HANDBOOK
OF ORGANIZATION
1992/1993
AND MEMBERSHIP
DIRECTORY

AMERICAN LIBRARY ASSOCIATION
Chicago and London 1992

"The best reading, for the largest number, at the least cost."
ALA motto; adopted, 1892 Conference

Resolved: "That this Association reinstate the use of this motto on appropriate occasions."
ALA Council, 1988

The ALA HANDBOOK OF ORGANIZATION

is a guide to the structure of the American Library Association. It provides names of current officials, committee members, Council members, and representatives. It also provides information regarding the units of ALA, such as divisions and round tables, and lists the periodicals of the association. Major staff members and staff offices are noted. Key documents, such as the Constitution, Bylaws, and Policies, are included.

The MEMBERSHIP DIRECTORY

includes the name and brief address of personal and organizational members. It is distributed annually without charge to organization and life members. Available for purchase. Address orders to Order Dept., ALA Hq.

Editors, Charles Harmon and Chere Elliott
Cover Design, Ellen Scanlon

International Standard Serial Number 0273-4605
International Standard Book Number 0-8389-5753-6
Library of Congress Catalog Card Number 80-649998
Copyright © 1992 by the American Library Association
Printed in the United States of America.

Published annually by the American Library Association, 50 E. Huron St., Chicago, IL 60611.

Postmaster: Please send notice of undeliverable copies on Form 3579 to Membership Services, American Library Association
50 E. Huron St., Chicago, IL 60611.

Contents

Honorary Members

Aiken, The Hon. George*
Allain, Alex P.
Asheim, Lester E.
Austin, Edwin C.*
Baker, Augusta
Barnard, Henry*
Becker, Joseph
Bishop, William Warner*
Bowker, Richard Rogers*
Brademas, John
Brown, Charles Harvey*
Bush, Barbara
Carnegie, Andrew*
Carson, Johnny
Chancellor, John Miller*
Chapman, Theodore S.*
Cheney, Frances Neel
Clapp, Verner Warren*
Clements, William L.*
Clift, David H.*
Cole, Fred C.*
Collins, Ross*
Coolidge, Elizabeth Sprague*
Dalton, Jack
Dix, William S.*
Douglas, The Hon. William O.*
Downs, Robert B.*
Eames, Wilberforce*
Eastman, Linda A.*
Eliot, Charles William*
Elliot, The Hon. Carl*
Ellsworth, Ralph E.
Evans, Charles*

_____
*Deceased

Evans, Luther H.*
Finley, John H.*
Fiske, Willard*
Fogarty, The Hon. John E.*
Ford, The Hon. William
Francis, Sir Frank*
Frase, Robert W.
Gaver, Mary V.
Gilman, Daniel Coit*
Grant, Edwin H.*
Grant, S. Hastings*
Guild, Reuben Aldridge*
Haines, Helen E.*
Hale, Edward Everett*
Harris, Ezekiel A.*
Haviland, Virginia*
Hill, Frank Pierce*
Hill, The Hon. Lister*
Hoover, Herbert Clark*
Hornback, Miriam L.*
Javits, The Hon. Jacob*
Jencks, Charles W.*
Joeckel, Carleton B.*
Jones, Clara Stanton
Jones, Virginia Lacy*
Keppel, Frederick P.*
Kilgour, Frederick
Krettek, Germaine
Lester, Robert MacDonald*
Liebaers, Herman
Low, Edmon*
Lydenberg, Harry Miller*
Martin, Allie Beth* (Special Centennial Honorary Membership)

Martin, Lowell A.
Melcher, Daniel*
Melcher, Frederick G.*
Metcalf, Keyes DeWitt*
Milam, Carl Hastings*
Moon, Eric
Moore, Bessie B.
Morton, Elizabeth Homer*
Nelson, Charles Alexander*
Owens, The Hon. Major
Pell, The Hon. Claiborne
Perkins, The Hon. Carl*
Powell, Lawrence Clark
Prince, Frederick O.*
Putnam, Herbert*
Rollins, Charlamae*
Rothrock, Mary U.*
Ruffner, Frederick Gale, Jr.
Shaw, Ralph R.*
Shaw, Spencer G.
Shera, Jesse H.*
Stevens, David H.
Stone, Elizabeth W.
Updike, Daniel Berkeley*
Upson, Anson Judd*
Vanderlip, Frank A.*
Vincent, Bishop John H.*
Wheeler, Joseph Lewis*
Wilson, Halsey William*
Wilson, Louis Round*
Young, Virginia G.

ALA Headquarters Telephone and Telefax Directory

ALA Headquarters' direct-dial telephone system features:
- **Direct inward dialing to all telephones.** Each staff member's phone has an individual telephone number that can be accessed directly by the caller and allows for incoming calls to bypass the switchboard.
- **Automated attendant.** The auto-attendant quickly answers incoming 800 toll-free calls and prompts callers to route themselves to a staff member or department.
- **Accurate timely messaging.** The 24-hour-a-day voice mail system eliminates the need for message-taking and provides time to leave accurate, complete messages that can be acted upon without endless telephone tag.

In addition, ALA Headquarters has retained its 312-944-6780 main telephone number as well as a members' toll-free number, 800-545-2433. ALA Headquarters' TDD number is (312) 944-7298.

Members who use the toll-free service are first connected to the automated attendant and can then dial the last four digits of the staff member's or office's direct-dial number, as listed below, to complete the call. All phones can be direct-dialed 24 hours a day with the prefix (312) 280-.

TELEPHONE DIRECTORY

Department Heads

Peggy Sullivan, Executive Director	3205
Roger H. Parent, Deputy Executive Director	3208
Peggy Barber, Associate Exec. Dir., Communications	3217
Ernest Martin, Associate Exec. Dir., Administrative Services	5058
JoAn Segal, Associate Exec. Dir., Programs	2518
Council Secretariat	3204

Divisions

American Association of School Librarians	4386
American Library Trustee Association	2161
Association of College & Research Libraries	2516
Association for Library Collections & Technical Services	5035
Association for Library Service to Children	2163

Association of Specialized & Cooperative Library Agencies	4398
Library Administration & Management Association	5038
Library & Information Technology Association	4270
Public Library Association	5752
Reference & Adult Services Division	4398
Young Adult Library Services Association	4391

Offices

Office for Accreditation	2432
Office for Intellectual Freedom	4223
Office for Library Outreach Services	4294
Office for Library Personnel Resources	4277
Office for Research & Statistics	4273
Office of the President	3213

Publishing Services

ALA Publishing Services	5416
American Libraries	4216
Book Links	5718
Booklist	5716
Library Technology Reports	4271

Marketing	2424
Reference Books Bulletin	5721

Other

Chapter Relations Office	4283
Conference Services Office	3225
Customer Services	5106
Data Processing—Mailing Lists	2460
Financial Services—Accounting	4239
Graphics Marketing	5047
Headquarters Library & Information Center	2153
Human Resources	2468
Human Resources Jobline	2464
Library/Book Fellows—International Relations	3200
Membership Services	4288
Public Information Office	5044
Public Programs	5055

Other Locations

Choice Magazine	(203) 347-6933
Washington Office	(202) 547-4440

TELEFAX DIRECTORY

ALA Headquarters (1st fl.-50 E.)	(312) 280-3255
ALA Headquarters (2HP)	(312) 280-3256
ALA Headquarters (4HP)	(312) 280-3257
ALA Headquarters (5HP)	(312) 280-3258
American Association of School Librarians	(312) 664-7459
American Libraries	(312) 440-0901

Association of College & Research Libraries	(312) 280-2520
Booklist	(312) 337-6787
Conference Services Office	(312) 280-3224
Customer Services	(312) 280-3224
Executive Office	(312) 944-3897
Headquarters Library & Information Center	(312) 440-9374

Office for Accreditation	(312) 280-2433
Public Information Office	(312) 944-8520
Public Library Association	(312) 280-5029
Publishing Services	(312) 944-2641
Young Adult Library Services Association	(312) 664-7459
Choice Magazine	(203) 346-8586
Washington Office	(202) 547-7363

ALA Ready-Reference Contacts
800-545-2433

Customer Services Office (see extensions below)

- Join ALA, a division, or round table (ext. 4287).
- Add division(s), round table(s), or section(s) (ext. 4287).
- Verify your ALA membership status (ext. 4288).
- Replace a lost or damaged membership card (ext. 4288).
- Request free *Handbook of Organization* (to ALA personal members) (ext. 4287).
- Correct your *Membership Directory* listing (ext. 4289).
- Subscribe to *Booklist, Library Personnel News, Library Systems Newsletter, Library Technology Reports, Newsletter on Intellectual Freedom, PR Activity Report, Rare Books and Manuscripts Librarianship,* or other periodicals (excluding *Book Links*) *not* included with membership (ext. 1548 or 1549).
- Change your address on subscriptions both included (ext. 4289) and not included (ext. 1545) with membership.
- Request replacement issues of subscription publications both included (ext. 4288) and not included (ext. 1545) with membership.
- Request free *ALA Graphics Catalog* (semi-annual) (ext. 5047).
- Order from the *ALA Graphics Catalog* (ext. 5048 or 5049).
- Order from the *ALA Books Catalog* (ext. 5108).

Many of the above services are available by telephone. VISA, MasterCard, or American Express is accepted. Before or after ALA office hours, leave messages for ALA Customer Services at (800) 545-2433, ext. 4299 or ext. 4298.

Conference Services Office   ext. 3225

- Reserve a meeting room or schedule a program at Midwinter Meeting or Annual Conference.
- Request information about exhibiting at ALA conferences and/or advertising in conference program.
  (Note: ALA division national conferences are administered by the division office staff.)

Chapter Relations Office   ext. 4283

- Request primary consultation on issues facing chapters.
- Request information for Chapter Relations Office database and clearinghouse.

- Request free subscription to *Chapter Relations Newsletter.*
- Request multiple copies of membership material for ALA student chapter use.

Information Center   ext. 2153

- Request free information on state and regional library associations (chapters).
- Receive free calendar of library association conferences.
- Request free list of ALA-accredited graduate library education programs.
- Request free *ALA Publications Catalog* (annual).
- Request free copy of "How to Publish in ALA Periodicals."
- Request copies of ALA policies, resolutions, and documents.
- Request information on ALA group insurance or credit card.
- Request additional ALA membership applications.
- Receive ALA awards information.
- Receive Midwinter Meeting or Annual Conference housing and registration information.

ALA Executive Office   ext. 3205

- Suggest ALA policies and projects.
- Request assistance regarding fair employment practices or related problems.

Data Processing   ext. 2460

- Mailing list rentals (Cheshire labels or pressure-sensitive).
- Request free ALA mailing list catalog.

ALA Washington Office

- Check status of federal legislation (regarding libraries).

Committee Involvement

- Volunteer for an ALA committee: write the ALA president-elect.
- Volunteer for a division or round table committee: write the appropriate president-elect.

American Library Association
50 E. Huron St., Chicago, IL 60611

Monday–Friday: 8:30 AM to 4:30 PM Central Time

ALA Washington Office
110 Maryland Ave. NE, Washington, DC 20002

Monday–Friday: 8:30 AM to 4:30 PM Eastern Time

Membership, Organization, Mission

Membership

The American Library Association, founded in 1876, is the oldest and largest national library association in the world. Its concern spans all types of libraries: state, public, school and academic libraries; special libraries serving persons in government, commerce and industry, the arts, the armed services, hospitals, prisons, and other institutions. With a membership of libraries, librarians, library trustees, and other interested persons from every state and many countries of the world, the Association is the chief advocate for the people of the United States in their search for the highest quality of library and information services. The Association maintains a close working relationship with more than 70 other library associations in the United States, Canada, and other countries, and it works closely with many other organizations concerned with education, research, cultural development, recreation, and public service.

On August 31, 1992, the Association had 3,090 organization members and 51,645 personal members—a total of 54,735.

Organization

Council, the governing body of ALA comprised of 100 members elected at large, 52 by chapters, 11 by divisions, and the 12 members of the Executive Board.

Executive Board, central management board of ALA comprised of the elected officers, the immediate past president, and 8 members elected by Council from among the members of that body.

ALA committees, appointed by the president, responsible for areas affecting all library and Association concerns. Number varies from year to year.

11 *divisions,* each responsible for a specified area of concern; each with an elected board of directors, and such committees and sections as are required to accomplish the division's goals.

17 *round tables,* each with an elected governing body, composed of members of the Association interested in the same field of librarianship not within the scope of any division.

57 *chapters,* autonomous units, each with its own elective structure, responsible for the promotion of library service and librarianship within its geographic area.

24 *affiliated organizations,* autonomous national or international organizations having purposes similar to ALA's and requesting affiliation.

Headquarters staff of approximately 260 employees, under the direction of an Executive Director who serves at the pleasure of the Executive Board.

Mission

The mission of the American Library Association is to provide leadership for the development, promotion, and improvement of library and information services and the profession of librarianship in order to enhance learning and ensure access to information for all.

(See ALA Policy Manual, Section One for Priority Areas and Goals.)

ALA Membership Organization

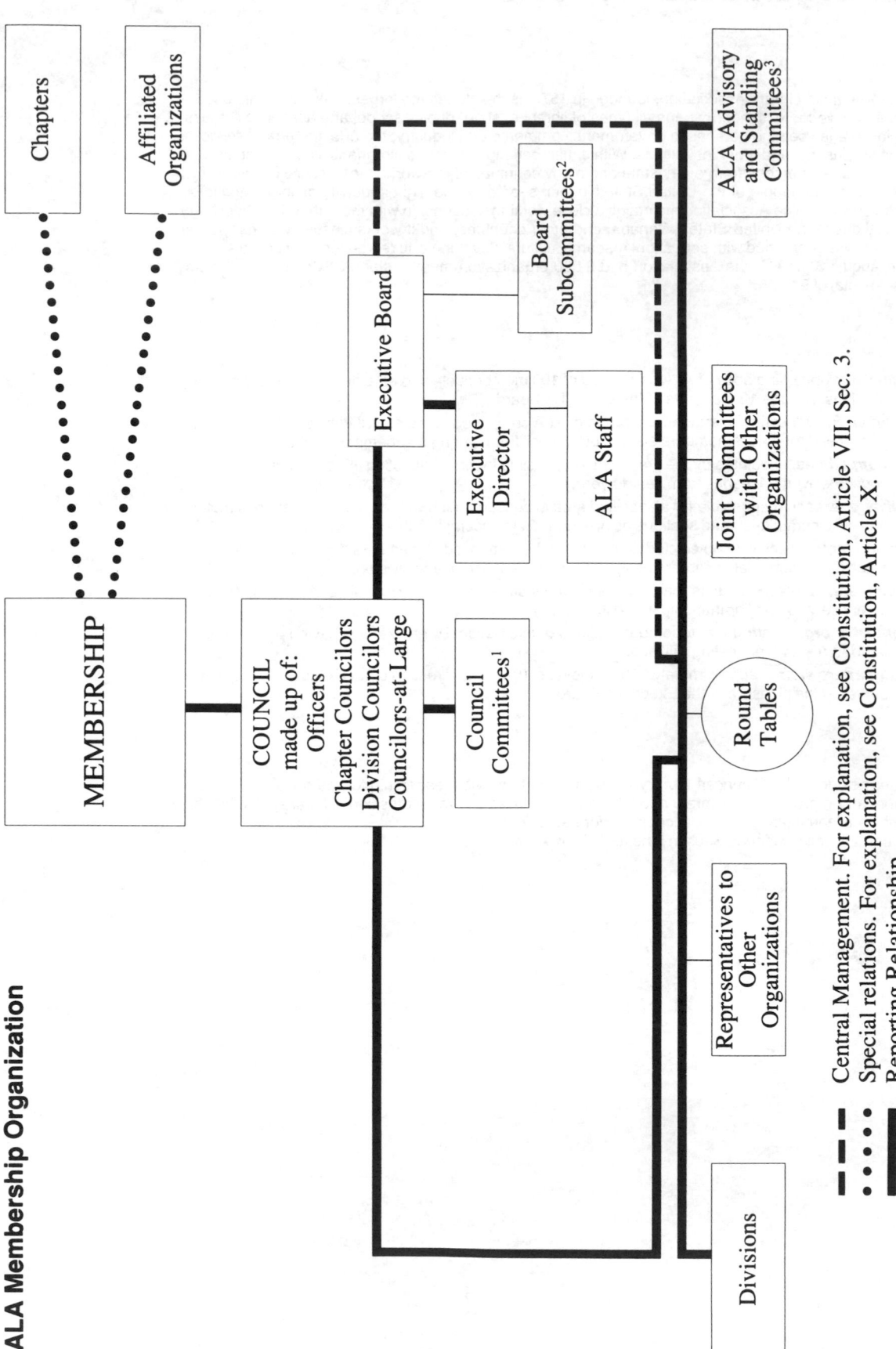

Chapters

Affiliated Organizations

MEMBERSHIP

COUNCIL made up of:
Officers
Chapter Councilors
Division Councilors
Councilors-at-Large

Council Committees[1]

Executive Board

Board Subcommittees[2]

Executive Director

ALA Staff

ALA Advisory and Standing Committees[3]

Joint Committees with Other Organizations

Round Tables

Representatives to Other Organizations

Divisions

– – – Central Management. For explanation, see Constitution, Article VII, Sec. 3.

• • • Special relations. For explanation, see Constitution, Article X.

——— Reporting Relationship

1. Committee on Committees; Council Orientation; Intellectual Freedom; International Relations; Legislation; Library Education; Minority Concerns; Organization; Pay Equity; Planning; Policy Monitoring; Professional Ethics; Program Evaluation and Support; Publishing; Resolutions; Women in Librarianship, Status of.

2. Administrative; Directions and Program Review; Finance and Audit; Office Program Reviews; Personnel.

3. Accreditation; "American Libraries"; Appointments; Awards; Chapter Relations; Conference Program; Constitution and Bylaws; Development Office; Library Outreach Services; Office for; Library Personnel Resources, Office for; Membership; Nominating; Public Information; Research and Statistics; Review, Inquiry, and Mediation; Standards; User Instruction for Information Literacy.

Officers and Executive Board

The Executive Board consists of the officers of the Association, the immediate past president, and 8 members elected by Council from its membership (4-year terms). The members of the Executive Board are members of Council as provided by the Constitution, Article VII, Section 1; Article VIII, Section 1; Bylaw Article III, Section 6(c); Bylaw Article IV, Section 2(e). The Executive Director is without vote, and the presiding officers of the Council may vote only in the case of a tie. The Executive Board acts for Council in the administration of established policies and programs. It serves as the management board of ALA, including headquarters operations, subject to review by Council, and makes recommendations with respect to policy and operation. (See Constitution, Article VII, Section 3.)

ALA OFFICERS

President
MARILYN L. MILLER
Dept. of Library & Information Studies
349 Curry Bldg.
University of North Carolina
Greensboro, NC 27412

President-elect
HARDY R. FRANKLIN
District of Columbia P.L.
901 G St. NW
Washington, D.C. 20001

Treasurer (1992–96)
ANN K. SYMONS
Juneau Douglas H.S. L.
Juneau, AK 99801

Executive Director
PEGGY SULLIVAN
ALA Headquarters
50 E. Huron St., Chicago, IL 60611

OTHER MEMBERS OF THE EXECUTIVE BOARD

Immediate Past Pres., Patricia Glass Schuman, Neal-Schuman Publishers, 100 Varick St., New York, NY 10013.

Term expiring 1993:
J. Dennis Day, P.L., 209 E. Fifth St., Salt Lake City, UT 84111
Agnes M. Griffen, Montgomery Cnty. Dept. of P. Ls., 99 Maryland Ave., Rockville, MD 20850

Term expiring 1994:
Nancy M. Bolt, State L., Dept. of Edu., 201 E. Colfax, Denver, CO 80203
Judith A. Sessions, King L., Miami Univ., Oxford, OH 45056

Term expiring 1995:
Betty J. Blackman, California State Univ.–Dominguez Hills Edu. Resources Ctr., 1000 E. Victoria St., Carson, CA 90747
Betty J. Turock, L. Inf. Studies, Rutgers Univ., 4 Huntington St., New Brunswick, NJ 08903

Term expiring 1996:
Cesar Caballero, El Paso Cmnty. Coll., El Paso, TX 79998
Bruce E. Daniels, Onondaga P.L. at the Galleries, 447 S. Salina St., Syracuse, NY 13202–2494

Secretariat: Emily I. Melton.

Liaisons

Chapter Relations Com.—Bruce E. Daniels.
Cultural Diversity, President's Com. on—Agnes M. Griffen.
Freedom to Read Foundation—Judith A. Sessions.
Publishing Com.—Nancy M. Bolt.

SUBCOMMITTEES OF THE BOARD

Administrative

To consist of the President of ALA, serving as chairperson, Vice-President, Treasurer, immediate Past President, and Executive Director. The Subcommittee shall assume the following responsibilities: Set meeting agendas; perform and delegate ceremonial activities as representatives of ALA; handle administrative communications of the organization and Board; coordinate ALA conference program planning; structure orientations for new Board members; share and alert the Executive Board to economic and political trends; recommend ALA's relationship with external organizations and individuals; assess ALA facilities; and perform general administrative duties of the Executive Board.

Ch., Marilyn L. Miller; Hardy R. Franklin; Patricia Glass Schuman; Peggy Sullivan; Ann K. Symons; staff liaison, Emily I. Melton.

Directions and Program Review

To consist of the immediate Past President of ALA, serving as chairperson, three members of the Executive Board, and the chairperson of the Council Committee on Planning, with the ALA Deputy Executive Director as resource person. This Subcommittee shall develop long- and short-range objectives for the general program of the Association from which operational strategies shall be developed by staff; relate financial projections to plans; review programs of all membership units and offices in relation to ALA Goals and Priorities; assess general programs of the Association and recommend that new activities and programs be initiated and/or that activities and programs no longer reflecting ALA Goals and Priorities be discontinued, and that, as appropriate, programs be merged, restructured, or realigned, subject to ratification by the full Board.

Ch., Patricia Glass Schuman; Hardy R. Franklin; Judith A. Sessions; Betty J. Turock; Planning Com. ch., Regina U. Minudri; staff liaison, to be appointed.

Finance and Audit

To consist of the Treasurer of ALA, serving as chairperson, three members of the Executive Board, and the chairperson of COPES, with the ALA Comptroller as resource person. This Subcommittee shall suggest measures to build the Association's financial resources; provide the Executive Board with interpretation of financial data needed for administrative decisions; serve as liaison to the endowment trustees; conduct audit reviews; review the treasurer's report; review and interpret the assumptions and procedures on which COPES operates; review financial projections; consider other matters related to finances and budget as appropriate and necessary; make recommendations to the Executive Board regarding the fiscal management of the Association (maintain communication with the Directions and Program Review Subcommittee); and perform general fiscal duties of the Executive Board.

Ch., Ann K. Symons; Nancy M. Bolt; Cesar Caballero; J. Dennis Day; COPES ch., Mary W. Ghikas; staff liaison: Peggy Sullivan; Roger Parent.

Office Program Reviews

Each Office will be reviewed at least at 5-year intervals under Procedures approved by the Executive Board in June 1989. Subcommittees shall be comprised of three Executive Board members, one of whom shall be a member of Directions and Program Review Committee, the Executive Director, Deputy Executive Director and other members as appropriate to individual office reviews.

Personnel

To consist of three members of the Executive Board. To review and recommend to the Executive Board personnel policies and practices for ALA staff and advise the Board on implementation of such policies and practices. The chairperson also chairs the Executive Director's Performance Evaluation Subcommittee, which consists of the chairs of DPR and F&A Subcommittees. The Associate Executive Director for Administrative Services serves as resource person for this phase of the Subcommittee's responsibilities. The Subcommittee also considers candidates for honorary membership and makes recommendations when appropriate and with discretion, under Bylaw Article 1, Section 1.A(6) and within the guide lines set forth in ALA Policy 2.1 and Executive Board procedure 212.2 (former policy compilation). The Subcommittee also considers and advises the Executive Board on special nominations and assignments of ALA representatives to outside bodies and/or activities as may be necessary from time to time, unless such nominations and assignments fall within the purview of an already established ALA unit. The Council–Executive Board Secretariat serves as staff resource person for this phase of the Subcommittee's activities.

Ch., Betty J. Blackman; Bruce E. Daniels; Agnes M. Griffen; staff liaison, Ernest Martin.

ENDOWMENT TRUSTEES

All receipts from life memberships and all gifts for endowment purposes are in the custody of 3 trustees, one of whom is elected by the Executive Board annually, for a 3-year term. The trustees have the authority to hold, invest, reinvest, and disburse endowment funds as directed by the Executive Board. (Constitution, Article IX, Section 1.)

Bernard A. Margolis, Pikes Peak L., Dist., 5550 N. Union Blvd., P.O. Box 1579, Pikes Peak, CO 80908 (1995).

Eric Moon, 5623 Palm Aire Dr., Sarasota, FL 34243 (1994).

Richard A. Olsen, Adams L., Rhode Island Coll., 600 Mt. Pleasant Ave., Providence, RI 02908 (1993).

Executive Board liaison: Ann K. Symons, Juneau Douglas H.S. L., Juneau, AK 99801.

Staff liaison: Peggy Sullivan.

CLERK OF THE AMERICAN LIBRARY ASSOCIATION IN THE COMMONWEALTH OF MASSACHUSETTS

Arthur Curley, Dir., P.L., Copley Sq., P.O. Box 286, Boston, MA 02117.

Council

The Council is the governing body of ALA. It delegates to the divisions of the Association authority to plan and carry out programs and activities in accord with policy established by Council. Only personal members of the Association may serve on Council. Two meetings are required each year, one at the annual conference of the Association and one not less than three months prior to annual conference. (See Article IV of the Bylaws.) Council determines all policies of the Association and its decisions are binding unless set aside by a three-fourths vote at any meeting of the Association membership or a majority vote by mail held upon petition of 200 members and requiring a minimum of one-fourth of the membership voting. (See Article VI of the Constitution.)

Officers and Members: The officers of the Association and Executive Board, including the immediate past president and treasurer, are members of the Council as provided in Bylaw Article III, Section 6(c) and IV, Section 2(e). The officers of Council are the president, the president-elect and the executive director.

Bylaw Article IV, Section 2(d) provides that there shall be 100 councilors at large who are elected by the Association at large, 25 being elected each year as provided in Bylaw Article III, Sec. 1(b), (c), (d) and Section 2(b).

Bylaw Article IV, Section 2(c) provides that each division of the Association shall be entitled to one councilor to be elected for a term of four years by the members of the division.

Bylaw Article IV, Section 2(b) provides that each state, provincial, and territorial chapter is entitled to one councilor, elected by the members of the chapter. Chapter representation is through state chapters unless chapters in a region choose to take representation through that regional chapter. In such case, the regional chapter shall elect one representative from each state or provincial chapter within that regional association. There is no current regional chapter representation.

The year following a name is the date of office term expiration.

OFFICERS OF THE COUNCIL

(Bylaw Article IV, Sec. 1(c))

Pres., Marilyn L. Miller
Pres.-elect, Hardy R. Franklin
Secy., Peggy Sullivan

COUNCILORS BY VIRTUE OF EXECUTIVE BOARD MEMBERSHIP

(Constitution Article VIII, Sec. 1, Bylaw Articles III, Sec. 6(C) and IV, Sec. 2.)

Immed. Past Pres., Patricia Glass Schuman
Treas., Ann K. Symons (1996)
Betty J. Blackman (1995)
Nancy M. Bolt (1994; at large 1993)
Cesar Caballero (1996)
J. Dennis Day (1993)
Bruce E. Daniels (1996; at large 1994)
Agnes M. Griffen (1993)
Judith A. Sessions (1994)
Betty J. Turock (1995)

COUNCILORS AT LARGE

Anderson, Mary Jane (1996)
Ashley, Roger S. (1994)
Atkinson, Ross W. (1995)
Balcom, Kathleen M. (1995)
Basone, Darlene Shiverdecker (1994)
Behrman, Sara T. (1994)
Biblo, Herbert (1996)
Biblo, Mary (1994)
Bingham, Rebecca T. (1994)
Boisse, Joseph A. (1994)
Bonnell, Pamela Gay (1994)
Boyd, Alex (1996)
Brown, Charles M. (1996)
Brown, Florence S. (1993)
Brynteson, Susan (1993)
Buck, Richard M. (1994)
Bunge, Charles A. (1996)
Cain, Carolyn L. (1996)
Caldwell-Wood, Naomi (1996)
Casey, Daniel W. (1995)
Cassell, Kay A. (1994)
Chaparro, Luis (1995)

Chen, Ching-chih (1993)
Conable, Gordon M. (1995)
Cooper, Ginnie (1995)
DeLoach, Marva L. (1993)
Dougherty, Linda Anne (1996)
Dresang, Eliza T. (1995)
Drescher, Judith A. (1995)
Dufault, Donna J. (1994)
Eaglen, Audrey B. (1995)
Eastman, Ann Heidbreder (1994)
Fox, Carol J. (1996)
Franklin, Robert (1996)
Futas, Elizabeth (1995)
Goldberg, Susan S. (1994)
Gomez, Martin J. (1996)
Gordon, Ruth I. (1995)
Gorman, Michael J. (1995)
Gregory, Mary Lou (1995)
Guerena, Salvador (1993)
Hales, John D. Jr. (1996)
Henington, David M. (1993)
Hill, Janet Swan (1993)
Hoadley, Irene B. (1994)
Holley, Robert P. (1995)
Horrocks, Norman (1995)
Hunt, Mary Alice (1994)
Hunter, Julie V. (1996)
Imhoff, Kathleen R. (1993)
Immroth, Barbara F. (1996)
Josey, E. J. (1996)
Kadanoff, Diane Gordon (1993)
Killeen, Erlene Bishop (1993)
Kimmel, Margaret M. (1993)
Kirkpatrick, Margaret L. (1994)
Kranich, Nancy C. (1996)
Leisner, Anthony B. (1993)
Lynch, Beverly P. (1993)
Malinconico, S. Michael (1994)
Margolis, Bernard A. (1993)
Marshall, Nancy H. (1993)
Matthews, Stephen L. (1993)
Meyers, Judith K. (1995)
Minudri, Regina U. (1994)
Morita, Ichiko T. (1995)
Morrison, Samuel F. (1996)
Negro, Antoinette (1994)
Nelson, Judy T. (1994)

O'Brien, Patrick M. (1995)
Perrault, Anna H. (1996)
Perry, Susan L. (1993)
Pritchard, Sarah M. (1994)
Rader, Hannelore B. (1996)
Reichel, Mary (1994)
Robbins, Jane (1995)
Roberts, William H. (1994)
Rohlf, Robert H. (1994)
Scilken, Marvin H. (1993)
Selverstone, Harriet S. (1995)
Shapiro, Beth J. (1995)
Sherman, Mary A. (1996)
Smith, Patricia H. (1996)
Somerville, Mary R. (1995)
Sorensen, Richard J. (1993)
Sprinkle-Hamlin, Sylvia Y. (1996)
Stripling, Barbara K. (1995)
Tseng, Sally C. (1993)
Tyson, John C. (1996)
Van Orden, Phyllis Jeanne (1993)
Warner, Gail P. (1995)
Weaver, Barbara F. (1993)
Whitney, Karen A. (1993)
Wilson, Betsy (1995)
Wilson-Lingbloom, Evie (1996)
Woolls, E. Blanche (1994)
Young, Christina C. (1996)

DIVISION COUNCILORS

AASL—Jane C. Terwillegar (1994)
ACRL—Rochelle Sager (1994)
ALCTS—Jean W. Farrington (1995)
ALSC—Frances V. Sedney (1996)
ALTA—Terri C. Jacobs (1995)
ASCLA—Suzanne J. LeBarron (1993)
LAMA—Rodney M. Hersberger (1993)
LITA—Donald E. Riggs (1993)
PLA—Linda Mielke (1994)
RASD—Gail A. Schlachter (1996)
YALSA—Pamela R. Klipsch (1995)

CHAPTER COUNCILORS

Alabama—Lee E. Pike (1994)
Alaska—Veda J. Arteaga (1997)
Arizona—David P. Snider (1994)

Arkansas—*Bob Razer (1992)
California—Linda M. Wood (1995)
Colorado—Eloise N. Fasold (1996)
Connecticut—*Marietta Johnson (1992)
Delaware—Catherine W. Wojewodski (1993)
District of Columbia—Robert R. Newlen (1993)
Florida—Lydia Acosta (1994)
Georgia—Charles E. Beard (1994)
Guam—Mark Goniwiecha (1994)
Hawaii—Florence H. Yee (1993)
Idaho—*Paul E. Holland, Jr. (1992)
Illinois—*Patricia M. Hogan (1992)
Indiana—Sara G. Laughlin (1995)
Iowa—Carol French Johnson (1995)
Kansas—Leroy M. Gattin (1995)
Kentucky—Ellen G. Hellard (1993)
Louisiana—Joy L. Lowe (1995)
Maine—Marilyn Clark (1994)
Maryland—Sandra S. Stephan (1994)
Massachusetts—Carolyn B. Noah (1993)

_____
*Successor to be elected.

Michigan— Beverly D. Papai (1994)
Minnesota—Janice Feye-Stukas (1995)
Mississippi—June M. Breland (1995)
Missouri—Marilyn A. McLeod (1993)
Montana—Deborah L. Schlesinger (1993)
Nebraska—Elizabeth J. Keefe (1995)
Nevada— Juanita P. Karr (1994)
New Hampshire—*Sherman Pridham (1992)
New Jersey—Elaine H. McConnell (1993)
New Mexico—Benjamin T. Wakashige (1993)
New York—Julie A. Cummins (1994)
North Carolina—Patricia A. Langelier (1993)
North Dakota—Betty A. Gard (1993)
Ohio—Steven Hawk (1996)
Oklahoma—Bettie Estes-Rickner (1996)
Oregon—Carol I. Hildebrand (1994)
Pennsylvania—Charles R. Peguese (1994)
Rhode Island—*Carol Drought (1992)
South Carolina—*Frankie H. Cubbedge (1992)
South Dakota—*Judith A. Johnson (1992)
Tennessee—Larry Romans (1996)
Texas—Gretchen L. Staas (1996)

Utah—Paul A. Mogren (1996)
Vermont—Sally G. Reed (1996)
Virginia—Thomas J. Hehman (1995)
Virgin Islands—*Fiolina B. Mills (1992)
Washington—Mary Y. Moore (1996)
West Virginia—Thomas M. Brown (1995)
Wisconsin—Patricia A. Bakula (1995)
Wyoming—Annette Anderson (1995)

Secretariat: Lois Ann Gregory-Wood

COMMITTEES OF COUNCIL

See individual committee listings for Council Committees: Committee on Committees, Council Orientation, Intellectual Freedom, International Relations, Legislation, Library Education, Minority Concerns, Organization, Pay Equity, Planning, Policy Monitoring, Professional Ethics, Program Evaluation and Support, Publishing, Resolutions, and Status of Women in Librarianship.

ALA Committees

Committees which are created by the Executive Board, Council, and the president are designated as ALA committees and committees of the Council. The Constitution provides for several types of committees: advisory, standing, special (limited to 2 years unless renewed by Executive Board or Council action), interdivisional, and joint. (See Bylaws, Article VIII.) By Council action, July 1969, the Executive Board and Council may also designate as ad hoc committees those committees appointed to pursue a designated project to a specific goal within a specific period, the life of the committee ending at the end of that specific time or the conclusion of the project.

Access to Information, Coordinating Committee on (special)

Established by Council, January 1989. To facilitate the development and maintenance of a comprehensive set of information access policies for the American Library Association in cooperation with all Association units; to draw together key persons within the Association to focus on access issues; to monitor access activities outside ALA which are of interest to the Association; to facilitate communications among ALA units on access issues and suggest areas where activity and/or coordination is required within the Association; to aggressively support and, when needed, develop coalitions to further ALA policies on access; to identify needed research on access issues and follow through; to advise ALA Council and Executive Board on programs, policies, and priorities in those areas of access not assigned to any other Council committee.

Ch., Gordon M. Conable (1994); Mary Treacy Birmingham (1993); Francis J. Buckley Jr. (1993); Maurice J. Freedman (1993); Stephen M. Hayes (1994); Barbara M. Jones (1994); Anita R. Schiller (1993); Patricia M. Wong (1993); staff liaisons: Eileen D. Cooke; Judith F. Krug; Mary Jo Lynch; Mattye L. Nelson.

Accreditation (standing)

To be responsible for the execution of the accreditation program of ALA, and to develop and formulate standards of education for librarianship for the approval of Council.

Ch., C. James Schmidt (1993); Luis Chaparro (1993); Roger G. Clark (1993); Robert B. Croneberger (1993); John A. Gray (1994); Elizabeth Hope Hayes (1994); Carol C. Kuhlthau (1994); Diane H. Mittermeyer (1994); Fred W. Roper (1994); Sherrie Schmidt (1993); Frank H. Spaulding (1993); Anne Woodsworth (1994); staff liaison, Prudence W. Dalrymple.

ALA Self-Study (special)

To develop a plan for a comprehensive organizational review, conduct the review, and prepare a final report with recommendation to Council by Annual Conference 1995.

Ch., F. William Summers (1995); Mary E. Arney (1995); Carolyn L. Cain (1995); Arthur Curley (1995); J. Dennis Day (1995); Mary W. Ghikas (1995); Gerald G. Hodges (1995); Althea H. Jenkins (1995); Regina U. Minudri (1995); Paul H. Mosher (1995); Susan E. Stroyan (1995); Karen A. Whitney (1995); staff liaison, Emily I. Melton (1995).

"American Libraries," Advisory

To be limited to advice to the editor on editorial matters.

Ch., Gail A. Schlachter (1993); Patricia W. Berger (1994); George R. Jaramillo (1994); Samuel F. Morrison (1993); Barbara K. Stripling (1994); Barbara Webb (1993); Roberta V. Webb (1993); staff liaison, Thomas M. Gaughan.

Appointments (advisory)

(Provided for in Bylaw Article VIII, Section 1.)

Ch., Hardy R. Franklin (1993); staff liaison, Emily I. Melton.

Awards (standing)

The ALA Awards Committee shall make recommendations to the Executive Board and the ALA Council on all policies relating to awards to be made or sponsored by ALA and its units. It shall administer the general awards, grants and scholarships presented in the name of the American Library Association, known as "ALA Awards." All such general ALA awards shall recognize achievements within the profession. The Committee shall review periodically the appropriateness of existing ALA Awards; shall recommend modification, elimination, or suspension of existing ALA Awards; and shall make recommendations with respect to proposed new ALA Awards. The Committee shall appoint juries to select recipients of ALA Awards (i.e., awards not administered by a unit of the Association), and shall coordinate the work of these juries and committees.

The Awards Committee shall be responsible for maintaining the *ALA Awards Manual,* which includes information for all awards presented by ALA or any of its units; shall provide general guidance regarding the procedural aspects of the Awards Program (such as information concerning deadline dates and publicity releases); and shall prepare, for each annual conference, a master list of awards recipients.

Each unit of ALA shall determine within the general policies governing awards new awards relating to its specific area of responsibility. Each unit shall review periodically the appropriateness of its existing awards; and shall modify, eliminate, or suspend its existing award(s) and shall handle all details and expenses with respect to its award(s).

Each unit will submit its proposals for new or existing unit awards to the ALA Awards Committee at a regular meeting of the Committee at least six months prior to the anticipated date of advertisement. The Awards Committee will review and provide assistance to the unit on questions of procedure and coordination with other ALA units. All new awards must be reported prior to implementation date to the Awards Committee, Executive Board and Council.

Each unit is also responsible for submitting complete records concerning its award(s) to the Awards Committee in order that the *ALA Awards Manual* may be maintained.

Ch., Robert S. Smith (1993); Rosemary H. Arneson (1994); David E. Ellefsen (1994); Clara G. Hoover (1994); Cynthia J. Johanson (1993); Diane Gordon Kadanoff (1993); Mary L. Larsgaard (1993); Virginia B. Moore (1993); Verna M. Muthoni (1994); staff liaison, JoAn S. Segal.

Billions of Books and Billions of Bucks, President's Committee on (special)

To serve as advisory board for Billions of Books and Billions of Bucks; to advise on implementation, evaluation, and follow-up. To investigate and propose activities and programs related to a national reading marathon, to work in developing information and training programs in concert with other ALA divisions, units, and committees. To establish liaison with other groups or professions concerned with promoting and/or supporting the development of reading. To advise on development and content of fact sheets, briefing books, and other "power tools" for use at national and local levels. To recommend agressive strategies for implementing the program.

Co-chs., David V. Loertscher (1995) and E. Blanche Woolls (1995); Nancy M. Bolt (1995); Pamela Gay Bonnell (1995); Retta B. Patrick (1995); Christy Tyson (1995); Diana D. Young (1995); ex officio, Hardy R. Franklin (1995); staff liaisons: Peggy Barber; Carol S. Nielsen; Susan Roman; Ann C. Weeks.

Chapter Relations (standing)

To promote the development and recognition of Chapters as integral components of ALA; to encourage discussion, activities and programs that support the mutual interests of ALA and the Chapters; to advise when requested on proposals and actions of other ALA units that may affect Chapters; to provide a forum wherein Chapters can share ideas and concerns of common interest and identify common needs and goals; to communicate these Chapter needs and goals to ALA and ALA goals, programs and priorities to the Chapters; to encourage and maintain a cooperative and supportive relationship among ALA, its units, and the Chapters; to formulate and review periodically requirements for Chapter status; and to serve as an advisory committee to the Chapter Relations Office.

Ch., Carol K. DiPrete (1993); Charles E. Beard (1993); Barbara A. Cunningham (1994); Danilo H. Figueredo (1993); Nann Blaine Hilyard (1993); Gilbert W. McNamee (1993); Merrilyn S. Ridgeway (1994); Exec. Bd. liaison, Bruce E. Daniels (1993); staff liaisons: Julie Ann Geissler; Gerald G. Hodges.

Chapter Booth (subcommittee)

Ch., Carolyn B. Noah (1993); Marilyn A. McLeod (1993).

Chapter Data Collection (subcommittee)

Ch., Danilo H. Figueredo (1993); Margaret S. Bauer (1993); Mary Sue Ferrell (1993); Nann Blaine Hilyard (1993); Juliana G. Huiskamp (1993).

Chapter Councilor Program (subcommittee)

Ch., Frankie H. Cubbedge (1993).

"Chapter Handbook" Revision (subcommittee)

Ch., Nann Blaine Hilyard (1993); Danilo H. Figueredo (1993).

Chapter Presidents-Elect Orientation (subcommittee)

Ch., Florence S. Brown (1993); Estelle M. Black (1993); Frankie H. Cubbedge (1993); Barbara A. Cunningham (1993); Marianne Gessner (1993); Katharine C. Hurrey (1993).

Editors' Interests (subcommittee)

To share among editors of chapter newsletters and journals common interests and concerns in their editorial responsibilities. To examine ways to strengthen and improve printed communication about issues and events in librarianship throughout the chapters.

The subcommittee may involve itself in surveys and other research studies on subjects related to publications; programs at ALA Annual Conferences on such topics as publication staff, acquisition of material to publish, editorial policies and procedures, advertising, technological innovations, layout and design; and a national chapter communique.

Ch., Frances B. Bradburn (1993); James H. Adams Jr. (1993); Nancy F. Carter (1993); Carol Cubberley (1993); Lesley S. J. Farmer (1993); Blaine H. Hall (1993); Patsy J. Hansel (1993); Ronald V. Norman (1993); Susan L. Richards (1993).

Library Education and Recruitment, Chapter Relations/SCOLE (interunit task force)

Ch., Joe F. Dahlstrom (1993); Tami Echavarria (1993); Marianne Gessner (1993); Josette A. Lyders (1993).

Committee on Committees (elected Council committee)

(See Bylaw, Article III, Section 6(a), 6(b), and 6(c), and Article VIII, Section 2.)

Ch., Hardy R. Franklin (1993); Kathleen M. Balcom (1993); Joseph A. Boisse (1993); Kay A. Cassell (1993); Margaret M. Kimmel (1993); staff liaison, Emily I. Melton.

Conference Program (standing)

To consist of the president, president-elect, the presidents of the divisions, the Executive Director of the Association, and three members-at-large with staggered terms, together with such other members as the committee may wish to add. To plan programs for the general sessions of the annual conferences; to insure, insofar as practicable, that the content of all program meetings of divisions, sections, round tables, and committees, together with the general sessions, present an integrated conference program with a minimum of duplication.

Members-at-large: Margaret L. Crist (1994); Jordan M. Scepanski (1995); Henrietta M. Smith (1993); staff liaison, Peggy Barber.

For New Orleans, 1993

Pres. and ch., Marilyn L. Miller (1993); Lizbeth Bishoff (ALCTS, 1993); Walt Crawford (LITA, 1993); Kathy Ann East (ALSC, 1993); Janice Beck Ison (ASCLA, 1993); Jacquelyn M. McCoy (ACRL, 1993); James G. Neal (LAMA, 1993); Elizabeth M. O'Donnell (YALSA, 1993); James R. Rettig (RASD, 1993); Aileen R. Schrader (ALTA, 1993); Elliot Shelkrot (PLA, 1993); Ruth Toor (AASL, 1993); staff liaison, Peggy Barber.

For Miami, 1994

Pres.-elect. and ch., Hardy R. Franklin (1994); Ann L. Donoghue (ALTA, 1994); Judith A. Druse (YALSA, 1994); Charles L. Gilreath (RASD, 1994); Thomas Kirk (ACRL, 1994); Carol F. L. Liu (LAMA, 1994); Tamara J. Miller (LITA, 1994); Barbara L. Perkis (ASCLA, 1994); Ellen M. Stepanian (ALSC, 1994); Pat Woodrum (PLA, 1994); E. Blanche Woolls (AASL, 1994); Jennifer A. Younger (ALCTS, 1994); staff liaison, Peggy Barber.

Local Arrangements—New Orleans, 1993

Ch., Mary Lee Sweat (1993); Germaine C. Age (1993); Elizabeth O. Bedikian (1993); Elizabeth E. Bingham (1993); Marguerite Rey Florent (1993); Margaret Friend (1993); Gwynette Goodman (1993); Hazel Moore (1993); Richard Snow (1993); Garland Strother (1993); Wilba Swearingen (1993); Eric M. Wedig (1993); staff liaison, Peggy Barber.

Poster Session

Organizes and promotes Poster Sessions at ALA Annual Conferences, reviews Poster Session applications, selects presenters, and compiles booklet of Poster Session abstracts. Poster Sessions were added to the Annual Conference program in 1982, and provide opportunity to selected individuals to present research findings and innovative programs on poster boards located in the exhibit area.

Ch., Katherine J. Harig (1993); Candace R. Benefiel (1993); Tammy Nickelson Dearie (1993); Cheryl A. Fields (1993); Thomas K. Fry (1993); Bee H. Gallegos (1993); Judith A. Harwood (1993); Barbara G. Preece (1993); Thyra K. Russell (1993); Suzanne Sweeney (1993); staff liaison, Paul Graller.

Constitution and Bylaws (standing)

To consider amendments to the Constitution and Bylaws and to make recommendations to the Association in accordance with the provisions of Articles XI and XII of the Constitution.

Ch., Thomas E. Alford (1993); John W. Berry (1993); Mary Alice Hunt (1994); Barbara J. Nemer (1994); Frances V. Sedney (1994); staff liaison, Emily I. Melton.

Council Orientation (special, Council)

To develop and carry out the Midwinter orientation for all new and continuing councilors and to manage the Council lounge at the Midwinter and Annual meetings.

Ch., Charles E. Beard (1993); Hannelore B. Rader (1993); Marvin H. Scilken (1993); Mary A. Sherman (1993); Phyllis Jeanne Van Orden (1993); J. Linda Williams (1993); Florence H. Yee (1993); staff liaison, Lois Ann Gregory-Wood.

Cultural Diversity, President's Committee on (special)

To work with relevant ALA units, committees, offices, task forces, affiliates, and staff to: (1) develop strategies and recommend an aggressive program to recruit members of minority and emerging majority populations to the profession; (2) gather data on existing cultural diversity activities within the association and the profession; (3) assess current efforts to implement and promote cultural diversity; (4) plan activities for the 1991–92 presidential year which will highlight the importance of cultural diversity; (5) suggest and develop tools and programs to encourage the recruitment, employment, retention, and advancement of culturally diverse staff at all levels at ALA headquarters and within the profession; (6) expand opportunities for members of culturally diverse groups to participate in leadership roles within ALA; (7) foster the development of multilingual and multicultural materials, collections, and services; (8) develop a comprehensive cultural diversity plan for ALA including a timeline and specific evaluation mechanisms.

Co-chs., Yolanda J. Cuesta (1993) and Gloria J. Leonard (1993); John L. Ayala (1993); Janice M. Beaudin (1993); Mario M. Gonzalez (1993); Susana A. Hinojosa (1993); Donnarae MacCann (1993); Abdul J. Miah (1993); Thomas C. Phelps (1993); Betty-Carol Sellen (1993); Vivian M. Sykes (1993); Andrew A. Venable Jr. (1993); Benjamin T. Wakashige (1993); Joyce C. Wright (1993); interns, Karen E. Downing (1993); Tracey J. Hunter (1993); Exec. Bd. liaison, Agnes M. Griffen (1993); staff liaisons: Margaret Myers; Mattye L. Nelson.

Development Office (advisory)

Basic priorities for the ALA Development Office shall be established by the Executive Director and Executive Board to support the initiatives and priorities of the Association. The Advisory Committee shall advise the staff on plans and strategies for building the ALA Endowment; shall assist the Development Office in identifying needs and priorities in fund-raising and grant activities; shall facilitate coordination of grant and development activities throughout the Association; and shall advise the Office on the development and implementation of Association policies and procedures on grants and fund-raising.

Ch., Pat Woodrum (1993); Albert W. Daub (1993); J. Dennis Day (1994); Gloria T. Glaser (1993); Susan S. Goldberg (1993); Stephen T. Kochoff (1993); Richard A. Olsen (1993); Frederick G. Ruffner Jr. (1993); ex officio, Ann K. Symons (1996); staff liaison, Peggy Barber.

Election (special)

To certify the results of the annual election of the Association. (See Bylaw Article III, Sec. 4(a).)

Ch. and members to be appointed in the spring of 1993. Staff liaison, Ernest Martin.

Intellectual Freedom (standing, Council)

To recommend such steps as may be necessary to safeguard the rights of library users, libraries, and librarians, in accordance with the First Amendment to the United States Constitution and the *Library Bill of Rights* as adopted by the ALA Council. To work closely with the Office for Intellectual Freedom and with other units and officers of the Association in matters touching intellectual freedom and censorship.

Ch., Candace D. Morgan (1994); Pamela Gay Bonnell (1993); Arthur Curley (1993); Joan Coachman Durrance (1993); Dianne McAfee Hopkins (1993); Barbara M. Jones (1994); Gayle Keresey (1994); Gene D. Lanier (1993); James S. McPhee (1993); William A. Moffett (1994); Betty-Carol Sellen (1993); Elizabeth Martinez Smith (1993); staff liaison, Judith F. Krug.

International Relations (standing, Council)

To promote the exchange of librarians between this and other countries; to encourage and facilitate the use of library and bibliographic techniques and knowledge throughout the world; to assist in the exchange of professional information, ideas, and literature between this and other countries; to coordinate the activities of other units of the Association within this field.

Ch., Nancy R. John (1994); Beverly P. Lynch (1993); Helen G. Maul (1993); James G. Neal (1994); Mary A. Sherman (1994); Evelyn V. Staton (1994); Robert D. Stueart (1993); Lucille C. Thomas (1993); staff liaison, Robert P. Doyle.

American–South Asian Librarians Conference (subcommittee)

To make all the conference arrangements with the help of the Indian Library Association; choose the conference theme; select paper topics to be presented by American librarians, library educators, and information science specialists; select speakers, assign them topics, and invite them to write and read papers at the conference; prepare the conference program; publicize the conference; apply for grants to cover the conference expenses; and arrange to publish the conference proceedings.

Ch., R. N. Sharma (1993); Ismail Abdullahi (1993); Jean S. Adelman (1993); Merry L. Burlingham (1993); Donald G. Davis Jr. (1993); J. Dennis Day (1993); Kul B. Gauri (1993); Abulfazal M. Fazle Kabir (1993); Averil J. Kadis (1993); Roger J. Long (1993); James H. Nye (1993); Andrew H. Wang (1993).

Bibliotheca Alexandrina (subcommittee)

To promote the international project of rebuilding the Library of Alexandria (Bibliotheca Alexandrina), to assist in raising funds to support the collection development and staffing of the Library, to make the American library community aware of the services the Alexandrian Library will provide to researchers and scholars.

Ch., Mohammed Aman (1993); Vinod Chachra (1993); Donald G. Davis Jr. (1993); George R. Ferguson (1993); Hardy R. Franklin (1993); Elinor M. Hashim (1993); Beverly P. Lynch (1994); Peter Paulson (1993).

Bogle International Library Travel Fund (subcommittee)

Responsible for administering funds accumulating as interest in the Bogle Memorial Fund.

Ch., Alexander Bloss (1993); Lesley C. Loke (1994); Joy L. Lowe (1993); Mary C. Mathews (1994); Loretta R. O'Brien (1993).

Chinese Libraries, Liaison with (ad hoc advisory)

To encourage and facilitate the development of exchange programs and other cooperative activities among libraries, librarians, and their associations in the United States and China.

Ch., Ching-chih Chen (1993); Wilfred W. Fong (1993); Hwa-Wei Lee (1993); Isabel A. Stirling (1994).

(John Ames) Humphry/OCLC/Forest Press Award Jury

The John Ames Humphry/OCLC/Forest Press Award for a Significant Contribution to International Librarianship consists of a prize of $1,000 and a certificate. The award is made to a librarian or another person who has made significant contributions to international librarianship, but "primary consideration will be given to contributions in the field of classification and subject analysis, and to work in Third World countries." Created on the occasion of the retirement of John Humphry as Executive Director of Forest Press, publisher of the Dewey Decimal Classification, the award recognizes Humphry's far-ranging work "to internationalize the English-language editions of Dewey and to ensure that translations were adapted to meet the needs of other cultures and countries."

Ch., Loretta R. O'Brien (1994); Dora Biblarz (1993); Barbara F. Immroth (1993); Beverly P. Lynch (1993).

International Federation of Library Associations and Institutions (subcommittee)

To maximize U.S. involvement in IFLA and to provide the mechanism for disseminating information to ALA members regarding elections to IFLA boards and committees.

Ch., Lucille C. Thomas (1993); Joseph F. Boykin (1993); Warren M. Tsuneishi (1993); Paul Vassallo (1993).

International Relations Committee— International Relations Round Table (subcommittee)

To prepare guidelines for exchanges with librarians throughout the world; to identify sources of funding for particular areas of the world; to compile a list of agencies and groups which sponsor exchanges and/or act as clearinghouses; to prepare a list of librarians who have been involved in international exchanges.

Ch., Opritsa A. Popa (1993); David L. Easterbrook (1994); Doina G. Farkas (1993); Kenneth L. Firestein (1993); Alfred Kagan (1993); Marta H. Kuszczak (1994); Wendy A. Miller (1994); Dallas Y. Shaffer (1993).

Japanese Libraries, Liaison with (ad hoc)

In coordination with its Japanese counterpart, to plan and implement U.S.-Japan binational conference(s) on librarianship in fulfillment of goals and objectives established by the ALA International Relations Committee. Serves as advisory to the ALA International Relations Committee.

Ch., Theodore F. Welch (1993); Kazuko M. Dailey (1993); Dorothy D. Gregor (1993); Mary F. Grosch (1993); Hideo Kaneko (1993); Charles Martell (1993); Hisao Matsumoto (1993); Jordan M. Scepanski (1993); Harold B. Shill (1993); Robert D. Stueart (1993).

U.S.-Armenian Libraries (subcommittee)

To establish relationships between the United States and Armenian libraries throughout the world; and to identify sources of funding for implementation of projects generated as a result of these relationships.

Ch., Sylva N. Manoogian (1993); Araxie P. Churukian (1993); Maurice J. Freedman (1993); Samuel Y. Fustukjian (1993); Ared Misirliyan (1994); Ann Dombourian Moore (1994); Lilia M. Vazquez (1993).

U.S.-Mexico Libraries (subcommittee)

Ch., Robert A. Seal (1993); Cesar Caballero (1993); Helen L. De Guevara (1993); Rhonda A. Rios Kravitz (1993); Helen G. Maul (1993); Sheila A. Milam (1994); Rhonda L. Neugebauer (1994); Elena Tscherny (1993).

U.S.-C.I.S.-Baltic States Library Cooperation (subcommittee)

To develop, enhance, and facilitate the cooperation among libraries, librarians, their societies and associations in the U.S. and the C.I.S.; to serve as a liaison with organizations and individuals who have been or would like to be involved in this activity; and to support all kinds of cooperation outlined in the Agreements and Protocols of the Commission on Library Cooperation of Learned Societies and the Library Council of the C.I.S.

Ch., Helen Teplitskaia (1993); Randall K. Barry (1993); Frank Elliott (1993); Carla D. Hayden (1994); Barbara F. Immroth (1993); Edward Kasinec (1993); Dennis A. Kimmage (1993); Harold M. Leich (1993); Madeleine M. Nichols (1993); Edward J. Valauskas (1993).

Legislation (standing, Council)

To have full responsibility for the Association's total legislative program on all levels—federal, state, and local. To recommend legislative policy and programs for Council approval and to take the necessary steps for implementation. To protest any legislation or executive policy adversely affecting libraries. To seek rulings and interpretations of laws and regulations affecting the welfare and development of libraries. To represent the ALA before executive and legislative branches of government as required at all levels. To provide a forum within ALA to gather information about needed legislation and to keep all units of the Association informed of the ALA legislative programs. To direct the activities of all units of the Association in matters relating to legislation.

Ch., Thomas L. Hart (1994); Charles E. Beard (1994); Francis J. Buckley Jr. (1994); Roberta G. Cade (1993); E. J. Josey (1994); Nancy C. Kranich (1993); Janet R. Moltzan (1993); Joan Ress Reeves (1993); Susan Rosenzweig (1994); Edward J. Valauskas (1994); staff liaison, Eileen D. Cooke.

Copyright (ad hoc subcommittee)

To set up and implement a mechanism for monitoring the effects on library services of compliance with the new copyright law, in preparation for the five-year review by the Register of Copyrights. To determine the kinds of data that should be collected for the review and how best to collect them. To serve as liaison with ALA divisions and other units and other library organizations, to receive information, serve as a sounding board, and relay information to the Legislation Committee on the various aspects of the copyright law that are unsettled or on which there is general lack of understanding among librarians.

Ch., Donald E. Riggs; Mary Hardin; Nancy H. Marshall; Patricia H. Mautino; Edward J. Valauskas; Paul Vassallo; David B. Walch; staff liaison, Eileen D. Cooke.

Government Information (ad hoc subcommittee)

Established by the American Library Association to identify other concerned organizations, investigate the problem, and seek legislative and executive efforts to examine the collection, analysis, and dissemination of government information vital to the well-being of the American public.

Ch., Nancy C. Kranich; Mary Birmingham; Thomas S. Blanton; Francis J. Buckley Jr.; Joan Coachman Durrance; Barbara Gloriod; Doria Beachell Grimes; Stephen M. Hayes; Barbara M. Jones; Katherine Mawdsley; James Nelson; Harold B. Shill; Robert A. Walter; staff liaison, Anne A. Heanue.

Legislation Assembly (subcommittee)

To act in an advisory and resource capacity to the ALA Legislation Committee. The individual members, named to the Assembly by the divisions and other units as determined by the Legislation Committee, shall serve as liaison to their divisions or units in matters relative to legislation.

Ch. and ACRL, Katherine Mawdsley; AASL, to be appointed; ALCTS, Jon Eldredge; ALSC, Marge Loch-Wouters; ALTA, Dorris D. Holmes; ASCLA, Barbara Will; COSWL, Estelle Black; FLRT, Phyllis Christenson; GODORT, Jan Fryer; LAMA, Robert Daugherty; LITA, Patrick Flannery; PLA, Don W. Barlow; RASD, James R. Cannon; SCOLE, to be appointed; YALSA, Jeri Baker; staff liaison, Carol Henderson.

Library Education (standing, Council)

To develop and recommend Association policies related to the educational preparation of all library personnel. To encourage other ALA units to establish education committees relevant to their specific fields of interest and to work closely with these units through the Library Education Assembly. To coordinate recommendations and policies concerning library education promulgated by ALA divisions, round tables, and other units to eliminate conflict or unnecessary duplication. To maintain communication and rapport, as appropriate, with other library organizations concerned with library education. To represent the Association to organizations and agencies outside the library field that are concerned with professional education and staff preparation. To identify needed research in the field of library education and to help promote its accomplishment. To act as a clearinghouse of information on all aspects of library education for the profession and public-at-large.

Ch., Ronald R. Powell (1994); Mary Biggs (1994); Nicholas C. Burckel (1994); Carolyn O. Frost (1994); Mary F. Lenox (1993); Jill L. Locke (1994); Susan B. Madden (1993); Albert J. Milo (1993); Darlene E. Weingand (1994); staff liaison, Margaret Myers.

Continuing Education (subcommittee)

To advise SCOLE on formation and implementation of overall Association policy on CE; to develop, review and promote adherence to standards/guidelines for good practice in CE; to design and coordinate comprehensive long-range planning and to evaluate the Association's effectiveness in meeting the CE needs of members; to promote the creation of a CE support system to serve members and ALA units; to maintain liaison with ALA units that have an interest in CE and with other providers of CE for the profession.

Ch., William L. Whitesides (1993); Gwen Arthur (1994); Daniel D. Barron (1993); Amy Bernath (1994); Duncan F. Smith (1994); SCOLE liaison, Jill L. Locke (1993).

International Library Education (subcommittee)

Responsible for the gathering and dissemination of information on library and information science education in other countries; for the promotion and exchange of information on curricula and teaching methods world wide; for carrying out specific projects, such as the Milam Lecture Series, and the Country Resource Panel list on equivalencies of qualifications in library and information science; and for advising and representing SCOLE in all matters pertaining to international library education.

Ch., Mohammed Aman (1993); Charles William Conaway (1993); John Corbin (1993); Shirley A. Fitzgibbons (1993); William Z. Nasri (1993); SCOLE liaison, Nicholas C. Burckel (1993).

"Library Education and Personnel Utilization" Policy Review, OLPR/SCOLE (interunit task force) (See p. 11.)

Library Education Assembly

To provide within ALA an opportunity for broad representation of the membership and for affiliated groups to exchange information, share ideas, and express concerns pertaining to education for library service with a view toward assisting the Standing Committee on Library Education in carrying out its charge. Representatives are appointed by ALA units and affiliates with education-related concerns; other library education groups plus members-at-large are also included. Meetings are held each Midwinter and Annual Conference.

Division Representatives

AASL—Elizabeth L. Marcoux.
ACRL—Rochelle R. Ballard; Larry R. Oberg; Elizabeth H. Park; Patricia Stinson Switzer.
ALCTS—Michael Elmore; Martha J. Hanson; Arno A. Kastner; Sally J. Rausch.
ALSC—Leslie Edmonds.
ALTA—Gloria F. Aguilar.
ASCLA—Donna Z. Pontau.
LAMA—Donald E. Wright.
LITA—Marcia K. Deddens.
PLA—June Lester.

RASD—Deborah A. Carver; Norman Howden; Genie McKee.
YALSA—to be appointed.

Round Table Representatives

AFLRT—to be appointed.
CLENERT—Darlene E. Weingand.
EMIERT—to be appointed.
FLRT—Lee R. McLaughlin.
GODORT—John B. Phillips.
ILERT—Ronald Sigler.
IRRT—Miles M. Jackson.
LHRT—Charles A. Seavey.
LIRT—Mary M. Nofsinger.
LRRT—to be appointed.
MAGERT—Charles A. Seavey.
NMRT—Dorothy Ann Branton.
SRRT—Carol R. Barta.
VRT—to be appointed.

Other Representatives

Chapter Relations Com.—Joe Dahlstrom.
Com. on Accreditation—C. James Schmidt.
User Instruction for Information Literacy—John C. Tyson.
Intellectual Freedom Com.—to be appointed.
OLOS—to be appointed.
OLPR—Maureen Sullivan.
SCOLE—Mohammed Aman; William L. Whitesides.
Staff liaison—Margaret Myers.

Library Outreach Services, Office for (standing, advisory)

To offer policy guidance to the Office; to advise and assist the Office in establishing programs and priorities; to examine and assist in coordinating the various relevant programs and activities within ALA; to recommend new programs; to provide a channel through which membership may make recommendations; and to issue reports and to promote any other activities that will improve the quality of library service to the rural and urban poor and to ethnic minority groups.

Ch., Virginia H. Mathews (1994); Thomas E. Alford (1994); Gloria J. Coles (1993); Martha L. Goddard (1994); Marjorie H. Li (1993); Deborah L. Schaeffer (1994); Dallas Y. Shaffer (1994); Linda L. Tse (1993); James C. Welbourne (1993); Gretchen M. Wronka (1994); staff liaison, Mattye L. Nelson.

ALA Minority Fellowship Advisory Board (subcommittee)

Ch., Maureen Sullivan (1993); Gloria J. Coles (1993); Yolanda J. Cuesta (1993); Judith A. Sessions (1993); ex officio: Virginia H. Mathews; Margaret Myers; Mattye L. Nelson; Susan Roman.

American Indians, Library Service for (subcommittee)

To promote the development of American Indian library services by serving as a focal point within ALA for issues related to American Indian library services; to encourage the implementation of ALA policy "Goals for Indian Library and Information Services;" to work with other ALA units to encourage the publication of bicultural materials, effective programming, the development of library personnel; and to advocate increased funding for American Indian library services.

Ch., John Aubrey (1993); Janice M. Beaudin (1993); Naomi Caldwell-Wood (1993); Virginia H. Mathews (1993); James H. May (1993); John R. McCracken (1993); Mary L. Nieball (1993); Lotsee Patterson (1993); Dennis Reed (1993); Maryalice Hedge Reszetar (1993); Sally Roggia (1993); Velma S. Salabiyc (1993); Rhonda Harris Taylor (1993).

Friends of Library Outreach
(subcommittee)

Ch., Clara S. Jones (1993).

Literacy Assembly

To establish a focal point with ALA that will emphasize the Association's continuing commitment to literacy beyond divisional and unit membership committees; to provide an opportunity for broad representation of the membership and affiliated groups to exchange information and share ideas, identify concerns and omissions, and coordinate programming; and, to develop and promote strategies for increased literacy activity within the Association.

Ch., Jane Heiser.

Division Representatives

AASL—to be appointed.
ACRL—Trish Ridgeway.
ALCTS—Anne Henley Cain.
ALSC—Helen Mae Mullen.
ALTA—Bonnie Bellamy.
ASCLA—to be appointed.
LAMA—Trellis C. Wright.
LITA—Joan Maier McKean.
PLA—Stewart L. Wells.
RASD—to be appointed.
YALSA—Ellen Libretto.

Round Table Representatives

AFLRT—to be appointed.
CLENERT—to be appointed.
EMIERT—Janice L. Lavery.
GODORT—Janita A. Jobe.
ILERT—to be appointed.
IRRT—Ernest A. DiMattia.
LHRT—to be appointed.
LIRT—Madeline A. Copp.
LRRT—to be appointed.
MAGERT—to be appointed.
NMRT—Jennifer Stone Abramson.
SORT—Donna Epps Ramsey.
SRRT—Denise E. Botto.
VRT—to be appointed.

Outside Representatives

REFORMA—Mario M. Gonzalez; Albert J. Milo.

Library Personnel Resources, Office for
(standing, advisory)

To advise the Office for Library Personnel Resources on activities, problems, and procedures related to library concerns in such areas as recruitment, utilization, education and training, and staff welfare. The committee will identify special areas of need or emphasis, suggest activities and programs, and stimulate programs and projects related to library personnel planning, development, and concerns. The committee will aid in communication and cooperation with other units of ALA and with other agencies, groups, and organizations within and beyond the library profession.

Ch., Maureen Sullivan (1993); Jennifer W. Arns (1993); Tami Echavarria (1994); Christine L. Hage (1994); Frances O. Painter (1994); Ruth J. Patrick (1994); Kitty Smith (1993); Lois Winkel (1993); 1 to be appointed; staff liaison, Margaret Myers.

"Library Education and Personnel Utilization" Policy Review, OLPR/SCOLE
(interunit task force)

To analyze comments received from the field on suggested changes for the policy and determine whether a revision should be recommended. To develop an action plan for further implementation of the policy statement.

Ch., Kitty Smith (OLPR); Patricia M. Paine (OLPR); Jane Robbins (SCOLE); Jana Varlejs (SCOLE).

Recruitment Assembly

To facilitate communication about activities related to recruiting for the profession among ALA units and other groups. To foster coordination and cooperation of recruitment efforts among ALA units and other groups. To avoid unnecessary duplication and enhance individual and collective recruitment efforts. To develop a multi-year systematic national recruitment plan as outlined in The Decade of the Librarian 1990–2000 and to assist in implementing and monitoring other recruitment strategies outlined in the plan. To expand the "Each One Reach One" network through publicity and involvement. To make recommendations for recruitment policies, programs, publications, or other activities to appropriate bodies. To communicate with other national library/information organizations with an interest in recruitment. To report to and advise the OLPR Advisory Committee and office on issues and activities related to recruitment.

Membership (standing)

To establish general policies, programs, and procedures to secure new members; to be responsible for the implementation of these programs; to coordinate membership promotion activities of all units and chapters of the Association; to coordinate the ALA committee internship program; to make recommendations concerning membership dues; and to serve the Association as a sounding board on membership.

Ch., Kay A. Cassell (1993).

Regional Representatives

California—Gail A. Schlachter (1993).
Canada—Gerald R. Brown (1994).
Hawaii—Florence Yee (1993).
Mid-Atlantic—to be appointed.
Midwestern—Darlene S. Basone (1994).
Mountain Plains—Phyllis A. Monyakula (1994).
New England—Harriet S. Selverstone (1993).
New York—Kay A. Cassell (1993).
Pacific Northwest—Susan B. Madden (1994).
Southeastern—Diana D. Young (1994).
Southwestern—Viki L. Ash-Geisler (1994).
Student rep.—Sandra E. Goldstein (1994).
Trustee rep.—Leroy D. Williams (1994).
Staff liaisons—Gerald G. Hodges and Julie Ann Geissler.

Membership Promotion Task Force

Along with the 12-member Membership Committee, these task force members—52 state and district representatives and their subcommittees, 11 division representatives, and the 17 round table representatives—are charged with promoting ALA membership within their respective units.

Division Representatives

AASL—to be appointed.
ALTA—to be appointed.
ALCTS—Barry Baker (1993).
ALSC—Joanne Foss (1993).
ACRL—Andrea C. Hoffman (1993).
ASCLA—Barbara Mates (1993).
LAMA—Robert A. Almony (1993).
LITA—Martha Hruska (1993).
PLA—Carole Dickerson (1993).
RASD—Linda Keir Simms (1993).
YALSA—Deborah Colter (1993).

Round Table Representatives

AFLRT—James F. Aylward (1993).
CLENERT—Cecy Keller (1993).
EMIERT—Bosiljka Stevanovic (1993).
ERT—Patricia H. Smith (1993).
FLRT—to be appointed.
GODORT—Linda B. Johnson (1993).
IFRT—Eric C. Welch (1993).
ILERT—to be appointed.
IRRT—Kathleen Gunning (1992).
LHRT—Nancy Becker Johnson (1993).
LIRT—Charlotte J. Files (1993).
LRRT—Mark Tucker (1993).
MAGERT—Katherine L. Rankin (1993).
NMRT—to be appointed.
SORT—to be appointed.
SRRT—Steven H. Murden (1993).
VRT—to be appointed.

State and District Chairpersons

State and District Chairpersons are appointed in October.

Minority Concerns (standing, Council)

To provide a mechanism that represents the interests and concerns of ethnic minority librarians; to work closely with the ALA Office for Library Outreach Services; to serve as liaison with the ALA office advisory committees, division boards or division committees, other membership units, the ALA affiliated ethnic minority associations and the nonaffiliated minority caucuses; to provide Council and Membership with reports and information needed for the establishment of policies and actions related to the interests and concerns of ethnic minority librarians; and to establish contacts with nonlibrary organizations whose purposes and activities are designed to serve the needs of ethnic minority groups.

Ch., Herman L. Totten (1993); Lydia A. Acosta (1994); Ingrid Betancourt (1994); Leon S. Bey (1994); Herbert Biblo (1993); Robert Caban (1993); Naomi Caldwell-Wood (1993); Ronald Rodriguez (1993); Fannette H. Thomas (1994); Phyllis Jeanne Van Orden (1994); ex officio, Patricia M. Wong (1993); staff liaison, Mattye L. Nelson.

Nominating—1993 Election (special)

(See Bylaw Article III.)

Ch., Mary R. Somerville (1993); Liz R. Miller (1993); Emily R. Mobley (1993); Jacqueline G.

Morris (1993); Thomas Shaughnessy (1993); staff liaison, Emily I. Melton.

Organization (standing, Council)

To advise and assist regarding structural and organizational concerns in ALA. To recommend to Council the establishment or discontinuance of divisions, roundtables, membership initiative groups, ALA committees, assemblies and joint committees, as the needs of the Association may require. To define the functions of these units, subject to the approval of Council. To recommend to Council the establishment, including the name and size, of other standing committees to consider matters of the Association that require continuity of attention by the members. To recommend to Executive Board the appropriate unit to appoint Official Representatives to outside organizations. To receive notification of the formation of interdivisional committees.

Ch., Karen A. Whitney (1993); William G. Asp (1994); Rebecca T. Bingham (1994); Melissa Buckingham (1993); Ginnie Cooper (1994); Joseph R. Edelen Jr. (1994); Marianne Gessner (1994); Salvador Guerena (1993); Suzine Har-Nicolescu (1993); W. Lee Hisle (1994); Gail P. Warner (1993); Ramonda S. Wertz (1994); J. Linda Williams (1993); staff liaison, JoAn S. Segal.

Pay Equity (standing, Council)

To promote the visibility of the pay equity issue as it affects library workers, both to the profession and to outside groups; to act as a resource on the issue for the association and its units; to develop and implement educational activities through conference programming, poster sessions, and publications; to continue active involvement and ALA representation in the National Committee on Pay Equity; to develop a national network of resource persons and provide information to state and local groups working to achieve pay equity; and to provide advisory support for pay equity litigation cases involving library workers.

Ch., Lourdes Y. Collantes (1993); Anne Henley Cain (1994); Robert Franklin (1993); Patricia M. Hogan (1993); Penelope S. Jeffrey (1994); Joyce E. Jelks (1994); Ivonne R. Jimenez (1994); Jessica A. Marshall (1994); Meralyn Meadows (1994); Sherman Pridham (1993); Sarah Barbara Watstein (1993); staff liaison, Margaret Myers.

Planning (standing, Council)

To provide the Association with a structured and identifiable mechanism for determining future trends and needs; to provide information and recommendations to assist in the periodic selection of priorities by the Association; to establish methods of evaluating Association progress toward the accomplishment of its priorities; to identify priority areas that are not being effectively addressed and to recommend appropriate action; to provide information and guidelines for program evaluation necessary to COPES in its budgetmaking process; to identify organizational issues related to Association priorities and refer such issues to COO.

Ch., Regina U. Minudri (1993); Patricia W. Berger (1993); Julie A. Cummins (1993); Bettie A. Estes-Rickner (1994); June M. Garcia (1994); Martin J. Gomez (1993); William A. Gosling (1993); staff liaison, Peggy Sullivan.

Planning and Budget Assembly (advisory to COPES and Planning)

To assist the Committee on Program Evaluation and Support and the ALA Planning Committee, there shall be a Planning and Budget Assembly which shall consist of one representative of each division, ALA committee, roundtable, and five councilors at large and five councilors from chapters. The representatives of the divisions, committees, and round tables shall be designated annually by each group; the Council representatives shall be elected by the Council for two-year staggered terms, none to extend beyond the regularly elected term on Council, from nominations submitted by the Council Committee on Committees. Additional nominations for the councilor members of the Planning and Budget Assembly may be made from the floor. The duties of the Planning and Budget Assembly are to provide guidance for program planning and evaluation, assist in periodic selection of goals, study the tentative summary planning document submitted by the Planning Committee and the balanced tentative budget submitted by the Committee on Program Evaluation and Support, raise questions concerning them, and offer suggestions to both committees.

Councilors-at-Large

Susan S. Goldberg (1993); Mary Lou Gregory (1994); William H. Roberts (1994); Mary R. Sommerville (1994); Gail P. Warner (1993).

Chapter Councilors

Lydia A. Acosta (1993); Lynette Anderson (1994); Carol I. Hildebrand (1994); Carolyn B. Noah (1993); Florence H. Yee (1993).

Division Representatives

AASL—Bernadette Winter.
ACRL—Jacquelyn A. McCoy.
ALCTS—Robert P. Holley; Jennifer A. Younger.
ALSC—Ellen G. Fader.
ALTA—Ann L. Donoghue.
ASCLA—Barbara L. Perkis.
LAMA—Ronald P. Naylor.
LITA—Paul Evan Peters.
PLA—Ronald A. Dubberly.
RASD—Charles L. Gilreath.
YALSA—Elizabeth M. O'Donnell.

ALA Committee Representatives

Access to Information—Gordon M. Conable.
Accreditation—C. James Schmidt.
American Libraries—Gail A. Schlachter.
Awards—Robert S. Smith.
Chapter Relations—Carol K. DiPrete.
Conference Program—Margaret L. Crist.
Constitution and Bylaws—Thomas E. Alford.
Council Orientation—Charles E. Beard.
Development—Pat Woodrum.
Intellectual Freedom—Candance D. Morgan.
International Relations—Nancy R. John.
Legislation—Thomas L. Hart.
Library Education—Ronald R. Powell.
Library Outreach Services—Virginia H. Mathews.
Library Personnel Resources—Maureen Sullivan.
Membership—Kay A. Cassell.
Minority Concerns—Herman L. Totten.
Nominating—Mary R. Sommerville.
Organization—Karen A. Whitney.

Pay Equity—Lourdes Y. Collantes.
Planning—Regina U. Minudri.
Policy Monitoring—Norman Horrocks.
Professional Ethics—Jeanne M. Isacco.
Program Evaluation and Support—Mary W. Ghikas.
Public Information—Elizabeth Futas.
Publishing—Sharon J. Rogers.
Research and Statistics—Barbara F. Immorth.
Resolutions—Judith R. Farley.
Review, Inquiry and Mediation—to be appointed.
Standards—Keith C. Wright.
User Instruction for Information Literacy—Marsha D. Broadway.
Women in Librarianship—Estelle M. Black.

Round Table Representatives

AFLRT—to be appointed.
CLENERT—Laura Kimberly.
EMIERT—to be appointed.
ERT—Nancy Schwartz.
FLRT—Lorie Stackpole.
GODORT—Julia F. Wallace.
IFRT—Thomas F. Budlong; Lois P. Mills.
ILERT—Susan N. Bjørner.
IRRT—Ernest A. DiMattia.
LHRT—Nancy Becker Johnson.
LIRT—Marilyn P. Whitmore.
LRRT—Elfreda A. Chatman.
MAGERT—Thornton P. McGlamery.
NMRT—Jennifer Stone Abramson.
SORT—Eleanor F. Pemberton.
SRRT—Roland C. Hansen.
VRT—Gary P. Handman.
Staff liaison—Roger H. Parent.

Policy Monitoring (standing, Council)

To monitor the accurate documentation and codification of ALA policy, as determined by formal action of Council; to prepare additions or changes in the ALA Policy Manual following each annual conference and midwinter meeting, as may be required by motions and resolutions adopted by Council; to review and advise on all unit organization policies to ensure that they are in compliance with Council approved Association-wide policies; to provide oversight by review prior to publication of the written text and Policy Manual numbers prepared by ALA staff and report to Council the accomplishment of Council's directives; to be responsible for keeping the Policy Manual accurate and up to date and to call Council's attention to out-dated items to be retired from the Manual or gaps in the presentation of Policies. (See ALA Policy 5.7.)

Ch., Norman Horrocks (1993); Stephen L. Matthews (1993); Sarah M. Pritchard (1993); staff liaison, Lois Ann Gregory-Wood.

Professional Ethics (standing, Council)

The Council Committee on Professional Ethics shall augment the *Statement on Professional Ethics* by explanatory interpretations and additional statements, prepared by this committee or elicited from other units of ALA. When units of the association develop statements dealing with ethical issues, a copy will be sent to the Committee on Professional Ethics for review so that it may be compared to the existing ALA Code of Ethics in order to determine whether or not conflicts occur.

Ch., Jeanne M. Isacco (1994); Roger S. Ashley (1994); Hans E. Bynagle (1994); Carolyn C.

Daniel (1993); Sara Fine (1993); Claire Oaks (1994); 1 to be appointed; staff liaison, Judith F. Krug.

Program Evaluation and Support
(standing, Council)

To evaluate the programs of the Association and submit a recommended budget to the Executive Board for action. (See Bylaw Article VIII, Sec. 2.)

Ch., Mary W. Ghikas (1993); N. Bernard Basch (1993); Joseph A. Boisse (1994); Margaret L. Crist (1994); Bruce E. Daniels (1994); Ann K. Symons (1996); Vivian R. Wynn (1996); staff liaison, Roger H. Parent.

Project Century 21 Advisory (special presidential)

The "Project Century 21: A Research and Action Program for Meeting the Information Needs of Society" will examine society's needs for information and the human resources that will be essential to deliver services through libraries and information agencies in the Information Age. The Advisory Committee will serve in an overall advisory role for all aspects of Project 21, including setting priorities, identifying funding sources and research teams and other project personnel, planning communication strategies, reviewing progress, and recommending future actions.

Ch., Jane Robbins (1994); Adele M. Fasick (1994); Carolyn O. Frost (1994); Suzanne H. Mahmoodi (1994); Thomas J. Michalak (1994); Pat Molholt (1994); Robert M. O'Neil (1994); Wayne A. Wiegand (1994); ex officio, Marilyn L. Miller (1994); staff liaison, Margaret Myers.

Public Information (standing, advisory)

To assist the Public Information Office (PIO) in identifying needs and priorities in the area of public awareness. To advise on development of promotional and marketing programs for libraries, librarians, and the American Library Association, including National Library Week and other national campaigns. To assist PIO in carrying out its responsibility for developing promotional tools for all types of libraries, coordinating media relations for the Association and providing public relations counsel to members and staff. To promote communication and cooperation throughout ALA, its chapters, and other library associations, also organizations beyond the library profession.

Ch., Elizabeth Futas (1993); Barbara D. Cooper (1994); Nancy A. Davenport (1993); Susan S. DiMattia (1994); Fred E. Goodman (1993); Dawn H. Heller (1994); Kathy L. Kelly (1994); Thomas C. Phelps (1993); Patricia H. Smith (1993); Kimberly K. Taylor (1993); staff liaison, Linda K. Wallace.

National Library Week (subcommittee)

To advise and assist the Public Information Advisory Committee and the Public Information Office in the planning, implementation, and evaluation of National Library Week promotion. To promote participation in NLW activities throughout ALA units and its chapters. To recommend policies and procedures for the Grolier National Library Week Grant and to promote applications. To serve as a jury for selection of the grant recipient.

Ch., Donna J. Dufault (1993); Carol S. Drought (1993); Beryl E. Eber (1993); Kathy L. Kelly (1994); John W. King (1994); Harriet Lapointe (1993); Deborah J. Leather (1993); LaDonne Roberts (1993); Amy K. Small (1994); Vivian R. Wynn (1994); staff liaison, Linda K. Wallace.

National Partners for Libraries and Literacy (subcommittee)

To establish and promote cooperative relations between ALA and appropriate national organizations, including associations and other library and nonlibrary groups. To promote support for activities related to ALA's public awareness goals. To disseminate library public relations materials and to gather information on library and literacy support programs. To strengthen public understanding and recognition of the importance of libraries to the nation.

Ch., Jean L. Preer (1993); Mary C. Chobot (1993); Eileen D. Cooke (1993); Evelyn M. Fass (1993); Mary K. Feldman (1993); Donald J. Fork (1993); Anne A. Heanue (1993); Mary Berghaus Levering (1993); John G. Lorenz (1993); Anne J. Mathews (1993); Maria Pedak-Kari (1993); Stephen Prine Jr. (1993); Barbara S. Roberts (1993); Sharon J. Rogers (1993); Mary June Roggenbuck (1993); Jane H. Roth (1993); Jacque-Lynne Schulman (1993); Gerald J. Sophar (1993); Elizabeth W. Stone (1993); Christina C. Young (1993); staff liaison, Linda K. Wallace.

Public Relations Assembly (subcommittee)

To provide a forum for the exchange of information about library public relations and marketing activities throughout the association and with other library groups and associations sharing an interest in library promotion. To promote cooperation and enhance the effectiveness of public relations activities throughout the association and to strengthen ALA's national public awareness efforts.

Ch. and members to be appointed.

Publishing (standing, Council)

To set the framework within which ALA publishing operates. To recommend publishing policies for the approval of Council; to advise and assist all units of the Association in their publishing activities; to give counsel and guidance on the administration of publishing services. To oversee publishing budget preparation and make recommendations on budgetary matters to COPES or other appropriate units. The committee shall control the use of the ALA imprint.

Ch., Sharon J. Rogers (1993); Linda D. Crowe (1993); Ann H. Eastman (1994); Diane J. Graves (1995); Marjorie Jones (1994); Eleanor R. Kulleseid (1994); Josette A. Lyders (1994); Michael J. Madden (1993); Beth J. Shapiro (1994); Raymond F. Vondran (1993); Exec. Bd. liaison, Nancy M. Bolt (1993); interim staff liaison, Evelyn Shaevel.

"Book Links" Advisory Board
(subcommittee)

To advise the editor of *Book Links: Connecting Books, Libraries, and Classrooms* on all matters pertaining to editorial policies of *Book Links* and to assist the editor in developing membership awareness of the programs of *Book Links*.

Ch., Ginny Moore Kruse (1994); Mary Ann Brown (1994); Dudley B. Carlson (1993); Barbara Z. Kiefer (1994); Retta B. Patrick (1993); staff liaison, Barbara Elleman.

"Booklist" Editorial Advisory Board
(subcommittee)

To advise the editors of *Booklist* on all matters pertaining to editorial policies of *Booklist;* to assist the editors of *Booklist* in developing membership awareness of the programs of *Booklist*.

Ch., Betty Carter (1993); R. Randall Enos (1994); Karen H. Harris (1993); Teresa Portilla Omidsalar (1993); Hilda W. Parfrey (1993); Ranae Pierce (1993); Marilyn L. Shackelford (1993); staff liaison, Bill Ott.

Carnegie Reading List and Whitney-Carnegie Grants (subcommittee)

To evaluate proposals submitted for the Carnegie Reading List and Whitney-Carnegie grants and make recommendations for awardees to the Publishing Committee for approval.

Ch., Marjorie Jones (1993); interim staff liaison, Evelyn Shaevel.

"Reference Books Bulletin" Editorial Board (subcommittee)

To provide authoritative, critical, timely evaluations of reference sources and to prepare these evaluations for publication.

Ch., Christine Bulson (1993); Edwina Amorosa (1993); Hampton M. Auld (1993); Susan C. Awe (1994); Kenneth L. Black (1993); Jerry J. Carbone (1994); Ron J. Chepesiuk (1993); Ann E. Cohen (1993); Sharon E. Cohen (1993); Lesley S. J. Farmer (1994); Elizabeth L. Fraser (1994); John P. Hall (1993); Robin Hoelle (1993); Sarah Sartain Jane (1994); Jane C. Jurgens (1993); Sue Kamm (1994); Marlene Kuhl (1993); Marvin D. Leavy (1993); Marilyn L. Long (1993); Carolyn M. Mulac (1993); Betty B. Page (1994); David N. Pauli (1993); Fannette H. Thomas (1994); Sarah Barbara Watstein (1993); A. Virginia Witucke (1994); interns: Rochelle Glantz (1993); Carol Sue Harless (1993); Thomas E. Klingler (1993); Kathleen Morrissey McBroom (1993); Elizabeth B. Nibley (1993); staff liaison, Sandy Whiteley.

Research and Statistics (standing)

To facilitate research and related activities in all units of the Association, especially activities related to library statistics; to advise the ALA Council and Executive Board on programs, policy, and priorities regarding research and related activities; to recommend procedures to achieve expeditious consideration of all ALA unit proposals for research and related activities by the ALA Executive Board; to encourage the establishment of divisional committees for the purpose of stimulating research and statistics; to maintain liaison with all units of the Association regarding research and related activities in the units; to identify questions regarding library service which need to be answered through research and promote the conduct of research to answer those questions; to review and make recommendations concerning national data collection efforts pertaining to libraries, recommending inclusions, definitions, procedures, and policies as appropriate; to serve as a base committee for liaisons from other associations and groups with shared concerns about library statistics; and to serve as an advisory committee for the Office for Research and Statistics.

Ch., Barbara F. Immroth (1993); Martin J. Dillon (1994); Janice Feye-Stukas (1993); Ronald G. Leach (1994); Murray S. Martin (1993); Richard W. Meyer (1994); Joseph J. Mika (1993); Barbara M. Robinson (1993); Marilyn L. Shontz (1994); Jo Bell Whitlatch (1994); Peter R. Young (1993); Craig S. Zapatos (1994); staff liaison, Mary Jo Lynch.

Research and Statistics Assembly (subcommittee)

To provide a forum for the exchange of information about library research and statistical activities throughout the association and with other library groups and associations sharing an interest in those topics; to enhance the effectiveness of research and statistical activities throughout the association; and to strengthen ALA's efforts to promote quality work in the areas of research and statistics.

The membership of the Assembly will include: the chairs of each division and section committee on research and/or statistics; the chairs of other ALA committees who request membership (e.g., RASD, MOPSS Evaluation Committee); and the chair of the Library Research Round Table (LRRT) and the Library History Round Table (LHRT).

Resolutions (standing, Council)

To provide an advisory and channeling function for all resolutions presented for Council's consideration, reviewing all resolutions submitted to Council pursuant to the criteria established by Council in Policy 5.4 (Guidelines for Preparation of Resolutions for Presentation to Council).

To advise the makers on how to bring their resolutions into compliance with the Guidelines adopted by Council. All resolutions shall go to Council with a notation that the resolution has been processed through the committee.

To determine the policy or nonpolicy nature of all resolutions to be presented to Council and transmit the resolutions with the appropriate indication. To review all resolutions passed by Membership to determine those that are clearly policy matters and therefore should be forwarded to Council for action. Any challenge to the determination of the Committee shall be voted on by councilors present at the meeting.

Ch., Judith R. Farley (1993); Alex Boyd (1993); Janice Feye-Stukas (1994); Janet Swan Hill (1994); Irene B. Hoadley (1994); Winona Jones (1993); Sharad Karkhanis (1993); Em Claire Knowles (1993); Bernard A. Margolis (1993); Carolyn Markuson (1994); Judith K. Meyers (1993); Barbara F. Weaver (1994); staff liaison, Emily I. Melton.

Review, Inquiry, and Mediation (standing)

Established by Council, January 1989. To be responsible for review, inquiry, and mediation as appropriate to tenure, status, fair employment practices (including discrimination and sexual harassment), due process, ethical practices, and the principles of intellectual freedom as set forth in policies adopted by the Council of ALA. The standing committee should be comprised of seven individuals from the membership plus a staff liaison appointed by the Executive Director; ex-

officio members are the directors of the Offices for Intellectual Freedom, and Library Personnel Resources.

Ch., to be appointed; Darrell L. Batson (1993); Anna A. Curry (1993); Donna O. Dziedzic (1993); Judith R. Farley (1993); Monteria Hightower (1993); Ronald S. Kozlowski (1993); Larry R. Oberg (1993); staff liaisons: Roger H. Parent; JoAn S. Segal; Jeniece N. Guy.

Standards (standing)

To review and approve new and revised standards and guidelines for consistency with ALA policies as codified in the ALA Policy Manual. To develop and distribute a procedures manual for the preparation of all standards and guidelines issued by ALA, thus enabling all units to follow common practices regarding procedures for the development of standards and guidelines. To monitor the activities of committees on standards in the various units to ensure that draft standards and guidelines are reviewed by all units that have a potential interest in the topic. To encourage units to monitor existing standards and guidelines for continued relevancy. To publish an annual list of ALA standards and guidelines. To sponsor a special collection in the Headquarters Library that contains: all standards and guidelines published by the American Library Association and other national and international library organizations, as well as standards applicable to librarianship from nonlibrary organizations and agencies international, national, regional, and state.

Ch., Keith C. Wright (1993); Elinor M. Hashim (1993); Sherman L. Hayes (1993); Jeanne M. Isacco (1993); Mary E. Jackson (1994); Dana J. Rizzotti (1994); Jo Ann V. Rogers (1994); Jane Bandy Smith (1994); Carol Starr (1993); staff liaison, Mary Jo Lynch.

User Instruction for Information Literacy (standing)

To review and coordinate on a continuing basis activities within ALA regarding instruction for users in acquiring, organizing, and using information; to submit formal annual written reports to the ALA membership and Council highlighting the Committee and ALA units and committees' activities on a regular basis; to promote research related to information literacy for access to information; and to encourage Association-wide conference programming inviting the cooperation of all ALA units and committees concerned with user instruction for information literacy.

Ch., Marsha D. Broadway (1994); James F. Bennett (1993); Christine E. King (1994); Mary Popp (1994); Amy D. Seetoo (1993); Alphonse F. Trezza (1993); John C. Tyson (1993); staff liaison, Andrew M. Hansen.

White House Conference on Library and Information Services, Ad Hoc ALA Committee on the 1991

To consult with ALA members, units, and affiliates to develop and track activities designed to implement the goals of the 1991 White House Conference; to recommend action to the Executive Board and Council on implementation, plans, and activities; to strengthen liaisons already established with the White House Conference on Library and Information Services Task Force (WHCLIST), the ALA Chapter Relations Committee, and other cooperating organizations by

undertaking joint projects, sharing information, and communicating with the states on implementation activities; to strengthen communications between the units and offices about White House Conference implementation activities so that ALA's work is coordinated; to take an active role in WHCLIST.

Ch., Carol Diehl (1994); Ann H. Eastman (1994); Cynthia W. Everett (1994); Judith G. Flum (1994); Carolyn M. Gray (1994); Nann Blaine Hilyard (1993); Karen L. Horny (1994); Thea J. Jones (1993); Allan M. Kleiman (1994); Sarah Ann Long (1994); Virginia H. Mathews (1994); Patricia A. Wand (1994); staff liaison, Charles Harmon.

Women in Librarianship, Status of (standing, Council)

To officially represent the diversity of women's interest within ALA and to ensure that the Association considers the rights of the majority (women) in the library field. To promote and initiate the collection, analysis, dissemination, and coordination of information on the status of women in librarianship. To coordinate the activities of ALA units that consider questions having special relevance for women. To identify lags, gaps, and possible discrimination in resources and programs relating to women. To help develop evaluative tools, guidelines, and programs in cooperation with other ALA units designed to enhance the opportunities and the image of women in the library profession, thus raising the level of consciousness concerning women. To establish contacts with committees on women within other professional groups and to officially represent ALA concerns at interdisciplinary meetings on women's equality. To provide Council and Membership with reports needed for the establishment of policies and actions related to the status of women in librarianship, and monitor ALA units to ensure consideration of the rights of women.

Ch., Estelle M. Black (1993); Mary Biblo (1993); Florence S. Brown (1994); Leslie B. Burger (1994); GraceAnne A. DeCandido (1993); Ruth I. Gordon (1994); Louise W. Greenfield (1994); Peter Hiatt (1993); Suzanne Hildenbrand (1994); Lynnda M. Wangsgard (1994); Fay Zipkowitz (1993); staff liaison, Margaret Myers.

Advancing Women in Library Management (subcommittee)

To recommend, support, and develop projects which encourage equal opportunity for women to advance in library management.

Ch., GraceAnne A. DeCandido (1993); Gillian D. Ellern (1993); Kay F. Jones (1993); Nancy L. Magnuson (1993); Hannah Stevens (1993).

Bibliography/Clearinghouse (task force)

To identify published materials on the status of women in librarianship; to compile, update, and issue a bibliography of these materials on a regular basis; to alert COSWL to pertinent information on the status of women in librarianship; to provide access to ephemeral materials through ALA Headquarters.

Co-chs., Lori A. Goetsch (1993) and Sarah Barbara Watstein (1993); Allison A. Cowgill (1993); Joan B. Fiscella (1993); Janice J. Kirkland (1993); Jean McManus (1993); Mary Beth Minick (1993); Sandra K. Peterson (1993); Mary

Ellen Shiflett (1993); Kristin L. Strohmeyer (1993); Mary I. Vela-Creixell (1993).

Minority Women Oral History Project
(task force)

To implement project to interview selected minority women on their personal experiences and perspectives on librarianship as a means of adding to library history the contributions of minority librarians.

Ch., Gail P. Warner (1993); Detrice A. Bankhead (1993); Cynthia J. Johanson (1993); Betty-Carol Sellen (1993); Mary I. Vela-Creixell (1993); Mary D. Walters (1993).

Your Right to Know, President's Committee on (special)

To serve as advisory board for "The Right to Know a United Voice" grant; to advise on implementation, evaluation, and follow-up. To seek additional sources of funding to support and enlarge a speakers network for ALA. To investigate and propose other Right to Know activities and programs, e.g., coalition building, "Fund for America's Libraries," training programs in concert with other ALA divisions, units, and committees. To establish liaison with other groups or professions concerned with promoting and/or supporting the right to know. To advise on development and content of fact sheets, briefing books, and other "power tools" for use at national and local levels. To recommend aggressive strategies for communicating the message "Your Right to Know: Librarians Make It Happen."

Ch., Margaret L. Crist (1993); Elizabeth A. Curry (1993); Carol K. DiPrete (1993); Joan Coachman Durrance (1993); Elizabeth Futas (1993); Margo W. Hart (1993); Nancy C. Kranich (1993); Patricia H. Mautino (1993); Kathleen de la Pena McCook (1993); Dorothy S. Puryear (1993); Joan Ress Reeves (1993); Merrilyn S. Ridgeway (1993); Rhea J. Rubin (1993); staff liaisons: Peggy Barber; Gerald G. Hodges.

Joint Committees

The following joint committees of the ALA with other organizations have been established by Council action, in accordance with Bylaws Article VIII, Section 6. In some instances, the joint committee involves another organization and ALA, but a unit of ALA makes the appointment of the ALA members and carries on the ALA share of the activities.

In other instances, the committee is a joint one with another association and a unit of ALA. In other instances, the committee is a joint one between another association and ALA, with no ALA unit involved.

American Association of Law Libraries—American Correctional Association—ASCLA Committee on Institution Libraries (joint)

To cooperate in the formulation and implementation of standards of library service in correctional institutions; to stimulate planning and provide guidance in the establishment and improvement of libraries in these institutions and other correctional services; to coordinate and strengthen such activities as each association now has under way; and to explore possibilities for future cooperation in carrying out the objectives held in common by both organizations.

Co-chs., Timothy Brown (ASCLA, 1993), Thea B. Chesley (ACA, 1993), and Judy Flaherty (AALL, 1993). ASCLA members: James Morgan (1993); Janice C. Stuter (1993); staff liaison, Andrew M. Hansen. AALL members: to be appointed. ACA members: to be appointed.

American Federation of Labor/Congress of Industrial Organizations—ALA, Library Service to Labor Groups, RASD

To initiate, develop, and foster, through the organizational structures of the ALA and the AFL-CIO, ways and means of effecting closer cooperation between the librarian and labor organizations and the large constituency represented by the labor organizations.

To serve as a catalyst for libraries and other institutions to enable them more effectively to fulfill both the expressed and unexpressed needs of the labor community; to encourage wider and more intensive patronage of library facilities by members of the labor community and their families; to keep librarians and labor educators aware of the needs and developments in the labor-library area so that programs, consistent with the goals of ALA and not inconsistent with the goals of the AFL-CIO, may be developed which are responsive to the current needs of both libraries and/or labor groups.

Through its publications and other available media, the joint committee disseminates to librarians, labor educators, and other interested parties, book lists, film lists, and suggested programs to meet the needs of the constituency the committee serves; and to provide leadership and assistance to librarians and labor organizations concerning the mutual endeavors, interests, and services available.

ALA—co-ch., Elaine Harger (1993); Billie M. Connor (1993); Mary F. Hicks (1994); Raymond H. Markey (1994); Shirley A. Maul (1994); Ruby U. Tyson (1993); staff liaison, Andrew M. Hansen.

AFL-CIO—co-ch., Anthony Sarmiento; Debra E. Bernhardt; Jodie Fine; Joan Goldman; Ellen S. Newton; Paula O'Connor; John Rogers; Steve A. Schwartz.

"Anglo-American Cataloguing Rules" Common Revision Fund

The committee administers the Common Revision Fund, which consists of royalties from the sale of authorized *AACR2* materials. The committee consists of three members, each of whom is appointed by the appropriate copyright holder. Members are appointed for terms of three years and may be reappointed. The committee meets annually.

ALA rep.—to be appointed.
Canadian Library Assn. rep.—Karen S. Adams, Canadian L. Assn., 200 Elgin St., Ste. 602, Ottawa, ON K2P 1L5 Canada.
Library Assn. rep.—to be appointed.

"Anglo-American Cataloguing Rules," Joint Steering Committee for Revision of (JSC)

1. To advise the editor of the abridged edition of *AACR2* and to approve the text of the said abridged edition prior to its publication.
2. To assess the use and sale of *AACR2* and the abridged edition and to advise users of *AACR2* and the abridged edition on implementation and adoption of the rules. To advise as required on the granting of permissions to translate.
3. To keep under review the need for amendment and revision of the second edition and abridgement, in the light of representations from users of the text; and to prepare any necessary amendments and revisions for publication by the copyright owners on an agreed schedule for the issue of amendment revision bulletins.
4. To act as a forum for discussion of proposals on rule interpretation so as to insure consistent use of *AACR2* and to promulgate agreed rule interpretations.
5. To define and propose appropriate activities associated with *AACR2* in accordance with the funding agreement made with the Council on Library Resources.
6. To maintain liaison with IFLA and the UBC office, in order to facilitate the interests of users of *AACR2* in any programs of international standardization in the cataloguing field carried out by those bodies.

Ch., Pat Oddy (British L.); secy., to be appointed; Rodney Brunt (Library Assn.); Diana Dack (Australian Com. on Catlg.); Janet Swan Hill (ALA, 1992); Ralph Manning (Canadian Com. on Catlg.); Sarah E. Thomas (L. of Congress).

Association for Educational Communications and Technology—AASL

To foster and develop through the organizational structure of AASL and AECT ways and means of effecting closer cooperation between the two organizations for the purpose of improving educational services for students and teachers and for the professional growth of the members of the associations.

AASL—ch., Drucilla Raines (1993); Patricia A. Berger (1994); Joyce E. Karon (1993); Jane A. Martinez (1994); Judith A. Walker (1994); staff liaison, Donald C. Adcock.

AECT—Gloria L. Davidson (1994); Donald P. Ely (1994); Paula Galland (1994); Suzanne G. Goodman (1994); Nancy Ellen Graf (1994); Doris J. Lusk (1993); Barbara Noble (1994); Linda Kay Rebstock (1994).

Association for Educational Communications and Technology—ACRL

To cooperate in the formulation, implementation, and revision of standards for community and junior college libraries and learning resource centers; to explore the advances in communications technology and the resultant effects upon learning resource centers; to suggest an appropriate legislative agenda for encouraging the improvement of libraries and learning resource centers at the community college level; to encourage cooperation between ACRL and AECT.

Co-chs., Marilyn M. McDonald (1993) and Gretchen H. Neill (1994); Susan M. Anderson (1994); Bernard Fradkin (1994); Susan M. Maltese (1993); Lois I. Marriott (1993); James O. Wallace (1993); staff liaison, Mary Taylor.

Association of American Publishers—ALA

To consist of the president, immediate past president, president-elect, and treasurer of ALA, plus two members-at-large to be appointed for two-year terms. (AAP membership to consist of a similar representative body.)

To discuss vital issues of mutual concern which affect the development and progress of both ALA and AAP. To provide for continuing communication and interchange of expert advice and information on matters not covered by or in the province of activities of any single unit of ALA.

ALA—pres., Marilyn L. Miller (1994); past. pres., Patricia Glass Schuman (1993); pres.-elect, Hardy R. Franklin (1995); treas., Ann K. Symons (1996); members-at-large: Audrey B. Eaglen (1993); E. Blanche Woolls (1994); staff liaison, Peggy Sullivan.
AAP—to be appointed.

Association of American Publishers—ALCTS

To consider mutual problems and to provide for the communication of ideas between members of the association and the division; to plan and sponsor meetings, seminars, studies, or other forms of communication on topics of common interest; and to encourage the exchange of ideas among publishers, wholesalers, and librarians, limited as always to appropriate and proper co-operation.

ALCTS—co-ch., Sally W. Somers (1994); Joanne S. Anderson (1994); Stuart F. Grinell (1993); Larry C. Price (1994); Joseph W. Raker (1994); Marla J. Schwartz (1994); Adelaide Weir Sukiennik (1994); Barbara A. Winters (1993); staff liaison: Karen Muller.

AAP—co-ch., Audrey D. Melkin (1993); Dimity S. Berkner (1993); Jack Burke (1993); John Chambers (1993); Robert Duran (1993); Dan Lundy (1993); Christine Nasso (1993); Marcia L. Purcell (1993); Shirley C. Sarris (1993); Peter E. Simon (1993); Joan Urban (1993); liaisons: Amy Miller (BISAC, 1993); Peter McCallion (SISAC, 1993); AAP staff liaison, Jerry Sirchia.

Children's Book Council—ALA

To explore mutual problems concerning content, format, distribution, and promotion of juvenile books and to propose cooperative action to resolve such problems.

ALA—co-ch., Judith Rovenger (1993); Bessie Condos Egan (1994); Lorrelle Henry (1993); Judith H. Higgins (1993); Louise L. Sherman (1994); Barbara L. Stein (1993); Kay E. Vandergrift (1994); Elizabeth S. Watson (1993); staff liaison, Susan Roman.

CBC—co-ch., Melanie Kroupa (1993); Marc Chesire (1994); Grace Clarke (1993); Sally Doherty (1994); Jazan Higgins (1994); Mimi Kayden (1995); Anne L. Okie (1993); Bonnie Ingber Verburg (1994); staff liaison, David S. Riederman.

Society of American Archivists—ALA (Joint Committee on Library-Archives Relationships)

The common purpose of archivists and librarians is to acquire, preserve, and deliver to users as needed the written and graphic record of man's intellect and experience. In order to enable such professionals to achieve these purposes, it is desirable to strengthen the relationship between the Society of American Archivists and the American Library Association, and to coordinate the goals and activities of the two organizations. To these ends, it is the function of this committee: (1) to foster and develop ways and means of effecting closer cooperation between the organizations; (2) to encourage the establishment of common standards; (3) to undertake such activities as are assigned to the committee by either of its parent bodies; (4) to initiate programs of a relevant and timely nature at the annual meetings of either or both parent bodies either through direct ALA/SAA Joint Committee sponsorship or by forwarding particular program plans to the appropriate unit of either parent body for action; and (5) to refer matters of concern to appropriate units of SAA or ALA.

ALA—co-ch., Robert M. Warner (1993); Charles B. Harrell (1993); Karen Nelson Hoyle (1994); William L. Joyce (1994); Robert S. Martin (1994); staff liaison, Charles Harmon.

SAA—co-ch., to be appointed; Karma A. Beal (1993); H. Thomas Hickerson (1994); Nancy McCall (1993); Mark A. Vargas (1993); staff liaison, Anne P. Diffendal.

Divisions

◆

American Association of School Librarians

◆

Membership as of August 31, 1992
Organization members   681
Personal members   6,726
Total   7,407

Ann C. Weeks, *executive director*
Barbara R. Herrin, *deputy executive director*
Donald C. Adcock, *coordinator for program support*
Marie Settem, *coordinator for membership and affiliate relations*

The American Association of School Librarians is interested in the general improvement and extension of library media services for children and young people. AASL has specific responsibility for: planning of program of study and service for the improvement and extension of library media services in elementary and secondary schools as a means of strengthening the educational program; evaluation, selection, interpretation, and utilization of media as it is used in the context of the school program; stimulation of continuous study and research in the library field and to establish criteria of evaluation; synthesis of the activities of all units of the American Library Association in areas of mutual concern; representation and interpretation of the need for the function of school libraries to other educational and lay groups; stimulation of professional growth, improvement of the status of school librarians, and encouragement of participation by members in appropriate type-of-activity divisions; conduct activities and projects for improvement and extension of service in the school library when such projects are beyond the scope of type-of-activity divisions, after specific approval by the ALA Council.

Board of Directors

Officers: pres., Ruth Toor (1994); pres.-elect, E. Blanche Woolls (1995); treas./financial officer, Bernadette G. Winter (1993); secy., Pamela W. Parman (1993); past pres., Dawn H. Heller (1993).

Other members: rgnl. dirs.: Helen R. Adams (1993); Jody Gehrig (1994); Marybeth Green (1995); Clara G. Hoover (1994); M. Ellen Jay (1995); Harriett S. Selverstone (1994); Philip M. Turner (1993); members: Deborah Roberts Coleman (1993); Cecile H. Dorr (1993); Lorrie M. Monprode-Holt (1994); Meb Norton (1994); Selvin W. Royal (1993); Joie L. Taylor (1995); Jane C. Terwillegar (1994); ex officio, Ann C. Weeks (1993).

Executive Committee

To act on policy and fiscal issues requiring action between meetings of the Board.

Pres., Ruth Toor (1994); pres.-elect, E. Blanche Woolls (1995); treas., Bernadette G. Winter (1993); past pres., Dawn H. Heller (1993); Pamela W. Parman (1993); ex officio, Ann C. Weeks (1993).

Publications

School Library Media Quarterly (quarterly). Sent to all AASL members. Subscription $40; $50 foreign annually to nonmembers. Ed., Mary Kay Biagini, Sch. of L. & Inf. Sci., 135 N. Bellefield Ave., Univ. of Pittsburgh, Pittsburgh, PA 15260.

AASL Presidential Hotline (semiannual). Sent to all AASL members. Not available by subscription.

COMMITTEES

UNIT I—Organizational Maintenance

Facilitator, Phyllis Heroy (1993).

Budget

To review budget requests submitted by committees, sections, and the Affiliate Assembly and prepare a preliminary budget based on AASL Board–accepted priorities for review and approval by the AASL Board; to review fiscal records and to propose modification of the current annual budget as needed.

Ch., Barbara J. Nemer (1993); treas., Bernadette G. Winter (1993); Roger S. Ashley (1994); M. Dorcas Hand (1993); Jerry R. Wicks (1993); ex officio: Lorrie M. Monprode-Holt (1993); E. Blanche Woolls.

Bylaws and Organization

To draft Bylaws; to consider amendments when needed; to evaluate all present and proposed committee function statements; to consider the committee size and terms of all committee members in relation to responsibility; and to update AASL Policy and Procedures Handbook. To recommend to the Board the establishment and dissolution of committees.

Ch., Carol A. Casey (1994); Beatrice E. Angus (1994); Geraldine W. Bell (1993); Emily S. Boyce (1993); Ethel C. Kutteroff (1993); Katherine Mills Olsen (1994).

Financial Planning and Fund Raising (special)

To investigate additional and alternative sources of funding and revenue for the division, consistent with the division's expressed values and priorities; to make recommendations to the Board of Directors on those funding approaches with the greatest potential for long-term success and greatest financial return; and to provide recommendations for revisions to the division's Long-Range Financial Plan.

Co-chs., Barbara Nemer (1992) and Bernadette (Bernie) G. Winter (1992); members to be appointed.

Identification of Future Conference Sites (task force)

To consider possible sites for the next three AASL National Conferences.

Ch., Jerry R. Wicks (1994); Donna Toler Baumbach (1994); Joyce M. Funk (1994); Lee D. Gordon (1994); Mary Lou Gregory (1994); Phyllis B. Heroy (1994); Marian E. Karpisek (1994); Janis Kessler (1994); Paula Kay Montgomery (1994).

Leadership Enhancement

To develop long- and short-range plans for improving the leadership and organizational management skills of current and potential AASL leaders.

Co-chs., Aileen Helmick (1993) and Jerry R. Wicks (1994); Jody Gehrig (1993); Marybeth Green (1993); Lucy M. Lyon (1993); Daniel J. Van Gesen (1994).

Long-Range Planning

To assist the Board in the identification of priorities, goals, and objectives for AASL as well as broad strategies for achieving them; to integrate AASL planning into the long-range planning cycle of ALA; and to develop a process for evaluating the division's movement toward these goals and objectives.

Ch., Hilda K. Weisburg (1993); Margaret A. Blake (1994); John D. Crowley (1993); Helen F. Flowers (1994); Lee D. Gordon (1993); Erlene Bishop Killeen (1994); Retta B. Patrick (1993); Charles R. White (1994); ex officio, E. Blanche Woolls (1993).

Membership

To advise and work with AASL staff on developing and implementing strategies for recruiting and maintaining professional and student members; to advise and work with AASL staff on special membership projects; to encourage student memberships by working directly with Educators of Library Media Specialists (ELMS) Section; to plan and assume responsibility for conference orientation session and to welcome and introduce new members to AASL goals and procedures.

Ch., Gail K. Dickinson (1993); Glenda D. Anderson (1994); Carolyn S. Brodie (1993); Nell J. Brown (1994); Rita M. Coleman (1994); Charlene K. Douglass (1994); Sheryl Egger (1993); Christa Even (1994); Judith J. Mahoney (1993); Jane C. Parker (1993); Christina B. Woll (1993).

Nominating—1993 Election

To prepare the annual slate for the AASL ballot; recommend AASL members to run for ALA offices and council to the ALA Nominating Committee; work with section nominating committees to prepare section ballots; and organize and conduct the AASL candidate's forum at ALA Midwinter.

Ch., Carolyn Markuson (1993); Roger S. Ashley (1993); Pauletta B. Bracy (1993); Mildred C. Lee (1993); Phyllis Jeanne Van Orden (1993).

UNIT II—Organizational Relationships

Facilitator, Marian Karpisek (1993).

American University Press Services, Inc.

To select suitable titles for secondary school use from the current publications of the members of the American Association of University Presses to be published in a catalog annually by the American University Press Services, Inc.

Ch., Janet P. Sarratt (1994); Betty Bankhead (1993); Priscilla B. Bennett (1994); Ethel C. Kutteroff (1993); Cheryl J. Mason (1993); Barbara H. Weathers (1994); Helen I. White (1993); Beverley A. von Kries (1994).

Association for Educational Communications and Technology—AASL (joint) (See listing under Joint Committees, p. 16)

International Relations

To encourage school library media center relationships with other countries; to promote international cooperation and multicultural understanding among school librarians and educators concerned with school library media centers; and to advise the ALA International Relations Committee on school library concerns and to coordinate joint school library activities with the ALA/IRC.

Ch., Ruth Cady (1993); Patricia F. Beilke (1994); Valerie J. Downes (1993); Jean E. Lowrie (1993); Stephen L. Matthews (1993); Marjorie N. Rosenthal (1994); Lucille C. Thomas (1994).

Legislation

To act in an advisory and planning capacity in cooperation with the ALA Legislation Committee in the area of school library legislation and to work with the ALA Washington Office; to inform the membership of AASL about pending school library legislation; to interpret total ALA legislative program to AASL membership; to plan for organization and action to all levels—national, state, and local.

Ch., Thomas L. Hart (1993); Beverly J. Bagan (1993); Ann W. Hanning (1993); Marjorie Horowitz (1994); Thea J. Jones (1993); Elaine B. Leggett (1993); Patricia H. Mautino (1993); Carol Diehl (1994).

Liaisons to Other Organizations

To establish an AASL presence at meetings of other educational associations; to establish sequential cooperative programs; to explore the possibility of joint publications; and to develop strong links between the leadership of their organizations with AASL.

American Assn. of School Administrators—to be appointed.
Assn. for Library Collection and Technical Services—Frances G. Corcoran (1993).
International Assn. of School Librarianship—Valerie J. Downes (1993).
International Reading Assn.—to be appointed.
Invent America—to be appointed.
National Assn. of Secondary School Principals—Dawn Heller (1993).
National Congress of Parents and Teachers—to be appointed.
National Council for the Social Studies—Christina B. Woll (1993).
National Council of Teachers of English—Hilda L. Jay (1994).
National Council of Teachers of Mathematics—to be appointed.

National Council for the Accreditation of Teacher Education

Administration and management of all ALA/AASL responsibilities for participation in NCATE.

Ch., Marilyn L. Shontz (1993); Shirley L. Aaron (1994); Thomas Downen (1993); Hilda L. Jay (1994); Josette A. Lyders (1994); Phyllis A. Monyakula (1994); Frances R. Roscello (1994).

School Library Statistics Program (advisory)

To provide advisory services concerning the collection, analysis, and dissemination of school library media statistics.

Ch., Jacqueline G. Morris (1993); M. Ellen Jay (1993); Mary D. Lankford (1993); David V. Loertscher (1993); Lucy M. Lyon (1993); Marjorie L. Pappas (1993); Anna R. Smink (1993).

UNIT III—Library Media Personnel Development

Facilitator, Jerry R. Wicks (1993).

Annual Conference Local Arrangements

To plan with the AASL Office, the AASL President, and the Annual Conference Planning Committee, the necessary local arrangements for the AASL program meetings and functions scheduled for the ALA Annual Conference. The chair serves as a member of the Annual Conference Program Planning Committee.

Co-chs., Marvene D. Dearman (1993) and Idella A. Washington (1993); Molly Bethea (1993); Earl D. Hart (1993); Mattic Jacks Mosley (1993); Mary Ellen Shiflett (1993).

Annual Conference Program Planning

To plan with the AASL Office and the AASL President the program meetings and functions to be scheduled for the AASL meetings at the ALA Annual Conference.

Ch., Judith M. King (1993); Sheila Berkelhammer (1993); Diane J. Biesel (1993); Marvene D. Dearman (1993); Thea J. Jones (1993); Mary D. Lankford (1993); Judith J. Mahoney (1993); Marianne S. Ramirez (1993); Idella A. Washington (1993).

Continuing Education/Professional Development

To serve as a planning and evaluation group for continuing education activities of AASL, recommending directions, policies, objectives, marketing strategies, publications activities, and evaluation in cooperation with AASL personnel in charge of professional development. The committee serves as an advisory group to the Board.

Ch., Elizabeth L. Marcoux (1993); Barbara J. Correll (1994); Ruth P. Curtis (1993); Carol J. Fox (1994); Robert J. Grover (1993); Carol A. Kearney (1993); Louise B. Miller (1994); Jane C. Parker (1994); Donald B. Reynolds Jr. (1994); Carol D. Stanke (1993); ex officio, Barbara R. Herrin (1993).

General Conference—Baltimore, 1992

To plan and develop the program for the divisional national conference and to act in an advisory capacity in the planning of the conference theme, format, registration, exhibits, and local arrangements.

Ch., Linda L. Cornwell (1993); James F. Bennett (1993); Irene Hildebrandt (1993); Thea J. Jones (1993); Lynn Mathieu (1993); Paula K. Montgomery (1993); Donnadine Spilman (1993); Valerie J. Wilford (1993); liaison, Elizabeth E. Elam (1993).

"Information Power" Revision Planning

Co-chs., Betty Bankhead (1993) and Delores Z. Pretlow (1993).

Professional Development Coordinating

To: (1) encourage communication among the groups planning continuing education activities

for the division; (2) coordinate professional development activities within the division according to the long-range plan developed by the Continuing Education/Professional Development Committee; (3) develop AASL continuing education activities in concert with the established priorities of AASL, the continuing education programs of ALA, and those of the profession; (4) serve as a clearinghouse as well as a forum for identification of or sounding board for continuing education ideas; and (5) determine the appropriate format, i.e., publication, concurrent program, etc., to address a continuing education need and/or a developmental sequence of planned interrelated association activities.

Ch., Elizabeth L. Marcoux (1993); Linda L. Cornwell (1993); Ruth P. Curtis (1993); Marvene D. Dearman (1993); Robert J. Grover (1993); Irene Hildebrandt (1993); Carol A. Kearney (1993); Judith M. King (1994); Virginia Nordstrom (1993); Carol D. Stanke (1993); Idella A. Washington (1993); ex officio, Mary K. Biagini (1994).

Publication Feasibility (special)

To explore the possibility of producing a new publication designed to communicate with members in a less formal and more timely basis about connections with other educational associations, new and evolving trends in education and in school library media programs, and other topics of current interest. The committee is asked to consider options for desktop publishing; to look at other publications, such as ASCD's *Curriculum Update*, as models for possible formats; and to suggest a time frame for development and publication. The committee is to make a progress report at 1993 Midwinter Meeting and a final recommendation at 1993 Annual Conference. The final report is to address whether the division should undertake such as project; the estimated costs, the anticipated content, the staff and members responsibilities; and the frequency of publication. The committee is to discuss this project with the Publications Committee.

Ch., M. Dorcas Hand (1993); Roger S. Ashley (1993); Marjorie Horowitz (1993); Ruth Jean Shaw (1993).

Publications

To review, analyze, coordinate, evaluate, and recommend for action all AASL publications, proposals, and manuscripts exclusive of the *Presidential Hotline*, the standards document, *School Library Media Quarterly*, and the *Focus on Issues and Trends* series.

Ch., Virginia Nordstrom (1993); Sybilla A. Cook (1994); Mary Lou Gregory (1994); Ken Haycock (1994); Judy M. Pitts (1994); Karen P. Smith (1993); Lillian M. Wehmeyer (1993); James Weigel (1993); Anne M. Wolter (1993); ex officio: Mary K. Biagini (1994); Eleanor R. Kulleseid (1994).

Publications Coordinating

To encourage communication and coordination of effort among the editors of the AASL divisional publications.

Ch., Virginia Nordstrom (1993); Mary K. Biagini (1994); Eleanor R. Kulleseid (1993).

Publications to Supplement "Information Power"

Ch., June Kahler (1993); Constance J. Champlin (1995).

Recruitment (special)

To develop coalitions with educational, administrative, and library associations to strengthen, support, and encourage recruitment into the school library media profession and to work with universities to support existing educational programs and to assist in establishing new ones. All recruitment activities should include a strong minority recruitment component.

Ch., Rita T. Adams (1993); Marie Harris Aldridge (1993); Dennis J. LeLoup (1993); Mary F. Lenox (1993); Virginia B. Moore (1994); Barbara R. Wallace (1993).

"School Library Media Quarterly" Editorial Board

To be responsible for manuscript development in cooperation with the editor; review manuscripts to recommend acceptance, request for revision, or rejection; and fulfill such other editorial and administrative duties as the editor shall deem necessary and proper.

Ch., Mary K. Biagini (1994); Roger S. Ashley (1994); Carol C. Kuhlthau (1994); Stephen L. Matthews (1994); Carole J. McCollough (1994); Jacqueline G. Morris (1994); Ellen M. Stepanian (1994); Christina C. Young (1994); ex officio, Eleanor R. Kulleseid (1994).

UNIT IV—Library Media Program Development

Facilitator, Drucilla (Drucie) Raines (1993).

Information Skills (special)

To identify competencies students require to effectively access, use, and apply information to solve problems, make decisions, or create new information; to examine models currently available and prepare a bibliography for school library media professionals to use in preparing a local information skills curriculum; to describe the process for school staff to use to ensure the integration of information skills into the overall K-12 curriculum.

Ch., Paula K. Montgomery (1993); Cecile H. Dorr (1993); Michael B. Eisenberg (1993); Carol Kroll (1993); Carol C. Kuhlthau (1993); Mary Jane McNally (1993); Judy M. Pitts (1993); Thomas J. Povhe (1993); Barbara K. Stripling (1993).

Integrating Literature Across the Curriculum (special)

To explore ways that school library media specialists can encourage the integration of literature in all pre-K–12 subject areas of the school curriculum; to identify ways to work with teachers to share the wealth of literature appropriate for subjects such as math and science, as well as the more traditional language arts and social studies areas; and to investigate means of disseminating this information in a variety of ways, including bibliographies and brochures, that offer examples for both AASL members and for members of the many educational groups with which we have established partnerships. The committee is to make progress reports at the 1993 Midwinter Meeting, the 1993 Annual Conference, and the 1994 Midwinter Meeting. A final report is to be made to the Board at the 1994 Annual Conference.

Phyllis K. Kennemer (1994); Mildred C. Lee (1994).

Intellectual Freedom

To prepare and gather materials that will advise the school library media specialist of available services and support both in formulating policies of intellectual freedom and for resisting local pressure and community action designed to impair the rights of users.

Ch., Mildred C. Lee (1993); Shirley L. Aaron (1993); Elaine Arciszewski (1994); Gayle Keresey (1994); Jean Kern (1994); Ginny Moore Kruse (1993); Gene D. Lanier (1994); Mary Ann Pellerin (1993); Rebecca S. Poole (1993); Elana Rabban (1993).

Literacy (special)

To examine the role of school library media specialists in promoting and encouraging literacy; to help students become literate through literature; to consider literacy activities for parents and students based on children's literature such as family literacy and programs carried out in schools; to identify models currently in the schools which could be replicated; to represent AASL at meetings with other groups both within ALA and outside of it who are concerned with developing literacy; to make progress reports at 1993 and 1994 Midwinter Meetings and at the 1993 Annual Conference with a final report due at the 1994 Annual Conference.

Research

To identify research needs; to coordinate research activities of the Association; to recommend general research program and priorities; to advise the Board about school library media research and development; to establish liaison and cooperate with the ALA Office for Research and Statistics; and to inform school library media professionals concerning the value and application of research techniques applicable in their situations.

Ch., Jane Bandy Smith (1993); Daniel D. Barron (1994); Daniel J. Callison (1993); Susan M. Easun (1994); Robert J. Grover (1994); Ken Haycock (1994); David V. Loertscher (1993); Mary Jane McNally (1994).

Role of Library Media Specialists in School Restructuring (special)

To study the variety of reports and models currently being prepared by many groups in the educational field about restructuring the schools for better learning; to identify the roles of library media specialists described in these reports; and to offer suggestions and ideas for ensuring that library media specialists are primary partners in the restructuring process. Based on the findings, the committee is to prepare a position paper to be issued to the AASL membership or published in *SLMQ* or in some other communication medium. The Committee is to make progress reports to the Board at the 1993 Midwinter Meeting, the 1993 Annual Conference, and the 1994 Midwinter Meeting. The final report and a position paper are to be presented to the Board at the 1994 Annual Conference.

Ch. and members to be appointed.

Site-Based Management (special)

To investigate the implications of the adoption of site-based management or other decision-making models in local schools and the possible effects of each on local, district, regional, and state

support for and operation of school library media programs; to draft a policy statement related to site-based management to be considered for adoption by the AASL Board of Directors, if deemed appropriate; to assess the continuing education and informational needs of members in relation to site-based management; and to prepare a final report that includes other suggested actions to be taken by AASL, by its Affiliate Associations, and by individual members.

Ch., Bettie Estes Rickner (1993); Phyllis Lacroix (1993); Carolyn K. Marcato (1993); Donna L. Peterson (1993); Betty S. Riley (1993); Linda A. Veltze (1993).

Technology

To coordinate the activities of the Technology subcommittees, review charges of existing subcommittees, and recommend to the Board the establishment and dissolution of subcommittees when appropriate.

Ch., Catherine Murphy (1993); Kathleen W. Craver (1994); Joyce E. Karon (1993); Neah J. Lohr (1994); Wendell Lotz (1994); Jane A. Martinez (1994); Betty J. Morris (1993); Michael E. Rayburn (1994); Frances R. Roscello (1994); Robert Ruezinsky (1994).

Whole Language (special)

To investigate ways that school library media specialists can work most effectively in schools where the whole language approach is implemented; to consider the implications and effects of the whole language movement on school library media programs; and to consider the effects of publishing and marketing trends on school library media programs' budgets. To draft a policy statement related to the whole language movement to be considered for adoption by the AASL Board of Directors, if deemed appropriate; to assess the continuing education and informational needs of members in relation to whole language methods; and to prepare a final report that includes other suggested actions to be taken by AASL, by its Affiliate Associations, and by individual members, and that identifies partnerships that could be developed by AASL and publishers and/or other educational associations.

Ch., Sharon Coatney (1993); Bernice E. Cullinan (1993); M. Jean Greenlaw (1993); Winona Jones (1993); Nancy Livingston (1993); Diane Person (1993); Bunny Yesner (1993).

UNIT V—Public Information

Facilitator to be appointed.

Awards

To coordinate the AASL awards committees; review criteria for new and continuing awards and make recommendations for change; advise on lists of contacts for each award; evaluate the need for new awards and seek funding in cooperation with the executive director to support these; circulate publicity related to individual awards in a timely fashion; coordinate the publicity related to award recipients; recommend publications concerning awards.

Ch., Karen J. Winsor (1994); Darlene Shiverdecker Basone (1994); Lois Farrell Fisher (1993); Clara G. Hoover (1993); Judith M. King (1994); Shirley D. Ross (1993); Janie R. Schomberg (1994).

Distinguished School Administrators Award, AASL/SIRS (subcommittee)

To review nominations for the selection of an administrator to receive the AASL Distinguished Library Service Award for School Administrators for the administration of a school or group of schools who has made an outstanding and sustained contribution toward furthering the role of the library and its development in elementary and/or secondary education.

Ch., Robert E. Barron (1993); Carol W. Franz (1993); Janice C. Ostrom (1993).

Distinguished Service Award, AASL/ Baker & Taylor (subcommittee)

To act in a planning capacity in cooperation with Baker & Taylor in the selection of an individual who will receive a cash award for providing an outstanding contribution to school librarianship and school library media program development.

Ch., Hilda L. Jay (1993); Beverly J. Bagan (1993); Kay Bland (1993); Helen F. Flowers (1993).

"Emergency Librarian" Periodical Award (subcommittee)

To administer the "Emergency Librarian" Periodical Award, given for an outstanding publication of a school library media association that is an affiliate member of AASL.

Ch., Laura D. Blanchard (1993); Judith L. Eller (1993); Judith Gray (1993); Daniel J. Van Gesen (1993).

Frances Henne Award (subcommittee)

To select the recipient of the Frances Henne Award, an annual grant to enable a school library media specialist with five or fewer years in the profession to attend an AASL regional conference or ALA Annual Conference. Award sponsored by the R. R. Bowker Company.

Ch., Sheila Salmon (1993); Kay Maynard (1993); Susan B. Preston (1993).

Information Plus Continuing Education Award (subcommittee)

To select the recipient of the AASL/Information Plus Scholarship Award, offered for the continuing education and professional development of an AASL member—building level library media specialist, supervisor, or educator. Purpose of the grant: to enable the AASL member to attend an ALA or AASL pre/post conference or an ALA/AASL-sponsored regional workshop.

Ch., Rose Mary Tobiassen (1993); Shelia K. Blume (1993); Cathy C. Bonnell (1993); Geneva T. Van Horne (1993); Jean N. Worley (1993).

Intellectual Freedom Award, AASL/SIRS (subcommittee)

To act in an advisory capacity in cooperation with Social Issues Resources Series, Inc., in the selection of an individual who will receive a cash award for upholding the principles of intellectual freedom as set forth in "Policies and Procedures for Selection of Instructional Materials."

Ch., Vicki H. Hardesty (1993); Elaine Arciszewski (1993); Mary Maude McCain (1993); Rebecca S. Poole (1993); Judy C. Roumillat (1993).

Leadership Development Award, ABC/ CLIO (subcommittee)

To select the recipient of the annual award, sponsored by ABC/CLIO, to enable an AASL affiliate organization to plan and implement a leadership development program.

Ch., Carol A. Kearney (1993); M. Elspeth Goodin (1993); Pamela Kramer (1993); Judy Reeves (1993); Maureen White (1993).

Microcomputer in the Media Center Award, AASL/Follett Software Company (subcommittee)

To select the recipients of the Follett Software Company awards for innovative use of the microcomputer in the school library media center in an elementary (K-6) and a secondary (7-12) setting.

Ch., Barbara J. Correll (1993); Linda C. Hartman (1993); Nancy P. Minnich (1993); Dennis A. Rumme (1993).

National School Library Media Program of the Year Award, AASL/Encyclopaedia Britannica Educational Corp. (subcommittee)

To act in an advisory capacity to the Encyclopaedia Britannica Companies and AASL in the selection of school districts to be given cash awards for demonstrating excellence in their school library media programs. The eligibility criteria will include schools and school systems from kindergarten through the 12th grade.

Ch., Diane D. Myers (1993); Suzanne W. Hawley (1993); Barbara Jeffus (1993); Paula K. Montgomery (1993); Bernice L. Yesner (1993).

School Librarian's Workshop Award (subcommittee)

To select the recipient of the annual award sponsored by the Library Learning Resources Company to provide financial assistance for the professional education of persons who plan to become school library media specialists working at the preschool, elementary, or secondary level (PS–12) in public or private educational settings.

Ch., Janie R. Schomberg (1993); Linda C. Bartone (1993); Carolyn S. Hayes (1993); Nadine E. Sarlin (1993).

National School Library Media Month

To promote recognition of School Library Media Month; to coordinate AASL efforts with other observances related to libraries.

Ch., Sara L. Stubbins (1993); Constance J. Champlin (1993); Laura E. Edwards (1994); Jane Humble (1993); Madeline Z. Ianni (1994); Roberta S. Kaiser (1994); Margaret L. Kirkpatrick (1993); Rocco A. Staino (1994).

Public Awareness

To gather, evaluate, and make available to school library media specialists public relations and promotional activities for school library media programs. To assist the AASL staff in developing, implementing, and evaluating an on-going public relations campaign for the association.

Ch., Doris M. Epler (1994); Deborah Roberts Coleman (1993); Harriet Lapointe (1993); Joseph J. Mattie (1993); Catherine L. Miller (1993);

Madeline F. Nixon (1994); Diane C. Pozar (1994); Kathleen A. Tobin (1993).

REPRESENTATIVES

ALA Appointments Com.—to be appointed.
ALA Conference Program Com. (New Orleans, 1993)—Ruth Toor.
ALA Legislation Assembly—Thomas Hart.
ALA Planning and Budget Assembly—Bernadette Winter.
ALCTS-CCS Cataloging of Children's Materials Com.—Frances G. Corcoran.
Freedom to Read Fdn.—Vicki Hardesty.
Library Education Assembly—Betty Marcoux.

SECTIONS

Educators of Library Media Specialists (ELMSS)
Non-Public Schools (NPSS)
Supervisors (SPVS)

Educators of Library Media Specialists Section (ELMSS)

The general purpose of this section shall be to provide a membership group for the exchange of ideas, for the review and study of curricula, and for the development of research activities for educators in colleges and universities whose programs focus on school library media education and training.

Executive Committee

Ch., Marilyn L. Shontz (1994); vice-ch., Mary Kathryn Holland (1995); secy., Julie I. Tallman (1993); past ch., Savan Wilby Wilson (1993); rep. to AASL Board, Selvin W. Royal (1993).

Committees

Bylaws

To review the ELMSS Bylaws and propose revisions to membership.

Ch. to be appointed; Barbara Erdman (1994); Aileen Helmick (1993); Elizabeth F. Howard (1993).

Nominating

Ch. to be appointed; Jody B. Charter (1994); Rosalind E. Miller (1993); Barbara L. Stein (1993).

Program

Ch., Dian E. Walster (1993); Janis H. Bruwelheide (1993); Janelle A. Paris (1993).

Non-Public Schools Section (NPSS)

The general purpose of this section shall be in accordance with that of the American Association of School Librarians. The specific purpose of this section shall be to provide a means for discussion of and action on the problems relating to all phases of non-public school librarianship.

Executive Committee

Ch., Karen Ann Wareham (1994); ch.-elect, Jacquelyn H. Thomas (1995); secy., Susan E. Hooper (1993); past ch., Mary Lou S. Treat (1993); rep. to AASL Bd., Meb Norton (1994).

Committees

Bylaws

Ch., to be appointed; Denise C. Miller (1993).

Nominating

Ch., Martha O. Myers (1993); M. Dorcas Hand (1993); Ann J. Kenney (1993).

Supervisors Section (SPVS)

The general purpose of this section shall be in accordance with that of the American Association of School Librarians. The specific purpose of this section shall be to provide a means for discussion of and action on the problems relating to all phases of school library supervision.

Executive Committee

Ch., June Kahler (1993); ch.-elect, Rebecca T. Bingham (1993); secy., Ann T. White (1993); past ch., Joyce B. Wallach (1993); rep. to AASL board, Joie L. Taylor (1993).

Committees

Bylaws

Ch., Mary M. Butler (1993); B Jo Morse (1994); Elizabeth A. Polk (1994); Joie L. Taylor (1994); Helen M. Tugwell (1993).

Critical Issues

Ch., Elizabeth Haynes (1993); Beverly J. Bagan (1994); Margaret Crank (1994); Amanda C. Lucas (1993); Mary Oppman (1993).

Nominating

Ch., Joyce B. Wallach (1993).

Program

Ch., Sharyl G. Smith (1993); Diane Durbin (1994); Jody Gehrig (1994); Donna L. Peterson (1993).

AFFILIATE ASSEMBLY

The Affiliate Assembly is composed of the representatives and delegates of the organizations affiliated with the American Association of School Librarians. The specific purpose of this assembly is to provide a channel for communication for reporting concerns of the affiliate organizations and their membership and for reporting the actions of the American Association of School Librarians to the affiliates.

Executive Committee

Ch., Deborah Roberts Coleman (1993); vice-ch./ch.-elect, James Weigel (1993); rec. secy., Daniel J. Van Gesen (1993); Rgn. I, Audrey J. Friend (1993); Rgn. II, Janice S. Dysart (1994); Rgn. III, Floyd C. Pentlin (1993); Rgn. IV, Roberts Ponis (1994); Rgn. V, Linda C. Bartone (1993); Rgn. VI, Idella A. Washington (1994); Rgn. VII, Barbara Jeffus (1993); ex officio: Affiliate Assembly reps to the bd.: Lorrie Monprode-Holt (1994); Cecile H. Dorr (1993); AASL pres., Ruth Toor (1993); immediate past ch., Lorrie Monprode-Holt (1992); immediate past rec. secy., Glenda D. Anderson (1992); exec. dir., Ann Carlson Weeks.

Committees

Bylaws

Ch. and members to be appointed.

Nominating—1993 Election

Ch. and members to be appointed.

State and Regional Affiliates

Alabama

Alabama Instr. Media Assn.—pres., Judy Reeves, 100 Snell Bridge Rd., Daleville, AL 36322. (Officers change Mar. 1993.)

Alaska

Alaska Assn. of Sch. Lns.—pres., Lois A. Petersen, P.O. Box 393, Kotzebue, AK 99752. (Officers change Mar. 1993.)

Arizona

Arizona State L. Assn., Sch. L. Media Div.—pres., Shirley A. Dresbach, 3041 E. Yucca St., Phoenix, AZ 85028. (Officers change Nov. 1993.)

Arkansas

Arkansas Assn. of Sch. L. Media Educators—pres., Grace Donaho, 405 Indian Trail, Springdale, AR 72764. (Officers change Nov. 1993.)

California

California Media & L. Educators Assn.—pres., Ellis Vance, Fresno Cnty. Off. of Edu., L., 1111 Van Ness Ave., Fresno, CA 93721-2000. (Officers change May 1993.)

Colorado

Colorado Edu. Media Assn.—pres., Roberta J. Ponis, 6997 Robb St., Arvada, CO 80004. (Officers change Feb. 1993.)

Connecticut

Connecticut Edu. Media Assn.—pres., Italia A. Negroni, 53 Blueberry Hill, Weston, CT 06883. (Officers change May 1993.)

Delaware

Delaware Sch. L. Media Assn.—pres., Margaret P. Dillner, 4 Orioles Nest., Glen Farms, Elkton, MD 21921. (Officers change Apr. 1993.)

District of Columbia

District of Columbia Assn. of Sch. Lns.—pres., Beverly J. Wheeler, 13905 Pond View Rd., Silver Spring, MD, 20905. (Officers change Aug. 1993.)

Florida

Florida Assn. for Media in Edu.—pres., Helen J. Tallman, 7601 S.W. 94th Ave., Miami, FL 33173. (Officers change Nov. 1993.)

Georgia

Georgia L. Assn., Sch. L. Media Div.—pres., Gordon N. Baker, 3087 Drexel Lane, Jonesboro, GA 30236. (Officers change Oct. 1993.)

Georgia L. Media Assn.—pres., Brenda W. Newbury, 4009 Braddock St., Martinez, GA 30907. (Officers change May 1993.)

Germany

L. Media Assn. of Germany—pres., Maureen Reed Booth, RMC Box #339, APO New York, NY 09220.

Hawaii

Hawaii Assn. of Sch. Lns.—pres., Linda Kim, 94-434 Holaniku St., Mililani, HI 96789. (Officers change May 1993.)

Illinois

Illinois L. Assn., Sch. L. Media Forum—pres., Karen Winsor, Dist. Media Svcs., Edgewood Middle Sch., 929 Edgewood Rd., Highland Park, IL 60035. (Officers change July 1993.)

Illinois Sch. L. Media Assn.—pres., Kathleen Shannon, 312 Osage, Park Forest, IL 60466. (Officers change July 1993.)

Indiana

Assn. for Indiana Media Educators—pres., Linda L. Mills, 913 Locust Ave., Batesville, IN 47006. (Officers change May 1993.)

Iowa

Iowa Edu. Media Assn.—pres., Ilene McLain, 2635 W. 43rd St., Davenport, IA 52806. (Officers change Apr. 1993.)

Kansas

Kansas Assn. of Sch. Lns.—pres., Judy Eller, 5201 N. St. Clair, Wichita, KS 67204. (Officers change June 1993.)

Kentucky

Kentucky Sch. Media Assn.—pres., Sarah (Sally) M. Livingston, 116 Heady Ave., Louisville, KY 40207. (Officers change Oct. 1993.)

Louisiana

Louisiana Assn. of Sch. Lns.—pres., Molly Bethea, 400 Ascot Ct., Bossier City, LA 71111. (Officers change July 1993.)

Maine

Maine Edu. Media Assn.—pres., Ellen T. Berrie, R.R.1, Box 844, S. Harpswell, ME 04079. (Officers change May 1993.)

Maryland

Maryland Edu. Media Org.—pres., Ann L. Hummer, 810 Belvedere Heights, Charles Town, WV 25414. (Officers change July 1993.)

Massachusetts

Massachusetts Assn. for Edu. Media—pres., Donna Guerin, 39 Jeanette Dr., Chicopee, MA 01013. (Officers change June 1993.)

Michigan

Michigan Assn. for Media in Edu.—pres., Barbara Wallace, 70 Poplar, Wyandotte, MI 48192. (Officers change Jan. 1993.)

Minnesota

Minnesota Edu. Media Org.—pres., Fran McDonald, Rt. 1, Box 173, Kasota, MN 56050. (Officers change May 1993.)

Mississippi

Mississippi L. Assn., Sch. Lns. Sect.—pres., Annette M. Wilson, 300-A Lindale St., Clinton, MS 39056. (Officers change Jan. 1993.)

Missouri

Missouri Assn. of Sch. Lns.—pres., Judy Mahoney, 1608 N.E. Rosewood Dr., Kansas City, MO 64118. (Officers change June 1993.)

Montana

Montana L. Assn., Sch. L. Media Div.—pres., Margaret A. Kernan, Helena H.S.L., 1300 Billings Ave., Helena, MT 59601. (Officers change July 1993.)

Nebraska

Nebraska Edu. Media Assn.—pres., Ella M. Epp, P.O. Box 286, Henderson, NE 68371. (Officers change July 1993.)

Nebraska L. Assn., Sch., Children's and Yng. Peop. Sect.—pres., Janice L. Kruse, Rt. 2, Box 285, Fremont, NE 68025. (Officers change Oct. 1993.)

Nevada

Nevada Sch. & Children's L. Assn.—pres., Edwin A. Iverson, 495 S. Bailey, Fallon, NV 89406. (Officers change Jan. 1993.)

New England

New England Edu. Media Assn.—pres., Harriet Lapointe, P.O. Box 287, Bristol, RI 02809. (Officers change Nov. 1993.)

New Hampshire

New Hampshire Edu. Media Assn.—pres., Susan D. Ballard, 55 Linda Lane, Manchester, NH 03104. (Officers change July 1993.)

New Jersey

Edu. Media Assn. of New Jersey—pres., Mary Jane Smith, 4 Wilbur Terr., Sayreville, NJ 08872. (Officers change June 1993.)

New Mexico

New Mexico L. Assn., Sch. L., Children's & YA's Servs. Div.—pres., Drew Harrington, 4404 De La Cruz N.W., Albuquerque, NM 87107. (Officers change Apr. 1993.)

New York

New York L. Assn., Sch. L. Media Sect.—pres., Judith Gray, 302 Pleasant St., Manlius, NY 13104-9771. (Officers change Nov. 1993.)

North Carolina

North Carolina Assn. of Sch. Lns.—pres., Nona Ann Pryor, R.R.1, Box 510, Randleman, NC 27317-9750. (Officers change Nov. 1993.)

North Dakota

North Dakota L. Assn., Youth Servs. Sect.—pres., Jacqueline M. Basaraba, 1815 29th. St. W., Williston, ND 58801. (Officers change Oct. 1993.)

Ohio

Ohio Edu. L./Media Assn.—pres., Anthony C. Marshalek, 4070 Tod Ave., N.W., Warren, OH 44485. (Officers change Jan. 1993.)

Oklahoma

Oklahoma Assn. of Sch. L. Media Specs.—pres., Jeanie Johnson, 12400 N.E. 10th., Choctaw, OK 73020. (Officers change July 1993.)

Oregon

Oregon Edu. Media Assn.—pres., Catherine L. Rooth, 733 Sacre Lane, Monmouth, OR 97361. (Officers change Oct. 1993.)

Pennsylvania

Pennsylvania Sch. Lns. Assn.—pres., Sally L. Myers, 337 Roley St., Belle Vernon, PA 15012. (Officers change July 1993.)

Rhode Island

Rhode Island Edu. Media Assn.—pres., Cheryl A. McCarthy, 69 Slocum Rd., Portsmouth, RI 02871. (Officers change June 1993.)

South Carolina

South Carolina Assn. of Sch. Lns.—pres., Judy Roumillat, 4515 Paramount Dr., Charleston, SC 29405. (Officers change June 1993.)

South Dakota

South Dakota L. Assn., Sch. Sect.—pres., Mary Gillick, 640 E. Hudson, Apt. 104, Spearfish, SD 57783. (Officers change Oct. 1993.)

Tennessee

Tennessee Assn. of Sch. Lns.—pres., Margaret Martin, 120 Rosebud Ln., Gray, TN 37615. (Officers change Oct. 1993.)

Texas

Texas Assn. of Sch. Lns.—pres., Laura Edwards, Coppell ISD, P.O. Box 1292, Coppell, TX 75019–1292. (Officers change Apr. 1993.)

Utah

Utah Edu. L. Media Assn.—pres., Michael J. Hirschi, 2045 W. 3875 S., Roy, UT 84067. (Officers change Mar. 1993.)

Vermont

Vermont Edu. Media Assn.—pres., Melissa Malcolm, Mt. Abraham Union H.S., Bristol, VT 05443. (Officers change May 1993.)

Virginia

Virginia Edu. Media Assn.—pres., Anne J. Madsen, 9535 Bay Front Dr., Apt. 302, Norfolk VA 23518. (Officers change May 1993.)

Washington

Washington L. Media Assn.—pres., Kathy Lemmer, 7412 84th St., Ct S.W., Tacoma, WA 98498. (Officers change Oct. 1993.)

West Virginia

West Virginia L. Assn., Sch. Sect.—pres., Martha Mae Danzig, Lewis Cnty H.S., Court Ave., Weston, WV 26452. (Officers change Dec. 1992.)

Wisconsin

Wisconsin Assn. of Sch. Lns.—pres., Ruth Dishnow, N4854 Sackett Dr., Medford, WI 54451. (Officers change Jan. 1993.)

Wisconsin Edu. Media Assn.—pres., Nelson Aakre, N6176 Summerglow Trail, Onalaska, WI 54650. (Officers change Apr. 1994.)

Wyoming

Wyoming L. Assn./School L. Media Sect.—pres., Barb Wegner, Cody Junior H.S., 920 Beck Ave., Cody, WY 82414. (Officers change Oct. 1993).

◆

American Library Trustee Association

◆

Membership as of August 31, 1992	
Organization members	303
Personal members	1,307
Total	1,610

Susan Roman, *executive director*

The American Library Trustee Association is interested in the development of effective library service for all people in all types of communities and in all types of libraries; it follows that its members are concerned, as policymakers, with organizational patterns of service, with the development of competent personnel, the provision of adequate financing, the passage of suitable legislation, and the encouragement of citizen support for libraries. ALTA recognizes that responsibility for professional action in these fields has been assigned to other divisions of ALA; its specific responsibilities as a division, therefore, are:

1. A continuing and comprehensive educational program to enable library trustees to discharge their grave responsibilities in a manner best fitted to benefit the public and the libraries they represent.

2. Continuous study and review of the activities of library trustees.

3. Cooperation with other units within ALA concerning their activities relating to trustees.

4. Encouraging participation of trustees in other appropriate divisions of ALA.

5. Representation and interpretation of the activities of library trustees in contacts outside the library profession, particularly with national organizations and governmental agencies.

6. Promotion of strong state and regional trustee organizations.

7. Efforts to secure and support adequate library funding.

8. Promulgation and dissemination of recommended library policy.

9. Assuring equal access of information to all segments of the population.

10. Encouraging participation of trustees in trustee/library activities, at local, state, regional and national levels.

Board of Directors

Officers: pres., Aileen R. Schrader (1994); vice-pres., Ann L. Donoghue (1995); 2d vice-pres., John W. A. Parsons (1993); secy., Holley Wilkinson (1993); past pres., Mary E. Arney (1993); parliamentarian, Ira B. Harkavy (1993).

Other members: councilor, Terri C. Jacobs (1995); council adms.: Esther W. Lopato (1993); Ruth Newell (1993); Carol K. Vogelman (1993); newsletter ed., Sharon A. Saulmon (1993); rgnl. vice-pres.: Wayne Coco (1993); Jack Cole (1993);

dees. The primary reason for the conference is education.

Ch., Cheryl J. Cooper (1994); Alma P. Dennis (1993); Gloria Dinerman (1993); Clifford Dittrich (1993); Robert W. Gibson Jr. (1993); Molly G. Glazer (1993); Jean T. Kreamer (1993); Barbara S. Prentice (1993); Rochelle Reagan (1993); Sharon A. Saulmon (1993); Wynne E. Weiss (1993); Leroy D. Williams (1993).

President's Program

To plan with the first vice-president/president-elect ways in which the ALA president's theme can be carried out in ALTA's Annual Conference program; to plan with the ALTA first vice-president the ALTA president's program.

Ch., Catherine S. Wallace (1994); Suzine Har-Nicolescu (1993); Gloria A. Weiss (1993).

Publications

To address all publishing concerns, future and existing, of the ALTA division.

Ch., Clifford Dittrich (1994); William G. Bridgman (1993); Jack Cole (1994); Suzine Har-Nicolescu (1994); Diane Hofstede (1993); Jean T. Kreamer (1994); Carolyn K. Landry (1993); Barbara S. Prentice (1993).

Resolutions

To receive committee resolutions and put in correct form for presentation to the ALTA board.

Ch. to be appointed; Jack Cole (1994); Charles E. Reid (1994); ex officio, Sharon A. Saulmon (1993).

Speakers Bureau

To maintain the operation, accuracy, and effectiveness of the ALTA Speakers Bureau.

Ch., Betty Paige Hanchey (1993); Richard A. Barry (1993); Helen Bolociuch (1993); Cheryl J. Cooper (1993); Helen S. Kolhman (1993); Roena Rand (1993); Sharon A. Saulmon (1994).

Special Functions

To plan and carry out ALTA's Gala and President's Reception at Annual Conference.

Ch., Ruth Newell (1994); Jayleen L. Angellotti (1994); Gail Dysleski (1994); William G. Murphy (1994).

Specialized Outreach Services

To focus on the needs of those who because of physical or mental handicaps are not being served or are underserved; to gather relevant information and resources pertinent to improvement in the quality and scope of outreach services for those unserved or underserved; and to use this information to make trustees more aware of their responsibility in this area.

Ch., Mrs. Floy Johnson (1994); Jayleen L. Angellotti (1994); Anthony Balestrieri (1993); Joanne Beegan (1993); Barbara Goldman (1994); Jean W. Greener (1993); Suzine Har-Nicolescu (1993); Arthur S. Kirschenbaum (1993); Athalie Kirschenbaum (1993); Lynnie G. Powell (1993); Ruth Showalter (1994); Carol K. Vogelman (1993); Catherine S. Wallace (1993); Gloria A. Weiss (1993); M. Jerry Weiss (1993); Marguerite W. Yates (1994); ex officio, Sharon A. Saulmon (1993).

Trustee Citations, Jury on

To annually select two outstanding trustees for distinguished service to library development whether on the local, state, or national level, and to administer the citations.

Ch., Ira B. Harkavy (1993); Bonnie Bellamy (1993); Robert Gaylor (1993); John W. A. Parsons (1993).

REPRESENTATIVES

ALA Com. on Organization—Ramona Wertz (1992).

ALA Com. on Professional Ethics—Judith M. Baker (1993).

ALA Fund-Raising Task Force—Wayne Moss (1993).

ALA Legislative Assembly—Dorris D. Holmes (1992).

ALA Literacy Assembly—Mrs. Floy Johnson (1992).

ALA Membership Com.—Barbara Cooper (1992).

ALA Membership Promotion Task Force—Leroy D. Williams (1992).

ALA Planning and Budget Assembly—Ann L. Donoghue (1993).

ALA Standing Com. on L. Edu.—Gloria Aguilar (1992).

FOLUSA—Roslyn S. Kurland (1993).

Freedom to Read Fdn.—Judith E. Petrou (1993).

PLA Bd. of Directors—Ramonda S. Wertz (1993).

PLA Membership Comm. Liaison—Leroy D. Williams (1993).

◆

Association for Library Collections & Technical Services

◆

Membership as of August 31, 1992
Organization members	982
Personal members	4,964
Total	5,946

Karen Muller, *executive director*

The Association for Library Collections & Technical Services is responsible for the following activities: acquisition, identification, cataloging, classification, and preservation of library materials; the development and coordination of the country's library resources; and those areas of selection and evaluation involved in the acquisition of library materials and pertinent to the development of library resources. ALCTS has specific responsibility for:

1. Continuous study and review of the activities assigned to the division.

2. Conduct of activities and projects within its area of responsibility.

3. Synthesis of activities of all units within the ALA that have a bearing on the type of activity represented.

4. Representation and interpretation of its type of activity in contacts outside the profession.

5. Stimulation of the development of librarians engaged in its type of activity, and stimulation of participation by members in appropriate type-of-library divisions.

6. Planning and development of programs of study and research for the type of activity for the total profession.

Board of Directors

Officers: pres., Lizbeth Bishoff (1994); pres.-elect, Jennifer A. Younger (1995); CRG ch., Jean Acker Wright (1994); div. councilor, Jean W. Farrington (1995); exec. dir., Karen Muller.

Other members: Marjorie E. Bloss (dir.-at-large, 1995); Mary M. Case (SS ch., 1993); Carol E. Chamberlain (AS ch., 1993); David Farrell (CMDS ch., 1993); Arnold Hirshon (past pres., 1993); Katha D. Massey (dir.-at-large, 1994); Lorraine H. Olley (PLMS ch., 1993); Jutta Reed-Scott (RLMS ch., 1993); Laverna M. Saunders (CRG vice-ch., 1994); Barbara B. Tillett (CCS ch., 1993); *ex officio*: Walter M. High (parliamentarian, 1993); Robert P. Holley (Budget & Finance ch., 1993); Richard P. Smiraglia (*LRTS* ed., 1993); Ann G. Swartzell (newsletter ed., 1995); Winston Tabb (L. of Congress liaison, 1993); John P. Webb (Planning ch., 1993).

Executive Committee: pres., Lizbeth Bishoff (1994); pres.-elect., Jennifer A. Younger (1995); past pres., Arnold Hirshon (1993); exec. dir., Karen Muller.

Publications

ALCTS Network News (ISSN 1056–6694) (irregular). Available through Bitnet and Internet. Free to members and nonmembers. To subscribe on Bitnet or Internet, send to LISTSERV @ UICVM.BITNET the message SUBSCRIBE ALCTS [Your first name—your last name]. Ed., Karen Muller.

ALCTS Newsletter (ISSN 1047–949X) (6 times a year). Sent to all ALCTS members. Subscriptions to nonmembers $25 a yr. ($35 foreign); single copies, $5. Ed., Ann G. Swartzell, 416 Library, Univ. of California, Berkeley, CA 94720.

Library Resources & Technical Services (ISSN 0024–2527) (quarterly). Sent to all ALCTS members. Subscriptions to nonmembers, $45 a yr.; single copies of journal issues, $14. Ed., Richard P. Smiraglia, Palmer School of L. & Inf. Science, Long Island Univ., Brookville, NY 11548.

COMMITTEES

Association of American Publishers—ALCTS (joint). (See listing under Joint Committees, p. 16.)

(Hugh C.) Atkinson Memorial Award, ACRL/ALCTS/LAMA/LITA (See listing on p. 44.)

Audiovisual

To consider the particular problems of audiovisual and other nonbook materials that fall within the division's mandate; to study and make recommendations on the acquisition, organization, and handling of these forms of materials and to work in conjunction with other division and section committees having the various functional responsibilities in order to keep a working relationship between form and function; to serve as the division's liaison with related committees within and outside ALA on matters falling within the responsibility of ALCTS.

Ch., Joan Swanekamp (1994); Eric R. Childress (1994); Josephine F. Davidson (1994); Janice M. DeSirey (1993); Anna S. Ferguson (1993); Richard L. Harwood (1993); Robert T. Ivey (1993); Daniel W. Kinney (1994); Johanne L. LaGrange (1993); Sheila A. Smyth (1994); cons., Patricia S. Vanderberg (1994); intern, John Oldick (1993).

Liaisons

AALL—Merle J. Slyhoff (1993).
AASL—Robert J. Skapura (1993).
CLA—Ganga B. Dakshinamurti (1994).
LC—Catherine R. Garland (1993).
LITA—David N. Nelson (1993).
MLA—James P. Cassaro (1993).
NLM—Alice E. Jacobs (1993).
OCLC—Glenn E. Patton (1993).
OLAC—Sheila A. Smyth (1993).
PLA—Shirley Evans (1993).
YALSA—Linda E. Sleeman (1993).

AV Producer/Distributor-Library Relations (subcommittee)

To encourage cooperation and the exchange of ideas among publishers/distributors of audiovisual information and librarians; to heighten the awareness of producers/distributors to the concerns of audiovisual librarians regarding consistent and accurate bibliographic descriptions of audiovisual materials; to provide a vehicle for two-way communication of concerns for the mutual benefit of both parties.

Ch., Richard L. Harwood (1993); Eric R. Childress (1993); Anna S. Ferguson (1993); Linda Hansen (1993); Robert T. Ivey (1993); Merle J. Slyhoff (1993); Joan Swanekamp (1993).

AV Standards (subcommittee)

To collect information from the library community regarding standards for audiovisuals, graphics, computer software, and other nonbook materials; to develop standards in conjunction with the National Information Standards Organization (NISO) for the identification, packaging, cataloging, and preservation of audiovisuals, graphics, computer software, and other nonbook materials, in which the unique requirements of these materials are addressed.

Ch., Johanne L. LaGrange (1993); Marilyn J. Craig (1993); Karen C. Driessen (1993); Robert T. Ivey (1993); Patricia S. Vanderberg (1993).

Best of LRTS Award

Annual citation to be given to the author(s) of the best paper published each year in the division's official journal. The recipient(s) shall meet the following criteria: (1) the content is a significant contribution about one or more issues addressed by ALCTS and its sections; (2) the statements in the paper are adequately supported by accurate data and/or documentation; (3) the writing style is clear and readable. Each of the papers published in the volume for the preceding calendar year is eligible for consideration with the exception of official reports and documents, obituaries, letters to the editor, and biographies of award winners. The jury may, at its discretion, invite recommendations from other readers. The jury may decide that there is no qualified article and not present an award.

Ch., William Z. Schenck (1993); Judith Hopkins (1993); Tom H. Ray (1993); Sally A. Rogers (1993); Diane Vizine-Goetz (1993).

Blackwell North America Scholarship Award

To review the literature published in the past calendar year and to select an author and article or book that the jury considers to be the best publication for the year on the field of acquisitions, collection development, and related areas of resources development in libraries. Materials may be considered in the second year following imprint date if such materials were published in the calendar year following the imprint date.

Ch., Edward A. Warro (1993); Betsy Kruger (1993); Helen I. Reed (1993); Craig A. Wilson (1993). 1 member to be appointed.

Budget and Finance

To submit a recommended annual budget for action to the ALCTS Board of Directors; to perform budget analyses and fiscal planning; to advise units requesting ALCTS funds; to review all requests for ALCTS funds; to advise the ALCTS Board on all fiscal matters of the division, including fiscal implications of all division publications and programs; and to represent ALCTS at the COPES Planning and Budget Assembly.

Ch., Robert P. Holley (1993); Carmel C. Bush (CRG rep., 1993); Charles R. Fenly (CCS rep., 1994); Lisa L. Fox (PLMS rep., 1994); Shirley W. Leung (RLMS rep., 1993); Jana L. Lonberger (SS rep., 1994); James R. Mouw (AS rep., 1993); Ann Thompson (CMDS rep., 1994); intern, Michael Samson (1993); ex officio: Jennifer A. Younger (1993); Karen Muller.

Catalog Form and Function

To study issues and to develop guidelines regarding the form and function of the catalog in its several formats, including issues arising from the structure of the catalog, filing order, authority control, record content, minimum level cataloging, retrospective conversion, command structure, search strategy, and record display. To develop programs as appropriate in these areas. To coordinate discussion of issues regarding all types of information in the catalog, including information relating to such areas as acquisitions, processing status, holdings, binding, circulation, and preservation, in addition to the information generated by descriptive and subject analysis of the collection. To provide liaison for those areas of interest between ALCTS and other ALA organizations that have an interest and concern for these activities.

Ch., Suzanne S. Striedieck (1993); Catherine S. Herlihy (1994); Colleen F. Hyslop (1993); Martin M. Kurth (1993); Barbara J. Anderson (CCS, 1994); Carol Cubberley (AS, 1994); Toby Heidtmann (PLMS, 1994); Norma K. Hendrickson (RLMS, 1993); Kathleen A. Schweitzberger (SS, 1994); Patricia O. Walker (CMDS, 1994); intern, Timothy V. Carstens (1993).

Commercial Technical Services

To study the relationship between libraries and commercial technical services which import and export bibliographic and other data to individual libraries or groups of libraries. To prepare recommendations and develop guidelines for users of commercial technical services. To encourage and facilitate the development of standards in the commercial technical service environment. To consider the particular problems of libraries as they relate to the evaluation and selection of vendors to perform any or all such services. To

provide a forum of communication between librarians and providers of commercial technical services. To work with other groups with related interest within and outside ALCTS.

Ch., Dawn L. Hale (1993); J. Randolph Call (1994); Marylou Colver (1994); Nancy A. Davey (1994); Marie A. Kascus (1994); Robert L. Watkins (1994); Gretchen Whitney (1993).

Conference Program—New Orleans, 1993

Ch., Lizbeth Bishoff (1993); Barry B. Baker (1993); Mary M. Case (SS, 1993); Carol E. Chamberlain (AS, 1993); Lorraine H. Olley (PLMS, 1993); Jutta Reed-Scott (RLMS, 1993); Kathy E. Tezla (CMDS, 1993); Barbara B. Tillett (CSS, 1993); Jean Acker Wright (CRG, 1993); staff liaison, to be announced.

Conference Program—Miami, 1994

Ch., Jennifer A. Younger (1994); Caroline L. Early (AS, 1994); Nancy E. Elkington (RLMS, 1994); Janet E. Gertz (PLMS, 1994); Connie McCarthy (CMDS, 1994); Miriam W. Palm (SS, 1994); Carlen M. Ruschoff (CCS, 1994); Laverna M. Saunders (CRG, 1994).

Duplicates Exchange Union

To facilitate the exchange of duplicate library materials among institutions participating in the program.

Ch., David E. Winchester (1994); Douglas A. DeLong (1993); Karen Matthews (1993); LaDonne Roberts (1994). 1 member to be appointed.

Education

To study and review the educational needs of resources and technical services librarians; to identify and propose methods and materials for recruitment to careers in the area; to explore and foster the development of curricula and continuing education programs; and to act as a catalyst in promoting communication between resources and technical service librarians and library educators.

Ch., Sally J. Rausch (1993); John Drew Racine (1993); Barbara J. Strauss (1993); Michael Elmore (SS, 1993); Sharlane T. Grant (PLMS, 1994); Arno A. Kastner (CCS, 1993); Elaine K. Rast (CRG, 1994); intern, Kathleen M. Kie (1993); cons.: Joyce L. Ogburn (1993); Patricia G. Oyler (1994); Nancy J. Williamson (1994). 3 members to be appointed.

International Relations

To identify knowledgeable individuals qualified to serve as representatives of the division at meetings of international organizations and as reviewers of documents emanating from such organizations and to submit lists of such names when called upon to do so; to encourage international organizations to appoint their committees and form specialized working groups in consultation with the appropriate library associations in order to determine the credibility and competence of the individuals proposed for appointment; to consult with the International Relations Officer in order to ascertain the names of individuals who may be attending or planning to attend international meetings which may have concerns of interest to ALCTS, enabling ALCTS to contact these individuals and to request that they monitor meetings, report to ALCTS, etc.; to identify likely sources of funding to support the participation of ALCTS in international activities, including the possibility of a fund to be developed in cooperation with other divisions; to identify expenses arising from participation in international activity and provide cost figures for the information and guidance of the Board; to participate in other activities as appropriate or as directed by the Board of Directors.

Ch., D. Whitney Coe (1993); Dora Biblarz (AS, 1993); Helga A. Borck (RLMS, 1994); Ruth C. Carter (CRG, 1994); Cecily A. Johns (CMDS, 1994); Frederick C. Lynden (CCS, 1993); Mark S. Roosa (PLMS, 1994); Sally C. Tseng (SS, 1993).

Legislation

To monitor legislative activity and identify those issues central to the concerns of the ALCTS membership. To identify appropriate ways in which to respond to relevant legislative issues. To raise awareness regarding library-related legislative activity, and to motivate political action within the ALCTS membership through a variety of means. To cooperate with other ALA legislation groups as appropriate.

Ch., Jonathan D. Eldredge (1994); Karen L. Horny (1993); Kate F. Nevins (1993); Stewart Bodner (AS, 1993); Deborah Fetch (CCS, 1993); John R. James (SS, 1994); Annette S. Morris (PLMS, 1994); Patricia A. Phillips (CRG, 1994); Barbara VanDeventer (CMDS, 1994); Joanna Walsh (RLMS, 1994).

Library Materials Price Index

To prepare and publish price indexes of library materials.

Ch., John M. Haar III (1993); Stephen J. Bosch (1993); Genevieve S. Owens (1993); Mark Sandler (1993).

"LRTS" Editor Search

Ch., John K. Duke (1993); Carol Pitts Hawks (1993); Jay H. Lambrecht (1993); William Z. Schenck (1993).

"LRTS" Editorial Board

The Editorial Board advises the editor on matters relating to editorial policies and journal content and assists in the selection of contributors and the evaluation of manuscripts.

Ch., Richard P. Smiraglia (1993); Thomas A. Bourke (RLMS, 1993); Gregory H. Leazer (1993); Miriam W. Palm (SS, 1993); Karen A. Schmidt (AS, 1993); Charles W. Simpson (CCS, 1993); D. Kathryn Weintraub (1993); Jean Acker Wright (CRG, 1993); indexer, Edward Swanson (1993); book review ed., Lawrence W. S. Auld (1993); ex officio: Ann G. Swartzell (1995); Karen Muller.

Development of Major Collections
(subcommittee)

To generate a series for the "Notes on Research" column in LRTS, on the topic of the development of historical collections.

Ch., Michael Ryan (1993); William L. Joyce (1993); Gregory H. Leazer (1993); ex officio, Richard P. Smiraglia (1993).

State of Copy Cataloging, The
(subcommittee)

To generate a series for the "Notes on Operations" column of LRTS, on the topic of the state of copy cataloging.

Ch., D. Kathryn Weintraub (1993); Gregory H. Leazer (1993); Margaret A. Rohdy (1993); ex officio, Richard P. Smiraglia (1993).

MARBI (Machine-Readable Bibliographic Information), ALCTS/LITA/ RASD
(interdivisional)

To encourage the creation of needed standards for the representation in machine-readable form of bibliographic information; to review and evaluate proposed standards; to recommend approval of standards in conformity with ALA policy (especially the ALA Standards Committee); to establish a mechanism for continuing review of standards (including the monitoring of further development); to provide commentary on the content of various implementations of standards to concerned agencies; to maintain liaison with concerned units within ALA and relevant outside agencies.

Ch., Florence Wilson (1993); Priscilla L. Caplan (LITA, 1993); Karen M. Drabenstott (RASD, 1994); Shelby E. Harken (ALCTS, 1994); William W. Jones Jr. (LITA, 1993); Patricia E. Luthin (ALCTS, 1993); Patricia Tegler (RASD, 1994); Beth A. Warner (RASD, 1994); Lawrence A. Woods (LITA, 1994); intern, Gary L. Strawn (1993); ex officio: Sally H. McCallum (1993); Young-Hee Queinnec (1993).

Membership

To develop and pursue a continuous campaign to recruit and retain members for ALCTS from among existing and potential ALA members; to provide a liaison between ALA membership services and ALCTS members.

Ch., Barry B. Baker (1993); Pamela M. Bluh (SS, 1993); Myron Chace (RLMS, 1994); Laverne C. Jenkins (AS, 1993); James Mason (PLMS, 1994); Robert McDonald (CCS, 1993); Judith A. Ranta (1994); Gordon S. Rowley (CMDS, 1994); interns: Mollie D. Niemeyer (1993); Jacquelene W. Riley (1993); liaison, Jane L. Tupin (NMRT, 1993); ex officio, Ann G. Swartzell (1995); staff liaison, Marie Rochelle.

Nominating

To nominate candidates for elective offices and to perform the duties specified in the bylaws.

Ch., Elaine K. Rast (1993); Joseph W. Barker (AS, 1993); Sharon C. Bonk (1993); Sherry Byrne (PLMS, 1993); Susan A. Davis (SS, 1993); Derry C. Juneja (CRG, 1993); Shirley W. Leung (RLMS, 1993); Louis A. Pitschmann (CMDS, 1993); Richard P. Smiraglia (CCS, 1993).

Organization and Bylaws

To advise the Board of Directors and through it the division on the establishment, functions, and discontinuance of sections, committees, and other groups as the needs of the division may require, and to advise the officers of the division and its sections and of affiliated groups, or groups seeking affiliation, for their consistency with the bylaws of the division and to report its findings to the Board of Directors; to recommend amendments to the bylaws of the division or any of its sections; to report upon proposals for amendments referred to the committee.

Ch., Arnold Hirshon (1993); Jennifer S. Banks (PLMS, 1994); Joan W. Hayes (CRG, 1993); Gail A. Kennedy (AS, 1994); Patricia A. McClurg (CMDS, 1993); Minna C. Saxe (SS, 1993); V. Louise Saylor (CCS, 1993); Ann G. Swartzell (RLMS, 1993); Katherine L. Walter (1993); staff liaison, Yvonne A. McLean.

(Esther J.) Piercy Award Jury

The jury shall, in correspondence and in meetings held at Midwinter, by review of the nominations and through such investigations as they may wish to make, award the Esther J. Piercy Award to recognize the contribution to those areas of librarianship included in library collections and technical services by a librarian with not more than ten years of professional experience who has shown outstanding promise for continuing contribution and leadership or decide that there is no qualified candidate for the year.

Ch., Frank A. D'Andraia (1993); Pamela M. Bluh (1993); Sarah A. Buchanan (1993); Trisha L. Davis (1993); Karen M. Hsu (1993); Patricia M. Thomas (1993).

Planning

To consider problems of technical services as a whole, including long-range division objectives and areas of new divisional interest, to undertake a systematic and continuing review once every five years or at the request of the ALCTS Board, whichever comes first, of all sections, committees, and other divisional-level units as to their charge, function, composition, size, and relevance to and success in forwarding the goals and objectives of ALCTS; and to recommend action to the ALCTS Board about the continuation or discontinuation of the unit reviewed.

Ch., John P. Webb (1993); Robert L. DeCandido (PLMS, 1993); Jean A. Pec (SS, 1993); Jack E. Pontius (RLMS, 1993); Edward Shreeves (CMDS, 1993); Judith D. Webster (AS, 1993). 2 members to be appointed.

Preservation Microfilming

To encourage the microfilming of deteriorated and deteriorating materials as a preservation technique; to collect and disseminate information about preservation microfilming activities, including selection criteria, cooperative approaches, production methods, storage, record control, and use of master microforms; to assist in ensuring the successful conduct of preservation microfilming programs by highlighting issues that impede or hamper activities and suggesting steps for ALCTS to take to focus attention on them or to resolve them; to propose educational programs and other projects as appropriate.

Ch. to be appointed; Julie E. Arnott (RLMS, 1993); Marjorie E. Bloss (1993); Mary H. Brennan-Kerr (CMDS, 1994); Margaret M. Byrnes (PLMS, 1993); Thomas F. R. Clareson (1994); Michael D. Esman (1994); Lydia Suzanne Kellerman (SS, 1993); Helen F. Schmierer (CCS, 1993); Errol S. Somay (1993); interns: Marda L. Johnson (1993); Erich J. Kesse (1993).

Program Initiatives

To coordinate the program planning of ALCTS except for annual conference planning; to develop the Division's plan of program offerings; to identify potential topics of interest to the ALCTS membership; to foster the development of programs on those topics that it or the ALCTS staff identify based on membership interactions; to assist others in developing topics and programs; to recommend groups to develop programs on selected topics; to advise the ALCTS staff on scheduling of programs.

Ch., Dorothy Keeton McKowen (1993); Bill Drewett (1994); Nancy R. John (1994); Julieann V. Nilson (1993); Janet G. Padway (1993); Nolan F. Pope (1994); John J. Riemer (1993).

Publications

To coordinate the association's publication program by (1) facilitating the expeditious handling of ALCTS publications by (a) reviewing, as rapidly as possible and prior to their submission to the ALCTS Board, all proposals for and manuscripts of publications originating in the division or any of its units, other than institute or promotional brochures, advertisements, publications lists (as opposed to bibliographies), and issues of existing journals (this includes proposals for serial publications and publications in any format); (b) suggesting an appropriate dissemination medium for each proposed publication; (c) identifying standards for content, format, and style for ALCTS publications; (d) insuring adherence to these and to appropriate editorial standards by assisting authors of ALCTS publications in the preparation of manuscripts; (e) reviewing ALCTS monographs-in-print and recommending to the appropriate section titles that need updating or revision, or suggesting possible subjects for publication; (f) recommending publishing priorities to the ALCTS Board; (g) assisting the ALA Publishing Committee and ALA Publishing Services in matters related to ALCTS publishing activites as requested; (h) reviewing and recommending to the Board proposed ALCTS endorsements of non-ALCTS publications; (2) providing a forum for discussion of editorial policy for the division's serial publications.

Ch., Bill E. Robnett (1994); Paula A. De Stefano (PLMS, 1993); Sylvia O. Martin (SS, 1993); Judith F. Niles (AS, 1993); Mary Faith Pankin (CCS, 1993); Elizabeth Patterson (RLMS, 1994); Anna H. Perrault (CMDS, 1993); ex officio: Richard P. Smiraglia (1993); Edward Swanson (1993); Ann G. Swartzell (1995).

Publisher/Vendor–Library Relations

To serve as the review and advisory committee on all matters of vendors of library materials—library relationships; to investigate these relationships; and to prepare recommendations and develop guidelines of acceptable performance for libraries and vendors for ordering and supplying of library materials.

Ch., Joseph W. Barker (1994); Mary M. Case (1993); Kay A. Granskog (1994); Joan Grant (1994); Wesley Lawton (1994); Michael W. Markwith (1993); Alexander M. Moyer (1993); Gary M. Shirk (1993); liaison, Kendall F. Svengalis (1993); intern, Michael T. Ryan (1993); cons., Helen I. Reed (1993).

Complaints (subcommittee)

To develop procedures and policies for maintaining and updating the "Gille" list, for handling complaints forwarded to PVLR, for publicizing results for inquiries regarding complaints re-

ceived by PVLR, and for considering whether there are programmatic and/or publication possibilities in this topic.

Ch., Gary M. Shirk (1993); Doina G. Farkas (1993); Julie A. Gammon (1993); Edna C. Laughrey (1993); Alexander M. Moyer (1993); Bob Rooney (1993); Kendall F. Svengalis (1993).

Research and Statistics

To explore, develop, and promote a research agenda, including statistics, which focuses on the current research needs in the areas of library collections and technical services; to develop activities and programs to stimulate quality research and to encourage improvement in research skills; to coordinate the activities of the division in the field of research and statistics; to maintain liaison with appropriate units of the Association and the division regarding research and statistics activities.

Ch., Sarah E. Thomas (1994); Robert Alan (SS, 1993); Marcia L. Anderson (CRG, 1993); Ruth C. Carter (1994); Myron B. Chace (RLMS, 1994); Sharon E. Clark (1993); Evelyn Frangakis (PLMS, 1994); Joe A. Hewitt (1994); Karen A. Schmidt (AS, 1994); Lynn F. Sipe (CMDS, 1994); Stephen E. Wiberley Jr. (1993); Nancy J. Williamson (CCS, 1993).

Scholarly Communication

To serve as the review and advisory committee on all matters of scholarly publishing; to investigate changes in methods for scholarly publishing and communication; to collect and review information from the library and scholarly community concerning guidelines and standards, and to promulgate guidelines concerning recommended practices that relate to scholarly communication; to consider mutual problems and to provide for the communication of ideas between members of ALCTS and scholarly associations and commercial and noncommercial scholarly presses; to plan and sponsor meetings, seminars, studies, or other forms of communication on topics related to changes and developments in scholarly communication; to encourage the exchange of ideas among scholars, librarians, and distributors of scholarly information.

Ch., Frederick C. Lynden (1993); Marshall Keys (1993); Paul J. Kobulnicky (1993); Gail McMillan (1994); Thomas J. Michalak (1994); Patricia A. Scarry (1993); cons., Nancy E. Gwinn (1994).

Technical Services Measurements

To provide a forum for studying, evaluating, and disseminating information related to the current and future measurement of technical services operations (i.e., output measures and costs, effectiveness and efficiency indicators, and factors that may affect the value of these indicators); to establish and maintain liaisons with related professional groups.

Ch., Kathleen R. Brown (1993); Ann Allan (1993); Cliff Glaviano (1994); Sandra Herzinger (1994); Jessica A. Marshall (1994); Dilys E. Morris (1994); Ronald J. Nimmer (1993); Linda J. Robinson (1994); Samson C. Soong (1993); cons.: Susanne Nevin (1993); Delmus E. Williams (1994). 2 members to be appointed.

TASK FORCES

Ethics

To review the ALA ethics statement in terms of ALCTS's areas of expertise and to recommend action related to the proposed Midwinter hearing on the ethics statement.

Ch., Gay N. Dannelly (1993); Gail A. Kennedy (1993); Stephen A. Marine (1993).

Nomination Procedures and Leadership

To recommend specific steps for the implementation of the report of the ALCTS task force on nominations procedures and leadership development.

Ch., Nancy R. John (1993); Carol E. Chamberlain (1993); Marcella Grendler (1993); Martha J. Hanson (1993).

Organizational Structure of ALCTS

To review the current division and section organizational structure of ALCTS, consulting widely within the division, and to recommend a new organizational model that will be appropriate to meet the needs of librarians in library collections and technical services during the late 1990s and after the year 2000; to report regularly to ALCTS Organization and Bylaws Committee; and to complete its work by 1993 Annual Conference.

Ch., Beth J. Shapiro (1993); William A. Gosling (1993); Mark S. Roosa (1994); Susan H. Vita (1993).

President's Program (1993)

Ch., Barry B. Baker (1993); Pamela P. Brown (1993); Jennifer A. Younger (1993).

DISCUSSION GROUPS

Acquisition of Library Materials (See Acquisitions Librarians/Vendors of Library Materials, p. 31.)

Acquisitions Administrators (See p. 31.)

Acquisitions Topics for Public Libraries (See p. 31.)

Authority Control in the Online Environment, LITA/ALCTS CCS (See p. 72.)

Automated Acquisitions/In-Process Control Systems

To provide a forum for the discussion of the development and implementation of automated acquisitions/in-process control systems in libraries; topics of discussion include, but are not limited to, automation of the traditional functions of order generation, receipt, check-in, claiming, cancellations, fund accounting, in-process control, and binding of monographs and serials; compatibility of these automated functions and integration with other online systems in the library; development of national levels of standardization for machine-readable acquisitions and in-process records; communication formats for the online systems in the library; development of national levels of standardization for machine-readable acquisitions and in-process records; communication formats for the online and tape transfer of order and vendor information; public access to in-process records and the need for authority control at the in-process stage; and integration of machine-readable in-process records with full and brief cataloging records. Also, to allow for the practical exchange of information on the implementation of various commercial and in-house acquisitions and processing systems in libraries.

Ch., Julia Gammon (1993); vice-ch., Rosann V. Bazirjian (1994).

Booksellers (See Acquisitions Librarians/ Vendors of Library Materials, p. 31.)

Catalog Management (See p. 33.)

Cataloging and Classification Research (See p. 33.)

Cataloging Norms (See p. 33.)

Chief Collection Development Officers of Large Research Libraries (See p. 34.)

Collection Development Librarians of Academic Libraries (See p. 34.)

Collection Management/Selection for Public Libraries (See p. 34.)

Computer Files

To provide a forum for the exchange of ideas among those persons working with or interested in computer file collections; to promote the availability, use, and bibliographic control of computer file collections; to strengthen communication and cooperation among computer file archivists, librarians, media specialists, and other persons working with computer file collections; and to contribute to the improvement of education and training of computer file archivists and librarians.

Ch., Colleen M. Thorburn (1993); vice-chs., Wilma I. Cromwell (1994) and Ann Sandberg-Fox (1994).

Copy Cataloging (See p. 33.)

Creative Ideas in Technical Services

Co-chs., Julieann V. Nilson (1993) and Janet G. Padway (1993).

Electronic Publishing

Ch., Richard P. Jasper (1993); vice-ch., Jean S. Callaghan (1993).

Gifts and Exchange (See p. 31.)

Heads of Cataloging Departments (See p. 33.)

Library Binding (See p. 36.)

Library-Vendor Relations (See p. 36).

Map Cataloging (See p. 33.)

MARC Holdings, LITA/ALCTS (interdivisional) (See p. 72.)

Microcomputer Support of Technical Services, LITA/ALCTS (interdivisional) (See p. 72.)

Newspaper

To provide a forum for the discussion of newspaper collection development and such man-

agement issues as the selection, preservation, stack maintenance, and bibliographic control.

Ch., Donnell L. Ruthenberg (1993).

Out of Print

To provide a forum for the discussion of techniques librarians can use: to influence publishers to keep more or specific books in print longer; to find and purchase books that are in the process of going out of print; and to locate books which were put out of print some time ago.

Ch., Barbara K. Nelson (1993); vice-ch., Floyd M. Zula (1993).

Physical Quality and Treatment (See p. 36.)

PLMS-RLMS (See p. 36.)

Pre-order and Pre-catalog Searching

To provide an informal forum for exchanging information and discussion techniques, new developments, problems, and emerging trends in the bibliographic searching of library materials to be acquired and/or cataloged.

Ch., Marsha Hamilton (1993); vice-ch., Nancy Boggess-Korekach (1993).

Preservation Administrators (See p. 36.)

Preservation Education and Outreach (See p. 36.)

Preservation of Library Materials (See p. 36.)

Public Service Managers of Microforms Facilities (See p. 37.)

Reproduction of Library Materials (See p. 37.)

Research Libraries (See p. 38.)

Retrospective Conversion, LITA/ALCTS (See p. 73.)

Role of the Professional in Academic Research Technical Services Departments

To provide a forum to discuss informally common problems concerning aspects of professional activity, both supervisory and nonadministrative, in the technical services area of academic research libraries.

Ch., Nancy Jean Gibbs (1993).

Serials Automation Interest Group, LITA/ ALCTS (See p. 73.)

Technical Services Administrators of Medium-sized Research Libraries

To meet and discuss informally problems within the field of technical services which are common to the administration of medium-sized research libraries. Open to technical services administrators in research libraries which do not qualify for the Technical Services Directors of Large Research Libraries Discussion Group, but with annual expenditures for library materials of at least $600,000 and a library of at least 1,000,000 volumes.

Ch., Deana L. Astle (1993).

Technical Services Directors of Large Research Libraries

To meet and discuss informally problems within the field of technical services which are common to the administration of large research libraries.

Ch., William A. Gosling (1993); vice-ch., Carol A. Mandel (1993).

Technical Services in Public Libraries

To provide a forum for the exchange of information and discussion of issues related to public library technical services functions; to be open to all librarians interested in technical services activities, including acquisitions, cataloging and classification, processing, preservation and bindery activities and technical services management.

Ch., Elisabeth A. Konrad (1993).

REPRESENTATIVES

Amer. Inst. for Consv. of Historic and Artistic Works—Constance L. Brooks (1993).
ALA Ad Hoc Com. on WHCLIS2—Karen L. Horny (1994).
ALA Com. on Research and Statistics—Sarah Thomas (1994).
ALA Legislation Assembly—to be appointed.
ALA Library Education Assembly—Sally J. Rausch (1993).
ALA Literacy Assembly—Cecily A. Johns (1993).
ALA Membership Promotion Task Force—Barry B. Baker (1993).
ALA Planning and Budget Assembly—Jennifer A. Younger (1993); Robert P. Holley (1992).
ALA Professional Ethics—Gay N. Dannelly (1993).
Com. on Preservation and Access—Constance Brooks (1993).
Freedom to Read Fdn. Board—John B. A. Hostage (1993).
Hugh C. Atkinson Memorial Award interdivisional—Thomas Leonhardt (1995).
Joint Advisory Com. on Nonbook Materials—Janice DeSirey (1993); Diane E. Hill (1993).
Joint Steering Com. for Revision of AACR2—Janet Swan Hill (1992).
Natl. Inf. Standards Org. (NISO): Standards Com. Z39 on Library Work, Documentation, and Related Publishing Practices—Myron B. Chace (1993); Alternate: Glenn E. Patton (1993).
Natl. Inst. for Conservation—Margaret S. Child (1993).

COUNCIL OF REGIONAL GROUPS

To encourage activities of regional group affiliates and assist them with information and advice relevant to their programs. The council shall consider problems common to or affecting the work of regional groups and shall recommend to the division such action as it deems to be in the interest of group activities.

Officers: ch., Jean Acker Wright (1994); vice-ch., Laverna M. Saunders (1994); past ch., Joan W. Hayes (1994).

Alabama L. Assn., Tech. Serv. RT— mod., Cathy Kellum, 6115 Stratford Ct., Huntsville, AL 35806.
Arizona State L. Assn., Clln. Devel. and Acq. RT—ch., Joddy McEuen, Dir., Pinal Cnty. L. Dist., P.O. Box E, Florence, AZ 85232.

Arkansas L. Assn., Resources and Tech. Serv. Div.—ch., Ellen Watson, Arkansas Coll. L., 2300 Highland Dr., Batesville, AR 72501.

California L. Assn., Tech. Serv. Chap—pres., Arlene Schwartz, Tech. Adv., Auto. Circ. Sys., Cnty of Los Angeles P.L., 7400 Imperial Hwy., P.O. Box 7011, Downey, CA 90241.

California (Northern) Tech. Proc. Group—ch., Evelyn Howard, Santa Clara Cnty. L., 1095 N. 7th St., San Jose, CA 95112-4434.

California (Southern) Tech. Proc. Group—pres., Derry C. Juneja, Riverside City and Cnty. P.L., P.O. Box 468, Riverside, CA 92502-0468.

Colorado L. Assn., Tech. Serv. and Automation Div.—ch., Gayle Abrahamson, Univ. of Southern Colorado, 2200 Bonforte Blvd., Pueblo, CO 81001-4901.

Connecticut L. Assn., Resources and Tech. Serv. Sect.—ch., Jane E. Murphy, Chief Tech. Serv. Ln., P.L., 1 Belden Ave., Norwalk, CT 06850.

District of Columbia L. Assn., Tech. Serv. Interest Group—John Page, Univ. of D.C., Learning Res. Div., 4200 Connecticut Ave. N.W., Washington, DC 20008.

Florida L. Assn., Tech. Serv. Caucus—ch., Terry Seebright, Olin L., 1000 Holt Ave., Rollins Coll., Winter Park, FL 32789.

Georgia L. Assn., Resources and Tech. Serv. Sect.—ch., David G. Anderson, Catalog Dept., Georgia State Univ. L., 100 Decatur St., SE, Atlanta, GA 30303–3081.

Illinois L. Assn., Resources and Tech. Serv. Forum—ch., Sheryl Nichin, P.L., 1224 W. Van Buren, Chicago, IL 60607.

Indiana L. Assn., Tech. Serv. Div.—ch., Bridgie B. Brelsford, Tippecanoe Cnty. P.L., 627 South St., Lafayette, IN 47901.

Iowa L. Assn., Resources and Tech. Serv. Forum—William Doering, Preus L., Luther Coll., Decorah, IA 52101-1060.

Kansas L. Assn., Resources and Tech. Serv. Sect.—ch., Charlene Grass, Farrell L., Kansas State Univ., Manhattan, KS 66506–7166.

Louisiana L. Assn., Tech. Serv. Interest Group—ch., Bobby Ferguson, State L., P.O. Box 131, Baton Rouge, LA 70821-0131.

Maryland L. Assn., Tech. Serv. Div.—pres., Joseph Boyce, Moore L., Coppin State Coll., 2500 W. North Ave., Baltimore, MD 21216.

Massachusetts L. Assn., Tech. Serv. Sect.—ch., Barbara Gibson, Head, Tech. Servs., Falmouth P.L., 123 Katherine Lee Bates Rd., Falmouth, MA 02540.

Metropolitan Area Collection Development Consortium—ch., Eleanor K. Pourron, Chief, Materials Mgt. Div., Arlington Cnty. Dept. of P.L., 1015 N. Quincy St., Arlington, VA 22201.

Michigan L. Assn., Tech. Serv. Forum—ch., Colleen Conway, Van Wylen L., Hope Coll., Holland, MI 49423-3698.

Minnesota L. Assn., Tech. Serv. Sect.—officers currently unknown.

Mississippi L. Assn., Tech. Serv. RT—ch., Missy Lee, Mgr., Tech. Proc., Information Services L., 3825 Ridgewood Road, Jackson, MS 39211.

Mountain Plains L. Assn., Tech. Serv. Sect.—ch., Rosario Garza, Auraria L., Lawrence at 11th St., Denver, CO 80204.

Nevada L. Assn., Collections, Automation, Preservation, Tech. Servs. & Acqs. in NV (CAPTAIN) Interest Group—ch., Diane Austin, Washoe Cnty. L. 301 S. Center St., P.O. Box 2151, Reno, NV 89505.

New England Tech. Serv. Lns.—pres., Cynthia Watters, Starr L. 6007, Middlebury Coll., Middlebury, VT 05753.

New Jersey L. Assn., Tech. Serv. Sect.—ch., Robert P. Rynkiewicz, P.L., 1 N. Tennessee Ave., Atlantic City, NJ 08401.

New York L. Assn., Sect. on Mgt. of Inf. Resources and Tech. (SMART)—pres., Jennifer Morris, Geneva Free L., 244 Main St., Geneva, N.Y. 14456-2370.

New York Tech. Serv. Lns.—pres., Marsha Clark, Bobst L., New York Univ., 70 Washington Sq. S., New York, NY 10012.

North Carolina L. Assn., Resources and Tech. Serv. Sect.—ch., Harry Tuchmayer, Coor., Main L. Serv., New Hanover Cnty. P.L., Wilmington, NC 28401.

North Dakota L. Assn. Tech. Serv. RT—ch., Margaret Blue, North Dakota State Univ. L., P.O. Box 5599 Univ. Station, Fargo, ND 58105.

Ohio L. Assn., Tech. Serv. Div.—Coord., Janet Harmon, Metropolitan L., 96 S. Grant Ave., Columbus, OH 43215-4781.

Ohio (Northern) Tech. Serv. Lns.—ch., Philip Tramdack, Automation Serv., Cleveland State Univ. L., 1860 E. 22nd St., Cleveland, OH 44115.

Ohio Valley Group of Tech. Serv. Lns.—ch., Pam Burton, Head, Serials Catlg., Ekstrom L., Univ. of Louisville, Louisville, KY 40208.

Oklahoma L. Assn., Tech. Serv. RT— ch., Linda Taylor, Oklahoma City Cmnty. Coll., 7777 S. May Ave., Oklahoma City, OK 73159.

Pennsylvania L. Assn., Tech. Serv. RT—ch., Janice H. Horn, 32 Barber St., Clarion, PA 16214-1603.

Potomac Tech. Proc. Lns.—ch., Margaret Warner, L. Media Ctr., Prince George's Cmnty. Coll., 301 Largo Rd., Largo, MD 20772.

South Carolina L. Assn., Tech. Serv. Sect.—ch., Martha Felts, Robert Scott Small L., Coll. of Charleston, Charleston, SC 29424.

Southeastern L. Assn. Resources and Tech. Serv. Sect.— ch., Judith Shelton, 3162 Stratford Green Pl., Avondale Estates, GA 30002; CRG rep., David G. Anderson, Head, Catalog Dept., Georgia State University Library, 100 Decatur St., SE, Atlanta, GA 30303–3081.

Tennessee L. Assn., Tech. Serv. RT—ch., Bob Ivey, Asst. Head, Catlg., Memphis State Univ. L., 2224 Sesame St., #4, Bartlett, TN 38134.

Texas L. Assn., Acq. and Clln. Devel. RT—ch., Janice Lange, Asst. Dir. for L. Clln. and Tech. Serv., Newton Gresham L., San Houston State Univ., Huntsville, TX 77341.

Texas Rgnl. Group of Catlgr. and Classifiers—ch., Mary Dabney Wilson, Univ. of Texas at Arlington L., P.O. Box 19497, Arlington, TX 76019.

Virginia L. Assn., Tech. Serv., Automation and Resources Forum—ch., Mary Haskell, Colonial Williamsburg Fdn. L., P.O. Box C, Williamsburg, VA 23187.

Washington L. Assn., Tech. Serv. Interest Group—ch., Emma de la Cruz, Bellingham P.L., P.O. Box 1197, Bellingham, WA 98227.

Wisconsin L. Assn., Tech. Serv. Sect.—ch., Marjorie Jo Tomczak, Head, Catlg. Dept., Milwaukee P.L., 814 W. Wisconsin Ave., Milwaukee, WI 53233–2385.

Affiliate Relations

Ch., Ann L. Denton (1993); Margaret R. Blue (1993); Mary Helen Faust (1993); Kathleen A. Schweitzberger (1993).

Speakers' Bureau

Ch., Dorothy H. Hope (1993); Debra Hackleman (1993); Derry C. Juneja (1993); Lee Marie Wisel (1993); Jean Acker Wright (1993).

Representatives

ALCTS Budget and Finance Com.—Carmel C. Bush (1993).

ALCTS Conference Program Com. (New Orleans, 1993)—Jean Acker Wright (1993).

ALCTS International Relations Com.—Ruth Carter (1994).

ALCTS Legislation Com.—Patricia A. Phillips (1994).

ALCTS *LRTS* Editorial Bd. —Jean Acker Wright (1993).

ALCTS Membership Com.—Kathleen A. Schweitzberger (1993).

ALCTS Nominating Com.—Derry C. Juneja (1993).

ALCTS Organization and Bylaws Com.—Joan W. Hayes (1993).

ALCTS Planning Com.—Doris H. Clark (1993).

ALCTS Research and Statistics Com.—Marcia L. Anderson (1993).

SECTIONS

Acquisitions (AS)
Cataloging and Classification (CCS)
Collection Management and Development (CMDS)
Preservation of Library Materials (PLMS)
Reproduction of Library Materials (RLMS)
Serials (SS)

Acquisitions Section (AS)

To contribute to library service and librarianship through encouragement, promotion of, and responsibility for those activities of ALCTS relating to the acquisition of all formats of information resources through purchase, lease, and other access methods, in all types of institutions.

Executive Committee

Ch., Carol E. Chamberlain (1993); ch.-elect, Caroline L. Early (1993); secy., Barbara C. Dean (1995); Carol Pitts Hawks (1994); Victoria A. Reich (1995); Kathryn A. Soupiset (1995); Barbara A. Winters (1994); ex officio: Karen Muller; Judith F. Niles (1993); Karen A. Schmidt (1993); Judith D. Webster (1993).

Committees

Acquisitions Organization and Management

To promote the development and practice of effective techniques and sound ethical, fiscal, and legal policies and procedures in acquisitions management, including relationships with suppliers; to further assess and encourage research into the role and organization of the acquisitions function within the library and the relationships among related areas such as accounting and purchasing offices and collection management.

Ch., Barbara A. Winters (1993); Rosann V. Bazirjian (1994); Christian M. Boissonnas (1994); Barbara C. Dean (1993); Laverne C. Jenkins (1993); Jan C. Maxwell (1994); Marilyn G. McSweeney (1993); Katina Strauch (1994); interns: David W. James (1993); Caroline A. Killens (1993); cons., Carol Pitts Hawks (1993).

Education

To further educational efforts in the area of acquisitions librarianship, ranging from library school instruction and practices to all types of continuing education; to encourage and coordinate programs, preconferences, and institutes; to identify the needs and to make recommendations for the content of such educational opportunities; to address issues related to the education and recruitment of acquisitions librarians; to establish liaison, as appropriate, between the committee and other bodies having similar interests.

Ch., Margaret Maes Axtmann (1993); John Corbin (1994); Edna C. Laughrey (1993); Joyce L. Ogburn (1993); John Oldick (1994); Patricia G. Oyler (1994); Karen A. Schmidt (1993); interns: Beth E. Jacoby (1993); Mary Beth Thomson (1993); cons., Barbara C. Dean (1994).

Mid-Atlantic Regional Institute (subcommittee)

To plan a Business of Acquisitions Institute for 1993.

Co-chs., Barbara C. Dean (1993) and Steve H. Murden (1993); Margaret M. Axtmann (1993); Stephen D. Clark (1993); Trisha L. Davis (1993); James T. Deffenbaugh (1993); Julia M. Gelfand (1993); Marilyn G. McSweeney (1993); Joyce L. Ogburn (1993); Eleanor K. Pourron (1993); Julie D. Pringle (1993); Karen A. Schmidt (1993); Sharon G. Sullivan (1993); Barbara A. Winters (1993).

Nominating

Ch., Joseph W. Barker (1993); Eileen D. Hardy (1993); Helen I. Reed (1993).

Policy and Planning

To coordinate the policy and planning activities of the Acquisition of Library Materials Section; to make recommendations regarding AS policy questions at the request of the AS Executive Committee; to consider acquisitions issues as a whole, including long-range section goals and objectives as well as new areas of interest; to review each standing section-level committee concerning its relevance to and success in forwarding the goals and objectives of the section.

Ch., Judith D. Webster (1994); Marsha S. Clark (1994); Caroline L. Early (1993); Barbara Henn (1993); Gail A. Kennedy (1994).

Publications

To coordinate the development and review of publications prior to submission to the AS Executive Committee; to refer proposals and manuscripts approved by the AS Executive Committee to the ALCTS Publications Committee and to expedite their progress through the publication process; to identify appropriate topics for new publications (including titles for the Acquisition Guides Series); to establish subcommittees to develop guides and other publications; to serve as consultant to other AS units that wish to prepare documents for publication.

Ch., Judith F. Niles (1993); Ellen J. Pletsch (1993); Sally W. Somers (1994); Kathryn A. Soupiset (1993); Christopher Sugnet (1994); intern, Stephen A. Marine (1993).

Foreign Book Dealers Directories Series (subcommittee)

To develop and edit new publications or revise existing publications on foreign book dealers, particularly those in the Third World.

Ch., Ellen J. Pletsch (1993); Janice Lynne Altstatt (1993); Thelma C. Diercks (1993); Doina G. Farkas (1993); David L. Marshall (1993); Patricia J. Masson (1993); Helen R. Miller (1993);

Sally W. Somers (1993); liaison, Doina G. Farkas (1993).

Guides (subcommittee)

To develop and edit new publications, or revise existing publications, which are guides for acquisitions librarians or others involved in operations associated with acquisitions departments in all types of libraries.

Ch., Kathryn A. Soupiset (1993); Starla G. Doescher (1993); Marsha Hamilton (1993); William E. Jarvis (1993); Mark Kovacic (1993); Jan C. Maxwell (1993); Lorenzo A. Zeugner Jr. (1993).

Technology for Acquisitions

To identify, study, and evaluate procedures, issues, and trends related to the selection, development, and implementation of acquisitions systems and related technologies by libraries and vendors of library materials; to identify the need for and to play an active role in the development of standards, and to encourage research and the general study of issues in this area; to make a continuing assessment of the state of the art and suggest the direction of change in the automation of acquisition processes.

Ch., Mita Nissley (1993); Doina G. Farkas (1993); William E. Jarvis (1994); Patricia J. Mason (1993); Joseph W. Raker (1993); Pamela Zager Rebarcak (1994); Helen I. Reed (1993); interns: Lynne Brown (1993); Martin L. Warzala (1993).

Discussion Groups

Acquisitions Librarians/Vendors of Library Materials

To stimulate and facilitate the free flow of ideas between and among acquisition librarians and vendors of library materials.

Co-chs., Judy Luther (1993) and Dorothy K. Marcinko (1993).

Acquisitions Administrators

To provide a forum for informal discussion of problems relating to administration of acquisitions departments (this may include but not be limited to issues and techniques, policy implementation, quality-control procedures, personnel and budget management, new developments in the discipline of acquisitions); to provide a reporting session on activity of other conference programs of interest to acquisitions librarians; to establish a network of acquisitions administrators to provide on-the-job direction and support for new acquisitions librarians and continuing education for existing acquisitions librarians.

Ch., Betsy Kruger (1993).

Acquisitions Topics for Public Libraries

To create a forum for discussion of issues relating to the unique aspects of acquisitions in large public libraries.

Ch., Mary Joanne Adetayo (1993).

Gifts and Exchange

To provide a forum for librarians to discuss gifts and exchanges. To consider legal issues, public relations matters, and administrative procedures which arise in the gifts and exchange process.

Ch., LaDonne Roberts (1993); vice-ch., Siew-Phek T. Su (1993).

Representatives

ALCTS Budget and Finance Com.—James R. Mouw (1993).
ALCTS Catalog Form and Function—Carol Cubberley (1994).
ALCTS Conference Program Com. (New Orleans, 1993)—Carol E. Chamberlain 1993).
ALCTS Conference Program Com. (Miami, 1994)—Caroline L. Early (1994).
ALCTS International Relations Com.—Dora Biblarz (1993).
ALCTS Legislation—Stewart Bodner (1993).
ALCTS *LRTS* Editorial Bd.—Karen A. Schmidt (1993).
ALCTS Membership Com.—Laverne C. Jenkins (1994).
ALCTS Nominating Com.—Joseph Barker (1993).
ALCTS Organization and Bylaws Com.—Gail A. Kennedy (1994).
ALCTS Planning Com.—Judith D. Webster (1993).
ALCTS Preservation Microfilming Com.—to be appointed.
ALCTS Publications Com.—Judith F. Niles (1993).
ALCTS Research and Statistics—Karen A. Schmidt (1994).
ALCTS CCS-CC:DA—Beth E. Jacoby (1993).
ALCTS CMDS—Gay Dannelley (1993).
ALCTS RLMS—Mark Knoblauch (1993).
ALCTS SS Acquisitions Com.—Lisa Peterson (1994).

Cataloging and Classification Section (CCS)

To contribute to library service and librarianship through encouragement, promotion of, and responsibility for those activities of the Association for Library Collections and Technical Services, a division of the American Library Association relating to the cataloging and classification of library materials in all types of institutions.

Executive Committee

Ch., Barbara B. Tillett (1993); ch.-elect, Carlen M. Ruschoff (1994); secy., William A. Garrison (1995); past ch., F. Kathleen Bales (1993); Alice J. Allen (1994); Jennifer B. Bowen (1995); David E. Gleim (1993); Judith A. Hudson (1993); Martha M. Yee (1994); ex officio: Joanne S. Anderson (DCEPC, 1996); Charles W. Simpson (*LRTS*, 1993); Karen Muller.

Committees

Cataloging: Asian and African Materials

1. To consider all aspects of problems in the bibliographic organization of materials issued in or dealing with Africa and Asia, with the exception of Asiatic U.S.S.R.
2. To review the use of the various ISBDs for describing materials written in nonalphabetic scripts or nonroman alphabets used in these areas and make recommendations concerning them to the Committee on Cataloging: Description and Access.
3. To review tables for romanization of languages used in these areas that are written in a nonroman script, for use in library catalogs. To transmit the approved tables through the official ALA liaison to the appropriate agency.

4. To consider problems in the bibliographic description of materials issued in these areas, especially those deriving from non-Western publishing traditions, and to make recommendations concerning them to the Committee on Cataloging: Description and Access.

5. To consider problems in establishing the form of heading for names of persons and of corporate bodies in these areas and make recommendations concerning them to the Committee on Cataloging: Description and Access.

6. To consider problems in established classification systems as they relate to these areas and make recommendations for change to the appropriate body for each classification system through the Subject Analysis Committee.

7. To consider problems in subject headings for materials dealing with these areas and make recommendations for change to the bodies responsible for specific lists of subject headings through the Subject Analysis Committee.

8. To communicate their findings to the library profession through committee reports, articles in professional journals, and any other channels that seem feasible or desirable.

Ch., Karl K. Kahler (1994); Ruby A. Bell-Gam (1993); Brenda E. Bickett (1993); Margaret R. D'Ambrosio (1994); Sarada Kotamraju (1994); James T. Maccaferri (1993); Yasuko Makino (1994); David P. Reynolds (1994); Doris J. Seely (1993); intern, Clare B. Dunkle (1994).

Cataloging: Description and Access

To make a continuing assessment of the state of the art and suggest the direction of change in the field of descriptive cataloging; to recommend solutions to problems relating not only to bibliographic description but also to choice and form of access points, other than subject access; to initiate proposals for additions to and revisions of the cataloging code currently adopted by ALA and to review proposals initiated by other groups or individuals; to develop official ALA positions on such proposals in consultation with other appropriate ALA units and organizations in the U.S.A.; to instruct the ALA Representative to the Joint Steering Committee for Revision of AACR (or successor organization) regarding the official ALA position and to suggest acceptable bases for negotiations; to develop official ALA positions on proposed international cataloging policies and standards pertaining to the committee's area of responsibility and to advise the official ALA representative; or, if there is *no official ALA representative*, to act as the clearinghouse within ALA for review of these policies and standards and to serve as the formal liaison between ALA and the originating organizations; to encourage the U.S. library and information services community to express opinions on issues under consideration through timely publication of agenda items in the community's press; to keep the profession informed by reporting committee actions promptly through appropriate communication channels.

Ch., Brian E. Schottlaender (1993); Nancy A. Davey (1993); John K. Duke (1993); Laurel Jizba (1993); Bruce Chr. Johnson (1994); Lee W. Leighton (1994); Ingrid Mifflin (1993); Frank E. Sadowski Jr. (1994); Mark R. Watson (1994); interns: Ann M. Fiegen (1993); Tamara S. Weintraub Frouin (1993).

Ex Officio Representatives

ALCTS—Karen Muller.
JSC—Janet Swan Hill.

L. of Congress—Sarah E. Thomas.
OCLC, Inc.—Glenn E. Patton.
Research Libraries Group, Inc.—Ed Glazier.

Non-Voting Liaisons from ALA Units

ACRL—to be appointed.
ALCTS-AV—Joan Swanekamp.
ALCTS-TSMC—Cliff Glaviano.
AS—Beth E. Jacoby.
CMDS—Matthew W. Wise.
CCS:AAM—Karl K. Kahler.
CCS:CCM—Dorothy M. Shields.
GODORT—Rhonda J. Marker.
IRRT—Elizabeth Widenmann.
LITA—Judith Hopkins.
MAGERT—Elizabeth U. Mangan.
MARBI—D. Sherman Clarke.
NMRT —Kathryn L. Sorury.
PLA—Judith H. Rossoff.
PLMS—Wilma I. Cromwell.
RASD—Noelle Van Pulis.
RLMS—Cecilia S. Sercan.
SS—Jean P. Altschuler.
SRRT—Sherry L. Kelley.

Non-ALA Liaisons

AALL—Regina T. Wallen.
AJL—Rita Lifton.
ARLIS/NA–Karen L. Meizner.
ARSC—Daniel Kinney.
ATLA—to be appointed.
CLA—Tina-Karen Forman.
IASSIST—Patricia S. Vanderberg.
Medical LA—Steven J. Squires.
Music LA—Philip Schreur.
SAA—to be appointed.
SLA—Dorothy McGarry.

Preconference on Bibliographic Control of Conference Proceedings, ALCTS CCS CC:DA/ACRL STS (joint subcommittee)

Co-chs., Olivia M. A. Madison (ALCTS, 1993) and Sara Shatford Layne (ACRL, 1993); Nirmala Bangalore (ACRL, 1993); Daniel W. Kinney (ALCTS, 1993); Joan Lussky (ACRL, 1993); David W. Mill (ALCTS, 1993); Colby Mariva Riggs (ALCTS, 1993); Rebecca S. Uhl (ACRL, 1993).

Cataloging of Children's Materials

To study the problems of and recommend action on all aspects of the cataloging of library materials for children.

Ch., Sharon R. Zuiderveld (1993); Marilyn Bethel (1993); Sharon Butera (1994); Sylvia C. Cornell (1994); Betty T. Furrie (1994); Susan Israilevich (1994); Catherine Murphy (1994); liaisons: Ann M. Case (Sears, 1993); Frances E. Corcoran (AASL, 1993); Jane E. Marton (LC, ALSC, 1993); Gregory R. New (LC, 1993); interns: Jeri Anne Townley (1993); Jianrong Wang (1993); cons.: Joycelyn Fobes Brand (1993); Michael J. Puma (1993); Karen H. Schambow (1993).

Conference Program—New Orleans, 1993

Ch., Barbara B. Tillett (1993); Alice J. Allen (1993); Judith A. Hudson (1993).

Education, Training, and Recruitment for Cataloging

To study and review the educational needs for cataloging and classification; to identify and propose methods and materials for recruitment to careers in cataloging; to explore and foster the development of curricula and continuing education programs; to act as a catalyst in promoting communication between catalogers and library educators; and to coordinate such work with the ALCTS Education Committee.

Ch., Arno A. Kastner (1993); Rick J. Block (1994); Allen Cohen (1994); David Fiste (1993); Francis Miksa (1994); Susanne Nevin (1994); Mary Dabney Wilson (1994); interns: Timothy V. Carstens (1993); Ling-Hwey Jeng (1993).

Margaret Mann Citation

To select the recipient of the Margaret Mann Citation for outstanding professional achievement in cataloging or classification either through publication of significant professional literature, participation in professional cataloging associations, or valuable contributions to practice in individual libraries.

Ch., Verna P. Urbanski (1993); Judith G. Fenly (1993); Dorothy McGarry (1993).

Nominating

Ch., Richard P. Smiraglia (1993); Michael Carpenter (1993); Ellen Siegel Kovacic (1993); Olivia M. A. Madison (1993); Marilyn H. McClaskey (1993).

Policy and Research

To be aware of the current status of research in cataloging and classification and to identify areas where research is needed. To encourage librarians to propose topics and problems in bibliographic control for discussion, research, and action. To consider and recommend to the CCS Executive Committee policies relevant to the Cataloging and Classification Section. To coordinate the work of the Policy and Research Committee with planning for ALCTS as a whole through participation of the committee chair in the work of the ALCTS Planning and Research Committee.

To maintain contact with and give assistance to the cataloging and classification editors of *Library Resources & Technical Services* and to the *ALCTS Newsletter*. To maintain a sustained channel of communication with the Library of Congress in matters relating to cataloging and classification.

Ch., Charles W. Simpson (1993); Judith Hopkins (1994); Karen M. Hsu (1994); Holley R. Lange (1994); Dallas R. Shawkey (1993); Philip M. Smith (1994); D. Kathryn Weintraub (1993); Cynthia Marie Whitacre (1994); interns: Gunnar S. Knutson (1993); Melinda Ann Reagor (1993); LC liaison, Sarah E. Thomas (1993).

Subject Analysis

To study problems and recommend improvements in patterns, methods, and tools for the subject analysis and organization of library materials, including particularly classification and subject headings systems, and to provide liaison for those areas of interest between CCS and other ALA and non-ALA organizations that have an interest in and concern for these activities.

Ch., Arlene G. Taylor (1993); Heeja H. Chung (1993); Martha O'Hara Conway (1994); Martin M. Kurth (1993); Mary C. Lasater (1994); Peter W. Lisbon (1993); Suzanne K. Lorimer (1993); Anita Schuneman (1994); Alva T. Stone (1993); interns: Gail P. Hueting (1993); Dee Shneiderman (1993); liaisons: Julianne Beall (LC, 1993); Ann M. Case (Sears, 1993).

DDC Life Sciences Schedule, Review (subcommittee)

Ch., Arnold Wajenberg (1993); members to be appointed.

DDC Public Administration Schedule, Review (subcommittee)

Ch., Martin M. Kurth (1993); Michele Behr (1993); Heeja H. Chung (1993); Jan DeSirey (1993); Mary Dabney Wilson (1993).

Guidelines on Subject Access to Individual Works of Fiction, Revision (subcommittee)

Ch., Patricia Thomas (1993); Jan DeSirey (1993); Linda Gabel (1993); Susan Hayes (1993); Sherry L. Kelley (1993); Mary Dabney Wilson (1993); Martha Yee (1993).

NISO Thesaurus Standard, Review (subcommittee)

To prepare comments on the NISO draft standard for monolingual thesauri which reflect the perspective of a broad range of members of the American library community, many of whom may not appreciate the potential importance of this work in librarianship.

Ch., Martin M. Kurth (1993); Barbara L. Berman (1993); Toni Petersen (1993); Paul G. Weiss (1993).

Program Planning, 1993 (subcommittee)

Ch. and members to be appointed.

Discussion Groups

Authority Control in the Online Environment, LITA/ALCTS CCS (See p. 72.)

Catalog Management

To discuss the various issues involved with cataloging, classification, and authority control after the initial cataloging has been performed. The group will provide a forum for exchanging information and discussing techniques, new developments, and problems in managing the bibliographic integrity of library catalogs.

Ch., Sheila V. Fehlman (1993); vice-ch., Robert J. Chipok (1993).

Cataloging and Classification Research

Ch., David E. Gleim (1993); vice-ch., Marilyn H. McClaskey (1993).

Cataloging Norms

To explore the possibility and usefulness of developing basic production norms for original cataloging and its component aspects. Two subtopics related to that purpose are: (1) basic terminology and (2) common statistical data.

Ch., Ann B. Vidor (1993).

Copy Cataloging

The purpose of the discussion group will be to meet at the Midwinter and Annual Conferences to discuss informally common problems concerning copy cataloging. Included will be discussions on quality control of copy cataloging, authority control, organization of copy cataloging units, work flows in copy cataloging, copy cataloging of all kinds of materials (monographs, serials, audiovisuals, etc.), staffing needs in copy cataloging, training of copy cataloging, effects of changes in cataloging rules on copy cataloging.

Ch., Sherry L. Kelley (1993); vice-ch., Cecilia S. Sercan (1993).

Heads of Cataloging Departments

To discuss policy, implementation, quality control of bibliographic and authority records, work flow, personnel including supervision, motivation and other issues of concern to the members of the group. The group will provide a forum for discussing techniques and exchanging information.

Ch., Sandra S. Herzinger (1993); vice-ch., Edward H. Baldridge (1993).

Map Cataloging, ALCTS CCS/MAGERT (interunit)

To discuss the basic issues relating to bibliographic control of maps and related materials. To discuss rules and standards covering such cataloging, as well as application of the rules and principles both in general and in response to specific problems, and various practicing options. The group will provide a forum for discussing matters of interest to beginners and experts alike. Because maps catalogers often have oversight responsibilities for a collection, discussions of administration of map cataloging, setting policy for map cataloging, etc., are also appropriate.

Ch., Michael Carpenter (1993); vice-ch., Karl Eric Longstreth (1993).

Representatives

ALA Library Education Assembly—Arno Kastner (1993).
ALCTS Budget and Finance Com.—Charles R. Fenly (1994).
ALCTS Catalog Form and Function Com.—Barbara J. Anderson (1994).
ALCTS Conference Prog. Com. (New Orleans, 1993)—Barbara B. Tillett.
ALCTS Conference Prog. Com. (Miami, 1994)—Carlen M. Ruschoff (1994).
ALCTS Education Com.—Arno Kastner (1993).
ALCTS International Relations Com.—Frederick C. Lynden (1993).
ALCTS Legislation Com.—Deborah Fetch (1993).
ALCTS *LRTS* Editorial Bd.—Charles Simpson (1993).
ALCTS Membership Committee—Robert McDonald (1993).
ALCTS Nominating Committee—Richard Smiraglia (1993).
ALCTS Organization and Bylaws Com.—V. Louise Saylor (1993).
ALCTS Planning Com.—Janet G. Padway.
ALCTS Preservation Microfilming Com.—Helen F. Schmierer (1993).
ALCTS Publications Com.—Mary Faith Pankin (1993).
ALCTS Research and Statistics Com.—Nancy J. Williamson (1993).
Assn. for Library and Information Science Education—to be appointed.
Decimal Classification Editorial Policy Com.—Joint Lake Placid Edu. Found./ALA—Patricia M. Thomas (1995); appointed by Lake Placid Edu. Found. from nominations by

ALCTS/CCS—Joanne S. Anderson (1996); Elaine Svenonius (1998); Helena M. VanDeroef (1997).
PLA Cataloging Needs of Public Libraries Com.—Derry C. Juneja (1993).
RASD Catalog Use Study Com.—Orthella Moman (1993).

Collection Management and Development Section (CMDS)

To contribute to library service and librarianship through encouragement, promotion of, and responsibility for those activities of ALCTS relating to collection management and development, selection, and evaluation of library materials in all types of institutions.

Executive Committee

Ch., David Farrell (1993); ch.-elect, Connie K. McCarthy (1993); secy., Kathryn Hammell Carpenter (1995); Dora Biblarz (1994); Bonita I. Bryant (1993); Gay N. Dannelly (1995); Samuel G. Demas (1995); Eugene L. Wiemers (1994); ex officio: Karen Muller; Edward Shreeves (P & P ch., 1993).

Committees

Administration of Collection Development

To address through continuing education programs, publications, and other means issues related to the administration of collection management and development, including but not limited to budgeting and fund allocation, organization and staffing, collection development policies, resource-sharing, preservation, and library development and fund-raising; to examine in greater detail matters raised in the CMDS discussion groups. To act as section liaison with other groups dealing with similar interests.

Ch., Bonita I. Bryant (1993); Barbara Allen (1994); Eileen D. Hardy (1994); Margaret Rogers Hunt (1994); Robert W. Kenselaar (1993); Bonnie MacEwan (1993); Mary Ellen Quinn (1994); Mark S. Sandler (1993); William J. Sittig (1994); liaison, Martha J. Hanson (1994); interns: Stephen Atkins (1993); John Oldick (1993).

Guide for Cooperative Collection Development (subcommittee)

Ch., Bart M. Harloe (1993); Romaine Ahlstrom (1993); Patricia L. Bril (1993); Steven L. Brown (1993); Cynthia Dobson (1993); Susan L. Fales (1993); Suzanne Fedunok (1993); Arlene M. Feiner (1993); Rhonna A. Goodman (1993); Patricia J. Masson (1993); Ellen J. Pletsch (1993); cons.: Bonita I. Bryant (1993); Sue O. Medina (1993).

Collection Development and Electronic Media

To address issues related to collection management and development of electronic media, their funding, and selection policies; to consider the adjustments an electronic environment requires of collection developers; to act as section liaison with other groups dealing with similar interests.

Ch., Peggy Johnson (1993); Michael E. Fineman (1994); Albert H. Joy (1993); Barbara Kornstein (1994); Patricia A. Promis (1993); Bill Robnett (1993); Kathy E. Tezla (1994); interns: Ewa E. Barczyk (1993); Bonnie J. Cox (1993).

Collection Development Practice in a Changing Environment

From the individual collection developer's perspective, to address through continuing education programs, publications, and other means issues related to the development and management of the collections in a changing environment, including but not limited to traditional and emerging techniques for selection, collection evaluation, weeding, serials review and cancellation, constituency liaison, nonprint media in collection development, and the intersection of collection development and management with preservation; to act as section liaison with other groups dealing with similar interests. May examine in greater detail matters raised in the CMDS discussion groups.

Ch., Merle L. Jacob (1993); Julie S. Alexander (1993); Edward H. Baldridge (1994); Michaelyn Burnette (1994); Maribeth Krupczak (1994); Janet W. Majilton (1993); Ellen J. Pletsch (1993); Cynthia Shelton (1994); Jane Treadwell (1994); interns: Kurt F. De Belder (1993); Julia M. Gelfand (1993); cons., Jasper G. Schad (1993).

Continuing Education

To coordinate educational program planning, both for stand-alone events (institutes, workshops) and for events associated with the annual conference (programs, pre-conferences) that will promote and enhance knowledge of collection management and development among librarians; to identify needed continuing education events or series of events and initiate their development or encourage other section committees to do so; to seek initial approval on all section program concepts from the Executive Committee, help planners as necessary to develop satisfactory program proposals, and present such proposals as it approves to the appropriate ALCTS bodies for final consideration and approval; as an informed authority on scheduling and planning processes for ALA conferences and for ALCTS-sponsored and other types of institutes, to advise on these matters to committees planning continuing education events, such advice to include orientation sessions on the ALCTS budget cycle for institute planners; to keep the Executive Committee informed about program development; to act as section liaison with other groups sponsoring continuing education programs related to collection development. Has oversight responsibility for the content and quality of continuing education events offered by the section.

Ch., Anthony W. Ferguson (1993); Jean A. Coberly (1993); James T. Deffenbaugh (1994); Gayle Garlock (1993); John M. Kelly (1994); Christopher Sugnet (1993); Marion Taylor (1994); Eugene L. Wiemers (1993); Phyllis Young (1994); cons., Jeanne G. Sohn (1993).

Advanced CMDI (subcommittee)

Ch., Gay N. Dannelly (1993); David Farrell (1993); Linda J. Gould (1993); Bonnie Mac-Ewan (1993); Jutta Reed-Scott (1993); Daniel T. Richards (1993); Barbara VanDeventer (1993); Eugene L. Wiemers (1993).

Canadian CMDI (subcommittee)

Co-chs., Gayle Garlock (1993) and Holly F. Melanson (1993); Jeanette Bourgoin (1993); Bonnie MacEwan (1993); Victor Nunn (1993); liaison, Terri M. Tomchyshyn (1993).

Preservation Issues in Collection Management Institute (subcommittee)

Ch., Sophia K. Jordan (1993); Samuel G. Demas (1993); Wanda V. Dole (1993); Martha J. Hanson (1993); Dorothy W. Wright (1993); staff liaison, Karen Muller.

Education for Collection Development

To promote appropriate, adequate, and innovative recruitment to and education for collection management and development in library schools. To work with collection development practitioners, libraries, library schools, and the Association for Library and Information Science Education to encourage mutual understanding of goals for education in collection development and management.

Ch., Patricia L. Bril (1993); John M. Budd (1994); Joan Grant (1994); Rose Mary Magrill (1993); Thomas E. Nisonger (1994); Cynthia L. Shamel (1994); Karin Wittenborg (1994); intern, Joseph C. Andrews (1993).

Nominating

Ch., Louis A. Pitschmann (1993); Joanne S. Anderson (1993); Eric J. Carpenter (1993).

Policy and Planning

To serve as a focal point or clearinghouse for activities and ideas relating to collection management in ALA and other organizations, the library profession at large, the scholarly world, and other communities; to draft or revise for Executive Committee approval an annual list of long-term section goals and maintain an ongoing list of trends and issues which are recommended to the Executive Committee as a focus for more immediate section activities; to review existing committees and discussion groups on a continuing basis, making sure that section activities are responsive to changing conditions and reflect the interests of a variety of library types, recommending changes in section structure as necessary; to coordinate the work of the Policy and Planning Committee with planning for ALCTS as a whole through the participation of the committee chair on the ALCTS Planning Committee.

Ch., Edward Shreeves (1993); Peter B. Allison (1993); Dora Biblarz (1994); Bart M. Harloe (1994); Patricia A. McClung (1993); Genevieve S. Owens (1993); Craig A. Wilson (1994).

Publications and Publicity

To initiate and refer to the appropriate CMDS committees suggestions for new or revised publications or, in the absence of an appropriate committee, develop the publication through a subcommittee of the Publications Committee; to review, advise on, and approve publication proposals and draft manuscripts produced as a result of section committee activity; to refer approved proposals and manuscripts to the ALCTS Publications Committee and monitor their progress through the publication process; to provide the section vice-chair with annual budget estimates for any publications to be issued by the section. Chair of this committee serves on the ALCTS Publications Committee.

Ch., Anna H. Perrault (1993); Joanne S. Anderson (1993); Suzanne H. Freeman (1993); Joan G. Hubbard (1994); William E. Jarvis (1994); Cecily A. Johns (1994); Dennis K. Lambert (1994).

Quantitiative Measures For Collection Management

To investigate and encourage the use of appropriate statistical techniques, based on information available from integrated library systems and elsewhere, to assist in the management of information resources. To explore, develop, and promote the use of quantitative measures in the analysis of library collections both in the local setting and on the national and international level. To coordinate the activities of the section on these topics, and to provide liaison with the relevant activities of other groups. To oversee, though a subcommittee or other appropriate structure, the North American Title Count, or its equivalent.

Ch., Lynn F. Sipe (1993); Robert L. Evensen (1994); Linda J. Gould (1994); Nancy E. Gwinn (1994); J. Dennis Hyde (1994); Holly F. Melanson (1994); Louis A. Pitschmann (1994); Florence J. Wilson (1994).

North American Title Count (subcommittee)

To coordinate and direct the development and production of statistics on collections growth, by subject classification, for participating libraries at agreed upon intervals, under the general direction of the Quantitative Measures for Collection Management Committee, and based upon the articulated needs of the membership of the Chief Collection Development Officers of Large Research Libraries Discussion Group and the Collection Development Librarians of Academic Libraries Discussion Group.

Ch., Dawn Bick (1993); Caroline L. Early (1993); Suzanne Fedunok (1993); Gayle N. Garlock (1993); Linda J. Gould (1993); Nancy E. Gwinn (1993); Cheryl A. Kern-Simirenko (1993); Robert W. Marek (1993); Gerald L. Newman (1993); Louis A. Pitschmann (1993); William J. Sittig (1993); John R. Yelverton (1993); rep., Chris Horak (1993).

Discussion Groups

Chief Collection Development Officers of Large Research Libraries

To discuss the various collection development and collection management issues of concern to large research libraries. To provide a forum for the exchange of information on new developments, techniques, and problems in managing the development of library collections.

Ch., Karin Wittenborg (1993); vice-ch., Dora Biblarz (1993).

Collection Development Librarians of Academic Libraries

To provide a forum for discussion of issues in collection development and collection management by academic and research libraries. The forum will act as an information network through discussions at the Midwinter and Annual Conferences of ALA.

Ch., Cheryl A. Kern-Simirenko (1993); vice-ch., Patricia Bril (1993).

Collection Management/Selection for Public Libraries

To provide a discussion forum for librarians and others whose interests include selection, collection development, and collection management in public libraries of all sizes.

Ch., Julie D. Pringle (1993); vice-ch., Nancy Thomas Musser (1993).

Representatives

ALCTS Budget and Finance Com.—Ann Thompson (1994).
ALCTS Catalog Form and Function—Patricia O. Walker (1994).
ALCTS Conference Program Com. (New Orleans, 1993)—Kathy E. Tezla (1993).
ALCTS Conference Program Com. (Miami, 1994)—Connie McCarthy (1994).
ALCTS International Relations Com.—Cecily Johns (1994).
ALCTS Legislation Com.—Barbara Van Deventer (1994).
ALCTS *LRTS* Editorial Bd.—Michael T. Ryan (1993).
ALCTS Membership Com.—Gordon S. Rowley (1994).
ALCTS Nominating Com.—Louis A. Pitschmann (1993).
ALCTS Organization and Bylaws Com.—Patricia A. McClung (1994).
ALCTS Planning Com.—Edward Shreeves (1993).
ALCTS Preservation Microfilming Com.—Mary H. Brennan-Kerr (1994).
ALCTS Publications Com.—Anna H. Perrault (1993).
ALCTS Research and Statistics Com.—Lynn F. Sipe (1994).
ALCTS CCS-CC:DA—Matthew W. Wise (1993).

Preservation of Library Materials Section (PLMS)

To advance the field of library preservation by exercising leadership in the establishment of sound preservation practices; advising and assisting the library profession in developing solutions to preservation problems; overseeing the implementation of the ALA Preservation Policy, serving as a source of information about preservation programs and initiatives throughout the Association, and coordinating preservation concerns among its various units; initiating cooperation among concerned individuals, institutions, industries, and organizations; promoting research in both administrative and technical aspects of the field; fostering the development of standards and specifications for materials, equipment, and techniques; promoting the education of practitioners, the library community, and the public at large; encouraging the establishment of local preservation programs; stimulating publication and dissemination of information; and advocating needs to government and funding agencies.

Executive Committee

Ch., Lorraine H. Olley (1993); ch.-elect, Janet E. Gertz (1993); secy., Marcella Grendler (1995); past ch., Lisa L. Fox (1993); member-at-large, Barbara A. Lilley (1994).

Committees

Conference Program

Ch., Lorraine H. Olley (1993); Janet E. Gertz (1993); ex officio, Karen Muller.

Education

To disseminate to the membership information on education opportunities in the preserva-

tion field through periodic updates of the *Preservation Education Directory*; to plan annual programs and other education activities for the section.

Ch., Martha J. Hanson (1994); Sharlane T. Grant (1994); Marcella Grendler (1993); Sophia K. Jordan (1994); Stephen A. Marine (1994); Regina A. Sinclair (1993); Katherine L. Walter (1993); interns: Lee Dirks (1993); Julie Allen Page (1993).

Management Strategies for Disaster Preparedness (subcommittee)

To plan a regional institute on disaster preparedness for 1993 or 1994.

Co-chs., Sheryl J. Davis (1994) and Linda B. Gunter (1994).

Preservation and Technical Services Program Planning (subcommittee)

To plan a series of programs on preservation and acquisitions, cataloging, collection management/development, and serials for 1994–95.

Ch., Stephen A. Marine (1993); Thomas F. R. Clareson (1993); Sophia K. Jordan (1993).

Preservation Education Needs (task force)

To explore preservation education opportunities and developments outside of ALA; to communicate with professional, institutional, and regional groups that provide or sponsor such activities; to consider the implications of the current educational scene for the development of preservation; and to identify gaps and deficiencies in preservation education.

Ch. Roxanna Herrick (1993); Lisa Biblo (1993); Sherry Byrne (1993); John Dean (1993); Martha J. Hanson (1993); Patricia E. Palmer (1993); Susan G. Swartzburg (1993); cons., Sally Buchanan (1993).

Preservation of Magnetic Media Institute (subcommittee)

To plan an institute on preservation of magnetic media.

Ch., Debra McKern (1993); Sheryl J. Davis (1993); Jan Merrill-Oldham (1993); Chris Paton (1993); Mark S. Roosa (1993); Patricia A. Smith (1993).

Public Libraries Program Planning (task force)

Ch., James W. Mason (1993); Romaine Ahlstrom (1993); Margaret S. Child (1993); Christopher D. G. Coleman (1993); Robert L. DeCandido (1993); Anne L. Reynolds (1993); Maxine K. Sitts (1993).

Library Binding Regional Institutes (ad hoc)

Co-chs., Sally Grauer (1994) and James W. Mason (1994); Thomas F. R. Clareson (1994); Carol E. Eyler (1993); Ivan E. Hanthorn (1994); Myra Jo Moon (1994); Connie J. Osborne (1994); Diane N. Paldan (1994); Katherine L. Walter (1994).

Nominating

Ch. Sherry Byrne (1993); Margaret S. Child (1993); Richard Frieder (1993).

Physical Quality and Treatment of Library Materials

To promote and support understanding, development, and use of appropriate methods and materials to preserve library collections in all formats by: (1) identifying issues; (2) appointing task forces to review draft standards, write guidelines, communicate with vendors, etc.; (3) fostering information exchange between librarians and vendors and/or developers of preservation supplies and services; (4) encouraging development and use of materials and manufacturing techniques that contribute to collection longevity.

Methods for preserving collections include, but are not limited to: proper storage environments and handling techniques; remedial and protective treatments such as conservation, protective housing, library binding, mass deacidification; and reformatting information onto stable media.

Ch., Wesley L. Boomgaarden (1993); Carol E. Eyler (1994); Ivan E. Hanthorn (1994); Joan ten Hoor (1993); Marcia A. Watt (1994); interns: Roxanna Herrick (1993); Susan Lunas (1993); Julie Smiley (1993); cons., Paul A. Parisi (1993).

Policy and Planning

To draft annual and long-range goals for the section and coordinate the planning activities of all section committees. To identify and recommend to the Executive Committee new activities to be undertaken by the section; to conduct periodic reviews of section effectiveness and recommend to the Executive Committee proposals for standards or research; to coordinate section planning with that of ALCTS through participation by the chairperson in the work of the ALCTS Planning and Research Committee.

Ch., Robert L. DeCandido (1993); John P. Baker (1993); Jennifer S. Banks (1994); Mary E. Cunningham-Kruppa (1994); Carolyn L. Harris (1993); interns: Evelyn Frangakis (1993); Robert B. Harriman Jr. (1993).

Preservation Management

To address issues related to the management of local and cooperative library preservation programs and to initiate action to aid libraries in their management. These include but are not limited to program funding, organization, policies, and procedures; budget, work flow, and personnel management; training of preservation staff; management information systems; bibliographic control issues as they pertain to preservation activities and selection of materials for preservation. To disseminate information about these issues to librarians. To monitor activities and emerging issues in collection management and development as they relate to preservation.

Ch., Richard Frieder (1993); Gerald J. Munoff (1993); Barclay W. Ogden (1994); Pamela I. Ploeger (1994); Duane A. Watson (1993); interns: Jeanne M. Drewes (1993); Don K. Thompson (1993).

Preservation of Scientific and Technological Research Records (subcommittee)

To build support and seek funding for preservation of the records of scientific and technological research.

Ch., Jennifer S. Banks (1993); Margaret S. Child (1993); Carolyn Morrow (1993); Karen Motylewski (1993).

Project Management Program (task force)

Co-chs., Cynthia D. Clark (1993) and Richard M. Peek (1993); John F. Dean (1993); Lee Dirks (1993); Carla J. Montori (1993).

Publications

To review, provide advice on, and approve proposals for publications and draft manuscripts which are produced as a result of the work of PLMS committees. To refer approved proposals and manuscripts to the ALCTS Publications Committee and monitor their progress through the publication process. To identify and refer to the appropriate PLMS committee suggestions for new or revised publications. To provide the section vice-chair with annual budget estimates for PLMS publications.

Ch., Paula A. DeStefano (1994); Thomas F. R. Clareson (1993); Karen Motylewski (1993); interns: Agnes B. Quigg (1993); James K. Wellvang (1993).

Discussion Groups

Cooperative Preservation Programs

To provide a forum for discussing issues related to planning, implementation, management, and evaluation of cooperative preservation programs, especially those at the state, regional, and national level.

Ch., Thomas F. R. Clareson (1993); secy., Katherine L. Walter (1993).

Library Binding

To provide a discussion and information forum between librarians and the commercial binding industry.

Ch., Carol E. Eyler (1993).

Library-Vendor Relations

To provide a forum for the exchange of information between librarians and binders and other suppliers; to work toward the solution of problems of mutual interest and concern.

Co-chs., Christine Allen (1993) and Karen Motylewski (1993).

Physical Quality and Treatment of Library Materials

To provide a forum for discussion of issues and new developments in such areas as preservation supplies and equipment, conservation treatments, environmental controls, and paper quality.

Ch., Gary Frost (1993); secy., Lisa Biblo (1993).

PLMS-RLMS

Co-chs., Carla J. Montori (1993) and Marcia A. Watt (1993).

Preservation Administrators

To provide a discussion forum specifically for preservation administrators, emphasizing issues of management, growth, personnel, and interdepartmental interactions.

Ch., Carla J. Montori (1993); vice-ch., Catherine A. Larson (1993); secy., Sara R. Williams (1993).

Preservation Course and Workshop

To discuss and share information on formal preservation instruction.

Ch., Margaret M. Byrnes (1993).

Preservation Education and Outreach

To provide a forum at the Annual Conference for the discussion of preservation education techniques for library staff and users and outreach efforts directed toward donors, the general public, policy and decision makers, or other groups. To share materials, strategies, and expertise in conducting preservation education and outreach efforts and to foster the development of new activities.

Ch., Julie Allen Page (1993).

Preservation of Library Materials

To discuss informally common problems concerning the preservation of library materials, including shelf-processing, storage environments and handling, binding, repair, restoration and other physical preservation techniques; and the preservation of information through reproduction and/or replacement of such materials.

Ch., Martha J. Hanson (1993).

Representatives

ALA Library Education Assembly—Martha J. Hanson (1993).
ALCTS Budget and Finance Com.—Lisa L. Fox (1994).
ALCTS Catalog Form and Function Com.—Toby Heidtman (1994).
ALCTS Conference Program Com. (New Orleans, 1993)—Lorraine H. Olley (1993).
ALCTS Conference Program Com. (Miami 1994)—Janet Gertz (1994).
ALCTS International Relations Com.—Mark S. Roosa (1994).
ALCTS Legislation Com.—Annette Morris (1993).
ALCTS *LRTS* Editorial 'Bd.—Carla Montori (1993).
ALCTS Membership Com.—James Mason (1994).
ALCTS Nominating Com.—Sherry Byrne (1993).
ALCTS Organization and Bylaws Com.—Jennifer S. Banks (1994).
ALCTS Planning Com.—Robert L. DeCandido (1993).
ALCTS Preservation Microfilming Com.—Margaret Byrnes (1993).
ALCTS Publications Com.—Paula DeStefano (1993).
ALCTS Research and Statistics—Evelyn Frangakis (1993).
ALCTS CCS CC:DA—Wilma I. Cromwell (1994).
ALCTS CMDS—Martha J. Hanson (1993).
ALCTS RLMS—Susan F. Blaine (1993).

Reproduction of Library Materials Section (RLMS)

To support individuals and organizations as they create, distribute, and use reproductions of library materials; to promote the standardization of techniques, methods, and products related to reproductions; to encourage study and research in areas related to this field; and to disseminate information and share knowledge about the management of reprographic facilities in libraries.

Executive Committee

Ch., Jutta Reed-Scott (1993); ch.-elect, Nancy E. Elkington (1993); secy., Phelix B. Hanible (1994); past ch., Debra McKern (1993); Robert B. Harriman Jr. (1994); Norma K. Hendrickson (1995); Jill A. Parchuck (1994); sect.-reps.: Myron B. Chace (1993); Sara J. Eichhorn (1993); Norman J. Shaffer (1993); ex officio: Jack E. Pontius (1993); Karen Muller.

Committees

Bibliographic Control of Microforms

To study and disseminate information about the bibliographic control of microforms; to coordinate the work of the committee with appropriate committees in other sections of ALCTS and with other appropriate agencies; to present bibliographic control issues to micropublishers and to monitor bibliographic control products and services provided by micropublishers and other agencies.

Ch., Robert B. Harriman Jr. (1993); Margaret A. Bellinger (1993); Janet A. Chin (1993); Crystal Graham (1994); Phelix B. Hanible (1993); Katha D. Massey (1993); Carol D. Unger (1993); Marcia A. Watt (1994); intern, Laurie Abbott (1993); cons., Norma K. Hendrickson (1993).

Conference Program, 1993

Ch., Jutta Reed-Scott (1993); Nancy E. Elkington (1993); ex officio: Karen Muller.

Copying

To study and disseminate information about the selection, administration, and use of reprographic methodologies and equipment in libraries, primarily the reproduction of copies of library materials (excluding audiovisual materials) by or for library users.

Ch., Sara R. Williams (1993); Jeffrey R. Hammond (1994); Craig W. Jensen (1993); Hari S. Rorlich (1994); Lorre B. Smith (1994).

Micrographic Equipment (subcommittee)

Ch., Karen Mokrzycki (1993); Jack E. Pontius (1993); Hari S. Rorlich (1993); Lorre B. Smith (1993); Susan Marie Szasz (1993).

Preservation Photocopying Guidelines (subcommittee)

Ch., Ann G. Swartzell (1993); Debi Core (1993); Fritz C. James (1993); Craig W. Jensen (1993); Karen E. Reilly (1993); Barbara R. Sagraves (1993).

Education

To serve as the programmatic arm of the section in the following ways: to study, review, and disseminate information on current education and training efforts that relate to the reproduction of library materials; to develop and update a document in which topics and issues suitable for developing into ALA/ALCTS programs, institutes, and preconferences are identified, and to perform all planning and implementation necessary (via special task forces and subcommittees) to ensure that such events occur in a timely fashion; to establish liaisons as needed with other committees, sections, or groups within ALCTS and ALA, including the Council of Regional Groups, that could be called upon as logical cosponsors of programmatic events; to develop and coordinate publications covering the field of concern to the membership of RLMS.

Ch., Suzanne C. Dodson (1993); Sara J. Eichhorn (1994); Catherine A. Larson (1994); Errol S. Somay (1993); Susan Cook Summer (1993).

Electronic Imaging Technologies

To facilitate the development of and assist in the implementation of electronic imaging technologies for the reproduction of library materials.

Ch., Patricia A. McClung (1993); Nancy Birk (1993); Lydia Suzanne Kellerman (1994); Mark S. Roosa (1994); Susan Marie Szasz (1993); Gary L. Wesley (1993); Dorothy W. Wright (1994); intern, William B. Keller (1993); cons., Judith M. Brugger (1994).

Micropublishing

To serve as a review and advisory committee on all matters relating to microforms and their use in libraries. To advise the Publisher/Vendor-Library Relations Committee on major problems relating to micropublisher-library relations. To evaluate and monitor the quality of micropublications and microform projects. To serve as a forum for discussion between librarians and micropublishers. To coordinate with other committees and sections matters of mutual concern and interest.

Ch., Virginia Steel (1993); Luella S. Allen (1994); M. Dina Giambi (1994); Charles R. Hixson III (1994); Louis A. Pitschmann (1994). 2 members to be appointed.

Nominating

Ch., Shirley W. Leung (1993); Martin Joachim (1993); Erich J. Kesse (1993).

Policy and Planning

To coordinate long-range planning for the section; to conduct periodic reviews of section activities and effectiveness; and to recommend appropriate changes. To identify and recommend to the Executive Committee new activities to be undertaken by the section. To coordinate the work of the section with planning for ALCTS as a whole through membership of the committee chairperson on the ALCTS Planning and Research Committee.

Ch., Jack E. Pontius (1993); Margaret M. Byrnes (1993); Suzanne C. Dodson (1993); Carla J. Montori (1993); Tom W. Sloan (1994).

Contract Negotiations for Commercial Reproductions of Library & Archival Materials (subcommittee)

Ch., Kenneth E. Carpenter (1993); Margaret A. Bellinger (1993); Phelix B. Hanible (1993); August A. Imholtz Jr. (1993); Barbara A. Lilley (1993); William E. Savage (1993); William Z. Schenck (1993); Judith Terrill-Breuer (1993); liaison, Cynthia G. Fox (1993).

Standards

To collect and review information from the library community regarding technical and service standards, as well as guidelines, recommended practices, and technical reports which relate to the reproduction of library materials; to review appropriate existing standards; to encourage and support the development of new standards; and to disseminate information encouraging their use and promoting awareness within both the library and publishing communities.

To forward needs for technical standards through ALA and the RLMS representative to the Association for Information and Image Management (AIIM), National Standards Council; and to provide guidance and support to the RLMS representative to AIIM/National Standards Council including providing additional sources of financial support.

To cooperate with the ALA Standards Committee.

Ch., Erich J. Kesse (1993); Thomas A. Bourke (1993); August A. Imholtz Jr. (1993); Judy A. Knop (1993); Lorraine M. Perrotta (1994); cons., Suzanne C. Dodson (1993).

Discussion Groups

PLMS-RLMS (See p. 36.)

Public Service Managers of Microform Facilities

To provide an informal forum for librarians who manage microform facilities or who are involved with public service aspects of microforms in which to exchange information and ideas and to discuss common problems.

Ch., Jean Alexander (1993).

Reproduction of Library Materials

To provide an informal forum for exchanging information and views and for discussing trends, problems, and developments in the area of reproduction of library materials.

Ch., Laurie Abbott (1993).

Representatives

ALA Copyright Subcom.—Helga Borck (1993).
ALCTS Budget and Finance Com.—Shirley W. Leung.
ALCTS Catalog Form and Function Com.—Norma K. Hendrikson (1993).
ALCTS Conference Program Com. (New Orleans, 1993)—Jutta Reed-Scott (1993).
ALCTS Conference Program Com. (Miami, 1994)—Nancy Elkington (1994).
ALCTS International Relations Com.—Helga Borck (1994).
ALCTS Legislation Com.—Joanna Walsh (1994).
ALCTS LRTS Editorial Bd.—Thomas A. Bourke (1993).
ALCTS Membership Com.—Myron Chace (1994).
ALCTS Nominating Com.—Shirley W. Leung (1993).
ALCTS Organization and Bylaws Com.—Ann G. Swartzell (1993).
ALCTS Planning Com.—Jack E. Pontius (1993).
ALCTS Preservation Microfilming Com.—Julie E. Arnott (1993).
ALCTS Publications Com.—Elizabeth Patterson (1994).
ALCTS Research and Statistics Com.—Myron B. Chace (1994).
ALCTS CCS CC:DA—Cecilia Sercan (1993).
ALCTS PLMS—Susan F. Blaine.
Assn. for Information and Image Management (AIIM) National Standards Council—Norman J. Shaffer (1993); alt.—Myron B. Chace (1993).
RASD Interlibrary Loan Com.—Sara J. Eichhorn (1993).

Serials Section (SS)

To contribute to library service and librarianship through the distribution of information concerning serials literature by reports and free discussion at general meetings and through publication; to encourage specialized training for librarians in the field of serials; and to coordinate the activities within the Association for Library Collections and Technical Services and within the American Library Association with respect to serials.

Executive Committee

Ch., Mary M. Case (1993); ch.-elect, Miriam W. Palm (1993); secy., Eleanor I. Cook (1994); past ch., Suzanne L. Thomas (1993); Julia C. Blixrud (1993); October R. Ivins (1994); Minna C. Saxe (1995); liaisons: Susan A. Davis (1993); Betty Landesman (1993); Joyce G. McDonough (1993); ex officio: Jean A. Pec (1993); Karen Muller.

Committees

Acquisitions

To serve as a review and advisory committee for all matters concerning the acquisition of serials and act as a clearinghouse for issues of mutual concern to libraries and the serials industry; to identify, study, and make recommendations or referrals on issues concerning the acquisition of serials; to gather, organize, and disseminate information about advances in the serials acquisition field; to communicate committee findings through appropriate channels; to identify and suggest formal liaison with other ALA committees.

Ch., Richard L. Brumley (1993); Marifran Bustion (1994); Julia A. Gammon (1994); Joyce G. McDonough (1993); Marla J. Schwartz (1994); interns: Donna D. Alsbury (1993); Winifred Gelenter (1993); cons: Gary J. Brown (1993); October R. Ivins (1993); Leslie C. Knapp (1993).

Bowker/Ulrich's Serials Librarianship Award

To select the recipient of the Award for distinguished contributions to serials librarianship, including but not limited to those made within the previous three years, demonstrated by such activities as leadership in serials-related activities through participation in professional associations and/or library education programs, contributions to the body of serials literature, conduct of research in the area of serials, development of tools or methods to enhance access to or management of serials, or other advances leading to a better understanding of the field of serials.

Ch., Rexford R. Bross Jr. (1993); Patrick F. Callahan (1993); Marilyn L. Norstedt (1993).

Education

To further educational efforts in the area of serials librarianship ranging from library school instruction and practices to all types of continuing education; to identify the needs and to make recommendations for the content of such educational opportunities; to communicate these to all appropriate persons or bodies; and to establish liaison, as appropriate, between the committee and other bodies having similar interests.

Ch., Michael Elmore (1993); Beverley Geer-Butler (1993); Cynthia K. Hepfer (1994); Pamela Zager Rebarcak (1994); Helen H. Wilkes (1994); interns: Sharon L. Mason (1993); Beatrice L. McKay (1993).

First Step Award

To select the winner of the SS First Step Award grant.

Ch., Elaine K. Rast (1993); Michele J. Crump (1993); Sally W. Somers (1993).

Nominating

Ch., Susan A. Davis (1993); Marcia L. Anderson (1993); Frank E. Sadowski Jr. (1993).

Policy and Research

To recommend long-range policies and plans for research in areas that need to be studied; to keep informed as to research in progress in the area of its responsibilities. To coordinate the work of the Policy and Research Committee with planning for the ALCTS as a whole through participation (by the committee chairperson) in the work of the ALCTS Planning and Research Committee, and a written report to the chairperson of that committee. The chairperson of the Policy and Research Committee serves as a nonvoting ex officio member of the Section Executive Committee.

Ch., Jean A. Pec (1993); Jeanne M. K. Boydston (1993); Edith Gewertz (1994); Odette F. Shepherd (1993); James Williams (1994); LC liaison, Kimberly W. Dobbs (1993); interns: June D. Chressanthis (1993); David Lucas Graves (1993).

Serials Cataloging, to Study

To identify, discuss, and propose solutions to problems related to serials cataloging. To make recommendations to the Committee on Cataloging: Description and Access and other appropriate bodies regarding changes to, or the interpretation of, the catalog code and appropriate communications formats which will enhance access to serials; to serve as a forum for discussion of all issues related to serials cataloging and to promote the exchange of information among the committee, the Library of Congress, CC:DA, MARBI, and the entire serials cataloging community; to distribute minutes of the meeting through available sources; to establish liaison, as appropriate, between the committee and other bodies having similar interests.

Ch., Eleanor I. Cook (1993); Norma J. Fair (1994); Taemin Park (1994); Elizabeth N. Steinhagen (1993); Ann B. Vidor (1993); liaisons: Jean P. Altschuler (1993); Dorothy Glasby (1993); interns: Carolyn C. Havens (1993); Wei Zhang (1993).

Serials Standards, to Study

To monitor serial standards by providing a forum for the discussion of developing standards, of revisions to existing standards, and of the implementation of standards; to suggest to the appropriate organizations the need for additional standards as they affect serials; to provide input into the standard-making process where appropriate (e.g., NISO standards); to develop channels of communication with appropriate groups (e.g., NISO, LITA/TESLA, SISAC, CONSER, MARBI, etc.); to further develop and coordinate serial standards activities within the American Library Association; and to communicate findings to the appropriate persons or organizations.

Ch., Karen D. Darling (1993); Valerie Bross (1994); Ruth E. Christ (1994); Margot S. Krissiep (1993); Frank H. Sun (1994); interns: Eugene H. Dickerson Jr. (1993); Sharon K. Scott (1993).

Union Lists of Serials

To address and study matters relating to union lists of serials, with special attention being given to evaluating trends or developing standards. The committee is further charged with coordinating and disseminating information on union lists of serials issues and concerns.

Ch., Betty Landesman (1993); Linda A. Arnold (1993); Mechael D. Gago (1994); Robert L. Watkins (1994); Susan M. Williams (1994); intern, Cathy Kellum (1993); cons., Cecelia N. Boone (1993).

Worst Serial Title Change of the Year

To solicit nominations from the library community for the annual Worst Serial Title Change awards. Primary consideration will be given to changes of title although other variations in publication, such as changes in format, frequency, and numbering, may also be considered.

To evaluate the nominations and assign awards as appropriate.

To prepare humorous descriptions for the awards and reasons for selection. To choose an individual to present the awards in the spirit intended at the annual meeting of the Association of Library Collections and Technical Services. To disseminate news of the awards to appropriate liaisons and publications.

Ch., Rosanna O'Neil (1993); Anne M. Gordon (1994); Margaret Mering (1993); interns: Adriana M. Pilecky-Dekajlo (1993); Linda L. Rosenstein (1993).

Discussion Group

Research Libraries

To provide an informal forum for presentation and discussion of matters of current interest and concern to those interested in serials in research libraries. To share progress reports on current projects and developments related to serials on national, regional and local levels.

Ch., Rita L. Echt (1993).

Representatives

ALA Library Edu. Assembly—Michael Elmore (1993).
ALCTS Budget and Finance Com.—Jana Lonberger (1994).
ALCTS Catalog Form and Function—Kathleen A. Schweitzberger (1994).
ALCTS Conference Program Com. (New Orleans, 1993)—Mary M. Case (1993).
ALCTS Conference Program Com. (Miami, 1994)—Miriam W. Palm (1994).
ALCTS International Relations Com.—Sally C. Tseng (1993).
ALCTS Legislation Com.—John R. James (1993).
ALCTS LRTS Editorial Bd.—Miriam Palm (1993).
ALCTS Membership Com.—Pamela Bluh (1994).

ALCTS Nominating Com.—Susan A. Davis (1993).
ALCTS Organization and Bylaws Com.—Minna C. Saxe (1993).
ALCTS Planning Com.—Jean A. Pec (1993).
ALCTS Preservation Microfilming Com.—Susan Kellerman (1993).
ALCTS Publications Com.—Sylvia O. Martin (1993).
ALCTS Publisher/Vendor–Library Relations Com.—Richard L. Brumley (1993).
ALCTS Research and Statistics Com.—Robert Alan (1993).
ALCTS AS Acquisitions Organization & Management Com.—Julia Gammon (1994).
ALCTS CCS-CC:DA—Jean P. Altschuler (1993).
North American Serials Interest Group—Susan A. Davis (1993).
Serials Industry Systems Advisory Com. (SISAC): Minna C. Saxe (1993); Betty Landesman (1993); Joyce McDonough (1993).

----◆----

Association for Library Service to Children

----◆----

Membership as of August 31, 1992
Organization	480
Personal	3,129
Total	3,609

Susan Roman, *executive director*
Eileen Fitzsimons, *deputy executive director*
Stephanie Dodge, *program officer*

The Association for Library Service to Children is interested in the improvement and extension of library services to children in all types of libraries. It is responsible for the evaluation and selection of book and nonbook library materials for and the improvement of techniques of library service to children from preschool through the eighth grade or junior high school age, when such materials and techniques are intended for use in more than one type of library. ALSC has specific responsibility for:

1. Continuous study and critical review of activities assigned to the division.

2. Conduct of activities and carrying on of projects within its area of responsibility.

3. Cooperation with all units of ALA whose interests and activities have a relationship to library service to children.

4. Interpretation of library materials for children and of methods of using such materials with children, to parents, teachers, and other adults, and representation of the librarians' concern for the production and effective use of good children's books to groups outside the profession.

5. Stimulation of the professional growth of its members and encouragement of participation in appropriate type-of-library divisions.

6. Planning and development of programs of study and research in the area of selection and use of library materials for children for the total profession.

7. Development, evaluation, and promotion of professional materials in its area of responsibility.

Board of Directors

Pres., Kathy Ann East (1994); pres.-elect, Ellen M. Stepanian (1995); past pres., Linda A. Perkins (1993); Rita Auerbach (1995); Therese G. Bigelow (1994); Gayle Cole (1993); Carla D. Hayden (1993); Steven L. Herb (1993); Elizabeth F. Howard (1994); Penny S. Markey (1994); Gretchen M. Wronka (1995); div. councilor, Frances V. Sedney (1996).

Executive Committee

To facilitate the actions of the Board of Directors between Board meetings and to consider such items that require interim decisions for the association; to review agendas for the meetings of the Board of Directors and for the annual business meeting of the association and may make recommendations to the Board regarding items reviewed and under consideration. All actions are to be reported at the next regular meeting of the Board and are subject to Board review.

Pres., Kathy Ann East (1994); pres.-elect, Ellen M. Stepanian (1995); past pres., Linda A. Perkins (1993); div. councilor, Frances V. Sedney (1996).

Publications

ALSC Newsletter (semiannual). Sent to all ALSC members. Not available by subscription. Ed., Anitra T. Steele, ALSC/ALA, 50 E. Huron St., Chicago, IL 60611.

Journal of Youth Services in Libraries (quarterly). Sent to all ALSC members. Subscription, $40 a yr. ($50 foreign). Issued jointly with YALSA. Co-eds., Donald J. Kenney, Virginia Tech. Univ. L., P.O. Box 90001, Blacksburg, VA 24061-0434, and Linda J. Wilson, Dept. of Ed. Studies, Radford Univ., 206A Russell Hall, Radford, VA 24142.

PRIORITY GROUPS

PRIORITY GROUP I—Child Advocacy

To identify and promulgate the rights of children, both within and outside the profession. To evaluate current or proposed policies, programs, and activities of ALA and its constituent bodies that affect service to children, and to recommend appropriate action. To submit evaluations of proposed national legislation affecting children with recommendation for action. To identify, evaluate, and recommend ways of working with other organizations and groups concerned with children on the local, state, and national levels. Priority group consultant, committee chairpersons, and discussion group leaders will review annually the function of each of the committees and make any recommendation necessary to meet the responsibilities of this priority group. To maintain liaison with ALA committees, divisions, round tables, and other ALSC priority groups with common concerns.

Cons., Ann L. Kalkhoff (1994).
Boy Scouts of America, Advisory
Legislation
Mass Media, Liaison With
National Organizations Serving the Child, Liaison With

PRIORITY GROUP II—Evaluation of Media

To evaluate, to establish standards for, and to encourage the availability of materials for children. Priority group consultant, committee chairpersons, and discussion group leaders will review annually the function of each of the committees and discussion groups and make any recommendations necessary to meet the responsibilities of this priority group. To maintain liaison with ALA committees, divisions, round tables, and other ALSC priority groups with common concerns.

Cons., Margaret A. Bush (1993).
Computer Software Evaluation
Film and Video Evaluation
Notable Children's Books
Recording Evaluation
Selection of Children's Books and Materials from Various Cultures

PRIORITY GROUP III— Professional Development

To identify and recommend any program, activity, or award pertaining to recruitment, improving professional education, continuing education, and the status of librarians serving children. To review any suggested program, award, or activity referred by the Board for research, analysis, or feasibility study. Priority group consultant, committee chairpersons, and discussion group leaders will review annually the function of each of the committees and make any recommendations necessary to meet the responsibilities of this priority group. To maintain liaison with ALA divisions, committees, round tables, and other ALSC priority groups with common concerns.

Cons., Patsy L. Weeks (1994).
ALSC/Econo-Clad Literature Program Award
ALSC Scholarships: Melcher and Bound to Stay Bound
Arbuthnot Honor Lecture
Distinguished Service to ALSC Award
Education
Managing Children's Services (committee)
Managing Children's Services (discussion group)
Putnam & Grosset Group Awards Selection
State and Regional Leadership (discussion group)
Teachers of Children's Literature (discussion group)

PRIORITY GROUP IV—Social Responsibilities

To identify areas in which service to children should be extended or improved. To recommend policies, programs, and activities that (1) provide children access to information necessary to their development as individual members of a democratic society, and (2) further the international exchange of professional knowledge and materials. Priority group consultant, committee chairpersons, and discussion group leaders will review annually the function of each of the committees and make any recommendation necessary to meet the responsibilities of this priority group. To maintain liaison with ALA committees, divisions, round tables, and other ALSC priority groups with common concerns.

Cons., Eliza T. Dresang (1993).
Children with Special Needs, Library Service to
Intellectual Freedom
International Relations
Preschool Services and Parent Education
Preschool Services (discussion group)
Social Issues in Relation to Materials and Services for Children (discussion group)

PRIORITY GROUP V—Planning and Research

To study needs in service to children in relation to the responsibilities and organizational structure of the division. To recommend research projects, to review program plans, to prepare budgets, and to advise on ALSC publications. Priority group consultant, committee chairpersons, and discussion group leaders will review annually the function of each of the committees and make any recommendation necessary to meet the responsibilities of this priority group. To maintain liaison with ALA committees, divisions, round tables, and other ALSC priority groups with common concerns.

Cons., Jill L. Locke (1994).
Caldecott Medal Calendar
Collections of Children's Books for Adult Research (discussion group)
Grants
Local Arrangements
Membership
National Reading Program
Nominating
Organization and Bylaws
Planning and Budget
Preconference Planning
Publications
Research and Development
Special Collections, National Planning of
Storytelling (discussion group)

PRIORITY GROUP VI—Awards

To nominate or select recipients of the awards based on the award criteria. Priority group consultant and committee chairpersons will review annually the procedures of each of the committees and make any recommendations necessary to meet the responsibilities of this group. To maintain liaison with ALA committees, divisions, round tables, and other ALSC priority groups with common concerns.

Cons., Ruth I. Gordon (1993).
(Mildred L.) Batchelder Award Selection
(Randolph) Caldecott Award Selection
(Andrew) Carnegie Award Selection
(John) Newbery Award Selection
(Laura Ingalls) Wilder Award

COMMITTEES

ALSC/ALTA (interdivisional)

To identify trends in library service to children and propose guidelines for action and board approval; to propose cooperative projects such as publications, continuing education programs, and reciprocal columns in division newsletters; to encourage trustees in cooperation with their children's librarians to act as advocates for public library service to children and families/caregivers; and to increase the visibility of trustees and to recognize their support to children's resources and programs in libraries.

Co-chs., Ruth Newell (1993) and Maria B. Salvadore (1993); Ralph S. Brown (1993); Lucille Hall (1993); Romona Howard (1993); Amy Kellman (1994); 2 to be appointed.

ALSC/Association of Booksellers for Children (joint)

To consider issues of concern common to both groups in order to effect change that will benefit both librarians and booksellers who work with children's books.

Co-chs., Marilyn P. Hollinshead (1993) and Caroline Ward (1993); Wendy Barish (1993); Anne Bustard (1993); Floyd C. Dickman (1994); Carol J. Erdahl (1993); Mimi Kayden (1994);

Ellen Krieger (1993); Mary D. Lankford (1993); John Mason (1993); Barbara A. Maxwell (1993); Theresa M. Schmitz (1993); Amy E. Spaulding (1993); Patricia T. Wroclawski (1993).

Arbuthnot Honor Lecture

To choose annually an individual of distinction who shall prepare and present a paper which shall be a significant contribution to the field of children's literature; to select a host institution and make appropriate arrangements for the presentation of the lecture; to arrange for publication of lecture in *Journal of Youth Services in Libraries.*

Ch., Marilyn Berg Iarusso (1993); Marian Drabkin (1993); Glenn E. Estes (1993); Anne Lundin (1993); Bette J. Peltola (1993).

(Mildred L.) Batchelder Award Selection, 1993

To make selection of the book to receive the Mildred L. Batchelder Award.

Ch., Eva-Maria Lusk (1993); Viki L. Ash-Geisler (1993); Mary Rinato Berman (1993); Joanna R. Long (1993); Hilda W. Parfrey (1993).

(Mildred L.) Batchelder Award Selection, 1994

Ch. and members to be appointed.

(Louise Seaman) Betchel Fellowship

To select annually up to three (3) librarians, the number to be determined by the income available and the qualifications of the applicants, to be awarded Fellowship(s) in the amount of $3,750 to read and study at the Baldwin Library of the George A. Smathers Libraries, University of Florida, for a period of at least one month.

Ch. and members to be appointed.

Boy Scouts of America (advisory)

To advise the Boy Scouts of America in revising publications (excluding *Boys' Life*); to advise the Boy Scouts of America in selecting media for BSA bibliographies in accord with established criteria; to explore and carry out other kinds of cooperation with the Boy Scouts of America in areas of concern to ALSC.

Ch., Nancy P. Zimmerman (1993); Elizabeth A. Blatz (1994); Barbara L. Flynn (1994); Judith V. Lechner (1994); Anne M. Smart (1993); cons., Nancy Hackett (1993).

(Randolph) Caldecott Award Selection, 1993

To select from the books published the preceding year within the terms, definitions, and criteria governing the awards, the most distinguished American picture book for children.

Ch., Jane Botham (1993); Melody L. Allen (1993); Laurel C. Chase (1993); Susan W. Faust (1993); Carole Fiore (1993); Sharon M. Harvey (1993); Rita J. Hoffmann (1993); Janet K. Irving (1993); April L. Judge (1993); Fay L. Matsunaga (1993); Helen Mae Mullen (1993); Sue McCleaf Nespeca (1993); Jane H. Pan (1993); Rivkah K. Sass (1993); Sally Anne M. Thompson (1993).

(Randolph) Caldecott Award Selection, 1994

Ch., Maria B. Salvadore (1994); Donna L. Bessant (1994); R. Randall Enos (1994); Dona Helmer (1994); Debra A. McLeod (1994); Cathryn

M. Mercier (1994); Jewell K. Stoddard (1994); Kathy Toon (1994).

Caldecott Medal Calendar, 1994

To recommend illustrations for the Caldecott Medal Calendar to the Executive Director of ALSC. Three recommendations with bibliographic data and annotations should be listed in priority order for the cover and for each month.

Ch., Mary Lou White (1993); Gratia Banta (1993); Letitia A. Wilson (1993).

(Andrew) Carnegie Award Selection, 1993

To select from the videos produced the preceding year within the terms, definitions, and criteria governing the award, the most distinguished American video for children.

Ch., Marina Starr LaTronica (1993); Kimberlin H. Badertscher (1993); Mary Ann Gilpatrick (1993); Rochelle Glantz (1993); Celia Holm (1993); Janet R. Moltzan (1994); Paula R. Moore (1993); Sandra M. Wilkie (1993); 1 to be appointed.

(Andrew) Carnegie Award Selection, 1994

Ch. and members to be appointed.

Children with Special Needs, Library Service to

To explore the areas which need to be developed by libraries to meet the needs of materials and library programs for exceptional children, and to explore the ways in which library training programs can prepare librarians in these areas. To offer specific leadership in discovering, developing, and disseminating information about library materials, programs, and facilities for children with special needs, that is, those children who require a modification of customary delivery of library services to meet their needs. To develop and maintain guidelines for selection of materials to such children. To discuss and suggest ways in which library education programs can prepare librarians to serve these children.

Ch., Cynthia K. Richey (1994); Mary Anne Corrier (1994); Sherry Des Enfants (1993); Susan H. Galloway (1993); James E. Massey (1994); Gretchen V. Swibold (1994); Maureen White (1994).

Computer Software Evaluation

To define and develop guidelines and criteria for the evaluation and selection of computer software. To recommend to the Board a means of publishing and sharing the recommendations made through the application of the selected guidelines and evaluative criteria. To identify and suggest to the Board cooperative projects within and without the American Library Association involving computer software accessible to children within their homes and libraries.

Ch., Civia M. Tuteur (1993); Cecily R. Pilzer (1993); Margaret R. Tassia (1993); Joanne Troutner (1993); Carol Ann Wilson (1993); Judy E. Zuckerman (1993).

Distinguished Service to ALSC Award

To administer an award to recognize an individual who has made a significant contribution to children's services and ALSC.

Ch., Gayle Cole (1993); Margery Cuyler (1994); Ginny Moore Kruse (1993); Zena B. Sutherland (1994).

Econo-Clad Literature Program Award

To select annually the recipient of the ALSC/ Econo-Clad Literature Program Award, given to an individual who has developed and implemented a unique and outstanding library program for children involving reading and the use of literature with children.

Ch., Trevelyn Jones (1993); Nell Colburn (1994); Margo H. Daniels (1994); Monique A. King (1993).

Education

To review the elements considered essential to the initial and continuing education of children's librarians. To explore, evaluate, and make recommendations concerning the current status of professional education in regard to library service to children. To establish a liaison with library educators for conveying recommendations and ideas from ALSC membership in order to preserve the quality of education for librarians who will be working with children. To recommend the initiation of programs to fill identified needs to the Board for implementation. To summarize annually for the Board concerns for library education and continuing educations solicited and/or gathered from ALSC committees and members. To review, as appropriate, the ALSC guidelines for the evaluation of proposals for continuing education programs. To represent ALSC at appropriate ALA committees, councils and assemblies, and to coordinate the activities of the committee with those of SCOLE.

Ch., Leslie Edmonds (1993); Carol A. Doll (1994); Mary J. Fellows (1994); Audrey J. Gorman (1994); Marion Hanes Rutsch (1993).

Film and Video Evaluation

To select, annotate, and present for publication annually a list of notable films, videotape and video disc recordings of interest to children, available for use in homes and libraries, produced in the two calendar years prior to the date of their selection. To reevaluate and to recommend change as needed in the ALSC criteria for notable films, videotape and video disc recordings of interest to children. To identify titles for consideration by other committees evaluating for specific clientele or purpose. To carry on other film and video evaluation projects as assigned by the ALSC Board. To implement the Film and Video Recommendation Policy and Procedures.

Ch., Debra A. McLeod (1993); Jacqueline M. Albers (1993); Vicki Beck Ford (1994); Paula Hayes (1993); Patricia A. McLaughlin (1993); Jacqueline G. Morris (1993); Grace O'Connor (1994); Jasmine Y. Posey (1993); Louise L. Sherman (1994); Flo Starkey (1994); Barbara D. Widem (1994).

Grants

To develop and maintain a listing of possible grants for ALSC projects and committees; to inform membership, through program(s) and/or publications, how to find sources of grant funds, and techniques for writing grant proposals; to assist ALSC Board and committees in locating sources of grant funds for specific purposes; and to provide assistance and advice to ALSC Board and committees considering applying for grant funds.

The Grants Committee and the Research and Development Committee shall meet regularly to discuss issues of mutual concern. At a minimum: (a) Chairpersons and/or the two committees shall meet at least once during Midwinter and Annual Conferences, and (b) the committee chairpersons shall communicate during the year, as appropriate.

Ch., Laurel C. Chase (1993); Kimberlin H. Badertscher (1994); Carol Kroll (1993); Effie Lee Morris (1993); Nora Jane Natke (1994); Carolyn B. Noah (1993); Rose Mary Olszewski (1993).

Intellectual Freedom

To serve as a liaison between the division and the ALA Intellectual Freedom Committee and all other groups within the association concerned with intellectual freedom. To advise the division on matters before the Office for Intellectual Freedom and their implication for library service to children and to make recommendations to the ALA Intellectual Freedom Committee for changes in policies involving library service to children; to promote in-service and continuing education programs in the area of intellectual freedom for those who select library materials for children.

Ch., Susan Hagen Land (1993); Janet Hildebrand (1993); Connie C. Rockman (1993); Nancy Seiner (1994); Elizabeth S. Watson (1994); Marie Turner Wright (1993); Gail Zachariah (1993).

International Relations

Within the association's field of responsibility, to encourage and facilitate the use of library techniques and knowledge throughout the world; to exchange professional information, ideas, and literature; to act as liaison with international organizations; to have responsibility for the preparation of a biannual bibliography of children's books published in the United States which would reflect the cultural diversity and/or pluralistic nature of the lifestyles and peoples of the U.S.A.; to keep the ALSC Board informed of those projects of ALA which are of international scope and suggest ways in which service to children might be incorporated.

Ch., Marsha L. Cutler (1993); Adele R. Bennett (1994); Joan M. Blumenstein (1993); John K. DeBacher (1993); Diane Driessen (1994); Monique A. King (1994); Margaret L. Kirkpatrick (1993); 2 to be appointed.

"Journal of Youth Services in Libraries" Editorial, ALSC/YASD (interdivisional)

To determine editorial policies for JOYS, subject to review by the joint ALSC/YALSA Boards; to suggest themes for forthcoming issues; to recommend resource people for articles and reviews; to review material submitted for publication upon request by the editor(s).

Co-chs. and eds., Donald J. Kenney (1994) and Linda J. Wilson (1994); Elizabeth G. Acerra (YALSA, 1994); M. Dorcas Hand (YALSA, 1993); Amy Kellman (ALSC, 1993); Marjorie Lewis (YALSA, 1993); Evelyn C. Walker (ALSC, 1994); 1 to be appointed.

"Journal of Youth Services in Libraries" Refereed Journal Evaluation Process, ALSC/YALSA (ad hoc interdivisional)

To design an evaluation process for the refereed journal of ALSC and YALSA—Journal of Youth Services in Libraries.

Ch., Barbara M. Barstow (ALSC, 1994); Barbara Hull (YALSA, 1994); Marjorie Jones (ALSC, 1993); Kathleen A. Staerkel (ALSC, 1993); Mary Elizabeth Wendt (YALSA, 1994).

Legislation

To serve as a channel of communication to legislative matters between the ALA Legislation Committee and the division, recommending to the ALSC Board changes as necessary in federal, state, and local legislation proposed by the ALA Legislation Committee, and advise on ALSC interests in the proposals before ALA Council. To call to the attention of the ALA Legislation Committee and to recommend to the ALSC Board endorsement or revision of legislation affecting children that might be proposed or supported by the ALA Legislation Committee.

Ch., Marge Loch-Wouters (1993); Roslyn Beitler (1993); Louise Howton (1994); Christine Jenkins (1993); Kathy H. Latrobe (1993); Phillis M. Wilson (1993); Diana D. Young (1994).

Local Arrangements—New Orleans, 1993

Ch. and members to be appointed.

Managing Children's Services

To identify issues relating to the management of children's services; to determine if these issues are being addressed by other divisions or committees; to cooperate as appropriate; and to initiate action to address these issues. Issues may be referred to the Committee by the ALSC Board or the Managing Children's Services Discussion Group.

Ch., Kathy Toon (1993); Berry G. Bateman (1993); Rosanne Cerny (1994); Bessie Condos Egan (1994); Marlene K. Lee (1993); Gene Nelson (1994); Marie C. Orlando (1993); Lynne R. Pickens (1994); Deborah A. Sherman (1993); Janice A. Yee (1993).

Mass Media, Liaison with

To initiate and maintain professional relationships with persons and organizations involved in the production and promotion of films, programs, and materials for children to be disseminated through the mass media. To maintain an active liaison with Action for Children's Television (ACT) and other appropriate groups. To develop and maintain, in the major geographic areas where production of mass media (programs and films) is centered, cadres of ALSC members willing and able to prepare selective bibliographies. To arrange, on request, for these members to develop specific bibliographies on related or specific programs or films in accord with criteria established.

Ch., Virginia McKee (1993); LaVerne Brown (1993); Heather E. Caines (1993); Barbara A. Genco (1994); April L. Judge (1993); Sandra M. Wilkie (1994); 1 to be appointed.

Membership

To plan campaigns for recruiting new members for ALSC at the national, regional, state, and local level. To plan and assume responsibility for conference orientation sessions and to welcome and introduce new members to ALSC purposes and procedures.

Ch., Joanne Foss (1993); Debra S. Gold (1994); Marilyn Long Graham (1993); Diane S. Marton (1994); Caroline L. Shepard (1993); Crystal L.

Weirich-Faris (1993); Mary-Kay Will (1993); Barbara S. Wortman (1993); 1 to be appointed.

National Organizations Serving the Child, Liaison with

To explore, recommend, initiate, and implement ways of working with other organizations that work with and for children.

Ch., Ione S. Cowen (1993); Roxanne Chadwick (1993); Sonia J. Church (1993); Karen L. Harvey (1994); Elizabeth A. Long (1994); Vicky L. Rose (1994); Katherine Todd (1994).

National Organizations Serving the Child, Liaison with, Task Force to Examine the Structure and Function of (task force)

To look into the structure and function of the Liaison with National Organizations Serving the Child Committee and to prepare a report for discussion by the ALSC Executive Committee at the November 1992 fall planning meeting.

Ch. to be appointed; Linda Ward Callaghan (1994); Marjorie Jones (1994); Helen Mae Mullen (1994).

National Reading Program

To work with ALA Graphics to prepare materials and recommend themes for the annual national reading programs each year.

Ch., Mollie B. Bynum (1993); Laurina Cashin (1993); Kathy Ann East (1993); Denise L. Krell (1993); Jill L. Locke (1994); Kathryn McClelland (1994); Hedra L. P. Peterman (1993); Caroline F. Vicchiarelli (1993); Deborah L. Wright (1994).

(John) Newbery Award Selection, 1993

To select from the books published the preceding year within the terms, definitions, and criteria governing the awards, the most distinguished contribution to American literature for children.

Ch., Sara L. Miller (1993); Joan L. Atkinson (1993); Carol J. Fox (1993); Susan L. Golden (1993); Suzanne W. Hawley (1993); Chrystal C. Jeter (1993); Amy Kellman (1993); Susan Knorr (1993); Virginia McKee (1993); Linda K. Murphy (1993); Judith Rovenger (1993); Karen Stanley (1993); Anitra T. Steele (1993); Vivian M. Sykes (1993); Kathryn M. Weisman (1993).

(John) Newbery Award Selection, 1994

Ch., Mary Ann Paulin (1994); Raymond W. Barber (1994); Barbara M. Barstow (1994); Barbara A. Genco (1994); Susanna S. Loftis (1994); Sarah M. McCarville (1994); Dianne L. Monson (1994); Kemie Nix (1994); 7 to be appointed.

Nominating—1993

Ch., Linda Abby Fein (1993); Floyd C. Dickman (1993); Janet Hildebrand (1993); Amy E. Spaulding (1993).

Notable Children's Books

To select, annotate, and present for publication annually the list of notable children's books of the preceding year.

Ch., Karen B. Breen (1993); Pamela Petrick Barron (1994); Michael Cart (1994); Judith F. Davie (1993); Kathleen F. Odean (1993); John

E. Peters (1994); Connie Pottle (1994); Susan Reisner (1994); Mercier C. Robinson (1994).

Organization and Bylaws

To develop for presentation to the Board of Directors a plan for the structure and function of each new committee or discussion group. To study, review, and, if necessary, make recommendations to the Board for revision of structure or function, addition, or discontinuation of committees and discussion groups. To make recommendations to the Board on organizational matters affecting ALSC as a whole, and to serve as liaison with the ALA Committee on Organization upon request of the Board. To serve, upon request, in an advisory capacity to priority group consultants, committees, and discussion groups on organizational matters in ALSC or between ALSC and other ALA divisions. To consider, develop, and present to the Board, and subsequently to membership, suggested amendments to the Bylaws. To assist in interpretation of the Bylaws to the Board, the membership, and the ALA Constitution and Bylaws Committee.

Ch., Wendy D. Caldiero (1993); Nancy Hackett (1993); Kathleen A. Staerkel (1994); Jane C. Terwillegar (1994); Barbara D. Widem (1993).

Planning and Budget

To prepare and submit to the ALSC Board an annual budget based on the priorities established by the Board; to review for the ALSC Board division activities for fiscal implications; to review for the ALSC Board, on a regular basis, the dues structure and other income activities of the division; to prepare and submit to the ALSC Board periodic analysis of the finances of the division; to review ALSC's fiscal relationship to ALA and other divisions and to act as liaison for the ALSC Board to the Planning and Budget Assembly.

Ch., Ellen G. Fader (1993); past pres., Linda A. Perkins (1993); Bd. rep., Steven Herb (1993); Ellen M. Stepanian (1993); Carol A. Tarsitano (1994).

Preconference Planning, 1993

Ch., Phyllis Jean Van Orden (1993); Jerry A. Bryan (1993); Helen Mae Mullen (1993); Carolyn B. Noah (1993); Linda L. Woodbury (1993).

Preschool Services and Parent Education

To recommend action for coordinated community service to early childhood, recommend media lists, and encourage training workshop action programs to get families of young children into closer library involvement. To draw up plans for adult, young adult, and children's departments to work together recruiting and training volunteers to work with small children and books. To initiate activities or projects in these areas appropriate to ALSC's field of responsibility.

Ch., Janice D. Smuda (1993); Amy L. Cohn (1994); Laura B. Culberg (1994); Linda L. Plevak (1994); Carol S. Spann (1994); Nan Sturdivant (1993); Letitia A. Wilson (1994); Susan A. Zeigler (1993).

Preservation of ALSC History (task force)

To explore the feasibility of collecting ALSC history from many of the well-known and respected children's specialists and to report back to the Board on a plan of action.

Co-chs., Jane Botham (1993) and Maria B. Salvadore (1993); Augusta Baker (1993); Carolyn W. Field (1993); Lillian N. Gerhardt (1993); Effie Lee Morris (1993).

Publications

To provide for continuity and balance in ALSC publications by coordinating and advising on all materials to be formally published by ALSC with the exception of *Journal of Youth Services in Libraries*. To promote and stimulate media of current and continuing interest for ALSC members, and to assist in the expedition of their timely publication. To prepare for Board consideration policies and general guidelines for ALSC publications, including procedures for submission of ideas, preparation of the manuscript, and completion of actual publication process. To establish guidelines for, receive, consider, and advise on all proposals for specific publications for committees, discussion groups, etc., prior to their submission to the ALSC Board of Directors. To develop and present to the Board of Directors proposals for new publications whose need in the ALSC publication program has become apparent. To regularly review previous publications and present proposals to the Board for revision or elimination. To report to the ALSC Board of Directors at each conference on the current status of the ALSC publications program, including projects both projected and in progress.

Ch., Pat R. Scales (1993); Carole J. De Jardin (1994); Marilyn P. Hollinshead (1993); June Kahler (1993); Carol K. Phillips (1994).

Publications Based on Membership Booth Letters (task force)

To prepare three publications based on letters received for the ALSC Membership Booth.

Ch. to be appointed; Marilyn P. Hollinshead (1993); June Kahler (1993).

Putnam & Grosset Group Awards Selection

To select annually, in accord with the terms of the award, four children's librarians who work directly with children, to receive the awards.

Ch., Blanka R. Saracevic (1993); Jo Anne Cypra-Sherlock (1993); Carla J. Kozak (1994).

Recording Evaluation

To select, annotate, and present for publication an annual list of notable audio recordings, disc or tape form, of interest to children. To reevaluate and recommend change as needed in the ALSC criteria for selection of recordings of interest to children. To identify titles for consideration by other committees evaluating for a specific clientele or purpose. To carry on other audio recording evaluation projects as assigned by the ALSC Board.

Ch., Elizabeth M. Simmons (1993); Kathy J. Heinrich (1994); Anne Meridian (1994); Penny Peck (1994); Marilyn P. Phillips (1993); Susan J. Pine (1993); Elizabeth M. Rosen (1993); John J. Sigwald (1993); 1 to be appointed.

Research and Development

To discover areas of library service to children in need of study and development; to devise possible projects in line with the responsibilities of the division that would explore these needs; to serve as liaison to the ALA Research Committee; to evaluate and to recommend research projects to the Board for action.

Ch., Virginia A. Walter (1993); Jerry A. Bryan (1994); Patricia J. Cianciolo (1994); Linda Abby Fein (1993); Janet A. Jerauld (1993); Loriene Roy (1993); Valerie Talbert (1994).

Scholarships: Melcher and Bound to Stay Bound

To select recipients and alternates for the annual ALSC Scholarships: Frederic G. Melcher and Bound to Stay Bound for professional education of librarians to work with children; to publicize the scholarship to potential candidates; and to advise the ALSC Board on needed changes in terms or administration of the scholarship.

Ch., Dudley B. Carlson (1993); Adele R. Bennett (1993); Theresa Black Chekon (1993); Doris J. Crabtree (1994); Lauren L. Wohl (1994).

"Selecting Materials for Children and Young Adults" Revision, ALSC/YALSA
(interdivisional task force)

To revise *Selecting Materials for Children and Young Adults* (ALA, 1977) by Midwinter meeting 1994.

Ch., Kay E. Vandergrift (1994); Maureen A. Connelly (YALSA, 1994); Jane A. Hannigan (1994); Gloria A. Waity (1994).

Selection of Children's Books and Materials from Various Cultures

To encourage the meeting of a variety of language and cultural needs by libraries and librarians serving children. To be responsible for the preparation of bibliographies of books and materials currently available for children in languages other than English, and English-language books originally published in other countries or produced by other cultures. To continue to explore the recommendations for effective acquisitions methods.

Ch., Doris C. Dale (1993); Gratia Banta (1993); Junko Yokota Lewis (1993); Suzanne Lo (1994); Lucrece Louisdhon (1994); Cathy A. Robinson (1993); Rivka K. Sass (1993).

Social Issues in Relation to Materials and Services for Children

To formulate a charge for the Social Issues Committee and to bring it to the Board for action during the Annual Conference 1992.

Ch., Kathleen T. Horning (1993); Grace W. Ruth (1994); Anitra T. Steele (1994).

Special Collections, National Planning of

To maintain lists of special collections of children's books now available in libraries; to encourage the creation of new collections and the strengthening of existing collections; to identify types of collections that need to be established; to establish criteria for evaluation of special collections; to explore and suggest ways in which special collections can be used locally, nationally, and internationally.

Ch., Corinne Camarata (1993); Ethel N. Ambrose (1994); Elizabeth F. Howard (1993); Dolores Blythe Jones (1993); Helen Mae Mullen (1994); Linda K. Murphy (1994); Evelyn M. Wagner (1993).

(Laura Ingalls) Wilder Award Selection, 1995

To select nominees for the Wilder Award, established by ALSC to give recognition each three years to an author or illustrator whose books published in the U.S. have over a period of years made a substantial and lasting contribution to literature for children.

Ch. and members to be appointed.

DISCUSSION GROUPS

Collections of Children's Books for Adult Research

To provide a forum for the discussion and study of specific collections of materials for children in terms of their research value.

Convenor, Philip Sadler (1993).

Managing Children's Services

To provide a forum for discussion of concerns of ALSC members that relate to managing children's services, to provide an opportunity to share management expertise, and to lend support to children's specialists, especially those new to ALA/ALSC.

Co-convenors, Carol K. Phillips (1993) and Carol Ann Wilson (1993).

Preschool Services

To provide a forum for discussion of concerns that relate to preschool services.

Convenor, Sue McCleaf Nespeca (1993).

Social Issues in Relation to Materials and Services for Children

To provide a forum for the discussion of the effect of social issues on library service to children and for the discussions of social issues and concerns as reflected in materials for children; to publicize and invite participation in such discussions so that awareness of such issues may be as broad as possible; to disseminate, with Board approval, the outcomes of the discussion of these concerns.

Co-convenors, Joanna R. Long and Anitra T. Steele.

Storytelling

To provide an on-going opportunity for sharing interest(s) in the art of storytelling in all its diversified forms and methods.

Co-convenors, Rita Auerbach (1993) and Mary Ann Gilpatrick (1993).

Teachers of Children's Literature

To provide a forum for the identification, investigation, discussion, and dissemination of ideas and information relating to the teaching of children's literature; to recommend to the ALSC Board methods of developing communication and cooperation with other groups of the same or similar interests within and outside of ALA.

Convenor, Rebecca R. James (1993).

REPRESENTATIVES

AASL National Conference—Baltimore, 1992—to be appointed.
ALA Annual Conference Program (New Orleans, 1993)—Kathy A. East.
ALA Appointments Com.—Ellen M. Stepanian.
ALA Budget & Planning Assembly—Ellen G. Fader.
ALA Fund-Raising Task Force—Therese Bigelow.
ALA Legislative Assembly—Marge Loch-Wouters.
ALA Library Education Assembly—Leslie Edmonds.
ALA Literacy Assembly—Helen Mae Mullen.
ALA Membership Promotion Task Force—JoAnne Foss.
ALA Planning Com.—Ellen G. Fader.
ALA Professional Ethics Com.—to be appointed.
ALCTS-CCS Cataloging of Children's Materials—Jane Marton, 1 to be appointed.
ASCLA Com. to Revise the Standards for Libraries at Institutions for the Mentally Retarded—Marilyn Karrenbrock, 1 to be appointed.
ASCLA Decade of Disabled Persons Com.—Cynthia K. Richey.
PLA Service to Children Com.—Marilyn Iarusso.
RASD Reference Services for Children and Young Adults—Elizabeth Overmyer.
White House Conference on Library and Information Services Task Force—Virginia Mathews.

LIAISONS WITH OTHER NATIONAL ORGANIZATIONS

4-H Programs Extension Service—Elizabeth M. Simmons.
American Assn. for Gifted Children—to be appointed.
Assn. for Childhood Education International—to be appointed.
Assn. for Children and Adults with Learning Disabilities—Clara Nalli Bohrer.
Assn. for the Care of Children's Health—Maria B. Salvadore.
Big Brothers and Big Sisters of America—Helen Mae Mullen.
Boy Scouts of America—Caroline S. Parr.
Boys Clubs of America—to be appointed.
Camp Fire, Inc.—Anitra T. Steele.
The Child Welfare League of America—Ethel N. Ambrose.
Children's Defense Fund—Effie Lee Morris.
Freedom to Read Fdn.—Susan Hagen Land.
Girl Scouts of America—to be appointed.
Girls Clubs of America—to be appointed.
International Reading Assn.—Clara Nalli Bohrer.
National Assn. for the Education of Young Children—Toni A. Bernardi.
National Assn. for the Perpetuation and Preservation of Storytelling—Elizabeth M. Simmons.
National Coalition to Support Sexuality Education (SIECUS)—Harriet Selenstone.
Natl. Committee for the Prevention of Child Abuse—to be appointed.
National Multiple Sclerosis Soc.—to be appointed.
Parent Cooperative Preschool International—Blair B. Christolon.

Parents Without Partners—Lucy C. Marx.
Puppeteers of America—Frances J. McCurdy.
Reading Is Fundamental—to be appointed.
Salvation Army—to be appointed.

Association of College and Research Libraries

Membership as of August 31, 1992
Organization members 1,143
Personal members 9,594
Total 10,737

Althea H. Jenkins, *executive director*
Cathleen Bourdon, *deputy director*
Patricia E. Sabosik, *editor and publisher*, Choice
Mary Ellen Kyger Davis, *editor and publisher*, C&RL News
Mary Taylor, *program officer*

The mission of ACRL is to foster the profession of academic and research librarianship and to enhance the ability of academic and research libraries to serve effectively the library and information needs of current and potential library users.

The major goals of ACRL are:
1. To contribute to the total professional development of academic and research librarians;
2. To enhance the capability of academic and research libraries to serve the needs of users;
3. To promote and speak for the interests of academic and research librarianship;
4. To promote study, research, and publications relevant to academic and research librarianship.

In order to accomplish these goals, the ACRL carries out a variety of activities and programs, including: encouraging research and publication; strengthening educational programs in librarianship, including continuing education programs; developing and supporting standards; developing and distributing informational material to its members; cooperating with other organizations and agencies—particularly those related to higher education and librarianship; promoting the use of library services and collections; supporting legislation of value to higher education and librarianship; advancing the profession.

Board of Directors

Pres., Jacquelyn A. McCoy (1994); pres.-elect, Thomas Kirk (1995); past pres., Anne K. Beaubien (1993); Karin E. Begg Borei (1994); Eileen Dubin (1993); Evan Ira Farber (1993); Ray E. Metz (1995); Linda L. Phillips (1995); Shelley E. Phipps (1994); Barbara J. Wittkopf (1994); councilor, Rochelle Sager (1994); Budget & Finance Com. rep., Thomas M. Peischl (1994); ex officio: Mary Sue Ferrell (1993); Althea H. Jenkins (1993).

Executive Committee

To act for the Board of Directors and make decisions on matters which require action before the next Board meeting, have been specifically delegated by the Board to the Executive Committee, or affect the budget and require immediate action; to act for the Board in the administration of established policies and programs, and to make recommendations to the Board with respect to matters of policy and operations; to review ACRL activities and programs and recommend priorities.

Pres., Jacquelyn A. McCoy (1994); pres.-elect, Thomas Kirk (1995); past pres., Anne K. Beaubien (1993); councilor, Rochelle Sager (1994); Budget & Finance Com. rep., Thomas M. Peischl (1994); ex officio, Althea H. Jenkins (1994).

Publications

ACRL Publications in Librarianship (formerly *ACRL Monograph Series*) (occasional). Standing or single orders available from Order Dept., ALA. Ed., Jonathan A. Lindsey, Baylor Univ., Waco, TX 76793.

Choice (monthly, 11 issues a yr., combined July-Aug. issue). $155 a yr. ($170 foreign); single copies, $15. *Choice Reviews-on-Cards:* $235 a yr. ($255 foreign); single copies, $25. Ed. and publisher, Patricia E. Sabosik, 100 Riverview Ctr., Middletown, CT 06457.

College & Research Libraries (6 bimonthly journal issues). Sent to all ACRL members. Subscriptions, $50 a yr. (PUAS countries, $55; other countries, $60); single copies, $14. Ed., Gloriana St. Clair, Pennsylvania State Univ., University Park, PA 16802; bk. review eds., Stephen R. Lehmann; Robert A. Walther; res. notes ed., Larry R. Oberg.

College & Research Libraries News (11 monthly issues, July-Aug. combined). Sent to all ACRL members. Subscriptions, $25 a yr. (PUAS countries, $30; other countries, $35); single copies, $6.50. Ed., Mary Ellen Kyger Davis, ACRL, 50 E. Huron St., Chicago, IL 60611.

Rare Books and Manuscripts Librarianship (2 issues). Subscriptions, $30 a yr. (PUAS countries, $35; other countries, $40); single copies, $15. Ed., Alice D. Schreyer, Asst. Dir. of Ls. for Spec. Clln., Univ. of Delaware L., Newark, DE 19717-5267.

COMMITTEES

Academic Library Statistics

Define the statistical needs of academic libraries; examine whether or how these needs are now being met; suggest ways ACRL could aid academic librarians and the profession by generating and/or disseminating these statistics; determine costs of such activities.

Ch., Richard W. Meyer (1993); Ray English (1993); Carol G. Henderson (1993); Lee C. Ketcham (1993); Elizabeth Salzer (1994); Marsha J. Stevenson (1993); Arthuree R. M. Wright (1994); interns, Chestalene Pintozzi (1993); Agnes Haigh Widder (1993); staff liaison, Mary Taylor.

Academic Status

To recommend appropriate policy and/or action on matters in academic libraries insofar as such matters affect the status of academic librarians; to be informed on all aspects of the status of academic librarians; and to develop standards, guidelines, procedures and programs for the attainment and protection of appropriate status.

Ch., Larry R. Oberg (1993); Gemma S. Devinney (1994); Janice C. Fennell (1993); Rena K. Fowler (1993); Caroline D. Harnly (1993); Douglas B. Highsmith (1994); Susan M. Kroll (1993); Douglas K. Lehman (1993); Thomas H. Patterson (1993); interns: Gillian F. Mendle (1993); W. Bede Mitchell (1993); staff liaison, Cathleen Bourdon.

Access Policy Guidelines (task force)

To review the 1975 Access Policy Guidelines and determine if the guidelines should remain in effect, be revised, or rescinded. In reviewing the Access Policy Guidelines, the task force will determine its relationship to the "ACRL Guidelines for the Preparation of Policies on Library Access" and the "Extended Campus Library Services Guidelines." If a revision is deemed needed, prepare drafts and share with the ACRL Standards and Accreditation Committee. Hold hearings on the proposed revisions and publish draft in *C&RL News* for comments. Submit the final draft to the Standards and Accreditation Committee for review. Final draft will be approved by the ACRL Board of Directors and the ALA Standards Committees. Final report due 1993, Annual Conference.

Ch., Kathleen Gunning (1993); Peter V. Deekle (1993); Helen B. Josephine (1993); David N. King (1993); Nancy P. O'Brien (1993); Carolyn Robison (1994); Natalie M. Schatz (1993); staff liaison, Mary Taylor.

ACRL Academic or Research Librarian of the Year Award

To recognize an individual member of the library profession who is making an outstanding national or international contribution to academic or research librarianship and library development.

Ch., Paul E. Dumont (1993); Mignon S. Adams (1993); Charles C. Curran (1993); Wendy Pradt Lougee (1993); Derrie B. Roark (1993); Carolyn Robison (1993); ex officio: Althea H. Jenkins (1993); Jacquelyn A. McCoy (1993); staff liaison, Mary Taylor.

ACRL & AECT Joint Committee (See listing under Joint Committees, p. 16)

"ACRL Publications in Librarianship" Editorial Board

To encourage research, writing and nonprint media production that may be appropriate for the *ACRL Publications in Librarianship* series; to solicit topics and, without guarantee of publication, to suggest them to appropriate authors; to review all materials submitted and approve them for publication in the *Publications in Librarianship* series.

Ed. and ch., Jonathan A. Lindsey (1993); Barbara B. Moran (1993); Stephen E. Wiberley Jr. (1993); ex officio: Anne K. Beaubien (1993); Althea H. Jenkins (1993); Karen S. Seibert (1994); staff liaison, Mary Taylor.

Appointments (1992) and Nominations (1993)

To recommend to the president-elect appointments to ACRL committees for the year of his or her term of office and to nominate the ACRL slate of candidates for president-elect and ACRL rep-

resentative on the ALA Council (when appropriate) the year following his or her term of office.

Ch., Hiram L. Davis (1993); Stephanie R. Bangert (1993); Deborah J. Grimes (1993); Sandra S. Kerbel (1993); Douglas K. Lehman (1993); Michael Ann Moskowitz (1993); Ronald Rodriguez (1993); John Sheridan (1993); Barbara Williams-Jenkins (1993); staff liaison, Cathleen Bourdon.

Appointments (1993) and Nominations (1994)

Ch., Pamela Snelson (1994); Betsy Baker (1994); Stanton F. Biddle (1994); Melvin R. George (1994); Marilyn M. McDonald (1994); Larry R. Oberg (1994); staff liaison, Cathleen Bourdon.

Association for Educational Communications and Technology—ACRL (joint) (See listing under Joint Committees, p. 16.)

(Hugh C.) Atkinson Memorial Award, ACRL/ ALCTS/LAMA/LITA (interdivisional)

To honor the life and accomplishments of Hugh C. Atkinson, and to recognize outstanding accomplishments of an academic librarian who has worked in the areas of library automation or library management and has made contributions (including risk taking) toward the improvement of library services or to library development or research. The award is jointly sponsored by the Association of College and Research Libraries (ACRL), the Library Administration and Management Association (LAMA), the Library and Information Technology Association (LITA), and the Association for Library Collections and Technical Services (ALCTS) and is funded by an endowment created by divisional, individual, and vendor contributions given in memory of Hugh C. Atkinson.

Ch., Nancy R. McAdams (1993); Willis M. Hubbard (1994); Thomas W. Leonhardt (1995); William Gray Potter (1996); staff liaison: Mary Taylor.

Audiovisual

To provide assistance in the planning, selection and use of audiovisual materials, technologies and services; to encourage cooperation with other committees and associations as appropriate; to further cooperation between audiovisual specialists and librarians in the academic environment; to promote the use of audiovisual materials as a resource for, as well as an appropriate topic for, scholarly research.

Ch., Imogene I. Book (1994); Marianna R. Fitzgerald (1993); Martin Goldberg (1994); Gary P. Handman (1993); Dennis A. Norlin (1993); J. Fred Olive III (1993); Pal V. Rao (1994); Lorre B. Smith (1994); interns: Isaac S. Call (1993); Stephen D. Fitt (1993); staff liaison, Cathleen Bourdon.

Budget and Finance

(1) To submit a recommended budget for the ACRL division to the ACRL Board of Directors for action; (2) to submit a recommended budget for division publications, including *Choice*, to the ACRL Board of Directors for action; (3) to advise the ACRL Board of Directors on questions regarding the fiscal matters of the division or its publications.

Ch., Thomas M. Peischl (1994); Mignon S. Adams (1995); Camila A. Alire (1995); Anna Lou Ashby (1994); David R. Brink (1995); Charles Martell (1993); Neil J. McElroy (1994); Keith W. Russell (1994); Helen H. Spalding (1996); intern, William Miller (1993); ex officio: Althea H. Jenkins (1993); Thomas Kirk (1993).

"Choice" Editorial Board

The Board serves in an advisory capacity to the Editor and the Publisher on the *Choice* programs.

Ch., W. Lee Hisle (1994); George R. Graf (1993); Victoria L. Hanawalt (1994); Norma J. Hervey (1994); Norma G. Kobzina (1994); Gary B. Thompson (1994); Esther Williams (1994); Christine deVallet (1994); ex officio: Anne K. Beaubien (1993); Althea H. Jenkins (1993); Patricia E. Sabosik (1993); Karen S. Seibert (1994).

Colleagues

To seek out, develop and nurture relationships with private sector companies, corporations, agencies, organizations and groups interested in supporting ACRL's mission in fostering the profession of academic and research librarianship; to involve Colleagues in ACRL programs and projects; to link Colleagues with ACRL leadership and members for mutual benefit; to recognize Colleagues' support; and to coordinate the work of the committee with the ACRL office.

Ch., Helen H. Spalding (1993); Vita C. Balsino (1993); Pierre V. Burke (1993); A. Beverley Gass (1993); Helen E. Gbala (1993); William R. Mott (1993); Eleanor H. Pinkham (1993); staff liaison, Cathleen Bourdon.

"College & Research Libraries" Editorial Board

The Editorial Board serves in an advisory capacity to the editor on the contents of the journal issues, and board members form the core of referees, reviewing manuscripts submitted for possible publication.

Ch., Gloriana St. Clair (1993); Ross W. Atkinson (1993); Karyle S. Butcher (1993); Larry L. Hardesty (1993); Rod Henshaw (1993); Peter Hernon (1993); Irene B. Hoadley (1993); Margaret A. Holleman (1993); James G. Neal (1994); Larry R. Oberg (1993); Emma B. Perry (1993); Ruth J. Person (1993); Donald E. Riggs (1993); ex officio: Anne K. Beaubien (1993); Althea H. Jenkins (1993); Karen S. Seibert (1994); staff liaison, Mary Ellen Kyger Davis.

"College & Research Libraries News" Editorial Board

The Editorial Board serves in an advisory capacity to the editor on all policy matters concerning editorial content or format.

Ch., Jonathan D. Eldredge (1993); Zenaida Fernandez (1994); Irene M. Hoffman (1994); Willis M. Hubbard (1994); Robert S. Martin (1994); Pamela Snelson (1994); ex officio: Anne K. Beaubien (1993); Mary Ellen Kyger Davis (1993); Althea H. Jenkins (1993); Karen S. Seibert (1994); Gloriana St. Clair (1993).

Conference Program Planning— New Orleans, 1993

To plan for the ACRL Conference program for the year in which the chair is ACRL President; to

review and advise on section, committee, and discussion group conference program proposals; and to make recommendations to the ACRL Board concerning requests for funding and meeting space for conference programs.

Ch., Jacquelyn A. McCoy (1993); Mignon S. Adams (1993); Ceres B. Birkhead (1993); Ray P. Boylan (1993); Karen E. Cargille (1993); Jo Ann Carr (1993); Doris H. Clack (1993); Virginia L. Daley (1993); Maija M. Lutz (1993); Sharon B. Mader (1993); Gary L. Menges (1993); Molly F. Molloy (1993); Micheline C. Nilsen (1993); Colleen J. Power (1993); Derrie B. Roark (1993); Carolyn Robison (1993); Caroline J. Tibbetts (1993); staff liaison, Cathleen Bourdon.

Conference Program Planning—Miami, 1994

Ch., Thomas Kirk (1994); Noreen S. Alldredge (1994); Lori L. Arp (1994); Barbara J. Brown (1994); Kathryn L. Creely (1994); Jackie M. Dooley (1994); Katharine K. Elsasser (1994); Janet S. Fore (1994); Betty J. Glass (1994); Margaret A. Holleman (1994); Lynn B. LaBrake (1994); Madeleine M. Nichols (1994); Judith Segal (1994); Leena Siegelbaum (1994); James H. Spohrer (1994); Charles D. Spornick (1994); William C. Welburn (1994); staff liaison, Cathleen Bourdon.

Constitution and Bylaws

To study and review current policies and activities of ACRL in order to propose necessary revisions in the ACRL Constitution and Bylaws; to review the bylaws of ACRL units; to draft proposals for revision of the ACRL Constitution and Bylaws upon request of ACRL units, staff, and members; to monitor proposals and changes in the ALA Constitution and Bylaws and to alert ACRL if it may be affected.

Ch., Richard J. Wood (1994); Robert G. Anderl (1993); Nicholas C. Burckel (1994); Joseph J. Harzbecker (1994); William G. Jones (1994); Darlene P. Nichols (1993); Aline E. Soules (1994); interns: Richard Bradberry (1993); Shelley J. Heaton (1993); staff liaison, Cathleen Bourdon.

Copyright

To elicit the concerns of ACRL members on copyright and gather information about copyright issues that impinge upon academic libraries; to bring before the ACRL Board issues and problems that may require legal action or interpretation on the part of ACRL; to represent ACRL when necessary in forums about copyright; to work with and appoint liaisons to ACRL Government Relations Committee, ALA's Copyright Subcommittee, and, when appropriate, other library or education copyright organizations.

Ch., Kristine R. Brancolini (1993); Sarah E. Cox-Byrne (1994); Dennis East (1993); Neil J. McElroy (1994); Derrie B. Roark (1993); Catherine E. Welsh (1993); interns: Dennis A. Norlin (1993); Richard N. Shaw (1993); staff liaison, Mary Ellen Kyger Davis.

Doctoral Dissertation Fellowship

To select a doctoral student in the field of academic librarianship whose research indicates originality, creativity, and interest in scholarship. The purpose of the fellowship is to foster re-

search by encouraging and assisting doctoral students with dissertation research.

Ch., Roger W. Durbin (1993); Richard C. Dickey (1994); Gabriele Divay (1993); Tamara U. Frost-Trujillo (1994); Abigail M. Studdiford (1993); Michael C. Walker (1994); interns: Johnny L. Johnson (1993); Lawrence J. McCrank (1993); staff liaison, Mary Taylor.

Government Relations

To take a direct and active role in formulating objectives and in planning and coordinating support for legislative action at the national level which may affect the welfare of academic and research libraries.

Ch., Katherine F. Mawdsley (1993); vice-ch., Carol Burroughs Hammond (1994); David W. Bretthauer (1993); Meredith Gillette (1993); Joan L. Heath (1993); Timothy D. Jewell (1994); George T. Johnson (1994); Kerry A. Keck (1994); Nancy M. Koller (1993); Lynn W. Livingston (1993); Henry N. Mendelsohn (1993); Gretchen H. Neill (1993); Connie E. Salyers (1994); Patricia A. Wand (1994); interns: Dolores Blythe Jones (1993); Birdie O. Weir (1993); staff liaison, Althea H. Jenkins.

Image (task force)

To identify ways ACRL represents the role of the academic librarian, and to provide suggestions for enhancing the presentation of role, particularly as it relates to recruiting talented people to librarianship. Final report due at the 1993 ALA Annual Conference.

Ch., Pamela J. Cravey (1993); Sheila A. Delacroix (1993); Rhonda A. Rios Kravitz (1993); Gary M. Pitkin (1993); Sarah Barbara Watstein (1993); Marilyn P. Whitmore (1993).

International Relations

To encourage international cooperation and understanding among academic librarians and educators concerned with academic libraries, to advise the ALA International Relations Committee (IRC) on academic library concerns, to carry out international academic library activities recommended by the ALA/IRC and the ACRL Board, to coordinate the international relations activities of ACRL, and to improve communications regarding these activities.

Ch., Maureen D. Pastine (1994); Charles William Conaway (1993); David L. Easterbrook (1994); Diane K. Harvey (1993); Martin A. Kesselman (1994); Amy Lewontin (1993); D. E. Perushek (1993); Donna Taxco Tang (1993); Craig A. Wilson (1994); Sandra da Conturbia (1994); interns: Talbott W. Huey (1993); Emilie Ngo-Nguidjol (1993); Kristin D. Vogel (1993); staff liaison, Cathleen Bourdon.

Intellectual Freedom (task force)

To read and analyze documents on intellectual freedom and make recommendations to the Board. To identify and recommend action on issues of intellectual freedom in higher education. To recommend how the association should (or should not) respond to "political correctness". To recommend if the association should establish a standing committee on intellectual freedom. Final report due to the Board in June 1994.

Ch., Judy Gibson Noyes (1994); Noreen S. Alldredge (1994); Charles E. Beard (1994); Ellen

Johnson (1994); Nancy H. Marshall (1994); Arthuree R. M. Wright (1994); staff liaison, Cathleen Bourdon.

(Samuel) Lazerow Fellowship for Research in Acquisitions or Technical Services

To foster advances in acquisitions or technical services by providing a fellowship for research, travel, or writing to a librarian currently working in acquisitions or technical services in an academic or research library.

Ch., Betty Landesman (1993); Julia A. Gammon (1993); Betty J. Glass (1993); Dalia Lapatinskas Hagan (1994); Richard E. Sapon-White (1993); Laverna M. Saunders (1994); intern, Judy Jeng (1993); staff liaison, Mary Taylor.

Membership

To propose directions, strategies, and programs for recruiting and retaining members; to serve as a link between ACRL and local chapters by coordinating membership promotional efforts and disseminating information; to advise ACRL staff on the implementation of membership policies and recruitment activities.

Ch., Andrea C. Hoffman (1993); Rick J. Block (1994); Starla G. Doescher (1994); Mary Ann Griffin (1994); John C. Hepner (1994); Betsy N. Hine (1993); Margaret C. Landrum (1994); Arlene E. Luchsinger (1994); Laura M. Osegueda (1994); Elaine Peterson (1994); Linda J. Piele (1994); Brenda D. Sloan (1994); Phoebe Timberlake (1993); Eveline L. Yang (1993); interns: Ellie E. Marsh (1993); Susanna J. Turner (1993); staff liaison, Cathleen Bourdon.

"MLA Bibliography" Scope and Overlap

To identify subject areas in which the *MLA Bibliography* replicates bibliographic coverage provided by other, similar reference sources, and to identify those sources, as well as to identify subject areas within the defined scope of the *MLA Bibliography* which are not being adequately covered, either within the *Bibliography* or elsewhere. The information provided by this analysis process will be used by the Modern Language Association to help ensure an allocation of bibliographic resources that will best serve the needs of humanities scholars in the coming years.

Ch., Elaine A. Franco (1993).

New Publications Advisory Board

To encourage research, writing, and nonprint media production that may be appropriate for a separately published title by ACRL; to solicit topics and, without guarantee of publication, to suggest them to appropriate authors; to review all manuscripts/materials submitted for possible publication as a separate ACRL-published title; to serve as an advisory body to the ACRL publications officer.

Ch., Eleanor H. Pinkham (1995); Brian E. Coutts (1995); Cynthia S. Faries (1995); A. Beverley Gass (1993); Paula Murphy (1993); Lorelei A. Tanji (1995); ex officio: Anne K. Beaubien (1993); Althea H. Jenkins (1993); Jonathan A. Lindsey (1993); Karen S. Seibert (1994); Mary Taylor (1993).

Orientation

To plan the Annual Conference orientation program for new officers and chairs.

Ch., Anne K. Beaubien (1993); Melvin R. George (1993); Claudette S. Hagle (1993); Michael D. Kathman (1993); Marilyn M. McDonald (1993); Rochelle Sager (1993); Helen H. Spalding (1993); staff liaison, Cathleen Bourdon.

Planning

To develop and ensure implementation of plans and strategies that will help the Association achieve its goals and objectives.

Ch., Mary Sue Ferrell (1993); Meredith A. Butler (1993); Larry L. Hardesty (1994); Kriza A. Jennings (1995); William L. Joyce (1993); Carol M. Kelley (1993); Sandra S. Kerbel (1993); William J. Pfannenstiel (1993); Sandra Ready (1995); David B. Walch (1995); interns: Susan S. Baughman (1993); Elinor F. Bridges (1993); ex officio: Anne K. Beaubien (1993); Thomas Kirk (1995); Jacquelyn A. McCoy (1994); staff liaison, Cathleen Bourdon.

President's Program Planning— New Orleans, 1993

Ch., Jordan M. Scepanski (1993); Hiram L. Davis (1993); Joanne R. Euster (1993); Charles Martell (1993); Barbara B. Moran (1993); Barbara J. Wittkopf (1993); staff liaison, Althea H. Jenkins.

President's Program Planning—Miami, 1994

Ch. and members to be appointed; staff liaison, Althea H. Jenkins.

Professional Education

To promote the professional competence, growth, and development of academic librarians through the educational process.

Ch., Rochelle R. Ballard (1994); Lorene B. Brown (1994); Deborah A. Carver (1994); Victoria L. Hanawalt (1993); M. Charlotte Hess (1993); Richard E. Sapon-White (1994); interns: Allison V. Level (1993); Cynthia L. Shamel (1993); staff liaison, Cathleen Bourdon.

Professional Liaison

To coordinate, recommend the budget for, and oversee the activities of designated liaisons to target associations and in support of individuals working with other professional associations. To identify and promote strong relationships between libraries and institutional, administrative, research, and instructional units. To cooperate with other ACRL committees on related projects.

Ch., Barbara J. Ford (1994); Noreen S. Alldredge (1994); Anne Marie Allison (1994); Susan M. Anderson (1993); Bradley F. Baker (1993); Elaine K. Didier (1993); Jean A. Major (1994); William Miller (1994); interns: Rhea Bradley (1993); Elaine M. Coppola (1993); staff liaison, Cathleen Bourdon.

Publications

To oversee and coordinate all publications of ACRL; to consider suggestions for publications and to advise as to means of publishing; to maintain standards; to review the work of the various publications and their boards; and to stimulate and encourage research and writing which might lead to publication under ACRL auspices.

Ch., Karen S. Seibert (1994); Betty K. Bryce (1993); Jennifer Cargill (1993); Brian E. Coutts (1994); Suzanne H. Freeman (1993); A. Bev-

erley Gass (1993); Margaret A. Holleman (1994); David U. Kim (1994); Richard Hume Werking (1994); interns: Naomi J. Lederer (1993); Helene C. Williams (1993); ex officio: Mary Ellen Kyger Davis (1993); Jonathan A. Lindsey (1993); Patricia E. Sabosik (1993); Gloriana St. Clair (1993); staff liaison, Mary Taylor.

Publications (task force)

To plan the future direction of the ACRL Publishing Program including *Choice*. Report due at Midwinter Meeting, 1993.

Ch., Michael D. Kathman (1993); Christine DeVallet (1993); Larry L. Hardesty (1993); Leslie A. Manning (1993); Pamela Snelson (1993); ex officio: Patricia E. Sabosik; Mary Taylor; Mary Ellen Kyger Davis.

Racial and Ethnic Diversity

To initiate, advise and mobilize support for appropriate action related to issues of racial and ethnic diversity in academic librarianship including the recruitment, advancement and retention of underrepresented groups to academic librarianship and the promotion of quality academic library and information services for members of racial and ethnic groups.

Ch., Susana A. Hinojosa (1994); Deborah Abston (1994); Gladys Chaw (1994); Em Claire Knowles (1993); Ichiko T. Morita (1993); Joan G. Rapp (1993); Samson C. Soong (1994); Vivian M. Sykes (1994); William C. Welborn (1994); interns: Indra M. David (1993); Rhonda A. Rios Kravitz (1993); staff liaison, Cathleen Bourdon.

"Rare Books and Manuscripts Librarianship" Editorial Board

Ed. and ch., Alice D. Schreyer (1993); Sidney E. Berger (1995); James N. Green (1993); Ann S. Gwyn (1993); Eleanor H. Pinkham (1994); Michael T. Ryan (1993); Larry E. Sullivan (1994); Daniel H. Traister (1993); ex officio, Anne K. Beaubien (1993); Althea H. Jenkins (1993); Karen S. Seibert (1994); staff liaison, Mary Ellen Kyger Davis.

Research

To explore, develop, and promote a research agenda which focuses on the current and future research needs of academic/research libraries and of the association; to develop programs and other activities which will assist in the accomplishment of the needed research; to develop activities and programs to encourage improvement in research skills among academic/research librarians.

Ch., Vicki Gregory (1993); Sara J. Clausen (1993); Deborah C. Greene (1993); Sharad Karkhanis (1993); Thomas A. Peters (1993); Maxine H. Reneker (1993); Patricia E. Renfro (1993); R. N. Sharma (1993); Michael V. Sullivan (1993); interns: George V. Hodowanec (1993); Elizabeth S. Smith (1993); staff liaison, Mary Taylor.

(K. G.) Saur Award for Best "College and Research Libraries" Article

To recognize and reward the most outstanding article published in *College and Research Libraries* (C&RL) during the preceding volume year.

Ch., Anne Woodsworth (1993); William Baker (1993); D. Whitney Coe (1993); Diane E. Murray (1993); James F. Williams II (1994); staff liaison, Mary Taylor.

Social Issues (task force)

To prepare a set of recommendations to guide ACRL on response (or nonresponse) to social issues. Recommendations will be made to the ACRL Board at the 1993 ALA Annual Conference.

Ch., Cerise Oberman (1993); Bonnie Jackson Clemens (1993); Pamela J. Cravey (1993); Sallie H. Ellison (1993); Betsy N. Hine (1993); Nancy Bird Luikart (1993); Robert S. Martin (1993); Carol A. Rudisell (1993); staff liaison, Cathleen Bourdon.

Standards and Accreditation

To direct the development of standards and guidelines adopted and promoted by the Association, and to establish and maintain appropriate liaisons with accrediting agencies and other organizations that monitor and evaluate the performance of academic libraries.

Ch., Lynn K. Chmelir (1993); William L. Cohn (1994); Carolyn Dusenbury (1994); V. Sue Hatfield (1994); W. Lee Hisle (1994); Barton M. Lessin (1994); Diane C. Parker (1994); Janice Lucas Peyton (1994); Norma N. Yueh (1994); interns: Louise S. Sherby (1993); Donald G. Sweet (1993); staff liaison, Mary Taylor.

Vocational Interest Inventories (task force)

To update and improve the librarian profile in standard vocational interest inventory tests such as Strong and SIGI+. Final report due at the 1993 ALA Annual Conference.

Ch., Mary Jane Scherdin (1993); Sheila A. Delacroix (1993); Deborah J. Grimes (1993); Carol G. Henderson (1993); Susan R. Jurow (1993); Sandra J. Pfahler (1993); Maureen Sullivan (1993).

REPRESENTATIVES

ALA Com. on Appointments—Thomas Kirk.
ALA Com. on Professional Ethics—Lorene B. Brown (1993).
ALA Conference Program Planning Com. (New Orleans, 1993)—Jacquelyn A. McCoy.
ALA Conf. Program Planning (Miami, 1994)—Thomas Kirk.
ALA Legislation Assembly—Katherine F. Mawdsley (1993).
ALA Literacy Assembly—Trish Ridgeway (1993).
ALA Membership Promotion Task Force—Andrea C. Hoffman (1993).
ALA Planning and Budget Assembly—Jacquelyn A. McCoy.
ALA Standing Com. on Library Education (SCOLE)—Larry R. Oberg (1993); Patsy Haley Stann (1993); Rochelle R. Ballard (1994).
ALCTS Com. on Cataloging: Description and Access—Norma H. Martin (1994).
Amer. Assn. for Higher Education—to be appointed.
Amer. Assn. for the Advancement of Science—to be appointed.
Amer. Assn. of University Professors—to be appointed.
Amer. Chemical Society—Arleen N. Somerville (1993).
Amer. Council on Education—to be appointed.

ASCLA L. Serv. to People Who Are Mentally Ill—Dennis A. Norlin.
Assn. for Asian Studies, Com. on East Asian Ls.—to be appointed.
Assn. of American Colleges—to be appointed.
Coalition of Networked Information—Thomas Kirk (1993), Noreen S. Aldredge (1993).
Consortium of Affiliates for International Programs—to be appointed.
Freedom to Read Fdn.—to be appointed.
LC Cataloging in Publication Advisory Group—Robert P. Holley (1993).
Modern Language Assn.—to be appointed.
National Forum on Information Literacy—Barbara J. Ford (1993).

SECTIONS

Afro-American Studies Librarians (AFAS)
Anthropology and Sociology (ANSS)
Arts (ARTS)
Asian and African (AAS)
Bibliographic Instruction (BIS)
College Libraries (CLS)
Community and Junior College Libraries (CJCLS)
Education and Behavioral Sciences (EBSS)
Extended Campus Library Services (ECLSS)
Law and Political Science (LPSS)
Rare Books and Manuscripts (RBMS)
Science and Technology (STS)
Slavic and East European (SEES)
University Libraries (ULS)
Western European Specialists (WESS)
Women's Studies Section (WSS)

Activity Sections Council (ASC)

Consists of two of the three officers of chair, vice-chair/chair-elect, or past chair of each ACRL type-of-activity section as designated by the section.

Ch., Robert B. Marks Ridinger (1993); secy., Micheline C. Nilsen (1994); staff liaison: Cathleen Bourdon.

Afro-American Studies Librarians Section (AFAS)

To study librarianship and collection development as it progresses and relates to the Afro-American Studies collection; to conduct an ongoing evaluation and discussion of research in the area of Afro-American Studies collections; to focus on areas such as resource sharing, archival materials, bibliographic control, retrospective collecting/purchasing, mechanized information, retrieval selection policies and procedures, oral history, and others as they relate to collection development and librarianship of Afro-American Studies.

Executive Committee

Ch., Doris H. Clack (1994); ch.-elect, William C. Welburn (1995); secy., Joyce E. Jelks (1993); past ch., Stanton F. Biddle (1993); Rochelle R. Ballard (1994); Michael C. Walker (1994).

Newsletter ed., William C. Welburn (1993).

Committees

Conference Program Planning—New Orleans, 1993

Ch., Alma Dawson (1993); Emma B. Perry (1993); Lou Helen Sanders (1993).

Constitution and Bylaws

Ch., Michael C. Walker (1994); Marcelle Elaine Hughes (1993); Delores T. McCoy (1994); Mark G. R. McManus (1993); Marcellus Turner (1993).

Membership

Ch., Diana L. Brice (1994); Fred J. Hay (1994); Harry R. Murphy (1994); Clarence Toomer (1993); Dorothy A. Washington (1993).

Nominating (1993 Elections)

Ch., Rochelle R. Ballard (1993); Kathleen E. Bethel (1993); Belinda S. Daniels (1993).

Anthropology and Sociology Section (ANSS)

Represents librarians and specialists working in anthropology, sociology, and related fields.

Executive Committee

Ch., Maija M. Lutz (1994); ch.-elect, Kathryn L. Creely (1995); secy., Janet L. Steins (1993); past ch., Robert B. Marks Ridinger (1993); Pauline D. Manaka (1993); J. Christina Smith (1994).

Newsletter co-eds., Fred J. Hay (1994) and James Williams (1992).

Liaison

ACRL Board—Lynne M. Schmelz-Keil.

Committees

Bibliography

To review and analyze the current state of bibliographic control of publications in anthropology and sociology; to identify specific areas needing improved bibliographic control; to communicate these needs to publishers and make recommendations for improvements; to disseminate information about the bibliography of these fields to the section membership.

Ch., David E. Carpenter (1994); Myra Anderson (1994); Joan R. Berman (1993); Shari T. Grove (1994); Brenda W. McCallum (1993); Cheryl Terrass Naslund (1994); Ellen D. Sutton (1993); Noel D. Young (1994).

Conference Program Planning—New Orleans, 1993

Ch., Margaret R. Dittemore (1993); Helen E. Ives (1993); Isabel del Carmen Quintana (1993); Alice Reviere Smith (1993).

Conference Program Planning—Miami, 1994

Ch. and members to be appointed.

Liaison

To identify organizations and professional bodies active in the fields of anthropology, sociology and affiliated fields of the social sciences that issue publications; to contact these groups and maintain communications about their information needs and publications.

Ch., Fred J. Hay (1993); Gregory A. Finnegan (1993); J. Christina Smith (1993).

Nominating (1993 Elections)

Ch., Janet L. Steins (1994); David Lonergan (1994); Ann L. Wood (1994).

Nominating (1994 Elections)

Ch. and members to be appointed.

Publications

To serve as the editorial board of the section newsletter, *ANSS Currents,* and to consider other publication projects and needs.

Ch., James Williams (1994); Fred J. Hay (1994); David M. Hovde (1994); Irene W. Hurlbert (1994); Stephen E. MacLeod (1994); Ellie E. Marsh (1994); Nancy S. Skipper (1993); Gary B. Thompson (1994).

Review and Planning

To prepare the regularly scheduled review of the Section mandated by ACRL, and to review and make recommendations regarding the Section's goals, future directions, policies and procedures.

Ch., Robert B. Marks Ridinger (1993); Kathryn L. Creely (1995); Lynne M. Schmelz-Keil (1993); Janet L. Steins (1993); ex officio: Maija M. Lutz (1994).

Discussion Group

Anthropology Librarians

Co-convenors, Gregory A. Finnegan (1993) and Nancy S. Skipper (1993).

Sociology Librarians

Ch., Irene W. Hurlbert (1993).

Arts Section (ARTS)

Represents librarians and specialists working in or interested in the field of visual arts and performing arts; provides an umbrella organization for the promotion of library service in this field through discussion of problems, exchange of information, and the carrying out of suitable projects.

Executive Committee

Ch., Micheline C. Nilsen (1994); ch.-elect, Madeleine M. Nichols (1995); secy., Carolyn A. Sheehy (1993); past ch., Kim N. Fisher (1993).

Newsletter ed., Betty K. Bryce (1994).

Committees

Bylaws Revision (ad hoc)

Ch., Roland C. Hansen (1994); Stephen C. Bloom (1994); Kim N. Fisher (1994).

Conference Program Planning—New Orleans, 1993

Co-chs., Rhea Bradley (1993) and Judy Harvey Sahak (1993); Bonnie Biggs (1993); Betty K. Bryce (1993); Sandra Mooney (1993); Sheryl R. Moore (1993); Lynn Barstis Williams (1993); ex officio, Micheline C. Nilsen (1993).

Conference Program Planning—Miami, 1994

Ch. and members to be appointed.

Government and Private Sector Activities

To monitor government and private sector activities that influence arts librarianship in all areas including grant funding and legislation.

Ch., William F. Coscarelli (1994); Joan F. Cheverie (1994); Paula L. Epstein (1994); Stephen Allan Patrick (1993); Marsha J. Stevenson (1993); Christine A. Whittington (1994); Janice Woo (1994).

Membership

Ch., Bonnie Biggs (1994); Paula L. Epstein (1994); Ann L. Jones (1994); Gina R. Overcash (1994); Donald G. Sweet (1994); Lorelei A. Tanji (1994); Elizabeth L. Townsend (1994).

Nominating (1993 Elections)

Ch., Stephen Allan Patrick (1993); Mary S. Bopp (1993); JoAn D. Kunselman (1993).

Nominating (1994 Elections)

Ch. and members to be appointed.

Planning

Ch., Stephen C. Bloom (1994); Allen Cohen (1994); Paula Murphy (1994); Judy Harvey Sahak (1994); Timothy Shipe (1994); Charles R. Smith (1994).

Publications

To coordinate all publications associated with the section and to serve as an advisory unit to the Executive Committee. The Committee shall identify publication needs; stimulate research and writing; and oversee development and production of the *Arts Newsletter* and selected projects.

Ch., Betty K. Bryce (1994); Suzanne H. Freeman (1994); Elizabeth A. Ginno (1994); Roland C. Hansen (1994); Alice N. Loranth (1994); David P. Malone (1994); Carolyn A. Sheehy (1994); Jane E. Sloan (1994); Peggy Warren-Wenk (1994); Lynn Barstis Williams (1994).

Consultants List (subcommittee)

Ch., Carolyn A. Sheehy (1994); Alice N. Loranth (1994); Peggy Warren-Wenk (1994).

Technology in the Arts

To keep informed of uses of technology in libraries and archives which provide information or collect materials on the visual and performing arts.

Co-chs., Howard Besser (1993) and Henry J. DuBois (1994); Frederick B. Gardner (1994); Deborah C. Greene (1994); Kimberly A. Hale (1994); Brigitte J. Kueppers (1994); Vickie E. Mick (1994); Karl F. Miller (1994); Madeleine M. Nichols (1994); Loanne L. Snavely (1994); Lynn Barstis Williams (1993).

Discussion Group

Dance Librarians

Ch., Mary S. Bopp (1993).

Asian and African Section (AAS)

Represents librarians and specialists in the fields of Asian and African area studies and acts for ACRL, in cooperation with other professional groups, in those areas of library service that require knowledge of Asian and African languages and cultures.

Executive Committee

Ch., Ray P. Boylan (1994); ch.-elect, Katharine K. Elsasser (1995); secy., Elise L. Chin (1993);

past ch., Merry L. Burlingham (1993); Gregory A. Finnegan (1993); Christine H. Guyonneau (1993); Donald Clay Johnson (1994).

Bibliographic Instruction Section (BIS)

To foster the profession of academic and research librarianship and to enhance the ability of academic and research bibliographic instruction librarians to serve effectively the library and information needs of current and potential library users.

Executive Committee

Ch., Sharon B. Mader (1994); ch.-elect, Lori L. Arp (1995); secy., Beth S. Woodard (1993); past ch., Mary Ellen Litzinger (1993); Claudette S. Hagle (1993); Linda S. Muroi (1994); Margaret R. Wells (1995).

Newsletter ed., Bee Gallegos (1994).

Committees

Advisory Council

Composed of the Executive Committee and Chair of each BIS committee; to provide coordination of section activities, communication between committees, and advice to the Executive Committee.

Ch., Sharon B. Mader (1994); Lori L. Arp (1995); Katherine Anne Branch (1993); Luella Davis (1993); Ree DeDonato (1993); Karen E. Downing (1993); Bee H. Gallegos (1994); Esther S. Grassian (1993); Bonnie G. Gratch (1993); Claudette S. Hagle (1993); Randall B. Hensley (1993); Susan J. Hoffman (1993); Mary Ellen Litzinger (1993); Abigail A. Loomis (1993); Sandra A. Martin (1993); Linda S. Muroi (1994); Elizabeth H. Park (1993); Sara Penhale (1993); Mary J. Petrowski (1993); Kathy Pletcher (1993); Lynn E. Randall (1993); Harvey M. Sager (1993); Margaret R. Wells (1995); Beth S. Woodward (1993); Diane M. Zabel (1994).

Awards

Ch., Mary Ellen Litzinger (1993); Patricia D. Arnott (1993); Ellen Broidy (1994); Carolyn Dusenbury (1993); Denise D. Green (1993); Barbara A. MacAdam (1994); Sharon B. Mader (1993); Phyllis L. Ruscella (1993); Ann S. Waggoner (1994); Karen A. Williams (1994); intern, Ann Pederson (1993).

Communication

To facilitate communication of information about the section and its activities to members through a newsletter; to produce annually a handbook as a resource for officers and committee members; to conduct regular orientation activities for prospective or new committee members; and to pursue other appropriate channels of communication outside as well as within the section.

Ch., Sara Penhale (1993); Jo Ann Calzonetti (1993); Leslie J. Canterbury (1994); Marilyn A. Grant (1994); Ann S. Masnik (1993); Elizabeth B. Nibley (1993); Nancy Shepard (1993); David Voros (1994); Carol Z. Womack (1994); intern, Kristin D. Vogel (1993); ex officio, Bee H. Gallegos (1994).

Conference Program Planning—New Orleans, 1993

Ch., Elizabeth H. Park (1993); Madeline A. Copp (1993); Susan G. Miller (1993); Robert F. Rose

(1993); N. Janell Rudolph (1993); Carol A. Wright (1993).

Conference Program Planning—Miami, 1994

Ch. and members to be appointed.

Continuing Education

To provide and promote continuing education in the area of academic bibliographic instruction in conjunction with annual conferences and on an ongoing basis; to investigate new technologies for providing continuing education to the widest possible audience; and to suggest and encourage continuing education activities in academic bibliographic instruction.

Ch., Diane M. Zabel (1994); Barbara E. Beaton (1994); Susan E. Clark (1994); Madeline A. Copp (1993); Rebecca D. Dixon (1994); Bee H. Gallegos (1993); Lynn M. Klekowski (1994); Naomi J. Lederer (1993); Michael D. Muchow (1993); Jill Newby (1993); Susan M. Norrisey (1994); Bonnie Osif (1993); Catherine S. Palmer (1993); Jennifer L. Sturgis (1993); William R. Taylor (1994); Deborah G. Tenofsky (1993); Claibourne George Williams (1994); Charlene C. York (1993); intern, Judith M. Arnold (1993).

Education for Bibliographic Instruction

To explore, encourage, and foster the development and expansion of the study of bibliographic instruction in library schools; to promote communication between librarians working in the area of bibliographic instruction and library schools; and to survey and report to the Executive Committee on the status of library education in bibliographic instruction.

Ch., Elizabeth H. Park (1993); Christine C. Avery (1994); Shirley R. Black (1993); Cathryn M. Canelas (1993); Elizabeth A. Frick (1993); Esther S. Grassian (1994); Jessica Grim (1993); Sheila S. Intner (1993); Trudi E. Jacobson (1994); Craig A. Mulder (1993); Marcella L. Stark (1994); Nancy L. Taylor (1993); intern, Kevin G. Ketchner (1993).

Emerging Technologies in Instruction

To promote and facilitate the use of emerging technologies in bibliographic instruction; to act as a resource and information-sharing vehicle for those who use electronic technologies in bibliographic instruction. Principal areas of interest include new or innovative applications of these technologies in bibliographic instruction.

Ch., Harvey M. Sager (1993); Maureen S. Connors (1993); Lee B. Dalzell (1994); Linda G. DeFato (1994); William P. Kane (1994); Cheryl M. LaGuardia (1994); Daniel R. Lee (1993); Amy Lewontin (1993); Marcia J. Martin (1994); Molly E. Molloy (1993); Marilyn G. Naito (1993); Judith M. Pask (1993); Carol A. Wright (1993); intern, Mark E. Andersen (1993).

Evaluating BI Handbook (task force)

Ch., Lynn E. Randall (1993); Valerie J. Feinman (1993); Monica G. Fusich (1993); Sandra Ready (1993); Diana D. Shonrock (1993); Karen A. Williams (1993).

Guidelines for BI (task force)

To review the "Guidelines for BI" and recommend whether they should be withdrawn.

Ch., Susan J. Hoffman (1993); Mary Ellen Bobp (1993); Ree DeDonato (1993); Irene W. Hurlbert (1993); Linda L. Parker (1993).

Instruction for Diverse Populations

To identify, study, and promote issues relating to bibliographic instruction and diversity, including but not limited to issues of gender, age, cultural background, race, ethnicity, disability, and sexual orientation; to promote equal access to instructional services, materials, and technology regardless of individual differences.

Ch., Karen E. Downing (1993); Mary Beth Allen (1993); Marcelle Elaine Hughes (1993); Poping Lin (1993); Lisa Melendez (1994); Dennis A. Norlin (1993); Jennie Saisakorn Sandberg (1994); Kwasi Sarkodie-Mensah (1993); Benjamin T. Wakashige (1994); intern, Karen M. Beavers (1993).

Management of Bibliographic Instruction Services

To identify and study issues relating to the management of bibliographic instruction services; to act as a resource and information-sharing vehicle for those who administer bibliographic instruction programs; to facilitate and encourage improvement in the management and evaluation of bibliographic instruction services.

Ch., Abigail A. Loomis (1993); Susan Broyles (1993); Marsha Forys (1993); Paul A. Frisch (1994); Rebecca Jackson (1993); Scott B. Mandernack (1994); Nancy Newins (1993); Kristin R. Ramsdell (1993); intern, Cheryl C. Albrecht (1993).

Nominating (1993 Elections)

Ch., Ree DeDonato (1993); Carolyn Dusenbury (1993); Cerise Oberman (1993).

Nominating (1994 Elections)

Ch. and members to be appointed.

Planning

To assist the BIS Executive Committee in the development of the BIS Strategic Plan; to facilitate the planning process, including committee reviews; and to monitor and extend the ongoing BIS plan within the framework of the ACRL Strategic Plan and the continuing interests of the section.

Ch., Sandra A. Martin (1993); Alison H. Armstrong (1994); Suzanne M. Byron (1994); Barbara M. Conant (1994); Linda J. Durfee (1993); Jack Forman (1993); J. David Martin (1993); Barbara R. Stevens (1994); intern, Kay M. Nagel (1993).

Policy

To advise the Executive Committee concerning policy and procedures for the section; to identify and suggest policy issues affecting the section that the Executive Committee should address; to respond to requests from the Executive Committee in regard to policies, procedures, issues and publications affecting the section; and to review bylaws and committee charges periodically, or as requested, to ensure that they reflect the aims and activities of the section.

Ch., Mary J. Petrowski (1993); Marilee Birchfield (1993); Evelyn Brass (1993); H. Scott Davis (1993); Margaret L. Fast (1994); Martin

Goldberg (1993); Carolyn A. Meanley (1993); Carl D. Phillips (1994); Linda Sharp (1994); Georgann K. Shaw (1994); Sister Anita Talar (1993); intern, Mari Ellen Leverence (1993).

Sourcebook for Bibliographic Instruction (task force)

To serve as the editorial board for the proposed publication *Sourcebook for Bibliographic Instruction.*

Ch., Katherine Anne Branch (1993); Barbara M. Conant (1993); Cynthia H. Roberts (1993); Kimberly Spyers-Duran (1993).

Strategic Options for Professional Education (ad hoc task force)

To investigate and identify strategic options, such as certification, which may influence and/or encourage library schools and employers to offer and develop education and continuing education for bibliographic instruction; to make recommendations to the Executive Committee on their facility and political usefulness for the Section in influencing library schools and employers; and to recommend a process of implementation within the Section.

Ch., Esther S. Grassian (1993); Elizabeth A. Frick (1993); Abigail A. Loomis (1993); Diane M. Zabel (1993).

Teaching Methods

To identify and promote teaching methods and materials useful to practicing bibliographic instruction librarians; to provide a forum for librarians interested in both the theoretical and practical aspects of teaching methods and the broader issues of instructional design and delivery.

Ch., Randall B. Hensley (1993); Andrea M. Bartelstein (1993); Catherine Gale Burrow (1994); Jody L. Caldwell (1993); Cynthia S. Faries (1993); Stanley D. Nash (1994); William A. Orme (1994); Holly D. Rogerson (1993); Loanne L. Snavely (1993); Alphonse N. Vinh (1993); Margaret R. Wells (1994); intern, Elizabeth S. Smith (1993).

College Libraries Section (CLS)

To advance college librarianship and the development of library service in four-year undergraduate institutions.

Executive Committee

Ch., Mignon S. Adams (1994); ch.-elect, Barbara J. Brown (1995); secy., Michael J. LaCroix (1993); past ch., Mary Lee Sweat (1993); Mary K. Sellen (1994); Pamela Snelson (1994).

Newsletter ed., Jonathan D. Lauer (1993).

Liaisons

ACRL Academic Status Com.—Larry R. Oberg (1993).
ACRL Government Relations Com.—Sarah Pedersen (1993).
ACRL Racial and Ethnic Diversity Com.—Sarah Pedersen (1993).
ACRL Standards and Accreditation Com.—Lynn K. Chmelir (1993).

Committees

CLIP Notes

To oversee the CLIP Notes program (College Libraries Information Packet), an ongoing publication.

Ch., James R. Cubit (1993); Patricia S. Butcher (1993); Andrea C. Hoffman (1994); Lawrie H. Merz (1993); Allen S. Morrill (1994); Karen A. Nuckolls (1994); intern, Carol Goodson (1993).

College Library Leadership (ad hoc)

Ch., Larry L. Hardesty (1993); Caroline M. Coughlin (1993); Evan Ira Farber (1993); Bart M. Harloe (1993); Mary K. Sellen (1993); Carolyn A. Sheehy (1993).

Conference Program Planning—New Orleans, 1993

Ch., John G. Jaffe (1993); Pauline W. Lee (1993); Evelyn C. Minick (1993); Darla H. Rushing (1993); Gary B. Thompson (1993).

Conference Program Planning—Miami, 1994

Ch. and members to be appointed.

Continuing Education (ad hoc)

Ch., Victoria A. Montavon (1994); Rebecca D. Dixon (1994); Lee C. Ketcham (1994); Lynn W. Livingston (1994); Susan L. Myers (1994).

Fringe Benefits Study (ad hoc)

To continue the work of the Real Income Committee in regard to non-compensation fringe benefits for college librarians. The committee will work in close cooperation with the ACRL Academic Status Committee.

Ch., Larry J. Frye (1993); Sue A. Burkholder (1993); B. Anne Commerton (1993); William R. Delzell (1993); Walter D. Morrill (1993).

Medium-sized Academic Libraries (ad hoc)

Ch., David B. Walch (1994); E. Dale Cluff (1994); Ralph E. Russell (1994).

National Advisory Council

Ch., Elizabeth W. Kaschins (1993); Robin Paul Benke (1993); Alan D. Boyd (1993); Kristina C. Brockmeier (1993); Helen G. Guenter (1993); Dene L. Clark (1993); Susan L. Craig (1993); Victoria L. Hanawalt (1993); Kathleen M. Hays (1993); Jack King (1993); Walter D. Morrill (1993); Karen A. Nuckolls (1993); Larry R. Oberg (1993); Lynn E. Randall (1993); Stuart P. Stelzer (1993); Ronelle K. H. Thompson (1993); Paul Vincent (1993); Myra J. Wilson (1993); Joan H. Worley (1993).

Newsletter

Ch., Jonathan D. Lauer (1993); Robin Paul Benke (1993); Norma J. Hervey (1993); Damon D. Hickey (1993); John J. Montag (1994).

Nominating (1993 Elections)

Ch., Sarah Pedersen (1993); Michael D. Kathman (1993); Nancy L. Magnuson (1993); Judy Gibson Noyes (1993).

Nominating (1994 Elections)

Ch. and members to be appointed.

Planning

To ensure that the CLS Strategic Plan is responsive to the needs of the CLS membership; to monitor how CLS meets the established plan; to suggest additions or revisions to the plan; to ensure that the CLS Strategic Plan is consistent with the ACRL Strategic Plan; to suggest to other CLS committees how they can contribute to the fulfillment of the Strategic Plan; to complete the annual ACRL Strategic Planning Inventory; and to complete the Section's five-year review.

Ch., Mary K. Sellen (1993); Sherman L. Hayes (1993); Norma J. Hervey (1993); Soo Kyung Lee (1994); Eugene S. Mitchell (1993); Walter D. Morrill (1993); Edward D. Starkey (1993).

Recruiting for College Librarianship (ad hoc)

To investigate strategies that the section can use to promote recruiting for college librarianship and make recommendations to the CLS Executive Committee.

Ch., Jean W. Haley (1994); Indra M. David (1994); Claudette S. Hagle (1994); Neil J. McElroy (1994); Sandra Ready (1994).

Research and Publication on College Librarianship (ad hoc)

To investigate ways that the section can encourage research and publishing on college libraries and librarianship and make recommendations to the CLS Executive Committee.

Ch. and members to be appointed.

Standards

To monitor the implementations of the 1986 College Library Standards.

Ch., Diane C. Parker (1993); Barbara D. Bryan (1993); Paul Coleman (1994); Janice C. Fennell (1994); Dalia Lapatinskas Hagan (1993); Ada D. Jarred (1993); P. Grady Morein (1994); Norma N. Yueh (1993).

Discussion Group

College Library Directors

Co-chs., Susan McCarthy Campbell (1993) and Billy Pennington (1993).

College Science Librarians

Ch., Esther Williams (1994).

Community and Junior College Libraries Section (CJCLS)

To contribute to library service and librarianship through activities that relate to libraries and learning resource centers that support the educational programs in community and junior colleges and equivalent institutions.

Executive Committee

Ch., Derrie B. Roark (1994); ch.-elect, Margaret A. Holleman (1995); secy., Susan M. Anderson (1993); past ch., Paul E. Dumont (1993); arch., Rosemary Henderson (1993).

Newsletter ed., Rebecca Kiel (1994).

Committees

Awards

Ch., Paul E. Dumont (1993); Susan M. Anderson (1993); Susan M. Maltese (1994); Charles R. Peguese (1993); James O. Wallace (1994).

Bibliographic Instruction

Ch., Wanda K. Johnston (1993); Lynnette Anderson (1994); Theresa S. Byrd (1993); Karen

C. Desaulniers (1993); Karen D. Jessee (1993); M. Ann Miller (1994); Robert C. Myers (1993); Cynthia L. Shamel (1994); Cary L. Sowell (1994); Marcia Suter (1993); Julie B. Todaro (1993).

Book Review

Ch., Karen Fischer (1994); Karl B. Johnson (1994); Maryann Laun (1994); Dale F. Luchsinger (1994); Terri L. Propes (1994).

Conference Program Planning—New Orleans, 1993

Ch., Douglas K. Lehman (1993); Susan M. Anderson (1993); Isaac S. Call (1993); Steven W. Hagstrom (1993); Margaret C. Landrum (1993); Lenora C. Lockett (1993); J. Richard Madaus (1993); Derrie B. Roark (1994); Cary L. Sowell (1993).

Conference Program Planning—Miami, 1994

Ch. and members to be appointed.

Library Technology Training (ad hoc)

Ch., Marilyn M. McDonald (1994); David R. Dowell (1994); Karl B. Johnson (1994); Jimmie Anne Nourse (1994); Robert A. Veihman (1994); Rudy Widman (1994).

Literacy across the Curriculum

To keep abreast of literacy projects developed at community and junior colleges; to investigate and disseminate information about integrating library skills into literacy projects; to develop a network with literacy projects at public libraries, high schools and four-year colleges and universities with the intention of developing a model program for community and junior college LRCs.

Ch., Gregory Golden (1994); Imogene I. Book (1993); Lenora C. Lockett (1994).

Local Arrangements—New Orleans, 1993

Ch., Lenora C. Lockett (1993); Carol Craft (1993); Harolyn S. Cumlet (1993); Pamela Harton (1993); Denise C. Repman (1993); Pamela C. Straub (1993); Constance Varnado (1993); Genevieve S. Wheeler (1993).

Membership/Communications

To increase the personal membership of the Section and to encourage participation in the Section and ACRL. Also to form communication links for the Section and to distribute information relative to two-year college librarians and libraries.

Ch., William J. Pfannenstiel (1993); Steven W. Hagstrom (1994); Kate D. Hickey (1993); Derrie B. Roark (1994); Marcia Suter (1993).

Nominating (1993 Elections)

Ch., Lenora C. Lockett (1993); Carol G. Henderson (1993); Dale F. Luchsinger (1993); Lois I. Marriott (1993).

Nominating (1994 Elections)

Ch. and members to be appointed.

Planning and Procedures

To do long-range planning, to propose activities, to update the *Procedures Handbook*, and make proposed revisions in the Bylaws of the Section.

Ch., Karl B. Johnson (1993); Paul E. Dumont (1994); Rosemary Henderson (1994); Marilyn M. McDonald (1994).

Procedures Manual (ad hoc)

Ch., Lois I. Marriott (1993).

Research and Publications (ad hoc)

Ch., A. Beverley Gass (1994); Susan M. Anderson (1993); Imogene I. Book (1993); Jennie Boyarski (1993); Isaac S. Call (1993); Terry Hancox (1994); Kate D. Hickey (1994); Margaret A. Holleman (1994); Cary L. Sowell (1994).

Services to Special Needs Students

To promote and enhance services to students in special populations, including but not limited to the physically disabled and those who need further preparation for academic and career programs.

Ch., Cay Gasque (1994); Terry Hancox (1994); Rita J. Jones (1994); Susan M. Maltese (1994).

Technology

To explore, collect, and disseminate information on new technologies and their application for community and junior college learning resource centers; to provide channels of communications for sharing this information with the goal of developing optimal application of these new technologies to a broad range of community and junior colleges; and to establish liaison with and work with other groups within and outside CJCLS having similar concerns about the utilization of new technologies in libraries.

Ch., Douglas K. Lehman (1993); Susan M. Anderson (1993); Jennie Boyarski (1993); Isaac S. Call (1993); Jay B. Clark (1994); Mary Dolven (1994); Kul B. Gauri (1994); Kate D. Hickey (1993); Margaret A. Holleman (1993); Mary Ann Miller (1993); Judith K. Ohles (1993); Derrie B. Roark (1993).

Education and Behavioral Sciences Section (EBSS)

Represents librarians and specialists in the fields of education and behavioral sciences.

Executive Committee

Ch., Jo Ann Carr (1994); ch.-elect, Judith Segal (1995); secy., Pam M. Baxter (1993); past ch., Barbara Kemp (1993); Thomas Tollman (1994); Sara E. Williams (1993).

Newsletter ed., Laverna M. Saunders (1993).

Liaison

ACRL Board—Leslie B. Bjorncrantz (1993).

Committees

25th Anniversary Celebration (ad hoc)

To plan and implement in coordination with the Conference Planning Committee a celebration to be held at the 1993 Annual Conference to commemorate the twenty-fifth anniversary of EBSS.

Ch., Laurene E. Zaporozhetz (1993); Sue Kopp (1993); Linda B. Richardson (1993); Michael L. Tillman (1993); Janet E. Welch (1993); Sara E. Williams (1993).

Bibliographic Instruction for Educators

To provide a forum for librarians interested in bibliographic instruction in education; to identify the issues and problems encountered by librarians serving schools, colleges, and departments of education in colleges and universities; to develop approaches and solutions to those problems and to recommend appropriate actions to the EBSS Executive Committee; to make distinctive contributions as education library specialists to the field of bibliographic instruction.

Ch., Patricia E. Libutti (1993); Jill Althage (1993); Gemma S. Devinney (1993); Anaclare F. Evans (1993); Mary Gouke (1993); Bonnie G. Gratch (1993); Mary Beth Minick (1994); Claudia J. Morner (1994); Carolynn L. Myers (1994); Nancy O'Hanlon (1993); Prue Stelling (1994); Thomas Tollman (1994).

Conference Program Planning—New Orleans, 1993

Ch., Jo Ann Carr (1993); Prue Stelling (1993).

Conference Program Planning—Miami, 1994

Ch. and members to be appointed.

Curriculum Materials

To examine areas of concern in curriculum materials administration; to explore the possibilities for improving curriculum materials administration (including selection, acquisition, classification, reference and retrieval, automation aspects, circulation, personnel, facilities, national and regional needs, cooperation, and continuing education); and to recommend to the EBSS Executive Committee alternative actions for making such improvements.

Ch., Kay Tavill (1993); Margaret Adlum (1993); Mary Ellen Collins (1993); Sue Kopp (1993); Janet K. Lawrence (1993); Patricia E. Libutti (1993); Michael L. Tillman (1994); Janet Stoeger Wilke (1994); Marlys Youngck (1993).

Distinguished EBSS Librarian Award (ad hoc)

To develop, plan and implement the EBSS Distinguished Librarian award to coincide with the 25th anniversary of EBSS at the 1993 Annual Conference.

Ch., Laurene E. Zaporozhetz (1993); Ruth E. Bauner (1993); Eva L. Kiewitt (1993); Virginia Nordstrom (1993); Nancy P. O'Brien (1993).

Government Policy

Ch., James L. Hodson (1993); Mary Alice Baish (1994); Leslie B. Bjorncrantz (1993); Marianna R. Fitzgerald (1994); Mary M. Gilles (1993); Marilyn A. Hicks (1994); Helen E. Ives (1993); Ann W. Latta (1994); Daniel J. Mollner (1994).

Membership and Orientation (ad hoc)

To propose strategies for recruitment, retention, and orientation of members in EBSS. To promote active interest in and support for the section and to enhance members' effectiveness.

Ch., Adele S. Dendy (1993); Pam M. Baxter (1993); Mary M. Harrison (1994); Barbara Kemp (1994); Connie L. Phelps (1993); Joyce K. Thornton (1994).

Nominating (1993 Elections)

Ch., Tara L. Fulton (1993); Kathleen M. McGowan (1993); Sally Willson Weimer (1993).

Nominating (1994 Elections)

Ch. and members to be appointed.

Problems of Access and Control of Education Materials

To review problems of the subject access systems for education literature and to recommend to the EBSS Executive Committee effective ways of improving such systems.

Ch., Allison Kaplan (1993); Karin Duran (1994); Bee H. Gallegos (1994); Jacqueline B. Hambric (1993); Carolyn L. Myers (1993); Elizabeth B. Nibley (1993); Laverna M. Saunders (1993); Ronald C. Toifel (1994); Lola Varughese (1994); Judith A. Walker (1993).

Curriculum Materials Centers Directory Revision (ad hoc subcommittee)

Ch., Laverna M. Saunders (1993); Beth G. Anderson (1994); Janet K. Lawrence (1994); Rolland H. McGiverin (1994); Donald V. Osier (1994).

Psychology/Psychiatry

To provide a forum for librarians interested in psychology and psychiatry to become more active in EBSS; to address problems and areas of interest specific to psychology and psychiatry.

Ch., Paul G. Fehrmann (1993); Richard Feinberg (1993); Gail F. Latta (1994); Cynthia R. Levine (1993); Jennie Saisakorn Sandberg (1993); Cindy S. Saur (1994); Sally A. Strickler (1994); Ellen D. Sutton (1993); Christy L. Zlatos (1994).

Publications

To investigate the avenues of publishing open to the section; to assume primary responsibility for the *EBSS Newsletter*; to clarify to the section the procedures required by ACRL and ALA for publishing; to review all EBSS publications and to provide written procedural guidance during initial planning stages and prior to any submission for funding or publication; to assist the section and its committees in finding appropriate areas for publishing projects as approved by the EBSS Executive Committee.

Ch., Nancy P. O'Brien (1993); Ruth E. Bauner (1994); Eleanor R. Kulleseid (1994); Dorothy M. Persson (1993); Kay Tavill (1993); Janet E. Welch (1993); ex officio, Laverna M. Saunders (1993).

Reference Sources and Services

To produce publications, sponsor programs, and conduct projects to improve academic library reference services in education and the behavioral sciences; to encourage communication among and the professional development of reference librarians working in these areas; to serve as resource persons and advocates to publishers and vendors producing reference materials in these disciplines, including those accessed via computer and other new technologies; to provide liaison with other ALA groups as appropriate.

Ch., to be appointed; Margaret K. Cook (1994); Cheryl Asper Elzy (1993); Carol A. Ingalls

(1994); Helen E. Ives (1994); Kathleen M. McGowan (1993); Alice J. Perez (1994); Patricia O. Rice (1993); David E. Shontz (1993); Charles B. Thurston (1993); Mary M. Wright (1994).

Social Work/Social Welfare

To provide a forum for librarians who serve social work/social welfare fields in academic settings; to sponsor discussions and programs; to produce publications to meet the needs of this clientele; and to undertake liaison activities with other professional organizations as appropriate.

Ch., Jennifer Kuehn (1993); Corryn Crosby-Muilenburg (1994); Francine M. DeFranco (1993); Donna L. Ferullo (1993); Rebecca L. Johnson (1993); Jane W. Johnson (1993); Angela S. W. Lee (1994); Darlene P. Nichols (1993); Helen Sue Schub (1994); Judith Segal (1993); Mary J. Stanley (1993).

Extended Campus Library Services Section (ECLSS)

To advance extended campus library services, extended campus librarianship and the development of extended campus library support programs; to contribute to librarianship through programming and publication to represent extended campus library activity; to promote understanding of extended campus library services within the profession and the academic community.

Executive Committee

Ch., Colleen J. Power (1994); ch.-elect, Lynn B. LaBrake (1995); secy., Kathleen M. O'Connor (1993); past ch., Barton M. Lessin (1993); Marie A. Kascus (1993); Carol M. Moulden (1994).

Newsletter ed., Kenneth E. Marks (1994).

Committees

Center for Off-Campus Library Services (advisory)

Ch., Colleen J. Power (1993); Marie A. Kascus (1993); Gloria Lebowitz (1993); Alexander L. Slade (1993).

Communications

To develop and issue a section newsletter; to provide a formal communication channel with ECLSS members, appropriate ACRL/ALA units and outside agencies; to make regular submissions to C&RL News; and to determine other appropriate journals for ECLSS news, investigate requirements for submission, and make appropriate submissions.

Ch., Kenneth E. Marks (1993); Ann Coder (1994); Nicoletta C. Hary (1993); Fred W. Jenkins (1993); Gloria Lebowitz (1993); Deborah J. Willis (1994).

Conference Program Planning—New Orleans, 1993

Ch., Gerard B. McCabe (1993); Michael B. Binder (1993); Mem Catania (1993); Gwendolyn J. Chandler (1993); Monica H. Collier (1993); Lynn M. Klekowski (1993); Jeremy W. Sayles (1993).

Conference Program Planning—Miami, 1994

Ch. and members to be appointed.

Guidelines

To promulgate the 1990 ECLS Guidelines both within the library profession and to outside agencies; to serve as an information resource regarding the use of the Guidelines; and to recommend and participate in a review of the Guidelines at such time that it is deemed needed.

Ch., A. Virginia Witucke (1993); Stephanie R. Bangert (1993); Janice R. Bradley (1993); Nicoletta C. Hary (1993).

Membership

To promote membership in the section; and to develop and maintain a membership list.

Ch., H. Maynard Lowry (1993); Janet Feldmann (1993); Robert P. Morrison (1994); Carol M. Moulden (1993); Kim E. Schultz (1994).

Nominating (1993 Elections)

Ch., Joyce V. Rumery (1993); Gwendolyn J. Chandler (1993).

Nominating (1994 Elections)

Ch. and members to be appointed.

Planning

Co-chs., Lynn B. LaBrake (1993) and Jerilyn A. Marshall (1993); Ann Blauer (1994); Nancy J. Burich (1993); James A. Damico (1993); Carol M. Greene (1994); Joyce V. Rumery (1994); Christie D. Vernon (1993).

Research

Ch., Marie A. Kascus (1994).

Discussion Group

Extended Campus Library Services

Ch., Christie D. Vernon (1993).

Law and Political Science Section (LPSS)

Represents librarians and specialists in the fields of law and political science.

Executive Committee

Ch., Caroline J. Tibbetts (1994); ch.-elect, Charles D. Spornick (1995); secy., Graham R. Walden (1993); past ch., Patricia A. McCandless (1993); Catherine F. Doyle (1994); Elizabeth A. Sibley (1993); Judy L. Solberg (1993).

Newsletter ed., Karen Whittlesey-First (1994).

Liaisons

AALL—James Hart (1994).

Committees

Bibliographies

To work on strategies for better communication with publishers and vendors in the field of law and political science. To plan the writing and publication of bibliographies that will be of value to academic libraries.

Ch., Brian B. Carpenter (1993); Dene L. Clark (1994); Mary Jeanetta Drueke (1994); James W. Hart (1994); M. Charlotte Hess (1993); Mary M. Koenig (1994); Barbara L. Morgan (1993);

Elizabeth A. Sibley (1993); Kenneth G. Walter (1994); Catherine Seitz Whitaker (1993).

Conference Program Planning—New Orleans, 1993

Ch., Caroline J. Tibbetts (1993); Sybil A. Boudreaux (1993); Ronald J. Heckart (1993); Rosemary Allen Little (1993).

Conference Program Planning—Miami, 1994

Ch. and members to be appointed.

Library Instruction

Ch., William A. Orme (1994); Laura M. Bartolo (1993); Renata G. Coates (1993); Judith E. O'Dell (1993); Robert W. Schriek (1993); Elizabeth A. Sibley (1993); Janet E. Spahr (1993); Sandra da Conturbia (1993).

Membership

Ch., Robert W. Schriek (1993); Kate E. Adams (1993); Beth A. Kremer (1993); ex officio, Elizabeth A. Sibley (1993).

Nominating (1993 Elections)

Ch., Jeanne Bohlen (1993); Charles D. Spornick (1993); ex officio, Caroline J. Tibbetts (1993).

Nominating (1994 Elections)

Ch. and members to be appointed.

Preconference Planning

Ch., James W. Hart (1994); Laura M. Bartolo (1994); Jeanne Bohlen (1994); Dene L. Clark (1994).

Publications

To facilitate communication with and about the section and its activities through the section newsletter. Committee members review and plan newsletter content, review and establish newsletter policies, solicit/submit articles, book reviews, and other pertinent information of interest to section members, and assist the editor in the production of the newsletter; revise and distribute annually the section manual; investigate other avenues of publishing open to the section and assist the section and its committee in finding appropriate areas for publishing projects that have been approved by the LPSS Executive Committee.

Ch., Stephen J. Stillwell Jr. (1994); Sever M. Bordeianu (1993); Barbara A. Burg (1993); Paula J. Popma (1994); ex officio, Karen L. Whittlesey-First (1994).

Review and Planning

To study the implications of the ACRL Strategic Planning Task Force report as a guide for future section activities. To prepare, every five years, a Section Review document to be submitted to the ACRL Planning Committee.

Ch., Marifran Bustion (1994); James W. Hart (1993); Charles D. Spornick (1993).

Rare Books and Manuscripts Section (RBMS)

Represents librarians and specialists concerned with the care, custody, and use of rare books, manuscripts, and archives and provides its members with a means of communication via publications, programs, and meetings.

Executive Committee

Ch., Gary L. Menges (1994); ch.-elect, Jackie M. Dooley (1995); secy., Elizabeth L. Johnson (1993); past ch., Cathy Henderson (1993); arch., John N. Hoover (1993); Nancy H. Burkett (1994); Robert S. Martin (1993); Charles B. McNamara (1995).

Newsletter ed., Stephen Ferguson (1993); asst. ed., Daryl Morrison (1993).

ACRL Board—Gary L. Menges (1993).
ACRL Professional Education—Kathryn N. Morgan (1994).
ALCTS—Charlotte B. Brown (1994).
GODORT—Connell B. Gallagher (1994).
WESS—Craig S. Likness (1994).
MAGERT/GODORT Committee on Rare Documents—Connell B. Gallagher (1994).

Committees

RBMS Award Committee (ad hoc)

To investigate the feasibility of establishing an annual RBMS award to recognize outstanding contributions to the field of rare books and manuscripts and the activities of RBMS.

Ch. and members to be appointed.

Bibliographic Standards

To serve as the ALA representative of rare book, manuscript and other special collections librarians and curators in all matters involving standards for providing intellectual access to and bibliographic description of those collections; to provide a centralized forum for discussion of issues relating to special collections technical processing, such as description cataloging and provision of intellectual access; to propose and/or develop necessary tools to support these activities; to develop ALA positions on, and provide a continuing review of bibliographic standards for, special collections; to serve as the formal liaison between the special collections community and appropriate units within ALA as well as organizations outside ALA, such as bibliographical networks, for the establishment of standards whereby the unique requirements of special collections may be addressed; and to disseminate information pertinent to librarians and others responsible for providing intellectual access to special collections.

Ch., Laura Stalker (1994); Jain Fletcher (1994); Elizabeth Herman (1994); Eric Holzenberg (1993); Elizabeth L. Johnson (1994); Rita A. Lunnon (1994); Eve R. Pasternak (1993); Deborah A. Ryszka (1993); Jocelyn A. Sheppard (1994); Joe Springer (1993).

Conference Program Planning—New Orleans, 1993

Ch., Gary L. Menges (1993); Jackie M. Dooley (1993); M. Susan Taraba (1993); Hugh Wilburn (1993).

Conference Program Planning—Miami, 1994

Ch., Bradley D. Westbrook (1994).

Education and Professional Development

To address all educational issues relevant to rare books and manuscripts librarianship; to analyze and assess education needs of section members; to develop model curricula programs and publications in response to identified professional education needs; to initiate, coordinate, and publicize continuing education activities in RBMS; in coordination with conference and pre-conference planning committees, to initiate and coordinate educational programs at section conferences and pre-conferences; to promote education opportunities between RBMS and other ACRL sections, ALA divisions, and other professional organizations as appropriate.

To investigate the feasibility of establishing an externally funded internship or fellowship program as a means of providing post-MLS training opportunities for new professionals.

Ch., Kathryn N. Morgan (1994); Lois Fischer Black (1994); Isaac M. Gewirtz (1994); Gretchen L. Lagana (1994); Martha Landis (1994); Richard H. F. Lindemann (1994); Janie C. Morris (1994); Daryl Morrison (1994); Judy Harvey Sahak (1994); Yvonne Schofer (1993); Rita H. Warnock (1994); Bradley D. Westbrook (1993).

Ethical Standards Review (ad hoc)

Ch., Beverly P. Lynch (1993); Susan M. Allen (1993); Sidney E. Berger (1993); David W. Corson (1993); Ellen S. Dunlap (1993); Sidney F. Huttner (1993); Alexandra Mason (1993); Alice D. Schreyer (1993); Daniel H. Traister (1993).

Exhibition Catalogs Awards

To recognize annually outstanding exhibition catalogs published by American and Canadian institutions in conjunction with exhibits of books and/or manuscripts. Catalogs are judged and selected on the level of accuracy and consistency of presentation, their clarity, originality, quality of design, and usefulness and relevance to the intended audience. The chair of the committee is to monitor the contractual conditions of the award.

Ch., Marvin J. Taylor (1994); William E. Brown Jr. (1993); Mark G. Dimunation (1994); Peter E. Hanff (1994); Kristin E. Jacobsen (1994); Mary Catharine Johnsen (1994); Tina A. Oswald (1993); Theresa A. Salazar (1994); Elaine B. Smyth (1993).

Guidelines on Archives and Manuscripts Review (ad hoc)

To revise "Guidelines on Manuscripts and Archives" (1977).

Ch., Robert Blesse (1994); Cathy Henderson (1994); Austin Hoover (1994); Margaret J. Kimball (1994).

Information Exchange

To hold a scheduled meeting during ALA Midwinter Meeting and at the end of ALA Annual Conference program for the reporting and discussion of timely RBMS and RBMS-related information; to foster the exchange of information among the RBMS membership.

Ch., Donald Farren (1994); Emily A. Bergman (1994).

Interlibrary Loan of Rare and Unique Materials (ad hoc)

To develop guidelines for the interlibrary loan of rare and unique materials as an addendum to the ALA guidelines on interlibrary loan.

Ch., H. Thomas Hickerson (1993); Lori N. Curtis (1994); Peggy E. Daub (1993); Scott H. Duvall (1994); Connell B. Gallagher (1993); Richard H. F. Lindemann (1994); Alice N. Loranth (1994); Susanne McNatt (1993); Daniel Meyer (1994); Judith A. Overmier (1994).

Nominating (1993 Elections)

Ch., Daniel H. Traister (1993); Susan M. Allen (1993); Samuel A. Streit (1993).

Nominating (1994 Elections)

Ch. and members to be appointed.

Planning (ad hoc)

To recommend an agenda to the Executive Committee regarding the future direction of RBMS and to investigate the possibility of the need for a standing RBMS Planning Committee.

Ch., Alice D. Schreyer (1993); Terry Belanger (1993); Lisa M. Browar (1993); William L. Joyce (1993); Sally S. Leach (1993); William A. Moffett (1993); Peter M. VanWingen (1993).

Preconference Program Planning—New Orleans, 1993

Ch., Patricia Bozeman (1993); Barbara J. Brown (1993); Nancy H. Burkett (1993); David W. Corson (1993); Emily Epstein (1993); William L. Joyce (1993); Sally S. Leach (1993); Janice E. Matthiesen (1993); Robert E. Parks (1993); Yvonne Schofer (1993); Jocelyn A. Sheppard (1993); Elaine B. Smyth (1993); Thomas M. Verich (1993); ex officio: Wilbur E. Meneray (1993); Gary L. Menges (1993); Kathryn N. Morgan (1993).

Preconference Program Planning—Local Arrangements, New Orleans, 1993

Ch., Wilbur E. Meneray (1993).

Preconference Program Planning—Miami, 1994

Ch., Jennifer B. Lee (1994).

Preconference Planning—Local Arrangements, Miami, 1994

Co-chs., William E. Brown Jr. (1994) and Nora J. Quinlan (1994).

Program Planning

To adopt a long-range view of conference planning activities: (1) identifying potential themes, topics, and sites of program interest to RBMS; (2) facilitating the conversion of these ideas into conference programs; (3) initiating and responding to program proposals shared with other sections or organizations; (4) serving as an agent of continuity for conference planning; (5) addressing issues in conference programs; (6) maintaining the preconference program planning manual.

Ch., Sally S. Leach (1993); Patricia Bozeman (1995); Cathy Henderson (1993); Sidney F. Huttner (1994); Jennifer B. Lee (1996); Robert S. Martin (1994); Charles B. McNamara (1993); Gary L. Menges (1995); Bradley D. Westbrook (1996); Elizabeth H. Witherell (1993); David S. Zeidberg (1993).

Publications

To investigate the avenues of publishing open to the section; to clarify to the section the procedures required by ACRL and ALA for publishing within and outside their auspices; to assist the section and its committees in finding appropriate areas for publishing projects that have been approved by the RBMS Executive Committee. In particular, to direct suitable material to the RBMS Newsletter; to represent the section's viewpoints on publishing to ACRL and ALA.

Ch., John N. Hoover (1994); Sidney E. Berger (1994); Catherine Denning (1993); Daryl Morrison (1994); Anne E. Moss (1994); Richard W. Oram (1994); John Bloomberg Rissman (1994); Daniel J. Slive (1994); ex officio, Alice D. Schreyer (1994).

Rare Books and Manuscripts Librarianship Award

To grant a biennial award for the best article published in *RBML* for the two preceding publication years. Award to be made in accordance with "Policies and Procedures for RBMS Standing Committee for the Rare Books and Manuscripts Librarianship Award."

Ch., Richard W. Oram (1994); Nancy H. Burkett (1994); John N. Hoover (1994); Jennifer B. Lee (1994); Alice D. Schreyer (1994).

Security

To ensure *Guidelines for Security of Rare Books, Manuscripts, and Other Collections'* widespread dissemination; to develop other guidelines, especially as regards procedures for dealing with suspected thieves while on the premises, and (if apprehended) their subsequent prosecution; to serve as needed as a resource for RBMS members and others who have experienced book or manuscript thefts; to serve as a liaison with other units within ALA having a concern with the theft of books and manuscripts; and to serve as a liaison between RBMS and the Antiquarian Booksellers Association of America (ABAA), the Society of American Archivists (SAA) (working as appropriate through the SAA/ALA Joint Committee), and with related organizations with a concern for the theft of books and manuscripts; to serve as a liaison with *Bookline Alert: Missing Books and Manuscripts* (BAM-BAM), and with other existing or future undertakings concerned to discourage the theft of books and manuscripts; and to undertake other duties and functions regarding the security of books and manuscripts as directed by the Executive Committee of RBMS.

Ch., Susan M. Allen (1993); George Arnold (1994); Lois Fischer Black (1994); Fraser Cocks (1994); Jennifer B. Lee (1993); Eric C. MacDonald (1994); Jean M. Rainwater (1993).

Discussion Groups

Curators and Conservators

To add to the body of information on Curator/Conservator relations and to encourage the education of curators and conservators about their respective professions; to provide a forum for discussion about topics of mutual interest; to identify, recommend, and facilitate creation of continuing education seminars through the Education and Professional Development Committee; to publicize issues concerning curators and conservators by encouraging the publication of relevant articles in appropriate journals.

Ch., Sidney E. Berger (1993).

Manuscripts and Other Formats

Co-chs., L. Rebecca Johnson (1993) and Timothy D. Murray (1993).

MARC for Special Collections

To provide an open forum for presentation and discussion of any topic or issue which involves rare book or special collections cataloguing, especially topics or issues which also involve automation.

Ch., Stephen R. Young (1993).

Science and Technology Section (STS)

Represents librarians and specialists in the fields of science and technology.

Executive Committee

Ch., Karen E. Cargille (1994); ch.-elect, Janet S. Fore (1995); secy., Janet Chisman (1993); past ch., Beverlee A. French (1993).

Newsletter co-eds., Kathy Fescemyer (1994) and Martha E. Lyle (1994).

Liaison

ACRL Board—Beverlee A. French (1993).

Committees

STS Council

Ch., Karen E. Cargille (1994); Carole S. Armstrong (1994); Jeanne E. Boyle (1994); Judith Carter (1993); Janet Chisman (1993); Deborah Dawson (1993); Thomas P. Dowling (1993); Ann M. Eagan (1994); Kathy Fescemyer (1994); Michael E. Fineman (1994); Janet S. Fore (1993); Beverlee A. French (1993); Caroline D. Harnly (1993); Sara Shatford Layne (1994); Harry P. Llull (1993); Martha E. Lyle (1994); Laura M. Osegueda (1993); Amy L. Paster (1993); Lois M. Pausch (1993); Colleen J. Power (1993); J. Robin Raquet (1994); Billie J. Reinhart (1994); Dorothy D. Smith (1993); Dawn E. Talbot (1994); Marlena M. Wald (1993); LeAnn C. Weller (1993); Katherine M. Whitley (1994); Esther Williams (1994); Julia A. Zimmerman (1993).

Comparison of Science/Technology Libraries

To collect, analyze and distribute comparative information on North American academic science and technology libraries.

Ch., Harry P. Llull (1993); Karen Croneis (1993); David S. Curry (1993); Julie M. Hurd (1993); Dency B. Kahn (1993); Kimberly B. Kelley (1993); Thomas L. King (1993); Bernard H. Lettington (1994); Mengxiong Liu (1993); Bonnie Osif (1994); Mara Pinckard (1993); Nancy R. Simons (1994); Peri I. Switzer (1994).

Conference Program Planning—New Orleans, 1993

Ch., Julia A. Zimmerman (1993); John P. Abbott (1993); Nirmala S. Bangalore (1993); Sheila R. Curl (1993); Johnny L. Johnson (1993); Gail E. Marredeth (1993); Kathleen L. Neeley (1993); Jill Newby (1993); Connie L. Phelps (1993); Amy W. Shannon (1993); Mara L. Sprain (1993); Crit Stuart (1993); Marlena M. Wald (1993).

Conference Program Planning—Miami, 1994

Ch. and members to be appointed.

Continuing Education

To coordinate, promote, and encourage all continuing education efforts within the Science and Technology Section; to act as the initial contact for individuals and groups wishing to plan science and technology related continuing education programs; to maintain channels of communication and review proposals for workshops, new discussion groups, and preconferences; to develop guidelines and recommendations for the membership in planning future continuing education activities.

Ch., Laura M. Osegueda (1993); Ruth Hafter (1994); Susan M. Norrisey (1994); Nestor L. Osorio (1993); Maria A. Porta (1994); Billie J. Reinhart (1993); Peri I. Switzer (1993).

Forum on Emerging Issues and Research

To plan forums for ALA meetings, where STS committees and STS members can present ideas, research in progress, and recent accomplishments.

Ch., Katherine M. Whitley (1994); Lori A. Bronars (1993); Janet Chisman (1993); Sheila G. Johnson (1994); Kenneth Luker (1993); Richard W. Meyer (1993); Richard E. Sapon-White (1993); Shirley R. Scott (1993); Michael V. Sullivan (1993).

Legislation

To serve as a focus for STS member concerns about science and technology legislative issues and to cooperate with other ACRL and ALA legislative groups as appropriate.

Co-chs., Dorothy D. Smith (1993) and LeAnn C. Weller (1993); James E. Alloway (1993); Michael J. Haddock (1993); Barry Hartigan (1993); Douglas E. Jones (1995); Allison V. Level (1995); Locke J. Morrisey (1994); Catherine W. Wojewodzki (1993).

Membership

To maintain a history of members' participation and maintain lists of volunteers for the nominating committee's use and for the vice-chair to assure a balance of appointments, both in the number of appointments of each individual member and in percentages of experienced versus new members. Create and update a recruitment brochure. Publish the list of committees and their members for the Executive Committee.

Ch., Thomas P. Dowling (1993); Marjo Andrews Gray (1993); Joseph J. Harzbecker (1993); Norma G. Kobzina (1994); Mengxiong Liu (1993); Lynn Sorensen Sutton (1994).

Newsletter

Co-chs., Kathy Fescemyer (1994) and Martha E. Lyle (1994); Alena F. Chadwick (1994); Eleanor S. Elder (1993); Lynn M. Llull-Kaczor (1993); Mary J. Markland (1994); Nancy Shepard (1993); Theresa S. Spence (1993); Rebecca S. Uhl (1994); Julia A. Zimmerman (1993).

Nominating (1993 Elections)

Ch., Colleen J. Power (1993); Eleanor R. Mathews (1993); Lee M. Murray (1993).

Nominating (1994 Elections)

Ch. and members to be appointed.

Oberly Award for Bibliography in the Agricultural Sciences

Ch., Amy L. Paster (1993); JoAnn DeVries (1993); Michael J. Haddock (1994); Cynthia S. Kaag (1994); Gerard McKiernan (1994); Sarah E. Thomas (1993).

Planning

To provide long-range direction for the section. Propose new activities, review suggestions from the membership, and perform section reviews as required.

Ch., Deborah Dawson (1993); John P. Abbott (1993); Emerson Hilker (1994); Laura M. Osegueda (1994); Lois M. Pausch (1993); Susanne J. Redalje (1993); Helen F. Smith (1993).

Preconference—New Orleans, 1993

Ch., Caroline D. Harnly (1993); Denise Beaubien Bennett (1993); Michael D. Cramer (1993); Eileen Dubin (1993); Julia M. Gelfand (1993); William J. Goff (1993); Johnny L. Johnson (1993); Sandra H. Kajiwara (1993); Mary J. Markland (1993); Thomas W. Ricks (1993); Marlena M. Wald (1993).

Preconference on Bibliographic Control of Conference Proceedings, ALCTS CCS CC:DA/ ACRL STS (joint subcommittee) (See p. 32)

Publisher/Vendor Relations

To serve as a channel for exchanging information between science and technology publishers and vendors and science and technology librarians.

Co-chs., Michael E. Fineman (1994) and Billie J. Reinhart (1994); Sallie H. Barringer (1993); Eleanor I. Cook (1993); Julia A. Gammon (1993); Marilyn A. Grant (1993); Robert F. Nardini (1994); Ann C. Paietta (1993); Virginia I. Rodes (1993); Cynthia A. Steinke (1993); Peri I. Switzer (1993); Marcia L. Tuttle (1994).

Subject and Bibliographic Access to Science Materials

To provide a forum for exchange of information of use to librarians (column in *STS Signal*, discussion groups). Serve as a channel/clearinghouse for concerns, problems, issues. For issues that can be resolved, propose projects, present them to the Planning Committee.

Ch., Judith Carter (1993); Nirmala S. Bangalore (1994); Sharon S. Chadwick (1993); Ann J. Hope (1993); Joan P. Lussky (1993); F. Douglas Martin (1993); Amy L. Paster (1994); Robert G. Sabin (1993); Christina Sokol (1993); Thomas R. Zogg (1993); intern, Mary C. Lasater (1993).

Discussion Groups

College Science Librarians

Co-chs., J. Robin Raquet (1994) and Esther Williams (1994).

General

To provide a forum for discussion of issues of concern to STS librarians not under the responsibility of any of the standing committees.

Co-chs., Janet S. Fore (1993) and Marlena M. Wald (1993).

Heads of Science and Technology Libraries

Co-chs., Carole S. Armstrong (1994) and Jeanne E. Boyle (1994).

Science Databases

Co-chs., Ann M. Eagan (1994) and Dawn E. Talbot (1994).

Slavic and East European Section (SEES)

Represents librarians and specialists in the fields of Slavic and East European studies and is concerned with those aspects of library service which require knowledge of Slavic and East European languages.

Executive Committee

Ch., Molly F. Molloy (1994); ch.-elect, Leena Siegelbaum (1995); past ch., Tatjana Lorkovic (1993); Alena Aissing (1994); Tatiana Goerner-Barr (1993); Michael Markiw (1994).

Newsletter ed., Harold M. Leich (1993).

Liaison

ACRL Board—Tatjana Lorkovic (1993).

Committees

Automated Bibliographic Control

To study and disseminate information about automated bibliographic control of Slavic and East European materials; to coordinate the work of the committee with appropriate sections of ALCTS and other divisions; to present bibliographic control issues and monitor online bibliographic control products and services.

Ch., Dena J. Schoen (1994); Alena Aissing (1994); Jacqueline J. Byrd (1993); Joanna K. Dyla (1993); Michael Markiw (1994); Susan Cook Summer (1993).

Conference Program Planning—New Orleans, 1993

Ch., Molly F. Molloy (1993); Michael Markiw (1993); Susan Cook Summer (1993).

Conference Program Planning—Miami, 1994

Ch. and members to be appointed.

Continuing Education on Slavic and East European Librarianship in North America

To advance the theoretical and practical aspects of Slavic and East European librarianship in North America; to maintain liaison with the ACRL Professional Education Committee.

Ch., Ruth Wallach (1993); Kristin A. Antelman (1993); Mieczslaw Buczkowski (1994); Jacqueline J. Byrd (1993); Laszlo L. Kovacs (1993); Cathy M. Zeljak (1994).

Newsletter Editorial Board

Ch., Harold M. Leich (1994); Sandra L. Levy (1994); Molly F. Molloy (1994); Mary P. Stuart (1994).

Nominating (1993 Elections)

Ch., Sandra L. Levy (1993); Harold M. Leich (1993); Viveca Seymour (1993).

Nominating (1994 Elections)

Ch. and members to be appointed.

Preservation of Slavic Materials and Special Collections

To investigate and report on preservation and conservation issues as they relate to collections in the area of Slavic and East European librarianship.

Ch., Susan K. Burke (1994); Anthony E. Anderson (1994); Sandra L. Levy (1994); Viveca Seymour (1994).

University Libraries Section (ULS)

To advance university librarianship, university library service, and the development of university libraries.

Executive Committee

Ch., Carolyn Robison (1994); ch.-elect, Noreen S. Alldredge (1995); secy., Lori A. Goetsch (1993); past ch., Joseph J. Branin (1993); William J. Crowe (1994); Jill B. Fatzer (1993); Beverlee A. French (1995); Kent H. Hendrickson (1995); David W. Lewis (1994); Judy A. Sackett (1993).

Liaisons

ACRL Government Relations—Paula D. Watson.
C&RL News—Sylvia Curtis.

Committees

Communications

Ch., Jill B. Fatzer; Rhea Bradley (1994); Bonnie Osif (1994); Angela Men-Lin Yang (1994); interns, Ellie E. Marsh (1994); Karen S. Seibert (1994).

Conference Program Planning—New Orleans, 1993

Ch., Carolyn Robison (1993); Rosie L. Albritton (1993); James A. Cogswell (1993); Jill B. Fatzer (1993); Barbara A. Lockett (1993); D. W. Schneider (1993); Sharon Kay Womack (1993).

Conference Program Planning—Miami, 1994

Ch. and members to be appointed.

Current Topics Planning

To organize informal discussion meetings and presentations on well-defined issues and problems of current interest to university libraries and librarians.

Ch., Eddy Hogan (1993); Jane A. Conrow (1993); Elaine K. Didier (1993); Thomas K. Fry (1994); John M. Haar III (1993); intern, Patricia M. Larsen (1994).

Nominating (1993 Elections)

Ch., Maxine H. Reneker (1993); Donald G. Frank (1993); John C. Hepner (1993).

Nominating (1994 Elections)

Ch. and members to be appointed.

Organization and Bylaws

To study the organizational structure of other sections within ACRL and other divisions of ALA and to develop a plan for changes in the ULS organization which will assure responsiveness to the needs of the members and broaden the opportunities of members to participate in the work of the section. To monitor proposals and changes in the ACRL Constitution and Bylaws and Strategic Plan and to alert ULS if it may be affected. To serve the ULS Executive Committee in an advisory capacity in all matters specified above.

Ch., Sharon M. Britton (1993); Cynthia Crooker (1993); Aline E. Soules (1994); intern, Aubrey W. Kendrick (1994).

Policy and Planning

To review and make recommendations to the Executive Committee regarding the section's future direction, goals and objectives, and policies. To develop and oversee implementation of plans and strategies that will help the section achieve these goals and objectives. To serve in an advisory capacity to the Executive Committee on matters of policy that may arise from time to time. To prepare and, subsequently, maintain and revise a policies and procedures manual for the section. To take responsibility for preparation of the section review and the Strategic Planning Inventory according to ACRL timetables.

Ch., Louise S. Sherby (1994); Sandra L. Gallup (1994); Charles E. Kratz Jr. (1993); Dennis K. Lambert (1994); Doris Ann Sweet (1993); intern, Elizabeth S. Smith (1994).

Discussion Group

Librarians in Higher Education and Campus Administration (ad hoc)

To address the issues of librarians who are increasingly involved in all aspects of higher education (accreditation, curriculum planning, student and academic support services, computer services, funding, etc.) and who hold positions or are interested in university-level campus administration.

Ch., James A. Estrada (1993); Indra M. David (1994); Wendy Pradt Lougee (1994); Judy Luther (1994); Danielle Mihram (1994); Mara R. Saule (1994).

Western European Specialists Section (WESS)

To represent librarians and others who specialize or are otherwise professionally involved in the acquisition, organization, and use of information sources originating in or relating to Western European countries; to promote the improvement of library services in support of study and research activities in Western European affairs.

Executive Committee

Ch., Ceres B. Birkhead (1994); ch.-elect, James H. Spohrer (1995); secy., Thomas M. Izbicki (1993); past ch., John R. Kaiser (1993); Craig S. Likness (1993).

Newsletter ed., Jeffry K. Larson (1995).

Liaison

ACRL Board—John Kaiser (1993).

Committees

ARL Project Advisory (ad hoc)

Ch., Barbara L. Walden (1994); David Jay Cooper (1994); Charles S. Fineman (1994); Mary Jane Parrine (1994); Assunta Pisani (1994).

Conference Program Planning—London, 1994

Ch., Charles S. Fineman (1994); Terry L. Allison (1994); Diana Chlebek (1994); Kurt F. De Belder (1994); Kathryn A. Gabriel (1994); Catharine M. E. Halls (1994).

Conference Program Planning—New Orleans, 1993

Ch., Richard Hacken (1993); Peter B. Allison (1993); John M. Cullars (1993); Kurt F. De Belder (1993); Craig S. Likness (1993); Michael Markiw (1993); Ann P. Snoeyenbos (1993); ex officio, Thomas M. Izbicki (1993).

Conference Program Planning—Miami, 1994

Ch. and members to be appointed.

Martinus Nijhoff International West European Specialists Study Grant

(For description, see Awards, p. 120.)

Ch., John M. Cullars (1993); Mary Jane Parrine (1993); Charles G. Spetland (1993); cons.: Marian Reijnen (1994).

Nominating (1993 Elections)

Ch., Mary Jane Parrine (1993); James Campbell (1993); Stephen R. Lehmann (1993).

Nominating (1994 Elections)

Ch. and members to be appointed.

Publications

To develop and coordinate the publishing efforts of the Section. To oversee and generally assist the editor in the production of the section's Newsletter. To organize and edit the Newsletter's bibliographic features.

Ch., Tom D. Kilton (1993); Marifran Bustion (1993); Diana Chlebek (1994); John M. Cullars (1994); Gretchen E. Holten (1993); Thomas M. Izbicki (1994); Stephen R. Lehmann (1993); Lawrence J. McCrank (1993); Susanne F. Roberts (1994); Leena Siegelbaum (1994); interns: Fred W. Jenkins (1994); Vivian Mei-Sheng Lo Chou (1993); Heleni Marques Pedersoli (1994); ex officio, Jeffry K. Larson (1995).

Newsletter (subcommittee)

Ch., Stephen R. Lehmann (1993); Sandra A. Fraser (1993); Gail P. Hueting (1994); Craig S. Likness (1994); Michael P. Olson (1993); Julie M. Still (1994); ex officio, Jeffery K. Larson (1995).

Research and Planning

To identify areas where there is a need for library related research in European Studies and assist in disseminating the results of that research through program and publications. To organize and promote the continuing education activities of the section. To appoint WESS liaisons to other groups, with the approval of the Executive Committee. To plan and review the activ-

ities of the section under the direction of the Executive Committee.

Ch., Charles S. Fineman (1993); Anthony E. Anderson (1993); Kathryn A. Gabriel (1994); Nancy L. Herron (1993); Danielle Mihram (1994); Reinhart Sonnenburg (1993); James H. Spohrer (1994); Phillip W. Wilkin (1993); Leona L. Wise (1994); interns: Jennalyn W. Tellman (1994); Dennis K. Lambert (1994).

Discussion Groups

Classical, Medieval, and Renaissance

To provide a discussion and information-sharing forum for librarians with particular interests in Western Europe (including Greece) in the ancient, medieval, and early modern periods.

Ch., Fred W. Jenkins (1993).

College and Medium-sized Libraries

To discuss topics of current interest pertaining to the acquisition, organization, and use of Western European materials as these relate to the special situations of smaller library collections.

Ch., Gretchen E. Holten (1993).

General

To discuss topics of current interest relating to the acquisition, organization and use of Western European materials.

Ch., Craig S. Likness (1993).

Germanists

To provide a discussion and information-sharing forum for librarians with particular interests in the German-speaking nations or in any aspect of German studies.

Ch., Barbara L. Walden (1994).

Romance Languages

To discuss topics of current interest relating to the acquisition, organization, and use of materials emanating from the Romance languages speaking countries of Western Europe or pertaining to any aspect of the study of these countries.

Ch., Frank Di Trolio (1993).

Scandinavian

To discuss topics of current interest relating to the acquisition, organization, and use of materials emanating from the Nordic countries of Western Europe or pertaining to any aspect of Scandinavian study.

Co-chs., Louis A. Pitschmann (1994) and Sem C. Sutter (1993); secy., Merry B. Schellinger (1993).

Women's Studies Section (WSS)

To discuss, promote and support Women's Studies collections and services in academic and research libraries; to investigate and develop bibliographic instruction, faculty liaison, and database searching in this cross-disciplinary field; to encourage cooperative collection development and access for Women's Studies materials; to foster cooperation among Women's Studies librarians, scholars, students, and publishers; to work with other ALA groups to promote library and information service to women.

Executive Committee

Ch., Virginia L. Daley (1994); ch.-elect, Betty J. Glass (1995); secy., Kristine J. Anderson (1993); past ch., Jacquelyn Marie (1993); Argent S. Gibson (1993); Rita Pellen (1993).

Newsletter ed., Wendy M. Thomas (1994).

Committees

Collection Development and Bibliography

To monitor collection development issues and resources in women's studies, including the content and use of evaluative techniques such as the conspectus, and the nature and availability of reference tools in print, microform, electronic and other formats. To recommend and implement projects to meet needs in this area including bibliographies, guides, instructional materials and other programs.

Ch., Betty H. Day (1993); Sara N. Brownmiller (1994); Judith A. Hudson (1994); Carol Ritzen Kem (1994); Pauline D. Manaka (1993); Rita Pellen (1994); Cynthia Shelton (1993); Ruth Wallach (1994).

Communications

To facilitate communication about the Section and its activities through a newsletter; to produce annually an updated version of the WSS brochure; to create and conduct regular orientation sessions for new or perspective WSS members; to communicate with other women's groups, both inside and outside of ALA, to further the goals of the WSS.

Ch., Bonnie J. Cox (1993); Argent S. Gibson (1994); Jessica Grim (1994); Emilie Ngo-Nguidjol (1994); Kristin R. Ramsdell (1993); Kathryn M. Ryan-Zeugner (1993).

Conference Program Planning—New Orleans, 1993

Co-chs., ,Sarah Barbara Watstein (1993) and Sally Willson Weimer (1993); Sybil A. Boudreaux (1993); Leta Hendricks (1993); Deborah A. Murphy (1993); Mary M. Nofsinger (1993); Deborah G. Tenofsky (1993); ex officio, Virginia L. Daley (1993).

Conference Program Planning—Miami, 1994

Ch. and members to be appointed.

Nominating (1993 Elections)

Ch., Joan Ariel (1993); Linda A. Krikos (1993); Pauline D. Manaka (1993).

Nominating (1994 Elections)

Ch. and members to be appointed.

Publications

Ch., Grace Jackson-Brown (1993); Abbie J. Basile (1994); Ellen Broidy (1994); Lori A. Goetsch (1994); Kay F. Jones (1993); Linda A. Krikos (1993); Jeannie Miller (1994); Sarah Pedersen (1993); Nancy M. Stanley (1994).

Technical Services

To monitor technical services issues and practices having an impact on Women's Studies; to recommend and implement projects to meet needs in this area.

Ch., Kristin H. Gerhard (1994); Susanne Nevin (1993); G. Margaret Porter (1994); Francoise S. Puniello (1994); Charlotte C. Rubens (1994); Mila C. Su (1994); Deborah G. Tenofsky (1994); Suzanne Tronier (1993); Priscilla C. Yu (1993).

ACRL DISCUSSION GROUPS

Academic Librarians' Association

Ch., Roberta J. Kramer (1993).

Australian Studies

Ch., Murray S. Martin (1994).

Canadian Studies

Ch., Louis A. Vyhnanek (1993).

Electronic Library Development in Academic Libraries

Ch., Craig A. Summerhill (1993).

English and American Literature

Ch., William Baker (1993).

Exhibits and Displays

Ch., Michael M. Miller (1993).

Fee-based Information Service Centers in Academic Libraries

Ch., Diane Richards (1993).

Fundraising and Development

Ch., Laura H. Maurer (1994).

Heads of Public/Readers Services

Ch., Claudette S. Hagle (1993).

Home Economics/Human Ecology Librarians

Ch., Judy M. Nixon (1993).

Journal Costs in Academic Libraries

Ch., Marcia L. Tuttle (1993).

Librarians of Library Science Collections

Ch., Patricia Stinson Switzer (1993).

Performance/Output Measures for Academic Libraries

Ch., Patricia M. Kelley (1993).

Personnel Administrators and Staff Development Officers of Large Research Libraries

Co-chs., Barbara Irene Dewey (1993) and Gail V. Oltmanns (1993).

Philosophical, Religious and Theological Studies

Ch., Edward D. Starkey (1993).

Popular Culture and Libraries

Ch., Douglas B. Highsmith (1993).

Public Relations in Academic Libraries

Ch., Linda Sharp (1993).

Research

Ch., Darrell L. Jenkins (1993).

Undergraduate Librarians

Ch., J. Louise Malcomb (1994).

ACRL CHAPTERS

Chapters Council

The Chapters Council shall consist of the president (chair) and vice-president (vice-chair) of each ACRL chapter or delegate who is a member of the executive board of the chapter. Each member of the Chapters Council shall be a member of the national Association and be knowledgeable about both chapter and national ACRL activities.

Ch., Susan Kay Phillips (1994); ch.-elect, Rena K. Fowler (1995); secy., Karyle S. Butcher (1993); past ch., Susan S. Baughman (1993).

Newsletter eds., Gail Junion-Metz (1993) and Ray E. Metz (1993).

Committees

ACRL Presidential Candidate Forum

Ch., Marian C. Winner (1993).

Chapter Support

To investigate the criteria and guidelines for proposals for special/extra programming funds; to review the proposals submitted; to allocate the resources; and to provide supervisory/evaluative controls and oversight.

Ch., Susan Kay Phillips (1994).

Nominating

Ch., Karen A. Nuckolls (1993).

Orientation

To plan, organize, and conduct the Chapters Council Orientation meeting at the Midwinter and Annual Conference in order to introduce the purpose of the Chapters Council to new members and to provide continuity.

Ch., Rena K. Fowler (1993).

Chapter Officers

Alabama

Pres., Eric A. Kidwell; vice-pres., Charles Skewis.
(Officers change Apr. 1993.)

Arizona

Pres., Eileen R. Shackelford; vice-pres., Virginia Sylvester.
(Officers change Nov. 1992.)

Arkansas

Pres., Henry Terrill; vice-pres., Jody B. Charter.
(Officers change Nov. 1992.)

California

Pres., Kathleen Dunn; vice-pres. (south), Venita Jorgensen; vice-pres. (north), Stephanie Bangert.
(Officers change Jan. 1993.)

Colorado

Pres., Orlando Archibeque.
(Officers change Oct. 1992.)

Delaware Valley

Pres., Joy Collins; vice-pres., Evelyn C. Minick.
(Officers change May 1993.)

Florida

Pres., Derrie Roark; vice-pres., Douglas K. Lehman.
(Officers change July 1993.)

Georgia

Pres., J. Allen Spivey; vice-pres., John R. Yelverton.
(Officers change Oct. 1993.)

Illinois

Pres., Karen A. Becker; vice-pres., Joyce C. Wright.
(Officers change June 1993.)

Indiana

Pres., JoAnn M. Arnold; vice-pres., Philip H. Young.
(Officers change June 1993.)

Iowa

Pres., Jill C. Miller; vice-pres., Catherine Rod.
(Officers change Dec. 1992.)

Kansas

Pres., John M. Stratton; vice-pres., Henry Stewart.
(Officers change July 1993.)

Kentucky

Pres., Cynthia F. Atkins; vice-pres., Cynthia L. Etkin.
(Officers change Oct. 1992.)

Louisiana

Pres., Peter B. Kaatrude; vice-pres., Catherine R. Nelson.
(Officers change Jan. 1993.)

Maryland

Pres., Stephen P. Labash; vice-pres., Diane L. Fishman.
(Officers change June 1993.)

Michigan

Pres., Timothy F. Richards; vice-pres., Aline Soules.
(Officers change June 1993.)

Minnesota

Pres., Margaret L. Johnson; vice-pres., Merry B. Schellinger .
(Officers change Jan. 1993.)

Mississippi

Pres., Patricia H. Matthes; vice-pres., Susanna Turner.
(Officers change Dec. 1992.)

Missouri

Pres., Barbara L. Schade; vice-pres., Linda Bigelow.
(Officers change Oct. 1992.)

Montana

Pres., Elaine Peterson.
(Officers change June 1993.)

Nebraska

Pres., Janice S. Boyer; vice-pres., Ruth Rasmussen.
(Officers change Oct. 1992.)

Nevada

Pres., Shelley J. Heaton; vice-pres., Thomas R. Mirkovich.
(Officers change Oct. 1992.)

New England

Pres., Michael Ann Moskowitz; vice-pres., Lynda C. Leahy.
(Officers change May 1993.)

New Jersey

Pres., Anita Talar.
(Officers change May 1993.)

New Mexico

Pres., Tracey Kimball; vice-pres., Kathy Flanary.
(Officers change Sept. 1992.)

New York, Eastern

Pres., Elaine M. Coppola; vice-pres., Mary E. Cahill.
(Officers change Apr. 1993.)

New York, Greater Metropolitan

Pres., Janet Wagner; vice-pres., Helen Sue Schub.
(Officers change Jan. 1993.)

New York, Western/Ontario

Pres., David Bertuca; vice-pres., Cynthia Singleton.
(Officers change Sept. 1992.)

North Carolina

Pres., Susan M. Squires; vice-pres., Plummer A. Jones.
(Officers change Nov. 1993.)

North Dakota

Pres., Frances Beth Fisher; vice-pres., Pat Berntsen.
(Officers change Sept. 1992.)

Ohio

Pres., Alison Scott Ricker; vice-pres., Gary Hunt.
(Officers change July 1993.)

Oklahoma

Pres., Mary Jane Hamilton; vice-pres., Alberta Mayberry.
(Officers change Jan. 1993.)

Oregon

Pres., Karyle S. Butcher; vice-pres., Jan Marie Fortier.
(Officers change Oct. 1992.)

Pennsylvania, Western

Liaison: Barbara G. Richards.

South Dakota

Pres., Patricia M. Anderson.
(Officers change Oct. 1992.)

Tennessee

Pres., Sharon C. Parente; vice-pres., Ray Hall.
(Officers change June 1993.)

Texas

Pres., Carol M. Kelley; vice-pres., Joe F. Dahlstrom.
(Officers change Apr. 1993.)

Utah

Pres., Larry J. Ostler.

Virginia

Pres., Berna Heyman; vice-pres., Carol Pfeiffer.
(Officers change Nov. 1992.)

Washington

Pres., Timothy D. Jewell.
(Officers change June 1993.)

Wisconsin

Pres., Linda Piele; vice-pres., Meredith Gillette.
(Officers change Jan. 1993.)

Association of Specialized and Cooperative Library Agencies

Membership as of August 31, 1992
Organization members   308
Personal members   896
Total   1,204

Andrew M. Hansen, *executive director*
Joanne Crispen, *deputy executive director*

The Association of Specialized and Cooperative Library Agencies represents state library agencies, specialized library agencies, and multitype library cooperatives.

State library agencies are those organizations created or authorized by the state government to promote library services in the state through the organization and coordination of a variety of library services.

Specialized library agencies are those organizations that provide materials and services to meet the information needs of persons whose access to library services and materials is limited because of confinement, sensory, mental, physical, health, or behavioral conditions.

Multitype library cooperatives are combinations, mergers, or contractual associations of two or more types of libraries (academic, public, special, or school) crossing jurisdictional, institutional, or political boundaries, working together to achieve maximum effective use of funds to provide library and information services to all persons above and beyond those that can be provided through one institution. Such cooperative agencies may be designed to serve a community, a metropolitan area, a region within a region, or may serve a statewide or multistate area.

Within the interests of these types of library organizations, the Association of Specialized and Cooperative Library Agencies has specific responsibility for:

1. Development and evaluation of goals and plans for state library agencies, specialized library agencies, and multitype library cooperatives to facilitate the implementation, improvement, and extension of library activities designed to foster improved user services, coordinating such activities with other appropriate ALA units.

2. Representation and interpretation of the role, functions, and services of state library agencies, specialized library agencies, and multitype library cooperatives within and outside the profession, including contact with national organizations and government agencies.

3. Development of policies, studies, and activities in matters affecting state library agencies, specialized library agencies, and multitype library cooperatives relating to (a) state and local library legislation, (b) state grants-in-aid and appropriations, and (c) relationships among state, federal, regional, and local governments, coordinating such activities with other appropriate ALA units.

4. Establishment, evaluation, and promotion of standards and service guidelines relating to the concerns of this association.

5. Identifying the interests and needs of all persons, encouraging the creation of services to meet these needs within the areas of concern of the association, and promoting the use of these services provided by state library agencies, specialized library agencies, and multitype library cooperatives.

6. Stimulating the professional growth and promoting the specialized training and continuing education of library personnel at all levels in the areas of concern of this association and encouraging membership participation in appropriate type-of-activity divisions within ALA.

7. Assisting in the coordination of activities of other units within ALA that have a bearing on the concerns of this association.

8. Granting recognition for outstanding library service within the areas of concern of this association.

9. Acting as a clearinghouse for the exchange of information and encouraging the development of materials, publications, and research within the areas of concern of this association.

Board of Directors

Pres., Janice Beck Ison (1994); pres.-elect, Barbara L. Perkis (1995); past pres., Duane F. Johnson (1993); Nancy Bolin (1993); Alan D. Lewis (1993); Laurence A. Miller (1994); Diana R. Tope (1994); sect. reps.: Thea B. Chesley (1993); Keith Michael Fiels (1993); Barbara J. Goral (1993); Anthony W. Miele (1993); div. councilor; Suzanne J. LeBarron (1993); ed., Thomas J. Dorst (1993); ex officio: Joanne L. Crispen (1993); Andrew M. Hansen (1993); Rod Wagner (1994).

Publications

Interface (quarterly). Sent to all ASCLA members. Subscriptions, $15 a yr. Single copies of issues, $4. Ed., Thomas J. Dorst, Illinois State Library, 300 S. Second St., Springfield, IL 62701.

COMMITTEES

American Association of Law Libraries— American Correctional Association— ASCLA Committee on Institution Libraries

(joint) (See listing under Joint Committees, p. 16.)

Americans with Disabilities Act Assembly

To facilitate communication among ALA units and other groups concerning the Americans with Disabilities Act—the legislation and its regulations; to foster coordination and cooperation of efforts to meet the challenges presented by the ADA legislation and its regulations among ALA units and other groups; to act as a clearinghouse on information concerning ADA issues such as employment and access to programs, services, and facilities for persons with disabilities; to report to and advise the ASCLA/LSSPS Executive Committee, the ASCLA Board, and the ASCLA Office on issues, activities, programs and materials related to the ADA legislation and its regulations to be shared with all ALA units and other groups.

Ch., Kathleen O. Mayo (1993); sect. rep., Michael G. Gunde (1993).

Awards

To administer and publicize the awards presented in the name of the Association of Specialized and Cooperative Library Agencies; to review periodically the appropriateness of existing ASCLA awards; to make recommendations to the ASCLA Board of Directors with respect to proposed new ASCLA awards; to modify, eliminate, or suspend existing awards when necessary; to handle all details and expenses with respect to the presentation of awards and coordinate this activity with the Conference Program Coordination Committee; to appoint, with assistance from the officers of appropriate units as needed, juries to select for recommendation to the Awards Committee recipients of ASCLA awards and coordinate the work of these juries; to select, subject to approval of the ASCLA Board of Directors, recipients of awards; to submit information concerning ASCLA to the ALA Awards Committee in order that the *ALA Awards Manual* be maintained; to report new awards prior to implementation date for information to the ALA Awards Committee, Executive Board, and Council.

Ch., Bridget Later Lamont (1994); Arthur Curley (1993); Elizabeth A. Curry (1993); Joe B. Forsee (1993); Howard F. McGinn (1993); Fred D. Neighbors (1993); Lisa M. Scholl (1993); Trish Skaptason (1993); Nettie B. Taylor (1993).

Awards Jury (subcommittee)

To select recipients for the ASCLA Leadership Achievement, the Exceptional Service, the ASCLA Service, and the ASCLA Professional Achievement awards.

Ch. to be appointed.

National Organization on Disability Award Jury (subcommittee)

Ch., Leslie Rosen (1993); Elizabeth Crenshaw (1993); Sherrie Dux-Ideus (1993).

Conference Program Coordination

To coordinate, facilitate, and provide continuity in conference programming of the general

sessions of the association for the ALA Annual Conference. To review proposed programs of all units of the association for each ALA Annual Conference, for the purpose of avoiding duplication, ensuring appropriate cosponsorship within and outside the division, and complying with ALA conference program guidelines. To present to the ASCLA Board of Directors at the required time a recommendation and budget proposal for division, section, and other unit programs for each ALA Annual Conference.

Ch., Mary Y. Moore (1993); Leslie B. Burger (1993); Sandra M. Ellison (1994); Brenda M. Pacey (1994); Beverly D. Papai (1993); Sandra Souza (1994); Sandra S. Stephan (1994); sec. reps: Keith Michael Fiels (1993); Mary E. Flournoy (1993).

1993 Preconference on Cost/Benefit Analysis for Cooperative Services (subcommittee)

Ch., Gordon C. Barhydt (1993); Elizabeth A. Curry (1993).

President's Program (1993) (subcommittee)

Ch., Alice M. Calabrese (1993); Fred E. Goodman (1993); Kate F. Nevins (1993).

Institute for Public Library Development, PLA/ASCLA (interdivisional) (See p. 75.)

Legislation

To develop policies, studies, and activities relating to state and federal library legislation; to relate state and federal legislation to local government; to coordinate these legislative activities with appropriate ALA units. The chairperson shall serve as liaison to the ALA Legislation Assembly.

Ch., Barbara H. Will (1993); Alice M. Calabrese (1994); Alan D. Lewis (1993); Barbara T. Mates (1993); Stephen Prine (1994); Nettie B. Taylor (1993); sect. reps.: Keith Michael Fiels (1994); Vibeke Lehmann (1993); Anthony W. Miele (1993).

Library Personnel and Education

To identify issues of concern to ASCLA members in the areas of library personnel and education, including administration, recruitment, staff development, library education and continuing education; to articulate and recommend ASCLA positions and policies in these areas; and to assure that ASCLA's program addresses this program as appropriate. The chairs shall serve as the representative of the association to the ALA Library Education Assembly and as the Association's liaison with the Office for Library Personnel Resources.

Ch., Donna Z. Pontau (1993); Steven A. Baughman (1993); Docia M. Blalock (1993); Nancy J. A. Busch (1993); Diane T. Johnson (1994); Timothy P. Lynch (1994); Ida D. McGhee (1993); Valerie J. Wilford (1994).

Membership Promotion

To establish general policies and procedures to secure new and continuing members; to develop and actively pursue an on-going membership recruitment program for ASCLA; to coordinate membership promotion activities of all sections within the association; to make recommendations to the ASCLA Board of Directors concerning membership dues; to represent AS-CLA on the ALA Membership Promotion Task Force.

Ch., Barbara T. Mates (1993); Barbara Allen (1994); Carl Beery (1994); Michael G. Gunde (1994); Laura J. Hodges (1994); Kate F. Nevins (1994); Donna Z. Pontau (1994); sect. reps.: Martha A. Caterson (1993); Jane Raifsnider (1993); Rod Wagner (1993).

Mentoring with Tribal Libraries (ad hoc)

To study the feasibility of developing and, if possible, testing a program of mentoring with, and networking among, tribal libraries and librarians; and to report back to the ASCLA Board no later than the 1992 ALA Conference.

Ch. and members to be appointed.

Nominating (1993)

Ch., William G. Asp (1993); Ann Joslin (1993); Nancy P. Knepel (1993); Kathleen O. Mayo (1993); sect. reps.: John M. Day (1993); Dottie R. Hiebing (1993); Alan D. Lewis (1993).

Organization and Bylaws

To maintain constant review of the association's organization and structure; to recommend to the ASCLA Board of Directors the establishment, functions, and discontinuance of committees, sections, discussion groups, or other subordinate units as the needs of the association may require; to develop bylaws and review all proposed bylaw amendments for recommendation to the ASCLA Board of Directors; to serve the ASCLA Board of Directors in an advisory capacity in all matters specified above, and to undertake special projects that are not within the scope of any other existing subordinate unit.

Ch., Rod Wagner (1994); Timothy Brown (1993); Patricia A. Tumulty (1993); sect. reps.: Sally J. Drew (1993); Martha N. Roblee (1993); Stewart L. Wells (1993).

Planning and Budget

To develop short- and long-range plans, at the direction of the Board of Directors, for the division; to recommend priorities, activities, and programs to further the division's goals and purposes. To review, in light of short- and long-range planning, financial requests from sections, committees, and officers for new and continuing programs; to review the financial status, and to prepare the annual budget for the support of the division activities; to present to the ASCLA board at its Midwinter Meeting the committee's recommendation for the annual budget and its priorities in funding; to consult with the ASCLA executive director in budget preparation and revision throughout the year; to identify and consider new revenue areas which might be developed by the division; to recommend funding needed for new program areas under consideration as a result of the planning process.

Co-chs., Duane F. Johnson (1993) and Barbara L. Perkis (1993); Nancy Bolin (1994); Thea B. Chesley (1994); Janice Beck Ison (1994); Anthony W. Miele (1994); Annette M. Milliron (1994); Vincent P. Schmidt (1993); Diana R. Tope (1993); Rod Wagner (1993); sect. reps.: Bill Crowley (1993); Mary W. Ghikas (1993); Barbara J. Goral (1993).

Program Development

To develop a plan for the division to sponsor and cosponsor programs at the meetings of allied organizations.

Ch. and members to be appointed.

Publications

To coordinate policies and activities of the publications program of ASCLA, other than *Interface;* to establish and maintain guidelines and criteria for procedures as well as style, format, and content for the ASCLA publications; to review proposed publications and recommend to the Board of Directors procedures for publication and distribution of individual projects; to assist ASCLA headquarters staff in preparing items for publication, including editorial advice; to identify and recommend new or revised ASCLA publications to appropriate units of the division and the Board of Directors; to maintain a liaison with *Interface* and ALA Publishing Services.

Ch. to be appointed; Jan L. Ames (1993); Bill Crowley (1993); Shirley George (1993); Joanne M. Kepics (1994); Kathleen O. Mayo; Jane F. Moore (1993); Sandra Souza (1993); sect. reps.: Sally J. Drew (1993); Susan H. Galloway (1993); Edwin S. Gleaves (1993); ex officio, Thomas J. Dorst (1993).

Research

To coordinate the activities of the division in the field of research; to keep membership informed about research in the areas of concern to the division; to recommend to the Board of Directors research needs and methods to facilitate research activities; to review and approve all survey instruments to be used by ASCLA units in research prior to distribution; to provide a liaison to the ALA Office for Research and the Library Research Round Table.

Ch., Jeannette P. Smithee (1993); Emily H. Ferren (1993); Ethel E. Himmel (1994); Ann Joslin (1993).

Serials Advisory

The Committee will serve in an advisory capacity to the Editors in all matters relating to the content of the newsletters. The Committee will develop guidelines to assist the Editors. It will review periodically overall editorial policy and, when needed, recommend changes to the ASCLA Board of Directors. In the event of a vacancy in the position of the Editor, the committee will recommend to the ASCLA Executive Board candidates for appointment as the new editor and any necessary change in policy.

Ch., Leslie B. Burger (1994); Thea B. Chesley (1993); Laurence A. Miller (1994); JoEllen Ostendorf (1993); Clarence R. Walters (1994); sec. rep., Sally J. Drew (1993); ex officio; Thomas J. Dorst (1993).

Standards Review

To direct the development of standards and guidelines appropriate to the institutions and activities represented in ASCLA; to review and forward with recommendations for action by the ASCLA Board of Directors on standards and guidelines developed by standards subcommittees; to appoint, in consultation with appropriate units, subcommittees to develop specified standards and guidelines; to maintain constant com-

munications with the ALA Standards Committee relative to policy and formatting and to seek approval by the ALA Standards Committee on these matters prior to ASCLA Board adoption of standards and guidelines; to maintain continuous study for currency and relevance of existing standards and guidelines appropriate to the institutions and activities represented in ASCLA; to maintain liaison with other divisions of ALA in all matters pertaining to standards; to maintain liaison with other standard-setting agencies and closely related professional organizations for consistency in standard setting on the part of all concerned.

Ch., Lorraine S. Summers (1993); Martha J. McDonald (1994); Linda N. Springer (1993); Linda Lucas Walling (1993); Anthony G. Yankus (1994); sect. rep., H. Neil Kelley (1994).

Library Standards for Juvenile Correctional Institutions (subcommittee)

Ch. to be appointed.

Standards for Libraries at Institutions for the Mentally Retarded (ad hoc subcommittee)

Co-chs., Marilyn M. Irwin (1993) and Ruth E. O'Donnell (1993); Carol Adams (1993); Marilyn Karrenbrock (1993); Linda Lucas Walling (1993); Dennis A. Norlin (ACRL, 1994); Stewart L. Wells (PLA, 1994).

REPRESENTATIVES

ALA Conference Program: New Orleans, 1993—Janice Beck Ison.
ALA Legislation Assembly—Barbara H. Will.
ALA Library Education Assembly—Donna Pontau.
ALA Membership Promotion Task Force—Barbara Mates.
ALA Planning and Budget Assembly—Barbara Perkis; Duane A. Johnson.
ALCTS-CCS Cataloging: Description and Access Com.—to be appointed.
American Correctional Assn.—to be appointed.
Assn. of Radio Reading Services—to be appointed.
Freedom to Read Fdn.—to be appointed.
Government Documents Round Table (GODORT)—to be appointed.
Interagency Council on Library Resources for Nursing—Frederic C. Pachman.
Library of Congress/NLS Cost Study Committee—Donna O. Dziedzic.
New Members Round Table (NMRT)—to be appointed.
RASD Interlibrary Loan Com.—to be appointed.

SECTIONS

Libraries Serving Special Populations (LSSPS)
Multitype Library Networks and Cooperatives (Multi-LINCS)
State Library Agency (SLAS)

Libraries Serving Special Populations Section (LSSPS)

To improve the quality of library service for people with special needs including those who are blind, physically handicapped, deaf, developmentally disabled, impaired elderly, in prisons or in health care facilities, or confined in other types of institutions; to improve library service for their families and for professionals working with them;

to foster awareness of these populations and their needs in the library community and among the general public. To carry out this charge, the Section will provide forums, membership activity groups and discussion groups to stimulate activities, to discuss issues, and to exchange ideas concerning quality library services for these special populations. The forums will assist libraries in initiating and improving these services, foster library programming, serve as a liaison with other agencies concerned with these populations, encourage the production of materials about these services and for these populations, encourage instruction in library schools regarding these populations and services, serve as a clearinghouse for ideas and resources, develop standards of service, monitor legislation affecting library service for these populations, and encourage their participation in libraries, in librarianship, and in ALA.

Executive Committee

Ch., Barbara J. Goral (1995); secy., Lance C. Finney (1994); past ch., John M. Day (1993); Timothy Brown (1993); Thea B. Chesley (1993); Emily H. Ferren (1993); Allan M. Kleiman (1993); Leslie Rosen (1993); Rhea J. Rubin (1994).

Committees

Francis Joseph Campbell Award

To select a person who has made an outstanding contribution to the advancement of library service for the blind and physically handicapped to receive the Francis Joseph Campbell citation and medal, to oversee the casting of the medal and the printing of the citation, and to arrange for the printing of the awards program activity, in cooperation with the ASCLA Awards Committee. When the award is given at a meal function, the chairperson is responsible for working closely with the Local Arrangements Subcommittee and for the advance ticket sale.

Ch., H. Neal Kelley (1993); J. L. Anjier (1993); Frederick Duda (1993); Lance C. Finney (1993); Donna S. Foust (1993); Lisa M. Scholl (1993).

Nominating (1993)

Ch., John M. Day (1993); Anne E. Feiler (1993); Barbara J. Goral (1993); Elliott E. Kanner (1993); Vibeke Lehmann (1993); Rhea J. Rubin (1993).

Organization and Bylaws

Ch., Stewart L. Wells (1993); Anne E. Feiler (1993); Donna Z. Pontau (1993); Linda Lucas Walling (1993).

Planning

Ch., Barbara J. Goral (1993); Timothy Brown (1993); Ann E. Eccles (1993); Susan H. Galloway (1993); Michael G. Gunde (1993); Rhea J. Rubin (1993).

Forums

Bibliotherapy Forum (BF)

To bring together and disseminate information on existing concepts and practices in bibliotherapy; to stimulate the further development and use of the techniques and materials of bibliotherapy as a library service; to discuss issues and topics in the area of bibliotherapy.

Ch., Rhea J. Rubin (1993).

Library Service to the Blind and Physically Handicapped Forum (LSBPHF)

To extend and improve library service to those unable to read or use standard printed materials because of physical limitations; to provide a symposium for the exchange of ideas and personnel; to acquaint all librarians whose service communities may include blind and physically handicapped readers with the forum and to enlist their cooperation in meeting those objectives.

Ch., Leslie Rosen (1993); ch.-elect, Michael Gunde (1994).

Library Service to the Deaf Forum (LSDF)

To promote library and information service to deaf persons by: fostering deaf awareness in the library community and in the deaf and hearing populations at large; monitoring and publicizing legislation and funding developments related to library and information services for deaf persons; encouraging employment and career opportunities for deaf persons in libraries, and encouraging their participation in the American Library Association; stimulating the production, distribution, and collection of materials in formats that are readily accessible to deaf persons and that accurately portray deaf persons; and developing and operating a clearinghouse of information on services for deaf persons to assist libraries in collection development and programming. These functions shall be carried out in cooperation with other ALA units and national organizations, as appropriate.

Ch., Emily H. Ferren (1993); ch.-elect, Susan H. Galloway (1994).

Library Service to the Impaired Elderly Forum (LSIEF)

To improve the quality of library service to the impaired elderly, including those with physical handicaps, emotional problems, those in institutions, in group living situations and the homebound who cannot avail themselves of traditional library service; to develop standards of library service in this area; to cooperate with organizations representing other disciplines working with the elderly; to develop innovative techniques of service with the frail elderly; to support and foster library programming for specific needs in this area; to encourage and develop instruction pertinent to establishing on-going programs in library schools and continuing education courses; to serve as a clearinghouse for information, ideas, materials, programs, and human resources available for library service to the impaired elderly; and to raise the awareness of other ALA divisions of the needs of this group.

Ch., Allan M. Kleiman (1993); ch.-elect, Ann E. Eccles (1994).

Library Service to Prisoners Forum (LSPF)

To raise the consciousness level of people within the library and correctional communities regarding the urgent and particular library and information needs of all prisoners; to encourage and assist librarians to begin, expand, and improve library service to prisoners and correctional staff; to serve as a clearinghouse for information, ideas, materials, programs, and human resources for correctional library services; to contribute to and promote cooperation among the

library communities and correctional agencies and organizations; to initiate and support pertinent legislation; and to contribute to and promote the adoption and improvement of standards for correctional library service.

Ch., Timothy Brown (1994).

Membership Activity Groups

Library Service to Developmentally Disabled Persons (LSDDP)

To promote and extend effective library services to developmentally disabled persons at their level of need by sharing information among practitioners currently providing service to this population and by providing information and guidance to those librarians who have unserved or inadequately served populations of developmentally disabled persons in their area.

Ch., Marilyn M. Irwin (1993).

Library Services to People Who Are Mentally Ill

To explore ways in which libraries of all types can initiate or improve services to the mentally ill; to encourage publication of articles and bibliographies on library services for the mentally ill; to provide the opportunity for information exchange between members at ALA meetings.

Ch., Thomas E. Hecker (1993).

Discussion Group

Academic Librarians Assisting the Disabled (ALAD)

To provide a forum for sharing information and experiences concerning services to users with disabilities in academic libraries; to build an information network among those responsible for providing such services; to encourage their improvement; to promote dialogue between librarians and vendors regarding the needs of users with disabilities; and to increase the awareness and cooperation of all academic librarians in better serving this special population.

Ch., John W. King (1993).

Multitype Library Networks and Cooperatives Section (Multi-LINCS)

To study, improve, promote, and represent the interests and activities of libraries involved in statewide, multistate and national coordination of cooperatives and multitype library systems and information networks designed to provide a nationwide information delivery system which equalizes access to information resources. To provide a forum for discussions, programs, and planning designed to stimulate and assist members to achieve effective coordination of library resources and services through multitype library cooperation.

Executive Committee

Ch., Keith Michael Fiels (1994); vice ch./ch.-elect, Mary W. Ghikas (1995); secy., Elizabeth A. Curry (1994); past ch., Martha J. McDonald (1993); John J. Hammond (1994); Jane Raifsnider (1993); Louella V. Wetherbee (1995).

Committees

Membership (ad hoc)

Ch., Jane Raifsnider (1993); Joanne M. Kepics (1993); Sara G. Laughlin (1993); Laurence A. Miller (1993); Ann T. Parent (1993); Frank Rodgers (1993); Melissa Stockton (1993).

Nominating (1993)

Ch., Dottie Hiebing (1993); Nancy P. Knepel (1993); Katherine Jagoe Massey (1993).

Planning

To develop short- and long-range plans for the section and to make recommendations for activities to the Executive Committee. To review the section's organizational structure and Bylaws and to make recommendations to the Executive Committee as appropiate.

Ch., Linda L. Fuchs (1994); Keith Michael Fiels (1994); David J. Karre (1993); Martha J. McDonald (1993); William Miller (1994); Joan Neumann (1994); Karen Liston Newsome (1994); Barbara H. Will (1994).

Planning for Multitype Library Organizations (ad hoc)

Ch., Janice Beck Ison (1993); Gordan C. Barhydt (1993); Steven A. Baughman (1993); Linda D. Crowe (1993); Elizabeth A. Curry (1993); Tony Gangloff (1993); Dottie Hiebing (1993); Ethel E. Himmel (1993); Karen Hyman (1993); Joan Neumann (1993); Bill Strader (1993); Sondra Vandermark (1993); Keith Washburn (1993); Valerie Wilford (1993).

Program (1993)

To coordinate Multi-LINCS programming activities with other appropriate units of ASCLA; to plan and produce appropriate programs according to the priorities of the section; to cooperate with other ALA units in carrying out programs related to multitype library cooperation.

Ch., Holly Clark Carroll (1993); Anita Anker Branin (1993); Susan M. Fayad (1993); Timothy P. Lynch (1993); Brenda M. Pacey (1993); Debra Park (1993); Sondra H. Vanderman (1993).

Publications (ad hoc)

The publications committee shall coordinate the section's publications programs in ways to include, but not be limited to, the following activities: (1) reviewing publications proposed by section committees and serving in a consulting role when appropriate; (2) assuring that section publications are produced in a consistent, recognizable format, and that they are easily identified as publications; (3) identifying areas where section publications might be useful, and consulting with the appropriate committees on their production; and (4) providing liaison to the ASCLA Publications Committee. The publications committee shall collect, publicize, and disseminate materials on multitype cooperation published by multitype library cooperatives in order to assist members in developing programs and publications.

Ch., Sally J. Drew (1993); Elizabeth A. Curry (1993); Rhonna A. Goodman (1994); Annette M. Milliron (1993); David S. Simmons (1993); Jeanette P. Smithee (1993); Amy E. Spaulding (1993); Roger D. Sween (1993); Richard E. Willson (1993); Catherine C. Wilt (1993).

Discussion Groups

Cooperative Collection Development

Charge to be developed.

Ch., Terry L. Weech (1993).

Interlibrary Cooperation

To provide a forum for discussion of interests in interlibrary cooperation and the statewide development of library service, emphasizing the interdependence of all types of libraries.

Ch., Keith E. Washburn (1993).

International Networking

To provide a forum for exchange of information relating to the internationalization of bibliographic databases and multitype library cooperation within and among the nations of the world.

Ch., Sherry K. Little (1993).

Network Assembly

A forum for communicating national updates related to networking. The Library of Congress Network Advisory Committee (NAC) serves as an informal connection between ASCLA, NAC, and other national groups. Special network problems and developments and updates of national significance are addressed in the Multi-LINCS Network Assembly.

Co-chs., Maureen L. Canick (1994) and Gregory Pronevitz (1994); Kathleen L. Bloomberg (1994).

Network Management

Charge to be developed.

Co-chs., Steven A. Baughman (1993) and Elizabeth A. Curry (1993).

Rural Library Cooperatives

To provide a forum for discussions of common interests of those working in and with rural networks.

Ch., John Christenson (1993).

State Library Agency Section (SLAS)

To develop and strengthen the unique role and functions of state library agencies in providing leadership and services that foster and improve the delivery of library services. To stimulate the continued professional development of state library agency personnel in discharging their unique functions in such areas as statewide planning and evaluation, services to state governments and legislatures, services to local libraries, services to users with special needs, etc.

Executive Committee

Ch., Anthony W. Miele (1994); ch.-elect, Bill Crowley (1995); secy., Yolanda J. Cuesta (1994); past ch., J. Gary Nichols (1993); Sandra Cooper (1994); Edwin S. Gleaves (1995); Howard F. McGinn (1993).

Committees

Conference Program

Ch., Sondra Vandermark (1993); Leslie B. Burger (1993); Michelle M. Gardner (1993).

Nominating (1993)

Ch., Fred D. Neighbors (1993); Sally J. Drew (1993); Charles Ray Ewick (1993).

Planning

Ch., Bill Crowley (1993).

Discussion Groups

Consultants for Service to Children and Young People

To provide a forum for persons concerned with statewide service to children and young people.

Ch., Grace Worcester Greene (1993).

General Consultants

To identify general consultants in ASCLA/SLAS and to provide a forum for discussion of common concerns, such as the defining of the role of consultants, the improvement of consulting skills, and the day-to-day practical problems of consultants.

Ch., Anthony W. Miele (1993).

Information Needs of State Government

To provide a forum for persons on the state level involved with the development and provision of library service to state governments and state agencies.

Ch., Marilyn E. Douglas (1993).

LSCA Coordinators

Ch., Loretta L. Flowers (1993).

Specialized Services Consultants

To provide a forum for state library agency consultants with responsibility for services and programs for special needs populations (the educationally, culturally, and socioeconomically disadvantaged in urban and rural areas, the elderly, ethnic minorities, persons with limited English speaking ability, and disabled persons) and to exchange information among members about the special concerns of these consultants at the state level.

Ch., Ruth E. O'Donnell (1993).

State Agency Consultants to Institutional Libraries

To provide a forum for persons from state library agencies and those in other state agencies with responsibilities for institutional services and programs and to exchange information among members about special concerns of institutional consultants at the state level.

Ch., Gloria A. Spooner (1993).

Library Administration and Management Association

Membership as of August 31, 1992
Organization members 811
Personal members 4,286
Total 5,097

Karen Muller, *executive director*
Elizabeth Dreazen, *deputy executive director*

The Library Administration and Management Association provides an organizational frame work for encouraging the study of administrative theory, for improving the practice of administration in libraries, and for identifying and fostering administrative skill. Toward these ends, the division is responsible for all elements of general administration which are common to more than one type of library. These may include organizational structure, financial administration, personnel management and training, buildings and equipment, and public relations.

LAMA meets this responsibility in the following ways:

1. Study and review of activities assigned to the division with due regard for changing developments in these activities.

2. Initiating and overseeing activities and projects appropriate to the division, including activities involving bibliography compilation, publication, study, and review of professional literature within the scope of the division.

3. Synthesizing the activities of other ALA units which have a bearing upon the responsibilities or work of the division.

4. Representing and interpreting library administrative activities in contacts outside the library profession.

5. Aiding the professional development of librarians engaged in administration and encouraging their participation in appropriate type-of-library divisions.

6. Planning and developing programs of study and research in library administrative problems which are most needed by the profession.

Board of Directors

Pres., James G. Neal (1994); pres.-elect, Carol F. L. Liu (1995); past pres., Susan E. Stroyan (1993); div. councilor, Rodney M. Hersberger (1993); *dirs.-at-large*: Anders C. Dahlgren (1993); Charles E. Kratz Jr. (1994); *sect. chs.*: Cathy J. Audley (FRFDS, 1993); Lee B. Brawner (BES, 1993); Phyllis E. Jaynes (LOMS, 1993); Carolyn Kacena (SS, 1993); Sandra A. Scherba (PRS, 1993); Gisela M. Webb (PAS, 1993); Jacqueline M. Zelman (SASS, 1993); *ex officio*: sect. vice-chs.: Carol L. Anderson (BES, 1994); Teresa A. Edwards (SASS, 1994); Joline Ridlon Ezzell (FRFDS, 1994); Michael S. Freeman (LOMS, 1994); John J. McGinnis (PRS, 1994); Joseph A. Starratt (SS, 1994); Ann F. Stone (PAS, 1994); Organization ch., Gerard B. McCabe (1993); Budget & Finance ch., Ronald P. Naylor (1993); ed., Diane J. Graves (1995); ed., Fred M. Heath (1993); assoc. ed., Joan R. Giesecke (1997); exec. dir., Karen Muller.

Executive Committee

Pres., James G. Neal (1994); pres.-elect, Carol F. L. Liu (1995); past pres., Susan E. Stroyan (1993); councilor, Rodney M. Hersberger (1993); exec. dir., Karen Muller.

Publications

Library Administration & Management (quarterly). Mailed to all LAMA members. Available by subscription. $50 a yr. ($60 foreign). Ed., Diane J. Graves, 4043 Wolf Rd., Western Springs, IL 60558; assoc. ed., Joan R. Giesecke, 5515 Sherman St., Lincoln, NE 68506.

COMMITTEES

(Hugh C.) Atkinson Memorial Award, ACRL/ALCTS/LAMA/LITA (See p. 44.)

Budget and Finance

To submit a recommended annual budget for action to the LAMA Board of Directors; to perform budget analyses and fiscal planning; to advise units on requesting LAMA funds; to review all requests for LAMA funds; to advise the LAMA Board on all fiscal matters of the division, including the fiscal implications of all division publications and programs; and to represent LAMA at the COPES Planning and Budget Assembly.

Ch., Ronald P. Naylor (1993); H. Harrison Heath (1994); Kathryn J. Hoffman (1994); Barbara Leonard (1994); Barton M. Lessin (1994); Roderick MacNeil (1994); Ryoko Toyama (1994); ex officio: Carol F. L. Liu (1994); James G. Neal (1994).

Cultural Diversity

To work with LAMA Membership Committee, vice-president/president-elect, and others to promote increased membership and participation in LAMA, its committee work, programs, and other activities by members of ethnic minority groups; to recommend efforts LAMA should make to lead libraries in improving services to a culturally diverse population, in developing equitable personnel policies and practices, in creating job/promotional/training opportunities for members of ethnic minorities, and in fostering the enlightened management of a culturally diverse workforce; to maintain liaisons and develop joint projects with established ALA units and affiliates and other organizations having similar concerns; to inform and advise LAMA and its units on matters related to cultural diversity; to present programs and carry out other appropriate activities.

Ch., Liz R. Miller (1993); Christina Young Allen (1993); Clarence E. Chisholm (1993); Denyvetta Davis (1993); Anthony M. Dos Santos (1994); Rodney M. Hersberger (1993); Raul A. Huerta (1993); Rebecca R. Martin (1994); Mimi McBride (1993); Pal V. Rao (1994); Joyce G. Taylor (1993); Virginia F. Toliver (1994); Darlene M. Ziolkowski (1994).

Editorial Advisory Board

To support the Editor of *Library Administration & Management* in publishing a high-quality professional magazine. The Board is responsible for editorial planning in coordination with the Editor; advising the Editor as requested; staying abreast of current LAMA membership interests as well as current issues in library administration and management; encouraging contributions from LAMA sections, task force, and discussion group members; assisting the Editor and Associate Editor in soliciting material as needed; assisting the Editor and Associate Editor in planning theme issues and suggesting contributing authors for those issues; and providing an annual evaluation of the Editor and Associate Editor to the Board of Directors.

Ch., Jonathan D. Eldredge (1993); Saul J. Amdursky (1993); Edward Garten (1993); Jane W. Greenfield (1993); Jasper G. Schad (1994); Karen S. Seibert (1994); Carolyn A. W. Snyder (1994); Kate Storms (1993); ed., Diane J. Graves (1995); assoc. ed., Joan R. Giesecke (1997); ex officio, James G. Neal (1993).

Education

To monitor issues related to education and continuing education for librarians and prepare the LAMA position as necessary; to develop a list of competencies for library administrators; to develop a continuing strategy to track LAMA's response to education issues; and to work with LAMA's liaisons to the Literary Education Assembly, the Literacy Assembly, and the Accreditation Standard Revision Committee.

Ch., Susanne Henderson (1993).

Governmental Affairs

To identify, monitor, and address executive and judicial branch issues, as well as those of the legislative branch, which affect divisional interests; to support the ALA legislative program by more actively involving the division in it; to encourage the collection and analysis of appropriate data to support LAMA's governmental efforts; and to inform LAMA members about appropriate governmental issues.

Ch., Robert A. Daugherty (1993); James B. Casey (1994); William M. Cochran (1994); David E. Ellefsen (1994); Robert W. Frase (1994); Carol M. Kelley (1993); Judith N. Long (1993); Eileen B. Longsworth (1993); June H. Martin (1993); Joan S. McConkey (1994); Dana E. Smith (1993); Diane Harvey Smith (1994); Bernadette R. Storck (1994); Steven Unger (1994).

Membership

To recruit new LAMA members and retain current members; to channel information regarding LAMA activities between members and LAMA headquarters; to market LAMA resources at local, state, and regional conferences; to schedule and staff the LAMA booth at ALA Conferences; to provide orientation to LAMA for National Membership Services Network Representatives.

To plan and conduct in conjunction with the LAMA Orientation Committee an orientation and social hour for members and potential members at the Annual Conference.

Ch., Robert A. Almony (1993); Sara T. Behrman (1994); Marcia L. Boosinger (1994); Anita R. Clamurro (1993); Sharon E. Clark (1994); Lynn Scott Cochrane (1993); Edward Garten (1994); Steven Hawk (1993); Elizabeth Hope Hayes (1994); Dottie R. Hiebing (1994); William G. Jones (1994); Roy L. Joynes (1993); Janet S. Kinney (1994); William Miller (1994); Kate W. Ragsdale (1993); Ellen Derey Safley (1994); Dallas R. Shawkey (1994); Aline E. Soules (1993); Laine Stambaugh (1994); Carolyn M. Tynan (1994); Lamar Veatch (1994); Patricia Wilson (1994); intern, Nancy F. Bierschenk (1993).

Nominating—1993 Elections

Ch., Robert F. Moran Jr. (1993); Lynn Scott Cochrane (1993); Jane W. Greenfield (1993); Malcolm K. Hill (1993); Trellis C. Wright (1993).

Nominating—1994 Elections

Ch. and members to be appointed.

Organization

To recommend to the LAMA Board of Directors changes in the LAMA Bylaws, establishment and discontinuance of any LAMA section or discussion group, establishment or discontinuance of standing committees, and the sizes and names of committees. The LAMA COO also defines the functions of each section and committee subject to the approval of the board.

Ch., Gerard B. McCabe (1994); Mary M. Gilles (1994); Maggie Gordon (1994); Aubrey W. Kendrick (1993); Norma H. Martin (1994); Robert F. Moran Jr. (1993); Thomas M. Peischl (1994); Cordelia W. Swinton (1994); John J. Vasi (1994); Mark Watson (1994).

Orientation

To develop and implement a formal orientation program for all division and section officers and committee members. Purpose of the program is to provide all LAMA members with sufficient information to help them contribute effectively to LAMA's programs; and, in particular, to help division and section officers and committee members to operate effectively.

To plan and conduct in conjunction with the LAMA Membership Committee an orientation and social hour for members and potential members at the Annual Conference.

Ch., Sharon L. Stewart (1993); Carol L. Anderson (1994); Rosemary H. Arneson (1994); Jeffrey S. Berger (1994); Joan F. Cheverie (1993); Mary M. Harrison (1993); Carl Heffington (1994); Barton M. Lessin (1994); Roderick MacNeil (1993); Norman L. Nelson (1994); Joan Reyes (1993); Marilyn H. Shaver (1994); Cecilia D. Stafford (1994).

Program

To develop criteria for LAMA Annual Conference programs; to review Annual Conference program plans approved by section executive committee chairs; to recommend approval of Annual Conference programs to the Board; to suggest themes for future Annual Conference programs; to serve as LAMA liaison with similar committees of other divisions.

Ch., Rod Henshaw (1993); Michael J. Abaray (1994); Susan M. Anderson (1993); Cheryl A. Bernero (1993); Jennifer Cargill (1994); Melissa Carr (1994); C. Colleen Cook (1993); Clifford H. Haka (1994); Ann Hamilton (1993); Malcolm K. Hill (1994); Joan S. Howland (1993); Rebecca R. Martin (1993); Salvatore M. Meringolo (1994); Beverly B. Moore (1993); Harold D. Neikirk (1993); Sharon L. Stewart (1994); Philip Tramdack (1994); ex officio: Carol F. L. Liu (1995); James G. Neal (1994); Susan E. Stroyan (1993).

Publications

To oversee and coordinate the publishing program of LAMA by: analyzing LAMA publications, identifying gaps and duplicates, and recommending publishing policy for the approval of the LAMA Board; overseeing publishing budget preparation; recognizing publishing priorities; and maintaining high publishing standards; reviewing the work of various continuing publications, their editors and their boards; advising and assisting the sections and LAMA membership in their publishing activities; and encouraging research in the theory and practice of library management which might result in an expanded publication program.

Ch., Charles B. Lowry (1993); Judith A. Adams (1994); Beverly J. Bagan (1993); Martha J. Bailey (1993); H. Scott Davis (1994); Kathleen G. Fouty (1993); George R. Jaramillo (1994); Gillian M. McCombs (1993); Richard W. Murphy (1993); ex officio: Diane J. Graves (1995); Susan Oberlander (1994).

Recognition of Achievement

To encourage, recognize, and commend excellence in service to LAMA and its sections. To establish, revise, and publicize selection criteria for the awards; to promote, encourage, and receive nominations from individual members or section Executive Committees; to evaluate nominations and recommend no more than three nominees for each award to the LAMA Board at the Midwinter Meeting each year; to determine the award format and plan the award ceremony. The awards shall be a Certificate of Appreciation for a significant contribution to the goals of LAMA over a period of several years and a Certificate of Special Thanks for a specific significant single contribution to the goals of LAMA.

Ch., Dale S. Montanelli (1993); June D. Chressanthis (1994); Susan E. Henderson (1994); William G. Jones (1993); Larry T. Nix (1994); Carolyn A. W. Snyder (1993); John J. Vasi (1994).

Small Libraries Publications Series

To prepare and/or recommend new or revised materials to be published for the guidance of personnel in small libraries.

Ch., Marcia L. Thomas (1993); Elinor F. Bridges (1994); Larayne J. Dallas (1993); Patricia E. Dick (1994); George V. Hodowanec (1994); Rashelle S. Karp (1994); Ruth Chamberlain Kowal (1994); John M. Robson (1994); ex officio, Susan Oberlander (1994).

Special Conferences and Programs

To provide leadership and coordinate the development of LAMA programming, apart from Annual Conferences, based on the continuing education needs of the members of the division and the profession at large; to initiate and develop specific program plans in cooperation with various ALA units; to review and report to the LAMA Board of Directors and to sections the potential programming implications of developments in library management; to review and recommend to the LAMA Board program proposals submitted by LAMA sections and committees or by private consultants and trainers according to LAMA Board approved criteria; to establish links with other professional associations and agencies involved in similar kinds of educational program activities.

Ch., Katherine Anne Branch (1993); Jan E. Baaske (1994); James R. Coffey (1994); Kathryn J. Deiss (1994); Connie Vinita Dowell (1994); Michael P. Kinch (1994); Doris A. Miller (1994); Jo Ann Pinder (1993); Marcia S. Rettig (1994); Judy Riggle (1994); Donald E. Wright (1993); Joyce Crawford Wright (1993).

TASK FORCES

Managing in a Networked Information Environment

To develop a set of strategies for shaping LAMA's leadership role and focusing LAMA programs in the area of networked information.

Ch., Jacqueline M. Zelman (1994).

Professional Certification, PLA/LAMA
(See p. 76.)

State/Regional Chapters

To explore and develop joint ventures with natural allies within state and regional organizations in the areas of administration and management.

Ch., Janice T. Koyama (1993); Richard L. Harwood (1993); Karen L. Horny (1993); Charles E. Kratz Jr. (1993); Lamar Veatch (1994).

White House Conference Follow-up

Ch., Danuta A. Nitecki (1993); Cecil P. Beach (1993); Annie Brewer (1993); Lynn Scott Cochrane (1993); Ann H. Eastman (1993); Elaine Graham Estes (1993); John D. Hales Jr. (1993); Edward R. Johnson (1993); Samuel F. Morrison (1993); Janet M. Welch (1993); Trellis C. Wright (1993).

DISCUSSION GROUPS

Assistants-to-the-Director

To provide a forum for individuals whose job assignments cause them to function as assistant to the director. The forum acts as an information network for the solution of common problems and emphasizes the working role with the director and staff responsibilities within the library.

Ch., John P. Culshaw (1993); secy./ch.-elect, Lynn M. Accardo (1994).

Library Storage

To provide a forum for exchanging ideas on the planning, design, development, operation, management and/or dismantling of library collection storage.

Ch., Claire Q. Bellanti (1993).

Middle Management

To provide a forum to examine and encourage the study of library administration, especially on the middle management level, and to encourage the improvement of such management in libraries. The Middle Management Discussion Group carries out these functions through discussions, programs, and preconferences at Midwinter and the Annual Conferences of the ALA and through publishing materials of interest to middle managers.

Ch., Sue A. Dietl (1993).

Women Administrators

To provide a forum for discussion of problems of particular concern to women in administrative positions.

Ch., Susan H. Anthes (1993).

REPRESENTATIVES

ALA Intellectual Freedom Com.—Patricia H. Latshaw (1993).

ALA Legislation Assembly—Robert A. Daugherty (1993).

ALA Library Education Assembly—Donald E. Wright (1993).

ALA Literacy Assembly—Trellis C. Wright (1993).

ALA Membership Com.—Robert A. Almony Jr. (1993).

ALA National Library Week—to be appointed.

ALA Planning and Budget Assembly—Ronald P. Naylor (1993).

ALA Professional Ethics Com.—Melissa A. Laning (1993).

ASCLA Decade of Disabled Persons Com. (interdivisional)—Sara B. Appelbaum (1993).

Freedom to Read Fdn.—Pamela Gay Bonnell (1993).

Friends of Libraries USA—Debra Park (1993).

SECTIONS

Buildings and Equipment (BES)
Fund Raising and Financial Development (FRFDS)
Library Organization and Management (LOMS)
Personnel Administration (PAS)
Public Relations (PRS)
Statistics (SS)
Systems and Services (SASS)

Buildings and Equipment Section (BES)

The section on Buildings and Equipment exercises responsibility for matters relating to library structure for all types of libraries, including their design, construction, alteration, and equipment. Illustrative of the fields of interest covered are library site selection; building planning and architecture; the interior organization of library buildings; library furniture and equipment; decoration of interiors; ventilation, air conditioning, and lighting; maintenance of library buildings and property; bookmobile planning and design; and other pertinent areas of interest.

Executive Committee

Ch., Lee B. Brawner (1994); ch.-elect, Carol L. Anderson (1995); secy., Gerard B. McCabe (1993); past ch., Elizabeth K. Gay (1993); Nancy R. McAdams (1993); Claudya B. Muller (1994).

Committees

Architecture for Public Libraries

To study, evaluate, and recommend in matters relating to public library structures, including their design, construction, and alteration. Its scope includes: library site selection; building planning and architecture; interior organization of library buildings; decoration of interiors; ventilation, air conditioning, and lighting; maintenance of library buildings and property; bookmobile planning and design.

Ch., Daniel L. Walters (1993); Jeffrey S. Berger (1994); Linda L. Cumming (1994); Mary L. Jensen (1994); Carolynn K. Johnson (1993); M. Kathleen T. Koppe (1994); Ella M. Melik (1993); David L. Michaels (1994); Kathryn Page (1994); Philip A. Place (1993); Janice M. Ridgeway (1994); Emelie J. Shroder (1994); Cy H. Silver (1994); George R. Stewart (1993); Jason R. Stone (1994); Anthony Tappe (1993); Richard L. Waters (1994); Anne Watts (1994).

Buildings for College and University Libraries

To study, evaluate, and recommend in matters relating to college and university structures,
including their design, construction, and alteration. Its scope includes: library site selection; building planning and architecture; interior organization of library buildings; decoration of interiors; ventilation, air conditioning, and lighting; maintenance of library buildings and property.

Ch., Carolyn A. W. Snyder (1993); Claire Q. Bellanti (1994); Min-Min Chang (1993); Robert E. Danford (1994); Ronald F. Dow (1993); Lynn M. Fortney (1994); Anne S. Hudson (1993); David P. Jensen (1993); Jane G. Johnson (1993); James R. Kennedy (1994); James M. Kusack (1994); Tess Midkiff (1993); Dale S. Montanelli (1994); Jay Martin Poole (1994); Kate W. Ragsdale (1993); Marion T. Reid (1994); Robert L. White (1993).

Equipment

To study, evaluate, and recommend in matters relating to library furniture and equipment for all types of libraries.

Ch., Elizabeth C. Habich (1993); Wendell A. Barbour (1993); Karen Havill Bingham (1993); Joan L. Clark (1993); Joseph H. Green (1994); B. Frank Hemphill (1993); Helmut Hutter (1993); Nancy Jaeger (1993); Michael J. LaCroix (1993); Sharon Lane (1994); Andrea A. Michaels (1993); Sarah C. Michalak (1993).

Functional Space Requirements

To assess the current status of national space allocation standards and guidelines; to develop new standards for physical space requirements for libraries in conjunction with other ALA units and external organizations such as AIA, ANSI, ASTM, and NISO.

Ch., Deborah B. Dancik (1993); Deborah B. Babel (1994); Joseph W. Barnes (1994); Mary M. Gilles (1994); Merri A. Hartse (1993); H. Harrison Heath (1993); Edgar L. Hillsman (1994); Anne S. Hudson (1994); Florence M. Mason (1993); Sheryl B. Owens (1994); Pal V. Rao (1994); Stanley J. Wilder (1994); Janice Skinner Yeager (1994).

Library Buildings Awards

To administer the joint ALA–American Institute of Architects awards program for the recognition of excellence in architectural design and planning of libraries; to interpret and publicize the results to the library profession; to assist in the selection and preparation of award jurors.

Ch., Anders C. Dahlgren (1993); Carol L. Anderson (1994); Charles Forrest (1993); Melvin R. George (1994); H. Harrison Heath (1993); Deborah Jacobs (1994); Lynda M. Lee (1994); Sul H. Lee (1994); Melody S. Linger (1994); Kathryn Courtland Millis (1993); Judy E. Myers (1994); Kenneth G. Sivulich (1993); Charles R. Smith (1994).

Library Buildings Consultant List

To prepare for issuance a biennial publication of LAMA-BES, *Library Buildings Consultant List;* to establish minimum eligibility criteria; working with the LAMA Executive Director, to issue a public invitation to prospective library building consultants; to compile and edit the list of qualified respondents; and to prepare the final copy for publication.

Ch., Gail A. Kennedy (1993); Mary C. Cooper (1994); James A. Estrada (1993); Karen Kinney (1994); Gloria J. Stockton (1994).

Nominating—1993 Elections

Ch., Carol L. Anderson (1993); Andrea A. Michaels (1993); Lamar Veatch (1993).

Nominating—1994 Elections

Ch. and members to be appointed.

Publications

To oversee and coordinate the publishing program of the LAMA Buildings and Equipment Section by: recommending appointments of editors and editorial boards to BES Executive Committee, analyzing BES needs, identifying gaps and duplicates, and recommending publishing policy for the approval of the BES Executive Committee; coordinating publishing activities with the LAMA Publishing Committee and other LAMA and ALA committees and groups; recognizing publishing priorities and maintaining high publishing standards, approving and reviewing the work of various continuing publications, their editors and committees; advising and assisting the BES research in the theory and practice of library buildings and equipment which might result in an expanded publication program.

Ch., Lamar Veatch (1994); Patricia S. Butcher (1994); Kazuko M. Dailey (1993); Catherine F. Doyle (1993); Ron G. Martin (1994); Nancy R. McAdams (1994); Claudia J. Morner (1994); William E. Sannwald (1993).

Safety and Security of Library Buildings

To deal with issues related to the safety and security of persons and property in library buildings; to promote safety measures in building design, interior organization, alteration, equipment and furnishings selection, and collection maintenance.

Ch., Phyllis L. Cutler (1994); Charles A. Baughan (1994); Sandra J. Beidler (1993); J. Craig Buthod (1993); Susan E. Cirillo (1994); Claire A. Colombo (1993); Kazuko M. Dailey (1994); Frank J. DeRosa (1993); Trudi M. Di Trolio (1994); Helen R. Goldstein (1994); Erla P. Heyns (1993); Stephanie Hillman (1994); James R. Kennedy (1994); Lora L. Lennertz (1994); Kenneth E. Marks (1994); Murray S. Martin (1993); Larry J. Ostler (1994); Stuart F. Rosselet (1994).

School Library Media Facilities

To study, evaluate, and disseminate information in matters relating to school library media facilities. Its scope includes: the facilities planning process; interior organization of instructional resource centers; interior design; renovation and remodeling; and provision for instructional equipment and furnishings.

Ch., Steven W. Hagstrom (1994); Phyllis D. Fisher (1994); M. Elspeth Goodin (1994); Edward H. Healey (1994); Anne Masters (1994); Retta B. Patrick (1994); Jacqueline C. Sanders (1993); Cherrill M. Whitlow (1993).

Discussion Group

Library Facilities Planning

To provide a forum for members whose interests include the development or coordination of building planning, and for members appointed or elected to serve on committees with building planning responsibilities, for library construction, expansion, or renovation. This forum will act as an information and support network to identify and discuss common problems and explore alternative solutions.

Ch., Donald G. Kelsey (1993).

Fund Raising and Financial Development Section (FRFDS)

The Fund Raising and Financial Development section exercises responsibility for matters pertaining to fund raising and resource development for libraries. Illustrative of the fields of interest are foundation, trust, and endowment development and administration; annual giving and direct-mail fund raising programs; capital campaign planning and implementation, grantsmanship; and other areas of fund raising activity. The section addresses these areas by providing a forum for discussion; serving as a clearinghouse for the exchange of related ideas, information, and techniques; and providing a source for the research and development of guides, aids, and publications relating to financial resource development.

Executive Committee

Ch., Cathy J. Audley (1994); ch.-elect, Joline Ridlon Ezzell (1995); secy., James A. Swan (1994); past ch., Christian Esquevin (1993); Dwight F. Burlingame (1994); Susan F. Gregory (1993).

Committees

Clearinghouse

To assist with the formation of a clearinghouse for fund-raising information at the library of the American Library Association.

Ch., Anne J. Borland (1993); Erla P. Heyns (1993).

Fund Fare

To plan and coordinate all activities to support the Fund Fare program at the annual conference.

Co-chs., Deborah Jacobs (1993) and Catherine S. Van Hoy (1993); Dorothy E. Christiansen (1993); Andrea Lapsley (1994); Terri Mc-Dermot (1994); Donald J. Schabel (1993).

Nominating—1993 Elections

Ch., Mary E. (Molly) Raphael (1993); members to be appointed.

Nominating—1994 Elections

Ch., Eugene T. Neely (1994); Claire Oaks (1994); Gene Rollins (1994).

Program

To plan and coordinate all programs presented by the section at the Annual Conference, special institutes, seminars, and preconferences as determined relevant to the continuing education needs of the members of the section. The chair serves as liaison to the LAMA Program Committee.

Ch., Jack F. Bulow (1993); Jerry W. Brownlee (1993); Rhonna A. Goodman (1994); Susan F. Gregory (1994); Deborah Jacobs (1994); Gene Rollins (1993).

Publications

Ch., Allan J. Dyson (1993); Dwight F. Burlingame (1993); Kenneth E. Flower (1993); Ann L. Koch (1993); Andrea Lapsley (1994); Marjorie H. Li (1993); Cheryl A. Napsha (1994).

Trends, Marketing, and Project Development

To gather and disseminate information on trends, theories, and techniques for library fund raising; to develop new projects related to fund raising in libraries to be undertaken by the section.

Ch., Elizabeth E. Bingham (1994); Rebecca R. Bostian (1993); Connie Vinita Dowell (1994); Elizabeth A. Fuseler (1994); Fay A. Golden (1994); Fred M. Heath (1994); Jeffrey R. Krull (1993); P. Grady Morein (1994); Eugene T. Neely (1994); Claire Oaks (1994).

Discussion Group

Development Issues

To provide an informal forum for members to exchange information on fund-raising issues and to seek solutions to common problems.

Ch., Dennis East (1994).

Library Organization and Management Section (LOMS)

The Library Organization and Management section investigates issues pertaining to efficient library operations in all types of libraries and disseminates information on management issues to all its members, the LAMA membership, and all librarians. Issues of ongoing interest are specified in the section's standing committees and discussion groups.

Executive Committee

Ch., Phyllis E. Jaynes (1994); ch.-elect, Michael S. Freeman (1995); secy., M. Sue Baughman (1993); past ch., Paul M. Gherman (1993); E. Anne Edwards (1993); Virginia L. Lowell (1993); Donna L. McCool (1994); Dorothy M. Persson (1994).

Committees

Comparative Library Organization

To collect information regarding library organizations and structures; to conduct or sponsor educational programs regarding library organization trends, developments, and theories; and to conduct and/or recommend research related to this concern.

Ch., Thomas L. Wilding (1994); Joseph C. Andrews (1993); Denise D. Bedford (1994); Karyle S. Butcher (1993); Maidel K. Cason (1994); David R. Dowell (1993); Sherman L. Hayes (1993); Joe A. Hewitt (1994); Jeffrey L. Horrell (1994); Connie Keller (1994); Deborah J. Leather (1993); Arlene E. Luchsinger (1994); Lawrence J. McCrank (1994); Roxanne J. Sellberg (1993); Marsha J. Stevenson (1993); Charles C. Stewart (1994); Mary Jane Vakili (1994).

Financial Management

To conduct and sponsor educational programs for librarians and officials, to conduct or recommend research, and to encourage or sponsor publications related to the financial management of libraries.

Ch., Ronald F. Dow (1993); Richard J. Coughlin (1994); John G. Crane (1994); Ray English (1993); Kenneth E. Flower (1993); Dalia Lapatinskas Hagan (1994); Steven W. Hagstrom (1994); Nancy Jaeger (1993); Patricia M. Kelley (1993); Michael J. LaCroix (1993); Virginia L. Lowell (1993); Louise S. McAulay (1994); Phil S. Parsons (1993); Renee Schwartz (1994); Richard Hume Werking (1994).

Nominating—1993 Elections

Ch., Joan S. McConkey (1993); E. Anne Edwards (1993); Virginia L. Lowell (1993); Richard M. Parker (1993).

Nominating—1994 Elections

Ch. and members to be appointed.

Planning and Evaluation of Library Services

To provide a forum in which individuals interested in both the theoretical and practical aspects of planning and evaluation of library services may exchange information; to analyze existing methodologies and ideas regarding the planning and evaluation of library services; to assist other interested individuals with information regarding the planning and evaluation of library services; to introduce innovative approaches to improve the process of planning and evaluation of library services.

Ch., Karen M. Bohrer (1993); Greg Anderson (1993); Ellory Christianson (1993); Lynn Scott Cochrane (1993); Roger W. Durbin (1993); David S. Ferriero (1994); David Fiste (1993); Janice L. Flug (1994); Yves Paul Fortin (1993); Frances J. Maloy (1994); James L. Mullins (1993); Michael H. Shelley (1994); Karen Chittick Stabler (1993); Linda L. Wilson (1993).

Risk Management and Insurance

To encourage the development and availability of adequate library insurance, to conduct an educational program for librarians and officials regarding library insurance, and to encourage and/or prepare informational materials for publication.

Ch., Dorothy M. Persson (1993); Ajaye Bloomstore (1993); Andrew R. Bonamici (1994); Edward Garten (1993); Germaine C. Linkins (1993); Robert E. Pillow (1993); Deborah L. Rinderknecht (1993); Martha Steele (1993); Phyllis W. Trammell (1994); Kay E. Vyhnanek (1993).

Discussion Groups

Fiscal and Business Officers

Ch., Thomas L. Wilding (1993).

Leadership

To provide a forum for members whose interests include consideration of research on leadership and development of leadership in libraries.

Ch., Tess Midkiff (1993).

Research on Organization and Management

Ch., Rod Henshaw (1993).

Personnel Administration Section (PAS)

The section on Personnel Administration exercises responsibility for general personnel administration in all types of libraries. Illustrative of the fields of interest are the recruitment and promotion of able people to positions at all levels of library service, certification of librarians, fair employment practices, equal employment opportunities, classification and pay plans, in-service training of all professional and nonprofessional workers (including those at supervisory levels), principles of tenure and intellectual freedom, personnel administration, relations between libraries and pertinent municipal and educational agencies, staff management, ethics, personnel measurement and guidance, and staff welfare programs, including all types of benefits.

This section is concerned with general personnel administration information, education, techniques, theories, practices, guidance materials, and research; it is not responsible for those specific but related duties of other ALA units.

Executive Committee

Ch., Gisela M. Webb (1994); ch.-elect, Ann F. Stone (1995); secy., Blanche Wysor Anderson (1993); past ch., J. Linda Williams (1993); Susan R. Jurow (1994); Janet T. Paulk (1993).

Committees

Economic Status and Staff Welfare

To advocate the development and practice of sound and equitable personnel policies and procedures in libraries in the areas of wage and salary administration, job classification systems, staff benefits programs, and staff welfare. These responsibilities are carried out through research activities, programs, and publications, and by liaison with other related and interested ALA units.

Ch., Priscilla Neill (1993); David Fiste (1993); Donald G. Frank (1994); Sarah E. Hamrick (1993); Barbara Baxter Jenkins (1994); Kathleen Joyce Kruger (1993); Steven J. Mayover (1993); Joan Reyes (1993); Marilyn H. Shaver (1994); W. Randall Wilson (1993).

Nominating—1993 Elections

Ch., Melissa Carr (1993); Maidel K. Cason (1993); Suellyn Hunt (1993).

Nominating—1994 Elections

Ch. and members to be appointed.

Publications

To coordinate and facilitate, as appropriate, publication activities of the section and its committees; to identify new opportunities for publications and the updating of existing publications; to serve as liaison on publication projects with other LAMA and ALA committees and groups; to undertake and carry out section level publications projects, such as the Personnel consultants list; to advise the section executive committee on a regular basis on the status of section publication projects.

Ch., Thomas L. Wilding (1994); Deborah B. Babel (1994); Patricia A. Brill (1994); Deborah A. Carver (1993); Janice E. Haraz (1994); Michael J. LaCroix (1993); Deborah L. Schaeffer (1993); Kimberly Spyers-Duran (1994); Teri R. Switzer (1994).

Staff Development

To facilitate and promote effective staff development programs in order to maximize staff abilities to successfully perform their responsibilities and thereby improve overall library effectiveness. Cooperating with other ALA units, the Committee devises appropriate means for exchanging information and highlighting research. Areas of staff development in which the Committee has an ongoing concern are needs assessment, goals and objectives, policy statements, responsibilities of staff development personnel, program design, successful learning activities, available resources, and evaluation techniques.

Ch., Robert R. Newlen (1994); Margaret Maes Axtmann (1993); Marilee A. Birchfield (1993); Rebecca R. Bostian (1993); Julie A. Brewer (1993); Mary Frances Burns (1993); Janice H. Burrows (1994); Gail K. Dickinson (1994); Erlene Bishop Killeen (1993); Pat L. Weaver-Meyers (1993); Stanley J. Wilder (1994); Carol Z. Womack (1993).

Supervisory Skills

To address the ongoing personnel needs of library supervisors by providing support to include, but not be limited to programs, publications, media material and workshops. Committee membership is to be representative of all types of libraries and to concentrate on first and second level supervisors.

Ch., George Lupone (1994); Gwen Arthur (1994); Stella Bentley (1993); June M. Breland (1993); June L. DeWeese (1993); Judy Jeng (1993); Sharon A. Lincoln (1993); Jan C. Maxwell (1994); Myrna Joy McCallister (1994); A. Christine Mote (1993); Ann C. Paietta (1994); Thomas H. Patterson (1993); Roberta L. Pitts (1994); Melinda Ann Reagor (1993); Joyce Crawford Wright (1993); Doris Zbornik (1993).

Discussion Group

Union Relations for Managers

To provide a forum for managers from unionized libraries, those who are approaching such situations, and those who are in nonunionized libraries but wish to raise their consciousness concerning supervision within the unionized environment, discuss negotiation and administration of collective bargaining agreements, grievance and arbitration procedures, and other issues related to the challenge of supervising within the unionized environment.

Co-chs., Diane Young Turner (1993) and Denise M. Weintraub (1993).

Public Relations Section (PRS)

The Public Relations Section provides a framework and impetus for the study of public relations theory and policies; for improving the practice of public relations in public, school, college and university, and special libraries; for serving as public relations liaison between the division and other ALA units; and for identifying those aspects of public relations about which the profession needs to be informed and educated so as to conduct appropriate programs and institutes.

The Public Relations Section meets these responsibilities in the following ways:

1. Reviews association, division, and section activities to identify changing public relations developments and needs.

2. Initiates and oversees activities and projects appropriate to the section, especially those relating to friends of libraries, public relations institutes, the John Cotton Dana Awards, publications, and public relations services to libraries, state libraries, and state library associations.

3. Presents and interprets library public relations to interested groups outside the profession, especially people in library service areas.

4. Aids the professional public relations development of librarians and other library public relations professionals by encouraging the exchange of ideas and participation in relevant programs, institutes, and other continuing education opportunities.

5. Uses all appropriate media to facilitate communication about public relations theory and practice among library and library-support groups and associations.

Executive Committee

Ch., Sandra A. Scherba (1993); ch.-elect, John J. McGinnis (1995); secy., Carol G. Walters (1993); Judith A. Gibbons (1994); Evelyn R. Olivier (1993).

Committees

Education and Training

To provide continuing education in public relations skills and techniques by developing programs and workshops for individuals responsible for public relations at their library. Programs may focus on the application of public relations skills to any aspect of library work.

Ch., Richard E. Rubin (1993); Katharina J. Blackstead (1994); Carol J. Brown (1994); Laureen Cardon (1993); Howard R. Downey (1993); Mildred H. Fry (1993); Pamela A. Grudzien (1993); Sarah E. Hamrick (1993); Kathleen R. Imhoff (1994); Mary Mayer-Hennelly (1993); Nancy P. O'Brien (1994); Janice C. Thenell (1993); Carol A. Zoppel (1994).

Governmental Advocacy Skills

To address the need for education and information in the legislative, administrative, and regulatory processes at all levels of government. To develop programs for the improvement of public relations skills needed to work effectively with legislators and regulators and to provide a forum for the exchange of information in these areas.

Ch., V. Louise Saylor (1993); Linda A. Brammer (1994); James B. Casey (1994); William M. Cochran (1994); David E. Ellefsen (1994); Connell B. Gallagher (1994); Louise S. McAulay (1994); Beth J. Mullaney (1994); Marilyn McKinley Parrish (1993); Nancy N. Powell (1993); Linda K. Reida (1994); Kenneth G. Walter (1994); Doris Zbornik (1993).

John Cotton Dana Library Public Relations Award

To recommend policies and procedures for John Cotton Dana Awards; to serve on jury for selection of winners of awards. The John Cotton Dana Library Public Relations Awards are given by the H.W. Wilson Co. in a contest sponsored jointly with the Public Relations Section of the Library Administration and Management Association.

Ch., Jeanne M. Thorsen (1993); Floyd C. Dickman (1993); Robyn C. Frank (1993); Kathleen R. Imhoff (1994); Patricia H. Latshaw (1994); John J. McGinnis (1993); Julia C. Peterson

(1994); Amy K. Small (1994); Sharyl G. Smith (1994); Lisa A. Wolfe (1993).

Nominating—1993 Elections

Ch., Patricia H. Latshaw (1993); Madeline S. Brookshire (1993); Blane K. Dessy (1993).

Nominating—1994 Elections

Ch., Jeanne M. Thorsen (1994); Charles E. Beard (1994); Evelyn R. Olivier (1994).

Publications

To develop publications on public relations. To encourage publications on the management of public relations skills based on the programs created by the PR section and the work of the committees. To assist individuals and PRS committees as they prepare material for submission to the LAMA Publications Committee. To develop public relations packets. To serve as reporter to *Library Administration & Management* and *Cognotes* for PRS.

Ch., Denise A. Forro (1993); Paula C. Banks (1994); Dorothy E. Christiansen (1994); Patricia E. Dick (1994); Ann Hamilton (1994); Connie J. Hines (1993); Rashelle S. Karp (1994); Debora Meskauskas (1993); Beth K. Steele (1994).

Recognition

To study ways in which the Public Relations Section can recognize outstanding service of its own members, to recognize companies and nonlibrary organizations which support the public relations work of libraries and library advocates and suggest to the PRS Board appropriate forms of recognition for each.

Ch., Carol J. Heller (1993); Margaret Chartrand (1994); Lawrence J. Corbus (1994); Corinne A. Frisch (1993); Marian E. Karpisek (1993); Melvin J. Klatt (1993).

Swap and Shop

To plan, coordinate and implement the Swap and Shop event at the annual conference of ALA. The committee will solicit the donation of public relations materials from libraries of all types for free distribution at the event. The event is open to all those registered for the conference. A best of show competition may be a part of the event.

Ch., Carol G. Walters (1994); Paula C. Banks (1993); Nancy F. Bierschenk (1993); Frances P. Black (1994); Paula D. DeRonde (1994); Nancy A. Downs (1994); Rheena B. Elmore (1994); Corrine A. Frisch (1993); Charles A. Hansen (1994); Bobbie Hirko (1993); Sarah K. Kelley (1994); Helen L. Lotos (1994); Jan H. McManus (1994); Sandra A. Scherba (1993); Susan Uebelacker (1994); Sandra M. Wilkie (1994); Roni L. Willis (1994); Kathleen L. Zaenger (1993).

Trends Awareness

To identify trends affecting libraries or developments in public perception of libraries, such as changes in readership patterns, the growth or decline of continuing education, or issues in intellectual freedom. To develop environmental scanning techniques to forecast policy issues affecting library science and to indicate public relations solutions where appropriate.

Ch., Kriza A. Jennings (1994); Beverly L. Cain (1993); Holly Clark Carroll (1993); Robyn C. Frank (1993); Judith A. Gibbons (1994); Molly R. Giles (1994); Carol J. Heller (1994); Steven J. Mayover (1993); Donna L. Riegel (1993); Linda A. Stith (1994).

Discussion Groups

Marketing Applications

To provide a forum for exchanging ideas on the application of marketing techniques appropriate to libraries.

Ch., Lorelei Starck (1994).

Public Relations Management

To provide a forum for those persons responsible for public relations in their libraries, to permit sharing of the ways they elicit support of the PR program from library directors, trustees, funding agencies, and library staff.

Ch., Katharina J. Blackstead (1993).

Statistics Section (SS)

The Statistics Section exercises overall responsibility for all matters pertaining to needs for and uses of statistical measurement of library resources, services, and facilities, regardless of type of library or functional activity. This section works with other organizations, agencies, and associations in planning and advising in areas of library statistical concerns; recommends and/or prepares guidelines, standards, and tools to be used in statistical activities; and recommends inclusions, definitions, procedures, and policies concerning library statistics.

Executive Committee

Ch., Carolyn Kacena (1994); ch.-elect, Joseph A. Starratt (1995); secy., Marsha J. Stevenson (1993); past ch., Keith Curry Lance (1993); Nancy Lee Myers (1994); Daniel O. O'Connor (1993).

Committees

Data Collection for Library Managers

To investigate current data collection methodologies and techniques for library managers; to identify needs for standard definitions of data elements and forms; to provide resources for library managers to develop skill in data collection; to promote proven methodologies; to encourage adherence to national standards at the local level.

Ch., Raul A. Huerta (1994); Darla Cottrill (1993); Rodger S. Harris (1993); Patricia L. Holsworth (1993); Myoungja L. Kwon (1994); Alice L. Lubrecht (1994); Deborah L. Rinderknecht (1993); Rita A. Scherrei (1994); D. W. Schneider (1993); Michael H. Shelley (1994); Linda S. Vertrees (1993).

Data Collection for Library Managers: Comparability of Reference Statistics (task force)

To identify and define comparable and practically collectible areas of reference data and work toward the development of national norms for reference service statistics.

Ch. to be appointed.

Development of Cost Analysis Standards (task force)

Ch., Susan Webreck Alman (1993).

Nominating—1993 Elections

Ch., Linda L. Parker (1993); Janis C. Keene (1993); Wayne Mullin (1993).

Nominating—1994 Elections

Ch. and members to be appointed.

Publication of Cost Analysis Forms Kits (task force)

Ch., Barton M. Clark (1993).

Using Statistics for Library Planning and Evaluation

To identify and disseminate information about the effective uses of statistics in library planning and evaluation; to recognize excellence in the use of statistics in planning and evaluation; to provide resources to develop skills in the generation, analysis, and use of statistics for planning and evaluation; to identify needed research and statistical tools in the areas of library planning and evaluation; to promote the formal education of librarians in statistical methodologies appropriate for planning and evaluation; to work with other LAMA sections and ALA divisions as appropriate.

Ch., Mary Ann Sheble (1994); Ed Averette (1994); Wanda V. Dole (1994); Elizabeth R. Higbee (1993); Mary Ellen L. Jacob (1994); Chui-Chun Lee (1994); Mary S. Page (1994); Valerie A. Samuelson (1993); Jan Walsh (1993); Robert H. Wittorf (1994).

Using Statistics for Library Presentations and Communications

To identify and disseminate examples of effective uses of statistics in budget justifications and other types of library presentations and communications; to provide resources to develop skills in effective development and uses of statistics for presentation and communication; to identify needs for research and methodologies for using statistics in presentations and communications; to promote formal professional education in skills necessary to using statistics in presentations and communications; to work with other LAMA sections and ALA divisions as appropriate.

Ch., John M. Budd (1994); Denise D. Bedford (1993); Co-Ming Chan (1994); Reginald P. Coady (1994); Carol Cubberley (1994); Rodger S. Harris (1994); Christie M. Koontz (1993); Carol J. Mueller (1993); Nancy Lee Myers (1993); Katy A. Sherlock (1993); Mary Ann Tricarico (1994); Craig S. Zapatos (1994).

Systems and Services Section (SASS)

The purpose of the section shall be to study and evaluate the application of new technology in services, and the management thereof, for the improvement of library services and systems. Within this context, the section shall foster research, develop and promote continuing education opportunities, disseminate information, and provide a forum for the discussion of related management issues pertinent to all types of libraries.

Executive Committee

Ch., Jacqueline M. Zelman (1994); ch.-elect, Teresa A. Edwards (1995); secy., Julia A. Woods (1994); past ch., Judith Paquette (1993); Marjorie G. Easton (1993); Cathy C. Miesse (1994).

Committees

Acquisitions Systems

To study and evaluate procedures and issues relating to the management of acquisitions systems and to provide a forum for discussion of related problems in all kinds of libraries.

Ch., Marilyn D. Schroeder (1993); Pamela M. Bluh (1993); Cynthia M. Coulter (1994); Jeanne Harrell (1993); William E. Jarvis (1993); Barbara Leonard (1994); Marilyn Lewis (1994); Patricia J. Masson (1993); Tim McAdam (1994); Joseph W. Raker (1993).

Circulation Services

To study and evaluate procedures and issues related to the management of circulation and access services in all types of libraries. To promote research and publication in the area of circulation and access services, facilitate communication between practitioners, and serve as an advocate for the interests of circulation and access services managers.

Ch., Margaret Hogue (1993); Anita R. Clamurro (1994); Ellen R. Cordes (1993); John B. Harer (1994); Estrella M. Iglesias (1993); Lora L. Lennertz (1994); Susan Marks (1993); Lesley A. Milner (1994); Matthew S. Moore (1993); Robert E. Pillow (1993); Thomas E. Smith (1993); Cordelia W. Swinton (1994).

Conference Program

To plan programs to be presented by the section at the ALA Annual Conference; to coordinate other programming; to oversee, through a subcommittee appointed by the SASS chair, preconferences sponsored by SASS.

Ch., Paul M. Anderson (1993); Greg Anderson (1993); Josephine Crawford (1993); Corryn Crosby-Muilenburg (1993); Linda Sue Dobb (1994); Ruth M. Katz (1993); Charles E. Kratz Jr. (1993); Richard Luce (1994); Cathy C. Miesse (1994).

Management Practices

To collect, organize, and disseminate information on management practices for all types of libraries in the area of systems and services. The focus of work will be on the management of technology related to these two areas—on applications rather than theory. Activities will include but not be limited to the encouragement of research, the development of standards, and the general study of issues in this area.

Ch., Jeanne E. Boyle (1993); Susan H. Anthes (1994); Emily Batista (1993); Kathleen M. Carney (1994); E. Anne Edwards (1994); Eddy Hogan (1994); W. Bede Mitchell (1993); Nancy R. Nelson (1994); Joan Reyes (1994); Hannah Stevens (1994); Lorenzo A. Zeugner Jr. (1993).

Nominating—1993 Elections

Ch., Ronald P. Naylor (1993); John Michael Bruer (1993); Sol M. Hirsch (1993); Elizabeth M. Valadie (1993).

Nominating—1994 Elections

Ch. and members to be appointed.

Publications and Bibliography

To conduct and disseminate research and to coordinate and facilitate publications of the section and its activities. Reviews publications proposed by other committees of SASS and makes appropriate recommendations to the SASS Executive Committee.

Ch., Ronald P. Naylor (1993); Mary M. Deane (1994); Merri A. Hartse (1993); Karen A. Hatcher (1994); Arlene E. Luchsinger (1994); Gregg E. Sapp (1993); Mary Jane Scherdin (1993); Laura A. Sill (1993).

Discussion Group

Circulation/Access Services

To provide a forum for the regular discussion of current issues pertaining to the management of circulation and access services operations in all types of libraries.

Co-chs., Ellen R. Cordes (1993) and Susan Marks (1993).

◆

Library and Information Technology Association

◆

Membership as of August 31, 1992
Organization members 872
Personal members 4,654
Total 5,526

Linda J. Knutson, *executive director*

Vision Statement

The Library and Information Technology Association envisions a world in which the complete spectrum of information technology is available to everyone. People in all their diversity will have access to a wealth of information technology in libraries, at work, and at home. In this world everybody can realize their full potential with the help of information technology. The very boundaries of human relations will expand beyond the limitations of time and space we experience today. The outer limits are still unknown; what is known is that the exploration will be challenging.

Mission Statement

LITA provides its members, other ALA divisions and members, and the library and information science field as a whole with a forum for discussion, an environment for learning, and a program for action on the design, development, and implementation of automated and technological systems in the library and information science field.

Function Statement

LITA is concerned with the planning, development, design, application, and integration of technologies within the library and information environment, with the impact of emerging technologies on library service, and with the effect of automated technologies on people. Its major focus is on the interdisciplinary issues and emerging technologies. LITA disseminates information, provides educational opportunities for learning about information technologies and forums for the discussion of common concerns, monitors new technologies with potential applications in information science, encourages and fosters research, promotes the development of technical standards, and examines the effects of library systems and networks.

Strategic Planning Goals

To provide opportunities for professional growth and performance in areas of information technology.

To influence national and international level initiatives relating to information and access.

To promote, participate in, and influence the development of technical standards related to the storage, dissemination, and delivery of information.

To strengthen the association and assure its continued success.

Officers and Board of Directors

Pres., Walt Crawford (1994); pres.-elect, Tamara J. Miller (1995); past pres., Paul Evan Peters (1993); Ching-chih Chen (1993); Michele I. Dalehite (1995); Katharina E. Klemperer (1994); Linda D. Miller (1994); Gail M. Persky (1993); Jean Armour Polly (1995); Nolan F. Pope (1994); div. councilor, Donald E. Riggs (1993); ex officio: Bylaws & Organization ch., Berna L. Heyman (1993); Linda J. Knutson.

Executive Committee

The Executive Committee is empowered to act for the Board of Directors between regular meetings of the Board. The decisions and actions of the Executive Committee are subject to review by the Board at its next regular meeting.

Ch., Walt Crawford (1994); Katherina E. Klemperer (1993); Tamara J. Miller (1995); Paul Evan Peters (1993); Donald E. Riggs (1993); ex officio, Linda J. Knutson.

Publications

Information Technology and Libraries (ITAL) (quarterly). Sent to all LITA members. Available on subscription, $45 a yr. Single copies $15. For information or to send manuscripts, contact the editor. Ed., Thomas W. Leonhardt, Dir. of Tech. Servs., Univ. of Oklahoma L., 401 W. Brooks St., Norman, OK 73019-0528; Managing ed., Marjorie E. Bloss, Dir. of Tech. Servs. Div., Ctr. for Research Ls., 6050 S. Kenwood Ave., Chicago, IL 60637; Book Review ed., Susan B. Harrison, Assoc. Dir., P.L., 455 Fifth Ave., New York, NY 10016; Software Review ed., George S. Machovec, Hd., L. Tech. & Sys., Univ. L., Arizona State Univ., Tempe, AZ 85287; Advertising ed., Stuart M. Foster, *Choice*, 100 Riverview Ctr., Middletown, CT 06457.

LITA Newsletter (quarterly). Sent to all LITA members. Available on subscription, $25 a yr. Single copies, $8. Ed., Walt Crawford, Research Libraries Group, 1200 Villa St., Mountain View, CA 94041-1100; Assoc. ed., Linda A. Driver, College of Notre Dame Library, 1500 Ralston Avenue, Belmont, CA 94002.

COMMITTEES

(Hugh) Atkinson Memorial Award, ACRL/ALCTS/LAMA/LITA (See p. 44.)

Budget Review

With the assistance of the Executive Director of LITA, the Budget Review Committee reviews the divisional budget requests and the final budget proposal; makes recommendations for changes as needed; and presents the budget to the LITA Board of Directors.

Ch., Paul Evan Peters (1993); Walt Crawford (1994); Katharina E. Klemperer (1993); Tamara J. Miller (1995); Paul Evan Peters (1993); ex officio, Linda J. Knutson.

Bylaws and Organization

The Bylaws and Organization Committee maintains the bylaws of the division and reports to the division board, committees, and interest groups on changes proposed to the bylaws.

Amendments to the bylaws may be proposed by the Board of Directors or, in writing to the Board of Directors, by any Division committee, or by petition signed by ten members of the Division. Proposed amendments shall be presented in writing to the executive director at least ninety days prior to the date at which they are to be acted upon; they shall then be referred by the executive director to the Bylaws and Organization Committee, which shall report upon them to the Division membership.

The Committee advises the Board of Directors, and through it the division membership, on the establishment, functional definition, and discontinuance of committees, interest groups, and other organization entities as the needs of the division require. The Bylaws and Organization Committee shall recommend the name and size of division committees, and may recommend special regulations concerning the composition of each committee and the appointment and terms of office of its members. Petitions for interest groups must be resubmitted to the Bylaws and Organization Committee every three years and reapproved by the LITA Board; otherwise, the Bylaws Committee shall recommend to the Board that the interest group be dissolved. This mechanism will provide for the dissolution of interest groups where member activity has fallen off.

On an annual basis, the Bylaws and Organization Committee reviews the functions of the division, committees, and interest groups and submits a report to the LITA Board for review at the ALA Midwinter Meeting.

Ch., Berna L. Heyman (1993); Dennis R. Brunning (1994); Donna L. Hirst (1993); Christopher G. Lewis (1994); David R. McDonald (1994); Ruby E. Miller (1994); Tamara J. Miller (1993); Charles A. Skewis (1993); Helen Citron Wiltse (1993); intern, Elaine M. Henjum (1993).

Education

To encourage basic education programs (including academic continuing education and staff development programs) relating to library and information technology through such means as: (1) identifying topics where there is a need for basic education and orientation; (2) bringing to the attention of the LITA committees and interest groups, and to the attention of the library and information technology educational community in general, the need for programs related to such topics; (3) planning and offering programs in this regard where no other means for LITA to address such needs can be found; (4) gathering and publishing information on basic educational needs and programs; and (5) encouraging research on education matters pertaining to technological subjects; to oversee the LITA/CLSI Scholarship in Library and Information Technology Subcommittee and the LITA/OCLC Minority Scholarship Subcommittee.

Ch., Nancy N. Pope (1993); Larry E. Compton (1994); William P. Kane (1994); Neal K. Kaske (1994); Michael E. D. Koenig (1993); Myoungja L. Kwon (1993); J. Andrew Magpantay (1993); S. Michael Malinconico (1993); Myrna Joy McCallister (1994); Karen Chittick Stabler (1993); intern, Judith Hopkins (1993).

LITA/CLSI Scholarship (subcommittee)

To select the recipient of the LITA/CLSI Scholarship, to be awarded annually according to the guidelines for the LITA/CLSI Scholarship established by the LITA Board.

Ch., Janet C. Woody (1993); past ch., Howard Besser (1993); William A. Boyd (1993); Pat Ensor (1993); John Popko (1993); CLSI liaison, Richard M. Poter (1993).

LITA/OCLC Minority Scholarship (subcommittee)

Ch., Marchita Phifer (1993); past ch., Kriza A. Jennings (1993); Sonya A. Kirkwood (1993); Nan Li (1993); OCLC liaison, Kate F. Nevins (1993).

Financial Development (ad hoc)

Ch., Jo-Ann Michalak (1993); James Michael (1994); Louella V. Wetherbee (1993); Florence J. Wilson (1993); Bd. liaison, Nolan F. Pope (1993); ex officio, Linda J. Knutson.

Gaylord Award for Achievement in Library and Information Technology

To select the recipient of the LITA/Gaylord Award for Achievement in Library and Information Technology, chosen to recognize achievement in the area of library and information technology. The award may be made in recognition of distinguished leadership, notable development of applications of technology, superior accomplishment in research or education, or original contribution to the literature in the field.

Ch., Jeanne M. Somers (1993); Corrie V. Marsh (1993); Jean Armour Polly (1993); Karen A. Schmidt (1993); Gaylord liaison, Nancy Schoonmaker (1993).

International Relations

To establish ways in which LITA can complement, or otherwise add to, ALA's international relations policy objectives. Among specific areas of interest are: the use of library technology to encourage the free flow of information and documents worldwide; the education of LITA members in international matters; contributions to the proposed ALA international "information clearing house"; work with U.S., foreign, and international bodies with shared interests in library technology; and LITA participation (collective and individual) in international conferences and other endeavors.

Ch., Charles Martell (1993); Michael J. Gorman (1994); Evelyn S. Murphy (1994); Sachie Noguchi (1993); Karen J. Starr (1994); Jian-Zhong Zhou (1994); Bd. liaison, Ching-chih Chen (1993); intern, Elaine Hartman (1993).

"ITAL" Editorial Board

To serve in an advisory capacity to the editor on the contents of the journal issues; to form the core of referees, reviewing manuscripts submitted for possible publication.

Ch. and ed., Thomas W. Leonhardt (1993); Alice J. Allen (1993); Rao Aluri (1994); Frank A. D'Andraia (1993); Karen Markey Drabenstott (1994); Patrick Flannery (1994); R. Bruce Miller (1993); Dilys E. Morris (1993); V. Louise Saylor (1993); Craig A. Summerhill (1993); managing ed., Marjorie E. Bloss (1993); book rev. ed., Susan B. Harrison (1993); software rev. ed., George S. Machovec (1993); advertising ed., Kurt R. Murphy (1993); intern, Randy L. Pederson (1993); ex officio: Walt Crawford (1994); William Gray Potter (1993).

Leadership Development

To plan and organize leadership development events for LITA committee and interest group officers; to stand ready to offer advice to LITA officers and staff, as needed and requested, on orientation events for committee and interest group officers.

Ch., Elizabeth L. Lane (1993); Nancy H. Evans (1993); Denise A. Forro (1994); Richard E. Gates (1994); George T. Rickerson (1993); Bd. liaison, Michele I. Dalehite (1993); ex officio, Craig A. Summerhill (1993).

Legislation and Regulation

The Legislation and Regulation Committee monitors legal and regulatory development of information and communications technologies; acts as technical advisor to the ALA Committee on Legislation in legislative and regulatory matters dealing with communications technologies; reviews pending drafts, statements, or information concerning technology-related laws and regulations; identifies issues affecting libraries; provides position statements on these issues as needed; and develops strategies as appropriate for effecting resolution of these issues. Members of this committee should expect to be called upon to provide testimony before Congressional committees and regulatory agencies as needed.

Ch., Patrick Flannery (1993); Marilyn H. Boria (1994); James J. Maloney (1994); Corrie V. Marsh (1993); Dennis J. Reynolds (1994); Mark Scott (1994).

Library Research (task force)

To investigate the needs and interests of LITA members in the research area, whether those needs are being met by existing ALA and divisional bodies, and whether LITA should take action in this area.

Co-chs., Carl E. Bengston (1993) and Gary S. Lawrence (1993); Don L. Bosseau (1993); Lloyd Davidson (1993); Miriam A. Drake (1993); Neal K. Kaske (1993); Thomas A. Peters (1993).

LITA/Library Hi Tech Award

The LITA/*Library Hi Tech* Award will be awarded to an individual or institution for a single seminal work, or a body of work, taking place within (or continuing into) the five years preceding the award, that shows outstanding achievement in communicating to educate practitioners within the library field in library and information technology.

Ch., Marcia K. Deddens (1993); Clifford A. Lynch (1993); William A. Muller III (1993).

MARBI (Machine-Readable Bibliographic Information), ALCTS/LITA/RASD (See p. 27.)

Membership

To develop methods to encourage, expand, and promote membership in LITA, and to implement those methods; to coordinate membership promotion activities of the LITA interest groups; and to serve as LITA liaison to the ALA Membership Committee. It advises the Board of Directors on policies relating to membership and dues.

Ch., Martha Hruska (1993); James E. Alloway (1994); Carl E. Bengston (1993); Linda S. Birtley (1993); Carol A. Brierty (1993); Thomas Joe Harris (1994); Jamie K. Hurley (1993); Billie R. Peterson (1993); Jane T. Sessa (1994); Bd. liaison, Gail M. Persky (1993); intern, Ann M. Fiegen (1993).

National Conference (1992) Steering

Ch., Betty G. Bengston (1993); Gordon C. Barhydt (1993); Pamela P. Brown (1993); Gail M. Dow (1993); Daniel H. Iddings (1993); Lois M. Kershner (1993); Thomas W. Leonhardt (1993); Carol A. Parkhurst (1993); Louella V. Wetherbee (1993); Bd. liaison, R. Bruce Miller (1993); ex officio: exhibits mgr., Sandra J. Donnelly (1993); Linda J. Knutson.

Conference Evaluation (subcommittee)

Ch., Lois M. Kershner (1993); Louella V. Wetherbee (1993).

Exhibits (subcommittee)

Ch., Pamela P. Brown (1993); ex officio: Sandra J. Donnelly (1993).

Local Arrangements (subcommittee)

Ch., Gail M. Dow (1993); Darmae J. Brown (1993); Elizabeth E. Brown (1993); Dayna Evers Buck (1993); Susan M. Fayad (1993); Rosario Garza (1993); Mohamed Hamdy (1993); Brenda G. Hawley (1993); Marit S. MacArthur (1993); Barbara B. MacDonald (1993); Bernard A. Margolis (1993); Ree Mobley (1993); Jeanette Mosey (1993); Gretchen Redfield (1993); Mara L. Sprain (1993); Nancy E. Tucker (1993); Patricia M. Wallace (1993).

Program Planning (subcommittee)

Ch., Daniel H. Iddings (1993); Marcia M. Anderson (1993); Pamela Q. J. Andre (1993); Mark A. Beatty (1993); Patricia H. Earnest (1993); Susan Baerg Epstein (1993); Joan L. Kuklinski (1993); David G. Lewis (1993); Nancy K. Roderer (1993); Roberta J. Wallis (1993); Barbara A. Winters (1993).

Showcase (subcommittee)

Ch., Barbara A. Winters (1993); Roberta A. Corbin (1993); Toni L. Lambert (1993); Marti Scheel (1993); Janet C. Woody (1993).

Publications (subcommittee)

Ch., Thomas W. Leonhardt (1993); Alice J. Allen (1993); Rao Aluri (1993); Catherine F. Doyle (1993).

Publicity (subcommittee)

Ch., Carol A. Parkhurst (1993); Barry B. Baker (1993); Tamara J. Miller (1993); Susan S. Starr (1993); Virginia G. Voedisch (1993); Judy Kulp Zelenski (1993).

Nominating

To present at least two candidates for each office to be filled at the next election; to select the candidates in such a manner as to assure as broad a representation as possible of different types and sizes of libraries, types of service, and geographic distribution of membership.

Ch., James J. Kopp (1993); Charles W. Bailey Jr. (1993); Elizabeth D. Nichols (1993).

Program Planning

The Program Planning Committee recommends to the Board of Directors action to be taken on programs proposed by the interest groups and committees for ALA annual conferences and LITA institutes. The committee coordinates and reviews program plans submitted by the committees and interest groups to ensure that sufficient planning has occurred and a realistic budget has been prepared. The committee works closely with the Education Committee and the Emerging Technologies Interest Group to identify program topics of interest to LITA membership and works with appropriate interest groups and committees in encouraging the planning of such programs. The committee may itself plan and execute institutes, programs and preconferences of interest to the division. Since preconferences and institutes generate revenue which is instrumental to the support of the LITA division activities in general, the Program Planning Committee encourages a sufficient number of preconferences and institutes to contribute to the economic stability of the division. A member of the committee serves on the program committee of any preconference or institute.

Ch., Barbra B. Higginbotham (1993); Patricia H. Earnest (1994); Pat Ensor (1993); Gerald M. Furi (1994); Mary L. Johnson (1993); Lynne D. Lysiak (1993); Linda D. Miller (1993); Scott P. Muir (1994); John Popko (1994); Linda J. Robinson (1994); Jeanne M. Somers (1994); ERT liaison, Pamela P. Brown (1993); Bd. liaison, Linda D. Miller (1993); intern, Carol Godson (1993).

Publications

The Publications Committee represents the broad publishing interests and concerns of all committees and interest groups of the division; it proposes and recommends division-wide publication policies to the LITA Board; and it advises and guides the editorial practices and operational details of the division's publications. (Committee function statement is currently under review by committee.)

Ch., William Gray Potter (1993); Charles W. Bailey Jr. (1994); Terry P. Dawson (1993); James J. Kopp (1993); Marilyn Lutz (1994); Dennis M. McGreer (1994); R. Bruce Miller (1993); William A. Muller III (1994); Julieann V. Nilson (1994); Brian H. Sealy (1994); Diane R. Tebbetts (1993); Thomas C. Wilson (1994); Grace

J. Agnew (000 ed., 1994); Michael J. Gorman (000 ed., 1994); Ann J. Hope (000 ed., 1995); Bd. liaison, Katharina E. Klemperer (1993); intern, Milton T. Wolf (1993).

Newsletter (subcommittee)

Ch. and ed., Walt Crawford (1994); assoc. ed., Linda A. Driver (1994).

Silver Celebration

Ch., Stephen R. Salmon (1993); Henriette D. Avram (1993); Nancy L. Eaton (1993); Donald P. Hammer (1993); Lois M. Kershner (1993); Carol A. Parkhurst (1993); ex officio: Walt Crawford; (1993); Linda J. Knutson.

Technical Standards for Library Automation (TESLA)

TESLA encourages, supports, and where appropriate establishes technical standards relating to library/information technologies and telecommunications; and it serves as a clearinghouse for such standards and information about such standards. In the area of library automation, it transmits proposed standards and recommendations to standards development committees through appropriate ALA representatives to the American Library Association Standards Committee and ANSI Committee; arranges for appropriate standards publicity; cooperates with the ALA Standards Committee; and encourages and supports technical communications between the library community and its suppliers in the business machine, computer, and telecommunications industries.

Ch., Sylvia M. Carson (1993); Joan M. Aliprand (1994); Sylvia C. Cornell (1994); Mark T. Hinnebusch (1994); Phyllis H. Johnson (1993); Betty Landesman (1993); Leslie B. Pearse (1994); Ellen C. Rappaport (1993); Rose Marie Saenz (1993); Beth Sandore (1994); intern, Douglas A. Kranch (1993); ex officio, Paul Evan Peters (1993).

Technology and Access

To work with the LITA Board, LITA Interest Groups, other ALA units, and the ALA Coordinating Committee on Access to Information to encourage a broad social and technical perspective on the effects of information technologies on freedom and equality of access to information.

The primary concern focuses on: the technical aspects of new information technologies which may increase or decrease access; the distribution models within which the technology is deployed; the economic, technological, and political control of information; confidentiality of personal data and access to data; and the economics of the production and provision of information.

To prepare position papers; develop tools to assist ALA members evaluate the social consequences of information technologies; and publicize technology and access issues.

Ch., Carolyn M. Gray (1993); Mary Alice Ball (1993); Catherine A. Dixon (1994); Charles W. Husbands (1994); Katherine B. Kott (1994); Patricia J. Mullen (1993); Marti Scheel (1994); C. James Schmidt (1993); Jacquelyn E. Siminitus (1993); Bd. liaison, Jean Armour Polly (1993); intern, Judy E. Myers (1993).

Ten Days to 2000

To jointly present with the Ontario Library Association a series of international technology conferences or symposia that will assist libraries in North America to further discover and utilize technologies that improve service effectiveness.

Ch., Paul Evan Peters (1993); Richard G. Akeroyd Jr. (1993); Kenneth E. Dowlin (1993); Carolyn M. Gray (1993); Susan K. Martin (1993); Peter R. Young (1993).

INTEREST GROUPS

Interest Group coor.: Craig A. Summerhill (1993).

Adaptive Technologies

To promote the availability and use of adaptive technologies for disabled persons, allowing them equal access to all types of library materials and services.

Ch., Christopher G. Lewis (1993); vice-ch., Dennis R. Norlin (1993); secy., Joan Maier McKean (1993); staff liaison, Linda J. Knutson.

Artificial Intelligence/Expert Systems

To act as a forum for discussion and exchange of ideas on the application of artificial intelligence and expert systems techniques in the field of library and information science to disseminate the information on artificial intelligence and expert systems to ALA members; to encourage research on the application of AI and expert systems to library and information science problems.

Ch., Gail F. Latta (1993); vice-ch., Douglas A. Kranch (1993); secy., Martin A. Kesselman (1993); past ch., Denise D. Bedford (1993); Pamela R. Mason (1993); staff liaison, Linda J. Knutson.

Authority Control in the Online Environment, LITA/ALCTS CCS (interdivisional)

To provide a forum for discussion of a variety of issues related to authority control for online catalogs and for international sharing of authority of data.

The goals of the interest group on authority control would be to raise the level of awareness on authority control issues, to encourage ideas for new approaches to authority control, to promote significant research on authority control, and to influence policy decisions related to authority control.

Ch., Joan E. Schuitema (1992); vice-ch., Karen S. Calhoun (1993); secy., Daniel V. Pitti (1993); past ch., Deborah J. Husted (1993); Linking Bibliographic Records (ad hoc) ch. to be appointed; Online Maintenance (ad hoc) ch., Douglas Koschik (1993); Patron Interaction (ad hoc) ch., Deborah A. Ryszka (1993); Series Authorities (ad hoc) ch., Kathryn M. Harcourt (1993); Subject Authorities (ad hoc) ch., Susan M. Moore (1993); Uniform Titles (ad hoc) ch., Joan Swanekamp (1993); staff liaison, Linda J. Knutson.

Customized Applications for Library Microcomputers

To serve as a forum for sharing information on the development, use, and distribution of customized applications of commercial off-the-shelf software; to improve the productivity of libraries and librarians.

Co-chs., Stephen R. Westman (1993); vice-ch., Andy D. Boze (1993); secy., Denise D. Bedford (1993).

Desktop Publishing

To inform and instruct the library community about the capabilities and potentialities of desktop publishing.

Ch., Pat Ensor (1993); vice-ch., Xiaoyan Shen (1993).

Distributed Systems

To provide a forum to facilitate communication and enhance understanding of the development, implementation, and problems related to distributed systems; to raise the level of awareness of the complexities related to implementation; to educate the group members and LITA membership on the structure and application of distributed systems through programs and discussions at ALA and LITA conferences; and to share experiences in the development, planning and implementation process.

Ch., Sandra K. Millard (1993); vice-ch., Deborah C. Masters (1993); secy., Kathleen A. Wakefield (1993); past ch., Charles Forrest (1993).

Electronic Mail/Electronic Bulletin Boards

To provide a forum for the interest group to explore questions and problems relating to access to electronic messages and information.

Co-chs., Stuart J. Glogoff (1993) and Dawn E. Talbot (1993); vice-ch., Ray E. Metz (1993); secy., Gail A. Wanner (1993).

Emerging Technologies

To identify new technologies in order to promote discussion of their impact on library automation; to be a critical technology watch within LITA.

Ch., Colby M. Riggs (1993); vice-ch., Richard E. Gates (1993); secy., Elena C. Carvajal (1993).

Human/Machine Interface

To provide a forum for sharing information on the following issues: transaction logs and transaction log analysis in online systems; staffing concerns such as training, turnover, sabotage, and productivity; the effects of multiple interfaces on library users, training, and productivity; standard command languages and functions for end-users; effects of the interface on user attitudes toward the system; and coping with existing systems vs. designing or redesigning systems.

Ch., Laine Farley (1993); past ch., Mary G. McMahon (1993).

Hypertext/Hypermedia

To provide a forum for the discussion of hypertext-based applications in libraries.

Ch., E. Paige Weston (1993); vice-ch., Judy E. Myers (1994).

Imagineering

To promote imaginative forecasting and planning for future information systems and technologies by the examination and analysis of science fiction themes and works.

Co-ch., Roberta J. Wallis (1993) and Milton T. Wolf (1993).

Library Consortia/Automated Systems

To discuss issues pertinent to the technology of implementing and running shared library processing and retrieval systems among consortia libraries, such as database configuration, patron files, shared files across institutions, direct patron access, loan policies, authority files, licensing and contracts, retrieval systems, multiple libraries linking different systems, etc.

Ch., Elaine Hartman (1993); vice-ch., Bernard G. Sloan (1993); secy., Thomas P. McGinn (1993); past ch., Michele I. Dalehite (1993).

MARC Holdings, LITA/ALCTS (interdivisional)

To provide a forum to educate the library community on the MARC holdings format, its purpose, its use, development, and implementation, as well as to encourage the use and implementation of the format.

Ch., Christina P. Meyer (1993); vice-ch., Kathryn A. Loafman (1993).

Microcomputer Support of Technical Services, LITA/ALCTS (interdivisional)

To discuss applications of microcomputers to library technical processing, including but not limited to cataloging, acquisitions, serials control, collection management, materials processing, and preservation.

Ch., Anna M. Wang (1993); vice-ch., Betsy Gamble (1993).

Microcomputer Users

To provide a forum for library and information professionals to discuss and explore emerging technologies in microcomputing; to present programs on broad topics having to do with microcomputer technology issues; and to provide a support network for LITA members interested in microcomputers.

Ch., Gerald M. Furi (1993); vice-ch., Birong A. Ho (1993).

Online Catalog

To provide a forum for the discussion of developments and problems of interest to individuals who are actively engaged in planning, developing, and installing or operating online library catalogs.

Ch., Mary E. Engle (1993); vice-ch., Jeffrey R. Rehbach (1993); past ch., Elizabeth Patterson (1993).

Optical Information Systems

To facilitate communication and enhance understanding of information systems incorporating laser videodisc, compact disc read only memory (CD-ROM), optical cards, tapes, and optical digital data discs. To make available to library professionals information on the kinds, uses, features, availability, and suppliers of optical information products and systems and to provide a voice for the library community to express its concerns and suggestions to suppliers regarding content, standards, software, workstations, etc.

Ch., Lorre B. Smith (1993); vice-ch., Pamela R. Mason (1993); secy., Michelle B. Cadoree (1993); past ch., Ka-Neng Au (1993).

Programmer/Analyst

To afford opportunities for members to discuss and exchange ideas concerning the development of computer programs.

Ch., Priscilla L. Caplan (1993); vice-ch., William W. Jones Jr. (1993); secy., Charles W. Husbands (1993).

Retrospective Conversion, LITA/ALCTS
(interdivisional)

The Retrospective Conversion LITA/ALCTS Joint Interest Group provides information to those preparing for, or involved in, the process of retrospective conversion, with emphasis on the most current details available on technology and programming changes or advances.

Co-chs., Birong A. Ho (1993) and Cheryl M. Rogers (1993); vice-ch., Rosario Garza (1993).

Serials Automation, LITA/ALCTS
(interdivisional)

The purpose of this group will be to discuss the application of computers to the control of serials in libraries, specifically their acquisition, bibliographic control, and inventory control.

Ch., Margaret Mering (1993); vice-ch., Elizabeth Davis Ten Have (1993); secy., Karen H. Wilhoit (1993); past ch., Marcia Anderson (1993).

Small Integrated Library Systems

To provide a forum for librarians in small-sized school, public, academic, and special libraries to discuss and share information about the capabilities and potentials of the technology for small integrated library systems.

Ch., Gregory J. Zuck (1993); vice-ch., Bruce Flanders (1993).

Telecommunications

To monitor for library purposes current developments in the use of telecommunications facilities; to disseminate information to ALA members on the current state of the art; and to encourage studies and development of applications for use in libraries.

Ch., Peter Burslem (1993).

Vendor/User

To provide a forum and the opportunity to discuss matters of mutual interest or concern with regard to the planning, development, implementation, or application of various automated products and services in the library environment including related activities that bear on vendors and users in these matters.

Ch., Gretchen L. Freeman (1993); vice-ch., Anita Cook (1993).

REPRESENTATIVES

ALA Chapter Relations Com.—Martha Hruska (1993).
ALA Copyright Subcom.—Jerome Yavarkovsky (1993).
ALA Education Com./Education Assembly—Nancy N. Pope (1993).
ALA Ethics Com.—Charles W. Husbands (1993).
ALA Legislation Assembly—Patrick Flannery (1993).
ALA Library Literacy Assembly—Joan Maier McKean (1993).
ALA Membership Promotion Task Force—Martha Hruska (1993).
ALA Planning and Budget Assembly—Paul Evan Peters (1993).
ALA Planning Com.—Gail M. Persky (1993).
ALA Public Relations Assembly—Carol A. Parkhurst (1993).
ALA Recruitment Assembly—to be appointed.
ALA Standards Com.—Joan M. Aliprand (1993).
ALCTS Audiovisual Com.—David N. Nelson (1993).
ALCTS CCS—Com. on Cataloging: Description and Access—Judith Hopkins (1993).
American National Standards Inst. (ANSI), Com. X3, Information Processing—Paul Evan Peters (1993).
American Soc. for Information Science (ASIS)—Patricia H. Ernest (1993).
ERT—Pamela P. Brown (1993).
Freedom to Read Fdn.—Ronald Sigler (1993).
NMRT—James E. Alloway (1993).
RASD-MARS—Peggy A. Seiden (1993).

REPRESENTATIVES AND LIAISONS TO LITA

ASIS—Nolan F. Pope (1993).
Library of Congress—Louis Drummond (1993).
NMRT—Jenifer Abramson (1993).
RASD-MARS—James J. Maloney (1993).

———◆———

Public Library Association

———◆———

Membership as of August 31, 1992
Organization members	712
Personal members	6,558
Total	7,270

Executive director, to be appointed.
Bridget A. Bradley, *deputy executive director*
Sandra Causey Garrison, *program officer*

Charge from Council (1978)

The Public Library Association has specific responsibility for:

1. Conducting and sponsoring research about how the public library can respond to changing social needs and technical developments.

2. Developing and disseminating materials useful to public libraries in interpreting public library services and needs.

3. Conducting continuing education for public librarians by programming at national and regional conferences, by publications such as the newsletter, and by other delivery means.

4. Establishing, evaluating, and promoting goals, guidelines, and standards for public libraries.

5. Maintaining liaison with relevant national agencies and organizations engaged in public administration and human services such as Na-

tional Association of Counties, Municipal League, Commission on Post-Secondary Education.

6. Maintaining liaison with other divisions and units of ALA and other library organizations such as the Association of American Library Schools and the Urban Libraries Council.

7. Defining the role of the public library in service to wide range of user and potential user groups.

8. Promoting and interpreting the public library to a changing society through legislative programs and other appropriate means.

9. Identifying legislation to improve and to equalize support of public libraries.

Mission Statement (1991)

The Public Library Association will advance the development and effectiveness of public library service and public librarians.

Program Assumptions (1991)

PLA exists to provide a diverse program of communication, publication, advocacy, and continuing education. The program priorities are determined by PLA members and may include some areas or concerns also identified as priorities by ALA. The primary staff program responsibility is to facilitate members' activities and initiatives by providing coordination and support.

As a division we are effective when we:

1. Provide leadership for the improvement of public libraries.

2. Provide an effective forum for discussing issues of concern to public librarians.

3. Provide relevant, high-quality continuing education through publications, workshops, and programs.

4. Provide opportunities for developing and enhancing individual professional networking.

5. Develop and disseminate policy statements on matters affecting public libraries.

6. Communicate effectively with the non-library world about matters impacting public library service.

7. Maintain a stable membership and financial base.

Priority Concerns (1991)

Adequate funding for public libraries.
Improved management of public libraries.
Recognition of the importance of all library staff in providing quality public service.
Recruitment, education, training, and compensation of public librarians.
Effective use of technology.
Intellectual freedom.
Improved access to library resources.
Effective communication with the non-library world.

Board of Directors

Officers: pres., Elliot Shelkrot (1994); pres.-elect, Pat Woodrum (1995), past pres., June M. Garcia (1993).

Other members: dirs.-at-large: Rick J. Ashton (1995); Ginnie Cooper (1994); Fran C. Freimarck (1993); Martin J. Gomez (1994); Victor Frank Kralisz (1993); Donna Barrett Schremser (1995); sect. reps.: ALLS pres., Mary Jo Ryan (1993); CIS past pres., C. Amoes Hunt (1994); MLS pres., Anne Marie Gold (1993); MPLSS pres., Will S. Bricker II (1993); PLSS pres., Donald A. Best (1993); SMLS rep., John Allyn

Moorman (1994); ALTA rep., Ramonda (Mandy) S. Wertz (1993); Affiliates Network rep., Christine L. Hage (1993); councilor, Linda Mielke (1994); ex officio: Budget and Finance ch., Ronald A. Dubberly (1993); exec. dir., Eleanor J. Rodger (1993).

Executive Committee

Pres., Elliot Shelkrot (1994); pres.-elect, Pat Woodrum (1995); past pres., June M. Garcia (1993); ex officio: Ronald A. Dubberly (1993); Eleanor J. Rodger (1993).

Publications

Public Libraries (bimonthly), sent to all PLA members. Subscriptions, $50 a yr., Canada and foreign $60 a yr., single copies, $10. Feature ed., Ellen Altman, 1936 E. Belmont Drive, Tempe, AZ 85284; Managing ed., Sandra Causey Garrison, PLA, 50 E. Huron St., Chicago, IL 60611.

COMMITTEES

1994 National Conference

Ch., Susan S. Goldberg (1994); Local Arrangements ch., Ronald A. Dubberly (1994); Exhibitor's Ad. ch., Mary L. Shapiro (1994); Program Ch., Sandra S. Nelson; Bd. rep., Martin J. Gomez (1994).

Exhibitor's Advisory (subcommittee)

Ch., Mary L. Shapiro (1994); Stephen T. Kochoff (1994); Julie L. Lahann (1994); Marcia L. Purcell (1994); William Sannwald (1994); Shirley C. Sarris (1994).

Local Arrangements (subcommittee)

Ch., Ronald A. Dubberly (1994); Steven R. Bedworth (1994); John M. Hilinski (1994); Angie Stuckey (1994).

Program (subcommittee)

Ch., Sandra S. Nelson (1994); Marilyn H. Boria (1994); Harriet Henderson (1994); Laura G. Johnson (1994); Sheldon B. Kaye (1994); Joseph J. Keenan Jr. (1994); Donna Mancini (1994); Brooke E. Sheldon (1994); Susan M. Veltfort (1994); Vivian R. Wynn (1994).

Audiovisual

To facilitate the selection, management, and marketing of audiovisual materials and services in public libraries.

Ch., Dorothy M. Liegl (1994); Elizabeth G. Acerra (1994); Norman Belk (1993); Debra A. Gumulauski (1994); Ralph E. Huntzinger (1994); Phil S. Parsons (1993); Elizabeth C. Orsburn (1994); Ronald Sigler (1993).

Awards

To assist with promotion of existing PLA awards, suggestion and review of proposed awards, coordination of the awards ceremony, and other necessary activities.

Ch. to be appointed; Judith P. Anderson (1994); Shirley May Byrnes (1994); Elizabeth A. Crabb (1993); Cynthia Czesak (1993); Melanie J. Deutsch (1993); Cecil Hixon (1993); Chrystal C. Jeter (1993).

Baker & Taylor Video

To present an annual $1,000 award to a public library demonstrating both excellence and inno-

vation in library programming with video as well as the ability to market and promote the use of these services to the library's users.

Ch., Phyllis Y. Massar (1994); Karen M. Bohrer (1994); Georgette D. Clark (1994); Kathleen M. Kilgen (1993); Philip C. Levering (1993); James E. Massey (1994); Phil S. Parsons (1994); Linda A. Stith (1993).

Budget and Finance

To submit a recommended budget for action to the PLA Board of Directors; to advise the PLA Board on all fiscal matters of the division, including the fiscal implications of the division's publications and programs.

Ch., Ronald A. Dubberly (1993); Linda P. Elliott (1993); Ronald S. Kozlowski (1993); Thomas C. Phelps (1994).

Business Council

To support public library service to business.

Ch., Michael J. Wirt (1994); Linda Holman Bentley (1993); Cindy L. Brennan-Gibbon (1994); Stephen D. Coffman (1994); Jo Ellen Flagg (1993); Thomas L. Johnson (1994); Susan V. McKimm (1993); John A. Philbrick III (1994); Marcella J. Ratzlaff (1994); Martha A. Shearer (1993); Mary A. Sherman (1993); Susan J. Strehl (1994); Richard L. Waters (1994).

Bylaws and Organization

To review the goals, organization, and structure of PLA and its committees and sections; to recommend to the PLA Board establishment and/or dissolution of committees and sections (including names, charge and function, and size); to study and review all committee and section charges and activities at the direction of the PLA Board; to make recommendations to the PLA Board for revisions to the *PLA Organization Manual;* to consider amendments to the Bylaws; and to make recommendations to the PLA Board on other organizational matters affecting PLA as a whole.

Ch., Judith M. Foust (1994); Susan Bolesta (1993); Donna M. Cranmer (1993); Louise S. McAulay (1994); Adelle McCarty (1993); Donna L. Morris (1993); Diane Purtill (1993).

Cataloging Needs of Public Libraries

1. To implement the goals of the Public Library Association as they relate to technical services.
2. To advance the professional interests of public librarians in technical services.
3. To promote research and publications in this area.
4. To provide forums for the discussion of issues in technical services as they relate to public libraries.
5. To cooperate with and to represent PLA with other units of the American Library Association and with other national and international organizations in these areas.

Ch., Ellen Slotoroff Zyroff (1993); Kristi L. Boyd (1993); Sandra A. Collins (1993); Barbara B. Elliott (1994).

Children, Service to

To alert PLA to current issues in children's services in public libraries and suggest appropriate action and responses to those issues; to advo-

cate children's services interests in program planning and publications of PLA; to identify training needs and resources for public library staff serving children; to maintain a relationship with the Association for Library Service to Children and work with that Division in any appropriate manner, as directed by the PLA Board.

Ch., Lucinda Frances Ware (1993); Bessie Condos Egan (1993); Debra H. Engel (1994); Marilyn Berg Iarusso (1993); Susan Kaminow (1993); Edward M. Kieczykowski (1993); Curtis L. Kiefer (1994); Penny S. Markey (1994); Effie Lee Morris (1993); Valerie Rowe-Jackson (1994).

CLSI International Study Grant

To annually select the recipient for the PLA/CLSI International Study Grant, which is an award of up to $5,000 and a citation presented to a librarian with a demonstrated interest in and commitment to furthering international public library cooperation. The purpose of the grant is to support a study tour abroad that will (1) stimulate interest among public librarians in the development of an international study project with public libraries outside the United States or (2) enable a staff member of a United States public library to attend an IFLA Conference, to visit and study public libraries in the host country or surrounding region, and to improve international understanding among public libraries worldwide.

Ch., Louise A. Sevold (1993); Leroy M. Gattin (1993); Rosemary S. Martin (1993).

Common Concerns, ALTA/PLA (See p. 24.)

Conference Program Coordinating

To coordinate conference programs sponsored by PLA at Annual Conferences; to ensure broad coverage, diversity, and limited duplication of programs; to provide PLA units with planning information; to receive conference program requests and review them for adherence to established procedures and budgets. To encourage the presentation of successful programs at various levels; to submit program requests along with the committee's recommendations to the PLA Board for its action.

Ch., James B. Alsip (1993); Daniel J. Barr (1994); Clara Nalli Bohrer (1994); Mary Jo Detweiler (1993); Harriet Henderson (1993).

Education of Public Librarians

To review periodically the elements considered essential to the initial and continuing education of public librarians; to establish continuing liaison with library educators for conveying both these recommendations and ideas from practitioners in public libraries to library schools on a regular basis.

Ch., June Lester (1993); Ellen Altman (1993); Edwin S. Gleaves (1993); Cecil Hixon (1993); Theresa C. Huang (1993); Kenneth D. Shearer Jr. (1993).

Executive Assembly

To enhance communication among the PLA and PLA section officers; to discuss issues of common concern and interest; to provide continuity and support for section activities; and to expedite accomplishment of the organization's goals and objectives.

Ch., June M. Garcia (1993); Donald A. Best (1993); Will S. Bricker II (1993); Roberta A. E. Cairns (1993); Jean T. Curtis (1993); Marianne C. Fairfield (1993); Fran C. Freimarck (1993); Anne Marie Gold (1993); Marilyn L. Hinshaw (1993); C. Amoes Hunt (1993); Kathleen R. Imhoff (1993); Marlys H. O'Brien (1993); Patricia L. Owens (1993); Kathryn M. Panares (1993); Donna L. Riegel (1993); Mary Jo Ryan (1993).

50th Anniversary Committee (special)

To plan the 50th anniversary celebration of PLA in 1994.

Ch. and members to be appointed.

Fund Raising (special)

In conjunction with LAMA and ACRL, to conduct an annual inventory of public library fund raising efforts and disseminate the findings to the professional library community.

Ch., to be appointed; Bettye Black (1993); Robert E. Cannon (1993); Emily Jackson (1993); Andrew A. Venable Jr. (1993).

Goals, Guidelines, and Standards for Public Libraries (see Planning and Evaluation Committee.)

Hot Topics

To prepare PLA President's Hot Topics program for the 1992 ALA Annual Conference.

Ch. and members to be appointed.

Institute for Public Library Development, PLA/ASCLA (special interdivisional)

Charge to be developed.

Ch., Sandra S. Nelson (1994); Elizabeth A. Funk (1994); Douglas P. Hindmarsh (1994); Bridget Later Lamont (1994).

Intellectual Freedom

To serve as liaison between PLA and the ALA Office of Intellectual Freedom, the ALA Intellectual Freedom Committee, the Freedom to Read Foundation, the ALA Intellectual Freedom Round Table, and other units with ALA activities related to intellectual freedom; to advise PLA on matters relating to intellectual freedom and their implication for public library service and to make recommendations for action to the PLA Board; and to prepare and gather materials which will advise the public librarian of available services and support both in formulating policies of intellectual freedom and for resisting local pressure and community action designed to impair the rights of users.

Ch., Loretta R. O'Brien (1994); Lesley D. Boughton (1993); Elinor Green Hunter (1994); Brenda Johnson (1993); Patricia Latch (1994); Mary L. Lawson (1993); Kenton L. Oliver (1994); Jan W. Sanders (1993).

International Relations

To promote international understanding among public librarians in order to improve the quality of public library practices. To promulgate the free flow of relevant information between American public librarians and their counterparts in various parts of the world.

Ch., David M. Henington (1993); Anthony M. Dos Santos (1994); Theresa C. Huang (1994);

Charles W. Hunsberger (1994); Joseph J. Keenan Jr. (1993); Chung-Sook Charlotte Kim (1994); Kimberly A. Lafferty-Cohen (1994); Patricia Wilson (1994).

Leadership Development

To facilitate communication within PLA and to transmit essential organizational information to PLA leadership through a formal orientation for all Division and section officers and committee members.

Ch., Fran C. Freimarck (1993); Marilyn H. Boria (1993); Elizabeth A. Crabb (1994); Janis C. Keene (1993); Victor Frank Kralisz (1994); Rosemary S. Martin (1993); Ross W. McLachlan (1994); Norman V. Plair (1993).

Legislation

To formulate and recommend to the Public Library Association Board of Directors legislative objectives which promote and enhance public libraries and librarianship. To take appropriate steps to increase the awareness of public librarians and public library supporters in the legislative process and to motivate their participation in legislative activity at all levels of government. To monitor legislation at the various levels of government and to inform the PLA Board and membership of legislation relevant to public libraries and to recommend action as appropriate. To maintain a liaison relationship with the ALA Legislation Committee, the Legislation Assembly, and other groups with like interests.

Ch., Sarah Ann Long (1993); Francis J. Buckley Jr. (1993); Lawrence J. Corbus (1993); Glen R. Dunlap (1994); Laura G. Johnson (1994); Robert M. Justin (1994); Joseph F. Shubert (1994); Nettie B. Taylor (1994); Andrew A. Venable Jr. (1994); Clarence R. Walters (1993); Evie Wilson-Lingbloom (1993).

(Allie Beth) Martin Award

To select the recipient for the Allie Beth Martin Award each year. The recipient shall be a librarian who, in a public library setting, has demonstrated: (1) extraordinary range and depth of knowledge about books or other library materials, and (2) distinguished ability to share that knowledge.

Ch., Charles M. Brown (1993); Barbara A. Genco (1992); John D. Hales Jr. (1993); Victoria L. Jenkins (1993); Pat C. Kelker (1993); Elaine H. McConnell (1993); Stephen C. Skidmore (1994).

Membership

To develop and pursue an aggressive and continuous campaign to recruit and retain members for PLA from among existing and potential ALA members.

Ch., Carole Dickerson (1993); Howard R. Downey (1993); Curtis L. Kiefer (1994); Gloria J. Leonard (1994); Harry R. Wachstein (1994); Stephen D. Wood (1993).

Multilingual Materials and Library Service

To collect and disseminate information on existing multilingual public library collections; to develop guidelines for establishment of foreign language material collections and services in public libraries; and to investigate the viability of cooperative acquisition programs.

Ch., John W. Cunningham Jr. (1993); Natalia Bezugloff (1993); Pamela A. Martin-Diaz (1993); Sheryl J. Nichin (1993); Nita Vegamora Norman (1994); David L. Searcy (1994); Eva Weiner (1993); Kenneth A. Yamashita (1993); Marie F. Zielinska (1993).

National Achievement Citation

To select recipients of National Achievement Citations, which recognize excellent or innovative public library service from amongst the applications submitted by public libraries; to review criteria, forms and procedures for awarding the National Achievement Citation and propose revisions to the PLA Awards Committee as necessary; to assist in the promotion of the National Achievement Citation program and encourage public libraries to apply.

Ch., Dorothy S. Puryear (1993); Susan R. Gallinger (1993); Charles D. Hanson (1994); Joyce V. Misner (1994); Kay K. Runge (1994).

National Organizations, Liaison with

To establish an ongoing relationship with (1) National Association of Counties; (2) National League of Cities; (3) National Association of Towns and Townships; (4) National Civic League; and (5) International City Management Association; and to encourage PLA and local public library participation in the activities/programs/publications of these organizations.

Ch., John D. Christenson (1993); Thomas E. Alford (1994); Alex Boyd (1993); Donnell J. Gaertner (1993); David Macksam (1993); Richard E. Ostrander (1994); Patricia L. Owens (1994); Stephen C. Skidmore (1994).

National Science Foundation Invitational Conference (special advisory)

To serve as an advisory group on the development of the program for an invitational conference which will be conducted in the fall of 1993 by PLA with support from the National Science Foundation. To recommend to the PLA Executive Committee individuals who should be considered as attendees at the conference.

Ch., Elliot Shelkrot (1994); Laura J. Isenstein (1994).

Nominating—1993

Ch., Carolyn Anthony (1993); Alex Boyd (1993); James H. Fish (1993); Honore L. Francois (1993); Bernard F. Vavrek (1993).

Nominating—1994

Ch., Donald J. Sager (1994); Lee B. Brawner (1994); Linda D. Crowe (1994); Ronald S. Kozlowski (1994); June Lester (1994).

PLA Partners

To encourage and develop relationships between the Public Library Association and the private sector for the support of PLA activities and services; to develop a recognition program for those vendors or others who contribute to the partners program; and to develop procedures for working with the PLA office for coordination of these activities.

Ch., LaDonna T. Kienitz (1993); Judith A. Drescher (1993); Stephen T. Kochoff (1993); Ronald S. Kozlowski (1994); Marcia C. Romanansky (1994); Kay K. Runge (1993); Mary L. Shapiro (1994); Paul K. Sybrowsky (1993).

Planning and Evaluation

To develop tools which assist public libraries in community based planning, measurement of performance, and evaluation of programs and services. To encourage effective management by assisting librarians in the use of these tools and processes. To evaluate and revise these tools on a regular basis. To monitor and review the work of other units related to this charge, and give approval (when appropriate).

Note: The name of the Goals, Guidelines, and Standards for Public Libraries Committee was changed by the PLA Board at the 1992 Annual Conference to the Planning and Evaluation Committee.

Ch., Karen J. Krueger (1993); Barbara J. Barber (1993); Philip M. Clark (1993); William M. Duncan (1993); Toni A. Garvey (1994); Jeanette H. Judkins (1994); Nolan Lushington (1993); Kathleen S. Reif (1994); Merna L. Smith (1993); Nancy M. Smith (1994); Elizabeth F. Stroup (1993).

Policy Manual (advisory)

Note: The Public Policy for Public Libraries section was created by the PLA Board at the 1992 Annual Conference. Therefore, the Policy Manual (Advisory) Committee will discontinue at the end of the 1993 Midwinter Meeting.

To research policies commonly needed by public libraries; identify the issues to be considered when establishing the respective policies; and disseminate the results of the work.

Ch., Jo Ann Pinder (1993); Barbara E. Chernik (1993); Toni A. Garvey (1993); James T. Giles (1993); Mary Jane Kepner (1993); Frances L. McClure (1993); June L. Mikkelsen (1993); Joel C. Rosenfeld (1993); Marcia L. Thomas (1994).

Political Effectiveness

To identify the characteristics and behaviors which constitute political effectiveness; to recommend methods (programs, publications, training, etc.) which could be used to enhance the political effectiveness of public librarians; to discuss the desirability of creating an award or other mechanism to recognize individuals who have been politically effective at the local, state, or national level. (Draft charge.)

Ch., Catherine A. O'Connell (1993); Daniel J. Bradbury (1993); Lee B. Brawner (1993); Ralph M. Edwards (1993); Ann M. Friedman (1993); Sharon A. Hammer (1993); Martha M. Makosky (1993); Patrick O'Brien (1993); Carol Starr (1993).

President's Program—1993

Ch., Barbara Webb (1993); Alex Boyd (1993); Will S. Bricker II (1993); Judith M. Foust (1993); Linda Mielke (1993).

President's Program—1994

Ch., Cathy J. Audley (1994); Thomas E. Alford (1994); A. Michael Deller (1994); Martha Greene (1994); Stephen T. Kochoff (1994); William Sannwald (1994); Mary A. Sherman (1994); William J. Wilson (1994); Michael J. Wirt (1994).

Professional Certification, PLA/LAMA (interdivisional task force)

To define and validate public library management competencies; to develop appropriate criteria and methods for recognizing the achievement of these competencies; to identify existing and potential opportunities which could lead to the achievement of these competencies; to propose a certification program based on the above to the Boards of Directors of PLA and LAMA.

Ch., Liz R. Miller (1994); Thomas A. Childers (1994); Catherine A. Dixon (1993); Ronald A. Dubberly (1993); Kenna J. Forsyth (1994); Suellyn Hunt (1993); Anthony B. Leisner (1993); Suzanne H. Mahmoodi (1994); Dallas Y. Shaffer (1993); F. William Summers (1993).

"Public Libraries" Advisory Board

To be responsible for publication development, developing editorial policy, evaluating the publication and its responsiveness to audience interests, and advising the Executive Director on the selection and evaluation of the Editor.

Ch., William Sannwald (1993); William T. Balcom (1993); Don W. Barlow (1994); Anne Marie Gold (1994); Carolyn Rowe Hale (1994); John H. Martin Jr. (1994); Patricia L. Owens (1993); Claudia B. Sumler (1994).

Public Library Data Service

To provide timely, reliable, useful, statistical, and descriptive information about public library resources, services, and performances in library specific formats. This information serves as a management tool for planning, policy formulation, evaluation, comparative analysis, and resource management.

Ch., Sheldon B. Kaye (1993); Jane S. Eickhoff (1994); Keith Curry Lance (1993).

Public Library History

To serve as a focal point within PLA for the discussion of issues related to the history of public libraries. To coordinate activities with the ALA Library History Round Table. To enhance the knowledge of public librarians about public library history. To provide information which would enable public librarians to save and share information about the history of their own institutions.

Ch., Donald J. Sager (1994); George S. Bobinski (1994); Elaine Graham Estes (1994); Donald D. Foos (1994); Averil J. Kadis (1994).

Public Library Services to the Homeless

To gather information on public library service to the homeless and to share it with the public library community; to make policy recommendations to the PLA Board on standards and ethics of library service to homeless people.

Ch., Ernestine L. Hawkins (1993); Joan Jackson (1994); Jane B. Lego (1993); Raymond Santiago (1994); Catherine M. Sullivan (1993).

Publications

To initiate and coordinate the publication of materials and the production of resources pertinent to the role of public library service; to work with PLA sections and committees to evaluate the need for revision of published materials; to aid in originating new publications, and in defining the purpose, audience, and scope of each publication; to ensure representation at meetings of the ALA Publishing Committee; to review publications in the public library field, especially publications of the division, to ensure that they are current and relevant to member needs.

Ch., Christine L. Hage (1993); Clara Nalli Bohrer (1993); Malcolm K. Hill (1993); Lyn W. Hopper (1993); Sue Jackson Luce (1993); Thomas C. Phelps (1994); Daniel G. Zack (1993); Norman L. Maas (sect. rep., 1993).

Research

To foster a research climate in public libraries and make it known to members; to identify needed research; to explore, develop, and promote a research agenda which focuses on the current research needs of public libraries and the association; to develop activities and programs to encourage the improvement of research skills among public librarians.

Ch. to be appointed; Frances A. Dowd (1993); Keith Curry Lance (1994); Jane F. Moore (1993); William H. Ptacek (1993); Kenneth D. Shearer Jr. (1994); Katherine Todd (1993); Nancy L. Wilcox (1993).

Retail Outlets in Public Libraries

To gather information including staffing patterns, management, and financial net on established gift shops, bookstores, restaurants and other retail outlets in public libraries and to make information available to the library community.

Ch. to be appointed; Donna Joy Burke (1994); Christy Connelly (1993); A. Michael Deller (1994); Linda P. Elliott (1993); Sally A. Fry (1994); Averil J. Kadis (1994); Sheldon B. Kaye (1993); Mary L. McGalliard (1994); Henry W. Moeller (1994); Elena Tscherny (1993).

Service Clubs, Liaison with

To establish liaison with the national headquarters of selected national and international service clubs. To encourage national and international service clubs to be aware of and support the services of local libraries. To encourage public librarians to participate with local service clubs in mutually beneficial projects. To create a mechanism to recognize outstanding examples of local service club/public library cooperative projects. To develop and implement projects approved by the PLA Board and various service clubs.

Ch., Faye Clow (1993); Jackie Beach (1993); Ernest A. DiMattia Jr. (1994); Helen G. Maul (1994); Lorraine I. O'Dell (1993); Lucie P. Osborn (1993); J. Robert Verbesey (1993).

Strategic Issues and Directions (special)

To identify issues which PLA should address in the next three to five years; to consider whether PLA is organized to effectively address those issues and, if not, to identify organizational options which could address them; to consult with and inform divisional leadership as appropriate; to identify priority action areas and prepare recommended action strategies for the PLA Board to consider.

Ch., Charles W. Robinson (1993); Melissa Buckingham (1993); Ginnie Cooper (1993); J. Dennis Day (1993); Fran C. Freimarck (1993); Luis Herrera (1993); Jeanne M. Holmes (1993); Amy Owen (1993); Gretchen M. Wronka (1993).

Technology in Public Libraries

To consider the impact of technology on the public library as an institution; to collect and disseminate information on technology applications in public libraries; to provide channels of communication for the sharing, among public librarians and others, of information about technology and of the experience gained in its use, with the aim of developing optimal applications of technology to public library services; to work toward achieving the goals of the Public Library Association as they relate to the use of technology in public library services; and to establish liaison with and work with other groups within and outside PLA and ALA having similar concerns about the utilization of technology in public libraries.

Ch., to be appointed; Michael P. Coyle (1994); Susan B. Harrison (1993); William H. Kneedler (1993); Parke P. Lightbown (1993); Jean Armour Polly (1994); John A. Richardson (1994); J. Maurice Travillian (1994); Robert Ward (1994).

(Leonard) Wertheimer Multilingual Award

To select a person, group, or organization in recognition of work they have done in enhancing and promoting multilingual public library service.

Ch., Carmen L. Martinez (1993); Javier Corredor (1994); Susan J. Freiband (1994); Matthew C. Kubiak (1993); Bosiljka Stevanovic (1994); Rita A. Torres (1994); Tamiye M. Trejo-Meehan (1993); Margaret C. Wong (1993); Marie F. Zielinska (1993).

Young Adult Services in Public Libraries, YALSA/PLA (special interdivisional)
(See p. 92.)

DISCUSSION GROUPS

Adult Services Coordinators in Public Libraries

Ch., Barbara B. Shapiro (1993).

Audiovisual

To provide public librarians with a forum to discuss issues related to audiovisual services in public libraries in order to exchange ideas, information, and experience and to offer guidance to librarians with audiovisual questions and concerns.

Ch., James E. Massey (1993).

Bookmobile Service

Ch., Miriam L. Morris (1993).

Cost Finding

Ch. to be elected.

Humanities Programming

Ch., Patricia L. Bates (1993).

Popular Materials Library

Ch. to be elected.

Preschoolers' Door to Learning

Ch. to be elected.

Public Library Service Evaluation

To provide a mechanism and forum through which public libraries can share experiences and identify available resources related to evaluation of library services; to provide an opportunity for practitioners to meet with researchers to explore and discuss public library evaluation needs and problems.

Ch. to be elected.

Total Quality Management

To provide opportunities for public librarians involved in the application of Total Quality Management, Total Quality Service, or Total Quality Improvement to meet and share their experience. To provide opportunities for public librarians to meet with TQ practitioners and experts to hear about principles and techniques that can be used in public settings.

Ch., M. Sue Baughman (1993).

REPRESENTATIVES

ALA Appointments Com.—Pat Woodrum (1993).
ALA-ASCLA Decade for the Disabled Planning Com.—Alice L. Hagemeyer (1993).
ALA Chapter Relations Com.—to be appointed.
ALA Conference Program (New Orleans 1993)—Elliot Shelkrot (1993).
ALA Conference Program (Miami 1994)—Pat Woodrum.
ALA International Relations Assembly—David M. Henington.
ALA Legislation Assembly—Sarah Ann Long (1993).
ALA Legislation Com., Copyright Subcom.—Sarah Ann Long (1993).
ALA Library Education Assembly—June Lester (1993).
ALA Literacy Assembly—to be appointed.
ALA Membership Promotion Task Force—Carole Dickerson (1993).
ALA Planning and Budget Assembly—Ronald A. Dubberly (1993).
ALA Professional Ethics—Melissa Buckingham (1993).
ALCTS Audiovisual Com.: Cataloging in Publications for Audiovisual Materials Interdivisional Group—Dorothy M. Liegl (1993).
ALCTS Com. on Cataloging: Description and Access—to be appointed.
ALCTS Preservation of Library Materials Section Executive Com.—to be appointed.
Alliance of Information and Referral Systems—to be appointed.
ALTA Board—Carolyn Anthony (1993).
Freedom to Read Fdn.—Loretta R. O'Brien.
Joint Meetings of Division IFC—Elliot Shelkrot (1993).
Library of Congress CIP Advisory Group—to be appointed.
U.S. President's Com. on Employment of People with Disabilities—Alice L. Hagemeyer (1993).

AFFILIATES NETWORK

The Affiliates Network is comprised of the representatives of the organizations affiliated with the Public Library Association. The mission of the Affiliates Network shall be to serve as a communications link between the Board of Directors of the Public Library Association and state and multistate public library associations.

Executive Committee

Pres., Dorothy S. Elliott (1993); vice-pres., Lorraine Sano Jackson (1993); secy., Ronald H. Gorsegner (1993); rep. to PLA Bd., Christine L. Hage (1993).

State and Multistate Affiliates

Arizona

Arizona State L. Assn.—David Gunckel, Sierra Vista P.L., 2950 E. Tacoma, Sierra Vista, AZ 85635-1399.

Colorado

Colorado L. Assn.—Donna R. Jones, Arkansas Valley Rgnl. L. Sys., 635 W. Corona, Ste. 113, Pueblo, CO 81004.

Delaware

Delaware L. Assn.—Yvonne Puffer, Newark Free P.L., 750 Library Ave., Newark, DE 19711-7146.

Illinois

Illinois L. Assn.—Jane B. Shaw, Lisle L. Dist., 777 Front St., Lisle, IL 60532-3599.

Iowa

Iowa L. Assn.—Ann Conner Johnson, Scott Cnty. L. Sys., 215 N. 2nd St., Eldridge, IA 52748-1284.

Kansas

Kansas L. Assn.—Rosanne E. Gable, SW Kansas L. Sys., 1001 2nd Ave., Dodge City, KS 67801-4484.

Massachusetts

Massachusetts L. Assn.—Louise R. Brown, Wayland Free P.L., 5 Concord Rd., Wayland, MA 01778-1999.

Michigan

Michigan L. Assn.—Christine L. Hage, Rochester Hills P.L., 210 W. University Dr., Rochester, MI 48063-4589.

Minnesota

Minnesota L. Assn.—Pat Christianson, Minnesota L. Assn., 1315 Lowry N., Minneapolis, MN 55411.

Mississippi

Mississippi L. Assn.—Jane C. Bryan, Jackson-George Rgnl. L. Sys., 3214 Pascagoula, Pascagoula, MS 39567.

Missouri

Missouri Library Assn.—Dorothy Sanborn Elliott, River Bluffs Rgnl. L., Tenth & Felix Sts., St. Joseph, MO 64501.

Montana

Montana L. Assn.—Bill Kochran, Montana L. Assn., 925 Burlington Ave., Billings, MT 59101.

New Jersey

New Jersey L. Assn.—Lorraine San Jackson, South Brunswick P.L., 110 Kingston Lane, Monmouth Junction, NJ 08852.

Ohio

Ohio L. Assn.—Steven Hawk, Akron-Summit P.L., 55 S. Main, Akron, OH 44326.

Oklahoma

Oklahoma L. Assn.—Andy Peters, Pioneer L. Sys., 121 Webster, Norman, OK 73069.

Oregon

Oregon L. Assn.—Robert R. Wilson, Ashland Br., Jackson Cnty. L. Sys., Gresham & Siskiyou Blvd., Ashland, OR 97520.

South Carolina

South Carolina L. Assn.—Joann Olson, South Carolina State L., P.O. Box 11469, Columbia, SC 29211.

Texas

Texas L. Assn.—Margaret Samples, Nicholson Mem. L. Sys., 625 Austin St., Garland, TX 75040–6365.

Utah

Utah L. Assn.—Howard R. Downey, Provo City P.L., 425 W. Center St., P.O. Box 1849, Provo, UT 84603.

Washington

Washington L. Assn.—Michael Wirt, Spokane Cnty. L., 4322 N. Argonne Rd., Spokane, WA 99212-1853.

Wisconsin

Wisconsin L. Assn.—Ron Gorsegner, Nicolet L. Sys., 575 Pine St., Green Bay, WI 54301.

Wyoming

Wyoming L. Assn.—Marsha Wright, Campbell Cnty. P.L., 2101 4-J Rd., Gillette, WY 82716.

SECTIONS

Adult Lifelong Learning (ALLS)
Community Information (CIS)
Marketing of Public Library Services (MPLSS)
Metropolitan Libraries (MLS)
Public Library Systems (PLSS)
Public Policy for Public Libraries (PPPLS)
Small and Medium-sized Libraries (SMLS)

Adult Lifelong Learning Section (ALLS)

To promote public library advisory, instructional, and informational programs and services relating to literacy, and basic education, continuing education, lifestage/role training and career choice/planning; to advocate the use of library-based self-directed study as well as more traditional learning modes; to stimulate continued professional growth in these areas; to provide a forum for the exchange of related research, strategies, techniques, and activities; and to create an environment for the discussion of the expanding educational role of the public library.

Executive Committee

Officers: pres., Mary Jo Ryan (1994); pres.-elect, Kathryn M. Panares (1995); secy., Marilyn G. Genther (1993); past pres., Marianne C. Fairfield (1993).

Committees

Advancement of Literacy Award

To select on an annual basis, as appropriate, a publisher, bookseller, hardware and/or software dealer, foundation, or similar group (i.e., not an individual), which has made a significant contribution to the advancement of adult literacy and to award a symbol of this contribution at the annual meeting of the American Library Association.

Ch., Barbara G. Fellows (1993); Barbara J. Barber (1993); Margaret P. Forehand (1993); S'Ann Freeman (1993); Jane C. Heiser (1993).

Basic Education and Literacy Services

To identify, assemble, and make available resources useful in developing, implementing, and maintaining literacy activities; to cooperate with other ALA divisions, sections, committees, and offices concerned with literacy and basic skills activities in libraries; to assist the Office of Library Outreach Services in providing information to public libraries about library literacy programs; to make librarians aware of the value of cooperation with other agencies in the formation and execution of literacy programs; to generate ideas for section and committee programs and publications.

Ch., Rhea B. Lawson (1993); Sally C. Anderson (1993); Barbara J. Barber (1993); Sarah J. Batt (1993); Jean U. Brinkman (1993); Mildred E. Dotson (1993); Jean W. Greener (1993); Donnie C. Griffin (1993); Laurie Gruenbeck (1993); Ernestine L. Hawkins (1993); Carl Heffington (1993); Margaret O. Herman (1993); Sandra B. Lockett (1993); Edward P. Miller (1993); Marcella J. Ratzlaff (1993); Janice F. Rosen (1993); Jenny L. Ryan (1993); Jan W. Sanders (1993); Jan K. Schroeder (1993).

Conference Program—1993

Co-chs., Carolyn Morgan Burrier (1993) and Susan Scheps (1993).

Conference Program—1994

Co-chs., Vera A. Green (1994) and Caryl Jean E. Mobley (1994).

Continuing and Independent Learning Services

To identify, assemble, and make widely available information about existing continuing and independent learning services and resources in public libraries; to keep up with developments in continuing and independent learning in other types of libraries and in other fields; to promote public library involvement in continuing and independent learning; to cooperate with other ALA divisions, sections, offices, and committees concerned with different aspects of continuing and independent learning; to generate ideas for section programs and publications.

Ch., Caryl Jean E. Mobley (1994); William T. Balcom (1993); Jean Coberly (1994); Margaret D. Cooper (1993); Edward V. Elenausky (1993); Nora A. Jones (1993); William L. Kingery (1993); Karen E. Maki (1993); Penny Pace-Cannon (1993); Kathleen M. Savage (1993); Marilyn J. VanGieson (1993).

Helpline

Charge to be developed.

Ch., Vera A. Green (1993).

Job and Career Information Services

To encourage the development of job and career information services in public libraries; to provide continuing education and information about these services to the library community; to act as liaison with other agencies providing related services; to develop guidelines for the provision of job and career information services by public libraries; to act as ALLS liaison with other units of PLA and ALA working with these and related areas; to generate ideas for section programs and publications.

Co-chs., Steve Oserman (1993) and Ruth S. Schwab (1993); Marianne C. Fairfield (1994); Virginia L. Fore (1993); Janice E. Haraz (1993); Margaret O. Herman (1994); Carol French Johnson (1993); Mark Legget (1995); James Lyons (1993); Terry McLaughlin (1993); Jeanne M. Patterson (1993); Erlinda J. Regner (1993); Frances E. Roehm (1993); Suzanne S. Schlaf (1994); Lynda F. Whitton (1993).

Membership

Ch., Marilyn G. Genther (1993); Judith C. Cooper (1993); Anne J. Hofmann (1993); Dorothy M. Lettus (1993).

Nominating—1993

Ch., June E. Eiselstein (1993); Jane C. Heiser (1993); Jeanne M. Patterson (1993).

Nominating—1994

Ch., Marianne C. Fairfield (1994); Virginia L. Fore (1994); Mary Jo Ryan (1994).

Organization and Bylaws

To review the goals, organization, and structure of ALLS and its committees; to recommend to the ALLS Executive Committee establishment of committees (including names, charges, function, and size) and/or discontinuance of committees; to study and review section and committee charges at the direction of the ALLS Executive Committee; to prepare and revise the section's procedures manual; to serve as liaison with the PLA Organization Committee; to consider amendments to the section bylaws and to make recommendations to the ALLS Executive Committee; to prepare revisions of the bylaws at the direction of the ALLS Executive Committee; to monitor the PLA Bylaws and inform the Executive Committee of any changes therein which would reflect upon ALLS bylaws or activities.

Ch., Dorothy O. Ahonen (1993); Richard G. Rekowski (1994).

Parent Education Services

To identify, assemble, and make widely available information about existing parent education services and resources in public libraries and also in other fields; to promote and publicize services to parents of children and young adults with special needs; to encourage increased participation of librarians representing all age level specialties in parent education services; to identify and cooperate with other ALA divisions, sections, committees, and offices concerned with parent education services in libraries; to generate ideas for programs and publications.

Co-chs., Carolyn Morgan Burrier (1993) and Susan Scheps (1993); Connie Adams Bush (1993); Mary Anne Corrier (1993); Jennifer J. Davis (1993); Madeleine Fisher (1994); Nancy Hackett (1993); Susan Kaminow (1993); Gayle S. Leach (1993); Sarah M. McCarville (1993); Carol K. Phillips (1993); Robin B. Rains (1993);

Valerie Rowe-Jackson (1993); JoEllen E. Sarff (1993).

Publications

To develop a plan, including priority areas and a timetable, for a series of publications on the various elements of alternative educational programs, similar to the "Small Library Series"; to be the section liaison with the PLA Publications Committee, "Public Libraries" Advisory Board; to review and approve all manuscripts to be submitted for publication by the section; to locate and contact appropriate authors for specified subject areas; to prepare guidelines for editing and for manuscript preparation; to be responsible for the development and preparation of flyers, brochures, and other information publications about the section; to work with section committees on the production of publications; to identify other publication possibilities.

Ch., Nancy Fisher (1993); Wendy D. Caldiero (1993); Vera A. Green (1994); Jane C. Heiser (1993); Jane B. Lego (1993); John A. Lonsak (1993); JoEllen E. Sarff (1993); Hedy L. Werner (1993).

Publishers Liaison

To inform publishers that librarians have a growing interest in professional and learning materials in areas of adult education: literacy, GED, career information, and various other areas; to encourage publishers to produce and market more titles on these subjects; to encourage jobbers to carry more adult education materials; to encourage publishers of adult education materials to exhibit at library conferences; to generate ideas for section programs and publications.

Ch., Lorraine Sano Jackson (1993); Barbara J. Barber (1994); Jane B. Lego (1994); Laurabelle McCaffery (1993); Susan A. McCarthy (1993); Jenny L. Ryan (1994); Lynn M. Stainbrook.

Discussion Group

Literacy

Ch., June E. Eiselstein (1993).

Community Information Section (CIS)

To promote public library programs and services furthering the provision of community information; to provide a forum for the exchange of program ideas developed to address identified community information needs; and to explore the role of the public library in actively providing community information to identified target groups.

Executive Committee

Officers: pres., David L. Searcy (1994); pres.-elect, Marlys H. O'Brien (1995); secy., Cynthia Cobb (1993); past pres., C. Amoes Hunt (1993); Norman L. Maas (1993); Cecilia Staudt (1994).

Committees

1994 National Conference

Ch., Anne J. Hofmann (1994); Honore L. Francois (1994); Jane Light (1994); Norman L. Maas (1994); Beth E. Wladis (1994).

Conference Program—1993

Ch., Marlys H. O'Brien (1993); Frances P. Black (1993); Mildred E. Dotson (1993); Carolyn L. Garnes (1993).

Conference Program—1994

Ch. and members to be appointed.

Education and Training

To identify and encourage the development of a curriculum relevant to community information services in library schools; and to promote and offer continuing education opportunities in community information services by library schools, state library agencies, and regional library associations.

Ch., Trish Skaptason (1993); Jean Drabbe Barnett (1993); Lillie J. Dyson (1994); S'Ann Freeman (1993); Cecil Hixon (1994); Lyn W. Hopper (1993); Brenda M. Hunter (1993); Stella I-Hua Shang (1994); Catherine A. Wright (1994).

Nominating—1993

Ch., Mary L. Cass (1993); Cecil Hixon (1993), Amy M. Levine (1993).

Nominating—1994

Ch. and members to be appointed.

Planning and Organization

To determine the organizational needs of the section with regard to committee structure including, but not limited to, a review of the charges of all standing committees; a recommendation for a mechanism to handle future bylaws and changes; and an investigation of the need for a Long-Range Planning and Evaluation Committee.

Ch., Beth E. Wladis (1994); Lillie J. Dyson (1994); Honore L Francois (1993).

Promotion

To study and disseminate ideas and methods for promoting community information and referral in public libraries; to develop strategies for promoting the Community Information Section.

Ch., Jane Raifsnider (1993); Francesca L. Hary (1994); Ernestine L. Hawkins (1994); Susan A. McCarthy (1994); Ann H. Scheffer (1994).

Service Development

To assist libraries in the development and implementation of community information services; to prepare aids for community assessment, service development, training, evaluation, and cooperation with other human service organizations.

Ch., Stephen Russo (1993); Emily R. Guss (1994); Janet Hawkins Guydon (1994); Karen E. Maki (1993); Ann H. Mallard (1993); Miriam L. Morris (1993); Steve W. Schaefer (1993); Angie Stuckey (1993).

Technologies

To collect and disseminate information about the array of technologies available and appropriate to the provision of community information.

Ch., Lynn Bellehumeur (1993); Anne Cain (1994); William A. Ellett (1993); Nora B. Jacob (1993); Patrick J. McClintock (1994); Janice F. Rosen (1994); Marguerite J. Scott (1994); Phyllis W. Trammell (1994); Marcia M. Trent (1994).

Marketing of Public Library Services Section (MPLSS)

To provide a forum for discussion of marketing issues related to public libraries including the relationship of the library to its environment, strategic marketing planning, marketing research and community analysis, and marketing segmentation and targeting; to educate librarians in all elements of the marketing mix including pricing issues, distribution strategies, and promotion; to integrate strategic marketing planning with the PLA Planning Process and with the use of marketing and audit and control systems.

Executive Committee

Officers: pres., Will S. Bricker II (1993); pres.-elect, Patricia L. Owens (1995); secy., Jane S. Eickhoff (1993); past-pres., Roberta A. E. Cairns (1993).

Committees

1994 National Conference Program

To plan and manage the upcoming PLA National Conference Program for the section, reviewing prior national and Annual Conference programs, and to pass information on to the next National Conference Program Committee.

Ch., Anne T. Parent (1994); Jean M. Tabor (1994).

Conference Program—1993

Ch., Bonnie E. Williams (1993); Will S. Bricker II (1993); Audra L. Caplan (1993); Philip S. Fleming (1993); Penelope S. Jeffrey (1993); Annelie W. Menzies (1993); Donna G. Soto (1993); Jean M. Tabor (1993); Phyllis W. Trammell (1993); Antoinette Lynn Walder (1993).

Conference Program—1994

Ch., Bonnie E. Williams (1994); Audra L. Caplan (1994); Penelope S. Jeffrey (1994); Lesley C. Loke (1994); Annelie W. Menzies (1994); Susan J. Paznekas (1994); Donna G. Soto (1994); Jean M. Tabor (1994); Antoinette Lynn Walder (1994).

Distribution of Library Services

To educate and inform public librarians on the need to consider a range of practices and structures in choosing among product and service delivery alternatives, based on an analysis of community needs.

Ch., John A. Lonsak (1993); Richard Chartrand (1993); Jannette Engel (1993); Anne E. Haley (1993); Betty J. Long (1993); Carol A. Tarsitano (1993); Sharon L. Winkle (1993).

Education

To explore mechanisms for responding to members' requests for information about marketing and to make recommendations to the MPLSS Executive Committee.

Ch. and members to be appointed.

Market Research, Community Analysis, and Planning

To identify and publicize currently accepted market research and planning methodologies that are appropriate for library users, and to foster an understanding of their use in public libraries.

Co-chs., Anne E. Foley (1993) and Mary Ann Tricarico (1994); Susan Bolesta (1994); Ernestine L. Hawkins (1994); Clara Mayer (1994); Sandra H. Neville (1994); Geneva B. Pullen (1993); Anne M. Roman (1993); Nancy H. Sherwin (1994).

Membership

To promote membership in the section within PLA and ALA, to represent membership interests within PLA, and to identify and recommend individuals for committee appointments to the vice-president/president-elect.

Co-chs., Carol Boutilier (1992) and J. Nicholas Fogarty (1991); Lynne G. Degen (1992); Joe McKenzie (1992); Suzanne R. Rickles (1993); Elizabeth Talbot Silva (1992); Wicky Sleight (1992); Nancy M. Smith (1992); Carol A. Tarsitano (1993).

Nominating—1993

Ch., Jan Buvinger (1993); Lillie J. Dyson (1993); Debra D. Peterson (1993); Barbara J. Pickell (1993).

Nominating—1994

Ch., Roberta A. E. Cairns (1994); Barbara J. Pickell (1994).

Organization and Bylaws

Ch., Nicholas G. Spillios (1993); Deborah F. O'Connor (1993); Robert Wood (1994).

Product and Service Management

To promote an understanding of the use and application of marketing principles as they relate to the review of existing products and services in public libraries and to the identification of new products and services.

Ch., Lillian H. Snyder (1993); Marilyn P. Barr (1993); Mary E. Donor (1994); Jane M. Gottfried (1993); Phyllis Kauffman (1994); Cecy Keller (1993); Anna M. Martinez (1993); Stephanie Sarnoff (1993); Nadia P. Taran (1994); Patricia Dwyer Wanninger (1993).

Promotion of Library Services

To educate librarians on the need for systematic planning to facilitate decision-making about promotional materials used by librarians.

Ch., Bobbie Hirko (1994); Anne Henley Cain (1993); Jennifer J. Davis (1993); Michele M. Gendron (1993); Lee J. Olivier (1994); Penny Pace-Cannon (1993); Lorelei Starck (1994); Linda A. Stith (1994); Carol G. Walters (1994).

Publication

To foster the publication of materials for the guidance, training, and education of personnel interested in applying marketing principles to public library services.

Ch., Richard T. Wells (1993); S'Ann Freeman (1993); Krysta A. Tepper (1993); Linda L. Wilson (1993).

Revenue and Pricing Issues in Public Libraries

To educate and inform the public library community on how pricing as a marketing concept relates to public library service.

Ch., Joseph H. Green (1994); Edward W. Byers (1993); Curtis L. Kiefer (1994); Ann S. Miller (1994); William D. Rubin (1993); Jerry A. Thrasher (1993).

Metropolitan Libraries Section (MLS)

To encourage the improvement of public library service in metropolitan areas and to provide a forum for discussion of issues distinctive to public libraries with a single board or serving a single jurisdiction in metropolitan areas.

Executive Committee

Officers: pres., Anne Marie Gold (1994); pres.-elect., Jean T. Curtis (1995); secy., Janis C. Keene (1993); past-pres., Marilyn L. Hinshaw (1993); Carolyn Anthony (1993); Anna Horn (1995); Judith L. Williams (1994).

Committees

1994 National Conference

Ch., Dianne J. Chrisman (1994); Bobbie Hirko (1994).

Collection Management

To collect and disseminate information on all aspects of collection management, including issues related to resource allocations, collection policies and practices, vendor relations, special collections, etc.

Ch., Claudia B. Sumler (1993); Sara B. Appelbaum (1993); Elinor L. Barrett (1993); Anne Henley Cain (1993); Jane Dayton (1994); Jane S. Eickhoff (1994); Ann E. Irvine (1993); Edward M. Kieczykowski (1993); Richard M. Parker (1993); Diane Purtill (1993); Barbara S. Roberts (1994); Mary L. Shapiro (1993); Bonnie E. Williams (1993); Lila B. Wisotzki (1993).

Communications and Membership

To publicize the activities and programs of the Metropolitan Libraries Section; to produce and recommend lists of ALA Annual Conference programs of particular interest to Metropolitan Libraries Section members; to act as liaison to the editor of the Metropolitan Libraries Section column in *Public Libraries*; to work with the Metropolitan Libraries Section representative on the PLA Membership Committee to retain and recruit members for MLS; to develop publicity about Metropolitan Libraries Section activities with the intent of retaining and recruiting MLS members.

Ch. to be appointed; Anthony M. Dos Santos (1994); Joan L. Clark (1993); Cecil Hixon (1994); Kathleen S. Johnson (1993); Carol M. Johnson (1993); Joseph Philip Rice (1993); Nancy Tessman (1993); John S. Wallach (1993).

Conference Program—1993

Ch. Stephen C. Klein (1993); Mary S. des Bordes (1993); James W. Hoogstra (1993); Theresa C. Huang (1993); Alison B. Landers (1993).

Conference Program—1994

Ch., Charles W. Hunsberger (1994); Lesley C. Loke (1994).

Nominating—1993

Ch., William Sanwald (1993); Carol J. Brown (1993); Claudya B. Muller (1993); K. Lynn Schule (1993).

Nominating—1994

Ch., Ramon R. Hernandez (1994); Sylvia Coker (1994); E. Paulette Smith-Epps (1994).

Organization and Planning

To review the goals, organization, and structure of MLS and its components; to recommend to the MLS Executive Committee establishment of committees (including names, charges, function, and size) and/or discontinuance of committees; to study and review section and committee charges at the direction of the MLS Executive Committee; to prepare and revise the Section's procedures manual; to serve as liaison with the PLA Bylaws and Organization Committee; to consider amendments to the section bylaws and to make recommendations to the MLS Executive Committee; to prepare revisions of the bylaws at the discretion of the MLS Executive Committee; to monitor the PLA Bylaws and inform the Executive Committee of any changes therein which would reflect upon MLS bylaws and activities.

Ch., Jo Ann Pinder (1993); Cathy R. Butler (1994); Joan L. Clark (1993); Ann M. Friedman (1994); Janet E. Larson (1993); Suzanne R. Rickles (1994); John S. Wallach (1993).

Service to Multicultural Populations

To develop strategies, guidelines, and manuals for providing services to special populations.

Ch., Rose Marie Kennedy (1993); Robert J. Belvin (1993); Judith A. Castiano (1994); Kenneth L. Cromer (1993); S'Ann Freeman (1993); Michele M. Gendron (1993); Donnie C. Griffin (1994); Theresa C. Huang (1994); Ann E. Irvine (1994); Mary L. Lawson (1993); B. Kathy Leitle (1993); Sylva N. Manoogian (1993); Susan A. McCarthy (1993); Annette C. Salo (1993); David L. Searcy (1994); Merna L. Smith (1993); Nancy L. Snauffer (1994); Thomas B. Wall (1994); Patricia M. Wong (1993); Kenneth A. Yamashita (1993).

Table Talk

To develop a forum for informal discussion on timely topics for both the ALA Annual Conference and for the PLA National Conference.

Ch., Bonnie Birman (1994); Jean Drabbe Barnett (1993); Donna Joy Burke (1994); William A. Knott (1993); Donna L. Morris (1993); K. Lynn Schule (1993); Lillian H. Snyder (1993); Leslie A. St. John (1993).

Workload Measures and Staffing Patterns

To review available data and produce a document on work assignments and activity indexes in order that libraries may better allocate staff and justify staffing requirements.

Ch., K. Lynn Schule (1993); Reginald P. Coady (1993); Judith Coleman (1993); Mary K. Conwell (1994); Lawrence J. Corbus (1993); Mary Anne Corrier (1994); Catherine A. Dixon (1994); Laura G. Johnson (1993); Irene M. Padilla (1994).

Discussion Groups

Branch Coordinators

Ch. to be appointed.

Branch Managers

Ch., Susan Kaminow.

Business Managers

Ch., M. Jacqueline Nytes.

Central Libraries

Human Resources

Ch., Debbra M. Buerkle.

Urban County Libraries

Ch., Melissa J. Sibley.

Volunteer Coordinators

Ch. to be appointed.

Public Library Systems Section (PLSS)

To encourage improved library service through the involvement of public libraries in multijurisdictional library systems and the participation of public libraries in multitype library systems; to provide a forum for discussion of problems distinctive to public library systems and to public library participation in library systems; to provide continuing education and information to the personnel of public library systems and to other public library personnel involved with library systems; to interpret the role of public library systems and public library involvement in library systems to the public and the profession; to cooperate with other units of the American Library Association and other organizations that are concerned with the development of library systems, and to relate to other cooperative ventures of concern to public libraries.

Executive Committee

Officers: pres., Donald A. Best (1994); pres-elect, Kathleen R. Imhoff (1995); secy., Bonnie E. Williams (1993); past pres., Donna L. Riegel (1993); Eric S. Anderson (1995); Donna Joy Burke (1994); Laurel C. Chase (1994); Linda P. Elliott (1995); Steve W. Schaefer (1993); Mary L. Tipton (1993).

Committees

1994 National Conference

Ch., Steve W. Schaefer (1994); Bonnie E. Williams (1994).

Conference Program—1993

Ch., Donald A. Best (1993); Rebecca Erwin Cawley (1993); Katherine E. Davis (1993); Rosanne E. Goble (1993).

Conference Program—1994

Ch., Carl Heffington (1994); members to be appointed.

Nominating—1993

Ch., Stephen Dix (1993); Ronald H. Gorsegner (1993); Norman V. Plair (1993).

Nominating—1994

Ch., Donna L. Riegel (1994); members to be appointed.

Planning and Bylaws

To work with the PLSS Executive Board in determining and recommending goals, objectives, priorities, and long-range plans for the section; strategies for achieving them; and to evaluate the progress of the section toward reaching them. To recommend revisions of the Bylaws for clarification, improvement and consistency with PLA Bylaws.

Ch., Cathy Caine (1993); Angie Stuckey (1993).

Public Policy for Public Libraries Section (PPPLS)

To meet the needs of public librarians and public libraries for public policy guidance from the Public Library Association on major issues affecting public library services and to develop public policy statements about such issues. (Draft charge.)

Committees

Transition Committee

Ch., Fran Freimarck (1993); Jane S. Eickhoff (1993); Sharon A. Hammer (1993); John Allyn Moorman (1993); Jo Ann Pinder (1993).

Small and Medium-sized Libraries Section (SMLS)

To encourage the improvement of public library service in small and medium-sized public libraries by considering solutions to problems unique to libraries of this type, such as acquisition and allocation of resources, equality of service to community groups, management of the library program, and to provide a forum for discussion of these and other problems distinctive to small and medium-sized public libraries.

Executive Committee

Officers: pres., Penny E. Albright (1994); pres.-elect, Jan Walsh (1995); secy., Ruth A. Magnussen (1993); past pres., Annette M. Milliron (1993); Deborah F. O'Connor (1994); Donald B. Reynolds Jr. (1995); Linda Sickles (1993); rep. to PLA Bd., John Allyn Moorman (1994).

Committees

1994 National Conference Program

To develop a program for the 1994 PLA National Conference in Atlanta; to identify and recruit speakers and presenters; and to follow through with arrangements for the Program. (Draft charge.)

Ch., Donald B. Reynolds Jr. (1994); Sandra O. Newell (1994); Annabel K. Stephens (1994).

Anniversary Celebration

Charge to be developed

Ch., Matthew C. Kubiak (1993).

Branch Libraries

To provide a forum for discussion for branch librarians; to gather ideas and information useful to branch libraries; and to disseminate that information through programs and publications.

Ch., Mary J. Miller (1993); Michael Charton (1993); Michael B. Clegg (1993); Emily R. Guss (1993); Marcia Vierck (1993).

Bylaws

To develop bylaws and respond to the changing needs of the membership and reflect changes in PLA and ALA.

Ch., Ellen G. Hellard (1993); Sara G. Bailey (1994); Cynthia A. Josephs (1993); Carol Starr (1993).

Conference Program—1993

Ch., Gordon S. Welles (1993); Carol L. Bowling (1993); Ruth Ellen Faklis (1993); Carl Stone (1993).

Conference Program—1994

Co-chs., Caryl Jean E. Mobley (1994) and Julia R. Rinehart (1994); Sandra O. Newell (1994).

Excellence in Small and/or Rural Public Library Service Award

To annually select the recipient of the award, a $1,000 honorarium, to a public library serving a population of 10,000 or less that demonstrates excellence of service to its community as exemplified by an overall service program or a special program of significant accomplishment.

Ch., John D. Hales Jr. (1993); Cynthia Czesak (1993); Marianne Kotch (1993); James C. Powers (1993); Laureen F. Riedesel (1993).

Ideas Exchange

To solicit practical ideas appropriate to small and medium-sized libraries, and to develop and maintain a distribution network for that information.

Ch., Catharine Cook (1993); Diane A. Bronson (1993); John D. Christenson (1994); Lynne C. Handy (1994); Philip C. Levering (1993).

Membership

To develop a continuous program of promoting SMLS in order to recruit and maintain members for SMLS and to represent SMLS on PLA Membership Committee.

Ch., Miriam L. Morris (1993); Elizabeth W. Estes (1993); Lyn W. Hopper (1993); Jo K. Potter (1993); Ted Schmidt (1993).

Nominating—1993

Ch., John D. Hales Jr. (1993); Matthew C. Kubiak (1993); Jan Walsh (1993).

Nominating—1994

Ch., Jule Fosbender (1994); Carl Heffington (1994).

Planning

To develop a structure and an evolving plan of action for SMLS to channel the section's activity in ways which best serve the changing needs of the membership; to evaluate proposed activities to determine the relationship of those activities to the section's adopted plan, and to provide recommendations to the SMLS Executive Committee; to incorporate any changes in PLA organization, the goals of the division, and the issues facing the profession as a whole into the ongoing planning process, and to confer annually with the SMLS Executive Committee regarding changes in the section's plan of action.

Ch., Jule Fosbender (1994); John D. Hales Jr. (1993); Marianne Kotch (1993); Margaret Bachman Reid (1993); David Stelts (1993); James A. Swan (1993); Nancy Tessman (1993); Gordon S. Welles (1994).

Publications (see Ideas Exchange Committee.)

Rural Library Services

To develop, coordinate, and provide information on service, education, research, and publications particularly pertinent to libraries serving rural populations.

Ch., Annabel K. Stephens (1993); Jackie Beach (1994); Barbara Jean Elliott (1993); Sally L. Houghton (1993); Patricia La Caille John (1993); Jerome W. Krois (1994); Martha G. Lawson (1994); Timothy P. Lynch (1994); Helen G. Maul (1993); Margaret Bachman Reid (1993); Donald B. Reynolds Jr. (1993); Marcia L. Thomas (1994); Larry R. Thorne (1993); Bernard F. Vavrek (1993); Connie D. Wilcox (1994).

University Press Books for Public Libraries

To work in cooperation with the American Association of University Presses to develop policies and procedures for the annual publication of *University Press Books for Public Libraries*; to receive, evaluate, select, and annotate material for inclusion in this publication; to assist the AAUP in editorial work on and distribution of the publication; and to evaluate the utilization and effectiveness of this publication to public libraries.

Ch., James C. Powers (1993); Jeffrey R. Herold (1993); Nann Blaine Hilyard (1993); Carolyn M. Moore (1993); William A. Muller III (1993); Joyce M. Trent (1993); Susan S. Whittle (1994).

———————◆———————

Reference and Adult Services Division

———————◆———————

Membership as of August 31, 1992
Organization members   975
Personal members   4,583
Total   5,558
Andrew M. Hansen, *executive director*

The Reference and Adult Services Division is responsible for stimulating and supporting in every type of library the delivery of reference/information services to all groups, regardless of age, and of general library services and materials to adults. This involves facilitating the development and conduct of direct service to library users, the development of programs and guidelines for service to meet the needs of these users, and assisting libraries in reaching potential users.

The specific responsibilities of RASD are:

1. Conduct of activities and projects within the division's areas of responsibility;

2. Encouragement of the development of librarians engaged in these activities, and stimulation of participation by members of appropriate type-of-library divisions;

3. Synthesis of the activities of all units within the American Library Association that have a bearing on the type of activities represented by the division;

4. Representation and interpretation of the division's activities in contacts outside the profession;

5. Planning and development of programs of study and research in these areas for the total profession; and

6. Continuous study and review of the division's activities.

Board of Directors

Officers: Pres., James R. Rettig (1994); pres.-elect, Charles L. Gilreath (1995); secy., Sandra S. Leach (1993).

Other members: past pres., Susan S. DiMattia (1993); dirs.-at-large: Anita K. Evans (1994); Linda Friend (1995); Mark Leggett (1995); Judith P. Reid (1993); Susan M. Riehm (1993); Nancy H. Sherwin (1994); ex officio (voting): councilor, Gail A. Schlachter (1996); BRASS ch., Catherine R. Friedman (1993); CODES ch., Mary L. Goodyear (1993); CSRG ch., John C. Hepner (1993); HS ch., Michael B. Clegg (1993); MARS ch., Carol M. Tobin (1993); MOPSS ch., Emily Johnson Batista (1993); SUPS ch., Allan M. Kleiman (1993); ex officio (nonvoting): *RASD Update* ed., Jane P. Kleiner (1994); *RQ* eds., Connie Van Fleet (1994) and Danny P. Wallace (1994); exec. dir., Andrew M. Hansen.

Executive Committee

To establish the agenda for board meetings and otherwise facilitate the work of the board; to consider budget proposals and make recommendations to the board; to be responsible for orientation of new RASD officers, board members, and committee chairs; to review all RASD program proposals and make recommendations to the board; and to take action on matters that require decisions between meetings of the board.

Pres., James R. Rettig (1994); pres.-elect, Charles L. Gilreath (1995); secy., Sandra S. Leach (1993); past pres., Susan S. DiMattia (1993); Gail A. Schlachter (1996); ex officio, Andrew M. Hansen (1993).

Publications

RASD Update (quarterly). Sent to all division members. Available on subscription, $15 a yr.; single copies, $4. Ed., Jane Kleiner, Reference Servs., LSU Ls., Middleton Bldg., Baton Rouge, LA 70803-7010.

Roundup (semi-annual). Newsletter of the RASD Council of State and Regional Groups (CSRG). Sent to RASD affiliates; not available by subscription. Ed., John C. Hepner, P.O. Box 507, Denton, TX 76202-0507.

RQ (quarterly). Sent to all division members. Subscriptions $42 a yr. (foreign, $52); single copies, $12. Co-eds., Danny P. Wallace and Connie Van Fleet; Louisiana State Univ., Baton Rouge, LA 70803-3290.

COMMITTEES

Access to Information

To investigate and make recommendations regarding any aspect of access to information or intellectual freedom relating to the interests of RASD and to the responsibilities of public service librarians.

Ch., Carolyn J. Radcliff (MARS, 1993); William R. Kinyon (1993); Alice J. Perez (1993); Frances E. Roehm (1993); Patricia P. Timberlake (1994); Kerranne Gilmour-Biley (BRASS, 1994); David L. Langenberg (HS, 1993); Noelene P. Martin (MOPSS, 1994); James D. Neeley (CODES, 1993); Louise S. Sherby (SUPS, 1994).

American Federation of Labor/Congress of Industrial Organizations—ALA, Library Service to Labor Groups (See listing under Joint Committees, p. 16.)

Awards Coordinating

To coordinate the activities of the awards committees of the division and its sections by assisting in orientation of new committee chairs, serving as a clearinghouse for information pertinent to policies and procedures of awards committees, and to assist the Board of Directors and/or section executive committees to develop new awards.

Ch., Peter McCallion (1994); Larayne J. Dallas (1994); Merle L. Jacob (1994); Carolyn M. Mulac (1993); Tom J. Muth (1993); Linda J. Sammataro (1994).

Behavioral Guidelines for Reference and Information Services (ad hoc)

To draft a set of behavioral guidelines for librarians to follow when providing reference and information services. These guidelines will recommend the behaviors an individual should exhibit when responding to another individual's information needs. The guidelines should rest on the profession's collective research on these matters, supplemented, where the research literature at this time is silent or self-contradictory, by sound professional judgment.

Ch., David A. Tyckoson (1994); Laura J. Isenstein (1994); Jane P. Kleiner (1994); Neel Parikh (1994); Rebecca J. Whitaker (1994); Jo Bell Whitlatch (1994); Hope H. Yelich (1994).

Conference Program—New Orleans, 1993

Ch., Johannah Sherrer (1993); Charles R. Anderson (1993); Barbara E. Beaton (1993); Geraldine King (1993); Beverly P. Lynch (1993); Delores D. Meglio (1993); Christine Nasso (1993).

Conference Program Coordinating

To coordinate the approval and implementation of programs presented or sponsored by RASD units and committees at ALA conferences.

Ch., Theodora T. Haynes (1994); Joyce E. Jelks (1993); James R. Kuhlman (1994); Anne L. Buchanan (BRASS, 1993); Kelly Janousek (MOPSS, 1994); Julia M. Rholes (MARS, 1994); Edward J. Russo (HS, 1993); Martha Eszes Smith (CODES, 1994).

Dartmouth Medal

Responsible for administering an annual award honoring achievement in creating reference works outstanding in quality and significance.

Ch., Mary Ellen Quinn (1993); Marie C. Ellis (1993); Susan Hagen Land (1993); Martha Landis (1993); ex officio, Ref. Bks. Bull. ch., Christine Bulson (1993).

Denali Press Award

To administer an annual award that recognizes achievement in creating reference works, outstanding in quality and significance, that provide information specifically about ethnic and minority groups in the United States.

Ch., Ingrid Betancourt (1993); Katherine M. Dahl (1993); Carolyn M. Gates (1993); Mario M. Gonzalez (1993); Joyce E. Jelks (1993).

Facts On File Grant

To select a library to receive a grant for imaginative programming which would make current affairs more meaningful to an adult audience.

Ch., Ree DeDonato (1993); Robert Caban (1993); Anna M. Donnelly (1993); Richard W. Grefrath (1993); Judith A. Koor (1993).

Finance

To advise the vice-president/president-elect and the RASD Board of Directors on budgetary matters.

Ch., Charles L. Gilreath (1993); Barbara E. Butler (BRASS, 1994); Nancy B. Crane (MARS, 1994); Michael A. Golrick (1993); Mario M. Gonzalez (SUPS, 1994); A. Craig Hawbaker (MOPSS, 1994); Patricia E. Kenly (1994); Gillian F. Mendle (CODES, 1994); Margaret Ann Reinert (HS, 1994).

Gale Research Award for Excellence in Reference and Adult Services

Responsible for administering an annual award presented to a library or library system for developing an imaginative and unique library resource to meet patrons' needs.

Ch., Christine C. Avery (1993); Jean S. Adelman (1993); Michael A. Golrick (1993); Patricia Groh (1993); Marsha L. Spyros (1993).

Legislation

To make recommendations to the RASD Board with regard to proposed or actual legislation with implications for library reference and adult services; to recommend to the RASD Board areas of concern involving library reference and adult services where legislative solutions are appropriate; and to serve as a channel of communication between the RASD Board and other appropriate units of ALA for the above-mentioned concerns.

Ch., James R. Cannon (1994); Anita K. Evans (1994); Ken Schott (1994); Steven D. Zink (1994).

MARBI (Machine-Readable Bibliographic Information), ALCTS/LITA/ RASD (See p. 27.)

Membership

1. To serve as the public relations arm of RASD, with the aim of promoting increased membership and retaining existing members in the division.
2. To represent RASD and its Board on the ALA Membership Promotion Task Force. The chairperson of the RASD Membership Committee shall assume this responsibility.
3. To be responsible for the concepts to be used in future RASD membership promotional brochures. This activity will be in coordination with the Executive Director of RASD and the Council of State and Regional Groups (CSRG).

4. To be responsible for planning the graphic design of the Annual Conference RASD booth and for coordinating the staffing of the booth. This activity will be in cooperation with the RASD Executive Director.
5. To be responsible for communicating the activities and needs of the Membership Committee to all RASD Committees.

Ch., Linda Keir Simons (1994); Eva M. Greenberg (SUPS, 1994); Jacqueline B. Hambric (1993); Marcia J. Martin (MARS, 1993); Tom J. Muth (HS, 1993); David Null (1994); Christine Roysdon (1994); Bruce A. Shuman (MOPSS, 1994); Felix Eme Unaeze (BRASS, 1994).

(Margaret E.) Monroe Library Adult Services Award

Responsible for administering an annual citation honoring a librarian who has made a distinguished contribution to library adult services.

Ch., Diane C. Strauss (1993); Barbara T. Balbirer (1993); Patricia M. Hogan (1993); Carl Stone (1993); Kathleen A. Sullivan (1993).

(Isadore Gilbert) Mudge Citation

Responsible for administering an annual citation to an individual who has made a distinguished contribution to reference librarianship.

Ch., Virginia Boucher (1993); Nancy Fisher (1993); Jeanne Gelinas (1993); Joanne Harrar (1993); Karen A. Sendi (1993).

Nominating—1993

Ch., Gail A. Schlachter (1993); Deborah H. Bryson (BRASS, 1993); Cathryn M. Canelas (CODES, 1993); Linda Friend (MARS, 1993); Una M. Gourlay (MOPSS, 1993); Margaret Ann Reinert (HS, 1993).

Nominating—1994

Ch. and members to be appointed.

Organization

To serve the Board of Directors in an advisory capacity by reviewing division organization and activities with the purpose of assisting the division in avoiding duplication of effort and making sure that the activities of RASD are compatible with the goals of the division and the goals of ALA as a whole. To undertake special projects which do not fall within the scope of existing committees.

Ch., Ted P. Sheldon (1994); John M. Budd (CODES, 1994); Janice M. Del Negro (1994); Peggy D. Glover (1994); Glenda J. Hughes (1994); Mark Leggett (1995); Alice C. Littlejohn (BRASS, 1994); William D. Michel (MOPSS, 1994); Bernard F. Pasqualini (MARS, 1993); Judith P. Reid (HS, 1993); ex officio, Susan S. DiMattia (1993).

Committee Reviews (subcommittee)

To oversee the procedures relating to the review of RASD committees as designated by the RASD Organization Committee.

Co-chs., John M. Budd (1994) and Karen J. Chapman (1994).

RASD Policy Handbook (subcommittee)

To oversee the compilation and updating of an RASD policy and procedure handbook for use by

the RASD Organization Committee. The handbook should include all Board policies and procedures, Division and Section Bylaws, Division and Section Committee and Discussion Group Descriptive Statements, and other documents as appropriate.

Co-chs., Peggy D. Glover (1993) and Bernard F. Pasqualini (1993).

Planning

To recommend to the Board goals, objectives, and priorities for the division as well as broad strategies for achieving them, and to evaluate the movement of the division and its units towards these goals and objectives.

Ch., Elaine Z. Jennerich (MOPSS, 1994); Diane F. Carothers (HS, 1994); Charles F. Cummings (HS, 1993); William J. Galaway (CODES, 1993); Mary L. Goodyear (CODES, 1994); Jane P. Kleiner (MARS, 1994); Kathleen Kluegel (MARS, 1993); Susan T. Newman (BRASS, 1994); Susan M. Riehm (1993); Robert F. Rose (MOPSS, 1994); Nancy H. Sherwin (1994); Roberta L. Tipton (BRASS, 1994).

Publications

To recommend to the RASD Board policy and steps to implement policy concerning *RQ, RASD Update*, and any other publishing activity originating with the division. The role of the RASD Publications Committee is to provide advice and recommendations regarding publications to RASD units and the RASD Board. Any RASD unit that wishes to publish an item is responsible for planning the publication, requesting board approval, and working with the RASD Director to take care of details involved in the actual publication.

Ch., Sandra Goldstein Hirsh (1993); Lucinda J. Angell (1993); Patricia S. Butcher (MOPSS, 1994); Robert Franklin (1994); Charles M. Getchell (HS, 1993); Lucy T. Heckman (BRASS, 1993); Danise Gianneschi Hoover (MARS, 1993); Peter McCallion (1993); Vivian M. Pisano (SUPS, 1994); Carol A. Wright (CODES, 1994).

Reference Service Press Award

To administer an annual award to be given to the author of the best article published in *RQ* in the preceding two volumes.

Ch., Ellen Derey Safley (1993); Kay A. Cassell (1993); Gary M. Klein (1993).

"RQ" Editorial Advisory Board

The Editorial Board members serve as advisors to the editor on the contents of the journal issues, and review manuscripts submitted for consideration for publication.

Co-chs., Connie J. Van Fleet (1994) and Danny P. Wallace (1994); James A. Benson (1994); Charles A. Bunge (1993); Jane P. Kleiner (1993); James R. Kuhlman (1994); J. David Martin (1993); Nancy C. Pack (1993); Ilene F. Rockman (1994); Richard E. Rubin (1993); Felix Eme Unaeze (1994); Anna L. Yount (1994).

(John) Sessions Memorial Award

To administer an annual award recognizing a library or library system that has made a significant effort to work with the labor community and by so doing has brought recognition to the community through the library of the history and contribution of the labor movement to the development of this country.

Ch., Barbara Hull (1993); Joan R. Berman (1993); Barbara C. Silver (1993); Ruby U. Tyson (1993).

(Louis) Shores–Oryx Press Award

Responsible for administering an annual award to recognize excellence in the reviewing of books and other materials for libraries.

Ch., Jack Forman (1993); Susan C. Awe (1993); Richard Bleiler (1993); Ann C. Holt (1993); Elaine Z. Jennerich (1993).

Standards and Guidelines

Responsible for advising the RASD Board of Directors on standards and guidelines for the delivery of reference information services and of general library services and materials to adults.

Ch., Mary E. Jackson (1993); Larayne J. Dallas (MOPSS, 1994); Franklin P. Gavett (MARS, 1994); Glenda S. Neeley (BRASS, 1993); Charles D. Patterson (1993); Karen J. Rupp-Serrano (CODES, 1994); Thomas B. Wall (1993); Sarah Barbara Watstein (1994); Roberta V. Webb (1993); Curt B. Witcher (HS, 1994).

COUNCIL OF STATE AND REGIONAL GROUPS

To encourage activities of state and regional RASD affiliated groups, to provide a forum for the exchange of information and advice relevant to their programs, and to facilitate cooperation among these groups and between them and the division.

Ch., John C. Hepner (1993).

Alabama—Ref. & Adult Serv. R.T.
Arkansas—Ref. Serv. Div.
California—Ref. & Info. Serv. Chap.
Colorado—Public L. Div.
Connecticut—Ref & Adult Serv. Sect.
District of Columbia—Ref. Interest Group
Hawaii— Spec. & Ref Sect.
Illinois—Ref. Forum
Iowa—Adult & Ref. Serv. Forum
Kansas—Public L. Sect.
Louisiana—Ref. Interest Group
Maine—Academic & Res. Ls.
Maryland—Pub. Serv. Div.
Massachusetts—Adult Serv. R.T.
Michigan—Ref. Caucus
Minnesota—Ref. & Adult Serv. Sect.
Missouri—Ref. & Inf. Serv. Council.
Nebraska—College & Univ. Sect.
New Hampshire—Ref. & Adult Serv.
New Jersey—Ref. Sect.
New York—Ref. & Adult Serv. Sect.
North Carolina—Ref. & Adult Serv.
Ohio—Ref. & Inf. Serv. Div.
Oklahoma—Ref. R.T.
South Carolina—P. Serv. Sect.
Tennessee—Ref. R.T.
Texas—Ref. R.T.
Washington—Ref. Interest Group
Wisconsin—Ref. & Adult Serv. Sect.
Wyoming—Ref. Interest Group.

REPRESENTATIVES

ALA Legislation Assembly—James R. Cannon.
ALA Membership Promotion Task Force—Linda Keir Simons.
ALA Professional Ethics—Kenneth L. Fersti.
ALCTS-CCS—Orthella Polk Moman.
Coalition of Adult Education Organizations— Andrew M. Hansen; Christina C. Young.
Documentation Abstracts, Inc.—David M. Pilachowski.
Freedom to Read Fdn.—Patricia P. Timberlake.
L. of Congress—to be appointed.
LIRT—Gretchen E. Pearson.
Literacy—to be appointed.

SECTIONS

Business Reference and Services (BRASS)
Collection Development and Evaluation (CODES)
History (HS)
Machine-Assisted Reference (MARS)
Management and Operation of Public Services (MOPSS)
Services to User Populations (SUPS)

Business Reference and Services Section (BRASS)

Represents the subject interests of reference librarians, business information specialists, and others engaged in providing business reference/information services. The section seeks to serve as a medium for the sharing of information and concerns among interested librarians, publishers, and other suppliers of business reference sources and through its programs and projects to help improve the sources and techniques of business reference and information.

Executive Committee

Ch., Catherine R. Friedman (1994); ch.-elect, Timothy A. Dixon (1995); secy., Wendy Diamond (1994); past ch., Priscilla C. Geahigan (1993); mbrs.-at-large: Linda Becketti (1993); Barbara E. Butler (1995); Susan J. Strehl (1994); ex officio, James R. Rettig (1993).

Business Reference in Academic Libraries

To study, promote, and support the role of business reference in academic libraries.

Ch., Peter Zachary McKay (1994); Mark Anderson (1994); Barbara E. Butler (1993); Katherine M. Dahl (1994); Donna L. Gilton (1993); Mary Ellen Hurt (1993); Trudi E. Jacobson (1994); Carol H. Krismann (1994); Jeffrey Bryan Levy (1993); Carol S. Lunce (1993); Thomas R. Mirkovich (1994); intern, Karen F. Cary (1993).

Creative Financing for Academic Business Libraries (ad hoc subcommittee)

To survey business librarians to determine successful strategies for raising funds to augment academic business library budgets; to present findings to full committee at the Midwinter meeting 1993.

Ch., Mary Monroe (1993); Kerranne Gilmour-Biley (1993); Elizabeth C. Jackson (1993); Stanley P. Lyle (1993).

Business Reference in Public Libraries

To study, promote, and support the role of business reference in public libraries.

Ch., Norman R. Wyckoff (1994); James R. Cannon (1993); Kay S. Clark (1993); Irwin D. Faye (1994); Thomas L. Johnson (1993); Mark Leggett (1994); Susan V. McKimm (1993); Richard L. Shelton (1994); Wicky Sleight (1994); Don Willis (1994); intern, Kathy J. Anderson (1994).

Business Reference Sources

To study and identify the need for and improvement in business reference sources, both print and electronic, and to promote communication between business reference librarians and the providers of business information.

Ch., Gordon J. Aamot Jr. (1993); John V. Ganly (1993); A. Craig Hawbaker (1993); Peter B. Ives (1994); Susan G. Neuman (1993); Ruth S. Schwartz (1994); Robert E. Sears (1994); Dennis E. Smith (1994); Diane C. Strauss (1994); intern, Brenda M. Scherr (1993).

Conference Program—New Orleans, 1993

Ch., Joanne A. Kosanke (1993); Paul D. Deane Jr. (1993); Tom Diamond (1993); Marilyn L. Hankel (1993); Katherine S. Laurence (1993); Anne B. Thatcher (1993).

Disclosure Student Travel Award

To administer an annual travel award to enable a student enrolled in an ALA-accredited master's degree program to attend the ALA Annual Conference.

Ch., Dennis R. Smith (1993); Pam Craychee (1993); Deborah H. Bryson (1993).

Education

To study and review the educational needs of business reference librarians and other librarians involved in providing business reference services; to explore and encourage the development of curriculum and continuing education programs in the area; and to promote communication between the profession and library educators.

Ch., Sharmon H. Kenyon (1994); Lynn C. Hattendorf (1994); Patricia E. Kenly (1994); Carol H. Krismann (1993); Lydia E. LaFaro (1993); Christina K. Morrow (1993); Richard T. Paustenbaugh (1994); Lee E. Pike (1993); Judith M. Wiza (1994); Carol Z. Womack (1993); intern, Bobray J. Bordelon (1993).

Gale Research Award for Excellence in Business Librarianship

To administer an annual award that recognizes an individual who has distinguished him- or herself in the field of business librarianship.

Ch., Violette Y. Brooks (1993); Kelly Janousek (1993); William R. Taylor (1993).

Nominating—1993

Ch., Deborah H. Bryson (1993); Peter B. Ives (1993); Nancy H. Sherwin (1993).

Nominating—1994

Ch. and members to be appointed.

Planning

To advise the BRASS Executive Committee on the present and future priorities and directions of the section; to formulate goals and objectives and the strategies for achieving them; and to evaluate the progress of the section and its units toward these goals and objectives.

Ch., Judy M. Nixon (1994); Karen J. Chapman (1993); Susan L. Kendall (1994); Peter Zachary McKay (1994); Susan G. Neuman (1994); ex officio: Timothy A. Dixon (1993); Roberta L. Tipton (1994).

Publications

To provide advice and recommendations regarding BRASS publications to the BRASS Executive Committee. To provide coordination of BRASS publication efforts and work closely with the RASD Publications Committee through the BRASS representative.

Ch., Thomas E. Hecker (1994); Susan C. Awe (1993); Leslie M. Haas (1994); Theodora T. Haynes (1993); Lucy T. Heckman (1993); Sylvia Ortiz (1994); Edgar Williamson (1994).

Discussion Group

Business Reference Services

To provide a forum for informal dialogue and idea exchange among those involved or interested in reference service to business clientele in an academic, public, or special library; to encourage informal contacts among business librarians; and to foster a group identity within ALA. (1986)

Ch., Anne L. Buchanan (1993).

Representatives

SLA Business & Finance Div.—to be appointed.

Collection Development and Evaluation Section (CODES)

(1) To develop the professional skills and knowledge of reference and adult services librarians who are involved in Collection Development and Evaluation (CD/E); (2) to gather and disseminate pertinent information to such librarians, and to facilitate communication among them; (3) to provide continuing education and training opportunities, and to represent the interests of RASD members working in CD/E; (4) to serve as an advisory body to the RASD Board on CD/E issues affecting reference and adult services librarians; and (5) to maintain liaison with existing units of RASD and ALCTS having related concerns.

Executive Committee

Ch., Mary L. Goodyear (1994); ch.-elect, Merle L. Jacob (1995); secy., Bonnie MacEwan (1994); past ch., William J. Galaway (1993); Caroline C. Long (1994); Judith B. Quinlan (1993).

Scheduling Coordinator: to be appointed.

Committees

Adult Library Materials

(1) To study all types of library materials, print and nonprint, useful to adults at all reading and comprehension levels to determine availability of these materials; (2) to explore and encourage new ways to stimulate the effective use of various types of library materials; (3) to develop model materials selection policies that reflect new priorities resulting from emerging and changing adult needs and interests; (4) to develop criteria for the selection, evaluation, and use of adult materials.

Ch., Harriet Gottfried (1993); Robert J. Bellinger (1993); Lenora Berendt (1994); Jean A. Coberly (1994); Anna M. Donnelly (1993); Ellen Ellickson (1994); Mary Ellen Collins (1993).

Bibliography

Responsible for surveys of the field of bibliography, disseminating information, studying needs, and advising on projects under way or under consideration.

Ch., Christine C. Avery (1993); Richard Bleiler (1994); Carole J. De Jardin (1994); Joan B. Fiscella (1994); Kathryn K. Kaya (1993); Mary M. Koenig (1994); Diane M. Zabel (1993); cons., William A. McHugh (1993).

Collection Development Policies

To encourage libraries to establish and regularly review collection priorities, develop systematic approaches to collection development and management, and document these priorities in written policies; to inform CODES members specifically and RASD members in general concerning new documents, trends, methodologies, and developments in collection management; and to provide methods of communication among CODES members and other relevant ALA organizations concerning collection development and management.

Ch., Kathleen A. Sullivan (1993); Suzanne Fedunok (1994); Patricia A. Kreitz (1994); James R. Kuhlman (1994); Patricia A. Promis (1994); Mary Ellen Quinn (1993); Terence M. Walton (1994); Christy L. Zlatos (1993); intern, Lise S. Snyder (1993).

Collection Evaluation Techniques

To identify, analyze, develop, and disseminate information and materials relating to techniques of evaluation of library print and nonprint collections in all types of libraries; to encourage research on methods of evaluation of such collections; to be a forum for discussion of collection evaluation concerns; to maintain liaison and share information with existing ALA units which have related concerns.

Ch., Cynthia S. Kaag (1993); Rhea Bradley (1993); Albert H. Joy (1994); Carol M. Kelley (1994); Collette G. Mak (1994); Nancy L. Pearl (1993); Dorothy E. Pittman (1993); Stephen Russo (1994); Karen Chittick Stabler (1993); Katherine M. Von Wald (1994); intern, Leilani S. Freund (1993).

Computer-based Methods and Resources

To provide a forum for discussion of issues relating to electronic resources in collection development and to serve as an advisory committee for concerns in this area; to produce information materials; to serve as a communication mechanism for gathering, organizing, and disseminating information about developments in the field.

Ch., Debora L. Cheney (1993); Eugenia D. Bryant (1993); Linda B. Gunter (1993); Suzanne D. Gyeszly (1993); Aubrey W. Kendrick (1994); Christopher W. Nolan (1994); Diane Harvey Smith (1994); Katina Strauch (1994); intern, Ellen Johnson (1993).

Conference Program—1993

Ch., Gerald J. Schafer (1993); Steve Alleman (1993); Ann E. Irvine (1993); Bonnie MacEwan (1993); Jane A. Dodd (1993).

Continuing Education

To identify the collection development continuing education needs of reference and adult services librarians to encourage and facilitate educational opportunities of such librarians.

Ch., Genie McKee (1994); Sharon Lee Cann (1993); Gale M. Chun (1994); Tami Echavarria (1993); Joseph J. Harzbecker (1994); Patricia M. Mount (1994); Gina R. Overcash (1994).

Liaison with Users

To build coalitions of librarians responsible for collection development and public services, especially coordinated liaison networks. A particular concern is the orientation, training, and education of liaisons, including formal and informal efforts. The focus will be on liaison work in all types of libraries in order to identify not only shared concerns but also the unique problems and opportunities of different environments.

Ch., Gail F. Latta (1994); Shirley Branden (1993); Marilyn Carbonell (1993); Peggy H. Cover (1994); Merle L. Jacob (1994); Marlene Kuhl (1994); Carol A. McAllister (1994); Chestalene Pintozzi (1994); Mary A. Ryan (1994); Mara L. Sprain (1993); cons., Diane M. Zabel (1993).

Nominating—1993

Ch., Cathryn M. Canelas (1993); Nancy O'Hanlon (1993); Marcia L. Rogers (1993).

Notable Books Council

To compile an annual list of Notable Books for use by the general reader and librarians who work with adult readers. The purpose of the list is to call attention to books published during the year which are significant additions to the world of books. (Committee appointments expire after Midwinter Meeting each year.)

1993 list: Ch., Tom H. Ray (1993); Amy B. Cohen-Rose (1993); Peggy Goodwin (1993); Harriet Gottfried (1994); Paula O. Green (1993); David K. Isaacson (1993); Ellen Loughran (1993); Eleanor Mitchell (1993); Nancy L. Pearl (1994); Peyton L. Penkowsky (1994); Margaret K. Powell (1994). *1994 list:* Ch., Tom H. Ray (1994).

Notable Books Council Publicity (subcommittee)

Ch., Marilyn Souders (1993); Marilyn L. Shackelford (1993).

Publications

To provide advice and recommendations regarding section documents and publications to CODES committees and to the CODES Executive Committee and to facilitate the publication process.

Ch., Sandra Kay Snell (1993); Katherine M. Dahl (1994); Rosemary A. Franklin (1994); Lynn C. Hattendorf (1994); Ann E. Irvine (1994); Joan S. Meador (1994); Nancy O'Hanlon (1993); Sydney J. Pierce (1994).

Reference Collection Development and Evaluation

To consider issues, problems, and trends relative to the development and evaluation of reference collections and to develop guides and guidelines for the practice of reference collection development. To coordinate with all relevant ALA committees and sections matters of mutual concern and interest.

Ch., Deborah D. Costa (1994); Gary O. Allen (1993); Daniel H. Gann (1993); Robert V. Labaree (1994); Barbara J. Pilvin (1993); Judith B. Quinlan (1994); Charles G. Spetland (1993); David A. Tyckoson (1993); Mary Jane Vakili (1994); Lola N. Warren (1994); M. Suzanne Wise (1993); Fred Yuengling (1994).

Reference Sources

To have responsibility for both the annual lists of reference sources recommended for small and medium-sized libraries and the quadrennial editions of *Reference Sources for Small and Medium-sized Libraries* or its successor. (Committee appointments expire after Midwinter Meeting each year.)

1993 list: Ch., Scott E. Kennedy (1993); Rebecca L. Johnson (1994); Dale Luchsinger (1994); Donald W. Maxwell (1994); Joyce A. McKnight (1993); Marguerite S. Mroz (1993); Razia Nanji (1994); Laurie Radde (1993); Deborah Thomas (1993); RBB rep., Rashelle S. Karp (1993). *1994 list:* Ch., Dale F. Luchsinger (1994).

Reference Tools Advisory

To implement the RASD Policy for Advising Publishers of Reference Sources and Vendors of Reference Services.

Ch., Thomas Gilson (1993); Linda G. DeFato (1993); Ann C. Holt (1993); Joan S. Meador (1994); Karen R. Snure (1994); Mila C. Su (1994); intern, Alice J. Perez (1993).

Materials Reviewing

To monitor, improve, moderate and encourage both the process and the skills of professionals involved in producing evaluative reviews of materials that may be selected for library collections; to maintain liaison and share information with existing ALA units and committees with related concerns.

Ch., David F. Kohl Jr. (1993); Heather Cameron (1993); Marie A. Garrett (1994); Richard T. Paustenbaugh (1994); Adam L. Schiff (1993); John P. Schmitt (1994); Graham R. Walden (1994); intern, Suzanne Nimitz (1993); ex officio, Nora K. Rawlinson (1993).

Staffing and Organization of Collection Development/Evaluation

To identify and study issues and trends related to staffing and organization of library collection development and evaluation activities; to collect, analyze, and disseminate information on staffing and organization of collection development and evaluation; and to develop guidelines and methods to advance and improve the staffing and organization of collection development and evaluation.

Ch., Susan L. Fales (1994); Merry L. Burlingham (1994); Cathryn M. Canelas (1993); Jeffrey Nathan Gatten (1994); Irene W. Hurlbert (1994); Elizabeth Kislitzin (1993); Jonathan Grant Pair (1993); Marcia L. Rogers (1993); Terence M. Walton (1993).

Small and Medium-sized Libraries (ad hoc)

To determine what collection management resources are available for librarians in small and medium-sized libraries of all types; to investigate options for RASD CODES; and to report to the CODES Executive Committee at the 1993 Midwinter Meeting.

Ch., Elizabeth J. McNeer (1993); Abby R. Kratz (1993); Georgine N. Olson (1993); Tedine J. Roos (1993).

Wilson Indexes

To study the periodical indexes published by the H. W. Wilson Company, to prepare questionnaires and voting lists as these may be required by which subscribers may elect titles to be indexed, to make recommendations to the subscribers and to the H. W. Wilson Company concerning these periodicals, and to advise the H. W. Wilson Company on problems, including policy matters, arising in the preparation of these indexes.

Ch., Phyllis Y. Massar (1993); Barbara J. Alper (1994); Karen Havill Bingham (1994); Stewart Bodner (1994); Jeanne Gelinas (1993); Kathleen M. Kehoe (1994); Carolyn Markuson (1994); Sandy Maxfield (1994); Lisa A. Romero (1994); Suzanne D. Sutton (1994).

Discussion Groups

Collection Development and Evaluation in Public Libraries

To serve as a forum for communication on collection development and evaluation in public libraries. (1988)

Co-chs., Georgianna S. Miles (1993) and Nancy L. Pearl (1993).

Dual Assignments

To facilitate communication concerning library personnel who have collection development and evaluation assignments as part of their professional duties. (1988)

Co-chs., Steve Alleman (1993) and Milton H. Figg (1993).

Representatives

ALCTS-RS, Collection Management & Development Com.—to be appointed.

History Section (HS)

To represent the subject interests of reference librarians, archivists, bibliographers, genealogists, historians and others engaged in historical reference or research. The History Section brings together representatives of history collections in all formats from all types of libraries, archives, and historical societies.

Reflecting the section's broad representation, its objectives are to identify common problems and to recommend solutions that can enhance service to all users. The section, through its programs and projects, helps improve the materials and methods for historical reference and research services.

Executive Committee

Ch., Michael B. Clegg (1994); ch.-elect, Carla Rickerson (1995); secy., Daniel W. Barthell (1993); past ch., Nancy Huling (1993); mbrs.-at-large: Diane F. Carothers (1993); Ruth A. Carr (1994); Margaret Ann Reinert (1995).

Committees

Bibliography and Indexes

To improve the usefulness of bibliographies and indexes through the evaluation both of specific publications and the pattern and effectiveness of coverage in all fields of history; to promote enhanced availability of historical works and information; and to serve as liaison among bibliographers, indexers, publishers, and professional associations.

Ch., Richard D. Van Orden (1994); Samuel J. Boldrick (1994); Charles F. Cummings (1993); Martin A. Cavanaugh (1994); Carl A. Hanson (1994); John D. Haskell Jr. (1994); Jean Schmidt Kiesel (1993); David A. Lincove (1993); Margaret Ann Reinert (1993); Agnes Haigh Widder (1994); Hope H. Yelich (1994).

Genealogical Publishing Company Award

To administer an annual award to encourage, recognize and commend professional achievement in Historical Reference and Research Librarianship.

Ch., Tom J. Muth (1993); Diane F. Carothers (1993); Nancy Huling (1993); Judith P. Reid (1993).

Genealogy

To provide a forum serving the interests of genealogists and of librarians whose work is in, or related to, the field of genealogy. To train and assist librarians, especially in History Departments and public libraries, who provide service to genealogists.

Ch., Raymond S. Wright III (1994); Ralph J. Crandall (1993); Michael D. Kirley (1993); David L. Langenberg (1993); Michele C. McNabb (1993); Barbara A. Musselman (1993); Steven W. Myers (1994); Keith F. Rose (1993); Bradley W. Steuart (1993); David T. Thackery (1993); ex officio, Curt B. Witcher (1993).

Historical Events

To select a single historical event or topic annually that facilitates development of materials, such as brochures or bibliographies, that will meet the needs of reference and public service librarians on a national level.

Ch., Paul A. Mogren (1994); Marilyn Carbonell (1993); John D. Haskell Jr. (1993); J. Ingrid Lesley (1993).

History of History (ad hoc)

Ch., Margaret Ann Reinert (1993); Diane F. Carothers (1993); Joyce E. Jelks (1993).

Local History

Seeks to provide a specific forum for those interested in and/or responsible for library services in local history through discussion groups, bibliographies, guidelines, and professional training programs; and to develop a network of local history resources and professionals who review and update techniques in the management of local history collections.

Ch., Curt B. Witcher (1993); Myra Anderson (1994); Norma J. Carmack (1993); Diane F. Carothers (1993); Priscilla C. Ciccariello (1993); George S. Hawley (1993); Stephen K. Kendall (1994); Tom J. Muth (1993); James C. Powers (1994); Carla Rickerson (1993); Frances E. Roehm (1994).

Nominating —1993

Ch., Carla Rickerson (1993); Margaret Ann Reinert (1993).

Discussion Groups

Genealogy and Local History

To provide a forum for the exchange of information about library services in local history and genealogy. To create and foster an environment for creativity and growth by acting as a catalyst for new ideas and problem-solving initiatives.

Ch., Diane R. Parkinson (1993).

History in Libraries

Ch., Paul A. Mogren (1993).

Machine-Assisted Reference Section (MARS)

Represents the interests of those concerned with attaining the highest possible quality in planning, developing, managing, teaching, or conducting all forms of computer-based reference and information services in libraries.

The responsibilities of the section are: (1) to conduct activities and projects within the section's areas of interest; (2) to be a means of sharing experience and information among interested librarians from all types of libraries and information services; (3) to seek to synthesize the activities of other units within the American Library Association that have a bearing on machine-assisted reference services; (4) to be a forum for discussion between librarians and the producers and suppliers of computerized reference and information services in a variety of formats; (5) to represent the needs and interests of the wide diversity of library users.

Executive Committee

Ch., Carol M. Tobin (1994); ch.-elect, Louis E. Drummond Jr. (1995); secy., Susan E. Hocker (1994); past ch., Jane P. Kleiner (1993); mbrs.-at-large: Sally Wayman Kalin (1994); Bernard F. Pasqualini (1995); Patricia Riesenman (1993); ex officio, RASD pres., James R. Rettig (1993).

Scheduling Coordinator works with the ALA Conference Arrangements Office and the MARS chair, vice-chair/chair-elect, and committee chairs to arrange Midwinter Meeting and Annual Conference meetings of MARS committees, including MARS Executive Committee, with as few conflicts as possible. Duties include communicating MARS meeting requests to the ALA Conference Arrangements Office, informing committee chairs of changes needed, and providing interim and final master lists of MARS meetings to all chairs involved. The Scheduling Coordinator also works with the MARS committee chairs and the chair of the RASD Membership Committee to arrange MARS staffing of the RASD booth at the Annual Conference—Janice D. Simmons-Welburn (1993).

Committees

Awards (ad hoc)

Ch., Linda Friend (1993).

Conference Program—1993

Ch., James E. Crooks (1993); Greg W. Byerly (1993); Marilyn A. Grant (1993); Pamela C. Sieving (1993); Carol M. Tobin (1993); Andrea Weinschenk (1993).

Conference Program—1994

Ch. and members to be appointed.

Education, Training, and Support

To create, collect, analyze, and disseminate information and materials on the development, implementation, and evaluation of education, training, and support for all groups of users of electronic reference services. These users include primary (on-site) and remote users, library staff, and library science educators and students.

Ch., Norman Howden (1994); Sara N. Brownmiller (1994); Martin P. Courtois (1994); Linda B. Gunter (1994); Sara Jane Lyon (1993); Randy L. Pederson (1994); Rosario Poli (1993); Barbara S. Roberts (1994); Janice D. Simmons-Welburn (1994); Marcella L. Stark (1994); interns: E. Alan Armstrong (1993); Chin-Wen C. Yu (1992).

Local Systems and Services

To create, collect, analyze, and disseminate information and materials on the development, implementation, and evaluation of local systems and services in any format; and to gather and share with the library profession information on new technologies and ethical issues relating to such systems and services. Local systems and services to be considered may include, but are not limited to, the following: provision of reference services via electronic mail; document delivery; expert systems; local area networks; locally mounted (third-party produced) databases; locally developed databases; public access catalogs; nonbibliographic databases.

Ch., Denise Beaubien Bennett (1994); Mark T. Day (1994); Elliot J. Kanter (1993); Kenneth R. Murr (1994); Laurie A. Preston (1994); Jayare Roberts (1994); Helen F. Smith (1994); David M. Strickler (1994); Melissa D. Trevvett (1993); interns: Mary A. Ryan (1993); Nancy P. Shires (1993).

Management

To create, collect, analyze, and disseminate information on all aspects of management of electronic resources for reference services. These aspects include planning, personnel, budget, organization, evaluation, facilities management, coordination, and promotion.

Ch., Mary M. Mintz (1993); Karen Berrish (1993); David M. Hovde (1993); Zsuzsa Koltay (1993); Pamela J. Lowe (1993); Marcia J. Martin (1993); Wilba Swearingen (1993); Stanley J Wilder (1994); intern, Lee B. Dalzell (1993).

Nominating—1993

Ch., Linda Friend (1993); Elliot J. Kanter (1993); Paula J. Swope (1993).

Nominating—1994

Ch. and members to be appointed.

Planning

To serve in an advisory capacity to the MARS Executive committee regarding goals, objectives, and priorities for the section as well as broad strategies for achieving them, and to evaluate the progress of the section and its units towards these goals and objectives.

Ch., Kathleen Kluegel (1994); Louis E. Drummond Jr. (1994); Linda Friend (1993); Elliot J. Kanter (1993); Jane P. Kleiner (1994); Bernard F. Pasqualini (1993); Peggy A. Seiden (1993).

Products and Services

To create, collect, analyze, evaluate, and disseminate information on, and coordinate the concerns of individuals or organizations involved in selecting, acquiring, and evaluating electronic reference products and services.

Ch., Rebecca J. Whitaker (1993); Sandra S. Ballasch (1994); Cynthia S. Faries (1994); Eric R. Loehr (1994); Catherine S. Palmer (1993); J. Robin Raquet (1994); Jayare Roberts (1994); Charles G. Spetland (1993); Christine A. Whittington (1994); intern, Xia Li (1993).

Public Libraries

To create, collect, and disseminate information on all aspects of electronic reference services in public libraries, and to represent interests of librarians concerned with planning, managing, or conducting electronic reference services in public libraries.

Ch., Nancy E. Bodner (1993); Margaret O. Herman (1994); James J. Maloney (1993); Lori J. Morse (1994); Rebecca J. Whitaker (1993); Patrick W. Wood (1993).

Publications

To provide advice and recommendations regarding section documents and publications to MARS committees and the MARS Executive Committee, and to facilitate the publication process.

Ch., Danise Gianneschi Hoover (1993); Byron P. Anderson (1993); Susan C. Awe (1994); Pat Hawthorne (1993); Pamela C. Sieving (1994).

Publications Awards (ad hoc)

Ch., Susan Hocker (1993).

User Access to Services

To create, collect, analyze, evaluate, and disseminate information and materials on access to electronic reference services and their impact on users. Electronic reference services and their delivery systems include (but are not limited to) mediated electronic searching, end-user searching, automated systems interfaces, networks, and gateways.

Ch., E. Paige Weston (1994); Sheila M. Barham (1994); Laine Farley (1994); Sheryl Horner (1993); Sally Wayman Kalin (1994); Stanley P. Lyle (1994); Karen R. Snure (1994); Kimberly Spyers-Duran (1994); Sally Willson Weimer (1994); intern, Lise M. Dyckman (1993).

Representatives

From LITA—to be appointed.
To LITA—James J. Maloney (1993).

Discussion Groups

Hot Topics in MARS

Ch., Elliot J. Kanter (1993).

Managers in MARS

Ch., Janice D. Simmons-Welburn (1993).

Management and Operation of Public Services Section (MOPSS)

Represents the interests of librarians engaged in direct service to their libraries' publics and of those responsible for the administration of public services in all types of libraries. The responsibilities of the section are: (1) to conduct activities and projects within the section's areas of interest; (2) to be a means of sharing experience and information among interested librarians from all types of libraries and information services; (3) to seek to synthesize the activities of other units within ALA that have a bearing on the management and operation of public services in libraries; (4) to represent the needs and interests of the wide diversity of library users.

Executive Committee

Ch., Emily Batista (1994); ch.-elect, Karen Liston Newsome (1995); secy., Kathryn J. Deiss (1994).

Committees

Catalog Use

To focus on the use of catalogs in reference service, including such aspects as communicating, evaluating, improving, studying, and teaching the use of catalogs in all forms; to monitor and communicate significant continuities and changes in the use of catalogs; to identify and examine critical issues and problems in catalog use; to provide opportunities for librarians to propose and discuss innovative solutions to catalog use problems; to join with librarians in other specialties to produce improvements in library service.

Ch., Linda L. Thompson (1994); Orthella Polk Moman (1993); Ellen E. Crosby (1993); Karen M. Drabenstott (1993); Carol M. Foggin (1993); Patricia A. Lawton (1994); Lorna Peterson (1993); Susanna J. Turner (1994); intern, Jonathan Miller (1993).

Cooperative Reference Service

Cooperative reference service extends a library's information service capability through interaction with other libraries or information centers. It is a process through which information assistance is provided, at least in part, by referring the user or the user's question to library/information personnel at another institution according to a system of formally established protocols. The purpose of the committee is to study, promote, and support cooperative reference service at all levels.

Ch., William M. Havener (1994); Susan K. Gore (1993); Donna R. Hogan (1994); Barbara R. Morland (1993); Mary M. D. Parker (1993); Carol A. Patrick (1993); Edmund F. Santa Vicca (1994); Janice D. Simmons-Welburn (1993); Martha Eszes Smith (1994); intern, Gillian F. Mendle (1993).

Electronic Information Request Form Pilot Project (subcommittee)

Ch., Janice D. Simmons-Welburn (1993); Julia M. Gelfand (1993); William M. Havener (1993); Edmund F. Santa Vicca (1993).

Model Outline for Cooperative Reference Service Manual (ad hoc subcommittee)

Ch., Mary M. D. Parker (1993); Donna R. Hogan (1993); Gillian F. Mendle (1993); Carol A. Patrick (1993); Martha Eszes Smith (1993).

Evaluation of Reference and Adult Services

To collect, analyze, and disseminate information to the RASD membership and profession on qualitative evaluation and quantitative measurements of service which will be used to assist in responsible managerial planning and decision making in reference and adult services; to support research in this area.

Ch., Beth S. Woodard (1994); Juleigh M. Clark (1993); Carole J. De Jardin (1994); Helen M. Gothberg (1993); Mary Ann Higdon (1994); Geraldine King (1993); Ralph A. Lowenthal (1993).

Fee-based Reference Services

To address the pros and cons of and alternatives to fee-based reference services in libraries; to serve as a forum for discussion of specific problems related to fee-based services in libraries; to act as an information clearinghouse for all groups in ALA with interest in fee-based or contracted reference services and alternatives to such services.

Ch., Pamela A. Noyes (1994); Zsuzsa Koltay (1993); Eric R. Loehr (1994); Anita Samuel (1994); Linda Keir Simons (1993); Jeffrey Smith (1994); Joseph M. Winkler (1994); intern, Alvetta S. Pindell (1993).

Interlibrary Loan

To consider current aspects of interlibrary loan service and to recommend solutions to interlibrary loan problems.

Ch., Mary L. Williamson (1994); Anthony E. Barnes (1994); Allison A. Cowgill (1994); Kathryn J. Deiss (1994); Una M. Gourlay (1994); Mary U. Hardin (1994); Lorna R. Newman (1993); Karen Liston Newsome (1993); Libby P. Soifer (1993); Kay E. Vyhnanek (1993); Margaret G. Whittier (1993); interns, Judy Ann Jerabek (1993); Lynn Wiley (1993).

Management of Reference

To identify and study issues relating to the management of reference services and to disseminate information on reference management in all types of libraries.

Ch., Carolyn M. Mulac (1993); Allen Louise Antone (1993); Sara B. Appelbaum (1994); Lee B. Dalzell (1994); Lisa E. Moeckel (1993); Mary M. Nofsinger (1993); Robert F. Rose (1994); Jane S. Row (1993); Karen H. Wielhorski (1994); intern, Anthony M. Dos Santos (1994).

Nominating—1993

Ch., Una M. Gourlay (1993); Charles D. Patterson (1993); Bruce A. Shuman (1993).

Professional Development

To encourage and promote effective professional development among reference and adult services librarians, and to coordinate with all relevant ALA committees.

Ch., Deborah A. Carver (1994); Gwen Arthur (1994); Bobray J. Bordelon (1994); Lynn W. Livingston (1994); Judith K. Ohles (1993); Billie J. Reinhart (1993); Karen J. Rupp-Serrano (1994); Stephen Russo (1994); Karen Chittick Stabler (1994).

Research and Statistics

To focus on current research needs and statistical procedures in the fields of reference and adult services.

Ch.,Marilyn K. Von Seggern (1994); Susan J. Beck (1994); Sharon Bostick (1994); Thomas J. Cashore (1994); Geraldine King (1993); Susan Klingberg (1993); James R. Kuhlman (1994); Marjorie E. Murfin (1993); Gail A. Schlachter (1994); Jo Bell Whitlatch (1993).

Discussion Groups

Interlibrary Loan

To provide a forum for discussion of issues pertaining to interlibrary loan and resource sharing among all types of libraries. (1985)

Co-chs., Andrew H. Bullen (1993) and Mary A. Hollerich (1993); Margaret G. Whittier (1993).

Performance Standards for Reference/ Information Librarians

To provide a forum for the informal exchange of information and the discussion of common challenges relating to performance issues in reference services; to serve as a vechicle for raising awareness of performance standards and their use in the provision of quality reference service. (1988)

Ch., Juleigh M. Clark (1993).

Reference Services in Large Research Libraries

To provide a forum for the discussion of issues of mutual interest to heads of reference departments in large research libraries. (1985)

Ch., Barbara E. Beaton (1993).

Reference Services in Medium-sized Research Libraries

To provide a forum for sharing of information and experience of reference librarians from those libraries smaller than the 54 largest Association of Research Libraries, whether academic or public. (1985)

Ch., David A. Tyckoson (1993).

Services to User Populations Section (SUPS)

Represents the interests of librarians serving diverse populations in all types of libraries. The responsibilities of the section are: (1) to conduct activities and projects within the section's areas of interest; (2) to be a means of sharing experience and information among interested librarians from all types of libraries and information services; (3) to seek to synthesize the activities of other units within the American Library Association that have a bearing on the provision of services to the diverse populations served by libraries; (4) to represent the needs and interests of the wide diversity of library users.

Executive Committee

Ch., Allan M. Kleiman (1994); ch.-elect, Mario M. Gonzalez (1995); secy., Elaine R. Lyon (1994).

Committees

Adults, Services to

(1) To identify the library and program interests of adults; (2) to collect and disseminate information on existing library programs and services; (3) to develop guidelines for programs and

services to meet specific interests and needs of adults; (4) to serve as a consultant for libraries with adult programming and/or services problems; (5) to create ad hoc subcommittees as needed to accomplish the above goals.

Ch., to be appointed; Celia C. Gibson (1993); Elaine R. Lyon (1993).

Aging Population, Library Service to

To explore ways of providing information and education on the subject and its problems for the profession and the layperson who work with this group facilitating the use of library service by the aged, continually exploring ways of making library service to the aged more effective.

Ch., Howard O. Zogott (1993); Edward P. Miller (1993); Robert C. Myers (1993); Nancy C. Pack (1993).

Literacy

To explore the issue of literacy as it relates to programs and services of libraries and to develop products and programs which will assist libraries and librarians in dealing with this issue.

Ch. and members to be appointed.

Nominating Committee—1993

Ch. and members to be appointed.

Reference Services for Children and Young Adults

To identify the reference/information needs of children and young adults and to suggest effective methods to meet those needs; to collect and disseminate related information; to identify all types of materials which meet these needs and to stimulate their publication; to develop guidelines for effective delivery of services; to support research, publication, and training programs; to represent the reference/information needs and interests of children and young adults; and to act as a liaison to other units with common concerns.

Ch., Leslie Edmonds (1993); Marsha D. Broadway (1993); May Brottman (1993); Judith H. Higgins (1993); Deborah J. Mason (1993); Elizabeth C. Overmyer (1993).

Spanish-Speaking, Library Services to the

To improve library services to the Spanish-speaking and Hispanic culture groups at both the local and national levels.

Ch., Susan J. Freiband (1993); Vivian M. Pisano (1993); Edward Erazo (1993); Maria E. Martinez (1993); Molly E. Molloy (1993).

Discussion Group

Women's Materials and Women Library Users

To serve as a forum for the sharing of information and exchanging of ideas about women's materials and resources and library services to women in all types of libraries. (1986)

Ch. to be appointed.

Young Adult Library Services Association

Membership as of August 31, 1992
Organization members   462
Personal members   1,761
Total   2,223

Ann C. Weeks, *executive director*
Linda Waddle, *deputy executive director*

The goal of the Young Adult Library Services Association is to advocate, promote, and strengthen service to young adults as part of the continuum of total library service. The following concerns and activities are interdependent in fulfilling the goal of YALSA. The Young Adult Library Services Association:

1. Advocates the young adult's right to free and equal access to materials and services, and assists librarians in handling problems of such access.

2. Evaluates and promotes materials of interest to adolescents through special services, programs, and publications, except for those materials designed specifically for curriculum use.

3. Identifies research needs related to young adult service and communicates those needs to the library academic community in order to activate research projects.

4. Stimulates and promotes the development of librarians and other staff working with young adults through formal and continuing education.

5. Stimulates and promotes the expansion of young adult service among professional associations and agencies at all levels.

6. Represents the interests of librarians and staff working with young adults to all relevant agencies, governmental or private, and to industries that serve young adults as clients or consumers.

7. Creates and maintains communication links with other units of the ALA whose developments affect service to young adults.

Board of Directors

Pres., Elizabeth M. O'Donnell (1994); pres.-elect, Judith A. Druse (1995); past pres., Mary Elizabeth Wendt (1993); Betty Carter (1994); Elizabeth E. Elam (1995); Jennifer Jung Gallant (1993); Constance P. Lawson (1994); Amy L. Oxley (1995); Pamela G. Spencer (1993); div. councilor, Pamela R. Klipsch (1995).

Executive Committee

To act for the Board of Directors between Board meetings on items that require interim action; to review agendas for the Board meet ings and to make recommendations to the Board regarding items reviewed and under consideration by the Board; to review YALSA activities and programs and recommend division priorities in relation to activities and programs.

Pres., Elizabeth M. O'Donnell (1994); pres.-elect, Judith A. Druse (1995); past pres., Mary Elizabeth Wendt (1993); div. councilor, Pamela R. Klipsch (1995); exec. dir., Ann C. Weeks (1994).

Publication

Journal of Youth Services in Libraries (quarterly). Sent to all YALSA members. Subscriptions, $40 a yr. ($50 Foreign). Issued jointly with ALSC. Eds., Donald J. Kenney, Virginia Tech. Univ. L., Blacksburg, VA 24061-0434, and Linda J. Wilson, Dept. of Ed. Studies, Radford Univ., 206A Russell Hall, Radford, VA 24142.

COMMITTEES

Best Books for Young Adults

To select from the year's publications those adult and young adult books significant for young adults; to annotate the selected titles.

Ch., Deborah D. Taylor (1993); John W. Callahan (1993); Helen F. Flowers (1993); Elizabeth B. Fowler (1993); Betsy Fowler (1993); Di Herald (1993); Ralph M. Jimenez (1993); Bonnie Kunzel (1993); Rosemary W. Moran (1993); Joel Shoemaker (1993); Leila Joy Sprince (1993); Evelyn C. Walker (1993); Laura R. Weber (1993); cons., Sally C. Estes; adm. asst., Lucy C. Marx (1993).

Budget and Finance

To prepare and submit a recommended annual budget for the division to the YALSA Board; to advise the YALSA Board on all fiscal matters relating to the division; and to review all activities and programs for fiscal implications.

Ch., JoAnn G. Mondowney (1993); Judith A. Druse (1993); Jack Forman (1994); Elizabeth M. O'Donnell (1993); Mary Elizabeth Wendt (1993).

Computer Applications to Young Adult Services

To investigate the impact of computer technology on youth library services.

Ch., Nancy P. Zimmerman (1993); Linda H. Bertland (1993); Elissa L. Glick (1993); Barbara B. Kiffmeyer (1993); Delores T. McCoy (1993); Rebecca J. Pasco (1994).

Conference Grant—Baker & Taylor/YALSA, 1993

To select annually in accord with the terms of the grant two young adult librarians who work directly with teenagers (1 school librarian and 1 public library young adult librarian) to receive the grant, which is to provide financial assistance in attending an ALA Annual Conference.

Ch., Ranae Pierce (1993); Susan Meck (1993); Amy L. Oxley (1993).

Directions for Library Service to Young Adults Revision (task force)

To revise the publication, *Directions for Library Service to Young Adults* by Midwinter Meeting 1993.

Ch., Marilee Foglesong (1993); Joan Atkinson (1993); Donna Bacon (1993); Mary K. Chelton (1992); Nyla L. Fujii (1993); Cynthia Glunt (1993); Julia Losinski (1993); Gail A. Richmond (1993); Jana Varlejs (1993).

Division Promotion

To develop and pursue an aggressive and continuous campaign to promote YALSA.

Ch., Paul F. Anderson (1993); Carolyn A. Caywood (1993); Sandra A. Farrell (1993); Juanita R. Foster (1994); Marsha Korobkin (1993); Susan B. Madden (1993); Elizabeth M. Reed (1993); Anne Sheehan (1994).

Econo-Clad Award for Young Adult Reading or Literature Program

To select annually, when a suitable winner is indicated, the recipient of the Econo-Clad Award for Young Adult Reading or Literature Program.

Ch., Jody Stefansson (1993); Audra Caplan (1993); Karlan K. Sick (1993).

Education

To explore, evaluate, and make recommendations concerning the current status of library school curriculum in regard to library service to young adults. To explore, evaluate, and make recommendations about continuing education for librarians working with young adults. To maintain liaison with the ALA Committee on Library Education and other related ALA units.

Ch. to be appointed; Patricia Feehan (1994); Elizabeth M. Rosen (1993); Bruce L. Siebers (1993); Maureen White (1993); 3 to be appointed.

(Margaret A.) Edwards Award, 1993

To select a living author or co-author whose book or books, over a period of time, have been accepted by young people as an authentic voice that continues to illuminate their experiences and emotions, giving insight into their lives. The book or books should enable them to understand themselves, the world in which they live, and their relationship with others and with society.

Ch., Marion H. Hargrove (1993); Ellin Chu (1993); Patrick Scott Jones (1993); Mary I. Purucker (1993); Janet P. Sarratt (1993).

(Margaret A.) Edwards Award 1994

Ch., Judy T. Nelson (1994); Frances B. Bradburn (1994); Beryl E. Eber (1994); Brenda M. Hunter (1994); Karlan K. Sick (1994).

Genre Lists

To prepare a revised and updated edition of the genre lists and a tip sheet for each, which will include background information suggestions for utilization of material with young adults.

The coordinator is to work with chairs and members of the eight Genre List Committees, serving as a consultant to each committee; to edit the annotations for each genre list and tip sheet; and to work with the YALSA Deputy Executive Director and other office staff to prepare materials for publication.

Coor., Karlan K. Sick (1993).

Fantasy

Ch., Merilyn L. Grosshans (1993); Toni A. Bernardi (1993); Penelope P. Hayne (1993); Catherine M. G. MacRae (1993); Judith Rodriguez (1993); Jeanette C. Smith (1993); Gloria A. Waity (1993).

Humor

Ch., Judy Sasges (1993); Jana R. Fine (1993); Lily J. Helwig (1993); Mary L. Keefer (1993); Nona Ann Pryor (1993); Susan J. Rosenkoetter (1993); Marcia L. Wright (1993).

Romance

Ch., Doris C. Losey (1993); Mary J. Arnold (1993); Nancy Bard (1993); Susan Farber

(1993); Juanita R. Foster (1993); Marva C. Webster (1993); Meg Wolfe (1993).

Sports

Ch., Helen A. Vandersluis (1993); Paul F. Anderson (1993); Barbara T. Balbirer (1993); Maureen A. Connelly (1993); Brenda S. Kilmer (1993); Nora Jane Natke (1993); Susan M. Veltfort (1993).

Genrecon Institute (ad hoc)

To develop a proposal for an institute based on, but not limited to, program elements from the 1991 Genrecon Preconference that would be made available on request to state library associations and other groups. To report about the feasibility of the project to the Board by Annual Conference 1993.

Ch., Christy Tyson (1993); Sharon Bart (1993); Pamela G. Spencer (1993).

Intellectual Freedom

To serve as a liaison between the division and the ALA Intellectual Freedom Committee and all other groups within the Association concerned with intellectual freedom; to advise the division on matters pertaining to the First Amendment of the U.S. Constitution and the ALA Library Bill of Rights and their implication to library service to young adults and to make recommendations to the ALA Intellectual Freedom Committee for changes in policy on issues involving library service to young adults; to prepare and gather materials which will advise the young adult librarian of available services and support for resisting local pressure and community action designed to impair the rights of young adult users.

Ch., Patricia Muller (1993); Darice McKay (1994); A. Jeanie McNamara (1994); Gail A. Richmond (1994); Roger Sutton (1994); Susan Uebelacker (1993); Geneva T. Van Horne (1994); Laura R. Weber (1994).

"Journal of Youth Services in Libraries" Editorial, ALSC/YALSA (interdivisional)
(See p. 41.)

"Journal of Youth Services in Libraries" Refereed Journal Evaluation Process, ALSC/YALSA (ad hoc interdivisional)
(See p. 41.)

Legislation

To serve as a liaison between the ALA Legislation Committee and the division. To inform and instruct librarians working with young adults of pending legislation, particularly that which affects young adults, and to encourage the art of lobbying. To recommend to the YALSA Board endorsement or revision of legislation affecting young adults which might be proposed or supported by the ALA Legislation Committee.

Ch., Jeri C. Baker (1993); Naomi K. Angier (1993); Larry D. Condit (1994); James Edward Cook (1993); Carole J. De Jardin (1994); Judith G. Flum (1993); Cathleen A. Friedmann (1993); Dierdre R. O'Hagan (1993).

Local Arrangements—New Orleans, 1993

To handle YALSA local arrangements for the ALA Annual Conference, in close cooperation with the YALSA president and staff.

Ch., Cathleen Friedmann (1993); members to be appointed.

Long-Range Planning

To make recommendations to the YALSA Board for division long-range plans; to monitor and evaluate current long-range plans, and make recommendations to the Board for updating the plans.

Ch., Helen J. Tallman (1993); Brenda M. Hunter (1993); Jo Ann Kingston (1993); Connie H. Lawson (1993); Joy L. Lowe (1993).

Look, Listen, Explain (ad hoc)

To revise the monograph Look, Listen, Explain.

Ch., to be appointed; Stephen J. Crowley (1994); Marijo Duncan (1994); Lily J. Helwig (1994); Constance P. Lawson (1994).

Media Selection and Usage

To study and promote the use of all media as related to libraries and to cooperate with agencies having similar functions; to prepare or to have prepared selected lists on subjects of current importance; to promote programming in areas of immediate interest to youth using library materials of all types; to keep the YALSA Board informed of all proposals and projects in this area.

Ch., Sandra Payne (1993); Susan Baldwin (1993); Connie Adams Bush (1993); Beryl E. Eber (1993); Hazel Moore (1993); Sandra Payne (1994); Sharon A. J. Suggs (1993); Hazel A. Yliniemi (1993); 2 to be appointed.

Membership Recruitment

To develop and pursue an aggressive and continuous campaign to recruit and retain members for YALSA.

Ch., Deborah J. Colter (1994); Susan S. Cannady (1993); Larry D. Condit (1993); Maureen A. Connelly (1994); Brenda Freitas-Obregon (1993); Andrea M. Howe (1993); Amy L. Oxley (1993); Caryn G. Sipos (1994); Bunni Union (1993); Rose O. Ward (1994).

National Organizations Serving the Young Adult Liaison

To explore, recommend, initiate, and implement ways of working with other organizations that work with and for young adults.

Ch., Ann C. Theis (1993); Lucinda K. Bereznay (1993); Betty H. Grebey (1993); Karen L. Gregory (1993); Bill Stack (1993).

Nominating—1993 Election

To prepare the slate for annual elections of YALSA officers and directors, and in so doing, to provide for representation of types of libraries, special interests, and geographical locations of the division membership.

Ch., Nancy Bard (1993); S. Chapple Langemack (1993); Kathy H. Latrobe (1993).

Organization and Bylaws

1. To revise the Bylaws in order to clarify them and, when necessary, to recommend revision and amendment to improve them for the effective management of the division, for the achievement of its stated objectives, and to keep them in harmony with ALA Constitution and Bylaws.

2. To study and review committee functions, recommending changes in committee structure; to advise on the organization manual; and to make recommendations on other organizational matters.

Ch. to be appointed; Margaret J. Fleesak (1993); Virginia Golodetz (1994); Marion H. Hargrove (1993); Lily J. Helwig (1994); Barbara J. Kruger (1993); Dolores Maminski (1993); Maureen A. Toole (1993); Helen A. Vanderslvis (1994).

Outreach

To address the needs of young adults who face barriers of access to library and information services because of economic, social, cultural, or legal factors; to identify, promote, and develop resources to assist service providers to young adults in overcoming barriers of access to libraries and information services; and to foster public and professional awareness of the needs of these young adults.

Ch., Mary E. Flournoy (1993); James Edward Cook (1993); Margaret J. Fleesak (1994); Susan Rosenzweig (1993); John V. Snow (1993); Shannon E. Van Kirk (1993); Marybeth Webb-Ozmun (1993); 1 to be appointed.

Outstanding Books for the College Bound—Biographies

To prepare a revised and updated edition of the list published in 1991.

Ch. to be appointed; Meryll J. Cohen (1994); Susan E. Dunn (1994); Ellen H. Ramsay (1994); Nancy E. Strong (1994); 3 to be appointed.

Outstanding Books for the College Bound—Fiction

To prepare a revised and updated edition of the list published in 1991.

Ch., Julie K. De Matteis (1994); Kathleen Bognanni (1994); Barbara G. Hall (1994); Phyllis E. Saunders (1994); Robyn H. Smith (1994); Lois A. Snider (1994); Marcia M. Trent (1994).

Outstanding Books for the College Bound—Fine Arts

To prepare a revised and updated edition of the list published in 1991.

Ch., Frances L. Novack (1994); Susan Baird (1994); Virginia Golodetz (1994); 4 to be appointed.

Outstanding Books for the College Bound—Nonfiction

To prepare a revised and updated edition of the list published in 1991.

Ch., Betty B. Lazarus (1993); Jeff Blair (1994); Meryll J. Cohen (1994); Andrea M. Howe (1994); Ann C. Sparanese (1994); Jody Stefansson (1994); Alice F. Stern (1994).

Outstanding Books for the College Bound—Theater

To prepare a revised and updated edition of the list published in 1991.

Ch., Jo Ann Kingston (1994); Naomi K. Angier (1994); Marijo Duncan (1994); Rhonda R. Glazier (1994); Florenz W. Maxwell (1994); Meg Wolfe (1994); 1 to be appointed.

Oversight

To review current activities of committees. To identify procedural problems within committees. To make recommendations to the YALSA Board regarding the implementation of the division's goals and objectives, as needed.

Ch., Helen J. Tallman (1993); Kay Brunton Covode (1993); Jo Ann G. Mondowney (1993); Jana R. Fine (1993); Maureen Toole (1993); 1 to be appointed.

Preconference—New Orleans, 1993

To plan, organize, and present a YALSA preconference at the 1993 Annual Conference in New Orleans.

Ch., Judy Sasges (1993); Marilee Foglesong (1993); Barbara G. Hall (1993).

Program Planning Clearinghouse and Evaluation

To review, facilitate and coordinate, and evaluate the planning for all conference and nonconference program proposals and to make overall recommendations to the YALSA Board on the package of programs.

Ch., Kay Brunton Covode (1993); Nancy Bard (1993); Julie K. De Matteis (1994); Lily J. Helwig (1994); Rosemary Kneale (1993); Susan J. Rosenkoetter (1993); Linda J. Wilson (1994).

Public Ear: Popular Music and Teenagers (ad hoc)

To develop this NEH grant into a training tool for young adult librarians in the field.

Ch., Frances B. Bradburn (1993); Katherine R. Cagle (1993); Matthew A. Kollasch (1993); Gary Morrison (1993); Sandra Payne (1993).

Public Relations

To develop and implement an overall public relations stategy; to promote the publications, programs and materials of the Division and to endeavor to enhance the reputation of the Yound Adult Library Services Association and of young adult library services and materials.

Ch. to be appointed; Rosemary S. Chance (1993); Timothea McDonald (1993); Anne B. Prusha (1993); 4 to be appointed.

Publications

To develop a publications program in the areas of young adult services and materials, identify topics to be covered and potential authors; to oversee and coordinate the YALSA publications program; to regularly review all YALSA publications and make recommendations to the YALSA Board regarding those needing revision or elimination.

Ch., Jana R. Fine (1993); Beth Nancy French (1993); Karen H. Harris (1993); Barbara Hull (1993); Eugene E. LaFaille (1993); 1 to be appointed.

Publishers Liaison

To create a better understanding between publishers and librarians in the library's use of materials with teenagers, in order that such materials be supplied more effectively.

Ch., Jill Smilow (1993); Judith P. Brill (1993); Lillian N. Gerhardt (1994); Constance A. John-

son (1993); Lucy C. Marx (1993); Barbara J. Nosanchuk (1993); Frances L. Novack (1994); Stephen Roxburgh (1993); Jan M. Srneoz (1993); 1 to be appointed.

Recommended Books for the Reluctant Young Adult Reader

To prepare an annual annotated list of recommended books appropriate for reluctant young adult readers.

Ch., Nellie C. Ward (1993); Mary J. Arnold (1993); Peter Muller Butts (1993); Deborah Y. Carton (1993); Marijo Duncan (1993); Patrick Scott Jones (1994); Nancy Reich (1994); Susan Rosenzweig (1994); Rochelle S. Sides (1994); Susan K. Thornton (1993).

Recommended Books for the Reluctant Young Adult Reader Policies and Procedures (ad hoc)

To evaluate policies and procedures governing the Recommended Books for the Reluctant Young Adult Reader Committee; to hold an open forum at the 1992 Annual Conference; and to report with recommendations to the YALSA Board at the 1993 Midwinter Meeting.

Ch., Barbara R. Hawkins (1993); Barbara A. Carmody (1993); Jane Chandra (1993); Judith A. Druse (1993); Janet P. Sarratt (1993).

Research

To stimulate, encourage, guide, and direct the research needs of young adult library service and to compile abstracts and disseminate research findings.

Ch., Kathy H. Latrobe (1993); Janice A. Hogan (1993); Mary L. Keefer (1993); Donald J. Kenney (1994); Judith Rodriguez (1993); 2 to be appointed.

Resource Directory (ad hoc)

To explore the feasibility of a Resource Directory; to develop proposals for implementation of a Resource Directory; and to report to the Board by Annual Conference 1993.

Ch., Mary K. Chelton (1993); members to be appointed.

Selected Films and Videos for Young Adults

To select from the past two years' films and videos those titles significant for young adults, to annotate the selected titles for publication.

Ch., Anne C. Raymer (1993); Stella F. Baker (1993); Rosemary S. Chance (1994); Catherine M. Clancy (1993); Rhonda R. Glazier (1993); Mary Huebscher (1993); Andrew W. Hunter (1993); Betty B. Lazarus (1993); Phyllis Singer (1994); Karen P. Smith (1993); Mary Jane Tacchi (1994); Drue Wagner-Mees (1994).

"Selecting Materials for Children and Young Adults" Revision, ALSC/YALSA (interdivisional) (See p. 42.)

Special Needs, Library Service to Young Adults with

To identify and promote the library programs, resources, and services that meet the special needs of young adults with physical, mental, learning, emotional disabilities or in special facilities such as hospitals, group homes, detention centers or jails, runaway shelters and homeless shelters; to serve as a liaison to other groups with similar interests such as ALSC Library Service to Children with Special Needs and ASCLA Libraries Serving Special Populations Section.

Ch. to be appointed; Nancy L. Carver-Russell (1993); Eva-Maria Lusk (1994); Amy L. Oxley (1993); John V. Snow (1993); 4 to be appointed.

(Amelia Elizabeth) Walden Award (ad hoc)

To develop criteria and procedures for the Amelia Elizabeth Walden Award and report to the Board by Annual Conference 1993.

Ch., Caryn G. Sipos (1993); Barbara Hawkins (1993); Bunni Union (1993).

White House Conference (interdivisional)

To develop, implement, and coordinate strategies for the 1991 WHCLIS youth recommendations and report to the YALSA Board semi-annually.

Ch., Virginia H. Mathews (1994); Jeri C. Baker (1994); Judith G. Flum (1994).

Young Adult Services in Public Libraries, YALSA/PLA (special interdivisional)

To develop an in-house training needs assessment instrument for public library managers to measure young adult training needs among their staff. To prepare for publication a self-training manual for public library generalists serving young adults. To prepare a grant proposal for a model invitational training conference for public library administrators and relevant state library personnel on establishing and managing young adult services within the roles delineated by *Planning and Role Setting for Public Libraries.* To develop a training workshop and/or preconference outline for use by PLA at national conferences and regional workshops. To recommend a permanent structural response within PLA to respond to public library issues regarding the young adult clientele. To recommend on-going collaborative activities between PLA and YALSA for public librarians serving young adults.

Note: The Committee will complete its charge at the end of the 1993 Midwinter Meeting.

Ch., Sally D. Arrivee (PLA, 1993); Sandra Ann Farrell (YALSA, 1993); Brenda Hunter (PLA, 1993); Alison Landers (PLA, 1993); Rosemary W. Moran (YALSA, 1993); Elizabeth O'Donnell (YALSA, 1993); Jim Rosinia (YALSA, 1993).

Youth Participation

To establish guidelines and/or procedures to involve young adults in the decision-making process which directly affects their access to information and library service at local, state, and national levels; to provide continuing education and public professional awareness of youth participation.

Ch., Candace V. Conklin (1993); Barbara Blosveren (1993); May Brottman (1993); Elaine M. McGuire (1994); Ranae Pierce (1993); Karen G. Schneider (1994).

REPRESENTATIVES

ALA Appointments Com.—Judith Druse.
ALA Budget Assembly—Jo Ann G. Mandowney.
ALA Diversity Com.—Mary Flournoy.
ALA Legislation Assembly—Jeri Baker.
ALA Library Education Assembly—to be appointed.
ALA Literacy Assembly—Ellen V. Libretto.
ALA Membership Promotion Task Force—Deborah Colter.
ALA Miami Conference Com.—Judith Druse.
ALA New Orleans Conference Com.—Elizabeth O'Donnell.
AASL National Conference—Elizabeth Elam.
ALA Professional Ethics Com.—Anne C. Raymer.
ALA Research and Statistics Com.—Kathy Latrobe.
Freedom to Read Fdn.—Patricia Muller.
LAMA Patron Behavior and Library Usage Com. (ad hoc)—Sandra Anne Farrell and Susan Uebelacker.
RASD Reference Services to Children Com.—Judith Rodriquez.

LIAISONS WITH OTHER NATIONAL ORGANIZATIONS

Adolescent Pregnancy Prevention Network.
American Natl. Red Cross/Red Cross Youth.
American Youth Work Ctr.
Child Welfare League of America.
Ctr. for Early Adolescence.
Family Resource Coalition.
Future Homemakers of America.
Junior Achievement.
Natl. Com. for Citizens in Education.
Natl. Council of La Raza.
Natl. Council of Teachers of English.
Natl. Ctr. for Youth Law.
Natl. Ctr. on Institutions and Alternatives.
Planned Parenthood Federation of America.

SIECUS (Sex Information and Education Council of the U.S.).

YALSA MEMBERSHIP RECRUITMENT STATE NETWORK

Alabama—Joan Atkinson.
Alaska—Ann Symons.
Arizona—Marijo Duncan.
Arkansas—to be appointed.
California—Laura R. Weber.
Colorado—Nancy Knepel.
Connecticut—Barbara L. Blosveren.
Delaware—to be appointed.
District of Columbia—Susan Uebelacker.
Florida—to be appointed.
Georgia—Rosie Meadows Thigpen.
Hawaii—Brenda Freitas-Obregon.
Idaho—to be appointed.
Illinois—to be appointed.
Indiana—Rebecca Gitin Ristow.
Iowa—Matthew Kollasch.
Kansas—Margaret L. Kirkpatrick.
Kentucky—Lucy Marx.
Louisiana—Patsy Perritt.
Maine—to be appointed.
Maryland—Susan Uebelacker.
Massachusetts—to be appointed.
Michigan—to be appointed.
Minnesota—Juanita Foster.
Mississippi—Iris Collins.
Missouri—to be appointed.
Montana—to be appointed.
Nebraska—to be appointed.
Nevada—Merilyn Grosshans and Joyce Dixon.
New Hampshire—Elizabeth O'Donnell.
New Jersey—Rose O. Ward.
New Mexico—to be appointed.
New York—to be appointed.
North Carolina—to be appointed.
North Dakota—to be appointed.
Ohio—to be appointed.
Oklahoma—Marybeth Webb-Ozmun.
Oregon—Naomi Angier.
Pennsylvania—Cheryl Napsha.
Rhode Island—Susan Rosenzweig.
South Carolina—to be appointed.
South Dakota—Donna Gilliland.
Tennessee—Beverly Youree.
Texas—Sharon Temple.
Utah—Ranae Pierce.
Vermont—Virginia Golodetz.
Virginia—Carolyn Caywood.
Washington—Susan Madden.
West Virginia—Anita Trout.
Wisconsin—Gloria A. Waity.
Wyoming—Marcia Wright.
U.S. Territories—to be appointed.
Canada—to be appointed.

Round Tables

A round table is a membership unit established to promote a field of librarianship not within the scope of any single division. Although it cannot commit the Association by any declaration of policy, a round table may recommend policy and action to other units. Members of ALA may join those round tables for which they are eligible by payment of the specified dues. (Bylaws Article VII.)

Armed Forces Libraries Round Table (AFLRT)

To promote quality library service to the Armed Forces community; to promote armed forces libraries in the military services, within ALA, and to nonmilitary libraries and library organizations; and to promote professional growth by providing continuing education and information to personnel who staff armed forces libraries.

Officers and Executive Committee

Pres., Myrtis Ann Parham (1993); vice-pres., Marsha L. W. Dreier (1993); secy.-treas., Patricia L. Alderman (1993); past pres., James F. Aylward (1993); dir. at large, Jolaine Lamb (1993); Air Force rep., Annette Gohlke (1993); Army rep., Lorna Andrle Dodt (1993); Marine-Navy rep., Karen E. Pollok (1995); staff liaison: Patricia A. Muir.

Committee Chairpersons

Awards—Belinda Pugh (1993).
Bylaws—Marian D. Fontish (1993).
Civil Service—Marilyn J. Smith (1993).
Conference Programs and Arrangements—Mary Nell Wooten (1993).
Membership—James F. Aylward (1993).
Network (ad hoc)—Sarah A. Mikel (1993).
Newsletter ed.—Karen E. Pollok (1993).
Nominating, 1993—to be appointed.
Oral History—Alice R. Roy (1993).
Planning—Pearce S. Grove (1993).
Programs and Arrangements—Mary Nell Wooten (1993).
Public Relations—Karen E. Pollok (1993).
Publications—co-chs., Karen E. Pollok (1993) and Elizabeth R. Snoke (1993).

Publication

Armed Forces Libraries Round Table of ALA Newsletter (quarterly). Free to round table members; unavailable by subscription. Ed., Karen E. Pollok, Naval Air Station Oceana, Station Library-Bldg. 416, Virginia Beach, VA 23460.

Membership

Any member of ALA interested in the purpose of the round table may become a personal member of the Armed Forces Libraries Round Table by paying the separate personal membership for AFLRT. As of August 31, 1992: 16 organizational members; 253 personal members; 269 total members.

Dues

ALA members, $10; corporate membership $10; special student rate $3.

Continuing Library Education Network and Exchange Round Table (CLENE RT)

(1) To provide a forum for the exchange of ideas and concerns among library and information personnel responsible for continuing library education, training, and staff development; (2) to provide learning activities and material to maintain the competencies of those who provide continuing library education; (3) to provide a force for initiating and supporting programs to increase the availability of quality continuing library education; (4) to create an awareness of, and sense of need for, continuing library education on the part of employees and employers.

Officers and Executive Board

Pres., Laura Kimberly (1994); pres.-elect, Kenna J. Forsyth (1995); secy., Sharon A. Taber (1993); past-pres., Darlene E. Weingand (1993); staff liaison, Margaret Myers.

Other members: Mary C. Bushing (1994); Catherine J. Hoy (1994); Miriam Pollack (1993); Rhea J. Rubin (1993); Rivkah K. Sass (1993); Gloria A. Waity (1994); ex officio, Marie E. Bryan (*CLENExchange* ed.).

Committee Chairpersons and Others

Booth/Suite—coor., Mildred H. Fry (1993).
Long Range Planning—Duncan F. Smith (1993).
Membership—Cecy Keller (1993).
Nominations—Kitty Smith (1993).
Program—Diane E. Johnson (1993).
Publications—Linda H. Reida (1993).
Publicity—Miriam Pollack (1993).
Telephone Consultations—co-chs., Kenna J. Forsyth (1993) and Gail J. McGovern (1993).

Liaisons

IFLA—Darlene E. Weingand (1993).
LAMA-PAS—to be appointed.
SCOLE-LEA—Darlene E. Weingand (1993).
SCOLE-CE—Duncan F. Smith (1993).

Publication

CLENExchange (quarterly). Free to members; available by subscription $20 a yr. ($25 foreign). Ed., Marie E. Bryan, P.L., 250 First St., Woodland, CA 95695.

Membership

Open to all ALA members. As of August 31, 1992: 70 organization members; 281 personal members; 351 total members.

Dues

Individual members, $15; organization members, $50.

Ethnic Materials and Information Exchange Round Table (EMIERT)

To serve as a source of information on ethnic collections, services, and programs; to organize task forces, institutes, and workshops to carry out the functions of the round table; to develop for annual conferences, forums, symposia, and programs that deal with the key issues of ethnicity and librarianship; to maintain a liaison with the Office for Library Outreach Services and cooperate with other ALA units including the caucuses in joint projects for betterment of outreach services; to disseminate the work of the round table through a program of publications.

Officers

Ch., Patricia F. Beilke (1993); vice-ch./ch.-elect, Kay A. Averette (1995); treas., Nancy L. Snauffer (1993); secy., Barbara L. Flynn (1993); staff liaison, Mattye L. Nelson.

Members-at-large: Chung-Sook Charlotte Kim (1993); Janice L. Lavery (1994); Marilyn Rehnberg (1994); Stella I-Hua Shang (1993); Bosiljka Stevanovic (1994); Tamiye M. Trejo-Meehan (1993); Vladimir Wertsman (1994).

Committee Chairpersons

Conference Programming—Kay A. Averette (1995) and Louise Y. Zwick (1993).
Constitution and Bylaws—Marie E. Zielinska (1993).
Membership—Bosiljka Stevanovic (1994).
Nominating—Robert K. Foy (1993).
Public Relations—Francesca L. Hary (1993).
Publications and *Bulletin*—David Cohen (1993).

Task Force Chairpersons

Building Coalitions for Ethnicity—Keith Jemison (1993).
Children's Services—Oralia Garza Cortes (1993).
Collection Development—Araxie P. Churukian (1993).
Ethnic Research—Wei Chi Poon (1993).
Jewish Librarians—Susan J. Freiband (1993) and Martin Goldberg (1993).
Library Education—to be appointed.
Publishing and Minority Materials—Vladimir Wertsman (1994).

Representatives and Liaisons

ALA Goal Award—to be appointed.
Election Process—to be appointed.
IRRT—to be appointed.
Literacy Assembly—to be appointed.
Minority Concerns Com.—to be appointed.
OLPR Recruitment Project—to be appointed.
Planning and Budget Assembly—to be appointed.

Publication

EMIE Bulletin (quarterly). Free to round table members; $10 a yr. to non-ALA members; $15 to institutions; back issues $1.50 each. Subscriptions available from ALA/EMIERT, 50 E. Huron St., Chicago, IL 60611. Ed., David Cohen, Grad. Sch. of L. & Inf. Studies, Queens Coll., City Univ. of New York, 65–30 Kissena Blvd., Flushing, NY 11367.

Membership

Open to all ALA members. As of August 31, 1992: 91 organization members; 632 personal members; 723 total members.

Dues

Personal, $10; sustaining, $10; student, $2.50; institutional, $15.

Exhibits Round Table (ERT)

(1) To act as an interface between exhibitors and the Association; (2) to provide a clearing-house for information on all state and regional library association conferences having commercial exhibits; (3) to maintain an up-to-date exhibits procedure manual to aid library exhibitions; and (4) to study convention procedures to set standards for booth rental, space assignment, exhibit hours, and sufficient information for exhibitors to plan an effective display.

Officers and Executive Board

Ch., Nancy E. Schwartz (1994); vice-ch., Patricia H. Smith (1995); treas., Gary Winter (1994); secy., John E. Ison (1994); past ch., Roger J. Long (1993); staff liaison Paul Graller.

Other members: Carl Grant (1993); B. Allison Gray (1993); Joseph H. Green (1993); Michael G. O'Brien (1993); Melissa J. Sibley (1993); Dean O. Tuggle (1993); Bonnie Clayton Zelter (1993).

Committee Chairpersons and Others

By-Laws Review/Revision—John E. Ison (1993) and Nancy E. Schwartz (1993).
Cross-Aisle Regulation Review—to be appointed.
Display Rules—Carl Grant (1993) and Dean O. Tuggle (1993).
Flyer Series—to be appointed.
FYI Newsletter—Carl Grant (1993).
Kohlstedt Exhibit Awards—Michael G. O'Brien (1993).
Membership—Patricia H. Smith (1993).
Nominating—Melissa J. Sibley (1993).

Membership

Open to all library associations, interested librarians, and firms or individuals exhibiting at library meetings. As of August 31, 1992: 90 organization members; 135 personal members; 225 total members.

Dues

Commercial membership for commercial firms, $30; institutional membership for libraries and library associations, $10; personal membership for individuals, librarians, and nonlibrarians, $10.

Federal Librarians Round Table (FLRT)

To promote library and information service and the library and information profession in the federal community; to promote appropriate utilization of federal library and information resources and facilities; to provide an environment for the stimulation of research and development relating to the planning, development, and operation of federal libraries and information activities.

Officers and Executive Board

Pres., Shirley Loo (1994); pres.-elect, Dan Orr Clemmer (1995); secy.-treas., Laurie S. Stackpole (1994); staff liaison, Patricia A. Muir.

Other members: Kathryn L. Earnest (1993); Lee R. McLaughlin (1994); staff liaison, Patricia Muir.

Committee Chairpersons

A-76 Task Force—to be appointed.
Awards—Kathryn L. Earnest (1993).
Membership—Katherine P. Sites (1993).
Nominating—Sami W. Klein (1993).
Personnel—Louise Nyce (1993).

Liaisons

AFLRT—Nina F. Jacobs (1993).
FLICC—Gail L. Kohlhorst (1993).
GODORT—Doria Beachell Grimes (1993).
Legislation Assembly—Phyllis R. Christenson.
NTIS—Christine E. Baldwin (1993).
SCOLE—Lee R. McLaughlin (1993).

Publications

The Federal Librarian. Free to round table members. Published 4 times a year. Ed., Gail L. Kohlhorst, General Services Admin. L., Rm. 1033, 18th & F Sts., NW, Washington, DC 20405.

Membership

Open to all ALA members. As of August 31, 1992: 80 organization members, 349 personal members; 429 total members.

Dues

Personal, $8; institutions, $10.

Government Documents Round Table (GODORT)

(1) To provide a forum for discussion of problems, concerns, and for exchange of ideas by librarians working with government documents; (2) to provide a force for initiating and supporting programs to increase availability, use, and bibliographic control of documents; (3) to increase communication between documents librarians and other librarians; (4) to contribute to the extension and improvement of education and training of documents librarians.

Executive Officers

Ch., Julia F. Wallace (1994); ch.-elect, Duncan M. Aldrich (1995); treas., Diane L. Garner (1993); secy., Carolyn W. Kohler (1993); past ch., Linda M. Kennedy (1993); publications ch., Herbert A. Somers (1993); staff liaison, Patricia A. Muir.

Task Force Coordinators

Federal Documents—ch., Linda Kopecky (1993).
International Documents—ch., Helen M. Sheehy (1993).
State and Local Documents—ch., Atifa R. Rawan (1993).

Committee Chairpersons and Others

Awards—Jan B. Swanbeck (1993).
Bylaws—Eleanor L. Chase (1993).
Cataloging—Rhonda J. Marker (1993).
Education—Michele T. McKnelly (1993).
Government Information Technology—Raeann S. Dossett (1993).
Legislation—Janice A. Fryer (1993).
Membership—Linda B. Johnson (1993).

Nominating—Rosemary Allen Little (1993).
Program—Duncan M. Aldrich (1993).
Publications—Herbert A. Somers (1993).
Statistical Measurement—Laura G. Harper (1993).

Publications

Documents to the People (bimonthly). Free to members; available by subscription, $20 a year. Ed., Mary Redmond; assoc. ed., Benjamin T. Amata; advertising mgr., Jill Moriearty; distribution mgr., Sinai P. Rocha.

Liaison

Freedom to Read Foundation—Lois P. Mills (1993).

Membership

Any personal member of ALA may elect to become a personal member of the round table, with the right to vote, upon payment of annual dues. Any group organized regionally or locally to work on problems of government documents will be welcome to designate an official liaison who is a member of ALA to the Round Table. As of August 31, 1992: 251 organization members; 1,063 personal members; 1,314 total members.

Dues

Personal members, $15; organization members, $15.

Independent Librarians Exchange Round Table (ILERT)

To provide a network for librarians working outside traditional library settings; to foster understanding of the services provided by individuals who have chosen alternative careers within the profession; to provide programs, publications, and related activities addressing the needs of the members.

Steering Committee

Pres., Vee Friesner Carrington (1994); pres.-elect, Susan N. Bjørner (1995); secy.-treas., Mary B. Vanderpoorten (1993); past pres., Carol A. Berger (1993); Murray S. Martin (1994); Ronald Sigler (1993); Kate Storms (1994); staff liaison, Margaret Myers.

Committees

Membership—Kate Storms.
Nominating—Carol A. Berger (1993).
Program—Vee Friesner Carrington (1993).

Liaisons

Library Education Assembly—Ronald Sigler.
Meeting Program—Vee Friesner Carrington.
Membership—Kate Storms.
Planning and Budget Assembly—Susan N. Bjørner.
Professional Ethics—Susan N. Bjørner.
Recruitment Assembly—Carol A. Berger.

Publications

Ilert Alert (semiannually). Free to round table members; subscriptions, $8. Ed., Susan N. Bjørner; prod. assistance, Susan Dunn.

Membership

Open to all ALA members. As of August 31, 1992: 44 organization members; 216 personal members; 260 total members.

Dues

Personal members, $8; organization members, $8.

Intellectual Freedom Round Table (IFRT)

To provide a forum for the discussion of activities, programs and problems in intellectual freedom of libraries and librarians; to serve as a channel of communications on intellectual freedom matters; to promote a greater opportunity for involvement among the members of the ALA in defense of intellectual freedom; to promote a greater feeling of responsibility in the implementation of ALA policies on intellectual freedom.

Executive Committee (officers, directors, standing committee chairpersons, and liaisons)

Ch. and program ch., Thomas F. Budlong Jr. (1993); ch.-elect, Pamela Gay Bonnell (1994); treas., Lois P. Mills (1993); secy., Fay A. Golden (1994); dirs.: Sue Kamm (1993); Martha Merrill (1993); Alice P. Naylor (1994); Richard E. Rubin (1994); staff liaison, Anne E. Penway.

Publication

IFRT Report (irregular). Free to members; not available by subscription. Ed., Paul C. Vermouth Jr.

Committee Chairpersons

Immroth Memorial Award—Douglas Koschik (1993).
Membership Promotion—Eric C. Welch (1993).
Nominating—Frances M. McDonald (1993).
(Eli M.) Oboler Award—Doug Rippey (1994).
Organization and Bylaws—Sue Kamm (1993).
Program—Thomas F. Budlong Jr. (1993).
Publications—Paul C. Vermouth Jr. (1993).
State Program Award—Susan M. Beck (1993).

Liaisons

ALCTS Subject Analysis Com.—Charles L. Brunk (1994).
IFC—Gene D. Lanier (1994).
Freedom to Read Foundation—Pamela Gay Bonnell (1993).

Membership

Any personal member of ALA who is interested in the purposes of this round table shall be eligible for personal membership upon payment of annual dues. A personal member shall have the right to vote. Any institutional member of ALA may become an institutional member of the round table upon payment of annual dues. Institutional members shall be nonvoting members. As of August 31, 1992: 169 organization members; 2,253 personal members; 2,422 total members.

Dues

Individual members, $10; institutions, $10; student members, $1.

International Relations Round Table (IRRT)

To develop the interests of librarians in activities and problems in the field of international library relations; to serve as a channel of communication and counsel between the International Relations Committee and the members of the Association; and to provide hospitality and information to visitors from abroad. The IRRT ar-ranges programs and business meetings and appoints representatives to attend meetings of the other professional groups.

Officers: Ch., Ernest A. DiMattia Jr. (1993); ch.-elect, Mohammed M. Aman (1994); past ch., Hannelore B. Rader (1993); secy., Leona L. Wise (1994).

Members-at-large: Anne E. Haley (1993); Helen G. Maul (1994).

Publication

International Leads (quarterly). Sent free to all IRRT members. Subscription to nonmembers, $12 a volume. Ed., Robert P. Doyle, ALA, 50 E. Huron St., Chicago, IL 60611.

Committee Chairpersons

Hospitality (ad hoc)—to be appointed.
Membership—to be appointed.
Nominating—to be appointed.
Planning, Structure and Programs (ad hoc)—to be appointed.
Program (ad hoc)—to be appointed.
Reception (ad hoc)—to be appointed.

Area Chairpersons

East Asia—to be appointed.
Latin America—to be appointed.
Middle East and North Africa—to be appointed.
South Asia—to be appointed.
Southeast Asia—to be appointed.

Representatives

ALCTS-CCS Com. on Cataloging: Description and Access—to be appointed.
Freedom to Read Fdn.—to be appointed.
Library Education Assembly—to be appointed.

Membership

Open to all ALA members. As of August 31, 1992: 80 organization members; 748 personal members; 828 total members.

Dues, $7.

Library History Round Table (LHRT)

To encourage research and publication on library history and promote awareness and discussion of historical issues in librarianship.

Officers

Ch., Joanne E. Passet (1994); ch.-elect, Mark Tucker (1995); secy.-treas., Nancy Becker Johnson (1993); past ch., Mary Niles Maack (1993); members-at-large: Barbara B. Brand (1994); Laurel Grotzinger (1993); staff liaison, Charles Harmon (1993).

Committees

1993 Program—Joanne E. Passett (1993).
1994 Program—Mark Tucker (1994).
Justin Winsor Prize—Robert S. Martin (1993).
Library History Seminar X Planning—Gordon B. Neavill (1994).
Newsletter—eds., Edward Goedeken (1994) and David Hovde (1994).
Nominating—Marion T. Casey (1993).
Phyllis Dain Dissertation Award—Mary Niles Maack (1993).
Publications—John V. Richardson Jr. (1993).
Research—Judith A. Overmier (1993).

Representatives

ALA Membership Promotion Task Force—Nancy Becker Johnson.
American Assn. for State and Local History—Nancy M. Godleski.
American Society for Information Science—Robert V. Williams.
Assn. for the Bibliography of History—Kenneth J. Potts.
Freedom to Read Foundation—Charles C. Stewart.
Libraries & Culture—Michele V. Cloonan.
Library Education Assembly—Charles A. Seavey.
Natl. Coordinating Com. for the Promotion of History—Steven W. Sowards.
Society of American Archivists—Robert S. Martin.

Publication

LHRT Newsletter (semiannually). Distributed to members; unavailable by subscription. Ed., David M. Hovde, HSSE L., Stewart Center, Purdue Univ., West Lafayette, IN 47907; and Edward Goedeken, Acqs. Dept., L. Offices, Stewart Center, Purdue Univ., West Lafayette, IN 47907.

Membership

Open to all ALA members. As of August 31, 1992: 59 organization members; 331 personal members; 390 total members.

Dues, $12; students, $5.

Library Instruction Round Table (LIRT)

To provide a forum for discussion of activities, programs, and problems of instruction in the use of libraries; to contribute to the education and training of librarians for library instruction; to promote instruction in the use of libraries as an essential library service, and to serve as a channel of communication on library instruction between the ALA divisions, ALA and ACRL committees, state clearinghouses, Project LOEX, other organizations concerned with instruction in the use of libraries, and members of the Association.

Officers

Pres., Timothy P. Grimes (1994); pres.-elect, Emily M. Okada (1995); treas., Marilynn P. Whitmore (1993); secy., Carol B. Penka (1993); past pres., Dianne C. Langlois (1993); archivist, Lynn E. Randall (1993); staff liaison, Jeniece Guy.

Committee Chairpersons

Computer Applications—Catherine Gale Burrow (1993).
Conference Program—Kari M. Lucas (1993).
Continuing Education—H. Scott Davis (1993).
Elections/Nominations—Thelma H. Tate (1993).
Liaison—Barbara M. Conant (1993).
Long Range Planning—Elizabeth J. Dailey (1993).
Organization and Bylaws—Dianne C. Langlois (1993).
Public Relations/Membership—Charlotte J. Files (1993).
Publications—Paul Frantz (1993).
Research—Rebecca L. Gardner (1993).

Task Force Chairpersons

Instructional Materials—Robert A. Kuhner (1993).

LIRT Fifteenth Anniversary—J. Randolph Call (1993).

Professional Associations Networking—Gail L. Egbers (1993).

Publicity Coordinator—Charles V. Dintrone (1993).

Publication

Library Instruction Round Table News (quarterly). Distributed to members; unavailable by subscription. Ed., Kwasi Sarkodie-Mensah, Snell L. Rm. 273, Northeastern Univ., 360 Huntington Ave., Boston, MA 02115; Newsletter/Production, Emily M. Okada, Main L. W121, Indiana Univ., Bloomington, IN 47405.

Membership

Open to all ALA members. As of August 31, 1992: 200 organization members; 922 personal members; 1,122 total members.

Dues

Personal members, $10; organizational affiliates, $15.

Library Research Round Table (LRRT)

To contribute toward the extension and improvement of library research; to provide public program opportunities for describing and evaluating library research projects and for disseminating their findings; to inform and educate ALA members concerning research techniques and their usefulness in obtaining information with which to reach administrative decisions and solve problems; and expand the theoretical base of the field. To serve as a forum for discussion and action on issues related to the literature and information needs for the field of library and information science.

Steering Committee

Ch., Elfreda A. Chatman (1994); ch.-elect, Mary Biggs (1993); secy.-treas., Kathleen Garland (1994); past ch., Wayne A. Wiegand (1994); members-at-large: Vicki Gregory (1994); Robert S. Martin (1995); staff liaison, Mary Jo Lynch.

Committee Chairpersons

Doctoral Students—Marion Paris (1993).
Endowment Fund—Arthur P. Young (1993).
L. & Inf. Sci. Literature (task force)—Judith Dye (1993).
Membership Promotion—Mark Tucker (1993).
Nominating—Roger C. Greer (1993).
Program—co-chs., Elfreda A. Chatman (1993) and Barbara B. Moran (1993).
Research Forums—Jo Bell Whitlatch (1993).
Shera Award—David W. Carr (1993).

Membership

Open to ALA members. As of August 31, 1992: 98 organization members; 629 personal members; 727 total members.

Dues

Personal, $10; organizations or institutions, $10; doctoral students, free.

Map and Geography Round Table (MAGERT)

(1) To provide a forum for the exchange of ideas by persons working with or interested in map and geography collections; (2) to provide a forum to increase the availability, use, and bibliographic control of map and geography collections; (3) to increase communication and cooperation between map and geography librarians and other librarians; and (4) to contribute to the improvement of education and training of map and geography librarians.

Officers

Ch., Thornton P. McGlamery (1994); ch.-elect, April Carlucci (1995); treas., Margaret S. Brill (1993); secy., Jenny M. Johnson (1993); past ch., Jim Walsh (1993); staff liaison, JoAn S. Segal.

Committee Chairpersons

Archives—Barbara Weatherall (1993).
Audio-Visual—Daniel T. Seldin (1993).
Cataloging and Classification—Christine E. Kollen (1993).
Constitution and Bylaws—Jenny M. Johnson (1993).
Education—Jim O'Donnell (1993).
Geographic Information Technology—Nancy J. Butkovich (1993).
Honors Awards—Jim Walsh (1993).
Membership—Katherine L. Rankin (1993).
Nominating—Jim Walsh (1993).
Program (New Orleans, 1993)—Thornton P. McGlamery (1993).
Program (Miami, 1994)—April Carlucci (1994).
Publications—Peter L. Stark (1993).

Task Force/Group Coordinators

Cartographic Statistics—Charles A. Seavey (1993).
Cartographic Users Advisory (CUAC)—Margaret S. Brill (1995).
Exhibits—Harry Davis (1993).
Maps in Small Libraries—Ann Sanders (1993).
Research Libraries Acquisitions Group (RLAG)—Mary L. Larsgaard (1993).

Representatives and Liaisons

ACRL-RBMS—Peter L. Stark.
ALCTS-CCS CC:DA—Elizabeth U. Mangan.
Anglo-American Cataloguing Com. for Cartographic Materials—Nancy J. Edstrom.
Com. on Southern Map Libraries—Ann Sanders.
Freedom to Read Fdn.—Alice C. Hudson.
GODORT—David A. Cobb.
IFLA—Gary W. North.
L. of Congress Geography and Map Div.—Elizabeth U. Mangan.
LITA—Thornton P. McGlamery.
Library Education Assembly—Charles A. Seavey.
MARBI—Susan Moore.
Natl. Technical Inf. Serv.—Jim Walsh.
North American Cartographic Information Society—Paul Stout.
Northeast Map Organization—Thornton P. McGlamery.
Special Libraries Assn., Geog. and Map Div.—Jim Gillespie.
U.S. Geological Survey—Wendy R. Hassibe.
Western Assn. of Map Ls.—Greg Armento.

Publications

base line. Bimonthly newsletter. Free to members; $15 to nonmembers, foreign, $20. Ed., Nancy J. Butkovich, Physical Sci. L., Penn. St. Univ., Univ. Park, PA 16802; subsc. mgr., Arlyn K. Sherwood, Ref. Dept., State L., Springfield, IL 62156.

Meridian. Semiannual, refereed journal. Free to members; $20 to nonmembers (foreign, $25), $25 to institutions (foreign, $30). Ed., Charles A. Seavey, Grad Sch. L. Sci., Univ. of Arizona, Tucson, AZ 85721. subsc. mgr., Christine E. Kollen, Map L., Univ. of Arizona, Tucson, AZ 85721.

Occasional Paper series. No. 1, *Exploration and Mapping of the American West: Selected Essays,* 1986; No. 2, *A Guide to Historical Map Resources for Greater New York City,* by Jeffrey A. Kroessler, 1988; No. 3, *Mapping the Transmississippi West, 1540–1861: An Index to the Cartobibliography,* by Charles A. Seavey, 1992. Contact: Kathryn Womble, FM-25, Map Clln., Suzzallo L., Univ. of Washington, Seattle, WA 98195.

Open File Reports. Contact: James A. Coombs, Meyer L., Southwestern Missouri State Univ., Springfield, MO 65804-0095.

Circulars. No. 1, *Cartographic Citations: A Style Manual,* by Suzanne M. Clark, Mary Larsgaard, and Cynthia M. Teague, 1992. Contact: Kathryn Womble, FM-25, Map Clln., Suzzallo L., Univ. of Washington, Seattle, WA 98195.

Guide to U.S. Map Resources, 2nd ed. Compiled by David A. Cobb. Contact: ALA Order Dept.

Membership

Any personal member of ALA interested in the purpose of this round table may elect to become a personal member, with voting rights, upon payment of annual dues. Institutional members of ALA may become institutional members of the round table upon payment of annual dues. Other groups interested in map and geography collections may associate with the round table as an affiliate member. As of August 31, 1992: 83 organization members; 359 personal members; 442 total members.

Dues

Personal member, $15; affiliate groups and institutions, $45.

New Members Round Table (NMRT)

To help the individual member to become oriented to the profession and to encourage membership participation in its organizations, national, state, and local; to promote a greater feeling of responsibility for the development of library service and librarianship; and to assist actively in the recruitment of qualified persons for the profession.

Executive Committee (officers and committee chairpersons)

Pres., Jenifer Stone Abramson (1994); pres.-elect, Joanna M. Burkhardt (1995); treas., Joni L. Gomez (1994); secy., Elizabeth M. Fordon (1993); past pres., James R. Mouw (1993); dirs.: Joan Kaplowitz (1993); Kathleen M. Kie (1994); Beatrice L. McKay (1994); J. Christina Smith (1993); staff liaison, JoAn S. Segal.

Publication

Footnotes (quarterly). Free to members; not available by subscription. Ed., Darlene P. Nichols.

Affiliates Council

Pres., Diane M. Tureski (1993); vice-pres., Dorothy Ann Branton (1993).

Committee Chairpersons

3M/NMRT Professional Development Grant—Heleni Marques Pedersoli; (1993).
Archivist—Robert A. Dunkelberger (1993).
Booth—Lora L. Lennertz (1993).
Cognotes—Terri L. Pedersen-Summey (1993).
Com. on Governance—Cynthia S. Church (1993).
Exhibitor Contact and Relations—Elaine Yontz (1993).
Grassroots Grants—Anne M. Gordon (1993).
Handbook—Clare B. Dunkle (1993).
Leadership Development—Joycelyn H. Claer (1993).
Library School Outreach—Suzanne M. Byron (1993).
Local Arrangements—Michael J. Coleman (1993).
Membership Meeting Program—co-chs., Judy M. Rudner (1993) and Rita Yribar (1993).
Membership Promotion and Relations—Lorelei A. Tanji (1993).
Midwinter Activities—co-chs., John P. Culshaw (1993) and Robert L. Wick (1993).
Minorities Recruitment—Joan Reyes (1993).
Nominating—Patricia A. Brill (1993).
(Shirley) Olofson Memorial Award—Richard C. Dickey (1993).
Orientation—co-chs., Dorothy Ann Branton (1993) and Steven P. Kerchoff (1993).
President's Program—Barbara A. Walchle (1993).
Publicity—Stephanie L. Sterling (1993).
Resources—co-chs., Elizabeth M. Fordon (1993) and Laura A. Sill (1993).
Scholarship—Angela R. Jones (1993).

Liaisons

ALA liaisons coor.—J. Christina Smith.
AASL Membership Com.—to be appointed.
ALA Membership Com.—Lorelei A. Tanji.
ALCTS-CCS CC:DA—Kathryn Sorury.
ALCTS Membership Com.—Selina Wang.
ALSC Membership Com.—Denise Krell.
ASCLA Membership Com.—Jane Tupin.
ERT—Elaine Yontz.
Freedom to Read Fdn.—Joanna Burkhardt.
Intellectual Freedom Com.—Joyce G. Taylor.
LAMA Membership Com.—Laura A. Sill.
LAMA-PAS—Susan Schmidt.
LAMA-PAS Staff Development—Deborah Tuma-Church.
LAMA-PAS Supv. Skills Com.—Dorothy Ownes.
Library Education Assembly—Dorothy Ann Branton.
LITA—Louise Ratliff.
PBA—Joni Gomez.
PLA Membership Com.—Patricia A. Brill.
Professional Ethics—Kimberly Robles.
RASD-MARS—Necia Parker.
YALSA Membership Com.—Deborah Colter.

Membership

Individual membership is open to any librarian or student in a library school who has been a member of ALA for 10 or fewer years; affiliate memberships are open to municipal, state, or regional groups; institutional memberships are open to any library or institution and carry a *Footnotes* subscription but no vote. As of August 31, 1992, 77 organization members; 865 personal members; 942 total members.

Dues

Individual members, $10; affiliates, $10; institutions, $10.

Social Responsibilities Round Table (SRRT)

To provide a forum for the discussion of the responsibilities of libraries in relation to the important problems of social change which face institutions and librarians; to provide for exchange of information among all ALA units about library activities with the goal of increasing understanding of current social problems; to act as a stimulus to the Association and its various units in making libraries more responsive to current social needs; to present programs, arrange exhibits, and carry out other appropriate activities.

Action Council

Coor., Stephen J. Stillwell Jr. (1993); secy., Debra L. Gilchrist (1993); treas., Roland C. Hansen (1993).

Members-at-large: Sherre H. Dryden (1994); Carolyn L. Garnes (1993); Dorothy Granger (1995); Carol Greenholz (1993); Alfred Kagan (1995); Steven H. Murden (1994); Becky A. Ray (1995); Mark C. Rosenzweig (1993); Theresa A. Tobin (1995); ex officio: John C. Sandstrom (1993); Thomas L. Wilding (1993).

Committee Chairpersons

Archives—Denise E. Botto (1994).
Conference Arrangements and Programs—to be appointed.
Membership/Recruitment—Steven H. Murden (1994) and Stephen J. Stillwell Jr. (1994).

Liaisons

ALA Membership Promotion Task Force—Steven H. Murden.
ALCTS-CCS Committee on Cataloging—Sherry L. Kelly.
Freedom to Read Foundation—Daniel C. Tsang.
Library Education Assembly—Carol R. Barta.
Literacy Assembly—Denise E. Botto.
Planning and Budget Assembly—Roland C. Hansen.

Task Force Coordinators

Alternatives in Print—Sylvia Curtis (1992), and Jackie Eubanks (1992).
Civil Rights—Donnarae MacCann (1992).
Coretta Scott King Award—Henrietta M. Smith (1992).
Environment—Patricia Cruse (1993).
Feminist—Madeline Tainton (1992).
Gay and Lesbian—Roland C. Hansen (1992) and Karen L. Whittlesey-First (1993).
International Human Rights—David L. Williams (1992).
Library Unions—Elaine M. Harger (1992).
Migration, Refugees and the Homeless—Julie A. Hersberger (1993) and Sherill Weaver Wozniak (1993).
Peace Information Exchange—Stephen J. Stillwell Jr. (1992).

Regional Affiliate Members

Kansas SRRT—Carol Barta.
Minnesota SRRT—Sanford Berman.
Oregon SRRT—to be appointed.
Progressive Librarians Guild—Elaine M. Harger.
Washington SRRT—Christine M. Livingston (1993).

Publications

GLTF Newsletter. Newsletter of the SRRT Gay and Lesbian Task Force. Quarterly. Subscrip-tions: $5 to SRRT members; $10 to non-SRRT members and institutions. Make checks payable to: ALA/SRRT/GLTF; send to 50 E. Huron St., Chicago, IL 60611. Ed., Kathy Anderson, Atlantic Cnty. L. Sys., 2 S. Farragut Ave., Mays Landing, NJ 08330.

SRRT Newsletter. Free to members; $10 to non-ALA members; $20 to institutions; $2 per back issue. Subscriptions available from SRRT Clearinghouse, 50 E. Huron St., Chicago, IL 60611. Ed., Thomas L. Wilding, Massachusetts Inst. of Tech. Ls., Cambridge, MA 02139. Clearinghouse Editorial Board: Mark C. Rosenzweig, John C. Sandstrom, Theresa A. Tobin.

Women in Libraries. Newsletter of the SRRT Feminist Task Force; $5 to individuals; $8 to institutions (prepaid); $10 to institutions (invoiced). Ed., Abbie J. Basile, 486 Ashland Ave., #3, Buffalo, NY 14222. Make check payable to: ALA/SRRT Feminist Task Force, 50 E. Huron Street, Chicago, IL 60611.

Membership

Open to all ALA members. As of August 31, 1992: 98 organization members; 1,753 personal members; 1,851 total members.

Dues

Personal members, $10; organizational members, $20; student members, free.

Staff Organizations Round Table (SORT)

To encourage the formation of staff organizations; to act as a clearinghouse for information about staff organizations; to bring staff organizations of library employees into closer relationship so as to foster mutual cooperation; to cooperate with all ALA units that are set up to study and act upon personnel matters.

Steering Committee

Officers: ch., Donna Epps Ramsey (1993); ch.-elect, Leon S. Bey (1994); secy., Allison L. Gould (1993).

Members-at-large: budget off., Eleanor F. Pemberton; staff liaison, Jeniece Guy.

Publication

SORT Bulletin (semiannually). Free to round table members only. Not available by subscription. Ed., Yvonne Beever (1993).

Committee Chairpersons

Budget Officer—Eleanor F. Pemberton (1993).
Bylaws—to be appointed.
Membership Promotion—Peggy G. Earheart (1993).
Program, 1993—Donna Epps Ramsey (1993).
Publicity—Orvella F. Fields (1993).
SORT Directory Update—to be appointed.

Representatives and Liaisons

Freedom to Read Foundation—Kay K. Ikuta.
Literacy Assembly—Yvonne Beever.
SRRT—Leon S. Bey.

Membership

Any personal member of the Association may become a personal member of the Staff Organizations Round Table by paying the separate personal membership fee for SORT. This entitles the members to annual subscription to the *SORT Bulletin*, to run for or be appointed to the SORT Steering Committee, and to vote in SORT elections.

A library staff organization wishing to join SORT as an organizational member must pay the round table fee. However, to be an organizational member of SORT, the staff organization need not be situated in a library which is an organizational member of ALA. Such a staff organization may itself become a member of ALA by paying the annual dues of the Association plus the appropriate dues of the round table.

As of August 31, 1992: 99 organization members; 117 personal members; 216 total members.

Dues

Organizational membership, $6. Personal membership, $3.

Video Round Table (VRT)

A broad-based group bringing together ALA members who have an interest in and/or responsibility for video collections, and providing a unified voice for video advocacy in the areas of legislation, professional guidelines for collections, and other issues specifically related to video and libraries.

Officers

Ch., Gary P. Handman (1994); ch.-elect, Mary A. Keelan (1995); treas., Merle J. Slyhoff (1993); secy., Mary Patricia Lora (1993); staff liaison, JoAn S. Segal.

Committee Chairpersons

Bylaws—Jean T. Kreamer (1993).
Gala Program—Joseph S. Clark (1993).

Membership—Kristine R. Brancolini (1993).
Newsletter—Carleton L. Jackson (1993).
Nominating—Sally E. Mason-Robinson (1993).
Program—Jean T. Kreamer (1993).

Membership

Open to all ALA members. As of August 31, 1992: 12 organization members; 169 personal members; 181 total members.

Publication

Video Round Table News (irregular). Free to round table members. Ed., Carleton L. Jackson.

Dues

Personal members, $12; organization members, $25.

Membership Initiative Groups

A membership initiative group is a short-term organizational vehicle that provides for prompt, organized membership activity on topical issues in librarianship of mutual interest.

A group of members, having identified their common concern for some aspect of librarianship, would register the following with the Committee on Organization: a statement of purpose; at least 100 signatures of ALA members in good standing; the names and addresses of designated organizers. "Guidelines for Membership Initiative Groups" is available from Dep. Exec. Dir., ALA Hq.

Library Support Staff Interests

To provide a forum within ALA for addressing a wide variety of issues relating to library support staff, including but not limited to basic preparation and continuing education, career development, job duties and responsibilities and other related issues.

Steering Committee

Co-chs., Annamarie Kehnast (1993) and Debbie A. Wolcott (1993); staff liaison: Margaret Myers.

Members-at-large: Betty Arnold (1993); Judy Barickman (1993); Karen L. Blatman-Byers (1993); Pat Clingman (1993); Peggy Earheart (1993); Mary Farris (1993); Virginia Gerster (1993); Meralyn Meadows (1993); Tobi Oberman (1993); Julie Wokinson (1993).

ALA Student Chapter Groups

Since 1980, when the first ALA Student Chapter was created at the University of Michigan—Ann Arbor, students at 35 additional universities have established chapters in 24 states. Student Chapters sponsor programs and activities such as library tours, career information sharing, newsletters, and an annual joint meeting. Each chapter sends a representative to ALA Annual Conference, where the student puts in 20 hours working with ALA staff in exchange for hotel and meal expenses.

In cooperation with a faculty advisor, ALA student members at the master's level and beyond are eligible to form official ALA Student Chapter groups at schools offering ALA-accredited programs of library and information science. For a detailed brochure on how to start a chapter, write Julie Ann Geissler, Chapter Relations Office, ALA, 50 E. Huron St., Chicago, IL 60611, or call 800-545-2433.

Alabama

ALA Student Chapter, Sch. of L. & Inf. Studies, Univ. of Alabama, P.O. Box 870252, Tuscaloosa, AL 35487-0252.
Pres., to be elected; faculty advisor, Ronald D. Doctor.

Arizona

ALA Student Chapter, L. Student Org., Sch. of L. Sci., Univ. of Arizona, 1515 E. 1st St., Tucson, AZ 85719.
Pres., Barb Kesel; faculty advisor, Gretchen Whitney.

California

ALA Student Chapter, Sch. of L. & Inf. Studies, Univ. of California, 102 South Hall, Berkeley, CA 94720.
Pres., to be elected; faculty advisor, Charlotte Nolan.

ALA Student Chapter, c/o Prof. Nancy Maack, Grad. Sch. of L. & Inf. Sci. Bldg., Univ. of California, 405 Hilgard Ave., Los Angeles, CA 90024-1520.
Pres., to be elected; faculty advisor, Nancy Maack.

Florida

ALA Student Chapter, Sch. of L. & Inf. Studies, Florida State Univ., Tallahassee, FL 32306-2048.

Ch., Patty Patterson; faculty advisor, Alphonse F. Trezza.

ALA Student Chapter, Div. of L. & Inf. Sci., Univ. of South Florida, CIS 1040/4202 Fowler Ave., Tampa, FL 33620.
Pres., to be elected; faculty advisor, Vicki Gregory.

Georgia

ALA Student Chapter, Sch. of L. & Inf. Studies, Atlanta Univ., James P. Brawley Dr. at Fair St. SW, Atlanta, GA 30314.
Pres., Edna S. Dixon; faculty advisor, Almeta G. Woodson.

Hawaii

ALA Student Chapter, Sch. of L. & Inf. Studies, Univ. of Hawaii, Hamilton L., 2550 The Mall, Honolulu, HI 96822.
Pres., A. Lani Teshima-Miller; faculty advisor, Sally Roggia.

Illinois

ALA Student Chapter, Northern Illinois Univ., Dept. of L. & Inf. Studies, DeKalb, IL 60115-2854.
Ch., to be elected; faculty advisor, Cosette N. Kies.

ALA Student Chapter, Grad. Sch. of L. & Inf. Sci., Rosary Coll., 7900 W. Division St., River Forest, IL 60305.

Pres., to be elected; faculty advisor, Tze-chung Li.

ALA Student Chapter, Grad. Sch. of L. & Inf. Sci., Univ. of Illinois, 410 David Kinley Hall, 1407 W. Gregory Dr., Urbana, IL 61801.
Pres., to be elected; faculty advisor, Leigh Estabrook.

Kansas

Elsie Pine L. Club, Sch. of L. & Inf. Mgmt., Emporia State Univ., Emporia, KS 66801.
Pres., Mary Story-Huffman; faculty advisor, Martha L. Hale.

Louisiana

ALA Student Chapter, Sch. of L. & Inf. Sci., Louisiana State Univ., 267 Coates Hall, Baton Rouge, LA 70803.
Pres., Marsha Curry; faculty advisor, Michael Carpenter.

Massachusetts

ALA Student Chapter, Grad. Sch. of L. & Inf. Sci., Simmons Coll., 300 The Fenway, Boston, MA 02115–5898.
Pres., Constance Drapeau; faculty advisor, Em Claire Knowles.

Michigan

ALA Student Chapter, Sch. of L. and Inf. Studies, Univ. of Michigan, 580 Union Dr., Ann Arbor, MI 48109-1346.

Pres., Jill Holman; faculty advisor, Margaret T. Taylor.

ALA Student Chapter, L. Sci. Prog., Wayne State Univ., 106 Kresge L., Detroit, MI 48202.
Ch., Lisa Lutes; faculty advisor, Carole McCollough.

Mississippi

ALA Student Chapter, Sch. of L. Sci., Univ. of Southern Mississippi, Southern Sta., Box 5146, Hattiesburg, MS 39406.
Ch., to be elected; faculty advisor, Onva Boshears.

New Jersey

ALA Student Chapter, Dept. of L. & Inf. Studies, Sch. of Comm., Inf., & L. Studies, Rutgers Univ., 4 Huntington St., New Brunswick, NJ 08903.
Co-chs., to be elected; faculty advisor, Kay E. Vandergrift.

New York

ALA Student Chapter, Palmer Sch. of L. & Inf. Sci., Long Island Univ.—C. W. Post Campus, Brookville, NY 11548.
Pres., to be elected; faculty advisor, to be appointed.

ALA Student Chapter, Grad. Sch. of L. & Inf. Sci., Queens Coll., CUNY, Rosenthall Rm. 254, Flushing, NY 11367.
Pres., Linda Zoppa; faculty advisor, Karen P. Smith.

ALA Student Chapter, Sch. of Inf. Sci. & Policy, State Univ. of New York, (SUNY), Draper 113, 135 Western Ave., Albany, NY 12222.
Ch., to be elected; faculty advisor, Vincent J. Aceto.

North Carolina

ALA Student Chapter, Sch. of L. & Inf. Sciences, North Carolina Central Univ., P.O. Box 19586, Durham, NC 27707.

Pres., Ivan T. Mosley; faculty advisor, Pauletta B. Bracy.

ALA/SCALA, Dept. of L. & Inf. Studies, Univ. of North Carolina, CB3360, Chapel Hill, NC 27599-3360.
Pres., Jeannie A. Dilger; faculty advisor, Edward G. Holley.

ALA/LISSA, Dept. of L. & Inf. Studies, Univ. of North Carolina, 349 Curry Bldg., Greensboro, NC 27412.
Pres., Amy Boykin; faculty advisor, James V. Carmichael.

Ohio

ALA Student Chapter, Sch. of L. Sci., Kent State Univ., P.O. Box 5190, Kent, OH 44242.
Ch., to be elected; faculty advisor, Carolyn Brodie.

Oklahoma

ALA Student Chapter, Sch. of L. & Inf. Studies, Univ. of Oklahoma, Norman, OK 73019.
Pres., Jeffrey Wilhite; faculty advisor, Judith Overmier.

Pennsylvania

ALA Student Chapter, Dept. of L. Sci., Clarion Univ. of Pennsylvania, 166 Carlson L. Bldg., Clarion, PA 16214.
Pres., Robert Harrison; faculty advisor, James T. Macaferri.

ALA Student Chapter, Coll. of Inf. Studies, Drexel Univ., Philadelphia, PA 19104.
Ch., to be elected; faculty advisor, Thomas Childers.

ALA Student Chapter, Sch. of L. & Inf. Sci., Univ. of Pittsburgh, 135 N. Bellefield Ave., Rm. 505, Pittsburgh, PA 15260.
Pres., to be elected; faculty advisors: Susan W. Alman and Mary K. Biagini.

South Carolina

ALA/LIS²A, Grad. Sch. of L. & Inf. Sci., Univ. of South Carolina, Columbia, SC 29208.

Pres., to be elected; faculty advisor, Charles C. Curran.

Tennessee

GSLIS ALA Student Chapter, Univ. of Tennessee, 804 Volunteer Blvd., Rm. 108, Knoxville, TN 37996.
Pres., to be elected; faculty advisors: Gary Purcell and Marilyn H. Karrenbrock.

Texas

GLISA, Sch. of L. & Inf. Studies, Texas Woman's Univ., P.O. Box 22905, Denton, TX 76204.
Pres., Darlean Spangenberger; faculty advisor, Adeline Wilkes.

ALA Student Chapter, Grad Sch. of L. & Inf. Sci., Univ. of Texas, Austin, TX 78712-1276.
Pres., Kristin Trefts; faculty advisor, Barbara Immroth.

Utah

ALA/GRADALIS, Sch. of L. & Inf. Sciences., Brigham Young Univ., 5042 HBLL, Provo, UT 84602.
Pres. Jan Porter; faculty advisor, Nathan M. Smith.

Washington

ALA Student Chapter, Grad. Sch. of L. & Inf. Sci., Univ. of Washington, 133 Suzzallo L., FM-30, Seattle, WA 98195.
Ch., to be elected; faculty advisor, Carol Doll.

Wisconsin

ALA Student Chapter, Sch. of L. & Inf. Studies, Univ. of Wisconsin, 4220 Helen C. White Hall, 600 N. Park St., Madison, WI 53706.
Co-ch., Robert Peterson; faculty advisor, Darlene Weingand.

ALA Student Chapter, Sch. of L. & Inf. Sci., Univ. of Wisconsin, Enderis Hall, P.O. Box 413, Milwaukee, WI 53201.
Pres., Keith Costas; faculty advisor, James H. Sweetland.

Chapters

Gerald G. Hodges, *Director, Chapter Relations Office*
Julie Ann Geissler, *Assistant Director, Chapter Relations Office*

Council may establish one chapter of ALA in any state, province, territory, or region if so requested by a majority of the ALA members residing in the area. However, only one chapter is permitted in any state, province, or territory. Chapter membership is not limited to members of ALA. The purpose of a chapter is to promote general library service and librarianship within its geographic area and to cooperate in the promotion of general and joint enterprises within ALA and other library groups. (Bylaws Article V.)

Each state, provincial, territorial, or regional chapter shall be the final authority within ALA in respect to all programs and policies which concern only the area for which the chapter is responsible, provided they are not inconsistent with program and policies established by Council.

Alabama Library Assn.—pres., Jane Keeton, Birmingham P. & Jefferson Cnty. Free L., 2100 Park Place, Birmingham, AL 35203; pres.-elect, Deborah J. Grimes, Shelton State Cmnty. Coll. L., 202 Skyland Blvd., Tuscaloosa, AL 35405; exec. dir., Barbara F. Black, Alabama L. Assn., 400 S. Union St., Stc. 255, Montgomery, AL 36104; (205) 262-5210. (Officers change Apr. 1993.)

Alaska Library Assn.—pres., Clara Sitter, Univ. of Alaska, 3211 Providence Dr., Anchorage, AK 99508; pres.-elect, Maurine Canarsky, 1009 Pedro St., Fairbanks, AK 99701; exec. secy., Isabelle Mudd, Alaska L. Assn., P.O. Box 71061, Fairbanks, AK 99707-1061; (907) 479-4522. (Officers change Mar. 1993.)

Arizona Library Assn.—pres., Judith Register, Mustang Br. L., 10101 N. 90th St., Scottsdale, AZ 85258; pres.-elect, Nancy Cummings, Yuma Cnty. L. Dist., 350 3rd Ave., Yuma, AZ 85364; exec. secy., Jim Johnson, Arizona L. Assn., 13832 N. 32nd St. D-1, Phoenix, AZ 85032; (602) 971-3885; FAX: (602) 482-1011. (Officers change Nov. 1992.)

Arkansas Library Assn.—pres., Margaret Crank, Arkansas Dept. of Educ., #4 Capitol Mall, Room 405B, Little Rock, AR 72201; pres.-elect, Kathy Sanders, Univ. of Arkansas, Ottenheimer L., 2801 S. University, Little Rock, AR 72204; exec. dir., Sherry Walker, Arkansas L. Assn., 1100 N. University #109, Little Rock, AR 72207-6344; (501) 661-1127; FAX: (501) 663-1218. (Officers change Nov. 1992.)

California Library Assn.—pres., Neel Parikh, San Francisco P. L., Civic Ctr., San Francisco, CA 94102; pres.-elect, Luis Herrera, San Diego P. L., 820 E St., San Diego, CA 92101; exec. dir., Mary Sue Ferrell, California L. Assn., 717 K St., Ste. 300, Sacramento, CA 95814-3477; (916) 447-8541; FAX: (916) 447-8394. (Officers change Nov. 1992.)

Colorado Library Assn.—pres., Judy Zelenski, Central Colorado L. Sys., 4350 Wadsworth #340, Wheatridge, CO 80033; pres.-elect, Rick Friddle, Pikes Peak Cmnty. Coll., 5675 S. Academy Blvd., Colorado Springs, CO 80906-5488; office mgr., Roger Baker, Colorado L. Assn., 114 Pinecliffe Rd., Pinecliffe, CO 80471; (303) 642-0203; FAX: (303) 642-0201. (Officers change Nov. 1992.)

Connecticut Library Assn.—pres., Peter Chase, Plainville P. L., 56 E. Main St., Plainville, CT 06062; pres.-elect, Sandra Ruess, Gilford Free P. L., 67 Park St., Gilford, CT 06437; exec. dir., M. Suzanne C. Berry, Connecticut L. Assn., 638 Prospect Ave., Hartford, CT 06105; (203) 232-4825; FAX: (203) 232-0819. (Officers change July 1993.)

Delaware Library Assn.—pres., Robert Wetherall, Dover P.L., 45 S. State St., Dover, DE 19901; (302) 736-7030; FAX: (302) 736-0985; pres.-elect, to be elected; mailing address: Delaware L. Assn., P.O. Box 1843, Wilmington, DE 19899. (Officers change May 1993.)

District of Columbia Library Assn.—pres., Susan Fifer Canby, National Geographic Soc., 1146 16th St. NW, Washington, DC 20036; (202) 857-7787; FAX: (202) 429-5735; pres.-elect, Hardy R. Franklin, M. L. King Mem. L., 901 G St. NW, Washington, DC 20001; mailing address: Dist. of Columbia L. Assn., P.O. Box 14177, Benjamin Franklin Sta., Washington, DC 20044. (Officers change Sept. 1992.)

Florida Library Assn.—pres., Ann W. Williams, Alachua Cnty. L. Dist., 401 E. University Ave., Gainesville, FL 32601; pres.-elect, Susan Anderson, St. Petersburg Jr. Coll., 8580 66th St. N., Pinellas Park, FL 34665-1299; exec. secy., Marjorie Stealey, Florida L. Assn., 1133 W. Morse Blvd., Ste. 201, Winter Park, FL 32789-3788; (407) 647-8839. (Officers change July 1993.)

Georgia Library Assn.—pres., Sharon Self, Hardaway High Sch., 2901 College Dr., Columbus, GA 31995; (404) 649-0748; FAX: (404) 649-0754; pres.-elect, Donna D. Mancini, Dekalb Cnty. P. L., Admin. Offices, 215 Sycamore St., Decatur, GA 30030; mailing address: Georgia L. Assn., c/o Robert J. Richardson, Young Harris Coll., P.O. Box 39, Young Harris, GA 30582; (Officers change Oct. 1993.)

Guam Library Assn.—pres., Linda Schlekau, Upi Elem. Sch., Yigo, P.O. Box DE, Agana, GU 96910; (671) 653-1371 or (671) 734-9186 or 9105; FAX: (671) 653-5305 or (671) 734-6882; pres.-elect, Joanne Tarpley, R. F. Kennedy Mem. L., UOG Sta., Mangilao, GU 96923; mailing address: Guam L. Assn., P.O. Box 22515 GMF, Barrigada, GU 96921. (Officers change May 1993.)

Hawaii Library Assn.—pres., Floriana Cofman, Hawaii Kai P. L., 249 Lunalilo Home Rd., Honolulu, HI 96825; (808) 395-2310; pres.-elect, Kenneth Herrick, Univ. of Hawaii at Hilo, 50-I Malaai Rd., Hilo, HI 96720. (Officers change Mar. 1993.)

Idaho Library Assn.—pres., Betty Holbrook, Pocatello P.L., 812 E. Clark, Pocatello, ID 83201; (208) 232-1263; FAX: (208) 232-9266; pres.-elect, Pat Stewart, Moscow Jr. High Sch., L., Moscow, ID 83843; mailing address: Idaho L. Assn., c/o Camille Wood, Treas., Univ. of Idaho L., Moscow, ID 83843. (Officers change Oct. 1992.)

Illinois Library Assn.—pres., W. Randall Wilson, Parlin-Ingersoll P. L., 205 W. Chestnut St., Canton, IL 61520; vice-pres., Barbara Meyers, Blue Island P. L., 2433 York St., Blue Island, IL 60406; exec. dir., Barbara Cunningham, Illinois L. Assn., 33 W. Grand Ave. #301, Chicago, IL 60610; (312) 644-1896; FAX: (312) 644-1899. (Officers change July 1993.)

Indiana Library Fed.—pres., Beverly A. Martin, Johnson Cnty. P. L., 401 S. State St., Franklin, IN 46131; pres.-elect, Sandy Sawyer, Fulton Cnty. P. L., R. R. 6, Box 162, Rochester, IN 46975; exec. dir., Linda Kolb, Indiana L. Fed., 1500 N. Delaware St., Indianapolis, IN 46202; (317) 636-6613; FAX: (317) 634-9503. (Officers change May 1993.)

Iowa Library Assn.—pres., Juliana Huiskamp, Cresco P. L., 320 N. Elm, Cresco, IA 52136; pres.-elect, Dottie Persson, Univ. of Iowa, Psychology L., Iowa City, IA 52242; exec. asst., Naomi Stovall, Iowa L. Assn., 823 Insurance Exch. Bldg., Des Moines, IA 50309; (515) 243-2172 (also FAX). (Officers change Jan. 1993.)

Kansas Library Assn.—pres., Kenton L. Oliver, Olathe P. L., 201 E. Park, Olathe, KS 66061; pres.-elect, Kay Bradt, Baker Univ., 606 8th, Baldwin, KS 66066; exec. secy., Leroy Gattin, Hutchinson P. L., 901 N. Main, Hutchinson, KS 67501; (316) 663-5441; FAX: (316) 663-1215. (Officers change July 1993.)

Kentucky Library Assn.—pres., Rose M. Gabbard, Lee Cnty. High Sch. L., Fairground Ridge, Beattyville, KY 41311; pres.-elect, Candace B. Wilson, Russell Cnty. Jr. High Sch., 2258 S. Hwy. 127, Russell Springs, KY 42642-4010; exec. secy., Tom Underwood, Kentucky L. Assn., 1501 Twilight Trail, Frankfort, KY 40601; (502) 223-5322. (Officers change Oct. 1992.)

Louisiana Library Assn.—pres., Earl Hart, Univ. of New Orleans, Coll. of Educ.—L. Sci. Prog., Lake Front Dr., New Orleans, LA 70148; pres.-elect, Grace G. Moore, State L. of Louisiana, P.O. Box 131, Baton Rouge, LA 70808; office mgr., Carol McMahon, Louisiana L. Assn., P.O. Box 3058, Baton Rouge, LA 70821; (504) 342-4928; FAX: (504) 342-3547. (Officers change July 1993.)

Maine Library Assn.—pres., Barbara Rice, Bangor P. L., 145 Harlow St., Bangor, ME 04401; vice-pres., Valerie Osborne, Old Town P. L., Old Town, ME 04468; exec. secy., Cathy Callahan, Maine Municipal Assn., Community Dr., Augusta, ME 04330; (207) 623-8429. (Officers change May 1994.)

Maryland Library Assn.—pres., John G. Ray, Loyola Notre Dame L., 200 Winston Ave., Baltimore, MD 21212; pres.-elect, Diana Cunningham, Univ. of Maryland, Health Sci. L., 111 S. Green St., Baltimore, MD 21201; assn. mgr., Dinah Kappus, Maryland L. Assn., 400 Cathedral St., 3rd Fl., Baltimore, MD 21201; (410) 727-7422. (Officers change July 1993.)

Massachusetts Library Assn.—pres., Bonnie O'Brien, Shrewsbury P. L., 609 Main St.,

Shrewsbury, MA 01545; vice-pres., Monica Grace, Framingham P.L., 49 Lexington St., Framingham, MA 01701; exec. secy., Barry Blaisdell, Massachusetts L. Assn., Countryside Offices, 707 Turnpike St., North Andover, MA 01845; (508) 686-8543. (Officers change July 1993.)

Michigan Library Assn.—pres., Jean Houghton, Univ. of Detroit—Mercy, Main L., 4001 W. McNichols, Detroit, MI 48221; pres.-elect, Francis Buckley, Detroit P. L. Public Serv., 5201 Woodward Ave., Detroit, MI 48202; exec. dir., Marianne Gessner, Michigan L. Assn., 1000 Long Blvd., Ste. 1, Lansing, MI 48911; (517) 694-6615; FAX: (517) 694-4330. (Officers change Nov. 1992.)

Middle Atlantic Regl. Library Fed.—pres., Katharine C. Hurrey, Southern Maryland Regl. L. Assn., P.O. Box 459, Charlotte Hall, MD 20622; (410) 934-9442; FAX: (410) 884-0438; vice-pres., Ernest R. Kallay, Clarksburg—Harrison P. L., 404 W. Pike St., Clarksburg, WV 26301. (Officers change May 1994.)

Midwest Fed. of Library Assns.—pres., Patricia Llerandi, Schaumburg Township L., 32 W. Library Ln., Schaumburg, IL 60194; (708) 885-3373; ext. 150; FAX: (708) 885-8271; pres.-elect, to be elected. (Officers change Nov. 1995.)

Minnesota Library Assn.—pres., Janet Kinney, Coll. of St. Catherine, 2004 Randolph Ave., St. Paul, MN 55105; pres.-elect, David Barton, Viking L. Sys., 317 N. Cascade, Fergus Falls, MN 56537; admin. secy., JoAnne Kelty, N. Regl. L. Sys., 1315 Lowrey Ave. N., Minneapolis, MN 55411-1398; (612) 521-1735. (Officers change Jan. 1993.)

Mississippi Library Assn.—pres., Kendall P. Chapman, Oswalt L., Copiah-Lincoln Cmnty. Coll., Wesson, MS 39191; pres.-elect, Sherry Laughlin, Univ. of Southern Mississippi, Cook Mem. L., Hattiesburg, MS 39406-5053; exec. secy., Sharon Buchanan, Mississippi L. Assn., P.O. Box 20448, Jackson, MS 39209-1448; (601) 352-3917. (Officers change Jan. 1993.)

Missouri Library Assn.—pres., Kurt Lamb, Mexico-Audrain Cnty. L., 305 W. Jackson, Mexico, MO 65265; pres.-elect, Annie Linnemeyer, Springfield-Greene Cnty. L., 397 E. Central, Springfield, MO 65801; exec. coord., Jean Ann McCartney, Missouri L. Assn., 1015 E. Broadway, Ste. 215, Columbia, MO 65201-4907; (314) 449-4627 (also FAX). (Officers change Oct. 1992.)

Montana Library Assn.—pres., Steve Cottrell, Bozeman P.L., 220 E. Lamme, Bozeman, MT 59715; (406) 586-4788; FAX: (406) 587-7785; pres. elect, Jane Howell, Eastern Montana Coll., 1500 N. 30th St., Billings, MT 59101-0298. (Officers change July 1993.)

Mountain Plains Library Assn.—pres., Corky Walters, Wyoming State L., Supreme Ct. Bldg., Cheyenne, WY 82002-0650; pres.-elect, Bunny Morrison, Skyview High Sch., 1775 High Sierra Blvd., Billings, MT 59105; exec. secy., Joseph R. Edelen, Univ. of South Dakota, L., Vermillion, SD 57069; (605) 677-6082. (Officers change Oct. 1992.)

Nebraska Library Assn.—pres., Sharon McCaslin, Peru State Coll., L., Peru, NE 68421; pres.-elect, Sarah Watson, Benson Br. L., 2918 N. 60th St., Omaha, NE 68104; exec. secy., Fiona Turnbull, Bellevue Coll. L., Galvin Rd. at Harvell Dr., Bellevue, NE 68005; (402) 293-2011. (Officers change Nov. 1992.)

Nevada Library Assn.—pres., Leona Wright, Sierra View Br. L., 4001 S. Virginia St., Reno, NV 89509; pres.-elect, Wendy Starkweather, Univ. of Nevada, L., 4505 Maryland Pkwy., Las Vegas, NV 89154; exec. secy., Carol Madsen, Nevada State L. & Arch., Capitol Complex, 401 N. Carson, Carson City, NV 89710; (702) 887-2620; FAX: (702) 887-2630. (Officers change Jan. 1993.)

New England Library Assn.—pres., Patricia Holloway, SE Connecticut L. Assn., Avery Pt., Groton, CT 06340; pres.-elect, Nancy Vincent, Keene P. L., 60 Winter St., Keene, NH 03431; exec. secy., Barry Blaisdell, New England L. Assn., Countryside Offices, 707 Turnpike St., North Andover, MA 01845; (508) 685-5966 (also FAX). (Officers change Sept. 1992.)

New Hampshire Library Assn.—pres., Margaret Marschner, Conway P. L., Box 2100, Conway, NH 03818; (603) 447-5552; FAX: (603) 447-6921; pres.-elect, Ann Tomentozzi, Howe P. L., 13 E. South St., Hanover, NH 03755. (Officers change May 1993.)

New Jersey Library Assn.—pres., Jane L. Crocker, Gloucester Cnty. Coll. L., Tanyard Rd., Sewell, NJ 08080; pres.-elect, Norma Blake, Gloucester Cnty. L., 200 Holly Dell Dr., Sewell, NJ 08080; exec. dir., Patricia A. Tumulty, New Jersey L. Assn., 4 W. Lafayette, Trenton, NJ 08608; (609) 394-8032; FAX: (609) 394-8164. (Officers change May 1993.)

New Mexico Library Assn.—pres., Drew Harrington, Albuquerque Acad. L., 6400 Wyoming NE, Albuquerque, NM 87109; (505) 828-3218; FAX: (505) 828-3119; pres.-elect, Alison E. Almquist, Wherry Elem. Sch., Inez Elem. Sch., Albuquerque, NM 87116; (505) 268-2434. (Officers change Apr. 1993.)

New York Library Assn.—pres., Janet M. Welch, Rochester Regl. L. Council, 302 N. Goodman St., Village Gate, Rochester, NY 14607; pres.-elect, Sheryl Egger, West Irondequoit Sch. Dist., 260 Cooper Rd., Rochester, NY 14617; exec. dir., Susan L. Keitel, New York L. Assn., 252 Hudson Ave., Albany, NY 12210; (518) 432-6952; FAX: (518) 427-1697. (Officers change Nov. 1992.)

North Carolina Library Assn.—pres., Janet Freeman, Meredith Coll., Campbell L., 3800 Hillsborough St., Raleigh, NC 27607-5298; pres.-elect, Gwendolyn Jackson, Southeastern Tech Asstc. Ctr., 2013 Lejeune Blvd., Jacksonville, NC 28546; admin. asst., Martha Fonville, State L. of North Carolina, 109 E. Jones St., Rm. 27, Raleigh, NC 27601-1023; (919) 839-6252 (also FAX). (Officers change Oct. 1993.)

North Dakota Library Assn.—pres., Marcella Schmaltz, Bismarck State Coll., L., 1500 Edwards Ave., Bismarck, ND 58501. (701) 224-5450; FAX: (701) 224-5551; vice-pres., Jan Hendrickson, McLean-Mercer Regl. L., Hazen Br., Main St., Hazen, ND 58545. (Officers change Oct. 1993.)

Ohio Library Assn.—pres., Patricia Latshaw, Akron-Summit Cnty. P.L., 55 S. Main St., Akron, OH 44326-0001; pres.-elect, Alan Hall, P. L. of Steubenville & Jefferson Cnty., 407 S. 4th St., Steubenville, OH 43952; interim exec. dir., Lynda Murray, Ohio L. Assn., 67 Jefferson Ave., Columbus, OH 43215; (614) 221-9057; FAX: (614) 221-6234. (Officers change Nov. 1992.)

Oklahoma Library Assn.—pres., Edward R. Johnson, Oklahoma State Univ., Stillwater, OK 74078-0375; pres.-elect, Janis Keene, Tulsa City-Cnty. L., 400 Civic Ctr., Tulsa, OK 74103; exec. dir., Kay Boies, Oklahoma L. Assn., 300 Hardy Dr., Edmond, OK 73013; (405) 348-0506; FAX: (405) 348-7027 (at *Kinko's*). (Officers change July 1993.)

Oregon Library Assn.—pres., Maureen Sloan, Oregon Grad. Inst., 19600 N.W. Von Neumann Dr., Portland, OR 97006; (503) 690-1060; pres.-elect, Deborah Jacobs, Corvallis-Benton Cnty. P. L., 645 N.W. Monroe Ave., Corvallis, OR 97330; mailing address: Oregon L. Assn., 1270 Chemeketa St. N.E., Salem, OR 97301. (Officers change Sept. 1992.)

Pacific Northwest Library Assn.—pres., Don Miller, Seattle P. L., c/o Greenlake L., 7364 E. Greenlake Dr. N., Seattle, WA 98115; (206) 684-7545; pres.-elect, June Pinnell-Stephens, Fairbanks North Star Borough P. L. & Regl. Ctr., Noel Wien L., 1215 Cowles St., Fairbanks, AK 99701. (Officers change Oct. 1992.)

Pennsylvania Library Assn.—pres., Diane L. Ambrose, Beaver Cnty. Fed. L. Sys., 1260 N. Brodhead Rd., Monaca, PA 15061; pres.-elect, Christine Roysdon, Lehigh Univ., Fairchild-Martindale L. 8A, Bethlehem, PA 18015; exec. dir., Margaret S. Bauer, Pennsylvania L. Assn., 3107 N. Front St., Harrisburg, PA 17110; (PA) (800) 622-3308 *or* (717) 233-3113; FAX: (717) 233-3121. (Officers change Oct. 1992.)

Rhode Island Library Assn.—pres., Judith Paster, 52 Seaview Ave., Cranston, RI 02905; (401) 467-8898; pres.-elect, Janet A. Levesque, Cumberland P. L., 1464 Diamond Hill Rd., Cumberland, RI 02864; mailing address: Rhode Island L. Assn., 300 Richmond St., Providence, RI 02903. (Officers change Nov. 1992.)

South Carolina Library Assn.—pres., David Cohen, Coll. of Charleston L., 38 Gibbes St., Charleston, SC 29401; pres.-elect, Claude W. Blakely, c/o Greenville Cnty. L., 300 College St., Greenville, SC 29601; exec. secy., Drucilla Raines, South Carolina L. Assn., P.O. Box 219, Goose Creek, SC 29445; (803) 764-3668. (Officers change Oct. 1992.)

South Dakota Library Assn.—pres., Leon Raney, Briggs L., South Dakota State Univ., Brookings, SD 57007; (605) 688-5106; pres.-elect, Terri Davis, Deadwood P. L., 435 Williams St., Deadwood, SD 57732; mailing address: South Dakota L. Assn., P.O. Box 673, Pierre, SD 57501. (Officers change Oct. 1992.)

Southeastern Library Assn.—pres., James E. Ward, Crisman Mem. L., Lipscomb Univ., Box 4146, Nashville, TN 37204-3951; pres.-elect, Gail Lazenby, Cobb Cnty. P. L., 266 Roswell St., Marietta, GA 30060; exec. secy., Claudia Medori, Southeastern L. Assn., P.O. Box 987, Tucker, GA 30085-0987; (404) 939-5080 (also FAX). (Officers change Dec. 1992.)

Tennessee Library Assn.—pres., Patricia Watson, Knox Cnty. P. L., 500 W. Church Ave., Knoxville, TN 37902; pres.-elect, Carolyn Daniel, McGavock High Sch. L., 3150 McGavock Pike, Nashville, TN 37214; exec. secy., Betty Nance, Tennessee L. Assn., P.O. Box 120085, Nashville, TN 37212; (615) 297-8316; FAX: (615) 269-1807. (Officers change July 1993.)

Texas Library Assn.—pres., James Stewart, Victoria P. L., 302 N. Main, Victoria, TX 77901-6592; pres.-elect, E. Dale Cluff, Texas Tech Univ. Ls., Lubbock, TX 79409-0002; exec. dir., Patricia H. Smith, Texas L. Assn., 3355 Bee Cave Rd. #603, Austin, TX 78746; (512) 328-1518; FAX: (512) 328-8852. (Officers change Mar. 1993.)

Utah Library Assn.—pres., Randy J. Olsen, 3080 Lee L., Brigham Young Univ., Provo, UT 84602; pres.-elect, Marian Karpisek, Salt Lake Sch. Dist., 1430 Andrew Ave., Salt Lake City, UT 84104; exec. secy., Don Trottier, Utah L. Assn., 2150 S. 300 W., Ste. 16, Salt Lake City, UT 84115; (801) 466-5888 *or* (801) 782-6409. (Officers change May 1993.)

Vermont Library Assn.—pres., Paula Baker, Rutland Free L., 10 Court St., Rutland, VT 05701; (802) 773-1860; pres.-elect, Laurel Stanley, Lyndon State Coll. L., Lyndonville, VT 05851; mailing address: Vermont L. Assn., Box 803, Burlington, VT 05402-0803. (Officers change May 1993.)

Virgin Islands Library Assn.—pres. of *St. Thomas* L. Assn., Lorraine Galiber Gundel, P.O. Box 10272, St. Thomas, VI 00801; (809) 774-9991 *or* (809) 776-0211; pres. of *St. Croix* L. Assn., Wallace Williams, P.O. Box 2720, Christiansted, St. Croix, VI 00820; (809) 773-5715; FAX: (809) 773-5327. (Officers change June 1993.)

Virginia Library Assn.—pres., Steve Matthews, Currier L., Foxcroft Sch., Middleburg, VA 22117; pres.-elect, Liz Hamilton, Campbell Cnty. P. L., P.O. Box 310, Rustburg, VA 24588; exec. dir., Deborah Trocchi, Virginia L. Assn., 669 S. Washington St., Alexandria, VA 22314-4109; (703) 519-7853; FAX: (703) 519-7732. (Officers change Dec. 1992.)

Washington Library Assn.—pres., Barbara Tolliver, King Cnty. L. Sys., 300 8th Ave. N., Seattle, WA 98109; (206) 684-9000; pres.-elect, Randall Hensley, Univ. of Washington Ls., OUGL, DF-10, Seattle, WA 98195; mailing address: Marge Burns, Correspondence Secy., Washington L. Assn., 1232 143rd Ave. SE, Bellevue, WA 98007. (Officers change Aug. 1993.)

West Virginia Library Assn.—pres., Pam Ford, Marshall Univ., Morrow L., 400 Hal Greer Blvd., Huntington, WV 25755-2060; (304) 736-9038; pres.-elect, Matt Onion, Cabell Cnty. P. L., 455 9th St. Plaza, Huntington, WV 25701; mailing address: West Virginia L. Assn., c/o Frederic Glazer, West Virginia L. Comm., Sci. & Cultural Ctr., Charleston, WV 25305. (Officers change Nov. 1992.)

Wisconsin Library Assn.—pres., Kathy Pletcher, Univ. of Wisconsin, Green Bay, L., 2420 Nicolet Dr., Green Bay, WI 54301; pres.-elect, Mildred N. Larson, Phillips Mem. P. L., 400 Eau Claire St., Eau Claire, WI 54701; exec. dir., Larry J. Martin, Wisconsin L. Assn., 4785 Hayes Rd., Madison, WI 53704; (608) 242-2040; FAX: (608) 242-2050. (Officers change Jan. 1993.)

Wyoming Library Assn.—pres., Dorothy Middleton, East High Sch., 2800 E. Pershing Blvd., Cheyenne, WY 82001; vice-pres., Laurn Wilhelm, Univ. of Wyoming L., UW Sta., Laramie, WY 82071; exec. secy., Ray Lansing, Wyoming L. Assn., P.O. Box 1387, Cheyenne, WY 82003; (307) 632-7622; FAX: (307) 634-9391. (Officers change Sept. 1992.)

Affiliates

Under Article X, Section 1, of the Constitution and upon application formally made by the proper officers, the Council has affiliated with the American Library Association the following national organizations of kindred purposes. Some of these societies meet annually at the time and place of ALA meetings. ALA recommends to those of its members to whom such connection is appropriate, membership also in these organizations.

NB: For affiliates of American Assn. of School Librarians, see p. 22.

American Association of Law Libraries

Headquarters: 53 W. Jackson Blvd., Room 940, Chicago, IL 60604; (312)939-4764.

Pres., Carolyn Ahearn, Shaw Pittman Potts & Trowbridge, 2300 N St. NW, Washington, DC 20037; (202) 663-8500; pres.-elect, Mark Estes, Holme, Roberts & Owen, 1700 Lincoln St., Ste. 4100, Denver, CO 80203; (303) 861-7000; exec. dir., Judith Genesen, Hq.

Officers change July 1993.

American Indian Library Association (AILA)

Pres., Naomi Caldwell-Wood, 291 Williams St., Providence, RI 02906; (401) 421-2598; pres.-elect, Rhonda Harris Taylor, 707 W. Tyler, Bullard, TX 75757; (903) 586-2471, ext. 52. Secy., Lisa Mitten, (412) 648-7723; FAX: (412) 648-1245; EMAIL: LMITTEN@PITTVMS.

Officers change July 1993.

American Society for Information Science

Headquarters: 8720 Georgia Ave. #501, Silver Spring, MD 20910-3602; (410) 495-0900.

Pres., Ann E. Prentice, Office of the Provost, Univ. of South Florida, 4202 E. Fowler Ave., Acad. Affairs, Adm. 226, Tampa, FL 33620-6100; (813) 974-2154; pres.-elect, Jose-Marie Griffiths, Hq.; exec. dir., Richard B. Hill, Hq.

Officers change Oct. 1992.

Asian/Pacific American Librarians Association

Pres., Marjorie H. Li, Rutgers. The State Univ. of New Jersey, New Brunswick, NJ 08803; (908) 932-5904; FAX: (908) 932-5888; BIT: "MLI@ZODIAC"; pres.-elect/vice pres., Ravindra N. Sharma, Dir., Univ. of Evansville, 1800 Lincoln Ave. Evansville, IN 47722; (812) 479-2485.

Officers change June 1993.

Association for Library and Information Science Education

Headquarters: 4101 Lake Boone Trail, Ste. 201, Raleigh, NC 27607; (919) 787-5181.

Pres., Adele M. Fasick, Univ. of Toronto SLIS, 140 St. George St., Toronto, ON, CANADA M5S 1A1; (416) 978-3202; FAX: (201) 846-0468; pres.-elect, Timothy Sineath, Univ. of Kentucky, Coll. of L. & Info. Sci., 502 M.I. King S., Lexington, KY 40506-0391; (606) 257-8100; FAX: (606) 257-1563; exec. dir., Sally Nicholson, Hq.

Officers change Jan. 1993.

Association of Research Libraries

Headquarters: 1527 New Hampshire Ave., NW, Washington, DC 20036; (202) 232-8056, ext. 450.

Pres., Arthur Curley, Copley Sq., Boston, MA 02117, (617) 536-5400, ext. 450; pres.-elect, Susan Nutter, North Carolina State Univ., Box 7111, Raleigh, NC 27695-7111; (919) 737-7188; FAX: (919) 737-3628; exec. dir., Duane Webster, Hq.

Officers change Oct. 1992.

Black Caucus of ALA

Pres., Alex Boyd, Dir., Newark P.L., 5 Washington St., Newark, NJ 07101; (201) 733-7780; newsl. ed., George C. Grant, Dir. of L. Serv., Rollins Coll., Olin L., 1000 Holt Ave., Campus Box 2744, Winter Park, FL 32789-4499; (407) 646-2676; FAX: (407) 646-1515.

Officers change July 1993.

Canadian Library Association

Headquarters: 200 Elgin St., Ste. 602, Ottawa, ON, K2P 1L5 Canada; (613)232-9625.

Pres., Margaret Andrewes, R.R. 3, Beamsville, ON L0R 1B0 Canada; pres.-elect, Francoise Hebert, 7 Thornwood Rd., #302, Toronto, ON M4W 2R8; exec. dir., Karen Adams, Hq.

Officers change June 1992.

Chinese-American Librarians Association

Headquarters: c/o Univ. of Colorado Health Sciences Ctr., 4200 E. 9th Ave., Denver, CO 80262; (303) 270-6444.

Pres., Roy Chang, Western Illinois Univ. L., Macomb, IL 61455; (309) 298-2731; pres.-elect, Carl Chan, Cataloging Ln., Academic L., Defense Lang. Inst., Monterey, CA 93944-5007; (408) 647-5578; exec. secy., Eveline Yang, Hq.

Officers change June 1992.

Council on Library/Media Technicians, Inc.

Headquarters: P.O. Box 951, Oxen Hill, MD 20750; (202) 662-6156.

Pres., Beverly Patton, Boehringer Mannheim, 9115 Hague Road, Indianapolis, IN 46250; (317) 576-7519; pres.-elect, to be elected; exec. secy., Ava J. Everett, Gen. Rdng. Rm. Div., L. of Congress, First and Independence Ave., SE, Washington, DC 20540.

Officers change June 1992.

Friends of Libraries USA

Headquarters: American L. Assn., 50 E. Huron St., Chicago, IL 60611; (215) 790-1674.

Pres., Joseph Fitzsimmons, Hq; exec. dir., Sandy Dolnick, 1326 Spruce St. #1105, Philadelphia, PA 19107; staff liaison, Peggy Barber.

Officers change June 1993.

Laubach Literacy International, Laubach Literacy Action (LLI/LLA)

Headquarters: 1320 Jamesville Ave., Box 131, Syracuse, NY 13210; (315) 422-9121.

Pres., Robert F. Caswell; CEO; exec. dir., Peter Waite, Hq.

Officers: no terms.

Literacy Volunteers of America, Inc.

Headquarters: 5795 Widewaters Pkwy., Syracuse, NY 13214; (315) 445-8000.

Ch., William H. Wilson, Hq.; pres., Helen Jinx Crouch, Hq.

Officers change November 1992.

Medical Library Association

Headquarters: 6 N. Michigan Ave., Ste. 300, Chicago, IL 60602; (312) 419-9094.

Pres., Jacqueline D. Bastille; pres.-elect, June Fulton, Med. Doc. Sect., ISI, 3501 Market St., Philadelphia, PA 19104; (215) 386-0100, ext. 1189; exec. dir., Carla J. Funk, Hq.

Officers change May 1993.

Music Library Association

Headquarters: c/o Academic Services, Inc., P.O. Box 487, Canton, MA 02021; (812) 855-2970.

Pres., Don L. Roberts, Music L., Northwestern Univ., 1935 Sheridan Rd., Evanston, IL 60208-2300; (708) 491-3434; pres.-elect, Michael Ochs, W.W. Norton, 500 5th Ave., New York, NY 10036; (212) 354-5500; exec. secy., Richard Griscom, Univ. of Louisville, Music L., 2301 S. 3rd St., Louisville, KY 40292; (502) 588-5659.

Officers change Feb. 1993.

National Librarians Association

Headquarters: P.O. Box 486, Alma, MI 48801; (517) 463-7227.

Pres., Alvin R. Bailey; pres.-elect, Matthew C. Kubiak, Dir., Bloomington P.L., 205 E. Olive St., Bloomington, IL 61701; (309) 828-6091; FAX: (309) 828-7312; secy., Peter A. Dollard, Hq.

Officers change July 1993.

Oral History Association

Headquarters: 1093 Broxton Ave. #720, Los Angeles, CA 90024; (213) 825-0597.

Pres., Terry Birdwhistle, Oral History Prog., Univ. of Kentucky L., Lexington, KY 40506-0039, (606) 257-1466; pres.-elect, A.L. Broussard, Texas A & M Univ., Dept. of History, College Sta., TX 77843; (409) 845-7151; exec. secy., Richard C. Smith, Hq.

Officers change Oct. 1992.

REFORMA (National Association to Promote Library Services to the Spanish Speaking)

Pres., Martin Gomez, P.L., 125 14th St., Oakland, CA 94612; (415) 273-3281; pres.-elect, to be elected.

Officers change June 1992.

Sociedad de Bibliotecarios de Puerto Rico

Headquarters: Univ. of Puerto Rico Sta., P.O. Box 22898, Rio Piedras, PR 00931; (809) 758-2525, ext. 1224.

Pres., Auria Jimenez de Banekinto, Hq.; pres.-elect, to be elected.

Officers change Oct. 1992.

Theatre Library Association

Headquarters: 111 Amsterdam Ave., New York, NY 10023; (212)870-1644.

Pres., James Poteat, Hq.; vice-pres., Bob Taylor, Billy Rose Theatre Clln., Hq.; exec. secy., Richard M. Buck, Hq.

Officers change Jan. 1993.

Ukrainian Library Association of America
(Ukraïns'ke Bibliotechne Toverystvo Ameryky)

Headquarters: European Div., L. of Congress, Washington, DC 20540; (202) 707-8483.

Pres., Bohdan Yasinsky, Hq.; pres.-elect, Jurij Dobczansky, Hq.; exec. secy., Valentina Limonchenko.

Officers change June 1992.

Urban Libraries Council

Headquarters: 500 E. Marylyn Ave. D-50, State College, PA 16801; (814) 237-0194; FAX: (814) 238-3847.

Pres., Robert C. Wilburn, Colonial Williamsburg Fdtn., P.O. Box 1776, Williamsburg, VA 23187-1776; (804) 220-7401; vice-pres., James R. Dawe, 750 B St., Ste. 2100, San Diego, CA 92101; (619) 685-3003; exec. dir., Keith Doms, Hq.

Officers change June 1992.

Representatives to Other Organizations

ALA has had for many years official representation to outside organizations. It also cooperates with other organizations in the establishment of councils, joint committees, and other groups that can work together in activities of mutual interest. When the work of an outside organization falls within the field of responsibility of one division, that division names the ALA representative. When an organization to which ALA does not now have representation asks for a representative, the decision of whether to make the appointment is made by the Committee on Organization. If the need for immediate action arises, the president makes the decision, based upon staff analysis and recommendation, and subject to later review by COO. Appointments made by the divisions are so indicated.

4-H Programs Extension Service—Elizabeth M. Simmons, ALSC.

Adolescent Pregnancy Prevention Network (Children's Defense Fund)—Linda Waddle, YALSA.

Alliance of Information and Referral Systems—to be appointed, PLA.

American Association for Gifted Children—to be appointed, ALSC.

American Association for Higher Education (AAHE)—to be appointed, ACRL.

American Association for State and Local History—Nancy M. Godleski, LHRT.

American Association for the Advancement of Science—to be appointed, ACRL; Consortium of Affiliates for International Programs—to be appointed, ACRL; Sect. on Information, Computing, and Communication Com. T—Jay K. Lucker, ALA.

American Association of University Professors (AAUP)—to be appointed, ACRL.

American Chemical Society (ACS)—Arleen N. Somerville, ACRL.

American Correctional Association—to be appointed, ASCLA.

American Council on Education—to be appointed, ACRL.

American Institute for Conservation of Historic and Artistic Works—Constance L. Brooks, ALCTS.

American National Red Cross/Red Cross Youth—to be appointed, YALSA.

American National Standards Institute (ANSI): Accredited Standards Com. on Information Processing (X3)—Paul E. Peters, LITA; Accredited Standards Com. on Instructional Audiovisual Systems (PH7)—Howard S. White, LTR.

American Society for Information Science—Patricia H. Earnest, LITA; Robert V. Williams, LHRT.

American Youth Work Center—to be appointed, YALSA.

Anglo-American Cataloguing Committee for Cartographic Materials—Nancy J. Edstrom, MAGERT.

Association for Asian Studies, Committee on East Asian Libraries—to be appointed, ACRL.

Association for Childhood Education International—to be appointed, ALSC.

Association for Children and Adults with Learning Disabilities—Clara Nalli Bohrer, ALSC; to be appointed, AASL.

Association for Educational Communications and Technology—to be appointed.

Association for Information and Image Management (AIIM)—Norman J. Shaffer, ALCTS; alt., Myron Chace, ALCTS-RLMS.

Association for Library and Information Science Education—Standing Com. on Library Education (SCOLE).

Association for Supervision and Curriculum Development—M. Ellen Jay, AASL.

Association for the Bibliography of History—Kenneth J. Potts, LHRT.

Association for the Care of Children's Health—Maria B. Salvadore, ALSC.

Association of American Colleges (AAC)—to be appointed, ACRL.

Association of Radio Reading Services, Inc.—to be appointed, ASCLA.

Big Brothers and Big Sisters of America—Helen Mae Mullen, ALSC.

Boy Scouts of America—Caroline S. Parr, ALSC.

Boys Clubs of America—to be appointed, ALSC.

Camp Fire, Inc.—Anitra T. Steele, ALSC.

Cartographic Users' Advisory Council—Margaret S. Brill, MAGERT.

Center for Early Adolescence—to be appointed, YALSA.

Chief Officers of State Library Agencies (COSLA)—Andrew M. Hansen, ASCLA.

Child Welfare League of America—Ethel N. Ambrose, ALSC.

Children's Defense Fund—Effie Lee Morris, ALSC.

Coalition of Adult Education Organizations—Andrew M. Hansen, Christina C. Young, RASD.

Coalition of Networked Information—Thomas Kirk, Noreen S. Aldredge, ACRL.

Council of National Library and Information Associations—Lucille C. Thomas, ALA.

Council of Professional Associations on Federal Statistics (COPAFS)—Peter B. Allison, Jean Stratford, Rachel Senner Van Wingen, GODORT.

Day Care and Child Development Council of America—James W. Hoogstra, ALSC.

Decimal Classification Editorial Policy Committee (Joint Lake Placid Education Foundation/ALA)—Patricia M. Thomas, ALCTS. Appointed by Lake Placid Edu. Fdn. from nominations by ALCTS-CCS—Joanne S. Anderson; Elaine F. Svenonius; Helena M. Van Deroet.

Documentation Abstracts, Inc.—David M. Pilachowski, RASD.

Family Resource Coalition—to be appointed, YALSA.

Federal Library and Information Center Committee—Adelaide Del Frate.

Federation of Organizations for Professional Women—Com. on the Status of Women in Librarianship.

Freedom to Read Foundation—(see p. 167).

Future Homemakers of America—Lily Helwig, YALSA.

Girl Scouts of America—to be appointed, ALSC.

Girls Clubs of America—to be appointed, ALSC.

Illuminating Engineers Society, Subcommittee on Library Lighting—Howard S. White, LTR.

Interagency Council on Library Resources for Nursing—Frederic C. Pachman, ASCLA.

International Association of School Librarianship—Valerie J. Downes, AASL.

International Board on Books for Young People, U.S. Section, Executive Board—Phyllis Van Orden, Susan Roman, Mary Lou White, ALSC.

International Federation of Library Associations and Institutions (IFLA)—Marilyn L. Miller, ALA.

Section on Acquisition and Exchanges—Katina Strauch (1993).

Section of Administrative Libraries—Judith R. Bernstein (1995).

Section of Art Libraries—Stephen C. Bloom (1995).

Section on Bibliography—Robert Holley (1993).

Section of Biological and Medical Science Libraries—Eleanor Mathews (1993).

Section on Cataloging—Olivia Madison (1993); Nancy Regina John (1995).

Section of Children's Libraries—Shirley A. Fitzgibbons (1993).

Section on Classification and Indexing—Julianne Beall (1993); Pat Molholt (1995).

Section on Conservation—Mark Roosa (1995).

Section on Education and Training—Robert D. Stueart (1993).

Section on Geography and Map Libraries—David A. Cobb (1995).

Section on Government Information and Official Publications—Linda Eileen Williamson (1993).

Section on Information Technology—Donald E. Riggs (1993); Ching-chih Chen (1995).

Section on Interlending and Document Delivery—Rodney M. Hersberger (1993).

Section on Library Buildings and Equipment—David Kaser (1993); David C. Weber (1995).

Section on Library Services to Multicultural Populations—Charles T. Townley (1993); E. J. Josey (1995).

Section on Library Theory and Research—Beverly P. Lynch (1993); Darlene E. Weingand (1995).

Section on Libraries Serving the Disadvantaged Persons—Janice M. Beaudin (1993).

Section on National Libraries—Henriette Avram (1995).

Section on Public Libraries—J. Dennis Day (1993).

Section on Rare and Precious Books and Documents—Michael T. Ryan (1993).

Section on School Libraries—Mary Biblo (1993).

Section on Science and Technology Libraries—Martin Kesselman (1995).

Section on Serials Publications—Ruth C. Carter (1995).

Section on Statistics—Raymond L. Carpenter (1993).

Section on University Libraries and other General Research Libraries—Hwa-Wei Lee (1993); Joseph A. Boissé (1995).

International Reading Association (IRA)—Clara Nalli Bohrer, ALSC; to be appointed, AASL.

Invent America—to be appointed, AASL.

Joint Advisory Committee on Nonbook Materials—Janice De Sirey; Diane Hill, ALCTS.

Joint Council on Educational Telecommunications (JCET), Board of Directors—Eileen D. Cooke, ALA.

Joint Steering Committee for Revision of AACR—Janet Swan Hill (1992), ALCTS.

Junior Achievement—Alice Stern, YALSA.

Libraries and Culture—Michele V. Cloonan, LHRT.

Library of Congress/NLS Cost Study Committee—Donna O. Dziedzic, ASCLA.

Library of Congress Cataloging in Publication Advisory Group—Marion T. Reid, ALA; Robert P. Holley, ACRL; to be appointed, PLA.

Library of Congress Geography and Map Div.—Elizabeth U. Mangan, MAGERT.

Library of Congress Network Advisory Committee—Joseph F. Shubert, ALA.

Modern Language Association (MLA)—to be appointed, ACRL.

National Association for the Education of Young Children—Toni A. Bernardi, ALSC.

National Association for the Perpetuation and Preservation of Storytelling—Elizabeth M. Simmons, ALSC.

National Association of Secondary School Principals—Dawn Heller, AASL.

National Center for Technology Software, National Advisory Board—to be appointed, AASL.

National Center for Youth Law—Carlos L. Najera, YALSA.

National Center on Institutions and Alternatives—Ann M. Chambers, YALSA.

National Coalition to Support Sexuality Education (SIECUS)—Harriet Selenstone, ALSC.

National Commission on Resources for Youth—to be appointed, YALSA.

National Committee for Citizens in Education—Deborah Church, YALSA.

National Committee on Pay Equity—Com. on Pay Equity.

National Committee for the Prevention of Child Abuse—to be appointed, ALSC.

National Congress of Parents and Teachers—to be appointed, AASL.

National Coordinating Committee for the Promotion of History—Steven W. Sowards, LHRT.

National Council for the Accreditation of Teacher Education: Board of Examiners—Roger S. Ashley, AASL; Pauletta B. Bracy, AASL; Marilyn W. Greenberg, AASL; Selvin W. Royal, AASL; Laurene E. Zaporozhetz, ACRL. Specialty Area Studies Board—Marilyn L. Miller, AASL.

National Council for the Social Studies—Christine B. Woll, AASL.

National Council of La Raza—Carlos L. Najera, YALSA.

National Council of Teachers of English—Hilda L. Jay AASL; Deborah Church, YALSA.

National Council of Teachers of Mathematics—to be appointed, AASL.

National Forum on Information Literacy—Patricia S. Breivik, ALA; Barbara J. Ford, ACRL.

National Information Standards Organization (NISO): Standards Com. on Library Work, Documentation and Related Publishing Practices (Z39)—Myron Chase, ALCTS; alt., Glenn E. Patton, ALCTS.

National Institute for Conservation—Margaret S. Child, ALCTS.

National Juvenile Law Center—Susan Rosenzweig, YALSA.

National Multiple Sclerosis Society—to be appointed, ALSC.

National Women's Studies Association—Com. on the Status of Women in Librarianship.

National Technical Information Service—Jim Walsh, MAGERT.

North American Cartographic Information Society—Paul Stout, MAGERT.

North American Serials Interest Group—Susan A. Davis, ALCTS-SS.

Northeast Map Organization—Thornton P. McGlamery, MAGERT.

Parent Cooperative Preschool International—Blair B. Christolon, ALSC.

Parents Without Partners—Lucy C. Marx, ALSC.

Planned Parenthood Federation of America—Lily Helwig, YALSA.

Puppeteers of America—Frances J. McCurdy, ALSC.

Reading Is Fundamental (RIF)—to be appointed, ALSC.

Salvation Army—to be appointed, ALSC.

Serials Industry Systems Advisory Committee (SISAC): Identification Code Subcom.—Minna C. Saxe; Order and Claim Formats Subcom.—Joyce McDonough; Membership and Publicity Subcom.—Betty Landesman, ALCTS-SS.

Sex Information and Education Council of the U.S. (SIECUS)—Deborah Church, YALSA.

Society of American Archivists—Robert S. Martin, LHRT.

Special Libraries Association, Geog. and Map Div.—Jim Gillespie, MAGERT.

U.S. Board on Books for Young People—Angeline Moscatt; Helen Mae Mullen.

U.S. Geological Survey—Wendy R. Hassibe, MAGERT.

U.S. Mission to the United Nations—Jane P. Franck.

U.S. President's Committee on Employment of People with Disabilities—Alice L. Hagenmeyer, PLA.

Western Association of Map Libraries—Greg Armento, MAGERT.

ALA Memberships in Other Organizations

Alliance of Information and Referral Systems (PLA)

Alliance of Nonprofit Mailers (Administrative Services)

American Council on Education

American National Standards Institute

American Society of Information Science (LITA)

American Standards Committee (ASC) X3, Information Processing Systems (LITA)

Association for Library and Information Science Education (Office for Accreditation)

Chicago Book Clinic (Publishing)

Coalition for Adult Education

Committee for Education Funding (Washington Office)

Council of National Library and Information Associations

Council on Postsecondary Accreditation

Federation of Organizations for Professional Women (Committee on the Status of Women in Librarianship)

First Amendment Congress (OIF)

Freedom to Read Foundation

Illinois OCLC Users Group (Headquarters Library)

Independent Sector

International Association of School Librarians (AASL)

International Federation of Library Associations and Institutions

Literacy Volunteers of America (OLOS)

National Coalition Against Censorship (OIF)

National Committee on Pay Equity (Committee on Pay Equity)

National Council for the Accreditation of Teacher Education

National Humanities Alliance

National Information Standards Organization

National Institute for the Conservation of Cultural Property (ALCTS)

National Women's Studies Association (Committee on the Status of Women in Librarianship)

Public Service Satellite Consortium

Society of National Association Publications (*American Libraries*)

Special Libraries Association (Headquarters Library)

U.S. Board on Books for Young People

ALA Headquarters

Headquarters: 50 E. Huron St., Chicago, IL 60611; (312) 944-6780
Peggy Sullivan, *executive director*
Washington Office: 110 Maryland Ave., NE, Washington, DC 20002; (202) 547-4440
Eileen D. Cooke, *director*
Choice Office: 100 Riverview Ctr., Middletown, CT 06457; (203) 347-6933
Patricia E. Sabosik, *editor/publisher*
(See directory on page v for additional telephone and telefax numbers.
Unless otherwise noted, the personnel listed below are located at
ALA Headquarters in Chicago.)

EXECUTIVE OFFICE

Executive Director: Peggy Sullivan.
Deputy Executive Director: Roger H. Parent.
Executive Board Secretariat: Emily Melton.
Council Secretariat: Lois Ann Gregory.
Office of the President: Carol Nielsen.
Headquarters Library and Information Center: librarian, Charles Harmon; reference librarian, Reneé Prestegard.
Library Fellows Program and International Relations Office: director, Robert P. Doyle.
Planning and Budgeting Director: Gregory Calloway.

ADMINISTRATIVE SERVICES

Associate Executive Director, Administrative Services: Ernest Martin.
Chapter Relations Office Director: Gerald G. Hodges.
Chapter Relations Assistant Director: Julie Ann Geissler.
Customer Services Director: Gerald G. Hodges.
Customer Relations Manager: Krista Rodino.
Data Processing Manager: Richard Roman.
Controller: Russell Swedowski.
Human Resources Acting Director: Louise Brewer.
Information Processing Manager: Ofelia Condei.
Membership Services Director: Gerald G. Hodges.
Membership Promotion Manager: to be appointed.
Membership Relations Manager: Eugenia A. Porter.
Office Services Manager: Maribeth Haney.
Reprographics & Distribution Center Manager: Lee Patenaude.

COMMUNICATIONS

Associate Executive Director, Communications: Peggy Barber.
Director of Marketing: Marcia J. Kuszmaul.

ALA Graphics

Director: Marcia J. Kuszmaul.
Marketing & Production Assistant: Chris Martin.

Conference Services

Conference Services Director: Paul Graller.
Planning & Scheduling Manager: to be appointed.
Conference Editorial & Production Manager: Pier A. London.
Conference Coordinator: Gloria Gray.

Development Office

Director: Delstene Atkinson.

Public Information Office

Director: Linda Wallace.
Public Information Officer: Pamela Goodes.

Public Programs

Humanities Grant Administrator: Deborah Robertson.

PROGRAM SERVICES

Associate Executive Director: JoAn S. Segal.

Divisional

American Association of School Librarians: executive director, Ann C. Weeks; deputy executive director, Barbara R. Herrin; coordinator for program support, Donald C. Adcock.
American Library Trustee Association: executive director. Susan Roman.
Association for Library Collections and Technical Services: executive director, Karen Muller; deputy executive director, to be appointed.
Association for Library Service to Children: executive director, Susan Roman; deputy executive director, Eileen Fitzsimons; program officer, Stephanie Dodge.
Association of College and Research Libraries: executive director, Althea H. Jenkins; deputy executive director, Cathleen Bourdon; program officer, Mary Taylor; ed., *C&RL News*, Mary Ellen Kyger Davis.
Association of Specialized and Cooperative Library Agencies: executive director, Andrew M. Hansen; deputy executive director, Joanne L. Crispen.
Library Administration and Management Association: executive director, Karen Muller; deputy executive director, Elizabeth Dreazen.
Library and Information Technology Association: executive director, Linda J. Knutson; interim program officer, Rob Carlson.
Public Library Association: executive director, to be appointed; deputy executive director, Bridget Bradley; program officer, Sandra Causey Garrison.
Reference and Adult Services Division: executive director, Andrew M. Hansen; program officer, to be appointed.
Young Adult Library Services Association: executive director, Ann C. Weeks; deputy executive director, Linda L. Waddle.

Round Tables

Armed Forces Libraries Round Table: staff liaison, Patricia A. Muir.
Continuing Library Education Network and Exchange Round Table: staff liaison, Margaret Myers.
Ethnic Materials Information Exchange Round Table: staff liaison, Mattye L. Nelson.
Exhibits Round Table: staff liaison, Paul Graller.
Federal Librarians Round Table: staff liaison, Anne A. Heanue.
Government Documents Round Table: staff liaison, Patricia A. Muir.
Independent Librarians Exchange Round Table: staff liaison, Margaret Myers.
Intellectual Freedom Round Table: staff liaison, Anne E. Levinson.
International Relations Round Table: staff liaison, Robert P. Doyle.
Library History Round Table: staff liaison, Charles Harmon.
Library Instruction Round Table: staff liaison, Jeniece Guy.
Library Research Round Table: staff liaison, Mary Jo Lynch.
Map and Geography Round Table: staff liaison, JoAn S. Segal.
New Members Round Table: staff liaison, JoAn S. Segal.
Social Responsibilities Round Table: staff liaison, Mattye L. Nelson.
Staff Organizations Round Table: staff liaison, Jeniece Guy.
Video Round Table: staff liaison, JoAn S. Segal.

Offices

(See pp. 111–12 for statements of purpose.)

Office for Accreditation: director, Prudence W. Dalrymple.
Office for Intellectual Freedom: director, Judith F. Krug; assistant director, Anne E. Levinson.
Office for Library Outreach Services: director, Mattye L. Nelson; Bell Atlantic/ALA Family Literacy Project director, Margaret Monsour; ALA Minority Fellow, 1992/93, to be appointed.
Office for Library Personnel Resources: director, Margaret Myers; assistant director, Jeniece Guy.
Office for Research and Statistics: director, Mary Jo Lynch.
Washington Office: director, Eileen D. Cooke; deputy director, Carol C. Henderson; associate director, Anne A. Heanue.

ALA PUBLISHING

Associate Executive Director, Publishing: to be appointed.
Associate Publisher, New Products: Arthur Plotnik.

108

Operations Manager: Robert G. Hershman.

ALA Books and Publishing Services

General Manager: David M. Epstein.
Senior Editor: Herbert Bloom.
Editor: Bonnie J. Smothers.
Managing Editor: to be appointed.
Production Manager: Dianne M. Rooney.
Project Editor: Mary Huchting.
Director of Manufacturing: Eileen Mahoney.
Production Editors: Amy I. Brown, Bruce Frausto, Josephine Gibson-Porter, Daniel L. Lewis, Beverly Thymes, Donovan Vicha.

American Libraries

Editor: Thomas Gaughan.
Managing Editor: Leonard Kniffel.

Senior Editor, production: Edith McCormick.
Senior Editor, news/articles: Gordon Flagg.
Associate Editor: Beverly Goldberg.
Associate Editor, LEADS: Jon Kartman.
Assistant Editor: Susan Carton.
Editorial Assistant: Georgia Okotete.

Booklist/Reference Books Bulletin/Book Links

Editor: Bill Ott.
Managing Editor: Stuart Whitwell.
Adult Books Editor: John Mort.
Editor, Books for Youth: Sally Estes.
Audiovisual Media Editor: Irene Wood.
Reference Books Bulletin Editor: Sandra Whiteley.

Book Links editor: Barbara Elleman.

Library Technology Reports

Editor: Howard S. White.

Marketing Services

Marketing Director: Evelyn Shaevel.
Marketing Manager (Journals): Danea Rush.
Marketing Manager (Books): Kathy A. Repholz.
Design and Production Manager: Ellen Scanlon.
Copyright, Rights and Permissions: to be appointed.
Advertising Traffic Manager: Cheryl Daszkiewicz.

ALA Offices: Statements of Purpose

Headquarters Library and Information Center

The Headquarters Library maintains collections of current professional literature and unique, Association-related materials that enable it to participate in a wide range of activities, including interlibrary cooperation, resource-sharing, and the provision of materials and information to ALA staff, Association members, the library profession at large, and the general public. While the primary goal of the Headquarters Library is to serve as an information resource center for ALA staff as they conduct the work of the Association and serve the membership, the library also functions as one of the key referral and response points for information requests coming into Headquarters by mail and telephone. The library is charged with the responsibility of maintaining the official records and publications of the Association, and in this capacity, it collects archival materials, works with staff in record and file maintenance, and serves as a liaison to the ALA Archives in Urbana.

Office for Accreditation

The purpose of the Office for Accreditation is to provide leadership in the development of standards for accreditation and to develop and maintain procedures for the implementation of the ALA accreditation function. In carrying out this purpose, the office performs the following functions: provides secretariat support for the Committee on Accreditation; gives assistance and support to library schools throughout the accreditation cycle (self-study, site visit, annual reporting); offers consultation and advice for programs considering application for initial accreditation; assists employers by providing information on the status of degrees held by applicants; provides information to prospective students on availability and location of accredited programs; maintains relationships for the Association with external oversight bodies, including the Council on Postsecondary Accreditation and the U.S. Department of Education; disseminates information to members and to the public on the role and function of accreditation, the ALA accreditation program, and graduate library education.

Office for Intellectual Freedom

The Office for Intellectual Freedom is charged with implementing ALA policies concerning the concept of intellectual freedom as embodied in the *Library Bill of Rights*, the Association's basic policy on free access to libraries and library materials. The goal of the office is to educate librarians and the general public about the nature and importance of intellectual freedom in libraries. To effect this goal, the office undertakes information, support, and coordination activities. These include distributing materials and information, preparing regular and special publications, maintaining the OIF exhibit, supervising liaison with the Freedom to Read Foundation (a separate corporation) and the LeRoy C. Merritt Humanitarian Fund (a trust), serving as liaison to the Intellectual Freedom Committee, coordinating activities of state intellectual freedom committees, and cooperating with other organizations whose purposes are similar to ALA's regarding intellectual freedom. All of these activities are carried on in accordance with the responsibility of the office to recommend, develop, implement, and maintain a total program for ALA in the area of intellectual freedom.

Office for Library Outreach Services

The office has a threefold statement of purpose: to promote the provision of library service to the urban and rural poor, of all ages, and to those people who are discriminated against because they belong to minority groups such as American Indians, Asians, Blacks, Latinos/Hispanics, Appalachians; to encourage the development of user-oriented informational and educational library services to meet the needs of the urban and rural poor, ethnic minority groups, the underemployed, school dropouts, the semiliterate and illiterate and those isolated by cultural differences; and to ensure that librarians and others have information, access to technical assistance, and continuing education opportunities to assist them in developing effective outreach programs.

Office for Library Personnel Resources

The Office for Library Personnel Resources combines ALA staff activities in library education, recruitment, and staff welfare to assist librarians and libraries in areas concerned with the rights, interests, and obligations of library personnel. The office serves as a major component within ALA that concerns itself with librarianship as a profession; with the individual's career goals; and the provision within library schools and libraries of policies and practices that enable staff to develop professionally.

Office for Public Information

The Public Information Office directs a year-round public awareness campaign for libraries and librarians at the national level, develops promotional materials to assist librarians with their public relations programs at the local level, coordinates media relations for the Association, and provides public relations counsel to members and communications support services to ALA and its units.

Office for Research and Statistics

The Office for Research and Statistics is charged with carrying out four functions in order to improve the effectiveness of the library profession: (1) To collect and interpret data to support and inform decision-making at ALA; (2) to collect or facilitate the collection of consistent and pertinent statistical data and other research results related to libraries and librarians; (3) to monitor ongoing research related to libraries and disseminate information about such studies within and outside the profession; (4) to facilitate quality research design in the studies and collection of data initiated by the ALA Executive Board, Council, Offices, Committees, Divisions, Round Tables, and other ALA units and to provide technical assistance.

Washington Office

The staff of the Washington Office acts as the link between ALA members and the federal government by relaying news of important government actions affecting libraries to the membership, and by supplying information and assistance to government agencies and Congress. The office makes official comment on proposed federal regulations concerning libraries and librarians, supports legislation benefiting libraries and library service, and works for meaningful appropriations levels for federal library-related programs. In addition, the office assists librarians in their contacts with government agencies and Congress, and works closely with state library associations, ALA units, and others in compiling data on library needs nationwide.

Periodicals Published by ALA

AASL Presidential Hotline. AASL. Semiannually. Free to members; not available by subscription.

ALA Washington Newsletter. ALA Washington Office. Irregular (minimum of 12 issues). Subscriptions, $25 a yr. Eds., Eileen D. Cooke, Carol C. Henderson.

ALCTS Network News. Irregular. Available through, BITNET and INTERNET. Free to members and nonmembers. To subscribe on BITNET or INTERNET, send to LISTSERV@UICVM.BITNET the message SUBSCRIBE.ALCTS [your first name—your last name]. Ed., Karen Muller.

ALCTS Newsletter. 6 times a year. Sent to all ALCTS members. Subscriptions to nonmembers, $25 a yr. ($35 foreign); single copies, $5. Ed., Ann G. Swartzell, 416 Library, Univ. of California, Berkeley, CA 94720.

ALSC Newsletter. Semiannually. Sent to all ALSC members; not available by subscription. Ed., Anitra T. Steele, ALSC/ALA, 50 E. Huron St., Chicago, IL 60611.

ALTA Newsletter. 6 issues a yr. Free to members; not available by subscription. Ed., Sharon A. Saulmon, 12228 High Meadow Ct., Oklahoma City, OK 73170.

American Indian Libraries Newsletter. Newsletter of the OLOS Advisory Committee's Subcommittee on Library Service for American Indian People in cooperation with the American Indian Library Association. Semiannual. Free to OLOS Advisory Committee members and members of the American Indian Library Association. Subscriptions: $5 to individuals; $7 to institutions; $10 overseas; $2 per back issue. Make checks payable to AILN; send to Charles Townley, Box 30006, Dept. 3475, Univ. L., New Mexico State Univ., Las Cruces, NM 88003. Eds., Mary W. Lockett and Lotsee Patterson, Univ. of Oklahoma, Sch. of L. & Inf. Studies, 401 W. Brooks, Rm. 120, Norman, OK 73019.

American Libraries. ALA. 11 issues a yr.; combined July-Aug. issue. Free to members. Single copies, $6. Available by subscription to organizations in U.S., Canada, and Mexico, $60 a yr.; other foreign, $70. Ed., Thomas Gaughan, ALA Hq.

Armed Forces Libraries Round Table of ALA Newsletter (quarterly). Free to round table members; unavailable by subscription. Ed., Karen E. Pollok, Naval Air Station Oceana, Station Library-Bldg. 416, Virginia Beach, VA 23460.

base line. MAGERT. Bimonthly newsletter. Free to round table members. Subscriptions: nonmembers, $15; foreign, $20. Ed., Nancy J. Butkovich, Physical Sci. L., Penn. St. Univ., Univ. Park, PA 16802; subsc. mgr., Arlyn K. Sherwood, Ref. Dept., State L., Springfield, IL 62756.

Book Links. ALA Publishing Serv., a *Booklist* publication. 6 issues a yr. Bimonthly Sept. through July. Subscriptions: U.S., Canada, and Mexico, $18; other countries, $22 a yr. Single copies, $3.50. Ed., Barbara K. Elleman.

Booklist. ALA Publishing Serv. 22 issues a yr. Semimonthly Sept. through May, monthly June through Aug. Subscriptions: U.S. and possessions, $60 a yr.; Canada and Mexico, $75 a yr.; and other countries, $75 a yr.; single copies, $4.50. Ed., Bill Ott.

Choice. ACRL. Monthly; 11 issues a yr., combines July-Aug. issue. Subscriptions: U.S., $155 a yr.; foreign, $170; single copies, $15. Ed., Patricia E. Sabosik.

Choice Reviews-on-Cards. $235 a yr.; foreign, $255; single copies, $25. Available only to subscribers of *Choice.*

CLENExchange. Quarterly. Free to members. Subscriptions: $20 a yr.; foreign, $25. Ed., Marie E. Bryan, P.L., 250 First St., Woodland, CA 95695.

College & Research Libraries. 6 bimonthly issues. Sent to all ACRL members. Subscriptions: $50 a yr.; Canada and Mexico, $55; other countries, $60. Single copies, $14. Ed., Gloriana St. Clair; bk. review eds., Stephen R. Lehmann; Robert E. Walther; res. notes ed., Larry R. Oberg.

College & Research Libraries News. 11 monthly issues; July-Aug. combined. Sent to all ACRL members. Subscriptions: $25 a yr.; Canada and Mexico, $30; other countries, $35. Single copies, $6.50. Ed., Mary Ellen Kyger Davis, ACRL, ALA Hq.

Documents to the People. GODORT. Bimonthly. Free to GODORT members. Subscriptions, $20 a yr. Ed., Mary Redmond; assoc. ed., Benjamin T. Amata; advertising mgr., Jill A. Moriearty; distribution mgr., Sinai P. Rocha.

EMIE Bulletin. EMIERT. Quarterly. Free to round table members. Subscriptions: $10 a yr. to non-ALA members; $15 to institutions; back issues, $1.50 each. Available from ALA/EMIERT, 50 E. Huron, Chicago, IL 60611. Ed., David Cohen, Grad. Sch. of L. & Inf. Studies, Queens Coll., City Univ. of New York, 65-30 Kissena Blvd., Flushing, NY 11367.

The Federal Librarian. FLRT. 4 issues a year. Free to round table members. Ed., Gail L. Kohlhorst, General Services Adm. L., Rm. 1033, 18th and F Sts., NW, Washington, DC 20405.

Footnotes. NMRT. Quarterly. Free to members; not available by subscription. Ed., Darlene P. Nichols.

FYI. ERT. Distributed free to members; not available by subscription. Lists states and regional library association meetings, dates, exhibit chairpersons, information on their association's exhibits, and news of interest to exhibitors. Ed., Carl Grant, Data Research Associates, Inc., 1276 N. Warson Rd., St. Louis, MO 63132-1806.

GLTF Newsletter. Newsletter of the SRRT Gay and Lesbian Task Force. Quarterly. Subscriptions: $5 to SRRT members; $10 to non-SRRT members and institutions. Make checks payable to: ALA/SRRT/GLTF; send to 50 E. Huron St., Chicago, IL 60611. Ed., Kathy Anderson, Atlantic City L. Sys., 2 S. Farragut Ave., Mays Landing, NJ 08330.

IFRT Report. IFRT. Irregular. Free to members; not available by subscription. Ed., Paul C. Vermouth Jr., MIT Libraries, Rm. 145-222, Massachusetts Institute of Technology, Cambridge, MA 02139.

Ilert Alert. ILERT. Semiannually. Free to all ILERT members. Subscriptions: $8 a yr. Ed., Susan N. Bjørner; prod. asst., Susan Dunne.

Information Technology and Libraries (ITAL). Quarterly. Sent to all LITA members. Subscriptions, $45 a yr.; Canada and Mexico, $50; other foreign countries, $55. Single copies, $15. For information or to send manuscripts, contact the editor. Ed., Thomas W. Leonhardt, Dir. of Tech. Serv., Univ. of Oklahoma L., 401 W. Brooks St., Norman, OK 73019-0528.

Interface. ASCLA. Quarterly newsletter. Sent to all ASCLA members. Subscriptions, U.S., $15 a yr; Canada and Mexico, $25 a yr.; other foreign countries, $25. Single copies, $4. Ed., Thomas J. Dorst, State L., 300 S. Second St., Springfield, IL 62701.

International Leads. IRRT. Quarterly. Sent to all IRRT members. Subscriptions, $12 a vol. Ed., Robert P. Doyle, ALA, 50 E. Huron St., Chicago, IL 60611.

Journal of Youth Services in Libraries. ALSC/YALSA. Quarterly. Sent to all ALSC and YALSA members. Subscriptions: $40 U.S.; $50 foreign. Co-eds., Donald J. Kenney, Virginia Tech. Univ. L., Blacksburg, VA 24061-0434, and Linda J. Wilson, Dept. of Ed. Studies, Radford Univ., 206A Russell Hall, Radford, VA 24142.

LHRT Newsletter. LHRT. Semiannual. Distributed to members; unavailable by subscription. Eds., David M. Hovde, HSSE L., Stewart Center, Purdue Univ., West Lafayette, IN 47907 and Edward Goedeken, Acqs. Dept., L. Offices, Stewart Center, Purdue Univ., West Lafayette, IN 47907.

Library Administration & Management. LAMA. Quarterly. Sent to all LAMA members. Subscriptions: $50 a yr.; foreign, $60. Ed., Diane J. Graves, 4043 Wolf Rd., Western Springs, IL 60558; assoc. ed., Joan Giesecke, 5515 Sherman St., Lincoln, NE 68506.

Library Instruction Round Table News. LIRT. Quarterly. Distributed to round table members; unavailable by subscription. Ed., Kwasi Sarkodie-Mensah, Snell L., Rm. 273, 360 Huntington Ave., Northeastern Univ., Boston, MA 02115; production, Emily M. Okada, Main L., W121, Indiana Univ, Bloomington, IN 47405.

Library Personnel News. OLPR. Quarterly. Subscriptions: $20 a yr.; single copies and back issues, $3.50. Eds., Margaret Myers, Jeniece Guy, ALA Hq.

Library Resources & Technical Services. ALCTS. Quarterly. Sent to all ALCTS members. Subscriptions to nonmembers, $45 a yr. Single copies, $14. Ed., Richard P. Smiraglia, Palmer Sch. of L. & Info. Sci., Long Island Univ., Brookville, NY 11548.

Library Systems Newsletter. LTR. Monthly. Subscriptions: $40 a yr.; foreign, $50. Order from LTR, ALA Hq. Ed. in chief, Howard S. White, ALA Hq.

Library Technology Reports. LTR. Bimonthly. Subscriptions: $185 a yr.; foreign, $215. Single issue: $30 for subscribers; $45 for nonsubscribers. Order from LTR, ALA Hq. Ed., Howard S. White, ALA Hq.

LITA Newsletter. LITA. Quarterly. Sent to all LITA members. Subscriptions: $25 a yr; Canada and Mexico, $30; other foreign countries, $40. Single copies, $8. Ed., Walt Crawford, Res. Ls. Group, 1200 Villa St., Mountain View, CA 94041-1100.

Memorandum. OIF. Monthly. Subscriptions, $20 a yr. Subscription and editorial mail should be addressed to ALA Office for Intellectual Freedom, ALA Hq.

Meridian. MAGERT. Semiannually. Free to MAGERT members. Subscriptions: $20 (foreign, $25); $25 to institutions (foreign, $30). Ed., Charles A. Seavey, Grad Sch. L. Sci., Univ. of Arizona, Tucson, AZ 85721; sub. mgr., Christine E. Kollen, Map L., Univ. of Arizona, Tucson, AZ 85721.

Newsletter on Intellectual Freedom. IFC. 6 issues a yr. Subscriptions: $40 a yr. (inc. index) U.S., Canada and Mexico; other foreign, $50. 5 or more subscriptions to the same address, $36 each. Single copies and back issues, $8 each. Ed., Judith F. Krug, ALA Hq.

PR Activity Report. Quarterly. Subscriptions: $25 with annual Library Publicity Book; Canada and Mexico, $30; other foreign, $35. Single copy, $7. ALA Public Information Office.

Public Libraries. PLA. Bimonthly. Sent to all PLA members. Subscriptions: $50 a yr., Canada and foreign, $60 a yr.; single copies, $10. Feature ed., Ellen Altman, 1936 E. Belmont Dr., Tempe, AZ 85284; managing ed., Sandra Causey Garrison, PLA/ALA.

Rare Books and Manuscripts Librarianship. ACRL. 2 issues a yr. Subscriptions: $30 a yr.; Canada and Mexico, $35; other countries, $40; single copies, $15. Ed., Alice D. Schreyer, Asst. Dir. of Ls. for Spec. Cllns., Univ. of Delaware L., Newark, DE 19717-5267.

RASD Update. RASD. Periodically. Sent to all members. Subscriptions, $15 a yr.; single copies, $4. Ed., Jane Kleiner, Ref. Serv., LSU Ls., Middleton Bldg., Baton Rouge, LA 70803-7010.

Reference Books Bulletin. Ed., Sandra Whiteley. Published in *Booklist.*

Roundup (semi-annual). Newsletter of the RASD Council of State and Regional groups (CSRG). Sent to RASD affiliates; not available by subscription. Ed., John C. Hepner, P.O. Box 507, Denton, TX 76202-0507.

RQ. RASD. Quarterly. Sent to all RASD members. Subscriptions: $42 a yr.; foreign, $52. Single copies, $12. Co-eds., Danny P. Wallace and Connie J. Van Fleet, Louisiana State Univ., Baton Rouge, LA 70803-3290.

School Library Media Quarterly. AASL. Quarterly. Sent to all AASL members. Subscriptions: $40; foreign, $50. Eds., Mary K. Biagini, Sch. of L. & Inf. Sci., 135 N. Bellefield Ave., Univ. of Pittsburgh, Pittsburgh, PA 15260.

SORT Bulletin. SORT. Semiannually. Free to round table members. Not available by subscription. Ed., Yvonne Beever.

SRRT Newsletter. SRRT. Free to round table members. Subscriptions: $10 to non-ALA members; $20 to institutions; $2 per back issue. Subscriptions available from SRRT Clearinghouse, ALA, 50 E. Huron St., Chicago, IL 60611. Ed., Thomas L. Wilding, Massachusetts Inst. of Tech. Ls., Cambridge, MA 02139. Clearinghouse Editorial Bd.: Mark C. Rosenzweig, John C. Sandstrom, Theresa A. Tobin.

Trustee Digest. ALTA. Quarterly. Sent to participants in the ALTA Affiliation Subscription Program. Affiliation fee, $75 a yr. Not available to nonaffiliates. Ed., Sandra Cooper, State L., Gray Bldg., Tallahassee, FL 32301-0250.

Video Round Table News. Irregular. Free to all round table members. Ed., Carleton L. Jackson.

Women in Libraries. Newsletter of the SRRT Feminist Task Force. Subscriptions: $5 to individuals; $8 to institutions (prepaid); $10 to institutions (invoiced). Make checks payable to: ALA/SRRT Feminist Task Force; send to 50 E. Huron St., Chicago, IL 60611. Ed., Abbie J. Basile, 486 Ashland St., #3, Buffalo, NY 14222.

ALA Awards for 1993

Through its awards program, the American Library Association seeks to honor those who have rendered distinguished service to libraries and librarianship. Such recognition is made for individual achievement of a high order in some area of librarianship, for effective participation in library affairs, and for writings and illustrations that enrich our collections. In addition, recognition and assistance are given to individuals and groups selected to conduct special studies, and scholarships are awarded to promising candidates seeking to enter the profession or for advanced study. The winners of the ALA awards for individual achievement constitute a Hall of Fame for librarianship. The juries and committees making the selections are charged with the responsibility of maintaining the high standards established by their predecessors in selecting individuals who have furthered to a notable degree the purposes for which libraries were created.

The winner of each award is selected according to the stated terms of the particular award. Apart from these limitations, no member of the profession shall be either selected for or excluded from receiving any award on the basis of the position held. It is the intent of the ALA Awards Program to recognize the living rather than to honor the dead; therefore, awards are not made posthumously except in situations where a death occurs between the time nominations are closed and the winners announced. Retired librarians may be honored by the ALA awards unless otherwise excluded by the terms of the award for which they have been nominated. For purpose of awards, the term "librarian" is not limited to those with formal library degrees but includes anyone occupying a recognized library position.

Following is a list of current awards, including citations, grants, and scholarships. These are grouped into two categories: ALA Awards and Scholarships, and Awards Administered by ALA Units.

Every ALA member is invited to nominate candidates.

1992 ALA AWARDS

Carroll Preston Baber—Christine Koontz and F. William Summers
Beta Phi Mu—Guy Garrison
Melvil Dewey—Michael Gorman
Equality—Susan Searing
Gale Research Financial Development—Oliver Wolcott Library, Litchfield, Conn.
Grolier Foundation—Effie Lee Morris
G. K. Hall Library Literature—not awarded.
Joseph W. Lippincott—John N. Berry III

Bessie Boehm Moore—Mohawk Valley Library Association
Herbert W. Putnam—Louise S. Robbins
H. W. Wilson Library Periodical—North Carolina Libraries
H. W. Wilson Library Staff Development—City University of New York Central Office, New York, N.Y.
World Book-ALA Goal Award—Washington Library Association and Idaho Library Association

---

◆

ALA Awards and Scholarships

◆

AWARDS

ALA Goal Awards

(See World Book—ALA Goal Awards, p. 116.)

(Carroll Preston) Baber Research Grant

An annual cash award of up to $7,500 and a citation presented to one or more librarians or library educators who will conduct innovative research that could lead to an improvement in services to any specified group(s) of people. Donated by Eric R. Baber. Administered by a jury of the ALA Awards Committee.

Deadline for applications is March 1, 1993. Jury ch., Susan E. Searing, Memorial L., Univ. of Wisconsin, 728 State St., Madison, WI 53706. Staff liaison, Mary Jo Lynch.

Beta Phi Mu Award

An annual award consisting of $500 and a citation of achievement, presented to a library school faculty member or to an individual for distinguished service to education for librarianship. The nominations must be accompanied by a specific statement of the qualifications of the nominee. Supporting evidence or testimonials are welcomed. Donated by Beta Phi Mu Interna-

tional Library Science Honorary Society. Administered by the ALA Awards Committee.

Deadline for nominations is December 1, 1992. Send nominations to the jury ch., Mimi Pechansky, Queens Coll. L., Flushing, NY 11367. Staff liaison, JoAn S. Segal.

(Melvil) Dewey Medal

An engraved medal and a citation presented annually to an individual or a group for recent creative professional achievement of a high order, particularly in those fields in which Melvil Dewey was actively interested, notably: library management, library training, cataloging and classification, and the tools and techniques of librarianship. Donated by OCLC Forest Press, Inc. Administered by the ALA Awards Committee.

Deadline for nominations is December 1, 1992. Send 5 copies of the nomination to the jury ch., Nancy Fisher, 939 Stuart Dr. S., Euclid, OH 44121. Staff liaison, JoAn S. Segal.

Equality Award

A certificate and a cash award of $500 given to an individual or group for an outstanding contribution towards promoting equality between women and men in the library profession. The contribution may be either a sustained one or a single outstanding accomplishment. The award may be given for an activist or scholarly contribution in such areas as pay equity, affirmative action, legislative work, and nonsexist education. Donated by the Scarecrow Press, Inc. Administered by the ALA Awards Committee.

Deadline for nominations is December 1, 1992. Send nominations to the jury ch., Sherre H. Dryden, Central L., Vanderbilt Univ., 419 21st Ave., S., Nashville, TN 37240-0007. Staff liaison, JoAn S. Segal.

Gale Research Company Financial Development Award

An annual award of $2,500 and a certificate presented to a library organization that exhibited meritorious achievement in carrying out a library financial development project to secure new funding resources for a public or an academic library entity. The criteria for selection of an award winner are: evidence of the need and appropriateness of the financial goal; the use of innovative, creative, and well-organized development methods; the success of the effort in meeting or exceeding the goal within a reasonable expenditure of fundraising monies; and the involvement of library supporters, who might include boards of trustees and library friends groups or their equivalent. Donated by the Gale Research Company. Administered by the ALA Awards Committee.

Deadline for applications is December 1, 1992. Jury ch., Louise Blalock, Dir., New Canaan P.L., 151 Main St., New Canaan, CT 06840. Staff liaison, JoAn S. Segal.

Grolier Foundation Award

An annual award consisting of $1,000 and a citation of achievement presented to a librarian who has made an unusual contribution to the stimulation and guidance of reading by children and young people. The award is given for outstanding work with children and young people through high school age, for continuing service, or in recognition of one particular contribution of lasting value. Donated by the Grolier Foundation. Administered by the ALA Awards Committee.

Deadline for nominations is December 1, 1992. Send 5 copies of the nomination statement to the jury ch., Donna J. Dufault, North Kingston Free P.L., 100 Boone St., North Kingston, RI 02852. Staff liaison, JoAn S. Segal.

(G. K.) Hall Award for Library Literature

An award consisting of $500 and a citation, presented to an individual who makes an outstanding contribution to library literature issued during the three years preceding the presentation. The award will be given only when a title merits such recognition. Donated by G. K. Hall & Co., Inc. Administered by the ALA Awards Committee.

Deadline for nominations and applications is October 1, 1992. Further information and application forms are available from the staff liaison, JoAn S. Segal. Completed applications should be sent to the jury ch., Louise S. Sherby, Assistant Dir. for Public Serv., Nichols L., Univ. of Missouri—Kansas City Libraries, 5100 Rock Hill Rd., Kansas City, MO 64110-2499.

(Joseph W.) Lippincott Award

An award consisting of $1,000 and a citation of achievement, presented annually to a librarian for distinguished service to the profession of librarianship, such service to include outstanding participation in the activities of professional library associations, notable published professional writing, or other significant activity on behalf of the profession and its aims. Donated by Joseph W. Lippincott, Jr. Administered by the ALA Awards Committee.

Deadline for nominations is December 1, 1992. Send nominations to the jury ch., Nancy Kellum-Rose, 1408 W. Carmen, #3, Chicago, IL 60640. Staff liaison, JoAn S. Segal.

(Bessie Boehm) Moore Award

An annual award consisting of $1,000 and a citation of achievement, presented to a library organization that has developed an outstanding and creative program for public library services to the aging. The criteria for selection of an award winner are: library's effectiveness in meeting program goals; percentage of targeted population reached by the program; program's recognition of diversity among the aging population; library's coordination with state and local agencies serving the aged; intergenerational aspects of the program; effective use of existing resources; involvement of community in program; potential for adoption in other libraries. Donated by Bessie Boehm Moore. Administered by the ALA Awards Committee.

Deadline for applications is December 1, 1992. Jury ch., Miriam L. Morris, Lane P.L., N. 3rd and Buckeye St., Hamilton, OH 45011. Staff liaison, JoAn S. Segal.

(Herbert W.) Putnam Honor Award

An award of $500 presented as a grant-in-aid to an American librarian of outstanding ability for travel, writing, or any other use that might improve his or her service to the library profession or to society. The $500 grant is made possible by the income received from the Herbert W. Putnam Honor Fund. Administered by the ALA Awards Committee.

Award will not be given in 1993. Staff liaison, JoAn S. Segal.

(H. W.) Wilson Library Periodical Award

An annual award consisting of $1000 and a certificate, presented to a periodical published by a local, state, or regional library, library group, or library association in the United States or Canada which has made an outstanding contribution to librarianship. (This excludes publications of ALA, CLA, and their divisions.) All issues for the calendar year prior to the presentation of the award will be judged on the basis of sustained excellence in both content and format, with consideration being given to both purpose and budget. The award is presented only in those years when a periodical merits such recognition. Donated by the H. W. Wilson Company. Administered by the ALA Awards Committee.

Deadline for nominations is December 1, 1992. Send 3 copies of all issues of the journal published in the 1990 calendar year to the jury ch., Kay K. Runge, Director, Davenport P.L., 321 Main St., Davenport, IA 52801. Staff liaison, JoAn S. Segal.

(H. W.) Wilson Library Staff Development Grant

A cash grant of $2,500 awarded to a library organization to assist it in a current or proposed program designed to further the goals and objectives of the library organization. The criteria for selection of a grant winner include: clearly defined documentation of need in relation to staff development, a well-defined program to meet the organization's needs, and the commitment and demonstrated ability to implement the program. Donated by the H. W. Wilson Company. Administered by the ALA Awards Committee.

Deadline for applications is December 1, 1992. Further information, application forms, and guidelines are available from the staff liaison, JoAn S. Segal. Completed applications should be sent to the jury ch., Jennifer W. Arns, U.S. General Accounting Office, 10 Causeway St., Rm. 575, Boston, MA 02222-1030.

World Book-ALA Goal Awards

World Book-ALA Goal Awards are two annual grants of $5,000 made by World Book, Inc., to encourage and advance the development of public, academic, and/or school library service and librarianship through recognition and support of programs which implement the Goal and Objectives of ALA.

All applications for grants must be submitted by March 1, 1993. The proposals are judged by a jury of the Awards Committee. The programs selected as award recipients will be announced at the ALA Annual Conference, New Orleans, 1993.

Units of the Association eligible for grants under the award are: ALA offices, ALA committees, ALA joint committees, ALA divisions, ALA round tables, and ALA chapters. Applications for grants from units within a division must be approved by the governing board of the division.

Further information, application forms, and application guidelines are available from the staff liaison, JoAn S. Segal. Jury ch., Kay A. Cassell, N.Y.P.L., 455 5th Ave., New York, NY 10016.

SCHOLARSHIPS

ALA Scholarship Program—David H. Clift Scholarship

ALA Scholarship Program, approved by the ALA Council, January 1969, provides the David H. Clift Scholarship in the amount of $3,000 to be given annually to a worthy student to begin a program of library education at the graduate level without regard to race, creed, color, national origin, or sex. The recipient must be a U.S. or Canadian citizen and must enter a formal program of graduate study leading to a master's degree at a graduate library education program accredited by the ALA. Funded by interest from the ALA Scholarship Endowment, two awards are given annually. Administered by the ALA Awards Committee and the Office for Library Personnel Resources.

Completed applications must be postmarked by Jan. 5, 1993. Jury ch., Joseph H. Green, Director, Nassau L. Sys., 900 Jerusalem Ave., Uniondale, NY 11553. Application and recommendation forms are available from the staff liaison, Margaret Myers.

ALA Scholarship Program—Louise Giles Minority Scholarship

Established in 1972 by the ALA Council, and named in memory of Louise Giles in 1977, the Minority Scholarship is a $3,000 cash award made to a worthy student who is a U.S. or Canadian citizen and is also a member of a principal minority group (American Indian or Alaskan native, Asian or Pacific Islander, black, Hispanic). The recipient must enter a formal program of graduate study leading to a master's degree at a graduate library education program accredited by ALA. Funded by interest from the ALA Scholarship Endowment, two awards are given annually. Administered by the ALA Awards Committee and the Office for Library Personnel Resources.

Completed applications must be postmarked by Jan. 5, 1993. Jury ch., Ilse Moon, 5623 Palm Aire Dr., Sarasota, FL 34243. Application and recommendation forms are available from the staff liaison, Margaret Myers.

ALA Scholarship Program—Tony Leisner Scholarship

Awarded for the first time in 1993, the scholarship is donated by and named for ALA member, Tony Leisner. The $3,000 award will support a library employee who wishes to attain a master's degree in librarianship at a program accredited by ALA. Administered by the ALA Awards Committee and the Office for Library Personnel Resources.

Completed applications must be postmarked by January 5, 1993. Jury ch., John Berry, Univ. of Illinois at Chicago L., P.O. Box 8198, Chicago, IL 60680. Application and recommendation forms are available from the staff liaison, Margaret Myers.

Awards Administered by ALA Units

ALA INTERNATIONAL RELATIONS COMMITTEE

The John Ames Humphry/OCLC/Forest Press Award

The $1,000 award is made to a librarian or other person who has made significant contributions to international librarianship. The contributions may include publication of significant professional literature, participation in library organizations, the introduction of new technologies or theories, or outstanding teaching. Primary consideration will be given to contributions in the field of classification and subject analysis, and to work in Third World countries, but the award is not limited to these areas. Donated by the OCLC/Forest Press.

Deadline for nominations is January 1, 1993. Jury ch., Loretta Randle O'Brien, Dep. Dir., Carnegie L., 4400 Forbes Ave., Pittsburgh, PA 15213.

Bogle International Library Travel Fund

A $500 award to assist ALA members to attend their first international library conference.

Applications and further information are available from Robert P. Doyle, ALA Headquarters. Deadline of January 1, 1993, for completed applications to be submitted to Alex Bloss, Hd. of Acq. Dept., Univ. of Illinois at Chicago L. (M/C 234), P.O. Box 8194, 801 S. Morgan St., Chicago, IL 60680.

ALA NATIONAL LIBRARY WEEK COMMITTEE

Grolier National Library Week Grant

An annual $2,000 cash award for a promotional program supporting the goals of National Library Week to be conducted in the year in which the grant is presented. Donated by Grolier Educational Corporation. Administered by the National Library Week Committee of the American Library Association.

Deadline for application forms is December 1, 1992. The winner will be announced at the 1993 ALA Midwinter Meeting. Application forms and further information are available from the staff liaison, Linda Wallace, ALA Public Information Office.

ALA PUBLISHING COMMITTEE

Carnegie Reading List Awards

Carnegie Reading List Awards are granted to official units of the American Library Association such as ALA divisions, committees, or round tables. The awards are based on a special fund established by Andrew Carnegie in 1902 and are "to be applied to the preparation and publication of such reading lists, indexes, and other bibliographical and library aids as will be especially useful in the circulating libraries of this country." The awards are for the creation of the lists; the cost of paper and printing is to be covered by sales to libraries. Priority will be given to proposals that (1) encourage use of library/information center

materials, (2) disseminate information about ways to promote reading, and (3) provide for distribution of such lists to appropriate potential users. The awards are chosen annually by the ALA Publishing Committee.

Proposals are accepted year round and are evaluated at the Committee's October meeting.

Whitney-Carnegie Awards

Whitney-Carnegie Awards are granted to individuals for preparation of guides to research resources. The aids must be aimed at a scholarly audience but have general applicability. The awards cover costs appropriate to the preparation of a useful product, including the cost of research and compilation. Whitney-Carnegie Awards do not generally cover the purchase of equipment or production costs. $5,000 is the maximum amount awarded; the amounts and number of awards are at the Publishing Committee's discretion and vary from year to year. Preference is given to projects for which the American Library Association can serve as publisher.

Proposals are accepted year round and are evaluated at the Committee's October meeting.

AMERICAN ASSOCIATION OF SCHOOL LIBRARIANS

Distinguished School Administrators Award, AASL/SIRS

An annual grant of $2,000 presented to a person directly responsible for the administration of a school or group of schools who has made an outstanding and sustained contribution toward furthering the role of the library and its development in elementary and/or secondary education. Sponsored by the American Association of School Librarians and Social Issues Resources Series, Inc.

Deadline for nominations is February 1, 1993. Nominations should be made on forms available from AASL. Jury ch., Robert E. Barron, 142 Stonington Hill Rd., P.O. Box 112, Voorheesville, NY 12186.

Distinguished Service Award, AASL/Baker & Taylor

An annual award of $3,000 presented to the individual who has demonstrated excellence and provided an outstanding national or international contribution to school librarianship and school library media development. Donated by Baker & Taylor.

Deadline for nominations is February 1, 1993. Nominations should be made on forms available from AASL. Jury ch., Hilda Jay, 10450 Lottsford Rd. #2108, Bowie, MD 20721.

"Emergency Librarian" Periodical Award

An annual grant of $500 presented to a school library media association that is an affiliate of AASL in recognition of an outstanding publication in the field of school librarianship. The award celebrates the efforts of AASL affiliates to promote excellence in school library media programs through publications for members. Donated by the publishers of *Emergency Librarian*. Administered by the American Association of School Librarians.

Deadline for applications is February 1, 1993. Applications are available from AASL. Jury ch.,

Laura D. Blanchard, 36 Fairway Lakes, Myrtle Beach, SC 29577.

Frances Henne Award

An annual grant of $1,250 to enable a school library media specialist with five or fewer years in the profession to attend an AASL regional conference or ALA Annual Conference. Sponsored by the R. R. Bowker Company.

Deadline for applications is February 1, 1993. Applications available from AASL. Jury ch., Sheila Salmon, 39-39 45th St., Sunnyside, NY 11104.

Information Plus Continuing Education Award

The Information Plus Continuing Education Scholarship provides financial assistance for the continuing education and professional development of a school library media specialist, supervisor, or educator. The $500 grant will enable an AASL member to attend an ALA or AASL pre/post conference or an ALA- or AASL-sponsored regional workshop. The Information Plus Continuing Education Scholarship is made possible through a donation from Information Plus, and is administered by the American Association of School Librarians.

Deadline for applications is February 1, 1993. Applications available from AASL. Jury ch., Rose Mary Tobiassen, 21 Sunrise Dr., Middletown, NY 10940.

Intellectual Freedom Award, AASL/SIRS

An annual award consisting of $2,000 and an engraved plaque presented to a school library media specialist at any level who has upheld the principles of intellectual freedom. The award also provides a grant of $1,000 and a framed certificate to a school library media center designated by the recipient. Donated by Social Issues Resources Series, Inc.

Deadline for nominations is February 1, 1993. Nominations should be made on forms available from AASL. Jury ch., Vicki H. Hardesty, 156 E. Jefferson St., Bluffton, OH 45817.

Leadership Development Award, ABC/CLIO

An annual grant of up to $1,750 to enable AASL Affiliate Organizations to plan and implement leadership development programs. Sponsored by ABC/CLIO.

Deadline for applications is February 1, 1993. Applications available from AASL. Jury ch., Carol A. Kearney, 54 Suburban Ct., West Seneca, NY 14224.

Microcomputer in the Media Center Award, AASL/Follett Software Company

The Microcomputer in the Media Center Award is designed to recognize and honor school library media specialists who have demonstrated innovative approaches to microcomputer applications in their respective libraries or media centers.

There are two award categories: (1) for the innovative use of the microcomputer in the school library media center in an elementary (K-6) setting; (2) for the innovative use of the microcomputer in the school library media center in a secondary (7-12) setting. Two national winners may be recommended, one in each category. Each recipient librarian will receive a $1,000 cash award and travel to the award ceremony; and each recipient library will receive a $500 cash award.

Deadline for applications is February 1, 1993. Applications available from AASL. Jury ch., Barbara J. Correll, 1004 Guava Isle, Ft. Lauderdale, FL 33315.

National School Library Media Program of the Year Award, AASL/Encyclopaedia Britannica Educational Corp.

Cash awards presented annually for outstanding achievement in exemplary school library media programs. Schools or districts representing elementary schools, secondary schools, or a combination of both may apply. Donated by Encyclopaedia Britannica Educational Corporation. Administered by the American Association of School Librarians.

Deadline for nominations is February 1, 1993. Nominations should be made on forms available from AASL. Jury ch., Diane D. Myers, Fulton Cnty. Schs., 786 Cleveland Ave. S.W., Atlanta, GA 30315.

Research Grant, AASL/The Highsmith Co., Inc.

An annual grant of $2,500 (up to $5,000 may be awarded to two or more researchers for a joint or group project) presented to one or more AASL members who are school library media specialists, library educators, or library information science/education professors to conduct innovative research aimed at measuring and evaluating the impact of school library media programs on learning and education. Sponsored by the American Association of School Librarians and The Highsmith Co., Inc.

Deadline for nominations is February 1, 1993. Nominations should be made on forms available from AASL. Jury ch., Jane Bandy Smith, 2033 Ellen St., Montgomery, AL 36106.

School Librarian's Workshop Award

An annual grant of $2,500 to provide financial assistance for the professional education of persons who plan to become school library media specialists working at the preschool, elementary, or secondary levels (PS-12) in public or private educational settings. Donated by the Library Learning Resources Company. Administered by the American Association of School Librarians.

Deadline for applications is February 1, 1993. Applications available from AASL. Jury ch., Janie R. Schomberg, 2210 Fletcher, Urbana, IL 61801.

AMERICAN LIBRARY TRUSTEE ASSOCIATION

ALTA/Gale Outstanding Trustee Conference Grant

A grant of $750 each to two trustees, enabling their first-time attendance at the ALA Annual Conference. The grant is awarded to two public library trustees who have demonstrated qualitative interests and efforts in supportive service of the local public library.

Deadline for applications is December 1, 1992. Applications should be sent to Ronald G. Harley, 14840 Massasoit, Oak Forest, IL 60452.

ALTA Major Benefactors Honor Award

An annual award consisting of a citation to recognize benefactors to public libraries. The recipient may be any person or persons, institution, agency, or organization. The significance of the gift will be measured from the point of view of the recipient library.

Deadline for nominations is December 1, 1992. Nominations should be made on forms available from the committee ch., Ronald G. Harley, 14840 Massasoit, Oak Forest, IL 60452.

Literacy Award

An annual award given to that individual who in a volunteer capacity has done an outstanding job in making contributions toward the extirpation of illiteracy. This award is given and administered by ALTA.

Deadline for nominations is December 1, 1992. Nominations should be sent to Ronald G. Harley, 14840 Massasoit, Oak Forest, IL 60452.

Trustee Citations

An ALA citation presented to each of two outstanding trustees, in actual service during part of the calendar year preceding the presentation, for distinguished service to library development whether on the local, state, or national level. Equal consideration is to be given to trustees of small and large public libraries. Administered by the American Library Trustee Association.

Deadline for nominations is December 1, 1992. Send 5 copies of nominations to Ronald G. Harley, 14840 Massasoit, Oak Forest, IL 60452.

ARMED FORCES LIBRARIES ROUND TABLE

Armed Forces Library Achievement Citation

An annual citation presented to members of the Armed Forces Libraries Round Table who have made significant contributions to the development of armed forces library service, and to organizations encouraging an interest in libraries and reading. Donated and administered by the Armed Forces Libraries Round Table.

Deadline for nominations is December 1, 1992. Send nominations to the jury ch., Belinda Pugh, Base L. Bldg. 1066, Naval Submarine Base, Kings Bay, GA 31547-5000. Staff liaison, Patricia A. Muir.

Armed Forces Library Certificate of Merit

This award shall be presented in recognition of special contributions to Armed Forces Libraries. Recipients need not be librarians or members of the association.

Deadline for nominations is December 1, 1992. Send nominations to the jury ch., Belinda Pugh, Base L. Bldg. 1066, Naval Submarine Base, Kings Bay, GA 31547-5000. Staff liaison, Patricia A. Muir.

Armed Forces Library Newsbank Scholarship Award

The purpose of the award is to recognize members of the Armed Forces Libraries Round Table who have given exemplary service in the area of library support for off-duty education programs in the armed forces.

Deadline for nominations is December 1, 1992. Send nominations to the jury ch., Belinda Pugh, Base L. Bldg. 1066, Naval Submarine Base, Kings Bay, GA 31547-5000. Staff liaison, Patricia A. Muir.

ASSOCIATION FOR LIBRARY COLLECTIONS & TECHNICAL SERVICES

Best of "LRTS" Award

An annual citation to be given to the author(s) of the best paper published each year in the division's official journal. The paper chosen shall meet the following criteria: (1) the content is a significant contribution about one or more issues addressed by ALCTS and its sections; (2) the statements in the paper are adequately supported by accurate data and/or documentation; (3) the writing style is clear and readable. Each of the papers published in the volume for the preceding calendar year is eligible for consideration with the exception of official reports and documents, obituaries, letters to the editor, and biographies of award winners. The jury may, at its discretion, invite recommendations from other readers. The jury may decide that there is no qualified article and not present an award.

Deadline for nominations is December 1, 1992. Send information to the jury ch., William Z. Schenck, 7909 Sycamore Dr., Falls Church, VA 22042.

Blackwell North America Scholarship Award

An annual award consisting of a citation given to the winner and a $2,000 scholarship that is donated by Blackwell North America to the library school of the winner's choice. The citation is presented to the author(s) of an outstanding monograph, published article, or original paper in the field of acquisitions, collection development, or related areas of resources development in libraries.

Deadline for submitting entries is December 1, 1992. Nominations should be sent to the jury ch., Edward A. Warro, Loyola Univ., Cudahy Mem. L., 6525 Sheridan Rd., Chicago, IL 60626.

First Step Award, Serials Section/Wiley Professional Development Grant

The purpose of the grant is to provide librarians new to the serials field with the opportunity to broaden their perspective and to encourage professional development in ALA Conference and participation in Serials Section activities. All ALA members with five or fewer years' professional experience in the serials field, who have not previously attended an ALA Annual Conference, are eligible. A $1,500 grant donated by John Wiley & Co. is applicable toward round trip transportation, lodging, registration fees, etc. Eligible applicants may apply more than once.

Deadline for submitting entries is December 1, 1992. Nominations should be sent to the jury ch., Elaine K. Rast, Northern Illinois Univ., Univ. L., Dekalb, IL 60115-2868.

(Margaret) Mann Citation

An annual citation made to a cataloger or classifier, not necessarily an American, for outstanding professional achievement cataloging or classification, either through publication of significant professional literature, participation in professional cataloging associations, introduction of new techniques of recognized importance, or outstanding work in the area of teaching within the past five years. Donated and administered by the Cataloging and Classification Section, Association for Library Collections & Technical Services.

Deadline for nominations is December 1, 1992. Send nominations, with resume of achievement on which nomination is based, to the jury ch., Verna P. Urbanski, Univ. of N. Florida, Carpenter L., P.O. Box 17605, Jacksonville, FL 32245-7605.

(Esther J.) Piercy Award

An annual citation presented in recognition of a contribution to librarianship in those areas of librarianship included in library collections and technical services by a librarian with not more than ten years of professional experience who has shown outstanding promise for continuing contributions and leadership in any of the fields comprising technical services by such means as: (a) leadership in professional associations at local, state, regional, or national level; (b) contributions to the development, application, or utilization of new or improved methods, techniques, and routines; (c) a significant contribution to professional literature; (d) conduct of studies or research in the technical services. The award will be given each year in which the jury believes there is a qualified recipient. Donated and administered by the Association for Library Collections & Technical Services.

Deadline for nominations is December 1, 1992. Send information to the jury ch., Frank A. D'Andraia, Univ. of North Dakota, Chester Fritz L., Grand Forks, ND 58202-0175.

Serials Section Bowker/Ulrich's Serials Librarianship Award

An annual award consisting of a citation and a $1,500 cash award for distinguished contributions to serials librarianship included but not limited to those made within the previous three years, demonstrated by such activities as leadership in serials-related activities, through participation in professional associations and/or library education programs, contributions to the body of serials literature, conduct of research in the area of serials, development of tools or methods to enhance access to or management of serials, other advances leading to a better understanding of the field of serials.

The award may be divided among two or more individuals who have participated in the achievement for which it is granted. Nominations and supporting documentation should be sent no later than December 1, 1992, to the jury ch., Rexford R. Bross Jr., Univ. of Toledo, Carlson L., 2801 W. Bancroft St., Toledo, OH 43606-3399.

ASSOCIATION FOR LIBRARY SERVICE TO CHILDREN

ALSC/Econo-Clad Literature Program Award

One annual $1,000 award to help defray the cost of ALA Conference attendance, presented to a member of the Association for Library Service to Children who has developed and implemented a unique and outstanding library program for children involving reading and the use of literature with children. The recipient must be a librarian who works directly with children and

whose program, targeted at and designed for children, has taken place within the past 12 months in a public library or school library media center. The program's purpose must be to bring children and books together to encourage development of life-long reading habits in young people.

Completed applications must be submitted by December 1, 1992. Jury ch., Trevelyn Jones, School Library Journal, 249 W. 17th St., New York, NY 10011. Applications available from staff liaison, Susan Roman.

(Mildred L.) Batchelder Award

A citation presented to an American publisher for a children's book considered to be the most outstanding of those books originally published in a foreign language in a foreign country and subsequently published in English in the United States during the preceding year. The award is made annually unless no book of that particular year is deemed worthy of the award. Donated and administered by the Association for Library Service to Children.

Announcement is made at the ALA Midwinter Meeting. The citation is presented to the publisher or representative during the ALA Annual Conference.

1993—Ch., Eva-Maria Lusk, W. 4333 Osage Way, Spokane, WA 99208. Staff liaison, Susan Roman.
1994—Ch., to be appointed.

(Louise Seaman) Bechtel Fellowship Award

For librarians, with at least twelve years of work at a professional level in a children's library collection, to read and study at the Baldwin Library of the George Smathers Libraries, University of Florida. Must be an ALSC member and have an MLS from ALA accredited program. Donor: Bechtel Fund, $3,750.

1993—Ch., to be appointed. Staff liaison, Susan Roman.

Bound to Stay Bound Books Scholarship

Two annual $5,000 scholarships established to assist individuals who wish to work in the field of library service to children. The scholarships may be used for study toward the MLS or graduate study beyond the MLS degree at an ALA-accredited library school. Donated by Bound to Stay Bound Books, Inc. Administered by ALSC.

Completed applications must be submitted by March 1, 1993. Jury ch., Dudley B. Carlson, 17 James Ct., Princeton, NJ 08540. Applications available from staff liaison, Susan Roman.

(Randolph) Caldecott Medal

A medal presented annually to the illustrator of the most distinguished American picture book for children published in the United States in the preceding year. The recipient must be a citizen or resident of the United States. Donated by Daniel Melcher. Administered by the Association for Library Service to Children.

Final selection is made by the Randolph Caldecott Award Committee and the winner is announced at the ALA Midwinter Meeting. The medal is presented at the ALA Conference.

1993—Ch., Jane Botham, 2579 N. Maryland Ave., Milwaukee, WI 53211. Staff liaison, Susan Roman.

1994—Ch., Maria B. Salvadore, D.C. P.L., 901 G St. NW, Washington, DC 20001.

(Andrew) Carnegie Medal

A medal presented annually to the American producer for the outstanding video production for children released in the United States in the previous calendar year. Administered by the Association for Library Service to Children. Medal endowed by the Carnegie Corporation of New York.

Final selection is made by the Andrew Carnegie Medal Committee, and the winner is announced at the ALA Midwinter Meeting. The medal is presented at the ALA Annual Conference.

1993—Ch., Marina Starr LaTronica, Berkeley P.L., 2090 Kitredge, Berkeley, CA 94704. Staff liaison, Susan Roman.
1994—Ch., to be appointed.

Distinguished Service to ALSC Award

To honor an ALSC member who has made significant contributions to, and an impact on, library service to children and/or ALSC. $1,000 award plus service pin.

1993—Ch., Gayle Cole, Stockton-San Joaquin County P.L., 605 N. El Dorado St., Stockton, CA 95202. Staff liaison, Susan Roman.

(Frederic G.) Melcher Scholarship

Two annual $5,000 scholarships established by the Association for Library Service to Children to encourage and assist people who wish to enter the field of library service to children. They are awarded to qualified candidates who have been accepted for admission to a graduate library school program accredited by the ALA. Donated by the ALSC in honor of Frederic G. Melcher. Administered by ALSC.

Completed applications must be submitted by March 1, 1993. Jury ch., Dudley B. Carlson, 17 James Ct., Princeton, NJ 08540. Applications available from staff liaison, Susan Roman.

(John) Newbery Medal

A medal presented annually to the author of the most distinguished contribution to American literature for children published in the United States in the preceding year. The recipient must be a citizen or resident of the United States. Donated by Daniel Melcher. Administered by the Association for Library Service to Children.

Final selection is made by the John Newbery Award Committee and the winner is announced at the ALA Midwinter Meeting. The medal is presented at the ALA Annual Conference.

1993—Ch., Sara L. Miller, 52-6 Foxwood Dr., Pleasantville, NY 10570. Staff liaison, Susan Roman.
1994—Ch., Mary Ann Paulin, 1205 Joliet, Marquette, MI 49855.

Putnam & Grosset Group Award

Four annual $600 awards presented to four children's librarians to enable them to attend ALA's annual conference. The recipients must be members of the Association for Library Service to Children, work directly with children, have one to ten years of library experience, and never have attended an ALA Annual Conference. Donated by Putnam & Grosset Group. Administered by ALSC.

Completed applications must be submitted by December 1, 1992. Jury ch., Blanka R. Saracevic, New Brunswick Free P.L., 60 Livingston Ave., New Brunswick, NY 08901. Applications available from staff liaison, Susan Roman.

(Laura Ingalls) Wilder Medal

A medal presented to an author or illustrator whose books, published in the United States, have, over a period of years, made a substantial and lasting contribution to children's literature. Donated and administered by the Association for Library Service to Children. ALSC members will be solicited to submit nominations to the Wilder Committee for its consideration. The winner is announced at ALA's Midwinter Meeting and the medal is presented at the ALA Annual Conference.

Presented every three years, this award will next be given in 1995.

1995—Ch., to be appointed.

ASSOCIATION OF COLLEGE AND RESEARCH LIBRARIES

ACRL Academic or Research Librarian of the Year Award

An annual award of $3,000 presented to the individual who has made an outstanding national or international contribution to academic and research librarianship and library development. Donated by Baker & Taylor Books. Administered by the Association of College and Research Libraries.

Deadline for award nominations for the 1993 award is December 1, 1992. Send nominations to ACRL.

ACRL Doctoral Dissertation Fellowship

An annual award of $1,000 presented to a doctoral student in the field of academic librarianship whose research is significant and demonstrates originality and creativity. The purpose of the fellowship is to foster research in academic librarianship by encouraging and assisting doctoral students in the field with their dissertation research. Recipients of the fellowship must be active doctoral students in the academic librarianship area in a degree-granting institution who have completed all their coursework and had their proposal accepted by the institution. Funded by the Institute for Scientific Information. Administered by the Association of College and Research Libraries.

Deadline for submission of proposals for the 1993 award is December 1, 1992. Send proposals to ACRL.

BIS Bibliographic Instruction Publication of the Year Award

An annual award of an appropriate citation to recognize an outstanding publication related to bibliographic instruction. Eligible publications include journal articles, books, and book chapters. Submitted publications may be authored by one or more individuals, group, organization, or committee. BIS publications are not eligible for consideration for the award. Publication year is defined as September through August of the year preceding the year the award is given.

Deadline for nomination is December 1, 1992. Submit publications for consideration to the Publications Awards Subcommittee ch., Karen

A. Williams, Hd., Ctrl. Ref., Univ. of Arizona L., Tucson, AZ 85721.

(Miriam) Dudley Bibliographic Librarian Award

An annual award of $1,000 presented to a librarian who has made an especially significant contribution to the advancement of bibliographic instruction. Nominees should have achieved distinction in such areas as planning and implementation of a bibliographic instruction program that has served as a model for other programs; research and publication that have had a demonstrable impact on the concepts and methods of teaching and information-seeking strategies in a college or research institution; active participation in organizations devoted to the promotion and enhancement of academic bibliographic instruction and promotion, development, and integration of education for bibliographic instruction in ALA-accredited library schools or professional continuing education programs that have served as models for other courses and programs. Nominees need not necessarily meet all the criteria. Funded by Mountainside Publishing Company on behalf of their publication *Research Strategies*, a journal of library concepts and instruction.

Deadline for nominations in letter form for the 1993 award is December 1, 1992. Send nominations to the jury ch., Mary Ellen Litzinger, Instr. Spec., Pattee L., Pennsylvania State Univ., University Park, PA 16802.

EBSCO Community College Learning Resources Library Achievement Awards

Two annual awards to recognize significant achievement in the areas of: (1) Program Development and (2) Leadership. Individuals or groups from two-year institutions, as well as the two-year institutions themselves, are eligible to receive the awards, which are printed citations and $500.

Nominees for the Program Award should demonstrate significant achievement in development of a unique and innovative learning resources/library program.

Nominees for the Leadership Award should demonstrate significant achievement in advocacy of learning resources/library programs or services or leadership in professional organizations that are associated with the mission of community, junior and technical colleges.

Deadline for award nominations is December 1, 1992. Nominations should be sent to the award jury chair and be made on a form available from the award jury ch., Paul E. Dumont, Dallas Cnty. Community Coll. Dist., Dist. Serv. Ctr., 4343 N Hwy. 67, Mesquite, TX 75150-2095.

(Samuel) Lazerow Fellowship for Research in Acquisitions or Technical Services

An annual award of $1,000 established to foster advances in acquisitions or technical services by providing librarians in those fields a fellowship for research, travel, or writing. Research projects in collection development or the compilation of bibliographies will not be supported by this fellowship. Proposals are judged on their potential significance, originality, and clarity. Funded by the Institute for Scientific Information. Administered by the Association of College and Research Libraries.

Deadline for submission of proposals for the 1993 award is December 1, 1992. Send proposals to ACRL.

(Katharine Kyes Leab and Daniel J.) Leab "American Book Prices Current" Exhibition Catalogue Awards

Three annual awards for the best catalogue published by American or Canadian institutions in conjunction with exhibitions of books and/or manuscripts will be granted in the spring of 1993. Catalogues published between September 1, 1991 and August 31, 1992 are eligible.

The entries will be divided into three budget categories: expensive, moderately expensive, and inexpensive, based upon production costs of the catalogues. Catalogues may be of varying formats, styles, and scope, but each must represent, either comprehensively or selectively, an exhibition that has taken place. Criteria for selecting winners will include the level of accuracy and consistency of presentation in the catalogue, its clarity, quality of design, and usefulness to the intended audience. The awards will take the form of printed citations to the institutions organizing the exhibitions.

Endowed by Katharine Kyes Leab and Daniel J. Leab. Administered by the Association of College and Research Libraries, Rare Books and Manuscripts Section.

Deadline for submission is September 30, 1992, to the ACRL-RBMS Com. for Awards for Exhibition Catalogues. Send nominations or inquiries to the jury ch., Marvin J. Taylor, Spec. Clln. Ln., Health Science L., Columbia Univ., 701 W. 168th St., New York, NY 10032.

Martinus Nijhoff International West European Specialist Study Grant

An annual grant for an ALA member to study some aspect of West European studies, librarianship, or the booktrade. The grant covers air travel to and from Europe, transportation in Europe, and lodging and board for no more than fourteen consecutive days. Maximum amount of 10,000 Dutch guilders is awarded per year. The primary criterion for awarding the grant is the significance and utility of the proposed project as a contribution to the study of the acquisition, organization, or use of library materials from or relating to Western Europe. A report of no fewer than 4,000 words on the research resulting from the study trip must be submitted to ACRL within six months of the trip's termination. If the report is suitable for publication, ACRL is given first rights of refusal. Administered by the Western European Specialists Section, ACRL. Funded by Martinus Nijhoff International. Application guidelines are available from ACRL.

Deadline for applications for the 1993 grant is December 1, 1992. Send applications to ACRL.

Oberly Award for Bibliography in the Agricultural Sciences

A biennial award given in odd-numbered years, consisting of a citation and a cash award from the income of the Oberly Memorial Fund, presented for the best English language bibliography in the field of agriculture or one of the related sciences in the two-year period preceding the year in which the award is made. The bibliographies are judged on accuracy, scope, usefulness, format, and special features such as explanatory introductions, annotations, and indexes.

Made possible by a fund established in memory of Eunice Rockwood Oberly. Administered by the Association of College and Research Libraries, Science and Technology Section.

Deadline for nominations is December 1, 1992. Send nominations to the jury ch., Amy L. Paster, E205 Pattee L., Pennsylvania State Univ., University Park, PA 16802.

Rare Books & Manuscripts Librarianship Award

A biennial $1,000 cash award to stimulate and increase the contribution of articles of superior quality to the ACRL journal, *Rare Books & Manuscripts Librarianship*. Any article published in RBML during the two preceding volume years is eligible. The winning articles will be selected on the basis of significance, originality, timeliness, thoroughness, and pertinence to issues relating to the theory and practice of special collections librarianship. Other criteria include clarity of thought and expression.

Articles for RBML may be submitted to Alice D. Schreyer, Univ. of Chicago L., Chicago, IL 60637.

(K. G.) Saur Award for Best "C&RL" Article

An annual award of $500 presented to the author to recognize the most outstanding article published in *College and Research Libraries* during the preceding volume year. The winning article will be selected on the basis of originality, timeliness, relevance to ACRL areas of interest and concern, and quality of writing. Donated by K. G. Saur. Administered by the Association of College and Research Libraries.

Articles for *C&RL* may be submitted to Gloriana St. Clair., Asst. Dean for Acc. Serv., E506 Pattee L., Pennsylvania State Univ., University Park, PA 16802.

ASSOCIATION OF SPECIALIZED AND COOPERATIVE LIBRARY AGENCIES

ASCLA Exceptional Service Award

A citation presented to recognize exceptional service to patients, to the homebound, to medical, nursing, and other professional staff in hospitals, and to inmates, as well as to recognize professional leadership, effective interpretation of programs, pioneering activity, and significant research of experimental projects. Donated and administered by the ASCLA.

Jury ch., to be appointed.

ASCLA Leadership Achievement Award

A citation presented to recognize leadership and achievement in the following areas of activity: consulting, multitype library cooperation, and state library development. The award recognizes sustained activity that has been characterized by professional growth and effectiveness, and has enhanced the status of these areas of activity.

Jury ch., to be appointed.

ASCLA Professional Achievement Award

A citation presented to one or more ASCLA members for professional achievement within the areas of consulting, networking, statewide services and programs. The criteria include: Record of accomplishment in the development or promotion of statewide library services and programs, or services and programs of multitype library organizations; Contributions which improve and enhance the status of state library agencies

or multitype library organizations; Evidence of initiative in dealing with issues and challenges facing state library agencies or multitype library organizations.

Jury ch., to be appointed.

ASCLA Service Award

A citation presented to recognize an ASCLA personal member for outstanding service and leadership to the division. The award recognizes sustained leadership and exceptional service through participation in activities which have enhanced the stature, reputation, and overall strength of ASCLA; representation of ASCLA to other appropriate organizations, institutions, or governmental agencies.

Jury ch., to be appointed.

ASCLA/National Organization on Disability Award

An annual award of $1,000 and a certificate are given to a library organization in recognition of either a specific innovative, creative, and well-organized program of services for persons who are disabled or for a library that has made its total services more accessible through changing physical and/or attitudinal barriers. Donated by the J.C. Penney Co. through the National Organization on Disability. Administered by the Association of Specialized and Cooperative Library Agencies.

Deadline for nominations is December 1, 1992. Send nominations to the jury ch., Leslie M. Rosen, American Fdn. for the Blind, 15 W. 16th St., New York, NY 10011.

Francis Joseph Campbell Citation

An annual award consisting of a citation and a medal presented to a person who has made an outstanding contribution to the advancement of library service for the blind and physically handicapped. This contribution may take the form of an imaginative and constructive program in a particular library; a recognized contribution to the national library program for blind persons; creative participation in library associations or organizations that advance reading for the blind; a significant publication or writing in the field; imaginative contribution to library administration, reference, circulation, selection, acquisitions, or technical services; or any activity of recognized importance. Donated and administered by the Libraries Serving Special Populations Section of ASCLA.

Deadline for nominations is December 1, 1992. Send nominations to the jury ch., H. Neil Kelley, Illinois State L., 300 S. Second, Springfield, IL 62701-1796.

EXHIBITS ROUND TABLE

Kohlstedt Exhibit Award

The Kohlstedt Exhibit Award is a citation given each year recognizing the best single, multiple, and island booth displays at the annual conference. The criteria on which judgment is made are as follows: clear identification of exhibitor and product or service offered, availability of staff, and accessibility of product or service; effective use of design elements, such as colors, shapes, and textures, and effectiveness of graphics in communicating about product or service; neat, un-

cluttered appearance, and arrangement of booth(s) for convenient flow of traffic.

The award citation is named after Donald W. Kohlstedt in recognition of his hard work for better library conference exhibits. It is administered by the Kohlstedt Committee of ERT.

All booths in each year's annual conference exhibits are eligible for the awards whether their companies or organizations are members of ERT or not. Six librarians judge the exhibits on the first day the exhibits are open. Ch., James M. O'Brien, Suburban L. Sys., 125 Tower Dr., Burr Ridge, IL 60521-5720. Staff liaison, Barbara A. Macikas.

FEDERAL LIBRARIANS ROUND TABLE

The Federal Librarians Achievement Award

An annual citation and gift for leadership or achievement in the promotion of library and information science in the federal community. Donated and administered by the Federal Librarians Round Table.

Deadline for nominations is December 29, 1992. Jury ch., Kathryn L. Earnest, 6045A Essex House Sq., Alexandria, VA 22310.

GOVERNMENT DOCUMENTS ROUND TABLE

(James Bennett) Childs Award

An annual award consisting of an engraved plaque presented to a librarian or another individual for distinguished contributions to documents librarianship. Donated and administered by the Government Documents Round Table.

Deadline for nominations is December 1, 1992. Send nominations to the jury ch., Jan B. Swanbeck, Doc. Dept., L. West, Univ. of Florida, Gainesville, FL 32611.

CIS/GODORT/ALA "Documents to the People" Award

An annual award consisting of a citation of achievement and a cash stipend of $2,000 to be used to promote professional advancement in the field of librarianship. The award is presented to the individual and/or library, organization, or other appropriate noncommercial group that has most effectively encouraged the use of government documents and information in support of library services. Donated by the Congressional Information Service, Inc. Administered by the Government Documents Round Table.

Deadline for nominations is December 1, 1992. Send nominations to the jury ch., Jan B. Swanbeck, Doc. Dept., L. West, Univ. of Florida, Gainesville, FL 32611.

Readex/GODORT/ALA Catharine J. Reynolds Grant

An annual award to present grants to documents librarians for travel and/or study in the field of documents librarianship or in an area of study that will directly benefit their performance as documents librarians. Supported by a $2,000 contribution from the Readex Corporation. Administered by the Government Documents Round Table.

Deadline for nominations is December 1, 1992. Send nominations to the jury ch., Jan B. Swanbeck, Doc. Dept., L. West, Univ. of Florida, Gainesville, FL 32611.

INTELLECTUAL FREEDOM ROUND TABLE

(John Phillip) Immroth Memorial Award for Intellectual Freedom

An annual award consisting of $500 and a citation presented to an intellectual freedom fighter who has made a notable contribution to intellectual freedom and demonstrated remarkable personal courage. Donated and administered by the Intellectual Freedom Round Table.

Deadline for nominations is December 1, 1992. Send nominations to the jury ch., Douglas Koschik, 4083 Wakefield, Berkley, MI 48072. Staff liaison, Anne Penway.

(Eli M.) Oboler Memorial Award

A biennial award of $1,500 presented to the author or authors of an article (including a review article), a series of thematically connected articles, a book, or a manual, published on the local, state, or national level, in English or in English translation. The works to be considered must have as their central concern one or more issues, events, questions, or controversies in the area of intellectual freedom, including matters of ethical, political, or social concerns related to intellectual freedom. The work or works need not have appeared in the "library press," nor have been written by a librarian. The work must have been published within the two-year period ending the December prior to the ALA Annual Conference at which the award is given. Donated by HBW Associates, Inc. Administered by the Intellectual Freedom Round Table.

Deadline for nominations is December 1, 1993. Jury ch., Doug Rippey, 503 E. Oak St., Lafayette, CO 80026-2522. Nominated works should be submitted in triplicate to IFRT staff liaison, Anne Penway, ALA Headquarters.

State Program Award

An annual award consisting of $1,000 and a citation presented to the state library association intellectual freedom committee, state library media association intellectual freedom committee, or state intellectual freedom coalition that has implemented the most successful and creative state IFC project during the calendar year. Donated by Social Issues Resources Series, Inc. (SIRS). Administered by the Intellectual Freedom Round Table.

Deadline for nominations is December 1, 1992. Send nominations to the jury ch., Susan M. Beck, 731 Packard St., Apt. 118, Ann Arbor, MI 48104. Staff liaison, Anne Penway.

INTERDIVISIONAL AWARD

Hugh C. Atkinson Memorial Award

An annual award consisting of an unrestricted cash prize and a plaque established to honor the life and accomplishments of Hugh C. Atkinson, one of the major innovators in modern leadership, and to recognize outstanding achievement (including risk-taking) by academic librarians that has contributed significantly to improvements in the area of library automation, library management, and/or library development or research. Nominees must be librarians employed in a university, college, or community college library in the year prior to application for the award and must have a minimum of five years of professional experience in an academic library. Individuals may nominate themselves or be nominated by others. The award is jointly sponsored by the ACRL, LAMA, LITA, and ALCTS and is funded by an endowment created by divisional, individual, and vendor contributions given in memory of Hugh C. Atkinson.

Deadline for submission of nominees is December 1, 1992. Nominations should be made in letter form outlining how the candidate meets the above criteria and should be accompanied by a current copy of the candidate's vita. Nominations should be sent to Hugh C. Atkinson Memorial Award, ACRL.

LIBRARY ADMINISTRATION AND MANAGEMENT ASSOCIATION

AIA/ALA-LAMA Library Buildings Award Program

An award presented by the American Institute of Architects and the Library Administration and Management Association, a division of ALA, formed to encourage excellence in the architectural design and planning of libraries. Awards are made to all types of libraries. Citations are presented to the winning architectural firms and to libraries.

The AIA/ALA-LAMA Library Buildings Award Program is held biennially. The next program will be conducted in 1993; entries will be accepted in the fall of 1992. Application forms are available after July 1, 1992, from the LAMA, ALA Headquarters. Staff liaison, Karen Muller.

John Cotton Dana Public Relations Awards

An annual citation made to libraries or library organizations of all types submitting materials representing the year's public relations program or a special project completed during the year 1992. Donated by the H. W. Wilson Company, the awards program is sponsored jointly with the Public Relations Section of the Library Administration and Management Association.

The deadline for receipt of scrapbooks and audiovisual materials is February 1, 1993. Information and entry forms are available from John Cotton Dana Public Relations Award Contest, H. W. Wilson Company, 950 University Ave., Bronx, NY 10452-9978. Send entries to the above address. Staff liaison, Karen Muller.

Recognition of Achievement Awards

Presented annually to encourage, recognize, and commend excellence in service to LAMA and its sections. The awards shall be a Certificate of Appreciation for a significant contribution to the goals of LAMA over a period of several years, and a Certificate of Special Thanks for a single, specific, significant contribution to the goals of LAMA. The LAMA Recognition of Achievement Committee establishes, revises, and publicizes the selection criteria for the awards, receives and evaluates nominations, and recommends no more than three nominees for each award to the LAMA Board at the Midwinter Meeting each year.

Deadline for nominations is December 1, 1992. Nominations should be made on forms available from LAMA. Staff liaison, Elizabeth Dreazen.

LIBRARY AND INFORMATION TECHNOLOGY ASSOCIATION

LITA/CLSI Scholarship in Library and Information Technology

To award the LITA/CLSI Scholarship in Library and Information Technology to a beginning student at the master's degree level in an ALA-accredited program in library and information science with emphasis on library automation. The purpose of the scholarship is to encourage the entry of qualified persons into the library automation field who plan to follow a career in that field and who evidence leadership in, and a strong commitment to, the use of automated systems in libraries.

The LITA/CLSI Scholarship was established by the Library and Information Technology Association and C.L. Systems (CLSI) in 1984. The scholarship is a cash award of $2,500.

Deadline for submitting applications for scholarship is April 1, 1993. Requests for applications should be addressed to LITA.

LITA/Gaylord Award for Achievement in Library and Information Technology

An annual award of $1,000 presented to recognize achievement in library and information technology. The award is intended to recognize distinguished leadership, notable development or application of technology, superior accomplishments in research or education, or original contributions to the literature of the field. Donated by Gaylord Bros., Inc., Syracuse, N.Y. Sponsored and administered by the Library and Information Technology Association.

Deadline for nominations is December 15, 1992. Send nominations to LITA. Staff liaison, Linda J. Knutson.

LITA/Library Hi Tech Award

The LITA/*Library Hi Tech* Award will be awarded to an individual or institution for a single seminal work, or body of work, taking place within (or continuing into) the five years preceeding the award, that shows outstanding achievement in communicating to educate practitioners within the library field in library and information technology. The award of $1,000 is presented at ALA Annual Conference.

Deadline for receipt of nominations in the LITA Office is December 1, 1992.

LITA/OCLC Minority Scholarship in Library and Information Technology

To award the LITA/OCLC Scholarship in Library and Information Technology to a student to begin or continue a master's level ALA-accredited program in library automation and the information sciences. The purpose of the scholarship is to encourage a qualified member of a principal minority group with a strong commitment to the use of automation in libraries to enter the library automation field and follow a career in that field. The recipient must be a U.S. or Canadian citizen and a qualified member of a principal minority group, that is, an American Indian or Alaskan native, Asian or Pacific Islander, African-American, or Hispanic. The LITA/OCLC Minority Scholarship was established by the Library and Information Technology Association and OCLC in 1991. The scholarship is a cash award of $2,500.

Deadline for submitting applications for the scholarship is April 1, 1993. Requests for applications can be addressed to LITA.

LIBRARY HISTORY ROUND TABLE

Justin Winsor Prize Essay

An award of $500 established and administered by the Library History Round Table of the American Library Association to encourage excellence in research in library history. The winner will be offered the privilege of being invited to submit his or her paper for publication in a future issue of *Libraries and Culture.*

The essays submitted should be manuscripts not previously published, not previously submitted for publication, and not currently under consideration for publication in another form. Essays should embody original historical research on a significant subject of library history, should be based on source materials and manuscripts if possible, and should use good English composition and superior style. They should be organized in form similar to that of articles published in *Libraries and Culture,* with footnotes, spelling, and punctuation conforming to the rules of *The Chicago Manual of Style* (13th ed., Chicago: University of Chicago Press, 1982). Papers should not exceed 35 typewritten pages in length, and should be submitted in three copies.

Manuscripts should be forwarded to Robert S. Martin, Louisiana State Univ. L., Baton Rouge, LA 70803.

Phyllis Dain Library History Dissertation Award

An award of $500 and a certificate given every two years by the Library History Round Table of the American Library Association to recognize outstanding dissertations treating the history of books, libraries, librarianship, or information science. Dissertations are eligible if they are completed during the designated period and have been submitted by the author along with a letter of support from the doctoral advisor or another faculty member at the institution where the degree was granted.

Entries are judged on: clear definition of the research questions and/or hypotheses; use of appropriate source materials; depth of research; superior quality of writing; ability to place the subject within its broader historical context; and significance of the conclusions.

For entry requirements and more information, contact: Charles Harmon, ALA Hq.

LIBRARY RESEARCH ROUND TABLE

Jesse H. Shera Award for Research

An award established by the Library Research Round Table to encourage excellence in library research. An award of $500 is presented annually to the person submitting the best completed paper. Entries are judged on the following points: definition of the research problem, application of research methods, clarity of the reporting of the research, and significance of the conclusions. Research papers completed in the pursuit of an academic degree are not eligible. Research papers submitted in the competition must not exceed 50 pages; only one research paper per entrant will be considered. The Shera Award Committee judges the entries and selects the winner. Donated by the Library Research

Round Table. The winner of the competition presents the research paper at one of the LRRT Research Forums at the next ALA Annual Conference.

Deadline for submitting entries is February 1, 1993. Send three copies of the research paper to Shera Award Com. ch., David Carr, SCLIS—Rutgers Univ., 4 Huntington St., New Brunswick, NJ 08903. Staff liaison, Mary Jo Lynch.

MAP AND GEOGRAPHY ROUND TABLE

MAGERT Honors Award

An award established by the Map and Geography Round Table to recognize outstanding contributions by a MAGERT personal member to map librarianship, MAGERT, and/or a specific MAGERT project. The award includes a citation and cash award of $25. Donated and administered by the Map and Geography Round Table.

Deadline for nominations is December 1, 1992. Submit nominations to the past ch., Jim Walsh, 161 Boutelle St., Fitchburg, MA 01420.

NEW MEMBERS ROUND TABLE

3M/NMRT Professional Development Grant

The purpose of the 3M/NMRT Professional Development grant is to encourage professional development and participation by new librarians in national ALA and NMRT activities. Cash awards are presented to librarians to attend an Annual Conference of ALA. The recipients must be current members of ALA and the New Members Round Table. Eligible applicants may apply more than once and may have attended previous ALA conferences. Administered by NMRT.

Deadline for applications is November 15, 1992. For more information, contact the ch., Heleni Marques Pedersoli, 3259 McKeldin L., Univ. of Maryland, College Park, MD 20742. Staff liaison, JoAn S. Segal.

NMRT EBSCO Scholarship

To be awarded in 1993 for the 1993-94 academic year. The scholarship is a cash award of $1,000, made possible through the support of EBSCO Subscription Services.

To be eligible, applicants must enroll at a library school accredited by ALA and plan to begin graduate studies in the fall of 1993 in a formal program of library education leading to the master's degree; must be a U.S. or Canadian citizen and a member of ALA and NMRT or must join prior to acceptance of the award.

Deadline for applications is December 15, 1992. Additional information and/or applications are available from the ch., Angela R. Jones, Univ. of South Mississippi, McCain L. & Archives, So. Sta., Box 5148, Hattiesburg, MS 39406-5148. Staff liaison, JoAn S. Segal.

Shirley Olofson Memorial Award

An annual cash award of up to $500 made to individuals to attend their second Annual Conference of ALA. The recipients must be members of ALA and be potential or current members of the New Members Round Table. Donated by New Members Round Table. Administered by NMRT.

Deadline for nominations is December 1, 1992. Send nominations to the jury ch., Richard C.

Dickey, Ref. Dept., Willis L., Univ. of North Texas L., P.O. Box 5188, Denton, TX 76203-5188. Staff liaison, JoAn S. Segal.

PUBLIC LIBRARY ASSOCIATION

Advancement of Literacy Award

An award presented to an American publisher, bookseller, hardware and/or software dealer, foundation, or similar group (i.e., not an individual) that has made a significant contribution to the advancement of adult literacy. Donated by *Library Journal.* Administered by the Adult Lifelong Learning Section, Public Library Association.

Deadline for nominations is December 1, 1992. Information and forms available from PLA. Jury ch., Barbara G. Fellows, Metropolitan L., 96 S. Grant Ave., Columbus, OH 43215-4781. Staff liaison, Sandra Causey Garrison.

Excellence in Small and/or Rural Public Library Service Award

An award to provide recognition and a $1,000 honorarium to a public library serving a population of 10,000 or less that demonstrates excellence of service to its community as exemplified by an overall service program or a special program of significant accomplishment. Sponsored by Ebsco Subscription Services. Administered by the Public Library Association.

Deadline for nominations is December 1, 1992. Information and forms available from PLA. Jury ch., John D. Hales Jr., Suwanee River Regl. L., 207 Pine Ave., Live Oak, FL 32060. Staff liaison, Sandra Causey Garrison.

Library Video Award

The Library Video Award provides recognition and a $1,000 honorarium to a public library demonstrating excellence and innovation in library programming with video and the ability to market and promote the use of these services to library users. Donated by Baker & Taylor Video. Administered by the Public Library Association.

Deadline for nominations is December 1, 1992. Information and forms available from PLA. Jury ch., Phyllis Y. Massar, Ferguson L., 1 P.L. Plaza, Stanford, CT 06904. Staff liaison, Sandra Causey Garrison.

(Allie Beth) Martin Award

An award of $3,000 and a citation presented to a librarian who, in a public library setting, has demonstrated an extraordinary range and depth of knowledge about books or other library materials and has exhibited a distinguished ability to share that knowledge. Donated by Baker & Taylor Books. Administered by the Public Library Association.

Deadline for nominations is December 1, 1992. Information and forms available from PLA. Jury ch., Charles M. Brown, Arlington Cnty. P.L., 1 Courthouse Plaza, Suite 402, 2100 Clarendon Boulevard, Arlington, VA 22203. Staff liaison, Sandra Causey Garrison.

National Achievement Citation

A citation is presented to a public library for significant, innovative activities that improve the organization, management, or services of public libraries. In addition to national recognition for each public library, program applications become a resource for PLA members who need information on new and innovative programs and how they were established. Any public library may apply; the chief officer of the library must authorize the application. There is a $30 application fee. Administered by the Public Library Association.

Deadline for nominations is December 1, 1992. Information and forms available from PLA. Jury ch., Dorothy S. Puryear, 99-07 23rd Ave., East Elmhurst, NY 11369. Staff liaison, Sandra Causey Garrison.

PLA/CLSI International Study Grant

A grant of up to $5,000 and a citation presented to a librarian with a demonstrated interest in and commitment to furthering international public library cooperation. The purpose of the award is to (1) support a study project in a public library or libraries outside the United States requiring a minimum of three months and a maximum of six months; or (2) to attend the IFLA conference and visit and study public libraries in the host country or surrounding region for two weeks or longer, before or after the IFLA conference. Donated by CLSI, Inc. Administered by the Public Library Association.

Deadline for nominations is December 1, 1992. Information and forms available from PLA. Jury ch., Louise A. Sevold, P.L., 3450 Lee Rd., Shaker Heights, OH 44120. Staff liaison, Sandra Causey Garrison.

(Leonard) Wertheimer Multilingual Award

A $1,000 award presented to a person, group, or organization in recognition of work that enhances and promotes multilingual public library service. Supported by the NTC Publishing Group. Administered by the Public Library Association.

Deadline for nominations is December 1, 1992. Information and forms available from PLA. Jury ch., Carmen L. Martinez, Los Angeles P.L., 630 W. 5th St., Los Angeles, CA 70071. Staff liaison, Sandra Causey Garrison.

REFERENCE AND ADULT SERVICES DIVISION

Dartmouth Medal

A medal presented to honor achievement in creating reference works outstanding in quality and significance. Creating reference works may include, but not be limited to, writing, compiling, editing, or publishing books or the provision of information in other forms for reference use, e.g., a databank. Bestowal of the award shall normally relate to works that have been published or otherwise made available for the first time during the calendar year preceding the presentation of the award. Donated by Dartmouth College, Hanover, N.H. Administered by the Reference and Adult Services Division.

Deadline for nominations is December 15, 1992. Send nominations to the jury ch., Mary Ellen Quinn, Harold Washington L. Ctr., 400 S. State St., #108, Chicago, IL 60605. Staff liaison, RASD Program Officer.

Denali Press Award

An annual award of $500 and a plaque to recognize achievement in creating reference works, outstanding in quality and significance, that provide information specifically about ethnic and minority groups in the United States. Outstanding contributions will be judged in part on accuracy, scope, usefulness, format, special features, and access as well as the gap in the literature filled by the work. Donated by the Denali Press. Administered by the Reference and Adult Services Division.

Deadline for nominations is December 13, 1992. Send nominations to the jury ch., Ingrid Betancourt, Newark P.L., 5 Washington St., P.O. Box 630, Newark, NJ 07101-0630. Staff liaison, RASD Program Officer.

Disclosure Student Travel Award, Business Reference and Services Section

An annual travel award of $1,000 that will enable a student enrolled in an ALA-accredited master's degree program to attend the ALA Annual Conference. The applicant shall have a demonstrated interest in pursuing a career as a business reference librarian and the potential to be a leader in the profession. The applicant shall be willing to participate in BRASS activities. Applicants who have received previous or concurrent ALA-sponsored travel awards are not eligible. Donated by Disclosure Incorporated. Administered by Reference and Adult Services Division Business Reference and Services Section.

Deadline for applications is December 15, 1992. Jury ch., Dennis R. Smith, 3185 Morningside Drive, Allison Park, PA 15101. Staff liaison, RASD Program Officer.

Facts On File Grant

A cash grant of up to $2,000 awarded to a library for imaginative programming that would make current affairs more meaningful to an adult audience. The grant will be awarded for projects to be conducted in an informal setting—whether in a public, academic, or school library—and will emphasize quality rather than the magnitude of the project. Programs, bibliographies, pamphlets, and innovative approaches of all types and in all media will qualify. Donated by Facts On File, Inc. Administered by the Reference and Adult Services Division.

Deadline for applications is December 15, 1992. Jury ch., Ree DeDonato, Ref., New York Univ. Bobst L., 70 Washington Square S., New York, NY 10012. Applications should be made on forms available from the staff liaison, RASD Program Officer.

Gale Research Award for Excellence in Business Librarianship, Business Reference and Services Section

An annual award of $1,000 and a citation made to an individual who has distinguished him- or herself in the field of business librarianship. Contributions should lie in a variety of endeavors, such as writing a seminal book or articles in business librarianship, developing an imaginative and successful program centered around business within a library, teaching business librarianship, or in other activities that encourage librarians to excel in business librarianship. Donated by Gale Research, Inc. Administered by the Reference and Adult Services Division Business Reference and Services Section.

Deadline for nominations is December 15, 1992. Jury ch., Violette Y. Brooks, 6235 S. Rhodes Ave., Chicago, IL 60637. Staff liaison, RASD Program Officer.

Gale Research Award for Excellence in Reference and Adult Services

An annual award of $1,000 and a citation presented to a library or library system for developing an imaginative and unique library resource to meet patrons' reference needs. Donated by Gale Research, Inc. Administered by the Reference and Adult Services Division.

Deadline for nominations is December 15, 1992. Jury ch., Christine C. Avery, E108 Pattee L., Pennsylvania State Univ., University Park, PA 16802. Staff liaison, RASD Program Officer.

Genealogical Publishing Company Award, History Section

An annual $1,000 cash award and a citation to encourage, recognize, and commend professional achievement in historical reference and research librarianship. The recipient shall be selected for exceptional accomplishment related to bibliography, book reviewing, indexing, professional association leadership, programs, and training that has furthered the quality of librarianship in history and the related subject interests of librarians, archivists, bibliographers, genealogists, historians, and others engaged in historical reference or research. Donated by the Genealogical Publishing Company. Administered by the Reference and Adult Services Division History Section.

Deadline for nominations is December 15, 1992. Jury ch., Tom J. Muth, 1311 Buchanan, Topeka, KS 66604. Staff liaison, RASD Program Officer.

(Margaret E.) Monroe Library Adult Services Award

A citation to be given at the ALA Annual Conference to a librarian who has made significant contributions to and an impact on library adult services. The person may be a practicing librarian, a library and information science researcher or educator, or a retired librarian who has brought distinction to the profession's understanding and practice of services for adults. Type of library affiliation is not a consideration in identifying possible recipients. "Adult" is defined to exclude young adults. Donated and administered by the Reference and Adult Services Division.

Deadline for nominations is December 15, 1992. Jury ch., Diane C. Strauss, 2028 Sprunt Ave., Durham, NC 27705. Staff liaison, RASD Program Officer.

(Isadore Gilbert) Mudge Citation

A citation to be given at the Annual Conference of the ALA to a person who has made a distinguished contribution to reference librarianship. The contribution may take the form of an imaginative and constructive program in a particular library, the writing of a significant book or articles in the reference field, creative and inspirational teaching of reference service, active participation in professional associations devoted to reference services, or other noteworthy activities which stimulate reference librarians to more distinguished performance. Donated and administered by the Reference and Adult Services Division.

Deadline for nominations is December 15, 1992. Jury ch., Virginia Boucher, 845 Lincoln Pl., Boulder, CO 80302. Staff liaison, RASD Program Officer.

Reference Service Press Award

An annual award of $1,000 presented to recognize the most outstanding article published in *RQ* during the preceding two volume years and to reward the author. The winning article will be selected on the basis of originality, timeliness, relevance to RASD areas of interest and concern, and quality of writing. "Article" is defined here to include any submitted or any invited column written by one or more individuals or by a committee, organization, or other group. Donated by Reference Service Press, Inc. Administered by the Reference and Adult Services Division.

Deadline for nominations is December 15, 1992. Jury ch., Ellen Derey Safley, Ref., Univ. of Texas at Dallas, P.O. Box 830643, Richardson, TX 75083-0643. Staff liaison, RASD Program Officer.

(John) Sessions Memorial Award

A plaque to be presented to a library or library system in recognition of significant efforts to work with the labor community. Such efforts may include outreach projects to local labor unions; the establishment of, or significant expansion of, special labor collections; initiation of programs of special interest to the labor community; or other library activities that serve the labor community. Donated by the AFL/CIO. Administered by the Reference and Adult Services Division.

Deadline for nominations is December 15, 1992. Jury ch., Barbara Hull, 35-20 Corporal Stone St., Bayside, NY 11361. Nominations should be made on forms available from the staff liaison, RASD Program Officer.

(Louis) Shores-Oryx Press Award

An annual award of $1,000 presented to an individual, to a team of individuals, or to an organization to recognize excellence in reviewing of books and other materials for libraries. The award may be given to reviewers, review editors, review media, teachers, or organizations, etc., that through their activities have furthered the quality and professionalism of reviews and the reviewing process. The award recipient should be selected for significant achievement related to reviewing of materials to help librarians make selection decisions. Donated by Oryx Press. Administered by the Reference and Adult Services Division.

Deadline for nominations is December 15, 1992. Jury ch., Jack Forman, 4175 Porte De Palmas, #171, San Diego, CA 92122. Staff liaison, RASD Program Officer.

SOCIAL RESPONSIBILITIES ROUND TABLE

Gay and Lesbian Book Award

An annual award honoring an English language book or books of exceptional merit relating to the gay/lesbian experience. The form of the award is not fixed but is designated by the Gay Book Award Committee each year as appropriate. Presentation of the award is made at the ALA Annual Conference.

Literature and nonfiction titles, including book-length bibliographies, are eligible. Nominations may be made by any individual not affiliated with the publisher; each nomination must include a brief statement of reasons for nomination. Administered by the SRRT/Gay and Lesbian Task Force.

Deadline for nominations is December 31, 1992. Send nominations to Susan Hoffman, 180 Wilson L., Univ. of Minnesota, Minneapolis, MN 55455. Staff liaison, Mattye L. Nelson.

Social Issues Resources Series, Inc., Peace Award

An annual award given to a library, which in the course of its educational and social mission, or to a librarian, who in the course of professional activities, has contributed significantly to the advancement of knowledge related to issues of international peace and security. The contribution may be in the form of, but is not limited to: a bibliographical compilation, research and publication of an original historical nature, or a nonprint media creation, display, or distribution.

The award, presented at the ALA Annual Conference, consists of $500 and a commemorative plaque donated by Social Issues Resources Series, Inc. The award is administered by the SRRT/Peace Information Exchange Task Force.

Nominations must be received by January 6, 1993, by the chair of the SRRT/Peace Information Exchange Task Force, Stephen J. Stillwell Jr. CSIA L., Harvard Univ., 79 John F. Kennedy St., #369, Cambridge, MA 02138. Further information available from staff liaison, Mattye L. Nelson.

SRRT Coretta Scott King Award

The award (or awards), given to a black author and to a black illustrator for an outstandingly inspirational and educational contribution, is designed to commemorate the life and work of the late Dr. Martin Luther King, Jr., and to honor Mrs. Coretta Scott King for her courage and determination in continuing to work for peace and world brotherhood. Book(s) must be published one year prior to year of award presentation.

The award is presented at the ALA Annual Conference. The award consists of a plaque and a cash award of $250 donated by Johnson Publications to the author and $250 to the illustrator. Sets of encyclopedias are also donated: *Britannica* to the author and *World Book* to the illustrator.

Deadline for nominations is December 31, 1992. Award winners will be announced February 1, 1993. Send nominations to the jury ch., Barbara Jones-Clark, 26130 W. 12-Mile Rd., Ste. 115, Southfield, MI 48034. Staff liaison, Mattye L. Nelson.

YOUNG ADULT LIBRARY SERVICES ASSOCIATION

(Margaret A.) Edwards Award

An award given to an author or co-author whose book or books, over a period of time, have been accepted by young adults as an authentic voice that continues to illuminate their experiences and emotions, giving insight into their lives. The award will be given next in 1993 in New Orleans. The award consists of $1,000 cash and a citation donated by *School Library Journal*.

Final selection of the next award will be made by the Margaret A. Edwards Award Committee and announced at the 1993 ALA Midwinter Meeting. Ch., Marion H. Hargrove, 61 St. Andrews Rd., Severna Park, MD 21146.

(Frances) Henne YALSA/*Voice of Youth Advocates (VOYA)* Research Grant

An annual grant of $500 to provide seed money for small-scale projects that will encourage significant research that will have an influence on library service to young adults. Applicants must be members of YALSA, although the research project may be undertaken by an individual, an institution, or a group. Grants will not be given for research leading to a degree. Donated by *Voice of Youth Advocates (VOYA)*. Administered by YALSA.

Completed applications must be received by December 14, 1992. Mail all proposals and/or requests for information to: Henne YALSA/VOYA Research Grant, YALSA Office, ALA Hq.

YALSA/Baker & Taylor Conference Grants

Two annual grants of $1,000 each awarded to young adult librarians who work directly with young adults in either a public library or a school library, to enable them to attend ALA's Annual Conference. Candidates must be members of YALSA, have 1-10 years of library experience, and never have attended an ALA Annual Conference. Donated by Baker & Taylor Books. Administered by YALSA.

Completed applications must be received by December 14, 1992, by the YALSA/Baker & Taylor Conference Grants Com., YALSA.

YALSA/Econo-Clad Reading or Literature Program Award

An annual award given to a member of YALSA who has developed and implemented a unique and outstanding library program for young adults involving reading and the use of literature. The $1,000 award is to be used to help defray the cost of ALA Conference attendance by the winner.

Completed applications must be received by December 1, 1992, by YALSA/Econo-Clad Award chair. Further information available from the YALSA deputy executive director.

Constitution and Bylaws

CONSTITUTION

Article I. Name

Sec. 1. The name of this body shall be the American Library Association.

Article II. Object

Sec. 1. The object of the American Library Association shall be to promote library service and librarianship.

Article III. Membership

Sec. 1. Members. Any person, library, or other organization interested in library service and librarianship may become a member upon payment of the dues provided for in the Bylaws. The Executive Board may suspend a member for cause after hearing by a two-thirds vote of the members of the Executive Board and may reinstate a member by a three-fourths vote of the members of the Executive Board.

Article IV. Divisions and Round Tables

Sec. 1. Divisions and Round Tables of the Association may be organized and supported as provided in the Bylaws.

Article V. Meetings

Sec. 1. Meetings shall be held as provided for in the Bylaws.

Article VI. Council

Sec. 1. (a) The Council of the American Library Association shall be the governing body of the Association. The Council shall delegate to the several divisions of the Association authority to plan and carry out programs and activities within assigned fields of responsibility and in accord with general Council policy.

(b) The Council shall determine all policies of the Association, and its decisions shall be binding upon the Association, except as provided in Sec. 4 (c) of this Article.

Sec. 2. Councilors shall be chosen as specified in the Bylaws of the Association.

Sec. 3. Seventy-five voting members of the Council shall constitute a quorum.

Sec. 4. (a) The Association by a vote at a membership meeting may refer any matter to the Council with recommendations and may require the Council to report on such matter at any specified session of the Association.

(b) Any question of policy may, by a majority vote of the Council, be submitted to the Association to be voted upon either at a membership meeting or by mail as the Council may determine.

(c) Any action of the Council may be set aside by a three-fourths vote at any membership meeting of the Association, or by a majority vote by mail in which one-fourth of the members of the Association have voted. Such vote by mail shall be held upon petition of two hundred members of the Association.

Article VII. Executive Board

Sec. 1. The Executive Board shall consist of the officers of the Association, the immediate past president, and eight members elected by the Council from among the members of that body, as provided in the Bylaws.

Sec. 2. A vacancy in the elected membership of the Executive Board, including a vacancy created by the election of a member to the office of president-elect or treasurer, shall be filled by Executive Board appointment, the person so appointed to serve until the following annual election.

Sec. 3. The Executive Board shall report on its activities not later than the next meeting of the Council. The Executive Board shall act for the Council in the administration of established policies and programs. It shall serve as the central management board of the American Library Association, including headquarters, subject to review by the Council, and shall make recommendations with respect to matters of policy and operations.

Sec. 4. A majority shall constitute a quorum of the Executive Board.

Article VIII. Officers and Committees

Sec. 1. Officers. Only personal members shall have the right to hold office. The officers of the Association shall be a president, a president-elect, who shall serve as vice-president, an executive director, and a treasurer. The president-elect and the treasurer shall be elected as provided for in the Bylaws, the president-elect for a term of one year and the treasurer for a term of four years. The executive director shall be appointed by the Executive Board, and shall hold office at its pleasure.

Sec. 2. Vacancy. When a vacancy occurs in the office of president-elect, the Nominating Committee shall reconvene to nominate candidates whose names shall be submitted to the membership for election by mail vote.

Sec. 3. Duties of Officers. The president, president-elect, executive director, and treasurer shall perform the duties pertaining to their respective offices and such other duties as may be approved by the Executive Board. The president-elect shall serve the first year after election as vice-president, the second year as president, and the third year as immediate past president. The president, for the Executive Board, and the executive director for the headquarters staff, shall report annually to the Council. The executive director shall be in charge of headquarters and its personnel; shall carry out the activities provided for in the budget; and shall perform such other duties as may be assigned to the office.

Sec. 4. Appointments. The Executive Board shall appoint all other officers and all committees of the Association not otherwise provided for and shall fix the compensation of all paid officers and employees. Only personal members of the Association shall be appointed to committees except by authorization of the Executive Board.

Sec. 5. Terms of office. All officers and all elected members of the Executive Board shall serve until the adjournment of the meeting at which their successors are chosen.

Article IX. Endowment Funds

Sec. 1. Receipts from life memberships and all gifts for endowment purposes shall, subject to conditions attached thereto, constitute endowment funds. Such funds shall, subject to conditions legally incident thereto, be in the custody of three trustees, one of whom shall be elected by the Executive Board annually to hold office for three years from the date of election and until a successor shall be elected. If any trustee resigns, dies, becomes incapacitated, or is removed from office, a successor may be elected by a majority vote of the Executive Board at any meeting, and such successor shall serve for the remainder of the term of the original trustee and until a successor is elected. The trustees shall have authority to hold, invest, reinvest, disburse, and otherwise deal with endowment funds in accordance with such directions as may be given them by the Executive Board of the Association. The principal of and income from endowment funds shall be expended under the directions of the Executive Board but no such expenditures shall be made except in accordance with any conditions imposed by the donors of any such funds nor for any purposes which are not in consonance with the approved policy of the Association nor shall principal be expended unless expressly permitted by the terms of the gift, or any amendment or modification thereof. No action shall be taken with reference to investment, reinvestment, or other principal transaction with respect to securities held in the endowment fund, except upon a resolution adopted by or written order signed by a majority of the trustees.

Article X. Affiliated Organizations and Chapters

Sec. 1. The Council may by vote affiliate with the American Library Association or with any subdivision thereof upon its request, any national or international organization having purposes similar to those of the Association or its subdivision. The dues of affiliated organizations shall be as provided in the Bylaws.

Sec. 2. The Council may by vote affiliate the Association, or any subdivision thereof upon its request, with any national or international organization having purposes similar to those of the Association or its subdivision; provided, however, that no subdivision of the Association may separately affiliate itself with an organization with which the Association as a whole is affiliated.

Sec. 3. By action of the Council, and in accordance with the Bylaws of the American Library Association, any legally constituted state, provincial, regional, or territorial library association may become a chapter of the American Library Association and receive such rights and privileges as provided in the Bylaws of the Association and under such conditions as may be provided in the Bylaws.

Article XI. Bylaws

Sec. 1. All proposals for amending the Bylaws shall originate in the Council. A proposed amendment or new bylaw shall become effective when it shall have been approved by a majority of the members of the Council present and voting at a meeting of the Council, followed by ratification by the members of the Association either by a vote by mail of a majority of the members of the Association voting, or by a majority vote of the members present and voting at a membership meeting of the Association. The Council, on approving a proposed amendment, shall specify whether a vote for ratification shall be taken at a membership meeting of the Association or by mail, and if a mail vote is ordered, the Council shall fix the time for the beginning and closing of the balloting. If a vote at a membership meeting is ordered, at least one month's written notice shall be given to the Association of the text of the proposed amendment or new bylaw.

Article XII. Amendments

Sec. 1. All proposals for amending the Constitution shall originate in the Council. A proposed amendment shall become effective when it shall have been approved by a majority of the members of the Council present and voting at two consecutive meetings held not less than two months apart, followed by ratification by the members of the Association either by a vote by mail of a majority of the members of the Association voting, or by a majority vote of the members present and voting at a membership meeting of the Association. The Council, on approving a proposed amendment for the second time, shall specify whether a vote on ratification shall be taken at a membership meeting of the Association or by mail, and if a mail vote is ordered, the Council shall fix the time for the beginning and closing of the balloting. If a vote at a membership meeting is ordered, at least one month's written notice shall be given to the Association of the text of the proposed amendment.

BYLAWS

Article I. Membership

Sec. 1. Classification of Membership. Membership of the Association shall consist of:

A. Personal Members

1. Regular Members—includes librarians, other library employees, and others employed in library service or related activities.

2. Trustees and Associate Members—includes those not employed in library and information services or related activities who through their personal commitment and support promote library and information services; i.e., members of governing boards, advisory groups, friends and special citizen caucuses, and/or individuals interested in participating in the work of the Association.

3. Foreign Librarians—librarians who do not hold U.S. citizenship and who are not employed in the U.S. or its possessions.

4. Student Members—members who are enrolled at least half-time in a program of library and information science in a four-year undergraduate or a graduate school.

5. Other Members—those who are inactive, retired, or unemployed, or are employed full- or part-time in library service or related activities at a salary of less than $10,000 per annum.

6. Honorary Members—persons nominated by the Executive Board and elected for life by the Council.

7. Life Members—all who have purchased life membership in the Association.

8. Continuing Members—those persons who have had twenty-five years of consecutive membership in the Association, who are members at the time of retirement from library service or related activities, and who have applied for such membership for life.

B. Chapter Members—any legally constituted state, provincial, territorial, or regional library association that has been granted chapter status by action of Council under Article V, Section 1(c) of the Bylaws.

C. Organization Members

1. Library and Library School Members—nonprofit libraries and nonprofit schools conducting programs of library education.

2. All other nonprofit organizations—Library associations, affiliated organizations, foreign organizations, and nonprofit organizations other than libraries and library schools.

D. Special Members—patrons of the ALA, sustaining, contributing, and subscribing—persons and organizations, except nonprofit libraries and library schools, electing to pay dues set in accordance with Section 2 of this Article.

Sec. 2. Dues, Rights, and Privileges. Only personal members of the Association shall have the right to vote and hold office, personal insurance privileges, and membership rates at Conferences. Personal members shall receive *American Libraries, the Handbook of Organization* and discounts on ALA monographs. All personal members shall be eligible for membership in any division upon payment of annual dues as established by the division.

The dues to be paid shall be as follows:

A. Personal Members
Five-year dues schedule:

	1985	1986	1987	1988	1989
1. Regular Members:	$55	$60	$65	$70	$75
3rd year of membership	$44	$48	$52	$56	$60
2nd year of membership	$36	$39	$42	$46	$49
1st year of membership	$28	$30	$33	$35	$38
2. Trustee and Associate Members:	$25	$27	$29	$32	$34
3. Foreign Librarians:	$33	$36	$39	$42	$45
4. Student Members (Eligibility is limited to no more than three calendar years.):	$14	$15	$16	$18	$19
5. Other Members:	$20	$21	$23	$25	$26

6. Honorary Members: No dues.

7. Life Members: No dues; Membership Directory upon request. Life members prior to 1983 may continue to select two divisional memberships annually at no cost. Designation of divisional memberships may be changed at the end of each membership year. Divisions will receive proportionate reimbursement for divisional memberships selected by life members.

8. Continuing Members: No dues. Divisional memberships as established by the divisions.

B. Chapter Members
Dues and perquisites shall be set by Council upon recommendation by the Executive Board.*

C. Organization Members
Organization dues and perquisites shall be set by Council upon recommendation by the Executive Board.*

D. Special Members
The special membership entitles the holder to request any perquisites available to a regular organization member. Dues and perquisites shall be set by Council upon recommendation by the Executive Board.*

Sec. 3. Members falling into two or more categories of membership shall pay the highest applicable dues and shall receive corresponding privileges. The Executive

---

* See ALA Policy #12.

Board shall have the authority to make adjustments in the scale of dues for cases not clearly covered in Sec. 2.

Sec. 4. Upon approval of the Executive Board special promotional membership rates may be made available from time to time.

Sec. 5. The classification to which any personal member belongs, except Honorary, Life, and Special Members, shall not be specified in the Directory and shall be regarded as confidential.

Sec. 6. Unpaid dues. Members whose dues are unpaid upon the expiration date of their membership year and who shall continue such delinquency for one month after notice of the same has been sent, shall be dropped from membership. Lapsed members may be reinstated upon payment of dues for the current year.

Sec. 7. (a) Fiscal Year. The fiscal year of the Association shall end August 31. The fiscal year shall govern all business and activities of the Association except as otherwise provided in the Constitution and Bylaws.

(b) Conference Year. The conference year shall be that period beginning with the adjournment of an annual conference of the Association and ending with the adjournment of the next succeeding annual conference.

(c) Membership Year. The membership year for the Association and for the divisions shall be twelve consecutive months, effective the first day of the month following receipt of dues payment.

Sec. 8. The ALA dues schedule shall be reviewed at least every five years at the discretion of the Executive Board.

Article II.   Meetings

Sec. 1. Annual Meetings. There shall be an annual conference of the Association at such place and time as may be determined by the Executive Board. For all persons attending any meeting or conference there may be a registration fee as fixed by the Executive Board.

Sec. 2. Special Meetings. Special meetings of the Association may be called by the Executive Board, and shall be called by the President on request of not less than five percent of the voting members of the Association as of the previous July 1, such request to be filed with the executive director at least ninety days before the proposed meeting. At least one month's notice shall be given, and only the business specified in the call shall be transacted.

Sec. 3. Regional Meetings. The Executive Board may arrange for regional meetings to include such chapters, divisions, library associations, and such other organizations as may desire to join in such a meeting, provided that the Executive Board may not call a regional meeting in the area covered by a regional chapter without the consent of such chapter.

Sec. 4. Membership Meetings. A membership meeting consists of the voting members of the Association with authority to act as set out in Article VI, Sections 4(a) and 4(c) of the Constitution. A membership meeting shall be held during the annual conference and at such other times as may be set by the Executive Board, Council or by membership petition as provided for in Article II, Section 2, of the Bylaws.

Sec. 5. Votes by Mail. Votes by mail, both of the Association and of the Council, may be authorized by the Executive Board between meetings. For votes by Council, fifty percent of the voting membership shall constitute a quorum and a three-fourths majority of those voting shall be required to carry. For votes by the Association twenty-five percent of the voting membership shall constitute a quorum and a majority of those voting shall be required to carry.

The Executive Board shall have authority to set the time limit during which votes will be recorded but if no such time limit is set no vote shall be counted unless received within thirty days from the day the text of the ballot or question voted upon was mailed properly addressed to those entitled to vote on the matter involved. In the case of a vote by mail by the Association, the Executive Board may designate publication of the ballot or question submitted in the official journal of the Association as the appropriate method of submitting the matter to the members for their determination.

Sec. 6. Quorum. Two hundred members shall constitute a quorum at membership meetings.

Article III.   Nominations and Elections

Sec. 1. (a) Prior to each annual conference of the Association, the Executive Board, upon recommendation of the Committee on Appointments, shall appoint an ALA Nominating Committee, no one of whom shall be a member of the Board, to nominate candidates for elective positions.

(b) Such committee shall nominate candidates from among the general membership for the position of president-elect annually; for the position of treasurer, whenever this is required by Article VIII, Sec. 1 of the Constitution; members of Council as provided in sections (c) and (d) below; and to fill vacancies.

(c) Such committee shall nominate annually not less than fifty candidates for twenty-five members-at-large of the Council for four-year terms. The position of the candidates on the ballot shall be determined by lot conducted by the Nominating Committee.

(d) Such committee shall also nominate and place on the ballot candidates for a vacancy in the membership of Council, representing the Association at large as provided in Sec. 1 (c) of this Article, to complete an unexpired term.

(e) No person may be nominated for or serve on the Council unless that person is a personal member of the American Library Association; no candidate may accept nomination from more than one group.

Sec. 2. (a) The ALA Nominating Committee shall report its nominations in the *American Libraries* not less than three weeks before the midwinter meeting of the Council. At that meeting, the names of the candidates shall be announced.

(b) No person shall be nominated by the committee whose written consent has not been filed with the executive director of the Association.

Sec. 3. (a) Nominations determined as herein provided shall be placed before the members of the Association on a printed ballot which shall be prepared under the direction of the Nominating Committee and which shall be known as the "Official Ballot."

(b) The ALA Nominating Committee shall also include on the official ballot other nominations filed with the executive director by petition of any twenty-five members of the Association at least four months before the annual conference, provided written consent of these nominees shall have been filed with the executive director of the Association.

(c) The professional address of each nominee shall be given on the Official Ballot.

Sec. 4. (a) The Executive Board shall appoint a Committee on Election which shall have charge of the conduct of the regular elections of the Association and the divisions, and the counting and tabulation of all votes cast.

(b) At least six weeks prior to the annual conference the executive director shall mail a copy of the ballot to each member of the Association in good standing. Ballots shall be marked and returned to the executive director in sealed envelopes bearing on the outside the words, "Official Ballot."

Sec. 5. For each office the candidate receiving the largest number of votes shall be elected and shall be so reported to the Association by the Committee on Election. In the case of a tie vote the successful candidate shall be determined by lot conducted by the Committee on Election. In the event that a candidate for election to Council withdraws from candidacy in the period between the mailing of ballots and the beginning of the new term of office, and the candidate is successful in the election, the Council seat affected will remain vacant until filled in the following annual election.

Sec. 6. (a) There shall be a Council Committee on Committees made up of four Councilors elected for one-year terms by Council as provided for in Article III, Sec. 6(b) of the Bylaws. The president-elect shall be the fifth member of this committee and its chairperson.

(b) The four elected members of the Council Committee on Committees shall be elected by ballot of the Councilors present and voting at the annual conference from a list of eight candidates submitted by the president-elect and included in the agenda mailed to Councilors before the annual conference. Additional nominations for the Committee on Committees may be made by Councilors from the floor.

(c) Such committee shall nominate annually candidates for two members of the Executive Board for four-year terms for election by the Council from among the members of the Council who are serving by virtue of election to it, as provided in Article IV, Sec. 2(b), (c), and (d) of the Bylaws, and who will have served at least one year preceding their prospective terms as Executive Board Members. Additional nominations for the Executive Board may be made by Councilors from the floor. Upon election to the Executive Board the member shall continue to serve as a member of the Council for the duration of the term for which elected to the Council and thereafter as a voting member ex officio for the duration of the term for which elected to the Executive Board.

Article IV.   Council

Sec. 1. (a) Council membership requirement. No person, including a representative of a state, provincial, or territorial chapter, may serve on the Council unless a personal member of the American Library Association.

(b) Meetings. The Council shall hold at least two meetings each year. Such meetings shall be held, one at the time and place of the annual conference of the Association and one not less than three months before the next annual conference, at a time designated by the Executive Board. The latter shall be called the midwinter meeting. Other meetings may be called by the president and shall be called upon request of twenty members.

(c) Officers. The president, president-elect, and the executive director of the Association shall serve as officers of the Council, the executive director serving as its secretary. The presiding officer may vote only in case of a tie and the executive director shall not have the right to vote.

Sec. 2. (a) All personal members of the ALA shall be eligible for nomination to Council from their respective constituencies, as indicated in Article IV, Sec. 2(b), (c), and (d), without regard to any other prerequisites.

(b) Each state, provincial, and territorial chapter shall be entitled to one councilor to be elected for a term of four years by the members of the chapter.

(c) Each division of the Association shall be entitled to one councilor to be elected for a term of four years by the members of the divisions.

(d) One hundred councilors shall be elected by the Association at large, twenty-five being elected each year as provided in Article III, Sec. 1(c) of the Bylaws.

(e) All members of the Executive Board shall automatically be members of the Council.

(f) No person shall serve simultaneously as a member of the Council elected by a chapter or a division and as a member elected by the Association at large. A person who is a member by virtue of being a member of the Executive Board may simultaneously be a regularly elected member according to paragraphs (b), (c), and (d), but such person shall have but one vote.

Sec. 3. All elected councilors shall serve for terms of four years or until their successors are selected and qualified.

Sec. 4. Each chapter shall accredit its councilor to the secretary of the Council in advance of the first meeting after the election.

Sec. 5. A vacancy in the membership of Council representing the Association at large shall be filled at the following election to complete the unexpired term.

Sec. 6. A vacancy in the membership of Council representing a state, provincial or territorial chapter, or a division of the Association may be filled by the chapter or division on an interim basis. Each chapter or division shall accredit its interim councilor to the secretary of the Council in advance of the first meeting after selection. The interim councilor shall serve as a voting member until the next regularly scheduled election or for a maximum of one year, by which time an election shall have been held to elect a successor.

Article V. Chapters

Sec. 1.(a) The purpose of a chapter is to promote general library service and librarianship within its geographic area, to provide geographic representation to the Council of the American Library Association, and to cooperate in the promotion of general and joint enterprises with the American Library Association and other library groups.

(b) The Council may establish a chapter of the American Library Association in any state, province, territory, or region in which a majority of the ALA members residing within the area involved and voting on the issue favors such action; provided, however, that the total number of persons voting on the issue shall not be less than ten percent of the total number of ALA members residing within the area. A regional chapter may consist of any area composed of three or more contiguous states or provinces.

(c) Any legally constituted state, provincial, territorial, or regional library association may, at its request, be designated a chapter of the American Library Association provided the membership of the association applying for chapter status has expressed approval of the application; and providing a majority of the ALA members residing in the area involved voting on the issue is in favor of such action 'ovided, however, that the total number of persons voting on the issue shall not be less than ten percent of the total number of ALA members residing within the area involved, and provided that there is no conflict in principle between the constitution and bylaws of the association involved and the Constitution and Bylaws of the American Library Association, and that copies of the chapter constitution and bylaws, and subsequent amendments to them are filed with the American Library Association and dues are paid in accordance with Article I of the Bylaws.

(d) No more than one chapter of the American Library Association shall exist in any state, province, or territory.

(e) In establishing regional chapters, no state, provincial, or territorial association may be included in more than one such region.

Sec. 2. A chapter may admit members who are not members of the American Library Association.

Sec. 3. Each state, provincial, territorial, or regional chapter shall be the final authority within the American Library Association in respect to all programs and policies which concern only the area for which the chapter is reponsible provided they are not inconsistent with any programs and policies established by the ALA Council. Any chapter may establish committees and boards which parallel national committees and boards in order to carry out over-all programs within its own area and to maintain liaison between its members and the national committees and boards. State, pro-

vincial, and territorial chapters may establish local chapters within the respective areas involved.

Sec. 4(a) Any chapter may withdraw from chapter status provided the issue has been submitted to a vote of the chapter membership and is favored by a majority of the members voting; and provided further that notice of withdrawal is sent to the executive director of the American Library Association.

(b) A chapter may be dissolved by the Council and shall be dissolved if it becomes inactive or fails to comply with the provisions of this Article.

Article VI. Divisions

Sec. 1. The Council may establish divisions under the following conditions:

(a) The Council may authorize the organization as a division of any group of not less than 500 members of the Asssociation who are interested in the same field of librarianship, upon petition of such group. Under exceptional circumstances, the Council may admit as divisions, groups having fewer than 500 members.

(b) The Council by a vote of two consecutive meetings may discontinue a division when, in the opinion of the Council, the usefulness of that division has ceased.

Sec. 2. (a) The purpose of a division is to promote library service and librarianship within and for a particular type of library or as it relates to a particular type of library activity, and to cooperate in the promotion of general and joint enterprises within the Association and with other library groups. Each division shall represent a field of activity and responsibility clearly distinct from that of other divisions.

(b) A division shall have authority to act for the ALA as a whole on any matter determined by Council to be the responsibility of the division.

Sec. 3.(a) Divisions are of two distinct kinds; "Type-of-library " divisions and "Type-of-activity" divisions.

(b) Type-of-library divisions focus attention upon planning in and evaluation of all functions as they contribute to the services of the library. Type-of-library divisions are interested in the general improvement and extension of service to the clientele and agencies served. Each such division has specific responsibility for: (1) Planning of programs of study and service for the type of library as a total institution; (2) Evaluation and establishment of standards in its field; (3) Synthesis of the activities of all units within the Association that have a bearing on the type of library represented; (4) Representation and interpretation of its type of library in contacts outside the profession; (5) Stimulation of the development of librarians engaged in its type of library, and stimulation of participation of members in appropriate type-of-activity divisions; and (6) Conduct of activities and projects for improvement and extension of service in its type of library when such projects are beyond the scope of type-of-activity divisions, after specific approval by the Council.

(c) Type-of-activity divisions focus attention upon study and development of such functions as reference, cataloging, personnel administration, etc., as they apply to all types of libraries. Type-of-activity divisions are interested in the improvement and extension of their functions. Each such division has specific responsibility for: (1) Continuous study and review of the activities assigned to the particular division; (2) Conduct of activities and projects within its area of responsibility; (3) Synthesis of the activities of all units within the Association that have a bearing on the type of activity represented; (4) Representation and interpretation of its type of activity in contacts outside the profession; (5) Stimulation of the development of librarians engaged in its type of activity, and stimulation of participation by members in appropriate type-of-library divisions; and (6) Planning and development of programs of study and research for the type of activity for the total profession.

(d) Type-of-activity divisions may develop and adopt technical standards as official ALA standards. Type-of-activity divisions may participate in the development of nontechnical standards by type-of-library divisions but nontechnical standards may be adopted, or approved as official ALA standards, only by type-of-library divisions.

Sec. 4. (a) Each division shall be organized under a board of directors with overlapping terms and with authority to make decisions between conferences of meetings of the division.

(b) Each division may establish such committees, sections, and other subordinate units as may be required to discharge properly the responsibilities assigned to it, but no committee, section, or other unit devoted to an activity assigned to a type-of-activity division shall be established in a type-of-library division.

(c) A division may affiliate with itself regional, state, or local groups interested in the same field of library service or librarianship. Such groups may admit members who are not members of the division or of the Association.

Sec. 5. (a) A division shall accept as members all members of the Association who elect membership in that division according to the provisions of Article I of the Bylaws. Only members of this Association may be members of a division.

(b) Only personal members of a division shall have the right to vote and to hold office.

Sec. 6. (a) Each division shall establish annual dues. Funds so collected shall be subject to the provisions of paragraphs (b), (c), and (d).

(b) All dues paid for membership in divisions may be put to the credit of the division. Additional allotments may be made on the basis of need as determined by the Executive Board upon recommendation of the Committee on Program Evaluation and Support.

(c) All divisional funds are to be in the custody of the Executive Board, to be accounted for and disbursed by its designated officer on authorization of the division officers.

(d) A division shall have the right by vote of its members to impose additional fees. Funds so collected shall be subject to the provisions of paragraphs (a) and (b).

Sec. 7. No division shall incur expense on behalf of the Association except as authorized, nor shall any division commit the Association by any declaration of policy, except as provided in Sec. 2(b) of this Article.

Sec. 8. (a) A division may: Issue publications; hold meetings; organize sections; retain or adopt a distinctive name; appoint committees to function within the field of its activities; in general, carry on activities along the lines of its interests. Divisions shall exercise editorial and managerial control over their periodicals. The ALA Publishing Committee will be informed of plans for any new division periodical prior to publication. Materials prepared for publication by a division not intended for inclusion in a division periodical must be offered to ALA Publishing Services for first consideration.

(b) A division may be authorized to arrange a non-business national divisional conference under such conditions as the Executive Board may prescribe.

Sec. 9. (a) Each division shall be governed by the provisions of the Constitution and Bylaws of the Association to the extent to which they are applicable. To guide the officers and members in conducting the affairs of a division which are peculiar to itself, the division shall adopt a constitution and/or bylaws which shall not be in conflict with those of the Association. Such documents shall provide appropriate rules governing the holding of meetings, the conduct of mail votes, the constitution of a quorum, the conduct of nominations and elections, the establishment and appointment of committees, the procedure for their own amendment.

(b) A section shall be governed by the constitution and/or bylaws of the division of which it is a part. It may adopt bylaws of its own provided that they are not inconsistent with the Constitution and Bylaws of the Association or with those of the division.

Article VII.   Round Tables

Sec. 1. The Council may establish round tables under the following conditions:

(a) The Council may authorize the organization as a round table of any group of not less than 100 members of the Association who are interested in the same field of librarianship not within the scope of any division, upon petition of such group which shall include a statement of purpose.

(b) The Council may discontinue a round table when, in the opinion of the Council, the usefulness of that round table has ceased.

Sec. 2. No round table shall incur expense on behalf of the Association except as authorized, nor shall any round table commit the Association by any declaration of policy.

Sec. 3. Round tables may charge annual dues, limit their membership, and may, subject to approval of the Publishing Committee, issue publications. All round table funds are to be in the custody of the Executive Board, to be accounted for and disbursed by its designated officer on authorization of the round table officers.

Sec. 4. A round table may affiliate with itself regional, state, or local groups interested in the same field of library service or librarianship. Such groups may admit members who are not members of the round table or of the Association.

Sec. 5. Any member of the Association may become a member of any round table by complying with the requirements for membership. The members of each round table shall, either by a mail ballot or at its final session at each annual conference, choose officers to serve until the close of the next annual conference. Only personal members shall have the right to vote and hold office.

Article VIII.   Committees

Sec. 1. Advisory Committees. (a) There shall be a Committee on Appointments to be comprised of the presidents-elect of the divisions and the president-elect of the Association, who shall serve as chairperson, to advise the president-elect of the Association on nominations for committee appointments.

Sec. 2. Committees of the Council. (a) There shall be a Committee on Program Evaluation and Support consisting of six members appointed by the Council Committee on Committees on a staggered basis. The regular term of office shall be four years with members ineligible for reappointment. The chairperson shall be designated annually by the president-elect from the members. The treasurer of the Association shall serve on the Committee ex officio, but with voting privilege. The Committee shall evaluate the programs of the Association and submit a recommended budget to the Executive Board for action. To assist the Committee on Program Evaluation and Support and the ALA Planning Committee, there shall be a Planning and Budget Assembly which shall consist of one representative of each division, ALA committee, and round table and five councilors at large and five councilors from chapters. The representatives of the divisions, committees, and round tables shall be designated annually by each group; the Council representatives shall be elected by the Council for two-year staggered terms, none to extend beyond the regularly elected term on Council, from nominations submitted by the Council Committee on Committees. Additional nominations for the Councilor members of the Planning and Budget Assembly may be made by Councilors from the floor. The duties of the Planning and Budget Assembly are to provide guidelines for program planning and evaluation, assist in periodic selection of goals, to study the tentative sum-

mary planning document submitted by the Planning Committee and the balanced tentative budget submitted by the Committee on Program Evaluation and Support, raise questions concerning them, and offer suggestions to both committees.

(b) There shall be a Committee on Organization which shall recommend to the Council the establishment or discontinuance of divisions, round tables, and committees, as the needs of the Association may require. Such committee shall define the functions of each division, round table, and committee subject to the approval of the Council. The Committee on Organization shall also authorize membership initiative groups.

(c) Other committees of the Council shall include the following:

    Intellectual Freedom Committee
    International Relations Committee
    Legislation Committee
    Library Education Committee
    Minority Concerns
    Orientation Committee
    Pay Equity
    Planning Committee
    Policy Monitoring
    Professional Ethics Committee
    Publishing Committee
    Resolutions Committee
    Status of Women in Librarianship

(d) Appointments to the committees of the Council will be made by the Council Committee on Committees. The appointments shall be reported to Council by the following Annual Conference, at the end of which the new members will take up their duties. The chairpersons of the committees of the Council will be designated by the chairperson of the Committee on Committees, who is the president-elect. The committee size and length of terms shall follow the policy in force at the time appointments are made.

(e) Membership of the committees of the Council may consist of both Councilors and non-Councilors. No member, either Councilor or non-Councilor, shall serve on more than one of the committees or subcommittees of the Council simultaneously except as that member represents the parent committee as a member of the subcommittee. Subcommittees of the committees of the council shall exist at the will of each Council committee.

(f) If a vacancy occurs in the committees of the Council before time for the regular appointment of new members, it shall be filled by appointment made by the President, and the new appointee shall serve until the expiration of the term of the member replaced. If the committee member creating the vacancy is a member of Council, the new appointee must also be a Councilor.

Sec. 3. Standing Committees. (a) The Council, upon recommendation of the Committee on Organization, may establish standing committees to consider matters of the Association that require continuity of attention by the members. The Committee on Organization shall recommend the name and size of each such committee. Unless otherwise recommended by the Committee on Organization and approved by the Council, members of standing committees shall be appointed for terms of two years, and may be reappointed for a second but not a third consecutive term; but in no case shall a person serve on a committee for more than four consecutive years. Appointments shall be made in such manner as to provide continuity in membership.

(b) The standing committees shall include administration committees with functions and size to be determined by the Council, such as:

    Constitution and Bylaws Committee
    Membership Committee

(c) The standing committees shall include general committees of the Association with functions and size to be determined by the Council, such as:

    Accreditation Committee
    Awards Committee

Sec. 4. Special Committees. (a) All other committees authorized by the Council, and interim committees authorized by the Executive Board, shall be special committees. The life of a special committee shall be limited to two years unless the Council or the Executive Board, whichever has authorized such committee, shall otherwise provide. The term of appointment for members of a special committee shall end with the adjournment of the annual conference unless the Councilor or Executive Board, whichever has authorized such committee, shall provide for a different or a longer term. Members of special committees whose terms expire shall be eligible for reappointment, except for the members of the Nominating Committees. Members of juries charged with making selections for awards shall be eligible for reappointment, but the number of members to be reappointed shall be limited to a minority in any single year.

(b) The special committees shall include the following administration committees with functions and size to be determined by the Council, such as:

    Conference Program Committee
    Election Committee
    Nominating Committee

Sec. 5. Interdivisional committees and other committees formed by two or more distinct units within the Association may be established as required by the groups concerned with notification to the Committee on Organization.

Sec. 6. Joint Committees. (a) The Council, on the recommendation of the Committee on Organization, may establish joint committees, either standing or special, with other organizations when the functions of the proposed committee cannot be appropriately delegated to a single division or ALA committee.

(b) Joint committees of the divisions or round tables with organizations outside the Association may be established only with the approval of the Council and upon the recommendation of the Committee on Organization.

Sec. 7. The committee membership year shall be the same as the conference year. Not less than two weeks prior to the midwinter meeting the president-elect shall report to the Executive Board for the Committee on Appointments. At a meeting prior to or during the midwinter meeting of the Council, the Executive Board shall consider the nominations and make its decisions as to appointments.

Sec. 8. (a) The Executive Board shall designate the chairperson of each committee annually except for the committees of council, which chairpersons are designated as set out in Article VIII, Sec. 2(d) of the Bylaws.

(b) Any vacancy occurring on a committee, except for committees of Council, shall be filled by appointment by the Executive Board until the expiration of the conference year in which the vacancy occurs, at which time appointment to fill out the unexpired term shall be made. Vacancies on the committees of the Council shall be filled as set out in Article VIII, Sec. 2(f) of the Bylaws.

(c) Any member of a committee, except for members of the committees of the Council, may be removed by a three-fourths vote of the Executive Board upon recommendation of either the chairperson of the committee, the chairperson of the Committee on Appointments, the board of directors of a division, or the president of the Association. Any member of a Council committee may be removed by action of the Council's Committee on Committees.

Sec. 9. Votes in the Executive Board, as well as in committees, may be taken by mail, electronic system, or conference call, provided that all members are canvassed simultaneously. An affirmative vote from two-thirds of the full body shall be required. Each committee shall have the authority to set a time limit within which the votes of its members shall be recorded, but if no such time limit is set no vote shall be counted unless received within 30 days from the day the text of the matter voted upon was mailed properly addressed to those entitled to vote on the matter involved.

Sec. 10. No committee shall incur expense on behalf of the Association except as authorized, nor shall any committee commit the Association by any declaration of policy.

Article IX. Finances

Sec. 1. Except for projects supported by grants to the Association, annual estimates of income shall be based upon the unexpended balance remaining from the previous year plus anticipated revenues for the next budget year. In no case may expenditures be budgeted in excess of the estimates of income arrived at in this manner except for projects supported by grants to the Association.

Sec. 2. An audit of all accounts shall be made annually by a commercial auditor.

Sec. 3. A report shall be made annually to the membership, by a duly authorized member of the Executive Board, detailing receipts and expenditures, explaining the Association's fiscal status, and reporting on the audit.

Article X. Notices by Mail

Sec. 1. Publication of notices in the *American Libraries* shall be considered sufficient to fulfill the requirement of notice by mail.

Article XI. Parliamentary Authority

Sec. 1. *Robert's Rules of Order Newly Revised*, in the latest edition, shall govern the Association in all cases to which it can be applied and in which it is not inconsistent with the Constitution, the Bylaws, or special rules of order of the Association.

As amended June, 1989.

INDEX

The initial letter *C* indicates Constitution; *B*, Bylaws.

ALA Policy Manual

CONTENTS

INTRODUCTION

The ALA POLICY MANUAL includes the brief statements of policies adopted by the ALA Council.

The full text of pertinent position statements, policies, and procedures is retained in the "Current Reference File" maintained at ALA Headquarters. Documents no longer pertinent to the ALA POLICY MANUAL will be retained in an historical file at the ALA Headquarters. Both of these files will be available at the ALA Headquarters and at the Midwinter and Annual meetings.

The ALA POLICY MANUAL is divided into two sections: Organization and Operational Policies, and Positions and Public Policy Statements.

Where ALA has made a position statement applicable to the operation of libraries, ALA accepts that statement for its own relevant operations.

Section ONE **Organization and Operational Policies**

1. MISSION, PRIORITY AREAS, GOALS

1.1 INTRODUCTION

Any organization as large, diverse, and dynamic as ALA must periodically reassess priorities in order to make progress in selected areas determined to be of prime concern to its members. The diversity of the membership dictates a wide range of interests that frequently overlap or complement one another. Nonetheless, we can identify overriding priorities that ALA should pursue vigorously within the United States and coordinate with groups abroad. Only such focusing of efforts and the subsequent allocation of Association funds and evaluation of its activities can ensure needed progress within the profession.

ALA recognizes its broad social responsibilities. The broad social responsibilities of the American Library Association are defined in terms of the contribution that librarianship can make in ameliorating or solving the critical problems of society; support for efforts to help inform and educate the people of the United States on these problems and to encourage them to examine the many views on and the facts regarding each problem; and the willingness of ALA to take a position on current critical issues with the relationship to libraries and library service set forth in the position statement.

ALA promotes the creation, maintenance, and enhancement of a learning society, encouraging its members to work with educators, government officials, and organizations in coalitions to initiate and support comprehensive efforts to ensure that school, public, academic, and special libraries in every community cooperate to provide lifelong learning services to all.

(*See also* Library Personnel Practices [54]; Intellectual Freedom [53]; Legislation [51]; and Services and Responsibilities of Libraries [52]; "Current Reference File": Realities, a report from the ALA Task Force on Excellence in Education.)

1.2 Mission

The mission of the American Library Association is to provide leadership for the development, promotion, and improvement of library and information services and the profession of librarianship in order to enhance learning and ensure access to information for all.

1.3 Priority Areas and Goals

Priority Area A. Access to information

ALA will promote efforts to ensure that every individual has access to needed information at the time needed and in a format the individual can utilize, through provision of library and information services.

Goals:

1) All individuals have equal access to libraries and information services.

2) Instruction in information use is available to all.

3) Government information is widely and easily available.

4) Library collections are developed, managed, and preserved to provide access for users to the full range of available knowledge and information.

5) Access to information is facilitated by bibliographic organization.

6) Library use is high.

7) Fees are not a barrier to library access and service.

Priority Area B. Legislation/funding

ALA will promote legislation at all levels that will strengthen library and information services. Means will be developed for facilitating the effective competition of libraries for public funds as well as for funds from the private sector.

Goals:

1) Libraries have adequate funding from public sources (local, state, federal).

2) ALA members are well informed about opportunities for raising funds from private sources.

3) Reliable and timely statistics and information about all sources of library funding are available.

4) Congress consistently approves legislation favorable to libraries.

5) Local governing authorities and state legislatures consistently approve ordinances and legislation favorable to libraries.
6) Information about legislation with potential impact on libraries and library service is easily available.

Priority Area C. Intellectual freedom

ALA will promote the protection of library materials, personnel, and trustees from censorship; the defense of library personnel and trustees in support of intellectual freedom and the Library Bill of Rights; and the education of library personnel, trustees, and the general public to the importance of intellectual freedom.
   Goals:
   1) First Amendment rights are secure.
   2) Persons whose First Amendment rights are challenged have adequate support.

Priority Area D. Public awareness

ALA will promote the role of librarians and the use of libraries and their resources and services as well as the awareness of their importance to all segments of society.
   Goals:
   1) ALA provides information about libraries to all.
   2) Librarians are recognized as proactive professionals responsible for ensuring the free flow of information and ideas to present and future generations of library users.
   3) Libraries are recognized as proactive agencies essential to the cultural, educational, and economic life of society.

Priority Area E. Personnel resources

ALA will promote the recruitment, education, professional development, rights, interests, and obligations of library personnel and trustees.
   Goals:
   1) Library and information science education meets the changing library and information needs of society.
   2) Master's level programs are effectively accredited.
   3) Librarians and all other library personnel are paid equitable and attractive salaries.
   4) Librarians have a variety of opportunities for professional development and continuing education.
   5) Workshops and conferences conducted by ALA are available to librarians, trustees, and others interested in libraries.
   6) Job information, placement, and career services are readily available to librarians.
   7) Effective library personnel policies are established and used.
   8) Librarianship recruits a racially and ethnically diverse group of high caliber persons.
   9) Librarians uphold the ALA Code of Ethics.
   10) Librarians are proactive professionals who ensure the free flow of information and ideas.

Priority Area F. Library services, development, and technology

ALA will promote the availability of information tools and technologies which assist librarians in providing services responsive to the changing needs of society.
   Goals:
   1) Guidelines, standards, and codes are formulated and promoted to facilitate effective library service.
   2) Professional resources in a variety of formats are produced by ALA.
   3) Statistics about libraries are collected regularly and distributed promptly.

4) Research related to libraries and librarianship is conducted and results are widely disseminated.
5) Information and advisory services about libraries and librarianship are available from ALA in response to requests.
6) ALA encourages cooperative activities to improve service to library users.
7) ALA promotes access to information via technological means.
8) Librarians are able to use technology effectively.
9) Library funds are managed effectively.
10) Librarians practice effective public relations.
11) Libraries are proactive agencies which meet the challenges of social, economic, and environmental change.

1.4   ALA Organizational Support Goals

In order to address these priorities, ALA will use its resources wisely and maintain a flexible structure that promotes the diverse interests and broad participation of members and units.

Organizational Area A. ALA roles and relationships

The size and complexity of ALA with its many and diverse units creates difficulties in coordinating roles and responsibilities. ALA has an opportunity to recognize diversity as a strength and build on it.
   Goals:
   1) The activities and programs of ALA are coordinated.
   2) ALA speaks with one voice for the profession.

Organizational Area B. ALA finances

ALA maintains financial stability.
   Goals:
   1) ALA obtains a significant amount of income from sources other than dues.
   2) ALA maintains adequate cash reserves.
   3) New markets are developed for ALA's products and services.
   4) ALA has a continuously updated multiyear financial plan.
   5) ALA provides accurate and timely financial reports to members, officers, and staff.

Organizational Area C. ALA human resources

A large, stable, and involved membership is essential to the health and effectiveness of ALA. The development of new leaders must be continuous in the Association. ALA must maintain staff with a high level of expertise and commitment.
   Goals:
   1) ALA membership is large and stable.
   2) Large numbers of members are involved in the work of the Association.
   3) ALA leaders are effective.
   4) ALA responds to the needs and interests of members.
   5) ALA staff provides a high level of expertise and service.
   6) Members are fully informed about ALA activities.
   7) State library associations/chapters are fully informed about ALA activities.
   8) Appropriate and timely data about the ALA membership are available.
      Adopted by ALA Council, July 1, 1986
   (*See* "Current Reference File": ALA Strategic Long Range Plan.)

2.   MEMBERSHIP

2.1   Honorary ALA Membership

The ALA Executive Board has sole authority to nominate honorary members. In making

nominations, it shall give consideration to those recommended to it by the boards of divisions. Divisions may confer honorary membership only upon those chosen as honorary members of ALA.

2.2   Membership: Suspension of

The Executive Board shall suspend from membership in the American Library Association any member who or which shall have been found by competent government authority to have violated any federal, state, or local civil rights law, such suspension to continue until such time as the Executive Board has been satisfied that the member is in full compliance with the law.

3.   TRUSTEES

3.1   Trustees and the American Library Association

The American Library Association reaffirms its interest in building a strong lay membership component of the Association in order to provide more effective leadership and guidance for American libraries.

3.2   Fair Representation on Library Boards

The American Library Association supports fair demographic, age group, socio-economic, ethnic, and racial minority representation on the governing boards of public libraries.

3.3   Reimbursement of Conference Expenses of Trustees

The American Library Association supports reimbursement of conference and meeting expenses incurred by trustees in the course of participation in ALA as legitimate and desirable budget expenditures by the local public library.

4.   ELECTIONS AND APPOINTMENTS AND ATTENDANT RESPONSIBILITIES

4.1   Vote Tallies: Publication

A complete report of the votes cast for the candidates for Councilor-at-Large and officers of ALA shall be listed in *American Libraries*.

4.2   Candidates: Statements of Concern

The ALA ballots for the positions of ALA officers and Councilors shall be accompanied by a short statement of the candidates' professional concerns.

4.3   Executive Board Vacancies

When a vacancy exists on the Executive Board for which an election is to be held, the two candidates receiving the highest and second highest number of votes are elected to regular four-year terms and the candidate receiving the third highest number of votes is elected to fill the vacancy. The same procedure applies should there be more than one vacancy.

4.4   Nominations and Appointments: Restrictions

No person shall accept nomination or appointment which could result in simultaneous service in any two or more of the following categories:
1) President of a division
2) President-elect of a division
3) Chair of a section of a division
4) Chair-elect of a section of a division
5) Chair of an ALA Committee
(*See also* 5.1 for further limitations on members of Council.)

4.5   Offices and Appointments: Restrictions

No member of the American Library Association may serve simultaneously on more than three committees or on one governing board/committee and two committees. Governing board/committee responsibilities which entail ex officio membership on other governing boards or committees are not in conflict with this policy.

(*See also* 5.1 for further limitations on members and Council and 4.4 above.)

4.6   Requirements for Committee Service

Members of all ALA and unit committees are expected to attend all meetings. Failure to attend two consecutive meetings or groups of meetings (defined as all meetings of a committee that take place at one Midwinter Meeting or Annual Conference) without an explanation acceptable to the committee chair constitutes grounds for removal upon request by the chair to and approval of the appropriate appointing official or governing board.

(*See also* 5.1 for limitation on service by members of Council.)

4.7   Conflict of Interest: Executive Board

Members of the Executive Board shall not use their Board or Association relationships for their personal gain. To ensure recognition of this responsibility, any Board member aware of a conflict of interest with a matter coming before the Board or any of its committees shall bring this to the attention of the Board or committee, shall not vote on the subject or attempt to influence the vote of others and shall not be counted in determining the quorum if that has not already been established for the meeting. These points shall be recorded in the Minutes of such meetings.

(*See* "Current Reference File" for full statement adopted by Council, June 30, 1980, which is read at every first meeting of the new Board.)

4.8   Members Serving as Independent Contractors

ALA may secure the services of members on a fee for service basis as independent contractors. Members who serve as independent contractors will enter into contractual arrangements to provide services to ALA or any of its units or components. In the Association-contractor relationship, the contract will include mutually agreed-upon parameters for the work of the member contractor. The member as contractor reports to and is accountable to the Association's project director. The contractual arrangement may also provide for reimbursement of expenses.

5.   COUNCIL

5.1   Limitation on Committee Service

No member of Council may serve on more than one non-Council-related Association activity, excluding Council membership.

This policy shall be explained to future nominees for Council.

5.2   Relationships of Executive Board and Council

Matters of policy or operations requiring Council actions shall normally be referred first to the Executive Board, which shall make recommendations to the Council.

A report of the Board's position shall go also to the bodies submitting the reports upon which the recommendations were made.

The Executive Board shall send to members of Council copies of the full minutes of all its meetings, together with any explanatory or other statements on matters coming before Council for action.

Written action reports of Council committees shall be made available on the same basis in time to the Executive Board and Council whether or not reports are issued at or between conferences and whether or not the Board acts on such reports during the conference at which received.

The Executive Board in its review of reports of Council committees should report in its recommendations particularly on organizational and administrative implications, if possible in writing.

If it elects to do so, Council may exercise its right to act upon policy recommendations of its committees without benefit of Executive Board discussion of the recommendations.

5.3   Motions for Council Action

A Council motion which has fiscal implications must be submitted to the Executive Director 24 hours before it is to be voted on.* The Committee on Program Evaluation and Support shall provide estimated fiscal information, or indicate that there is insufficient time to get such information, or that the motion is not specific enough to enable COPES to estimate the costs involved. If a resolution would impose specific assignments on a division, it will be reviewed by COPES with the division board of directors to assess the financial needs in that assignment; COPES will report to Council recommended budgetary adjustments necessary to implement that assignment. COPES' report on all resolutions with fiscal implications will be given to Council prior to final Council action.

5.4   Council Resolutions: Guidelines for Preparation of Resolutions to Council

The following guidelines are addressed to individuals and units preparing resolutions to come before Council:

1) A resolution should be complete so that, upon passage, it becomes a clear and formal expression of the opinion or will of the assembly.

2) The resolution should show clearly the initiating individual or unit.

3) The resolution should address only one topic or issue.

4) The terms used in a resolution should be readily understandable or have specific definition.

5) The intent, objective, or goal of the resolution should be clear to all. The resolution should make clear whether it sets forth a general policy, an ALA viewpoint, or a call for specific action.

6) All ALA position statements shall set forth their relationship to libraries and library service.

7) If the resolution calls for a specific action or a course of action in certain circumstances, the resolution should specify the resources needed to carry out the directive.

8) A Council resolution which has fiscal implications must be submitted to the Executive Director 24 hours before it is to be voted on so that COPES can provide fiscal information as required in 5.3.*

9) The Rules of Council require submission of resolutions 24 hours prior to presentation to Council to allow time for reproduction and distribution.*

10) All resolutions must be submitted by a voting member of Council; memorial resolutions, tributes, and testimonials may be exempted from this guideline.

11) No resolution, except those from ALA committees, which has not been reviewed by the Council Committee on Resolutions may be accepted for inclusion on the agenda until so reviewed.

12) The mover of a resolution shall state whether the resolution amends or creates policy and

_____

*If there is less than 24 hours between the adjournment of Council II and Council III's convening hour, resolutions may be submitted within 90 minutes following adjournment of Council II. (Adopted by Council July 1988)

shall identify the policy being changed and/or indicate the portion of the resolution to be cited as policy. If a policy set forth conflicts with another policy, provision to resolve the conflict shall be made.

13) If the resolution calls for a specific action or program with a timetable, the timetable shall be clear and achievable.

14) If the resolution is addressed to or refers to a specific group or groups, it shall name the groups. Sponsors of the resolution shall provide to the Council Secretariat the names and addresses of all such named groups.

15) Memorial resolutions, tributes, and testimonials will be presented to Council at the beginning of the last session of Council at each Midwinter Meeting, and to the membership at the beginning of the last Membership Meeting at each Annual Conference:

a) Presiding officer will read the names of persons/organizations recognized by a formal resolution; the names will be displayed on the screen and copies of each resolution will be available at the information table.

b) *American Libraries* will carry an annual "memorial page," noting members who have died since the previous list, with appropriate notations.

The *Annual Conference Program* will also include a "memorial page" listing those members who have died since preparation of the previous Conference Program.

5.5   Reporting the Implementation of Council Actions and Resolutions

At the first Council meeting of each Annual Conference and Midwinter Meeting, the ALA Executive Board or its delegate shall report to Council on the status of implementation of motions and resolutions passed by Council during the preceding year. The report shall be entered in the Council minutes.

5.6   Policies on Council Procedures

5.6.1   *Attendance*

At each Council meeting, attendance shall be taken by checklist or roll call.

5.6.2   *Council-Board Session*

At each Midwinter Meeting, there shall be at least one session of Council with the Executive Board for information only, to be held prior to other meetings of Council.

At each annual Conference, there shall be at least one joint session of Membership and Council with the Executive Board, for information only, to be held prior to other meetings of Council and Membership.

5.6.3   *Agenda*

The Executive Director, as Secretary of the Council, shall mail the agenda for a Council meeting, including such documentation as has been provided by members and units, to reach Council members not later than two weeks before such meetings. Minority reports shall be given to Council.

5.6.4   *Reports*

Matters and reports of a purely informational nature will be distributed to Council in writing. Oral reports will be confined to matters requiring Council action or which are requested by the Council or by the Executive Board.

5.6.5   *Reports of Divisions*

Annual reports from ALA division presidents shall be submitted to Council in writing for inclusion in the record of Council meetings.

5.6.6   *Recorded Votes*

Action of the Council on matters of policy will be on roll call vote if the presiding officer so determines or on request from a Councilor. Results of roll call votes shall be published in *American Libraries* for the information of the membership. Results of other recorded votes shall be reported to membership.

5.6.7 *Minutes*

Minutes of Council meetings shall be approved for distribution by the President and President-elect and distributed promptly. Council members shall be requested to submit additions or corrections within 10 days of receipt of the minutes, such additions and corrections to be placed on the agenda of Council's next meeting, at which formal approval of the minutes shall take place.

5.7 *Policy Manual*/Monitoring Committee

Policy adopted by ALA Council shall be incorporated into a manual in simple, clear language, indexed for easy access, and made available in a format easily reproduced and updated. A Policy Monitoring Committee shall have prepared additions or changes in the Manual following each Annual Conference or Midwinter Meeting as may be required by motions and resolutions adopted by the Council following the guidelines (5.4), and shall review these additions and changes prior to publication. In instances of long reports and resolutions, it is the responsibility of the issuing committee to include an abstract statement or the exact language for the Policy Manual. The Policy Monitoring Committee will report to Council on the accomplishment of Council directives. The committee shall be responsible also for bringing to the attention of Council updated items to be retired from the Manual, and gaps in the presentation of policies upon which Council may wish to act.

6. UNITS, COMMITTEES, ETC.

6.1   Chapters

6.1.1 *ALA Responsibilities to Chapters*

A statement of summary of conditions governing Chapter affiliations as stated in various ALA policies and the Constitution and Bylaws shall be sent to each Chapter for its acceptance as a certified statement of agreement between the Chapter and ALA.

6.1.2 *Effect of Unpaid Dues on Chapter Status*

A Chapter which has not paid its dues as of March 1 of each year, and which continues such delinquency for one month after notice has been sent, is no longer a member and no longer entitled to have a Councilor, until such time as the Chapter resumes payment of dues.

6.1.3 *Library Issue Caucuses*

Chapter Councilors and Councilors-at-Large should work together to establish library issue caucuses at state and regional library association and type-of-library association meetings with the goal of identifying, developing information, and communicating recommendations on library issues to ALA Council and/or other appropriate bodies.

6.2   New Units of ALA

6.2.1 *Petitions for Establishment of New Units of ALA*

Minimum acceptable standards for petitions requesting the establishment of new divisions, round tables, and other units of ALA are:

1) The purpose of the petition shall be clearly stated on a single sheet attached to each group of signature pages.

2) Each signature page shall contain this statement: "I favor this petition to . . ."

3) Petitioners shall sign and give library affiliation legibly. Failure to do so may result in the invalidation of the petition.

4) Information about this format and a sample petition will be supplied from ALA headquarters to anyone inquiring.

5) Petitioners shall be personal members of ALA.

6.3   Round Tables of ALA: Role and Function

Round Tables are provided for in the ALA Bylaws, Article VII.

1) *Role of Round Tables in ALA*. Round Tables may conduct continuing educational activities; study and discuss topics of concern to the Round Table; work with other ALA units on joint projects; issue publications with the advice, assistance, and approval of the ALA Publishing Committee; conduct projects and programs in the areas of the Round Table's purpose and recommend activities and policies to units of the Association, including Council.

2) *Policy Functions*. As noted in the ALA Constitution, Article VI, and the Bylaws, Article VII, three bodies—Council, the divisions, and the membership—have authority to determine and act for ALA in matters of policy. Recommendations of Round Tables regarding a lack of policy, a new policy, or changes in policy shall be forwarded to the appropriate body for action.

3) *Finances*. Round Tables shall not incur expenses on behalf of the Association except as authorized. Funds of Round Tables are in the custody of the ALA Executive Board, to be accounted for and disbursed by its designated officer only upon authorization of the Round Table officers.

Any formal solicitation of funds by any ALA unit from outside organizations, agencies, groups of individuals, or others must be authorized by the ALA Executive Board or Executive Director. Acceptance of unsolicited funds shall be authorized by the Executive Director to assure that the terms and conditions are consistent with ALA policies. Contracts, grant agreements, project proposals, and similar financial documents shall be signed by the ALA Executive Director for all ALA activities and units.

4) *ALA Services to Round Tables*. ALA will supply to Round Tables such support services as: staff liaison and related staff services; maintenance of Round Table membership and subscription records; accounting services to include preparation of monthly budget reports and bill payment; preparing, distributing, and counting ballots for annual election of Round Table officers; services of the conference Arrangements Office, to include scheduling and announcement of Midwinter and Annual Conference meetings and other special events; cartage of materials to ALA meetings; services of the Public Information Office, including preparation and distribution of press releases; specialized reference services of the ALA Headquarters Library; use of the ALA mailroom for routine and special mailings; storage of supplies, documents, and equipment at the ALA warehouse organization and storage of Round Table documents at ALA Headquarters Library and archives.

Round Tables shall deposit at least two copies of all periodicals and other Round Table publications in the ALA Headquarters Library.

Charges for data processing services, reproduction of materials, mailings, and similar support services will be charged to the Round Table at the same rate as to other units.

Staff liaison services are made available to Round Tables to aid the officers and members in coordinating projects and programs with other units, in handling financial obligations and records, in orienting new Round Table officers and groups, in determining procedures to expedite or conduct Round Table projects and programs, in administrative or secretarial phases of Round Table activities, and in planning activities.

5) *Round Table Services to ALA*. The ALA Round Tables through their programs and services implement and enhance the overall ALA program, further the Association's Goals and Priorities, and provide an added dimension to the ALA structure. All Round Tables are membership units which provide an additional avenue for membership discussion, opinion, and response. It is not currently possible for Round Tables to bear a charge which will cover the complete direct and indirect costs of services from ALA. ALA has adopted a schedule of charges based on a Round Table's total dues income. The assessment of each Round Table shall be based on the best estimate of services performed recently by Headquarters staff.

6.4   Divisions

6.4.1 *Policies of the American Library Association in Relation to its Membership Divisions*

I. Preamble

The American Library Association (ALA) is unique among American associations in the manner in which it is structured. It is one association, with indivisible assets and a single set of uniform administrative, financial, and personnel policies and procedures. It is governed by one Council, from which its Executive Board is elected, and is managed by an Executive Director who serves at the pleasure of that Board.

It is also the home for eleven Divisions, each of which has:

- a statement of responsibility developed by its members and approved by ALA Council;
- a set of goals and objectives established by its members, which drive its activities;
- an Executive Director and other personnel as necessary to carry out its programs;
- responsibility for generating revenue to support staff and carry out its programs; and,
- a separate Board of Directors, elected by its members, and responsible to ALA Council.

Divisions and all other units of ALA are inextricably interrelated in structure, personnel, resources, overall mission, and operations. All members of Divisions are first members of ALA. Their voluntary selection of Division membership is an indication of their special interests, in addition to their general concern for libraries and librarianship, and it demands the commitment of the Divisions to serve those special interests.

By this commitment, expressed in publications, conference programming, advisory services, and other educational activities germane to their mission statements, the Divisions serve the American Library Association as a whole. By supporting Division operations through the provision of space and services, ALA gives tangible evidence of its recognition of the importance of Divisions in meeting the needs of its members.

The nature of the relationships among the various ALA units is a dynamic one. Divisions and ALA are committed to maintaining a collaborative style of interaction and to remaining flexible enough to address the ever-changing issues facing libraries and librarians.

This collaborative model implies mutuality in all relationships, the ability of any aggregation of units to work together for the common good, and the co-existence of Division autonomy and ALA unity.

This policy document implies the need for a mutual understanding of the differences between Divisions and other ALA units, differences which are balanced by a similarity of interest and activity. It underscores the Divisions' willingness to support and contribute to ALA as a whole and their recognition of the interdependence of all ALA units.

These policies must be based on an appreciation by the total membership and by other ALA units of the Divisions' contributions to ALA as a whole. An activity carried out by a Division is an ALA activity. Division staff members are ALA staff members and represent ALA as well as their own Divisions in work with members and the general public. Division officers and members must recognize the value to the Division of the services provided by ALA, and ALA members and units must recognize the value to ALA as a whole of the services provided by Divisions.

Divisions are integrally involved in the decision-making process of the Association. They exercise their decision-making prerogatives through the following means:

- Full authority within those areas of responsibility designated by ALA Council (ALA Bylaws, Article VI, Section 2b)
- Representation on ALA Council to raise issues and to set policy (ALA Bylaws, Article IV, Section 2c; ALA Policy 5.4)
- Representation on the Planning and Budget Assembly (ALA Bylaws, Article VIII, Section 2)
- Negotiation of performance objectives of Division Executive Directors with the ALA Deputy Executive Director (ALA Policy 6.4.1 VII)
- Day-to-day involvement of Division staff in the operations and deliberations of the Association
- Representation on Association-wide bodies including the Legislative Assembly, the Library Education Assembly, and the Membership Promotion Task Force
- Participation in the planning process.

In sum, this document is designed to continue a cooperative framework in which the inevitable questions of organizational relationships can be addressed and resolved.

II. Current Organizational Values of ALA

This statement reflects the current organizational values of the American Library Association and was developed through reference to existing ALA documents.

A. Unity

ALA is one association. It has a single set of administrative, financial, and personnel policies and procedures, as well as indivisible assets. All members of Divisions are members of ALA. Divisions and all other ALA units are inextricably interrelated in structure, personnel, resources, overall mission, and operations.

B. Diversity

ALA has a stake in the work of each of its Divisions. Division activities and services are of value and importance to the Association. They provide for a rich and diverse program that gives opportunities to all segments of the profession for involvement, leadership, and participation in activities that carry out the mission, goals, and priorities of the Association.

C. Authority

Recognizing the significant contribution, resources, and expertise of its Divisions, ALA delegates to each Division the authority and responsibility to represent the Association in designated areas. Each Division provides unique programs and services to its members, to all members of the Association, to the profession of librarianship, to the broader educational community, and to the public at large.

D. Autonomy

ALA provides leadership for the development, promotion, and improvement of library service. ALA values the strength and effectiveness of its Divisions. Divisions are best able to carry out their missions when their members have the autonomy, independence, and freedom to pursue goals and objectives of particular concern to them, as well as to participate democratically in the Division's direction, governance, and financial decisions.

E. Collaboration/Cooperation

ALA and its Divisions have opportunities through the Association's unique governance and administrative structure to stimulate and build on one another's strengths and resources to advance shared, as well as diverse, goals.

III. Purpose, Scope, Implementation, Review Process, and Definitions

A. Purpose and Scope

Divisions have a substantial degree of autonomy and responsibility; however, the corporate and legal entity is the American Library Association. Any responsibilities not specifically delegated to Divisions remain within the authority of the Executive Board and ALA Council. The principal intent of this document is to define the policies governing the relationship between ALA and its membership Divisions.

In addition to the ALA Constitution and Bylaws and other ALA Policies, this document provides a framework of guiding principles for that relationship. As a policy document, its adoption and approval of revisions are the responsibility of the ALA Council. ALA has other policies and procedures that govern the relationships with other organizational units.

B. Implementation

Implementation of these policies will be carried out under the direction of the ALA Executive Director, working with the department heads and Division executive directors. Major operational decisions made in that implementation will be codified in documents referred to as "Operational Practices."

C. Review Process

To make this Agreement responsive to the needs of the Association, it shall be reviewed on an annual basis by those responsible for the governance of ALA and its membership Divisions. Changes may be recommended by Division leadership, ALA staff and management, or other interested parties at any time; however, COPES shall initiate the review process annually according to the following schedule:

Fall COPES Meeting—At this meeting, COPES develops agenda of major emerging issues and requests input from Divisions. The annual indirect cost study shall be available.

Midwinter—Divisions discuss any operating agreement issues identified by COPES and raise other operating agreement issues to be discussed by COPES at its Spring meeting. The Planning and Budget Assembly (PBA) may be used as a forum for PBA participants to identify operating agreement issues of concern.

Spring COPES Meeting—Mandated discussion of operating agreement issues raised by Divisions, ALA staff and management, and/or other interested parties. COPES recommends mechanism and time table for cooperative actions with Divisions to address proposed changes.

Annual—Operating agreement is a mandated item on PBA agenda. Division Boards review any COPES recommendations and respond to COPES. COPES forwards any necessary recommendations to Executive Board for action by Council.

Any changes undertaken in this Operating Agreement shall be implemented consistent with the budget cycle of ALA and its Divisions and shall be done in such a manner as to minimize negative impact on the program of ALA and of the Divisions.

Roles of Key Parties to operating agreement

Division Boards: identify problem areas and issues; initiate actions necessary for revisions; work with Division staff and other Divisions as appropriate to explore problems and solutions; make recommendations to COPES to initiate revisions.

COPES: identify problem areas and issues; communicate information concerning the operating agreement through PBA to Council and to ALA at large; work with Division leaders and ALA management to recommend solutions and consequent revisions to operating agreement.

ALA Management: identify problem areas and issues and work with the Division Executive Directors to explore problems and solutions. Review policies and make recommendations as appropriate to COPES and Executive Board.

Division Executive Directors: identify problem areas and issues and review as appropriate with management and Division Boards.

D. Definitions

The following definitions are guidelines for members and staff in the development, review, and implementation of these policies:

- *Policies:* Guiding principles that provide the framework for the relationship between ALA and its membership Divisions. Policies reflect the views and thinking of membership, and provide a guide to action to achieve the goals of the American Library Association. Policies are adopted by the Council of the American Library Association.
- *Operational Practices:* Definitions of the manner or method of implementing policies. Operational Practices (1) deal with terms under which services will be provided free of charge or at a cost; (2) define roles and responsibilities in policy implementation; and (3) reflect other issues contained in the "Policies" document that may require negotiation between departments and membership Divisions.

  Operational Practices are developed by the ALA Executive Director with the ALA Department Heads in consultation with the Division executive directors and appropriate personnel in the department responsible for the activity described. Department personnel will provide draft copies of those procedures for review and comment to appropriate ALA staff members whose work will be affected by those procedures. Copies of Operational Practices are supplied to appropriate membership units responsible for the governance of ALA and its membership Divisions.

  Detailed information about implementation of the policies outlined throughout this document are found in the Operational Practices for the Implementation of Policies of the American Library Association in Relation to Its Membership Divisions.
- *ALA Basic Services:* Those services made available to all ALA members at no additional charge beyond their ALA dues. Dues provide the primary support for basic services. Basic services may be supported by dues or other options as approved by the Executive Board. Basic ALA services include: *American*

Libraries, information/advisory services, support for governance/member groups, public/professional relations, administration of awards and scholarships, membership promotion/retention, executive/administrative/financial services; offices: research, personnel resources, outreach services, government relations, intellectual freedom, accreditation; Headquarters Library.

- *Division Basic Services:* Those services made available to all Division members at no additional charge beyond their Division dues. Dues provide the primary support for basic services. Basic services may be supported by dues or other options as determined by Division Boards. Basic Division services include: periodical publications designated as perquisites of membership, information/advisory services, support for governance/member groups, public/professional relations, administration of awards and scholarships, membership promotion/retention, executive/administrative/financial services.

- *Overhead:*
  a) Internal: that overhead rate applied to units of ALA, e.g., the annual overhead rate paid by divisions for revenue-generating activities identified in this policy document.
  b) External: that overhead rate applied for the purposes of external reporting, e.g., grants and taxes.
- *Fund Balance:* Accumulated net revenue.

IV. Use of ALA Services

All ALA Divisions must use exclusively the following services provided by the ALA Administrative Services Department: Personnel, Membership Services, telephone, insurance, purchasing, Fiscal Services Department, Legal Counsel, and Archives. ALA Divisions must be housed in properties owned or leased by the Association.

V. Financial

Divisions are governed by prevailing ALA fiscal policies and procedures. Divisions shall participate in formulating and revising these policies and procedures.

A. Dues

Divisions have the right to establish their own personal and organizational dues structures and set membership perquisites. (ALA Bylaws, Article I, Section 2; Article VI, Section 6)

Discount and special promotion dues authorized by the ALA Executive Board apply only to that portion of dues applying to ALA membership. Divisions receive proportionate reimbursements for "free" Division choices of continuing and life members. (ALA Bylaws, Article I, Section 2 A.7)

B. Council Actions with Fiscal Implications

Council resolutions that would impose specific assignments on a Division shall be reviewed by COPES with the Division Board of Directors to assess any financial implications of that assignment. COPES shall report back to Council with recommendations as to any budgetary adjustments necessary to implement such assignments prior to final Council action on that item. (ALA Policy 5.3)

C. Services and Charges

The fiscal arrangements between ALA and its membership Divisions in regard to charges for services can be categorized in five ways. The five categories are defined below. Specific examples of the services in each category are given.

1. ALA provides to Divisions at no direct charge the following services of ALA Departments and Offices:

a. Administrative Services Department
- Office space and related services
- Telephone services: switchboard, 800 number, and internal service, as defined in an Operational Practice
- Distribution services
- Basic furniture and equipment (as defined in an Operational Practice) for each regular Division staff member
- Equipment maintenance on equipment supplied by ALA
- Membership services
- Personnel services
- Purchasing
- Data processing (as defined in an Operational Practice)
- Storage and warehouse space
b. Communications Department
- Conference Arrangements, including:
  —Staff travel costs and per diem for Midwinter Meetings and Annual Conferences
  —Equipment (e.g., AV and computers including the cost of labor), supplies, services, and space for programs, meetings and offices at the Midwinter Meeting and Annual Conference (as defined in an Operational Practice)
  —Exhibit space at Annual Conference
- Public information services, including the preparation and distribution of news releases
c. Fiscal Services Department
- Accounting
- Financial systems
- Planning and budgeting
- Business expense (insurance, legal, audit)
- Credit and collections
d. Publishing Department
- Copyright service
- Rights and permissions
e. Executive Office
f. Washington Office
g. Office for Intellectual Freedom
h. Office for Library Outreach Services
i. Office for Library Personnel Resources
j. Office for Research
k. Headquarters Library

2. ALA charges Divisions for the actual costs of the following services of ALA departments:
a. Administrative Services
- Specialized data processing, as defined in an Operational Practice
- Equipment maintenance for equipment purchased by the Division over which the Division exercises sole use and control
- Printing and duplication, as defined in an Operational Practice
- Telephone services not specified in V.C.1.a., as defined in an Operational Practice
- Postage for special mailings, as defined in an Operational Practice
b. Fiscal Services
- Overhead on non-dues revenue-generating activities. The rate will be set annually according to an ALA Operational Practice and will be assessed as explained below on non-dues revenue at a composite rate.
- Overhead will be assessed at 100% of the ALA composite rate (at the end of a four-year phase-in period, beginning in 1991 and ending in 1994) on revenue from:
  —registration fees
  —exhibit space rental
  —meal functions, except for separately-ticketed events.
  (The schedule for phase-in of the ALA composite overhead rate on revenues is:
  —50% of the ALA composite rate in 1991 and 1992

  —75% of the ALA composite rate in 1993
  —100% of the ALA composite rate in 1994)
- Overhead will be assessed at 50% of the ALA composite rate (at the end of a five-year phase-in period, beginning in 1991 and ending in 1995, in equal annual increments) on revenues from:
  —net sales of materials
  —subscriptions
  —advertising except in those publications which are provided to Division members as a perquisite of membership
  —other miscellaneous fees.
- Overhead will not be assessed on revenues from:
  —dues
  —donations
  —interest income
  —ALA royalties to Divisions
  —travel expense reimbursements from outside organizations
  —separately-ticketed events at conferences (e.g., tours and meal functions)
  —advertising in those publications which are provided to Division members as a perquisite of membership
c. Publishing
- Subscription and order billing services
- Central Production Unit Services
- Marketing Services

3. ALA and the Divisions share the costs of the following:
- Division Leadership Enhancement Program
- Awards promotion

4. Divisions assume total responsibility for the following costs:
- Division personnel compensation
- Projects and activities of the Divisions except as specified in this agreement
- Membership group support (governance—boards, committees, etc.)
- Furnishings and equipment purchased by Divisions and over which they have sole control and use

See also Section IX, Annual Conference and Midwinter Meeting.

5. Divisions may:
- Purchase services or products from other ALA units and outside agencies, consistent with ALA policy

D. Fund Balances

1. ALA Divisions build and maintain fund balances appropriate to their needs. A fund balance is defined as accumulated net revenue.

2. Divisions will not receive interest on fund balances or deferred revenue.

E. Endowments

Divisions may establish endowments or add to existing Division endowments from any source including existing fund balances once the Division has reached a minimum fund balance as determined by the Division and approved in accordance with the budget review process and approved financial plan. The establishment of Division endowments will follow the guidelines outlined in ALA policy. The use of the interest from these Division endowments will be subject to Division Board approval and applicable ALA policy.

F. Furniture and Equipment

ALA will provide basic furniture and equipment to each regular Division staff member.

Divisions will retain sole control and use of all furniture and equipment purchased with Division funds.

Divisions may acquire additional furniture and equipment in two ways:

1. Above the capitalization limit:

a. Divisions have authority to purchase capital equipment outright by paying the full price to ALA, with ALA taking the depreciation.
b. Divisions can purchase furniture and equipment through ALA budget request process by paying the scheduled depreciation, subject to ALA priorities and approvals.
2. Below the capitalization level, Divisions have the authority to purchase equipment outright.

G. Division Budget Review

Division Boards have responsibility for developing and approving budgets and multi-year program and financial plans, which are then reviewed by ALA management and COPES. Annual budgets are approved by the ALA Executive Board. Divisions also have the responsibility to alert the Association of any planned activities that could have a potential negative impact upon the fiscal stability of the Association.

H. Divisions with Small Revenue Bases/Number of Members

ALA Council has assigned specific responsibilities to Divisions. To carry out these responsibilities, each Division requires a base of operating revenue. ALA recognizes that each Division must have staff and must provide basic services to its members as defined in Section III. When a Division's current revenue from dues and other sources excluded from overhead is not sufficient, ALA recognizes its obligation to provide supplemental financial support up to a maximum of 50% of the funding required. This support would be provided only as a result of a well-planned process that is an integral part of the annual budget process that includes review by COPES and approval by the Executive Board. This type of support would not be available to a Division, which, at the end of a fiscal year happened to find itself in a deficit position.

Annually COPES and the Executive Board will determine and approve the specific amount of funding required to provide a minimum level of staff and basic services, compare this amount to the Division's estimated revenue, and allocate an appropriate General Fund supplement.

Divisions must generate from dues and other revenue excluded from overhead at least 50% of the funding required to provide basic services. If a Division is unable to meet this 50% level for two consecutive years, its status as a Division must be referred to Council by the Executive Board, with an appropriate recommendation. Money from the General Fund will not be used to offset expenses for non-dues revenue-generating products and services. Divisions may retain the net revenue from these activities to initiate and support other similar activities in the future.

I. Association Finances

The Divisions will be kept informed about the Association's financial health and will be involved in meaningful consultation when there is potential impact on Divisions, collectively or individually.

J. Other

1. Credit and Collections
   Management will provide effective credit and collection policies and services to the Divisions. Divisions will be charged for their bad debts in accordance with ALA policy.
2. Unrelated Business Income Taxes (UBIT)
   To the extent that Divisions incur unrelated business income, they will assume responsibility for paying the resulting taxes.

VI. Publishing Activities

The ALA Publishing Committee has the responsibility for control of the ALA imprint.

A Division may publish materials in three ways: through ALA Publishing Services, on its own, or through an outside publisher. Materials prepared by a Division for other than its own publication must be offered to ALA Publishing Services for first consideration. A Division has the right to accept or reject ALA's offer and pursue other publishing opportunities.

Divisions exercise editorial and managerial control over their periodicals.

The ALA Publishing Committee shall be informed of plans for any new Division periodicals prior to publication.

A Division may purchase production and distribution services from the Central Production Unit. A Division may also purchase marketing services from the Publishing Services Department.

ALA Publishing Services pays royalties to Divisions for Division-generated materials. Divisions may negotiate with ALA Publishing Services on royalties and other variables of publishing An "Intra mural Agreement of Publishing Responsibility" is signed by the Division Executive Director and the Director of Publishing Services for each publishing project.

ALA has the sole right to record and market tapes of programs at ALA conferences with the advance consent of the units and speakers. Divisions receive royalties from the sale of tapes of a Division's conference programs. Divisions have the right to record and market tapes of Division preconferences, programs at ALA Annual Conferences which ALA chooses not to record, Division national conferences and regional institutes.

VII. Personnel

All ALA personnel are responsible to the ALA Executive Director, and through the Executive Director to the entire membership. Unlike other ALA personnel, Division Executive Directors are also responsible to Division Boards and through those Boards to the memberships of their respective Divisions.

All ALA employees are subject to ALA's personnel policies. Each Division shall be responsible for generating the income required for the salaries, wages, and benefits of Division employees.

Each Division Executive Director serves as an ALA Program Director, a senior professional position, and is responsible for advising on ALA plans and preparing recommendations on priorities and alternatives, especially as they relate to the Division's priorities, goals, and objectives. The Division Executive Director meets regularly with other ALA staff members and communicates, cooperates, and coordinates Division activities with those of other ALA units.

The assignment of the appropriate grade for Division staff is made according to ALA personnel policies. The determination of the appropriate staffing pattern (number and position descriptions) shall be made by the Division Executive Director and the Division Board in consultation with the ALA Executive Director.

The recruitment, appointment, and termination of Division Executive Directors shall be a process involving consultation by the ALA Executive Director with the Division Board of Directors or its designates.

Each Division's Board of Directors shall annually review the performance of the Division's Executive Director based upon a single set of goals and objectives as agreed upon by the Division Board, Deputy Executive Director, and Division Executive Director. The Division Board shall convey its recommendation to the Deputy Executive Director, to whom the ALA Executive Director has delegated the responsibility for evaluating the performance of Division Executive Directors. The Deputy Executive Director shall discuss the confidential report of the performance review with the Division's President upon request.

Division Executive Directors shall have the authority to select, evaluate, and recommend termination of all Division employees, consistent with ALA personnel policies and procedures.

Assignments of Division staff to ALA internal committees are arrived at in the context of Division priorities and are kept at a reasonable level.

VIII. Division National Conferences, Preconferences, and Related Activities

Divisions may conduct preconferences, workshops, institutes, seminars, and Division national conferences, in accordance with ALA Policy, at intervals determined by Division program priorities and supported by sound financial management. A Division is responsible for all costs incurred in planning and carrying out such activities. (ALA Policy 7.2.2)

Division National Conferences shall be defined as "non-business conferences removed in time and place from the American Library Association's Annual Conference" and Midwinter Meeting in order "to view and explore areas of divisional concerns in depth." Proposals for Division National Conferences should be made to the ALA Executive Board at least two years in advance of the anticipated meeting date following a prescribed proposal outline. ALA state and regional chapters in the geographical area of a proposed conference shall be notified in writing of a desired conference at least four months prior to submitting the request to the Executive Board. Such notice shall seek the cooperation of the chapters with respect to scheduling and programming to the extent feasible. In the event of a conflict with the ALA state or regional chapters and the proposed divisional conference, the ALA Executive Board shall make the decision.

IX. Annual Conference and Midwinter Meeting

ALA provides the support necessary for Divisions to conduct business and plan and present Conference programs. Some Conference program costs may be borne by the Division except financial support for staffing and equipment as described in Section V.C.1.b. Recognizing that conference programming benefits all attendees, financial support in the form of General and Special Allocations from ALA to Divisions and other units for Annual Conference programming shall be provided; this support will be arrived at as the result of an explicit and equitable process in which the Divisions participate. Meal functions and special events must be self-supporting.

X. Special Projects of Divisions

Divisions may seek external (non-ALA) funding to pursue projects to enhance Division program priorities. Division Boards of Directors have the responsibility for assessing programmatic impact and must approve all requests for funding external projects. Additionally, all proposals and contracts for such funds are signed by the Executive Director of ALA in the name of the Association. All special projects are reviewed, approved, and conducted in accordance with established ALA policies and procedures and the conditions of the grant or contract.

All costs for projects funded through grants or contracts from outside agencies or organizations should be covered by project funding.

XI. Planning

Each Division has autonomy in its own planning processes within its area of responsibility as designated by ALA Council, subject to present and future ALA policies. They have the responsibility to develop and implement a planning process to guide their program and allocate their resources within the areas of responsibility assigned to them by the ALA Council. Since Divisions contribute to the formulation of ALA goals, it may be expected that many of the priorities and activities reflected in the plans will also be a part of Division priorities and activities. Further, each Division has responsibility for providing ALA with a multi-year financial plan consistent with ALA's existing financial policies and resting on multi-year program plans reflecting the priorities of the Division's members.

Divisions have a responsibility to assist and inform the Planning Committee of their strategic plans on a regular basis, and to inform the Planning Committee of their work through timely and comprehensive reporting to the annual Action Inventory.

6.5   Units

A unit is any membership group within the American Library Association which has a distinct organizational entity. Committees and subcommittees which are appointive groups are excluded from this definition of *unit*.

6.6   Committees

6.6.1   *Types of Committees*

1) *Standing.* A standing committee is a committee with long-term objectives so closely interwoven with the total program and development of policy of the Association or its subdivisions that it should have a continuing life.

2) *Special.* A special committee is a committee established to study various aspects of policy, planning, and administration. It should have a specific assignment and make recommendations based on that assignment. Its life should depend on the need for continued study in its area of assignment, but in accordance with the Bylaws it is normally limited to a two-year existence.

3) *Ad Hoc.* An ad hoc committee is a committee appointed to pursue a designated project to a specific goal within a specific time period. The life of the committee ends at the end of that specific time or at the conclusion of the project.

6.6.2   *Kinds of Committees*

The following kinds of committees will be one of the three types defined above: standing, special, or ad hoc, depending on the life and objectives of the committee established.

1) *Advisory.* An advisory committee evaluates programs, policies, or projects and recommends courses of action. It may function either within the structure of ALA or with an outside organization.

2) *Coordinating.* A coordinating committee receives information from two or more sub-units and supervises the integration of the work of those units.

3) *Interdivisional.* An interdivisional committee, composed of members from two or more divisions of the Association, promotes projects or programs in which there is overlapping interest.

4) *Joint.* A joint committee develops and carries out programs of mutual interest, exchanges information, or discusses matters of mutual concern with an organization or organizations outside ALA.

6.7   Subcommittees

Subcommittees in the ALA structure may be formed by a parent group to carry out specific duties. Such subcommittees are appointed by the chair of the parent committee, but are not limited to members of the parent committee; they do not have a separate life and must report to the parent committee for action. They can be abolished by decision of the parent committee.

6.8   Commissions

A commission is a body of persons from ALA members and recognized authorities in other fields who are appointed by the ALA president or president-elect and approved by the Executive Board for the purpose of considering, investigating, or recommending action on certain matters or subjects as assigned. A commission may be created only after existing ALA structures such as special or joint committees are considered, and only when the subject requires such a broadbased body. A commission has a limited term of existence, reports regularly to the President and to the Executive Board, and is advisory to the association. Commission report(s) may be published by ALA but will not be considered ALA policy until officially adopted by Council.

6.9   Task Forces

A task force is an action-oriented membership group whose charge is to address specific goals, complete a specific task, or to consider a particular issue. There may be a designated time frame defined by the nature of the task or set forth in the function statement. Functions of a task force may include the following: (1) gathering information and making recommendations; (2) studying an issue and preparing a report; (3) carrying out a specific project or activity; (4) conducting programs at conferences; (5) establishing committees or other subunits. A task force is used to address critical, urgent, or ongoing situations which require a strong, visible organizational effort and/or activist response.

6.10   Discussion Groups

Definition to be proposed to Council by the Committee on Organization in 1993.

7.   CONFERENCES AND MEETINGS

7.1   Facilities

7.1.1   *Non-Discrimination Practices in Facilities Used by ALA*

There shall be no discrimination, including that based on race, origin, color, sex, or creed, in the use of any facilities used by ALA. This policy shall become a part of ALA contracts for the use of space.

7.1.2   *Equal Employment Practices in Facilities*

The American Library Association will meet only in facilities complying with equal employment and non-discrimination laws. A statement confirming an investigation by staff of such compliance shall be a part of pre-registration materials.

7.1.3   *Conference Arrangements for the Handicapped*

Local arrangements committees, headquarters staff, exhibitors, and others involved in the planning and execution of conferences and meetings of the Association shall be aware of and sensitive to the problems of conference participants who are handicapped, in the selection, planning, and layout of all conference facilities, especially meeting rooms and exhibit areas.

The Association of Specialized and Cooperative Library Agencies Library Service to the Deaf Forum is responsible for coordinating interpretive services to the deaf. This includes determining meetings to be interpreted with assistance from all units, in identifying programs of particular interest to the deaf, engaging interpreters, and publicizing the schedule of interpretive meetings. The Conference Arrangements Office will work with a liaison from the ASCLA Library Service to the Deaf Forum to assure that a minimum of 35 hours of interpretive service shall be provided for from the general fund at both Midwinter Meeting and Annual Conference. ALA also encourages all units to provide interpreters for unit programs that can be shown to be of particular interest to deaf conferees.

7.1.4   *Services and Rooms for Non-ALA Groups*

The Executive Board in consultation with the Conference Arrangements Office shall develop and adopt a schedule of fees to be charged for space and service at conferences and meetings to small ad hoc groups, non-profit, and commercial organizations. Chapters shall not be charged a fee. Payment at the time space is reserved is required.

7.1.5   *Non-Smoking in Meetings*

Smoking is prohibited at Midwinter Meetings, Annual Conferences, regional/national conferences, continuing education programs, exhibits, and other gatherings sponsored by the ALA.

7.1.6   *Placement Service at Conference and Midwinter Meetings*

The American Library Association shall provide a staffed placement service at Annual Conferences and Midwinter meetings, such placement services to be in, or immediately adjacent to, the official conference sites.

(*See* "Current Reference File": Placement Service Guidelines.)

7.1.7   *Annual Conference: Location*

Selection of the sites for the ALA Annual Conference shall be made by the Executive Board in consultation with the Conference Arrangements Office.

7.1.8   *Midwinter Meeting Sites*

Sites for Midwinter Meetings of the Association shall be selected by the Executive Board in consultation with the Conference Arrangements Office.

7.1.9   *Fire Protection in Conference Hotels*

The Conference Arrangements Office shall obtain information from conference hotels concerning their compliance with National Fire Protection Association standards. A statement concerning their compliance shall be a part of preregistration materials.

7.2   Finances: Workshops, Institutes, etc.

7.2.1   *Fees for Institutes, Workshops, etc.*

There shall be preferential registration fees for ALA members at institutes, workshops, etc., sponsored by ALA and/or its units. However, an additional preferential rate may be extended to members of the sponsoring unit(s).

7.2.2   *Financing of Institutes, Workshops, etc.*

All institutes, workshops, etc., sponsored by ALA and/or its units shall be self-supporting and shall include provision for ALA administrative costs.

7.3   Exhibits/Exhibitors

7.3.1   *Rules and Regulations for Exhibits/Exhibitors*

Rules and regulations for exhibitors at Midwinter Meetings and Annual Conferences shall be developed by the Conference Arrangements Office and reviewed and adopted by the Executive Board. Rules and regulations so adopted shall be a part of the contracts for space.

Exhibitors may appeal decisions of the Conference Arrangements Office regarding rules and regulations to the Executive Board.

7.3.2   *Admissions to Exhibits*

Admission to exhibits at the Annual Conference or Midwinter Meeting is by registration badge. Complimentary exhibit passes may be issued to those not attending the conference or meeting under rules developed by the Conference Arrangements Office.

Exhibitors are entitled to visitor badges for issuance to their customers.

7.3.3   *Exhibit Space for Professional Groups*

The American Library Association Conference management shall, at each annual conference, provide a reasonable amount of exhibit space for the use of ALA groups. The amount of such space set aside in any one year shall be determined by the conference management, which shall also determine locations and space allocations.

No rental fee shall be charged to the ALA groups assigned space, and the Association will bear the expense of setting up the regulation backwall for one booth or equivalent for each group. ALA groups having their own funds are to pay fees for rental of such booth furnishings selected if furnishings have to be rented and to pay the cost of backwalls in excess of one unit.

No rental fee for space may be accepted from any group within the Association for the purpose of granting preference in the allocation of space.

Exhibits of other professional and non-library organizations and government agencies may be accommodated as liberally as possible but not at the expense of groups within the Association.

7.4 Regulations and Guidelines: Conferences and Meetings

7.4.1 *Registration at Conferences and Midwinter Meetings*

ALA members may attend general membership and council meetings, whenever and wherever held, by showing either a conference badge for the day of the meeting or a current membership card. Registration badges shall be shown for admission to all other meetings.

Registration at Annual Conferences and Midwinter Meetings is required of all those attending all other meetings of the Association, its units, committees, etc., except as specifically waived by action of the Executive Board.

7.4.2 *Preferential Registration Fees*

At Annual Conferences and Midwinter Meetings, there shall be a preferential registration fee for ALA members.

7.4.3 *Open Meetings*

All meetings of the American Library Association and its units are open to all members and to members of the press. Registration requirements apply. Closed meetings may be held only for the discussion of matters affecting the privacy of individuals or institutitons.

(*See also* "Current Reference File": Interpretive Statement on Open Meetings Policy.)

7.4.4 *Distribution of Materials at ALA Council and Membership Meetings*

Permission for the distribution of materials within the ALA Council and Membership Meeting areas, if the material is not official documentation, must be granted by the Executive Director or the ALA President.

7.4.5 *Media Access to Information*

National library media, and other media making a request, shall receive all information and documentation that is sent to Council and Executive Board prior to meetings of these bodies except, in the opinion of the Executive Board, anything affecting the privacy of individuals or institutions, and shall receive all information presented to those registering at meetings of the Association.

7.4.6 *Purpose of Annual Conferences*

Annual Conferences of the Association are an association-wide activity pertinent to all members regardless of divisional affiliation. The ALA Annual Conference shall be devoted primarily to providing a range of program activities for its membership and to conduct the business of the Association. Agendas of Membership Meetings shall provide priority to discussion of membership resolutions.

(*See* "Current Reference File": 1985–86.)

7.4.7 *Purpose of Midwinter Meetings*

The ALA Midwinter Meeting is convened for the primary purpose of expediting the business of the Association through sessions of its governing and administrative delegates serving on boards, committees, and Council. Programs designed for the continuing education and development of the fields of library service shall be reserved for Annual Conference except by specific authorization of the Executive Board acting under the provisions of the ALA Constitution. Hearings seeking membership reactions and provisions for observers and petitioners at meetings of Council, committees, and boards are to be publicized; programs of orientation or leadership development to Association business are encouraged; assemblies of groups of individuals for information sharing vital to the development of Association business shall be accepted as appropriate to the purposes of the Midwinter Meeting.

(*See* "Current Reference File": 1989–90 CD#30.)

7.4.8 *Meetings of the Executive Board*

The ALA Executive Board shall meet during the weeks beginning with the last Mondays in April and October, subject to availability of its members. Dates shall be selected and published well in advance.

7.4.9 *Conference Planning Calendar*

The American Library Association will establish and maintain a ten-year advance planning calendar of religious observances considered to be most obligatory to practitioners of major groups and will circulate the document annually to all units and affiliates as well as to other agencies that indicate an interest in its receipt. ALA shall advise all units that the scheduling of events of interest to libraries and their staffs should avoid these dates and allow for travel time free of conflict with them.

(*See* "Current Reference File": 1986–87 CD #14.)

7.4.10 *Conference Program Planning*

Planning for major conference programs shall follow the constraints imposed upon divisional conference planning. Communication among membership divisions, committees, and staff engaged in such planning shall be maintained throughout the process.

7.4.11 *Parliamentarian*

The American Library Association shall employ a parliamentarian who is not a member of ALA for the Council and Membership meetings of the Association.

8. FINANCES

8.1 Management of ALA Funds

8.1.1 *Purchasing Policy/Conflict of Interest*

No purchase of goods and securities nor procurement of services, insurance, or other intangibles shall be made through firms, companies, or agencies with which officers, members of the Executive Board, or fund trustees are associated as partners, directors, or in a managerial capacity, except as such purchases relate to procurement of professional materials such as publications.

8.1.2 *Short-Term Investments*

The Executive Director and the Controller of the American Library Association are authorized to make short-term investments of such funds as are available for this purpose.

8.1.3 *Property Transactions: Authorization to Sell Real Estate*

The ALA Executive Board is authorized from time to time to sell, mortgage, or otherwise dispose of any and all real estate now or hereafter owned by the American Library Association or any part thereof or any interest therein. The officers of the Association, at the direction of the Executive Board, are authorized to make, execute, acknowledge, and deliver all appropriate instruments of conveyance, mortgages or otherwise so authorized concerning such real estate.

8.1.4 *Authorization to Overspend Budgeted Funds*

The Executive Director is authorized to overspend line amounts in the General Funds Budget but not in excess of the total General Funds budgeted figure. The Executive Director may not incur any salary commitment in excess of the current year's commitments.

8.1.5 *Authority to Borrow Money*

The President and the Executive Director are authorized and directed, from time to time as in their judgment the needs of ALA require, to borrow from any bank or other lender chosen by them, for the use and benefit of ALA, a sum or sums not exceeding $1,000,000 in the aggregate remaining unpaid. The indebtedness shall be evidenced by a promissory note or notes which shall be corporate obligations only and shall mature and be payable not more than one (1) year after date. The Executive Board shall be informed of each transaction.

8.1.6 *Limitations on ALA Funding of Divisions*

Divisions which impose additional fees under the ALA Bylaws, Article VI, Section 6(b) and (d) or otherwise raise additional funds for divisional programs and activities shall not obligate the Association to the continuation of the programs for which continuous funding is not or cannot be provided.

8.1.7 *Unrestricted Bequests*

Regardless of size, every restricted or unrestricted bequest will be acknowledged appropriately in ALA publications and news releases unless publication of the bequest is restricted by the donor. Any unrestricted bequest in excess of $15,000 will be routinely added to the ALA quasi-endowment funds income which may be used for the general support of Association programs. Unrestricted bequests of less than $15,000 will be invested with a separate record maintained of the principal and earnings of each such bequest. Upon review of proposals prepared by any program or administrative unit, the Executive Board will determine how the principle and interest of each such bequest are to be used.

(*See also* "Current Reference File": Policy for Unrestricted Bequests.)

8.2 Support for Officers and Executive Board

8.2.1 *Expenses of the ALA President*

The annual ALA budget shall include an item sufficient to cover all travel and other expenses incidental to the discharge of the official duties of the President, including attendance at regular meetings of the Association.

8.2.2 *Expenses of Members of the Executive Board*

The American Library Association will pay expenses of members of the Executive Board to Midwinter Meetings, Annual Conferences, and interim meetings of the Executive Board when such expenses are not paid by the member's institution.

8.2.3 *Released Time for the ALA President*

ALA approves in principle the provision by the ALA President's institution of up to one-quarter released time including the cost of fringe benefits for the President of ALA.

8.3 Disaster Aid

In case of a natural disaster which inflicts serious physical damage on a number of libraries, the President of the Association is empowered to appoint at once an ad hoc committee to assist the stricken libraries.

ALA will make use of existing budgetary mechanisms including the Executive Director's contingency fund to respond to the need for financial assistance which may occur during the year as a result of natural disasters.

(*See* "Current Reference File," 1989–90 CD#80.)

8.4   Council Receipt of ALA Budgets

Councilors will be provided with summary sheets of the ALA annual budget, with the understanding that any Councilor will receive the full budget upon request.

8.5   Endowment Funds

8.5.1 *Endowment Funds: Withdrawals*

The Executive Board shall make withdrawals from the Carnegie Endowment Fund only when the need is so great that the purposes and programs of the Association would otherwise be seriously impaired; such withdrawals to be considered only with specific repayment schedules and interest rates set at the time of the withdrawal.

In preparation of the ALA annual budget, COPES is authorized to include as income a withdrawal from the endowment funds of up to six percent (6%) of a five-year average of the market value of the Association's securities less the amounts returned as interest and dividends or up to six percent (6%) of the current market value less the amount returned as interest and dividends.

8.5.2 *Endowment Funds: Combining*

The Executive Director of ALA is empowered to combine endowment funds subject to advice from the Association's legal counsel, and upon approval by the Executive Board.

9. RELATIONSHIPS TO OTHER ORGANIZATIONS

9.1   The Use of ALA's Name and Joint Relationships

The American Library Association is a nonprofit organization operated in the interest of libraries and to promote library service and membership.

All ALA units are responsible to Council which determines policies. Council's actions, however, may be overset by the membership. Therefore, primarily and ultimately the responsibility for the use of the American Library Association name rests with the aggregate membership.

The Association is governed by Council and administered by the Executive Board, which in its role as central management board, appoints the executive director, who is in charge of headquarters and its personnel.

The executive director delegates authority within ALA headquarters to ALA's department heads, who, in carrying out their assigned duties, are called upon to use ALA's name and, in that name, to commit the Association to programs, activities, and binding agreements.

Divisions are empowered by ALA's bylaws "to act for the ALA as a whole on any matter determined by Council to be the responsibility of the division." Authority for acting on behalf of the division rests with that division's executive board.

Round tables, membership initiative groups, and committees, do not have this constitutional authority.

The American Library Association's Executive Board, divisions, executive director, and department heads (consisting of the deputy executive director and the associate executive directors for the Washington Office, Administrative Services, Publishing Services, Commu-

nication Services, and Fiscal Services) who must use ALA's name in executing their responsibilities or in entering into joint relationships with other organizations abide by state ALA policies and the following principles:

1. ALA's primary objective for entering into joint relationships with other organizations and business enterprises should be:

   1) To help the Association achieve its mission to promote and improve library and information services and librarianship, or to assist libraries in achieving their mission.

   2) To fulfill a specific need related to current ALA goals and objectives or to contribute in a significant way to the cooperating organization while using ALA's name and its resources effectively.

   3) To benefit as much as possible from a reciprocal relationship in the form of finances, expertise, experience, public relations, or other advantages.

2. Joint relationships should be entered into with other organizations and business enterprises whose strength and reputation have been evaluated.

3. Effective joint relationships are based on the following criteria:

   1) The relationship is, as much as possible, reciprocal in that there are mutual needs and a sharing of purposes.

   2) The structure and level of the relationship represents the best method of accomplishing the purpose or meeting the need.

   3) The appropriate personnel are available and the time and talent are being or will be used effectively.

   4) Costs in time and money are justified by the results.

   5) Useful reporting devices are designed and used.

   6) The need for the relationship is evaluated periodically.

4. Formal joint relationships require a written agreement which, among other things, specifies that ALA retains control of the use of its name and that reports and evaluations be made periodically.

5. Joint relationships with other organizations or business enterprises do not necessarily imply ALA endorsement of their policies, products, or services.

6. None of the American Library Association's published reports, findings, etc., shall be circulated under the imprint of the cooperating agency without the permission of the Association. The ALA Publishing Committee shall control the use of the ALA imprint.

While endorsements, or boycotts, by the American Library Association are not explicitly authorized in the Constitution and Bylaws, implicit authorization can be derived from the Constitution, Article VI (a) and (b). Such endorsements (example: Policy Manual 57.3) and boycotts (example: Policy Manual 57.3) have taken place.

Commendations honoring outstanding efforts of an individual, institution, or organization may be issued in the name of the Association by Council or units designated by Council through a formal resolution. (See Policy Manual 5.4.15: Memorial resolutions, tributes, and testimonials.)

9.2   Affiliation with other Organizations

Criteria have been set up to guide the Council in considering applications for affiliation with

ALA of national and international organizations which must be not for profit, have interests consistent with those of ALA, have sufficiently large membership and length of existence to ensure continued support under constitutions and bylaws not in conflict with ALA's, and do not discriminate in membership on the basis of race, creed, color, sex, age, physical handicaps, or national origin.

(*See* "Current Reference File" for full text.)

9.3   Definition of Affiliate

An affiliate is a group having purpose or interests similar to those of the Association or its Divisions/Round Tables which has made successful formal application for affiliate status to Council (national or international group) or Division/Round Table (local, state or regional groups). No subdivision of the Association may separately affiliate itself with an organization with which ALA as a whole is affiliated. [See also policy 9.2]

9.4   Representatives and Liaisons

Official representatives to outside organizations serve either at the request of Council or at the direct request of an ALA unit whose approved budget includes membership dues and whose representative plays a active role in the governance or affairs of the outside organization. Should an outside organization request an official representative from the Association, the request goes to the Executive Board and Council. If approved, the Committee on Organization (COO) identifies the appropriate ALA unit and makes this recommendation to the Executive Board. In the case of potential or actual involvement of more than one ALA unit, COO refers the appointment to the Executive Board Personnel Subcommittee.

An official representative to an outside organization is a member of the Association who is appointed to an outside organization for the purpose of fully participating in their meetings or in the establishment of Councils, joint committees and other groups which work together in activities of mutual interest.

A representative to another ALA unit is an appointed member of an ALA unit whose duties include attending meetings of other ALA units for such purpose as communication or information dissemination.

A liaison is a member of an ALA unit appointed by the unit to perform networking or coordinating functions with units inside or with organizations outside the Association. The liaison has no formal role in the governing structure of the other unit or organization.

9.5   Relationships with Organizations Violating Human Rights

The American Library Association shall have no affiliation with, memberships in, or formal relationships with organizations which violate ALA principles and commitments to human rights and social justice as set forth in ALA's policies, procedures, and position statements and the Universal Declaration of Human Rights.

9.6   Racist Institutions: Opposition to Support of

Public, academic, or school libraries which provide services or materials to racist institutions conceived for the purpose of circumventing desegregation of public schools may be censured by the American Library Association under procedures to be developed and approved by Council.

10. HEADQUARTERS AND PUBLICATIONS

10.1   *American Libraries*: Editorial Policy

Because *American Libraries* is the official organ of the American Library Association, the editor has a particular responsibility to convey to the membership and other readers full and accurate information about the activities, purposes, and goals of the Association. In order to carry out this responsibility, the editor may have access to privileged information. The editor must assume an obligation to represent the best interests of the Association and its units fairly and as fully as possible within the scope of the journal and with due regard to the editor's prerogatives in producing a balanced and readable publication.

ALA encourages publication in the news columns of *American Libraries* of news about all matters of import to libraries and librarians. The editor is guaranteed independence in gathering, reporting, and publishing news according to the principles of the Association's policies on intellectual freedom.

Statements of official ALA positions on any matters shall be clearly identified as such when published in *American Libraries*. The editor must be free to analyze and interpret such matters as his or her judgment dictates, and such analysis and interpretation should appear over the editor's signature.

News and views have their place in *American Libraries*, and every opportunity shall be assured for expression of diverse views when members believe such views run counter to their own, or when news is considered to be inaccurately or not fully reported. Signed interpretative comment shall be encouraged. Columns of *American Libraries* shall be kept scrupulously and faithfully open to expression of all viewpoints of interest and concern to the library profession.

10.2 Responsibility for Content of ALA Publications

As a publisher, the American Library Association and its member units establish goals and set policies for publication programs. The purpose and scope for each major publication will be clearly specified.

It is the responsibility of each member unit to communicate to its membership and its editors the purpose of the publication, its specific format, and to identify the audience for which it is intended.

Consistent with ALA's traditional dedication to the freedom of expression, free flow of ideas, and policies on intellectual freedom and ethics, all member units shall endorse and apply the principles of freedom of the press to their publication program.

It is the responsibility of each member unit to appoint editors with experience or training in editorial theory and practice. Such editors, whether headquarters staff, contractors, or volunteers, shall be responsible for determining the content and style of the publication consistent with the goals and policies of the sponsoring unit.

The decision as to appropriate material for inclusion in the publication shall rest with the editor guided by the ALA Constitution, its Bylaws, and relevant policies as adopted by the ALA Council and the unit which sponsors the publication.
(*See* "Current Reference File": 1989–90 CD#47.1.)

10.3 Sex-Stereotyping Terminology

Publications and official documents of the American Library Association shall avoid terminology which perpetuates sex stereotypes. Existing publications and official documents, as they are revised, shall be changed to avoid such terminology.

ALA will establish guidelines for editing all future publications and official documents and for review of all future advertising copy to insure that discriminatory remarks and sex-stereotyping terminology of any kind are eliminated.

10.4 Reproduction of Articles

The American Library Association may enter into agreements with various organizations engaged in the business of providing copies of copyrighted articles to persons requesting them. The copies are sometimes available in magnetic tape, in microform, and in hard copy.

ALA has developed criteria by which the agreements may be evaluated so as to assure uniform and nondiscriminatory treatment by ALA and the protection of the interests of ALA in its journals and publications and their contents. Any agreements made in accordance with these criteria do not imply any restriction on the use of copyrighted materials in ALA journals and publications for the noncommercial purpose of scientific or educational advancement. ALA Publishing Services has the responsibility for administering this policy and for securing approval of appropriate ALA units.
(*See* "Current Reference File" for full text and statement of criteria.)

10.5 Executive Board Review

The Executive Board shall review administrative decisions made in the internal management of Headquarters by the Executive Director, and the Executive Director shall be authorized to carry out the provisions of the budget including hiring and firing of staff without submitting matters previously authorized or individual appointments to the Executive Board except in the form of reports of action. Any action by the Executive Director shall be subject to review by the Executive Board upon request of any member of the Executive Board.

11. AWARDS

11.1 Presentation of Awards

Any award in a field covered by an ALA division shall be presented at a session of that division. No recognition of these awards will be made at ALA general sessions.

General awards shall be presented at general sessions. The chair of the ALA Awards Committee shall read a citation of no more than 300 words; the award will be presented by ALA's presiding officer; there are no speeches of acceptance.

Donors of awards are not invited to present awards in person. Potential donors shall be notified of these policies before ALA accepts the award from the donor.

11.2 Administrative Costs of Awards

Effective in 1990, minimum ALA awards shall be $1,000; minimum scholarships shall be $3,000. In considering new awards, the Awards Committee shall add a cost for administration. For awards from an outside source, the standard overhead should be requested. For awards by a unit of ALA, administrative costs estimated by the unit shall be included in the proposal and in budget requests as needed.

12. ORGANIZATION MEMBERSHIP DUES AND PERQUISITES

The Bylaws, Article I, Section 2–B, C, and D, authorize Council to set the dues and perquisites of Chapters, Organization Members, and Special Members. The dues and perquisites established effective with the 1985 Membership Year are as follows:

Chapter Members: Dues $50 annually.

Organization Members

1. Library and Library School

Library's Budget	Dues
Under $50,000	$ 70
$50,000–$199,999	$110
$200,000–$499,999	$330
$500,000–$999,999	$550
$1,000,000–$2,000,000	$770
Over $2,000,000	$900

2. All other Nonprofit Organization Members (library associations, affiliated organizations, foreign organizations, and nonprofit organizations other than libraries and library schools): Dues $50 annually. For members joining ALA under Bylaw 1.2 B–C, the perquisites of membership shall be *American Libraries, ALA Handbook of Organization and Membership Directory*, eligibility for division and round table membership, eligibility for insurance, and discounts on library materials.

Special Members:

Patrons of ALA: Dues $1,000 annually
Sustaining Members: Dues $500 annually
Contributing Members: $300 annually
Subscribing Members: $150 annually

The special membership entitles the holder to request any perquisites available to a regular organization member.

Section TWO **Positions and Public Policy Statements**

50. NATIONAL INFORMATION SERVICES AND RESPONSIBILITIES

50.1 Support for "Goals for Action" of the National Commission on Libraries and Information Science

The American Library Association concurs in concepts and recommendations contained in "Goals for Action," a report of the National Commission on Libraries and Information Science, and commits the Association and its units to maximum cooperation with the National

Commission in implementation and further development of "Goals for Action."

50.2 Equal Rights Amendment Legislation

The American Library Association supports the equality of women both in the profession and in society at large. To this end the Association (a) supports implementation of the national plan of action as amended at the National Women's Conference in Houston in November 1977; (b) supports through employment practices policy the equal treatment of women in the work place; (c) supports the Equal Rights Amendment legislation; (d) supports the elimination of sex-stereotyping terminology through avoiding the use of such terminology in ALA publications and (e) supports adherence to affirmative action policies through its support of the enforcement of such policies in its library school accreditation standards and guidelines.

50.3   ALA Support for the White House
        Conference on Library and Information
        Services
        The American Library Association is on record as supporting the recommendations of the 1979 White House Conference on Library and Information Services.

50.4   Free Access to Information
        The American Library Association asserts that the charging of fees and levies for information services, including those services utilizing the latest information technology, is discriminatory in publicly supported institutions providing library and information services.
        The American Library Association shall seek to make it possible for library and information service agencies which receive their major support from public funds to provide service to all people without additional fees and to utilize the latest technological developments to insure the best possible access to information, and ALA will actively promote its position on equal access to information.

50.5   Bibliographic Data Bases
        The American Library Association supports open access to information, including the information contained in online data bases, and encourages data base providers and other organizations to minimize restrictions placed on their members' use of bibliographic records maintained in their online data bases.
        (*See* "Current Reference File": 1984–85 CD#41.)

50.6   Funding for Community Access Cable
        Programming
        Libraries should work cooperatively with other groups in promoting the widest possible access to communications and information, including community access cablecasting. The American Library Association, in order to support stable sources of funding for community access channels, endorses the following principles articulated by Open Channel and Publicable, two organizations with knowledge and experience in community access cablecasting:
        1) That a portion of cable revenues be designated to provide financial and technical assistance for community access programming.
        2) That this support be sufficient to promote genuine access.
        3) That this assistance increase as the cable operator's revenue increases.
        4) That the specific structures, funding formulas, and monitoring arrangements be left to the local community.

50.7   Literacy
50.7.1 *Literacy and State Library Agencies*
        The American Library Association supports the achievement of national literacy through educational activities utilizing the historical and cultural experience of libraries and librarians.

The American Library Association urges state library agencies to address the problems of illiteracy and give high priority to solutions in their short- and long-range plans for library development and the use of federal and state funds.

50.7.2 *Literacy and the Role of Libraries*
        The American Library Association reaffirms and supports the principle that lifelong literacy is a basic right for all individuals in our society and is essential to the welfare of the nation. ALA advocates the achievement of national literacy through educational activities utilizing the historical and cultural experiences of libraries and librarians.
        ALA confirms that libraries of all types, as appropriate to their mission, have the responsibility to make literacy a high priority in planning and budgeting for library services. As pioneer and equal partners in the national literacy movement, libraries will continue to take a strong leadership role and must join with other literacy providers to urge local, state, federal, and private agencies to promote active development of literacy on a policy level and to support funding of the literacy services in libraries.

50.8   Nominations to the Posts of Librarian of
        Congress and of Archivist of the United
        States
        The privilege of reviewing nominations made by the President of the United States to the highest government posts in their respective professions is one accorded the major national professional organizations. The American Library Association strongly supports the extension of a similar privilege to ALA, enabling it to review the recommendations and nominations for the positions of Librarian of Congress and of Archivist of the United States whenever new appointments to those posts are under consideration.
        (*See* "Current Reference File": July 1975 CD #58, 1986–87 CD#18.)

50.9   Financing of Libraries
        In order to assist libraries facing severe economic problems resulting from inflation, the American Library Association will engage in a broad media information program to make the public aware of the benefits to be gained through tax support of libraries, and will simultaneously explore public financing alternatives for libraries facing financial problems.

50.10   NCLIS Membership
        The American Library Association supports the appointment of members to the National Commission on Libraries and Information Science in an expeditious manner with appointees who fully meet the requirements of the statute.
        (*See* "Current Reference File": 1989–90 CD#59.)

50.11   Disarmament and Conflict Solving
        Information in Libraries
        Libraries should make available and readily accessible information on possibilities for disarmament and alternative ways of solving conflicts.

50.12   Nuclear Freeze, the Arms Race and National
        Security
        The American Library Association supports the concept of a nuclear freeze on the development and deployment of nuclear weapons. It urges libraries to establish balanced up-to-date collections of library materials on national security in the nuclear age, on nuclear arms, and the movements for disarmament and a nu-

clear moratorium. The Association furthermore urges libraries to stimulate public interest in these issues and make information available about various courses of action concerned individuals may take.
        (*See* "Current Reference File.")

50.13   Environmental Issues
        The American Library Association urges librarians and library governing boards to collect and provide information on the condition of our Earth, its air, ground, water, and living organisms from all available sources.
        (*See* "Current Reference File": 1989–90 CD#48.)

50.14   National Library Symbol
        The American Library Association endorses the symbol recommended by the ALA President's Task Force and promotes its use.

50.15   Trade Publishers Discounts
        The American Library Association supports the concept of equal discounts on equal volume orders for all buyers.
        (*See* "Current Reference File": 1983–84 CD#32.)

51.   FEDERAL LEGISLATIVE POLICY

A democratic society depends on the federal government ensuring the right of all its citizens of access to a comprehensive range of knowledge and a diversity of communications media. Through declaration of policy, by legislation, regulation, and the appropriation of financial support, the Executive Branch and the Congress of the United States have responded to citizen requests for a federal role in support of libraries as vital institutions serving the needs and well-being of individuals and the nation. Thus, while most libraries are local institutions, under local control, the federal government plays an essential role in helping ensure access to resources and services to all.

Open government is vital to a democracy. Federal policymakers must continue to recognize the unique role of libraries, their existing delivery systems, and inherent community base in the dissemination of information to the public. Recognizing the constraints of national security, privacy, efficient decision-making, and costs, the federal government must continue to assume special responsibility to ensure that information produced by the government is accessible to the people through the nation's libraries.

The federal government also must provide leadership in developing new technologies and services. Federal action can stimulate local pilot programs for innovative services designed for specific user groups, programs which require specialized materials, and education programs for library personnel.

Emerging technology is altering the profile of library service. The federal government has initiated and facilitated cooperation, encouraged resource sharing among all types of libraries, and established standards and practices for development of quality library networks that extend beyond state and national boundaries.

The Department of Education, through its mandate to assist librarians across the country, raises standards of service and develops new programs to benefit library users. The Department not only administers effective grant programs to public libraries, elementary and secondary school libraries, academic and research libraries, but also provides leadership, technical assistance, and dissemination of information. These functions must continue.

The federal government also plays a critical role in the compilation and timely dissemination of statistical information about libraries which is essential to long-range planning and library development.

In an age of international communication and interchange of resources, the federal government is pivotal in the development of libraries as institutions that transcend national boundaries. International protocols, participation in international organizations, transnational data flow and monetary policies are inherently within the domain of the federal government.

In all, this federal role complements, without supplanting, the basic responsibilities of state and local governments and institutions in the assurance of quality library and information services.

The Federal Legislative Policy of the American Library Association, the product of an ongoing revision program, was adopted by Council in July, 1987. The entire text, from which the preceding is taken, is available free from the ALA Washington Office, 110 Maryland Avenue NE, Box 54, Washington, DC 20002.

Sections of the Policy are: (1) *The Federal Government's Role in Library and Information Services.* (2) *Access to Information:* Public Access to Federal Information; Equal Access to Library Service. (3) *Intellectual Freedom.* (4) *Federal Policies:* Postal Rates and Quality of Postal Services; Taxation; Copyright; Preservation of Library Materials. (5) *Federal Programs:* Federal Libraries: A National Resource; Bibliographic and Reference Service; National Commission on Libraries and Information Science; U.S. Department of Education; National Archives and Records Administration; National Endowment for the Arts and Humanities; Federal Support for State Library Agencies; Federal Aid to Libraries, Systems, Education Agencies and Institutions; School Library Media Centers; Technical, Professional, and Vocational Institution Libraries; College and Research Libraries; Public Libraries; Service to Persons in Institutions; Federal Support for Library Facilities. (6) *Information Technologies:* National Library and information Networks; Technical Standards and Copyright Protection; Telecommunications and Broadcast Media; Information Technology Education. (7) *Personnel Development, Research, and Education:* Education of Librarians and Information Specialists; Research in Library and Information Science; Personnel Policies and Employment Standards; Education for Library Users. (8) *White House Conference on Library and Information Services.* (9) *Equal Rights Amendment.* (10) *International Programs:* United Nations; United Nations Educational, Scientific and Cultural Organization; Organization of American States; International Exchange of Persons; International Flow of Publications, Florence Agreement; United States Libraries and Information Centers Abroad; International Copyright; International Postal Policy; Economic and Educational Development Programs. (11) *Existing Federal Laws Affecting Librarians, Libraries and Their Users.*

52.   SERVICES AND RESPONSIBILITIES OF LIBRARIES

52.1   Service to Detention Facilities and Jails
The American Library Association encourages public libraries and systems to extend their services to residents of jails and other detention facilities within their taxing areas. ALA instructs its Association of Specialized and Cooperative Library Agencies in cooperation with the Public Library Association, the American Library Trustee Association, and other interested units to design a plan to assist public libraries in extending their services to local jails and detention facilities.

52.2   Preservation
52.2.1   *Preservation Policy. National Information Services and Responsibilities Permanence and Durability of Information Products.*

The American Library Association, with its history of concern and action in the preservation of information resources, affirms that such preservation is central to libraries and librarianship. In particular, ALA affirms that the preservation of library resources is essential to protect the public's right to the free flow of information as embodied in the First Amendment to the Constitution and the Library Bill of Rights.

The Association's preservation concerns are not limited to information recorded on paper but include information disseminated on other media such as film, magnetic tape, and digital disks. ALA believes that manufacturers, publishers and purchasers of information in any medium must address the usability, durability and longevity of resources published and disseminated in both electronic and traditional formats. These issues include the permanence of the medium itself, its intelligibility and readability over time, the threat to information posed by technical obsolescence, the long-term retention of information resident in commercial databases, and the security of library and commercial databases.

1) The American Library Association and its Divisions will work closely with standards-setting organizations to identify and develop needed preservation standards and to promote compliance. The ALA further affirms that, while preservation guidelines and standards emanating from the Divisions are helpful, they should be a prelude to official national and international standards. An official standard developed through consensus of all parties, including commercial organizations, has a greater chance of implementation than a guideline or standard developed and promulgated solely by a professional association. The Association will establish and promote links with trade associations, publishers, and publishing associations to develop, promote and publicize standards for the permanence and durability of all information media.

2) In respect to the permanence of information products printed on paper, ALA urges publishers to use paper meeting standards promulgated by the American National Standards Institute (ANSI) and the International Standards Organization (ISO) for all publications of enduring value. A statement of compliance should be included on the verso of the title page of a book or in the masthead or copyright area of a periodical as well as in catalogs, advertising and bibliographic references. In addition, ALA will work with electronic publishers to develop guidelines governing the preservation of data, so that information will not be lost when publishers can no longer economically retain and desseminate it.

3) The impermanence of archival collections threatens our ability to understand our past. Repositories around the country collect materials from individuals, local governments, and private and public institutions to document political, economic, cultural and social history. Much of this material was, however, created as a record of current activities and events rather than as permanent documentation. Although citizens may know about the impermanent nature of newsprint, many are unaware that color photographs, video tape, and magnetic media are even less enduring. Libraries and other repositories have an obligation to inform their users, administrators, and local officials about the ephemeral nature of these materials and to recommend more permanent documentation techniques. The Association will help to stimulate public interest in this issue and will provide information about more lasting options.

52.2.2   *Recycled Paper*
The American Library Association urges all publishers, including the government, to use recycled paper for publications normally issued on nonpermanent paper and urges librarians to dispose of discarded paper so that it is available for recycling.

52.3   School Libraries
52.3.1   *Instruction in Use of Libraries in Teacher Training*
The American Library Association and its American Association of School Librarians division favor the introduction or development of instruction in the use of libraries and of printed and audiovisual materials in all teacher training programs.

52.3.2   *School Libraries as Instructional Materials Centers*
The school librarian, in addition to offering individual reading guidance and support of the school curriculum, should be ready to serve as both teacher and instructional materials specialist, providing and aiding in the selection of printed materials, other media, and the equipment necessary for effective use in classroom and library.

52.3.3   *School Libraries: Materials Selection Policy Statements*
As a basis for excellence in materials selection for school libraries, the American Library Association recommends that every school district have a materials selection policy, formally adopted by the school board, which states the responsibility of the professional personnel for selection, the criteria used in selection of all types of library materials, and procedures for consideration of criticism of particular materials, following the principles of the School Library Bill of Rights.
(*Note:* The Revision Committee recommends that the three sections be referred to the American Association of School Librarians for any desired changes of terminology and integration with the Intellectual Freedom section as currently under revision.)

52.4   Confidentiality of Library Records
The ethical responsibilities of librarians, as well as statutes in most states and the District of Columbia, protect the privacy of library users. Confidentiality extends to "information sought or received, and materials consulted, borrowed, acquired," and includes database search records, reference interviews, circulation records, interlibrary loan records, and other personally identifiable uses of library materials, facilities, or services.

The American Library Association recognizes that law enforcement agencies and officers may occasionally believe that library records contain information which may be helpful to the investigation of criminal activity. If there is a reasonable basis to believe such records are necessary to the progress of an investigation or prosecution, the American judicial system provides the mechanism for seeking release of such confidential records: the issuance of a court order, following a showing of good cause based on specific facts, by a court of competent jurisdiction.

The American Library Association strongly recommends that the responsible officers of each library, cooperative system, and consortium in the United States:

1) Formally adopt a policy which specifically recognizes its circulation records and other records identifying the names of library users with specific materials to be confidential.

2) Advise all librarians and library employees that such records shall not be made available to any agency of state, federal, or local government except pursuant to such process, order, or subpoena as may be authorized under the authority of, and pursuant to, federal, state, or local law relating to civil, criminal, or administrative discovery procedures or legislative investigatory power.

3) Resist the issuance or enforcement of any such process, order, or subpoena until such time as a proper showing of good cause has been made in a court of competent jurisdiction.

52.5   Library Services for Youth

52.5.1 *Youth Services*

The American Library Association recognizes that the future of libraries and of society itself depends upon the preparedness of youth to carry adult responsibilities for business, government, parenthood and other leadership. Children and young adults cannot fulfill their potential or that of society without high quality library opportunities through both public and school libraries. ALA is committed to the support and development of resources and services for children and young adults through both school and public libraries.

52.5.2 *Sex Education Materials in Libraries*

ALA affirms the right of youth to comprehensive, sex-related education, materials, programs, and referral services of the highest quality; affirms the active role of librarians in providing such; and urges librarians and library educators to reexamine existing policies and practices and assume a leadership role in seeing that information is available for children and adolescents, parents, and youth-serving professionals.

52.5.3 *Selective Service Information in Libraries*

Librarians should have available information on the full range of alternatives within and without the military services for those young persons who are facing the prospect of conscription.

52.6   Instruction in the Use of Libraries

In order to assist individuals in the independent information retrieval process basic to daily living in a democratic society, the American Library Association encourages all libraries to include instruction in the use of libraries as one of the primary goals of service. Libraries of all types share the responsibility to educate users in successful information location, beginning with their childhood years and continuing the education process throughout their years of professional and personal growth.

53.   INTELLECTUAL FREEDOM

Texts of policies are available from the Office of Intellectual Freedom, ALA Headquarters, 50 E. Huron Street, Chicago, IL 60611.

53.1   Library Bill of Rights

The American Library Association affirms that all libraries are forums for information and ideas, and that the following basic policies should guide their services.

1) Books and other library resources should be provided for the interest, information, and enlightenment of all people of the community the library serves. Materials should not be excluded because of the origin, background, or views of those contributing to their creation.

2) Libraries should provide materials and information presenting all points of view on current and historical issues. Materials should not be proscribed or removed because of partisan or doctrinal disapproval.

3) Libraries should challenge censorship in the fulfillment of their responsibility to provide information and enlightenment.

4) Libraries should cooperate with all persons and groups concerned with resisting abridgment of free expression and free access to ideas.

5) A person's right to use a library should not be denied or abridged because of origin, age, background, or views.

6) Libraries which make exhibit spaces and meeting rooms available to the public they serve should make such facilities available on an equitable basis, regardless of the beliefs or affiliations of individuals or groups requesting their use.

Adopted June 18, 1948. Amended February 2, 1961, June 27, 1967, and January 23, 1980, by the ALA Council.

53.1.1   Challenged materials which meet the criteria for selection in the materials selection policy of the library should not be removed under any legal or extra-legal pressure. Adopted 1971, revised 1990.

(*See* "Current Reference File": Challenged Materials: An Interpretation of the Library Bill of Rights: 1989–90 CD#61.2.)

53.1.2   Expurgation of any parts of books or other library resources by the library, its agent, or its parent institution is a violation of the Library Bill of Rights because it denies access to the complete work, and, therefore, to the entire spectrum of ideas that the work was intended to express.

(*See* "Current Reference File": Expurgation of Library Materials: An Interpretation of the Library Bill of Rights, revised 1990. 1989–90 CD#61.3.)

53.1.3   Members of the school community involved in the collection development process employ educational criteria to select resources unfettered by their personal, social, or religious views. Students and educators served by the school library media program have access to resources and services free of constraints resulting from personal, partisan, or doctrinal disapproval and which reflect the linguistic pluralism of the community. School library media professionals resist efforts by individuals to define what is appropriate for all students or teachers to read, view, or hear. Adopted 1986, revised 1990.

(*See* "Current Reference File": Access to Resources and Services in the School Library Media Program: An Interpretation of the Library Bill of Rights: 1989–90 CD#61.1.)

53.1.4   Denying minors access to certain library materials and services available to adults is a violation of the Library Bill of Rights. Librarians and governing bodies should maintain that parents—and only parents—have the right and the responsibility to restrict the access of their children—to library resources. Adopted 1972, amended 1981, 1992.

(*See* "Current Reference File": Free Access to Libraries for Minors: An Interpretation of the Library Bill of Rights.)

53.1.5   Evaluation of library materials is not to be used as a convenient means to remove materials presumed to be controversial or disapproved of by segments of the community.

(*See* "Current Reference File": Evaluating Library Collections: An Interpretation of the Library Bill of Rights.)

53.1.6   Attempts to restrict library materials violate the basic tenets of the Library Bill of Rights. Policies to protect library materials for reasons of physical preservation, protection from theft, or mutilation must be carefully formulated and administered with extreme attention to the principles of intellectual freedom. Adopted 1973, amended 1981, 1991.

(*See* "Current Reference File": Restricted Access to Library Materials: An Interpretation of the Library Bill of Rights.)

53.1.7   Describing or designating certain library materials by affixing a prejudicial label to them or segregating by a prejudicial system is an attempt to prejudice attitudes and, as such, is a censor's tool; such practices violate the Library Bill of Rights. A variety of private organizations promulgate rating systems and/or review materials as a means of advising either their members or the general public concerning their opinions of the contents and suitability or appropriate age for use of certain books, films, recordings, or other materials. For the library to adopt or enforce any of these private systems, to attach such ratings to library materials, to include them in bibliographic records, library catalogs, or other finding aids, or otherwise to endorse them would violate the Library Bill of Rights. Adopted 1951, amended 1971, 1981, 1990.

(*See* "Current Reference File": Statement on Labeling: An Interpretation of the Library Bill of Rights.)

53.1.8   Libraries maintaining exhibit spaces and bulletin boards for outside groups and individuals should develop and publish statements governing use to assure that space is provided on a equitable basis to all groups which request it. A publicly supported library may limit use of its exhibit space to strictly "library related" activities, provided that the limitation is clearly circumscribed and is viewpoint neutral. Libraries may include in this policy rules regarding the time, place, and the manner of use of the exhibit space, so long as the rules are content neutral and are applied in the same manner to all groups wishing to use the space. Adopted 1991.

(*See* "Current Reference File": Exhibit Spaces and Bulletin Boards: An Interpretation of the Library Bill of Rights.)

53.1.9   Libraries maintaining meeting room facilities should develop and publish statements governing use. These statements can properly define time, place, or manner of use; such qualifications should not pertain to the content of a meeting or to the beliefs or affiliations of the sponsors. If meeting rooms in libraries supported by public funds are made available to the general public for non-library sponsored events, the library may not exclude any group based on the subject matter to be discussed or based on the ideas that the group advocates. A publicly supported library may limit use of its meeting rooms to strictly "library related" activities, provided that the limitation is clearly circumscribed and is viewpoint neutral. Adopted 1991.

(*See* "Current Reference File": Meeting Rooms: An Interpretation of the Library Bill of Rights.)

53.1.10 A policy on library initiated programming should set forth the library's commitment to free access to information and ideas for all users. Library staff select programs based on the interests and information needs of the community. Libraries serving multilingual and multicultural communities make efforts to accommodate the information needs of those for whom English is a second language. Adopted 1982, amended 1990.

(*See* "Current Reference File": Library-Initiated Programs as a Resource: An Interpretation of the Library Bill of Rights.)

53.1.11 American libraries exist and function within the context of a body of laws derived from the United States Constitution, defined by statute, and implemented by regulations, policies, and procedures established by their governing bodies and administrations. These regulations, policies, and procedures reflect the function and character of the library, define its operations, and protect its mission and the rights of its users. Such policies and procedures affect access, and must not become a convenient means for removing or restricting access to controversial materials; limiting access to facilities, programs, or exhibits; or for discriminating against specific individuals or groups of library patrons. Administrative policies and procedures which infringe on equitable access to library buildings, services, and resources, the privacy of the individual, or the right to read, violate the Library Bill of Rights. Adopted 1982 as Administrative Policies and Procedures Affecting Access to Library Resources and Services; amended with title change 1991.

(*See* "Current Reference File": Regulations, Policies, and Procedures Affecting Access to Library Resources and Services: An Interpretation of the Library Bill of Rights.)

53.1.12 Librarians have a professional responsibility to be inclusive, not exclusive, in collection development and in the provision of interlibrary loan. Access to all materials legally obtainable should be assured to the user and policies should not unjustly exclude materials even if offensive to the librarian or the user. Collection development should reflect the philosophy inherent in Article 2 of the Library Bill of Rights. A balanced collection reflects diversity of materials, not equality of numbers. Collection development responsibilities include selecting materials in the languages in common use in the community which the library serves. Collection development and the selection of materials should be done according to professional standards and established selection and review procedures.

Librarians have an obligation to protect library collections from removal of materials based on personal bias or prejudice, and to select and support the acquisition of materials on all subjects that meet, as closely as possible, the needs and interest of all persons in the community

which the library serves. This includes materials that reflect political, economic, religious, social, minority, and sexual issues.

(*See* "Current Reference File": Diversity in Collection Development: An Interpretation of the Library Bill of Rights: 1989–90 CD#61.3.)

53.1.13 The American Library Association believes that freedom of expression is an inalienable human right, necessary to self-government, vital to the resistance of oppression, and crucial to the cause of justice, and further, that the principles of freedom of expression should be applied by libraries and librarians throughout the world. Adopted 1989.

(*See* "Current Reference File": The Universal Right to Free Expression: An Interpretation of the Library Bill of Rights: 1990–91 CD#18.1.)

53.1.14 Recognizing that libraries cannot act *in loco parentis,* policies which set minimum age limits for access to videotapes and/or audiovisual material and equipment with or without parental permission abridge library use for minors. Nevertheless, ALA acknowledges and supports the exercise by parents of their responsibility to guide their own children's viewing, using published reviews of films and videotapes and/or reference works which provide information about the content, subject matter, and recommended audiences.

53.2 **Freedom to View**

The American Library Association endorses Freedom to View, a statement of the American Film and Video Association.

(*See* "Current Reference File": Freedom to View, revised 1990; 1989–90 CD#61.5.)

53.3 **Freedom to Read**

The American Library Association endorses Freedom to Read, a joint statement by the American Library Association and the Association of American Publishers.

(*See* "Current Reference File": Freedom to Read.)

53.3.1 *Linguistic Pluralism*

The American Library Association opposes all language laws, legislation, and regulations which restrict the rights of citizens who speak and read languages other than English, and those language laws, legislation, and regulations which abridge pluralism and diversity in library collections and services. The Association works with state associations and other agencies in devising ways to counteract restrictions arising from existing language laws and regulations, and encourages and supports the provision of library resources and services in the languages in common use in each community in the United States.

53.4 **Governmental Intimidation**

The American Library Association opposes any use of government prerogatives which leads to the intimidation of the individual or the citizenry from the exercise of free expression. ALA encourages resistance to such abuse of government power, and supports those against whom such governmental power has been employed.

54.   LIBRARY PERSONNEL PRACTICES

54.1   Library Education and
Personnel Utilization

To meet the goals of library service, both professional and supportive staff are needed in libraries. The library occupation is much broader than that segment of it which is the li-

brary profession. The library profession has responsibility for defining the training and education required for the preparation of personnel who work in libraries at any level, supportive or professional.

Skills other than those of librarianship have an important contribution to make to the achievement of superior library service. There should be equal recognition in the professional and supportive ranks for those individuals whose expertise contributes to the effective performance of the library and promotion of the most effective utilization of personnel at all levels.

The title "librarian" carries with it the connotation of "professional" in the sense that professional tasks are those which require a special background and education.

(*See* "Current Reference File": ALA Library Education and Personnel Utilization: A Public Policy Statement.)

54.2   Librarians: Appropriate Degrees

The master's degree from a program accredited by the American Library Association is the appropriate professional degree for librarians.

(*See* "Current Reference File": Historical Note on the Use of Terminology Pertaining to Degree Programs Accredited by the American Library Association.)

54.2.1 *Academic Librarians*

The master's degree in library science from a library school program accredited by the American Library Association is the appropriate terminal professional degree for academic librarians.

54.2.2 *School Library Media Specialists*

The master's degree in librarianship from a program accredited by the American Library Association or a master's degree with a specialty in school library media from an educational unit accredited by the National Council for the Accreditation of Teacher Education is the appropriate first professional degree for school library media specialists. (Adopted July 6, 1988, by ALA Council.)

54.3   Equal Employment Opportunity

The American Library Association is committed to equality of opportunity for all library employees or applicants for employment, regardless of race, color, creed, sex, age, physical or mental handicap, individual life-style, or national origin; and believes that hiring disabled individuals in all types of libraries is consistent with good personnel and management practices. Key factors in the selection of library personnel are training, knowledge, job interest, and the particular physical or mental abilities to do a specific job. Modification of the work environment should be considered if necessary to assist an individual in performing the job.

(*See* "Current Reference File": ALA Equal Employment Opportunity Policy: A Public Policy Statement on Employment; also, Employment of the Handicapped.)

54.3.1 *Affirmative Action Plans*

Member libraries and library schools with 15 or more staff shall formulate written affirmative action plans and shall submit these plans to OLPR for review.

54.4   Comparable Rewards

The American Library Association supports salary administration which gives reasonable and comparable recognition to positions having administrative, technical, subject, and linguistic requirements. It is recognized that all such specialist competencies can be intellectually vigorous and meet demanding professional operational needs. In administering such a policy, it can be a useful guide that, in major libraries, as many nonadministrative specialties be assigned to the top classifications as are administrative staff. Whenever possible there should be as many at the top rank with less than 30 percent administrative load as there are at the highest rank carrying over 70 percent administrative load.

54.5 Faculty Status of College
and University Librarians

Where the role of college and university librarians, in teaching and research, requires them to function essentially as part of the faculty, this functional identity should be recognized by granting of faculty status. Faculty status for librarians entails the same rights and responsibilities as for other members of the faculty.

(See "Current Reference File" for text of full statement.)

54.6 Fair Employment Practices in Libraries
and Among Suppliers to Libraries

The American Library Association Council instructs the Library Administration and Management Association to:

1) Guide libraries in the process of soliciting fair employment practice information from suppliers.
2) Advise libraries on the enforcement of fair employment practice laws in their employment practices and policies.
3) Submit an annual report to Association membership on the status of such actions.

54.7 Security of Employment
for Library Employees

Security of employment means that, following the satisfactory completion of a probationary period, the employment of a library employee under permanent appointment* carries with it an institutional commitment to continuous employment. Job competence, in accordance with the aims and objectives of the library, should be the criterion for acceptable performance for a library employee with permanent appointment. Library employees shall not be terminated without adequate cause and then only after being accorded due process.

Employing anyone for successive, limited periods with the intent to avoid the granting of permanent appointment is deemed unethical.

Security of employment, as an elementary right, guarantees specifically:

1) Intellectual freedom, defined as freedom to assume the responsibility placed upon a person by a democratic society to educate oneself and to improve one's ability to participate usefully in activities in which one is involved as a citizen of the United States and of the world, and institutional adherence to the *Library Bill of Rights*.
2) Appointments and promotions based solely on merit without interference from political, economic, religious, or other groups.
3) A sufficient degree of economic security to make employment in the library attractive to men and women of ability.
4) The opportunity for the library employee to work without fear of undue interference or dismissal and freedom from discharge for

*Permanent appointment in different types of libraries is variously called tenure, continuous appointment, career service, regular contract, etc.

racial, political, religious, or other unjust reasons.

54.8 The Library's Pay Plan

Libraries should have a well-constructed and well-administered pay plan based on systematic analysis and evaluation of jobs in the library and which will assure equal pay for equal work.

(See "Current Reference File": The Library's Pay Plan: A Public Policy Statement.)

54.9 Permanent Part-Time Employment

The right to earn a living includes a right to part-time employment on a par with full-time employment, including prorated pay and fringe benefits, opportunity for advancement and protection of tenure, access to middle- and upper-level jobs, and exercise of full responsibilities at any level.

ALA shall create more voluntarily chosen upgraded permanent part-time jobs in its own organization and supports similar action on the part of all libraries.

54.10 Equal Opportunity
and Salaries

The American Library Association supports and works for the achievement of equal salaries and opportunity for employment and promotion for men and women.

The Association fully supports the concept of comparable wages for comparable work that aims at levels of pay for female-oriented occupations equal to those of male-oriented occupations; ALA therefore supports all legal and legislative efforts to achieve wages for library workers commensurate with wages in other occupations with similar qualifications, training, and responsibilities.

ALA particularly supports the efforts of those library workers who have documented, and are legally challenging, the practice of discriminatory salaries, and whose success will benefit all library workers throughout the nation.

54.11 Collective Bargaining

The American Library Association recognizes the principle of collective bargaining as one of the methods of conducting labor-management relations used by private and public institutions. The Association affirms the right of eligible library employees to organize and bargain collectively with their employers, or to refrain from organizing and bargaining collectively, without fear of reprisal.

(See "Current Reference File": Collective Bargaining, Statement of Guidelines.)

54.12 Residency and Citizenship Requirements

The American Library Association is opposed to any rule, regulation or practice, imposed as a condition of new or continued employment in any library, a requirement of residence or U.S. citizenship except where a demonstrable danger to national security is involved.

54.13 Drug Testing

The American Library Association opposes mandatory drug testing of library employees and advocates employee assistance programs as the best way for library employers to respond to performance deficiencies due to drug use.

(See "Current Reference File": 1987–88 CD #61.)

54.14 Program of Review, Inquiry and Mediation

There shall be a Program of Action for Review, Inquiry and Mediation for the purpose of supporting professional standards and ethics as defined in ALA policies. There shall be a Standing Committee on Review, Inquiry and Mediation which is assigned responsibility for

review, inquiry and mediation regarding tenure, status, fair employment practices (including discrimination and sexual harassment), due process, ethical practices, and the principles of intellectual freedom as set forth in policies adopted by the Council of ALA.

(See "Current Reference File": 1989–90 CD#75.)

54.15 Institutional Support of ALA Members
to Attend ALA Conferences

The American Library Association supports the principle of giving preference, in libraries, to members of ALA in providing financial support and administrative leave to attend ALA Conferences. ALA supports encouraging staff in both administrative and non-administrative positions in libraries to attend the annual ALA Conference.

54.16 On Professional Ethics

Since 1939, the American Library Association has recognized the importance of codifying and making known to the public and the profession the principles which guide librarians in action. This latest revision of the Code of Ethics reflects changes in the nature of the profession and in its social and institutional environment. It should be revised and augmented as necessary.

Librarians significantly influence or control the selection, organization, preservation, and dissemination of information. In a political system grounded in an informed citizenry, librarians are members of a profession explicitly committed to intellectual freedom and the freedom of access to information. We have a special obligation to ensure the free flow of information and ideas to present and future generations.

Librarians are dependent upon one another for the bibliographical resources that enable us to provide information services, and have obligations for maintaining the highest level of personal integrity and competence.

Code of Ethics

1) Librarians must provide the highest level of service through appropriate and usefully organized collections, fair and equitable circulation and service policies, and skillful, accurate, unbiased, and courteous responses to all requests for assistance.
2) Librarians must resist all efforts by groups or individuals to censor library materials.
3) Librarians must protect each user's right to privacy with respect to information sought or received, and materials consulted, borrowed, or acquired.
4) Librarians must adhere to the principles of due process and equality of opportunity in peer relationships and personnel actions.
5) Librarians must distinguish clearly in their actions and statements between their personal philosophies and attitudes and those of an institution or professional body.
6) Librarians must avoid situations in which personal interests might be served or financial benefits gained at the expense of library users, colleagues, or the employing institution.

Adopted June 30, 1981, by ALA Membership and ALA Council.

54.17 Gay Rights

The American Library Association Council reaffirms its support for equal employment opportunity for gay librarians and library workers. The Council recommends that libraries reaffirm their obligation under the *Library Bill*

of Rights to disseminate information representing all points of view on this topic.
(*See also* 54.3.)

54.18   Advertising Salary Ranges

Salary ranges shall be given for positions listed in any placement services provided by ALA and its units. A regional salary guide delineating the latest minimum salary figures recommended by state library associations shall be made available from any placement services provided by ALA and its units.

All ALA and unit publications printing classified job advertisements shall list the salary ranges established for open positions and shall include a regional salary guide delineating the latest minimum salary figures recommended by state library associations for library positions.

54.19   Reproduction of Noncommercial Educational and Scholarly Journals

ALA encourages authors writing primarily for purposes of educational advancement and scholarship to reserve to themselves licensing and reproduction rights to their own works in the publishing contracts they sign.

ALA, in cooperation with other educational organizations, urges publishers to adopt and include in their journals or similar publications a notice of a policy for the noncommercial reproduction of their materials for educational and scholarly purposes.

54.20   AIDS Screening

The American Library Association opposes mandatory AIDS screening of library employees and advocates employee assistance programs as the best way for library employers to respond to performance deficiencies related to [such illness as] AIDS and AIDS-Related Complex (ARC)."
(*See* "Current Reference File": 1988–89 CD#22.)

54.21   Loyalty Oaths

The American Library Association strongly protests loyalty programs which inquire into a library employee's thoughts, reading matter, associates, or membership in organizations, unless a particular person's definite actions warrant such investigation. We condemn loyalty oaths as a condition of employment and investigations which permit the discharge of an individual without a fair hearing. We hold that in a fair hearing the accused is furnished a statement of the charges against him, is allowed to see the evidence against him, is given an opportunity to prepare and to present his defense and to question his accusers with the aid of legal counsel, is presumed innocent until proven guilty and is given the opportunity, if adjudged guilty, of judicial review. We also condemn negative loyalty oaths as a condition of election or appointment of library trustees.

54.22   Shield Laws

The American Library Association supports the enactment by Congress of a broad and effective federal shield law. The Association exhorts its chapters to work vigorously for the enactment of broad and effective shield laws in every state.

55.   STANDARDS AND GUIDELINES

55.1   Adoption of Standards

Standards, guidelines, criteria, etc., adopted by ALA units other than divisions as provided in the Constitution and Bylaws become ALA policy only when adopted by Council.

From time to time, ALA adopts standards and guidelines for the information and use of the public as represented in the library services of the nation.
(*See* "Current Reference File": ALA Standards Manual, Items 5.1–5.5. For a complete list of standards and guidelines adopted by ALA units with order information, see pp. 154–56.)

55.2   Standards of Accreditation in Library Education: Appeals Procedure

An institution of library education may file a written appeal against any accreditation decision, by the Committee on Accreditation, which does not result in accreditation. The details of the appeals procedure shall be adopted by the Executive Board as implementation of this policy, and the procedure shall be a part of the information supplied to institutions participating in the accreditation process.
(*See* "Current Reference File": Executive Board Appeal Procedure.)

56.   LIBRARY EDUCATION

56.1   The American Library Association supports the provision of library services by professionally qualified personnel who have been educated in graduate programs within institutions of higher education. It is of vital importance that there be professional education available to meet the social needs and goals of library services. Therefore, the American Library Association supports the development and continuance of high quality graduate library/information science educational programs of the quality, scope and availability necessary to prepare individuals in the broad profession of information dissemination.

56.2   Affirmative Action

The American Library Association encourages ALA-accredited programs of library science to continue to implement their affirmative action programs in admissions and in employment in the wake of the Bakke case decision by the Supreme Court.
(*See* "Library Education to Meet the Needs of Spanish-Speaking People" [59.4], "Standards of Accreditation in Library Education: Appeals Procedure" [55.1], "Standards and Guidelines" [55].)

56.3   Continuing Education

The American Library Association is committed to a national comprehensive long-range plan for continuing education to improve the quality of library service with appropriate support from ALA funds. Standards for libraries and library education and guidelines for services developed by any ALA unit should include a significant continuing education component where appropriate.
(*See* "Current Reference File": Continuing Education.)

57.   INTERNATIONAL RELATIONS

57.1   Policy Objectives

The ALA Charter states that the Association was formed "for the purpose of promoting library interest throughout the world by exchanging views, reaching conclusions and inducing cooperation in all departments of bibliothecal science and economy." The commitment in the area of international relations is carried out, in part, through the activities and programs of ALA's International Relations Office.

The American Library Association establishes these objectives and responsibilities for its international relations programs:
1) To encourage the exchange, dissemination, and access to information and the unrestricted flow of library materials in all formats throughout the world (ALA Priority Area A: Access to Information).
2) To promote and support human rights and intellectual freedom worldwide (ALA Priority Area C: Intellectual Freedom).
3) To foster, promote, support and participate in the development of international standards relating to library and information services, including informational tools and technologies (ALA Priority Area F: Library Services, Development, and Technology).
4) To promote legislation and treaties that will strengthen library, information and telecommunications services worldwide (ALA Priority Area B: Legislation and Funding).
5) To encourage involvement of librarians, information specialists, and other library personnel in international library activities and in the development of solutions to library service problems that span national boundaries (ALA Priority Area F: Library Services, Development, and Technology).
6) To promote the education of librarians, information specialists, and other library personnel in such ways that they are knowledgeable about librarianship in the international context (ALA Priority Area E: Personnel Resources).
7) To promote public awareness of the importance of the role of librarians, libraries, and information services in national and international development (ALA Priority Area D: Public Awareness).
(*See* "Current Reference File" for full text, including implementation: 1989–90 CD#14.)

57.2   Selection of Consultants to Serve Abroad

The American Library Association, serving the public interest, assigns a high priority to the development of libraries, librarianship, and information services throughout the world. ALA reaffirms its continuing desire to foster international library development in all countries, and in return hopes to continue to learn from its participation.

In response to requests for assistance from abroad, ALA must be able to recommend librarians and information specialists who are both highly qualified and sensitive to cultural and national differences. ALA will therefore apply its approved guidelines and criteria in recommending, nominating, and selecting international consultants.
(*See* "Current Reference File" for full text and guidelines and criteria.)

57.3   Abridgment of the Rights of Freedom of Foreign Nationals

Threats to the freedom of expression of any person become threats to the freedom of all; therefore ALA adopts as policy the principles of Article 19 of the Universal Declaration of Human Rights adopted by the United Nations General Assembly. The Association will address the grievances of foreign nationals where the infringement of their rights of free expression is clearly a matter in which all free people should show concern. Resolutions or other documents attesting to such grievances will be brought to the attention of the Executive Board and Council by the ALA International Relations Committee.

(See "Current Reference File": Policy on Abridgment of the Rights of Freedom of Foreign Nationals and Freedom of Expression of Foreign Nationals; Abridgement of Human Rights in South Africa: 1985–86 CD#58.)

57.4   Article 19 of the United Nations' Universal Declaration of Human Rights

Everyone has the right to freedom of opinion and expression; this right includes freedom to hold opinions without interference and to seek, receive and impart information and ideas through any media regardless of frontiers.
(See "Current Reference File": 1990–91 CD#24 and CD#76.)

58.   PUBLIC RELATIONS

58.1   Policy Objectives

Through public information programs, and through its publications and membership activities, the ALA seeks to keep the American public aware of libraries in order to encourage their greater use, and to stimulate citizen support. It is ALA's policy to engage in public information programs that are primarily national in scope, that benefit all types of libraries and their constituents, and that, in turn, inspire local or special libraries to engage in promotion and education activities in their own communities.

Through its Public Information Office, ALA will maintain a close relationship with the library press, both national and international, and sustain a steady flow of information about the organization and its activities, as well as major developments affecting the library profession. Through its Washington Office, ALA seeks to inform the United States legislature and the various federal agencies about events generally, and legislation specifically, which influence library-related activities.
(See "Current Reference File" for full statement.)

58.2   Public Information Office Responsibility

The responsibility for implementing national public information programs and for coordinating ALA contact with the national and international media, rests with the Public Information Office of the Association with support by the Public Relations (LAMA) Section and other appropriate groups.

59.   MINORITY CONCERNS

The American Library Association promotes equal access to information for all persons and recognizes the urgent need to respond to the increasing racial and ethnic diversity among Americans. African-Americans, Hispanic Americans, Asian Americans, Native Americans, and other minorities have critical and increasing needs for information and library access. They are affected by a combination of limitations including illiteracy, language barriers, economic distress, cultural isolation, and discrimination in education, employment, and housing. Therefore, the role played by libraries to enable minorities to participate fully in a democratic society is crucial. Libraries must utilize multivariate resources and strategies to empower minority people. Concrete programs of recruitment, training, development, and upward mobility are needed in order to increase and retain minority personnel within librarianship. Within the American Library Association, the coordinating mechanisms for pro-

grams and activities dealing with minorities in various ALA divisions, offices, and units should be strengthened, and support for minority liaison activities should be enhanced.

59.1   Policy Objectives

The American Library Association shall implement these objectives by:
1) Promoting the removal of all barriers to library and information services, particularly fee charges and language barriers.
2) Promoting the publication, production, and purchase of print and nonprint materials that present positive role models of cultural minorities.
3) Promoting full funding for existing legislative programs in support of minority education and training, and to explore alternative funding sources for scholarships, fellowships, and assistantships to encourage minority recruitment into librarianship.
4) Promoting training opportunities for librarians, including minorities, in order to teach effective techniques for generating tripartite public funding for upgrading library services to minorities.
5) Promoting the incorporation of minority programs and services into the regular library budgets in all types of libraries, rather than the tendency to support these activities solely from "soft monies" such as private grants or federal monies.
6) Promoting equity in funding adequate library services for minority populations, in terms of professional and nonprofessional personnel, materials, resources, facilities, and equipment.
7) Promoting supplemental support for library resources on cultural minorities by urging local, state, and federal government, and the private sector, to provide adequate funding.
8) Promoting increased public awareness of the importance of library resources and services in all segments of society, especially in minority communities.
9) Promoting the determination of output measures through the encouragement of community needs assessments, giving special emphasis to assessing the needs of cultural minorities.
10) Promoting increased staff development opportunities and upward mobility for minority librarians.
(See 1.3 A and "Current Reference File": *Equity at Issue* [1985–86 CD #30] adopted by Council June 1986.)

59.2   Combating Prejudice, Stereotyping, and Discrimination

The American Library Association actively commits its prestige and resources to a coordinated action program that will combat prejudice, stereotyping, and discrimination against individuals and groups in the library profession and in library service because of race, sex, creed, color, or national origin.

Nothing in the Resolution on Prejudice, Stereotyping, and Discrimination authorizes censoring, expurgation, or labeling of materials. Actions and programs to raise the awareness of library users to any problem or condition would not be in conflict with the *Library Bill of Rights* when they are free of any element of advocacy. Both documents respect the rights of all who use libraries to do so freely and without being subjected to any pressures from any sources within the institution.
(See "Current Reference File" for full Resolution on Prejudice, Stereotyping, and Dis-

crimination, a revision of the Resolution on Racism and Sexism Awareness.)

59.3   Goals for Indian Library and Information Services

The American Library Association and the National Indian Education Association support guidelines designed to meet the informational needs and to purvey and promote the rich cultural heritage of American Indians.
1) All library and information services must show sensitivity to cultural and social components existent in individual Indian communities.
2) Indian representation through appointment to local boards and creation of local advisory committees concerning service to and about American Indians are essential for healthy, viable programs.
3) Materials which meet informational and educational needs and which present a bicultural view of history and culture must be provided in appropriate formats, quality, and quantity to meet current and future needs.
4) Library programs, outreach and delivery systems must be created which will insure rapid access to information in a manner compatible with the community's cultural milieu.
5) American Indian personnel trained for positions of responsibility are essential to the success of any program.
6) Continuing funding sources for library and information services must be developed.
(See "Current Reference File" for full adopted text.)

59.4   Library Education to Meet the Needs of Spanish-Speaking People

The American Library Association will take steps through its Committee on Accreditation to encourage graduate library schools seeking accreditation or reaccreditation to assure that course content reflects the cultural heritage and needs of the Spanish-speaking people of the United States and will encourage such schools to include bilingual/bicultural persons on their faculties.

59.5   Ethnic and Cultural Minorities in State, Municipal, and County Agencies

The American Library Association urges and supports the recruiting, hiring, and promotion of ethnic and cultural minorities within the state, municipal, and county library structure, especially in the areas of administration and consultation.
(See "Current Reference File": 1989–90 CD#98. See also 53.1.11, 54.3, 54.3.1, 56.2.)

60.   LIBRARY SERVICES FOR THE POOR

The American Library Association promotes equal access to information for all persons, and recognizes the urgent need to respond to the increasing number of poor children, adults, and families in America. These people are affected by a combination of limitations, including illiteracy, illness, social isolation, homelessness, hunger, and discrimination, which hamper the effectiveness of traditional library services. Therefore it is crucial that libraries recognize their role in enabling poor people to participate fully in a democratic society, by utilizing a wide variety of available resources and strategies. Concrete programs of training and development are needed to sensitize and prepare library staff to identify poor people's needs and deliver relevant services. And within the American Library Association the coordinating mechanisms of programs and activities dealing with poor people in various divisions, offices, and units should be strengthened, and support for low-income liaison activities should be enhanced.

60.1 Policy Objectives

The American Library Association shall implement these objectives by:

1) Promoting the removal of all barriers to library and information services, particularly fees and overdue charges.

2) Promoting the publication, production, purchase, and ready accessibility of print and nonprint materials that honestly address the issues of poverty and homelessness, that deal with poor people in a respectful way, and that are of practical use to low-income patrons.

3) Promoting full, stable, and ongoing funding for existing legislative programs in support of low-income services and for proactive library programs that reach beyond traditional service-sites to poor children, adults, and families.

4) Promoting training opportunities for librarians, in order to teach effective techniques for generating public funding to upgrade library services to poor people.

5) Promoting the incorporation of low-income programs and services into regular library budgets in all types of libraries, rather than the tendency to support these projects solely with "soft money" like private or federal grants.

6) Promoting equity in funding adequate library services for poor people in terms of materials, facilities, and equipment.

7) Promoting supplemental support for library resources for and about low-income populations by urging local, state, and federal governments, and the private sector, to provide adequate funding.

8) Promoting increased public awareness— through programs, displays, bibliographies, and publicity—of the importance of poverty-related library resources and services in all segments of society.

9) Promoting the determination of output measures through the encouragement of community needs assessments, giving special emphasis to assessing the needs of low-income people and involving both anti-poverty advocates and poor people themselves in such assessments.

10) Promoting direct representation of poor people and anti-poverty advocates through appointment to local boards and creation of local advisory committees on service to low-income people, such appointments to include library-paid transportation and stipends.

11) Promoting training to sensitize library staff to issues affecting poor people and to attitudinal and other barriers that hinder poor people's use of libraries.

12) Promoting networking and cooperation between libraries and other agencies, organizations, and advocacy groups in order to develop programs and services that effectively reach poor people.

13) Promoting the implementation of an expanded federal low-income housing program, national health insurance, full-employment policy, living minimum wage and welfare payments, affordable day care, and programs likely to reduce, if not eliminate, poverty itself.

14) Promoting among library staff the collection of food and clothing donations, volunteering personal time to anti-poverty activities and contributing money to direct-aid organizations.

15) Promoting related efforts concerning minorities and women, since these groups are disproportionately represented among poor people.

INDEX
Originally compiled by Pamela Hori; updated by Charles Harmon

Appendixes

A. ALA Documents

CHARTER

Commonwealth of Massachusetts

Be it known, that whereas Justin Winsor, C. A. Cutter, Samuel S. Green, James L. Whitney, Melvil Dui, Fred B. Perkins and Thomas W. Bicknell, have associated themselves with the intention of forming a corporation under the name of the American Library Association for the purpose of promoting the library interests of the country by exchanging views, reaching conclusions, and inducing cooperation in all departments of bibliothecal science and economy; by disposing the public mind to the founding and improving of libraries; and by cultivating good will among its own members, and have complied with the provisions of the statutes of this Commonwealth in such case made and provided, as appears from the certificate of the President, Treasurer and Executive Board of said corporation, duly approved by the Commissioner of Corporations, and recorded in this office.

Now, therefore, I, Henry B. Peirce, Secretary of the Commonwealth of Massachusetts, do hereby certify that said Justin Winsor, C. A. Cutter, Samuel S. Green, James L. Whitney, Melvil Dui, Fred B. Perkins and Thomas W. Bicknell, their associates and successors, are legally organized and established as, and are hereby made an existing corporation under the name of the American Library Association, with the powers, rights, and privileges, and subject to the limitations, duties, and restrictions, which by law appertain thereto.

Witness my official signature hereunto subscribed, and the seal of the Commonwealth of Massachusetts hereunto affixed this tenth day of December in the year of Our Lord one thousand eight hundred and seventy-nine.

HENRY B. PEIRCE
Secretary of the Commonwealth

NOTE: The changes in the first paragraph italicized below were approved by Henry F. Long, Commissioner of Corporations and Taxation of the Commonwealth of Massachusetts, on February 6, 1942:

Be it known that, whereas Justin Winsor, C. A. Cutter, Samuel S. Green, James L. Whitney, Melvil Dui, Fred B. Perkins and Thomas W. Bicknell, have associated themselves with the intention of forming a corporation under the name of the American Library Association for the purpose of promoting library interests *throughout the world* by exchanging views, reaching conclusions and inducing cooperation in all departments of bibliothecal science and economy; by disposing the public mind to the founding and improving of libraries; and by cultivating good will among its own members, *and by such other means as may be authorized from time to time by the Executive Board or Council of the American Library Association,* and have complied with the provisions of the statutes of this Commonwealth in such case made and provided, as appears from the certificate of the President, Treasurer and Executive Board of said corporation, duly approved by the Commissioner of Corporations, and recorded in this office.

STANDARDS AND GUIDELINES*

NOTE: This list includes documents entitled "standards" and "guidelines" as well as other documents of a similar nature entitled "statements," "rules," and "criteria." The intent is to include documents prepared and endorsed by ALA units for the purpose of helping others improve library service.

Academic Libraries

See Colleges and Universities

Access

"AASL Statement on Confidentiality of Library Records." American Association of School Librarians. From *Information Power: Guidelines for School Library Media Programs.* Chicago: ALA, 1988. 1 p. AASL.

"Access Policy Guidelines." Association of College & Research Libraries. Reprinted from *College & Research Libraries News,* Nov. 1975. 2 pp. $1.00. ACRL.

"Guidelines for the Preparation of Policies on Library Access." Association of College and Research Libraries. Reprinted from *College & Research Libraries News,* June 1990. 6 pp. $1.00. ACRL.

Accreditation

"Standards for Accreditation of Master's Programs in Library and Information Studies." Adopted by the Council of the American Library Association, 1992. ALA Committee on Accreditation. OA.

Aging, Services to

"Guidelines for Library Service to Older Adults." Reference and Adult Services Division. Reprinted from *RQ,* Summer 1987. 4 pp. Headquarters Library.

Archives

See Rare Books, Manuscripts, and Archives.

Audiovisual Materials

"Guidelines for Audiovisual Services in Academic Libraries." Association of College and Research Libraries. Reprinted from *College & Research Libraries News,* Oct. 1987. 4 pp. $1.00. ACRL.

Bibliographic Control

ALA Filing Rules. Resources and Technical Services Division, Filing Committee, 1980. 50 pp. $10.00. ISBN 0-8389-3255-X. Order Dept.

ALA Rules for Filing Catalog Cards, 2d ed., abridged. Pauline A. Seely, ed. Resources and Technical Services Division, 1968. 104 pp. $10.00. ISBN 0-8389-0001-1. Order Dept.

Anglo-American Cataloguing Rules, 2d ed. Michael Gorman and Paul W. Winkler for the Joint Steering Committee for Revision of AACR. Resources and Technical Services Division. Rev. 1988. 677 pp. Paperback: $27.50. ISBN 0-8389-3360-2. Hardcover: $37.50,

---

*Where no price is given, a single copy may be obtained from issuing unit on request by including a self-addressed mailing label and 50¢ postage.

ISBN 0-8389-3346-7. Ring-binder: $48.00, ISBN 0-8389-3361-0. Order Dept.

"Guidelines for a Database Search Guide." Reference and Adult Services Division. *RQ,* Summer 1987. Headquarters Library.

"Guidelines for Cataloging Microform Sets." Association for Library Collections & Technical Services, 1989. 1 p. Headquarters Library.

"Guidelines for Standardized Cataloging of Children's Materials." Resources and Technical Services Division, 1982 (rev. 1983). Reprinted in *Cataloging Correctly for Kids: An Introduction to the Tools.* Rev. ed. by Sharon Zuiderveld. ALA, 1991. Headquarters Library.

"Guidelines for the Preparation of a Bibliography." Rev. 1992. Reference and Adult Services Division, 1992. To be published in *RQ.* Headquarters Library.

"Guidelines for the Subject Analysis of Audiovisual Materials." Association for Library Collections & Technical Services, 1992. 3 pp. Headquarters Library.

"Guidelines on Subject Access to Individual Works of Fiction, Drama, etc." Association for Library Collections & Technical Services, 1990. 40 pp. $8.00. ISBN 0-8389-3386-6. Order Dept.

"Guidelines on Subject Access to Microcomputer Software." Resources and Technical Services Division, 1986. 27 pp. $6.00. ISBN 0-8389-0452-1. Order Dept.

Bibliographic Instruction

"Model Statement of Objectives for Academic Bibliographic Instruction." Association of College and Research Libraries. Reprinted from *College & Research Libraries News,* May 1987. 6 pp. $1.00. ACRL.

Blind and Physically Handicapped

Revised Standards and Guidelines of Service for the Library of Congress Network of Libraries for the Blind and Physically Handicapped. Association of Specialized and Cooperative Library Agencies. 1984. 55 pp. $6.50. ISBN 0-8389-3306-8. Order Dept.

Children's Services

"Competencies for Librarians Serving Children in Public Libraries." Association for Library Service to Children. *Journal of Youth Services in Libraries,* Spring 1989. Pamphlet. $2.00. ALSC.

"Output Measures for Public Library Service to Children: A Manual of Standardized Procedures." Part of the Public Library Development Program. By Virginia Walter. (Not a standard or guideline, but allied to public library standards development.) 1992. 129 pp. $20. ISBN 0-8389-3404-8. Order Dept.

Collection Management and Development

Guide for Writing a Bibliographer's Manual. Resources and Technical Services Division, 1987. Collection Management & Development Guides, No. 1. 32 pp. $7.00. ISBN 0-8389-3343-2. Order Dept.

Guide for Written Collection Policy Statements. Resources and Technical Services Division, 1989. Collection Management & Development Guides, No. 3. 32 pp. $7.00. ISBN 0-8389-3371-8. Order Dept.

Guide to Budget Allocation for Information Resources. Edward Shreeves, ed. Association for Library Collections & Technical Services, 1991. Collection Management & Development Guides, No. 4. 23 pp. $7.00. ISBN 0-8389-3397-1. Order Dept.

Guide to Performance Evaluation of Library Materials Vendors. Resources and Technical Services Division, 1989. Acquisition Guidelines, No. 5. 24 pp. $6.00. ISBN 0-8389-3369-6. Order Dept.

Guide to Review of Library Collections: Preservation, Storage, and Withdrawal. Lenore Clark, ed. Association for Library Collections & Technical Services, 1991. 41 pp. $7.00. ISBN 0-8389-3396-3. Order Dept.

Guide to the Evaluation of Library Collections. Barbara Lockett, ed. Resources and Technical Services Division, 1989. Collection Management & Development Guides, No. 2. 25 pp. $7.00. ISBN 0-8389-3370-X. Order Dept.

"Guidelines for Developing Beginning Genealogical Collections and Services." Reference and Adult Services Division. 1992. To be published in *RQ*. Headquarters Library.

"Guidelines for Liaison Work." Reference and Adult Services Division, 1992. To be published in *RQ*. Headquarters Library.

"Guidelines for Preservation, Conservation, and Restoration of Local History and Local Genealogical Materials." Reference and Adult Services Division, 1992. To be published in *RQ*. Headquarters Library.

Colleges and Universities

"Guidelines for Branch Libraries in Colleges and Universities." Association of College and Research Libraries. Reprinted from *College & Research Libraries News*, Oct. 1975. 3 pp. $1.00. ACRL.

"Guidelines for Extended Campus Library Services." Association of College and Research Libraries. Reprinted from *College & Research Libraries News*, Apr. 1990. 3 pp. $1.00. ACRL.

"Mission of an Undergraduate Library: Model Statement." Association of College and Research Libraries. Reprinted from *College & Research Libraries News*, Oct. 1987. 3 pp. $1.00. ACRL.

"Standards for College Libraries." Association of College and Research Libraries. Reprinted from *College & Research Libraries News*, Mar. 1986. 12 pp. ACRL.

"Standards for University Libraries and Evaluation of Performance." Association of College and Research Libraries. Reprinted from *College & Research Libraries News*, Sept. 1989. 13 pp. ACRL.

Community and Junior Colleges

"Standards for Community, Junior, and Technical College Learning Resources Programs." Association of College and Research Libraries/Association for Educational Communications and Technology. Reprinted from *College & Research Libraries News*, Sept. 1990. 11 pp. ACRL.

Cooperative Library Systems

See Networks of Libraries

Correctional Institutions

Library Standards for Adult Correctional Institutions. Association of Specialized and Coop-

erative Library Agencies, Standards Review Committee, Library Standards for Adult Correctional Institutions ad hoc subcommittee, 1992. 4 pp. $15.00. Order Dept.

Library Standards for Jails and Detention Facilities. Association of Specialized and Cooperative Library Agencies, 1981. 8 pp. $1.50. ISBN 0-8389-5598-3. Order Dept.

Editing and Publishing

"Guidelines for Authors, Editors, and Publishers of Literature in the Library and Information Field." Adopted by ALA Council, June 1983. CD #38 (1982–83). Headquarters Library.

"Guidelines for Editors of Historical and Genealogical Bulletins and Family Newsletters." Reference and Adult Services Division. Reprinted from *RQ*, Winter 1986. 2 pp. Headquarters Library.

"Guidelines for Reprinting or Republishing Books of Historical Interest." Reference and Adult Services Division. *RQ*, Fall 1984. Headquarters Library.

"Guidelines for the Preparation of a Bibliography." Rev. 1992. Reference and Adult Services Division, 1992. To be published in *RQ*. Headquarters Library.

Education for Library Service

"Criteria for Programs to Prepare Library Media Technical Assistants." Adopted by the Library Education Division, ALA, 1971. Rev. ed. adopted by ALA Council, June 1979. Standing Committee on Library Education.

"Guidelines for Practice and Principles in the Design, Operation, and Evaluation of Standard Field Experiences in Library and Information Science." Adopted by ALA Council, June 1984. 7 pp. Standing Committee on Library Education.

"Guidelines for Quality in Continuing Education for Information, Library, and Media Personnel." Adopted by ALA Council, Jan. 1988. 21 pp. Standing Committee on Library Education.

"Library Education and Personnel Utilization: A Statement of Policy." Office for Library Personnel Resources. Adopted by ALA Council, June 30, 1970. Rev. 1976. 8 pp. ISBN 0-8389-5482-0. OLPR.

"Position Statement on Preparation of School Library Media Specialists." American Association of School Librarians. From *Information Power: Guidelines for School Library Media Programs*. Chicago: 1988. 1 p. AASL.

"Standards for Accreditation of Master's Programs in Library and Information Studies." Adopted by the Council of the American Library Association, 1992. ALA Committee on Accreditation. OA.

"Statement on History in Education for Library and Information Science." Library History Round Table, 1989, 1 p. Headquarters Library.

"Statement on the Terminal Professional Degree for Academic Librarians." Association of College and Research Libraries, 1975. 1 p. $1.00. ACRL.

Ethnic Groups

"Guidelines for Multilingual Materials Collection and Development and Library Services." Reference and Adult Services Division. Reprinted from *RQ*, Winter 1990. 4 pp. Headquarters Library.

"Guidelines for Library Services to Hispanics." Reprinted from *RQ*, Summer 1988. 5 pp. Headquarters Library.

Handicapped

See Blind and Physically Handicapped
See Institutional Library Services

Information Services

"Guidelines for a Database Search Guide." Reference and Adult Services Division. *RQ*, Summer 1987. Headquarters Library.

"Guidelines for Developing Beginning Genealogical Collections and Services." Reference and Adult Services Division, 1992. To be published in *RQ*. Headquarters Library.

Guidelines for Establishing Community Information and Referral Services in Public Libraries, 3d ed. Public Library Association, 1989. 25 pp. $15, $13 (ALA members), $10 (PLA members). ISBN 0-8389-7365-5. Order Dept.

"Guidelines for Medical, Legal, and Business Responses at a General Reference Desk." Reference and Adult Services Division. Reprinted from *RQ*, Summer 1992. Headquarters Library.

"Guidelines for Use of the Information Request Form." Reference and Adult Services Division. Reprinted from *RQ*, Summer 1988. 2 pp. Headquarters Library.

"Information Services for Information Consumers: Guidelines for Providers." Reference and Adult Services Division. Supersedes the 1976 and 1979 statement entitled "A Commitment to Information Services: Developmental Guidelines." Reprinted from *RQ*, Winter 1990. 4 pp. Headquarters Library.

Institutional Library Services

See also Correctional Institutions

"Standards and Guidelines for Client Library Services in Residential Mental Health Facilities." Association of Specialized and Cooperative Library Agencies, 1987. 29 pp. $10.00. ISBN 0-8389-7137-7. ASCLA.

"Standards for Libraries at Institutions for the Mentally Retarded." Association of Specialized and Cooperative Library Agencies, 1981. 32 pp. $5.00, $4.50 (ASCLA members). ISBN 0-8389-6460-5. ASCLA.

Interlibrary Loan

"Guidelines and Procedures for Telefacsimile Transmission of Interlibrary Loan Requests." Reference and Adult Services Division. Reprinted from *RQ*, Winter 1990. 2 pp. Headquarters Library.

"Guidelines for Packing and Shipping Microforms." Association for Library Collections & Technical Services, 1989. 1 p. Headquarters Library.

Library Technology Program

See Technical Standards and Specifications

Manuscripts

See Rare Books, Manuscripts, and Archives.

Networks of Libraries

"Standards for Cooperative Multitype Library Organizations." Association for Specialized and Cooperative Library Agencies, 1990. 15 pp.

$10, $8 (ASCLA members). ISBN 0-8389-7399-X. ASCLA.

Personnel Issues

"Guidelines and Procedures for the Screening and Appointment of Academic Librarians." Association of College and Research Libraries. Reprinted from *College & Research Libraries News*, Sept. 1977. 4 pp. $1.00. ACRL.

"Guidelines for Academic Status for College and University Libraries." Association of College and Research Libraries. Reprinted from *College & Research Libraries News*, Mar. 1990. 2 pp. $1.00. ACRL.

"Guidelines for Liaison Work." Reference and Adult Services Division, 1992. To be published in *RQ*. Headquarters Library.

"Guidelines for Library Affirmative Action Plans." Office for Library Personnel Resources, 1976. OLPR.

"Joint Statement on Faculty Status of College and University Librarians." Association of College and Research Libraries/American Association of University Professors/Association of American Colleges. Reprinted from *College & Research Libraries News*, Feb. 1974. 1 p. $1.00. ACRL.

"Library Education and Personnel Utilization: A Statement of Policy." Office for Library Personnel Resources. Adopted by ALA Council, June 30, 1970. Rev. 1976. 8 pp. ISBN 0-8389-5482-0. OLPR.

"The Master's Degree for Library and Information Professionals." Office for Library and Personnel Resources. Adopted by ALA Council, July 1992. 3 pp. OLPR.

"Model Statement of Criteria and Procedures for Appointment, Promotion in Academic Rank, and Tenure for College and University Librarians." Association of College and Research Libraries. Reprinted from *College & Research Libraries News*, May 1987. 8 pp. $1.00. ACRL.

"Position Statement on Appropriate Staffing for School Library Media Centers." American Association of School Librarians. From *Information Power: Guidelines for School Library Media Programs*. Chicago: 1988. 1 p. AASL.

"Standards for Ethical Conduct for Rare Book, Manuscript, and Special Collections Libraries." Reprinted from *College & Research Libraries News*, Mar. 1987. 2 pp. $1.00. ACRL.

"Standards for Faculty Status for College and University Librarians." Association of College and Research Libraries. Reprinted from *College & Research Libraries News*, May 1992. 2 pp. $1.00. ACRL.

"Statement on Collective Bargaining." Association of College and Research Libraries, 1975. 1 p. $1.00. ACRL.

"Statement on the Terminal Professional Degree for Academic Librarians." Association of College and Research Libraries, 1975. 1 p. $1.00. ACRL.

Physically Handicapped

See Blind and Physically Handicapped

Planning

"Mission of an Undergraduate Library: Model Statement." Association of College and Research Libraries. Reprinted from *College & Research Libraries News*, Oct. 1987. 3 pp. $1.00. ACRL.

Planning and Role Setting for Public Libraries. Prepared for the Public Library Development Project by Charles R. McClure, Amy Owen, Douglas L. Zweizig, Mary Jo Lynch, and Nancy A. Van House. (Not a standard or guideline, but allied to public library standards development.) 1987. 117 pp. $18.00. ISBN 0-8389-3341-6. Order Dept.

Planning Guide for Information Power: Guidelines for School Library Media Programs. American Association of School Librarians, 1988. 40 pp. $7.00. ISBN 0-8389-7255-1. Order Dept.

Preservation

"ALA Preservation Policy." Adopted by ALA Council, June 1991. Headquarters Library.

"Guidelines for Preservation, Conservation, and Restoration of Local History and Local Genealogical Materials." Reference and Adult Services Division, 1992. To be published in *RQ*. Headquarters Library.

"Guidelines for Preservation Photocopying of Replacement Pages." Association for Library Collections & Technical Services, 1990. 3 pp. Headquartes Library.

Public Libraries

See also Planning.

Output Measures for Public Libraries: A Manual of Standardized Procedures, 2d ed. Prepared for the Public Library Development Project by Nancy A. Van House, Mary Jo Lynch, Charles R. McClure, Douglas L. Zweizig, and Eleanor J. Rodger. (Not a standard or guideline, but allied to public library standards development.) 1987. 99 pp. $18.00. ISBN 0-8389-3340-8. Order Dept.

Output Measures for Public Library Service to Children: A Manual of Standardized Procedures. Part of the Public Library Development Program. By Virginia Walter. (Not a standard or guideline, but allied to public library standards development.) 1992. 129 pp. $20. ISBN 0-8389-3404-8. Order Dept.

Publishing

See Editing and Publishing

Rare Books, Manuscripts, and Archives

"Guidelines for Borrowing Special Collections Materials for Exhibition." Association of College and Research Libraries. Reprinted from *College & Research Libraries News*, May 1990. 5 pp. $1.00. ACRL.

"Guidelines for the Security of Rare Book, Manuscript, and Other Special Collections." Association of College and Research Libraries. Reprinted from *College & Research Libraries News*, Mar. 1990. 3 pp. $1.00. ACRL.

"Guidelines on the Selection of General Collection Materials for Transfer to Special Collections." Association of College and Research Libraries. Reprinted from *College & Research Libraries News*, Sept. 1987. 4 pp. $1.00. ACRL.

"Guidelines Regarding Thefts in Libraries." Association of College and Research Libraries. Reprinted from *College & Research Libraries News*, Mar. 1988. 4 pp. $1.00. ACRL.

"Preparation of Archival Copies of Theses and Dissertations." Resources and Technical Services Division, 1984. 24 pp. $6.00. ISBN 0-8389-0449-1. Order Dept.

"Standards for Ethical Conduct for Rare Book, Manuscript, and Special Collections Libraries." Reprinted from *College & Research Libraries News*, March 1987. 2 pp. $1.00. ACRL.

Reference Services

See Information Services

School Library Media Centers

Information Power: Guidelines for School Library Media Programs. Prepared jointly by the American Association of School Librarians and the Association for Educational Communications and Technology. 1988. 172 pp. $14.00. ISBN 0-8389-3352-1. Order Dept.

"Position Statement on Flexible Scheduling." American Association of School Librarians, June 1991. 1 p. Single copy free with self addressed envelope. AASL.

"Sample Statement on the Role of the School Library Media Program." American Association of School Librarians, Oct. 1990. 1 p. Single copy free with self addressed envelope. AASL.

State Library Services

Standards for Library Functions at the State Level, 3d ed. Association of Specialized and Cooperative Library Agencies, 1985. 44 pp. $6.75. ISBN 0-8389-3317-3. Order Dept.

Statistics

Statistics for Managing Library Acquisitions. By Eileen D. Hardy. Resources and Technical Services Division, 1989. Acquisitions Guidelines, No. 6. $7.00. ISBN 0-8389-3374-2. Order Dept.

Young Adult Services

"Young Adults Deserve the Best." Competencies for Librarians Serving Youth." Rev. ed. 1991. Young Adult Library Services Association. 4 pp. Single copies free. 25 copies/$10.00. YALSA.

B. Calendars

SPECIAL EVENTS

International Federation of Library Associations and
  Institutions (IFLA):

  Aug. 1993, Barcelona, Spain
  Aug. (3d wk.) 1994, Havana, Cuba
  Aug. 22–26, 1995, Istanbul, Turkey
  Aug. (3d wk.) 1994, Beijing, China

Children's Book Week: Nov. 16–22, 1992
National Library Week: Apr. 18–24, 1993;
  Apr. 17–23, 1994
Banned Books Week: Sept. 25–Oct. 2, 1993

FUTURE ALA MEETINGS

Midwinter Meeting

Cities	Dates
Denver	Jan. 22–28, 1993
Los Angeles	Feb. 4–10, 1994
Cincinnati	Jan. 20–26, 1995

Annual Conference

Cities	Dates
New Orleans	June 24–July 1, 1993
Miami	June 23–30, 1994
Chicago	June 22–29, 1995

EXECUTIVE BOARD

In addition to the Midwinter and Annual Meetings, the
Executive Board normally meets on Wednesday and
Thursday during the weeks that begin with the last
Monday of the months of April and October.

EXHIBIT INFORMATION

Complete information on ALA Midwinter Meeting and
Annual Conference exhibits is mailed on the following
schedule:

Midwinter Meeting	April of preceding year
Annual Conference	September of preceding year

If you are interested in exhibiting at ALA meetings and
do not receive exhibit information within 14 days after
these mailings, please contact the ALA Conference
Services Office.

AWARDS, CITATIONS, AND SCHOLARSHIPS

See pp. 115–25 for deadlines for applications.

1993 ELECTION SCHEDULE

Petitions of nominations for ballots must be received at ALA Hq. not later than	Feb. 26, 1993
Last day ballots accepted for in-house printing	Mar. 12, 1993
Membership dues payment cutoff for receipt of ballots	Mar. 31, 1993
Ballot mailing completion	Apr. 30, 1993
Ballot return must be received at ALA Hq. not later than	June 4, 1993
Distribution of election results	June 9, 1993

ALA OFFICES CLOSED (holidays)

Nov. 26, 1992	Jan. 18, 1993
Nov. 27, 1992	Feb. 15, 1993
Dec. 24, 1992	May 31, 1993
Dec. 25, 1992	July 5, 1993
Jan. 1, 1993	Sept. 6, 1993

LIBRARY ASSOCIATIONS' CONFERENCES

Date	Association	Place
November 1992		
November	California Media & Library Educators Assn.	Sacramento
Nov. 4–7	Georgia Library Assn.	Savannah
(joint conf.)	Georgia Council of Media Organizations	
Nov. 4–7	Ohio Library Assn./OELMA	Columbus
Nov. 12–14	Virginia Library Assn.	Richmond
Nov. 13–16	Literacy Volunteers of America	Orlando
Nov. 14–18	California Library Assn.	Long Beach
January 1993		
Jan. 13–15	South Carolina Assn. of School Librarians	Charleston
Jan. 14–18	Assn. for Educational Communications & Technology	New Orleans
Jan. 22–28	ALA Midwinter Meeting	Denver
February 1993		
February	Art Libraries Society of North America	TBA
March 1993		
March/April	Delaware Library Assn.	TBA
Mar. 5–7	Michigan Assn. for Media in Education	Sugar Loaf
Mar. 6–8	Alaska Library Assn.	Nome
Mar. 9–13	Texas Library Assn.	San Antonio
Mar. 17–20	New Mexico Library Assn.	Las Vegas
Mar. 17–21	Public Library Assn. Cluster Workshops	Chicago
Mar. 22–26	Louisiana Library Assn.	Shreveport
Mar. 24–27	Kansas Library Assn.	Overland Park
Mar. 26–27	Hawaii Library Assn.	Kohala Dist.
Mar. 30–Apr. 3	Oklahoma Library Assn.	Oklahoma City
April 1993		
April/May	Council of Planning Librarians	Chicago
(joint conf.)	American Planning Assn.	
Apr. 1–3	Oregon Library Assn.	Eugene
Apr. 4–6	Missouri Assn. of School Librarians	Lake Ozark
Apr. 12–15	Catholic Library Assn.	New Orleans
(joint conf.)	National Catholic Education Assn.	
Apr. 13–16	Alabama Library Assn.	Huntsville
Apr. 14–15	Connecticut Library Assn.	Cromwell
Apr. 21–23	New Jersey Library Assn.	Long Branch
Apr. 21–24	Washington Library Assn.	Tacoma
Apr. 27–May 1	Illinois Library Assn.	Springfield
Apr. 28–May 1	Tennessee Library Assn.	Nashville
Apr. 29–30	Wisconsin Educational Media Assn.	Appleton

LIBRARY ASSOCIATIONS' CONFERENCES (cont.)

Date	Association	Place
May 1993		
May 4–6	Indiana Library Assn.	Indianapolis
May 6–7	SOLINET	Atlanta
May 10–12	New Hampshire Library Assn.	Waterville Valley
May 10–13	Florida Library Assn.	Daytona Beach
May 11–15	School Library Media Div., Montana Library Assn.	Kalispell
May 12–14 (tent.)	Utah Library Assn.	Cedar City
May 13–14	Maryland Library Assn.	Pikesville
May 14–20	Medical Library Assn.	Chicago
May 16–18	Maine Library Assn.	Orono
May 19–20	Vermont Library Assn.	TBA
June 1993		
June	Rhode Island Library Assn.	TBA
June 5–10	Special Libraries Assn.	Cincinnati
June 24–July 1	ALA Annual Conference	New Orleans
June 28	Theatre Library Assn.	New Orleans
July 1993		
July 8–11	Canadian Library Assn.	Toronto
July 11–13	Church & Synagogue Library Assn.	Houston
July 17–22	American Assn. of Law Libraries	Boston
August 1993		
August 22–28	International Federation of Library Assns.	Barcelona, Spain
August 11–14	Pacific Northwest Library Assn.	Kalispell
(joint conf.)	Montana Library Assn.	
September 1993		
Sept. 2–5	Society of American Archivists	New Orleans
Sept. 23–25	School Library Media Section, North Dakota Library Assn.	Williston
Sept. 26–28	New England Library Assn.	Burlington, Vt.
Sept. 26–29	Pennsylvania Library Assn.	Philadelphia
Sept. 30–Oct. 2	Nevada Library Assn.	Elko
Sept. 30–Oct. 4	Mountain Plains Library Assn.	Aspen
(joint conf.)	Colorado Library Assn.	
October 1993		
October	American Society for Information Science	Columbus, Ohio
October	Illinois Media School Library Assn.	Effingham
October	Minnesota Library Assn.	Rochester
October/November	Georgia Library Assn.	Jekyll Island
Oct. 6–8	Idaho Library Assn.	Moscow
Oct. 6–9	South Dakota Library Assn.	Brookings
Oct. 11–13	Arkansas Library Assn.	Hot Springs
Oct. 13–15	Iowa Library Assn.	Ames
Oct. 14–16	West Virginia Library Assn.	Huntington
Oct. 19–22	North Carolina Library Assn.	Winston-Salem
Oct. 20–23	Michigan Assn. for Media in Education	Kalamazoo
Oct. 27–29	Mississippi Library Assn.	Natchez
Oct. 27–30	Ohio Library Assn./OELMA	Cleveland
November 1993		
Nov. 3–5	Wisconsin Library Assn.	Green Bay
Nov. 3–7	New York Library Assn.	Niagara Falls
(joint conf.)	Ontario Library Assn.	
Nov. 13–16	California Library Assn.	Oakland

C. Forms

BEQUEST TO THE AMERICAN LIBRARY ASSOCIATION

I give to the American Library Association, an educational association organized under the laws of the Commonwealth of Massachusetts, the sum of _____ to be used for the general purposes of said association. [Alternatives for suggested use of funds: (a) to be added to and become a part of the general endowment fund of said Association; (b) to be used as the Governing Board of said Association from time to time shall decide. It is my wish, but I do not direct, that said sum be used for _____.]

PETITION PROCEDURES

The Bylaws of the American Library Association provide for petitions: *to call a special meeting of the Association* [Article II, Sec. 2]; *to propose additional nominees for the ballot* [Article III, Sections 2(b) and 3(b)]; *to call a special Council meeting* [Article IV, Sec. 1(b)]; *to request establishment of a division* [Article VI, Sec. 1(a)], *or a round table* [Article VII, Sec. 1(a)].

Council, upon recommendation of the Committee on Organization, established in January 1967 the following guidelines for the preparation of petitions:

1. The purpose of the petition shall be clearly stated on a single sheet attached to each group of ten signature pages.

2. Each signature page shall contain this statement: "I favor this petition to. . . ."

3. Petitioners shall sign and give library affiliation legibly. Failure to do so may result in the invalidation of the petition.

4. Information about this format and a sample petition will be supplied from ALA headquarters to anyone inquiring.

5. Petitioners shall be personal members of ALA.

The following petitions are samples of the desired form in which they should appear.

PETITION TO CALL A MEETING

The purpose of this petition is to request that a special meeting of the American Library Association (or of Council) be called

on _____.
    (date)

According to the Bylaws, Article II, Section 2, _____ signatures of 5 percent of the voting membership as of July 1 are
                                        (number)

required to call such a meeting. All signatures must be those of personal members of ALA.

The purpose of the meeting to be called is

_____

_____

_____

_____

I favor this petition to call a meeting of _____ on _____.
                                                                                    (date)

Name _____   Library _____

PETITION PROPOSING ADDITIONAL NOMINATION

The purpose of this petition is to add the name of _____ to the nominees appearing on

the official ballot of the American Library Association for the office of _____, _____.
(dates of term)

According to the Bylaws, Article III, Section 3(b), 25 signatures of personal members are required to add a name to the official

ballot.

I favor the petition to add the name of _____ to the ballot for the office of _____,

_____.
(dates of term)

[Please write legibly]

Name _____ Library _____

PETITION FOR THE ESTABLISHMENT OF A DIVISION OR ROUND TABLE

The purpose of this petition is to request the establishment of _____

_____

_____

in the American Library Association.

According to the Bylaws, Article _____, Section _____, _____ signatures are required for the establishment

of _____. All signatures must be those of personal members of ALA.

The statement of function and responsibility of the unit proposed is: _____

_____

_____.

I favor this petition to establish _____

_____

_____

in the American Library Association.

Name _____ Library _____

These sample petition forms may be mechanically reproduced for use by members.

Application for Organization Membership   1993

All ALA Organization Members Receive: Tangible benefits that include: *American Libraries* (11 issues per year), *ALA Membership Directory, ALA Handbook of Organization* and discounts on library materials, and eligibility for Library Professional Liability Insurance.

Organization membership does not include personal member perquisites such as reduced conference rates, group health insurance or voting privileges.

If you have questions call ALA Membership Services (312) 944-6780, 800-545-2433; FAX (312) 944-2641.

Please Note:
Membership cards will be mailed in advance of any publications, which should begin arriving in six to eight weeks.

Your ALA organization membership will be in effect for twelve full months following the receipt of correct ALA dues. Each year, you will receive a membership renewal to continue membership.

Journals
$30 of dues is for annual subscription to American Libraries magazine; price to non-member organizations is $60.

$20 of AASL dues is for a one-year subscription to *School Library Media Quarterly;* non-member price is $40.

$22.50 of ALCTS dues is for a one-year subscription to *Library Resources & Technical Services;* non-member price is $45. $12.50 of ALCTS dues is for a one-year subscription to *ALCTS Newsletter;* non-member price is $25.

$25 of ACRL dues is for a one-year subscription to *College and Research Libraries;* non-member price is $50. $12.50 of ACRL dues is for a one-year subscription to *C&RL News;* non-member price is $25.

$7.50 of ASCLA dues is for a one-year subscription to *Interface;* non-member price is $15.

$25 of LAMA dues is for a one-year subscription to *Library Administration and Management;* non-member price is $50.

$22.50 of LITA dues is for a one-year subscription to *Information Technology and Libraries;* non-member price is $45. $12.50 of LITA dues is for a one-year subscription to *LITA Newsletter;* non-member price is $25.

$25 of PLA dues is for a one-year subscription to *Public Libraries;* non-member price is $50.

$21 of RASD dues is for a one-year subscription to *RQ;* non-member price is $42. $7.50 of RASD dues is for a one-year subscription to *RASD Update;* non-member price is $15.

$20 of YALSA and ALSC dues is for a one-year subscription to *Journal of Youth Services in Libraries;* non-member price is $40.

Date of
Application: _____

| | Day | Month | Year |

Library _____

Mailing Address _____

_____

City and State _____   Zip _____

Telephone Number _____

Your Name _____

Position _____

For membership received before July 15, the above information will appear in the next issue of the ALA Membership Directory.

Special note regarding mailing list rentals:

From time to time, ALA rents its membership lists to selected organizations offering services or products related to libraries. If you do not wish to be included in these mailings, please check this box: M ☐

Send completed application with payment or purchase order to:

American Library Association
Membership Services
50 East Huron Street
Chicago, Illinois 60611

Membership Dues

Select your type of membership by checking the appropriate box.
U.S. Library or Library School—dues based on annual operating expenditure for personnel and library materials for the previous fiscal year.

Dues		Library's Budget
☐ L1	$ 70	Under $50,000
☐ L2	$110	$50,000–$199,999
☐ L3	$330	$200,000–$499,999
☐ L4	$550	$500,000–$999,999
☐ L5	$770	$1,000,000–$1,999,999
☐ L6	$900	Over $2,000,000

CH **$50**
☐ **Chapter Members** State and Regional Library Associations that have been granted chapter status by the ALA Council.

FL **$50**
☐ **Foreign Library or Foreign Library School** including Canadian libraries which belong to the Canadian Library Association.

NP **$50**
☐ **Non-profit Organizations** Library associations, affiliated organizations, chapters, and non-profit organizations other than libraries or library schools.

Basic Dues   **A$** _____

(Continued)

Divisions

Another benefit of membership in ALA is eligibility for membership in our Divisions and their subsections. Each of our eleven Divisions focuses on a special type of library or library service and publishes its own member publication. The Divisions are also involved in improving overall library service, establishing guidelines and standards, and working with the Washington Office in a combined effort to pass positive legislation.

Any ALA organization member can belong to any division by remitting the dues, as listed, for that division.

Please check the boxes at the left for your Division and section selections.

☐ **$35**
American Association of School Librarians (AASL) Publications: *School Library Media Quarterly. AASL Presidential Hotline* (semi-annual)
Sections: ($5.00 each)
☐ Supervisors
☐ Non-Public Schools
☐ Educators of Library Media Specialists

☐ **$40**
American Library Trustee Association (ALTA) Publication: *The ALTA Newsletter* (bimonthly)

☐ **$35**
Association for Library Collections & Technical Services (ALCTS) Publications: *Library Resources & Technical Services* (quarterly journal) and *ALCTS Newsletter* (six issues per year)
Sections: (No charge)
☐ Acquisitions
☐ Collection Management and Development
☐ Cataloging and Classification
☐ Serials
☐ Reproduction of Library Materials
☐ Preservation of Library Materials

☐ **$35**
Association for Library Service to Children (ALSC) Publications: *Journal of Youth Services in Libraries* (quarterly journal). Newsletter (semi-annual)

☐ **$50**. (State Library Agencies, **$500**)
Association of Specialized and Cooperative Library Agencies (ASCLA) Publication: *Interface* (quarterly)
Sections: (No charge)
☐ Libraries Serving Special Populations (Including forums for Bibliotherapy, Library Service to the Blind and Physically Handicapped, Library Service to the Deaf, Library Service to the Impaired Elderly and Library Service to Prisoners.)
☐ Multitype Library Networks & Cooperatives
☐ State Library Agency.

☐ **$35**
Library Administration and Management Association (LAMA) Publication: *Library Administration and Management* (Issued Quarterly)
Sections: (No charge)
☐ Buildings and Equipment
☐ Library Organization & Management
☐ Personnel Administration
☐ Public Relations
☐ Systems and Services
☐ Statistics
☐ Fund Raising and Financial Development

☐ **$50**
Library and Information Technology Association (LITA) Publications: *Information Technology and Libraries* (quarterly), *LITA Newsletter* (quarterly)

☐ **$35**
Public Library Association (PLA) Publication: *Public Libraries* (Issued bimonthly)
Sections: (No charge)
☐ Public Library Systems
☐ Metropolitan Libraries
☐ Small and Medium-sized Libraries
☐ Community Information
☐ Adult Lifelong Learning
☐ Marketing of Public Library Services
☐ Public Policy for Public Libraries

☐ **$35**
Association of College and Research Libraries (ACRL) Publications: *College & Research Libraries* (bimonthly journal) and *C&RL News* (11 issues per year)
Sections: (One free section from category 1 and two free sections from category 2. Additional sections are $2 each.)
Category 1
☐ Community and Junior College Libraries
☐ University Libraries
☐ College Libraries
Category 2
☐ Science and Technology
☐ Arts
☐ Law and Political Science
☐ Slavic and East European
☐ Education and Behavioral Sciences
☐ Extended Campus Library Services
☐ Asian and African
☐ Anthropology and Sociology
☐ Rare Books and Manuscripts
☐ Bibliographic Instruction
☐ Western European Specialists
☐ Women's Studies
☐ Afro-American Studies Librarian

☐ **$35**
Reference and Adult Services Division (RASD) Publications: *RQ* (quarterly journal): *RASD Update* (quarterly)
Sections: (No charge)
☐ Business Reference and Services
☐ Collection Development and Evaluation
☐ History
☐ Machine-Assisted Reference Services
☐ Management and Operation of Public Services
☐ Services to User Populations

☐ **$35**
Young Adult Library Services Association (YALSA) Publication: *Journal of Youth Services in Libraries* (quarterly journal)

Add Division and Section dues and record on line B.

Total Division and Section Membership Dues   B$_____

Round Tables

Only ALA members are eligible to join Round Tables.

Round Tables	Dues
☐ Armed Forces Libraries Round Table	$10
☐ Continuing Library Education Network and Exchange	$50
☐ Ethnic Materials Information Exchange	$15
☐ Exhibits	$10
☐ Federal Librarians	$10
☐ Government Documents	$15
☐ Independent Librarians Exchange	$ 8
☐ Intellectual Freedom	$10
☐ International Relations	$ 7
☐ Library History	$12

Round Tables	Dues
☐ Library Instruction	$15
☐ Library Research	$10
☐ Map and Geography	$45
☐ New Members	$10
☐ Social Responsibilities	$20
☐ Staff Organizations	$ 6
☐ Video	$25
Total Round Table Dues	**C$**_____

Make check payable to American Library Association for exact amount shown on Line D. Dues paid to ALA are deductible for Income Tax purposes. **Your cancelled check is your receipt.** If an invoice is requested, membership privileges are effective upon payment of invoice.
☐ Check enclosed   ☐ Please send invoice (Purchase order enclosed)

TOTAL DUES (Total of A, B & C)   **D$**_____

Application for Personal Membership

General Information

As An ALA Member You Will Receive:

Tangible benefits such as *American Libraries* (11 issues per year), discounts on ALA publications and graphics, member rates at ALA conferences, voting and committee privileges, insurance privileges, eligibility to join round tables and divisions, and a copy of the *ALA Handbook of Organization* (upon request).

Professional support through active national programs in legislation, intellectual freedom, standards, research and more.

Information and interaction for professional development.

A voice in the future of your profession.

If you have any questions call ALA Membership Services (312) 944-6780, 800-545-2433; FAX (312) 944-2641.

Please Note:

Membership cards will be mailed in advance of any publications, which should begin arriving in six to eight weeks.

Your ALA membership will be in effect for twelve full months following the receipt of correct ALA dues. Each year, you will receive a membership renewal to continue membership.

Journals

$30 of dues is for annual subscription to *American Libraries* magazine; price to non-member organizations is $60.

$20 of AASL dues is for a one year subscription to *School Library Media Quarterly*; non-member price is $40.

$22.50 of ALCTS dues is for a one year subscription to *Library Resources & Technical Services*; non-member price is $45. $12.50 of ALCTS dues is for a one year subscription to the *ALCTS Newsletter*; non-member price is $25.

$25 of ACRL dues is for a one year subscription to *College and Research Libraries*; non-member price is $50. $12.50 of ACRL dues is for a one year subscription to *C&RL News*; non-member price is $25.

$7.50 of ASCLA dues is for a one year subscription to *Interface*; non-member price is $15.

$25 of LAMA dues is for a one year subscription to *Library Administration and Management*; non-member price is $50.

$22.50 of LITA dues is for a one year subscription to *Information Technology and Libraries*; non-member price is $45. $12.50 of LITA dues is for a one year subscription to *LITA Newsletter*; non-member price is $25.

$25 of PLA dues is for a one year subscription to *Public Libraries*; non-member price is $50.

$21 of RASD dues is for a one year subscription to *RQ*; non-member price is $42. $7.50 of RASD dues is for a one year subscription to *RASD Update*; non-member price is $15.

$20 of YALSA and ALSC dues is for a one year subscription to *Journal of Youth Services in Libraries*; non-member price is $40.

Date

_____

Name: First   Initial   Last

_____

Mailing Address

_____

_____

City and State   Zip

_____

Home Telephone

The following information will appear in the next issue of the ALA Membership Directory if this application is received before July 15.

_____

Your Position

_____

_____

Place of Employment/Institution

_____

_____

City and State   Zip

Mail to ☐ Home ☐ Office

If you are using this form for renewal of your membership, please enter your current ALA Membership Number here:

_____

Special note regarding mailing list rentals:

From time to time, ALA rents its membership lists to selected organizations offering services or products related to libraries. If you do not wish to be included in these mailings, please check this box: M ☐

Send completed application to:

American Library Association
Membership Services
50 East Huron Street
Chicago, Illinois 60611

Basic Dues

Regular Members—librarians, other library employees and others employed in library service or related activities.

☐ R **$38** First Year

☐ R **$49** Second Year

☐ R **$60** Third Year

☐ R **$75** Fourth and Later Years

☐ ST **$19.00**

Student members—members who are enrolled at least half-time in a program of library and information science in a four year undergraduate or graduate school. Limited to three years.

☐ NS **$26.00**

Other members—those who are inactive, retired, or unemployed, or are employed full- or part-time in library service or related activities at a salary of less than $10,000 per annum.

☐ F **$45.00**

Foreign Librarians—librarians who do not hold U.S. citizenship and who are not employed in the U.S. or U.S. Possessions, regardless of salary.

☐ TR **$34.00**

Trustee and Associate Members—includes those not employed in library and information services or related activities who through their personal commitment and support promote library and information services; i.e., members of governing boards, advisory groups, friends and special citizen caucuses, and/or individuals interested in participating in the work of the Association.

Basic Dues   **A$** _____

(Continued)

Divisions

All ALA personal members are eligible for membership in any division. Division Membership dues are additional to ALA dues.
Check boxes below for divisions and sections selected.

☐ **$35.** ALA student member, **$15**
American Association of School Librarians (AASL)
Publications: *School Library Media Quarterly*, *AASL Presidential Hotline* (semi-annual)
Sections: ($5.00 each)
☐ Supervisors
☐ Non-Public Schools
☐ Educators of Library Media Specialists

☐ **$40**
American Library Trustee Association (ALTA)
Publication: *The ALTA Newsletter* (bimonthly)

☐ **$35.** ALA Student member, **$15**
Association for Library Collections & Technical Services (ALCTS)
Publications: *Library Resources & Technical Services* (quarterly journal) and *ALCTS Newsletter* (six issues per year)
Sections: (No charge)
☐ Acquisitions
☐ Collection Management and Development
☐ Cataloging and Classification
☐ Serials
☐ Reproduction of Library Materials
☐ Preservation of Library Materials

☐ **$35.** ALA Student member, **$15**
Association for Library Service to Children (ALSC) Publications: *Journal of Youth Services in Libraries* (quarterly journal), *ALSC Newsletter* (semi-annual)

☐ **$35.** ALA Student member, **$15**
Library and Information Technology Association (LITA)
Publications: *Information Technology and Libraries* (quarterly)
LITA Newsletter (Quarterly)

☐ **$35**
Association of College and Research Libraries (ACRL)
Publications: *College & Research Libraries* (bimonthly journal), *C&RL News* (11 issues per year)
Sections: (one free section from category 1 and two free sections from category 2. Additional sections are $2 each)
Category 1
☐ Community and Junior College Libraries
☐ University Libraries
☐ College Libraries
Category 2
☐ Science and Technology
☐ Arts
☐ Law and Political Science
☐ Slavic and East European
☐ Education and Behavioral Sciences
☐ Extended Campus Library Services
☐ Asian and African
☐ Anthropology and Sociology
☐ Rare Books and Manuscripts
☐ Bibliographic Instruction
☐ Western European Specialists
☐ Women's Studies
☐ Afro-American Studies Librarian

☐ **$20** First-year member
☐ **$15** ALA Student member
☐ **$30** Renewing member
Association of Specialized and Cooperative Library Agencies (ASCLA) Publication: *Interface* (quarterly)
Sections: (No charge)
☐ Libraries Serving Special Populations (Including forums for Bibliotherapy, Library Service to the Blind and Physically Handicapped, Library Service to the Deaf, Library Service to the Impaired Elderly and Library Service to Prisoners.)
☐ Multitype Library Networks & Cooperatives
☐ State Library Agency

☐ **$35.** ALA Student member, **$15**
Young Adult Library Services Association (YALSA)
Publication: *Journal of Youth Services in Libraries* (quarterly journal)

☐ **$35.** ALA Student member, **$15**
Library Administration and Management Association (LAMA)
Publication: *Library Administration and Management* (quarterly)
Sections: (No charge)
☐ Buildings and Equipment
☐ Library Organization & Management
☐ Personnel Administration
☐ Public Relations
☐ Systems and Services
☐ Statistics
☐ Fund Raising and Financial Development

☐ **$35.** ALA Student member, **$10**
Public Library Association (PLA)
Publication: *Public Libraries* (bimonthly journal)
Sections: (No charge)
☐ Public Library Systems
☐ Metropolitan Libraries
☐ Small and Medium-sized Libraries
☐ Community Information
☐ Adult Lifelong Learning
☐ Marketing of Public Library Services
☐ Public Policy for Public Libraries

☐ **$35.** ALA Student member, **$15**
Reference and Adult Services Division (RASD)
Publications: *RQ* (quarterly journal), *RASD Update* (quarterly)
Sections: (No charge)
☐ Business Reference and Services
☐ Collection Development and Evaluation
☐ History
☐ Machine-Assisted Reference Services
☐ Management and Operation of Public Services
☐ Services to User Populations

Add Division and Section dues and record on line B.

Total Division and Section Membership Dues   B$ _____

Round Tables

Only ALA members are eligible to join Round Tables. Check boxes for Round Tables selected.

Membership in the New Members Round Table is limited to persons having 10 or fewer years of membership in ALA.

Round Tables	Dues
☐ Armed Forces Libraries Round Table	$10
AFLRT ALA Student Members	$ 3
☐ Continuing Library Education & Network Exchange	$15
☐ Ethnic Materials Information Exchange	$10
☐ EMIERT ALA Student Members	$2.50
☐ Exhibits	$10
☐ Federal Librarians	$ 8
☐ Government Documents	$15
☐ Independent Librarians Exchange	$ 8
☐ Intellectual Freedom	$10
☐ IFRT ALA Student Members	$ 1

Round Tables	Dues
☐ International Relations	$ 7
☐ Library History	$12
☐ LHRT ALA Student Members	$ 5
☐ Library Instruction	$10
☐ Library Research	$10
☐ LRRT Doctoral Students	FREE
☐ Map & Geography	$15
☐ New Members	$10
☐ Social Responsibilities	$10
☐ SRRT ALA Student Members	FREE
☐ Staff Organizations	$ 3
☐ Video	$12
Total Round Table Dues	**C$ _____**

Total Dues

Add amounts on lines A-C and place total on D.

Make check payable to American Library Association for exact amount shown on Line D. Dues paid to ALA are deductible for Income Tax purposes. **Your cancelled check is your receipt.**

Total D$ _____

Please charge my membership dues (line D) to
VISA ☐   Master Card ☐
American Express ☐

card number

☐☐☐☐☐☐☐☐☐☐☐☐☐☐☐☐☐☐

expiration date _____

signature _____

Application for Special Membership

General Information

All ALA special members receive tangible benefits that include: *American Libraries* magazine (11 issues per year), *ALA Handbook of Organization & Membership Directory*, discounts on ALA publications and graphics, eligibility for division and round table memberships, eligibility for insurance and special member recognition programs.

Journals

$30 of dues is for annual subscription to *American Libraries* magazine; price to non-member organizations is $60.

$20 of AASL dues is for a one year subscription to *School Library Media Quarterly*; non-member price is $40.

$22.50 of ALCTS dues is for a one year subscription to *Library Resources & Technical Services*; non-member price is $45.

$12.50 of ALCTS dues is for a one year subscription to *ALCTS Newsletter*; non-member price is $25.

$25 of ACRL dues is for a one year subscription to *College and Research Libraries*; non-member price is $50. $12.50 of ACRL dues is for a one year subscription to *C&RL News*; non-member price is $25.

$7.50 of ASCLA dues is for a one year subscription to *Interface*; non-member price is $15.

$25 of LAMA dues is for a one year subscription to *Library Administration & Management*; non-member price is $50.

$22.50 of LITA dues is for a one year subscription to *Information Technology and Libraries*; non-member price is $45. $12.50 of LITA dues is for a one year subscription to *LITA Newsletter*; non-member price is $25.

$25 of PLA dues is for a one year subscription to *Public Libraries*; non-member price is $50.

$21 of RASD dues is for a one year subscription to *RQ*; non-member price is $42. $7.50 of RASD dues is for a one year subscription to *RASD Update*; non-member price is $15.

$20 of YALSA and ALSC dues is for a one year subscription to *Journal of Youth Services in Libraries*; non-member price is $40.

Date of Application: Day   Month   Year

Firm

Mailing Address

City and State   Zip

Telephone

Your Name

Position

Special note regarding mailing list rentals: From time to time, ALA rents its membership lists to selected organizations offering services or products related to libraries. If you do not wish to be included in these mailings, please check this box: M ☐

Send completed application to:

**American Library Association
Membership Services
50 East Huron Street
Chicago, Illinois 60611**

Membership Dues

Select your type of membership by checking the appropriate box.

Special Membership Dues Categories

☐ Firm Membership (or)

☐ Individual Membership

☐ Patrons of the ALA	$1000.00
☐ Sustaining	500.00
☐ Contributing	300.00
☐ Subscribing	150.00

Basic Dues   **A$** _____

Make check payable to American Library Association for the exact amount shown on Line D. Dues paid to ALA are deductible for Income Tax purposes. Your cancelled check is your receipt. If an invoice is requested, membership privileges are effective upon payment of invoice.

☐ Check enclosed

☐ Please send invoice (purchase order enclosed)

Total Dues (Total of A, B, & C)   D$ _____

Please note: Membership cards will be mailed in advance of any publications, which should begin arriving in six to eight weeks. Membership is in effect for twelve full months following receipt of correct ALA dues.

If you have questions, call ALA Membership Services at (312) 280-4298. Call toll-free (800) 545-2433, ext. 4298. FAX only (312) 944-2641.

For memberships received before July 15, the above information will appear in the next issue of the ALA Membership Directory.

(Continued)

Divisions

Another benefit of membership in ALA is eligibility for membership in our divisions and their subsections. Each of our eleven divisions focuses on a special type of library or library service and publishes its own member publication. The divisions are also involved in improving overall library service, establishing guidelines and standards, and working with the Washington Office in a combined effort to pass positive legislation.

Any ALA special member can belong to any division by remitting the dues, as listed, for that division.

Please check the boxes at the left for your Division and Section selections.

☐ **$35.00 AASL**
American Association of School Librarians
Publications: *School Library Media Quarterly* and *AASL Presidential Hotline* (semi-annual)
Sections: ($5.00 each)
☐ Educators of Library Media Specialists (ELMSS)
☐ Non-Public Schools (NPSS)
☐ Supervisors (SPVS)

☐ **$40.00 ALTA**
American Library Trustee Association
Publication: *The ALTA Newsletter* (bimonthly)

☐ **$35.00 ALCTS**
Association for Library Collections & Technical Services
Publications: *Library Resources & Technical Services* (quarterly journal) and *ALCTS Newsletter* (six issues per year)
Sections: (no charge)
☐ Acquisitions (AS)
☐ Cataloging and Classification (CCS)
☐ Collection Management and Development (CMDS)
☐ Preservation of Library Materials (PLMS)
☐ Reproduction of Library Materials (RLMS)
☐ Serials (SS)

☐ **$35.00 ALSC**
Association for Library Service to Children
Publications: *Journal of Youth Services in Libraries* (quarterly) and *ALSC Newsletter* (semi-annual)

☐ **$35.00 ACRL**
Association of College and Research Libraries
Publications: *College and Research Libraries* (bimonthly journal), and *C&RL News* (11 issues per year)
Sections: (You may choose one type of library section and two types of activity sections. Additional sections, $2.00)
Type of library sections
☐ College Libraries (CLS)
☐ Community and Junior College Libraries (CJCLS)
☐ University Libraries (ULS)
Type of activity sections
☐ Afro-American Studies Librarian (AFAS)
☐ Anthropology and Sociology (ANSS)
☐ Arts (ARTS)
☐ Asian and African (AAS)
☐ Bibliographic Instruction (BIS)
☐ Education and Behavioral Sciences (EBSS)
☐ Extended Campus Library Services (ECLSS)
☐ Law and Political Science (LPSS)
☐ Rare Books and Manuscripts (RBMS)
☐ Science and Technology (STS)
☐ Slavic and East European (SEES)
☐ Western European Specialists (WESS)
☐ Women's Studies (WSS)

☐ **ASCLA**
☐ **$30.00 Individual**
☐ **$50.00 Organization**
Association of Specialized and Cooperative Library Agencies
Publication: *Interface* (quarterly journal)
Sections: (No charge)
☐ Libraries Serving Special Populations (LSSPS)
Forums:
☐ Bibliotherapy, ☐ Library Services to the Blind and Physically Handicapped, ☐ Library Service to the Deaf, ☐ Library Service to the Impaired Elderly, ☐ Library Service to Prisoners
☐ Multitype Library Networks and Cooperatives (MLNCS)
☐ State Library Agency (SLAS)

☐ **$35.00 LAMA**
Library Administration and Management (quarterly journal)
Sections: (no charge)
☐ Buildings and Equipment (BES)
☐ Fund Raising and Financial Development (FRFDS)
☐ Library Organization and Management (LOMS)
☐ Personnel Administration (PAS)
☐ Public Relations (PRS)
☐ Statistics (STATS)
☐ Systems and Services (SASS)

☐ **$50.00 LITA**
Library and Information Technology Association
Publications: *Information Technology and Libraries* (quarterly journal) and *LITA Newsletter* (quarterly)

☐ **$35.00 PLA**
Public Library Association
Publication: *Public Libraries* (bimonthly journal)
Sections: (No charge)
☐ Adult Lifelong Learning (ALLS)
☐ Community Information (CIS)
☐ Marketing of Public Library Services (MPLSS)
☐ Metropolitan Libraries (MLS)
☐ Public Library Systems (PLSS)
☐ Small and Medium-sized Libraries (SMLS)
☐ Public Policy for Public Libraries (PPPLS)

☐ **$35.00 RASD**
Reference and Adult Services Division
Publications: *RQ* (quarterly journal) and *RASD Update* (quarterly)
Sections: (no charge)
☐ Business Reference and Services (BRASS)
☐ Collection Development and Evaluation (CODES)
☐ History (HS)
☐ Machine-Assisted Reference Services (MARS)
☐ Management and Operation of Public Services (MOPSS)
☐ Services to User Populations (SUPS)

☐ **$35.00 YALSA**
Young Adult Library Services Association
Publication: *Journal of Youth Services in Libraries* (quarterly)

Add division and section dues and record on line B.

Total Division and Section Membership Dues   **B$** _____

Round Tables

Only ALA members are eligible to join Round Tables.

Round Tables	Dues
☐ Armed Forces Libraries Round Table (AFLRT)	$10.00
☐ Continuing Library Education Network and Exchange (CLENERT)	
☐ Individual	$15.00
☐ Organization	$50.00
☐ Ethnic Materials Information Exchange Round Table (EMIERT)	
☐ Individual	$10.00
☐ Organization	$15.00
☐ Exhibits Round Table (ERT)	
☐ Individual	$10.00
☐ Organization	$30.00
☐ Federal Librarians Round Table (FLRT)	
☐ Individual	$ 8.00
☐ Organization	$10.00

Round Tables	Dues
☐ Government Documents Round Table (GODORT)	$15.00
☐ Independent Librarians Round Table (ILERT)	$ 8.00
☐ Intellectual Freedom Round Table (IFRT)	$10.00
☐ International Relations Round Table (IRRT)	$ 7.00
☐ Library History Round Table (LHRT)	$12.00
☐ Library Instruction Round Table (LIRT)	
☐ Individual	$10.00
☐ Organization	$15.00
☐ Library Research Round Table (LRRT)	$10.00
☐ Map and Geography Round Table (MAGERT)	
☐ Individual	$15.00
☐ Organization	$45.00

Round Tables	Dues
☐ New Members Round Table (NMRT)	$10.00
☐ Social Responsibilities Round Table (SRRT)	
☐ Individual	$10.00
☐ Organization	$20.00
☐ Staff Organizations Round Table (SORT)	
☐ Individual	$ 3.00
☐ Organization	$ 6.00
☐ Video (VRT)	$12.00
Total Round Table Dues	**C$**

D. Other Organizations

COALITION FOR LITERACY

The Coalition for Literacy brings together organizations whose objectives include providing communication among coalition members, stimulating public awareness, encouraging the availability of national information and referral services and providing a forum for the discussion of national literacy initiatives.

Ch., Richard Lynch, Amer. Bar. Assn., 1800 M St., NW, Washington, DC 20036; staff liaisons: Peggy Barber, Mattye Nelson, ALA Hq.

COALITION ON GOVERNMENT INFORMATION

The Coalition on Government Information, initiated by ALA in 1986, is composed of public interest and library organizations united in their concern about the public's right to be well informed about the activities of the federal government. The coalition's objectives include: (1) developing support for improved access to government information; (2) focusing national attention on efforts that limit access to government information; (3) identifying organizations and individuals who are concerned with limitations on access, and encouraging them to advocate appropriate actions to improve access to government information; and (4) alerting the public to the importance of government information through public awareness campaigns.

Ch., Nancy C. Kranich (ALA rep.); staff liaison: Anne A. Heanue.

Publication

Coalition on Government Information Newsletter. Free to member organizations. Subscription $10.00 per year available through the ALA Washington Office, 110 Maryland Ave., NE, Washington, DC, 20002. Published quarterly. Ed., Anne A. Heanue.

Membership

Alaska State Library
American Association for the Advancement of Science
American Association of Law Libraries
American Association of University Professors
American Civil Liberties Union
American Library Association
The American Physical Society
American Society for Information Science
American Society of Access Professionals
American Society of Journalists and Authors
Association for Library and Information Science Education
Association of Public Data Users
Association of Research Libraries
Center for Citizen Access to Government Information
Center for Study of Responsive Law
The Chicago Committee to Defend the Bill of Rights
Coalition for the Right to Know
Council of Professional Associations on Federal Statistics
First Amendment Center
Fund for Open Information and Accountability
Government Accountability Project
Inter-Agency Committee on Dissemination of Statistics
Iowa Freedom of Information Council

Librarians for Nuclear Arms Control
Long Island Library Resources
Maryland State Department of Education, Division of Library Development and Services
Media Alliance
Medical Library Association
METRONET
Metropolitan Council of the Twin Cities Area
Minnesota State Planning Agency
National Association of Counties
National Association of Government Communicators
National Association of Housing and Redevelopment Officials
National Committee Against Repressive Legislation
National Consumers League
National Coordinating Committee for the Promotion of History
National Education Association
National Newspaper Association
National Security Archive
New York Library Association
OMB Watch
People for the American Way
The Progressive
Project Censored
Public Citizen
Right to Know, Data Center
Special Libraries Association
Taxpayer Assets Project
Women in Communications, Inc.
World University Service–U.S.

FREEDOM TO READ FOUNDATION

(A separate corporation, working in close liaison with ALA. Its secretariat is located in the OIF, ALA Hq.)

To promote and protect freedom of speech and freedom of the press; to protect the public right of access to libraries; to support the right of libraries to collect and make available any creative work they may legally acquire; and to supply legal counsel and otherwise support libraries and librarians suffering injustices due to their defense of speech and freedom of the press.

Pres., Gordon M. Conable, Monroe Cnty. L. Sys., 3700 S. Custer, Monroe, MI 48161 (1993); vice-pres., J. Dennis Day (1994); treas., Roger L. Funk (1994); dirs.: Patricia W. Berger (1994); Nat Hentoff (1993); Barbara F. Immroth (1994); Burton Joseph (1993); Ginny Moore Kruse (1994); Susan M. Pavsner (1993); Russell Shank (1993); Linda Steinman (1993).

Ex officio: pres. ALA, Marilyn L. Miller; pres.-elect, ALA, Hardy R. Franklin; ch., IFC, Candace D. Morgan; exec. dir, ALA, Peggy Sullivan; exec. dir. and secy., Judith F. Krug.

Unit reps.: ALA Exec. Bd., Judith Sessions; AASL, Vicki Hardesty; ACRL, to be appointed; ALCTS, John Hostage; ALSC, Susan Hagen Land; ALTA, Judith E. Petrau; ASCLA, to be appointed; CRC, Charles Beard; GODORT, Lois P. Mills; IFRT, Pamela Gay Bonnell; IRRT, to be appointed; LAMA, Pamela Gay Bonnell; LHRT, Charles C. Stewart; LITA, Ronald Sigler; MAGERT, Alice C. Hudson; NMRT, Joanna M. Burkhardt; OLOS, Marie C. Harris; PLA, Loretta R. O'Brien; RASD, Patricia P. Timberlake; SORT, Kay K. Ikuta; SRRT, Daniel C. Tsang; YALSA, Patricia Muller.

FRIENDS OF LIBRARIES U.S.A.

(An affiliate of ALA. Its secretariat is located in the ALA Hq., Communications Dept., 50 E. Huron St., Chicago, IL 60611.)

To encourage and assist the formation and development of Friends of Library groups in the United States; to promote the development of excellent library service for all residents of the United States; to provide a means for Friends of Library groups to have access to information and ideas that will prove useful to them in the operation of their organizations; to make the public aware of the existence of Friends of Library groups, and of the services they perform.

Officers. pres., Joseph J. Fitzsimmons; vice-pres., Michael E. Strauss; secy., Jane Rutledge; treas., Patricia Lawrence.

Board members: Doris Bass; Walli Beall; Dale D. Buboltz; Johnny Carson; Ernestine F. Clark; Lucy Core; Rennie Davant; Roger Downward; Jonathan D. Eldredge; Rod Gauvin; Elizabeth Geiser; Ann Hartman; Martha Kemplin; Julie Lahann; Natalie Lang; Harriet Larson; Marianne Lubar; William R. Mott; Evy Nordley; Joni L. Olmstead; Barbara S. Prentice; Larry C. Price; Marcia L. Purcell; Bernie Rath; Patricia Glass Schuman; James L. Smith; Phyllis B. Steckler; Louise Stern; Gary E. Strong; Robert Wedgeworth; Jane Winslow; Barbara Wunsch.

Liaisons: Peggy Barber; Gloria Gray, ALA; ex officio: John Cole; Robbie Kurland, ALTA.

Exec. Dir.: Sandy Dolnick, 1326 Spruce St., #1105, Philadelphia, PA 19107.

Distinguished board members: Sandy Dolnick; Joan Hood; James Houck; Frank Miller; Frederick G. Ruffner; Richard Torbert; Cecil Young.

Publications

Friends of Libraries U.S.A. National Notebook is the official newsletter of the organization. It is available only to members.

MERRITT HUMANITARIAN FUND*

The LeRoy C. Merritt Humanitarian Fund was established as a special trust in memory of Dr. LeRoy C. Merritt. It is devoted to the support, maintenance, medical care, and welfare of librarians who, in the Trustees' opinion, are: (1) discriminated against on the basis of sex, sexual preference, race, color, creed, or place of national origin; (2) denied employment rights; or (3) threatened with loss of employment or discharged because of their stand for the cause of intellectual freedom, including promotion of freedom of the press, freedom of speech, and the freedom of librarians to select items for their collections from all the world's written and recorded information.

Ch., Christine Jenkins (1993); Sherrie S. Bergman (1994); Sarah Pritchard (1995); secy. and staff liaison, Judith F. Krug, ALA Hq.

---

*Information about the Merritt Humanitarian Fund (trust) is included in the handbook as an item of interest to librarians; the trust is not an American Library Association fund.

NATIONAL FORUM ON INFORMATION LITERACY

The National Forum on Information Literacy is a coalition which focuses national attention on the importance of information literacy to individuals, to the economy, and to an informed citizenry. It promotes public awareness and supports the role of education in the development of information literate people. Its activities include: (1) identifying organizations whose purposes can be enhanced through the promotion of information literacy and inviting membership or affiliation in the Forum; (2) encouraging member organizations and individuals to advocate appropriate actions to promote information literacy; (3) providing a national forum for the exchange of ideas and programs to create public awareness of the need for information literacy and specifying examples of how information literacy may affect individuals; (4) developing a public awareness program to alert citizens to the importance of information literacy; (5) monitoring emerging trends and patterns and encouraging research and demonstration projects; and (6) promoting the establishment of a clearinghouse to gather and disseminate information on information literacy programs.

ALA rep., Patricia S. Breivik; staff liaison: Ann C. Weeks.

NATIONAL PARTNERS FOR LIBRARIES AND LITERACY

The Partners are 62 national organizations that join with ALA in promoting libraries and literacy through their publications and other activities at the local and national levels. The program is administered by a subcommittee of the Public Information Advisory Committee.

Adult Literacy Initiative, U.S. Department of Education
American Association for Adult and Continuing Education
American Association for the Advancement of Science
American Association of Community and Junior Colleges
American Association of Retired Persons
American Booksellers Association
American Council on Education
American Federation of Labor–Congress of Industrial Organizations
American Foundation for the Blind
American Library Association
American Mothers, Inc.
American Physical Society
American Society for Information Science
American Society of Association Executives
Association for Library & Information Science Education
Association for Retarded Citizens
Association of American Publishers
Blinded Veterans Association
Business Council for Effective Literacy
Camp Fire, Inc.
Catholic Library Association
Center for the Book, Library of Congress
Church and Synagogue Library Association
Coalition of Adult Education Organizations
Common Cause
Council for the Advancement of Experimental Learning
Federal Bar Association
Friends of Libraries, U.S.A.
General Federation of Women's Clubs
Home and School Institute, Inc.
International Reading Association
Laubach Literacy Action
League of Women Voters
Librarians of Library Science Collections
Lions Clubs International
Literacy Volunteers of America, Inc.
Medical Library Association
National Adoption Center
National Agricultural Library
National Association of Independent Schools
National Association of Women Lawyers
National Council of Senior Citizens
National Council on the Aging
National Council on Vocational Education
National Education Association
National 4-H
National Governors' Association
National Home Study Council
National Library of Medicine
National Organization on Disability
National Parents and Teachers Association
National Rehabilitation Association
People for the American Way
Reading Is Fundamental
Short Story International
Special Libraries Association
State Services Organization
U.S. Association of Evening Students
U.S. Government Printing Office
U.S. Small Business Administration, Office of Advocacy
Universal Serials and Book Exchange
Women's American Organization for Rehabilitation Through Training
Women's Equity Action League
Women's National Book Association

E. ALA Group Insurance and Credit Card Addresses

ALA Group Insurance (includes hospital indemnity, major medical, disability income, term life insurance)
  Godwins Inc./Frank B. Hall Consulting Co.
  261 Madison Ave.
  New York, NY 10016
  1-800-431-2052; in New York State,
    1-800-942-1905

ALA Automobile & Homeowners Insurance
  GEICO—Government Employees
    Insurance Co.
  Geico Plaza
  Washington, DC 20076
  1-800-368-2734 (24 hrs.)

ALA Libraries' Errors & Omissions Insurance Plan
  Albert H. Wohlers & Co.
  1440 N. Northwest Hwy.
  Park Ridge, IL 60068-1400
  1-800-323-2106; in Illinois,
    1-312-698-2221, ext. 234

ALA Credit Card
  MemberCard
  c/o Maryland Bank, N.A.
  P.O. Box 15464
  Wilmington, DE 19885-9440
  1-800-847-7378

F. Acronyms and Abbreviations

ACRONYMS

AA—Affiliate Assembly (AASL)
AAAS—American Association for the Advancement of Science
AAC—Association of American Colleges
AACJC—American Association of Community and Junior Colleges
AACR—*Anglo-American Cataloguing Rules*
AAHE—American Association for Higher Education
AALL—American Association of Law Libraries
AAM—Asian & African Materials (ALCTS)
AAP—Association of American Publishers
AAS—Asian and African Section (ACRL)
AASA—American Association of School Administrators
AASL—American Association of School Librarians
AAUP—American Association of University Presses; American Association of University Professors
ABA—American Booksellers Association
ABAA—Antiquarian Booksellers of America Association
ACA—American Correctional Association
ACE—American Council on Education
ACRL—Association of College and Research Libraries
AECT—Association for Educational Communications and Technology
AEPI—American Educational Publishers Institute
AFAS—Afro-American Studies Librarians Section (ACRL)
AFL/CIO—American Federation of Labor/Congress of Industrial Organizations
AFLRT—Armed Forces Libraries Round Table
AIA—American Institute of Architects
AIIM—Association for Image and Information Management
AILA—American Indian Library Association
AL—*American Libraries*
ALA—American Library Association
ALAD—Academic Librarians Assisting the Disabled (ASCLA)
ALCTS—Association for Library Collections and Technical Services
ALISE—Association for Library and Information Science Education
ALLS—Adult Lifelong Learning Section (PLA)
ALSC—Association for Library Service to Children
ALTA—American Library Trustee Association
ANSI—American National Standards Institute
ANSS—Anthropology and Sociology Section (ACRL)
AOTE—Associated Organizations of Teachers of English
ARL—Association of Research Libraries
ARLIS/NA—Art Libraries Society of North America
ARTS—Arts Section (ACRL)
AS—Acquisitions Section (ALCTS)
ASC—Activity Sections Council (ACRL)
ASCA—American School Counselors Association
ASCD—Association for Supervision and Curriculum Development
ASCLA—Association of Specialized and Cooperative Library Agencies

ASIS—American Society for Information Science
ASTM—American Standards of Testing Materials
ATLA—American Theological Library Association
AUPS—American University Press Services

BES—Buildings and Equipment Section (LAMA)
BF—Bibliotherapy Forum (ASCLA)
BIS—Bibliographic Instruction Section (ACRL)
BRASS—Business Reference and Services Section (RASD)

CAEO—Coalition of Adult Education Organizations
C&RL—*College & Research Libraries*
C&RL News—*College & Research Libraries News*
CBC—Children's Book Council
CC:AAM—Committee on Cataloging: Asian and African Materials (ALCTS-CCS)
CC:DA—Committee on Cataloging: Description and Access (ALCTS-CCS)
CCS—Cataloging and Classification Section (ALCTS)
CIS—Community Information Section (PLA); Congressional Information Service
CJCLS—Community and Junior College Libraries Section (ACRL)
CLA—Canadian Library Association; Catholic Library Association
CLENE RT—Continuing Library Education Network and Exchange Round Table
CLR—Council on Library Resources
CLS—College Libraries Section (ACRL)
CMDS—Collection Management and Development Section (ALCTS)
CNLIA—Council of National Library and Information Associations
CODES—Collection Development and Evaluation Section (RASD)
COLT—Council on Library/Media Technicians
CONSER—Cooperative Online Serials Program
COO—Committee on Organization
COPES—Committee on Program Evaluation and Support
COSLA—Chief Officers of State Library Agencies
COSWL—Committee on Status of Women in Librarianship
CRC—Chapter Relations Committee
CRG—Council of Regional Groups (ALCTS)
CRL—Center for Research Libraries
CUAC—Cartographic Users Advisory Council

DEU—Duplicates Exchange Union (ALCTS)
DPR—Directions and Program Review

EB—Encyclopaedia Britannica
EBSS—Education and Behavioral Sciences Section (ACRL)
ECLSS—Extended Campus Library Services Section (ACRL)
EIC—Education Information Center (PLA)
ELMSS—Educators of Library Media Specialists Section (AASL)

EMIERT—Ethnic Materials Information Exchange Round Table
ERIC—Education Resources Information Center
ERT—Exhibits Round Table

F&A—Finance and Audit Committee (ALA)
FLRT—Federal Librarians Round Table
FOLUSA—Friends of Libraries USA
FRFDS—Fund Raising and Financial Development Section (LAMA)
FTRF—Freedom to Read Foundation

GODORT—Government Documents Round Table

HCLF—Health Care Libraries Forum (ASCLA)
HS—History Section (RASD)

IASSIST—International Association for Social Science Information Service and Technology
IBBY—International Board on Books for Young People
IFC—Intellectual Freedom Committee
IFLA—International Federation of Library Associations and Institutions
IFRT—Intellectual Freedom Round Table
IG—Interest Group
ILERT—Independent Librarians Exchange Round Table
IRA—International Reading Association
IRC—International Relations Committee
IRRT—International Relations Round Table
IRS—Internal Revenue Service (U.S.)
ITAL—*Information Technology and Libraries*

JCET—Joint Council on Educational Telecommunications
JOYS—*Journal of Youth Services in Libraries*
JSC—Joint Steering Committee for Revision of *Anglo-American Cataloguing Rules*

LAMA—Library Administration and Management Association
LC—Library of Congress
LHRT—Library History Round Table
LIRT—Library Instruction Round Table
LITA—Library and Information Technology Association
LLA—Laubach Literacy Action
LLI—Laubach Literacy International
LOMS—Library Organization and Management Section (LAMA)
LPSS—Law and Political Science Section (ACRL)
LRC—Learning Resource Center
LRRT—Library Research Round Table
LRTS—*Library Resources & Technical Services*
LSBPHF—Library Service to the Blind and Physically Handicapped Forum (ASCLA)
LSCA—Library Services and Construction Act
LSDDP—Library Service to Developmentally Disabled Persons (ASCLA)
LSDF—Library Service to the Deaf Forum (ASCLA)
LSIEF—Library Service to the Impaired Elderly Forum (ASCLA)

LSPF—Library Service to Prisoners Forum (ASCLA)
LSSPS—Libraries Serving Special Populations Section (ASCLA)
LTR—Library Technology Reports

MAGERT—Map and Geography Round Table
MARBI—Machine-Readable Bibliographic Information
MARC—Machine-Readable Cataloging
MARS—Machine-Assisted Reference Section (RASD)
MLA—Medical Library Association; Modern Language Association; Music Library Association
MLS—Metropolitan Libraries Section (PLA)
MOPSS—Management and Operation of Public Services Section (RASD)
MPLSS—Marketing of Public Library Services Section (PLA)
Multi-LINCS—Multitype Library Networks and Cooperatives Section (ASCLA)

NASSP—National Association of Secondary School Principals
NCATE—National Council for Accreditation of Teacher Education
NCLIS—National Commission on Libraries and Information Science
NCPT—National Congress of Parents and Teachers
NCTE—National Council of Teachers of English
NCTM—National Council of Teachers of Mathematics
NIC—National Institute for Conservation
NISO—National Information Standards Organization (formerly, ANSI Z–39)
NLW—National Library Week
NMA—National Micrographics Association
NMRT—New Members Round Table
NPSS—Non-Public School Section (AASL)
NTIS—National Technical Information Service

OA—Office for Accreditation
OCLC—Online Computer Library Center
OIF—Office for Intellectual Freedom
OLAC—Online Audiovisual Catalogers
OLOS—Office for Library Outreach Services
OLPR—Office for Library Personnel Resources
ORS—Office for Research and Statistics

PAS—Personnel Administration Section (LAMA)
PIO—Public Information Office
PLA—Public Library Association
PLMS—Preservation of Library Materials Section (ALCTS)
PLSS—Public Library Systems Section (PLA)
PPC—Process Planning Committee
PPPLS—Public Policy for Public Libraries Section (PLA)
PRS—Public Relations Section (LAMA)
PVLR—Publisher/Vendor–Library Relations Committee (ALCTS)

RASD—Reference and Adult Services Division
RBB—Reference Books Bulletin
RBML—Rare Books and Manuscript Librarianship
RBMS—Rare Books and Manuscripts Section (ACRL)
REFORMA—National Association to Promote Library Services to the Spanish Speaking
RIF—Reading Is Fundamental
RLG—Research Libraries Group
RLIN—Research Libraries Network
RLMS—Reproduction of Library Materials Section (ALCTS)

SAA—Society of American Archivists
SASS—System and Services Section (LAMA)
SCOLE—Standing Committee on Library Education
SCRIM—Standing Committee on Review, Inquiry, and Mediation

SEES—Slavic and East European Section (ACRL)
SIECUS—Sex Information and Education Council of the U.S.
SISAC—Serials Industry Systems Advisory Committee
SLA—Special Libraries Association
SLAS—State Library Agency Section (ASCLA)
SLMES—School Library Media Educators Section (AASL)
SLMQ—School Library Media Quarterly
SLRP—Strategic Long-Range Planning
SMLS—Small and Medium-sized Libraries Section (PLA)
SMSA—Standard Metropolitan Statistical Area
SORT—Staff Organizations Round Table
SPVS—Supervisors Section (AASL)
SRRT—Social Responsibilities Round Table
SS—Serials Section (ALCTS); Statistics Section (LAMA)
STS—Science and Technology Section (ACRL)
SUPS—Services to User Population Section (RASD)

TESLA—Technical Standards for Library Automation
TLA—Theatre Library Association

ULS—University Libraries Section (ACRL)
USBE—Universal Serials and Book Exchange, Inc.

VOYA—Voice of Youth Advocates
VRT—Video Round Table

WESS—Western European Specialists Section (ACRL)
WHCLIS—White House Conference on Library and Information Services
WSS—Women's Studies Section (ACRL)

YALSA—Young Adult Library Services Association

ABBREVIATIONS

AB — Alberta
Acad. — Academy, academic
Acc. — Accessions
Acq. — Acquisitions
Ad. — Adult
Add. — Address
Adm. — Administrator, administrative, administration
Adv. — Adviser, advisory
Affil. — Affiliated
Agr. — Agriculture, agricultural
AK — Alaska
AL — Alabama
Amer. — American
Anly. — Analyst
AR — Arkansas
Arch. — Architecture, architectural
Archv. — Archive(s)
Assn. — Association
Assoc. — Associate
Asst. — Assistant
Atten. — Attendant
AV — Audiovisual
AZ — Arizona

B&PH — Blind & Physically Handicapped
BC — British Columbia
Bd. — Board

Bibl. — Bibliography, bibliographer, bibliographic, bibliographical
Biog. — Biography
Biol. — Biology, biological
Bk. — Book
Bkmob. — Bookmobile
Bks. — Books
Bldg. — Building
Br(s). — Branch(es)
Bull. — Bulletin
Bur. — Bureau
Bus. — Business

CA — California
CAN — Canada
Catlg. — Catalog, cataloging
Catlgr. — Cataloger
CE — Continuing Education
Ch. — Chairperson; Children('s)
Chap. — Chapter
Chem. — Chemistry
Cir. — Circle
Circ. — Circulating, circulation
Clln. — Collection(s)
Cmnty. — Community
Cnty. — County
CO — Colorado
Co. — Company

Coll. — College
Com. — Committee
Comm. — Commission
Commr. — Commissioner
Commun. — Communication
Cons. — Consultant(s)
Consol. — Consolidated
Consv. — Conservation, conservationist, conservator
Contrib. — Contributing
Coop. — Cooperative, cooperating
Coor. — Coordinator, coordinating
Corp. — Corporation
Corr. — Correspondence, correspondent, corresponding
Ct. — Court
CT — Connecticut
Ctr. — Center
Ctrl. — Central
Cur. — Curriculum
Cura. — Curator

DC — District of Columbia
DE — Delaware
Dep. — Deputy
Dept. — Department, departmental
Devel. — Development
Dir. — Director

Disc. — Discussion
Dist. — District
Div. — Division, divisional
Doc. — Documents, documentation

Econ. — Economics
Ed. — Editor, editorial
Edu. — Education, educational
Elem. — Elementary
Emer. — Emerita, emeritus
Engr. — Engineer, engineering
Exch. — Exchange
Exec. — Executive
Experim. — Experiment, experimental
Ext. — Extension

Fr. — Free
Fdn. — Foundation
Fed. — Federal
Fedn. — Federation
Fict. — Fiction
Fl. — Floor
FL — Florida
For. — Foreign

GA — Georgia
Gen. — General
Geog. — Geography, geographical
Govt. — Government, governmental
Gr. — Grade
Grad. — Graduate
GU — Guam

Hd. — Head
HI — Hawaii
Hist. — History, historical
Hosp. — Hospital
Hq. — Headquarters
H. S. — High school
Hum. — Humanities
Hwy. — Highway

IA — Iowa
ID — Idaho
IL — Illinois
IMC — Instructional materials center
IN — Indiana
Ind. — Industry, industrial
Indp. — Independent
Inf. — Information
Inst. — Institute, institution, institutional
Instr. — Instructor, instruction, instructional
Inter-L. — Interlibrary
Intl. — International

Jr. — Junior
Jt. — Joint
Juv. — Juvenile

KS — Kansas
KY — Kentucky

L(s). — Library(ies)
LA — Louisiana
Lab. — Laboratory
Lang. — Language
LB — Labrador
Lect. — Lecturer
Legis. — Legislative
Lit. — Literature
LLC — Library learning center
Ln(s). — Librarian(s)
Lnship. — Librarianship
LRC — Learning resources center

MA — Massachusetts
Maint. — Maintenance
Math. — Mathematics
MB — Manitoba
MD — Maryland
ME — Maine
Mech. — Mechanical
Med. — Medicine, medical
Mem. — Memorial
Memb. — Membership
Metro. — Metropolitan
Mgr. — Manager
Mgt. — Management
MI — Michigan
Misc. — Miscellaneous
MN — Minnesota
MO — Missouri
Ms(s). — Manuscript(s)
MS — Mississippi
MT — Montana
Mun. — Municipal
Mus. — Museum

Nat. — Natural
Natl. — National
NB — New Brunswick
NC — North Carolina
ND — North Dakota
NE — Nebraska
NF — Newfoundland
NH — New Hampshire
NJ — New Jersey
NM — New Mexico
Nom. — Nominating
NS — Nova Scotia
NT — Northwest Territories
Nurs. — Nurses, nursing
NV — Nevada
NY — New York

Off. — Office
Offr. — Officer
OH — Ohio
OK — Oklahoma
ON — Ontario
OR — Oregon
Ord. — Order
Org. — Organization(s), organizational

P. — Public
PA — Pennsylvania
PE — Prince Edward Island
Peop. — People's
Per. — Periodical(s)
Pers. — Personnel
Phil. — Philosophy
Phys. Hndcpd. — Physically Handicapped
Pict. — Picture
Pkwy. — Parkway
Pl. — Place
PR — Puerto Rico
Prelim. — Preliminary
Prep. — Preparatory, preparations
Pres. — President
Presv. — Preservation
Prin. — Principal
Proc. — Processes, processing
Prof. — Professor, professional
Prog. — Program
Prgmr. — Programmer
Proj. — Project
Prov. — Provincial
Psych. — Psychology
Publ. — Publisher, publishing
Pubn. — Publication(s)

QC — Quebec (also PQ)

Rdng. — Reading
Rdr. — Reader(s)
Rec. — Record, recording
Ref. — Reference
Regis. — Registration
Rel. — Relations
Rep(s). — Representative(s)
Res. — Research
Rev. — Reviser
Rgn. — Region
Rgnl. — Regional
RI — Rhode Island
Rm(s). — Room(s)
Rt. — Route

S. — South
SC — South Carolina
Sch(s). — School(s)
Sci. — Science, scientific
SD — South Dakota
Sect. — Section
Secy. — Secretary
Sel. — Selection
Sem. — Seminary
Ser. — Serial(s)
Serv. — Service(s)
SK — Saskatchewan
Soc. — Society, social
Spec. — Special, specialist
Sq. — Square
Sr. — Senior
Sta. — Station
Stat. — Statistics, statistical
Stu. — Student
Subcom. — Subcommittee
Subj. — Subject
Subsc. — Subscription, subscribing
Supp. — Support
Supt. — Superintendent
Supv. — Supervisor, supervisory, supervising
Surg. — Surgeon(s)
Sys. — System(s)

TBA — to be announced
Tchr. — Teacher
Tech. — Technical, technology, technological
Terr. — Terrace
Theo. — Theology, theological
TN — Tennessee
Tr. — Trail; Trustee
Treas. — Treasurer
Twp. — Township
TX — Texas

Univ. — University
UT — Utah

VA — Virginia
Vet. — Veteran(s)
VI — Virgin Islands
Voc. — Vocational
VT — Vermont

WA — Washington
WI — Wisconsin
Wk. — Work
WV — West Virginia
WY — Wyoming

YA — Young Adult
Yng. — Young
YT — Yukon Territory

G. General Information about ALA

ALA PRESIDENTS, TREASURERS, SECRETARIES, AND EXECUTIVE DIRECTORS

Presidents

Justin Winsor	1876–85
(d. October 22, 1897)	
William Frederick Poole	1885–87
(d. March 1, 1894)	
Charles Ammi Cutter	1887–89
(d. September 8, 1903)	
Frederick Morgan Crunden	1889–90
(d. October 28, 1911)	
Melvil Dewey	1890–July
(d. December 26, 1931)	1891
Samuel Swett Green	July–Nov.
(d. December 8, 1918)	1891
William Isaac Fletcher*	1891–92
(d. June 6, 1917)	
Melvil Dewey	1892–93
(d. December 26, 1931)	
Josephus Nelson Larned	1893–94
(d. August 15, 1913)	
Henry Munson Utley	1894–95
(d. February 16, 1917)	
John Cotton Dana	1895–96
(d. July 21, 1929)	
William Howard Brett	1896–97
(d. August 24, 1918)	
Justin Winsor	July–Oct.
(d. October 22, 1897)	1897
Herbert Putnam	Jan.–Aug.
(d. August 14, 1955)	1898
William Coolidge Lane	1898–99
(d. March 18, 1931)	
Reuben Gold Thwaites	1899–1900
(d. October 22, 1913)	
Henry James Carr	1900–1
(d. May 21, 1929)	
John Shaw Billings	1901–2
(d. March 11, 1913)	
James Kendall Hosmer	1902–3
(d. May 18, 1927)	
Herbert Putnam	1903–4
(d. August 14, 1955)	
Ernest Cushing Richardson	1904–5
(d. June 3, 1939)	
Frank Pierce Hill	1905–6
(d. August 28, 1941)	
Clement Walker Andrews	1906–7
(d. November 20, 1930)	
Arthur Elmore Bostwick	1907–8
(d. February 13, 1942)	
Charles Henry Gould	1908–9
(d. July 30, 1919)	
Nathaniel Dana Carlile Hodges	1909–10
(d. November 25, 1927)	
James Ingersoll Wyer	1910–11
(d. November 1, 1955)	
Theresa West Elmendorf	1911–12
(d. September 4, 1932)	
Henry Eduard Legler	1912–13
(d. September 13, 1917)	
Edwin Hatfield Anderson	1913–14
(d. April 29, 1947)	
Hiller Crowell Wellman	1914–15
(d. February 3, 1956)	

Mary Wright Plummer	1915–16
(d. September 21, 1916)	
Walter Lewis Brown	1916–17
(d. October 16, 1931)	
Thomas Lynch Montgomery	1917–18
(d. October 1, 1929)	
William Warner Bishop	1918–19
(d. February 19, 1955)	
Chalmers Hadley	1919–20
(d. May 11, 1958)	
Alice S. Tyler	1920–21
(d. April 18, 1944)	
Azariah Smith Root	1921–22
(d. October 2, 1927)	
George Burwell Utley	1922–23
(d. October 4, 1946)	
Judson Toll Jennings	1923–24
(d. February 8, 1948)	
Herman H. B. Meyer	1924–25
(d. January 16, 1937)	
Charles F. D. Belden	1925–26
(d. October 23, 1931)	
George H. Locke	1926–27
(d. January 28, 1937)	
Carl B. Roden	1927–28
(d. October 25, 1956)	
Linda A. Eastman	1928–29
(d. April 5, 1963)	
Andrew Keogh	1929–30
(d. February 14, 1953)	
Adam Strohm	1930–31
(d. October 30, 1951)	
Josephine Adams Rathbone	1931–32
(d. May 17, 1941)	
Harry Miller Lydenberg	1932–33
(d. April 16, 1960)	
Gratia A. Countryman	1933–34
(d. July 26, 1953)	
Charles H. Compton	1934–35
(d. March 17, 1966)	
Louis Round Wilson	1935–36
(d. December 9, 1979)	
Malcolm Glenn Wyer	1936–37
(d. December 31, 1965)	
Harrison Warwick Craver	1937–38
(d. July 26, 1951)	
Milton James Ferguson	1938–39
(d. October 23, 1954)	
Ralph Munn	1939–40
(d. January 22, 1975)	
Essae Martha Culver	1940–41
(d. January 2, 1973)	
Charles Harvey Brown	1941–42
(d. January 19, 1960)	
Keyes D. Metcalf	1942–43
(d. November 3, 1983)	
Althea H. Warren	1943–44
(d. December 21, 1958)	
Carl Vitz	1944–45
(d. January 28, 1981)	
Ralph A. Ulveling	1945–46
(d. March 21, 1980)	
Mary U. Rothrock	1946–47
(d. January 30, 1976)	
Paul North Rice	1947–48
(d. April 16, 1967)	
Errett Weir McDiarmid	1948–49
Milton E. Lord	1949–50
(d. February 1985)	

Clarence R. Graham	1950–51
(d. January 28, 1989)	
Loleta Dawson Fyan	1951–52
(d. April 1990)	
Robert Bingham Downs	1952–53
(d. February 24, 1991)	
Flora Belle Ludington	1953–54
(d. March 23, 1967)	
L. Quincy Mumford	1954–55
(d. August 15, 1982)	
John S. Richards	1955–56
(d. December 1979)	
Ralph R. Shaw	1956–57
(d. October 17, 1972)	
Lucile M. Morsch	1957–58
(d. July 3, 1972)	
Emerson Greenaway	1958–59
(d. April 1990)	
Benjamin E. Powell	1959–60
(d. March 11, 1981)	
Frances Lander Spain	1960–61
Florrinell F. Morton	1961–62
(d. January 1990)	
James E. Bryan	1962–63
Frederick H. Wagman	1963–64
Edwin Castagna	1964–65
(d. November 26, 1983)	
Robert Vosper	1965–66
Mary V. Gaver	1966–67
(d. December 31, 1991)	
Foster E. Mohrhardt	1967–68
Roger McDonough	1968–69
William S. Dix	1969–70
(d. February 22, 1978)	
Lillian M. Bradshaw	1970–71
Keith Doms	1971–72
Katherine Laich	1972–73
Jean E. Lowrie	1973–74
Edward G. Holley	1974–75
Allie Beth Martin	1975–Apr.
(d. April 11, 1976)	1976
Clara Stanton Jones	Apr. 11–
(Acting President)	July 22, 1976
Clara Stanton Jones	July 1976–77
Eric Moon	1977–78
Russell Shank	1978–79
Thomas J. Galvin	1979–80
Peggy A. Sullivan	1980–81
Elizabeth W. (Betty) Stone	1981–82
Carol A. Nemeyer	1982–83
Brooke E. Sheldon	1983–84
E. J. Josey	1984–85
Beverly P. Lynch	1985–86
Regina Minudri	1986–87
Margaret E. Chisholm	1987–88
F. William Summers	1988–89
Patricia Wilson Berger	1989–90
Richard M. Dougherty	1990–91
Patricia G. Schuman	1991–92
Marilyn L. Miller	1992–93

Treasurers

Melvil Dewey	1876–77
Charles Evans	1877–78
Melvil Dewey	1878–79
Frederick Jackson	1879–80
Melvil Dewey	1880–81
Frederick Jackson	1881–82
James Lyman Whitney	1882–86
Henry James Carr	1886–93

---

*Mr. Fletcher served as President 1891–92; on May 21, 1892 the Executive Committee accepted the resignation of K. August Linderfelt, who was elected October, 1891, with the stipulation that his name would be expunged from the presidential rolls.

George Watson Cole	1893–95
Edwin Hatfield Anderson	1895–96
George Watson Cole	1896 (Sept.–Nov.)
Charles Knowles Bolton	1896–97
Gardner Maynard Jones	1897–1906
George Franklin Bowerman	1906–7
Anderson Hoyt Hopkins	1907–8
Purd B. Wright	1908–10
Carl B. Roden	1910–20
Edward D. Tweedell	1920–27
Matthew S. Dudgeon	1927–41
Rudolph H. Gjelness	1941–47
Harold F. Brigham	1947–49
R. Russell Munn	1949–52
Raymond C. Lindquist	1952–56
Richard B. Sealock	1956–60
Arthur Yabroff	1960–64
Ralph Blasingame	1964–68
Robert B. McClarren	1968–72
Frank B. Sessa	1972–76
William Chait	1976–80
Herbert Biblo	1980–84
Patricia Glass Schuman	1984–88
Carla J. Stoffle	1988–92
Ann K. Symons	1992–96

Secretaries

Melvil Dewey	1879–90
William E. Parker and Mary Salome Cutler	1890–July 1891
Frank Pierce Hill	1891–95
Henry Livingston Elmendorf	1895–96
Rutherford Platt Hayes	1896–97
Melvil Dewey	1897–98
Henry James Carr	1898–1900
Frederick Winthrop Faxon	1900–2
James Ingersoll Wyer	1902–9
(Edward C. Hovey, executive officer, 1905–7)	
Chalmers Hadley	1909–11
George Burwell Utley	1911–20
Carl H. Milam	1920–48
Harold F. Brigham (interim)	July–Aug., 1948
John MacKenzie Cory	1948–51
David H. Clift	1951–58

Executive Directors

David H. Clift (emeritus; d. October 12, 1973)	1958–72
Robert Wedgeworth	1972–85
Thomas J. Galvin	1985–89
Linda F. Crismond	1989–92
Peggy Sullivan	1992–

ALA CONFERENCES, 1876–1992

Date	Place	Attendance	Annual Membership
1876, Oct. 4–6	Philadelphia	103	
1877, Sept. 4–6	New York	66	
1877, Oct. 2–5	London (International)	21*	
1878	No Meeting		
1879, June 30–July 2	Boston	162	
1880	No Meeting		
1881, Feb. 9–12	Washington, D.C.	70	
1882, May 24–27	Cincinnati	47	
1883, Aug. 14–17	Buffalo	72	
1884	No Meeting		
1885, Sept. 8–11	Lake George, N.Y.	87	
1886, July 7–10	Milwaukee	133	
1887, Aug. 30–Sept. 2	Thousand Island, N.Y.	186	
1888, Sept. 25–28	Catskill Mountains, N.Y.	32	
1889, May 8–11	St. Louis	106	
1890, Sept. 9–13	Fabyans (White Mountains)	242	
1891, Oct. 12–16	San Francisco	83	
1892, May 6–21	Lakewood, Baltimore, and Washington D.C.	260	
1893, July 13–22	Chicago	311	
1894, Sept. 17–22	Lake Placid, N.Y.	205	
1895, Aug. 13–21	Denver and Colorado Springs	147	
1896, Sept. 1–8	Cleveland	363	
1897, June 21–25	Philadelphia	315	
1897, July 13–16	London (International)	94*	
1898, July 5–9	Lakewood-on-Chautauqua	494	
1899, May 9–13	Atlanta	215	
1900, June 6–12	Montreal	452	874
1901, July 3–10	Waukesha	460	980
1902, June 14–20	Boston and Magnolia, Mass.	1,018	1,152
1903, June 22–27	Niagara Falls, N.Y.	684	1,200
1904, Oct. 17–22	St. Louis	577	1,228
1905, July 4–8	Portland	359	1,253
1906, June 29–July 6	Narragansett Pier, R.I.	891	1,844
1907, May 23–29	Asheville, N.C.	478	1,808
1908, June 22–27	Lake Minnetonka, Minn.	658	1,907
1909, June 28–July 3	Bretton Woods, N.H.	620	1,835
1910, June 20–July 6	Mackinac Island	533	2,005
1910, Aug. 28–31	Brussels (International)	46*	
1911, May 18–24	Pasadena	582	2,046
1912, June 26–July 2	Ottawa, Canada	704	2,365
1913, June 23–28	Kaaterskill, N.Y.	892	2,563
1914, May 25–29	Washington, D.C.	1,366	2,905
1915, June 3–9	Berkeley	779	3,024
1916, June 26–July 1	Asbury Park, N.J.	1,386	3,188
1917, June 21–27	Louisville	824	3,346
1918, July 1–6	Saratoga Springs	620	3,380
1919, June 23–27	Asbury Park, N.J.	1,168	4,178
1920, June 2–7	Colorado Springs	553	4,464
1921, June 20–25	Swampscott, Mass.	1,899	5,307
1922, June 26–July 1	Detroit	1,839	5,684
1923, Apr. 23–28	Hot Springs	693	5,669
1924, June 30–July 5	Saratoga Springs	1,188	6,055
1925, July 6–11	Seattle	1,066	6,745
1926, Oct. 4–9	Atlantic City	2,224	8,848
1927, June 20–27	Toronto	1,964	10,056
1927, Sept. 26–Oct. 1	Edinburgh (L.A. Jubilee)	82*	
1928, May 28–June 2	West Baden, Ind.	1,204	10,526
1929, May 13–18	Washington, D.C.	2,743	11,833
1929, June 15–30	Rome and Venice (International)	70*	
1930, June 23–28	Los Angeles	2,023	12,713
1931, June 22–27	New Haven	3,241	14,815
1932, Apr. 25–30	New Orleans	1,306	13,021
1933, Oct. 16–21	Chicago	2,986	11,880
1934, June 25–30	Montreal	1,904	11,731
1935, May 20–30	Madrid, Seville, and Barcelona (International)	42*	
1935, June 24–29	Denver	1,503	12,241
1936, May 11–16	Richmond	2,834	13,057
1937, June 21–26	New York	5,312	14,204
1938, June 13–18	Kansas City, Mo.	1,900	14,626
1939, June 18–24	San Francisco	2,869	15,568
1940, May 26–June 1	Cincinnati	3,056	15,808
1941, June 19–25	Boston	4,266	16,015
1942, June 22–27	Milwaukee	2,342	15,328
1943	No meeting		14,546
1944	No meeting		14,799
1945	No meeting		15,118
1946, June 16–22	Buffalo	2,327	15,800
1947, June 29–July 5	San Francisco	2,534	17,107
1948, June 13–19	Atlantic City	3,752	18,283

*American attendance.

ALA CONFERENCES, 1876–1992 (cont.)

Date	Place	Attendance	Annual Membership
1949, Regional Conferences		(Attendance not recorded)	19,324
Aug. 22–25	(Far West) Vancouver, Canada		
Sept. 2–5	(Trans. Miss.) Fort Collins		
Oct. 3–6	(Middle Atlantic) Atlantic City		
Oct. 12–15	(New England) Swampscott, Mass.		
Oct. 26–29	(Southeastern) Miami Beach		
Nov. 9–12	(Midwest) Grand Rapids		
Nov. 20–23	(Southwestern) Fort Worth		
1950, July 16–22	Cleveland	3,436	19,689
1951, July 8–14	Chicago	3,612	19,701
1952, June 29–July 5	New York	5,212	18,925
1953, June 21–27	Los Angeles	3,258	19,551
1954, June 20–26	Minneapolis	3,230	20,177
1955, July 3–9	Philadelphia	4,412	20,293
1956, June 17–23	Miami Beach	2,866	20,285
1957, June 23–30	Kansas City, Mo.	2,953	20,326
1958, July 13–19	San Francisco	4,400	21,716
1959, June 21–27	Washington, D.C.	5,346	23,230
1960, June 19–24	Montreal (ALA-CLA Joint)	4,648	24,690
1961, July 9–15	Cleveland	4,757	25,860
1962, June 17–23	Miami Beach	3,527	24,879
1963, July 14–20	Chicago	5,753	25,502
1964, June 28–July 4	St. Louis	4,623	26,015
1965, July 3–10	Detroit	5,818	27,526
1966, July 10–16	New York	9,342	31,885
1967, June 25–July 1	San Francisco	8,116	35,289
1968, June 23–29	Kansas City, Mo.	6,849	35,666
1969, June 22–28	Atlantic City	10,399	36,865
1970, June 28–July 4	Detroit	8,965	30,394
1971, June 20–26	Dallas	8,087	29,740
1972, June 24–30	Chicago	9,700	29,610
1973, June 24–30	Las Vegas	8,539	30,172
1974, July 5–13	New York	14,382	34,010
1975, June 29–July 5	San Francisco	11,606	33,208
1976, July 18–24	Chicago (Centennial)	12,015	33,560
1977, June 17–23	Detroit	9,667	33,767
1978, June 25–30	Chicago	11,768	35,096
1979, June 24–30	Dallas	10,650	35,524
1980, June 29–July 4	New York	14,566	35,257
1981, June 26–July 2	San Francisco	12,555	37,954
1982, July 10–15	Philadelphia	12,819	38,050
1983, June 25–30	Los Angeles	11,005	38,862
1984, June 23–28	Dallas	11,443	39,290
1985, July 6–11	Chicago	14,160	40,761
1986, June 26–July 3	New York	16,530	42,361
1987, June 27–July 2	San Francisco	17,844	45,145
1988, July 9–14	New Orleans	16,530	47,249
1989, June 24–29	Dallas	17,592	49,483
1990, June 23–28	Chicago	19,982	50,509
1991, June 29–July 4	Atlanta	17,764	52,893
1992, June 25–July 2	San Francisco	19,261	54,735

*American attendance

ALA MEMBERSHIP BY STATES

United States	1988	1989	1990	1991	1992
Alabama	501	522	506	584	563
Alaska	182	186	204	202	207
Arizona	703	758	749	792	825
Arkansas	278	285	256	280	284
California	4,120	4,226	4,290	4,507	5,215
Colorado	634	654	728	753	852
Connecticut	954	999	1,019	1,071	1,069
Delaware	155	174	171	176	193
District of Columbia	503	500	463	472	503
Florida	1,558	1,684	1,749	1,916	1,845
Georgia	891	971	1,001	1,450	1,234
Hawaii	251	253	244	287	355
Idaho	114	127	120	111	125
Illinois	3,314	3,381	3,762	3,849	3,937
Indiana	1,152	1,245	1,322	1,353	1,354
Iowa	665	689	725	729	718
Kansas	539	607	625	632	653
Kentucky	466	492	495	538	556
Louisiana	929	848	754	782	776
Maine	199	232	231	226	234
Maryland	1,483	1,528	1,551	1,591	1,650
Massachusetts	1,634	1,733	1,700	1,733	1,737
Michigan	1,733	1,772	1,860	1,911	1,912
Minnesota	823	833	873	885	856
Mississippi	347	335	282	312	266
Missouri	725	804	826	857	873
Montana	110	107	111	122	134
Nebraska	270	301	307	315	341
Nevada	185	191	200	212	241
New Hampshire	262	272	256	275	297
New Jersey	1,557	1,657	1,679	1,769	1,895
New Mexico	237	277	292	302	298
New York	4,243	4,356	4,360	4,437	4,525
North Carolina	1,203	1,249	1,295	1,400	1,374
North Dakota	95	98	101	105	124
Ohio	1,913	1,975	2,125	2,206	2,237
Oklahoma	493	550	539	512	533
Oregon	475	480	503	516	616
Pennsylvania	1,941	1,954	2,008	2,113	2,175
Rhode Island	248	285	276	294	312
South Carolina	518	561	568	696	657
South Dakota	113	119	127	139	137
Tennessee	643	633	612	681	645
Texas	2,196	2,640	2,477	2,480	2,615
Utah	308	350	389	320	370
Vermont	143	163	168	164	194
Virginia	1,475	1,570	1,562	1,583	1,635
Washington	889	903	965	1,051	1,183
West Virginia	191	201	220	220	218
Wisconsin	987	1,018	1,095	1,140	1,175
Wyoming	122	123	120	118	113
Total U.S.	45,670	47,871	48,861	51,169	52,836
U.S. Territories	107	118	118	140	245
Canadian and foreign	1,472	1,494	1,530	1,584	1,654
Grand total	47,249	49,483	50,509	52,893	54,735

As of August 31

ALA MEMBERSHIP—AUGUST 31, 1992

Personal members	51,645
Organizational members	3,090
Total	54,735

General Index

In this index the word *committee* does not usually appear as part of the committee name. When page numbers following a topic are not consecutive, the page number given first has the most complete description of the entry. Most main headings in the text of the ALA Constitution and Bylaws and the ALA Policy Manual have been indexed here; complete indexes appear on pages 131–132 and 151–153.

Index of Persons

Included in this index are addresses of ALA members whose names appear in the Handbook of Organization. (For a fuller explanation of addresses used, see Introduction.) The page numbers on which the names appear are given as usual.

Craver, Kathleen W., 20 • 4506 Chancery Court NW • Washington, DC 20007

Cravey, Pamela J., 45, 47 • Georgia State University • Pullen Library • 100 Decatur Street S.E. • Atlanta, GA 30303-3081 • 404/651-2198; Fax: 404/651-2508; E-mail: LIBPJC@GSUVM1

Crawford, Josephine, 69 • 409 N Eau Claire-210 • Madison, WI 53705

Crawford, Walt, 8, 69, 70, 71, 113 • Research Libraries Group Inc. (RLG) • 1200 Villa Street • Mountain View, CA 94041-1100 • 412/691-2227; Fax: 415/964-0943

Craychee, Pam, 84 • Carnegie Library of Pittsburgh • East Plaza 500 Grant St. • 4400 Forbes Avenue • Pittsburgh, PA 15213-4080

Creely, Kathryn L., 45, 47, 48 • University of California-San Diego • Central Library 0175-R • La Jolla, CA 92093-0175

Crenshaw, Elizabeth, 59 • 598 Carlton Avenue • Brooklyn, NY 11238 • 212/340-0843

Crispen, Joanne L., 58, 59, 108 • American Library Association • 50 East Huron Street • Chicago, IL 60611-2795 • 312/280-4396

Crist, Margaret L., 8, 12, 13, 15 • University of Michigan • 818 Hatcher Graduate Library • Ann Arbor, MI 48109-1205

Crocker, Jane Lopes, 102 • Gloucester County College • Library Media Center • Tanyard Rd. RR #4, Box 203 • Sewell, NJ 08080

Cromer, Kenneth L., 80 • 1026 King Ave • Lorain, OH 44052-1153 • 216/244-1192

Cromwell, Wilma I., 29, 32, 36 • 1508 San Antonio-N • Menlo Park, CA 94025

Croneberger, Robert B., 7 • Carnegie Library of Pittsburgh • 4400 Forbes Avenue • Pittsburgh, PA 15213-4080

Croneis, Karen, 54 • Washington University Libraries • Campus Box 1061 • 1 Brookings Drive • Saint Louis, MO 63130-4899

Crooker, Cynthia, 56 • 325 Willow St. • New Haven, CT 06511 • 203/432-1705

Crooks, James E., 87 • University of California-Irvine Library • P.O. Box 19557 • Irvine, CA 92713 • 714/856-4123; E-mail: JECROOKS@UCI

Crosby, Ellen E., 88 • 2716 Partridge Dr So • Hopkins, SC 29061 • 803/777-6938

Crosby-Muilenburg, Corryn, 52 • 1181 Tilley Court • Arcata, CA 95521 • 707/826-4955

Crowe, Linda D., 13, 62, 75 • Peninsula Library System • 25 Tower Road • San Mateo, CA 94402

Crowe, William J., 55 • University of Kansas • Library • Lawrence, KS 66045-2800 • 913/864-3601

Crowley, Bill, 60, 62 • State Library of Ohio • 65 S. Front St. • Columbus, OH 43266-0334

Crowley, John D., 18 • Joel Barlow High School • 100 Black Rock Turnpike • West Redding, CT 06896

Crowley, Stephen J., 90 • Putnam County Library System • Palatka Public Library • 601 College Road • Palatka, FL 32177-3873

Crump, Michele J., 38 • 3510 NW 4TH St. • Gainesville, FL 32609-2266 • 904/392-0355

Cruse, Patricia, 97 • 1944 Tulip St. • Baton Rouge, LA 70806-6638 • 504/388-2570

Cubbedge, Frankie H., 6, 8 • University of South Carolina at Aiken • Gregg-Graniteville Library • 171 University Parkway • Aiken, SC 29801

Cubberley, Carol, 8, 26, 31, 68 • University of Southern Mississippi • Cook Memorial Library • Box 5053 Southern Station • Hattiesburg, MS 39406-5053 • 601/266-4248

Cubit, James R., 50 • Williams College • Sawyer Library • Williamstown, MA 01267

Cuesta, Yolanda J., 8, 10, 62 • California State Library • Library Development Services Bureau • 1001 6th St, Suite 300 • Sacramento, CA 95814-3324 • 916/322-0372

Culberg, Laura B., 42 • 4510 North Greenview • Chicago, IL 60640 • 312/747-4614

Cullars, John M., 56 • University of Illinois at Chicago • University Library • P.O. Box 8198 • Chicago, IL 60680 • 312/996-2730

Cullinan, Bernice E., 20 • Tudor Lane • Sands Pt, NY 11050 • 516/883-8537

Culshaw, John P., 64, 97 • 50 S. Boulder Cir-#5028 • Boulder, CO 80303-4264 • 303/492-0487

Cumlet, Harolyn S., 50 • 3625 Clematis St • New Orleans, LA 70122-4724

Cumming, Linda L., 65 • 1369 S.Vine • Denver, CO 80210 • 303/640-8893

Cummings, Charles F., 83, 86 • 54 Richmond Street • Newark, NJ 07103-3424

Cummings, Nancy R., 101 • 2724 Pinewood • Yuma, AZ 85364-6817

Cummins, Julie A., 6, 12 • New York Public Library • Children's Coor • 455 Fifth Ave. • New York, NY 10016

Cunningham, Barbara A., 7, 8, 101 • Illinois Library Association • 33 West Grand Ave. -301 • Chicago, IL 60610-4306

Cunningham, Diana S., 101 • 319 Walgrove Rd • Reistertown, MD 21136 • 410/328-7378

Cunningham, John W., 75 • 979 N 5th St • Philadelphia, PA 19123 • 215/686-5425

Cunningham-Kruppa, Mary E., 35 • University of Texas Libraries • General Libraries • PCL 3200 • PCL 1.114 • Austin, TX 78713-7330

Curl, Sheila R., 54 • 3175 N Price Rd-#2087 • Chandler, AZ 85224 • 602/965-7609

Curley, Arthur, 4, 7, 9, 59, 104 • Boston Public Library • Copley Square • P.O. Box 286 • Boston, MA 02117

Curran, Charles C., 44, 100 • University of South Carolina • College of Library & Information Science • Columbia, SC 29208

Curry, Anna A., 14 • Enoch Pratt Free Library • 400 Cathedral Street • Baltimore, MD 21201-4484

Curry, David S., 54 • University of Iowa Libraries • Hardin Library for Health Sci • Iowa City, IA 52242-1379 • 319/335-9871; Fax: 319/335-9897; E-mail: CADDAVTS@UIAMVS.BITNET

Curry, Elizabeth A., 15, 59, 61, 62 • 2224 Seagrape Circle • Coconut Creek, FL 33066

Curry, Marsha A., 99 • 6813 Bayou Pines Drive • Biloxi, MS 39532

Curtis, Jean T., 80 • Detroit Public Library • 5201 Woodward Avenue • Detroit, MI 48202

Curtis, Lori N., 53 • University of Tulsa • McFarlin Library • 600 S. College • Tulsa, OK 74104-3189

Curtis, Ruth P., 19 • P.O. Box 90225 • Lafayette, LA 70501 • 318/984-2646

Curtis, Sylvia, 55, 97 • University of California • UCSB Library • Santa Barbara, CA 93106-9010

Cutler, Marsha L., 41 • 4621 Coran Lane • Las Vegas, NV 89108 • 702/382-3493

Cutler, Phyllis L., 65 • 71 School St • Williamstown, MA 01267 • 413/597-2502

Cuyler, Margery, 40 • Holiday House Inc. • 425 Madison Ave • New York, NY 10017

Cypra-Sherlock, Jo Anne, 42 • 522 Shalamar Place • Irving, TX 75061 • 214/721-2458

Czesak, Cynthia, 74, 81 • 106 Ridgewood Rd • Clifton, NJ 07012 • 201/772-5500

D'Ambrosio, Margaret R., 32 • 808 E Street SE • Washington, DC 20003-2842 • 202/357-3161

D'Andraia, Frank A., 27, 70, 119 • 204 27th Ave. South • Grand Forks, ND 58201 • 701/777-2617

da Conturbia, Sandra, 45, 52 • 2011 Langford • College Station, TX 77840 • 409/845-5741

Dack, Diana, 16 • Principal Librarian • National Library of Australia • Integrated Library Mgt. System • Canberra ACT 2600 • Australia

Dahl, Katherine M., 83, 84, 85 • Western Illinois University Libraries • Reference Dept. • Macomb, IL 61455 • 309/298-2742; Fax: 309/298-2781

Dahlgren, Anders C., 63, 65 • 5814 Dorsett Dr. • Madison, WI 53711 • 608/266-3874

Dahlstrom, Joe F., 8, 10, 58 • University of Houston-Victoria Library • 2602 North Ben Jordan • Victoria, TX 77901-5699

Dailey, Elizabeth J., 95 • Onondaga County Public Library • Betts Branch • 4862 S. Salina St. • Syracuse, NY 13205

Dailey, Kazuko M., 9, 65 • University of California-Davis Library • Davis, CA 95616

Dakshinamurti, Ganga B., 26 • 934 Crestview Park Drive • Winnipeg MB,R2Y 0V7 CAN • 204/474-8927

Dale, Doris C., 42 • Southern Illinois University • Dept. of Curriculum & Instr. • Carbondale, IL 62901

Dalehite, Michele I., 69, 70, 72 • Florida Center for Library Automation • 2002 NW 13th Street.,#320 • Gainesville, FL 32609

Daley, Virginia L., 45, 57 • Duke University • William R. Perkins Library • Durham, NC 27706

Dallas, Larayne J., 64, 82, 84 • 8118 Cardin Drive • Austin, TX 78759 • 512/495-4503

Dalrymple, Prudence W., 7, 108 • American Library Association • 50 East Huron Street • Chicago, IL 60611-2795

Dalzell, Lee B., 49, 87, 88 • 123 Park St • Williamstown, MA 01267 • 413/597-2021

Damico, James A., 52 • University of South Alabama Library • 307 University Blvd. • Downtown Branch • Mobile, AL 36688

Dancik, Deborah B., 65 • University of Alberta • Rutherford Library North • Edmonton AB,T6G 2J4 CAN

Danford, Robert E., 65 • #5 DeWitt Drive • Sidney, NY 13838 • 607/431-4449

Daniel, Carolyn C., 12, 102 • 1309 Clearview Dr • Mt Juliet, TN 37122

Daniels, Belinda S., 47 • 506 So Cherry St • Kernersville, NC 27284

Daniels, Bruce E., 3, 4, 5, 7, 13 • Onondaga County Public Library • at the Galleries • 447 South Salina Street • Syracuse, NY 13202-2494

Daniels, Margo H., 40 • Branch Librarian • Reston Regional Library • 11925 Bowman Towne Drive • Reston, VA 22090-3306

Dannelly, Gay N., 28, 29, 31, 33, 34 • Ohio State University Libraries • 1858 Neil Avenue Mall • Columbus, OH 43210-1286 • 614/292-6151; Fax: 614/292-7859

Danzig, Martha Mae, 23 • Lewis County Board of Education • Central Elementary School • Lewis County High School • Weston, WV 26452-0000

Darling, Karen D., 38 • University of Oregon • Library • Eugene, OR 97403-1299 • 503/346-3063; Fax: 503/346-3094

Daszkiewicz, Cheryl, 108 • American Library Association • 50 East Huron Street • Chicago, IL 60611-2729

Daub, Albert W., 8 • 1 Hill Hollow Rd • Watchung, NJ 07060 • 908/548-8600

Daub, Peggy E., 53 • 1506 Arborview • Ann Arbor, MI 48103

Daugherty, Robert A., 10, 63, 65 • University of Illinois at Chicago • University Library • P.O. Box 8198 • Chicago, IL 60680 • 312/996-2734; Fax: 312/996-0901

Davant, Rennie, 167 • Friends of Libs USA (FOLUSA) • 1326 Spruce Street, #1105 • Philadelphia, PA 19107-5829

Davenport, Nancy A., 13 • 5606 Dawes Ave • Alexandria, VA 22311 • 202/707-8883

Davey, Nancy A., 26, 32 • 6052 Pillory Drive • Indianapolis, IN 46254-5040 • 317/298-6570

David, Indra M., 46, 50, 56 • 1330 Fieldway Drive • Bloomfield Hills, MI 48013-2043

Davidson, Gloria L., 16 • T. C. Williams High School • 3330 King Street • Alexandria, VA 22302 • 703/824-6848; Fax: 703/998-7284

Davidson, Josephine F., 26 • 185 Crestwood Drive • Athens, GA 30605 • 404/542-0585

Davidson, Lloyd, 70 • Northwestern University Library • Mudd Library for Science & Engineering • 2233 Sheriden Rd. • Evanston, IL 60208

Davie, Judith F., 41 • 1605 Bear Hollow Rd • Greensboro, NC 27410 • 919/370-8346

Davis, Denyvetta, 63 • 2220 N.E. 25 • Oklahoma City, OK 73111 • 405/424-1437

Davis, Donald G., 9 • University of Texas at Austin • Graduate School of Library & Information Sciences • Austin, TX 78712-1276

Davis, H. Scott, 49, 64, 95 • 322 Potomac • Terre Haute, IN 47803 • 812/237-2604

Davis, Harry O., 96 • 704 S. Murrie Drive • Carbondale, IL 62901-2472 • 618/453-2705

Davis, Herbert A., 24 • P O Box 108-Old Court & Falls Rds. • Brooklandvl, MD 21022

Davis, Hiram L., 44, 46 • Michigan State University Libraries • East Lansing, MI 48824-1048 • 517/355-2341; Fax: 517/353-9806

Davis, Jennifer J., 78, 80 • North Central Library Cooperative • 27 North Main St. • Mansfield, OH 44902 • ; Fax: 419/526-2145

Davis, Katherine E., 81 • Lakeland Library Cooperative • 60 Library Plaza NE • Grand Rapids, MI 49503

Davis, Luella, 48 • Emory University Libraries • Robert W. Woodruff Library • Reference Department • Atlanta, GA 30322-2870 • 404/727-0146

Davis, Mary Ellen K., 43, 44, 45, 46, 108, 113 • American Library Association • Assn of Coll and Res Libs • 50 East Huron Street • Chicago, IL 60611-2795 • 312/280-2511; Fax: 312/280-7663

Davis, Sheryl J., 35 • 1556 Campus Ave • Redlands, CA 92374

Davis, Susan A., 27, 37, 38, 107 • 7721 Lewiston Rd • Batavia, NY 14020 • 716/636-2784

Davis, Terri L., 102 • P.O. Box 272 • Deadwood, SD 57732-0272

Davis, Trisha L., 27, 31 • 117 East New England Ave. • Worthington, OH 43085 • 614/292-6314

Dawe, James R., 24, 105 • Seltzer Caplan Wilkins & McMahon • 2100 Symphony Towers • 750 B Street • San Diego, CA 92101-8177

Dawson, Alma, 47 • P.O. Box 80411 • Baton Rouge, LA 70898

Dawson, Deborah, 54, 55 • 1415 Sheridan • Laramie, WY 82070 • 307/766-4264

Dawson, Terry P., 71 • 907 N Fair • Appleton, WI 54911 • 414/832-6168

Day, Betty H., 57 • 1204 Goth Lane • Silver Spg, MD 20905 • 301/405-9117

Day, J. Dennis, 3, 4, 5, 7, 8, 9, 76, 106, 167 • Salt Lake City Public Library • 209 E 500 South • Salt Lake City, UT 84111

Day, John M., 60, 61 • Gallaudet University Library • 800 Florida Avenue N.E. • Washington, DC 20002

Day, Mark T., 87 • 2536 East 8th St • Bloomington, IN 47408 • 812/855-8028

Dayton, Jane, 80 • Carnegie Library of Pittsburgh • 4400 Forbes Avenue • Pittsburgh, PA 15213-4080

De Belder, Kurt F., 34, 56 • 1 Washington Sq. Vlg. • Apt. 13-H • New York, NY 10012 • 212/998-2515

De Guevara, Helen L., 9 • 2 East 8th Street #1010 • Chicago, IL 60605 • 312/606-0555

De Jardin, Carole J., 42, 85, 88, 90 • Appleton Public Library • 225 N. Oneida St. • Appleton, WI 54911-4780

de la Cruz, Emma, 30 • Bellingham Public Library • P.O. Box 1197 • Bellingham, WA 98227-1197

De Matteis, Julie K., 91 • 3337 N Chatham Rd-#I • Ellicott City, MD 21042

Dean, Barbara C., 30, 31 • Fairfax County Public Library • 13135 Lee Jackson Hy-Suite 115B • Fairfax, VA 22033-1909 • 703/222-3139; Fax: 703/222-3193

Dean, John F., 35, 36 • 1433 Coddington Rd • Brooktondale, NY 14817 • 607/255-9687

Deane, Mary M., 69 • 11233 SW 114th Lane Cir. • Miami, FL 33176 • 305/348-2488

Deane, Paul D., 84 • 315 Lincoln Lane • Arlington Heights, IL 60004

Dearie, Tammy Nickelson, 8 • University of California-San Diego • Central University Library • La Jolla, CA 92093-0175

Dearman, Marvene D., 19 • 1471 Chevelle Drive • Baton Rouge, LA 70806 • 504/357-6464

DeBacher, John K., 41 • Big Rapids Community Library • 426 South Michigan • Big Rapids, MI 49307-2090

Schafer, Gerald J., 85 • 2054 Clarkson Street • Denver, CO 80205 • 303/556-8370
Schambow, Karen H., 32 • 401 W Jackson • Woodstock, IL 60098
Schaner, Marian E., 108 • 223 Bartlett Ave. • Sharon Hill, PA 19079-1305
Schatz, Natalie M., 44 • Tufts University-Fletcher • School of Law & Diplomacy • Edwin Ginn Library • Medford, MA 02155-7082 • 617/628-7010; Fax: 617/628-5508
Scheel, Marti, 71 • 15-J Laurel Hill Rd • Greenbelt, MD 20770
Scheffer, Ann H., 79 • 1664 Ridge Top Way • Clearwater, FL 34625 • 813/462-6800
Schellinger, Merry B., 56, 58 • 2929-45th Ave.S. • Minneapolis, MN 55406
Schenck, William Z., 26, 27, 37, 118 • 7909 Sycramore Dr. • Falls Church, VA 22042 • 202/287-7050
Scheps, Susan, 78 • 1285 Giesse Dr • Mayfield Hts, OH 44124
Scherba, Sandra A., 63, 67, 68 • Cromaine Library • 3688 N. Hartland Rd. • Hartland, MI 48353-0950
Scherdin, Mary Jane, 47, 69 • 6111 Winnequah Road • Madison, WI 53716 • 608/262-8025
Scherr, Brenda M., 84 • 1613 N. Quinn St-Apt 104 • Arlington, VA 22209-2850 • 202/687-7534
Scherrei, Rita A., 68 • 4133 St. Claire Ave. • Studio City, CA 91604 • 213/825-1201
Schiff, Adam L., 86 • 2 Midcrest Way • San Francisco, CA 94131 • 415/750-7104
Schiller, Anita R., 7 • 7109 Monte Vista • La Jolla, CA 92037
Schlachter, Gail A., 5, 7, 11, 12, 82, 83, 88 • Reference Services Press • 1100 Industrial Road • Suite 9 • San Carlos, CA 94070
Schlaf, Suzanne S., 78 • 215 Walters Ln. • Itasca, IL 60143
Schlekau, Linda C., 101 • 59 Golden Shower • Dededo, GU 96912
Schlesinger, Deborah L., 6 • 507 5th Ave • Helena, MT 59601
Schmaltz, Marcella, 102 • Director Library • Bismarck State College Library • 1500 Edwards Ave. • Bismarck, ND 58501-1276
Schmelz-Keil, Lynne M., 47, 48 • Harvard University • Tozzer Library • 21 Divinity Avenue • Cambridge, MA 02138 • 617/495-2253; Fax: 617/495-0403; E-mail: DIXON@HARVARDA
Schmidt, C. James, 7, 12, 71 • 244 Forest Avenue • Palo Alto, CA 94301
Schmidt, Karen A., 27, 28, 30, 31, 70 • R R 2 Box 157 • Bloomington, IL 61704 • 217/333-1054
Schmidt, Sherrie, 7 • 8485 E. McDonald-#382 • Scottsdale, AZ 85250 • 602/965-3956
Schmidt, Susan H., 97 • 3510 N Pine Grove-Apt. 510 • Chicago, IL 60657
Schmidt, Ted, 81 • 2706 Hartsel Court • Loveland, CO 80538
Schmidt, Vincent P., 60 • 3712-5 Greggory Way • Santa Barbara, CA 93105
Schmidtmann, Nancy K., 61 • 149 Orchard St • Plainview, NY 11803 • 516/772-1058
Schmierer, Helen F., 27, 33 • 100 E Manning St-#2B • Providence, RI 02906-4347 • 401/863-2064
Schmitt, John P., 86 • 2743 Garden Dr. • Fort Collins, CO 80526 • 303/491-1859
Schmitz, Theresa M., 40 • The Children's Bookshop • 237 Washington St. • Brookline, MA 02146
Schneider, D. W., 55, 68 • Louisiana State University Libraries • Middleton Library • Baton Rouge, LA 70803-3342
Schneider, Karen G., 92 • 301 West Green St., Apt. 1W • Champaign, IL 61820
Schoen, Dena J., 55 • Hoover Institution on War, • Revolution & Peace Library • 115 Hoover Tower • Stanford University • Stanford, CA 94305-6010
Schofer, Yvonne, 53 • University of Wisconsin-Madison • Memorial Library • 728 State St. • Madison, WI 53706
Scholl, Lisa M., 59, 61 • Illinois Regional Library for • The Blind & Physically Handicapped • 1055 West Roosevelt Road • Chicago, IL 60608
Schomberg, Janie R., 20, 21, 118 • 2210 Fletcher Street • Urbana, IL 61801 • 217/384-3612
Schoonmaker, Nancy, 70 • Gaylord Borthers • P.O. Box 4901 • Syracuse, NY 13221-4901
Schott, Ken, 83 • University of Nevada-Las Vegas • James R. Dickinson Library • 4505 Maryland Parkway • Las Vegas, NV 89154
Schottlaender, Brian E., 32 • 1002 Keniston St. • Los Angeles, CA 90019-1707
Schrader, Aileen R., 8, 23, 24 • 47 Sandpiper St., Unit. B • Newport Beach, CA 92660
Schremser, Donna Barrett, 73 • Huntsville-Madison County • Public Library • P O Box 443 • Huntsville, AL 35804
Schreyer, Alice D., 44, 46, 53, 54, 114 • University of Chicago Library • 1100 E. 57th St. • Chicago, IL 60637-1502 • 312/702-8705; Fax: 312/702-0853
Schriek, Robert W., 52 • 42 Ridge Road • North Arlington, NJ 07032 • 201/648-5676
Schroeder, Jan K., 78 • 5756 North Shore Drive • Duluth, MN 55804 • 218/723-3821
Schroeder, Marilyn D., 69 • 11717 Briary Branch Ct. • Reston, VA 22091 • 202/662-9182
Schub, Helen Sue, 52, 58 • 40 Harrison St-8d • New York, NY 10013
Schuitema, Joan E., 72 • Northwestern University Library • 1935 Sheridan Road • Evanston, IL 60208-2300
Schule, K. Lynn, 80 • 320 York Rd • Towson, MD 21204 • 301/887-6177
Schulman, Jacque-Lynne A., 13 • P.O. Box 8086 • McLean, VA 22106-8086
Schultz, Kim E., 52 • Central Michigan University • 755 W. Big Beaver, Suite 222 • Troy, MI 48084
Schuman, Patricia Glass, 3, 5, 16, 167 • Neal-Schuman Publishers, Inc. • 100 Varick Street • New York, NY 10013
Schuneman, Anita, 32 • 503 E. Oak St. • Lafayette, CO 80026 • 303/492-4534
Schwab, Ruth S., 78 • 68 Cedar Dr E • Briarcliff Manor, NY 10510 • 914/941-2416
Schwartz, Marla J., 17, 37 • 5403 Glenwood Rd • Bethesda, MD 20817 • 202/885-2680
Schwartz, Nancy E., 12, 94 • H. W. Wilson Company • 950 University Avenue • Bronx, NY 10452
Schwartz, Renee, 66 • 4448 North Richmond • Chicago, IL 60625 • 312/996-3850
Schwartz, Ruth S., 84 • 168 Cherry Lane • River Edge, NJ 07661 • 201/692-2276
Schwartz, S Arlene, 30 • 7137 Stewart & Gray Rd • Apt 36 • Downey, CA 90241 • 310/940-8555
Schwartz, Steve A., 16 • Service Employees International Union • Library • 1313 L Street N.W. • Washington, DC 20005
Schweitzberger, Kathleen A., 26, 30, 38 • P.O. Box 12793 • Overland Park, KS 66282-2793 • 816/235-2227
Scilken, Marvin H., 5, 8 • 330 W 28th St • Apt. 9F • New York, NY 10001 • 201/673-0153
Scott, Marguerite J., 79 • 1253 South 50th St • Birmingham, AL 35222
Scott, Mark, 70 • Massachusetts Institute of Technology Libraries • (MIT) • Room 10-500 • Cambridge, MA 02139
Scott, Sharon K., 38 • P.O. Box 9697 • Reno, NV 89507 • 702/784-4578
Scott, Shirley R., 54 • Oregon State University • William Jasper Kerr Library • Corvallis, OR 97331-4501
Seal, Robert A., 9 • University of Texas at El Paso Library • El Paso, TX 79968-0582 • 915/747-5683; Fax: 915/747-5327; E-mail: FG00@UTEP
Sealy, Brian H., 71 • 437 Spring St • Ann Arbor, MI 48103 • 313/763-3420
Searcy, David L., 75, 79, 80 • Atlanta-Fulton Public Library • East Atlanta Branch • 457 Flat Shoals Ave. SE • Atlanta, GA 30316 • ; Fax: 404/688-4267
Searing, Susan E., 115 • 2142 Oakridge Ave • Madison, WI 53704 • 608/265-2727
Sears, Robert E., 84 • RR 2, Box 307 • Oakland City, IN 47660
Seavey, Charles A., 10, 96, 114 • University of Arizona • Graduate Library School • 1515 East 1st Street • Tucson, AZ 85721
Sedney, Frances V., 5, 8, 39 • Harford County Library • Riverside Business Park • 1221A Brass Mill Road • Belcamp, MD 21017
Seebright, Terence F., 30 • Student • Rollins College • Olin Library • 1000 Holt Ave., Campus Box 2744 • Winter Park, FL 32789-4499
Seely, Doris J., 32 • 1530 S 6th St • Chase House Apt-702 • Minneapolis, MN 55454
Seetoo, Amy D., 14 • 2907 Logan Court • Ann Arbor, MI 48108 • 313/761-4700
Segal, JoAn S., 7, 12, 14, 96, 98, 108, 115, 116, 123 • American Library Association • 50 East Huron Street • Chicago, IL 60611-2795 • 280-2518
Segal, Judith, 45, 51, 52 • 2946 Oakcrest Ave SW • Roanoke, VA 24015 • 703/362-6592
Seibert, Karen S., 44, 45, 46, 55, 63 • 1724 E. Woodward #203 • Auston, TX 78741 • 602/523-9036
Seiden, Peggy A., 73, 87 • Pennsylvania State University • New Kensington • 3550 Seventh St Road • New Kensington, PA 15068 • 412/339-6036; Fax: 412/339-6039
Seiner, Nancy, 41 • 5415 Plainfield St • Pittsburgh, PA 15217
Seldin, Daniel T., 96 • 800 N Smith Rd. • Apt. 5S • Bloomington, IN 47408 • 812/855-1108
Self, Sharon W., 101 • 10501 Whitesville Rd • Fortson, GA 31808 • 404/649-0748
Sellberg, Roxanne J., 66 • 2823 124th Place NE • Bellevue, WA 98005 • 206/543-1828
Sellen, Betty-Carol, 8, 9, 15 • 9615 McAlpine Road • Silver Spring, MD 20901
Sellen, Mary K., 49, 50 • Chapman College • Clarke Memorial Library • 333 N Glassell St • Orange, CA 92666
Selverstone, Harriet S., 5, 11, 18 • 31 Bonnie Brook Rd • Westport, CT 06880 • 203/838-4481
Sendi, Karen A., 83 • 4915 New England Lane • Apt. 104 • Sylvania, OH 43560 • 419/537-2852
Senner, Rachel, 106 • 220 East 7th-Box 697 • Freeman, SD 57029
Sercan, Cecilia S., 32, 33, 37 • 211 Bryant Avenue • Ithaca, NY 14850 • 607/255-4247
Sessa, Jane T., 71 • 643 S 21st St • Arlington, VA 22202 • 202/272-7550
Sessions, Judith A., 3, 5, 10, 167 • Miami University • Acq Dept. • 271 King Library • Oxford, OH 45056
Settem, Marie-Louise H., 18 • American Library Association • 50 E. Huron St. • Chicago, Il 60611-2729
Sevold, Louise A., 74, 124 • 1209 Stoney Run Trail • Broadview Hts, OH 44147 • 216/749-9383
Seymour, Viveca, 55 • Stanford University • Hoover Instution Library • Stanford, CA 94305-6011 • 415/723-2065; Fax: 415/723-1687
Shackelford, Eileen R., 57 • 2610 Barbara Ave • Yuma, AZ 85365 • 602/344-7660
Shackelford, Marilyn L., 13, 85 • 5619 S Madison Pl • Tulsa, OK 74105-7809 • 918/250-7307
Shaevel, Evelyn, 13, 109 • American Library Association • 50 East Huron Street • Chicago, IL 60611-2795 • 312/280-2428
Shaffer, Dallas Y., 9, 10, 76 • Monterey County Free Libraries • 26 Central Avenue • Salinas, CA 93901
Shaffer, Norman J., 36, 37, 106 • 3001 Veazey Terr. NW-Apt 1432 • Washington, DC 20008 • 202/707-1608
Shamel, Cynthia L., 34, 46, 50 • 1730 Robinhood Rd • Vista, CA 92084
Shang, Stella I-Hua, 79, 93 • 35-27 171 Street • Flushing, NY 11358 • 212/379-6733
Shank, Russell, 167 • 12919 Montana Avenue • Apt. 101 • Los Angeles, CA 90049 • 213/206-7496
Shannon, Amy W., 54 • University of Oklahoma Libraries • University Libraries • 401 W. Brooks St. • Norman, OK 73019
Shapiro, Barbara B., 77 • 465 Broadway • Hastings-Hudson, NY 10706 • 212/340-0948
Shapiro, Beth J., 5, 13, 28 • Rice University • Fondren Library • P.O.Box 1892 • Houston, TX 77251-1892 • 713/542-4022
Shapiro, Mary L., 74, 76, 80 • Baker & Taylor Books • 652 E. Main St. • P.O. Box 6920 • Bridgewater, NJ 08807-0920
Sharma, R.N., 9, 46, 104 • Director • University of Evansville • 1800 Lincoln Ave. • Evansville, IN 47722-0001
Sharp, Linda, 49, 57 • 1356 Sunnymede • South Bend, IN 46615
Shaughnessy, Thomas, 12 • 5705 Wycliffe Rd. • Ednia, MN 55436 • 612/624-1807
Shaver, Marilyn H., 64, 67 • Rt. 12, Box 196 • Bedford, IN 47421 • 812/855-8196
Shaw, Georgann K., 49 • 847 N Elm • Greenville, IL 62246
Shaw, Jane B., 24, 77 • Lisle Library District • 777 Front St. • Lisle, IL 60532
Shaw, Richard N., 45 • Technical College of the Low Country • P.O. Box 1288 • 100 South Ribaut Road • Beaufort, SC 29902
Shaw, Ruth Jean, 19 • 5430 E 32nd Ave • Anchorage, AK 99508
Shawkey, Dallas R., 32, 63 • Brooklyn Public Library • Catalog Department • Grand Army Plaza • Brooklyn, NY 11238 • 718/780-7859
Shearer, Kenneth D., 74, 76 • 1205 Leclair • Chapel Hill, NC 27514
Shearer, Martha A., 74 • 1547 Dieffenbach Road • Evansville, IN 47720
Sheble, Mary Ann, 68 • University of Alabama • Catalog Dept. Box • Tuscaloosa, AL 35487-0266
Sheehan, Anne, 89 • 7 Steadman Road, Apt. #116 • Lexington, MA 02173-7130
Sheehy, Carolyn A., 48, 50 • 1350 N. Lake Shore Dr. • Apt. 1618 • Chicago, IL 60610 • 708/420-3402
Sheehy, Helen M, 94 • Pennsylvania State University • Pattee Library • C207 Documents Section • University Park, PA 16802
Sheldon, Brooke E., 74 • University of Texas at Austin • Graduate School of Library & Information Sciences • Austin, TX 78712-1276
Sheldon, Ted P., 83 • 10715 W 71st St • Shawnee, KS 66203
Shelkrot, Elliot, 8, 73, 74, 75, 77 • Free Library of Philadelphia • Logan Square • Philadelphia, PA 19103
Shelley, Michael H., 68 • 9915 Natick Rd • Burke, VA 22015 • 202/707-6367
Shelton, Cynthia, 34, 57 • 16174 Alcima Avenue • Pacific Palisades, CA 90272 • 213/825-1324
Shelton, Judith M., 30 • 3162 Stratford Green Pl. • Avondale East, GA 30002-1341
Shelton, Richard L., 84 • 3162 Stratford Green Pl • Avondale Est, GA 30002 • 404/729-1028
Shen, Xiaoyan, 72 • University of the Pacific • 3601 Pacific Ave. • Stockton, CA 95211
Shepard, Caroline L., 41 • North Carolina State Library • 109 E Jones St • Raleigh, NC 27601-2807
Shepard, Nancy, 48, 54 • • , • ; Fax: 509/335-2534; E-mail: SHEPARD@WSUVM1
Shepherd, Odette F., 38 • 3201 Coppertree Drive • At the Stands • Bloomington, IN 47401 • 812/855-5672
Sheppard, Jocelyn A., 53 • 86 South Wade Avenue, Apt. 2 • Washington, PA 15301 • 304/829-7339
Sherby, Louise S., 47, 56, 82, 116 • University of Missouri • Miller-Nichols Library • 5100 Rockhill Rd. • Kansas City, MO 64110 • 816/235-1530; Fax: 816/333-5584; E-mail: LSSHERBY@UMKCVAX1
Sheridan, John, 44 • 1731 N Nevada Ave • Colorado Spg, CO 80907
Sherlock, Katy A., 68 • 1206 W. Daniel Street • Champaign, IL 61821-4514 • 217/333-1980
Sherman, Deborah A., 41 • Medina County District Library • 210 S Broadway • Medina, OH 44256
Sherman, Louise L., 17, 40 • Anna C. Scott School • Highland St. • Leonia, NJ 07605 • 201/461-9100
Sherman, Mary A., 5, 8, 9, 74, 76 • Pioneer Library System • 225 North Webster • Norman, OK 73069

ALA Membership Directory 1992

This edition of the ALA MEMBERSHIP DIRECTORY lists all members as of August 1992.

To facilitate reference, public libraries and city schools and school districts are listed by city, town, or village (example: Chicago Public Library).

Each member's division and round table affiliations, if any, are indicated after the entry. Members who purchased life memberships in ALA are indicated by "Life." Continuing members are indicated by "Continuing." Classifications of members are noted in Bylaws, Article I.

The ALA MEMBERSHIP DIRECTORY is not intended to serve as a mailing list of ALA members. Requests for information on the rental of ALA membership lists should be addressed to Administrative Services, ALA.

Sustaining Members

Faxon Company
Grolier Educational Corporation
Information Access Company
World Book Publishing

Patrons

Apple Computer, Inc.
The Baker and Taylor Company
Brodart Company
Donovan Publishing Company
Gale Research Company
Government Employees Insurance Co. (GEICO)
IBM ACIS
National Register Publishing Co.
Omnigraphics, Inc.
Rittenhouse Financial Services, Inc.
Salem Press
The H. W. Wilson Company

Contributing Members

Books on Tape
Curley Publishing Inc.
Eastern Book Company
Godwins/Frank B. Hall Consulting Co.
Harper Collins Children's Books
Harper Collins Publishers
The Hillier Group
Kent Adhesive Product Company (KAPCO)
Millbrook Press, Inc.
Perma-Bound Books/Hertzberg-New Method, Inc.
Peterson's
Scarecrow Press, Inc.
Schweitzer-Sortiment
Showbest Fixture Company

Subscribing Members

ABT Associates, Inc.
Academic Press
Addison-Wesley Publishing Company
Aerospace Corporation
African Books Collective Ltd.
Altschul Group Corporation
Ameritech Information Systems
The Annenberg-CPB Project
Apollo Moving Specialist
Ashgate Publishing Company
Audio Editions
Auto-Graphics, Inc.

Avec Technical Services, Inc.
Bailey & Gardner, A.I.A.
Baker and Taylor Video
Russ Bassett Company
BC Inventar, Inc.
Beacham Publishing, Inc.
Ovid H. Bell—Ovid Bell Press, Inc.
Blackwell North America
Blanton & Moore Company
Book It!
Borroughs Manufacturing Corp.
Boston Edison
Bound to Stay Bound Books, Inc.
Leon L. Bram—Funk & Wagnalls, Inc.
John M. Brenner—Wood Knapp Video
Bullfrog Films
Business One Irwin
CBIS
Chicago One Stop, Inc.
Chicago Women in Publishing
Chronicle Books
Churchill Films
CLSI, Inc.
Commodore Business Machines
CompCare Publishers
Congressional Quarterly, Inc.
Council for Bibliographic and Information Technologies (CoBIT)
Coutts Library Services, Inc.
George F. Cram Company
CRC Press
Custom Manufacturing Inc.
D. S. Limited
Dalkey Archive Press
Data Research Associates, Inc.
Data Trek, Inc.
Davis & Henderson, Ltd.
Dearborn Trade
Delta Lithograph Company
Demco Inc.
Disclosure Incorporated
Documents Index
Norma J. Draper—Information Strategies Group
Bobbea Duran-Molloy—Select Video Publishing
Duncan Systems Specialists
Dymaxian Research Limited
DYNIX, Inc.
Educational Communications, Inc.
Elsevier Science Publishing Co.
Emery-Pratt Company
Enem Systems Inc.
Estey Co.
Evan Tercy Associates P.C., Architects
EZ-Reader, Inc.
Fanlight Productions
Far West Data Control, Inc.
Facts of File
FENCO, Division of United Hospital Supply Corp.

Films Incorporated
Follett Software Company
Forest House Publishing Company
Freline, Inc.
Frontier Press Company
Gaylord Brothers
General Automation, Inc.
Globe Pequot Press
Gould Evans Architects, P.A.
Greenhaven Press
Greenwood Publishing Group
Gressco, Ltd.
Griffin Technology, Inc.
Hallenbook
Harcourt Brace Jovanovich Publishers
Henry Holt & Company
Hidell Architects
Highlights for Children, Inc.
Hotho & Company
HRD Group
Idaho Power Company
Idea House Publishing Company
Ideals Publishing Corporation
Infocentre Corporation
Ingram Library Service
Innovative Interfaces, Inc.
Internal Revenue Service
Intertec Publishing Corporation
Interweave Press
The Irish Times, Ltd.
January Productions
JD Store Equipment, Inc.
David Kerin—Ebsco Subscription Services
Kingsley Library Equipment Co.
Kintronics, Inc.
Lectorum Publications, Inc.
Lexecon
Library Binding Institute
Library Bureau Inc.
Macmillan Library Services, Division of Macmillan Publishing Company
Marburger Stempel-Erzeugung
Marshall, O'Toole, Gerstein, Murray, & Bicknell
Martinus Nijhoff International
MCB & Associates, Ltd.
Meridiar Data, Inc.
Merritt McCallum Cieslak Architects
Midwest Micro Information Systems
MJ Industries, Inc.
Moonbeam Publications, Inc.
MPI Home Video
K.R. Montgomery & Associates
Mulder's Red Carpet Moving & Storage
Multnomah Press
Steven J. Nash Publishing
New Age Publishing & Retailing Alliance (NAPRA)
John Noonan—AIG Financial Products Corp.
Roy Oakley—Live Oak Media
Ohio Bus Sales, Inc.

Orchard Books, Division of Franklin Watts
The Oryx Press
Pan Asian Publications
Pegasus Publishing Company, Inc.
Pleasant Company
Popular Culture, Inc.
Susan K. Prather—Krames Communications
Prentice Hall Press
Public Affairs Information Service
Quality Books, Inc.
REI America, Incorporated
Reference Press, Incorporated
Retro Link Associates
R.J. Reynolds Tobacco Company
Norman Ross Publishing, Inc.
Routledge, Chapman & Hall
John Rowe—Filmakers Library

Sage Publications
Susan M.Q. Severston—Chadwyck-Healey, Inc.
Signature Books
Silo Music
Simon & Schuster Books for Young Readers
Society for Visual Education, Inc.
Software AG
Southeastern Library Network (SOLINET)
Spacesaver Corporation
Spoken Arts, Inc.
Steck-Vaughn Company
Patricia W. Stevens—Maxwell Online
Stewart, Tabori & Chang
SVS, Inc.
The Talman Company
Texwood Furniture Corporation

Thorndike Press
Time Being Books
TPS Electronics
Troll Associates
Tundra Books
Union Carbide-Nova Tran
USA Today
Video Trend, Inc.
Virginia Library Technical Services, Inc. (VTLS)
Walker & Company
The Walt Disney Company
Western Publishing Company
Janet P. Whaley—Maxwell Online
Winnebago Software Corporation
Workman Publishing Company, Inc.

Personal Members

Aagaard James S. • Director, ISDO • Northwestern University Library • Evanston, IL 60208-2300 • LITA

Aagaard Mary-Lou • Trustee • Glenview Public Library • Glenview, IL 60025

Aakre Judith • ICC • CESA #4 • Onalaska, WI 54650

Aakre Nelson E. • AV-IMC Media Specialist • Logan High School • La Crosse, WI 54603 • AASL

Aamot Carolyn H. • Head Gift Processing Section • University of Washington • Seattle, WA 98195

Aamot Gordon J. Jr. • Head, Bus. Admin Library • University of Washington Suzzallo Library • Seattle, WA 98195 • ACRL RASD GODORT IRRT

Aaron Amira • Lexington, MA 02173 • ACRL LITA

Aaron Kathleen F. • Reference Coordinator • Inland Library System • Riverside, CA 92502 • ASCLA PLA RASD

Aaron Shirley L. Dr. • Professor • Florida State University School of Library and Information Studies • Tallahassee, FL 32306-2048 • AASL LITA YALSA IFRT

Aaronian Jan M • Branch Librarian • Contra Costa County Library Martinez Library • Martinez, CA 94553

Aaronson Kristina • Director • Somerville Public Library • Somerville, NJ 08876

Aarstad Jonette • Asst. Reference Librarian • University of Evansville • Evansville, IN 47722 • ACRL

Abadie James E. Sr • Trustee • Ascension Parish Library • Donaldsonville, LA 70346-2535 • ALTA PLA SRRT

Abar Ellen L. • Coordinator of Library Services • Allegany Community College • Cumberland, MD 21502-2596

Abaray Michael J. • Technical Services Librarian • Evansville-Vanderburgh County Public Library • Evansville, IN 47708-1694 • LAMA

Abarr Dawn J. • Librarian • Belton High School • Belton, MO 64012 • AASL

Abate Anne K. • Librarian • Dinsmore & Shohl Library • Cincinnati, OH 45202-3172

Abayhan Zubay • Durham, NC 27705 • ILERT

Abbasi Roza M. • Librarian II • Fort Worth Public Library Diamond Hill/Jarvis Branch • Fort Worth, TX 76106

Abbaticchio Donna L. • Dept. Hd., History & Social Sci. • New York Public Library Mid-Manhattan Branch • New York, NY 10016 • RASD

Abbe Bernice E. • Enfield, CT 06082

Abbey Leonard • Trustee • Farmers Branch Public Library • Farmers Branch, TX 75234 • ALTA

Abbott Dorothy D. • Pensacola, FL 32526

Abbott George L. • Syracuse University Library E. S. Bird Library • Syracuse, NY 13244-2010 • ACRL LITA ERT

Abbott Heidi • Director • Citrus County Library System • Crystal River, FL 32623-0635 • LAMA PLA

Abbott Joan E. • Librarian • Bicentennial Elementary School • Nashua, NH 03062 • AASL ALSC

Abbott John C. • Special & Research Coll Libn • Southern Illinois University • Edwardsville, IL 62026 • ACRL RASD *Life*

Abbott John P. • Hd of Natural Resources Library • North Carolina State University D. H. Hill Library • Raleigh, NC 27695-7111 • ACRL

Abbott Julia A. • Bookmobile Librarian • South Brunswick Public Library • Monmouth Junction, NJ 08852

Abbott Kent • Catalog Librarian • Stanford University Jackson Library • Stanford, CA 94305 • ACRL ALCTS

Abbott Kristin • Bibliographic Servs. Librarian • Northeastern University Burlington Campus Library • Burlington, MA 01803 • ACRL

Abbott Laurie • Preservation Program Officer • Research Libraries Group Inc. (RLG) • Mountain View, CA 94041-1100 • ALCTS

Abbott Lisa T. • Documents Librarian • North Carolina State University D. H. Hill Library • Raleigh, NC 27695-7111 • LITA GODORT

Abbott Mary L. • Teacher-Librarian • Pleasant Ridge Elementary • Cincinnati, OH 45213 • AASL

Abbott Monica M. • Library Chairperson • Barlett School • Winchester, MA 01890 • AASL ALSC

Abbott Ruth Junkin • Austin, TX 78731 • AASL ALSC *Life*

Abbott Thomas E. • Director of Learning Resources • University of Maine at Augusta Learning Resources Center • Augusta, ME 04330 • ACRL LITA

Abbott Vondra Shaw • Library Consultant • Office of Catholic Schools • Louisville, KY 40204 • AASL

Abdallah Cendrella • Information Specialist • American Insurance Services Group • New York, NY 10038

Abdel-Motey Yaser Yousef Dr. • Professor • College of Basic Education • Idailiya, 73251, Kuwait • LITA

Abdmishani Beatriz P. • Library Director • William B. Harlan Memorial Library • Tompkinsville, KY 42167

Abdoo Ann R. • Coor. Adult Services Division • Southfield Public Library David Stewart Memorial Library • Southfield, MI 48037-2055 • PLA

Abdullahi Ismail • Hattiesburg, MS 39401 • IRRT

Abdulle Ali D. • Student • State University of New York School of Information & Library Sci • Albany, NY 12203

Abed Donna M. • Delaware Technical Community College Wilimington Campus Library • Wilimington, DE 19801-2499 • ACRL

Abel Charlene • Librarian • DePaul University Library • Chicago, IL 60604-2287 • RASD

Abel Gene M. • Trustee • Knoxville Knox County Public Library • Concord, TN 37922 • ACRL ALTA *Life*

Abel Joanne E. • Assistant Reference Librarian • Durham County Library • Durham, NC 27702 • PLA IFRT SRRT

Abel Joseph A. • Student • University of Hawaii School of Library & Information Studies • Honolulu, HI 96822 • LHRT

Abelack Joan S. • Chief Librarian • Styvesant High School • New York, NY 10003 • AASL

Abell Carol E. • West Lafayette, IN 47907

Abell Millicent D. • University Librarian • Yale University Sterling Memorial Library • New Haven, CT 06520 • *Life*

Abels Florence • San Diego, CA 92122 • *Life*

Aber Jeanne • Dallas, TX 75231

Aberman Jennifer M. • Head of Adult Services • La Porte County Public Library • La Porte, IN 46350 • PLA

Abernathy Mary Jo • Chilton/Clanton Public Library • Clanton, AL 35045

Abeyta Sally B. • Librarian • Clatskanie Library District • Clatskanie, OR 97016 • PLA

Abid Ann B. • Cleveland Museum of Art • Cleveland, OH 44106 • ACRL ALCTS LITA RASD

Abilock Debbie • Librarian • Nueva Center for Learning • Hillsborough, CA 94010 • AASL ALSC YALSA

Abisognio Paula • Levittown, NY 11756 • ALCTS PLA

Able Ellen Hanscom • Bala Cynwyd, PA 19004

Ableidinger Rose Ann • Library Media Specialist • Elvehjem Elementary School • Madison, WI 53716 • AASL ALSC

Abler Susan S. • Student • University of California Los Angeles Graduate School of Library & Information Science • Los Angeles, CA 90024 • NMRT

Abmayr Marie T. F.M.I. Sister • Archbishop Mitty High School Library Media Center • San Jose, CA 95129 • AASL YALSA

Abner Judith • Branch Manager • Meyers Park Library • Charlotte, NC 28207

Abney Sylvia B. • Mosinee, WI 54455

Abraham Kristin • Librarian • Tabernacle Baptist School • Concord, CA 94521

Abraham Midhart D. • Middle East Librarian • University of Arizona Library • Tucson, AZ 85721 • ACRL IFRT

Abraham Penny C. Ms. • School Librarian • Greenville Elementary School • Baton Rouge, LA 70806 • AASL

Abraham Sandra H. • Librarian II • East Baton Rouge Parish Library Jones Creek Branch • Baton Rouge, LA 70817

Abraham Susan • Cataloger • John Carroll University Grasselli Library • University Heights, OH 44118

Abrahamian Dro M. • Wayne State University • Detroit, MI 48202 • RASD

Abrahams Barbara • School Media Specialist • North Broad Street School • Oneida, NY 13421 • AASL

Abrahams Sherry L. • Information Librarian • University of Alaska Elmer E. Rasmuson Library • Fairbanks, AK 99775-1005 • ALCTS LITA *Life*

Abrahamson Ed • Trustee • Huntington Public Library • Huntington, NY 11743 • ALTA

Abrahamson Edythe B. • Program Chair • Minneapolis Public Library & Information Center • Minneapolis, MN 55401-1992

Abrahamson Wendy K. • Student • Pratt Institute Graduate School of Library & Information Science • Brooklyn, NY 11205 • RASD IFRT LHRT SRRT

Abram Stephen K. • Toronto ON, M6P 4E1 Canada • LAMA LITA

Abram Wiley K. • Olathe, KS 66062

Abramoff Carolann P. • Children's Librarian • Collier County Public Library • Naples, FL 33940 • ALSC PLA IFRT

Abramowitz Marilyn N. • Mineola High School • Garden City Park, NY 11040 • AASL

Abrams Ann Carol • Temple Israel Library • Boston, MA 02215

Abrams Anne Frances • Adult Services Librarian • Boise Public Library • Boise, ID 83702-0715

Abrams Brian S. • Social Sciences Librarian • Idaho State University Eli M. Oboler Library • Pocatello, ID 83209-8089 • IFRT LIRT SRRT

Abrams Josephine C. • Phoenix, AZ 85014 • PLA YALSA

Abrams Marlene • Portland, OR 97214

Abrams Martha • Lynwood, CA 90262 • NMRT

Abrams Mary Louise • Paramus Public Library • Paramus, NJ 07652 • LAMA PLA

Abrams Roger E. • Cincinnati, OH 45236 • IFRT

Abrams Wanda • Student • State University of New York (SUNY) School of Information & Library Studies • Buffalo, NY 14260

Abramson Debora R. • Baton Rouge, LA 70802 • ASCLA *Continuing*

Abramson Jenifer Stone • Task Force Librarian • University of California Library • Los Angeles, CA 90024 • ALCTS ALSC LAMA LIRT NMRT

Abramson Martin • Trustee • Peninsula Public Library • Lawrence, NY 11559

Abramson Sherle E. • Williamsburg, VA 23185

Abrell Diana F. • Anna Porter Public Library • Gatlinburg, TN 37738

Abrera Josefa B. • Associate Professor • Indiana University School of Library and Information Science • Bloomington, IN 47405 • ALCTS LITA IRRT LRRT

Absher Linda S. • Student • University of California-Berkeley School of Library & Information Studies • Berkeley, CA 94720

Absi Joann E. • Librarian • Roland-Grise Middle School • Wilmington, NC 28403 • AASL

Abston Deborah • Assistant Librarian • Arizona State University Hayden Library • Tempe, AZ 85287-1006 • ACRL ALCTS

Aby Stephen H. • University of Akron University Library & Learning Resource • Akron, OH 44325-1707 • ACRL IFRT

Acampora Susan • College of New Rochelle Gill Library • New Rochelle, NY 10805

Acanfora Lisa E. • Garner, NC 27529 • AASL

Accardi Joseph J. • Assoc. University Librarian • Northeastern Illinois University Library • Chicago, IL 60625 • LITA

Accardo Lynn M. • University of New Orleans Earl K. Long Library • New Orleans, LA 70148 • LAMA

Accurso Diana L. • Social Science Reference Ln. • Auburn University Ralph Brown Draughon Library • Auburn, AL 36849-5606

Ace Susan • Librarian • Mariner High School • Everett, WA 98204 • AASL

Acerra Elizabeth G. • Brooklyn Public Library Spring Creek Branch • Brooklyn, NY 11207 • PLA YALSA IFRT VRT

Acerri Federico U. • Head of Reference • Wayne Cnty Intermediate Sch Dist • Wayne, MI 48184 • LITA

Aceves- Foster Gary • Wheeler, AFB, HI 96786

Achamire Thelma P. • Wenatchee Valley College North Library • Omak, WA 98841 • ACRL

Achebo Nubi • Assistant Professor • Iowa State University Library • Ames, IA 50011-2140 • ACRL

Acheson David • Supervisor, Cataloging Services • Rand Corporation Library • Santa Monica, CA 90406-2138

Achildiyev Anna • Student • Pratt Institute Graduate School of Library & Information Science • Brooklyn, NY 11205

Achille Karen • Children's Librarian • Vineyard Haven Public Library • Vineyard Haven, MA 02568 • ALSC

Acker Sandra Benet • Music Librarian • University of Victoria McPherson Library • Victoria BC, V8W 3H5 Canada • ACRL

Ackerman Caryl • Director • Oceanside Free Library • Oceanside, NY 11572 • PLA

Ackerman Kathy • Trustee • East Lansing Public Library • East Lansing, MI 48823 • ALTA

Ackerman Marilyn • Brooklyn, NY 11215 • SRRT

Ackerman Page • Santa Monica, CA 90402 • ACRL

Ackerman Roxane • Director • Gay Head Public Library • Gay Head, MA 02535 • LITA YALSA EMIERT

Ackerman Sonya Lea • Tonopah, NV 89049 • AFLRT

Ackerman Susan H. • Assistant Librarian • Sidney Memorial Public Library • Sidney, NY 13838 • YALSA

Ackerson Linda G. • Sci. & Engr. Ref. Libraries • University of Alabama Amelia Gayle Gorgas Library • Tuscaloosa, AL 35487-0266 • ACRL

Ackert-Herzig Ruby • School Librarian • Hyde Park Elementary School • Hyde Park, VT 05655 • AASL

Ackler Susan • Librarian • New Hope-Solebury Junior-Senior High School • New Hope, PA 18938 • YALSA

Ackley Donald A. • Director/Media Service • Orange Coast College • Costa Mesa, CA 92628-5005 • ACRL

Acklin Kay • Reference Librarian • Hinsdale Central High School Library • Hinsdale, IL 60521 • AASL

Ackroyd-Kelly Elaine • Technical Services Librarian • Centenary College Taylor Memorial Library • Hackettstown, NJ 07840 • ACRL

Acosta Idalia P. • Head, Cataloging Branch • United States Department of Agriculture National Agricultural Library • Beltsville, MD 20705-2351 • ALCTS FLRT

Acosta Lydia A. • Director • University of Tampa Kelce Library • Tampa, FL 33606 • ACRL ALCTS ASCLA LAMA LITA RASD

Acs Imre Dr • Cleveland, OH 44120 • GODORT

Acuna Gilbert M. • Student • University of California-Berkeley School of Library & Information Studies • Berkeley, CA 94720 • IFRT

Adair Lolita • Trustee • Akron-Summit County Public Library • Akron, OH 44326-0001 • ALTA

Adair Patricia S. • Librarian • L. J. Price Middle School Atlanta Public Schools • Atlanta, GA 30315

Adair Torsten • Omaha, NE 68114-2230 • ALCTS NMRT

Adam Anthony J. • Assistant Reference Librarian • John B. Coleman Library • Prairie View, TX 77446 • ACRL RASD

Adam Joan H. • Director • Sequoyah Regional Library • Canton, GA 30114 • PLA

Adames Dora L. Fma Sr • L Media Coor • Villa Madonna School • Tampa, FL 33602

Adamick Lucille F. • Trustee • Eisenhower Public Library District • Harwood Heights, IL 60656 • ALTA

Adamovich Shirley Gray • Durham, NH 03824 • PLA CLENE LHRT

Adams Barbara • Reference Librarian • Duquesne University Library • Pittsburgh, PA 15282

Adams Barbara K. • Reference Librarian • University of Mississippi John Davis Williams Library • University, MS 38677 • ACRL

Adams Bray Jessica • Prairieville, LA 70769-4303 • ASCLA LAMA LITA

Adams Bruce A. • Branch Librarian • Public Library of Charlotte & Mecklenburg County Northwest Branch • Charlotte, NC 28216 • RASD

Adams Carol • Institutional Consultant • Virginia State Library & Archives • Richmond, VA 23219 • ASCLA

Adams Carol L. • Associate Librarian • University of Regina • Regina SK, S4S 0A2 Canada • ACRL ALCTS LAMA LITA RASD CLENE ERT LIRT SORT

Adams Carol V. • Librarian • Perryville High School • Perryville, AR 72126 • AASL

Adams Carole M. • Los Angeles County Public Library Marina Del Rey Branch • Marina del Rey, CA 90292

Adams Charles J. • Hopland, CA 95449

Adams Charles W. • Hanover, MA 02339

Adams Christina S. • Library Assistant • Phoenix Public Library Yucca Branch • Phoenix, AZ 85015

Adams Colleen B. • Head Librarian • Dade Christian School • Miami, FL 33015 • AASL

Adams Cynthia C. • Reference Librarian • Univ of North Carolina Hum Dep • Chapel Hill, NC 27514 • ACRL

Adams Deanna • Student • Brigham Young University School of Library & Information Sciences • Provo, UT 84602 • ALSC

Adams Diane M. • Student • University of Washington Graduate School of Library and Information Science • Seattle, WA 98195 • ALSC YALSA

Adams Earlean • Board Member • Prichard Public Library • Prichard, AL 36610

Adams Elaine P. Dr. • President • Northeast College Houston Community College System • Houston, TX 77270-7849

Adams Eleanor • Brooklyn, NY 11239 • IFRT

Adams Elizabeth C. • Media Specialist • A C Flora High School • Columbia, SC 29204 • AASL YALSA

Adams Elizabeth F. • PSI, International Inc. • Rockville, MD 20852 • LITA

Adams Gail D. • Librarian • Enterprise High School • Redding, CA 96002 • AASL

Adams Glenda C. • Rancho Cordova, CA 95670

Adams Gustave C. • Miami, FL 33126 • AASL RASD *Life*

Adams Helen R. • High School Media Specialist • Rosholt Public Schools • Rosholt, WI 54473 • AASL

Adams Ida G. • Assistant Director • Florida A&M University • Tallahassee, FL 32307 • ACRL

Adams J. Robert • Head Librarian • Wesleyan University Olin Memorial Library • Middletown, CT 06459 • ACRL LAMA

Adams Jacqueline M. • Materials Managment Coor. • Carroll County Public Library • Westminster, MD 21157 • IFRT

Adams January V. • Reference Librarian • Somerville Public Library • Somerville, NJ 08876

Adams Jennifer S. • Reference Librarian • Anne Arundel County Public Library Provinces Branch • Severn, MD 21144

Adams Joan • Trustee • Las Vegas-Clark County Library District Flamingo Library • Las Vegas, NV 89119 • ALTA

Adams John A. • Student • Dalhousie University School of Library & Inf. Studies • Halifax NS, B3H 4H8 Canada

Adams John M. • Orange County Public Library • Santa Ana, CA 92705

Adams Joyce • Socorro High School • Socorro, NM 87801

Adams Judith A. • Director • State University of New York (SUNY) at Buffalo • Buffalo, NY 14260 • ACRL LAMA LRRT

Adams Julia • Tennessee Wesleyan College • Athens, TN 37303 • RASD IFRT

Adams June B. • Bridgewater, NJ 08807 • ALCTS PLA RASD ILERT

Adams Kate E. • Chair, General Services Dept. • University of Nebraska-Lincoln University Libraries • Lincoln, NE 68588-0410 • ACRL RASD

Adams Kathryn G. • Librarian • Lincoln City Libraries • Lincoln, NE 68508

Adams Kay T. • Assistant Director Tech. Service • Southeastern Louisiana Univ • Hammond, LA 70402 • ALCTS

Adams Leonard R. • Government Documents Librarian • University of Massachusetts University Library • Amherst, MA 01003 • ACRL GODORT

Adams Libby • Librarian • Sacred Heart Academy • New Orleans, LA 70115 • AASL

Adams Liese • North Olmsted, OH 44070 • LITA

Adams M.L. Phoebe • Head Librarian • Sierra Club William E. Colby Memorial Library • San Francisco, CA 94109 • ACRL SRRT

Adams Marcia L. • Smithsonian Institution Libraries Natural Museum of American History • Washington, DC 20560 • LITA

Adams Mary Anne H. • Manager Research Library • Ortho Diagnostics Systems • Raritan, NJ 08869

Adams Mary L. • Huntington, WV 25727-2726 • AASL YALSA

Adams Michael • Assistant Director • Fairleigh Dickinson University Florham-Madison Campus Library • Madison, NJ 07940 • ACRL

Adams Mignon S. • Director • Philadelphia College of Pharmacy & Science-Joseph W. England Library • Philadelphia, PA 19104-4491 • ACRL LAMA LIRT

Adams Ora M. • Elementary Librarian • Orr Elementary School • Tyler, TX 75702

Adams Patsy H. • Librarian/Media Specialist • Corner School • Warrior, AL 35180 • AASL YALSA

Adams Raquel K. • Salt Lke Cty, UT 84103

Adams Rita T. • Director • Loomis Chaffee School • Windsor, CT 06095 • AASL ALCTS LAMA LITA LIRT

Adams Rose M. • Palo Alto, CA 94306 • SRRT

Adams Ruth L. • Surry, ME 04684 • ALSC   *Continuing*

Adams Sharon D. • Children's Librarian • Public Library of Columbus and Franklin County Shepard Branch Lib. • Columbus, OH 43219

Adams Sherry S. • Librarian • Houston Chronicle • Houston, TX 77210 • RASD

Adams Stanley E. • Special Projects Coordinator • Illinois State Library • Springfield, IL 62701-1796 • ASCLA LAMA GODORT

Adams Steven E. • Trustee • Mid-Wisconsin Federated Library System • Fond du Lac, WI 54935-5510 • ALTA

Adams Sue M. • Student • University of Arizona Graduate Library School • Tucson, AZ 85721 • PLA SRRT

Adams Susan L. • Head of Central Children's Serv. • Pack Memorial Library • Asheville, NC 28801

Adams Tyna Elizabeth • Librarian • Midlothian Middle School • Midlothian, TX 76065

Adams Valarie • Asst. Prof/Cataloging Libn • University of Tennessee T Carter & M Rawlings Lupton Lib • Chattanooga, TN 37403

Adams Wanda K. • Horton High School • Horton, KS 66439 • AASL YALSA

Adamshick Margery I. • Student • State University of New York (SUNY) School of Information & Library Studies • Buffalo, NY 14260 • AASL

Adamshick Robert • Chicago, IL 60626

Adamski Julia M. • Student • University of Illinois Graduate School of Library and Information Science • Urbana, IL 61801

Adamson Danette Cook • Catalog Libn/Music Bibliographer • California State Polytech University • Pomona, CA 91768

Adamson James P. • Resident Treatment Worker • Mental Health Institute • Cherokee, IA 51012

Adamson Margaret W. • Student • Emporia State University School of Library & Information Management • Emporia, KS 66801

Adamson Martha C. • Asst. & Dir. Systems & Tech. • University of Texas Southwestern Medical Center at Dallas Library • Dallas, TX 75235-9049 • LITA

Adamson Stauney F. • Springfield, OR 97477

Adan Adrienne H. • Los Angeles, CA 90025

Adatto Shelley R. • Librarian • Seattle Public Library • Seattle, WA 98104-1193

Adcock Betty L. • Librarian • Lincoln/Webster Elementary School • Clinton, IL 61727 • AASL

Adcock Briley Queen • Director • Linebaugh Public Library • Murfreesboro, TN 37130

Adcock Donald C. • Coordinator Program Support AASL • American Library Association • Chicago, IL 60611-2795 • AASL ALSC YALSA

Addamus Carmelita B. • Librarian • Naval Support Activity Library • New Orleans, LA 70142-5000 • AFLRT

Addison Carolyn E. • Los Angeles, CA 90018

Addison Florence • Brewster, MA 02631 • ALSC PLA   *Continuing*

Addison Jane G. • Librarian • M.D. Anderson Cancer Center Research Medical Library • Houston, TX 77030

Addison Janet V. • Library Catalog Dept. • Purdue University Libraries • West Lafayette, IN 47907-1530 • ALCTS

Addison Maeives • Baltimore County Public Library Essex Area Branch • Essex, MD 21221

Addlesperger Boyd • Lexington, OH 44904

Addona Gina • Bristol-Myers Squibb Company Research Library • Wallingford, CT 06492

Addor Margaret H. • Librarian • Titusville Middle School • Poughkeepsie, NY 12603 • AASL

Addotta Salvatore M. • Assistant Library Director • Placentia Library District • Placentia, CA 92670 • PLA

Addy K. Janyce • Midhurst ON, L0L 1X0 Canada • ALSC

Addy Mary L. • Director • Bolivar-Harpers Ferry Library • Harpers Ferry, WV 25425

Adelman Jean S. • Librarian • University of Pennsylvania Libraries Museum Library • Philadelphia, PA 19104-6324 • ACRL RASD IRRT

Adelman Loretta • Librarian • Crestwood High School • Dearborn Heights, MI 48127 • AASL

Adelsperger R J. • Spec Clln Ln & Cura of Rare Bks • University of Illinois at Chicago University Library • Chicago, IL 60680 • ACRL RASD   *Life*

Adeniran Dixie D. • Director • Ventura County Library Services Agency • Ventura, CA 93003 • ALTA LAMA LITA PLA

Ader Elizabeth R. • Head/Access Services • University of Missouri-Kansas City Library • Kansas City, MO 64110-2499 • ACRL LAMA LITA CLENE IFRT IRRT

Aderholdt Sarah W. • Student • University of Illinois Graduate School of Library and Information Science • Urbana, IL 61801

Adetayo Mary Joanne • Chief Acquisitions • District of Columbia Public Library Martin Luther King Memorial Library • Washington, DC 20001 • ALCTS

Adin Kathleen B. • Kingston City Schools • Kingston, NY 12401

Adkesson Ann • Library Director • Barclay Public Library District • Warrensburg, IL 62573 • PLA

Adkins Edna F. • Media Specialist • Jenkins High School • Savannah, GA 31406 • AASL

Adkins Lorna B. • Student • San Jose State University Division of Library & Information Science • San Jose, CA 95192-0029 • RASD EMIERT IFRT LHRT

Adkins Marjorie R. • Chicago, IL 60643 • PLA EMIERT

Adkins Myra • Saint Peter's School • Chattanooga, TN 37415 • AASL ALSC

Adkins Roger W. • Media/Technology Director • Educational Service Unit-#16 • Ogallala, NE 69153 • AASL

Adkisson Marge • Branch Manager • Dakota County Library • Eagan, MN 55123 • SRRT

Adler A. Emmeli • Seattle, WA 98116 • ACRL LITA RASD EMIERT GODORT IFRT IRRT LIRT NMRT SRRT

Adler Beverly S. • Student • Emporia State University School of Library & Information Management • Emporia, KS 66801 • AASL

Adler Leah D. • Head Librarian • Yeshiva University Libraries • New York, NY 10033 • ACRL ALCTS

Adler Lois • Oak Park, IL 60302

Adler Lorna R. • Director • Larchmont Public Library • Larchmont, NY 10538 • LAMA PLA RASD YALSA

Adler Prudence S. • Asst. Executive Director, ARL • Association of Research Libraries (ARL) • Washington, DC 20036 • GODORT

Adler Sue • Modesto Junior College Library • Modesto, CA 95350 • ACRL LITA

Adler Tobi K. • Far Rockaway, NY 11691

Adley Sharon K. • Head, Circulation Services • Lake County Public Library • Merrillville, IN 46410-5382 • SORT

Adlum Margaret • Social Sci & Edu Ln • University of Massachusetts at Boston Joseph P. Healey Library • Boston, MA 02125-3393 • AASL ACRL

Admire Leslie Quinlan • Los Angeles County Municipal Courts • Los Angeles, CA 90012

Adrian Anna • Student • University of Arizona Graduate Library School • Tucson, AZ 85721

Adrian Lydia L. • Tampa-Hillsborough County Public Library West Tampa Branch • Tampa, FL 33607 • AASL

Adriance Lois • Consultant • Northeast Kansas Library System • Shawnee Mission, KS 66204-2217 • ALSC ALTA PLA

Adrianopoli Barbara C. • Director of Extension Services • Schaumburg Township District Library • Schaumburg, IL 60194 • PLA SRRT

Adrion Mary • Media Spec Ln • Kent Intermediate School District Educational Services Center • Grand Rapids, MI 49505 • AASL

Adshead Mona • Auburn, MA 01501 • Continuing

Ady Dawn S. • Saint John's River Community College Orange Park Center Library • Orange Park, FL 32073

Ady Marilyn M. • Reference Librarian • Tarpon Springs Public Library • Tarpon Spring, FL 34689 • ACRL

Aebischer Joanne • Automation Library System Coor. • Chemeketa Cooperative Regional Library Servies • Salem, OR 97309-7070 • LITA

Affleck Delburt E. • Head, Education Branch Library • University of Regina • Regina SK, S4S 0A2 Canada • AASL ACRL LITA RASD

Affleck Mary Ann • Director • Greater Hartford Community College • Hartford, CT 06105 • ACRL RASD

Afifi Marianne • Student • University of California Los Angeles Graduate School of Library & Information Science • Los Angeles, CA 90024

Afulezi Uju N. • Student • Pratt Institute Graduate School of Library & Information Science • Brooklyn, NY 11205

Afuso Pauline S. • Student • University of California-Los Angeles Graduate School of Library & Information Science • Los Angeles, CA 90024-1520

Agbafe Peter C. • Branch Manager • Saint Louis Public Library Lashly Branch • St. Louis, MO 63108 • LAMA PLA

Agbim Ngozi P. • Chief Librarian • LaGuardia Community College • Long Island City, NY 11101 • ACRL ALCTS ASCLA LAMA LITA RASD YALSA EMIERT GODORT IFRT LIRT MAGERT

Age Germaine C. • Community Awareness Coordinator • New Orleans Public Library • New Orleans, LA 70140 • PLA

Agenbroad James E. • Senior Systems Analyst • Library of Congress • Washington, DC 20541 • ACRL ALCTS LITA

Agent Susan M. • Coordinator for Database Mgmt • University of Delaware Library • Newark, DE 19717-5267 • ALCTS LAMA

Aggertt Debra • Director • Ashland Public Library • Ashland, IL 62612

Agnello Jane • E Islip, NY 11730

Agnew Andrew John • Glen Ellyn, IL 60137

Agnew Ellen Y. • Richmond, VA 23221

Agnew Grace J. • Atlanta-Fulton Public Library • Atlanta, GA 30303 • LITA

Agosta Karin E. • Trade Sales Manager • W. H. Freeman & Company • New York, NY 10010

Agosta Leigh • Media Specialist • Iroquois Middle School • Mt. Clemens, MI 48044 • AASL

Agostas Josephine R. • Davidson Fine Arts • Augusta, GA 30901

Agresti Risa • Olney, MD 20832

Agriesti Roseann C. • Duluth, MN 55804

Aguayo Jorge • Washington, DC 20008 • ACRL ALCTS
Continuing

Aguilar Dane E. • Reference Librarian • Eastern New Mexico University Golden Library • Portales, NM 88130 • LIRT

Aguilar Gloria F. • Trustee • Farmers Branch Public Library • Farmers Branch, TX 75234 • ALTA

Aguilar Irene G. • Children's Librarian • San Antonio Public Library Brookhollow Branch • San Antonio, TX 78232

Aguilar Nina W. • Denver, CO 80220 • LITA RASD AFLRT NMRT SRRT

Aguilar William • University Librarian • California State University • San Bernardino, CA 92407 • ACRL

Aguino Leticia E. • Falls Church, VA 22044 • LITA

Aguirre Maria E. • New Hyde Park, NY 11040

Ahadi Gisela • Catalog Librarian • Washington University Libraries • Saint Louis, MO 63130-4899 • ALCTS

Ahearn John J. • Media Specialist • Xavier University • New Orleans, LA 70125

Ahearn Julia • School Library Media Specialist • Cypress Trails CES • Royal Palm Beach, FL 33404

Ahern Catherine • Reference Librarian • Russell Library • Middletown, CT 06457 • SRRT

Ahern Karolyn • Coordinator Instructional Media • Vergennes Union High School • Vergennes, VT 05491 • AASL

Ahern Kathleen S. • Librarian • Barrington Public Library District • Barrington, IL 60010

Ahern Patricia C. • Trustee • Palatine Public Library • Palatine, IL 60067 • ALTA

Ahern Patricia F • Student • Massachusetts Institute of Technology Libraries (MIT) • Cambridge, MA 02139

Ahern Zilpha S. • System Librarian • Dayton & Montgomery County Public Library • Dayton, OH 45402-2103

Ahl Ruth • Library Director • Waukesha County Technical College • Pewaukee, WI 53072 • ACRL RASD

Ahlers Eleanor E. • Prof Emeritus • University of Washington Graduate School of Library and Information Science • Seattle, WA 98195 • Continuing

Ahlers Glen-Peter Sr. • University of Arkansas Libraries • Fayetteville, AR 72701-1201 • LAMA

Ahlquist Bernice • Cherry Hill, NJ 08003

Ahlschwede Stephanie M. • Nashville, TN 37212-4120 • PLA

Ahmann Cynthia J. • Branch Head • Madison County Public Library • Richmond, KY 40475 • PLA

Ahmed Syed Sakil • Dhaka-1219, Bangladesh • RASD IFRT NMRT

Ahmed Terry T. • Buffalo, NY 14215

Ahn Hyonah K. • Ref/AV Resource • Chicago Public Library Sulzer Regional Library • Chicago, IL 60625 • PLA

Ahonen Dorothy O. • Public Services Librarian II • Cuyahoga County Public Library Bay Village Branch • Bay Village, OH 44140-2194 • ALSC PLA

Ahouse John • Curator,American Literature • University of Southern California Doheny Library • Los Angeles, CA 90089-0182 • ACRL

Ahrens Carol • Director • North Merrick Public Library • North Merrick, NY 11566

Ahrens Christine • San Francisco Public Library Ortega Branch • San Francisco, CA 94122

Ahronheim Judith R. • Cataloger • University of Michigan • Ann Arbor, MI 48109-1205 • ALCTS LITA

Ahtola A. Anneli • Head Librarian • Tampere University Library • SF-13131 Hameenlinna, Finland • ACRL

Aiau Kathleen Malie • Solana Beach, CA 92075 • IFRT

Aiello Helen M. • Serials Librarian • Wesleyan University Olin Memorial Library • Middletown, CT 06459 • ACRL ALCTS

Aikawa Hiroko • Cataloger • Cleveland Public Library • Cleveland, OH 44114-1271

Aiken Jay R. • Bridgeport Public Library • Bridgeport, CT 06604

Aiken Mary Miss • Children's Librarian • Greenville County Library • Greenville, SC 29601 • ALSC ASCLA LAMA PLA RASD YALSA   *Life*

Aiken Sheila • Library Media Specialist • Underhill Central School • Underhill Center, VT 05490 • AASL

Aikens Antonell K. • Trustee • District of Columbia Public Library Martin Luther King Memorial Library • Washington, DC 20001

Aikin Louisa A. • Scottsdale, AZ 85258

Aikman Nancy R. • Librarian I • Alberta Research Council Devon Branch Library • Devon AB, T0C 1E0 Canada

Aillet-Crochet Jan • Librarian • Our Lady of Fatima School • Lafayette, LA 70503 • AASL

Ailslieger Sharon • Wichita, KS 67235

Ainslie Karen L. • Carmel, IN 46032

Airoldi Melissa • Technical Services Librarian • Austin Community College DAO LRS • Austin, TX 78752 • LITA

Airozo Diana • Washington, DC 20009 • SRRT

Airth Elizabeth J. • Librarian • University of Texas Libraries General Libraries • Austin, TX 78713-7330 • ACRL

Aissing Alena • University of Florida Libraries • Gainesville, FL 32611 • ACRL

Aitkens Jane E H • McGill University Library Systems Office • Montreal PQ, H3A 1Y1 Canada • ACRL LITA

Aivaliotis Vasilios A. • Reference Librarian • Incarnate Word College Library Saint Pius X Library • San Antonio, TX 78209 • ACRL

Ajami Sandra A. • Technical Services Librarian • Warner Pacific College Otto F. Linn Library • Portland, OR 97215

Ajibero Matthew I. Dr. • Bayero University • Kano, Nigeria W. Africa

Ajifu Beth C. • Student • University of Hawaii School of Library & Information Studies • Honolulu, HI 96822 • RASD IFRT SRRT

Akana Sandra • Kailua, HI 96734

Akard Linda B. • Technical Services Librarian • Virginia Intermont College J. F. Hicks Library • Bristol, VA 24201 • ALCTS

Ake Janet L. • Farmers Branch Public Library • Farmers Branch, TX 75234 • ALSC YALSA

Ake Mary • Head Librarian • Whitman Elementary School Library • Littleton, CO 80120 • AASL

Aked Michael J. • Lansing, MI 48911 • RASD LIRT

Akeman Maryjo • Trustee • Granite City Public Library District • Granite City, IL 62040

Akenhead Lisa M. • Student • University of Pittsburgh School of Library and Information Science • Pittsburgh, PA 15260

Aker Julia Kathleen • Children's Librarian • Jackson County Public Library • Seymour, IN 47274 • ALSC

Akerlof Carol R. • Washtenaw Community College • Ann Arbor, MI 48106

Akers Judith A. • Librarian • Oakton School • Evanston, IL 60202 • AASL

Akerson Amelia • Librarian • Upton Town Library • Upton, MA 01568

Akins Neil W. • Head Librarian • Stony Brook School • Stony Brook, NY 11790

Akinwole Barbara S. • Reference Business Serv. Cons. • North Carolina State Library • Raleigh, NC 27601-2807 • PLA RASD

Al-Husaini Pamela P. • Alvord, TX 76225 • AASL ACRL

Al Sadat Amira A. H. • Cataloger • University of Pittsburgh Hillman Library • Pittsburgh, PA 15260 • ILERT IRRT

Al-Adwani Jamila • Student • Columbia University School of Library Service • New York, NY 10027

Al-Aghbary Mohamed • Educator • Educational Research & Development Center • Sana'a, Yemen • AASL ALCTS PLA

Al-Arfaj Khaled A. • Student • Indiana University School of Library and Information Science • Bloomington, IN 47405

Al-Ashqar Mohammed M. • Student • Texas Woman's University School of Library & Information Studies • Denton, TX 76204

Al-Dobaian Saad A. • Assistant Professor • King Saud University College of Arts • Riyakh, Saudi Arabia • ACRL ALCTS PLA

Al-Mufaraji Moosa N. • Reference Librarian • Sultan Qaboos University Library • Muscat, Sultanate, Oman

Al-Qallaf Charlene L. • Al-diayah 35451, Kuwait • ACRL ALCTS LAMA RASD

Al-Qattan Ahmad M. • Director of Libraries • Qatar University Library • Doha, Qatar • ACRL ALCTS LAMA LITA RASD

Al-Wardi Mohammed • Deputy Director • Sultan Qaboos University Library • Muscat, Sultanate, Oman • LITA

AlFaramawy Gamaluddin M. • Librarian • King Abdulaziz Public Library • Riyadh 11622, Saudi Arabia • ACRL

Ala Judy Mrs. • Librarian • Glenbard West High School Library • Glen Ellyn, IL 60137

Alabaster Carol • Collection Development Coor. • Phoenix Public Library • Phoenix, AZ 85004

Alaimo Rosina R. • School Library Media Specialist • Maple West Elementary School • Williamsville, NY 14221 • AASL

Alamillo Joseph • Trustee • Hammond Public Library • Hammond, IN 46320 • ALTA

Alan Robert • Head,Serials Department • University of California Shields Library • Davis, CA 95616 • ALCTS LAMA LITA

Alanen-Mosher Robin L. • Librarian • Battle Creek Health System Professional Library • Battle Creek, MI 49016 • ASCLA

Alaniz Miguel J.C. • Library Director • City of Inglewood Public Library • Inglewood, CA 90301-1771 • PLA

Alarid Jeanette M. • Librarian III • Phoenix Public Library Yucca Branch • Phoenix, AZ 85015 • PLA

Alatorre Yiyuk E. • El Paso, TX 79949

Alban Barbara E. • Datalib Program Manager • Centel Federal Systems, Inc. • Reston, VA 22091-1506 • LITA

Albanese Jeanne M. • Northeastern University School of Law Library • Boston, MA 02115 • ACRL ALCTS

Albang Betty A. • Petaluma, CA 94954 • AASL

Albano Christine A. • Librarian II • Cleveland Public Library Eastman Branch • Cleveland, OH 44111

Albaugh Sandra N. • Librarian • Carol Morgan School • Sant Domingo, Dominican Republic • AASL ALSC

Albee Barbara L. • Student • University of Pittsburgh School of Library and Information Science • Pittsburgh, PA 15260

Alberi Elaine L. • Library Media Specialist • Traphagen School • Mt. Vernon, NY 10552 • AASL

Alberico Ralph • Head of Undergraduate Library • University of Texas Libraries General Libraries • Austin, TX 78713-7330 • ACRL LITA

Albers Jacqueline M. • Cuyahoga County Public Library Parma-Snow Branch • Parma, OH 44134-2789 • ALSC

Albert Ann L. • K-8 Librarian • Prairie Valley Community School • Farnhamville, IA 50538

Albert Myra F. • Voorheesville, NY 12186

Albert Robin P. • Herndon, VA 22070 • LITA

Albert Ronald E. • Directort • Long Beach City College • Long Beach, CA 90808 • ACRL ALCTS LITA *Life*

Albertine Mary Ann • Librarian • Harwich Elementary School • Harwich, MA 02645 • AASL ALSC

Alberts Edith C. • Student • Rutgers University School of Communication Information & Library Studies • New Brunswick, NJ 08903

Albertson Christopher • City Librarian • Tyler Public Library • Tyler, TX 75702 • PLA

Albertson Joan G. • Student • Southern Connecticut State University School of Libray Science & Instructional Technology • New Haven, CT 06515

Albin Lynn • Student • Northern Illinois University Department of Library & Information Studies • DeKalb, IL 60115

Albin Michael W. • Chief Order Division • Library of Congress • Washington, DC 20541 • ACRL IRRT LHRT

Albitz Rebecca S. • Media Services Librarian • University of Iowa Libraries • Iowa City, IA 52242-1379 • ACRL VRT

Albosta Diane H. • Director • Episcopal High School • Alexandria, VA 22302 • AASL

Albotins Ilga E. • Student • University of Western Ontario School of Library & Information Science • London ON, N6G 1H1 Canada • ACRL IFRT SRRT

Albracht J. Thomas • Manhattan, KS 66502

Albrecht Cheryl C. • Head, Langsam Library Services • University of Cincinnati • Cincinnati, OH 45221-0033 • ACRL RASD LIRT

Albrecht Lisa A. • Dubuque, IA 52001-4357 • ALSC

Albrecht Lois K. • Consultant • Foresight Inc Planning & Development Consultants • Camp Hill, PA 17011 • ALTA ASCLA LAMA PLA CLENE

Albrecht Mary L. • Media Specialist • Dixie Hollins High School Library • St Petersburg, FL 33709 • YALSA

Albrecht Sterling J. • Director • Brigham Young University Harold B. Lee Library • Provo, UT 84602 • ACRL

Albrethsen Karen • Spring Creek Elementary School • Elko, NV 89801 • AASL LITA

Albright Bruce • Dallas, TX 75230

Albright Carol R. • Tallahassee, FL 32303

Albright Corabelle L. • Big Pine, CA 93513

Albright Elaine M. • Director • University of Maine Raymond H. Fogler Library • Orono, ME 04469 • ACRL LITA

Albright Eric D. • Reference Librarian • Northwestern University Galter Health Sciences Library • Chicago, IL 60611 • ACRL RASD

Albright Esta Lee • Public Service Librarian • Hartnell College Library-Media Technology • Salinas, CA 93901

Albright John B. • Online Computer Systems Inc. • Germantown, MD 20874 • ACRL ALCTS LITA RASD LHRT LRRT *Life*

Albright Karin Zitzewitz • Cataloging Dept. Intern • University of Chicago Library • Chicago, IL 60637-1502 • ALCTS

Albright Penny E. • Team Leader • DYNIX Inc. • Provo, UT 84606 • PLA

Albright Rick • Jakarta 12430, Indonesia • AASL

Albright Thomas E. • E Lansing, MI 48823 • Life

Albritton Nancy F • Young Adult Librarian • East Baton Rouge Parish Library • Baton Rouge, LA 70806-7699 • YALSA

Albritton Rosie L. • University of Illinois Graduate School of Library and Information Science • Urbana, IL 61801 • ACRL LAMA

Albury Karen S. • Director • Milton-Union Public Library • West Milton, OH 45383 • PLA

Albyn Carole L. • Friendswood, TX 77546-3401

Alcaraz Emilia R • Gainesville, FL 32609

Alcorn Cynthia W. • Librarian • Grand Lodge Of Massachusetts Ancient Free & Accepted Masons Library • Boston, MA 02111 • ACRL ALCTS RASD

Alcott Martha • Chappaqua Library • Chappaqua, NY 10514

Alden Gail M. • Branch Manager • Jefferson County Public Library Evergreen Branch • Evergreen, CO 80439 • IFRT

Alderfer Jane B. • Archivist Librarian • Childrens Museum • Oak Ridge, TN 37830

Alderman Belle Dr. • Senior Lecturer in Librarianship • University of Canberra • Belconnen ACT 2616, Australia

Alderman Patricia L. • Fort Myer Library • Ft. Myer Library, VA 22211-5050 • PLA AFLRT FLRT

Alderson Karen A. • Marion, IA 52302

Aldred Richard W. • Catalog Librarian • Haverford College James P. Magill Library • Haverford, PA 19041 • IRRT

Aldrich Duncan M. • Sparks, NV 89434 • ACRL GODORT

Aldrich Jerry • Whitemore Asst. Manager • Salt Lake County Library System • Salt Lake City, UT 84121-3188 • ALSC LITA PLA RASD YALSA ERT

Aldrich Linda Wilson • Librarian • Fireman's Fund Insurance Library • Novato, CA 94998 • AASL

Aldridge Betsy B. Ph.D. • Shawnee, OK 74801-1626 • ACRL IFRT LRRT SRRT

Aldridge Deanne • Librarian • Dahlstrom Middle School • Buda, TX 78610 • AASL IFRT

Aldridge Ethel S. • California State Library • Sacramento, CA 94237-0001

Aldridge Jacquelin C. • Student • University of California-Berkeley School of Library & Information Studies • Berkeley, CA 94720

Aldridge Marie Harris • Supervising Director • District of Columbia Public Schools • Washington, DC 20020 • AASL

Aldrman Sylvia J,. • Librarian • J. L. Stanford Middle School • Palo Alto, CA 94306 • AASL

Aleccia Janet A. • Librarian • Joint Commission • Oak Brook Terrace, IL 60181

Aleman Diana M. • Film Librarian • Atlanta-Fulton Public Library • Atlanta, GA 30303 • PLA IFRT

Alesandrini Barbara • Berkeley, CA 94703 • RASD IFRT NMRT

Alessi Dana L. • Dir. Ntl Academic Sales • Baker & Taylor Books • Charlotte, NC 28217 • ACRL ALCTS LAMA

Alevizos Theodore Esq • Alevizos & Alevizos • Boston, MA 02108 • ACRL LAMA *Life*

Alexa Cynthia M. • Regional Children's Serv Mgr • Cuyahoga County Public Library Maple Heights Regional Branch • Maple Heights, OH 44137 • ALSC

Alexander-Manifold Alan B. • Systems Implementation Manager • Purdue University • West Lafayette, IN 47907 • LITA

Alexander Adrian W. • Faxon Company Inc. • Westwood, MA 02090 • ACRL ALCTS LITA

Alexander Barbara B. • Head, Documents/Maps • Texas A & M University Sterling C. Evans Library • College Station, TX 77843-5000 • ACRL LAMA GODORT NMRT

Alexander Barbara J. • Library Trustee • Zion-Benton Public Library District • Zion, IL 60099

Alexander Carolyn Inez • Chief Librarian • United States Army Technical Information Center • Ft. Hunter Liggett, CA 93928-5021 • LAMA LITA *Life*

Alexander Constance • Technical Services Librarian • Douglas County Library • Minden, NV 89423

Alexander E. Mona • Saint Petersburg, FL 33705 • Continuing

Alexander Elinor • Berkeley, CA 94708 • GODORT

Alexander Helen Davis • Father Ryan High School • Nashville, TN 37204-3500 • AASL

Alexander Jamie S. • Student • Drexel University College of Information Studies • Philadelphia, PA 19104-2875 • LITA IFRT SRRT

Alexander Janet E. • Student • Widener University Wolfgram Library • Chester, PA 19013

Alexander Jean • Regional Adminstrator • County of Los Angeles Public Library West County Region 300 • Carson, CA 90745 • LAMA PLA

Alexander Jean M. • Northwestern University Library • Evanston, IL 60208-2300 • ACRL

Alexander Joan • Trustee • Commack Public Library District • Commack, NY 11725 • ALTA

Alexander Johanna A. • Reference Documents Librarian • California State University • Bakersfield, CA 93311

Alexander Judith L. • School Librarian • Edmonds School District • Lynnwood, WA 98036-7400

Alexander Julie S. • Asst Dir for Clln Devel • University of Texas at Arlington • Arlington, TX 76019-0497 • ALCTS

Alexander Karen E. • Librarian • Miami Tribe of Oklahoma • Miami, OK 74355 • ASCLA

Alexander Laurel • New York, NY 10304 • IFRT

Alexander Lee C. • University of Wisconsin-Milwaukee School of Library & Information Science • Milwaukee, WI 53201

Alexander Lesley B. • Student • University of California Los Angeles Graduate School of Library & Information Science • Los Angeles, CA 90024 • PLA IFRT SRRT

Alexander Linda • Mt. Ranier, MD 20712

Alexander Linda Baldwin • Teaching Fellowship • East Carolina University Joyner Library • Greenville, NC 27858-4353

Alexander Liz C. • Documents Coordinator • Illinois State Library • Springfield, IL 62701-1796 • ALCTS GODORT

Alexander Margaret K. • Veterinary Medical Librarian • Tuskegee University • Tuskegee Institute, AL 36088 • ACRL

Alexander Marian L. • Head of Technical Services • Western Washington University Wilson Library • Bellingham, WA 98225 • ACRL ALCTS

Alexander Mary H. • Englewood, FL 34223

Alexander Rachel • Columbus, OH 43214 • AASL ALSC

Alexander Rebecca • Settle, WA 98118-1834

Alexander Shirley B. • Documents Librarian • Abilene Christian University Margaret & Herman Brown Library • Abilene, TX 79699 • GODORT

Alexander Stacie L. • Student • University of North Carolina at Chapel Hill School of Information and Library Science • Chapel Hill, NC 27599-3360 • PLA

Alexander Susanna • Jefferson City, MO 65109 • Continuing

Alexander Suzanne E. • Kokomo Tribune • Kokomo, IN 46901

Alexander Virginia Alice • Descriptive Cataloging Division • Library of Congress • Washington, DC 20541 • ACRL ALCTS *Life*

Alexander William D. • Director • South Portland Public Library • South Portland, ME 04106 • PLA YALSA

Alfano Bernadine M. • Trustee • Crestwood Public Library District • Crestwood, IL 60445

Alfano Joseph A. • Trustee • Crestwood Public Library District • Crestwood, IL 60445

Alfieri Cindy R. • Student • University of California-Berkeley School of Library & Information Studies • Berkeley, CA 94720 • LITA CLENE IRRT LHRT LRRT NMRT

Alfonso Ernesto L. Mr. • Ft. Lauderdale, FL 33312

Alfonso Milagros M. • Librarian • Roosevelt School • New Brunswick, NJ 08901 • AASL

Alford Kathleen E. • Librarian Administrative Serv. • Largo Public Library • Largo, FL 34640

Alford Larry P. • Assoc Univ Ln for Admin Services • University of North Carolina Walter Royal Davis Library • Chapel Hill, NC 27599-3924 • ACRL LAMA

Alford Mary A. • Assistant Director • Brazoria County Library System • Angleton, TX 77515 • ALSC

Alford Sylvia L. • Baltimore County Public Library • Towson, MD 21204

Alford Thomas E. • Assistant City Librarian • Los Angeles Public Library • Los Angeles, CA 90071 • ACRL LAMA PLA YALSA EMIERT ERT IFRT SRRT *Life*

Algaze Selma • Adult/Reference Services Coor. • Broward County Division of Libraries Broward County Library • Fort Lauderdale, FL 33301 • LAMA PLA

Alger Beatrice • District Librarian • United States Army Corps of Engineers • Sacramento, CA 95814

Alger Sallie J. • Reference Associate • Andrews University James White Library • Berrien Springs, MI 49104-1400

Alghamdi Saad A. • Student • Indiana University School of Library and Information Science • Bloomington, IN 47405

Algier-Baxter Aimee T. • Librarian • Santa Clara University Michel Orradre Library • Santa Clara, CA 95053

Alhadeff Norma R. • Librarian • Atlanta International School • Atlanta, GA 30342 • AASL

Ali Farooq • Santa Clara, CA 95051

Ali Rajah • San Bernardino, CA 92405

Ali Shamim • Subject Specialist & Collector • Metropolitan Toronto Library • Toronto ON, M4W 2G8 Canada • ACRL

Aliapoulios Janet • Resource Center Director • Greeley School • Winnetka, IL 60201 • AASL ALSC

Alibhai Mehrun • Cataloging Librarian • Carleton University Library • Ottawa ON, K1S 5J7 Canada • LITA

Alice Marie Sr. • Librarian • Saint Mary Our Mother School • Horseheads, NY 14845

Alikhan Victoria • Library Associate • Chicago Public Library West Addison Branch • Chicago, IL 60634

Aliprand Joan M. • Library System Analyst • Research Libraries Group Inc. (RLG) • Mountain View, CA 94041-1100 • LITA IRRT

Alire Camila A. • Dean • University of Colorado at Denver Auraria Library • Denver, CO 80204 • ACRL LAMA

Alire Wilifred L. • Librariain • Kings River Cmnty College Library • Reedley, CA 93654

Alix Cleta M. • Campbell, CA 95008-3136

Alkaabi Mohammed A. • Student • University of Arizona Graduate Library School • Tucson, AZ 85721 • AASL ALSC

Alkhoudairy Merveit • Manager • Denver Public Library • Denver, CO 80204-2602 • ALTA

Alkhoudairy Tawfik • Reference Librarian • Kern County Library Taft Branch • Taft, CA 93268 • PLA

Alkire Cheryl • Librarian • Post Falls Junior High School • Post Falls, ID 83854

Allaback Patricia A. • Librarian • Cate School McBean Library • Carpinteria, CA 93014-5005 • AASL LIRT

Allain Alex P. • Trustee • Saint Mary Parish Library • Franklin, LA 70538 • AASL ACRL ALCTS ALSC ALTA ASCLA LAMA LITA RASD YALSA *Honorary*

Allan Ann • Assistant Professor • Kent State University School of Library & Information Science • Kent, OH 44242-0001 • ALCTS LRRT

Allan Ann P. • Falmouth, ME 04105

Allan Joyce E. • Huntington, WV 25705 • AASL

Allan Linda L. • Catalog Unit Supervisior • Western Kentucky University Helm-Cravens Library • Bowling Green, KY 42101 • ACRL

Allan Margaret H. • Cataloger • University of Pennsylvania Library Van Pelt-Dietrich Library Center • Philadelphia, PA 19104-6206 • ACRL ALCTS

Allan Mark A. • Student • University of North Texas School of Library & Information Sciences • Denton, TX 76203 • ACRL NMRT

Allan Nancy P. • Reference Librarian • Barrington Public Library District • Barrington, IL 60010

Allan Pamela G. • Circulation Librarian • Northfield Mount Hermon School Dolben Library • Northfield, MA 01360 • AASL

Allard Paul • Librarian • Fairfax County Public Library George Mason Regional Branch • Annandale, VA 22003 • ALCTS

Allard Winona • Director • Santa Monica Public Library • Santa Monica, CA 90401 • PLA

Allcock Jana C. • Student • Texas Woman's University School of Library & Information Studies • Denton, TX 76204

Allcorn Linda G. • Director • Boonslick Regional Library • Sedalia, MO 65301 • PLA

Alldredge Noreen S. • Dean • Montana State University • Bozeman, MT 59717-0332 • ACRL LAMA

Alldridge Laura A. • Catalog Maintenance Supervisor • Cuyahoga County Public Library • Cleveland, OH 44134-2792

Allee Cathy A. • Children's Librarian • Santa Maria Public Library • Santa Maria, CA 93454

Alleman Kathryn L. • Portsmouth Public Library • Portsmouth, NH 03801

Alleman Steve • Associate Librarian • University of New Orleans Earl K. Long Library • New Orleans, LA 70148 • RASD

Allen-Flaherty Barbara A. • Director • Billerica Public Library • Billerica, MA 01821

Allen-Olsen Dena G. • Info Spec Tele Ref • Salt Lake County Library System • Salt Lake City, UT 84121-3188 • ALSC PLA CLENE

Allen Alice J. • Asst Univ Lb Tech Serv • University of Oregon Library • Eugene, OR 97403-1299 • ALCTS LAMA LITA

Allen Anne • Librarian • U S Navy Naval Base L • Charleston, SC 29407

Allen Barbara • Networkiong Consultant • Illinois State Library • Springfield, IL 62701-1796 • ALCTS ASCLA

Allen Barbara F.H. • Reference Librarian • University of Northern Iowa Donald O. Rod Library • Cedar Falls, IA 50613-3675 • ACRL

Allen Bonnie J. • Beaverton, OR 97006 • ACRL ALCTS LAMA LITA

Allen Bryce L. • Assistant Professor • University of Illinois Graduate School of Library and Information Science • Urbana, IL 61801 • ACRL RASD

Allen Caroline A. • Library Director • Sumner Memorial High School • East Sullivan, ME 04607 • PLA

Allen Carolyn • Head of Children's Dept. • Farmington Community Library • Farmington Hills, MI 48334

Allen Cassandra R. • Head of Collection Access Sect. • National Library of Medicine • Bethesda, MD 20894 • ACRL LAMA

Allen Catherine • Ann Arbor, MI 48104 • ACRL PLA RASD IFRT

Allen Christina Young • Director of Technical Services • Glen Ellyn Public Library • Glen Ellyn, IL 60137 • LAMA

Allen Christine • Sales & Marketing Mgr. • University Products, Inc. • Holyoke, MA 01041 • ALCTS

Allen Christine M. • Riverside Unified School District • Riverside, CA 92506

Allen Constance E. • Trustee • Zion-Benton Public Library District • Zion, IL 60099

Allen David R. • Lutherville, MD 21093

Allen David Y. • Associate Librarian • State University of New York (SUNY) Frank Melville Jr. Memorial Library • Stony Brook, NY 11794-3300 • ACRL GODORT MAGERT

Allen Debra • Orangeburg County Library • Orangeburg, SC 29115-1367 • LITA

Allen Diane • Assistant Professor • University of North Texas • Denton, TX 76203 • AASL

Allen Donald R. • Humanities Reference Librarian • Saint Louis Public Library • St. Louis, MO 63103-2389

Allen Dorothy B. • Santa Fe, NM 87501-4149 • ASCLA YALSA *Life*

Allen Dorothy L W • Downers Grv, IL 60516

Allen Edna Dr. • Trustee • East Saint Louis Public Library • East St. Louis, IL 62201 • ALTA

Allen Edward S. • Student • Louisiana State University School of Library & Information Science • Baton Rouge, LA 70803-3290 • PLA SRRT

Allen Edwin J. • Acquisition Librarian • Wesleyan University Olin Memorial Library • Middletown, CT 06459 • ACRL

Allen Eileen E. • Marcellus, NY 13108

Allen Elizabeth R. • Director • Schlow Memorial Library • State College, PA 16801 • ALSC LAMA PLA RASD

Allen Forrest P. • Student • University of South Carolina College of Library & Information Science • Columbia, SC 29208 • SRRT

Allen Frances Ott • German Cataloger • University of Cincinnati Langsam Library • Cincinnati, OH 45221-0033 • ACRL ALCTS LHRT

Allen Francis P. • Sarasota, FL 33577 • Continuing

Allen Frank R. • Research Assistant • University of Tennessee-Knoxville Graduate School of Library & Information Science • Knoxville, TN 37996-4330

Allen Gloria • Trustee • Pine Mountain Regional Library • Manchester, GA 31816

Allen James A. • Little Rock, AR 72211

Allen Joan C. • Assistant Librarian • Old Sturbridge Village Research Library • Sturbridge, MA 01566-0200 • ACRL

Allen Justus P. Jr. • Librarian • Woburn Senior High School Harlow Library • Woburn, MA 01801 • AASL

Allen Karen B. • Student • University of Kentucky College of Library & Information Science • Lexington, KY 40506-0391

Allen Karyn • Social Law Library • Boston, MA 02108 • LITA

Allen Kathy H. • Librarian • Griffithville Public School • Griffithville, AR 72060 • AASL

Allen Kay C. • Branch Collection Manager • Cleveland Public Library • Cleveland, OH 44114-1271 • PLA

Allen Laurie C. • Head, Stevenson Library • Vanderbilt University Library • Nashville, TN 37240-0007 • ACRL LAMA

Allen Lenore M. • Brooklyn Public Library Williamsburg Branch • Brooklyn, NY 11240

Allen Lucia W. • Alicia, AR 72410 • AASL

Allen Luella S. • Head, Media Services Department • University of Delaware Morris Library • Newark, DE 19717-5267 • ACRL ALCTS VRT

Allen Lynne B. • Oviedo, FL 32765

Allen M. Kathryn • Director • Justice Public Library • Justice, IL 60458 • RASD

Allen Magaret Joy • El Granada, CA 94018

Allen Marjorie • Smithville High School Smithville Junior High School • Smithville, TX 78957 • AASL YALSA

Allen Mary Beth • University of Illinois Library • Urbana, IL 61801 • ACRL ASCLA IRRT

Allen Mary M. • Student • University of Arizona Graduate Library School • Tucson, AZ 85721

Allen Maureen A. • North Tonawanda, NY 14120 • RASD IFRT

Allen Maxine B. • Trustee • Johnson County Library • Shawnee Mission, KS 66201 • ALTA

Allen Melody L. • Supv., Young Readers Services • Rhode Island Department of State Library Services • Providence, RI 02903-4222 • ALSC

Allen Mildred J. • Lake Shore Middle School • Jacksonville, FL 32210 • AASL

Allen Myrna • Br Hd • Dayton & Montgomery County Public Library Burkhardt Avenue Branch • Dayton, OH 45431 • ALSC

Allen Nancy H. • Dean of the Library • University of Denver Penrose Library • Denver, CO 80208 • ACRL LAMA

Allen Norene F. • Marcive, Inc. • San Antonio, TX 78265 • LITA

Allen Pamela K. • Student • University of North Texas School of Library & Information Sciences • Denton, TX 76203

Allen Patricia J. • Director • Sanibel Public Library • Sanibel, FL 33957 • LAMA PLA

Allen Robert P. • Incarnate Word College • San Antonio, TX 78209-9367

Allen Robert S. • Physics/Earth & Atmosphere Ln. • Purdue University Libraries • West Lafayette, IN 47907 • ACRL MAGERT

Allen Ronald • Director • Washington University Libraries • Saint Louis, MO 63130-4899 • ACRL RASD

Allen Rose M. • Library Assistant • Mount Prospect Public Library • Mount Prospect, IL 60056

Allen Sandra D. • Coordinator of Cataloging Serv. • Kutztown University Rohrbach Library • Kutztown, PA 19530-0721 • ACRL LITA

Allen Sandra E. • Resources Librarian • Poynter Institute for Media Studies • St. Petersburg, FL 33701 • LITA

Allen Sandra L. • Minneapolis, MN 55417 • ACRL

Allen Sarah E. • Spartanburg, SC 29302 • ACRL

Allen Sharon • Director • Humbolt County Library • Winnemucca, NV 89445 • PLA

Allen Sharon A. • Student • Syracuse University School of Information Studies • Syracuse, NY 13244-4100 • ACRL

Allen Sharon M. • Manlius, NY 13104

Allen Sharon S. • Student • Wright State University • Dayton, OH 45435 • AASL LITA

Allen Stanley R. • Social Law Library • Boston, MA 02108 • ALCTS

Allen Stephanie O. • Phoenix, AZ 85003-1245

Allen Susan M. • Head, Special Collections • Claremont Colleges Libraries Honnold/Mudd Library • Claremont, CA 91711 • ACRL

Allen Susan M. • Director of Libraries • The Nichols Middle School • Buffalo, NY 14216 • AASL

Allen Suzan G. • Trustee • Lafayette Parish Public Library • Lafayette, LA 70502-3427 • ALTA

Allen Vicki M • Freedom, CA 95019

Allen Virginia M. • Systems Coordinator • Lamar University Gray Library • Beaumont, TX 77710 • LAMA LITA

Allen Walter C. • Associate Professor Emeritus • University of Illinois Graduate School of Library and Information Science • Urbana, IL 61801 • LAMA IFRT

Allen Wendy L. • Librarian II • Enoch Pratt Free Library Hamilton Branch • Baltimore, MD 21214

Allender Robert K. • Regional Librarian • Kentucky Department for Libraries & Archives Lake Cumberland Regional Office • Columbia, KY 42728-1487 • PLA

Allensworth James H. • Reference Librarian • Mountain Valley Library System • Sacramento, CA 95814 • RASD

Allerhand Lorraine • Cataloger • University of Southern California • Los Angeles, CA 90033 • ALCTS

Allerton Ellen M. • Raleigh, NC 27612-6501

Allex Wendy K. • Head of Cataloging • Lee County Library System Processing Center • Fort Myers, FL 33912 • ALCTS

Alley Brian • Dean of Library Services • Sangamon State University Norris L. Brookens Library • Springfield, IL 62794-9243 • ACRL ALCTS

Alley Katherine S. • Machias, ME 04654

Alliprandine Judith Neale • Head, Acquisitions Unit. • Jefferson County Public Library Library Service Center • Wheat Ridge, CO 80033 • ALCTS

Allison Anne Marie • Director of Libraries • University of Central Florida Library • Orlando, FL 32816-0666 • ACRL LAMA IFRT

Allison Beverly E. • Teacher/Librarian • Tusculum View Elementary School • Greeneville, TN 37743

Allison Claudia A. • Bonny Kate Elementary School • Knoxville, TN 37920

Allison Dee Ann K. • Serials Librarian • University of Nebraska Love Library • Lincoln, NE 68588-0410 • ACRL ALCTS

Allison Evelyn F. • Reference Librarian • Bucks County Community College Library • Newtown, PA 18940-0999 • ACRL RASD GODORT IFRT SRRT

Allison Peter B. • Social Science Bibliographer • University of Connecticut Homer Babbidge Library • Storrs, CT 06269-1005 • ACRL ALCTS GODORT

Allison Scott • Librarian • University of Alberta Cameron Library • Edmonton AB, T6G 2J8 Canada • ACRL

Allison Susan • Librarian • Lewiston High School • Lewiston, ME 04240 • AASL

Allison Susan • Richardson Public Library • Richardson, TX 75080

Allison Terri M. • Librarian • Carrollton Public Library • Carrollton, TX 75006 • RASD NMRT

Allison Terry L. • Collection Librarian • California State University San Marcos • San Marcos, CA 92069-0001 • ACRL ALCTS IRRT SRRT

Allison Theodore R. • Director • Bellevue Public Library • Bellevue, OH 44811

Allman Meribeth • Bowie, MD 20715

Allman Miriam H. • Boston, MA 02116 • ACRL ALCTS LITA IFRT

Allman Nadine C. • Library Assisant II • Chemeketa Community College • Salem, OR 97309

Allmand Linda F. • Director • Fort Worth Public Library • Fort Worth, TX 76102 • LAMA IFRT

Allmond Linette V. • Supervising Librarian • New York Public Library Melrose Branch • Bronx, NY 10451

Allon Robert B. Dr. • Bellcore • Morristown, NJ 07920 • LITA

Alloway James E. • University of Michigan Libraries • Ann Arbor, MI 48109-1205 • ACRL LITA

Allred Curtis • Honolulu, HI 96822 • PLA

Allred Vanessa L. • Student • Florida State University School of Library and Information Studies • Tallahassee, FL 32306-2048

Allsop Mary Beth • Supv., Technical Services • Lorain Public Library • Lorain, OH 44052 • ALCTS

Allsup-Miller Judith M. • Student • University of Rhode Island Graduate School of Library & Information Studies • Kingston, RI 02881-0815 • ALCTS

Allwardt Richard E. • Assistant Director • Mansfield-Richland County Public Library • Mansfield, OH 44902-1295 • LAMA

Allyn Anderson A. Sr. • Trustee • Geauga County Public Library • Chardon, OH 44024

Alman Susan Webreck • University of Pittsburgh School of Library and Information Science • Pittsburgh, PA 15260 • LAMA

Almarez Carol S. • Eagle Rock, VA 24085 • AASL

Almarzouk Martha Garcia • Extension Services Coordinator • Santa Ana Public Library • Santa Ana, CA 92701 • LAMA EMIERT

Almeroth Lillian • Library Trustee • Bellwood Public Library • Bellwood, IL 60104 • ALTA

Almes June • Assoc. Prof. • Lock Haven Univ of Pennsylvania Stevenson Library • Lock Haven, PA 17745 • AASL

Almgren Shelly D. • Assistant Librarian • Panhandle State University • Goodwell, OK 73939

Almony Robert A. • Asst Dir for Adm Serv • University of Missouri Libraries-Columbia Elmer Ellis Library • Columbia, MO 65201-5149 • ACRL LAMA

Almquist Alison E. • School Librarian • Wherry Elementary School Inez Elementary School • Albuquerque, NM 87106 • AASL ALSC

Alms Brian R • Kankakee Junior High School • Kankakee, IL 60901 • AASL YALSA

Almstedt Kirsten Ann • Children's Librarian • Burlington Public Library • Burlington, WA 98233-1998

Almy Iris E. • Cumberland, ME 04021 • ALCTS RASD *Continuing*

Alonso Cynthia G. • Tampa, FL 33610

Alonzi Mary S. • Wilmette, IL 60091

Alonzo Shirley P. • Librarian I • Chicago Public Library • Chicago, IL 60605 • PLA

Alper Barbara J. • Director • Bergen Community Coll • Paramus, NJ 07652 • ACRL RASD

Alper Jerry W. • President • Jerry Alper Inc • Eastchester, NY 10707 • ACRL

Alper Laurie C. • Reference Librarian • New Haven Free Public Library • New Haven, CT 06510

Alpert Mark R. • Staff Development/Soc Sci Biblio • Brandeis University Goldfarb Library • Waltham, MA 02254 • ACRL

Alqudsi Taghreed • Professor • Kuwait University • Al-Khalidia, Kuwait • LITA

Alred Clayton Dr. • Associate Dean of LRC • Odessa College M H Fly Learning Resource Center • Odessa, TX 79764 • ACRL ALCTS LAMA LITA RASD IFRT LIRT SRRT

Alrutz Thomas J. • Assoc. Dir. Central Lib Servs. • The New York Public Library • New York, NY 10016 • LAMA PLA

Alsbury Donna D. • User Services Librarian • Florida Center for Library Automation • Gainesville, FL 32609 • ACRL ALCTS LITA

Alsfeld Vincent Mrs. • Head Librarian • Wilton Public-Gregg Free Library • Wilton, NH 03086

Alshanbari Humod A. • Student • Indiana University School of Library and Information Science • Bloomington, IN 47405

Alsip James B. • Public Services Librarian • Baltimore County Public Library • Towson, MD 21204 • PLA

Alsip Sharon R. • Hampton, VA 23669

Alsobrook Anne K. • H Grady Bradshaw Chambers County Library • Valley, AL 36854

Alsop Joan B. • Trustee • Loudoun County Public Library • Leesburg, VA 22075 • ALTA

Alston Florence • Temple Hills, MD 20748 • AASL

Alston Gayle G. • Dallas, TX 75220

Alston Jane C. • Library Coordinator • Southwestern Educational Society • Mayaguez, PR 00683 • AASL

Alston Leonard R. • Trustee • Roosevelt Public Library • Roosevelt, NY 11575 • ALTA

Alston Mary Y. Ms. • Media Specialist • Northeast Guilford Senior High School • McLeansville, NC 27301 • AASL

Alston Paula Knoll • Reference Librarian • Chesapeake Public Library • Chesapeake, VA 23320 • PLA

Alston Regina L. • Philadelphia, PA 19141 • ALSC

Alston Sandra • Librarian • University of Toronto • Toronto ON, M5S 1A5 Canada • ACRL

Alston-Reeder Lizzie Ann • Head of Branch Services • High Point Public Library • High Point, NC 27261 • PLA EMIERT

Alsum Mariann B. • Reference Librarian • Saint Mary's College Fitzgerald Library • Winona, MN 55987

Alsup Anne M. • Student • University of Rhode Island Graduate School of Library & Information Studies • Kingston, RI 02881-0815

Alsworth Frances W. • Edmond, OK 73034

Altan Susan • Library Director • Columbus School for Girls • Columbus, OH 43209 • AASL

Altemus Leard R. • Student • Syracuse University School of Information Studies • Syracuse, NY 13244-4100

Altenberger Alicja • Head Cataloger/Reference Ln. • Harvard University Gutman Library-Research Center • Cambridge, MA 02138 • ACRL ALCTS

Altenbernd Kerry D. • Lawrence, KS 66044-3729 • IFRT

Altenhofen Mary Clare • Assistant Librarian • Massachusetts Institute of Technology Libraries (MIT) • Cambridge, MA 02139 • ACRL IRRT

Alter Forrest H. • Ann Arbor, MI 48103 • Continuing

Alter Patricia A. • FPO, AP 96522-0002

Althage Jill • Cir Materials Ctr Coord/Ed Bibl • Northeastern Illinois University Library • Chicago, IL 60625 • ACRL

Altman Ellen • University of Arizona Graduate Library School • Tucson, AZ 85721 • PLA LRRT

Altman James A. • Student • Long Island University Palmer School of Library & Info. Sci. • Brookville, NY 11548

Altman Lillian Fried • San Diego, CA 92103 • Continuing

Altman Marie A. • Bridgeport, CT 06606 • Life

Altman Mary Anne • Supervising Librarian • New York Public Library Chatham Square Regional Branch • New York City, NY 10002 • PLA

Altmann Thomas F. • Librarian IV • Milwaukee Public Library • Milwaukee, WI 53233

Altoma Amal A. • Department Head/Circulation • Monroe County Public Library • Bloomington, IN 47408

Altomara Rita • Director • Fort Lee Public Library • Fort Lee, NJ 07024 • LAMA PLA RASD YALSA

Altschiller Donald • Bibliographic Services Librarian • Northeastern University • Boston, MA 02115 • ACRL RASD GODORT

Altschuler Jean P. • Arnold & Porter Library • Washington, DC 20036 • ALCTS LITA

Altshuler Alyssa • Student • University of South Carolina College of Library & Information Science • Columbia, SC 29208 • ACRL PLA AFLRT EMIERT FLRT

Altstadt Patricia A. • Library Media Specialist • Littleton Public Schools Franklin Elementary School • Littleton, CO 80121 • AASL

Altstatt Janice Lynne • Head of Acquisitions • University of Pennsylvania Library Van Pelt-Dietrich Library Center • Philadelphia, PA 19104-6206 • ALCTS

Altuna-Esteibar Belen • Spain Biblioteca Nacional • 28071 Madrid, Spain • LITA

Aluri Rao • Burr-Brown Corporate Library • Tucson, AZ 85734 • LITA

Aluzzo Adrienne A. • Detroit, MI 48224

Alva-Gerdes Aida E. • Student • University of New Mexico General Library • Albuquerque, NM 87131

Alvarado Meijuan Zou • Technical Services Librarian • Northern Arizona University Cline Library • Flagstaff, AZ 86011-6022

Alvarez-Galvan Irene • Senior Librarian • Los Angeles Public Library System Cahuenga Branch • Los Angeles, CA 90029 • PLA

Alvarez Amando M. • Student • Denver Public Library • Denver, CO 80203-2165

Alves Catherine Mello • East Providence, RI 02914

Alvin Glenda M. • Acq./Clln Devlp Libn • University of Central Arkansas Torreyson Library • Conway, AR 72032 • ALCTS

Alzawawi Altaf A. • Librarian • Kuwait Foundation for the Advancement of Sciences • Safat, 13113, Kuwait

Alzo Nancy A. • Senior Assistant Ln./Head Catlg. • State Univ of NY Coll at Potsdam Frederick W. Crumb Memorial Library • Potsdam, NY 13676 • ALCTS

Alzofon Sammy R. • St Petersburg, FL 33731-0743 • LITA RASD

AmRhein Richard • Music Librarian • University of Nevada-Las Vegas James R. Dickinson Library • Las Vegas, NV 89154 • ACRL

Amabile Helen M. • Dep Chief L Prog Div • U S Inf Agency • Washington, DC 20547 • IRRT

Amadife Nkechi G. • Student • University of Rhode Island Graduate School of Library & Information Studies • Kingston, RI 02881-0815

Amador Rochelle D. • Student • Wayne State University Library Science Program • Detroit, MI 48202

Amalaha Okezie E. • Atlanta, GA 30305

Amamasi Innocent C. • Student • Akwa Ibom University • Uyo, Nigeria W. Africa • ALCTS LITA

Aman Maryjo • Head, Educational & Cur. Clln • University of Wisconsin-Milwaukee Golda Meir Library • Milwaukee, WI 53201 • ALSC

Aman Mohammed • Dean • University of Wisconsin-Milwaukee School of Library & Information Science • Milwaukee, WI 53201 • ACRL ALCTS IRRT

Amann Michael R. • Baltimore County Public Library • Towson, MD 21204 • ALTA PLA

Amann Sharon A. • San Antonio, TX 78245 • ALSC PLA RASD AFLRT IFRT NMRT SRRT

Amara Margaret F. • Librarian • Center for Advanced Study in the Behavioral Sciences • Stanford, CA 94305

Amaral Anne • Catalog Librarian • University of Nevada-Reno Noble H. Getchell Library • Reno, NV 89557 • ACRL ALCTS LITA

Amari Francesca L. • Communications Manager • Grand Rapids Public Library • Grand Rapids, MI 49503-3093 • LAMA PLA IFRT NMRT

Amaru Paul F. • Librarian • Hackensack High School • Hackensack, NJ 07601 • AASL LITA

Amastae Sharon S. • Camino Real Middle School Library • El Paso, TX 79907 • AASL YALSA

Amata Benjamin T. • Government Documents Librarian • California State University-Sacramento Library • Sacramento, CA 95819-6039 • GODORT

Amato Kimberly Allen • Asst to the Dean, Cult Affairs • University of Maine Raymond H. Fogler Library • Orono, ME 04469 • LITA

Amato Sara E. • Assistant Librarian • Willamette University Mark O Hatfield Library • Salem, OR 97301 • LITA

Amaya Rene D. • Literacy Librarian • Los Angeles County Public Library • Downey, CA 90242

Ambardekar Raj P D • Librarian • Middle Georgia College Roberts Memorial Library • Cochran, GA 31014

Amberg Barbara A. • Student • San Mateo County Free Library System Sanchez Branch • Pacifica, CA 94044 • ALSC

Amberg Carol • Head Librarian • Burke, Williams & Sorensen • Los Angeles, CA 90017

Ambrose Carol • Adult Services • Worth Public Library District • Worth, IL 60482

Ambrose David W. • Media Director • Cuyahoga Heights High School • Cleveland, OH 44125 • AASL

Ambrose Diane L. • Director • Beaver County Federated Library System • Monaca, PA 15061 • PLA

Ambrose Ethel N. • Coordinator of Children's Serv • Central Arkansas Library System • Little Rock, AR 72201-4698 • ALSC PLA SRRT *Life*

Ambrose Mary Salter • West Hills, CA 91307

Ambrose Susan • Quintilla Geer Bruton Memorial Library • Plant City, FL 33566 • ALCTS

Amdursky Saul J. • Director • Kalamazoo Public Library • Kalamazoo, MI 49007-5270 • ASCLA LAMA LITA PLA

Ameel Jane Byers • Director • Waukesha Public Library • Waukesha, WI 53186 • LAMA PLA

Ameika Martha S. • Media Specialist • Mount Zion Elementary School • John's Island, SC 29455

Amelkin Brian A. • Student • Saint John's University Division of Library & Information Science • Jamaica, NY 11439 • PLA

Amelung Richard C. • Head of Technical Service • Saint Louis University Omer Poos Law Library • St. Louis, MO 63108-3478 • ACRL ALCTS

Amendola Michele M. • Extension Services Librarian • Napa City-County Library • Napa, CA 94559-3396 • PLA IFRT

Amer Rosalie C. • Automation/Technical Service Ln. • Cosumnes River College Library • Sacramento, CA 95823-5799 • ACRL ALCTS LITA IRRT

Amerman Ami D. • Student • Indiana University School of Library and Information Science • Bloomington, IN 47405

Ames Anne V • Evening Circulation Supervisor • Keene State College Mason Library • Keene, NH 03431 • ALCTS

Ames Charlotte A. • Bibliographer • University of Notre Dame Theodore M. Hesburgh Library • Notre Dame, IN 46556 • ACRL *Life*

Ames Diane P. • Student • University of California-Berkeley School of Library & Information Studies • Berkeley, CA 94720 • ACRL EMIERT IFRT SRRT

Ames Jan L. • Director • Washington Library for the Blind & Physically Handicapped • Seattle, WA 98129 • ASCLA

Ames Kathryn • Director • Athens Regional Library • Athens, GA 30606 • LAMA PLA

Ames Mark J. • Grand Haven, MI 49417

Ames Patricia A. • Librarian • United States Naval Air Systems Command Technical Information & Reference Center • Washington, DC 20361 • FLRT

Ames Sandra K • Payson Junior High School • Payson, UT 84651 • AASL

Ames Sandra L. • Prairie Village, KS 66207 • AASL

Amey Ellen B. • Librarian/Media Specialist • Hart Junior High School Library • Washington, DC 20032 • AASL

Amey Lorne J. • Professor • Dalhousie University School of Library & Inf. Studies • Halifax NS, B3H 4H8 Canada • YALSA

Amick Charles W. Mr • Yonkers, NY 10704 • ACRL ALSC *Life*

Amicone Janice L. • Librarian • Downingtown Area Schools • Downingtown, PA 19335

Amin Shamima • Catalog Dept. • University of Florida • Gainesville, FL 32605

Amison Mary Veronica CHS Sr. • College of Saint Francis Xavier • New York, NY 10011 • AASL ALSC

Ammenheuser Zonia • Librarian • Pleasant Hill Elementary School • Austin, TX 78745

Ammerman Robert C. • Head Librarian • Germantown Public Library • Germantown, OH 45327 • PLA

Ammon Bette D. • Missoula Public Library • Missoula, MT 59802 • YALSA

Ammons Douglas L. • Municipality of Metropolitan Seattle • Seattle, WA 98104

Ammons Shirley A. • Branch Head • Amarillo Public Library • Amarillo, TX 79189 • AASL

Amodeo Anthony J. • Associate Librarian • Loyola Marymount University Charles Von Der Ahe Library • Los Angeles, CA 90045 • ACRL RASD LIRT

Amores Irene D. Dr. • Director of Libraries • Polytechnic University of the Philippines • Manila, Philippines

Amorosa Edwina • Sherman, CT 06784

Amorosi Madeline A. • Branch Librarian • Boston Public Library Dudley Branch • Roxbury, MA 02119

Amos Billie E. • Camden Point, MO 64018 • PLA

Amos Lynn A. • Art Dir./Wilson Lib. Bulletin • H. W. Wilson Company • Bronx, NY 10452 • LAMA

Amos Macie E. • Librarian • Riley Hospital Riley Family Library • Indianapolis, IN 46223

Amos Thomas L. • Curator of Rare Books • Saint Johns University Alcuin Library • Collegeville, MN 56321-7155 • ACRL

Amoscato Guy T. • Reference Librarian • Corpus Christi State University • Corpus Chrsti, TX 78412 • ACRL

Ampulski Shirley A. • Cataloger • Library of Michigan • Lansing, MI 48909 • ALCTS IFRT SRRT

Amrhein John K. • Dean of Library Services • California State Univ Stanislaus • Turlock, CA 95380

Amrhein Kathleen M. • Pittsburgh, PA 15221 • ALSC PLA

Amsberry Dawn • Student • San Jose State University Division of Library & Information Science • San Jose, CA 95192-0029 • ALSC

Amsel Don G. • Student • Simmons College Graduate School of Library & Information Science • Boston, MA 02115 • LITA SRRT

Amundson Constance R. • Student • University of South Florida School of Library & Information Science • Tampa, FL 33620

Anakani Ejikeme • Abia State University Library • Uturu, Abia, Nigeria W. Africa

Anama Shirley Mrs. • Trenton, NJ 08610

Anastasio Helen O. • Student • Southern Connecticut State University School of Libray Science & Instructional Technology • New Haven, CT 06515

Ances Marlayne R. • Haddonfield, NJ 08033 • ACRL

Andelson Eric • Student • Kent State University School of Library & Information Science • Kent, OH 44242-0001 • IFRT

Anderl Robert G. • Head of Information Access Svs • University of Alaska Elmer E. Rasmuson Library • Fairbanks, AK 99775-1005 • ACRL LITA

Anderle Donald F. • Assistant Director • Getty Center for the History of Art Humanities Library • Santa Monica, CA 90401-1455 • ACRL

Anderman Lynea • Library Director • Warren County Community College • Washington, NJ 07882-9605 • ACRL ALCTS ALTA LAMA RASD IFRT LHRT LIRT

Andermann Patricia • Director • Kinderhook Regional Library • Lebanon, MO 65536 • LAMA PLA

Anders Mary Edna • Northport, AL 35476 • Continuing

Anders Vicki • Hd Automated Info Retrieval • Texas A & M University Sterling C. Evans Library • College Station, TX 77843-5000 • ACRL RASD

Andersen-Pusey Vavene J. • Aztec, NM 87410 • AASL FLRT LIRT

Andersen Althea F. • Division Manager • Clearwater Public Library • Clearwater, FL 34623 • PLA

Andersen Beth E. • Hd Circ Servs & Browsing Lib. • Ann Arbor Public Library • Ann Arbor, MI 48104 • PLA

Andersen Carol • Govt. Documents Librarian • Highline Community College • Des Moines, WA 98198-9800 • GODORT

Andersen Deanie • Librarian • South High School Library • Denver, CO 80210 • AASL

Andersen Kirsten • White House Station, NJ 08889 • RASD

Andersen Mark E. • Mangement Reference Librarian • Northwestern University Library • Evanston, IL 60208-2300 • ACRL RASD

Andersen Rosamond B. • Webb City, MO 64870 • AASL YALSA *Life*

Andersen Thomas K. • Head Government Pubns. • California State Library • Sacramento, CA 94237-0001 • GODORT

Andersen Torris Jr. • Reference Librarian • Rutgers University Libraries Archibald Stevens Alexander Library • New Brunswick, NJ 08903 • GODORT NMRT

Anderson-Currie Stephanie J. • Student • University of South Carolina College of Library & Information Science • Columbia, SC 29208 • RASD

Anderson-Story Janet S. • Student • Kansas State University Libraries • Manhattan, KS 66506-7166

Anderson A. Gerald • Ref/Scandinavian Librarian • University of Washington Suzzallo Library • Seattle, WA 98195 • ACRL RASD

Anderson A. J. • Professor • Simmons College Graduate School of Library & Information Science • Boston, MA 02115

Anderson Albert Jr • Head Librarian • Worchester Ploytechnic Institute Library • Worcester, MA 01609 • ACRL ALCTS LITA RASD

Anderson Allison H. • Branch Librarian • Spartanburg County Public Library Westside Branch • Spartanburg, SC 29301

Anderson Ann T. • Design & Architecture Senior High School • Miami, FL 33137 • AASL

Anderson Anne E. • Student • Emporia State University School of Library & Information Management • Emporia, KS 66801

Anderson Anthony E. • Librarian III • University of Southern California Doheny Library • Los Angeles, CA 90089-0182 • ACRL GODORT IRRT

Anderson Arlene L. • Branch Manager • Baltimore County Public Library Arbutus Branch • Baltimore, MD 21227-2598 • PLA

Anderson Barbara D. • Student • University of Pittsburgh School of Library and Information Science • Pittsburgh, PA 15260

Anderson Barbara J. • Head, Cataloging Services • Virginia Commonwealth University • Richmond, VA 23284-2033 • ALCTS

Anderson Barbara L. • Forsyth County Public Library • Winston-Salem, NC 27101 • PLA

Anderson Barbara L. • County Librarian • San Bernardino County Library • San Bernardino, CA 92415 • PLA

Anderson Barbara S. • Charleston Southern University L Mendel Rivers Library • Charleston, SC 29411 • ACRL GODORT

Anderson Barbara S. • Wauwatosa, WI 53222

Anderson Belinda V. • Trustee • Memphis-Shelby County Public Library and Information Center • Memphis, TN 38104-4025

Anderson Beth G. • Director • University of Delaware Education Resource Center • Newark, DE 19716-2901 • AASL ACRL

Anderson Betsy L. • Librarian • Sterling Municipal Library • Baytown, TX 77520 • PLA IFRT NMRT SORT

Anderson Betty • Murrysville, PA 15668

Anderson Blanche Wysor • Public Services Division Chief • Arlington County Department of Libraries • Arlington, VA 22201 • ACRL LAMA PLA

Anderson Brooke E. • Library Media Specialist • Roosevelt Junior High School • Zanesville, OH 43701 • YALSA

Anderson Byron P. • Ln., Coor. Computer Access Servs • Northern Illinois University University Libraries • DeKalb, IL 60115-2868 • RASD SRRT

Anderson C. Leonard • Librarian/Media Specialist • Grant High School • Portland, OR 97212 • AASL

Anderson Carl A. • Asst. Dir. for Tech. Services • Temple University Health Science Center Library • Philadelphia, PA 19140 • ACRL LITA

Anderson Carol L. • Associate Librarian • State University of New York (SUNY) University Libraries • Albany, NY 12222 • LAMA

Anderson Carolyn S. • School Library Media Spec. • Haverhill Elementary School • Portage, MI 49002 • AASL

Anderson Catherine • Library Media Specialist • West Side Elementary • Rossville, GA 30741 • AASL

Anderson Charles H. • Central Library Manager • Chesapeake Public Library • Chesapeake, VA 23320 • PLA

Anderson Charles R. • Assistant Director for Pubn Serv • Evanston Public Library • Evanston, IL 60201 • PLA RASD

Anderson Charlotte • Trustee • Minneapolis Public Library & Information Center • Minneapolis, MN 55401-1992 • ALTA PLA

Anderson Charlotte K. • Professor, Asst Librarian Emer. • University of New Hampshire Library • Durham, NH 03824 • ACRL

Anderson Chris M. • Student • University of Illinois Graduate School of Library and Information Science • Urbana, IL 61801

Anderson Christine D. • Anchorage, KY 40223

Anderson Clifford D. • Coor for Prospect Res • University of California University Advancement • Santa Cruz, CA 95064 • LITA RASD *Life*

Anderson Clint J. • Circulation/Curriculum Librarian • Southwestern Adventist College Findley Memorial Library • Keene, TX 76059 • ACRL

Anderson Colleen D. • P-time Student/P-time Ref Help • Bryant College Hodgson Memorial Library • Smithfield, RI 02917 • RASD

Anderson Connie J. • Business/Economics Librarian • Southern Oregon State Coll Library • Ashland, OR 97520 • ACRL RASD LIRT

Anderson David C. • Information Specialist • University of California-Davis Library • Davis, CA 95616

Anderson David G. • Head, Catalog Department • Georgia State University Pullen Library • Atlanta, GA 30303-3081 • ACRL ALCTS

Anderson David W. • Media Center Director • Thornton Academy • Saco, ME 04072 • AASL LITA

Anderson Debbie • Pershing Elementary School • Fort Leonard Wood, MO 65473 • AASL

Anderson Deborah • Librarian • South Mountain Community College Library • Phoenix, AZ 85040

Anderson Debra A. • Coordinator of Library Svs • Aultman Hospital Library • Canton, OH 44710

Anderson Donna Ann • Children's Librarian • Westfield Memorial Library • Westfield, NJ 07090 • YALSA

Anderson Doretta D. • Media Specialist • DeKalb County Schools Nancy Creek Elementary • Chamblee, GA 30319 • AASL

Anderson Dorothy J. • Assistant Dean • University of California Los Angeles Graduate School of Library & Information Science • Los Angeles, CA 90024 • ACRL LAMA *Life*

Anderson Dorrine A. • Gladstone, MI 49837

Anderson Douglas • Furman University • Greenville, SC 29613-0600

Anderson Ed • Trustee (Commissioner) • Redondo Beach Public Library • Redondo Bch, CA 90277

Anderson Elaine K. • Adult Services Librarian • Houston Lighting & Power Company Library • Houston, TX 77251

Anderson Eleanor • Librarian • Granite High School Library • Salt Lake City, UT 84106 • AASL

Anderson Elizabeth C. • Reference Librarian • Newport Beach Public Library • Newport Beach, CA 92660 • PLA

Anderson Ellen Patton • Student • University of South Florida School of Library & Information Science • Tampa, FL 33620

Anderson Elma • Periodicals Librarian • Marywood College Library Learning Resources Center • Scranton, PA 18509 • AASL ALCTS LITA *Life*

Anderson Eric S. • Director • Ohio Valley Area Libraries (OVAL) • Wellston, OH 45692 • PLA

Anderson Esta D. • Student • University of Washington Graduate School of Library and Information Science • Seattle, WA 98195

Anderson Frank • Trustee • Everett Public Library • Everett, WA 98201

Anderson Gail Erwin • Seaside Pk, NJ 08752 • AASL ALSC *Life*

Anderson Glenda D. • Film Librarian • Knox County Schools • Knoxville, TN 37901 • AASL

Anderson Glenda E. • Research Librarian • City of Savannah Municipal Research Library • Savannah, GA 31402 • ACRL RASD GODORT MAGERT

Anderson Gordon B. • Director, Slavic Section • University of Kansas Library • Lawrence, KS 66045-2800 • ACRL MAGERT

Anderson Grant A. • Manager, Library Division • Church of Jesus Christ of Latter-Day Saints • Salt Lake City, UT 84150 • ACRL LAMA RASD

Anderson Greg • Assoc. Dir Systems & Planning • Massachusetts Institute of Technology Libraries (MIT) • Cambridge, MA 02139 • LAMA LITA

Anderson H. Jean Miss • Cleveland, OH 44106 • ALSC YALSA *Continuing*

Anderson Hank • J. Walter Thompson • Chicago, IL 60611 • RASD IFRT SRRT

Anderson Harriet L. • Supervisor • Madison Public Library • Madison, WI 53703 • PLA

Anderson Helen J. • Slavic Bibliographer/Reference • McGill University Libraries • Montreal PQ, H3A 1Y1 Canada • ACRL

Anderson Helen Miss • Wakefield, MA 01880 • PLA YALSA *Continuing*

Anderson Herschel V. • Director • Mesa Public Library • Mesa, AZ 85201-6768 • PLA

Anderson Ivy L. • Head of Systems & Access Srvs • Brandeis University Main Library • Waltham, MA 02254-9110 • ACRL LITA

Anderson Jacqulyn • Baptist Sunday School Board • Nashville, TN 37234 • LITA YALSA

Anderson James D. • Associate Dean/Professor • Rutgers University School of Communication Information & Library Studies • New Brunswick, NJ 08903 • ALCTS LITA SRRT

Anderson James F. • Director • First Regional Library • Hernando, MS 38632 • LAMA PLA

Anderson James H. • Brigham Young University School of Library & Information Sciences • Provo, UT 84602

Anderson Janet A. • Campus Services Librarian • Utah State University Merrill Library • Logan, UT 84322-3000 • ACRL

Anderson Janet I. • District Department Head • Stamford Public Schools Educational Media Dept. • Stamford, CT 06905 • AASL

Anderson Janet J. • Libraian/English Teacher • Provo High School • Provo, UT 84604 • AASL

Anderson Janice • Assoc. Director for Tech Service • Georgetown University Law Center Edward Bennett Williams Library • Washington, DC 20001-1417 • ACRL ALCTS LAMA LITA

Anderson Janice C. • Access Information Associates Inc. • Bellaire, TX 77401 • LITA ILERT

Anderson Jean • Director of Library Services • Palm Beach Community College • Belle Glade, FL 33430

Anderson Jean B. • Student • Emporia State University School of Library & Information Management • Emporia, KS 66801

Anderson Jean R. • Planning Officer • Broward County Division of Libraries Broward County Library • Fort Lauderdale, FL 33301

Anderson Jeanmarie • Santa Rita, GU 96915

Anderson Jewette L. • Montgomery, AL 36104

Anderson Jill E. • Reference Librarian • Homewood Public Library District • Homewood, IL 60430

Anderson Joan C. • Reference Librarian • Carnegie Library of Pittsburgh • Pittsburgh, PA 15213-4080 • Life

Anderson Joanne S. • Supervising Librarian • San Diego Public Library • San Diego, CA 92101 • ALCTS RASD

Anderson John F. • Tucson, AZ 85737 • ALTA PLA *Life*

Anderson John T. • Reference Librarian • Palm Beach County Public Library System Greenacres City Branch • Greenacres City, FL 33463

Anderson Judith L. • Assistant Cataloger • James Madison University Carrier Library • Harrisonburg, VA 22807 • ACRL ALCTS LITA

Anderson Judith P. • Regional Branch Manager • Fairfax County Public Library Pohick Regional Branch • Burke, VA 22015 • LAMA PLA SORT

Anderson Judy A. • Student • University of Arizona Graduate Library School • Tucson, AZ 85721 • LITA

Anderson Julie E. • Marietta, GA 30066 • NMRT

Anderson Julie S. • Librarian • Miramonte High School • Orinda, CA 94563 • AASL RASD YALSA

Anderson Karen A • Circulation Librarian • Decatur Public Library • Decatur, IL 62523

Anderson Karen B. • Reference Department • California State University • Northridge, CA 91330 • ACRL

Anderson Karen E. • Reference Librarian • Whitman College Penrose Memorial Library • Walla Walla, WA 99362-9982 • ACRL RASD IFRT LIRT

Anderson Karen M • Community Services Specialist • Public Library of Des Moines • Des Moines, IA 50308-1791

Anderson Karen T. • Deputy Director • Fountaindale Public Library District • Bolingbrook, IL 60440 • PLA

Anderson Kari J. • Reference Librarian • University of Washington Suzzallo Library • Seattle, WA 98195 • ACRL NMRT

Anderson Kathleen • Community Relations Librarian • Atlantic County Library • Mays Landing, NJ 08336 • SRRT

Anderson Kathleen B. • Student • University of Washington Graduate School of Library and Information Science • Seattle, WA 98195

Anderson Knute E. • Student • San Jose State University Division of Library & Information Science • San Jose, CA 95192-0029 • IFRT SRRT

Anderson Kristen L. • Science Reference Librarian • University of Hawaii Thomas Hale Hamilton Library • Honolulu, HI 96822

Anderson Kristine J. • Humanities Bibliographer • Purdue University • West Lafayette, IN 47907 • ACRL

Anderson Lemoyne W. • Ft Collins, CO 80524 • ACRL ALCTS *Life*

Anderson Linda A. • Librarian • Hong Kong International School • Hong Kong, Hong Kong • AASL

Anderson Linda C. • Student • University of Rhode Island Graduate School of Library & Information Studies • Kingston, RI 02881-0815 • PLA

Anderson Lois A. • Chapel Hill, NC 27516 • ALSC

Anderson Lori L. • Librarian • Saguache City Public Library • Center, CO 81125

Anderson Lorraine I. • Librarian • Baltimore County Public Library • Towson, MD 21204

Anderson Lou • Fort Collins, CO 80526-1968 • ACRL

Anderson Lynn R. • Student • Brigham Young University School of Library & Information Sciences • Provo, UT 84602

Anderson Lynnette • Director • Casper College Goodstein Foundation Library • Casper, WY 82601 • ACRL

Anderson M. Elaine • Education Technology Consultant • Apple Computer Inc. • Chicago, IL 60631 • AASL

Anderson Marcia L. • Head of Aquisitions • Arizona State University Libraries • Tempe, AZ 85287-1006 • ALCTS LITA

Anderson Margaret Ann • Wichita, KS 67203 • PLA

Anderson Maria Patricia • Technical Services Center • Newport News Public Library System • Newport News, VA 23607 • ALCTS PLA

Anderson Mark • Reference/Information • Fairfax County Public Library • Fairfax, VA 22033-1909 • EMIERT

Anderson Marlene K. • Washington University Olin Library • Saint Louis, MO 63130 • ALCTS

Anderson Mary Gay • International/Doc. Librarian • University of Florida Libraries • Gainesville, FL 32611-2047 • ACRL GODORT

Anderson Mary Jane • Waukegan Public Library • Waukegan, IL 60085 • ALSC PLA

Anderson Mary P. Mrs. • Linton Cambs, United Kingdom • Life

Anderson Mary Sieminski • Head of Technical Services • Clark University Robert Hutchings Goddard Library • Worcester, MA 01610

Anderson Meredith Lou • Intermediate School Librarian • Louise Black Intermediate School • Weslaco, TX 78596 • AASL LAMA

Anderson Monica L. • Plymouth, MI 48170 • LAMA

Anderson Myra • Bibliographer,Social Sciences • University of California Rivera Library • Riverside, CA 92517 • ACRL ALCTS CLENE EMIERT

Anderson Nancy D. • Urbana, IL 61801 • ACRL

Anderson Nancy E. • Reference Librarian • Northern Illinois Library System • Rockford, IL 61108

Anderson Nancy E. • School Library Media Specialist • Glenn Stephens Elementary Madison Metropolitan School District • Madison, WI 53706

Anderson Nancy K. • University Librarian • Howard Payne University • Brownwood, TX 76801 • ACRL LIRT

Anderson P. Genene • Adult Services Librarian • Rockford Public Library • Rockford, IL 61101-1061 • PLA RASD

Anderson Patricia A. • Dimondale, MI 48821

Anderson Patricia A. • Director • New Rochelle Public Library • New Rochelle, NY 10801

Anderson Patricia T. • Stuart, FL 34997

Anderson Paul F. • Young Adult Librarian • Fremont Main Library • Fremont, CA 94538 • YALSA

Anderson Paul M. • Head Access Services Department • University of Delaware Library • Newark, DE 19717-5267 • LAMA

Anderson Pauline H. • Broadalbin, NY 12025 • AASL

Anderson R. Patricia • Acting Program Director • Boston Public Schools • Boston, MA 02108 • AASL ALSC YALSA LIRT

Anderson Rachael K. • Director Health Sciences Lib • University of Arizona Arizona Health Sciences Center Library • Tucson, AZ 85724 • ACRL LAMA

Anderson Rebecca K. • Student • University of South Carolina College of Library & Information Science • Columbia, SC 29208 • ALCTS LITA SRRT

Anderson Richard N. • Library Systems Analyst • Stanford University • Stanford, CA 94305-6011 • LITA

Anderson Robert P. • National Agricultural Library • Beltsville, MD 20705-2351 • ACRL LHRT LIRT

Anderson Roger W. • Database Manager • Cooperative Computer Services • Wheeling, IL 60090 • ALCTS

Anderson Rosemary • Head of Children's Department • Bexley Public Library • Columbus, OH 43209 • ALSC IFRT

Anderson Rowena R. • Library Assistant • Clayton State College • Morrow, GA 30260

Anderson Ruby Nell • Librarian • Scottsboro Junior High School Library • Scottsboro, AL 35768

Anderson Sally C. • Director • Vermont Reading Project • Chester, VT 05143 • PLA

Anderson Sally K. • H S L Media Spec • Messalonskee H S • Oakland, ME 04963 • AASL LITA

Anderson Sally S. • Student • University of South Florida School of Library & Information Science • Tampa, FL 33620 • AASL

Anderson Sara Ellen • Elgin, IL 60123 • AASL

Anderson Sarah A. • Serials & Reference Librarian • North Park College & Theo Sem Consolidated Library • Chicago, IL 60625 • RASD

Anderson Sharon McClure • Government Document Librarian • University of California-San Diego • La Jolla, CA 92093-0175 • GODORT

Anderson Susan M. • Director Libraries • Saint Petersburg Junior College • St. Petersburg, FL 33733 • ACRL

Anderson Terry Ann • Student • Chadron State College Reta E. King Library • Chadron, NE 69337

Anderson Thomas Earl • Branch Head • Montgomery City-County Library Main Branch • Montgomery, AL 36104

Anderson Vartouhi S. • Librarian/Children's Services • Oakland Public Library • Oakland, CA 94612 • ALSC

Anderson Vera K. • Student • University of Michigan School of Information and Library Studies • Ann Arbor, MI 48109-1092

Anderson Verlyn D. • Library Director • Concordia College Carl B. Ylvisaker Library • Moorhead, MN 56562 • LAMA ILERT

Anderson Viola C. • Cleveland, OH 44106 • Continuing

Anderson Virginia • Librarian • Indiana State University Cunningham Memorial Library • Terre Haute, IN 47809

Andis Virginia R. • Planning Consultant • Indiana State Library • Indianapolis, IN 46204-2296

Andrade Kathleen M. • City Librarian • Lodi Public Library • Lodi, CA 95240 • LAMA

Andre Pamela Q. J. • Associate Dir. For Automation • United States Department of Agriculture National Agricultural Library • Beltsville, MD 20705-2351 • ALCTS LITA

Andre Priscilla W. • Head Administrative Services • Northwestern University Library • Evanston, IL 60208-2300 • LAMA

Andrea Marcy S. • Student • University of South Florida School of Library & Information Science • Tampa, FL 33620 • LITA

Andres Jean E. • Children's Librarian • Tippecanoe County Public Library • Lafayette, IN 47901 • ALSC

Andres Mark F. • Reference Librarian • Temple University Japan • Tokyo 192-03, Japan

Andres Stanley • Trustee • Ocean County Library System • Toms River, NJ 08753

Andresen Leila H. • Trustee • Alameda County Library System • Fremont, CA 94538 • ALTA

Andresen Tish C. • Deputy Director, Public Service • Pierce County Rural Library District • Tacoma, WA 98446 • LAMA PLA

Andrew David G. • Escondido, CA 92026 • NMRT

Andrew Mary • Cook Memorial Library • Libertyville, IL 60048

Andrew Melanie J. • Adult Services • Cuyahoga County Public Library Nordonia Hills Branch Library • Northfield, OH 44067

Andrew Paige G. • Cataloging Dept. • University of Georgia Libraries • Athens, GA 30602 • MAGERT

Andrew Stephanie • Librarian • Iowa City Public Library • Iowa City, IA 52240

Andrews Ann U. • Librarian • Memphis-Shelby County Public Library Bartlett Branch • Bartlett, TN 38134 • ALSC

Andrews Barbara A. • Student • Simmons College Graduate School of Library & Information Science • Boston, MA 02115 • LITA RASD

Andrews Barbara P. • Librarian • Nantucket Atheneum Library • Nantucket, MA 02554-0808

Andrews Charles Dr • Dean of Library Services • Hofstra University Axinn Library • Hempstead, NY 11550 • ACRL

Andrews Donna D. • Reference Librarian • Watertown Public Library • Watertown, WI 53094

Andrews Elizabeth • Brewer, ME 04412

Andrews Francine T. • St. Ignatius High School • Cleveland, OH 44113 • AASL

Andrews Helen R. Mrs • Erie, PA 16502 • Continuing

Andrews Janet A C Dr. • Head, Technical Services • Winter Park Public Library • Winter Park, FL 32789 • ALCTS LITA LRRT *Life*

Andrews Joanna M. • Head Technical Services • McGill University • Montreal PQ, H3A 1Y1 Canada • LAMA LITA

Andrews Joseph C. • Hd., Acqs. & Clln. Development • University of Central Florida Library • Orlando, FL 32816-0666 • ACRL ALCTS LAMA

Andrews Joyce D. • Trustee • Fairfax County Public Library • Fairfax, VA 22033-1909

Andrews Judith C. • Social Science Ref. Librarian • Southern Oregon State Coll Library • Ashland, OR 97520 • ACRL GODORT MAGERT

Andrews Judith K. • Science Librarian • University of the Pacific Science Library • Stockton, CA 95211 • ACRL RASD

Andrews Karen L. • Math/Computer Science Libn. • University of California Engineering & Math Science Library • Los Angeles, CA 90024-1598 • ACRL LITA

Andrews Linda R. • Director • Hoover Public Library • Birmingham, AL 35216 • ALSC ALTA LAMA PLA RASD IFRT

Andrews Lynn J. • Librarian • Redwood City Public Library • Redwood City, CA 94063-1868

Andrews Margaret • Library Assoc/Reference Dept. • Salem State College Library • Salem, MA 01970

Andrews Margaret A. • Communications Coordinator • Utlas International • Etobicoke, ON, M8X 2X2 Canada • IRRT

Andrews Margaret B. • Rochester, NY 14610 • ACRL RASD *Continuing*

Andrews Margaret D. • Base Librarian • Base Library/ FL5699 Unit 7235 • APO, AE 09846 • PLA AFLRT FLRT IFRT

Andrews Marilyn I. • Government Publication Section • University of Regina • Regina SK, S4S 0A2 Canada • ACRL LAMA GODORT

Andrews Mark Joseph • Customer Service Rep. • Columbia Library System (CTB) • Monterey, CA 93940 • LITA

Andrews Nan • LMC Director • Rhinelander High School • Rhinelander, WI 54501 • AASL YALSA

Andrews Patricia A. • Washington, DC 20024

Andrews Patricia L. • Librarian • Laguna Elementary School • Scottsdale, AZ 85258

Andrews Phyllis C. • Asst Director for Public Srvs • University of Rochester Rush Rhees Library • Rochester, NY 14627-0055 • ACRL LAMA RASD

Andrews Rebecca F. • Librarian • Southern State Community College Learning Resource Center (South) • Sardinia, OH 45171 • ACRL LAMA LRRT

Andrews Rosalyn M. • Plainsboro, NJ 08536

Andrews S. E. Ms. • University of British Columbia • Vancouver BC, Canada

Andrews Sandra D. • Piedmont Open Middle School • Charlotte, NC 28210 • AASL ALSC

Andrews Sara W. • Director • Marlboro College Rice Library • Marlboro, VT 05344 • ACRL

Andrews Sarah K. • Lansingburg, NY 12182 • AASL PLA

Andrews Shirley G. • Head of Art & Music Dept. • Peoria Public Library • Peoria, IL 61602 • RASD

Andrews Susanne V. • Hd of Public Servs & Circ. • University of Massachusetts-Dartmouth Library • North Dartmouth, MA 02747

Andrews Theodora A. • Pharmaceutical Svs Bibliographer • Purdue University Libraries • West Lafayette, IN 47907 • ACRL

Andrews Virginia L. • Head, Automation Depratment • Texas Tech University Libraries • Lubbock, TX 79409-0002 • ACRL LITA

Andrews Winifred E. • Alhambra, CA 91801 • AASL YALSA *Continuing*

Andrilli Ene • Rdr Serv Ln • St Joseph Coll Univ • Philadelphia, PA 19131 • ACRL

Andronik Catherine M. • Bedford Middle Sch • Westport, CT 06880 • AASL

Andrus Simone A. • Student • Indiana University School of Library and Information Science • Bloomington, IN 47405 • ACRL RASD IFRT SRRT

Andrzejewski Renee • Librarian Assistant • Buffalo & Erie County Public Library • Buffalo, NY 14203

Anell Esther W. Miss • Bibl & Asst Prof Emerita • University of Illinois Library • Urbana, IL 61801 • Life

Anemaet Josephine C. • Catalog Librarian • Oregon State University William Jasper Kerr Library • Corvallis, OR 97331-4501 • ACRL SRRT

Anesi Andrea J. • Student • Syracuse University School of Information Studies • Syracuse, NY 13244-4100

Anfuso Mary F. • Librarian • Kollsman • Merrimack, NH 03054

Angel Lisbeth A. • Library Media Specialist • Willard Elementary School • Berlin, CT 06037 • AASL

Angel Michael R. • Associate Director of Libraries • University of Manitoba Elizabeth Dafoe Library • Winnipeg MB, R3T 2N2 Canada • ACRL

Angele Elizabeth D • Librarian • German Cultural Center • Chicago, IL 60611 • ACRL LITA

Angelette Gwendolyn D. • Librarian • Lacache Middle School • Chauvin, LA 70344

Angeletti Lois R. • Cataloging Librarian • Virginia State Library & Archives • Richmond, VA 23219 • ALCTS

Angeley Michele A. • Student • Florida State University Library Science Library • Tallahassee, FL 32306-2047

Angelini June M. • School Library Media Specialist • Saw Mill Elementary School • North Bellmore, NY 11710

Angelini Margo L. • Ann Arbor, MI 48103

Angelis Jane • Director • Illinois Integerenerational Initiative • Carbondale, IL 62901 • RASD

Angell Alice • Global Studies Magnet School • Greensboro, NC 27408 • AASL

Angell Lucinda J. • Information Specialist • Kraft General Foods • Glenview, IL 60025 • LAMA RASD

Angell Lynn E. • Westlake Village, CA 91362

Angell Richard S. • Bethesda, MD 20816 • ALCTS *Life*

Angellotti Jayleen L. • Trustee • Chicago Heights Public Library • Chicago Heights, IL 60411 • ALTA

Angelo Alice M. • Circulation Librarian • Trinity College Library • Hartford, CT 06106 • ACRL

Angelo Constance • Oak Lawn, IL 60453

Angelos Sandra B. • Systems Analyst • Blue Shield of California • San Francisco, CA 94133

Angelucci Andrea • Media Specialist • Nova Middle School • Davie, FL 33314 • AASL

Angeo Joseph • Media Specialist • Chatham Junior Senior High School • Chatham, MA 02633 • AASL

Angier Naomi K. • Young Adult Specialist • Multnomah County Library Administrative Offices • Portland, OR 97212 • YALSA IFRT

Angilello-Turner Jo-Ann • Student • Queens College Graduate School of Library & Information Studies • Flushing, NY 11367 • AASL ACRL PLA RASD

Angiolillo Amedeo • President and CEO • Academic & Entertainment Video Corporation • New York, NY 10022

Anglada Juliana • Associate Librarian • Dwight-Englewood School • Englewood, NJ 07631

Angle Melanie J. • Marietta, GA 30064

Anglin Richard V. • Director • Ramapo Catskill Library System • Middletown, NY 10940 • LAMA PLA

Angolia Christine • Govt. Doc. Reference Librarian • University of Missouri Miller-Nichols Library • Kansas City, MO 64110 • ACRL GODORT

Angus Beatrice E. • School Library System Director • Madison-Oneida BOCES School Library System • Sherrill, NY 13461 • AASL

Angus Carolyn R • Associate Director • George Stone Center for Childrens Books • Claremont, CA 91711-6188 • YALSA

Angus Evalene K. Mrs • Hialeah, FL 33012 • Continuing

Anhalt Joy L. • Head of Technical Services • Tinley Park Public Library • Tinley Park, IL 60477 • ALCTS

Anish Louise Miss • School Librarian • Piscataway Township School District • Piscataway, NJ 08854 • AASL

Anish Michele • Cataloger • Institute of Human Relations Blaustein Library • New York, NY 10022

Anjier J. L. Mrs • Coordinator, Special Services • State Library of Louisiana • Baton Rouge, LA 70821

Ankersen Elizabeth L. • Assistant Librarian • Queens Borough Public Library • Jamaica, NY 11432 • ALCTS

Ankner Thomas C. • Student • Rutgers University School of Communication Information & Library Studies • New Brunswick, NJ 08903

Anliker Julia H. • Librarian • SFB Morse Elementary School • Poughkeepsie, NY 12601 • AASL

Annable Dorothy Miss • Woburn, MA 01801 • AASL PLA *Continuing*

Annan Beatrice E. • Providence, RI 02905 • Continuing

Annan Isaac B. • Reference Librarian • Paterson Free Public Library Danforth Memorial Library • Paterson, NJ 07501

Annand Katherine • Largo, FL 34644

Annett Adele M. • Head Serial Catalog Section • University of Toronto Robarts Library • Toronto ON, Canada • ALCTS

Annett Susan E. • Santa Monica Public Library • Santa Monica, CA 90401 • PLA VRT

Annicchiarico Julie • Trustee • Rapid City Public Library • Rapid City, SD 57701-3630

Annichiarico Mark • Assoc. Book Review Editor • Library Journal Cahners Publishing Company • New York, NY 10011

Annis Ethan J. • Student • University of North Carolina at Chapel Hill School of Information and Library Science • Chapel Hill, NC 27599-3360 • NMRT SRRT

Anoff Karen A. • Student • Rosary College Graduate School of Library & Information Science • River Forest, IL 60305 • AASL

Ansari Mary • Asst. University Librarian • University of Nevada Reno Library • Reno, NV 89511 • ACRL

Ansart Dorothy • Student • Rutgers University School of Communication Information & Library Studies • New Brunswick, NJ 08903 • NMRT

Anselmo Priscilla M. • Senior Library Media Specialist • Ridgefield High School Library • Ridgefield, CT 06877 • AASL

Ansett John • Book House • Jonesville, MI 49250 • LITA

Anshien Carol M • Asst. Branch & Reference Ln. • New York Public Library Countee Cullen Regional Library • New York, NY 10030 • EMIERT

Ansley Kathleen Mrs. • Library Media Specialist • W.C. Walker Elementary School • Crestview, FL 32536

Anspach Karen • Systems Analyst Designer • Data Trek, Inc. • Carlsbad, CA 92008 • ALCTS LITA

Anstee Anna May • Head of Technical Services • Helen M. Plum Memorial Library • Lombard, IL 60148 • ALCTS LITA PLA

Antczak Janice • Professor • Brookdale Community College • Lincroft, NJ 07738 • ALSC

Antelman Kristin A. • University of Delaware Library • Newark, DE 19717-5267 • LITA

Anthes Harriet C. • Cataloger • Harvard College Library Widener Memorial Library • Cambridge, MA 02138

Anthes Susan H. • Associate Director Public Serv • University of Colorado-Boulder University Libraries • Boulder, CO 80309 • ACRL LAMA GODORT MAGERT

Anthony Angela • National Association of Insurance Commissions • Kansas City, MO 64105

Anthony Carolyn • Director • Skokie Public Library • Skokie, IL 60077-3680 • LAMA PLA

Anthony Kay C • District Librarian • Coalinga-Huron Library District • Coalinga, CA 93210 • PLA

Anthony Nancy • Trustee • Metropolitan Library System • Oklahoma City, OK 73102 • ALTA PLA

Anthony Paul L. • Asst. Prof. & Hd. of Circulation • Southern Illinois University • Edwardsville, IL 62026 • ACRL

Anthony Robert G. Jr. • Clln Devlp Libn • University of North Carolina • Chapel Hill, NC 27599-3930 • ACRL RASD LHRT

Anthony Victoria Mark • Darien High School • Darien, CT 06820 • AASL

Antico Linda J. • Reference Librarian • Alrington County Library Central • Arlington, VA 22201

Antigo Dolores A. • Library Director • Brooke County Public Library • Wellsburg, WV 26070 • PLA

Antill Deborah A. • Cleveland, OH 44144 • ALCTS

Antin Patricia • Librarian II • New York Public Library • New York, NY 10018-2788 • ACRL NMRT

Antipa Susan M. • Dir. of Learning Resources • Sierra Nevada College • Incline Village, NV 89450 • ACRL

Antolin Laura K. Dranoff • Chicago, IL 60660

Anton Bette B. • Health Sciences Librarian • University California-Berkeley • Berkeley, CA 94720

Anton Lorraine Illan • Librarian • Green Tree School • Philadelphia, PA 19144 • AASL

Antone Allen Louise • Head of Reference Department • Appalachian State University Carol Grotnes Belk Library • Boone, NC 28608 • RASD

Antonelli Monika J. • Student • University of North Texas School of Library & Information Sciences • Denton, TX 76203 • IFRT SRRT

Antonetti Martin • Librarian • The Grolier Club Library • New York, NY 10022 • ACRL

Antonietti Barbara • Trustee • Calumet City Public Library • Calumet City, IL 60409-4003 • ALTA

Antoniewicz Carol M. • Reference Libn./Bibliographer • Washington University Libraries • Saint Louis, MO 63130-4899 • LITA RASD

Antonowicz Ruslana • Student • Pratt Institute Graduate School of Library & Information Science • Brooklyn, NY 11205

Antonucci Ronald J. • Student • Kent State University School of Library & Information Science • Kent, OH 44242-0001

Antonuccio Steven J. • Colorado Springs, CO 80918-1857

Antrim Kimberlee K. • Tactical Training Group Pacific Tactical Library Code: 206 • San Diego, CA 92147-5080

Antrim Patricia A. • Librarian • Ashland Community College • Ashland, KY 41101 • ACRL GODORT SRRT

Antrim Priscilla J. • Stevensville, MT 59870

Anunson Margaret L. • Budget Officer • University of Wisconsin-Madison Memorial Library • Madison, WI 53706

Aoyama Karen • Battelle-Seattle Research Center • Seattle, WA 98105 • RASD

Apel Catherine D. • Huntington, WV 25705 • AASL

Apel H. W. • Chief Technical Librarian • U.S. Army Corp of Engineers Ohio River Division • Cincinnati, OH 45201 • AASL FLRT

Aper Debra L. • K-6 School Librarian • John Adams School • Decatur, IL 62521 • AASL

Apley Shirley A. • Sioux Falls, SD 57105

Apo Brian T. • Student • University of Hawaii • Manoa, HI 96789

Aponte Jose Antonio • Principal Admin. Librarian • San Juan Capistrano Regional Library • San Juan Capistrano, CA 92675

Apostol Jeanne • Library of Congress • Washington, DC 20541 • VRT

Apostolos Margaret M. • Microtext & Per Ln • Kutztown University Rohrbach Library • Kutztown, PA 19530-0721 • ACRL ALCTS

Appel-Mosesof Rhoda • Springfield, NJ 07081

Appel Anne M. • County Librarian • Marin County Free Library • San Rafael, CA 94903 • ALSC ASCLA LAMA LITA PLA RASD

Appel Barbara E. • Tamarac, FL 33321

Appel Bernice M. RSM Sr. • Library Director • Gwynedd Mercy College Lourdes Library • Gwynedd Valley, PA 19437 • ACRL LAMA

Appel Fern • Los Angeles, CA 90035 • SRRT

Appelbaum Elliot L. • Lexington, KY 40511

Appelbaum Sara B. • Manager, Public Services • Tampa-Hillsborough County Public Library • Tampa, FL 33602 • PLA RASD

Appell Alice J. • Long Beach, CA 90803 • Life

Apperson Frances • Jones, AL 36749 • ACRL ALCTS *Life*

Apple Hope • Skokie Public Library • Skokie, IL 60077-3680 • ILERT

Applebaum Edmond L. • College Pk, MD 20740 • ACRL ALCTS *Life*

Applegate Howard L. • Secretary of the College • Lebanon Valley College • Annville, PA 17003 • ACRL *Life*

Appleton Brenda F. • Vancouver Community College • Vancouver BC, V5T 4N3 Canada

Appling Jane B. • Newport Public Library • Newport, OR 97365 • PLA

Aprigliano Patricia A. • Riva, MD 21140

Aprill Susan E. • New York, NY 10009 • IFRT LHRT LRRT MAGERT SRRT

Apted Janis E. • Head, Library Devlp. • University of Michigan Libraries • Ann Arbor, MI 48109-1205 • LAMA

Apter Elaine A. • Wymore Career Educational Center • Eatonville, FL 32751 • AASL

Aquila Salvatore A. • Coordinator, Database Operations • University of Victoria McPherson Library • Victoria BC, V8W 3H5 Canada • ALCTS LITA

Aquilina Lynore • Student • State University of New York (SUNY) at Buffalo • Buffalo, NY 14260

Arab Dorothy W. • Student • Anchorage Municipal Libraries Z. J. Loussac Library • Anchorage, AK 99503

Arakawa Steven R. • Processing Services Department • Yale University Sterling Memorial Library • New Haven, CT 06520 • ACRL ALCTS LITA IFRT

Araki Elizabeth A. • Lakewood, CO 80226 • LITA

Aramayo Susan B. • Country Library Director • American Embassy • APO, AE 09080 • LAMA IRRT

Arant Iris Simpson Mrs. • Media Specialist • Orangeburg School District Five Belleville Middle School • Orangeburg, SC 29115

Arasanyin Frank O. • Student • Rutgers University School of Communication Information & Library Studies • New Brunswick, NJ 08903

Araujo Fernanda • Student • University of Kentucky • Lexington, KY 40506-0056 • ACRL RASD

Araujo Mercedes • Vancouver, BC, V6H 1N9 Canada • SRRT

Aravena Joyce C. • Baton Rouge, LA 70810

Arbaugh Linda E. • Librarian • Santa Clara County Free Library Milpitas Community Library • Milpitas, CA 95035 • Life

Arbus Rose • New York, NY 10128

Arcan Pinar • Washington, DC 20008

Arcand Janet L. • Ames, IA 50010 • ACRL ALCTS

Arcari Ralph D. • Director • University of Connecticut Health Center Lyman Maynard Stowe Library • Farmington, CT 06032

Arceneaux Muriel D. • Retired Teacher • Terrebonne Parish School Board • Houma, LA 70360

Arceneaux Nelly T. • Librarian • L J Alleman Middle School • Lafayette, LA 70503 • AASL

Archbold Barbara C. • Regional Coordinator • King County Library System • Seattle, WA 98109-5191 • PLA

Archdale Michael D. • Wibaux, MT 59353 • AASL

Archer Colleen S. • Branch Head • Toledo-Lucas County Public Library • Toledo, OH 43624

Archer J. Douglas • Reference Librarian • University of Notre Dame Theodore M. Hesburgh Library • Notre Dame, IN 46556 • ACRL RASD IFRT LIRT

Archer John A. Jr. • Carmel Valley, CA 93924-9729 • IRRT

Archer Katherine Jean • Student • Drexel University College of Information Studies • Philadelphia, PA 19104-2875 • RASD

Archer Polly • Assistant Director • Pacific Grove Public Library • Pacific Grove, CA 93950 • RASD

Archibald Gail • Trustee • Bellwood Public Library • Bellwood, IL 60104 • ALTA

Archibald Pamela P. • Clarence Public Library • Clarence, NY 14031

Archibeque Orlando • Social Science Bibliographer • University of Colorado at Denver Auraria Library • Denver, CO 80204 • ACRL

Archuleta Alyce J. • Supervisor/Librarian • San Diego Public Library • San Diego, CA 92101 • PLA

Archuleta Lena L. • Denver, CO 80206-2024 • ALTA *Life*

Arciszewski Elaine • Media Specialist • Morristown High School • Morristown, NJ 07960 • AASL

Arciszewski Katherine • Student • Long Island University Palmer School of Library & Information Science • Greenvale, NY 11548

Ard Harold J. • Manager • Forth Worth Public Library Wedgewood Branch • Fort Worth, TX 76133

Ard Paula M. • Student • University of North Carolina at Chapel Hill School of Information and Library Science • Chapel Hill, NC 27599-3360

Arden Michael G. • Assistant Librarian • U S Air Force Base Library • APO San Francisco, CA 96239 • AFLRT

Arden Sandra • Southfield, MI 48076

Ardrey Richard L. • Director • Indiana University at Kokomo Learning Resources Center • Kokomo, IN 46904-9003 • ACRL

Ardrey William C. Rev • Trustee • Detroit Public Library • Detroit, MI 48202 • ALTA

Arduengo Richard R. • Assistant Chief of Branches • Houston Public Library • Houston, TX 77002 • LAMA PLA

Ardueser Winifred G. • Librarian • Wray High School • Wray, CO 80758 • AASL

Arenales Duane W. • Chief Technical Service Div. • National Library of Medicine • Bethesda, MD 20894 • ALCTS

Arendes Karen V. • Sales Representative • DYNIX,Inc. • Santa Ana, CA 92707 • LITA

Arendt Katherine A. • Catalog Librarian • Patent and Trademark Office • Crystal City, VA 22202

Arestad Sheila • Federal Way, WA 98003-4001

Argabright Sandra S. • Student • University of Missouri-Columbia School of Library & Informational Science • Columbia, MO 65211 • EMIERT SRRT

Argentati Carolyn D. • Hd, Natural Resoruces Library • North Carolina State University • Raleigh, NC 27695-7111 • ACRL LITA

Argentieri Elizabeth J.D. • Student • University of Rochester Rush Rhees Library • Rochester, NY 14627-0055

Argue Patricia • Teacher • Westbury High School • Westbury, NY 11590

Arguinzoniz Maria de la Luz • 03900 Mexico DF 19, Mexico • ALCTS

Arhipov Sergei D. • Primary Consultant • MGL Corporation • Trevose, PA 19053 • ACRL

Ariail Julius F. • Library Director • Georgia Southern University Library • Statesboro, GA 30460-8074

Ariaratnam Lakshmi • Reference and Instruction Libn. • California State University-Chico Meriam Library • Chico, CA 92929-0295 • ACRL RASD LIRT

Arias Marie E. • Librarian • Thomas Jefferson High School • San Antonio, TX 78201 • AASL

Ariel Joan • Librarian • University of California-Irvine Library • Irvine, CA 92713 • ACRL SRRT

Ariel Marie • Cataloger/Librarian • Cambridge Public Schools • Cambridge, MA 02138 • ALCTS SRRT

Arington Edwina F. • Shawnee Correctional Center • Vienna, IL 62995 • ASCLA

Ariss Jose O. • Bogota, Colombia • LITA

Arist Suzanne • Volunteer • Evanston Public Library • Evanston, IL 60201

Ark Winfred C. • Student • San Jose State University Division of Library & Information Science • San Jose, CA 95192-0029 • RASD SRRT

Arkwright Patti A. • Children's Librarian • Narragansett Public Library • Narragansett, RI 02882 • ALSC

Arlen Shelley A. • Reference • University of Oklahoma Libraries University Libraries • Norman, OK 73019 • ACRL

Armato Rosemary • Database Manager • Boston University Mugar Memorial Library • Boston, MA 02215

Armbrecht P. II Conrad • Trustee • Mobile Public Library • Mobile, AL 36602 • ALTA

Armbrister Ann • Tallahassee, FL 32301 • ALCTS LITA CLENE

Armbruster Carol • French/Italian Area Specialist • Library of Congress • Washington, DC 20541 • ACRL

Armbruster Joan • Assistant Director • Olean Public Library • Olean, NY 14760 • PLA

Armbruster Katherine • Miami, FL 33172 • ALSC

Armento Greg • Senior Assistant Librarian • California State University-Long Beach University Library & Learning Resources • Long Beach, CA 90840-1901 • ACRL MAGERT

Armer Deborah M. • Student • Rosary College Graduate School of Library & Information Science • River Forest, IL 60305

Armes Patricia S. • Dallas, TX 75243

Armington Patricia B. • Head Librarian • Mount Carmel Academy • New Orleans, LA 70124 • AASL

Armistead Julia B. • Knoxville, TN 37919 • Continuing

Armistead Leslie K. • Library Manager • Career Action Center • Palo Alto, CA 94306

Armistead Peter S. • Cataloger • Winter Park Public Library • Winter Park, FL 32789

Armistead Sally J. • Head of Technicl Services • Catonsville Community College • Baltimore, MD 21228

Armitage Elizabeth D. • Engineering Librarian • Case Western Reserve University Sears Library • Cleveland, OH 44106 • ACRL LITA RASD

Armitage Katherine Y. • Director • Haywood County Public Library • Waynesville, NC 28786 • ALSC PLA RASD IFRT

Armitage Stephen H. • Librarian • Westport Public Library • Westport, CT 06880 • ALSC RASD

Armitage Thomas E. • Library Director • Cedar Rapids Public Library • Cedar Rapids, IA 52401 • LAMA

Armor Karen L. • Children's Program Librarian • Santa Clara County Free Library Campbell Public • Campbell, CA 95008

Armour Andrea W. • Springfield, PA 19064

Armour James • Collection Development Officer • Northern Arizona University • Flagstaff, AZ 86011-6022 • ACRL ALCTS GODORT IFRT

Armour Margaret G. • Columbus, OH 43204

Armour Rayne S. • Technical Services Librarian • College of Lake County Learning Resource Center • Grayslake, IL 60030

Armstrong-Player Jewel • Library Program Office • United States Army Materiel Command • Alexandria, VA 22333 0001 • LITA AFLRT FLRT

Armstrong Alison H. • Instruction/Reference Ln. • University of Nevada-Las Vegas James R. Dickinson Library • Las Vegas, NV 89154 • ACRL LIRT

Armstrong Carole S. • Head Science Librarian • Michigan State University Libraries • East Lansing, MI 48824-1048 • ACRL ALCTS LAMA *Life*

Armstrong Carolyn Y. • Automation/Circulation Libn. • Dalton Regional Library • Dalton, GA 30720

Armstrong Dan • Director • Palatine Public Library • Palatine, IL 60067 • PLA

Armstrong E. Alan • Electronic Ref. Servs. Librarian • Virginia Polytechnic Inst & State Univ University Libraries • Blacksburg, VA 24062-9001 • ACRL RASD

Armstrong E. W. • Teacher-English, Dept. Head • North Salinas High School • Salinas, CA 93906

Armstrong Grace E. • Creighton, PA 15030 • ACRL PLA LIRT

Armstrong Jeanne M. • Tucson, AZ 85716

Armstrong Joanne E. • Baltimore, MD 21210 • AASL *Life*

Armstrong John C. • Gulf Coast Community College • Panama City, FL 32401 • ACRL

Armstrong Johnny Lynn • Shane-Armstrong Information Systems • Fayetteville, AR 72702

Armstrong Judy C. • Ramsey High School • Birmingham, AL 35205 • AASL IFRT

Armstrong Mary Lu • Supervisor for Media Svcs • Cobb County Public Schools • Marietta, GA 30060 • AASL

Armstrong Patti • Trustee • Johnson County Library • Shawnee Mission, KS 66201 • ALTA

Armstrong Rhonda K. • Chattanooga, TN 37405 • RASD IFRT NMRT

Armstrong Robert W. • Birmingham, MI 48025 • ALCTS PLA *Life*

Armstrong Rodney • Director • Boston Athenaeum • Boston, MA 02108 • ACRL LAMA *Life*

Armstrong Ruth C. • Orlando, FL 32804-4434 • CLENE ILERT SORT

Armstrong Virgil • Houston Public Library • Houston, TX 77002

Arn Nancy L. • Librarian • Barton Library • El Dorado, AR 71730 • PLA

Arnall Janet • Librarian • Madison High School • San Diego, CA 92117-3299 • AASL

Arndt Arleen • Technical Service Librarian • Adrian College Shipman Library • Adrian, MI 49221 • ACRL ALCTS ALSC

Arndt Phillip • Audio Visual Librarian • Rosary College • River Forest, IL 60305-1066

Arndt Theresa S. • Student • State University of New York (SUNY) School of Information & Library Studies • Buffalo, NY 14260

Arneja Harbhajan S. • Reader Services Librarian • Dominican College Library • Blauvelt, NY 10913

Arnesen Sandra L. • Student • Emporia State University Emporia in the Rockies • Denver, CO 80204 • LITA

Arneson Dorothy A. • Branch Manager • Kansas City Public Library Westport Branch • Kansas City, MO 64111 • LAMA PLA

Arneson Jo Ann • Librarian • Oak Knoll School Library • Menlo Park, CA 94025

Arneson Rosemary H. • Director • Queens College Everett Library • Charlotte, NC 28274 • ACRL LAMA

Arnett Earlene H. • Librarian • Scott County Public Library • Georgetown, KY 40324 • PLA

Arnett Stanley K. II • Head of Adult Services • Saint Clair County Library System • Port Huron, MI 48060-4098 • MAGERT

Arney Mary E. • Trustee • Kansas City Public Library • Kansas City, MO 64106 • ALTA PLA

Arney Roberta T. • University of Texas at El Paso Library • El Paso, TX 79968-0582

Arnholter Ellen P. • Dallas, TX 75211-1806 • NMRT

Arnold Alexandria • Assistant Director • Summit Public Library • Summit, NJ 07901

Arnold Amy E. • Collection Development Libn. • AUM Library & Resource Center (LRC) • Montgomery, AL 36117-3596

Arnold Arlene • Media Coordinator • Pleasant Grove Junior High School • Pleasant Grove, UT 84062 • AASL

Arnold Betty C. • Library Supervisor • Pennsylvania State University E506 Pattee Library • University Park, PA 16802 • ACRL

Arnold Carole • Director • Dolores Public Library • Dolores, CO 81323 • PLA LRRT SRRT

Arnold Catherine J. • Library Director • Lucy Boyle Public Library • Blackfoot, ID 83221 • PLA

Arnold Cynthia • Librarian/Media Specialist • Lincoln Academy • Newcastle, ME 04553 • AASL

Arnold Donna W. • Computer Oper Coor/Ln • Oceanside Public Library • Oceanside, CA 92054

Arnold Fern Edith • Highland, IN 46322 • PLA *Life*

Arnold George • Univ Archvst & Hd of Spec Cllns • The American University Library • Washington, DC 20016-8046 • ACRL IFRT

Arnold Gwenyth L. • Youth Services Librarian • Palatine Public Library • Palatine, IL 60067 • ALSC PLA

Arnold Hilda • Drakesboro, KY 42337

Arnold Janice E. • Regional Adult Services Manager • Cuyahoga County Public Library Parma Regional • Parma, OH 44129-3199 • PLA

Arnold Jessie B. • Assistant Library Director • Alcorn State University Library • Lorman, MS 39096

Arnold JoAnn M. • Indiana University-Purdue University Walter E. Helmke Library • Fort Wayne, IN 46805-6514 • ACRL ALCTS

Arnold Judith M. • Saint Xavier University • Chicago, IL 60655 • ACRL RASD

Arnold Kathryn • Chattanooga, TN 37415

Arnold Linda A. • Section Mngr/Res Sharing MC175 • Online Computer Library Center (OCLC) • Dublin, OH 43017-3395 • ALCTS

Arnold Marianne S. • Colorado Spg, CO 80918 • AASL

Arnold Marilyn J. • Children's Librarian • Oak Park Public Library • Oak Park, IL 60301 • YALSA

Arnold Mary • Library Trustee • Glenview Public Library • Glenview, IL 60025

Arnold Mary J. • Young Adult Librarian • Medina County District Library • Medina, OH 44256 • YALSA

Arnold Michael S. • Assistant Director • South Brunswick Public Library • Monmouth Junction, NJ 08852 • LITA PLA

Arnold Patricia L. • Media Specialist • Bancroft Elementary School Minneapolis Public Schools • Minneapolis, MN 55407 • AASL IFRT

Arnold Paula N. • Norwich University Library • Northfield, VT 05663

Arnold Ruth • Director • Staunton Public Library Technical Services • Staunton, VA 24401

Arnold Sharon H. • Fullerton, CA 92633 • PLA

Arnold Veronica A. • Student • Texas Woman's University School of Library & Information Studies • Denton, TX 76204

Arnost Eleanor M. • Head of Technical Services • Hewlett Woodmere Public Library • Hewlett, NY 11557-2301 • ALCTS PLA

Arnott Amy L. • St. Louis, MO 63121

Arnott Julie E. • Preservation Education Officer • Southeastern Library Network (SOLINET) • Atlanta, GA 30309-2955 • ALCTS

Arnott Patricia D. • Associate Reference Librarian • University of Delaware Library • Newark, DE 19717-5267 • ACRL

Arnoux Yvette • Evanston, IL 60202

Arns Jennifer W. • Technical Information Specialist • U.S. General Accounting Office • Boston, MA 01950 • RASD FLRT

Arny Philip H. • TLC Coordinator • University of Washington Health Science Library & Info Center • Seattle, WA 98195 • LITA IFRT NMRT SRRT

Aroeste Jean L. • Assoc Univ Ln Ref & Clln Devel • Princeton University Library • Princeton, NJ 08544 • ACRL ALCTS RASD

Aroksaar Richard • Assistant Regional Librarian • National Park Service • Seattle, WA 98112

Arola Barbara J. • Media Specialist • Matteson School District #162 • Park Forest, IL 60466 • AASL

Aroldi Susan A. • Saddle Rvr, NJ 07458 • AASL

Aronson Mimi S • Librarian II-Adult Services • Phoenix Public Library Mesquite Branch • Phoenix, AZ 85032

Arosio Charlyne M. • Librarian • Obrien Middle School • Reno, NV 89503 • AASL

Arp Lori L. • Head of Central Reference • University of Colorado Norlin Library • Boulder, CO 80309-0184 • ACRL RASD

Arpaia William C. • Library Media Specialist • Platt Regional Vocational Technical School • Milford, CT 06460

Arps Jane F. • Longfellow School Library • Sheboygan, WI 53081 • ALSC

Arps Louisa W. • Denver, CO 80217 • Continuing

Arreola Miguel A. • Library Director • Instituto Technologico Estudios Superiores De Monterrey • Monterrey NL 64849, Mexico • ACRL ALCTS LAMA LITA

Arret Linda L. • Automated Reference Services • Library of Congress • Washington, DC 20541 • ALCTS LITA RASD

Arriaga Joaquin E. • New York Public Library • New York, NY 10016 • SRRT

Arrington Irene C. • Chicago, IL 60649

Arrington Lillian M. • School Library Media Specialist • Spring Valley JHS • Chestnut Ridge, NY 10977 • AASL

Arrivee Sally D. • Director • Brandon Township Library • Ortonville, MI 48462 • LAMA PLA YALSA

Arrowood Donna J. • Sunnyvale, CA 94088-2376

Arrowood Donna K. • Student • University of North Carolina Department of Library & Information Studies • Greensboro, NC 27412-5001 • ALSC NMRT

Arroyo Josie C. • Student • Sam Houston State University Department of Library Science • Huntsville, TX 77341-2236

Arsenault A. • Media Specialist • Harwich Middle School • Harwich, MA 02645 • AASL YALSA

Arsenault Kathy • Collection Development Librarian • University of South Florida • Saint Petersburg, FL 33701 • ACRL ALCTS

Arsenault Rochelle K. • School Librarian • Los Angeles Unified School District Venice High School • Los Angeles, CA 90036

Arsenty Richard • Science Librarian • State University of New York College at Purchase Library (SUNY) • Purchase, NY 10577-2826 • ACRL

Artale Anthony • Head of ILL • New York Medical College Medical Sciences Library • Valhalla, NY 10595

Arteaga Veda J. • Librarian • Ketchikan High School Library • Ketchikan, AK 99901 • AASL YALSA

Arter Patricia Y. • Student • Brigham Young University Harold B. Lee Library • Provo, UT 84602 • ASCLA SRRT

Arth J M. • University of Minnesota Bio-Medical Library • Minneapolis, MN 55455 • ACRL

Arthaud Rebecca • Columbia, MO 65203 • PLA

Arthur Barbara J. • School Library Systems Director • WWHE BOCES Media Center • Hudson Falls, NY 12839 • AASL YALSA

Arthur Gwen • Information Services • Bowling Green State University Jerome Library • Bowling Green, OH 43403 • ACRL LAMA RASD CLENE LIRT

Arthur Kathleen • University of Chicago • Chicago, IL 60637

Arthur Susan • Special Services Coordinator • Jacksonville Public Libraries Main Library • Jacksonville, FL 32202 • ASCLA

Artus Katherine J • Student • Emporia State University Emporia in the Rockies • Denver, CO 80204

Arvanites Jane M. • Albany, NY 12206

Arvey Martha M. • Fairbanks, AK 99708

Ary Gennean • Chandler, OK 74834 • AASL

Arya Usha M. • Head Librarian • Marine Corps Recruit Depot Library • San Diego, CA 92140

Arzu Angela R. • Duarte, CA 91010 • ALSC

Asantewa Doris • Librarian • Johns Hopkins University • Rockville, MD 20850 • ACRL

Asare Shirley A. • Senior Librarian • Georgia Regional Library for the Blind & Physically Handicapped • Atlanta, GA 30310

Asawa Edward E. • Acquisitions Librarian • Los Angeles County Public Library • Downey, CA 90242 • ALCTS

Asch R. Christopher • New York Public Library • New York, NY 10018-2788

Asche Jeanine • Librarian II • Half Moon Bay Branch Library SMCO Library • Half Moon Bay, CA 94019

Aschmann Althea • Head of Technical Services • Xavier University • New Orleans, LA 70125 • ACRL

Asfour Karen R. • Trafalgar Middle School • Cape Coral, FL 33991 • AASL

Ash-Geisler Viki L. • Children's Coordinator • Corpus Christi Public Library • Corpus Christi, TX 78401 • ALSC

Ash Lee • Bethany, CT 06524 • ACRL ALCTS LAMA PLA RASD IFRT LHRT MAGERT SRRT

Ash Shereen L. • San Anselmo, CA 94960

Ash Teresa M. • Owner • Rivershore Reading Store • Rock Island, IL 61201 • LAMA ERT

Ashbridge Carole L. • School Media Specialist • Sackets Harbor Central School • Sackets Harbor, NY 13685 • AASL

Ashburn Frances L. • Humanities Prog in Pub Libs • Let's Talk About It • Camden, SC 29020 • PLA ILERT

Ashby Anna Lou • Assoc Curator of Printed Books • Pierpont Morgan Library • New York, NY 10016 • ACRL ALCTS LHRT

Ashby Barbara A. • Barrington, RI 02806-4860 • AASL

Ashby Lois C. • Student • Louisiana State University School of Library & Information Science • Baton Rouge, LA 70803-3290

Ashcraft Carolyn • County Librarian • Saline County Public Library • Benton, AR 72015 • PLA

Ashcraft Darrel E. • Reference Librarian • Taunton Public Library • Taunton, MA 02780 • RASD

Ashe James C. • Librarian • John Jermain Memorial Library • Sag Harbor, NY 11963 • PLA

Ashe James Casey • AV Librarian • Tulsa City-County Library System • Tulsa, OK 74103

Ashe Kathleen M. • Head Cataloger • Traverse des Sioux Library System • Mankato, MN 56002-0608 • ALCTS

Ashe Lyn S. • Library Director • Rogers Memorial Library • Southampton, NY 11968 • PLA

Ashe Martha Irene • Houston, TX 77013 • AASL

Ashe Mary • San Francisco, CA 94118 • ACRL RASD

Ashe Patricia • Yuma, AZ 85364

Asheim Lester Prof • Professor,Emeritus • University of North Carolina at Chapel Hill School of Information and Library Science • Chapel Hill, NC 27599-3360 • ACRL PLA IFRT IRRT LIRT SRRT *Honorary*

Ashford Marguerite K. • Head Librarian • Punahou School • Honolulu, HI 96822 • AASL YALSA

Ashford Richard K. • Chevy Chase, MD 20815

Ashford Verna F. • ALTA Program Officer • American Library Association • Chicago, IL 60611-2795

Ashkar Carolyn S. • Knoxville, TN 37917 • ILERT

Ashley Deloris • Librarian • San Jose Medical Center Health Science Library • San Jose, CA 95112 • ASCLA LAMA LITA

Ashley Katherine E. • Wyncote Church Home • Wyncote, PA 19095 • ALSC YALSA *Continuing*

Ashley Lois A. • Student • Wayne State University Library Science Program • Detroit, MI 48202 • PLA

Ashley Lowell E. • Principal Cataloger • Virginia Polytechnic Institute and State University, Newman Library • Blacksburg, VA 24061-0434 • ACRL ALCTS LITA IRRT SRRT

Ashley Patricia N.R. • Pittsburgh, PA 15213

Ashley Roger S. • Director • Model High School • Bloomfield Hills, MI 48304 • AASL ALTA LIRT

Ashley Sally W. • Ln • Scarborough High School • Scarsborough, ME 04074 • AASL

Ashley Teresa E. • Reference Librarian • Austin Community College Northridge Campus • Austin, TX 78714 • ACRL RASD LIRT

Ashlock Larilyn • Englewood Public Library • Englewood, CO 80110

Ashmore Nancy Kay • FPO, AE 09420

Ashton-Beazie Janet • Director • Victor Valley College Library • Victorville, CA 92392 • ACRL

Ashton Charles J. • Children's Services Manager • Redwood City Public Library • Redwood City, CA 94063-1868 • PLA

Ashton Fran • Childrens Librarian • Edgewater Public Library • Edgewater, FL 32132

Ashton Jean W. • Director of Library • New York Historical Society Library • New York, NY 10024-5194 • ACRL

Ashton Patricia M. • Media Specialist • Pleasant Grove Elementary School • Pensacola, FL 32507 • AASL

Ashton Rick J. • City Librarian • Denver Public Library • Denver, CO 80203-2165 • LAMA PLA

Ashworth Cari M. • Student • Indiana University • Bloomington, IN 47405

Ashworth Sara J. • Youth Services Librarian • Saint Louis Public Library • Saint Louis, MO 63103-2389 • ALSC

Askuvich S. Jay • Sales Manager • Midwest Library Service • Bridgeton, MO 63044 • ACRL ALCTS LITA PLA ERT

Asmuth Gretchen W. • Preston, Gates, Ellis, etal • Washington, DC 20006

Asp William G. • Director • Office of Library Development & Services • Saint Paul, MN 55101 • ASCLA CLENE

Aspinall Karen • Getty Center Resources Collections • Santa Monica, CA 90401 • ALCTS

Assaf Nancy Corbin • Branch Librarian • San Diego Public Library Scripps Miramar Ranch Library Center • San Diego, CA 92131

Asselin Claudette M. • Brookline, MA 02146-6335 • RASD

Astbury Effie C. • Montreal PQ, H3G 1Y2 Canada • Continuing

Astle Deana L. • Head,Technical Services • Clemson University Robert Muldrow Cooper Library • Clemson, SC 29634-3001 • ACRL ALCTS

Aston Margaret C. • Holder ACT 2611, Australia • Continuing

Aston Rollah A. • Director • Eastern New Mexico University LRC • Roswell, NM 88201 • IFRT

Astorga Alicia M. • Director of Libraries • Ursuline Academy High School • Wilmington, DE 19806 • AASL

Astorino Monica C. • MMI Preparatory School Library • Freeland, PA 18224 • AASL

Atchison Fred Jr. • Director • North Central Kansas Ls • Manhattan, KS 66502 • PLA

Atchison Lillian E. • Administrative Librarian • University Sr H S • University City, MO 63130 • AASL YALSA

Aten Jean C. Mrs • Librarian • Pauoa School Library • Honolulu, HI 96822 • AASL ALSC *Life*

Athan Mary-Kay • University of California Los Angeles Graduate School of Library & Information Science • Los Angeles, CA 90024

Athearn Ruth C. • Library Trustee • San Juan Island Public Library • Friday Harbor, WA 98250

Athens Jean M. • Adult Services Librarian • San Ramon Library • San Ramon, CA 94583

Athy Doris Jean • Director • Thomas Jefferson Library • Jefferson City, MO 65101 • LAMA PLA

Atkins Cynthia F. • Director, of Library Services • Hopkinsville Community College Library • Hopkinsville, KY 42241-2100 • ACRL

Atkins Daniel E. • Dean of Professor • University of Michigan School of Information and Library Studies • Ann Arbor, MI 48109-1092

Atkins Donna A. • Head Documents Librarian • Kennedy Space Center Library • Kennedy Space Center, FL 32899

Atkins Frances Catherine • Children's Librarian • Sacramento Public Library Southgate Community Branch • Sacramento, CA 95823

Atkins Gene D. • Head of Technical Services • Thomas Branigan Memorial Library • Las Cruces, NM 88001 • SRRT

Atkins Gregg T. • Director of Library Services • College of San Mateo Library • San Mateo, CA 94402 • ACRL ASCLA LAMA LITA

Atkins Judith • ILL & Asst Ref. • Greenfield Public Library • Greenfield, MA 01301

Atkins Lori K. • Student • University of North Texas School of Library & Information Sciences • Denton, TX 76203

Atkins Mary Ann • Automation Coor./Consultant • Bur Oak Library System • Shorewood, IL 60436 • LITA

Atkins Millie • Managing Editor • University Microfilms International • Ann Arbor, MI 48106-1346 • AASL

Atkins Priscilla • Student • Ball State University • Munice, IN 47304 • ACRL

Atkins Rodney • Sr. Librarian/Circ. & Media • Tyler Public Library • Tyler, TX 75702

Atkins Stephen • Head, Resource Development • Texas A & M University Sterling C. Evans Library • College Station, TX 77843-5000 • ACRL ALCTS LAMA LRRT

Atkins Thomas V. • Chief Librarian • Hunter College Library • New York, NY 10021 • ACRL LITA

Atkinson Jane W. • Student • Georgia State University • Atlanta, GA 30303-3083 • AASL

Atkinson Joan L. • Associate Professor • University of Alabama School of Library & Information Studies • Tuscaloosa, AL 35487-0252 • AASL ALSC YALSA IFRT LRRT

Atkinson Margaret H. • Jenison, MI 49428 • ALCTS ALTA *Life*

Atkinson Nancy I. • Moscow, ID 83843 • ACRL ALCTS *Continuing*

Atkinson Norma M. • Laredo, TX 78043

Atkinson Robert L. • Fermi Laboratory Library • Batavia, IL 60510

Atkinson Ross W. • Asst Univ Ln for Clln Devel • Cornell University Library • Ithaca, NY 14853 • ACRL ALCTS LAMA

Atkisson Elizabeth K. • FPO, AE 09619-3000

Atlas Michel • University of Louisville Libraries • Louisville, KY 40292 • ACRL

Ator-James Carrie S. • Coordinator/Educational Media • Ohio University Libraries • Athens, OH 45701-2978 • ACRL

Attalai Christine Koskimaki • Librarian • High Park Montessori School • Toronto ON, M6P 2CP Canada • AASL

Attarian Lorraine B. • St. Mary Medical Center • Long Beach, CA 90801

Attig John C. • Associate Ln/Cataloger • Pennsylvania State University E506 Pattee Library • University Park, PA 16802 • ACRL ALCTS LITA RASD MAGERT

Attinello E. F. • Librarian II • Chicago Public Library • Chicago, IL 60605

Attwood Ray • Trustee • British Library Information Sciences (BLISS) • London, England

Atwell Pat R. • Ln • Broken Arrow Elementary Shawnee Mission School District • Shawnee, KS 66401 • AASL

Atwood Donna J • Children's Librarian • Olathe Public Library • Olathe, KS 66061 • ALSC PLA

Atwood Emily V. • Librarian • Dr. Nixon Elementary School • El Paso, TX 79934 • AASL ALSC

Atwood Joanne • Seoul American High School • APO, AP 96205-0005

Atwood Judy J. • Librarian • Middle Georgia Regional Library • Macon, GA 31201

Atwood Laura J. • Munster, IN 46321

Au Eleanor Chong • Head Special Collection • University of Hawaii Thomas Hale Hamilton Library • Honolulu, HI 96822 • ACRL

Au Ka-Neng • Microcomputers Systems Librarian • Rutgers University John Cotton Dana Library • Newark, NJ 07102 • LITA RASD

Au-Yeung Sylvia M.L. • The Hong Kong and Shanghai Banking Corporation, GHO Library • Hong Kong, Hong Kong • LITA

Aubitz Karen L. • Library Media Specialist • Westtown-Thornbury Elementary School • West Chester, PA 19382

Aubrey Daurene V. • Head Librarian • Bermuda College Library • Devonshire, Bermuda • ACRL LAMA LITA LIRT

Auchstetter Rosann M. • Indiana University • Bloomington, IN 47405

Aucoin Barbara A. • Middle School Librarian • Sacred Heart Academy • New Orleans, LA 70115 • AASL

Aucoin Ronald G. • Librarian • Adams & Reese • New Orleans, LA 70139

Aucoin Sharilynn A. • Library Manager I • State Library of Louisiana • Baton Rouge, LA 70821-0131 • VRT

Aud Thomas L. • Director • Jackson-Madison County Library • Jackson, TN 38301 • PLA

Audette Mary L. • Marlboro Public Library • Marlboro, MA 01752

Audia Christina • Bibliographic Database Manager • Detroit Public Library Acq Dept • Detroit, MI 48202-4093 • ALCTS

Audley Cathy J. • Mgr of Pub Rel Dept/Development • Tulsa City-County Library System • Tulsa, OK 74103 • LAMA PLA

Auer Margaret E. • Director of Libraries • University of Detroit-Mercy Main Library • Detroit, MI 48221 • ACRL ALCTS LAMA LITA RASD

Auerbach Rita • Librarian • Stratford Avenue School • Garden City, NY 11530 • AASL ALSC IFRT SRRT

Auerbach Robert S. • Greenbelt, MD 20770 • Continuing

Auerswald Paul E. • Editor and Publisher • Foreign Policy Bulletin • Washington, DC 20016 • ALCTS GODORT IRRT

Aufdemberge Sara L. • Hayden High School • Topeka, KS 66606 • AASL

Aufdenkamp JoAnn • Business/Econmics Librarian • Northern Illinois University University Libraries • DeKalb, IL 60115-2868 • RASD

Aufderhaar Kathleen E. • Bowling Green, OH 43402

Aufses Harriet W. • Librarian • Hunter College High School L • New York, NY 10128 • AASL

Auge Mary L. • Lisle, IL 60532-2425

Augelli John F. • Director • Stillwater Public Library • Stillwater, OK 74074 • PLA

Auger Brian K. • Regional Librarian • Montgomery County Department of Public Libraries • Rockville, MD 20850

Aughinbaugh Dianne T. • Media Specialist • Cascade School • Cascade, MD 21719 • AASL

Aughinbaugh Patricia B. • Director • Saint Francis College • Loretto, PA 15940

Augur James K. • Library Science Student • University of Michigan School of Information and Library Studies • Ann Arbor, MI 48109-1092 • PLA

August Robert L. • Librarian • Library of Congress • Washington, DC 20541

Augustine Joan • Berkeley, CA 94703-1038 • LRRT SRRT

Augustine Lynne A. • Assistant Product Manager • Dun & Bradstreet, Inc. • New Provicence, NJ 07974 • ACRL RASD

Augustine Rolf S. • Cataloger • University of California McHenry Library • Santa Cruz, CA 95064 • ACRL ALCTS RASD

Augustine Sheryl • Newburgh Free Library • Newburgh, NY 12550

Augustyn Frederick J. Jr • Student • Library of Congress • Washington, DC 20541 • LHRT LRRT

Auh Y John • Chief Librarian • Wagner College Library and Learning Resources Center • Staten Island, NY 10301 • ACRL

Aul Billie K. • Senior Librarian • New York State Library State Education Department • Albany, NY 12230 • SRRT

Auld Hampton M. • Branch Manager • Carroll County Public Library North Carroll Branch • Greenmount, MD 21074

Auld Lawrence W. S. • Associate Professor • East Carolina University Department of Library & Information Studies • Greenville, NC 27858-4353 • ALCTS

Auld Vivian A. • Computer Resources Coordinator • Louisiana State University School of Library & Information Science • Baton Rouge, LA 70803-3290

Aulston Frances P. • Student • Drexel University College of Information Studies • Philadelphia, PA 19104-2875

Ault Robert D. • Student • Kent State University School of Library & Information Science • Kent, OH 44242-0001

Auma De Jesus • Reference Librarian • Seton Hall University Law Library • Newark, NJ 07102

Aumann Katherine M. • Columbus, OH 43202 • Continuing

Aumiller Tina M. • Information Access Services • University Park, PA 16802

Auriene Patricia J. • Director of Technical Services • Fountaindale Public Library District • Bolingbrook, IL 60440 • PLA

Aust-Keefer Mary Beth • Director of Lib. & AV Services • Edison State Community College • Piqua, OH 45356 • ACRL LAMA

Aust Karen M. • Gulfport Public Library • Gulfport, FL 33707 • RASD

Austen Barbara E. • Museum Curator • Suffolk County Historical Society • Riverhead, NY 11901

Austen Christine A. • Mount Sinai, NY 11766 • AASL

Auster Ethel Dr. • Faculty of Lib & Inf Sci • University of Toronto Faculty of Library & Information Science • Toronto ON, M5S 1A1 Canada • ACRL LITA RASD

Austgen Beth • Librarian • St Charles H S • St Charles, IL 60174

Austhof Bart A. • Geography/Map Librarian • University of Nebraska Love Library • Lincoln, NE 68588-0410 • ACRL MAGERT

Austin B. • AT&T Bell Laboratories • Murray Hill, NJ 07974 • ACRL LITA

Austin Dale M. • Student • Northeastern Illinois University Library • Chicago, IL 60625 • RASD SRRT

Austin Deborah R. • Preservation Officer • Fort Worth Public Library • Fort Worth, TX 76102 • ALCTS LIRT

Austin Debra E. • Librarian • Data Research • Saint Louis, MO 63132 • LITA

Austin Deronica Mrs. • Trustee • Yonkers Public Library • Yonkers, NY 10701 • ALTA

Austin Diane A. • Media Specialist • Lively Vocational-Technical H.S. • Tallahassee, FL 32308

Austin Gary L. • Student • University of Hawaii School of Library & Information Studies • Honolulu, HI 96822 • ACRL PLA RASD

Austin Josephine S. • Janesville, WI 53546 • PLA RASD *Continuing*

Austin Judith P. • Hd of Local Hist & Genealogy Rdn • Library of Congress • Washington, DC 20541 • RASD

Austin Lisa M. • Student • University of North Carolina Department of Library & Information Studies • Greensboro, NC 27412-5001 • AASL

Austin Mary C. • Spruce Pine, NC 28777 • ALSC

Austin Nancy A. • Head of Cataloging • Stanford University Lane Medical Library • Stanford, CA 94305-5323 • ACRL LITA

Austin Ronald E. • Reference Librarian • University of Michigan Graduate Library Reference • Ann Arbor, MI 48109 • ACRL RASD

Austin Rosemary • Library Director • Blackfeet Community College • Browning, MT 59417 • ACRL

Austin Roxanna • Decatur, GA 30033 • Continuing

Austin Steve • Trustee • Boulder Public Library • Boulder, CO 80306

Austrino Kathleen M. • Assistant Supervisor • Reuben McMillan Free Library Association Youngstown & Mahoning Cnty P L • Youngstown, OH 44503

Austrom Elizabeth C. • Dist. Principal-Curriculum Res. • Vancouver School District • Vancouver BC, Canada • AASL YALSA

Austveg Kari • Dallas, TX 75240

Auth Judith M. • Library Director • Riverside City & County Public Library • Riverside, CA 92502-0468 • PLA

Autry Brick • Cape Girardeau, MO 63701

Avant Julia King Dr. • Director • Lincoln Parish Library • Ruston, LA 71270 • PLA

Avenick Karen • Assistant Director • Camden County Library Echelon Urban Center • Voorhees, NJ 08043 • PLA RASD CLENE

Avera Victoria • Smithsonian Institution Libraries • Washington, DC 20560 • ALCTS FLRT

Averette Ed • Library Budget & Operations Mgr • San Diego State University Love Library • San Diego, CA 92182-0511 • LAMA

Averette Kay A. • LibrariaN Division Hd PRE/ID • Akron-Summit County Public Library • Akron, OH 44326-0001 • YALSA EMIERT SRRT

Averre Amy A. • Librarian • Husson College Library • Bangor, ME 04401 • ACRL

Avers Janet Johnson • FPO, AP 96306-1602

Avery-Sublett Janet M. • Audio Visual Librarian • Angelina College • Lufkin, TX 75902

Avery Barbara E. • School Librarian • Sunnyslope Elementary School • Phoenix, AZ 85020 • AASL

Avery Bonnie E. • Forestry Librarian • Oregon State University William Jasper Kerr Library • Corvallis, OR 97331-4501

Avery Bonny • Librarian • Troy Public Library • Troy, MI 48084 • ALSC

Avery Christine C. • Business Librarian • Pennsylvania State University Pattee Library • University Park, PA 16802 • ACRL RASD

Avery Ernest L. Jr. • University of Pittsburgh School of Library and Information Science • Pittsburgh, PA 15260 • LIRT LRRT

Avery Gail W. • Regional Branch Librarian • District of Columbia Public Library Chevy Chase Branch • Washington, DC 20015 • PLA IFRT

Avery Galen • Supervisor,Govt Procurement Ctr • Toledo-Lucas County Public Library • Toledo, OH 43624

Avery Joan C. • Librarian • Los Angeles Public Library System Atwater Branch • Los Angeles, CA 90039

Avery M. Leonilda Sister • Librarian • Saint Rose of Lima School • N. Syracuse, NY 13212 • AASL

Avery Marianne K. • Assistant Director • Newark Public Library • Newark, NJ 07101-0630 • PLA

Avery Maude E. Miss • Providence, RI 02906 • Continuing

Avery T. M. Jr. Mr. • Kitty Hawk, NC 27949-3806 • ACRL ALCTS *Life*

Aviles Elizabeth R. • Louisville, KY 40207 • NMRT

Avitabile Susan L. • Consultant • Batterymarch Financial Management • Boston, MA 02210

Avner Jane A. • University of Washington • Seattle, WA 98195 • ACRL ALSC LRRT

Avram Henriette D. • Silver Spgs, MD 20903 • ACRL ALCTS LITA *Life*

Awagain Kenneth K. • Public Services Libraian • McNeese State University Lether E. Frazar Memorial Library • Lake Charles, LA 70609

Awe Susan C. • Branch Manager • Jefferson County Public Library Arvada Branch • Arvada, CO 80002 • RASD

Awkard Julita C. • Librarian • Florida A & M University School of Nursing • Tallahassee, FL 32307 • ACRL

Awo Isaie • Student • Emporia State University School of Library & Information Management • Emporia, KS 66801

Axam John Arthur • Philadelphia, PA 19141 • PLA SRRT

Axdal Joan • Cottage Grove, MN 55016 • LITA

Axeen Marina E. Dr • Ball State University Bracken Library • Muncie, IN 47306-0160 • ACRL *Life*

Axel-Lute Melanie • Children's Librarian • South Orange Public Library • South Orange, NJ 07079 • ALSC

Axelrad Ronald H. • Archivist • Jewish Historical Society of Central Jersey • New Brunswick, NJ 08901 • ACRL ERT

Axelrod Adelina Azevedo • Student • Simmons College Graduate School of Library & Information Science • Boston, MA 02115

Axelrod Jerold • Trustee • Commack Public Library District • Commack, NY 11725 • ALTA

Axt Randolph William • Board of Trustees • Superior Public Library • Superior, WI 54880 • Life

Axtmann Margaret Maes • Asst. Director Tech. Serv. • University of Minnesota Law Library • Minneapolis, MN 55455 • ALCTS LAMA LITA

Ayala-Schueneman Maria • Government Documents Librarian • Texas A & I University James C. Jernigan Library • Kingsville, TX 78363 • GODORT

Ayala Barbara • Student • San Jose State University Division of Library & Information Science • San Jose, CA 95192-0029

Ayala Jacqueline L. • San Diego, CA 92110-5501

Ayala John L. • Dean Learning Resources • Fullerton College • Fullerton, CA 92634 • ACRL SRRT

Aycock Ann B. • Librarian • Vista Verde Middle School • Phoenix, AZ 85032

Aydell Mary Alice • Trustee • Ascension Parish Library • Donaldsonville, LA 70346-2535 • ALTA PLA

Ayer Carol A. • Technical Information Officer • Intermountain Research Station • Ogden, UT 84401 • FLRT

Ayer Valerie V. • Stone Mountain, GA 30083 • ILERT

Ayers Barbara K. • Librarian • Putnam/Northern Westchester BOCES School Library System • Yorktown Hts, NY 10598 • AASL

Ayers Janet • Northwestern University Library Mudd Library for Science & Engineering • Evanston, IL 60208 • ACRL ALCTS LITA RASD

Ayers Leighann • Head Serials Cataloging • University of Michigan Libraries Technical Services • Ann Arbor, MI 48109 • LITA

Ayers Virginia F. • Librarian • Evanston Township High School • Evanston, IL 60204 • AASL

Aylward James F. • Director • United States Navy Naval Education & Training Center Main Library • Newport, RI 02841-5002 • AFLRT FLRT

Aylward Judith • Librarian • Kansas City Public Library • Kansas City, MO 64106 • ALSC

Aylward Susan L. • Assitant Library Director • North Kingstown Free Library • North Kingstown, RI 02852

Ayotte Marie Blanche Sr • Librarian • Sacred Heart Academy • Stamford, CT 06902

Ayres Anne M. • Student • University of Tennessee-Knoxville Graduate School of Library & Information Science • Knoxville, TN 37996-4330 • ALSC IFRT

Ayres Carolyn D. • Childrens Librarian • Port Washington Public Library • Port Washington, NY 11050

Ayres Dorothy • Englewood, CO 80110 • ALSC *Continuing*

Ayres Shirley • Librarian • Telos Corporation • Shrewsbury, NJ 07703

Azar Ella-Paula • Student • University of Rhode Island Graduate School of Library & Information Studies • Kingston, RI 02881-0815

Azeltine Mary R. • Cedar Rapids Public Library • Cedar Rapids, IA 52401

Azen Linda • Seal Beach, CA 90740 • ACRL RASD MAGERT NMRT

Azmi Hesham M. • Giza, Egypt • LITA

Azralon Allene B. • Technical Librarian • Hewlett-Packard Company • Rockville, MD 20850

Azusenis Helen V. • Librarian • Cleveland Public Library • Cleveland, OH 44114-1271 • LAMA PLA

Azzata Gerry • Preservation Supervisor • Harvard University • Cambridge, MA 02138 • ACRL SRRT

Azzoli Barbara E. • Student • Rutgers University School of Communication Information & Library Studies • New Brunswick, NJ 08903

Baade Harley D. • Houston, TX 77018

Baars William A. • Portland, OR 97213

Baarson Elaine M • Library Manager,Information Svs • Tucson-Pima Library • Tucson, AZ 85701 • PLA RASD SRRT

Baaske Jan E. • Administrative Assistant • Indian Trails Public Library District • Wheeling, IL 60090 • LAMA

Babayan Suzanne • Librarian • Dearborn Park Elementary School • Seattle, WA 98108

Babb Melissa B. • Lansing, KS 66043 • AASL

Babb Sandra T. • Library Director • Burleson Public Library • Burleson, TX 76028 • PLA

Babbitt Dennis L. • Director • Madison-Jefferson County Public Library • Madison, IN 47250 • PLA

Babbitt Susan • Director of Libraries • Tulsa Public Schools • Tulsa, OK 74147-0208 • AASL

Babcock James M. • Harsen Island, MI 48028 • ACRL RASD *Life*

Babcock Judith A. • Media Specialist • Miami Killian Senior High School • Miami, FL 33176

Babcock Lucy Ann • El Reno, OK 73036 • ALSC RASD *Continuing*

Babcock Melinda J. • Oxford University Press-OED • Oxford, United Kingdom • ACRL RASD

Babcock Rosa B. • Librarian-LRC • El Centro College • Dallas, TX 75202

Babcock Warren E. • Reference Librarian • Utah State University Merrill Library • Logan, UT 84322-3000

Babcock William D. • Library Director • Markham Public Library • Markham, IL 60426 • PLA

Babel Deborah B. • Clemson University • Cleson, SC 29634 • ACRL LAMA

Baber Carolyn D. • Head, Government Publications • San Diego State University Library • San Diego, CA 92182-0511 • ACRL GODORT

Baber Elizabeth A. • Head of Data Base Management • Rice University Fondren Library • Houston, TX 77251-1892 • LITA

Babikow Mary Beth • Librarian • Baltimore County Public Library • Towson, MD 21204 • LAMA PLA

Babin Denise L. • Student • Louisiana State University School of Library & Information Science • Baton Rouge, LA 70803-3290 • PLA

Babits Ann C. • East Brunswick Public Library • E. Brunswick, NJ 08816

Babou Robin L. • Student • San Jose State University Division of Library & Information Science • San Jose, CA 95192-0029 • ACRL ALCTS RASD IFRT LRRT NMRT SRRT

Babula Martie • Coordinator, Tech. Processing • Maine Township High School East • Park Ridge, IL 60068 • ALCTS LITA

Baburek Milton Jr. • Librarian & Chairman • Proviso East High School Library • Maywood, IL 60153

Baca Nancy D. • Alameda County Library System • Fremont, CA 94538 • ALCTS LAMA LITA PLA EMIERT

Bacak Laverne • Branch Librarian • Wharton County Library El Campo Branch • El Campo, TX 77437

Bacchus Anetta I. • Teacher Librarian • Scarborough Board of Education Professional Library 2 • Scarborough ON, M1P 4N6 Canada • ACRL

Bach Barbara S. • Minneapolis, MN 55422 • YALSA

Bach Harriette H. • Librarian • Hennepin County Library Southdale-Hennepin Area Library • Edina, MN 55435

Bach Nancy C. • Librarian • Van Hise Middle School • Madison, WI 53705 • AASL YALSA IFRT

Bacha Arden K. • West Fork, AR 72774 • PLA

Bacharach Ruth B. • Librarian • King County Library System Shoreline Branch • Seattle, WA 98155

Bachelder Lisa J. • Reference Librarian • Princeton University Firestone Library • Princeton, NJ 08544

Bachemin Anatalie W. • School Librarian • Fannie Williams Middle School New Orleans Public Schools • New Orleans, LA 70126 • AASL YALSA

Bachich Jan • Automation Systems Coordinator • Sacramento Public Library • Sacramento, CA 95814

Bachman Neal K. • Kansas City Kansas Public Library • Kansas City, KS 66101

Bachman Sandra Lee • Catalog Librarian • Burbank Public Library • Burbank, CA 91502

Bachmann Christine • Director • Central Lake Township Library • Central Lake, MI 49622

Bachmann Donna L. • Coordinator of Access Services • University of Puget Sound Collins Memorial Library • Tacoma, WA 98416 • ACRL

Bachmann Jean M. • Head Technical Services • Elyria Public Library • Elyria, OH 44035 • ALCTS ILERT

Bachus Orval Jr. Mr. • Port Huron, MI 48060 • SRRT

Back Carol J. • K-12 Librarian • Cheyenne Wells School • Cheyenne Wells, CO 80810 • AASL

Back Gary A. • Librarian • Nathan Hale High School • West Allis, WI 53227

Backes Cindy A. • Librarian • Saint Teresa School • Pittsburgh, PA 15209 • AASL

Backes John • Assoc. Dean, Instr. Res./Comp. • North Seattle Community College • Seattle, WA 98103 • ACRL

Backhus Daine • Reference Librarian • Pikes Peak Library District • Colorado Springs, CO 80901

Backman Carroll H. Mrs. • Matthews, NC 28105 • LAMA

Backus Claudia • Waukesha Public Library • Waukesha, WI 53186 • ALSC

Backus Linda K. • Scott & White Memorial Hospital Medical Library • Temple, TX 76508

Bacmeister Elena Snell • Bibliographic Assistant/Serials • Johns Hopkins University Milton S. Eisenhower Library • Baltimore, MD 21218 • ACRL

Bacon Carey H. • Blaine School Libraries • Blaine, WA 98230 • AASL ALSC YALSA

Bacon Carol E. • Director • Littlefield Library • Tyngsboro, MA 01879-0218 • PLA

Bacon Carolyn J. • Briar Crest Accelerated School • St. Ann, MO 63074

Bacon Dalli C. • Head Librarian • Convent of The Sacred Heart • New York, NY 10028 • AASL

Bacon Grace W. • Middletown, CT 06457 • ACRL RASD *Continuing*

Bacon Lois C. • Business Analyst/Information Ser • Faxon Company Inc. • Westwood, MA 02090 • ACRL ALCTS

Bacon Phoebe Edwards • National Cathedral School • Washington, DC 20016 • ALSC

Bacsanyi Karen H. • Librarian • Wayne State University • Detroit, MI 48202 • ACRL RASD

Bade Debra K. • Reference/Special Projects Ln. • Cable News Network (CNN) • Atlanta, GA 30348

Baden Diane G. • Head, of Bibliographic Services • Minuteman Library Network • Framingham, MA 01701 • ALCTS LITA

Baden Marla M. • Reference Center Director • Tri-ALSA • Fort Wayne, IN 46801

Bader Kathleen D. • Director • Snow Library • Orleans, MA 02653 • ALCTS LAMA PLA

Badertscher David A. • Head of Technical Services • Washington & Lee University • Lexington, VA 24450

Badertscher Kimberlin H. • Indianapolis, IN 46278 • ALSC IFRT

Badics Joseph A. • University of Michigan School of Information and Library Studies • Ann Arbor, MI 48109-1092

Badillo Zwinda • Aguadilla, PR 00605

Bading Kathryn E. • Catalog/Maintainance Librarian • Trinity University • San Antonio, TX 78212 • ALCTS LITA

Badion Norman • Supervisor Reference-AV Dept. • Napa City-County Library • Napa, CA 94559-3396

Badough Rose Marie • Librarian • Naaman Forest High School • Garland, TX 75040 • AASL YALSA

Badrampour Ailyn C. • Miami-Dade Public Library West Kendall Regional Library • Miami, FL 33186

Badrinarayan Archana • Livingston, NJ 07039

Baechtold Marguerite • Kalamazoo, MI 49008 • Continuing

Baehr Betty B. Miss • Chevy Chase, MD 20815 • LAMA RASD *Life*
Baehr Carl W. • Librarian • Trinity Memorial Hospital Fine Library • Cudahy, WI 53110
Baek Heh Young • Student • University of Wisconsin School of Library & Information Studies • Madison, WI 53706 • ACRL EMIERT
Baer Eleanora A. • Saint Louis, MO 63144 • AASL
Baer Elizabeth • Oxford, OH 45056 • ALCTS *Continuing*
Baer Joyce • Branch Supervisor • Public Library of Cincinnati & Hamilton County Pleasant Ridge • Cincinnati, OH 45213
Baer Laurel E. • Librarian • Wayne County Public Library • Wooster, OH 44691
Baer Lisa C. • Student • Brigham Young University School of Library & Information Sciences • Provo, UT 84602
Baer Nadine L. • Serial Cataloger • University of Rhode Island Library • Kingston, RI 02881-0803 • ACRL ALCTS
Baer Rebecca A. • Middle School Librarian • School District U-46 • Elgin, IL 60120
Baer Robert L. • Director • Enumclaw Public Library • Enumclaw, WA 98022 • PLA YALSA SRRT
Baernthaler Klaus • Reference Librarian • Salve Regina College Library • Newport, RI 02840 • ACRL RASD
Baerveldt Larry R. • Assistant Librarian/Reference • Hanover College Duggan Library • Hanover, IN 47243-0287 • RASD LIRT
Baerwald Diane A. • Los Angeles, CA 90049
Baesler Alice • Board Member • Lexington Public Library • Lexington, KY 40507 • ALTA
Baetge Dorothy C. • Director of Media Services • Pasadena Independent School District • Pasadena, TX 77502 • AASL
Baez Maureen L. • Adult Services Librarian • Tampa-Hillborough Cnty P L Sys Riverview Branch Library • Riverview, FL 33569
Bagan Beverly J. • Executive Director • Virginia State Library & Archives • Richmond, VA 23219 • AASL LAMA
Bagavan Sandhya • Natick, MA 01760
Bagby Charlotte A. • Oakland, CA 94602
Bagby Dallas M. • Medical Librarian • Saint Boniface General Hosp. Helene Fuld Library • Winnipeg MB, R2H 2A7 Canada • ACRL IRRT
Bagby Felicia R. • ARCO • Los Angeles, CA 90071 • ALCTS
Bagby Pamela Mae • Librarian • Castlewood Library • Englewood, CO 80112
Bagby Ross F. • Columbus, OH 43220
Bagg Deborah L. • Asst. Managing Librarian • King County Library System Federal Way Public Library • Federal Way, WA 98003 • ASCLA
Baggs Robert N. Jr • Library Director • Ocean City Free Public Library • Ocean City, NJ 08226-3071
Bagley-Stanton Beth • New Baltimore, MI 48047
Bagley Laurie J. • Research Director • Saint Luke's Hospital Medical Library • San Francisco, CA 94110
Bagley Michaeleen M. • Librarian • Monfort Elementary School • Greeley, CO 80631 • AASL ALSC
Baglivo Megan Del • Serials Services Librarian • Hartford Graduate Center • Hartford, CT 06120
Bagnall Whitney S. • Special Collections Librarian • Columbia University • New York, NY 10027-7297 • ACRL
Bagnasco Nancy • Wayne State University Library Science Program • Detroit, MI 48202 • PLA
Bagwell Linda • Branch Head • Amarillo Public Library East Branch • Amarillo, TX 79103 • ACRL
Bahbah Johnny A. • Student • Brigham Young University School of Library & Information Sciences • Provo, UT 84602
Bahm Barbara • Librarian • Tonganoxie High School • Tonganoxie, KS 66086 • AASL
Bahnsen Kay E. • Reference Librarian • Bloomingdale Public Library • Bloomingdale, IL 60108 • PLA
Bahnsen Wendy S. • King of Prussia, PA 19406 • ACRL ERT
Bahr Alice H. • Director • Spring Hill College Thomas Byrne Memorial Library • Mobile, AL 36608 • ACRL LAMA
Bahr Amy • Franconia, NH 03580 • PLA
Bahr Nancy I. • Plymouth, MI 48170
Bahre Stephen A. • Library Director • Merrimack College McQuade Library • North Andover, MA 01845 • ACRL
Bahrenfuse Susan J. • Grinnell College • Grinnell, IA 50112-0811 • ACRL ALCTS LITA IFRT
Baia Wendy • Serial Dept. • University of Colorado Norlin Library • Boulder, CO 80309-0184 • LITA
Baier Helgard B. • Graduate Student • Louisiana State University School of Library & Information Science • Baton Rouge, LA 70803-3290 • IFRT
Baier Norman S. • Simsbury, CT 06070 • LAMA
Baiera Patricia A. • Media Specialist • Hubbard Elementary School • East Berlin, CT 06023 • AASL
Bailey Alberta S. • Head of Public Services • University of Arkansas Mullins Library • Fayetteville, AR 72701 • LAMA LITA
Bailey Alvin R. • Director • Denison Public Library • Denison, TX 75020 • PLA
Bailey Ann C. • Director • Bradford Memorial Library • El Dorado, KS 67042 • PLA
Bailey Barbara J. • Head Reference Librarian • Welles-Turner Memorial Library • Glastonbury, CT 06033
Bailey Bertha M. • Pittsburgh, PA 15206 • AASL YALSA *Life*
Bailey Billy D. • Student • University of Kentucky College of Library & Information Science • Lexington, KY 40506-0391
Bailey Brenda K. • Denver, CO 80203-3622 • LITA
Bailey Carol A. • Atlantic Beach, FL 32233
Bailey Catherine Miss • Indianapolis, IN 46240 • ALSC ASCLA *Continuing*
Bailey Charles W. Jr • Assistant Director for Systems • University of Houston Libraries • Houston, TX 77204-2091 • ACRL ALCTS LITA
Bailey Cheryl M. • Library Director • University of Mary Library • Bismarck, ND 58504 • ACRL
Bailey Christine D. • University of Chicago Library • Chicago, IL 60637-1502
Bailey D. Jean • Library Media Specialist • Lithonia High School • Lithonia, GA 30058 • AASL
Bailey Darlene L. • Childrens Librarian • Sacramento Public Library North Sacramento-Hagginwood Branch • Sacramento, CA 95815
Bailey Deborah A. • Librarian • West Middle School • Rockford, IL 61103 • AASL
Bailey Deborah L. • Assistant Reference Librarian • Arkansas State University Dean B. Ellis Library • State University, AR 72467-2040 • ACRL LHRT
Bailey Don L. • Information Specialist • Lake Lanier Regional Library System Forsyth County Branch • Cumming, GA 30130
Bailey Dorothy C. • Atlanta, GA 30345
Bailey Edgar C. Jr. • Director • Providence College Phillips Memorial Library • Providence, RI 02918 • ACRL
Bailey Eleanor F. • Media Specialist • Winter Haven Senior High School • Winter Haven, FL 33880 • AASL YALSA
Bailey Evelyn M. • Brunswick, ME 04011 • Continuing
Bailey Gail C. • Staff Specialist • Maryland State Department of Education Division of Library Development & Services • Baltimore, MD 21201 • AASL
Bailey Gary • Adminstrator • Eckhart Public Library • Auburn, IN 46706
Bailey George M. • Claremont, CA 91711 • ACRL RASD *Life*
Bailey Jeffrey R. • Arkansas State University Dean B. Ellis Library • State University, AR 72467-2040
Bailey Jennifer S. • Student • Indiana University School of Library and Information Science • Bloomington, IN 47405 • ALCTS IFRT SRRT
Bailey Julia • Assistant Director • Sumter County Library • Sumter, SC 29150
Bailey Karen R. • Student • Southern Connecticut State University School of Libray Science & Instructional Technology • New Haven, CT 06515 • SRRT
Bailey Kay • Supervisory Librarian • COMFLEACT Yokosuka Library • FPO, AP 96349-1111 • AFLRT
Bailey Leeta L. • Amherst College Library • Amherst, MA 01002 • ACRL
Bailey Leslie • John Cooper School • Woodlands, TX 77381 • AASL
Bailey Loreen R. • School Librarian • Wilchester Elementary School • Houston, TX 77079
Bailey Lucille E. • Carmel, NY 10512 • ACRL
Bailey Lugene • Reference Service Librarian • Central State University Hallie Q Brown Memorial Library • Wilberforce, OH 45384
Bailey M. Susan • Columbia, MD 21044-1692
Bailey Madeleine J. • Director of Library Services • Mount Royal College Library • Calgary AB, T3E 6K6 Canada • ACRL
Bailey Margaret J. • User Education LIbrarian • Southern Methodist University Fondren Library • Dallas, TX 75275-0135 • LIRT
Bailey Martha J. • Life Sciences Librarian • Purdue University Libraries Life Sciences Library • West Lafayette, IN 47907-1323 • ACRL LAMA
Bailey Melanie D. • Student • Portland State University School of Education • Portland, OR 97207 • AASL SRRT
Bailey Nancy P. • Bimingham, AL 35223
Bailey Pamela J. • Manager-Training Support & Adm. • OCLA Pacific Network • Rancho Cucamonga, CA 91730
Bailey Patti L. • Technical Service Librarian • Deschutes County Library • Bend, OR 97701 • LITA
Bailey Paul D. • Urbana, IL 61801
Bailey Rebecca F. • Libraian III • Warioto Regional Library Center • Clarksville, TN 37041-0886
Bailey Robert G. • Methodist Country House • Wilmington, DE 19807 • ACRL *Continuing*
Bailey Roberta J. • Deputy Publisher • Simon & Schuster Young Books • Hemel Hempstead Hert, United Kingdom
Bailey Ruth A. • Librarian • Knox High School • Knox, IN 46534
Bailey Sara G. • Library Director • West Palm Beach Public Library • West Palm Beach, FL 33401 • LAMA PLA
Bailey Sara M. • Pitman, NJ 08071
Bailey Shelia M. • Head Librarian • Rowan-Cabarnes Community College • Salisbury, NC 28144
Bailey Sherryl L. • Director • Boston University Corp Education Center • Tyngsboro, MA 01879 • ACRL
Bailey Susan B. • Assistant Head/Catalog Librarian • Emory University Libraries Robert W. Woodruff Library • Atlanta, GA 30322-2870 • ALCTS
Baillif Janet M. • Conrad High School • West Hartford, CT 06107
Baillio O. Dallas Jr. • Director • Mobile Public Library • Mobile, AL 36602 • LAMA PLA
Bain Evelyn S. • Librarian • National Library of Medicine • Bethesda, MD 20894 • ALCTS
Bain George W. • Head Archives & Special Cllns. • Ohio University Vernon R. Alden Library • Athens, OH 45701-2978 • ACRL
Bain Janice W. • Head of Access Services Dept. • University of Central Florida Library • Orlando, FL 32816-0666 • ACRL LAMA
Bain Leslie E. III • Librarian • North High School Library • Evansville, IN 47711 • AASL
Bain Michael Lee • East Point, GA 30344 • ACRL
Baine Martha S. • Dallas, TX 75205 • ACRL ALCTS LITA
Baines Grace A. • Head of Bibliographic Services • Buffalo & Erie County Public Library • Buffalo, NY 14203 • ALCTS LITA
Bair Alice • Crystal Lake, IL 60014
Baird-Joshi Susan D. • Student • University of Washington Graduate School of Library and Information Science • Seattle, WA 98195 • LITA NMRT
Baird Alexandra G. • Huntsville, AL 35801 • PLA RASD
Baird Cynthia • Childrens Librarian • South San Francisco Public Library • South San Francisco, CA 94080
Baird Dennis W. • Social Science Librarian • University of Idaho Library • Moscow, ID 83843 • GODORT MAGERT
Baird Dorothy • Dana Point, CA 92629 • AASL
Baird Jane H • Anchorage, AK 99516
Baird Judilee A. • Director • Mineral County Public Library • Hawthorne, NV 89415
Baird Lynn Norris • Head of Serials Department • University of Idaho Library • Moscow, ID 83843 • ALCTS
Baird Morna S. • Librarian • San Jose Mercury News Library • San Jose, CA 95091
Baird Patricia M. • San Diego, CA 92128 • Continuing
Baird Susan • Head, Patron Services Dept. • Oak Lawn Public Library • Oak Lawn, IL 60453 • PLA YALSA VRT
Baish Mary Alice • Reference/Documents Librarian • The American University Library • Washington, DC 20016-8046 • ACRL GODORT
Baiter Jamey • Southern Illinois University • Edwardsville, IL 62026
Bajabir Patricia C. • Cataloger • Kenosha Public Library • Kenosha, WI 53142-5799
Bajema Bruce D. • San Rafael, CA 94901 • LITA PLA *Life*
Bajt Mary F. • Chicago Public Library Harold Washington Library • Chicago, IL 60605 • ALSC
Bajzatt Magdaline • Library Board President • Whiting Public Library • Whiting, IN 46394 • LITA
Baker-Madsen Marilyn B. • Director • Hayward Public Library • Hayward, CA 94541 • PLA
Baker Amy J. • Columbiana, OH 44408
Baker Anne H. • Burke, VA 22015
Baker Anne L. • Librarian • Blennerhassett Junior High School • Parkersburg, WV 26101 • AASL
Baker Augusta Mrs. • Lecturer • University of South Carolina College of Library & Information Science • Columbia, SC 29208 • AASL ACRL ALCTS ALSC ALTA ASCLA LAMA LITA PLA RASD YALSA *Honorary*
Baker Barbara • Associate Dean • Durham Tech Community College • Durham, NC 27703 • ACRL
Baker Barbara E. • Branch Librarian • Muncie Public Library Kennedy Branch Library • Muncie, IN 47304
Baker Barbara E. • Department Head A-V • Lima Public Library • Lima, OH 45801 • PLA
Baker Barbara K. • Library Director • Newcastle Public Library • Bowmanville ON, L1C 3A8 Canada • LITA PLA RASD
Baker Barbara L. • Library Media Specialist • John Campbell Elementary • Selah, WA 98942 • AASL

Baker Barry B. • Asst. Dir. for Technical Service • University of Georgia Libraries • Athens, GA 30602 • ACRL ALCTS LITA

Baker Becky • Director • Seward Public Library • Seward, NE 68434

Baker Bob • Asst Vice Chancellor/Inf Servs. • Pima Community College • Tucson, AZ 85709 • ACRL

Baker Bradley F. • Director • Northeastern Illinois University Library • Chicago, IL 60625 • ACRL

Baker Calvin L. • Manager-Corp Rds & Lib Svs • Energen Corporation • Birmingham, AL 35203 • LAMA LITA GODORT

Baker Carl • Librarian • Los Angeles County Museum of Art Art Research Library • Los Angeles, CA 90036 • ACRL ALCTS

Baker Carol A. • Port Townsend, WA 98368

Baker Carol M. • Bibliographic Coordinator • University of Calgary Libraries • Calgary AB, T2N 1N4 Canada • ALCTS

Baker Caroline F. • Muskegon, MI 49441

Baker Carolyn B. • Childrens Librarian • Beatrice Public Library • Beatrice, NE 68310 • ALSC

Baker Diane L. • Library Development Officer • Nevada State Library & Archives • Carson City, NV 89710

Baker Donald E. • Director • Ohio Township Public Library System • Newburgh, IN 47630 • PLA SRRT

Baker Donna • Elementary Librarian • McMurray Elementary School • Gainesville, TX 76240 • AASL

Baker Doris C. • University Librarian • Florida State University Robert M. Strozier Library • Tallahassee, FL 32306-2047 • ALCTS

Baker Doris M. • School Lib/Media Specialist • Plantsville School • Southington, CT 06489

Baker Dorothy C. • Pittsburg, NH 03592

Baker Douglas • Director • Kenosha Public Library • Kenosha, WI 53142-5799

Baker Elaine M. • Plainfield Public Library • Plainfield, NJ 07060 • LITA

Baker Elizabeth C. • Assistant Librarian • Indiana University • Bloomington, IN 47405 • ACRL LIRT SRRT

Baker Elizabeth E. • Xenia, OH 45385 • ALSC PLA *Life*

Baker Emily F. • Collection Devel. Librarian • Olathe Public Library • Olathe, KS 66061

Baker Esther M. • East Peoria, IL 61611 • AASL YALSA *Life*

Baker Gayle S. • University of Tennessee John C. Hodges Library • Knoxville, TN 37996-1000 • ACRL LITA RASD

Baker Gordon N. • Library Media Specialist • Eagle's Landing High School • McDonough, GA 30253 • AASL

Baker Helen M. • Branch Librarian • Kansas City Public Library • Kansas City, MO 64106

Baker James E. • Technical Services Librarian • Oak Lawn Public Library • Oak Lawn, IL 60453 • LITA

Baker Jane H. • Librarian • Chicago Public Library Harold Washington Library • Chicago, IL 60605 • GODORT

Baker Janet R. • Library Director • Gale Free Library • Holden, MA 01520 • PLA

Baker Janice O. Miss • Alexandria, VA 22301-1228 • ACRL ALCTS *Life*

Baker Jean M. • Student • Connecticut College • New London, CT 06320-4196

Baker Jean S. • Public Services Librarian • Siena Heights College Library • Adrian, MI 49221 • ACRL

Baker Jeanetta R. • Media Center Librarian • McDonald Creative Services • Oak Brook, IL 60521 • ALCTS LAMA LITA CLENE

Baker Jeanne Arnold • Head, Rapid Cataloging Unit. • University of Maryland College Park Theodore R. McKeldin Library • College Park, MD 20742-7011 • ALCTS LITA

Baker Jeanne C. • Lower School Librarian • Greenhill School • Dallas, TX 75244-3698 • AASL

Baker Jennifer S. • Lynnwood, WA 98036-7602

Baker Jeri C. • Young Adult Spec, Current Clln • Dallas Public Library • Dallas, TX 75201 • PLA YALSA

Baker Joan H. • Librarian • Bulkley Richardson and Gelinas • Springfield, MA 01103

Baker John P. • Chief of Conservation Division • New York Public Library • New York, NY 10018-2788 • ACRL ALCTS

Baker Judith A. • Berkeley, CA 94708 • ALCTS LITA

Baker Judith M. • Trustee • Acorn Public Library District • Oak Forest, IL 60452 • ALTA PLA

Baker Kimberly A. • Lansing, KS 66043

Baker Laverne S. Mrs. • Los Angeles, CA 90045 • AASL YALSA *Life*

Baker Lavonne • Tucson, AZ 85745 • AASL

Baker Lawrence W. • Gale Research, Inc. • Detroit, MI 48226

Baker Lesli A. • Austin, TX 78744

Baker Linda L. • Academic • El Centro College • Dallas, TX 75202 • ACRL

Baker Margaret • Library Media Teacher • Red Bank Elementary School • Clovis, CA 93612 • AASL

Baker Marjorie C. • Director Librarian/Media Service • Chestnut Hill Academy • Philadelphia, PA 19118 • AASL

Baker Mary H. • Librarian • Lee High School • Jonesville, VA 24263 • AASL

Baker Nancy • Public Service Librarian • Hinds Community College McLendon Library • Raymond, MS 39154 • ACRL RASD LIRT

Baker Nancy • Trustee • Bucyrus Public Library • Bucyrus, OH 44820

Baker Nancy L. • Director of Libraries • Washington State University • Pullman, WA 99164-2112 • ACRL LAMA LITA

Baker Nettie L. Mrs. • Director • University of Dallas William A. Blakley Library • Irving, TX 75062 • ACRL LAMA CLENE SORT

Baker Pamela S. • Cataloger • Saint Francis College • Fort Wayne, IN 46808

Baker Paul B. • Student • North Carolina Central University • Durham, NC 27707

Baker Paula J. • Rutland Free Library • Rutland, VT 05701-4058 • PLA

Baker Penny L. • Vineland, NJ 08360 • ACRL LAMA

Baker Roberta • Fairland High School • Fairland, OK 74343 • AASL

Baker S. Michele • Law Library Manager • Windle Turley P.C. • Dallas, TX 75206

Baker Sandra A. • School Library Media Specialist • Cicero-North Syracuse High School • Cicero, NY 13039 • AASL

Baker Sarah W. • Serials Cataloging/Catgl Hd. • Indiana State University Cunningham Memorial Library • Terre Haute, IN 47809 • ALCTS LAMA LITA

Baker Shari A. • Media Specialist • Walker School • Marietta, GA 30062 • AASL

Baker Sharon L. • Associate Professor • University of Iowa School of Library & Information Science • Iowa City, IA 52242

Baker Shirley K. • Dean of University Libraries • Washington University Libraries • Saint Louis, MO 63130-4899 • ACRL ALCTS LITA

Baker Stella F. • Community Relations Manager • Contra Costa County Library • Pleasant Hill, CA 94523 • PLA YALSA

Baker Susan J • Learning Resources Specialist • Bremerton School District • Bremerton, WA 98312 • AASL

Baker Susan Jacobs • Librarian • Cobb County Public Library System Kennesaw Branch • Kennesaw, GA 30144 • ACRL

Baker Susan M. • Librarian • Wickenburg High School Library • Wickenburg, AZ 85358 • AASL

Baker Susan S. • Library Manager • Hewlett-Packard Company Signal Analysis Division Library • Rohnert Park, CA 94928 • LITA

Baker Sylva S. • Wallingford, PA 19086

Baker Sylvia C. • Supervising Librarian • Palo Alto City Library • Palo Alto, CA 94303 • PLA RASD

Baker Theresa A. • Student • Indiana University School of Library and Information Science • Bloomington, IN 47405

Baker Therese D. • Western Kentucky University Helm-Cravens Library • Bowling Green, KY 42101 • ACRL

Baker Thomas • Student • Rutgers University School of Communication Information & Library Studies • New Brunswick, NJ 08903 • LITA

Baker Thomas R. • Librarian • Smithsonian Institution Libraries • Washington, DC 20560

Baker Thurbert E. • Library Trustee • DeKalb County Public Library • Decatur, GA 30030 • ALTA

Baker Trina D. • Student • University of California-Berkeley School of Library & Information Studies • Berkeley, CA 94720

Baker Vicki Ann • Henderson State University Huie Library • Arkadelphia, AR 71923 • ACRL MAGERT NMRT

Baker Wendy • Enoch Pratt Free Library • Baltimore, MD 21201-4484

Baker William • Associate Professor • Northern Illinois University University Libraries • DeKalb, IL 60115-2868 • ACRL

Baker Zachary M. • Head Librarian • Yivo Inst for Jewish Research Library • New York, NY 10028 • ACRL

Bakeraitis Dolores • Bay City, MI 48708 • Continuing

Bakke Celia D. • Head of Cataloging Department • San Jose State University Clark Library • San Jose, CA 95192-0028 • ALCTS

Bakken Gena J. • Northwood, IA 50459-1744 • PLA YALSA *Continuing*

Bakken Mary Ann • Saint Charles Public Library • St. Charles, IL 60174

Bakker Connie • Director/Learning Resoures Ctr. • Ohio State University Newark • Newark, OH 43055 • ACRL NMRT

Bakker Jan • Director of Special Library • North Central Regional Educational Laboratory • Oak Brook, IL 60521 • LAMA LITA

Bakula Claudia J. • Associate University Libn • Northern Arizona University • Flagstaff, AZ 86011-6022 • LITA

Bakula Patricia A. • Youth Librarian • Maude Shunk Public Library • Menomonee Falls, WI 53051 • ALSC PLA

Baky John S. • Director of Library Services • La Salle University Connelly Library • Philadelphia, PA 19141 • ACRL LAMA LIRT LRRT

Bala Karen • Trustee • Calumet City Public Library • Calumet City, IL 60409-4003 • RASD

Bala Maureen T. • Tacoma, WA 98467

Balaam Deborah • University of Puget Sound School of Education • Tacoma, WA 98416

Balaban Naomi • Pittsburgh, PA 15217

Balaban Robin M. • Librarian • Cummins & White • Los Angeles, CA 90017

Balachandran M. • Head of Commerce Library • University of Illinois Library • Urbana, IL 61801

Balalamenti Kay • Brooklyn Public Library • Brooklyn, NY 11238

Balan Susan M. • Pilot Mountain, NC 27041 • AASL

Balaraman Kanala • Doctoral Candidate • University of Hawaii School of Library & Information Studies • Honolulu, HI 96822

Balas Janet L. • Library Info. Systems Analyst • Monroeville Public Library • Monroeville, PA 15146-3381 • LITA

Balatti David R. • Chief, Subject Analysis Div. • National Library of Canada • Ottawa, ON, K1A 0N4 Canada • ALCTS

Balay Robert • New Haven, CT 06511

Balazs Joe • Director • Adams County Library • Adams, WI 53910

Balbirer Barbara T. • Trustee • Lincolnwood Public Library District • Lincolnwood, IL 60646 • RASD YALSA IRRT

Balcerowski Beverly • St. Francis, WI 53235 • RASD

Balch Earl • Library Systems Department • University of California-San Diego Central University Library • La Jolla, CA 92093-0175 • LITA

Balch Louise • Librarian • Tupelo High School Library • Tupelo, MS 38801 • AASL

Balch Priscilla K S • Library Media Specialist • Midwood High School • Brooklyn, NY 11210 • AASL

Balcom Karen S. • Systems Librarian • San Antonio College Library • San Antonio, TX 78212 • ACRL LAMA LITA LRRT

Balcom Kathleen J. • Head of Children's Services • Racine Public Library • Racine, WI 53402

Balcom Kathleen M. • Director • Arlington Heights Memorial Library • Arlington Heights, IL 60004-5966 • LAMA PLA IFRT

Balcom William T. • Library Administrator • Villa Park Public Library • Villa Park, IL 60181 • LAMA PLA RASD IFRT SRRT

Balcombe Judith A. • Director Law Library • Collin County Law Library • McKinney, TX 75069 • LITA

Balconi William J. Brother • Librarian • John Carroll University Jesuit Community • Cleveland, OH 44118 • ACRL

Baldarotta Anthony • Urbana, IL 61801 • Continuing

Baldauf Gretchen S. • Substitute Librarian & Teacher • Central School District • Amherst, NY 14226

Balderrama Sandra • Supervising Librarian • Oakland Public Library • Oakland, CA 94612 • PLA EMIERT

Baldini Lois D. • Director • North Haven Memorial Library • North Haven, CT 06473 • PLA

Baldock Margaret R. • Assistant Director of Libraries • University of Saskatchewan Library • Saskatoon SK, S7N 0W0 Canada • ACRL ALCTS LAMA

Baldonado Chuck • Albuquerque Technical Vocational Institute • Albuquerque, NM 87106

Baldridge Edward H. • Head Cataloger • Miami-Dade Community College North Campus Library • Miami, FL 33167 • ACRL ALCTS

Baldridge Sherie W. • Librarian • Paso Robles Elementary School District Flamson Middle School • Paso Robles, CA 93446

Baldridge Suzanne L. • Student • University of Oklahoma School of Library & Information Studies • Norman, OK 73019 • PLA RASD AFLRT IFRT NMRT SRRT

Baldridge Wanda E. • Lewisville, TX 75067

Balducci Tito O. • Florida A & M University School of Nursing • Tallahassee, FL 32307 • LAMA

Baldwin Brenda C. • Labat-Anderson Inc. • San Francisco, CA 94105

Baldwin Christine E. • Reference Librarian • Army Logistics Library • Fort Lee, VA 23801-6047 • PLA AFLRT FLRT

Baldwin David A. • Head of Administrative Services • University of New Mexico General Library • Albuquerque, NM 87131 • LAMA

Baldwin Dee F. • Director of Library Services • Westark Community College • Fort Smith, AR 72913 • ACRL LAMA IRRT MAGERT

Baldwin Elizabeth • Homer, NY 13077

Baldwin Geraldine S. • Library Director • Alice & Hamilton Fish • Garrison, NY 10524 • PLA IFRT

Baldwin Gil • Chief, Library Division • U.S. Government Printing Office Library Program Service • Washington, DC 20401 • FLRT GODORT

Baldwin James A. • Head of Acquisitions • Indiana University-Purdue University at Indianapolis Library (IUPUI) • Indianapolis, IN 46202 • ACRL ALCTS MAGERT

Baldwin Janet M. • Malvern, PA 19355-9608

Baldwin Julia F. • Documents Librarian • University of Toledo William S. Carlson Library • Toledo, OH 43606-3399 • ACRL GODORT

Baldwin Lora K. • Indiana University East Library Learning Resources Center • Richmond, IN 47374-1289 • ACRL

Baldwin Martha Lynne • Library Manager • United States Navy Naval Air Station Library • Jacksonville, FL 32212-0052 • AFLRT

Baldwin Paul E. • Associate Librarian • Simon Fraser University W. A. Bennett Library • Burnaby BC, V5A 1S6 Canada • ACRL ALCTS LITA

Baldwin Robert D. • Director of Learning Resources • Allegany Community College • Cumberland, MD 21502-2596

Baldwin Susan • Branch Librarian • DeKalb County Public Library Brookhaven Branch • Atlanta, GA 30319 • YALSA IFRT

Baldwin Susan R. • Bellvue, WA 98004 • PLA

Baldwin Susan W. • Ferguson Library • Stamford, CT 06902

Baldwin Trudy Taylor • Supv. of Library Media Services • Timberlane Regional School District • Atkinson, NH 03811 • AASL ALSC YALSA

Balentine Don • Librarian • Oil Trough Elementary • Oil Trough, AR 72564 • ALSC

Bales F. Kathleen • Research Libraries Group Inc. (RLG) • Mountain View, CA 94041-1100 • ALCTS LITA

Balestrieri Anthony • Library Trustee • Paramus Public Library • Paramus, NJ 07652 • ALTA PLA

Balgopal Shyamala • Reference Librarian • University of Illinois • Urbana, IL 61801

Balis Michelle E. • Children's Librarian • Corpus Christi Public Library • Corpus Christi, TX 78401 • ALSC

Balius Sharon A. • University of Michigan • Ann Arbor, MI 48109-1205 • ALCTS

Balk Judith A. • Chester, NH 03036

Balkema Kathleen A. • Youth Services Coordinator • Royal Oak Public Library • Royal Oak, MI 48068 • ALSC

Balkenberg Joan • Lamar Elementary School • Houston, TX 77009 • AASL

Balkin Ruth • Partner/Librarian • Balkin Library Management Services • Rochester, NY 14609 • ILERT

Ball Alan • Columbia Computing Services • Vancouver BC, V6M 1M2 Canada • AASL LITA

Ball Alice D. • Washington, DC 20015 • ALCTS IRRT

Ball Ardella P. • Asst Prof of Library Science • Armstrong State College Library Media • Savannah, GA 31419 • AASL

Ball Candace M. • Student • Simmons College Graduate School of Library & Information Science • Boston, MA 02115

Ball Dannie J. • Director • Iberville Parish Library • Plaquemine, LA 70764

Ball Diane • Trustee • Daniel Boone Regional Library • Columbia, MO 65205-1267 • ALTA

Ball Edna B. • Student • San Jose State University Division of Library & Information Science • San Jose, CA 95192-0029

Ball Eileen • Librarian • Orford High School • Orford, NH 03777

Ball Evelyn H. • Branch Library Head • Hartford Public Library Mark Twain Branch • Hartford, CT 06105 • PLA SRRT

Ball Gayle M. • Map Cataloger • Miami University Brill Science Library • Oxford, OH 45056

Ball John Leslie • Librarian • University of Toronto Scarborough College-Bladen Library • Scarborough ON, M1C 1A4 Canada • ACRL LITA

Ball Joyce • California State University-Sacramento Library • Sacramento, CA 95819-6039

Ball Linda • Tustin, CA 92680

Ball Mary Alice • Head of Library Systems • Loyola University E.M. Cudahy Memorial Library • Chicago, IL 60626 • ACRL LITA IRRT

Ball Michael J. • Librarian • Grand Rapids Public Library • Grand Rapids, MI 49503-3093 • ALCTS

Ball Patricia B. • Pittsburgh, PA 15217

Ballantyne Lygia Maria • New Delhi-LOC Department of State-USIS New Delhi • Washington, DC 20521-9000 • ACRL

Ballard Arlene K. • Substitute Media Specialist • Dougherty County Board of Education • Albany, GA 31703 • AASL

Ballard Elizabeth B. • Washington, DC 20007

Ballard Jane W. • Student • University of South Carolina College of Library & Information Science • Columbia, SC 29208 • RASD IFRT SRRT

Ballard Lynn • Mildred B. Harrison Regional Library • Columbiana, AL 35051 • RASD

Ballard Melody • Administrative Assistant • Arizona State University Department of Education Library Science • Tempe, AZ 85287

Ballard Patricia I. • Head, Monographs Catlg Dept • Winthrop College Ida Jane Dacus Library • Rock Hill, SC 29733 • ALCTS

Ballard Rochelle R. • Reference Librarian • University of Central Florida Library • Orlando, FL 32816-0666 • ACRL SRRT

Ballard Susan D. • Director • Londonderry School District • Londonderry, NH 03053 • AASL

Ballard Susan M. • Ritter Public Library • Vermilion, OH 44089 • PLA SRRT

Ballard Terry • Library Assistant • Adelphi University Swirbul Library • Garden City, NY 11530 • LITA

Ballard Thomas H. • Jackson, MS 39211-5849 • ACRL LAMA PLA RASD

Ballard Thomas P. • Sacramento Public Library • Sacramento, CA 95814

Ballasch Sandra S. • Reference Librarian • University of Iowa Libraries • Iowa City, IA 52242-1379 • ACRL RASD

Ballenger Mabel F. • Supervisor/Technical Serv Dept • Daniel Boone Regional Library • Columbia, MO 65205-1267

Ballenger Sherry A. • Science Indexer • H. W. Wilson Company • Bronx, NY 10452 • ACRL

Baller Cheryl R. • Saint Paul, MN 55106

Ballinger Barbara • Oak Park, IL 60302

Ballinger Zetha V. • Dematha High School • Hayattsville, MD 20781

Balliot Robert L. • Director • University of Pittsburgh at Bradford • Bradford, PA 16701

Ballou Eleanor F. • Chief Librarian • United States Air Force Base Hickam Air Force • Honolulu, HI 96853 • AFLRT

Ballou Patricia K. • Chester, VT 05143 • ACRL

Balmaseda Luis • Student • University of California-Los Angeles Graduate School of Library & Information Science • Los Angeles, CA 90024-1520

Balmer Carolyn • Librarian • Ridgebury Elementary School • Ridgebury, CT 06877

Balmer Mary • Director of Special Projects • Connecticut University • Storrs, CT 06268 • ACRL LAMA

Balog Rita J. • Director/Librarian • Harbor-Topky Memorial Library • Ashtabula, OH 44004

Balonis Marie J. • Librarian • Webster Elementary School • Mesa, AZ 85201 • AASL

Balsam Debra M. • Librarian • Taylor Elementary School • Arlington, VA 22207 • ALSC

Balsam Frances • Fort Worth Public Library • Fort Worth, TX 76102 • ALCTS

Balsano Christine • Assistant Librarian • Downers Grove North High School • Downers Grove, IL 60516 • AASL

Balsiger Linda A. • Librarian • University of Wisconsin • Madison, WI 53706 • ACRL LAMA

Balsino Vita C. • Marketing Director Academic Lib. • Baker & Taylor Books • Bridgewater, NJ 08807 • ACRL ALCTS

Balthis Charles • Cataloger • Mary Washington College Library Simpson Library • Fredericksburg, VA 22401-4664

Baltins Vivija N. • Evanston, IL 60204 • AASL ACRL *Life*

Balusek Charlotte E. • San Antonio, TX 78223 • AASL

Bambakidis Elli • Adults Reference Librarian • Dayton & Montgomery County Public Library • Dayton, OH 45402-2103

Bambenek Jill E. • Student • College of Saint Catherine • Saint Paul, MN 55105 • ALSC

Bana Joseph J. • Euclid, OH 44132

Banach Patricia S. • Head Serials Automation Section • University of Massachusetts • Amherst, MA 01003 • LITA

Banach Therese Sister • Villa Joseph Marie High School • Holland, PA 18966 • AASL YALSA

Banas-Marti Kathleen A. • Librarian • Connecticut University • Storrs, CT 06268

Banas Warren J. • Monarch of Chicago • Chicago, IL 60639

Bancroft Elizabeth • National Intelligence Book Center • Washington, DC 20037 • ALCTS LITA RASD GODORT

Band Charles E. • Haywood County Public Library • Waynesville, NC 28786 • PLA

Band Richard • Director • Lancaster County Library • Lancaster, SC 29720 • PLA

Banda Anne E. • Student • University of Wisconsin-Milwaukee School of Library & Information Science • Milwaukee, WI 53201 • ACRL

Bandel Frances L. • Los Angeles, CA 90004 • Continuing

Bandelin Janis • Head of Public Services • Mercer University Main Library • Macon, GA 31207 • ACRL RASD

Bandre Carol E. • Children's Librarian • Dunham Public Library • Whitesboro, NY 13492 • ALSC

Bandy Vicki • Media Specialist • Papillion High School • Papillion, NE 68046

Bandziukas Vytas • Student • Catholic University of America School of Library and Information Science • Washington, DC 20064 • LITA

Bane Linda Celet • Potomac State College Library • Keyser, WV 26726 • ACRL ASCLA RASD IFRT LIRT LRRT

Banfield Becky • Assistant Librarian • Northwestern University Joseph Schaffner Library • Chicago, IL 60611 • ACRL

Banfield Jacqueline K. • Assistant Library Director • Sherman Public Library • Sherman, TX 75090-5975 • PLA

Banfill Christine • Cataloger • University of Ottawa Libraries Morisset Library • Ottawa ON, K1N 9A5 Canada

Bangalore Nirmala S. • Assistant Catalog Librarian • University of Illinois at Chicago University Library • Chicago, IL 60680 • ACRL ALCTS

Bange Stephanie D. • FPO San Francisco, CA 96654-2906

Bangert Stephanie R. • Library Director • Saint Mary's College of California • Moraga, CA 94575 • ACRL LAMA

Banghart Sandra M. • Scotia, NY 12302-1515 • PLA

Bangs Dawn L. • Library Director • Eleanor Ellis Public Library • Phelps, WI 54554

Banicki Cynthia A. • DA Library Program Manager • United States Army Headquarters, Department of the Army • Washington, DC 20310-0107 • AFLRT

Banister Karon K. • High School Librarian • Cairo High School • Cairo, IL 62914

Banitt Inga T. • Student • University of Wisconsin-Madison School of Library & Information Studies • Madison, WI 53706 • ALSC IFRT

Bankhead Betty • Library Media Coordinator • Cherry Creek High School • Englewood, CO 80111 • AASL LITA

Bankhead Detrice A. • Assistant University Librarian • University of California Library • Santa Barbara, CA 93106 • ACRL LAMA

Bankhead Sheila W. • Reference Librarian • Bay County Public Library Association NW Regional Lib System • Panama City, FL 32401-2625

Banks Benjamin F. • Trustee • Grand Ledge Public Library • Grand Ledge, MI 48837 • ALTA IFRT

Banks Bonita R. • Children's Librarian • Amos Memorial Public Library • Sidney, OH 45365 • ALSC

Banks Elizabeth S. • Curator • Frederick Law Olmsted National Historic Site • Brookline, MA 02146 • ACRL ALCTS LAMA FLRT

Banks Jennifer S. • Hd, Presv & Coll Mgt Servs • Massachusetts Institute of Technology Libraries (MIT) • Cambridge, MA 02139 • ACRL ALCTS

Banks Marlyn • Student • University of Michigan School of Information and Library Studies • Ann Arbor, MI 48109-1092 • ALCTS LAMA

Banks Nancy R. • Media Specialist • Riffenburgh School • Fort Collins, CO 80525 • AASL

Banks Paul N. • Research Scholar • Columbia University School of Library Service • New York, NY 10027 • ACRL ALCTS

Banks Paula C. • Public Information Officer • Medina County District Library • Medina, OH 44256 • LAMA PLA

Banks Robert E. • Student • Emporia State University School of Library & Information Management • Emporia, KS 66801 • LITA

Banks Roderick E. • Associate Director • University of New Brunswick • Fredericton NB, E3B 5H5 Canada

Banks Sherman • Trustee • Central Arkansas Library System • Little Rock, AR 72201-4698 • ALTA

Bankston Audrey N. • Reference Librarian • Georgia Institute of Technology • Atlanta, GA 30332 • LIRT

Bannahan Erin • Branch Manager • Washoe County Library Sierra View Branch • Reno, NV 89502 • PLA

Banner Linda T. • Reference Librarian • Inland Library System Reference Center • Riverside, CA 92502 • PLA

Bannerot Frederick G. III Dr • Trustee • Kanawha County Public Library • Charleston, WV 25301 • ALTA

Bannick Barbara B. • Head of Reference • Somerville Public Library • Somerville, MA 02143 • PLA RASD

Bannigan Bernice G. • New Hartford, NY 13413 • Continuing

Bannister Frances M. • Hebrew Day School of Central Florida • Maitland, FL 32751 • AASL ALSC

Bannon Mary J. • Student • Catholic University of America Library School Library • Washington, DC 20064

Bannon Susan H. • Assistant Professor • Auburn University • Auburn, AL 36849 • AASL ALSC

Bansemer Ellen M. • Student • University of Maryland College of Library and Information Services • College Park, MD 20742-4345 • RASD

Banta Brady M. • Louisiana State University School of Medicine • Shreveport, LA 71130-3932 • ACRL LHRT

Banta Gratia • Children Librarian Asst Director • Germantown Public Library • Germantown, OH 45327 • ALSC

Bantz-Gustafson Susan K. • Chicago Public Library • Chicago, IL 60605

Bantz Elizabeth R. Miss • University of California • Berkeley, CA 94720 • ACRL ALCTS RASD *Life*

Bao Elaine Y • Chicago, IL 60615

Bao Jane H. • Student • San Jose State University Division of Library & Information Science • San Jose, CA 95192-0029

Bao Xue-ming • Literacy Librarian • Paterson Free Public Library Danforth Memorial Library • Paterson, NJ 07501

Baptiste Syria E. • Oakland, CA 94621

Baraloto Ronald Anthony • Trustee • Montgomery County Department of Public Libraries • Rockville, MD 20850 • ALTA PLA

Barancik Susan L. • Children's Librarian • Evansville-Vanderburgh County Public Library • Evansville, IN 47708-1694 • ALSC PLA

Baranko Elaine T. • Detroit, MI 48227

Baranowski George V. • Albany, CA 94706

Baranyar Jean • Notre Dame Catholic High School • Fairfield, CT 06432

Baratta Rosemarie • Long Beach, NY 11561 • Continuing

Barbacovi Joanie • Trustee • Everett Public Library • Everett, WA 98201

Barban Leslie Stuart • Children's Librarian • Richland County Public Library • Columbia, SC 29201

Barbaree Mark C. • Piedmont Hospital Sauls Memorial Library • Atlanta, GA 30309 • IFRT

Barbee Lynda L. • Librarian • Sullivan South High School • Kingsport, TN 37663 • AASL

Barbee Norman N. • Washington, DC 20013

Barbee Suzi Sam • Owner • Suzi and Vic Enterprises • Fort Worth, TX 76118

Barber Barbara J. • Associate Director • Topeka Public Library • Topeka, KS 66604-1374 • PLA

Barber Gloria K. • Assoc. Spec. Library/Media • Virginia Department of Education • Richmond, VA 23216 • AASL ALTA

Barber Helen M. • Assoc Prof/Asst Ref Libn • New Mexico State University Library • Las Cruces, NM 88003-0006 • ACRL RASD YALSA *Life*

Barber Henry A. III Mrs. • Arcadia, CA 91006 • Continuing

Barber Ione M. Mrs • Tujunga, CA 91042 • Continuing

Barber Patricia L. • Comanche, OK 73529

Barber Peggy • Associate Executive Director • American Library Association • Chicago, IL 60611-2795

Barber Raymond W. • Director of Libraries • William Penn Charter School • Philadelphia, PA 19144 • AASL ALSC YALSA

Barber Richard • Student • Sam Houston State University Department of Library Science • Huntsville, TX 77341-2236 • AASL

Barber Tanya A. • Smyrna, GA 30080-6415

Barberena Elsa • Cordinadora de Bibliotecas • Unam Facultad de Filosofia y Letras • Mexico DF, Mexico

Barbour Suzannah • Ross School • Ross, CA 94957 • AASL ALSC

Barbour Wendell A. • Director • Christopher Newport College Captain John Smith Library • Newport News, VA 23606 • ACRL LAMA

Barbula P. Marvin Dr. • Director of Media Services • San Diego County Office of Education • San Diego, CA 92111 • AASL

Barch Bethany H. • Student • Randolph-Macon College McGraw-Page Library • Ashland, VA 23005

Barchas Sarah E • Elementary School Librarian • Unified School District • Tucson, AZ 85717-0400 • AASL EMIERT

Barclay-Pereira Susan • Director, Learning Resources • Durham College • Oshawa ON, L1H 7L7 Canada • ACRL

Barclay Donald A. • New Mexico State University Library • Las Cruces, NM 88003-0006 • ACRL LIRT

Barclay Julius P. • Charlottesvle, VA 22901 • Continuing

Barclay Sylvia • Library Media Specialist • Avon High School • Avon, CT 06001 • AASL

Barcus Christine • Coordinator of Technical Serv. • Uncle Remus Regional Library System • Madison, GA 30650 • PLA

Barczak M. Jessie • Washington, DC 20001 • IRRT

Barczyk Ewa E. • Asst. Dir. for Collection Mgmt. • University of Wisconsin-Milwaukee Golda Meir Library • Milwaukee, WI 53201 • ACRL ALCTS

Bard Beatrice A. • Maumee, OH 43537

Bard Lauara B. • Monroe, NY 10950 • ALSC

Bard Nancy • Librarian/Director • Thomas Jefferson High School for Science & Technology • Alexandria, VA 22312 • AASL YALSA

Bard Therese Bissen • Associate Professor • University of Hawaii Thomas Hale Hamilton Library • Honolulu, HI 96822 • AASL ALSC

Barde Rogers R. Ms. • Librarian • Mesa Alta Junior High School • Bloomfield, NM 87413 • AASL

Bardeen Marjorie R. • Lancaster, PA 17603

Barding Kathleen A. • Librarian • Morrison & Hecker • Kansas City, MO 64108

Bare Rebecca S. • Academia Menonita • Caparra Heights, PR 00920 • AASL

Barefoot Gary F. • Librarian • Mount Olive College Moye Library • Mount Olive, NC 28365-1699 • RASD

Barevich Rachel • Manager • Richmond Hill Public Library • Richmond Hill, GA 31324

Barfield William B. • Science & Tech. Ref. Lib • Public Library of Charlotte & Mecklenburg County • Charlotte, NC 28202

Bargar Sherie K. • Media Specialist • Maitland Middle School • Maitland, FL 32751 • AASL

Bargeman Gregory • Student • Catholic University of America School of Library and Information Science • Washington, DC 20064

Barham Sheila M. • Head of Reference • University of Central Arkansas Torreyson Library • Conway, AR 72032 • RASD

Barhydt Gordon C. • Director • Central Colorado Library System • Wheat Ridge, CO 80033 • ASCLA

Baringer Jeanine • Pine Island, MN 55963

Baringer Sally E. • Mankato, MN 56001-2580 • AASL

Barish Wendy • New York, NY 10021

Bark Catherine M. • Student • University of Oklahoma School of Library & Information Studies • Norman, OK 73019 • EMIERT

Barkema Lori A. • Director • LeMars Public Library • LeMars, IA 51031

Barker Anne D. • Extension Supervisor • Aiken-Bamberg-Barnwell-Edgefield Regional Library System (ABBE) • Aiken, SC 29802

Barker Anne K. • Student • University of Illinois Graduate School of Library and Information Science • Urbana, IL 61801 • ACRL IFRT

Barker Barbara L. • Hilton Head Island, SC 29926 • AASL

Barker Gloria • Norton, MA 02766

Barker Iris A. Mrs. • Branch Library Manager • Queens Borough Public Library South Jamaica Branch • Jamaica, NY 11433 • PLA EMIERT

Barker Jeffrey C. • South Tama Middle School • Toledo, IA 52342 • AASL YALSA

Barker Joseph W. • Head of Acquisition Department • University of California-Berkeley University Library • Berkeley, CA 94720 • ALCTS

Barker L. E. • Tucson, AZ 85745 • IFRT SRRT

Barker Lillian H. • Laurel, MD 20707 • Continuing

Barker Margaret M. • Maple Shade, NJ 08052

Barker Mary S. Schmidt • Head Librarian/Director • William H. Aitkin Memorial Lib • Croswell, MI 48422 • ALTA LAMA PLA IFRT

Barker Patrick G. • Oakland, CA 94618

Barker Robin • Assistant Director Support Serv. • Whatcom County Library System • Bellingham, WA 98226-9092

Barker Sallie A. • Librarian • Salisbury School • Salisbury, MD 21802-2295

Barkley Bruce Owen • Library Director • Galesburg Public Library • Galesburg, IL 61401 • LAMA PLA

Barkley Daniel C. • Government Documents/Microtext • Wake Forest University Z Smith Reynolds Library • Winston Salem, NC 27109-7777 • GODORT MAGERT

Barkley Donna J. • Cincinnati, OH 45224

Barkley Elaine • Reference Librarian • Montgomery County Department of Public Library/ Bethesda Regional Library • Bethesda, MD 20814 • PLA

Barkley Laura P. • Oakland, CA 94610 • Continuing

Barkley Linda C. • Off Campus Reference Ln. • University of Redlands Armacost Library • Redlands, CA 92374-3758 • ACRL PLA YALSA IRRT

Barksdale Bonnie K. • Librarian • Sunny Hills High School • Fullerton, CA 92633 • AASL

Barlak Pamela M. • Volunteer Coor/Public Relations • Bethel Park Public Library • Bethel Park, PA 15102-2790

Barlow Cara • Winchester Public Library • Winchester, MA 01890 • LAMA PLA RASD

Barlow Deborah L. • Fine Arts Ln., General Ref. • North Texas State University Willis Library • Denton, TX 76203 • ACRL

Barlow Diane L. • University of Maryland College of Library and Information Services • College Park, MD 20742-4345 • LITA

Barlow Don W. • Westerville Public Library • Westerville, OH 43081 • LAMA PLA

Barlow Esther A. • Chicago, IL 60614 • Continuing

Barlow Jennifer G. • Museum of Our National Heritage • Lexington, MA 02173 • IFRT

Barlup Jacqueline H. • Waynesboro Area Senior High School • Waynesboro, PA 17268 • AASL

Barmer Andy M. • Jacksonville, FL 32205

Barmer Theresa D. • Jacksonville Public Libraries Main Library • Jacksonville, FL 32202 • LITA PLA

Barna Mary L. • Director • Interboro United Districts Library • Peckville, PA 18452

Barnard Jane A. • Librarian • Tempe Public Library • Tempe, AZ 85282

Barnard Madelene A. • Bradenton, FL 33505

Barnard Mary S. • Lancaster County Library • Lancaster, PA 17602 • PLA IFRT

Barnard Melissa J. • Head of Extension Section • Lansing Public Library • Lansing, MI 48933

Barnard Patricia S. • Student • Texas Woman's University School of Library & Information Studies • Denton, TX 76204 • AFLRT

Barnard Sandra K. • Redding, CA 96001

Barnard Susan B. • Assistant to the Dean • Kent State University Libraries • Kent, OH 44242 • ACRL

Barnard Walter M. • Humanities Bibliographer • Columbia University Libraries • New York, NY 10027 • ACRL

Barnard William S. • Student • Towson State University • Towson, MD 21204 • LITA SORT SRRT

Barndt Jeanine • Supervisor of Technical Services • Pacific Lutheran University Mortvedt Library • Tacoma, WA 98447 • ALCTS

Barnekow Dana Hendrix • Collection Development Ln. • Southwestern University A. Frank Smith Junior Library Center • Georgetown, TX 78626

Barnello Inga H. • Social Sciences References Ln. • LeMoyne College • Syracuse, NY 13214 • ACRL

Barner Charlene K. • Student • Clarion University of Pennsylvania Rena M. Carlson Library • Clarion, PA 16214

Barnes Anne E. • Librarian • Leedshill-Herkenhoff Inc • Albuquerque, NM 87102

Barnes Anthony E. • Interlibrary Loans Librarian • New Orleans Public Library • New Orleans, LA 70140 • RASD

Barnes Arlene M • Library Assistant II • University of Colorado at Denver Auraria Library • Denver, CO 80204 • ALCTS LITA

Barnes Belvina M. Mrs. • Teacher/Librarian • Bermuda Institute • Southampton, Bermuda • AASL

Barnes Carolyn F. • Library Director • Burnham Memorial Library • Colchester, VT 05446

Barnes Catherine L. • York University Scott Library • North York, ON, M3J 1P3 Canada

Barnes Christina M. • Student • University of Southern Mississippi School of Library Science • Hattiesburg, MS 39406-5146

Barnes Clarence • Librarian • Benjamin Franklin Middle School • Baltimore, MD 21225 • AASL

Barnes Dolly • Community Library Supervisor • Santa Clara County Free Library Saratoga Commmunity Library • Saratoga, CA 95070

Barnes Everett Wayne • Education/Psychology Librarian • University of Missouri Libraries-Columbia Elmer Ellis Library • Columbia, MO 65201-5149 • ACRL

Barnes Jacqueline • Wake Forest High School • Wake Forest, NC 27587 • AASL

Barnes Jan Ezkovich • Assistant Head Acquisition • New Orleans Public Library • New Orleans, LA 70140

Barnes Joseph W. • Library Director • Shepherd College Ruth Scarborough Library • Shepherdstown, WV 25443-1568 • ACRL LAMA

Barnes Judith A. • Medical Librarian • Lansing General Hospital Library • Lansing, MI 48910-3490

Barnes Karen B. • Student • University of Washington Graduate School of Library and Information Science • Seattle, WA 98195 • SRRT

Barnes Kristi A. • Student • University of Illinois Graduate School of Library and Information Science • Urbana, IL 61801 • PLA

Barnes Laura L. • Student • University of Illinois Graduate School of Library and Information Science • Urbana, IL 61801 • ALSC PLA IFRT NMRT SRRT

Barnes Margaret M. • Assistant Director • Bensenville Community Public Library • Bensenville, IL 60106 • PLA SRRT

Barnes Maxine Miss • Evanston Public Library • Evanston, IL 60201 • Continuing

Barnes Ned M. • Trustee • Spokane Public Library Comstock Building Library • Spokane, WA 99201-0976 • ALTA

Barnes Pamela M. • Library of Congress • Washington, DC 20541

Barnes Richard G. Sr. • Trustee • Jackson-Hinds Library System • Jackson, MS 39201 • ALTA

Barnes Roy E. • Serial Librarian • University of Toledo • Toledo, OH 43606 • ALCTS

Barnes Susan Clark • Librarian • Newport News • Arlington, VA 22202

Barnes Susan J. • Head of Public Services • Cornell University Albert R. Mann Library • Ithaca, NY 14853-4301 • ACRL LITA

Barnett-Leeson Carol A. • Children's Librarian • County of Los Angeles Public Library Lancaster Library 101 • Lancaster, CA 93534 • ALSC

Barnett Carlene S. • Seattle, WA 98146 • ALSC EMIERT

Barnett Caroline M. • Children's Services Librarian • Memphis-Shelby County Public Library Highland Branch • Memphis, TN 38111 • ALSC

Barnett Cassandra G. • School Library Media Specialist • Leverett Elementary School • Fayetteville, AR 72701 • AASL

Barnett David • Forest, VA 24551-1221

Barnett David A. • Student • University of North Carolina School of Library Science • Chapel Hill, NC 27599-3360 • LITA

Barnett Jean Drabbe • Mgr, Popular Lib & Film Section • Multnomah County Library Central Branch • Portland, OR 97205 • PLA VRT

Barnett Judith B. • Associate Professor/Cataloger • University of Rhode Island Library • Kingston, RI 02881-0803 • ACRL ALCTS

Barnett Judith M. • Library Media Specialist • Sierra High School Library Media Center • Colorado Spgs, CO 80916 • AASL

Barnett Karen J. • Student • Catholic University of America John K. Mullen of Denver Memorial Library • Washington, DC 20064 • AFLRT FLRT SRRT

Barnett Karen S. • New York, NY 10128

Barnett Leigh D. • Episcopal School of Dallas • Dallas, TX 75229

Barnett Michael S. • Automation Librarian • Mankato State University Memorial Library • Mankato, MN 56002-8400 • LITA

Barnett Michelle M. • Bossier City, LA 71112

Barnett Paul G. • Fairfield, VA 24435 • RASD

Barnett Sally D. • Head/Children & Youth Services • Huntsville-Madison County Public Library • Huntsville, AL 35804 • ALSC PLA

Barney Alan F. • College Librarian • Barat College Library • Lake Forest, IL 60045

Barney Anita R. • Assistant Administrator • Southwestern Connecticut Library Council • Bridgeport, CT 06604 • LITA

Barney Katharine M. • Clerk • Patagonia Public Library • Patagonia, AZ 85624

Barnhardt Maria G. • Robins AFB, GA 31098-1150 • AASL ALSC

Barnhart Deanna Fitt • Librarian • San Mateo County Office of Education • Redwood City, CA 94065-1064 • AASL

Barnhart Linda S. • Music Collection Dept. 0175Q • University of California-San Diego Central University Library • La Jolla, CA 92093-0175 • ALCTS LITA

Barnhouse Nancy J. • Newark, NJ 07104

Barnicle Sara Morrison • AV Librarian • Oceanside Public Library • Oceanside, CA 92054

Barnidge Janys L. • Tallahassee Community College • Tallahassee, FL 32304

Barns Jacqueline Suzanne • Student • University of Oklahoma School of Library & Information Studies • Norman, OK 73019

Barnum Amy • Librarian • New York State Historical Association • Cooperstown, NY 13326 • ACRL LAMA

Baron Doris S. • Librarian • Saint Martin's Episcopal School Library Martin Family Library • Metairie, LA 70003 • AASL

Barone Louise • Summit Public Library District • Summit, IL 60501

Barr-Reddick Constance • David Weir School • Fairfield, CA 94533

Barr Daniel J. • Niagara Falls Public Library • Niagara Fls, NY 14305 • PLA

Barr Janet L. Dr. • Director • BOCES I SLS • Riverhead, NY 11901-2763 • AASL

Barr Jeffrey A. • California Historical Society • San Francisco, CA 94109 • ACRL

Barr Linda S. • Chillicothe & Ross County Public Library • Chillicothe, OH 45601 • LAMA LITA IFRT

Barr Marilyn P. • Children's Librarian • Free Library of Philadelphia Ritner Children's Branch • Philadelphia, PA 19148 • ALSC PLA LIRT

Barr Patricia K. • Roosevelt Middle School • Decatur, IL 62522 • YALSA

Barr Virginia L. • Reference Specialist • University of California McHenry Library • Santa Cruz, CA 95064 • ACRL RASD

Barr William E. • Catalog Librarian • Eastern Washington University • Cheney, WA 99004 • ACRL ALCTS

Barraco Gail • Student • Syracuse University School of Information Studies • Syracuse, NY 13244-4100

Barrall Karen • Blairstown Township Elementary School • Blairstown, NJ 07825

Barratt Margaret M. • Novato, CA 94949-5879

Barreca D. Nora • Staff Librarian/Social Sciences • Carnegie Library of Pittsburgh • Pittsburgh, PA 15213-4080

Barrera Brenda J. • San Diego, CA 92130

Barreras Dolly M. • Catalog Department • Sacred Heart Coll • Santurce, PR 00907

Barrett Barbara K. • Hillside Junior High School • Boise, ID 83703 • AASL

Barrett Buckley Barry • Head, Library Technical Svs. • California State University • San Bernardino, CA 92407 • ACRL ALCTS

Barrett Darryl D. • Librarian 2 • Minneapolis Public Library & Information Center • Minneapolis, MN 55401-1992 • ACRL

Barrett Donald J. • Assistant Director • United States Air Force Academy Academy Library (DFSEL) • USAF Academy, CO 80840 • ACRL LAMA AFLRT FLRT

Barrett Dwight D. • Cranston, RI 02905 • AASL

Barrett Elinor L. • Head of Public Services • Daniel Boone Regional Library • Columbia, MO 65205-1267 • PLA IFRT

Barrett James • Cataloger • University of Rhode Island Library • Kingston, RI 02881-0803 • ACRL ALCTS LITA

Barrett John C. • Public Library Consultant • New Hampshire State Library • Concord, NH 03301 • PLA

Barrett Judy A. • Head Librarian • Morristown-Beard School • Morristown, NJ 07962-1999 • AASL

Barrett Lenna M. • Pryor, OK 74361 • Continuing

Barrett M. Joanne • Student • Brigham Young University School of Library & Information Sciences • Provo, UT 84602 • ALSC PLA

Barrett Marguerite B. • Rutgers University Art Library Voorhees Hall • New Brunswick, NJ 08903

Barrett Mary • Detroit, MI 48224

Barrett Michael • California State University Oviatt Library • Northridge, CA 91328-1289

Barrett Minnie Evetta • Youth Services Librarian • Waukegan Public Library • Waukegan, IL 60085 • ALSC

Barrett Molly • Library Director • Coquille Public Library • Coquille, OR 97423

Barrett Patricia L. • Wantagh, NY 11793

Barrett Shirley A. • Trustee • Oak Lawn Public Library • Oak Lawn, IL 60453 • ALTA PLA

Barrett Theresa • Catonsville Community College • Baltimore, MD 21228

Barrett Viola T. • Lafayette, CO 80026

Barrette Elise D. Mrs. • Johnson City, TN 37604 • Continuing

Barrette Linda J. • John A Logan College • Carterville, IL 62918 • ACRL

Barrick Judy H. • Director • Liturgy Library • Lincoln, NE 68503-0221 • ALCTS NMRT

Barrick Susan K. • Assistant Director • Southwest Public Libraries • Grove City, OH 43123 • LAMA PLA

Barrie Diane L. • Student • University of California-Los Angeles (UCLA) • Los Angeles, CA 90024-1450

Barringer Mary Ann • East Chicago Public Library • E. Chicago, IN 46312

Barringer Sallie H. • Newport, KY 41071

Barrio Elena J. • Coordinator Children's Service • Uncle Remus Regional Library System • Madison, GA 30650

Barron Cloma G. • Farmerville, LA 71241 • Continuing

Barron Daniel D. • Associate Professor • University of South Carolina College of Library & Information Science • Columbia, SC 29208 • AASL CLENE IFRT IRRT LIRT

Barron Deborah A. • Student • University of Texas at Austin Graduate School of Library & Information Sciences • Austin, TX 78712-1276

Barron Joan R. • Voorheesville, NY 12186

Barron Lynn S. • Hammond School Upper School Library • Columbia, SC 29209 • AASL

Barron Margaret P. • Reference Librarian • Cuyahoga Community College Metropolitan Campus LRC • Cleveland, OH 44115 • RASD

Barron Pamela Petrick • Associate Professor • University of South Carolina College of Library & Information Science • Columbia, SC 29208 • ALSC

Barron Robert E. • Chief, Bur. of Sch. L Media • State Education Department Bureau of School Library/Media Programs • Albany, NY 12234 • AASL YALSA

Barron Sandra M. • LMC Director • Tomball High School • Tomball, TX 77375 • AASL YALSA IFRT

Barron Sandra R. • Student • University of Texas at Austin Graduate School of Library & Information Sciences • Austin, TX 78712-1276 • ALSC PLA AFLRT FLRT

Barron Shelley • LeGrand Pioneer Heritage Library • LeGrand, IA 50142

Barron Shirley • E Derry, NH 03041

Barrow Carroll J. • Director • Richland Hills Public Library • Richland Hills, TX 76118 • PLA

Barrow Deborah L. • Library Automation Mgr • Chula Vista Public Library • Chula Vista, CA 91910 • LITA

Barrows Pamela • Government Documents Librarian • New Orleans Public Library • New Orleans, LA 70140 • GODORT

Barry Carol J. • Associate Librarian • Elmhurst College A. C. Buehler Library • Elmhurst, IL 60126 • ACRL

Barry Carol L. • Assistant Professor • Louisiana State University School of Library & Information Science • Baton Rouge, LA 70803-3290 • LITA

Barry Diane M. • Washington County Cooperative Library Service • Aloha, OR 97006 • ASCLA

Barry Janice R.F. Dr. • Adjunct Professor • Alabama State University Levi Watkins Learning Center Library • Montgomery, AL 36195-0301 • LITA

Barry Jeffrey S. • Graduate Student • University of Tennessee-Knoxville Graduate School of Library & Information Science • Knoxville, TN 37996-4330 • ACRL

Barry Julia • California Division of Mines & Geology • Sacramento, CA 95814-0131

Barry Maureen • Librarian • Burlington Public Library • Burlington ON, L7R 1J4 Canada

Barry Pamela A. • Juvenile Librarian • Indianapolis Marion County Public Library • Indianapolis, IN 46206 • YALSA

Barry Randall K. • MARC Standards Specialist • Library of Congress • Washington, DC 20541

Barry Richard A. • Trustee • Queens Borough Public Library • Jamaica, NY 11432 • ALTA PLA

Barry Richard J. • Information Specialist • American Nurse's Association • Washington, DC 20024-2571

Barry Sharan M. • Student • Cresthaven Elemetary School • Silver Spring, MD 20903 • AASL

Barry Sheila A. • Student • Catholic University of America School of Library and Information Science • Washington, DC 20064

Barstow Barbara M. • Assistant Children's Manager • Cuyahoga County Public Library • Cleveland, OH 44134-2792 • ALSC PLA

Barstow Sandra M. • Head of Acquisitions Department • University of Wyoming • Laramie, WY 82071 • ALCTS

Barsumyan Silva • Fairview, NJ 07022

Bart Muriel • Forest Hills, NY 11375

Bart Sharon • Branch Libraries Administrator • Miami-Dade Public Library System • Miami, FL 33130-1504 • PLA YALSA

Barta Carol R. • Access Services Librarian • Avila College Hooley-Bundschu Library • Kansas City, MO 64145 • SRRT

Bartel Joan • Assistant Director Central Lib. • Los Angeles Public Library • Los Angeles, CA 90071 • LAMA

Bartels Janet • Librarian • Goffstown Public Library • Goffstown, NH 03045

Bartelstein Andrea M. • University of Washington Libraries Odegaard Undergraduate Library • Seattle, WA 98195 • ACRL SRRT

Bartelt Kathryn R. • Collection Management Librarian • University of Evansville • Evansville, IN 47722 • ACRL

Bartenbach Bill K. • Director, Special Projects • Engineering Information Inc • New York, NY 10017 • LITA IFRT IRRT

Bartenbach Martha A. • Asst. to the Director • Nassau Library System • Uniondale, NY 11553

Barth Edward W. • Rockville, MD 20853 • AASL LAMA *Life*

Barth J. A. Mrs • Stockton, CA 95207-6568 • Continuing

Barth John E. • Catalog Librarian • Saint Thomas Aquinas College Library Lougheed Library • Sparkill, NY 10976 • ALCTS

Barthe Margaret R. • Director • Haines City Public Library • Haines City, FL 33844

Barthel Hetty H. • Branch Services Librarian • Juneau Public Libraries • Juneau, AK 99801 • PLA

Barthell Daniel W. • Reference Librarian • George Washington University Gelman Library • Washington, DC 20052 • ACRL RASD

Bartholomew Alan A. • Director of the Library • Albertus Magnus College Library • New Haven, CT 06511 • ACRL

Bartholomew Daphne S. • Librarian • Poultney Public Library • Poultney, VT 05764

Bartholomew Patricia J. • Sioux City, IA 51104

Bartko Yvonne O. • Honolulu, HI 96825

Bartkowiak Dale E. • Director • Marshfield Public Library • Marshfield, WI 54449 • LAMA PLA

Bartle Matthew W. • Hilbert College McGrath Library • Hamburg, NY 14075
Bartlett Ann E. • Head Librarian • Central High School Library • Cpe Girardeau, MD 20746 • AASL
Bartlett Billye M. • 6510 Clemons Ridge Rd. • Cookeville Junior High School • Cookeville, TN 38501 • AASL
Bartlett Diane L. • Livermore Public Library • Livermore, CA 94550
Bartlett Dorma M. • Associate Director • University of Wisconsin-Green Bay Library Learning Center • Green Bay, WI 54311 • ACRL ALCTS LITA
Bartlett Elizabeth • Franklin County Library • Louisburg, NC 27549
Bartlett James E. • New York, NY 10024
Bartlett Jane U. • Manager Info Tech Prog. • United States Government Printing Office • Washington, DC 20401 • LITA RASD GODORT
Bartlett Jay P. • Market Development Manager • Information Access Company • Foster City, CA 94404 • LITA RASD
Bartlett Kathleen • Asst. Dir., Public Services • Missoula Public Library • Missoula, MT 59802
Bartlett Mabel • New London, CT 06320
Bartlett Mark C. • Student • Dalhousie University School of Library & Inf. Studies • Halifax NS, B3H 4H8 Canada • IFRT SRRT
Bartley David G. • Mgr of ERC Support Service • Dallas County Community College District District Service Center • Mesquite, TX 75150-2095 • ACRL ALCTS LITA IFRT
Bartley Joyce • Midway Schools Unified School District #433 • Denton, KS 66017 • AASL
Bartley Linda • Library of Congress • Washington, DC 20541 • ALCTS
Bartolini Laurie • Reference Librarian • Lincoln Library • Springfield, IL 62701
Bartolini R Paul Mr. • Knoxville, TN 37920 • ALTA PLA *Life*
Bartolotti Maria T. • Reference Librarian • Tredyffrin Public Library • Strafford, PA 19087 • RASD
Barton Barbara I. • Librarian • Eight Mile Rock High School • Pinedale Grand Is., Bahamas
Barton Carolyn • San Antonio, TX 78234 • PLA
Barton David J. • Director • Viking Library System • Fergus Falls, MN 56537
Barton Holly H. • Student • University of Rhode Island Graduate School of Library & Information Studies • Kingston, RI 02881-0815 • AASL
Barton Jean E. • Topeka, KS 66610
Barton John F. Jr. Mr. • Circulation Librarian • Western Connecticut State University • Danbury, CT 06810 • ACRL LITA RASD LIRT *Life*
Barton Marlin C. • Sales Representative • Schwartz-Hill Book Company • Bethel, CT 06801
Barton Mary A. • Instruction/Reference Librarian • Moorhead State University Livingston Lord Library • Moorhead, MN 56563-2989 • ACRL
Barton Miriam G. • School Librarian • Cedarcest Southmoor Elementary School • Baton Rouge, LA 70816
Barton Nancy E. • Assistant Director • Denison Public Library • Denison, TX 75020 • PLA
Barton Phillip K. • Director • Rowan Public Library • Salisbury, NC 28144 • LAMA PLA
Barton Richard B. Mr. • Assistant Director • Detroit Public Library • Detroit, MI 48202 • ACRL RASD *Life*
Barton Virginia L. • Chehalis, WA 98532
Bartone Linda C. • Education Assoc/Library Media • South Carolina State Department of Education Curriculum Division • Columbia, SC 29201 • AASL ALSC YALSA
Bartosh Julia M. • Trustee • Crestwood Public Library District • Crestwood, IL 60445
Bartoshesky Patricia A. • Librarian • Saint Edumon's Academy • Wilmington, DE 19810-4199 • AASL
Bartovic Anna • Education Indexer • H. W. Wilson Company • Bronx, NY 10452 • ACRL
Bartow Virginia L. • Manager, Master Microform Coll. • New York Public Library • New York, NY 10018-2788 • ACRL ALCTS LITA
Bartram Joan G. • Collection Development Libn. • Salve Regina University Library • Newport, RI 02840 • ACRL ALCTS
Bartram Sharon V. • Librarian • Brown Public Library • Northfield, VT 05663 • PLA
Bartusiewicz Pamela • Riverdale Public Library • Riverdale, IL 60627 • PLA YALSA
Bartuska Florence C. • Granger, IN 46530 • EMIERT SRRT
Bartz Alice P. • Jenkintown, PA 19046 • AASL ALSC *Continuing*
Bartz Joachim Mr. • Sales Manager • Starkmann Library Services Ltd. • London NW8 8AE, England • ACRL
Bartz Mary Ann • Library Director • Waldorf College Voss Memorial Library • Forest City, IA 50436 • ACRL
Bary Paul • University of Maryland Libraries • College Park, MD 20742
Barzdukas Daiva • Assistant Coodinator • Library of Congress • Washington, DC 20541
Barzelatto Elba G. • Manager Information Services • Princeton Public Library • Princeton, NJ 08542
Barzelay Mary S. Bandyk • Branch Manager • Webster College • New Port Richey, FL 34652 • LAMA
Basby Joan A. • Student • University of Alabama School of Library & Information Studies • Tuscaloosa, AL 35487-0252 • AASL
Basch N. Bernard • Chicago, IL 60611 • ACRL ALCTS
Bascom Julie Hunter • Edward A. White Elementary School • Fort Benning, GA 31905 • ALSC PLA
Basefsky Stuart M. • Document Librarian • Duke University William R. Perkins Library • Durham, NC 27706 • GODORT
Basel Joy Mrs. • Librarian • Williamsburg Schools Library • Williamsburg, KS 66095 • AASL
Bashaw Marjorie K. • Student • Kent State University School of Library & Information Science • Kent, OH 44242-0001 • ALSC PLA RASD IFRT SRRT
Basher Karen W. • Angola, NY 14006 • NMRT
Basile Abbie J. • Assistant Librarian • University of Michigan Graduate Library Reference • Ann Arbor, MI 48109 • ACRL SRRT
Basile Anne J. • Sylvanie, OH 43560 • ACRL
Basile Barbara L. • Librarian • Chicago Public Library West Lawn Branch • Chicago, IL 60629
Basioli Maja Mp • Reference-Adm. Librarian • Seton Hall University Law Library • Newark, NJ 07102
Baskakova Marina G. • Librarian • Thomas College LRC • Thomasville, GA 31792
Baskett James A • Library Trustee • DeKalb County Public Library Adminstration Building • Decatur, GA 30030 • ALTA
Baskin Jeffrey L. • Director • William F. Laman Public Library • North Little Rock, AR 72114 • PLA
Basone Darlene Shiverdecker • Librarian/Media Specialist • Walnut Hills High School • Cincinnati, OH 45207 • AASL YALSA
Bass Corinne • New Orleans, LA 70115 • Continuing
Bass Doris • Director, Marketing Services • Scholastic Inc. • New York, NY 10003 • AASL ALSC PLA ERT
Bass Erica B. • Student • University of Alabama McLure Education Library • Tuscaloosa, AL 35487-0266
Bass Linnea M. • Buffalo Grove High School Library • Buffalo Grove, IL 60089 • LIRT
Bass Lisa J. • Student • Queens College Grad Sch of Lib & Inf Studies • Flushing, NY 11367 • LITA
Bass Martha L. • Elementary School Specialist • Fremont Re-1 Schools • Canon City, CO 81212 • AASL ALSC
Bass Rae B. • Public Service Librarian-Ch Serv • Seattle Public Library Henry Branch • Seattle, WA 98102 • ALSC
Bassam Bertha • Toronto ON, M4T 1M5 Canada • Continuing
Basse Mary A. • Anna, IL 62906 • AASL
Bassett Katherine A. • Media Specialist • Ocean City Intermediate School • Ocean City, NJ 08226 • LITA
Bassett Mary Ruth • Wawa, PA 19063-5531 • Continuing
Bassham Mia W. • Wilkes-Barre, PA 18702 • IRRT
Bassily-Ayad Wadie Zaky • Library Consultant • Alexandria New Library • Alexandria, Egypt • CLENE IRRT
Bassington Sally J. • Barbican Library Barbican Centre • London EC2Y 8DS, United Kingdom
Bassman George D. • Saint Louis, MO 63105
Basso Cheryl L. • Librarian • Saint Mary School • Plainfield, IL 60544 • ALSC
Basso Donna • Student • Saint John's University Division of Library & Information Science • Jamaica, NY 11439 • AASL
Bastacky Debbie • Circulation Technician • Howard County Public Library • Columbia, MD 21044
Bastian Jeannette B. • Virgin Islands Division of Libraries Archives & Museums • Saint Thomas, VI 00802
Bastos-Connelly Madalena M. • Community Library Manager • Malibu Library • Malibu, CA 90265
Basu Debabrata • Miami University Brill Science Library • Oxford, OH 45056 • RASD
Basu Patricia Lyons • Director • Sacred Heart Major Seminary • Detroit, MI 48206 • ACRL ALCTS LAMA
Batchelder Mildred L. • Evanston, IL 60201 • ALSC YALSA *Continuing*
Batchelor Frederica A. • Dept. Head-Library Systems • University of Connecticut Homer Babbidge Library • Storrs, CT 06269-1005 • ACRL LITA
Batchelor Steve • Trustee • Anderson County Library • Anderson, SC 29622-4047
Bateman Berry G. • Natchez, MS 39121 • ALSC
Bateman Denise H. • Technical Services Librarian • Bolivar County Library Robinson-Carpenter Memorial Library • Cleveland, MS 38732
Bateman Douglas Mrs. • Director • Lowndes County Library System • Columbus, MS 39701
Bateman R. James • Trustee • Peoria Public Library • Peoria, IL 61602 • ALTA
Bates Charles E. • Director • Pueblo Library District McClelland Library • Pueblo, CO 81004-1997 • ALTA LAMA PLA
Bates Christopher • Trustee • Hennepin County Library • Minnetonka, MN 55343 • ALTA
Bates Daniel G. • Librarian • United States Army Corps of Engineers Technical Library • New Orleans, LA 70160-0267
Bates Darlene • District Librarian • Vista Unified School District • Vista, CA 92084-3404 • AASL
Bates Henry E. Jr • Library Director • Mendocino County Library • Ukiah, CA 95482 • RASD
Bates Hugh A. • Trustee • Ontario Library Service-Escarpment • Hamilton ON, L8K 1N7 Canada
Bates Ieva • Children's Librarian/Branch Head • Ann Arbor Public Library Nellie S. Loving Branch • Ann Arbor, MI 48104 • PLA
Bates Karla • Assistant Director • Muskegon County Library • Muskegon, MI 49442-1094
Bates Marcia J. Dr. • Professor • University of California Los Angeles Graduate School of Library & Information Science • Los Angeles, CA 90024 • RASD
Bates Nancy F. • Director • Davidson County Library System • Lexington, NC 27292 • ALSC LAMA PLA
Bates Patricia L. • Adult Program Coordinator • Howard County Library • Columbia, MD 21044
Bates Rosalie A. • Northern Tioga School District Westfield Elementary School • Westfield, PA 16950 • AASL
Bates Wilma H. • Media Coordinator • Weaver Educational Center • Greensboro, NC 27401 • AASL
Batesel Sarah D. • Assistant Director • Mayville State University Library • Mayville, ND 58257
Bathaiian Seyed Mahmoud • Student • University of Shiraz School of Science • Shiraz, 71454, Iran • ALCTS
Batich Dorothy • Reference Librarian • Clark Public Library • Clark, NJ 07066
Batista David E. • Reference Librarian • Rutgers University • Camden, NJ 08102
Batista Emily • Head of Circulation Services • University of Pennsylvania Library Van Pelt-Dietrich Library Center • Philadelphia, PA 19104-6206 • ACRL LAMA RASD
Batiuk Ann Wilder • City University of New York Graduate School Mina Rees Library • New York, NY 10036-8099
Batsis Katherine • Educational Media Specialist • North Dover Elementary School • Toms River, NJ 08755
Batson Darrell L. • Extension Administrator • Las Vegas-Clark County Library District Flamingo Library • Las Vegas, NV 89119 • ASCLA
Batson John O. III • Student • Louisiana State University School of Library & Information Science • Baton Rouge, LA 70803-3290 • PLA IFRT NMRT SRRT
Batt Fred • Assoc Univ Pub Services Ln • California State University-Sacramento Library • Sacramento, CA 95819-6039 • ACRL LAMA
Batt Sarah J. • Manager, Literacy Services • Indianapolis Marion County Public Library • Indianapolis, IN 46206 • PLA
Battaglia Bonnie • Reference Catalog Librarian • El Dorado County Library • Placerville, CA 95667
Battaglia Nancy • Learning Center Director • The Lane School • Hinsdale, IL 60521
Battell Gertrude S. • Saint Paul, MN 55108 • ACRL RASD *Life*
Batterson Jack A. • Columbia, MO 65203
Battey Jean D. • Poohs End RFD • Chelsea, VT 05038 • AASL
Battin Marcia S. • S Pasadena, CA 91030 • IFRT
Battin Patricia • President • Commission on Preservation & Access • Washington, DC 20036 • ACRL
Battistella Maureen S. • Medical Librarian • Baptist Medical Center • Birmingham, AL 35211
Battle Alice H. • North Olympic Library System • Port Angeles, WA 98362
Batton Delma H. • Dover, DE 19901 • Continuing
Batts Nathalie C. • Towson, MD 21286 • Life
Batty Barbara D. • Port Neches, TX 77651 • AASL ACRL LAMA YALSA *Life*
Batty Carol A. • Access Coordinator • Washtenaw Community College • Ann Arbor, MI 48106 • ACRL
Batway Darwyn J. • Tacoma, WA 98407-4503
Batzdorff S. M. Mrs. • Santa Rosa, CA 95405 • Continuing
Baucom Charles V. • Director • York College • York, NE 68467 • ACRL
Baucom Marsha • Norcross Public Library • Norcross, GA 30071

Bauer Amy • Trustee • Mid-Wisconsin Federated Library System • Fond du Lac, WI 54935-5510 • ALTA

Bauer Barbara B. • Easton Area Public Library • Easton, PA 18042 • RASD

Bauer Beverly • District Media Coor. • Roseville Area Schools District #623 Curriculum Center • Roseville, MN 55113-4594 • AASL

Bauer Beverly • K-12 Media Specialist • University Lake School • Hartland, WI 53029 • AASL

Bauer Brad • Librarian I • Anaheim Public Library Euclid Branch • Anaheim, CA 92802 • NMRT

Bauer Caroline Feller Dr. • Miami Beach, FL 33140 • ALSC   Life

Bauer Carolyn J. Dr. • Oklahoma State Univ L • Stillwater, OK 74078-0375 • AASL ALSC

Bauer Christine J. • Student • University of Wisconsin-Milwaukee School of Library & Information Science • Milwaukee, WI 53201

Bauer Elizabeth I. • Middleton, WI 53562-4235

Bauer Francie L. • Science Referece Librarian • Vanderbilt University Library • Nashville, TN 37240-0007 • ACRL LITA

Bauer Helen C. • Student • Drexel University College of Information Studies • Philadelphia, PA 19104-2875

Bauer Karen L. • Hayes, VA 23072

Bauer Ken A.H. • Computer Systems Specialist • University of Northern Iowa Donald O. Rod Library • Cedar Falls, IA 50613-3675 • LITA

Bauer Marilyn A. • Oregon State Library • Salem, OR 97310-0640 • IFRT

Bauer Mary • Buffalo, NY 14214

Bauer Mary B. • Coordinator/Children Service • Prince George's County Memorial Library System • Hyattsville, MD 20782-2098 • ALSC PLA

Bauer Sarah A. • San Antonio, TX 78217-5408 • RASD

Bauer, CAE Margaret S. • Executive Director • Pennsylvania Library Association • Harrisburg, PA 17110

Baugh Georgia A. • Saint Louis University Pius XII Memorial Library • St. Louis, MO 63108 • AASL ACRL

Baugh Janice E. • Librarian • Pikes Peak Library District • Colorado Springs, CO 80901

Baughan Charles A. • Asst Dir For Support Serv • Johns Hopkins University Milton S. Eisenhower Library • Baltimore, MD 21218 • LAMA

Baugher Monica A. • Miami, FL 33155 • PLA IFRT

Baughman Carol H. • Children's Services Consultant • Kentucky Department for Libraries & Archives • Frankfort, KY 40602-0537 • ALSC ASCLA

Baughman James C. • Professor • Simmons College Graduate School of Library & Information Science • Boston, MA 02115 • AASL ALTA   Life

Baughman M. Sue • Branch Chief • Maryland State Department of Education Division of Library Development & Services • Baltimore, MD 21201 • ASCLA LAMA PLA

Baughman Steven A. • Manager, Member & Network • Southeastern Library Network (SOLINET) • Atlanta, GA 30309-2955 • ASCLA

Baughman Susan S. • Director • Clark University Robert Hutchings Goddard Library • Worcester, MA 01610 • ACRL

Baum Audrey V. • Librarian • Kirkwood Public Library • Kirkwood, MO 63122 • PLA

Baum Christina D. • Cottage Grove, MN 55016

Baum Linda T. • Youth Services Librarian • Trenton Public Library • Trenton, MI 48183 • ALSC

Baum Marsha L. • Columbia, SC 29212 • ACRL ALCTS LAMA GODORT

Baum Nathan • Reference Librarian • State University of New York (SUNY) Frank Melville Jr. Memorial Library • Stony Brook, NY 11794-3300 • ACRL RASD

Baum Rachel R. • Director • Ravena Free Library • Ravena, NY 12143

Baum Winifred E. • Oak Park, IL 60302 • Continuing

Bauman Marian • Librarian-in-Charge • George Washington High School • New York, NY 10040 • AASL

Baumann Charles H. • University Librarian Emeritus • Eastern Washington University • Cheney, WA 99004 • ACRL LITA

Baumann Melinda J. • Student • Syracuse University School of Information Studies • Syracuse, NY 13244-4100 • IFRT SRRT

Baumann Nancy L. • Athens, GA 30605

Baumann Richard J. • Milwaukee, WI 53218

Baumbach Donna Toler • Associate Professor • University of Central Florida Department of Education Services • Orlando, FL 32816-0992 • AASL

Baumbach Joyce • Student • University of North Texas • Denton, TX 76203

Baumgardner Janet R. • Librarian • Chesterfield County Public Library Midlothian Branch • Midlothian, VA 23113

Baumgartner Harriet May • Washington, DC 20010 • LITA RASD   Life

Baumgartner Marsha K. • Librarian • Livonia Public Schools • Livonia, MI 48154-5474 • AASL

Baumgartner Steve M. • Vice President • Book Dymanics, Inc. • Linden, NJ 07036 • PLA RASD YALSA

Baumholtz Steven • Serials Cataloger • Harvard University • Cambridge, MA 02138

Baumruk Robert • Berwyn, IL 60402 • PLA GODORT   Continuing

Baumwart Kathleen E. • Librarian • Davis-Monthan AFB Library United States Air Force • Davis- Monthan, AZ 85707-5000 • AFLRT FLRT

Baun Grace M. • Assistant Librarian • R E Lee High School • Springfield, VA 22014 • AASL

Baun Luise • Director • Mountain Home Public Library • Mountain Home, ID 83647

Bauner Ruth E. • Education & Psychology Librarian • Southern Illinois University Delyte W. Morris Library • Carbondale, IL 62901-6632 • ACRL RASD

Baur Janet L. • Student • Long Island University Palmer School of Library & Information Science • Greenvale, NY 11548 • AASL

Baur Patricia S. • Library Commissioner • Yorba Linda Public Library • Yorba Linda, CA 92686 • ALTA

Baur Susan R. • Librarian/A-V Coordinator • Owego Free Academy Library • Owego, NY 13827 • AASL YALSA

Bausch Claire • Director • Abilene Public Library • Abilene, TX 79601-5793 • LAMA

Bausch Donna K. • Norfolk, VA 23507

Bausom Nancy J. • Danville, CA 94526

Bausser Janet J. • Raleigh, NC 27604

Bautz Karen L. • Springfield, VA 22150 • LAMA PLA Life

Bavin Ann L. • Children Librarian/Assoc Dir. • Marvin Memorial Library • Shelby, OH 44875 • ALSC

Baxter Anne Maria • Boardman, OH 44512

Baxter Barbara • Supervising Librarian/Reference • Fremont Main Library • Fremont, CA 94538 • PLA

Baxter Carol • Librarian • Gulliver Prep School • Miami, FL 33156

Baxter Cynthia L. • Asst/In Catlg Dept • Indiana University School of Library and Information Science • Bloomington, IN 47405 • ALCTS

Baxter Frank L. • Brockton Public Library • Brockton, MA 02401

Baxter Kathleen Nee • Ursuline Academy • Dedham, MA 02026 • YALSA

Baxter M. Veanna • District Coor. Media Services • Conestoga Valley School District • Lancaster, PA 17601 • AASL

Baxter Margot S. • Audio-Visual Librarian • Manlius Library • Manlius, NY 13104

Baxter Pam M. • Purdue University Libraries • West Lafayette, IN 47907 • ACRL

Baxter Vicki • Trustee • Birmingham Public Library • Birmingham, AL 35203 • ALTA

Bay Flora P. • Norman, OK 73072 • IRRT

Bayard Laura • University of Notre Dame Library • Notre Dame, IN 46556 • ALCTS LAMA

Bayard Mary Ivy • Hd, Administrative Services Dept • Temple University Paley Library • Philadelphia, PA 19122 • ACRL LAMA

Bayer Bernard I. • Student • University of North Carolina at Chapel Hill School of Information and Library Science • Chapel Hill, NC 27599-3360

Bayer Paula Entin • Practice Inf. Operations Coor. • McKinsey & Company • New York, NY 10022

Bayha Christi A. • Student • University of Washington Graduate School of Library and Information Science • Seattle, WA 98195

Bayless Bernie J. • Assistant Editor • H. W. Wilson Company • Bronx, NY 10452 • RASD

Bayless June E. • Newport Beach, CA 92663 • Continuing

Bayless M. L. • Administrator • Mississippi Bend Area Education Agency • Bettendorf, IA 52722 • AASL

Baylis J. E. • President • Franklin Fixtures, Inc. • Brewster, MA 02631 • LAMA

Bayne Karen L. • Library Media Specialist • Bear Creek Elementary School • Baltimore, MD 21222 • AASL

Baynes Patricia L. • Student • State University of New York (SUNY) School of Information & Library Studies • Buffalo, NY 14260

Bayone Lillian • Brookline, MA 02146

Bayruns Kristin • Catalog Librarian • Moore College of Art Library • Philadelphia, PA 19103

Bayster Kathryn L. • Reference Librarian • Passaic Township Public Library • Stirling, NJ 07980

Bazan Lorraine R. • Reference Librarian/Bus Bibl • Santa Clara University Michel Orradre Library • Santa Clara, CA 95053 • ACRL

Bazar Sandra F. • Supervisor-Media Services • Lenape High School Library • Medford, NJ 08055 • AASL ALCTS LAMA LITA YALSA EMIERT IFRT LIRT SRRT

Bazaz Diane M. • Information Services • Hewlett-Packard Company • Burlington, MA 01803

Baze Mary Pierce • Puyallup, WA 98373 • AASL YALSA   Life

Bazillion Richard J. • Director of Library Services • Brandon University John E. Robbins Library • Brandon MB, R7A 6A9 Canada • ACRL

Bazirjian Rosann V. • Head, Bibliographic Srvs Dept • Syracuse University Library E. S. Bird Library • Syracuse, NY 13244-2010 • ACRL ALCTS

Beach Anne N. • Louisville, CO 80027

Beach Barbara J. • Senior Editor-New Product Dev. • Gale Research, Inc. • Detroit, MI 48226 • LITA PLA RASD

Beach Cecil P. • Director of Public Services • Broward County Florida Government Center #433 • Fort Lauderdale, FL 33301 • ASCLA LAMA PLA

Beach Daniel R. • School Library Media Specialist • Concord Elementary School • Anderson, SC 29621

Beach Earle C. • Business Manager • Temple University Paley Library • Philadelphia, PA 19122 • LAMA

Beach Jackie • Director • Edgecombe County • Tarboro, NC 27886 • LAMA PLA IFRT NMRT

Beach James H. • Assistant Professor • Harvard University • Cambridge, MA 02138 • LITA

Beach Jane • Director • Cooperstown Public Library • Cooperstown, PA 16317

Beach Regina L. • Ypsilanti, MI 48197 • ACRL

Beach Robert F. • Mars, PA 16046-8203 • Continuing

Beacher Karen L. • State University of New York (SUNY) School of Information & Library Studies • Buffalo, NY 14260

Beacom Marjorie • Santa Ana, CA 92706

Beacom Matthew L. • Yale University Sterling Memorial Library • New Haven, CT 06520 • ACRL LITA

Beadle Elizabeth L. • Somerset County Library • Bridgewater, NJ 08807

Beagle Brian D. • Toronto ON, M4R 1Y8 Canada

Beal Billy C. • Head Librarian • Meridian Community College • Meridian, MS 39307 • ACRL LITA SRRT

Beal Donna M. • Grand Forks, ND 58201 • AASL

Beal George • Newbury Public Library • Newbury, NH 03255

Beal Karma A. • Archivist • National Institute of Standards & Technology • Gaithersburg, MD 20899 • ALCTS

Beal Margaret D. • Jefferson, MD 21755 • AASL

Beal Sarell W. • Associate Professor • Eastern Michigan University Library Center of Educational Resources • Ypsilanti, MI 48197 • LIRT   Life

Beale Nancy Torres • Assistant Department Hd, Access • University of California-San Diego Central University Library • La Jolla, CA 92093-0175

Beall Deborah S. • Phoenix, AZ 85020

Beall Jeffrey • Cataloger • Harvard College Library • Cambridge, MA 02138

Beall Julianne • Assistant Editor • Library of Congress • Washington, DC 20541 • AASL ACRL ALCTS LAMA LITA PLA RASD FLRT GODORT IFRT IRRT LRRT SORT SRRT   Life

Beall Mary E. • Student • Wayne State University Library Science Program • Detroit, MI 48202

Beam Barbara S. • Serials Librarian • Illinois State Library • Springfield, IL 62701-1796 • ALCTS SRRT

Beaman Diane C. • Troy, NH 03465 • LIRT

Beaman Patricia L. • Southside Elementary School • Elko, NV 89801

Beamer Julie A. • Automation Librarian • Roanoke College Library • Salem, VA 24153 • LITA

Beamer Lisa M. • Childrens Librarian • Newark Free Library • Newark, DE 19711-7146 • ALSC PLA

Beamguard E P. Mrs • Montgomery, AL 36111

Bean Bobby G. • John Hope Elementary School • Atlanta, GA 30312 • AASL YALSA

Bean Delphine L. • Librarian • H. M. Smith Elementary School Library • Las Vegas, NV 89117

Bean Douglas J. • Library Director • Middletown Public Library • Middletown, OH 45044 • PLA

Bean Ethelle S. • Director • Dakota State University Karl E. Mundt Library • Madison, SD 57042-1799 • ACRL LAMA

Bean Kim L. • Director • Samuels Public Library • Front Royal, VA 22630 • PLA

Bean Lester O. • Librarian • Hillsboro High School • Hillsboro, OR 97123

Bean Norma P. • Associate Director • Texas Southern University • Houston, TX 77004

Bean Rick J. • Assistant Reference Librarian • DePaul University O'Hare Campus • Des Plaines, IL 60018 • ACRL

Beane Joel W. • Director • Kingwood Public Library • Kingwood, WV 26537

Beard Charles E. • Director of Libraries • West Georgia College Irvine Sullivan Ingram Library • Carrollton, GA 30118 • ACRL LAMA PLA

Beard Christine A. • Librarian • Ridgely Middle School • Lutherville, MD 21093 • AASL

Beard Craig W. • Head of Reference Services • University of Alabama at Birmingham Mervyn H. Sterne Library • Birmingham, AL 35294-0014

Beard Cynthia H. • Reader Services Librarian • Mobile College J.L. Bedsole Library • Mobile, AL 36663-0220 • ACRL

Beard Dorothy A. • Director • Mount Dora Public Library • Mount Dora, FL 32757 • PLA

Beard John R. • New York, NY 10027 • Continuing

Bearden Eithne M. • Reference Librarian • La Salle University Connelly Library • Philadelphia, PA 19141 • ACRL

Bearden Joan L. • Department Chair • Florida Community College Kent Campus Library • Jacksonville, FL 32205 • ACRL LITA

Bearden Joseph M. • Branch Library Administrator • Dallas Public Library • Dallas, TX 75201 • LAMA PLA

Bearden Kayron F. • Roswell, GA 30075

Bearden Martha B. • Children's Librarian • Bellaire City Library • Bellaire, TX 77401-4498 • ALSC

Bearden William L. • Assistant Director • Stockton State College • Pomona, NJ 08240 • ALCTS LITA

Bearman Toni Carbo • Dean • University of Pittsburgh School of Library and Information Science • Pittsburgh, PA 15260 • SRRT

Bearre Denise M. • Student • Wayne State University Library Science Program • Detroit, MI 48202 • IFRT

Bearse Margaret M. • Special Collections • University of Kansas Spencer Research Library • Lawrence, KS 66045-2800 • ACRL ALCTS

Beary Camille A. • Student • Arkansas College • Batesville, AR 72501

Beasley Augie E. • Media Specialist • East Mecklenburg High School • Charlotte, NC 28212 • AASL

Beasley Barbara K. • Library Head • Metropolitan Library System Bethany Branch • Bethany, OK 73008

Beasley Carla H. • Norcorss, GA 30093 • PLA

Beasley Carol Tom • Library Consultant • Uvalde CISD • Uvalde, TX 78801 • AASL

Beasley Debra A. • Cataloger • Utah State University Merrill Library • Logan, UT 84322-3000

Beasley James F. • Coordinator Title II • Tennessee State Library & Archives • Nashville, TN 37243-0312

Beasley James L. • Documents Librarian • University of South Dakota • Vermillion, SD 57069 • RASD GODORT LHRT

Beasley Nancy R. • Cartersville, GA 30120

Beasley Sarah E. • Reference Librarian • Oregon State University William Jasper Kerr Library • Corvallis, OR 97331-4501 • ACRL

Beasley Secundra • Senior Sales Clerk • Smithsonian Museum Shops • Washington, DC 20019 • ACRL

Beaton Barbara E. • Coordinator,Information Center • University of Michigan Libraries Reference Office • Ann Arbor, MI 48109 • ACRL RASD

Beatrice Sharon D. • Hibberd Middle School Richards Community Schools • Francesville, IN 47946 • AASL

Beattie Alexander F. • Reference-Government Documents • State University of New York (SUNY) Penfield Library • Oswego, NY 13126-3514 • ACRL GODORT

Beattie Barbara C. • Reference Librarian • Lee County Library System • Fort Myers, FL 33901

Beattie Betsy • Canadian Studies Librarian • University of Maine Raymond H. Fogler Library • Orono, ME 04469 • ACRL NMRT

Beattie Constance N. • Wilmington, DE 19806

Beattie Kathleen M. • Victoria 3053, Australia • ALCTS LITA RASD

Beattie Margaret • Central Rappahannock Regional Library Wallace Memorial Library • Fredericksburg, VA 22401

Beattie Marilyn S. • Director • Orange Public Library • Orange, CT 06477

Beatty-Oliver Denise • Director of Marketing • Dun & Bradstreet • Parsippany, NJ 07054 • RASD

Beatty Diane G. • Director • Apache County Library • St. Johns, AZ 85936 • PLA

Beatty Joseph H. Rev. • Trustee • Free Library of Philadelphia • Philadelphia, PA 19103 • ALTA

Beatty Leona Jean • Hingham, MA 02043 • PLA

Beatty Mark A. • ILL Coordinator • Council of Wisconsin Libraries Inc. • Madison, WI 53706 • LITA LIRT

Beatty Peggy R. • Branch Supervisor • Middletown Public Library Union Township Branch • West Chester, OH 45069 • PLA

Beatty William K. • Professor of Medical Bibliograph • Northwestern University Medical School • Chicago, IL 60611 • ACRL ALCTS *Life*

Beaubien Anne K. • Cooperative Access Services Head • University of Michigan Libraries • Ann Arbor, MI 48109-1205 • ACRL

Beauchamp Ilka M. • Student • Sam Houston State University Department of Library Science • Huntsville, TX 77341-2236

Beauchel Virginia Dr. • Head Librarian • Santa Rita High School • Tucson, AZ 85730 • AASL YALSA

Beaulac Lillian Sr • Anna Maria College Mondor-Eagen Library • Paxton, MA 01612 • ACRL

Beaumont Jane • Library Information Systems Cons • Beaumont & Associates • Toronto, ON, M4V 2S9 Canada • LITA

Beauregard John • Librarian • Gordon College Jenks Learning Resource Center • Wenham, MA 01984-1895 • ACRL RASD

Beauregard Susan L. • Student • Simmons College Graduate School of Library & Information Science • Boston, MA 02115

Beaver Holly • Hinkle Creek Elementary School • Noblesville, IN 46060 • AASL

Beaver Kathleen M. • Reference Librarian • Alverno College Library Media Center • Milwaukee, WI 53234-3922 • GODORT

Beaver Lucile E. • Arlington, VA 22202 • Continuing

Beaver Robin J. • Media, PA 19063 • AASL

Beavers Karen M. • Minority Library Intern • University of Minnesota • Minneapolis, MN 55455 • ACRL SRRT

Beavers Kathy • Area Librarian • Windsor Woods Area Library • Virginia Beach, VA 23452 • LAMA PLA

Beavers Paul J • Student • University of Michigan School of Information and Library Studies • Ann Arbor, MI 48109-1092

Beavers Peggy J. • ARS Coordinator • United States Department of Agriculture National Agricultural Library • Beltsville, MD 20705-2351 • ACRL LITA FLRT

Beavin Helen I. Ms • Young Adult Librarian • Naperville Public Libraries • Naperville, IL 60540 • YALSA

Beavin Kristi Thomas • Children's Librarian • Arlington County Department of Libraries • Arlington, VA 22201 • ALSC

Bebber Diane P. • Deputy Director, Support Svs. • San Diego Public Library • San Diego, CA 92101 • ALCTS LAMA LITA

Bebout Lois • Austin, TX 78703

Becham Gerald C. • Director • La Grange Memorial Library • La Grange, GA 30240 • PLA

Bechanan H. Gordon Mr. • Blacksburg, VA 24060 • ACRL ALCTS *Life*

Bechtel Carol A. • InterLibrary Loan Librarian • Environmental Protection Agency Headquarters Library • Washington, DC 20460

Bechtel Joan M. • Dickinson College Library Boyd Lee Spahr Library • Carlisle, PA 17013 • ACRL ALCTS LAMA LITA

Bechtler Ora F. • Bookmobile/Outreach Supv. • Greenville County Library • Greenville, SC 29601

Beck Allisa L. • Reference Librarian • University of Southern Mississippi Cox Library • Long Beach, MS 39560 • ACRL

Beck Arthur R. • Advertising/Promotion Manager • American Library Association-ACRL Choice Magazine • Middletown, CT 06457

Beck Barbara E. • Technical Services Department • Evanston Public Library • Evanston, IL 60201 • ALCTS CLENE *Life*

Beck Colleen • Librarian/Dept. Chair • Miramar College Learning Resource Center • San Diego, CA 92126 • ACRL

Beck Donald K. Jr. • Architect • Beck Associates Architects Citizens Tower • Oklahoma City, OK 73106 • LAMA

Beck Jeffrey A. • Reference Libraian • William Penn College Wilcox Library • Oskaloosa, IA 52577 • ACRL SRRT

Beck Julianne V. • Head of Library • Toronto French School • Toronto ON, M4N 1TY Canada

Beck Kathryn M. • Librarian I • Appleton Public Library • Appleton, WI 54911-4780

Beck M. A. • Department Chair Media • Cherry Hill High School East • Cherry Hill, NJ 08003 • AASL

Beck M. Clare • Government Documents Librarian • Eastern Michigan University Library Center of Educational Resources • Ypsilanti, MI 48197 • ACRL GODORT

Beck Margaret V. • Austin, MN 55912 • AASL ALSC *Life*

Beck Marianne J. • Archivist • Wartburg College Engelbrecht Library • Waverly, IA 50677-9987

Beck Maureen A. • Resource Services Librarian • Johns Hopkins University Milton S. Eisenhower Library • Baltimore, MD 21218 • ACRL LITA

Beck Melissa M. • University of California-Los Angeles (UCLA) • Los Angeles, CA 90024-1450 • ACRL ALCTS LITA

Beck Patricia • Childrens Librarian • Whittier Public Library Whittwood Branch • Whittier, CA 90603 • ALSC

Beck Sara R. • Manager, Bus., Sci., Tech. Dept. • Saint Louis Public Library • St. Louis, MO 63103-2389 • ACRL

Beck Susan E. • Del Mar College Library • Corpus Christi, TX 78404 • ACRL

Beck Susan J. • Ref Ln/Coor of Online Servs • Rutgers University Paul Robeson Library • Camden, NJ 08101-3990 • RASD

Beck Susan M. • Director • Hancock School Public Library • Hancock, MI 49930 • AASL ALSC PLA YALSA IFRT

Beck Teresa A. • Reference Librarian • East Chicago Public Library • E. Chicago, IN 46312 • RASD

Beck William L. • Dean of Library Services • California University of Pennsylvania • California, PA 15419 • ACRL

Beckemeier DeWayne • Librarian • Poplar Bluff Public Library • Poplar Bluff, MO 63901 • PLA

Becker Alan • Head-Fine Arts/AV • Broward County Division of Libraries Broward County Library • Fort Lauderdale, FL 33301

Becker Barbara J. • Media Specialist • Robert Lucas Elementary School • Iowa City, IA 52245 • AASL

Becker Barbara S. • Grand Island, NE 68801

Becker Brian L. • Librarian Chief • North Dakota State Hospital Health Sciences Library • Jamestown, ND 58402

Becker Carolyn S. • Silverlake, OH 44224 • AASL

Becker Daniel J. • Architect • Zimmerman Design Group • Milwaukee, WI 53213

Becker Dorothy • Librarian • Smithtown High School West • Smithtown, NY 11787 • AASL

Becker Edna • Schaumburg, IL 60193 • ALSC PLA *Continuing*

Becker Gregory • Westminster, MD 21158 • PLA

Becker John T. • Academic Librarian • Texas Tech University Texas Tech Library • Lubbock, TX 79409

Becker Joseph • Pacific Palisades, CA 90272 • AASL ACRL ALCTS ALSC ALTA ASCLA LAMA LITA PLA RASD YALSA AFLRT CLENE EMIERT ERT FLRT GODORT IFRT ILERT IRRT LHRT LIRT LRRT MAGERT NMRT SORT SRRT VRT *Honorary*

Becker Josephine • San Antonio, TX 78280-8066 • LAMA PLA ILERT

Becker Joyce • County Librarian • Colusa County Free Library • Colusa, CA 95932

Becker Judith E. • Technical Services Supervisor • West Springfield Public Library • West Springfield, MA 01089

Becker Karen A. • Library Instruction Coordinator • Northern Illinois University University Libraries • DeKalb, IL 60115-2868 • ACRL

Becker Lauren L. • Pembroke Pines, FL 33024 • ALSC IFRT

Becker Linda O. • Cambridge, MA 02142 • LITA

Becker Mary P. • Miami, FL 33186 • AASL *Life*

Becker Mildred C. • Chesterfield, MO 63017 • ALSC PLA *Continuing*

Becker Patti M. • Head Cataloger • Marquette University Memorial Library • Milwaukee, WI 53233 • ALCTS LRRT

Becker Richard L. • Student • Rosary College Graduate School of Library & Information Science • River Forest, IL 60305

Beckerdite L. A. • Librarian Grade 3 • Chicago Public Library Midwest Branch • Chicago, IL 60622

Beckerman Edwin P. • Princeton, NJ 08540 • PLA IFRT

Beckert Doris L. • Head of Reference Service Dept. • American River College Library • Sacramento, CA 95841 • RASD LIRT

Beckert Helen V. • Chicago, IL 60613

Beckett Karen W. • Library Branch Manager • Irving Public Library Northwest Branch • Irving, TX 75062 • ALSC PLA

Becketti Linda • Librarian • Johnson County Library • Shawnee Mission, KS 66201 • LAMA PLA RASD

Becking Mara Swanson • Media Specialist • Chesterton High School • Chesterton, IN 46304 • AASL YALSA

Beckley Jean D. • Milwaukee Public Schools Doerfler School • Milwaukee, WI 53215 • AASL ALSC

Beckman Margaret • Beckman Associates Library Consultants Inc. • Waterloo, ON, N2L 1C5 Canada • ACRL LAMA

Beckmann William • St. Charles, IL 60174 • AASL

Becknell Karen S. • Media Specialist • Hiller Elementary School • Madison Heights, MI 48071 • AASL

Beckner M Caroline • Arlington, VA 22209

Beckwith Bobbie C. • Trustee • Indianapolis Marion County Public Library • Indianapolis, IN 46206

Beckwith Ellen • Media Generalist • Atkinson Academy • Atkinson, NH 03811 • AASL

Beckwith Jane • Delta High School • Delta, UT 84624 • AASL

Beckwith Judy • Student • Allen County Public Library Dupont Branch • Ft. Wayne, IN 46825 • ALSC PLA

Beckwith Lucille A. • Calgary AB, T2J 4V1 Canada

Becton Betty G. • Wallingford Elementary School • Wallingford, PA 19086 • AASL ALSC

Becton Edna L. • Librarian • Langley Junior High School • Washington, DC 20002 • AASL

Beczak Judith A. • Staff Librarian • Carnegie Library of Pittsburgh Knoxville Branch • Pittsburgh, PA 15210

Beda Joanne • Elmhurst, IL 60126 • AASL

Beda Margaret C. • Virginia Beach, VA 23454 • Continuing

Bedan Lucille D. • Librarian • Rosati-Kain High School Library • St Louis, MO 63108 • AASL

Bedard Laura A. • Special Collection Librarian • Georgetown University Law Center Edward Bennett Williams Library • Washington, DC 20001-1417 • ACRL

Bedeian Lynda K. • Librarian • Episcopal Junior Senior High School • Baton Rouge, LA 70816 • AASL ALSC YALSA

Bedford Dale J. • Reference Librarian • Clifton Public Library • Clifton, NJ 07011

Bedford Denise D. • Senior Analyst • Information International • Oak Ridge, TN 37831 • ACRL ALCTS ASCLA LAMA LITA FLRT ILERT

Bedford Ruth A. • Schaumburg, IL 60194 • Continuing

Bedi Victoria • Librarian • Rockingham Free Public Library • Bellows Falls, VT 05101 • LITA PLA

Bedient Douglas • Director,Learning Resources Serv • Southern Illinois University Delyte W. Morris Library • Carbondale, IL 62901-6632

Bedikian Elizabeth O. • Head of Ctrl Library Public Serv • New Orleans Public Library • New Orleans, LA 70140 • PLA

Bedle Margaret • Caravel Academy Librarry • Bear, DE 19701

Bednar Carol • Acting Govt. Doc. Coordinator • California State University • Fullerton, CA 92634 • ACRL ALCTS GODORT

Bednar Marie L. • Hd,Bibliographic Support Servs. • Pennsylvania State University Libraries • University Park, PA 16802 • ACRL ALCTS

Bednarek Daniel P. • Systems Librarian • Harvard University • Cambridge, MA 02138 • LITA

Bedor Donna A. • Reference/Periodicals Librarian • Fort Lewis College Library • Durango, CO 81301 • ACRL

Bedsole Dan T. • Director • Randolph-Macon College McGraw-Page Library • Ashland, VA 23005 • ACRL

Bedunah Virginia • Director • Lincoln Township Public Library • Stevensville, MI 49127 • ALSC PLA

Bedwell Rose L. • Camp Verde, AZ 86322-3209 • ALSC

Beebe Richard J. • Technical Support Specialist • County of Los Angeles Public Library South County Region 500 • Norwalk, CA 90650 • PLA RASD

Beebe Robert W. • Librarian II • San Antonio Public Library • San Antonio, TX 78205

Beech Valerie • Reference Librarian • Indiana University at South Bend Franklin D. Schurz Library • South Bend, IN 46634 • ACRL

Beechem Patricia • Librarian-Circulation • Grand Rapids Public Library • Grand Rapids, MI 49503-3093 • LITA PLA CLENE SORT

Beecher John W. • Director of Libraries • North Dakota State University Library • Fargo, ND 58105-5599 • ACRL LAMA LITA IRRT *Life*

Beecher Sally • Hd, General Reference Services • Boston Public Library • Boston, MA 02117 • RASD

Beechey Mary E. • Big Flats, NY 14814 • AASL

Beegan Joanne • Trustee • Poplar Creek Public Library Dist • Streamwood, IL 60107 • ALTA

Beehler Sandra • Acquisitions Librarian • Cornell University Law School Library • Ithaca, NY 14853-4901

Beeko Stephen • Technical Services Librarian • Texas State Technical College Library • Waco, TX 76705 • ALCTS IRRT

Beeler Margery D. • Assistant Director • Schenectady County Public Library • Schenectady, NY 12305 • PLA

Beeler Mary Glenda F. • Librarian/Legal Worker • Joseph Beeler, P.A. • Miami, FL 33137 • ACRL RASD SRRT

Beeman John A. • Snohomish, WA 98290-7953 • PLA

Beene Lonnie P. • Bibliographic Control Librarian • St. Mary's University Academic Library • San Antonio, TX 78228

Beer Patience C. • Head of Adult Services • Independence Township Library • Clarkston, MI 48346 • PLA RASD

Beere Elizabeth A. • Student • University of North Carolina School of Library Science • Chapel Hill, NC 27599-3360

Beerman Sandy J. • Librarian • Rosemead High School • Rosemead, CA 91770 • AASL

Beers Cally • Student • O'Melveny & Myers Law Library • Los Angeles, CA 90071-2899

Beers Catherine M. • Student • Kutztown University Library Science Department • Kutztown, PA 19530 • AASL ALSC

Beers Lisa L. • American College for the Applied Arts • Atlanta, GA 30326

Beery Carl • Assistant Director • Saint Joseph County Public Library • South Bend, IN 46601 • ASCLA PLA

Beery Gen A. • Librarian • Wolf Point Public Schools • Wolf Point, MT 59201 • ALSC

Beeson Ann M. • Marketing Manager • Mead Data Central Inc. • Dayton, OH 45401 • PLA

Beeson Sandra J. • Coor of Media Processing Serv • Northern Virginia Community College Annandale Campus • Annandale, VA 22003

Beetem Doris • Houston, TX 77035

Beethe Mary • K-12 Librarian • Unified School District #488 • Bern, KS 66408 • AASL

Beeton Elizabeth D. • Asst Dir Sys & Tech Supp Div • Metropolitan Toronto Reference Library • Toronto ON, M4W 2G8 Canada • ALCTS LAMA LITA PLA RASD

Beezley Jo A. • Head, Government Documents • Pittsburg State University • Pittsburgh, KS 66762 • GODORT

Begg Karin E. • Associate University Librarian • Boston College • Chestnut Hill, MA 02167 • ACRL LAMA LITA

Begg Nancy • Delmar, NY 12054

Beggs Linda P. • Plainview, AR 72857

Begley Jane • Library Media Specialist • E.J. Dillon Middle School • Phoenix, NY 13135 • AASL

Beglo Jo • Ottawa ON, K1Y 3X7 Canada

Behem Gloria A. • Librarian • Chester Public School • Chester, MT 59522 • AASL

Behike Robert E. • Oak Creek, WI 53154

Behler Patricia A. • Assoc Library Services Youth • Missouri State Library • Jefferson City, MO 65102

Behling Linda M. • Coordinator, Adult Services • Fort Bend County Library System • Richmond, TX 77469 • PLA RASD

Behlman Pia C. • Teacher • Southern Connecticut State University School of Libray Science & Instructional Technology • New Haven, CT 06515

Behm Kathlyn F. • Director Learning Resources Ctr. • Southern Illinois University • Edwardsville, IL 62026

Behnke Diane D. • Student • Wayne State University Library Science Program • Detroit, MI 48202

Behr Michele D. • Catalog Librarian • Carnegie-Mellon University Libraries Hunt Library • Pittsburgh, PA 15213 • ALCTS

Behra Robert • Cataloger • University of Texas • Austin, TX 78712-1276 • ACRL ALCTS LHRT SRRT

Behrendt Kathleen • Children's Librarian • Berwyn Public Library System • Berwyn, IL 60402 • ALSC

Behrens Elizabeth • College Librarian • Sir Wilfred Grenfell College • Corner Brook NF, Canada • ACRL LAMA RASD LIRT

Behrens Janet Louise • Sigourney, IA 52591 • PLA

Behrman Sara T. • Director • Mideastern Michigan Library Coop. • Flint, MI 48502 • LAMA PLA

Behroozi Jaleh • San Jose, CA 95117

Beidl Mary Beth • Coord. Library Information Syst. • Brooklyn Public Library • Brooklyn, NY 11238 • LAMA LITA PLA

Beidler Sandra J. • Head, Special Collections • University of North Dakota Chester Fritz Library • Grand Forks, ND 58202-0175 • LAMA

Beidler Susan K. • Collection Management Serv Ln • Lycoming College Library • Williamsport, PA 17701-5192 • ACRL ALCTS RASD

Beiers Katherine • Assistant University Librarian • University of California-Santa Cruz Library • Santa Cruz, CA 95064 • ACRL

Beihl Renee M. • Librarian • Fort Collins Public Library • Ft. Collins, CO 80524-2990

Beilby Mary L. • Mc Graw, NY 13101

Beile Esther L. • Media Specialist • Crete Elementary School • Crete, NE 68333 • AASL

Beilke Patricia F. • Prof of Library & Info Science • Ball State University Department of Secondary Education • Muncie, IN 47306 • AASL ALSC PLA EMIERT IRRT LIRT

Beiman Frances M. • Supervising Librarian • Newark Public Library • Newark, NJ 07101-0630 • PLA

Bein Ann • Catalog Librarian • University of California-Los Angeles (UCLA) • Los Angeles, CA 90024-1450 • ALCTS

Bein Miriam • Director • Mountainside Public Library • Mountainside, NJ 07092 • PLA

Beinhoff Lisa A. • University of Redlands Armacost Library • Redlands, CA 92374-3758 • GODORT LRRT

Beiriger Elizabeth A. • Tacoma, WA 98467 • AASL ALSC *Life*

Beisenherz Nona Kay • Special Services Librarian • Loyola University Loyola Law School Library • New Orleans, LA 70118 • ACRL

Beiser Karl A. • Library Systems Coordinator • Maine State Library • Bangor, ME 04402

Beisswenger D. Andrew • University of Alabama School of Library & Information Studies • Tuscaloosa, AL 35487-0252

Beitler Roslyn • Program Manager • Smithsonian Resident Assoc Prog • Washington, DC 20560 • ALSC

Beitzel Amy C. • Canfield, OH 44406

Bejnar Thaddeus • Law Librarian • New Mexico State Library • Santa Fe, NM 87503

Belair Paula M. • Branch Coordinator • Scranton Public Library Albright Memorial Library • Scranton, PA 18509-3248 • PLA NMRT SRRT

Belan Judy • Special Collections Librarian • Augustana College Library • Rock Island, IL 61201 • ACRL

Belanger Anne-Marie • Record Maintance/Products Lib • Concordia University Libraries • Montreal PQ, H3G 1M8 Canada • ACRL ALCTS

Belanger Betty • Reference Head • Athens Regional Library • Athens, GA 30606 • PLA

Belanger David L. • Assistant System Administrator • Delaware County Library System • Brookhaven, PA 19015 • LITA

Belanger Janet B. • P 3 Acquisitions Librarian • Boston Public Library • Boston, MA 02117 • ALCTS

Belanger Judy • Trustee • Addison Public Library • Addison, IL 60101-2499 • AASL ALSC ALTA

Belanger Maryann M. • Assistant Librarian • Princeton University • Princeton, NJ 08544-2098 • ACRL

Belanger Sandra • Librarian • San Jose State University Clark Library • San Jose, CA 95192-0028 • ACRL RASD LRRT

Belanger Terry • University Professor • University of Virginia Alderman Library • Charlottesville, VA 22903-2498 • ACRL LHRT

Belastock Tjalda N. • Associate Director • Bentley College Solomon R. Baker Library • Waltham, MA 02154-4705 • ACRL LITA

Belcastro Patricia A. • Deputy Director • Rocky River Public Library • Rocky River, OH 44116-2699 • LAMA PLA

Belcher Faye • Library Consultant • Morehead State University Camden-Carroll Library • Morehead, KY 40351 • ACRL *Continuing*

Belcher Nancy S. • Head of Juvenile Services • West Des Moines Public Library • West Des Moines, IA 50265 • ALSC PLA

Belcher Sheila W. • Seattle, WA 98125

Beleu Steve • Head of U.S. Gov't Info Division • Oklahoma Department of Libraries • Oklahoma City, OK 73105-3298 • GODORT MAGERT

Belflower Elizabeth D. • Auke Bay, AK 99821

Belfor Pamela S. • Student • Emporia State University Emporia in the Rockies • Denver, CO 80204 • ALSC GODORT

Belgum Kathie C. • Executive Law Librarian • University of Iowa Libraries • Iowa City, IA 52242-1379

Belich Daniel G. • Library Assistant • Harvard University • Cambridge, MA 02138

Beline Jayne W. • Director • Parsippany-Troy Hills Public Library Parsippany Branch • Parsippany, NJ 07054-4036 • LAMA PLA

Belisle Germain • Sherbrooke PQ, J1K 1V2 Canada • Continuing

Belk Norman • Coordinator Community Service • Greenville County Library • Greenville, SC 29601 • PLA

Belkin Betsey • Director • Ursuline College Ralph M. Besse Library • Pepper Pike, OH 44124 • ACRL

Bell-Abbott Karen D. • Librarian II • Detroit Public Library Jefferson Branch • Detroit, MI 48224 • YALSA

Bell-Russel Danna C • Marymount University Reinsch Library • Arlington, VA 22207-4299 • ACRL

Bell-Smith Cynthia • Judson Fundamental Magnet School • Shreveport, LA 71109

Bell Ann M. • Great Falls, MT 59401

Bell Barbara L. • Documents/Reference Librarian • College of Wooster Andrews Library • Wooster, OH 44691 • ACRL GODORT

Bell Barbara S. • Wicomico Senior High School • Salisbury, MD 21801 • AASL

Bell Becky • Sales Manager • Medialog Inc. • Alexandria, KY 41001 • AASL

Bell Carol • President • Friends of Hugh Embry Library • Dade City, FL 33526

Bell Carol A. • Albuquerque, NM 87109 • AASL NMRT

Bell Carole R. • Asst Hd of Serials & Acq • Northwestern University Library • Evanston, IL 60208-2300 • ACRL ALCTS NMRT

Bell Cecelia L. • Health Science Librarian • Mississippi Baptist Medical Center J. Manning Hudson Health Sci Lib • Jackson, MS 39202

Bell Cecilia E. • Student • Western Kentucky University Library Media Education • Bowling Green, KY 42101 • AASL IFRT SRRT

Bell David B. • Head Librarian • Myrtle Beach High School • Myrtle Beach, SC 29577 • AASL

Bell Don C. • Reference Librarian • Shelton State Community College Junior College Division Library • Tusacaloosa, AL 35405 • SRRT

Bell Dorothy J. • Site Coordinator • Tampa-Hillsborough County Public Library West Tampa Branch • Tampa, FL 33607

Bell Ellen • Director • Washington County Public Library • Marietta, OH 45750 • PLA
Bell Ellen J. • Children's Librarian • North Babylon Public Library • North Babylon, NY 11703
Bell Esther T. • Library Clerk • Evans County Library • Claxton, GA 30417
Bell George • Trustee • Oregon State Library • Salem, OR 97310-0640 • ALTA
Bell Geraldine W. Dr. • President • Birmingham Public & Jefferson County Free Library • Birmingham, AL 35203 • AASL ALTA PLA
Bell Gladys Smiley • Kent State University Libraries • Kent, OH 44242 • ACRL LITA RASD
Bell Janice B. • Southern University John B. Cade Library • Baton Rouge, LA 70813
Bell Jo Ann G. • Director of Library Services • Richardson Independent School District • Richardson, TX 75081 • AASL ALSC YALSA
Bell Jo Ann H. • Director • East Carolina University Health Sciences Library • Greenville, NC 27858-4354 • ACRL
Bell Judith H. • Director • Jamestown Philomenian Library • Jamestown, RI 02835 • PLA
Bell Leroy Jr. • Montgomery, AL 36117
Bell Leslie • Member Services Coordinator • Northwest Kansas Library Systems • Norton, KS 67654
Bell Mabel Boyd Mrs. • Howard Beach, NY 11414 • ALSC PLA *Continuing*
Bell Martha S. Miss • Roanoke, VA 24012 • ACRL *Continuing*
Bell Mary E. • Associate Library Director • Community College of the Finger Lakes Library • Canandaigua, NY 14424 • ACRL
Bell Mary J. • Knoxville, TN 37917 • Continuing
Bell Mary K. • Library Media Specialist • West Junior High School • Wisconsin Rapids, WI 54494 • AASL
Bell Mertys W. • Greensboro, NC 27407 • ACRL
Bell Michael • Director • LaJoya ISD • LaJoya, TX 78560 • AASL
Bell Nancy E. • District Librarian • Woodland High School • Woodland, ME 04694
Bell Naomi • Children's Librarian • Chatham-Effingham-Liberty Regional Library (CEL) • Savannah, GA 31499-4301
Bell Ovid H. • Chairman of Board • Ovid Bell Press, Inc • Fulton, MO 65251 • ACRL *Subscribing*
Bell Peggy S. • Student • Kansas State University Farrell Library • Manhattan, KS 66506-1200 • EMIERT
Bell Phyllis A. • Chief, Documents Cataloging Dept • Air University Library • Maxwell AFB, AL 36112 • LITA FLRT
Bell Rebecca L. • Automation Coordinator,Tds/PALS • Traverse des Sioux Library System • Mankato, MN 56002-0608 • ALCTS LITA
Bell Rebecca L. • Senior Technical Services Ln • Country Music Foundation Library and Media Center • Nashville, TN 37203 • ALCTS
Bell Robert David • University Center at Tulsa • Tulsa, OK 74106 • ACRL LITA RASD GODORT NMRT
Bell Ruth V. • Director of Library Service • Blue Valley Unified School District • Overland Park, KS 66223 • AASL ALCTS ALSC LAMA LITA YALSA LIRT
Bell Sabra J. • Librarian • South Conway Elementary School • Conway, SC 29526 • AASL
Bell Sally • Farmer City, IL 61842
Bell Susan H. • Nashville, TN 37211 • ERT VRT
Bell Suzanne S. • Rochester Institute of Technology Wallace Memorial Library • Rochester, NY 14623-0887
Bell Thomas R. • Reference Librarian • Hinsdale Public Library • Hinsdale, IL 60521
Bell Valeria A. • Health Sciences Librarian • Grady Memorial Library Piedmont Hall Library • Atlanta, GA 30335
Bell W. Michael • Head/Acquisitions/Fund Acct • Tennessee University Library at Chattanooga • Chattanooga, TN 37403
Bell Walter F. • Assistant Reference Librarian • University of North Texas • Denton, TX 76203 • ACRL RASD
Bell-Gam Ruby A. • African Studies Bibliographer • UCLA Library University Research Library • Los Angeles, CA 90024-1575 • ACRL ALCTS IRRT
Bellaire Nancy • Chief • Monroe County Library System Bedford Branch • Temperance, MI 48182
Bellamy Bonnie • Trustee • Brooklyn Public Library • Brooklyn, NY 11238 • ALTA
Bellamy Lois M. • Systems Librarian • University of Tennessee-Memphis Health Sciences Center Library • Memphis, TN 38163 • LITA
Bellamy Patricia C. • Reference Librarian • University of Toronto Robarts Library • Toronto ON, Canada • ACRL NMRT
Bellante Angela • Jefferson High School • Daly City, CA 94014
Bellanti Claire Q. • Head, Acess Services • University of California-Los Angeles University Research Library • Los Angeles, CA 90024 • LAMA
Bellanti Robert • Management Librarian • University of California Los Angeles Management Library (UCLA) • Los Angeles, CA 90024-1460 • ACRL
Bellardo Trudi • Associate Professor • Catholic University of America School of Library and Information Science • Washington, DC 20064
Bellas Susan • Hillsboro, OH 45133
Bellavance Jean B. • Librarian-Elementary Division • Gwynedd-Mercy Academy • Spring House, PA 19477 • AASL
Belle Penny M. • Oxford, OH 45056 • IFRT SRRT
Bellehumeur Lynn • Chief of Technical Services • Milwaukee Public Library • Milwaukee, WI 53233 • ALCTS LITA PLA
Belles Melinda • Reference Librarian • Vigo County Public Library • Terre Haute, IN 47807 • PLA RASD
Bellin Bernard E. • Library Coordinator • Franklin Public Library • Franklin, WI 53132 • LAMA PLA
Bellinger Barry • Asst Editor of Class Schedules • Library of Congress • Washington, DC 20541
Bellinger Christina • Cataloging Team Manager • University of New Hampshire Library • Durham, NH 03824 • ACRL ALCTS
Bellinger Margaret A. • Vice Pres., Editorial & Preserv. • Research Publications • Woodbridge, CT 06525 • ACRL ALCTS
Bellinger Robert J. • Associate Chief • Donnell Library Center • New York, NY 10019 • PLA RASD
Bellino Annette M. • Student • Rosary College Graduate School of Library & Information Science • River Forest, IL 60305
Bellitti-LaSita Laura J. • Head of Young Adult Services • Riverhead Free Library • Riverhead, NY 11901 • YALSA
Belluomini Michele A. • Free Library of Philadelphia West Philadelphia Regional • Philadelphia, PA 19139
Belnap Rey • Library/Media Coordinator • Tooele High School • Tooele, UT 84074 • AASL
Beloher Ellen H. • Student • University of South Carolina College of Library & Information Science • Columbia, SC 29208 • ALCTS IFRT SRRT
Belsches Jane F. • Dothan City School District • Dothan, AL 36301 • AASL ALSC
Belsley Nancy C. • PPG Industries, Incorporated • Iowa City, IA 52240
Belton Joyce F. • Student • University of Pittsburgh School of Library and Information Science • Pittsburgh, PA 15260
Belvin Carolyn J. • Children's Librarian • Ocean County Public Library • Toms River, NJ 08753 • PLA
Belvin Diana D. • Librarian • Given Memorial Library • Pinehurst, NC 28374
Belvin Robert J. • New Brunswick Free Public Library • New Brunswick, NJ 08901 • LAMA PLA YALSA LRRT
Belz James A. • Head of Public Services • Rollins College Olin Library • Winter Park, FL 32789-4499 • ACRL LAMA IFRT SRRT
Bem Rosemarie L. • Librarian • Veterans Administration Outpatient Clinic Library • Martinez, CA 94553
Bembenek Elizabeth M. • Chicago Ridge, IL 60415
Bemenick Carolyn J. • Arlington, VA 22202 • ACRL
Bemont Susie L. • Vestal, NY 13850
Ben-Simon Julie E. • Head of Acquisitions • King County Library System • Seattle, WA 98109-5191 • PLA
Ben-Ami Frank Y. • Student • Wayne State University Library Science Program • Detroit, MI 48202 • ALCTS LITA
Ben-Dor Sue E. • Circulation Librarian • Fairleigh Dickinson University Weiner Library • Teaneck, NJ 07666
Benaicha Hedi • Arabic Bibliographer • Princeton University • Princeton, NJ 08544-2098 • ACRL ALCTS IRRT
Benaud Claire-Lise • University of New Mexico General Library • Albuquerque, NM 87131 • ALCTS
Benbrook Donna M. • Frederick County Public Library C. Burr Artz Library • Frederick, MD 21701
Bencic Linda J. • Librarian • Albuquerque Public Library Juan Tabo Branch • Albuquerque, NM 87111
Bencini Debra L. • Wading River, NY 11792 • PLA SRRT
Bencivenga Linda L. • Elementary Librarian • Forest Avenue School • Middletown, RI 02840 • AASL
Benckart Amy M. • Bookmobile Librarian • Erie County Library System • Erie, PA 16501
Bend Steven H. • Student • University of Pittsburgh School of Library and Information Science • Pittsburgh, PA 15260
Benda Constance M. • Librarian • Saint James/Seton School • Omaha, NE 68134 • AASL
Benda Janice M. • Director • Saxton B. Little Free Library, Inc. • Columbia, CT 06237
Bender-Lamb Sylvia L. • Senior Librarian • California Division of Mines & Geology • Sacramento, CA 95814-0131 • ACRL LAMA MAGERT
Bender Betty W. • Cheney, WA 99004 • LAMA
Bender Cynthia Froelich • Asst Head/General Info Dept. • Enoch Pratt Free Library • Baltimore, MD 21201-4484 • LAMA PLA RASD
Bender Evelyn • Elkins Park, PA 19117 • AASL YALSA
Bender Helen F. • Boston Public Library • Boston, MA 02117 • RASD
Bender Joann M. • Student • University of Kentucky College of Library & Information Science • Lexington, KY 40506-0391 • PLA
Bender Linda K. • Refernce Librarian • Clark County Public Library Park Branch • Springfield, OH 45501
Bender Mary C. • Cataloger of Serials • Mississippi State University Mitchell Memorial Library • Mississippi State, MS 39762 • ALCTS
Bender Miriam • Sylvania, OH 43560
Bender Nancy White • Library Media Specialist • Public Schools • Lexington, MA 02173 • AASL
Bender Nathan E. • Montana State University • Bozeman, MT 59717-0332 • ACRL
Bender Ruth E • Reference Librarian • Elkhart Public Library • Elkhart, IN 46516-3184
Bender Shirley R. • Ln • Horace Mann School • Bronx, NY 10471 • AASL
Bender Virginia L. • Bozeman, MT 59715
Bendick Jeanne • Guilford, CT 06437
Bendig Deborah L. • Sr. Product Support Specialist • Online Computer Library Center (OCLC) • Dublin, OH 43017-3395 • RASD
Bendig Mark W. • Res Scientist Off Of Res • Online Computer Library Center (OCLC) • Dublin, OH 43017-3395
Bendix Dorothy • Phildelphia, PA 19103 • PLA RASD *Life*
Bendix Linda A. • Head-Technical Services • Manitowoc Public Library • Manitowoc, WI 54220 • PLA
Bendror Jack • President • Mekatronics, Inc. • Port Washington, NY 11050
Benedetti Joan M. • Museum Librarian • Craft & Folk Art Museum • Los Angeles, CA 90036 • ACRL EMIERT
Benedetti Marie M. • Librarian • Telephonics Corporation • Farmingdale, NY 11735
Benedict Diane G. • Birmingham, MI 48301
Benedict K. C. • Associate Librarian • College of Eastern Utah San Juan Center Library • Blanding, UT 84511 • ACRL
Benedict Linda C. • A-V & Automation Consultant • Wayne County Library System • Newark, NY 14513 • PLA VRT
Benedict Marjorie A. • Librarian • State University of New York (SUNY) University Libraries • Albany, NY 12222 • ACRL
Beneduce Ann K. • Princeton, NJ 08540 • ALSC
Benedum Patricia L. • Supervisor Lib Media Svs/IMC • Monongalia County Board of Education • Morgantown, WV 26505 • AASL
Benefiel Candace R. • Reference Librarian-Humanities • Texas A & M University Sterling C. Evans Library • College Station, TX 77843-5000 • ACRL RASD IFRT LIRT LRRT
Benemann William E. • Head of Bancroft Cataloging • University of California-Berkeley Bancroft Library • Berkeley, CA 94720 • ACRL
Benenfeld Alan R. • Director • Northeastern University Libraries • Boston, MA 02115 • ACRL ALCTS LAMA LITA RASD LRRT
Benetz E. Steven • Director • Eustis Memorial Library • Eustis, FL 32726 • LAMA PLA
Benford Joseph M. • Library Supervisor I • Free Library of Philadelphia Oak Lane Branch • Philadelphia, PA 19126 • PLA
Bengel Ellyn • Trustee • East Central Arkansas Regional Library • Wynne, AR 72396
Bengston Carl E. • Library Director • Dominican College of San Rafael Archbishop Alemany Library • San Rafael, CA 94901 • ACRL LAMA LITA
Bengstron William A. • President • Port Jefferson Free Library • Pt. Jefferson, NY 11777-1897
Bengtson Ardell M. • Dakota County Library System Wescott Library • Eagan, MN 55123 • ALCTS
Bengtson Betty G. • Director of University Libs. • University of Washington Suzzallo Library • Seattle, WA 98195 • ACRL ALCTS LAMA LITA
Bengtson Marjorie • Assistant/Documents Librarian • University of Illinois at Chicago University Library • Chicago, IL 60680 • ACRL LITA RASD GODORT MAGERT
Benham Barbara L. • Libn./Media Specialist • Episcopal High Sch Lib • Jacksonville, FL 32207 • AASL
Benham Frances • University Librarian • Saint Louis University Pius XII Memorial Library • St. Louis, MO 63108 • ACRL ALCTS LAMA RASD
Benham Hiltraut H. • Student • University of Oklahoma School of Library & Information Studies • Norman, OK 73019
Benham Kenneth W. • Springfield, OH 45504

Benidir Samia • Arlington, VA 22201

Benigno Dorothy B. • Levittown, NY 11756 • PLA

Benitez-Sharpless Mercedes • Librarian • Lafayette College Kirby Library • Easton, PA 18042-1797 • ACRL

Benitez Valerie J. • Beale Memorial Library • Bakersfield, CA 93301

Benjamin Bernice S. • Trustee • Central Arkansas Library System • Little Rock, AR 72201-4698 • ALTA

Benjamin Harriet S. • Branch Library Manager • Queens Borough Public Library Jackson Heights Branch • Jackson Heights, NY 11372

Benjamin Jeanne E. • Indiana University at South Bend Franklin D. Schurz Library • South Bend, IN 46634 • ACRL

Benjamin Lillie M. • Dublin, GA 31040 • AASL

Benjamin Marian J. • Technical Services Supervisor • Mansfield-Richland County Public Library • Mansfield, OH 44902-1295 • IFRT

Benjamin Muriel N. • Student • University of Rhode Island Graduate School of Library & Information Studies • Kingston, RI 02881-0815 • AASL ALSC

Benjamin Patricia A. • Clark University • Worcester, MA 01610 • IFRT

Benjamin Peggy J. • Librarian • North Pocono School District Higgh School 9-12 • Moscow, PA 18444 • AASL

Benjamin Susan A. • Sherman Oaks, CA 91403 • NMRT

Benjumea Joan • Oakland Public Schools • Oakland, CA 94606

Benke Louise F. • Laporte, CO 80535 • ALSC

Benke Robin Paul • Director of Library Services • Clinch Valley College John Cook Wyllie Library • Wise, VA 24293 • ACRL IFRT IRRT

Benkert Alan G. • Director • Groton Public Library • Groton, CT 06340

Benn James R. • Library Systems Consultant • Auto-Graphics • Niantic, CT 06357-2330 • ASCLA PLA

Benne Mae M. • Professor,Emeritus • University of Washington Graduate School of Library and Information Science • Seattle, WA 98195 • ALSC   *Continuing*

Benner Evangeline A. • Branch Manager • Baltimore County Public Library Loch Raven Branch • Towson, MD 21204 • ALSC LAMA PLA RASD

Benner Faith • Librarian • Vestavia Hills High School • Vestavia Hills, AL 35216

Bennett-Speed Carolyn • Fredericksburg, VA 22401

Bennett Adele R. • Children's Librarian • Brentwood Public Library • Brentwood, NY 11717 • AASL ALSC

Bennett Agnes H. • Turlock, CA 95380-1422 • Continuing

Bennett Al • Literacy Cons • California State Library Library Development Services Bureau • Sacramento, CA 95814-3324

Bennett Alma • Columbia, MO 65202 • ACRL RASD   *Life*

Bennett Betty B. • Nacogdoches, TX 75961 • ACRL RASD   *Life*

Bennett Betty L. • Fairmont, WV 26554

Bennett Carolyn L. • Beatrice, NE 68310 • ASCLA

Bennett Carson W. • Ventura, CA 93003 • ACRL

Bennett Cheryl W. • Student • University of Arizona Graduate Library School • Tucson, AZ 85721

Bennett Christine H. • Reference Librarian • Monroe County Library System • Monroe, MI 48161

Bennett Claire D. • Associate Reference Librarian • Southern Connecticut State University Hilton C. Buley Library • New Haven, CT 06515 • ACRL RASD

Bennett Clara T. • Trustee • Hicksville Free Public Library • Hicksville, NY 11801 • ALTA

Bennett Connie J. • Mesa County Public Library • Grand Junction, CO 81502 • LITA

Bennett Cynthia A. • Library Director • Lewisville Public Library • Lewisville, TX 75029 • LAMA LITA PLA RASD YALSA

Bennett David B. • Library Automation Coordinator • Robert Morris College Library • Coraopolis, PA 15108-1189 • LITA

Bennett Dean L. • Brigham Young University Harold B. Lee Library • Provo, UT 84602

Bennett Deborah A. • Denton, MD 21629 • PLA

Bennett Deborah L. • Librarian • N.A. Chaderjian School • Stockton, CA 95213-9014

Bennett Denise Beaubien • Reference Librarian • University of Florida Libraries • Gainesville, FL 32611-2047 • ACRL RASD

Bennett E Kenneth • Collection Development Librarian • California State University-Dominguez Hills Library • Carson, CA 90747 • ACRL IFRT SRRT

Bennett Elizabeth A. • Seminole County Library System Technical Services • Sanford, FL 32771

Bennett Frank • Assistant Director • Peach Public Libraries • Fort Valley, GA 31030

Bennett George E. • Caneadea, NY 14717 • ACRL

Bennett H. Michael • Deputy Branch Manager • Hilton Head Public Library • Hilton Head, SC 29928 • PLA

Bennett Helen H. • Dover, DE 19901 • AASL LAMA IRRT   *Continuing*

Bennett Jack A. • Associate Professor • Georgia Southern University Henderson Library • Statesboro, GA 30460 • AASL

Bennett James F. • Librarian-Media Specialist • Shoreham-Wading Senior High School Library Media Center • Shoreham, NY 11786 • AASL ALSC LAMA YALSA IFRT   *Life*

Bennett Jane A. • Trustee • Clark County Public Library • Springfield, OH 45501-1080 • ALTA

Bennett John A. • Library Services Associate • Man Tech Enviornmental Technology Incorporation • Research Triangle Pk, NC 27709

Bennett Josephine • New York, NY 10021

Bennett Judith K. • Branch Manager • Memphis-Shelby County Public Library Raleigh Branch • Memphis, TN 38128 • PLA

Bennett Judy K. • Children's Librarian • Wichita Public Library • Wichita, KS 67202 • YALSA

Bennett Kathryn G. • School Librarian • Warner Public School Nashville Public Schools • Nashville, TN 37205

Bennett Linda S. • Librarian • Kent Middle School • Kentfield, CA 94904

Bennett Lora L. • Youth Services/Reference Info • King County Library System Shoreline Branch • Seattle, WA 98155 • ASCLA PLA

Bennett M. A. • Branch Librarian • Atlanta-Fulton Public Library Southwest Regional Library • Atlanta, GA 30331 • LAMA PLA

Bennett Marion Rev. • Trustee • Las Vegas-Clark County Library District • Las Vegas, NV 89101 • ALTA

Bennett Marsha K. • Special Projects Librarian II • Boston Public Library • Boston, MA 02117 • ACRL ALCTS LITA YALSA

Bennett Mary • Librarian • State Historical Society of Iowa • Iowa City, IA 52240

Bennett Mary L. • Media Center Director • Hubbard High School • Hubbard, OH 44425 • AASL YALSA

Bennett Mary L. • School Librarian • Lamar Consolidated Independent School District Jackson Middle School • Rosenberg, TX 77471 • AASL

Bennett Mary P. • Omaha, NE 68154

Bennett Nancy Ann • Tucson, AZ 85733-4222

Bennett Peggy E. • Director of Libraries • Southern Missionary College McKee Library • Collegedale, TN 37315 • ACRL

Bennett Phyllis J. • Altoona, PA 16602

Bennett Priscilla B. • Associate Professor/Media Educ • West Georgia College Library Media Program • Carrollton, GA 30118 • AASL ALSC

Bennett Richard F. • University of Florida • Gainesville, FL 32605 • ACRL LAMA

Bennett Rowland F. • Director • Maplewood Memorial Library • Maplewood, NJ 07040 • ACRL ALCTS ALSC LAMA PLA RASD YALSA

Bennett Samuel J. • Kansas City, MO 64109 • PLA

Bennett Sandra E. • Elementary Librarian • Townley Elementary School • Irving, TX 75060 • AASL

Bennett Scott • Johns Hopkins University Milton S. Eisenhower Library • Baltimore, MD 21218 • ACRL

Bennett Sylvia C. • Cataloger • Duke University William R. Perkins Library • Durham, NC 27706 • ALCTS LITA

Bennett Yvonne S. • Assoc. Libn. for Bibliographic • Medgar Evers College • Brooklyn, NY 11225 • ACRL LIRT SRRT

Bennetts Jean • District Librarian • Stanley Intermedia School • Lafayette, CA 94549 • AASL

Benning Susan P. • Salisbury, MD 21801

Bennington April A. • Public Services Librarian • University of Texas Cancer Center Research Medical Library • Houston, TX 77030

Bennion Bruce C. • Faculty Member • University of Southern California • Los Angeles, CA 90033

Bennison Nancy D. • Student • Simmons College Graduate School of Library & Information Science • Boston, MA 02115 • SRRT

Bennorth Barbara L. • Hd, Technology & Bus • Bridgeport Public Library • Bridgeport, CT 06604

Benny Robert K. • Minneapolis, MN 55445 • LAMA

Beno Cynthia L. • Prince William County Public Library Central Branch • Prince William, VA 22192 • RASD GODORT

Benoff Symme J. • Las Vegas, NV 89119

Benoit Christine M. • Biddleford Pool, ME 04006 • AASL ALSC

Benoit Graham M. • Director • Owatonna Public Library • Owatonna, MN 55060 • LAMA PLA

Benoski Kathy Carberry • Littlestown High School Library • Littlestown, PA 17340 • AASL YALSA

Benshoof Anne T. • Librarian • Glen Rock Public Library • Glen Rock, PA 17327

Bensing K. M. • Benjamin Rose Institute • Cleveland, OH 44120

Bensinger Claire • Cataloger • University of New Mexico General Library • Albuquerque, NM 87131

Benson Amy F. • Cambridge, MA 02140

Benson Charlotte W. • Library Media Specialist • Carmen Arace School • Bloomfield, CT 06002 • AASL

Benson Christine • Student • University of South Florida School of Library & Information Science • Tampa, FL 33620

Benson Dorris A. • Librarian • East High School • Anchorage, AK 99508 • AASL YALSA

Benson Geraldine M. • Documents Librarian • Millersville University of Pennsylvania • Millersville, PA 17551-0302 • ACRL GODORT

Benson Helen P. • Lancaster, PA 17603 • ALCTS

Benson Holly • Toronto Public Library • Toronto ON, M5S 2E4 Canada

Benson J. Arthur • Government Service/Ref Librarian • County of Los Angeles Public Library Valencia Library 113 • Valenica, CA 91355

Benson James A. • Saint John's University Division of Library & Information Science • Jamaica, NY 11439 • ACRL RASD

Benson Jeanne E. • Reference Librarian • Riverside City & County Public Library Marcy Branch Library • Riverside, CA 92506

Benson Joan L. • Motorbooks International • Osceola, WI 54020

Benson Joyce • San Antonio, TX 78212-2375

Benson Karl • Head Librarian • Boyle County Public Library • Danville, KY 40422 • PLA

Benson Kitty P. • Student • University of North Carolina School of Library Science • Chapel Hill, NC 27599-3360 • ALSC

Benson Laura M. • Media Director • High Point City School District • High Point, NC 27261 • AASL

Benson Laurel D. • Librarian • Rochester Independent School District #535 • Rochester, MN 55904

Benson Mariana • Library Coordinator • Matteson School District #162 Huth Upper Grades Center • Matteson, IL 60443 • AASL

Benson Mary Margaret • Technical Service Librarian • Linfield College Northup Library • McMinnville, OR 97128 • ALCTS   *Life*

Benson Nancy F. • Student • Southern Connecticut State University School of Libray Science & Instructional Technology • New Haven, CT 06515 • AASL

Benson Rebecca A. • Reidville, NC 27320 • SRRT

Benson Sandra J. • Hudson Junior High School • Hudson, WI 54016 • AASL YALSA

Benson Sarah S. • Student • Brigham Young University Harold B. Lee Library • Provo, UT 84602 • AASL

Benson Steven W. • Richardson Public Library • Richardson, TX 75080

Bent Barbara E. • Palo Alto, CA 94301 • ALSC PLA   *Continuing*

Bent Nancy P. • Brookfield, IL 60513

Bentin Douglas G. • Program Coordinator • Metropolitan Library System • Oklahoma City, OK 73102 • PLA IFRT

Bentke Delores A. • Branch Librarian • Houston Public Library Hillendahl Branch • Houston, TX 77080

Bentley Donna G. • Children's Coordinator • Ontario City Library • Ontario, CA 91764 • ALSC

Bentley Linda Holman • Librarian II • Phoenix Public Library • Phoenix, AZ 85004 • PLA IRRT

Bentley Linda R. • Denver, CO 80210 • LITA

Bentley Lorraine K. • Library Media Specialist • Saint Andrews Apostle School • Silver Spring, MD 20902 • AASL ALSC

Bentley Margaret S. • Librarian • Pembroke Public Library • Pembroke, MA 02359

Bentley Stella • University of California UCSB Library • Santa Barbara, CA 93106-9010 • ACRL ALCTS LAMA RASD

Bently Terry • Branch Manager • OCE-USA Inc. • Pittsburgh, PA 15205

Benton Bleue J. • Director • Hillside Public Library • Hillside, IL 60162 • LAMA PLA IFRT SRRT

Benton Charles • Chairman • Public Media Inc. • Chicago, IL 60640 • VRT

Benton Mildred C. Miss • Silver Spring, MD 20906 • ACRL ALCTS   *Continuing*

Benton Rebecca L. • Librarian • Arthur Middleton School • Waldorf, MD 20602 • AASL

Bentz Dale M. • Iowa City, IA 52245-4414 • ACRL ALCTS LAMA LITA   *Life*

Bentz Donald N. • Tucson, AZ 85704 • AASL ACRL   *Life*

Benware Gretchen L. • Librarian • Central Arkansas Library System Sherwood Public Library • Sherwood, AR 72116

Benyo Patricia A. • Grandview School Derry Area School District • Derry, PA 15627 • AASL

Benyon Elizabeth V. • Decatur, IL 62522 • Continuing

Benz Sara L. • Reference Librarian • Mayor Salvatore Mancini Union Free Public Library • North Providence, RI 02904

Benzel Julia M. • Teacher • Millard Public School • Omaha, NE 68022 • ALSC

Bequette Neva L. • Kennewick, WA 99337 • Continuing

Berberich Patricia L. • Chief Librarian • Hartford Public Library • Hartford, CT 06103-3003 • LAMA PLA

Bercik Mary Ellen • Supervisor, Reference & Network • Apple Computer, Inc. Library • Cupertino, CA 95014 • RASD

Berdan Emma • Head of Acquisitions • San Diego State University Library • San Diego, CA 92119-2120

Berdan Meg Shands • Edison Elementary School • Kingston, NY 12401

Berecka Alan M. • McLennan Community College Library • Waco, TX 76708 • ACRL

Berendt Lenora • Librarian II • Salt Lake City Public Library • Salt Lake City, UT 84111 • PLA RASD EMIERT GODORT IFRT LIRT

Berenguer Lowell T. • Systems Librarian • United States Air Force Air University Library • Maxwell AFB, AL 36112-5564 • LITA FLRT

Bereznay Lucinda K. • Cuyahoga County Public Library Fairview Park Regional Branch • Fairview Park, OH 44126-2189 • PLA YALSA

Berg Becky • Trustee • Bellevue Public Library • Bellevue, NE 68005 • ALTA

Berg Dave C. • Media Specialist • Fergus Falls High School Media Center • Fergus Falls, MN 56537 • AASL EMIERT

Berg Edna B Mrs • Trustee • Bozeman Public Library • Bozeman, MT 59715 • Continuing

Berg Elizabeth R. • St. Simons Island, GA 31522

Berg Jean H. • Mount Vernon, MO 65712

Berg John Leonard • Student • University of Wisconsin-Madison School of Library & Information Studies • Madison, WI 53706 • SRRT

Berg Josephine F. • Ln. Grade I, Reference Dept. • Texas A & M University Sterling C. Evans Library • College Station, TX 77843-5000 • ACRL RASD GODORT LIRT

Berg Katharina B.L. • Sao Paulo, Brazil • LITA

Berg Mark R. • Circulation Dept. • Boston College O'Neill Library • Chestnut Hill, MA 02167 • ACRL LITA GODORT

Berg Mary • Catalog Librarian • Appomattox Regional Library • Hopewell, VA 23860

Berg Patricia M. • Mission Viejo, CA 92692-4914

Berg Priscilla A. • Media Director • Totino-Grace High School • Fridley, MN 55432 • AASL

Berg Rita Johann • Media Center Director • Bishop Noll Institute • Hammond, IN 46327 • AASL

Berg Sally A. • Student • University of Arizona Graduate Library School • Tucson, AZ 85721

Berg Sharon • Librarian • Anacapa Middle School • Ventura, CA 93003 • AASL

Bergacker Dawn E. • Imperial Holly Corporation Center Technical Library • Colorado Spring, CO 80918 • LITA IRRT

Bergan Helen • Alexandria, VA 22302

Bergantino Geraldine • Librarian • West Milford Township High School • West Milford, NJ 07480

Bergart Sharlene • Library Media Specialist • Cecille B. DeMille Middle School • Long Beach, CA 90808 • AASL

Bergdorf Randolph S. • Peninsula Library & History Society • Peninsula, OH 44264

Berge Anna M.S. • Student • University of California-Berkeley School of Library & Information Studies • Berkeley, CA 94720

Berge Martha Miss • Appleton, WI 54911 • ACRL *Continuing*

Bergelt Robert L. • Petersburg, VA 23803 • Life

Bergen Esther Lou Miss • Atlanta, GA 30307 • Continuing

Bergen Patricia H. • Media Specialist • Greensboro Public Schools • Greensboro, NC 27402 • AASL ALSC

Berger B. Megan • Librarian • Grove City Middle School • Grove City, PA 16127

Berger Barbara J. • Findlay, OH 45840

Berger Carol A. • Consultant • C. Berger & Company • Carol Stream, IL 60188 • ALCTS LAMA FLRT ILERT

Berger Christopher T. • Reference Librarian • California State Library • Sacramento, CA 94237-0001 • RASD

Berger Claudia • Librarian • Berkeley Public Library North Branch • Berkeley, CA 94707

Berger Ellen J. • Branch Manager • Miami-Dade Public Library System Coconut Grove Branch • Miami, FL 33133

Berger Esther Mrs. • Ann Arbor, MI 48105 • Continuing

Berger Florie G. • Palo Alto, CA 94306 • ACRL LHRT

Berger George Combs • Alexandria, VA 22314-2610

Berger Harold L. • Indexer-Social Sciences • H. W. Wilson Company • Bronx, NY 10452 • ACRL

Berger Jeffrey S. • Dept. Asst.-Ext Servs Dept. • Queens Borough Public Library • Jamaica, NY 11432 • LAMA

Berger Joan S. • Librarian • Archbishop Howard School • Portland, OR 97213

Berger Kenneth W. • Reference Ln and Bibliographer • Duke University William R. Perkins Library • Durham, NC 27706

Berger Marianne • Geneva, IL 60134 • ACRL

Berger Mary Frances L. Sr • Circulation Librarian • Loyola University E.M. Cudahy Memorial Library • Chicago, IL 60626 • ACRL LAMA RASD

Berger Michael G. • Assistant Director • University of California Division of Library Automation • Oakland, CA 94612-3550 • LITA RASD LIRT LRRT

Berger Miles P. • Trustee • Newark Public Library • Newark, NJ 07101-0630 • ALTA PLA

Berger Monica • Student • Columbia University Library Service Library • New York, NY 10027 • ALCTS IFRT SRRT

Berger Patricia A. • Librarian • Byran Hills High School • Armonk, NY 10504 • AASL

Berger Patricia W. • Dir. Office of Inf. Serv. • National Institute of Standards & Technology • Gaithersburg, MD 20899 • FLRT

Berger Paula S. • University of Chicago Library • Chicago, IL 60637-1502 • ALSC

Berger Pearl • Dean of Libraries • Yeshiva University Libraries • New York, NY 10033 • ACRL

Berger Shirley A. • School Librarian • J. B. Young Jr. High School • Davenport, IA 52803 • AASL YALSA

Berger Sidney E. • Head of Special Collection • University of California Rivera Library • Riverside, CA 92517 • ACRL

Berger Teresa • Honolulu, HI 96826 • PLA

Bergeron Jeanette M. • Columbia, SC 29204

Bergeron Nancy K. • Durham, NH 03824

Bergeron Patricia D. • Children's Librarian • Kanawha County Public Library • Charleston, WV 25301 • ALSC PLA

Bergeron Peter L. • Coor of Sch Ls & H S Ln. • Longmeadow High School • Longmeadow, MA 01106 • AASL SRRT

Berges Cherry L. • Student • Clarion University of Pennsylvania • Clarion, PA 16214 • ALCTS LAMA PLA RASD

Bergeson Michael E. • Seattle, WA 98112

Berggren Kathy • Director • Graves Public Library District • Mendota, IL 61342

Berghausen Judith • North Fairmount • Cincinnati, OH 45225 • AASL

Bergholz Donna C. • Head, Serials Cataloging Section • Duke University William R. Perkins Library • Durham, NC 27706 • ALCTS LAMA

Bergin Carol • Librarian • Saint Bartholomew School Library • Bethesda, MD 20817

Bergin Edward A. • Alexandria, VA 22304

Bergin Joyce Williams • Director of Library • Robert S. Kerr Enviromental Research Laboratory • Ada, OK 74820 • ACRL FLRT GODORT

Bergin Marilyn J • Senior Asst. Librarian • California State University-Long Beach University Library & Learning Resources • Long Beach, CA 90840-1901

Bergin Melissa C. • Student • State University of New York at Albany School of Information Science & Policy • Albany, NY 12222 • AASL

Bergin Virginia M. • Student • University of South Florida School of Library & Information Science • Tampa, FL 33620 • RASD

Berglund Marjorie • President, System Library Board • Western Illinois Library System • Galesburg, IL 61401 • ALTA

Berglund Patricia • Resource Librarian • San Francisco Unified Schools • San Francisco, CA 94102

Bergman Betty L. • Assistant Director • Waterloo Public Library • Waterloo, IA 50701

Bergman Emily A. • Catalog Librarian • Gene Autry Western Heritage Museum • Los Angeles, CA 90027-1462 • ACRL ALCTS LIRT

Bergman Julia E. • City College of San Francisco • San Francisco, CA 94112

Bergman Linda M. • Fairfax, VA 22031

Bergman Sherrie S. • Librarian • Wheaton College Wallace Library • Norton, MA 02766 • ACRL ALCTS LAMA SRRT

Bergman Virgil • Trustee • Escondido Public Library • Escondido, CA 92025 • ALTA

Bergmann Allison M. • Forest Hills, NY 11375 • ACRL

Bergmann Elizabeth • Humanities Reference • Carnegie Library of Pittsburgh • Pittsburgh, PA 15213-4080 • PLA

Bergmann Sue A. • Branch Manager • Dekalb County Public Library • Decatur, GA 30032 • PLA

Bergquist Christine • Assistant Director • Wilbraham Public Library • Wilbraham, MA 01005

Bergsing Patricia M. • City Librarian • Burlingame Public Library • Burlingame, CA 94010 • ALCTS ALTA LAMA LITA PLA RASD

Bergsten Beth • Ware Elementary School • Fort Riley, KS 66442 • AASL

Bergstresser Louise • Librarian • New York Public Library • New York, NY 10016 • RASD

Bergstrom Charlotte • Librarian • Manlius Pebble Hill School • De Witt, NY 13214 • AASL

Bergstrom Elizabeth A. • Student • Emporia State University Emporia in the Rockies • Denver, CO 80204

Bergstrom Margie • Librarian • Nuclear Age Resource Center • Cleveland, OH 44122 • ILERT IRRT SRRT

Bergstrom Rita • Maryland Elementary School • Phoenix, AZ 85015 • AASL

Bergup Bernice I. • Reference Librarian • University of North Carolina Walter Royal Davis Library • Chapel Hill, NC 27599-3924 • ACRL RASD

Berhanu Aslaku • Librarian • Temple University Paley Library • Philadelphia, PA 19122

Berhe Annette C. • Head Librarian • Lemoyne-Owen College • Memphis, TN 38126

Bering Carol G. • Prog Admin for Technical Servs. • Fort Collins Public Library • Ft. Collins, CO 80524-2900

Bering Susan A. • Vallejo, CA 94591-8444

Berinstein Paula • Woodland Hills, CA 91364 • ILERT

Berk Jack M. • Director • Bethlehem Area Public Library • Bethlehem, PA 18018-5888 • LAMA LITA PLA RASD

Berk Lawrence S. • Director • Florida Keys Community College Library • Key West, FL 33040

Berke Sheila E. • Miami, FL 33176 • PLA IFRT

Berkebile Sue Ann • Assistant Director • Rogers Memorial Library • Southampton, NY 11968 • PLA RASD

Berkeland John M. • Student • University of Iowa School of Library & Information Science • Iowa City, IA 52242 • NMRT

Berkeley Edmund Jr. • Director,Special Clln Dept. • University of Virginia Alderman Library • Charlottesville, VA 22903-2498 • ACRL

Berkelhammer Sheila • School Library Representative • H.W. Wilson Company • Bronx, NY 10452 • AASL IFRT

Berkey Ada E. • Scottsdale, AZ 85251 • ACRL RASD *Life*

Berkey Virginia A. • Eugene, OR 97405 • AASL

Berkman Dulcie • International Falls, MN 56649 • AASL ALSC

Berkner Dimity S. • Director, Marketing & Sales • Columbia University Press • New York, NY 10025 • ACRL ALCTS LITA PLA RASD

Berkov Ellen • Severna Park, MD 21146

Berkowitz Nancy M. • Senior Book Reviewer • Department of Media Service School District • Lansing, MI 48911 • ALSC YALSA

Berkowitz Robert E. • Library Media Specialist • Wayne Central Middle School • Ontario Center, NY 14520 • AASL

Berkowitz Susan • Half Hollow Hills Community Public Library • Dix Hills, NY 11746 • ALTA

Berkwitz Rebecca • Collection Management Asst. • Brandeis University Goldfarb Library • Waltham, MA 02254

Berlin Gregory • Great Lakes Adventist Academy • Cedar Lake, MI 48812 • AASL

Berliner Barbara • Supervising Librarian • The New York Public Library • New York, NY 10016 • LAMA RASD

Berling John G. • Dean, Learning Resources Serv. • Saint Cloud State University Centennial Hall LRC • St. Cloud, MN 56301-4498 • AASL ACRL

Berlowitz Sara B. • Head, Bibliographic Processing • San Francisco State University J. Paul Leonard Library • San Francisco, CA 94132 • ALCTS

Berlund Sharon L. • Student • University of Hawaii School of Library & Information Studies • Honolulu, HI 96822 • LITA RASD NMRT

Berman Arthur • Director Learning Resources Ctr • East Arkansas Cmnty Coll • Forrest City, AR 72335-9598 • ACRL

Berman Barbara L. • Pennsylvania State University Pattee Library • University Park, PA 16802 • ALCTS

Berman Clarice H. • School Library Media Specialist • Bryam Hills School District Crittenden Middle School • Armonk, NY 10504 • AASL IFRT

Berman Francine J. • Southfield, MI 48076 • AASL IFRT

Berman Herbert • Trustee • Queens Borough Public Library • Jamaica, NY 11432 • ALTA PLA

Berman Jennifer A. • Student • University of California-Los Angeles (UCLA) • Los Angeles, CA 90024-1450

Berman Joan R. • Reference Librarian • Humboldt State University Library • Arcata, CA 95521 • ACRL ALCTS LITA RASD GODORT

Berman Mary Rinato • Regional Librarian • New York Public Library Belmont Branch • Bronx, NY 14058 • ALSC

Berman Sanford • Head Cataloger • Hennepin County Library • Minnetonka, MN 55343 • SRRT

Berman Susan • Good Shepard Center • Baltimore, MD 21227-2770 • AASL

Berman Susan F. • Assistant Director • North Kingstown Free Library • North Kingstown, RI 02852

Berman Susan R. • Fountain Valley, CA 92708 • PLA SRRT

Bern Alan • Student • University of California-Berkeley University Library • Berkeley, CA 94720 • ACRL PLA RASD EMIERT IFRT LHRT SRRT

Bernard Judith L. • Student • Northern Illinois University Department of Library & Information Studies • DeKalb, IL 60115 • EMIERT

Bernard Matilda M. Sr. • Librarian • St. Ursula Academy • Cincinnati, OH 45206

Bernard Patrick S. • Principal Editor • Library of Congress • Washington, DC 20541 • ALCTS

Bernard Rose Sr. • Cathedral High School • Springfield, MA 01118

Bernardi Toni A. • Coordinator of Childrens Serv • San Francisco Public Library • San Francisco, CA 94102 • ALSC PLA YALSA IFRT

Bernardis Tim • Little Big Horn College Library • Crow Agency, MT 59022 • ACRL EMIERT

Bernardo Anthony J. • Lib. Services Asst. I • Yale University Sterling Memorial Library • New Haven, CT 06520

Bernath Sharon E. • Adams Elementary School • Livonia, MI 48154

Berne Ellen • Library Director • Winsor School Library • Boston, MA 02215

Berner Andrew J. • Director • University Club Library • New York, NY 10019 • ACRL

Berner Cynthia K. • Coor. of Extension Services • Wichita Public Library • Wichita, KS 67202 • ASCLA LAMA PLA

Berner Karen • Shaw AFB, SC 29152

Bernero Cheryl A. • Account Services Manager • EBSCO Subscription Services • Cary, IL 60013 • ACRL LAMA

Berney Mary E. • Student • University of Illinois Graduate School of Library and Information Science • Urbana, IL 61801

Bernhagen Ann R. • Churchville, NY 14428

Bernhard Nell Ms. • Librarian • Harlandale Middle School • San Antonio, TX 78214 • AASL ALSC   *Life*

Bernhard Patricia • Director • Henrietta Public Library • Rochester, NY 14623 • PLA

Bernicchi Judith F. • Technical Services Librarian • Foreign Mission Board,SBC Jenkins Research Library • Richmond, VA 23230 • ALCTS LITA IRRT MAGERT

Bernier Jennifer S. • Legislative Office Building Legislative Library • Hartford, CT 06106 • IFRT NMRT

Bernier Loretta M. • Librarian • Lyme-Old Lyme Junior Senior High School • Old Lyme, CT 06371

Bernier Theresa Nackley • Student • James Madison University Carrier Library • Harrisonburg, VA 22807 • AASL

Berning Robert W. • Director • Carlisle Public Library • Carlisle, IA 50047

Berninghausen D. K. • Sun City, AZ 85351 • ACRL LAMA   *Life*

Berns Rona L. • Los Angeles Public Library Branch Library Services • Los Angeles, CA 90013

Bernstein Adriana Bennett • Library Director • Kenilworth Free Public Library • Kenilworth, NJ 07033 • PLA NMRT

Bernstein Amy J. • Simmons College Graduate School of Library & Information Science • Boston, MA 02115

Bernstein Bernard • Trustee • Commack Public Library District • Commack, NY 11725 • ALTA

Bernstein Bonnie S. • Student • Edward R. Murrow High School • Brooklyn, NY 11230 • AASL

Bernstein Elayne P. • President of the bd of Trustees • Great Neck Library • Great Neck, NY 11024

Bernstein Gail R. • Librarian • P.S. 225 Queens Seaside Elementary School • Rockaway Park, NY 11694

Bernstein Hermine • Student • Southern Connecticut State University School of Libray Science & Instructional Technology • New Haven, CT 06515 • RASD

Bernstein Joan E. • Moorestown, NJ 08057 • LITA ILERT

Bernstein Judith • Director • University of New Mexico • Albuquerque, NM 87131 • ACRL LAMA RASD

Bernstein Sharon C. • South Georgia Regional Library for the Blind • Valdosta, GA 31601 • ASCLA

Bernstein Toby N. • Principal Cataloger • Northeastern University • Boston, MA 02115 • ACRL ALCTS

Bernthal Rebecca • Librarian • University of Nebraska • Lincoln, NE 68588 • ACRL RASD

Berntsen Patricia O. • Asst Dir for Public Services • University of North Dakota Chester Fritz Library • Grand Forks, ND 58202-0175 • ACRL

Berow Shirley E. • Glendale, AZ 85308-5118 • AASL

Berringer Virginia • Cataloger • University of Akron Bierce Library • Akron, OH 44325-1706 • ALCTS LITA VRT

Berrios Lily del C. • Project Architect • Sizemore Floyd Architects, Inc. • Atlanta, GA 30308

Berrish Karen • Library Support Manager • VTLS, Inc. • Blacksburg, VA 24060 • ACRL RASD

Berry Anne B. Miss • Vancouver BC, CANADA Canada • ACRL ALCTS   *Continuing*

Berry Barbara • Indexer • H. W. Wilson Company • Bronx, NY 10452 • ACRL

Berry Carol • Edison Elementary School • Kennewick, WA 99336

Berry Diana M. • Deputy Director • Cayman Islands Public Library • British, West Indies

Berry Diane • Mid-York Library System • Utica, NY 13502 • ALCTS LITA PLA

Berry Gayle C. • Librarian/Public Service • Clarkson University • Potsdam, NY 13676 • ACRL RASD

Berry Grace F. • Director • Pope County Library System • Russellville, AR 72801 • LAMA PLA

Berry Jane D. • Young Adult Librarian • Glenview Public Library • Glenview, IL 60025 • YALSA

Berry Janet C. • Coordinator of Catalog Service • Arkansas State Library • Little Rock, AR 72201 • ALCTS

Berry Janice • Glen Alpine Elementary School • Glen Alpine, NC 28628

Berry Jary A. • Lausanne Collegiate School Goodman Library • Memphis, TN 38119 • AASL

Berry Jean A. • Willow, AK 99688-0062 • AASL

Berry John D. • Librarian • United States Food & Drug Administration C.D.E.R. Medical Library • Rockville, MD 20857

Berry John N. III • Editor in Chief • Library Journal Cahners Publishing Company • New York, NY 10011 • ACRL ALCTS ALTA ASCLA LAMA LITA PLA RASD ERT IFRT IRRT SORT SRRT

Berry John W. • University of Illinois at Chicago University Library • Chicago, IL 60680 • ACRL LAMA IRRT

Berry Leona P. • Hoisington, KS 67544 • Continuing

Berry Louise Parker • Director • Darien Library • Darien, CT 06820-4497 • ALTA LAMA PLA RASD SRRT

Berry Marge • Assistant Director • LaPorte County Public Library • LaPorte, IN 46350 • PLA

Berry Marilyn P. • Head Librarian • Bad Axe Public Library • Bad Axe, MI 48413

Berry Mary A. • Professor • Sam Houston State University Department of Library Science • Huntsville, TX 77341-2236

Berry Mary J. • Librarian • Porterville Developmental Center • Porterville, CA 93258

Berry Nancy R. • Covina, CA 91723

Berry Paul L. • Prt Republic, MD 20676

Berry Susan O. • Student •University of Kentucky College of Library & Information Science • Lexington, KY 40506-0391 • PLA

Berry Teresa U. • Knoxville, TN 37938 • ACRL

Berry Wanda A. • Director • DeSoto Parish Library • Mansfield, LA 71052 • LAMA PLA IFRT

Berryhill Ellen K. • Library Media Specialist • Columbus School/Webster School/ • Bridgeport, CT 06604 • AASL

Berryhill Mary M. • Reference Librarian • Elsie Quirk Public Library • Englewood, FL 34223 • PLA RASD

Berryman Barbara P. • School Librarian • Holy Innocents' Episcopal School • Atlanta, GA 30327 • AASL

Berryman Karan Ann • Director • Andrew College Pitts Library • Cuthbert, GA 31740

Berson Janis K. • Arlington Heights, IL 60004 • RASD

Berstein Noreen H. • Youth Service's Director • Williamsburg Regional Library • Williamsburg, VA 23185 • ALSC YALSA

Bertalmio Lynne S. • Director • Stillwater Public Library • Stillwater, MN 55082 • LAMA PLA

Bertchume Gary • Bibliographic Analyst • Columbia University Libraries • New York, NY 10027 • ALCTS LITA

Berteaux Susan S. • Document Librarian • Woods Hole Oceanographic Institution • Woods Hole, MA 02543 • LITA

Berthiaume Dennis A. • Saint Anselm College Geisel Library • Manchester, NH 03102-1310 • ACRL LITA RASD GODORT IRRT MAGERT

Bertland Linda H. • Stetson Middle School • Philadelphia, PA 19134 • AASL YALSA

Bertoia James • Sparwood BC, V0B 2G0 Canada

Bertolucci Katherine • Consultant • Isis Information Services • Oakland, CA 94611 • AASL ALCTS LAMA LITA EMIERT ILERT SRRT

Bertolucci Ysabel R. • Health Science Librarian • Kaiser Permanente Medical Center • Oakland, CA 94611

Bertone Maria • Trustee • Suffolk Cooperative Library System • Bellport, NY 11713 • ALTA

Bertovich Jennifer L. • Clarion, PA 16214 • AASL

Bertram Carla E. • Glendale, CA 91202

Bertram Dora R. • Assistant Law Librarian • Washington University Libraries • Saint Louis, MO 63130 • GODORT

Bertram Gwendolyn M. • Sales Representative • Faxon Company,Inc. • Westwood, MA 02090

Bertram Lucille • Head of Reference • Teaneck Public Library • Teaneck, NJ 07666 • RASD

Bertrand Beverly Page • Librarian • Grand Blanc High School • Grand Blanc, MI 48439 • AASL

Bertrand Carol M. • Northwestern College Library • Lima, OH 45805

Bertrand Deanne S. • Boothbay Harbor, ME 04538

Bertrand H Louise • Manager of Media Processing Ctr • Baltimore County Public Schools • Baltimore, MD 21234 • AASL

Bertrand Robert W. • Head Reference Department • Lima Public Library • Lima, OH 45801 • RASD

Bertuca David J. • Head Serials Management • State Univ of New York-Buffalo • Amherst, NY 14260 • ACRL

Berube Daniel • Albany, NY 12203

Berwind Anne May • Head of Information Service Dept • Austin Peay State University • Clarkville, TN 37044 • ACRL GODORT

Besant Larry Mr. • Morehead State University Camden-Carroll Library • Morehead, KY 40351 • AASL ACRL ALCTS ASCLA LAMA LITA PLA RASD CLENE GODORT LIRT SORT

Besch Carol J. • Manchester, MO 63021

Besemer Diana • Crawford County R-II School • Cuba, MO 65453 • AASL

Besemer Susan P. • Director of Library Services • State University of New York College Daniel A. Reed Library • Fredonia, NY 14063 • ACRL LAMA   *Life*

Beserra Christine E. • Student • University of Illinois Graduate School of Library and Information Science • Urbana, IL 61801 • IFRT SRRT

Beshers Olga E. • Cataloging Department • University of Miami Libraries Richter Library • Coral Gables, FL 33124

Beske Venice N. Brown • Documents Librarian • Wyoming State Library • Cheyenne, WY 82002-0650 • GODORT

Besore Mary O. Mrs. • Atlantic City, NJ 08401 • Continuing

Bess Joan M. • Head Librarian • Culver Academies Library • Culver, IN 46511 • AASL YALSA IFRT

Bessa Maria C. • Student • University of Missouri-Columbia School of Library & Informational Science • Columbia, MO 65211

Bessant Donna L. • Coordinator IMC/Libraries • Monterey Peninsula Unified School District • Monterey, CA 93940 • AASL ALSC

Bessant Ruth Pralle • Technical Services Librarian • Ripon College Library • Ripon, WI 54971

Besser Howard • Information Systems Mgr • Canadian Centre for Architecture • Montreal PQ, H3H 2S6 Canada • ACRL LITA SRRT

Besserman Frances A. • Librarian • Kishwaukee College • Malta, IL 60150 • ACRL

Bessler Joanne M. • South Bend, IN 46617 • ACRL LAMA LRRT

Best Barbara D. • Youth Librarian • Maui Library District • Wailuku, HI 96793 • ALSC YALSA

Best Cari • Editorial Director • Weston Woods Studios Inc • Weston, CT 06883 • AASL ALSC

Best Dee • Director Library Services • Davidson County Community College Learning Resource Center • Lexington, NC 27293

Best Donald A. • Director • Cadillac-Wexford Public Library • Cadillac, MI 49601-0700 • ALSC ALTA ASCLA LAMA LITA PLA RASD YALSA CLENE

Best Gladys E B • Reference Librarian • Abilene Public Library • Abilene, TX 79601-5793 • IFRT

Best Joyce R. • University City, MO 63130 • AASL

Best Julia W. • Serials Librarian • University of North Carolina Law Library • Chapel Hill, NC 27599

Best Kathleen M. • New Carrollton, MD 20784-3350 • ACRL

Best Laurel S. • Director • Smyrna Public Library • Smyrna, GA 30080

Best Mittie S. • Montgomery, AL 36105

Best Rickey D. • Archivist/Spec Collections Libn • Auburn University at Montgomery • Montgomery, AL 36117-3596 • ACRL

Besterfeldt Judith • Head Librarian • Scott Foresman & Company • Glenview, IL 60025 • ALSC

Beszhak Nancy R. • Elementary Media Specialist • Kegonsa Elementary School • Stoughton, WI 53589 • AASL

Betancourt Ingrid • Principal Librarian • Newark Public Library • Newark, NJ 07101-0630 • RASD

Betancourt Maria I. • University of South Florida School of Library & Information Science • Tampa, FL 33620 • RASD SRRT

Betcher William M. • Associate Dean • Ohio University Vernon R. Alden Library • Athens, OH 45701-2978 • ACRL

Beth Amy • Earlham College Lilly Library • Richmond, IN 47374 • IFRT

Beth Jacqueline • Reference Librarian • Alameda County Library Castro Valley Branch • Castro Valley, CA 94546

Bethea Florence • Marion, SC 29571 • Continuing

Bethea Molly • Librarian • Airline High School Library • Bossier City, LA 71111 • AASL

Bethel Kathleen E. • African-American Studies Ln. • Northwestern University Library • Evanston, IL 60208-2300 • ACRL

Bethel Marilyn • Director of Children's Services • Broward County Library Century Plaza Branch • Deerfield Beach, FL 33441 • ALCTS ALSC

Bethel Patricia R. • Head Librarian • Hoffman Estates High School • Hoffman Estates, IL 60195 • AASL

Bethel Rebecca • Bloomington, IN 47401

Bethune Marjorie • Head of Technical Services • Milton Public Library • Milton ON, L9T 2L5 Canada • LITA

Betonte Gary R. • Student • University of Pittsburgh School of Library and Information Science • Pittsburgh, PA 15260

Bett Bruce • Systems Manager/Reference Ln • Madonna University Library • Livonia, MI 48150 • LITA

Bettencourt Ronald J. • Cataloger • B M C Durfee High School • Fall River, MA 02720 • AASL ALCTS

Betts Bobby • Trustee • East Saint Louis Public Library • East St. Louis, IL 62201 • ALTA

Betts Judith H. • Miami Sunset Senior High School • Miami, FL 33183 • AASL

Betts Robert E. • Saint Petersburg, FL 33705-1502 • ACRL ALCTS *Continuing*

Betts Salome • Atlanta, GA 30305

Betty C. Michelle • Student • San Jose State University Division of Library & Information Science • San Jose, CA 95192-0029

Betz-Zall Jonathan R. • Children's Librarian • Sno-Isle Regional Library Edmonds Branch • Edmonds, WA 98020 • ALSC EMIERT SRRT

Betz Mary C. • George Gershwin Intermediate School • Brooklyn, NY 11207 • AASL

Beunderman Ellen S. • Librarian • Internation School of Paris • Paris 75016, France • AASL

Beury Barbara S. • Librarian • New Albany High School Library • New Albany, IN 47150 • AASL

Beuthel Ellengail • Librarian • Denver Public School District Professional Library • Denver, CO 80205 • ALCTS

Bever David P. • Teacher • Saint Thomas Lutheran School • E Detroit, MI 48021

Bever Diane J. • Head of Reference Services • Indiana University at Kokomo Learning Resources Center • Kokomo, IN 46904-9003 • LAMA

Beverage Stephanie L. • Southwest Sales Representative • Midwest Library Service • Bridgeton, MO 63044 • ALCTS

Beveridge David C. • Assistant Director • National Geographic Society Library • Washington, DC 20036 • ALCTS LITA

Beveridge Mary • Head Public Services • Drake University Cowles Library • Des Moines, IA 50311 • ACRL

Beverly Camille M. • Media Librarian • Jefferson County Junior High School • Fayette, MS 39069 • LIRT

Beverly Martha • Library Trustee • Kalamazoo Public Library • Kalamazoo, MI 49007-5270 • ALTA PLA

Bevier RuthAnne • Pasadena, CA 91106

Bevilacqua Ann F. • Manchester, CT 06040 • LIRT

Bevington Elizabeth H. • Terre Haute, IN 47804 • ACRL *Continuing*

Bevins Connie C. • Georgetown, KY 40324 • AASL

Bevis Dorothy • Oakland, CA 94611-2137 • ALCTS RASD *Continuing*

Bewley Gladys P. • Haddonfield, NJ 08033

Bewley Jean G. • Library Media Specialist • Smith Road Elementary School • N Syracuse, NY 13212 • AASL ALSC

Bewley Joan M. • John F. Kennedy University • Orinda, CA 94563 • SRRT

Bey Jacqueline S • Administrative Librarian • Army Explosives Safety Technical Library USADACS • Savanna, IL 61074-9639 • AFLRT

Bey Leon S. • Reference Librarian • Dayton & Montgomery County Public Library • Dayton, OH 45402-2103 • SORT SRRT

Beye Sandra L. • Adult Services Librarian • Bloomington Public Library • Bloomington, IL 61702-3308 • ALCTS LITA PLA RASD

Beyer Carol • Director • Wood-Ridge Memorial Library • Wood-Ridge, NJ 07075

Beyer Linda M. • Beloit Public Library • Beloit, WI 53511

Beyers Catherine • Harry Spence School • La Crosse, WI 54601 • AASL ALSC

Beynen Bert K. • Librarian • Public Library of Des Moines • Des Moines, IA 50308-1791

Bezanson Deborah • Arlington, VA 22203 • ACRL RASD

Bezera Elizabeth A. • Assoc. Dir. for Public Services • Emerson College Library • Boston, MA 02116 • ACRL

Bezirgan Basima • Middle East Catlgr/Arabic Spec. • University of Chicago Library • Chicago, IL 60637-1502 • ACRL IRRT

Bezugloff Natalia • Head Foreign Literature Dept • Cleveland Public Library • Cleveland, OH 44114-1271 • ACRL PLA

Bhashyam-Tambe Ranjan D. • Administrative Librarian • Naval Air Station • Alameda, CA 94501-5051 • AFLRT

Bhatia Harjeet K. • Technical Services Dept. Head • Berwyn Public Library • Berwyn, IL 60402 • ALCTS CLENE

Bhatia Sharmila • Archivist I • South Carolina Dept. of Archives and History • Columbia, SC 29211-1669

Bhatt Jay J. • Student • Drexel University College of Information Studies • Philadelphia, PA 19104-2875 • LIRT SRRT

Bhattacharya Rakhi • New Brunswick, NJ 08903-5063

Bhide Vidya G. • Student • State University of New York School of Information & Library Sci • Albany, NY 12203 • SRRT

Bhniya M. A. • Student • Pratt Institute Graduate School of Library & Information Science • Brooklyn, NY 11205

Bi Zhiwei • Student • Kent State University School of Library & Information Science • Kent, OH 44242-0001

Biagianti Arthur S. • Director/Librarian • Case Western Reserve University School of Applied Social Sciences • Cleveland, OH 44106 • ACRL

Biagini Mary K. • Associate Dean • University of Pittsburgh School of Library and Information Science • Pittsburgh, PA 15260 • AASL ALSC YALSA CLENE

Bialac Verda H. • Assistant Director • Omaha Public Library • Omaha, NE 68102

Bialek Janka • Reference Librarian • William K. Sanford Town Library • Loudonville, NY 12211

Bianchi-Barteletti Marcia B. • Aloha, OR 97006

Bianchi Jo Ann M. • Beaumont, TX 77706

Bianchi Rosemary E. • Kenosha, WI 53140

Bianchi Stephanie • Albany, OR 97321-9340

Bianco Christina M. • Assistant Librarian Director • Crest Hill Public Library Des Plaines Valley Public Library Dist. • Crest Hill, IL 60435

Bias Peggy Sue • Director • Putnam County Library • Hurricane, WV 25526 • LAMA PLA

Biastre Robert • Librarian • North Plainfield Library • North Plainfield, NJ 07060

Bibbee Robert G. • Head, Business Information Ctr • Chicago Public Library • Chicago, IL 60605 • RASD

Bibel Barbara M. • Reference Librarian • Oakland Public Library • Oakland, CA 94612 • RASD EMIERT

Biblarz Dora • Assoc Dean for Coll Devel • Arizona State University Libraries • Tempe, AZ 85287-1006 • ACRL ALCTS IRRT

Bible Amanda R. • Director • Columbus Cnty Public • Whiteville, NC 28472 • ALSC ALTA LAMA PLA RASD IFRT

Biblo Herbert • Long Island Library Resource Council • Stony Brook, NY 11794-3399 • AASL ACRL ALCTS ASCLA LAMA LITA PLA RASD EMIERT GODORT IFRT IRRT SORT SRRT

Biblo Lisa • Harvard University Library • Cambridge, MA 02138-2901 • ACRL ALCTS SRRT

Biblo Mary • Librarian • University of Chicago Lab School Library • Chicago, IL 60637 • AASL ALSC EMIERT IFRT SRRT

Bick Dawn • Assistant Executive Director • Houston Academy of Medicine Texas Medical Center Library • Houston, TX 77030 • ALCTS

Bickel Bernice M. • Head of Children Services • Evansville-Vanderburgh County Public Library • Evansville, IN 47708-1694 • ALSC

Bickerstaff Kevin • Manchester M29 0PA, United Kingdom

Bickett Brenda E. • Arabic Materials Specalist • Georgetown University Joseph Mark Lauinger Library • Washington, DC 20057-1006 • ACRL ALCTS IRRT

Bickford Christina R. • Media Services Librarian • Barnard College • New York, NY 10027 • ACRL

Bickford David L. • Business & Sciences • Phoenix Public Library • Phoenix, AZ 85004 • RASD NMRT

Bickford Jane T. • Adult Librarian • Boston Public Library Connolly Branch • Jamaica Plain, MA 02130-1895

Bickham J. L. • Huntington, WV 25701-3631

Bickham Nancy M. • Saint Francisville, LA 70775 • AASL ALSC

Bickhaus Cynthia L. • Denton, TX 76201 • AASL ALSC

Bickley Dorothy B. • West Carrollton Senior High School • W Carrollton, OH 45449 • AASL ALSC

Bickley Thomas F. • Director of Education • Houston Academy of Medicine Texas Medical Center Library • Houston, TX 77030 • LIRT

Bicknell Kenneth D. • Cataloging Librarian • Southwest Museum Braun Research Library • Los Angeles, CA 90041-0558 • SRRT

Bicknell Mary B. • Student • Simmons College Graduate School of Library & Information Science • Boston, MA 02115 • RASD

Bicknell Sarah D. • Manatee County Public Library System Island Branch • Holmes Beach, FL 34217

Bicknell Tracy • Central Reference Services • University of Nebraska Love Library • Lincoln, NE 68588-0410 • RASD

Bickoff Marcia • Librarian • Southern Connecticut State University Hilton C. Bulev Library • New Haven, CT 06515

Bicksler Sandra • Media Specialist • Anne Arundel County Public School Library Media Services • Annapolis, MD 21401 • AASL

Bicsak Ilona M. • Head Cataloging W.Copy Dept. • Columbia University Library Service Library • New York, NY 10027

Bida Larissa • Mohawk, NY 13407 • Continuing

Biddinger Diane N. • Student • University of Washington Graduate School of Library and Information Science • Seattle, WA 98195 • PLA

Biddison Donald G. • Head Reference Department • University of Wisconsin-Milwaukee Golda Meir Library • Milwaukee, WI 53201 • ACRL RASD

Biddle Michaelle L. • Assistant Director • Wesleyan University Olin Memorial Library • Middletown, CT 06459

Biddle Stanton F. • Baruch College • New York, NY 10010 • ACRL LAMA *Life*

Bidlack Russell E. • University of Michigan School of Information and Library Studies • Ann Arbor, MI 48109-1092 • Continuing

Bidnick Richard • Pike County Public Library • Milford, PA 18337-1398

Bidwell Lynne H. • Supv. Tech. Servs/Acqs. Serials • Apple Computer • Cupertino, CA 95014 • ALCTS

Biebush Barbara • Reference Librarian • Sonoma State University Ruben Salazar Library • Rohnert Park, CA 94928 • ACRL

Biek David Eugene • Managing Librarian • Tacoma Public Library • Tacoma, WA 98402 • LAMA

Biel Audrey C. • Dearborn, MI 48120 • PLA YALSA *Life*

Bielaczyc Donna A. • Youth Services Librarian • Mark Twain Library Association • Redding, CT 06875

Bielawski Marvin F. • Systems Librarian • Princeton University • Princeton, NJ 08544-2098 • LITA

Bielefeld Kathryn M. • Librarian I • Hudson Area Branch Library • Hudson, FL 34667

Bielefield Arlene C. • East Hampton Public Library • East Hampton, CT 06424 • LAMA PLA

Bielich Paul S. • Library Media Specialist • Northwestern High School • Detroit, MI 48208 • AASL

Bielitz Gerda E. • First Asst Aud Hd of Ctrl Lib • Grosse Pointe Public Library Central Branch • Grosse Pointe, MI 48236 • PLA

Bielmeier Sonia L. • Director • Brookfield Public Library • Brookfield, WI 53005 • ALCTS ALSC LITA PLA RASD

Bielsky Katherine H. • Catalog Department Head • College of Charleston Robert Scott Small Library • Charleston, SC 29424 • ACRL ALCTS

Bieniek Cynthia S. • Detroit, MI 48224

Bieniek Marian Owen • Martinsburg, WV 25401

Bierbaum Esther G. • Faculty • University of Iowa School of Library & Information Science • Iowa City, IA 52242 • ACRL ALCTS LITA LRRT

Bierbower Amy E. • Library Assistant • University of Texas Libraries General Libraries • Austin, TX 78713-7330 • ALCTS

Bierey Donald W • Student • San Jose State University Clark Library • San Jose, CA 95192-0028 • LITA

Bierman JoAnn • Assistant Documents Librarian • Oklahoma State University Library • Stillwater, OK 74078-0375 • RASD GODORT

Bierman Kenneth J. • Assistant Director • Oklahoma State University Library • Stillwater, OK 74078-0375 • ACRL LITA

Bierschenk Nancy F. • Associate Executive Director • Houston Academy of Medicine Texas Medical Center Library • Houston, TX 77030 • ACRL LAMA

Biersdorf Ruth F. • Lathrup Village, MI 48076 • ALSC IFRT

Bieschke Gail D. • Student • Rosary College Graduate School of Library & Information Science • River Forest, IL 60305 • AASL

Biesel David B. • Haworth, NJ 07641 • ACRL

Biesel Diane J. • Haworth, NJ 07641 • AASL *Continuing*

Biesterfeld Patty • Technical Services Coordinator • Traverse des Sioux Library System • Mankato, MN 56002-0608 • LITA

Bieszad Gail G. • Dake Junior High School • Rochester, NY 14617 • AASL

Bifano Helen L. • Media Specialist • Parker High School • Janesville, WI 53545 • AASL

Biffer Ava M • Student • Central Connecticut State University • New Britain, CT 06050 • AASL

Bigbee Donna B. • Oklahoma City, OK 73162

Bigelow Alice T. • Media Coor • Bartlett Yancey Senior High School • Yanceyville, NC 27379 • AASL

Bigelow Jane M. • Student • Emporia State University Emporia in the Rockies • Denver, CO 80204 • LITA

Bigelow Linda K. • Director of Learning Resources • Jefferson College Library • Hillsboro, MO 63050 • ACRL

Bigelow Lynne A. • Bookmobile Librarian • Iosco-Arenac District Library • Tawas City, MI 48763

Bigelow Therese G. • Director • Wayne County Public Library • Goldsboro, NC 27530 • ALSC LAMA PLA

Biggar Joan I. • Managing Librarian • Tucson Pima Library • Tucson, AZ 85726 • PLA

Bigger Marcia E. • Librarian • Vandercook Lake Junior Senior High School • Jackson, MI 49203 • AASL

Biggerstaff Judi • Library Director • William T. Cozby Public Library • Coppell, TX 75019 • LAMA PLA

Biggley Margery P. • Jarrettsville, MD 21804 • AASL

Biggs-Williams E. Ann • Librarian • Jefferson Davis Community College Leigh Library • Brewton, AL 36426-2116 • ACRL

Biggs Bonnie • Assistant to the Director • California State University San Marcos • San Marcos, CA 92096 • ACRL

Biggs Debra R. • Librarian • P.B.S. Inc. • Ann Arbor, MI 48108 • ACRL

Biggs F. Susan • L Coor • Pattonville School District • Maryland Heights, MO 63043 • AASL

Biggs Mary • Dean of the Library • Trenton State College Roscoe L. West Library • Trenton, NJ 08650-4700 • ACRL LRRT

Biglin Karen E. • Technical Services Librarian • Scottsdale Community College Library • Scottsdale, AZ 85256

Bignell Mary Franich • Santa Cruz, CA 95062

Bigwood David P. • Student • University of North Texas School of Library & Information Sciences • Denton, TX 76203 • GODORT IFRT

Bihler Charles H. • Coordinator/Media Service • Greenwich Public Schools • Greenwich, CT 06830 • AASL

Bildersee Adele • Oxnard, CA 93035

Bileckyj Peter A. • Reference Librarian • Wilson County Public Library • Wilson, NC 27893 • LITA RASD

Biles Paula • Head Librarian • Manatee Community College Library Sara Scott Harllee Library • Bradenton, FL 34206

Bilinski Donald S. Rev • Administrator • Provincial Depository Library • Lake Geneva, WI 54162 • Continuing

Billah Muhammed M. • Cataloging Librarian • Saint John's University Division of Library & Information Science • Jamaica, NY 11439

Billard Gerard • Librarian II • County of Los Angeles Public Library Cudahy Library 632 • Cudahy, CA 90201 • PLA SRRT

Biller Florence E. • Jacksonville, FL 32257 • Continuing

Billerbeck Amy E. • Student • Indiana University School of Library and Information Science • Bloomington, IN 47405

Billerbeck Barbara J. • Fremont, MI 49412 • AASL ALSC

Billet Katherine A. • Librarian • Dallastown Elementary School • Dallastown, PA 17313 • AASL

Billeter Anne • Adult Services Coordinator • Jackson County Library System • Medford, OR 97501 • PLA RASD

Billings Alison • Ontario Library Association • Toronto ON, M5C 1M3 Canada

Billings Anne • Dallas, TX 75205-4317 • PLA

Billings Carol D. • Director • Law Library of Louisiana • New Orleans, LA 70112 • LAMA

Billings Mary W. • Reference Librarian • Hartford Public Library • Hartford, CT 06103-3003

Billings Pennie • University of Texas Southwestern Medical Center at Dallas Library • Dallas, TX 75235-9049 • ACRL

Billings Rolland G. Dr • Director of Media Services • Public Schools • Ann Arbor, MI 48104 • AASL LAMA *Life*

Billingsley Barbara • Children Librarian • Rochester Public Library • Rochester, NY 14604 • ALSC

Billington James H. • Library of Congress • Washington, DC 20541

Billinsky Christyn G. • Instructor • University of South Carolina College of Library & Information Science • Columbia, SC 29208

Bills Diane M. • Reference Library I • Stockton-San Joaquin County Public Library • Stockton, CA 95202

Bills Linda G. • TRI- College Consortium • Bryn Mawr College Canaday Library • Bryn Mawr, PA 19010 • ALCTS LITA

Bills Rebecca A. • Information Management Serivces Inc. • Dellslow, WV 26531 • ALCTS LITA ILERT

Billy George J. • Chief Librarian • United States Merchant Marine Academy • Kings Point, NY 11024-1699 • ACRL

Bilsland Mary Jane • Serials Librarian • Saskatoon Public Library • Saskatoon SK, SN5 OJ6 Canada

Bilsland Stacia • High School Librarian • Tenino High School • Tenino, WA 98589 • AASL LIRT

Bilyeau Amy M. • Student • University of Michigan School of Information and Library Studies • Ann Arbor, MI 48109-1092

Bilz Rachelle M. • Lake Ridge Academy • N. Ridgeville, OH 44039 • YALSA

Bina Marcella A. • Children Librarian • Cuyahoga County Public Library Parma Heights Branch • Parma Heights, OH 44130-3086 • ALSC IFRT

Binder Connie D. • Independent Librarian • National Geographic Society Library • Washington, DC 20036 • ACRL ALCTS LITA ILERT

Binder Laurie Twist • Library Media Specialist • Herman Badillo Community School • Buffalo, NY 14201 • AASL

Binder Michael B. • Dean of Libraries • Western Kentucky University College Heights • Bowling Green, KY 42101 • ACRL LAMA LITA

Bingenheimer Susan A. • Eustis Memorial Library • Eustis, FL 32726

Bingham Elizabeth E. • Head of Adult Services • East Baton Rouge Parish Library • Baton Rouge, LA 70806-7699 • LAMA PLA ERT IFRT

Bingham F. Keith • Public Services Librarian • University of the Virgin Islands The Ralph M. Paiewonsky Library • Saint Thomas, VI 00802 • ACRL

Bingham III Ralph S. • Student • Rutgers University School of Communication Information & Library Studies • New Brunswick, NJ 08903

Bingham James L. • Director • University of Kansas Medical Center A.R. Dykes Library • Kansas City, KS 66103 • LITA

Bingham Jane M. • Professor of Children's Lit. • Oakland University • Rochester, MI 48309-4401 • ALSC

Bingham Janice • Rossville, KS 66533 • AASL

Bingham Karen Havill • Asst. Dir. for Adm. Services • Case Western Reserve University • Cleveland, OH 44106-7151 • ACRL LAMA RASD

Bingham Marie B. • Head, Catalog Department • University of Alabama Amelia Gayle Gorgas Library • Tuscaloosa, AL 35487-0266

Bingham Phyllis A. • North Andover, MA 01845

Bingham Rebecca T. • Director of Library Media Serv. • Jefferson County Public School • Louisville, KY 40209 • AASL ALSC

Bingham Robbie B. • Associate Professor • Virginia State University School of Education • Petersburg, VA 23803 • ACRL ALCTS LRRT

Bingley Dorothy • Trustee • Prairie Trails Public Library District • Burbank, IL 60459 • ALTA

Binion Celious • Librarian • Burke School • Chicago, IL 60619

Binkins Robert M. • Student • Drexel University College of Information Studies • Philadelphia, PA 19104-2875

Binkle Margaret M. • Student • University of Western Ontario School of Library & Information Science • London ON, N6G 1H1 Canada

Binkley Dorothy • Librarian • Wesley Hosp Nurs & Med L • Wichita, KS 67012 • Continuing

Binkley Mary A. • Circulation Librarian • Harding University • Searcy, AR 72149-0928

Binkley Susan • Norman, OK 73069

Binns Elliott M. • Reference Technical Services • Community College of Allegheny County South Campus Library • West Mifflin, PA 15122 • ACRL

Birch Grace M. • Town Librarian • Trumbull Library • Trumbull, CT 06611 • ALTA PLA

Birch Tobeylynn • Director of the Library • California School of Professional Psychology Los Angeles Campus Library • Alhambra, CA 91803-1360 • ACRL ALCTS LIRT

Birchenall Martha P. • Assistant Librarian-Serials • Augusta College Reese Library • Augusta, GA 30910

Birchfield Marilee • Instructional Services Librarian • Northwestern University Library • Evanston, IL 60208-2300 • ACRL LAMA LIRT

Birchfield Martha J. • Director • Lexington Community College Library • Lexington, KY 40506-0235 • ACRL

Birck Gwendolyn • Cocoa Beach, FL 32931-4097

Birckhead Janet • Long Branch, NJ 07740

Bird Clarence T. Dr. • Reference Librarian • Tampa-Hillsborough County Public Library • Tampa, FL 33602

Bird Debbie • Library Director • Cambridge Community Library • Cambridge, WI 53523

Bird Jan • Trustee • Baldwin Public Library • Birmingham, MI 48012-3002

Bird Jane • Media Specialist • North Central High School Lib • Indianapolis, IN 46240 • AASL

Bird Margaret W. • Librarian • Garber High School Library • Essexville, MI 48732 • AASL

Bird Mary K. • Wichita Public Library • Wichita, KS 67202

Bird Nora J. • Public Services Librarian • Teikyo Post University Traurig Library • Waterbury, CT 06708 • ACRL

Bird Sherilyn M. • Assistant Librarian • Southern Methodist University • Dallas, TX 75275 • ACRL

Bird Virginia K. • Director • Union County Public Library • Lake Butler, FL 32054 • ALSC PLA

Birden Cynthia L. • Childrens Coordinator • West Florida Regional Library • Pensacola, FL 32501 • ALSC

Birdsall Douglas G. • Texas Tech University Libraries • Lubbock, TX 79409-0002 • ACRL LAMA

Birdsong Gail E. • Branch Manager • Baltimore County Public Library White Marsh Branch • Baltimore, MD 21236 • PLA

Birdsong Karen A. • Librarian • Upper School Library • Baltimore, MD 21210 • AASL

Bires Mary • Saint Louis, MO 63108 • Continuing

Birk Nancy • Assoc Curator of Special Clln • Kent State University Library • Kent, OH 44242 • ACRL ALCTS IRRT

Birkam Anne Marie • Librarian • Public Libraries of Saginaw • Saginaw, MI 48605 • GODORT

Birkby Paul D. • Student • State University of New York (SUNY) School of Information & Library Studies • Buffalo, NY 14260 • AASL IFRT

Birkel Paul E. • San Francisco, CA 94131 • Continuing

Birkett Maureen G. • Assistant Children's Librarian • South Holland Public Library • South Holland, IL 60473 • ALSC

Birkett Patricia D. • Student • Louisiana State University School of Library & Information Science • Baton Rouge, LA 70803-3290

Birkhead Ceres B. • Coordinator,Library Instruction • University of Utah Marriott Library • Salt Lake City, UT 84112-1179 • ACRL RASD IRRT LIRT

Birkinshaw Scott B. • Assoc. Professor of Lib Sci • Weber State University Stewart Library • Ogden, UT 84408-2901 • ACRL

Birkman John P. • Student • University of Texas at Austin Graduate School of Library & Information Sciences • Austin, TX 78712-1276

Birkner Sandra L. • Technical Services • Sno-Isle Regional Library • Marysville, WA 98271-9164

Birks Florence E. • Daytona Beach, FL 32020 • ALCTS PLA *Continuing*

Birlem Lynne W. • Director Media Services • Wellesley Public Schools • Wellesley, MA 02181 • AASL

Birman Bonnie • Regional Librarian • New York Public Library Jefferson Market Branch Library • New York, NY 10011 • LITA PLA RASD

Birmingham Elisabeth • Student • Middlesex County College Library • Edison, NJ 08818-3050 • ACRL

Birmingham Frank R. Dr. • Department Chairperson • Mankato State University Library Media Education Department • Mankato, MN 56003 • AASL IFRT

Birmingham John T. • Oberlin, OH 44074

Birmingham Mary Treacy • Director • METRONET • Saint Paul, MN 55101 • AASL ASCLA PLA

Birnbaum Henry • University Librarian • Pace University • New York, NY 10038 • ACRL ALCTS LITA *Life*

Birnbaum Wendy G. • Library Media Specialist • Ridgedale Middle School • Florham Park, NJ 07932 • AASL YALSA

Biro Juliane • Children Librarian • Mount Kisco Public Library • Mount Kisco, NY 10549 • ALSC

Birt Barbara • Trustee • Grand Island Memorial Library • Grand Island, NY 14072

Birtcher Martha • Librarian • Public Library of Catasauqua • Catasauqua, PA 18032 • LAMA

Birtciel Kathleen L. • Librarian II • Phoenix Public Library Ironwood Branch • Phoenix, AZ 85041 • ALSC

Birtha Jessie M. • Philadelphia, PA 19119 • ALSC *Continuing*

Birtley Linda S. • Dir. of Legal Support Servs. • Hinshaw & Culbertson • Chicago, IL 60601 • LITA NMRT

Bisaillon Blaise • Director • Forbes Library • Northampton, MA 01060 • PLA

Bisbee Helen F. • Librarian • Grand Rapids Public Library • Grand Rapids, MI 49503-3093 • ALCTS

Biscardi Francine • Montebello, CA 90640

Bischof Phyllis B. • Africana Librarian • University of California-Berkeley University Library • Berkeley, CA 94720 • ACRL

Bischoff Mary R. • Director • Jesuit-Krauss-McCormick Library • Chicago, IL 60615 • LAMA

Bishai Elizabeth • Cataloger • Harvard College Library Widener Memorial Library • Cambridge, MA 02138 • ALCTS

Bisher Kathryn • Library Media Specialist • Napoleon High School • Napoleon, OH 43545

Bishoff Lizbeth • Online Computer Library Center (OCLC) • Dublin, OH 43017-3395 • ALCTS LAMA LITA

Bishop Ann P. • University of Illinois Graduate School of Library and Information Science • Urbana, IL 61801 • ALCTS LITA LRRT

Bishop Barbara A. • Manager,New Products Group • Silver Platter Information • Norwood, MA 02062-5026

Bishop Barbara A. • Humanities Reference Librarian • Auburn University Ralph Brown Draughon Library • Auburn, AL 36849-5606 • ACRL

Bishop Clifford M. • Assistant Librarian • University of Illinois Undergraduate Library • Urbana, IL 61801 • ACRL RASD

Bishop David F. • Librarian • University of Illinois Library • Urbana, IL 61801 • ACRL ALCTS LITA

Bishop Edith P. • Costa Mesa, CA 92626 • LAMA PLA YALSA   *Continuing*

Bishop Elizabeth • Ryerson Polytech Institute • Toronto ON, M5B 2K3 Canada • ACRL

Bishop Esther E. • Legislative Librarian • Maryland Department of Legislative Reference Library • Annapolis, MD 21401-1991

Bishop Faira L. • Librarian • Eastside School • Clinton, MS 39056 • AASL

Bishop Genevieve K. • Bradenton, FL 34209 • AASL

Bishop Howard E. Mrs • Grass Valley, CA 95949 • ALSC

Bishop J. Catherine • Cataloger • Johns Hopkins University Milton S. Eisenhower Library • Baltimore, MD 21218 • ACRL ALCTS LITA

Bishop James P. Rev. • Milwaukee, WI 53202 • ACRL

Bishop Jean • Head of Public Services • Montana Colleg of Mineral Science and Technology Library • Butte, MT 59701 • ACRL

Bishop Jean E. • Pikes Peak Library District • Colorado Springs, CO 80901

Bishop John M. • Student • University of Texas at Austin Graduate School of Library & Information Sciences • Austin, TX 78712-1276 • PLA IFRT ILERT IRRT

Bishop Karen E. • Librarian • Theodore Roosevelt High School • San Antonio, TX 78218 • AASL LIRT

Bishop Laura D. • Norcross, GA 30092 • AASL

Bishop Mary J. • Student • Indiana University School of Library and Information Science • Bloomington, IN 47405 • IFRT SRRT

Bishop Mary L. • Crawfordsville, IN 47933

Bishop Meredith J. • Childrens Librarian • Finney Library • Milwaukee, WI 53208 • ALSC

Bishop Minnie S. • Mobile, AL 36617

Bishop Nancy D. • Covenant Medical Center Library • Urbana, IL 61801 • ASCLA

Bishop Rebecca L. • Student • Catholic University of America School of Library and Information Science • Washington, DC 20064 • PLA YALSA

Bishop Rosemarie M. • Library Media Specialist • Grissom High School • Huntsville, AL 35802

Bishop Rudine Sims • Professor • Ohio State University College of Education • Columbus, OH 43210 • ALSC EMIERT SRRT

Bishop Teresa H. • Davidson, NC 28036 • PLA

Biske Carol • Training Supervisor • McDonald's Corporation • Oak Brook, IL 60521-1921

Bisom Diane B. • Librarian • University of California-Irvine Library • Irvine, CA 92713 • ALCTS LITA

Bison Ruth L. • Reference • William T. Cozby Public Library • Coppell, TX 75019

Bissell Joann S. • Signal Mountain, TN 37377

Bissessar Carmen Toni • Children's Librarian • Oakland Public Library • Oakland, CA 94612 • ALSC EMIERT

Bissett Claudia L. • Northboro, MA 01532 • ALCTS

Bissey Mary E. • Librarian • Champaign Public Library & Information Center • Champaign, IL 61820-5193

Bisso Arthur J. • Director • Hart County Library • Hartwell, GA 30643

Bitler Cherie M. • Salt Lake County Library Systems Sandy Library • Sandy, UT 84092

Bitner Harry • Hackensack, NJ 07601 • Continuing

Bitte Ines • Reference Librarian • Pikes Peak Library District • Colorado Springs, CO 80901 • RASD

Bitterolf Faith A. • Librarian • Winchester-Thurston School • Pittsburgh, PA 15213 • AASL

Bittle Ilene • Henderson, NV 89015 • AASL

Bittner Bobbie I H • Conroe, TX 77385 • Continuing

Bittner Debora H. • Library Systems Analyst • Carlyle Systems Inc. • San Mateo, CA 94608 • ALCTS

Bittner Sharon L. • Student • University of Missouri-Columbia School of Library & Informational Science • Columbia, MO 65211 • AFLRT IFRT NMRT

Bivens Carolyn T. • University Librarian • Florida A&M University S.H. Coleman Memorial Library • Tallahassee, FL 32307 • ACRL

Bivens Cathy L. • Student • Indiana University School of Library and Information Science • Bloomington, IN 47405 • RASD

Bivens Lydia R. • Judson High School Library • Converse, TX 78109 • AASL YALSA

Bixler Linda V. • Student • Texas Woman's University Mary Evelyn Blagg-Huey Library • Denton, TX 76204-1715

Bizub Dale J. • Student • University of Pittsburgh School of Library and Information Science • Pittsburgh, PA 15260

Bizub Johanna C. • Library Director • Sills Cummis, et al. • Newark, NJ 07102-5400 • LAMA RASD

Bjoin Cheryl J. • Watonwan County Library • St. James, MN 56081

Bjorgo Maynard • Thunder Bay ON, P7B 5E3 Canada • PLA RASD   *Life*

Bjork Priscilla • Tempe, AZ 85283-4544

Bjorklund Edith M. • Milwaukee, WI 53210

Bjorklund Katharine B. • Reference Librarian • Los Alamos County Library • Los Alamos, NM 87544 • RASD

Bjorkquist Donna M. • Librarian • Maple Grove Junior-Senior High School • Bemus Point, NY 14712

Bjorkquist Donna R. • Librarian • Saint Paul Public Library • St. Paul, MN 55102

Bjorncrantz Leslie B. • Cur. Librarian/Core Librarian • Northwestern University Library • Evanston, IL 60208-2300 • ACRL LITA RASD

Bjorner Susan N. • Bjorner & Associates • Woodbury, CT 06798 • LITA RASD CLENE ILERT LIRT LRRT

Blacher Lynette • Buffalo, NY 14222

Blachowicz Maralyn • Education Librarian • Wichita State University Ablah Library • Wichita, KS 67208 • ACRL

Black A. Fiona • Student • Dalhousie University School of Library & Inf. Studies • Halifax NS, B3H 4H8 Canada • PLA RASD

Black Ann E. • Terre Haute, IN 47805

Black Anna Marie • Children's Librarian • Dixon Homestead Library • Dumont, NJ 07628 • ALSC

Black Bette-Jean D. • Student • University of Rhode Island Graduate School of Library & Information Studies • Kingston, RI 02881-0815 • AASL

Black Byron P. • Student • Indiana University School of Library and Information Science • Bloomington, IN 47405

Black Carl Monroe • Fort Worth, TX 76119 • ALCTS PLA   *Continuing*

Black Carol • Library Branch Manager • Irving Public Library Southwest Branch • Irving, TX 75060 • ALSC

Black Carol M. Dr • Lamar University-Port Arthur Gates Library • Port Arthur, TX 77640 • AASL RASD LIRT

Black Carolyn J. • Librarian • Kingsbury High School • Memphis, TN 38122 • IFRT

Black Carolyn R. • Librarian • Texarkana Public Library • Texarkana, TX 75501 • ALCTS YALSA

Black Catharine E. • South Plainfield High School • South Plainfield, NJ 07080

Black Christina S. • Sleepy Hollow Elementary School • Falls Church, VA 22042 • AASL

Black Daryl A. • Adult Services Librarian • Santa Fe Public Library Oliver LaFarge Branch • Santa Fe, NM 87505 • IFRT

Black Diane R. • Student • University of South Carolina College of Library & Information Science • Columbia, SC 29208

Black Dorothy C. • School Media Specialist • Windsor Spring Elementary School • Augusta, GA 30906 • AASL

Black Elizabeth • Manager, Bibliographic Services • Utlas International • Etobicoke, ON, M8X 2X2 Canada • LITA

Black Estelle M. • Librarian • Rockford Public Library • Rockford, IL 61101-1061 • LAMA PLA SRRT

Black Frances P. • Director • Southwest Public Libraries • Grove City, OH 43123 • LAMA PLA IFRT

Black Jack M. • Columbia University Library Service Library • New York, NY 10027 • PLA

Black Jane L. • University of Windsor Leddy Library • Windsor ON, N9B 3P4 Canada • LITA IRRT

Black Janet • Student • University of Hawaii School of Library & Information Studies • Honolulu, HI 96822 • IFRT SRRT

Black Jean P. • Portland, OR 97210 • ACRL   *Continuing*

Black JoAnn J. • Media Specialist • Lincoln High School • Tallahassee, FL 32301 • AASL

Black John B. Dr. • Chief Librarian • University of Guelph Library • Guelph ON, N1G 2W1 Canada • ACRL LITA IRRT

Black Junivee • South Hutchinson, KS 67505

Black Kenneth L. • Head of Public Services • Rosary College • River Forest, IL 60305-1066

Black Larry D. • Executive Director • Columbus Metropolitan Library • Columbus, OH 43215 • LAMA PLA IFRT

Black Lea • Library Technician • Little Hoop Community College • Fort Totten, ND 58335

Black Leah C. • Cataloging/Reference Librarian • Michigan State University Libraries • East Lansing, MI 48824-1048 • ACRL ALCTS RASD ILERT

Black Leigh S. • Saint John's Episcopal School • Albilene, TX 79605

Black Lois • Assistant Director • North Bellmore Public Library • N. Bellmore, NY 11710

Black Lois Fischer • Special Collections Librarian • New York Academy of Medicine Library • New York, NY 10029 • ACRL

Black Patricia S. • Student • Rosary College Graduate School of Library & Information Science • River Forest, IL 60305

Black Robert E. • Little Rock, AR 72204 • ASCLA PLA

Black Robert S. • Reference Librarian • Missouri Southern State College Library • Joplin, MO 64801 • ACRL LIRT

Black Shirley R. • University of Detroit-Mercy Outer Drive Library • Detroit, MI 48219-3599 • ACRL LIRT

Black Susan A. • Librarian • Richard Bennett Elementary School • Bellevue, WA 98008 • AASL

Black Thelma U. • Pasadena, CA 91106

Black Tracy • Monmouth, OR 97361

Black William K. • Library Devel & Project Mgr. • Iowa State University Library • Ames, IA 50011-2140 • ACRL LAMA

Black William P. • Library Director • Chatham Hall School for Girls Edmund J. and Lucy Lee Library • Chatham, VA 24531

Black William R. • Plainboro, NJ 08536 • ALCTS

Blackaby Sandra L. • Director of Library Services • Walla Walla Community College Library • Walla Walla, WA 99362 • ACRL

Blackburn-Foster Brenda • West Chester, PA 19380-3630

Blackburn Barbara S. • President • Cleveland County Memorial Library • Shelby, NC 28150 • PLA

Blackburn Clayton E. • Post Librarian • United States Army Leighton Army Library • APO, AE 09244 • ALCTS LITA PLA AFLRT FLRT

Blackburn F M. Mr • Georgetown, TX 78626 • ACRL LAMA   *Life*

Blackburn Joann D. • Mount Lebanon School District • Pittsburgh, PA 15243 • AASL ALSC

Blackburn Joseph L. • Catalog Librarian • Texas Tech University Health Sciences Center Library • Lubbock, TX 79430

Blackburn Patricia H. • Coordinator-Learning Resources • Peterborough County Board of Education • Peterborough, ON, K9J 7A1 Canada • AASL

Blackburn Reeves S. • Librarian • Spartanburg Day School • Spartanburg, SC 29302

Blacker Marilyn E. • Student • Emporia State University Emporia in the Rockies • Denver, CO 80204 • IFRT

Blackford Bland • Colonial Williamsburg Foundation • Williamsburg, VA 23187 • NMRT

Blackham Margaret Ann • Media Coordinator • Rock Canyon Elementary School • Provo, UT 84604 • AASL

Blackledge Ella Haw • San Mateo, CA 94402

Blackman Betty J. • Dean • California State University-Dominguez Hills Library • Carson, CA 90747 • ACRL LAMA

Blackman Gordon • Bossier Parish Library • Bossier City, LA 71111

Blackman Marcia H. • Ref. Librarian/Adult Services • East Meadow Public Library • East Meadow, NY 11554-1700 • RASD

Blackman Normandy S. • Librarian • Backus Junior High School • Washington, DC 20017

Blackman Sally J. • Student • University of Arizona Graduate Library School • Tucson, AZ 85721

Blackmon Zenobia L. • Montgomery, AL 36116 • SRRT

Blackshear Martha • Headland, AL 36345 • Continuing

Blackshear Orrilla • Madison, WI 53705 • Continuing

Blackstead Katharina J. • Library Advancement Officer • University of Notre Dame Libraries • Notre Dame, IN 46556 • ACRL LAMA

Blackston Jeanette • Pittsburgh, PA 15221-1256

Blackwelder Teresa S. • Washington, DC 20008 • AASL ALSC

Blackwell Jean C. • Salisbury, NC 28144

Blackwell Kathryn • Minneapolis, MN 55427 • Continuing

Blackwell Richard Miles • Blackwell's B.H. Blackwell Ltd. • Oxford, OX1 3BQ England • ACRL ALCTS LITA *Life*

Blackwell Steve • Media Specialist • Charlotte High School • Punta Gorda, FL 33950 • AASL

Blackwell Terri • Acquisitions Librarian • Abilene Public Library • Abilene, TX 79601-5793

Blackwood Deborah R. • Greensboro, NC 27403

Blackwood Phyllis D. • North Loop Elementary School • EL Paso, TX 79915 • AASL

Blaes Evelyn R. • Serials Department • The American University Library • Washington, DC 20016-8046 • ALCTS

Blaha Diane M. • Sturdy Memorial Hospital • Attleboro, MA 02703

Blaha Janet • Santa Clara County Free Library Milpitas Community Library • Milpitas, CA 95035

Blaha Linda N. • Regional Childrens Serv Manager • Cuyahoga County Public Library Parma Regional • Parma, OH 44129-3199 • ALSC

Blain Del • Director • Washtenaw Community College • Ann Arbor, MI 48106 • ACRL LAMA

Blaine Susan F. • Head,Preservation Services Dept. • Smithsonian Institution Libraries • Washington, DC 20540 • ALCTS

Blaine William M. Jr • Trustee • Mount Prospect Public Library • Mount Prospect, IL 60056

Blair Amy Grobbel • Librarian II • Michigan State University Libraries • East Lansing, MI 48824-1048 • ACRL

Blair Angela W. • Dallas, TX 75217

Blair Charles J. D. • Student • University of Chicago Graduate Library School • Chicago, IL 60637 • LITA

Blair Elaine • Librarian • Dale B Davis School • Carrollton, TX 75007 • AASL

Blair Jeff • Librarian • Olathe South High School • Olathe, KS 66062 • YALSA

Blair Joan • Digital Equipment Corporation • Marlboro, MA 01752 • ACRL

Blair Joann M. • Estill Springs, TN 37330

Blair Julia • Iowa City, IA 52240 • GODORT

Blair Kathryn E. • Library Media Specialist • Littleton Public Schools Superintendent of Schools • Littleton, MA 01460 • AASL

Blair Lynne M. • Director • Rhodes College Burrow Library • Memphis, TN 38112 • ACRL ALCTS LAMA LITA RASD

Blair Madeline S. • Washington, DC 20037

Blair Mary Ann • Adult Services • Winthrop Public Library • Winthrop, MA 02152 • PLA

Blair Nancy E. • Adult Services/Reference • Goodnow Library • Sudbury, MA 01776-2383 • RASD

Blair Sharon • Librarian • Albert R. Lewis Elementary School • Pickens, SC 29671 • AASL

Blair Thea Q. • Catalog Librarian • Orange Public Library • Orange, CA 92666

Blake-Muccing Fay Blake • Lauderhill, FL 33313 • CLENE NMRT

Blake Dorothy W. • Atlanta, GA 30317 • AASL *Continuing*

Blake Jill Elizabeth • Archival/Presv. Librarian • Hertzberg Museum • San Antonio, TX 78232

Blake John • Librarian • Las Lomas High School Library • Walnut Creek, CA 94596 • AASL

Blake John N. • United States Department of Education • Washington, DC 20208 • ACRL

Blake Julie C. • Student • Indiana University School of Library and Information Science • Bloomington, IN 47405

Blake Margaret A. • Special Media Services • Mobile County Public Schools • Mobile, AL 36633

Blake Mary K. • Emporia, VA 23847 • ALCTS

Blake Michael R. • Head of Reference • Harvard University Library • Cambridge, MA 02138-2901 • ACRL RASD

Blake Norma E. • Director • Gloucester County Library • Sewell, NJ 08080

Blakely Claude William • Greenville County Library • Greenville, SC 29601 • ALTA

Blakely Cora J. • Librarian Media Specialist • Central High School • West Helena, AR 72390 • AASL

Blakely Florence • Durham, NC 27705 • ALCTS RASD *Life*

Blakely Julia D. • Arlington, VA 22204 • ACRL

Blakely Linda M. • Statesville High School • Statesville, NC 28677 • AASL

Blakeman Betsy • Campbellsville Elementary School • Campbellsville, KY 42718

Blakesley Elizabeth A. • Student • Indiana University School of Library and Information Science • Bloomington, IN 47405

Blakesley S. Lynn • Waubonsee Community College Library • Sugar Grove, IL 60554 • LAMA

Blakesley Suzanne • Librarian • Timpview High School Library • Provo, UT 84604

Blakey Jane B. • Bibliographic Services Coor. • Tennessee State Library & Archives • Nashville, TN 37243-0312 • ALSC

Blakey Patricia B. • Librarian • Marvelwood School • Cornwall, CT 06753 • RASD LIRT

Blakley Alma • Branch Head • Gary Public Library John F Kennedy Branch • Gary, IN 46409 • PLA

Blakley Lee A. • Assistant Librarian • Elmhurst Public Library • Elmhurst, IL 60126

Blalock Louise • Director • New Canaan Library • New Canaan, CT 06840 • LAMA PLA SRRT

Blalock Mary Beth • Nashville, TN 37211 • ACRL LAMA

Blanchard J Richard • Univ. Librarian Emeritus • University of California-Davis Library • Davis, CA 95616 • ACRL *Continuing*

Blanchard Jill M. • Student • Simmons College Beatley Library • Boston, MA 02115 • EMIERT IFRT

Blanchard Laura D. • Coordinator, Media Services • Horry County Schools • Conway, SC 29526 • AASL

Blanchard Margaret B. • Director • Central North Carolina Regional Library • Burlington, NC 27215 • ALSC PLA RASD

Blanchard Mark A. • Product Support Specialist • Online Computer Library Center (OCLC) • Dublin, OH 43017-3395 • RASD

Blanchard Mary Ann • Teacher • Orange County Public Schools • Orlando, FL 32801

Blanchard Robert T. • Reference Librarian • Warren-Newport Public Library District • Gurnee, IL 60031

Blanchard Susan M. • School Liaison • Greenwich Library • Greenwich, CT 06830

Blanchard Woodie • Trustee • Western Plains Library System • Clinton, OK 73601

Blanchette Amy C. • Librarian • Mount Saint Charles Academy Library • Woonsocket, RI 02895 • AASL

Blanco Jeanette • Pittsburgh, PA 15228

Bland Catherine V. • Petersburg, VA 23803 • ACRL

Bland Elizabeth A. • Library Assistant • von Briesen & Purtell • Milwaukee, WI 53202-4470 • ACRL NMRT

Bland Kay • Director of Media Technology • Pulaski County Special School District • Little Rock, AR 72216 • AASL

Bland Rodney L. • Director • Weatherford Public Library • Weatherford, TX 76086-5098 • PLA

Blander Murray • Adult Service Librarian • North Bellmore Public Library • N. Bellmore, NY 11710

Blandy Susan Griswold • Professor/Asst. Librarian • Hudson Valley Community College Dwight Marvin Library • Troy, NY 12180 • ACRL

Blank Annette C. • Baltimore, MD 21206 • ALSC *Continuing*

Blank Charles S. • Director • Washington County Free Library • Hagerstown, MD 21740

Blanke Leonella Jameson Ms. • Kalamazoo, MI 49008 • AASL ALSC *Life*

Blanke Nedra V. • Head Technical Services • Orange County Library System Orlando Public Library • Orlando, FL 32801-2471

Blankenburg Judith B. • Assistant Professor • James Madison University • Harrisonburg, VA 22807 • AASL

Blankenburg Julie J. • Assistant Librarian • United States Forest Service Forest Products Laboratory • Madison, WI 53705-2398 • ALCTS

Blankenhorn Janet • Librarian • State College Area School District • State College, PA 16801 • AASL

Blankenship Edith G. • Program Director Information Svs • Utah State Library • Salt Lake City, UT 84115-2579 • ASCLA

Blankenship Emily F. • Student • Florida State University • Tallahassee, FL 32306-2047

Blankenship Lisa • University of Northern Colorado James A. Michener Library • Greeley, CO 80639 • ACRL IFRT LIRT

Blankenship Maria E. • Campbell, CA 95008 • ACRL IFRT

Blankenship Sandra R. • Shelby, NC 28150

Blankenship William J. • Director • Saint Marys Public Library • Saint Marys, GA 31558 • LAMA RASD CLENE LIRT

Blankinship Carmen • Senior Assistant Librarian • Cornell University Library • Ithaca, NY 14853-5301 • LAMA GODORT IFRT IRRT

Blankmeyer Carol L. • Student • San Jose State University Division of Library & Information Science • San Jose, CA 95192-0029

Blanton Carmen T. • Media Specialist • Gettys D. Broome High School • Spartanburg, SC 29302 • AASL YALSA

Blanton Cheryl • Librarian • Mobile Public Library Cottage Hill Branch • Mobile, AL 36609 • VRT

Blanton Linda Ann Heck • Technical Services Librarian • Johnson City Public Library • Johnson City, TN 37601-5771 • ALCTS PLA

Blanton Thomas S. • Executive Director • National Security Archive • Washington, DC 20036 • FLRT GODORT IFRT

Blaschek Jack A. • Trustee • Schiller Park Public Library • Schiller Park, IL 60176-1699 • ALTA

Blascovich Mary Jo • Librarian • Schuylkill Elementary School • Phoenixville, PA 19460 • AASL

Blasingame Ralph • Professor Emeritus • Rutgers University School of Communication Information & Library Studies • New Brunswick, NJ 08903 • ACRL PLA *Life*

Blasinski Clare M. • Librarian • Milwaukee Public Library • Milwaukee, WI 53233

Blasius Anne M. • Arlington, VA 22207-3226

Blaszka Donna M. • Library Director • Sayreville Free Public Library • Parlin, NJ 08859 • PLA

Blatchley Jeremy • Bryn Mawr College Canaday Library • Bryn Mawr, PA 19010

Blatman-Byers Karen L. • Library Technician III • McNeil Island Corrections Center • Steilcoom, WA 98388

Blatt Leslie S. • Library Media Specialist • Manchester Regional High School Library • Haledon, NJ 07508 • AASL YALSA

Blatz Elizabeth A. • Supervising Branch Librarian • New York Public Library Kips Bay Branch • New York, NY 10016 • ALSC

Blau Donna L. • Library Trustee • Franklin Park Public Library District • Franklin Park, IL 60131 • ALTA PLA

Blauer Ann • Head of Informational Services • University of South Alabama Baldwin County Branch • Fairhope, AL 36532 • ACRL

Blauer Katherine • Regional Marketing Manager • Online Computer Library Center (OCLC) • Washington, DC 20037 • LAMA LITA

Blauet Doris • Medical Librarian • Flint Osteopathic Hospital • Flint, MI 48502

Blauvelt III Arthur A. • Trustee • Timberland Regional Library • Olympia, WA 98501 • ALTA

Blauvelt Lucille L. • Verona, NJ 07044 • Continuing

Blauvelt Marion • Associate Librarian • State Univ of NY Coll at Potsdam Frederick W. Crumb Memorial Library • Potsdam, NY 13676 • ACRL GODORT

Blaylock James C. • Director • Baptist Missionary Association Theological Seminary /Kellar Library • Jacksonville, TX 75766-5414

Blazakis E. Lillie • Allentown High School • Allentown, NJ 08501

Blazek Daniel R. • Student • University of Miami Libraries Richter Library • Coral Gables, FL 33124

Blazek David M. • Florida State University School of Library and Information Studies • Tallahassee, FL 32306-2048

Blazek Ronald D. • Professor • Florida State University School of Library and Information Studies • Tallahassee, FL 32306-2048 • ACRL PLA RASD LHRT LRRT *Life*

Bleakley Karen • Librarian • KPMG Peat Marwick • Washington, DC 20036 • LITA

Blechl Susan • Director • Dickinson County Library • Iron Mtn, MI 49801

Blecic Deborah D. • Resident Librarian • University of Illinois at Chicago • Chicago, IL 60680

Bledsoe Cynthia L. • Student • Dorchester County Library • Saint George, SC 29477 • PLA

Bledsoe Kathleen E. • Special Collections, Librarian • Marshall University James E. Morrow Library • Huntington, WV 25755-2060

Bledsoe Linda S. • School Librarian • Pearl B. Larsen Elementary School • St. Croix, VI 00820 • AASL

Bledsoe Robert V. • Interlibrary Loan Librarian • Tulane University Howard-Tilton Memorial Library • New Orleans, LA 70118

Bledsoe Susan A. • Library Director • American Graduate School of International Management Barton K Yount Memorial Library • Glendale, AZ 85306 • ACRL IFRT

Blegen Dennis A. • Children's Librarian • Sacramento Public Library • Sacramento, CA 95814

Blegen John C. • Executive Librarian • Glenview Public Library • Glenview, IL 60025 • LAMA LITA PLA

Bleier Carol S. • Student • University of Pittsburgh School of Library and Information Science • Pittsburgh, PA 15260

Bleiler Richard • Humanities Reference Bibl. • University of Alabama at Birmingham Mervyn H. Sterne Library • Birmingham, AL 35294-0014 • ACRL RASD

Bleiweis Maxine A. • Director • Lucy Robbins Welles Library • Newington, CT 06111 • LAMA

Blendermann Frances V. • Media Specialist • Harpers Choice Middle School • Columbia, MD 21044 • AASL

Blenk Carol A. • Childrens' Services Coordinator • Osceola County Library System BVL Library • Kissimmee, FL 34743 • PLA

Blenkinsopp Heather M. • Asst. Head of Technical Services • Mercy College Libraries • Dobbs Ferry, NY 10522 • ACRL ALCTS LITA

Blenkush Marge A. • South Saint Paul, MN 55075-2902

Bleses Judith M. • Librarian • Edwin D. Smith Elementary School • Dayton, OH 45419 • AASL ALSC

Blesse Robert • Head of Special Collections Dept • University of Nevada-Reno Noble H. Getchell Library • Reno, NV 89557 • ACRL

Blessing Candace L. • School Library Media Spec. • Ephrata Senior High School Media Center • Ephrata, PA 17522 • AASL

Blessington Elizabeth L. • Children's Librarian • Brighton Memorial Library • Rochester, NY 14618 • ALSC

Blest Kathy • Librarian • Evangelical Christian Academy • Madrid 28022, Spain • ALSC

Blevins James • Trustee • East Saint Louis Public Library • East St. Louis, IL 62201 • ALTA

Blevins Jane E. • Collection Department Librarian • Palm Beach County Library System • West Palm Beach, FL 33406 • ALCTS PLA

Blevins Kimberly S. • East Liverpool, OH 43920 • ALSC

Blevins Melissa F. • Student • Middle Tennessee State University Library • Murfreesboro, TN 37132 • AASL

Blewett Daniel K. • Bibliographer/Reference Ln. • Loyola University E.M. Cudahy Memorial Library • Chicago, IL 60626 • ACRL MAGERT

Bley Mary F. • Reference Librarian • Library of Congress • Washington, DC 20541 • ALSC

Blickley Kathy W. • Littleton, CO 80122

Blickley LaVerne • Trustee • Grand Rapids Public Library • Grand Rapids, MI 49503-3093

Blietz Cynthia S. • Alsip-Merrionette Park Library District • Alsip, IL 60658 • RASD

Blight Marilyn • Media Generalist • Hanover High School • Hanover, NH 03755 • AASL

Blinn Marjeanne B • Reference Librarian • Palos Verdes Library District • Pls Vrd Pnsla, CA 90274 • PLA RASD

Bliss Anthony S. • Rare Book Librarian • University of California-Berkeley Bancroft Library • Berkeley, CA 94720 • ACRL

Bliss Jennifer W. • Red Bluff, CA 96080 • PLA CLENE IFRT NMRT

Bliss Joanne F. • Community Library Manager • County of Los Angels Public Library Long Beach • Long Beach, CA 90036

Bliss Nonie J. • Denton, TX 76204-0403

Bliss Russell C. • Consultant • Natalie Wargin Design • Chicago, IL 60618

Blitch Sara L. • Columbia, SC 29210

Blixrud Julia C. • Program Officer • Council on Library Resources • Washington, DC 20036-2117 • ACRL ALCTS LITA

Blocher Carolyn S. • Student • Northern Illinois University Department of Library & Information Studies • DeKalb, IL 60115

Blocher John W. • Student • University of Arizona Graduate Library School • Tucson, AZ 85721

Block David • Ibero-American Bibliographer • Cornell University • Ithaca, NY 14853-5301

Block Jennifer M. • Williamsville, NY 14221

Block Joann R. • Librn For Blind & Phys Hndcpd • Broward County Division of Libraries Broward County Library • Fort Lauderdale, FL 33301

Block Judy F. • Ann Arbor, MI 48103-2076

Block Lois • Williamsville, NY 14221

Block Patricia L. • Kensington, CA 94707 • LITA

Block Paula K. • Nashua, NH 03062

Block Rick J. • Head, Cataloging Dept. • Tufts University Arts & Sciences Library • Medford, MA 02155 • ACRL ALCTS LITA

Block Sandra S. • Miami, FL 33186 • AASL

Blockcolski Lewis • Assistant Director • Enid & Garfield County Public Library • Enid, OK 73702 • PLA

Blodgett-Klein Nancy • Trustee • Arlington Heights Memorial Library • Arlington Heights, IL 60004-5966

Blodgett Anita Jan • County Archivist • Saint Mary's County Records Center & Archives • Leonardtown, MD 20650

Blodgett Elizabeth • Naples, NY 14512

Blodgett Marjorie L. • Auburn, CA 95603 • ALSC PLA IFRT

Blodgett Teresa K. • Coor. Computer Asst Search Serv. • Texas Tech University Libraries • Lubbock, TX 79409-0002

Bloesch Ethel B. • Assistant To Director • University of Iowa School of Library & Information Science • Iowa City, IA 52242

Blohm Carol H. • Reference Librarian • Arlington Heights Memorial Library • Arlington Heights, IL 60004-5966 • PLA

Blomeyer Elizabeth A. • Washington, DC 20008

Blommel Henry H. • Connersville, IN 47331

Blomquist Carol A. • Teacher • Dent Elementary School • Escalon, CA 95320

Blomquist Daniel E. • Director,REMC21 • Marquette-Alger Intermediate School District • Marquette, MI 49855 • AASL LITA

Blomquist Laura • Head Education/Psychology Ln. • Ohio State University Education Psychology Library • Columbus, OH 43210 • ACRL ALCTS LAMA LITA LRRT

Blomquist Paul • Student • Denver Public Library • Denver, CO 80203-2165 • LITA

Blomstedt Erik R. • Director • Three Rivers Public Library • Channahon, IL 60410-0300 • PLA

Blomstrom Nancy • Reference Librarian • Housatonic Cmnty Coll • Bridgeport, CT 06608

Blonz Barbara • Trustee • Morton Grove Public Library • Morton Grove, IL 60053 • ALTA

Blood Richard W. • Assistant Director • San Francisco State University J. Paul Leonard Library • San Francisco, CA 94132 • LITA

Blood Susan • Technical Services Librarian • Charles Sturt University Riverina • Wagga Wagga NSW 2650, Australia • LITA

Bloodworth Velda Jean • Reference Librarian • Rollins College Olin Library • Winter Park, FL 32789-4499 • ACRL

Bloom Beth S. • Student • Rutgers University School of Communication Information & Library Studies • New Brunswick, NJ 08903

Bloom Charles • Arcata, CA 95521

Bloom Marshall S. • Library Assistant • Southfield Public Library David Stewart Memorial Library • Southfield, MI 48037-2055

Bloom Stephen C. • Director of University Libraries • University of the Arts Libraries • Philadelphia, PA 19102 • ACRL LAMA LHRT

Bloom Susan P. • Simmons College Center for the Study of Children's Literature • Boston, MA 02115 • YALSA

Bloom Vickey S. • Grosse Pointe Public Library Central Branch • Grosse Pointe, MI 48236

Bloom Wendy B. • Mount Kisco Public Library • Mount Kisco, NY 10549 • YALSA

Bloomberg-Rissman Kathryn • Riverside, CA 92507

Bloomberg Kathleen L. • Associate Director/Library Devel • Illinois State Library • Springfield, IL 62701-1796 • ASCLA

Bloomquist Mary J. • McNeese State University Lether E. Frazar Memorial Library • Lake Charles, LA 70609

Bloomsburgh Esther • Newtown Square, PA 19073

Bloomstone Ajaye • Mary Bird Perkins Cancer Center Clinical Oncology Library • Baton Rouge, LA 70809 • ALCTS LAMA

Bloomstrand Nancy L. • Rockfrord, IL 61111-7818 • AASL

Bloss Alexander • ALCTS,Deputy Exec. Director • American Library Association • Chicago, IL 60611-2795 • ALCTS

Bloss Carl H. • Library Media Specialist • Conshohocken Elementary School Library • Conshohocken, PA 19428-1991 • AASL

Bloss Marjorie E. • Center for Research Libraries • Chicago, IL 60637 • ACRL ALCTS LITA IRRT

Blosser John P. • Student • University of Illinois Graduate School of Library and Information Science • Urbana, IL 61801 • LITA SRRT

Blossic Audrey J. • Library Director • Springfield Township Library • Springfield, PA 19064 • LAMA PLA RASD

Blossom Carole A. • Casper, WY 82601

Blossom Katherine E. • Medical Librarian • Virginia Beach General Hospital • Virginia Beach, VA 23454 • ACRL IFRT NMRT

Blosveren Barbara • Young Adult Librarian • Stratford Library Association • Stratford, CT 06497 • YALSA

Blote Larry • Trustee • Rapid City Public Library • Rapid City, SD 57701-3630

Blough Lauren M. • Circulation Systems Coordinator • Queens Borough Public Library • Jamaica, NY 11432

Blouin Robert J. • Head Serials/Circulation • Westfield State College Ely Memorial Library • Westfield, MA 01086 • ACRL

Blount Billie Ruth • Frankfurt American High School • APO, AE 09228 • AASL

Blount Edward F. • Berwick, ME 03901-2536 • Continuing

Blower Paul E. • Chief Librarian • Orillia Public Library • Orillia ON, Canada • ALSC LAMA PLA RASD

Blowers Mel E. • Univ Librn & Assoc Prof Of Bibl • North Carolina University Ramsey Library • Asheville, NC 28804 • ACRL ALCTS LAMA LITA RASD YALSA

Blowney Steven P. • Student • State University of New York (SUNY) Thomas E. Dewey Graduate Library • Albany, NY 12222 • RASD

Bloy Jonathan P. • Oak Creek Public Library • Oak Creek, WI 53154

Blubaugh Penny L. • Community Services,Young Adult • Eisenhower Public Library District • Harwood Heights, IL 60656 • YALSA EMIERT IFRT SRRT

Blue Jackalie L. • Vice President • Science Applications International Corporation • Albuquerque, NM 87106 • GODORT

Blue Kathryn J. • Hd, Bibliographic Control Dept • College of William & Mary Earl Gregg Swem Library • Williamsburg, VA 23187-8794 • ACRL ALCTS LITA IFRT MAGERT

Blue Margaret L. • Chula Vista Public Library • Chula Vista, CA 91910 • ALCTS LITA PLA

Blue Margaret R. • North Dakota State University Library • Fargo, ND 58105-5599 • ACRL ALCTS LAMA LITA IFRT LRRT   Life

Blue Philip Y. • Reference Librarian • Dowling College • Oakdale, NY 11769

Blue Richard I. • Big Bend, WI 53103 • ACRL

Bluel Marcia • Branch Librarian • Brooklyn Public Library Sheepshead Bay Branch • Brooklyn, NY 11235 • LAMA

Bluemel Nancy G. • Library Coordinator • Sherman Independent School District • Sherman, TX 75090 • AASL

Bluh Pamela M. • Asst Director for Tech Services • University of Maryland at Baltimore Marshall Law Library • Baltimore, MD 21201 • ALCTS LAMA

Bluhdorn Frances L. • Royal Australian Historical Society • Sydney NSW 200, Australia • ALCTS LAMA LITA IRRT LIRT LRRT

Blum Annette • Charleston County Library • Charleston, SC 29403

Blum Fred • Reference Librarian • Eastern Michigan University Library Center of Educational Resources • Ypsilanti, MI 48197 • ACRL

Blum Irma • Philadelphia, PA 19119

Blum Ken • University of California Los Angeles Graduate School of Library & Information Science • Los Angeles, CA 90024

Blum Patricia • Hawaii State Library System Library for the Blind & Phys Hndcpd • Honolulu, HI 96815-3894 • ASCLA NMRT

Blum Peter • Waterbury, CT 06710

Blumberg Catherine • Asst. Library Director • Mill Valley Public Library • Mill Valley, CA 94941 • PLA

Blumberg Janet L. • Coordinator of Bibl. Services • Seattle Public Library • Seattle, WA 98104-1193

Blume Lenore • Reference Ln./Branch Supv. • Palos Verdes Library District • Pls Vrd Pnsla, CA 90274 • PLA

Blume Scott • Hd Childrens Serv • Bellingham Public Library • Bellingham, WA 98227

Blume Shelia K. • Library Media Speicialist • Kensington Community/School Library • Kensington, KS 66951 • AASL

Blumenfeld Lea • Branch Head/Children's Librarian • Carnegie Library of Pittsburgh Hazelwood Branch • Pittsburgh, PA 15207 • ALSC EMIERT

Blumenkrantz Robert P. • Librarian I • Stockton-San Joaquin County Public Library • Stockton, CA 95202

Blumenshine Joyce M. • District Librarian • Yupiit School District • Akiachak, AK 99551-9999

Blumenstein Joan M. • Senior Librarian • Orange Public Library • Orange, CA 92666 • ALSC IRRT

Blumenthal Caroline • Reference Librarian • Georgia State University Pullen Library • Atlanta, GA 30303-3081 • ACRL RASD

Blumentritt Leetta D. • Rochester, MN 55906

Blumhardt Kathryn A. • Bridgeport, CT 06606 • AASL ACRL IFRT LIRT LRRT SRRT

Blundell Catherine • Assistant Librarian • Bodleian Library • Oxford OXI 3BG, England

Blutt Judith A. • Lombard, IL 60148

Bly Linda D. • Asst. Director for Public Servs. • Central Arkansas Library System • Little Rock, AR 72201-4698 • ALCTS LAMA PLA RASD

Bly Matthew • Computer Operations • Public Library of Charlotte & Mecklenburg County • Charlotte, NC 28202

Blythe Carolyn • Librarian • Deer Park Public Library • Deer Park, NY 11729 • LITA

Blythe Jane Merit • Reference Library • Rochester Hills Public Library • Rochester, MI 48307 • PLA RASD

Blythe Lois J. • Head, Adult Services • Burlington Public Library • Burlington, IA 52601

Boagni Thomas J. • Student • Louisiana State University School of Library & Information Science • Baton Rouge, LA 70803-3290

Boardman April • Clear Fork Elementary School • Lockhart, TX 78644 • AASL

Boardman Cynthia A. • Long Island University Palmer School of Library & Information Science • Greenvale, NY 11548

Boardman Muriel • Piedmont, CA 94611

Boardman Richard C. • Head, Map Collection • Free Library of Philadelphia • Philadelphia, PA 19103 • MAGERT

Boatman Sandra L. • Chester, VA 23831 • PLA

Boatright George S. • Circulation Librarian • Texas A & I University James C Jernigan Library • Kingsville, TX 78363

Boatright Marylynn C. • Lebanon Middle School • Lebanon, IN 46052 • YALSA VRT

Boaz Martha T. • Prof Emeritus & Dean Emeritus • Southern California University School of Library Science • Los Angeles, CA 90089-0182 • ACRL LAMA   Life

Boaz Ruth L. • Memphis, TN 38122 • AASL ASCLA   Life

Boaz Valerie J. • Student • Kent State University School of Library & Information Science • Kent, OH 44242-0001

Bobbitt Margaret S. • Hilton Head Island, SC 29928-4684 • Continuing

Bobeen Jeanette E. • Youth Services Coordinator • Sioux City Public Library • Sioux City, IA 51101-1203 • ALSC IFRT

Bobick James E. • Head, Science & Technology Div. • Carnegie Library of Pittsburgh • Pittsburgh, PA 15213-4080 • ACRL RASD

Bobinets Deborah L. • Asst. Law Libn./Circulation Svs. • University of Akron • Akron, OH 44325-1707 • ACRL ALCTS LAMA RASD GODORT

Bobinski George S. • Dean • State University of New York School of Information & Library Studies • Amherst, NY 14260 • LHRT

Bobinski Mary F. • Director • Amherst Public Library • Amherst, NY 14228

Bobo Doris A. • Media Specialist • Carole Highlands Elementary School • Takoma Park, MD 20912 • AASL

Bobo Paul D. • Associate Librarian • University of Tulsa McFarlin Library • Tulsa, OK 74104-3189

Bobowicz Stephen A. P. • Head Technical Services • Western New England College D'Amour Library • Springfield, MA 01119 • ACRL ALCTS

Bobp Mary Ellen • Senior Assistant Librarian • California State University • San Bernardino, CA 92407 • ACRL

Bobzien Barbara • Technical Services Librarian • Janesville Public Library • Janesville, WI 53545-3971 • ALCTS

Bobzin Dorothy H. • Student • University of South Florida School of Library & Information Science • Tampa, FL 33620 • AASL

Boc Noelle E. • Student • University of Texas at Austin Graduate School of Library & Information Sciences • Austin, TX 78712-1276

Bocamazo Michael F. • Middle Village, NY 11379

Bocchieri Anthony G. • Trustee • Copiague Memorial Public Library • Copiague, NY 11726 • ALTA

Bochenek Edmund L. • Dearborn, MI 48128 • ACRL

Bocher Robert F. • Automation Consultant • Wisconsin Division for Library Services • Madison, WI 53707 • LITA PLA

Boches Naomi • Young Adult Librarian • Catholic High School of Baltimore • Baltimore, MD 21213 • AASL YALSA

Bock D. Joleen Dr. • Mount Olive College Moye Library • Mount Olive, NC 28365-1699 • ACRL ALCTS *Life*

Bock Deborah E. • Johnson Free Public Library • Hackensack, NJ 07601

Bock Elizabeth • Santa Rosa, CA 95403 • LAMA PLA AFLRT FLRT IFRT *Life*

Bockman Glenda C. • Librarian • Ancilla College Gerald J. Ball Library • Donaldson, IN 46513

Bockmon Karen W. • Children's & Young Adult Ln • Phoenix Public Library • Phoenix, AZ 85004

Bockoven Francy K. • Technical Services Librarian • Glendora Public Library • Glendora, CA 91740

Bockrath D. L. • Coordinator Urban Services • Buffalo & Erie County Public Library • Buffalo, NY 14203

Bockstruck Lloyd D. • Librarian • Dallas Public Library • Dallas, TX 75201 • Life

Boctor Margaret • Librarian Cataloger • Saint Michaels College Library • Toronto ON, M5S 1J4 Canada • ACRL ALCTS

Bodak Trudy B. • Map Librarian • York University Libraries • North York ON, M3J 1P3 Canada • ACRL ALCTS MAGERT

Bodart Joni Richards Dr. • Littleton, CO 80123 • YALSA

Bodbout Melissa B. • Librarian • Mary Cheney Library • Manchester, CT 06040

Boden Dana W.R. • Subject Specialist Librarian • University of Nebraska C Y Thompson Library • Lincoln, NE 68583-0717 • ACRL LAMA LIRT LRRT NMRT

Boden Pam • Trustee • Western Plains Library System • Clinton, OK 73601

Boden Rosemary • Asst Dir-Children's Librarian • Ohio Valley District Free Public Library • Manchester, OH 45144

Bodenheimer Carol E. • Winston-salem, NC 27104 • IFRT

Bodenheimer Lisa • Monographs Cataloger • Clemson University R. M. Cooper Library • Clemson, SC 29634-3001 • ACRL ALCTS NMRT

Bodi Sonia E. • Head of Reference • North Park College & Theo Sem Consolidated Library • Chicago, IL 60625 • ACRL

Bodien Carol M. • Collections Development Ln. • Bemidji State University A. C. Clark Library • Bemidji, MN 56601-2699

Bodiford Heather H. • Orlando, FL 32812

Bodnar Janice C. • Student • Texas Woman's University School of Library & Information Studies • Denton, TX 76204 • IFRT SRRT

Bodnar Linda E. • Huntington Beach, CA 92648

Bodnar Marilyn G. • Reader Services Librarian • Pennsylvania College of Technology Learning Resources Center • Williamsport, PA 17701 • ACRL

Bodner Nancy E. • Arlington Heights Memorial Library • Arlington Heights, IL 60004-5966 • PLA RASD

Bodner Stewart • Ln III Per Sect Res Ls • New York Public Library Division P • New York, NY 10163-2240 • ALCTS

Bodo Carolyn • Tampa, FL 33618

Bodre Margaret S. • Mukilteo, WA 98275

Boe Michael K. • Minneapolis Institute of Arts • Minneapolis, MN 55404 • ACRL

Boehm J. William • California State University • Fullerton, CA 92634

Boehm Ross H. • Librarian • Sacramento City USD • Sacramento, CA 95608

Boehm Simmie R. • Library Media Specialist • Sacramento City USD • Sacramento, CA 95608

Boehme Vada • Librarian • Barton Creek Elementary-Eanes ISD • Austin, TX 78733 • AASL

Boehmer Elaine • Bremerton, WA 98310

Boehmke Mary Ann R. • Reference Librarian • University of Idaho Library • Moscow, ID 83843

Boehnen Elisabeth R. • Wisconsin Department of Health & Social Service Library • Madison, WI 53707-7925

Boehning Karen S. • Head of Collection Management • Oshkosh Public Library • Oshkosh, WI 54901 • ALCTS LAMA LITA PLA

Boehr Diane L. • Library Services Consultant • Costabile Associates Inc • Bethesda, MD 20814

Boekhoff Terri A. • Iowa City, IA 52240

Boelke Joanne H. • Reference/Instruction Librarian • Mankato State University Memorial Library • Mankato, MN 56002-8400 • ACRL LAMA

Boenders Karina M. • Manager,Computer Services • Town of Markham Public Libraries Technical Services Department • Markham Ontario, L3R 9X7 Canada • LITA

Boeringer Margaret J. • University of Arkansas at Little Rock Law Library • Little Rock, AR 72201

Boerner Nancy S. • Library Associate • Indiana University • Bloomington, IN 47405 • ACRL

Boerner Susan • Librarian • Capitol Institute of Technology Librery • Laurel, MD 20708 • LAMA

Boersma Kathrine • Superior, NE 68978

Boerth Joanne • Librarian • Forest Ridge School Library • Bellevue, WA 98006 • AASL

Boese Linda S. • Public Services Librarian I • Cuyahoga County Public Library Mayfield Regional Branch • Mayfield Village, OH 44143-2179 • ALSC IFRT

Boese Robert A. • Director • East Central Regional Library • Cambridge, MN 55008

Boesen Mary M. • Coordinator of Media Services • Highland Park High School-IMC • Highland Park, IL 60035 • AASL YALSA

Boettcher Cheryl M. • Student • University of California-Los Angeles Graduate School of Library & Information Science • Los Angeles, CA 90024-1520 • ALCTS IRRT LHRT LRRT

Boettcher Jennifer C. • Student • State University of New York School of Information & Library Sci • Albany, NY 12203 • GODORT IFRT IRRT SRRT

Boettcher Joel W. • Librarian • Lutheran High School of Kansas City • Kansas City, MO 64125 • YALSA

Boettcher Myron D. • Director of Library Services • Concordia Teachers College Link Library • Seward, NE 68434 • LITA

Bofetta Patrick K. • Flagstaff, AZ 86001

Bogage Alan • Reference Specialist • Howard County Library • Columbia, MD 21044

Bogan Mary E. • Special Collections Librarian • Emporia State University William Allen White Library • Emporia, KS 66801 • ACRL ALCTS ALSC

Bogan Ruth A. • Cook Memorial Library • Libertyville, IL 60048 • ALCTS LITA

Bogan Terri L. • Student • Pacific Christian College • Fullerton, CA 92631 • ACRL

Bogard Barbara • Volunteer • National Park Service • Seattle, WA 98112

Bogart Gary • Supervising Branch Librarian • New York Public Library • New York, NY 10016 • LAMA

Bogatz June H. • Meriden, CT 06450 • PLA

Bogeest Margaret • Bridgewater, CT 06752

Bogel Ingrid E. • Assistant Director • Conservation Center for Art & Historic Artifacts • Philadelphia, PA 19102

Bogel Roberta A. • Student • San Jose State University Division of Library & Information Science • San Jose, CA 95192-0029 • AASL ALSC PLA

Bogenschneider Duane R. • Gurnee, IL 60031

Bogey Daniel P. • Director • Clearfield County Public Library • Curwensville, PA 16833

Boggess-Korekach Nancy • Vanderbilt University Library • Nashville, TN 37240-0007 • ALCTS

Boggess Jennylind C. • System Librarian • National Institutes of Health Library • Bethesda, MD 20892 • LITA

Boggins Mel • Dir. of Placement & CE. • University of Texas at Austin Graduate School of Library & Information Sciences • Austin, TX 78712-1276 • CLENE

Boggs Virginia M. • AV Materials Specialist • Skokie Public Library • Skokie, IL 60077-3680 • ALCTS LITA

Boggus Tamara K. • Children Librarian • Cobb County Public Library System Merchant's Walk Branch • Marietta, GA 30068

Bogie Thomas M. • Dallas, TX 75214 • Continuing

Bogier Edward • Director Chief Facilities • Enoch Pratt Free Library • Baltimore, MD 21201-4484

Bogin Frederick D. • BI Librarian/Bibliographer • Brooklyn College Library • Brooklyn, NY 11210 • ACRL

Bogis Nana E. • Director • Free Public Library of Monroe Township • Williamstown, NJ 08094

Bogle Carlene M. • Chair, Public Services Dept. • Loma Linda University Del E. Webb Memorial Library • Loma Linda, CA 92350 • ACRL

Bogle Clara M. • Deputy City Librarian • Richmond Public Library • Richmond, VA 23219

Bogle Janet L. • Atlanta-Fulton Public Library Hobgood-Palmer Branch • Fairburn, GA 30213 • PLA

Bogle Myrle C. • Brazosport College Library • Lake Jackson, TX 77566 • ACRL NMRT

Bogle Robert G. • Automation Librarian • University of Texas at El Paso Library • El Paso, TX 79968-0582 • ACRL

Bognanni Kathleen • Supervising Librarian • Des Moines Public Library Franklin Avenue Branch • Des Moines, IA 50310 • PLA YALSA

Bognar Dorothy McAdoo • Head Music Librarian • University of Connecticut Cookson Music Library • Storrs, CT 06269-1153 • ACRL

Bognaski Mary L. • Librarian • Litchfield Middle School • Litchfield, NH 03051

Bogner Claudia L. • Mgr. Technical Processing Svs. • OCLC Incorporation • Dublin, OH 43017 • ALCTS

Bohachevsky Roman S. • Director • Fort Bend County Library System • Richmond, TX 77469 • LAMA PLA

Bohannan April J. • University of North Carolina at Chapel Hill School of Information and Library Science • Chapel Hill, NC 27599-3360

Bohdan Jacqueline • Librarian • Our Lady Queen of Heaven School • Lake Charles, LA 70605 • AASL

Bohl Janet • Coordinator • Broome-Delaware-Tioga BOCES School Library System • Binghamton, NY 13905-1699 • AASL

Bohlen James A. • Technical Services Administrator • El Paso Public Library • El Paso, TX 79901

Bohlen Jeanne • United States Institute of Peace • Washington, DC 20005-1708 • ACRL ALCTS LAMA LITA RASD FLRT SRRT

Bohling Raymond A. • Engineering Bibliographer • University of Minnesota Walter Library • Minneapolis, MN 55455 • ACRL LAMA *Life*

Bohman Amy Apel • Innovative Interfaces, Inc. • Berkeley, CA 94710 • LITA

Bohman Jean E. • Marathon Area Elementary School • Marathon, WI 54448 • AASL

Bohmfalk Pamela P. • Dodge City Middle School • Dodge City, KS 67801 • AASL YALSA

Bohn Melvin M. • Reference Librarian • University of Nebraska • Omaha, NE 68182 • ACRL LITA RASD

Bohn Sue-Ellen J. • Head of Copy Cataloge • Stanford University • Stanford, CA 94305-6011 • ALCTS

Bohne David R. • Director • San Leandro Library • San Leandro, CA 94577 • PLA

Bohnsack Regina • Student • Rutgers University School of Communication Information & Library Studies • New Brunswick, NJ 08903

Bohrer Clara Nalli • Director • West Bloomfield Township Public Library Public Library • W. Bloomfield, MI 48033 • ALSC LAMA PLA

Bohrer Karen M. • Head of Adult Services • Lucy Robbins Welles Library • Newington, CT 06111 • LAMA PLA RASD

Boieru Olga • Westlake, OH 44145

Boies Kay A. • Executive Director • Oklahoma Library Association • Edmond, OK 73013

Boing Frank M. • Student • University of North Carolina Department of Library & Information Studies • Greensboro, NC 27412-5001 • AASL IFRT

Boing Jessica S. • Librarian • Salem Academy Library • Winston-Salem, NC 27101

Boisse Joseph A. • Director • University of California UCSB Library • Santa Barbara, CA 93106-9010 • ACRL LAMA RASD SRRT

Boissevain Ellen V. • Arlington, VA 22203 • FLRT

Boissonnas Christian M. • Acquisitions Librarian • Cornell University Library • Ithaca, NY 14853 • ALCTS

Boissy Robert W. • Electronic Data Enterchange Spec • Faxon Company Inc. • Westwood, MA 02090 • LITA

Boisvert Marianne • Acquisitions Supervisor • Family History Library • Salt Lake City, UT 84150 • ALCTS

Bojack Elizabeth D. • Spring, TX 77379

Bojda Janice E. • Librarian • Lansing Public Library • Lansing, IL 60438 • ALSC LAMA PLA

Bokan Kathleen H. • Saratoga Springs, NY 12866

Bokelman Julee L. • Student • University of Wisconsin School of Library & Information Studies • Madison, WI 53706 • RASD IFRT LHRT

Bolas Deborah W. • Lake Oswego, OR 97034

Bolch Leona P. • Branch Manager,Librarian III • Atlanta-Fulton Public Library Alpharetta Branch • Alpharetta, GA 30201 • LAMA LITA PLA

Bold Frances Ann • Decimal Class Specialist • Library of Congress • Washington, DC 20541 • PLA YALSA IRRT

Bolden Barbara F. Mrs • Tech Serv Coordinator • Rockingham County Public Library • Eden, NC 27288 • PLA

Bolden-Marshall Valerie M. • Library Associate • Western New England College D'Amour Library • Springfield, MA 01119

Bolding Julie • Student • University of Illinois Graduate School of Library and Information Science • Urbana, IL 61801

Boldra Alice Amick • Inglewood, CA 90301 • PLA YALSA *Life*

Boldrick Samuel J. • Manager, Florida Collection • Miami-Dade Public Library System • Miami, FL 33130-1504 • RASD SRRT

Bolduc Francois • Project Manager • National Archives of Canada Informatics Branch • Ottawa, ON, K1A 0N3 Canada

Bolear Bernadette C. • Student • University of Texas at Austin Graduate School of Library & Information Sciences • Austin, TX 78712-1276

Bolef Doris • Oak Park, IL 60304 • ALTA

Bolek Ann D. • Physical Science Bibliographer • University of Akron • Akron, OH 44325-1707 • ACRL

Bolesta Susan • Administrative Librarian I • Free Library of Philadelphia • Philadelphia, PA 19103 • LAMA PLA

Bolgiano Melissa G. • Librarian • Hewitt Elementary School Library • Hewitt, TX 76643

Bolick Lynne • Reference Services Librarian • Catawba County Library • Newton, NC 28658 • RASD

Bolig David • Information Specialist/Education • Michigan State University Libraries • East Lansing, MI 48824-1048 • ACRL

Bolin Cathy D. • Fort Worth, TX 76116 • AASL

Bolin Ellen • Librarian • Saint Mary's School • New Albany, IN 47150 • AASL

Bolin Nancy • Columbia, MD 21044 • ASCLA PLA

Bolin Robert L. • Ln • University of Idaho Library • Moscow, ID 83843 • LHRT

Bolin Ruth A. • Library Director • Suffern Free Library • Suffern, NY 10901-5694

Boling Bruce D. • Principal Cataloger • University of New Mexico General Library • Albuquerque, NM 87131 • ACRL

Boling Sarah J. • Cataloging Specialist • New England School of Law Library • Boston, MA 02116 • ACRL

Bolis Christine E. • Student • Indiana University School of Library and Information Science • Bloomington, IN 47405 • AASL ALSC

Bolko Barbara A. • Librarian • McIntosh College Library • Dover, NH 03820 • ACRL

Boll Jacqueline • Reference Librarian • Fullerton College William T. Boyce Library • Fullerton, CA 92634 • ACRL

Bollati Mary T. ASCJ Sr • Librarian • Cor Jesu Academy • St Louis, MO 63123

Bollenbacher Beverly • Sweetwater Public Library • Sweetwater, TN 37874 • PLA

Bolles Charles A. • State Librarian • Idaho State Library • Boise, ID 83702 • ASCLA LAMA

Bollet Joan M. • San Jose, CA 95117 • PLA

Bollig Martha J. • Johnson Controls, Inc. • Milwaukee, WI 53202

Bolling Frances G. • Simpsonville, SC 29681

Bolling Thomas E. • Reference Librarian • University of Washington Libraries Odegaard Undergraduate Library • Seattle, WA 98195

Bollinger Dorian Martyn • Mgr.,Technical Information Res. • The Upjohn Company Technical Library • Kalamazoo, MI 49001 • ALCTS LRRT

Bollinger Mary Faith • Caldwell, ID 83605

Bollman Louise P. • Reference Librarian • King County Library System • Seattle, WA 98109-5191 • IFRT

Bollman Mary A. • Childrens Librarian • Lake Forest Library • Lake Forest, IL 60045 • ALSC

Bolluyt Linda B. • Library Director • Spirit Lake Public Library • Spirit Lake, IA 51360

Bolner Myrtle S. • Librarian • Louisiana State University Libraries Troy H. Middleton Library • Baton Rouge, LA 70803-3342 • ACRL GODORT IFRT LIRT

Bolociuch Helen • Trustee • Stickney-Forest View Library • Stickney, IL 60402 • ALTA

Bologna Patricia G. • Reference Librarian • Curry College Library • Milton, MA 02186 • ACRL

Bolotin Miriam A. • Washington Grove, MD 20880 • RASD

Bolster Kathryn • Librarian • Canterbury School Library • New Milford, CT 06776 • AASL LIRT

Bolt Janice A. • Professor • Chicago State University Department of Library Science & Communication Media • Chicago, IL 60628 • AASL ACRL ALSC

Bolt Nancy M. • Deputy State Librarian • Colorado State Library Department of Education • Denver, CO 80203 • AASL ASCLA LAMA PLA

Bolte Rebecca J. • Librarian • Seminole County Library System Central Branch • Casselberry, FL 32707

Bolte William F. • Director • Jeffersonville Township Public Library • Jeffersonville, IN 47131-1548

Boltjes Janet D. • Student • University of South Carolina College of Library & Information Science • Columbia, SC 29208 • AASL PLA

Bolton Addie • Trustee • Franklin Parish Library • Winnsboro, LA 71295 • ALTA

Bolton Mae W. • Library Services Manager • Berkeley Public Library • Berkeley, CA 94704 • ALCTS

Bolton Mary Ann F. • Director • Iowa Western Community College Learning Resource Center • Council Bluffs, IA 51502

Bolton Susan • Information Services • University of Lethbridge Library • Lethbridge AB, T1K 3M4 Canada

Boman Mary R. • Jonesboro, GA 30236 • AASL

Bomar Cora Paul • Associate Professor, Emeritus • University of North Carolina • Greensboro, NC 27412-5001 • AASL ACRL ALSC *Life*

Bomarc M. Deloris • Saint Mary's College of Maryland Library • St. Mary's City, MD 20686

Bombay Catharine Dawn • Student • University of Western Ontario School of Library & Information Science • London ON, N6G 1H1 Canada

Bomgardner Barbara-Ann • Columbus, NJ 08022 • PLA RASD *Life*

Bomhold Catharine A. • Student • University of Illinois Graduate School of Library and Information Science • Urbana, IL 61801

Bonam Robert O. • Trustee • Rochester Hills Public Library • Rochester, MI 48307 • ALTA

Bonamici Andrew R. • University of Oregon Library • Eugene, OR 97403-1299 • LAMA

Bonanno-Glose Mary P. • Student • Long Island University Palmer School of Library & Information Science • Greenvale, NY 11548 • ACRL

Bonanno Barbara A. • Assistant Librarian • Hilbert College McGrath Library • Hamburg, NY 14075 • ACRL

Bonanno Estherine C. • Public Library Director • Port Jefferson Free Library • Pt. Jefferson, NY 11777-1897 • PLA

Bonario J. Stephen • Sr. Library Assistant • University of Houston Libraries • Houston, TX 77204-2091 • ACRL LAMA NMRT

Bonaro Cynthia M. • Branch Librarian • Pierce County Library Sumner Branch • Sumner, WA 98390

Bonath Gail J. • Assistant Librarian for Tech Svs • Grinnell College • Grinnell, IA 50112-0811 • ACRL ALCTS LITA

Bonazinga Angela • Director • Brighton Memorial Library • Rochester, NY 14618 • LAMA PLA IFRT SRRT

Bond Carole J. • Director • City of Hialeah Library Division • Hialeah, FL 33012 • LAMA PLA YALSA IFRT ILERT SRRT

Bond Catherine B. • Librarian • Conestoga Senior High School • Berwyn, PA 19312 • AASL

Bond Della R. • Mill Creek, WA 98012-1245

Bond Gillian F. • Student • Dalhousie University School of Library & Inf. Studies • Halifax NS, B3H 4H8 Canada

Bond Julia W. • Ref Ln • Atlanta University Center Robert W. Woodruff Library • Atlanta, GA 30314 • ACRL RASD LRRT

Bond Kenneth E. • Trustee • Baldwin Public Library • Birmingham, MI 48012-3002

Bond Marvin A. • Chief, Info. System & Equip. • National Institute of Standards & Technology • Gaithersburg, MD 20899 • LITA FLRT

Bond Ollie P. • Librarian • Bertie County Schools • Windsor, NC 27983

Bondareff Hyla • Champaign, IL 61821

Bondi Joseph • Broadview Public Library District • Broadview, IL 60153 • ALSC

Bonds Armenda • Media Specialist • Sandy Creek High School • Tyrone, GA 30290 • AASL

Bonds Armenda L. • Media Specialist • Sandy Creek High School • Tyrone, GA 30290

Bonds Pat N. • Librarian • Zula B. Wylie Library • Cedar Hill, TX 75104 • LAMA PLA

Bonds Patricia N. • Librarian/Media Specialist • Duke Ellington School of the Arts • Washington, DC 20007 • AASL ACRL YALSA EMIERT NMRT

Bone Jennifer M. • Ch Ln • Keene Public Library • Keene, NH 03431

Boner M. Christopher • Director • Callaway Educational Association Coleman Library • La Grange, GA 30240 • ALTA LAMA LITA PLA IFRT SORT

Bonett Susan P. • Director • Trails Regional Library • Warrensburg, MO 64093 • AASL ACRL ALCTS ALSC LAMA LITA PLA RASD

Bonfili Barbara D. • Duval County Public Schools • Jacksonville, FL 32207 • AASL YALSA

Bongero Agnes A • Student • Henry Ford Hospital Library Sladen Library • Detroit, MI 48202

Bongiorno Connie M. • Student • Wayne State University Library Science Program • Detroit, MI 48202 • AASL

Bongiorno Nunzia A. • Assistant Head,Cataloging Office • The New York Public Library • New York, NY 10016

Bonhomme Mary S. • Assoc. Dir. Potter Engr. Edu. • Purdue University Libraries • West Lafayette, IN 47907

Bonifanti Georgeanne E. • Media Specialist • Manchester School • Manchester Center, VT 05255 • AASL

Bonilla Roger B. • Senior Librarian • Palo Alto City Library • Palo Alto, CA 94303

Bonin Helene B. • Assistant Serials Librarian • Central Connecticut State University Elihu Burritt Library • New Britain, CT 06050 • ACRL

Bonin Kenneth R. • Laurentian University Library • Sudbury ON, PE3 2C6 Canada • ACRL LAMA

Bonitch Yolanda • Supervising Community Specialist • New York Public Library Donnell Library Center • New York, NY 10019 • ALSC EMIERT

Bonjour Barbe M. • Director • Riverhead Free Library • Riverhead, NY 11901 • LAMA

Bonk Sharon C. • Assistant Director • State University of New York (SUNY) University Libraries • Albany, NY 12222 • ACRL ALCTS LAMA RASD

Bonnell-Kangas Nancy • Columbus Metropolitan Library • Columbus, OH 43215

Bonnell Cathy C. • Librarian • Ironwood Elementary School • Phoenix, AZ 85023 • AASL

Bonnell Claudia J. • Student • Rosary College Graduate School of Library & Information Science • River Forest, IL 60305

Bonnell Pamela Gay • Plano, TX 75024-2469 • LAMA PLA IFRT

Bonnelli Ann E. • Coor. Children's/Youth Servs. • Detroit Public Library • Detroit, MI 48202 • ALSC

Bonner Bester D. • Dir. Library Media Svs. Branch • District of Columbia Public Schools • Washington, DC 20002 • AASL

Bonner Erin G. • Librarian/Archivist • Museum of Contemporary Art • Los Angeles, CA 90012 • NMRT

Bonner Evelyn K. Dr. • Director Learning Resources • Sheldon Jackson College Library • Sitka, AK 99835 • ACRL LRRT

Bonner Melrita R. • Branch Librarian • Central Arkansas Library System Southwest Branch • Little Rock, AR 72209

Bonner Patricia • Branch Manager • Spokane Public Library Hillyard Branch • Spokane, WA 99207

Bonner Robert J. • Indianapolis, IN 46205

Bonnett Teresa • Albany, CA 94706 • YALSA

Bonnilla de Gaviria Maria C. • Director • Universidad Del Pacifico Biblioteca • Lima, 11, Peru • ACRL LAMA

Bonnin Jean F. • Conservateur • Bibliotheque Municipale • St. Etienne Ledea I, France • LITA

Bonniwell Elizabeth H. • South Carolina Department of Mental Health Crafts-Farrow State Hospital • Columbia, SC 29203

Bonsal Richard I. • Trustee • Montclair Free Public Library • Montclair, NJ 07042

Bonta Bruce D. • History/Area Studies Librarian • Pennsylvania State University Pattee Library • University Park, PA 16802 • RASD IRRT

Bonzi Dee Schwartz • Tampa, FL 33617-8358

Boocker Joan A. • Student • Wayne State University Library Science Program • Detroit, MI 48202

Booher Anita C. • Media Specialist • Park City High School • Park City, UT 84060 • AASL

Book Imogene I. • Director • Denmark Technical College Learning Resource Center • Denmark, SC 29042 • ACRL

Booker Marjorie L. Miss • Wilmington, DE 19805 • AASL YALSA *Continuing*

Booker Nell H. • Library Media Specialist • Rosebank Elementary School • Nashville, TN 37216 • AASL EMIERT LIRT

Bookless Marie T. • Plymouth, MI 48170 • PLA RASD

Boomgaarden Wesley L. • Preservation Officer • Ohio State University Libraries • Columbus, OH 43210-1286 • ACRL ALCTS

Boon Belinda • Library Director • Bastrop Public Library • Bastrop, TX 78602-0670 • PLA IFRT

Boone Beth A. • Charlotte, NC 28211 • ALCTS

Boone Blanche • Trustee • Gary Public Library • Gary, IN 46402 • ALTA

Boone Cecelia N. • Ed IV • MINITEX Lib Info Network University of Minnesota • Minneapolis, MN 55455-0414 • ALCTS LITA

Boone Diana Sue • Bellevue Public Library • Bellevue, NE 68005 • ALCTS

Boone Donna • Thorntown Public Library • Thorntown, IN 46071

Boone Jon A. • Rapid City, SD 57702 • ACRL

Boone Louise V. • Winton, NC 27986

Boone Mary L. • Training Officer • United States Information Agency (USIA) • Washington, DC 20547 • LAMA IRRT

Boone Morell D. • Dean • Eastern Michigan Univ • Ypsilanti, MI 48197 • ACRL

Boord Miller • Lynchburg, VA 24502-4238 • ACRL   *Life*

Boore Beatrice B. Mrs • Altadena, CA 91001 • ACRL PLA   *Life*

Boosinger Marcia L. • Bibliographic Instruction Librn • Auburn University Ralph Brown Draughon Library • Auburn, AL 36849-5606 • ACRL LAMA LIRT NMRT

Booth-Poor Elizabeth • Assistant Director • Bartholomew County Library Cleo Rogers Memorial Library • Columbus, IN 47201

Booth Bonnie D. • Board Member • Jacksonville Public Libraries Main Library • Jacksonville, FL 32202

Booth Judith B. • Technical Librarian • Martin Marietta Energy Systems • Oak Ridge, TN 37831 • RASD

Booth Judy E. • Reference Librarian • Newport Beach Public Library • Newport Beach, CA 92660 • PLA

Booth Maureen A. • Manager-Information Center • The Tobacco Institute • Washington, DC 20006 • LAMA LITA RASD

Booth Patricia B. • Librarian • Jay Shideler Elementary School • Topeka, KS 66610 • AASL

Booth Robert • Trustee • Chicago Heights Public Library • Chicago Heights, IL 60411 • ALTA

Booth Robert Edmund Dr • Grosse Pointe, MI 48230

Booth Vicki M. • North Vancouver BC, V7N 2P2 Canada

Boothroyd Patricia • Student • Southern Connecticut State University School of Libray Science & Instructional Technology • New Haven, CT 06515 • AASL

Boozer Ted • Business Manager • Dallas Public Library • Dallas, TX 75201 • PLA

Bopp Barbara A. • Seattle, WA 98115 • ACRL

Bopp Ginger • Toledo, OH 43606

Bopp Mary S. • Assistant Librarian • Indiana University at Bloomington University Libraries • Bloomington, IN 47405 • ACRL LIRT

Bopp Richard E. • Reference Librarian • University of Illinois Library • Urbana, IL 61801 • ACRL RASD

Boral John • Owner • Business to Business Direct • Westfield, MA 01085 • ALCTS

Borash Joan A. • Anchorage, AK 99508

Borch Kathleen • Student • University of Wisconsin-Milwaukee School of Library & Information Science • Milwaukee, WI 53201 • ALSC

Borchelt Louise • Blacksburg, VA 24060 • PLA *Continuing*

Borchert Carol Ann • Catalog Librarian • Furman University • Greenville, SC 29613-0600 • NMRT

Borchert Doris F. • Assistant Librarian • Pacific Oaks College • Pasadena, CA 91103 • SRRT

Borchuck Fred P. • Director • East Tennessee State University Sherrod Library • Johnson City, TN 37614 • ACRL

Borck Helga A. • Chief, Copy Services • New York Public Library • New York, NY 10018-2788 • ALCTS LAMA

Borck Liba • Jerusalem, Israel • ACRL

Borck Patricia A. • Head, of Public Services • Macon College Library • Macon, GA 31297

Bordeianu Sever M. • University of New Mexico General Library • Albuquerque, NM 87131 • ACRL

Bordelon Bobray J. • Business Reference Specialist • New Mexico State University Library • Las Cruces, NM 88003-0006 • RASD

Borden Joan S. • Somerset, NJ 08873 • AASL

Borden Joseph C. • West Lafayette, IN 47906 • Continuing

Borden Julie J. • Student • University of Arizona Graduate Library School • Tucson, AZ 85721

Borden Renee G. • Silver Spring, MD 20910 • AASL ALSC PLA

Borders F. Joyce • Richland County Public Library Northeast Branch • Columbia, SC 29208

Borders Florence E. • Archivist • Southern University in New Orleans Leonard S. Washington Library • New Orleans, LA 70126

Bordonaro Salvatore • Library Director • Lackawanna Public Library • Lackawanna, NY 14218

Borea Marilyn • Trustee • Minneapolis Public Library & Information Center • Minneapolis, MN 55401-1992 • ALTA PLA

Borer Alan B. • Assistant Manager • Toledo-Lucas County Public Library Sanger Branch • Toledo, OH 43606

Bores Barbara • Acquisitions Librarian • Villanova University Falvey Memorial Library • Villanova, PA 19085-1699 • ACRL

Borgeaud Michel • Gerant Managing Director • Borgeaud Bibliotheques • Montrouge Cedex, France

Borgen Denise M. • Maple Valley, WA 98038 • LITA

Borger Ruth A. • Student • San Jose State University Division of Library & Information Science • San Jose, CA 95192-0029 • LITA RASD

Borgman Betty C. • Farmington, MI 48335

Borgman Christine • Associate Professor • University of California Los Angeles Graduate School of Library & Information Science • Los Angeles, CA 90024

Borgstrom Amy • Student • Kent State University School of Library & Information Science • Kent, OH 44242-0001 • ACRL

Boria Marilyn H. • Administrative Librarian • Elmhurst Public Library • Elmhurst, IL 60126 • LAMA LITA PLA

Borin Jacqueline M. • Reference Librarian • California State University San Marcos • San Marcos, CA 92096 • ACRL

Boring Joan W. • Supervisor, Information Ref. • Middletown Public Library • Middletown, OH 45044

Borissov Michele M. • Student • Wayne State University Library Science Program • Detroit, MI 48202 • PLA

Bork Harry J. • Director • Fox Lake District Library • Fox Lake, IL 60020

Bork Suzanne M. • Kirkwood Elementary School • Coralville, IA 52241 • AASL

Borland Anne J. • Vice President • Foundation Center • New York, NY 10003 • LAMA

Borman Roberta H. • Media Specialist • Severna Park Middle School • Severna Pk, MD 21146 • AASL

Born Gerald M. • Hammond, IN 46320 • ACRL PLA   *Life*

Born Judy • Manatee Community College Library Sara Scott Harllee Library • Bradenton, FL 34206 • ACRL

Born Kathleen • Marketing Mgr., Academic Div. • EBSCO Subscription Service • Birmingham, AL 35201 • ACRL ALCTS LITA

Borne Barbara • Young Adult/Reference Librarian • Wallingford Public Library • Wallingford, CT 06492

Borne Lisa L. • Literacy Coordinator • Assumption Parish Library • Napoleonville, LA 70390 • PLA

Bornemann Cheryl • Librarian • Fond du Lac Public Library • Fond du Lac, WI 54935

Bornholdt Ruth E. • Substitute Librarian • Abington School District • Abington, PA 19001

Bornt Phyllis • Coordinator Of Branch • Schenectady County Public Library • Schenectady, NY 12305 • PLA

Borod Elizabeth A. • Director • Metropolitan Cleveland Educational Resource Center • Cleveland, OH 44134

Borowick Elaine C. • Acquisitions/Serials Librarian • Merrimack College McQuade Library • North Andover, MA 01845

Borowiec Joanna K. • Learning Center Coordinator • Polish Welfare Association Learning Center • Chicago, IL 60641 • ACRL

Borowski Joseph F. • Elgin, IL 60120

Borrego Diana • Children's Librarian • San Jose Public Library East San Jose Carnegie Library • San Jose, CA 95112

Borrelli Barbara A. • U S Tobacco • Nashville, TN 37202 • IFRT

Borrero-Saks Marisol • Project Manager • New York Public Library • New York, NY 10018 • ALCTS

Borress Lewis R. • Asst Chief Ln./Catlg. Servs. • Port Authority of NY & NJ Library • New York, NY 10048 • LITA

Borthwick Howard H. • Sun City West, AZ 85375 • Continuing

Borthwick J. Scott • Lyndhurst, OH 44124 • ACRL PLA RASD LIRT NMRT

Bortner Karen R. • Student • University of North Texas School of Library & Information Sciences • Denton, TX 76203 • YALSA IFRT

Borzumato Theresa M. • Director of Marketing • Farrar Straus Giroux Inc • New York, NY 10003 • ALSC YALSA ERT

Bos Susan K. • Cataloging Coordinator • The Upjohn Company Technical Library • Kalamazoo, MI 49001 • ALCTS

Bosca David T. • Director • American Council for the Arts Information Services • New York, NY 10022-4201 • Life

Bosch Allan W. • Kenyon College Olin Library • Gambier, OH 43022 • ACRL LAMA LITA

Bosch Stephen J. • Acquisitions Librarian • University of Arizona Library • Tucson, AZ 85721 • ALCTS

Bosco E Carole • Volunteer Librarian • Saint Andrew School Library • Clifton, NJ 07009

Boshears Onva K. Jr • Professor, Library Science • University of Southern Mississippi School of Library Science • Hattiesburg, MS 39406-5146 • ACRL ALCTS RASD

Bosley Jennifer L. • Denver, CO 80231

Bosma Patricia A. • Asst Hd Selection/Acq Section • National Library of Medicine • Bethesda, MD 20894 • ALCTS

Bosman Ellen M. • Student • Indiana University Northwest Library • Gary, IN 46408 • ACRL

Boss Jacqueline A. • Librarian • Colorado Division of Wildlife • Fort Collins, CO 80526 • ASCLA

Boss Richard W. • Senior Consultant • Information Systems Consultants Inc. • Washington, DC 20036 • ACRL ALCTS LITA PLA

Bossard Carolyn D. • Reference Librarian • Steele Memorial Library • Elmira, NY 14901-2799 • RASD

Bosscher Scott • Rose Records • Chicago, IL 60604

Bosse Maurice • Commander/Director Library Serv • Massachusetts Maritime Academy • Buzzards Bay, MA 02532

Bosseau Don L. • Director of Library • San Diego State University Library • San Diego, CA 92119-2120 • ACRL LITA

Bosshardt Margaret E. • Director • Marshall-Lyon County Library • Marshall, MN 56258 • LAMA PLA RASD

Bosshart Judith J. • Library Director • Davenport College Kalamazoo Branch Library • Kalamazoo, MI 49007 • ACRL

Bosteels Mary Jo • Children Librarian • Alameda County Library Pleasanton Branch • Pleasanton, CA 94566

Bostian Rebecca R. • Radford University John P. McConnell Library • Radford, VA 24142 • ACRL LAMA

Bostick Paula A. • Governments Documents Librarian • University of North Texas • Denton, TX 76203

Bostick Sharon • Assistant Director • University of Toledo William S. Carlson Library • Toledo, OH 43606-3399 • ACRL RASD LRRT

Bostley Jean R. Sister • Saint Joseph Central High School Library • Pittsfield, MA 01201 • AASL

Bostrom David W. • Minneapolis, MN 55417 • LITA RASD IFRT SRRT

Bostrom Laura P. • Director • Withers Memorial Public Library • Nicholasville, KY 40356 • PLA

Bostwick Dawn S. • Director • Bradford County Public Library • Starke, FL 32091

Bostwick June • Cataloger • Philadelphia College of Bible LRC • Langhorne, PA 19047-2992 • ALCTS

Bostwick Margaret G. • Catalog Librarian • University of Florida Libraries • Gainesville, FL 32611-2047 • ALCTS

Boswell Carolyn S. • Acquisitions Associate • Georgia College Ina Dillard Russell Library • Milledgeville, GA 31061 • ACRL

Boteler Jennifer L. • Boise, ID 83706 • ALSC RASD

Botero Cecilia • Librarian • University of Florida Libraries • Gainesville, FL 32611-2047 • ALCTS

Botes Doris L. • Reference Librarian • Algonquin Area Public Library District • Algonquin, IL 60102 • RASD

Botham Barbara • Children's Librarian II • Oak Park Public Library • Oak Park, IL 60301 • ALSC

Botham Jane • Coordinator of Children's Serv • Milwaukee Public Library • Milwaukee, WI 53233 • ALSC PLA SRRT

Bothwell Judith L. • Library Media Specialist • Gildersleeve School • Portland, CT 06480 • AASL

Botos Gary A. • Head of Reference Department • Kirkwood College Library • Cedar Rapids, IA 52406 • IFRT

Bott Susan M. • Student • University of Washington Graduate School of Library and Information Science • Seattle, WA 98195

Botta Jean Clancy • Dir of Correctional Lib Servs • New York State Department of Correctional Services • Albany, NY 12226 • ASCLA EMIERT SRRT

Bottaro Timothy S. • Sioux City Public Library • Sioux City, IA 51101-1203 • ALTA

Botten Mary A. • Redlands, CA 92373 • ALSC YALSA
Continuing

Bottge Lynn M. • St. Louis, MN 55416

Botto Denise E. • Acquisitions Librarian • Southern Connecticut State University Hilton C. Buley Library • New Haven, CT 06515 • ACRL ALCTS ALTA SRRT

Bottoms Laura S. • Oral Roberts University Library • Tulsa, OK 74171 • ACRL LAMA RASD LIRT

Bottoms Rita B. • Head, Special Collections • University of California-Santa Cruz Library • Santa Cruz, CA 95064 • ACRL

Botts Joy • Director • Pauline Haass Public Library • Sussex, WI 53089 • ALCTS PLA

Botuck Joan H. • Legislative Calendar Clerk • United States House of Representatives Committee on Public Works and Transportation • Washington, DC 20515

Bouboussis Nayiri • Automation Proj Ln • Berkeley Public Library • Berkeley, CA 94704 • LITA

Bouchard Celia D. • User Education/Ref Librarian • Saint Louis University Medical Center Library • St. Louis, MO 63104

Bouchard Cynthia C. • Long Beach, MS 39560-3854

Bouchard James F. • Director • Lima Public Library • Lima, OH 45801 • LAMA PLA IFRT

Bouchard Marcel A. • Canton, NY 13617

Bouche Nicole L. • University of California-Berkeley Bancroft Library • Berkeley, CA 94720 • ACRL

Boucher Janet A. • Indiana, PA 15701 • AASL

Boucher Pauline A. • Tufts University Nils Yngve Wessell Library • Medford, MA 02155 • ACRL GODORT LIRT

Boucher Teresa L. • San Mateo County Library • San Mateo, CA 94402

Boucher Virginia • Boulder, CO 80302 • ACRL RASD ILERT *Continuing*

Boudon Johanna B. • Learning Resource Specialist • Shoreline School District #412 Ridgecrest • Seattle, WA 98177

Boudreau-Gaudet Isabelle • Raymond, Chabot, Martin, Pare • Montreal PQ, H3B 4L8 Canada

Boudreau Allan • New York, NY 10012-1601 • ALTA PLA *Life*

Boudreau Barbara A. • Student • State University of New York at Albany School of Information Science & Policy • Albany, NY 12222 • PLA SRRT

Boudreau Berthe • Professor • Universite De Moncton Centre de Ressources Pedagogiques • Moncton NB, E1A 3E9 Canada • AASL

Boudreau Ingeborg • Portland, OR 97229 • ACRL LITA *Life*

Boudreau Suzanne M. • Schaumburg Township District Library • Schaumburg, IL 60194

Boudreaux Sybil A. • Reference Services Dept. • University of New Orleans Earl K. Long Library • New Orleans, LA 70148 • ACRL RASD

Boughton Lesley D. • Director • Carbon County Library • Rawlins, WY 82301 • PLA

Boula Lillian • Allegan, MI 49010-0081 • AASL LITA *Life*

Boulanger Mary E. • Reference Librarian • University of Wisconsin-Milwaukee Golda Meir Library • Milwaukee, WI 53201 • LITA RASD

Bouldin Lucy W. • Librarian • Storey County Library • Virginia City, NV 89440

Boule Suzanne E. • Branch Manager • Palm Beach County Library System Okeechobee Boulevard Branch • West Palm Beach, FL 33417 • RASD

Boultbee Paul G. • Collection Mgmt./Ref. Librarian • Red Deer College • Red Deer AB, Canada • ACRL ALCTS

Boulware Ann M. • Personnel Director • New Orleans Public Library • New Orleans, LA 70140

Bouma Ray H. • Villa Park, IL 60181 • AASL

Bounds Nancy Boykin • Head of Cataloging • Sam Houston State University Newton Gresham Library • Huntsville, TX 77341-2281

Bourbeau Ann M. • Co-Director • Springfield City Library • Springfield, MA 01103 • PLA

Bourbulas Helen • Director of Media Center • Oak Lawn Community High School • Oak Lawn, IL 60453 • AASL

Bourdon Cathleen • ACRL Deputy Exec. Director • American Library Association • Chicago, IL 60611-2795 • ACRL

Bourdon Lisa A. • Supv. Sci. & Bus. Services • Miles Inc. Science & Business Information Services • Elkhart, IN 46515 • ACRL LITA

Bourgault Jean-Daniel • Montreal PQ, H4A 2L8 Canada • PLA

Bourgeois Cornell J. • Trustee • Ascension Parish Library • Donaldsonville, LA 70346-2535 • ALTA PLA

Bourgeois Joann • Trustee • West Baton Rouge Parish Library • Port Allen, LA 70767

Bourgeois June K. • First Assistant • Houston Public Library Montrose Branch • Houston, TX 77002

Bourgo Jerrie L. • Kirkwood College Library • Cedar Rapids, IA 52406

Bourke Dorothea L. • Student • Clark-Atlanta University School of Library & Information Studies • Atlanta, GA 30314-4391 • SRRT

Bourke Jacqueline K. • Germantown, TN 38138

Bourke Samuel C. • Supervisor Librarian • Camp Walker Library • APO San Francisco, CA 96218-0074 • ALSC LAMA LITA PLA RASD AFLRT FLRT

Bourke Thomas A. • Chief Microforms Division • New York Public Library • New York, NY 10018-2788 • ALCTS LITA

Bourne Frances T. • Venice Area Public Library • Venice, FL 34285

Bourne Sarah E. • Librarian • Commonwealth of Massachusetts Office of Management Information Systems Library • Boston, MA 01801

Bourne Sheila • North Carolina Central University Law Library • Durham, NC 27707

Bourque Barbara J. • Student • Southern Connecticut State University School of Libray Science & Instructional Technology • New Haven, CT 06515

Bourque Gail E. • Principal Librarian • Ocean County Library Point Pleasant Beach Library • Point Pleasant Beach, NJ 08742

Bourrie Sharon D. • Student • Rutgers University School of Communication Information & Library Studies • New Brunswick, NJ 08903

Bourrie Susan E. • Student • University of Michigan School of Information and Library Studies • Ann Arbor, MI 48109-1092 • ALSC

Bousfield Brenda Lee • Syracuse University Library E. S. Bird Library • Syracuse, NY 13244-2010 • ACRL

Bouthillier Mary M. • School Media Specialist • Plainfield High School Library • Central Village, CT 06332 • AASL YALSA

Boutilier Carol • Mount Olive Public Library • Budd Lake, NJ 07828 • PLA

Bovarnick Esther W. • Reader Services Librarian • United States Merchant Marine Academy • Kings Point, NY 11024-1699 • ACRL

Bovee Dena K. • Dublin, OH 43017

Bovino Jana K. • Reference Libraian • Downers Grove Public Library • Downers Grove, IL 60515 • IFRT NMRT

Bovy Karen A. • Minneapolis, MN 55410 • AASL EMIERT

Bow Judith W. • Head, Talking Book Program • Ohio State Library • Colubus, OH 43266-0334 • ASCLA

Bowden Ann Dr. • Austin, TX 78703-1040 • ACRL

Bowden Delores M. • Librarian • Moxee Community Library • Moxee, WA 98936

Bowden Jim M. • Carmel, IN 46033 • ALCTS GODORT

Bowden John M. • Southwest State University • Marshall, MN 56258

Bowden Linda F. • Doniphan, NE 68832 • ACRL

Bowden Michael L. • Richmond, IN 47375-2534 • ACRL LITA RASD SRRT

Bowden Philip L. • DeVry Institute of Technology • Lombard, IL 60148 • ACRL

Bowden Virginia M. • Library Director • University of Texas Health Science Center Briscoe Library • San Antonio, TX 78284-7940 • ACRL LAMA LRRT

Bowdoin Anne C. • Circulation Librarian • Plymouth Public Library • Plymouth, MA 02360

Bowdoin Sally • Librarian/Catlaoger • Brooklyn College Library • Brooklyn, NY 11210

Bowell Daniel J. • Director of the Library • King College Library • Bristol, TN 37620 • ACRL ALCTS LITA RASD

Bowen Carolyn F. • Reference Librarian • University of Georgia Libraries • Athens, GA 30602 • ACRL RASD

Bowen Christopher F. • Library Director • Downers Grove Public Library • Downers Grove, IL 60515 • LAMA PLA IFRT LRRT SRRT

Bowen Cynthia W. • Baytown, TX 77520 • RASD

Bowen Dorothy N. Dr. • Wilmore, KY 40390-1108 • ACRL IRRT

Bowen Ellen C. • Stamford, CT 06905

Bowen Emily • Trustee • Westminster Public Library • Westminster, CO 80030-4970

Bowen Jennifer B. • Assoc. Head of Tech. Services • Eastman School of Music Sibley Music Library • Rochester, NY 14604 • ALCTS LITA

Bowen Johanna E. • Ser Ln • State University of New York College at Cortland • Cortland, NY 13045 • ALCTS LITA

Bowen Joy S. • Bethesda, MD 20817

Bowen Kay • Sales Support • Geac Computers, Ltd. • Markham ON, L3R 4T5 Canada • LITA

Bowen Kay A. • Childrens Librarian • Wayne County Public Library • Wooster, OH 44691 • ALSC

Bowen Kristie G. • Pagosa Springs, CO 81147

Bowen Louise E. • Doerun, GA 31744 • AASL

Bowen Mary E. • Falls Church, VA 22043 • RASD

Bowen Melissa D. • Florence, SC 29501 • PLA

Bowen Rebecca L. • Cupertino, CA 95014 • IFRT LHRT SRRT

Bower Janet L. • Denver, CO 80227-3244

Bower Jim • Foundation Advisor • Marketing/Communications • Gilroy, CA 95020 • PLA

Bower Merry D. • Nonbook Catlgr • Kansas State University Farrell Library • Manhattan, KS 66506-1200

Bower Rachel E. • Librarian/Cataloger • Fairmont State College Library • Fairmont, WV 26554

Bower Shirley N. • Student • University of Tennessee-Knoxville Graduate School of Library & Information Science • Knoxville, TN 37996-4330

Bower Wayne E. • Associate Director • Albuquerque Public Library • Albuquerque, NM 87102 • ALCTS LITA PLA

Bowers Averill A. Ms. • Grand Junction, CO 81503 • IFRT

Bowers Doris Ms. • Murrysville, PA 15668 • ACRL LAMA LITA

Bowers Elizabeth A. • Librarian • Weld County Library District • Greeley, CO 80631

Bowers Herbert E. • Waleska, GA 30183-9780 • ALCTS LITA *Life*

Bowers Karen A. • Stafford, VA 22554 • PLA

Bowers Kathryn A. • Cataloger • Library of Congress, Motion Picture Broadcast & Recorded Sound Division • Washington, DC 20541

Bowers Linda S. • Nashville, TN 37214 • AASL ALSC

Bowers Lois M. • Bonita Spring, FL 33923

Bowers Nancy S. • Research Librarian • Nevada Legislative Counsel Bureau • Carson City, NV 89710

Bowers Patti L. • University of North Carolina Department of Library & Information Studies • Greensboro, NC 27412-5001

Bowers Tamara L. • Central School Napoleon City School • Napoleon, OH 43545 • AASL

Bowers Thermutis T. • Cleveland Heights, OH 44118

Bowers Virginia • Muleshoe Independent School District Dillman Elementary School • Muleshoe, TX 79347 • AASL

Bowersox Kathlyn A. • University of Nebraska-Lincoln University Libraries • Lincoln, NE 68588-0410

Bowie Cathryn E. • Houston, TX 77008

Bowie Claire D. • New York, NY 10003 • Continuing

Bowie Melvin M. • Associate Professor • University of Georgia Department of Instructional Technolgy • Athens, GA 30602 • AASL

Bowie Shirley • Library Officer • Socorro High School Bill Sybert Library • El Paso, TX 79927 • AASL

Bowker Sara • Technical Information Analyst • Nissan Research & Development, Inc. • Farmington Hill, MI 48333-9200 • LITA

Bowles Carol A. • Technical Services Librarian • San Mateo County Library • San Mateo, CA 94402 • ALCTS LITA

Bowles Gladys M. Miss • Spokane, WA 99204 • PLA RASD *Continuing*

Bowles Karen S. • Associate Director • Stratford Library Association • Stratford, CT 06497 • LAMA

Bowles Suzanne • Librarian • Grand Ledge Public Library • Grand Ledge, MI 48837 • LAMA PLA

Bowlgy Barbara J. • Student • Columbia University Library Service Library • New York, NY 10027 • RASD IFRT

Bowling Barbara L. • School Library Media Specialist • Crump Elementary School • Montgomery, AL 36116 • AASL

Bowling Carol L. • Head Librarian • Lane Public Library • Hamilton, OH 45011 • PLA RASD

Bowling Kathleen • Librarian • Anchorage Public Schools • Anchorage, KY 40223 • AASL

Bowman A. Louise • Blacksburg, VA 24060 • Continuing

Bowman Barbara E. • Student • Emporia State University School of Library & Information Management • Emporia, KS 66801 • ALCTS LITA RASD

Bowman Bonita F. • Student • Concord College Library • Athens, WV 24712

Bowman Cheryl K. • Librarian • Upper Sandusky Middle School • Upper Sandusky, OH 43351 • ALSC

Bowman Elizabeth • Librarian • Millbrook School • Millbrook, NY 12545

Bowman James R. • Elementary Librarian • Enfield Public Schools Bd of Educ/Business Office/Admn Bldg • Enfield, CT 06082 • AASL

Bowman James R. • Library of Congress • Washington, DC 20541 • Life

Bowman Jane B. • West Milford, WV 26451 • ALSC ASCLA *Life*

Bowman Jean O. • Librarian,Traveling Library • King County Library System • Seattle, WA 98109 • ASCLA PLA

Bowman Joan H. • Children's/Assisstnat Branch • Bucks County Free Library Bensalem Branch • Bensalem, PA 19020

Bowman Kathleen A. • Middle/Upper School Librarian • The Linfield School • Temecula, CA 92592 • AASL YALSA

Bowman Leslie Ann • Head Technical Services • Philadelphia College of Pharmacy & Science-Joseph W. England Library • Philadelphia, PA 19104-4491 • ACRL ALCTS

Bowman Mark • Head of Cataloging Services • North Dakota State Library • Bismarck, ND 58505 • ALCTS NMRT

Bowman Martha A. • Director of Libraries • University of Missouri Libraries-Columbia Elmer Ellis Library • Columbia, MO 65201-5149 • ACRL ALCTS LAMA

Bowman Mary • Head of Acquisitions • DePaul University Libraries • Chicago, IL 60614 • ALCTS

Bowman Mary Ellen • Supv. Librarian/Adult Services • Yorba Linda Public Library • Yorba Linda, CA 92686

Bowman Mary Lynn • Student • University of Oklahoma School of Library & Information Studies • Norman, OK 73019 • ALCTS NMRT

Bowman Michael S. • Portland State University Library • Portland, OR 97207 • LITA RASD

Bowman Nancy G. • Greensboro, NC 27405 • AASL

Bowman Phyllis M. • Pikes Peak Library District • Colorado Springs, CO 80901-1579

Bowman Robert M. • Reference Librarian • King County Library System • Seattle, WA 98109-5191 • PLA RASD NMRT

Bowra Richard A. • Director • Dauphin County Library System • Harrisburg, PA 17101 • PLA

Bowser Anita • Trustee • Michigan City Public Library • Michigan City, IN 46360 • ALTA
Bowser Susan L. • Elizabethtwn, PA 17022 • ALSC PLA
Box Florence O. • Librarian • Starkville High School • Starkville, MS 39759 • AASL YALSA
Box Susan C. • Bartlesville, OK 74006
Boyadjian Ani • Glendale Public Library • Glendale, CA 91205
Boyajian Joanne G. • Librarian • Ontario City Library • Ontario, CA 91764
Boyarski Jennie • Director of Library Services • Paducah Community College Library • Paducah, KY 42002-7380 • ACRL
Boyarsky Karen R. • Beverly Hills High School Library • Beverly Hills, CA 90212
Boyce Ann • Young Adult/Children • Weber County Library Southwest Branch • Roy, UT 84067-2696 • YALSA
Boyce Barbara S. • Associate Librarian • Tufts University-Fletcher School of Law & Diplomacy • Medford, MA 02155-7082 • ACRL LAMA IRRT
Boyce Bert R. Dr • Professor & Dean • Louisiana State University School of Library & Information Science • Baton Rouge, LA 70803-3290
Boyce Emily S. • Professor • East Carolina University Department of Library & Information Studies • Greenville, NC 27858-4353 • AASL LITA
Boyce Harold W. Dr • Administrator • Eastern Indiana ALSA • Anderson, IN 46016-2701
Boyce Judy I. • Baton Rouge, LA 70808 • ALTA PLA RASD YALSA
Boyce Linda Neal • College of William & Mary • Williamsburg, VA 23185 • AASL ALSC LIRT
Boyce Lois B. • Cherry Hill High School West • Cherry Hill, NJ 08002 • AASL
Boychuk Elaine K. • Associate Librarian • Dalhousie University Library • Halifax NS, Canada • ACRL ALCTS LAMA LITA
Boyd Alan D. • Head of Cataloging & Libr. Sys. • Oberlin College Library • Oberlin, OH 44074 • ACRL LITA
Boyd Alex • Director • Newark Public Library • Newark, NJ 07101-0630 • LAMA PLA
Boyd Barbara Gray • Bremerton, WA 98310 • Continuing
Boyd Betty J. • Library Director • York High School Library • Elmhurst, IL 60126 • AASL
Boyd Charles H. • Assistant Director • Tulsa Junior College • Tulsa, OK 74119 • ACRL LIRT
Boyd J. L. III Dr. • Head Librarian • Trinity Valley School Library • Fort Worth, TX 76133
Boyd Janet E N • Pkepin, WI 54759-0377 • AASL ALSC *Life*
Boyd John • Assist. Librarian • Watterson College • Louisville, KY 40218
Boyd John D. • Student • Kent State University School of Library & Information Science • Kent, OH 44242-0001
Boyd Joseph D. • Student • University of British Columbia School of Library, Archival & Information Studies • Vancouver BC, V6T 1Z1 Canada • SRRT
Boyd Joseph W. • Albert Whitman & Company • Morton Grove, IL 60053-2723 • AASL ALSC ERT
Boyd Julia G. • Director • Upper Cumberland Regional Library • Cookeville, TN 38501 • PLA
Boyd Kathryn E. • Student • University of Illinois Graduate School of Library and Information Science • Urbana, IL 61801 • IFRT
Boyd Kenneth A. • Director of Instr Media Center • Asbury Theological Seminary B. L. Fisher Library • Wilmore, KY 40390 • ACRL LITA
Boyd Kristi L. • Coordinator of Technical Servs. • Alexandrian Public Library • Mount Vernon, IN 47620 • PLA
Boyd Lee E. • Whitehall Public Library • Pittsburgh, PA 15236
Boyd Lisa M. • Studrnt-Ph. D. in African Amer. • University of Maryland • Baltimore, MD 21228 • ACRL
Boyd Lori • Lovett School • Atlanta, GA 30327 • AASL
Boyd Margaret M. • Central Federal Services Inc. • Reston, VA 22091 • LAMA LITA PLA RASD
Boyd Marie • Principal Librarian • Upland Public Library • Upland, CA 91786
Boyd Marilyn G. • North Hollywood, CA 91606-1311 • ALSC
Boyd Mary A. • Easley, SC 29642
Boyd Maurice • Washington, DC 20024 • IFRT
Boyd Pat • Media Specialist • West End Elementary School • Midgeville, GA 31061
Boyd Ronald E. • Dallas, TX 75209
Boyd Ruth E. • Special Collections Consultant • Denver Public Library • Denver, CO 80204-2602
Boyd Sandra E. • Missippi Department of Archives & History • Jackson, MS 39205-0571 • RASD
Boyd Susan H. • Assistant Director • Vail Public Library • Vail, CO 81657 • LITA
Boyd Sylvia A. • Head, Reference Department • Bridgeport Public Library • Bridgeport, CT 06604
Boyd Virginia • Brunswick, GA 31520-5101
Boyd William A. • Assistant Professor • Clark-Atlanta University School of Library & Information Studies • Atlanta, GA 30314-4391 • LITA
Boyd William D. • Associate Professor • University of Southern Mississippi School of Library Science • Hattiesburg, MS 39406-5146 • ALCTS LHRT LRRT
Boydston Jeanne M. K. • Asst. Prof./Serials Catlgr. • Iowa State University Library • Ames, IA 50011-2140 • ALCTS
Boye Inger • Zephyr Cove, NV 89448-3816 • Continuing
Boyer Anita • Head of Technical Services • Alsip-Merrionette Park Library District • Alsip, IL 60658 • ALCTS PLA
Boyer Calvin J. Dr. • University of California-Irvine Library • Irvine, CA 92713 • ACRL LAMA
Boyer Dona A. • Director • Kent Public Library • Carmel, NY 10512 • PLA
Boyer Ellen M. • Librarian • Circle High School Library • Towanda, KS 67144 • AASL YALSA
Boyer Harold N. • Library Director • Marple Public Library • Broomall, PA 19008
Boyer Janice S. • Asst Dir for Administrative Serv • University of Nebraska at Omaha University Library • Omaha, NE 68182-0237 • ACRL
Boyer Karen S. • New Lenox, IL 60451 • IFRT
Boyer Kathenne G. • Librarian • Conewago Township Elementary School • Hanover, PA 17331 • AASL
Boyer Laura M. • Reference Librarian • California State Univ Stanislaus • Turlock, CA 95380 • ACRL RASD
Boyer Lois • Librarian • Barkley Elementary • Phoenixville, PA 19460 • AASL
Boyer Philip E. • Manager, Library Systems • Washington State University • Pullman, WA 99164-1230 • LITA
Boyer Robert E. • Coord Support Services • Nicholson Memorial Library • Garland, TX 75040-6365 • ALCTS LAMA LITA PLA GODORT IFRT
Boyer Ruth R. • University of California-Irvine Library • Irvine, CA 92713 • ACRL ALCTS LITA IRRT
Boyer Yvonne • Vanderbilt University Library • Nashville, TN 37240-0007
Boyes Laura K. • King County Library System Shoreline Branch • Seattle, WA 98155
Boykin Dianne C. • Student • Charleston Southern University L Mendel Rivers Library • Charleston, SC 29411
Boykin Joseph F. • Director of Libraries • Clemson University Robert Muldrow Cooper Library • Clemson, SC 29634-3001 • ACRL LAMA LITA
Boykin Laura H. • Montgomery County Library System • Conroe, TX 77301
Boykin Lucile A. • Dallas, TX 75231 • Continuing
Boykin Myrtle I. • Librarian • San Francisco Unified Schools • San Francisco, CA 94102 • AASL YALSA
Boykin Sally C. • Librarian • Benedictine High School • Richmond, VA 23221 • AASL LIRT
Boylan Lorena A. • Director of Library Services • Saint Charles Borromeo Seminary Ryan Memorial Library • Overbrook, PA 19096-3012 • ACRL LAMA
Boylan Maryanne • Student • University of Michigan School of Information and Library Studies • Ann Arbor, MI 48109-1092 • SRRT
Boylan Ray P. • Center for Research Libraries • Chicago, IL 60637 • ACRL ALCTS
Boyle Brendan W. • New York Public Library Todt Hill-Westerleigh Branch • Staten Island, NY 10314
Boyle Helen D. • Sales Rep Ulverscroft/Charnwood • Large Print Books • Guilford, CT 06437 • PLA
Boyle Jeanne • Palos Heights Public Library • Palos Heights, IL 60463
Boyle Jeanne E. • Rutgers University Libraries Library of Science & Medicine • Piscataway, NJ 08855-1029 • ACRL LAMA GODORT
Boyle Lawrence C. • Reference Librarian • Franklin Park Public Library District • Franklin Park, IL 60131 • PLA RASD
Boyle Thomas E. • Library Director • Midland Lutheran College • Fremont, NE 68025 • ACRL
Boylen Kathryn L. • Troy, NY 12180 • AASL
Boyles Emily D. • San Francisco Public Library Catalog Department • San Francisco, CA 94102
Boyles Linda • Hq. Patron Services Coor. • Alachua County Library District • Gainesville, FL 32601 • ALSC PLA
Boylls Virginia W. • Branch Manager • San Diego Public Library University Community Branch • San Diego, CA 92122 • ALSC PLA
Boylston Robert Mrs • Trustee • Manatee County Public Library System • Bradenton, FL 34205
Boyse Carol D. • Systems Educator • New Mexico State University Library • Las Cruces, NM 88003-0006 • ACRL LITA
Boyvey Mary R. Dr • Austin, TX 78731 • Continuing
Boze Andy D. • PC/LAN Coordinator • University of Notre Dame Libraries • Notre Dame, IN 46556 • LITA
Bozeman Patricia • Head Special Collections • University of Houston Libraries • Houston, TX 77204-2091 • ACRL
Bozich Stephen J. • Baker & Taylor • Momence, IL 60954
Bozman Barbara • Children's Librarian • Los Angeles Public Library Will & Ariel Durant Branch • Los Angeles, CA 90046 • SRRT
Bozone Billie R. • Amherst, MA 01002
Braby Ellen J. • Librarian • Santa Monica Public Library • Santa Monica, CA 90401 • ALSC
Brace Debra A. • Student • Louisiana State University School of Library & Information Science • Baton Rouge, LA 70803-3290
Brace Joyce • Librarian • Toll Junior High School • Glendale, CA 91202 • AASL
Brace William • Associate Professor • Rosary College Graduate School of Library & Information Science • River Forest, IL 60305 • ACRL RASD *Life*
Bracewell E. Ellen • Smyrna, GA 30080 • ALSC PLA YALSA
Bracewell R Grant • Librarian • Emmanuel College • Toronto ON, M5S 1K7 Canada • ACRL LITA
Brachfeld Laura B. • Student • Rutgers University School of Communication Information & Library Studies • New Brunswick, NJ 08903
Brachmann Kathleen A. • Dunedin Public Library • Dunedin, FL 34698-7998 • PLA
Brack Lillie Henderson • Coordinator of Reference Servs • Kansas City Public Library • Kansas City, MO 64106 • RASD GODORT
Brackeen Elizabeth L. • Student • University of North Texas School of Library & Information Sciences • Denton, TX 76203 • SRRT
Brackin C. Lynn • Student • University of North Carolina Walter Clinton Jackson Library • Greensboro, NC 27412-5201
Brackins Betty J. • Librarian • Baton Rouge Magnet High School • Baton Rouge, LA 70806
Brackwinkle Hilda L. • Flagler Beach, FL 32136 • Continuing
Bracy Pauletta B. • Associate Porfessor • North Carolina Central University School of Library & Information Science • Durham, NC 27707 • AASL IFRT
Bradbeer Gayle E. • Student • Emporia State University School of Library & Information Management • Emporia, KS 66801 • LITA RASD
Bradberry Richard • Library Director • Delaware State College William C. Jason Library • Dover, DE 19901 • ACRL
Bradburn Frances B. • Assistant Prof.of Media & Tech. • East Carolina University Joyner Library • Greenville, NC 27858-4353 • ALSC YALSA
Bradburn Teri C. • Overland, MO 63114 • ACRL PLA
Bradbury Corinne L. • Technical Services Supervisor • City of Commerce Public Library • Commerce, CA 90040 • ALCTS
Bradbury Daniel J. • Director • Kansas City Public Library • Kansas City, MO 64106 • LAMA PLA
Bradbury Jobeth • Kansas City Kansas Public Library West Wyandotte Branch • Kansas City, KS 66112
Bradbury John F. • Decatur, IL 62526 • AASL ALSC *Life*
Bradbury Kathleen G. • Media Department Manager • Fort Worth Public Library • Fort Worth, TX 76102
Bradbury Lisa • New Brunswick, NJ 08901 • PLA
Bradbury Phil • Library Educational Institute, Inc. • New Albany, PA 18833
Braddock Donna L. • Director • Corbit-Calloway Memorial Library • Odessa, DE 19730
Braddock Jean H. • Student • University of Alabama School of Library & Information Studies • Tuscaloosa, AL 35487-0252
Brademas John Hon • President • New York University • New York, NY 10036 • AASL ACRL ALCTS ALSC ALTA ASCLA LAMA LITA PLA RASD YALSA *Honorary*
Braden Margaret Kelly • Supervisor • Allen County Public Library Aboite Branch • Fort Wayne, IN 46804 • PLA
Braden Mark E. • Librarian • Occidental College Library • Los Angeles, CA 90041
Bradfield Marjorie A. • Detroit, MI 48238 • Continuing
Bradford Barry D. • New Orleans, LA 70124 • PLA NMRT
Bradford Daniel L. • Washington, DC 20032
Bradford Daniel R. • Emporia State University School of Library & Information Management • Emporia, KS 66801 • PLA
Bradford J Edward • Wood Haven, NY 11421 • ACRL ALCTS LITA *Life*
Bradford Jane T. • Reference Librarian • Stetson University DuPont-Ball Library • De Land, FL 32720-3769 • ACRL IFRT IRRT LHRT

Bradford John P. • Indian Prairie Public Library District • Willowbrook, IL 60517 • PLA RASD
Bradford Liz • Dallas, TX 75244
Bradford Maureen • Fort Worth, TX 76133
Bradfute Rachelle H. • Student • University of Michigan School of Information and Library Studies • Ann Arbor, MI 48109-1092
Bradigan Pamela S. • Head of Reference Services • Ohio State University Health Sciences Library • Columbus, OH 43210 • ACRL RASD
Bradleigh Simone M. • ILL Librarian • El Camino Hospital Library • Mountain View, CA 94039-7025
Bradley Ann E. • Cape Coral, FL 33904 • ALSC PLA RASD
Bradley Betsy A. • District Librarian • Southeast Island School District • Ketchikan, AK 99901
Bradley Bruce E. • Linda Hall Library • Kansas City, MO 64110 • ACRL
Bradley C. Diane • Social Science Reference Libn. • Auburn University Ralph Brown Draughon Library • Auburn, AL 36849-5606 • ACRL
Bradley Colleen P. • Student • University of South Carolina College of Library & Information Science • Columbia, SC 29208
Bradley Darlene L. • Temple City, CA 91780
Bradley Doreen R. • Redford, MI 48239 • IFRT SRRT
Bradley Doris A. • Serials Catalog Librarian • University of North Carolina at Charlotte J. Murrey Atkins Library • Charlotte, NC 28223 • ACRL ALCTS LITA
Bradley Florene J. • Director • Columbia-Lafayette Ouachita Calhoun Regional Library • Magnolia, AR 71753 • LAMA PLA
Bradley Heather L. • Newbury Elementary School • Newbury, OH 44065 • Life
Bradley Jan • Far Eastern Economic Review Library • Hong Kong, Hong Kong
Bradley Jan • Librarian II • Clearwater Public Library • Clearwater, FL 34623
Bradley Janice R. • Hd, Extended Campus Library Svs. • Washington State University Library • Pullman, WA 99164-5610 • ACRL
Bradley Jannette • Ref./Technical Services Libn. • College of Saint Francis Library Science Program • Joliet, IL 60435
Bradley Joan L. • Librarian • John F. Kennedy High School • Somers, NY 10589
Bradley Judith • Student • Wayne State University Library Science Program • Detroit, MI 48202
Bradley Kate • Acquisitions Librarian • Bellevue Community College • Bellevue, WA 98007
Bradley Larry C. • Director • Fort Scott Cmnty College • Fort Scott, KS 66701 • ACRL LITA
Bradley Linda K. • Indiana, PA 15701
Bradley Lynn H. • Media Specialist • Eastside Elementary School • Douglasville, GA 30134
Bradley M. B. • Acquisitions Supervisor • Denver Public Library • Denver, CO 80204-2602
Bradley Melissa K. • Cypress, CA 90630
Bradley Murray L. • Naval Research Laboratory • Washington, DC 20375 • ACRL
Bradley Pamela T. • Student • University of Alabama School of Library & Information Studies • Tuscaloosa, AL 35487-0252 • AASL
Bradley Peggy I. • Library Director • Howe Community Library • Howe, TX 75059 • AASL PLA
Bradley Ruth B. • Librarian • Hialeah High School Library • Hialeah, FL 33013 • AASL YALSA *Life*
Bradley Ruth T. • Ch Ln • Harvey Public Library • Harvey, IL 60426
Bradley Susanne A. • USD-333 Junior Senior High School • Concordia, KS 66901 • AASL YALSA
Bradley Theora • Trustee • Portsmouth Public Library • Portsmouth, OH 45662
Bradley Violet • Trustee • Bridgeview Public Library • Bridgeview, IL 60455 • ALTA
Bradner Margaret • Foxboro, MA 02035
Bradshaw Ann • Dallas, TX 75208 • ALCTS IFRT
Bradshaw Deloris • Librarian • South Aiken High School • Aiken, SC 29801 • AASL
Bradshaw Graham S. • Hist & Medieval Book Selector • University of Toronto Robarts Library • Toronto ON, Canada • ACRL
Bradshaw James R. • Technical Services Librarian • Morningside College Library • Sioux City, IA 51106 • ALCTS IFRT
Bradshaw Lillian M. • Dallas, TX 75214 • Continuing
Bradshaw Martha G. • Rockledge, FL 32955
Bradshaw Patricia E. • Yucca Valley, CA 92284
Bradsher Charles A. • Student • University of South Carolina College of Library & Information Science • Columbia, SC 29208
Bradt Elizabeth • Reno, NV 89509 • PLA RASD
Bradt Kathleen R. • Associate Director • Baker University Library • Baldwin, KS 66006 • ACRL ALCTS RASD LIRT
Bradway Paula S. • Ely, IA 52227 • AASL
Bradwell Carol S. • Chief, Catalog Division • District of Columbia Public Library Martin Luther King Memorial Library • Washington, DC 20001 • ALCTS
Brady Ben • Director • Ouachita Parish Public Library • Monroe, LA 71201 • ALSC PLA
Brady Betty Ann • Children's Librarian • Orange County Library System East Orange Branch • Orlando, FL 32807 • ALSC
Brady Christopher P. • Student • Middlebury College • Middlebury, VT 05753-6062
Brady David • Trustee • Bedford Park Public Library District • Bedford Park, IL 60501 • PLA
Brady Dianne C. • Head of Children's Services • East Baton Rouge Parish Library • Baton Rouge, LA 70806-7699
Brady Eileen • Reference Librarian • University of North Florida Library Science Program • Jacksonville, FL 32216
Brady Jean S. • Librarian II • Yale University Sterling Memorial Library • New Haven, CT 06520 • ACRL ALCTS CLENE
Brady Josiah B. • Collection Development Mgr. • El Paso Public Library • El Paso, TX 79901
Brady Julia A. • Librarian • Bensenville Community Public Library • Bensenville, IL 60106 • ALSC
Brady Lila • Rockford, IL 61107
Brady Lynn A. • Dobbs Ferry, NY 10522
Brady Marie T. • Dir. Library/Media Department • Arlington Public Schools • Arlington, MA 02174 • AASL
Brady Mary C. • West Nyack Free Library • West Nyack, NY 10994 • RASD
Brady Mary M. • Librarian/Director • Boerne Public Library • Boerne, TX 78006 • PLA
Brady Mary T. • New York, NY 10028
Brady Patricia A. • San Francisco, CA 94109
Brady Susan • Yale University Sterling Memorial Library • New Haven, CT 06520 • ACRL
Brady Thelma I. • Media Center Specialist • Olney Public School • Coalgate, OK 74538 • NMRT
Braeckel Kathleen • Evergreen, CO 80439 • LITA
Braga Maria T. • Newark, NJ 07104
Bragg Alethea • Head Arlington Branch Librarian • Memphis-Shelby County Public Library Arlington Branch • Arlington, TN 38002 • PLA
Bragg Mary Jane • Fullerton, CA 92631 • Continuing
Bragg Teresa C. • Malheur County Library • Ontario, OR 97914 • LAMA PLA
Braglia Nancy L. • Youth Services Librarian • Rochester Hills Public Library • Rochester, MI 48307 • ALSC
Brahm Walter T. • Dublin, OH 43017 • Continuing
Brahme Maria E.I • Automation/Systems • Auto-Graphics Incorporation • Pomona, CA 91768
Braid James Andrew • British Library Document Supply Center • West Yorkshire, England • LITA
Braigen Milla B. • Asst Ed Applied Sci & Tech • H. W. Wilson Company • Bronx, NY 10452 • ACRL
Brainard Blair A. • Reference Librarian • Radford University John P. McConnell Library • Radford, VA 24142 • ACRL LIRT
Brainard Elsie • Director • Truro Public Library • North Truro, MA 02652
Braine Nghei F. • Mobile, AL 36608
Brake Thomas W. • Charlotte, NC 28211
Brakel Lisa E. • Student • Indiana University School of Library and Information Science • Bloomington, IN 47405 • NMRT
Braley Barbara M. • Head Librarian • Grafton Public Library • Grafton, MA 01519 • PLA
Bram Leon L. Mr. • Funk & Wagnalls Corporation • Mahwah, NJ 07495-0017 • Subscribing
Bramble Laura E. • Director • Washington Township Public Library • Plainfield, IN 46168 • PLA
Bramblett Scott A. • Lake Lanier Regional Library System Lilburn Public Library • Lilburn, GA 30247
Bramlett Carol G. • Library Consultant • Lubbock Independent School District • Lubbock, TX 79401 • AASL ALSC
Bramlett Doran A. • Owner • Doran A. Bramlett Associate • Mount Pleasant, SC 29464
Bramlett Suzanne M. • K-12 Librarian • Anthony Independent School District • Anthony, TX 79821 • AASL
Brammer Linda A. • Administrator • Cecil County Public Library • Elkton, MD 21921 • ALTA LAMA PLA
Branan Julia D. • Dean, Academic Affairs • Salem Community College Library • Carneys Point, NJ 08069
Branberg Donna • Trustee • Anderson County Library • Anderson, SC 29622-4047
Branch Brenda S. • Director • Austin Public Library • Austin, TX 78768 • LAMA PLA
Branch Katherine Anne • Yale University Kline Science Library • New Haven, CT 06511-8142 • ACRL LAMA
Branch Sonya M. • Director • Lafayette Parish Public Library • Lafayette, LA 70502-3427 • ALCTS ALSC ALTA ASCLA LAMA YALSA CLENE
Branch Susan B. • Reference Librarian • Worthington Public Library • Worthington, OH 43085 • IFRT
Branche-Brown Lynne C. • Acquisitions Librarian • Pennsylvania State University E506 Pattee Library • University Park, PA 16802 • ACRL ALCTS LITA
Branciforte Eileen • Cromwell Belden Public Library • Cromwell, CT 06416
Brancolini Kristine R. • Indiana University at Bloomington University Libraries • Bloomington, IN 47405 • ACRL VRT
Brand Barbara B. • Head, Interlibrary Loan Dept. • State University of New York (SUNY) Frank Melville Jr. Memorial Library • Stony Brook, NY 11794-3300 • LHRT
Brand Barbara J. • Baton Rouge, LA 70808
Brand Elaine • Student • University of Maryland College of Library and Information Services • College Park, MD 20742-4345 • AASL
Brand Joanna • Librarian (BI) • Orange Coast College • Costa Mesa, CA 92628-5005 • ACRL LIRT
Brand Joshua M. • Brand Ventures Group • Marlboro, NJ 07746
Brand Joycelyn Fobes • Manager • Catalog Card Company • Edina, MN 55435-5111 • AASL ALCTS ALSC LITA ERT
Brandau Christie • Asst. State Librarian • State Library of Iowa • Des Moines, IA 50319 • PLA
Brandau Doris K. • Head of Circulation Dept • Atlanta-Fulton Public Library Buckhead Branch • Atlanta, GA 30305 • LAMA
Brandeau John H. • Chief Librarian • Cuny Hiroshima College • Hiroshima 731-15, Japan • ACRL
Brandeis Robert C. • Chief Librarian • Victoria University • Toronto ON, Canada • ACRL
Brandel Pamela • Library Services Coordinator • Demco Inc. • Madison, WI 53707
Branden Shirley • Head Reference Department • University of Delaware Library • Newark, DE 19717-5267 • RASD
Brandi Melinda S • Student • Salt Lake County Library System Riverton Branch • Riverton, UT 84065
Brandin-Fiske Linnea • West Hartford, CT 06107 • ALSC
Brandow Sylvia A. • Head of Extension Services • Bloomington Public Library • Bloomington, IL 61702-3308 • PLA
Brandt Charlton J. • Project Director • Illinois Early Childhood Intervention Clearinghouse • Springfield, IL 62704
Brandt Diane T. • Student • University of California Los Angeles Graduate School of Library & Information Science • Los Angeles, CA 90024 • ACRL
Brandt Dorothy M. • Librarian • Newington Forest Elementary School • Springfield, VA 22153 • AASL ALSC
Brandt Garnet • Southern Prairie Area 15 Industrial Airport • Ottumwa, IA 52501 • AASL
Brandt Janet • Technical Service Librarian • Red Wing Public Library • Red Wing, MN 55066 • ALCTS LITA
Brandt Laurel J. • Melvindale, MI 48122
Brandt Lilly • Evanston, IL 60201 • LAMA LITA IFRT IRRT
Brandt Michael H. • Columbus, OH 43209 • RASD
Brandt Paula O. • Coordinator Curriculum Lab • University of Iowa Cur Lab • Iowa City, IA 52242 • AASL ALSC IFRT
Brandt Steven R. • Director • Fresno Pacific College Hiebert Library • Fresno, CA 93702 • ACRL
Brandwein Larry • Director • Brooklyn Public Library • Brooklyn, NY 11238 • LAMA PLA
Brangwin Nelda F. • Bellevue, WA 98006 • AASL ALSC
Branham Eula Lee • Margaret Mitchell School • Atlanta, GA 30327 • AASL
Branham Jennie P. Mrs • New York, NY 10037
Branin Anita Anker • Assistant Director • MINITEX Lib Info Network University of Minnesota • Minneapolis, MN 55455-0414 • ALCTS ASCLA LITA
Branin Joseph J. • University of Minnesota Meredith Wilson Library • Minneapolis, MN 55455 • ACRL ALCTS
Brannick Anne K. • Maryknoll, NY 10545-0311
Brannigan Gypsy M. • Dallas, TX 75229
Branning Katherine A. • New York, NY 10012
Brannon Kathleen • PALINET Library Network • Philadelphia, PA 19104 • NMRT
Brannon Shirleigh • Librarian • Solano County Library Vacaville Branch • Vacaville, CA 95688
Branscomb Carol J. • Columbus, OH 43214
Branscomb Lewis C. Prof • Emeritus • Ohio State University Libraries • Columbus, OH 43210-1286 • ACRL LAMA *Life*
Bransford Eleanor • Cataloger • Greensboro Public Library • Greensboro, NC 27402 • ALCTS

Branson Barbara • Catalog Department • Duke University William R. Perkins Library • Durham, NC 27706 • ALCTS LITA

Branson Jody • Medical Librarian • Humana Hospital University • Louisville, KY 40202 • IFRT SRRT

Branson Margaret S. • Consultant • Wisconsin Division for Library Services • Madison, WI 53707 • ASCLA

Brant Mary Jean • Trustee • City of Commerce Public Library • Commerce, CA 90040 • ALTA

Brant Susan L. • Librarian • Nicolet Area Technical College Learning Resources Center • Rhinelander, WI 54501 • ACRL IFRT IRRT

Brant Virginia A. • Crestline, OH 44827 • AASL

Brantigan-Stowell Martha • Wellesley, MA 02181 • ACRL ALCTS

Brantley Burnelle W. • Ruston, LA 71270

Brantley Juanita • Bloomington, IN 47401

Brantley Mildred • Chicago, IL 60628

Branton Dorothy Ann • Assistant Cataloger • University of Southern Mississippi Cook Memorial Library • Hattiesburg, MS 39406-5053 • ACRL ALCTS NMRT

Branton Mary K. • Student • University of North Texas School of Library & Information Sciences • Denton, TX 76203

Branzburg Marian G. • Librarian Section Coor-Children • Oak Park Public Library • Oak Park, MI 48237

Brar Navjit K. • Library Assistant • California State University • Fullerton, CA 92634

Brasel Michael L. • Univbersity Librarian • Brenau College Trustee Library • Gainesville, GA 30501

Brasfield Alice R. • Kansas City, MO 64130 • Continuing

Brash Janice M. • Medford, MA 02155 • AASL

Brasher Rose Anne • Director of Library Service • Temple Junior College • Temple, TX 76504 • ACRL RASD

Brasile Laurie • Multi-Media Services Coordinator • Early Childhood Training Center • Omaha, NE 68144-4910

Brass Debra A. • Student • Kent State University School of Library & Information Science • Kent, OH 44242-0001 • PLA

Brass Evelyn • University of Houston Libraries • Houston, TX 77204-2091 • ACRL

Brassell Daniel P. • Director • Durango Public Library • Durango, CO 81301 • ALCTS PLA

Brasseur Jill A. • Winnetka Public Library District • Winnetka, IL 60093

Brassington Dereck • Business Subject Specialist • Villanova University Falvey Memorial Library • Villanova, PA 19085-1699

Bratcher Perry R. • Automation Librarian • Northern Kentucky University Steely Library • Highland Heights, KY 41099-6101 • ALCTS LITA

Brathovde Jennifer • Librarian • Library of Congress • Washington, DC 20541

Brattin Barbara C. • Fairfield, OH 45014-5283

Bratton Ethel • Librarian • Donnell Library Center • New York, NY 10019 • CLENE

Bratton John Thomas • Head Of Technical Services • Eastern Montana College Library • Billings, MT 59101-0298 • ACRL ALCTS *Life*

Bratton Phyllis Ann K • Director • Jamestown College Raugust Library • Jamestown, ND 58401 • ACRL IFRT

Bratton Sally H. • Student • University of Oklahoma School of Library & Information Studies • Norman, OK 73019 • AASL ALSC IFRT

Brauch Patricia O. • Associate Librarian Information • Brooklyn College Library • Brooklyn, NY 11210 • ACRL

Braucher-Watton Paulette • Librarian • North Pennsylvania Sch Dist • Lansdale, PA 19446 • AASL

Braude Robert M. Ph.D. • Asst. Dean for Info.Resources • Cornell University Medical College Library • New York, NY 10021-4896 • ACRL

Braude Sharon K. • Student • Queens College Graduate School of Library & Information Studies • Flushing, NY 11367 • IFRT SRRT

Brauer Patricia K. • Katy, TX 77450 • LITA

Brauer Regina • Librarian • Hunter College Elementary School • New York, NY 10028 • AASL ALSC

Braun Anne M. • Library/Media Specialist • Howard Eccles School • Canby, OR 97013 • AASL

Braun Beverly J. • Hartnell College Learning Resources Center • Salinas, CA 93901 • ACRL

Braun Janice E. • Oakland, CA 94606 • ACRL

Braun Karin R. • Santa Claus, IN 47579 • AASL

Braun Linda W. • Children's Librarian • Westwood Public Library • Westwood, MA 02090 • ALSC IFRT

Brauner Jeanette A • Children's Librarian • Plumas County Library • Quincy, CA 95971 • ALSC

Braunig Nancy E. • Student • Spring Independent School District Salyers Elementary • Spring, TX 77373 • AASL

Braunstein Barry A • Assistant Editor • H. W. Wilson Company • Bronx, NY 10452 • RASD

Braunstein Kent • Trustee • The Bryant Library • Roslyn, NY 11576

Brautigam David K. • Acquisitions Librarian • Westminster College McGill Library • New Wilmington, PA 16172-0001 • ALCTS

Brautigam Faith J. • Gail Borden Public Library • Elgin, IL 60120 • ALSC

Brautigam Patsy R. • Sugar Land, TX 77478

Bravata Virginia P. • Tickfaw, LA 70466

Braverman Miriam • New York, NY 10025

Bravy Gary J. • Media Reference Librarian • Georgetown University Law Center Edward Bennett Williams Library • Washington, DC 20001-1417 • ACRL GODORT

Brawn Elizabeth • Los Altos, CA 94022-1020 • Continuing

Brawner Lee B. • Executive Director • Metropolitan Library System • Oklahoma City, OK 73102 • ALCTS ALTA ASCLA LAMA LITA PLA IFRT

Braxton Ann B. • Greensboro, NC 27406

Bray Ethel E. • Library Administrator • Seneca Nation Library • Irving, NY 14168

Bray June A. • Teacher/Librarian • High Sch Lib • Somers, CT 06071 • AASL

Bray Lessell M. • Student • Appalachian State University Carol Grotnes Belk Library • Boone, NC 28608 • AASL

Bray Margaret M. Miss • Saginaw, MI 48603-2104 • Continuing

Bray Pamela N. • Memphis-Shelby County Public Library and Information Center • Memphis, TN 38104-4025

Bray Richard D. • Student • San Jose State University Division of Library & Information Science • San Jose, CA 95192-0029

Bray Sandra M. • Arizona State University Libraries • Tempe, AZ 85287-1006 • ACRL ALCTS LAMA

Brayboy Larry S. • Student • Wayne State University Library Science Program • Detroit, MI 48202 • GODORT IFRT SRRT

Brayton Roy • Archive Manager • Brooklyn Hospital Center • Brooklyn, NY 11201 • ALCTS ERT

Brazell Beckie S. • Librarian • Alameda County Library Union City Branch • Union City, CA 94587

Brazil Colleen S. • Student • University of Washington Graduate School of Library and Information Science • Seattle, WA 98195 • SRRT

Brazil Mary Jo • Gerontology Librarian • Vintage Health Library • Berkeley, CA 94704 • RASD

Brazile Orella R. • Dir of the Library • Southern University Shreveport-Bossier City Campus • Shreveport, LA 71107 • ACRL

Brazill Maria • Peace Dale, RI 02883

Brazington Barbara C. • Student • University of Arizona Library • Tucson, AZ 85721 • PLA RASD NMRT

Breach Elaine C. • Monographic Cataloger • Washington State University Library • Pullman, WA 99164-5610

Breashears Lucy D. • Student • Oak Ridge Central School • Ravenden Spring, AR 72460 • AASL

Breaux Ann-Marie • Harvard College Library Lamont Library • Cambridge, MA 02138 • ALCTS

Brech Maria • Librarian • Mahopac Library • Mahopac, NY 10541

Brecher Laura • Librarian • Johnson, Bromberg & Leeds Law Library • Dallas, TX 75201

Brechner Ritalynne • Director,Overseas Students Prog • University of Haifa Library • Haifa 3199, Israel

Brecht Celeste D. • Media Specialist • Severna Park High School • Severena Park, MD 21146 • AASL

Breckenridge L. L. Mrs • Coordinator Grade 2 • Free Library of Philadelphia • Philadelphia, PA 19103 • ALSC

Bredehoft Linda • Winfield, KS 67156

Bredengerd Linda J. • Library Assistant • University of Pittsburgh at Bradford • Bradford, PA 16701

Breder Linda M. • Children's Services Librarian • Randolph Township Free Public Library • Randolph, NJ 07869 • ALSC

Bredeson Jim • Director • University of Wisconsin Center Baraboo-Sauk County Library • Baraoo, WI 53913

Bredeson Peggy Z. • Director • Beloit Public Library • Beloit, WI 53511 • LAMA PLA

Breed Clara E. • Spring Valley, CA 91977-5899 • PLA *Continuing*

Breeden Barbara K. • Reference/Interlibrary Loan Ln • United States Naval Academy Nimitz Library • Annapolis, MD 21402-5029 • ACRL RASD AFLRT FLRT GODORT LIRT

Breeden Mary K. • Hd Non-bk Serv • University of Tennessee T Carter & M Rawlings Lupton Lib • Chattanooga, TN 37403 • ACRL VRT

Breeden Wendy R. • Winter Park, FL 32789

Breeding Marshall M. • Lib. Networks & Microcomp. Anal • Vanderbilt University Library • Nashville, TN 37240-0007 • LITA

Breeding Noreen Aboutok • Albuquerque Public Library Wyoming Regional Branch • Albuquerque, NM 87110

Breedlove W. Stephen • Reference/ILL Librarian • La Salle University Connelly Library • Philadelphia, PA 19141 • RASD

Breen Allison • Wichita Fls, TX 76308

Breen Baerbel B. • Houston, TX 77096

Breen Karen B. • Library Power • New York, NY 10016 • AASL ALSC

Breen Kevin E. • Librarian • Williamsburg Regional Library • Williamsburg, VA 23185

Breen M. Frances Dr. • Plattsburgh, NY 12901 • ACRL LAMA LIRT

Breen Patricia • Library Media Specialist • Poughkeepsie Middle School • Poughkeepsie, NY 12601

Breen Sonja • Beatty Community Library • Beatty, NV 89003

Breetz Dalarna T. • Asst. Dir. Field Services Div. • Kentucky Department for Libraries & Archives • Frankfort, KY 40602-0537 • LAMA PLA IFRT

Bregman Adeane A. • Reference Bibliographer • Boston College O'Neill Library • Chestnut Hill, MA 02167 • ACRL LIRT

Bregman Steven H. • Director • Bellmore Memorial Library • Bellmore, NY 11710 • PLA

Bregzis Ilze • Head of Technical Services • Ontario Institute for Studies in Education Library • Toronto ON, M5S 1V6 Canada • ACRL ALCTS LITA

Bregzis Ritvars • Toronto ON, M6S 2W5 Canada • ALCTS LITA *Continuing*

Breheny Mary R. • Librarian/Media Specialist • Bellwood Elementary School • Richmond, VA 23237

Breidt Cheryll Kae • Librarian • Pinehurst-Kingston Free Library District • Pinehurst, ID 83850

Breier Christin A. • Evening Supervisor • Siena College • Loudonville, NY 12211-1462

Breimeier Lois • Arcadia, MI 49613

Breit Anitra D. • Director • Walla Walla County Library • Walla Walla, WA 99362

Breit Roslind • School Library Media Specialist • Smithtown High School East • Saint James, NY 11780 • AASL

Breitbard Ronda E. • New York, NY 10023-6566 • ACRL ALCTS MAGERT

Breitenbach Wanda G. • Associate Director • University of Baltimore Langsdale Library • Baltimore, MD 21201 • ACRL LAMA

Breitenwischer Rosalyn E. • Serial Cataloger • University Microfilms International • Ann Arbor, MI 48106-1346 • ALCTS

Breitfeller Linda M. • Library Trainee • Middle Country Public Library • Centereach, NY 11720 • ACRL SRRT

Breiting Amelia R. • Search Analyst • Northeastern University Dodge Library • Boston, MA 02115 • RASD

Breitman Marilyn F. • Librarian • Joseph Kushner Hebrew Academy • West Caldwell, NJ 07006 • AASL

Breivik Patricia Senn • Assoc. Vice Pres. Inf. Resources • Towson State University • Towson, MD 21204 • ACRL LIRT

Brekelbaum Barbara J. • Librarian • Saint Gregory School • Plantation, FL 33324 • AASL

Brekke Elaine C. • Washington State University Owen Science & Engineering Library • Pullman, WA 99164-3200

Breland Anita L. • Senior Industry Representative • IBM ACIS • Milford, CT 06460 • ACRL LITA IRRT

Breland June M. • Coordinator of Acq. Serv. • Mississippi State University Mitchell Memorial Library • Mississippi State, MS 39762 • ACRL LAMA LIRT

Brelsford Bridgie B. • Head/Technical Services • Tippecanoe County Public Library • Lafayette, IN 47901

Bremer Elizabeth L. • Mililani, HI 96789

Bremer Julius J. • Librarian • Cleveland Public Library • Cleveland, OH 44114-1271

Bremer Robert V. • Quality Controll Librarian • Online Computer Library Center (OCLC) • Dublin, OH 43017-3395 • ALCTS MAGERT

Bremer Suzanne W. • Chief Executive Officer • Broadbased Information Services, Inc. • Somerville, MA 02143-2018 • ILERT

Bremer Thomas A. • Assistant Director CMRS • North Dakota State University Library • Fargo, ND 58105-5599 • LAMA RASD

Bremner Patricia A. • Student • University of Texas at Austin Graduate School of Library & Information Sciences • Austin, TX 78712-1276

Bren Barbara R. • Reference Librarian • University of Wisconsin-Whitewater Harold Andersen Library • Whitewater, WI 53190 • RASD GODORT

Brenkosh Shirley V. • Albuquerque, NM 87111

Brennan-Gibbon Cindy L. • Director • Camas Public Library • Camas, WA 98607 • LAMA PLA IFRT

Brennan-Kerr Mary H. • Chief Clln Devlp Officer • University of Texas at Austin General Libraries • Austin, TX 78713-7330 • ACRL ALCTS

Brennan-Milczarski Vivian • Student • State University of New York at Albany School of Information Science & Policy • Albany, NY 12222 • AASL

Brennan Charlotte A. • Director Learning Resources • Yavapai College Library • Prescott, AZ 86301 • ACRL ALCTS

Brennan Christopher P. • Asst Librarian For Tech Services • Colgate Rochester Divinity Sch • Rochester, NY 14620 • ALCTS LITA

Brennan David P. • Student • Saint Francis Medical Center School of Nursing Library • Pittsburgh, PA 15201

Brennan Deborah B. • Saunderstown, RI 02874 • ILERT

Brennan Lisa R. • Student • University of Washington Graduate School of Library and Information Science • Seattle, WA 98195

Brennan Mary A. • Librarian • West Carroll Parish Library • Oak Grove, LA 71263

Brennan Mary E. S S J Sr. • Librarian • College of Our Lady of the Elms Alumnae Library • Chicopee, MA 01013-2839 • ACRL ALCTS ALSC RASD

Brennan Mary Eleanor • Cataloging Coordinator • AT&T Bell Laboratories • Holmdel, NJ 07733-1988 • LITA IFRT

Brennan Mary Margaret • University School • Shaker Heights, OH 44122 • AASL

Brennan Patricia B.M. • Rhode Island College James P Adams Library • Providence, RI 02908 • ACRL RASD LIRT

Brennan Sheila A. • Media Director • Academy of the Holy Angels High School • Richfield, MN 55423

Brennan Terrence F. • Director of Library Services • Chadron State College Reta E. King Library • Chadron, NE 69337

Brenneise Harvey R. • Head, Reference Librarian • Andrews University James White Library • Berrien Springs, MI 49104-1400 • RASD

Brenneman Melissa J. • Student • University of Tennessee-Knoxville Graduate School of Library & Information Science • Knoxville, TN 37996-4330 • IFRT

Brennemann Aeola • Alliance, NE 69301 • ALSC PLA *Continuing*

Brenner Barbara • Collection Development Libn • Marist College Library • Poughkeepsie, NY 12601

Brenner Eric • Skyline College Library • San Bruno, CA 94066 • ACRL LITA

Brenner Howard • Brooklyn Law School Library • Brooklyn, NY 11201

Brenner John M. • Regional Sales Manager • Wood Knapp Video • Marietta, GA 30068 • VRT *Subscribing*

Brenner Lanelle N. • Vice-President Board of Trustees • Evansville-Vanderburgh County Public Library • Evansville, IN 47708-1694 • ALTA

Brenner Lawrence • Senior Medical Librarian • Boston City Hospital Health Sciences Library • Boston, MA 02118

Brenner Willis F. • Documents Librarian • Arkansas State University Dean B. Ellis Library • State University, AR 72467-2040 • ACRL RASD GODORT

Brent Carol L. • Manager Serials Data Management • University Microfilms International • Ann Arbor, MI 48106-1346 • LITA

Brent Gloria W. • Library Media Specialist • McKinley Senior High School • Washington, DC 20002 • AASL

Brent Nancy E. • Librarian • Kermit Independent School District Kermit High School • Kermit, TX 79745

Brereton Mary M. • Associate Editor • H. W. Wilson Company • Bronx, NY 10452 • AASL ASCLA

Breshears Shirley • Parma School District-#137 • Parma, ID 83660 • AASL YALSA

Bresien Patricia A. • Clinical Reference Librarian • Metro Health Saint Lukes's Medical Center • Cleveland, OH 44104

Bresler Riva T. Miss • Daly City, CA 94015 • Continuing

Breslin Catherine A. • Librarian • University of Utah • Salt Lake City, UT 84112

Bresnahan Beverly • Central Middle School Kent County Learning Resource Center • Dover, DE 19901 • AASL

Bresnahan Lori A. • Student • Syracuse University School of Information Studies • Syracuse, NY 13244-4100 • AASL

Bressler Anne S. • Student • University of California-Berkeley School of Library & Information Studies • Berkeley, CA 94720

Bressman Anne S. • Cherry Hill, NJ 08003

Brest Jennifer • Children's Librarian • Norwalk Public Library • Norwalk, OH 44857 • ALSC

Brethauer Caroline M. • Librarian • Maryknoll School • Honolulu, HI 96822 • AASL

Breting Elizabeth C. • Coordinator, Youth Services • Kansas City Public Library • Kansas City, MO 64106 • ALSC PLA

Bretscher Susan M. • Our Lady Of Lourdes Hospital • Binghamton, NY 13905 • ASCLA

Brett George H. II • Program Manager • University of North Carolina • Chapel Hill, NC 27599 • ACRL LITA

Brett Linda K. • Student • University of North Carolina at Chapel Hill School of Information and Library Science • Chapel Hill, NC 27599-3360

Brett Lorraine E. • Instruction Material Center • Vigo County School Corp Instructional Materials Center Library • Terre Haute, IN 47803 • AASL

Brett William H. • Oakland, CA 94807

Bretthauer David W. • Assistant Librarian • Southern Connecticut State University Hilton C. Buley Library • New Haven, CT 06515 • ACRL ALCTS LITA LRRT

Brettschneider Sharon E. • Director • Connecticut State Library Willimantic Library Service Center • Willimantic, CT 06226

Bretz Cinda Sue • Director • Willard Memorial Library • Willard, OH 44890 • PLA

Bretz Linda M. • Rochester Public Library • Rochester, NY 14604 • PLA IFRT

Brewer Anna C. • Media Specialist • Independent School District Pillow Elementary School • Austin, TX 78702 • AASL

Brewer Annie • Whitefoord Press • Dearborn, MI 48124 • ACRL ALCTS ALSC ASCLA LAMA LITA PLA RASD YALSA CLENE ERT FLRT GODORT ILERT LRRT

Brewer Calvin R. • Stillwater, OK 74075 • Continuing

Brewer Jeaneice • Memphis, TN 38128 • ACRL ALCTS *Life*

Brewer Joseph M. • Student • University of Arizona Graduate Library School • Tucson, AZ 85721 • IFRT SRRT

Brewer Julie A. • University of Delaware Library • Newark, DE 19717-5267 • ACRL LAMA NMRT

Brewer Patsy Carol • Pine Forest Regional Library • Richton, MS 39476 • PLA

Brewer Rosellen E. • Part-time Researcher • Monterey Bay Area Cooperative Library System • Monterey, CA 93940 • PLA RASD NMRT

Brewer Shirley J. • Bookmobile Librarian • San Jose Public Library • San Jose, CA 95113 • PLA NMRT

Brewer Tony • Library Director • Longmont Public Library • Longmont, CO 80501 • LAMA PLA

Brewin C. Kelly • Al AIN, United Arab Emirates • ACRL IRRT

Brewster Doris H. • Medical Librarian • Mercy Hospital • Janesville, WI 53545 • ASCLA IFRT

Brewster Ellen I. • Silver Spring, MD 20902

Brewster Evelyn S. • Denver, CO 80231 • Continuing

Brewster Marie M. • Libn II Ref & Pub Service • Buffalo & Erie County Public Library • Buffalo, NY 14203 • RASD

Brewster Olive N. • San Antonio, TX 78210

Brewster Ruth J. • Baco Raton, FL 33429

Brewster Steven E. • Adult Services Coordinator • Orange County Public Library • Santa Ana, CA 92705 • ACRL ALCTS LAMA LITA PLA RASD YALSA CLENE IFRT IRRT SRRT

Brewton Jewwll • Scottsboro Public Library • Scottsboro, AL 35768

Breyfogle Donna H. • Collections Management Libraries • University of Manitoba • Winnipeg MB, R3T 2N2 Canada • ACRL ALCTS

Brezden Zenia • Warren, MI 48091

Breznay Ann Marie • Sytstems Librarian • University of Utah Marriott Library • Salt Lake City, UT 84112-1179 • ACRL LITA

Breznitsky Lynda K. • Scotch Plains, NJ 07076 • AASL

Brian Ray • San Francisco, CA 94114 • ALCTS LITA *Life*

Briand Mary B. • Library Services Administrator • Harris Electronic Systems Sector ATT: Harris ESS Library,3A-8544 • Melborne, FL 32902

Briant Susan L. • Librarian • Roselle Park Veteran Memorial Library • Roselle Park, NJ 07204 • PLA

Brice Diana L. • Chicago Public Library Carter G. Woodson Regional Library • Chicago, IL 60628 • ACRL LAMA PLA SRRT

Brice John J. III • Meadville Public Library • Meadville, PA 16335

Brich George M. • Director • Elkhart Public Library • Elkhart, IN 46516-3184 • LAMA PLA

Brick Sarah E. • Assistant Professor of Lib. Serv • Northeastern Oklahoma State University John Vaughan Library-LRC • Tahlequah, OK 74464 • ACRL LIRT

Bricker Karin K. • Senior Librarian • Mountain View Public Library • Mountain View, CA 94041 • PLA

Bricker Will S. II • Branch Manager • Free Library of Philadelphia • Philadelphia, PA 19103 • PLA

Brickner Margaret • Acquisitions Librarian (Acting) • City College of San Francisco • San Francisco, CA 94112

Bridegam Willis E. • Librarian • Amherst College Library • Amherst, MA 01002 • ACRL ALCTS *Life*

Briden Altamae • Findlay-Hancock County Public Library • Findlay, OH 45840 • PLA RASD

Briden Judith S. • Arkansas State University Dean B. Ellis Library • State University, AR 72467-2040 • ACRL RASD

Bridge Frank Robert • Automation Consultant • Walton Bridge Consulting Inc. • Austin, TX 78759 • LAMA LITA

Bridgeford Grace L. • Media Specialist • School District of Kansas City,MO AV Film/ Video Library • Kansas City, MO 64120

Bridgers Jeffrey W. • Student • University of Missouri-Columbia School of Library & Informational Science • Columbia, MO 65211 • LITA

Bridges Anne E. • Reference Librarian • University of Tennessee Library • Knoxville, TN 37996-1000 • ACRL

Bridges Elinor F. • Director of Library Services • Pembroke State University Mary Livermore Library • Pembroke, NC 28372 • ACRL LAMA

Bridges Kathyrn A. • Hannibal, MO 63401

Bridges Peggy B. • Gainesville, FL 32607

Bridges Rebecca J. • Barnwell Elemntary School • Alapharetta, GA 30202

Bridges Vontella R. • Reader Services Librarian • DeKalb College South Campus Learning Resources Center • Decatur, GA 30034 • ACRL

Bridgman Alicemae • Grand Rapids, MI 49503

Bridgman Amy R. • Public Librarian (Part-time) • Escondido Public Library • Escondido, CA 92025 • LRRT

Bridgman William G. • Director • Sandhill Regional Library System • Rockingham, NC 28379-4995 • ALTA PLA

Bridgwater Dorothy W. • Hamden, CT 06517 • ACRL RASD *Continuing*

Bridwell Eugene E. • Special Collection Librarian • Simon Fraser University W. A. Bennett Library • Burnaby BC, V5A 1S6 Canada • ACRL

Briell Robert D. • Director • Warren-Trumbull County Public Library • Warren, OH 44483

Brier David J. • Student • University of Michigan School of Information and Library Studies • Ann Arbor, MI 48109-1092

Brierty Carol A. • Morehead State University Camden-Carroll Library • Morehead, KY 40351 • LITA

Brigell Bruce C. • Assistant Director • Ventress Memorial Library • Marshfield, MA 02050

Briggs Anne F. • Director • Kent County Public Library • Chestertown, MD 21620 • PLA IFRT

Briggs Barbara M. • Simmons College Graduate School of Library & Information Science • Boston, MA 02115

Briggs E. Beatrice • Stonington, IL 62567

Briggs Kate H. • Holiday House Inc. • New York, NY 10017 • ALSC

Briggs Madge H. • Sch Lib Media Specialist • Brookside School • Ossining, NY 10562 • AASL

Briggs Margaret I. Miss • Minneapolis, MN 55403 • AASL RASD *Continuing*

Briggs Mary Kay • APO, AP 96319-4905 • AFLRT

Briggs Mary S. • Library Media Teacher • LaCosta Heights Elementary School • Carlsbad, CA 92009 • AASL

Briggs Nancy B. • Media Specialist • Brighton High School/Area Schools • Brighton, MI 48116 • AASL

Briggs Nathalie E. • Kingston, RI 02881 • Continuing

Briggs Rebecca L. • Student • State University New York at Buffalo School of Inf. & Library Studies • Buffalo, NY 14260 • IFRT

Bright Alice • Head,Cataloging • Carnegie-Mellon University Libraries Hunt Library • Pittsburgh, PA 15213 • ACRL ALCTS

Bright Cynthia A. • Librarian • Bannockburn School • Deerfield, IL 60015 • AASL

Bright Elizabeth J. • Hopkinton, MA 01748 • AASL

Bright Franklyn F. • Madison, WI 53705 • LAMA

Brightharp Wilma S. • Branch Manager • Atlanta-Fulton Public Library West Hunter Branch • Atlanta, GA 30314 • PLA

Brightly Lillian • Media Specialist • Mountain View School • Mendham, NJ 07945 • AASL

Bril Patricia L. • Collection Department Officer • California State University • Fullerton, CA 92634 • ACRL ALCTS LAMA

Briley Anne S. • Greenville, NC 27858-3918

Briley Dorothy • Clarion Books • New York, NY 10003 • ALSC YALSA

Brill Alison • Denver, CO 80206 • LAMA LITA IFRT IRRT

Brill Ellen F. • Cataloger • Denver Public School District Professional Library • Denver, CO 80205

Brill Judith P. • Supervising Branch Librarian • New York Public Library Sixty-Seventh Street Branch • New York, NY 10021 • YALSA

Brill Margaret S. • Public Documents & Map Dept. • Duke University William R. Perkins Library • Durham, NC 27706 • RASD GODORT MAGERT

Brill Patricia A. • Adminstrative Assistant • Rolling Meadows Library • Rolling Meadows, IL 60008 • LAMA NMRT

Brilmyer Catherine W. • Librarian • Roosevelt High School • Gary, IN 46407

Brilz Linda L. • Youth Services Librarian • Boise Public Library • Boise, ID 83702-0715 • YALSA

Brimsek Tobi A. • Assistant Executive Director • Special Libraries Association • Washington, DC 20009 • LITA

Brin Beth L. • Science-Engineering Libn. • University of Arizona Library • Tucson, AZ 85721 • ACRL

Brindamour Patricia K. • Library Assistant II • University of Connecticut Homer Babbidge Library • Storrs, CT 06269-1005

Brindza Stephen M. • Reference Librarian • Saint Clairsville Public Library • St. Clairsville, OH 43950

Brink Clarence Jr • Reference Librarian • Vigo County Public Library • Terre Haute, IN 47807 • RASD

Brink David R. • Business Bibliographer • University of Akron • Akron, OH 44325-1707 • ACRL

Brink Mary L. • Executive Director • Nioga Library System • Lockport, NY 14094 • ALSC PLA

Brinkerhoff Kathie • Business Reference Librarian • University of Oregon Library • Eugene, OR 97403-1299 • RASD

Brinkler Bartol • Librarian • Harvard College Library Widener Memorial Library • Cambridge, MA 02138 • ACRL ALCTS   *Life*

Brinkley Linda L. • University of North Carolina School of Library Science • Chapel Hill, NC 27599-3360

Brinkman Antoinette M. • Evansville, IN 47715

Brinkman Jean U. • Literacy Services Coordinator • Jacksonville Public Libraries Main Library • Jacksonville, FL 32202 • PLA

Brinton Keven H. • Student • Brigham Young University School of Library & Information Sciences • Provo, UT 84602

Brisbane Mary Jane F. • Decatur, GA 30030 • AASL

Brisbin John A. • Director • Manchester City Library • Manchester, NH 03101 • ACRL LAMA LITA PLA RASD YALSA

Briscoe Peter M. • Chief Clln Devel Offr • University of California Rivera Library • Riverside, CA 92517 • ACRL ALCTS

Brisfjord Inez L. • Associate Professor • Long Island University Palmer School of Library & Info. Sci. • Brookville, NY 11548 • IRRT

Briska Boniface • Assistant Librarian Emeritus • State University of New York (SUNY) University Libraries • Albany, NY 12222

Briskin Sylvia M. • Youth Services Librarian • Riverside City & County Public Library Central Branch • Riverside, CA 92502

Briskman Holle • Mobile Public Library • Mobile, AL 36602 • ALTA

Brisson Patricia M. • Reference Librarian • Phillipsburg Free Public Library • Phillipsburg, NJ 08865 • RASD

Brisson Roger O. • Senior Asst. Librarian • Pennsylvania State University E506 Pattee Library • University Park, PA 16802 • ACRL

Bristol Carolyn S. • Parkwood-Upjohn School • Kalamazoo, MI 49001

Bristol Ruth A. • Cockeysville, MD 21030 • Continuing

Bristow Ann • Head Reference Department • Indiana University at Bloomington University Libraries • Bloomington, IN 47405 • ACRL LITA

Bristow Barbara A. • Humanities Index • H. W. Wilson Company • Bronx, NY 10452 • ACRL

Britain Annette B • Reference/Interlibrary Loan Libn • Kemp Public Library • Wichita Falls, TX 76301 • PLA NMRT

Britain Karla • Associate Librarian • Union College Library • Lincoln, NE 68506-4386 • ACRL ALCTS

Britt Robin • Trustee • Greensboro Public Library • Greensboro, NC 27402 • ALTA

Britt Sheelah • Head of Administrative Services • Massachusetts Institute of Technology Libraries (MIT) • Cambridge, MA 02139 • LAMA

Brittain Cynthia E. • Reference Librarian • Contra Costa County Library Concord Branch • Concord, CA 94519

Brittain Kirk D. • Limon, CO 80828 • LITA

Brittain Maxine Hollye • Librarian • Greenhill School • Dallas, TX 75244-3698 • AASL

Britten William A. • Systems Librarian • University of Tennessee Library • Knoxville, TN 37996-1000 • ACRL LITA

Britting Paula M. • Director • Dover Town Library • Dover, MA 02030

Britto Mary M. • Childrens Librarian • Glencarlyn Branch Library • Arlington, VA 22204 • ALSC

Britton Anne Putman • Librarian • Scottsdale Community College Library • Scottsdale, AZ 85256 • ACRL

Britton Constance J. • Librarian • Ohio Agricultural Research and Development Center Library • Wooster, OH 44691-6900 • ACRL

Britton Helen H. • Long Beach, CA 90807 • Continuing

Britton Janice B. • Librarian • Rayville High School • Rayville, LA 71269 • AASL

Britton Ruth • Social Work Librarian • University of Southern California • Los Angeles, CA 90033 • ACRL

Britton Scott R. • Circulation Supervisor • Northeastern University • Boston, MA 02115

Britton Sharon M. • Asst. Univ. Libn. for Pub Svs. • University of New Hampshire Library • Durham, NH 03824 • ACRL

Brizendine Margaret • Librarian • Library Media Specialist Edwards-Knox School Library • Russell, NY 13684

Broad Lillian • Trustee • North Bellmore Public Library • N. Bellmore, NY 11710 • ALTA

Broadbent H. E. III • Executive Director • Pittsburgh Regional Library Center • Pittsburgh, PA 15221 • ASCLA

Broadbent J. Elaine • Salt Lake City, UT 84103 • ALCTS LITA

Broadhead Eunice • Public Services Librarian • Boulder City Library • Boulder City, NV 89005

Broadhead Margaret • Chief Librarian • Victoria College • Burwood VIC 3125, Australia • AASL ACRL ALCTS LAMA LITA RASD YALSA

Broadman Diana • Librarian • Arcadia High School • Phoenix, AZ 85018 • AASL CLENE

Broadnax Lavonda Kay • Chief Librarian • District of Columbia General Hospital Medical Library • Washington, DC 20003 • LAMA

Broadus Robert N. • University of North Carolina at Chapel Hill School of Information and Library Science • Chapel Hill, NC 27599-3360 • ACRL ALCTS LAMA LRRT

Broadwater Barbara S. • Tazewell, VA 24651-0356

Broadwater Deborah H. • Serials Librarian • Vanderbilt University Medical Center Library • Nashville, TN 37232 • ALCTS

Broadway Dale E. • Columbia, MO 65203

Broadway Marsha D. • Assistant Professor • Brigham Young University School of Library & Information Sciences • Provo, UT 84602 • ALSC RASD

Broadwin John • Collection Development Librarian • Foothill College Library • Los Altos Hills, CA 94022-4599 • ACRL

Brock-Johnston Carol A. • Gaithersburg, MD 20878

Brock Amy A. • Head of Children's Section • New Orleans Public Library • New Orleans, LA 70140 • ALSC

Brock Edith Grace • Mt Lake Park, MD 21550 • PLA

Brock Elma • Head Media Specialist • Fort Rucker Elementary School • Ft. Rucker, AL 36352 • AASL

Brock Heather L. • Student • University of Alabama School of Library and Information Studies • Tuscaloosa, AL 35487

Brock Joan • Manager • Manukau Libraries • Private Bag Manukau, New Zealand • PLA

Brock Kathy T. • Coordinator of Media Services • Douglas County Public Schools • Douglasville, GA 30133 • AASL

Brock Lynn A. • Student • San Jose State University Division of Library & Information Science • San Jose, CA 95192-0029

Brock Lynn A. Mr. • Cedarville College Centennial Library • Cedarville, OH 45314 • AASL ACRL ALCTS LAMA RASD

Brock Martha A. • Head Children's Department • Lima Public Library • Lima, OH 45801

Brock Ruthie H. • Reference Librarian • University of Texas at Arlington • Arlington, TX 76019-0497 • PLA RASD GODORT

Brockenbrough Mary A. • Evening Supervisor • Harvard University • Cambridge, MA 02138 • ACRL

Brockhage Mary C. • Librarian/Chapter I Tchr • San Mateo/Foster City School District Borel Middle School • San Mateo, CA 94402 • AASL YALSA

Brockington Catherine B. • Vicksburg, MI 49097-9411 • AASL

Brockman Wanda Z. • Seattle, WA 98103 • Continuing

Brockman William • English Librarian • University of Illinois Library • Urbana, IL 61801 • ACRL

Brockmeier Kristina C. • Director of Library Service • Clayton State College • Morrow, GA 30260 • ACRL   *Life*

Brockmeyer-Klebaum Donna M.C. • Librarian • University of Alberta Cameron Library • Edmonton AB, T6G 2J8 Canada • ACRL

Brockway Mary • Librarian • La Lumiere School • La Porte, IN 46350

Broda John W. • Student • Queens College Grad Sch of Lib & Inf Studies • Flushing, NY 11367 • PLA

Brodak Elizabeth W. • Grand Junction, CO 81505 • LITA

Brodar Meldine N. • Student • Drexel University College of Information Studies • Philadelphia, PA 19104-2875 • AASL

Broderick Bridgid M. • Student • Florida State University School of Library and Information Studies • Tallahassee, FL 32306-2048 • PLA IFRT SRRT

Broderick Dorothy M. • Scarecrow Press, Inc. • Metuchen, NJ 08840 • PLA YALSA IFRT

Broderick Linda M. • Assoc Ln/spec Cllns Catlgr • University of California UCSB Library • Santa Barbara, CA 93106-9010

Broderick Therese L. • Librarian • Albany Public Library • Albany, NY 12210 • PLA RASD CLENE

Broderson Margaret • Asst Dean for Library Services • Scott Community College • Bettendorf, IA 52722 • ACRL

Brodhead Heather • Student • University of Pittsburgh School of Library and Information Science • Pittsburgh, PA 15260

Brodhurst Corrine • C'sted, St. Croix, VI 00824-0242 • AASL ALSC

Brodie Carolyn S. Dr. • Assistant Professor • Kent State University School of Library & Information Science • Kent, OH 44242-0001 • AASL ALSC YALSA SRRT

Brodie Debra • Library Director • Hillsboro Public Library • Hillsboro, OR 97123 • PLA

Brodie Heather A. • Ashby, MA 01431

Brodie Kay L. • Administrator • Chesapeake College Library • Wye Mills, MD 21679

Brodney Kay • Head Life Science Section • Library of Congress • Washington, DC 20541 • ACRL RASD   *Life*

Brodnick Corinne • Shepard School • Old Bridge, NJ 08857 • AASL

Brodnitz Gaya J. • Media Specialist • Lacey Township High School Library • Lanoka Harbor, NJ 08734 • AASL

Brodsky Joan B. • Highland Pk, IL 60035

Brodson Diane E. • Head of Acquisitoins • Arlington Heights Memorial Library • Arlington Heights, IL 60004-5966 • ALCTS PLA

Brodt James W. • Librarian • Reading-Fleming Middle School • Flemington, NJ 08822 • AASL

Brody Arthur • Brodart Company • San Diego, CA 92127-1798 • AASL ACRL ALCTS ASCLA LAMA LITA PLA RASD

Brody Catherine T. • Director of Archives • New York Technical College Archives • Brooklyn, NY 11201-2983 • ACRL

Brody Eleanor • Adult Services Librarian • Pittsford Community Library • Pittsford, NY 14534

Brody Julia J. • Pleasantville, NY 10570

Brody Laura • Columbia University Libraries • New York, NY 10027

Brodziski Ann M. • Graduate Student • University of Wisconsin-Milwaukee School of Library & Information Science • Milwaukee, WI 53201

Broenkow Kyle W. • Student • University of California Los Angeles Graduate School of Library & Information Science • Los Angeles, CA 90024 • PLA

Broering Naomi C. • Medical Center Librarian • Georgetown University J V Dahlgren Memorial Library • Washington, DC 20007

Brogan Martha L. • New Haven, CT 06515 • ACRL IRRT

Brogan Thomas W. • Librarian I • Brooklyn Public Library Canarsie Branch Library • Brooklyn, NY 11236 • ACRL

Brogden Stephen • Deputy Director • Thousand Oaks Library • Thousand Oaks, CA 91362 • LAMA PLA

Broidy Ellen • Librarian • University of California-Irvine Library • Irvine, CA 92713 • ACRL EMIERT LIRT SRRT

Broman Susan B. • Valenica, CA 91355

Bromberg Peter J. • Student • Rutgers University School of Communication Information & Library Studies • New Brunswick, NJ 08903

Bromley Patricia J. • Supervisor Specialist • Toledo-Lucas County Public Library • Toledo, OH 43624 • ALCTS PLA

Bromschwig Suzanne • Supervisor • Saint Louis County Library • St. Louis, MO 63131

Bronars Lori A. • Sci Ref Ln & Database Coor. • Yale University Kline Science Library • New Haven, CT 06511-8142 • ACRL RASD

Bronson Barbara • Walnut Creek, CA 94595 • Continuing

Bronson Diane A. • Director • Chestatee Regional Library • Gainesville, GA 30505-2399 • ALCTS ALSC ALTA LAMA LITA PLA RASD IFRT

Bronson Joan R. • Library Associate • Annapolis & Anne Arundel County Public Library • Annapolis, MD 21401-7042

Bronson Margaret W. • Media Specialist • Stevenson High School • Livonia, MI 48152 • AASL

Bronson Que A. • Chief of Public Services • Montgomery County Department of Public Libraries • Rockville, MD 20850

Bronsteader Muirl • La Grange Highlands School District 106 • La Grange, IL 60525 • AASL YALSA

Bronstein Alice S. • Gloucester County Library • Sewell, NJ 08080

Bronstein Arthur • Trustee • Boulder Public Library • Boulder, CO 80306

Bronstein Dorothy J. • Director • Virgin Islands Regional Library for the Visually and Physically Handicapped • Frederiksted, VI 00820 • ASCLA

Brook Barbara • Principal Librarian • Orange County Public Library Heritage Park Regional Library • Irvine, CA 92720

Brook Judith D. • Acting Library Administrator • Mercer University Monroe F. Swilley Jr Library • Atlanta, GA 30341 • ACRL RASD

Brooke F. Dixon Jr. • Vice Pres.,Division General Mgr. • EBSCO Subscription Service • Birmingham, AL 35201 • ACRL ALCTS LAMA

Brooke Lee • Oak Park, IL 60303

Brooker Valerie A. • Main Library Director • Santa Fe Public Library • Santa Fe, NM 87501

Brooker Virginia L. • Librarian • Midlands Technical College • Columbia, SC 29202

Brooking Diana M. • Madison, WI 53705

Brookins Joni L. • Technical Services Librarian • Warsaw Community Public Library • Warsaw, IN 46580

Brookins Naomi A. • Head Librarian • Washington High School • Chicago, IL 60617 • AASL

Brookman Jo Anne • Head,Carlson Health Sciences Lib • University of California-Davis Carlson Health Sciences Library • Davis, CA 95616-5291 • ACRL ALCTS

Brooks-Barr John M. • Library Director • Upper Arlington Public Library • Upper Arlington, OH 43221 • PLA

Brooks Alfred C. • Vice President • The Davey Company • Jersey City, NJ 07306

Brooks Beverly • Library Trustee • Zion-Benton Public Library District • Zion, IL 60099

Brooks Burton H. • Executive Director • Michigan Association for Media in Education • Grand Haven, MI 49417 • AASL LITA   Life

Brooks Cathleen S. • Thousand Oaks, CA 91360

Brooks Charles E. • University of Tulsa McFarlin Library • Tulsa, OK 74104-3189 • ACRL RASD IFRT NMRT

Brooks Clifford J. • Elmwood Park Memorial Junior-Senior High School • Elmwood Park, NJ 07407 • AASL

Brooks Constance L. • Chief of Preservation Dept • Stanford University Libraries Cecil H. Green Library • Stanford, CA 94305-6004 • ACRL ALCTS

Brooks Harry F. • United States D.O.I Bureau of Mines Library • Albany, OR 97321-2198

Brooks Helen L. • Springdale, UT 84767

Brooks Jane R. • Library/Media Specialist • West Morris Mendham High School • Mendham, NJ 07945 • AASL

Brooks Janet E. • Materials Selector • Metropolitan L Sys Downtown • Oklahoma City, OK 73102 • ALSC IFRT VRT

Brooks Jean • Russell, KS 67665

Brooks Jean S. • Jefferson Cty, MO 65109

Brooks Judith A. • Librarian • Oakland Schools • Waterford, MI 48328

Brooks Julie B. • Director • Sandusky Library • Sandusky, OH 44870 • LAMA

Brooks Kathleena • Library Director • Hitchcock Public Library • Hictchcock, TX 77563

Brooks L. Gordon • Soc Sci & Religion Subj Spec • Los Angeles Public Library • Los Angeles, CA 90071 • RASD GODORT IFRT

Brooks Laura • Redford, MI 48239 • ACRL ALCTS RASD IFRT SRRT

Brooks Laurie C. • Director • TST BOCES School Library System • Ithaca, NY 14850 • AASL

Brooks Leon B. • Database Coordinator • Trenton State College Roscoe L. West Library • Trenton, NJ 08650-4700

Brooks Margaret M. • Los Altos, CA 94024 • RASD

Brooks Maria M. • Branch Librarian • District of Columbia Public Library Martin Luther King Memorial Library • Washington, DC 20001

Brooks Mary Ann • Stockton-San Joaquin County Public Library • Stockton, CA 95202 • RASD LIRT

Brooks Nancy Mrs. • Baltimore County Public Library • Towson, MD 21204 • ALTA PLA

Brooks Paul • Group Manager • Family History Service Centers • Salt Lake City, UT 84150

Brooks Phyllis • Lexington, MA 02173

Brooks Robert M. • Navesink, NJ 07752 • ACRL

Brooks S. Barbara A. • Librarian • College of Saint Catherine • Saint Paul, MN 55105

Brooks Susan R. • Librarian • Sisseton Wahpeton Community College • Sisseton, SD 57262

Brooks Violette Y. • Librarian • Chicago Transit Authority Anthon Memorial Library • Chicago, IL 60654 • RASD EMIERT SRRT

Brookshier Doris • Special Collections Librarian • Central Missouri State University Ward Edwards Library • Warrensburg, MO 64093 • ACRL

Brookshire Madeline S. • Public Relations Director • Cuyahoga County Public Library • Cleveland, OH 44134-2792 • LAMA PLA

Brookstein Fran • Librarian • Wescott School • Northbrook, IL 60062

Broome Douglas G. • Cambellsville, KY 42718-2702

Broome Joellen • Technical Librarian • University of Nevada-Las Vegas James R. Dickinson Library • Las Vegas, NV 89154 • RASD

Broome Robin M. • Aurora, CO 80012 • SRRT

Broome Susan G. • Mercer University Main Library • Macon, GA 31207

Broomfield Sandra J. • Branch Librarian • Wellesley Free Library • Wellesley, MA 02181-5989 • PLA

Brophy Faye R. • Librarian • University of Southern Mississippi Cox Library • Long Beach, MS 39560 • ACRL

Brophy Mary J. • La Crescenta, CA 91214-2946

Brose Friedrich K. • Riverside Community College Library • Riverside, CA 92506

Brose Katherine A. • Oakland, CA 94610 • Continuing

Brosnihan Lauren M. • Library Instruction Coordinator • Connecticut College • New London, CT 06320-4196 • ACRL LIRT

Bross Anita K. • Librarian • Princeton High School • Cincinnati, OH 45246 • AASL

Bross Rexford R. Jr. • Head of Monographs • University of Toledo William S. Carlson Library • Toledo, OH 43606-3399 • ALCTS

Bross Valerie • California Polytechnic State University Robert E. Kennedy Library • San Luis Obispo, CA 93407 • ALCTS LITA   Life

Brostrom David • Director • Vaughn Public Library • Ashland, WI 54806 • PLA

Brotemarkle MaryAnn • Children's Librarian • Dorothy Bramlage Public Library • Junction City, KS 66441 • ALSC NMRT

Brothen Linda L. • Asst. Dir. for Public Services • University of Wisconsin • Madison, WI 53706

Brothers Joyce D. • Reference/Tech. Services Libn. • Narragansett Public Library • Narragansett, RI 02882 • RASD

Brothers Katherine I. • Library Technician, II • East Baton Rouge Parish Library • Baton Rouge, LA 70806-7699

Brotman Suzanne S. • Real Estate Agent • Pearce-Jannarone Inc. • Vineland, NJ 08360

Broton Cecilianne Sr • Librarian & Instructor • Calumet College • Hammond, IN 46394 • Continuing

Brottman May • Media Specialist • Glenbrook North High School • Northbrook, IL 60062 • AASL LITA RASD YALSA LIRT

Brough Randy • Director • Franklin Public Library • Franklin, NH 03235 • PLA

Broughton Angela C. • Library Principal Associate • Atlanta-Fulton Public Library Kirkwood Branch • Atlanta, GA 30317 • PLA

Broughton Doris • Librarian • Oak Ridge Elementary School • Arlington, VA 22202 • AASL

Brouillard Donna M. • TAP Resource Teacher • School District #109 • Deerfield, IL 60015 • AASL

Broun Kevin D. • Sr. Information Specialist • Apple Computer, Inc. Library • Cupertino, CA 95014 • LITA RASD

Brouse Ann G. • Head Of Technical Service Dept. • Steele Memorial Library • Elmira, NY 14901-2799 • ALCTS PLA

Broussard Harry C. • Technical Services Operations • University of New Mexico General Library • Albuquerque, NM 87131 • LITA

Brow Ellen H. • Basque Studies Librarian • University of Nevada-Reno Noble H. Getchell Library • Reno, NV 89557 • ACRL ALCTS RASD GODORT LIRT

Brow Judith Ann • Reference Librarian • Delta College Learning Resources Center • University Center, MI 48710 • ACRL ALCTS RASD GODORT

Browar Lisa M. • Asst Dir for Rare Bks & Ms • New York Public Library • New York, NY 10018-2788 • ACRL

Browder Mack • Trustee • Memphis-Shelby County Public Library and Information Center • Memphis, TN 38104-4025

Browder Martha H. • Librarian • Waynesboro High School Library • Waynesboro, VA 22980 • AASL YALSA   Continuing

Browdy Vivian H. • Senior Library Associate • Atlanta-Fulton Public Library West End Branch • Atlanta, GA 30310 • AASL

Brower Nancy D. • Assistant Director • Butte County Library • Oroville, CA 95966 • PLA

Brown-Byrne Linda R. • Student • University of Missouri-Columbia School of Library & Informational Science • Columbia, MO 65211

Brown-May Patricia • Kalamazoo, MI 49001-5416

Brown Amelie • Legal Information Center • University of California Hastings College of the Law Library • San Francisco, CA 94102

Brown Andrea P. • Reference Librarian • Henrico County Public Library Tuckahoe Area Library • Richmond, VA 23229

Brown Anita Fay • Elementary Librarian • Cuyahoga Falls Board of Education • Cuyahoga Falls, OH 44221 • AASL

Brown Anita P. • Librarian • Camden Catholic High School • Cherry Hill, NJ 08002

Brown Ann • Cache, OK 73527 • PLA IFRT

Brown Annee P. • Student • University of South Carolina College of Library & Information Science • Columbia, SC 29208 • AASL ALSC

Brown Annie • Branch Head • Gary Public Library Tolleston Branch • Gary, IN 46404-2297 • PLA

Brown Atlanta T. • Wilmington, DE 19808

Brown Barbara A. • Librarian • Grace A Dunn Middle School • Trenton, NJ 08610 • AASL

Brown Barbara A. • Philadelphia, PA 19131

Brown Barbara B. • Harwinton, CT 06791

Brown Barbara E. • DeKalb, IL 60115

Brown Barbara Elizabeth • Ottawa ON, K2B 8G5 Canada • ACRL ALCTS LITA   Continuing

Brown Barbara J. • Lexington, VA 24450 • ACRL LAMA LITA

Brown Barbara J. • Librarian • Des Moines Public Library Franklin Avenue Branch • Des Moines, IA 50310

Brown Barry • Science Librarian • University of Montana Library • Missoula, MT 59812 • ACRL

Brown Basak U. • Librarian • Ankara Base Library • APO New York, AE 09822

Brown Bettye • Reference Librarian • State Community College of E. St. Louis Senator Kenneth Hall LRC • East Saint Louis, IL 62201

Brown Beverly Cyr • Milton, MA 02186

Brown Brenda • Librarian • The Branson School • Ross, CA 94957 • AASL

Brown Brian Patrick • Acting Branch Librarian • District of Columbia Public Library Cleveland Park Branch • Washington, DC 20008

Brown Candice • Extension Services Manager • Arapahoe Library District • Littleton, CO 80121 • PLA IFRT

Brown Caren R. • Director • West Orange Free Public Library • West Orange, NJ 07052 • PLA

Brown Carl M. • Librarian • Orange County Library System Orlando Public Library • Orlando, FL 32801-2471 • PLA

Brown Carlene Perry • Cataloger • University of California-Berkeley University Library • Berkeley, CA 94720

Brown Carol • Franics W. Parker School • San Diego, CA 92103 • AASL ALSC

Brown Carol J. • Self-Employed • Carol Brown Associates • Houston, TX 77096 • LAMA PLA

Brown Carolyn P. • Chevy Chase, MD 20815 • LITA FLRT

Brown Carolyn T. • Assoc. Ln for Cultural Affairs • Library of Congress • Washington, DC 20541 • AASL YALSA

Brown Catherine M. • University of California Library • Los Angeles, CA 90024 • ACRL LIRT

Brown Charles A. • Librarian • Valley Grande Academy • Weslaco, TX 78596 • LAMA

Brown Charles L. • Manager • Louisville Free Public Library • Louisville, KY 40203-2257 • RASD

Brown Charles M. • Director of Libraries • Arlington County Department of Libraries Office of the Director • Arlington, VA 22201 • LAMA PLA RASD

Brown Charlotte B. • Archivist • Franklin & Marshall College Library • Lancaster, PA 17604-3003 • ACRL ALCTS

Brown Christopher • Librarian • Vermilion Parish Library • Abbeville, LA 70510 • PLA

Brown Clara M. • Gainesville, GA 30501 • ACRL RASD   Continuing

Brown Cynthia A. • Yreka Union School District Jackson Street School • Yreka, CA 96097 • AASL

Brown Cynthia J. • Saint Louis, MO 63119

Brown Dale W. • Supervisor of Lib Media Servs • Arlington Public Schools • Arlington, VA 22207 • AASL ALSC

Brown Darmae J. • Systems Coordinator • Aurora Public Library • Aurora, CO 80012 • LITA

Brown David B. • Asst. Head, Information Svs. • Fountaindale Public Library District • Bolingbrook, IL 60440

Brown David Carl • Librarian • U.S. Marine Corps James Carson Breckinridge Library • Quantico, VA 22134-5050 • ACRL RASD FLRT   Life

Brown Diana Mignery • Saint Charles Public Library • St. Charles, IL 60174

Brown Diane M. • Southeastern Library Network (SOLINET) • Atlanta, GA 30309-2955

Brown Dilek S. Mrs. • International Monetary Fund & World Bank • Washington, DC 20433

Brown Donald • Los Angeles, CA 90039 • NMRT

Brown Donald R. • Myerstown, PA 17067 • Continuing

Brown Donna L. • Head of Technical Services • Kokomo Howard County Public Library • Kokomo, IN 46901 • ALCTS

Brown Donna M. • Assistant Director • Stockton-San Joaquin County Public Library • Stockton, CA 95202 • LAMA PLA

Brown Doris R. • Director • DePaul University Libraries • Chicago, IL 60614 • ACRL LAMA

Brown E. G. • Serials/Collection Devlp Ln • Canisius College Andrew L. Bouwhuis Library • Buffalo, NY 14208-1098 • ALCTS

Brown Edna Earle G. • Associate Director • Georgia Southern University Library • Statesboro, GA 30460-8074 • ACRL ALCTS LAMA

Brown Elinor D. • Oak Ridge, TN 37830

Brown Elisabeth Potts • Quaker Bibliographer • Haverford College James P. Magill Library • Havertord, PA 19041 • ACRL

Brown Elizabeth A. • Library Media Specialist • Valparaiso High School • Valparaiso, IN 46383 • AASL IFRT

Brown Elizabeth A. • Assistant Professor Emeritus • University of Minnesota O. Meredith Wilson Library • Minneapolis, MN 55455-0414

Brown Elizabeth E. • Littleton, CO 80123 • LITA RASD *Continuing*

Brown Elizabeth W. • Harvard College Library Widener Memorial Library • Cambridge, MA 02138 • ALCTS NMRT

Brown Elmita R. • Children's Librarian • County of Los Angeles Public Library Gardena Library 313 • Gardena, CA 90247

Brown Emma Lee • Reference Librarian • West Chester University Francis Harvey Green Library • West Chester, PA 19383 • ACRL

Brown Ernestine Miss • Seattle, WA 98105 • ACRL RASD *Continuing*

Brown Eulalie W. • Head Govt. Publication Dept. • University of New Mexico General Library • Albuquerque, NM 87131 • ACRL GODORT

Brown Eva R. • Assistant Director • Chicago Library System, 10S-15 • Chicago, IL 60605 • ASCLA

Brown Florence S. • Chief, Extension Division • Enoch Pratt Free Library • Baltimore, MD 21201-4484 • LAMA PLA

Brown Freddiemae E. • Asst Chief Branch Services • Houston Public Library • Houston, TX 77002 • PLA

Brown Gary J. • Regional Manager • Faxon Company Inc. • Westwood, MA 02090 • ACRL ALCTS

Brown Gay • Orient, OH 43146

Brown George C. Rev • Framingham, MA 01701-6407

Brown Georgia W. • Director of Libraries • Southern University John B. Cade Library • Baton Rouge, LA 70813 • ACRL

Brown Gerald R. • Chief Librarian • Winnipeg School Division No. 1 Teachers Resource Center • Winnipeg MB, Canada • AASL EMIERT

Brown Glenda • Technical Service Librarian • Waukegan Public Library • Waukegan, IL 60085

Brown Gloria Primm • Program Officer • Carnegie Corporation of New York • New York, NY 10022 • ALSC YALSA

Brown Gregory H.B. • Reference Libn/Social Sci Dept • Toledo-Lucas County Public Library • Toledo, OH 43624 • PLA IFRT SRRT

Brown H. Glenn • Providence, RI 02906-3321 • ACRL *Continuing*

Brown Harriett B. • New York, NY 10025 • Continuing

Brown Helen R. • Murfreesboro, TN 37130

Brown Huey P. • Trustee • West Baton Rouge Parish Library • Port Allen, LA 70767

Brown Ina A. • Manager, Information Svs Dept. • AT&T Bell Laboratories • Murray Hill, NJ 07974 • ILERT

Brown Jack Perry • Director • Art Institute of Chicago Ryerson & Burnham Library • Chicago, IL 60603 • ACRL ALCTS LAMA LITA

Brown Jacqueline D. • Director of Information Serv. • Princeton University • Princeton, NJ 08544-2098 • ACRL LITA

Brown James M. • Student • Clarion University of Pennsylvania College of Library Science • Clarion, PA 16214 • LRRT

Brown James R. III • Librarian • Glen Cove Public Library • Glen Cove, NY 11542

Brown Jane • Supervisor of Public Services • Mesquite Public Library • Mesquite, TX 75149 • PLA

Brown Janet Dagenais • Wichita State University Library • Wichita, KS 67208

Brown Janet E. • Endicott, NY 13760 • ACRL SRRT

Brown Janette J. • Librarian • Moore Memorial Public Library • Texas City, TX 77590 • ALCTS

Brown Janis F. • Associate Director Educational • University of Southern California Norris Medical Library • Los Angeles, CA 90033-4582 • LITA

Brown Jeanne • Architecture Librarian • University of Nevada-Las Vegas James R. Dickinson Library • Las Vegas, NV 89154 • ACRL

Brown Jo • Student • Catholic University of America Library School Library • Washington, DC 20064

Brown Joanne E. • Wisconsin Regional Primate Research Center Primate Center Library • Madison, WI 53715 • ACRL IFRT

Brown Joanne L. • Student • Drexel University College of Information Studies • Philadelphia, PA 19104-2875

Brown Johanna B. • Head Loan Services • California Polytechnic State University Robert E. Kennedy Library • San Luis Obispo, CA 93407 • ACRL LAMA RASD

Brown Josef B. • Trustee • Prince George's County Memorial Library System • Hyattsville, MD 20782-2098 • ALTA

Brown Joyce A. • Director • Brewerton Free Library • Brewerton, NY 13029

Brown Joyce Lea • Children's Librarian • Oakland Park City Library • Oakland, FL 33334

Brown Judith A. • Prof Library Media Specialist • Carroll High Sch Lib • Southlake, TX 76092-9405 • AASL

Brown Judith A. • Fort Meyers, FL 33907

Brown Judith B. • Librarian • Landon Lower School • Bethesda, MD 20817 • AASL ALSC

Brown Judith Lynn Wilson • Indianapolis, IN 46229

Brown June E. • Alfred, NY 14802

Brown Karen E. • Youth Services Manager • Monterey Public Library • Monterey, CA 93940

Brown Karen E. • Reading, MA 01867 • PLA

Brown Karen L. • Acquisitions Librarian • Patrick J. Stapleton Library Indiana University of Pennsylvania • Indiana, PA 15705 • ALCTS LITA

Brown Karen M. • Bryant Adult Education Center • Alexandria, VA 22306 • AASL YALSA IFRT

Brown Katherine M. • Muncie, IN 47303 • Continuing

Brown Katherine S. • Coordinator • North Texas Library System • Fort Worth, TX 76107-2921

Brown Kathleen • Student • San Jose State University Division of Library & Information Science • San Jose, CA 95192-0029

Brown Kathleen R. • Acquisitions Librarian • North Carolina State University D. H. Hill Library • Raleigh, NC 27695-7111 • ACRL ALCTS LAMA LITA LRRT

Brown Kathryn E. • Librarian • Union-Endicott School District • Endicott, NY 13760

Brown Kay • Coor. of Children's Services • Greene County Public Library • Xenia, OH 45385 • ALSC PLA

Brown Kay Klayman • Head of Reference • State Univ of NY Coll at Potsdam Frederick W. Crumb Memorial Library • Potsdam, NY 13676 • ACRL

Brown Kent L. Jr. • Highlights For Children • Honesdale, PA 18431 • AASL ALSC

Brown LaVerne • Manager • Dallas Public Library Preston Royal Branch • Dallas, TX 75229-5599 • ALSC PLA

Brown Ladd II • Acquisition/Services Librarian • Georgia State University College of Law Library • Atlanta, GA 30303-3092 • ALCTS

Brown Lee C. • Librarian Emeritus • Harvard College Library Widener Memorial Library • Cambridge, MA 02138 • ACRL ASCLA *Continuing*

Brown Linda • Librarian • Wickenburg Public Library • Wickenburg, AZ 85358

Brown Linda A. • Head of Reference Department • Hamilton College Burke Library • Clinton, NY 13323 • ACRL RASD

Brown Linda M. • Haledon, NJ 07508 • ALCTS

Brown Lorelle R. • Coordinator of Reference Service • East Chicago Public Library • E. Chicago, IN 46312 • LAMA

Brown Lorene B. • Associate Professor • Clark-Atlanta University School of Library & Information Studies • Atlanta, GA 30314-4391 • ACRL LITA

Brown Louise R. • Director • Wayland Free Public Library • Wayland, MA 01778-1999 • LAMA LITA PLA RASD

Brown Lozella P. • Librarian • Philander Smith College M. L. Harris Library • Little Rock, AR 72202

Brown Lucinda A. • Director • Boone County Public Library • Florence, KY 41042

Brown Luther Dr. • Dean, Emeritus • St. Cloud State University • Saint Cloud, MN 56301 • ACRL LAMA *Life*

Brown Lyn S. Dr • Director • Philadelphia College of Bible LRC • Langhorne, PA 19047-2992 • ACRL

Brown Lynne • Chief Librarian • Chatham Public Library • Chatham ON, N7M 2G6 Canada • LAMA PLA RASD

Brown M. Audrey • Enoch Pratt Free Library Herring Run Branch • Baltimore, MD 21213

Brown M. Sharon • Social Sciences Bibliographer • University of Toronto John Robarts Library • Toronto ON, M5S 1A5 Canada • ACRL GODORT

Brown M. Suzanne • Asst. Chair & Assoc. Univ. Libn. • University of Florida Libraries • Gainesville, FL 32611-2047 • ACRL RASD

Brown Mabel E. • Conesville, IA 52739 • Continuing

Brown Malore I. • Children's Librarian I • Chicago Public Library Harold Washington Library • Chicago, IL 60605 • ALSC SRRT

Brown Margaret A. • Hd,Ref Services & Young Adults • Naperville Public Libraries • Naperville, IL 60540 • PLA RASD

Brown Margaret C. • Newtown, PA 18940 • ALCTS PLA *Life*

Brown Margaret C. • Trustee • DeKalb County Public Library • Decatur, GA 30030 • ALTA

Brown Margaret S. • Library Media Specialist • F. Douglass High School • Atlanta, GA 30318

Brown Margery P. • Cromwell, CT 06416 • Continuing

Brown Marie H. • Encino, CA 91316

Brown Marion E. • Toronto ON, M6G 3Z5 Canada • Continuing

Brown Mark N. • Curator of Manuscripts • Brown University Library • Providence, RI 02912 • ACRL

Brown Martha S. • Professional Development Officer • American Association of Law Libraries • Chicago, IL 60604 • ACRL ALCTS LAMA LITA CLENE

Brown Mary A. • Assistant Librarian • Purdue University Veterinary Medical Library • W. Lafayette, IN 47907

Brown Mary Ann • School Librarian • Mangum Primary School • Bahama, NC 27503 • AASL ALSC

Brown Mary Ann • Librarian • Grandview C-4 School District • Kansas City, MO 64145 • AASL

Brown Mary O. • Cataloger • Warren Wilson College Martha Ellison Library • Swannanoa, NC 28778

Brown Mary Sue • Library Administrator • Woodridge Public Library • Woodridge, IL 60517 • LAMA PLA

Brown Melinda C. • Librarian • Cambridge School • Weston, MA 02193 • AASL

Brown Melva J. • Librarian • Baton Rouge Magnet High School • Baton Rouge, LA 70806

Brown Melvin Marlo • Reference Librarian • Tennessee Technological University University Library • Cookeville, TN 38505 • NMRT

Brown Merrikay Everett • Branch Manager • Lewisville Branch Library • Lewisville, NC 27023 • PLA

Brown Michael A. • Automation Consultant • Texas Department of Human Services Rendential Child Care Licensing • Houston, TX 77024

Brown Michele T. • Thousand Oaks, CA 91360

Brown Mildred Ootsey • Baton Rouge, LA 70811

Brown Muriel W. • Part-time Librarian • Hockaday Private School • Dallas, TX 75229 • ALSC

Brown Nancy E. • Lit. AV Ln. • Downers Grove Public Library • Downers Grove, IL 60515 • PLA IFRT

Brown Nancy H. • Student • Burroughs Wellcome Company • Research Triangle Pk, NC 27709

Brown Nancy J. • Librarian • Moore Elementary School • Franklin, TN 37064 • AASL

Brown Nancy Jo • Database Manager • Old Colony Library Network • Canton, MA 02021 • ALCTS LITA

Brown Nell J. • Director of Media • Wadsworth Elementary School • Palm Coast, FL 32137 • AASL

Brown Norma-Jean V. • Student • Louisiana State University School of Library & Information Science • Baton Rouge, LA 70803-3290 • PLA

Brown Norman B. • Asst Dir Spec Clln • University of Illinois Library • Urbana, IL 61801 • ACRL ALCTS

Brown Pamela J. • Baltimore County Public Library • Towson, MD 21204 • PLA

Brown Pamela M. • Children's Librarian • Sonoma County Library Rohnert Park-Cotati Branch • Rohnert Park, CA 94928 • ALSC

Brown Pamela P. • Technical Services Head • Arlington Heights Memorial Library • Arlington Heights, IL 60004-5966 • ALCTS LITA

Brown Patricia B. • Navistar International Transportation Corp. • Melrose Park, IL 60660

Brown Patricia L. • Division Director • Savage Information Services • Torrance, CA 90505 • ILERT

Brown Paula D. • Head of Adult Services • Chula Vista Public Library • Chula Vista, CA 91910 • PLA

Brown Paula V. • Avon Grove Elementary School • West Grove, PA 19311 • AASL

Brown Peter B. • Catalog Librarian • Professional Media Services • Gardena, CA 90248 • ALCTS LITA

Brown Philip L. • Head of Document Department • South Dakota State University Briggs Library • Brookings, SD 57007 • ACRL GODORT

Brown Phyllis B. • Supervisor • Fayette County Margaret Mitchell Public Library • Fayetteville, GA 30214 • LAMA PLA

Brown Phyllis J. • Head of Acquistions • Idaho State University Eli M. Oboler Library • Pocatello, ID 83209-8089 • ACRL ALCTS

Brown Phyllis M. Miss • Sitka, AK 99835 • Continuing

Brown Phyllis N. • Information Services Coordinator • U. S. Secret Service • Washington, DC 20223

Brown Picken • Trustee • William Leonard Public Library District • Robbins, IL 60472 • ALTA
Brown R Warner • Trustee • Elmhurst Public Library • Elmhurst, IL 60126 • ALTA PLA
Brown R. Roslyn • Youth Service Coordinator • Central Florida Regional Library • Ocala, FL 32671
Brown Ralph S. • President • American Standard Car Company • Crystal Lake, IL 60014 • ALSC ALTA
Brown Raymond R. • Trustee • Akron-Summit County Public Library • Akron, OH 44326-0001 • ALTA
Brown Rebecca K. • Media Specialist • Duval County Board of Education Justina Road Elementary School • Jacksonville, FL 32210 • AASL
Brown Rene L. • Librarian • Maryview Hospital Health Sciences Library • Portsmouth, VA 23707
Brown Richard C. • Personnel Administrator • Richland County Public Library • Columbia, SC 29201
Brown Ricki Val • Headquarters Librarian • Cumberland County Public Library and Information Center • Fayetteville, NC 28301 • LAMA PLA
Brown Rita • Mariner High School • Cape Coral, FL 33909
Brown Robin • Student • Syracuse University School of Information Studies • Syracuse, NY 13244-4100 • RASD IFRT NMRT SRRT
Brown Ronald • Student • Clark-Atlanta University School of Library & Information Studies • Atlanta, GA 30314-4391
Brown Rosanna N. • Director • Lassen College • Susanville, CA 96130
Brown Rowland C W • Columbus, OH 43221
Brown Ruth Eleanor • Burdett, NY 14818 • ALCTS PLA *Continuing*
Brown Ruth M. • Children's Librarian • Los Angeles Public Library Pio Pico Korea Town Branch • Los Angeles, CA 90006 • PLA
Brown Ruth Marilyn • Cataloging Librarian • Wingate College • Wingate, NC 28174 • ALCTS
Brown Salazar Mary Jane • Washington, DC 20003-3017 • ALSC
Brown Sandra L. • Director • Mount Marty College Library • Yankton, SD 57078 • ACRL
Brown Sandra L. • Bolivar, MO 65613 • LAMA
Brown Sarah C. • Director • New Castle Public Library • New Castle, DE 19720 • PLA
Brown Sharon D. • Serials Librarian • National Library of Medicine • Bethesda, MD 20894
Brown Sheila • Adult Services • Cranberry Public Library • Mars, PA 16046
Brown Sheila A. • Student • San Jose State University Division of Library & Information Science • San Jose, CA 95192-0029
Brown Shelley Q. • Student • University of South Carolina College of Library & Information Science • Columbia, SC 29208
Brown Sherry Kelly M. • Student • University of South Carolina College of Library & Information Science • Columbia, SC 29208 • AASL
Brown Steven A. • Document Delivery Lib-Sci Lib • University of Georgia Libraries • Athens, GA 30602 • ACRL
Brown Steven L. • Director • Brazoria County Library System • Angleton, TX 77515 • ALCTS LAMA IFRT
Brown Susie Avis • South Daytona, FL 32019 • Continuing
Brown Sylvia A. • Branch Librarian • United States District Court Library • Madison, WI 53703 • FLRT GODORT
Brown Tamiko G. • Montgomery, AL 36110
Brown Thomas • Trustee • Schiller Park Public Library • Schiller Park, IL 60176-1699 • ALTA
Brown Thomas M. • Librarian • Concord College Library • Athens, WV 24712 • ACRL ALCTS RASD
Brown Timothy • Librarian • Washington State Penitentiary • Walla Walla, WA 99362 • ASCLA
Brown Timothy A. • University Librarian • Boise State University Library • Boise, ID 83725 • ACRL
Brown Vicki L. • Goldsboro, NC 27530 • ALCTS
Brown Vickie B. • Woodruff Primary School • Woodruff, SC 29388
Brown Virginia E. • Technical Services Coordinator • Irving Public Library System • Irving, TX 75015-2288 • PLA
Brown Virginia K. • Middle School Media Specialist • Mohave Middle School • Scottsdale, AZ 85250 • AASL
Brown William A. III • Assistant Director • Portsmouth Public Library • Portsmouth, VA 23704
Brown William E. Jr. • Head, Archives & Special Clln. • University of Miami Libraries Richter Library • Coral Gables, FL 33124 • ACRL
Browne Berks • University of Regina • Regina SK, S4S 0A2 Canada • ACRL ALCTS LITA
Browne Blanche G. • Coordinator • Jim Cherry Center • Atlanta, GA 30329 • AASL
Browne Eleanore B. • Media Specialist • Jupiter Community High School • Jupiter, FL 33458 • AASL
Browne Elizabeth • School Librarian • Pennbrook Schools • North Wales, PA 19454 • AASL
Browne Elizabeth L. • Librarian • Memorial University Queen Elizabeth II Library • St Johns NF, A1B 3Y1 Canada • ALCTS LITA
Browne Gretchen • Rockville Center, NY 11570
Browne Joseph P. Rev • Librarian • University of Portland Clark Memorial Library • Portland, OR 97203-5798
Browne Lynda S. • National Research Council Library • Washington, DC 20418 • LITA
Browne Sharon H • Southwestern School • Windsor, NC 27983 • AASL IFRT
Browne Steven J. • Student • University of Iowa School of Library & Information Science • Iowa City, IA 52242 • PLA
Brownell Barbara A. • Technical Processing Spec. • Online Computer Library Center (OCLC) • Dublin, OH 43017-3395 • ACRL ALCTS
Brownell Catherine • Circulation Librarian • Renton Public Library • Renton, WA 98055-2126 • LITA
Brownell Daphne M. • De Land, FL 32724 • Life
Brownell Richard G. • Adult Services • Solano County Library Vacaville Branch • Vacaville, CA 95688 • RASD
Browning Ann F. • Winston-Salem, NC 27104 • ALCTS
Browning Elizabeth K. • Coor Of L Serv • Henrico County Public Schools • Richmond, VA 23223 • AASL
Browning Garry A. • Support Services Supervisor • Oregon State University William Jasper Kerr Library • Corvallis, OR 97331-4501
Browning Henrietta S. Mrs. • Reference • Hillsdale Free Public Library • Hillsdale, NJ 07642
Browning Irene • Trustee • Richmond Public Library • Richmond BC, V6X 2E3 Canada
Browning Marilyn • Science Reference Librarian • University of Hawaii Library • Honolulu, HI 96822 • MAGERT
Browning Marvin T. • Head of Technical Services • College of Mount Saint Joseph • Cincinnati, OH 45233-1671 • ALCTS
Browning Medora E. • Reference Librarian • Free Library of Philadelphia • Philadelphia, PA 19103 • PLA
Browning Robert X. • Dir.,Public Affairs Video Arch • Purdue University • West Lafayette, IN 47907 • LITA GODORT
Browning Ruth H. • Reference Department Head • Upper Arlington Public Library • Upper Arlington, OH 43221 • RASD SRRT
Browning Sandra B. • Greenville, SC 29615
Browning Susan M. • Cirrculation Librarian • Dade County Library System Coral Gables Branch Library • Coral Gables, FL 33134 • PLA
Brownlee Bobbie J. • Librarian • Kialing Junior High School • Austin, TX 78702 • AASL
Brownlee Diane T. • Reference Librarian • Santa Ana Public Library • Santa Ana, CA 92701
Brownlee Evelyn L • Supervisor, Libraries • E.I. du Pont de Nemours & Company • Wilmington, DE 19880-0301 • ACRL ALCTS LAMA LITA RASD
Brownlee Jerry W. • Director • Palm Beach County Library System • West Palm Beach, FL 33406 • LAMA PLA
Brownmiller Sara N. • Coor. Electronic Resources • University of Oregon Library • Eugene, OR 97403-1299 • ACRL RASD
Brownson Bruce B. • President • Congressional Staff Directories • Mount Vernon, VA 22121 • LITA FLRT GODORT
Brownstein Valarie R. • Rochester, NY 14612
Broyles Elizabeth C. • Librarian • University of Texas at San Antonio-Library • San Antonio, TX 78249 • ACRL
Broyles Linda S. • Mishawaka, IN 46545
Broyles Susan • Hd. Instruction & Info Servs. • Arizona State University Hayden Library • Tempe, AZ 85287-1006 • ACRL LAMA LIRT
Brozena Susan A. • Senior Librarian/Children's Dept • Hamilton Township Public Library • Trenton, NJ 08619 • ALSC PLA
Brozinski Susan A. • Student • Forest Elementary School • Farmington, MI 48331 • AASL
Brubacher Lois • Media Specialist • Hesston Middle School • Hesston, KS 67062 • AASL
Brubaker Jana P. • DeKalb, IL 60115 • IFRT SRRT
Brubaker Maryellen • Library Director • Cortez City Library • Cortez, CO 81321
Bruce Anne • Trustee • Loudoun County Public Library • Leesburg, VA 22075 • ALTA
Bruce Bonny K. • Student • University of Arizona Graduate Library School • Tucson, AZ 85721 • ALSC PLA RASD
Bruce Dennis L. • County Librarian • Spartanburg County Public Library • Spartanburg, SC 29304 • PLA
Bruce Gerald G. • Reference Librarian • Lancaster County Library • Lancaster, PA 17602 • MAGERT
Bruce Judith A. • Austin, TX 78727 • SRRT
Bruce Mary J. • Midland, MI 48640 • AASL
Bruce Mary Jo • Media Specialist • Bloom Elementary School Library • Louisville, KY 40204 • AASL
Bruce Mary Jo • Student • Texas Woman's University School of Library & Information Studies • Denton, TX 76204 • LITA EMIERT NMRT
Bruce Patricia A. • Media Specialist • Forestville High School • Forestville, MD 20745 • AASL YALSA
Bruce Robert Keady • Head of History Dept • Minneapolis Public Library & Information Center • Minneapolis, MN 55401-1992 • ACRL PLA RASD CLENE IRRT MAGERT *Life*
Bruce Susan D. • Librarian • Powell Middle School • Littleton, CO 80121
Bruce Valerie M. Sr. • Librarian • Bishop Dunne High School Library • Dallas, TX 75224
Bruch Harriet Hagen • Curriculum Materials Edu. Libn. • Hofstra University Libraries • Hempstead, NY 11550 • AASL ACRL ALSC
Bruckner Jeanne L. • United States Army Library Kelley Barracks • APO New York, NY 09107
Bruder William P. • Architect/President • William P. Bruder Architect Ltd. • New River, AZ 85027 • LAMA
Brudi Gina M. • San Antonio, TX 78216-2961
Brudny Jennifer G. • Hackenstack, NJ 07601
Brudvig Glenn L. • Library Director • California Institute of Technology • Pasadena, CA 91125 • ACRL LAMA LITA
Brue Theresa • Caledonia-Mumford Central School Elementary Library • Caledonia, NY 14423
Brueggeman Peter • Head of Public Services • University of California Scripps Institute of Oceanography • La Jolla, CA 92093-0175 • ACRL MAGERT
Brueggen Pamela L. • Tampa, FL 33624-5023
Bruer John Michael • Associate Director • New York Public Library • New York, NY 10018-2788 • LAMA
Bruere Lisa • St. Louis, MO 63188 • ALCTS PLA
Bruggeman Lora L. • Student • University of Illinois Graduate School of Library and Information Science • Urbana, IL 61801 • PLA IFRT
Brugger Arden R. • Reference Librarian • Jacksonville Public Libraries Main Library • Jacksonville, FL 32202 • Life
Brugger Jane • Charleston, WV 25304 • Continuing
Brugger Judith M. • Catalog Management Librarian • Cornell University • Ithaca, NY 14853-5301 • ALCTS LITA
Brugger Susan • Legal Assistant • Davenport, Evans, Hurwitz and Smith • Sioux Falls, SD 57101-1030 • IFRT
Brugnolotti Phyllis T. • Head Librarian • New York City Collegiate School • New York, NY 10024
Bruguier Elsa A. • Student • Rutgers University School of Communication Information & Library Studies • New Brunswick, NJ 08903
Bruhn Valerie Mrs. • Manager, Technical Services • Vaughan Public Libraries • Maple ON, L6A 1T1 Canada • LITA
Bruins Sara E. • Student • University of Wisconsin-Madison School of Library & Information Studies • Madison, WI 53706 • ALCTS LITA
Brum Laura L. • George Mason University Fenwick Library • Fairfax, VA 22030 • RASD
Bruman Janet L. • INLEX, Inc. • Monterey, CA 93942 • ALCTS LITA
Brumback Elsie L. • Media & Technology Director • North Carolina State Department of Public Instruction • Raleigh, NC 27603-1712 • AASL
Brumback Una Marie Sr • Head Librarian • Avila College Hooley-Bundschu Library • Kansas City, MO 64145 • ACRL
Brumbaugh D. • Student • Kent State University School of Library & Information Science • Kent, OH 44242-0001 • PLA SRRT
Brumley Richard L. • Head, Acquisitions Dept. • California Polytechnic State University Robert E. Kennedy Library • San Luis Obispo, CA 93407 • ACRL ALCTS
Brumm Janet • Cataloging Librarian • Wayne State College U S Conn Library • Wayne, NE 68787 • ALCTS
Brummer Kristine E. • Student • University of Wisconsin-Milwaukee School of Library & Information Science • Milwaukee, WI 53201
Brunat Alice L. • Bloomington, MN 55438 • Continuing
Brundage Louise A. • Public Services Director • Hamden Library • Hamden, CT 06518 • PLA IFRT
Brundige Nancy F. • Los Angeles, CA 90064
Brundin Robert E. Dr • Professor • University of Alberta • Edmonton, AB T6G 2J4 Canada
Brune Bonnie J. • Klamath County School District Instructional Media Center • Klamath Falls, OR 97603 • AASL LIRT

Bruneau Deborah G. • Adult Services Supervisor • Westfield Athenaeum • Westfield, MA 01085
Brunell David H. • Director • Bibliographical Center for Research • Denver, CO 80222 • LITA
Bruner David L • Librarian I • Southwest Texas State University Learning Resource Center • San Marcos, TX 78666-4604 • ACRL ALCTS
Bruner Gilda • Library Director • Greenwood Lake Public Library • Greenwood Lake, NY 10925
Bruner Katharine E. • Chattanooga, TN 37405 • AASL
Brunet Louis • Director • College De Maisonneuue Bibliotheque • Montreal PQ, Canada • ACRL LITA RASD
Brunet Patrick J. • Library Manager • Western Wisconsin Technical College • La Crosse, WI 54602-0908 • ACRL RASD
Brunett Sally • Trustee • Metropolitan Library System • Oklahoma City, OK 73102 • ALTA PLA
Bruning Jean • Ithaca, NY 14850 • ALSC *Continuing*
Bruning Martha • Director • Pittsylvania County Public Library • Chatham, VA 24531 • PLA
Brunk Charles L. • Cataloging Librarian • University of Wisconsin • Milwaukee, WI 53201 • ACRL ALCTS IFRT
Brunken Phyllis • Media/Technical Director • Educational Serv Unit #7 Library • Columbus, NE 68601 • AASL LITA
Brunkow Jeanne M. • Fort Collins, CO 80525
Brunner A. Mila N • Houston, TX 77095-3513
Brunner Eileen • Librarian/Director • Columbia County Public Library • Lake City, FL 32055 • PLA
Brunner Karen B. • Librarian • Riker Danzig Scherer Hyland Perretti • Morristown, NJ 07960 • LAMA RASD
Brunner Rickie L. • Books & Serials Librarian • Alabama Department of Archives & History Library • Montgomery, AL 36130 • ACRL ALCTS LAMA LITA *Life*
Bruno Cynthia A. • Public Service Librarian II • Metropolitan Library System in Oklahoma Southern Oaks Branch • Oklahoma City, OK 73139-7299 • LITA
Bruno Elaine S. • Head of Circulation • Cairo American College • APO, AE 09839-4900
Bruno Frances Jean • Librarian • Middletown Township Free Public Library • Middletown, NJ 07748 • ALSC
Bruno Frank A. • Student • Brigham Young University Hawaii Campus • Laie, HI 96762
Bruno Thomas • Assistant Area Librarian • Dumbarton Public Library County of Henrico • Richmond, VA 23228 • Life
Brunot Eugenia Miss • Pittsburgh, PA 15226 • AASL ASCLA *Continuing*
Bruns Phyllis • Senior MARC Standards Spec • Library of Congress • Washington, DC 20541
Brunsman Patricia • Director • Nanuet Public Library • Nanuet, NY 10954 • LAMA
Brunson Crenetha S. • Serial Cataloger • Library of Congress • Washington, DC 20541
Brunswick John R. • North Olmsted, OH 44070 • ACRL IFRT NMRT
Brunton David W. • Personnel/Purchasing Director • Arapahoe Library District • Littleton, CO 80121 • LAMA PLA IFRT
Brunton F Elaine • Chula Vista, CA 91910-6418 • AASL
Brunvand Amy • Science Reference Librarian • Fort Lewis College Library • Durango, CO 81301 • GODORT MAGERT
Bruseau Laurence Lynn • Staff Member/Tech Serv Dept • Portland State University Library • Portland, OR 97207
Brush Maryanne • Assistant to the Director • Jefferson County Public Library • Lakewood, CO 80215 • LAMA
Bruss Heidi Luise • Suburban Library System • Burr Ridge, IL 60521
Bruton D. Jane • Wilmington College Library • New Castle, DE 19720 • ALCTS
Bruursema Shirley A. • Library Board Chair • Kent County Library System • Grand Rapids, MI 49503
Bruwelheide Janis H. • Associate Professor • Montana State University • Bozeman, MT 59717-0332 • AASL
Bryan Ann • School Librarian • Gainesville High School • Gainesville, FL 32609 • AASL
Bryan Anna R. • Coordinator Special Clln • University of Delaware Library • Newark, DE 19717-5267 • ACRL ALCTS
Bryan Arthur L. • Director • Wadleigh Memorial Library • Milford, NH 03055
Bryan Barbara D. • University Librarian • Fairfield University Gustav & Dagmar Nyselius Library • Fairfield, CT 06430-7524 • AASL ACRL ALCTS LAMA LITA RASD
Bryan Barnabas Jr Mrs • New York, NY 10022 • Life
Bryan Carol L. • Charleston, WV 25306 • LAMA
Bryan Cheryl G. • Director • Brewster Ladies Library Association • Brewster, MA 02631
Bryan Cynthia A. • Branch Manager • Calcasieu Parish Pub Lib Sys Sulphur Branch • Sulphur, LA 70663
Bryan Dean • Lead Cataloger • Scottsdale Public Library • Scottsdale, AZ 85251
Bryan Eunice Von Ende • East Sullivan, NH 03445 • PLA RASD *Continuing*
Bryan James E. • Longwood, FL 32779 • Continuing
Bryan Jane • Grandview, MO 64030 • AASL
Bryan Jane C. • Director • Jackson-George Regional Library System • Pascagoula, MS 39567 • PLA
Bryan Jane G. • Head Reference Department • University of Pennsylvania Library Van Pelt-Dietrich Library Center • Philadelphia, PA 19104-6206 • ACRL RASD GODORT
Bryan Jennifer L. • Student • Indiana University School of Library and Information Science • Bloomington, IN 47405
Bryan Jerry A. • Regional Sales Manager • Book Wholesalers Inc. • Lexington, KY 40511 • ALSC
Bryan Joyce • Gulf Breeze, 32561
Bryan M. Virginia • Student • University of Wisconsin-Madison School of Library & Information Studies • Madison, WI 53706
Bryan Marie E. • Woodland Public Library • Woodland, CA 95695 • ALSC LAMA LITA PLA CLENE
Bryan Michael G. • Librarian II • Tampa-Hillsborough County Library System Ruskin Branch • Ruskin, FL 33570 • ALSC
Bryan Sarah J. • Asst. Librarian • University of Central Arkansas Torreyson Library • Conway, AR 72032 • ALCTS
Bryan Susan M. • Librarian • Warwick Veterans Memorial High School • Warwick, RI 02886 • AASL
Bryan Virginia S. Ms. • Librarian • Bossier Parish Community College Library • Bossier City, LA 71108 • ACRL LAMA
Bryan William W. • Peoria Heights, IL 61614 • PLA *Continuing*
Bryant Bonita I. • Asst. Director Collection Devlp. • State University of New York (SUNY) University Libraries • Albany, NY 12222 • ACRL ALCTS
Bryant Darcel A. • Head Cataloger • Hampton University Collis P. Huntington Memorial Library • Hampton, VA 23668 • LAMA
Bryant David S. • Director • Free Public Library of Belleville Township • Belleville, NJ 07109 • LAMA PLA
Bryant Deloris V. • School Library Media Specialist • Hugoton High School • Hugoton, KS 67951 • AASL
Bryant Dorothy G. • Leicester, NC 28748 • Continuing
Bryant Douglas • Trustee • Cumberland County Public Library and Information Center • Fayetteville, NC 28301
Bryant Douglas W. • Dartmouth College Biomedical Lib. Dartmouth-Hitchcock Medical Center • Hanover, NH 03756 • ACRL LAMA *Life*
Bryant Elizabeth A. • Library Media Specialist • Happy Hollow School • Wayland, MA 01778 • AASL
Bryant Ellen K. • Young Adult & Reference Libn • Glencoe Public Library • Glencoe, IL 60022-1597 • RASD
Bryant Eugenia D. • Public Services & Asst. Director • Morton Grove Public Library • Morton Grove, IL 60053 • PLA RASD
Bryant Franja • Children's Librarian • King County Library System Lake Hills Branch • Bellevue, WA 98007 • ALSC
Bryant Josephine • Chief Executive Officer • North York Public Library • North York ON, M2N 5N9 Canada • LAMA PLA
Bryant Judith W. • Head of Children's Room • Jersey City Public Library • Jersey City, NJ 07302-3499 • PLA IFRT SRRT
Bryant Laura • Director • Galax-Carroll Regional Library • Galax, VA 24333 • PLA
Bryant Linda L. • School Librarian • Whilesville Elementary School • Monks Corner, SC 29461 • AASL PLA
Bryant Lorraine • Minneapolis, MN 55412 • ALSC SRRT
Bryant Marion K. • Librarian • Muskogee Public Library • Muskogee, OK 74401
Bryant Robyn B. • Eagle County Public Library • Eagle, CO 81631 • ALSC
Bryant Virginia M. • Cataloging Librarian • Library of Congress • Washington, DC 20541 • ALCTS
Bryant Vylinda Ann • Student • University of Iowa School of Library & Information Science • Iowa City, IA 52242 • AASL
Bryant William • Contract Specialist • District of Columbia Public Library Martin Luther King Memorial Library • Washington, DC 20001
Bryce Betty K. • Reference Librarian • University of Alabama • Tuscaloosa, AL 35487-0266 • ACRL IRRT
Bryd Shirley T. • Head Librarian • Salem Junior High School • Virginia Bch, VA 23464 • AASL
Bryden David L. • High Point College • High Point, NC 27262
Bryfonski Dedria A. • Gale Research, Inc. • Detroit, MI 48226 • ALCTS RASD
Bryner Barbara K. • Librarian • Brimfield Elementary School Library • Kent, OH 44240 • AASL
Brynteson Susan • Director of Libraries • University of Delaware Library • Newark, DE 19717-5267 • ACRL ALCTS LAMA LITA PLA RASD GODORT IFRT MAGERT
Bryson Barbara • Student • University of Hawaii School of Library & Information Studies • Honolulu, HI 96822
Bryson Deborah H. • Reference Librarian • Southern California University Crocker Business Library • Los Angeles, CA 90089-0182 • RASD IFRT
Bryson Juliette • Ashland, KY 41101 • Continuing
Bryson Kathleen C. • Library Director • Transylvania University Library • Lexington, KY 40508 • ACRL
Bryson Linda C. • Student • University of North Texas School of Library & Information Sciences • Denton, TX 76203 • RASD
Bryson Ronald • Regional Library Administrator • Kentucky Department for Libraries & Archives Kentuckiana Region • Eminence, KY 40019 • ACRL
Bryson Shauna • Manager of Library Services • LS, Inc. • New York, NY 10017 • ILERT
Bryson Susan A. • Reference Librarian • High Point Public Library • High Point, NC 27261 • PLA RASD SRRT
Bryson Verena • Trustee • South Carolina State Library • Columbia, SC 29211 • ALTA
Brzezinski Tom • Media Specialist • Clemens Crossing Elementary School • Columbia, MD 21044-4138
Brzozowski Margery E. • Director of Library Services • Grand Canyon University Fleming Library • Phoenix, AZ 85061 • ACRL LAMA LITA
Brzustowicz Richard J. Jr. • Seattle, WA 98145
Buak Susan Jarvis • Cobb County Public Library System • Marietta, GA 30060
Bubelis Dona • Seattle Public Library • Seattle, WA 98104-1193
Bubert Jane M. • Linsly Institute Coudon Library • Wheeling, WV 26003
Bublick Raisa L. • Hd Ln • Rocky Hill High School • Rocky Hill, CT 06067
Buboltz Dale D. • Library Media Center Director • South Gate Junior High School • South Gate, CA 90280 • AASL LAMA
Bubolz Jocelyn • Director • Elm Grove Public Library • Elm Grove, WI 53122-0906 • ALTA LAMA LITA PLA RASD CLENE IFRT SRRT
Bucalo Stephanie • Student • Saint John's University Division of Library & Information Science • Jamaica, NY 11439 • AASL ACRL PLA
Buchan Patricia C. • Director • All Children's Hospital Medical Library #766 • Saint Petersburg, FL 33731-8920
Buchanan Anissa J. • Student • Murray State University Department of Elementary & Secondary Education • Murray, KY 42071-3309
Buchanan Anne L. • Purdue University Krannert Management & Economics Library • West Lafayette, IN 47907 • RASD
Buchanan Barbara G. • Administrative Librarian • United States Department of Agriculture National Agricultural Library • Beltsville, MD 20705-2351
Buchanan Dana • Children's Librarian • Webster Groves Public Library • Webster Grvs, MO 63119 • ALSC
Buchanan Dawn E. • Traverse City, MI 49684
Buchanan F G. • Trustee • Metropolitan Library System • Oklahoma City, OK 73102 • ALTA
Buchanan Holly Shipp • Louisville, KY 40204 • ACRL
Buchanan J. Paul • Dir. of Computing & Telecom. • Washington University Libraries • Saint Louis, MO 63130-4899 • ACRL LITA
Buchanan Jack • City Librarian • Santa Maria Public Library • Santa Maria, CA 93454 • PLA
Buchanan Jan • Partin Elementary School • Oviedo, FL 32765 • AASL
Buchanan Lori E. • User Education Librarian • Austin Peay State University • Clarkville, TN 37044 • ACRL LIRT
Buchanan Margie S. • Air Training Command Librarian • HQ Air Training Command USAF • Randolph AFB, TX 78150-5001 • AFLRT
Buchanan Mary G. • Freelance Indexer • Scarsdale Public Library • Scarsdale, NY 10583
Buchanan Midori M. • Cruz Bay, VI 00831-0536 • AASL
Buchanan N K. • Boulder, CO 80303 • PLA
Buchanan Nancy E. • Reference Librarian • Pima Community College West Campus LRC • Tucson, AZ 85709
Buchanan Nancy L. • Reference Dept. • Texas A & M University Sterling C. Evans Library • College Station, TX 77843-5000 • ACRL RASD
Buchanan Nancy Officer • Librarian • Cumberland County Elementary School • Burkesville, KY 42717
Buchanan Raymond F. • Director • Fairport Public Library • Fairport, NY 14450 • PLA
Buchanan Sarah A. • Assoc. Professor • University of Pittsburgh Hillman Library • Pittsburgh, PA 15260 • ACRL ALCTS
Buchanan William C. Dr. • Library Director • Jefferson State Junior College Allen Library • Birmingham, AL 35215
Buchberger Ellen M. • Reference & Inter-Librarian • Wisconsin Valley Library Service • Wausau, WI 54401

Buchen Richard W. • Southwest Museum Braun Research Library • Los Angeles, CA 90041-0558 • ACRL ALCTS EMIERT IRRT SRRT

Bucher Eric M. • Lake Worth, FL 33461-1434

Bucher Katherine T. Dr • Old Dominion University Library • Norfolk, VA 23529-0256 • AASL

Bucher Margaret • Trustee • River Bluffs Regional Library • Saint Joseph, MO 64501

Buchholz Lucy D. Mrs • Media Specialist • Walton Middle School Media Center • Charlottesville, VA 22901 • AASL ALSC *Life*

Buchholz Patty M. • Librarian • Margureite Hahn Elementary School • Rohnert Park, CA 94928

Buchstein Frederick • Cleveland Heights-University Heights Public Library • Cleveland Heights, OH 44118

Buchta Tom • Dean • College of Lake County Learning Resource Center • Grayslake, IL 60030 • ACRL LAMA

Buchwald Carole R. • Reference Back-Up • South Texas Library System • Corpus Christi, TX 78401

Buciak Beverly A. • Reference Librarian • Alsip-Merrionette Park Library District • Alsip, IL 60658 • AASL PLA RASD YALSA

Buck Anne M. • Librarian • New Jersey Institute of Technology Van Houten Library • Newark, NJ 07102 • ACRL LAMA LITA

Buck Dayna Evers • Project Manager • GEAC Computers Inc. • Englewood, CO 80111 • LAMA LITA

Buck Jean L. • Technical Librarian • Wolfram Research Inc. • Champaign, IL 61826

Buck Jeremy R. • Deputy Director • Dayton & Montgomery County Public Library • Dayton, OH 45402-2103 • PLA IFRT

Buck Kathryn L. • Crete, NE 68333 • Continuing

Buck Lawrene S. • LMS Director • Foyil Public School • Foyil, OK 74031 • AASL

Buck Mary M. • Student • University of Pittsburgh School of Library and Information Science • Pittsburgh, PA 15260

Buck Patricia K. • Assistant Librarian • Philadelphia School District Pedagogical Library • Philadelphia, PA 19103

Buck Richard M. • Asst. to the Exec. Dir. • New York Public Library Performing Arts • New York, NY 10023 • IFRT SRRT

Buck Sandra • Library Media Teacher • Scandinavian Middle School • Fresno, CA 93726 • AASL YALSA

Buck Stefanie • Student • University of Hawaii School of Library & Information Studies • Honolulu, HI 96822

Buckalew Sue M. • Media Specialist • Bethesda Elementary School • Lawrenceville, GA 30245

Buckardt Kate • Reference Librarian • Darien Library • Darien, CT 06820-4497

Buckholz Margaret N. • Skykomish, WA 98288

Buckingham Betty • Consultant Education Media • State Department of Education • Des Moines, IA 50319 • AASL

Buckingham Dorothea N. • Student • University of Hawaii School of Library & Information Studies • Honolulu, HI 96822

Buckingham Jeanette F. • Collections Coordinator • John W. Scott Health Sciences Library University of Alberta Library • Edmonton AB, T6G 2R7 Canada • ACRL ALCTS RASD

Buckingham Jeanette M. • Library Media Specialist • Roosevelt Elementary School • Ames, IA 50010 • AASL

Buckingham Melissa • Head, Community Services,OWA/YA • Free Library of Philadelphia • Philadelphia, PA 19103 • ASCLA PLA

Buckingham Rebecca M. • East Area Supervisor • Sno-Isle Regional Library Snohomish Branch • Marysville, WA 98290 • ALSC

Buckland Lawrence F. • President • Inforonics Inc. Library • Littleton, MA 01460 • LITA

Buckland Michael K. • Professor • University of California-Berkeley School of Library & Information Studies • Berkeley, CA 94720 • ACRL *Life*

Buckland Tessa S. • Director • Library Management & Services • Austin, TX 78703

Buckles Terry • Washington State University • Pullman, WA 99164-1230

Buckley Bonnie J. • Head of Planning Research & Proj • Nevada State Library & Archives • Carson City, NV 89710

Buckley Claire K. • Director • South Burlington Community Library • South Burlington, VT 05403 • AASL PLA

Buckley Francis J. Jr. • Assoc Director for Public Serv • Detroit Public Library • Detroit, MI 48202 • ALCTS LAMA PLA RASD GODORT IFRT

Buckley James • Hd Ln • Torrance Public Library • Torrance, CA 90503 • LAMA PLA YALSA

Buckley Jeanne M. • Student • Simmons College Graduate School of Library & Information Science • Boston, MA 02115 • IFRT

Buckley Jonathan S. • Literacy Coordinator/Reference • Kings County Library • Hanford, CA 93230

Buckley Louise A. • Government Publications Libn • Rutgers University Libraries Archibald Stevens Alexander Library • New Brunswick, NJ 08903 • RASD GODORT

Buckley Mary L. • Librarian • Mount Blue Junior High School • Farmington, ME 04938 • AASL

Buckley Virginia • Editor Director • Lodestar Books • New York, NY 10014 • YALSA

Bucklin Susan • Children's Librarian • Rye Public Library • Rye, NH 03870 • ALSC YALSA

Buckman Thomas R. • Senior Advisor • The Foundation Center • New York, NY 10003 • ACRL ASCLA *Life*

Buckmaster Sara L. • Breaux Bridge, LA 70517

Bucknall Carolyn F. • Austin, TX 78701 • ALCTS

Bucknall Tim • Librarian • University of North Carolina • Chapel Hill, NC 27599-3902 • ACRL

Buckner Antoinette G. • City Librarian • Sierra Madre Public Library • Sierra Madre, CA 91024 • LAMA PLA

Buckner Cindy L. • Librarian • Telesec Library Services • Wheaton, MD 20902

Buckner Rebecca M. • Director • Gadsden-Etowah County Library Gadsden Public Library • Gadsden, AL 35901-3101

Buckner Regina E. • Western Michigan University Libraries Dwight B. Waldo Library • Kalamazoo, MI 49008 • LITA

Buckner William D. • Assistant Librarian • Cushman, Darby & Cushman • Washington, DC 20036 • ALCTS

Buckwalter Robert L. • Assoc. Libn for Clln. Services • Harvard Law School Library • Cambridge, MA 02138 • ACRL ALCTS

Bucy Elizabeth • Lewisville, TX 75067

Buczkowski Mieczslaw • Cataloger/Slavic Bibliographer • University of Colorado • Boulder, CO 80309 • ACRL

Buda Janet E. • Dorchester, MA 02122

Buda Michele K. • Cataloger • California State University Hayward Library • Hayward, CA 94542 • ACRL ALCTS LITA

Budd John M. • Louisiana State University School of Library & Information Science • Baton Rouge, LA 70803-3290 • ACRL ALCTS LAMA RASD LHRT LRRT

Budge Ronnie L. • Library Director • Jackson County Library System • Medford, OR 97501

Budge William D. • Business Reference Librarian • California State University-Sacramento Library • Sacramento, CA 95819-6039 • RASD

Budington William S. • Colorado Springs, CO 80903 • ACRL RASD *Life*

Budlong Thomas F. Jr. • Oper. Manager Reg Serv Team • Atlanta-Fulton Public Library Southwest Regional Library • Atlanta, GA 30331 • LAMA LITA PLA RASD IFRT

Budny Mary Ann • Buffalo & Erie County Public Library • Buffalo, NY 14203

Budwig Judith • West Nottingham Academy • Colora, MD 21917

Buehl Ann • Oregon, WI 53575

Buehler Barbara • Director • Allen Public Library • Allen, TX 75002 • ALSC PLA

Buehler Kelly A. • Student • University of Toronto Faculty of Library & Information Science • Toronto ON, M5S 1A1 Canada • PLA

Buehler Peter J. • Student • Massachusetts Institute of Technology Libraries (MIT) • Cambridge, MA 02139 • IFRT

Buehler Srthur R. • John Dewey Middle School • Denver, CO 80221

Bueler Roy David • Coor. Instructional Resources • Tacoma Public Schools • Tacoma, WA 98401 • AASL

Buell Carol Dick • Hanahauoli School • Honolulu, HI 96822

Buenavenyura Nenita • San Jose State University Division of Library & Information Science • San Jose, CA 95192-0029

Buerkle Debbra M. • Pikes Peak Library District • Colorado Springs, CO 80901 • LAMA PLA

Buermann Yvonne L. • Librarian Media Specialist • Cottage Grove High School • Cottage Grove, OR 97424 • AASL

Bueschlen Wava • Director • Summit Christian College • Ft Wayne, IN 46807 • ACRL

Bueter Rita VanAssche • Mgr., Clln Dev & Standing Ord • Blackwell North America • Blackwood, NJ 08012 • ALCTS LITA

Buetow Christine K. • Student • University of Illinois Graduate School of Library and Information Science • Urbana, IL 61801 • EMIERT IFRT SRRT

Buettner John F. • Tr • Cuyahoga County Public Library • Cleveland, OH 44134-2792 • LAMA PLA

Buettner Kathleen L. • Librarian, Youth Services • Monterey Public Library • Monterey, CA 93940

Buettner Vicki J. • Head Librarian • OSU-OKC OK State University-OK City Campus • Oklahoma City, OK 73107

Buffalomeat Nellie K • Director • Haskell Indian Junior College • Lawrence, KS 66046-4800 • ACRL

Buffington Cynthia Davis • Philadelphia Rare Books & Manuscripts Co • Philadelphia, PA 19124 • ACRL

Buffington Karyl • Coffeyville Public Library • Coffeyville, KS 67337

Buffy Stephen Curtis • Reference Librarian • Sonoma County Library • Santa Rosa, CA 95404

Bufkin Anne G. • Collection Development Manager • Orange County Library System Orlando Public Library • Orlando, FL 32801-2471 • ALCTS LAMA PLA

Bugala Christine M. • Technical Services Librarian • C. Berger & Company • Carol Stream, IL 60188

Bugbee Bruce A. • Missoula, MT 59803

Bugg Louise M. • Director of Automated Systems • Wayne State University Purdy Library • Detroit, MI 48202 • ACRL ALCTS LITA

Bugher Kate • Librarian • Edgewood High School • Madison, WI 53711 • AASL

Bugnone Cheryl • Librarian • Kinsman Free Public Library • Kinsman, OH 44428

Buhmann Michael W. • Reference Librarian • Mount Prospect Public Library • Mount Prospect, IL 60056

Buhr Doris A. • Los Fresnos, TX 78566 • AASL

Buhrman Jan • Librarian • Oak Bluffs School • Oak Bluffs, MA 02557 • AASL

Buhrow Paula J. • Burlington, IA 52601

Buhse Moira B. • Head Librarian • Westmont Public Library • Westmont, IL 60559 • LAMA PLA

Bui-Burton Kim L. • Monterey Public Library • Monterey, CA 93940

Buice Dorothy A. • Dallas, TX 75231

Buker Kathleen M. • Reference Librarian • Leavenworth Public Library • Leavenworth, KS 66048

Bukovac Jamie P. • Assistant Director • Downers Grove Public Library • Downers Grove, IL 60515 • LAMA PLA

Bukovsky JoAnn M. • Board Trustee • Stickney-Forest View Library • Stickney, IL 60402 • ALTA

Bukowski Joyce S. • McCord Memorial Library • North East, PA 16428

Bulaong Grace F. • Chief Librarian • Ontario Institute for Studies in Education Library • Toronto ON, M5S 1V6 Canada • ACRL LITA

Bulat Mary Lee • Torrington, CT 06790

Bulazo Lydianne • Library Consultant • Viking Library System • Fergus Falls, MN 56537 • PLA

Bulbulian Francis • Vice President • Leonard Parker Associates Architects • Minneapolis, MN 55403

Bull Capers B. Jr. • Adult Services Librarian • Orangeburg County Library • Orangeburg, SC 29115-1367 • RASD

Bull Darlene • Coor Fiction & Supports Serv • Joliet Public Library • Joliet, IL 60431 • PLA

Bull Elizabeth K. • Student • Central High Sch Lib • Cornwall, NY 12518 • AASL

Bull Gregory D. • Viterbo College Library • La Crosse, WI 54601

Bull Judith G. • Media Services Coordinator • North Saint Paul-Maplewood-Oakdale School District • Maplewood, MN 55109 • AASL

Bull Judy • Board President • Washington County Library • Woodbury, MN 55125 • ALTA

Bull Mary R. • Reference Librarian • South Carolina State Library • Columbia, SC 29211 • RASD

Bull Susie • Asst Dir • Ricks Memorial Library • Yazoo City, MS 39194

Bullard Deborah • Librarian • Marist School • Atlanta, GA 30319

Bullard Kathy Ellen • Director • Woonsocket Harris Public Library • Woonsocket, RI 02895 • LAMA PLA

Bullard Rita J. • Librarian • Eastern Michigan University Library Center of Educational Resources • Ypsilanti, MI 48197 • ACRL

Bullard Sharon W. • Head,Circulation Dept • University of California UCSB Library • Santa Barbara, CA 93106-9010 • ACRL LAMA

Bullen Andrew H. • Student • University of Illinois Graduate School of Library and Information Science • Urbana, IL 61801 • LITA

Buller Anne Christine • Librarian • Hesston Public Library • Hesston, KS 67062 • PLA

Buller Nell L. • Music Librarian • Dalhousie University Killam Library • Halifax NS, B3H 4H8 Canada • ACRL

Bullian Lana D. • Tampa, FL 33615 • PLA

Bullis Barbara J. • Circulation Supervisor • El Dorado County Library • Placerville, CA 95667

Bullock Deborah P. • School Library Media Specialist • Fairfax County Public Schools Woodburn Elementary • Falls Church, VA 22042 • AASL

Bullock Helen C. Miss • San Jose, CA 95129 • ALSC YALSA *Continuing*

Bullock Jane M. • Raleigh, NC 27604

Bullock Judy Y. • Librarian • Jacksonville Public Libraries Main Library • Jacksonville, FL 32202 • PLA
Bullock Ruth M. • Social Studies Librarian • New Trier High School • Winnetka, IL 60093 • ACRL EMIERT
Bullock Susan • Director • Meriden Public Library • Meriden, CT 06450 • PLA
Bulman Elaine M. • Student • Indiana University School of Library and Information Science • Bloomington, IN 47405
Bulman Learned T. • Wharton, NJ 07885 • ACRL PLA YALSA *Life*
Bulow Jack F. • Associate Director • Birmingham Public Library • Birmingham, AL 35203 • LAMA PLA
Bulson Christine • State University of New York (SUNY) Milne Library • Oneonta, NY 13820 • ACRL
Bulthuis Claudia B. • Cataloger • Oak Park Public Library • Oak Park, IL 60301
Bumbalough Bruce L. • Northwest Kansas Library Systems • Norton, KS 67654 • ALTA ASCLA LAMA PLA RASD
Bumbera Alice P. • Librarian • Crosswicks Library Company • Crosswicks, NJ 08515
Bumgardner Katherine A. • Assistant Librarian • New Port Richey Public Library • New Port Richey, FL 34652 • YALSA
Bunce Nan • Reference Libn./YA Librarian • South Country Library • Bellport, NY 11713 • YALSA
Bunch David E. • Trustee • Cabell County Public Library • Huntington, WV 25701 • ALTA PLA
Bunch Robert C. • Student • Jones High School • Coldspring, TX 77331 • AASL SRRT
Bunco Merle Ann • Serials Librarian • Southern Connecticut State University Hilton C. Buley Library • New Haven, CT 06515 • ACRL
Bundy Annalee M. • Barrington, RI 02806
Bundy Debbe • Fairbury Junior-Senior High School • Fairbury, NE 68352
Bundy Mary Thames • South Texas Library System • Corpus Christi, TX 78401 • ASCLA PLA
Bundy Sharon L. • Student • University of Arizona Graduate Library School • Tucson, AZ 85721
Bundza Maira • Latvian Studies Center • Kalamazoo, MI 49006 • ACRL
Bunge Charles A. • Professor • University of Wisconsin School of Library & Information Studies • Madison, WI 53706 • RASD
Bunge Mary-Beth B. • Administrative Director • Cornell University • Ithaca, NY 14853-5301 • ACRL LITA
Bunge Rosalie • Media Specialist • Normandale Community College Learning Resource Center • Bloomington, MN 55431
Bunker Geraldine R. • Systems Librarian • University of Washington Suzzallo Library • Seattle, WA 98195 • LITA
Bunker Lisa W. • Library Asst. II • El Paso Public Library Lower Valley Branch • El Paso, TX 79915 • ALSC
Bunker Martin E. • Portland, ME 04103-3723
Bunn Diane • Seattle, WA 98115
Bunn Dumont C. • Macon, GA 31204 • ACRL
Bunn Scott M. • Supervisor of Libraries • Charles County Public Library • La Plata, MD 20646 • AASL
Bunnell William I. • Mercersburg Academy Albert M Swank Library • Mercersburg, PA 17236 • AASL ALCTS
Bunner Kimberly S. • Public Services Librarian • Parlin-Ingersoll Library • Canton, IL 61520 • RASD
Bunshaft Marilyn • Community Services Specialist • East Meadow Public Library • East Meadow, NY 11554-1700 • SORT
Bunt Gail • Cataloger • University of Saskatchewan Library • Saskatoon SK, S7N 0W0 Canada • ALCTS LITA
Bunt Kathy • Lakeland Area Education Agency • Cylinder, IA 50528 • AASL
Bunte Linda J. • Student • Rutgers University School of Communication Information & Library Studies • New Brunswick, NJ 08903 • LITA PLA IFRT NMRT SRRT
Bunte W Hazel • Hastings, MI 49085 • Continuing
Bunten Paul S. • New York, NY 10025 • AASL
Bunting Alison • University of California-Los Angeles (UCLA) • Los Angeles, CA 90024-1450
Bunton Granville A. • Library Personnel Officier • University of Louisville Ekstrom Library • Louisville, KY 40292 • LAMA
Burak Eugene D. • Student • Queens College Grad Sch of Lib & Inf Studies • Flushing, NY 11367
Burbank Richard D. • Music Catalog Coordinator • University of Illinois • Urbana, IL 61801 • ALCTS
Burch John R. • Gov't Docs/Ref. Libn. • Southern Arkansas University Magale Library • Magnolia, AR 71753 • ACRL PLA RASD IFRT
Burch Kathryn A. • Student • University of Washington Graduate School of Library and Information Science • Seattle, WA 98195 • AASL ALSC PLA
Burch Marcia T. • Librarian • Claremont Junior High School • Claremont, NH 03743 • AASL
Burch Margaret A. • Trustee • Baldwin Public Library • Birmingham, MI 48012-3002
Burchell Patricia M. • Metropolitan Toronto Reference Library • Toronto ON, M4W 2G8 Canada • ALCTS
Burcher Hilda B. • Librarian • Saint Agnes Saint Stephen's School • Alexandria, VA 22302 • AASL
Burchett Judy W. • Elementary Librarian • Washington County Board of Education • Springfield, KY 40069 • AASL
Burchfield Jane • Reference Librarian • Bucknell University Bertrand Library • Lewisburg, PA 17837-2086 • ACRL
Burck Benjamin A. • New York Public Library • New York, NY 10018-2788 • IFRT
Burckel Nicholas C. • Assoc Dean for Clln & Services • Washington University Libraries • Saint Louis, MO 63130-4899 • ACRL ALCTS *Life*
Burdash David H. • Director • Wilmington Institute Library • Wilmington, DE 19801 • LAMA LITA PLA
Burden William Mrs. • Director • Bernardsville Public Library • Bernardsville, NJ 07924 • LAMA PLA
Burdett Pamela D. • Asst Librarian for Public Serv • Stetson University College of Law Charles A. Dana Law Library • Saint Petersburg, FL 33707 • RASD SRRT
Burdette Connie • San Jose State University Clark Library • San Jose, CA 95192-0028 • ALCTS
Burdette Sally D. • Reference • Walkersville Public Library • Walkersville, MD 21793
Burdick David P. • Extension/Outreach Librarian • Pine Bluff & Jefferson County Library System • Pine Bluff, AR 71601 • PLA
Burdick Kathryn • Student • Indianapolis Marion County Public Library • Indianapolis, IN 46206 • YALSA LIRT
Burdick Lois B. • Tallahassee, FL 32304 • ACRL LAMA
Burdick Susan Elizabeth • Reference/Gov't Documents Libn. • Rodale Press,Inc Library • Emmaus, PA 18098 • ACRL
Burdick Vanroy R. • Director • California College of Arts & Crafts Library • Oakland, CA 94618
Burdine Judith • Librarian/Director • Pulaski County Public Library • Somerset, KY 42501 • PLA
Burek Ann J. • Colorado Springs, CO 80917 • LITA IFRT
Burford Judith H. • Trustee • DeSoto Parish Library • Mansfield, LA 71052
Burford Robert S. • Customer Services Representative • CLSI, Inc. • Newtonville, MA 02160 • ALCTS PLA
Burg Corinne • Sewanee, TN 37375 • Continuing
Burg Roxanne • Children's Librarian • City of Commerce Public Library • Commerce, CA 90040 • ALSC
Burgan Anne Shaw • Hartford, CT 06105 • PLA
Burgan Myrna • Trustee • East Cleveland Public Library • East Cleveland, OH 44112
Burgard Daniel E. • Librarian • Oklahoma State University Edmon Low Library • Stillwater, OK 74078-0375 • IFRT
Burgart John L. • Curriculum Supervisor • Dubuque Community School District • Dubuque, IA 52001 • AASL YALSA
Burgart Kristine J. • Student • Indiana University School of Library and Information Science • Bloomington, IN 47405 • ACRL
Burge Peggy M. • High School Librarian • Mission San Jose High School • Fremont, CA 94539 • AASL
Burgee Donna • Palm Coast, FL 32137
Burgee Rebecca C. • Librarian • Westgate Elementary School • Falls Church, VA 22043
Burger Leslie B. • Library Consultant • Library Development Solutions • Cranbury, NJ 08512 • ASCLA
Burgeson Clair D. Jr • Sloatsburg, NY 10974
Burgeson Diane M. • Librarian II • Rochester Hills Public Library • Rochester, MI 48307 • ALCTS
Burgess Barbara J. • Media Specialist • Hoglan Elementary School • Marshalltown, IA 50158 • AASL *Life*
Burgess Dean • Director • Portsmouth Public Library • Portsmouth, VA 23704 • LAMA PLA
Burgess Eileen E. • Hyattsville, MD 20781
Burgess Frederick R. • Librarian • Gary Public Library • Gary, IN 46402
Burgess Irene • Trustee • Fairfax County Public Library • Fairfax, VA 22033-1909
Burgess Jo • Student • Indiana University at Bloomington University Libraries • Bloomington, IN 47405-9998
Burgess Kathleen E. • Head,Extension Services • Gary Public Library • Gary, IN 46402 • ALSC PLA
Burgess Larry E. • Library Director • A.K. Smiley Public Library • Redlands, CA 92373
Burgess Marguerite B. • Norfolk Public Library Larchmont Branch • Norfolk, VA 23508
Burgess Michael • Chief Cataloger • California State University John M. Pfau Library • San Bernardino, CA 92407
Burgess Robert S. • Professor Emeritus • State University of New York at Albany School of Information Science & Policy • Albany, NY 12222 • ACRL RASD *Life*
Burgess Rosanne R. • Bay City Public Library • Bay City, TX 77414 • PLA
Burgess Sue • LRC Specialist • Madison Middle School (Abilene Independent School District) • Abilene, TX 79605 • AASL
Burgess William E. • Modoc Press Inc • Santa Monica, CA 90401
Burgett James E. • Lexington, KY 40504 • ACRL IRRT
Burgett Mary L. • Director,Division of Proc Svs • Rice University Fondren Library • Houston, TX 77251-1892 • ALCTS LITA
Burgett Shelley W. • University of Louisville Libraries • Louisville, KY 40292
Burghduff Betty K. • Librarian • Clear Lake United Methodist Church • Houston, TX 77062-5299
Burgin Robert E. • North Carolina Central University • Durham, NC 27707
Burgio Bonnie • Assistant District Attorney • Jefferson County District Attoney's Office • Watertown, NY 13601 • ACRL
Burgis Grover C. • Director • Brampton Public Library • Brampton ON, Canada • ALCTS LAMA LITA PLA RASD
Burglechner William J. • Vice President-Sales • Data Research Associates Inc. • Saint Louis, MO 63132
Burgman Carolyne C. • Media Specialist • Clarke Middle School • Athens, GA 30606 • AASL
Burgoyne Mary Beth • Librarian • Mesa Public Library • Mesa, AZ 85201-6768 • RASD
Burhanna Kenneth J. • Student • Kent State University School of Library & Information Science • Kent, OH 44242-0001 • SRRT
Burhans Barbara C. • Alexandria, VA 22302 • ACRL RASD FLRT SRRT *Continuing*
Burhans Robert L. • President-Board of Trustee • Peoria Public Library • Peoria, IL 61602 • ALTA
Buri Trudie L. • Adult Services/Deputy Director • Wissahickon Valley Public Library • Ambler, PA 19002 • PLA
Burian Joanne G. • Librarian II Adult Services • Phoenix Public Library • Phoenix, AZ 85004 • RASD
Burich Nancy J. • Librarian • University of Kansas Regents Center Library • Shawnee Msn, KS 66206 • ACRL
Burk Anne P. • Youth Services Librarian • Livermore Public Library • Livermore, CA 94550 • ALSC PLA
Burk Bartley A. • Staff Librarian • University of Notre Dame • Notre Dame, IN 46556 • ACRL
Burk Daniel P. • Librarian II-Business Dept. • Toledo-Lucas County Public Library • Toledo, OH 43624 • RASD
Burk John H. • Student • San Jose State University Division of Library & Information Science • San Jose, CA 95192-0029 • ALCTS LITA IFRT LRRT
Burk Joyce A. • Barstow, CA 92311 • RASD
Burk Roberta L. • Student • Northern Illinois University Department of Library & Information Studies • DeKalb, IL 60115 • PLA RASD
Burka Margaret K. • Children's Librarian • Lakeside Congregation for Reform Judaism Library • Highland Park, IL 60035 • ALSC NMRT
Burkart Marcia • Carlthrop Elementary School • Santa Monica, CA 90402 • AASL
Burke Adrienne J. • Librarian • Long Branch High School Library • Long Branch, NJ 07740 • AASL
Burke Anne M. • Trustee • Merrick Public Library • Merrick, NY 11566 • PLA IFRT
Burke Barbara L. • Asst Clln Serv Ln • Colorado State University William E. Morgan Library • Fort Collins, CO 80523 • LITA
Burke Carol A. • Assistant Director • Colville Public Library • Colville, WA 99114
Burke Carole R. • Interlibrary Loan • University of Alabama Amelia Gayle Gorgas Library • Tuscaloosa, AL 35487-0266 • ACRL LAMA
Burke Carolyn E. • Greensboro, NC 27410 • AASL ALSC
Burke Catherine A. • Director of Libraries • Holland Hall School • Tulsa, OK 74136 • AASL LITA
Burke Cynthia • Long Island University Brooklyn Center • Brooklyn, NY 11201
Burke Dale C. • Technical Services Librarian • Edmonds Community College Library • Lynnwood, WA 98036 • ACRL
Burke Donna Joy • Branch Librarian • Broward County Library Hallandale Branch • Hallandale, FL 33009 • PLA
Burke Elaine A. • Librarian • Indian Trails Public Library District • Wheeling, IL 60090 • PLA
Burke Elizabeth A. • Student • Catholic University of America School of Library and Information Science • Washington, DC 20064 • AASL YALSA
Burke Helen S. • Minneapolis Public Library & Information Center • Minneapolis, MN 55401-1992 • ACRL RASD FLRT GODORT

Burke Jan • Campbell County School District • Gillette, WY 82717 • AASL

Burke Jane A. • President • NOTIS Systems, Inc. • Evanston, IL 60201-3622 • ACRL LITA ERT

Burke John J. • Student • University of Tennessee-Knoxville Graduate School of Library & Information Science • Knoxville, TN 37996-4330 • SRRT

Burke Joseph A. • Information Sys. Coordinator • United States Air Force Europe Hq USAFE/MWCL • APO, AE 09012 • PLA AFLRT

Burke Julie K. • Instructor/Laboratory Coor. • Kent State University School of Library & Information Science • Kent, OH 44242-0001 • LITA

Burke June • Librarian • Lincoln College McKinstry Library • Lincoln, IL 62656 • ACRL RASD LIRT LRRT

Burke Lynne • Technical Services Librarian • New England Historic Genealogical Society • Boston, MA 02116 • ALCTS LITA

Burke Lynne T. • Minneapolis, MN 55410-1908

Burke Marianne • Assistant Librarian/ Tech Servs • Boston Library Consortium • Boston, MA 02117 • ACRL LITA

Burke Mary E. • Coral Gables, FL 33134

Burke Maureen A. • Reference/Documents Librarian • Selby Public Library • Sarasota, FL 33577 • GODORT

Burke Patricia P. • Prince William County Public Library Central Branch • Prince William, VA 22192 • ALCTS LITA

Burke Phyllis A. • Englishtown, NJ 07726 • AASL

Burke Pierre V. • Dallas, TX 75214-1639 • ACRL PLA RASD

Burke Rebecca J. • Head Government Documents • Arizona State University Hayden Library • Tempe, AZ 85287-1006 • ACRL LAMA GODORT

Burke Rick • Librarian • University of Judaism Library • Los Angeles, CA 90077 • ACRL LITA

Burke Scott • Woodstock High School Library • Woodstock, IL 60098 • AASL

Burke Susan C. • Reference Librarian • Ela Area Public Library District • Lake Zurich, IL 60047 • PLA

Burke Susan K. • Assistant Slavic Librarian • University of Washington Suzzallo Library • Seattle, WA 98195 • ACRL

Burke Terri L. • Student • Rutgers University School of Communication Information & Library Studies • New Brunswick, NJ 08903 • PLA

Burke Timothy • Siena College • Loudonville, NY 12211-1462 • ACRL

Burkes Ceasar D. • Trustee • Cleveland Public Library • Cleveland, OH 44114-1271 • ALTA

Burkett Donald E. • Senior Librarian • New York State Library State Education Department • Albany, NY 12230 • ALCTS GODORT

Burkett Elisabeth A. • Media Specialist/Librarian • Oakton Elementary School • Oakton, VA 22184 • AASL ALSC RASD LIRT

Burkett Janet A. • Head of Technical Services • North Georgia College Stewart Library • Dahlonega, GA 30597-3001 • GODORT

Burkett Nancy H. • Librarian • American Antiquarian Society • Worcester, MA 01609-1634 • ACRL LAMA

Burkett Phyllis • Director • Crowley Ridge Regional Library • Jonesboro, AR 72401 • PLA

Burkhalter Walter S. • Library Director • Orange Public Library • Orange, TX 77630

Burkhardt B. • Linwood Middle School • North Brunswick, NJ 08092

Burkhardt Barbara J. • Student • Rutgers University School of Communication Information & Library Studies • New Brunswick, NJ 08903

Burkhardt Joanna M. • Library Director • University of Rhode Island College of Continuing Education Library • Providence, RI 02908 • ACRL IFRT NMRT

Burkheart Sue • Murfreesboro, TN 37129-1765

Burkholder Debbie • Rock Creek Valley Elementary • Rockville, MD 20853

Burkholder Jennifer • Summit, NJ 07901 • AASL

Burkholder Sue A. • Director • Southern Oregon State Coll Library • Ashland, OR 97520 • ACRL ALCTS LAMA

Burkitt Jeannine P • Librarian • Waverly High School Library • Waverly, OH 45690

Burkle Kathryn E. • Student • Valley City State University Allen Memorial Library • Valley City, ND 58072

Burks Alice Anne • Director of Extension Service • Thomas Jefferson Library • Jefferson City, MO 65101 • PLA

Burks Doris Taylor • Pontiac, MI 48342

Burks Elizabeth • Apache Junction Public Library • Apache Junction, AZ 85219

Burks Freda A. • Librarian • Trinity High School • Euless, TX 76039 • AASL YALSA

Burks Suzan K. • Catalog Librarian • Gonzaga University Crosby Library • Spokane, WA 99258 • ACRL

Burleigh Rebecca R. • Wabbaseka School Library • Wabbaseka, AR 72175

Burley Cheryl J. • Data & Inf. Resource Libn • University of Michigan Information Technology Division-CIESIN • Ann Arbor, MI 48109-2016 • ACRL

Burlingame Ann Mary • Head Children's Services • Wake County Public Library North Regional Library • Raleigh, NC 27615

Burlingame Connie • Librarian • Area High School • Towanda, PA 18848 • AASL IFRT

Burlingame Dwight F. • Director of Academic Programs • Center on Philanthropy • Indianapolis, IN 46202 • ACRL LAMA   *Life*

Burlingham Esther • State College, PA 16801 • Continuing

Burlingham Merry L. • South Asia Librarian • University of Texas Libraries General Libraries • Austin, TX 78713-7330 • ACRL ALCTS RASD EMIERT IRRT

Burman Celeste M. • Ann Arbor, MI 48109 • PLA SRRT

Burman Kay W. • Manager, Resource Center • Colorado Technical College • Colorado Springs, CO 80907 • ACRL

Burmeister Florence E. • Macedonia, OH 44056-1001 • Life

Burn Barbara • Des Moines, IA 50313 • ACRL ALCTS LAMA RASD IFRT LIRT SRRT

Burnam Paul • Public Services Librarian • Ohio Wesleyan University • Delaware, OH 43015 • ACRL LIRT

Burnett Bescye P. • Deputy Director • Cleveland Heights-University Heights Public Library • Cleveland Heights, OH 44118 • LAMA PLA LIRT

Burnett Billie M. • Lexington, KY 40502 • AASL ALSC

Burnett James E. • Adult Services Librarian • San Jose Public Library Almaden Branch • San Jose, CA 95120 • LITA

Burnett James J. • Ouachita Parish Public Library • Monroe, LA 71201

Burnett Karen E. • Coor. of Libs, Media & Tech • Fremont Union High School District • Sunnyvale, CA 94087 • AASL YALSA

Burnett Kathleen M. • Assistant Professor • Rutgers University School of Communication Information & Library Studies • New Brunswick, NJ 08903 • ACRL ALCTS LITA

Burnett Michael S. • Library Director • Northville Public Library • Northville, NY 12134

Burnett Rosa S. • Dir Of L • State Technical Institute • Memphis, TN 38134

Burnett Stephen G. • Lincoln, NE 68507

Burnett Walter M. • Trustee • New Orleans Public Library • New Orleans, LA 70140 • ALTA

Burnette Frances A. • Lima, OH 45805 • Continuing

Burnette Michaelyn • Humanities Librarian • University of California-Berkeley University Library • Berkeley, CA 94720 • ACRL ALCTS RASD

Burnham-Kidwell Debbie • Library District Director • Mohave County District Library • Kingman, AZ 86401 • ALCTS

Burnham Helen • Croton-on-Hudson, NY 10520

Burnham John P. • Bookstore Manager • University of Maine • Farmington, ME 04938 • ACRL YALSA   *Life*

Burnham Ruth M. • Librarian • Kent Denver School • Englewood, CO 80110

Burns Ada • Library Director • California School of Professional Psychology Library • San Diego, CA 92121-3205 • ACRL

Burns Ann • Librarian • University of Queensland Library • St. Lucia, QLD 4072, Australia • IRRT

Burns Barbara D. • Media Spec • Saint Martha's School Library • Sarasota, FL 34236 • AASL

Burns Barbara K. • Head of Reference Service • Crown Point Community Library • Crown Point, IN 46307 • LIRT

Burns Betty L. • High School Librarian • Maquoketa Community Schools • Maquoketa, IA 52060

Burns Carol A. • Brecksville, OH 44141 • ALSC

Burns Carol J. • Director of Technical Services • Multnomah County Library • Portland, OR 97212 • ALCTS LITA

Burns Christa J. • Reference Librarian • Pace University • White Plains, NY 10603

Burns Deborah A. • Library Associate-Children's • Chicago Public Library Avalon Branch • Chicago, IL 60617 • ALSC

Burns Georganne • Acquisitions Librarian • Tennessee Technological University University Library • Cookeville, TN 38505

Burns Grant F. • Reference Librarian • University of Michigan • Flint, MI 48502-2186 • IFRT

Burns Janice • Acting Director • Finney County Public Library • Garden City, KS 67846 • PLA CLENE

Burns Jinny • Senior, Librarian • Douglas County Library System • Roseburg, OR 97470

Burns Joanne C. • Aston, PA 19014-2758

Burns Joyce S. • Librarian II • Atlanta-Fulton Public Library Southwest Regional Library • Atlanta, GA 30331 • AASL ALSC PLA

Burns Karen M. • Administrator • Southwest Iowa Regional Library System • Council Bluffs, IA 51503 • LITA PLA RASD

Burns Mary Florence Sr. • Trustee • Brooklyn Public Library • Brooklyn, NY 11238 • ALTA

Burns Mary Frances • Assistant Administrative Ln. • Palatine Public Library • Palatine, IL 60067 • LAMA

Burns Mary H. • Seattle, WA 98121-1456

Burns Mary M. • Librarian • Framingham State College Henry Whittemore Library • Framingham, MA 01701 • ALSC

Burns Ollie H. • Member of Lib Board of Control • Ouachita Parish Public Library • Monroe, LA 71201 • ALTA

Burns Pamela J. • Bessemer, AL 35023

Burns Patricia A. • Media Specialist • Crary Middle School • Waterford, MI 48328 • AASL

Burns Richard K. • Hatboro, PA 19040

Burns Richard P. • Kaneohe Public Library • Kaneohe, HI 96744 • IFRT

Burns Robert G. • Librarian • Pingry School • Martinsville, NJ 08836 • AASL

Burns Tracie M. • Field Acct. Services Manager • EBSCO Subscription Services • Shrewsbury, NJ 07702-4321 • AASL

Burns Violanda O. • Head, Management Library • University of Rochester Rhees Library • Rochester, NY 14627-0055 • LAMA RASD

Burnside Frances Miss • Rochester, MI 48063 • Continuing

Buro Richard W. • Temple ISD Instructional Media Center • Temple, TX 76504 • AASL

Burow Eleanore • Trustee • Bridgeview Public Library • Bridgeview, IL 60455 • ALTA

Burr Angela T. • Librarian • Saint George's School • Spokane, WA 99205 • AASL

Burr Annette • Librarian • Virginia Polytechnic Inst & State Univ University Libraries • Blacksburg, VA 24062-9001 • ACRL

Burr Charlotte A. • Reference Librarian • Ripon College Library • Ripon, WI 54971 • ALTA

Burr Elizabeth • Springfield, IL 62702 • ALSC ASCLA   *Continuing*

Burr Robert L. • Director • Gonzaga University Crosby Library • Spokane, WA 99258 • ACRL ALCTS LAMA LITA RASD GODORT LIRT LRRT

Burrell C. S. • Ocean County Library System • Toms River, NJ 08753

Burrell Carolyn • Librarian • Antelope Valley College • Lancaster, CA 93536 • ACRL

Burrell Cora Sue • Librarian • Hanalei Elementary School • Hanalei, HI 96714 • AASL

Burrell Renee K. • Librarian • Salvation Army School Hicks Memorial Library • Atlanta, GA 30310

Burrer Esther • Columbus, OH 43229 • AASL YALSA   *Continuing*

Burress Elizabeth A. • Librarian • Campbellsville High School • Campbellsville, KY 42718

Burress Lee A. III • Rockford Public Library • Rockford, IL 61101-1061 • ALSC IFRT NMRT SRRT

Burrier Carolyn Morgan • Librarian • Stow Public Library • Stow, OH 44224 • ALSC PLA

Burrier Donald H. Jr • Director • Elyria Public Library • Elyria, OH 44035

Burright Nancy • Trustee • Northwest Regional Library Systems • Sioux City, IA 51102 • ALTA

Burris Marie T. • Winter Haven, FL 33884 • Continuing

Burritt Elaine • Branch Supervisor • Weld County Library District • Greeley, CO 80631

Burroughs Betty • Menasha, WI 54952

Burroughs Christine • Owego, NY 13827 • MAGERT

Burrow Barbara A. • Director • Cotuit Public Library • Cotuit, MA 02635

Burrow Catherine Gale • Ref. Ln. & Coor. of Lib. Instr. • Claremont Colleges Libraries Honnold/Mudd Library • Claremont, CA 91711 • ACRL RASD LIRT

Burrows Janice H. • Library Human Resources Director • University of California-Berkeley University Library • Berkeley, CA 94720 • ACRL LAMA

Burrows Robert P. • Senior Consultant • NOTIS Systems, Inc. • Evanston, IL 60201-3622 • ACRL LAMA LITA

Burrows Thomas W. • Cataloger • Naperville Public Libraries • Naperville, IL 60540

Burrus Steve R. • Architect • Sherman, Carter, Barnhart Architects • Lexington, KY 40507

Burruss-Ballard Marsha A. • Director • Principia College Marshall Brooks Library • Elsah, IL 62028 • ACRL LAMA RASD

Bursick Michele Z. • Pittsburgh, PA 15243

Bursik Carol J. • Systems Librarian • Department of Defense Pentagon Library • Washington, DC 20310 • LITA FLRT

Bursk Mary Ann • Assistant Branch/Children's Libn • Bucks County Free Library Lower County Branch • Levittown, PA 19057 • ALSC

Burslem Peter • Systems Librarian • University of Maryland at Baltimore Marshall Law Library • Baltimore, MD 21201 • LITA

Burson Betsy L. • Director • Arlington Public Library • Arlington, TX 76010 • LAMA PLA

Burson Max M. • Reference/Interlibrary Loan • Cameron University • Lawton, OK 73505 • ACRL

Burson Phyllis S. • Corpus Chrsti, TX 78404 • Continuing

Burstein Susan • Library Media Specialist • Portland Middle School Library • Portland, CT 06480

Burt David W. • Student • University of Washington Graduate School of Library and Information Science • Seattle, WA 98195

Burt Janet C. • Library Coordinator K-12 • Manchester Public Schools Manchester High School • Manchester, MA 01944

Burt Janet K. • Childrens' Librarian • Greenfield Public Library • Greenfield, IN 46140 • ALSC

Burton Arlynn R. • Regional Librarian • Cuyahoga County Public Library Parma Regional • Parma, OH 44129-3199 • PLA

Burton Elizabeth Hesse • Genzyme Corporation Information Services • Cambridge, MA 02139

Burton Jay L. • Adult Services Librarian • Park City Public Library • Park City, UT 84060 • ALCTS

Burton Jean Piper • Asst. Cataloging Librarian • West Chester University Francis Harvey Green Library • West Chester, PA 19383 • ACRL ALCTS

Burton Lewis R. • Trustee • Pikes Peak Library District • Colorado Springs, CO 80901 • ALTA PLA

Burton M Ethel Miss • Montgomery, AL 36107 • ACRL ALCTS *Continuing*

Burton Marybeth S. • Plainsboro, NJ 08536 • LAMA LITA

Burton Pamela Kaye • Serials Cataloger • University of Louisville Ekstrom Library • Louisville, KY 40292

Burton Patricia H. • Student • University of Texas at Austin Graduate School of Library & Information Sciences • Austin, TX 78712-1276

Burton Robert E. • Northport, MI 49670-9737 • ACRL IFRT

Burton Susan • Librarian • Prescott College Library • Prescott, AZ 86301 • ACRL RASD

Burton Terry I. • Brandon, FL 33510-3833

Burtt Robert • Mars, PA 16046

Burvill Sheila A. • Head Catlg. & Classification • Canada Institute for Science and Technical Information • Ottawa ON, K1A 0S2 Canada • ALCTS LAMA LITA

Burwell Olivia B. • Greensboro, NC 27410 • ALTA PLA *Continuing*

Burwinkel Julie A. • Media Coordinator • Ursuline Academy • Cincinnati, OH 45242 • AASL NMRT

Bury Pamela • Supervising Librarian • Goleta Library • Goleta, CA 93117

Bury Peter • Glenview Public Library • Glenview, IL 60025

Busby Christine N. • Student • Rosary College Graduate School of Library & Information Science • River Forest, IL 60305

Busch Ann E. • Children's Librarian • Roseville Public Library • Roseville, MI 48066 • ALSC PLA

Busch B. J. • Associate Librarian • University of Alberta Library • Edmonton AB, T6G 2J8 Canada • ACRL LAMA

Busch Barbara • Supv. Technical Inf. Spec. • Defence Technical Information Center • El Segundo, CA 90245-4320 • AFLRT FLRT

Busch Joseph A. • Systems Project Manager • Getty Art History Info Prog Information Program • Santa Monica, CA 90401-1455 • LITA

Busch Judith • Library Media Specialist • Norwich High School Library • Norwich, NY 13460 • AASL IFRT

Busch Kathleen M. • Head of Children's Services • New Canaan Library • New Canaan, CT 06840 • ALSC

Busch Mary J. • Librarian • Lukens Steel Company Technical Library • Coatesville, PA 19320 • Continuing

Busch Nancy J A • Nebraska Library Commission • Lincoln, NE 68508 • ASCLA

Buscher Patricia K. • Senior Reference Librarian • Escondido Public Library • Escondido, CA 92025 • RASD

Buschman Isabel M. • Cataloger • University of Wyoming Coe Library • Laramie, WY 82071-3334 • ALCTS

Buschmon John E. • Associate Prof.-Librarian • Rider College • Lawrenceville, NJ 08648-3099 • ACRL

Buser Robin A. • Columbus, OH 43213 • ALCTS PLA

Bush Barbara Mrs. • Washington, DC 20500 • AASL ACRL ALCTS ALSC ALTA ASCLA LAMA LITA PLA RASD YALSA *Honorary*

Bush Bonnie • Mount Laurel Library • Mt. Laurel, NJ 08054-9539 • LAMA

Bush Carmel C. • Assistant Director of Tech Serv • Colorado State University William E. Morgan Library • Fort Collins, CO 80523 • ACRL ALCTS LAMA GODORT

Bush Caryn M. • Reference Librarian • Loyola University E.M. Cudahy Memorial Library • Chicago, IL 60626 • RASD IFRT NMRT

Bush Connie Adams • Popular Materials & Services • Daniel Boone Regional Library • Columbia, MO 65205-1267 • ALSC PLA YALSA

Bush Earl T. • Head, Circulation Services • University of Tennessee Library • Knoxville, TN 37996-1000

Bush Emily W. • Norwick, VT 05055-1308 • ALSC

Bush Gayla S. • Reference Librarian • Farmers Branch Public Library • Farmers Branch, TX 75234

Bush Joyce F. • Senior Librarian • White Plains Public Library • White Plains, NY 10601 • RASD

Bush Kimberley M. • Student • Clarion University of Pennsylvania College of Library Science • Clarion, PA 16214

Bush M. A. Jody • Assistant Director • Berkeley Public Library • Berkeley, CA 94704 • PLA SRRT

Bush Margaret A. • Associate Professor • Simmons College Graduate School of Library & Information Science • Boston, MA 02115 • ALSC PLA

Bush Mary E. • Librarian • Broughton Hospital • Morganton, NC 28655 • ASCLA

Bush Mary M. • Asst Coor, Instructional Servs • Multnomah Education Service District • Portland, OR 97216

Bush Nancy W. Dr. • Professor, Library Science • University of South Alabama Library • Mobile, AL 36688 • AASL ACRL ALSC LHRT LRRT *Life*

Bush Patricia A. • Management Bibliographer • Northwestern University Library • Evanston, IL 60208-2300 • ACRL RASD MAGERT *Life*

Bush Rhoda H. • Reference Librarian • Montgomery County Department of Public Libraries Kensington Branch • Kensington, MD 20895 • PLA RASD

Bush Virginia M. • Librarian • Minneapolis Public Library Hosmer Branch • Minneapolis, MN 55408

Bushallow Lara A. • Student • State University of New York (SUNY) School of Information & Library Studies • Buffalo, NY 14260 • SRRT

Bushing Mary C. • Montana State University • Bozeman, MT 59717-0332 • ACRL ALCTS CLENE

Bushing Vera Rose • Valparaiso, IN 46383 • Continuing

Bushlin Lenore • Broomall, PA 19008

Bushnell Judith A. • Librarian • State University of New York (SUNY) College at Geneseo Milne Library • Geneseo, NY 14454-1498

Bushnell Pat • Richards School Library • Whitefish Bay, WI 53217

Bushong Sara • Bowling Green State University • Bowling Green, OH 43403

Busker Sally S. • Trustee • Montgomery County Dept of Pub Lib Davis Community Library • Bethesda, MD 20817-1699 • ALTA PLA

Buskey John L. • Director of Library • Alabama State University Levi Watkins Learning Center Library • Montgomery, AL 36195-0301

Busko Robert W. • Student • University of South Carolina College of Library & Information Science • Columbia, SC 29208 • LITA PLA IFRT SRRT

Buss Greg A. • Trustee • Richmond Public Library • Richmond BC, V6X 2E3 Canada

Buss Jeanne C. • Student • Indiana University School of Library and Information Science • Bloomington, IN 47405

Buss William M. • Urbana, IL 61801

Busse Catherine G. • Trustee • West Baton Rouge Parish Library • Port Allen, LA 70767

Bussell Mari E. • Library Personnel Officer • University of Florida Libraries • Gainesville, FL 32611 • LAMA

Bussey Carla V. • Washington, DC 20002

Bustamante Corazon R. • Senior Librarian • New York Public Library Mid-Manhattan Branch • New York, NY 10016

Bustamante Patricia S. • Branch Supervisor/Librarian II • Richland County Public Library • Columbia, SC 29201

Bustard Anne • Toad Hall Bookstore • Austin, TX 78705 • ALSC

Bustion Marifran • Head, Acqusitions Deaprtment • George Washington University Gelman Library • Washington, DC 20052 • ACRL ALCTS LRRT

Bustos Roxann R. • Asst. Head of Public Services • Augusta College Reese Library • Augusta, GA 30910 • RASD LIRT

Buswell Christa H. • Chief Library Services • Veterans Administration Center Wadsworth Medical Library • Los Angeles, CA 90073 • LITA FLRT

Buswell Rosalind • Springfield, MA 01109 • Continuing

Butchart Lorraine K. • Technical Services Librarian • Jackson District Library • Jackson, MI 49201 • LAMA PLA

Butchart Sheila L. • Beaufort High School • Beaufort, SC 29902

Butcher Cherie J. • Student • University of Michigan School of Information and Library Studies • Ann Arbor, MI 48109-1092

Butcher Jane • Trustee • Boulder Public Library • Boulder, CO 80306

Butcher Karyle S. • Asst. Dir. for Research & Ref. • Oregon State University William Jasper Kerr Library • Corvallis, OR 97331-4501 • ACRL LAMA RASD LRRT

Butcher Madeleine K. • Trustee • Free Library of Philadelphia • Philadelphia, PA 19103 • ALTA

Butcher Patricia S. • Asst Director of Public Services • Trenton State College Roscoe L. West Library • Trenton, NJ 08650-4700 • ACRL LAMA RASD

Butera Sharon • Cataloger • Elementary School District 64 District Media Center • Park Ridge, IL 60068 • ALCTS ALSC

Buthmann E • Library Media Specialist • Arlington Central School District • Poughkeepsie, NY 12603 • AASL

Buthod J. Craig • Deputy City Librarian • Seattle Public Library • Seattle, WA 98104-1193 • PLA

Butkis John F. Rev • Regional Adult Serv. Coor. • County of Los Angeles Public Library Central County Region 600 • Montebello, CA 90640

Butkovich Nancy J. • State College, PA 16803 • ACRL MAGERT

Butlein Jayne G. • Librarian • CPU Computer People Unlimited • Milwaukee, WI 53203

Butler Alice E. • Student • University of British Columbia School of Library, Archival & Information Studies • Vancouver BC, V6T 1Z1 Canada • ALCTS LITA PLA RASD NMRT

Butler Barbara A. • Oregon Institute of Marine Biology • Charleston, OR 97420

Butler Barbara E. • Reference Librarian • University of Nevada-Reno Noble H. Getchell Library • Reno, NV 89557 • ACRL RASD

Butler Broadus N. • Silver Spring, MD 20903

Butler Carol • Librarian • Nabisco Brand,Inc Information Center • East Hanover, NJ 07936 • LITA

Butler Cathleen M. • Weston County Library • Newcastle, WY 82701

Butler Cathy R. • Branch Manager • Public Library of Annapolis & Anne Arundel County Crofton Branch • Crofton, MD 21114 • PLA

Butler Clifford B. • Sunland Developmental Center • Marianna, FL 32446

Butler Dorothy D. • Poway, CA 92064 • ALSC

Butler Elizabeth A. • Branch Manager • Fairfax County Public Library George Mason Regional Branch • Annandale, VA 22003

Butler Harry A. • Collection Development Librarian • University of Dallas William A. Blakley Library • Irving, TX 75062 • ACRL ALCTS

Butler Jamie F. • Oak Ridge, TN 37830 • AASL ALSC PLA RASD

Butler Jane C. • Shaker Heights, OH 44120

Butler Jane C. • United States Army Engineer District, Mobile • Mobile, AL 36628 • ALCTS LAMA LITA FLRT

Butler Joan M. • DB Administrator • University of Michigan Libraries • Ann Arbor, MI 48109-1205

Butler John P. • Queens, NY 11327 • PLA

Butler Judy M. • Circulation Librarian • David Lipscomb University University Library • Nashville, TN 37204-3951 • ACRL LITA LIRT

Butler Julene • Library Use Instruction Coord. • Brigham Young University • Provo, UT 84602 • ACRL RASD

Butler Kathleen J. • Student • University of Pittsburgh School of Library and Information Science • Pittsburgh, PA 15260

Butler Lori J. • Pittsburgh, PA 15243

Butler Lynne G. • Northbrook Public Library • Northbrook, IL 60062 • LAMA

Butler M Flo • Los Alamos, NM 87544

Butler Mark H. • Student • University of California-Berkeley School of Library & Information Studies • Berkeley, CA 94720 • LITA

Butler Mary M. • Media Specialist • Bellevue Public Schools Avery School • Bellevue, NE 68005 • AASL

Butler Mary S. • Arlington Heights Memorial Library • Arlington Heights, IL 60004-5966 • RASD

Butler Meredith A. • Director of University Libraries • State University of New York (SUNY) University Libraries • Albany, NY 12222 • ACRL ALCTS LAMA

Butler Nancy • Weeks Transitional School • Des Moines, IA 50315

Butler Patricia • School Librarian • Bridgewater-Raritan School District • Bridgewater, NJ 08807 • AASL

Butler Rachel C. • Oklahoma City Community College Learning Resources Center • Oklahoma City, OK 73159 • MAGERT

Butler Rebecca P. • Student • University of Wisconsin-Madison School of Library & Information Studies • Madison, WI 53706

Butler Robert S. • Student • Wayne State University Library Science Program • Detroit, MI 48202
Butler Robert W. • South Fallsburg, NY 12779-0600
Butler Shelley J. • Minneapolis, MN 55417
Butler Tina • Ohio Dominican College • Columbus, OH 43219 • AASL
Butlerworth Jane R. • Student • Clarion University of Pennsylvania College of Library Science • Clarion, PA 16214 • ACRL
Butlien Allison • Student • Long Island University Palmer School of Library & Information Science • Greenvale, NY 11548 • AASL ALSC EMIERT IFRT SRRT
Butsch Monica M. • Librarian I • Enoch Pratt Free Library • Baltimore, MD 21201-4484
Butt Men-Sze • Music Cataloger • City University of New York Graduate School Mina Rees Library • New York, NY 10036-8099
Butt Rhonda R. • High School Library • Berlin, WI 54923
Buttars Ann • Asst Curator/Associate Ln. • Utah State University Merrill Library • Logan, UT 84322-3000 • ACRL
Butterfield Nancy E. • Head of Technical Services • Keene State College Mason Library • Keene, NH 03431 • ACRL ALCTS LITA RASD
Butterwick Nigel B. • Associate Librarian • Queens University of Belfast • Belfast, BT7 1LS United Kingdom • ACRL
Buttlar Lois J. • Associate Professor • Kent State University School of Library & Information Science • Kent, OH 44242-0001
Button Carol J. • Library Assistant III • University of Alaska Wildlife Library • Fairbanks, AK 99775 • ACRL
Butts Joan D. • District Library Media Spec • Unified School District 417 District Media Center • Council Grv, KS 66846 • AASL
Butts Peter Muller • East Lansing Public Schools • East Lansing, MI 48823 • AASL YALSA SRRT
Butts Sharon E. • Supervisory Librarian • Library of Congress • Washington, DC 20541
Butz Helen S. • Concord, NH 03301 • ACRL ALCTS
Butzler Margaret L. Mrs. • Bethel Park Public Library • Bethel Park, PA 15102-2790 • YALSA
Buvinger Jan • Director • Charleston County Library • Charleston, SC 29403 • PLA
Buxbaum Sharolyn • Assistant Business Librarian • Michigan State University Libraries • East Lansing, MI 48824-1048 • RASD
Buxton David T. • Asst. Dir for Automation Serv. • Gonzaga University Crosby Library • Spokane, WA 99258 • LITA
Buyserie Eileen • Administrative Secretary • Chemeketa Community College • Salem, OR 97309
Buzonas Edward J. Jr • Espyville, PA 16414
Buzzard Patricia A. • Grants Pass, OR 97526
Buzzell Bonnie Good • Brown University Rockefeller Library • Providence, RI 02912 • ACRL LAMA
Buzzelli James • Trustee • Frederick County Public Library C. Burr Artz Library • Frederick, MD 21701 • ALTA
Buzzeo Toni • West Buxton, ME 04093 • AASL
Byadoo Joseph K. • Norcross, GA 30071
Byars E Gaye • Montgomery, AL 36111
Bybee Cheryl A. • Health Careers High School • San Antonio, TX 78229 • AASL YALSA
Bybee Jane • Columbia, MO 65201 • ACRL ALCTS *Life*
Byer Dorothy J. • Media Specialist • Smoky Hill High School • Aurora, CO 80015 • AASL LITA IFRT LIRT LRRT
Byer Moira • Volunteer Coor. Family Res. Ctr. • Children's Hospital • Boston, MA 02115 • ALSC
Byergo Frederick H. • Head Librarian • Cook Memorial Library • Libertyville, IL 60048 • LAMA PLA
Byerly Diane • Librarian • Withrow Senior High School Library • Cincinnati, OH 45208 • AASL
Byerly Edna Mary • Mt. Vernon, IA 52314
Byerly Eleanor L. • Ohio Wesleyan University • Delaware, OH 43015 • LITA
Byerly Greg W. • Head of Systems • Kent State University School of Library & Information Science • Kent, OH 44242-0001 • ACRL LITA RASD
Byerly Imogene M. • Greenbelt, MD 20770
Byers Bertina • Leavenworth, KS 66027
Byers Cheryl L. • Ann Arbor, MI 48108 • ALCTS
Byers Edward W. • Director • Reading Public Library • Reading, MA 01867-2550 • LAMA PLA GODORT
Byers Geralyn • Cheshire Public Library • Cheshire, CT 06410
Byers Laura • East Canaan, CT 06024 • ACRL
Byers Lorena Garloch • Pittsburgh, PA 15219-1604 • ACRL ALCTS *Life*
Byers Marie P. • Reference Librarian • David Lipscomb University University Library • Nashville, TN 37204-3951 • ACRL
Byers Rosemarie • Director • Grace A. Dow Memorial Library • Midland, MI 48640 • LAMA LITA PLA
Byford John • Reader Services • British Library • London, WC1B 3DG United Kingdom • IRRT
Bykoski Cara • Library Technical Assistant • Cheshire Public Library • Cheshire, CT 06410
Byler Anne Meyer • Champaign Public Library & Information Center • Champaign, IL 61820-5193
Bynagle Hans E. • Director • Whitworth College Library • Spokane, WA 99251 • ACRL
Bynum Jean Davis • Westminster Schools-Bynum • Atlanta, GA 30327 • AASL
Bynum Mollie B. • Teacher's Librarian • Chester Valley Elementary School • Anchorage, AK 99504 • AASL ALSC
Byram Carole • Media Specialist • Comanche County Unified School District #300 • Coldwater, KS 67029 • AASL
Byrd Beverly P. • Tallahassee, FL 32308
Byrd Caroline • Assistant Director • St. Mary's University Academic Library • San Antonio, TX 78228 • LAMA
Byrd Charlotte V. • Library Media Specialist • Patapsco High School • Baltimore, MD 21222 • AASL
Byrd Frederick E. Judge • Trustee • Detroit Public Library • Detroit, MI 48202 • ALTA
Byrd Gary D. • Assistant Dir. Health Sci. Lib. • University of North Carolina • Chapel Hill, NC 27599 • ACRL
Byrd Jacqueline J. • Cataloger • Indiana University at Bloomington University Libraries • Bloomington, IN 47405-9998 • ACRL ALCTS
Byrd Karen R. • Lawrenceburg, TN 38464 • ACRL
Byrd Lois W. • Media Specialist • Athens High School Media Center • Troy, MI 48098 • AASL
Byrd Margaret • School Media Specialist • Erwin Open School Library • Greensboro, NC 27405 • AASL
Byrd Myona S. • Librarian • Williamsburg Independent School • Williamsburg, KY 40769 • LIRT
Byrd Pamela L. • Taylors, SC 29687-8814 • AASL ALSC
Byrd Rachel • Library Media Specialist • Lakeside High School Library • Hot Springs, AR 71901 • AASL
Byrd Robert L. • Director of Special Collections • Duke University William R. Perkins Library • Durham, NC 27706 • ACRL
Byrd Samuel D. III • Boston, MA 02118-3117 • ALCTS
Byrd Sherry L. • Minneapolis, MN 55410
Byrd Susan Gray • Reference Librarian • Miami Dade Community College • Miami, FL 33176 • ACRL
Byrd Susan W. • Richmond, VA 23221
Byrd Theresa S. • LRC Director • J Sargeant Reynolds Cmnty Coll • Richmond, VA 23241 • ACRL
Byre Calvin S. Dr • Humanities Reference Librarian • University of Oklahoma Libraries University Libraries • Norman, OK 73019 • ACRL
Byrne Christina A. • Engineering Reference Librarian • University of Washington Engineering Library • Seattle, WA 98195 • ACRL LITA RASD
Byrne Deborah J. • Southeast Metropolitan Board of Cooperative Services (SEMBCS) • Littleton, CO 80120
Byrne Elizabeth M. • Littleton, CO 80121
Byrne Karen L. • Delaware Valley College Sci & Agr Krauskopf Memorial Library • Doylestown, PA 18901 • ACRL LAMA
Byrne Kristine M. • Student • San Jose State University Division of Library & Information Science • San Jose, CA 95192-0029
Byrne Margaret A. • Base Librarian • Offutt Air Force Base Library • Offutt AFB, NE 68113-5000 • PLA AFLRT
Byrne Mary Ann • Los Angeles, CA 90069
Byrne Mary B. • Hd, Technical Services Dept. • Glencoe Public Library • Glencoe, IL 60022-1597 • ALCTS
Byrne Monica R. • Rock Lake Middle School • Longwood, FL 32750 • AASL
Byrne R. Joan • Reference Librarian/Asst. Dir. • Dodge City Public Library • Dodge City, KS 67801 • PLA RASD
Byrne Roseanne • Principal Librarian • Hennepin County Library • Minnetonka, MN 55343
Byrne Sherry • Preservation Librarian • University of Chicago Library • Chicago, IL 60637-1502 • ALCTS
Byrne Timothy L. • University of Colorado-Boulder University Libraries • Boulder, CO 80309 • LITA GODORT
Byrnes Ellen L. • Portland, OR 97220
Byrnes James M. • Charles E. Miller Library • Ellicott City, MD 21043
Byrnes Margaret M. • Bethesda, MD 20814 • ALCTS
Byrnes Sherri L. • Librarian • Dover High School Library • Dover, NJ 07801
Byrnes Shirley May • Public Library Consultant • South Central Library System • Madison, WI 53704 • PLA *Life*
Byrns Susan J. • Librarian • Oregon Middle School • Oregon, WI 53575 • AASL
Byron Suzanne M. • Head of User Education • University of North Texas • Denton, TX 76203 • ACRL RASD LIRT NMRT
Byrum John D. Jr. • Chief,Rgnl & Coop Catlg Div. • Library of Congress • Washington, DC 20540 • ALCTS
Caballero Cesar • Head Special Collection • University of Texas at El Paso Library • El Paso, TX 79968-0582 • LAMA
Caban Belen F. • Reference Specialist • Columbus Metropolitan Library Whetstone Branch Library • Columbus, OH 43214
Caban Robert • Head of Reference • Dekalb County Public Libraries Decatur Library • Decatur, GA 30030 • PLA RASD ILERT
Cabe Linda S. • Rockledge, FL 32955
Cabe Nancy W. • Trustee • Atlanta-Fulton Public Library • Atlanta, GA 30303 • PLA
Cabeen Shirley • Librarian • Los Angeles Public Library Palisades Branch • Pacific Palisades, CA 90272 • PLA
Cabell Leo W. Jr • Boulder, CO 80302 • Continuing
Cabezas Connie P. • Reference Librarian • Saint Edwards University Scarborough Phillips Library • Austin, TX 78704
Cabot Robin R. • Consultant • Arizona State Library Department of Library Archives & Public Records • Phoenix, AZ 85007
Cabrales Arthur K. • Librarian II • Las Vegas-Clark Cnty Lib Dist Spring Valley Library • Las Vegas, NV 89101
Caccese Vincent P. • Reference-Collection Development • University of California-Davis Library • Davis, CA 95616 • ACRL
Cacciola Lisa J. • Wayne Public Library • Wayne, NJ 07470
Cace Elga M. • Regional Librarian • New York Public Library Fordham Library Center • Bronx, NY 10458 • LAMA PLA RASD
Cackowski Irene • Director • Monroe Township Public Library • Jamesburg, NJ 08831 • PLA
Cadbury Elizabeth • Trustee • Pemberton Community Library Association • Pemberton, NJ 08068-1208
Cade Barbara C. • Atlanta, GA 30339 • AASL
Cade Roberta G. • Director • Division of Library Development • Albany, NY 12203 • ASCLA
Cadone Joy S. • Deputy County Librarian • Alameda County Library System • Fremont, CA 94538 • LAMA PLA
Cadoree Michelle B. • Science Reference Librarian • Library of Congress • Washington, DC 20541 • LITA RASD
Cadorette Margaret K. • Arnold, MD 21012
Cadra Laura A. • Reference Librarian • University of California L.A. Library Law Library • Los Angeles, CA 90024-1302
Cady George B. • Librarian • Baker High School Library • Baldwinsville, NY 13027 • AASL
Cady Maria E. • Media Specialist • Fulton Elementary School • Hempstead, NY 11550 • AASL
Cady Ruth • Librarian Media Specialist • Saint Anthony High School • Long Beach, CA 90801 • AASL IRRT LIRT
Cady Steven R. • Librarian • San Francisco Public Library Mission Branch • San Francisco, CA 94110 • EMIERT
Cady Susan A. • Assoc. Dir for Tech Services • Lehigh University Libraries Linderman Library 30 • Bethlehem, PA 18015-3067 • ACRL LITA LHRT
Caffee Jackie D. • Disabled Service Librarian • San Diego Public Library • San Diego, CA 92101 • ASCLA
Caffee Raymond • Saint Lawrence, SD 57373
Caffey Helen P. Miss • Mesilla Park, NM 88047 • ALSC PLA *Continuing*
Caforio Carla • Relocation Specialist • Bay State Moving Systems • Shrewsbury, MA 01745
Cage Alvin C. • Library Director • Stephen F. Austin State University Steen Library • Nacogdoches, TX 75962
Cagle Carolyn • Librarian • Westorchard Elementary School • Chappaqua, NY 10514 • AASL
Cagle Carroll K. • Media Specialist • Dalton Public Schools • Dalton, GA 30720 • AASL
Cagle R. Brantley Jr • Librarian • McNeese State University Lether E. Frazar Memorial Library • Lake Charles, LA 70609 • ASCLA GODORT MAGERT
Cahill Alice M. • Brighton, MA 02135 • ASCLA LAMA *Life*
Cahill James J. • Director • Margate City Library • Margate, NJ 08402
Cahill Mary E. • Reference & Interlibrary Loan Ln • Union College Schaffer Library • Schenectady, NY 12308 • ACRL SRRT
Cahill Nancy M. • Media Specialist • Cromwell Middle School • Cromwell, CT 06416 • AASL YALSA
Cahill Suzanne L. • Elementary School Librarian • Schulze Elementary School • Irving, TX 75060 • AASL
Cahn Joseph M. • Student • University of California Los Angeles Graduate School of Library & Information Science • Los Angeles, CA 90024 • RASD SRRT
Cahoon Andrea R. • Director • Ringwood Public Library • Ringwood, NJ 07456 • PLA SRRT
Cahoon Herbert T F • New York, NY 10028 • ACRL *Continuing*

Cai Wei • Student • Emporia State University School of Library & Information Management • Emporia, KS 66801

Caiger Anne • Manuscripts Librarian • University of California-Los Angeles (UCLA) • Los Angeles, CA 90024-1450 • ACRL

Cain Anne Henley • Assistant County Librarian • Contra Costa County Library • Pleasant Hill, CA 94523 • ALCTS PLA RASD

Cain Beverly L. • Manager of Reference/Adult Serv. • Medina County District Library • Medina, OH 44256 • LAMA RASD

Cain Carol J. • Student • Rutgers University School of Communication Information & Library Studies • New Brunswick, NJ 08903

Cain Carolyn L. • Director • La Follette High School • Madison, WI 53716 • AASL CLENE

Cain Charlene C. • Governments Documents Librarian • Louisiana State University Law Center Library • Baton Rouge, LA 70803-1010 • GODORT

Cain Jean A. S. • Sewickley, PA 15143

Cain Karyn E. • Student • University of Michigan School of Information and Library Studies • Ann Arbor, MI 48109-1092

Cain Linda J. • Associate Provost • University of Cincinnati Libraries • Cincinnati, OH 45221-0033 • ACRL

Cain Mark E. • Xavier University • Cincinnati, OH 45207 • ACRL LITA

Cain Melissa M. • Director of Development • University of North Carolina at Chapel Hill School of Information and Library Science • Chapel Hill, NC 27599-3360 • LAMA

Cain Vernon W. • President & CEO • Dawson Subscription Service • Mt. Morris, IL 61054 • ACRL PLA

Caine Cathy • Director • North Central Library Cooperative • Mansfield, OH 44902 • LAMA PLA

Caine William C. • Conserssion Specialist • Data Research Associates Inc. • Saint Louis, MO 63132 • ALCTS

Cairney Anna L. • Benedictine College North Campus Library • Atchison, KS 66002 • ACRL

Cairns Phyllis J. • Washington Library for the Blind & Physically Handicapped • Seattle, WA 98129 • ASCLA

Cairns Roberta A. E. • Director • East Providence Public Library Central Library • East Providence, RI 02914 • ALSC LAMA PLA RASD YALSA

Cairns Virginia L. • Ref. & Interlibrary Loan Ln. • Mercer University Main Library • Macon, GA 31207 • NMRT

Cairo Christine M. • Coordinator of Children's Serv. • Indianapolis Marion County Public Library • Indianapolis, IN 46206 • ALSC

Cairo Nelida A. • Reference Librarian • Instituto Tecnologico De Santo Domingo (INTEC) • Santo Domingo, DN, Dominican Republic

Cal Daria B. • Seattle, WA 98118

Calabrese Alice M. • Executive Director • Chicago Public Library • Chicago, IL 60605 • ASCLA LITA PLA

Calabro Susanne M. • Librarian • Bluford Elementary School • Greensboro, NC 27401 • AASL ALSC

Calamari Diane B. • Arden, NC 28704

Calantore Susan • Student • Rutgers University School of Communication Information & Library Studies • New Brunswick, NJ 08903

Calaway Lorna L. • Student • Arizona State University-West Fletcher Library • Phoenix, AZ 85069-7100 • LITA

Calbert Jack L. • Social Sciences Bibliographer • Tulane University Howard-Tilton Memorial Library • New Orleans, LA 70118

Calbreath Susan G. • Children's Coordinator • Lake Lanier Regional Library Lawrenceville Branch • Lawrenceville, GA 30245 • YALSA

Calcagno Eva D. • Automation Program Specialist • Washington County Cooperative Library Service • Aloha, OR 97006 • ALCTS LITA RASD

Calcagno Jeffrey A. • Corporate Library Blackwell North America • Lake Oswego, OR 97035 • ALCTS LITA

Calcaterra Lori Ms. • Library Director • Parks College of Saint Louis University • Cahokia, IL 62206 • ACRL LAMA

Calderon Federman • Columbia University Health Sciences Library • New York, NY 10032 • ALCTS

Calderon Lucy L. • Miami, FL 33144

Caldiero Wendy D. • Assistant Coordinator • New York Public Library Manhattan Borough Office • New York, NY 10019 • ALSC PLA

Caldor Selina • Clarksburg, MD 20871 • Continuing

Caldwell-Ries Michele A. • Portland, OR 97225

Caldwell-Wood Naomi • Nathan Bishop Middle School • Providence, RI 02906 • AASL LITA

Caldwell Angela R. • Lexington, KY 40517 • AASL SRRT

Caldwell Cora Lou • Idaho State School for the Deaf & Blind • Gooding, ID 83330 • AASL ALSC

Caldwell George H. • Senior Spec In U S Govt Doc • Library of Congress • Washington, DC 20541 • ACRL RASD FLRT GODORT *Life*

Caldwell Ila M. • Media Specialist • Macedonia Middle School Berkeley County • Moncts Corner, SC 29461

Caldwell Jana • Technical Services Coordinator • Indiana University School of Library and Information Science • Bloomington, IN 47405

Caldwell Jane • Collection Development Coor • Catawba County Library • Newton, NC 28658 • PLA RASD IFRT

Caldwell Jean L. • Librarian I • Seminole County Library System Central Branch • Casselberry, FL 32707 • NMRT

Caldwell Jody L. • Head, Reference Department • Drew University • Madison, NJ 07940-4007 • ACRL RASD LIRT

Caldwell Lora • Village School • Pacific Palisades, CA 90272 • AASL

Caldwell Lou A. • Staff Training & Development • Houston Public Library • Houston, TX 77002 • LAMA PLA RASD CLENE

Caldwell Martha R. • Stockton-San Joaquin County Public Library • Stockton, CA 95202

Caldwell Mary S. • Ft Lauderdale, FL 33304

Caldwell Melinda K. • Computer Services • Public Library of Cincinnati and Hamilton County • Cincinnati, OH 45202

Caldwell Richard Clark • Museum of History • Seattle, WA 98112 • ACRL LITA RASD

Caldwell Rossie B. • Orangeburg, SC 29115 • Continuing

Cale William E. • Cataloger • Morgan State University Soper Library • Baltimore, MD 21239-4098 • ALCTS

Calef Daniel Carr • Chief Librarian • Yorkton Public Library • Yorkton, SK, S3N 0L9 Canada

Calemme Sandra M. • University of Detroit Mercy Library • Detriot, MI 48219-3599

Calender David W. • School Library Media Specialist • Wichersham Elementary School • Lancaster, PA 17602 • AASL

Caley Charlotte A. • Assistant Director • Jefferson County Public Library • Louisville, GA 30434

Caley Diane • Library Administrator • Ward County Public Library • Minot, ND 58701

Calhoun Becky • Reference Librarian • Henderson County Public Library • Hendersonville, NC 28739 • RASD

Calhoun Elizabeth Gray • Technical Services • University of Michigan Libraries • Ann Arbor, MI 48109-1205

Calhoun Ellen • Government Documents Librarian • Rutgers University Libraries Library of Science & Medicine • Piscataway, NJ 08855-1029 • GODORT

Calhoun Jean F. • Trustee • Concordia Parish Library • Ferriday, LA 71334 • ALTA

Calhoun John C. • Collection Development Librarian • University of Arkansas at Little Rock Library & Information Science Programs • Little Rock, AR 72204

Calhoun Karen S. • Manager • Online Computer Library Center (OCLC) • Dublin, OH 43017-3395 • LITA

Calhoun Laurie R. • Washington, DC 20009 • ACRL RASD

Calhoun Mary I. • Cataloging Librarian • Florida Institute of Technology Library • Melbourne, FL 32901

Calhoun Patrick T. • University of South Carolina • Columbia, SC 29208 • LITA

Calhoun Wanda J. • Director • East Central Georgia Regional Library Augusta-Richmond County • Augusta, GA 30901 • LAMA

Cali Joseph J. • Librarian • Antioch College • Yellow Spring, OH 45387

Caliendo Lorraine • American Marketing Association • Chicago, IL 60606 • LAMA RASD

Califf John Mark • Librarian • Drew University • Madison, NJ 07940-4007 • ACRL ALCTS

Calimano Ivan E. • Head of Copy Cataloger • University of Southern California • Los Angeles, CA 90033 • ALCTS

Calixto Beatriz V. • Student • University of Texas at Austin Graduate School of Library & Information Sciences • Austin, TX 78712-1276 • LITA LRRT

Calk Jo Frances M. • Library Systems Specialist 3 • Western Library Network (WLN) • Lacey, WA 98503 • ALCTS LITA SRRT

Calkins Kay • Senri International School • Mino City,Osaka 562, Japan • AASL

Call Isaac S. • Dir. of Instr. Supp. Service • Broward Community College • Fort Lauderdale, FL 33314 • ACRL

Call J. Randolph • Coordinator of Cataloging • Detroit Public Library • Detroit, MI 48202 • ALCTS LITA LIRT *Life*

Callaghan Anne C. • Preschool Services Coordinator • Glenview Public Library • Glenview, IL 60025 • PLA

Callaghan Jean S. • Serials Librarian • Wheaton College Wallace Library • Norton, MA 02766 • ACRL ALCTS

Callaghan Linda Ward • Head of Children's Services • Naperville Public Libraries • Naperville, IL 60540 • ALSC EMIERT

Callaghan M. Hilary • Student • Wayne State University Library Science Program • Detroit, MI 48202

Callaghan Richard J. • Senior Reference Librarian • South Hadley Library System • South Hadley, MA 01075

Callaghan Teresa Mary • Chestnut Hill, MA 02167 • ALSC YALSA *Life*

Callaham Betty E. • Columbia, SC 29205 • Continuing

Callahan Arlene M. Sr. • Library Director • Rivier College Regina Library • Nashua, NH 03060 • ACRL ALCTS LAMA LITA

Callahan Christopher J. • Student • State University of New York at Albany School of Information Science & Policy • Albany, NY 12222 • AASL

Callahan Daren J. • Carbondale, IL 62901-2030 • ACRL

Callahan Diane R. • Hudson, NH 03051-4411

Callahan John . • Systems Librarian • University of Lowell Lydon Library • Lowell, MA 01854 • ACRL MAGERT

Callahan John J. III • Library Services Manager • Hernando County Library System • Brooksville, FL 34601

Callahan John W. • Coordinator-Young Adult Services • Stark County District Library • Canton, OH 44702 • YALSA

Callahan Mary Virginia Mrs. • Librarian • Underwood Elementary School Library • Andrews, TX 79714 • ALSC

Callahan Nancy R. • Reference Librarian • Thomas Branigan Memorial Library • Las Cruces, NM 88001

Callahan Patricia • Associate Director for Tech Svs. • University of Pennsylvania Libraries Biddle Law Library • Philadelphia, PA 19104-6279 • ALCTS LITA

Callahan Patricia A. • Head Children's Services • Jericho Public Library • Jericho, NY 11753

Callahan Patrick F. • University of Cincinnati • Cincinnati, OH 45221-0033 • ALCTS

Callahan Virginia • Librarian • Underwood Elementary School Library • Andrews, TX 79714 • ALSC

Callanan Ellen M. • Head Cataloger • New Jersey Institute of Technology Van Houten Library • Newark, NJ 07102 • ACRL

Callard Carole C. • Supervisor • Library of Michigan • Lansing, MI 48909 • RASD FLRT GODORT

Callavini Cheryl A. • Children's Librarian • Jacksonville Public Library Regency Square Branch • Jacksonville, FL 32225

Callaway Duryea H. • Interlibrary Loan Librarian • Wayne State University • Detroit, MI 48202

Callaway Susan A. • Business Manager • Salt Lake City Public Library • Salt Lake City, UT 84111

Callen James D. • Student • University of Oklahoma School of Library & Information Studies • Norman, OK 73019 • SRRT

Callender Rebecca L. • Columbus Metropolitan Library Hilltonia Branch • Columbus, OH 43223 • PLA

Callender Ross D. • Library Technician • Library of Congress • Washington, DC 20541

Calleton Pamela B. • Student • San Jose State University Clark Library • San Jose, CA 95192-0028

Callicoat Sharon E. • Children's Librarian • Milton-Union Public Library • West Milton, OH 45383 • ALSC

Callis Felicity C. • Media Specialist • East Lee County Junior High School • Sanford, NC 27330 • AASL

Callison Daniel J. • Indiana University School of Library and Information Science • Bloomington, IN 47405 • AASL LIRT

Callison Helen L. • W Columbia, SC 29169 • AASL *Continuing*

Callison Patricia G. • Librarian • Monroe County Public Library • Bloomington, IN 47408

Calmes Leslie S. • Tucson, AZ 85716

Calote Carol • Librarian • Cerritos College Library • Norwalk, CA 90650 • ACRL LIRT

Calpestri Suzanne H. • Head,Cooperative Services • University of California-Berkeley University Library • Berkeley, CA 94720 • ACRL LAMA RASD

Caltabiano Marilyn • Library Director • Memorial Library of Radnor Township • Wayne, PA 19087 • LAMA PLA

Caltrider Janet E. • Tawas City, MI 48763 • AASL

Caltvedt Sarah C. • Head of Adult Services • Elmhurst Public Library • Elmhurst, IL 60126 • PLA RASD

Calub Laura N. • Rosenberg, TX 77471 • ALCTS

Calvani Patricia L. • Director • York County Library System • York, PA 17402-9004 • LAMA PLA NMRT

Calvano Mary F. • Earie, PA 16506

Calvert Donna B. • Library Consultant • West Virginia Library Commission • Charleston, WV 25305 • PLA

Calvert Herta M. • Student • San Jose State University Division of Library & Information Science • San Jose, CA 95192-0029

Calvert Hildegund M. • Circulation Supervisor • Ball State University Library Department of Library Services • Muncie, IN 47306

Calvi Elise Thall • Harvard University • Cambridge, MA 02138 • ALCTS

Calvin Alva F. • Wilmington, DE 19809

Calvin Bruce C. • Information Specialist • American Society for Training and Development • Alexandria, VA 22313 • RASD

Calvin Diane L. • Government Documents Librarian • Ball State University Library Department of Library Services • Muncie, IN 47306 • ACRL GODORT

Calzonetti Jo Ann • University Librarian • West Virginia University Charles C. Wise Jr. Library • Morgantown, WV 26506 • ACRL GODORT

Cama Maryann • Poland, OH 44514

Camacho Nancy S. • National Library of Medicine • Bethesda, MD 20894 • ASCLA

Camarata Corinne • Director of Children's Serv. • Port Washington Public Library • Port Washington, NY 11050 • ALSC

Cambre Pamela • Student • Louisiana State University School of Library & Information Science • Baton Rouge, LA 70803-3290

Cambron Barbara A. • Eliahu Academy • Louisville, KY 40218 • ALSC

Camden Beth Picknally • Head, Copy Cataloging • University of Virginia Alderman Library • Charlottesville, VA 22903-2498 • ALCTS LITA

Camenga Carol H. • Student • University of South Florida School of Library & Information Science • Tampa, FL 33620 • PLA RASD

Camenga John F. • Librarian II • Tampa-Hillsborough County Public Library • Tampa, FL 33602 • ACRL GODORT MAGERT

Camerman Virginia • Senior Librarian, Ref. Services • New York State Library State Education Department • Albany, NY 12230

Cameron-Miller Brenda L. • Fort Vancouver Regional Library • Vancouver, WA 98663 • LAMA LHRT

Cameron Alexander A. • Chief Executive Officer • Town of Pickering Public Library • Pickering ON, L1V 2R6 Canada

Cameron Constance B. • Assistant Librarian • Bryant College Hodgson Memorial Library • Smithfield, RI 02917 • RASD

Cameron Dee B. • Librarian • Burnet Elementary School • El Paso, TX 79901

Cameron H. Charles • Department Head • Newfoundland Public Library Service Arts & Culture Centre • St. John's NF, A1B 3A3 Canada • RASD

Cameron Hazel • Business Librarian • University of Victoria McPherson Library • Victoria BC, V8W 3H5 Canada • LITA

Cameron Heather • ABC-CLIO, Inc. • Denver, CO 80209 • AASL ACRL PLA RASD ERT

Cameron Jayne B. • Media Specialist • Wiley Elementary School • Greensboro, NC 27406

Cameron Jeremiah • Trustee • Kansas City Public Library • Kansas City, MO 64106 • ALTA

Cameron Lucille • Dean • University of Rhode Island Library • Kingston, RI 02881-0803 • ACRL

Cameron Margaret A. • Chief Librarian • Deakin University • Victoria 3217, Australia • ACRL RASD

Cameron Mary • Children's Librarian • Chapel Hill Public Library • Chapel Hill, NC 27514 • ALSC

Cameron Mary • Dir., Alumni & Public Relations • University of North Carolina School of Library Science • Chapel Hill, NC 27599-3360

Cameron Robert F. • Circulation Coordinator • Loyola University Library • New Orleans, LA 70118 • SRRT

Cameron Virginia S. • Librarian • Stewart Library • Grinnell, IA 50112 • YALSA

Camille Damon • Asst. Exec. Dir. for Lib Svs. • Houston Academy of Medicine Texas Medical Center Library • Houston, TX 77030

Camins Ruth • Assistant Director • Oradell Public Library • Oradell, NJ 07649

Cammack Bruce P. • Texas Tech University Libraries • Lubbock, TX 79409-0002 • ACRL

Cammack Nancy M. • Sullivan's School • FPO, AP 96349-0005

Cammarata Paul J. • Librarian • State University of New York (SUNY) Frank Melville Jr. Memorial Library • Stony Brook, NY 11794-3300 • ACRL LITA RASD GODORT

Camp James E. • Head of Record Control • Cobb County Public Library System • Marietta, GA 30060

Camp Maryann L. • Student • Rutgers University School of Communication Information & Library Studies • New Brunswick, NJ 08903

Camp Roxanne • Acqs. Firm Order Supervisor • San Jose State University Clark Library • San Jose, CA 95192-0028

Camp Thomas E. • Associate Librarian • University of the South Jessie Ball duPont Library • Sewanee, TN 37375-4005 • ACRL

Campa Josephine Dr. • Media Specialist • Watkins Mill Elementary School • Gaithersburg, MD 20860 • ALSC *Life*

Campana Janice H. • Branch Librarian • Cleveland Heights-University Heights Public Library Noble Neighborhood Branch • Cleveland Heights, OH 44121-2208

Campbell Anna Fay • Brewster Middle School • Camp Lejeune, NC 28542 • AASL YALSA

Campbell Anna M. • St. LTA • Florida State University • Tallahassee, FL 32306-2047

Campbell Barbara J. • Campbell, CA 95008 • ALTA PLA
Life

Campbell Barbara S. • Media Specialist • Farmington High School Library • Farmington, CT 06032 • AASL ACRL LITA RASD

Campbell Bernard Dr • Trustee • Mid-Continent Public Library • Independence, MO 64050 • ALTA

Campbell Bertha M. • Branch Librarian • Atlanta-Fulton Public Library • Atlanta, GA 30303 • ALSC

Campbell Bettye W. • Library Media Coordinator • Richard Campus-Community High School District 218 • Oak Lawn, IL 60453 • Life

Campbell Bonnie • President • Campbell Consulting Ltd. • Toronto ON, M6G 3L8 Canada • LITA

Campbell Bonnie Heather • Senior Librarian • Jacksonville Public Library Highlands Branch • Jacksonville, FL 32218-4712 • PLA

Campbell Brian G. • Systems & Planning Director • Vancouver Public Library • Vancouver BC, V6Z 1X5 Canada • LITA IFRT SRRT

Campbell Cameron J. • Head, Serials Cataloging Section • University of Chicago Library • Chicago, IL 60637-1502

Campbell Carl S. • Librarian III • Phoenix Public Library Acacia Branch • Phoenix, AZ 85020 • ASCLA PLA

Campbell Carol A. • Parish Librarian • Saint Thomas Church Library • Sunnyvale, CA 94086

Campbell Caroline C. • District Librarian • District Library Media Center • East Peoria, IL 61611 • AASL

Campbell Cassandra • Children Services • Hilton Head Public Library • Hilton Head, SC 29928

Campbell Catherine A. • Brigham Young University School of Library & Information Sciences • Provo, UT 84602

Campbell Christine M. • Librarian • J.R. Tucker High School • Richmond, VA 23294 • AASL

Campbell Colleen F. • Student • University of Montana • Missoula, MT 59801 • ALCTS

Campbell Dana A. • Fort Vancouver Regional Library • Vancouver, WA 98663

Campbell Deirdre A. • Morgan Hill, CA 95037

Campbell Diana L. • Owner • Imaginasium Village of Colonial Peddlers • Carlisle, PA 17013

Campbell Dolores • Combee Elementary School • Lakeland, FL 33801

Campbell Don James • Student • San Jose State University Division of Library & Information Science • San Jose, CA 95192-0029

Campbell Donna M. • Chief Librarian • Agawam Public Library • Agawam, MA 01001 • ALCTS ALSC PLA

Campbell Douglas G. • Director of Library Services • Northwestern Michigan College Mark & Helen Osterlin Library • Traverse City, MI 49684 • ACRL

Campbell Elizabeth L. • Mesa County Public Library • Grand Junction, CO 81502 • IFRT VRT

Campbell Garnett S. • Student • University of Missouri-Columbia School of Library & Informational Science • Columbia, MO 65211 • LITA

Campbell Gloria L. • Regional Manager • Memphis-Shelby County Public Library and Information Center • Memphis, TN 38104-4025 • PLA

Campbell Gregor R. • President-Owner • Campbell-Logan Bindery, Inc • Minneapolis, MN 55401 • ALCTS

Campbell James • North Europe Bibliographer • University of Virginia Alderman Library • Charlottesville, VA 22903-2498 • ACRL ALCTS LITA

Campbell Janet • Literature Cataloger • California State University-Long Beach University Library & Learning Resources • Long Beach, CA 90840-1901 • ACRL ALCTS

Campbell Jerry D. • Vice-Provost for Lib. Affairs • Duke University William R. Perkins Library • Durham, NC 27706 • ACRL ALCTS LAMA

Campbell Joan • Chicago, IL 60614 • Life

Campbell Joan M. • Student • Drexel University College of Information Studies • Philadelphia, PA 19104-2875

Campbell John D. • Director • Pathfinder Library System • Montrose, CO 81402 • ASCLA

Campbell John L. • Online Service Coordinator • University of Georgia Libraries • Athens, GA 30602 • ACRL RASD

Campbell Kristen A. • Base Librarian • Scott Air Force Base Library • Scott AFB, IL 62225 • ALSC PLA AFLRT

Campbell Lee Ann • Dellslow, WV 26531-0067 • RASD ILERT

Campbell Lucy B. • Portsmouth, VA 23704

Campbell Marilyn Ida • Columbus, OH 43209

Campbell Marta S. • Westport Public Library • Westport, CT 06880 • RASD YALSA

Campbell Mary E. • Technical Services Librarian • Idaho State Library • Boise, ID 83702 • ALCTS VRT

Campbell Mary G. • Student • University of Missouri-Columbia School of Library & Informational Science • Columbia, MO 65211 • PLA RASD

Campbell Mary J. • Greensboro, NC 27406 • AASL

Campbell Mary K. • Fayetteville, NC 28305 • YALSA IFRT

Campbell Mary S. • Elementary Librarian • Foster Heights Elementary School • Bardstown, KY 40004 • AASL ALSC   *Life*

Campbell Nancy F. • Reference Librarian • Northern Kentucky University Steely Library • Highland Heights, KY 41099-6101 • ACRL

Campbell Patricia • West Allis Public Library • West Allis, WI 53214

Campbell Patricia G. • Head-Reference, Adult Services • South Country Library • Bellport, NY 11713 • PLA RASD

Campbell Patricia J. • Fallbrook, CA 92028 • YALSA

Campbell Peter Scott • Librarian-Social Sciences • Queens Borough Public Library • Jamaica, NY 11432

Campbell R Carolyn • Lib Learning Center Specialist • Community Unit School District #200 Longfellow Elementary Street • Wheaton, IL 60187 • AASL ALSC

Campbell R. R. • School Librarian • School District U-46 • Elgin, IL 60120 • AASL

Campbell Rick • Trustee • Central Arkansas Library System • Little Rock, AR 72201-4698 • ALTA

Campbell Sandra M. • Reference Librarian • University of Alberta Library • Edmonton AB, T6G 2J8 Canada • ACRL LAMA

Campbell Sharon • Director • Ella Johnson Memorial Pub Lib District • Hampshire, IL 60140 • LAMA PLA LIRT

Campbell Sharon L. • Rochester Hills, MI 48306

Campbell Sheila R. • Upper Arlington, OH 43220

Campbell Stanley • Director of Libraries • Centre College of Kentucky Doherty Library • Danville, KY 40422-1394 • ACRL ALCTS RASD

Campbell Susan McCarthy • Director • York College of Pennsylvania Schmidt Library • York, PA 17403 • ACRL

Campbell Susan T. • Chesapeake Public Library • Chesapeake, VA 23320

Campbell Sylvia • Substitute Librarian • Sonoma County Library • Santa Rosa, CA 95404

Campbell Ted T. • Director • Stuttgart Public Library • Stuttgart, AR 72160

Campbell Teresa W. • Charlestown-Clark County Library • Charlestown, IN 47111

Campbell Thelma • Librarian I/Bldg Mgr. • Broward County Division of Libraries West Regional Branch • Plantation, FL 33324

Campbell Vivian L. • Assoc Law Ln for Clln Devel • Georgetown University Law Center Edward Bennett Williams Library • Washington, DC 20001-1417 • ACRL ALCTS

Campeau Katherine • Librarian • Bozeman Senior High School Library • Bozeman, MT 59715

Camper Cathryn A. • Ln./Technology & Science Dept. • Minneapolis Public Library & Information Center • Minneapolis, MN 55401-1992 • SRRT

Campion Carol-Mae • Librarian • Lackawanna Junior College Seeley Memorial Library • Scranton, PA 18503 • ACRL

Campion Eleanor E. • Newtown, PA 18940 • Continuing

Campione Patricia Ms. • Trustee • Summit Public Library District • Summit, IL 60501

Campos Brigida A. • Student • University of California-Berkeley School of Library & Information Studies • Berkeley, CA 94720 • EMIERT

Canaan Sibyl • Cold Spring, NY 10516 • PLA

Canada Dee A. • Graduate Student • University of Southern Mississippi School of Library Science • Hattiesburg, MS 39406-5146 • AASL

Canada Mary W. • Durham, NC 27701 • ACRL RASD *Life*

Canadee Amy A. • Reference Librarian • Ritter Public Library • Vermilion, OH 44089 • RASD

Canady Iris • Teacher • Dadeville High School • Dadeville, AL 36853

Canales Herbert G. • Director • Corpus Christi Public Library • Corpus Christi, TX 78401 • PLA

Canarsky Maurine • Media Librarian • Fairbanks North Star Borough Public Library & Regional Center-Noel Wien Library • Fairbanks, AK 99701 • LAMA PLA RASD VRT

Canavan Roberta • Director • Linden Free Public Library • Linden, NJ 07036 • PLA

Canby Susan Fifer • Library Director • National Geographic Society Library • Washington, DC 20036 • LAMA MAGERT

Candaras Barbara P. • Student • State University of New York (SUNY) School of Information & Library Studies • Buffalo, NY 14260

Cande Lorraine • Media Specialist • Floral Park-Bellerose School Library • Floral Park, NY 11001 • AASL

Candir Julie B. • Des Plaines, IL 60016

Canelas Cathryn M. • Reference Librarian • Iowa State University Library • Ames, IA 50011-2140 • ACRL RASD

Canelas Dale B. Ms • Director of Libraries • University of Florida Libraries • Gainesville, FL 32611-2047 • ACRL LAMA *Life*

Canevari de Paredes Donna A. • University of Saskatchewan Library • Saskatoon SK, S7N 0W0 Canada • ACRL RASD

Canfield Cheryl L. • Reference Librarian • Hutchinson Public Library • Hutchinson, KS 67501 • RASD IFRT

Canfield Dee • Manager, Talking Book Center • River Bend Library System • Coal Valley, IL 61240 • ASCLA IFRT

Canfield Laurie • Children's Librarian • Solano County Library Vacaville Branch • Vacaville, CA 95688 • ALSC

Canfield Ruth • Student • University of North Carolina School of Library Science • Chapel Hill, NC 27599-3360

Cangiano Barbara • Library Systems Analyst • Columbia University Libraries Butler Library • New York, NY 10027 • ACRL

Canham-Eaton Clare • Media Specialist • Ann Arbor Public School • Ann Arbor, MI 48104 • AASL

Canick Maureen L. • Head, Loan Reference Section • Library of Congress • Washington, DC 20541 • ASCLA RASD

Cann Sharon Lee • Student • Georgia State University Pullen Library • Atlanta, GA 30303-3081 • AASL ACRL ALCTS RASD

CannCasciato Daniel G. • Catalog Librarian • University of Oregon Library • Eugene, OR 97403-1299

Cannady Beverly • Library Director • Verona Public Library • Verona, WI 53593 • PLA YALSA

Cannady Susan S. • Librarian • Grimsley High School • Greensboro, NC 27408 • AASL YALSA

Cannallo Kathy • Librarian • Hawaii Department of Education Special Instructional Programs & Services Branch • Honolulu, HI 96816 • AASL

Cannan Judith A. • Chief Tech Proc & Automation Instr Off • Library of Congress • Washington, DC 20541 • ALCTS

Cannell Jeffrey Wm. • Branch Head • Cumberland County Public Library and Information Center, Eutaw Branch • Fayetteville, NC 28314-1936 • LAMA PLA

Cannetti Margaret T. • Lexington Pk, MD 20653

Canney Michele R. • Librarian • Le Jardin Academy • Kailua, HI 96734 • AASL

Cannon Carol A. • Librarian III, Asst. Hd. • Chicago Public Library Carter G. Woodson Regional Library • Chicago, IL 60628

Cannon Charlotte F. • Richmond, KY 40475

Cannon Donald M. • Assoc. Ed., Cumulative Bk. Index • H. W. Wilson Company • Bronx, NY 10452 • ACRL

Cannon Ellen C. • Student • University of North Carolina at Chapel Hill School of Information and Library Science • Chapel Hill, NC 27599-3360

Cannon James R. • Reference Librarian • Indianapolis Marion County Public Library • Indianapolis, IN 46206 • PLA RASD

Cannon Marcia D. • Media Specialist • Myakka City Schools • Myakka City, FL 34251 • AASL

Cannon Marion J. • Media Specialist/President • Orange County Classroom Teacher's Association • Orlando, FL 32804 • AASL

Cannon Patricia A. • Northern Illinois University Department of Library & Information Studies • DeKalb, IL 60115 • IFRT

Cannon Robert E. • Director • Public Library of Charlotte & Mecklenburg County • Charlotte, NC 28202 • LAMA PLA

Cannon Tyrone H. • Sr. Associate Univ. Librarian • Boston College Libraries • Chestnut Hill, MA 02167 • ACRL LAMA RASD

Cano Margarita • Community Relations Coordinator • Miami-Dade Public Library System • Miami, FL 33130-1504 • PLA

Canon Carrie A. • Head Librarian • Saint Charles Parish Library • Destrehan, LA 70047 • ALSC

Canosa-Albano Jean M. • Springfield, MA 01119

Canterbury Leslie J. • Reference Librarian • University of Redlands Armacost Library • Redlands, CA 92374-3758 • ACRL

Cantlon Michael B. • Decimal Class Specialist • Library of Congress • Washington, DC 20541 • ACRL ALCTS LITA RASD IFRT

Cantoni Sylvia T. • Librarian • IBM Corporation IBM Library • Charlotte, NC 28257-0201

Cantor Mel L. • Director • Monterey Public Library • Monterey, CA 93940 • LAMA PLA

Cantrall Rebecca J. • Pittsburgh, PA 15219 • Continuing

Cantrell Barbara D. • Student • Texas Woman's University School of Library & Information Studies • Denton, TX 76204

Cantrell Clyde Hull Dr • Director Emeritus of Libraries • Auburn University Ralph Brown Draughon Library • Auburn, AL 36849-5606 • ACRL ALCTS LAMA RASD *Life*

Cantrell Gloria • Librarian • McCall Public Library • McCall, ID 83638

Cantrell Ida Beth • Executive Director • Thomas Brothers Maps • Los Angeles, CA 90017 • MAGERT

Cantwell Jacqueline F. • Librarian • Gibson, Dunn & Crutcher • San Francisco, CA 94104

Cantwell Mary Louise • Collection Development Librarian • Grandview Heights Public Library • Columbus, OH 43212 • RASD

Canzano Deborah J. • Project Librarian • New York State Library Division of Library Development • Albany, NY 12230

Cap Maria • Los Angeles County Law Library • Los Angeles, CA 90012

Capan Mary Ann • Technical Instructor • Western Illinois University Department of Media & Educational Technology • Macomb, IL 61455 • YALSA

Capano Laura M. • Children's Librarian • Howard County Library • Columbia, MD 21044 • ALSC

Caparros Ilona S. • Public Services Librarian • Rutgers University Libraries • New Brunswick, NJ 08903 • ACRL ALCTS RASD

Cape Stephen H. • Indiana University Lilly Library • Bloomington, IN 47405 • ACRL ALCTS

Capella Jeanne • Junior Librarian • Atlantic County Library • Mays Landing, NJ 08336 • PLA

Capelle-Cook Donna J. • Syracuse University • Syracuse, NY 13244 • ACRL

Capen Elizabeth D. • Librarian • Rock Springs High School Library • Rock Springs, WY 82901 • AASL

Capizzi Susan A. • Librarian II • Auburn-Placer County Library • Auburn, CA 95603-3789 • RASD

Caplan Audra L. • Public Service Libraian • Baltimore County Public Library • Towson, MD 21204 • PLA YALSA

Caplan Carol • Miami, FL 33102-5573 • AASL

Caplan Donald H. • Partner • Patterosn, Kirk, Wallace • Toronto ON, M5H 3Y2 Canada • ACRL LAMA PLA CLENE NMRT

Caplan Ellen R. • Sr. Quality Control Librarian • Online Computer Library Center (OCLC) • Dublin, OH 43017-3395 • ACRL ALCTS MAGERT

Caplan Fredda E. • Iowa City, IA 52246 • YALSA EMIERT IFRT

Caplan Priscilla L. • Head Systems Devel Division • Harvard University • Cambridge, MA 02138 • LITA

Caplan Victoria F. • Chicago Public Library • Chicago, IL 60605 • IFRT IRRT SRRT

Capone Theresa • Cataloger • John Jay College of Criminal Justice • New York, NY 10019 • ALCTS

Capoor Asha • Groug Dir./Lib Svs & Data Base • Baker & Taylor Books • Bridgewater, NJ 08807-0920 • ACRL ALCTS LITA

Caporale Ted • Westland, MI 48185

Capozzoli Lisa M. • Student • University of Maryland College of Library and Information Services • College Park, MD 20742-4345 • SRRT

Cappadonna Mary S. • Technical Processing Librarian • Oceanside Public Library • Oceanside, CA 92054

Cappas Lucille • Senior Librarian • Los Angeles Public Library Venice Branch • Venice, CA 90291 • PLA

Cappas de Pinero Belsie I. • Coor. of Continuing Edu. L. Sys. • University of Puerto Rico • Rio Piedras, PR 00931

Cappelson Sharon E. • Student • Pratt Institute Graduate School of Library & Information Science • Brooklyn, NY 11205

Cappetta Michele • Principal Librarian • Newark Public Library • Newark, NJ 07101-0630 • PLA

Capps Paullean P. • Northeast Arkansas Regional Library • Paragould, AR 72450

Capps Rosemary • Librarian • Rider High School • Wichita Falls, TX 76308 • AASL YALSA

Cappuzzello Paul G. • Senior Marketing Representative • OCLC Incorporation • Dublin, OH 43017 • ASCLA RASD

Caputo Anne S. • Mgr., Academic Programs • Dialog Information Service Inc. • Arlington, VA 22209 • AASL ACRL

Caputo Christine D. • Free Library of Philadelphia Mantua Branch • Philadelphia, PA 19104 • AASL ALSC

Caputo Jill E. • Media Manager • Sugarloaf School • Sugarloaf, FL 33042 • ALSC

Caputo L. Corinne • Alpine, TX 79830

Cara James • Supervising Librarian • Berkeley Public Library • Berkeley, CA 94704 • PLA IFRT

Carabateas Clarissa D. • Nassau, NY 12123

Carabell Janet L. • Lyons, CO 80540 • LITA

Caracuzzo Alexander J. • Student • University of Rhode Island Graduate School of Library & Information Studies • Kingston, RI 02881-0815

Caravello Patti Schifter • Reference Librarian • University of California-Los Angeles University Research Library • Los Angeles, CA 90024 • ACRL LIRT

Carberry Pamela M. • Library Director • Theodore Austin Cutler Mem Library Saint Louis Public Library • St Louis, MI 48880

Carbone Jerry J. • Assistant Director • Brooks Memorial Library • Brattleboro, VT 05301

Carbone Linda Wilkens • Resources Center Manager • YWCA of Boulder County • Boulder, CO 80302

Carbone Lisa S. • Student • State University of New York (SUNY) Central Technical Services • Buffalo, NY 14260

Carbonell Marilyn • Asst Dir. for Collection Devel. • University of Missouri-Kansas City Library • Kansas City, MO 64110-2499 • ACRL ALCTS LAMA RASD SRRT

Card Judy • Staff Development Officer • Memphis-Shelby County Public Library and Information Center • Memphis, TN 38104-4025 • PLA CLENE

Card Sandra • Asst to Head,Online Catlg/Bibl • State University of New York at Binghamton Libraries (SUNY) • Binghamton, NY 13902-6012 • ALCTS

Card Sandra E. • Automated Systems Coordinator • California State University-Los Angeles John F. Kennedy Memorial Library • Los Angeles, CA 90032-8300 • ACRL ALCTS LITA

Cardenas-Parra Yolanda • Library Section Supervisor • City of Commerce Public Library • Commerce, CA 90040

Cardenas Patricia A. • Assistant Librarian • University of Illinois Library • Urbana, IL 61801 • ACRL IRRT

Carder Linda L. • Reference Librarian • Southeast Missouri State University • Cape Girardeau, MO 63701

Cardew Catherine • Rochester, NY 14610 • Continuing

Cardillo Edna D. • Dorchester, MA 02122

Cardman Elizabeth R. • Student • University of Illinois Graduate School of Library and Information Science • Urbana, IL 61801

Cardman Helen-Andrea • Children's Librarian • Champaign Public Library & Information Center • Champaign, IL 61820-5193

Cardon Laureen • Circulation Librarian • Brigham Young University Harold B. Lee Library • Provo, UT 84602 • LAMA

Cardona Joanne S. Ms • Librarian • Moorestown Friends School • Moorestown, NJ 08057 • YALSA

Cardone Debra • Crossroads School for Arts & Science • Santa Monica, CA 90404

Cardoza Frances A. • Library Director • Rogue Community College Library • Grants Pass, OR 97527 • ACRL

Cardwell Carolyn • Database Licensing Specialist • UMI Data Courier Inc. • Louisville, KY 40202 • LITA

Caren Loretta • Okemos, MI 48864 • ACRL LAMA

Caretti Susan Pashel • Pittsburgh, PA 15210-1948

Carew Ann M. • Director • Mary Morgan Elementary School • Byron, IL 61010

Carew Virginia M. • Student • Queens College Grad Sch of Lib & Inf Studies • Flushing, NY 11367 • RASD

Carey Audrey Lane • Trustee • Oregon State Library • Salem, OR 97310-0640 • ALTA

Carey Barbara J. • Coordinator of Library Services • Butte County Office Education • Oroville, CA 95965 • AASL ALSC

Carey Cathy A. • Adult Services Librarian • Rochester Hills Public Library • Rochester, MI 48307 • YALSA

Carey Francis J. • Assistant Librarian • Duke University William R. Perkins Library • Durham, NC 27706

Carey Jan M. • Librarian • Hibbing Community College Library • Hibbing, MN 55746

Carey Joan • Outreach Services • Oregon Health Science University Library • Portland, OR 97207 • ACRL LITA

Carey Kjestine • Reference Librarian • Montana State University • Bozeman, MT 59717-0332

Carey Lynne • Ames Public Library • Ames, IA 50010

Carey Marilyn • Librarian • Muncie Central High School Library • Muncie, IN 47305 • AASL

Carey Marsha C. • Law Librarian • United States Department of Justice Main Library • Washington, DC 20530

Carey Paula A. • Science Bibliographer • Boston University Mugar Memorial Library • Boston, MA 02215 • ACRL

Cargile Cathy A. • Student • University of Pittsburgh School of Library and Information Science • Pittsburgh, PA 15260

Cargile Michele L • Northport, AL 35476

Cargill Jennifer • Dean of Libraries • Louisiana State University Libraries Middleton Library • Baton Rouge, LA 70803-3342 • ACRL LAMA

Cargille Douglas A. • Head, Collection Development • San Diego State University Library • San Diego, CA 92119-2120 • ACRL ALCTS

Cargille Karen E. • Head, Acquisitions Dept. • University of California-San Diego Library 0175A • La Jolla, CA 92093-0175 • ACRL ALCTS

Cargo Margaret C. • Librarian • Troy High School • Fullerton, CA 92631

Carhart Cindy • Young Adult Librarian • Hayward Public Library • Hayward, CA 94541

Carhart Forrest F. Jr • Denver, CO 80222 • ACRL LAMA *Life*

Carhart Jo-Ann • Librarian • East Islip Public Library • East Islip, NY 11730-2896 • YALSA

Cariappa Victoria B. • Gale Research Inc. • Detroit, MI 48226-4094

Carignan Yvonne A. • Lloyd House Alexandria Library • Alexandria, VA 22314

Carinci Judith E. • Special Projects Librarian • Widener University School of Law Library • Wilmington, DE 19803-0475 • ALCTS

Carini Helen H. • Senior Librarian • Ocean County Library System • Toms River, NJ 08753 • ALCTS

Carl Annmarie C. • N. Catasauqua, PA 18032

Carl George W. Jr. • Camden, NC 27921

Carl Herbert A. • Exeter, NH 03833 • ACRL PLA *Life*

Carl Pauline L. • School Librarian • Branchburg Township School District • Somerville, NJ 08876 • AASL ALSC

Carlanita M. Sr. • Director of Library Services • Alvernia College • Reading, PA 19607 • ACRL

Carlblom Sheila O. • Northwestern College Library • Saint Paul, MN 55113 • ACRL

Carlborg Edith M. Miss • Providence, RI 02906 • ACRL ALCTS *Continuing*

Carlborg Kenneth J. • Research Associate • University of Illinois • Urbana, IL 61801

Carle Daria O. • Science Librarian • University of Colorado-Boulder University Libraries • Boulder, CO 80309 • ACRL NMRT

Carle Patricia M. • Pittsburgh, PA 15224

Carlen Claudia Sr • Ann Arbor, MI 48105 • Continuing

Carlesimo Cheryl • Development • Robbit Ears Production • Rowyton, CT 06853 • ALSC YALSA

Carlet Patricia N. • Edgartown School • Edgartown, MA 02539 • AASL

Carleton Patricia A. • Saint Louis Public Library Divoll Branch • St. Louis, MO 63107 • PLA YALSA

Carley Lawana J. • Scottsbluff, NE 69361 • AASL YALSA *Life*

Carlin Don • Austin Peay State University • Clarkville, TN 37044 • ACRL LITA

Carlin Kimberly A. • Cohoes, NY 12047

Carlin Mary M. • Webster, NY 14580

Carlisle Carol • Simsbury, CT 06070 • AASL

Carlisle Hilda B. • Auburn, AL 36830 • AASL

Carlisle Sarah A. • Adelia M. Russell Library • Alexander City, AL 35010

Carlisle Scott G. • Rare Book Cataloger • Princeton University Library • Princeton, NJ 08544 • ACRL

Carlo Donald E. • Reference Librarian • Bloomfield Public Library • Bloomfield, NJ 07003

Carlotta Mary Sr. • Santa Catalina School Library • Monterey, CA 93940 • AASL

Carlsen Cliff • Trustee • Multnomah County Library • Portland, OR 97212 • ALTA

Carlsen Linda • Gallup Public Library • Gallup, NM 87301

Carlson-Young Karen L. • Assistant Head • Harvard College Library Widener Memorial Library • Cambridge, MA 02138 • ALCTS LAMA

Carlson Albert P. • Director of LRC • Patrick Henry Community College • Martinsville, VA 24115-5311 • ACRL GODORT IFRT LIRT SRRT

Carlson Barbara J. • H. W. Wilson Company • Bronx, NY 10452 • RASD

Carlson Claudette J. • Branch Head • Chicago Public Library West Belmont Branch • Chicago, IL 60634 • PLA

Carlson Constance P. • Trustee • Bettendorf Public Library • Bettendorf, IA 52722 • ALTA

Carlson David C. • Student • University of California-Berkeley School of Library & Information Studies • Berkeley, CA 94720 • LITA

Carlson David H. • Executive Director • Triangle Research Libraries Network • Chapel Hill, NC 27599-3940 • ACRL LITA

Carlson Diane B. • Director • Willow School Primary Library • Homewood, IL 60430

Carlson Diane K. • Media Specialist • Duluth Public Schools Teacher's Resource Center • Duluth, MN 55802

Carlson Dudley B. • Manager, Youth Services • Princeton Public Library • Princeton, NJ 08542 • ALSC LAMA PLA

Carlson Elizabeth • Spokane, WA 99207 • ALSC *Continuing*

Carlson Esther K. • Redford, MI 48239 • Continuing

Carlson G. Kay • Assistant Librarian • Umatilla County Library Special Library District • Pendleton, OR 97801-0530

Carlson George • Documents Librarian • Santa Clara University Michel Orradre Library • Santa Clara, CA 95053 • ACRL GODORT IFRT

Carlson Jane M. • Irving Elementary School • Indianola, IA 50125 • AASL

Carlson Judith • Admin Assistant • Alameda County Library System • Fremont, CA 94538 • LITA

Carlson Judith E. • Technical Services Librarian • Adams State College Library • Alamosa, CO 81102 • ACRL LITA

Carlson Judy • Librarian • Nisqually Middle School • Olympia, WA 98503 • AASL

Carlson Julia F. • Derwood, MD 20855 • FLRT

Carlson Kathleen A. • Elementary School Librarian • Sunny Hills Elementary School • Issaquah, WA 98027 • AASL

Carlson Kathleen N • Library Assistant II • Maricopa County Library District • Phoenix, AZ 85032

Carlson Linda G. • Reader Services Librarian • Johns Hopkins University School of Advanced International Studies • Washington, DC 20036 • RASD

Carlson Margaret W. • Children's Librarian • Saint John the Baptist Parish Library • LaPlace, LA 70068

Carlson Mary G. • Marysville, KS 66508

Carlson Mary Kay • Senior Librarian • Pikes Peak Library District • Colorado Springs, CO 80901-1579

Carlson Maude C. Mrs • Long Beach, CA 90807 • Continuing

Carlson Melinda Suzanne • Librarian • USA Today • Arlington, VA 22209

Carlson Melvin A. Jr • Sr Catlgr/Asst Hd Catlg Dep • University of Massachusetts Library • Amherst, MA 01003 • ACRL ALCTS

Carlson Nancy • Librarian • Picacho Middle School • Las Cruces, NM 88001 • AASL

Carlson Ralph • President • Carlson Publishing Inc. • Brooklyn, NY 11202-0067 • ACRL RASD

Carlson Robert P. • Program Officer LITA • American Library Association • Chicago, IL 60611-2795 • LITA

Carlson Sandra Louise • Head, Central Branch Services • Kitsap Regional Library • Bremerton, WA 98310 • ALSC PLA

Carlson Shawn M. • Student • University of Wisconsin-Milwaukee Golda Meir Library • Milwaukee, WI 53201

Carlson Sue • Lake Lanier Regional Library Lawrenceville Branch • Lawrenceville, GA 30245-4707

Carlson Susan R. • White City Schools • White City, KS 66872 • AASL

Carlson Susan Stillwater • Georgetown Township Public Library • Jenison, MI 49428 • PLA

Carlson Terri L. • Librarian I • San Diego County Library Vista Branch • Vista, CA 92083-6686

Carlson Virginia A. • Children's Librarian • Pikes Peak Library District • Colorado Springs, CO 80901 • ALSC

Carlson Virginia R. • Automation Librarian • Johnson County Library • Shawnee Mission, KS 66201

Carlson William Hugh Mr • Corvallis, OR 97330 • Continuing

Carlton Colleen A. • Operations Manager • University of California-Los Angeles (UCLA) • Los Angeles, CA 90024-1450 • LAMA

Carlton Janet R. • Librarian • Virginia Polytechnic Institute and State University • Falls Church, VA 22042-1287 • ACRL

Carlton Timothy J. • Descriptive Cataloger • Library of Congress • Washington, DC 20541

Carlucci April • Assistant Chief,Map Division • New York Public Library • New York, NY 10018-2788 • MAGERT

Carlucci Marie T. • Library/Media Specialist • Aire Libre Elementary School • Phoenix, AZ 85022 • AASL ALSC IFRT

Carmack Bob D. • Director • University of Wisconsin-Superior Jim Dan Hill Library • Superior, WI 54880 • ACRL LAMA

Carmack Mona D. • Director • Johnson County Library • Shawnee Mission, KS 66201 • LAMA PLA

Carmack Norma J. • Documents Librarian • Trinity University • San Antonio, TX 78212 • RASD GODORT LIRT

Carman Carol A. • Cataloger • Maryland Department of Legislative Reference Library • Annapolis, MD 21401-1991 • GODORT

Carman Florence E. • Milford, CT 06460

Carman Frances E. • Cleveland, OH 44106 • Continuing

Carman Margaret L. • Cobb County Public Library Stratton Branch • Marietta, GA 30064 • PLA IFRT

Carmean Joseph C. • Iowa City, IA 52240-3038

Carmichael Gary • Saco, MT 59261

Carmichael James V. Jr • Greensboro, NC 27408 • ACRL RASD IFRT LHRT

Carmichael Michael • Trustee • Bloomfield Township Public Library • Bloomfield Hills, MI 48302-2437 • ALTA

Carmichael Wendy J. • Acting Head, Catlg. Section • British Columbia Legislative Library • Victoria BC, V8V 1X4 Canada • ALCTS LITA

Carmichael Yvonne D. • Carmel, NY 10512 • ACRL

Carmody Barbara A. • Tahoma Junior High School • Maple Valley, WA 98038 • AASL YALSA IFRT

Carmody Claire • Niles, IL 60714-4432

Carmody Jean C. • Elementary Librarian • Oak Creek Schools • Oak Creek, WI 53154 • Continuing

Carnahan Anne D. • Head of Children's Services • Darien Library • Darien, CT 06820-4497 • ALSC

Carnahan Christie K. • .... • Logansport Cass County Public Library Logansport Public Library • Logansport, IN 46947

Carnahan Mabel A. • Branch Manager • Jacksonville Public Library Regency Square Branch • Jacksonville, FL 32225 • CLENE

Carnahan Paul A. • Librarian • Vermont Historical Society • Montpelier, VT 05609-0901 • ACRL

Carnal Judith L. • Director of Media Services • Metropolitan School District Perry Township • Indianapolis, IN 46227 • AASL ALSC

Carnall Kathleen • Director • Porter Public Library • Westlake, OH 44145 • LAMA PLA

Carnell Brett • Cataloger • Library of Congress • Washington, DC 20541

Carnelli Sandra R. • Head, Adult Services • Waukegan Public Library • Waukegan, IL 60085 • RASD

Carnes Judith • Reference Librarian • Yale University Social Science Library • New Haven, CT 06520

Carnes Vanda M. • Technical Services Dept. • Citrus County Library System • Crystal River, FL 32629 • LITA

Carney John M. • Student • University of California Los Angeles Graduate School of Library & Information Science • Los Angeles, CA 90024 • LITA

Carney Karen M. • Assoc. Libn./Technical Services • Ulster Cnty Cmnty Coll • Stone Ridge, NY 12484 • ACRL ALCTS

Carney Kathleen M. • Head of Cataloging • Boston College Libraries • Chestnut Hill, MA 02167 • ALCTS LAMA LITA

Carney Patricia • Harpeth Hall School Library • Nashville, TN 37215 • YALSA

Carney Patrick J. • Librarian • United States Marine Corps Base Library • Camp Pendltn, CA 92055 • ALCTS LAMA LITA PLA RASD AFLRT FLRT GODORT

Carney Sheila M. • Columbia University Libraries • New York, NY 10027

Carnovsky Ruth F. • Oakland, CA 94606 • ACRL ALCTS *Life*

Caro Carol B. • Automation Librarian • Boston College • Chestnut Hill, MA 02167 • LITA SRRT

Carol Barbara B. • Head, Technical Services • Pueblo Library District McClelland Library • Pueblo, CO 81004-1997

Carolla Marianne • New Haven Free Public Library • New Haven, CT 06510 • PLA RASD

Carollo Michael T. • Consultant • Southwest Iowa Regional Library System • Council Bluffs, IA 51503 • LAMA PLA CLENE

Carollo Monica G. • Milwaukee, WI 53217 • AASL ALSC

Caron Mary L. • Illinois Benedictine College Lownik Library • Lisle, IL 60532 • ACRL LAMA RASD

Carosella Claudia C. • Newtown Square, PA 19073 • AASL

Carothers Diane F. • Communications Librarian • University of Illinois • Urbana, IL 61801 • RASD

Carotta Mary • Holland, MI 49424

Carparelli Felicia A. • Chicago, IL 60613

Carpender Jane F. • Young Adult Librarian • Park Ridge Public Library • Park Ridge, IL 60068-4188 • YALSA

Carpentar Robert E. • Hampton, VA 23663

Carpenter Angelica • Director • Palm Springs Public Library • Palm Springs, FL 33461 • PLA

Carpenter Beth A. • Student • University of Iowa School of Library & Information Science • Iowa City, IA 52242

Carpenter Betty • Librarian • Arbutus Elementary School Library • Baltimore, MD 21228 • AASL ALSC

Carpenter Brian B. • Texas A & M University Sterling C. Evans Library • College Station, TX 77843-5000 • ACRL GODORT

Carpenter Carole H. • Milford, DE 19963 • AASL

Carpenter David E. • Collections Development • Vanderbilt University Central Library • Nashville, TN 37240-0007 • ACRL

Carpenter Donna J. • Springfield, MA 01104

Carpenter Elizabeth • Student • University of South Carolina College of Library & Information Science • Columbia, SC 29208 • SRRT

Carpenter Eric J. • Collection Development Ln • Oberlin College Library • Oberlin, OH 44074 • ACRL ALCTS

Carpenter Gai • Director • Hampshire College Harold F. Johnson Library Center • Amherst, MA 01002 • ACRL LITA

Carpenter Janella • Newport, TN 37821

Carpenter Jennifer • Public Library of Cincinnati & Hamilton County Green Township Branch • Cincinnati, OH 45248

Carpenter Jennifer K. • Information Services Manager • Rowan Public Library • Salisbury, NC 28144 • PLA

Carpenter Jo A. • Librarian • Thibodaux Elementary School Library • Thibodaux, LA 70301

Carpenter Judith A. • Syracuse, NY 13215 • AASL LHRT

Carpenter Kathryn Hammell • Bibliographer for the Health Sci • University of Illinois at Chicago University Library • Chicago, IL 60680 • ACRL ALCTS LAMA

Carpenter Kenneth E. • Assistant Director for Research • Harvard University • Cambridge, MA 02138 • ACRL ALCTS

Carpenter Lee • Wellesley, MA 02181

Carpenter Lydia S. • Library Div. Manager Br. Serv. • Stockton-San Joaquin County Public Library • Stockton, CA 95202 • LAMA PLA IFRT

Carpenter Michael • Louisiana State University School of Library & Information Science • Baton Rouge, LA 70803-3290 • ALCTS LAMA LITA IRRT LHRT LRRT MAGERT

Carpenter Myra • Norwalk, OH 44857 • AASL *Continuing*

Carpenter Ray • Professor • University of North Carolina at Chapel Hill School of Information and Library Science • Chapel Hill, NC 27599-3360 • ACRL IRRT

Carpenter Sandra J. • Hamilton School District • Hamilton, KS 66853 • AASL

Carpenter Stacey T. • Student • Catholic University of America School of Library and Information Science • Washington, DC 20064 • LITA NMRT SRRT

Carpenter Stewart T. • Student • University of Southern Mississippi School of Library Science • Hattiesburg, MS 39406-5146

Carpenter Susan L. • Staff Librarian • Carnegie Public Library • Pittsburgh, PA 15219

Carpenter Zoe I. • Assoc Ln-Catlgr • John Hopkins University Applied Physics Laboratory • Laurel, MD 20707-6099 • ALCTS

Carpentier Louise J. • Elementary School Librarian • Cedar Menor Elementary School • St. Louis Park, MN 55426 • AASL ALSC

Carper Anna M. • Elizabethtwn, PA 17022 • Continuing

Carper Jeanette V. • Student • University of Texas at Austin Graduate School of Library & Information Sciences • Austin, TX 78712-1276

Carper John M. • Assistant Librarian • Harvard College Library • Cambridge, MA 02138 • ACRL

Carper Myrta Thomas • Asheboro, NC 27203 • Continuing

Carpineta Anthony • Hyattsville, MD 20782

Carr Barbara J. • Student • Clarion University of Pennsylvania College of Library Science • Clarion, PA 16214 • SRRT

Carr Betty H. • Coordinator Reference Inf. • Manchester City Library • Manchester, NH 03104-6199

Carr Bobbie • Associate Director • Naval Postgraduate School Dudley Knox Library • Monterey, CA 93943-5002

Carr Carol L. • Catalog Librarian • Whitman College Penrose Memorial Library • Walla Walla, WA 99362-9982 • ACRL

Carr Caryn J. • Head, Reader Services • Lock Haven University George B Stevenson Library • Lock Haven, PA 17745-2390 • ACRL LAMA RASD LIRT

Carr Charles E. • Readers Advisor • Burlington County Library • Mount Holly, NJ 08060-1394 • PLA

Carr David W. • Associate Professor • Rutgers University School of Communication Information & Library Studies • New Brunswick, NJ 08903 • ACRL PLA RASD IFRT LRRT SRRT

Carr Deborah E. • Assistant Staff Manager • Bell South Corporation • Atlanta, GA 30367 • ACRL ALCTS ASCLA LITA NMRT

Carr Diana • Library Media Specialist • Maxwell AFB Elementary School • Maxwell AFB, AL 36112 • AASL

Carr Diane R. • Student • University of Tennessee-Knoxville Graduate School of Library & Information Science • Knoxville, TN 37996-4330

Carr Donna L. • Student • University of Arizona Graduate Library School • Tucson, AZ 85721 • PLA EMIERT SRRT

Carr Dorothy • Director • South Salem Library • South Salem, NY 10590 • PLA

Carr Emily • Librarian for Govt. Docs. • George Mason University Law Library • Arlington, VA 22201 • ACRL GODORT

Carr Gabrielle • Senior Reference Librarian • Indiana University Southeast Library Southeastern Campus Library • New Albany, IN 47150-6405 • ACRL

Carr Jean • Head Librarian • North Central High School Lib • Indianapolis, IN 46240 • AASL

Carr Jo Ann • Director • IMC • Madison, WI 53706 • ACRL

Carr Josephine S. • Sarasota, FL 34231

Carr Judith G. • Librarian • Baltimore County Public Library • Towson, MD 21204 • PLA

Carr Kathi • Media Specialist • North Charleston High School • North Charleston, SC 29406 • AASL

Carr Kathy M. • Reference Librarian • University of Washington Suzzallo Library • Seattle, WA 98195 • ACRL

Carr Linda K. • Collection Adminstrator • Boston University Mugar Memorial Library • Boston, MA 02215 • ACRL ALCTS RASD

Carr Mary Faye • Media Specialist • North Hardin High School Library • Radcliff, KY 40160 • AASL YALSA

Carr Mary M. • Director of Library Services • North Idaho College Library • Coeur d'Alene, ID 83814 • ACRL

Carr Melissa • Head of Regional Services • Daniel Boone Regional Library • Columbia, MO 65205-1267 • LAMA PLA

Carr Patricia M. • Coor. Audiovisual Services • Portland Public Schools • Portland, OR 97208-3107 • AASL LITA

Carr Richard D. • Asst. Dir. for Access Services • Medical College of Wiconsin Libraries • Milwaukee, WI 53226 • ACRL

Carr Robert P. • Branch Librarian • Mohave County Library System Bullhead City Public Library • Riviera, AZ 86442 • PLA

Carr Ruth A. • Division Chief • New York Public Library • New York, NY 10018-2788 • RASD IFRT

Carr Ruth R. • Science Fiction & Mystery Bookshop • Atlanta, GA 30306 • ACRL

Carr SallyAnn • Information Resource Manager • American Chiropractic Association • Arlington, VA 22209 • IRRT

Carr Sharon L. • Oak Park, IL 60302 • AASL

Carr Sharon T. • Consultant • El Paso Independent School District • El Paso, TX 79904 • AASL

Carr Timothy B. • Arlington, VA 22206 • ACRL

Carraher Gail D. • Reference Librarian • Northeast Texas Community College Learning Resource Center • Mount Pleasant, TX 75455

Carrasquillo Denise • East Chicago, IN 46312 • PLA

Carrea Alexandra • North Vancouver, BC, V7N 2J7 Canada • NMRT SRRT

Carreau Janice E. • Librarian • Westerly High School Library • Westerly, RI 02891 • AASL YALSA

Carreno Angela M. • Social Science Bibliographer • New York University Elmer Holmes Bobst Library • New York, NY 10012 • ACRL ALCTS GODORT

Carreon Sylvia A. • San Antonio, TX 78237

Carretti Mary • St Louis, MO 63117 • Continuing

Carriar Nancy L. • Head-Public Services • University of Minnesota-Duluth Library • Duluth, MN 55812-2495 • ACRL LAMA RASD LIRT

Carrick Bruce R. • Vice President • H. W. Wilson Company • Bronx, NY 10452 • AASL ACRL ALSC

Carrick Jennifer D. • Des Peres, MO 63131 • ACRL

Carrick Kathryn F. • Vermilion, OH 44089-1923

Carrico Diane F. • Lexington, KY 40504 • ACRL

Carrico Mona S. • Denton, TX 76201

Carrier Esther J. • Reference Librarian • Lock Haven University George B Stevenson Library • Lock Haven, PA 17745-2390 • ACRL

Carrier Joan W. • Cpe Elizabeth, ME 04107 • GODORT

Carrier Katheryn A. • Reference Librarian • Traverse Area District Library • Traverse City, MI 49684 • RASD

Carrier R. Timothy • Branch Manager • Clermont County Public Library Williamsburg Branch • Williamsburg, OH 45176

Carrigan Barbara A. • Baltimore County Public Library • Towson, MD 21204 • PLA

Carrigan Dennis P. • Assistant Dean • University of Kentucky College of Library & Information Science • Lexington, KY 40506-0391 • ALCTS LAMA PLA

Carrigan Esther E. • Technical Services Librarian • Texas A & M University Medical Sciences Library • College Station, TX 77843 • ALCTS LITA

Carrigan John L. • Information Specialist • City of Hope Medical Center Department of Library Service • Duarte, CA 91010 • ACRL

Carrigan Marietta • Library Media Specialist • Richland High School • Richland, WA 99352 • AASL

Carrillo Sherry J. • Assistant Director • Florida International University • Miami, FL 33199 • ACRL IFRT

Carrington Bessie M. • Reference Librarian • Duke University William R. Perkins Library • Durham, NC 27706 • LITA RASD

Carrington Virginia Friesner • Waterbury, CT 06704 • ACRL CLENE ILERT

Carrison Dale K. • MSUS/PALS Director • Mankato State University Memorial Library • Mankato, MN 56002-8400 • ACRL ALCTS LAMA LITA *Life*

Carriveau Kenneth L. Jr. • Student • University of North Carolina • Chapel Hill, NC 27599-3930 • LAMA LITA

Carroll Annie L. • Children's Librarian • Chicago Public Library Carter G. Woodson Regional Library • Chicago, IL 60628 • ALSC

Carroll Barbara A. • Instructional Resource Ctr. Ln. • Florida International University North Miami Campus • North Miami, FL 33181 • ACRL RASD

Carroll Barbara Tuttle • Eau Claire, WI 54701

Carroll Bonnie C. • President • Information International • Oak Ridge, TN 37831 • GODORT

Carroll Brenda L. • Director • Holdrege Public Library • Holdrege, NE 68949 • LAMA PLA

Carroll Celia G. • Automation Coordinator • Santa Monica Public Library • Santa Monica, CA 90401 • LITA PLA

Carroll Charles • Account Manager • Data Research Associates, Inc. • Salt Lake City, UT 84123 • LITA

Carroll E. Colteen • Camden, AR 71701

Carroll Eireann M. • Product Manager • Dialog Information Service Inc. • Palo Alto, CA 94304 • ACRL

Carroll Elaine • Trustee • Paramus Public Library • Paramus, NJ 07652 • ALTA PLA

Carroll Elizabeth A. • Agency Manager • Memphis-Shelby County Public Library and Information Center • Memphis, TN 38104-4025

Carroll Elizabeth A. • Reference Librarian • The American University Library • Washington, DC 20016-8046 • IFRT LIRT

Carroll Hardy • Western Michigan University Libraries Dwight B. Waldo Library • Kalamazoo, MI 49008 • LRRT

Carroll Holly Clark • Executive Director • NOLA Regional Library System • Warren, OH 44483 • ASCLA LAMA PLA YALSA

Carroll John • Trustee • Elmhurst Public Library • Elmhurst, IL 60126 • ALTA PLA

Carroll John P. • Trustee • Schiller Park Public Library • Schiller Park, IL 60176-1699 • ALTA

Carroll Kelley • Melrose, MA 02176

Carroll Lois Elaine • Mission College LRS • Santa Clara, CA 95054

Carroll Marian • Normal, IL 61761 • GODORT

Carroll Nancy A. • Public Services Librarian • Clarke College Schrup Library • Dubuque, IA 52001 • ACRL LITA

Carroll Nancy L. • Student • University of Washington Graduate School of Library and Information Science • Seattle, WA 98195 • ACRL ALCTS RASD IFRT LHRT SRRT

Carroll Roger Lee • Manager • Dallas Public Library • Dallas, TX 75201

Carroll Ruth P. • Director of Libraries • Saint Francis Hospital & Medical Center • Hartford, CT 06105 • ASCLA LAMA LITA

Carroll Susan W. • Librarian • J. W. Coon Elementary School Media Center • Fayetteville, NC 28304 • AASL

Carroon Barbara P. • Trustee • Jackson-Hinds Library System • Jackson, MS 39201 • ALTA

Carrpan Jean M. • Bellcore • Piscataway, NJ 08854 • ACRL LITA

Carruthers Dorothy • Student • McGill University Graduate School of Library & Information Studies • Montreal PQ, H3A 1Y1 Canada • PLA

Carruthers Joan • Reference Department • York University Libraries • North York ON, M3J 1P3 Canada • ACRL

Carruthers Ralph H. • Somers, NY 10589-1114 • LITA PLA *Continuing*

Carson Anne R. • Reference Librarian • Cornell University • Ithaca, NY 14853-5301

Carson C Herbert • University of Rhode Island Graduate School of Library & Information Studies • Kingston, RI 02881-0815 • AASL

Carson Doris M. • Salina, KS 67401 • Continuing

Carson Howard C. • Vice President • EBSCO Subscription Services • Springfield, VA 22151-4148 • ALCTS FLRT

Carson Janet • Area Supervisor,Documents Div. • Carleton University Library • Ottawa ON, K1S 5J7 Canada • ACRL LITA LIRT

Carson Johnny Mr. • Host • The Tonight Show • Burbank, CA 91523 • AASL ACRL ALCTS ALSC ALTA ASCLA LAMA LITA PLA RASD YALSA *Honorary*

Carson Josephine R. Mrs • Brown University Science Library Bio-Medical • Providence, RI 02912 • Continuing

Carson Justine H. • Editorial Director • Institute for Scientific Information • Philadelphia, PA 19104 • ACRL

Carson Lois • Media Specialist • Atlanta Public Schools • Atlanta, GA 30324

Carson Lynn • Madison, WI 53703-2361

Carson Mary K. • Curriculum Supervisor • Springfield Public Schools Curriculum Resource Center • Springfield, MO 65802 • AASL

Carson Sheila • Branch Manager • Free Library of Philadelphia Haddington Branch • Philadelphia, PA 19151 • ALSC

Carson Sylvia M. • Library Systems Specialist • Pennsylvania State University Pattee Library • University Park, PA 16802 • LITA

Carson Thomasine • Administrator • North Las Vegas Public Library • North Las Vegas, NV 89030 • ALSC PLA

Carstater Mary Esther Sr • Librarian and AV Specialist • Our Lady of Mercy High School • Rochester, NY 14610 • AASL

Carstens Cathleen S. • Children's Librarian • Wood Library • Canandaigua, NY 14424-1295

Carstens Jane Ellen • Professor of Library Science • University of Southwestern Louisiana Department of School Librarianship • Lafayette, LA 70504 • AASL ALSC YALSA

Carstens Timothy V. • Head of Cataloging • Western Carolina University Hunter Library • Cullowhee, NC 28723-9002 • ACRL ALCTS

Cart Michael • Los Angeles, CA 90046 • ALSC PLA YALSA

Cartee Lewis D. Jr. • Tulane University Howard-Tilton Memorial Library • New Orleans, LA 70118 • ACRL LITA

Cartelli Alessandra J. • Library Supervisor • Arthur Andersen & Company • Philadelphia, PA 19103

Carter Alfred • Trustee • Western Plains Library System • Clinton, OK 73601

Carter Ann M. • Director • Saint Vincent de Paul High School • Petersburg, VA 23805 • AASL

Carter Anne L. • Trustee • Oregon State Library • Salem, OR 97310-0640 • ALTA

Carter Annie Jo • Nashville, TN 37204 • Continuing

Carter Barbara N. • Media Director/Librarian • Harrison-Washington Community Schools • Gaston, IN 47342 • AASL

Carter Barbara W • Knox County Public Library System • Knoxville, TN 37902

Carter Betty • Media Specialist • D. Russel Lee Career Center • Hamilton, OH 45011 • AASL

Carter Betty • Texas Woman's University School of Library & Information Studies • Denton, TX 76204 • AASL YALSA

Carter Catherine • Principal Catlg.,Catlg. Dept. • Pennsylvania State University E506 Pattee Library • University Park, PA 16802 • ACRL ALCTS LITA   Life

Carter Christina E. • California State University,Fresno Henry Madden Library • Fresno, CA 93740-0034 • ACRL RASD EMIERT LIRT

Carter Coatest A. • Montgomery, AL 36110 • Continuing

Carter Constance • Head of Science & Reference • Library of Congress • Washington, DC 20541 • ACRL RASD

Carter Darline L. • Director • West Islip Public Library • West Islip, NY 11795-3999 • LAMA PLA

Carter Erik W. • Tigard Public Library • Tigard, OR 97223 • IFRT

Carter Gail W. • Covington, GA 30209 • AASL ALSC

Carter Harriet I. • Westerville, OH 43081 • PLA   Life

Carter Helen L. • Baltimore County Public Library Rosedale Area Branch • Baltimore, MD 21237 • PLA

Carter Jack • Los Alamos National Lab Lib • Los Alamos, NM 87545-0020

Carter Janet D. • Reference Librarian • University of California-Los Angeles Biomedical Library • Los Angeles, CA 90024-1798 • ACRL ALCTS RASD

Carter Janet K. • Community Services/PR Libn • Bradley Memorial Library • Columbus, GA 31907

Carter Janet L. • Student • University of California-Berkeley School of Library & Information Studies • Berkeley, CA 94720 • ACRL LITA RASD IFRT

Carter Jeanette • Information Services Coordinator • Iowa City Public Library • Iowa City, IA 52240 • RASD

Carter Jeanne M. • Trustee • Metropolitan Library System • Oklahoma City, OK 73102 • ALTA PLA

Carter Judith • Library Liaison Officer • AMIGOS Bibliographic Council,Inc. • Dallas, TX 75251-2104 • ACRL

Carter Judith C. • Penn Manor School Dist • Millersville, PA 17551

Carter Kathleen E. • Cataloging • University of Alberta Cameron Library • Edmonton AB, T6G 2J8 Canada • ALCTS

Carter Kathryn A. • Student • University of Michigan School of Information and Library Studies • Ann Arbor, MI 48109-1092

Carter Laura Lee • International Documents Libn. • University of Colorado • Boulder, CO 80309 • GODORT

Carter Leslie • Librarian • Clark High School • Plano, TX 75023 • AASL YALSA

Carter Mary • Los Angeles, CA 90045 • ALCTS LITA

Carter Mary E. • Student • Clarion University of Pennsylvania College of Library Science • Clarion, PA 16214

Carter Michael • Teacher • Orchard Hills Elementary School • Novi, MI 48375 • AASL LITA IFRT

Carter Nancy F. • Music Librarian • University of Colorado-Boulder University Libraries • Boulder, CO 80309 • ACRL ALCTS

Carter Naomi • Assistant Librarian • Bainbridge College • Bainbridge, GA 31717 • ACRL

Carter Patricia B. • Media Specialist • Constable Middle School • Kendall Park, NJ 08824 • AASL

Carter Peggy C. • Reference Librarian • Las Positas College • Livermore, CA 94550

Carter Rosalie M. • Chairman of the Board • Electronic Bookshelf, Inc. • Frankfort, IN 46041 • AASL

Carter Rosalyn C. • Librarian • Riverdale Elementary School Media Center • Riverdale, MD 20737

Carter Ruth C. • Assistant Dir for Tech Serivces • University of Pittsburgh Hillman Library • Pittsburgh, PA 15260 • ACRL ALCTS LAMA LITA

Carter Sharon Kay • Information Specialist • Saint Paul Fire and Marine Insurance Company • St. Paul, MN 55102 • LITA RASD   Life

Carter Stephanie E. • Student • La Sierra University Library • Riverside, CA 92515

Carter Thomas L. • Loyola Marymount University Charles Von Der Ahe Library • Los Angeles, CA 90045 • ACRL RASD

Carter Ulysses B. • Board Member • Jacksonville Public Libraries Main Library • Jacksonville, FL 32202

Carter Vivian H. • Director of Children's Services • Normal Public Library • Normal, IL 61761 • ALSC

Carter William L. • Librarian I • Omaha Public Library • Omaha, NE 68102 • PLA

Carter Yvonne B. • Administrative Librarian • United States Department of Education Office of Educational Res & Improvement • Washington, DC 20208-5571 • AASL ACRL

Carterette Patricia • Librarian I • Cleveland Heights-University Heights Public Library Noble Neighborhood Branch • Cleveland Heights, OH 44121-2208 • PLA

Carterette Robert • Automated Systems Manager • Cleveland Public Library • Cleveland, OH 44114-1271 • LITA

Cartland Mary P. • Student • Rosary College Graduate School of Library & Information Science • River Forest, IL 60305

Cartledge Connie L. • Archivist • Library of Congress • Washington, DC 20541

Cartmell G E. Mrs • Flushing, NY 11355 • Continuing

Cartmell Mary Janet • School Librarian • Tates Creek Middle School • Lexington, KY 40517 • AASL

Cartner Margaret F. • Reference Librarian • Center for Creative Leadership Library • Greensboro, NC 27438-6300 • RASD SRRT

Carton Deborah Y. • Young Adult/Reference Librarian • Berkeley Public Library North Branch • Berkeley, CA 94707 • YALSA

Carton Roderick J. • Cataloger • H.W. Wilson Company • Bronx, NY 10452 • ACRL

Carton Stephen E. • Vice President • Online Computer Systems Inc. • Germantown, MD 20874 • ALCTS ASCLA

Cartularo Teresa C. • Reference Librarian • Widener University Wolfgram Library • Chester, PA 19013 • ACRL

Cartwright Dolores A. • Saint Joseph's College Callahan Library • Patchogue, NY 11772

Cartwright James F. • University of Hawaii Library • Honolulu, HI 96822 • ACRL

Carty Kevin J. • Jamestown, RI 02835-1325 • ACRL

Carus Marianne • Publisher & Editor-in-Chief • Cricket and Ladybug Magazines • Peru, IL 61354 • ALSC

Caruso Carl J. • Executive Director • Broadview Public Library District • Broadview, IL 60153 • LAMA PLA

Caruso Helen B. • Student • Louisiana State University School of Library & Information Science • Baton Rouge, LA 70803-3290 • RASD

Caruso Jo Anne • Macomb, IL 61455-9508

Caruso Joan F. • Chief of Extension Services • Queens Borough Public Library • Jamaica, NY 11432

Caruso Joy-Louise • Manager of Information Services • CPC International Inc. Moffett Technical Library • Argo, IL 60501

Caruso Nicholas • California, PA 15419

Caruso Paula M. • Student • Louisiana State University School of Library & Information Science • Baton Rouge, LA 70803-3290 • RASD IFRT NMRT

Caruso Rose M. • Rockville, MD 20850 • ACRL LAMA RASD LRRT

Caruthers Lynn • Signal Mt., TN 37377 • AASL

Caruthers Terry Lee • Branch Manager • Knox County Public Library System Burlington Branch Library • Knoxville, TN 37914 • ALSC PLA

Carvajal Elena C. • Librarian • Electronic Data Systems (EDS) • Plano, TX 75024

Carvajal Jane J. • Microcomputer Instructor/Tech • Metropolitan Library System • Oklahoma City, OK 73102 • LITA PLA CLENE

Carvalho Marci • Student • Emporia State University School of Library & Information Management • Emporia, KS 66801

Carvell Linda • Head Librarian • Lancaster Country Day School • Lancaster, PA 17603 • AASL

Carver-Russell Nancy L. • Head Librarian • Maryvale High School • Phoenix, AZ 85033 • ALSC YALSA

Carver Anne W. • Supervisor of Media Services • Beaufort County School District • Beaufort, SC 29901-0309 • AASL

Carver Beverly J. • Ref. & User Education Librarian • Southern Methodist University Fondren Library • Dallas, TX 75275-0135 • ACRL

Carver David C. • Librarian II, Cataloger • Akron-Summit County Public Library • Akron, OH 44326-0001 • ALCTS GODORT

Carver Deborah A. • Asst. Director for Public Servs. • University of Oregon Library • Eugene, OR 97403-1299 • ACRL LAMA RASD

Carver Gloria C. • Director • East Longmeadow Public Library • East Longmeadow, MA 01028 • PLA

Carver Molly • Librarian • Sandusky Library • Sandusky, OH 44870 • IFRT

Carver Pam K. • Lubbock, TX 79413-5707

Carver Scherel H. • Assistant City Librarian • Tyler Public Library • Tyler, TX 75702 • LAMA

Cary Elizabeth E. • Student • Clarion University of Pennsylvania College of Library Science • Clarion, PA 16214

Cary Karen F. • Reference Librarian • Virginia Commonwealth University • Richmond, VA 23284-2033 • ACRL ALCTS RASD

Cary Linda L. • Librarian • Elkhart Public Library • Elkhart, IN 46516-3184 • ALCTS

Cary Mary E. • La Crosse, WI 54601 • IFRT ILERT

Cary Mary K. • Director of Admissions & Student • University of Michigan School of Information and Library Studies • Ann Arbor, MI 48109-1092

Cary Maxine M. • Sunnyvale, CA 94087

Cary Meredith B. Mrs • Western Washington University Wilson Library • Bellingham, WA 98225 • ACRL RASD Life

Cary Paul A. • Reference Librarian • Cleveland Institute of Music • Cleveland, OH 44106 • RASD

Casabonne Richard J. • Casabonne Associates • New York, NY 10016 • AASL

Casale Michael A. Mr. • Director of Instructional Media • Beverly Public Schools • Beverly, MA 01915 • AASL ALSC YALSA

Casalini Mario • Director • Casalini Libri • Firenze, Italy • ACRL LITA

Casamajor Julia M. • Coordinator of Information • Livermore Public Library • Livermore, CA 94550 • PLA

Casas Mayra • Automated Services Librarian • Miami-Dade Public Library System • Miami, FL 33130-1504 • LITA

Casas de Faunce Maria • Granada 18010, Spain • ALCTS

Casazza Rosa T. • Librarian • Richmond Public Library • Richmond, CA 94804 • ALSC

Cascanet Valerie R. • Library Media Specialist • Watertown High School • Watertown, NY 13601 • AASL IFRT

Casciero Albert J. • Director • University of the District of Columbia Learning Resources Division • Washington, DC 20008

Cascio Suzanne L. • Reference Librarian • Manhattanville College Library • Purchase, NY 10577-0560 • ACRL LIRT LRRT

Case Ann M. • Associate Dir of Indexing Serv • H. W. Wilson Company • Bronx, NY 10452 • AASL ACRL ALCTS ALSC LAMA LITA PLA RASD YALSA

Case Barbara S. • Special Collections Librarian • California State University-Los Angeles John F. Kennedy Memorial Library • Los Angeles, CA 90032-8300 • ACRL RASD

Case Bonnie N. • Director • Highland Park Library • Dallas, TX 75205 • LAMA PLA YALSA

Case Edith A. • Cleveland, OH 44113-1812 • LAMA PLA
                                                        Continuing

Case Frances K. • Director • South Carolina State Library Department for Blind & Handicapped • Columbia, SC 29202 • ASCLA

Case Marjorie • Seattle, WA 98101 • Continuing

Case Mary M. • Hd. of Serials & Acq. Servs. • Northwestern University Library • Evanston, IL 60208-2300 • ALCTS LAMA

Case Patricia J. • Resolution Trust Corporation Public Reading Room • Washington, DC 20434 • FLRT IFRT SRRT

Case Robert N. • Director • Lancaster County Library • Lancaster, PA 17602 • ALCTS ALSC ALTA ASCLA LAMA LITA PLA RASD YALSA EMIERT GODORT IFRT SORT SRRT

Casebolt Jody M. • Media Specialist • Triton High School • Erwin, NC 28339 • AASL YALSA

Casellas Gilbert F. • Trustee • Free Library of Philadelphia • Philadelphia, PA 19103 • ALTA

Casement Susan • University of California-Davis Agricultural Economics Library • Davis, CA 95616 • Life
Casetta Prima • Getty Center Resources Collections • Santa Monica, CA 90401 • ALCTS
Casey Anne M. • Off-Campus Library Servs. Ln. • Central Michigan University Charles V. Park Library 315 • Mount Pleasant, MI 48859 • ACRL
Casey Barbara C. • Coordinator • State Department of Education • Oklahoma City, OK 73105 • AASL YALSA
Casey Carin M. • Student • Simmons College Center for the Study of Children's Literature • Boston, MA 02115
Casey Daniel W. • Trustee • Solvay Public Library • Solvay, NY 13209 • AASL ACRL ALTA ASCLA LAMA LITA PLA RASD CLENE EMIERT ERT FLRT GODORT IFRT IRRT LIRT SRRT
Casey Dawn M. • Honolulu, HI 96815
Casey Diane Dates • Assistant Technical Services Ln • Moraine Valley Community College Library • Palos Hills, IL 60465 • ALCTS
Casey Genevieve M. • Professor Emerita • Wayne State University Library Science Program • Detroit, MI 48202 • Continuing
Casey Helen W. • Assistant Librarian • Brooks County Library Ed Rachal Memorial Library • Falfurrias, TX 78355 • ALCTS ALSC PLA RASD YALSA
Casey James B. • Director • Oak Lawn Public Library • Oak Lawn, IL 60453 • LAMA
Casey Joseph O. • Assistant Editor • H.W. Wilson Company • Bronx, NY 10452 • ACRL
Casey Judith R. • Trustee • Pikes Peak Library District • Colorado Springs, CO 80901 • ALTA
Casey Judy F. • Head Extension Services Dept. • Aurora Public Library • Aurora, IL 60505-4299 • PLA
Casey Julia K. • Student • Wayne State University Library Science Program • Detroit, MI 48202
Casey Kathleen • Saint Louis, MO 63143 • ACRL
Casey Kathy • Senior Librarian • Hunts Point Regional Library • Bronx, NY 10459 • IFRT IRRT SRRT
Casey Marion T. • Emeryville, CA 94608 • LHRT
Casey Mary Agnes SSJ Sr • Librarian • Saint Aloysius High School • Jersey City, NJ 07306 • AASL
Casey Mary Anne • Asst Deputy Dir Subject Depts • Buffalo & Erie County Public Library • Buffalo, NY 14203 • RASD
Casey Mary H. • Consultant • Information Systems Consultant Inc. • South Salem, NY 10590 • LITA
Casey Phyllis A. Miss • St Louis, MO 63108 • ASCLA YALSA *Continuing*
Casey Susan E. • Palo Alto, CA 94306
Casey Terry Mr. • Trustee • Columbus Metropolitan Library • Columbus, OH 43215 • ALTA PLA
Casey Wayne T. • Cataloger • Foreign Mission Board Southern Baptist Convention • Richmond, VA 23230 • ACRL
Casey William F. • Dir. Health Sciences Library • Nassau County Medical Center Library • East Meadow, NY 11554 • ASCLA
Cash Patricia E. • Academic Librarian • Defense Language Institute • Lackland AFB, TX 78236 • AFLRT
Cashin Ann M. • Manhattan, KS 66502
Cashin Laurina • Dir.,Sales, & Mkt.,Child. Div. • Yankee Book Peddler • Contoocook, NH 03229 • ALSC PLA YALSA
Cashin Mary Ann • Assistant Librarian • Augusta College Reese Library • Augusta, GA 30910
Cashman Joyce S. • Las Vegas-Clark County Library District East Las Vegas Branch • Las Vegas, NV 89121 • PLA YALSA
Cashore Thomas J. • Business Librarian • University of Notre Dame Theodore M. Hesburgh Library • Notre Dame, IN 46556 • ACRL RASD
Casida Elizabeth A. • Student • Texas Woman's University School of Library & Information Studies • Denton, TX 76204 • EMIERT SRRT
Casillo Salvatore • Technical Information Ctr Coor. • Toledo Edison • Oak Harbor, OH 43449
Casini Barbara P. • Director of Educational Res • Moss Rehabilitation Hospital Library • Philadelphia, PA 19141 • Life
Caskey Frances C. • Clemson, SC 29631
Casler Robert G. • Print Media Specialist • Ag. Communciations/Computer Support • Tucson, AZ 85719 • ACRL
Caso Gasper • State Librarian/Director • State Library of Massachusetts • Boston, MA 02133 • LAMA
Cason Maidel K. • Assistant Director-Adm Services • University of Delaware Library • Newark, DE 19717-5267 • ACRL LAMA IFRT IRRT SRRT
Cason Wanda Brown • Head Catalog Department • Wake Forest University Z Smith Reynolds Library • Winston Salem, NC 27109-7777 • ACRL
Casorso Tracy M. • Special Projects Librarian • North Carolina State University D. H. Hill Library • Raleigh, NC 27695-7111 • ACRL LITA
Casper Christianne L. • Monographic Acquistions Libn. • University of Miami Libraries Richter Library • Coral Gables, FL 33124
Caspers Jean S. • Curriculum Center Librarian • Gonzaga University Crosby Library • Spokane, WA 99258
Caspers Mary E. • Assistant Reference Librarian • South Dakota State University Briggs Library • Brookings, SD 57007 • ACRL RASD
Caspole Catherine P. • Primary School Librarian • W.W. Ashurst Elementary School • Quantico, VA 22134 • AASL ALSC
Casraiss Teresa W. • Cataloging Librarian • Library of Congress • Washington, DC 20541
Cass Richard R. • Director • West Caldwell Public Library • West Caldwell, NJ 07006
Cassady Michael R. • Student • Kent State University School of Library & Information Science • Kent, OH 44242-0001 • ACRL
Cassagne Gail A. • Libraian III • New Orleans Public Library • New Orleans, LA 70140
Cassaro James P. • Cornell University Music Library • Ithaca, NY 14853-4101 • ACRL ALCTS LAMA
Cassavant Judith A. • Head Cataloger • Worcester Public Library • Worcester, MA 01608 • ALCTS
Cassel Jeris F. • Piscataway, NJ 08854-3055 • ACRL LITA RASD LIRT LRRT
Cassel Steven L. • Librarian • State Library of Ohio • Columbus, OH 43266-0334
Cassel Susan D. • Supervising Branch Librarian • New York Public Library Pelham Bay Branch • Bronx, NY 10461 • EMIERT
Cassell Jenna • President • Sign Enchancers, Inc. • Salem, OR 97304 • ASCLA VRT
Cassell Judy A. • Librarian • Coca Cola Company Marketing Information Center • Atlanta, GA 30301
Cassell Kay A. • Assoc. Dir. for Programs & Svs. • The New York Public Library • New York, NY 10016 • PLA RASD SRRT
Cassell Peggy F. • Student • Emporia State University School of Library & Information Management • Emporia, KS 66801 • AASL
Cassell Rebecca • Librarian • Lincoln Park High School • Chicago, IL 60614 • AASL
Casselman Margaret H. • High School Librarian • Franklin Senior High School • Franklin, LA 70538 • AASL YALSA
Cassen M. Anne • School Librarian • Fort Wingate Elementary School • Fort Wingate, NM 87466 • AASL LIRT
Casserly Mary F. • University of Maine Raymond H. Fogler Library • Orono, ME 04469 • ACRL
Cassidy-VanHoff Lucy A. • Amityville, NY 11701
Cassidy James T. Mrs. • Columbia, MO 65203
Cassidy Kathleen Sr. • Reference Librarian • College of Mount Saint Vincent Elizabeth Seton Library • Bronx, NY 10471 • ACRL
Cassidy Michael J. • Cassidy Cataloging Services • Kearny, NJ 07032 • LITA
Cassidy Susan • Head Librarian • Fountain Valley School • Colorado Springs, CO 80817 • AASL
Cassidy Terence W. • South Eastern Pennsylvania Transportation Authority Library (SEPTA) • Philadelphia, PA 19107 • ACRL ALCTS *Life*
Cassie Sue • Children's Librarian • Franklin Public Library • Franklin, WI 53132
Cassman Pearl S. • Milwaukee, WI 53202 • AASL ACRL *Life*
Cassner Mary E. • Library Specialist • University of Nebraska • Lincoln, NE 68588 • EMIERT IFRT SRRT
Casson Edward B. • Cataloger • Los Angeles Southwest College Learning Resources Center • Los Angeles, CA 90047 • ALCTS SRRT
Cassoni Brenda L. • Kenmore Mercy Hospital • Kenmore, NY 14217
Cast Melissa A. • Student • University of Missouri-Columbia School of Library & Informational Science • Columbia, MO 65211 • ALCTS SRRT
Castagnozzi Carol A. • Head Public Service • California State University Hayward Library • Hayward, CA 94542 • ACRL
Castano Sylvia E. • Assistant Director • University of Houston Law Libraries • Houston, TX 77204-6390 • IFRT
Castay Gail • Trustee • Saint John the Baptist Parish Library • LaPlace, LA 70068 • ALTA
Castellan Edward Jr. • Trustee • Melrose Park Public Library • Melrose Park, IL 60160
Castellano Arthur G. • Trustee • Copiague Memorial Public Library • Copiague, NY 11726 • ALTA
Castellarin Sheila A. • Trustee • Columbus Metropolitan Library • Columbus, OH 43215 • LAMA PLA
Castellucci Art • West Chester, PA 19382 • AASL
Castelluzzo Julie • New York, NY 10003 • LITA
Castiano Judith A. • Outreach Services Librarian • San Diego Public Library • San Diego, CA 92101 • PLA
Castiglione Carol J. • Blount County Public Library • Maryville, TN 37801
Castillo-Speed Lillian • Library Coordinator • California University Chicano Studies Library • Berkeley, CA 94720
Castillo Nina M. • Harrisburg Area Community College McCormick Library • Harrisburg, PA 17110
Castillo Pamela A. • Petaluma Regional Library • Petaluma, CA 94952
Castle Mary K. • Hd of Acq. & Collection Devel. • University of Texas at Arlington • Arlington, TX 76019-0497 • ALCTS
Castle Miriam • Columbia University Libraries Butler Library • New York, NY 10027 • ACRL ERT
Castleberry Susan U. • Houston, TX 77041
Castles Ethel M. • Librarian-Reference • Albertus Magnus College Library • New Haven, CT 06511
Castleton Tatiana R. • Head of Central Children Section • Stockton-San Joaquin County Public Library • Stockton, CA 95202 • ALSC
Casto Susan B. • Special Assistant to Supt. • Killeen Independent School District • Killeen, TX 76540
Castonguay Russell • Jet Propulsion Laboratory Library • Pasadena, CA 91109
Castor Nancy J. • San Francisco, CA 94118
Castro Julio E. • Asst. Coor. of Automated Cir Svs • Miami-Dade Public Library West Kendall Regional Library • Miami, FL 33186
Castro Rafaela G. • Berkeley, CA 94702
Casullo Joanne M. • Coordinator of Library Services • Legislative Reference Library • Lincoln, NE 68509
Caswell Jean Louise • Systems Librarian • Rice University Fondren Library • Houston, TX 77251-1892
Caswell Jerry V. • Asst. Dir. for Automated Sys. • Iowa State University Library • Ames, IA 50011-2140 • LITA
Caswell Lucy S. • Columbus, OH 43214 • ACRL
Caswell Mary C. • Library Technician • U S Army Res Inst • Alexandria, VA 22333
Catalanello Mary Ann • De Kalb Public Library • De Kalb, IL 60115 • PLA
Cataldo Lucia M. • Media Specialist • Loudonville Elementary School • Loudonville, NY 12211 • AASL
Catalon Carolyn W. • Cataloger • University of Alabama at Birmingham Mervyn H. Sterne Library • Birmingham, AL 35294-0015 • ALCTS
Catanese Peter • Junior High Librarian • Indiana Area Junior High School Library • Indiana, PA 15701
Catania Mem • Librarian • University of Central Florida-Brevard • Cocoa, FL 32922 • ACRL ALCTS
Cate Gwen • Learning Resource Librarian • Tahoka ISD • Tahoka, TX 79373 • AASL
Catelain Ken • Trustee • Palatine Public Library • Palatine, IL 60067 • ALTA
Cater Judy J. • Director Library/Media Center • Palomar Community College Library • San Marcos, CA 92069 • ACRL
Caterina Ann M. • Staten Island, NY 10308
Caterson Martha A • Reference Librarian • The American University Library • Washington, DC 20016-8046
Cates Dan R. • Des Moines, IA 50322-5126 • LITA
Cates Judith M. • Media Coordinator • Southern Guilford High School • Greensboro, NC 27406 • AASL
Catherall Lynette • Library Director • Springville Public Library • Springville, UT 84663 • PLA
Catherman Mary H. • Student • University of North Carolina School of Library Science • Chapel Hill, NC 27599-3360
Catlett Dianne B. • Director • George H & Laura E Brown Library • Washington, NC 27889 • PLA
Catlin Jolien • Orchard Park Presbyterian Church Library • Indianapolis, IN 46280
Catlin Wesley R. • Library Tech. • Sacramento Public Library Literacy Service • Sacramento, CA 95820 • RASD
Catoggio Michael • Law Librarian II • Alaska Court Libraries • Anchorage, AK 99501
Caton Anne Mast • Bethalto Public Library • Bethalto, IL 62010 • ALSC
Catrone Deborah J. • Librarian II • Akron-Summit County Public Library Ellet Branch • Akron, OH 44312
Catt Martha • Director • Hussey-Mayfield Memorial Public Library • Zionsville, IN 46077 • PLA
Cattrell Betty J. • Librarian • Haysville Community Library • Haysville, KS 67060 • PLA
Catucci Louis V. • Director • West New York Public Library • West New York, NJ 07093
Caudillo Ellen Antoinette • Student • Texas Woman's University School of Library & Information Studies • Denton, TX 76204 • ACRL ALCTS GODORT
Caudle Violet K. • Outreach Librarian • Iredell County Library • Statesville, NC 28677
Caughey Ann L. • Cataloger • Tacoma Public Schools • Tacoma, WA 98401 • AASL
Caughman Ginger • Trustee/Vice President Lib. Br. • Saint Charles Parish Library • Luling, LA 70070 • ALTA

Caulfield Elizabeth A. • Student • Louisiana State University School of Library & Information Science • Baton Rouge, LA 70803-3290

Caulkins Lorna W. • Director • Stewart Library • Grinnell, IA 50112 • PLA IFRT

Causey Enid R. • Director of Library • Charleston Southern University L Mendel Rivers Library • Charleston, SC 29411

Causey Iris K. • Librarian/Adult Inf. Serv. • Prince William Public Library Chinn Park Regional Library • Prince William, VA 22192 • ALSC PLA

Cauthen Shirley P. • Editor • Christians Listening • Van Wyck, SC 29744

Cavallo Kay L. • Kearnersville, NC 27284 • AASL

Cavan Mary Lee Miss • Newton, NJ 07860 • AASL ALSC   *Life*

Cavanagh Eileen • Senior Librarian • Hennepin County Library • Minnetonka, MN 55343

Cavanagh Janet Muldoon • Head-Circ/Reserve Librarian • State University of New York (SUNY) • Stony Brook, NY 11794-2225 • ACRL LAMA LHRT

Cavanagh Joseph M. A. • Library Systems/Planning Officer • State University of New York (SUNY) Frank Melville Jr. Memorial Library • Stony Brook, NY 11794-3300

Cavanagh Rita W. • Head, Children's Services Dept. • Oak Park Public Library • Oak Park, IL 60301 • ALSC

Cavanagh Shirley Bickoff • Librarian • Southern Connecticut State University Hilton C. Buley Library • New Haven, CT 06515 • GODORT

Cavanaugh Barbara Bernoff • Pennsylvania Hospital Medical Library • Phildelphia, PA 19107 • ACRL ASCLA IFRT ILERT SRRT

Cavanaugh Bonnie B. • Librarian • Middle School Library Colony Middle School • Palmer, AK 99645 • AASL

Cavanaugh Marianne L. • Associate Librarian • Saint Louis Art Museum Richardson Memorial Library • St. Louis, MO 63110 • ALCTS LITA

Cavanaugh Martin A. • Reference Librarian/ Bibl. • Washington University Libraries • Saint Louis, MO 63130-4899 • ACRL LITA RASD

Cavanaugh Nancy J. • United States Department of Education • Washington, DC 20208 • ASCLA EMIERT

Cavanaugh Trish • Comm Relations Manager • E. P. Foster Library • Ventura, CA 93001

Cave Carol J. • Student • University of Kentucky College of Library & Information Science • Lexington, KY 40506-0391 • AASL

Caven Mary P. • Media Specialist • Duluth Public Library • Duluth, MN 55802

Cavender E. Eugenia • Director • Dalton Regional Library • Dalton, GA 30720

Cavender Lucile P. Mrs • Attleboro, MA 02703 • ACRL ASCLA   *Continuing*

Caver Mildred H. • Librarian • Oakland Unified School District • Oakland, CA 94609

Cavey Sandra • Librarian I • Sacramento Public Library Carmichael Regional Branch • Carmichael, CA 95608

Cavil Dolores J. • Librarian • Bayou Road Elementary School La Marque Independent School District • La Marque, TX 77568 • AASL

Cavill Marianna K. • Lexington, KY 40503 • PLA IFRT SRRT

Cavin Cara • Library Media Director • Verona Country View Elementary • Verona, WI 53593 • AASL

Cavin Elaine E. • Preservation Division • University Microfilms International • Ann Arbor, MI 48106-1346 • ALCTS

Cavinee Deeanna R. • Pittsburgh, PA 15217 • LAMA PLA LRRT

Cawiezel Marilyn • Board President • Lisle Library District • Lisle, IL 60532 • ALTA

Cawley Daniel D. • Bexley, OH 43209

Cawley James F. • Bucks County Free Library • Doylestown, PA 18901 • ALTA

Cawley Rebecca Erwin • Northland Library Cooperative • Alpena, MI 49707 • ASCLA LAMA PLA RASD

Cawn Mary Ann • Martin Marietta Energy Systems • Oak Ridge, TN 37873

Caylor Lawrence M. • University of Lowell O'Leary Library • Lowell, MA 01854 • ACRL

Cayme Teodora B. • Manila Standard Library Kamahalan Publishing Corporation • Manila, Philippines

Cayton Janice M. Mrs • Markham Elementary School • Fort Belvoir, VA 22060

Caywood Carolyn A. • Librarian • Virginia Beach Public Library Bayside Area Library • Virginia Beach, VA 23455 • ALSC PLA YALSA IFRT

Caywood Gladys • Newport News, VA 23602 • AASL ALSC   *Continuing*

Cayz James • Senior Librarian-Automation Serv • State Librarian Delaware Division of Libraries • Dover, DE 19901 • LITA

Cazaudebat Carol W. • Versailles, KY 40383 • PLA

Cazayoux Vivian • Associate Librarian • State Library of Louisiana • Baton Rouge, LA 70821 • Continuing

Cazeaux Isabelle • Professor of Music • Bryn Mawr College • Bryn Mawr, PA 19010 • ACRL ALCTS   *Life*

Cazzulino Clara P. • Media Specialist • Shelter Rock Elementary School • Manhasset, NY 11030 • AASL

Cearbaugh Linda S • Carnegie Middle School • Raleigh, NC 27610 • AASL

Cecchini Linda R. • Serials Librarian • University of Wisconsin-Eau Claire William D. McIntyre Library • Eau Claire, WI 54702 • ACRL ALCTS

Cedarblade Edna G. • Denver, CO 80209 • AASL YALSA   *Continuing*

Cedarface Mary Jane M. • Rutgers University Libraries • New Brunswick, NJ 08903 • ACRL

Cederoth Pat • Children's Services Librarian • Oswego Public Library District • Oswego, IL 60543 • ALCTS ALSC PLA

Cegielski Carla S. • Perry, OH 44081

Celeste Eric • Massachusetts Institute of Technology Libraries (MIT) • Cambridge, MA 02139

Celestre Marie • Customer Services Librarian • Western Library Network (WLN) • Lacey, WA 98503 • LITA

Celigoj Carmen Z. • Director • Kent Free Library • Kent, OH 44240 • LAMA PLA

Celis Lydia R. • Catalog Librarian • Cleary, Gottlieb, Steen & Hamilton • New York, NY 10006 • ALCTS

Celizic Gayle D. • Roosevelt Elementary School • Euclid, OH 44119

Celli John P. • Assistant Chief • Library of Congress • Washington, DC 20541

Celmer Mary L. • Trustee • Acorn Public Library District • Oak Forest, IL 60452 • ALTA

Cenacveira Jacquelyn P. • Sherman Oaks, CA 91413

Centanne Sharon Marie • Student • University of South Florida School of Library & Information Science • Tampa, FL 33620 • AASL ACRL ALCTS ASCLA LITA PLA RASD LHRT MAGERT NMRT

Centeno Patricia A. • Branch Head • Chicago Public Library Mayfair Branch • Chicago, IL 60630 • PLA

Center Helen N. • Michigan Cty, IN 46360

Center Robert J. • Trustee • Michigan City Public Library • Michigan City, IN 46360 • ALTA

Centinaro Martha • Head Librarian • Dormont Public Library • Pittsburgh, PA 15216-2594

Centing Richard R. • Hd Eng/Theatre Commun L State Un • Ohio State University Libraries • Columbus, OH 43210-1286

Centner Catherine • Jamesburg, NJ 08831

Cenzer Pamela • Science Librarian, Serials • University of Florida Libraries • Gainesville, FL 32611-2047 • ACRL RASD

Ceppaglia Deborah M. • Student • State University of New York (SUNY) School of Information & Library Studies • Buffalo, NY 14260 • ACRL LHRT

Ceppos Karen F. • Professor • San Jose State University Division of Library & Information Science • San Jose, CA 95192-0029 • LAMA LRRT

Cerabona Kathryn A. • Assistant Librarian • Glenbard West High School Library • Glen Ellyn, IL 60137

Ceraldi Katherine C. • Burke County Public Library • Morganton, NC 28655

Ceravolo Teresa • Head Librarian • Birmingham Public Library Parke Memorial Branch • Birmingham, AL 35205 • PLA

Ceresa Mario A. • Detroit College of Law • Detroit, MI 48201

Cerini-Lopis Elizabeth • Librarian • Liberty High School • Issaquah, WA 98027 • AASL YALSA LIRT

Cernak David • Chicago, IL 60656

Cerny Kathy M. • Student • University of Arizona Graduate Library School • Tucson, AZ 85721

Cerny Rosanne • Coordinator For Children's Servs • Queens Borough Public Library • Jamaica, NY 11432 • ALSC

Cerritelli Ellen M. • Villanova University School of Library Science • Villanova, PA 19083 • AASL YALSA

Cerrone Bettyjane L. • Indexer/Relations Guide • H.W. Wilson Company • Bronx, NY 10452 • ACRL

Cerulli-Rosen Franca • Hd, Interlibrary Loan Services • Jefferson County Public Library • Lakewood, CO 80215 • ALCTS PLA RASD

Cerullo Joseph D. • Vice President • IMR Limited Valmont Industrial Park • West Hazelton, PA 18201 • ACRL ALCTS

Cervantes David M. • Librarian I • Phoenix Public Library Palo Verde Branch • Phoenix, AZ 85031 • PLA

Cervenka Patricia A. • Associate Director • Creighton University Law Library • Omaha, NE 68178-0340

Cervera Barbara R. • University of Connecticut Homer Babbidge Library • Storrs, CT 06269-1005 • ACRL LAMA LITA

Cervera Jorge L. • Storrs, CT 06268

Cesario Virginia N. • Monterey, MA 01245 • Continuing

Cesarz Thomas J. • Head of Access Services • Northeastern University Libraries • Boston, MA 02115 • ACRL

Ceterski Joseph E. • Information Coodinator • Rensselaer Polytechnic Institute • Troy, NY 12180 • ACRL LITA IFRT

Cettomai Phyllis J. • Director • Reed Memorial Library • Ravenna, OH 44266

Cetwinski Thomas C. • University of Illinois at Chicago University Library • Chicago, IL 60680 • LAMA

Cevallos Elena E. • Ref/Coor. CD-ROM End User Servs. • Hofstra University Axinn Library • Hempstead, NY 11550 • ACRL RASD

Chace Laura L. • Library Director • Cincinnati Historical Society Library • Cincinnati, OH 45203

Chace Myron B. • Hd Spec Serv Sect/Photo-Dup Serv • Library of Congress • Washington, DC 20541 • ALCTS

Chach Maryann • Archivist • Shubert Archive/Lyceum Theatre • New York, NY 10036 • ACRL

Chad Barry L. • Student • University of Pittsburgh School of Library and Information Science • Pittsburgh, PA 15260

Chadderdon Philip M. • Knoxville High School • Knoxville, IL 61448 • AASL

Chadley Otis A. • Reference Librarian • State University of New York at Albany School of Information Science & Policy • Albany, NY 12222 • ACRL

Chadsey Kathy A. • Children's Librarian • Tillamook County Library • Tillamook, OR 97141 • ALSC

Chadwick Alena F. • Iowa City, IA 52240 • ACRL MAGERT   *Life*

Chadwick Janina A. • Head of Circulation Department • Bexley Public Library • Columbus, OH 43209

Chadwick Rhonda J. • North Provdence, RI 02911-3214 • ACRL

Chadwick Roxane • Montgomery County Public Library Wheaton Regional Branch • Wheaton, MD 20902-1997 • ALSC PLA

Chadwick Sharon S. • Physical Science Librarian • Humboldt State University Library • Arcata, CA 95521 • ACRL

Chaet Mark • Reference Librarian • Library Management Systems • Sherman Oaks, CA 91423

Chaffee David E. • Trustee • Pikes Peak Library District • Colorado Springs, CO 80901 • ALTA

Chaffee Elaine L. • Lundahl Junior High School Learning Center • Crystal Lake, IL 60014

Chaffee Judith A. • Barneveld, NY 13304 • AASL

Chaffee Keith • Student • Los Angeles Public Library Serials Division • Los Angeles, CA 90033 • PLA RASD IFRT NMRT SRRT

Chaffee R Lance • Reference Librarian • Olean Public Library • Olean, NY 14760 • LITA

Chaffin Nancy J. • Texas A & M University Sterling C. Evans Library • College Station, TX 77843-5000 • ACRL ALCTS

Chafin Karen S. • Librarian • John I. Burton High School • Norton, VA 24273 • AASL

Chagala Georgia • Rancho Bernardo High School • San Diego, CA 92128 • AASL

Chait William • Hiltn Head Is, SC 29928 • LAMA PLA *Life*

Chakeres Patricia H. • Student • Saint John's University Division of Library & Information Science • Jamaica, NY 11439 • AASL

Chaklosh Cynthia L. • Green Valley, AZ 85614-2815 • ALSC PLA   *Life*

Chakraborty Khana • Scotch Plains, NJ 07076

Chale Donna M. • Media Specialist • Warsaw Middle School • Pittsfield, ME 04967 • AASL

Chaleff Jane • Children's Librarian • Rogers Memorial Library • Southampton, NY 11968 • ALSC

Chalfant Margarete Elsa • Seattle, WA 98103 • GODORT   *Continuing*

Challacombe Elaine M. • Asst. Librarian/Curator • University of Minnesota Bio-Medical Library • Minneapolis, MN 55455 • ACRL

Challener Marcee M. • Collection Development Ln. • Tampa-Hillsborough County Public Library • Tampa, FL 33602 • LAMA PLA RASD

Challinor Joan R. Dr. • Radcliffe College Schlesinger Library • Cambridge, MA 02138 • ALTA

Chalmees John P. • Austin, TX 78741 • ACRL

Chalmers Lois M. • Takoma Park, MD 20912

Chalmers Mary T. • Librarian • Strafford High School • Goose Creek, SC 29445

Chalmers Patricia L. • The University of King's College The Library • Halifax NS, B3H 2A1 Canada • ACRL LHRT

Chalnick Teresa C. • Special Events Coordinator • Broward County Division of Libraries Broward County Library • Fort Lauderdale, FL 33301

Chamberlain Barbara Jean • Student • San Jose State University Division of Library & Information Science • San Jose, CA 95192-0029 • AASL PLA

Chamberlain Carol E. • Chief, Acquisitions Department • Pennsylvania State University Pattee Library • University Park, PA 16802 • ACRL ALCTS

Chamberlain Cynthia • Swansea, MA 02777-4220 • ALSC

Chamberlain Donna L. • IMC Coordinator • County Superintendent of Schools Office • Susanville, CA 96130 • AASL

Chamberlain Dorothy E. • Arlington, VA 22205 • Continuing

Chamberlain Erna B. • Original Cataloger • State University of New York at Binghamton Libraries (SUNY) • Binghamton, NY 13902-6012 • ACRL

Chamberlain Kim P. • Student • Clark-Atlanta University School of Library & Information Studies • Atlanta, GA 30314-4391

Chamberlain Mary Jo • Librarian • Green Valley Elementary School • Roanoke, VA 24018 • AASL

Chamberlain Mitchell E. • Collection Management Librarian • Middle Tennessee State University Library • Murfreesboro, TN 37132 • ACRL

Chamberlain William R. • Director of General Library Div • Virginia State Library & Archives • Richmond, VA 23219

Chamberland Eleanore • Suttons Bay, MI 49682 • ALTA PLA

Chamberland Fayth C. • Children's Librarian • Concord Free Public Library • Concord, MA 01742

Chamberlin Charles E. • Deputy Director of Libraries • University of Washington • Seattle, WA 98195 • ACRL LAMA LITA

Chamberlin Cynthia C. • Library Director • Nutley Free Public Library • Nutley, NJ 07110 • LAMA PLA

Chamberlin Leslie • Napa, CA 94559-0071

Chambers Carolyn J. • Interim Library Director • Shasta County Library • Redding, CA 96001 • PLA

Chambers Cathy L. • Student • University of California-Los Angeles Graduate School of Library & Information Science • Los Angeles, CA 90024-1520 • ACRL SRRT

Chambers Cynthia D. • Jamaica, NY 11432

Chambers Donald A. • Mililani, HI 96789

Chambers Elizabeth • Claremont, CA 91711 • Continuing

Chambers Frances • Reference Librarian • City College of New York (CUNY) • New York, NY 10031 • ACRL IRRT

Chambers Holly E. • Senior Assistant • State Univ of NY Coll at Potsdam Frederick W. Crumb Memorial Library • Potsdam, NY 13676 • ACRL LITA RASD LIRT SRRT

Chambers Jeannine L. • Librarian I • University of Washington Suzzallo Library • Seattle, WA 98195 • ALSC RASD

Chambers Jo Nelle • Librarian • Galena High School Library • Galena Park, TX 77547 • AASL YALSA

Chambers Joan L. • Director of Libraries • Colorado State University William E. Morgan Library • Fort Collins, CO 80523 • ACRL ALCTS LAMA LITA RASD

Chambers Marybeth • Senior Catalog Librarian • Northern Arizona University • Flagstaff, AZ 86011-6022 • ALCTS

Chambers Paula H. • School Library Media Specialist • West Bainbridge Elementary School • Bainbridge, GA 31717 • AASL

Chambers Saundra R. • Supervisory-Branch Manager • Wake County Library System Richard B. Harrison Branch • Raleigh, NC 27610

Chambers Sydney • Gonzaga University Crosby Library • Spokane, WA 99258 • LITA SRRT

Chambers Tom • Trustee • Grand Rapids Public Library • Grand Rapids, MI 49503-3093

Chamley Rhonda J. • Coordinator of Adult Services • Cape Girardeau Public Library • Cape Girardeau, MO 63701 • PLA

Chammou Eliezer • Near East Cataloger • University of California-Los Angeles (UCLA) • Los Angeles, CA 90024-1450 • ALCTS MAGERT

Chamness Berry M. • Cataloging Librarian • Bryn Mawr College • Bryn Mawr, PA 19010 • ALCTS SRRT

Champagne Anne E. • State College, PA 16801-6051 • ACRL

Champagne Carol C. • Toledo-Lucas County Public Library • Toledo, OH 43624

Champagne Danielle • Bibliotheque Municipale de Brossard • Brossard, PQ, J4Z 2B4 Canada • ALSC

Champagne Julie W. • Director • Saint James Parish Library • Lutcher, LA 70071 • ALSC PLA RASD IFRT NMRT

Champagne Thomas E. • Ross & Hardies • Chicago, IL 60601 • ALCTS SRRT

Champlin Constance J. • Coor, Media Services • MSD Washington Township • Indianapolis, IN 46240 • AASL ALSC

Champlin Maria A. • YPL- Department Head • Las Vegas-Clark County Library District • Las Vegas, NV 89101

Champlin Peggy • Los Angeles, CA 90077

Chan Alice K. • Cataloger • University of Alberta • Edmonton AB, T6G 2J8 Canada

Chan Anthony P. • Library Associate • State Library of Ohio • Columbus, OH 43266-0334 • LITA

Chan Betty M. • Student • University of Washington Graduate School of Library and Information Science • Seattle, WA 98195 • LITA PLA RASD ILERT

Chan Carl C. • Head, Public Services • Defense Language Institute Learning Resources Center • Presidio of Monterey, CA 93944-5007 • ALCTS EMIERT FLRT

Chan Co-Ming • Head Cataloger • Oklahoma State University Library • Stillwater, OK 74078-0375 • LAMA

Chan Connie Yee • Reference Librarian • Alhambra Public Library • Alhambra, CA 91801

Chan Corinne M. • Newton, MA 02168

Chan Dominic C.K. • Senior Adm. Officer • University of Macau Student Counselling Office • Macau, Hong Kong

Chan Florence M. • San Mateo, CA 94402

Chan Grace Y. • Sugarland, TX 77478

Chan Lillian L. • Department Chair of Science Dept • San Diego State University Library • San Diego, CA 92119-2120 • ACRL

Chan Lois M. • Professor • University of Kentucky Libraries • Lexington, KY 40506-0039 • ALCTS LITA *Life*

Chan Moses C. • Information Consultant • North Carolina Foreign Language Center • Fayetteville, NC 28301

Chan Stella P. • Coordinator of Library Services • Skyline College Library • San Bruno, CA 94066 • ACRL

Chan Vivian C.Y. • Librarian I • San Francisco Public Library • San Francisco, CA 94102

Chan Wai-Kwan • Mississauga ON, L5M 4K7 Canada

Chan Winnie S. • Automatic Sys. Maint. Coor. • University of Illinois Library • Urbana, IL 61801 • ALCTS LITA

Chance Homer R. • Pueblo West, CO 81007 • Continuing

Chance Martha S. Mrs • White Springs, FL 32096 • Life

Chance Rosemary S. • Instructor • Sam Houston State University Department of Library Science • Huntsville, TX 77341-2236 • AASL YALSA

Chancellor Martha • Library Media Specialist K-12 • Saint Ansgar High School • Saint Ansgar, IA 50472 • AASL

Chancey Linda N. • Director • Bartow Public Library • Bartow, FL 33830 • PLA

Chancey Monty R. • Librarian • Meadowlawn Middle School • Saint Petersburg, FL 33703 • AASL

Chandler Ann R. • Assoc. Director Public Services • Stephen F. Austin State University Steen Library • Nacogdoches, TX 75962

Chandler Bertha A. • Director • Boyden Library • Foxboro, MA 02035 • LAMA PLA IRRT

Chandler Beverly • Coordinator • Vanier Cegep • St. Laurent PQ, ZH4L 3X9 Canada • ACRL LAMA LITA

Chandler Bonnie L. • Librarian III • Columbus Metropolitan Library • Columbus, OH 43215

Chandler Cheryle C. • Live Oak, FL 32060

Chandler Constance P. • Manager, RS & S • Bibliographical Center for Research • Denver, CO 80222

Chandler Cynthia S. • Sr. Librarian/Branch Manager • DeKalb Public Library System Reid H. Cofer Branch • Tucker, GA 30084 • PLA RASD

Chandler Dorothy S. • Director • Raleigh County Public Library • Beckley, WV 25802-1876

Chandler Gayle L. • Exhibit Coordinator • Delaware Technical & Community College • Georgetown, DE 19947

Chandler Gwendolyn J. • Ln • Florida Community College at Jacksonville Downtown Campus Learning Res Center • Jacksonville, FL 32202 • ACRL

Chandler Maureen P. • Bergen Community Coll • Paramus, NJ 07652 • ACRL

Chandler Mildred C. • Harvard, MA 01451 • Continuing

Chandler Rod R. II • Los Angeles, CA 90046

Chandler Stacie Browne • Head of Technical Services • Plymouth Public Library • Plymouth, MA 02360

Chandler Vivian L. • Reference Librarian • Atlanta Metropolitan College • Atlanta, GA 30310

Chandler Yvonne J. • Doctoral Student • University of Michigan School of Information and Library Studies • Ann Arbor, MI 48109-1092 • LRRT

Chandra Jane • Ben L. Smith High School • Greensboro, NC 27407 • AASL YALSA

Chandra Yasmin • Student • University of British Columbia School of Library, Archival & Information Studies • Vancouver BC, V6T 1Z1 Canada

Chandrasekhar Ratna • Acting Director • Bridgewater State College Clement C. Maxwell Library • Bridgewater, MA 02325

Chaney Charles C. • Branch Librarian • Cleveland Public Library Walz Branch • Cleveland, OH 44102 • PLA

Chaney Daniel W. • Aurora, IL 60506

Chaney Robin Bell • Circulation/Aduio Visual Mgr • Waterloo Public Library • Waterloo, IA 50701 • LITA

Chaney Ruth E. • Trustee • Bonita Springs Public Library • Bonita Springs, FL 33923

Chaney Suzanne • Reference Librarian • University of Texas Libraries General Libraries • Austin, TX 78713-7330 • RASD

Chaney Suzanne F. • Fredericton NB, E3B 5L7 Canada • ACRL RASD *Life*

Chang Amy • Head of Access Services Dept. • Texas Tech University Libraries • Lubbock, TX 79409-0002 • ACRL

Chang Ann Han-Chih • Cataloging Librarian • John B. Coleman Library • Prairie View, TX 77446 • ACRL

Chang Bao-Chu • Cary, NC 27511

Chang Chia-Ching • Head,Serials Dept. • Bucknell University Bertrand Library • Lewisburg, PA 17837-2086 • ACRL ALCTS LITA

Chang Chia-Hsiu • Student • University of Pittsburgh School of Library and Information Science • Pittsburgh, PA 15260

Chang Ching-Tung • Student • University of South Carolina College of Library & Information Science • Columbia, SC 29208

Chang Christine F. • Librarian • West Virginia University Department of Library Science • Morgantown, WV 26506-6069

Chang Cindy Hsu • Cataloger • Elmhurst Public Library • Elmhurst, IL 60126

Chang Daphne • Technical Services Librarian • Hillside Free Public Library • Hillside, NJ 07205 • LITA

Chang David • Head Librarian • Sussex County Community College • Newton, NJ 07860 • ACRL LIRT

Chang Helen S. • Springfield, VA 22153 • ASCLA

Chang Henry C. Dr. • Director of Library Service • Los Angeles Sight Center Library Conference Center • Los Angeles, CA 90029 • ASCLA LAMA

Chang Heui-Ju • Cataloging Librarian • Yale University Sterling Memorial Library • New Haven, CT 06520

Chang Hsin-Wei Grace • Aurora, CO 80014

Chang Hui-Yee • Assistant Catalog Librarian • New Mexico State University Library • Las Cruces, NM 88003-0006 • ALCTS

Chang Hung-Yun • Senior Librarian • New York Public Library Donnell Library Center • New York, NY 10019 • RASD

Chang Isabelle C. • Shrewsbury, MA 01545 • Continuing

Chang Lianmaan • Taitung 95004 R.O.C., Taiwan • AASL

Chang Ling-Li • Loyola University E.M. Cudahy Memorial Library • Chicago, IL 60626 • ALCTS

Chang Linh H. • Ann Arbor, MI 48104

Chang Margaret A. • Librarian • Buxton School • Williamstown, MA 01267 • ALSC

Chang Min-Min • Director of the Library • Hong Kong University of Science & Technology University Library • Kowloon, Hong Kong • ACRL ALCTS LAMA LITA RASD

Chang Robert Chen • Los Angeles, CA 90020

Chang Robert H. • Director of Library Services • University of Houston-Downtown William I Dykes Library • Houston, TX 77002

Chang Rosalind • Childrens Librarian • San Francisco Public Library Ortega Branch • San Francisco, CA 94122 • ALSC

Chang Roy T. • Cataloging Coordinator • Western Illinois University Libraries • Macomb, IL 61455 • LITA

Chang Shirley L. • Asso Prof/Ref/Catlg Librarian • Lock Haven Univ of Pennsylvania Stevenson Library • Lock Haven, PA 17745

Chang Sylvia M. • Saint Mary's College Alumni Memorial Library • Orchard Lake, MI 48324 • ACRL ALCTS EMIERT IRRT

Chang Theresa S. • Technical Services Librarian • Gallaudet University Library • Washington, DC 20002 • ALCTS

Chang Tohsook P. • Cataloging/Assoc. Prof. • University of Alaska • Anchorage, AK 99508

Chang Tony H. • Chinese Catlg Libn./Bibliograph • Washington University Libraries • Saint Louis, MO 63130-4899

Chang de Huang Mei S. • Student • University of Illinois Graduate School of Library and Information Science • Urbana, IL 61801

Channing Rhoda K. • Director • Wake Forest University Z Smith Reynolds Library • Winston Salem, NC 27109-7777 • ACRL LAMA LITA

Chapa Joan I. • Manager, Gpo Services • Marcive, Inc. • San Antonio, TX 78265 • GODORT

Chaparro Catherine F. • Carnegie Library of Pittsburgh • Pittsburgh, PA 15213-4080 • PLA EMIERT IFRT SRRT

Chaparro Luis • Director-Learning Resources • El Paso Community College • El Paso, TX 79998 • ACRL ALCTS ALTA LAMA LITA RASD EMIERT IRRT SRRT

Chapin Damaris B. • Marblehead, MA 01945 • SRRT

Chapin James B. Dr. • Trustee • Queens Borough Public Library • Jamaica, NY 11432 • ALTA PLA

Chapin Joan R. • Rahway, NJ 07065 • ALSC

Chapin Patricia • Redmond, WA 98053 • ACRL ALCTS LITA

Chapin Richard E. • Director Emeritus • Michigan State University Libraries • East Lansing, MI 48824-1048 • ACRL LAMA   *Life*

Chaplin Hattie M. • Washington, DC 20008

Chapman Bert T. • Reference/Documents Librarian • Lamar University Gray Library • Beaumont, TX 77710 • ACRL GODORT

Chapman Beth M. • Salem, OR 97302-1818

Chapman Catherine A. • Student • University of South Florida School of Library & Information Science • Tampa, FL 33620 • PLA

Chapman Ellen L. • Reference Librarian • University of Hawaii Thomas Hale Hamilton Library • Honolulu, HI 96822

Chapman Greta J. • Library Director • Lincoln County Free Library • Libby, MT 59923

Chapman James E. • Librarian • Canandaigua Academy • Canandaigua, NY 14424 • AASL

Chapman Karen J. • Business Reference Librarian • University of Alabama • Tuscaloosa, AL 35487-0266 • ACRL RASD

Chapman Katherine • Lubbock, TX 79424

Chapman Keith D. • Rice University Fondren Library • Houston, TX 77251-1892

Chapman Kendall P. • Director of Learning Services • Copiah-Lincoln Junior College Evelyn W. Owsalt Library • Wesson, MS 39191

Chapman Marcia C. • Librarian • Houston Public Library Robinson-Westchase Branch • Houston, TX 77042 • IFRT

Chapman Mary • Associate Librarian Tech. Serv • New York University Library of the School of Law • New York, NY 10012-1099 • ALCTS LITA

Chapman Mary • Dynix Library Systems, Inc. • Waterloo, ON, N2J 2M1 Canada

Chapman Mary A. • Head of Reference-Interloan • Huron Valley Library System • Ann Arbor, MI 48107 • PLA

Chapman Nancy C. • Student • University of South Carolina College of Library & Information Science • Columbia, SC 29208 • AASL

Chapman Susan E. • Reference & User Services Branch • National Agricultural Library Reference Section • Beltsville, MD 20705 • ACRL

Chapman Toni • Pelham Public Library • Pelham, NH 03076

Chapnik Ann • Media Specialist • Needham Public Schools • Needham, MA 02192 • AASL

Chappelear Nancy M. • Zanesville, OH 43701

Chappell Nell C. • Rice University Fondren Library • Houston, TX 77251-1892

Chapple-Sokol Angie • Student • State University of New York (SUNY) Thomas E. Dewey Graduate Library • Albany, NY 12222 • SRRT

Chapple Cecilia • Head Librarian • Milwaukee Public Library Martin L. King Branch • Milwaukee, WI 53212 • PLA EMIERT SRRT

Charbonneau Carol-Anne • United States Air Force Intelligence Command-General Library • San Antonio, TX 78243-5000 • AFLRT

Charbonneau Gary W. • Assistant Library • Indiana University • Bloomington, IN 47405 • LITA

Charbonneau Janice M. • Trustee • Central Massachusetts Regional Library System • Worcester, MA 01608-2074

Charbonneau Sylvia • Portage, IN 46368

Charette Sharon J. • Director of LRC • New England Institute of Technology Learning Resources Center • Warwick, RI 02886

Charles-Hanvey Carole A. • Student • University of Missouri-Columbia School of Library & Informational Science • Columbia, MO 65211

Charles Carolyn • Adult Services Librarian • Cuyahoga County Public Library Solon Branch • Solon, OH 44139 • NMRT

Charles Deborah A. • Newspaper Librarian • The Royal Gazette • Hamilton, HM08, Bermuda

Charles Elizabeth D. • Executive Director • Rice University Fondren Library • Houston, TX 77251-1892 • LAMA

Charley Susan J. • Associate Director Central Serv. • North Country Library System • Watertown, NY 13601

Charlton Mary A. • Baltimore County Public Library Loch Raven Branch • Towson, MD 21204 • PLA

Charnes Alan N. • General Manager • Colorado Alliance of Research Libraries • Denver, CO 80210

Charney Hayley Horn • Student • University of Maryland College of Library and Information Services • College Park, MD 20742-4345 • ACRL

Charney Madeleine • Student • University of Rhode Island Graduate School of Library & Information Studies • Kingston, RI 02881-0815

Chart Maria G. • Chicago Public Library Harold Washington Library • Chicago, IL 60605

Charter Jody B. • Associate Professor • University of Central Arkansas Department of Educational Media & Library Science • Conway, AR 72032-5001 • AASL ACRL

Chartier Marie C. • Library Director • Bugbee Memorial Library • Danielson, CT 06239 • PLA

Chartoff Faye M. • Vice President of Operations • Innovative Interfaces, Inc. • Berkeley, CA 94710

Charton Michael • Parsippany-Troy Hills Public Library Lake Hiawatha Branch • Lake Hiawatha, NJ 07034 • PLA

Chartrain Mary A. • Stockton-San Joaquin County Public Library • Stockton, CA 95202 • RASD

Chartrand Margaret • Ottawa ON, K1V 0H4 Canada • LAMA

Chartrand Richard • Director • East Alton Public Library • East Alton, IL 62024 • LAMA PLA

Chase Allison L. • Student • Emporia State University School of Library & Information Management • Emporia, KS 66801 • AFLRT SRRT

Chase Amy M • Student • University of Michigan School of Information and Library Studies • Ann Arbor, MI 48109-1092

Chase Anne Wenz • Director of Library • College of Mount Saint Joseph • Cincinnati, OH 45233-1671 • ACRL

Chase Barbara Sendker • Reference Librarian • Medina County District Library • Medina, OH 44256 • RASD

Chase Carmela A. • Director • Tuxedo Park Library • Tuxedo Park, NY 10987 • PLA

Chase Clarie • Young Adult Librarian • Cuyahoga County Public Library Bay Village Branch • Bay Village, OH 44140-2194 • YALSA

Chase Eleanor L. • Librarian Govt. Publications • University of Washington Suzzallo Library • Seattle, WA 98195 • ACRL GODORT

Chase Hope L. • Head of Children's Services • Howard County Library • Columbia, MD 21044 • ALSC PLA

Chase Judith Helfer • Klamath Falls, OR 97603 • ALCTS

Chase Julie Anne • Director • Dane County Library Service • Madison, WI 53703

Chase Laurel C. • Irving Public Library • Irving, TX 75060 • ALSC

Chase Linda S. • Chevy Chase, MD 20815 • ACRL ALCTS

Chase Margaret A. • Branch Librarian • Evansville-Vanderburgh County McCollough Branch Library • Evansville, IN 47715 • PLA

Chase Melissa A. • Library Circulation Assistant • Jonathan Bourne Public Library • Bourne, MA 02532

Chase Peter F. • Director • Plainville Public Library • Plainville, CT 06062 • PLA

Chase William C. • Klamath Falls, OR 97603

Chasse Emily Schuder • Online Search Servs. Librarian • Central Connecticut State University Elihu Burritt Library • New Britain, CT 06050 • ACRL

Chastain Sharon J. • Student • University of Washington Graduate School of Library and Information Science • Seattle, WA 98195

Chatfield Linda L. • Student • Simmons College Graduate School of Library & Information Science • Boston, MA 02115 • ALSC PLA YALSA

Chatfield Margaret • Norfolk, VA 23505

Chatfield Mary • Head Librarian • Harvard Business School Baker Library • Boston, MA 02163 • ACRL

Chatham Nancy G. • Librarian • Mercy Academy • Louisville, KY 40204 • AASL

Chatman Beverly • Jonesboro, TN 37659

Chatman Elfreda A. • Associate Professor • University of North Carolina at Chapel Hill School of Information and Library Science • Chapel Hill, NC 27599-3360 • PLA LRRT

Chatterton Leigh A. • Member Services Librarian • NELINET Inc. • Newton, MA 02162 • ACRL

Chatton Barbara • Associate Professor of Lib Sci • University of Wyoming • Laramie, WY 82071 • YALSA

Chau Mayying • Student • Wayne State University Library Science Program • Detroit, MI 48202

Chau Weihsin • Brookline, MA 02146

Chauffe Dolores L. • Head Librarian • Hahnville High School Library • Boutte, LA 70039 • AASL YALSA

Chauhan Ram • Director • East Saint Louis Public Library • East St. Louis, IL 62201

Chaussee Mary Jane • Assistant Director • Bismarck Veterans Memorial Public Library • Bismarck, ND 58501

Chauvin Laurel S. • New Orleans, LA 70119

Chavez-Samaniego Carmen • Librarian • Library of Congress • Washington, DC 20541

Chavez Frances • Trustee • Prince William Public Library System Administrative Support Center • Prince William, VA 22192-5073

Chavez Gilbert T. • Librarian II Cataloger • San Bernardino County Library Rancho Cucamonga Branch • Cucamonga, CA 91730

Chavez Joan • Lincoln Elementary School • Lancaster, CA 93534

Chavez Linda • Los Angeles County Public Library East Los Angeles Branch • Los Angeles, CA 90022

Chaw Gladys • College of San Mateo Library • San Mateo, CA 94402 • ACRL

Chawziuk Joan T. • School Librarian • Fairgrounds Elementary School • Nashua, NH 03060

Cheatham Bertha M. • Chappaqua, NY 10514 • AASL ALSC

Cheatham Gary L. • Reference Librarian • Northeastern Oklahoma State University John Vaughan Library-LRC • Tahlequah, OK 74464

Cheatham Gordon K. • Copperas Cove, TX 76522

Cheatham Mary L. • Director • Mid-Arkansas Regional Library • Malvern, AR 72104 • PLA

Cheatwood Luci • Media Specialist • Montebello Elementary School • Baltimore, MD 21214 • AASL

Check Walter A • Librarian • Antelope Valley High School • Lancaster, CA 93535 • AASL

Chee Kathleen A. • Librarian • Hawaii Pacific University Meader Library • Honolulu, HI 96813-3192 • ACRL LITA

Cheek Belinda L. • Technical Services • North Central College Oesterle Library • Naperville, IL 60540

Cheeseman Margaret • Portland, IN 47371 • ASCLA PLA   *Life*

Chekon Theresa Black • Coordinator Childrens Service • Sacramento Public Library • Sacramento, CA 95814 • ALSC

Chekouras R. A. • Chicago, IL 60640

Chelariu Ana Radu • Director • Palisades Park Public Library • Palisades Park, NJ 07650 • PLA

Chelmow Linda • Williamsburg, VA 23185

Chelton Mary K. • Milltown, NJ 08850 • PLA YALSA IFRT

Chen Agnes M. • Youth Services Librarian • Contra Costa County Library El Cerrito Branch • El Cerrito, CA 94530

Chen Barbara A. • Associate Dir of Indexing Serv. • H. W. Wilson Company • Bronx, NY 10452 • LITA RASD

Chen Carrie C. • Catalog Service Librarian • Eastern Illinois University Booth Library • Charleston, IL 61920-3099

Chen Cecilia M. • Cataloger • California State University-Dominguez Hills Library • Carson, CA 90747 • ACRL ALCTS

Chen Chih-Hui • Assistant Cataloger/Database Mgr • University of Maryland-Eastern Shore Frederick Douglass Library • Princess Anne, MD 21853 • LITA

Chen Ching-chih • Professor & Associate Dean • Simmons College Graduate School of Library & Information Science • Boston, MA 02115 • LITA IRRT LRRT

Chen Chiou-Sen • Bridgewater, NJ 08807 • ALCTS

Chen Diana • Childrens Librarian • Fort Lee Public Library • Fort Lee, NJ 07024

Chen Effie Y H • Asst. Interlibrary Svs Libn • Princeton University • Princeton, NJ 08544-2098

Chen Gwen A. • Children's Librarian • Lake County Library • Lakeport, CA 95453 • ALSC

Chen Huijie • Graduate Student • Indiana University School of Library and Information Science • Bloomington, IN 47405 • ACRL

Chen Ida K. • Trustee • Free Library of Philadelphia • Philadelphia, PA 19103 • ALTA

Chen Jie-Hong • Student • University of Southern Mississippi School of Library Science • Hattiesburg, MS 39406-5146

Chen Jieru • Student • University of Illinois Graduate School of Library and Information Science • Urbana, IL 61801

Chen Kao-Chung • Cataloging • National Institute of the Arts • Taipei, 24702, Taiwan • ACRL ALCTS LITA

Chen Kimberly Y.F. • Revelle Hawkins Public School • Bellevue, WA 98004

Chen Kwei-Ying Kay • Acquisition Librarian • Boston Public Library • Boston, MA 02117

Chen Laura F. • Hd,General Catlg Unit • New Mexico State University Library • Las Cruces, NM 88003-0006

Chen Liang-Han Mr. • Branch Library Manager • Queens Borough Public Library Forest Hills Branch • Forest Hills, NY 11375 • PLA

Chen Lilian L. • Head of Cataloging Department • University of Saint Thomas • Houston, TX 77006

Chen Lily • Adult Services Librarian • Ridgefield Park Public Library • Ridgefield Park, NJ 07660

Chen Majorie • Circulation Librarian • Miami-Dade Public Library System West Dade Regional Library • Miami, FL 33165

Chen Meei-Ling • Syracuse, NY 13210 • LITA

Chen Mingliang • Hampton, VA 23663-2344

Chen Peiling • Student • Florida State University School of Library and Information Studies • Tallahassee, FL 32306-2048

Chen Robert P. • Documents Coordinator • Eastern Illinois University Booth Library • Charleston, IL 61920-3099 • GODORT

Chen Shangyu • Student • Saint John's University Division of Library & Information Science • Jamaica, NY 11439

Chen Shu-hsien L. Mrs • University of Georgia Department of Instructional Technolgy • Athens, GA 30602 • AASL LRRT

Chen Veronica L. • Director of Library Services • Butler County Community College Library • Butler, PA 16003-1203 • ACRL

Chen Xiao K. • Student • University of South Florida School of Library & Information Science • Tampa, FL 33620

Chen Yueh-Lin • Student • Queens College Graduate School of Library & Information Studies • Flushing, NY 11367

Chen Yvonne • Advocate, Reference Services • Seattle Public Library • Seattle, WA 98104-1193 • PLA RASD

Chenault Elizabeth A. • Rare Book Collection Librarian • University of North Carolina • Chapel Hill, NC 27599-3902 • ACRL

Chenevert Susan R. • Librarian I • East Baton Rouge Parish Library • Baton Rouge, LA 70806-7699 • PLA

Cheney Catherine P. • Trustee • York Public Library • Yorktown, VA 23692

Cheney Craig H. • Regional Sales Manager • Book Wholesalers Inc. • Lexington, KY 40511 • YALSA

Cheney Debora L. • Documents Librarian/Cataloger • Pennsylvania State University Pattee Library • University Park, PA 16802 • ACRL RASD GODORT

Cheney Debra M. • Dover, NH 03820 • AASL

Cheney Frances N. • Newberry, SC 29108-9310 • AASL ACRL ALCTS ALSC ALTA ASCLA LAMA LITA RASD YALSA   *Honorary*

Cheney Harold W. Jr • Asst Dean for Lib Sys/Auto Res • Indiana State University Cunningham Memorial Library • Terre Haute, IN 47809 • LITA

Cheney Nancy W. • Regional Marketing Manager • OCLC Online Computer Library Center • Dublin, OH 43017-3395 • ALCTS

Cheney Patricia S. • Student • Wayne State University • Detroit, MI 48202

Cheng Alice Hua Liang • Muncie, IN 47304 • ALCTS

Cheng Annie H. • Children's Librarian • San Jose Public Library Almaden Branch • San Jose, CA 95120

Cheng Charmian S. • Chinese Catlg/ Hd of Public Serv • Princeton University Gest Oriental Library & East Asian Clln • Princeton, NJ 08540

Cheng Ching-Yi Jasmine • Boca Raton, FL 33433

Cheng Cynthia Jean • Penn Valley Community College Library • Kansas City, MO 64111

Cheng George C. • Reference Librarian • San Francisco State University J. Paul Leonard Library • San Francisco, CA 94132

Cheng Juliana M. • Regional Manager • Los Angeles Public Library Northeast Region • Los Angeles, CA 90042 • PLA

Cheng Louise M. • Librarian/Indexer • Labat-Anderson Incorporated EPA Superfund Records Center • San Francisco, CA 94105

Cheng Phyllis S. • Catalog Librarian • Portsmouth Public Library • Portsmouth, VA 23704

Cheng Po-Ying • 4 Wah Lok Path, Hong Kong • VRT

Cheng Rosemary • Honolulu, HI 96828 • ALSC

Cheng Xiao J. • Student • Southern Connecticut State University School of Libray Science & Instructional Technology • New Haven, CT 06515

Chenoweth Rose M. • Director • Goshen Public Library • Goshen, IN 46526 • LAMA PLA

Chenoweth Susan J. • Valrico, FL 33594

Chepesiuk Ron J. • Head Special Collections • Winthrop College Ida Jane Dacus Library • Rock Hill, SC 29733 • IRRT

Chepko Karen D. • Student • Florida State University School of Library and Information Studies • Tallahassee, FL 32306-2048 • AASL ACRL LITA

Cherbosque Cathy A. • Student • University of California-Los Angeles (UCLA) • Los Angeles, CA 90024-1450 • ACRL

Cheresnowski Linda M. • Secretary/Treasurer • Ski S Market Inc • Clintonville, PA 16372 • AASL ALSC

Cherniack Jay Mrs. • Trustee • Omaha Public Library • Omaha, NE 68102 • ALTA

Chernik Barbara E. • Kenosha, WI 53143 • PLA

Chernofsky Jacob L. • Editor • AB Bookmans Weekly • Clifton, NJ 07015 • ACRL ALCTS RASD ERT IFRT IRRT LHRT MAGERT

Chernow Paige A. • Student • University of California-Berkeley University Library • Berkeley, CA 94720

Chernowski-Mancuso Ellen M. • Monroe Community College LeRoy V. Good Library • Rochester, NY 14623-0701 • LITA NMRT

Cherny Cynthia J. • Milwaukee, WI 53211 • IRRT LRRT

Cherry Chanie M. • Librarian • South Mississippi Regional Library • Columbia, MS 39429 • RASD

Cherry Ed • Samford University Library • Birmingham, AL 35229

Cherry Philip III • Administrative Officer • Public Library of Charlotte & Mecklenburg County • Charlotte, NC 28202 • LAMA

Cherry Virginia R. • Stony Creek, VA 23882

Cherup Nadya • Librarian II • Detroit Public Library • Detroit, MI 48202

Chervenak Joseph F. • Manager,Library Services • National Renewable Energy Laboratory • Golden, CO 80401 • LITA

Chervenie Paul B. • Library Supervisor I • Enoch Pratt Free Library • Baltimore, MD 21201-4484

Chervinko James S. • Cataloger • Southern Illinois University Delyte W. Morris Library • Carbondale, IL 62901-6632 • ACRL

Chery Marc A. • Chicago, IL 60626 • SRRT

Chesbro Melinda S. • Systems Librarian • University of Colorado-Boulder University Libraries • Boulder, CO 80309 • LITA

Chesham Jane • Public Services Librarian • Bellwood Public Library • Bellwood, IL 60104 • PLA

Chesher Catherine H. • Student • University of Michigan School of Information and Library Studies • Ann Arbor, MI 48109-1092

Chesher Joyce A. Ms. • Corporate Librarian • DFW Airport Board Library • DFW Airport, TX 75261 • LITA

Chesire Esther E. Miss • Albuquerque, NM 87104 • ACRL RASD   *Continuing*

Cheski Richard • State Librarian • State Library of Ohio • Columbus, OH 43266-0334 • ASCLA

Chesky Pamela • Student • Rutgers University School of Communication Information & Library Studies • New Brunswick, NJ 08903 • AASL

Chesley Ed A. • Librarian • Appalachian Bible College • Bradley, WV 25818 • ACRL

Chesley Thea B. • Coordinator of Library Services • Illinois Department of Corrections • Springfield, IL 62794-9277 • ASCLA NMRT

Chesney Jane E. • The Woodlands, TX 77380 • AASL

Chesnut Barbara A. • Trustee • Havelock Aluminum • Lincoln, NE 68507 • ALTA

Chesser Linda R. • Student • Northern Illinois University Department of Library & Information Studies • DeKalb, IL 60115

Chesser Sally A. • Network Consultant • Kentucky Library Network • Frankfort, KY 40602 • ASCLA LITA

Chesser Susan G. • Baton Rouge, LA 70806

Chessman Rebecca L. • Dist Librarian • School District • Belmont, CA 94002 • AASL ALSC

Chest Sarah A. • Henry Highland Garnet School for Success PS 175/IS 275 • New York, NY 10030 • AASL

Chester Mary J. • Librarian • Saint Rose Primary Resource • St. Rose, LA 70087

Chestnut Barbara L. • Hershey, PA 17033 • AASL

Chetner Sylvia R. S. • Librarian • John W. Scott Health Sciences Library University of Alberta Library • Edmonton AB, T6G 2R7 Canada • ACRL

Cheung Hiu-Ling • Student • University of South Florida School of Library & Information Science • Tampa, FL 33620 • LITA

Cheuvront Florence Z. • Rialto, CA 92376

Cheverie Joan F. • Government Doc./Microforms Libn • Georgetown University Joseph Mark Lauinger Library • Washington, DC 20057-1006 • ACRL LAMA GODORT

Chew Katherine Lex • APO, AE 09012

Chew Susan M. • Middle School Librarian • Episcopal Junior Senior High School • Baton Rouge, LA 70816 • AASL

Chewning Miriam D. • Student • University of South Carolina College of Library & Information Science • Columbia, SC 29208

Chezem Joan • Librarian • Cincinnati Country Day School • Cincinnati, OH 45243 • AASL

Chiang Belinda • Head, Cataloging Dept. • Queens College Benjamin S. Rosenthal Library • Flushing, NY 11367-0904 • ALCTS

Chiang Hsingfang • Richardson, TX 75082

Chiang Hsiu-Ying • Senior Cataloger • National Central Library • Taipei, 100, Taiwan • ALCTS LITA

Chiang Katherine S. • Cornell University Albert R. Mann Library • Ithaca, NY 14853-4301 • ACRL

Chiang Kathy • Taipei, Taiwan

Chiang Nancy S. • Head, Technical Services • Hartwick College Stevens German Library • Oneonta, NY 13820

Chiang Pi-lien • St. Paul, MN 55108

Chiang Veronica T. • Librarian/Tech Serv/Exhibits • California State University • Fullerton, CA 92634 • LITA

Chiappisi Andrea L. • Reference Librarian • Corvallis-Benton County Public Library • Corvallis, OR 97330-4728

Chiaverotti Betty • Branch Librarian Supervisor • Warren Public Library • Warren, MI 48092 • PLA

Chichester Joy M. • Midland, MI 48640

Chickering F. William • Pratt Institute Library • Brooklyn, NY 11205 • AASL ACRL ALCTS LAMA LITA PLA RASD YALSA FLRT

Chickering Susan R. • National Gallery of Art Library • Washington, DC 20565 • LITA

Chicorel Eva Marietta • Director • American Library Publishing Company • Sedona, AZ 86340 • AASL ACRL   *Life*

Chidiac Sheila • Children's Librarian • Leonia Public Library • Leonia, NJ 07605

Chie Margarita E. • Student • University of California Los Angeles Graduate School of Library & Information Science • Los Angeles, CA 90024

Chien Shou-Fen T. • Stow, OH 44224

Chijioke Mary Ellen • Friends Historical Library of Swathmore College • Swarthmore, PA 19081 • ACRL ALCTS LITA

Chikiasuye June • Coor, Instructional Materials • San Lorenzo Unified School District • San Lorenzo, CA 94580 • AASL

Chikombah Rosemary T. • Harare, Zimbabwe

Chilcoat Nancy L. • Branch Manager • Lake Lanier Regional Library Mountain Park Branch • Lilburn, GA 30247

Chilcote Sanford M. • Regional Librarian • Labrador and Northern Regional Library Offices • Labrador City NF, A2V 2J8 Canada • IRRT

Child Margaret S. • Washington, DC 20009 • ALCTS

Childers Martha P. • Head of Cataloging • San Diego County Law Library • San Diego, CA 92101-3999 • ALCTS PLA GODORT IFRT

Childers Sumie Y. • Catalog Librarian • La Mesa Spring Valley School District • La Mesa, CA 92041 • LITA

Childers Thomas A. • Prof Information Studies • Drexel University College of Information Studies • Philadelphia, PA 19104-2875 • LAMA PLA RASD LRRT

Childers Virginia • Media Specialist • Symington Elementary School • Kansas City, MO 64134 • AASL

Childres Betty P. • Kennesaw State College • Marietta, GA 30061

Childres Sydney D. • Knoxville, TN 37917 • IFRT

Childress Carol B. • Statesville High School • Statesville, NC 28677

Childress Eric R. • Elon College Iris Holt McEwen Library • Elon College, NC 27244-0187 • ACRL ALCTS LITA IFRT

Childrey Cynthia A. • Sr. Ref/Bibliographic Instr. • Northern Arizona University Cline Library • Flagstaff, AZ 86011-6022 • ACRL RASD SRRT

Childs Mimi P. • Media Specialist • Muscogee County School District • Columbus, GA 31904

Childs Tracey D. • Philadelphia, PA 19150 • PLA

Chiles Michael • Trustee • Montclair Free Public Library • Montclair, NJ 07042

Chilian Linda L • Assistant Technical Inf. Serv. • Glaxo Inc. • Zebulon, NC 27597

Chilmonczyk Dianne M. • Co Chief Catalog Department • Stanford University • Stanford, CA 94305-6011 • ALCTS

Chilson Shirley E. • Head of Information Services • Waukesha Public Library • Waukesha, WI 53186 • RASD

Chilton Christine M. • Branch Librarian • Tulsa City-County Library Martin East Regional Library • Tulsa, OK 74129 • PLA

Chilton Kathryn B. • Library Media Specialist • Orlando Junior High School • Orlando Park, IL 60462 • AASL ALSC

Chilton Lisa M. • Library-Technician II • Washington State University • Pullman, WA 99164-2112 • ALSC

Chilton Nelle • Kanawha County Public Library • Charleston, WV 25301 • ALTA

Chin Bess • School Librarian • Redwood High School • Larkspur, CA 94939 • YALSA

Chin Elise L. • Head Cataloging Librarian • University of Washington East Asia Library • Seattle, WA 98195 • ACRL

Chin Janet A. • Sr Cataloger Research Collection • University Microfilms International • Ann Arbor, MI 48106-1346 • ALCTS IFRT

Chin Janet M. • Librarian • Hockessin Public Library • Hockessin, DE 19707 • LAMA PLA

Chin Linda S. • Student • San Jose State University Division of Library & Information Science • San Jose, CA 95192-0029

Chin Loretta • Coordinator Learning Resource • Alameda County Schools Learning Resources • Hayward, CA 94544

Chin Siew-Ben • Wheaton, IL 60189

Chin Warrick Hwa-ruey • Algoma University College Library Arthur A. Wishart Library • Sault St. Marie ON, P6A 2G4 Canada • LITA

Chinault Jane • Assistant Librarian • Airport High School Library • West Columbia, SC 29170 • AASL

Chinery Dorothy H. • Librarian • Rutherford County Schools Smyrna West School • Smyrna, TN 37130

Ching Carolyn S. H. • Student • University of Hawaii School of Library & Information Studies • Honolulu, HI 96822 • IFRT SRRT

Ching Edith I. • Student • Saint Albans School • Washington, DC 20016 • YALSA

Ching Ellen K. Y. • Eugene, OR 97405 • Continuing

Ching Eng K. • Toronto ON, M6C 1G5 Canada

Ching Winnie • Tackan Elementary School • Nesconset, NY 11767

Chinik Mildred K. • Pittsburgh, PA 15236 • Continuing

Chipman Ernestine L. • Reference Librarian • Johnson & Gibbs P.C. • Dallas, TX 75202 • LITA RASD

Chipok Robert J. • Catalog Maintenance Librarian • New York University Elmer Holmes Bobst Library • New York, NY 10012 • ALCTS LITA

Chirakos Helen F. • Retrospective Conversion Libn. • Ohio State University Law Library • Columbus, OH 43210 • IFRT

Chirieleison Georgia A. • Head of Children's Services • Fairfax County Public Library Patrick Henry Branch • Vienna, VA 22180 • ALSC

Chisaki Jane M. • Children's Librarian • Alameda Free Library • Alameda, CA 94501 • ALSC

Chisenhall Mary B. • Student • University of Kentucky College of Library & Information Science • Lexington, KY 40506-0391

Chisenhall Patricia J. • Hennepin County Library Brookdale Branch • Brooklyn Center, MN 55430

Chisholm Margaret E. • Director • University of Washington Graduate School of Library and Information Science • Seattle, WA 98195

Chisholm de Cruz Margo L. • Reference Librarian • Crowell & Moring Law Library • Washington, DC 20004

Chism Betty L. • County Librarian & Director • Modoc County Library School Media Centers • Alturas, CA 96101 • AASL

Chisman Janet • Lib User Education Coor. • Washington State University Owen Science & Engineering Library • Pullman, WA 99164-3200 • ACRL RASD

Chisman Janet M. • Information Center Librarian • Kentucky Department for Libraries & Archives • Frankfort, KY 40602-0537 • RASD

Chisum Gloria Twine Dr • Trustee • Free Library of Philadelphia • Philadelphia, PA 19103 • ALTA

Chitty M Elizabeth • Director • Fairchilde International Library Institute • Plainfield, NJ 07060-1609 • ACRL ILERT IRRT

Chitwood Julius R. • Rockford, IL 61104-1246 • LAMA LITA PLA RASD ILERT IRRT *Life*

Chiu Cathy • East Asian Librarian • University of California Library • Santa Barbara, CA 93106 • ACRL

Chiu Kai-Yun • Library Company of the Baltimore Bar • Baltimore, MD 21202 • LAMA

Chiu Norine • Chicago, IL 60626

Chizak Kathleen S. • Coordinator of Libraries • Sosquehanna Valley Schools • Conklin, NY 13748 • AASL

Chlebek Diana • Arts, Language & Lib Biblio • University of Akron University Library & Learning Resource • Akron, OH 44325-1707 • ACRL

Chmelir Lynn K. • College Librarian • Linfield College Northup Library • McMinnville, OR 97128 • ACRL

Chmurynsky Susan E. • Library/Media Specialist • E. Kentwood High School • Grand Rapids, MI 49501 • AASL YALSA

Cho Chansik • Student • Rutgers University School of Communication Information & Library Studies • New Brunswick, NJ 08903

Cho Horton Keiko • Coordinator, Interlibrary Loan • University of Houston Libraries • Houston, TX 77204-2091 • RASD SORT

Cho Yong-Ja • International Development Research Center Information Division • Ottawa ON, K1G 3H9 Canada • ACRL

Choate Beverly H. • Library Media Specialist • Alief Independent School District Hearne Elementary • Houston, TX 77083 • AASL IFRT

Choate Jackie Ms. • Vermilion Parish Library • Abbeville, LA 70510

Chobot Karen M. • John Moritz Library • Omaha, NE 68114

Chobot Mary C. Dr. • Mary C. Chobot & Associates • Annandale, VA 22003-4166 • CLENE ILERT LRRT

Chodacki Roberta A. • East Carolina University Joyner Library • Greenville, NC 27858-4353

Chodorow Julius Mr. • Trustee • The Bryant Library • Roslyn, NY 11576

Choe Judy • Subject Cataloger • Library of Congress • Washington, DC 20541

Choe Sung-In • Associate Librarian • University of California UCSB Library • Santa Barbara, CA 93106-9010

Choi Eunhee • Illinois Department of Employment Security • Chicago, IL 60605

Choi Hyesik • Norman, OK 73072

Choi Hyonggun • Alhambra, CA 91801 • ACRL

Choi Ilze Anna • Adult/Young Adult Librarian • Jefferson Parish Library West Bank Regional Branch • Harvey, LA 70058

Choice Nancy J. • Head, Admin & Borrower Services • Annapolis & Anne Arundel County Public Library • Annapolis, MD 21401-7042 • LAMA PLA YALSA *Life*

Choldin Marianna Tax • Professor • University of Illinois Library • Urbana, IL 61801 • ACRL IFRT LHRT

Choncoff Mary • Tempe, AZ 85282

Chong Eleanor Hung • Student • University of New South Wales • Kensington NSW 2033, Australia

Chong Pearl • School Librarian • Saint Hubert Catholic High School • Philadelphia, PA 19136 • AASL

Chong Sam • California Newsreel • San Francisco, CA 94103 • VRT

Chong Sue C. • Supv. Library Tech • Pearl Habor Naval Shipyard • Pearl Harbor, HI 96860-5350 • PLA FLRT

Chook Mindi • Student • University of South Florida School of Library & Information Science • Tampa, FL 33620

Chopko Roberta • Boonton, NJ 07005 • ALTA

Choppin Joy B • Librarian • Georgetown Prep School • Rockville, MD 20852 • AASL

Chopra Linda • Reference Librarian • Cleveland Heights-University Heights Public Library • Cleveland Heights, OH 44118 • PLA

Choquette Mary Beth • Hollis, NH 03049 • AASL

Choszczyk E. Annette • Library Manager • Arapahoe Library District Glendale Library • Denver, CO 80222

Chou Chih-hua • Reference Librarian • Lake Jackson Public Library • Lake Jackson, TX 77566

Chou Chiu-chuang • Data Librarian • University of Wisconsin Data & Program Library Service • Madison, WI 53705

Chou Margaret Yu-Lan • Chinese Cataloger • Ohio State University Libraries • Columbus, OH 43210-1286 • ACRL ALCTS

Chou Marian T. • Children's Librarian • Indianapolis-Marion County Public Library Shelby Branch • Indianapolis, IN 46203-4236 • ALSC

Chou Michaelyn P. Dr. • Librarian V • University of Hawaii Thomas Hale Hamilton Library • Honolulu, HI 96822 • ACRL RASD EMIERT

Chou Pei Hua • Director Learning Resources • Cuyamaca College • El Cajon, CA 92019

Chou Penny L. • Media Specialist • P.K. Yonge Lab School • Gainesville, FL 32601 • AASL

Chou Yi-Chih • Student • University of Michigan School of Information and Library Studies • Ann Arbor, MI 48109-1092

Chou Yi-Wen • Pittsburgh, PA 15213

Chow Diana • Trustee • Alhambra Public Library • Alhambra, CA 91801

Chow Donna S. • Director of Public Library • Autauga-Prattville Public Library • Prattville, AL 36067 • ALSC EMIERT

Chow Ruey-hwa • Coordinator Tech Processes • Dayton & Montgomery County Public Library • Dayton, OH 45402-2103

Chowdhury Mostaque A. Md. • Student • Pratt Institute Graduate School of Library & Information Science • Brooklyn, NY 11205

Chowning Ricki L. • Media Director • East Grand Rapids High School • Grand Rapids, MI 49506 • AASL YALSA IFRT

Choy Fatt-Cheong • Chief Librarian • Singapore Armed Forces Singapore Command & Staff College • Singapore 2879, Singapore • AFLRT

Choy Natalie • Librarian • Hong Kong International School • Tai Tam, Hong Kong

Chressanthis June D. • Serials Cataloger • Mississippi State University Mitchell Memorial Library • Mississippi State, MS 39762 • ALCTS LAMA

Chris Veronica A. • Acquisitions Librarian • Seton Hall University Law Library • Newark, NJ 07102

Chrisman Diane J. • Deputy Director • Buffalo & Erie County Public Library • Buffalo, NY 14203 • PLA

Chrisman Vicki L. • Iberia Parish Library • New Iberia, LA 70560

Chrismore Tina L. • Library Assistant • Fluor Daniel, Inc. • Chicago, IL 60606 • LAMA IRRT

Christ Caryl • Reference & Young Adult • Smithtown Library Nesconset Branch • Nesconset, NY 11767

Christ Ruth E. • Serials Librarian • University of Iowa Libraries • Iowa City, IA 52242-1379 • ACRL ALCTS LITA IRRT

Christel Mark A. • Student • Rutgers University School of Communication Information & Library Studies • New Brunswick, NJ 08903 • NMRT

Christenberry H. Faye • Ref./Bibl Instr. Librarian • Berea College Hutchins Library • Berea, KY 40404 • ACRL

Christenbury Leila Dr. • Teacher Education • Virginia Commonwealth University • Richmond, VA 23284

Christensen Adele • Media Center Director • Highland Public Schools • Highland, WI 53543

Christensen Beth E. • College Librarian • Saint Olaf College Halvorson Music Library • Northfield, MN 55057 • ACRL

Christensen Beverly J. • Library Media Specialist • Shoultes Elementary School • Marysville, WA 98271 • AASL

Christensen Catherine • Student • Johnson & Johnson • New Brunswick, NJ 08903

Christensen Diane K. • Sutter Creek, CA 95685-0668

Christensen Helen M. Dr • School Library Consultant • California Department of Education Library • Sacramento, CA 95807 • AASL YALSA *Life*

Christensen John T. • Student • DePaul University Libraries • Chicago, IL 60614 • SRRT

Christensen Laura • Trustee • Denver Public Library • Denver, CO 80203-2165 • ALTA PLA

Christensen Nancy • Librarian • Madison Middle School • North Platte, NE 69101 • AASL

Christensen Pamela R. • Library Director • Peter White Public Library • Marquette, MI 49855 • LAMA

Christensen Paul M. Dr. • Librarian • North Kitsap High School • Poulsbo, WA 98370 • AASL

Christensen Phyllis K. • Wausaw, WI 54402 • ALCTS RASD

Christensen R M. • Ontario, CA 91761 • ACRL ALCTS RASD *Life*

Christensen Rebecca S. • Student • University of Michigan School of Information and Library Studies • Ann Arbor, MI 48109-1092 • ALSC

Christensen Richard L. • Circulation Librarian • Illinois State University Milner Library • Normal, IL 61761-0900

Christensen Rita A. Baguio • Children's Librarian • Kirkwood Public Library • Kirkwood, MO 63122

Christensen Ross Alan • Reference Librarian • Hawaii State Library • Honolulu, HI 96813 • RASD

Christensen Susan J. • Denver, CO 80211 • PLA

Christensen Verda Mae • Salt Lake City Public Library • Salt Lake City, UT 84111 • ALTA

Christenson John D. • Director • Traverse des Sioux Library System • Mankato, MN 56002-0608 • ASCLA PLA

Christenson Phyllis R. • Dir., Information Services Ctr. • U. S. General Accounting Office • Washington, DC 20548 • FLRT GODORT

Christenson Shirley J. • District Media Center Coor • Anoka-Hennepin Independent School District #11 • Anoka, MN 55303 • AASL

Christian Clifford • Trustee • Maywood Public Library • Maywood, IL 60153 • ALTA

Christian Diane M. • Head of Young Peoples Department • Aurora Public Library • Aurora, IL 60505-4299 • ALSC

Christian Elaine J. • North Carolina State Library • Raleigh, NC 27601-2807

Christian Gayle R. • Reference/Documents Librarian • Georgia State University Pullen Library • Atlanta, GA 30303-3081 • ACRL RASD GODORT IFRT

Christian Judith A. • Media Specialist • Fairfax County Public Schools • Alexandria, VA 22310 • AASL

Christian Mariel L. • Student • North Carolina Central University • Durham, NC 27707

Christian Michael A. • Librarian • National Society Sons of the American Revolution • Louisville, KY 40203

Christiani Linnea J. • Manager, Vendor Relations • Information Access Company • Foster City, CA 94404 • LITA RASD

Christians Priscilla • Student • University of Illinois School of Library Information Science • Champaign, IL 61820

Christiansen Christine J. • Serials Acquisitions Librarian • University of Miami Libraries Richter Library • Coral Gables, FL 33124 • IFRT

Christiansen Claire B. • Community Library Coordinator • Timberland Regional Library • Olympia, WA 98501 • LAMA PLA

Christiansen Dorothy E. • Hd, Special Clln & Archives • State University of New York (SUNY) University Libraries • Albany, NY 12222 • ACRL ALCTS LAMA RASD

Christiansen Gloria • Neligh Educational Service Unit, #8 • Neligh, NE 68756

Christiansen Hugo W. • Asst Chief Shared Catlg Div • Library of Congress • Washington, DC 20541

Christiansen Irene • Librarian • Glenview Public Library • Glenview, IL 60025 • LAMA

Christiansen Paula • Salt Lake City, UT 84116

Christianson Elin • Hobart, IN 46342 • ACRL LAMA RASD

Christianson Ellory • University of Minnesota Meredith Wilson Library • Minneapolis, MN 55455 • LAMA

Christianson Marilyn C. • Coordinator of Reference • University of North Texas • Denton, TX 76203 • ACRL

Christie Rebecca A. • Washington Department of Natural Resources Division of Geology & Earth Resources • Olympia, WA 98504

Christine Barbara S. • Chief Acquisitions Librarian • United States Air Force CFSC (CFSC-CR-L) • Alexandria, VA 22302 • LITA AFLRT
Christman Kathleen S. • Student • Syracuse University School of Information Studies • Syracuse, NY 13244-4100 • AASL
Christman Marilyn • Trustee • Pittsford Community Library • Pittsford, NY 14534
Christner Lee • Reference Librarian • University of Richmond • Richmond, VA 23173 • LIRT
Christner Terry A. • Public Information Officer • Hutchinson Public Library • Hutchinson, KS 67501 • YALSA
Christolon Blair B. • Manassas, VA 22111 • ALSC
Christopher Frances • Edina, MN 55436 • PLA YALSA *Life*
Christopher Irene • Librarian • Boston University Alumni Medical Library • Boston, MA 02118 • ACRL LAMA RASD
Christopher Lynn • Acquisitions/Catlg Libn • United States News & World Report Library-451 • Washington, DC 20037 • ALCTS
Christopher S. J. Mr. • Lacey, WA 98503 • Continuing
Christopher Sandra C. • Assistant Library Director • Burbank Public Library • Burbank, CA 91502
Christopher Vandy M. • Southwest Regional Library • Fort Worth, TX 76109 • PLA
Christy Ann K. • System Analyst • Library of Congress • Washington, DC 20541 • LITA
Christy Kathleen • Director of Library/LRC • Belmont Technical College • Saint Clairsville, OH 43950 • ILERT IRRT
Chritsman Frances G. • Assistant Librarian • University of Cambridge Syndicate CED Libarary • Cambridge, CB1 2EU, England • RASD
Chrostowski Jennifer A. • Sterling Heights, MI 48310
Chrzastowski Tina E. • Chemistry Librarian • University of Illinois Chemistry Library • Urbana, IL 61801 • ACRL
Chshti Sarfraz H. • Librarian • Pakistan Administrative Staff College • Lahore, Pakistan
Chu Cheng O. • Cataloger • University of California-Davis Library • Davis, CA 95616
Chu Clara M. • Acting Asst. Professor • University of California-Los Angeles (UCLA) • Los Angeles, CA 90024-1450 • EMIERT
Chu Ellin • Young Adult Consultant • Monroe County Library System • Rochester, NY 14604 • YALSA
Chu Felix • President • Transmission Books & Microforms • Taipei ROC, Taiwan
Chu Felix T. • Western Illinois University Libraries • Macomb, IL 61455 • ACRL
Chu Nancy L. • Assistant Professor • Western Illinois University Department of Media & Educational Technology • Macomb, IL 61455 • ALSC
Chu Patrick S.Y. • Acquisitions Librarian • Hong Kong University of Science & Technology University Library • Kowloon, Hong Kong • ALCTS
Chua Boonleng • Hayward, CA 94541
Chuang Marita • Branch Head • Chicago Public Library Roosevelt Branch • Chicago, IL 60608
Chubbuck Judith A. • Omaha, NE 68123 • PLA RASD
Chudowsky Valentine • Senior Librarian • Yale University Sterling Memorial Library • New Haven, CT 06520
Chudy Sylvia • Media Specialist • Dawson Educational Cooperative • Arkadelphia, AR 71923 • AASL
Chulak C.B. Powell • Systems Librarian • The Acad of the New Church The Swedenborg Library • Bryn Athyn, PA 19009 • LAMA PLA
Chulski Marie Duber • Head Reference & Information • Monroe County Library System • Monroe, MI 48161 • LAMA PLA RASD IFRT
Chumas Donna L. • Director • Patchogue-Medford High School • Medford, NY 11763 • AASL
Chuml Thecla Sr • Librarian • Loyola Marymount University-Orange Loyola Marymount Library • Orange, CA 92668-3998 • ACRL
Chun Gale M. • Librarian • Cuyahoga County Public Library Parma Heights Branch • Parma Heights, OH 44130-3086 • PLA RASD SORT
Chun Geri K. • Student • University of California Los Angeles Graduate School of Library & Information Science • Los Angeles, CA 90024 • AASL
Chun Karen • Pearl City, HI 96782 • PLA
Chun Kyungmi • Student • University of North Texas School of Library & Information Sciences • Denton, TX 76203
Chun Stephen B. T. • Montgomery, AL 36111 • ACRL ALCTS LITA RASD GODORT
Chung Catherine L. • Languages Librarian • Phoenix Public Library • Phoenix, AZ 85004
Chung Chih-Wen • Student • University of Pittsburgh School of Library and Information Science • Pittsburgh, PA 15260 • ACRL LITA
Chung Fen-Fang • Madison, WI 53705 • ALCTS
Chung Heeja H. • Head of Cataloging Department • Westchester Library System • Elmsford, NY 10523 • ALCTS
Chung Jay J. • City Librarian • Racine Public Library • Racine, WI 53402 • ALCTS ALSC ALTA LAMA LITA RASD GODORT
Chung Lan-Seng F. • Cordova, TN 38018 • ACRL
Chung Sejin • Serials Librarian • Michigan State University Libraries • East Lansing, MI 48824-1048 • LITA
Chung Sheue-jen Jenny • Catolguer • National Chengchi University Mucha District • Taipei, Taiwan • ACRL
Chupela Dolores C. • Children's Librarian • Edison Free Public Library • Edison, NJ 08817 • ALSC
Church Annette B. • Librarian • Westside Elementary School • Rio Linda, CA 95673 • AASL
Church Barry S. • Chief Librarian • Grimsby Public Library • Grimsby ON, Canada • PLA
Church Jeanne • Trustee • Timberland Regional Library • Olympia, WA 98501 • ALTA
Church Joyce N. • School Library Media Specialist • Otselic Valley Central School Junior & Senior High School • South Otselic, NY 13155-0161 • AASL
Church Sonia J. • Manager,Children's Serv Div • Ventura County Library Services Agency • Ventura, CA 93001 • ALSC
Church Van E. • Reference Librarian • Orange County Library System Orlando Public Library • Orlando, FL 32801-2471
Churchill Lisa • Librarian • Gresham Middle School • Birmingham, AL 35243 • AASL
Churchill Richard J. • Central Connecticut State University Elihu Burritt Library • New Britain, CT 06050 • ACRL GODORT
Churchill Susan Mrs. • Trustee • King County Library System • Seattle, WA 98109-5191 • ALTA LAMA PLA
Churchman Alice • Coordinator of Media Studies • Board of Education • Etobicoke ON, Canada • AASL
Churchwell Charles D. Dr • Dean • Clark-Atlanta University School of Library & Information Studies • Atlanta, GA 30314-4391 • ACRL *Life*
Churgay Lenore • Dearborn Department of Libraries Henry Ford Centennial Library • Dearborn, MI 48126 • LAMA PLA
Churma Thomas P. • Serials Librarian • Hawaii State Library • Honolulu, HI 96813 • ALCTS SRRT
Churukian Ann E. • Vassar College Library • Poughkeepsie, NY 12601
Churukian Araxie P. • Librarian • University of California Rivera Library • Riverside, CA 92517 • ACRL ALCTS EMIERT IRRT
Chute Mary L. • Franklin, MA 02038 • PLA IFRT
Chvatal Donald P. • Auto-Graphics Incorporation • Pomona, CA 91768 • ACRL ALCTS LITA
Chwalek Adele R. • Director of Libraries • Catholic University of America John K. Mullen of Denver Memorial Library • Washington, DC 20064 • ACRL LAMA
Chweh Steven Seokho Dr • Mission Viejo, CA 92691
Chylinski Manya S. • Boston, MA 02116 • LITA RASD IFRT
Cia Patricia K. • Student • University of British Columbia School of Library, Archival & Information Studies • Vancouver BC, V6T 1Z1 Canada • ALCTS PLA
Ciacci K Jane • Head,Cataloging Dept • University of Chicago Library • Chicago, IL 60637-1502 • ACRL ALCTS IRRT
Ciallella Carol A. • Director of Library Services • Miami Memorial Library • Miami, AZ 85539 • PLA RASD
Ciallella Emil A. • Director • Gila County Library District • Miami, AZ 85539 • LAMA
Cianchette Robert M. • Reference Librarian • Davidge Data Systems Corporation • New York, NY 10005
Cianciolo Patricia J. Dr. • Professor • Michigan State University Libraries • East Lansing, MI 48824-1048 • ALSC
Ciani Amerigo T. • Scotts Valley, CA 95066
Ciarfella Roberta • Boston, MA 02109 • ACRL LAMA
Cibbarelli Pamela • Huntington Beach, CA 92648 • LITA ILERT
Cicchetti Christina R. • Curriculum Librarian • La Sierra University Library • Riverside, CA 92515
Ciccone Amy Navratil • Head Librarian • University of Southern California • Los Angeles, CA 90033 • ACRL
Ciccone Michael J. • Student • State University of New York at Albany School of Information Science & Policy • Albany, NY 12222
Cichanowicz Edana McCaffery • Head,Reference Services • Riverhead Free Library • Riverhead, NY 11901 • RASD
Cichowski Stephanie • Trustee • Bridgeview Public Library • Bridgeview, IL 60455 • ALTA IFRT
Cicola William D. • Library Director • Copiague Memorial Public Library • Copiague, NY 11726 • ALTA LAMA LITA PLA RASD
Ciejka Patricia A. • University of Texas Medical Branch Moody Medical Library • Galveston, TX 77555-1035
Cienava Stanley • Asst. Prof. of English • Onondaga Community College Sidney B Coulter Library • Syracuse, NY 13215
Ciesar Lorraine • Library Board Member • Whiting Public Library • Whiting, IN 46394
Cieszynski Izabela M. • Dir of Libraries and Inf Servs. • Newport News Public Library System • Newport News, VA 23607 • LAMA LITA PLA
Cifra Ann M. • Sewickley Public Library • Sewickley, PA 15143
Cihon Alice • Manager-Information Serv • Spencerstuart • Chicago, IL 60611 • LITA
Ciliberti Anne C. • Executive Director • B-P Regional Library Cooperative • Hawthorne, NJ 07456 • ASCLA LITA PLA
Cilluffo Mary • Bloomingdale, IL 60108 • Continuing
Cimermanis Ilze V. • Falls Church, VA 22044
Cimino Maria • New York, NY 10011 • ALSC YALSA *Continuing*
Cinciarelli John V. • Library/Media Specialist • Ferris High School • Jersey City, NJ 07302 • AASL
Cincore Vera R. • Librarian • Compton Unified Sch Dist • Compton, CA 90220 • LIRT LRRT
Cincotta Barbara • Student • Rutgers University School of Communication Information & Library Studies • New Brunswick, NJ 08903 • AASL
Cincotta Margaret A. • East Meadow Public Library • East Meadow, NY 11554-1700 • RASD
Cinquemani Frank L. • Upr Montclair, NJ 07043 • RASD *Continuing*
Cinquino Connie M. • Westminster, MD 21157
Ciolli Antoinette • Brooklyn, NY 11228 • ACRL *Continuing*
Ciorciari Ann A. • Student • Southern Connecticut State University School of Libray Science & Instructional Technology • New Haven, CT 06515
Ciparelli Peter F. • Assistant Director • Manchester Public Library • Manchester, CT 06040 • LAMA NMRT
Cipolla Wilma Reid • Buffalo, NY 14226
Ciporen Fred • Vice President/Gorup Publisher • Library Journal Cahners Publishing Company • New York, NY 10011
Ciraula Joan Sister • Cataloging Librarian • Marywood College Library Learning Resources Center • Scranton, PA 18509 • RASD
Cirillo Susan E. • Associate University Librarian • University of Massachusetts-Dartmouth Library • North Dartmouth, MA 02747 • ACRL LAMA LITA
Cirullo Betty • Librarian • Immaculate Conception Academy • San Francisco, CA 94110 • AASL
Cisco Dan E. • Honnolulu, HI 96814 • LITA RASD
Cisler Steve A. • Senior Scientist • Apple Computer, Inc. Library • Cupertino, CA 95014 • LITA
Ciszek Margaret W. • Student • Rosary College Graduate School of Library & Information Science • River Forest, IL 60305
Ciucki Marcella A. • Chief of Technical Services • Lake County Public Library • Merrillville, IN 46410-5382
Ciurczak Alexis K. • Public Services Librarian • Palomar Community College Library • San Marcos, CA 92069 • ACRL ILERT IRRT
Civkin Shelley J. • Librarian • Richmond Public Library • Richmond BC, V7C 4N1 Canada
Claassen Janet W. • Fresno, CA 93710
Clabo Carrie A. • Librarian • Pigeon Forge Primary School • Pigeon Forge, TN 37863-9799 • AASL ALSC
Clack Carolyn • Elmira, NY 14905 • AASL
Clack Doris H. Dr. • Professor • Florida State University School of Library and Information Studies • Tallahassee, FL 32306-2048 • ACRL ALCTS
Clack Mary E. • Serial Records Librarian • Harvard College Library Widener Memorial Library • Cambridge, MA 02138 • ACRL ALCTS LAMA
Claer Joycelyn H. • Coord of Pub Servs/Outreach • Kilgore College R C Watson Library • Kilgore, TX 75662
Claerbout Diane S. • San Mateo County Library • San Mateo, CA 94402
Claiborne Ian W. • Judge • Pointe Coupee Parish Library • New Road, LA 70760 • ALTA
Clamme Rosalie A. • Director • Jay County Public Library • Portland, IN 47371
Clampit Lucy L. • Sherwood Elementary School • Houston, TX 77043 • AASL
Clamurro Anita R. • Assoc. Hd. Libn., Access Servs. • Massachusetts Institute of Technology Libraries (MIT) • Cambridge, MA 02139 • ACRL LAMA
Clancy Anne F. • Assistant Librarian • Clear Lake High School Clear Creek Independent School District • Houston, TX 77058 • AASL YALSA

Clancy Bridget Arthur • Librarian • University of Pennsylvania • Philadephia, PA 19104 • ACRL ALCTS

Clancy Catherine M. • Head,YA Services/General Library • Boston Public Library • Boston, MA 02117 • YALSA

Clancy Marguerite A. • Assistant to Director • South Hadley Library System • South Hadley, MA 01075

Clancy Ron • Chief Librarian • New Westminster Public Library • New Westminster BC, V3M 2B3 Canada

Clanton-Green Kimberly E. • Las Vegas-Clark County Library Rainbow Branch • Las Vegas, NV 89108

Clanton Kay • Director • Washington County Library System • Greenville, MS 38701 • ALSC ALTA LAMA PLA

Clapham Thomas Jr • Head of Adult Services • Cherry Hill Free Public Library • Cherry Hill, NJ 08034 • RASD

Clapp David F. • Assistant Director for Ext. Serv • Chattanooga-Hamilton County Bicentennial Library • Chattanooga, TN 37402 • LAMA PLA

Clapper Thomas H. • Committee Staff • Oklahoma State Senate • Oklahoma City, OK 73105

Clare Allen J. D.D.S. • Trustee • Coalinga-Huron Library District • Coalinga, CA 93210

Clarence Judy • California State University Hayward Library • Hayward, CA 94542 • ACRL RASD LIRT

Clareson Thomas F. R. • AMIGOS Preservation Service Mgr. • AMIGOS Bibliographic Council,Inc. • Dallas, TX 75251-2104 • ALCTS

Clariday Sandra C. • Director of Library • Tennessee Wesleyan College • Athens, TN 37303 • ACRL ALCTS

Clarie Thomas C. • Reference Librarian • Southern Connecticut State University Hilton C. Buley Library • New Haven, CT 06515 • ACRL RASD IRRT

Clark Alan • Reference Librarian • Emory University Libraries Robert W. Woodruff Library • Atlanta, GA 30322-2870 • ACRL LIRT

Clark Alan B. Mr • Director • Albuquerque Public Library • Albuquerque, NM 87102 • LAMA PLA *Life*

Clark Alice S. • Davis, CA 95616

Clark Alleda • Librarian • Livermore Public Library • Livermore, CA 94550 • PLA

Clark Barbara C. Dr • Dean of Learning Resources • Pitt Community College • Greenville, NC 27835-7007 • ACRL LAMA IFRT

Clark Barbara H. • Central Region Manager • Los Angeles Public Library Angeles Mesa Branch • Los Angeles, CA 90043

Clark Barbara Lee • Assistant Head of Extension • Columbus Metropolitan Library • Columbus, OH 43215

Clark Barbara S. • Educ Research Librarian • State University of New York (SUNY) College at Geneseo Milne Library • Geneseo, NY 14454-1498 • ACRL

Clark Barton M. • Director of Departmental Lib Svs • University of Illinois Library • Urbana, IL 61801 • ACRL LAMA LITA LRRT

Clark Betty S. • Assistant Director • Durham County Library • Durham, NC 27702

Clark Blair B. • Culver, IN 46511 • AASL ALCTS

Clark Carlenea K. • Serials Cataloger • Public Library of Cincinnati and Hamilton County • Cincinnati, OH 45202

Clark Carol P. • Head Librarian • R E Lee High School • Springfield, VA 22150 • AASL

Clark Carolyn L. • Librarian, Film Department • Atlanta-Fulton Public Library • Atlanta, GA 30303 • ACRL PLA EMIERT LIRT SRRT

Clark Charlene K. • Development & Promotion Coor • Texas A & M University Sterling C. Evans Library • College Station, TX 77843-5000 • LAMA

Clark Charlotte L. • Sr. Children's Librarian • Queens Borough Public Library • Jamaica, NY 11432 • ALSC PLA EMIERT IFRT

Clark Charlotte R. • Carbondale, IL 62901

Clark Cynthia D. • Head of Serials Dept. • University of California General Library • Irvine, CA 92713 • ALCTS LAMA

Clark Cynthia L. • Reston, VA 22091

Clark David L. • Chairman • Los Angeles City Historical Society • Los Angeles, CA 90041 • LITA

Clark David S. • Director • Indian Valley Public Library • Telford, PA 18969 • PLA

Clark Deborah K. • Library Director • Alhambra Public Library • Alhambra, CA 91801 • LAMA PLA

Clark Deborah K. • Media Specialist • Maple Elementary • Indianapolis, IN 46234 • AASL

Clark Dene L. • Reference Librarian • University of Colorado at Denver Auraria Library • Denver, CO 80204 • ACRL SRRT

Clark Denise L. • Public Services Librarian • North Idaho College Library • Coeur d'Alene, ID 83814 • RASD

Clark Donna • Wilkinson Library • Telluride, CO 81435

Clark Edith • Librarian • Coldspring Area Public Library • Coldspring, TX 77331

Clark Edith M. • Davidson, NC 28036 • PLA RASD *Continuing*

Clark Elaine M. • Director • South Orange Public Library • South Orange, NJ 07079 • SRRT

Clark Elizabeth B. • Student • Florida State University School of Library and Information Studies • Tallahassee, FL 32306-2048 • LITA LRRT SRRT

Clark Ellen • San Antonio Public Library • San Antonio, TX 78205

Clark Ellen B. • Wilmette Public Library • Wilmette, IL 60091

Clark Emma • Supervising Reference Librarian • Richmond Public Library • Richmond, CA 94804 • RASD

Clark Ernestine F. • Volunteer Coordinator • Metropolitan L Sys Downtown • Oklahoma City, OK 73102 • PLA

Clark Georgette D. • Asst. Coor.-Public Serv Support • Brooklyn Public Library • Brooklyn, NY 11238 • PLA RASD YALSA

Clark Georgia H. • Fayetteville, AR 72703-5172 • Continuing

Clark Gerald • Manager of Library Computer Sys • University of Chicago Library • Chicago, IL 60637-1502 • LITA

Clark Geraldine • New Rochelle, NY 10801 • Continuing

Clark Hazel C. • Cinnaminson, NJ 08077 • Continuing

Clark Heidi G. • Children's Librarian • County of Los Angeles Public Library Valencia Library 113 • Valenica, CA 91355 • ALSC

Clark Helen E. • Libraria II • Phoenix Public Library Saguaro Branch • Phoenix, AZ 85008 • PLA

Clark Helen T. • Las Vegas, NV 89122

Clark Jay B. • Library Director • San Jacinto College Lee Davis Library • Pasadena, TX 77505-2007 • ACRL LAMA LITA *Life*

Clark Jeffrey M. • Geography & Map Division Ln • Library of Congress • Washington, DC 20541 • MAGERT

Clark Joan B. • Public Services Librarian • Rockford College • Rockford, IL 61108-2393 • ACRL

Clark Joan L. • Head of Main Library • Cleveland Public Library • Cleveland, OH 44114-1271 • LAMA PLA

Clark John K. • Head Librarian • Springfield City Library Forest Park Branch • Springfield, MA 01108 • PLA RASD

Clark Joseph S. • Librarian II • New Orleans Public Library • New Orleans, LA 70140 • VRT

Clark Joyce R. • Carson City, NV 89703 • GODORT IFRT

Clark Juleigh M. • Reference Librarian • Virginia Commonwealth University • Richmond, VA 23284-2033 • RASD

Clark Karen A. • Independent Sales Rep. • Brodart Company • Williamsport, PA 17705

Clark Katharine E. • Head, Life Sciences Library • Pennsylvania State University Pattee Library • University Park, PA 16802 • ACRL LITA

Clark Kathleen A. • Student • University of Illinois Graduate School of Library and Information Science • Urbana, IL 61801

Clark Kathleen E. • Student • University of Washington Graduate School of Library and Information Science • Seattle, WA 98195 • IFRT SRRT

Clark Kathleen L. • Adult Services Librarian • Baldwin Public Library • Birmingham, MI 48012-3002

Clark Kathleen L. • Children's Librarian • Mountain View Public Library • Mountain View, CA 94041 • ALSC

Clark Kay S. • Akron-Summit County Public Library • Akron, OH 44326-0001 • RASD

Clark Laura A. • APO, AP 96555-2526 • AASL

Clark Lewis J. • Vershire, VT 05079-9801 • ACRL

Clark Linda A. • Student • University of Texas at Austin Graduate School of Library & Information Sciences • Austin, TX 78712-1276 • ACRL

Clark Linda L. • Librarian • East Coast Bible Coll • Charlotte, NC 28214 • ACRL

Clark Maeve K. • Asst. Director/Head Adult Serv. • Carnegie-Stout Public Library • Dubuque, IA 52001 • PLA

Clark Maperal • Assistant Director • Macon County-Tuskegee Public Library • Tuskegee, AL 36083 • PLA EMIERT NMRT

Clark Margaret E. • Wausau, WI 54401 • ALCTS *Continuing*

Clark Margaret G. • Program Services • Kansas City Public Library • Kansas City, MO 64106 • ERT

Clark Margaret L. • Senior Librarian • East Orange Public Library • East Orange, NJ 07018 • ALSC

Clark Margaret M. • Cleveland, OH 44118 • AASL ALSC *Continuing*

Clark Marguerite M. • Forest Grove, OR 97116 • AASL YALSA *Life*

Clark Maria • Principal Catalog Librarian • Yale University Sterling Memorial Library • New Haven, CT 06520 • ACRL IFRT IRRT

Clark Marie L. • Head of Public Documents & Maps • Duke University William R. Perkins Library • Durham, NC 27706 • ACRL GODORT SRRT

Clark Marilyn • Librarian • Mark & Emily Turner Memorial Library • Presque Isle, ME 04769 • PLA IFRT

Clark Marilyn L. • Children's Coordinator • Toledo-Lucas County Public Library • Toledo, OH 43624 • ALSC PLA

Clark Marilyn P. • Library Media Specialist • Dryden Middle School • Juneau, AK 99801 • AASL

Clark Marsha S. • Monographic Acquisitions Ln • New York University Elmer Holmes Bobst Library • New York, NY 10012 • ALCTS

Clark Martha W. • Bassett, VA 24055

Clark Mary Anne • Librarian • Lakeview School • Phoenix, AZ 85029 • AASL

Clark Mary Elizabeth • Instructor/Biblio Records Libn • University of Tennessee T Carter & M Rawlings Lupton Lib • Chattanooga, TN 37403

Clark Mary J. • Reference Librarian • Crane Public Library • Quincy, MA 02169 • PLA RASD

Clark Mary L. • Student • Rosary College Graduate School of Library & Information Science • River Forest, IL 60305 • ALCTS LITA

Clark Mary-Beth • Vancouver BC, V6R 1W5 Canada • ACRL LAMA LITA RASD EMIERT IRRT

Clark Nancy B. • Librarian • Clarkston High School Library • Clarkston, GA 30021 • AASL

Clark Nancy K. • Librarian • Junior High School Library • Mascoutah, IL 62258 • AASL

Clark Norah M. Miss • Toronto ON, Canada • Continuing

Clark Offie E. • Chairman • Maryland Advisory Council on Libraries • Baltimore, MD 21201 • ALTA

Clark Palmer Price Mrs • Fairfax, VA 22033 • Continuing

Clark Patricia • Littleton, CO 80121-2247

Clark Patricia A. • Librarian II • Los Angeles Public Library • Los Angeles, CA 90071 • ACRL PLA RASD FLRT IFRT

Clark Patricia A. • Librarian • E.W. Oliver Elementary • Riverdale, GA 30296 • ALSC

Clark Patricia G. • Student • University of Illinois Graduate School of Library and Information Science • Urbana, IL 61801

Clark Patricia H. • Springfield, VA 22151 • PLA

Clark Patty C. • Media Coordinator • Randleman Middle School • Randleman, NC 27317 • AASL

Clark Philip M. • Saint John's University Division of Library & Information Science • Jamaica, NY 11439 • LAMA LITA PLA LRRT

Clark Phyllis I. • Director • Lapeer County Library • Lapeer, MI 48446 • PLA

Clark Robert L. • Director • Oklahoma Department of Libraries • Oklahoma City, OK 73105-3298

Clark Ruth E. • Media Specialist • Zion Central Junior High School • Zion, IL 60099 • AASL YALSA

Clark Sharon E. • Asst. Director of Automated Serv • University of Illinois Library • Urbana, IL 61801 • ALCTS LAMA LITA

Clark Stephen D. • Acquisitions Librarian • College of William & Mary Earl Gregg Swem Library • Williamsburg, VA 23187-8794 • ALCTS

Clark Susan E. • Reference Librarian • University of the Pacific • Stockton, CA 95211 • ACRL LIRT

Clark Susan G. • Reference/Adult Services Ln • Zion-Benton Public Library District • Zion, IL 60099 • PLA RASD

Clark Suzanne M. • Librarian • University of Vermont Bailey Howe Library • Burlington, VT 05405-0036 • GODORT MAGERT

Clark Tanya Marie • Dublin, CA 94568

Clark Terry Mrs. • Assoc. Ln. (Sys) • Carleton University Library • Ottawa ON, K1S 5J7 Canada • ACRL LAMA LITA

Clark Thomas • Director • Milford Town Library • Milford, MA 01757

Clark Tommy A. • Asst. Dir. for User Services • Valdosta State College Library • Valdosta, GA 31698-0001

Clark Valerie A. • Head, Adult Reference Serv. • Niles Public Library • Niles, IL 60648 • PLA

Clark Violet Wuerfel • Trustee • McGregor Public Library • Highland Park, MI 48203 • ALTA

Clark Virginia G. • Reference Librarian • Great River Regional Library • Saint Cloud, MN 56301

Clark Virginia M. • Trustee • Addison Public Library • Addison, IL 60101-2499 • ALTA

Clarke Ann H. • Orangeburg, SC 29115 • AASL ACRL

Clarke Becky • Director • H. W. Wilson Company • Bronx, NY 10452 • LITA RASD

Clarke Catherine M. • Pittsburg, CA 94565

Clarke Charlotte C. • Librarian II-Adult & Ref. Servs. • Ramsey County Public Library • Shoreview, MN 55126 • RASD

Clarke Christine M. • Catalog Librarian • Syracuse University Library E. S. Bird Library • Syracuse, NY 13244-2010

Clarke D. Sherman • Assistant Librarian/Cataloger • Amon Carter Museum Library • Fort Worth, TX 76113 • ACRL ALCTS LITA SRRT

Clarke Danielle • Hopewell Junction, NY 12533 • RASD IFRT

Clarke David E. • Storrington RH20 4NF, England

Clarke Donatta R. • Student • University of Texas at Austin Graduate School of Library & Information Sciences • Austin, TX 78712-1276 • ALSC

Clarke Dorothy J. • Librarian • The Pingree School • S Hamilton, MA 01982

Clarke Elizabeth D. • Charleston, WV 25312

Clarke Jessica C. • Head Technical Services Dept. • Rosenberg Library • Galveston, TX 77550 • ALCTS LITA

Clarke Joan E. • Library Media Specialist • Wethersfield High School • Wethersfield, CT 06109

Clarke Joan S. • Dir of Instructional Resources • Saint Charles County Community College Library • St. Peters, MO 63376-2866 • ACRL ALCTS LITA

Clarke Joy A. • Library Media Specialist • Denver Public Schools Kunsmiller Middle School • Denver, CO 80219

Clarke Katherine M. • Reference Librarian • Sandia Prep School • Albuquerque, NM 87113 • AASL

Clarke Paula F. • Student • San Jose State University Division of Library & Information Science • San Jose, CA 95192-0029

Clarke Robert F. Dr. • Miami, FL 33186-3545 • ACRL ALCTS   Life

Clarke Shirlee M. • Librarian • Industrial Design Corporation • Portland, OR 97201

Clarke Susan A. • Media Specialist • Rampart High School • Colorado Spring, CO 80920 • AASL

Clarke Tobin deLeon Ed.D • Director of Learning Resource • San Joaquin Delta College Goleman Library • Stockton, CA 95207 • ACRL

Clarke Vashti G. • Student • Pratt Institute Graduate School of Library & Information Science • Brooklyn, NY 11205

Clarkson Jane S. • Florida State University Robert M. Strozier Library • Tallahassee, FL 32306-2047 • ALCTS

Clarkson Mary C. • Head of Circulation • Trinity University • San Antonio, TX 78212 • LAMA YALSA LIRT

Clarkson Roberta D. • School Media Specialist • Seneca Middle School • Seneca, SC 29679 • AASL

Clarkson Wendy CR • System Adminstrator • Somerset County Library • Bridgewater, NJ 08807

Clary Ann Roane • Washington, DC 20015

Clary Lillian • Allan Hancock College Learning Resources Center • Santa Maria, CA 93454 • RASD

Clashy Irene M. • Elementary School Librarian • Kennedy School • Somerville, MA 02144

Clasper James W. • University of Cincinnati Libraries • Cincinnati, OH 45221-0033 • ACRL LITA

Claspy Lois • Adult Services Librarian • Cuyahoga County Public Library Middleburg Heights Branch • Middleburg Heights, OH 44130

Clasquin Frank F. • Dedham, MA 02026 • ALCTS

Classen Joanne E. • Denver, CO 80222 • PLA RASD Life

Claus-Smith Diane K. • Librarian • North Salem High School • Salem, OR 97301

Clausen Carol • Senior Catlgr, Hist of Med. Div. • National Library of Medicine • Bethesda, MD 20894 • ACRL ALCTS

Clausen Mary Ethel • Librarian • Kenai Peninsula College • Soldotna, AK 99669 • ACRL

Clausen Sara J. • Tyler, TX 75703 • ACRL

Claussen Frederick Thomas • Hd, Preservation Microfilm Lab. • New York Public Library • New York, NY 10018 • ALCTS

Claussen Margaret M. • Supervisor • Illinois Valley Library System • Pekin, IL 61554

Claver M. Peter Sr. • Tuskegee Inst, AL 36088 • AASL

Claveria Aida • Children's Librarian • Jersey City Public Library • Jersey City, NJ 07302-3499

Claxton Gary R. • Regional Head Adult Section • Cuyahoga County Public Library Fairview Park Regional Branch • Fairview Park, OH 44126-2189 • PLA RASD SRRT

Clay Carolyn M. • Oakland, KY 42159 • AASL IFRT

Clay Connie L. • Director • Princeton Public Library Mercer Memorial Library • Princeton, WV 24740

Clay Edwin S. III • Director • Fairfax County Public Library Administrative Offices • Fairfax, VA 22030 • LAMA PLA

Clay Genevieve J. • Head,Central Serials • Eastern Kentucky University John Grant Crabbe Library • Richmond, KY 40475-3121 • ALCTS

Clay Rena M. • Memphis, TN 38111

Clay Rudolph Jr • Reference Dept.-Supervisor • Washington University Olin Library • Saint Louis, MO 63130 • ACRL RASD EMIERT

Clayborne Jon Lee • Director of Market Development • H. W. Wilson Company • Bronx, NY 10452 • LAMA LITA RASD AFLRT LIRT SRRT

Clayman Ida H. • Colonial Hgts, VA 23834 • ALCTS

Claypool B Joyce • Houston, TX 77060

Claypool Teresa • Training Specialist • Hewlett-Packard Company • San Diego, CA 92123

Clayton Christine E. • Encinitas, CA 92024 • Life

Clayton Frances • El Paso, TX 79902 • Continuing

Clayton Georgia L. • Media Specialist • Lincoln Fundamental School • Davenport, IA 52803

Clayton Laurence K. • Student • University of Michigan Libraries Information and Library Studies • Ann Arbor, MI 48109

Clayton Lesley J. • Student • University of South Florida School of Library & Information Science • Tampa, FL 33620 • IFRT SRRT

Clayton Marguerite V. • Pine Bluff, AR 71603 • Continuing

Clayton Sue N. • Clln. Devel. & Management • Manatee Community College Library Sara Scott Harllee Library • Bradenton, FL 34206 • SRRT

Claytor Linda H. • Arlington, TX 76012

Cleary Daniel E. • Research Librarian • Time Warner Inc • New York, NY 10020

Cleary Patia • Librarian • Irwin County High School Library • Ocilla, GA 31774

Cleary Robert O. • President • Rancho Santa Fe Library Guild • Rancho Santa Fe, CA 92067

Cleaver Betty • Director • Ohio State University Edgar Dale Educational Center • Columbus, OH 43210 • AASL ACRL LRRT

Cleaver Margaret V. • Librarian • Santa Monica Public Library • Santa Monica, CA 90401

Clegern Nadine Y. • Supervising Librarian • Aetna Life & Casulty Eng. Information Center W101 • Windsor, CT 06095 • LAMA LITA RASD ILERT NMRT

Clegg Melaine B. • Student • Rutgers University School of Communication Information & Library Studies • New Brunswick, NJ 08903 • ACRL ALSC ASCLA PLA SRRT

Clegg Michael B. • Branch Operation Mgr. • Allen County Public Library • Fort Wayne, IN 46801-2270 • PLA RASD

Cleinman Caroline M. • School Library Media Specialist • Schenevus Central School • Schenevus, NY 12155 • AASL

Cleland Abby H. • Graduate Student • Abbeville-Greenwood Regional Library • Greenwood, SC 29646

Cleland Camille S. • Head of Technical Services • Skokie Public Library • Skokie, IL 60077-3680 • ALCTS LITA

Cleland Carole • Federal Deposit Insurance Corp L • Washington, DC 20429 • ALCTS FLRT

Cleland Elizabeth • Vernon Area Public Library • Prairie View, IL 60069

Cleland Kathryn M. • Social Sciences Librarian • Swarthmore College Library • Swarthmore, PA 19081 • ACRL

Cleland Mary E. • Public Services Librarian • Geneva College McCartney Library • Beaver Falls, PA 15010 • ACRL

Cleland Mary V. • Willamette University College of Law Library • Salem, OR 97301

Clem Betty • Trustee • Western Plains Library System • Clinton, OK 73601

Clem Harriet M. • Director/Clerk-Treasurer • Rodman Public Library • Alliance, OH 44601 • AASL PLA

Clem Lucy Y. • Children's Librarian • Evansville-Vanderburgh County North Branch Library • Evansville, IN 47710 • ALSC

Clemens Bonnie Jackson • Director of the Libraries • Claremont Colleges Libraries Honnold/Mudd Library • Claremont, CA 91711 • ACRL LAMA LITA

Clemens Lawrence E. • Reference Librarian • U S Naval Academy Nimitz Library • Annapolis, MD 21402 • ACRL

Clemensen Beth E. • West High School • Davenport, IA 52804

Clement Anne A. • Bureau of Business Practice • Waterford, CT 06386 • RASD

Clement Charles R. • International Reference • Family History Library • Salt Lake City, UT 84150

Clement Evelyn G. Dr. • Memphis, TN 38111 • ACRL LAMA LITA   Life

Clement Gail P. • Student • Florida International University • Miami, FL 33199 • ACRL

Clement Joan W. • Cinnaminson, NJ 08077

Clement Lucinda W. • Media Specialist • Farmington High School • Farmington, MI 48336 • AASL YALSA Life

Clement Marchyne R. • Circulation Librarian • Edison Community College Univ. of S Florida Learning Resources Center • Fort Myers, FL 33906-6210 • ACRL

Clement Margaret A. • Student • State University of New York at Albany School of Information Science & Policy • Albany, NY 12222 • RASD

Clement Martha L. • Tilton School • Tilton, NH 03276 • ALSC

Clement Richard W. • University of Kansas Spencer Research Library • Lawrence, KS 66045-2800 • ACRL LHRT

Clements Cynthia L. • Richland College • Dallas, TX 75243-2199 • ALCTS

Clements Diane • Librarian • Saint Cecilia Academy • Nashville, TN 37205 • AASL

Clements Mary T. • Student • University of South Florida School of Library & Information Science • Tampa, FL 33620

Clements Pamela H. • Greenbrier Primary School • Chesapeake, VA 23320

Clements Susan M. • Readers Advisor • Alabama Public Library Service • Montgomery, AL 36130 • ASCLA

Clementson Susan B. • Rosman High School • Rosman, NC 28772 • AASL

Cleminshaw Barbara B. • Librarian II • Onondaga County Public Library at the Galleries • Syracuse, NY 13202-2494 • PLA

Clemmer Dan Orr • Chief Readers Services • United States Department of State Library • Washington, DC 20520 • FLRT GODORT

Clemmer Joel G. • Director • DeWitt Wallace Library MacAlester College • Saint Paul, MN 55105 • ACRL LAMA

Clemmons Jean Marie • United States Air Force Base Library • Mather AFB, CA 95655 • RASD

Clendening Denise D. • Houston, TX 77084 • NMRT

Clendinning David • Assistant University Librarian • Florida State University Robert M. Strozier Library • Tallahassee, FL 32306-2047 • LAMA

Clennell William H. • Asst. Secretary Pers Officer • Bodleian Library • Oxford OXI 3BG, England • LAMA LHRT

Cleveland Edith F. • Akron, OH 44303 • RASD

Cleveland John • Manager-Branch Library • Toledo-Lucas County Public Library West Toledo Branch • Toledo, OH 43613 • PLA

Cleveland Louise • Librarian • Unionville Middle School Library • Unionville, PA 19375 • AASL

Cleveland Mary L. • Director of Library Services • Texas College • Tyler, TX 75702 • ACRL

Clevenger Judy Beth • Director • Scott-Sebastian Regional Library • Greenwood, AR 72936 • PLA

Cleverdon Carrie L. • Student • University of Alabama School of Library & Information Studies • Tuscaloosa, AL 35487-0252 • IFRT

Click Philip • Trustee • Queens Borough Public Library • Jamaica, NY 11432 • ALTA PLA

Clifford Ann T. • Director • Pasadena Public Library • Pasadena, TX 77506-4895 • PLA

Clifford Anne • Librarian • Coronado Public Library • Coronado, CA 92118

Clifford Anne E. • Canisius College Andrew L. Bouwhuis Library • Buffalo, NY 14208-1098 • ACRL LITA RASD

Clifford Arthur S. • Administrator • University of Massachusetts Library • Amherst, MA 01003 • LAMA

Clifford Katherine A. • Trustee • Bellwood Public Library • Bellwood, IL 60104 • ALTA PLA

Clifford Sandra R. • Assistant Librarian • Winsor School Library • Boston, MA 02215 • AASL

Clifton Janet R. • Library Aid-Children's Librarian • Harford County Library • Belcamp, MD 21017 • ALSC

Clifton Shari C. • Student • University of Oklahoma School of Library & Information Studies • Norman, OK 73019 • NMRT SRRT

Cline-Howley Pamela • Memorial University Queen Elizabeth II Library • St Johns NF, A1B 3Y1 Canada • ACRL ALCTS LITA

Cline Barbara A. • Librarian • Salisbury Township School District • Allentown, PA 18106 • AASL

Cline Bonnie K. • Student • University of Washington Graduate School of Library and Information Science • Seattle, WA 98195 • PLA

Cline Carrie L. • Librarian • Maries County R-1 School • Vienna, MO 65582

Cline Cheryl L. • Hombrechtikon, Switzerland

Cline Elaine R. • Director • Augsburg College George Sverdrup Library • Minneapolis, MN 55454 • ACRL LAMA

Cline Elizabeth • Arlington County Department of Libraries • Arlington, VA 22201 • RASD

Cline Gloria S. • Assistant Director • University of Southwestern Louisiana Libraries • Lafayette, LA 70503 • ACRL

Cline Helen • Hennessey, OK 73742

Cline Herman H. • Associate Professor Ref Ln • City College of New York (CUNY) • New York, NY 10031 • IRRT

Cline James D. • Assistant Director • Porter County Public Library • Valparaiso, IN 46383 • ASCLA PLA IFRT

Cline Jonathan A. • Dayton & Montgomery County Public Library • Dayton, OH 45402-2103

Cline Lynn S. • Head of Acquisitions Clln Devel • Southwest Missouri State University Library • Springfield, MO 65804-0095 • ACRL ALCTS LITA

Cline Nancy M. • Dean of University Libraries • Pennsylvania State University Libraries • University Park, PA 16802 • ACRL LAMA GODORT

Cline Patricia • Reference Librarian • Illinois State University Milner Library • Normal, IL 61761-0900 • ACRL LITA

Cline Raymond D. • Director • Port Arthur Public Library • Port Arthur, TX 77642-3136 • PLA

Cline Susan C. • Fort Sill, OK 73503 • AASL

Cline William Vern • Roseville, MI 48066 • Continuing

Clingan Maria M Ambrose • Bloomfield, NJ 07003 • AASL ALSC

Clingman Patricia A. • Admin. Secretary • Dayton & Montgomery County Public Library • Dayton, OH 45402-2103

Clodfelter Cherie A. • Chair • University of Dallas Department of Education • Irving, TX 75062 • ALSC

Cloner Joshua D. • Reference Librarian • Los Angeles County Public Library East Los Angeles Branch • Los Angeles, CA 90022

Cloonan Michele V. • Professor • University of California-Los Angeles Graduate School of Library & Information Science • Los Angeles, CA 90024-1520 • ACRL ALCTS LHRT

Clopine John J. • Sarasota, FL 34231 • ACRL LAMA *Life*

Close Carl Reeves • Student • University of Texas at Austin Graduate School of Library & Information Sciences • Austin, TX 78712-1276

Close Martha H. • Wexford, PA 15090

Close Mary Ellen • Director • Community Library • Salem, WI 53168 • PLA VRT

Clotfelter Kathleen • Librarian • Hillel Community Day School • North Miami Beach, FL 33180

Clothey Phillip Warren • Student • University of Pittsburgh School of Library and Information Science • Pittsburgh, PA 15260 • ACRL IFRT IRRT

Clothier Mary E. • Student • University of Wyoming • Laramie, WY 82071

Cloud Angela S. • Student • Indiana University School of Library and Information Science • Bloomington, IN 47405

Cloudman Katherine • Reference Librarian • Chandler Public Library • Chandler, AZ 85225 • PLA

Cloudsley Donald H. • Director • Buffalo & Erie County Public Library • Buffalo, NY 14203 • PLA

Clough Andrea M. • Student • State University New York at Buffalo School of Inf. & Library Studies • Buffalo, NY 14260

Clough Anne • School Library Media Specialist • Dodge Elementary School • East Amhurst, NY 14209 • AASL

Clough Beth • Student • Towson State University • Towson, MD 21204

Clough Debra L. • Fairlee Public Library • Fairlee, VT 05045

Clough Elaine B. • Thousand Oaks, CA 91360 • ACRL RASD GODORT *Continuing*

Clough Jeanette M. • Reference Librarian • Getty Center Resources Collections • Santa Monica, CA 90401 • ACRL

Clough Merle • Snake River Senior High School • Blackfoot, ID 83221 • AASL

Clougherty Leo • Chemistry/Botany & Biology Ln • University of Iowa Libraries • Iowa City, IA 52242-1379 • ACRL

Clouten Keith H. • Ln • Canadian Union College Library • College Heights AB, T0C 0Z0 Canada • ACRL

Clow Faye • Director • Bettendorf Public Library • Bettendorf, IA 52722 • ASCLA PLA

Clower Susan W. • Northeastern University • Boston, MA 02115 • ACRL

Clowers Francis M. • Director • Shoreline Community College Ray W Howard Library Media Center • Seattle, WA 98133 • ACRL LITA

Clubb Barbara H. • Director • Libraries & Community Information • Toronto ON, M7A 2R9 Canada • ALTA ASCLA LAMA PLA IRRT SRRT

Cluff E. Dale • Director • Texas Tech University Libraries • Lubbock, TX 79409-0002 • ACRL

Clum Audna T. • Troy, NY 12182

Clumpner Krista E. • Head of Tech Services & Systems • Northern Michigan University Lydia M. Olson Library • Marquette, MI 49855 • ACRL ALCTS IFRT

Clunan Kathleen K. • Library Director • Lynn University • Boca Raton, FL 33431 • ACRL

Clune John R. • Chief Librarian • Kingsborough Community College Library • Brooklyn, NY 11235 • ACRL LAMA

Clutz Linda J. • Student • University of Iowa School of Library & Information Science • Iowa City, IA 52242 • PLA

Clyburn Tamara K. • Library Media Specialist • Baron DeKalb Elementary School • Camden, SC 29020 • AASL IFRT NMRT

Clyburn Vera M. • Alexandria, VA 22310 • ALCTS

Clyde Gioia M. • Circulation Librarian • Reuben Hoar Library • Littleton, MA 01460

Clymer Theodore • Carmel, CA 93922-2138

Cnudde Susan H. • State Library of Florida Division of Library & Information Services • Tallahassee, FL 32399-0250

Coachman Dorothea L. • Schenectady, NY 12304-3615 • AASL

Coady Reginald P. • Director • Dearborn Department of Libraries Henry Ford Centennial Library • Dearborn, MI 48126 • LAMA PLA

Coady Teresa R. • Medical Librarian • The Hertzler Clinic • Halstead, KS 67056

Coakley Dorothy J. • Librarian • San Francisco Public Library Bernal Branch • San Francisco, CA 94110 • ALSC YALSA

Coakley Margaret R. • Community Relations Coordinator • Central Arkansas Library System • Little Rock, AR 72201-4698

Coakley Nancy • Librarian • Our Lady of the Assumption School • Atlanta, GA 30319 • AASL

Coan Cynthia J. • Pima Air Museum Library • Tucson, AZ 85706

Coan La Verne Z. • Literature Associate • Parke-Davis Pharmaceutical Research Library • Ann Arbor, MI 48105 • RASD

Coaston Shirley A. • Head Librarian • Laney College Library • Oakland, CA 94607 • ACRL SRRT

Coates Augusta M. • Silver Spring, MD 20906 • AASL ALSC *Life*

Coates Patricia L. • University of Arizona Library • Tucson, AZ 85721 • ALCTS LITA LIRT

Coates Renata G. • Asst. Head, Reference Services • University of California-San Diego Central University Library • La Jolla, CA 92093-0175 • ACRL RASD

Coatney Sharon • Library Media Specialist • Oak Hill School • Overland Park, KS 66052 • AASL

Coats Jacqueline A. • Head Acquisitions Librarian • University of Chicago Library • Chicago, IL 60637-1502

Cobb Carole • Trustee • Thomas Jefferson Library • Jefferson City, MO 65101 • ALTA

Cobb Cynthia • Fayetteville, NC 28303 • LAMA PLA

Cobb David A. • Harvard Map Collection • Harvard College Library • Cambridge, MA 02138 • ACRL GODORT MAGERT

Cobb David H. • Media Specialist • Airport High School Library • West Columbia, SC 29170 • AASL

Cobb Eileen F. • Director of Main Library • Broward County Division of Libraries Broward County Library • Fort Lauderdale, FL 33301

Cobb Elizabeth R. • Librarian • Northwest H S-RI Sch Dist • House Springs, MO 63051 • AASL YALSA

Cobb Flora S. • Instr. Sci. Ref/Clln Devel. Ln. • Va Polytechnic Inst & State Univ Universities Libraries • Blacksburg, VA 24061-0434 • RASD NMRT SRRT

Cobb Judith • Reference Services Librarian • Ball State University Library Department of Library Services • Muncie, IN 47306 • ACRL RASD

Cobb Karen Bosch • Associate County Librarian • Fresno County Free Library • Fresno, CA 93721-2285

Cobb Marilyn R. • New Trier High School • Winnetka, IL 60093 • AASL

Cobb Martha S. • Media Specialist • Congaree Elementary School Lexington County District #2 • West Columbia, SC 29169 • AASL

Cobb Mary Louise • Wake Forest University School of Law Library • Winston-Salem, NC 27109 • ACRL ALCTS LITA GODORT

Cobb Nell Miss • Fayetteville, NC 28301 • PLA RASD *Continuing*

Cobb Sandra U. • Hampton, VA 23661 • AASL

Cobb Sylvia R. • Serials/Government Documents Ln. • Oklahoma Baptist University • Shawnee, OK 74801-2590 • ACRL GODORT

Cobbe Lucy C. • Dallas, TX 75243

Coberly Jean A. • Coordinator Resource Div • Seattle Public Library • Seattle, WA 98104-1193 • ALCTS PLA RASD

Coble Gerald M. • Gulf Breeze, FL 32561 • ACRL PLA *Life*

Coble James W. • Libn. Dir. of Library Systems • Duke University William R. Perkins Library • Durham, NC 27706 • LITA

Cobos Ana Maria • Stanford University • Stanford, CA 94305-6011 • ACRL

Coburn Catherine W. • Children's Librarian • Windsor Public Library • Windsor, CT 06095

Coburn Leonard • Urbana, IL 61801 • ACRL RASD *Life*

Coburn Louis • Coconut Creek, FL 33066 • LITA PLA IRRT *Continuing*

Coburn Michael Fr. • Trustee • Maywood Public Library • Maywood, IL 60153 • ALTA

Coburn Morton • Director Library Programs • Chicago Public Library • Chicago, IL 60605 • LAMA PLA

Coburn Susan I. • Head of Reference Department • Toledo-Lucas County Public Library • Toledo, OH 43624 • PLA RASD

Cochenour Donnice K. • Serials Librarian • Colorado State University William E. Morgan Library • Fort Collins, CO 80523 • ACRL ALCTS

Cochran Ann T. • Student • University of South Carolina College of Library & Information Science • Columbia, SC 29208

Cochran Carolyn • Dir. Learning Rescource Cntr. • DeVry Institute of Technology Learning Resource Center • Irving, TX 75038-4299 • ACRL LITA LIRT

Cochran Cindy A. • Coordinator • Lincoln City Libraries • Lincoln, NE 68508 • LITA

Cochran Debra Lee • ARKnet Library Project • University of Arkansas Mullins Library • Fayetteville, AR 72701

Cochran Helen J. • Library Associate • Atlanta-Fulton Public Library Roswell Branch • Roswell, GA 30075

Cochran Jean D. Miss • Director • East Central Georgia Regional Library Augusta-Richmond County • Augusta, GA 30901 • Continuing

Cochran Judith J. • Learning Center Teacher • Hillcrest School • Downers Grove, IL 60521 • AASL

Cochran Karen L. • Librarian • Boiling Springs Junior Senior High School • Boiling Springs, PA 17007 • AASL

Cochran Radeen Mrs. • Librarian • Marlborough Elementary School • Green Lane, PA 18054 • AASL

Cochran Richard • Director • Saint Michael's College • Colchester, VT 05439-2525 • ACRL ALCTS LAMA LITA RASD

Cochran Stephen L. • Student • Indiana University School of Library and Information Science • Bloomington, IN 47405 • ALCTS SRRT

Cochran William M. • Director • Parmly Billings Library • Billings, MT 59101 • LAMA PLA IFRT LHRT

Cochrane Joseph • Student • San Jose State University Division of Library & Information Science • San Jose, CA 95192-0029 • IRRT MAGERT

Cochrane Linda L. • Director, Learning Res Ctr. • Chemeketa Community College • Salem, OR 97309 • ACRL

Cochrane Lynn Scott • Dean for Lib & Learning Serv • Marymount University Reinsch Library • Arlington, VA 22207-4299 • ACRL LAMA

Cochrane Pauline • Washington, DC 20016-2143 • ALCTS LITA *Life*

Cocke John R. • Randolph, VT 05060

Cocke Lucy S. • Director • Mount Vernon College • Washington, DC 20007

Cocker Martha A. • Student • University of Kentucky College of Library & Information Science • Lexington, KY 40506-0391 • RASD

Cockett Lynn • Children's Librarian • Elmwood Park Public Library • Elmwood Park, NJ 07407-2799 • ALSC YALSA

Cockram Alison R. • Student • University of North Carolina Department of Library & Information Studies • Greensboro, NC 27412-5001

Cocks Anna R. • Elkhart, IN 46514-4162 • Continuing

Cocks Fraser • Curator, Special Collections • University of Oregon Library • Eugene, OR 97403-1299 • ACRL

Coco Carolyn M. • Student • Louisiana State University School of Library & Information Science • Baton Rouge, LA 70803-3290

Coco Wayne • Architect • Avoyelles Parish Library • Marksville, LA 71351 • ALTA

Cocozzoli Gary • Lawrence Technological University Library • Southfield, MI 48075 • ACRL

Codair Frederick C.E.X. Bro. • Bishop Fenwick High School • Peabody, MA 01960

Coddington Amy E. • University of Kansas Spencer Research Library • Lawrence, KS 66045-2800

Codell Cindy D. • Librarian • Clark Middle School • Winchester, KY 40391 • AASL ALSC IFRT

Coder Ann • Hd, Gen & Humanities/Soc Sci Ref • University of Hawaii Thomas Hale Hamilton Library • Honolulu, HI 96822 • ACRL

Codina Merce • Student • Indiana University School of Library and Information Science • Bloomington, IN 47405

Cody Charles J. • Librarian I • Columbus Metropolitan Library • Columbus, OH 43215 • IFRT

Cody Gwendalyn F. • Trustee • Fairfax County Public Library • Fairfax, VA 22033-1909

Cody Sandra J. • Catalog Maintenance, Head • Ohio State University Libraries • Columbus, OH 43210-1286

Cody Sara E. • Extension Librarian • Dalton Regional Library • Dalton, GA 30720

Coe D. Whitney • Anglo-American Bibliographer • Princeton University • Princeton, NJ 08544-2098 • ACRL ALCTS LITA *Life*

Coe Gloria M. • Director of Library • Goldey Beacom College Library • Wilmington, DE 19808

Coe Joyce E. • School Librarian • Lynn/Urquides Elementary School • Tucson, AZ 85713 • AASL ALSC

Coe Judy • Circulation Manager • York County Library • Rock Hill, SC 29730 • IFRT

Coe Leslie B. • Reference Librarian • East Baton Rouge Parish Library • Baton Rouge, LA 70806-7699 • PLA RASD

Coe Miriam • Baton Rouge, LA 70802-8416 • Continuing

Coe Tamala M. • Youth Servs Library Assoc II • Veterans Memorial Library City of Mount Pleasant Library • Mount Pleasant, MI 48858 • ALSC NMRT

Coelho Jill Young • Acquisitions Librarian • Harvard College Library Widener Memorial Library • Cambridge, MA 02138 • ACRL ALCTS LAMA SORT

Coelho Linda J. • Student • University of Rhode Island Graduate School of Library & Information Studies • Kingston, RI 02881-0815

Coffee Leona Rose • NLM Associate • National Library of Medicine • Bethesda, MD 20894

Coffee William N. • Hinsdale, IL 60521

Coffey Carol Y. • Student • Louisiana State University School of Library & Information Science • Baton Rouge, LA 70803-3290 • PLA RASD

Coffey Clare A. • Memphis-Shelby County Public Library Germantown Branch • Germantown, TN 38138 • ALSC YALSA

Coffey Donald • Principal • White Station High School Library • Memphis, TN 38117

Coffey James R. • Technical Services Librarian • Rutgers University Paul Robeson Library • Camden, NJ 08101-3990 • ACRL LAMA LITA

Coffey Lyle S. • Information Resources Specialist • Los Angeles County Office of Education • Downey, CA 90242 • ALCTS

Coffey Michaela M. • Technical Services Librarian • Vincennes University Shake Learning Resources Library • Vincennes, IN 47591 • ACRL

Coffey Monica A. Ph.D. • Cataloger/Data Entry Supervisor • Saint Louis University Pius XII Memorial Library • St. Louis, MO 63108 • ACRL

Coffey Nancy Applegate • Senior Librarian, Support Svs. • Torrance Public Library • Torrance, CA 90503 • LAMA LITA

Coffey Patrick • Matteson, IL 60443 • PLA

Coffey Sue E. • Serial Librarian • Midwestern State University George Moffett Library • Wichita Fls, TX 76308 • ACRL

Coffie Patricia R. • Director • Waverly Public Library • Waverly, IA 50677 • PLA

Coffin Susan M. • Asst. Dir. Children's Ln. • Belfast Free Library • Belfast, ME 04915

Coffindaffer Clarence L. • Davis & Elkins College Library • Elkins, WV 26241 • ACRL IFRT LRRT

Coffman Catherine E. • Page • Tucson Public Library G. Freeman Woods Branch • Tucson, AZ 85719 • PLA

Coffman Joseph W. • Professor • Texas Woman's University School of Library & Information Studies • Denton, TX 76204 • ACRL

Coffman Pat • Branch Manager • Clay County Public Library Orange Park Branch • Orange Park, FL 32073

Coffman Stephen D. • Director • County of Los Angeles Public Library Norwalk Library 501 • Norwalk, CA 90650 • PLA RASD

Cofrancesco James R. • Asst. Librarian Public Services • Herkimer Cnty Cmnty Coll • Herkimer, NY 13350 • ACRL

Cogan Sarah W. • Librarian, Computer Services • Eastern Michigan University Library Center of Educational Resources • Ypsilanti, MI 48197

Coggins Hal Q. • Student • University of North Carolina at Chapel Hill School of Information and Library Science • Chapel Hill, NC 27599-3360 • LRRT

Coggins Jennifer M. • Student • University of Texas at Austin Graduate School of Library & Information Sciences • Austin, TX 78712-1276

Coggins Margaret • Library Media Specialist • Kennedy Elementary School • Lawrence, KS 66044 • AASL

Coghlan Colleen L. • Tenants Harbor, ME 04860-0030

Cogliser LuAnn L. • Watertown High School Library • Watertown, CT 06795 • AASL

Cogswell James A. • Division Head • University of Minnesota Meredith Wilson Library • Minneapolis, MN 55455 • ACRL LAMA

Cohan Harriet C. • Miami, FL 33180-3043

Cohen-Rose Amy B. • Research Librarian • Houghton Mifflin Company Library • Boston, MA 02108 • RASD

Cohen A. J. Dr. • White Plains City School District • White Plains, NY 10605 • AASL

Cohen Aaron • Architect A I A • Aaron Cohen Associates • Croton-On-Hudson, NY 10520 • LAMA

Cohen Allen • Head of Catalog Department • University of California UCSB Library • Santa Barbara, CA 93106-9010 • ACRL ALCTS LITA

Cohen Alma O. • Trustee • Free Library of Philadelphia • Philadelphia, PA 19103 • ALTA

Cohen Ann E. • Assistant Division Head • Rochester Public Library • Rochester, NY 14604 • PLA RASD

Cohen Arlene N. • Director • White Pine County Public Library • Ely, NV 89301 • PLA

Cohen Beatrice • Media Specialist • Overland High School • Aurora, CO 80012

Cohen Beth F. • Director, Lib for AIDS Resources • Rolling Stone Magazine Library • New York, NY 10104

Cohen Betty E. • Student • Southern Connecticut State University School of Libray Science & Instructional Technology • New Haven, CT 06515

Cohen Bill • Publisher • The Haworth Press • Binghamton, NY 13904-1580 • AASL ACRL ALCTS ALSC ASCLA LAMA LITA PLA RASD YALSA GODORT IFRT LRRT SRRT

Cohen Charlotte E. • Student • American Graduate School of International Management Barton K Yount Memorial Library • Glendale, AZ 85306

Cohen Christina M. • Ref Ln & Archivist • Deerfield Academy • Deerfield, MA 01342

Cohen David • Adjunct Professor • Queens College Grad Sch of Lib & Inf Studies • Flushing, NY 11367 • EMIERT IFRT SRRT   *Continuing*

Cohen David J. • Director • College of Charleston Robert Scott Small Library • Charleston, SC 29424 • ACRL

Cohen Deatra • Student • San Jose State University Division of Library & Information Science • San Jose, CA 95192-0029 • ACRL

Cohen Donna K. • Rollins College Olin Library • Winter Park, FL 32789-4499

Cohen Edward S. • Head of Reference • Western Carolina University Hunter Library • Cullowhee, NC 28723-9002 • RASD

Cohen Elaine • Aaron Cohen Associates • Croton-On-Hudson, NY 10520

Cohen Ellen Y. • General Accounting Manager • Harvard College Library Widener Memorial Library • Cambridge, MA 02138

Cohen Frances L. • School Librarian • Conestoga Senior High School • Berwyn, PA 19312 • AASL LITA YALSA LIRT LRRT

Cohen Gilbert • Springfield, NJ 07081 • ACRL RASD

Cohen Harriet A. • Head, Newspaper & Periodicals • Indianapolis Marion County Public Library • Indianapolis, IN 46206 • PLA

Cohen Harriet E. • Youth Services Librarian • San Diego Public Library San Carlos Branch • San Diego, CA 92119 • ALSC

Cohen Ilene L. • Children's Librarian • Santa Monica Public Library Fairview Branch Library • Santa Monica, CA 90405

Cohen Inez Shor • City College of San Francisco • San Francisco, CA 94112

Cohen Jane L. • Reference Librarian • Defense Systems Management College Library • Fort Belvoir, VA 22060-5426

Cohen Jean N. • Audiovisual Services • Allen County Public Library • Fort Wayne, IN 46801 • PLA SORT VRT

Cohen Jennifer E. • Yorktown Hts, NY 10598 • AASL

Cohen Joan G. • Hillside, NJ 07642 • NMRT

Cohen Josh • New Paltz, NY 12561 • LAMA IFRT

Cohen Kathleen • Assistant Dir. of Library • University of North Florida • Jacksonville, FL 32216 • ACRL ALCTS

Cohen Leonard • Homer, NY 13077 • ACRL RASD   *Life*

Cohen Linda E. • Childrens Librarian • Thomas Crane Public Library • Quincy, MA 02171

Cohen Linda M. • Dept. Hd, Sci & Tech Dept. • Birmingham Public Library • Birmingham, AL 35203

Cohen Lucy R. • Mgr Pers & Payroll Serv • University of Michigan Libraries • Ann Arbor, MI 48109-1205 • ACRL LAMA

Cohen Lynne D. • Audiovisual Librarian • Brookline High School Burack Library • Brookline, MA 02146

Cohen Mark B. • Denver, CO 80210 • ACRL

Cohen Martha J. • King County Library System White Center Library • Seattle, WA 98146 • YALSA

Cohen Martin • Kalamazoo, MI 49008 • RASD   *Life*

Cohen Martin Dr. • Asst. Technical Services Ln. • McGill University Libraries • Montreal PQ, H3A 1Y1 Canada • ALCTS

Cohen Martin J. • Information Services Librarian • Saint Mary's College of California • Moraga, CA 94575 • LITA RASD

Cohen Meryll J. • Head of Youth Services • Broward County Division of Libraries West Regional Branch • Plantation, FL 33324 • YALSA

Cohen Millard • St. Louis, MO 63141-9050

Cohen Morris L. • Yale University Law Library • New Haven, CT 06520 • ACRL

Cohen Nancy • VP & Librarian • Kidder, Peabody & Co Inc • New York, NY 10005 • LITA

Cohen Naomi S. • Saint Josephs University Drexel Library • Philadelphia, PA 19131-1395

Cohen Nathan M. • Arlington, VA 22205 • Continuing

Cohen Pauline M. • Librarian • University School Upper Campus • Hunting Valley, OH 44022 • AASL

Cohen Rebecca • Childrens Services • Newport Public Library • Newport, OR 97365 • ALSC

Cohen Renee G. • Matawan, NJ 07747

Cohen Sharon E. • Reference/ILL Librarian • Bank Street College of Education Library • New York, NY 10025 • ACRL RASD

Cohen Sharon L. • Library Coordinator • Burbank Public Library • Burbank, CA 91502 • PLA

Cohen Steven • Cataloger • Pratt Institute Graduate School of Library & Information Science • Brooklyn, NY 11205

Cohen Susan E. • Sudent • San Jose State University Division of Library & Information Science • San Jose, CA 95192-0029 • RASD EMIERT IFRT SRRT

Cohen Thelma • Media Specialist • Wootton High School • Rockville, MD 20850 • AASL

Cohen Vicky E. • Frenchtown, NJ 08825

Cohick Keith B. • Librarian • University of Pittsburgh Johnstown Campus Library • Johnstown, PA 15904

Cohn-Brown Clare A. • Art/Architecture Librarian • New York Institute of Technology • Old Westbury, NY 11568 • ACRL

Cohn-Madanick Patricia E. • Children's Librarian • Warner Library • Tarrytown, NY 10591 • ALSC

Cohn-Stickgold Judy R. • Librarian • Los Angeles Unified School District Granada Hills High School • Granada Hills, CA 91344 • YALSA

Cohn Emma • Bronx, NY 10458 • Continuing

Cohn Jeanette • Director • Rockaway Township Free Public Library • Rockaway, NJ 07866 • ALSC PLA RASD

Cohn Jeffrey R. • Trustee • Long Beach Public Library • Long Beach, NY 11561 • ALTA

Cohn John M. Dr • Director of Library Services • County College of Morris S H Masten Learning Resource Center • Randolph Township, NJ 07869-2086 • ACRL ALCTS LAMA LITA RASD ILERT

Cohn Sherrill • Savage Information Services • Torrance, CA 90505 • ALCTS

Cohn William L. • West Virginia State College Drain-Jordan Library • Institute, WV 25112-1002 • ACRL

Cohon Mary Ellen • Trustee • Morton Grove Public Library • Morton Grove, IL 60053 • ALTA

Cohrs Cynthia I. • Assoc. Info. Scientist • R.W. Johnson Pharmaceutical Research Institute • Raritan, NJ 08869 • ALCTS

Cohrs Joyce S. • Cobb County Public Library System • Marietta, GA 30060 • PLA

Coil Dorothy • Life Science Librarian • University of Notre Dame Libraries • Notre Dame, IN 46556 • ACRL

Coil Muriel J. • Reference Librarian • Northern Arizona University • Flagstaff, AZ 86011-6022

Coit Shirley • Townsend, MA 01469

Cokain Deborah Ann • District Library Coor. • Clearview Junior and Senior High School • Lorain, OH 44052 • AASL

Coker Janis L. • Library Director • Schiller International University Florida Campus Library • Dunedin, FL 34698 • ACRL

Coker Julianne • Student • University of Missouri-Columbia School of Library & Informational Science • Columbia, MO 65211

Coker Mary Dowdle Mrs • Little Rock, AR 72207-5061 • AASL YALSA   *Continuing*

Coker Sylvia • Branch Manager • Enoch Pratt Free Public Library Walbrook Branch • Baltimore, MD 21216 • PLA

Colaianni Lois Ann • Associate Director • National Library of Medicine • Bethesda, MD 20894

Colaianni Midge L. • Head of Serials • Idaho State University Eli M. Oboler Library • Pocatello, ID 83209-8089

Colburn Nell • Children's Selections Librarian • Prince George's County Memorial Library System • Hyattsville, MD 20782-2098 • ALSC PLA

Colburn Virginia • Youth Services Librarian • Warsaw Community Public Library • Warsaw, IN 46580 • PLA

Colby Diana C. • Program Librarian • Santa Clara County Free Library Saratoga Commmunity Library • Saratoga, CA 95070 • ALSC EMIERT

Colby Michael D. • Music Cataloger • University of California Shields Library • Davis, CA 95616

Colcord Evelyn H. • Somerville, MA 02144 • Continuing

Coldiron Ralph • Trustee • Lexington Public Library • Lexington, KY 40507 • ALTA

Coldren Ellen Sue • Fitzsimons Army Medical Center • Aurora, CO 80045 • LITA

Coldwell Charles P. • Managing Libn./Art,Music & Media • Seattle Public Library • Seattle, WA 98104-1193 • PLA

Cole Barbara W. • Assistant Director • State Library of Pennsylvania Department of Education • Harrisburg, PA 17105 • ASCLA PLA

Cole Cathy • Director • Fort Scott Public Library • Fort Scott, KS 66701

Cole Charlene J. • Director • Coleman Library • Tougaloo, MS 39174

Cole Christopher H. • Head Technical Services • Maricopa County Library District • Phoenix, AZ 85032

Cole D. John • Associate Dean of LRC • Delta College Learning Resources Center • University Center, MI 48710 • ACRL LAMA LITA LIRT SORT

Cole David H. • Technical Services Coordinator • Great River Regional Library • Saint Cloud, MN 56301

Cole Diane D. • Student • Kent State University School of Library & Information Science • Kent, OH 44242-0001

Cole Elizabeth M. • S Wellfleet, MA 02663 • Continuing

Cole Frances D. • Director • West Baton Rouge Parish Library • Port Allen, LA 70767 • PLA

Cole Gayle • Coordinator of Youth Services • Stockton-San Joaquin County Public Library • Stockton, CA 95202 • ALSC PLA   *Life*

Cole Grace • Boulder, CO 80303 • AASL

Cole Heather E. • Librarian • Harvard College Library Lamont Library • Cambridge, MA 02138 • ACRL LAMA

Cole Jack • Trustee • Hennepin County Library • Minnetonka, MN 55343 • ALTA

Cole James P. • Asst. Chief-Info & Ref. • Library of Congress • Washington, DC 20541 • LAMA

Cole Janice L. • Salem School • Salem, CT 06420-3804 • AASL

Cole Joan E. • Regional Manager • Queens Borough Public Library • Jamaica, NY 11432 • ALSC LAMA

Cole John Y. • Director • Library of Congress Center for the Book • Washington, DC 20540 • LHRT   *Life*

Cole Karen • Hays, KS 67601 • ACRL

Cole Lynn • Roanoke County Public Library • Roanoke, VA 24018 • PLA

Cole Maud D. • Astoria, NY 11105

Cole Maureen T. • Student • University of South Florida School of Library & Information Science • Tampa, FL 33620

Cole Mitzi M. • Reference Librarian • Scottsdale Public Library • Scottsdale, AZ 85251

Cole Norma • Librarian • Reber Memorial Library • Raymondville, TX 78580

Cole Patricia A. • Elementary School Media Spec • Edward Morley School • West Hartford, CT 06119 • AASL

Cole Sally • Gary Hutton Design • San Francisco, CA 94110

Cole Sarah L. • Librarian • North East Multi-Regional Training • North Aurora, IL 60542

Cole Susan B. • Tahoe City, CA 96145 • PLA

Cole Teresa D. • Student • University of Alabama School of Library & Information Studies • Tuscaloosa, AL 35487-0252

Cole Timothy W. • Assistant Librarian • University of Illinois Library • Urbana, IL 61801 • LITA

Cole Vija V. • Library Media Specialist • Third Ward Elementary School • Griffin, GA 30223 • AASL LIRT

Coleburn Jacqueline • Processing Librarian • Library of Congress • Washington, DC 20541 • ALCTS

Coleman-Sherwood Sandra • Assistant Children's Librarian • Waukegan Public Library • Waukegan, IL 60085 • ALSC RASD

Coleman Alice L. • Director • Texarkana Public Library • Texarkana, TX 75501 • LAMA PLA

Coleman Annie H. • Coordinator • Allen University J. S. Flipper LRC • Columbia, SC 29204 • ACRL EMIERT LIRT NMRT

Coleman Barbara K. • Media Spec • Emerson Middle Sch • Lakewood, OH 44107 • AASL LITA

Coleman Brenda W. • Graduate Student • University of Southern Mississippi School of Library Science • Hattiesburg, MS 39406-5146

Coleman Christopher D G • Preservation Librarian • University of California-Los Angeles (UCLA) • Los Angeles, CA 90024-1450 • ACRL ALCTS

Coleman Connie T. • Trustee • Baltimore County Public Library • Towson, MD 21204 • ALTA PLA IFRT

Coleman Deborah L. • Student • Simmons College Graduate School of Library & Information Science • Boston, MA 02115

Coleman Deborah Roberts • Director of Media Services • Barnwell Elementary School • Barnwell, SC 29812 • AASL

Coleman Elizabeth H. • South Hadley, MA 01075 • Continuing

Coleman Faith • Associate Archivist • Ford Foundation • New York, NY 10017 • ACRL

Coleman Francis N. • Associate Director & Head • Mississippi State University Mitchell Memorial Library • Mississippi State, MS 39762 • ACRL ALCTS LAMA

Coleman Henry E. Jr. • Richmond, VA 23220 • ACRL ALCTS   *Continuing*

Coleman J Gordon Jr • Assoc. Prof & Asst. Dean • University of Alabama School of Library & Information Studies • Tuscaloosa, AL 35487-0252 • AASL

Coleman James M. • Reader Advisor • Alabama Public Library Service • Montgomery, AL 36130

Coleman James W. • Senior Program Officer • Research Libraries Group Inc. (RLG) • Mountain View, CA 94041-1100 • ACRL

Coleman Jean A. • Winter Park, FL 32792 • Continuing

Coleman Jean Ellen • New York, NY 10002 • EMIERT SRRT

Coleman Judith • Deputy Director • Cuyahoga County Public Library Administration Building • Parma, OH 44134-2792 • LAMA PLA

Coleman Kathleen Devaney • Librarian • Sunnyvale Public Library • Sunnyvale, CA 94088-3714 • ALSC

Coleman Kathleen L. • Librarian • San Diego State University Library • San Diego, CA 92119-2120 • ACRL RASD

Coleman Keith A. • Axtell Independent School District • Axtell, TX 76624 • AASL YALSA

Coleman Ken • Reference Librarian • Randolph Public Library • Asheboro, NC 27203 • PLA RASD

Coleman L. Zenobia Ms. • Childersburg, AL 35044 • ACRL ALCTS   *Continuing*

Coleman Laura • Fort Worth, TX 76133

Coleman Margaret • Portland, OR 97222 • Continuing

Coleman Margaret A. • Birdville Independent School District • Fort Worth, TX 76117 • AASL

Coleman Melody E. • Library Director • Calumet Park Pub Library • Calumet Park, IL 60643 • PLA

Coleman Michael J. • Louisiana State University Medical Center Library • New Orleans, LA 70112-2223 • ALCTS NMRT

Coleman Monica • Automated Services Librarian • Long Beach City College • Long Beach, CA 90808 • ACRL LITA

Coleman Paul • Library Director • Adrian College Shipman Library • Adrian, MI 49221 • ACRL LAMA MAGERT

Coleman Rita M. • School Media Specialist • David M. Cox Elementary School • Henderson, NV 89014 • AASL

Coleman Ronald L. • Library Trustee • Granite City Public Library District • Granite City, IL 62040

Coleman Sandra S. • Administrative Dean • Harvard Law School • Cambridge, MA 02138

Coleman Shelley J. • Lutheran Medical Library • Wheat Ridge, CO 80033 • LITA

Coleman Shirley F. • Serials Catalog Librarian • Purdue University Libraries • West Lafayette, IN 47907-1530 • ALCTS

Coleman Valerie M. • Librarian • Chaminade University • Honolulu, HI 96816

Coles Betty • Decatur, GA 30035

Coles Elizabeth L. • Trustee • Cleveland Public Library • Cleveland, OH 44114-1271 • ALTA

Coles Gloria J. • Director • Flint Public Library • Flint, MI 48502 • LAMA PLA SRRT

Coles Jayne P. Mrs. • Head Librarian • Fort Myers Beach Public Library • Ft. Myers Beach, FL 33931

Coletta Theresa C. • Regional Library Director • Avery-Mitchell Yancey Regional Library • Spruce Pine, NC 28777 • PLA IFRT

Coletti Donna J • Librarian • Smithsonian Institution Astrophysical Observatory Library • Cambridge, MA 02138

Coletti Martin L. • Student • San Jose State University Division of Library & Information Science • San Jose, CA 95192-0029

Coley Betty A. • Librarian • Baylor University Armstrong Brown Library • Waco, TX 76798-7152 • ACRL LRRT

Colfax Claire L. • Los Angeles, CA 90049 • ACRL

Colgan Larry J. • Cataloging Assistant • DePaul University Libraries • Chicago, IL 60614 • ACRL ALCTS

Colgin Jill U. • School Librarian • Brock ISD • Weatherford, TX 76087

Colish Louis • Library Service Assistant • West Kildonan Library • Winnipeg MB, R2V 0N3 • ACRL PLA RASD

Coll John D. • San Francisco, CA 94131

Collantes Augurio L. • Hostos Community College • Bronx, NY 10451

Collantes Lourdes Y. • Associate Librarian • State University of New York (SUNY) College at Old Westbury Library • Old Westbury, NY 11568 • ACRL EMIERT

Collard R. Michael • Jonesboro, IL 62952-0357

Collazo Maria L. • San Juan, PR 00936-7344

Collett Connie • Head Librarian • Greene County Public Library Yellow Springs Community Library • Yellow Springs, OH 45387

Collier Carol M. • Greensview Elementary School • Upper Arlington, OH 43220 • AASL

Collier Frank • Vice President • Carr McLean Limited • Toronto ON, Canada • AASL ACRL ALCTS ASCLA LAMA LITA ERT

Collier Kathryn • Media Specialist • Sycamore Junior High School • Cincinnati, OH 45242 • AASL

Collier Mark • Ref./Biblio. Instr Libn • Western Maryland College Hoover Library • Westminster, MD 21157-4390

Collier Monica H. • Detroit Metro Regional Librarian • Central Michigan University • Troy, MI 48084 • ACRL

Collignon Mary Ann • Williamsburg Regional Library • Williamsburg, VA 23185 • ALSC PLA

Colling Michael L. • Student Librarian III • Los Angeles Public Library West L.A. Rgnl. Branch • Los Angeles, CA 90025 • EMIERT IFRT SRRT

Collings Terry R. • Development Officer • Seattle Public Library • Seattle, WA 98104-1193 • LAMA

Collini Robert A. • Student • Simmons College Graduate School of Library & Information Science • Boston, MA 02115 • ACRL PLA RASD NMRT

Collins-Turner Kathryn • Media Specialist • Urie Elementary School Uinta District #6 • Lyman, WY 82937

Collins Adeline T. • Cleveland, TN 37312

Collins Barbara D. • Head Librarian • Central High School • Knoxville, TN 37918 • AASL LIRT

Collins Betsy R. • Daniel Boone Regional Library • Columbia, MO 65205-1267 • PLA

Collins Bobbie L. • Wake Forest University Z Smith Reynolds Library • Winston Salem, NC 27109-7777 • ACRL

Collins Boyd R. • Christendom College • Front Royal, VA 22630

Collins Bruce • Librarian • University City Public Library • University City, MO 63130 • PLA RASD

Collins Carol A. • Asst. Supv. of Circulation • Waukegan Public Library • Waukegan, IL 60085 • PLA

Collins Carol J. • Student • Rutgers University School of Communication Information & Library Studies • New Brunswick, NJ 08903 • AASL EMIERT

Collins Catherine D. • Niigata 959-26, Japan • ACRL LAMA IRRT

Collins Cathy E. • Student • University of South Florida School of Library & Information Science • Tampa, FL 33620 • AASL

Collins Cheryl • Senior Librarian • Los Angeles Public Library • Los Angeles, CA 90047 • PLA

Collins Elizabeth H. • Centerville, MD 21617 • Continuing

Collins Elizabeth M. • Middle School Librarian • Poquoson Middle School • Poquoson, VA 23665 • AASL

Collins Eugenia A. • Atlanta, GA 30318 • PLA RASD *Life*

Collins Evron S. • Clln Devel/Map Librarian • Bowling Green State University Jerome Library • Bowling Green, OH 43403 • ACRL LAMA GODORT MAGERT   *Life*

Collins Geraldine • University of North Florida Thomas G. Carpenter Library • Jacksonville, FL 32245-7605

Collins Grace M. Mrs • Vista, CA 92083 • Continuing

Collins Helen J. • Valencia, CA 91355

Collins Iris • Media Specialist • Harrison Central Elementary School • Gulfport, MS 39503 • AASL

Collins Jacquelyn • Warwick, NY 10990

Collins Janice Ann • Assistant Librarian • Clausen Miller Gorman Caffrey & Witous P.C. Library • Chicago, IL 60603

Collins Jean D. • University Library Director • Northern Arizona University • Flagstaff, AZ 86011-6022

Collins Jennifer • Student • University of California-Berkeley School of Library & Information Studies • Berkeley, CA 94720 • ALSC

Collins Joan E. • Corporate Librarian • John Fluke Mfg. Company Inc. • Everett, WA 98206-9090 • LAMA

Collins John William III • Librarian • Harvard University Gutman Library-Research Center • Cambridge, MA 02138 • ACRL

Collins Joy S. • Head of Information Srvs Dept. • Drexel University W. W. Hagerty Library • Philadelphia, PA 19104 • ACRL

Collins Judith Ann • Salinas, CA 93908 • ILERT

Collins Leonora T. • Olympic High School • Charlotte, NC 28210 • AASL IFRT

Collins Linda E. • Wheaton College Wallace Library • Norton, MA 02766 • LAMA

Collins Mary Anne • Librarian • Ingram Tom Moore H. S. Library • Ingram, TX 78025 • AASL

Collins Mary Ellen • Associate Professor • Purdue University Libraries • West Lafayette, IN 47907-1530 • ACRL RASD

Collins Mary Frances • Director, Central Tech. Services • University of Minnesota O. Meredith Wilson Library • Minneapolis, MN 55455-0414 • ACRL ALCTS

Collins Melanie H. • Director • Harnett County Public Library System • Lillington, NC 27546 • LITA PLA NMRT

Collins Mianda • Lake Lanier Regional Library Lawrenceville Branch • Lawrenceville, GA 30245-4707

Collins Mitzi L. • Library of Congress • Washington, DC 20541 • ALCTS

Collins Myrtis Cochran • Associate Reference Librarian • University of California-Berkeley University Library • Berkeley, CA 94720 • ACRL RASD NMRT

Collins Patricia A. • Media Generalist • Danville Elementary • Danville, NH 03819 • AASL

Collins Patricia L. • Librarian/Media Specialist • Cook Elementary School • Austin, TX 78102 • AASL ALSC IFRT

Collins Patrick • Student • Florida State University School of Library and Information Studies • Tallahassee, FL 32306-2048 • ALCTS LITA

Collins Pauline P. • Latin American Specialist • University of Massachusetts Library • Amherst, MA 01003 • ACRL

Collins Sadie • Trustee • Prince William Public Library System Administrative Support Center • Prince William, VA 22192-5073

Collins Sandra • Media Coordinator • South Rowan High School • China Grove, NC 28023 • AASL IFRT

Collins Sandra A. • Associcate Director • Weber County Library • Odgen, UT 84401 • ALCTS ALSC LAMA PLA IFRT SRRT

Collins Sara J. • Virginiana Librarian • Arlington County Dept of Libraries Columbia Pike Branch • Arlington, VA 22204

Collins Sarah F. • Library Director • Foundation Center • New York, NY 10003 • LAMA

Collins Sharon E. • Pt. Jefferson Stn, NY 11776 • ACRL

Collins Sheila B. • Student • State University of New York (SUNY) School of Information & Library Studies • Buffalo, NY 14260

Collins Shelley A. • Las Vegas, NV 89130 • YALSA

Collins Susan E. • Librarian • Roxbury Public Library • Succasunna, NJ 07876 • ALCTS

Collins Thunga T. • Carrollton, TX 75006

Collins Tim • Wayne, NJ 07470 • ALTA

Collins Violet Kulcke • Ouachita Parish Public Library • Monroe, LA 71201 • ALTA

Collins William P. • Alexandria, VA 22306

Collinsworth Barbara L. • Mio, MI 48647 • ACRL

Collum Dale E. • Student • Florida State University School of Library and Information Studies • Tallahassee, FL 32306-2048 • RASD

Collum Garry B. • Student • University of North Texas School of Library & Information Sciences • Denton, TX 76203 • SRRT

Collura Ruth L. • Public Service Librarian • Community College of Allegheny County South Campus Library • West Mifflin, PA 15122 • ACRL

Colmer Mary W. • Moss Point, MS 39563 • ACRL ALCTS
Life

Colombo Charles A. • Interlibrary Loan Assistant • Widener University School of Law • Harrisburg, PA 17110-9450

Colombo Claire A. • Circulation Librarian • University of Georgia Libraries • Athens, GA 30602 • ACRL LAMA

Colombo Mary Elizabeth • Director • B F Jones Memorial Library Aliquippa District Center • Aliquippa, PA 15001 • ALSC LAMA PLA RASD YALSA

Colon Carlos • Reference Supervisor • Shreve Memorial Library • Shreveport, LA 71120-1523

Colon Nancy • School Librarian • Saint Johns School • Santurce, PR 00907-1560 • AASL

Colpaert Nancy J. • Head of Collection Services • Monroe County Library System • Monroe, MI 48161

Colpitts Kinne • Reference Librarian • University of Arkansas Libraries • Fayetteville, AR 72701-1201 • ACRL MAGERT

Colson Elizabeth A. • Director,Cataloging Dept. • Houston Academy of Medicine Texas Medical Center Library • Houston, TX 77030

Colson Judith K. • Head of Collections Development • University of New Brunswick • Fredericton NB, E3B 5H5 Canada • ACRL RASD

Colson Margaret • Saratoga, CA 95070 • ALSC

Colt James N. • Associate Professor of Education • North Carolina Agricultural & Technical State University • Greensboro, NC 27411

Colt Pamela B. • Somerville Public Library • Somerville, MA 02143

Colter Deborah J. • Indianapolis Marion County Public Library • Indianapolis, IN 46206 • YALSA NMRT

Colter Pityllis • Literacy Executive Director • El Centro Public Library • El Centro, CA 92243-2973

Coltman Ellen • Lake Lanier Regional Library Buford-Sugar Hill Branch • Buford, GA 30518

Colton Norma W. • York Public Library • Yorktown, VA 23692

Coltrin Sue Ellen • Librarian • Tucson Unified School District Rincon/University High Schools • Tucson, AZ 85711 • AASL

Colucci Eugene V. • Buffalo, NY 14223 • IFRT

Colucio Ann B. • River Edge, NJ 07661

Colver Marylou • Senior Account Manager • Blackwell North America • Lake Oswego, OR 97034 • ALCTS

Colvin-Harrison Laura • Washington, DC 20024 • ACRL ALCTS
Life

Colvin Emsie D. • Birmingham, AL 35211 • Continuing

Colvin Gloria P. • Reference Librarian • Duke University • Durham, NC 27708

Colvson Mark H • Reference Librarian • University of Pennsylvania Library Van Pelt-Dietrich Library Center • Philadelphia, PA 19104-6206 • RASD

Colwell Carolyn J. • Assistant Reference Librarian • Georgetown University Joseph Mark Lauinger Library • Washington, DC 20057-1006 • ACRL RASD

Colwell Patricia E. • Ashland, OR 97520-2607

Combs Adele W. • Asst Univ Libn for Public Serv. • Northwestern University Library • Evanston, IL 60208-2300 • ACRL LAMA LITA RASD

Combs Brenda R. • Wilkesboro, NC 28697 • AASL

Combs Cinda S. • Library Assistant • Mission Viejo Library • Mission Viejo, CA 92691

Combs Darra R. • University Hospital Health Sciences Library • Augusta, GA 30910-3599

Combs Mary C. • Reference Services • University of Minnesota • Minneapolis, MN 55455 • ACRL RASD

Combs Patricia A. • School Library Media Spec. • La Plata Senior High School Media Center • La Plata, MD 20646 • ACRL

Comeau Amy R. • Head Librarian • Haight Gardner Poor & Havens • New York, NY 10007

Comeau Reginald A. Dr. • Director of Learning Resources • New Hampshire Technical College • Manchester, NH 03102-8518

Comeaux Connie B. • Librarian • Jeanerette Elementary School • Jeanerette, LA 70544 • AASL

Comen Diane B. • Palatine, IL 60067 • AASL ALSC PLA

Comeno Doris • Head of Technical Services • LaPorte County Public Library • LaPorte, IN 46350

Comer Cynthia H. • Head of Reference • Oberlin College Library • Oberlin, OH 44074 • ACRL LAMA RASD

Comer Marian Dr. • Trustee • Gary Public Library • Gary, IN 46402 • ALTA

Comerford Sandra S. • Head of Circulation • Wittenberg University Thomas Library • Springfield, OH 45501 • LITA

Comes James F. • Science Librarian • Ball State University • Munice, IN 47304 • ACRL LITA

Comfort Christy • Laurel, MD 20707 • AASL

Comfort Kathy • Bellarmine Prep High School • Tacoma, WA 98405

Comins Dorothy • Ann Arbor, MI 48105 • ACRL ALCTS
Life

Comissiong Barbara L W • Gardens Valsayn, Trinidad • ACRL LAMA

Comly Mary E. • No Liberty, IA 52317

Commerton B. Anne • Sunset Beach, NC 28468 • ACRL

Comparin Ida • Associate Director • Montgomery-Floyd Regional Library • Christiansburg, VA 24073 • PLA

Compton Annilee • Media Coordinator • Whitfield County Public School • Dalton, GA 30720 • AASL

Compton Bruce • Automation Librarian • Louisiana State University Libraries Middleton Library • Baton Rouge, LA 70803-3342 • LITA

Compton Christopher • Santa Rosa, CA 95409-6106

Compton Deborah F. • Community Activies Librarian • Asheville-Buncombe Library System • Asheville, NC 28801

Compton Judy • Trustee • Prince William Public Library System Administrative Support Center • Prince William, VA 22192-5073

Compton Lanell Miss • Head of Catalog Department • Arkansas State Library • Little Rock, AR 72201 • PLA RASD
Life

Compton Larry E. • New Mexico State Library • Santa Fe, NM 87503 • LITA

Compton Susan M. • McKinney Memorial Public Library • McKinney, TX 75069 • PLA

Comras Rema • Miami Beach, FL 33139

Comstock Dan • Los Alamos, NM 87544 • SRRT

Comstock Edna M. • Coordinator, Inf. Exchange • Maine State Library • Augusta, ME 04333 • AASL

Comstock Evelyn B. • Sunnyvale, CA 94086-7622 • ALSC

Comstock MaryAnn • Student • University of Rhode Island Graduate School of Library & Information Studies • Kingston, RI 02881-0815 • ACRL RASD IFRT LHRT NMRT

Conable Gordon M. • Director • Monroe County Library System • Monroe, MI 48161 • LAMA PLA IFRT
Life

Conable Irene H. • Airport High School • Carleton, MI 48117 • AASL

Conant Audrey • Library Media Specialist • Wayne School • Wayne, ME 04284 • AASL

Conant Barbara M. • Park Forest, IL 60466 • ACRL LIRT

Conant Veronika A. • Acting Head • Hunter College Library • New York, NY 10021 • ACRL RASD

Conaty Barbara • Library of Congress • Washington, DC 20541 • ALCTS

Conaway Brenda L. • Children's Services Supervisor • Carroll County Public Library • Westminster, MD 21157 • ALSC

Conaway Charles William • Associate Professor • Florida State University School of Library and Information Studies • Tallahassee, FL 32306-2048 • ACRL IRRT
Life

Conaway Eve E. • Huntsville, AL 35803 • ALSC YALSA

Conaway Margaret G. • Senior Librarian • San Jose Public Library • San Jose, CA 95113

Conaway Tara L. • Director • Zeeland Public Library • Zeeland, MI 49464

Concannon Tom • Ridgefield, CT 06877

Concato Dolores M. • Librarian • Hazel Park High School • Hazel Park, MI 48030 • AASL

Concklin Smiley Betty A. • Librarian • Lehigh Acres Public Library • Lehigh Acres, FL 33936 • ALSC PLA

Condic Kristine Salomon • Oakland University • Rochester, MI 48309-4401 • ACRL

Condit Larry D. • Reference Center • Santa Clara County Free Library Cupertino Public Library • Cupertino, CA 95014 • RASD YALSA

Condit Martha O. • Florham Pk, NJ 07932 • AASL ALSC
Continuing

Condit Nancy E. • Catalog Librarian • University of Arizona Arizona Health Sciences Center Library • Tucson, AZ 85724 • ALCTS

Condon Scott M • Edmonds, WA 98026-3614

Condron Lyn • Texas Woman's University Mary Evelyn Blagg-Huey Library • Denton, TX 76204-1715

Condry Linda C. • Head, Tech Servs/Automation • Marion Public Library • Marion, OH 43302 • PLA MAGERT

Conduitte Catherine J. • Librarian Grade 5 • Miami-Dade Public Library System West Dade Regional Library • Miami, FL 33165 • PLA

Cone Patricia A. • St. Petersburg, FL 33708

Conesa Lillian S. • Miami, FL 33126 • ALCTS

Conescu Marcia • Manhasset Public Library • Manhasset, NY 11030

Congdon Charles C. • Professor Emeritus • Octagon Press, LTD London • Oak Ridge, TN 37831 • ACRL

Congdon Gertrude P. • Shawnee Mission, KS 66205 • Continuing

Congdon Nell A. • Head of Inf. & Ref. Division • New Orleans Public Library • New Orleans, LA 70140 • RASD IFRT

Congelosi Catherine • Circulation & Clln Devel Supv • Bershire Athenaeum Pittsfield Public Library • Pittsfield, MA 01201

Conger Joan E. • Student • University of Texas at Austin Graduate School of Library & Information Sciences • Austin, TX 78712-1276 • ACRL ALSC LAMA RASD

Conger Mary Jane • Assistant Cataloging Librarian • University of North Carolina Walter Clinton Jackson Library • Greensboro, NC 27412-5201 • ALCTS

Congleton Robert • Serials Acquisitions Librarian • Temple University Paley Library • Philadelphia, PA 19122 • LIRT

Conitz Allison • San Marcos, CA 92069

Conkey Edith B. • San Francisco, CA 94116 • AASL YALSA
Life

Conklin Candace V. • Tampa-Hillsborough County Public Library Thonotosassa Branch • Thonotosassa, FL 33592 • YALSA

Conklin Harriet • Librarian • Kewanee Public Library • Kewanee, IL 61443

Conklin Honor • Albany, NY 12203-1514 • ACRL SRRT

Conklin Nancy M. • Head Librarian • Horseheads Free Library Ruth B Leet Library • Horseheads, NY 14845 • PLA

Conklin Robert C. • Student • Indiana University School of Library and Information Science • Bloomington, IN 47405 • PLA

Conklin Thomas • Editor • Silver Moon Press • New York, NY 10011

Conkling Diedre • Lincoln County Library District • Newport, OR 97365 • LAMA PLA SRRT

Conlan Eileen • Clearwater, FL 34621

Conley Kathleen M. • Library Tech. Asst. III • Illinois State University Milner Library • Normal, IL 61761-0900

Conley Sally J. • Student • Rutgers University School of Communication Information & Library Studies • New Brunswick, NJ 08903

Conlin David B. • Lawrence, KS 66064

Conlin Marie A. • Reference Librarian • Saint Louis County Library • St. Louis, MO 63131

Conlon Alice C. • Houston, TX 77005 • AASL ALSC

Conlon James F. • Librarian • Franklin County Technical High School • Turner Falls, MA 01326

Conlon Kathryn E. • Henderson County Public Library • Hendersonville, NC 28739

Conmy Peter T. • City Librarian Emeritus • Oakland Public Library • Oakland, CA 94612 • LAMA LHRT

Conn Joseph W. • West Branch School • Bradford, PA 16701

Connair Karen L. • Library Director • Base Library Andrew AFB • Washington, DC 20334 • FLRT

Connaway Lynn S. • Grand Junction, CO 81503 • ALCTS LRRT

Connayhan Stephen J. • Student • Catholic University of America Libraries • Washington, DC 20064 • LITA

Conneen Olga F. • Children's Librarian • Bethlehem Area Public Library • Bethlehem, PA 18018-5888 • ALSC

Connell Carol M. • New Fairfield Free Public Library • New Fairfield, CT 06812

Connell Kari E. • Student • University of Texas at Austin Graduate School of Library & Information Sciences • Austin, TX 78712-1276 • AASL

Connell Patricia J. • Director • Altoona Area Public Library • Altoona, PA 16602-3693 • ALTA LAMA PLA YALSA

Connell Robert H. • Librarian • Capitol Region Library Council • Windsor, CT 06095 • LAMA LITA

Connell Suzan D. • Adult Resources Coordinator • Lincoln City Libraries • Lincoln, NE 68508 • PLA IFRT SRRT

Connell Suzanne Mclaurin • Southport, NC 28461-3706 • Continuing

Connell Tschera Harkness • Kent State University School of Library & Information Science • Kent, OH 44242-0001 • ACRL ALCTS LITA

Connellan Catherine J. • Director-Media Services • Troy School District • Troy, MI 48083 • AASL

Connellan Cathy • Trustee • Rochester Hills Public Library • Rochester, MI 48307 • ALTA

Connelly Christy • Friends' Shop Mgr/Buyer • Public Library of Cincinnati and Hamilton County • Cincinnati, OH 45202 • PLA

Connelly Dolores • Melrose Park Public Library • Melrose Park, IL 60160

Connelly Maureen A. • Youth Librarian • New York Public Library Aguilar Branch • New York, NY 10029 • YALSA

Connelly Patricia J. • Kirkpatrick Middle School • Fort Worth, TX 76106 • AASL

Conner Connie L. • Student • Kent State University School of Library & Information Science • Kent, OH 44242-0001 • ALCTS

Conner Kelly A. • Maine University Blake Library • Fort Kent, ME 04743 • ACRL

Conner Leola Mae • Branch Manager • Newport Beach Public Library Corona del Mar Branch • Corona del Mar, CA 92625

Conner Phyllis H. • S.L. Lewis Elementary School • College Park, GA 30349 • AASL

Conner Ronald C. • Reference Librarian • Arlington Heights Memorial Library • Arlington Heights, IL 60004-5966 • RASD

Conner Rosalind Kaplan • Head of Technical Services • Four County Library System • Vestal, NY 13850

Conning Carmela A. • Kemmerer, WY 83101 • AASL

Connolly Elizabeth J. • Bronx, NY 10458 • Continuing

Connolly Laura H. • Technical Information Spec • Roy F. Weston, Inc. • Albuquerque, NM 87108

Connolly Susan C. • Library Associate • Tacoma Public Library • Tacoma, WA 98402 • GODORT

Connolly Sybil D. • Windsor Hills Elementary • Oklahoma City, OK 73127 • AASL ALSC

Connor Anne C. • Senior Librarian • Los Angeles Public Library West L.A. Rgnl. Branch • Los Angeles, CA 90025 • ALSC PLA

Connor Billie M. • Hd of Science, Tech and Patents • Los Angeles Public Library • Los Angeles, CA 90071 • ACRL PLA RASD GODORT IFRT SRRT

Connor Carol J. • Director • Lincoln City Libraries • Lincoln, NE 68508 • LAMA LITA PLA

Connor Elizabeth Miss • Claremont, CA 91711 • Continuing

Connor Evelyn • Director Branch Libraries • Denver Public Library • Denver, CO 80203-2165 • PLA IFRT

Connor Jean L. Miss • Delmar, NY 12054 • ASCLA PLA
Life

Connor Patricia A. • Marian College Library • Indianapolis, IN 46222 • ALCTS

Connor Sharon C. • Librarian • Brookfield Elementary School • Chantilly, VA 22021 • AASL

Connor Sharon E. • Student • Catholic University of America School of Library and Information Science • Washington, DC 20064

Connors Elizabeth A.S. • Librarian • Mentor Public Library • Mentor, OH 44060 • PLA

Connors Jean M. • Law Librarian • U S Department of Energy Bonneville Power Administrative Library • Portland, OR 97208

Connors Kathleen M. • Librarian • Thrall Library • Middletown, NY 10940 • PLA GODORT

Connors Lavinia M. • Director of Library Media • Belmont Public Schools • Belmont, MA 02178 • AASL

Connors Linda E. • Coor of Collection Development • Drew University • Madison, NJ 07940-4007 • ACRL

Connors Maureen S. • Reference Librarian • George Mason University Libraries • Fairfax, VA 22030 • ACRL

Connors Nancy J. • Media Specialist • Westside Middle School • Omaha, NE 68114

Connors Sheila S. • Student • University of Wisconsin-Superior Jim Dan Hill Library • Superior, WI 54880

Connors Theresa M. • Spring Hill College Thomas Byrne Memorial Library • Mobile, AL 36608

Connors William E. • Director • State University of New York College at New Paltz Sojourner Truth Library • New Paltz, NY 12561 • ACRL LAMA

Connorton Judy • Archives Librarian • City College of New York (CUNY) • New York, NY 10031 • ACRL

Conover Craig R. • Union City, CA 94587 • Life

Conover Janet G. • Hayward Public Library • Hayward, CA 94541 • PLA
Life

Conover Kathryn H. • Media Specialist • William T. Dwyer High School • Palm Beach Gardens, FL 33418 • AASL

Conover Mary • Middle School Librarian • Glassboro Intermediate School • Glassboro, NJ 08028

Conover Robert W. • Library Director • City of Commerce Public Library • Commerce, CA 90040 • LAMA PLA RASD

Conrad Claudia P. • Library Assistant/Clerk • Sacramento City College Library • Sacramento, CA 95822 • ALCTS

Conrad Darla • St. Petersburg, FL 33713

Conrad Deborah K. • Network Administrator • Southeastern Automated Libraries, Inc. • South Dartmouth, MA 02748 • LITA

Conrad Eva • North Miami, FL 33181 • GODORT

Conrad Frances M. • Director • Shelter Rock Public Library • Albertson, NY 11507 • LAMA PLA

Conrad Gertrude C. • Media Coordinator • Derita Elementary School • Charlotte, NC 28262 • AASL

Conrad Jim H. • Univ. Archv. & Oral Historian • East Texas State University Library • Commerce, TX 75428

Conrad Kay Ann • Head, Reference Department • Fond du Lac Public Library • Fond du Lac, WI 54935

Conrad Leigh E. • Scottsdale Public Library • Scottsdale, AZ 85251

Conrad Marc A. • Student • Indiana University School of Library and Information Science • Bloomington, IN 47405 • ACRL SRRT

Conrad Melinda S. • Adult Services Supervisor • Chandler Public Library • Chandler, AZ 85225 • PLA RASD

Conrad Neily • Branch Manager • Public Library of Charlotte & Mecklenburg County Matthews Branch • Matthews, NC 28105 • PLA

Conrad Patricia A. • Adult Services-Head • Freeport Public Library • Freeport, IL 61032 • NMRT

Conrad R. Victor • Supv. Publications Devel/Lib. • Thiorol Corporation • Brigham City, UT 84302-0707 • ALCTS LAMA

Conrad Scott • Beloit Public Library • Beloit, WI 53511

Conrath Gail H. • Reference Librarian • Downers Grove Public Library • Downers Grove, IL 60515 • PLA

Conrow Jane A. • Asst. Dean of Libraries/Planning • Arizona State University Libraries • Tempe, AZ 85287-1006 • ACRL LAMA

Conroy Cathleen H. • Serials Librarian • Harvard Law School Library • Cambridge, MA 02138 • ALCTS

Conroy Christine • Cataloging Department • Boston College O'Neill Library • Chestnut Hill, MA 02167 • ALCTS LITA

Conroy Margaret M. • Coordinator,Cooperative Services • Great River Library System • Quincy, IL 62301-3997

Conroy Patricia Regan • Director • Alexandria Public Library • Alexandria, MN 56308-1790

Conser Mary C • Supervisor/AV & Circulation • Lorain Public Library • Lorain, OH 44052 • PLA VRT

Consoli Joseph P. • Humanities Bibliographer • Rutgers University Libraries • New Brunswick, NJ 08903 • ACRL

Constance Joseph • Director of Library • Saint Anselm College Geisel Library • Manchester, NH 03102-1310 • ACRL LAMA

Constant Jane I. • Reference Librarian • B M C Durfee High School • Fall River, MA 02720 • AASL

Constantinides Judith H. • Children's Librarian • East Baton Rouge Parish Library • Baton Rouge, LA 70806-7699 • ALSC

Conte Joyce A. • Director • East Detroit Memorial Library • East Detroit, MI 48021-2390

Conte Margaret T. • Teacher-Librarian • Allen Creek School • Rochester, NY 14618

Contee Richard • Trustee • Phoenix Public Library • Phoenix, AZ 85004 • ALTA

Conti-White Linda • Trustee • Loudoun County Public Library • Leesburg, VA 22075 • ALTA

Conti Louise M. • Branch Manager • Atlanta-Fulton Public Library Roswell Branch • Roswell, GA 30075 • PLA

Convery Marjorie • Vineyard Haven Public Library • Vineyard Haven, MA 02568 • PLA CLENE

Conway Anne W. • Head Adult Services • Cuyahoga County Public Library Berea Branch • Berea, OH 44017-2524 • RASD SORT

Conway Colleen M. • Hope College Van Wylen Library • Holland, MI 49423 • ACRL ALCTS NMRT

Conway Elizabeth E. • Head, Circulation Department • Rutgers University John Cotton Dana Library • Newark, NJ 07102 • ACRL NMRT

Conway Jane E. • Fine Arts Librarian • Ann Arbor Public Library • Ann Arbor, MI 48104

Conway Jeanne W. • Associate Librarian • Gallaudet University Library • Washington, DC 20002

Conway Lauren K. • Reference Librarian • Lansing Public Library • Lansing, MI 48933

Conway Linda J. • Shore Regional High School • W Long Branch, NJ 07764 • AASL LITA

Conway Martha O'Hara • Library of Congress • Washington, DC 20541 • ALCTS

Conway Mary E. • Librarian/Media Specialist • Toll Gate High School Library • Warwick, RI 02886

Conway Melissa • Arlington, VA 22201 • ACRL

Conway Michael J. • Automation Services Coordinator • Michigan Library Consortium • Lansing, MI 48911 • RASD

Conway Paul L. • Yale University Sterling Memorial Library • New Haven, CT 06520 • ALCTS

Conway Sue E. • Hockessin, DE 19707

Conwell George J. • Supervising Librarian • Brooklyn Public Library King's Highway Branch • Brooklyn, NY 11229

Conwell Mary K. • Associate Director • New York Public Library Manhattan Borough Office • New York, NY 10019 • PLA

Conzola Kim E. • Student • State University of New York (SUNY) School of Information & Library Studies • Buffalo, NY 14260

Coo Losu Marcus Ekundayo • Librarian Division Head • Rubber Research Institute of Nigeria • Benin City, Nigeria W. Africa • ACRL LITA

Cook-Wood Holly M. • Director • College of the Albemarle • Elizabeth City, NC 27909 • ACRL

Cook Anita I. • Associate Professor • University of Nebraska-Lincoln University Libraries • Lincoln, NE 68588-0410 • ACRL LITA

Cook Anita S. • Technical Services Librarian • Grand Rapids Community College Library • Grand Rapids, MI 49503

Cook Ann H. • Head of Youth Services • Winter Park Public Library • Winter Park, FL 32789 • ALSC

Cook B. Donald • Trustee • Massachusetts Board of Library Commissioners • Boston, MA 02215-2070

Cook Beth A. • Southwestern Heights High School • Kismet, KS 67859 • AASL

Cook C. Colleen • College Stn, TX 77845 • ALCTS LAMA

Cook C. Donald Prof • Toronto ON, M5R 2X3 Canada • ACRL ALCTS LITA
Life

Cook Candace • Oxford, OH 45056 • AASL ASCLA LIRT

Cook Catharine • Director • Enid & Garfield County Public Library • Enid, OK 73702 • PLA

Cook Cathy L. • Student • University of Missouri-Columbia School of Library & Informational Science • Columbia, MO 65211

Cook Charles T. • Director • Portsmouth Public Library • Portsmouth, OH 45662

Cook Cheryl C. • Customer Service Analyst • Library of Congress • Washington, DC 20541

Cook Daraka S. • Public Services Librarian • Catonsville Community College • Baltimore, MD 21228 • ACRL

Cook Dawn Mather • Boston, MA 02130

Cook Deborah A. • Head of Loan Services • Southern Oregon State Coll Library • Ashland, OR 97520

Cook Donald C. • Associate Director • State University of New York (SUNY) Frank Melville Jr. Memorial Library • Stony Brook, NY 11794-3300 • ACRL ALCTS LITA RASD

Cook Douglas L. • Media Librarian • Shippensburg University Lehman Memorial Library • Shippensburg, PA 17257-2299

Cook Eleanor I. • Serials Librarian • Appalachian State University Carol Grotnes Belk Library • Boone, NC 28608 • ACRL ALCTS LITA

Cook Gail F. • Librarian • California State University-Dominguez Hills Library • Carson, CA 90747 • ACRL

Cook Glenn S. • George C. Marshall Research Library • Lexington, VA 24450 • ACRL ALCTS

Cook Grace H. • Trustee • Saint John the Baptist Parish Library • LaPlace, LA 70068 • ALTA

Cook Harry F. • Bradenton, FL 34209 • Continuing

Cook Ilse Mary • Educational Media Spec. K-12 • Platte Canyon High School • Bailey, CO 80421 • YALSA

Cook James Edward • Young Adult Librarian • Dayton & Montgomery County Public Library • Dayton, OH 45402-2103 • YALSA SORT SRRT

Cook Jane Dyer • Branch Librarian • Stockton-San Joaquin County Public Library Margaret K. Troke Branch • Stockton, CA 95207 • ALSC

Cook Janet • Librarian • Public School #101 • Forest Hills, NY 11375 • AASL

Cook Jean G. • Ames, IA 50010

Cook Jean K. • Student • State University of New York (SUNY) School of Information & Library Studies • Buffalo, NY 14260 • ALCTS RASD SRRT

Cook Jeannine S. • Stony Brook, NY 11790 • ALSC LAMA PLA

Cook Jill A. • Helene Fuld Medical Center Medical Library • Trenton, NJ 08638

Cook Juanita • Director, Learning Resources • Southern Arkansas University -Tech Library Tech Station • Camden, AR 71701-1148 • ACRL

Cook June A. • Juneau, AK 99801 • ACRL

Cook Karen J. • Mt. Vernon, IN 47620 • ALCTS LITA PLA IFRT NMRT

Cook Kevin L. • Carrollton, GA 30117-3034 • ACRL GODORT

Cook Kim N. Mr. • Library Director • Kent State University Library Ashtabula Campus Library • Ashtabula, OH 44004 • LAMA LRRT

Cook Kimberly • Assistant Librarian • Elk Township Library • Peck, MI 48466-0268 • PLA

Cook Laraine E. • Santa Clara Elementary School • Eugene, OR 97404

Cook Lynn F. • Classification/Catalog Librarian • Schenectady County Public Library • Schenectady, NY 12305

Cook Margaret K. • Assistant Librarian • Southern Illinois University Delyte W. Morris Library • Carbondale, IL 62901-6632 • ACRL

Cook Marion E. • Farmington, CT 06032 • Continuing

Cook Marjorie L. • Library Director • Summer Institute of Linguistics • 1099 Manila, Philippines • ALCTS

Cook Marsha • Library/Media Specialist • Pennichuck Junior High • Nashua, NH 03090 • AASL

Cook Mary E. • Philadelphia, PA 19131-5605

Cook Merribeth • St Louis, MO 63119

Cook Nancy E. • Madison, SD 57042

Cook Pamela D. • Research Libraries Group Inc. (RLG) • Mountain View, CA 94041-1100

Cook Peggy C. • Goffstown, NH 03045

Cook Peggy Royster • Branch Manager • Norman Public Library • Norman, OK 73069 • PLA IFRT

Cook Robin J. • Photo Librarian • Labat-Anderson Incorporated • Arlington, VA 22201

Cook Rosemond F. • La Jolla, CA 92037

Cook Ruth A. • Librarian • Pond Springs Elementary School • Austin, TX 78729

Cook Sally • Phoenix, AZ 85021

Cook Sybilla A. • Roseburg, OR 97470 • AASL ALSC LIRT *Continuing*

Cook Wendell E. • Southern County Services • Atlanta, GA 30346 • LAMA PLA IFRT

Cook Wendy M. • Duncan, OK 73533 • PLA SRRT

Cooke Anna Lee • Jackson, TN 38301 • Continuing

Cooke Annie C. Mrs • Rumford, RI 02916 • LAMA PLA *Continuing*

Cooke Barbara L. • Information Specialist • Van Kampen Merritt • Oakbrook Terrace, IL 60181 • RASD LRRT

Cooke Bette L. • Director of the Library • Saint Mary of the Plains College Library Science Program • Dodge City, KS 67801 • ACRL YALSA

Cooke Constance • Director • Queens Borough Public Library • Jamaica, NY 11432 • LAMA PLA

Cooke Eileen D. • Associate Executive Director • American Library Association Washington Office • Washington, DC 20002 • LAMA PLA *Life*

Cooke George W. • Franklin Lakes Public Library • Franklin Lakes, NJ 07417 • ALCTS PLA RASD EMIERT

Cooke Grace Mrs. • Board of Trustees • East Orange Public Library • East Orange, NJ 07018 • ALTA

Cooke Joan F. • Outreach Services Librarian • Finger Lakes Library System • Ithaca, NY 14850 • ALSC PLA

Cooke Marcia L. • Head of Access Services • Aurora University Library • Aurora, IL 60506

Cooke Susan • Thunderbird High School • Phoenix, AZ 85023 • AASL LITA

Cookingham Peter O. • Librarian & Project Manager • Michigan State University Libraries • East Lansing, MI 48824-1048 • LITA

Cookingham Robert M. • Director of Administrative Serv • Brooklyn College Library • Brooklyn, NY 11210 • ACRL

Cooklock Richard A. • River Falls, WI 54022 • Continuing

Cooksey Elizabeth B. • Georgia State University Pullen Library • Atlanta, GA 30303-3081 • SRRT

Cookston James S. Dr. • Baton Rouge, LA 70808 • AASL YALSA IRRT *Life*

Cooley Dan • Dover Public Library • Dover, OH 44622 • LAMA PLA

Cooley David Sears • Boston, MA 02116 • PLA RASD *Life*

Cooley Laurel J. • Editor • H. W. Wilson Company • Bronx, NY 10452 • YALSA

Cooley Marney • Director • Tecumseh Public Library • Tecumseh, MI 49286 • LAMA PLA

Coolidge-Harshbarger Amy • Indianapolis, IN 46219

Coolidge Daurel L. • Rogue Community College Library • Grants Pass, OR 97527 • AASL

Coolidge Martha B. • Atlanta, GA 30319 • ACRL LITA RASD

Coombs Elisabeth • Pittsboro, NC 27312

Coombs James A. • Map Librarian • Southwest Missouri State University Library • Springfield, MO 65804-0095 • MAGERT

Coombs Leonard A. • Associate Collections Archivist • Michigan Historical Collection • Ann Arbor, MI 48109 • ACRL

Coon Carol E. • Goverment Documents Manager • San Francisco Public Library • San Francisco, CA 94102 • RASD GODORT

Coon Jeffrey A. • Reference Librarian • Indiana University at Kokomo Learning Resources Center • Kokomo, IN 46904-9003 • RASD GODORT

Coon Wendell B. • Pasadena, CA 91101-1259 • PLA FLRT *Life*

Cooney Jane Hanson • President • Books for Business Ltd • Toronto ON, M4V 1A2 Canada

Cooney Joan D. • Reference Librarian • Hofstra University Axinn Library • Hempstead, NY 11550 • ACRL RASD

Cooney Mary K. • Master's Student • Saint Petersburg Junior College M.M. Bennett Library • Pinellas Park, FL 34665 • RASD IFRT

Cooney Mata-Marie H.J. • Librarian • Truckee Meadows Community College Learning Resources Center • Reno, NV 89512 • ACRL

Coonin Bryna R. • Assistant Head Reference Dept. • North Carolina State University D. H. Hill Library • Raleigh, NC 27695-7111 • RASD GODORT

Coonley Linda • Branch Manager • Johnson County Library • Shawnee Mission, KS 66201 • PLA

Coons Bill • Reference • Cornell University School of Hotel Administration Library • Ithaca, NY 14853-6902 • ACRL LITA RASD

Coons Elinor J. • Librarian • Star Hill School Library • Dover, DE 19901

Coons Martha E. • Student • State University of New York at Albany School of Information Science & Policy • Albany, NY 12222 • RASD SRRT

Cooper-Fedler Pamela A. • Devel & External Rel Offr • Texas Tech University Texas Tech Library • Lubbock, TX 79409 • ACRL LAMA

Cooper Alice M. Miss • Gilman, IL 60938 • ACRL RASD *Life*

Cooper Annie M. • Hd Libn.,Sch of Labor & Ind Rel • Michigan State University Libraries • East Lansing, MI 48824-1048 • ACRL LAMA

Cooper Arthur G. • Librarian • Mineola Middle School • Mineola, NY 11501 • AASL

Cooper Barbara D. • Public Affairs Director • Omnigraphics Inc. • Fort Lauderdale, FL 33301 • ALTA

Cooper Carol D. • R. R. Bowker • New Providence, NJ 07974 • ACRL ALCTS LITA

Cooper Carol V. • Chatham, NJ 07928

Cooper Catherine • Assistant Director • Lee Whedon Memorial Library • Medina, NY 14103

Cooper Cheryl J. • Library Director • Saint Mary Parish Library • Franklin, LA 70538 • ALTA PLA

Cooper Christy • Rensselaer, NY 12144

Cooper Collins Peggy S. • Collection Development Libn. • Western Oregon State College Library • Monmouth, OR 97361 • ACRL ALCTS

Cooper Cynthia W. • Student • North Texas State University Willis Library • Denton, TX 76203 • ALCTS

Cooper David L. • Director • Noblesville-Southeastern Public Library • Noblesville, IN 46060 • LAMA PLA SRRT

Cooper Eileen • Director • Widener University School of Law Library • Wilmington, DE 19803-0475 • ACRL IFRT

Cooper Elizabeth A. • San Antonio College Library • San Antonio, TX 78212

Cooper Elizabeth C. • Oklahoma City, OK 73122 • Continuing

Cooper Ginnie • Director • Multnomah County Library • Portland, OR 97212 • LAMA PLA RASD *Life*

Cooper Hilma F. • Director • Cheltenham Township Library • Glenside, PA 19038-4586 • ALSC PLA IFRT

Cooper Hope I. • Coordinator,Technical Services • Birmingham Public & Jefferson County Free Library • Birmingham, AL 35203 • ALCTS

Cooper Jacquelyn B. • Branch Librarian • Providence Public Library Rochambeau Branch • Providence, RI 02906

Cooper James P. • West Georgia Regional Library • Carrollton, GA 30117 • PLA

Cooper Joanne S. • Erie, PA 16504

Cooper Jonathan D. • Chief,Catalog Section • State Historical Society of Wisconsin • Madison, WI 53706 • ALCTS

Cooper Judith C. • Development Officer • Prince George's County Memorial Library System • Hyattsville, MD 20782-2098

Cooper Judith K. • Student • Northeastern Illinois University Library • Chicago, IL 60625 • ACRL IFRT

Cooper Judy L. • School Media Consultant • Kentucky Department of Education • Frankfort, KY 40601

Cooper Karen L. • Librarian • Syosset Public Library • Syosset, NY 11791 • AASL RASD

Cooper Katharyn • Sacramento, CA 95864

Cooper L. Gayle • Specialist for Rare Book Catlg. • University of Virginia Alderman Library • Charlottesville, VA 22903-2498 • ACRL

Cooper Lillian P. • Wickenburg, AZ 85358 • ACRL

Cooper Lily P. • Student • University of South Carolina College of Library & Information Science • Columbia, SC 29208 • AASL

Cooper Marcia Allen • Montgomeryvle, PA 18936

Cooper Margaret D. • Director • Stow Public Library • Stow, OH 44224 • LAMA PLA

Cooper Margery Jane • Library Manager • Salt Lake County Library System West Jordan Branch • West Jordan, UT 84084 • ALSC PLA

Cooper Marianne • Director • Queens College Grad Sch of Lib & Inf Studies • Flushing, NY 11367 • ACRL LRRT

Cooper Mary C. • President • Cooper Information • Cambridge, MA 02138 • LAMA

Cooper Mary Frances • Chief, Central Library • Minneapolis Public Library & Information Center • Minneapolis, MN 55401-1992 • ACRL PLA RASD

Cooper May E. • Oean Grove, NJ 07756 • Continuing

Cooper Nancy C. • Reference Librarian • Arlington County Department of Libraries • Arlington, VA 22201

Cooper Naomi Z. • Library Media Specialist • John Jay High School • Brooklyn, NY 11215 • AASL

Cooper Patricia J. • Archv., United Way Production • United Way of America • Alexandria, VA 22314

Cooper Paul F. • Silver Spg, MD 20901

Cooper Rebecca R. • Student • Black Hills State University • Spearfish, SD 57799-9548

Cooper Regina • Head, Collection Development • Huntsville-Madison County Public Library • Huntsville, AL 35804

Cooper Richard A. • Manager of Eductional Technology • Arkansas College • Batesville, AR 72501

Cooper Richard S. • Director/Finance, Planning & Adm • University of California San Francisco Library • San Francisco, CA 94143-0840 • LAMA

Cooper Sandra M. • Chief Bureau of Library Devel. • State Library of Florida Division of Library & Information Services • Tallahassee, FL 32399-0250 • ALTA ASCLA LAMA PLA CLENE

Cooper Sarah H. • Director • Southern California L for Social Studies & Res • Los Angeles, CA 90044

Cooper Sharon M. • Student • Emporia State University School of Library & Information Management • Emporia, KS 66801

Cooper Susan A. Dr. • Assistant Professor • University of Kentucky College of Library & Information Science • Lexington, KY 40506-0391

Cooper Sylvia Jane • Tulsa Regional Medical Center L.C. Baxter Library • Tulsa, OK 74127

Cooper Tracy • Trustee • Pikes Peak Library District • Colorado Springs, CO 80901 • ALTA

Cooper Veronica Dr. • School Media Center Supervisor • Chesterfield County School District Office • Chesterfield, VA 22907 • AASL

Cooper Virginia R. • Youth Services Librarian • Henrietta Public Library • Rochester, NY 14623 • YALSA

Cooper Wilhemina A. • Student • University of South Carolina College of Librarianship • Columbia, SC 29208 • PLA EMIERT SRRT

Cooper William C. • Director • Laurens County Library • Laurens, SC 29360-2647 • ALCTS ALSC LAMA LITA PLA RASD YALSA

Cooper William E. • Kern County Library System • Bakersfield, CA 93301 • Life

Cooperman Estelle R. • Trustee • Morton Grove Public Library • Morton Grove, IL 60053 • ALTA

Coopey Barbara B. • Asst Librarian-Inter-L Loan • Pennsylvania State University Pattee Library • University Park, PA 16802

Cooprider Pearl M. • Gig Harbor, WA 98335

Coover Deborah A. • Director • Pioneer Library System • Newark, NY 14513 • LAMA LITA PLA

Coover Robert W. • San Jose, CA 95135 • ACRL LAMA *Life*

Copans Ruth S. • Librarian • Skidmore College Lucy Scribner Library • Saratoga Springs, NY 12866

Cope Alora M. • Librarian • Alora Cope & Associates • LaGrange Park, IL 60525

Cope Jeanette M. • Reference Librarian • Buckeye Valley High School • Delaware, OH 43015

Cope Robert S. • President • Auto-Graphics Inc. • Pomona, CA 91768 • LITA

Cope Sandra • Children Librarian • Waukesha Public Library • Waukesha, WI 53186 • ALSC

Copeland Alice T. • Madison, NJ 07940 • ALCTS

Copeland Betty L. • Librarian • Saint Michaels Catholic Academy • Austin, TX 78735 • AASL

Copeland Charlotte B. • Student • University of Southern Mississippi School of Library Science • Hattiesburg, MS 39406-5146

Copeland Claudia M. • Branch Manager • Terrell County Library • Dawson, GA 31742

Copeland David R. • Bibliographic Assistant • Southern Methodist University DeGolyer Library & Fikes Hall • Dallas, TX 75275-0396

Copeland Ella G. • Dir./Lib Learning Resources Ctr • Ohio State University • Wooster, OH 44691 • ACRL LIRT

Copeland Eugene L. • Trustee • Denver Public Library • Denver, CO 80203-2165 • ALTA PLA

Copeland Jacqueline D. • Irvington, NY 10533

Copeland L. Griffin • Librarian • Florida College Chatlos Library • Temple Terrace, FL 33617-5578

Copeland Lynn • Manager, Library Systems • Simon Fraser University W. A. Bennett Library • Burnaby BC, V5A 1S6 Canada • LITA

Copeland Nora S. • Catalog Librarian • Colorado State University William E. Morgan Library • Fort Collins, CO 80523 • ACRL ALCTS LITA

Copeland Robert M. • Prog Administrator Ref Servs • Fort Collins Public Library • Ft. Collins, CO 80524-2990

Copeland Wilda L. • Manager • Metropolitan Library System Capitol Hill Branch • Oklahoma City, OK 73109

Copenhaver Jane • Librarian • Saint John School • Saint John, ND 58369

Coplan Kate M. • Baltimore, MD 21208 • LAMA PLA *Continuing*

Copley Helen Marie G. • Inf. Specialist/Consultant • Circle Incorporation • McLean, VA 22102 • ALCTS LITA

Copp Madeline A. • University of Washington Suzzallo Library • Seattle, WA 98195 • ACRL LIRT

Copp Patricia • Merced County Library • Merced, CA 95340

Copp Roberta VH • South Carolina Dept. of Archives and History • Columbia, SC 29211-1669

Coppel Lynn M. • Reference Librarian • California State University • Fullerton, CA 92634 • ACRL RASD IFRT SRRT

Coppola Elaine M. • Associate Librarian • Syracuse University Library E. S. Bird Library • Syracuse, NY 13244-2010 • ACRL

Coppola Judy J. • Reference Coordinator • Michigan State University Libraries • East Lansing, MI 48824-1048 • ACRL

Coppola Linda L. • Humanities/Printing Ref. Ln. • Rochester Institute of Technology Wallace Memorial Library • Rochester, NY 14623-0887 • ACRL LIRT

Coppola Susan B. • Canton High School • Canton, MA 02021 • AASL YALSA

Copsey Mark J. • Technical Services Librarian • Walla Walla College Peterson Memorial Library • College Place, WA 99324

Corbaci Margarita • Reference Librarian • Saint Joseph County Public Library • South Bend, IN 46601 • ASCLA RASD *Life*

Corbeil Donna L. • Senior Librarian • Oakland Public Library West Oakland Branch • Oakland, CA 94607

Corbert Andrew C. • Marketing Manager • Kluwer Academic Publishers • Norwell, MA 02061

Corbett Ann L. • Mount Holly, NJ 08060

Corbett Dorothy H. • Director • Bethel Park Public Library • Bethel Park, PA 15102-2790

Corbett Elizabeth M. • Santa Rosa, CA 95404

Corbett John • Automation/Tech. Serv. Assoc. • Ramapo Catskill Library System • Middletown, NY 10940 • LITA

Corbett Lynn D. • Supervisor-Library Legal Records • United Gas Pipeline Company Law Library • Houston, TX 77251 • LAMA

Corbett Orcena • Santa Rosa, CA 95409 • ALCTS *Life*

Corbett Thomas B. • Reference Librarian • University City Public Library • University City, MO 63130 • LITA

Corbett Wilma Jean • Akron, OH 44313 • AASL YALSA

Corbin-Muir Susan R. • Student • University of Iowa School of Library & Information Science • Iowa City, IA 52242 • AASL ALSC

Corbin Evelyn D. • Palm Coast, FL 32137-8457

Corbin John • University of North Texas School of Library & Information Sciences • Denton, TX 76203 • ALCTS LITA

Corbin John • Dallas Fort Worth School of Law • Irving, TX 75062

Corbin Patricia L. • Library Media Specialist • Mogollon High School Media Center • Heber, AZ 85928 • AASL ILERT IRRT

Corbin Roberta A. • Bibliographic Systems Manager • University of California-San Diego • La Jolla, CA 92093-0175 • LITA

Corbin Shirley M. • University of Guam • Mangilao, GU 96923 • ACRL

Corbitt Gordon K. • Hartsville, SC 29550 • ACRL LITA ILERT IRRT

Corbo Lucille A. • Scranton, PA 18504

Corbridge Ruth • Librarian • Millard Fillmore Library • Fillmore, UT 84631

Corbus Lawrence J. • Corbus Library Consultants • Chesterland, OH 44026 • LAMA PLA

Corbus Lesley • Student • San Jose State University Division of Library & Information Science • San Jose, CA 95192-0029 • PLA

Corcoran Dennis R. • Director • Ventress Memorial Library • Marshfield, MA 02050

Corcoran Frances E. • Coor Instr Mat Ctr • Des Plaines Public School District-62 • Des Plaines, IL 60016 • AASL ALCTS LIRT

Corda Arthur • Director Library/Media Services • South Central Community College • New Haven, CT 06511

Cordalis Mimi E. • School Librarian • Kyrene de la Paloma School • Tempe, AZ 85284 • AASL

Cordaro Barbara • Library Director • West Milford Township Library • West Milford, NJ 07480 • LAMA PLA

Cordell Rosanne M. • South Bend, IN 46614

Cordell Sylvia Y. • Head of Learning Center • Atlanta-Fulton Public Library • Atlanta, GA 30303 • PLA

Corder Marlene F. • Library Media Teacher • E. A. Hall Middle School • Watsonville, CA 95076 • AASL

Corderman Cynthia D. • Fullerton, CA 92631

Cordes Ellen R. • Head of Circulation Department • Yale University Sterling Memorial Library • New Haven, CT 06520 • ACRL LAMA

Cordoba Carlos A. • Centro De Investigacoines Bibliotecologicas • 1002 Buenos Aires, Argentina • AASL ALSC

Cordon Garcia Jose Antonio • Subdirector • Universidad De Salamanca E.U. Biblioteconomia Y Doc • 37007 Salamanca, Spain • RASD LRRT

Cordon Myrt M. • Assistant Director • San Luis Obispo City-County Library • San Luis Obispo, CA 93403 • PLA

Cordova Martha H. • Librarian • Monument Elementary School • Bennington, VT 05201 • AASL

Cordray Dorothy • Library Media Specialist • Marshall High School • Marshall, TX 75670 • AASL

Core Debi • Marketing Manager • LBS/Archival Products • Des Moines, IA 50305

Core Irene • Trustee • Clinton Public Library • Clinton, IA 52732 • ALTA

Core Sheila A. • Reference Librarian • Surry Community College Learning Resources Center • Dobson, NC 27017 • ACRL RASD LIRT *Life*

Corey Dorothy A. • Student • University of Wisconsin-Milwaukee School of Library & Information Science • Milwaukee, WI 53201

Corey James F. • Florida Center for Library Automation • Gainesville, FL 32609 • LITA

Corey Karen M. • Reader Service Librarian • Purdue University Calumet The Library • Hammond, IN 46323-2094

Corey Linda Kay • Washburn Rural Middle School • Topeka, KS 66619 • AASL

Corlee Lisa • Cataloger • University of Nevada Reno Library • Reno, NV 89511 • LITA

Corlee Michael C. • Microcomputer Specialist • University of Nevada Reno Library • Reno, NV 89511 • LITA

Corless Lucinda • Media Specialist • St. John Neumann School • Lilburn, GA 30247 • AASL

Corley Carol N. • Ft Worth, TX 76112-4196

Corliss Bonita C. • Reference Librarian • Seattle Public Library • Seattle, WA 98104-1193

Corn Joan • Librarian • Woodlands High School • Hartsdale, NY 10530

Corne Denice M. • Trustee • Saint John the Baptist Parish Library • LaPlace, LA 70068 • ALTA

Corneiro Nina • St Thomas, VI 00804 • Continuing

Cornelius John C. • Head of Cataloging • National Archives, The • Washington, DC 20408 • ALCTS FLRT GODORT

Cornelius Mary Ellen • Head, Youth Services Department • Lynchburg Public Library • Lynchburg, VA 24501

Cornell Barbara M. • Librarian • Conant Public Library • Sterling, MA 01564 • PLA

Cornell Charles R. • Editor-Biography Index • H. W. Wilson Company • Bronx, NY 10452 • RASD

Cornell Christine A. • Records Clerk • First of America Bank • Kalamazoo, MI 49009 • ACRL

Cornell Dolores S. • Homstead Middle School • Homestead, FL 33030 • AASL

Cornell Evan L. • Student • University of Pittsburgh School of Library and Information Science • Pittsburgh, PA 15260 • SRRT

Cornell Patricia C. • United States Coast Guard TNG Center • Petula, CA 94952-5000

Cornell Sylvia C. • Assistant Director • Jacksonville Public Libraries Main Library • Jacksonville, FL 32202 • ALCTS LITA

Corner Dean • Asst. Director Centrl Services • Broome County Public Library • Binghamton, NY 13901 • PLA

Cornett Linda B • Student • Clarion University of Pennsylvania College of Library Science • Clarion, PA 16214

Cornick Donna P. • Online/Reference Serv Librarian • University of North Carolina Walter Royal Davis Library • Chapel Hill, NC 27599-3924 • ACRL RASD

Cornish Alan K. • Student • Louisiana State University School of Library & Information Science • Baton Rouge, LA 70803-3290

Cornish Dorothy • Librarian Middle School • Elmwood Elementary School • Syracuse, NY 13207

Cornn Jean • Branch Manager • Atlanta-Fulton Public Library Hapeville Branch • Hapeville, GA 30354 • ASCLA

Cornog Martha • Manager, Membership Services • American College of Physicians • Philadelphia, PA 19106 • IFRT SRRT

Cornue Deborah A. • Adult Services Librarian • San Francisco Public Library Mission Branch • San Francisco, CA 94110 • EMIERT

Cornwall Scot J. • Cura Res L Stacks • Boston Public Library • Boston, MA 02117 • ACRL ALCTS PLA *Life*

Cornwall Susan E. • Library Tehnician • Capital Systems Group Inc. • Rockville, MD 20874

Cornwell Gary • Associate Librarian • University of Florida Libraries • Gainesville, FL 32611-2047 • GODORT

Cornwell Linda L. • Learning Resources Consultant • Indiana Dept of Education • Indianapolis, IN 46204 • AASL

Cornwell Wilna J. Miss • Pasadena, CA 91101-1259 • AASL YALSA *Life*

Corona Linda Ann • Elem. School Media Specialist • Wilson Elementary School • Westfield, NJ 07039 • AASL NMRT

Coronado Deborah M. • Sioux City Public Library • Sioux City, IA 51101-1203

Corr Suzanne D. • Student • University of North Carolina at Chapel Hill School of Information and Library Science • Chapel Hill, NC 27599-3360 • ALCTS

Corradini Diane • Adult Services Librarian • Herrick Public Library • Holland, MI 49423

Correa Eda M. • Orlando, FL 32839

Correa Lisa • Arongen Elementary School • Clifton Park, NY 12065 • AASL

Corredor Javier • Branch Manager • County Department of Libraries Columbia Pike Branch Library • Arlington, VA 22204 • PLA EMIERT

Correia Kathleen A. • California State Library • Sacramento, CA 94237-0001

Correll Barbara J. • Ft Lauderdale, FL 33315 • AASL

Correll Emily C N • Coopers & Lybrand • Atlanta, GA 30309

Corrick L. Grace • Library Media Chairperson • Blue Valley North High School • Overland Park, KS 66209 • AASL

Corrier Mary Anne • Borough Coordinator • New York Public Library Branches Staten Island Borough Office • Staten Island, NY 10301 • ALSC LAMA PLA

Corriere Patrick J. • Govt. Publications Libn • Chicago Public Library • Chicago, IL 60605 • GODORT SRRT

Corrigan Carol A. • Coram, NY 11727 • AASL

Corrigan Deni Donich • Director • Hearst Free Library • Anaconda, MT 59711

Corrigan Jerome K. • Forest Heights, MD 20745 • PLA RASD *Life*

Corrigan Judith L. • University of Michigan School of Information and Library Studies • Ann Arbor, MI 48109-1092

Corrigan Maripat • Head of Technical Service • Lincolnwood Public Library District • Lincolnwood, IL 60646 • ALCTS

Corrigan Maureen F. • Head of Tax Librarian • Arther Andersen & Company • New York, NY 10105 • LAMA

Corrigan Susan L. • Orem, UT 84058

Corrigan Thomas D. • Trustee • Cleveland Public Library • Cleveland, OH 44114-1271 • ALTA

Corrsin Stephen D. • Associate Librarian • Brooklyn College Library • Brooklyn, NY 11210 • ACRL

Corry Annette B. • Fairfax, VA 22031

Corry Donna L. • Librarian • Flora Carnegie Library • Flora, IL 62839-0216

Corry Emmett Bro. • Director • Saint John's University Division of Library & Information Science • Jamaica, NY 11439 • AASL

Cors Paul B. • Catalog Librarian • University of Wyoming • Laramie, WY 82071 • ACRL ALCTS IFRT

Corsaro Julie A. • Children's Librarian • Chute Middle School • Evanston, IL 60645 • ALSC EMIERT

Corsi Elena • Librarian I • Chicago Public Library • Chicago, IL 60605 • ALCTS RASD

Corsi Julie • Palos Heights Public Library • Palos Heights, IL 60463

Corsiglia Annette • Youth Services Librarian • Palatine Public Library • Palatine, IL 60067 • PLA NMRT

Corson Cornelia M. • Head Librarian • The Spence School • New York, NY 10128 • AASL YALSA IFRT

Corson David W. • Cornell University 213 Olin Library • Ithaca, NY 14853-5301 • ACRL

Cortelyou Catherine E. • Public Services Librarian • Institute of Transportation Studies • Berkeley, CA 94720 • ACRL ASCLA

Cortelyou Shirley R. • Student • State University of New York (SUNY) School of Information & Library Studies • Buffalo, NY 14260 • AASL

Cortes Oralia Garza • Austin, TX 78723 • ALSC EMIERT

Cortez Edwin M. Dr. • Librarian • University of Wisconsin School of Library & Information Studies • Madison, WI 53706 • LITA

Cortner Della M. • Kansas City, MO 64113 • Continuing

Corum Fred M. • Fresno, CA 93726-1122 • ALCTS

Corum Susan L • Dean Learning Resources • Saddleback College • Mission Viejo, CA 92692 • ACRL

Corvi Marlene W. • Portland, OR 97221-3059 • LITA

Corwin Dean W. • University of Nebraska Love Library • Lincoln, NE 68588-0410 • ALCTS

Corwin Donald K. • Trustee • Suffolk Cooperative Library System • Bellport, NY 11713 • ALTA

Corwin James A. • San Dimas, CA 91773 • PLA

Corwin Karen S. • Los Angeles County District Attorney Busch Law Library • Los Angeles, CA 90012

Corwin Lynn • Instructional Service • Klamath County School District Instructional Media Center • Klamath Falls, OR 97603 • AASL

Cory John F. • Assistant Library Director • Cranston Public Library • Cranston, RI 02920 • PLA

Cory Karen A. • Student • University of Western Ontario School of Library & Information Science • London ON, N6G 1H1 Canada

Cory Lisa J. • Librarian • Veterans Affairs Medical Center Library Service • Mountain Home, TN 37684

Cory Rose • Hoffman Ests., IL 60195

Cory Salome K.A • Librarian • Congregation Emanu-El • New York, NY 10021-6596 • IFRT

Cosanzo Anna Marie • Librarian • Notre Dame High School • Easton, PA 18042

Cosby Debra G. • Adminstrative Assistant • Rice University Fondren Library • Houston, TX 77251-1892

Cosby Neva W. • Librarian • Sacramento Public Library Literacy Service • Sacramento, CA 95820

Cosby Shirlene D. • Trustee • Memphis-Shelby County Public Library and Information Center • Memphis, TN 38104-4025

Coscarelli William F. • Dept Head Fine Arts/Media • University of Georgia Libraries • Athens, GA 30602 • ACRL ALCTS SRRT

Cosgriff John C. Jr • Science & Technology Librarian • Virginia Polytechnic Institute and State University, Newman Library • Blacksburg, VA 24061-0434 • ACRL RASD

Cosgrove Alma C. • Hampton, VA 23669

Cosgrove Helen V. M. • Milwaukee Area Technical College North Campus • Mequon, WI 53092 • Continuing

Cosgrove Julia M. • Conroe, TX 77302-1148

Coshland Helen J. • Tucson, AZ 85718-7307 • Continuing

Cosmai Brenda K. • Kissimmee, FL 34744 • AASL

Cosmann Richard S. • Brooklyn, NY 11231

Cosner Renna H. • Fredericksburg, VA 22405

Cosper Mary F. • Assistant Director • Terrebonne Parish Library • Houma, LA 70360

Cossman Ollie • Director • Community Lib Assn Inc • Ketchum, ID 83340

Costa Betty L. • Hayden, CO 81639 • LITA

Costa Deborah D. • Reference Librarian • University of California-Los Angeles (UCLA) • Los Angeles, CA 90024-1450 • ACRL LAMA RASD

Costa Kathy • Childrens' Coordinator • Santa Fe Public Library Oliver LaFarge Branch • Santa Fe, NM 87505 • ALSC

Costa Robert N. • City Librarian • Richmond Public Library • Richmond, VA 23219 • PLA

Costa de Ramos Carmen M. • Westbury, NY 11590

Costabile Mary R. • Assistant to Director • American Library Association Washington Office • Washington, DC 20002

Costabile Salvatore L. • Costabile Associates Inc • Bethesda, MD 20814 • FLRT

Costales Cindy • Literacy Coordinator • South State Cooperative Library System • Downey, CA 90241 • PLA

Costanzo Jane E. • Media Center Specialist • John Kennedy School • Batavia, NY 14020 • AASL LIRT

Costello Colleen M. • Head of Youth Services • Vernon Area Public Library • Prairie View, IL 60069

Costello Irene • Trustee • Niles Public Library • Niles, IL 60648 • ALTA

Costello Joan M. • Head Librarian, Administrator • Osterhout Free Library • Wilkes Barre, PA 18701

Costello Lilla Wood • Hingham, MA 02043

Costello Lorraine W. • Trustee • Paramus Public Library • Paramus, NJ 07652 • ALTA PLA

Costello Louise A. • Media Specialist • Forest Glen Middle School • Coral Springs, FL 33067 • AASL ALSC YALSA

Costello M. Rita • Librarian-Clln. Devel. • University of California Los Angeles Management Library (UCLA) • Los Angeles, CA 90024-1460 • RASD SORT

Costello Mary I. • Anaheim, CA 92804 • PLA

Costello Nancy M. • Worthington, OH 43085

Costello Patricia • Librarian II • Enoch Pratt Free Library Light Street Branch • Baltimore, MD 21230 • YALSA

Costello Richard J. • Severna Pk, MD 21146

Costello S. Janice • Educational Librarian • Jacksonville State University Library • Jacksonville, AL 36265 • ACRL

Costello Stanley J. • Student • University of Kentucky College of Library & Information Science • Lexington, KY 40506-0391

Costello Suzanne T. • Indianapolis Marion County Public Library • Indianapolis, IN 46206 • ALSC

Costello Thomas M. • President • Springfield Library/ Museums Association • Springfield, MA 01103 • LAMA PLA

Coster Kathy J. • Program Manager • Baltimore County Public Library • Towson, MD 21204 • PLA VRT

Costich Lisa M. • Assistant Manager • Allen County Public Library Little Turtle Branch • Ft. Wayne, IN 46825

Costigan Mary • Librarian • Free Library of Philadelphia Wyoming Avenue Branch • Philadelphia, PA 19120

Costin Michael J. • Sr Sub-Ln Tech Serv • University of Hong Kong • Hong Kong, Hong Kong • ACRL IRRT

Costner Mary Sandra • Librarian • Mooneyham Public Library • Forest City, NC 28043 • PLA

Cote Camille • Associate Professor • McGill University School of Library Science • Montreal PQ, Canada • ALCTS YALSA

Cote Donna G. • Director • Central Rappahannock Regional Library Wallace Memorial Library • Fredericksburg, VA 22401 • ALCTS ALSC ALTA LAMA LITA PLA YALSA CLENE IFRT LIRT SORT SRRT

Cote Sarah W. • Jacksonville, FL 32208 • Continuing

Cotham James S. • Head,McClung Historical Clln. • Knox County Public Library System • Knoxville, TN 37902-2505

Cothran Jean S. • Greenwood, SC 29649 • ACRL ALSC *Continuing*

Cothroll Victoria • University of Wisconsin Library and Learning Resources • Whitewater, WI 53190

Cotilla Linda • Churchville, PA 18966 • ACRL LAMA

Cotner Alsa K. • Head Librarian • Hutcheson & Grundy L.L.P. • Houston, TX 77042

Cotner Cynthia Snyder • Public Services Coordinator • Lincoln University Inman E. Page Library • Jefferson City, MO 65102-0029 • ACRL

Cotner Mark E. • Student • University of Oklahoma School of Library & Information Studies • Norman, OK 73019 • ALCTS LITA

Cotrim Flavita • Head Librarian • American School-Rio Library • APO Miami, FL 34030 • AASL RASD YALSA

Cottam Keith M. • Director • University of Wyoming • Laramie, WY 82071 • ACRL

Cotter Kimberly A. • Federal Govt. Sales & Mktg Rep • EBSCO Subscription Services • Springfield, VA 22151-4148 • ALCTS ASCLA AFLRT FLRT

Cotter Mary S. • Cataloger • East Carolina University Health Sciences Library • Greenville, NC 27858-4354 • ALCTS

Cotter Michael G. • Documents Librarian • East Carolina University Joyner Library • Greenville, NC 27858-4353 • ACRL GODORT

Cottey Kathryn A. • University of Arizona Graduate Library School • Tucson, AZ 85721

Cottingham Elsie E. • Technical Services Librarian • Anderson University • Anderson, IN 46012 • ACRL ALCTS LITA RASD GODORT

Cottingham Gwedolyn S. • Media Specialist • Jacskon Academy School Library • East Orange, NJ 07017 • AASL ALSC EMIERT VRT

Cotton Daniel Page • Cataloger • Clark University Robert Hutchings Goddard Library • Worcester, MA 01610 • LITA

Cotton Kathy L. • Branch Head • Lake County Public Library • Merrillville, IN 46410-5382 • PLA

Cotton Ruth • Atlanta-Fulton Public Library Sandy Springs Branch • Sandy Springs, GA 30328 • PLA

Cottone Joan • Associate Librarian • State University of New York (SUNY) College at Geneseo Milne Library • Geneseo, NY 14454-1498 • ALCTS

Cottrell Constance S. • Atlanta, GA 30318

Cottrell E. Emma • Chattahoochee Tech • Marietta, GA 30060

Cottrell Jean • Johnson City, TN 37604

Cottrell Linda D. • Tucson, AZ 85718

Cottrell Steve G. • Director • Bozeman Public Library • Bozeman, MT 59715 • PLA

Cottrill Darla • Management Analyst • Ohio State Library • Colubus, OH 43266-0334 • LAMA

Coty Patricia A. • Mgr. Information Services • State University of New York (SUNY) National Center Earquake Engineering Res • Buffalo, NY 14260

Couch Nena L. • Ohio State University Lawrence & Lee Theatre Research Inst. • Columbus, OH 43210-1230 • ACRL

Couch Wilson • Director • Alice Lloyd College McGaw Library & Learning Center • Pippa Passes, KY 41844 • ACRL

Coughenour Stacey A. • Pittsburgh, PA 15227

Coughlan Margaret N. • Reference Specialist in Chls Lit • Library of Congress • Washington, DC 20541 • ALSC

Coughlin Caroline M. • Director • Drew University • Madison, NJ 07940-4007 • ACRL

Coughlin June M. • Sandusky, OH 44870

Coughlin Mary H. • Shape Elementary School • APO, AE 09708 • AASL YALSA FLRT

Coughlin Richard J. • Administrative Serv. Librarian • Boston College O'Neill Library • Chestnut Hill, MA 02167 • ACRL LAMA

Coughlin Robert M. • Trustee • Euclid Public Library • Euclid, OH 44123-2091 • ALTA

Coughlin Ruth E. • Student • University of Hawaii School of Library & Information Studies • Honolulu, HI 96822

Coughlin Violet L. • Professor Emeritus • McGill University Graduate School of Library Science • Montreal PQ, Canada • Continuing

Coulombe Dominique C. • Head,Catalog Librarian • Brown University Rockefeller Library • Providence, RI 02912 • ALCTS LITA CLENE

Coulson Donna C. • Coordinator of Technical Serv • Houston Community College • Houston, TX 77004 • ALCTS

Coultas Simon T. • Reference Librarian • Charleston County Library • Charleston, SC 29403

Coulter Cynthia M. • Head, Acquisitions Dept. • University of Northern Iowa Purchasing Off • Cedar Falls, IA 50614 • ACRL ALCTS LAMA IFRT

Coulter Margaret C. • New Paltz, NY 12561 • Continuing

Coulter Patricia • Program Manager • ERIC Department of Education • Washington, DC 20002

Coulthart Lois H. • Vienna, VA 22181 • AASL

Coulton Martha J. • Centerville, OH 45459 • ACRL

Coumbe Robert E. • Director • Trenton Free Public Library • Trenton, NJ 08608

Councill Mildred S. • Mount Olive, NC 28365-2626 • Continuing

Councilman-Lempe Linda S. • District Librarian/ Teacher • Maricopa Unified School District 20 • Maricopa, AZ 85239 • AASL

Counts Teresa • Trustee • Topeka Public Library • Topeka, KS 66604-1374

Coup William A. • Reference Audio-Visual Ln. • Boynton Beach City Library • Boynton Beach, FL 33435

Coupe Jill M. • Co-Head, Resource Serv. Dept. • Johns Hopkins University Milton S. Eisenhower Library • Baltimore, MD 21218 • ACRL

Coupe Sandra L. • Librarian • Federal Bureau of Investigation FBI Academy Library • Quantico, VA 22135 • LAMA FLRT

Couper R. W. • Trustee • Woodrow Wilson National Fellowship Foundation • Princeton, NJ 08540

Courier Daniel J. • Senior Project Manager • Educational Technology Foundation • Indianapolis, IN 46203

Coursey Michael E. • Cataloger I • Johns Hopkins University Milton S. Eisenhower Library • Baltimore, MD 21218 • ACRL

Courteau Barbara • Librarian • H.B. Fuller Co. • Vadnais Heights, MN 55110 • LITA

Courtland Christine • Librarian • Wade Carpenter Middle School • Nogales, AZ 85621
Courtney Diane • Adult/Young Adult Media Cons. • Westchester Library System • Elmsford, NY 10523 • RASD YALSA
Courtney Ina • Children's Librarian • Free Library of Philadelphia Southwark Branch • Philadelphia, PA 19147 • ALSC
Courtney June M. • Head Technical Service Dept. • Reading Public Library • Reading, PA 19602 • ALCTS
Courtney Keith • Sales Director • Taylor & Francis • Basingstoke Hants, United Kingdom • ALCTS
Courtney Marjorie S. • John Burroughs School • Saint Louis, MO 63124
Courtney Ralph E. • Grand Forks, ND 58201-8723 • IFRT
Courtois Joyce • Houston, TX 77036
Courtois Martin P. • Database Coordinator • Michigan State University Libraries • East Lansing, MI 48824-1048 • ACRL RASD
Courtright Diane R. • Library Media Specialist • Calvin Coolidge School • Binghamton, NY 13904
Courtright Harry • System Administrator • Delaware County Library System • Brookhaven, PA 19015 • PLA
Courtright Rosemary • Information Librarian • Kitsap Regional Library • Bremerton, WA 98310 • RASD
Cousineau Carl A. • Automation Coordinator • Oakland Public Library • Oakland, CA 94612 • LITA
Cousineau J Ann • Administrative Librarian • Solano County Library • Fairfield, CA 94533 • LAMA PLA
Cousineau Laura K. • Student • North Carolina Central University School of Library & Information Science • Durham, NC 27707 • RASD
Coussement B Mrs • Media Specialist • Westfield School • Glen Ellyn, IL 60137 • AASL ALSC
Couston George • Schaumburg, IL 60195 • Continuing
Coutant Patricia C. • Fine Arts & Recreation Dept. Hd. • Jacksonville Public Libraries Main Library • Jacksonville, FL 32202 • ALSC PLA RASD IFRT
Coutinho Jessica • Student • University of South Carolina College of Library & Information Science • Columbia, SC 29208
Couts Mona C. • Head,Info Tech Servs • University of North Carolina • Chapel Hill, NC 27599 • ALCTS LITA
Couts Pat • Mustang High School • Mustang, OK 73064
Coutts Brian E. • Head, Dept. of Lib Pub Svs • Western Kentucky University Helm-Cravens Library • Bowling Green, KY 42101 • ACRL
Coutts Cynthia L. • Student • University of California Los Angeles Graduate School of Library & Information Science • Los Angeles, CA 90024 • RASD
Couture Norma • New Haven, CT 06515-2208
Coval Margaret • Assistant Director • Colorado Endowment For The Humanities • Denver, CO 80202
Covell Judy A. • Technical Services Coordinator • Timberland Regional Library • Olympia, WA 98501 • PLA
Cover Linda K. • Librarian • Woodview Elementary School • Houston, TX 77055
Cover Peggy H. • Head Reference • Model High School • Bloomfield Hills, MI 48304 • ACRL RASD
Covert-Vail Lucinda • San Francisco State University • San Francisco, CA 94132 • IRRT
Covert Nadine • Spec Cons/Critical Inventory • Program for Art on Film • New York, NY 10021 • ACRL ALCTS LITA
Covey Harriett R. • Claremont, CA 91711
Covey Helen Claire • Student • University of Alabama School of Library & Information Studies • Tuscaloosa, AL 35487-0252 • ALCTS LITA PLA NMRT SRRT
Covey Marjorie A. • Director, IMC • Marion Education Services District • Salem, OR 97303
Covey William C. III • Head, System Office • University of Florida Libraries • Gainesville, FL 32611-2047 • LITA
Covici Anna Propp • LaJolla, CA 92037
Covington Laura A. • Media Director • Isidore Newman School Library • New Orleans, LA 70115 • AASL
Covington Paula A. • Latin Amer & Iberian Bibl • Vanderbilt University Library Jean & Alexander Heard Library • Nashville, TN 37240-0007 • ACRL
Covington R. Dean • Library Director • Arkansas College • Batesville, AR 72501 • ACRL
Covington S. Annelle • Librarian • Chisholm Trail Middle School • Round Rock, TX 78681 • AASL
Covington Tommy • Branch Librarian • Northeast Regional Library Ripley Library Branch • Ripley, MS 38663 • IFRT SRRT
Covington Veronica P. • Huntsville, TX 77340
Covode Kay Brunton • Pass Christian Public Library • Pass Christian, MS 39571 • YALSA LIRT
Covone Maureen D. • Haworth, NJ 07641
Cowan Beatrice K. • Librarian • San Diego Academy Library • National City, CA 91950 • AASL
Cowan Christina M. • Mankato, MN 56002
Cowan James L. • Student • University of California-Berkeley School of Library & Information Studies • Berkeley, CA 94720 • ACRL LITA IFRT SRRT
Cowan Nancy W. • Raleigh, NC 27612 • ALCTS PLA
Cowan Sherna L. • Community Library Manager • County of Los Angeles Public Library Rowland Heights Branch • Rowland Heights, CA 91748
Coward David R. • Youth Services Supervisor • Kansas City Kansas Public Library • Kansas City, KS 66101
Cowart-Stucki Elizabeth R. • Western Library Network (WLN) • Lacey, WA 98503-0888 • LITA
Cowdrey Rosalynde G. • Librarian • Sandalwood Senior High School • Jacksonville, FL 32216
Cowen Ione S. • Head, Main Children's Room • Akron-Summit County Public Library • Akron, OH 44326-0001 • ALSC
Cowen Linda L. • Library Media Specialist • Truman Elementary School • Norman, OK 73072 • AASL
Cowens Cynthia • New York, NY 10025 • YALSA
Cowgill Allison A. • Head Reference Librarian • Nevada State Library & Archives • Carson City, NV 89710 • ACRL RASD
Cowgill Benjamin • Trustee • Lexington Public Library • Lexington, KY 40507 • ALTA
Cowin Audena L. • Librarian • Conackamack Middle School • Piscataway, NJ 08854 • AASL
Cowles Christine A. • Administrative Assistant • Cattermole Memorial Library • Fort Madison, IA 52627
Cowles Diane M. • Children's Librarian • Seattle Public Library Beacon Hill Branch • Seattle, WA 98144
Cowley Anne M. • Secondary Librarian • Chambersburg Area School District • Chambersburg, PA 17201
Cowling Joanne E. • Director • La Grande Public Library • La Grande, OR 97850 • ALSC PLA
Cox-Byrne Sarah E. • Hartford, CT 06105-2277 • ACRL LITA
Cox Ann C. • Glade Spring, VA 24340
Cox Barbara • Salt Lake City, UT 84112 • ACRL MAGERT
Cox Barbara J. • Midland, TX 79705 • AASL
Cox Bonnie J. • Humanities Bibliographer • University of Kentucky • Lexington, KY 40506-0056 • ACRL ALCTS SRRT
Cox Catherine P. • Automation Assistant • DeAnza College Learning Center • Cupertino, CA 95014 • ACRL IFRT NMRT
Cox Charles W. • Hattiesburg, MS 39401 • LITA RASD
Cox Denise • Media Specialist • Nikiski Elementary School • Nikiski, AK 99635 • AASL LIRT LRRT
Cox Dorothy • Southern Illinois University Dept. of Curriculum & Instr. • Carbondale, IL 62901 • AASL RASD YALSA
Cox Helen A. • Director • Book Group, The Utah Humanites Resource Center • Salt Lake City, UT 84111-2908
Cox Janice E. • Assistant Executive Director • Indiana Cooperative Library Services Authority (INCOLSA) • Indianapolis, IN 46278 • ALCTS LAMA LITA
Cox Jeannette R. • Circulation Librarian • Florida State University Robert M. Strozier Library • Tallahassee, FL 32306-2047 • LAMA
Cox Jennifer L. • Reference Librarian • University of Arizona Library • Tucson, AZ 85721
Cox Joanne R. • Library Director • Lillie M. Evans Library District • Princeville, IL 61559
Cox Joyce M. • Spokane, WA 99212
Cox Juanita • Trustee • Bellwood Public Library • Bellwood, IL 60104 • ALTA
Cox Judith E. • Ninilchik Elementary/High School Library • Ninilchik, AK 99639
Cox Judith L. • Administrative Support Librarian • Gallaudet University Library • Washington, DC 20002 • ACRL ALCTS ASCLA LAMA
Cox Karen A. • Oakland, CA 94619
Cox Katherine L. • Student • Wayne State University • Detroit, MI 48202 • LITA RASD SRRT
Cox Linda H. • Director • Blair Academy Scribner Library • Blairstown, NJ 07825-0600 • AASL ACRL
Cox Linda N. • Northwestern State University Watson Memorial Library • Natchitoches, LA 71497
Cox Lucy I. • Librarian • Our Lady of Grace School • Encino, CA 91316 • AASL ALSC
Cox Marilee A. • Student • San Jose State University Division of Library & Information Science • San Jose, CA 95192-0029
Cox Marjorie • New Castle, IN 47362 • AASL
Cox Mary Sue • Greenville, SC 29615 • Continuing
Cox Pat • Director of Marketing • Saint Louis County Library • St. Louis, MO 63131 • ALSC LAMA PLA
Cox Robert L. • Student • University of South Carolina College of Library & Information Science • Columbia, SC 29208
Cox Ruth M. Miss • Colorado Springs, CO 80909 • ALSC PLA *Continuing*
Cox Shelley M. • Rare Book Librarian • Southern Illinois University Delyte W. Morris Library • Carbondale, IL 62901-6632 • ACRL
Cox Virginia C. • Media Specialist • Cowpens Junior High School • Cowpens, SC 29330 • AASL
Cox William H. Jr • Rochester, NY 14620 • ACRL PLA *Life*
Cox William J. • Library Aide • Asotin Junior-Senior High School • Asotin, WA 99403
Coxe Christina M. • Student • University of Southern Mississippi School of Library Science • Hattiesburg, MS 39406-5146 • PLA
Coxe Elizabeth L. • Student • University of Tennessee-Knoxville Graduate School of Library & Information Science • Knoxville, TN 37996-4330
Coy Jo Ann • Librarian • Clearwater High School • Clearwater, KS 67026 • AASL YALSA
Coyan Noreen • Trustee • State Library of Iowa • Des Moines, IA 50319 • ALTA
Coyle-Kidwell Mary L. • Asst. Mgr., Inf and Pubn Serv. • Mitre Corp Library • Mc Lean, VA 22102 • LITA RASD
Coyle Ann M. • Librarian • Loyola Academy Resource Center • Wilmette, IL 60091 • AASL
Coyle John R. Jr. • Trustee • Ramapo Catskill Library System • Middletown, NY 10940
Coyle Karen E. • Bibliographic Analyst • University of California Division of Library Automation • Oakland, CA 94612-3550 • ALCTS LITA
Coyle Michael P. • Deputy Dir. for Public Servs. • Free Library of Philadelphia • Philadelphia, PA 19103 • PLA
Coyle Patricia F. • Honolulu, HI 96822 • AASL NMRT
Coyle Patrick • Assistant Librarian • California State University-Dominguez Hills Library • Carson, CA 90747
Coyle Robert J. • President • Ruzica Library Bindery Inc. • Greensboro, NC 27403
Coyle Thomas J. • Director • Hillsdale Free Public Library • Hillsdale, NJ 07642 • PLA
Coyne John Robert • Head of Reference Services • Schaumburg Township District Library • Schaumburg, IL 60194 • PLA IFRT
Coyne Richard J. • Vice President • Eastern Book Company • Portland, ME 04112 • ACRL ALCTS LITA
Crabb Elizabeth A. • Coordinator • Northeast Texas Library System • Garland, TX 75040-6304 • ASCLA LAMA PLA
Crabb Patricia M. • Head, Circulation Services • University of West Florida John C. Pace Library • Pensacola, FL 32514 • ACRL
Crabbe Nancy • San Carlos, CA 94070 • PLA
Crabill Robert E. • Student • San Jose State University Division of Library & Information Science • San Jose, CA 95192-0029
Crabtree Anna Beth • St Johns Regional Health Center Medical Library • Springfield, MO 65804
Crabtree Clara J. • Bahama, NC 27503 • AASL*Continuing*
Crabtree Doris J. • Cuyahoga County Public Library Berea Branch • Berea, OH 44017-2524 • ALSC IFRT
Crace Sallye C. • Librarian I • Jefferson County Public Schools • Louisville, KY 40232
Craddock Mariam N. • Oklahoma Cty, OK 73118 • LAMA PLA *Continuing*
Craft Anne H. • Coordinator of Media Services • Gwinnett County Public Schools • Lawrenceville, GA 30245 • AASL
Craft G. Jan • Onenta, AL 35121
Craft Guy Calvin • Dean,Lib & Learning Resources • Chicago State University Paul & Emily Douglas Library • Chicago, IL 60628
Craft Margaret E. • Asst Dir for Special Services • University of Scranton Harry & Jeanette Weinberg Memorial • Scranton, PA 18510-4700 • ACRL LAMA
Crafts George T. • French & Italian Bibl • University of Virginia Library • Charlottesville, VA 22903
Cragan Barbara J. • Librarian • Barrington High School • Barrington, IL 60010 • AASL
Craig Allison • Vice President • Ontario Library Association • Toronto ON, M5C 1M3 Canada
Craig Christina L. • M'film Service Coordinator • Southeastern Library Network (SOLINET) • Atlanta, GA 30309-2955 • ALCTS
Craig Genevieve K. • Shafter, CA 93263 • AASL
Craig James L. • Biological Science Librarian • University of Massachusetts Library • Amherst, MA 01003 • ACRL ALCTS LAMA CLENE LIRT MAGERT
Craig James Pat • Director Medical Center Library • Louisiana State University School of Medicine • Shreveport, LA 71130-3932
Craig Jane B. • Head of Reference • Palm Beach County Library System • West Palm Beach, FL 33406
Craig Jean E. • University of Pennsylvania Library Van Pelt-Dietrich Library Center • Philadelphia, PA 19104-6206 • ACRL ALCTS
Craig Jeanette Frances • Sacramento, CA 95818 • AASL YALSA *Continuing*

Craig John R. Jr. • CBA/Atlanta • Atlanta, GA 30305-1503
Craig Karen • Lexington, KY 40517-3801 • IFRT
Craig Laurie G. • Director of Lib. Serv. • Highland Elementary School • Kissimmee, FL 34741
Craig Louise L. • Research Librarian • The Boeing Company Renton Technical Library • Seattle, WA 98124 • RASD
Craig Marillyn F. • Collection Development • Vanderbilt University Library • Nashville, TN 37240-0007 • ACRL ALCTS RASD
Craig Marilyn J. • Bibliographic Services Div Ln. • University of Houston Libraries • Houston, TX 77204-2091 • ALCTS LITA
Craig Pamela J. • Media Special • Riverside Middle School • Dearborn Heights, MI 48152
Craig Patricia F. • Arlington Heights Memorial Library • Arlington Heights, IL 60004-5966 • ALSC
Craig Ruth L. • Student • San Jose State University Division of Library & Information Science • San Jose, CA 95192-0029
Craig Susan K. • Assistant Director • Iowa City Public Library • Iowa City, IA 52240 • LITA PLA
Craig Susan L. • Director of the Library • Aurora University Library • Aurora, IL 60506 • ACRL LAMA
Craigmile Robert L. • Student • Indiana University School of Library and Information Science • Bloomington, IN 47405 • SRRT
Crain Carolyn • City Librarian • San Marino Public Library • San Marino, CA 91108 • PLA
Crain Laura L. • Bloomington, IN 47401 • IFRT
Crain William H. • Curator • University of Texas Ransom Humanities Research Center • Austin, TX 78713 • ACRL
Cram Laura E. • Teacher • University of South Australia • Adelaide, SA 5000, Australia • PLA YALSA
Cram Mary Esther • Branch Head • Troy Public Library • Troy, MI 48084 • PLA IFRT SRRT
Cramblitt Valerie A. • Assistant Librarian • Enoch Pratt Free Library • Baltimore, MD 21201-4484
Cramer Anne O. • Eastern Virginia Medical School Moorman Memorial Library • Norfolk, VA 23501 • ACRL ALCTS LAMA LITA
Cramer Dorothy M. • Bellevue, WA 98005 • ACRL ASCLA *Continuing*
Cramer Elizabeth E. • Student • Kent State University School of Library & Information Science • Kent, OH 44242-0001 • ACRL
Cramer Jane A. • Librarian • Brooklyn College Library • Brooklyn, NY 11210 • GODORT
Cramer Jeffrey S. • Circulation Systems Librarian • Boston Public Library • Boston, MA 02117
Cramer Mary M. • Smith & Nephew Richards Inc. • Memphis, TN 38116 • ALCTS LITA RASD ILERT
Cramer Michael D. • Acquisitions Librarian • Virginia Polytechnic Inst & State Univ University Libraries • Blacksburg, VA 24062-9001 • ACRL ALCTS
Cramer Patricia Thompson • Director • Westfield Athenaeum • Westfield, MA 01085 • ALSC LAMA PLA
Cramer Robert N. • Trustee • Camden Free Public Library • Camden, NJ 08103 • LITA
Cramer Sharon L. • Asst. Desert Regional Mgr • Friends of Desert Libraries Indio Library • Indio, CA 92201
Cramer Suzanne • Student • University of Arizona Graduate Library School • Tucson, AZ 85721 • LITA
Crammer Marjorie A. • Children's Age-Level Specialist • Prince George's County Memorial Library System New Carrollton Branch Library • New Carrollton, MD 20784 • ALSC
Crampton Wanda J. • Library Administrator • Peninsula Community Library • Traverse City, MI 49684
Crandall Michael D. • Seattle, WA 98103
Crandall Paul D. • Librarian • Michigan Biotechnology Institute • Lansing, MI 48910
Crane Amy R. • Student • University of South Florida School of Library & Information Science • Tampa, FL 33620 • ALSC
Crane Gerri G. • Director • Lyons Public Library • Lyons, KS 67554-2721
Crane Hugh M. • Assistant Head of Reference • Cambridge Public Library • Cambridge, MA 02138 • RASD GODORT
Crane Jean M. • Librarian • Bloomsburg Area Middle School • Bloomsburg, PA 17815 • AASL
Crane John G. • Administrative Serv Librarian • Dartmouth College Library Baker Memorial Library • Hanover, NH 03755-3525 • LAMA
Crane Karen R. • State Librarian • Alaska State Library • Juneau, AK 99811-571 • ASCLA LAMA PLA
Crane Lois F. • Wichita Art Museum • Wichita, KS 67203 • ALCTS
Crane Marilyn C. • Catalog Librarian • Loma Linda University Del E. Webb Memorial Library • Loma Linda, CA 92350 • ALCTS
Crane Nancy B. • Head of Reference Department • University of Vermont Bailey Howe Library • Burlington, VT 05405-0036 • ACRL RASD
Crane Rachel L. • Student • University of Missouri-Columbia School of Library & Informational Science • Columbia, MO 65211 • ALSC
Crane Richard A. • Library Director • Maude Shunk Public Library • Menomonee Falls, WI 53051 • LAMA PLA
Craner Linda E. • SE Regional Sales Executive • Brodart Company • Williamsport, PA 17705 • LITA
Crank Margaret • Library Media Services Supvr. • Arkansas Department of Education • Little Rock, AR 72201 • AASL
Cranmer Donna M. • Head Technical Services • Sioux Falls Public Library • Sioux Falls, SD 57102 • PLA
Crannell Philip A. • Gee & Jenson Engr Arch Plamers Inc • West Palm Beach, FL 33416-4600
Cranston Alyce M. • Minneapolis, MN 55401 • Continuing
Cranston Linda A. • Head Technical Services • University of New Hampshire Library • Durham, NH 03824 • ALCTS MAGERT
Cranwell Elizabeth C. • Director • Northeast Regional Library • Corinth, MS 38834 • LAMA PLA
Crase Nancy L. • Library Technician • Telesel Library Services • Washington, DC 20006
Cravens Sally A. • Documents Librarian • University of Florida Libraries • Gainesville, FL 32611-2047 • ACRL RASD GODORT
Cravens Vickie L. • Kinderhook Regional Library • Lebanon, MO 65536 • ALCTS PLA
Craver Kathleen W. • Head Librarian • National Cathedral School • Washington, DC 20016 • AASL YALSA
Cravey Pamela J. • Head of Circulation/Assoc Prof • Georgia State University Pullen Library • Atlanta, GA 30303-3081 • ACRL
Crawford-Oppenheimer Christine • Bibliographic Services Coor. • Southeastern New York Library Resources Council • Highland, NY 12528
Crawford Anne M. • Librarian I • Phoenix Public Library Cholla Branch • Phoenix, AZ 85051-1598 • ASCLA PLA RASD IFRT ILERT
Crawford Anthony R. • Archivist/Curator of Manuscripts • Kansas State University Farrell Library • Manhattan, KS 66506-1200 • ACRL
Crawford Barbara • Albany, NY 12205
Crawford Carolyn • Santa Barbara, CA 93105 • Continuing
Crawford Charles J. • Vashon, WA 98070
Crawford Christiana K. • Village School • Gorham, ME 04038
Crawford Christine A. • Prospect Heights, IL 60070-1246
Crawford Cindy • Circulation Supervisor • Needham Free Public Library • Needham, MA 02194
Crawford Cynthia L. • Media Center Director • Brady Elementary School • Little Rock, AR 72205
Crawford Daniel R. • Manchester, IA 52057
Crawford Doris L. • Saint Elizabeth Hospital Medical Center School of Nursing Library • Youngstown, OH 44501 • ACRL
Crawford Dorothy C. • San Antonio Public Library Thousand Oaks Branch • San Antonio, TX 78233
Crawford Eleanor • Head, Genealogy Dept. • Orange County Library System Orlando Public Library • Orlando, FL 32801-2471
Crawford Elizabeth Mrs • Charlotte, NC 28203 • Continuing
Crawford Geraldine H. • Dearborn, MI 48127
Crawford Gregory A. • Student • Rutgers University School of Communication Information & Library Studies • New Brunswick, NJ 08903 • ACRL RASD
Crawford John • Sun City Ctr, FL 33570 • Continuing
Crawford Josephine • University of Wisconsin Center for Health Sciences Library • Madison, WI 53706 • ALCTS LAMA LITA
Crawford Julia L. • Albany, GA 31707 • PLA RASD *Continuing*
Crawford Julie A. • Student • Wayne State University Library Science Program • Detroit, MI 48202
Crawford Laura B. • Director • Amesbury Public Library • Amesbury, MA 01913
Crawford Lucille V. • Jacksonville, IL 62650 • ALCTS LITA *Continuing*
Crawford Lura E. Miss • Bushnell, FL 33513 • AASL ALSC *Continuing*
Crawford Lynn D. • Supervising Libn./Technical Svs. • Burlington County Library • Mount Holly, NJ 08060-1394 • ALCTS PLA
Crawford Marianne C. • Student • San Jose State University Division of Library & Information Science • San Jose, CA 95192-0029 • RASD NMRT
Crawford Miriam • Philadelphia, PA 19104 • ACRL IFRT SRRT *Continuing*
Crawford Mona L. • Columbus, GA 31904-2127 • ACRL NMRT
Crawford Patricia A. • Student • University of Rhode Island Graduate School of Library & Information Studies • Kingston, RI 02881-0815 • ACRL RASD
Crawford Sherrida J. • Head of Circulation • Valdosta State College Library • Valdosta, GA 31698-0001 • ACRL
Crawford Shirley A. • Librarian I • Atlanta-Fulton Public Library • Atlanta, GA 30303 • LAMA YALSA
Crawford Susan Young Dr • Professor & Library Director • Washington University School of Medicine • St Louis, MO 63110 • ACRL LITA
Crawford Virginia • Norwalk, CT 06850 • AASL
Crawford Walt • Principal Analyst • Research Libraries Group Inc. (RLG) • Mountain View, CA 94041-1100 • LITA
Crawford Wray Ann • Librarian • Bunker Hill Elementary School • Indianapolis, IN 46227 • AASL
Crawley Marian H. • Branch Administrator • Indianapolis-Marion County Public Library Southport Branch • Indianapolis, IN 46227-8899 • PLA
Cray Jean C. • Director Instructional Mat Ctr • Hinsdale South High School • Darien, IL 60559 • AASL
Craychee Pam • Department Head Business • Carnegie Library of Pittsburgh • Pittsburgh, PA 15213-4080 • RASD
Crayne Janet I. • Slavic Cataloger-Instr. Status • University of Virginia Alderman Library • Charlottesville, VA 22903-2498 • ACRL
Crayton James E. • Assoc Dean Community Skills Ctr • Pasadena Area Community College District • Pasadena, CA 91101
Creamer Geraldine M. • Sayreville, NJ 08872
Creamer Thomas • Student • University of Maryland College of Library and Information Services • College Park, MD 20742-4345 • ACRL RASD IFRT SRRT
Crean Louise A. • Loyola High School • Los Angeles, CA 90006 • AASL
Creaser Linda A. • Coordinator of BI • Ferris State University • Big Rapids, MI 49307 • ACRL
Creech John K. • Reference Librarian • Western Carolina University Hunter Library • Cullowhee, NC 28723-9002 • ACRL
Creecy Rachel A. • Hong Kong Baptist Theological Seminary • Kowloon, Hong Kong • ACRL ALCTS *Life*
Creecy Richard B. L. Jr. • Cataloger • H.W. Wilson Company • Bronx, NY 10452 • ALCTS
Creed Daniel J. • Student • Rosary College Graduate School of Library & Information Science • River Forest, IL 60305 • IFRT
Creed Susan • Children's Librarian • North Spokane Library • Spokane, WA 99218
Creedon Jennifer M. • Plattsburgh, NY 12901
Creedon Michael E. • Student • San Jose State University Division of Library & Information Science • San Jose, CA 95192-0029
Creek David J. • Young Adult Librarian • Rochester Public Library Arnett Branch • Rochester, NY 14619
Creek Leon J. • Serial Cataloger/Phil Bibl • University of Rochester Rush Rhees Library • Rochester, NY 14627 • ALCTS RASD
Creekmore Verity V. • Library Media Specialist • Sheridan Elementary School • Organgeburg, SC 29135 • AASL
Creel R. Allyson • Orem, UT 84057
Creelman M. Gwendolyn • Head of Cataloging • Mount Allison University Ralph Pickard Bell Library • Sackville NB, E0A 3C0 Canada • ALCTS LITA
Creely Kathryn L. • University of California-San Diego • La Jolla, CA 92093-0175 • ACRL
Creeron Carolyn E. • Deltona, FL 32725
Crehore Mary P. • Adult Services, Head • Amherst Public Library • Amherst, OH 44001 • RASD
Creider Laurence S. • Cataloger • University of Pennsylvania Library Van Pelt-Dietrich Library Center • Philadelphia, PA 19104-6206 • ALCTS
Creighton Alice S. • Head of Special Collections • U S Naval Academy Nimitz Library • Annapolis, MD 21402 • ACRL
Creighton Beatrice • Editor-in-Chief • Lothrop Lee & Shepard Books • New York, NY 10019 • AASL YALSA *Life*
Creighton Elizabeth Ms. • Head, Technical Services Dept. • Meriden Public Library • Meriden, CT 06450
Creighton Melissa I. • Cataloger Librarian • Richland County Public Library • Columbia, SC 29201 • ALCTS LITA
Creighton Sherry L. • Assistant Manager • Dallas Public Library Audelia Road Branch • Dallas, TX 75238-1999 • ALSC
Crell Bonnie • Principal Librarian • California Youth Authority • Sacramento, CA 95823
Crelling Sharon M. • Milwaukee, WI 53212-1747

Crenshaw Elizabeth • Librarian Project Access • The New York Public Library • New York, NY 10016 • ASCLA
Crenshaw Faith M. • School Librarian • Scottsdale Christian Academy • Phoenix, AZ 85032-5531
Crenshaw Gwendolyn L. • Head Librarian • Kent Denver School • Englewood, CO 80110
Crenshaw Jan C. • Head Librarian • San Jacinto College North Library • Houston, TX 77049 • ACRL
Crenson Alene L. • Public Services Librarian • Baltimore County Public Library Catonsville Branch • Catonsville, MD 21228 • PLA
Crescenzi Jean D. • Rutgers University Paul Robeson Library • Camden, NJ 08101-3990 • ACRL RASD
Crescimanno Terry A. • Student • Southern Connecticut State University School of Libray Science & Instructional Technology • New Haven, CT 06515 • PLA
Crescimano Linda J. • Pine Crest Upper School Library • Ft Lauderdale, FL 33308 • AASL ALCTS LITA YALSA
Crespi Maria B. • Student • University of South Florida School of Library & Information Science • Tampa, FL 33620
Crespin Yolanda C. • Librarian • Saint Anthony Hospital Systems Medical Reference Library • Denver, CO 80204
Cress Ann • Jefferson County Public Library • Lakewood, CO 80215 • ALSC
Cress Elizabeth J. • Assistant Director • Poplar Creek Public Library Dist • Streamwood, IL 60107 • PLA
Cressman Pamela • Librarian • Central Bucks High School, West • Doylestown, PA 18901 • AASL
Cressman Shawne Diaz • Allentown, PA 18102 • ALCTS
Crest Sarah Elizabeth • Baltimore, MD 21218 • ACRL LIRT
Cresto Kathleen M. • Senior Librarian • Thousand Oaks Library • Thousand Oaks, CA 91362
Creswell Gwendolyn S. • Director • Georgia Southwestern College James Earl Carter Library • Americus, GA 31709 • ACRL
Creth Sheila D. • Librarian • University of Iowa Libraries • Iowa City, IA 52242-1379 • ACRL LAMA LITA
Cretini Blanche M. • Coordinator of User Services • State Library of Louisiana • Baton Rouge, LA 70821 • ASCLA
Creve Heidi S. • Student • University of California Los Angeles Graduate School of Library & Information Science • Los Angeles, CA 90024 • IFRT
Creveling Alice J. • Librarian • Shawnee Mission North High School • Shawnee Mission, KS 66202 • AASL YALSA
Crew Hilary S. • Rutgers University School of Communication Information & Library Studies • New Brunswick, NJ 08903 • YALSA
Crews Joyce • Senior Librarian • Mill Valley Public Library • Mill Valley, CA 94941
Crews Kenneth D. • San Jose State University School of Business • San Jose, CA 95192-0070
Cribben Mary Margaret Sr • Associate Professor • Villanova Univ Grad Dept of L Scie • Villanova, PA 19085 • Continuing
Cribbin Ruth P. • Stone Mtn, GA 30083 • ACRL
Cribbs Jane L. • Librarian • Lordstown Elementary School • Warren, OH 44485 • AASL
Crichton Deirdre M. • Librarian • Mississauga Public Library • Mississauga ON, L5B 2N6 Canada • ALSC PLA
Crider Lissa Ann • Librarian • Windward School • Los Angeles, CA 90066
Crider Pamela • Young Adult Librarian • San Jose Public Library Almaden Branch • San Jose, CA 95120
Cridland Nancy C. • History Librarian • Indiana University at Bloomington University Libraries • Bloomington, IN 47405-9998 • ACRL
Crimmin Wilbur B. • Librarian • Hartford Public Library • Hartford, CT 06103-3003 • PLA IFRT
Crimmins Peggy • MIS Training/Support Specialist • Adams Twelve Five Star School District • Northglenn, CO 80233 • LITA
Crinion Jacquelyn • Collection Development Spec. • University of Texas at San Antonio-Library • San Antonio, TX 78249 • ACRL ALCTS
Cripe Carolyn R. • Reference Librarian • Tri-State University Perry T. Ford Library • Angola, IN 46703 • RASD
Crippen Davis • Trustee • Ramapo Catskill Library System • Middletown, NY 10940 • ALSC
Crippin Linda M. • New Brighton, MN 55112
Crisco Mary E. • Automated Circ Control Coor • Harford County Library • Belcamp, MD 21017 • LITA
Crislip Marion P. • Director • Graves County Library • Mayfield, KY 42066 • LAMA PLA
Crisman Mary F Borden • Tacoma, WA 98406 • RASD
Crismond Linda F. • Northfield, IL 60093 • LAMA LITA PLA
Crisp Brandee • Arlington Heights, IL 60005-1362 • PLA RASD IFRT LIRT NMRT SRRT
Crisp Jeanne • Washington State Library • Olympia, WA 98504-2470 • LITA
Crisp Marlou • Milpitas, CA 95035
Crisp Mary Mrs. • Trustee • Sears Store • Robbinsville, NC 28771 • ALTA
Crisp Vincent • Trustee • Nantahala Regional Library • Murphy, NC 28906 • ALTA
Crispen Joanne L. • RASD/ASCLA Deputy Exec. Dir. • American Library Association • Chicago, IL 60611-2795 • ASCLA
Crispin Brenda D. • Librarain I • Oxnard Public Library • Oxnard, CA 93030
Crispino Marie • Head Circulation Librarian • Scranton Public Library Albright Memorial Library • Scranton, PA 18509-3248 • PLA RASD IFRT
Criss Janice G. • Director • Baldwin Borough Public Library • Pittsburgh, PA 15227-3638 • PLA
Criss Laura A H • Coral Gables, FL 33146
Crissinger John D. • Library Director • Ambassador College Library Roy Hammer Library Building • Big Sandy, TX 75755 • ACRL LAMA MAGERT
Crist Lynda L. • Jefferson Davis Association • Houston, TX 77251-1892
Crist Margaret L. • Asst. Dir. for Public Services • University of Michigan • Ann Arbor, MI 48109-1205 • ACRL LAMA LITA RASD
Cristobal Hope A. • Trustee • Nieves M. Flores Memorial Library • Agana, GU 96910 • ALTA
Critchlow Therese E. • Princeton Public Library • Princeton, NJ 08542
Crites Lynn • Library Director • Farmington Public Library • Farmington, MO 63640 • PLA
Crnkovich Philip • Reference Librarian • Lancaster County Library • Lancaster, PA 17602 • RASD LHRT
Croal Mary M. • Library Director • Norwell School Library • Norwell, MA 02061 • AASL YALSA
Croasdale Hud • Trustee • Prince William Public Library System Administrative Support Center • Prince William, VA 22192-5073
Crocker Jane Lopes • Director • Gloucester County College Library Media Center • Sewell, NJ 08080 • ACRL
Crocker Joann M. • University of Nebraska Medical Ctr McGoogan Library of Medicine • Omaha, NE 68198-6705 • ALCTS LITA
Crocker Judith A. • Library Media Specialist • Chamisa Elementary School • Los Alamos, NM 87544 • AASL ALSC
Crocker Marilyn E. • Librarian • Dewey School • Evanston, IL 60201
Crocker Mary E. • Houston Public Library • Houston, TX 77002 • ASCLA
Crocker Shelli R. • Biomedical Librarian • University of Kansas Medical Center A.R. Dykes Library • Kansas City, KS 66103 • LITA
Crocker Susan O. • Franklin Lakes Public Library • Franklin Lakes, NJ 07417 • LAMA PLA
Crocker Wayne M. • Director of Library Service • Petersburg Public Library • Petersburg, VA 23803 • PLA
Crockett Darla J. • Academic Coordinator • University of California-Berkeley School of Library & Information Studies • Berkeley, CA 94720
Crockett Denise J. • Principal • Naremco Services Inc. • New York, NY 10165 • LAMA LITA
Crockett Mary Lou • Los Angeles Public Library • Los Angeles, CA 90071 • ALTA
Crockett Sharon W. • Collection Management Librarian • Congressional Research Service • Washington, DC 20540 • IFRT
Croft Betty M. E. • Maryville, MO 64468 • ACRL ALCTS *Life*
Croft Elizabeth G. • Librarian-Cataloger • Price Waterhouse Information Ctr. • New York, NY 10022 • ALCTS
Croft Jeannette M. • Phoenix, AZ 85020
Crohan Catherine L. • Serials Librarian • Siena College • Loudonville, NY 12211-1462 • ACRL ALCTS IFRT SRRT
Cromer Donna E. • University of New Mexico Centennial Science & Engineering Library • Albuquerque, NM 87131
Cromer Kenneth L. • Assistant Director • Lorain Public Library • Lorain, OH 44052 • PLA
Crompton Marie E. • Director of Media Services • Salem School District Media Center • Salem, NH 03079
Cromwell Wilma I. • Menlo Park, CA 94025 • ALCTS LITA IFRT SRRT
Croneberger Robert B. • Carnegie Library of Pittsburgh • Pittsburgh, PA 15213-4080 • LAMA LITA PLA IFRT SRRT
Croneis Karen • Washington University Libraries • Saint Louis, MO 63130-4899 • ACRL LAMA SRRT
Cronenwett Philip N. • Chief of Special Collections • Dartmouth College Library Baker Memorial Library • Hanover, NH 03755-3525 • ACRL
Cronin Lucille D. • Trustee • Clark County Public Library • Springfield, OH 45501-1080 • ALTA
Cronin Mary J. • University Librarian • Boston College Libraries • Chestnut Hill, MA 02167 • ACRL
Cronk Ellen L. • Ref. Ln./Supp. Staff Supv. • University of Rochester Library • Rochester, NY 14627 • ACRL RASD CLENE
Cronkhite Janet • Librarian • United Samanitans Medical Center • Danville, IL 61832
Cronn Katherine H. • Library Media Specialist • Oneida Senior High School • Oneida, NY 13421 • AASL
Crook David M. • Northeast Magnet High School • Wichita, KS 67214
Crook Judy L. • Library Director • Colorado Mountain College-Spring Valley Library • Glenwood Springs, CO 81601 • ACRL LAMA RASD
Crook Kathleen P. • Iberia Parish Library • New Iberia, LA 70560
Crook Mark A. • Section Manager • OCLC Incorporation • Dublin, OH 43017 • RASD
Crook Virginia M. • Head, Reference Librarian • Black Gold Coop Library System • San Luis Obispo, CA 93403 • RASD
Crooker Cynthia • Cataloging Team Leader • Yale University Sterling Memorial Library • New Haven, CT 06520 • ACRL ALCTS
Crooks Constance A. • Librarian Grade 2 • Milwaukee Public Library • Milwaukee, WI 53233 • PLA
Crooks James E. • Data Services • University of California-Irvine Library • Irvine, CA 92713 • ACRL LITA RASD
Crooks Sylvia A. • Instr/Adms & Placement Officer • University of British Columbia • Vancouver BC, V6T 1Z1 Canada • PLA RASD
Croom Philip • Richmond, VA 23223
Croom Sue • Librarian • Pioneer Memorial Library • Fredericksbrg, TX 78624 • PLA
Crosby-Muilenburg Corryn • Chair,Information Serivces • Humboldt State University Library • Arcata, CA 95521 • ACRL LAMA RASD
Crosby Barbara A. • Wenatchee, WA 98801-1684 • SRRT
Crosby Ellen E. • University of South Carolina College of Library & Information Science • Columbia, SC 29208 • ALCTS LITA RASD
Crosby Joel • City Council Liaison • Spokane Public Library Comstock Building Library • Spokane, WA 99201-0976 • ALTA
Crosby Kathryn A. • Managing Libraian • King County Library System Vashon Library • Vashon, WA 98070 • ALSC PLA
Crosby Kay M. • Bakersfield, CA 93309-3630
Crosby Linda K. • Aqquisition Clerk • Chemeketa Community College • Salem, OR 97309
Crosby Lucile Z. Miss • Phoenix, AZ 85020 • Continuing
Crosby Marilyn D. • Student • University of South Carolina College of Library & Information Science • Columbia, SC 29208
Crosby Theresa • Library Technician • North Hennepin Community College Library • Brooklyn Park, MN 55445
Crose Michael A. • Asst. Director Management Serv. • Timberland Regional Library • Olympia, WA 98501 • LAMA
Cross-Briscoe Marcia P. • Asst. Govt. Documents Librarian • Atlanta-Fulton Public Library • Atlanta, GA 30303 • PLA GODORT
Cross Dorothy A. • Alexandria, VA 22310-2609 • Continuing
Cross Geraldine P. • Decatur, GA 30033
Cross James Edward • Archivist • Clemson University R. M. Cooper Library • Clemson, SC 29634-3001 • ACRL RASD
Cross Jennie B. • Library Services Director • Oakland Schools • Waterford, MI 48328 • GODORT
Cross Jennifer D. • Student • University of Pittsburgh School of Library and Information Science • Pittsburgh, PA 15260
Cross Lorna • Burlington, VT 05401
Cross Mary R. • Head, Technical Services • Columbia College J. Drake Edens Library • Columbia, SC 29203 • ALCTS
Cross Patricia H. • Programmer/Analyst • University of California-Los Angeles (UCLA) • Los Angeles, CA 90024-1450 • ACRL LAMA NMRT
Crossey Constance M. • Library Specialist III • University of Pittsburgh Hillman Library • Pittsburgh, PA 15260 • ALCTS
Crossey Nancy J. • Pikes Peak Library District • Colorado Springs, CO 80901
Crossland Brent L. • Trustee • Crossland's Meats • Bowen, IL 62316 • ALTA PLA
Crossland Howard • Media Specialist • Trenton Board of Education Woodrow Wilson Elementary • Trenton, NJ 08638 • AASL
Crossley Patricia A. • Beavercreek, OH 45434
Crossley Winnifred M. • Petoskey, MI 49770-2430 • ALSC YALSA *Life*

Crossman Barbara • Library Director • Jacksonville Public Library • Jacksonville, TX 75766 • PLA

Crossman Cheryl A. • The Boeing Company Renton Technical Library • Seattle, WA 98124 • ALCTS

Crosson Vicky L. • Library Consultant • Texas State Library • Austin, TX 78711 • ALSC

Crott E. Renee • Director • Holmes County Library • Millersburg, OH 44654 • PLA

Crotteau Mark D. • Student • Washington State University Library • Pullman, WA 99164-5610 • ALCTS

Crotts Carolyn • Librarian • Unified School District, #102 • Cimarron, KS 67835 • AASL LITA YALSA

Crotts Joe • Head of Access Services • California State University-Chico Meriam Library • Chico, CA 92929-0295 • Life

Crouch Chris A. • Media Specialist • Three Chopt Elementary School • Richmond, VA 23229 • AASL

Crouch Jacob F. III • Librarian I • Atlanta-Fulton Public Library • Atlanta, GA 30303 • PLA RASD

Crouch Kathryn J. • Richmond, KY 40475 • PLA

Crouch Lora E. • Salt Lake City, UT 84102 • RASD
Continuing

Crouch M Lois Miss • Sioux City, IA 51106 • Continuing

Crouch Marilyn C. • Director of Library Services • El Dorado County Library • Placerville, CA 95667

Crouch Milton H. • Asst Director of Reader Serv • University of Vermont Bailey Howe Library • Burlington, VT 05405-0036 • ACRL LITA RASD

Crouch Polly • King, NC 27021 • AASL LIRT

Croughan Catlin M. • Development Consultant • Library Foundation of San Francisco • San Francisco, CA 94104

Crouse A. Lorraine • Extension/Outreach Specialist • Kansas City Public Library • Kansas City, MO 64106 • ASCLA PLA

Crouse Kathryn E. • Student • Syracuse University School of Information Studies • Syracuse, NY 13244-4100 • RASD

Crouse Kathy A. • Head of Adult Services • Tipton County Public Library • Tipton, IN 46072 • PLA RASD YALSA

Crouse Richard R. • Riva, MD 21140

Crouze T. Joan • Mgr., Corporate Resource Center • SunHealth Corporation • Charlotte, NC 28266-8800

Crow Rebecca N. • Head, Current Collections Div. • Dallas Public Library • Dallas, TX 75201

Crow Rochelle • Head of Acquisitions & Catalog • University of Alabama at Birmingham Mervyn H. Sterne Library • Birmingham, AL 35294-0014 • LITA

Crow Sherry R. • Schaumburg Township District Library • Schaumburg, IL 60194 • AASL ALSC

Crowder Carolyn J. • Library Manager • Ida Hilton Public Library • Darien, GA 31305

Crowe-Crawford Maryjeanne • Adminstrative Librarian • Glenwood-Lynwood Public Library • Glenwood, IL 60425 • PLA

Crowe Edith L. • Librarian • San Jose State University Clark Library • San Jose, CA 95192-0028 • ACRL RASD IFRT LIRT SRRT

Crowe Elaine N. • Reference Librarian • Shasta College Library • Redding, CA 96099 • ACRL

Crowe John P. • Asst. Director/Head Reference • Cora J Belden Library • Rocky Hill, CT 06067 • PLA

Crowe Kathryn M. • Assistant Reference Librarian • University of North Carolina • Greensboro, NC 27412-5001 • ACRL

Crowe Lillie E. • Warner Robins, GA 31088 • AASL

Crowe Linda D. • Director • Peninsula Library System • San Mateo, CA 94402 • ASCLA SRRT

Crowe Martha J. • Cornell University Library • Ithaca, NY 14853 • LITA

Crowe Mary • Librarian • Benicia High School • Benicia, CA 94510 • AASL

Crowe Susan B. • Manager • Aerospace Corp • Los Angeles, CA 90009-2957 • ACRL ALCTS LITA

Crowe Virginia M. Dr. • Dean of Library & Media Services • Shippensburg University Lehman Memorial Library • Shippensburg, PA 17257-2299 • ACRL

Crowe William J. • Dean of Libraries • University of Kansas Library • Lawrence, KS 66045-2800 • ACRL LITA LHRT

Crowell Nancy E. • Librarian • Scarborough Public Library • Scarborough, ME 04074 • ALSC LAMA PLA IFRT

Crowell Ruth Anne Stirk • Librarian • Lyman High School Library • Longwood, FL 32750 • AASL

Crowley-Hodina Carolyn • Chief Librarian • United States Air Force Western Space & Missle Center • Vandenberg AFB, CA 93437 • PLA

Crowley Bill • State Library of Ohio • Columbus, OH 43266-0334 • ASCLA

Crowley Ellen T. • Vice Pres. & Publ, General Ref. • Gale Research, Inc. • Detroit, MI 48226 • RASD

Crowley John D. • Joel Barlow High School • West Redding, CT 06896 • AASL ALCTS LITA

Crowley Julie Moore • Cataloger/Librarian • Saint Leo College • Saint Leo, FL 33574-2128

Crowley Kim M. • Weidman, MI 48893

Crowley Rhea A. • Children's Librarian • Boyle County Public Library • Danville, KY 40422 • ALSC

Crowley Sandra C. • Librarian • Lincoln High School • Vincennes, IN 47591-0216 • AASL

Crowley Stephen J. • Director • Putnam County Library System • Palatka, FL 32177-3873 • YALSA

Crowley Terence Dr. • Professor • San Jose State University Division of Library & Information Science • San Jose, CA 95192-0029 • ACRL PLA RASD GODORT LRRT SRRT

Crown Colette K. • Ledyard, CT 06339-1327 • LITA SRRT

Crown Faith W. • New Hope, PA 18938-9607

Crown Jeanne • Warrenton, VA 22186 • AASL

Crowner Dee • Library Director • North Liberty Community Library • North Liberty, IA 52317

Crownfield Eleanor Bostwick • Catalog Librarian/Asst. Prof • University of Northern Iowa Donald O. Rod Library • Cedar Falls, IA 50613-3675 • ACRL ALCTS LITA IFRT

Crowther Eleanor • Trustee • Loudoun County Public Library • Leesburg, VA 22075 • ALTA

Crowther Jason R. • Librarian • The Leelanau School Library • Glen Arbor, MI 49636 • AASL ILERT

Croxen Mary B. • Cataloger • Harvard University Frances L Loeb Library • Cambridge, MA 02138 • LITA IFRT

Crozier Mary Ann • Coordinator of Children's Servs. • Bucks County Free Library • Doylestown, PA 18901 • ALSC

Crozier Virginia • Kailua, HI 96734 • Continuing

Crudele Charles • Reference Librarian • Cherry Hill Free Public Library • Cherry Hill, NJ 08034 • LITA

Cruikshank Renee R. • Reference Librarian • Anderson University • Anderson, IN 46012

Cruikshank Rosamond • Fitchburg, MA 01420-9656 • Continuing

Crum Mark Dr. • Kalamazoo, MI 49001 • Continuing

Crum Mary Jane • Eastern Guilford High School • Gibsonville, NC 27249 • AASL

Crum Patricia Ann • Director • Martin County Public Library • Inez, KY 41224 • LAMA PLA

Crum Shutta K. • Youth Specialist Librarian • Ann Arbor Public Library • Ann Arbor, MI 48104

Crumb Debra A. • Librarian • Washington State Library • Olympia, WA 98504-2470 • ASCLA

Crumb Lawrence N. • Reference Librarian • University of Oregon Library • Eugene, OR 97403-1299 • ACRL RASD

Crumb Lois King • San Luis Obispo, CA 93401 • LAMA PLA
Life

Crumley Sean Emmett • Student • Indiana University School of Library and Information Science • Bloomington, IN 47405 • LITA RASD LIRT

Crump Joyce A. • LAC/Harbor-UCLA Medical Center Parlow Library • Torrance, CA 90509

Crump Michele J. • Head of Receiving Unit • University of Florida Libraries • Gainesville, FL 32611-2047 • ALCTS

Crump Quita • Market Research • Alumax Inc. Market Research Library • Norcross, GA 30092-2812 • LITA

Crumrin Robin • Noblesville, IN 46060-8672

Crumrine Katherine • Pittsburgh, PA 15226 • LAMA PLA
Continuing

Cruse James M. • Asst. Chief Access Serv. • Stanford University • Stanford, CA 94305-6011 • LITA

Cruse Patricia • Librarian • Louisiana State University Libraries Middleton Library • Baton Rouge, LA 70803-3342 • ACRL GODORT

Crutchfield B. Jr. • Assoc Prof & Dir of L Serv • West Virginia Wesleyan College Annie Merner Pfeiffer Library • Buckhannon, WV 26201-2998 • ACRL LIRT

Cruz Aguigui Ignacio • Trustee • Nieves M. Flores Memorial Library • Agana, GU 96910 • ALTA

Cruz Aurora • Student • State University of New York at Albany School of Information Science & Policy • Albany, NY 12222

Cruz Delia • Reference Librarian • International American University of Puerto Rico • Hato Rey, PR 00919

Cruz Lucy S. • Taos, NM 87571 • AASL

Cruz Prudenciana C. • Student • National Library of the Philippines • Manila, Philippines

Cruz Rosario M. • Miami, FL 33183

Cruz Sobeida • Trustee • Yonkers Public Library • Yonkers, NY 10701 • ALTA

Cryan Anne • Moraga, CA 94556 • PLA

Cryan Meike E. • Library Director • Liberty Public Library • Liberty, NY 12754 • PLA

Cryor Lea • Bakersfield, CA 93309

Cseh Eugene F. • Head, Acquisitions Department • University of Connecticut Homer Babbidge Library • Storrs, CT 06269-1005 • ALCTS

Csicsay Carol • Buffalo, NY 14220

Cubbedge Frankie H. • Dean • University of South Carolina at Aiken Gregg-Graniteville Library • Aiken, SC 29801

Cubberley Carol • Director of Technical Services • University of Southern Mississippi Cook Memorial Library • Hattiesburg, MS 39406-5053 • ALCTS LAMA

Cubit James R. • Assistant College Librarian • Williams College Sawyer Library • Williamstown, MA 01267 • ACRL LAMA IFRT

Cucchiara Anthony M. • Asst. Prof./Archivist • Brooklyn College Library • Brooklyn, NY 11210

Cuccia Carol M. • Arlington, VA 22203 • AASL

Cuccia Kevin D. • Science Librarian • Louisiana Technical University Prescott Memorial Library • Ruston, LA 71270-9985 • ACRL

Cucciarre Barbara L. • Director, Resource Center • Magnificat High School • Rocky River, OH 44116

Cuddigan Maureen • Branch Children's Librarian • Dakota County Library System Burnsville Branch Library • Burnsville, MN 55337 • ALSC PLA

Cudney Cheryl L.R. • Media Specialist • Keystone Middle School • Lagrange, OH 44050

Cudnohfsky Susan A. • University of Washington • Seattle, WA 98195

Cuebas Ana E. • Mayaguez, PR 00708

Cuellar Margaret • Librarian • Johnston High School • Austin, TX 78721 • AASL

Cuesta Yolanda J. • Chief of Library Devel Services • California State Library Library Development Services Bureau • Sacramento, CA 95814-3324 • PLA

Cugino Priscilla A. • Librarian • Clayton Davenport School • Cardiff, NJ 08232 • AASL

Cukurs Ruth • Elementary School Librarian • Baxter Elementary School • Anchorage, AK 99504

Culberg Laura B. • Head Librarian • Chicago Public Library Harold Washington Library • Chicago, IL 60605 • ALSC

Culbert Merle M. • Media Services Coordinator • Manhattan Beach City School District • Manhattan Beach, CA 90266 • AASL

Culbertson Cheryl W. • Trustee • Atkinson Public Library District • Atkinson, IL 61235-0633 • ALTA

Culbertson Grace • Student • Texas Woman's University School of Library & Information Studies • Denton, TX 76204 • AASL ALSC NMRT

Culbertson Judith Diehl • Assistant Professor • Shippensburg University Lehman Memorial Library • Shippensburg, PA 17257-2299 • ACRL ALCTS
Life

Culbertson Lillian D. • Downers Grove, IL 60515 • ALCTS LITA

Culbertson Linda A. • Children's Librarian • Cleveland Heights-University Heights Public Library • Cleveland Heights, OH 44118 • ALSC

Culbertson Mary A. • Library Director • Birchard Public Library of Sandusky County • Fremont, OH 43420

Culbertson Michael R. • Librarian • Colorado State University William E. Morgan Library • Fort Collins, CO 80523 • ACRL

Culbreath Ethelrene • Librarian • Atlanta-Fulton Public Library • Atlanta, GA 30303

Culhane Mary T. • Pembroke Pines, FL 33026 • CLENE

Culkin Patricia B. • Vice President • Colorado Alliance of Research Libraries • Denver, CO 80210 • LITA

Cullarin Edgardo C. • Librarian • Carlos P. Romulo Memorial Library and Museum • Tarlac, Tarlac 2300, Philippines

Cullars John M. • University of Illinois at Chicago University Library • Chicago, IL 60680 • ACRL

Cullen Ellen N. • Media Specialist • Notre Dame Prep High School • Towson, MD 21204 • AASL YALSA

Cullen Geraldine • Terryville, CT 06786-0118

Cullen Lawrence R. • Librarian • North Hennepin Community College Library • Brooklyn Park, MN 55445 • ACRL

Cullen Mary Jo • Trustee • Arlington Heights Memorial Library • Arlington Heights, IL 60004-5966 • ALTA

Cullen Mary Sister • Calumet College • Whiting, IN 46394 • ACRL

Cullen Mary Sue • Longfellow Intermediate School • Falls Church, VA 22043 • AASL

Cullen Rosemary L. • Curator of the Harris Collection • Brown University Library • Providence, RI 02912 • ACRL

Cullen T. H. Mrs. • Bradenton, FL 34203 • Continuing

Cullers Sandra M. • Supervisor School Improvement • Missouri Department of Elementary and Secondary Education • Jefferson City, MO 65102 • AASL

Cullimore R. Holliday • University of California-Berkeley Institute of Governmental Studies • Berkeley, CA 94720

Cullinan Bernice E. • Professor • New York University Elmer Holmes Bobst Library • New York, NY 10012 • AASL

Cullinan Katherine L. • Reference Librarian • Elmhurst Public Library • Elmhurst, IL 60126 • PLA

Cullinane Jane F. • Connecticut State Library • Hartford, CT 06106 • ALCTS
Cullinane Phyllis A. • Simmons College Graduate School of Library & Information Science • Boston, MA 02115
Culliver Linda Redd • Librarian • Rancho High School • North Las Vegas, NV 89030 • AASL *Life*
Cullop Mary H. • Librarian • Veterans Administration Medical Center Library • Salisbury, NC 28144
Cullum Laura L. • Sanford, FL 32271 • AASL
Culmer-Nier Lessie A. • Catalog Librarian • Drew University • Madison, NJ 07940-4007 • ACRL ALCTS LITA
Culmer Carita M. • Clln. Development & Space Proj. • Phoenix College Library • Phoenix, AZ 85013 • ACRL
Culotta Betty W. • Millboro, VA 24460 • AASL ALTA
Culotta John • Trustee • Melrose Park Public Library • Melrose Park, IL 60160
Culotta Wendy A. • Sci-Tech Librarians • California State University-Long Beach University Library & Learning Resources • Long Beach, CA 90840-1901 • ACRL ALCTS
Culp Bryan A. • Student • University of Tennessee-Knoxville Graduate School of Library & Information Science • Knoxville, TN 37996-4330
Culp Carol Ann • Lakewood, OH 44107 • RASD
Culp Gwen R. • Manager of Customer Svs. Sales • Western Library Network (WLN) • Lacey, WA 98503-0888 • ALCTS LITA
Culp Joan • Stewart Elementary School • Huntsville, TX 77340 • AASL ALSC
Culpepper Betty M. • Librarian • Library of Congress • Washington, DC 20541 • LAMA RASD
Culpepper Jetta C. • Head of Acquisitions • Murray State University Harry Lee Waterfield Library • Murray, KY 42071-3309 • ACRL
Culshaw John P. • Central Reference Librarian • University of Colorado • Boulder, CO 80309 • LAMA NMRT SRRT
Culver Colette A. • District Librarian/Media Coor. • Pleasant Hill High School Library District #1 • Pleasant Hill, OR 97455 • AASL
Cumberbatch-Lavender G. A. • Nashville, TN 37211
Cumings Susan M. • Fairfax, VA 22037-0001 • AASL LAMA YALSA
Cumming Leighton H. • World Bank • Washington, DC 20433
Cumming Linda L. • Dir. of Central Library • Denver Public Library • Denver, CO 80203-2165 • LAMA PLA
Cummings Dana D. • Head Technical Services • Berkeshire Athenaeum • Pittsfield, MA 01201 • ALCTS LITA
Cummings Elizabeth • Phoenix, AZ 85020 • Continuing
Cummings Esther S. • Libn-Ref. Div. Supervisor • Burlingame Public Library • Burlingame, CA 94010
Cummings Gary J. • Director • Henry Carter Hull Library • Clinton, CT 06413
Cummings Gary K. • Reference Librarian • Ontario City Library • Ontario, CA 91764 • ALCTS LITA RASD
Cummings John P. • Associate Director • United States Naval Academy Nimitz Library • Annapolis, MD 21402-5029 • ACRL AFLRT FLRT
Cummings Laura • New York, NY 10025 • Continuing
Cummings Mary Bowling • Reference Librarian • Shawnee State University Library • Portsmouth, OH 45662-4303 • ACRL IFRT LIRT SRRT
Cummings Nancy L. • Reference Librarian • Cornell University Library • Ithaca, NY 14853 • NMRT
Cummings Nancy W. • School Library Media Specialist • Fairport Central Schools Johanna Perrin Middle School • Fairport, NY 14450 • AASL
Cummings Peggy A. • President • Literary Research Company • Sedalia, CO 80135
Cummings Sarah N. • Children's Librarian • Sweetwater County Library Systems • Green River, WY 82935 • ALSC
Cummins A. Blair • Locust Valley Library • Locust Valley, NY 11560 • PLA
Cummins Carol O. • Student • University of Rhode Island Library • Kingston, RI 02881-0803
Cummins Carol P. • Circulation Librarian • Virginia Theological Seminary • Alexandria, VA 22304-5201
Cummins Ellen M. • University of Missouri-Saint Louis • St. Louis, MO 63121-4499
Cummins Julie A. • Coordinator of Children's Servs. • New York Public Library • New York, NY 10016 • ALSC PLA
Cummins Lynn M. • Catalof Librarian, ACQS • California State University • Northridge, CA 91330 • ACRL ALCTS LITA RASD *Life*
Cummins Milla L. • Student • University of Wisconsin-Milwaukee School of Library & Information Science • Milwaukee, WI 53201 • ACRL PLA
Cummiskey Patricia A. • Anchorage, AK 99517
Cunha George M. • Conservation Cons & Tchr • University of Kentucky College of Library & Information Science • Lexington, KY 40506-0391 • ACRL ALCTS
Cuniff Wanda • Librarian • T.J. Risk Library Media Center(Middle School) • Nacogdoches, TX 75961
Cunningham-Kruppa Mary E. • Preservation Officer • University of Texas Libraries General Libraries • Austin, TX 78713-7330 • ALCTS
Cunningham Allen • Director • Livingston Parish Library • Livingston, LA 70754 • PLA
Cunningham Allison C. • Jacksonville, FL 32216
Cunningham Ann Marie • Executive Director • National Federation of Abstracting & Information (NFAIS) • Philadelphia, PA 19102
Cunningham Barbara A. • Executive Director • Illinois Library Association • Chicago, IL 60610-4306
Cunningham Betty D. • Librarian • Phoenix Public Library Mesquite Branch • Phoenix, AZ 85032
Cunningham Beverly • North Kingstown, RI 02852 • PLA
Cunningham Cynthia Altick • Reference Librarian • University of Washington Suzzallo Library • Seattle, WA 98195 • ACRL LIRT
Cunningham Danny H. • Assistant Library Director • Nicholson Memorial Library • Garland, TX 75040-6365
Cunningham Diana S. • University of Maryland at Baltimore Health Sciences Library • Baltimore, MD 21201 • ACRL LAMA
Cunningham Diane • Reference Librarian • National Institute of Standards & Technology • Gaithersburg, MD 20899
Cunningham Diane • Pebble Beach, CA 93953
Cunningham Eileen M. • Oswego, NY 13126 • AASL ALSC
Cunningham Gloria S. • Librarian • Mansfield Township School District • Port Murray, NJ 07865 • AASL
Cunningham James L. • Visiting Reference Librarian • Northern Illinois University • DeKalb, IL 60115-2854 • ACRL AFLRT
Cunningham Jay L. • Asst Chief for Technical Serv • California State Library • Sacramento, CA 94237-0001 • ACRL ALCTS LITA
Cunningham John W. Jr • Planning Implementation Coor. • Free Library of Philadelphia • Philadelphia, PA 19103-1189 • PLA IFRT SRRT
Cunningham Julie • Public Services Assistant Dean • Saint John's University Library • Jamaica, NY 11439 • ACRL LAMA RASD
Cunningham Karen L. • Reference Librarian • King County Library System Redmond Library • Redmond, WA 98052 • PLA NMRT
Cunningham Katharine S. • Head Librarian • Trinity School Upper School Library • New York, NY 10024 • AASL YALSA
Cunningham Katherine V. • Manager, User Services • NOTIS Systems, Inc. • Evanston, IL 60201-3622 • LITA
Cunningham L. Kay • Memphis-Shelby County Public Library and Information Center • Memphis, TN 38104-4025
Cunningham Marcia A. • Librarian • San Luis Obispo City-County Library • San Luis Obispo, CA 93403
Cunningham Mary Ann • Giessen Elementary School • APO, AE 09169 • AASL ALSC
Cunningham Mel C. • Director • Johnson County Community College Library • Overland Park, KS 66210 • ACRL ALCTS LAMA LITA RASD
Cunningham Patricia A. • Library Media Specialist • Chickasha Public Schools • Chickasha, OK 73018 • AASL
Cunningham Patricia A. • East Lake High School • Tarpon Springs, FL 34689 • AASL YALSA
Cunningham Penny S.C. Sr. • Saint Mary-Basha Catholic School Library • Chandler, AZ 85224 • AASL
Cunningham Robert L. • Library & Information Services • NELINET Inc. • Newton, MA 02162 • ACRL ALCTS LITA IFRT SRRT
Cunningham Sharon K. • New York, NY 09716
Cunningham Veronica Colley • Preservation Librarian • State University of New York (SUNY) University Libraries • Albany, NY 12222 • ALCTS SRRT
Cunningham Virginia P. • Coordinator of Online Services • University of South Florida Library • Tampa, FL 33620-5600 • ACRL
Cunningham William D. • Mitchellville, MD 20721 • ASCLA LAMA
Cuomo Elia R. • Huntington Sta., NY 11746
Cupman Margaret E. • San Francisco, CA 94116 • ALSC
Cupps Candace C. • National Institutes of Health Library • Bethesda, MD 20892 • IFRT
Curasi Suzanne C. • Coordinator of Acquisitions • University of Wisconsin-Milwaukee Golda Meir Library • Milwaukee, WI 53201 • ACRL ALCTS
Curci-Gonzalez Lucy • Head Librarian • Morgan & Finnegan Library • New York, NY 10154
Curia Patricia • San Jose, CA 95112 • PLA
Curl Margo Warner • College of Wooster Andrews Library • Wooster, OH 44691 • ACRL ALCTS LITA IRRT
Curl Olive Ann G. • Lincoln Elementary School • Jackson, TN 38301 • AASL ALSC
Curl Sheila R. • Science Reference Libn • Arizona State University Libraries • Tempe, AZ 85287-1006 • ACRL
Curlee Faye S. • Media Specialist • Norton Elementary School • Snellville, GA 30278
Curlee Mary Anne • Student • University of South Carolina College of Library & Information Science • Columbia, SC 29208
Curley Arthur • Director • Boston Public Library • Boston, MA 02117 • ACRL ALCTS ASCLA LAMA LITA PLA YALSA IFRT IRRT SRRT
Curley Elmer F. • Reference/Bibliography Librarian • University of Nevada-Las Vegas James R. Dickinson Library • Las Vegas, NV 89154 • ACRL ALCTS
Curley Kathleen • School District Co-Ordinator • Yellow Springs Village School District • Yellow Spg, OH 45387 • AASL ALSC
Curley Kathleen F. • Acting Director • Pima Community College Downtown Campus • Tucson, AZ 85703-0027
Curley Maxine • Branch Supervisor • Mesa County Public Library • Grand Junction, CO 81502 • ALSC
Curley Thomas E. Ph. D. • Trustee • Queens Borough Public Library • Jamaica, NY 11432 • ALTA PLA
Curlin Carolyn L. • Media Specialist • Gladys Noon Spellman Elementary School • Cheverly, MD 20784
Curnow Janine • Assistant Reference Librarian • Pennsylvania State University Heindel Library • Middletown, PA 17057 • ACRL SRRT
Curol Helen • Librarian • McNeese State University Lether E. Frazar Memorial Library • Lake Charles, LA 70609 • RASD
Curole Mary G. • Librarian • South Lafourche High School • Galliano, LA 70354
Curr L. James • University of Maryland • College Park, MD 20742-2411
Curran Charles C. • Professor • University of South Carolina College of Library & Information Science • Columbia, SC 29208 • PLA LRRT
Curran Francis J. • Media Director • Hanover Middle School • Hanover, MA 02339 • AASL
Curran Joseph L. • Director • Trinity Catholic High School Library • Newton, MA 02158-1494
Curran Nancy E. • Coordinator • District Learning Resource Center • Decatur, IL 62522 • AASL
Curren Catherine E. • Student • Houston Public Library • Houston, TX 77002
Current Karen M. • Richmond, MI 48062 • AASL
Currie Constance J. • Student • Wayne State University Library Science Program • Detroit, MI 48202
Currie Jean • Special Projects Director • South Central Research Library Council • Ithaca, NY 14850 • ASCLA
Currie Susan Annah • Access Services Librarian • Cornell University • Ithaca, NY 14853-5301 • LAMA
Currie William W. • Bowling Green State Univ Firelands Campus • Huron, OH 44839 • ACRL
Currier Nell • Paris, TN 38242 • AASL ALSC *Life*
Curry Ann Q. • Trustee • Atlanta-Fulton Public Library • Atlanta, GA 30303
Curry Anna A. • Director • Enoch Pratt Free Library • Baltimore, MD 21201-4484 • LAMA PLA IFRT
Curry David S. • Coordinator, Science Libraries • University of Iowa Libraries • Iowa City, IA 52242-1379 • ACRL IRRT
Curry Doris M. • Hugoton, KS 67951 • AASL
Curry Elaine M. • Medical Librarian • Hazleton General Hospital Medical Library • Hazelton, PA 18201
Curry Elizabeth A. • Executive Director • South East Florida Library Information Network (SEFLIN) • Fort Lauderdale, FL 33301 • ALCTS ASCLA LITA PLA
Curry Janet S. • Media Specialist • Bryden Elementary School • Beachwood, OH 44122 • AASL
Curry Janette M. • Librarian • Mobile Public Library • Mobile, AL 36602
Curry Juanita V. • Mid-Continent Public Library • Independence, MO 64050
Curry M. Caroline • Student • University of South Carolina College of Library & Information Science • Columbia, SC 29208 • ACRL
Curry Marsha A. • Student • Louisiana State University School of Library & Information Science • Baton Rouge, LA 70803-3290 • PLA RASD
Curry Marsha J. • Evamere School • Hudson, OH 44224
Curry Maureen E. • Director • Olean Public Library • Olean, NY 14760 • PLA
Curry Shirley • Trustee • Bridgeview Public Library • Bridgeview, IL 60455 • ALTA
Curtin Jean P. • Educational Media Specialist • Keansburg High School • Keansburg, NJ 07734 • AASL
Curtin Kathleen Sr. • Librarian • Saint Agnes Academy School Library • College Point, NY 11369 • AASL
Curtin Matthew T. • Reference Librarian • Edinburg Public Library • Edinburg, TX 78539-4596 • RASD NMRT
Curtin Mimi Veblen • La Mesa, CA 91942

Curtin Nancy • Assistant to the Director • Port Washington Public Library • Port Washington, NY 11050
Curtis Annette M. • Student • San Jose State University Division of Library & Information Science • San Jose, CA 95192-0029 • ACRL GODORT
Curtis Annette W. • Mid-Continent Public Library • Independence, MO 64050 • RASD
Curtis Bill • Senior Vice President • Harris Publishing Company • Twinsburg, OH 44087-1999
Curtis Donna R. • Heizer Jr. High School • Hobbs, NM 88240 • AASL LITA
Curtis Donnelyn • New Mexico State University Library • Las Cruces, NM 88003-0006 • RASD NMRT
Curtis George A. • Rock Island, IL 61201 • Continuing
Curtis Howard W. • Director • Haverhill Public Library • Haverhill, MA 01830 • PLA
Curtis Jean T. • Director • Detroit Public Library • Detroit, MI 48202 • LAMA PLA YALSA SRRT
Curtis Jeffrey A. • Student • Kent State University School of Library & Information Science • Kent, OH 44242-0001 • SRRT
Curtis John T. • Student • Kent State University School of Library & Information Science • Kent, OH 44242-0001
Curtis Karen L. • Oak Park, IL 60302
Curtis Kathy W. • Troy Public Library • Troy, MI 48084
Curtis Lori N. • Special Collections Librarian • University of Tulsa McFarlin Library • Tulsa, OK 74104-3189 • ACRL
Curtis Margaret D. • Reference Librarian • Chattanooga-Hamilton County Bicentennial Library Eastgate Br • Chattanooga, TN 37411
Curtis Marilyn D. • Assistant Cataloger • Redwood Library & Athenaeum • Newport, RI 02840-3292
Curtis Marsha Morrell • Trustee • Euclid Public Library • Euclid, OH 44123-2091 • ALTA
Curtis Mary A. • Tacoma, WA 98499 • Continuing
Curtis Michael A. • Technical Services Librarian • Benedictine College North Campus Library • Atchison, KS 66002
Curtis Nancy R. • University of Arkansas for Medical Science Library • Little Rock, AR 72205-7186 • ACRL LIRT
Curtis Peter H. • Greenbelt, MD 20770 • ACRL MAGERT
Curtis Rita • Student • Durango Public Library • Durango, CO 81301 • ALSC
Curtis Rita H. • Martinez, GA 30907 • AASL
Curtis Ruth • Asst. Prof. Sch. Inf. Studies • Syracuse University School of Information Studies • Syracuse, NY 13244-4100 • AASL
Curtis Ruth P. • Librarian • Acadiana High School • Lafayette, LA 70506 • AASL
Curtis Sylvia • Acting Studies Librarian • University of California UCSB Library • Santa Barbara, CA 93106-9010 • ACRL RASD EMIERT IRRT LIRT SRRT
Curva Ramon C. • Student • Queens College Graduate School of Library & Information Studies • Flushing, NY 11367
Curzon Susan C. • Director of Libraries • California State University • Northridge, CA 91330 • PLA
Cuseo Allan A. • Librarian • Greece Arcadia High School • Rochester, NY 14612 • YALSA SRRT
Cusher Helen • Retired Teacher-Librarian • Adams County Library Reeder Branch • Reeder, ND 58649
Cushing Charles M. • Adult Service Librarian • Hamilton Public Library • Hamilton ON, L8N 4E4 Canada • LITA PLA RASD IFRT SRRT
Cushing Helen G. • New York, NY 10022 • ACRL ALCTS *Continuing*
Cushing Margaret A. • Librarian • Orange County Library System Orlando Public Library • Orlando, FL 32801-2471
Cushman Jerome • Senior Lecturer • University of California Los Angeles Graduate School of Library & Information Science • Los Angeles, CA 90024
Cushman Rosalie • Community Coordinator • West Des Moines Public Library • West Des Moines, IA 50265
Cushmore Carole L. • Silver Burdett Press, Inc. • New York, NY 10023-7706 • AASL YALSA
Cushwa Susan • Middletown High School • Middletown, DE 19709 • AASL
Cusimano Lori L. • Student • Louisiana State University School of Library & Information Science • Baton Rouge, LA 70803-3290
Custer Benjamin A. • Bethesda, MD 20817 • ACRL ALCTS *Life*
Custer Deborah P. • Head Librarian • Kent Library Association Kent Memorial Library • Kent, CT 06757-0127 • PLA
Custis Charlotte • Manager • Ameritech Information Systems • Dublin, OH 43017 • ALCTS LITA
Cutburth Dennis • Adjunct Professor • Rutgers University School of Communication Information & Library Studies • New Brunswick, NJ 08903 • LITA
Cutchin Cheryl E. • Media Specialist • McKendree Elementary School • Lawrenceville, GA 30243 • AASL
Cuthbert Martha Mrs. • Rochester City School District #6 School Library • Rochester, NY 14605 • AASL YALSA
Cuthbertson Richard • Trustee • West Des Moines Public Library • West Des Moines, IA 50265
Cutler Diane M. • Branch Manager • Kent County Library System Cascade Branch • Grand Rapids, MI 49546
Cutler Dorothy R. • Olympia, WA 98502 • ASCLA PLA *Life*
Cutler Juanita A. • Oconomowoc, WI 53066-2602
Cutler Kay A. • Instructional Services Librarian • University of Virginia Library • Charlottesville, VA 22903 • ACRL
Cutler Kirsten G. • Children's Librarian • Sonoma County Library Petaluma Regional Branch • Petaluma, CA 94952
Cutler Marsha L. • Storyteller Librarian • Las Vegas-Clark County Library District Las Vegas Library • Las Vegas, NV 89101 • ALSC
Cutler Mary Ellen • Media Coordinator • Eastern Randolph High School • Ramseur, NC 27316-8422 • AASL
Cutler Phyllis L. • Director • Williams College Sawyer Library • Williamstown, MA 01267 • ACRL LAMA
Cutrezzula Denise D. • Student • University of Pittsburgh School of Library and Information Science • Pittsburgh, PA 15260 • SRRT
Cutright Patricia J. • La Grande, OR 97850-1338
Cutshall Tom C. • Indiana University School of Library and Information Science • Bloomington, IN 47405
Cutting Gregory F. • Head of Reference Services • Lake Oswego Public Library • Lake Oswego, OR 97034 • RASD
Cuttitta Patricia • Media Specialist • Mill River Union High School • North Clarendon, VT 05759 • AASL
Cuyjet Stephanie • Technical Services Librarian • Mesa College Library • San Diego, CA 92111 • ALCTS
Cuyler Margery • Holiday House Inc. • New York, NY 10017 • ALSC YALSA
Cveljo Katherine • Denton, TX 76201 • Continuing
Cychowski Lucille M. • Student • Drexel University College of Information Studies • Philadelphia, PA 19104-2875
Cylkowski Kathleen M. • Librarian • Bishop McGuinness Memorial High School Library • Winston-Salem, NC 27103 • AASL
Cypra-Sherlock Jo Anne • Librarian • Irving Public Library System • Irving, TX 75015-2288 • ALSC EMIERT NMRT
Cypress Donna A. • Student • Towson State University • Towson, MD 21204 • AASL ALSC EMIERT LRRT NMRT SRRT
Cyr Charlotte M. • Media Specialist • Millinocket Middle School • Millinocket, ME 04462 • YALSA
Cys John M. • Student • University of North Texas School of Library & Information Sciences • Denton, TX 76203
Cytrynbaum Mary L. • Senior Information Specialist • Amoco Production Company Library • Denver, CO 80201 • LITA
Cyzyk Mark D. • Student • University of Maryland College of Library and Information Services • College Park, MD 20742-4345
Czaja Pamela M. • N. Tonawanda, NY 14120
Czarnecki Cary J. • Assistant Director • Oak Park Public Library • Oak Park, IL 60301
Czarnecki Emma-Louise • Bloomfield, NJ 07003
Czarnezki Mary E. • Library Media Specialist • Edgerton Elementary School • Hales Corners, WI 53130 • AASL
Czarski Charles M. • Maysville Community College Library • Maysville, KY 41056
Czechowski Leslie • Assistant to Director • Stewart Library • Grinnell, IA 50112
Czekala Barbara C. • Reference Librarian • The Bryant Library • Roslyn, NY 11576
Czerny Susan G. • Collection Development • Kutztown University Rohrbach Library • Kutztown, PA 19530-0721
Czerwiec Nancy • Trustee • Oak Lawn Public Library • Oak Lawn, IL 60453 • ALTA
Czerwinski Karen L. • Student • Drexel University College of Information Studies • Philadelphia, PA 19104-2875
Czesak Cynthia • Clifton Public Library • Clifton, NJ 07011 • LAMA PLA
Cziffra Elizabeth S. • Princeton University • Princeton, NJ 08544-2098 • ACRL ALCTS LAMA LITA RASD GODORT ILERT
Czisny Julie A. • Thousand Oaks, CA 91361 • ACRL
Czopek Vanessa • Tempe, AZ 85283 • ALSC LAMA IFRT
D'Adamo Margaret A. • Baltimore, MD 21214 • AASL
D'Agostino Carla J. • Martinsville, NJ 08836
D'Alessandro Edward A. • Spec Asst Constitutent Services • Library of Congress • Washington, DC 20541
D'Ambrosio Margaret R. • Librarian • Smithsonian Institution Libraries • Washington, DC 20540 • ALCTS LITA
D'Ambrosio Tom • Student • Indiana University School of Library and Information Science • Bloomington, IN 47405 • AASL
D'Amico Nancy Bunims • Salem Public Library • Salem, MA 01970-3298 • LITA SRRT
D'Amours Helen • Head Librarian • Langley High School • McLean, VA 22101 • AASL
D'Andraia Dana D. • Yankee Book Peddler • Contoocook, NH 03229 • ACRL ALCTS
D'Andraia Frank A. • Director • University of North Dakota Chester Fritz Library • Grand Forks, ND 58202-0175 • ACRL ALCTS LAMA LITA
D'Andrea Joan M. • Bibliography Instruction Coor. • Saint John's University Library • Jamaica, NY 11439 • ACRL LIRT
D'Andrea Steven • Head of Computer Services • Upper Arlington Public Library • Upper Arlington, OH 43221
D'Angelo Kathleen • Allentown, PA 18104 • AASL ALSC YALSA
D'Angelo Kathleen T. • Asst. Acquisition Librarian • University of North Carolina Walter Clinton Jackson Library • Greensboro, NC 27412-5201
D'Annunzio Rebecca T. • Professional Librarian • Adamston Elementary School Lib • Clarksburg, WV 26301 • AASL
D'Arrigo Carol A. • Student • Queens College Graduate School of Library & Information Studies • Flushing, NY 11367 • AASL
D'Astarte Mona S. • Online Customer Services • Information Access Company • Foster City, CA 94404 • IFRT SRRT
D'Aversa Concettina M. • Librarian Technical Service • Moraine Valley Community College Library • Palos Hills, IL 60465 • ACRL ALCTS LITA
D'Avis Marcelyn H. • Student • University of Arizona Graduate Library School • Tucson, AZ 85721
D'Eliso Mary A. • Children's Librarian • Monroe County Public Library • Bloomington, IN 47408
D'Onofrio Erminio • Documents Librarian • New York Public Library • New York, NY 10018-2788 • ACRL LAMA RASD GODORT IFRT
D'Orazio Antonette K • Student • Rutgers University School of Communication Information & Library Studies • New Brunswick, NJ 08903 • ALSC
D'Urso Lawrence A. • Mount Prospect Public Library • Mount Prospect, IL 60056 • PLA
da Conturbia Sandra • Documents/Microtext Ref. Libn. • Texas A & M University Sterling C. Evans Library • College Station, TX 77843-5000 • ACRL GODORT IRRT
Da Cunha Murilo Bastos • Brasilia DF 71500, Brazil • ACRL LITA
da Silva Carol M. • Aptos, CA 95003 • PLA
Daane Jeanette K. • Tempe, AZ 85282
Dabbs Susan C. • Townsend Junior High School • Tucson, AZ 85712
Dabek Joan R. • Head of Circulation • University of Houston Libraries • Houston, TX 77204-2091 • LAMA
Dabkowski Charles T. • Serials Librarian • Niagara University Library • Niagara University, NY 14109
Dabrishus Michael J. • Curator of Special Collection • University of Arkansas Libraries • Fayetteville, AR 72701-1201 • ACRL
Dadson Theresa • Acquisition Librarian • University of Maryland-Eastern Shore Frederick Douglass Library • Princess Anne, MD 21853
Daenzer Terry R. • Salisbury State University Blackwell Library • Salisbury, MD 21801 • GODORT IRRT
Dagg Carole • Coor. Community Services • Everett Public Library • Everett, WA 98201 • ERT
Daggett Connie S. • Autryville, NC 28318 • AASL
Dagher Nadia A. • Senior Librarian • Thousand Oaks Library Newbury Park Branch • Newbury Park, CA 91320 • ALCTS
Dagle Nancy • Asst. Dir. For Technical Service • Bucknell University Bertrand Library • Lewisburg, PA 17837-2086 • ACRL ALCTS LAMA LITA
Dague Ann M. • Kokomo, IN 46901 • ALSC
Dahill Judith M. • New York, NY 10002 • ACRL
Dahl Judy A. • Beaverton, OR 97006 • AASL ALSC LIRT
Dahl Karen J. • Student • Dalhousie University School of Library & Inf. Studies • Halifax NS, B3H 4H8 Canada • AASL ALSC NMRT
Dahl Katherine M. • Reference Dept. • Western Illinois University Libraries • Macomb, IL 61455 • ACRL RASD EMIERT IFRT LIRT SRRT
Dahl Kim A. • Student • University of Wisconsin School of Library & Information Studies • Madison, WI 53706 • AASL
Dahl Ruth • Viola H. Nelson School East Maine School District • Niles, IL 60648 • AASL
Dahlager Becky B. • Kailua Kona, HI 96740 • AASL
Dahlgreen Marykay • Children's Librarian • King County Library System Des Moines Library • Des Moines, WA 98198 • ALSC IFRT

Dahlgren Anders C. • Cons Public Library Construction • Wisconsin Division for Library Services • Madison, WI 53707 • LAMA PLA NMRT

Dahlin Deborah C. • Department Head • Birmingham Public Library • Birmingham, AL 35203

Dahlin Therrin C. • Head, Documents & Maps Dept. • Brigham Young University • Provo, UT 84602 • GODORT

Dahlke Hazel C. • Circulation Department Head • Manitowoc Public Library • Manitowoc, WI 54220 • PLA

Dahlsrom Sandra • Trustee • Timberland Regional Library Hoquiam Branch • Hoquiam, WA 98550

Dahlstrom Joe F. Dr. • Director • University of Houston Victoria Library • Victoria, TX 77901-5699 • ACRL

Dahmer Elinor • Librarian • Edison School Library • Morton Grove, IL 60053 • AASL   *Life*

Dahms-Stinson Nancee J. • Librarian I-Branch Library • Saint Stephens Library • Hickory, NC 28601 • ALSC PLA IFRT NMRT

Dai Wei-ling • Head, Serials Dept. • University of California Library • Santa Barbara, CA 93106 • ALCTS LITA IRRT

Daigle Karen • Lincoln, NE 68510

Daigneault Audrey I. • Media Specialist • Pleasant Valley School • Groton, CT 06340 • AASL

Dailey Becky • Thomas Street Elementary School • Tupelo, MS 38801 • AASL

Dailey Elizabeth J. • Children's Librarian • Onondaga County Public Library Betts Branch • Syracuse, NY 13205 • PLA IFRT LIRT

Dailey Kazuko M. • Associate University Librarian • University of California-Davis Library • Davis, CA 95616 • ACRL ALCTS LAMA LITA

Dailey Lucinda A. • Library Assistant I • University of Missouri Libraries-Columbia Elmer Ellis Library • Columbia, MO 65201-5149 • ACRL ALCTS LITA RASD GODORT IFRT ILERT LIRT SORT

Daily Ann P. • Student • University of Texas at Austin Graduate School of Library & Information Sciences • Austin, TX 78712-1276

Daily Jay E. Dr • Professor • University of Pittsburgh School of Library and Information Science • Pittsburgh, PA 15260 • ACRL ALCTS   *Life*

Daily Pamela S. • Brandon, FL 33510 • ALSC PLA

Daily Patricia • Moorestown, NJ 08057

Dain Phyllis • Professor • Columbia University School of Library Service • New York, NY 10027 • ACRL ALCTS LHRT LRRT

Daines Richard • Student • Drexel University College of Information Studies • Philadelphia, PA 19104-2875

Dais Romeo • Reference • Madison Public Library • Madison, WI 53703 • RASD GODORT

Daitch-Holzberg Merrie • Anne Hutchinson Elementary School • Eastchester, NY 10707 • AASL

Dajani Nabila • Cherry Hill, NJ 08003

Dajin Sun • Pittsburgh, PA 15213-4317

Dakan Norman E. • San Antonio, TX 78239-3913 • AFLRT FLRT

Dake Mary G. • Director • Hartford Public Library • Hartford, IL 62048

Dakin Elizabeth • Cleveland, MS 38732 • ACRL   *Continuing*

Dakshinamurti Ganga B. • Coor.,Bibliographic Database • University of Manitoba Libraries Elizabeth Dafoe Library • Winnipeg MB, R3T 2N2 Canada • ACRL ALCTS LAMA LITA CLENE LRRT SORT

Dal Bianco Tracey A. • Student • University of Western Ontario School of Library & Information Science • London ON, N6G 1H1 Canada • ACRL

Dal Canton Helene H. • Reference Librarian • Andrew Carnegie Free Library • Carnegie, PA 15106

Dal-hyun Choe • Chairperson • Kyungpook National University • Taegu 702-701, South Korea • ALCTS LITA

Dalbello-Lovric Marija • Student • University of Toronto Faculty of Library & Information Science • Toronto ON, M5S 1A1 Canada • ACRL EMIERT

Dalbey Alice F. • San Rafael, CA 94901

Dalbotten Mary S. • Learning Resources & Strategies • Minnesota Department of Education • Saint Paul, MN 55101 • AASL YALSA IFRT

Dalby Mary Ellen • Colorado Springs, CO 80915 • ACRL ALCTS   *Life*

Dalby Richard F. • Librarian • Emerson Junior High School • Colorado Springs, CO 80909 • AASL ALSC   *Life*

Dale Charles F. • Collingswood, NJ 08107

Dale Doris C. • Professor • Southern Illinois University Dept. of Curriculum & Instr. • Carbondale, IL 62901 • AASL ALCTS ALSC   *Life*

Dale Mary C. • Librarian • Colorado School of Mines Arthur Lakes Library • Golden, CO 80401

Dale Nancy E. • Media Librarian • Saint Anthony Medical Center • Rockford, IL 61108

Dale Paula R. • Elkhart, IN 46514

Dalehite Michele I. • Asst. Dir for Library Services • Florida Center for Library Automation • Gainesville, FL 32609 • ACRL LITA

Dalen Eleanor • Information Specialist • Ernst & Young Resource Center • Chicago, IL 60606 • LAMA

Dalessandro Anne B. • Santa Fe, NM 87505 • AASL ALSC

Daley Deborah D. • Student • University of Wisconsin-Milwaukee School of Library & Information Science • Milwaukee, WI 53201

Daley Diane R. • Reference Librarian • Chase Manhatten Bank • New York, NY 10081

Daley Virginia L. • Women's Studies Archivist • Duke University William R. Perkins Library • Durham, NC 27706 • ACRL SRRT

Dalgliesh Archie D. • Reference Librarian • University of Michigan School of Information and Library Studies • Ann Arbor, MI 48109-1092

Dalhaimer Kim M. • Asst. Ref. Lib./Extension Servs. • Mead Public Library • Sheboygan, WI 53081 • RASD

Dallas Larayne J. • University of Texas Libraries • Austin, TX 78713 • LAMA RASD

Dallavalle Ann M. • Pasadena, CA 91107

Dallman Glenn R. • Clearwater, FL 34625-2521 • *Continuing*

Dallmann Dianne J. • Student • Texas Woman's University School of Library & Information Studies • Denton, TX 76204

Dalman Ruth Mrs. • Student • University of Missouri-Columbia School of Library & Informational Science • Columbia, MO 65211

Dalpiaz Patricia • Harpursville High School Library • Harpursville, NY 13787 • AASL

Dalquist Janet A. • University Library Bibliographer • Michigan Technological University J. R. Van Pelt Library • Houghton, MI 49931-1295 • ACRL ALCTS RASD

Dalrymple Christie • Media Specialist • The University School of Nova University • Fort Lauderdale, FL 33314 • AASL

Dalrymple Connie D. • Site Librarian • Eastman Kodak Company • Rochester, NY 14650-1121

Dalrymple Dana R. • Austin, TX 78753 • PLA

Dalrymple Julie • Children's Program Librarian • Santa Clara County Free Library Cupertino Public Library • Cupertino, CA 95014 • ALSC PLA

Dalrymple Prudence W. • Dir. Office for Accreditation • American Library Association • Chicago, IL 60611-2795 • LRRT

Dalrymple Tamsen • Reference Services Division • Online Computer Library Center (OCLC) • Dublin, OH 43017-3395 • RASD

Dalstrom Ruth • Coordinator/Library Media • Goliad ISD • Goliad, TX 77963 • AASL

Dalton Ann L. • Children's Librarian • Seattle Public Library Mobile Services • Seattle, WA 98102

Dalton Anna D. • Librarian • Lowell High School • San Francisco, CA 94132 • AASL

Dalton Bonnie B. • Corinth High School • Corinth, MS 38834 • AASL

Dalton Carolyn J. • Media Chairman • William Fremd High School • Palatine, IL 60067 • AASL

Dalton Elizabeth • System Librarian • Derby High School • Derby, CT 06418

Dalton Jack • New York, NY 10027 • AASL ACRL ALCTS ALSC ALTA ASCLA LAMA LITA PLA RASD YALSA   *Honorary*

Dalton Janet N. • West Sunbury, PA 16061-0322

Dalton Kathleen J. • Reference Librarian • Susquehanna University • Selinsgrove, PA 17870 • ACRL RASD LIRT

Dalton Lisa K. • Information Services Coordinator • Rockingham County Public Library Eden Branch • Eden, NC 27288 • PLA RASD GODORT

Dalton Marian L. • Systems Engineer • IBM • Portland, ME 04112 • LITA

Dalton Marylee • Technical Services Librarian • University of Michigan Law Library • Ann Arbor, MI 48109-1210 • ALCTS LITA

Dalton Phyllis I. • Scottsdale, AZ 85254 • ASCLA   *Continuing*

Dalton Robert S. • Humanities Reference • University of North Carolina Davis Library CB#3922 • Chapel Hill, NC 27599 • ACRL RASD

Dalton Susan E. • Media Specialist • Lost Mountain Middle School • Kennesaw, GA 30144 • AASL YALSA

Daltry Carolyn C. • Library Media Specialist • John Rolfe Middle School • Richmond, VA 23223 • AASL

Daly Darleen G. • Assistant Head, Catalog Dept. • University of Cincinnati • Cincinnati, OH 45221-0033 • ALCTS LAMA

Daly Elizabeth T. • Sheffield, MA 01257

Daly Frank • Director, Marketing • Baker & Taylor Books • Bridgewater, NJ 08807-0920 • AASL ACRL PLA YALSA ERT

Daly Jamie C. • Student • University of Tennessee-Knoxville Graduate School of Library & Information Science • Knoxville, TN 37996-4330 • AASL

Daly John G. • Librarian • Los Altos Public Library • Los Altos, CA 94022

Daly Kathleen Evans • Assistant Director • Ann Arbor Public Library • Ann Arbor, MI 48104 • LAMA PLA

Daly Leva M • Tucson, AZ 85748

Daly Loretta C. • Marketing Manager • Turner Subscriptions • New York, NY 10003 • AASL PLA

Daly Sally A. Sr. • Librarian • Saint Timothy School • Philadelphia, PA 19149 • AASL ALSC

Daly Simeon Rev • Head Librarian • Saint Meinrad College & School of Theology Archabbey Library • Saint Meinrad, IN 47577 • ACRL

Dalzell Lee Ann • Assistant Librarian/Cataloger • Georgia Southwestern College James Earl Carter Library • Americus, GA 31709

Dalzell Lee B. • Reference • Williams College Sawyer Library • Williamstown, MA 01267 • ACRL RASD LIRT

Daman Doris A. • Assistant Librarian • Warren Township Public Library • Warren, NJ 07059

Dambergs Ingrida • Head Cataloger • Union College Schaffer Library • Schenectady, NY 12308 • ACRL ALCTS LRRT

Dameron Janet L. • Lincoln Co. R. I. School • Silex, MO 63377

Dameron Sharon • Librarian • East Peoria Community High School • East Peoria, IL 61611 • AASL

Dames Barbara B. • Inter-Library Loan Librarian • Harvard College Library Widener Memorial Library • Cambridge, MA 02138 • RASD

Damewood Eleanor F. • Librarian • MacArthur High School • San Antonio, TX 78216 • AASL YALSA

Damico James A. • Director of University Libraries • University of South Alabama Library • Mobile, AL 36688 • ACRL LAMA

Damien Yvonne M. • Reference/Bibliographer • Loyola University E.M. Cudahy Memorial Library • Chicago, IL 60626 • ACRL

Damko Ellen E. • University of Akron Bierce Library • Akron, OH 44325-1706

Damkot Sharon • Essex Elementary School Learning Center • Essex Juction, VT 05452 • AASL

Damman Bonita • Waukegan, IL 60085-2313 • AASL YALSA   *Continuing*

Damon Gene A. • Associate Dean • Colorado Alliance of Research Libraries • Denver, CO 80210 • ACRL LITA

Damon Linda • Trustee • Boulder Public Library • Boulder, CO 80306

Damon Martha J. • Student • University of Arizona Graduate Library School • Tucson, AZ 85721

Damron Georgia F. • Pikeville, KY 41501

Dana Mary Hunt Miss • South Casco, ME 04077 • *Continuing*

Danant Joelle • Coordinator • National Clearinghouse on Development Education • New York, NY 10038 • ACRL LAMA IRRT SRRT

Dance Betty A. • Librarian • Utah State University Merrill Library • Logan, UT 84322-3000 • ACRL LIRT

Dancer Andrew III • Director • Catskill Public Library • Catskill, NY 12414 • PLA

Dancer Rusty M. • Outreach Librarian • Craighead County Library • Jonesboro, AR 72401

Danchak Caroline R. • Cataloger • Trinity College Library • Hartford, CT 06106

Dancik Deborah B. • Head, Hum & Social Sci • University of Alberta Rutherford Library North • Edmonton AB, T6G 2J4 Canada • ACRL LAMA RASD

Dancy Billie E. • Library Director • South San Francisco Public Library • South San Francisco, CA 94080 • LAMA PLA

Dandridge Juanita M. • Trustee • Ascension Parish Library • Donaldsonville, LA 70346-2535 • ALTA PLA

Dandy Cora P. • Student • Florida State University School of Library and Information Studies • Tallahassee, FL 32306-2048 • AASL

Dane Carol B. • Massachusetts Board of Library Commissioners • Boston, MA 02215-2070

Dane Lena P. • Cranston, RI 02921 • SRRT

Dane M. Stephen • General Manager • Kluwer Academic Publishers • Norwell, MA 02061

Dane Mardy • Trustee • Euclid Public Library • Euclid, OH 44123-2091 • ALTA

Danecourt Annora E. K. • Johns Hopkins University Milton S. Eisenhower Library • Baltimore, MD 21218

Danegger Anne N. • Fox Lake, IL 60020 • ALTA PLA   *Continuing*

Daneri Mary Louise • Reference Librarian • Baltimore County Public Library Cockeysville Branch • Cockeysville, MD 21030 • PLA RASD

Danford Robert E. • College Librarian • Hartwick College Stevens German Library • Oneonta, NY 13820 • ACRL ALCTS LAMA LITA VRT

Danicic Lawrence J. • Serials Supervisor • Cleveland Public Library • Cleveland, OH 44114-1271 • ALCTS
Daniel Bridget S. • Apex, NC 27502 • ALSC
Daniel Carla • Delaware Valley High School • Milford, PA 18337
Daniel Carol O. • Chairman of the Library • John Burroughs School • Saint Louis, MO 63124
Daniel Carolyn C. • Head Libraian • McGavock High School • Nashville, TN 37214 • AASL
Daniel Donna • Galion, OH 44833 • Life
Daniel Eileen • Head of Reference • York University Libraries • North York ON, M3J 1P3 Canada • ACRL
Daniel Evelyn H. • Professor • University of North Carolina at Chapel Hill School of Information and Library Science • Chapel Hill, NC 27599-3360 • AASL LRRT
Daniel Joann P. • Director • Concordia College Library • Selma, AL 36761 • ACRL LAMA
Daniel Judy A. • Library Media Specialist • Drexel R-4 School • Drexel, MO 64742 • AASL
Daniel Kay M. • Christ Church Episcopal School Lower School Library • Greenville, SC 29601 • AASL
Daniel Lynn C. • Managing Librarian • Seattle Public Library • Seattle, WA 98104-1193 • PLA
Daniel Mary H. • Reference Services Librarian • Christopher Newport College Captain John Smith Library • Newport News, VA 23606 • RASD IRRT LIRT
Daniel Wilbur • Public Services Supervisor • Oxnard Public Library • Oxnard, CA 93030 • ALSC LAMA PLA
Daniels Ann • Carmel, IN 46032 • AASL
Daniels Annette • Platteville, WI 53818 • AASL
Daniels Belinda S. • Reference Librarian • Guilford Technical Community Coll Learning Resources Center • Jamestown, NC 27282-0309 • ACRL RASD
Daniels Bruce E. • Director • Onondaga County Public Library at the Galleries • Syracuse, NY 13202-2494 • AASL ASCLA PLA YALSA IFRT SRRT
Daniels Cindy • Saint Mary's Academy High School Library • Portland, OR 97201 • YALSA
Daniels Esther J. • Public Services Librarian • University of Washington Bothell Branch Campus • Bothell, WA 98021 • ACRL LIRT
Daniels Frances Betsye • Media Coordinator • Lynn Road Elementary • Raleigh, NC 27612 • AASL
Daniels Jeanne L. • Madison, WI 53704
Daniels Jerome P. • Director • University of Wisconsin-Platteville Elton S. Karrmann Library • Platteville, WI 53818-3099 • ACRL
Daniels Julian A. Mr. • Media Specialist • Southside Junior High School • Greenwood, SC 29646 • AASL
Daniels Marilyn L. • Health Services Librarian • Latrobe Area Hospital • Latrobe, PA 15650
Daniels Stephen • Trustee • Downers Grove Public Library • Downers Grove, IL 60515 • ALTA
Daniels Susan C. • West Allis Public Library • West Allis, WI 53214
Daniels Susan F. • Student • University of Illinois Graduate School of Library and Information Science • Urbana, IL 61801 • ACRL
Daniels Sylvia Hope • President, Friends of The • Chicago Public Library • Chicago, IL 60605 • PLA
Danielson Connie • Media Specialist • Fairfield Middle School • Fairfield, IA 52556 • AASL YALSA
Danielson Laura E. • Student • University of California Los Angeles Graduate School of Library & Information Science • Los Angeles, CA 90024
Danielson Wilfred • Librarian Cataloger • United States Government Printing Office • Washington, DC 20401 • FLRT GODORT
Danigelis Anita • Reference Librarian • Fletcher Free Library • Burlington, VT 05401 • PLA
Danky James P. • Newspapers & Per. Librarian • State Historical Society of Wisconsin • Madison, WI 53706 • IRRT LHRT SRRT
Danley Elizabeth B. • Youth Services Librarian • Pasco County Library System • Hudson, FL 34667 • AASL ALSC
Dann Laura J. • Librarian • Clearwater Public Library • Clearwater, FL 34623
Dann Priscilla Davis • Children's Librarian • Cuyahoga County Public Library South Euclid-Lyndhurst Branch • South Euclid, OH 44121-4087
Dannecker Joyce H. • Assistant Library Director • Bay County Public Library Association NW Regional Lib System • Panama City, FL 32401-2625 • PLA RASD IFRT
Dannelly Gay N. • Assistant Professor • Ohio State University Libraries • Columbus, OH 43210-1286 • ACRL ALCTS RASD
Dannen Willena M. • Cataloger • Spokane Public Library Comstock Building Library • Spokane, WA 99201-0976
Danner Richard A. • Law Librarian & Professor of Law • Duke University Law Library • Durham, NC 27706 • ACRL ALCTS LAMA LITA RASD GODORT
Dannis L Klimecki • Trustee • Warren Public Library • Warren, MI 48092
Dano Pamela A. • Young Adult Librarian • Baldwinsville Public Library • Baldwinsville, NY 13027-2485 • YALSA
Danowski Alyson B • InterLibrary Loan Specialist • Center for Naval Analyses • Alexandria, VA 22302-0268
Dansker George L. • Serials Librarian • New Orleans Public Library • New Orleans, LA 70140
Danton J. Periam • Professor • University of California-Berkeley School of Library & Information Studies • Berkeley, CA 94720 • ACRL LAMA *Life*
Danzig Alexis • Student • Brooklyn Law School Library • Brooklyn, NY 11201 • AASL IFRT ILERT LHRT SRRT
Danziger Margaret C. • Assistant Director • Toledo-Lucas County Public Library • Toledo, OH 43624 • PLA
Daragan Patricia A. • Head Librarian • Coast Guard Academy Library (d1) • New London, CT 06320 • ACRL LITA AFLRT FLRT
Darbee Leigh • Curator of Printed Collections • Indiana Historical Society Library • Indianapolis, IN 46202 • ACRL
Darby Christine M. • Student • Syracuse University School of Information Studies • Syracuse, NY 13244-4100 • ACRL
Darby Della Holland • Student • University of South Carolina • Columbia, SC 29208 • IFRT SRRT
Darby Mark L. • Cataloging Asst./Archivist • Institute For Advanced Studies Library • Princeton, NJ 08543-0631
Darcy William E. • Librarian • United States Air Force Ramstein Base Library • APO New York, NY 09094-5000 • AFLRT
Dardarian Candace Marie • Faculty Library Chairperson • Harding Street Elementary School • Sylmar, CA 91342
Dardis Marjorie M. • Librarian • Marana High School Library • Tucson, AZ 85743
Dare Jean • Trustee • Cuyahoga County Public Library Parma-Snow Branch • Parma, OH 44134-2789
Dare Philip M. • Head Librarian • Lexington Theological Seminary Bosworth Memorial Library • Lexington, KY 40508 • ACRL
Daris Annouck F. • Manager • International Libraries Service Center • Bruxelles 1050, Belgium • PLA
Daris Claude • Periodical Librarian • Free University of Brussels • Brussels 1050, Belgium • ACRL ALCTS
Dark Maxine • Broken Arrow, OK 74012 • Continuing
Darke Barbara H. Mrs • Clarksville, TN 37040
Darley Roxanna • Reference Librarian • Sutter County Library • Yuba City, CA 95991 • PLA
Darling John B. • Chapel Hill, NC 27514
Darling Karen D. • Head, Serials Department • University of Oregon Library • Eugene, OR 97403-1299 • ALCTS LITA
Darling Louise • Los Angeles, CA 90049
Darling Pamela W. • Philadelphia, PA 19116 • ALCTS
Darling Philip W. • Chicago, IL 60613
Darmer Marie E. • Tucsoon, AZ 85718
Darnell Barbara • Circulation Librarian • Huntsville-Madison County Public Library • Huntsville, AL 35804
Darnell Jennifer A. • Student • Indiana University School of Library and Information Science • Bloomington, IN 47405 • AASL ALSC IFRT
Darr Allan • Trustee • Everett Public Library • Everett, WA 98201
Darr Karleen L. • Head of Technical Services • University of California-Davis Carlson Health Sciences Library • Davis, CA 95616-5291 • ALCTS
Darragh Fred K. Jr. • Trustee • Darragh Investment Company • Little Rock, AR 72211 • ALTA
Darrah Betsy D. • Reference Librarian • University of Washington Suzzallo Library • Seattle, WA 98195 • ACRL RASD
Darrah Claudia • Children's Librarian • San Antonio Public Library Ed Cody Branch • San Antonio, TX 78230
Darrow Barbara M. • Librarian • Chicago Public Library Austin Branch • Chicago, IL 60644 • PLA
Darrow Bonnie • Librarian • Upper Arlington Schools • Columbus, OH 43220 • AASL
Darrow Marilyn K. • Willits, CA 95490
Darrow Sheila L. • Student • Kent State University School of Library & Information Science • Kent, OH 44242-0001 • ACRL
Dartt Florence R. • General Librarian • Long Beach Public Library • Long Beach, CA 90802-4482
Darvin Barbara Mrs. • Amagansett Union Free School District • Amagansett, NY 11930
Das Sulekha • Whippanong Public Library • Whippany, NJ 07981 • PLA
Dasgupta Krishna Mrs • Coor. Online Search & Tech Svs • Worcester State College • Worcester, MA 01602
Dasgupta Wen • Technical Services • Grand Rapids Public Library • Grand Rapids, MI 49503-3093
Dash Barbara L. • Annandale, VA 22003 • NMRT
Dashiell Marilyn • Reference Librarian • West Chicago Public Library District • West Chicago, IL 60185
Daso Judith A. • Document Librarian • Ohio University Vernon R. Alden Library • Athens, OH 45701-2978 • GODORT
Dassoff Christine • Pacific Graduate School of Psychology Library • Palo Alto, CA 94303 • LAMA
Datchuck Evelyn S. • San Diego, CA 92114
Dattalo Elmo F. • Head Librarian • Morrison & Foerster • Washington, DC 20006
Dattulo Annette • Librarian • Holden Elementary School • Chicago, IL 60608 • AASL
Daub Albert W. • President • Scarecrow Press, Inc. • Metuchen, NJ 08840
Daub Peggy E. • Head, Spec Clln & Arts Libs • University of Michigan Libraries • Ann Arbor, MI 48109-1205 • ACRL
Daubenas Jean D. • Acquisitions Librarian • Saint John's University Library • Jamaica, NY 11439 • ACRL RASD
Daubenspeck Anita T. • Director • Ridgefield Library • Ridgefield, CT 06877 • PLA
Dauber Sheila • Library Media Specialist • South Orange Middle School • South Orange, NJ 07079 • AASL
Daubert Madeline J. • Tampa, FL 33618 • LAMA
Daugherty Doris A. • Director of Information Services • North Dakota State Library • Bismarck, ND 58505
Daugherty Karen S. • Student • Rosary College Graduate School of Library & Information Science • River Forest, IL 60305 • AASL
Daugherty Robert A. • Circulation Librarian • University of Illinois at Chicago University Library • Chicago, IL 60680 • ACRL ALCTS LAMA LITA
Daughtry Maryjane • Children's Librarian • Sheppard Memorial Library • Greenville, NC 27858 • ALSC
Daughtry Sarah B. • Assistant Director • Prichard Public Library • Prichard, AL 36610 • PLA
Daughtry Wesley N. • Student • East Carolina University Department of Library & Information Studies • Greenville, NC 27858-4353
Daum Freddie M. • Reference Librarian • Norcross Public Library • Norcross, GA 30071
Daume Mary R. • Monroe, MI 48161-2257 • ALTA ASCLA LAMA IFRT *Continuing*
Daun-Bedford Sheri L. • Head of Young People's Services • Woodridge Public Library • Woodridge, IL 60517 • ALSC
Dauphin Linda Sue • Coordinator Library Automation • Fairfax County Public Schools • Annandale, VA 22003 • LITA
Dauphinais Helaine V. • Director • Thompson Library • Thompson, CT 06277 • PLA
Dausch Ann Sheridan • Children's Librarian • Somerville Public Library • Somerville, MA 02143
Dausch Carol E. • Librarian • Baltimore County Public Library Essex Area Branch • Essex, MD 21221 • ALSC PLA
Dausch Linda S. • Student • Indiana University School of Library and Information Science • Bloomington, IN 47405
Dautrich Mary Jane Ward • Topton, PA 19562 • Continuing
Davenport Charles R. • Knox County Public Library System • Knoxville, TN 37902-2505
Davenport Charlotte M. • Student • Catholic University of America Library School Library • Washington, DC 20064 • AASL
Davenport Cynthia A. • Children's/Young Adult Librarian • McKinney Memorial Public Library • McKinney, TX 75069
Davenport Diane L. • Library Manager, Reference • Berkeley Public Library • Berkeley, CA 94704
Davenport Diane M. • Reference Librarian • County College of Morris Masten Learning Resource Center • Randolph, NJ 07869-2086 • ACRL LIRT
Davenport Janet L. • Bus/ Sci/ Tech Ln • Omaha Public Library • Omaha, NE 68102 • RASD
Davenport Jean • Houston, TX 77036
Davenport John B. • Head of Special Clln • University of Saint Thomas O'Shaughnessy Library • Saint Paul, MN 55105 • ACRL ALCTS RASD
Davenport John N. • Librarian II • District of Columbia Public Library Woodridge Regional Branch • Washington, DC 20018
Davenport June • Librarian • San Pedro Elementary School • Robstown, TX 78380 • AASL ALSC
Davenport Kenneth M. • Student • Northeastern Iowa Regional Library System • Waterloo, IA 50701 • LITA IFRT ILERT MAGERT
Davenport Lawrence B. • Director • Warren Public Library • Warren, MI 48092 • PLA
Davenport Nancy A. • Asst. Dir., Congressional Res. • Library of Congress • Washington, DC 20541 • LAMA PLA FLRT
Davenport Steven L. • Audio/Visual Librarian • Lexington Public Library • Lexington, KY 40507 • PLA FLRT IRRT NMRT VRT
Davey Beryl P. • Omaha, NE 68144

Davey Carroll A. • Student • State University of New York at Albany School of Information Science & Policy • Albany, NY 12222

Davey Nancy A. • Director, Processing Center • Indiana Cooperative Library Services Authority (INCOLSA) • Indianapolis, IN 46278 • ALCTS *Life*

Davi Susan A. • Associate Librarian • University of Delaware Morris Library • Newark, DE 19717-5267

David Indra M. • Associate Library Dean • Oakland University • Rochester, MI 48309-4401 • ACRL LAMA LRRT

Davidge Gwendolyn E. • Head, Serial Records • University of Michigan Libraries • Ann Arbor, MI 48109-1205 • ALCTS LITA GODORT

Davidoff Donna J. • Stu • State University of New York College at Buffalo, E. H. Butler Library • Buffalo, NY 14222-1095 • ACRL

Davidoff Marcia • Orlando, FL 32803-4257

Davidowitz Merna • School Librarian • Manhattan Day School • New York, NY 10023-1602 • AASL

Davids-Puzzo Anne-Marie • Librarian • Blanchet High School Lib • Seattle, WA 98103 • AASL

Davidson Ann C. • Philadelphia, PA 19130

Davidson Catherine A. • U.S. District Court Library • Anchorage, AK 99513

Davidson Charlotte H. • Librarian-Children • Atlanta-Fulton Public Library • Atlanta, GA 30303 • AASL ALSC

Davidson D. Helen • APO, AE 09033 • ALCTS ALSC PLA FLRT

Davidson Dona • Public Services Librarian • University Center at Tulsa • Tulsa, OK 74106

Davidson Donald C. • Goleta, CA 93117 • ACRL *Continuing*

Davidson Dorothy • Periodicals Librarian • Springfield-Greene County Library • Springfield, MO 65801

Davidson Elizabeth • Professor Library Science • Southeastern Louisiana University Linus A. Sims Memorial Library • Hammond, LA 70402 • Continuing

Davidson Gloria L. • Head Librarian • T. C. Williams High School • Alexandria, VA 22302 • AASL

Davidson Jeanne R. • Reference Librarian • Augustana College Library • Rock Island, IL 61201 • ACRL

Davidson Josephine F. • Head, Nonbook Cataloging Section • University of Georgia Libraries • Athens, GA 30602 • ACRL ALCTS LITA MAGERT

Davidson Laura B. • Librarian • Gwinnett University System Center • Lawrenceville, GA 30243 • LITA RASD

Davidson Leanne B. • Cataloging Services Librarian • Ball State University Bracken Library • Muncie, IN 47306-0160 • ACRL ALCTS

Davidson Lisa L. • Bloomington, IN 47408 • LITA IFRT

Davidson Lloyd • Northwestern University Library Mudd Library for Science & Engineering • Evanston, IL 60208 • ACRL LITA

Davidson Martha W. • Assoc. Dir. for Tech. Services • Simmons College Beatley Library • Boston, MA 02115 • ACRL ALCTS LITA

Davidson Mary W. • Librarian • University of Rochester Sibley Library, Eastman School of Music • Rochester, NY 14604-2505 • LAMA

Davidson Nancy M. • Reference Librarian Coordinator • Winthrop College Ida Jane Dacus Library • Rock Hill, SC 29733 • ACRL LIRT

Davidson Sherrie K. • School Librarian • Theodor Herzl Jewish Day School • Denver, CO 80231-3816 • AASL

Davidsson Robert • Govt Info Svs Libn II • Palm Beach County Library System • West Palm Beach, FL 33406

Davie Judith F. • Director School Media Program • Greensboro Public Schools • Greensboro, NC 27402 • AASL ALSC

Davies-Smith Alayna • Director • Lewis & Clark Community College Reid Memorial Library • Godfrey, IL 62035 • ACRL

Davies Donna J. • Senior Librarian • Weston Public Library • Weston, MA 02193

Davies Dorothy • Director • Manchester Township Library • Manchester, MI 48158

Davies Frederica A. • Student • Kentucky State University Blazer Library • Frankfort, KY 40601

Davies Gordon D. • Media Specialist • Bethesda Elementary School • Bethesda, MD 20814 • AASL

Davies Jean • Trustee • Timberland Regional Library • Olympia, WA 98501 • ALTA

Davies Jo • Sequim, WA 98382

Davies Jonell • Librarian • Kensler Elementary School • Wichita, KS 67212 • AASL

Davies Leslie C. • School Librarian • Westridge Elementary School • Rock Springs, WY 82902 • AASL

Davila Daniel • Chief Librarian • Hostos Community College • Bronx, NY 10451

Davis-Millis Nina • Associate Humanities Librarian • Massachusetts Institute of Technology Libraries (MIT) • Cambridge, MA 02139 • ACRL

Davis-Shockley Kay • Port Jefferson Sta., NY 11776

Davis Ann • Assistant Director • Saint Bernard Parish Library • Chalmette, LA 70043

Davis Ann M. • Librarian • Morse School of Business • Hartford, CT 06103

Davis Anna G. • Lee County Library • Leesburg, GA 31763

Davis Anna M. • Director • Bayport Blue Point Public Library • Blue Point, NY 11715 • PLA

Davis Anne C. • Information Specialist • University of Michigan • Ann Arbor, MI 48109-1205 • LITA IRRT LRRT

Davis Anne M. • San Francisco, CA 94109 • ACRL PLA *Life*

Davis Arline • Belmont, MA 02178 • ACRL

Davis Barbara • Coordinator, Professional Lib. • Durham County Schools • Durham, NC 27701 • AASL

Davis Barbara • Library/Media Services Coor. • North East Independent School District • San Antonio, TX 78217 • AASL

Davis Barbara • Director • Lake Geneva Public Library • Lake Geneva, WI 53147 • PLA

Davis Barbara J. • Library Media Specialist • Deer Creek Elementary School • Edmond, OK 73034 • AASL

Davis Benita D. • Coordinator Special Services • Maine State Library • Augusta, ME 04333 • PLA

Davis Betty B. • Assoc. Dean for Tech. Services • Indiana State University Cunningham Memorial Library • Terre Haute, IN 47809 • ACRL ALCTS LAMA LITA

Davis Bryan T. • Assistant Director • Cedar Rapids Public Library • Cedar Rapids, IA 52401 • LITA PLA

Davis Burns • Information Resources Librarian • Nebraska Library Commission • Lincoln, NE 68508

Davis C. Roger Dr. • Northampton, MA 01060-2115 • ACRL ALCTS SRRT

Davis Carolyn W. • Librarian • Delaware Technical & Community College Terry Campus • Dover, DE 19901 • ACRL

Davis Carroll Nelson • Serials Cataloger • Columbia University Libraries Butler Library • New York, NY 10027 • ALCTS LITA

Davis Catherine Sr. • Librarian • Notre Dame Elementary School • Belmont, CA 94002

Davis Charles E. • Chair Public Services • La Sierra University Library • Riverside, CA 92515 • ACRL RASD

Davis Charles H. Dr. • Professor • University of Illinois Graduate School of Library and Information Science • Urbana, IL 61801 • ACRL RASD LRRT

Davis Charles W. Jr. • Trustee • Spokane County Library District • Spokane, WA 99212-1853

Davis Christopher J. • Student • Purdue University • West Lafayette, IN 47907

Davis Clara • Trustee • Bossier Parish Library • Bossier City, LA 71111

Davis Clarke S. • Director • Nashua Public Library • Nashua, NH 03060 • LAMA LITA

Davis Clayla C. • Library Director • St. Helena Public Library • St Helena, CA 94574 • LAMA

Davis David Michael • City Librarian • Colton Public Library • Colton, CA 92324

Davis Denise • Branch Head Librarian • Carroll County Public Library Eldersburg Branch • Eldersburg, MD 21784 • PLA SRRT

Davis Denise M. • Reference Librarian • University of Maryland Hornbake Library • College Park, MD 20742

Davis Dennis A. • Fond du Lac, WI 54935-6221 • LAMA LITA PLA

Davis Denyvetta • Library Head • Metropolitan Library System Ralph Ellison Library • Oklahoma City, OK 73111 • LAMA SRRT

Davis Diana J. • West Covina, CA 91792 • LITA

Davis Dolores D. • Student • Glassboro State College • Glassboro, NJ 08028

Davis Donald G. Jr • Professor • University of Texas at Austin Graduate School of Library & Information Sciences • Austin, TX 78712-1276 • ACRL RASD IRRT LHRT

Davis Donna L. • Student • University of Texas at Austin Graduate School of Library & Information Sciences • Austin, TX 78712-1276 • PLA

Davis Donna Z. • Librarian • Greater Latrobe High School Library • Latrobe, PA 15650 • AASL

Davis Dorothy F. • Student • University of North Texas School of Library & Information Sciences • Denton, TX 76203

Davis Dorothy Gae • Associata Librarian • University of Michigan • Flint, MI 48502-2186 • RASD GODORT SRRT

Davis Dorothy N. • Director of Library-Media Servs • Groton-Dunstable Regional School Systems • Groton, MA 01450 • AASL LIRT

Davis Douglas A. • Associate Dean • California State University Oviatt Library • Northridge, CA 91328-1289 • ACRL LAMA

Davis E. Renette Mrs. • Serial Cataloger • University of Chicago Library • Chicago, IL 60637-1502 • ALCTS

Davis Eleanor H. • Honolulu, HI 96822 • Continuing

Davis Elizabeth A. • Music Librarian • Columbia University Music Library • New York, NY 10027

Davis Elizabeth A. • Wilmington, DE 19899

Davis Elizabeth H. Miss • Kansas City, MO 64114 • Continuing

Davis Ellen B. • School Librarian • Christian Brothers High School Library • Memphis, TN 38120

Davis Ellison C. • Reference Librarian • Shoreline Community College Ray W Howard Library Media Center • Seattle, WA 98133 • ACRL RASD LIRT NMRT

Davis Enid A. • Los Altos, CA 94022 • PLA

Davis Estelle A. • Science/Engineering Library • City College of New York (CUNY) • New York, NY 10031 • ACRL

Davis Frances A. • Owensboro Community College • Owensboro, KY 42303 • ACRL

Davis Francis R. Rev • Corning, NY 14830

Davis G. Kevin • Adult Services Dept. • Warrenville Public Library District • Warrenville, IL 60555

Davis Gail A. • Bourgade Catholic High School • Phoenix, AZ 85017 • AASL

Davis Gerald F. • Director • Springfield College Babson Library • Springfield, MA 01109 • ACRL

Davis Glenda G. • Media Specialist • Continental Colony • Atlanta, GA 30331

Davis Gloria Jean • Public Library of Annapolis & Anne Arundel County Crofton Branch • Crofton, MD 21114 • PLA

Davis Gordon S. • Assistant Librarian • Old Dominion Animal Hosp • Mc Lean, VA 22101

Davis Gwendolyn J. • Asst. Ln Computer Coordinator • Mokena Community Public Library District • Mokena, IL 60448 • ALCTS

Davis H. Scott • Head, Dept. of Lib. Instruction • Indiana State University • Terre Haute, IN 47809 • ACRL LAMA LIRT

Davis Harry O. • Map & Assistant Science Ln. • Southern Illinois University Delyte W. Morris Library • Carbondale, IL 62901-6632 • ACRL GODORT MAGERT

Davis Hazel M. • Student • University of Arizona Graduate Library School • Tucson, AZ 85721 • PLA IFRT LHRT SRRT

Davis Herbert A. • Baltimore County Public Library • Towson, MD 21204 • ALTA PLA IFRT

Davis Hiram L. • Director of Libraries • Michigan State University Libraries • East Lansing, MI 48824-1048 • ACRL ALCTS LAMA LITA EMIERT SORT

Davis Inez W. • Oak Ridge, TN 37830-7526 • Continuing

Davis Irene Mrs • Houston, TX 77025 • Continuing

Davis Jack H. • The Reading Circle • Columbus, OH 43201 • AASL

Davis James • Los Angeles, CA 90034 • ACRL

Davis Jane B. • Fort Collins Public Library • Ft. Collins, CO 80524-2990 • PLA

Davis Janet M. • Principal Reference Librarian • Warren County Library • Belvidere, NJ 07823 • RASD

Davis Janice J.K. • Madison, WI 53705

Davis Janice S. • Irving, TX 75062

Davis Jannie • Library Director • United States Base Library/FL 4420 • APO, AE 09097 • AFLRT FLRT

Davis Jennifer J. • North Central Library Cooperative • Mansfield, OH 44902 • LAMA PLA CLENE EMIERT IFRT

Davis Jennifer J. • Dauenport, IA 52802 • ALCTS

Davis Jennifer Nason • Johnson, Stokes & Master Library • Central, Hong Kong • ACRL LITA

Davis Jinnie Y. • Asst. Dir. for Planning & Res. • North Carolina State University D. H. Hill Library • Raleigh, NC 27695-7111 • ACRL LAMA LITA LRRT

Davis Joan • Librarian • Immaculate Heart Academy LMC • Westwood, NJ 07675 • AASL

Davis Joan C. • Uvalde, TX 78801

Davis Jody H. • Children's Librarian • Everett Public Library • Everett, WA 98201

Davis Joseph D. • Student • Stanly County Public Library • Albemarle, NC 28001 • ALSC

Davis Joy Vee • Atlanta-Fulton Public Library Peachtree Branch • Atlanta, GA 30309 • PLA IRRT

Davis Joyce • Jefferson Schools Hurd Road Elementary • Monroe, MI 48161

Davis Joyce • Dodge City, KS 67801 • ALSC PLA *Life*

Davis Joyce N. • Director of Library • Catawba College Library • Salisbury, NC 28144 • ALCTS LAMA LITA

Davis Judith A. • Vineland, NJ 08360 • AASL

Davis Julie C. • Boise Public Library • Boise, ID 83702-0715

Davis Karen Jean • Student • Central State University Library • Edmond, OK 73034-0193 • AASL

Davis Karen Joan • Student • Syracuse University School of Information Studies • Syracuse, NY 13244-4100 • ACRL ALCTS LRRT

Davis Karen L. • Evanston, IL 60201 • AASL

Davis Karen Sue • Cedar Falls High School • Cedar Falls, IA 50613-2389 • AASL YALSA

Davis Karyn Y. • Student • Wayne State University • Detroit, MI 48202

Davis Katherine E. • Administrator • Lakeland Library Cooperative • Grand Rapids, MI 49503 • LAMA PLA

Davis Kathleen E. • Gunn Memorial Public Library • Yanceyville, NC 27379

Davis Kathleen R. • Head,Interlibrary Loan • Columbia University Libraries Butler Library • New York, NY 10027

Davis Kathy L. • Senior Librarian • Tigard Public Library • Tigard, OR 97223 • YALSA

Davis Kathy M. • Director of Libraries • DePauw University Roy O. West Library • Greencastle, IN 46135-0037 • LAMA LITA

Davis Laura L. • Student • Indiana University School of Library and Information Science • Bloomington, IN 47405

Davis Leslie C. • Student • Glaxo Inc. • Research Tri. Pk., NC 27709 • LITA SRRT

Davis Leticia H. • Arlington, VA 22203 • AASL

Davis Lila C. • Librarian • King George High School • King George, VA 22485

Davis Linda J. • Librarian I • High Point Public Library • High Point, NC 27261 • PLA RASD

Davis Linda S. • Teacher-Librarian • Western Canada High School • Calgary, AB, T2S 0B5 Canada • AASL

Davis Lucille G. • Romulus, MI 48174 • ASCLA PLA
Continuing

Davis Luella • Emory University Libraries Robert W. Woodruff Library • Atlanta, GA 30322-2870 • ACRL

Davis Lynda C. • Director • Maryland Department of Legislative Reference Library • Annapolis, MD 21401-1991

Davis Marcie L. • Instructor Librarian • Florida State University Robert M. Strozier Library • Tallahassee, FL 32306-2047

Davis Maribelle M. • Director • Plano Public Library System • Plano, TX 75086-0356 • LAMA PLA

Davis Marie A. • Philadelphia, PA 19119 • Continuing

Davis Marilyn J. • Huntington Beach, CA 92646 • SRRT

Davis Marjorie E. • School Librarian • Scurry-Rosser Independent School District • Scurry, TX 75158-9734

Davis Marjorie F. • Cincinnati, OH 45215 • Continuing

Davis Marlys Cresap • Missouri State Library • Jefferson City, MO 65102 • LAMA PLA IFRT

Davis Marta A. • Assistant Humanities Librarian • Southern Illinois University Delyte W. Morris Library • Carbondale, IL 62901-6632

Davis Martha Elaine • Technical Services Librarian • Guilford Technical Community Coll Learning Resources Center • Jamestown, NC 27282-0309 • AASL ACRL

Davis Martha Elizabeth • Sedalia Elementary School • Sedalia, NC 27342 • AASL

Davis Martha H. • Reidsville, NC 27320 • Continuing

Davis Mary • Hattiesburg, MS 39401

Davis Mary B. • Librarian • Huntington Free Library and Reading Room • Bronx, NY 10461 • ACRL

Davis Mary B. • Ponte Vedra Beach, FL 32082

Davis Mary Ellen K. • Dir. of Commun., Ed. & Publ. • American Library Association • Chicago, IL 60611-2795 • ACRL

Davis Mary L. • Assoc Univ Ln • University of North Florida Thomas G. Carpenter Library • Jacksonville, FL 32245-7605

Davis Mary R. • Student • State University of New York at Albany School of Information Science & Policy • Albany, NY 12222

Davis Melody • Youth Services Coordinator • Sidney Memorial Public Library • Sidney, NY 13838 • ALSC

Davis Mildred W. • Hammond, LA 70401 • ACRL ALCTS
Life

Davis Mimi D. • Reference Librarian • Plano Public Library System W.O. Haggard Library • Plano, TX 75075 • IFRT

Davis Nancy A. • Fairfax, VA 22032

Davis Nancy P. • Library Assistant • Roanoke County Public Library Hollins Branch Library • Roanoke, VA 24019 • ALSC CLENE

Davis Natalia G. • Branch Manager • Brooklyn Public Library Windsor Terrace Branch • Brooklyn, NY 11218 • PLA EMIERT

Davis Pamela N. • Jackson, TN 38301

Davis Patricia J. • Student • University of Texas at Austin Graduate School of Library & Information Sciences • Austin, TX 78712-1276

Davis Patrick J. • Student • University of Texas at Austin Graduate School of Library & Information Sciences • Austin, TX 78712-1276 • IFRT SRRT

Davis Philip M. • Reference Librarian • Fort Worth Public Library • Fort Worth, TX 76102

Davis Phyllis B. • South Central Library System • Madison, WI 53703 • LITA SRRT

Davis Phyllis K. • Librarian • Gastineau School Library • Juneau, AK 99801 • AASL ALSC

Davis Randall M. • Blackshear, GA 31516 • ACRL ASCLA LITA PLA RASD

Davis Regina M. • Software Specialist • Data Research Associates Inc. • Saint Louis, MO 63132

Davis Robert H. Jr. • Student • New York Public Library • New York, NY 10018-2788 • ACRL ALCTS

Davis Ronda • Western Regional Education Center • Canton, NC 28716-4489 • AASL

Davis Ronnie E. • Br Mgr • Alameda County Library Albany Branch • Albany, CA 94706

Davis Rose P. • Reference Librarian • Mississippi State University Mitchell Memorial Library • Mississippi State, MS 39762

Davis Ruth F. • Librarian • Delaware City Commodore Macdonough Elementary School • New Castle, DE 19720

Davis Sally • Madison, WI 53717 • Continuing

Davis Sandra B. • Librarian II • Chicago Public Library • Chicago, IL 60605

Davis Sara Bond • Atlanta, GA 30314 • Continuing

Davis Sarah Marie • Coralville, IA 52241 • ACRL
Continuing

Davis Shelagh • Brighton, MI 48116-2885

Davis Sheri Ann R. • Branch Manager • Jacksonville Public Library Murray Hill Branch • Jacksonville, FL 32205 • PLA YALSA

Davis Sheryl J. • Head, Acquisitions/Serials Dept • University of California Rivera Library • Riverside, CA 92517 • ACRL ALCTS

Davis Shirley B. • Head Curriculum Library • East Texas State University Library • Commerce, TX 75428

Davis Stephen P. • Assistant Director for Lib. Sys. • Columbia University Libraries • New York, NY 10027 • LITA

Davis Susan A. • Head, Periodicals • State University of New York (SUNY) Central Technical Services • Buffalo, NY 14260 • ALCTS

Davis Susan M. • Franktown, CO 80116

Davis Susan M. • Periodicals & ILL Librarian • Gallaudet University Library • Washington, DC 20002 • ALCTS RASD SRRT

Davis Susan W. • Preservation Librarian • Vanderbilt University Library • Nashville, TN 37240-0007 • ALCTS

Davis Sylvia S. • Ref. & Biblo. Instr. Libn. • Catonsville Community College • Baltimore, MD 21228 • ACRL

Davis Teresa • Librarian • Phelps Dunbar • New Orleans, LA 70130

Davis Terri L. • Library Director • Deadwood Public Library • Deadwood, SD 57732

Davis Trisha L. • Ohio State University Libraries • Columbus, OH 43210-1286 • ALCTS LITA

Davis Vona Lee • Hermosa Beach, CA 90254

Davis Wendy E. • Highland Park, IL 60035 • AFLRT

Davis William H. • Seattle, WA 98118

Davis William P. • Senior Associate • Missouri State Library • Jefferson City, MO 65102 • ASCLA PLA EMIERT IFRT SRRT

Davis William T. • Librarian/Media Specialist • Don Lugo High School • Chino, CA 90815 • AASL LIRT

Davis Wylma P. • Assistant Head Librarian & Lect. • Virginia Military Institute J.T.L. Preston Library • Lexington, VA 24450 • ACRL GODORT

Davish William Rev. • Reference Librarian • Loyola College • Baltimore, MD 21210 • ACRL RASD *Continuing*

Davison Alison H. • Law Librarian • ITT Hartford Insurance • Hartford, CT 06115

Davison Chice A. • Librarian • Antelope Valley College • Lancaster, CA 93536 • ACRL RASD LIRT

Davison Dorothy J. • Librarian • New York Public Library New Dorp Regional Library • Staten Island, NY 10306

Davison Frieda M. • Assistant University Librarian • San Francisco State University J. Paul Leonard Library • San Francisco, CA 94132 • LAMA RASD

Davison Jennifer A. • Student • University of Wisconsin School of Library & Information Studies • Madison, WI 53706

Davison Jo Ann G. • Librarian • Gilman School Library • Baltimore, MD 21210 • AASL ACRL IFRT

Davison Ruth M. • Indiana University • Bloomington, IN 47405 • GODORT

Davitt Theresa B. • Law Librarian • New England Telephone • Boston, MA 02107 • LITA

Davy Edgar W. • Head Dewey Library • Massachusetts Institute of Technology Libraries (MIT) • Cambridge, MA 02139 • ACRL

Daw Lenore E. • Fresno, CA 93727 • AASL

Dawe James R. • Chairman, Bd. of Commissioners • Seltzer Caplan Wilkins & McMahon • San Diego, CA 92101-8177 • ALTA

Dawe Kathleen T. • Library Media Specialist • Harriman Heights Elementary School • Harriman, NY 10926 • AASL

Dawe Virginia P. • Head Librarian • Germantown Academy • Fort Washington, PA 19034 • AASL LAMA YALSA LIRT

Dawes Trevor A. • Access Services Coordinator • Columbia University Science & Engineering Division Libraries • New York, NY 10027 • ACRL

Dawkins Diantha D. • Librarian • Lee Freshman Library • Midland, TX 79705 • AASL LITA LIRT

Dawood Rosemary • Head, Literature & Language • Chicago Public Library • Chicago, IL 60605

Dawson Aleena R. Mrs • Belleair Bluffs, FL 34616 • Continuing

Dawson Alma • Baton Rouge, LA 70898 • ACRL LIRT

Dawson Anne • Saratoga, CA 95070

Dawson Barbara J. • Assistant Librarian • Cincinnati Historical Society Library • Cincinnati, OH 45203

Dawson Bunny S. • Librarian • Oromondale Elementary School • Portola Valley, CA 94028 • AASL

Dawson Deborah • Head of Science Library • University of Wyoming • Laramie, WY 82071 • ACRL ALCTS

Dawson Elizabeth Anne • Supervisor Library Section • Los Angeles City Schools • Los Angeles, CA 90044 • Continuing

Dawson F. Lawrence • Director • Beloit Corporation Research Center Technical Library • Rockton, IL 61072-1595 • IFRT

Dawson George H. Jr. • Director • Refugio County Public Library • Refugio, TX 78377 • PLA NMRT

Dawson Jan E. • Gillette, WY 82717-0682 • RASD GODORT

Dawson Jean • Trustee • Franklin Park Public Library District • Franklin Park, IL 60131

Dawson John Minto • Newark, DE 19713 • ACRL   *Life*

Dawson Judy Kay • Reference Librarian • Jefferson State Junior College Allen Library • Birmingham, AL 35215

Dawson Julie Eng • Serials Librarian • Princeton Theological Seminary • Princeton, NJ 08542

Dawson Luna E. Miss • Cleveland, OH 44124 • Continuing

Dawson Muir • President • Dawsons Book Shop • Los Angeles, CA 90004 • ACRL

Dawson Patrick J. • Reference Librarian • University of California General Library • Irvine, CA 92713 • ACRL RASD EMIERT

Dawson Ruth C. Mrs • Crete, IL 60417 • AASL YALSA
Continuing

Dawson Shirley F. • Librarian • Monterey County Library Castroville Branch • Castroville, CA 95012

Dawson Terry P. • Assistant Director • Appleton Public Library • Appleton, WI 54911-4780 • LAMA LITA PLA

Day Angela M. • Windsor Public Library • Windsor, VT 05039

Day Betty H. • Bibliographer • University of Maryland College Park Theodore R. McKeldin Library • College Park, MD 20742-7011 • ACRL ALCTS

Day Carol L. • Library Media Specialist • L.B. Haynes Elementary • Niantic, CT 06357 • AASL ALSC

Day Christina M. • Hardin County Library • Savannah, TN 38372

Day Elizabeth B. • Santa Barbara County School • Santa Barbara, CA 93160-6307 • AASL

Day Helen M. Miss • Buffalo, NY 14223 • PLA *Continuing*

Day J. Dennis • Director • Salt Lake City Public Library • Salt Lake City, UT 84111 • AASL ACRL ALSC LAMA LITA PLA YALSA GODORT IFRT IRRT

Day Janet V. • Director • Woodbridge Town Library • Woodbridge, CT 06525 • PLA

Day Jeanette Mrs • East Catholic High School • Manchester, CT 06040 • AASL

Day John M. • Director • Gallaudet University Library • Washington, DC 20002 • ACRL ASCLA

Day Margaret A. • Information Specialist • Applied Science Associates Inc. • Butler, PA 16003

Day Marilyn K. • Student • Sam Houston State University Department of Library Science • Huntsville, TX 77341-2236

Day Mark T. • Associate Librarian/Reference • Indiana University at Bloomington University Libraries • Bloomington, IN 47405 • ACRL LITA RASD IFRT

Day Melvin S. • President • M. Day Consultants International Inc. • Washington, DC 20016

Day Nancy Jane • Laurens, SC 29360 • AASL YALSA
Continuing

Day Nancy K. • Librarian for Processing Serv. • Linda Hall Library • Kansas City, MO 64110 • ACRL

Day Normayne • School Library Media Specialist • Lake Orion High School • Lake Orion, MI 48360 • AASL

Day Pamela A. • Minnesota Legislative Reference Library • Saint Paul, MN 55155

Day Roy E C • Coordinator of Adult Services • Chatham-Effingham-Liberty Regional Library (CEL) • Savannah, GA 31499-4301

Day Sandra L. • Franklin Sherman Elementary School • McLean, VA 22101 • AASL ALSC

Day Serenna F. • Senior Ln Children Lit Dept. • Los Angeles Public Library • Los Angeles, CA 90071 • ALSC EMIERT IFRT

Day Thomas Lee • Bookmobile/outreach Supervisor • Clark County Public Library • Springfield, OH 45501-1080

Dayanandan Anne M. • Madras Christian College • Madras 600 059, India • ALCTS

Daye Katherine H. • YA Librarian • Jacksonville Public Libraries Main Library • Jacksonville, FL 32202

Dayhoff Alice J. • Student • Toledo-Lucas County Public Library • Toledo, OH 43624

Dayo Ayo • Children's Services Supervisor • Prince William Public Library Chinn Park Regional Library • Prince William, VA 22192 • ALSC

Dayton Diane • Head Librarian • The Westminster Schools • Atlanta, GA 30327 • AASL LIRT

Dayton Jane • Head of Branch Libraries • Carnegie Library of Pittsburgh • Pittsburgh, PA 15213-4080 • LAMA PLA

de Angeli Marianne • Librarian • Jenkintown High School Library • Jenkintown, PA 19046 • YALSA

De Antoniis Paul J. Rev. • Archmere Academy Library • Claymont, DE 19703

De Are Carolyn M. • Head of Reference • Wheaton Public Library • Wheaton, IL 60187-5376

de Bear Richard • Library Building Consultant • Library Design Associates Inc • Plymouth, MI 48170 • LAMA

De Belder Kurt F. • New York University Elmer Holmes Bobst Library • New York, NY 10012 • ACRL ALCTS LITA

de Berge Linda • Librarian II • Phoenix Public Library Palo Verde Branch • Phoenix, AZ 85031 • PLA

De Boer Alice • Librarian • Lansing Public Schools • Lansing, IL 60438

de Bruijn Maria C.A. • Student • Queens College Graduate School of Library & Information Studies • Flushing, NY 11367 • ACRL IRRT

de Castro Deborah F. • Bronx, NY 10475 • NMRT

De Cecco Susanna H. • Libraraian • Widener University School of Law • Harrisburg, PA 17110-9450 • ALCTS

De Ceunynck Harriet • Principal Cataloger • Hunter College Library • New York, NY 10021 • ALCTS GODORT

de Cuenca Pilar A. • Librarian • Public School 25 The Bilingual School • Bronx, NY 10455 • ALSC

De Falco Daniela • El Paso, TX 79912-4250

De Frage Ann • Branch Librarian • Contra Costa County Library West Regional Headquarters • El Sobrante, CA 94803 • PLA

De Francesco Laura J. • Assistant Dir. for Support Serv. • Danbury Public Library • Danbury, CT 06810 • PLA

de Freitas Claudette C. • Student • University of Toronto Faculty of Library & Information Science • Toronto ON, M5S 1A1 Canada • LITA

de Goede Trudy • Social Sciences Libn./Bibl. • University of Texas at Arlington • Arlington, TX 76019-0497 • ACRL MAGERT

de Groat Greta G. • Western Library Network (WLN) • Lacey, WA 98503-0888

De Guevara Helen L. • Director of Libraries • Mexican Cultural & Educational Institute of Chicago/Program for Mexican • Chicago, IL 60601 • LAMA IRRT

de Havenon Georgia • Student • Queens College Grad Sch of Lib & Inf Studies • Flushing, NY 11367

De Jardin Carole J. • Supv-Ch Serv. • Appleton Public Library • Appleton, WI 54911-4780 • ALSC RASD YALSA

de Klerk Ann M. • Director • Bucknell University Bertrand Library • Lewisburg, PA 17837-2086 • ACRL LAMA LITA

de Krafft Linda Joy • Elementary Librarian • Smithfield Elementary Library • East Strousburg, PA 18301

de La Fontaine John F. • Occidental College Library • Los Angeles, CA 90041 • LITA RASD

De La Garza Mary L. • Incarnate Word College • San Antonio, TX 78209-9367

De Langeron D. Andrualt • Indexer • H. W. Wilson Company • Bronx, NY 10452 • ACRL

de Long Laurie • Highland Park, NJ 08904

de Lyon Friel Linda • Methuen High School Media Center • Methuen, MA 01844 • AASL

De Matteis Julie K. • Librarian • Baltimore County Public Library Catonsville Branch • Catonsville, MD 21228 • ALSC YALSA

De Melle Walter E Jr • Librarian • Hotchkiss Sch Edsel Ford Mem L • Lakeville, CT 06039 • AASL RASD

De Milia Carl R. • New Milford Public Library • New Milford, CT 06776

de Onis Johanna Mrs • Alexandria, VA 22312

de Ortego y Gasca Felipe Dr. • Scholar in Residence • Texas Woman's University School of Library & Information Studies • Denton, TX 76204 • EMIERT

de Peters Ana Margarita • Librarian • The American School Library • San Salvador, El Salvador •

De Quesada Raul • Trustee • Distribuidora del Libro, Inc. (D.D.L. Book Inc.) • Miami, FL 33166

de Rochefort-Reynolds Denise • Director • Frank Carlson Library • Concordia, KS 66901 • PLA

De Rose Dominick • Trustee • Johnson Free Public Library • Hackensack, NJ 07601 • AASL ACRL ALTA LAMA PLA RASD YALSA GODORT

De Rouen Noemie M. • Librarian Grade 3 • State Library of Louisiana • Baton Rouge, LA 70821

De Rousse Kay • Teacher • Beach Park School District #3 • Zion, IL 60099 • AASL

de Sciora Edward • Director • Port Washington Public Library • Port Washington, NY 11050 • LAMA PLA   *Life*

de Sciora Susan O. • Director • Hewlett Woodmere Public Library • Hewlett, NY 11557-2301 • LAMA LITA

de Scossa Catriona • Associate Professor • University of Alberta • Edmonton, AB T6G 2J4 Canada • ACRL

de Stefano Daniel A. • Head Librarian • Nahant Public Library • Nahant, MA 01908

de Trenck Alexandra • Asst. Mgr. Library Relations • H. W. Wilson Company • Bronx, NY 10452 • LAMA ERT

de Usabel Frances E. • Library Consultants Special Serv • Wisconsin Division for Library Services • Madison, WI 53707 • ACRL ASCLA SRRT

De Waelsche T. Matthew • Archives of the Episcopal Church • Austin, TX 78768

DeAbreu Stephanie T. • Chief, Development Office • Enoch Pratt Free Library • Baltimore, MD 21201-4484

DeAngelis Paul A. • Director • Somerville Public Library • Somerville, MA 02143

DeAngelo Karen J. • Waterford, NY 12188-1079

deAraujo Georgia R. • Assistant Library Director • Boyle County Public Library • Danville, KY 40422

DeBacher John K. • Library Director • Big Rapids Community Library • Big Rapids, MI 49307-2090 • ALSC PLA

DeBacher Richard D. • Librarian • Southern Illinois University Press • Carbondale, IL 62902-3697 • IFRT

DeBartolo Jack Jr., FAIA • Anderson Debartolo Pan Inc. • Phoenix, AZ 85014-2443 • LAMA

deBear Christopher J. • Treasurer/Sales • Library Design Associates, Inc. • Columbus, OH 43226 • LAMA

deBear Richard S. Jr. • Vice President • Library Design Associates, Inc. • Columbus, OH 43226 • LAMA

DeBeau-Melting Linda • University of Minnesota O. Meredith Wilson Library • Minneapolis, MN 55455-0414 • ACRL ALCTS LAMA LITA SRRT

DeBeer Kathleen A. • Sun City, AZ 85351

DeBell Charlotte H. • Library/Media Generalist • North Londonderry School Library Media Center • Londonderry, NH 03053 • AASL

DeBellis Mary M. • Student • Queens College Grad Sch of Lib & Inf Studies • Flushing, NY 11367 • PLA

DeBenedictis Nicholas • Trustee • Free Library of Philadelphia • Philadelphia, PA 19103 • ALTA

DeBlauw Robert • Littleton Public School • Littleton, CO 80120 • LITA

DeBlois Lillian N. • Tucson, AZ 85715

DeBolt Vicki L. • Assistant Librarian • Dwyer-Mercer County Public Library • Celina, OH 45822

DeBonis M. Elaine • Information Resource Analyst • Hudsons Bay Company • Toronto, ON, M6A 3B3 Canada • LITA

deBruijn Deb • University of Calgary Libraries • Calgary AB, T2N 1N4 Canada • LITA

DeBuse Raymond • Senior Consultant • Woodard Bay Co. • Lacey, WA 98503 • LITA

DeCamps Alice Loraine • Head, Bus., Science Technology • Richmond Public Library • Richmond, VA 23219 • GODORT

DeCandido GraceAnne A. • Exec. Editor, News & Features • School Library Journal • New York City, NY 10011 • AASL PLA SRRT

DeCandido Robert L. • Head Shelf & Binding Prep Office • New York Public Library Conservation Division • New York, NY 10018 • ALCTS LAMA

DeCaprio Albert A. • Assistant County Librarian • San Bernardino County Library • San Bernardino, CA 92415 • LITA

DeCaria Mary • Librarian • Bethune-Cookman College Swisher Library • Daytona Beach, FL 32115 • ACRL

DeCastro Elinore H. • Chief Ln & Prof, Lib Sci Dept. • Philippine Normal College • Manila, Philippines

DeCecco Mary E. • Student • San Jose State University Division of Library & Information Science • San Jose, CA 95192-0029

DeCelles Linda M. • Preservation Recon Cataloger • University of Chicago Library • Chicago, IL 60637-1502

deChambeau Aimee L. • Student • University of Pittsburgh School of Library and Information Science • Pittsburgh, PA 15260 • RASD IFRT NMRT

DeChant Ruth E. • Student • Emporia State University Emporia in the Rockies • Denver, CO 80204

DeDecker Sharon K. • Santa Barbara, CA 93110 • RASD

DeDonato Ree • Hd General & Humanities Ref • New York University Elmer Holmes Bobst Library • New York, NY 10012 • ACRL LAMA LITA RASD

DeFato Linda G. • Reference Librarian • Arizona State University Libraries • Tempe, AZ 85287-1006 • ACRL RASD

DeFazio Patricia Malone • Student • State University of New York at Albany School of Information Science & Policy • Albany, NY 12222

DeFelice Barbara J. • Reference Librarian • Dartmouth College Kresge Physical Sciences Library • Hanover, NH 03755 • ACRL RASD MAGERT

DeFelice Linda • Reference Librarian • Gloucester County College Library Media Center • Sewell, NJ 08080

DeFeo Marie E. • Student • State University of New York at Albany School of Information Science & Policy • Albany, NY 12222

DeFilippo Georgene A. • Children's Librarian • Bethel Park Public Library • Bethel Park, PA 15102-2790 • ALSC

DeFoe Helene B. • Library Director • Mashpee Public Library • Mashpee, MA 02649 • PLA

DeFoe Mary K. • Baton Rouge, LA 70808 • PLA

DeForest Emily H. • Librarian • Kenai Community Library • Kenai, AK 99611 • PLA

DeForest Janet L. • Andalusia, AL 36420

DeFrain Patricia M. • Librarian III • Milwaukee Public Library • Milwaukee, WI 53233 • ACRL GODORT

DeFrance Duffy • Children's Librarian • Musser Public Library • Muscatine, IA 52761 • ALSC PLA RASD IFRT

DeFranco Francine M. • Social Work Librarian • University of Connecticut H. B. Trecker Library • West Hartford, CT 06117 • ACRL

DeFranks Lucille M. • Project Coordinator • Buffalo & Erie County Public Library • Buffalo, NY 14203

DeGeer Mary E. • Children's Librarian • Bartlesville Public Library • Bartlesville, OK 74003

DeGennaro Richard • Librarian • Harvard College Library Widener Memorial Library • Cambridge, MA 02138 • ACRL LITA   *Life*

DeGraff Kathryn • Special Collections Librarian • DePaul University Libraries • Chicago, IL 60614 • ACRL ALCTS

DeGraff Margaret H. • Student • Anna S. Kuhl Elementary School • Port Jervis, NY 12771 • AASL

DeGrandis Paul J. Jr. • Cleveland Public Library • Cleveland, OH 44114-1271 • ALTA

deGuzman Johanna T. • Student • University of Pittsburgh School of Library and Information Science • Pittsburgh, PA 15260 • ALSC

DeHaan Elizabeth A. • Librarian • Humane Society of the United States • Washington, DC 20037 • ACRL

DeHart Brian P. • Student • University of Illinois Graduate School of Library and Information Science • Urbana, IL 61801

DeHoll Cheryl • Student • University of South Carolina College of Library & Information Science • Columbia, SC 29208

DeHoogh Doris • Librarian • Hesston High School • Hesston, KS 67062 • AASL YALSA

DeJesus Deborah Mrs. • Trustee • Yonkers Public Library • Yonkers, NY 10701 • ALTA

DeJesus Lisa G. • Librarian • Alameda County Library Pleasanton Branch • Pleasanton, CA 94566 • PLA

DeJohn William T. • Director • MINITEX Lib Info Network University of Minnesota • Minneapolis, MN 55455-0414 • ACRL ASCLA LAMA LITA SRRT

DeJong Linda • Media Specialist • Ford Elementary School • Denver, CO 80239 • AASL

DeJonker Debra A. • Assistant Director • Haverhill Public Library • Haverhill, MA 01830 • RASD

DeLaGarza P. J. Mr • Washington, DC 20003 • ACRL ALCTS   *Life*

DeLaGraza Luis Alberto • Student • University of California-Berkeley School of Library & Information Studies • Berkeley, CA 94720

DeLaPena Rita A. • Library Relations Rep. • H.W. Wilson Company • Bronx, NY 10452

DeLanty Cynthia A. • Student • Long Island University Palmer School of Library & Information Science • Greenvale, NY 11548

DeLapp Larry R. • Roswell, GA 30076-1519

DeLauche Jean E. • Director • Alverno College Library Media Center • Milwaukee, WI 53234-3922 • ACRL LAMA LITA

DeLoach Marva L. • Adm. Ln for Reference Services • Oakland Public Library • Oakland, CA 94612 • ACRL ALCTS LAMA LITA PLA RASD SRRT

DeLong Dianne S. • Cataloging Librarian • Illinois State University Milner Library • Normal, IL 61761-0900 • ACRL

DeLong Douglas A. • Acquisition Librarian • Illinois State University Milner Library • Normal, IL 61761-0900 • ALCTS MAGERT

DeLong Edward J. • Head of Media Services • Southwest Missouri State University Library • Springfield, MO 65804-0095

DeLong Kathleen M. • Education Librarian • University of Alberta Library • Edmonton AB, T6G 2J8 Canada
DeLong Priscilla E.S. • Media Specialist • Rosemary Hills Elementary School • Silver Spring, MD 20910 • AASL
deLong Suzanne • Tucson, AZ 85713
DeLuca Carolyn J. • Student • University of Illinois Graduate School of Library and Information Science • Urbana, IL 61801
DeLucia Esther P. • Glastonbury, CT 06033 • AASL
DeLuz Mary N. • Library Assistant • San Diego Public Library • San Diego, CA 92101 • PLA
DeMarco JoEllen • Librarian • Log College Middle School • Warmister, PA 18974 • AASL
DeMarco Joseph R. • Saint Joseph's Preparatory School Student's Library • Philadelphia, PA 19130 • AASL YALSA LIRT
DeMarinis Ellen S. • Bibliographer/Social Wk Liaison • University of Pennsylvania Library Van Pelt-Dietrich Library Center • Philadelphia, PA 19104-6206 • ACRL
DeMiller Anna L. • Hd., Soc Sci & Humanites Dept • Colorado State University • Fort Collins, CO 80523 • ACRL LITA
DeMonet Patricia B. • Columbus, GA 31904
DeMoss Barbara E. • Librarian • Saint Paul's School • Oakland, CA 94602
DeNamur Ruth M • Plano, TX 75023
DeNigris Peter J. • Trustee • Babylon Public Library • Babylon, NY 11702 • ALTA
DeNoble Augustine Rev. • Saint Benedict, OR 97373 • Continuing
DeOliveira Vilma • Librarian • East Baton Rouge Parish Library • Baton Rouge, LA 70806-7699
DePalma Michelle • Oakdale, NY 11769 • AASL
DePetro Thomas G. • Aviation & Engineering Librarian • Wichita State University Library • Wichita, KS 67208 • IRRT
DePew John N. • Professor • Florida State University School of Library and Information Studies • Tallahassee, FL 32306-2048 • ACRL ALCTS RASD *Life*
DePorter Laura J. • Student • Catholic University of America School of Library and Information Science • Washington, DC 20064 • RASD
DePriest Jeanette Dr. • Sun Lakes, AZ 85248 • ALSC *Continuing*
DeQuasie Clarise A. • Catalog Librarian • Vanderbilt University Library Jean & Alexander Heard Library • Nashville, TN 37240-0007 • ALCTS
deRecinos Donna D. • Supervisor Media Services • Flood Middle School • Stratford, CT 06497 • AASL
DeReu Murriel L. • Marion, NY 14505-0003 • PLA
DeReus Julie M. • Grinnell, IA 50112-1654
DeRicco Gretchen S. • Director Learning Resources • Western Nevada Community College • Carson City, NV 89703 • ACRL
DeRochi Helen • Media Specialist • Alderman Elementary School • Greensboro, NC 27407 • AASL
DeRonde Paula D. • Community Outreach Coordinator • Toronto Public Library • Toronto ON, M5A 4L2 Canada • LAMA PLA
DeRoode Clifford • Librarian • Paris Study Center • Paris 75015, France • ACRL LAMA RASD
DeRosa Frank J. • Dir. Facilities Mgmt & Risk Ctrl • Brooklyn Public Library • Brooklyn, NY 11238 • LAMA
DeSalvo Nancy N. • Coordinator of Children's Serv • Farmington Public Library • Farmington, CT 06034 • ALSC
DeSantis John C. • Russian Cataloger • Amherst College Library • Amherst, MA 01002 • ACRL SRRT
DeSantis M. Carmel Sr. • Syosset, NY 11791 • AASL
DeSelms Marilyn K. • School Librarian • John F. Kennedy School • Phoenix, AZ 85040 • AASL
DeShay Claudia H. • Librarian I • University of Texas Southwestern Medical Center at Dallas Library • Dallas, TX 75235-9049 • AASL ALSC EMIERT SRRT
DeSirey Janice M. • Cataloger • Hennepin County Library • Minnetonka, MN 55343 • ALCTS PLA SRRT
DeSmith Elaine • Library Director • University of Southern Mississippi Cox Library • Long Beach, MS 39560 • ACRL
DeSoto Randy A. • Administrative Librarian • Saint John the Baptist Parish Library • LaPlace, LA 70068 • LAMA PLA SRRT
DeStefano Deborah K. • Librarian • Information Enterprises • Austin, TX 78763
DeStefano Kimberly A. • Student • State University of New York at Albany School of Information Science & Policy • Albany, NY 12222 • AASL
deStigter Beth A. • Media Specialist • Amerman Elementary School • Northville, MI 48716 • AASL
deVallet Christine • Assistant Librarian • Yale University • New Haven, CT 06520 • ACRL
DeVelbiss Elizabeth • Berkeley, CA 94707 • Continuing
DeVine Dianne M. • El Paso, TX 79927 • NMRT
DeVine Gail • Librarian • Frost Middle School LMC • Louisville, KY 40272 • AASL
DeVinney Cora E. • Director • Troy Public Library • Troy, MI 48084 • ASCLA LAMA PLA *Continuing*
DeVoss Elaine F. • Librarian • Loomis Chaffee School • Windsor, CT 06095 • AASL
DeVries Dana J. • Riverside, IL 60546 • IFRT
deVries Eileen • Librarian • Culinary Institute of America • Hyde Park, NY 12538-1499 • ACRL
DeVries Hendrik R. • Librarian • Pacific Islands Bible College • Agana, GU 96910-0338 • ACRL
DeVries JoAnn • Reference/Bibliographer • University of Minnesota Saint Paul Campus Libraries • Saint Paul, MN 55108 • ACRL
DeWaelsche Catherine A. • Librarian • Parkway School District • Chesterfield, MO 63017 • AASL ALSC YALSA
DeWalt Mary M. • Milwaukee, WI 53212
DeWeese Beverly J. • Librarian • Milwaukee Public Library • Milwaukee, WI 53233 • RASD
DeWeese June L. • Head of Access Services • University of Missouri Libraries-Columbia Elmer Ellis Library • Columbia, MO 65201-5149 • ACRL LAMA
DeWeese Keith P. • Audio-Visual Librarian • Chicago Public Library Sulzer Regional Library • Chicago, IL 60625
DeWell Helen M. • Lloyd C. Bird High School • Chesterfield, VA 23832 • AASL
DeWitt B R • Miami, FL 33187 • AASL
DeWitt Gerald T. • Champaign, IL 61821
DeWitt Melinda A. • Student • University of Washington Graduate School of Library and Information Science • Seattle, WA 98195
deWolfe Becky • Library Media Specialist • Sabin Junior High School • Colorado Springs, CO 80917 • AASL IFRT *Life*
DeWitt Robert H. • Fort Collins, CO 80525-1420 • Continuing
DeYoung-Galassini Kathleen • Student • Rosary College Graduate School of Library & Information Science • River Forest, IL 60305
DeYoung Alma J. • Administrative Librarian • South Holland Public Library • South Holland, IL 60473 • LAMA LITA PLA
DeYoung Charles D. • Librarian • Michigan City Public Library • Michigan City, IN 46360 • LAMA PLA *Life*
DeYoung Gail O. • Librarian • Kent County Library System East Grand Rapids Branch • East Grand Rapids, MI 49506 • PLA
Deacon Mary Dale • Dean of Libraries • University of Nevada-Las Vegas James R. Dickinson Library • Las Vegas, NV 89154 • ACRL LAMA RASD
Deacon William W. • Librarian • Mid-Continent Public Library Grandview Branch • Grandview, MO 64030 • PLA
Deacy Linda L. • Douglas County Library • Minden, NV 89423
Deadder Patricia • Reno, NV 89511 • GODORT
Deady Eleanor M. • Student • Simmons College Graduate School of Library & Information Science • Boston, MA 02115 • LITA RASD ERT IFRT SRRT
Deakyne William J. • Director • East Lyme Public Library • Niantic, CT 06357-1100
Deal Carl W. • Director of Library Collection • University of Illinois Library • Urbana, IL 61801 • ACRL
Deal Glynda I. • District Librarian • Taft 1st District Schools • Taft, TX 78390 • AASL
Deale H Vail • Director of Libraries Emeritus • Beloit College Libraries Colonel Robert H. Morse Library • Beloit, WI 53511 • ACRL LAMA *Life*
Dealleaume William A. • New York State Library State Education Department • Albany, NY 12230
Dean Barbara C. • Fairfax County Public Library • Fairfax, VA 22033-1909 • ALCTS
Dean Barbara C. • Midland Lutheran College • Fremont, NE 68025 • AASL
Dean Beth W. • Adult Services Librarian • Huntsville-Madison County Public Library • Huntsville, AL 35804 • PLA YALSA IFRT
Dean Delight • Library Director • Shelby Township Library • Shelby Township, MI 48316 • PLA IFRT SRRT
Dean Esther M. • Student • University at Albany Libraries • Albany, NY 12222 • PLA
Dean Frances C. • Rockville, MD 20851 • IFRT
Dean Hazel Miss • Inglewood, CA 90301 • ALCTS *Continuing*
Dean Jane • Branch-Head • Wichita Public Library • Wichita, KS 67202
Dean John F. • Dir. Preservation & Conservation • Cornell University • Ithaca, NY 14853-5301 • ACRL ALCTS
Dean Judith A. • Stanford University • Stanford, CA 94305-6011
Dean Julia A. • South Side High Library • Memphis, TN 38106
Dean LeAnn F. • Reference Librarian • University of Minnesota-Morris Rodney A Briggs Library • Morris, MN 56267 • ACRL
Dean Martha L. • Director • San Joaquin County Office of Education Instructional Media Center • Stockton, CA 95213-9030 • AASL
Dean Mary M. • Reference Librarian • Lansing Public Library • Lansing, MI 48933
Dean Russell W. • Librarian • Snow College Lucy A Phillips Library • Ephraim, UT 84627 • ACRL
Dean Sylvia H. • Trustee • Cumberland County Public Library and Information Center • Fayetteville, NC 28301
Dean Winifred F. • Business & Social Science Libn. • Cleveland State University Library • Cleveland, OH 44115 • ACRL ALCTS RASD IFRT LIRT
Deane Catherine Hill • Head Children's Services • Mount Prospect Public Library • Mount Prospect, IL 60056 • ALSC PLA
Deane Mary M. • Library Systems Coordinator • Florida International University • Miami, FL 33199 • LAMA LITA
Deane Paul D. Jr • Arlington Heights, IL 60004 • PLA RASD
Deane Roxanna L. • Chief, Washingtoniana Division • District of Columbia Public Library Martin Luther King Memorial Library • Washington, DC 20001
Dearborn Susan C. • Marking & Sales Support Cons. • CLSI, Inc. • Newtonville, MA 02160 • AASL ACRL LAMA LITA PLA FLRT NMRT
Deardorff Claudia M. • Librarian • Ventura County Library Service Agency • Ventura, CA 93002 • GODORT
Deardorff Jan • Corvallis School District 509-J Central I M C • Corvallis, OR 97330 • AASL ALCTS LAMA EMIERT
Deardorff Thomas • Coor. for Access Services • University of Washington • Seattle, WA 98195 • ACRL LITA IFRT
Dearie Tammy Nickelson • Infomations Access Librarian • University of California-San Diego Central University Library • La Jolla, CA 92093-0175 • ACRL LAMA LITA
Dearman Marvene D. • Librarian • Istrouma Middle Magnet • Baton Rouge, LA 70805 • AASL
Dearman Susan M. • Librarian/Director • Fort Walton Beach Public Library • Fort. Walton Beach, FL 32548 • PLA
Dearnaley Carolyn • Rider College • Lawrenceville, NJ 08648-3099 • ACRL IFRT
Dearnbarger Dennis • United States Government Printing Office • Washington, DC 20401 • ACRL GODORT
Dearstyne Susan V. • Albany, NY 12203
Dearth Betty J. • Manitoba Research Council • Winnipeg, R2J 3T4 Canada
Deaton Nancy S. • Information Consultant • AIHRS • Orlando, FL 32817 • ACRL
Deaven Paul • Media Specialist • Dakota County Library System Wescott Library • Eagan, MN 55123 • PLA VRT
Deaver Margaret A. • Library Book Center • Wichita, KS 67216 • AASL ALSC YALSA
Deaver Tracy H. • Mgr., Conversion Services • Sirsi Corporation • Huntsville, AL 35801 • ALCTS LITA
Debreczeni Joyce E. • Palm Springs, CA 92264-9159 • ALSC PLA YALSA
Debreczeny Gillian Mrs • Librarian • University of North Carolina at Chapel Hill School of Information and Library Science • Chapel Hill, NC 27599-3360 • IRRT
Debus Karl E. • Head, Monographic Acquisitions • United States Department of Agriculture National Agricultural Library • Beltsville, MD 20705-2351 • ALCTS FLRT
Debusman Amelia O. • Coordinator Extension Serv. • Louisville Free Public Library • Louisville, KY 40203-2257 • PLA
Decina Grace H. • Media Specialist • Yonkers Public Schools • Yonkers, NY 10705 • AASL
Deckelbaum David M. • Reference Librarian • University of California-Los Angeles (UCLA) • Los Angeles, CA 90024-1450 • ACRL MAGERT
Decker Antoinette T. • Glendale, CA 91205
Decker Carol Lee • Librarian • Estell Manor School Library • Estell Manor, NJ 08319
Decker Charlotte J. • Children's Assistant • Public Library of Cincinnati and Hamilton County • Cincinnati, OH 45202 • ALSC
Decker Gary • Santa Cruz City-County Library System • Santa Cruz, CA 95060 • RASD
Decker Judy J. • Bookmobile Librarian • Quincy Public Library • Quincy, IL 62301 • ALSC
Decker Ralph W. Jr • Registrar • Southwestern Library • Winfield, KS 67156 • ACRL ALCTS *Life*
Decker Susan L. • Childrens Librarian • Sherborn Library • Sherborn, MA 01770
Decker Terri • Head of Technical Services • Ector County Library • Odessa, TX 79761 • ALCTS
Decker William H. • Sales Consultant • Brodart Company • Williamsport, PA 17705

Deckert Carol A. • Redford Township Public Library • Redford, MI 48239

Decoteau Earline M. • Library Director • Ascension Parish Library • Donaldsonville, LA 70346-2535 • PLA

Dedas Lyn W. • Assistant Director • Spokane County Library District • Spokane, WA 99212-1853 • LAMA PLA

Deddens Marcia K. • Director of Library Systems • University of Cincinnati Central Library • Cincinnati, OH 45221-0033 • LITA

Dede Bonnie A. • Librarian • University of Michigan Libraries • Ann Arbor, MI 48109-1205 • ACRL ALCTS IFRT

Dederick Donald H. • Technical Services Librarian • State University of New York • Brooklyn, NY 11203 • ACRL

Dedich Laura R. • Librarian • Southfield Public Library David Stewart Memorial Library • Southfield, MI 48037-2055 • PLA

Dedina Hana E. • Slavic Languages Cataloger • Cornell University Library • Ithaca, NY 14853 • ACRL IRRT

Dee Cheryl R. Ph. D. • Library Director • Watson Clinic Library • Lakeland, FL 33804

Deegan Rosemary L. • Hd., Ref. & Clln. Development • Albright College • Reading, PA 19612-5234 • ACRL

Deeken Jo Anne • Head of Acquisitions • Clemson University R. M. Cooper Library • Clemson, SC 29634-3001 • ACRL ALCTS LAMA

Deekle Peter V. • Director • Susquehanna University • Selinsgrove, PA 17870 • ACRL

Deemer Pamela E. • Dir of Cataloging Services • Emory University Law Library • Atlanta, GA 30322 • ALCTS

Deemer Selden S. • Library Systems Manager • Emory University Libraries Robert W. Woodruff Library • Atlanta, GA 30322-2870

Deener Darlene • Ursuline College Ralph M. Besse Library • Pepper Pike, OH 44124 • ACRL

Deeney Marian A. • Library Consultant • State Library of Florida Division of Library & Information Services • Tallahassee, FL 32399-0250

Deer Karen J. • Student • Wayne State University Library Science Program • Detroit, MI 48202

Deering Andy J. • Librarian • Riverton Branch Library • Riverton, WY 82501

Deering Carol A. • Aurora, IL 60504

Deering Carol L. • Assistant Librarian • Central Wyoming College Library • Riverton, WY 82501

Deering Ronald F. Dr. • Librarian • Southern Baptist Theological Seminary Library • Louisville, KY 40280 • ACRL ALCTS LAMA LITA RASD

Dees Leslie M. • Cataloger • DeKalb County School System • Atlanta, GA 30329 • ACRL ALCTS

Dees Margaret N. • Urbana, IL 61801 • AASL   *Life*

Dees Suzanne • Director • Superiorland Library Cooperative • Marquette, MI 49855 • ASCLA LAMA PLA

Deese Susan A. • Director, CAPS • University of New Mexico General Library • Albuquerque, NM 87131 • ACRL

Deeter Shirley • Boulder, CO 80303-3546

Deever Gladys M. • Kansas City, MO 64111 • ALSC   *Continuing*

Defassio Sharon • Library Director • Mary Meuser Memorial Library • Easton, PA 18042

Defendorf Gail • Manhattan, KS 66502-4024 • ALCTS

Deffenbaugh James T. • College of William & Mary Earl Gregg Swem Library • Williamsburg, VA 23187-8794 • ACRL ALCTS

Degatano Jeanne M. • Media Specialist • Thomas Jefferson Middle School • Edison, NJ 08817 • AASL

Degen Evelyn W. • Huntington, NY 11743

Degen Lynne G. • Manager • Harford County Library Bel Air Branch • Bel Air, MD 21014 • PLA

Degener Christie T. • Serials Librarian • University of North Carolina • Chapel Hill, NC 27599 • ALCTS

Degenhardt Barbara L. • Librarian • Lane Public Library Fairfield Branch • Fairfield, OH 45014

Degrassi-Rosenthal Deborah • Children's Librarian • Bellmore Memorial Library • Bellmore, NY 11710 • ALSC

Degutis Alan N. • Head, Catalog Services • American Antiquarian Society • Worcester, MA 01609-1634 • ACRL ALCTS LITA

Deheck M. • Library Media Specialist • Bechtel Elementary School Media Center • APO, AP 96377 • AASL ALSC YALSA   *Life*

Dehler Susan J. • Special Collections Archivist • Vigo County Public Library • Terre Haute, IN 47807

Dehn Mary B. • Assistant to the Director • Great Neck Library • Great Neck, NY 11024

Deibel Donna R. • Springfield, VA 22152 • AASL

Deich Ione • Director • Hutchinson Memorial Library • Randolph, WI 53956

Deily Carole C. • Reference Librarian • Plano Public Library System • Plano, TX 75086-0356 • RASD

Deily Robert Howard Dr. • Slingerlands, NY 12159 • ACRL ALSC   *Life*

Deisher Christine • Librarian • Lajes Elementary School • APO New York, 09406 • AASL

Deisher Elizabeth G. • Librarian • Colonial Elementary School • Blue Ridge, VA 24064 • AASL

Deisley Candace E. • Children's Librarian • Albany Public Library Pine Hills Branch • Albany, NY 12203 • ALSC PLA

Deiss Kathryn J. • Head of Interlibrary Loan • Northwestern University Library • Evanston, IL 60208-2300 • ACRL LAMA RASD

Deiters Pamela J. • Administrator • Tinley Park Public Library • Tinley Park, IL 60477 • PLA

Dekker Harold • Library Board Commissioner • Grand Rapids Public Library • Grand Rapids, MI 49503-3093

del Castillo Eduardo C. • Library Assistant • Littler Mendelson Fastiff & Tichy • San Francisco, CA 94108 • ALCTS NMRT

Del Guidice Robin • Head of Children's Services • Somerset County Library • Bridgewater, NJ 08807 • ALSC PLA IFRT

Del Negro Janice M. • Children's Services • Harold Washington Library Center Chicago Public Library • Chicago, IL 60605 • ALSC

Del Sordo Jean S. • Dorchester County Public Library • Cambridge, MD 21613 • PLA

Del Valle Heida C. • Librarian • Academia Perpetuo Socorro Library • Miramar, PR 00907

Del Vecchio Steve • The New York Public Library • New York, NY 10016 • ALSC PLA SRRT

DelCervo Diane M. • Executive Editor • Research Publications • Woodbridge, CT 06525 • ALCTS

DelGiudice Donna M. • Librarian • Woodward-Clyde Consultant Library • Wayne, NJ 07470-0290 • GODORT MAGERT

DelMar Patricia F. • Associate Director • Long Beach Public Library • Long Beach, CA 90802-4482 • PLA

Delacroix Sheila A. • Minority Fellow • American Library Association • Chicago, IL 60611-2795 • ACRL

Delahaye D. Caroline • Student • Louisiana State University School of Library & Information Science • Baton Rouge, LA 70803-3290

Delamarter Ralph L. • Director • Deschutes County Library • Bend, OR 97701 • PLA

Delana Genevieve A. • Skokie, IL 60076 • ACRL   *Continuing*

Delaney-Lehman Maureen • Lake Superior State University Library • Sault Sainte Marie, MI 49783

Delaney Anita B. • Palo Alto, CA 94301

Delaney Elizabeth J. • New York Public Library Schomburg Center for Research in Black Culture • New York, NY 10037 • ALCTS

Delaney Helen M. • Chevy Chase, MD 20815

Delaney Jeanne • Regional Adult Serv Manager • Cuyahoga County Public Library Maple Heights Regional Branch • Maple Heights, OH 44137 • LAMA PLA

Delaney Joan M. • Student • Wayne State University Library Science Program • Detroit, MI 48202 • SRRT

Delano Diane • Student • Louisiana State University School of Library & Information Science • Baton Rouge, LA 70803-3290 • LAMA

Delap Kay E. • Engineering Librarian • Teradyne Inc. • Boston, MA 02118

Delehanty Susan F. • Library Clerk • New York State Library State Education Department • Albany, NY 12230

Delfausse Abigail W. • Asst Prof & Catalog Librarian • Skidmore College • Saratoga Springs, NY 12866

Delfausse Kristine • Ft. Lauderdale, FL 33308 • ALSC

Delfino Erik C. • Network Librarian • Library of Congress • Washington, DC 20541 • LITA FLRT

Delgado Carlos R. • Student • University of California-Berkeley School of Library & Information Studies • Berkeley, CA 94720

Delgado Idalia • Boynton Beach, FL 33437-2843 • ACRL LAMA   *Life*

Delia George P. • Associate Professor • University of Minnesota Carolson School of Management • Minneapolis, MN 55455 • ACRL PLA LRRT

Delia Joseph G. • Public Services Manager • Jackson District Library • Jackson, MI 49201 • PLA VRT

Delieato Constance G. • Birmingham, MI 48009

Deligans Sylvia • Student • University of Hawaii School of Library & Information Studies • Honolulu, HI 96822 • PLA SRRT

Delivuk John A. • Automation Librarian • Geneva College McCartney Library • Beaver Falls, PA 15010 • LITA

Delke Theresa J. • Greenfield, WI 53220 • ALCTS LAMA PLA IFRT

Dell Deborah J. • Houston, TX 77065-4139

Della-Cava Olha T. • Librarian • Columbia University School of Library Service • New York, NY 10027 • ACRL LRRT

Della-Terza Mollie • Head of Technical Services • Harvard College Houghton Library-Rare Books & Manuscripts • Cambridge, MA 02138 • ACRL ALCTS LITA

Della Sala Carolyn • Plainfield Public Library • Plainfield, NJ 07060

Dellamonica Antonia • Assistant Librarian • Mineral County Public Library • Hawthorne, NV 89415

Dellamore Jack • • Gaylord Brothers • Syracuse, NY 13221 • LAMA ERT

Dellapina Carol A • Reference Librarian • Midway College Marrs Library • Midway, KY 40347 • ACRL

Dellaria Janet • Geneva, IL 60134

Deller A. Michael • City Librarian • Livonia Public Library • Livonia, MI 48154-3045 • ALSC LAMA PLA

Delli Bertrun H. • Editor of Art Index • H. W. Wilson Company • Bronx, NY 10452 • ACRL

Delmont Mary K. Ms. • Librarian • State University of New York College at Buffalo, E. H. Butler Library • Buffalo, NY 14222-1095 • ACRL RASD

Deloatch Karen L. • Public Service Librarian • Greater Hartford Community College • Hartford, CT 06105 • ACRL RASD

Delougaz Nathalie • Descriptive Cataloger Specialist • Library of Congress • Washington, DC 20541 • ALCTS

Delozier Eric P. • Pennsylvania State University College of Medicine • Hershey, PA 17033

Delp Maryellen • Librarian-Cataloger • Florida State Archives • Tallahassee, FL 32301

Delrossi Dolores • Librarian • Paulsboro High School • Paulsboro, NJ 08057

Deluca Lucy A. • Federal Document Librarian • University of Connecticut Homer Babbidge Library • Storrs, CT 06269-1005 • RASD GODORT

Delude Carolyn M. • Library Director • Westborough Public Library • Westborough, MA 01581

Delury Michael J. • Head of Reference Services • Manitowoc Public Library • Manitowoc, WI 54220 • PLA

Delzell Robert F. • Springfield, MO 65807 • ACRL   *Life*

Delzell William R. • Springfield, MA 01108 • ALCTS SRRT

Demacedo Maria L. • Biblioteca National Library • 1751 Lisbon, Portugal • ALCTS

Demaray Carolyn M. • San Diego, CA 92115

Demaree Annette L. • Johnson County Public Library White River Branch • Greenwood, IN 46142 • ALSC IFRT

Demaree Marta • Reference Librarian • Plano Public Library System L.E.R. Schimelpfenig Library • Plano, TX 75023-5108

Demaree Pauline • Director • Lorain Public Library • Lorain, OH 44052 • LAMA PLA

Demarest Robert C. • Director • Collier County Public Library • Naples, FL 33940 • LAMA PLA

Demas Samuel G. • Head Collection Development • Cornell University Albert R. Mann Library • Ithaca, NY 14853-4301 • ACRL ALCTS

Demas Tula A. • Librarian • Mount San Antonio College • Walnut, CA 91789 • ACRL

Demasco Anthony • Trustee • Massepequa Public Library • Massapequa, NY 11758 • ALTA PLA

Demchock Charlotte K. • Director • Satellite Beach Public Library • Satellite Beach, FL 32937 • PLA

Demeo Mary Ann • Librarian • Safety Harbor Public Library • Safety Harbor, FL 34695 • LAMA PLA

Demeo Mary Louise • West Hartford, CT 06119

Demeritt Annette K. • Juvenile Specialist • Houston Public Library • Houston, TX 77002 • ALSC

Demeter Marilyn P. • Cleveland Heights, OH 44118

Demetrakakes Jennifer A. • Head, Community Services • Ela Area Public Library District • Lake Zurich, IL 60047

Demeyere Dianne R. • Media Specialist • Thunderbird High School • Phoenix, AZ 85023 • AASL

Deming Joyce C. • Student • Emporia State University Emporia in the Rockies • Denver, CO 80204 • LITA PLA

Deminski Carol D. • Rahway, NJ 07065-2725 • LITA

Demlow Mary D. • Rociada, NM 87742-0844

Demme Nancy C. • Lawrenceville, NJ 08648 • PLA NMRT SRRT

Demmitt Joyce • Head Information Service • Howard County Library • Columbia, MD 21044 • PLA

Demo William J. • Ithaca, NY 14850 • ACRL

Demontigny Dorothy • Library Director • Quitman Public Library • Quitman, TX 75783

Demos Helen S. • Media Specialist • Orange Grove Elementary School • Charleston, SC 29407 • AASL

Demos John T. • Louisville, KY 40241 • Life

Dempsey Arlene C. • Library Supervisor • Dhahran Recreation Library • Dhahran, Saudi Arabia • PLA

Dempsey Laurence F. • Freeport, NY 11520

Dempsey Patricia • Branch Manager • Cuyahoga County Public Library Independence Branch • Independence, OH 44131 • PLA

Dempsey Paula R. • Oak Park, IL 60302-1427 • ACRL NMRT
Demski Kris • Northampton, MA 01060 • AASL ALSC
Demson Venetia V. • Milwaukee, WI 53207-1965
Demuth Elaine • Librarian • Great Bend Senior High School • Great Bend, KS 67530 • AASL YALSA
Denbo Jane P. • Student • California State University-Los Angeles John F. Kennedy Memorial Library • Los Angeles, CA 90032-8300 • AASL
Denboer Helen L. • Media Specialist • Montgomery County Public Schools Monocacy Elementary School • Rockville, MD 20850 • AASL
Denby Greg S. • Children's Librarian/Asst Mgr. • Columbus Metropolitan Library Karl Road Branch • Columbus, OH 43229 • ALSC PLA
Dendy Adele S. • Director of Libraries • Texas Southern University • Houston, TX 77004 • ACRL LAMA
Denecour Mary D • Sr. Administrative Librarian • Orange County Public Library El Toro Branch • El Toro, CA 92630
Denehy Carol C. • Page ACT 2614, Australia
Deng Margaret • Student • Queens College Graduate School of Library & Information Studies • Flushing, NY 11367 • LRRT SRRT
Dengle Caroline W. • Student • University of North Texas School of Library & Information Sciences • Denton, TX 76203 • ALSC EMIERT
Denham Mary Anne Hodel • Chief • State Library Resource Center • Baltimore, MD 21201-4484 • LITA
Denison Alan J. • The Boeing Company Renton Technical Library • Seattle, WA 98124 • ALCTS LITA
Denison Monica J. • Assistant Borough Coordinator • New York Public Library Branches Staten Island Borough Office • Staten Island, NY 10301 • PLA
Denk Deanna P. • Student • University of Tennessee-Knoxville Graduate School of Library & Information Science • Knoxville, TN 37996-4330 • ACRL LITA RASD IFRT
Denley-Laing Wanda L. • Librarian • Kinkaid School • Houston, TX 77024 • AASL
Denlinger Scott B. • Serials Technician • Talbot Research Library Fox Chase Cancer Center • Philadelphia, PA 19111 • ACRL
Denman-West Margaret W. • Cleveland, OH 44111 • AASL
Denman Lynn A. • Director • Sullivan BOCES School Library System • Liberty, NY 12754 • AASL
Denman Nancy L. • Student • University of Rhode Island Graduate School of Library & Information Studies • Kingston, RI 02881-0815 • AASL
Denmark Morris I. • Student • University of Pittsburgh School of Library and Information Science • Pittsburgh, PA 15260
Dennard Gladys S. • Atlanta-Fulton Public Library Dunbar Branch • Atlanta, GA 30312 • ALSC PLA RASD
Dennard Gloria J. • Director of Library Media Serv. • Jefferson County Board of Education Instructional Material Center/Foster • Bessemer, AL 35020 • AASL
Dennehy Margaret • School Librarian • St. Brigid School Library • New York, NY 10009 • ALSC IFRT
Denner Eileen • Head of Readers Services • Seton Hall University Law Library • Newark, NJ 07102 • LAMA
Denner Susan C. • Librarian I • Omaha Public Library Florence Branch • Omaha, NE 68112 • ALSC
Denney Elizabeth A. • Children's Librarian • Toledo-Lucas County Public Library Toledo Heights Branch • Toledo, OH 43609 • IFRT
Denney Lauren • La Porte, IN 46350
Denney Linda S. • El Toro, CA 92630 • LITA
Denning Catherine • Curator • Brown University Library • Providence, RI 02912 • ACRL
Denning Heather S. • Los Angeles Public Library Systems Eagle Rock Branch • Los Angeles, CA 90041
Denning Julie W. • Manager • Albuquerque Public Library Juan Tabo Branch • Albuquerque, NM 87111 • PLA
Dennis Alma P. Mrs. • Trustee • Birmingham Public Library • Birmingham, AL 35203 • ALTA
Dennis Anne Maull • Librarian • Lewes Junior High School Library • Lewes, DE 19958 • AASL LITA YALSA LIRT
Dennis Chandler • Trustee • Montclair Free Public Library • Montclair, NJ 07042
Dennis Deborah Ellis • Systems Librarian • Camden County Library Echelon Urban Center • Voorhees, NJ 08043
Dennis Debra A. • Children's Librarian • Los Angeles Public Library Mar Vista Branch • Los Angeles, CA 90066 • ACRL
Dennis Donald D. • University Librarian Emeritus • The American University Library • Washington, DC 20016-8046 • ACRL ALCTS *Life*
Dennis Everett J. • Panama City, FL 32413
Dennis Nancy • Outreach Librarian • Salem State College Library • Salem, MA 01970 • ACRL LAMA LRRT
Dennis Nancy K. • Librarian • Los Angeles Public Library • Los Angeles, CA 90071
Dennis Patricia A. • High School Librarian • Kotzebue High School • Kotzebue, AK 99752 • AASL
Dennis Robert G. • Librarian • Sumter High School Library • Sumter, SC 29154 • AASL
Dennis Scott L. • Reference/Collection Management • Marquette University Memorial Library • Milwaukee, WI 53233 • IFRT
Dennis Shirley A. • St. Louis, MO 63146 • RASD
Dennis Thomas A. • Student • University of Illinois Graduate School of Library and Information Science • Urbana, IL 61801 • RASD
Dennison Kathleen • Community Library Manager • Los Angeles County Library Leland R. Weaver Library • South Gate, CA 90208
Dennison Lynn C. • Pacific Palisades, CA 90272 • ACRL
Dennison Sharon A. • Philadelphia, PA 19126
Denniston Donna • Oklahoma Department of Libraries • Oklahoma City, OK 73105-3298
Denniston Susan W. • Adm. Lib. Children's Serv • Sunnyvale Public Library • Sunnyvale, CA 94088-3714 • ALSC PLA EMIERT
Denny Anne H. • Branch Manager • Tucson Public Library G. Freeman Woods Branch • Tucson, AZ 85719 • RASD
Denny C. A. • Branch Head • Riverside City & County Public Library Louis Robidoux Branch • Riverside, CA 92509 • PLA
Denny Emmett C. • Librarian • State Library of Florida Division of Library & Information Services • Tallahassee, FL 32399-0250
Denny Florence • Administrator,Computer & Tech • Suffolk Cooperative Library System • Bellport, NY 11713 • LITA
Denny Mary Charline • Meridian, ID 83642
Densmore Elizabeth S. • Ticonderoga, NY 12883
Denson Cynthia H. • School Librarian • Isidore Newman School Library • New Orleans, LA 70115 • AASL
Dent Nancy B. • Director of Library Development • New Mexico State University Library • Las Cruces, NM 88003-0006 • LAMA
Dentinger Patricia • Senior Librarian • Palo Alto City Library • Palo Alto, CA 94303
Dentinger Susan M. • University of Wisconsin-Madison Memorial Library • Madison, WI 53706 • LITA
Denton-Hill Kim • Sandia National Laboratories • Albuquerque, NM 87175-5800
Denton A. Wayne Dr • Director • Christian Brothers University Plough Library • Memphis, TN 38104 • ACRL
Denton Ann L. • Asst Hd, Acquisition Dept. • Memphis State University Main Library • Memphis, TN 38152 • ALCTS
Denton Laquitta B. • Arvada, CO 80004
Denue Gary N. • Director of Libraries • Southern Illinois University • Edwardsville, IL 62026 • ACRL
Denver Kathleen H. • Santa Barbara, CA 93108
Denyer Susannah • Head, Technical Services • Queen University • Kingston ON, Canada • ACRL ALCTS LITA
Depew Judith H. • Librarian • Florida State University Robert M. Strozier Library • Tallahassee, FL 32306-2047 • ACRL ALCTS LAMA RASD GODORT MAGERT
Depke Jennie • Library Media Center Director • Maple School Library Media Center • Northbrook, IL 60062 • AASL YALSA
Depp Mahnaz • Hd of Monographs/Invoicing Coor. • University of California-Santa Cruz Library • Santa Cruz, CA 95064 • ALCTS
Depp Roberta J. • Library Director • Welles-Turner Memorial Library • Glastonbury, CT 06033 • LAMA PLA
Deprisco R. P. • Pt St Lucie, FL 33485 • AASL YALSA *Life*
Deraska Norma N. • Cataloguer • Brookdale Community College • Lincroft, NJ 07738 • ALCTS
Derbyshire Ruth • Sebring, FL 33870 • ACRL ALCTS *Continuing*
Derck K. Lynn • Assistant Director • Bay County Library System • Bay City, MI 48708 • LAMA PLA IFRT SORT
Derenfeld Leslie C. • School Library Media Spec. • Martin Luther King Jr. Elementary School • Wyandanch, NY 11798
Derenzy Maureen • Director • Otsego County Library • Gaylord, MI 49735
Dering Carol • Media Chairman • J. B. Conant High School Professional Library • Hoffman Estates, IL 60194 • AASL
Derksen Charlotte R. • Earth Science Librarian • Stanford University Libraries Branner Earth Sciences Library • Stanford, CA 94305-2174 • ACRL MAGERT
Dermody Mary E. • High Bridge, NJ 08829 • ACRL
Dermont Scott V. • Librarian I • Ames Public Library • Ames, IA 50010
Derner Carol A. • Director • Lake County Public Library • Merrillville, IN 46410-5382 • LAMA PLA LIRT
Derrick Susan E. • Dept. Head, Business Sci. Doc. • Jacksonville Public Libraries Main Library • Jacksonville, FL 32202
Derrick Thomas E. • Library Media Specialist • Plaza Middle School • Kansas City, MO 64151 • AASL ALSC YALSA IFRT
Derrington Peggy D. • Library Media Specialist • Henry County High School • Paris, TN 38242 • AASL
Derryberry Marilyn Jo • Student • Kent State University School of Library & Information Science • Kent, OH 44242-0001
Dertien James L. • Librarian • Sioux Falls Public Library • Sioux Falls, SD 57102 • ALCTS LAMA LITA PLA RASD YALSA
Derum Claudia F. • Student • San Jose State University Division of Library & Information Science • San Jose, CA 95192-0029 • ACRL LITA RASD NMRT
Dery Joanne • Librarian • Montreal Museum of Fine Arts Library • Montreal PQ, H3G 1K3 Canada • ACRL ALCTS ASCLA LAMA LITA RASD
Dery Rita D. • Librarian • Steele Memorial Library • Elmira, NY 14901-2799
des Bordes Mary S. • Branch Head Librarian • New Orleans Public Library East New Orleans Regional • New Orleans, LA 70127 • PLA
Des Enfants Sherry • Youth Services Coor. • Dekalb County Public Library • Decatur, GA 30032 • ALSC PLA
DesMarais Susanna • Student • San Jose State University Division of Library & Information Science • San Jose, CA 95192-0029
DesRochers John A. • Librarian I • San Antonio Public Library • San Antonio, TX 78205 • RASD
Descaviah Diane • Ann Arbor, MI 48105-2133
Desch Carol Ann • Assistant to the Director • New York State Library Division 10C50 Cultural Education Center • Albany, NY 12230 • ASCLA LAMA PLA RASD *Life*
Deschene Dorice • Cincinnati, OH 45231-4206
Deschenes Alain • Librarian • Sobeco Group • Montreal PQ, H2Z 1Y7 Canada • LITA PLA
Deshautelles Angelle M. • Ascension Parish Library • Donaldsonville, LA 70346-2535 • PLA
Desiderio Dennis Owen • Librarian • New York Public Library Parkchester Branch Library • Bronx, NY 10462
Desilets Charlotte L. • District of Columbia Public Library Tenley Friendship Branch • Washington, DC 20016
Desimone Elaine • Library Media Specialist • Furnace Wood Elem Sch • Peekskill, NY 10566 • AASL
Desjardins Alvina • Fort Collins, CO 80522 • ACRL ALCTS *Life*
Desjarlais-Lueth Christine • Head,Collection Development • Brown University Library • Providence, RI 02912 • ACRL ALCTS RASD
Desmarais Norman • Acquisitions Librarian • Providence College Phillips Memorial Library • Providence, RI 02918 • LITA
Desmarais Robert N. • Trustee • York Public Library • Yorktown, VA 23692
Desmond Jean A. • Rocky River, OH 44116-1329
Desmond Kelly B. • Goldsboro, NC 27534-5433
Desmond Patricia E. • Hudson Public Library • Hudson, MA 01749 • PLA
Desmond Robert D. • Rehoboth Bch, DE 19971 • ALCTS *Life*
Desmuke Christine E. • Kansas State Historical Society Library • Topeka, KS 66612 • RASD GODORT NMRT
Desnoyers Martha S. • Librarian • Oyster School • Washington, DC 20008 • AASL ALSC IFRT
Despres Ted • Library Development Consultant • State Library of Ohio • Columbus, OH 43266-0334 • PLA
Dess Howard M. • Science Librarian • Rutgers University Libraries Library of Science & Medicine • Piscataway, NJ 08855-1029 • ACRL LRRT
Dessauer Phil E. • Tulsa, OK 74105 • ALTA
Dessino Jacquelyn A. • Reference Librarian • Tidewater Community College Virginia Beach Campus Library • Virginia Beach, VA 23456 • ACRL RASD
Dessouky Ibtesam • Streamwood, IL 60107
Dessy Blane K. • Acting Dir Librn Devel Staff • United States Department of Education • Washington, DC 20208 • LAMA
Detchon Evelyn B. • San Diego, CA 92103 • Continuing
Deterding Carole A. • Durango Public Library • Durango, CO 81301
Detlefsen Ann • Librarian • East High School • Des Moines, IA 50316 • AASL
Detrich Susanne K. • Chambersburg Area Middle School • Chambersburg, PA 17201 • AASL YALSA
Dettling Lisa • Student • Queens College Grad Sch of Lib & Inf Studies • Flushing, NY 11367 • SRRT
Dettmer Genevieve A. • Student • University of North Texas School of Library & Information Sciences • Denton, TX 76203

Detweiler Carolyn • Media Specialist • Saint James School • Washington, IA 52353 • AASL

Detweiler Mary Jo • Alexandria, VA 22307 • PLA

Detweiler Suzanne E. • Librarian • Hatboro-Horsham High School Library • Horsham, PA 19044 • AASL YALSA

Detwiler Bonnie M. • Section Head • Library of Congress • Washington, DC 20541 • ALCTS FLRT

Detwiler Doris J. • Detroit, MI 48204 • ACRL LAMA *Life*

Detzler Jack • Trustee • Saint Joseph County Public Library • South Bend, IN 46601 • ALTA

Deuel Marlene R. • Chief Deputy Director • Illinois State Library • Springfield, IL 62701-1796 • ASCLA LAMA PLA

Deutch Miriam B. • Access Service Librarian • Brooklyn College Library • Brooklyn, NY 11210

Deutsch James I. • Washington, DC 20037

Deutsch Melanie J. • Fiction Specialist • Cuyahoga County Public Library Parma Regional • Parma, OH 44129-3199 • PLA

Deutsch Patricia L. • Senior Librarian • Los Angeles Public Library • Los Angeles, CA 90071 • RASD

Devan Chris B. Mr • Librarian • Virginia Department of Mines, Minerals and Energy • Charlottesville, VA 22903 • LITA *Life*

Devenish-Cassell Ann W. • Member Services Librarian • NELINET Inc. • Newton, MA 02162 • RASD

Devens Lisa E. • Student • University of South Carolina College of Library & Information Science • Columbia, SC 29208

Devera Elisa • Adult/Young Adult Services Libn. • Sno-Isle Regional Library Lynnwood Branch • Lynnwood, WA 98036 • YALSA

Devereaux Barbara L. • Children's Librarian • Oak Park Public Library • Oak Park, IL 60301 • ALSC

Devereaux E. Janine • Base Librarian • U S Air Force Base Base Library • Charleston AFB, SC 29404 • AFLRT FLRT

Devereaux Margaret A. • Media/Collection Devlp. Libn. • Cayuga Community College,Bourke Memorial Library Learning Resources Center • Auburn, NY 13021

Devereaux Robert W. • Media Specialist • Clarkston Community Schools Bailey Lake Elementary School • Clarkston, MI 48016 • AASL

Devers Alice R. • District Consultant Librarian • Martin Memorial Library • York, PA 17401 • LAMA PLA

Devin Robin B. • Head Acquisitions • University of Rhode Island Library • Kingston, RI 02881-0803

Devine-Lebby Kathleen A. • Director • Girard Free Public Library • Girard, OH 44420 • PLA

Devine Judith W. • Area Librarian • Saint Paul Public Library Hayden Heights Branch • Saint Paul, MN 55106 • LAMA PLA

Devine Leah E. • Millbury, MA 01527

Devine Rosemary J. • Trustee • Sioux City Public Library • Sioux City, IA 51101-1203 • ALTA

Deviney Carol K. • Plano, TX 75074 • AASL IFRT

Devinney Gemma S. • Coor. Bibliographic Instr. • Lockwood Memorial Library • Buffalo, NY 14260 • ACRL RASD LIRT

Devita Helen • Rockville, MD 20853-1450 • ACRL PLA *Continuing*

Devitt Glenn E. • Director • Summit Public Library • Summit, NJ 07901 • LAMA LITA PLA

Devlin Barry T • Assistant Director • Ruth L. Rockwood Memorial Library • Livingston, NJ 07039

Devlin Eugene J. • Director • Berlin-Peck Memorial Library • Kensington, CT 06037 • PLA

Devlin Jean Ph.D • Southern Illinois University • Carbondale, IL 62901-6632

Devlin Mary K. • Western Region Manager • Faxon Company Inc. • Westwood, MA 02090 • ACRL ALCTS LAMA LITA

Devlin Peter J. • Head, Copy Cataloging • Northwestern University Library • Evanston, IL 60208-2300 • ACRL ALCTS LAMA

Devlin Roseyn J. • Librarian • Maryknoll School • Honolulu, HI 96822 • AASL

Devoe Jule C. • Director • Douglas Public Library • Douglas, AZ 85607 • LAMA PLA IFRT IRRT

Devoe Wilma • Literacy Coordinator • New Orleans Public Library • New Orleans, LA 70140

Devonshire Kathleen R. • Library Resource Specialist • Mercer County Community College Library • Trenton, NJ 08690 • LITA LIRT

Dew Barbara • Ottawa Library • Ottawa, KS 66067-2828 • ALSC ALTA LAMA LITA PLA RASD YALSA IFRT

Dew Stephen H. • Assistant Reference Librarian • University of North Carolina at Charlotte J. Murrey Atkins Library • Charlotte, NC 28223 • ACRL RASD

Dewald Nancy Hodge • Reference Librarian • Albright College • Reading, PA 19612-5234 • RASD

Dewdney Patricia • London ON, N6G 1H1 Canada • PLA RASD LIRT LRRT

Deweese Don B. • Adm. Asst. for Inf. Serv. • Fayetteville Pubic Schools • Fayetteville, AR 72702 • AASL

Deweese Eldonna • Editor, SBPI • Southwest Baptist University Estep Library • Bolivar, MO 65613 • ACRL

Dewey Barbara Brown • Librarian • Frank Porter Graham Elementary School • Chapel Hill, NC 27516 • AASL

Dewey Barbara Irene • Dir,Admin & Access Svcs • University of Iowa Libraries • Iowa City, IA 52242-1379 • ACRL ALCTS LAMA

Dewey Gene L. • Coordinator of Acquisitions • University of Wisconsin-Madison Memorial Library • Madison, WI 53706

Dewey Harry • Beltsville, MD 20705 • ALCTS LITA *Continuing*

Dewey Helen W. • Fairfax County Public Library Pohick Regional Branch • Burke, VA 22015 • PLA RASD

Dewey Margaret • Director • Cumberland County Library System • Carlisle, PA 17013 • ACRL ALTA PLA

Dewey Mary Lou • Carroll County Public Library • Westminster, MD 21157 • ALTA

Dewey Patrick • Director • Maywood Public Library • Maywood, IL 60153 • LITA PLA

Dewey Sallyann T. • Reference Librarian • Arlington County Department of Libraries • Arlington, VA 22201 • PLA RASD

Dewitz Margaret E. • West Bond, WI 53095 • PLA YALSA *Life*

Dewkett R. Ellen • Upper Savannah AHEC Self Memorial Hospital • Greenwood, SC 29646 • LITA

Dews Thomas M. Jr. • Kimberton Waldorf School • Kimberton, PA 19442 • AASL

Dexter Diane B. • North Scituate, RI 02857 • AASL

Dey Anita C. • Head of Reference Services • Saginaw Valley State University Melvin J. Zahnow Library • University Center, MI 48710 • RASD

Dey John L. • Kenosha, WI 53141-0397 • ACRL SRRT

Dey William L. • Director • Northeast Texas Community College Learning Resource Center • Mount Pleasant, TX 75455 • ACRL

Deyerle Kathryn • VideoTours Inc • Glastonbury, CT 06033

Deyoe Duane • Trustee • Boulder Public Library • Boulder, CO 80306

Deyoe Lois • Manhattan, KS 66502

Deyoe Nancy S. • Wichita State University Ablah Library • Wichita, KS 67208 • ACRL ALCTS *Life*

Di Felice Clara • Beaumont District Library • Beaumont, CA 92223

Di Loreto Joy • Assistant City Librarian • Bruggemeyer Memorial Library City of Monterey Park • Monterey Park, CA 91754 • PLA

Di Roma Edward • Garnerville, NY 10923 • RASD

Di Trolio Frank • Humanities Bibliographer • University of Florida Libraries • Gainesville, FL 32611-2047 • ACRL

Di Trolio Trudi M. • Assistant to the Director • University of Florida Health Science Center Library • Gainesville, FL 32610 • LAMA

DiBari Mary • Children's Librarian • Joint Free Public Library of The Chathams • Chatham, NJ 07928 • ALSC

DiBetta Crystal • School Librarian • Robert Hunter Library • Flemington, NJ 08822 • AASL

DiBiase Linda • University of Washington Suzzallo Library • Seattle, WA 98195 • ACRL ALCTS

DiBona Leslie F. • Head of Technical Services • United States Department of Education • Washington, DC 20208 • ALCTS LAMA

DiCicco Pauline E. • Librarian • Holy Cross High School Library • Flushing, NY 11358 • AASL

DiCrescenzo Bridgie B. • Stoneham, MA 02180 • LIRT

DiDonato Michele • Librarian • Bedford Hills Elementary School • Bedford Hills, NY 10507 • AASL

DiGiovanni Kathleen Leles • Reference Librarian • Oakland Public Library • Oakland, CA 94612

DiIorio Susan K. • Biglerville High School • Biglerville, PA 17307

DiJiulo Nancy L. • Walton Center School • Walton, NY 13856

DiMarino Alfred T. • Chief Librarian • Johns Hopkins Univ Bologna Ctr • Bologna 40126, Italy • ACRL

DiMartino Diane • Asst. Professor • Baruch College • New York, NY 10010 • ACRL LITA

DiMattia Ernest A. Jr. • President & Exective Director • Ferguson Library • Stamford, CT 06904 • ACRL LAMA LITA PLA ERT IFRT IRRT

DiMattia Susan S. • Stamford, CT 06903 • LAMA RASD ILERT

DiMuccio Mary-Jo Dr. • Sunnyvale, CA 94087

DiPaola Joseph F. Jr. • Garden City, NY 11530

DiPaolo Janet E. • Reference Librarian • University of Massachusetts at Boston Joseph P. Healey Library • Boston, MA 02125-3393

DiPardo Clarie H. • Lansdale, PA 19446 • ALCTS

DiPrete Carol K. • Director • Roger Williams College Library • Bristol, RI 02809-2921 • ACRL LAMA IFRT

DiRusso Richard V. • Adult Services Librarian • Green Valley Public Library • Green Valley, AZ 85614 • IRRT SRRT

DiSalvo Barbara A. • Cataloger • Cornell University Albert R. Mann Library • Ithaca, NY 14853-4301 • LITA

DiTata Joseph • Media Specialist • Greater Amsterdam School District Barkley/Bacon Elementary Schools • Amsterdam, NY 12010

DiThomas Grace • Student • State University of New York (SUNY) School of Information & Library Studies • Buffalo, NY 14260

DiTomasso Matthew • White Plains, NY 10606

Dial Carolyn E. • Librarian • Pine Island Public Library • Bokeelia, FL 33922

Dial David Emory • Berea, OH 44017-2343

Dial Marshall R. • Librarian • New Madrid County Library • Portageville, MO 63873

Dial Ron • Reference/Instruction Librarian • United States Air Force Air University Library • Maxwell AFB, AL 36112-5564 • RASD

Dialessi John L. • Student • State University of New York at Albany School of Information Science & Policy • Albany, NY 12222

Diambra Eileen F. • Eau Claire, WI 54701

Diamond Estelle L. • Buffalo, NY 14207 • SRRT

Diamond F. Anne • Statewide Library Programs • Library of Michigan • Lansing, MI 48909 • GODORT

Diamond Hilary • Coordinator • Holt Labor Library • San Francisco, CA 94102 • NMRT

Diamond Natalie M. • Librarian • Indiana Vocational Technical College • Evansville, IN 47710 • ACRL

Diamond Shela W. • School Media Librarian • Oldham County High School • Buckner, KY 40010 • AASL

Diamond Sherry • Administrative Librarian • West Allis Public Library • West Allis, WI 53214 • PLA

Diamond Timothy R. • Cleveland Public Library • Cleveland, OH 44114-1271 • IFRT

Diamond Tom • Business Reference Specialist • Louisiana State University Libraries • Baton Rouge, LA 70803 • RASD

Diamond Wendy • Reference Librarian • University of California-Berkeley Business-Social Sciences • Berkeley, CA 94720 • RASD

Diamondstein Ronni S. • Bedford Road School • Pleasantville, NY 10540 • AASL

Diana Joan P. • Head Librarian • Pennsylvania State University Wilkes Barre Campus • Lehman, PA 18627 • ACRL

Diange Victoria D. • Coor. Teacher & Media Center • Calvert County Public Schools • Prince Frederick, MD 20678 • AASL

Diaz Anna G. • Guaynabo, PR 00969 • ACRL ALCTS

Diaz Dixie A. • Mother Whiteside Memorial Library • Grants, NM 87020

Diaz Jose O. • Indiana University School of Library and Information Science • Bloomington, IN 47405

Diaz Joseph R. • Staff Develp./Recruitment Lib. • University of Arizona Library • Tucson, AZ 85721 • LAMA SRRT

Diaz Magna M. • School Librarian • Philadelphia School District Vare Middle School • Philadelpia, PA 19145

Diaz Nelson A. Hon • Trustee • Free Library of Philadelphia • Philadelphia, PA 19103 • ALTA

Diaz Theresa • Student • Drexel University College of Information Studies • Philadelphia, PA 19104-2875

Dibbern Daniel • Student • Queens College Grad Sch of Lib & Inf Studies • Flushing, NY 11367 • ACRL IFRT

Dibble Audrey • Oak Harbor, WA 98277 • ACRL

Dibble Katherine K. • Assistant Supervisor • Boston Public Library • Boston, MA 02117 • ACRL RASD

Dibert Merleen D. • Illinois State Library • Springfield, IL 62701-1796 • Life

Dibianco Phyllis R. • School Library Media Specialist • Yorktown High School • Yorktown Heights, NY 10598 • AASL

Dible Joan B. • Cataloging Associate Librarian • Stanford University • Stanford, CA 94305-6011 • ACRL ALCTS

Dicey Elizabeth S. • Student • Syracuse University School of Information Studies • Syracuse, NY 13244-4100 • AASL

Dicey Susan B. • Fork Shoals Elementary School • Pelzer, SC 29669 • AASL IFRT

Dichek Shirley • Oakland, CA 94610

Dick Jacqueline C. • Head Technical Services • Lee County Library System Processing Center • Fort Myers, FL 33912 • LITA

Dick Jeff T. • Audiovisual Librarian • Augustana College Library • Rock Island, IL 61201 • VRT

Dick Lianna R. • Student • Texas Woman's University School of Library & Information Studies • Denton, TX 76204

Dick Norma P. • Coor. of Library Media • Fresno Pacific College Hiebert Library • Fresno, CA 93702 • AASL

Dick Patricia E. • Head Librarian • Fort Stockton Public Library • Fort Stockton, TX 79735 • LAMA LITA PLA
Dick Shirley • Director • Keokuk Public Library • Keokuk, IA 52632 • ALSC LAMA PLA RASD
Dickau Norma • Associate Director • College of Saint Benedict Library • Saint Joseph, MN 56374 • ACRL
Dickens Janis L. • Head, Media Services • University of California McHenry Library • Santa Cruz, CA 95064 • LITA
Dickens Martha Hall • Moore, SC 29369
Dicker Joan • Supervising Librarian, Reference • Wayne Public Library • Wayne, NJ 07470 • PLA RASD
Dickerson Carol Lou • Director • Vanderbilt University Management Library • Nashville, TN 37203 • ACRL IFRT
Dickerson Carole • Director • Lake Oswego Public Library • Lake Oswego, OR 97034 • PLA IFRT
Dickerson D. Jean • Regional Manager • Queens Borough Public Library • Jamaica, NY 11432
Dickerson Dale A. • Cleveland Heights, OH 44121
Dickerson Eugene H. Jr. • Serials Librarian • Villanova University Falvey Memorial Library • Villanova, PA 19085-1699 • ACRL ALCTS SRRT
Dickerson Lon R. • Director • Timberland Regional Library • Olympia, WA 98501 • LAMA PLA IRRT *Life*
Dickert Paul • Trustee • San Jose Public Library • San Jose, CA 95113
Dickes Janis • Technical Service Librarian • Mount Mercy College J. Edward Lundy Library • Cedar Rapids, IA 52402
Dickey Adelle D. • Houston, TX 77036 • Continuing
Dickey David C. • Director • Taylor University Zondervan Library • Upland, IN 46989 • ACRL
Dickey Ellen E. • Student • North Carolina Central University • Durham, NC 27707 • ALSC
Dickey Jack W. • Iowa City, IA 52245
Dickey Joyce E. • Student • Emporia State University Emporia in the Rockies • Denver, CO 80204
Dickey Richard C. • University of North Texas • Denton, TX 76203 • ACRL NMRT
Dickhut Rachel S. • West DePere High School • DePere, WI 54115 • IFRT
Dickinson Ann R. • Librarian • Tucson-Pima Library • Tucson, AZ 85701 • YALSA
Dickinson Carolyn • Salt Lake City Public Library • Salt Lake City, UT 84111 • LITA PLA
Dickinson Dennis W. • College Librarian • Beloit College Libraries Colonel Robert H. Morse Library • Beloit, WI 53511 • ACRL ALCTS LAMA LITA GODORT
Dickinson Donald C. • Professor • University of Arizona Graduate Library School • Tucson, AZ 85721 • ACRL RASD LHRT SRRT
Dickinson Gail K. • Library Supervisor • Union-Endicott School District • Endicott, NY 13760 • AASL LAMA
Dickinson Janet • Garfield, AR 72732 • GODORT
Dickinson Julia B. • Reference Librarian • Hamilton College Burke Library • Clinton, NY 13323 • SRRT
Dickinson Linda • Reference Librarian • Hunter College Library • New York, NY 10021 • ACRL
Dickinson Luren E. • Director • Findlay-Hancock County Public Library • Findlay, OH 45840 • LAMA LITA PLA
Dickler Jan P. • Student • Drexel University College of Information Studies • Philadelphia, PA 19104-2875 • EMIERT IFRT SRRT
Dickman Floyd C. • Head, Library Development • State Library of Ohio • Columbus, OH 43266-0334 • ALSC ASCLA LAMA
Dickmeyer Dan E. • Santa Cruz, CA 95060-9653 • EMIERT IFRT SRRT
Dicks Mary M. • Unit Library Media Specialist • Yorkwood Community Unit #225 • Monmouth, IL 61462 • AASL
Dickson Barbara K. • Support Services Librarian • Cerritos Public Library • Cerritos, CA 90701 • LAMA PLA
Dickson Edward D. • Trustee • Euclid Public Library • Euclid, OH 44123-2091 • ALTA
Dickson Jane • Stephenville, TX 76401 • ACRL RASD
Dickson Jean E. • Curator, Polish Collection • Lockwood Memorial Library • Buffalo, NY 14260
Dickson Lance E. • Law Librarian • Stanford University Law School • Stanford, CA 94305 • ACRL ALCTS LITA RASD GODORT IFRT
Dickson Ron • Trustee • Richmond Public Library • Richmond BC, V6X 2E3 Canada
Dickson Theresa Jaye • Head Librarian • Pioneer Library System • Norman, OK 73069
Dickstein Ruth H. • Reference Librarian • University of Arizona Library • Tucson, AZ 85721 • ACRL RASD
Dicus Shawn M. • Director • Mount Carmel Public Library • Mount Carmel, IL 62863 • PLA
Didamo Martha M. • Librarian • Brownell-Talbot Preparatory School James Upper School Library • Omaha, NE 68132 • AASL
Didiano Filomena C. • Sterling, MA 01564 • LITA
Didier Elaine K. • Dir., Information Resources • University of Michigan Kresge Business Adm Library • Ann Arbor, MI 48109-1234 • ACRL LAMA
Diebold Barbara A. • Librarian • Buffalo Board of Education Follow Through School • Buffalo, NY 14072 • AASL
Diecidue Maria • Modern • St. Petersburg, FL 33709 • VRT
Diefenbach Dale Alan • Reference Librarian • Harvard Law School Library • Cambridge, MA 02138 • ACRL RASD
Diefendorf Elizabeth L. • Chief, General Research Div. • New York Public Library • New York, NY 10018-2788
Diefenthal Muzette Z. • Collection Management Librarian • Arlington Heights Memorial Library • Arlington Heights, IL 60004-5966 • RASD
Diegel Karen A. • Branch Librarian • Warren Public Library Arthur J. Miller Branch • Warren, MI 48092 • ALSC ASCLA
Diehl Carol • Director, Library Media Services • School District of New London • New London, WI 54961 • AASL LAMA YALSA
Diehl Dedra O. • Librarian • University of Iowa Library • Iowa City, IA 52242 • ASCLA
Diehl Katharine S. • Seguin, TX 78155 • ACRL *Life*
Diehl Susan J. • Chicago Ridge, IL 60415-1754
Dieman Janet S. • Cincinnati, OH 45243
Diener Margaret M. • Library Director • Justin-Siena High School • Napa, CA 94559-2243 • AASL ACRL
Dienes Jennie • Librarian I • University of Kansas Library • Lawrence, KS 66045-2800 • MAGERT
Dienes Susan K. • Adult Services Librarian • Dolton Public Library District • Dolton, IL 60419-1091
Diepen Sally • Director • Shelby Public Library • Shelby, MI 49455 • PLA
Dierauer Elizabeth D. • Bismarck, ND 58501 • IFRT SRRT
Dierauer Joyce • Director • Summit County Library • Frisco, CO 80443 • ALTA PLA
Dierbeck M. Anne • Learning Center Director • Winkelman School • Glenview, IL 60025 • ALSC
Diercks Eileen K. • Plainfield, IL 60544 • AASL
Diercks Thelma C. • Head, Monographs Department • University of Hawaii Library • Honolulu, HI 96822 • ACRL ALCTS LITA
Dierksen Deane C. • Director • Mary Riley Styles Public Library • Falls Church, VA 22046 • ALCTS ALSC LAMA LITA PLA RASD YALSA
Diesen Betty V. • Branch Library Manager • Whittier Public Library Whittwood Branch • Whittier, CA 90603
Diesenhaus Judith A. • Great Falls, VA 22066 • AASL
Diesing Laura A. • Supervisor of Branch • Cleveland Public Library • Cleveland, OH 44114-1271 • PLA
Diesing Terri C. Ms. • Trustee • Omaha Public Library • Omaha, NE 68102 • ALTA
Dieterle Ulrike • Reference Coordinator • University of Wisconsin-Platteville Elton S. Karrmann Library • Platteville, WI 53818-3099
Dietert Catherine A. • Student • University of South Florida School of Library & Information Science • Tampa, FL 33620
Dietl Sue A. • Head, Access Services • University of Notre Dame Theodore M. Hesburgh Library • Notre Dame, IN 46556 • ACRL LAMA
Dietrich Irma M. • Shawnee Mission, KS 66202 • Life
Dietrich Virginia L. • Oklahoma Department of Libraries • Oklahoma City, OK 73105-3298 • PLA RASD
Dietz Ann F. • Indexer • H. W. Wilson Company • Bronx, NY 10452
Dietz Kathryn Ann • Information Specialist • Kimberly-Clarke Corporation • Neenah, WI 54956 • ACRL ALCTS ALSC
Dietz Sharon D. • Librarian • Indian Valley Elementary School Library • Overland Park, KS 66210 • AASL
Dietze Andrea R. • Senior Library Specialist • Orange County Public Library Heritage Park Regional Library • Irvine, CA 92720
Diez Sydney B. • Decatur, GA 30033 • AASL
Diffenderfer Judy M. • Student • University of Pittsburgh School of Library and Information Science • Pittsburgh, PA 15260 • ACRL ALCTS
Digiambattista James V. • Director of Learning Resources • Hawaii Loa College • Kaneohe, HI 96744 • ACRL
Dilgarde Nikki • Reference Libn/Instructor • University of Colorado at Denver Auraria Library • Denver, CO 80204 • ACRL
Dilger Doris L. • Librarian • Southridge High School • Huntingburg, IN 47542
Dilger Jeannie A. • Student • University of North Carolina at Chapel Hill School of Information and Library Science • Chapel Hill, NC 27599-3360 • PLA YALSA
Dill Bart • Trustee • Elk Grove Village Public Library • Elk Grove Village, IL 60007 • ALTA
Dill Clara Roselle • Taylors, SC 29687
Dillahunt Shirley R. • Library Principal Assoc. • Atlanta-Fulton Public Library • Atlanta, GA 30303
Dillard Bonita Dickinson • Reference Librarian • Saint Charles City County Library K. Linneman Branch • St. Charles, MO 63301 • RASD IFRT SRRT
Dillard George L. • Coor. Circulation & Reference • Callaway County Public Library • Fulton, MO 65251
Dillard Georgia M. • Educational Services Librarian • Phoenix College Library • Phoenix, AZ 85013 • ACRL LIRT
Dillard Laura A. • Student • University of Oklahoma School of Library & Information Studies • Norman, OK 73019 • AASL
Dillard Nancy S. • Student • University of Alabama School of Library & Information Studies • Tuscaloosa, AL 35487-0252 • AASL
Dillard Thomas W. • Library Director • Charles A Cannon Memorial Library • Concord, NC 28025 • PLA
Dillard Tom W. • Trustee • Central Arkansas Library System • Little Rock, AR 72201-4698 • ALTA
Dillenschneider P. • Supervisor Librarian • Camden Free Public Library • Camden, NJ 08103 • ALCTS
Dillenseger Marie-Pierre • Cambridge, MA 02138 • LAMA
Diller Deborah • Director • Odell Public Library • Morrison, IL 61270 • PLA NMRT
Dilles Marilyn L. • Children's Librarian • Los Gatos Public Library • Los Gatos, CA 95032
Dillie Thomas W. • Student • University of Illinois Graduate School of Library and Information Science • Urbana, IL 61801 • PLA
Dillinger Mary A. • Librarian • Olivet Nazarene University Benner Library & Resource Center • Kankakee, IL 60901-0592 • RASD
Dillinger Susan D. • Library Director • New Port Richey Public Library • New Port Richey, FL 34652 • LAMA PLA
Dillner Margaret P. • Librarian • George Read Middle School • New Castle, DE 19720 • AASL IFRT
Dillon-Fast Jackie • Sierra Vista, AZ 85635 • ACRL LITA
Dillon Dennis J. • Reference Librarian • University of Texas Libraries General Libraries • Austin, TX 78713-7330 • ACRL
Dillon Douglas K. • Teacher • Lakota Freshmen School • West Chester, OH 45069
Dillon Howard • Director, Services • Columbia University Libraries • New York, NY 10027 • ACRL ALCTS LAMA LITA
Dillon Jane E. • Carrollton, TX 75006-2945 • PLA
Dillon John B. • European Humanities Bibl. • University of Wisconsin-Madison Memorial Library • Madison, WI 53706 • ACRL ALCTS *Life*
Dillon M. Laura Sr • Librarian • Immaculate Heart of Mary High School • Westchester, IL 60153
Dillon Martin J. • Director, Office of Research • Online Computer Library Center (OCLC) • Dublin, OH 43017-3395
Dillon Michele C. • Student • University of Arizona Graduate Library School • Tucson, AZ 85721
Dillon Michelle L. • Rodman Public Library • Alliance, OH 44601
Dillon Patricia M. • Information Specialist • Costabile Associates Inc • Bethesda, MD 20814
Dillon Vicki J. • System Analyst • State University of New York (SUNY) University Libraries • Albany, NY 12222 • LITA IFRT
Dillon Virginia • Wichita, KS 67220-3931 • LAMA
Dilmore Donald • Assistant to the Director of Lib • University of Lowell O'Leary Library • Lowell, MA 01854 • ACRL LAMA LRRT
Dilworth Ted A. • Hillcrest Elementary School • Odgen, UT 84404
Dimasi Elizabeth • San Pedro, CA 90732 • ASCLA PLA *Life*
Dimenstein Catherine J. • Tucson, AZ 85741
Diment Barbara J. • Library Media Specialist • Sante Fe Elementary School • Kansas City, MO 64138 • AASL
Diment Elna N. • School Librarian • Concord Elementary School • Edina, MN 55424 • ALSC
Diment Janie • Eugene, OR 97401 • AASL
Diment Mavis E. • District Librarian • Marcus Community School District • Marcus, IA 51035 • AASL ALSC YALSA
Dimick Barbara L. • Children Librarian • Madison Public Library • Madison, WI 53703 • ALSC PLA
Dimmich Kathleen • Librarian • Parkland High School • Orefield, PA 18069 • AASL
Dimmick Mary L. • Reference Librarian • University of Pittsburgh Hillman Library • Pittsburgh, PA 15260
Dimond Patricia N. • Assistant Director • Urbandale Public Library • Urbandale, IA 50322
Din Judy Sutliff • Albuquerque, NM 87112 • Life
Dinan Amy L. • Washington, DC 20003

Dinberg Donna J. • Head, Systems & Standards, UCD • National Library of Canada • Ottawa, ON, K1A 0N4 Canada • ACRL ALCTS LAMA LITA

Dindayal Joyce S. • Circulation Librarian • Fordham Law School Library • New York, NY 10023

Dineen Diane M. • Coor., Coop. Work/Study Prog. • University of Western Ontario School of Library & Information Science • London ON, N6G 1H1 Canada • LAMA PLA

Dineen Yvonne Darlene • West Valley, UT 84120

Diner Linda • Reference/Adult Services • William Jeanes Memorial Library • Lafayette Hl, PA 19444 • RASD

Dinerman Gloria • Consultant • The Library Co-op Inc. • Eolison, NJ 08820 • ALTA

Dinges Mary E. • Trustee • North Suburban District Library • Loves Park, IL 61111

Dingle Susan M. • Clarion University of Pennsylvania College of Library Science • Clarion, PA 16214 • ASCLA LAMA PLA RASD CLENE GODORT IFRT LRRT SRRT

Dingley Brenda L. • Head of Acquisitions • University of Missouri-Kansas City Library • Kansas City, MO 64110-2499 • ACRL ALCTS RASD

Dingman Stephen C. • San Antonio College Library • San Antonio, TX 78212

Dinkins Debbi • Tuscaloosa, AL 35405 • ACRL

Dinkins Michael J. • Reference Librarian • Timberland Regional Library Centralia Branch • Centralia, WA 98531

Dinkins Rebecca Elsea • Agnes Scott College • Decatur, GA 30030 • LIRT MAGERT

Dinnan Leo T. Mr • Westland, MI 48185 • LAMA PLA *Life*

Dinneen Erin G. • Morrisville High School • Morrisville, NY 13346 • AASL

Dinsmoor Margaret • Sacremento, CA 95814 • Continuing

Dinsmore Margaret V. • Trustees • Placentia Library District • Placentia, CA 92670 • ALTA

Dinsmore Roberta M. • Director • Punxsutawney Memorial Library • Punxsutawney, PA 15767

Dintrone Charles V. • San Diego State University Library • San Diego, CA 92182-0511 • ACRL RASD LIRT

Dinwoody Bryan • Director • Alma Public Library • Alma, MI 48801 • PLA

Dion Bette G • Librarian • East Providence High School Riverside Junior High • East Providence, RI 02914 • AASL

Dion Suzanne A. • Assistant News Editor • The Lowell Sun Publishing Co • Lowell, MA 01853 • LITA RASD

Dionisio Frances • Acquisitions Librarian • William Rainey Harper College Learning Resources Center • Palatine, IL 60067 • ACRL

Dionne JoAnn L. • Reference • Yale University Social Science Library • New Haven, CT 06520

Dionne Joseph R. • Director • Lawrence Public Library • Lawrence, MA 01841 • LAMA PLA EMIERT

Dionne Richard J. • Hamden, CT 06517 • ACRL LITA RASD

Directo-Narvas Constacia • Project Worker • Library Associates • Beverly Hills, CA 90210

Dirks Celia F. • Youth Services Librarian • Roseville Public Library • Roseville, CA 95678

Dirks Lee • Proj. Coordinator • Columbia University Libraries Butler Library • New York, NY 10027 • ALCTS

Dirks Martha W. • Wakeeney, KS 67672 • AASL

Dirksen Jean • Deputy Chief Librarian • Regina Public Library • Regina SK, S4P 3Z5 Canada • ACRL LAMA PLA

Dirksen Phyllis A. • Tucson, AZ 85741 • AASL

Dirtadian Helen H. • Utica, NY 13501

Disanto Joan • Board of Cooperative Educational Services • Canton, NY 13668 • AASL

Disbrow Laurel J. • Auburn, WA 98002-3569 • AASL

Disbrow Mary E. • Clinton, IA 52732 • Continuing

Disbrow Nancy J. • Assistant Professor • Southern Connecticut State University School of Library Science & Instructional Technology • New Haven, CT 06515 • ALSC

Disch Nancy J. • Student • University of Illinois Graduate School of Library and Information Science • Urbana, IL 61801

Discher Anne G. • Adult Services Department Ln • Jeffersonville Township Public Library • Jeffersonville, IN 47131-1548 • RASD

Dishnow Ruth E. • Medford, WI 54451 • AASL

Dissly Lois E. • Student • Emporia State University School of Library & Information Management • Emporia, KS 66801

Distasio William R. • Trustee • Massepequa Public Library • Massapequa, NY 11758 • ALTA PLA

Distefano Carmela • Caracas, Venezuela

Dittemore Margaret R. • Social Science Bibliographer • University of Pennsylvania Library Van Pelt-Dietrich Library Center • Philadelphia, PA 19104-6206 • ACRL IRRT

Dittgen Diane L. • Manatee County Public Library System • Bradenton, FL 34205

Dittmar Sue K. • Belleville, IL 62223-7377

Dittrich Clifford • Middle Country Public Library • Centereach, NY 11720 • ALTA

Ditzel Jan • Loveland, CO 80538-4142

Ditzler Carol J. • Head of Document Delivery Serv. • United States Department of Agriculture National Agricultural Library • Beltsville, MD 20705-2351

Divay Gabriele Dr • German Catalog & Bibliography • University of Manitoba • Winnipeg MB, Canada • ACRL

Divelbiss Mary L. • Library Media Specialist • Coolidge Elementary School • Enid, OK 73701 • AASL

Divelbiss Rosalie B. • Librarian • Saint Peter & Paul Grade School • Seneca, KS 66538

Diveley Ruth Miss • Los Angeles, CA 90041 • Continuing

Diver Bettie H. • Director • Dobbs Ferry Public Library • Dobbs Ferry, NY 10522

Divers Jacquelyn F. • Cave Spring Junior High School Library • Roanoke, VA 24018 • AASL

Dix Stephen • Mid-Michigan Library League • Cadillac, MI 49601 • LITA PLA

Dixon Angela V. • Science Reference Librarian • University of Georgia Science Library • Athens, GA 30602 • ACRL

Dixon Caitlin E. • Reference Library • Catholic University of America School of Library and Information Science • Washington, DC 20064 • ALSC PLA

Dixon Catherine A. • Assistant Director • Fort Worth Public Library • Fort Worth, TX 76102 • LAMA LITA PLA

Dixon Cheryl • Fairfield, CT 06430 • ALSC

Dixon Christopher O. • Documents Reference Librarian • Saint Josephs University Drexel Library • Philadelphia, PA 19131-1395 • GODORT

Dixon Clay G. • Student • University of Texas at Austin Graduate School of Library & Information Sciences • Austin, TX 78712-1276 • LHRT SRRT

Dixon Donnie P. • Librarian II • Atlanta-Fulton Public Library Roswell Branch • Roswell, GA 30075 • PLA

Dixon Edith M. • University of Wisconsin-Madison Memorial Library • Madison, WI 53706 • ACRL LITA

Dixon Edna S. • Student • Clark-Atlanta University School of Library & Information Studies • Atlanta, GA 30314-4391

Dixon Ellen R. • Champaign, IL 61826-6924

Dixon Henrietta L. • Cataloger • Chicago Public Library Harold Washington Library • Chicago, IL 60605 • ALCTS

Dixon Janet B. • Map Librarian • University of Arkansas Libraries • Fayetteville, AR 72701-1201 • MAGERT

Dixon Joyce K. • Young People's Library Coor • Las Vegas-Clark County Library District Las Vegas Library • Las Vegas, NV 89101 • ALSC YALSA

Dixon Lana S. • Reference Librarian • University of Tennessee Library • Knoxville, TN 37996-1000

Dixon Lynn M. • Young Adults Librarian • Harvey Public Library • Harvey, IL 60426

Dixon Pat M. • Student • University of Michigan School of Information and Library Studies • Ann Arbor, MI 48109-1092 • IRRT SRRT

Dixon Phyllis • Trustee • Rapid City Public Library • Rapid City, SD 57701-3630

Dixon Rebecca D. • University of Saint Thomas O'Shaughnessy-Frey Library • Saint Paul, MN 55105 • ACRL LAMA LITA

Dixon Susan G. • Librarian • Museum of Natural History • Santa Barbara, CA 93105 • ACRL ALCTS MAGERT SRRT

Dixon Theresa E. • Reference/Adult Programming • Minot Public Library • Minot, ND 58701

Dixon Timothy A. • Director • University of Georgia SBDC Connection • Athens, GA 30602 • RASD

Dixon Trudi A. • Student • Ohio Dominican College • Columbus, OH 43219 • SRRT

Dixson Maria A. • Director • George F. Johnson Memorial Library • Endicott, NY 13760 • PLA

Djevalikian Sonia • Saint Laurent PQ, H4L 2H2 Canada

Djorup Kristin N. • Sales Associate • Cooleys Marco Polo, Inc. • Wellesley, MA 02181 • IFRT

Doak Elaine M. • Oklahoma City, OK 73118-1914 • ACRL

Doak Genevieve • Branch Librarian • Glenwood Springs Branch Library • Glenwood Springs, CO 81601

Doak Mary M. • Lincoln, NE 68522 • ACRL

Doak Wesley • Sacramento, CA 95826-5143 • LITA IFRT *Life*

Doane Grayce S. • Oklahoma City, OK 73134 • AASL

Doares Juanita S. • New York, NY 10027 • ACRL ALCTS RASD SRRT

Dobb Linda Sue • Asst. University Librarian • San Francisco State University J. Paul Leonard Library • San Francisco, CA 94132 • ACRL LAMA LITA LRRT

Dobberstein Paul M. Rev. • Elmhurst, IL 60126 • PLA RASD GODORT

Dobberteen Sara J. • Minneapolis Public Library & Information Center • Minneapolis, MN 55401-1992

Dobbins Denise L. • Educational Media Specialist • Cleveland Elementary School • Englewood, NJ 07631

Dobbins Elsie T. • Caldwell, NJ 07006 • ALSC PLA *Continuing*

Dobbins Freda J. • Director • Pottawatomie-Wabaunsee Regional Library • Saint Marys, KS 66536 • LAMA PLA

Dobbs Ann R. • Branch Supervisor • Adams County Public Library Northglenn Branch • Northglenn, CO 80234

Dobbs Arta M. • Collection Mgr Librarian • University of Connecticut Health Center Lyman Maynard Stowe Library • Farmington, CT 06032 • ACRL ALCTS ASCLA

Dobbs Carolyn Ms • Trustee • Timberland Regional Library • Olympia, WA 98501 • ALTA

Dobbs Kimberly W. • Chief Serial Record Division • Library of Congress • Washington, DC 20541 • ALCTS

Dobbs Marjo • Reference • Louisiana State University Libraries Troy H. Middleton Library • Baton Rouge, LA 70803-3342 • ACRL RASD SRRT

Dobbs Robert J. Jr • Director • Cayuga-Onondaga Board of Cooperative Educational Services • Auburn, NY 13021 • AASL ALSC ASCLA

Dobi Hanko H. • University Librarian • University of New Haven Marvin K Peterson Library • West Haven, CT 06516 • ACRL LAMA LITA RASD

Dobkins Debra • Lake Lanier Regional Library Peachtree Corners Branch • Norcross, GA 30092

Dobkowski William • Kennedy Memorial Hospitals University Medical Center Barsky Memorial Library • Turnersville, NJ 08012 • SRRT

Dobrot Nancy L. • San Antonio, TX 78230 • AASL ALSC

Dobrozsi Jean • Assistant Director • Middletown Public Library • Middletown, OH 45044 • LAMA

Dobrunz Sally J. • Elementary Libraian • Bristol/Steger Elementary Schools • Saint Louis, MO 63119 • AASL ALSC *Life*

Dobrusky Karen • Reference Librarian • Barnard College Library • New York, NY 10027

Dobrzynski Terenita Sr • Director of Library • Villa Maria College Library • Buffalo, NY 14225 • ACRL

Dobson Cynthia • Head, Clln Develp Dept • Iowa State University Library • Ames, IA 50011-2140 • ALCTS

Dobson Joan L. • Assistant Manager, Special Clln • Dallas Public Library • Dallas, TX 75201 • PLA NMRT

Dobson Mary • Librarian • Raymore-Peculiar High School • Peculiar, MO 64078 • AASL

Dobucki Margaret E. • Student • Kent State University School of Library Science/Columbus Program • Columbus, OH 43210 • ALSC

Dobush Debbie B. • Librarian • Ravena Elementary School • Ravena, NY 12143 • AASL

Doby Lillian M. • Trustee • Montgomery County Department of Public Libraries • Rockville, MD 20850 • ALTA PLA IFRT

Dobyns Wynne M • San Jose Public Library • San Jose, CA 95113

Docheff Carol L. • Lafayette, CA 94549 • ALSC

Docken Lorie J. • OCLC Coordinator • University of Wisconsin-Madison Memorial Library • Madison, WI 53706 • ACRL

Dockens Elaine B. • Law Librarian • West on Hurd Library • Cleveland, OH 44113 • LITA

Dockswell Carol • Ref/Instr Servs Ln • Lynn University • Boca Raton, FL 33431

Dockter Irene • Trustee • North Dakota State Library • Bismarck, ND 58505

Dockter Sally • Reference Librarian • University of North Dakota Chester Fritz Library • Grand Forks, ND 58202-0175

Doctor David L. • Reference Librarian • Edmonds Community College Library • Lynnwood, WA 98036 • ACRL

Doctor Patrice F. • Lompoc, CA 93436

Doctor Ronald D. Dr. • Associate Professor • University of Alabama School of Library & Information Studies • Tuscaloosa, AL 35487-0252 • LITA PLA RASD

Dodd David G. • Public Services Librarian • Benicia Public Library • Benicia, CA 94510 • PLA RASD NMRT

Dodd Dorothy • Tallahassee, FL 32301 • Continuing

Dodd James A. Mr. • Director, Emeritus • Adrian College Shipman Library • Adrian, MI 49221 • ACRL LAMA *Life*

Dodd Jane A. • Business Reference Librarian • Texas A & M University Sterling C. Evans Library • College Station, TX 77843-5000 • RASD

Dodd Janet B. • Georgia Institute of Technology • Atlanta, GA 30332

Dodd Janice • Portland, OR 97214

Dodd Jeffrey • Iowa City, IA 52246 • ACRL

Dodd Patricia J. • Personnel/Labor Relations Mgr. • Brown University Library • Providence, RI 02912

Dodd Robin S. • Adult Reference Librarian • Toledo-Lucas County Public Library Maumee Branch • Maumee, OH 43537

Dodds Joanne L. • Assistant Director • Pueblo Library District McClelland Library • Pueblo, CO 81004-1997 • PLA

Dodendorf Mary S. • McMinnville, OR 97128 • Continuing

Dodge Christopher • Hennepin County Library • Minnetonka, MN 55343 • SRRT

Dodge Lynn • City Librarian • Lynchburg Public Library • Lynchburg, VA 24501 • ALSC PLA RASD

Dodge Stephanie • Program Officer • American Library Association • Chicago, IL 60611-2795 • ALSC

Dodson Charlotte • Trustee • Metropolitan Library System • Oklahoma City, OK 73102 • ALTA PLA

Dodson Howard • Assoc. Director/Chief • New York Public Library Center for Research in Black Culture • New York, NY 10037 • ACRL

Dodson James T. Mr • Director • University of Texas Southwestern Medical Center at Dallas Library • Dallas, TX 75235-9049 • ACRL LITA *Life*

Dodson Mary A. • Greensburg, PA 15601 • ALCTS

Dodson Snowdy D. • Chair, Technical Services Dept. • California State University-Northridge • Northridge, CA 91328-1292 • ACRL

Dodson Suzanne C. • Facilities & Preservation Mgr • University of British Columbia Library • Vancouver BC, V6T 1Z1 Canada • ACRL ALCTS

Dodt Lorna Andrle • Annandale, VA 22003 • RASD AFLRT FLRT

Dodwell Catherine M. • Ramsey, NJ 07446-0081

Doebbeling Mary • Coordinator • Southwest Regional Library • Fort Worth, TX 76109 • PLA

Doebler Chris A. • Trustee • Warren Public Library • Warren, MI 48092

Doel Julie M.B. • Student • State University of New York School of Information & Library Sci • Albany, NY 12203 • ACRL RASD IFRT NMRT SRRT

Doelling Donna L. • Tampa, FL 33624

Doennig David R. • Aministrative Librarian • Barry-Lawrence Regional Library • Monett, MO 65708

Doepker Bonita W. • Wright State University • Dayton, OH 45435 • ALCTS

Doerge Janet M. • Student • University of Pittsburgh School of Library and Information Science • Pittsburgh, PA 15260

Doering Elizabeth Amity • Library Supervisior I • Free Library of Philadelphia Education,Philosophy & Religion • Philadelphia, PA 19103 • LAMA

Doering William T. • Head of Technical Services • Luther College • Decorah, IA 52101 • ACRL LITA

Doerksen J. Ray • Associate Director • Grand Rapids Baptist College & Seminary Library • Grand Rapids, MI 49505 • ACRL LAMA CLENE

Doerner Sarah M. • Du Quoin, IL 62832

Doerning Madeleine • System Advisory Brd. Mem. Altr. • Alhambra Public Library • Alhambra, CA 91801

Doerr Thomas G. • Librarian • Denver Public Library • Denver, CO 80203-2165 • LITA

Doerrer David • Library Automation Coor. • University of West Florida John C. Pace Library • Pensacola, FL 32514 • ACRL LITA

Doerschuk Ernest Jr. • Leicester, NC 28748 • Continuing

Doescher Starla G. • Head, Acquisitions Dept. • University of Oklahoma Libraries University Libraries • Norman, OK 73019 • ACRL ALCTS

Doezema Linda A. • Coordinator Public Services • Houghton College Willard J Houghton Library • Houghton, NY 14744 • ACRL RASD

Doffek Pamala J. • Shalimar, FL 32579 • PLA

Doggett Marguerite • Kew Gardens, NY 11415 • Continuing

Doggett Rachel H. • Andrew Mellon Curator of Books • Folger Shakespeare Library • Washington, DC 20003-1094 • ACRL

Dohany Rose S. • Chelsea, MI 48118-9738 • YALSA

Doherty Brian J. • Harid Conservatory • Boca Raton, FL 33431

Doherty Dorothy J. • Reference Librarian • Wood County Dist Public Library • Bowling Green, OH 43402

Doherty Edmond J. • Reading, PA 19604 • Continuing

Doherty Joan A. • Chief Inf & Ref Division • Library of Congress • Washington, DC 20541

Doherty Mary A. • Library Director • Winn Parish Library • Winnfield, LA 71483 • PLA NMRT

Doherty Rebecca A. • Programmer/Analyst • University of California-Berkeley University Library • Berkeley, CA 94720 • ALCTS LITA

Doherty Teresa J. • Rockville, MD 20852-4616 • AASL YALSA *Life*

Dohner Jan • Dexter, MI 48130 • ASCLA

Dohring-Whitehead Martha E. • Middleport, NY 14105

Doi Makiko • Prof. of Librarianship • Central Washington University • Ellensburg, WA 98926 • ACRL ALCTS

Dokken Mimi S. • Adult Services Librarian • Vail Public Library • Vail, CO 81657

Dokorno Neil J. Student • Wallingford, CT 06492

Doksansky Florence Kell • Asst Univ Ln/P Serv & Clln Devel • Brown University Library • Providence, RI 02912 • ACRL ALCTS RASD *Life*

Doku Ishmael A.M. • Toronto ON, M6H 3A6 Canada

Dolak F J. Dr. • Head of Educational Resources PS • Ball State University Bracken Library • Muncie, IN 47306-0160 • ACRL

Dolan Anne Marie • Director • West Babylon Public Library • West Babylon, NY 11704 • PLA

Dolan Catherine E. • Student • Vail Public Library • Vail, CO 81657 • LITA PLA

Dolan Deirdre • W W Norton Company • New York, NY 10036

Dolan Elizabeth R. • Thomas Giordano Junior High School • Bronx, NY 10458 • YALSA

Dolan J. Joel Br. • Romeoville, IL 60441 • RASD *Continuing*

Dolan Kathleen A. • Kensington, MD 20895-1421 • LITA

Dolan Mary K. • Tomales, CA 94971

Dolan Patricia A. • Illinois Institute of Technology Paul V. Galvin Library • Chicago, IL 60616

Dolan Philip H. Mr • Seminole, FL 33542 • LAMA PLA *Continuing*

Dolan Robert T. • Director • College of Eastern Utah Library • Price, UT 84501 • ACRL ALCTS LAMA

Dolan Susan • Head of Children's Services • Webster Groves Public Library • Webster Grvs, MO 63119 • PLA

Dole Wanda V. • Asst. Dir. Clln Devel & Mgt • State University of New York (SUNY) Frank Melville Jr. Memorial Library • Stony Brook, NY 11794-3300 • ACRL ALCTS LAMA

Dolence Linda Eloise • Virginia Beach Public Library Central Library • Virginia Beach, VA 23452

Dolgin Jeanne R. • Ardsley, NY 10502

Dolin Jacqueline G. • Library Director • Harold D. Cooley Library • Nashville, NC 27856 • PLA

Doll Carol A. • Seattle, WA 98125 • AASL ALSC

Doll Dorothy L. • Student • University of Maryland College of Library and Information Services • College Park, MD 20742-4345

Dollard Peter A. • Library Director • Alma College • Alma, MI 48801 • ACRL ALCTS LITA RASD YALSA LIRT

Dollen Charles Rev Msgr • Poway, CA 92074-0867 • Continuing

Dollerschell Allen L. • Library Coordinator • Rochester Community College Goddard Library • Rochester, MN 55904 • ACRL

Dollisch Patricia A. • Student • University of Pittsburgh School of Library and Information Science • Pittsburgh, PA 15260

Dolmetsch Ellen L. • Student • Drexel University College of Information Studies • Philadelphia, PA 19104-2875

Dolnick Sandy F. • Executive Director • Friends of Libraries USA (FOLUSA) • Philadelphia, PA 19107

Dolven Mary • Director • Diablo Valley College Library • Pleasant Hill, CA 94523 • ACRL LITA

Domas Ralph E. • Online Search Service Coord. • San Antonio College Library • San Antonio, TX 78212 • ACRL LIRT

Domashevsky Vasyl • Chicago, IL 60639

Dombek Peg A. • Student • University of Washington Graduate School of Library and Information Science • Seattle, WA 98195

Dombourian Moore Ann • Base Librarian • United States Air Force McConnell Air Force Base • McConnell AFB, KS 67221 • ACRL LAMA AFLRT FLRT LIRT

Dombourian Sona J. • Assistant Director • Lafayette Parish Public Library • Lafayette, LA 70502-3427 • LITA PLA RASD

Dombroski Ellen M. Mrs. • Librarian • Paul VI High School • Fairfax, VA 22030

Dombrowski Janet E. • Student • University of Maryland College of Library and Information Services • College Park, MD 20742-4345 • ACRL NMRT SRRT

Dombrowski John H. • Goverment Documents Specialist • Wake Forest University Z Smith Reynolds Library • Winston Salem, NC 27109-7777 • ACRL GODORT

Dombrowski Mark A. • Librarian • Siena Heights College Library • Adrian, MI 49221 • ACRL SRRT

Dombrowsky Robin D. • Reference Librarian • Leesburg Public Library • Leesburg, FL 34748 • RASD

Domineske Alice M. • Librarian • Shawnee High School • Medford, NJ 08055 • AASL

Domingo Elsie G. • Librarian • Dover Junior High School • Dover, NH 03820 • AASL

Domingues Josephine B. • Springfield, VA 22152 • AASL SRRT

Domingues Larry • Branch Supervisor • Jefferson County Public Library Standley Lake Library • Arvada, CO 80005

Dominguez Patricia B. • The University of North Carolina Collection Development Department • Chapel Hill, NC 27599-3918 • ACRL ALCTS

Dominguez Rick R. • Librarian • Von Steuben High School • Chicago, IL 60625

Domney James M. • Librarian • Kaiser Permanente ISD Library • Pasadena, CA 91188

Domogauer Renee E. • Library Media Specialist • Anne Arundel County Public Schools Broadneck Senior High School • Annapolis, MD 21401 • AASL

Domowne Sylvia • Library Media Teacher • Berner Junior High School • Massapequa, NY 11758 • AASL

Doms Carol A. • Overland Park, KS 66204

Doms Keith • Executive Director • Urban Libraries Council • State College, PA 16801 • PLA IRRT

Donahoe Dorothy A. • Denver, CO 80220-3138 • ALCTS RASD *Continuing*

Donahoo Nancy S. • Director • Bedford Public Library • Bedford, VA 24523 • LAMA PLA

Donahue Katharine E.S. • University of California-Los Angeles Biomedical Library • Los Angeles, CA 90024-1798 • ACRL

Donahue Lora J. • Student • University of Illinois Graduate School of Library and Information Science • Urbana, IL 61801 • ALSC IFRT SRRT

Donahue Martha • Mansfield University Library • Mansfield, PA 16933 • ACRL

Donahue Sandra R. • Asst Ln/Hd of Tech Servs • Elmhurst College A. C. Buehler Library • Elmhurst, IL 60126 • ACRL ALCTS LITA

Donahue Therese M. • Library Media Specialist • John Jay Junior High School • Katonah, NY 10536 • AASL

Donahugh Robert H. • Youngstown, OH 44511 • ACRL RASD *Life*

Donald Elizabeth R. • Public Services Librarian • Brooks County Public Library • Quitman, GA 31643 • NMRT

Donaldson Anna Lea • Music/Reference Librarian • Hardin-Simmons University Richardson Library • Abilene, TX 79698

Donaldson Linda K. • Portsmouth Public Library • Portsmouth, OH 45662

Donaldson Marion F. • Library Director • Lawton Public Library • Lawton, OK 73501 • LAMA PLA

Donaldson Timothy P. • Access Services Manager • Jackson District Library • Jackson, MI 49201 • IFRT

Donato Amy T. • Youth Services • Bartlett Public Library District • Bartlett, IL 60103 • ALSC

Donavin Denise Perry • American Library Association • Chicago, IL 60611-2795 • ALSC

Dondero Ann M. • Youth Services Librarian • Forest Grove City Library • Forest Grove, OR 97116

Donegan Nora T. • Bronx, NY 10463 • ACRL RASD

Donegan Patricia Morris • Public Services Librarian • San Antonio College Library • San Antonio, TX 78212 • ACRL LIRT

Donegan Robert W. • Sales Manager • Kluwer Academic Publishers • Norwell, MA 02061

Donehoo Betsy E. • Sewickley, PA 15143

Donel John R. • Oregon State University William Jasper Kerr Library • Corvallis, OR 97331-4501 • ACRL

Donelan Carol • Supervisor • Saint Louis County Library • St. Louis, MO 63131

Donham Diane E. • University of California • Santa Cruz, CA 95064

Donham van Deusen Jean • District Library Media Coor. • Iowa City Community Schools • Iowa City, IA 52240 • AASL

Donica Wayne J. • Director • University of Science & Arts of Oklahoma • Chickasha, OK 73018 • ACRL

Donick Caroline H. • Easton Public Library • Easton, CT 06612 • PLA

Doniger Sheri B. • Trustee • Lincolnwood Public Library District • Lincolnwood, IL 60646

Donitz Hillary J. • New York City, NY 10010 • ALSC

Donley Barbara A. • Student • State University of New York at Albany School of Information Science & Policy • Albany, NY 12222

Donley Dennis L. • Librarian • Hurbert Hoover High School • San Diego, CA 92115

Donley Mary A. • Assistant Librarian • George Memorial Library • Richmond, TX 77469 • RASD EMIERT SRRT VRT

Donley Mary R. • Menomonie, WI 54751 • Continuing

Donne Mary C. • New Brunswick, NJ 08901

Donnell Leslie A. • Reference/Cataloging Libn • Harvard University JF Kennedy School of Government Library • Cambridge, MA 02138

Donnellan Margaret • City Librarian • Whittier Public Library • Whittier, CA 90602 • PLA

Donnelly Anna M. • Ref Librarian/Associate Prof. • Saint John's University Library • Jamaica, NY 11439 • ACRL LAMA RASD

Donnelly Arthur R. • Associate Director • University of Florida College of Law • Gainesville, FL 32611

Donnelly Caren • Coordinator Library Media • Hauppauge High School • Hauppauge, NY 11788 • AASL

Donnelly Christine S. • Student • University of South Florida School of Library & Information Science • Tampa, FL 33620 • RASD IFRT SRRT

Donnelly Eileen D. • Associate Information Spec. • Kraft General Foods • Tarrytown, NY 10591

Donnelly Kathleen • Librarian Director • Benesch, Friedlander et al • Cleveland, OH 44114 • LAMA

Donnelly Leslie • Richard L. Rice Elementary School • Marlton, NJ 08053

Donnelly Margaret L. • Student • San Jose State University Division of Library & Information Science • San Jose, CA 95192-0029

Donnelly Marie C. • Hawthorne, NY 10532

Donnelly Mary E. • Flushing, NY 11354

Donnelly Sandra J. • Downers Grove, IL 60515 • AASL ACRL LITA PLA ERT

Donnelly Sheila J. • Tucson, AZ 85712

Donner Rachel S. • Forest Hills, NY 11375

Donofrio Nancy E. • Birmingham, MI 48010

Donoghue Ann L. • Trustee • Acorn Public Library District • Oak Forest, IL 60452 • ALTA

Donoghue Elaine J. • Student • University of Rhode Island Graduate School of Library & Information Studies • Kingston, RI 02881-0815 • AASL ALSC

Donoghue Rosemary • Morris County Free Library • Whippany, NJ 07981 • RASD

Donohoe Laura E. • Indexer • H.W. Wilson Company • Bronx, NY 10452 • ALCTS

Donohoe Laurence • San Francisco, CA 94107-2610 • LITA NMRT

Donohoo Christine S. • Cuyahoga Fls, OH 44221

Donohue Joseph C. • Librarian • Foreign Service Institute • Arlington, VA 22209 • ACRL FLRT

Donohue Lee • Acton Memorial Library • Acton, MA 01720 • YALSA

Donohue Nancy W. • Library/Media Supervisor • Cherokee High School • Marlton, NJ 08053 • AASL

Donohue Patricia • Librarian • Metropolitan Learning Center • Portland, OR 97209

Donor Mary E. • Library Director • Jericho Public Library • Jericho, NY 11753 • PLA IFRT

Donovan David G. • Trustee • York Public Library • Yorktown, VA 23692

Donovan Donna M. • Marketing Consultant • Digital Equipment Corporation • Marlboro, MA 01752

Donovan Jerry J. • Reference Librarian • Federal Reserve Bank of Atlanta Research Library • Atlanta, GA 30301-1731 • ACRL

Donovan Joanne • Document Librarian • University of California-San Diego Central University Library • La Jolla, CA 92093-0175 • GODORT

Donovan Judy K. • Library Media Specialist • Oakridge High School • Muskegon, MI 49441 • AASL

Donovan Kathleen • Harvard University Gutman Library-Research Center • Cambridge, MA 02138

Donovan Mary E. • Indian Trail Learning Center • Highland Pk, IL 60035 • AASL

Donovan Maureen H. • Janpanese Studies Librarian • Ohio State University Libraries • Columbus, OH 43210-1286 • ACRL ALCTS LITA IRRT

Donovan Paul T. • Network Consultants • Digital Equipment Corporation • Tallahassee, FL 32308 • ACRL PLA RASD *Life*

Donovan Ruth H. • Reno, NV 89507

Donovan Sandra J. • Library Director • Laramie County Community College • Cheyenne, WY 82007 • ACRL LAMA

Donovan Susan M. • Milford, CT 06460

Donovan William A. • Chicago Public Library Harold Washington Library • Chicago, IL 60605

Dooe Frederick C. • Coordinator Technical Services • Belmont Public Library • Belmont, MA 02178

Dooley Catherine T. • Student • University of Rhode Island Graduate School of Library & Information Studies • Kingston, RI 02881-0815 • PLA IFRT

Dooley Jackie M. • Head of Collections Cataloging • Getty Center for the History of Art Humanities Library • Santa Monica, CA 90401-1455 • ACRL ALCTS

Dooley James J. • Student • Brigham Young University School of Library & Information Sciences • Provo, UT 84602 • ACRL RASD

Dooley John F. • Director • Seminole Community College Library • Sanford, FL 32773 • ASCLA GODORT

Dooley Leila A. • Carlsbad City Library • Carlsbad, CA 92008

Dooley Ruth W. • West Palm Beach, FL 33405

Dooley Sally Jo • Librarian • Esperero Canyon Middle School • Tucson, AZ 85718 • AASL

Dooley Sheila M. • Director • The Dalles City Wasco County Library • The Dalles, OR 97058

Doolittle Beth Deanne • Catalog Librarian • Montgomery County Library System • Conroe, TX 77301

Doolittle Elizabeth M. • Head of Public Services • Nicholls State University Allen J. Ellender Memorial Library • Thibodaux, LA 70310 • ACRL CLENE LIRT

Dooner Phyllis • Trustee • Pueblo Library District McClelland Library • Pueblo, CO 81004-1997 • PLA

Dooner Robert E. • University Hts., OH 44118 • PLA

Dooney Marcella G. • Cooper City, FL 33026 • AASL ACRL CLENE

Doorenbos Judith K. • Hd Bibl Search • University of Iowa Libraries • Iowa City, IA 52242-1379 • ALCTS

Dopp Bonnie Jo • Chief Biography Division • District of Columbia Public Library Martin Luther King Memorial Library • Washington, DC 20001 • RASD SRRT

Dopp Elizabeth A. • Coordinator Collections Mgmt • Rochester Institute of Technology Wallace Memorial Library • Rochester, NY 14623-0887 • IFRT SRRT

Doppke James A. • President • Glenview Public Library • Glenview, IL 60025

Doran Brenda O. • Library Director • Richland Parish Library • Rayville, LA 71269 • LAMA PLA RASD

Doran E. Marie • Librarian II, CLSI Coordinator • Peninsula Public Library • Lawrence, NY 11559 • PLA

Doran Kirk P. • Librarian • Dickinson College Library Boyd Lee Spahr Library • Carlisle, PA 17013

Doran Mary E. • University City, MO 63130

Doran Michael • University of Texas at Arlington • Arlington, TX 76019-0497 • ACRL

Doran Myrna • Media Generalist • Osseo Schools Maple Grove Junior High • Maple Grove, MN 55369 • AASL

Dore Eleanor G.F. • Asst. Cluster Chief • District of Columbia Public Library Martin Luther King Memorial Library • Washington, DC 20001

Doremus Douglas R. • Regional Sales Manager • Dun & Bradstreet • Parsippany, NJ 07054 • ACRL RASD

Dorer Suzann M. • Greenvale, NY 11548-1001 • LITA PLA RASD YALSA IFRT SRRT

Dorey Marcia A. • Northwest Missouri State University Owens Library • Maryville, MO 64468

Dorey Roberta J. • Periodicals Librarian • Deerfield Academy • Deerfield, MA 01342 • ACRL

Dorf William H. • Librarian • Cheyney University Leslie P. Hill Library • Cheyney, PA 19319 • ACRL

Dorfler Melayn • Daytona Beach, FL 32119-1575 • ACRL RASD GODORT

Dorfman Andrew • Regis University Dayton Memorial Library • Denver, CO 80221-1099 • ACRL

Dorgan Charity Anne • Gale Research, Inc. • Detroit, MI 48226 • RASD

Dorio Terrie N. • Children's Librarian I • Santa Monica Public Library Montana Avenue Branch • Santa Monica, CA 90403 • ALSC

Dority G. Kim • Englewood, CO 80112 • ACRL

Dorkey Virginia D. • Deputy Director • Prince William Public Library System Administrative Support Center • Prince William, VA 22192-5073

Dorman David • Hershey, PA 17033 • AASL YALSA *Life*

Dorman David C. • Head, Automated Services • Upper Hudson Library System • Albany, NY 12206 • LITA

Dormer Larry • Englewood, NJ 07631

Dormire Kornelia M. • Reference/Adult Servs. Librarian • Upper Saddle River Public Library • Upper Saddle River, NJ 07458-1699 • RASD

Dorn Suzanne M. • Library Director • Onondaga Free Library • Syracuse, NY 13215 • PLA IFRT

Dornberger Julie L. • Hd. of Children's Library • High Point Public Library • High Point, NC 27261 • ALSC PLA

Dornbush Kenneth J. • Fanwood, NJ 07023

Dorney Kristi D. • Media Specialist • Rosenwald Middle School • Panama City, FL 32401 • AASL

Dornfeld Ernst G. • King County Archives Records & Elections Division • Seattle, WA 98104 • GODORT

Dornfest Walter T. • Associate Professor • College of Staten Island Saint George Campus Library • Staten Island, NY 10301 • LAMA

Doro Edward Mr • Head Librarian • Monterey Inst of Intl Studies • Monterey, CA 93940 • ACRL LAMA *Life*

Dorothy Grace Sister • Saint Maria Goretti High School Library • Philadelphia, PA 19148

Dorr Cecile H. • Media Specialist • Laurel Bay School 2 • Laurel Bay, SC 29902 • AASL ALSC LIRT

Dorr Lilith J. • East Elementary School • Ankeny, IA 50021 • AASL

Dorr Ralze W. • University Librarian (Acting) • University of Louisville Libraries • Louisville, KY 40292 • ACRL LAMA

Dorr Robert W. • Library Assistant II/Cataloging • University of New Hampshire Library • Durham, NH 03824 • ACRL NMRT SORT

Dorrell Larry D. • Associate Professor • Central Missouri State University • Warrensburg, MO 64093 • AASL

Dorrian James J. • Mechanicsburg, PA 17055

Dorsett Helen M. • Librarian • Miami-Dade Public Library System North Dade Regional • Miami, FL 33056 • ALSC LAMA PLA

Dorsett Melissa H. • San Juan, PR 00906 • AASL

Dorsey-Jones Margaret F. • Regional Branch Librarian • District of Columbia Public Library Georgetown Regional Branch • Washington, DC 20007 • PLA

Dorsey Carol G. • Special Librarian • Industrial Testing Laboratories • New York, NY 10010

Dorsey Honnor • Head Librarian • Shepherdstown Public Library • Shepherdstown, WV 25443

Dorsey Leigh Ann • Asst. Circulation Librarian • University of Illinois at Chicago University Library • Chicago, IL 60680 • NMRT

Dorsey Mildred M. • Altadena, CA 91001-3306 • ALSC *Continuing*

Dorsey Richard H. • Oshkosh, WI 54901

Dorsey Sarah B. • Music Librarian • State University of New York College Daniel A. Reed Library • Fredonia, NY 14063

Dorsey Sheila • Assistant Director • Charleston County Library West Ashley Branch • Charleston, SC 29407

Dorsey Theresa M. • Clinton, MA 01510

Dorson Beverly A. • Media Specialist • Parma City Schools • Parma, OH 44129

Dorst Thomas J. • Illinois State Library • Springfield, IL 62701-1796 • ALCTS ASCLA

Dorton Louise • Darlington County Library • Darlington, SC 29532 • PLA

Dorwaldt Virginia M. • Librarian • Albany Academy • Albany, NY 12208 • AASL

Dos Santos Anthony M. • Branch Manager • Alameda County Library Castro Valley Branch • Castro Valley, CA 94546 • LAMA PLA RASD

Dose Claus D. • Student • Saint John's University Division of Library & Information Science • Jamaica, NY 11439

Doss Lou L • Student • University of North Carolina at Chapel Hill School of Information and Library Science • Chapel Hill, NC 27599-3360 • AASL ALSC

Doss Priscilla • Regional Library Manager • Metropolitan Library System Belle Isle Branch • Oklahoma City, OK 73112-7164

Doss Susan M. • Student • University of North Carolina at Chapel Hill School of Information and Library Science • Chapel Hill, NC 27599-3360

Dosse Carol H. • Student • University of Iowa School of Library & Information Science • Iowa City, IA 52242 • ALSC PLA

Dosser Doris E. • Reseda, CA 91335

Dossett Laura White • Student • University of South Florida School of Library & Information Science • Tampa, FL 33620 • SRRT

Dossett Raeann S. • University of Illinois Graduate School of Library and Information Science • Urbana, IL 61801 • GODORT

Doster Pamela • Librarian • Keiser College of Technology • Fort Lauderdale, FL 33309 • AASL

Doszkocs Tamas E. • Computer Scientist • National Library of Medicine • Bethesda, MD 20894 • LITA IRRT

Doszpoly Ivan • New York, NY 10028-0853 • IFRT

Dote Jean O. • Librarian • Ventura Cnty Lib Serv Agency Simi Valley Library • Simi Valley, CA 93063 • RASD

Dote Yasuko Grace • Librarian • University of California-Berkeley Giannini Foundation of Agricultural Economics • Berkeley, CA 94720 • ACRL ALSC

Dotson Carol • Tillamook County Library • Tillamook, OR 97141

Dotson Mildred E. • The New York Public Library • New York, NY 10016 • LAMA PLA

Dotterrer Ellen C. • Sr. Technical Inf. Specialist • Rohm & Haas Company • Spring House, PA 19477 • ALCTS LAMA LITA

Doty Julie C. • Lewisville, TX 75067

Doty Kristin E. • Student • Simmons College Graduate School of Library & Information Science • Boston, MA 02115 • ALCTS NMRT

Doty Madge R. • Lansing, MI 48910 • Continuing

Doty Marlene • Director • Berkeley College of Business Walter A. Brower Library • West Paterson, NJ 07424 • ACRL

Doty Mary • Trustee • Minneapolis Public Library & Information Center • Minneapolis, MN 55401-1992 • ALTA PLA

Doty Philip • Student • Syracuse University School of Information Studies • Syracuse, NY 13244-4100 • ACRL

Doty Yvonne Newcomb • Director of Library Services • Daytona Beach Community College • Daytona Beach, FL 32015 • ACRL

Doubek Stephanie A. • Hillsboro Public Library • Hillsboro, OR 97123

Doublestein Judith A. • Library Director • Oxford Public Library Addison Township Library • Oxford, MI 48371 • LAMA PLA

Douce Martha • President Board of Trustee • Newton Falls Public Library • Newton Falls, OH 44444-1694

Doucet Helen C. • Director Cur. Materials Center • McNeese State University Curriculum Materials Center • Lake Charles, LA 70609

Doucette Mary Ellen • West Allis, WI 53219

Doud Mary A. • Assistant Director for Pub. Serv • Kalamazoo Public Library • Kalamazoo, MI 49007-5270

Doudell Charlotte • Program Librarian • Santa Clara County Free Library • San Jose, CA 95112-4446

Doudna Eileen B. • Librarian • Nawcc Museum Inc. • Columbia, PA 17512

Doudna Patricia • Jacksonville, FL 32218

Dougherty Anna E. • Mitchellville, MD 20721 • Continuing

Dougherty Linda Anne • Branch Head • Chicago Public Library Clearing Branch • Chicago, IL 60638 • LAMA LIRT SRRT *Life*

Dougherty Patricia H. • Career Information Librarian • Enoch Pratt Free Library • Baltimore, MD 21201-4484 • PLA

Dougherty Perry • Librarian • Aikin Elementary School Library • Dallas, TX 75243

Dougherty Richard M. • University of Michigan School of Information and Library Studies • Ann Arbor, MI 48109-1092 • AASL ACRL ALCTS LAMA LITA RASD *Life*

Dougherty Roberta L. • Student • University of Michigan School of Information and Library Studies • Ann Arbor, MI 48109-1092 • ACRL LITA IRRT LHRT

Dougherty Ruth A. • Librarian • Indiana Girls School • Indianapolis, IN 46214 • AASL

Doughty Nancy M. • Librarian • Woodstock High School Library • Woodstock, IL 60098 • AASL

Douglas Alice W. • Director • Weston Public Library • Weston, MA 02193 • ALCTS ALSC ALTA LAMA LITA PLA RASD IFRT SORT

Douglas Andrea G. • Student • University of Rhode Island Graduate School of Library & Information Studies • Kingston, RI 02881-0815

Douglas Carolyn J. • Mount Saint Mary's College • Los Angeles, CA 90049

Douglas Delores • Media Coordinator • Centerville High School • Clifton, VA 22180 • AASL

Douglas J. Dee • Student • Georgia-Pacific Corporation • Atlanta, GA 30303

Douglas Jacqueline J. • Student • Saint John's University Division of Library & Information Science • Jamaica, NY 11439

Douglas Jeffery A. • Knox College Henry W. Seymour Library • Galesburg, IL 61402 • ACRL LHRT

Douglas Karen Rich • Greensburg, PA 15601

Douglas Kimberly • Head of Reader Services • California Institute of Technology • Pasadena, CA 91125 • ACRL

Douglas Marilyn E. • Ln • New York State Library State Education Department • Albany, NY 12230 • ASCLA LITA LRRT

Douglas Nancy E. • University of California Rivera Library • Riverside, CA 92517 • ACRL ALCTS

Douglas Sherri • Anchorage Municipal Libraries Z. J. Loussac Library • Anchorage, AK 99503 • ALSC

Douglas Susan • Media Specialist • Madison Elementary School • Janesville, WI 53545 • AASL

Douglas V Gail • Director • Schertz Public Library • Schertz, TX 78154

Douglas Worth • Asst. Supervisor, Branches • Boston Public Library • Boston, MA 02117 • LAMA PLA

Douglass Anne • Reference Librarian • Houston Public Library • Houston, TX 77002

Douglass Charlene K. • Ben Lomond, CA 95005 • AASL RASD

Douglass Janet C. • Shelbyville, IN 46176 • AASL YALSA

Douglass Leslie A. • Dialog Information Services Inc. • Philadelphia, PA 19103

Douglass Steven • Trustee • Memphis-Shelby County Public Library and Information Center • Memphis, TN 38104-4025

Douthitt Rita C. • Director • Paul Sawyier Public Library • Frankfort, KY 40601 • PLA

Doutt Margaret E. • Technical Services • East Carolina University Joyner Library • Greenville, NC 27858-4353 • ALCTS

Dove Allison K. • Public Services Librarian • Sierra Vista Public Library • Sierra Vista, AZ 85635

Dove H. Paul Jr. • Director of the Library • Francis Marion University James A. Rogers Library • Florence, SC 29501 • IFRT

Dove Harold R. • Library Director • Speer Memorial Library • Mission, TX 78572 • Life

Dover Leta Sowder • Muskogee, OK 74401 • Continuing

Dover Terese M. • Librarian • Bristol Consolidated School • Pemaquid, ME 04558 • ALSC

Doversberger Linda E. • Elkhart, IN 46514 • ACRL

Dow Barbara J. • Saint Louis, MO 63128 • LITA YALSA

Dow Gail M. • Director of Technical Services • Denver Public Library • Denver, CO 80204-2602 • ALCTS LAMA LITA PLA

Dow Karen L • Middletown, DE 19709 • PLA

Dow Kathleen L. • Student • University of Michigan School of Information and Library Studies • Ann Arbor, MI 48109-1092

Dow Marcia • Edison Junior/Senior High School Library • Lake Station, IN 46405

Dow Ronald F. • Assistant Dean of Libraries • Pennsylvania State University Pattee Library • University Park, PA 16802 • ACRL LAMA

Dow Sally Read • Children Librarian • Ossining Public Library • Ossining, NY 10562 • ALSC

Dow Victoria E. • Assistant Director • Tredyffrin Public Library • Strafford, PA 19087

Dowd Frances A. • Assistant Professor • Texas Woman's University School of Library & Information Studies • Denton, TX 76204 • PLA

Dowd Frank B. • Acqs & Spec Cllns Mgr • Montgomery County Department of Public Libraries • Rockville, MD 20850 • ALCTS

Dowd Mary Maxine • Graham & Dunn • Seattle, WA 98101-2390

Dowd Robert C. • New York State Newspaper Project New York State Library • Albany, NY 12230

Dowd Sheila T. • Berkeley, CA 94708 • ACRL ALCTS RASD

Dowding Martin R. • Coor. of Special Services • Saint Mary's University Patrick Power Library • Halifax NS, B3H 3C3 Canada

Dowdle Charlotte • Seattle, WA 98109

Dowdle Glen L. • Librarian • Safford City-Graham County Library • Safford, AZ 85546

Dowell Connie Vinita • Head of Reference Department • University of California UCSB Library • Santa Barbara, CA 93106-9010 • ACRL LAMA

Dowell Craig R. • Student • University of Texas at Austin Graduate School of Library & Information Sciences • Austin, TX 78712-1276

Dowell David R. • Pasadena City College • Pasadena, CA 91106 • ACRL LAMA

Dowell Gail K. • Student • San Jose State University Division of Library & Information Science • San Jose, CA 95192-0029

Dowell Loretta • San Francisco Public Library Ingleside Branch • San Francisco, CA 94112

Dowell Marilyn R. • Assistant Director • Irving Public Library System • Irving, TX 75015-2288 • PLA

Dowell Nancy E. Winkelmeier • Technical Service Coordinator • Vigo County Public Library • Terre Haute, IN 47807 • PLA

Dowis Connie • Librarian • Keytesville R-3 Schools • Keytesville, MO 65261 • AASL

Dowler Lawrence • Librarian • Harvard College Library Widener Memorial Library • Cambridge, MA 02138

Dowlin C. Edwin • Director • Eastern New Mexico University Golden Library • Portales, NM 88130 • ACRL LAMA

Dowlin Kenneth E. • City Librarian • San Francisco Public Library • San Francisco, CA 94102 • LAMA LITA PLA

Dowlin May • Portales, NM 88130-7046 • Continuing

Dowling Betty Mays • Conway, SC 29526

Dowling Mary • Librarian • Franklin School PS 157K • Brooklyn, NY 11205 • ACRL EMIERT

Dowling Mary A Leith • Librarian • Delta Junction School • Delta Junction, AK 99737 • AASL YALSA

Dowling Maureen D. • School Librarian • Frank Borman Jr. High School • Phoenix, AZ 85031 • YALSA

Dowling Rita C. • Graduate Student • Irving Elementary School • Garnett, KS 66032 • AASL ALSC

Dowling Thomas P. • Computer-Based Services Libn. • University of Washington Engineering Library • Seattle, WA 98195 • ACRL LITA

Downard Roger L. • Executive Director • Friends of the Library of Hawaii • Aiea, HI 96701

Downen Kathleen Z. • Indexer Appl Sci & Tech • H. W. Wilson Company • Bronx, NY 10452 • ACRL

Downen Thomas • Media Specialist • Savannah-Chatham County Board of Education • Savannah, GA 31401 • AASL YALSA

Downes Robin N. • Director of Libraries • University of Houston Libraries • Houston, TX 77204-2091 • ACRL LITA

Downes Valerie J. • Director of Media & L Service • Morton West High School • Berwyn, IL 60650 • AASL IRRT

Downey Barbara A. • Director • Baylor Health Sciences Library • Dallas, TX 75246 • ACRL

Downey Howard R. • Director • Provo City Public Library • Provo, UT 84601 • LAMA PLA

Downey Jean • San Francisco, CA 94132

Downey Joy Mrs. • Cobbs Lower Elementary School • Newark, DE 19713 • AASL

Downey Lawrence J. • Indianapolis, IN 46202 • Continuing

Downey Margaret A. • Cincinnati, OH 45238-1825 • ACRL ALCTS *Life*

Downey Maria C. • Student • Kent State University School of Library Science/Columbus Program • Columbus, OH 43210 • ALSC

Downey Mary I. • Milwaukee, OR 97222 • Continuing

Downing Alice C. • Assistant Librarian • University College • Galway City, Ireland

Downing Arthur • Librarian • New York Academy of Medicine Library • New York, NY 10029 • ACRL ALCTS LITA RASD SRRT

Downing Carolyn • School Librarian • Kalles Junior High School • Puyallup, WA 98371 • AASL

Downing David H. • Wyncote, PA 19095

Downing Elaine L. • Librarian • State University of New York College at Oneonta-Library • Oneonta, NY 13820-4014 • ACRL

Downing Jeff • Arlington, TX 76011

Downing Karen E. • Associate Librarian • University of Michigan Libraries • Ann Arbor, MI 48109-1205 • ACRL

Downing Kathleen M. • Allen Park Public Library • Allen Park, MI 48101

Downing Mary E. • Laramie, WY 82070

Downing Mary K. • Librarian • M. Alice Chapin Memorial Library • Marion, MI 49665

Downing Mary M. • Library Consultant • Western Illinois Library System • Galesburg, IL 61401 • AASL ALSC

Downing Merle Ellen • Inforonics Inc. Library • Littleton, MA 01460 • ALCTS LITA

Downing Mildred H. • Chapel Hill, NC 27514

Downing Nancy C. • Librarian • Mayfield Senior School Library • Pasadena, CA 91105

Downing Pamela J. • Librarian • Santa Cruz City-County Library System • Santa Cruz, CA 95060

Downs Alice • Librarian II • Detroit Public Library Acq Dept • Detroit, MI 48202-4093

Downs Jane B. • Urbana, IL 61801 • AASL ALSC

Downum Evelyn R. • Flagstaff, AZ 86001 • Continuing

Dowski Craig A. • Catalog Librarian • Hobart & William Smith Colleges Warren H. Smith Library • Geneva, NY 14456 • ALCTS LITA NMRT SRRT

Doyen Sally E. • Library Computer Coordinator • South Windsor School District • South Windsor, CT 06074 • AASL LRRT

Doyle Barbara J. • Personnel & Staff Devel Officer • University of Minnesota O. Meredith Wilson Library • Minneapolis, MN 55455-0414 • LAMA

Doyle Carol • Trustee • Prince William Public Library System Administrative Support Center • Prince William, VA 22192-5073

Doyle Carol D. • Document Librarian • University of California UCSB Library • Santa Barbara, CA 93106-9010 • ACRL

Doyle Catherine F. • Access Services Librarian • Christopher Newport College Captain John Smith Library • Newport News, VA 23606 • ACRL LAMA LITA

Doyle Christina • Moreno Valley United School District • Moreno Valley, CA 92388 • AASL

Doyle Clare • Cataloger • H.W. Wilson Company • Bronx, NY 10452 • ACRL

Doyle David • Trustee • Grand Rapids Public Library • Grand Rapids, MI 49503-3093

Doyle Dorothy • Olympia, WA 98501 • Continuing

Doyle Eileen • Head of Youth Services • Mentor Public Library • Mentor, OH 44060 • ALSC LAMA PLA

Doyle Elizabeth J. • Student • University of Michigan School of Information and Library Studies • Ann Arbor, MI 48109-1092

Doyle Francis R. • Law Librarian • Loyola University School of Law • Chicago, IL 60611 • ACRL ALCTS LITA

Doyle Greg Aw • Network Coordinator • Online Computer Library Center (OCLC) • Portland, OR 97283 • ALCTS

Doyle Herbert A. Jr. • Trustee • Fairfax County Public Library • Fairfax, VA 22033-1909

Doyle James D. • Head of Reference Dept • Sara Hightower Regional Library • Rome, GA 30161

Doyle James J. Brother • Head Librarian • Saint Anthony-on-Hudson Theological Seminary Library • Rensselaer, NY 12144 • ALCTS

Doyle James M. • Public Service Librarian • Macomb Community College South Campus M Thompson Learning Center • Warren, MI 48093-3896 • ACRL IRRT

Doyle Joanne C. • Reference Librarian • Wicomico County Free Library • Salisbury, MD 21801

Doyle Julie M. • Librarian • D. Eisenberg School • Las Vegas, NV 89129 • AASL

Doyle Kathleen M. • El Dorado High School Library • Placerville, CA 95667 • AASL

Doyle Laura M. • Student • University of Kentucky College of Library & Information Science • Lexington, KY 40506-0391

Doyle Mary A. • Head, Tech Svs, Aqc, Aut • Manchester City Library • Manchester, NH 03101

Doyle Mary S. • Librarian • North Carolina State University D. H. Hill Library • Raleigh, NC 27695-7111

Doyle Pamela B. • Library Technical Asst. Coor. • North Carolina Department of Community Colleges Library • Raleigh, NC 27603 • ACRL ALCTS

Doyle Patricia A. • Acquisition Librarian • Amarillo Public Library • Amarillo, TX 79189 • ASCLA

Doyle Patricia A. • Student • Indiana University School of Library and Information Science • Bloomington, IN 47405 • PLA SRRT

Doyle Patricia C. • Jacksonville, FL 32205 • ALCTS LAMA PLA

Doyle Patricia L. • McKinney, TX 75069

Doyle Richard • Director of Library Services • Coe College Stewart Memorial Library • Cedar Rapids, IA 52402-5092

Doyle Robert P. • Dir. Library/Book Fellows Prog. • American Library Association • Chicago, IL 60611-2795 • IRRT

Doyle Sarah S. • Librarian • Bright School • Chattanooga, TN 37405 • AASL

Doyle Susan Badger • Albuquerque, NM 87106

Doyle Theresa Sharon • Teacher-Librarian • Havergal College Upper School • Toronto ON, M5N 2H9 Canada • AASL

Dozier Beverly B. • Bookmobile Supervisor • Oceanside Public Library • Oceanside, CA 92054 • PLA RASD SORT

Dozier Etrulia P. • Librarian • Whittemore Middle School • Conway, SC 29527 • ALTA

Dozier Lois G. • Washington, DC 20024 • Continuing

Drabenstott Karen M. • Associate Professor • University of Michigan School of Information and Library Studies • Ann Arbor, MI 48109-1092 • ALCTS LITA RASD

Drabkin Jane S. • Public Services Librarian • United States Army • Fort Belvoir, VA 22060-5028 • AFLRT FLRT

Drabkin Marian • Science Education Librarian • University California-Berkeley • Berkeley, CA 94720 • ALSC

Drach Marian C. • Supv of Library & Media Services • Baltimore County Public Schools • Towson, MD 21204 • AASL ALSC   *Life*

Drach Priscilla L. • Children Service Manager • Cuyahoga County Public Library • Cleveland, OH 44134-2792 • ALSC

Draegert Edith • Waukegan Public Library • Waukegan, IL 60085 • LAMA PLA

Dragash Laura J. • Indiana Historical Society Library • Indianapolis, IN 46202

Dragotta Linda • Supv., Inf. Servs. Oper. & Plan • Air Products & Chemicals • Allentown, PA 18195-1501 • LITA

Dragutsky Paula • New York, NY 10023

Drake Diane I. • Riverside City & County Public Lib Moreno Valley Branch Library • Moreno Valley, CA 92553 • PLA RASD

Drake Donald E. • Executive Director • Northern Illinois Learning Resources Cooperative • Sugar Grove, IL 60554

Drake Dorothy M. • Spring Valley, CA 92077 • ACRL RASD   *Continuing*

Drake H. J. Rev. • Winnipeg MB, R3T 2M6 Canada • Continuing

Drake Karen K. • Library Manager • Chandler Public Library • Chandler, AZ 85225 • LAMA PLA

Drake Kathryn J. • Washington, DC 20397-0001 • ALSC LIRT

Drake Linda L. • Librarian • Kluge Children's Rehabilitation Center • Charlottesville, VA 22901 • ALSC

Drake Marian M. • Lake Park Public Library • Lake Park, FL 33403 • PLA

Drake Marjory H. • Ann Arbor, MI 48105 • ACRL ALCTS   *Continuing*

Drake Marsha J. • Student • Kent State University School of Library Science/Columbus Program • Columbus, OH 43210 • ASCLA

Drake Miriam A. • Dean & Director • Georgia Institute of Technology • Atlanta, GA 30332 • ACRL LITA LRRT

Drake Paul B. • Serials/ILL Librarian • Roger Williams College Library • Bristol, RI 02809-2921 • ACRL GODORT SRRT

Drake Sally H. • Inter-l Loan Ln • University of Hawaii Thomas Hale Hamilton Library • Honolulu, HI 96822

Drake Sylvia P. • San Francisco, CA 94123 • LITA ILERT

Drake Virginia H. • Catalog Coordinator • Johns Hopkins University Milton S. Eisenhower Library • Baltimore, MD 21218 • ALCTS LITA

Drake Vivian • Pittsburgh, PA 15232 • PLA   *Continuing*

Drane Marcia A. • Reference & Adult Services • Hudson Area Branch Library • Hudson, FL 34667 • RASD

Drapeau Constance M. • Student • Simmons College Graduate School of Library & Information Science • Boston, MA 02115 • ACRL PLA RASD IFRT LIRT NMRT SRRT

Draper James • Doraville Public Library • Doraville, GA 30340 • PLA

Draper Jennifer Stahl • Healdsburg, CA 95448

Draper Kathryn M. • Public Services Librarian • Sierra Vista Public Library • Sierra Vista, AZ 85635 • ALSC

Draper Larry • Senior Librarian • Church of Jesus Christ of Latter-Day Saints • Salt Lake City, UT 84150 • ACRL

Draper Nancy L. • Trustee • West Des Moines Public Library • West Des Moines, IA 50265

Draper Norma J. • Manager, Information Resources • Information Strategies Group • Vienna, VA 22182 • LITA GODORT   *Subscribing*

Drapp Laureen • Director • Norwalk Public Library • Norwalk, OH 44857 • IFRT

Dratch Gladys I. • Collection Devel. Librarian • Harvard University Gutman Library-Research Center • Cambridge, MA 02138 • ACRL ALCTS RASD

Draughon Betty Ann • Media Coordinator • Enka High School • Enka, NC 28728 • AASL

Dravet Jean M. • Schaumburg Township District Library • Schaumburg, IL 60194 • PLA YALSA

Drawbaugh Cynthia A. • Library Supervisor • Chambersburg Area School District • Chambersburg, PA 17201 • AASL

Drayson Pamela K. • Director of Library • Kansas City Kansas Community College Library • Kansas City, KS 66112-3098 • ACRL

Drayton Anita L. • Library Media Specialist • Dunbar High School Library • Washington, DC 20001 • AASL YALSA

Drees Kevin P. • Student • Emporia State University School of Library & Information Management • Emporia, KS 66801 • SRRT

Dreese Sidney • Drexel University W. W. Hagerty Library • Philadelphia, PA 19104 • ACRL LHRT

Dreesen Robert F. • Docent • Smithsonian Institution Libraries National Air & Space Museum Library • Washington, DC 20560

Dreher Cora L. • Assistant Librarian • Northeast Louisiana University Sandel Library • Monroe, LA 71209-0720 • ACRL RASD

Dreier Marsha L W • Librarian • United States Air Force Cannon Air Force Base • Cannon AFB, NM 88103 • AFLRT

Drennan Henry T. Mr. • Librarian • Morristown Centennial Library • Morrisville, VT 05661 • ASCLA PLA   *Life*

Drennen Nancy W. • Suffern, NY 10901

Dresang Eliza T. • Madison Metropolitan School District Media Processing, Rm 1108 • Madison, WI 53703 • AASL ALSC YALSA

Dresbach Debra • Librarian • Oak Grove Middle School • Decatur, IL 62526 • AASL

Dresbach Shirley A. • Library Media Center Director • Monte Vista School • Phoenix, AZ 85018 • AASL

Drescher Judith A. • Director • Memphis-Shelby County Public Library and Information Center • Memphis, TN 38104-4025 • LAMA PLA

Drescher Karen A. • Student • Rosary College Graduate School of Library & Information Science • River Forest, IL 60305

Drescher Robert A. • Executive Director • Cooperative Library Agency for Systems & Services (CLASS) • San Jose, CA 95112-4698 • ASCLA LITA PLA ERT

Dreshfield Eleanor • Catalog Librarian • Union Carbide Corporation • Cleveland, OH 44101

Dresp Donald F. • Director • Thomas Branigan Memorial Library • Las Cruces, NM 88001 • PLA

Dressel Janice H. • Associate Professor • Central Michigan University • Mount Pleasant, MI 48859 • ALSC

Dresser Herbert • Associate Archivist • First Church of Christ Scientist • Boston, MA 02115 • LITA

Dresser Sylvia L. • Deerfield, IL 60015 • AASL

Dressler Rona • Stony Brook, NY 11790 • RASD NMRT

Dressman Mary Lynn • Patchogue-Medford Library • Patchogue, NY 11772 • AASL

Drew Elaine Carol • Children's Librarian • Indianapolis Marion County Public Library • Indianapolis, IN 46206 • ALSC

Drew Jeri • Librarian • Watertown School District • Watertown, SD 57201 • AASL

Drew K C. • San Diego, CA 92122

Drew M. Falisa CSJ Sr. • Mount Saint Joseph Academy • Brighton, MA 02135 • AASL

Drew Sally J. • Wisconsin Department of Public Instruction Bureau of ILL & Resource Sharing • Madison, WI 53716 • ASCLA

Drewes Jeanne M. • Dir. of Instr. Access Serv. • Mary Washington College Library Simpson Library • Fredericksburg, VA 22401-4664 • ALCTS LIRT

Drewes Tom C. • Deerfield, IL 60015 • ASCLA LITA PLA ERT IFRT SRRT

Drewett Bill • Chief Systems Engineer • NOTIS Systems, Inc. • Evanston, IL 60201-3622 • ALCTS LITA

Drewry Elizabeth • Librarian • Columbiana Library • Columbiana, AL 35051

Drews Lois E. • Technical Services Center • ASARCO Inc. • Salt Lake City, UT 84119-4191

Drews Lucy • Reference Librarian • Palatine Public Library • Palatine, IL 60067 • RASD

Drexler Margreta • Library Media Specialist • Cherry Road School • Syracuse, NY 13219 • AASL

Drexler Susan G. • Rochester, NY 14620

Dreyer Norma S. • Tulsa, OK 74114 • AASL LITA

Dreyer Trudie R. • Librarian • Woodstock Public Library • Woodstock, IL 60098 • ALCTS

Drick Beverly K. • Acq Ln • Oakton Community College Library • Des Plaines, IL 60016

Drickamer Jewel • East Providence, RI 02915

Drickamer Karen D. • Curator of Manuscripts • Southern Illinois University Delyte W. Morris Library • Carbondale, IL 62901-6632 • ACRL RASD

Driessen Diane • Librarian • Wickliffe School • Upper Arlington, OH 43221 • AASL ALSC

Driessen Karen C. • Media Librarian • University of Montana Library • Missoula, MT 59812 • ACRL ALCTS

Driggers Rita K. • School Librarian • Elrod Elementary School Northside ISD • San Antontio, TX 78250 • AASL

Driggs Christopher G. • Senior Archives Assistant • Nevada State Library & Archives • Carson City, NV 89710

Driggs Tiffany J. • Student • Simmons College Graduate School of Library & Information Science • Boston, MA 02115

Driscoll Audrey A. • Cataloger • University of Saskatchewan Library • Saskatoon SK, S7N 0W0 Canada • ALCTS LITA

Driscoll Carol M. • Canada College Library • Redwood Cty, CA 94061

Driscoll Kay P. • Student • University of California Los Angeles Graduate School of Library & Information Science • Los Angeles, CA 90024 • ALSC

Driscoll Mary K. • Childrens Librarian • Sun Prairie Public Library • Sun Prairie, WI 53590

Driscoll Maxine C. • Program Administrator • San Francisco Unified Schools • San Francisco, CA 94102 • AASL

Driscoll Rosemarie • Librarian • Dr. Charles Murphy School • Oakdale, CT 06370 • AASL

Driscoll Rosemary • Providence Public Library • Providence, RI 02903-3283

Driscoll Sally S. • Student • Clarion University of Pennsylvania College of Library Science • Clarion, PA 16214 • IFRT

Driver Ben Carl Mr • New York, NY 10027 • ACRL ALCTS   *Life*

Driver Dale G. • Tucson, AZ 85719-2750 • LITA IFRT

Driver Linda A. • Library Director • College of Notre Dame Library • Belmont, CA 94002 • ACRL LITA RASD

Driver Mary Anne R • Extension Services Manager • Athens Regional Library • Athens, GA 30606

Drnec-Thompson Paula J. • Library Associate I • Baltimore County Public Library North Point Branch • Baltimore, MD 21222-3295 • NMRT

Drobney Joseph C. • Student • Clarion University of Pennsylvania College of Library Science • Clarion, PA 16214

Drobnicki John A. • Bellerose, NY 11426-2521 • IFRT

Droessler Judith B. • Reference/Cllns. Devel. Ln. • University of Lethbridge Library • Lethbridge AB, T1K 3M4 Canada

Droessler William F. • Monticello, AR 71655 • ACRL

Drone-Silvers Scott C. • Lake Land College • Mattoon, IL 61938 • LITA RASD IFRT

Drone Jeanette M. • Carmi, IL 62821

Dross Polly C. • Springfield-Greene County Library Kearney Branch • Springfield, MO 65802

Drost Carol A. • Willamette University Mark O Hatfield Library • Salem, OR 97301

Drought Carol S. • Deputy Director • Warwick Public Library • Warwick, RI 02886 • PLA

Drovdahl Michele Q. • Relocation Asst. Program Mgr • Moffett Field Library • Moffett Field, CA 94035 • PLA AFLRT FLRT

Druckenbrod Ellen C. • Student • Clarion University of Pennsylvania College of Library Science • Clarion, PA 16214 • PLA SRRT

Drudge Jo Lynn • Librarian • Rome City School • Rome City, IN 46784 • AASL YALSA

Druehl Suzanne E. • Acquisitions • Allen County Public Library • Fort Wayne, IN 46801 • ALCTS PLA IFRT

Drueke Mary Jeanetta • Subject Specialist • University of Nebraska Love Library • Lincoln, NE 68588-0410 • ACRL IFRT

Druesedow Elaine L. • Senior Cataloger • Duke University • Durham, NC 27708 • ALCTS

Druggish Richard S. • Concord College Library • Athens, WV 24712 • AASL

Druley Helen • Rushville, IN 46173

Drum Catherine S. • Library Media Specialist • East Intermediate School • Weymouth, MA 02189

Drum Lori I. • Raleigh, NC 27606

Drummey Peter • Librarian • Massachusetts Historical Society • Boston, MA 02215 • ACRL RASD LHRT MAGERT

Drummond Gloria • Waukegan, IL 60085

Drummond Herbert • Humanities Reference Librariran • California State University-Sacramento Library • Sacramento, CA 95819-6039

Drummond Louis E. Jr. • Head, Online Systems Team • Library of Congress • Washington, DC 20541 • LITA RASD

Drummond Paula C. • Head Adult Services Dept. • Ypsilanti District Library • Ypsilanti, MI 48197

Drummond Rebecca C. • Georgia State University Pullen Library • Atlanta, GA 30303-3081 • ACRL

Drungil Mary J. • Student • University of Illinois Graduate School of Library and Information Science • Urbana, IL 61801

Drury Donald V. • Library Director • Menlo School & College Library • Atherton, CA 94027-4185 • ACRL ALCTS

Drury Felix • Felix Drury Arch & Planners • New Haven, CT 06511

Druschel Pauline H. • Public Service Librarian • Novi Public Library • Novi, MI 48375 • ASCLA LAMA

Druse Judith A. • Curriculum/Media Librarian • Washburn University of Topeka Mabee Library • Topeka, KS 66621 • AASL ACRL YALSA IFRT

Dryden Donald W. • Nashville, TN 37212

Dryden Sherre H. • Asst. Dir. Ctrl & Sci Libs • Vanderbilt University Central Library • Nashville, TN 37240-0007 • SRRT

Dryer Barbara • Librarian • Lansdowne High School • Baltimore, MD 21227

Drzewiecki Iris M. • Elma, NY 14059 • ALSC

Du Corday Gerard M. • Vice President • Visions • Santa Ana, CA 92705

Du Mont Mary J. • Reference Librarian • Kent State University Library • Kent, OH 44242 • ACRL

Du Ning Yu • Student • Louisiana State University School of Library & Information Science • Baton Rouge, LA 70803-3290 • LITA

DuBois Henry J. • Acting Associate Director • California State University-Long Beach University Library & Learning Resources • Long Beach, CA 90840-1901 • ACRL ALCTS LAMA

DuBois Paul Z. • Dean • Winthrop College Ida Jane Dacus Library • Rock Hill, SC 29733 • ACRL

DuBose Nellita • Media Specialist • Stratford High School • Goose Creek, SC 29445

DuBose Stefanie P. • Student • University of South Carolina • Columbia, SC 29208

DuMont Rosemary Dr. • Dean • Kent State University School of Library & Information Science • Kent, OH 44242-0001 • ACRL PLA LRRT

DuQuette Patricia • Librarian • Benji Cosor Elementary School • Fallsburg, NY 12733

DuRea Mary V. • Oak Ridge, TN 37830

du Vair Suzanne M. • Madison, WI 53713

DuVall Mickey B. • Reference Librarian • Corpus Christi Public Library • Corpus Christi, TX 78401 • PLA

DuVernay Lisa A. • Temp Assistant Librarian • State University of New York (SUNY) Charles B. Sears Law Library • Buffalo, NY 14260

Duan Shu-Jy • Student • Ohio State University Dept of Edu Theory & Practice • Columbus, OH 43210-1177

Duba Vern • Consultant • East Central Regional Library • Cedar Rapids, IA 52401 • LAMA

Dubberly Ronald A. • Director • Atlanta-Fulton Public Library • Atlanta, GA 30303 • ALTA LAMA PLA IFRT

Dube Lindgale • Library Media Specialist • Bishop Ireton High School • Alexandria, VA 22314

Dubester Henry J. • Bethesda, MD 20817 • ALCTS LITA
Life

Dubin Eileen • De Kalb, IL 60115 • ACRL

Dubin Judith A. • Librarian • Schulze Elementary School • Detroit, MI 48221

Dubois Deborah L. • Mansfield-Richland County Public Library • Mansfield, OH 44902-1295 • ALSC

Dubois Rae E. • Head, Gift and Exchange • National Agricultural Library • Beltsville, MD 20705-2351 • ALCTS FLRT

Dubrawski Marion S. • Librarian & Media Spec. • Saint Dominic Savio High School Library • East Boston, MA 02128 • AASL

Duby Leesa G. • Montague, MA 01351 • ACRL IFRT NMRT SRRT

Ducar Lynn • Reference/Adult Srvs • Elgin Community College • Elgin, IL 60123 • ACRL

Ducey Mary-Gay • Children's Librarian • Oakland Public Library Rockridge Branch • Oakland, CA 94618 • ALSC SRRT

Duchow Sally M. • Reference Instruction Librarian • Danville Area Community College • Danville, IL 61832 • ACRL

Duck Patricia M. • Director of Library • University of Pittsburgh at Greensburg • Greensburg, PA 15601 • ACRL ALCTS

Duckor Ian S. • Student • State University of New York (SUNY) Thomas E. Dewey Graduate Library • Albany, NY 12222 • IFRT SRRT

Duckwall Larry • Alameda County Library Pleasanton Branch • Pleasanton, CA 94566 • PLA IFRT

Duckworth Paul M. • Collection Devel. Coordinator • Springfield-Greene County Library • Springfield, MO 65801 • ALCTS

Ducote M. J. Dr. • Supervisor • Caddo Parish Schools • Shreveport, LA 71101 • AASL

Ducote Melissa L. • Youth Services Librarian • Huntsville-Madison County Public Library • Huntsville, AL 35804 • YALSA NMRT

Duda Andrea L. • Assistant Librarian • University of California Science and Engineering Library • Santa Barbara, CA 93106 • ACRL LITA LIRT

Duda Elizabeth A. • Gail Borden Public Library • Elgin, IL 60120 • PLA

Duda Frederick • Talking Book Librarian • Manatee County Public Library System • Bradenton, FL 34205 • ASCLA

Dudash Joyce K. • Librarian-M.S. • South Amherst Middle School • Amherst, OH 44001

Dudczak Cynthia Shedd • Allen Road Elementary School • North Syracuse, NY 13212 • AASL

Dudding Jan • Librarian II • Volusia County Public Library • Daytona Beach, FL 32124

Dudek Edward F. • Library Director • Summit Public Library District • Summit, IL 60501

Dudgeon Edith M. • Whitewater, WI 53190 • Continuing

Dudley-Lewis Gwendolyn • Cerveny Middle School • Detroit, MI 48227

Dudley Beverly E. • Director • York Public Library • Yorktown, VA 23692 • PLA

Dudley Doreen S. • General Subjects Selector • University of Michigan Graduate Library Reference • Ann Arbor, MI 48109 • ALCTS

Dudley Joan M. • Greenfield Elementary School • Richmond, VA 23235 • AASL

Dudley Mimi • Sylmar, CA 91342 • ACRL

Dudley Norman H. • Sylmar, CA 91342 • ALCTS

Dudley Robyn A. • McClellanville, SC 29458 • LITA

Dudnik Laura S. • Head, Readers Advisory Dept. • Evanston Public Library • Evanston, IL 60201

Duesenberg Marie Miss • Assistant Director • Willard Public Library • Battle Creek, MI 49017 • Continuing

Duesterbeck Florence R. • Librarian • Saskatchewan Provincial Library • Regina SK, S7P 3V7 Canada

Duesterhoeft Diane M. • Urbana, IL 61801 • SRRT

Duet Theresa O. • Golden Meadow Lower Elementary School • Golden Meadow, LA 70357 • AASL

Duett Pamela S. • Librarian • United States Air Force RAF Bentwaters Base Library • Bentwaters, United Kingdom • AFLRT

Dufault Donna J. • Library Director • North Kingstown Free Library • North Kingstown, RI 02852 • ALCTS ALSC ALTA LAMA PLA RASD

Dufault Susan M. • Director • Hills Memorial Library • Hudson, NH 03051 • LITA

Duff Brenda G. • Asst. Head of Youth Services • Ela Area Public Library District • Lake Zurich, IL 60047 • ALSC

Duff Janet Hyde • Student • University of Rhode Island Graduate School of Library & Information Studies • Kingston, RI 02881-0815

Duff John B. • Commissioner • Chicago Public Library Harold Washington Library • Chicago, IL 60605 • LAMA PLA

Duff Margaret K. • Fountain Hills, AZ 85268 • ALSC

Duff Nathaniel • Trustee • McGregor Public Library • Highland Park, MI 48203 • ALTA

Duff Wanda P. • Library Media Specialist • Northwest High School • Omaha, NE 68134 • AASL

Duffel John A. • Business Manager • New Orleans Public Library • New Orleans, LA 70140

Duffel Patricia G. • Librarian • University of Iowa Hospitals and Clinics • Iowa City, IA 52242 • LITA RASD

Duffel Sarah C. • Clln. Devel. Coordinator • New Orleans Public Library • New Orleans, LA 70140 • ALCTS

Duffett Gorman L. • Director • John Carroll University Grasselli Library • University Heights, OH 44118 • ACRL

Duffey Polly J. • Circulation Manager • Alachua County Library District • Gainesville, FL 32601 • LAMA PLA VRT

Duffy Annette C. • Librarian • Oklahoma School of Science & Math • Oklahoma City, OK 73104 • AASL

Duffy Catherine S.C. Sister • Librarian • Cathedral Preparatory Seminary • New York, NY 10024

Duffy Jacqueline G. • Assistant Director • Porter Public Library • Westlake, OH 44145 • PLA

Duffy Joan R. • Project Director • Yale University Divinity School • New Haven, CT 06510

Duffy Karen Rollin • Assistant Director • Redwood City Public Library • Redwood City, CA 94063-1868 • LAMA PLA RASD

Duffy Kathleen E. • Supv. Librarian/Automation • Cape May County Library • Cape May Ct. House, NJ 08210 • LITA IFRT

Duffy Marguerite S. • Student • Indiana University School of Library and Information Science • Bloomington, IN 47405 • SRRT

Duffy Mary A. • Student • San Jose State University Division of Library & Information Science • San Jose, CA 95192-0029 • LITA RASD

Duffy Mary Anne Burns • Document & Map Librarian • West Chester University Francis Harvey Green Library • West Chester, PA 19383 • ACRL GODORT MAGERT

Duffy Mary F. • Salt Lake City, UT 84124

Duffy Mary H. • Jersey City, NJ 07306 • Continuing

Duffy Michelle • West Hartford Public Library • W. Hartford, CT 06107 • ALCTS

Duffy Paula A. • Librarian • Eastern Montana College Library • Billings, MT 59101-0298 • GODORT

Duffy Rebecca K. • Librarian • Lakeview High School Library • Lakeview, OR 97630

Duffy Rose E. Miss • Elmhurst, IL 60126 • PLA RASD
Continuing

Duffy Suzanne • Coordinator of Collection Devel. • Texas Tech University Libraries • Lubbock, TX 79409-0002 • ACRL ALCTS IFRT SRRT

Dugan Charlotte A. • Southwest Missouri State University Library • Springfield, MO 65804-0095 • ACRL RASD LIRT

Dugan M. P. • Director • Dougherty County Public Library • Albany, GA 31701-2533 • LAMA PLA

Dugan Maureen S. • Media Resources Teacher • Brevard County Schools • Melbourne, FL 32940-6699 • AASL ALSC YALSA

Dugan Robert E. • Associate University Librarian • Georgetown University • Washington, DC 20057-1006 • LITA

Dugas Mildred E. • San Diego, CA 92109 • Continuing

Dugdale Joan P. Mrs • Carmichael, CA 95608 • Continuing

Dugdale Timothy D. • Madison, WI 53715 • LITA RASD

Duggan Carol C. • Columbia, SC 29204

Duggan Doris A. • Librarian/Media Specialist • North Scituate School • North Scituate, RI 02857 • AASL

Duggan Kathleen P. • Assistant Librarian • Massachusetts Bay Community College Learning Resource Center • Wellesley, MA 02181 • ACRL

Duggan Mary Kay • Associate Professor • University of California Study Centre • London, SW1P 2HY, England

Duggan Michelle S. • Technical Reference Librarian • Library of Congress • Washington, DC 20541 • LITA

Duggan Theresa W. • Coor. of Inf. Technologies • Concord Public Schools Concord-Carlisle RSD • Concord, MA 01742-2699

Duggar David Charles • Reference Librarian • Louisiana State University School of Medicine • Shreveport, LA 71130-3932 • ACRL ALCTS GODORT

Duggleby Esther • Librarian • Chico State College Library • Chico, CA 95929 • ACRL ASCLA   *Continuing*

Duhamell Lynnette H. • Library Media Specialist • Portage High School East • Portage, IN 46368 • AASL

Duhart Queen E. • Media Spec • Montgomery County Public School Paint Branch High School • Burtonsville, MD 20866 • AASL

Duhig Mary C. • Point Park College Helen-Jean Moore Library • Pittsburgh, PA 15236

Duhrsen Lowell R. • Associate Dean • New Mexico State University Library • Las Cruces, NM 88003-0006 • ACRL

Dujmic Linda L. • Fine Arts Cataloger • Carnegie-Mellon University • Pittsburgh, PA 15213

Duke Barbara M. • Head, Education/Psych. Library • University of California Library • Los Angeles, CA 90024 • ACRL

Duke Cassandra L. • Student • University of North Texas School of Library & Information Sciences • Denton, TX 76203

Duke Deborah C. • Nigth Owl Supervisor • Enoch Pratt Free Library • Baltimore, MD 21201-4484 • LAMA PLA IFRT

Duke Gary K. • Reference Librarian • Richland College • Dallas, TX 75243-2199 • ACRL RASD LIRT NMRT

Duke Irma H. • Director • Phenix City-Russell County Library • Phenix City, AL 36867 • PLA

Duke Joan A R • Librarian • Sedona Public Library • Sedona, AZ 86336
Duke John K. • L Collections & Access Services • Virginia Commonwealth University • Richmond, VA 23284-2033 • ACRL ALCTS LITA
Dukelow Rosemary • Youth Services • Oakland Public Library West Oakland Branch • Oakland, CA 94607 • ALSC
Dukes Earnstein • Automation Services Manager • Fort Worth Public Library • Fort Worth, TX 76102 • LITA PLA
Dulac Ingrid • Media Specialist • Livingston Educational Service Agency • Howell, MI 48843
Duling Sandra C. • Reference Librarian • Castleton State College Calvin Coolidge Library • Castleton, VT 05735 • LIRT
Dulka John • Milwaukee, WI 53217 • Continuing
Dull Paula J. • Head Librarian • Parkway West High School Library • Ballwin, MO 63011 • AASL
Dumais Rosemary B. • Chrysler Museum Library • Norfolk, VA 23510-1587 • ALCTS
Dumas Elaine • Head Librarian • Little Rock Central High School • Little Rock, AR 72202 • AASL YALSA
Dumas Robert H. • Decatur, IL 62522 • Continuing
Dumas Thomas D. • Baton Rouge, LA 70809
Dumaux Sally A. • Special Collections Librarian • Frances Howard Goldwyn Hollywood Regional Library • Los Angeles, CA 90028 • PLA
Dummer Kathleen A. • Newcastle Middle School • Newcastle, WY 82701 • AASL
Dumond Paul • Trustee • Ramapo Catskill Library System • Middletown, NY 10940
Dumont Elinor • Librarian • American Bankers Association Library • Washington, DC 20036
Dumont Normand E. • Port Washington, NY 11050
Dumont Paul E. • Director Technical Service • Dallas County Community College District District Service Center • Mesquite, TX 75150-2095 • ACRL
Dunaway Barbara J. • Waterford, MI 48328 • PLA
Dunbar Amy D. • Student • Louisiana State University School of Library & Information Science • Baton Rouge, LA 70803-3290
Dunbar Carol W. • Student • University of Rhode Island Graduate School of Library & Information Studies • Kingston, RI 02881-0815 • AASL EMIERT
Dunbar Glynn M. • Baton Rouge, LA 70806
Dunbar Helen A. • Head of Branches • Alameda County Library System • Fremont, CA 94538 • LAMA PLA IFRT
Duncan Anne S. • Librarian • Francis W. Parker School • Chicago, IL 60614 • AASL
Duncan Cyd J. • Business Reference Librarian • Saint Joseph County Public Library • South Bend, IN 46601 • PLA
Duncan Cynthia B. • Norfolk, VA 23503 • ACRL RASD *Life*
Duncan Denise T. • Trustee • Zion-Benton Public Library District • Zion, IL 60099
Duncan Donna N. • RECON Project Manager • McGill University • Montreal PQ, Canada • ACRL ALCTS LAMA LITA
Duncan Elizabeth B. • Young Adult Librarian • Broward County Library Florida Center for the Book • Fort Lauderdale, FL 33301 • YALSA
Duncan Elizabeth C. • Head of Technical Service • Albany Law School Schaffer Library • Albany, NY 12208 • ACRL
Duncan Eve A. • Arlington, VA 22204 • LAMA
Duncan John E. • London N4 1AD, England
Duncan Joy A. • Library Technical Assistant • Barr Engineering Company • Minneapolis, MN 55437-1026 • ALCTS
Duncan Linda N. • Children's Specialist • Contra Costa County Library • Pleasant Hill, CA 94523
Duncan Lucy E. • Technical Services Librarian • Saint Philip's College LRC • San Antonio, TX 78203 • ALCTS
Duncan Marijo • Librarian II • Phoenix Public Library Cholla Branch • Phoenix, AZ 85051-1598 • PLA YALSA
Duncan Mary-Ruth Y. • National Defense University • Washington, DC 20319 • Life
Duncan Melanie C. • Student • Florida State University School of Library and Information Studies • Tallahassee, FL 32306-2048 • RASD
Duncan Samuel D. • Cataloger • Amon Carter Museum Library • Fort Worth, TX 76113
Duncan Sandra • Patent Supervising Librarian • Sunnyvale Public Library Patent Branch • Sunnyvale, CA 94086 • PLA
Duncan William L. • New Orleans, LA 70127 • Continuing
Duncan William M. • Director • Metropolitan Library Service Agency (MELSA) • Saint Paul, MN 55104-3083 • ASCLA LITA PLA
Dungan Helen V. • Technical Services Librarian • Lafayette College Skillman Library • Easton, PA 18042-1797 • ALCTS LITA
Dunham Catherine W. • Fairview Elementary School • Modesto, CA 95350-4044
Dunham Christopher S. • Student • Rutgers University School of Communication Information & Library Studies • New Brunswick, NJ 08903
Dunham Della M. • Chicago, IL 60620
Dunham John C. • Mission Viejo, CA 92692
Dunham Linda Predmore • Librarian • Spokane Cooperative Library Information System • Spokane, WA 99206 • LITA
Dunham Marian E. • Grinnell, IA 50112 • Continuing
Dunham Selma • Information Systems Coordinator • Northern State University • Aberdeen, SD 57401 • LITA
Dunhouse Marybeth • Coordinator of Res & Processing • Boston Public Library • Boston, MA 02117 • ALCTS ALSC
Dunikoski Alfred A. Ed.D • Dean, Learning Resources • William Rainey Harper College Learning Resources Center • Palatine, IL 60067 • ACRL
Dunkelberger Doris • School Library Media Specialist • Challenger & Atlantis Libraries • Mc Guire AFB, NJ 08641 • AASL
Dunkelberger John G. • Reference Librarian • Urbana Free Library • Urbana, IL 61801-3283 • RASD IFRT SRRT
Dunkelberger Robert A. • Assistant Archivist • University of Illinois Archives • Urbana, IL 61801 • NMRT
Dunker Marcia Lynn • Automation Coordinator • Cooperating Libraries in Consortium • Saint Paul, MN 55105 • LITA
Dunker Susan E. • Auburndale, MA 02166
Dunkin Barbara • Rocky Point, NY 11778
Dunkle Clare B. • Monographs Cataloger • Trinity University • San Antonio, TX 78212 • ALCTS NMRT
Dunkle Gladys L. • LRC Director • Palm Beach Community College -E • Palm Beach Gardens, FL 33410 • ACRL
Dunkle Rebecca M. • Librarian • University of Michigan Libraries • Ann Arbor, MI 48109-1205
Dunlap Connie • Ann Arbor, MI 48103 • ACRL ALCTS *Life*
Dunlap David M. • Senior Reference Librarian • Bucks County Free Library • Doylestown, PA 18901
Dunlap Ellen S. • Rosenbach Museum and Library • Philadelphia, PA 19103 • ACRL
Dunlap Glen R. • Trustee • Alabama Public Library Service • Montgomery, AL 36130 • ALTA PLA
Dunlap Leslie W. Dr. • Dean of Lib. Adm. Emeritus • University of Iowa Libraries • Iowa City, IA 52242-1379 • ACRL RASD *Life*
Dunlap Mitzi M. • Student • University of Pittsburgh School of Library and Information Science • Pittsburgh, PA 15260 • ACRL
Dunlavey Maryrita Elise • Silver Spring, MD 20902
Dunleavy Kathleen Ann • Palm Beach County Library System • Boca Raton, FL 33434
Dunlevy Loretta R. • Louisville Free Public Library • Louisville, KY 40203-2257
Dunlop Karen S. • Columbia, SC 29204
Dunman Susan • Head-Periodicals Department • Murray State University Harry Lee Waterfield Library • Murray, KY 42071-3309
Dunmire Kathryn Carey • Horizon Elementary School Media Center • Port Orange, FL 32119 • AASL
Dunmire Raymond V. • Montevallo, AL 35115 • ACRL ALCTS *Life*
Dunmire Suzanne K. • Student • University of Missouri-Columbia School of Library & Informational Science • Columbia, MO 65211 • PLA
Dunmore Leslie A. • Descriptive Cataloger • Library of Congress • Washington, DC 20541 • ALCTS LITA
Dunn Amy • Student • University of Washington Business Administration • Seattle, WA 98195
Dunn Bessie • Director • Waterloo Grant Township Public Library • Waterloo, IN 46793
Dunn Carol A. • AV Librarian • Findlay-Hancock County Public Library • Findlay, OH 45840 • VRT
Dunn Caroline • Greenwood, IN 46143 • ACRL *Continuing*
Dunn Carolyn • Director • Clatsop Community College Library • Astoria, OR 97103 • ACRL ALCTS RASD
Dunn Catherine Carver • New York Public Library • New York, NY 10018-2788
Dunn Christina J. • Adminstrative Librarian • United States Department of Education • Washington, DC 20208 • PLA
Dunn Donald J. • Librarian • Western New England College Law Library • Springfield, MA 01119 • ACRL ALCTS LITA RASD
Dunn Dorothy A. • Bridgewater, MA 02324
Dunn Elizabeth Bramm • Durham, NC 27705-5383
Dunn Elizabeth K. • Lenexa, KS 66215
Dunn Jean E. • Librarian/Media Specialist • Lafayette Elementary School • Lafayette, CO 80026 • AASL
Dunn Kate F. • School Library Media Specialist • West Pensacola Elementary School • Pensacola, FL 32506
Dunn Kathel • Student • University of North Carolina at Chapel Hill School of Information and Library Science • Chapel Hill, NC 27599-3360
Dunn Kathleen K. • Head, Reference Dept. • California State Polytech University • Pomona, CA 91768 • ACRL
Dunn Kay T. • Sarasota, FL 34232 • AASL EMIERT
Dunn Lisa G. • Reference Librarian • Colorado School of Mines Arthur Lakes Library • Golden, CO 80401 • ACRL RASD
Dunn Lucia S. • Librarian/Archivist • New Trier High School • Winnetka, IL 60093 • AASL RASD LIRT
Dunn Mary Joan • Manager, Information Center • Solicitor General of Canada • Ottawa, ON, K1G 4G4 Canada • ACRL ALCTS LAMA LITA RASD
Dunn Myra Turner • Glen Ellyn, IL 60137
Dunn Oliver C. Mr • West Lafayette, IN 47906 • ACRL LAMA *Life*
Dunn Pam • Library Consultant • Region VIII ESC • Mount Pleasant, TX 75455
Dunn Patrick F. • Acquisitions Librarian • East Tennessee State University • Johnson City, TN 37614 • ALCTS
Dunn Susan E. • Adult Services Coordinator • Warwick Public Library • Warwick, RI 02886 • PLA
Dunn Susan E. • Young Adult Outreach Librarian • Salem Public Library • Salem, OR 97309-5020 • YALSA
Dunn Susan M. • Lincoln, NE 68504 • ILERT
Dunn Susan S. • Washington, DC 20007
Dunn Thomas J. • Trustee • Mount Prospect Public Library • Mount Prospect, IL 60056
Dunnagan Lynn A. • Riley Family Library • Indianapolis, IN 46202-5200
Dunne Eileen J. • Circ. Coordinator-LRC Prog. • Cooper High School Library • Abilene, TX 79605
Dunne Mary Ellen • Bensenville Community Public Library • Bensenville, IL 60106 • PLA RASD
Dunne Virginia T. • Reference Librarian • Dominican College Library • Blauvelt, NY 10913
Dunnigan Virginia • Government Documents Librarian • Saint Thomas Aquinas College Library Lougheed Library • Sparkill, NY 10976 • RASD
Dunning Laura D. • Camarillo, CA 93012 • RASD
Duno Barbara L. • Bryn Mawr, PA 19010
Dunphy Marie Claire Sister • Librarian • Loretto Academy Library • El Paso, TX 79903
Dunphy Sandra J. • Bibliographic Servs. Librarian • Northeastern University • Boston, MA 02115 • ACRL
Dunseth Lisa M. • San Francisco, CA 94109
Dupont Donald P. • Trustee • Palatine Public Library • Palatine, IL 60067 • ALTA
Dupont Inge • Head of Reader Services • Pierpont Morgan Library • New York, NY 10016 • ACRL
Dupras Rheba A. • University of Alaska Elmer E. Rasmuson Library • Fairbanks, AK 99775-1005 • ACRL ALCTS LITA RASD LIRT LRRT
Dupre Maryann • Mount Clemens, MI 48043 • NMRT
Dupree Sandra • Assistant Libn-Reader Services • University of Arkansas Monticello Library • Monticello, AR 71655
Dupuis Alice A. • Circulation Manager • Miami-Dade Public Library System • Miami, FL 33130-1504 • PLA RASD
Dupuis Elizabeth A. • Student • University of Illinois Graduate School of Library and Information Science • Urbana, IL 61801 • PLA RASD
Dupuy Ernest J. • Editorial Division • Hammond, Inc. • Maplewood, NJ 07040 • MAGERT
Duquette Diane R. • Director • Kern County Library System • Bakersfield, CA 93301 • LAMA PLA
Duran-Molloy Bobbea • Director of Sales • Select Video Publishing • Englwood, CO 80112 • Subscribing
Duran Camille J. • West Hempstead, NY 11552 • ALSC
Duran Cheryl M. • Assistant Dean • University of California • Los Angeles, CA 90024-1573 • LRRT
Duran Karin • Reference Librarian • California State University • Northridge, CA 91330 • ACRL LIRT
Duran Kimberly Whittaker • Student • University of South Florida School of Library & Information Science • Tampa, FL 33620 • EMIERT SRRT
Duran Nancy • Student • University of Missouri-Columbia School of Library & Informational Science • Columbia, MO 65211
Duran Ninfa A. • Fullerton, CA 92632 • PLA
Duranceau Ellen Finnie • Assoc. Head for Serials Acq. • Massachusetts Institute of Technology Libraries (MIT) • Cambridge, MA 02139 • ALCTS
Durand Jo Anne • Reference Librarian • McNeese State University Lether E. Frazar Memorial Library • Lake Charles, LA 70609
Durand Joan • Library Director • Mount Saint Alphonsus Seminary Library • Esopus, NY 12429
Durand Joyce • Coordinator of Media Services • Rockdale County Schools • Conyers, GA 30207 • AASL

Durand Mary V. • Student • Wayne State University Library Science Program • Detroit, MI 48202 • PLA

Durand Winsley Jr. • Peoria Public Library • Peoria, IL 61602 • ALTA

Durant H. Lawrence • Senior Cataloger • Boston College Burns Library • Chestnut Hill, MA 02167 • ALCTS

Durbin Ann B. • School Media Librarian • Thomas Jefferson Middle School • Louisville, KY 40219

Durbin Diane • Librarian • Pearland High School • Pearland, TX 77581 • AASL

Durbin Emalee E. • Corvallis, OR 97339 • AASL YALSA
Life

Durbin Hugh • Library Director • Urbana University Swedenborg Memorial Libary • Urbana, OH 43078-2091 • AASL ACRL ALCTS

Durbin Lois Mrs. • Trustee • Topeka Public Library • Topeka, KS 66604-1374

Durbin Ramona J. • Annapolis, MD 21401 • Life

Durbin Roger W. Dr. • Associate Dean • University of Akron Bierce Library • Akron, OH 44325-1706 • ACRL LAMA LITA

Durda Mary E. • Needham Free Public Library • Needham, MA 02194

Duree Barbara J. • Chicago, IL 60620 • AASL YALSA *Life*

Durfee-Smith Tamara • Manager • Green Mountain Power Corporation Library Services • South Burlington, VT 05402 • RASD

Durfee Linda J. • Head of Reference Services • Tufts University Arts & Sciences Library • Medford, MA 02155 • ACRL

Durham Billie Mace • Southwestern Randolph Middle School • Asheboro, NC 27203 • AASL

Durham James G. • Asst. Manager-Children's Libn. • Columbus Metropolitan Library Franklinton Branch • Columbus, OH 43222 • ALSC

Durham Jennifer M. • Reference Librarian • Hudson Area Branch Library • Hudson, FL 34667

Durham Laura A. • Student • Indiana University School of Library and Information Science • Bloomington, IN 47405 • PLA IFRT

Durham Sharon M. • Saint Dominic School • Baltimore, MD 21214 • AASL

Durham Shawn E. • Student • State University of New York at Albany School of Information Science & Policy • Albany, NY 12222 • NMRT

Durivage Mary Jo • Medical Librarian • Veterans Administration Medical Center Library Service • Allen Park, MI 48101 • ASCLA PLA RASD FLRT SRRT

Durnell George • Supervisor-Readers Services • Saint Louis County Library • St. Louis, MO 63131 • PLA

Duron Carlos E. • California High School • Whittier, CA 90604

Durrance Joan Coachman • Associate Professor • University of Michigan School of Information and Library Studies • Ann Arbor, MI 48109-1092 • ACRL PLA RASD GODORT LRRT

Durrance Jocelyn M. • Adult Services Librarian • Pitkin County Library • Aspen, CO 81611

Dursema Judith C. • Librarian • Cavallini Middle School • Upper Saddle River, NJ 07458 • AASL

Duschaneck Trudy • Librarian Media Specialist • Preston Elementary School • West Harrison, NY 10604

Dusenberry Judith A. • Community Relations Coordinator • Moline Public Library • Moline, IL 61265

Dusenberry Mary D. • Central, SC 29630-9460 • AASL YALSA

Dusenbury Carolyn • Director of Library Services • California State University-Chico Meriam Library • Chico, CA 92929-0295 • ACRL LAMA RASD

Dusenbury Lee Anne • Children's Librarian • Marion County Library • Marion, SC 29571 • ALSC

Dusky Kathy L. Kit • Cataloger • Portland State University Library • Portland, OR 97207 • ACRL IFRT SRRT

Dust Donald • Trustee/Aide to the Mayor • Newark Public Library • Newark, NJ 07101-0630 • ALTA PLA

Duszak Thomas • Harrisburg, PA 17102-2916 • ACRL LITA

Dutchak Katheleen M. • Mgr., Administrative Services • Kitchener Public Library • Kitchener ON, N2H 2H1 Canada • LITA

Dutcher Harry J. • Director • Saratoga Springs Public Library • Saratoga Springs, NY 12861

Dutcher Henry • Longmeadow, MA 01106

Dutcher Milton E. Jr. • Branch Librarian • Baltimore County Public Library North Point Branch • Baltimore, MD 21222-3295 • PLA

Dutcher Roger • System Librarian • Beloit Public Library • Beloit, WI 53511 • PLA

Dutka June • Government Publication Librarian • University of Manitoba Libraries Elizabeth Dafoe Library • Winnipeg MB, R3T 2N2 Canada

Dutkiewicz Scott M. • Librarian • Griffin College • Bellevue, WA 98004

Dutler Sue A. • Head Librarian • Robert Morris College • Chicago, IL 60601

Dutta Gouri • North Carolina Central University James E. Shepard Memorial Library • Durham, NC 27707

Dutton J. W. • Kansas State University Farrell Library • Manhattan, KS 66506-1200 • ALCTS

Dutton Lee S. • Librarian Southeast Asia Clln. • Northern Illinois University University Libraries • DeKalb, IL 60115-2868 • ACRL

Dutton Margaret • Galveston, TX 77550 • Continuing

Dutton Mark R. • Sales Manager • Harbor Court Hotel • Baltimore, MD 21202

Dutton Paula T. • Librarian • Elmont Elementary School • Ashland, VA 23005 • AASL MAGERT

Duttweiler Robert Dr. • Director, Library & Media • Augusta Technical Institute • Augusta, GA 30906 • ACRL

Dutz Gloria M. • Librarian • Hamilton High School Library • Sussex, WI 53089

Duval Katherine B. • Acct. Executive • Data Research Associates, Inc. • Ashland, VA 23005

Duvall John E. • Admin Services Manager • Hogan & Hartson • Washington, DC 20004 • ALCTS

Duvall Scott H. • Chair Special Collections • Brigham Young University • Provo, UT 84602 • ACRL

Duvall Steven R. • Student • University of South Florida School of Library & Information Science • Tampa, FL 33620 • PLA

Dux-Ideus Sherrie • Director • University of Nebraska at Kearney Library • Kearney, NE 68849 • ASCLA PLA

Duyst Johanna • Librarian • Calvin College & Seminary Library • Grand Rapids, MI 49546 • ACRL ALCTS

Duzak Sandra J. • San Rafael, CA 94901

Duzinski Jennifer • Student • Experiment Intl Living • Brattleboro, VT 05301

Dvorchak Kathleen • Librarian • Ludow Public Schools • Belchertown, MA 01007 • AASL

Dvorzak Marie A. • Head, Geology-Geophysics Library • University of Wisconsin-Madison Geology-Geophysics Library • Madison, WI 53706 • ACRL ALCTS MAGERT

Dwelley Roberta K. • Howell Carnegie Disrict Library • Howell, MI 48843-2195 • ALSC

Dwiggins Cheryl • Yavapai County Library District • Prescott, AZ 86301

Dwinell Sheryl L. • Student • University of Wisconsin School of Library & Information Studies • Madison, WI 53706

Dwor-Frecaut Gary N. • Student • Catholic University of America School of Library and Information Science • Washington, DC 20064 • RASD

Dwork Barry F. • Student • University of Maryland College of Library and Information Services • College Park, MD 20742-4345

Dworkin Judith Daniels • Director • Amherst Public Library • Amherst, OH 44001 • PLA

Dworkin Rita A. • Head of Adult Services • East Meadow Public Library • East Meadow, NY 11554-1700 • RASD

Dworkin Victoria G. • Reference Service Librarian • Hawaii Pacific University Meader Library • Honolulu, HI 96813-3192 • ACRL RASD

Dwoskin Beth • Catalog Librarian • University Microfilms International • Ann Arbor, MI 48106-1346 • ALCTS LRRT

Dwoyer Nancy • Gloucester, VA 23061 • PLA

Dwyer Ann Kenna • Director • Cold Spring Harbor Library • Cold Spring Harbor, NY 11724-1315

Dwyer Catherine M. • Government Documents Librarian • State University of New York (SUNY) University Libraries • Albany, NY 12222 • GODORT

Dwyer Denise G. Dr. • Department Chair • Kenwood Academy • Chicago, IL 60615 • AASL LIRT LRRT

Dwyer Dianna S. • Collection Development Librarian • Glendale Community College Library/Media Center • Glendale, AZ 85302

Dwyer James R. • Bibliography Service Dept. Head • California State University-Chico Meriam Library • Chico, CA 92929-0295 • LITA IFRT LRRT SRRT

Dwyer Joanne K. • Student • Simmons College Graduate School of Library & Information Science • Boston, MA 02115

Dwyer Sharon K. • Director • Eau Gallie Public Library • Melbourne, FL 32935

Dwyre Katherine • Assistant Librarian • Worcester Public Library • Worcester, MA 01608 • Continuing

Dyal Carole • University of Connecticut Homer Babbidge Library • Storrs, CT 06269-1005 • ACRL ALCTS SRRT

Dyar Mary L. • Burnsville, MN 55337 • LAMA PLA *Life*

Dyck Ronald J. • Director, Technical Services • Etobicoke Public Libraries • Etobicoke ON, M9C 5G1 Canada • LITA

Dyckman A. Ann • Director of Library Personnel • Cornell University Library • Ithaca, NY 14853-5301 • LAMA

Dyckman Lise M. • Reference Librarian • New York University Elmer Holmes Bobst Library • New York, NY 10012 • ACRL RASD LIRT

Dye Cynthia H. • Children's Librarian I • Boston Public Library Egleston Square Branch • Roxbury, MA 02119 • ALSC

Dye Elizabeth Anne • Arlington, TX 76012 • AASL

Dye Judith • Head, SLIS Library • Indiana University School of Library and Information Science • Bloomington, IN 47405 • ACRL

Dye Margarette M. • Librarian • Paul, Hastings, Janofsky & Walker • Atlanta, GA 30303

Dyer-Hurdon Michelle M. • U.S. Army Corps of Engineers • Detroit, MI 48226

Dyer Barbara • Librarian • North Junior High Library • Boise, ID 83702

Dyer Barbara M. • Branch Manager • Farragut Branch Library • Knoxville, TN 37922 • PLA

Dyer Charles • Law Library Director • San Diego County Law Library • San Diego, CA 92101-3999 • LAMA LITA PLA

Dyer David J. • Trustee • Elmhurst Public Library • Elmhurst, IL 60126 • ALTA PLA

Dyer Dolores • Oakland Public Library • Oakland, CA 94612 • EMIERT

Dyer Esther R. • Dir. of Govt. & Cmnty. Affairs • Empire Blue Cross Blue Shield • New York, NY 10016 • Life

Dyer Gregory L. • Student • Indiana University School of Library and Information Science • Bloomington, IN 47405 • ALCTS LITA RASD

Dyer Jean • South Portland High Sch • S Portland, ME 04106 • AASL LIRT

Dyer Linda • Librarian • Iowa City Public Library • Iowa City, IA 52240

Dyer Nancy W. • Head Extension Dept. • Lancaster County Library • Lancaster, PA 17602 • PLA IFRT

Dyer Sandra Y. • Visiting Assistant Librarian • Indiana University • Bloomington, IN 47405

Dyer Susan K. • Director • Faxon Company Federal Information Services Division • Herndon, VA 22070 • LITA AFLRT FLRT

Dyer Victor E. II • Abbot Public Library • Marblehead, MA 01945

Dygert Michael H. • Director • Revere Public Library • Revere, MA 02151

Dykas Felicity A. • Kansas City, MO 64110 • SORT SRRT

Dyke Dorothy S. • Mesilla Pk, NM 88047

Dyke James P. Dr. • Mesilla Pk, NM 88047 • ACRL
Continuing

Dykeman Amy • Asst. Dir. for Technical Svs. • Georgia Institute of Technology Price Gilbert Memorial Library • Atlanta, GA 30332-0900 • ACRL ALCTS

Dykes Bobbie • Serials Librarian • Jefferson Parish Library Department • Metairie, LA 70010

Dykes Mary Beth E. • Librarian • Kyrene Centennial Middle School • Phoenix, AZ 85044 • YALSA

Dykhuis Randy • Hilliard, OH 43026 • LITA RASD IFRT

Dyki Janet L. • Librarian • Elk Township Library • Peck, MI 48466-0268 • PLA

Dyki Judy • Library Director • Cranbrook Academy of Art Library • Bloomfield Hills, MI 48303-0801 • ACRL LAMA LITA

Dykstra Anne • Brooklyn, NY 11218

Dykstra Kathleen • Branch Manager • Martin County Public Library • Stuart, FL 33494-2374 • AASL LAMA

Dykstra Kathleen Cole • Kingston, RI 02881 • PLA

Dykstra Larry D. • President • Spacemaster Systems Inc. • Zeeland, MI 49464 • LAMA ERT

Dykstra Mary E. • Director • Dalhousie University School of Library & Inf. Studies • Halifax NS, B3H 4H8 Canada

Dykstra Rita W. • East Schodack, NY 12063 • AASL

Dyla Joanna K. • Slavic Cataloger • University of California-Berkeley University Library • Berkeley, CA 94720 • ACRL IRRT

Dymek Mary J. • Director • South Windsor Public Library • South Windsor, CT 06074 • LAMA PLA

Dyment Alan R. • Dean, Academic Services • Mount Royal College Library • Calgary AB, T3E 6K6 Canada • ACRL

Dynin Alan L. • Atlanta, GA 30307-1705 • RASD

Dypolt Ruth E. • Student • University of Tennessee-Knoxville Graduate School of Library & Information Science • Knoxville, TN 37996-4330

Dysart Janice S. • Library Media Specialist • Central Columbia Middle School • Bloomsburg, PA 17815 • AASL

Dysart Marcia • Reference Librarian • Enoch Pratt Free Library • Baltimore, MD 21201-4484 • PLA RASD

Dysart Nancy Noechel • Trustee • Montgomery County Department of Public Libraries • Rockville, MD 20850 • ALTA PLA

Dysleski Gail • Friend • East Brunswick Public Library • E. Brunswick, NJ 08816 • ALTA

Dyson Allan J. • University Librarian • University of California-Santa Cruz Library • Santa Cruz, CA 95064 • ACRL LAMA IFRT

Dyson Jimothy J. • Director • Travis County Law Library • Austin, TX 78767 • ALCTS ASCLA LITA RASD

Dyson Karen D. • Library Instruction Librarian • Shippensburg University Lehman Memorial Library • Shippensburg, PA 17257-2299 • LIRT

Dyson Lillie J. • Baltimore, MD 21207 • PLA

Dyson Rick • Reference Librarian • Montana State University • Bozeman, MT 59717-0332

Dziatkowicz Patricia E. • Circulation Supervisior • Cuyahoga County Public Library Olmsted Falls Branch • Olmsted Falls, OH 44138

Dziedzic Donna O. • New Jersey State Library Department of Education • Trenton, NJ 08625-0520 • ASCLA

Dzurenko Jeanne M. • Supervisor of Business Services • Nashua Public Library • Nashua, NH 03060 • RASD

Dzurnak Elizabeth P. • Library Assistant • University of Connecticut H. B. Trecker Library • West Hartford, CT 06117

Eades Barbara L. • Audiovisual Ln/Health Sci Lib • West Virginia University Health Sciences Center Library • Morgantown, WV 26506 • ACRL LITA IFRT NMRT

Eades Beth • Knoxville, TN 37918 • AASL

Eads Charles R. • Greenwood, IN 46143 • LITA RASD

Eads Roberta L. • Reference Librarian • Indiana State Library • Indianapolis, IN 46204-2296

Eagan Ann M. • Physical Sciences Librarian • University of Nevada-Reno • Reno, NV 89557-0020 • ACRL ALCTS

Eagan Deborah L. • Laguna Elementary School Library • Laguna, NM 87026 • AASL LIRT

Eagan Florence L. • Kilmer Elementary School • Monument, CO 80132

Eagan Joseph M. • Head, Government Ref. Service • Enoch Pratt Free Library • Baltimore, MD 21201-4484 • SORT SRRT

Eager Nancy A. • Public Services Coordinator • Hayward Public Library • Hayward, CA 94541 • ALSC PLA

Eagle Opal Cole • Greencastle, IN 46135 • PLA YALSA   *Life*

Eagle Sherry • Aurora, IL 60507

Eaglen Audrey B. • Order Librarian • Cuyahoga County Public Library • Cleveland, OH 44134-2792 • YALSA SRRT

Eaglesfield Jaunette • Science Collections Coordinator • Michigan State University Libraries • East Lansing, MI 48824-1048 • ACRL ALCTS SRRT

Eakin Dottie • College Station, TX 77845 • ACRL LAMA LITA

Eames Charles • Reference Librarian • Okefenokee Regional Library • Waycross, GA 31502

Eames Nancy A. • Children's Librarian • Toledo-Lucas County Public Library Maumee Branch • Maumee, OH 43537

Eames Robert W. • Rochester, NY 14625 • ACRL PLA   *Life*

Ean Janice H. • Head Librarian • Forest Park Library • Seattle, WA 98155 • PLA

Eannel Lois • Children's Librarian • Middle Country Public Library • Centereach, NY 11720 • ALSC

Earheart Peggy G. • Supervisor of Monograph Maint • Vanderbilt University Library Jean & Alexander Heard Library • Nashville, TN 37240-0007 • SORT

Earl Susan R. • Public Services Librarian • Clayton County Library System • Jonesboro, GA 30236 • RASD

Earle Antoinette • Greensboro, NC 27406 • Continuing

Earle Elinor S. • Akron, OH 44304 • AFLRT   *Continuing*

Earle Mary E. • Akron, OH 44304-1551 • Continuing

Earles Helen M. Dr. • East Orange, NJ 07018 • AASL

Earley George E. • Kenosha, WI 53143 • Continuing

Earlin Luise • Elementary Librarian • Delaware Valley School District • Milford, PA 18337 • AASL

Early Caroline L. • Head, Acquisitions & Serials Br. • National Agricultural Library • Beltsville, MD 20705 • ACRL ALCTS LAMA LITA

Early Charles T. • Co-Head, Resource Services Dept. • Johns Hopkins University Milton S. Eisenhower Library • Baltimore, MD 21218 • ACRL RASD

Early Sharon M. • Library Media Coordinator • Lee's Summit School District #7 • Lee's Summit, MO 64063 • AASL ALSC LITA YALSA

Early Stephen T. • Cataloger/Deffered Cat. Proj. • Center for Research Libraries • Chicago, IL 60637 • ALCTS

Earnest Jeffrey D • Head, Music Technical Services • Stanford University • Stanford, CA 94305-6011 • ACRL ALCTS

Earnest Kathryn L. • Librarian • Department of Defense Pentagon Library • Washington, DC 20310 • LITA AFLRT FLRT

Earnest Marlene • Librarian • Vallivue Senior High School • Caldwell, ID 83605

Earnest Patricia H. • Manager/Technical Service • Anaheim Public Library • Anaheim, CA 92805 • LITA

Earnshaw Donald C. • Lees Summit, MO 64063 • Continuing

Earnshaw Merle • Branch Librarian • Phoenix Public Library Cholla Branch • Phoenix, AZ 85051-1598 • PLA

Easley Janet T. • Ocean Park, WA 98640 • ILERT

Eason Helga H. • Miami, FL 33168 • Continuing

Eason Lisa Harper • Director • Keller Public Library • Keller, TX 76248 • ALSC PLA YALSA

Eason Susan L. • Associate Archivist • Southwestern University A. Frank Smith Junior Library Center • Georgetown, TX 78626

East Dennis • Assistant Dean of Libraries • Bowling Green State University Jerome Library • Bowling Green, OH 43403 • ACRL LAMA

East Kathleen B. • Student • Southern Connecticut State University School of Libray Science & Instructional Technology • New Haven, CT 06515 • AASL

East Kathy Ann • Assistant Director • Wood County Dist Public Library • Bowling Green, OH 43402 • ALSC PLA

East Mona • Ann Arbor, MI 48106 • ACRL ALCTS   *Life*

Easter Sara • John R. Lowrance Middle School • Jacksboro, TX 76458 • AASL

Easter Susan B. • Student • University of North Carolina Department of Library & Information Studies • Greensboro, NC 27412-5001

Easterbrook Caroline B. • Senior Librarian • Jersey Public Library • Jersey C.I., United Kingdom

Easterbrook David L. • Curator of Africana • Northwestern University Library • Evanston, IL 60208-2300 • ACRL ALCTS IFRT IRRT SRRT

Easterday Nancy D. • Coordinator Technical Operations • Worthington Public Library • Worthington, OH 43085 • LITA

Easterly-Potter Anne P. • Sylvania, OH 43560 • Life

Easterly Ambrose • Dowelltown, TN 37059 • ACRL ALCTS LAMA LHRT   *Life*

Easterly Fannie P. • Student • Louisiana State University School of Library & Information Science • Baton Rouge, LA 70803-3290

Eastes Janice C. • Reference Librarian • Bentley College Solomon R. Baker Library • Waltham, MA 02154-4705

Eastham Ann C. • Madison, WI 53703

Eastman Ann H. • Executive Director • Eastman Associates • Green Valley, AZ 85614-4841 • LAMA

Eastman Danita R. • Carson Regional Library • Carson, CA 90745 • ALSC PLA

Eastman Franklin R. • Branch Manager • Newport Beach Public Library Mariners Branch • Newport Beach, CA 92660 • PLA

Eastman Jane M. • Cary Memorial Library • Lexington, MA 02173 • PLA

Easton Amy M. • Librarian • Boardman, Suhr, Curry & Field • Madison, WI 53703

Easton Marjorie G. • Systems Librarian • San Francisco State University J. Paul Leonard Library • San Francisco, CA 94132 • LAMA

Eastwold Carol L. • Albert Lea, MN 56007 • Continuing

Eastwood Beverly J. • Librarian • King Elementary School Lancaster School District • Lancaster, PA 17603

Eastwood Kelly • Student • University of North Texas School of Library & Information Sciences • Denton, TX 76203

Eastwood Phyllis M. • Children's Librarian • Falmouth Public Library • Falmouth, MA 02540

Easun M. Susan • University of Toronto Faculty of Library & Information Science • Toronto ON, M5S 1A1 Canada • AASL ALSC LRRT NMRT

Eatenson Ervin T. • Dallas, TX 75219 • Continuing

Eaton Andrew J. • Frankfort, MI 49635 • ACRL LAMA *Life*

Eaton Barbara • Library Service Institutions • Colorado State Library Department of Education • Denver, CO 80203 • ASCLA

Eaton Bernice • Head,Technical Services • Fort Valley State College H.A. Hunt Memorial Library • Ft. Valley, GA 31030 • ALCTS

Eaton Carolyn K. • Librarian • U.S. Army Corp of Engineers Ohio River Division • Cincinnati, OH 45201 • FLRT

Eaton Casindania P. • New York, NY 10011 • YALSA IFRT   *Continuing*

Eaton Doris A. • Student • Rutgers University School of Communication Information & Library Studies • New Brunswick, NJ 08903

Eaton E. Gale • University of Rhode Island Graduate School of Library & Information Studies • Kingston, RI 02881-0815 • AASL ALSC LITA

Eaton Edward A. III • Computer Programmer • Marcive, Inc. • San Antonio, TX 78265 • LITA

Eaton Katherine G. • Public Relations Librarian • University of Oregon Library • Eugene, OR 97403-1299 • ACRL

Eaton Kay S. • Houston, TX 77055 • ALCTS IRRT

Eaton Nancy L. • Director • Iowa State University Library • Ames, IA 50011-2140 • ACRL LITA

Eaton Rita • Trustee • East Orange Public Library • East Orange, NJ 07018 • ALTA IFRT

Eavenson Diane M. • Library Consultant • Costabile Associates Inc. • Bethesda, MD 20814

Ebbatson Patricia K. • Delaware County District Library • Delaware, OH 43015

Ebbers Frances A. • Librarian • Saint Edwards University Scarborough Phillips Library • Austin, TX 78704 • ACRL

Ebbinghouse Carol Price • Librarian • Western State university • Fullerton, CA 92631 • ACRL LAMA LITA RASD

Ebbitt Paula F. Ms. • Head of Circulation & Reserves • Harvard University JF Kennedy School of Government Library • Cambridge, MA 02138 • ACRL

Ebeling-Koning Blanche T. • Cura of Rare Bks & Lit Mss • University of Maryland College Park Theodore R. McKeldin Library • College Park, MD 20742-7011 • ACRL

Ebeling Nancy • Dennis Chavez Elementary School • Albuquerque, NM 87109 • AASL

Eber Beryl E. • Supervising Librarian • New York Public Library Manhattan Borough Office • New York, NY 10019 • YALSA

Eberhart George M. • Priority Publishing • Chicago, IL 60660 • ACRL

Eberhart Gwen • Houston, TX 77042-2709 • AASL

Eberhart Martha L. • Reference Librarian • University of Minnesota-Duluth Library • Duluth, MN 55812-2495

Eberly Elaine D. • Trustee • Henrico Public Library • Richmond, VA 23223 • ALTA

Ebersole W. Brian • Science Librarian • Claremont Colleges Libraries Honnold/Mudd Library • Claremont, CA 91711

Ebersole William Dale Junior • Serials Cataloger • University of Toledo • Toledo, OH 43606 • ALCTS

Eberspacher Debbie • Student • Emporia State University School of Library & Information Management • Emporia, KS 66801 • ALSC

Ebert Debby • Lewis Elementary School • Solon, OH 44139 • ALSC

Ebert John J. • Marian College of Fond du Lac Cardinal Meyer Library • Fond du Lac, WI 54935

Ebert Mary J. • Emporia, KS 66801 • PLA

Ebert Patrice Gaffney • Librarian • Charlotte & Mecklenburg Public Library Morrison Regional Library • Charlotte, NC 28211

Ebinger Meade • Wallingford, CT 06492 • ASCLA

Eble Mary M. • Westlake, OH 44145-3646

Ebrahim Husain Ahmed • Science Librarian • Florida State University • Tallahassee, FL 32306-2047 • IRRT

Ebright Madge • Paradise, CA 95969 • Continuing

Ebster Deborah M. • Public Services Librarian • Rock Valley College Educational Resources Center • Rockford, IL 61111

Eby James F. • Director, ERC • Tulare County Office of Education • Visalia, CA 93291 • AASL ALSC LITA

Eby Patricia • Salinas, CA 93907 • AASL ACRL ALCTS LAMA LITA PLA

Eccles Ann E. • Librarian • Hennepin County Library • Minnetonka, MN 55343 • ASCLA LAMA PLA RASD

Eccles Kim L. • Librarian (Part-time) • Horace W. Sturgis Library • Marietta, GA 30061 • ACRL

Echavarria Tami • University of California-San Diego Library 0175A • La Jolla, CA 92093-0175 • ACRL RASD NMRT

Echols Anne E. • Branch Head • Chicago Public Library Hamilton Park Branch • Chicago, IL 60621

Echt Rita L. • Head, Serials Acquisitions • Michigan State University Libraries • East Lansing, MI 48824-1048 • ACRL ALCTS LAMA

Echt Sandy A. • Indexer, Bus. Per. Index • H. W. Wilson Company • Bronx, NY 10452 • RASD

Eck Shannon A. • Student • University of Kentucky College of Library & Information Science • Lexington, KY 40506-0391

Eckardt Gladys • Sarasota, FL 34243

Eckart Violet L. • Director • Corydon Public Library • Corydon, IN 47112 • LAMA PLA

Eckelmeyer Karin A. • Slavic Cataloger • Stanford University Libraries Cecil H. Green Library • Stanford, CA 94305-6004 • ACRL ALCTS LITA

Eckels Patricia W. • Hanovr, NH 03755

Eckenrod J Victoria • Library Director • Seneca East Public Library • Attica, OH 44807 • PLA

Eckerman Nancy L. • Special Collections Librarian • Indiana University School of Medicine Ruth Lilly Medical Library • Indianapolis, IN 46220 • ACRL

Eckerson Gale • Supervisor of User Services • C/W Mars • Paxton, MA 01612 • LITA

Eckert Carolyn J. • Children's Services Manager • Fullerton Public Library • Fullerton, CA 92632 • ALSC

Eckert Daniel • Manager Learning Resources • Holy Family Medical Center Health Science Library • Manitowoc, WI 54221-1450

Eckert Julie A. • Corporate Librarian • Mead Corporation • Dayton, OH 45463 • NMRT
Eckert Mary E. • Head Librarian • Landon School • Bethesda, MD 20817 • AASL
Eckert Sharon S. • University of New England Jack S. Ketchum Library • Biddeford, ME 04005 • ALCTS
Eckhardt Fern L. • Librarian II • Phoenix Public Library • Phoenix, AZ 85004 • PLA
Eckhardt Su A • Media Coordinator • Smoky Hill High School • Aurora, CO 80015 • AASL
Eckhardt Vicki • Technical Services Librarian • Texas Lutheran College Blumberg Memorial Library • Seguin, TX 78155 • ACRL ALCTS RASD
Eckinger Linda • Independence, MO 64050
Eckles Elizabeth • Adm Ln • Wolfner Library for the Blind & Physically Handicapped • Jefferson City, MO 65109
Ecklund Kristin A. • California State University Oviatt Library • Northridge, CA 91328-1289 • ACRL ALCTS LITA RASD ILERT LIRT LRRT
Eckman Catherine A. • Assistant Reference Libraian • University of South Carolina • Columbia, SC 29208
Eckness June B. • Branch Manager & Reference • Broward County Library Fort Lauderdale Branch • Ft. Lauderdale, FL 33304
Eckols Ruth W. • Austin, TX 78703
Eckroade Carlene B. • Millersville University of Pennsylvania • Millersville, PA 17551-0302 • ACRL
Eckstein Adele L. • Director • West Hempstead Public Library • West Hempstead, NY 11552 • LAMA PLA
Eckstrand Tatyana L. • Asst. Librarian II Cataloger • University of California-San Diego Library 0175A • La Jolla, CA 92093-0175 • SRRT
Eckstrom David K. • Assistant Librarian • California Polytechnic State University Robert E. Kennedy Library • San Luis Obispo, CA 93407 • ACRL ALCTS RASD IFRT LIRT NMRT VRT
Eckstrom Luverne • Minneapolis, MN 55404 • Continuing
Eckwright Gail Z. • Humanities Librarian • University of Idaho Library • Moscow, ID 83843 • ACRL
Economos Lucia X. • Des Plaines, IL 60018
Ecsedy Brenda L. • Systems Librarian • Boston University Alumni Medical Library • Boston, MA 02118 • ACRL LITA
Edberg J Fyle • Bridgeport, CT 06604 • ACRL LITA *Life*
Edberg Ruth M. • Librarian/Media Specialist • Notre Dame High School Peter Chanel Library • Harper Woods, MI 48225 • AASL YALSA
Eddie Ann S. • Deputy Chief Executive Officer • Scarborough Public Library • Scarborough ON, M1P 4P4 Canada • LAMA LITA PLA RASD
Eddinsa Donna E. • Children's Librarian • Memphis-Shelby County Public Library Hollywood Branch • Memphis, TN 38108 • ALSC
Eddy Diane K. • Head Librarian • Ewa Beach Public and School Library • Ewa Beach, HI 96706
Eddy Ginger • Head Librarian • Sulphur High School • Sulphur, LA 70663 • AASL YALSA IFRT
Eddy Janet S. • Children's Librarian • Spokane Public Library Shadle Branch • Spokane, WA 99205
Eddy Lola N. • Decatur, GA 30033 • AASL YALSA *Life*
Eddy Lucy R. • New York, NY 10027 • Continuing
Ede Robin E. • Student • Florida State University School of Library and Information Studies • Tallahassee, FL 32306-2048 • PLA
Ede Stuart J. • Head of Records • British Library • W Yorkshire LS23 7BQ, United Kingdom • LITA
Edelblute Thomas • Student • University of Missouri-Columbia School of Library & Informational Science • Columbia, MO 65211 • ALCTS LITA
Edelen Joseph R. Jr. • Bibliographic Control Librarian • University of South Dakota I.D. Weeks Library • Vermillion, SD 57069-2390 • ACRL LITA *Life*
Edelman Bruce • Reference Librarian • Marion County Library • Marion, SC 29571 • PLA RASD
Edelman Hendrik • Professor/Library & Info Studies • Rutgers University School of Communication Information & Library Studies • New Brunswick, NJ 08903 • ACRL ALCTS
Edelman Michael • Personnel Officer • Free Library of Philadelphia • Philadelphia, PA 19103 • LAMA PLA
Edelstein Elizabeth • Chevron Research & Technology Company • Richmond, CA 94802-0627
Edelstein Judith A. • Coordinator of Public Services • Manhattan Public Library • Manhattan, KS 66502 • PLA YALSA SRRT
Eden Barbara J. • Principal Designer • Eden Design Associates, Inc. • Carmel, IN 46032
Eden David E. • Director • Thomas County Public Library System • Thomasville, GA 31792 • PLA
Edenbach Joan K. • Librarian • Middletown High School Library • Middletown, RI 02840
Edens Erika E. • Bloomington, IN 47401 • PLA
Edgar Lynne E. • Tucson, AZ 85712 • PLA EMIERT IFRT SRRT
Edge Carolyn D. Ms • Library Media Specialist • Washington Irving Middle School • Tarrytown, NY 10591 • AASL
Edgerly Joan S. • Media Specialist • Griswold Elementary School • Berlin, CT 06037 • AASL
Edgerton Janet Gebbie • Catalog Librarian • North Carolina State University • Raleigh, NC 27695-7111 • ALCTS
Edgerton Linda K. • Librarian • Windam Texitile & History Museum • Willimantic, CT 06226 • ALSC YALSA *Life*
Edgerton Margaret C. • Lancaster, SC 29720 • AASL
Edgerton Sylvelin A. • Assistant Librarian-Reference • University of California UCSB Library • Santa Barbara, CA 93106-9010 • ACRL RASD IFRT SRRT
Edgren-Krekovich Gale R. • Youth Services Librarian • Calumet City Public Library • Calumet City, IL 60409-4003 • ALSC
Edleman Joan • Library Media Specialist • George W. Hewlett High School • Hewlett, NY 11557 • AASL
Edlin Katherine C. • Assistant Director • Greenwich Library • Greenwich, CT 06830 • PLA
Edlund Norma L. • Director • Salida Regional Library • Salida, CO 81201 • PLA
Edlund Thomas K. • Salt Lake City, UT 84152
Edmanson Barbara W. • Argyle, TX 76226 • NMRT
Edminster Reuben William • McHenry Public Library District • McHenry, IL 60050-5796 • SRRT
Edminster Tami Maher • Student • Indiana University School of Library and Information Science • Bloomington, IN 47405 • AASL ALSC PLA
Edmond Veyshon C. • Student • University of Illinois Graduate School of Library and Information Science • Urbana, IL 61801
Edmonds Anne C. • Librarian • Mount Holyoke College Williston Memorial Library • South Hadley, MA 01075-1493 • ACRL
Edmonds Leslie • Youth Services Coordinator • Saint Louis Public Library • St. Louis, MO 63103-2389 • AASL ALSC PLA RASD YALSA LIRT LRRT
Edmonds Margaret • Librarian • Lewis-Palmer Elementary School • Monument, CO 80133 • AASL
Edmonds May H. • Deland, FL 32724 • ALSC PLA *Continuing*
Edmonds Susan L. • Technical Services Supervisor • Somerville Public Library • Somerville, MA 02143 • ALCTS
Edmondson C • Plano, TX 75023
Edmondson Carol A. • Upper School Librarian • Nichols School • Buffalo, NY 14216-3698 • AASL
Edmondson Ernestine B. • Automation/Technical Services • Chesapeake Public Library • Chesapeake, VA 23320 • ALCTS PLA
Edmondson Joan • Media Specialist • Rabun Gap-Nacoochee High School • Rabun Gap, GA 30568 • LITA
Edmonson Melissa C. • Lawton, OK 73505 • AASL
Edmunds Randa H. • Media Specialist • Kingsbury Elementary School • Sumter, SC 29154 • AASL ALSC NMRT
Edmunds Susan Hester • Public Information Librarian • Iberia Parish Library • New Iberia, LA 70560 • LAMA
Edmundson Margaret B. • Librarian • College of the Marshall Islands • Majuro, MH 96960 • PLA
Edmundson Martha M. • Youth Services Librarian • Denton Public Library • Denton, TX 76201 • ALSC IFRT
Edney James W. • Regional Librarian • Fleming County Public Library • Flemingsburg, KY 41041-1298
Ednie Harry • Public Service Librarian • Truckee Meadows Community College Learning Resources Center • Reno, NV 89512 • LAMA RASD
Edrington Rozanne A. • Butler, MO 64730 • NMRT
Edsall Shirley A. • Campbell, NY 14821-9742 • PLA YALSA IFRT *Life*
Edsall Thomas L. • Baltimore, MD 21203
Edstrom Catherine A. • Hales Corners, WI 53130 • LITA IFRT
Edstrom Nancy J. • Springfield, IL 62704-4927 • MAGERT
Edstrom Sharon M. • Littleton, CO 80122 • PLA
Edward Ian M. • Head Acquisitions Department • Memphis State University Main Library • Memphis, TN 38152 • ACRL
Edwards Alice P. • Concord, NC 28025-9230 • AASL ALSC
Edwards Andrea Y. • School Library Media Specialist • Cardozo High School • Washington, DC 20011 • AASL
Edwards Anne G. • Asst. Head, Ellis Ref Services • University of Missouri-Columbia Ellis Library • Columbia, MO 65201 • ACRL RASD
Edwards Betty • Library Manager • Motorola Codex • Mansfield, MA 02048 • LAMA LITA
Edwards Bonnie • Trustee • Henrico Public Library • Richmond, VA 23223 • ALTA
Edwards Burton V. • Rare Book Cataloger • University of Pennsylvania Library Van Pelt-Dietrich Library Center • Philadelphia, PA 19104-6206 • ACRL LHRT
Edwards Carol A. • Children's Program Supervisor • Buckham Memorial Library • Faribault, MN 55021 • ALSC YALSA EMIERT SRRT
Edwards Cynthia M. • Librarian • Woodstock Union High School • Woodstock, VT 05091 • AASL
Edwards Dale L. • Director of Library Services • Treasure Valley Community College • Ontario, OR 97914
Edwards Dana S. • California State University Hayward Library • Hayward, CA 94542 • ACRL LAMA
Edwards Dorothy D. • Librarian • Boy Scouts of America • Irving, TX 75015-2079
Edwards E. Anne • Assoc. Dean for Access Services • University of Alabama • Tuscaloosa, AL 35487-0266 • ACRL ALCTS LAMA LITA
Edwards Elaine F. • Reference Librarian • Cheshire Public Library • Cheshire, CT 06410
Edwards Estelle Z. • Reference Librarian • Smithtown Library • Smithtown, NY 11787
Edwards Frances B. • Houston, TX 77088-6918 • AASL
Edwards Gregory A. • Reference Library • Middletown Public Library Union Township Branch • West Chester, OH 45069
Edwards Guy P. • Freeport Memorial Library • Freeport, NY 11520
Edwards Harriet M. • Assistant Director • East Meadow Public Library • East Meadow, NY 11554-1700 • PLA SRRT
Edwards Jemeta • Lida Benton Elementary School • Monroe, LA 71202 • AASL
Edwards Jennifer L. • Natural History Museum of Los Angeles County • Los Angeles, CA 90007 • ACRL NMRT
Edwards John • Catalog Librarian • Teachers College-Columbia University Milbank Memorial Library • New York, NY 10027 • ALCTS LITA
Edwards John J. • Edwards Brothers Inc • Ann Arbor, MI 48106 • ACRL ALCTS *Life*
Edwards Jonathan C. • Ft. Lauderdale, FL 33315
Edwards Judy P. • Circulation Supervisor • Getty Center for the History of Art Humanities Library • Santa Monica, CA 90401-1455
Edwards Karlene K. • Librarian • Ironwood High School Library • Glendale, AZ 85304 • AASL LITA *Life*
Edwards Kathleen M. • Library Manager • Plano Public Library System • Plano, TX 75086-0356 • LITA PLA
Edwards Laura E. • Secondary Media Ctr. Director • Coppell Independent School District • Coppell, TX 75019 • AASL ALSC YALSA
Edwards Leroy V. • Supervisor • Dayton Board of Education Library/Media Telecomm Srvs • Dayton, OH 45427-3482 • AASL
Edwards Linda E. • Librarian • Waterford Elementary • Orlando, FL 32828 • AASL
Edwards Louise • Lake Otis Elementary School Library • Anchorage, AK 99508
Edwards Louise D. • Supervisior Cataloging Dept. • University of Guelph Library • Guelph ON, N1G 2W1 Canada • ACRL ALCTS
Edwards Margaret A. • Toledo, OH 43606
Edwards Marie M. • Librarian • Brogden Primary School • Dudley, NC 28333 • AASL
Edwards Mary E. • Media Specialist • Young Middle School • Pembroke Pines, FL 33028 • AASL
Edwards Mary E. • Student • University of California-Los Angeles (UCLA) • Los Angeles, CA 90024-1450 • LITA PLA RASD NMRT
Edwards Mary L. • Manager, Technical Services • Montgomery County Library System • Conroe, TX 77301 • ALCTS PLA CLENE
Edwards Merlyn J. Mrs. • Woodbridge Middle School • Woodbridge, VA 22191 • AASL
Edwards Ossia Mrs. • Trustee • Prichard Public Library • Prichard, AL 36610
Edwards Peggy • Baty Elementary School • Del Valle, TX 78617 • AASL
Edwards Ralph M. • City Librarian • Phoenix Public Library • Phoenix, AZ 85004 • LAMA PLA
Edwards Richard A. • Evergreen State College • Olympia, WA 98505
Edwards Ronald G. • Concordia University • Mequon, WI 53092-9990 • ACRL LHRT
Edwards Rosa • Supervisor • Wilson Memorial Hospital • Wilson, NC 27893 • ASCLA
Edwards Sally J. • Redondo Beach, CA 90277 • ALSC PLA
Edwards Samuel B. • Media Specialist • Calhoun County High School Library • Edison, GA 31746 • AASL
Edwards Sandra E. • Humanities Librarian • Rice University Fondren Library • Houston, TX 77251-1892 • ACRL
Edwards Shelly A. • Instructor/Analyst • Geac Computers Inc. • Dallas, TX 75244 • ALCTS LITA

Edwards Sherri L. • Director • Ohio State University-Mansfield Bromfield Learning Resources Center • Mansfield, OH 44906 • ACRL RASD LIRT

Edwards Shirley J. • Head of Indexing Branch • National Agricultural Library • Beltsville, MD 20705-2351 • LAMA LITA

Edwards Stephanie L. • Assistant Archivist/Librarian • Texas Tech University Southwest Collection-106 Math • Lubbock, TX 79409 • ACRL

Edwards Susan M. • Student • State University of New York at Albany School of Information Science & Policy • Albany, NY 12222 • ACRL NMRT

Edwards Teresa A. • Asst Dean of Univ Lib for Syst • Saint John's University Library • Jamaica, NY 11439 • ACRL LAMA LITA

Edwards Terry • Trustee • Spokane County Library District • Spokane, WA 99212-1853 • ALTA

Edwards Virginia K. • Children's Library Specialist • Mesa Verde Branch Library • Costa Mesa, CA 92626 • ALSC

Edwards Willie M. Mrs. • Coordinator of Reference Servs. • Wayne State University Purdy-Kresge Library • Detroit, MI 48202

Effinger Nancy E. • Director • Teton County Library • Jackson, WY 83001

Effron Barbara A. • Annadale, VA 22003-4020

Efird Deborah L. • Winston-Salem, NC 27103

Efird Frank K. Jr • Archivist II • Illinois State Archives Office of The Secretary of State • Springfield, IL 62756 • RASD GODORT

Efron Eva • Student • Saint John's University Division of Library & Information Science • Jamaica, NY 11439 • AASL YALSA

Eftekhari Luz Mrs. • Librarian • University of Tehran Library of the Faculty of Law & Political Science • Tehran, Iran • ACRL

Egal Sylvia I. • Student • Saint John's University Division of Library & Information Science • Jamaica, NY 11439

Egan Bessie Condos • Children & Youth Services Cons. • California State Library Library Development Services Bureau • Sacramento, CA 95814-3324 • ALSC PLA

Egan Elizabeth • Director • Gloucester City Library • Gloucester City, NJ 08030 • PLA

Egan Elizabeth M. • Consultant • Dialog Information Services • Chicago, IL 60601

Egan Gwen M. • Student • State University of New York (SUNY) Thomas E. Dewey Graduate Library • Albany, NY 12222

Egan Jill L. • Student • University of Michigan School of Information and Library Studies • Ann Arbor, MI 48109-1092 • AASL

Egan Marian D. • Joliet, IL 60435-3940

Egan Terence W. • Manuscript Division • University of California-Berkeley Bancroft Library • Berkeley, CA 94720 • ACRL

Egbers Gail L. • Ref./Bibl. Instr. Librarian • Pacific Lutheran University Mortvedt Library • Tacoma, WA 98447 • ACRL RASD LIRT

Egbert Stephen D. • Jacksonville Public Libraries Main Library • Jacksonville, FL 32202

Egdes Margaret • Student • University of Texas at Austin Graduate School of Library & Information Sciences • Austin, TX 78712-1276 • RASD

Egebrecht Linda • Technical Services Librarian • Park Ridge Public Library • Park Ridge, IL 60068-4188 • ALCTS LITA

Eger Stephany A. • Branch Manager • Albuquerque Public Library Ernie Pyle Branch • Albuquerque, NM 87106

Eggen J Archer • Green Valley, AZ 85614 • LAMA PLA *Life*

Egger-Price Kathleen • Extension Librarian • Anderson County Library • Anderson, SC 29622-4047

Egger Sheryl • Coordinator of Libraries • West Irondequoit School District • West Irondequoit, NY 14617 • AASL

Eggers Carolyn J. • Waverly, IA 50677

Eggers Goldie • Serials Librarian • Fullerton College William T. Boyce Library • Fullerton, CA 92634

Eggers Lolly P. • Director • Iowa City Public Library • Iowa City, IA 52240 • LAMA PLA IFRT

Eggers Sara H. • Princeton, NJ 08540

Eggers Thomas D. • Illinois Veterans Home • Quincy, IL 62301

Eggert Carolyn Kyes • County Commissioner • Indian River County Library • Vero Beach, FL 32960

Eggert Charlean • Law Librarian • Du Page County Law Library • Wheaton, IL 60187 • LAMA

Eggert Karen M. • Databse Administrator • Joint Bank-Fund Library • Washington, DC 20431 • ALCTS LITA

Eggert Nancy B. • Chicago, IL 60646

Eggleston Marcia M. • Librarian • Norwood-Norfolk Central School • Norwood, NY 13668 • AASL

Eggleston Suzanne M. • Fairfield, CT 06430 • ACRL IFRT LIRT NMRT

Eggum Janet M. • Library Director • Whitefish Bay Public Library • Milwaukee, WI 53217

Egizi Eileen P. • Librarian • Landis School Libray • Vineland, NJ 08360-8165 • AASL

Egleston Charles Lee • Bibliographer • University of California Rivera Library • Riverside, CA 92517 • ACRL

Egorshin Tanya • Phillips Junior College • Jackson, MS 39216

Ehernberger Diane • Bozeman, MT 59715 • AASL

Ehernberger Nicolette • Manager, Quick Reference • Saint Louis Public Library • St. Louis, MO 63103-2389 • PLA RASD

Ehler Charles • Head Librarian • South Winneshiek Community Schools • Calmar, IA 52132 • AASL

Ehlers Lesa R. • Mound, MN 55364 • NMRT

Ehlers Shirley A. • Library Media Specialist • Lawton-Bronson Community School • Lawton, IA 51030 • AASL YALSA

Ehlert Phyllis L. • Downriver Branch Supervisor • Sacramento Public Library Isleton Branch • Isleton, CA 95641

Ehlinger Clifford J. • Director of Media • Grant Wood Area Education Agency • Cedar Rapids, IA 52404

Ehlke Nancy K. • Annandale, VA 22003

Ehrenberg Ralph E. • Acting Chief Geog & Map Div • Library of Congress • Washington, DC 20541 • MAGERT

Ehrens Cheryl • Editor, Social Sciences Index • H. W. Wilson Company • Bronx, NY 10452 • LITA

Ehresman Colette P. • Arnold J. Tyler School • New Lenox, IL 60451 • AASL

Ehret Judith • Team Leader • Sonoma County Office of Education • Santa Rosa, CA 95403 • AASL

Ehrhardt Allyn • Librarian • Franklin University Library • Columbus, OH 43215 • ACRL RASD

Ehrhardt Margaret • Columbia, SC 29210 • AASL

Ehrhorn Jean H. • University of Hawaii Thomas Hale Hamilton Library • Honolulu, HI 96822 • ACRL LAMA

Ehrich Joan C. • Librarian • Marblehead Public Schools Business Office • Marblehead, MA 019445

Ehrig Ellen H. • Librarian • State University of New York (SUNY) College of Technology • Alfred, NY 14802-1193 • ACRL ALCTS RASD

Ehrlich Evelyn • Collection Services Dept. • New York University Elmer Holmes Bobst Library • New York, NY 10012 • ACRL LAMA

Ehrlichman Elizabeth • School Librarian • New York City Board of Education John Adams High School • Ozone Park, NY 11417 • AASL YALSA

Eiberson Harold • Oakland Gardens, NY 11364 • Continuing

Eich Berna • Sayville, NY 11782

Eichekberger Jeanne T. • State University of New York at Binghamton Libraries (SUNY) • Binghamton, NY 13902-6012

Eichelberger Marianne • Director • Newton Public Library • Newton, KS 67114 • PLA

Eichell Nanette • Director • Nevins Memorial Library • Methuen, MA 01844 • LAMA PLA

Eichenberg Robert A. • Media Specialist • Bradenton Southeast High School • Bradenton, FL 33508 • AASL IFRT

Eichfeld Kathleen M. • Reference Librarian • Calvert County Public Library • Prince Frederick, MD 20678

Eichholtz Lisa A. • Student • Syracuse University School of Information Studies • Syracuse, NY 13244-4100

Eichhorn Sara J. • Acting Head, Circulation Dept. • University of California-Irvine Library • Irvine, CA 92713 • ALCTS RASD

Eickhoff Jane S. • Baltimore County Public Library Pikesville Branch • Baltimore, MD 21208 • PLA

Eide Margaret Ann • Social Science Librarian • Eastern Michigan University Library Center of Educational Resources • Ypsilanti, MI 48197

Eidelman Diane L. • Documents Librarian • Suffolk Cooperative Library System • Bellport, NY 11713 • PLA GODORT

Eifert Phillip • Librarian • Dayton & Montgomery County Public Library Northtown-Shiloh Branch • Dayton, OH 45405

Eiffert Robert E. • Media Specialist • Myrtle Creek Elementary School • Myrtle Creek, OR 97457 • AASL

Eig Nathan G. • Denver, CO 80206 • Continuing

Eigabroady Helen M. • Director • Friends Free Library of Germantown • Philadelphia, PA 19144

Eike Claire M. • Librarian • San Diego Museum of Arts • San Diego, CA 92112-2107

Eilering Susan M. • University of Missouri-Columbia Ellis Library • Columbia, MO 65201 • ACRL

Eilers Marsha J. • Associate Director Ref. Serv. • Elkhart Public Library • Elkhart, IN 46516-3184 • PLA RASD

Eilert Mary Jean • Houston, TX 77057 • AASL RASD *Life*

Eilts John A. • Program Officer for Mid. Eastern • Research Libraries Group Inc. (RLG) • Mountain View, CA 94041-1100 • ACRL ALCTS IRRT

Eimas Evelyn N M • Westerville, OH 43081

Eimas Richard • Curator • University of Iowa Libraries • Iowa City, IA 52242-1379 • ACRL

Einhorn Deborah A. • Reference Librarian • Air Products & Chemicals • Allentown, PA 18195-1501

Eise Martha • Librarian • Saint Mary's School • Bridgeton, MO 63044 • AASL

Eisele Elizabeth A. • Media Specialist • Elkhart Central High School • Elkhart, IN 46516 • AASL

Eiselstein June E. • Director • New Britain Public Library • New Britain, CT 06050 • LAMA LITA PLA

Eiseman Fannie R. Mrs • Brooklyn, NY 11238 • AASL YALSA *Continuing*

Eisemann Ruth Elaine • Atlanta, GA 30345 • AASL

Eisen David J. • Director • Mishawaka-Penn Public Library • Mishawaka, IN 46544

Eisen Marc M • Director • East Orange Public Library • East Orange, NJ 07018 • LAMA PLA *Life*

Eisenbach E. R. • Los Angeles, CA 90049 • IFRT SRRT

Eisenbeis Kathleen M. • Harwood, MD 20776 • GODORT

Eisenbeiser Thomas • Ann Arbor, MI 48103 • IRRT

Eisenberg Michael B. • Associate Professor • Syracuse University School of Information Studies • Syracuse, NY 13244-4100 • AASL LRRT

Eisenberg Phyllis • Librarian • Piedmont Virginia Community College • Charlottesvle, VA 22901

Eisenhut Lynn • Children's Services Coordinator • Orange County Public Library • Santa Ana, CA 92705 • ALSC IFRT SRRT

Eisenman Jean S. • University of Missouri-Rolla Curtis Laws Wilson Library • Rolla, MO 65401 • ACRL RASD

Eisenmann Judith S. • Oak Park, IL 60304 • PLA YALSA

Eisenstadt Rosa M. • Librarian • Greenville Technical College Learning Resources Center • Greenville, SC 29606

Eisenstein Eva F. • Librarian • Evanston Hospital • Evanston, IL 60201 • RASD ILERT

Eisenstein Jill M. • High School Librarian • University School of Nashville • Nashville, TN 37212 • AASL

Eisert Debra • Branch Head • Lane Public Library Fairfield Branch • Fairfield, OH 45014 • PLA RASD

Eisinger Carol A • Librarian • College of DuPage Learning Resources Center • Glen Ellyn, IL 60137

Eisinger John H. • Burbank, CA 91506

Eismann Donald • Board of Trustees Member • Pierce County Rural Library District • Tacoma, WA 98446 • ALTA PLA

Eisnaugle Jennie M. • Children's Librarian • Dayton & Montgomery County Public Library Northmont Branch • Engelwood, OH 45322 • ALSC

Eisner Jane M. • Madison, WI 53705 • ACRL

Eisner Nadene S. • Librarian I-Ref. & YA • Chicago Public Library Blackstone Branch • Chicago, IL 60615

Eissinger Richard A. • Student • Texas A & M University • College Station, TX 77843-5000 • RASD

Eiten Keith D. • Acquisitions/Serials/Ref. Lib. • Central College Library • Pella, IA 50219

Ekanayaka Ranjith Charles • Executive Director • Tri-Star Group of Companies • Colombo, 4, Sri Lanka

Ekberg Eleanor • Tacoma, WA 98403 • ASCLA *Continuing*

Ekblad-Bean Pearl • Lake Bluff, IL 60044

Ekblad Ann M. • Metairie, LA 70002

Ekblad Howard J. • Metairie, LA 70002

Ekblad Judith A. • Young Peoples Librarian • Elmhurst Public Library • Elmhurst, IL 60126 • ALSC PLA

Ekblom Robert F. • Marketing Manager • Brodart Company • Williamsport, PA 17705

Ekdahl Janis K. • Assistant Director • Museum of Modern Art Library • New York, NY 10019-5498

Ekfelt Lynn Case • Archivist & Cura of Rare Bks & S • Saint Lawrence University Owen D. Young Library • Canton, NY 13617 • ACRL ALCTS LITA RASD

Ekhaml Leticia Dr • Assoc Prof of Media Education • West Georgia College Library Media Program • Carrollton, GA 30118 • AASL

Ekins Grace G. • Librarian-Cataloging • DeKalb College Central Campus Library • Clarkston, GA 30021-2396 • ACRL ALCTS

Ekland Patricia A. • Coor. Electronic Search Svs. • University of Victoria McPherson Library • Victoria BC, V8W 3H5 Canada • LITA

Eklund Janet R. • Elburn, IL 60119

Ekwinski Catherine J. • Yorkville, IL 60560 • LITA PLA

El-Hadidy Bahaa Dr. • Professor • University of South Florida School of Library & Information Science • Tampa, FL 33620 • LITA RASD IRRT

El-Hoshy Lynn M. • Policy Specialist • Library of Congress • Washington, DC 20541 • ALCTS

Elam Elizabeth E. • Young Adult Level Specialist • Prince George's County Memorial Library System • Hyattsville, MD 20782-2098 • AASL YALSA

Elam Lynn M. • Librarian • Waubonsee Community College Library • Sugar Grove, IL 60554

Elbert Carol A. • Ames Public Library • Ames, IA 50010 • ALSC

Elcock Harriet A. • Wichita, KS 67203 • Continuing

Elder Connie C. • Student • University of Pittsburgh School of Library and Information Science • Pittsburgh, PA 15260 • ALSC

Elder Eleanor S. • Head, Science & Engineering Div. • Tulane University Howard-Tilton Memorial Library • New Orleans, LA 70118 • ACRL

Elder Jane D. • Winter Park, FL 32792-2568 • Continuing

Elder Jean • Media Specialist • Putnam City High School • Oklahoma Cty, OK 73122 • AASL

Elder Kathryn • Film Librarian • York University Libraries • North York ON, M3J 1P3 Canada • ACRL

Elder Margaret E. • Denair, CA 95316 • Continuing

Elder Mary L. • Processing Librarian • Library of Congress • Washington, DC 20541 • ACRL ALCTS

Elder Natalie • East Orange, NJ 07017

Elder Nelda J. • Chair,Collection Development • Kansas State University Farrell Library • Manhattan, KS 66506-1200 • ACRL ALCTS

Elder Richard H. • Chief, Tech Services Division • Enoch Pratt Free Library • Baltimore, MD 21201-4484 • ALCTS LAMA LITA

Elder Sandra M. • School Library Media Generalist • Moultonboro Schools • Moultonboro, NH 03254 • AASL ALSC YALSA

Elderwind Jean M. • Librarian • Carnegie Public Library • Eureka Spg, AR 72632

Eldon Kathryn • Yuma, AZ 85366-4554

Eldred Heather A. • System Director • Wisconsin Valley Library Service • Wausau, WI 54401

Eldredge Jeffrey R. • Kauai Library District • Lihue, HI 96766 • PLA

Eldredge Jonathan D. • Chief Clln & Inf Res Devel • University of New Mexico Medical Center Library • Albuquerque, NM 87131 • ACRL ALCTS LAMA

Eldredge Mary • Associate Librarian • University of California Shields Library • Davis, CA 95616

Eldridge Carrie • Anchorage Municipal Libraries Z. J. Loussac Library • Anchorage, AK 99503 • ALSC YALSA

Eldridge Diane D. • Student • University of Pittsburgh School of Library and Information Science • Pittsburgh, PA 15260

Eldridge Elizabeth C. • Newark, DE 19711

Eldridge Joanne Nyota • Community Library Manager • County of Los Angeles Public Library Compton Library 531 • Compton, CA 90220 • LAMA PLA

Eldridge Sheryl H. • College Station, TX 77845

Eldridge Shirley G. • Tishomingo, OK 73460 • AASL

Elenausky Edward V. • Director • Emma S Clark Memorial Library • Setauket, NY 11733-2868 • PLA

Elewitz Leah Rae • Matawan, NJ 07747

Elffner Frances • Poudre School District R-1 • Fort Collins, CO 80521 • ALCTS LRRT

Elfstrand Stephen F. • Manager. Technical Services • James J. Hill Reference Library • Saint Paul, MN 55102

Elg Nancy • Library Supervisor • Micron Technology Library • Boise, ID 83706

Elgin Ramona R. • Reference Librarian • Schiller Park Public Library • Schiller Park, IL 60176-1699 • RASD

Elgin Susan R. • Assistant Director • Santa Cruz City-County Library System • Santa Cruz, CA 95060 • LAMA LITA PLA RASD

Eliason Elisabetha S. • Stanhope, NJ 07874

Eliassen Meredith M. • Student • Simmons College Graduate School of Library & Information Science • Boston, MA 02115 • LAMA RASD

Eliceiri Ellen M. • Head of Public Services • Webster University & Eden Theo Seminary & Reformed Historical Society • Webster Groves, MO 63119-3192 • ACRL LIRT

Elieson Victoria • Head Librarian • Sanger Public Library • Sanger, TX 76266

Elizabeth Mary Sr • Librarian • Moore Catholic High School • Staten Island, NY 10314

Elkhafaifi Hussein M. • Student • Brigham Young University School of Library & Information Sciences • Provo, UT 84602

Elkington Nancy E. • Preservation Program Officer • Research Libraries Group Inc. (RLG) • Mountain View, CA 94041-1100 • ACRL ALCTS

Elkins Anne M. • Consultant • North Carolina Department of Cultural Resources State Library • Raleigh, NC 27601-2807 • PLA IFRT

Elkins Linda Y. • Peabody Awards Librarian • University of Georgia Libraries • Athens, GA 30602 • ALCTS LITA

Elkins Patricia A • Closter, NJ 07624 • MAGERT

Elkordy Angela Bird • Librarian • Federal Reserve Bank of New York • New York, NY 10045

Ell Elizabeth L. • Chief Librarian • MidCon Management Corporation • Lombard, IL 60148

Ellair Jeffrey A. • Serials/Interlibrary Loan Ln. • Quincy College Brenner Library • Quincy, IL 62301-2699

Ellefsen David E. • Assistant Director • DYNIX Inc. • Provo, UT 84606 • LAMA IFRT

Elleman Barbara K. • Editor, Book Links • American Library Association • Chicago, IL 60611-2795 • AASL ALSC

Ellenberg Lisa B. • School Librarian • Catlin Gabel School Lower School Library • Portland, OR 97225 • AASL

Ellenberger Jack S. • Shearman & Sterling • New York, NY 10022 • LAMA LITA

Eller Augusta D. • Assistant City Librarian • Saint Clair Shores Public Library • St. Clair Shores, MI 48081 • RASD

Eller Barbara A. • Fayetteville, NC 28301 • AFLRT FLRT

Eller James • Associate Director • Wichita State University Ablah Library • Wichita, KS 67208 • LAMA

Eller Judith L. • School Library Media Specialist • Unified Sch Dist 439 • Sedgwick, KS 67135 • AASL YALSA

Ellermeyer Robert H. • Academic Librarian • Holy Family College Library • Philadelphia, PA 19114

Ellern Gillian D. • Coord of Library Automation • Western Carolina University Hunter Library • Cullowhee, NC 28723-9002

Ellero Nadine P. • Asst. Director for Bibl Control • University of Virginia Medical Center Claude Moore Health Sciences Library • Charlottesville, VA 22908

Ellert D. John • Adminstrative Assistant • Wichita Public Library • Wichita, KS 67202 • LITA

Ellett Robert O. Jr. • Armed Forces Staff College Library • Norfolk, VA 23511-6097

Ellickson Ellen • Quinnipiac College • Hamden, CT 06518 • ALCTS RASD LRRT

Elling Laura M. • Student • University of North Carolina at Chapel Hill School of Information and Library Science • Chapel Hill, NC 27599-3360

Ellingson Barbara • Librarian • Stowe Elementary School • Stowe, VT 05672 • AASL

Ellingson Jo Ann • Director • Saint Xavier University • Chicago, IL 60655 • ACRL LIRT

Ellingson LaVonne • Osceola Elementary School • Osceola, WI 54020

Ellington Marcia L. • Library Director • Wilton Manors Public Library • Wilton Manors, FL 33305

Ellington Sala S. • Athens, GA 30606 • AASL

Ellington Sandra L. • Raleigh, NC 27604-9596 • AASL

Ellingwood Sara • Children's Librarian • E. P. Foster Library • Ventura, CA 93001

Ellingwood Sue A. • Supv., Art/Music/Video Dept. • Saint Paul Public Library • St. Paul, MN 55102

Elliot Hugh • Dir. of Information Resources • USAssist • Washington, DC 20008

Elliot Jason M. • Student • New York Public Library • New York, NY 10018-2788 • ACRL GODORT

Elliott-Strange Valerie L. • Indianapolis Marion County Public Library • Indianapolis, IN 46206 • IFRT

Elliott Archie W. • Cataloger • Boston University Mugar Memorial Library • Boston, MA 02215 • LITA

Elliott Barbara B. • Librarian • Baltimore County Public Library • Towson, MD 21204 • PLA

Elliott Barbara Jean • Director • Bluffton-Wells County Public Library • Bluffton, IN 46714 • PLA

Elliott C. Danial • Library Director • Rosemont College Library • Rosemont, PA 19010-1699 • ACRL

Elliott Cherelynn A. • Palos Park, IL 60464-0218

Elliott Dorothy S. • Director • River Bluffs Regional Library • Saint Joseph, MO 64501 • LAMA PLA

Elliott Frank • Librarian for Public Services • G M I Engineering & Management Inst. Library • Flint, MI 48504-4898 • ACRL LAMA IRRT

Elliott Gloria J. • Manager • Los Angeles Public Library North Hollywood Regional Branch • North Hollywood, CA 91601

Elliott Greta K. • Technical Services Supervisor • Las Vegas-Clark County Library District • Las Vegas, NV 89101

Elliott Gwendolyn • Magnolia, DE 19962

Elliott Janet E. • Librarian • Loma Vista Intermedia School • Riverside, CA 92505

Elliott Jean Ann • Library Services Coordinator • Shepherd College Ruth Scarborough Library • Shepherdstown, WV 25443-1568 • AASL ACRL RASD YALSA

Elliott John J. • Head of Technical Service • Crystal Lake Public Library • Crystal Lake, IL 60014 • PLA

Elliott Kay M. • Iowa Department of Human Services Library • Des Moines, IA 50319 • ASCLA LAMA

Elliott Laura D. • Walden Books • Fremont, CA 94538

Elliott Lee • Vice President of Marketing • Millbrook Press Inc. • Brookfield, CT 06804 • AASL ALSC RASD YALSA IFRT IRRT SRRT

Elliott Linda P. • Director • Palos Verdes Library District • Pls Vrd Pnsla, CA 90274 • ALTA LAMA PLA ERT

Elliott Lirlyn J. • Librarian • Eric Williams Medical Services • Champs Fleurs, Trinidad

Elliott Lloyd Gene • Library Director • Greenville Technical College Learning Resources Center • Greenville, SC 29606 • ACRL

Elliott Lorraine T. • Austin, TX 78731

Elliott Louise M. • Library Media Specialist • Wolcott High School • Wolcott, CT 06716 • AASL

Elliott Margaret M. • Student • Syracuse University School of Information Studies • Syracuse, NY 13244-4100 • PLA RASD

Elliott Marian H. • Vice Chairman Bd. of Trustees • Jacksonville Public Libraries Main Library • Jacksonville, FL 32202

Elliott Mary E. • Head of Technical Services • Public Libraries of Saginaw • Saginaw, MI 48605 • LITA PLA IRRT

Elliott Maxine L. • Serials Cataloger • Clemson University R. M. Cooper Library • Clemson, SC 29634-3001 • ALCTS NMRT

Elliott Richard G. • Waldport, OR 97394-9477 • Continuing

Elliott Riette Bryant • Librarian • Walker College Irma D Nicholson Library • Jasper, AL 35501-4899 • ACRL

Elliott Sharon E. • Reference Libn./Bibliographer • Washington University Libraries • Saint Louis, MO 63130-4899 • ACRL RASD SRRT

Elliott Stephen R. • Student • Dalhousie University School of Library & Inf. Studies • Halifax NS, B3H 4H8 Canada • RASD LRRT

Elliott Susan A. • Automation Librarian • Alaska State Library • Juneau, AK 99811-571 • LITA

Ellis Allen W. • Reference Librarian • Northern Kentucky University Steely Library • Highland Heights, KY 41099-6101 • ACRL

Ellis Amy N. • Inf. Res. Coordinator • Fishbeck, Thompson, Carr & Huber • Ada, MI 49301

Ellis Carol P. • Student • Kent State University School of Library & Information Science • Kent, OH 44242-0001

Ellis Edward F. • Doctoral Student • University of Kentucky College of Education • Lexington, KY 40506

Ellis Elaine C. • Librarian • Whindham Southeast Supervisory Union • Brattleboro, VT 05301

Ellis Elizabeth G. • Salisbury, MD 21801-8328 • ACRL

Ellis Gloria B. • Library Director • Walsh College of Accountancy Business Administration • Troy, MI 48007-7006 • ACRL ALCTS LAMA GODORT

Ellis Gonzalez Carolyn S. • Bedford, IN 47421

Ellis Jack D. Dr • Morehead, KY 40351-1564 • Continuing

Ellis Jill C. • Western Nebraska Cmnty Coll Library • Scottsbluff, NE 69361 • ACRL

Ellis Jonette S. • Director • Enid Public Schools Central Library • Enid, OK 73701 • AASL IFRT

Ellis Karen S. • Coor. of Information Services • Victoria Public Library • Victoria, TX 77901 • YALSA

Ellis Kate M. • System Librarian • Harvard University • Cambridge, MA 02138 • ACRL LITA

Ellis Kathleen V. • Librarian • Berkeley Carroll Street School • Brooklyn, NY 11217 • AASL EMIERT

Ellis Kem B. • Head of Information Service • High Point Public Library • High Point, NC 27261 • PLA

Ellis Lawrence E. • Newberry College Wessels Library • Newberry, SC 29108

Ellis Madaleen J. • Chair Librarian • Newtown Square Public Library • Newtown Sq, PA 19073

Ellis Marie C. • English & Amer Lit Bibl. • University of Georgia Libraries • Athens, GA 30602 • ACRL RASD

Ellis Mark E. • Reference Librarian • East Tennessee State University Sherrod Library • Johnson City, TN 37614 • ACRL RASD

Ellis Mary J. • Bloomfield Hills, MI 48302

Ellis Nathan • Hialeah, FL 33014 • RASD LRRT

Ellis Patricia C. • Wilmington, NC 28412 • AASL

Ellis Patrick Brother • Trustee • Free Library of Philadelphia • Philadelphia, PA 19103 • ALTA

Ellis Peggy L. • Catawba County Library • Newton, NC 28658 • ALCTS

Ellis Rebecca • Adult Services Librarian • Cerritos Public Library • Cerritos, CA 90701

Ellis Ruth M. • Sacramento Public Library Central Branch • Sacramento, CA 95814 • RASD SRRT

Ellis Virginia M. • Francestown, NH 03043

Ellis William W. • Associate Librarian • Library of Congress • Washington, DC 20541

Ellisen Judith N. • Cataloger • Hayward Public Library • Hayward, CA 94541 • ALCTS PLA

Ellison Joseph W. • Circulation Desk Unit Head • University of Texas Libraries General Libraries • Austin, TX 78713-7330 • ACRL LITA NMRT

Ellison Rena • Library Supervisor • Wood County Board of Education • Parkersburg, WV 26101 • AASL

Ellison Sallie H. • Director • Wayne State University Purdy-Kresge Library • Detroit, MI 48202 • ACRL

Ellison Sandra M. • Public Library Consultant • Oklahoma Department of Libraries • Oklahoma City, OK 73105-3298 • ALTA ASCLA PLA

Ellison Virginia N. • Woodbury, NY 11797

Ellisor F. L. Page • Houston, TX 77042

Ellmann Gail M. • Coordinator of Learning Systems • State University of New York College at Buffalo, E. H. Butler Library • Buffalo, NY 14222-1095 • ACRL

Ells Michael J. • Student • Northern Illinois University Department of Library & Information Studies • DeKalb, IL 60115

Ellson Linda R. • Small Library Services • Battle Ground, WA 98604 • ALCTS LITA

Ellsworth Judith Love • Student • State University of New York at Albany School of Information Science & Policy • Albany, NY 12222 • ALSC

Ellsworth Marlene A. • Cadillac-Wexford Public Library • Cadillac, MI 49601-0700 • PLA RASD

Ellsworth Ralph E. • Boulder, CO 80302 • ACRL LITA *Honorary*

Elman Sarah Su-erh • Los Angeles, CA 90049

Elman Stanley A. • Pasadena, CA 91107 • LITA

Elmendorf Dorothy • Grand Rapids, MI 49506-4320 • RASD

Elmer Jan • Student • University of California-Berkeley School of Library & Information Studies • Berkeley, CA 94720

Elmer Linda M. • Librarian • Legislative Reference Bureau Library • Milwaukee, WI 53202-3567

Elmore Barbara • Director • Lake Villa Public Library District • Lake Villa, IL 60046 • ALCTS ALSC ALTA LAMA PLA RASD

Elmore Chloe Anne • Librarian • Moore High School • Louisville, KY 40228

Elmore Gleena • Librarian • Kendrick Memorial Library • Brownfield, TX 79316 • ALSC PLA

Elmore Kathy • Young Adult Coordinator • Danbury Public Library • Danbury, CT 06810 • YALSA

Elmore Kenneth C. • Brookline, ME 04616 • IFRT LRRT

Elmore Lisa E. • Branch Head • Forsyth County Public Library Kernersville Branch • Kernersville, NC 27284

Elmore Michael • Head, Copy Cataloging • New York University Elmer Holmes Bobst Library • New York, NY 10012 • ALCTS IFRT

Elmore Rheena B. • Student • University of Alabama School of Library & Information Studies • Tuscaloosa, AL 35487-0252 • LAMA

Elmouchi Joan • Auburn Hills Public Library • Auburn Hills, MI 48326

Elms Mary E. • Director • Carlsbad Public Library • Carlsbad, NM 88220 • PLA SORT

Elrod Frances • Wilson, NC 27893-3146 • Continuing

Elrod J. McRee • Victoria BC, V9B 5T7 Canada • ALCTS *Continuing*

Elrod Jennifer M. • Madison, WI 53711-3287 • ALSC IFRT

Elrod Melissa • Librarian • Northside Elementary School • Shreveport, LA 71107 • AASL

Elsasser Katharine K. • Team Leader • Library of Congress • Washington, DC 20541 • ACRL ALCTS

Elsbernd Mary E. • Collection Development Librarian • Northern Kentucky University Steely Library • Highland Heights, KY 41099-6101 • ACRL

Elsbree John J. • Dir. Off. of Pubn. & Bibl. Serv. • National Tech Inf Service • Falls Church, VA 22042 • GODORT

Else Carolyn J. • Director • Pierce County Rural Library District • Tacoma, WA 98446 • LAMA PLA

Else Willis I. • President • Genealogical System Inc. • Columbus, OH 43220 • LITA

Elsen Carol J. • Somerville, MA 02143

Elsen Marie K. • Associate Professor • Saint Cloud State University Centennial Hall LRC • St. Cloud, MN 56301-4498 • ACRL ALCTS *Life*

Elsener Paul • Director • Harborfields Public Library • Greenlawn, NY 11740 • ALSC ALTA LAMA LITA PLA YALSA

Elshami Ahmed M. • System Librarian • Temple University Paley Library • Philadelphia, PA 19122 • ACRL LITA

Elshoff Beth D. • Elementary Librarian • Muscatine Community School District • Muscatine, IA 52761 • ALSC

Elsner Jacqueline C. • Children's Librarian • Athens Regional Library • Athens, GA 30606

Elstein Herman • Librarian • Free Library of Philadelphia Northeast Regional Library • Philadelphia, PA 19149

Elstein Jacqueline • Librarian • University of Cape Town Graduate School of Business Library • Rondebosch 7700, South Africa • ACRL LAMA

Elston Jamie L. • Terrytown, LA 70056

Elsweiler John A. Jr. • Head of Reference • Utah State University Merrill Library • Logan, UT 84322-3000 • ACRL RASD

Elswick Rebecca E. • Fredericksbrg, VA 22401-3829

Elswick Stanley W. • Cataloging Librarian • National Oceanic & Atomospheric Administration (NOAA) Library & Information Servs. Div. • Rockville, MD 20852 • ALCTS

Eltzroth Elsbeth Lee • Visual Scene South • East Point, GA 30344

Elvir Karen M. • Marsh & McLennan, Incorporated • Dallas, TX 75201 • IFRT

Elwart Joan Potter • Trustee • Dearborn Department of Libraries Henry Ford Centennial Library • Dearborn, MI 48126

Elwell Irma F. • Librarian • Gloucester City Junior-Senior High School • Gloucester City, NJ 08030

Elwell Margaret • Part-time Clerk • San Jose Public Library • San Jose, CA 95113 • EMIERT SRRT

Ely Donald P. • Director • ERIC Clearinghouse on Information Resources Syracuse University • Syracuse, NY 13244 • AASL ALTA

Elzein Khadiga M. • Cataloger • Temple University Paley Library • Philadelphia, PA 19122 • ACRL ALCTS

Elzy Cheryl Asper • Head, Edu./Psychology/TMC Dir • Illinois State University Milner Library • Normal, IL 61761-0900 • ACRL

Emanoil Mary J. • Librarian • Toledo-Lucas County Public Library • Toledo, OH 43624 • LITA PLA SRRT

Emanuel Elinor N. • Librarian • Baltimore County Public Library Woodlawn Branch • Baltimore, MD 21207 • PLA

Emanuele Susan J. • Student • University of Pittsburgh School of Library and Information Science • Pittsburgh, PA 15260 • ACRL

Emard James J. • Student • University of Rhode Island Graduate School of Library & Information Studies • Kingston, RI 02881-0815 • ACRL LITA

Emberson Eileen J. • Library Services Manager • Chippewa Valley Technical College • Eau Claire, WI 54701 • ACRL LITA

Embrey Frances • Trustee • Prince William Public Library System Administrative Support Center • Prince William, VA 22192-5073

Embry Carmen F. • Coord. of Bibliographic Instr. • University of Louisville Ekstrom Library • Louisville, KY 40292

Emde Judith Z. • Assistant Science Librarian • University of Kansas Anschutz Science Library • Lawrence, KS 66045-2800 • ACRL

Emerick John L. • Boyertown Area School District • Boyertown, PA 19512 • AASL

Emerick Michael J. • Reading School District • Reading High School • Reading, PA 19604 • AASL

Emerson Arthur V. • Library of Congress • Washington, DC 20541

Emerson Carolyn • Acting Head, Reference Dept. • Emma S Clark Memorial Library • Setauket, NY 11733-2868 • RASD

Emerson Deborah • Librarian • Monroe Community College LeRoy V. Good Library • Rochester, NY 14623-0701

Emerson Debra L. • Librarian I • Colegio Franklin D. Roosevelt The American School of Lima Peru • APO Miami, FL 34031

Emerson Eileen M. • Fayetteville, NY 13066

Emerson Gloria J. • Interim Dean of CRCE • Institute of American Indian Arts • Santa Fe, NM 87504 • EMIERT

Emerson Gretchen A. • Elem. Library Media Specialist • Seminole Elementary School • Mount Clemens, MI 48043 • AASL ALSC

Emerson Karin E. • Reference Librarian • Marin County Free Library • San Rafael, CA 94903

Emerson Kathleen • Gateway Regional High School • Woodbury Heights, NJ 08097 • AASL

Emerson Patrick R. • Student • University of Iowa School of Library & Information Science • Iowa City, IA 52242

Emerson S. Kay • Librarian • Marine Corps Air Ground Combat Center • 29 Palms, CA 92278 • PLA AFLRT FLRT

Emerson Tamsen L. • Associate Librarian • University of Wyoming • Laramie, WY 82071

Emerson Toni C. • Student • University of Washington Graduate School of Library and Information Science • Seattle, WA 98195

Emerson William L. • Playa Del Rey, CA 90291 • ACRL LAMA *Life*

Emerton Bruce L. • Reference Librarian • California State Polytech University • Pomona, CA 91768 • ACRL RASD

Emery Carol A. • Librarian • United States Air Force Shaw Air Force Base Library • Shaw AFB, SC 29152 • AFLRT

Emery Esther W. • Librarian • Oak Creek Elementary School • Houston, TX 77068

Emery F Doreen • Reference Librarian • Marin County Free Library • San Rafael, CA 94903

Emery George J. • Student • State University of New York (SUNY) at Buffalo • Buffalo, NY 14260

Emery Glenn • Supervisior Librarian • Jacksonville Public Library Highlands Branch • Jacksonville, FL 32218-4712

Emery Karen E. • Student • Kent State University School of Library & Information Science • Kent, OH 44242-0001

Emery Margaret J. • Campus Librarian • University of Adelaide Roseworthy Campus • Roseworthy, Australia • LITA

Emmans Henry M. • Assistant Librarian • State University of New York (SUNY) Penfield Library • Oswego, NY 13126-3514

Emme Sandra J. • Branch Manager • Prince George's County Memorial Library System-Marlboro Branch • Marlboro, MD 20772 • LAMA LRRT

Emmert Betty • Director • Klamath County Public Library System • Klamath Falls, OR 97603

Emmert Donna • Library Director • Perry Public Library • Perry, IA 50220

Emmett James • Director • Emmett-HNK Inc. • Novato, CA 94947 • ALCTS

Emmons Kathy • Student • University of California-Berkeley School of Library & Information Studies • Berkeley, CA 94720 • LITA

Emmons Mark E. • Occidental College Library • Los Angeles, CA 90041 • ACRL IFRT LIRT

Emmons Mary Ellen B. • Director • Wasilla Public Library • Wasilla, AK 99654-7085 • ALCTS LAMA PLA EMIERT IFRT

Emmons Mildred G. • Atlanta, GA 30342

Emons Margaret L. • Student • University of Nebraska • Lincoln, NE 68588

Emory Johnny Lou Mrs. • Librarian • Bishop England High School • Charleston, SC 29401-3522

Emperado Mercedes L. • Federal Emergency Management Agency • Washington, DC 20472 • LAMA FLRT

Emrich Priscilla • Librarian • Murphy Memorial Library • Livingston, TX 77351

Emrick Ruth G. • Natchez, MS 39120

Emser S. Ellen • Student • Catholic University of America School of Library and Information Science • Washington, DC 20064

Encarnacion Jorge • Professor • University of Puerto Rico Graduate School of Librarianship • Rio Piedras, PR 00931 • ACRL

Encell Elizabeth • Benson High School • Omaha, NE 68104 • AASL

Enden Diana J. • Library Media Specialist • Jefferson High School • Portland, OR 97217 • AASL YALSA

Ender Deniz • Pearland, TX 77584

Enderle Karen H. • Louis Bennett Public Lib • Weston, WV 26452

Enders Joan • Library Media Specialist • Monticello Middle School • Longview, WA 98632 • AASL

Endres Heidi M. • Library Director • Cedarburg Public Lib • Cedarburg, WI 53012 • LAMA PLA

Endres Maureen D. • Student • Bowling Green State University • Bowling Green, OH 43403 • RASD LIRT SRRT

Enemuoh Tina E. • Student • University of Wisconsin School of Library & Information Studies • Madison, WI 53706

Eng Catherine • Paramus Public Library • Paramus, NJ 07652 • ALSC PLA

Eng Mamie • Librarian • Henry Waldinger Memorial Library • Valley Stream, NY 11582-3011

Engberg Linda L. • Librarian • Hennepin County Library • Minnetonka, MN 55343 • LAMA PLA CLENE

Engebretsen Imogene • Modesto City Schools • Modesto, CA 95351 • AASL ALSC

Engebretson Mary E. • Head of Reference Services • University of South Alabama Library • Mobile, AL 36688 • ACRL RASD

Engel Charles T. • Topeka Public Library • Topeka, KS 66604-1374

Engel Debra H. • Assistant Director • Pioneer Library System • Norman, OK 73069 • PLA

Engel Diane • Young Adult Services • Framingham Public Library • Framingham, MA 01701-8218

Engel Genevieve • Oakland, CA 94610 • LITA SRRT

Engel Jannette • Assistant Director • San Mateo County Library • San Mateo, CA 94402 • PLA CLENE

Engel Julie A. • Director of Learning Resources • DeVry Institute of Technology Learning Resource Center • Chicago, IL 60618 • ACRL SRRT

Engel Kevin R. • Science Librarian • Grinnell College • Grinnell, IA 50112-0811 • ACRL

Engel Sondra F. • Oxford, OH 45056 • AASL ILERT

Engelbert Alan • Director • Manitowoc Public Library • Manitowoc, WI 54220 • PLA

Engelbrecht Mary E. • Reston, VA 22094

Engeldinger Eugene A. • Director of Library Services • Carthage College John Mosheim Ruthrauff Library • Kenosha, WI 53141 • ACRL

Engelfried Steven • Childrens Librarian • Alameda County Library Pleasanton Branch • Pleasanton, CA 94566 • ALSC

Engelke Hans Dr • Assistant Dean • Western Michigan University Libraries Dwight B. Waldo Library • Kalamazoo, MI 49008 • ACRL ALCTS LAMA LITA

Engelkes Sheri L. • Student • University of Missouri-Columbia School of Library & Informational Science • Columbia, MO 65211

Engelman Alice H. • Assistant Director • Washington County Library • Woodbury, MN 55125 • LAMA PLA

Engels Mary G. • Director • Connecticut State Library Middletown Library Service Center • Middleton, CT 06457 • PLA

Engelstein Lena S. • New Haven, CT 06511 • Continuing

Engen Richard B. Mr. • Cleveland, OH 44120-3830 • ASCLA PLA *Life*

Engen Susan H. • Librarian • Follett Corporation • Juneau, AK 99801 • AASL

Engh Jane A. • Reference Coordinator • Traverse des Sioux Library System • Mankato, MN 56002-0608 • RASD

England Claire • Associate Professor • University of Toronto Faculty of Library & Information Science • Toronto ON, M5S 1A1 Canada

England Ellen E. • Fremont, CA 94555 • LITA

England Janet • Librarian • Greenwich Country Day School • Greenwich, CT 06830 • AASL

England Jeanie N. • Library Media Specialist • Doolittle Elementary School • Cheshire, CT 06410 • AASL

England Margaret J. • Pierre, SD 57501-3352 • GODORT

England Patricia W. • Director • Manlius Library • Manlius, NY 13104

Englander Claire L. • Indexer • University of California Division of Library Automation • Oakland, CA 94612-3550 • ALCTS MAGERT

Engle Carolyn • Assistant & Children's Librarian • Guthrie Public Library • Guthrie, OK 73044 • ALSC YALSA

Engle Constance B. • Hendersonville, NC 28739 • ALCTS LITA

Engle Emma P. • Clarksboro, NJ 08020 • Continuing

Engle Joyce C. • Head of Circulation Department • Hamilton Township • Trenton, NJ 08610

Engle Lucia S. • Belmar, NJ 07719 • Continuing

Engle Madge • Indianapolis, IN 46278

Engle Mary E. • Berkeley, CA 94705 • LITA SRRT

Engle Michael O. • Hd, Reference & Instuction • Cornell University • Ithaca, NY 14853-5301 • ACRL

Engle Monica W. • Senior Reference Librarian • Pikes Peak Library District • Colorado Springs, CO 80901 • LITA

Engle Sherry S. • Student • Clarion University of Pennsylvania College of Library Science • Clarion, PA 16214

Engle Virginia E. Miss • Akron, OH 44308-1419 • ACRL ALCTS *Continuing*

Engleman Roberta A. • Rare Book Cataloger • University of North Carolina Academic Affairs Library 080-A • Chapel Hill, NC 27514 • ACRL

Engler Dorothy Ms. • Retired • Fluvanna County Library • Fork Union, VA 23055

Engler Gretchen A. • Morgan Stanley & Co Inc • New York, NY 10020 • LAMA LITA LRRT

Engler Jean • Englewood, CO 80112

Engler Lois N. • Bismarck, ND 58501 • Continuing

Engler Martha C. • Dorchester, MA 02122 • ALSC PLA *Continuing*

Englesakis Marina F. • Librarian/Archivist • St. Michael's Hospital • Toronto ON, M5B 1W8 Canada

English Ada J. Mrs • Librarian Emeritus • Rutgers University Libraries Mabel Smith Douglass Library • New Brunswick, NJ 08903-0270 • ACRL LAMA *Continuing*

English Alice • Trustee • Bellwood Public Library • Bellwood, IL 60104 • ALTA

English Christine • Student • Northern Illinois University Department of Library & Information Studies • DeKalb, IL 60115 • AASL EMIERT

English David S.J. • Yuba City, CA 95991 • PLA FLRT GODORT

English Denise M. • Chicago, IL 60628

English Dorothy V. • Bainbridge, WA 98110 • ALSC

English Janet L. • Circulation Dept. Supervisor • Central State University Hallie Q Brown Memorial Library • Wilberforce, OH 45384

English John P. • Philadelphia, PA 19119-3137

English Marie • Carousel Book Fair • Salt Lake City, UT 84109

English Mary C. • Librarian. Cataloging Dept. • University of Notre Dame Libraries • Notre Dame, IN 46556 • ACRL ALCTS

English Melda D. • Librarian III • Cleveland Public Library Mount Pleasant Branch • Cleveland, OH 44115 • EMIERT

English Ray • Director of Libraries • Oberlin College Library • Oberlin, OH 44074 • ACRL LAMA

English Rita C. • Naples, FL 33942 • PLA YALSA *Life*

Engman Elizabeth F. • Elgin, IL 60120

Engstrand Eva J. • Reference Librarian • Huntington Public Library • Huntington, NY 11743 • LAMA RASD

Engstrand Joseph • Huntington Public Library • Huntington, NY 11743

Engstrom Ruth E. • Detroit, MI 48240 • Continuing

Enlow Cathy R. • Assistant Director/Adult Serv. • Brookings Public Library • Brookings, SD 57006-2077

Enlow Helen Hahn • Wooster, OH 44691 • Continuing

Enomoto Ginger T. • Librarian • Mililani-Uka Elementary School • Mililani, HI 96789 • AASL

Enomoto Wanda H. • Wahiawa, HI 96786

Enos R Randall • Children's Services Consultant • Ramapo Catskill Library System • Middletown, NY 10940 • ALSC YALSA

Enos Rosemary H. • Media Specialist • Havelock Elementary School New Bern-Craven County • Havelock, NC 28532

Enrich Rachel • Student • University of North Carolina School of Library Science • Chapel Hill, NC 27599-3360 • PLA RASD AFLRT

Enright-Hajek Maris • Chicago, IL 60611

Enright Adele M. • Librarian • Rio Hondo Community College Library • Whittier, CA 91101

Enright Dennis J. • Eisenhower Public Library District • Harwood Heights, IL 60656

Enright Joan • Director of Media • Harper High School • Chicago, IL 60636 • YALSA

Ensel Ellen H. • Reference Librarian • New Haven Free Public Library • New Haven, CT 06510 • LITA

Ensley Robert F. • Kaskaskia Library System • Smithton, IL 62285 • ASCLA LAMA LITA RASD SRRT

Ensor Pat • Coor., Electronic Inf. Services • Indiana State University Cunningham Memorial Library • Terre Haute, IN 47809 • LITA

Entlich Richard G. • Sr Sys Analyst/Tech Proj Leader • Cornell University Albert R. Mann Library • Ithaca, NY 14853-4301 • LITA

Entorf Regina P. • Special Collections Librarian • Wittenberg University Thomas Library • Springfield, OH 45501 • ACRL

Entrekin Paulette D. • Director • Laurel-Jones County Library • Laurel, MS 39440 • LAMA

Entz Bruce • Head Librarian • Tabor College Library • Hillsboro, KS 67063 • ACRL IFRT IRRT LHRT SRRT

Entzi Sara D. Mrs • Youngstown, OH 44512 • ASCLA PLA *Life*

Enujioke Emmanuel A. • Librarian/Assistant Dept Head • Atlanta-Fulton Public Library • Atlanta, GA 30303 • PLA

Enyart Michael G. • Director, Business Libraray • University of Wisconsin • Madison, WI 53706 • RASD

Enzmann Heidi J. • Audio Visual Librarian • Downey City Library • Downey, CA 90241

Epler Doris M. • Epler Enterprises, Inc. • Hummelstown, PA 17036 • AASL

Epling Susan S. • Research Assistant • University of Tennessee-Knoxville Graduate School of Library & Information Science • Knoxville, TN 37996-4330 • ALSC

Epp Mary Anne • Director of Library Services • Vancouver Community College • Vancouver BC, V5T 4N3 Canada • ACRL LAMA

Epperly Joyce • Parttime Librarian • Northeast Iowa Community College • Calmar, IA 52132 • ACRL

Eppinger Michelle C. • Student • University of Wisconsin-Milwaukee School of Library & Information Science • Milwaukee, WI 53201

Eppink Alice J. • Washington, DC 20016 • Continuing

Epple Margie • Coor. for Interlibrary Loan Svs. • Rutgers University Libraries Archibald Stevens Alexander Library • New Brunswick, NJ 08903 • ACRL LAMA

Epps Dorothy A. • Elementary Librarian • Sand Lake Elementary School • Anchorage, AK 99502 • AASL

Epps Helen • Macon, GA 31211

Epstein Connie C. • Port Washington, NY 11050 • AASL ALSC

Epstein Dena J. • Chicago, IL 60615 • Continuing

Epstein Emily • Kansas State University Farrell Library • Manhattan, KS 66506-1200 • ACRL

Epstein Eva H. Mrs • Newton Center, MA 02149 • AASL ALSC *Continuing*

Epstein Hank • Madison, WI 53711 • AASL LITA

Epstein Joanna • University of Chicago Library • Chicago, IL 60637-1502 • LITA

Epstein Lionel • Kensington, MD 20895 • ACRL

Epstein Paula L. • Reference Librarian • Columbia College Library • Chicago, IL 60605 • ACRL

Epstein Peter • Marketing Director • Video Project • Oakland, CA 94618 • PLA

Epstein Rheda • Technical Services Division Hd. • Palm Beach County Library System • Riviera Beach, FL 33404-9947 • ALCTS LAMA LITA PLA EMIERT

Epstein Sarah G. • Providence, RI 02906

Epstein Susan Baerg • President • Susan Baerg Epstein Ltd • Costa Mesa, CA 92626 • ACRL LITA PLA

Erazo Edward • Ref./Tech. Serv. Librarian • Saint Thomas University Law Library • Miami, FL 33054 • ACRL RASD

Erb Robert H. • Assistant Cataloger • Montgomery County Community College Learning Resource Center • Blue Bell, PA 19422-0758 • ACRL ALCTS

Erbst Jeannette R. • Director of Educational Media • Red Bank Catholic High School • Red Bank, NJ 07701

Ercelawn Ann • Serials Librarian • Vanderbilt University Library Jean & Alexander Heard Library • Nashville, TN 37240-0007 • ALCTS

Erdahl Carol J. • Co-owner • The Red Balloon Bookshop • Saint Paul, MN 55105 • ALSC

Erdman Barbara • Assistant Professor • Ohio State University • Columbus, OH 43210 • AASL

Erdman C. Sue • Adult Svs/Ref. Libn-Asst. Dir. • Bosler Free Library • Carlisle, PA 17013 • PLA

Erdman Eve • Prescott College Library • Prescott, AZ 86301 • IFRT

Erdman Marie G. • Student • University of Illinois Graduate School of Library and Information Science • Urbana, IL 61801

Erdt Terrence Dr. • Director • Purdue University Calumet Instructional Technologies Services • Hammond, IN 46323-2094

Erena Suzanne • Williamsburg, VA 23185

Erickson Ann • Pembroke Hill School • Kansas City, MO 64112 • AASL

Erickson Annamarie • Student • Rosary College Graduate School of Library & Information Science • River Forest, IL 60305

Erickson Carol A. • Student • University of Illinois Graduate School of Library and Information Science • Urbana, IL 61801

Erickson Charlene M. • Student • Indiana University School of Library and Information Science • Bloomington, IN 47405 • ALCTS IFRT

Erickson E. Walfred • Stuart, FL 34994 • ACRL LAMA *Continuing*

Erickson Estelle • 1st Assistant Catalog Department • Library Association of Portland • Portland, OR 97205 • Continuing

Erickson Jean M. • Librarian • Franklin Park Public Library District • Franklin Park, IL 60131 • ALCTS

Erickson Joanne L. • President • Friends of East Bridgewater Public Library • East Bridgewater, MA 02333

Erickson Lucie A. • Director • Weyauwega Public Library • Weyauwega, WI 54983 • PLA NMRT

Erickson Lynda L. • Acquisitions Librarian • Old Dominion University Library • Norfolk, VA 23529-0256 • ALCTS

Erickson Miriam • Media Director • Gibraltor High School • Fish Creek, WI 54212 • AASL

Erickson Muriel C. • Librarian • Pine River Public Library • Pine River, MN 56474

Erickson Nancy L. • Student • University of Michigan Libraries Information and Library Studies • Ann Arbor, MI 48109 • AASL

Erickson Patricia A. • Stoughton Public Library • Stoughton, WI 53589

Erickson Phyllis L. • Education Reference • Kansas State University Farrell Library • Manhattan, KS 66506-1200 • ACRL

Erickson Rodney • Acquisitions/Reference Librarian • Moorhead State University Livingston Lord Library • Moorhead, MN 56563-2989

Erickson Sandra E. • Senior Technical Librarian • General Railway Signal Corporation • Rochester, NY 14611

Erickson Virginia P. • Urbana, IL 61801

Ericsen Patricia G. • Librarian • Woodside Elementary School • Glen Burnie, MD 21461 • AASL

Ericson Randall L. • Assoc Univ Libn for Tech/Auto • Syracuse University Library E. S. Bird Library • Syracuse, NY 13244-2010 • ALCTS

Ericsson Paul A. • Head of Technical Services • Westport Public Library • Westport, CT 06880

Eriksen Mark J. • Public Services Librarian • Dakota State University • Madison, SD 57042-1799 • ACRL RASD LIRT MAGERT

Erisman Donna D. • Media Specialist • Oldtown School • Oldtown, MD 21555 • AASL

Erk Ruth P. • Smithtown Library • Smithtown, NY 11787

Erlandson Rhonda L. • Wilsonville, OR 97070 • IFRT

Erlich Martin • Orange, CA 92665

Ernest Douglas J. • Assistant Reference Librarian • Colorado State University William E. Morgan Library • Fort Collins, CO 80523

Ernestine M. Sr • Librarian • Saint Joseph Hill Academy Library • Staten Island, NY 10305

Ernst Alison A. • Associate Alumni Relations • Hampshire College Harold F. Johnson Library Center • Amherst, MA 01002

Ernst Carolyn A. • Manager Defense Sys. & Elec. • Texas Instruments Inc. • Lewisville, TX 75067 • ALCTS LAMA LITA

Ernst Christine M. • University of Kansas Medical Center A.R. Dykes Library • Kansas City, KS 66103 • ACRL RASD

Ernst Gordon E. Jr • Assistant Head of Cataloging • Western Michigan University Libraries Dwight B. Waldo Library • Kalamazoo, MI 49008 • ALCTS

Ernst Margaret M. • Circulation Librarian • Appleton Public Library • Appleton, WI 54911-4780 • PLA

Ernsthausen David G. • Business Reference Librarian • Wake Forest University Z Smith Reynolds Library • Winston Salem, NC 27109-7777 • RASD

Errico-Cox Lisa A. • Librarian • Queens Borough Public Library • Jamaica, NY 11432

Ersfeld William • Flushing, NY 11358

Erskine Eleanor S. • Coordinator Technical Services • Neumann College Library • Aston, PA 19014

Erskine M. Pauline • Lakewood, CO 80228-4327

Ertel Monica E. • Manager • Apple Computer, Inc. Library • Cupertino, CA 95014 • AASL LITA PLA

Ertell Irene E. • City Librarian • Tigard Public Library • Tigard, OR 97223 • LAMA

Ertl Charlene R. • Student • University of Rhode Island Graduate School of Library & Information Studies • Kingston, RI 02881-0815 • ALSC

Ervin Diane S. Dr. • Media Specialist • Southside High School • Greenville, SC 29605 • AASL

Ervin Natalie N. • Bellevue, WA 98008

Ervin Sherri • Gary, IN 46408-4532 • NMRT

Erwin Helen J. • American Antiquarian Society • Worcester, MA 01609-1634 • ACRL

Erwin Linda M. • South Texas Library System • Corpus Christi, TX 78401

Erwin Marie C. • School Media Specialist-Ln • Mount Everett Regional School • Sheffield, MA 01257 • AASL YALSA SRRT

Erwin Richard A. • Student • University of Illinois Graduate School of Library and Information Science • Urbana, IL 61801 • EMIERT IFRT IRRT SRRT

Erwin Sarah J. • Curator of Archival Clln • Thomas Gilcrease Institute of American History and Art • Tulsa, OK 74127

Erwin Stephen H. • Brookline, MA 02146

Esau Denis Frederick • Head Librarian • Saint Anthony Adult Education Center Library • Boksburg 1460, South Africa

Esbenshade Ranz C. • Knoxville, TN 37931 • ACRL RASD

Escheandia Pedro • Information Specialist • Apple Computer, Inc. Library • Cupertino, CA 95014 • ALCTS

Eschelbach Claudia A. • Columbus, OH 43232 • ALSC

Escobedo Armando J. • Reference Librarian • Miami-Dade Community College North Campus Library • Miami, FL 33167

Escoffier Alfred H. • Asst. City Librarian • Burlingame Public Library • Burlingame, CA 94010

Escoffier Deirdre M. • Children's Librarian • Locust Valley Library • Locust Valley, NY 11560 • ALSC

Escude Andrew J. • General Librarian • Louisiana State University Libraries Middleton Library • Baton Rouge, LA 70803-3342

Eshelman William R. • Proprietor • The Press at the Camperdown Elm • Wooster, OH 44691 • Continuing

Eskay Lalie F. • Brunswick Elementary School • Brunswick, MD 21771 • AASL

Eskoz Patricia A. • Cataloger • University of Colorado at Denver Auraria Library • Denver, CO 80204 • ALCTS

Eskridge Beverly M. • Students • University of Tennessee-Knoxville Graduate School of Library & Information Science • Knoxville, TN 37996-4330

Eskridge Nancy L. • Austin, TX 78745 • AASL

Esman Michael D. • Catalog Librarian • National Agricultural Library • Beltsville, MD 20705-2351 • ALCTS

Esparza Julia M. • Student • Indiana University School of Library and Information Science • Bloomington, IN 47405 • IFRT IRRT SRRT

Espeland Katharine H. • Student • University of California-Berkeley University Library • Berkeley, CA 94720

Espina Marina E. • Reference/Bibliographer • University of New Orleans Earl K. Long Library • New Orleans, LA 70148

Espinal Isabel R. • Reference Librarian • New Haven Free Public Library • New Haven, CT 06510

Espinas Deanna • Hawaii Department of Public Safety • Honolulu, HI 96813 • ASCLA

Espley John L. • Dir. of Customer Services • VTLS Inc. • Blacksburg, VA 24060 • ALCTS LITA

Espo Harold • District Sales Manager • Dialog Information Services, Inc. • New York, NY 10166 • ACRL

Esposito Denise • Fort Collins, CO 80526-4235

Esposito Joseph A. Jr. • Library Manager • Thunderbird Samaritan Medical Center Medical Library • Glendale, AZ 85306

Esposito Judith S. • Student • University at Albany Libraries • Albany, NY 12222 • AASL

Esposito Michael A. • Senior Librarian • New York State Library State Education Department • Albany, NY 12230

Esquevin Christian • Director of Library Services • Coronado Public Library • Coronado, CA 92118 • ALSC LAMA PLA

Esquibel Oresta • Associate Libn. for Public Svs. • Westminster College of Salt Lake City • Salt Lake City, UT 84105 • ACRL

Esquivel Cecelia M. • Librarian II • San Diego Public Library • San Diego, CA 92101 • ALSC RASD

Esquivel Junior • Highland Park High School • Dallas, TX 75205

Essency Janet E. • University of Chicago Library John Crerar Library • Chicago, IL 60637-1403 • ALCTS

Esser Patrick R. • Omaha Public Library • Omaha, NE 68102 • PLA

Essick James F. • Head Librarian • Silver City Public Library • Silver City, NM 88061 • PLA

Essig Mary L. • Student • University of Iowa School of Library & Information Science • Iowa City, IA 52242

Essman Mary Pat • Director • Lane Public Library • Hamilton, OH 45011

Estabrook Leigh • Dean • University of Illinois Graduate School of Library and Information Science • Urbana, IL 61801 • PLA SORT SRRT

Estelle Myron E. • Student • University of Kentucky College of Library & Information Science • Lexington, KY 40506-0391 • LITA PLA

Estepp Marjorie Vivian • Moorefield High School • Moorefield, WV 26836 • AASL

Estermann-Wiskot Yolanda • University of Michigan Libraries Information and Library Studies • Ann Arbor, MI 48109 • RASD

Estes Carol A. • Asst. Children's Librarian • Mission Viejo Library • Mission Viejo, CA 92691 • ALSC

Estes Cheri S. • Student • University of Kentucky College of Library & Information Science • Lexington, KY 40506-0391 • ALSC

Estes Donna S. Ms. • Trustee • Greensboro Public Library • Greensboro, NC 27402 • ALTA

Estes Elaine Graham • Director • Public Library of Des Moines • Des Moines, IA 50308-1791 • LAMA PLA

Estes Elizabeth W. • Assistant Director • Stanly County Public Library • Albemarle, NC 28001 • PLA IRRT

Estes Glenn E. • Professor and Asst. Director • University of Tennessee-Knoxville Graduate School of Library & Information Science • Knoxville, TN 37996-4330 • ALSC RASD

Estes Grace W. Miss • Janesville, WI 53545 • Continuing

Estes Hilda J. • Thomas Jefferson High School • Port Arthur, TX 77642 • AASL

Estes James A. • Student • Catholic University of America Library Science Library • Washington, DC 20064

Estes Marilyn Starke • Gallaudet University Library • Washington, DC 20002 • ASCLA

Estes Pamela Jean • Camden, AR 71701

Estes Sally C. • Booklist Ed, Books for Youth • American Library Association • Chicago, IL 60611-2795 • YALSA

Estevez Donna D. • Elem. Library Media Spec. • Tara Elementary School • Bradenton, FL 34203 • AASL

Estivill Assumpcio • Professor • Escola University of Bibliograhic • Barcelona, Spain • ALCTS LITA

Estra Hannah • Otis Public Library • Norwich, CT 06360

Estrada James A. • Director • University of Connecticut H. B. Trecker Library • West Hartford, CT 06117 • ACRL LAMA LITA

Estrin Chere • Estrin Publishing • Santa Monica, CA 90403

Estrin Jonathan W. • Pittsburgh, PA 15232 • ALCTS IFRT

Etcheson Kimberly B. • Kankakee Community College Learning Resources Center • Kankakee, IL 60901

Etchingham Barbara Y. • Librarian • Latin School of Chicago • Chicago, IL 60610 • AASL

Etchison Josephine P. • Frederick, MD 21701 • PLA RASD   *Continuing*

Etemad Behnam • Student • University of Oklahoma School of Library & Information Studies • Norman, OK 73019

Etheridge Lucy C. • Student • Louisiana State University School of Library & Information Science • Baton Rouge, LA 70803-3290 • SRRT

Etheridge Shirley L. • Lake Jackson, TX 77566

Etherington Don • President Conserv Div • Information Conservation Inc • Brown Summit, NC 27214-9745 • ALCTS

Etherington Thomas L. • Lenape High School Library • Medford, NJ 08055 • AASL

Etkin Elaine G. • State University of New York Agricultural & Technical College Library • Farmingdale, NY 11735 • ACRL ALCTS SRRT

Etschmaier Gale S. • Oakton, VA 22124-1401 • ACRL ALCTS

Ettl Lorraine • Public Service Librarian • University of North Dakota H.E.French Library of Health Sciences • Grand Forks, ND 58202-9002 • ASCLA

Eubanks Diane • Librarian • Seminole Community College Library • Sanford, FL 32773

Eubanks Elizabeth B. • Durham, NC 27712 • AASL

Eubanks Jackie • Associate Professor • Brooklyn College Library • Brooklyn, NY 11210 • ACRL RASD ILERT IRRT SRRT

Eubanks Margaret • Saint Paul, MN 55113 • Continuing

Eulberg Judith • Portage Turner High School • Portage, WI 53901 • AASL YALSA

Eurich Dawn R. • Student • University of Michigan School of Information and Library Studies • Ann Arbor, MI 48109-1092

Eury William L. • Bessemer Cty, NC 28016 • Continuing

Eussen Barbara • United States Army Fort Riley Post Library • Fort Riley, KS 66442

Euster Joanne R. • Vice-President for Univ Libs • Rutgers University Libraries • New Brunswick, NJ 08903 • ACRL IRRT

Eustis Joanne D. • Interim University Librarian • Virginia Polytechnic Inst & State Univ University Libraries • Blacksburg, VA 24062-9001

Evalds Victoria K. • Ardmore, PA 19003

Evanitsky Matoula A. • Branch Librarian • Mid-Continent Public Library Antioch Branch • Gladstone, MO 64119

Evans Anaclare F. • Head,Database Management Section • Wayne State University Purdy-Kresge Library • Detroit, MI 48202 • ACRL ALCTS LITA

Evans Anita K. • Public Services Coordinator • University of Wisconsin Murphy Library • La Crosse, WI 54601 • ACRL RASD

Evans Anne M. • School Librarian • Berkshire Farm Junior-Senior High School • Canaan, NY 12029 • AASL YALSA

Evans Barbara L. • Product Specialist • Data Research Associates Inc. • Saint Louis, MO 63132 • LAMA LITA

Evans Brenda J. • Adult Service Librarian • Novi Public Library • Novi, MI 48375 • ALCTS ALSC ALTA LAMA LITA PLA RASD

Evans Calvin D. • Area Librarian • McGill University Libraries • Montreal PQ, H3A 1Y1 Canada • ACRL

Evans Carol A. • Reston, VA 22090 • ALCTS LITA FLRT

Evans Carolyn M. • Andover, MA 01810-5018 • ALSC PLA

Evans Catherine G. • Librarian • Memphis University School Hyde Library • Memphis, TN 38119-5399 • AASL

Evans Charlotte E. • Assistant Librarian • University of Central Arkansas Torreyson Library • Conway, AR 72032

Evans Cheryl M. • Cataloging Librarian • Nevada State Library & Archives • Carson City, NV 89710

Evans Dana • Unified School District Library • Cloverdale, CA 95425

Evans David • Media Director • Bloomimgton Junior High School • Bloomington, IL 61701

Evans David G. • Librarian • Ohio State University Marion Regional Campus Library • Marion, OH 43302 • ACRL RASD

Evans Denise M. • Hayward Public Library • Hayward, CA 94541

Evans Dilys • Dilys Evans Fine Illustration • Norfolk, CT 06058 • ALSC

Evans Dorothy J. • Children's Librarian • Chicago Public Library South Shore Branch • Chicago, IL 60649 • ALSC SRRT

Evans Elizabeth M. • Online Services Ref Librarian • New York University Library of the School of Law • New York, NY 10012-1099

Evans Elizabeth Sandidge • Chesapeake Public Library Hillard Branch • Chesapeake, VA 23323

Evans G. Edward • Director • Loyola Marymount University Charles Von Der Ahe Library • Los Angeles, CA 90045 • ACRL ALCTS LAMA LITA IRRT   *Life*

Evans Gloria B. • Serials Librarian • Alabama A&M University J.F. Drake Memorial LRC • Normal, AL 35762

Evans Glyn T. • Assistant Provost • State University of New York Office of Library Services • Albany, NY 12246

Evans Gwynneth • Director, External Relations • National Library of Canada • Ottawa, ON, K1A 0N4 Canada • ACRL LAMA

Evans James David • Kennesaw State College • Marietta, GA 30061 • ACRL

Evans James M. • Cataloger • Louisiana Technical University Prescott Memorial Library • Ruston, LA 71270-9985 • ACRL ALCTS IFRT IRRT

Evans Jean D. • Bartlett Public Library District • Bartlett, IL 60103 • YALSA SRRT

Evans Joan H. • Library Media Specialist • Joppaview Elementary School • Perry Han, MD 21128 • AASL

Evans Judith L. • Manager, Main Library • Ontario City Library • Ontario, CA 91764 • PLA

Evans Judy I. • Development & Library Serv • Pikes Peak Library District • Colorado Springs, CO 80901 • LAMA

Evans June C. • High Point Public Library • High Point, NC 27261 • RASD

Evans Karen L. • Columbus, OH 43235

Evans Leigh • Decatur, GA 30030 • AASL

Evans Linda J. • Elementary Librarian • Ringgold School District Gastonville Elementary Center • Finleyville, PA 15332 • AASL

Evans Lori A M • Vacaville, CA 95687

Evans Lorraine • University of Denver Penrose Library • Denver, CO 80208 • LITA

Evans Malinda M. • Library Director • Vespasian Warner Public Library • Clinton, IL 61727 • ALSC PLA

Evans Marcia A. • Student • State University New York at Buffalo School of Inf. & Library Studies • Buffalo, NY 14260

Evans Margaret M. • Head,Technical Services • Hammond Public Library • Hammond, IN 46320 • ALCTS LITA

Evans Marie • Macon, GA 31211 • LAMA

Evans Marion R. • Singles Library Coordinator • Presbyterian Church • Solana Bch, CA 92075 • Continuing

Evans Mark D. • Director • Livingston & Wyoming County Library Systems • Avon, NY 14414 • PLA

Evans Mary M. • East Central University Linscheid Library • Ada, OK 74820-6899 • ACRL IFRT NMRT

Evans Melva E. • Children's Librarian • Atlanta-Fulton Public Library Dogwood Branch • Atlanta, GA 30318 • PLA

Evans Nancy • Librarian • Vernon Free Public Library • Vernon, VT 05354

Evans Nancy E. • Data Management • Olin Ordnance • Saint Petersburg, FL 33716 • ACRL ALCTS LITA SRRT

Evans Nancy H. • Head Librarian • Pennsylvania State University Ogontz Campus Library • Abington, PA 19001 • ACRL LAMA LITA LRRT

Evans Nancy L. • Conway County Library • Morrilton, AR 72110 • PLA

Evans Nelson H. • Document Librarian • Trenton State College Roscoe L. West Library • Trenton, NJ 08650-4700 • GODORT

Evans Patricia • Library Principal Associate • Atlanta-Fulton Public Library Peachtree Branch • Atlanta, GA 30309

Evans Patricia • Reid Reference Publication • Wilmette, IL 60091

Evans Patricia S. • Director • Victor Free Library • Victor, NY 14564 • PLA

Evans Robert W. • Key West, FL 33040 • ACRL ALCTS *Life*

Evans Russel C. • Catalog Librarian • Carroll College Library • Waukesha, WI 53186 • ACRL ALCTS

Evans Ruth A. • Schenectady, NY 12309 • ACRL

Evans Ruth D. • Cataloger • Alabama Public Library Service • Montgomery, AL 36130 • ALCTS GODORT

Evans Stephen P. • Raleigh, NC 27611 • ILERT

Evans Susan L. • Librarian • W.B. Simpson Elementary School • Camden-Wyoming, DE 19934 • AASL

Evans Teresa E. • Assistant Head of Serials • University of Rochester Rush Rhees Library • Rochester, NY 14627-0055 • ALCTS

Evans V. Tessa Perry • Assist Dir for Collection Develp • Fayetteville State University Chesnutt Library • Fayetteville, NC 28301 • EMIERT

Evard Susan R. • Student • San Jose State University Division of Library & Information Science • San Jose, CA 95192-0029

Evarts Lynn • Student • University of Wisconsin School of Library & Information Studies • Madison, WI 53706 • AASL

Evatt Jay C. • Soc Sci/Humanities Ref Libn. • University of Georgia Libraries • Athens, GA 30602 • ACRL

Eveland Ruth A. • Tenants Harbor, ME 04860

Evelev Leila L. • Librarian • Roeper City Country Schools • Bloomfield Hills, MI 48013 • ALSC

Even Christa • Library Media Director • De Kalb High School Library Media Center • DeKalb, IL 60115 • AASL

Evensen Dolores • Librarian • Hillsborough Community College Dale Mabry Campus • Tampa, FL 33630

Evensen Robert L. • Assoc Dir Clln Mgt & Tech Serv • Brandeis University Main Library • Waltham, MA 02254-9110 • ACRL ALCTS

Evensen Sharon L. • Library Director • Univ of North Dakota-Lake Region • Devils Lake, ND 58301

Everett Cynthia W. • Jackson-George Regional Library System • Pascagoula, MS 39567 • ALTA

Everett David D. • Assoc Director for Public Servs • Stetson University DuPont-Ball Library • De Land, FL 32720-3769 • ACRL RASD

Everett Edith H. • Gulfport, MS 39507

Everett Ellen • Reference Librarian • University of Chicago Library • Chicago, IL 60637-1502

Everett Janet Gilles • Branch Manager • Cuyahoga County Public Library Orange Branch • Pepper Pike Village, OH 44124 • ALSC PLA

Everett Sandra • Saint Louis Community College at Meramec • St Louis, MO 63122

Everett Willard R. • Minneapolis, MN 55401

Everhart Nancy • Tamaqua Area Senior High School • Tamaqua, PA 18252 • AASL

Everhart Paul R. • Head Librarian • Palatine High School • Palatine, IL 60067 • AASL

Everitt Roberta M. • Catskill, NY 12414 • AASL YALSA *Life*

Evermon Vandy L. • Technical Services Librarian • Columbia College Stafford Library • Columbia, MO 65202

Eversmeyer Pamela S. • Librarian • Ecole Classique • Metairie, LA 70006

Everson Francine • Technical Info Specialist • Foster Wheeler Enviresponse Inc, U.S. EPA • Edison, NJ 08837

Everstine Carrie K. • Fombell, PA 16123

Evert Carolyn S. • Caldwell Community College LRC • Hudson, NC 28638

Evins F. Jean • Librarian/Media Specialist • Mohave High School • Riviera, AZ 86442 • AASL

Evitts Beth A. • Director-Library Services • York Hospital • York, PA 17405 • ASCLA LAMA

Evitts Virginia A. • Trumbull, CT 06611

Evola Elizabeth • Student • Indiana University School of Library and Information Science • Bloomington, IN 47405

Evon Flora M. • Technical Information Specialist • Department of State • Washington, DC 20520

Ewald Robert B. • Descriptive Catalog Specialist • Library of Congress • Washington, DC 20541

Ewalt Rosalind Haynes • Serials Cataloger • Dallas County Community College District District Service Center • Mesquite, TX 75150-2095 • ALCTS

Ewbank Elberta J. • Vandalia, IL 62471 • PLA RASD *Life*

Ewbank Melinda J. • Information Services Librarian • Lane Public Library Fairfield Branch • Fairfield, OH 45014

Ewell Adele • Ann Arbor, MI 48104 • ACRL ALCTS *Continuing*

Ewell Diana L. • Reference/BI Librarian • Elon College Iris Holt McEwen Library • Elon College, NC 27244-0187 • ACRL

Ewell Martha N. • Asst. Librarian • I H Kempner High School • Sugerland, TX 77487

Ewen Eric P. • Head Catalog Librarian • University of San Francisco Richard A. Gleeson Library • San Francisco, CA 94117 • ALCTS

Ewen Sylvia S. • Great Neck, NY 11021 • Continuing

Ewick Charles Ray • Director • Indiana State Library • Indianapolis, IN 46204-2296 • ALTA ASCLA LAMA PLA

Ewick David L. • Director • Fulton County Public Library • Rochester, IN 46975

Ewick Joann • A-V Librarian • Johnson County Public Library White River Branch • Greenwood, IN 46142 • PLA

Ewing Becky • Library Coordinator • United Day School • Laredo, TX 78043

Ewing Caroline Massey • Trustee • Horry County Memorial Library • Conway, SC 29526 • ALTA

Ewing Frances K. • Presbyterian Hospital Medical Library • Albuquerque, NM 87125-6666

Ewing Jerry L. • Document Librarian • Washington University Olin Library • Saint Louis, MO 63130 • ACRL GODORT

Ewing Katherine • Reference Librarian • Hughes Hubbard & Reed Library • New York, NY 10005

Ewing M Keith • Reference Coordinator • Saint Cloud State University Centennial Hall LRC • St. Cloud, MN 56301-4498 • ACRL LAMA

Ewing Mark E. • Student • Wayne State University • Detroit, MI 48202 • ACRL PLA

Ewing Robert S. • City Librarian • San Bernardino Public Library • San Bernardino, CA 92410 • PLA

Exner Carol R. • Student • North Carolina Central University • Durham, NC 27707 • YALSA IFRT

Eyer Bruce J. • Director of Learning Resources • Yakima Public Schools • Yakima, WA 98902 • AASL

Eykholt Christine E. • Student • Indiana University School of Library and Information Science • Bloomington, IN 47405

Eyler Carol E. • Head of Tech Servs & Systems • Mercer University Main Library • Macon, GA 31207 • ACRL ALCTS

Eyler Neala R. • Librarian • Fairview Elementary School • New Cumberland, PA 17070-2309 • AASL

Eyman David H. • College Librarian • Skidmore College Lucy Scribner Library • Saratoga Springs, NY 12866 • ACRL LAMA LITA

Eysenbach Beth • Young Adult Librarian • Homewood Public Library District • Homewood, IL 60430 • YALSA

Eysie Loretta • Student • Simmons College Graduate School of Library & Information Science • Boston, MA 02115 • ALSC

Eyth Mary J. • Reference Librarian • Houston Public Library • Houston, TX 77002 • RASD

Ezell Charlaine L. • Lansing, MI 48906 • LAMA PLA CLENE

Ezell Johanna V. • Head Librarian • Pennsylvania State Univ • Mont Alto, PA 17237 • ACRL

Ezell Mancil C. • Director • Baptist Sunday School Board • Nashville, TN 37234

Ezydorski Robert J. • Support Services Supervisor • Phoenix Public Library • Phoenix, AZ 85004 • ALCTS PLA

Ezzell Joline Ridlon • Special Projects Librarian • Duke University William R. Perkins Library • Durham, NC 27706 • LAMA

Faber Elizabeth M. Miss • Watertown Public Library • Watertown, WI 53094 • Continuing

Faber Lillian R. • Library Media Specialist • Willow Bend School • Rolling Meadows, IL 60008 • AASL

Fabian George N. • School Librarian • East Orange High School • East Orange, NJ 07017

Fabian Merle G. • Head, Chemistry Library • Princeton University • Princeton, NJ 08544-2098

Fabio Adriane • Rare Book Cataloger • New York Academy of Medicine Library • New York, NY 10029 • ACRL

Fabiszewski Mary E. • Essex Institute Library • Salem, MA 01970

Fabre Alvin • Dr. (Education) • Pointe Coupee Parish Library • New Road, LA 70760 • ALTA

Fabugais Trisha • Milwaukee, WI 53211 • PLA

Facente Gary • Evanston, IL 60201

Facer Kathleen • Adult Service Librarian • Richmond Memorial Library • Batavia, NY 14020

Fackler Naomi P. • Collection Development Coor. • Texas A & M University Medical Sciences Library • College Station, TX 77843 • ALCTS LITA

Fadden Donald M. • Pittsburgh, PA 15213 • AASL

Fadell John E. • Lang & Lit Bibl./Ref Ln • University of Houston Libraries • Houston, TX 77204-2091 • ACRL

Fader Ellen G. • Head of Children's Services • Westport Public Library • Westport, CT 06880 • ALSC

Fadlalla Gerald J. • Director • Glen Rock Public Library • Glen Rock, NJ 07452-1795 • LAMA

Fagan Ann S. • Mesa, AZ 85203 • AASL

Fagan Carolyn M. • Librarian • Mt. Lebanon School District • Pittsburgh, PA 15228 • AASL

Fagan Charling C. • Library Director • Sarah Lawrence College Esther Raushenbush Library • Bronxville, NY 10708 • ACRL ALCTS

Fagan Christine S. • Collection Development Libn • Roger Williams College Library • Bristol, RI 02809-2921 • ALCTS

Fagan Judy M. • W. Newton, MA 02165

Fagan Matilda SR • Curriculum Laboratory Librarian • Incarnate Word College Library Saint Pius X Library • San Antonio, TX 78209

Fagan Michele L. • Manuscripts,Rare Books Curator • Memphis State University Main Library • Memphis, TN 38152

Fagan Sheila • Library/Media Teacher • Newberg High School • Newberg, OR 97132 • AASL

Fagerholm Judy • Peridicals Librarian • Palo Alto City Library • Palo Alto, CA 94303 • PLA IFRT

Fagerlin Virginia A. • Eastern Illinois University Booth Library • Charleston, IL 61920-3099

Fagerstrom David M. • University of Colorado-Boulder University Libraries • Boulder, CO 80309

Faggiani Irene • Bayport, NY 11705

Fagin Roberta E. • Menlo Park, CA 94025

Faherty Gladys W. • Frostburg, MD 21532 • Continuing

Faherty Robert L. • Director of Publications • Brookings Institution • Washington, DC 20036 • ALTA

Fahey Joan K. • Head Librarian • Saint Joseph County Public Library River Park Branch • South Bend, IN 46615 • PLA

Fahey Kathleen G. • Science Librarian • Southern Illinois University Delyte W. Morris Library • Carbondale, IL 62901-6632 • ACRL

Fahey Rosemary G. • Student • San Jose State University Division of Library & Information Science • San Jose, CA 95192-0029 • ACRL

Failli Joseph N. • 30122 Venezia, Italy • LITA

Fain Ellen T. • Sunnyside, NY 11104 • PLA

Fain Glenda M. • Library Assistant III • Butte County Library • Oroville, CA 95966 • NMRT SORT

Fain Margaret A. • Reference • University of South Carolina Coastal Carolina College Kimbel Library • Conway, SC 29526

Fain Sybil M. • Student • University of South Carolina College of Library & Information Science • Columbia, SC 29208 • AASL PLA LRRT

Fair Kathy L. • Head of Technical Services • Virginia Military Institute J.T.L. Preston Library • Lexington, VA 24450 • ACRL ALCTS LAMA LITA

Fair Norma J. • Cataloger • University of Missouri Libraries-Columbia Elmer Ellis Library • Columbia, MO 65201-5149 • ACRL ALCTS LITA

Fair Shana C. • Reference Librarian • Ohio University • Zanesville, OH 43701 • ACRL IFRT LIRT

Fairchild Constance A. • Assistant Reference Librarian • University of Illinois Library • Urbana, IL 61801 • ACRL RASD *Life*

Fairchild Helene B. • Trustee • Salt Lake City Public Library • Salt Lake City, UT 84111

Fairclough G. Thomas • Director • Burkburnett Library • Burkburnett, TX 76354

Fairclough Ian • Music Cataloger • Ball State University Bracken Library • Muncie, IN 47306-0160 • ALCTS

Fairfield Jay B. • Trustee • General Bookbinding Company • Chesterland, OH 44026 • ALCTS

Fairfield John R. • President • Information Conservation Inc • Brown Summit, NC 27214-9745 • ALCTS

Fairfield Marianne C. • Branch Librarian • Cuyahoga County Public Library Bay Village Branch • Bay Village, OH 44140-2194 • PLA

Fairfield Patricia D. • Librarian • Essex County College • Newark, NJ 07102 • ACRL ALCTS

Fairgrove Rowan • Ricoh California Research Center • Menlo Park, CA 94025 • IFRT

Fairhurst Jean B.F. • Children's Librarian • Stockton-San Joaquin County Public Library • Stockton, CA 95202 • ALSC

Fairley Craig R. • Asst. Mgr., Acquisitions Dept. • Metropolitan Toronto Reference Library • Toronto ON, M4W 2G8 Canada • ALCTS LITA

Fairley Elizabeth P. • Florida State University Robert M. Strozier Library • Tallahassee, FL 32306-2047 • ACRL ALCTS

Fairlie David W. • Student • State University New York at Buffalo School of Inf. & Library Studies • Buffalo, NY 14260 • AASL

Faix Euxine • Fork Union Military Academy • Fork Union, VA 23055 • AASL YALSA

Faklis Ruth Ellen • Director • Prairie Trails Public Library District • Burbank, IL 60459 • PLA

Fal Andrew J. • New Britain, CT 06051-1221

Falanga Rosemarie E. • Exploratorium • Sacramento, CA 94123 • AASL LITA

Falardeau E. R. Rev • Saint Charles Borromeo • Albuquerque, NM 87106

Falat Julie A. • Manitowoc Public Library • Manitowoc, WI 54220 • ALSC

Falcon Blanche B. • Glendale, CA 91201-1407

Falcone Celeste • Student • Ohio State University Edgar Dale Educational Center • Columbus, OH 43210

Falcone Cheryll L. • Fort Worth, TX 76180-8476 • AASL IFRT

Falcone Edward M. • Director • Ossining Public Library • Ossining, NY 10562 • LAMA PLA

Falcone Elena C. • Library Supervisor • Philip Morris, Inc. • New York, NY 10017 • LITA

Falconieri Marietta • Pre & Lower School Librarian • Brooklyn Friends School • Brooklyn, NY 11201 • AASL

Fales Susan L. • Librarian • Brigham Young University Harold B. Lee Library • Provo, UT 84602 • ACRL ALCTS RASD

Falgione Joseph F. • Associate Director Main Lib Serv • Carnegie Library of Pittsburgh • Pittsburgh, PA 15213-4080 • PLA

Falk Carolyn L. • Student • University of Pittsburgh School of Library and Information Science • Pittsburgh, PA 15260 • IRRT

Falk Diane M. • The World & I (Magazine) c/o Library • Washington, DC 20002 • RASD

Falk Irene J. • Nutley, NJ 07110

Falk Joyce Duncan Dr. • Santa Barbara, CA 93105-3708 • ACRL *Life*

Falk Louise • Onawa, IA 51040

Falk Patty K. • Student • University of Wisconsin-Milwaukee School of Library & Information Science • Milwaukee, WI 53201

Falk S. Steven • Installation Specialist • Data Research Associates Inc. • Saint Louis, MO 63132 • LITA

Falkinburg Barbara • Library Media Specialist • Mars Estates Elementary School • Baltimore, MD 21221 • AASL

Falkins Beth • Jonesboro, GA 30236 • LITA

Falkowski David A. • Student • Wayne State University Purdy Library • Detroit, MI 48202

Fall James E. • New York, NY 10003

Fall John • New York, NY 10010 • Continuing

Faller Martha L. • Circulation • Niagara County Community College Faculty Resource Center • Sanborn, NY 14132 • ACRL

Fallon Ellen • Student • University of Arizona Graduate Library School • Tucson, AZ 85721 • ACRL LITA GODORT

Fallon J. H. Mrs. • Canterbury School • Ft. Worth, IN 46804 • ALSC

Falls Anona J. • Jonestown, MS 38639-0068 • Continuing

Falls Waldtraut M. • Clinical Librarian • P. C. Associates Otolaryngoloy-Plastic Surgery • Brooklyn, NY 11209 • ASCLA

Falzone Paul L. • Librarian • Croswell-Lexington High School • Croswell, MI 48422 • AASL

Fan Diana Chon • Librarian • Brooklyn Public Library Sheepshead Bay Branch • Brooklyn, NY 11235

Fan Felicia C.S. • Lake Forest Library • Lake Forest, IL 60045

Fan Jianing • Provo, UT 84604

Fan Jiemin • Student • Florida State University School of Library and Information Studies • Tallahassee, FL 32306-2048

Fang Josephine R. Dr • Belmont, MA 02178 • ALCTS IRRT *Continuing*

Fannin Caroline M. • Director • Louis Bay Second Library • Hawthorne, NJ 07506 • PLA IFRT

Fannin Robin L. • Media Specialist • Crawford Middle School • Lexington, KY 40505 • AASL

Fanning Carol C. • Commack, NY 11725 • AASL

Fanning Erin C. • Adult Services Librarian • Stockton-San Joaquin County Public Library Manteca Branch • Manteca, CA 95336 • SRRT

Fanning Frances P. • Glendale, MO 63122

Fannon Elizabeth L. • Swoope, VA 24479

Fannon Mona Lisa • Software Specialist • Data Research Associates Inc. • Saint Louis, MO 63132

Fansher Virginia • Cincinnati, OH 45240 • Continuing

Fanslow Malinda C. • Librarian • Dobyns-Bennett High School • Kingsport, TN 37664 • AASL YALSA

Fanta David • Chapman & Cutler • Chicago, IL 60603

Farace Virginia K. • Director • Boynton Beach City Library • Boynton Beach, FL 33435 • ALCTS LAMA LITA PLA

Farago Kathleen M. • Cleveland, OH 44113

Faraone Maria B. • Faculty • Long Island University Palmer School of Library & Information Science • Greenvale, NY 11548

Farb Randy H. • Student • Jefferson Community College Library • Louisville, KY 40202

Farb Sharon • Special Porject Director • Career Resources Library UCLA Placement and Career Planning Center • Los Angeles, CA 90024-1573

Farber Amy E. • Sr. Cataloger, Research Library • Federal Reserve Bank of New York • New York, NY 10045 • ALCTS LITA

Farber Evan Ira • Librarian • Earlham College Lilly Library • Richmond, IN 47374 • ACRL ALCTS LAMA LITA RASD GODORT LIRT

Farber Susan • Young Adult Librarian • Ossining Public Library • Ossining, NY 10562 • RASD YALSA

Fareydoon-Nezhad Bahiyyih • Huntington, WV 25703

Farhat Elizabeth • Branch Librarian • Livonia Public Library • Livonia, MI 48154-3045 • LAMA PLA RASD

Faria Ronald L. • President • Data Recall • Campbell, CA 95008 • ALTA

Farias Elizabeth Hall • Fuquay-Varina, NC 27526

Faries Cynthia S. • Sr. Assistant Librarian • Pennsylvania State University Pattee Library • University Park, PA 16802 • ACRL RASD

Farin Nieves F. • Brookline, MA 02146 • Continuing

Farina John Jr. • Trustee • Deer Park Public Library • Deer Park, NY 11729

Fariss Linda C. • Librarian • Mount Horeb High School • Mt Horeb, WI 53572 • AASL

Fariss Susan T. • La Crosse, WI 54601

Fark Ronald K. • E. Greenwich, RI 02818 • SRRT

Farkas Andrew • Director of Libraries • University of North Florida Thomas G. Carpenter Library • Jacksonville, FL 32245-7605

Farkas Charles • Director • Braircliff Manor Public Library • Briarcliff Manor, NY 10510

Farkas Doina G. • Chair/Acquisitions Dept. • University of Florida Libraries • Gainesville, FL 32611-2047 • ALCTS IRRT

Farley Anne • Media Specialist • Illing Junior High School • Manchester, CT 06040 • AASL

Farley Charles E. Jr. • Vice President • Gaylord Information Systems • Syracuse, NY 13221 • LITA PLA

Farley Dawn Roberts • Director of Library Services • Traverse City Area Public Schools • Traverse City, MI 49684 • AASL

Farley Edward • Trustee • Macomb County Library • Mount Clemens, MI 48044 • ALTA

Farley Edward V. • Trustee • Macomb County Library • Mount Clemens, MI 48044 • ALTA

Farley John J. • Clifton Park, NY 12065

Farley Judith R. • Special Projects Manager • Library of Congress • Washington, DC 20541 • RASD FLRT SRRT

Farley Laine • University of California Division of Library Automation • Oakland, CA 94612-3550 • ACRL LITA RASD

Farley Marian D. • The Analytic Sciences Corporation Library • Reading, MA 01867

Farley Richard A. • Sedalia, MO 65301 • ACRL *Continuing*

Farley Stella S. • Floistell, MO 63348 • Continuing

Farmakis Lou • Division Chair Library Servs. • Paradise Valley Community College • Phoenix, AZ 85032 • LAMA

Farman Patricia • Librarian • Saint Anne Elementary School • St. Anne, IL 60964 • AASL

Farmer Donald • Librarian • Ocean View High School • Huntington Beach, CA 92647 • AASL

Farmer Eleanor • Trustee • Anderson County Library • Anderson, SC 29622-4047

Farmer Jill • Washington, DC 20008 • RASD

Farmer Kristina C. • Director • Babylon Public Library • Babylon, NY 11702 • ALSC PLA *Life*

Farmer Lesley S. J. • Director • San Domenico High School Library • San Anselmo, CA 94960 • AASL YALSA IRRT

Farmer Marjorie Dr • Trustee • Free Library of Philadelphia • Philadelphia, PA 19103 • ALTA

Farmer Michael James • Catalog Librarian • Ohio University Libraries • Athens, OH 45701-2978 • ACRL ALCTS MAGERT

Farmer Sandra L. • Houston, TX 77080

Farmer Susan M. • Student • Indiana University • Bloomington, IN 47405

Farmerie Linda M. • Childrens Librarian • Northland Public Library • Pittsburgh, PA 15237 • ALSC

Farnell Mary S. • Seaford, DE 19973

Farner Susan • Roswell, GA 30075 • ILERT NMRT

Farney Keitha J. • School Library Media Specialist • Beaver River Central School • Beaver FAlls, NY 13305

Farnham Shera M. • Libn. for Staff Devlp. • Phoenix Public Library • Phoenix, AZ 85004 • PLA

Farnsworth Alan W. • Assistant Librarian • Stratford Public School • North Stratford, NH 03590

Farnsworth Julie A. • Director • Salt Lake County Library System Holladay Library • Salt Lake City, UT 84117

Farnsworth Rose E. • Hartville, OH 44632

Farquharson H. Jean Mrs. • Paris ON, N3L 3E3 Canada • LAMA

Farr Carole P. • Media Specialist • East Central Elementary School • Rome, GA 30161 • AASL

Farr Patricia A. • Young Adult Services Coordinator • Central Rappahannock Regional Library Wallace Memorial Library • Fredericksburg, VA 22401 • YALSA

Farrar Blanche • Lincoln, NE 68503 • Continuing

Farrar Bruce S. • Head of Extension Services • Public Library of Nashville and Davidson County • Nashville, TN 37203-3585 • ALSC PLA

Farrar Karen • Trustee • Jefferson County Public Library • Lakewood, CO 80215 • ALTA

Farrar Mark • Stoneham, MA 02180 • LITA

Farrar Nancy L. • Sycamore School • Indianapolis, IN 46260

Farrell David • Asst. Univ. Libn. for Cllns. • University of California-Berkeley University Library • Berkeley, CA 94720 • ACRL ALCTS

Farrell Kathy L. • Head of Cataloging • Sonoma State University Ruben Salazar Library • Rohnert Park, CA 94928 • ACRL ALCTS

Farrell Mary E. • Fresno, CA 93726

Farrell Mary Ellen • Library Systems Coordinator • Illinois Library Computer System Office • Champaign, IL 61820 • LITA

Farrell Maureen • Library Coordinator • Minnesota Department of Corrections • St Paul, MN 55104 • ASCLA

Farrell Maureen C. • Map Librarian • Cleveland Public Library • Cleveland, OH 44114-1271 • MAGERT

Farrell Michele A. • Library Director • D'Youville College Library • Buffalo, NY 14201 • ACRL ALCTS LAMA
Farrell Sallie J. • Baton Rouge, LA 70808
Farrell Sandra A. • Branch Librarian • Free Library of Philadelphia South Philadelphia Branch • Philadelphia, PA 19145 • PLA YALSA IFRT
Farrell Sean A. • Assistant Director • Hattiesburg, Petal & Forrest County, The Library • Hattiesburg, MS 39401 • PLA
Farrell Thomas M. • Library Specialist • Palo Alto City Library • Palo Alto, CA 94303 • NMRT VRT
Farrell Vera A. • Library Media Specialist • Central School Elementary School Library • Livingston Manor, NY 12758
Farrell-Bergeron Frances • Warwick, RI 02886 • ILERT
Farrelly Deg • Media Librarian • Arizona State University West Campus Fletcher Library • Phoenix, AZ 85069 • ACRL VRT
Farren Donald • Assoc Dir for Spec Clln • University of Maryland Libraries • College Park, MD 20742 • ACRL LHRT MAGERT
Farrier George F. • Callahan, CA 96014
Farries Robert C. • Pueblo Library District McClelland Library • Pueblo, CO 81004-1997 • LITA
Farrington Hilari • Director • Stowe Free Library • Stowe, VT 05672 • PLA
Farrington Jean W. • Head Serials Department • University of Pennsylvania Library Van Pelt-Dietrich Library Center • Philadelphia, PA 19104-6206 • ACRL ALCTS LITA
Farrington Josephine B. • St Louis, MO 63119 • PLA *Continuing*
Farris Alice Hild • Librarian • Central High Sch Lib • Cheyenne, WY 82009 • AASL LAMA LITA YALSA *Life*
Farris Dale F. • Staff Development Coorporation • Saint Elizabeth Hospital Health Science Library • Beaumont, TX 77702
Farris Joyce L. • Catalog Librarian • Duke University Library Monographic Cataloging Department • Durham, NC 27706 • ALCTS
Farris Loretta • Director • Library Media Exam Center • Kingston, PA 18704-0649 • AASL
Farris Mary • Hot Springs, AR 71913 • IFRT NMRT
Farris Mary Elizabeth • Library Media Specialist • Cummings Elementary School • Memphis, TN 38106 • AASL
Farris Patricia B. • Librarian • Tallahassee 1st District Court of Appeal • Tallahassee, FL 32399-1850
Farris Peter • Student • San Jose State University Division of Library & Information Science • San Jose, CA 95192-0029 • SRRT
Farris Rodney A. • Library Media Specialist • Brewer Middle School • Brewer, ME 04412 • AASL ALSC
Farris Sally G. • Branch Librarian • Aiken County Public Library • Aiken, SC 29801 • PLA
Farrow Mildred H. • University of Chicago Library • Chicago, IL 60637-1502
Farrugia A. Denise • Head of Children's Services • Saint Charles Public Library • St. Charles, IL 60174 • ALSC
Farseth Kathryn • Librarian III • Milwaukee Public Library Center Street Branch • Milwaukee, WI 53210 • PLA
Farwell Sybil M. • Media Specialist • Sweetwater Elementary School • Miami, FL 33174 • AASL YALSA
Farynk Linda J. • Assistant University Librarian • Old Dominion University Library • Norfolk, VA 23529-0256 • ACRL LAMA RASD
Fasana Paul J. • Director,Research Libraries • New York Public Library Division P • New York, NY 10163 • ACRL
Fasano Diane Marie • Librarian • Lakeland Public Library • Lakeland, FL 33801 • ALSC LAMA PLA RASD YALSA CLENE LIRT
Fase Laura E. • Bain & Company, Inc. • San Francisco, CA 94114 • RASD
Fashing Margaret A. • LaSalle Language Academy • Chicago, IL 60614 • AASL
Fasick Adele M. • Professor • University of Toronto Faculty of Library & Information Science • Toronto ON, M5S 1A1 Canada • ALSC PLA EMIERT IFRT LRRT
Fasold Eloise N. • Director • Arapahoe Library District • Littleton, CO 80121 • ALSC LAMA PLA
Fast Daniel R. • Indianapolis Marion County Public Library • Indianapolis, IN 46206
Fast Margaret L. • Wichita State University Ablah Library • Wichita, KS 67208 • ACRL
Fatika Joan • Head of Circulation • Lane Public Library • Hamilton, OH 45011
Fattig Karl E. • Catalog Librarian • University of Nebraska Love Library • Lincoln, NE 68588-0410 • ACRL ALCTS LITA LHRT SRRT
Fatzer Jill B. • Director • University of New Orleans Earl K. Long Library • New Orleans, LA 70148 • ACRL LAMA LITA
Faule Jacques • Bibliotheque Publique D' Information • Paris Cedex 04, France
Faulhaber Cynthia B. • Partner • Miller, Canfield, Paddock and Stone • Detroit, MI 48226 • ASCLA LAMA
Faulk Gerard Jr • School Media Specialist • Wayland Alexander Elementary School • Hartford, KY 42347 • AASL LITA CLENE LIRT
Faulkner Beth A. • Chicago Heights Public Library • Chicago Heights, IL 60411
Faulkner Deborah F. • Adult Services Librarian • Indian Valley Public Library • Telford, PA 18969 • RASD
Faulkner Maggie • Trustee • Everett Public Library • Everett, WA 98201
Faulkner Sharon J. • Norwood, NC 28128-0072 • AASL EMIERT IFRT SRRT
Faurot Ellen F. • Director • Judson College • Marion, AL 36756 • ACRL
Fausser Jean Ann • Children's Books & Co. • Tulsa, OK 74137 • AASL ALSC YALSA
Faust Bradley D. • Student • Ball State University Bracken Library • Muncie, IN 47306-0160 • LITA
Faust Jeffrey B. • Student • Louisiana State University School of Library & Information Science • Baton Rouge, LA 70803-3290
Faust Judith • Associate Member • Diablo Valley College Library • Pleasant Hill, CA 94523 • ACRL
Faust Julia B. • Director • Riverside Public Library • Riverside, IL 60546 • ALSC LAMA PLA RASD
Faust Kathy • Asst Librarian for Tech Services • Northwestern School of Law Boley Library • Portland, OR 97219 • ACRL LITA
Faust Mary • Reference Librarian • Bishop Eustace Prep Sch Library • Pennsauken, NJ 08110 • AASL
Faust Mary Helen • Acquisitions Fiscal Control Ln • Ball State University Library Department of Library Services • Muncie, IN 47306 • ACRL ALCTS
Faust Susan W. • Katherine Burke School • San Francisco, CA 94121 • AASL ALSC
Faust Teresa R. • Wake Forest University Z Smith Reynolds Library • Winston Salem, NC 27109-7777
Fauver Marge E. • Student • University of Texas at Austin Graduate School of Library & Information Sciences • Austin, TX 78712-1276
Favell Judith E. • Reference Librarian • University of Wisconsin-River Falls Chalmer Davee Library • River Falls, WI 54022
Favini Robert J. • Reference Librarian • Bentley College Solomon R. Baker Library • Waltham, MA 02154-4705 • ACRL
Favretti Joy P. • Reference Librarian • Mansfield Public Library • Mansfield Center, CT 06250 • LITA
Fawcett-Brandon Pamela • Head of Technical Services • South Orange Public Library • South Orange, NJ 07079 • NMRT SRRT
Fawcett Bettye L. • Librarian • Connally High School • Waco, TX 76705 • AASL
Fawcett Georgene E. • Cataloger • University of Nebraska at Omaha University Library • Omaha, NE 68182-0237 • ACRL ALCTS LITA
Fawcett Patrick J. • Systems Librarian • University of Manitoba Libraries Elizabeth Dafoe Library • Winnipeg MB, R3T 2N2 Canada • LITA
Fawcett Rita • School Library Media Specialist • Oak Hills School • Beaverton, OR 97075 • AASL
Fawcett Susanne J. • Austin, TX 78723
Fawcett W. Peyton • Librarian • Field Museum of Natural History • Chicago, IL 60605-2498 • ACRL ALCTS RASD
Fax Elton C. • Trustee • Queens Borough Public Library • Jamaica, NY 11432 • ALTA PLA
Fay Kathleen J. • Administrator • Enoch Pratt Free Library • Baltimore, MD 21201-4484
Fay Nancy L. • Reference Librarian • Sparta Public Library • Sparta, NJ 07871
Fay Thomas • Telecommunications Specialist • Las Vegas-Clark County Library District Flamingo Library • Las Vegas, NV 89119
Fayad Susan M. • Colorado State Library Department of Education • Denver, CO 80203 • ASCLA LAMA LITA
Faye Elizabeth K. • Student • University of California Los Angeles Graduate School of Library & Information Science • Los Angeles, CA 90024 • LHRT
Faye Irwin D. • Librarian IV • Chicago Public Library Sulzer Regional Library • Chicago, IL 60625 • RASD
Faye Nina S. • Hyattsville, MD 20782 • IFRT SRRT
Fazio BingShan • Student • University of Arizona Graduate Library School • Tucson, AZ 85721
Feagin James R. • Student • Louisiana State University School of Library & Information Science • Baton Rouge, LA 70803-3290
Fearn Andrew S. • Canton, OH 44708 • ALCTS PLA RASD
Fearon John M • Indexer • H. W. Wilson Company • Bronx, NY 10452 • RASD
Feather Celeste • Circulation/Reference Librarian • Georgetown University Law Center Edward Bennett Williams Library • Washington, DC 20001-1417 • ACRL
Feather Pamela P. • Executive Director • Dupage Library System • Geneva, IL 60134 • PLA
Featheringham Gail • Student • Kent State University School of Library & Information Science • Kent, OH 44242-0001 • LITA
Feathers-Ebbinghaus Ruth • Academic Coordinator • DeVry Institute of Technology • Lombard, IL 60148
Feavel Paul T. • Asst. Devel. Officer • Seattle Public Library • Seattle, WA 98104-1193 • LAMA
Feazel Edythe J. • Technical Services Librarian • Indiana University at Kokomo Learning Resources Center • Kokomo, IN 46904-9003
Fecher Mary B. • Children's Librarian • Plymouth Public Library • Plymouth, IN 46563 • ALSC
Federgreen Dorothea • Branch Librarian • Chicago Public Library Rogers Park Branch • Chicago, IL 60626 • ALSC
Federhart Margaret S. • ACIS/Library Solutions • IBM Corporation • Boulder, CO 80301-9191 • ACRL LAMA LITA
Federici Yolanda D. • Chicago, IL 60643-4107 • Continuing
Federico Hilda W. • Head of Public Services • Jacksonville University Carl S. Swisher Library • Jacksonville, FL 32211
Federowski M. S. • Cass County Library • Cassopolis, MI 49031 • PLA
Federspiel Catherine M. • Student • Wayne State University Library Science Program • Detroit, MI 48202
Federspiel Pamela W. • Library Director • Shelby County Library District • Shelbyville, KY 40065
Fedigan Bonnie • Arroyo Elementary School • Glendale, AZ 85304 • AASL LHRT
Fedorijczuk Jaroslaw • Community College of Philadelphia • Philadelphia, PA 19130
Fedrick Mary Anne • Director • Marywood College Library Learning Resources Center • Scranton, PA 18509 • ACRL
Fedunok Suzanne • Assistant Director of Resources • State University of New York Bartle Library • Binghamton, NY 13902-6012 • ACRL ALCTS RASD
Fedyn Elizabeth M. • Oconomowoc, WI 53066
Fee Martha F. • Centerport, NY 11721
Fee Penny • Trustee • Sioux City Public Library • Sioux City, IA 51101-1203 • ALTA
Fee Victoria S. • Student • Kent State University School of Library & Information Science • Kent, OH 44242-0001 • SRRT
Feehan Ellen C. • Cataloger • University of Miami Libraries Richter Library • Coral Gables, FL 33124
Feehan Patricia E. • University of South Carolina College of Library & Information Science • Columbia, SC 29208 • YALSA
Feen Anne B. • Dover, MA 02030
Feen Sharon J. • Library/Media Specialist • Pinellas Technical Education Center • St. Petersburg, FL 33713
Feeney Ann M. • Student • Rosary College Graduate School of Library & Information Science • River Forest, IL 60305
Feeney Helen • Acting Co-Director • Everett Community College Library Media Center • Everett, WA 98201-1327 • RASD NMRT
Feeney Kevin E. • President • Pacific Administration & Design Assistance • Honolulu, HI 96813
Feenstra Terrence D. • Trustee • Sioux City Public Library • Sioux City, IA 51101-1203 • ALTA
Fegley Lynda R. • Cataloger • Baker & Taylor Books • Bridgewater, NJ 08807-0920
Fehlman Sheila V. • Head of Online Catalog Mgt. • Boston College Libraries • Chestnut Hill, MA 02167 • ACRL ALCTS SRRT
Fehner Cornelia • Orange, CA 92666 • PLA RASD *Life*
Fehr Jane B. • Serials Supervisor • Buena Vista College Ballou Library • Storm Lake, IA 50588 • ALCTS
Fehrmann Paul G. • Kent State University Libraries • Kent, OH 44242 • ACRL
Feicht Therese M. • Director • Ida Rupp Public Library • Port Clinton, OH 43452 • PLA
Feick Christina L. • Serials Specialist-USA • Blackwell's Periodicals Division U. S. Sales Office • Cold Spring, NY 10516 • ACRL ALCTS
Feider Christopher J. • Morningside College Library • Sioux City, IA 51106 • RASD
Feierstein Nancy S. • Public Services Librarian • Baltimore County Public Library Woodlawn Branch • Baltimore, MD 21207 • ALSC
Feight Julie • Student • Millersville University • Millersville, PA 17551
Feil Denise M. • Seattle, WA 98116
Feiler Anne E. • Deaf Services Librarian/Ref. • Chicago Public Library Sulzer Regional Library • Chicago, IL 60625
Feiler Marilyn L. • Library Director • Colorado Academy • Denver, CO 80235

Fein Linda Abby • Free Library of Philadelphia Northeast Regional Library • Philadelphia, PA 19149 • ALSC PLA
Fein Mollie • Baltimore County Public Library Essex Area Branch • Essex, MD 21221 • PLA IRRT
Feinberg Arthur • Trustee • Finkelstein Memorial Library • Spring Valley, NY 10977
Feinberg David G. • Tuscaloosa, AL 35404 • ACRL RASD
Feinberg Renee • Professor • Brooklyn College Library • Brooklyn, NY 11210
Feinberg Richard • State University of New York (SUNY) • Stony Brook, NY 11794-2225 • ACRL IFRT LIRT
Feinberg Sandra • Director • Middle Country Public Library • Centereach, NY 11720 • PLA
Feind Rebecca S. • Student • University of Missouri-Columbia Ellis Library • Columbia, MO 65201 • IFRT
Feiner Arlene M. • Chicago, IL 60657 • ALCTS LAMA *Life*
Feiner Joanne D. • Student • Slocum-Skewes School • Ridgefield, NJ 07647 • AASL
Feingold Judith A. • Cleveland Hts., OH 44118
Feinman Barbara F. • Library/Media Specialist • Pinellas County Schools Woodlawn Elementary School • St. Petersburg, FL 33704
Feinman Lynn • Student • University of Rhode Island Graduate School of Library & Information Studies • Kingston, RI 02881-0815
Feinman Valerie J. • Coordinator of BI • Adelphi University Swirbul Library • Garden City, NY 11530 • ACRL LITA RASD LIRT
Feinmark David P. • Acquisition/Collections Ln. • Washburn University of Topeka Mabee Library • Topeka, KS 66621 • ACRL ALCTS
Feinsilver Jeffrey M. • Baldwin, NY 11510 • ACRL RASD
Feinstein Barbara D. • Librarian • Washington School • Huntington Station, NY 11746 • AASL
Feix Charles • Assistant Librarian • Cynthiana-Harrison County Public Library • Cynthiana, KY 41031
Fekety Peter M. • Adult Services Librarian • Rockville Regional Library • Rockville, MD 20850 • PLA EMIERT SRRT
Felber Sue H. • Medical Librarian • Naples Community Hospital Medical Library • Naples, FL 33941-3029 • ACRL ASCLA LAMA
Felch Carol Ann • Lancaster Junior High School • Lancaster, TX 75146-3036 • AASL
Felchlin Marva R. • Burbank, CA 91506
Feld Norma • Assistant Director • Yeshiva University Cardozo School of Law Library • New York, NY 10003-3299 • ALCTS LITA
Felder-Hoehne Felicia H. • Reference Librarian • University of Tennessee John C. Hodges Library • Knoxville, TN 37996-1000
Felder Jimmie R. • Library Director • Hayneville Public Library • Hayneville, AL 36040-0425
Feldman Barbara • Highland Park, IL 60035
Feldman Devin • Student • Queensborough Community College Library • Bayside, NY 11364 • ACRL
Feldman Felice R. • Head Librarian • Notre Dame High School • St. Louis, MO 63125 • AASL
Feldman Iris S. • Librarian • Lawrence School Library • Brookline, MA 02146
Feldman Irwin • Library Director • Dharma Realm Buddhist University • Talmage, CA 95481
Feldman Jill • Student • Drexel University College of Information Studies • Philadelphia, PA 19104-2875 • ALCTS LAMA LITA RASD
Feldman Marianne • Portland, OR 97221
Feldman Mary K. • Takoma Pk, MD 20912 • CLENE ILERT
Feldman Sally M. • Administrator • Las Vegas-Clark County Library District Green Valley Library • Henderson, NV 89014 • PLA
Feldman Sari • Coordinator of Children Svs. • Onondaga County Public Library at the Galleries • Syracuse, NY 13202-2494 • PLA YALSA
Feldman William • Trustee • Free Public Library of Woodbridge • Woodbridge, NJ 07095 • ALTA ILERT
Feldmann Janet • Head Librarian • Indiana University-Purdue University Columbus Campus Library (IUPUI) • Columbus, IN 47203 • ACRL RASD IFRT LIRT
Feldshuh Muriel • Library Teacher • Brooklyn Public School #16 • Brooklyn, NY 11211 • AASL
Felgenhour Jerry L • Director Library Media Services • Ithaca City School District • Ithaca, NY 14850 • AASL
Feliciano Olga Edleen • Librarian III • Chicago Public Library • Chicago, IL 60607
Felix Sally T. • Administrator • Lackawanna County Library System • Scranton, PA 18503 • LAMA PLA
Feliz Zoe A. • El Paso, TX 79936 • AASL PLA RASD
Feller Judith M. • Documents Librarian • East Stroudsburg University Kemp Library • East Stroudsburg, PA 18301 • ACRL GODORT
Feller Siegfried • Pelham, MA 01002 • ACRL IRRT
Feller Sue A. • Old Bethpage, NY 11804
Fellin Octavia • Gallup, NM 87301
Fellman-Rips Nancy Ms. • Trustee • Omaha Public Library • Omaha, NE 68102 • ALTA
Fellows Barbara G. • Assistant Director • Columbus Metropolitan Library • Columbus, OH 43215 • PLA
Fellows Lois A. • School Librarian • Amelia County Middle School • Amelia, VA 23002 • AASL
Fellows Mary J. • Weston Public Library • Weston, OH 43569 • ALSC LAMA PLA
Felmet Joyce A. H. • Librarian • Pearl City Public Library • Pearl City, HI 96782 • ALSC PLA NMRT
Felmlee Cheryl A. • Acquisitions & Serials Librarian • Trinity Evangelical Divinity School Rolfing Library • Deerfield, IL 60015 • LITA
Felsing Robert H. • Orientalia Bibliographer • University of Oregon Library • Eugene, OR 97403-1299
Felsted Carla Martindell • Saint Edwards University Scarborough Phillips Library • Austin, TX 78704 • ACRL RASD CLENE EMIERT SRRT
Felter Alma • Eureka, IL 61530-0128 • PLA YALSA *Continuing*
Feltes Gretchen • Preservaton/Reference Librarian • New York University Library of the School of Law • New York, NY 10012-1099 • ALCTS
Feltes Mary Kay • Owatonna Public Library • Owatonna, MN 55060 • ALSC PLA
Felts Gloria J. • Librarian • Highland Junior High School • Hobbs, NM 88240 • AASL
Felts Martha Stackel • Assistant Catalog Librarian • College of Charleston Robert Scott Small Library • Charleston, SC 29424 • ALCTS GODORT
Feltz Carol J. • Librarian • Oak Hall Private School • Gainesville, FL 32607 • AASL
Fendel Mary Kay • Librarian • Piney Point Elementary School • Houston, TX 77063
Fenelon Claudia • Student • University of California-Berkeley School of Library & Information Studies • Berkeley, CA 94720
Feng Margaret S. • Cataloger • National Library of Medicine • Bethesda, MD 20894
Feng Yen Tsai • Chestnut Hill, MA 02167 • ACRL IRRT *Life*
Fenichel Barbara • Librarian • Moraga Branch Library • Moraga, CA 94556
Fenichel Carol H. PHD • Hahnemann University Library • Philadelphia, PA 19102 • ACRL ALCTS LITA RASD LRRT
Fenker Lois A. • Deputy Dir., Public Services • Corvallis-Benton County Public Library • Corvallis, OR 97330-4728
Fenlon Mary P. • Public Services Librarian • Kansas City Kansas Community College Library • Kansas City, KS 66112-3098 • IFRT
Fenly Charles R. • Asst Chief,Descriptive Cat Div • Library of Congress • Washington, DC 20541 • ALCTS
Fenly Judith G. • Washington, DC 20015 • ALCTS
Fennefos Myrtle • Vancouver, WA 98664 • Continuing
Fennell Catherine • Norristown, PA 19403
Fennell Janice C. • Director of Libraries & Professo • Georgia College Ina Dillard Russell Library • Milledgeville, GA 31061 • ACRL LAMA
Fennema David • Duke University William R. Perkins Library • Durham, NC 27706 • LAMA
Fenneman Nordica Miss • Chicago, IL 60640 • Continuing
Fenner David B. • Spacesaver Corporation • Fort Atkinson, WI 53538 • ACRL LAMA
Fenner Karen L. • Student • Emporia State University School of Library & Information Management • Emporia, KS 66801
Fenner Ruth E. • Rochester, MN 55904 • AASL ALSC *Life*
Fennessey Mary D. Dr • Northland College Dexter Library • Ashland, WI 54806-3999 • ACRL
Fennewald Joseph A. • Student • University of Missouri-Columbia College of Education • Columbia, MO 65211 • PLA EMIERT SRRT
Fenno-Smith Kyzyl M. • Seattle, WA 98112 • EMIERT IFRT LIRT SRRT
Fensin Anne B. • Assistant Director • Jefferson Parish Library Department • Metairie, LA 70010
Fenske David E. • Head, Music Library • Indiana University Music Library • Bloomington, IN 47401 • ACRL
Fenske Rachel F. • University of the Pacific • Stockton, CA 95211
Fenske Ruth E. • University of Illinois at Chicago Library of the Health Sciences • Urbana, IL 61801 • ACRL ALCTS LAMA LITA RASD LHRT LRRT SRRT
Fenstermann Duane W. • Archivist • Luther College • Decorah, IA 52101 • ACRL ALCTS LITA *Life*
Fentin Richard M. Mr. • Trustee • The Bryant Library • Roslyn, NY 11576
Fenton Elaine P. • Circuit Librarian • United States Court of Appeals • Atlanta, GA 30303 • LITA
Fenton Jo Ann • Librarian • Seattle Public Library • Seattle, WA 98104-1193
Fenton Lori R. • Student • Emporia State University School of Library & Information Management • Emporia, KS 66801 • MAGERT NMRT SRRT
Fenwick Carolsue R. • Kadena Elementary School • APO, AP 96367-5064
Fenwick Sara I. • St Petersburg, FL 33705 • ALSC *Continuing*
Ferber Pamela Gibbs • Branch Libraian • Jasper County Public Library • Rensselaer, IN 47978
Ferder Leon • Slavic Bibliographer • University of California-Los Angeles (UCLA) • Los Angeles, CA 90024-1450 • ACRL
Ferdula Tammy-Jo • Student • University of Rhode Island Graduate School of Library & Information Studies • Kingston, RI 02881-0815
Ference Gregory C. • Salisbury, MD 21801
Fergins Alicia B. • District of Columbia Public Library Martin Luther King Memorial Library • Washington, DC 20001
Ferguson Amy S. • Student • University of Southern Mississippi School of Library Science • Hattiesburg, MS 39406-5146
Ferguson Ann L. • Reference Librarian • Yale University Sterling Memorial Library • New Haven, CT 06520
Ferguson Anna S. • Assistant Coordinator Tech Serv • State Library of Louisiana • Baton Rouge, LA 70821 • ALCTS
Ferguson Anthony W. • Dir. , Resources & Spec. Cllns. • Columbia University Libraries Butler Library • New York, NY 10027 • ACRL
Ferguson Barbara • Librarian • Robeson High School • Chicago, IL 60620
Ferguson Cheryl • Librarian • Ebon Research Systems • Washington, DC 20011
Ferguson Chris D. • Head, Research Services Dept. • University of California-San Diego • La Jolla, CA 92093-0175 • ACRL RASD
Ferguson Constance • Librarian-Researcher • Valuation Counselors • Los Angeles, CA 90010
Ferguson Cynthia M. • Saint Mark's School of Texas • Dallas, TX 75230 • AASL YALSA
Ferguson Douglas • Automation Librarian • California State University Hayward Library • Hayward, CA 94542
Ferguson Eleanor A. • Fitzwilliam, NH 03447 • ASCLA PLA *Life*
Ferguson Ellen B. • Bloomington, IN 47401 • ALSC
Ferguson Eugene Hardin • Library Analyst • Library of Congress • Washington, DC 20541
Ferguson Gary L. • Reference Librarian • State Library of Louisiana • Baton Rouge, LA 70821 • RASD
Ferguson Jane M. • Adult Services & Reference • Manlius Library • Manlius, NY 13104 • RASD
Ferguson Janna K. • Fort Worth, TX 76133-2854
Ferguson John • Toms River, NJ 08755-2143
Ferguson John W. • Director • Mid-Continent Public Library • Independence, MO 64050 • LAMA PLA
Ferguson Katharine A. • Librarian • United States Army Post Library • Yuma Proving Ground, AZ 85365-9123 • AFLRT
Ferguson Linda K. • School Library Media Specialist • Fairfax County Public Schools Hunters Woods Elementary School • Reston, VA 22091
Ferguson Margaret M. • Editor-in-Chief • Farrar Straus Giroux Inc • New York, NY 10003
Ferguson Margaret S. • Reference Librarian • San Jose State University Clark Library • San Jose, CA 95192-0028 • ACRL PLA
Ferguson Margo • Reference Librarian • Elkhart Public Library • Elkhart, IN 46516-3184 • IFRT
Ferguson Marian T. • Viola Cobb Elementary School • Channelview, TX 77530 • AASL
Ferguson Mark S. • Student • University of Wisconsin-Madison School of Library & Information Studies • Madison, WI 53706 • LITA NMRT
Ferguson Rena Rae • Assistant Director • Idaho Falls Public Library • Idaho Falls, ID 83401 • PLA
Ferguson Sarah A. • Dean of Educational Resources • Brookhaven College Learning Resources Center • Farmers Branch, TX 75244 • RASD LIRT
Ferguson Stephen • Curator of Rare Books • Princeton University • Princeton, NJ 08544-2098 • ACRL
Ferguson Susan H. • Library Media Specialist • Vienna Elementary School • Vienna, VA 22180 • AASL LITA
Ferguson Virginia • Selwyn House Sch Lib • PQ Canada, H3Y 2H8 Canada
Fergusson David G. • Assistant Director-Headquaters • Forsyth County Public Library • Winston-Salem, NC 27101 • LAMA PLA
Ferington Karen A. • Niagara County Community College Faculty Resource Center • Sanborn, NY 14132 • ALCTS
Ferkin Susan B. • Ithaca, NY 14850 • LIRT

Ferl Terry Ellen • Librarian • University of California McHenry Library • Santa Cruz, CA 95064 • LITA
Ferlanti Vita L. • Head of Technical Services • Denville Free Public Library • Denville, NJ 07834
Ferlas Joanne B. • Reference & Adult Services • Fraser Public Library • Fraser, MI 48026 • PLA
Fermon Daniel A. • Bronx, NY 10458
Fernald Gail H. • Boulder, CO 80304
Fernander Curlean M. • Teacher Librarian • Government High School • Nassau, Bahamas • YALSA
Fernandes Kathleen F. • Montgomery County Department of Public Libraries Gaithersburg Regional Library • Gaithersburg, MD 20879
Fernandez B. Adele • Student • University of North Texas School of Library & Information Sciences • Denton, TX 76203
Fernandez Cheryl Wise • Irvine, CA 92715
Fernandez Joseph • DeKalb, IL 60115
Fernandez M. Louise Sr • Librarian • Cardinal Spellman High School • Bronx, NY 10466 • AASL
Fernandez Nenita • Head Catalog Librarian • Yale University Social Science Library • New Haven, CT 06520 • ALCTS IRRT
Fernandez Nora • Cataloger • Organization of American States (OAS) Columbus Memorial Library • Washington, DC 20006-4499
Fernandez Priscilla • Reference Library • Chaffey College • Alta Loma, CA 91701 • ACRL RASD
Fernandez Silvia • Ridgefield, NJ 07657
Fernandez Susana D. • Brookings, OR 97415
Fernandez Zenaida • Head Librarian • Miami Dade Community College Wolfson Campus LRC • Miami, FL 33132 • ACRL LAMA
Fernie W. Janet • Dallas, TX 75230
Ferrall Eleanor • Scottsdale, AZ 85257
Ferrandino Maya D. • Student • Florida State University School of Library and Information Studies • Tallahassee, FL 32306-2048
Ferrang Edward G. • Assistant Chief Extension Serv. • East Central Georgia Regional Library Augusta-Richmond County • Augusta, GA 30901 • PLA
Ferranti Mary L. • Student • University of Missouri-Columbia School of Library & Informational Science • Columbia, MO 65211
Ferrara Christine • Valley High School Library Media Center • Sacramento, CA 95823 • AASL
Ferrara Joyce A. • Librarian I • East Baton Rouge Parish Library • Baton Rouge, LA 70806-7699
Ferrara Pasquale Jr. • Trustee • East Islip Public Library • East Islip, NY 11730-2896
Ferrara Robert F. • Asst Chief,Branch Administration • Brooklyn Public Library • Brooklyn, NY 11238
Ferrare Carolina L. • Raven Elementary School • Raven, VA 24639 • AASL
Ferrarese Mary Ann • Senior Library Sys. Specialist • Library of Congress • Washington, DC 20541 • ALCTS LITA
Ferrari Elizabeth I. • Reference Librarian • Wilmette Public Library • Wilmette, IL 60091
Ferree Renate S. • Fairfield, CT 06430
Ferree Yvette S. • Mile High Center Law Library • Denver, CO 80290
Ferreira Judy A. • County Librarian • Stanislaus County Free Library • Modesto, CA 95354
Ferreira Valentino J. • Student • Long Island University Palmer School of Library & Information Science • Greenvale, NY 11548
Ferrell Judith C. • Reference Assistant • Elkhart Public Library • Elkhart, IN 46516-3184
Ferrell Mary Sue • Executive Director • California Library Association • Sacramento, CA 95814 • ACRL ERT *Life*
Ferren Emily H. • Extension Services Coordinator • Carroll County Public Library Westminster Branch • Westminster, MD 21157 • ALSC ASCLA
Ferrero Carol B. • Librarian • Detroit Public Library Lincoln Branch • Detroit, MI 48203 • LAMA SRRT
Ferrero Lucia N. • Scarsdale High School • Scarsdale, NY 10583 • IRRT
Ferretti Elisabete • New York, NY 10028
Ferreyra Steven R. • Student • University of Arizona Graduate Library School • Tucson, AZ 85721 • PLA
Ferriby Martha L. • Director • Veterans Memorial Library • Mt. Pleasant, MI 48858 • PLA
Ferriby Peter Gavin • Cataloging Department • Drew University • Madison, NJ 07940-4007 • ACRL
Ferrier Douglas M. • Dean of the Library • Texas Wesleyan University West Library • Fort Worth, TX 76105 • ACRL
Ferrier Kayne L. • Youth Specialist II • Grand Rapids Public Library • Grand Rapids, MI 49503-3093 • ALSC IFRT
Ferriero David S. • Associate Dir. for Pub. Servs. • Massachusetts Institute of Technology Libraries (MIT) • Cambridge, MA 02139 • ACRL LAMA
Ferries Carmen • McAllen, TX 78501 • AASL
Ferrigno Helen • Information Specialist • Digital Equipment Corporation • Merrimack, NH 03054
Ferring Geraldine • Walnut Creek, CA 94595 • Life
Ferris David A. • Curator of Rare Books • Harvard Law School Library • Cambridge, MA 02138 • ACRL
Ferris Jeffrey • Head Librarian • New Castle County Dept. of Libraries • Wilmington, DE 19808 • LAMA LITA PLA
Ferro-Nyalka Ruth R. • District Librarian • School District 105 • La Grange, IL 60525 • AASL YALSA
Ferron-Smith Diane • Westerly, RI 02891
Ferron April G. • Southern Connecticut State University School of Libray Science & Instructional Technology • New Haven, CT 06515
Ferry Janice M. • Librarian • Newport Beach Public Library Mariners Branch • Newport Beach, CA 92660 • PLA
Ferstl Kenneth L. • Assistant Professor • University of North Texas School of Library & Information Sciences • Denton, TX 76203 • ALCTS LITA PLA RASD
Ferullo Donna L. • Reference Librarian • Boston College • Chestnut Hill, MA 02167 • ACRL
Fescemyer Kathy • Agricultural Reference Libn. • Clemson University Robert Muldrow Cooper Library • Clemson, SC 29634-3001 • ACRL LIRT
Fessard Jacqueline A. • Reference Librarian/Archivist • Indiana University Southeast Library Southeastern Campus Library • New Albany, IN 47150-6405 • ACRL GODORT
Fessier Patricia • Assistant Librarian • St. Johns Seminary Edward Laurence Doheny Memorial Library • Camarillo, CA 93012
Fessler Vera F. • Associate Director • Fairfax County Public Library • Fairfax, VA 22033-1909 • LAMA LITA
Fetch Deborah • Head of Ordering Section • Pennsylvania State University E506 Pattee Library • University Park, PA 16802 • ACRL ALCTS LAMA
Fetchenhier LuJean D. • Student • College of Saint Catherine • Saint Paul, MN 55105
Fetner Carolyn G. • J. G. Dyer Elementary School • Lawrenceville, GA 30243 • AASL
Fetner Iris D. • Student • University of North Carolina School of Library Science • Chapel Hill, NC 27599-3360 • AASL
Fetsch Mary Jo Mrs. • Arcadia Elementary School • Arcadia, WI 54612 • AASL
Fetterhoff Patricia L. • Children's Librarian • Dayton & Montgomery County Public Library • Dayton, OH 45402-2103 • ALSC
Fetzer Mary K. • Government Pubns • Rutgers University Libraries • New Brunswick, NJ 08903 • ACRL GODORT
Feuerbach George R. • Agawam, MA 01001
Feuerbacher Cindy L. • Librarian II • Omaha Public Library Willa Cather Branch • Omaha, NE 68105 • ALSC
Feuerhelm Jill A. • Bailey Hill School • Eugene, OR 97405-1099 • AASL ALSC
Feuerman Francine • Peekskill, NY 10566 • LAMA
Feuka Theresa M. • Limerick, ME 04048-9795 • NMRT
Feulner Deborah A. • Librarian • Oak Ridge Military Academy • Oak Ridge, NC 27310 • AASL YALSA
Few John E. • Chair Dept. of Library Info Tech • City College of San Francisco • San Francisco, CA 94112 • ACRL
Fewster Warren J. Jr. • Manager,Fiscal Services • Baltimore County Public Library • Towson, MD 21204 • PLA
Feye-Stukas Janice • Library Consultant • Library Development & Services Minnesota State Library Agency • Saint Paul, MN 55101 • ASCLA LAMA PLA LRRT SRRT *Life*
Fialkoff Francine S. • Executive Director • Library Journal Cahners Publishing Company • New York, NY 10011
Fiawoo Pamela A. • Library Assistant • Rice University Fondren Library • Houston, TX 77251-1892 • NMRT
Fick Carol M. • Childrens Librarian • King County Library System White Center Library • Seattle, WA 98146
Fick Gary R. • University Librarian • Seattle Pacific University Weter Memorial Library • Seattle, WA 98119 • ACRL
Fick Jodi L. • Assistant Director • Minnehaha County Library • Crooks, SD 57020
Ficke Eleanore R. • Reston, VA 22090-4447
Fickes Jody • Owner • Adventures for Kids • Ventura, CA 93003 • ALSC
Ficks Judy A. • LCR Director • Meadowview School • Woodridge, IL 60517 • AASL
Fiddler Vera M. • Assistant Director-Info Services • Port Washington Public Library • Port Washington, NY 11050 • RASD IFRT
Fidel Raya • Associate Professor • University of Washington Graduate School of Library and Information Science • Seattle, WA 98195
Fidishun Dolores • Head of Audiovisual Services • Widener University Wolfgram Library • Chester, PA 19013 • ACRL
Fidler Josephine • Director of Libraries • Marshall University James E. Morrow Library • Huntington, WV 25755-2060 • ACRL LAMA
Fidler Linda M. • Madison, WI 53719-2047 • ACRL LAMA
Fiedler Lien Ms. • Senior Librarian(Cataloger) • Library of Congress • Washington, DC 20541
Fiegas Barbara E. • Vice President • E.B.S. Inc. Book Service • Lynbrook, NY 11563 • ACRL AFLRT
Fiegen Ann M. • Cataloger • University of Arizona Library • Tucson, AZ 85721 • ALCTS LITA
Fiehler Judith M. • Systems Analyst • Library of Congress • Washington, DC 20541 • LITA
Field Alida • Student • San Jose State University Division of Library & Information Science • San Jose, CA 95192-0029 • NMRT
Field Anne • Site Librarian • Mitchell Senior School • Atwater, CA 95301 • AASL
Field Carolyn W. • Philadelphia, PA 19144 • ALSC *Continuing*
Field Curtis L. • Library Director • Canadian Consulate General • New York, NY 10020
Field Dorothy • Marketing & Development Officer • Broward County Division of Libraries Broward County Library • Fort Lauderdale, FL 33301 • PLA
Field Judith • Northville, MI 48167 • RASD GODORT
Field Karen E. • Law Librarian • Ameritrust Corporation • Cleveland, OH 44101-0937
Field Kathryn L. • Portsmouth Public Library • Portsmouth, NH 03801 • ALCTS LAMA
Field Kathy M. • Murfreesboro, TN 37130
Field Margaret E. • Director • Woodstock Public Library • Woodstock, IL 60098 • ALSC PLA RASD
Field Mary N. • Librarian • North Cross School • Roanoke, VA 24014 • AASL
Field Oliver T. Dr. • Associate Professor • Denver University • Denver, CO 80210 • ACRL ALCTS *Life*
Field Ruth Graham • Louisville, KY 40205 • Continuing
Field Susan C. • Head, Government Documents Dept. • University of Georgia Libraries • Athens, GA 30602 • GODORT
Field Susan L. • Student • University of Michigan School of Information and Library Studies • Ann Arbor, MI 48109-1092 • LITA
Field William N. • Archivist Spec Cllns • Seton Hall University • South Orange, NJ 07079-2690 • ACRL
Fielden Stanley • Associate Librarian • University of Regina • Regina SK, S4S 0A2 Canada • ACRL
Fielder Amanda • Student • Indiana University School of Library and Information Science • Bloomington, IN 47405
Fielder Faith M. • Student • Texas Woman's University School of Library & Information Studies • Denton, TX 76204
Fielder Marce G. • Student • Emporia State University School of Library & Information Management • Emporia, KS 66801
Fielder Susan J. • Head of AV Services • Naperville Public Libraries • Naperville, IL 60540 • ALSC LITA VRT
Fielders Margaret G. • Columbus, OH 43230 • Continuing
Fielding Joyce C. • Rosary College • River Forest, IL 60305-1066
Fields Anne M. • Columbus, OH 43220-4870
Fields Barbara C. • Teacher/Librarian • Martin Luther King High School • Chicago, IL 60653 • AASL
Fields Carolyn B. • Reference Librarian • San Diego State University Library • San Diego, CA 92119-2120 • ACRL RASD LIRT
Fields Cheryl A. • Serial Records Section • National Library of Medicine • Bethesda, MD 20894 • FLRT
Fields Cheryl A. • Shreve, OH 44676
Fields Lynnette M. • Student • Southern Illinois University • Edwardsville, IL 62026
Fields Mary Alice S. • Library Consultant • Alabama Public Library Service • Montgomery, AL 36130 • LRRT
Fiels Keith Michael • Director • Massachusetts Board of Library Commissioners • Boston, MA 02215-2070 • ASCLA LITA
Fielstra Gerritt • St Petersburg, FL 33711
Fiering Norman • John Carter Brown Library • Providence, RI 02912 • ACRL
Fiero Janet L. • Librarian • Alice Independent School District Alice High School • Alice, TX 78332 • AASL
Fierstein Jacqueline • Brooklyn, NY 11235
Fife Barbara Hale • Associate Librarian • Weber County Library • Odgen, UT 84401
Fifield Carol • Information Center • G. Holmes Braddock Senior High School • Miami, FL 33186

Fifield Nancy R. • Librarian • Lincolnwood Elementary School • Evanston, IL 60201 • AASL

Figg Milton H. • Collection Development Librarian • University of Tennessee John C. Hodges Library • Knoxville, TN 37996-1000 • ACRL ALCTS RASD SRRT

Figliola Carl Dr. • Trustee • Queens Borough Public Library • Jamaica, NY 11432 • ALTA PLA

Figlioli Catherine M. • Peru, NY 12972

Figueredo Danilo H. • Library Director • Bloomfield College Library • Bloomfield, NJ 07003 • ACRL

Figueroa Lydeliz • Head Librarian • American Military Academy • Guaynabo, PR 00651-7884 • ALSC

Figur Maxine • Islip Middle School • Islip, NY 11751

Figurski Barbara J. • Worcester, MA 01606 • PLA

Fike Gail • Dover, NH 03820 • AASL

Fike Lynn M. • Library Assistant III • Fort Vancouver Regional Library • Vancouver, WA 98663

Filbert Tamara S. • Branch Manager • River Bluffs Regional Library Belt Library • Saint Joseph, MO 64506

Filby P. William • Savage, MD 20763

Filderman Marilyn M. • San Diego, CA 92103

Files Charlotte J. • Librarian • Mississippi Band of Choctaw Indians • Philadelphia, MS 39350 • AASL ALSC LIRT

Files Kathy M. • Beverly Hills Public Library • Beverly Hills, CA 90210

Files Patricia T. • Los Altos, CA 94024

Filipa Barbara Sporer • Senior Library Associate Spec. • Brown University John Hay Library, Box A • Providence, RI 02912

Filipczak Carol M. • Manager, Information Services • RM & D Advertising • Baltimore, MD 21201

Filipiak Dawn A. • Reference Librarian • Wheaton Public Library • Wheaton, IL 60187-5376 • LITA

Filipic Mary A. • Branch Manager • Cuyahoga County Public Library Parma-Snow Branch • Parma, OH 44134-2789 • LAMA PLA

Filipowicz Catherine A. • Librarian • Lincoln High School Library • Yonkers, NY 10704 • AASL

Filkins Jean • University of Redlands Armacost Library • Redlands, CA 92374-3758

Fillhart L. S. • Branch Librarian • Portsmouth Public Library Cradock Branch • Portsmouth, VA 23702

Fillion Gabriel G. • Student • University of Montreal Bibliotheques • Montreal, PQ, H3C 3J7 Canada

Filsinger Elaine G. • Librarian • Lock Haven University Clearfield Branch Library • Clearfield, PA 16830 • ACRL

Filstrup E. Christian • AUL/Collections • George Washington University Gelman Library • Washington, DC 20052 • ACRL ALCTS LAMA IRRT

Finan Patrick E. • Library Director • Portage County District Library Garrettsville Branch • Garrettsville, OH 44231 • PLA

Finch Carol S. • Children's Librarian • Phoenix Public Library Mesquite Branch • Phoenix, AZ 85032 • PLA

Finch Edith W. • Philadelphia, PA 19103

Finch Edward • Freeport High School • Freeport, IL 61032

Finch Frances • Canton, NY 13617

Finch Herbert • Assistant University Librarian • Cornell University Library • Ithaca, NY 14853 • ACRL

Finch Margaret M. • Paradise, CA 95969

Finch Martha B. • Berkeley, CA 94709 • Continuing

Finch Mildred Evelyn • Head, Technical Services • Henrico Public Library • Richmond, VA 23223 • LITA

Finch Nancy • Librarian • Rippowam Center • Stamford, CT 06905 • AASL

Finch Robert H. • Librarian II (Fine Arts) • Houston Public Library • Houston, TX 77002

Fincher Margaret A. • Librarian • Abramson School Library Media Center • New Orleans, LA 70127

Fincher Marian M. • University of Oregon Library • Eugene, OR 97403-1299

Fincke William J. • Interlibrary Loan Librarian • Lehigh University Libraries Fairchild-Martindale Library • Bethlehem, PA 18015 • ACRL

Finder Lisa N. • Student • Columbia University Preservation Department • New York, NY 10027

Findlay Gail O. • Regional Manager • Memphis-Shelby County Public Library and Information Center • Memphis, TN 38104-4025 • PLA

Findlay Kathryn A. • Notre Dame MS-High School • Wichita Falls, TX 76309

Findlay Margery W. • District Librarian • Rio Linda Union School District Library Services • Rio Linda, CA 95673 • ALSC

Findley Jeannette M. • Media Specialist • Saratoga Elementary School • Springfield, VA 22153 • AASL

Findley Naomi K. • Hoover Institution on War, Revolution & Peace Library • Stanford, CA 94305-6010 • ACRL ALCTS

Findly Elizabeth • Professor Emeritus, Lnship. • University of Oregon Library • Eugene, OR 97403-1299 • Continuing

Fine Fran • Trustee • Las Vegas-Clark County Library District Flamingo Library • Las Vegas, NV 89119 • ALTA

Fine Jana R. • Librarian II • Clearwater Public Library • Clearwater, FL 34623 • ALSC PLA YALSA

Fine Joan L. • West Hartford, CT 06107

Fine Karen • Children's Librarian • Warren Township Public Library • Warren, NJ 07059

Fine Ruth • Washington, DC 20016 • FLRT GODORT *Continuing*

Fine Sara • Faculty • University of Pittsburgh School of Library and Information Science • Pittsburgh, PA 15260 • SRRT

Finegan Jane S. • Tech Services Librarian • Eastchester Public Library • Eastchester, NY 10709

Fineman Charles S. • Humanities Bibliographer • Northwestern University Library • Evanston, IL 60208-2300 • ACRL ALCTS IRRT

Fineman Michael E. • University of California Science Library • Santa Cruz, CA 95064 • ACRL ALCTS

Finemel Sybil • Head Librarian • King David High School • Johannesburg, South Africa • AASL

Finer Eileen P. • Rockville, MD 20852

Fineran Mary Sr. • Librarian • Our Lady of Good Counsel High School • Newark, NJ 07104 • AASL VRT

Finestone Judith C. • Librarian • Pennsylvania School for the Deaf • Philadelphia, PA 19144 • ASCLA EMIERT

Finger Lori • Hilton Head Elementary School • Hilton Head, SC 29926 • AASL

Finger Marcia L. • Tampa, FL 33624

Fingerhood Dorothy A. • Student • New York State Newspaper Project c/o South Central Research Library Council • Ithaca, NY 14850 • ACRL

Fini Denice S. • Librarian I • Prince George's Cnty Memorial Lib Surratts-Clinton Branch • Clinton, MD 20745 • ALSC PLA

Fink David Seth • Student • Indiana University School of Library and Information Science • Bloomington, IN 47405

Fink Madonna Sr. • Reference Librarian • Saint Mary College DePaul Library • Leavenworth, KS 66048

Fink Molly R. • Graduate Student • Indiana University School of Library and Information Science • Bloomington, IN 47405 • ACRL

Fink Sylvia S. • Manager Technical Services • University of Alaska • Anchorage, AK 99508

Fink Teri • Eastmont Senior High School • E Wenatchee, WA 98801

Finkbeiner Andrew Finley • Student • University of Missouri Miller-Nichols Library • Kansas City, MO 64110

Finkbeiner Heidi • Librarian • John Hopkins University Applied Physics Laboratory • Laurel, MD 20707-6099 • Life

Finkbonner Jana M. • Circulation Services Manager • Lummi Library • Bellingham, WA 98226 • ALSC NMRT VRT

Finkelstein M. Mrs • Lancaster, PA 17603 • AASL YALSA

Finkelstein Norman • Librarian • Edward Devotion Library • Brookline, MA 02146

Finkelstein Robert • Trustee • Finkelstein Memorial Library • Spring Valley, NY 10977

Finkelston Candace H. • Director of Library Services • Saint Louis Community College at Meramec • St Louis, MO 63122 • LAMA

Finkle Dagmar • Library Media Specialist • Lester C. Noecker School • Roseland, NJ 07068 • AASL ALSC YALSA

Finkler Norman • Kensington, MD 20895 • Continuing

Finks Lee W. • Associate Professor • North Carolina Central University School of Library & Information Science • Durham, NC 27707

Finlay Barbara • McGill University Libraries • Montreal PQ, H3A 1Y1 Canada • ALCTS ASCLA

Finlay Mary • Librarian • Canada Department of National Defence Mobile Command Headquarters Library • St. Hubert PQ, J3Y 5T5 Canada • LITA RASD

Finley Alice R. • Assistant Director • Wayne County Public Library • Wooster, OH 44691

Finley Deborah A. Ph.D. • Trustee • Montgomery County Department of Public Libraries • Rockville, MD 20850 • ALTA PLA

Finley Elsie W. • Material Selector • Case Western Reserve Univ Freiberger Library • Cleveland, OH 44106-7151 • ACRL

Finley Kaye H. • Springfield, MO 65807-3452

Finley Mary M. • Reference Librarian/OLIB • California State University Oviatt Library • Northridge, CA 91328-1289 • ACRL RASD GODORT

Finley Meredith • Cataloger • Dayton & Montgomery County Public Library • Dayton, OH 45402-2103 • ALCTS

Finn Bette Marie • Atlanta, GA 30305

Finn Bonnie • Director • Bedford Public Library • Bedford, TX 76021 • LAMA

Finn Brenda M. • Circulation Supervisor/Records • Redwood Library & Athenaeum • Newport, RI 02840-3292

Finn Maureen D. • Marysville, OH 43040-9543

Finn Nilene T. • Librarian • IBM Corporation • San Jose, CA 95141 • LAMA LITA RASD CLENE LIRT LRRT NMRT

Finnegan Gregory A. • Reference Librarian • Dartmouth College Library Baker Memorial Library • Hanover, NH 03755-3525 • ACRL LITA RASD IRRT

Finnegan Mary J. • Reference Librarian • Salem Public Library • Salem, OR 97309-5020

Finnegan Robert F. • Reference Librarian • College of Lake County Learning Resource Center • Grayslake, IL 60030 • ACRL

Finnerty Jack • Director • Scranton Public Library Albright Memorial Library • Scranton, PA 18509-3248 • PLA

Finney Catherine L. • Humanitities Librarian • Colorado College Tutt Library • Colorado Springs, CO 80903 • ACRL

Finney Jeannette • Garrettsville, OH 44231 • Continuing

Finney Kay • Young Adult/Reference Librarian • Berkeley Public Library South Branch • Berkeley, CA 94703 • SRRT

Finney Lance C. • Director • Maryland State Library for the Blind & Physically Handicapped • Baltimore, MD 21201-2595 • ASCLA LAMA

Finney Nancy • Periodicals Librarian • College of the Sequoias • Visalia, CA 93277 • ACRL

Finney Patricia J. • Head, Stack Management Dept. • Center for Research Libraries • Chicago, IL 60637 • LAMA

Finney Wilma J. • Wayne, NJ 07470 • AASL

Finni John J. • Inforonics Inc. Library • Littleton, MA 01460 • LITA

Finnicum Susan K. • Magnolia, OH 44643 • AASL NMRT

Finnigan Georgia L. • President • The Information Store Inc. • San Franscisco, CA 94111 • LITA

Finnucan Lou Ann • Rutenberg Library • Fort Myers, FL 33919

Finster Vicki D. • Aloha, OR 97007 • AASL

Finzi John Charles • Assistant Dir., Library Resource • Library of Congress • Washington, DC 20541 • ACRL ALCTS *Life*

Fiol Maria A. • ESL Coordinator • Queens Borough Public Library • Jamaica, NY 11432 • PLA RASD EMIERT

Fiolek Anna • Bethesda, MD 20814 • ACRL

Fiordalisi Anne M. • Mayfield Heights, OH 44124

Fiore Carole • Youth Services Consultant • State Library of Florida Division of Library & Information Services • Tallahassee, FL 32399-0250 • ALSC ASCLA YALSA

Fiore Jannette C. • Assoc Director for Collections • Michigan State University Libraries • East Lansing, MI 48824-1048 • ACRL ALCTS

Fiorello Maureen F. • Library Director • Onslow County Public Library • Jacksonville, NC 28540 • LAMA

Fipps Susan R. • Library Systems Specialist • Indiana Cooperative Library Services Authority (INCOLSA) • Indianapolis, IN 46278 • LITA

Firebaugh Sharon A. • Twin Creeks Middle School Library • Spring, TX 77373

Firestein Kenneth L. • Asst Ln • University of California Shields Library • Davis, CA 95616

Firestone Barbara J. • Technicals Services Librarian • Sandia Prep School • Albuquerque, NM 87113

Firestone Bina • Moriches Elementary School • Morchies, NY 11951 • AASL

Firestone Kathryn L. • Student • University of Pittsburgh School of Library and Information Science • Pittsburgh, PA 15260 • ALSC

Firman Peggy A. • University of Puget Sound Collins Memorial Library • Tacoma, WA 98416 • ACRL ALCTS

Firth R Sylvia • Morgantown, PA 19543 • AASL

Fiscella Joan B. • Bibliographer • University of Illinois at Chicago University Library • Chicago, IL 60680 • ACRL ALCTS RASD LRRT

Fisch Donna K. • Media Librarian • Russell School • Lexington, KY 40508 • AASL

Fischbach Deborah K. • Library/Media Specialist • Lincolnview Local Schools • Van Wert, OH 45891 • LAMA

Fischbeck Lynn • Media Specialist • Sherwood Elementary School • Melbourne, FL 32935 • AASL

Fischelis Krista • Reference • Pasadena Public Library • Pasadena, CA 91101

Fischer Aletheia M. • Director • Merrimack School District School Library Program • Merrimack, NH 03054 • AASL

Fischer Barbara H. • Children's/YA Consultant • Virginia State Library & Archives • Richmond, VA 23219 • ALSC PLA

Fischer Catherine S. • Senior Government Docs Librarian • Hennepin County Library Southdale-Hennepin Area Library • Edina, MN 55435 • PLA GODORT

Fischer Christine M. • Bookmobile Assistant • Mason County Library • Scottville, MI 49454
Fischer Denise R. • Asst. City Librn./Public Servs. • Sterling Municipal Library • Baytown, TX 77520 • PLA
Fischer Eugene T. • Superintendent • West Florida Regional Library • Pensacola, FL 32501
Fischer Hans J. • Lawrence, KS 66044
Fischer Karen • Director of Library/Media Serv • Central Oregon Community College • Bend, OR 97701 • ACRL LAMA RASD
Fischer Laurel J. • Sherrodsville, OH 44675
Fischer Linda • Burlington, IA 52601 • AASL
Fischer Marijeanne • Library Trustee • Hammond Public Library • Hammond, IN 46320 • ALTA
Fischer Russell G. • Director • San Jose City College • San Jose, CA 95128 • LITA IFRT
Fischer William T. • Champaign, IL 61820-4825 • LITA PLA IFRT NMRT SRRT
Fischetti Mary P. Sister • Librarian • St. Jerome School • Philadelphia, PA 19136
Fischischweiger Thomas • Gainesville, FL 32605-4934
Fischler Barbara B. • Director of University Libraries • Indiana University-Purdue University at Indianapolis Library (IUPUI) • Indianapolis, IN 46202 • ACRL LAMA LITA
Fischli Irmgard Mrs. • Sandoz Pharma, Ltd. • 4002 Basle, Switzerland • ALCTS LAMA
Fiscus Judith A. • Richmond, VA 23229 • AFLRT
Fish Barbara • San Jose, CA 95124-1904
Fish Barbara M. • Hillandale Elementary School • Durham, NC 27705 • AASL
Fish Bonnie • School Librarian • Cameron High School Library • Cameron, MO 64429 • AASL
Fish Deanna • Director • Southwest Regional Library • Bolivar, MO 65613 • LAMA
Fish Elizabeth A. • Linden, NJ 07036 • GODORT
Fish Hilda B. • Library Director • Franklin County Library • Louisburg, NC 27549 • PLA
Fish James H. • San Jose Public Library • San Jose, CA 95113 • LAMA PLA
Fish Jocelyn M. • Calgary AB, T2S 0S7 Canada • NMRT
Fish Marie • Library Services Adminstrator • Glendale Public Library • Glendale, CA 91205 • PLA RASD
Fish Paula A. • Student • State University of New York at Albany School of Information Science & Policy • Albany, NY 12222 • EMIERT GODORT IFRT SRRT
Fishbein Patricia B. • Catalog Librarian • Susquehanna University • Selinsgrove, PA 17870 • ACRL ALCTS
Fishel Frederick C. • Head Film Division • Queens Borough Public Library • Jamaica, NY 11432 • PLA VRT
Fishel Teresa A. • Head of Reference • DeWitt Wallace Library MacAlester College • Saint Paul, MN 55105 • ACRL RASD
Fisher-Folks Robin C. • Atlanta, GA 30308 • RASD
Fisher Alice • Santa Monica, CA 90402
Fisher Allen • Library Assistant III • Willis, Graves & Associate • Austin, TX 78730
Fisher Becky R. • School Librarian • Edcouch-Elsa Independent School District Administrative Office • Elsa, TX 78538 • AASL
Fisher Carl D. • Arlington County Department of Libraries • Arlington, VA 22201 • ALCTS PLA
Fisher Carolyn H. • Director • Independent Schools Multi-Media Center Inc. • New York, NY 10023 • AASL
Fisher Diane Lewis • Library Manager • Krause Memorial Library • Rockford, MI 49341 • PLA
Fisher Donald W. Jr. • Reference Librarian • Allen County Public Library • Fort Wayne, IN 46801 • RASD
Fisher Edith M. Dr. • President • Tenge Enterprises • Encinitas, CA 92024 • ACRL
Fisher Eleanor W. • Librarian • Green Valley Elementary School Library • Monrovia, MD 21770 • AASL
Fisher Elise R. • Circulation Librarian • William Jewell College Curry Library • Liberty, MO 64068
Fisher Ellen R. • Librarian • Radnor Township School District • Wayne, PA 19087 • AASL
Fisher Florence I. Mrs • Peoria, IL 61614 • ALSC PLA *Continuing*
Fisher Frances Beth • Serials Librarian • North Dakota State University Library • Fargo, ND 58105-5599 • ACRL
Fisher Frances F. • Trustee • Muskegon County Library • Muskegon, MI 49442-1094
Fisher Frederick T. • Harvard Law School Library • Cambridge, MA 02138 • ACRL
Fisher Jane E. • Continuing Edu. Specialist • University of California-Berkeley Extension • Menlo Park, CA 94025 • CLENE
Fisher Janet B.P. • Bridgeport Public Library • Bridgeport, CT 06604
Fisher Janet L. • Asst. Div. Dir. Research Div. • Arizona State Library Department of Library Archives & Public Records • Phoenix, AZ 85007 • GODORT
Fisher Janet S. • Asst Dean for Learning Resources • East Tennessee State University James H. Quillen College of Medicine • Johnson City, TN 37614-0693
Fisher Joan W. • Frederick County Public Library C. Burr Artz Library • Frederick, MD 21701 • ASCLA PLA
Fisher Kathleen M. • San Francisco, CA 94122
Fisher Kim N. • Lemont, PA 16851-0461 • ACRL
Fisher Leslie R. • Technical Information Spec. • Lawrence Livermore Natl Lab • Livermore, CA 94550 • LITA
Fisher Lois Farrell • Chair, Library Department • New Trier High School • Winnetka, IL 60093 • AASL
Fisher Madeleine • Director • Bell Memorial Public Library • Mentone, IN 46539 • PLA
Fisher Margery • Librarian • Coleytown Middle School Library • Westport, CT 06880 • AASL
Fisher Marilyn D. • Milwaukee, WI 53209
Fisher Marshall • William Rainey Harper College Learning Resources Center • Palatine, IL 60067 • ACRL
Fisher Maureen • Rockford, IL 61107 • Continuing
Fisher Michael J. • Weslaco Public Library • Weslaco, TX 78596-6215 • PLA
Fisher Mildred L. • Librarian • Queens Borough Public Library • Jamaica, NY 11432
Fisher Nancy • Director • Wickliffe Public Library • Wickliffe, OH 44092 • PLA RASD EMIERT
Fisher Patricia A. • Assoc. Dir. for Public Services • University of Denver Penrose Library • Denver, CO 80208 • ACRL RASD
Fisher Patricia H. • Board of Trustees • Baltimore County Public Library • Towson, MD 21204 • ALTA PLA IFRT
Fisher Phyllis D. • Copiague, L. I., NY 11726 • AASL LAMA YALSA
Fisher Rebecca L. • Librarian I • Concord Pike Library • Wilmington, DE 19803 • ALSC
Fisher Robert E • Tucson, AZ 85747
Fisher Robert F. • Director • Robeson County Public Library • Lumberton, NC 28358
Fisher Roseann W. • Supv. Lib Media Services • Washington County Board of Education Instructional Resource Library • Hagerstown, MD 21740 • AASL
Fisher Sherry M. • Student • Murray State University • Murray, KY 42071-3309 • AASL
Fisher Steven P. • Special Collections Curator • University of Denver Penrose Library • Denver, CO 80208 • ACRL LHRT
Fisher Susan E. • Children's Librarian • Alameda County Library Dublin Branch • Dublin, CA 94568
Fisher Vicki I. • Student • Sam Houston State University Department of Library Science • Huntsville, TX 77341-2236 • AASL
Fisher William H. • Associate Professor • San Jose State University Division of Library & Information Science • San Jose, CA 95192-0029 • ACRL LAMA RASD
Fisher William T. • Reference Librarian • Hartford Graduate Center • Hartford, CT 06120
Fishler Claudia Dahldorf • Substitute Librarian • County of Los Angeles Public Library Culver City Library 330 • Culver City, CA 90230 • RASD
Fishler Esther B. • Ridgewood, NJ 07450
Fishman Diane L. • Columbia, MD 21045 • ACRL
Fishman Susan J. • Librarian • Weis Intermediate School • Galveston, TX 77551 • AASL ALSC
Fishwick Edward T. • Northwestern University Library • Evanston, IL 60208-2300 • ACRL RASD GODORT
Fisk Linda F. • Law Librarian • Berks County Law Library • Reading, PA 19601-3566
Fisk Mary M. • Director Resource Center • I. H. Springman Junior High School • Glenview, IL 60625 • AASL
Fiske Andrea H. • Librarian • Cordova Senior High School • Rancho Cordova, CA 95670
Fiske Carla B. • Monmouth County Library Eastern Branch • Shrewsbury, NJ 07702
Fiske Sally A. • Professional Associate • Baltimore County Public Library • Towson, MD 21204 • ALSC
Fisken Patricia B. • Music Librarian • Dartmouth College • Hanover, NH 03755 • ACRL
Fiste David • Head of Bibliographic Serv. Dept • Case Western Reserve University • Cleveland, OH 44106-7151 • ALCTS LAMA *Life*
Fister Barbara R. • Bibliographic Instruction Ln • Gustavus Adolphus College Folke Bernadotte Memorial Library • St Peter, MN 56082 • ACRL
Fitch Ann • Ramsey County Public Library Adminstrative Offices • Shoreview, MN 55126-5800 • PLA
Fitch Donna K. • Reference Unit Coordinator • Samford University Library • Birmingham, AL 35229
Fitch H Glen • Hillsdale, MI 49242 • Continuing
Fitch Katherine • Lake Braddock Secondary School • Burke, VA 22015 • YALSA
Fitch Lois R. • Trustee • Portsmouth Public Library • Portsmouth, OH 45662
Fitch Lucile H. • Chagrin Falls, OH 44022-5731 • ALSC PLA *Continuing*
Fitchen Richard • Stanford University Libraries Cecil H. Green Library • Stanford, CA 94305-6004 • ACRL
Fite Bethel • Tuscaloosa, AL 35401 • Continuing
Fite Karen Stanton • Assistant Inter-Library Loan Ln • Oklahoma Department of Libraries • Oklahoma Cy, OK 73105-3298 • RASD
Fite Vicki • Hurst, TX 76053 • ALCTS
Fitt Stephen D. • Head Nonbook Librarian • University of Nevada-Las Vegas • Las Vegas, NV 89154-7001 • ACRL LIRT VRT
Fitts Richard J. • Architect • Design Collaborator • Virginia Beach, VA 23452
Fitz Carolyn • Branch Librarian • Jacksonville Public Library Sys Fernandina Beach Branch • Fernandina Beach, FL 32034-4123
FitzGerald Patricia • Assistant Director • Johns Hopkins University Libraries William H Welch Medical Library • Baltimore, MD 21205 • ACRL LAMA
Fitzgerald-Fleck Katharine • Youth Services Librarian • Beloit Public Library • Beloit, WI 53511 • ALSC
Fitzgerald Adena H. • Associate Director • East Chicago Public Library • E. Chicago, IN 46312 • ALCTS ALSC LAMA PLA
Fitzgerald Allene R. • Pensacola, FL 32503 • ACRL RASD *Continuing*
Fitzgerald Carol H. • Director • Sussex County Department of Libraries • Georgetown, DE 19947 • PLA
Fitzgerald Carol M. • Student • Emporia State University School of Library & Information Management • Emporia, KS 66801 • LITA SRRT
Fitzgerald Claire M. • Fayettville, NC 28314 • ALSC
Fitzgerald Diana S. • Arlington, VA 22207
Fitzgerald Elizabeth • Reference Librarian • Providence Public Library • Providence, RI 02903-3283 • YALSA
Fitzgerald Gail • Central Programs, Inc. Gumdrop Books • Bethany, MO 64424
Fitzgerald Jane R. • Reference Librarian • Paul D. West Professional Library Fulton County Board of Education • East Point, GA 30344 • AASL
Fitzgerald Joseph E. • Managing Partner • Fitzgerald & Anthony Inc. • New York, NY 10169 • LITA
Fitzgerald Judy K. • Reno, NV 89523
Fitzgerald Kerry A. • Student • University of Michigan School of Information and Library Studies • Ann Arbor, MI 48109-1092
Fitzgerald Lora H. • Student • University of Pittsburgh School of Library and Information Science • Pittsburgh, PA 15260 • PLA RASD SRRT
Fitzgerald Marianna R. • Reference Librarian • Bowling Green State University Jerome Library • Bowling Green, OH 43403 • ACRL IRRT
Fitzgerald Michael • Chief Cataloger • Harvard College Library Widener Memorial Library • Cambridge, MA 02138 • ACRL ALCTS LITA *Life*
Fitzgerald Michelle • Athens, GA 30627-1912 • AASL
Fitzgerald Patricia M. • Student • Rutgers University School of Communication Information & Library Studies • New Brunswick, NJ 08903 • AASL
Fitzgerald Ruth F. • REMC XI Director • Berrien County ISD • Berrien Springs, MI 49003 • AASL ALSC
Fitzgibbons Shirley A. • Indiana University School of Library and Information Science • Bloomington, IN 47405 • AASL ALSC RASD YALSA IFRT LRRT
Fitzhugh Kenneth • Librarian/Director • Davenport College of Business Library • Grand Rapids, MI 49502
Fitzpatrick Gary L. • Sr Ref Librarian, Geog/Map Divis • Library of Congress • Washington, DC 20541 • MAGERT
Fitzpayne Elizabeth F. • Librarian • Malden Hospital Medical Library • Malden, MA 02148 • ACRL
Fitzsimmons Donald J. • Piscataway, NJ 08854 • IFRT
Fitzsimmons Kathy M. • Boone, IA 50036
Fitzsimmons Richard • Director • Pennsylvania State Univ Library • Dunmore, PA 18512
Fitzsimmons Suzanne D. • Ref Ln-Bibliographic Instruction • Saint Louis University Pius XII Memorial Library • St. Louis, MO 63108
Fitzwater Diana L. • Reference Librarian • College of Dupage Learning Resources Center • Glen Ellyn, IL 60137 • ACRL SRRT
Fitzwater Tracy A. • Port Angeles, WA 98362 • AASL
Fiumara Melisa A. • Student • University of Wisconsin-Madison School of Library & Information Studies • Madison, WI 53706 • RASD IFRT SRRT
Fivecoat Martha H. • Student • Kent State University School of Library Science/Columbus Program • Columbus, OH 43210 • LITA
Fix Dorothy D. • Naples, FL 33942 • Continuing
Fixell Audrey • Trustee • East Meadow Public Library • East Meadow, NY 11554-1700 • ALTA
Flack Anne T. • Substitute Librarian • Arlington County Department of Libraries • Arlington, VA 22201

Flack Cynthia A. • University of Georgia Libraries • Athens, GA 30602
Flack Leona • Trustee • Mid-Hudson Library System • Poughkeepsie, NY 12601
Flack Shirley J. • Director • Scottsbluff Public Library • Scottsbluff, NE 69361-2493 • ALSC LAMA PLA GODORT
Fladland Kathleen T. • Catalog Librarian • Virginia Commonwealth University • Richmond, VA 23284-2033 • LITA IFRT
Fladung Hans G. • Oak Park, IL 60302
Flagg Gordon E. • Senior Editor, American Libs • American Library Association • Chicago, IL 60611-2795
Flagg Jo Ellen • Branch Services Chief • Kanawha County Public Library • Charleston, WV 25301 • LAMA PLA
Flahel Suzette A. • Student • Drexel University College of Information Studies • Philadelphia, PA 19104-2875
Flaherty Beverley J. • Asst. Dir., Public Serv. • Anoka County Library • Blaine, MN 55434
Flaherty Franklin Jr. Mrs • Librarian • The Peck School • Morristown, NJ 07960 • AASL
Flaherty Patricia • Programmer/Analyst • Mankato State University • Mankato, MN 56002 • LITA
Flaherty Rosemary • Librarian • Watertown Library Association Oakville Branch • Oakville, CT 06779
Flaherty Susan • South Milwaukee, WI 53172
Flam Floris • Team Leader, CRS/CRD • Library of Congress • Washington, DC 20541 • LITA
Flanagan Catherine • Student • University of Maryland College of Library and Information Services • College Park, MD 20742-4345
Flanagan Gary L. • Cataloger • Morehead State University Camden-Carroll Library • Morehead, KY 40351 • ACRL SRRT
Flanagan Leo N. • Director • Silas Bronson Library • Waterbury, CT 06702-1981
Flanagan Lynn L. • Reference Librarian • Middle Tennessee State University Library • Murfreesboro, TN 37132 • ACRL
Flanagan Robert A. • Supervisor, Main Library • Camden County Library Echelon Urban Center • Voorhees, NJ 08043 • PLA
Flanders Bruce • Kansas State Library • Topeka, KS 66612-1593 • ASCLA LITA
Flanders Clover • Kalamazoo, MI 49006 • ACRL RASD *Life*
Flanders E. Lorene • Instruction Librarian • Georgia College Ina Dillard Russell Library • Milledgeville, GA 31061 • ACRL IRRT
Flanders Frances • Monroe, LA 71201-4648 • Continuing
Flanders Kristin • Head, Dept. Tech Services • Maywood Public Library • Maywood, IL 60153
Flandreau Suzanne • Librarian and Archivist • Center for Black Music Research • Chicago, IL 60605 • ACRL
Flaningam Rita Rice • Clarion University of Pennsylvania • Clarion, PA 16214
Flanner Caroline • Riviera Beach, FL 33404-6217
Flannery Ann H. • Cataloger • Science & Technology Information Center National Science Council • Taipei, Taiwan
Flannery Doriel P. • Ln-System Adm & Tech Servs • Mills College Library • Oakland, CA 94613
Flannery Michael A. • Assistant Professor of L. Sci. • Northern Kentucky University • Highland Heights, KY 41099-6101
Flannery Sharon A. • Librarian/Media Specialist • Patrick McGaheran School • Lebanon, NJ 08833 • AASL
Flansburg Craig • Regional Sales Manager • Faxon Company,Inc. • Westwood, MA 02090 • LITA
Flath Bruce A. • Library Director • California Institute of Integral Studies • San Francisco, CA 94117 • ACRL
Flatten Kay • Darlaston W Midlands, England • LITA
Flattery Winifred B. • Saint Paul's Lower School for Boys • Brooklandville, MD 21022 • AASL
Flavin James • Media Services • University of Florida College of Law • Gainesville, FL 32611
Flaxbart David W. • Librarian • University of Texas Libraries • Austin, TX 78713 • ACRL
Fleck Karen • Children's Librarian • Free Library of Philadelphia South Philadelphia Branch • Philadelphia, PA 19145
Fleck Nan J. • Homestead, FL 33035
Fleck Nancy W. • Student • University of Michigan School of Information and Library Studies • Ann Arbor, MI 48109-1092
Flecker Dale • Assoc Univ Ln for Planning & Sys • Harvard University Library • Cambridge, MA 02138-2901 • ACRL LITA
Fleeger Dale • Manager of Branch Libraries • Harris County Public Library • Houston, TX 77054 • PLA
Fleeger Karen L. • Librarian • Herbert Hoover Elementary School • Harrisburg, PA 17110 • AASL
Fleek Melanie G. • San Jose, CA 95113 • PLA NMRT
Fleenor Judy A. • Knoxville, TN 37938 • AASL
Fleesak Margaret J. • Supervising Branch Librarian • New York Public Library High Bridge Branch • Bronx, NY 10452 • YALSA
Fleet Frances A. • Librarian • Tiffin University Pfeiffer Library • Tiffin, OH 44883 • ACRL RASD
Fleetwood Thom • Mattituck Free Library • Mattituck, NY 11952
Fleharty Carrie L. • Student • Bartlesville Mid-High School Library • Bartlesville, OK 74006 • AASL YALSA
Fleischer Karen S. • Media Specialist • Highland Elementary School • Silver Spring, MD 20902 • AASL ALSC
Fleischer M. Constance • Student • University of Illinois School of Library Information Science • Champaign, IL 61820 • ALCTS
Fleischer Regina • Assistant Director • Wilmette Public Library • Wilmette, IL 60091
Fleischhauer Carl • Project Specialist • Library of Congress • Washington, DC 20541
Fleishauer Carol J. • Associate Director • Massachusetts Institute of Technology Libraries (MIT) • Cambridge, MA 02139 • ACRL ALCTS
Fleishhacker Joy F. • Children's Librarian • Brooklyn Children's Museum • Brooklyn, NY 11213 • ALSC
Fleisig Susan R. • Student • University of Rhode Island Graduate School of Library & Information Studies • Kingston, RI 02881-0815
Fleming Amy K. • Catalog Librarian • Harris County Public Library • Houston, TX 77054 • ALCTS
Fleming Ann E. • West Palm Beach, FL 33411 • ALCTS
Fleming Assunta M. • Jonesboro, GA 30236
Fleming Carol A. • Student • Carson Middle School Library • Pittsburgh, PA 15237
Fleming Catherine M. • Branch Manager • North Flint Public Library • Flint, MI 48504 • IFRT
Fleming Darby B. • Pt. Pleasant Beach, NJ 08742
Fleming Faith D. • Reference Librarian • Cornell University • Ithaca, NY 14853-5301 • ACRL
Fleming Jennifer E. • Student • University of Pittsburgh School of Library and Information Science • Pittsburgh, PA 15260 • ALSC
Fleming Katherine L. • Lexington, KY 40504 • ACRL SRRT
Fleming Kathleen A.C. • Library Media Specialist • Hazard Control Program • Bloomington, IN 47405
Fleming Lois D. PhD • Tallahassee, FL 32303
Fleming Margaret P. • Denver, CO 80210 • Continuing
Fleming Marie • Copyright Information Specialist • Library of Congress • Washington, DC 20541
Fleming Michael T. • Student • University of Texas at Austin Graduate School of Library & Information Sciences • Austin, TX 78712-1276
Fleming Paula M. • Children's Librarian • Boston Public Library South Boston Branch • Boston, MA 02127 • ALSC PLA YALSA
Fleming Sara • Student • University of Pittsburgh School of Library and Information Science • Pittsburgh, PA 15260
Fleming Shawna L. • Student • University of California-Berkeley School of Library & Information Studies • Berkeley, CA 94720
Fleming Thomas P. • Ln Med L Ret & Prof L Sci Emer • Columbia University Libraries Butler Library • New York, NY 10027 • ACRL ALCTS *Life*
Flemming Carolyn • Children's Services Coordinator • Glendale Public Library • Glendale, CA 91205 • ALSC
Flener Jane G. • Louisville, KY 40207 • ACRL RASD *Life*
Flesia Faye A. • Library & Media Director • University of Wisconsin • Waukesha, WI 53188
Flesner Mitchell R. • Student • Westmont Public Library • Westmont, IL 60559
Fletcher Buna K. • New Castle, DE 19720
Fletcher Emmanuelle • Student • University of Maryland College of Library and Information Services • College Park, MD 20742-4345
Fletcher Harriett • Columbus, OH 43214 • Continuing
Fletcher Homer L. • Cupertino, CA 95014
Fletcher Jain • Cataloger • University of California-Los Angeles (UCLA) • Los Angeles, CA 90024-1450 • ACRL ALCTS
Fletcher Lee T. • Head, Reference Department • New Albany-Floyd County Public Library • New Albany, IN 47150
Fletcher Marilyn P. • Serial Librarian • University of New Mexico General Library • Albuquerque, NM 87131 • ALCTS LITA
Fletcher Michele S. • Troy, OH 45373 • LAMA PLA
Fletcher Miles A. • Houston Public Library Kashmere Garden Branch • Houston, TX 77026 • LAMA
Fletcher Robert A. • Librarian • Briarwood Elementary School • Issaquah, WA 98027-7003 • AASL YALSA *Life*
Fletcher Ruth • Evergreen Heights Elementary School • Auburn, WA 98001
Fletcher Sandy • Head Librarian • Duncanville High School • Duncanville, TX 75116 • AASL
Fleury Ann M. • Principal Librarian • Tampa-Hillsborough County Library Northwest Branch • Tampa, FL 33624
Fleury Mary Ellen • Information Specialist • Texaco, Inc. • New Orleans, LA 70160 • GODORT MAGERT
Flexman Ellen R. • Librarian • Indianapolis-Marion County Public Library Southport Branch • Indianapolis, IN 46227-8899 • IFRT
Flibotte Kally P • Payson, AZ 85547
Flick Eileen M. • Student • University of California-Los Angeles (UCLA) • Los Angeles, CA 90024-1450
Flick K. A. • Librarian • Ramsey County Public Library Adminstrative Offices • Shoreview, MN 55126-5800
Flickema Laura M. • Student • Madonna University Library • Livonia, MI 48150
Flickinger Carol A. • Media Specialist • Newton Public Schools U.S.D. #373 • Newton, KS 67114
Fling Jacqueline A. • Project Manager • Labat-Anderson Incorporated • Arlington, VA 22201 • LAMA
Flink Charles E. • Audio-Visual Librarian • Chicago Public Library Harold Washington Library • Chicago, IL 60605
Flinn Cheryl • Librarian • Ridgewood High School • Norridge, IL 60634 • AASL
Flint Anne G. • Automation Project Manager • University of the South Jessie Ball duPont Library • Sewanee, TN 37375-4005
Flint Carolyn A. • Librarian III • East Baton Rouge Parish Library • Baton Rouge, LA 70806-7699 • PLA RASD
Flint Linda Crecy • Carson, CA 90746
Flint Ruth E. • Student • University of Kentucky College of Library & Information Science • Lexington, KY 40506-0391 • ACRL ALCTS RASD NMRT
Flintrup Walter • Trustee • Skokie Public Library • Skokie, IL 60077-3680 • ALTA PLA
Fliotsos Anne L. • Winthrop College Ida Jane Dacus Library • Rock Hill, SC 29733
Flis Cecilia C. • Adults Services Librarian • Margaret R. Grundy Memorial Library • Bristol, PA 19007
Flisher Olivia R. • Solvang, CA 93463 • ALSC PLA
Flocchini Ella L. • Director,Media Services • Klamath Falls Public Schools • Klamath Falls, OR 97601 • AASL
Flood-Partridge Lucelia • Adult Librarian • Atlanta-Fulton Public Library • Atlanta, GA 30303 • ALCTS PLA
Flood Carol J. • Director Library Service • Briarwood College • Southington, CT 06489-1007 • ACRL
Flood Francis J. • Associate Professor Emeritus • University of Missouri-Columbia School of Library & Informational Science • Columbia, MO 65211 • ACRL ALCTS LHRT
Flood Susan C. • Approval Plan Librarian • Auburn University Ralph Brown Draughon Library • Auburn, AL 36849-5606 • ACRL ALCTS
Flora Nima V. • Victoria 3150, Australia
Floren Marisol • Student • University of Illinois Graduate School of Library and Information Science • Urbana, IL 61801 • IRRT
Florent Marguerite Rey • Loyola University Loyola Law School Library • New Orleans, LA 70118
Flores Arturo A. • University of California-Santa Cruz Library • Santa Cruz, CA 95064
Flores David S. • Student • University of Wisconsin-Milwaukee School of Library & Information Science • Milwaukee, WI 53201
Flores Josephine M. • Livonia, MI 48154 • AASL
Flores Matilda A. • Librarian I • Temecula Library • Temecula, CA 92590
Flores Verdel L. • Los Angeles, CA 90008-1936
Flores Yolanda R. • Reference Librarian • Las Vegas-Clark County Library District Charleston Heights Branch • Las Vegas, NV 89107 • ASCLA RASD VRT
Florio Mary • Waterford School Library • St. Johnsbury, VT 05819 • AASL
Flory Bonita G. • Branch Librarian • Kenmore Library • Bothel, WA 98011
Flott Nancy F. Dr • Director of the Library • Cottey College • Nevada, MO 64772 • ACRL
Flournoy Mary E. • Young Adult Specialist • Free Library of Philadelphia • Philadelphia, PA 19103 • ASCLA YALSA
Flower Eric S. • Library Director • University of Hawaii-West Oahu • Pearl City, HI 96782 • LITA
Flower Kenneth E. • Assoc. Dir., Administrative Serv • Johns Hopkins University Milton S. Eisenhower Library • Baltimore, MD 21218 • ACRL LAMA LITA RASD
Flowers Ann A. • Editor • Horn Book Inc. • Boston, MA 02108 • ALSC
Flowers Eileen • Director • North Canton Public Laibrary • North Canton, OH 44720 • LAMA PLA
Flowers Fran P. • Librarian • Marist School • Atlanta, GA 30319 • ALCTS

Flowers Helen F. • Head Librarian • Bay Shore Senior High School Library • Bay Shore, NY 11706 • AASL YALSA

Flowers Jackie D. • Librarian • Unified School District #270 Plainville Elementary School • Plainville, KS 67663 • AASL

Flowers Janet L. • Head, Acquisitions • University of North Carolina • Chapel Hill, NC 27599-3902 • ACRL ALCTS LAMA

Flowers Jeanne P. • Ketchum, ID 83340

Flowers Kay A. • Rice University Fondren Library • Houston, TX 77251-1892 • ACRL LAMA LITA

Flowers Kelley F. • Library Associate • Clark-Atlanta University School of Library & Information Studies • Atlanta, GA 30314-4391

Flowers Pat • University of California Rivera Library • Riverside, CA 92517 • ACRL ALCTS LITA RASD

Flowers Sarah I. • Student • San Jose State University Division of Library & Information Science • San Jose, CA 95192-0029

Floyd Dora • Denton, TX 76205 • ACRL ALCTS *Continuing*

Floyd James E. • Bradley Junior High School • Cleveland, TN 37311 • AASL

Floyd Sheila D. • Government Documents • Southern University John B. Cade Library • Baton Rouge, LA 70813 • GODORT

Floyd William B. • System Development Librarian • University of North Texas • Denton, TX 76203 • ACRL LAMA LITA

Fluckiger Adrienne N. • Director • Seaford Public Library • Seaford, NY 11783 • PLA

Fluellen Gwendolyn F. • Curriculum Spec. Media Services • Atlanta Public Schools • Atlanta, GA 30310

Flug Janice L. • Head Acquisitions • The American University Library • Washington, DC 20016-8046 • ACRL ALCTS LAMA

Flum Judith G. • Branch Manager • Alameda County Library San Lorenzo Branch • San Lorenzo, CA 94580 • LAMA PLA YALSA EMIERT IFRT SRRT

Flynn B. A. • Student • State University of New York (SUNY) School of Information & Library Studies • Buffalo, NY 14260

Flynn Barbara L. • Head,Reference Services • University of Southwestern Louisiana Libraries • Lafayette, LA 70503 • ACRL RASD

Flynn Barbara L. • Head Film/Video Center • Chicago Public Library Harold Washington Library • Chicago, IL 60605 • ALSC EMIERT

Flynn Cornelia D. • Buffalo, NY 14209-1836 • PLA RASD *Continuing*

Flynn David A. • Tech. Servs. Coor/HRL • Indiana University • Bloomington, IN 47405

Flynn Elizabeth • Head of Cataloging • Berkeley Public Library • Berkeley, CA 94704 • ALCTS

Flynn Ida M. • University of Pittsburgh School of Library and Information Science • Pittsburgh, PA 15260 • LITA

Flynn Joan • Director Lib./ & A-V Media Serv. • Chaminade University • Honolulu, HI 96816

Flynn John Philip • Wright State University Library • Dayton, OH 45435 • RASD

Flynn Kellie J. • Decatur, IL 62522

Flynn Mark W. • Head of Cataloging • State Library of Florida Division of Library & Information Services • Tallahassee, FL 32399-0250 • ALCTS

Flynn Patricia • Trustee • Queens Borough Public Library • Jamaica, NY 11432 • ALTA PLA

Flynt Linda S. • Media Specialist • Mohonasen Central Schools • Rotterdam, NY 12303 • AASL

Flythe Mary D. • Children's Librarian • Craven-Pamlico-Carteret Regional Library • New Bern, NC 28560

Fobert John • Student • University of Rhode Island Graduate School of Library & Information Studies • Kingston, RI 02881-0815

Fobes Hazel W. • Asheville, NC 28804

Focht Ruth Ann • Librarian • Abington Senior High Library • Abington, PA 19001 • AASL

Focke Helen M. • La Verne, CA 91750 • Continuing

Foechterle Sariah A. • Vienna, VA 22181

Foerster Lauralee H. • Supervisor of Media Services • Lafayette School Corporation • Lafayette, IN 47905 • AASL

Foerster Sharon M. • Librarian • Paul VI High School • Haddonfield, NJ 08033 • AASL

Fogal Annabel E. • Cataloging Services Manager • Brodart Company • Williamsport, PA 17705 • ALCTS LITA PLA

Fogarty Catherine B. • Librarian • Grey Nuns Motherhouse Library • Yardley, PA 19067

Fogarty Eleanor A. • Student • University of Pittsburgh School of Library and Information Science • Pittsburgh, PA 15260

Fogarty J. Nicholas • Asst. Director • Cobb County Public Library System • Marietta, GA 30060 • PLA

Fogarty James S. • Schuylkill Intermediate Unit 29 • Marlin, PA 17951 • AASL

Fogarty Joseph P. • Trustee • Ramapo Catskill Library System • Middletown, NY 10940

Fogarty Molly E. • Branch Supervisor • Springfield Library/Museums Association • Springfield, MA 01103 • PLA

Fogec Barbara A. • Student • University of Wisconsin-Milwaukee School of Library & Information Science • Milwaukee, WI 53201

Fogel Robin B. • Student • Queens College Graduate School of Library & Information Studies • Flushing, NY 11367 • LITA

Fogelman Phyllis J. • President/Publisher • Dial Books for Young Readers • New York, NY 10014 • ALSC

Fogelman Sheldon • New York, NY 10016 • ALSC IFRT

Fogg Dana A. • Denton, TX 76204-1742 • ALCTS SRRT

Fogg Elizabeth C. • Director • Salem Free Public Library • Salem, NJ 08079 • LAMA PLA RASD YALSA

Foggin Carol M. • University of Tennessee Library • Knoxville, TN 37996-1000 • ACRL ALCTS RASD

Fogleman Linda W. • Gateway Education Center • Greensboro, NC 27405

Fogler Patricia Nuquist • Montgomery, AL 36117 • AFLRT

Foglesong Marilee • Coordinator, Young Adult Service • The New York Public Library • New York, NY 10016 • PLA YALSA IFRT

Folcarelli Ralph • Trustee • Suffolk Cooperative Library System • Bellport, NY 11713 • ALTA

Folda Linda W. • Tech. Services Librarian • Chapel Hill Public Library • Chapel Hill, NC 27514

Foley Anne E. • Chief of Staff • Chicago Public Library Harold Washington Library • Chicago, IL 60605 • LAMA LITA PLA

Foley Carol J. • Student • Syracuse University • Syracuse, NY 13244 • AASL SRRT

Foley Elizabeth • Riverside City & County Public Library Central Branch • Riverside, CA 92502

Foley Erin E. • Minneapolis Public Library & Information Center • Minneapolis, MN 55401-1992 • ACRL

Foley Harriet F. • Franklin, OH 45005-0345 • YALSA *Continuing*

Foley Katie • Columbia Basin College • Pasco, WA 99301 • ACRL LAMA RASD

Foley Lela W. • Student • University of Iowa School of Library & Information Science • Iowa City, IA 52242

Foley Margaret M. • Latham, NY 12110 • PLA *Continuing*

Foley Mary Donna • High School Librarian • Russell County High School • Russell Spring, KY 42642 • AASL

Foley Meredith A. • Assistant Director • Leominster Public Library • Leominster, MA 01453 • PLA

Foley Nancy A. • Coordinator of Adult Services • Seattle Public Library • Seattle, WA 98104-1193 • PLA SRRT

Foley Ray J. • Trustee • Clinton Public Library • Clinton, IA 52732 • ALTA

Foley Robert A. • Director • Fitchburg State College Library • Fitchburg, MA 01420 • ACRL LAMA

Folke Carolyn W. • Bureau Director • Department of Public Instruction Division for Library Services • Madison, WI 53707 • AASL IFRT

Folland David M. • Ann Arbor, MI 48103

Follender Rochelle K. • Librarian • Montgomery County Department of Public Library/ Bethesda Regional Library • Bethesda, MD 20814 • RASD

Follet Robert E. • Head Music Librarian • University of Arizona Library • Tucson, AZ 85721 • ACRL LAMA RASD

Follette Clara E. Miss • Weston, VT 05161-9702 • Continuing

Follick Edwin D. Dr. • Dean of Education • Cleveland Chiropractic College of Los Angeles • Los Angeles, CA 90004 • AASL ACRL *Life*

Follo Mary H. • Detroit College of Business Warren Campus Library • Warren, MI 48092-5209

Follstad Virginia P. • Library Director • Irvin L. Young Memorial Library • Whitewater, WI 53190 • LAMA PLA

Folmar Becky A. • Irving, TX 75060 • AASL

Folmer Fred • Independence, KY 41051-9242 • ACRL *Life*

Folsom Patti • School Librarian • Ponaganset High School Library • N Scituate, RI 02857 • AASL

Folsom Sandy L. • Serials Cataloger • Central Michigan University Charles V. Park Library 315 • Mount Pleasant, MI 48859 • ACRL ALCTS

Folsom Steven R. • Oklahoma State University Edmon Low Library • Stillwater, OK 74078-0375 • ACRL

Foltz Florence P. • Littleton, CO 80121-2424 • AASL YALSA *Continuing*

Foltz Lynn J. • Student • Wayne State University Library Science Program • Detroit, MI 48202 • PLA IFRT SRRT

Foltzer Maureen • Norfolk Public Schools Willard Elementary School • Norfolk, VA 23504

Fomerand Raissa • Wilson Library Bulletin • Larchmont, NY 10538 • ERT ILERT

Fong J. Yem • Head of CTRC • University of Colorado Norlin Library • Boulder, CO 80309-0184 • EMIERT

Fong Jeanne W. • University of California • Berkeley, CA 94720

Fong Nancy • San Leandro Library • San Leandro, CA 94577

Fong Wilfred W. • Milwaukee, WI 53211 • ACRL LITA IRRT SRRT

Fonnesbeck Beverley • Anchorage, AK 99507 • AASL

Fons Theodore A. • Library Assistant • Tufts University Nils Yngve Wessell Library • Medford, MA 02155

Fontaine Everett O. Mr • New York, NY 10033 • Continuing

Fontaine Ronald G. • Reference Librarian • Connecticut State Office of Policy & Management Library • Hartford, CT 06106

Fontalbert Terry • Trustee • Kanawha County Public Library • Charleston, WV 25301 • ALTA

Fontenot Frances M. • Bueche, LA 70720 • RASD

Fontenot Helen Sister • Director, Learning Resources • Our Lady of Holy Cross College Blaine S. Kern Library • New Orleans, LA 70131 • ACRL

Fontenot Linda H. • Elementary School Librarian • Martin Petitjean Elementary School • Rayne, LA 70578 • AASL ALSC

Fontenot Wridley A. Ph. D. Dr. • Assistant Director • Allen Parish Libraries Headquarters • Oberlin, LA 70655-0400

Fontes Patricia • Librarian • Westborough Middle School • Westborough, MA 01581 • AASL YALSA IFRT

Fontish Marion D. • Library Director • Lackland Base Library • Lackland AFB, TX 78236-5000 • AFLRT

Fooks S. Virginia • Williamsburg, VA 23185 • ALSC *Continuing*

Foos Donald D. • Tallahassee, FL 32304

Foote Elizabeth C. • NILS Publishing • Chatstworth, CA 91311

Foote Janet H. • Arlington, VA 22201

Foote Jody Bales • Southern Illinois University Delyte W. Morris Library • Carbondale, IL 62901-6632 • ACRL LIRT

Footracer Tevis Ann • Librarian • Campbell Hall • N Hollywood, CA 91607 • AASL YALSA SRRT

Foppiani Mary A. • Brookline, MA 02146

Forbes DeAnn • Library Media Teacher • Montezuma Creek Elementary School • Montezuma Creek, UT 84534 • AASL

Forbes Edith J. • Reference Librarian • Nassau Community College Library • Garden City, NY 11530 • ALSC

Forbes Harold M. Jr. • Associate Curator • West Virginia and Regional History Collection • Morgantown, WV 26506 • ACRL

Forbes John B. • Librarian • U S Natl Agricultural L • Beltsville, MD 20705 • RASD

Forbes LaVerne F. • Librarian-Lower Division • Berkeley Preparatory School • Tampa, FL 33615 • AASL

Forbes Leslie T. • Webster, TX 77598

Forbes Liane R. • Chattanooga, TN 37411 • AASL

Forbes Lydia B. • Librarian • Blackburn College Library • Carlinville, IL 62626

Forbes Marna S. • Student • University of Wisconsin School of Library & Information Studies • Madison, WI 53706

Forbes Martha E. • Student • University of South Florida School of Library & Information Science • Tampa, FL 33620

Forbes Mary E. • Student • University of Illinois Graduate School of Library and Information Science • Urbana, IL 61801 • PLA

Forbes Nancy R. • Palos Verdes Intermediate School Library • Palos Verdes Est., CA 90274 • YALSA

Forbus Bettye L. • Director • Houston Love Memorial Library • Dothan, AL 36303 • PLA

Forbush Carolyn J. • Lapeer, MI 48446 • AASL SRRT

Force Lorraine M. • Walnut Creek, CA 94595 • AASL YALSA IFRT

Force Ronald W. • Dean of Library Services • University of Idaho Library • Moscow, ID 83843 • ACRL

Force Stephen E. • Director, Computer Operations • H. W. Wilson Company • Bronx, NY 10452 • LITA

Forcier Peggy J. • Manager • Washington County Cooperative Library Service • Aloha, OR 97006 • PLA

Ford-Foster Barbara A. • Bowling Green State University Jerome Library • Bowling Green, OH 43403 • ACRL ALCTS LITA RASD LIRT

Ford Barbara J. • Dir. Univ. Library Services • Virginia Commonwealth University • Richmond, VA 23284-2033 • ACRL LAMA LITA RASD GODORT IFRT IRRT LRRT SRRT *Life*

Ford Bernard J. • Associate Director • University of Pennsylvania Library Van Pelt-Dietrich Library Center • Philadelphia, PA 19104-6206 • ACRL ALCTS

Ford Collette • Education Services Coord • University of California-Irvine Library • Irvine, CA 92713 • ACRL LIRT

Ford Elizabeth Ann • Order Librarian, Acq. Dept. • University of Iowa Libraries • Iowa City, IA 52242-1379 • ALCTS

Ford Freddie T. Mrs. • Media Specialist • Kittredge Magnet School for High Achievers • Atlanta, GA 30329 • AASL

Ford Janet L. • Director • Ritter Public Library • Vermilion, OH 44089 • LAMA PLA

Ford Jasmine B. • Bremerton, WA 98310 • Continuing

Ford Joseph B. • President • Joseph Ford & Associates Inc • Olympia, WA 98501 • LITA

Ford Karin E. • Assoc. Dir. Information Services • Idaho State Library • Boise, ID 83702 • ACRL ASCLA LAMA

Ford Lorrita E. • Student • Oakland Public Library • Oakland, CA 94612 • ALCTS PLA RASD EMIERT

Ford Madeline A. • Student • Baruch College Library • New York, NY 10010 • RASD

Ford Marcia Kay • Jay County Public Library • Portland, IN 47371 • ALCTS ALSC PLA

Ford Martha J. • New York Public School 113M • New York, NY 10026

Ford Michael W. Jr. • Student • University of Pittsburgh School of Library and Information Science • Pittsburgh, PA 15260

Ford Nita F. • Assistant Librarian • Mother Whiteside Memorial Library • Grants, NM 87020

Ford Pamela W. • Marshall University James E. Morrow Library • Huntington, WV 25755-2060 • ALCTS

Ford Peggy • Sacramento, CA 95818-3906 • AASL

Ford Robert B. Jr. • Cambria Hts, NY 11411 • ACRL LHRT LRRT

Ford Stephen W. • Grand Rapids, MI 49505-4578

Ford Steven J. • Lincoln County Public Library • Lincolnton, NC 28092

Ford Sylverna V. • Executive Director • Oakland Library Consortium Hunt Library • Pittsburgh, PA 15213-3890 • ACRL ASCLA LAMA

Ford Terence • New York, NY 10276-1115 • ACRL IRRT NMRT

Ford Tracey T. • Student • East Carolina University Department of Library & Information Studies • Greenville, NC 27858-4353 • AASL

Ford Vicki Beck • Librarian • Osage R-3 Schools • Westphalia, MO 65085 • ALSC

Ford William D. Hon. • U.S. House of Representatives • Washington, DC 20515 • AASL ACRL ALCTS ALSC ALTA ASCLA LAMA LITA PLA RASD YALSA *Honorary*

Forde Janet L. • College Librarian • Sir Arthur Lewis Community College • St. Lucia, West Indies • ACRL

Fordell Rose Mary • Trustee • Dearborn Department of Libraries Henry Ford Centennial Library • Dearborn, MI 48126

Fordham Cynthia • Paramus Public Library • Paramus, NJ 07652

Fordon Elizabeth M. • Young Adult/Children's Librarian • Huntington Public Library • Huntington, NY 11743 • ALSC YALSA NMRT

Fore Janet S. • Science Reference Librarian • University of Arizona Library • Tucson, AZ 85721 • ACRL RASD

Fore Virginia L. • Branch Manager • Enoch Pratt Free Library Govans Branch • Baltimore, MD 21212 • PLA

Forehand Margaret P. • Director • Chesapeake Public Library • Chesapeake, VA 23320 • ALSC PLA

Foreman Gertrude E. • Prof./Head, Public Services • University of Minnesota Bio-Medical Library • Minneapolis, MN 55455 • ACRL RASD

Foreman Iona L. • Macon, GA 31213

Foreman Robyn I. • Corrdinator, Borrower Services • Seattle Public Library • Seattle, WA 98104-1193 • LAMA PLA

Foreman Rose Ann • Librarian • Saint Paul Public Library • St. Paul, MN 55102 • PLA

Forfia Linda S. • Central Christian Academy • Wichita, KS 67226

Forgach L. Violet • Manager • The Glidden Company • Strongsville, OH 44136

Forger Garry • Computer Assisted Instr Coor • Crouse Irving Memorial Hospital Library • Syracuse, NY 13210

Forget Louis J. S. • Director Director • National Library of Canada Information Technical Services • Ottawa ON, K1A 0N4 Canada • ACRL LITA

Fork Donald J. • Administrative Librarian • United States Department of Education Office of Educational Res & Improvement • Washington, DC 20208-5571

Forker Carol L. • Idaho Falls Public Library • Idaho Falls, ID 83401 • LITA PLA

Forker Imogene • Whittier, CA 90605 • AASL YALSA EMIERT IFRT

Forkner Jane L. • Catalog Librarian • Topeka Public Library • Topeka, KS 66604-1374 • LITA

Forman Jack • Ref./Pub Services Librarian • Mesa College Library • San Diego, CA 92111 • ACRL RASD YALSA

Forman Tina-Karen • Head, Copy Cataloging Section • UCLA Library University Research Library • Los Angeles, CA 90024-1575 • ACRL

Forman Virginia • Paul H. Cale Elementary School • Charlottesville, VA 22901 • AASL IFRT

Formanack Gail M. • Librarian • Omaha Public Schools • Omaha, NE 68111 • AASL

Forney Brian • Reference Coordinator • Northern Arizona University Cline Library • Flagstaff, AZ 86011-6022

Forney Christopher D. • Asst. Branch Manager • Howard County Library • Columbia, MD 21044

Forrest Carl E. • Buffalo, NY 14223 • ACRL

Forrest Charles • Dir. Financial Mgt./Planning • Emory University Libraries Robert W. Woodruff Library • Atlanta, GA 30322-2870 • ACRL LAMA LITA RASD

Forrest Dan • Student • East Baton Rouge Parish Library • Baton Rouge, LA 70806-7699 • ACRL

Forrest Lee M. • Cataloger • Saint Louis University Plus XII Memorial Library • St. Louis, MO 63108 • ACRL

Forrest Linda A. • Student • Florida State University School of Library and Information Studies • Tallahassee, FL 32306-2048 • AASL

Forrest Rosamund • Torrance, CA 90505

Forrester Victoria W. • Librarian • Saint Mark's School • San Rafael, CA 94903

Forro Denise A. • Bancroft, MI 48414 • LAMA LITA

Forsberg Ruth • Librarian • Monterey County Free Libraries • Salinas, CA 93901 • ALCTS

Forsee Joe B. • Director • Georgia Department of Education Division of Public Library Services • Atlanta, GA 30303-3692 • ASCLA

Forsling Susan J. • Librarian • Northeast Hamilton Community School District • Blairsburg, IA 50034-0200 • AASL YALSA

Forsman Greta P. • Reference Librarian • Saint Louis University Pius XII Memorial Library • St. Louis, MO 63108 • ACRL

Forsman John • Tiburon, CA 94920

Forsman Rick B. • Director • University of Colorado Health Science Center, Denison Mem Lib • Denver, CO 80262 • LAMA LITA

Forster Barbara • Perez Yigo, GU 96929

Forster Mary L. • Student • University of Washington Graduate School of Library and Information Science • Seattle, WA 98195 • EMIERT IFRT SRRT

Forsyth Anita J. • Reference Librarian • Citrus College Hayden Memorial Library • Glendora, CA 91740-1899

Forsyth Ella M. • Dickinson College Library Boyd Lee Spahr Library • Carlisle, PA 17013

Forsyth John H. • Reference Libraian • Worthington Public Library • Worthington, OH 43085 • ACRL PLA RASD

Forsyth Kenna J. • Baltimore County Public Library • Towson, MD 21204 • LAMA PLA CLENE

Forsyth Melissa M. • Asst. Librarian • Prestonsburg Community College • Prestonburg, KY 41653-9502 • ACRL

Forsythe David N. • Associate Dir. for Field Service • State University of New York OCLC Library Network • Albany, NY 12246 • ACRL ALCTS

Forte Joseph E. • Library Director • Kansas Newman College Ryan Library • Wichita, KS 67213-2097 • ACRL

Forte Thomas A. • Executive Director • Glencoe Public Library • Glencoe, IL 60022-1597 • LAMA PLA

Fortenberry Ann • School Librarian • South Mississippi Regional Library • Columbia, MS 39429 • ALSC

Fortenberry Joyce W. • Student • Ohoopee Regional Library • Vidalia, GA 30474 • PLA

Forth Stuart Dr. • Dean Emeritus Univ. Libraries • Pennsylvania State University Libraries • University Park, PA 16802 • ACRL ALCTS *Life*

Fortier-Barnes Catherine A. • Serials Librarian • University of Massachusetts-Dartmouth Library • North Dartmouth, MA 02747 • ACRL

Fortier Jan Marie Dr. • Director • Marylhurst College Shoen Library • Marylhurst, OR 97036 • ACRL LAMA

Fortin Clifford C. Dr. • Hamel, MN 55340-9625 • Continuing

Fortin Maurice G. • Asst. Director for Pub. Svs. • University of North Texas • Denton, TX 76203 • ACRL LAMA RASD

Fortin Yves Paul • Library Consultant • University of Montreal Ecole De Bibliotheconomie • Montreal ON, Canada

Fortini Bernice • Librarian • Ressurection High School • Chicago, IL 60631 • AASL

Fortney Linda M. • Reference Librarian • Montgomery College • Rockville, MD 20850 • RASD

Fortney Lynn M. • Biomedical Mgr. Marketing Mgr • EBSCO Subscription Service • Birmingham, AL 35201 • ALCTS LAMA

Fortson Judith L. • Head Librarian • Hoover Institution on War, Revolution & Peace Library • Stanford, CA 94305-6010 • ALCTS

Fortunato Lynne A. • Librarian II • New York Public Library • New York, NY 10018-2788

Fortune Janet M. • Fairbanks, AK 99709 • AASL

Fortunoff Alan • President • Fortunoff • Westbury, NY 11590 • ACRL

Forys John W. • Engineering Librarian • University of Iowa Libraries • Iowa City, IA 52242-1379 • ACRL LITA

Forys Marsha • Reference Librarian • University of Iowa Libraries • Iowa City, IA 52242-1379 • ACRL LIRT

Fosbender Jule • Director • Adrian Public Library • Adrian, MI 49221 • ALSC LAMA LITA PLA RASD

Fosburg Marilyn • Woodstock Middle School • Woodstock, VA 22664

Fosgate Jennifer H. • Davenport, CA 95017

Foshee Marteyne • North Greene High School • Greenville, TN 37743

Foshee Sharon K. • Edmond, OK 73034 • ALSC NMRT

Foss E. Martin • Associate Librarian • Carleton University Library • Ottawa ON, K1S 5J7 Canada • ACRL LITA

Foss Joanne • Children's Coordinator • Lancaster County Library • Lancaster, PA 17602 • ALSC

Fosselman Steve • Administrator • Edith Abbott Memorial Library • Grand Island, NE 68801 • LAMA YALSA IFRT

Fossett Alice T. • Librarian • Boothbay Region Elementary School • Boothbay Harbor, ME 04538 • AASL

Foster Candice L. • Niceville, FL 32578 • AASL

Foster Colleen M. • Coor. of Adult Services • Stockton-San Joaquin County Public Library • Stockton, CA 95202 • LAMA PLA RASD

Foster Connie • Serials Librarian • Western Kentucky University Helm-Cravens Library • Bowling Green, KY 42101

Foster Elizabeth S. • Director, Technical Services • Reuben McMillan Free Library Association Youngstown & Mahoning Cnty P L • Youngstown, OH 44503 • ALCTS

Foster Eloise • Director • American Hospital Association Resource Center • Chicago, IL 60611 • ASCLA LAMA

Foster Emilia • Librarian/Sch Lib Media Spec • Department of Education • Hato Rey, PR 00919

Foster Erin E. • Student • University of Texas at Austin Graduate School of Library & Information Sciences • Austin, TX 78712-1276 • SRRT

Foster F Blanche • Terre Haute, IN 47807 • Continuing

Foster Francis M. D.D.S. Dr. • Richmond, VA 23220

Foster Imogene • Scottsville, KY 42164 • ACRL RASD *Life*

Foster Iva J. • Tempe, AZ 85282

Foster Jacqulyn G. • Daniel High School • Clemson, SC 29631

Foster James S. • Student • University of Texas at Austin Graduate School of Library & Information Sciences • Austin, TX 78712-1276 • LITA

Foster Joan • City Librarian • San Luis Obispo City-County Library • San Luis Obispo, CA 93403 • PLA

Foster Johanna M. • Associate Librarian • University of Windsor Leddy Library • Windsor ON, N9B 3P4 Canada • ACRL ALCTS LAMA

Foster Joy V. • Library Media Specialist • Auburn High and Middle School • Riner, VA 24149 • AASL

Foster Joyce M. • Director, Lib. Devel. • Arizona State University Libraries • Tempe, AZ 85287-1006 • ACRL LAMA

Foster Juanita R. • Librarian • Hennepin County Library Rockford Road Branch • Crystal, MN 55427 • ALSC YALSA

Foster Karen R. • Student • Widener University School of Law Library • Wilmington, DE 19803-0475

Foster Katharin • Head, Collection Dev • Ohio University Vernon R. Alden Library • Athens, OH 45701-2978 • ACRL ALCTS

Foster Leslie Anne • Govt. Publications Librarian • University of Wisconsin-Eau Claire William D. McIntyre Library • Eau Claire, WI 54702 • ACRL GODORT

Foster Lorris A. • The Woodlands, TX 77381

Foster Marsha G. • Marketing Consultant • Data Research Associates Inc. • Saint Louis, MO 63132 • LITA

Foster Mary E. Miss • Tucson, AZ 85701 • Continuing

Foster Pauline M. • Tuscaloosa, AL 35404 • AASL YALSA *Continuing*

Foster Robert E. • Librarian • Sacramento Public Library • Sacramento, CA 95814

Foster Robin J. • Director • Dadeville Public Library • Dadeville, AL 36853 • LAMA PLA

Foster Sallie L. • Tempe, AZ 85282 • LITA

Foster Susan A. • Asst. Children's Librarian • Lake County Public Library Munster Branch • Munster, IN 46321 • PLA CLENE MAGERT

Foster Tahirih A. • Kamuela, HI 96743

Foster Valerie N. • Assistant Librarian • American Postal Workers Union Library Information Center • Washington, DC 20005 • LITA FLRT

Foster William W. • Librarian I • Tampa-Hillsborough County Public Library North Tampa Branch • Tampa, FL 33604 • PLA

Foth Ellen K. Mrs • Cedar Grove, NJ 07009 • Continuing

Foth Nancy M. • Coordinator Adult Service • Toledo-Lucas County Public Library • Toledo, OH 43624 • LAMA LITA PLA

Fouchecourt Marilyn L. • Librarian • Naval Weapons Station Library • Charleston, SC 29408-7000 • AFLRT FLRT

Foucher Harriet A. • Branch Head • Highland County Library • Highland, CA 92346 • PLA

Fouchereaux Karen T. • Student • Indiana University School of Library and Information Science • Bloomington, IN 47405

Foudray Rita Schoch Dr. • Mgr., Interlibrary Loan • Dallas Public Library • Dallas, TX 75201 • LITA LRRT

Foulke Kathleen S. • Saint Michael's Country Day School • Newport, RI 02840 • AASL ALSC

Foulke Lori D. • De Kalb, IL 60115-4417 • EMIERT IRRT

Foulke Phyllis • Catholic Memorial High School • Waukesha, WI 53186 • AASL

Fountain Eugenia Ferris • Director of Library Services • Marian Court Junior College Library • Swampscott, MA 01907 • ACRL LITA LIRT

Fountain Joanna Dr. • Georgetown, TX 78626

Fourie Denise K. • Consultant • Library Concepts • San Luis Obispo, CA 93405 • ILERT

Fournier Anna-Marie • Consultant • Durham Board of Education • Whitby Ontario, L1N 2C3 Canada • AASL

Fournier Susan R. • Washington, DC 20002 • LAMA RASD

Fourre Doris • Trustee • Timberland Regional Library • Olympia, WA 98501 • ALTA

Foust Donna S. • Cincinnati, OH 45242 • ASCLA

Foust J'aime L. • Librarian • Queensbury High School • Queensbury, NY 12804

Foust John H. • Librarian • Ohio Valley College Learning Resources Center • Parkersburg, WV 26101 • ACRL ALSC

Foust Judith M. • Deputy Director • Brooklyn Public Library • Brooklyn, NY 11238 • PLA

Fouste Teresa N. • Williams, OR 97544 • ACRL

Fouts Judith F. • Finders Keepers Out of Print Book Search • Dallas, TX 75382-0247 • ALCTS

Fouty Gary • University of Minnesota Walter Library • Minneapolis, MN 55455 • ACRL

Fouty Kathleen G. • Science & Engineering Reference • University of Minnesota Institute of Technology Libraries • Minneapolis, MN 55455 • ACRL LAMA

Foutz Chloe V. • Library Director • Union College Library • Lincoln, NE 68506-4386 • ACRL LAMA RASD

Fowells Susan • Media Specialist • Covington Junior High School • Vancouver, WA 98664-1660 • AASL IFRT

Fowler Albert W. • Fairbanks, AK 99708-0548 • ACRL ALCTS SRRT

Fowler Anne • President • Friends of the Boone County Library • Harrison, AR 72601

Fowler Blanche F. • Media Specialist • Oakbrook Middle School • Ladson, SC 29456 • AASL ALSC

Fowler Brian R. • San Jose Public Library • San Jose, CA 95113

Fowler Carole F. • Director • Jervis Public Library Association • Rome, NY 13440

Fowler Elizabeth • St Charles, IL 60174

Fowler Elizabeth B. • Young Adult Librarian • Prince George County Memorial Library • Oxon Hill, MD 20745 • YALSA

Fowler Elizabeth P. • University of California-Berkeley School of Library & Information Studies • Berkeley, CA 94720

Fowler Ellen T. • Children's Librarian • King County Library System • Seattle, WA 98109-5191 • ALSC

Fowler Florence L. • Mill Valley, CA 94941 • ALSC ASCLA YALSA

Fowler James W. • Garland County Community College LRC • Hot Spg Natl, AR 71901 • ACRL LAMA LITA

Fowler Joseph W. • Manager,Magazines/Newspaper Div. • Columbus Metropolitan Library • Columbus, OH 43215 • ALCTS PLA RASD

Fowler Linda J. • Childrens Librarian • Burlington Public Library • Burlington, IA 52601

Fowler Louise D. • Western Connecticut State University • Danbury, CT 06810 • ACRL

Fowler Lucille L. • Trustee • Evansville-Vanderburgh County Public Library • Evansville, IN 47708-1694 • ALTA

Fowler Lynda B. • Media & Technology Coor. • Pitt County Schools • Greenville, NC 27858 • AASL

Fowler Lynne S. • Student • University of Michigan School of Information and Library Studies • Ann Arbor, MI 48109-1092 • ALSC PLA RASD

Fowler Mable L. • Librarian/Instr. in Catlg. Dept. • Georgia Southern University Henderson Library • Statesboro, GA 30460

Fowler Martha J. • Rochester, NH 03867

Fowler Mary B. • Honey Grove, TX 75446

Fowler Maryann K. • Columbia, SC 29209

Fowler Patricia M. • Director • Witherle Memorial Library • Castine, ME 04421 • ALSC LAMA PLA RASD

Fowler Rena K. • Arcata, CA 95521-9999 • ACRL LITA

Fowler Sonja • A Likely Story Bookstore • Oklahoma City, OK 73120

Fowler Susan G. • Student • Emporia State University School of Library & Information Management • Emporia, KS 66801 • LITA

Fowler Taena L. • Student • University of Iowa School of Library & Information Science • Iowa City, IA 52242 • NMRT

Fowler Yvonne G. • Chicago, IL 60619

Fowlie Les • Chief Librarian • Toronto Public Library • Toronto ON, M5A 4L2 Canada • LAMA PLA

Fox-Grimm Mary • Trustee • Montgomery County Dept of Pub Lib Davis Community Library • Bethesda, MD 20817-1699 • ALTA PLA

Fox Annie • Vail Public Library • Vail, CO 81657 • LITA IRRT

Fox Barbara Jean • Technical Librarian • White Sands Missile Range Post Library • White Sands MR, NM 88002 • FLRT

Fox Beth Wheeler • Director • Westbank Community Library • Austin, TX 78746 • PLA

Fox Bruce T. • Branch Librarian • Chicago Public Library North Austin Branch • Chicago, IL 60639

Fox Carol A. • Librarian • Unified School District • El Dorado, KS 67042 • AASL YALSA

Fox Carol J. • Youth Services Consultant • Illinois State Library • Springfield, IL 62701-1796 • AASL ALSC ASCLA

Fox Dexter L. • Automation Planning Specialist • Library of Congress Automation Planning & Liaison • Washington, DC 20540 • ALCTS LITA FLRT GODORT

Fox Elizabeth R. • Reference & Bibiographic Inst. • Adams State College Library • Alamosa, CO 81102 • ACRL

Fox Estella E. • Ft Thomas, KY 41075 • AASL YALSA *Life*

Fox Frances Jaunice • Phoenix, AZ 85015

Fox Gale M. • Webster Groves, MO 63119-4204

Fox Howard A. • Librarian • Seattle Public Library • Seattle, WA 98104-1193 • PLA

Fox James W. • Dir.,Ref. Svs. & Clln Mgmt • Southern Illinois University Delyte W. Morris Library • Carbondale, IL 62901-6632 • RASD

Fox Janet L. • Systems Analyst • University of Chicago Library • Chicago, IL 60637-1502 • ACRL ALCTS LITA

Fox Jean Joicey • San Antonio, TX 78238

Fox Jeanne W. • Library Director • H Leslie Perry Memorial Library • Henderson, NC 27536 • LAMA PLA

Fox Joan • Director • Granby Public Library • Granby, CT 06035 • PLA

Fox Judith A. • Head Cataloger • Washington University Libraries • Saint Louis, MO 63130-4899 • ALCTS LITA

Fox Kathleen A. • Technical Services Librarian • San Jose City College Library • San Jose, CA 95128 • ALCTS LITA

Fox Leandra C. • Portland, OR 97225 • RASD

Fox Leroy G. • Marshalltown, IA 50158

Fox Linda • Library Assistant • Cloquet Public Library • Cloquet, MN 55720 • ALSC

Fox Linda • Librarian • New Fairfield Free Public Library • New Fairfield, CT 06812 • ALTA PLA

Fox Linda J. • Head of Reference • Berkeley Heights Public Library • Berkeley Hts, NJ 07922

Fox Lisa L. • Preservation Program Development • Southeastern Library Network (SOLINET) • Atlanta, GA 30309-2955 • ALCTS

Fox Lynda D. • Branch Head • Ypsilanti District Library Peters Branch • Ypsilanti, MI 48198

Fox Lynne M. • University of Northern Colorado James A. Michener Library • Greeley, CO 80639

Fox M. Anne • International Librarian • Oregon State University William Jasper Kerr Library • Corvallis, OR 97331-4501 • ACRL IRRT

Fox Margaret M. • Media Center Director • Fenton High School Library • Bensenville, IL 60106 • AASL

Fox Mary A. • Assistant Catalog Librarian • Southern Illinois University Delyte W. Morris Library • Carbondale, IL 62901-6632 • ALCTS

Fox Mary Ann W. • Librarian • The Hun School of Princeton • Princeton, NJ 08540

Fox Mary P. • Coor of Technical Services • Dallas Baptist University Vance Memorial Library • Dallas, TX 75211

Fox Mary T. • Library Teacher • Clarkes School • Mulino, OR 97042

Fox Marylou Pierce • Director • Webster Groves Public Library • Webster Grvs, MO 63119 • LAMA PLA

Fox Merle U. Rev. • New Oxford, PA 17350 • Continuing

Fox Michael J. • Head of Processing • Minnesota Historical Society • Saint Paul, MN 55102 • ALCTS

Fox Monica L. • Personnel Officer • Spokane Public Library Comstock Building Library • Spokane, WA 99201-0976 • LAMA

Fox Paula Huey • Librarian • Hennepin County Library Southdale-Hennepin Area Library • Edina, MN 55435

Fox Richard M. • Senior Map Cataloger • Library of Congress • Washington, DC 20541 • GODORT MAGERT

Fox Robert E. Jr. • Ref./Bibl Instr Librarian • Clayton State College • Morrow, GA 30260 • ACRL SRRT

Fox Sharon A. • St. Louis, MO 63121 • SRRT

Fox Vicki • Head of Children's Service • Pikes Peak Library District • Colorado Springs, CO 80901 • ALSC PLA

Foy Lorraine • Childrens Librarian & Branch Mgr • Free Library of Philadelphis Whitman Branch • Philadelphia, PA 19148 • ALSC

Foy Robert K. • Hd, Art & Literature Dept. • New York Public Library Mid-Manhattan Branch • New York, NY 10016 • PLA EMIERT SRRT

Foyt Michelle S. • Librarian • Swiss Hospitality Institute • Washington, CT 06793

Fraas Julia M. • Jefferson City, MO 65109

Frachetti Suzanne M. • Student • Syracuse University School of Information Studies • Syracuse, NY 13244-4100

Fraction Nicolette • Associate Professor-Acquisitions • Hostos Community College • Bronx, NY 10451 • ACRL EMIERT

Fradenburgh Robin L. • Automated/Catl/Services Ln • University of Texas Libraries General Libraries • Austin, TX 78713-7330

Fradkin Bernard • Dean of Learning Resource Ctr. • College of DuPage Learning Resources Center • Glen Ellyn, IL 60137 • ACRL

Frakes Susan M. • Student • Clarion University of Pennsylvania College of Library Science • Clarion, PA 16214

Fraley Barbara L. • Director • Johnson County Library • Buffalo, WY 82834

Fraley Ruth Ann • Dir.,Office of Libs & Records • New York Office of Court Administration • Albany, NY 12222 • LAMA

Fralick Marsha • Chief,Technical Services • Minneapolis Public Library & Information Center • Minneapolis, MN 55401-1992 • ALCTS LITA

Frame Paul N. • Denver, CO 80220 • Continuing

Frame Ruth • Chicago, IL 60611 • ASCLA LAMA   *Life*

Frances Melodie M. • San Jose, CA 95112 • SRRT

Franceschelli Christopher • Dutton, Lodester, Cobblehill • New York, NY 10014-3658 • ALSC YALSA

Franceschi J. Michael • Library Director • Greenfield Public Library • Greenfield, MA 01301 • PLA

Franceschini Christina MC • St. Catharines ON, L2S 2C2 Canada

Franchetto Barbara • Service Director • Southern Ontario Library Service • Richmond Hill ON, L4B 1K5 Canada • LITA

Franchino Cathryn D. • Fairport Central Schools Johanna Perrin Middle School • Fairport, NY 14450 • AASL

Francis Barbara • President/Publisher • Pippin Press • New York, NY 10028

Francis Beth • Vice President • David O. Wiley Inc. • Phoenix, AZ 85004 • LAMA PLA ERT

Francis Beverly H. • Bernards Township Library • Basking Ridge, NJ 07920 • ALSC

Francis Denise H. • Reference Librarian • Bala-Cynwyd Library • Bala Cynwyd, PA 19004-3095

Francis Douglas J. • Librarian • Maple Ave Middle School Area School District • Littlestown, PA 17340 • AASL

Francis Frank Jr. • Library Director • Wiley College Thomas Winston Cole Sr. Library • Marshall, TX 75670 • ACRL LIRT

Francis Georgianna J. • Head, Technical Services • Asheville-Buncombe Library System • Asheville, NC 28801

Francis Helen C. • Mendham, NJ 07945 • Continuing

Francis Janet O. • Senior Cataloger • Brigham Young University Harold B. Lee Library • Provo, UT 84602 • ALCTS ALSC LIRT

Francis Marion W. • Mgr Germantown/Cordova Branches • Memphis-Shelby County Public Library and Information Center • Memphis, TN 38104-4025 • PLA

Francisco Marylynn • Reference Librarian • General Electric-Aerospace • Reston, VA 22090

Francisquelo Maria E. • Secretaria Tecnica • Centro De Investigacoines Bibliotecologicas • 1002 Buenos Aires, Argentina • LAMA CLENE LRRT

Franck Ilona G. • Louisville, KY 40205

Franck Jane P. • Teachers College-Columbia University Milbank Memorial Library • New York, NY 10027 • AASL ACRL ALCTS ALSC ASCLA LAMA LITA RASD GODORT IFRT IRRT LIRT LRRT

Franck Marga Mrs • Mason, MI 48854 • ACRL ALCTS *Continuing*

Franco Adrienne • Reference Librarian • Iona College Ryan Library • New Rochelle, NY 10801 • LRRT

Franco Elaine A. • Principal Cataloger • University of California Shields Library • Davis, CA 95616 • ACRL ALCTS SRRT *Life*

Franco Janis • Northford, CT 06472

Franco Julia • Glendale Public Library • Glendale, CA 91205 • NMRT

Franco Kathryn • Assistant Librarian • State University of New York (SUNY) Milne Library • Oneonta, NY 13820 • ACRL

Franco Marcela C. • Ypsilanti, MI 48197 • LITA SRRT

Francois Honore L. • Coordinator, Extension Services • Prince George's County Memorial Library System • Hyattsville, MD 20782-2098 • PLA

Francois Marian P. • Peace Corps Library • Washington, DC 20526

Francos Alexis • Lancaster, PA 17603

Francq Carole • Dir. of Collection Management • Indiana University School of Medicine Library • Indianapolis, IN 46202-5121 • LAMA LRRT

Frandina Mary Lou • Part time Librarian • Canisius College Andrew L. Bouwhuis Library • Buffalo, NY 14208-1098

Frandsen-Cantillas Caroline M. • Librarian • United States Air Force Castle Air Force Base • Castle, CA 95342-5000

Frandsen Rex • Director of Learning Resources • Brigham Young University Hawaii Campus • Laie, HI 96762

Frangakis Evelyn • Student • Columbia University Library Service Library • New York, NY 10027 • ACRL ALCTS

Frank Anne • Reference Librarian • University of California-Irvine Library • Irvine, CA 92713 • EMIERT SRRT

Frank Carol B. • Librarian • Ashland High School • Ashland, OR 97520 • AASL

Frank Donald G. • Head,Science/Engineering Library • University of Arizona Library • Tucson, AZ 85721 • ACRL LAMA RASD

Frank Elizabeth W. • Izmir, Turkey • AASL YALSA IRRT

Frank Ilene B. • Reference Dept. • University of South Florida Library • Tampa, FL 33620-5600 • ACRL ALCTS LAMA SRRT

Frank Julie K. • Student • Concordia University Klinck Memorial Library • River Forest, IL 60305-1499 • LITA

Frank Karen R. • Dillingham, AK 99576

Frank Kathleen • Greensboro, NC 27407

Frank Keiko H. • Seattle Public Library • Seattle, WA 98104-1193

Frank Kenneth • Assistant Librarian • Des Plaines Public Library • Des Plaines, IL 60016

Frank Larry J. • Director • Boyd County Public Library • Ashland, KY 41101 • LAMA PLA

Frank Marina G. • Palm Desert, CA 92260 • AASL

Frank Maureen Sherr • Director • Atlantic City Free Public Library • Atlantic City, NJ 08401 • LAMA PLA

Frank Polly P. • Instruction Coor/Reference Libn • Mankato State University Memorial Library • Mankato, MN 56002-8400 • ACRL

Frank Robyn C. • Head, Information Centers Branch • United States Department of Agriculture National Agricultural Library • Beltsville, MD 20705-2351 • LAMA

Frank Sandra G. • Chicago Public Library Scottsdale Branch • Chicago, IL 60652

Frank Sheryl J. • Librarian • Tolleson Public Library • Tolleson, AZ 85353

Frank Stephen K. • Librarian • Harry T. Truman High School • Bronx, NY 10475 • AASL

Frank Theodore Mrs. • Bethesda, MD 20816

Frank-de Ois Jan • Shenandoah Public Library • Shenandoah, IA 51601 • ALSC PLA YALSA

Franke Barbara B. • Volunteer Coordinator • Waukegan Public Library • Waukegan, IL 60085

Franke Eileen M. • Webster Groves, MO 63119

Frankel Elka R. • Student • State University of New York at Albany School of Information Science & Policy • Albany, NY 12222

Frankel Lloyd Mrs. • Trustee • Cabell County Public Library • Huntington, WV 25701 • ALTA PLA

Frankel Robert • Trustee • Schaumburg Township District Library • Schaumburg, IL 60194

Frankena Joann Koelln • Northern Illinois Library System • Rockford, IL 61108

Frankenfield Sharon L. • Student • Clarion University of Pennsylvania College of Library Science • Clarion, PA 16214

Frankenheim LaDonna • Brooklyn, NY 11234 • PLA

Frankfurth Mary • Children's Services Librarian • Wauwatosa Public Library • Wauwatosa, WI 53213 • ALSC

Frankie Suzanne • Dean • Oakland University • Rochester, MI 48309-4401 • ACRL

Frankle Raymond A. • Director • University of North Carolina at Charlotte J. Murrey Atkins Library • Charlotte, NC 28223 • ACRL LAMA

Franklin Barbara B. • Baltimore County Public Library Catonsville Branch • Catonsville, MD 21228 • RASD

Franklin Barbara W. • Franklin & Ackerman Chevy Chase Pavillion • Washington, DC 20015

Franklin Brinley R. • Associate Director/Admin. Servs. • University of Connecticut Homer Babbidge Library • Storrs, CT 06269-1005 • ACRL LAMA

Franklin Grace A. • Librarian I • Columbus Metropolitan Library • Columbus, OH 43215 • RASD IFRT

Franklin Hardy R. • Director • District of Columbia Public Library Martin Luther King Memorial Library • Washington, DC 20001 • ACRL ASCLA LAMA PLA RASD YALSA

Franklin Jennifer M. • Student • University of Western Ontario School of Library & Information Science • London ON, N6G 1H1 Canada

Franklin Laurel F. • Head Cataloger • City College of New York (CUNY) • New York, NY 10031 • ALCTS LITA

Franklin Louise • San Antonio, TX 78238 • PLA *Continuing*

Franklin Monquie A. • Student • Louisiana State University School of Library & Information Science • Baton Rouge, LA 70803-3290

Franklin Patricia C. • Teacher • Incline Middle School Library • Incline Village, NV 89450

Franklin Ralph W. • Yale University Beinecke Rare Book & Manuscript Library • New Haven, CT 06520 • ACRL

Franklin Robert • President • McFarland & Co Inc Publishers • Jefferson, NC 28640 • AASL ACRL LAMA PLA RASD IFRT IRRT SRRT

Franklin Robert D. • Charlottesville, VA 22901 • LAMA PLA *Life*

Franklin Rosemary A. • English Lit./ Bibl. & Ref. Ln. • University of Cincinnati Langsam Library • Cincinnati, OH 45221-0033 • ACRL RASD

Franko Mary A. • Gilbert, PA 18331

Frankowski Hazel • Librarian • Rockland Public Library • Rockland, ME 04841

Franks Anthony R.D. • Library of Congress • Washington, DC 20541

Franks Carolyn J. • Director • Ardmore Public Library • Ardmore, OK 73401-4398 • LITA PLA

Franks Dana L. • Librarian • Highline Community College • Des Moines, WA 98198-9800 • ACRL RASD

Franks Jeffrey A. • University of Central Florida Library • Orlando, FL 32816-0666

Franks Julie A. • Librarian • West Side Traditional Academy Elementary School • Pittsburgh, PA 15205

Franks Mildred Miles • Reference Librarian • University of Louisville Ekstrom Library • Louisville, KY 40292 • ACRL RASD

Franks Pauline B. • Uniontown, OH 44685-8732 • ACRL ALCTS LAMA LITA RASD *Life*

Frankson Marie S. • Librarian • Stroman High School Library • Victoria, TX 77901 • AASL EMIERT

Fransen Gary K. • Library Director • Coolidge Public Library • Coolidge, AZ 85228 • PLA

Fransen Pattie A. • Librarian I • Phoenix Public Library Cholla Branch • Phoenix, AZ 85051-1598 • PLA

Frantz Barbara • Indianapolis, IN 46220 • PLA RASD *Life*

Frantz Claudia Boycott • Severn School • Severna Park, MD 21146 • AASL

Frantz Jill K. • Student • Indiana University School of Library and Information Science • Bloomington, IN 47405 • ALSC

Frantz John C. • San Francisco, CA 94102 • LAMA PLA

Frantz Mary L. • Baltimore, MD 21234 • Life

Frantz Nancy R. • Needham, MA 02192

Frantz Paul • Library Instruction Coor. • University of Oregon Library • Eugene, OR 97403-1299 • LIRT

Frantz Pollyanne S. • Technical Services Librarian • Newton County Library Systems • Covington, GA 30209

Frantz Ray W. Jr • University Librarian • University of Virginia Alderman Library • Charlottesville, VA 22903-2498 • ACRL ALCTS *Life*

Franz Carol W. • Fairfax County Public Schools • Falls Church, VA 22041 • AASL ALSC

Franz David A. • Director • Ogdensburg Public Library • Ogdensburg, NY 13669 • PLA

Franz Patricia Sheppard • Public Services Librarian • Pamunkey Regional Library • Hanover, VA 23069 • PLA IFRT

Franzel Adeline • Collingswood, NJ 08108

Franzen John F. • Director • East Meadow Public Library • East Meadow, NY 11554-1700 • LAMA LITA PLA

Frary Mildred P. • Richardson, TX 75082 • AASL

Frase Robert W. • Falls Church, VA 22043 • ACRL ALCTS ALTA ASCLA LAMA LITA PLA RASD FLRT GODORT IFRT IRRT LHRT LIRT LRRT *Honorary*

Fraser Alex V. • Librarian • Chicago Public Library West Town Branch • Chicago, IL 60622

Fraser Alma C. • Aids Library of Philadelphia • Philadelphia, PA 19106 • ALCTS

Fraser Bessie F. • Montreal Association for the Blind • Montreal PQ, H4B 1R3 Canada • Continuing

Fraser Diana Lynn • Colton Public Library • Colton, CA 92324 • PLA RASD

Fraser Elizabeth L. • Kanawha County Public Library • Charleston, WV 25301

Fraser Emily Jean • Failure Analysis Associates • Menlo Park, CA 94025 • ACRL LAMA LITA RASD NMRT

Fraser James Dr. • Director • Fairleigh Dickinson University Florham-Madison Campus Library • Madison, NJ 07940

Fraser Joan • Data Control Coordinator • Carleton University Library • Ottawa ON, K1S 5J7 Canada • ALCTS LITA

Fraser Julijona L. • El Cerrito, CA 94530 • ALSC

Fraser Paula K. • Student • University of Washington Graduate School of Library and Information Science • Seattle, WA 98195 • AASL SRRT

Fraser Sandra A. • Reference Librarian • New York University Elmer Holmes Bobst Library • New York, NY 10012 • ACRL ALCTS SRRT

Fraser Susan M. • Serials & Exchange • The New York Botanical Gardens Library • Bronx, NY 10458-5126 • ACRL ALCTS LAMA RASD

Fraser Walter J. • Washington, DC 20003 • ACRL ALCTS *Life*

Frashier Anne E. • Malibu, CA 90265

Frasier Brenda A. • Wichita Falls, TX 76306-1206

Frasier David K • Assistant Librarian-Reference • Indiana University • Bloomington, IN 47405

Frasier Sally F. • Trustee • Tulsa City-County Library System • Tulsa, OK 74103 • ALTA

Fratis Suzanne • Library Specialist • Palo Alto City Library Mitchell Park Branch Library • Palo Alto, CA 94303

Fraucher Teresa L. • Palo Alto, CA 94303

Fraysse Susan • Dir. of Media Services • Gwinnett Technical Media Center • Lawrenceville, GA 30340

Frazee John D. • Librarian • Museum of Flight • Seattle, WA 98108 • ACRL ALCTS

Frazer Amelia W. • Director • Dare County Library • Manteo, NC 27954

Frazer Cynthia M. • Sapulp, OK 74066-8904

Frazer Judith H. • Plasma Physics Librarian • Princeton University • Princeton, NJ 08544-2098 • ACRL

Frazer Stuart L. • Reference Librarian • West Virginia State College Drain-Jordan Library • Institute, WV 25112-1002

Frazier Ann • Pace Academy • Atlanta, GA 30327 • AASL

Frazier Betty W. • Media Coordinator • Cumberland County Schools Pine Forest Junior High • Fayetteville, NC 28311

Frazier Judith B. • Senior Reference Specialist • Library of Congress • Washington, DC 20541

Frazier Kenneth L. • Director,General Lib System • University of Wisconsin-Madison Memorial Library • Madison, WI 53706

Frazier Margaret P. • Student • Rosary College Graduate School of Library & Information Science • River Forest, IL 60305 • PLA

Frazier Meg • Chicago, IL 60625-2813 • NMRT

Frazier Velma V. • Rockville, MD 20852

Freas Anne G. • Lancaster, PA 17603 • AASL

Freathy Margaret M. • Director • Emanuel Einstein Free Public Library • Pompton Lakes, NJ 07442 • LAMA CLENE

Frechette Dorothy B. • Deputy Director • Rhode Island Department of State Library Services • Providence, RI 02903-4222 • LITA

Freda Cecelia • EMS • Conover Road School • Colts Neek, NJ 07722 • AASL

Frederick Cary • New York, NY 10033

Frederick Janet E. • Auburn University • Auburn, AL 36849 • ACRL LITA

Frederick Linda E. • Documents/Serials Librarian • Principia College Marshall Brooks Library • Elsah, IL 62028 • GODORT

Frederick Loretta A. • Pikes Peak Library District • Colorado Springs, CO 80901

Frederick Terri M. • Public Relations Officer • Lorain Public Library • Lorain, OH 44052 • PLA
Fredericka Theresa M. • Lakewood, OH 44107 • AASL
Fredericks Catherine • Tucson, AZ 85704
Fredericks Linda C. • University of Washington Suzzallo Library • Seattle, WA 98195 • IRRT
Fredericks Valerie • Assistant Director • Darien Library • Darien, CT 06820-4497 • LAMA
Fredericksen Grant A. • Director • Illinois Prairie District Public Library • Metamora, IL 61548-0011 • LAMA LITA PLA
Frederickson Dennis C. • Reference Librarian • Spokane Public Library Comstock Building Library • Spokane, WA 99201-0976 • PLA RASD
Frederickson Marnie B. • Children's Library Assistant • Port Townsend Public Library • Port Townsend, WA 98368 • ALSC
Fredette Kathy A. • Director of Public Services • Topeka Public Library • Topeka, KS 66604-1374 • LAMA LITA PLA IFRT
Fredette Kevin L. • Microforms Librarian • University of California General Library • Irvine, CA 92713 • GODORT
Fredine Anne B. • Director • Moorhead Public Library • Moorhead, MN 56560
Fredrick Kathy • Media Specialist • R.B. Chamberlin High School • Twinsburg, OH 44087 • AASL
Fredrickson Karen • Librarian • Menlo Park Public Library • Menlo Park, CA 94025
Fredrickson Susan • Oak Ridge, TN 37830 • LITA
Freeborn Miriam • Trustee • Alhambra Public Library • Alhambra, CA 91801
Freeburn Jacqueline • Yonkers, NY 10710
Freed Ann • Perry Public Library • Perry, OH 44081
Freed Arlene R. • Reference Librarian • Hartford Hospital Health Sciences Libraries • Hartford, CT 06115
Freed Mary • Librarian • Richmond Montessori School Library • Richmond, VA 23229 • AASL
Freedman Annetta R. • Director, Media Services • Doherty Middle School • Andover, MA 01810
Freedman Ellen • Children's Librarian • Huntington Public Library • Huntington, NY 11743
Freedman Jack A. • Des Moines, IA 50312
Freedman Janet Dr. • Dean, Library Services • University of Massachusetts-Dartmouth Library • North Dartmouth, MA 02747 • ACRL SRRT
Freedman Joseph S. • Collection Devel. Librarian • Illinois Wesleyan University Sheean Library • Bloomington, IL 61702 • ACRL
Freedman Mary F. • Director • Pequot Library • Southport, CT 06490 • LAMA LITA PLA IFRT
Freedman Maurice J. • Director • Westchester Library System • Elmsford, NY 10523 • ALCTS ALTA ASCLA LAMA LITA PLA IRRT SRRT
Freedman Nora H. • Librarian • Jacksonville Public Library System Mandarin Branch • Jacksonville, FL 32257
Freedman Robert • Coordinator Tech. Services • Bethlehem Area Public Library • Bethlehem, PA 18018-5888 • ALCTS
Freegard Sarah A. • Student • Northern Illinois University Department of Library & Information Studies • DeKalb, IL 60115 • ALSC IFRT SRRT
Freeh Mary Beth A. • Head/Information & Instructional • Cedar Crest College Cressman Library • Allentown, PA 18104
Freel Robert B. • Public Service Supervisior • University of California-Los Angeles (UCLA) • Los Angeles, CA 90024-1450 • ACRL LAMA
Freeland Marija R. • Ann Arbor, MI 48103
Freeland Robert F. • Librarian • Linda Vista Bible College • El Cajon, CA 92021
Freeman Anita S. • Director • Randolph Township Free Public Library • Randolph, NJ 07869 • PLA
Freeman Arllyn D. • Student • Rosary College Graduate School of Library & Information Science • River Forest, IL 60305 • ALCTS LITA
Freeman Benny • Librarian • Dunklin County Library • Kennett, MO 63857
Freeman Carol P. • Evening Librarian (part-time) • Davidson County Community College Learning Resource Center • Lexington, NC 27293
Freeman Dennis R. • Mt Shasta, CA 96067 • ACRL
Freeman Ellen L. • Chief Service Librarian • Chicago Public Library Rogers Park Branch • Chicago, IL 60626 • ALSC
Freeman Ellen L. Miss • Geology Librarian • Indiana University & Indiana Geological Survey • Bloomington, IN 47405 • ACRL RASD *Life*
Freeman Evelyn B. • Associate Professor • Ohio State University Newark • Newark, OH 43055 • ALSC
Freeman Geoffrey T. • Architect • Shepley Bulfinch Richardson and Abbott • Boston, MA 02109 • ACRL LAMA LITA
Freeman Gretchen L. • Manager, Customer Support • DYNIX Inc. • Provo, UT 84606 • LITA
Freeman Helen C. • Cataloger • Sawyer Free Library • Gloucester, MA 01930
Freeman Iva M. • Library Director • Kendall College Library • Evanston, IL 60201 • ACRL
Freeman Janet L. • Head Librarian • Meredith College Carlyle Campbell Library • Raleigh, NC 27607 • ACRL *Life*
Freeman June A. • Director • Clifton Springs Library • Clifton Springs, NY 14432
Freeman Kevin A. • Stanford University • Stanford, CA 94305-3076 • ACRL ALCTS
Freeman Larry S. • Readers Services Librarian • Orangeburg-Calhoun Technical College • Orangeburg, SC 29115
Freeman Louise A. • Media Specialist • Hartsfield School • Tallahassee, FL 32301 • AASL
Freeman Lucile • Wheelers Trailer Park • Bozeman, MT 59715
Freeman Lucile C. • Librarian III • Montgomery County Department of Public Library/ Bethesda Regional Library • Bethesda, MD 20814 • PLA RASD YALSA IFRT
Freeman Lynne • Assistant Professor • Southwest Missouri State University Library • Springfield, MO 65804-0095 • ACRL RASD LHRT LIRT LRRT
Freeman Marjorie • Lynchburg College • Lynchburg, VA 24501
Freeman Michael S. • Director • Haverford College James P. Magill Library • Haverford, PA 19041 • ACRL LAMA IFRT
Freeman Nancy S. • Audio Visual Dept. Head • Huntington Public Library • Huntington, NY 11743
Freeman Pat S. • Instructor • Astronaut High School • Titusville, FL 32796
Freeman Patricia E. • Albuquerue, NM 87119
Freeman Paul • Honolulu, HI 96822
Freeman Robert G. • Stevens Institute of Technology S.C. Williams Library • Hoboken, NJ 07030
Freeman Robert S. • Student • Washington University Olin Library • Saint Louis, MO 63130
Freeman S'Ann Dr. • San Bernardino Public Library • San Bernardino, CA 92410 • PLA
Freeman Sandi • East Orange Public Library • East Orange, NJ 07018 • ALTA
Freeman Suzanne H. • Arts/Hum. Clln. Mgt. Librarian • Virginia Commonwealth University • Richmond, VA 23284-2033 • ACRL ALCTS
Freemon Betty W. • Student • West Georgia College Library Media Program • Carrollton, GA 30118 • AASL
Freeny Maralita L. • Associate Director for Br. Serv. • Prince George County Memorial Library System Hyattsville Branch • Hyattsville, MD 20782 • LAMA PLA
Freese Melanie L. • Catalog Librarian • Hofstra University Axinn Library • Hempstead, NY 11550 • ACRL ALCTS
Freeze B. • CNIB Library for the Blind • Toronto ON, M4G 3EB Canada
Freeze Barbara • Director of Production & Proc. • CNIB Library for the Blind • Toronto ON, M4G 3EB Canada
Freggiaro Diane C. • Senior Administrative Analyst • Stockton-San Joaquin County Public Library • Stockton, CA 95202
Freiband Susan J. • Associate Professor • University of Puerto Rico Graduate School of Library and Information Science • Rio Piedras, PR 00920 • PLA RASD EMIERT ILERT IRRT
Freiberger Norman S. • Trustee • Shelter Rock Public Library • Albertson, NY 11507 • ALTA
Freiburger Gary A. • Deputy Library Director • University of Maryland at Baltimore Health Sciences Library • Baltimore, MD 21201 • LITA
Freides Thelma • Head, Reader Services • State University of New York College at Purchase Library (SUNY) • Purchase, NY 10577-2826 • ACRL RASD GODORT LIRT
Freilich Judith • Media Specialist • Asher Holmes Elementary School • Morganville, NJ 07751 • AASL
Freilich Mary K. • Germantown, TN 38138
Freimarck Fran C. • Director • Pamunkey Regional Library • Hanover, VA 23069 • PLA
Freimer Gloria R. • Associate Professor • University of Toledo William S. Carlson Library • Toledo, OH 43606-3399 • ACRL
Freitag Anne K. • Anchorage, AK 99501 • IFRT
Freitag Rosalie • Madison Public Library • Madison, WI 53703
Freitag Susan D. • Student • University of Wisconsin-Milwaukee School of Library & Information Science • Milwaukee, WI 53201 • PLA
Freitas-Obregon Brenda • Statewide Program Coordinator • Hawaii State Public Library System • Honolulu, HI 96813 • PLA YALSA *Life*
Freitas Rhoda J.R. • Librarian • Moreno Valley High School • Moreno Valley, CA 92553
Freivalds Dace I. • Library Systems Specialist • Pennsylvania State University Libraries • University Park, PA 16802 • ACRL LITA
Fremd Lynn E. • Hyattsville, MD 20781 • ALCTS
French Beth Nancy • Interloan Dept Mgr • Cuyahoga County Public Library Administration Building • Parma, OH 44134-2792 • PLA
French Beverlee A. • Assistant Univ. Libn.-Sciences • University of California-Davis Library • Davis, CA 95616 • ACRL LITA
French Cavett H. • Adult Services Librarian • Northland Public Library • Pittsburgh, PA 15237 • RASD
French Charlotte • Trustee • Oklahoma City Community College Learning Resources Center • Oklahoma City, OK 73159 • ALTA PLA
French David W. • Student • University of Hawaii School of Library & Information Studies • Honolulu, HI 96822
French Frances S. • Reference Librarian • Memphis-Shelby County Public Library and Information Center • Memphis, TN 38104-4025 • RASD
French George W. Dr. • Trustee • Free Library of Philadelphia • Philadelphia, PA 19103 • ALTA
French Janet D. • Mechanicsville, PA 18934 • Continuing
French Jeffrey A. • Supv. Adult/Information Svs. • Cleveland Heights-University Heights Public Library • Cleveland Heights, OH 44118 • PLA
French Katharine E. • Rockford, IL 61103-4132 • YALSA EMIERT IRRT
French Linda S. • Media Spec • Springbrook High School • Silver Spring, MD 20904 • AASL
French Marienne • Jacksonville Public Libraries Main Library • Jacksonville, FL 32202 • ALCTS
French Marilyn S. • Librarian • La Roche Chemicals, Inc. • Baton Rouge, LA 70821
French Mark A. • New York, NY 10014
French Mary Jane • Head Librarian • Atlanta-Fulton Public Library Sandy Springs Branch • Sandy Springs, GA 30328 • PLA
French Michael F. • Director • Rossford Public Library • Rossford, OH 43460 • PLA
French Michael W. • Student • University of Kentucky • Lexington, KY 40506-0056
French Nancy • Las Vegas-Clark County Library District Las Vegas Library • Las Vegas, NV 89101 • ALSC YALSA
French Ruth B. • Granby, MA 01033
Frenn Mary C. • Reserve Supervisor • Marquette University Memorial Library • Milwaukee, WI 53233
Frensley Erika E. • Editor • M.D. Anderson Cancer Center Research Medical Library • Houston, TX 77030 • IFRT NMRT
Frere Penelope W. • Bell Buckle, TN 37020 • ACRL
Fret Marilyn • Head of Circulation • Waukegan Public Library • Waukegan, IL 60085 • PLA
Fretwell Shela S. • Waterloo, IA 50702 • RASD
Fretz Lynne K. • Dauphin County Library System • Harrisburg, PA 17101
Freund Leilani S. • University of Florida Libraries • Gainesville, FL 32611 • RASD
Freund Paula • Trustee • Long Beach Public Library • Long Beach, NY 11561 • ALTA YALSA
Freund Penny • Librarian • Prairie School • Racine, WI 53402 • AASL ALSC RASD YALSA IFRT LIRT
Frew Martha Gale • Columbus, OH 43214-1525 • AASL ALSC *Life*
Frew Roberta C. • Lanoka Harbor, NJ 08734-9107
Frewin Richard E. • Hd, Govt. Pubs Dept. • San Francisco State University J. Paul Leonard Library • San Francisco, CA 94132 • ACRL GODORT LIRT MAGERT
Frey Anita M. • Head of Reference • East Islip Public Library • East Islip, NY 11730-2896
Frey James E. • Student • Louisiana State University School of Library & Information Science • Baton Rouge, LA 70803-3290 • ACRL PLA RASD
Frey Jo Ann • Galileo High School • San Francisco, CA 94109
Frey Naida • Reference Librarian • Lake County Library • Lakeport, CA 95453
Frey P. Diane • Program Coordinator-Media Serv • School District of Lancaster • Lancaster, PA 17603 • AASL LAMA YALSA
Frey Roxanne C. • Wilmington Public Library District • Wilmington, IL 60481
Freyer Kenneth • Leeds, MA 01053 • Continuing
Freyou Denise S. • Acqusitions Librarian • East Baton Rouge Parish Library • Baton Rouge, LA 70806-7699
Frias Montoya Jose Antonio • Teacher • Universidad de Salamanca • Salamanca, 37007, Spain • ALCTS CLENE
Frick Elizabeth A. • Associate Professor • Dalhousie University School of Library & Inf. Studies • Halifax NS, B3H 4H8 Canada • ACRL RASD

Frick John H. • The Boeing Company Renton Technical Library • Seattle, WA 98124

Fricke Christine • Media Specialist • Fox Hill School Library • Kansas City, MO 64118 • AASL

Friddle Richard L. • Director of Learning Resources • Pikes Peak Community College • Colorado Springs, CO 80906 • ACRL

Fridell Jeanette H. • Media Specialist • Trunnell Elementary School • Louisville, KY 40214 • AASL

Fridlington Robert • President • Cranford Public Library • Cranford, NJ 07016 • ALTA

Fried Bobbi P. • Lexington, KY 40502

Fried Edith • Documents Librarian • Syracuse University Library E. S. Bird Library • Syracuse, NY 13244-2010 • GODORT

Fried Helen L. • Frankfort, IN 46041 • ACRL ALCTS   Life

Frieden Charles L. • Director of Circulation Service • University of Virginia Alderman Library • Charlottesville, VA 22903-2498

Frieden Janet C. • Head Librarian • Western Albemarle High School • Crozet, VA 22901 • AASL

Frieder Richard • Head, Preservation Dept. • Northwestern University Library • Evanston, IL 60208-2300 • ALCTS

Friedhaber-Hard Susan M. • School Librarian Media Spec. • Pioneer Central High School • Yorkshire, NY 14173 • AASL

Friedland Rhoda • Director • Rockville Centre Public Library • Rockville Centre, NY 11570 • PLA

Friedline Marie C. • Chicago, IL 60660-1236 • Life

Friedman Aileen • Book Producer • Woodberry Books • Mill Valley, CA 94941

Friedman Ann M. • Deputy Director • Montgomery County Department of Public Libraries • Rockville, MD 20850 • LAMA PLA EMIERT

Friedman Arlene • Onondaga County Public Library • Syracuse, NY 13202

Friedman Arthur L. • Professor,Media Ln • Nassau Community College Library • Garden City, NY 11530 • ACRL LAMA LITA IFRT

Friedman Catherine R. • Head, General Reference Div • San Diego State University General Reference Division • San Diego, CA 92182-0511 • ACRL RASD

Friedman Deborah S. • Cataloger • National Agricultural Library • Beltsville, MD 20705-2351

Friedman Fred T. • Research Library • United States Enviromental Protection Agency Region I • Boston, MA 02203

Friedman J. A. • Head of Cataloging • Virginia Beach Public Library Central Library • Virginia Beach, VA 23452

Friedman Janice M. • Great Neck North High School Library • Great Neck, NY 11023

Friedman Joseph P. • Librarian • Santa Rosa Junior College • Santa Rosa, CA 95401 • ACRL

Friedman Marcia R. • Kailua, HI 96734

Friedman Max Mrs. • La Jolla, CA 92037 • PLA RASD
Continuing

Friedman Sandra C. • Naval Weapons Center • China Lake, CA 93555 • LITA FLRT

Friedman Sarene A. • Libnrarian/Bibliotherapist • Saint Elizabeths Hospital Circulating Library • Washington, DC 20032 • ASCLA

Friedman Sylvia • North Miami Beach, FL 33162

Friedman Tova • Librarian • Yeshira University High School for Girls • Holliswood, NY 11423 • AASL

Friedmann Cathleen A. • Middle & Upper School Libn • Metarie Park Country Day • Metarie, LA 70005 • AASL YALSA IFRT

Friedmann Esther K. • Johnson Technical Institute Library • Scranton, PA 18508-1495 • ACRL

Friedrich Deborah • Librarian • Del Valljo Middle School Library • San Bernadino, CA 92404 • AASL

Friedrich Denise A. • Student • North Carolina Central University • Durham, NC 27707 • AASL

Friedrich Jacqueline K. • Student • North Texas State University Willis Library • Denton, TX 76203

Friedrich Judith M. • Librarian • Hennepin County Library Southdale-Hennepin Area Library • Edina, MN 55435 • RASD

Friedrichs Amy • Children's Services • Mead Public Library • Sheboygan, WI 53081

Friedrichs Annette M. • De Witt, NY 13214

Friedrichs Donald • Trustee • Livonia Public Library • Livonia, MI 48154-3045 • ALTA

Friend Audrey J. • Lexington, MA 02173-1217 • AASL

Friend Linda • Electronic Resource Spec. • Pennsylvania State University Libraries • University Park, PA 16802 • RASD

Friend Margaret • Automated Systems Librarian • Jefferson Parish Library Department • Metairie, LA 70010 • PLA

Fries Bea Ann • Librarian • Belleville Area College Library • Belleville, IL 62221 • ACRL

Fries Mary A. • Tacoma, WA 98403 • Continuing

Friesen-Lynn Laura L. • Student • University of California-Los Angeles (UCLA) • Los Angeles, CA 90024-1450 • NMRT

Friesen Elvin • Consultant • Hamilton County Office of Education • Cincinnati, OH 45231

Friesen Sharon A. • Fitzgerald Public Schools • Warren, MI 48091 • AASL ALSC YALSA

Friesen Susanne • Assistant Director • Goshen Public Library • Goshen, IN 46526 • ALCTS

Friesen Tracey D. • Reference Ln.-part time • Concordia University Libraries • Montreal PQ, H3G 1M8 Canada • ACRL NMRT

Friess Wanda • Educational Media Services • Maple Avenue School • Newark, NJ 07112 • AASL

Friggle Elizabeth S. • Greensboro, NC 27410

Friloux Margaret B. • Student • University of Pittsburgh School of Library and Information Science • Pittsburgh, PA 15260

Frisbie Mary Lee • Librarian • Brentwood Public Library • Brentwood, MO 63144 • LAMA PLA

Frisbie Michael J. • Mission, KS 66202

Frisbie Richard • Trustee • Arlington Heights Memorial Library • Arlington Heights, IL 60004-5966

Frisch Corrine A. • Head of Public Relations • Lincoln Library • Springfield, IL 62701 • LAMA

Frisch Paul A. • Head, Reference Department • Southwest Missouri State University Library • Springfield, MO 65804-0095 • ACRL LAMA RASD LHRT

Frischer Rita C. • Director, Library Services • Sinai Temple Blumenthal Library • Los Angeles, CA 90024 • AASL

Frischkorn Florine L. • St Paul, MN 55107 • ALSC PLA
Life

Frishett Julia S. • Reference/Youth Services Ln. • Pinellas Park Public Library • Pinellas Park, FL 34665

Fritch-Morris Stephen • Audiovisual Librarian • Redondo Beach Public Library • Redondo Bch, CA 90277

Frith Margaret H. • President • Putnam & Grosset Book Group • New York, NY 10016 • ALSC

Fritsch Barbara A. • Head of Children's Services • Stratford Library Association • Stratford, CT 06497

Fritsch David R. • Territory Manager • Faxon Company,Inc. • Westwood, MA 02090 • ALCTS

Fritsch Lisa Marie • Riverside City & County Public Library Central Branch • Riverside, CA 92502 • PLA IFRT

Fritschel Linda Ruth • Minneapolis Public Library & Information Center • Minneapolis, MN 55401-1992 • PLA RASD

Fritter Joanne • Head Librarian • Oak Brook Free Public Library • Oak Brook, IL 60521 • PLA

Fritts Carol • Library Media Specialist • Deep Run Elementary School • Elkridge, MD 21227 • AASL

Fritts Jack Jr. • Public Services Librarian • National-Louis University Division of Learning Resources • Evanston, IL 60201-1796 • ACRL LITA

Fritts Kathleen • Jesuit High School • Portland, OR 97225 • YALSA

Fritz Deborah A. • Library Automation Consultant • The MARC of Quality • Land O'Lakes, FL 34639 • LITA

Fritz Donald D. • Librarian • Lutheran High School East • Detroit, MI 48225 • AASL

Fritz Doreen K. • Student • Northern Illinois University Department of Library & Information Studies • DeKalb, IL 60115 • AASL

Fritz Rebecca B. • Reston, VA 22094

Frizzell Jane • Librarian • Bonny Eagle Junior High School • West Buxton, ME 04093 • AASL

Frizzell Jane C. • Wilton, IA 52778-9748

Frizzell Leigh • Fort Myers, FL 33902

Frizzell Robert • Director • Hendrix College Olin C. Bailey Library • Conway, AR 72032 • ACRL

Froehlich Nancy J. • Roslyn, NY 11577 • ACRL RASD IFRT

Froehlich Patricia H. • Albuquerque, NM 87107 • AASL

Frohlich Anne • Newberg, OR 97132 • ALCTS LITA

Frohmberg Katherine A. • Earthquake Engineering Research Center • Richmond, CA 94804 • ACRL ALCTS LITA

Frolund Tina L. • Seattle, WA 98102

Fromel Robert A. Mrs. • Chatham, NJ 07928

Fromme Catherine • Coor. Inf. Services • University of Oregon • Eugene, OR 97403

Frommeyer L. Ronald • Asst to the Dean & University Ln • University of Cincinnati Langsam Library • Cincinnati, OH 45221-0033 • ACRL

Fromowitz Joan K. • APO, AE 09842 • ALCTS LAMA

Fronius Sandra K. • Student • Kent State University School of Library & Information Science • Kent, OH 44242-0001 • PLA IFRT SRRT

Frontino Anne U. • Librarian • Haddonfield Public Library • Haddonfield, NJ 08033

Frontz Kim E. • Student • University of Arizona Graduate Library School • Tucson, AZ 85721

Frost Carolyn O. • Professor • University of Michigan School of Information and Library Studies • Ann Arbor, MI 48109-1092 • ALCTS

Frost Cynthia J. • Student • University of North Carolina at Chapel Hill School of Information and Library Science • Chapel Hill, NC 27599-3360 • PLA IRRT SRRT

Frost Ellen L. • Richardson, TX 75081

Frost Gary • Library Conservator • Booklab • Austin, TX 78754 • ALCTS

Frost Rebecca H. • Library Media Specialist • Scott Elementary School • Evansville, IN 47711 • AASL

Frost Rose • Director • Presque Isle County Library • Rogers City, MI 49779

Frost Stan • Librarian • California State University-Sacramento Library • Sacramento, CA 95819-6039 • ACRL LITA

Frost Sylvia J. • Head of Cataloging Department • University of Notre Dame Library • Notre Dame, IN 46556 • ALCTS LITA

Frost William J. • Reference Librarian • Bloomsburg University Harvey A. Andruss Library • Bloomsburg, PA 17815 • RASD LIRT

Frowert Mary Jane C. • Nokesville, VA 22123 • AASL

Froyen Gail E. • Media Specialist • University of Northern Iowa Purchasing Off • Cedar Falls, IA 50614 • AASL

Fruchtenicht Carolyn • Reference Librarian • Napa Valley College Library • Napa, CA 94558-6236 • ACRL ALCTS RASD

Fruge Donna R. • Librarian • Saint Michael Elementary School • Crowley, LA 70526

Fry Belita R. • Koch Library Services • Wichita, KS 67201 • ALCTS LITA

Fry Bernard M. • Bloomington, IN 47401

Fry Donna E. • Canton, OH 44708 • AASL YALSA

Fry Hazel A. • University of Calgary Library Sciences/Professions Area • Calgary, AB, T2N 1N4 Canada • ACRL LAMA

Fry James W. • State Librarian • Library of Michigan • Lansing, MI 48909 • ASCLA

Fry John J. • Student • University of Pittsburgh School of Library and Information Science • Pittsburgh, PA 15260 • ACRL

Fry Kaia M. • Director • Deerfield Public Library • Deerfield, WI 53531

Fry Mildred H. • Assistant Director • Cleveland Area Metropolitan Library System • Shaker Heights, OH 44122-5210 • LAMA CLENE

Fry Morel A. • Management Services Librarian • Old Dominion University Library • Norfolk, VA 23529-0256

Fry Ray M. • Senior Advisor for Library Prog. • United States Department of Education Office of Educational Res & Improvement • Washington, DC 20208-5571 • AASL ALSC PLA YALSA   Life

Fry Roy H. • Skokie, IL 60077 • Continuing

Fry Sally A. • Community Relations Coordinator • Orange County Library System Orlando Public Library • Orlando, FL 32801-2471 • PLA

Fry Thomas K. • College Librarian • University of California-Los Angeles (UCLA) • Los Angeles, CA 90024-1450 • ACRL LAMA

Fryar Linda S. • Librarian • United States Air Force Base Library • Sheppard Afb, TX 76311 • PLA AFLRT

Fryberger Nancy B. • Librarian • Warren Township Public Library • Warren, NJ 07059

Frycek Susan Lynn • Student • State University New York at Buffalo School of Inf. & Library Studies • Buffalo, NY 14260

Frydendall Karen • North Elementary School • Saint Peter, MN 56082 • AASL

Frydryk Teresa E. • John Snow Inc. • Boston, MA 02111

Frye Bettie E. • Asst Librarian, Hd of Tech Serv. • Abraham Baldwin Agricultural College Baldwin Library • Tifton, GA 31793-4401 • ALCTS

Frye Jayne C. • Red Bank, NJ 07701 • AASL YALSA

Frye Larry J. • Director • Wabash College • Crawfordsville, IN 47933 • ACRL

Frye Roberta D. • Librarian • Oakland Public Library • Oakland, CA 94612 • IFRT SRRT

Frye Stephanie D. • Student • Rosary College Graduate School of Library & Information Science • River Forest, IL 60305 • IFRT SRRT

Fryer Janice A. • Reference Department • Iowa State University Library • Ames, IA 50011-2140 • ACRL RASD GODORT

Frymann Joyce V. • Westport Public Library • Westport, CT 06880

Frymier Virginia Boggs • Manchester High School • Richmond, VA 23235

Frymire Jane K. • Senior Mgmt. Information Speclst • Hennepin County Library • Minnetonka, MN 55343 • LITA

Fu Clare Shu-Erh • Community College of Philadelphia Educational Resource Center • Philadelphia, PA 19130 • ACRL ALCTS

Fu James S. • Watsonville, CA 95076-9605

Fu Julie L W • Library Manager • County of Los Angeles Public Library Gardena Library 313 • Gardena, CA 90247

Fu Paul S. • Law Librarian • Ohio Supreme Court Law Library • Columbus, OH 43266 • ACRL ALCTS ASCLA LAMA LITA RASD

Fu Tina C. • Public Service • University of Wisconsin • Oshkosh, WI 54901 • ACRL

Fuchs Arlene • Brooklyn, NY 11214

Fuchs Curt Dr. • Coordinator, Lib/Media Comp Serv • Columbia Public Schools • Columbia, MO 65201 • AASL

Fuchs John M. • Director • Carmel Clay Public Library • Carmel, IN 46032 • PLA

Fuchs Linda L. • Chief, Library & Network Serv. • State Library of Florida Division of Library & Information Services • Tallahassee, FL 32399-0250 • ASCLA LITA IFRT

Fuchs Phyllis • Children's Librarian • Captain Curtis Memorial Library • Brunswick, ME 04011 • ALSC

Fuchs Rifki • Montreal PQ, H3S 1G2 Canada

Fuchs Suzanne M. • Student • Pratt Institute Graduate School of Library & Information Science • Brooklyn, NY 11205 • RASD LRRT SRRT

Fuderer Laura Sue • Rare Books Librarian • University of Notre Dame Libraries • Notre Dame, IN 46556 • ACRL

Fuentes Christina • Student • Queens College Graduate School of Library & Information Studies • Flushing, NY 11367 • AASL EMIERT IFRT SRRT

Fuentes Jerry • Trustee • San Antonio Public Library • San Antonio, TX 78205

Fuerst-Smith Cynthia • Youth Services Librarian • Bur Oak Library System • Shorewood, IL 60436 • ALSC

Fugate Cynthia S. • Campus Librarian • University of Washington Bothell Branch Campus • Bothell, WA 98021 • ACRL LAMA RASD SRRT

Fuhr Sandra L. • Redwood Falls, MN 56283

Fuhrmann Dorothy M. • Department Chair • Los Angeles City College • Los Angeles, CA 90029 • ACRL ALCTS LITA RASD

Fuhrmann Rhonda A. • U.S. Fish & Wildlife Service National Fisheries Research Center • LaCrosse, WI 54602-0818

Fuhs Doretta • Information Asst/Adult Servs • Skokie Public Library • Skokie, IL 60077-3680

Fujii Nyla L. • Dir. of Program Development • Hawaii State Public Library System Office of the State Librarian • Honolulu, HI 96813 • PLA

Fujii Raymond Y. • Head Librarian • Kaneohe Public Library • Kaneohe, HI 96744 • LITA PLA

Fujimoto Gail G. • Head Librarian • Midkiff Learning Center Kamehameha Schools • Honolulu, HI 96817 • AASL

Fujimoto Jan D. • Tucker, GA 30084

Fujimoto Keiko • Student • University of Illinois Graduate School of Library and Information Science • Urbana, IL 61801

Fujino Amy H. • Administrator • Hawaii State Public Library West Oahu Library District • Pearl City, HI 96782 • PLA

Fujitani Sharon • California Polytechnic State University Robert E. Kennedy Library • San Luis Obispo, CA 93407 • ACRL ALCTS LITA RASD GODORT LIRT

Fujiyoshi Grace H. • School Librarian • Kaimuki High School • Honolulu, HI 96816 • AASL

Fuke Stanley A. • School Library Consultant • Clark County School District • Las Vegas, NV 89121-5207 • AASL

Fukuda Fumiko • Honolulu, HI 96821

Fukuda Yukiko • Honolulu, HI 96821

Fukui Kimberly I. • Wilmington Public Library • Wilmington, DE 19801

Fukumoto Elaine M. • Los Angeles County Library Manhattan Beach Branch • Manhattan Beach, CA 90266 • PLA

Fukuyama Margaret N. • Vancouver BC, V6H 1R5 Canada • ALCTS LITA

Fulcher Jane M. • Avella, PA 15312

Fulk Mary C. • Librarian I • Edward Warrior Womens Correction Center • Taft, OK 74463 • ASCLA IRRT

Fullen Brenda J. • Alexandria, LA 71301 • AASL

Fullenwider Catherine H. • Truman Medical Center-West Clinical Laboratory • Kansas City, MO 64108

Fullenwider Nancy D. • Cataloger • University of Southern California Doheny Library • Los Angeles, CA 90089-0182 • Life

Fuller Cherry L. • Library Coordinator • Northwest Independent School District • Justin, TX 76247 • AASL

Fuller Crystal J. • Student • Murray State University Harry Lee Waterfield Library • Murray, KY 42071-3309

Fuller Daniel • School Librarian/Media Specialis • Follett Software Company • McHenry, IL 60050-5589 • AASL

Fuller David A. • Bakersfield, CA 93301-3447 • ACRL

Fuller Edward H. • Special Collections Librarian • Swarthmore College • Swarthmore, PA 19081

Fuller Elizabeth A. • Contra Costa County Library • Pleasant Hill, CA 94523

Fuller Elizabeth C. • Newport News, VA 23606 • LAMA PLA AFLRT *Life*

Fuller Elizabeth E. • Manuscript Cataloguer • Rosenbach Museum and Library • Philadelphia, PA 19103 • ACRL ALCTS LITA

Fuller Gaylin S. • Librarian • Tuzzy Consortium Library North Slope Borough • Barrow, AK 99723 • ACRL

Fuller Gloria A. • Upper Marlboro, MD 20772 • AFLRT FLRT

Fuller Helen • Long Beach, CA 90803 • ALSC LAMA *Continuing*

Fuller Howard J. III • Student • University of Wisconsin-Milwaukee School of Library & Information Science • Milwaukee, WI 53201

Fuller Joseph • Trustee • Peninsula Public Library • Lawrence, NY 11559

Fuller Kathryn W. • Bloomington, IN 47408 • ACRL RASD

Fuller Linda • North Carolina State University D. H. Hill Library • Raleigh, NC 27695-7111

Fuller Marcella • Serials Librarian • Vanderbilt University Library Jean & Alexander Heard Library • Nashville, TN 37240-0007 • ACRL ALCTS LRRT

Fuller Nancy F. • Head, Branch Libraries • University of Mississippi Dodge Library School of Pharmacy • University, MS 38677

Fuller Nancy L. • Plano, TX 75023-1804 • ALSC EMIERT

Fuller Paul Eugene • University of Kentucky • Lexington, KY 40506-0056 • LITA IFRT SRRT

Fuller Sandra • New London, WI 54961-0301

Fuller Sherlene • Fresno, CA 93721 • AASL

Fuller Sherrilynne • Director • University of Washington Health Science Library & Info Center • Seattle, WA 98195 • ACRL

Fuller Stephen H. • Chairman & Chief Executive Off. • World Book Publishing • Chicago, IL 60661 • Life

Fuller Susan A. • County Librarian • Santa Clara County Free Library • San Jose, CA 95112-4446 • PLA

Fullerton Anne F. • Reference & Collection Librarian • University of Waterloo Library • Waterloo ON, Canada • ACRL LAMA RASD

Fullerton Janet E. • Ferris State University • Big Rapids, MI 49307

Fulling Richard W. • Documents Librarian • Barton College Library • Wilson, NC 27893 • RASD GODORT

Fullington Angela L. • Carrboro, NC 27510-1420 • RASD IFRT SRRT

Fullum Joseph F. • Reference Librarian • Boston Public Library • Boston, MA 02117 • RASD

Fulmer Margaret • Librarian Emeritus • Whittier Public Library • Whittier, CA 90602 • ALSC PLA *Continuing*

Fulmer Russell F. • Golden, CO 80401 • LITA

Fulop Ivy Jackson • Memphis, TN 38122 • Continuing

Fulsaas Esther M. • Assoc. Librarian • University of California-Berkeley University Library • Berkeley, CA 94720 • ALCTS LITA

Fulton Elaine • Adult Services • De Kalb Public Library • De Kalb, IL 60115

Fulton Gloria • Associate Librarian • Humboldt State University Library • Arcata, CA 95521 • ACRL IRRT

Fulton M. Jane • Paducah, KY 42001

Fulton Marsha K. • Arthur Andersen • Saint Louis, MO 63101 • LITA

Fulton R. Steven • Technical Services Librarian • Texas Woman's University Mary Evelyn Blagg-Huey Library • Denton, TX 76204-1715 • ALCTS LITA

Fulton Tara L. • Loyola University E.M. Cudahy Memorial Library • Chicago, IL 60626 • ACRL LAMA

Fulton W. Bruce • Head of Technical Servs. Dept. • Mercy College Libraries • Dobbs Ferry, NY 10522 • ALCTS LITA SRRT *Life*

Fultz Norma J. • Assoc. Prof. of Lib. Svs. • Ball State University Bracken Library • Muncie, IN 47306-0160

Fultz Tamara Lee • Bloomington, IN 47401-4941

Fulwell Elizabeth A. • Director of Library • Niagara County Community College Faculty Resource Center • Sanborn, NY 14132

Funabiki Ruth Patterson • University of Idaho Law Library • Moscow, ID 83843 • ALCTS LITA

Funda Nura • Quick Information Specialist • McKinsey & Company • New York, NY 10022

Funderburke Wilhemina • Trustee • Roosevelt Public Library • Roosevelt, NY 11575 • ALTA

Funes Carolyn H. • Student • San Jose State University Division of Library & Information Science • San Jose, CA 95192-0029 • PLA

Fung Karen A. • Deputy Curator • Stanford University • Stanford, CA 94305-6011 • ACRL

Fung Margaret C. • Professor • National Cheng-Chih University • Taipei ROC, Taiwan • ACRL LAMA *Life*

Fung Tom H. • Librarian • Labat-Anderson Incorporated EPA Superfund Records Center • San Francisco, CA 94105

Funk Elizabeth A. • Asst. Dir./Advisory Svs & Cnt Ed • State Library of Pennsylvania Department of Education • Harrisburg, PA 17105 • ASCLA PLA

Funk Joyce M. • Librarian • Shawnee Heights Elementary School • Topeka, KS 66605 • AASL

Funk Nancy J. • Media Specialist • Mc Graw Elementary School • Mc Graw, NY 13101 • AASL ALSC

Funk Roger L. • Los Angeles, CA 90068-2827

Funke Claudia • Librarian/Rare Books • New York Public Library Division P • New York, NY 10163-2240 • ACRL

Funke John E. Jr. • Shreveport, LA 71101-4948

Funkhouser Brenda K. • Librarian • Eldorado Memorial Public Library District • Eldorado, IL 62930

Funkhouser Deborah D. • Student • Radcliffe College Schlesinger Library • Cambridge, MA 02138 • IFRT

Funkhouser Norma F. • Lecturer • Texas A & M University Medical Sciences Library • College Station, TX 77843 • LITA

Funkhouser Richard L. • Science Librarian • Purdue University Libraries • West Lafayette, IN 47907 • ACRL ALCTS *Life*

Furbush Eleanor S. • Eldredge Public Library • Chatham, MA 02633

Furgason Barbara J. • Branch Librarian • Contra Costa County Library Lafayette Branch • Lafayette, CA 94549

Furi Gerald M. • Assistant Director • Farmington Community Library • Farmington Hills, MI 48334 • LITA

Furl Michael • Library Director • Kankakee Public Library • Kankakee, IL 60901 • PLA

Furlong Elizabeth • Evanston, IL 60201

Furlong John T. • Student • University of Missouri-Columbia School of Library & Informational Science • Columbia, MO 65211 • SRRT

Furlong Robert E. • Indian Hill Library Manager • Bell Telephone Lab • Indian Hill, IL 60540 • LAMA LITA *Life*

Furlough Mary C. • Head Children's Services • William F. Laman Public Library • North Little Rock, AR 72114

Furman Holly J. • Business Information Center • Texaco Incorporated • White Plains, NY 10650 • ACRL ALCTS LAMA RASD

Furman Susan L. • Newberry Library • Chicago, IL 60610 • ACRL LITA

Furmanak Stan • Assistant Director • Lebanon County Library System • Lebanon, PA 17042

Furness Anne W. • Cambridge, MA 02138

Furniss Kevin • Catologer/Collections Librarian • Athabasca University Library • Athabasca AB, T0G 2R0 Canada • ACRL ALCTS RASD IFRT SRRT

Furr Barbara L. • Branch Librarian • Public Library of Cincinnati and Hamilton County Walnut Hills Branch • Cincinnati, OH 45206 • PLA

Furr Diana B. • Elementary Librarian • Seabourn Elementary School Library • Mesquite, TX 75149 • AASL ALSC

Furrie Betty T. • Cataloging Supervisor • San Diego City Schools, IMC • San Diego, CA 92123 • ALCTS

Fursa Edmond C. • Bloomfield, NJ 07003 • ACRL LAMA PLA RASD EMIERT IFRT IRRT LRRT SORT SRRT

Furst Sharon L. • Student • University of Maryland College of Library and Information Services • College Park, MD 20742-4345 • SRRT

Furtado Ernestina D. • New Bedford, MA 02740 • ACRL

Furth Elizabeth A. • Columbus, NJ 08022

Furuhashi Lynette • University of Hawaii Thomas Hale Hamilton Library • Honolulu, HI 96822

Furukawa Kathleen M. • Student • University of Hawaii School of Library & Information Studies • Honolulu, HI 96822 • ALCTS

Furukawa Marion K. • Trustee • Yakima Valley Regional Library • Yakima, WA 98901

Furumoto Viola • Honolulu, HI 96816

Furuta Kenneth R. • Government Documents Dept. • Arizona State University Hayden Library • Tempe, AZ 85287-1006 • ACRL GODORT

Furuyama Aileen T. • San Leandro, CA 94578

Fusaro Janiece B. • Librarian • Metropolitan State University • St Paul, MN 55108 • ACRL LITA *Life*

Fusco C • School Librarian • Whitman-Hanson Regional High School • Whitman, MA 02382 • AASL IFRT LIRT

Fuseler Elizabeth A. • Colorado State University William E. Morgan Library • Fort Collins, CO 80523 • ACRL LAMA

Fusich Monica G. • Lib. Instruction Coordinator • University of California Rivera Library • Riverside, CA 92517 • ACRL RASD

Fuson Charlotte A. • Belton, TX 76513 • AASL

Fussell Francoise Hipp • Lithia Springs, GA 30057

Fussler Herman • Chapel Hill, NC 27514 • ACRL ALCTS
Life

Fustukjian Samuel Y. • Director • University of South Florida Library • Tampa, FL 33620-5600 • ACRL IFRT

Futa Debra D. • Financial Services Adm. • Saint Joseph County Public Library • South Bend, IN 46601 • PLA

Futas Elizabeth • Director • University of Rhode Island Graduate School of Library & Information Studies • Kingston, RI 02881-0815 • RASD SRRT

Futo Yoshio I. • Director of Libraries • Portifical Gregorian University • Rome 00187, Italy

Futscher Joan M. • Solano County Library • Fairfield, CA 94533

Fyfe Phyllis A. • Educational Media Specialist • Township of Ocean Intermediate School • Ocean, NJ 07712 • AASL

Fyffe Karlene I. • Student • Queens College Benjamin S. Rosenthal Library • Flushing, NY 11367-0904

Fyffe Richard C. • Cura. of Literary & Cutur Archv. • University of Connecticut Homer Babbidge Library • Storrs, CT 06269-1005 • ACRL

Gaab Donna A. • Director • Cochise County Library District • Bisbee, AZ 85603 • PLA

Gaag Karen L. • The Andrews School • Willoughby, OH 44094 • AASL YALSA

Gaal Phyllis A. • Yuba City, CA 95991

Gaarder David • Librarian • Guam Territorial Law Library • Agana, GU 96910

Gab Helen • Trustee • Stickney-Forest View Library • Stickney, IL 60402 • ALTA

Gabay Wendie H. • Philadelphia, PA 19115 • SRRT

Gabbard Rose M. • Librarian • Lee County High School Library • Beattyville, KY 41311 • AASL YALSA

Gabbedon Alja Farie • Librarian • Dana Junior High School Los Angeles Unified Sch Dist • San Pedro, CA 90731 • AASL

Gabehart Alan Dale • Canyon, TX 79015 • ACRL LAMA

Gabel Judith A. • Library Board Member • Jacksonville Public Libraries Main Library • Jacksonville, FL 32202

Gabel Linda G. • Senior Quality Control Libn. • OCLC Incorporation • Dublin, OH 43017 • ALCTS LITA

Gabel Margaret • Cataloger • Elizabethtown College High Library • Elizabethtown, PA 17022 • ALCTS

Gabia Thomas J. • Asst. System Coordinator • Nassau Library System • Uniondale, NY 11553 • PLA SRRT

Gabianelli Linda R. • Children's Librarian • Prosser Public Library • Bloomfield, CT 06002 • ALSC

Gabl Donna M. • Madison, WI 53711

Gable Debra H. • Student • San Jose State University Division of Library & Information Science • San Jose, CA 95192-0029 • AASL

Gabler Charlene K. • District Children's Librarian • Minneapolis Public Library East Lake Branch • Minneapolis, MN 55406 • PLA

Gabor Barbara T. • Law Librarian • Adams, Duque & Hazeltine • Los Angeles, CA 90017 • ACRL RASD GODORT

Gaboriault Paul H. Dr. • Director • Superior Public Library • Superior, WI 54880 • ALCTS LAMA RASD

Gabriel Claire • Reference Librarian • New York Public Library • New York, NY 10018-2788 • ACRL RASD

Gabriel Joseph A. • Head, Technical Services • Harvard University Gutman Library-Research Center • Cambridge, MA 02138 • ACRL ALCTS

Gabriel K. M. • Student • University of Washington Graduate School of Library and Information Science • Seattle, WA 98195 • NMRT

Gabriel Katherine M. • Hanover, MA 02339

Gabriel Kathryn A. • Senior Assistant • University of Delaware Library • Newark, DE 19717-5267 • ACRL ALCTS

Gabriel Michael L. • Oak Park, IL 60302 • RASD

Gabriel Michael R. • Head Microforms & Media Dept. • Northern Illinois University University Libraries • DeKalb, IL 60115-2868 • ACRL

Gabriel Patricia M. • Cuyahoga Community College Eastern Campus • Warrensville, OH 44122 • ACRL NMRT

Gabriel Sheila J. • Asst. Librarian, Media Center • Muskingum College Library • New Concord, OH 43762 • IFRT VRT

Gabriele Daniel • Librarian • Barnard School • New York, NY 10033

Gabuzda Stella S. • Director • Ludington Library • Bryn Mawr, PA 19010 • PLA

Gackler D. Jane • Librarian I-Reference • Spokane Public Library Comstock Building Library • Spokane, WA 99201-0976 • RASD SRRT

Gad Carol L. • Teacher • Milwaukee Public Schools • Milwaukee, WI 53218 • ASCLA

Gadawski Sharon A. • Media Specialist • Our Lady of Mt. Carmel School • Niagara Falls, NY 14301

Gadd Jean F. • Akron, OH 44333-2231 • Continuing

Gaddie Sheila • Southfield, MI 48075 • ALCTS GODORT

Gaddis-Philips Karen • Sam Barlow High School • Gresham, OR 97080

Gaddis Dale W. • Director • Durham County Library • Durham, NC 27702 • PLA

Gaddis Sharon H. • Tucson, AZ 85749

Gade Christy H. • Librarian/Cataloger • California State University,Fresno Henry Madden Library • Fresno, CA 93740-0034 • ACRL ALCTS

Gade Rachel P. • Reference Librarian • Ramsey County Public Library • Shoreview, MN 55126 • RASD

Gademan Linda M. • School Librarian • John F. Kennedy Middle School • Enfield, CT 06082 • AASL

Gadikian Randolph L. • State University College at Buffalo • Buffalo, NY 14222-1095

Gadsden Charlyne C. • Assistant Branch Manager • Queens Borough Public Library • Jamaica, NY 11432

Gaeddert Jean • Adult Literacy Coordinator • Hutchinson Public Library • Hutchinson, KS 67501

Gaertner Donell J. • Director • Saint Louis County Library • St. Louis, MO 63131 • AASL ACRL ALCTS ALSC ALTA ASCLA LAMA LITA PLA RASD YALSA CLENE GODORT SRRT

Gaertner Leroy J. • Chicago, IL 60655 • AASL ALSC *Life*

Gaetano Darlene B. • Manager Automated Services • Downey City Library • Downey, CA 90241 • LITA

Gaffney Jane E. • P/T Librarian • Elmont Public Library • Elmont, NY 11003

Gaffney Jean • Branch Manager • Dayton & Montgomery County Public Library • Dayton, OH 45402-2103 • ALSC LAMA PLA

Gafvert Jane M. • Administration • State Librarian Delaware Division of Libraries • Dover, DE 19901 • LAMA

Gage Cheryl L. • Assistant Director • Fond du Lac Public Library • Fond du Lac, WI 54935 • LAMA LITA

Gage Louise F. • Librarian • Woolslair Elementary Gifted Ctr Pittsburgh Public Schools • Pittsburgh, PA 15224 • ALSC

Gagen Cynthia A. • Manager • Standard & Poor's Corp. • New York, NY 10004 • ACRL ALCTS LAMA LITA PLA RASD GODORT

Gagnier Donna • Coodinator Bibliographic Instr • Illinois Institute of Technology Paul V. Galvin Library • Chicago, IL 60616 • ACRL

Gagnier Gertrude CSC Sr. • Manchester, NH 03104

Gagnon Ronald A. • Network Administrator • North of Boston Library Exchange (NOBLE) • Beverly, MA 01915 • LITA

Gagnon Ruth • Librarian • Memorial Drive School • Farmington, NH 03835 • AASL

Gago Mechael D. • Hd., Serials Dept. Catlg Sect. • Indiana University • Bloomington, IN 47405 • ALCTS

Gahagan Karen A. • Information Services Director • National Committee on Property Insurance (NCPI) • Boston, MA 02110

Gaharan Susan Fogleman • Lake Primary School • Saint Amant, LA 70774 • AASL

Gahman Marilena N. • Detroit Public Library • Detroit, MI 48202

Gahran Christopher W. • A.V.P. Systems Development • DAIS Group, Inc. • New York, NY 10004 • ACRL RASD

Gaida Harriette H. • User Services Librarian • Middle Tennessee State University Andrew L. Todd Library • Murfreesboro, TN 37132 • GODORT

Gaige Deanna • San Francisco, CA 94123

Gainer Barbara S. • Librarian K-6 • Cochran Elementary School • Dallas, TX 75211 • AASL

Gaines Anne M. • Library Systems Specialist • Data Research Associates Inc. • Saint Louis, MO 63132

Gaines Berthe • Trustee • Boston Public Library • Boston, MA 02117 • ALTA

Gaines Carol L. • Asst. Director • Clinton Public Library • Clinton, SC 29325 • LITA

Gaines James E. Jr. Dr. • Head Librarian • Virginia Military Institute J.T.L. Preston Library • Lexington, VA 24450 • ACRL LAMA *Life*

Gaines Katherine S. • Abington Free Library • Abington, PA 19001 • Life

Gaines Lynn R. • Librarian • New Orleans Public Library • New Orleans, LA 70140

Gaines Mattie B. • Library Director • Thrall Library • Middletown, NY 10940 • PLA

Gaines Richard D. • Trustee • Rockford Public Library • Rockford, IL 61101-1061 • ALTA

Gainor Lawrence A. • Student • University of Texas at Austin Graduate School of Library & Information Sciences • Austin, TX 78712-1276 • RASD IFRT SRRT

Gaisford K. Janet • Manager Acquisitions • Metropolitan Toronto Reference Library • Toronto ON, M4W 2G8 Canada • LITA

Gaitskill Pamela M. • Director • Prairie State College • Chicago Hts, IL 60411 • ACRL

Galant Eleanore F. • Saratoga Springs, NY 12866 • ALTA PLA IFRT

Galaway Beryl T. Ms • Champaign, IL 61821 • Continuing

Galaway William J. • Head of Adult Services • Arlington Heights Memorial Library • Arlington Heights, IL 60004-5966 • LAMA PLA RASD SRRT

Galberach Karen • University Microfilms International • Ann Arbor, MI 48106-1346 • LITA

Galbraith Constance J. • Department Head • Carnegie Library of Pittsburgh Allegheny Regional Branch • Pittsburgh, PA 15212

Galbraith Marc R. • Director of Reference Division • Kansas State Library • Topeka, KS 66612-1593 • IFRT

Galbraith Paul J. • Student • Catholic University of America John K. Mullen of Denver Memorial Library • Washington, DC 20064 • PLA RASD

Galbraith Pauline • Lynwood, CA 90262

Galbraith William B. • Fairbanks North Star Borough Public Library & Regional Center-Noel Wien Library • Fairbanks, AK 99701

Galbreath Robert • Asst. Dir. for Clln. Mgt. • University of North Carolina Walter Clinton Jackson Library • Greensboro, NC 27412-5201 • ACRL ALCTS

Gale David J. • Senior Editor • Delacorte Press-Dell Publishing • New York, NY 10103 • ALSC YALSA

Gale Judy L. • Birmingham, MI 48025

Gale Julia M. • Student • Louisiana State University School of Library & Information Science • Baton Rouge, LA 70803-3290

Gale Mary R. • Salinas High School • Salinas, CA 93901 • AASL

Gale Robert J. • Head of Technical Services • Newark Public Library • Newark, OH 43055 • ALCTS

Gale Roswita W. • Montgomery County Department of Public Libraries Gaithersburg Regional Library • Gaithersburg, MD 20879

Gale Sarah E. • Acquisitions Department Head • Indiana State University Cunningham Memorial Library • Terre Haute, IN 47809 • ACRL ALCTS LITA

Galejs John E. • Ames, IA 50010 • ACRL ALCTS *Life*

Galer Sybil E. • Director • Letcher County Public Library • Whitesburg, KY 41858 • PLA

Galey Gail D. • Barnwell Elementary School • Barnwell, SC 29812 • AASL

Galfand Sidney • Wynnewood, PA 19096-2124 • AASL ALCTS *Life*

Galiger Sarah J. • Student • County of Los Angeles Public Library Lancaster Library 101 • Lancaster, CA 93534 • YALSA

Gallagher Connell B. • Asst. Dir for Research Clln. • University of Vermont Bailey Howe Library • Burlington, VT 05405-0036 • ACRL

Gallagher D. Nora • Adelphi University Swirbul Library • Garden City, NY 11530 • Continuing

Gallagher Daniel J. • Chairman Board of Trustees • Jacksonville Public Libraries Main Library • Jacksonville, FL 32202

Gallagher Dave • Trustee • Oak Lawn Public Library • Oak Lawn, IL 60453 • ALTA

Gallagher Dennis J. • Trustee • Denver Public Library • Denver, CO 80203-2165 • ALTA PLA

Gallagher Edward J. • Student • Rutgers University School of Communication Information & Library Studies • New Brunswick, NJ 08903

Gallagher Eileen L. • Librarian • Calloway Elementary School • Panama City, FL 32404

Gallagher Eileen M. • Associate Librarian • Montay College Library • Chicago, IL 60659-3115 • ACRL RASD

Gallagher Janet • Librarian • Rogers Elementary School • Rogers, MN 55374 • AASL

Gallagher Judith K. • New Providence, NJ 07974 • AASL

Gallagher Lynn • Thomas Nelson Community College Library • Hampton, VA 23670 • ACRL LAMA LITA LIRT

Gallagher Michael B. • Children's Librarian • University of California-Berkeley School of Library & Information Studies • Berkeley, CA 94720 • ALSC PLA IFRT SRRT

Gallagher W. Gregory • Librarian • The Century Association • New York, NY 10036

Gallahar Christine M. • Children's Librarian • Miami-Dade Public Library System • Miami, FL 33130-1504

Gallant Charlotte A. • Delaware, OH 43015 • Continuing

Gallant Elizabeth A. • Senior Librarian • Childrens Museum Museum Wharf • Boston, MA 02210

Gallant Jennifer Jung • Director • Saint John & West Shore Hospital Media Center • Westlake, OH 44145 • YALSA

Gallant Maureen P. • Hanover Street School • Lebanon, NH 03766

Gallant Patricia M. • Acadia University Library • Wolfville NS, B0P 1X0 Canada • LITA

Gallant Stephen L. • Adult/Services • Cuyahoga County Public Library South Euclid-Lyndhurst Branch • South Euclid, OH 44121-4087 • YALSA

Gallaugher Nancy • Gilbert, AZ 85234 • YALSA

Gallegos Bee H. • Information & Research Support • Arizona State University-West Fletcher Library • Phoenix, AZ 85069-7100 • ACRL

Gallemore Don S. • Library Consultant • Calcasieu Parish School Board • Lake Charles, LA 70601 • AASL LAMA LITA

Galletta Rosanne L. • Laurel, MD 20708-2437 • PLA

Galley Thomas C. • President, CEO • Internet Communications Corporation • Englewood, CO 80111 • LITA

Gallier Judith E. • Gulf Shores, AL 36547

Galligan Daniel L. • University of Chicago Library • Chicago, IL 60637-1502

Galligan Elaine K. • Student • Saint John's University Library • Jamaica, NY 11439 • EMIERT IFRT

Gallilee Patty • Librarian I Cataloger • University of Regina • Regina SK, S4S 0A2 Canada • ACRL ALCTS LITA

Gallina Marie E. • Palham Manor, NY 10803

Gallinger Susan R. • Director • Livermore Public Library • Livermore, CA 94550 • LAMA PLA

Gallivan A. M. • Student • Emporia State University Emporia in the Rockies • Denver, CO 80204 • LAMA PLA IFRT NMRT SRRT

Gallivan Barbara A. • Toronto ON, M8V 1P9 Canada

Gallivan Marion F. • Director • Villa Maria College Library • Erie, PA 16505-4494 • ALSC LAMA PLA   *Life*

Gallmeyer Marianne • Reference Librarian • Stanislaus County Free Library • Modesto, CA 95354

Gallo Nancy V. • Director • Pequannock Township Public Library • Pompton Plains, NJ 07444 • PLA

Galloway Barbara Joan • Director, Library Services • Miami-Dade Community College • Miami, FL 33176 • ACRL

Galloway Deborah N. • Director • Mendon Public Library • Honeoye Falls, NY 14472 • PLA

Galloway Elizabeth A. • V.P. Director of Library • Art Center College of Design • Pasadena, CA 91103 • ACRL

Galloway Illa • Trustee • Calumet City Public Library • Calumet City, IL 60409-4003 • ALTA

Galloway James W. Dr • Coordinator Reference Service • Texas Woman's University Mary Evelyn Blagg-Huey Library • Denton, TX 76204-1715

Galloway Karen • Bourbon County High School • Paris, KY 40361

Galloway Lucille E. • Chief Librarian • Burlington Public Library • Burlington ON, L7R 1J4 Canada • ALCTS ALSC ASCLA LAMA LITA PLA RASD

Galloway Margaret E. • Automated Serials Librarian • University of North Texas • Denton, TX 76203 • ACRL

Galloway Mary Alyce • Reference Librarian • Mid-America Nazarene College Mabee Library • Olathe, KS 66061

Galloway R Dean • Oakland, CA 94612 • Continuing

Galloway Rosalie • Librarian • Wheeling Country Day School • Wheeling, WV 26003

Galloway Susan H. • Librarian • Oklahoma School for the Deaf • Sulphur, OK 73086 • ALSC ASCLA

Galloway Susannah • Librarian • University of California-San Diego Central University Library • La Jolla, CA 92093-0175 • ACRL

Gallucci Barbara A. • Piscataway Township Free Pub Library John F Kennedy Memorial Library • Piscataway, NJ 08854

Gallucci Robert R. • Director • The Brookfield Library • Brookfield Center, CT 06805

Gallup Sandra L. • Database Activities • University of Connecticut Homer Babbidge Library • Storrs, CT 06269-1005 • ACRL ALCTS LITA

Gallups Jerry D. • Director • Saint Clair County Public Library System • Pell City, AL 35125

Galsworthy Peter R. • Ln Clln/On-Line/Ref • University of Western Ontario Allyn & Betty Taylor Library • London ON, N6A 3K7 Canada • ACRL

Galt Francis E. • Supervisor • Saint Paul Public Library • St. Paul, MN 55102 • PLA

Galura Rosario P. • Cataloger/Asst Prof of Biblio • University of Oklahoma School of Library & Information Studies • Norman, OK 73019

Galvan Jose P. • Young Adult Librarian • Los Angeles Public Library Will & Ariel Durant Branch • Los Angeles, CA 90046 • PLA

Galvez Joan M. • Alameda County Business Library • Oakland, CA 94612

Galvin George • Russell Library • Middletown, CT 06457

Galvin Hoyt R. Mr • Charlotte, NC 28211 • LAMA LITA   *Continuing*

Galvin Jeanne D. • Kingsborough Community College • Brooklyn, NY 11235 • LITA

Galvin Kathryn J. • Assistant to the Dean • State University of New York (SUNY) at Buffalo • Buffalo, NY 14260

Galvin Thomas J. • Rockefeller College State University of New York at Albany • Albany, NY 12222

Gamache Earleen P. • Director • Lincoln Public Library • Lincoln, RI 02865

Gamache Ellen K. • History Librarian • Albany Public Library • Albany, NY 12210 • RASD

Gamage Jeanne • Library/Media Services • York High School • York, ME 03909

Gamal Sandra Hodges Mrs. • Librarian • Cairo American College • APO, AE 09839-4900 • ALCTS RASD IRRT

Gamaluddin Ahmad F. • Professor • Clarion University of Pennsylvania College of Library Science • Clarion, PA 16214 • ACRL ALCTS LITA

Gamaluddin Constance • Reference Librarian • Clarion University of Pennsylvania College of Library Science • Clarion, PA 16214

Gambee Budd L. • Chapel Hill, NC 27514 • Continuing

Gambill Joy M. • Student • University of North Carolina at Chapel Hill School of Information and Library Science • Chapel Hill, NC 27599-3360

Gamble Betsy • Head, CTS Original Catlg Unit • Cornell University • Ithaca, NY 14853-5301 • ALCTS LITA IFRT

Gamble Daniel M. • Columbus, OH 43209 • ILERT

Gamble Holly A. • Branch Librarian • Euclid Public Library Upson Branch Library • Euclid, OH 44123

Gamble Marian L. • Director • Genesee District Library • Flint, MI 48504 • ALCTS ALTA ASCLA LAMA LITA PLA RASD

Gamble Robert A. • Head, Architecture Library • University of Texas at Arlington • Arlington, TX 76019-0497 • ACRL

Gambling Edna H. • Coordinator of Childrens Service • Orange County Public Library • Hillsborough, NC 27278 • ALSC

Gambrill Paula M. • Dayton, OH 45429 • PLA

Games Elizabeth M. • Wellesley College Library Margaret Clapp Library • Wellesley, MA 02181-8275

Gammell-Byas Denyce G. • Seward County Community College • Liberal, KS 67905-1137 • ACRL

Gammon Julia A. • Head, Acquisitions Department • University of Akron Bierce Library • Akron, OH 44325-1706 • ACRL ALCTS LITA

Gandara Nancy L. • Assistant Director • San Antonio Public Library • San Antonio, TX 78205 • PLA

Gandhi Villy Mrs. • Education Media Specialist • Lakeside Middle School • Pompton Lakes, NJ 07442

Gandy Norma B. • Memphis-Shelby County Public Library and Information Center • Memphis, TN 38104-4025 • LAMA PLA

Gandy Patricia • Library Director/Reference Lib • Perth Amboy Public Library • Perth Amboy, NJ 08861 • LAMA PLA RASD ERT LRRT

Gang Adrienne • Student • Pratt Institute Graduate School of Library & Information Science • Brooklyn, NY 11205 • LITA IFRT SRRT

Gangl Susan D. • Assistant Librarian • University of Minnesota Humanities/Social Sciences Library • Minneapolis, MN 55455 • ACRL LIRT

Gangone Lucy B. • Director • Somers Public Library • Somers, CT 06071 • PLA

Ganly John V. • Chief • New York Public Library • New York, NY 10018-2788 • ACRL RASD

Gann Daniel H. • Indianapolis, IN 46208 • PLA RASD

Gann Linda A. • Library Media Director • Jenks High School Library • Jenks, OK 74037 • AASL YALSA

Gann Sheila J. • Head, Technical Serv. • British Columbia Legislative Library • Victoria BC, V8V 1X4 Canada • ALCTS LITA

Gannett Katherine G. • Student • State University of New York School of Information & Library Sci • Albany, NY 12203

Gannon Dorothy A. • Library Manager • Creare Inc. • Hanover, NH 03755

Gans Alfred • ISA Australia • Toowong QLD 4066, Australia

Gans Marion • Beachwood, OH 44122 • Continuing

Gans Naomi Beth • Student • Long Island University Palmer School of Library & Information Science • Greenvale, NY 11548 • AASL

Ganske Karen • Library Director • Nampa Public Library • Nampa, ID 83651 • PLA

Gansmuller Karla J. • Librarian • Andrew Jergens Company Research Department • Cincinnati, OH 45214

Ganss Dawn S. • Library Coordinator • Westfield High School Library • Westfield, NJ 07090 • AASL

Gansz David C.D. • Student • University of Michigan School of Information and Library Studies • Ann Arbor, MI 48109-1092

Gant Donna J. • Virginia Beach Public Library Central Library • Virginia Beach, VA 23452 • YALSA

Gantz Ethel Jane • Muncie, IN 47304-2223 • ALCTS PLA   *Life*

Ganus Burnley C. • Student • Brevard College James A. Jones Library • Brevard, NC 28712

Ganyard Margaret E. • Manager Popular Library • Saint Louis Public Library • St. Louis, MO 63103-2389

Gao Wen • Alachua County Library District • Gainesville, FL 32601

Gao Xiaomeng • Student • University of Illinois Graduate School of Library and Information Science • Urbana, IL 61801

Gao Xiaoyun • Indexer • H. W. Wilson Company • Bronx, NY 10452 • RASD

Garbarino Susan J. • Los Angeles Valley College • Van Nuys, CA 91401

Garbelman Alicia D. • School Librarian • Lake Ridge Middle School • Woodbridge, VA 22192 • AASL

Garber Doris E. • Children's Librarian • Portsmouth Public Library • Portsmouth, OH 45662 • ALSC

Garber Marion H. • Oak Ridge, TN 37830 • Continuing

Garber Marvin I. • Librarian II • Chicago Public Library Sulzer Regional Library • Chicago, IL 60625 • LITA PLA

Garber Suzanne • Reference Librarian • Western New England College D'Amour Library • Springfield, MA 01119 • ALTA RASD

Garberding Paige L. • Student • University of Washington Graduate School of Library and Information Science • Seattle, WA 98195 • ASCLA PLA IFRT SRRT

Garceau Blair • Granger, IN 465360

Garcelon Eva M. • Administrative/Clerical • Kermit Lynch Wine Merchand • Berkeley, CA 94708-1317 • NMRT

Garces Vincente E. • Student • University of California-Berkeley Law Library • Berkeley, CA 94720-2499 • IFRT SRRT

Garcia-Bryson Maria E. • Student • Wayne State University • Detroit, MI 48202

Garcia Adrian E. • Director • GV Editores, S.A. • Mexico DF, 03330, Mexico • ACRL

Garcia Alice P. • San Francisco, CA 94110-6047 • ALCTS

Garcia Alice Terrell • San Antonio Area Library System • San Antonio, TX 78205 • ALSC ASCLA PLA

Garcia Anthony S. • Orange, CA 92667

Garcia Barbara D. • Cumberland County Public Library and Information Center • Fayetteville, NC 28301

Garcia Carmen Rebecca • Automation Specialist • Dynix Incorporated • Austin, TX 78767 • LITA

Garcia Enriqueta T. • Head Librarian • Alamo Heights Independent School Dist • San Antonio, TX 78209 • AASL

Garcia Garcia Alberto • Chief of the Process Department • Universidad de las Americas Puebla • 72820 Puebla, Mexico • ALCTS

Garcia Jania • University of Washington Graduate School of Library and Information Science • Seattle, WA 98195

Garcia Jorge A. • Librarian • Porter High School • Brownsville, TX 78520

Garcia Josefa • Librarian • Gateway Community College • Phoenix, AZ 85034

Garcia Joseph E. • Director • Kent County Library System • Grand Rapids, MI 49503 • LAMA PLA

Garcia June M. • Lib. Extension Services Admin. • Phoenix Public Library • Phoenix, AZ 85004 • ALSC LAMA PLA YALSA IFRT SRRT   *Life*

Garcia Leonora R. • Library Clerk • Mother Whiteside Memorial Library • Grants, NM 87020

Garcia Mary Jean • Librarian • Oliveria Middle School Library • Brownsville, TX 78521

Garcia Pamela P. • Los Angeles, CA 90042

Garcia Robert W. • Student • University of Western Ontario School of Library & Information Science • London ON, N6G 1H1 Canada

Garcia Sonja W. • Assistant Director, Human Res • University of South Florida Library • Tampa, FL 33620-5600 • LAMA SORT

Gard Betty A. • Head, Ref. & Research Serv. • University of North Dakota Chester Fritz Library • Grand Forks, ND 58202-0175 • ACRL RASD

Gardin Martha • Assistant Director • Greene County Public Library • Xenia, OH 45385 • LAMA PLA CLENE

Gardine Tila S. • Media Specialist • Moulton Udell School District • Moulton, IA 52572

Gardiner Kent L. Mr. • Miami Shores, FL 33138

Gardinier Holly A. • Mansfield University Library • Mansfield, PA 16933

Gardner-Flint Judith • Librarian • Johns Hopkins University Milton S. Eisenhower Library • Baltimore, MD 21218 • ACRL

Gardner-Westcott Katherine A. • Watertown Public Library • Watertown, MA 02172

Gardner Bonnie K. • Director • Weeks Public Library • Greenland, NH 03840

Gardner Carrie • Palmyna High School • Palmyna, NJ 08065

Gardner Carroll S. • Librarian • Henderson District Public Library • Henderson, NV 89015 • LAMA PLA YALSA

Gardner Catherine • Director of Lib & Inf Resources • Stanford University Libraries Cecil H. Green Library • Stanford, CA 94305-6004

Gardner Cecile • Brewster, MA 02631

Gardner Charles A. • Hastings, NE 68901 • Continuing

Gardner Dawn T. • Director of Youth Services • Flagstaff City-Coconino County Public Library • Flagstaff, AZ 86001 • ALSC

Gardner Donald B. • Salesperson • Bookshop Santa Cruz • Santa Cruz, CA 95060

Gardner E Helen • New York, NY 12180 • ASCLA

Gardner Elizabeth • Librarian • Southeastern Community College South Campus • Keokuk, IA 52632 • ACRL RASD

Gardner Frances M. • Associate Cataloging Librarian • University of Michigan Law Library • Ann Arbor, MI 48109-1210 • Continuing

Gardner Frederick B. • Dean of Library • California Institute of the Arts • Valencia, CA 91355 • ACRL LAMA SRRT

Gardner Jeffrey J. • Director, Info Resources • RFE/RL Research Institute Munich Office • New York, NY 10019 • ACRL

Gardner Joan M. • Tucson, AZ 85741-9390

Gardner Jodie A. • Student • University of Illinois Graduate School of Library and Information Science • Urbana, IL 61801 • IFRT

Gardner John R. • Director • Morley Library • Painesville, OH 44077 • PLA

Gardner Juanita H. • Trustee • Atlanta-Fulton Public Library • Atlanta, GA 30303 • PLA

Gardner Judy • Public Service Librarian • Rutgers University Libraries • New Brunswick, NJ 08903 • ACRL RASD

Gardner Katherine Ann • Reference Collection Specialist • Library of Congress • Washington, DC 20541 • RASD

Gardner Kerry A. • Public Services Librarian • Sul Ross State Bryan Wildenthal Memorial Library • Alpine, TX 79830

Gardner Laura • Library Media Specialist • Park Hills High School • Kansas City, MO 64153 • AASL

Gardner Laura • Kern County Library System • Bakersfield, CA 93301

Gardner Linda L. • Technical Services Coordinator • Alachua County Library District • Gainesville, FL 32601 • ALCTS PLA IFRT

Gardner Lucy • Director • Howard Community College • Columbia, MD 21044 • ACRL ALCTS LAMA LITA RASD

Gardner Mary Louise • Library Board Trustee • Sioux Falls Public Library • Sioux Falls, SD 57102

Gardner Melanie A. • Beltsville, MD 20705

Gardner Michelle M. • Deputy Commissioner • Kentucky Department for Libraries & Archives • Frankfort, KY 40602-0537 • ASCLA

Gardner Rachel • Assistant Librarian • Monmouth College Guggenheim Memorial Library • West Long Branch, NJ 07764 • ACRL LIRT

Gardner Rebecca L. • Reference Librarian • Rutgers University Libraries Mabel Smith Douglass Library • New Brunswick, NJ 08903-0270 • GODORT LIRT

Gardner Richard K. • Professor • University of Montreal Ecole de Bibliotheconomie • Montreal PQ, H3C 3J7 Canada • ACRL ALCTS

Gardner Ron • Columbus, OH 43221

Gardner Sally • Librarian • Glee Merritt Kelly Community Library • Wolcott, VT 05680 • PLA

Gardner Stan A. • Assistant State Librarian • Missouri State Library • Jefferson City, MO 65102 • ASCLA LAMA LITA

Gardner Susan • President • Herongate Group Inc • London, ON, N6A 4V8 Canada • LITA

Gardner Suzanne T. • Nantucket High School Library • Nantucket, MA 02554 • AASL

Gardner W. Jeanne • Director, LRC • Pueblo Community College Learning Resource Center • Pueblo, CO 81004-9998 • ACRL

Gardner Wanda P. • Library Director • Decorah Public Library • Decorah, IA 52101 • PLA

Gardner William M. • Director • Marquette University Memorial Library • Milwaukee, WI 53233 • ACRL

Gardy Thais • Mechanicsburg, PA 17055

Garelick Alexander L. • Coordinator of Library Services • Ocean County College-LRC • Toms River, NJ 08753 • ACRL ALCTS RASD

Garen Robert • Coor. Community Relations • Detroit Public Library • Detroit, MI 48202

Garey Anita • Berkeley, CA 94703

Garey Linda K. • Student • Indiana University School of Library and Information Science • Bloomington, IN 47405 • PLA RASD

Garfinkle Gail J. • Richmond, VA 23223 • ACRL

Gargan William M. • Deputy Associate Librarian • Brooklyn College Library • Brooklyn, NY 11210 • ACRL RASD IFRT

Gargani Frank • Seven Wolves Publishing • Los Angeles, CA 90034

Gargiulo Deborah L • Lemoyne, PA 17043

Garibaldi Antoine M. • Trustee • New Orleans Public Library • New Orleans, LA 70140 • ALTA

Garibay Pilar • School Librarian • Brownsville Independent School District • Brownsville, TX 78521 • AASL ALSC

Garity Joseph M. • Reference Librarian • University of San Francisco Richard A. Gleeson Library • San Francisco, CA 94117

Garitz Stella • Library Media Specialist • Watertown City Schools District Primary Schools • Watertown, NY 13601 • AASL

Garland Catherine R. • Automated Operations Coor • Library of Congress • Washington, DC 20541 • ALCTS LITA

Garland Charlotte • Des Moines, IA 50317 • ASCLA

Garland Diane D. • Tomball Intermediate School • Tomball, TX 77375 • AASL

Garland Jean L. • Librarian • Bartlett Public Libary • Bertlett, NH 03812-0366 • AASL ALSC

Garland Kathleen • University of Michigan School of Information and Library Studies • Ann Arbor, MI 48109-1092 • AASL ALSC LRRT

Garland Mary D. • Geneva, IL 60134

Garland Robert R. • Library Director • Mount Union College • Alliance, OH 44601 • ACRL LAMA

Garlick Karen • Senior Conservator • National Archives, The • Washington, DC 20408 • ALCTS

Garlock Gayle N. • Associate Librarian • University of Toronto Library • Toronto ON, M5S 1A5 Canada • ACRL ALCTS RASD

Garm Mary O. • Consultant Librarian • Scranton Public Library Albright Memorial Library • Scranton, PA 18509-3248 • PLA

Garman Pat • Library Manager • PRC Incorporation • McLean, VA 22102

Garn Frances L. • Middleton, WI 53562

Garn Karlene • Media Specialist • Ames High School • Ames, IA 50010 • AASL

Garnar William H. • Assistant Director • Louisville Free Public Library • Louisville, KY 40203-2257 • LAMA PLA

Garneau Michele C. • APO, AE 09026

Garner Carolyn L. • Pasadena, CA 91106 • RASD

Garner Diane L. • Harvard University • Cambridge, MA 02138 • GODORT MAGERT

Garner Elizabeth • Teacher-Librarian • Unified School District • Berkeley, CA 94708

Garner Francine E. • Media Specialist • Tucker Elementary School • Miami, FL 33133 • AASL

Garner Marianne • Librarian • University of California-Berkeley University Library • Berkeley, CA 94720

Garner Nancy • Southern Pine, NC 28387

Garnes Carolyn L. • Community Extension Librarian • Atlanta-Fulton Public Library • Atlanta, GA 30354 • LAMA PLA SRRT

Garnett Thomas • Systems Librarian • Smithsonian Institution Libraries • Washington, DC 20540 • LITA

Garnsey Alice M. • Mayville, MI 48744

Garofalo Denise A. • Automated Systems Manager • Mid-Hudson Library System • Poughkeepsie, NY 12601 • ALCTS LITA PLA

Garofalo Michael Peter • Reg. Adm. • County of Los Angeles Public Library East County Region 800 • West Covina, CA 91790 • PLA

Garonzik Joseph • Genealogical Publishing Co. • Baltimore, MD 21202 • RASD ERT SRRT

Garoogian Rhoda • Vice-President • Universal Reference Publications • Boca Raton, FL 33486 • ACRL LITA

Garoutte Jane A. • Business Manager • Elkhart Public Library • Elkhart, IN 46516-3184

Garralda John • Manager Uncover Project • Colorado Alliance of Research Libraries • Denver, CO 80210 • ACRL

Garretson Aline L. • Mansfield University Library • Mansfield, PA 16933 • ACRL

Garretson Henry C. Jr • Turin, NY 13473

Garrett Alberta H. • School Media Specialist • Highland Park Schools • Highland Park, MI 48203

Garrett Amy • Audiovisual • Carrollton Public Library • Carrollton, TX 75006 • RASD NMRT

Garrett Claudia Ruth • Claremont, CA 91711

Garrett Connie L. • Florida State Archives • Tallahassee, FL 32301

Garrett Inez R. • Cataloger • Alamogordo Public Library • Alamogordo, NM 88337 • PLA

Garrett Jane • Barcelona Elementary School • Albuquerque, NM 87105 • AASL

Garrett Janean • VA Medical Center • Kansas City, MO 64113

Garrett Jeffrey • Foreign Literature Bibliographer • Purdue University Libraries • West Lafayette, IN 47907 • ACRL LHRT

Garrett Laurel A. • Head Librarian • Ocosta School District • Westport, WA 98595 • AASL

Garrett LeAnn • Student • University of Hawaii School of Library & Information Studies • Honolulu, HI 96822 • ALCTS LITA LRRT

Garrett Linda • Head Librarian • Bryan Adams High School • Dallas, TX 75228 • AASL YALSA

Garrett Margaret S. • Head of Technical Services • State University of New York College at Purchase Library (SUNY) • Purchase, NY 10577-2826 • ACRL ALCTS

Garrett Marie A. • Reference Librarian • University of Tennessee John C. Hodges Library • Knoxville, TN 37996-1000 • ACRL RASD

Garrett Mary J. • Asst. Admin. Libn. • Northlake Public Library District • Melrose Park, IL 60164 • ALCTS PLA

Garrett Maryhelen W. • Off-Campus Library Services • Central Michigan University Charles V. Park Library 315 • Mount Pleasant, MI 48859 • ACRL

Garrett Melinda R. • Head, Audio-Visual Services • Mansfield-Richland County Public Library • Mansfield, OH 44902-1295 • PLA IFRT VRT

Garrett Pete Ed • Principal • Morris Architects • Houston, TX 77227-2715 • LAMA

Garrett Rebecca • Trustee • Atlanta-Fulton Public Library • Atlanta, GA 30303 • PLA

Garrett Sally C. • Reference Librarian • Patchogue-Medford Library • Patchogue, NY 11772 • ACRL ALCTS RASD   Life

Garrett Valerie A. • Baltimore, MD 21217

Garrett Willa J. • Reference Librarian • Southwest Missouri State University Library • Springfield, MO 65804-0095

Garrettson Victoria L. • Patients Librarian • Springfield Hospital Center Medical Library • Sykesville, MD 21784 • ASCLA

Garrick Cynthia • Yakima Valley Regional Library • Yakima, WA 98901 • RASD

Garrido Maria U. • Student • Florida State University School of Library and Information Studies • Tallahassee, FL 32306-2048

Garris Malinda J. • Student • Kent State University School of Library & Information Science • Kent, OH 44242-0001

Garris Penny • Children's Librarian • Pamunkey Regional Library • Hanover, VA 23069

Garrison-Terry Suzanne C. • Librarian-Reference Dept I.L.L. • Dowling College • Oakdale, NY 11769 • ACRL

Garrison Angelyn Geraci • Acting Director • Edgewood College Library • Madison, WI 53711 • ACRL EMIERT

Garrison Bernie J. • Librarian III • Columbus Metropolitan Library • Columbus, OH 43215

Garrison Brenda • Vice President • Grand Rapids Urban League • Grand Rapids, MI 49503

Garrison Catherine L. • Little Silver, NJ 07739

Garrison Cheryl • Branch Manager • Kent County Library System Walker Branch • Walker, MI 49504 • PLA

Garrison Frances S. • Mansfield University Library • Mansfield, PA 16933 • ACRL

Garrison Guy • Drexel University College of Information Studies • Philadelphia, PA 19104-2875 • ACRL PLA IRRT   Life

Garrison Jeanne B. • Health Sci Ln • Vineland Free Public Library • Vineland, NJ 08360

Garrison Judith A. • Western Michigan University Libraries Dwight B. Waldo Library • Kalamazoo, MI 49008

Garrison Michael G. • Director • Rocky River Public Library • Rocky River, OH 44116-2699 • PLA IFRT

Garrison Patricia A. • Houston, TX 77070

Garrison Reba • Student • University of Oklahoma School of Library & Information Studies • Norman, OK 73019 • AASL

Garrison Sandra Causey • PLA Program Officer • American Library Association • Chicago, IL 60611-2795 • PLA

Garrison Teresa J. • Assistant Director for Pub. Serv • Kansas City Kansas Public Library • Kansas City, KS 66101

Garrison William A. • Principal Cataloger • University of Colorado Norlin Library • Boulder, CO 80309-0184 • ACRL ALCTS LITA

Garrity Kathern • Librarian • Fairfield High School • Fairfield, CT 06430

Garrity William F. • Assistant to Director • University of Chicago Library • Chicago, IL 60637-1502 • ACRL LAMA

Garry Gerald F. • Divine Word College • Epworth, IA 52045 • ACRL

Garsnett Kay L. • Randolph AFB, TX 78148

Garson Kenneth W. • Reference Librarian • Drexel University W. W. Hagerty Library • Philadelphia, PA 19104 • ACRL RASD LRRT

Garten Edward • Director University Libraries • University of Dayton Roesch Library • Dayton, OH 45469 • ACRL ALCTS LAMA LITA RASD

Garthwait Abigail • Asa Adams Elementary • Orono, ME 04473 • AASL

Gartin Sara E. • Librarian • Bluffton-Wells County Public Library • Bluffton, IN 46714 • LITA

Gartrell Joyce Veenstra • Head,Serials Cataloging • Columbia University Libraries Butler Library • New York, NY 10027 • ACRL ALCTS LAMA LITA

Gartseff Catherine • Non-Book Cataloger • University of Georgia Libraries • Athens, GA 30602

Garty Anne E. • Asst. Director • Ciba-Geigy Corporation • Summit, NJ 07901 • LAMA LITA

Garver Lynn A. • Student • Kent State University School of Library & Information Science • Kent, OH 44242-0001 • AASL ALSC

Garver Ruth S. • Public Services Librarian • Kent County Library System East Grand Rapids Branch • East Grand Rapids, MI 49506 • AASL PLA RASD

Garvey Toni A. • Deputy Director • Loudoun County Public Library • Leesburg, VA 22075 • LAMA PLA

Garvin Eileen T. • Arlington, VA 22202

Garvin Susan L. • Librarian • Roosevelt School District #66 • Phoenix, AZ 85040 • AASL

Garwood Dorothy • Columbus, OH 43212

Garwood Kimberly S. • Headquarter Librarian • Jasper County Public Library • Rensselaer, IN 47978

Garwood Rosemary • Library Director • Wayne Public Library • Wayne, NJ 07470 • LAMA LITA PLA GODORT IFRT SORT

Garwood Sam • Assistant Librarian • University of Maine Raymond H. Fogler Library • Orono, ME 04469 • LITA

Gary Ellen • Librarian Associate Professor • Richard J. Daley College • Chicago, IL 60652

Gary Nellie M. • Defiance, OH 43512 • Continuing

Garypie Renwick • Director • Marshall Public Library • Marshall, MI 49068 • LAMA PLA *Life*

Garza-Mercado Ario • Library Adviser • Mexican Academic Clearing House • Mexico, D.F., Mexico

Garza E.Kim Seller • Tempe, AZ 85282 • PLA

Garza Ivett L. • Houston Public Library Montrose Branch • Houston, TX 77002 • SRRT

Garza Lynne • Reference Librarian • Baldwin Public Library • Birmingham, MI 48012-3002 • RASD

Garza M. Antoinette • Director of University Libraries • Our Lady of the Lake University • San Antonio, TX 78207-4666 • ACRL

Garza Noemi • Director of Libraries • Knoxville College • Knoxville, TN 37921 • ACRL LIRT

Garza Rosa • Student • Louisiana State University School of Veterinary Medicine Library • Baton Rouge, LA 70803-8414

Garza Rosario • Bibliographic Ctr for Research • Denver, CO 80222 • ALCTS LITA

Garza San Juanita • Trustee • Houston Public Library • Houston, TX 77002 • ALTA

Gashurov Irene • Reference Librarian/Clln Devel • University of Southern California Doheny Library • Los Angeles, CA 90089-0182 • ACRL

Gaskell Carolyn S. • Director of Libraries • Walla Walla College Peterson Memorial Library • College Place, WA 99324 • AASL ACRL ALCTS RASD YALSA

Gaskell Millicent R. • Morrestown, NJ 08057 • PLA RASD

Gaskins Rosa • Broward Community College North Campus • Coconut Creek, FL 33066

Gasque Cay • Assistant Dean, Library Systems • Florida Community College Kent Campus Library • Jacksonville, FL 32205 • ACRL LITA

Gass A. Beverley • Dean • Guilford Technical Community Coll Learning Resources Center • Jamestown, NC 27282-0309 • ACRL

Gass Frances M. • Librarian • Camden County High School • Camden, NC 27921 • AASL

Gass Patricia • Director • Little Dixie Regional Libraries • Moberly, MO 65270 • PLA

Gass Susan K. • Elementary Librarian • Shea Terrace Elementary School • Portsmouth, VA 23505 • AASL LIRT

Gasser Sharon • Acquisitions Librarian • James Madison University Carrier Library • Harrisonburg, VA 22807 • ACRL ALCTS

Gassett Stephen R. • Audiovisuals Librarian • East Central Oklahoma State University • Ada, OK 74820 • IFRT

Gassie Donald V. • Student • University of Hawaii School of Library & Information Studies • Honolulu, HI 96822

Gasteyer Lois • Trustee • Oak Lawn Public Library • Oak Lawn, IL 60453 • ALTA

Gaston Judy A. • Director • University of Minnesota Film & Video • Minneapolis, MN 55414 • ACRL

Gaston Michael K. • Director • Siuslaw Public Library • Florence, OR 97439 • PLA

Gata Sylvia • Librarian • Collegio Espiritu Santo Library • Hato Rey, PR 00919 • AASL

Gatch Milton McC. • Director • Burke Library Union Theological Seminary • New York, NY 10027 • ACRL

Gatenby Janifer L. • System Consultant • Library Automation Consultant • Neutral Bay NSW 2089, Australia • ACRL ALCTS LITA

Gater Dolores A. • San Francisco, CA 94116

Gater Helen L. • Director • Arizona State University-West Fletcher Library • Phoenix, AZ 85069-7100 • ACRL LAMA LITA

Gates Carolyn M. • Academic Appt. Librarian • University of California Library • Santa Barbara, CA 93106 • RASD MAGERT

Gates Connie M. • Dir of Libraries & Technology • Pittsford Central School District Media Center • Pittsford, NY 14534 • AASL

Gates James L. Jr. • Asst. Dir. for Technical Serv. • University of Florida College of Law • Gainesville, FL 32611

Gates Jean Key • Professor Emeritus • University of South Florida School of Library & Information Science • Tampa, FL 33620

Gates Joseph E. • Dover, DE 19901 • AASL

Gates Marlayna K. • Interlibrary Loan Librarian • New York University Elmer Holmes Bobst Library • New York, NY 10012 • ACRL RASD

Gates Mary D. • Ft Atkinson, WI 53538

Gates Patricia H. • Assistant Librarian • Leyden High Schools • Franklin Park, IL 60131 • AASL YALSA *Life*

Gates Richard E. • Director of Library Automation • University of California Library • Santa Barbara, CA 93106 • LITA

Gates Stephanie J. • Student • Lock Haven Univ of Pennsylvania Stevenson Library • Lock Haven, PA 17745 • AASL

Gates Stephen R. • Provo, UT 84606

Gates Wilfrid • Trustee • East Providence Public Library Central Library • East Providence, RI 02914 • ALTA

Gates William T. • Trustee • King County Library System • Seattle, WA 98109 • ALTA LAMA PLA

Gatewood Joan C. • Bronx, NY 10463 • ALCTS LAMA

Gatewood Sharon • Media Specialist • Central Intermediate School • Waterloo, IA 50701 • AASL

Gatlin Elizabeth B. • Student • Columbia University School of Library Service • New York, NY 10027

Gatsoff Martin • New York, NY 10116

Gatten Jeffrey Nathan • Stow, OH 44224-2707 • ACRL RASD

Gattin Leroy M. • Director • South Central Kansas Library System • Hutchinson, KS 67501 • LAMA LITA PLA

Gattin Martha A. • Hutchinson Community College • Hutchinson, KS 67501 • LITA

Gattuso-Mentz Karin A. • Librarian • Dr. Gertrude A. Barber Center Library • Erie, PA 16507 • AASL ALSC ASCLA

Gauch Patricia L. • Editor • Putnam & Grosset Group • New York, NY 10016

Gaudet Dodie • Head of Technical Services • Western Massachusetts Regional Library System • Hatfield, MA 01038 • ALCTS

Gaudet Jean Ann • Librarian • Potomac Senior High School • Dumfries, VA 22026 • AASL *Life*

Gaudio Beatrice C. • Librarian • Central High School • Manchester, NH 03104

Gaudioso Madeline • West Hills, CA 91304-4403 • ASCLA

Gauen Maureta D. • Branch Supervisor • Mesquite Public Library North Branch • Mesquite, TX 75150

Gaughan Iris G. • Media Coordinator • Rancocas Valley Regional High School • Mt Holly, NJ 08060

Gaughan Margaret M. • Children's Librarian • Kern County Library System Eleanor N. Wilson Branch • Bakersfield, CA 93304-5696

Gaughan Thomas M. • Editor, American Libraries • American Library Association • Chicago, IL 60611-2795 • ACRL

Gaugy Margaret • School Library Specialist • Fremont High School • Sunnyvale, CA 94087 • LITA

Gaul Kathleen A. • Asst Ref Database Searcher Ln • Indiana State University Cunningham Memorial Library • Terre Haute, IN 47809

Gaul Robert E. • Falls Church, VA 22044 • IRRT LHRT

Gaul Ruth L. • Hilton Head, SC 29926 • IFRT

Gaulden Fletcher E. • Vice President • Craig, Gaulden & Davis, Inc., • Greenville, SC 29602 • LAMA

Gaulke Mary F. Dr. • Days Creek, OR 97429

Gault Anne • Director • Val Verde County Library • Del Rio, TX 78840

Gault Mary Lou • Cuyahoga Falls, OH 44223

Gault Robin R. • Associate Director • Florida State University Law Library • Tallahassee, FL 32306-1034

Gaumond George R. • Director • Valdosta State College Library • Valdosta, GA 31698-0001 • ACRL LAMA

Gaunce Patricia A. • Branch Coordinator • West Wyandotte Library • Kansas City, KS 66112

Gaunt Eleanor M. • Librarian • Ipswich Public Library • Ipswich, MA 01938 • ALSC PLA

Gaunt Marianne I. • Assoc. Univ. Librarian • Rutgers University Libraries • New Brunswick, NJ 08903 • ACRL LAMA

Gauri Kul B. • Librarian • Macomb Community College South Campus M Thompson Learning Center • Warren, MI 48093-3896 • ACRL

Gaus Sharon M. • Atlanta-Fulton Public Library Roswell Branch • Roswell, GA 30075 • YALSA IFRT

Gause George R. Jr. • Special Collections • University of Texas-Pan American • Edinburg, TX 78539-2999

Gause J. Richard Jr. • Student • Orange County Library System Orlando Public Library • Orlando, FL 32801-2471

Gause Virginia Haynie • Reference Librarian • University of Texas-Pan American • Edinburg, TX 78539-2999 • LITA

Gauss Janet G. • Winston-Salem, NC 27101

Gauthier Doreen • Library Director • City of Lighthouse Point Library • Lighthouse Point, FL 33064-5100

Gauthier Dorothy J. • North Providence, RI 02911-3308

Gauthier Mark A. • Assistant Editor • H. W. Wilson Company • Bronx, NY 10452 • ACRL

Gauthier Paula J. • Branch Manager • Kent County Library System • Grand Rapids, MI 49503

Gave Marc • Publisher Children's Books • W. H. Freeman & Company • New York, NY 10010

Gavett Franklin P. • Head of Reference • Colgate University Everett Needham Case Library • Hamilton, NY 13346 • RASD

Gavrish Diane L Arrato • Merrimack Public Library • Merrimack, NH 03054

Gawler Ann C. • Onondaga County Public Library at the Galleries • Syracuse, NY 13202-2494

Gawron Carol J. • Special Services Adminstrator • Miami-Dade Public Library System • Miami, FL 33130-1504 • PLA

Gawron Marlene E. • Children's Librarian • Orange County Library System Orlando Public Library • Orlando, FL 32801-2471 • ALSC

Gay Cheri Y. • Media Specialist • Detroit Public Library • Detroit, MI 48202 • ERT

Gay Donna G. • Mansfield, MA 02048

Gay Eleanor S. • Librarian • Lyndon Institute, Inc. • Lyndon Center, VT 05850 • AASL YALSA IFRT

Gay Elizabeth K. • Central Library Director • Los Angeles Public Library • Los Angeles, CA 90071 • LAMA PLA IFRT

Gay Nora H. • Student • Texas Woman's University School of Library & Information Studies • Denton, TX 76204 • NMRT

Gay Stanley • Trustee • East Cleveland Public Library • East Cleveland, OH 44112 • ALTA

Gaydosh Ann • Head, Adult Services • North Plainfield Library • North Plainfield, NJ 07060

Gaylor Robert • Associate Professor and Curator • Oakland University • Rochester, MI 48309-4401 • ACRL ALTA

Gaylord Donald A. • Trustee • Pueblo Library District McClelland Library • Pueblo, CO 81004-1997 • PLA

Gaylord Joan P. • Princeton, NJ 08540

Gaylord Ruth A. • Librarian II Asst./Branch Mgr. • Lexington Public Library Northside Branch • Lexington, KY 40505

Gaymon Nicholas E. • Library Director • Florida A&M University S.H. Coleman Memorial Library • Tallahassee, FL 32307 • ACRL

Gaynor Donald • Vice-President of the Board • Roosevelt Public Library • Roosevelt, NY 11575 • ALTA

Gaynor Kathy A. • Friends University Library • Wichita, KS 67213 • ACRL ALCTS RASD LIRT

Gaynor Muriel A. • Library Media Specialist • King Philip Middle School • West Hartford, CT 06117 • AASL

Gaynor Nancy L. • Librarian • Illinois Institute of Technology Daniel F & Ada L. Rice Campus • Wheaton, IL 60187 • ACRL LITA RASD

Gayton Cheryl J. • Librarian • Commonwealth College • Virginia Beach, VA 23452 • ACRL NMRT

Gaza Elizabeth • Archivist • Virginia State Library & Archives • Richmond, VA 23219

Gazzano Julian • Trustee • Suffolk Cooperative Library System • Bellport, NY 11713 • ALTA

Gbala Helen E. • User Services Librarian • NOTIS Systems, Inc. • Evanston, IL 60201-3622 • ACRL ALCTS LAMA LITA CLENE

Gbur Jacqueline M. • Lancaster, PA 17601

Geahigan Priscilla C. • Reference Librarian • Purdue University Krannert Management & Economics Library • West Lafayette, IN 47907 • ACRL RASD

Gear James G. • Collegeville, PA 19426

Gear Nancy S. • Student • Florida State University School of Library and Information Studies • Tallahassee, FL 32306-2048 • ALSC

Gearhart Carol A. • Assistant Professor of Lib. Sci. • Kutztown University Rohrbach Library • Kutztown, PA 19530-0721 • AASL ALSC

Gearin Louvan B. • St. Louis, MO 63146 • Continuing

Gearty Thomas J. • Sr. Trainer & Cust. Supp. Spec. • Faxon Company Inc. • Westwood, MA 02090 • LITA

Geary James W. • Professor Library Administration • Kent State University Libraries • Kent, OH 44242 • ACRL RASD IFRT

Geary Kathleen A. • El Paso, TX 79902 • Life

Geary Patricia A. • Senior Staff Librarian • Carnegie Library of Pittsburgh • Pittsburgh, PA 15213-4080 • PLA RASD GODORT

Gebauer Jutta J. • Library Assistant • University of Texas Tarlton Law Library • Austin, TX 78705-5799

Gebauer William • New Orleans, LA 70118

Geberbauer Cheryl A. • Learning Center Teacher • Salt Creek School District Albright Middle Sch • Villa Park, IL 60181 • AASL

Gebert Sandra M. • Librarian • Lindenhurst Memorial Library • Lindenhurst, NY 11757

Gebhard Patricia • Santa Barbara, CA 93108 • ACRL RASD *Continuing*

Gebhardt Patricia V. • Asst. Dept. Head/Adult Servs. • Gail Borden Public Library • Elgin, IL 60120 • PLA

Gecker Terry P. • Bronx, NY 10463 • AASL

Geda Carolyn L. • Librarian • Institute for Social Research Library • Ann Arbor, MI 48106

Geddes Andrew • Albany, NY 12208 • ALTA LAMA PLA *Life*

Geddes Judy J. • Indianapolis, IN 46239

Gedeon Julie A. • Kent State University School of Library & Information Science • Kent, OH 44242-0001

Gee Charles B. • Director • Pine Mountain Regional Library • Manchester, GA 31816

Gee Christina W. • Longview, WA 98632

Gee Corrin • Ontario, CA 91764

Gee Fred T. • Bronx, NY 10463

Gee Pamela E. • Associate Director • Warren County-Vicksburg Public Library • Vicksburg, MS 39180 • YALSA

Geels Marilyn F. • Reference Librarian • City University of New York Graduate School Mina Rees Library • New York, NY 10036-8099

Geenen George J. • Kansas City, MO 64131 • ACRL RASD *Life*

Geer-Butler Beverley • Hd., Copy Cataloging Section • Ohio State University Libraries • Columbus, OH 43210-1286 • ALCTS LAMA

Geer Gary D. • Collection Management • University of South Carolina • Columbia, SC 29208 • ACRL

Geers Kathleen F. Mrs. • Librarian • Alburnett School • Alburnett, IA 52202 • AASL YALSA

Geers Sandra B. • School Librarian • Winslow Township School #3 • Sicklerville, NJ 08018 • AASL

Geffert Bryn • Student • University of Illinois School of Library Information Science • Champaign, IL 61820

Gegenhuber Susan K. • Principal Libn. for Support Svs. • Pasadena Public Library • Pasadena, CA 91101 • ALCTS PLA

Gegna Gail M. • Supv. Young Readers Serv. • Palos Verdes Library District • Pls Vrd Pnsla, CA 90274 • ALSC

Gehman Judy • Student • San Jose State University Division of Library & Information Science • San Jose, CA 95192-0029

Gehman Louise A. • Librarian • Wolfeboro Public Library • Wolfeboro, NH 03894 • PLA

Gehres Donna J. • Assistant Librarian • Gene Autry Western Heritage Museum • Los Angeles, CA 90027-1462

Gehres Eleanor M. • Head, Western History Division • Denver Public Library • Denver, CO 80203-2165

Gehri Vera M. • Webb High School IMC • Reedsburg, WI 53959 • AASL

Gehrig Jody • Library Media Consultant • Nevada Department of Education • Carson City, NV 89701 • AASL ILERT

Gehring Honore • Student • Long Island University Palmer School of Library & Information Science • Greenvale, NY 11548

Gehring Lillie A. • Librarian/Media Special • Groveport-Madison Middle School North • Columbus, OH 43232 • AASL

Gehrke Mary C. • Denver, CO 80214 • Life

Gehrman Gloria • Reference Librarian • King County Library System Fairwood Library • Renton, WA 98058 • PLA

Geib Jerry H.E. • Director • Ottumwa Public Library • Ottumwa, IA 52501 • PLA

Geibel Barbara E. • Menlo Park, CA 94025

Geiben Rodney F. • Librarian • Senior High School Library • Dunkirk, NY 14048 • YALSA

Geier Martha L. • Branch Librarian • Data Research Associates Inc. • Saint Louis, MO 63132

Geiger Betty J. • Educational Media Supervisor • Springfield City Schools • Springfield, OH 45503 • AASL

Geiger Grady E. • Librarian III • Auburn University Ralph Brown Draughon Library • Auburn, AL 36849-5606 • ACRL GODORT MAGERT

Geiger Nancy L. • Cedar Rapids, IA 52402

Geiger Richard G. • Library Director • San Francisco Chronicle • San Francisco, CA 94119

Geiken Nancy Lee • Library Media Specialist • Washington High School • Vinton, IA 52349 • AASL

Geiman Robert • V.P. for Administration • Masters College • Newhall, CA 91322-0878

Geisel Ann M. • Director • Peterborough Town Library • Peterborough, NH 03458

Geisel Mary C. • Minneapolis, MN 55418 • AASL ALSC

Geiser Cherie J. • Chair, General User Services • Kansas State University Farrell Library • Manhattan, KS 66506-1200

Geiser Elizabeth • New York, NY 10022

Geisey Barbara T. • Director • Wayne College Library University of Akron • Orrville, OH 44667 • ACRL RASD LIRT

Geisler Barbara R. • Librarian • San Francisco Performing Arts Library and Museum • San Francisco, CA 94102 • ACRL

Geisler Dennis W. • Librarian • East Primary Elementary School • Waynesville, MO 65583 • AASL

Geisler Penelope A. • La Grande, OR 97850

Geissler Anne-Marie • Westbrook, CT 06498

Geissler Julie Ann • Asst. Dir., Chapter Relations • American Library Association • Chicago, IL 60611-2795

Geistlinger Linda J. • Librarian III-Childrens Libn. • San Francisco Public Library • San Francisco, CA 94102 • ALSC SORT

Geitgey Gayle A. • District Media Specialist • Urbana City Schools • Urbana, OH 43078 • AASL

Geitgey Judy A. • Technical Information Specialist • Sandia National Laboratories • Albuquerque, NM 87185 • MAGERT

Gelb Linda • Lexington, MA 02173

Gelber Steve • Beverly Hills, CA 90212

Gelbert Marianne • Toms River, NJ 08755 • ALCTS

Gelbwasser Sherry E. • Student • State University of New York at Albany School of Information Science & Policy • Albany, NY 12222

Geldon Marjorie B. • Ashburton Elementary School • Bethesda, MD 20817 • AASL

Gelenter Winifred • Head, Serials Unit • United States Department of Agriculture National Agricultural Library • Beltsville, MD 20705-2351 • ALCTS

Gelfand Julia M. • Reference/Bibliographer • University of California-Irvine Library • Irvine, CA 92713 • ACRL ALCTS RASD IRRT MAGERT

Gelfand Morris A. • Proprietor • Stone House Press • Roslyn Harbor, NY 11576

Gelfius Larry William • Administration Librarian • Homewood Public Library District • Homewood, IL 60430 • LAMA PLA

Gelhausen Michael J. • Library Director • Hartford Public Library • Hartford, WI 53027-1596 • PLA

Gelinas Jeanne • Librarian • Hennepin County Library Westonka Library • Mound, MN 55364 • PLA RASD IFRT IRRT

Gell Carolyn J. • Learning Resources Librarian • Marymount School • Santa Barbara, CA 93103

Gellatly Peter • Editor-in-Chief • Haworth Press, Inc. • Seattle, WA 98115 • ACRL ALCTS LRRT

Geller Dennis P. • Trustee • Brookline Public Library • Brookline, MA 02146 • ALTA

Geller Linda G. • Elmwood Park, IL 60635-3516

Geller Marilyn • Serials Cataloger • Massachusetts Institute of Technology Libraries (MIT) • Cambridge, MA 02139 • ALCTS LITA

Gellman Margaret A. • Reasearch Librarian • Merrill Lynch • Princeton, NJ 08543

Gelover Karen • Student • Queens College Grad Sch of Lib & Inf Studies • Flushing, NY 11367

Gelston Betty W. • Student • University of Southern Mississippi School of Library Science • Hattiesburg, MS 39406-5146

Geltner Sharon • Librarian • University of Southern California • Los Angeles, CA 90033 • ACRL RASD GODORT

Gemmel Nancy C • Librarian • Texas Commission on Alcohol and Drug Abuse • Austin, TX 78701 • ACRL ASCLA LITA

Gemmell Lisa L. • Napa, CA 94558

Gemmett Kendra • School Library Media Specialist • Fred W. Hill Elementary School • Brockport, NY 14420

Genaway David C. • University Librarian • Youngstown State University William F. Maag Library • Youngstown, OH 44555 • ACRL LITA

Genco Barbara A. • Asst Coor Off of New Bks Selecti • Brooklyn Public Library • Brooklyn, NY 11238 • ALSC PLA RASD SORT SRRT

Genco Veronica L.B. • Palm Harbor, FL 34685 • ACRL

Gendron Jeanine M. • Hollywood, FL 33019 • AASL LITA

Gendron Michele M. • Curator, Special Collections • Free Library of Philadelphia • Philadelphia, PA 19103 • PLA LIRT

Generes Tasker • Trustee • Northbrook Public Library • Northbrook, IL 60062 • ALTA

Genereux Alice • Librarian • Southern Regional High School • Manahawkin, NJ 08050 • AASL

Genest Sue A. • Shelbyville, IN 46176 • ALSC

Genet Ellen M. • Student • Syracuse University School of Information Studies • Syracuse, NY 13244-4100 • AASL YALSA

Genett Mary E. • Library Associate • American Museum of Natural History Library • New York, NY 10024 • ALCTS

Gennarelli Clifford M. • Trustee • Paramus Public Library • Paramus, NJ 07652 • ALTA PLA

Genshaw Sarah K. • Branch Librarian • Lake County Public Library Schereville Branch • Schereville, IN 46375

Gensichen Thomas F. • University of Nebraska Medical Ctr McGoogan Library of Medicine • Omaha, NE 68198-6705 • ASCLA LITA

Gensler Rosemary • Trustee • Massepequa Public Library • Massapequa, NY 11758 • ALTA PLA

Genson Thomas J. • Assistant Director • Grand Rapids Public Library • Grand Rapids, MI 49503-3093 • LAMA PLA

Genther Marilyn G. • Director • Mount Prospect Public Library • Mount Prospect, IL 60056 • LAMA PLA RASD LIRT

Gentner James N. • Assistant Program Officer • Library of Congress • Washington, DC 20541 • ACRL ALCTS LITA

Gentry Margaret C. • Virginia Bch, VA 23455

Genzel Jane M. • New Berlin, WI 53151 • ALCTS PLA RASD LRRT

Geoffroy Melba Y. • Director • Danville Public Library • Danville, IN 46122 • PLA

Geoghegan Doris J. • Louisville University Law School Library • Louisville, KY 40292 • ALCTS

George Ancil • University of Pennsylvania Library Van Pelt-Dietrich Library Center • Philadelphia, PA 19104-6206 • ACRL SRRT

George Aubrey W. • Mamager for Public Services • Spokane Public Library Comstock Building Library • Spokane, WA 99201-0976 • PLA

George Betty J. • Special Services Librarian • District of Columbia Public Library Martin Luther King Memorial Library • Washington, DC 20001

George Bruce J. • Rochester, NY 14617

George Christine G. • Librarian • Bertie County Schools Aulander Elementary • Aulander, NC 27805 • AASL

George David L. Mrs • Saint Gregory Elementary School • South Euclid, OH 44121 • ALSC

George Edith E. • Librarian • South Western City Schools • Grove City, OH 43123 • AASL ALSC

George Edward R. • Essex County Public Library • Essex ON, N8M 1Y3 Canada • YALSA

George Jessica • Student • University of Illinois Graduate School of Library and Information Science • Urbana, IL 61801

George Karen A. • Bibliographic Cataloging Spec. • Dallas County Community College District District Service Center • Mesquite, TX 75150-2095

George Kathie B. • Assistant Librarian • University of Texas Tarlton Law Library • Austin, TX 78705-5799

George Kathy • Bernardsville Middle School • Bernardsville, NJ 07924 • AASL ALSC

George Lee Anne • Coordinator • George Washington University Gelman Library • Washington, DC 20052 • ACRL LAMA RASD

George Mary W. • Head, General & Hum. Ref. Div. • Princeton University Firestone Library • Princeton, NJ 08544 • ACRL RASD LIRT LRRT

George Melba G. • Librarian • Tuckahoe Middle School • Richmond, VA 23229 • AASL

George Melvin R. • University Librarian • Oregon State University William Jasper Kerr Library • Corvallis, OR 97331-4501 • ACRL LAMA

George Philip G. • Cataloger • Library of Congress • Washington, DC 20541

George Ruth H. • Milwaukee, WI 53209 • Continuing

George Shirley • City Librarian • Beaverton City Library • Beaverton, OR 97005 • LAMA PLA IFRT LRRT

George Susan C. • Physical Sciences Librarian • Dartmouth College Kresge Physical Sciences Library • Hanover, NH 03755 • ACRL LITA

George Tamara S. • Librarian • Cobb County Public Library System • Marietta, GA 30060 • PLA

Georgeff Mary D. • Student • State Historical Society of Wisconsin • Madison, WI 53706 • IFRT SRRT
Georgel Joyce • Elementary Librarian • Holy Angels Academy • Louisville, KY 40208
Georgiou Eleanor A. Mrs • Media Specialist • Academy Of Holy Names • Tampa, FL 33609 • AASL
Geppert Alida L. • Director • Southwest Michigan Library Coop • Paw Paw, MI 49079 • Life
Gepson Lolly H. • Northbrook Public Library • Northbrook, IL 60062 • ALSC
Geraci Diane • Social Science & Data Librarian • State University of New York at Binghamton University Libraries • Binghamton, NY 13902-6012 • ACRL LITA
Gerald Rebecca L. • Student • University of Pittsburgh School of Library and Information Science • Pittsburgh, PA 15260
Geraldino-Orban Amparo M. • Fairfield, CT 06430
Gerard Beverly R. • Librarian • Anadarko High School • Anadarko, OK 73005 • AASL
Gerard Diane E. • Student • State University New York at Buffalo School of Inf. & Library Studies • Buffalo, NY 14260
Gerard Sandra-Chell • Director • Cathedral High School • Los Angeles, CA 90012 • AASL YALSA LIRT
Gerber Brian • Graduate Student • State University of New York (SUNY) University Libraries • Albany, NY 12222
Gerber Geraldine B. • Librarian • Area High School Library • Selinsgrove, PA 17870 • AASL YALSA
Gerber Judith D. • Bellmore, NY 11710
Gerber Kathy • Marlette, MI 48453 • AASL
Gerber Susan H. • Manager, Audio-Visual Division • Columbus Metropolitan Library • Columbus, OH 43215 • PLA VRT
Gerbrandt Bianka M. • Librarian • Grayson County Public Library • Leitchfield, KY 42754-0512
Gerchman Lisa • Fuller School • Keene, NH 03431 • AASL
Gercken Richard • Assistant Director • Massillon Public Library • Massillon, OH 44646
Gerdes Carolyn • Maplewood, NJ 07040 • AASL
Gerdes Neil Wayne • Librarian • Meadville/Lombard Theo School • Chicago, IL 60637 • ACRL
Gerdes Sharman E. • Director • Monmouth Public Library • Monmouth, OR 97361 • PLA
Gerecke Lillian M. • Librarian • Fitchburg State College Library • Fitchburg, MA 01420
Gergen Michael • Principal • Don Bosco Technical Institute • Rosemead, CA 91770 • AASL
Gerhard Kristin H. • Catalog Librarian • Iowa State University Library • Ames, IA 50011-2140 • ACRL ALCTS
Gerhard Louise S. • Traphill, NC 28685 • PLA RASD
Gerhardt Lillian N. • Editor • School Library Journal • New York, NY 10011 • AASL ALSC YALSA LHRT
Gerhart Catherine A. • University of Washington Suzzallo Library • Seattle, WA 98195 • ALCTS
Gering Kathrine K. • Librarian • McBee High School • McBee, SC 29101 • AASL YALSA
Gerity Louise P. • Coordinator of Reference Servs. • Lewis & Clark College Aubrey R. Watzek Library • Portland, OR 97219 • ACRL
Gerke Ray • Hd, Ref & Adult Services • Concord Free Public Library • Concord, MA 01742 • ACRL RASD
Gerken Bonnie A. • Asst Coor Children's Services • Sno-Isle Regional Library • Marysville, WA 98271-9164
Gerlach Donald E. • Librarian • University of Wisconsin-Madison College Library Helen C. White Hall • Madison, WI 53706
Gerlach Gretchen J. • Media Specialist • Mayo Middle School Media Center • Paris, IL 61944
Gerlach William P. • Head, Monographs • North Dakota State University Library • Fargo, ND 58105-5599
Gerling Kathy J. • Student • University of Iowa School of Library & Information Science • Iowa City, IA 52242
Gerlock Joanna • Student • Rutgers University School of Communication Information & Library Studies • New Brunswick, NJ 08903 • AASL
Gerloff Karen • Reference Librarian • Anaheim Public Library • Anaheim, CA 92805
Germain Barbara L. • Director • Johnstown Public Library • Johnstown, NY 12095
Germain Claudia B. • Scotia, NY 12302
Germann Caro Ann • Kinkaid School • Houston, TX 77024 • AASL ALSC
Germano Diane • Mamaroneck, NY 10543
Germany Elizabeth • Chicago, IL 60615 • Continuing
Germer Jayne R. • Assistant Librarian • Cloud County Community College • Concordia, KS 66901 • ACRL LIRT
Germino Chris B. • Reclass, Project Manager • Vanderbilt University Central Library • Nashville, TN 37240-0007
Germovnik Francis Rev • Saint Thomas Seminary Library • Denver, CO 80210 • ACRL ALCTS
Gernart Jay • Trustee • Nantahala Regional Library • Murphy, NC 28906 • ALTA
Gerolemou Chris • Assistant Editor • H. W. Wilson Company • Bronx, NY 10452 • LITA
Geron Cary Ann • Huntsville, AL 35811
Gerow Margaret L. • Tucson, AZ 85718
Gerow Sandra • Director • Sturgis Public Library • Sturgis, MI 49091 • LAMA PLA
Gerrard Philip B. • New York, NY 10012 • IFRT
Gerrietts Jeanette A. • Library Media Specialist • Tripoli Community School • Tripoli, IA 50676 • AASL
Gerrity Mary T. • Camp Springs, MD 20748 • AASL
Gers Ralph • Library Consultant • Transform, Inc. • Columbia, MD 21044 • LAMA RASD CLENE LRRT
Gershevsky Ruth • Mercer Island, WA 98040 • Continuing
Gershman Bettie • Saint Louis County Library • St. Louis, MO 63131
Gersic Marge T. • Trustee • Fairfax County Public Library • Fairfax, VA 22033-1909 • ALTA
Gerson Mary B. • Media Specialist • Cuyahoga Heights Elementary School • Cleveland, OH 44125
Gerst Patricia S. • Radium Springs Middle School • Albany, GA 31705 • AASL
Gerstbacher Emily M. • Reference Librarian • Riverside City & County Public Library-Central • Riverside, CA 92502
Gerstle Steven • Hd, Reference & Library Instr. • State University of New York (SUNY) Penfield Library • Oswego, NY 13126-3514 • ACRL RASD EMIERT IFRT SRRT
Gerteis Joan D. • Fremont, CA 94539
Gertel Elliot H. • Reference Librarian • California State University • Fullerton, CA 92634 • ACRL
Gerth Karen R. • Librarian • Anaheim Public Library • Anaheim, CA 92805 • ACRL LIRT
Gertler Fred I. • System Implementation Librarian • Santa Clara University Michel Orradre Library • Santa Clara, CA 95053 • LITA
Gertz Janet E. • New York, NY 10025 • ALCTS
Gertzog Marsha K. • Peninsula Public Library • Lawrence, NY 11559
Gerwitz Laura E. • Student • University of Hawaii School of Library & Information Studies • Honolulu, HI 96822
Geske Roger J. • Trustee • Itasca Community Library • Itasca, IL 60143 • ALTA
Gessel Judith L. • Head of Reference • Sussex County Library System • Newton, NJ 07860-0076
Gessesse Kebede • Science & Enginineering Ref Ln • University of Alabama • Tuscaloosa, AL 35487-0266 • ACRL
Gessler Penny S. • Children's Librarian • Joplin Public Library • Joplin, MO 64801
Gessner Marianne • Executive Director • Michigan Library Association • Lansing, MI 48911 • ERT
Gesterfield K. Mrs • Springfield, IL 62703 • ASCLA PLA RASD
Getaz Joan • Director of LRC • Camden County College • Blackwood, NJ 08012 • ACRL
Getchell Charles M. • Wake Forest University Z Smith Reynolds Library • Winston Salem, NC 27109-7777 • RASD
Getchell Louise W. • Millersville, MD 21108-1482 • ACRL ALCTS *Continuing*
Getman Anne V. S. • Director • Whitman County Library • Colfax, WA 99111 • LAMA PLA
Getrost Christina D. • Student • Kent State University School of Library & Information Science • Kent, OH 44242-0001
Getson Carol A. • Student • Rosary College Graduate School of Library & Information Science • River Forest, IL 60305
Gettelman John • Assistant Library Director • Wauwatosa Public Library • Wauwatosa, WI 53213 • PLA
Gettis Rita R. • Lithonia, GA 30058
Gettler Laura • Librarian • Westlake High School Library Media Center • Atlanta, GA 30331 • AASL
Getty Mary J. • School Librarian/Media Spec • Mason County Board of Education Point Pleasant Junior High School • Point Pleasant, WV 25550 • AASL
Getty Sarah S. • Project Director • New England Foundation for Humanities • Boston, MA 02116-4802 • IRRT
Getty Soma • Trustee • Summit Public Library District • Summit, IL 60501
Getz Judy A. • Baltimore County Public Library • Towson, MD 21204 • LITA
Getz Malcolm • Director • Vanderbilt University Library Jean & Alexander Heard Library • Nashville, TN 37240-0007 • LITA
Getze Frederick B. • Associate Librarian • University of Delaware Library • Newark, DE 19717-5267 • ACRL RASD
Geu Glenda M. • Carnegie Public Library • Monte Vista, CO 81144 • ALSC
Geverdt Louella G. • Augsburg Elementary School • APO, AE 09178 • AASL ALSC
Gevins Adi • Student • University of California-Berkeley School of Library & Information Studies • Berkeley, CA 94720 • IFRT
Gewertz Edith • Head, Serial Cataloging • The New York Public Library • New York, NY 10016 • ALCTS LITA
Gewin Elizabeth Forster • Branch Librarian • Lake Lanier Regional Library System Forsyth County Branch • Cumming, GA 30130
Gewirtz Isaac M. • Special Collections Librarian • Southern Methodist University • Dallas, TX 75275 • ACRL
Gex Jeannie L. • Reference/Instruction Libararian • State University of New York (SUNY) Silverman Undergraduate Library • Buffalo, NY 14260 • ACRL LIRT
Geyer Richard D. • Adrian College Shipman Library • Adrian, MI 49221 • ACRL
Geyer Robert I. • College of DuPage • Glen Ellyn, IL 60137 • ACRL
Ghadrboland Shahla Sohail • Children's Librarian • Enoch Pratt Free Library Roland Park Branch • Baltimore, MD 21210
Ghassemi Ali • Denton, TX 76203
Gherman Paul M. • Special Asst to the Vice Pres • Virginia Polytechnic Institute & State University • Blacksburg, VA 24061-0434 • ACRL LAMA
Ghidella Catherine • Immaculate Conception Regional • Franklin, NJ 07461
Ghidiu Betty Lou • Student • State University of New York (SUNY) Thomas E. Dewey Graduate Library • Albany, NY 12222
Ghikas Mary W. • Western New York Library Resources Council • Buffalo, NY 14203 • AASL ALCTS ASCLA LAMA LITA PLA IFRT
Ghiorsi Laura P. • Dallas, TX 75252 • RASD
Gholz Mary Ethel • Librarian • Clawson Public Schools • Clawson, MI 48017 • AASL
Ghose Sreenanda • Student • University of Wisconsin-Milwaukee School of Library & Information Science • Milwaukee, WI 53201
Ghosh Subhra • Indexer • H. W. Wilson Company • Bronx, NY 10452 • ASCLA
Giacoma Pete J. • Director • Davis County Library • Farmington, UT 84025 • PLA
Giamalva Lolah C. • Blue Anchor, NJ 08037 • RASD
Giambalvo Jenny L. • Library Media Director • Spring Brook School • Naperville, IL 60565 • AASL
Giambi M. Dina • Asst Dir for Lib Tech Services • University of Delaware Library • Newark, DE 19717-5267 • ACRL ALCTS
Giambra Carolyn P. • Library Media Specialist • Williamsville North High School • Williamsville, NY 14221 • AASL
Gianitsaris Victoria • Student • University of Rhode Island Graduate School of Library & Information Studies • Kingston, RI 02881-0815
Giannella Anita R. • Adult Services Librarian • Glen Rock Public Library • Glen Rock, NJ 07452-1795 • PLA YALSA
Giannelli Silvia • Children's Librarian • Manlius Library • Manlius, NY 13104 • ALSC IFRT IRRT NMRT
Giannini Tula A. • Director • Adelphi University Library • Garden City, NY 11550 • ACRL
Gianoli Carol K. • School Librarian • Quigley Preparatory Seminary Library • Chicago, IL 60611-2093 • AASL
Gibbard Judith R. • Director • Patchogue-Medford Library • Patchogue, NY 11772 • PLA
Gibbens Carol • University of California UCSB Library • Santa Barbara, CA 93106-9010 • LITA
Gibbens Juannie M. • APO New York, NY 09605 • LAMA AFLRT
Gibberman Susan R. • Researcher/Cataloger • Walt Disney Imagineering • Glendale, CA 91221
Gibble Ginny • Lancaster, PA 17603
Gibbon Constance M. • Manager, Medical Library • Grant Hospital of Chicago • Chicago, IL 60614 • ACRL RASD
Gibbons Denise • Youth Services Libraian • East Providence Public Library Central Library • East Providence, RI 02914 • ALSC YALSA
Gibbons Donna • Librarian • Gemini Junior High School • Niles, IL 60648 • AASL IFRT LIRT
Gibbons Douglas F. • Director of Library Services • Museum of Television and Radio • New York, NY 10019 • LAMA LITA
Gibbons Hughes O. Mr • Translator Analyst • National Security Agency • Fort Meade, MD 20755 • Life
Gibbons Judith A. • Director • Woodford County Library • Versailles, KY 40383 • LAMA PLA
Gibbs George E. • Asst. Dean Tech. Servs./Cllns. • University of Kansas Watson Library • Lawrence, KS 66045-2800 • ACRL ALCTS LITA

Gibbs Jane • Librarian • Cleveland Public Library • Cleveland, OH 44114-1271 • ALCTS PLA *Continuing*

Gibbs Margareth • Peoria, IL 61615 • LAMA

Gibbs Marilyn Y. • Library Director • Claflin College H.V. Manning Library • Orangeburg, SC 29115 • ACRL LAMA NMRT

Gibbs Mary Ellyn G • Librarian • Thornwood High School • South Holland, IL 60473 • AASL YALSA IFRT LIRT

Gibbs Mary M. • Branch Room Coordinator • San Francisco Public Library • San Francisco, CA 94102

Gibbs Nancy Jean • Asst Hd of Acquisitions • North Carolina State University • Raleigh, NC 27695 • ALCTS LAMA

Gibbs Robert C. • Assistant University Librarian • Auburn University Ralph Brown Draughon Library • Auburn, AL 36849-5606 • ACRL ALCTS

Gibbs Sara Thompson • Head of Reference & Adult Serv • Cabell County Public Library • Huntington, WV 25701 • PLA

Gibbs Suzanne A. • Chester High School • Chester, PA 19013 • YALSA

Gibert Mary Evelyn • CDC Information Center • Centers for Disease Control • Atlanta, GA 30333

Gibian Germaine • Cleveland, OH 44112 • PLA YALSA *Life*

Gibney Barbara R. • Student • University of Maryland College of Library and Information Services • College Park, MD 20742-4345

Gibson Alison J. • Assistant Librarian • Tredyffrin Public Library • Strafford, PA 19087

Gibson Ann C. • Archivist, Assistant • Chase Manhattan • New York, NY 10081

Gibson Anne D. • Librarian • Terraset Elementary School • Reston, VA 22091 • AASL

Gibson Anne E. • Adult Services • Toronto Public Library Parkdale Branch • Toronto ON, M6K 1L6 Canada • PLA

Gibson Barbara H. • Director of Library Services • Farmington Public Library • Farmington, CT 06034 • ALSC PLA

Gibson Barbara J. • School Media Specialist • Forsyth Country Day School • Lewisville, NC 27023 • AASL EMIERT

Gibson Betty R. • Librarian • Catawba County Library • Newton, NC 28658 • LAMA PLA

Gibson Carol • Director • Oak Park Public Library • Oak Park, IL 60301 • PLA CLENE

Gibson Carol J. • System Coordinator • Manitowoc Calumet System • Manitowoc, WI 54220 • PLA RASD

Gibson Celestine W. • Branch Manager/Children's • Atlanta-Fulton Public Library Adams Park Branch Library • Atlanta, GA 30311 • ALSC

Gibson Celia C. • Coordinator of Adult Services • Indianapolis Marion County Public Library • Indianapolis, IN 46206 • PLA RASD

Gibson Claudia • Acquisitions Coordinator • Dodge City Public Library • Dodge City, KS 67801 • PLA

Gibson E. Bernice • University of Wisconsin School of Library & Information Studies • Madison, WI 53706

Gibson Elizabeth E. • Planning Consultant • California State Library Library Development Services Bureau • Sacramento, CA 95814-3324 • ASCLA LAMA PLA

Gibson Elizabeth G. • Butler Area Public Library • Butler, PA 16001 • ALSC

Gibson Elsie O. • Bensalem, PA 19020 • RASD YALSA *Life*

Gibson Emma C. • Reference • California State Polytech University • Pomona, CA 91768 • ACRL LIRT

Gibson Harold R. • Associate Director • Montclair State College Harry Sprague Library • Upper Montclair, NJ 07043 • ACRL

Gibson Ingrid D. • Washington, DC 20007

Gibson James C. • Head, User Education Program • Washington State University Library • Pullman, WA 99164-5610 • ACRL LIRT

Gibson Jesse E. • Chief of Technical Services • United States Patent & Trademark Office Library Programs • Washington, DC 20231

Gibson Jim Dr. • Director Special Programs • Ferndale School District #502 • Ferndale, WA 98226

Gibson Karla L. • Adult Services Librarian • Milford Township Library • Milford, MI 48381 • PLA RASD

Gibson Kristi N. • Pub. Relations Representative • Minneapolis Public Library & Information Center • Minneapolis, MN 55401-1992

Gibson Leesa L. • Student • Florida State University School of Library and Information Studies • Tallahassee, FL 32306-2048 • ALSC

Gibson M. Elizabeth • Information/Reference Librarian • Queens University Douglas Library • Kingston, ON, K7L 5C4 Canada • ACRL

Gibson Marvelyn L. D. • Media Specialist • Beecher Hills • Atlanta, GA 30311 • AASL

Gibson Mary J. • San Diego, CA 92103-4362 • Continuing

Gibson Merry Louise • Student • University of Texas at Austin Graduate School of Library & Information Sciences • Austin, TX 78712-1276 • ALSC

Gibson Nancy K. • Montclair Kimberley Academy • Montclair, NJ 07402

Gibson Norma J. • Librarian • University of Kentucky Libraries • Lexington, KY 40506-0039 • ACRL RASD LIRT

Gibson Robert C. • Graduate Student • University of Missouri-Columbia School of Library & Informational Science • Columbia, MO 65211 • LITA

Gibson Robert S. • Charlotte, NC 28213-3298 • Continuing

Gibson Robert W. Jr • London, TN 37774 • ALTA

Gick Francois • Librarian • Boston College High School • Dorchester, MA 02125

Gideon Charlotte • Library/Media Specialist • Traverse City Area Public Schools • Traverse City, MI 49684 • AASL

Gidney Margaret D. • Swannanoa, NC 28778 • ACRL ALCTS LITA

Giefer Marjorie • Director • Bower Elementary School • Warrenville, IL 60555 • AASL

Giegoldt Deborah D. • Weatherford, TX 76086 • AASL YALSA

Gier Elizabeth A. • Reference Librarian • Texas State Technical College Library • Waco, TX 76705

Gier Mary Ann • Marysville Public Library • Marysville, KS 66508

Giese JoAnn P. • Student • Rosary College Graduate School of Library & Information Science • River Forest, IL 60305 • RASD SRRT

Giesecke Joan R. • Associate Dean • University of Nebraska-Lincoln University Libraries • Lincoln, NE 68588-0410 • ACRL ALCTS LAMA

Giesinger Suzanne M. • Librarian II • Cleveland Public Library • Cleveland, OH 44114-1271 • PLA

Giessner Peter A. • Indexer • H. W. Wilson Company • Bronx, NY 10452 • ACRL

Giffard Susan A • Englewood Public Library • Englewood, NJ 07631 • ALSC PLA IFRT SRRT

Gifford Anne C. • Director of Library Services • Northwestern Connecticut Community College Library • Winisted, CT 06098 • ACRL

Gifford Becky J. • Vice-President • Savage Information Services • Torrance, CA 90505

Gifford Caroline J. • Serials Librarian • New York Public Library • New York, NY 10018-2788

Gifford Gwendolyn L. • Librarian • Pasco County Schools Fox Hollow Elementary • Port Richey, FL 34668

Gifford Jeri A. • High School Librarian • Academy of the Sacred Heart • Chicago, IL 60660 • AASL YALSA

Gifford Judith N. • Groton, CT 06340

Gifford Lawrence G. • Elementary Media Specialist • Franklin Elementary School Library • Rochester, MN 55904 • AASL ALTA

Gifford Martha • Reference Librarian • E. P. Foster Library • Ventura, CA 93001 • RASD

Gifford Nancy A. • Children's Librarian • Schenectady County Public Library • Schenectady, NY 12305 • ALSC

Gifford Olive R. • Gunnison, CO 81230 • AASL YALSA *Life*

Gifford Roger D. • Head Library Systems Development • University at Albany Libraries • Albany, NY 12222 • LITA

Gifford Theodore L. • Student • Miami University Edgar W. King Library • Oxford, OH 45056 • AASL

Gigax William R. • Library Supervisor • Library of Congress • Washington, DC 20541

Giglierano Joan • Columbus Metropolitan Library • Columbus, OH 43215 • RASD

Giglio Barbara • Media Specialist • Crosby High School • Waterbury, CT 06705

Gil Eduardo • Reference/Online Librarian • Montclair State College Harry Sprague Library • Upper Montclair, NJ 07043 • ACRL VRT

Gil Esther L. • Student • University of Arizona Graduate Library School • Tucson, AZ 85721 • ACRL ALCTS LAMA EMIERT

Gilbert Betsy J. • ILL • Rochester Public Library • Rochester, NY 14604

Gilbert Christine B. • Lenox, MA 01240 • Continuing

Gilbert Donna J. • Media Specialist • North High School • Westerville, OH 43081 • AASL

Gilbert Dorothy S. • Dorset, VT 05251

Gilbert Edith K. • Swanson Elementary School • Palmer, AK 99645 • AASL

Gilbert Ellen D. • Princeton, NJ 08540 • ACRL LHRT LRRT

Gilbert Helen E. • Head Librarian • McKendree College • Lebanon, IL 62254 • ACRL LAMA

Gilbert Jefferson • Director of Communications • Ontario Library Association • Toronto ON, M5C 1M3 Canada

Gilbert Luanne E. • Deputy County Librarian • Alameda County Library System • Fremont, CA 94538

Gilbert Marion M. • Rowayton, CT 06853 • AASL

Gilbert Mary A. • Saint Joseph County Public Library River Park Branch • South Bend, IN 46615 • ALSC

Gilbert Miriam • Trustee • Westview Press • Boulder, CO 80301 • ACRL

Gilbert Nancy L. • Assistant Director for Lib. Serv • United States Army Military History Institution • Carlisle, PA 17013-5008 • FLRT

Gilbert Ophelia R. • Curator, Res Clln in Literature • Central Missouri State University Ward Edwards Library • Warrensburg, MO 64093 • AASL LRRT

Gilbert Paula M. • Children's Services Librarian • Martin Memorial Library • York, PA 17401 • ALSC LAMA PLA

Gilbert Peter J • Reference Librarian • Lawrence University Seeley G. Mudd Library • Appleton, WI 54911 • ACRL LHRT

Gilbert Polly S. • Librarian • Saint Mark's School of Texas • Dallas, TX 75230

Gilbert Ruth • Library Media Specialist • Salem Central School District • Salem, NY 12865 • AASL

Gilbert Sara K. • Assistant Librarian • The Ellis School • Pittsburgh, PA 15206 • ALSC

Gilbert Sybil M. • Director • Harvin Clarendon County Library • Manning, SC 29102

Gilbert Virginia A. • Head, Collections Devel. Dept. • Duke University William R. Perkins Library • Durham, NC 27706 • ACRL ALCTS

Gilbertson Jean A. • Acting Director • University of Wisconsin Steenbock Memorial Library • Madison, WI 53706 • ACRL LAMA

Gilborne Jean E. • Geneseo, IL 61254 • Continuing

Gilchrist Alexander M. • Collection Management Officer • University of South Carolina • Columbia, SC 29208 • ACRL

Gilchrist Debra L. • Director of Library Services • Pierce College Library • Tacoma, WA 98498 • ACRL LIRT SRRT

Gildemeister Enrique E. • Lehman College Library • Bronx, NY 10468 • ALCTS LITA GODORT

Gilden Susanna C. • Admin, Services Manager • Oakland Public Library • Oakland, CA 94612 • PLA

Gildersleeve Hal • Lincoln, NE 68542 • ACRL ALCTS *Life*

Gildersleeve Robert G. • Northport, NY 11768 • ALCTS RASD *Life*

Gilderson-Duwe Jeffery A. • Overland Park, KS 66212 • RASD

Gileadi Ruth H. • Palm Harbor, FL 34683

Giles Carol A. • Saint Louis Public Library • St. Louis, MO 63103-2389 • PLA SRRT

Giles Cheryl A. • Oakland, CA 94619

Giles Claudia P. • Library Assistant • Chemeketa Community College • Salem, OR 97309

Giles James T. • Director • Cranston Public Library • Cranston, RI 02920 • LAMA PLA IRRT

Giles Marta-Marie G. • Librarian • Houston Public Library • Houston, TX 77002

Giles Molly R. • Cuyahoga County Public Library North Olmsted Branch • North Olmsted, OH 44070-3186 • LAMA

Giles Robbie L. • Head, Database Management • Washington State University Library • Pullman, WA 99164-5610 • ALCTS LITA NMRT

Gilg Rhonda K. • Student • University of Nebraska • Omaha, NE 68182

Gilham Laura B. • Mississippi County Christian Academy • Luxora, AR 72358 • LAMA

Gilheany Rosary S. • Director • Washington Public Library • Washington, NJ 07882 • PLA IFRT

Gilkeson Diane R. • Santa Maria Public Library • Santa Maria, CA 93454

Gilkeson Susan M. • Health Sciences Librarian • Texas Woman's University • Dallas, TX 75235 • NMRT

Gilkey Richard • Director • Portland Public Schools • Portland, OR 97208-3107 • AASL

Gill Bernard I. • Hillsboro, ND 58045 • ACRL LITA *Life*

Gill Calva A. Ms. • Northwest Elementary School • Lenox, GA 31637 • AASL

Gill Caroline • Palms Junior High School • Los Angeles, CA 90034

Gill Gerald L. • Associate Prof./Business Ref. Ln • James Madison University Carrier Library • Harrisonburg, VA 22807 • ACRL LITA RASD GODORT LIRT

Gill John T. • Student • Kent State University School of Library & Information Science • Kent, OH 44242-0001 • ACRL LITA IFRT

Gill Linda S. • Coordinator of User Services • Middle Tennessee State University Andrew L. Todd Library • Murfreesboro, TN 37132 • ACRL

Gillam Joyce E. • Audio Visual Librarian • Plano East Senior High School • Plano, TX 75074

Gillaspie Deborah L. • Chicago, IL 60615 • LITA IFRT LRRT

Gilleland Kathleen • Statesville, NC 28677

Gillen Betty E. • Circulation Department Head • Naperville Public Libraries • Naperville, IL 60540 • PLA

Gillen Carol T. • Student • Rutgers University School of Communication Information & Library Studies • New Brunswick, NJ 08903 • LITA NMRT

Gillentine Jane P. • Santa Fe, NM 87501 • ACRL

Gilles Mary E. • Director • Oakfield Public Library • Oakfield, WI 53065

Gilles Mary M. • Business Subject Specialist • Washington State University Library • Pullman, WA 99164-5610 • ACRL LAMA

Gillesby John Douglas • Albertson Learning Resource Ctr University of Wisconsin , Stevens Point • Stevens Point, WI 54481 • ACRL RASD

Gillespie Barbara • Manager of Extension Services • Medina County District Library • Medina, OH 44256

Gillespie David Lee • Gulfport, MS 39501 • AASL ALSC *Life*

Gillespie Joe • Sales Representative • Quality Books Inc. • Lake Bluff, IL 60044-2204

Gillespie John T. • New York, NY 10021 • AASL YALSA

Gillespie Marilyn • Supervising Librarian • Palo Alto City Library Downtown Branch • Palo Alto, CA 94301 • ASCLA PLA

Gillespie Pamela R. • NOTIS Mgr/Director of Commun. • Hunter College Library • New York, NY 10021 • ACRL

Gillespie Prentiss L. • Washington, DC 20010

Gillett Jonathan N. • President • Gordon and Breach, Inc. • New York, NY 10011 • ACRL PLA

Gillette Meredith • Director • Cardinal Stritch College • Milwaukee, WI 53217 • ACRL

Gillette Robert S. • Abilene Library Association • Abilene, TX 79699-8177

Gilley Ruth E. • Northridge, CA 91326 • Continuing

Gilley Sharon A. • Library Director • Lucius Beebe Memorial Library • Wakefield, MA 01880 • ALCTS ALSC LAMA LITA PLA RASD IFRT

Gilley T. Michael • Director • Wythe-Grayson Regional Library • Independence, VA 24348 • ALCTS LAMA RASD

Gillfillan Nancy M. • Library Director • Dixon Public Library • Dixon, IL 61021 • PLA

Gillham Cynthia • Collection Development Spec. • Grand Rapids Public Library • Grand Rapids, MI 49503-3093 • RASD

Gillham Mary A. • Princeton, IL 61356

Gillham Virginia A. • Director • Wilfrid Laurier University Library • Waterloo ON, N2L 3C5 Canada • ACRL LITA GODORT

Gilliam Bodil H. • Regional Library Officer • Benjamin Franklin Library • 06600 Mexico D.F., Mexico • LAMA RASD IRRT

Gilliam Joanne C. • Cleveland Heights, OH 44121

Gilliam Oliver • Trustee • Gary Public Library • Gary, IN 46402 • ALTA

Gilliard Dorothy S. • Librarian Grade 3 • Chicago Public Library • Chicago, IL 60605

Gillies Irene B. • Head Librarian • Eldredge Public Library • Chatham, MA 02633

Gillies Nancy B. High • Librarian III • University of Connecticut • Stamford, CT 06903 • ALCTS

Gillies Paige C. • Publishers Graphics • Bethel, CT 06801 • ALSC

Gillies Thomas • Olympia, WA 98502 • Continuing

Gilligan Janet M. • New Delhi-LOC Department of State-USIS New Delhi • Washington, DC 20521-9000 • IRRT

Gilligan Rose • New York, NY 10009 • Continuing

Gilliland Donna • School Library Coordinator • South Dakota State Library • Pierre, SD 57501-2294 • AASL YALSA

Gilliland Jane M. • Carnegie-Mellon University Libraries Hunt Library • Pittsburgh, PA 15213 • ACRL

Gilliland Paul M. Mr • Harrington, WA 99134 • ACRL ALCTS LITA *Life*

Gillingham Sandra A. • Reference Librarian • South Pasadena Public Library • South Pasadena, CA 91030

Gillion Sharron R. • Augusta, GA 30909 • AASL

Gillis Jane M. • Yale University Sterling Memorial Library • New Haven, CT 06520 • ACRL

Gillis Ruth J. • Grand Marais, MN 55604-0964

Gillis Theresa • Eastern Oregon State College Walter M. Pierce Library • LaGrande, OR 97850 • ACRL

Gillispie James E. • Govt. Pubs./Maps/Law Lib • Johns Hopkins University Milton S. Eisenhower Library • Baltimore, MD 21218 • GODORT MAGERT

Gillispie Mary Ann • James Hart Junior High School • Homewood, IL 60430 • AASL

Gillmore Donald W. • Systems Analyst • Access Innovations, Inc. • Albuquerque, NM 87196 • LITA

Gillmore Sally • Librarian • Mayfield High School • Cleveland, OH 44143 • AASL YALSA

Gillon Linda D. • Principal Librarian • Brandon Regional Library • Brandon, FL 33511 • LAMA

Gillson Lyn • Librarian • Los Angeles Public Library • Los Angeles, CA 90071 • LAMA PLA

Gilman Constance W. • Manassass, VA 22110 • LAMA

Gilman Lelde B. • Head of Collection Development • University of California Los Angeles Biomedical Library (UCLA) • Los Angeles, CA 90024 • ACRL *Life*

Gilman Nelson J. • Director • University of Southern California Norris Medical Library • Los Angeles, CA 90033-4582 • ACRL LITA *Life*

Gilmore Carolyn • Coordinator of Public Services • Dawson College • Westmount, PQ, H3Z 1A4 Canada

Gilmore Constance B. • Arapahoe School Library Media Center • Arapahoe, WY 82510 • AASL

Gilmore Diane M. • Southfield, MI 48075 • AASL YALSA *Life*

Gilmore Ellen M. • School Librarian • Pemetic Elementary School • Southwest Harbor, ME 04679 • AASL

Gilmore Frederick L. • Science Librarian • University of Michigan • Ann Arbor, MI 48109-1205 • ACRL

Gilmore Janis M. • Student • South Street Elementary School • Manorville, NY 11949

Gilmore Jeanne • Reference Librarian • Jefferson Parish Library • Metairie, LA 70010

Gilmore Joanne Rita • Director,Tech Services Dept. • Columbus Metropolitan Library • Columbus, OH 43215 • PLA

Gilmore Julia • Head of Technical Services • Kentucky Wesleyan College Library Learning Center • Owensboro, KY 42302 • ACRL ALCTS LAMA LITA GODORT IFRT

Gilmore Teresa • Reference Librarian • San Rafael Public Library • San Rafael, CA 94901 • RASD EMIERT

Gilmour-Biley Kerranne • Librarian • University of Colorado at Denver Auraria Library • Denver, CO 80204 • RASD NMRT

Gilmour David R. • Tacoma, WA 98406

Gilner David J. • Librarian • Hebrew Union College Library • Cincinnati, OH 45220 • LITA

Gilpatrick Mary Ann • Walla Walla, WA 99362 • ALSC YALSA IFRT

Gilpin Jean • Director • Washington Public Library • Washington, IA 52353 • PLA

Gilreath Charles L. • Associate Director for Pub. Serv • North Carolina State University D. H. Hill Library • Raleigh, NC 27695-7111 • ACRL RASD

Gilreath Julia • Student • Emporia State University School of Library & Information Management • Emporia, KS 66801 • LITA EMIERT SRRT

Gilson Myral A S • Mesa, AZ 85201 • AASL ALSC

Gilson Thomas • Head, Reference Services • College of Charleston Robert Scott Small Library • Charleston, SC 29424 • ACRL RASD

Gilstrap Deborah B. • Fargo, ND 58103

Gilton Donna L. • Asst. Prof.-Library Science • University of Rhode Island Graduate School of Library & Information Studies • Kingston, RI 02881-0815 • ACRL RASD EMIERT IRRT LIRT LRRT

Giltrow Peggy M. • New Mexico State Library • Santa Fe, NM 87503

Gimble Stephanie E. • Student • University of North Texas School of Library & Information Sciences • Denton, TX 76203

Gimmi Robert D. • Serials Librarian • Shippensburg University Lehman Memorial Library • Shippensburg, PA 17257-2299 • ACRL ALCTS

Ginanni Kathryn S. • Librarian • Old Dominion University Library • Norfolk, VA 23529-0256 • ACRL ALCTS

Ginder Bernice • Director, User Servs Computing • Rutgers University Libraries • Piscataway, NJ 08855-1179 • ACRL LITA

Ginder Jack Bro. • Librarian • St. Joseph High School • Jackson, MS 39213

Gingery James A. • Database Manager • Milwaukee County Federated Library System • Milwaukee, WI 53233 • LITA

Gingher Kimberly • Cloverdale Elementary School • Cloverdale, IN 46120 • AASL

Gingrich Linda • Student • Emporia State University School of Library & Information Management • Emporia, KS 66801

Ginnane Mary • Oregon State Library • Salem, OR 97310-0640 • PLA CLENE EMIERT IFRT

Ginnings April S • Student • University of Michigan School of Information and Library Studies • Ann Arbor, MI 48109-1092 • ACRL ALCTS

Ginno Elizabeth A. • Reference Librarian • California State University Hayward Library • Hayward, CA 94542 • ACRL NMRT

Ginoza Kathryn • Regional Collection Coordinator • County of Los Angeles Public Library North County Region Office 108 • Valencia, CA 91355 • PLA

Ginsberg Barbara • Children's Librarian • Dow's Lane Elementary School • Irvington, NY 10533 • AASL

Ginsberg Marjorie • Wycoff, NJ 07481

Ginsberg Victor • Regional Sales Manager • Book House • Jonesville, MI 49250

Ginsburg Coralie S. • Librarian • Skokie Public Library • Skokie, IL 60077-3680 • PLA IFRT

Ginsburg David D • Central Michigan University Charles V. Park Library 315 • Mount Pleasant, MI 48859 • ACRL

Ginsburg Mary Lou • Reference Librarian • Abington Free Library • Abington, PA 19001 • RASD

Ginsburg Rachel R. • Consultant • Publishers Development Group • New York, NY 10128 • RASD YALSA

Ginsky Carol A. • Onondaga County Public Library at the Galleries • Syracuse, NY 13202-2494

Ginsparg Suzanne M. • Librarian • North Chicago Public Library • North Chicago, IL 60064

Ginter Karen A. • Director, Search Service • Maxwell Online • McLean, VA 22102

Ginter Lucia K. • Librarian Associate • Levi E. Coe Library • Middlefield, CT 06455-0458 • ALSC YALSA

Ginther-Webster Kimberly M. • Computer Science Librarian • Carnegie Mellon University Libraries • Pittsburgh, PA 15213 • ACRL LITA SRRT

Ginther Carolyn • Library Media Specialist • Tredyffrin-Easttown Middle School • Berwyn, PA 19312 • AASL

Gioffre Betty Jo • Deputy Director • Lakewood Public Library • Lakewood, OH 44107 • LAMA

Giordano Barbara • Youth Service Coordinator • Melrose Park Public Library • Melrose Park, IL 60160

Giordano Frederick S. • Library Director • New City Library • New City, NY 10956 • LAMA PLA YALSA IFRT

Giordano Gerard • Phoenix Public Library • Phoenix, AZ 85004 • PLA

Giorgi Florence A. • Springfield, MA 01109 • PLA

Giorgis Cyndi • Tucson, AZ 85715 • AASL ALSC

Gipe Patricia H. • Defense Systems Management College Library • Fort Belvoir, VA 22060-5426 • LAMA PLA *Life*

Gipson Patricia • Holly Springs, MS 38635 • AASL

Giral Angela • Librarian • Columbia University Libraries Butler Library • New York, NY 10027 • ACRL LITA SRRT

Girard Louise H. • Associate Librarian • University of Saint Michael's College Library • Toronto ON, M5S 1J4 Canada • ACRL LAMA LITA IRRT

Girard Sherry L. • Eagle River, AK 99577 • AASL ALSC

Girard Valerie Valle • Children's Librarian • San Marino Public Library • San Marino, CA 91108

Giraud Mary Lousie • Houston, TX 77024 • Continuing

Gire Judith A. • Law Librarian • Franklin Pierce Law Ctr Library • Concord, NH 03301 • ACRL ALCTS LITA

Girill Ruth A. • Bank of America Research Library #3405 • San Francisco, CA 94137 • LITA RASD

Giroux Gail L. • Student • University of Pittsburgh School of Library and Information Science • Pittsburgh, PA 15260

Girres Ann O. • Librarian • St Thomas Academy • St Paul, MN 55120 • AASL

Girsdansky Christine W. • Richmondville, NY 12149

Girshick David • Technical Services Manager • Spokane County Library District Argonne Branch • Spokane, WA 99212-2100 • ALCTS

Gishlick Carolyn D. • Children's Librarian • Mercer County Library Hickory Corner Branch • East Windsor, NJ 08520 • ALSC

Gisondi Gary-Gabriel • Senior Info Systems Analyst • New York Public Library • New York, NY 10018 • LITA

Gisonny Karen A. • Librarian • New York Public Library • New York, NY 10018-2788 • ACRL SRRT

Giszczak Dennis P. • Student • University of Michigan Libraries Information and Library Studies • Ann Arbor, MI 48109

Gitler Robert L. Dr. • University Librarian-Emeritus • University of San Francisco Richard A. Gleeson Library • San Francisco, CA 94117 • ACRL LAMA IRRT *Life*

Gitner Fred J. • Library Director • French Institute-Alliance Francaise Library • New York, NY 10022 • ACRL ALCTS IRRT

Gittelsohn Marc • Del Mar, CA 92014 • ACRL *Continuing*

Gittings Jeanne A. • Librarian • United Medical Center Library Services • Moline, IL 61265

Gittings June • Librarian • Salk Institute • San Diego, CA 92186-5800

Giuliano Lillian C. • Director • Marlborough Public Library • Marlborough, MA 01752

Giunta Mary P. • Collection Management Librarian • Barnard College • New York, NY 10027 • ACRL ALCTS

Given Alida F. • Librarian • Clifton Elementary School • Clifton, VA 22024

Givens-Barnes Johnnie E. • President • Givens-Barnes Associates • Decatur, GA 30031 • ACRL ALCTS *Life*

Givens Beth M. • San Diego, CA 92104 • SRRT

Givhan Annetta Foster • Trustee • Free Library of Philadelphia • Philadelphia, PA 19103 • ALTA

Giving Ingrid J. • St. Paul, MN 55108

Gjelten Daniel R. • Head of Reference • University of Saint Thomas O'Shaughnessy-Frey Library • Saint Paul, MN 55105 • ACRL LITA

Gjersvik Randi • Technical University of Norway • N-7034 Trondheim, Norway • ACRL ALCTS RASD
Gjettum Pamela E. • Director • Exeter Public Library • Exeter, NH 03833
Glace John • Ocean County Library Brick Town Branch • Brick, NJ 08723 • LITA
Glackin Barbara C. • Western Iowa Tech Community College • Sioux City, IA 51106 • ALCTS
Gladding Claire T. • Winston-Salem, NC 27104-5210 • AASL
Gladieux Mary Beth Mrs. • Director • Kenrick-Glennon Seminary Library • Saint Louis, MO 63119 • ACRL ALCTS LRRT
Gladish Christine S. • Public Services • California State University-Los Angeles John F. Kennedy Memorial Library • Los Angeles, CA 90032-8300 • ACRL RASD
Gladish Wayne • California State University-Los Angeles John F. Kennedy Memorial Library • Los Angeles, CA 90032-8300 • ALCTS IFRT MAGERT
Gladstone Mark A. • Research Specialist • AT&T Information Research Center • Bernardsville, NJ 07924 • RASD GODORT
Gladstone Russell B. • Circulation/Reserve Supervisior • University of New Mexico Centennial Science & Engineering Library • Albuquerque, NM 87131
Gladysz Margean • Reference/Indexing • Kalamazoo Public Library • Kalamazoo, MI 49007-5270 • RASD
Glancy-Hobin Mary • Basking Ridge, NJ 07920 • AASL ALSC
Glancy Richard T. • Property Control • University of North Texas School of Library & Information Sciences • Denton, TX 76203 • ACRL
Glannon Ann M. • Acton, MA 01720 • ACRL
Glantz Rochelle • Arlington High School • Arlington, MA 02174 • AASL ALSC YALSA
Glasby Dorothy • Asst. Chief Serial Rec. Div. • Library of Congress • Washington, DC 20541 • ACRL ALCTS LITA
Glascoff Elisabeth D. • Asst. Director, Technical Servs • Governors State University University Library • University Park, IL 60466 • ACRL ALCTS LAMA GODORT
Glaser Earleen R. • Reference Librarian • Mercyhurst College Hammermill Library • Erie, PA 16546 • RASD
Glaser Gloria T. • New York, NY 10022 • ALTA
Glasgow Rose • Librarian • Margaret R. Grundy Memorial Library • Bristol, PA 19007
Glass Betty J. • Instructional Services Librarian • University of Nevada-Reno Noble H. Getchell Library • Reno, NV 89557 • ACRL LIRT
Glass Catherine C. • Head Cataloger • Millersville University of Pennsylvania • Millersville, PA 17551-0302 • ACRL
Glass Elizabeth • Department Head • South Plains College Lubbock Branch • Lubbock, TX 79401
Glass Helaine S. Mrs. • Librarian • Good Hope School • Glendale, WI 53209 • AASL
Glass Katherine F. • La Grange, GA 30240 • Continuing
Glass Nellie L. Miss • Fort Myers, FL 33908 • Continuing
Glass Phyllis F. • Benton Harbor, MI 49022
Glass Rick E. • Customer Service Rep. • Maxwell Online • McLean, VA 22102 • LITA
Glass Susanne R. • Director Cataloging Services • University of Virginia Alderman Library • Charlottesville, VA 22903-2498 • ACRL ALCTS
Glasser Anne • Children's Specialized Hospital • Mountainside, NJ 07091
Glasser Carole • Trustee • Kanawha County Public Library • Charleston, WV 25301 • ALTA
Glasser Jean M. • Student • Saint John's University Division of Library & Information Science • Jamaica, NY 11439 • AASL EMIERT SRRT
Glassman Nancy R. • Albert Einstein College of Medicine Gottesman Library • Bronx, NY 10461 • ACRL RASD
Glasson Holly • Miami, FL 33173 • AASL
Glasson Patricia A. • Student • Wichita State University Ablah Library • Wichita, KS 67208 • ACRL
Glast Lilianne • Dallas, TX 75230 • IFRT
Glastris Williams V. • Saint Louis County Library • St. Louis, MO 63131
Glatt Michelle L. • Student • University of Illinois School of Library Information Science • Champaign, IL 61820
Glauber Leni • Assistant Director • Scarsdale Public Library • Scarsdale, NY 10583
Glavash Keith • Head, Microreproduction Lab • Massachusetts Institute of Technology Libraries (MIT) • Cambridge, MA 02139 • ALCTS LITA
Glaviano Cliff • Head,Cataloging Department • Bowling Green State University William Jerome Library • Bowling Green, OH 43403-0175 • ACRL ALCTS LAMA
Glavin Paul J. • Lenox, MA 01240
Glaze III Edward F. • Trustee • Corpus Christi Public Library • Corpus Christi, TX 78401
Glaze Sue S. • Head Librarian • Huntingdon College Houghton Memorial Library • Montgomery, AL 36106
Glazer Frederic J. • State Librarian • West Virginia Library Commission • Charleston, WV 25305
Glazer Joan I. • Professor • Rhode Island College • Providence, RI 02908 • ALSC
Glazer Molly G. • Trustee • Cuyahoga County Public Library • Cleveland, OH 44134-2792 • ALTA
Glazer Patricia M. • Mgr. Information Resource Ctr. • Technology Concepts Inc. • Sudbury, MA 01776 • LITA
Glazer Suzanne M. • Director of Library Marketing • Random House Inc. • New York, NY 10003 • AASL ALSC PLA RASD YALSA IFRT
Glazier Ed • Bibl Quality Assur Off • Research Libraries Group Inc. (RLG) • Mountain View, CA 94041-1100 • ALCTS
Glazier Rhonda R. • Journalism Librarian • University of Missouri-Columbia Journalism Library • Columbia, MO 65203 • YALSA
Gleason Maureen L. • Deputy Director • University of Notre Dame Libraries • Notre Dame, IN 46556 • ACRL ALCTS LHRT
Gleason Natalie C. • Children's Librarian • Smithtown Library Commack Branch • Commack, NY 11725 • ALSC
Gleason Paula J. • Director Educational Media • Escambia County School District • Pensacola, FL 32503 • AASL ALCTS ALSC LAMA LITA
Gleason Robert W. • Assoc Prof Of Media Serv • Rockland Community College Library Media Center • Suffern, NY 10901 • ACRL
Gleason Ruth • Media Coordinator • Saint Charles Media Center • Bloomington, IN 47401 • ALSC
Gleason Ruth • LMC Director • Avoca West School • Glenview, IL 60025 • AASL
Gleason Susan J. • Director • Kimball Public Library • Atkinson, NH 03811 • LAMA PLA
Gleason Virginia Lee • Children's Librarian • Springfield-Greene County Library • Springfield, MO 65801 • ALSC
Gleaves Edwin S. • State Librarian and Archivist • Tennessee State Library & Archives • Nashville, TN 37243-0312 • ASCLA PLA IRRT
Gleb Mary L. • Librarian • McMurray Intermediate School • Vashon, WA 98070 • AASL
Gleboff Serge N. • Librarian II • The New York Public Library • New York, NY 10016 • ACRL
Gledhill William • Kutztown Area High School • Kutztown, PA 19530
Gleeson Joyce M. O.S.B. • Children's Librarian • Chicago Public Library Austin-Irving Branch • Chicago, IL 60634 • PLA
Gleeson Roberta R. • Coor.-Library Media Technology • Hacienda La Puente USD Media Center • City of Industry, CA 91716-0002 • AASL LITA
Gleiberman Pat • Periodicals/YA Librarian • Bellmore Memorial Library • Bellmore, NY 11710
Gleichmann Sandra K. • Reference Librarian II • Burlingame Public Library • Burlingame, CA 94010 • YALSA EMIERT
Gleim David E. • Assistant Head of Catlg Dept. • University of North Carolina • Chapel Hill, NC 27599-3914 • ACRL ALCTS LIRT
Gleim Sharon S. • Assistant Head, Serials Dept. • University of North Carolina Walter Royal Davis Library • Chapel Hill, NC 27599-3924
Glenn Chih-Tzu L. • Columbia, SC 29206
Glenn Clara C. • Saint Paul, MN 55107 • Continuing
Glenn Elaine D. • Student • Rosary College Graduate School of Library & Information Science • River Forest, IL 60305 • AASL
Glenn Elizabeth J. • Librarian II-YA • Prince William Public Library System Central Branch • Manassas, VA 22111 • YALSA
Glenn Gwenneth • Librarian • John F. Horgan Elementary School • West Warwick, RI 02893
Glenn Helen H. • Carson City, NV 89703
Glenn Judith A. • Oregon State University William Jasper Kerr Library • Corvallis, OR 97331-4501 • GODORT
Glenn Karen A. • Media Specialist • F.D. Roosevelt High School • Hyde Park, NY 12538
Glenn Michael D. • Local History Librarian,Ref Dept • Springfield-Greene County Library • Springfield, MO 65801
Glenn Rosemary M. • Children's Librarian • Atlanta-Fulton Public Library • Atlanta, GA 30303 • ALSC EMIERT
Glenn Suzanne • Voorhees, NJ 08043
Glenn Vivian • Morgan High School • McConnelsville, OH 43756 • AASL YALSA
Glennon Irene W. • Head Sci and Tech Cataloging • Virginia Polytechnic Inst & State Univ University Libraries • Blacksburg, VA 24062-9001 • ALCTS *Life*
Glesmann Jeanette P. • Librarian • Shore Country Day School • Beverly, MA 01915 • AASL
Glick Barbara I. • Student • East Carolina University Department of Library & Information Studies • Greenville, NC 27858-4353 • AASL
Glick Elissa L. • Senior Young Adult Librarian • New York Public Library Ninety-Sixty Street • New York, NY 10128 • YALSA
Glick Kenneth W. • North Haven, CT 06473
Glick Warren E. • Reference Librarian • District of Columbia Public Library Martin Luther King Memorial Library • Washington, DC 20001 • PLA RASD GODORT IFRT ILERT SRRT
Glickman Ronald • Trustee • Half Hollow Hills Community Public Library • Dix Hills, NY 11746 • ALTA
Glicksberg Barbara G. • Seattle, WA 98115 • RASD
Glickstein Eileen Agard • Director • Barnard College Library • New York, NY 10027 • ACRL
Glidden Georgia C. • Librarian • Saint Charles City-County Library • St. Peters, MO 63376-0529 • GODORT
Glikin Ronda • Humanities Librarian • Eastern Michigan University Library Center of Educational Resources • Ypsilanti, MI 48197
Glinka John L. • Lawrence, KS 66044 • ALCTS PLA *Life*
Glinskas Renate • Senior Library Technician • Santa Ana Public Library • Santa Ana, CA 92701
Glinski Kathleen G. • Hd. of Ref. & Adult Circulation • Putnam County Library • Cookeville, TN 38501
Glisczinski Diane M. • Milwaukee, WI 53207 • SRRT
Glise Laura Rugel • Newman, GA 30263
Glisson Patricia R. • Richmond Hill, GA 31324 • AASL
Glisson Peg • Librarian • Penfield Public Library • Penfield, NY 14526 • ALSC PLA
Glock Diane C. • Librarian Cataloging & Serials • General Electric Company Whitney Library KWF-116 • Schenectady, NY 12301
Gloeckner Paul B. Dr • Law Librarian • Schnader Harrison Segal & Lewis • Philadelphia, PA 19103 • ALCTS LITA GODORT
Glogoff Stuart J. • Head, Systems Dept. • University of Arizona Library • Tucson, AZ 85721 • LITA
Glogowski Maryruth P. • Associate Director • State University of New York College at Buffalo, E. H. Butler Library • Buffalo, NY 14222-1095 • ACRL
Glomski Jacqueline L. • Student • Columbia University School of Library Service • New York, NY 10027 • ACRL
Gloriod Barbara A. • Librarian • District of Columbia Public Library Martin Luther King Memorial Library • Washington, DC 20001
Gloss Carol A. • Asst. Ln., Catalog Dept. • State University of New York (SUNY) Charles B. Sears Law Library • Buffalo, NY 14260 • ASCLA SRRT
Glossi Suzann P. • School Library Media Specialist • Union-Endicott Central School District • Endicott, NY 13760 • AASL
Glotfelty Martha D. • Student • University of Alabama School of Library & Information Studies • Tuscaloosa, AL 35487-0252
Glotzbach Doris J. • Baltimore County Public Schools • Towson, MD 21204 • AASL
Glover Alda • Eight-Mile, AL 36613
Glover Barbara L. • Eastern Michigan Univ • Ypsilanti, MI 48197 • ALCTS
Glover Bernardette A.. • Branch Librarian • Pasadena Public Library Lamanda Park Branch • Pasadena, CA 91107 • PLA
Glover Frank J. • Reference Librarian • Sutro Library • San Francisco, CA 94132 • RASD
Glover Julie S. • Librarian & Association Pres. • G.B. Public Youth Library • Freeport, Bahamas
Glover Peggy D. • Deputy Director • Free Library of Philadelphia • Philadelphia, PA 19103 • PLA RASD
Glover Renee L. • Trustee • Atlanta-Fulton Public Library • Atlanta, GA 30303 • PLA
Gluck Carrie E. F. • Student • Rosary College Graduate School of Library & Information Science • River Forest, IL 60305
Gluck Myke H. • Syracuse, NY 13204-1844
Gluckman Adam D. • Asst for Interlibrary Loan • Clayton State College • Morrow, GA 30260
Glunt Cynthia L. • Young Adult Regional Manager • Cuyahoga County Public Library Mayfield Regional Branch • Mayfield Village, OH 44143-2179 • YALSA
Glunts Ira • Northampton, MA 01060
Glushenok George • Hd, Circ Serv Dept of Libraries • Sunnyvale Public Library • Sunnyvale, CA 94088-3714 • RASD
Gluss Vivian K. • Media Specialist • Stamford High School • Stamford, CT 06902 • AASL
Glynn Gail S. • Richmond, IN 47374 • AASL IFRT
Glynn Jeannette E. • Technical Library Manager • Bank of America Technical Library • Concord, CA 94520
Glynn Joseph A. • Sycamore, IL 60178
Gnadinger Jane E. • Librarian • Colonia High School • Colonia, NJ 07067

Gnat Jean M. • Associate Director • Indiana University-Purdue University at Indianapolis Library (IUPUI) • Indianapolis, IN 46202 • ACRL LAMA
Gnat Raymond E. • Director • Indianapolis Marion County Public Library • Indianapolis, IN 46206 • LAMA PLA *Life*
Gnau Roxane M. • Baltimore, MD 21236
Gnau Tara B. • Branch Supervisor • Dearborn Department of Libraries Esper Branch • Dearborn, MI 48126 • PLA EMIERT
Gnesin Stephanie L. • Morganville, NJ 07751
Gniewek Debra L. • Spruance School • Philadelphia, PA 19149 • AASL ALSC
Goad Sharon I. • Nicholls State University Allen J. Ellender Memorial Library • Thibodaux, LA 70310 • ACRL LAMA
Gober Kenneth E. • Harmong, RI 02829
Goble Anne • Houston, TX 77024
Goble Rosanne E. • Assistant Dir/Consultant • Southwest Kansas Library System • Dodge City, KS 67801 • PLA
Goblish Cheryl R. • Student • University of North Dakota Department of Library Science & Audiovisual Instruction • Grand Forks, ND 58202
Gochnawer Valerie • Librarian • Lake Park Public Library • Lake Park, IA 51347
Gocken Colleen • Librarian • College Center for Library Automation • Tallahassee, FL 32304 • LITA
Gockley Karen • Librarian • Essex Junction Educational Center • Essex Junction, VT 05452 • AASL
Godbey Esther Ruth • Omaha, NE 68114
Goddard Constance T. • Senior Librarian • Seattle Public Library • Seattle, WA 98104-1193
Goddard Joan B. • Branch Librarian • San Jose Public Library Empire Branch • San Jose, CA 95112 • ASCLA EMIERT IFRT SRRT
Goddard John R. • Associate Catalog Librarian • Cornell University Library • Ithaca, NY 14853-5301 • ACRL ALCTS
Goddard Martha L. • Deaf Services Librarian • San Francisco Public Library • San Francisco, CA 94102 • ASCLA PLA
Goddard Rosalind K. • Senior Librarian • Los Angeles Public Library Robertson Branch • Los Angeles, CA 90035
Goddard Susanne • Cataloging Librarian • Texas Tech University Libraries • Lubbock, TX 79409-0002 • ACRL ALCTS
Godden Irene P. • Associate Director • Colorado State University William E. Morgan Library • Fort Collins, CO 80523 • ACRL LITA
Godfrey James P. • Upper School Principal • Rye Country Day School • Rye, NY 10580
Godfrey Jon R. • Head Librarian • Smyth Public Library • Candia, NH 03034
Godfrey Lisa A. • Library Trustee • Kalamazoo Public Library • Kalamazoo, MI 49007-5270 • ALTA PLA
Godfrey Michael F. Mrs. • Saint Louis, MO 63109
Godfrey Michelle L. • Lexington, KY 40503 • PLA EMIERT SRRT
Godfrey Nancy N. • New Windsor, NY 12553 • LAMA
Godfrey Nina S. • Dallas, TX 75230
Godfrey Ruth A. • Librarian • Easton Elementary School • Morgantown, WV 26505 • AASL
Godin Christine C. • Johnson County Community College Library • Overland Park, KS 66210
Godleski Nancy M. • Student • Indiana University School of Library and Information Science • Bloomington, IN 47405 • RASD IFRT LHRT SRRT
Godow Michael D. • Student • Rosary College Graduate School of Library & Information Science • River Forest, IL 60305 • ALCTS LITA
Godreau Lillian Leon • Student • Stanford University • Stanford, CA 94305-6011 • LAMA LITA EMIERT ERT IFRT
Godsey James M. • Deputy Director • Rochester Public Library • Rochester, MN 55904-3777 • ALCTS LAMA PLA
Godshall Patti • Santa Ana, CA 92705
Godwin Frances • Colorado City, TX 79512 • Continuing
Godwin James L. • Library of Congress • Washington, DC 20541 • LITA
Godwin Joyce L. • Librarian • Sioux City Public Library Morningside Branch • Sioux City, IA 51106 • PLA
Godwin Mary Jo P. • Editor • H. W. Wilson Company • Bronx, NY 10452 • LAMA PLA ILERT
Godwin Ruta Pempe • Project Manager • National Science Foundation • Washington, DC 20550 • LAMA LITA
Goebel Heather L. • Reference Librarian • Phoenix Newspapers Library • Phoenix, AZ 85001 • Life
Goebes Carole A. • Lincoln, NE 68506-2452
Goedeken Edward • West Lafayette, IN 47906 • LHRT
Goehner Donna M. • Dean of University Libraries • Western Illinois University Libraries • Macomb, IL 61455 • ACRL LAMA
Goeke Joyce Kay • Librarian • Hilklsboro Junior High School • Hillsboro, IL 62049 • AASL
Goeke Sheila • Reference Librarian • Princeton Public Library • Princeton, NJ 08542
Goel Krishan S. • Librarian • U.S. Army Environmental Hygiene Agency Library • Aberdeen, MD 21010-5422
Goergen Lee P. • Student • Indiana University School of Library and Information Science • Bloomington, IN 47405
Goerke Beverly A. • Head Fiction/Browsing Sect. • Chicago Public Library Harold Washington Library • Chicago, IL 60605 • RASD
Goerner-Barr Tatiana • Cataloger • Stanford University Libraries Cecil H. Green Library • Stanford, CA 94305-6004 • ACRL ALCTS IFRT
Goers Steven D. • Des Moines, IA 50310
Goessman Cornelia • Baltimore, MD 21201
Goeters Elizabeth R. • Student • Clark-Atlanta University School of Library & Information Studies • Atlanta, GA 30314-4391
Goetsch Lori A. • Head Information Reference • Michigan State University Libraries • East Lansing, MI 48824-1048 • ACRL LAMA SRRT
Goettling Karen J. • Consultant • Washington State Library • Olympia, WA 98504-2470 • LAMA PLA
Goettsch Jane M. • Sioux Falls Public Library • Sioux Falls, SD 57102
Goetz Arthur H. • Administrator • Wicomico County Free Library • Salisbury, MD 21801 • PLA
Goetze Pamela R. • Student • University of North Carolina at Chapel Hill School of Information and Library Science • Chapel Hill, NC 27599-3360
Goetzfridt Nicholas J. • Reference Librarian • University of Guam • Mangilao, GU 96923
Goetzinger Emily C. • Louisville, KY 40215
Goff Betty J. • Director • Forked Deer Regional Library • Halls, TN 38040 • PLA
Goff David W. • Student • Clarion University of Pennsylvania College of Library Science • Clarion, PA 16214 • ACRL ALCTS LITA
Goff Dewey A. Jr • Strughold Aeromedical Library Armstrong Labatory (USAF) • Brooks AFB, TX 78235-500 • LITA FLRT GODORT
Goff Gorden F. • President • Palace Press • San Francisco, CA 94124
Goff Gwendolyn F. • Virginia State Library & Archives • Richmond, VA 23219
Goff Hugh L. • Sacramento, CA 95864
Goff Jennifer L. • Student • University of Michigan School of Information and Library Studies • Ann Arbor, MI 48109-1092 • ACRL ALCTS
Goff Linda J. • Library Instruction Librarian • California State University-Sacramento Library • Sacramento, CA 95819-6039 • ACRL LAMA LIRT
Goff Marilyn Marie • Library Director • United States Air Force • Brooks AFB, TX 78235-5000 • AFLRT
Goff William J. • Head Librarian • University of California Scripps Institute of Oceanography • La Jolla, CA 92093-0175 • ACRL
Goforth Allene M. • Asst. Agency Head Cataloging • Salt Lake City Public Library • Salt Lake City, UT 84111 • LITA PLA
Goforth Jean • Technical Proc. Librarian • Lee College Church of God School of Theology • Cleveland, TN 37311
Goforth Johanna A. • Prospect Hts, IL 60070-1905
Goggin Jacqueline M. • Prep School Librarian • Fairfield College Prep School Library • Fairfield, CT 06430
Goggin Margaret • Gainesville, FL 32605 • ACRL RASD IRRT *Continuing*
Gogolin Linda J. • Elementary Librarian • Hill City School District • Hill City, SD 57751 • AASL
Goheen Diane • Topeka West High School • Topeka, KS 66604 • YALSA
Gohlinghorst Monica A. • Council Bluffs, IA 51503
Gohlke Annette • Assistant Director • United States Air Force Libraries • Randolph AFB, TX 78150-6001 • LAMA AFLRT FLRT
Going Susan C. • Lander College Jackson Library • Greenwood, SC 29649
Goins Doris A. • Library Director • Kendallville Public Library • Kendallville, IN 46755 • PLA
Goins Rodney K. • Automation Coordinator • Harvard College Library Widener Memorial Library • Cambridge, MA 02138 • LITA
Gojmerac-Leiner Georgia • Student • Southern Connecticut State University School of Libray Science & Instructional Technology • New Haven, CT 06515 • ACRL SRRT
Golan Bernadette • Student • Indiana University School of Library and Information Science • Bloomington, IN 47405
Golar Alice • Trustee • Finkelstein Memorial Library • Spring Valley, NY 10977
Golata John • Trustee • Morton Grove Public Library • Morton Grove, IL 60053 • ALTA
Golbert Alice F. • Librarian • Hewlett Woodmere Public Library • Hewlett, NY 11557-2301
Gold Anne Marie • County Librarian • Contra Costa County Library • Pleasant Hill, CA 94523 • LAMA PLA
Gold Debby S. • Children's Librarian • Cuyahoga County Public Library Warrensville Branch • Warrensville Heights, OH 44128-4885 • ALSC
Gold Etta D. • Student • University of South Florida School of Library & Information Science • Tampa, FL 33620
Gold Jane M. • Periodical & AV Librarian • Joint Free Library of Morristown & Morris Township • Morristown, NJ 07960 • PLA RASD
Gold Marion • Literacy Coordinator • North York Public Library Fairview Regional Branch • North York, ON, M2J 4S4 Canada
Gold Marv H. • Librarian • Winslow Township Elementary School 5 • Cedar Brook, NJ 08018
Goldberg Barbara W. • Glen Rock, NJ 07452 • ALSC
Goldberg Beverly • Associate Editor • American Library Association • Chicago, IL 60611-2795
Goldberg Elizabeth D. • Miami, FL 33126 • ACRL ALCTS LITA
Goldberg Eric A. • Reference Librarian • Los Angeles County Public Library La Canada Flintridge Branch • La Canada Flintridge, CA 91011 • PLA RASD
Goldberg Harriet S. • Adult Services Librarian • Jeffersonville Township Public Library • Jeffersonville, IN 47131-1548
Goldberg Kay L. • Director,Library Services • Baptist Hospital East • Louisville, KY 40207 • LITA
Goldberg Linda B. • Louisville, KY 40207
Goldberg Lisbeth S. • Arlington County Department of Libraries • Arlington, VA 22201 • VRT
Goldberg Martin • Head Librarian • Pennsylvania State University Beaver Campus • Monaca, PA 15061 • ACRL EMIERT
Goldberg Phyllis • Trustee • State Library of Iowa • Des Moines, IA 50319 • ALTA
Goldberg Robert L. • Director • William Paterson College Library • Wayne, NJ 07470
Goldberg Ronnie A. • Asst Dir for Access Services • State University of New York at Binghamton University Libraries • Binghamton, NY 13902-6012 • ACRL LAMA LITA
Goldberg S. Tyler • Head, Serials Department • University of Louisville Ekstrom Library • Louisville, KY 40292 • ALCTS
Goldberg Sharon • Alhambra, CA 91803
Goldberg Susan • Trustee • Portland Public Library • Portland, ME 04101
Goldberg Susan S. • Minneapolis Public Library & Information Center • Minneapolis, MN 55401-1992 • PLA
Goldberg Sylvia M. • Library Assistant • University of California-Irvine Library • Irvine, CA 92713
Goldberg Terry • Sylvania, OH 43560
Goldberger David J. • Union, NJ 07083
Golden Dan W. • Tuxedo, NY 10987
Golden Diana L. • Librarian • Aubrey Junior/Senior High School • Aubrey, TX 76227
Golden Fay A. • Director • Liverpool Public Library • Liverpool, NY 13088 • LAMA PLA IFRT LIRT
Golden Gary A. Dr. • Director • Rutgers University Paul Robeson Library • Camden, NJ 08101-3990 • ACRL LITA
Golden Gregory • Head Librarian • Edmonds Community College Library • Lynnwood, WA 98036 • ACRL
Golden Judith A. • Library Director • Houston County Public Library System • Perry, GA 31069
Golden Margaret G. • Danbury, CT 06811 • SRRT
Golden Susan L. • Children's Literature Specialist • Appalachian State University Carol Grotnes Belk Library • Boone, NC 28608 • ALSC EMIERT
Goldenheim Anne J.C. • Student • University of Missouri-Columbia School of Library & Informational Science • Columbia, MO 65211 • AASL RASD
Goldenkoff Isabel M. • Reference Library • Syosset Public Library • Syosset, NY 11791
Golderman Gail M. • Student • State University of New York at Albany School of Information Science & Policy • Albany, NY 12222 • PLA RASD IFRT SRRT
Goldfarb Elizabeth • Field Librarian • The Library Power Project c/o Reader's Digest • New York, NY 10016 • AASL
Goldfarb Kathleen V. • Associate Univ Librarian • Florida State University Robert M. Strozier Library • Tallahassee, FL 32306-2047 • ALCTS LAMA
Goldfarb Stephen J. • Trustee • Atlanta-Fulton Public Library • Atlanta, GA 30303 • RASD SRRT
Goldfluss Harriet N. • Administrative Librarian • Marin County Free Library • San Rafael, CA 94903 • PLA

Goldhor Herbert • University of Illinois Graduate School of Library and Information Science • Urbana, IL 61801 • ALCTS PLA *Life*
Goldman Barbara • Trustee • Syosset Public Library • Syosset, NY 11791 • ALSC ALTA
Goldman Brenda Chasen • Tufts University • Medford, MA 02155 • ACRL ALCTS LAMA
Goldman Irene J. • Cigna Corporation • Bloomfield, CT 06002
Goldman Joan • Librarian II-Branch Manager • San Francisco Public Library • San Francisco, CA 94102 • RASD SRRT
Goldman Maurice S. • Director • Willingboro Public Library • Willingboro, NJ 08046 • ALSC ALTA LAMA LITA PLA RASD
Goldman Rebecca E. • Collections Development Libn. • University of Saint Thomas • Houston, TX 77006 • ACRL
Goldmanis Zane • Children's Librarian • Seattle Public Library Magnolia Branch • Seattle, WA 98199
Goldner Matthew R • Head Librarian • Tifton-Tift County Public Library • Tifton, GA 31794 • LITA PLA
Goldschmidt Eva M. • Assistant Librarian • French Institute-Alliance Francaise Library • New York, NY 10022
Goldschmidt Helen B. • Student • University of South Florida School of Library & Information Science • Tampa, FL 33620
Goldsmith A. A. Jr. Mr. • Clarksville, TN 37040-3837 • ACRL *Life*
Goldsmith David H. • Trustee • Prince George's County Memorial Library System • Hyattsville, MD 20782-2098 • ALTA
Goldsmith Jacklin • Lincoln, NE 68506
Goldsmith Joan M. • Santa Monica, CA 90403
Goldstein Bonnie Sterling • Reference Librarian • Rutgers University Libraries Livingston College Kilmer Area Library • Piscataway, NJ 08854
Goldstein Carole L. • Kew Gardens, NY 11415 • SRRT
Goldstein Diane M. • Circulation Librarian • Morris County Free Library • Whippany, NJ 07981 • PLA
Goldstein Doris E. • Pembroke Pines, FL 33026
Goldstein Doris R. • Palm Springs, CA 92264
Goldstein E. L. • Miami Beach, FL 33141 • Continuing
Goldstein Elliot • Publisher • Sirs, Incorporated • Boca Raton, FL 33427 • PLA IFRT
Goldstein Hilary A. • Young Adult Librarian • Shaker Heights Public Library Bertram Woods Branch • Shaker Hts., OH 44122 • YALSA IFRT
Goldstein Melvin S. • New York, NY 10021
Goldstein Michael H. • Student • University of Maryland College of Library and Information Services • College Park, MD 20742-4345
Goldstein Milton • Trustee • Hennepin County Library • Minnetonka, MN 55343 • ALTA
Goldstein Peter • Librarian • Harwich High School • Harwich, MA 02645 • AASL YALSA
Goldstein Rosalyn M. • Head of Cataloging & Serials • Widener University Wolfgram Library • Chester, PA 19013 • ACRL ALCTS LITA
Goldstein S. James • Architect & Engr Managing Partner • James Goldstein & Partners • Millburn, NJ 07041 • LAMA
Goldstein Sandra E. • University of California Los Angeles Graduate School of Library & Information Science • Los Angeles, CA 90024 • RASD LRRT NMRT
Goldwater Glenda • San Francisco Public Library West Portal Branch • San Francisco, CA 94127 • VRT
Gole Ralph • Student • University of Wisconsin-Milwaukee School of Library & Information Science • Milwaukee, WI 53201
Golembeske Beth • Librarian • Brownell Library • Little Compton, RI 02837
Golembeski Carol • Librarian • Waiakeawaena School • Hilo, HI 96720
Golenko Jane A. • Librarian • Pasadena High School • Pasadena, TX 77506 • AASL
Goley Elaine P. • Children's Librarian • Houston Public Library Collier Branch • Houston, TX 77092 • ALSC EMIERT
Golian L. M. • Boca Raton, FL 33428 • RASD NMRT
Golichowski Mary • Librarian • Park-Tudor School Library • Indianapolis, IN 46240 • AASL
Golinski-Foisy Antonia • Children's Librarian • Hubbard Memorial Library • Ludlow, MA 01056
Golla Katherine • Librarian • Indian Hills High School • Oakland, NJ 07436 • AASL
Golladay Carolyn S. • Media Technology Dept. • Teacher Resource Center • Newport News, VA 23601 • AASL
Gollop Claudia J. • Doctoral Student • University of Pittsburgh School of Library and Information Science • Pittsburgh, PA 15260
Golob Miriam R. • Director of Information Serv. • Whitehall Laboratories • New York, NY 10017
Golobic Gwen E. • Chicago, IL 60614
Golodetz Virginia • Burlington, VT 05401 • ALSC ALTA YALSA
Golomb Katherine A. • Director of Public Services • Ferguson Library • Stamford, CT 06902
Golovin Naomi E Title • San Jose, CA 95123
Golrick Michael A. • Scy/Treas • Government Documents Round Table • Enfield, CT 06082 • PLA RASD
Goltz Evelyn • Trustee • Oak Lawn Public Library • Oak Lawn, IL 60453 • ALTA
Golub Andrew J. • Director • University of New England Jack S. Ketchum Library • Biddeford, ME 04005 • ACRL LAMA
Gomba Vivian T. • Media Spec • Maryland City Elementary • Laurel, MD 20724 • AASL
Gomes Ginger R. • Librarian • Metairie Park Country Day Lower School • Metairie, LA 70005 • AASL
Gomes Maria Alexandria W. • McLean, VA 22101 • ALSC
Gomes Scarrain D. • La Jolla, CA 92037
Gomez Cheryl J. • Reference Librarian • University of California McHenry Library • Santa Cruz, CA 95064 • ACRL EMIERT
Gomez Joni L. • College Station, TX 77842 • NMRT
Gomez Lillian • Student • Queens College Graduate School of Library & Information Studies • Flushing, NY 11367 • AASL
Gomez Margaret • Trustee • East Chicago Public Library • E. Chicago, IN 46312 • PLA
Gomez Maria Eugenia • Librarian • European Southern Observatory • Santiago 19, Chile • ALCTS LITA
Gomez Martin J. • Director • Oakland Public Library • Oakland, CA 94612 • ALSC LAMA PLA EMIERT
Gomez Michael J. • A Wegener Institute Fur Polar Meeresforschung Bibliothek • 2850 Bremerhaven, Germany • LITA
Gomez Rebecca J. • Interlib Loan/ Ref Ln • Duke University William R. Perkins Library • Durham, NC 27706 • RASD
Gomez Sherry Kay • Librarian III • Kern County Library System • Bakersfield, CA 93301
Gomonda Goodson S. • Student • University of Pittsburgh School of Library and Information Science • Pittsburgh, PA 15260 • SRRT
Gonce Nancy H. • Associate Director, Pub Services • Towson State University • Towson, MD 21204 • LITA
Gonderinger Theresa J. • Assistant Librarian • Burges High School • El Paso, TX 79925 • AASL
Goniwiecha Mark C. • Assistant Professor • University of Guam • Mangilao, GU 96923 • AASL PLA RASD AFLRT EMIERT IFRT NMRT SRRT
Gonnerman Kristyn • Student • San Jose State University Division of Library & Information Science • San Jose, CA 95192-0029
Gonsalves Alfred A. • Assistant Director • Occidental College Library • Los Angeles, CA 90041 • ACRL EMIERT
Gonsenhauser Rachel • Student • State University of New York (SUNY) School of Information & Library Studies • Buffalo, NY 14260
Gonser Martin H.F. • Student • Saint John's University Division of Library & Information Science • Jamaica, NY 11439 • AASL
Gonsoulin Neva C. • Student • San Jose State University Division of Library & Information Science • San Jose, CA 95192-0029 • PLA SRRT
Gontarek Mary • Reference & AV Librarian • Owatonna Public Library • Owatonna, MN 55060
Gonzales Linda B. • Wauwatosa, WI 53222-3327 • ALCTS ASCLA RASD
Gonzales Lydia A. • Reference Librarian • Woodbury University Library • Burbank, CA 91510-7846
Gonzales Rosalie L. • School Librarian • Cornell School • Albany, CA 94706 • AASL
Gonzalez-Ruiz Elsa E. • School Librarian • Cupeyville School • Rio Piedras, PR 00928 • AASL
Gonzalez Alma • Acquisitions Librarian • Edinburg Public Library • Edinburg, TX 78539-4596 • PLA
Gonzalez Daniel • Cayey, PR 00633
Gonzalez Elisa R. • Librarian • Los Angeles Public Library • Los Angeles, CA 90071 • Life
Gonzalez Elizabeth M. • Woodbury, MN 55125
Gonzalez Estella V. • Saint Raphael's School • El Paso, TX 79925 • AASL
Gonzalez Frank • Mesa Community College Library • Mesa, AZ 85202
Gonzalez Irma G. • Administrator • Weslaco Independent School District • Weslaco, TX 78596 • AASL
Gonzalez Linda M. • Bethel Park, PA 15102 • IFRT LHRT SRRT
Gonzalez Lucia M. • Student • Miami-Dade Public Library System West Dade Regional Library • Miami, FL 33165 • ALSC EMIERT
Gonzalez Margarita • Librarian • University of Puerto Rico Medical Sciences Campus • San Juan, PR 00936
Gonzalez Mario M. • The New York Public Library • New York, NY 10016 • PLA RASD EMIERT SRRT
Goo Beryl Ms. • Children's Librarian • Aiea Public Library • Aiea, HI 96782
Gooch Donna R. • Student • Texas Woman's University School of Library & Information Studies • Denton, TX 76204 • SRRT
Gooch William D. • Director & Librarian • Texas State Library • Austin, TX 78711 • ASCLA
Goochey Susan • Media Specialist • Burwell Elementary School • Burwell, NE 68823
Good Dale L. • Editor • Compton's Encyclopedia • Chicago, IL 60604
Good Donna D. • AV Director, Librarian • Moses Brown Upper Middle Schools • Providence, RI 02906 • AASL YALSA
Good Linda A. • Librarian, Public Services • Iowa Central Community College Fort Dodge Center Library • Fort Dodge, IA 50501 • ACRL RASD
Good Noel C. • Support Services Manager • River Bluffs Regional Library Belt Library • Saint Joseph, MO 64506 • ALCTS LITA
Goodale Janine • Harbor City, CA 90710 • ALSC PLA
Goodchild Eleanor D. • Woodland Hills, CA 91364 • ACRL
Goode Clara J • Director • East Islip Public Library • East Islip, NY 11730-2896 • PLA
Goode Faye L. • Head Librarian • Covington High School • Covington, LA 70433 • AASL
Goode M Harriet • Jekyll Island, GA 31520 • ALCTS PLA *Life*
Goodell Barbara • Library Director • Wharton County Library • Wharton, TX 77488
Goodell John S. Dr. • Lecturer, Sch of Inf Systems • Queensland University of Technology • Brisbane, QLD 4001, Australia • ACRL ALCTS LITA *Life*
Gooden Susan W. • Librarian • Concord High School • Wilmington, DE 19810 • AASL
Goodenough Nancy J. • Santa Rosa, CA 95401 • Continuing
Goodenough Ruth • El Paso, TX 79930 • Continuing
Goodfellow Jacklyn • Librarian • Mountain El Sch Library • Los Alamos, NM 87544 • AASL
Goodfellow William D. • Head Reference Services • Oak Lawn Public Library • Oak Lawn, IL 60453 • RASD
Goodgion Laurel F. • Director • Portland Public Library • Portland, CT 06480 • ALSC PLA RASD
Goodhartz Gerald • Librarian • Kaye Scholer Fierman Hays Handler Law Library • New York, NY 10022 • ACRL ALCTS LAMA LITA RASD FLRT GODORT LIRT LRRT SORT
Goodier Darlene • Middleburg Elementary School • Middleburg, FL 32043
Goodin-Wellever Debra K. • Student • University of Washington Graduate School of Library and Information Science • Seattle, WA 98195 • LITA
Goodin John S. • Head, Technical Services • Indiana University Southeast Library Southeastern Campus Library • New Albany, IN 47150-6405 • ACRL
Goodin M. Elspeth Dr. • Library Director • Kittatinny Regional High School • Newton, NJ 07860 • AASL LAMA
Gooding V. Kathleen • Library Media Specialist • Houlton Elementary School • Houlton, ME 04730 • AASL
Goodkind Joan C. • Associate Head Librarian • Simon's Rock of Bard College Library • Great Barrington, MA 01230
Goodknight Sally • Taos, NM 87571 • IFRT
Goodlett Doris R. • Area Manager • Prince George's County Memorial Library System New Carrollton Branch Library • New Carrollton, MD 20784 • LAMA PLA
Goodman Andrea I. • Briarwood, NY 11435 • RASD
Goodman Barbara • Reference Librarian • Wilmette Public Library • Wilmette, IL 60091
Goodman Dottie D. • English Teacher/Dept. Chair • Alamo Heights Junior School • San Antonio, TX 78209
Goodman Elaine • Adult Reference Librarian • Freeport Memorial Library • Freeport, NY 11520
Goodman Elaine Mason • New Mexico State Library • Santa Fe, NM 87503
Goodman Gwynette • Circulation Librarian • Jefferson Parish Library • Metairie, LA 70010
Goodman Helen C. • El Paso, TX 79912 • IFRT
Goodman Joanne • Children's Librarian • Boston Public Library Fields Corner Branch • Dorchester, MA 02122 • SRRT
Goodman Laura S. • Brooklyn, NY 11234 • SORT
Goodman Linda E. • President • The Bilingual Publications Company • New York, NY 10012 • PLA EMIERT
Goodman Marcia M. • History of Science Librarian • University of Oklahoma History of Science Collection • Norman, OK 73019 • ACRL
Goodman Ora K. • Portland, OR 97210 • Continuing

Goodman Paulette M. • Library Director • Kennedy Junior High School • Lisle, IL 60532 • AASL YALSA

Goodman Rhonna A. • Assoc. Libn. for Development • New York Academy of Medicine Library • New York, NY 10029 • ASCLA LAMA YALSA

Goodman Roslyn • Bering Strait School District • Unalakleet, AK 99684 • AASL

Goodman Susan G. • Circ In/Earth Sciences Res Ln • Rutgers University Libraries Library of Science & Medicine • Piscataway, NJ 08855-1029 • ACRL MAGERT

Goodram E. Robin • La Mesa, CA 91942 • AASL

Goodram Richard J. • Associate University Librarian • San Diego State University Library • San Diego, CA 92182-0511

Goodrich Carolyn B. • Lower School Librarian • The Spence School • New York, NY 10128 • ALSC

Goodrich Diane Deaver • Librarian • Stone Robinson Elementary School • Charlottesvle, VA 22901 • AASL

Goodrich Jeanne D. • Deputy Director • Multnomah County Library Administrative Offices • Portland, OR 97212 • LAMA PLA

Goodrich Judith A. • Director • Logan County District Library • Bellefontaine, OH 43311 • PLA

Goodrich Margaret • F.H. Douglas Memorial Library of Native Arts • Denver, CO 80204 • LITA

Goodrich Margaret K. • Student • University of Michigan School of Information and Library Studies • Ann Arbor, MI 48109-1092 • ACRL PLA

Goodrich Mary P. • Greenwich, CT 06830-6589 • Continuing

Goodrich William A. • Director • Willard Public Library • Evansville, IN 47710

Goodroe Sally Bates • Children's Librarian • Houston Public Library • Houston, TX 77002 • ALSC

Goodrum Abby A. • Librarian • Cable News Network (CNN) • Atlanta, GA 30348 • SRRT

Goodsell Joan W. • Asst. Mgr. Creative Library • J Walter Thompson Co • New York, NY 10801 • LAMA LITA   *Life*

Goodson Carol • West Georgia College Irvine Sullivan Ingram Library • Carrollton, GA 30118 • ACRL LITA RASD

Goodson Jennifer C. • Reference Librarian • University of Oklahoma Robert M Bird Health Sciences Library • Oklahoma City, OK 73190

Goodson Luanne M. • Student • University of North Texas School of Library & Information Sciences • Denton, TX 76203

Goodson Martha Glynn • Staff Development Coordinator • DeKalb County Public Library • Decatur, GA 30030

Goodwater Leanna K. • Coor. of Collection Development • Santa Clara University Michel Orradre Library • Santa Clara, CA 95053 • ACRL

Goodwin Anne • Trustee • Laramie County Library System • Cheyenne, WY 82001-2799 • ALTA

Goodwin Bryan D. • Reference Librarian • Mount Holyoke College Williston Memorial Library • South Hadley, MA 01075-1493

Goodwin Carol F. • Director • Macomb County Library • Mount Clemens, MI 48044 • LAMA LITA PLA

Goodwin Claire C. • Student • Simmons College Graduate School of Library & Information Science • Boston, MA 02115

Goodwin Gail E. • Trustee • Maywood Public Library • Maywood, IL 60153 • ALTA

Goodwin Lynn M • School Media Specialist • Warrenville Elementary School • Warrenville, SC 29851 • AASL

Goodwin Marion L. • Moultonboro, NH 03254 • ALSC *Life*

Goodwin Peggy • Adult Librarian • Nicholson Memorial Library Walnut Creek Branch • Garland, TX 75042-7118 • RASD

Goodwin Timothy C. • Warren, OH 44483

Goodwin Vania M. • Head of Cataloging Department • Indiana University-Purdue University at Indianapolis Library (IUPUI) • Indianapolis, IN 46202 • ALCTS IRRT

Goodwyn Betty Ruth • Librarian • Mountain Brook High School • Mt. Brook, AL 35223 • AASL

Goodyear Judith • Librarian • Carroll Community College • Westminster, MD 21157 • ACRL RASD

Goodyear Mary L. • Asst Dir Clln Interpretation • Texas A & M University Sterling C. Evans Library • College Station, TX 77843-5000 • ACRL RASD LRRT SRRT

Goodykoontz Brian • Catalog Librarian • University Microfilms International • Ann Arbor, MI 48106-1346 • ALCTS IFRT

Goolabsingh David B. • Miami, FL 33157

Goold Judy L. • Associate Librarian • Anderson-Foothill Library • Salt Lake City, UT 84108

Goold Larry B. • Media Coordinator • Pocatello School District # 25 • Pocatello, ID 83201 • AASL

Goold Martha L. • Kent, OH 44240

Goostree Jane R. • Columbus State Community College Educational Resources Center • Columbus, OH 43215

Gootee Nancy Norcross • Music Librarian • Indianapolis Marion County Public Library • Indianapolis, IN 46206 • PLA

Gopel Maria G. • Human Resources Librarian • Princeton University • Princeton, NJ 08544-2098 • LAMA

Goral Barbara J. • Director • Colorado Talking Books • Denver, CO 80226 • ASCLA

Goral Miki • Reference Librarian • University of California-Los Angeles (UCLA) • Los Angeles, CA 90024-1450

Gorby Jerry W. • National Sales Manager • Nemschoff Chairs, Inc. • Sheboygan, WI 53081 • LAMA

Gorchels Clarence C. • Librarian • Paul Jensen Arctic Museum Research Library • Monmouth, OR 97361 • ACRL RASD   *Life*

Gordon-Kelter Janice • Houston, TX 77006

Gordon-Lewis Wendy R. • Laguna Niguel, CA 92677-5725 • ACRL

Gordon Anita • Freeport Memorial Library • Freeport, NY 11520

Gordon Ann R. • Detroit Public Library Downtown Branch • Detroit, MI 48226-2284

Gordon Anne M. • Database Management Librarian • Marquette University Memorial Library • Milwaukee, WI 53233 • ALCTS NMRT

Gordon Barbara P. • Catalog Librarian • Charlotte-Mecklenburg Schools • Charlotte, NC 28205 • ALCTS

Gordon Belle • Cincinnati, OH 45236 • Continuing

Gordon Carol D. • Documents Librarian • Milwaukee County Federated Library System • Milwaukee, WI 53233 • AASL GODORT

Gordon Catherine C. • El Cerrito, CA 94530

Gordon Dwain • Acquisitions Librarian • Central Arkansas Library System • Little Rock, AR 72201-4698 • ALCTS PLA RASD EMIERT IFRT

Gordon Elaine • CBI • H. W. Wilson Company • Bronx, NY 10452 • ALCTS

Gordon Elaine H. • Instruction Librarian • DePaul University Libraries • Chicago, IL 60614 • ACRL LIRT

Gordon Elizabeth B. • Library Director • Central Islip Public Library • Central Islip, NY 11722

Gordon Fannie R. • Milwaukee, WI 53216 • PLA RASD   *Life*

Gordon Gerald D. • Coordinator of Cataloging Servs • Radford University John P. McConnell Library • Radford, VA 24142 • ALCTS

Gordon Henry P. • Library Media Specialist • Herman Leimbach Elementary School • Sacramento, CA 95823 • AASL

Gordon Kathleen J. • Librarian • Anchorage Municipal Libraries Z. J. Loussac Library • Anchorage, AK 99503 • LITA

Gordon Kathryn B. • Library Media Specialist • Buffalo Public School (PS 57) • Buffalo, NY 14216

Gordon Lee D. • Eldorado High School • La Vegas, NV 89110 • AASL YALSA

Gordon Lewis A. • Borden Public Library District • Elgin, IL 60120 • ALTA LAMA LITA

Gordon Lilias S. • Las Vegas, NV 89104 • AASL

Gordon Linda L. • Librarian II • Atlanta-Fulton Public Library Northside Branch • Atlanta, GA 30327 • ALSC PLA

Gordon Lois E. • Reference Librarian • McConnell Air Force Base Library • McConnell AFB, KS 67221-5000

Gordon Lucille • New York, NY 10023 • ACRL RASD

Gordon Lynn S. • Milwaukee, WI 53211 • ALCTS IFRT NMRT

Gordon Maggie • Assistant to the University Ln. • University of California-Santa Cruz Library • Santa Cruz, CA 95064 • ACRL LAMA RASD LIRT

Gordon Margaret H. • Student • Kutztown University Library Science Department • Kutztown, PA 19530 • AASL

Gordon Marilyn C. • Librarian • Memphis University School Hyde Library • Memphis, TN 38119-5399

Gordon Mark • New York, NY 10032 • AASL LITA IFRT SRRT

Gordon Martha K. • Children's Services Supervisor • South Salem Library • South Salem, NY 10590 • ALSC

Gordon Martin • Acquisitions Librarian • Franklin and Marshall College • Lancaster, PA 17604

Gordon Muriel C. • Camden County Vocational / Technical Schools • Pennsauken, NJ 08109 • AASL

Gordon Nancy • Hunter School • Raleigh, NC 27601 • AASL ILERT

Gordon Patricia H. • Jackson County Library System • Medford, OR 97501 • YALSA

Gordon Ruth I. • Cloverdale, CA 95425-3115 • ALSC IFRT ILERT

Gordon Shirley S. • District Elementary Library Coor • Unified School District #389 • Eureka, KS 67045 • ALSC

Gordon Stacey L. • Presbyterian Church (USA) Synod of Alaska-Northwest • Seattle, WA 98109 • SRRT

Gordon Stacy • Daily News of Los Angeles • Woodland Hills, CA 91367

Gordon William R. • Director • Prince George's County Memorial Library System • Hyattsville, MD 20782-2098 • LAMA PLA

Gore Cynthia • Media Specialist • Stephen Decatur High School • Berlin, MD 21811 • AASL IFRT

Gore Herbert L. • Acquisitions Librarian • Pepperdine University Payson Library • Malibu, CA 90263 • ACRL ALCTS

Gore Mary W. • Student • Catholic University of America School of Library and Information Science • Washington, DC 20064 • AASL ALSC

Gore Sharon W. • Student • North Carolina Central University • Durham, NC 27707 • ACRL

Gore Susan K. • Interlibrary Loan Librarian • Western Kentucky University Helm-Cravens Library • Bowling Green, KY 42101 • ACRL RASD

Goree Pat • Springfield, MO 65807

Gorelangton Tim • Circulation Supervisor • Washoe County Library • Reno, NV 89505 • PLA

Gorena Elma E. • Edinburg, TX 78539

Gorgas Alice M. • Director • Riverview Public Library • Riverview, MI 48192 • LAMA PLA RASD

Gorham S. Jack • Student • Indiana University School of Library and Information Science • Bloomington, IN 47405

Gorman Audrey J. • Consultant • New Jersey State Library Department of Education • Trenton, NJ 08625-0520 • ALSC ASCLA YALSA GODORT

Gorman Helen Craig • Oxford, OH 45056

Gorman Janet L. • Director • Ralston Public Library • Ralston, NE 68127

Gorman Joanne E. • Portsmouth, RI 02871

Gorman Lorraine Dent • Arlington Heights Memorial Library • Arlington Heights, IL 60004-5966 • ALCTS

Gorman Maureen A. • Reference Librarian • Trenton State College Roscoe L. West Library • Trenton, NJ 08650-4700 • ACRL

Gorman Michael J. • Dean of Library Services • California State University,Fresno Henry Madden Library • Fresno, CA 93740-0034 • ACRL ALCTS LITA

Gormley Mark M. • Cleveland Heights, OH 44106 • ACRL ALCTS   *Life*

Gormley Maureen • Plymouth, MN 55441 • PLA

Gornish Stanley E. • Director of Development • Queens Borough Public Library • Jamaica, NY 11432 • LAMA

Gors Carina A. • San Antonio, TX 78213

Gorsegner Betty D. • Health Science Librarian • Saint Vincent Hospital • Green Bay, WI 54307 • YALSA

Gorski Stanley J. • Collection Librarian • Philadelphia College of Textiles & Science Senator John Pastore Library • Philadelphia, PA 19144 • ACRL LITA

Gorsky Martha J. • Media Specialist • Handke School Independent School District #728 • Elk River, MN 55330 • AASL

Gorsuch Christopher J. • Hd, Serials/Music Cataloging • Florida State University Robert M. Strozier Library • Tallahassee, FL 32306-2047 • ALCTS

Gorton Barbara A. • Periodicals Inter-L Loan Ln. • Hillsdale College Mossey Learning Resources Center • Hillsdale, MI 49242

Gorwitz Ann R. • Yorktown, VA 23693 • FLRT

Gosda David L. • New York State Library State Education Department • Albany, NY 12230 • ASCLA LITA

Gosda Patricia J. • Library Media Specialist • Niskayuna Middle School • Schenectady, NY 12309 • AASL

Gosdeck David M. • Librarian • Northwestern College • Watertown, WI 53094 • ACRL

Gosden George • Syosset, NY 11791

Gosebrink Jean E Meeh • Saint Louis Public Library • St. Louis, MO 63103-2389 • ACRL

Gosik Pamela • Librarian • Royal Oak Public Library • Royal Oak, MI 48068 • PLA RASD YALSA   *Life*

Gosling Marilyn A. • Librarian • Glen Oaks Community College • Centreville, MI 49032

Gosling Tara E. • Toledo-Lucas County Public Library Holland Branch Library • Holland, OH 43528

Gosling William A. • Asst. Director, Tech. Servs. • University of Michigan Libraries • Ann Arbor, MI 48109-1205 • ACRL ALCTS LAMA

Gosnell Charles F. • Professor & Research Consultant • New York University • New York, NY 10036 • ACRL ALCTS LAMA RASD   *Life*

Goss Anne S. • Dir., Health Sciences Lib. • Ohio University Libraries • Athens, OH 45701-2978

Goss Jeanne • Standard Rate nad Data Service • Wilmette, IL 60091 • RASD

Goss Marsha • Director • Villa De Matel Library • Houston, TX 77023

Goss Susan J. • Assistant Cataloging Librarian • Touro College Law School Library • Huntington, NY 11743

Gossage Wayne • Library Director • Gossage Regan Associates Inc. • New York, NY 10036 • ACRL ALCTS ALTA LAMA PLA RASD

Gosselin Donna • Trustee • Phoenix Public Library • Phoenix, AZ 85004 • ALTA

Gossen Eleanor A. • Social Sciences Bibliographer • State University of New York (SUNY) University Libraries • Albany, NY 12222 • ACRL

Gossman C. Ann • Librarian • El Monte High School • El Monte, CA 91731 • AASL

Gostas George F. • Santa Fe, NM 87501 • ACRL ALCTS *Life*

Goswitz Jody • School Librarian • Kettle Moraine School District • Wells, WI 53183

Gosz Kathleen M. • Director • Waukesha County Federated Library Systems • Waukesha, WI 53186 • PLA

Gothberg Helen M. • Associate Professor • University of Arizona Graduate Library School • Tucson, AZ 85721 • LAMA RASD

Gothe Jerry • Collection Development Officer • California State University,Fresno Henry Madden Library • Fresno, CA 93740-0034 • ACRL

Gothe Sandra L. • Associate Dean • California State University,Fresno Henry Madden Library • Fresno, CA 93740-0034 • ALCTS

Gothia Blanche OP Sr. • Media Coordinator • Saint Agnes Academy Library Learning Resource Center • Houston, TX 77036 • AASL LITA

Gotrik Glenn J. • Hinna, 4030, Norway

Gottardi M. Angela • Reference/Serials Librarian • Franklin Pierce College Library • Rindge, NH 03461-0060 • ACRL

Gottbrath Anne F. • Wakarusa Public Library • Wakarusa, IN 46573

Gottfried Harriet • Branch Librarian • New York Public Library Hudson Park Branch • New York, NY 10014 • PLA RASD SRRT

Gottfried Jane M. • Branch Librarian • Free Library of Philadelphia Lawncrest Branch • Philadelphia, PA 19111 • PLA

Gotti Margaret L. • Director • El Centro Public Library • El Centro, CA 92243-2973 • ALSC

Gottlich Gretchen L. • Newport News, VA 23606-1414 • LAMA

Gottlieb Delia • Media Consultant • Nassau Library System • Uniondale, NY 11553 • VRT

Gottlieb Harry F. • Silver Spring, MD 20902

Gottlieb Janice • Tamarac, FL 33321

Gottsch Cindy L. • Northwestern Oklahoma State University J. W. Martin Library • Alva, OK 73717

Gottschalk Tania H. • Reference & Extension Libn • University of Idaho Library • Moscow, ID 83843 • ACRL

Gottschall Faye • Student • State University of New York at Albany School of Information Science & Policy • Albany, NY 12222 • ALSC

Gotwals Joan I. • Vice Provost & Director of Libs. • Emory University Candler Library • Atlanta, GA 30322 • ACRL LAMA LITA RASD

Goudelock Carol V. • Inglewood, CA 90307-0722 • LITA ILERT

Goudie Allen R. • Librarian • United States Army 10th Mountain Division (LI) & Fort Drum • Fort Drum, NY 13602

Goudie Holly A. • Troy, MI 48083

Goudket Laura • Assistant Director • Freeport Memorial Library • Freeport, NY 11520 • PLA

Gough Cal • Ref Librarian/Sci Bk Selector • Atlanta-Fulton Public Library • Atlanta, GA 30303 • RASD SRRT

Gough Madge M. • Librarian • Saint Gregory School • San Mateo, CA 94403 • AASL NMRT

Gougnin Catherine A. • Student • Millersville University of Pennsylvania • Millersville, PA 17551-0302 • AASL

Gouke Mary • Referene Librarian • Ohio State University Libraries • Columbus, OH 43210-1286 • ACRL LIRT

Gouker David R. • Branch Svs. Supervising Libn. • Stockton-San Joaquin County Public Library • Stockton, CA 95202 • PLA RASD

Gould Allison L. • Oberlin College Library • Oberlin, OH 44074 • ACRL LAMA RASD CLENE GODORT SORT

Gould Douglas A. • Systems Librarian • Naval Postgraduate School Dudley Knox Library • Monterey, CA 93943-5002

Gould Henry H. • Providence, RI 02906

Gould Jacqueline E. • Clearview Regional Senior High School • Mullica Hill, NJ 08062 • AASL

Gould Judy • Traverse City, MI 49684 • AASL

Gould Kris J. • Childrens Librarian • Indianapolis Marion County Public Library • Indianapolis, IN 46206

Gould Laurel M. • General Mgr-Libs & Info Res • Public Service Electric & Gas Company Library • Newark, NJ 07101 • ALCTS LITA

Gould Linda J. • Associate Director,Lib Clln • University of Washington • Seattle, WA 98195 • ACRL ALCTS

Gould Martha B. • Director • Washoe County Library • Reno, NV 89505

Gould Terry E. • Student • Emporia State University Emporia in the Rockies • Denver, CO 80204

Goulden Teresa M. • Lexington, KY 40502 • PLA

Goulding Mary A. • Director,SLS Reference Services • Suburban Library System • Oak Lawn, IL 60453 • PLA RASD

Gourlay Una M. • Rice University Fondren Library • Houston, TX 77251-1892 • ACRL RASD

Gouwens Jodi • Fairbanks, AK 99708-4675 • LITA GODORT MAGERT

Gover Harvey R. • Library Director • Washington State University Tri-Cities • Richland, WA 99352 • ACRL LAMA RASD LIRT NMRT

Goverman Gloria • Reference & Young Adult • Field Library of Peekskill • Peekskill, NY 10566-2138

Govern James J. • Director • Stanly County Public Library • Albemarle, NC 28001 • LAMA PLA

Governs Molly K. • Kaneohe Elementary School • Kaneohe, HI 96744 • AASL

Gowan Carolyn • School Librarian • Sherburne Public Library • Sherburne, NY 13460 • ALSC PLA

Gowan Samuel C. • Associate Director • University of Florida Libraries • Gainesville, FL 32611-2047 • ACRL ALCTS LAMA

Gowdy Laura E. • Special Collections Librarian • Illinois State University • Normal, IL 61761 • ACRL RASD

Gower Virginia • Greenville, SC 29601

Gowings Dana I. • Cataloger • Salem-Teikyo University Benedum Library • Salem, WV 26426 • ALCTS LITA GODORT

Gowler Steve • Wofford College Sandor Teszler Library • Spartanburg, SC 29303-3663 • ACRL

Goyette Betty • Library Media Consultant • State Department of Education • Hartford, CT 06040 • AASL

Goykin Robert • Reference Librarian • Smithtown Library • Smithtown, NY 11787

Goyne Carol Lea • Head-Technical Services • San Diego State University Library • San Diego, CA 92119-2120

Gozzi Cynthia I. • Director of Technical Services • Stanford University • Stanford, CA 94305-6011 • ACRL ALCTS LAMA

Grabarek Daryl P. • Librarian • Brooklyn Public Library • Brooklyn, NY 11238

Grabbe Kaye A. • Librarian/Director • Lake Forest Library • Lake Forest, IL 60045

Grabe Lauralee F. • Head, Tech. Services Dept. • Creighton University Reinert-Alumni Memorial Library • Omaha, NE 68178 • ACRL ALCTS

Grabenstatter Christine N. • Manager,Cataloging Servs Sect • Online Computer Library Center (OCLC) • Dublin, OH 43017-3395 • ALCTS LITA

Grabenstein Joseph L. Bro. • Beltsville, MD 20705

Graber Reta K. • Collection Development Coor. • Hutchinson Public Library • Hutchinson, KS 67501

Grabill Cynthia M. • Elementary Librarian • Wellston School District • Saint Louis, MO 63121 • ALSC PLA

Grabner Linda L. • Teacher • Abney Elementary School • Slidell, LA 70445 • AASL

Grabowski Barbara V. • Lyons Township High School • LaGrange, IL 60525 • AASL

Grace Kathleen A. • Technical Service Librarian • Oshkosh Public Library • Oshkosh, WI 54901 • ALCTS PLA

Grace Loranne J. C. • Technical Service Director • Southern Missionary College McKee Library • Collegedale, TN 37315 • ALCTS

Grace Michael S J Bro • Bibliographic Librarian • Loyola University E.M. Cudahy Memorial Library • Chicago, IL 60626 • ACRL

Grace Michelle A. • Student • Coralville Public Library • Coralville, IA 52241

Grace Monica • Supervisor of Technical Services • Framingham Public Library • Framingham, MA 01701-8218 • ALCTS LITA

Grace Patrick J. • Government Documents Librarian • Oregon State University William Jasper Kerr Library • Corvallis, OR 97331-4501 • ACRL LAMA RASD GODORT IFRT SRRT

Grace Sara D. • Castleton, VT 05735 • AASL

Grace Theodore A. • Base Librarian • Marine Corps Base Base Library • Camp Lejeune, NC 28542 • AFLRT FLRT

Grace William Mason • Student • Rutgers University School of Communication Information & Library Studies • New Brunswick, NJ 08903 • ACRL LAMA

Gracechild Valerie • Boca Raton, FL 33433

Gracy David B. II • Professor • University of Texas at Austin Graduate School of Library & Information Sciences • Austin, TX 78712-1276 • ACRL ALCTS

Gradilone Thomas J. Msgr. • Trustee • Queens Borough Public Library • Jamaica, NY 11432 • ALTA PLA

Gradone Linda • Audio-Visual Librarian • Newton Free Library • Newton, MA 02159

Gradowski Gail A. • Santa Clara University Michel Orradre Library • Santa Clara, CA 95053 • ACRL RASD LIRT

Grady Agnes M. • Head, Cataloging Dept. • University of Tennessee John C. Hodges Library • Knoxville, TN 37996-1000 • ACRL ALCTS LAMA LITA GODORT

Grady Emma A. Miss • N. Palm Beach, FL 33408 • Continuing

Grady J. Yvonne • Midland, TX 79707 • AASL YALSA

Grady Jenifer L. • Student • University of North Carolina at Chapel Hill School of Information and Library Science • Chapel Hill, NC 27599-3360 • EMIERT

Grady Joni K. • Walhalla High School • Walhalla, SC 29691 • AASL YALSA IFRT

Grady Mamie • Head Librarian • Chicago Public Library-Illinois Regional Library for the Blind & Physically Handicapped • Chicago, IL 60608 • SRRT

Grady Phyllis A. • Librarian • Wayne Elementary School • Wayne, PA 19087 • AASL ALSC IFRT

Grady Rebecca I. • Librarian • East Central College • Union, MO 63084 • RASD

Graedel Laura H. • Student • University of Michigan School of Information and Library Studies • Ann Arbor, MI 48109-1092 • ALSC PLA IFRT NMRT

Graf Ellen M. • Special Project Librarian • Boston Public Library • Boston, MA 02117 • PLA

Graf George R. • Acquisitions Librarian • Trinity College Library • Hartford, CT 06106 • ACRL

Graf Ma. Antonieta Lic. • Director • Universidad Iberoamericana • Mexico D.F., Mexico • ACRL LAMA

Graff Diana • Library Director • Southern Utah University Library • Cedar City, UT 84720 • ACRL

Graff Heidi J. • Children's Librarian • Philadelphia City Institute Library • Philadelphia, PA 19103 • PLA

Graff Joan • Branch Head • Broward County Library Hollywood Branch • Hollywood, FL 33020 • SRRT

Grafstein Ann J. • School Librarian • Catholic Separate School Board • London, ON, N6A 4X5 Canada

Grafton Mona R. • Librarian • Mattoon Public Library • Mattoon, IL 61938 • LAMA

Grafton Nina Suzanne • Student • University of Southern Mississippi School of Library Science • Hattiesburg, MS 39406-5146

Gragg Victor D. Dr. • Trustee • Mid-Continent Public Library • Independence, MO 64050 • ALTA

Graham Aileen • Unified School District-383 • Manhattan, KS 66502 • AASL IFRT

Graham Alexis A. • Librarian III/Branch Manager • Austin Public Library Windsor Village Branch • Austin, TX 78723

Graham Allan B. • Mgr./Technical Serv Marketing • Corporate Library Blackwell North America • Lake Oswego, OR 97035 • ALCTS LITA

Graham Amy W. • Swarthmore College Library • Swarthmore, PA 19081

Graham Anne M. • New Castle Public Library • New Castle, PA 16101 • ALSC

Graham Aubry L. Mrs • Fairfax, VA 22031 • Continuing

Graham Barbara J. • Head, Library Services • H. B. Beal Secondary School • London ON, N6B 1W5 Canada • AASL YALSA

Graham Barbara S. • Assoc Dir for Admin & Programs • Harvard University • Cambridge, MA 02138 • ACRL LAMA

Graham Betty J. • Librarian II • Fairfax County Public Library • Fairfax, VA 22033-1907

Graham Carole S. • Principal • Wilson/Graham Design Group • North Hollywood, CA 91601

Graham Christine M. • Librarian • San Francisco State University J. Paul Leonard Library • San Francisco, CA 94132 • ACRL

Graham Crystal • University of California-San Diego Central University Library • La Jolla, CA 92093-0175 • ACRL ALCTS LITA IFRT

Graham Doris P. • Branch Librarian • Brooklyn Public Library Midwood Branch • Brooklyn, NY 11230 • PLA

Graham Earl C. • Batavia, IL 60510 • ALSC ASCLA *Continuing*

Graham Edward T. • Alice Lloyd College McGaw Library & Learning Center • Pippa Passes, KY 41844 • RASD

Graham Elaine • Puyallup, WA 98374 • ACRL

Graham Flora • Fairbanks, AK 99708 • ALSC

Graham Jack • Sales Representative • Quality Books Inc. • Lake Bluff, IL 60044-2204

Graham Joanne L. • Temple Hills, MD 207748 • RASD

Graham John J. • Trustee • Skokie Public Library • Skokie, IL 60077-3680 • ALTA PLA

Graham Joy W. • Extension Service Librarian • Deschutes County Library • Bend, OR 97701 • LAMA

Graham Kathleen • Trustee • Northlake Public Library District • Melrose Park, IL 60164 • ALTA

Graham Kelly • Librarian • Lakeridge High School • Lake Oswego, OR 97034 • AASL IFRT   *Life*

Graham Kent W. • Young Adult Librarian • Farmington Community Library • Farmington Hills, MI 48334

Graham Lee O. • Librarian • Northeast High School • Oklahoma City, OK 73111 • AASL IFRT

Graham Mae • Baltimore, MD 21207 • AASL ALSC   *Continuing*

Graham Marilyn J. • Director • Webster Public Library • Webster, NY 14580 • LAMA PLA

Graham Marilyn Long • Youth Svs Programming Spec. • Lee County Library System Processing Center • Fort Myers, FL 33912 • ALSC PLA

Graham Mark L. • Saratoga, CA 95070-4925

Graham Marlene • Adult Services • Waukegan Public Library • Waukegan, IL 60085 • RASD

Graham Martha • Trustee • Half Hollow Hills Community Public Library • Dix Hills, NY 11746 • ALTA

Graham Mary Kathleen • Head Librarian • Westchester Public Library • Westchester, IL 60154 • ALSC LAMA PLA RASD

Graham Paul M. • Technical Services/Reference • East Stroudsburg University Kemp Library • East Stroudsburg, PA 18301 • ACRL IFRT

Graham Peter S. • Associate Vice President • Rutgers University Libraries • Piscataway, NJ 08855-1179 • ACRL ALCTS LITA

Graham Robert J. • Director-LRC • West Virginia University Medical Center Library • Charleston, WV 26506

Graham Rosalyn L. • San Luis Obispo City-County Library • San Luis Obispo, CA 93403 • ALSC

Graham Rose • Rice University Fondren Library • Houston, TX 77251-1892

Graham Rumi Y. • Head, Collection Organization • University of Lethbridge Library • Lethbridge AB, T1K 3M4 Canada • ACRL

Graham Wendy L. • Environmental Restoration Mgt. • Yakima Indian Nation Library • Toppenish, WA 98948

Grahame Vicki A. • Cataloger • University of South Florida Library • Tampa, FL 33620-5600

Grainger William K. • Temple City, CA 91780 • Continuing

Gralapp Marcelee • Director • Boulder Public Library • Boulder, CO 80306 • LAMA PLA

Gramann Carol A. • Student • Louisiana State University School of Library & Information Science • Baton Rouge, LA 70803-3290 • ASCLA RASD GODORT

Grambo Marilyn R. • Branch Librarian • Hammond Public Library • Hammond, IN 46320

Gramley Sarah M. • Media Coordinator • Colfax Elementary School • Colfax, NC 27235 • AASL

Gramling Phillip W. • Library Associate • University of Alabama at Birmingham • Birmingham, AL 35294

Grams Carol L. • Smoky Hill High School • Aurora, CO 80015 • AASL

Grams T. C. W. • Tucson, AZ 85712-0652 • Continuing

Granade J Warner • Assistant Librarian • University of Virginia Clemons Library • Charlottesville, VA 22904-0100 • ACRL

Granade Vicki • Flagstaff City-Coconino County Public Library • Flagstaff, AZ 86001 • LITA

Granados Cecilia • Bogota DE, Colombia • RASD

Granberg Margaret D. • Trustee • West Des Moines Public Library • West Des Moines, IA 50265

Grandal Sylvia N • Catalog Librarian • Kanawha County Public Library • Charleston, WV 25301

Grandy-Berquist Patricia • Librarian • Beltzhoover Elementary School • Pittsburgh, PA 15210 • AASL

Grandy Cnythia L. • Big Lake, TX 76932 • LAMA

Granger Diana L. • Personnel Director • Fairfax County Public Library • Fairfax, VA 22033-1909 • LAMA PLA

Granger Dorothy • Head Librarian • Pacific Oaks College • Pasadena, CA 91103 • ACRL SRRT

Granger Karen J. • Lake Crystal, MN 56055 • AASL ALCTS IFRT

Granger Mary S. Miss • Newark, NY 14513 • LAMA PLA   *Continuing*

Granger Pat E. • East Cary Middle School • Cary, NC 27511 • AASL

Granitz Adrienne D. • Circulation Supervisor • Piedmont Virginia Community College • Charlottesvle, VA 22901

Grannan Judith A. • Student • Indiana University • Bloomington, IN 47405 • ACRL

Grannis Mabel V. • Lansing, MI 48912

Granskog Kay A. • Head of Monographic Acquisitions • Michigan State University Libraries • East Lansing, MI 48824-1048 • ALCTS

Grant Alicia D. • Assistant Librarian • University of Houston Libraries • Houston, TX 77204-2091 • LIRT NMRT

Grant Anita H. • Ohio University Vernon R. Alden Library • Athens, OH 45701-2978 • ACRL

Grant Carl • Vice-President • Data Research Associates Inc. • Saint Louis, MO 63132 • ACRL LAMA LITA ERT

Grant Doris E. • Librarian • Marblehead High School Library • Marblehead, MA 01945 • AASL

Grant Elizabeth M. • University of the South Jessie Ball duPont Library • Sewanee, TN 37375-4005

Grant George C. • Director of Library Service • Rollins College Olin Library • Winter Park, FL 32789-4499 • ACRL

Grant Helen B. • Head, Branch Service Dept. • Knox County Public Library System • Knoxville, TN 37902-2505 • PLA

Grant Henry L.S. • Manhasset, NY 11030 • LITA

Grant Isabelle F. Miss • Champaign, IL 61820 • ACRL   *Continuing*

Grant Jo Ann Mrs. • Director • Anderson Community Schools • Anderson, IN 46016 • AASL

Grant Joan • Dir of Collection Management • New York University Elmer Holmes Bobst Library • New York, NY 10012 • ACRL ALCTS

Grant Julienne E. • Student • Rosary College Graduate School of Library & Information Science • River Forest, IL 60305 • EMIERT IRRT SRRT

Grant Lana S. • Norman, OK 73071 • PLA EMIERT

Grant Leslie S. • Media Specialist • Cone Elementary School • Greensboro, NC 27405 • AASL

Grant Lisa M. • Student • University of Illinois Graduate School of Library and Information Science • Urbana, IL 61801

Grant Margaret Mrs • Tampa, FL 33612 • Continuing

Grant Marilyn A. • Reference Librarian • Boston College • Chestnut Hill, MA 02167 • ACRL LAMA LITA RASD GODORT LIRT

Grant Mary A. • Cataloger • University of Wisconsin-Milwaukee Golda Meir Library • Milwaukee, WI 53201 • ACRL ALCTS

Grant Nancy A. • Supv. General Adult Services • Nashua Public Library • Nashua, NH 03060

Grant Robert S. • Director of Sales • Worden Company • Holland, MI 49423 • LAMA

Grant Ruth H. • New London, NH 03257 • ACRL ALCTS   *Continuing*

Grant Sharlane T. • Head, Preservation Department • Arizona State University Libraries • Tempe, AZ 85287-1006 • ACRL ALCTS

Grant Susan M. • Student • Texas Woman's University School of Library & Information Studies • Denton, TX 76204

Grant Thirza E. Miss • Chapel Hill, NC 27514 • Continuing

Grant Wallace C. • DeKalb, IL 60115

Grantano Cheryl K. • Lib. III, Circ. & Systems Supv • South San Francisco Public Library • South San Francisco, CA 94080

Grantham Ann V. • Media Specilaist • Clayton County Board of Education Haynie Elementary School • Morrow, GA 30206 • AASL

Grants Yvette M. • Reference Specialist • Cuyahoga County Public Library Parma Regional • Parma, OH 44129-3199

Grappone Teresa M. • Briarwood, NY 11435 • AASL

Grasela James W. • Librarian • Apponequet Regional High School • East Freetown, MA 02717 • AASL

Grass M Winifred Sr • Saint Joseph's College Library • Brooklyn, NY 11205 • ACRL LAMA

Grassian Esther S. • Reference Instrucion Librarian • University of California-Los Angeles (UCLA) • Los Angeles, CA 90024-1450 • ACRL LIRT

Gratch Bonnie G. • Student • Syracuse University School of Information Studies • Syracuse, NY 13244-4100 • ACRL

Grathwol Mary J. • Sante Fe, NM 87501

Gration Selby U. • Director of Libraries • State University of New York College at Cortland • Cortland, NY 13045 • ACRL

Gratke Paul • Milwaukee, WI 53207 • ASCLA PLA   *Life*

Grattan Robert III • Bibliotheque Americaine A Paris • Paris 75007, France • LITA IRRT

Gratz Robin J. • Library Director • Manchester College • North Manchester, IN 46962

Graubart Marilyn • Business Reference Librarian • University of Missouri-Kansas City Library • Kansas City, MO 64110-2499 • ACRL

Graudin Shirley • Executive Editor • Open Court Publishing Company • Chicago, IL 60605 • ALSC

Grauel Helen J. • Coordinator • Saint Louis Public Schools Office of Library Services • St. Louis, MO 63107 • AASL YALSA

Grauer Sally • Executive Director • Library Binding Institute • Edina, MN 55439 • ALCTS

Graunke Cheryl L. • Library of Congress • Washington, DC 20541 • LITA

Graupner Eunice N. • University of Wisconsin School of Business Library • Madison, WI 53706 • ACRL

Graversen Louise • Tacoma Public Schools • Tacoma, WA 98401

Graves Ben M. • Director • Calloway County Public Library • Murray, KY 42071 • ALSC LAMA PLA

Graves Charjean Laughlin • Clarksdale, MS 38614

Graves David Lucas • Senior Serials Cataloger • Library of Congress • Washington, DC 20541 • ACRL ALCTS

Graves Diane J. • Loyola University • Chicago, IL 60611 • ACRL ALCTS LAMA

Graves Elizabeth A. • Tampa-Hillsborough County Public Library • Tampa, FL 33602

Graves Frances M. • Sacramento, CA 95816

Graves Fred H. • New York, NY 10022 • Continuing

Graves Gail Tait • Head, Reference Department • University of Mississippi John Davis Williams Library • University, MS 38677 • ALCTS

Graves Howard E. Jr • Head Catlgr/Systems Librarian • Hofstra University Axinn Library • Hempstead, NY 11550 • LITA

Graves James T. • Adult Services • Tampa-Hillsborough County Public Library • Tampa, FL 33602 • IFRT

Graves Judith M. • Edina, MN 55439

Graves Kathryn A. • Librarian I, Reference Dept. • University of Kansas Library • Lawrence, KS 66045-2800 • ACRL LHRT

Graves Nell H. • Brookview Elementary School • Jacksonville, FL 32216 • AASL

Graves Sandra S. • Student • Louisiana State University School of Library & Information Science • Baton Rouge, LA 70803-3290

Graves Sheila L. • Sr. Academic Specialist • IBM • Baltimore, MD 21202 • ACRL LITA

Graves Sid F. Jr. • Director • Carnegie Public Library • Clarksdale, MS 38614 • RASD

Gravier Frances M. • Student • University of California McHenry Library • Santa Cruz, CA 95064 • ACRL

Gravois James M. • Auburn University Ralph Brown Draughon Library • Auburn, AL 36849-5606 • ACRL GODORT

Gravois Marie E. • Student • Louisiana State University School of Library & Information Science • Baton Rouge, LA 70803-3290

Grawemeyer Jane • Data Research Associates Inc. • Saint Louis, MO 63132 • ALCTS LITA

Gray Allan • Director • Northwest Library District (NORWELD) • Bowling Green, OH 43402 • ASCLA PLA

Gray Allyson • Director • Lasell College • Newton, MA 02166

Gray Alma Long • Baltimore, MD 21211-2104 • Continuing

Gray Anke V. • Cataloging Division • University of Washington Suzzallo Library • Seattle, WA 98195 • ALCTS LITA MAGERT

Gray Arthur • President • CPE Risk Management • Dolton, IL 60419-2759

Gray B. Allison • Head of Children's Dept. • South Country Library • Bellport, NY 11713 • ALSC

Gray Barbara E. • Library Assistant • Ursuline Academy High School • Wilmington, DE 19806 • AASL

Gray Barbara J. • Detroit, MI 48221 • PLA

Gray Barry J. • Technical Services Librarian • Mercyhurst College Hammermill Library • Erie, PA 16546 • ALCTS

Gray Beth B. • Director • East Hampton Library • East Hampton, NY 11937 • PLA

Gray Betsy Ms. • Evanston, IL 60201 • ALSC

Gray Beverly A. • Head African Section • Library of Congress • Washington, DC 20541

Gray Bonnie M. • Student • University of Rhode Island Graduate School of Library & Information Studies • Kingston, RI 02881-0815 • AASL

Gray Candace R. • Media Specialist • Academy of Liberal Arts & Sciences • Kansas City, MO 64113

Gray Carolyn M. • Assoc Dir Tech & Rdr Serv • Brandeis University Main Library • Waltham, MA 02254-9110 • ACRL LITA

Gray Catherine T. • Division Chief • Brooklyn Public Library • Brooklyn, NY 11238 • PLA YALSA

Gray Cynthia A. • Library Director • Palestine Public Library • Palestine, TX 75801 • PLA

Gray Cynthia L. • McIntosh Middle School • Sarasota, FL 34232

Gray David R. • Davis & Elkins College Library • Elkins, WV 26241 • SRRT

Gray Deborah G. • Pinellas Park, FL 34666 • YALSA IFRT

Gray Doris K. • Plainview, NY 11803

Gray Dorothy A. • Reference Librarian • University of Louisville Ekstrom Library • Louisville, KY 40292 • ACRL

Gray Dorothy L. • Dir of Information Services • National Association of Industrial & Office Pks (NAIOP) Information Center • Arlington, VA 22202 • RASD

Gray Douglass P. • Systems Librarian • Eastern Shore Regional Library • Salisbury, MD 21801

Gray Gabriella S. • Student • University of California-Los Angeles Graduate School of Library & Information Science • Los Angeles, CA 90024-1520

Gray Gayle E. • Student • University of Kentucky College of Library & Information Science • Lexington, KY 40506-0391 • AASL

Gray Geraldine Hall • Loyola-Notre Dame Library, Inc. • Baltimore, MD 21212 • ACRL

Gray Gloria D. • Conference Coordinator • American Library Association • Chicago, IL 60611-2795

Gray Gloria M. • Richardson, TX 75080

Gray Gwendolyn • Librarian • University of Missouri-Columbia Ellis Library • Columbia, MO 65201 • RASD

Gray Isabelle J. Mrs. • Media Specialist • M.A. Milam Elementary School • Hialeah, FL 33012

Gray Judith • Librarian • Nottingham High School Library • Syracuse, NY 13224-1647 • AASL

Gray Julie • Dist/Media Library Tech. Spec. • Temecula Valley Unified School District • Temecula, CA 92591 • AASL

Gray Karen S. • Assistant Executive Director • Great River Library System • Quincy, IL 62301-3997 • LITA

Gray Libby Cooke • Librarian • McClintock Junior High School • Charlotte, NC 28212 • AASL

Gray Liebe • Los Angeles Public Library Lincoln Heights Branch • Los Angeles, CA 90031 • YALSA

Gray Madeline D. • Chapel Hill, NC 27514-2003

Gray Margaret C. • Kanoehe, HI 96744 • Continuing

Gray Margaret S. • Weimar, TX 78962 • YALSA

Gray Marjo Andrews • University of San Diego Copley Library • San Diego, CA 92110 • ACRL LAMA

Gray Marlene R. • Kohler, WI 53044

Gray Mary Ann • Reference Librarian • County College of Morris Masten Learning Resource Center • Randolph, NJ 07869-2086 • ALCTS

Gray Maurine E. • Director • Beaumont Public Library • Beaumont, TX 77704 • ALCTS ALSC LAMA LITA PLA RASD

Gray Nancy A. • Reference Librarian • University of Arkansas at Little Rock Ottenheimer Library • Little Rock, AR 72204 • ACRL RASD

Gray Patricia B. • Senior Librarian • Norfolk Public Library Kirn Memorial Library • Norfolk, VA 23510

Gray Paul W. • Dean of Comp. Svs./Univ Libn • Azusa Pacific University • Azusa, CA 91702

Gray Phyllis A. • Bal Harbour, FL 33154

Gray Raymond L. • Yardley, PA 19067

Gray Robert • Student • State University of New York (SUNY) School of Information & Library Studies • Buffalo, NY 14260

Gray Robert G. • Librarian • White Pine High School • Ely, NV 89301 • AASL

Gray Roberta C. • Library Director • Westbrook College Library • Portland, ME 04103 • ACRL

Gray Suzanne K. • Sharon, MA 02067

Gray Tomysena F. • First Church of God Christian School • Los Angeles, CA 90043 • AASL

Gray Victoria M. • Director,Editorial Operations • Information Access Company • Foster City, CA 94404 • ACRL ALCTS LITA RASD

Gray Wayne D. • Central Library Administrator • Dallas Public Library • Dallas, TX 75201 • PLA

Graybeal Earl E. • Librarian • State Services Organization Library • Washington, DC 20001 • SRRT

Grayson Barbara E. • Graduate Student • University of Washington Graduate School of Library and Information Science • Seattle, WA 98195 • ALCTS

Grayson Dianne B. • University of Southern Indiana • Evansville, IN 47712

Graziani Mary E. • United States Geological Survey • Reston, VA 22092

Grazier Margaret H. • Detroit, MI 48221 • AASL ALSC *Life*

Grazier Robert T. Mr • Detroit, MI 48221 • ACRL ALCTS *Life*

Grazier Todd A. • Bethel Park, PA 15102 • SRRT

Grazioli Margaret • Director • Secaucus Free Public Library • Secaucus, NJ 07094

Grazulis Terese Lilija • Director • Melvindale Public Library • Melvindale, MI 48122 • PLA CLENE IFRT IRRT

Greany Patty C. • Meadowview, VA 24361

Grear Robert M. • Adult Services Librarian • Dayton & Montgomery County Public Library • Dayton, OH 45402-2103 • NMRT SRRT

Greathouse Janet C. • Director • Calera Public Library • Calera, AL 35040

Greathouse Madeleine M. M. • Newcastle NB, E1V 3M5 Canada

Greaves F. Landon Jr. • Library Director • Southeastern Louisiana University Linus A. Sims Memorial Library • Hammond, LA 70402 • ACRL LAMA

Greaves Susan J. • Map Librarian • Cornell University • Ithaca, NY 14853-5301 • MAGERT

Grebey Betty H. • Library Coordinator • Downingtown Area Schools • Downingtown, PA 19335 • AASL ALCTS YALSA ERT *Life*

Grebles Shelley • Reference Coordinator • Scottsdale Public Library • Scottsdale, AZ 85251 • PLA RASD

Greco Gloria T. • Retired Director • College of New Rochelle Gill Library • New Rochelle, NY 10805

Greco Mary E. • Librarian • University of California-Los Angeles (UCLA) • Los Angeles, CA 90024-1450 • ACRL

Greco Steve J. • Trustee • Schiller Park Public Library • Schiller Park, IL 60176-1699 • ALTA

Greeley Joseph M. • Student • University of Tennessee-Knoxville Graduate School of Library & Information Science • Knoxville, TN 37996-4330

Greeley Nancy P. • Rialto Unified School District • Rialto, CA 92376

Green Aida R. • Sevierville, TN 37864

Green Alan A. • Graduate Student • State University of New York (SUNY) School of Information & Library Studies • Buffalo, NY 14260 • ACRL LITA RASD IFRT

Green Andrea L. • Student • University of North Texas School of Library & Information Sciences • Denton, TX 76203

Green Ann • Howard County Library • Columbia, MD 21044 • PLA

Green Anne Carey • Trustee • Akron-Summit County Public Library • Akron, OH 44326-0001 • ALTA

Green Arlene R. • Media Specialist • Hazel Park High School • Hazel Park, MI 48030 • AASL

Green Barbara G. • Providence, RI 02906

Green Becky Spiro • Acquistions & Cataloging • Huntington Library • San Marino, CA 91108

Green Bradley A. • Director • Lane Memorial Library • Hampton, NH 03842

Green Brian P. • Albuquerque, NM 87111

Green Carol C. • Head Librarian • University of Washington Forest Resources Library AQ-15 • Seattle, WA 98195 • ACRL

Green Carol D. • Serials Librarian • University of Southern Mississippi Cook Memorial Library • Hattiesburg, MS 39406-5053 • NMRT

Green Deborah P. • Coordinator of Children's Svs. • Iowa City Public Library • Iowa City, IA 52240 • ALSC

Green Debra L. • Library Director • Fred L. Fisher Library • Belleville, MI 48111

Green Denise D. • Public Services Librarian • Ohio Wesleyan University • Delaware, OH 43015 • ACRL GODORT LIRT

Green Diana H. • Publisher • Parents Choice • Newton, MA 02168

Green Diane M. • Librarian • Saint Joseph's Catholic School • Jacksonville, FL 32258

Green Diane T. • Middle School Librarian • Salem Public Schools • Salem, OR 97302 • AASL

Green Felita S. • Information Services Librarian • Richland County Public Library • Columbia, SC 29201 • NMRT

Green G. David • Head Librarian • Loyola University • Chicago, IL 60611 • ACRL IFRT

Green Gary A. • Head of Technical Services • Kalamazoo Public Library • Kalamazoo, MI 49007-5270

Green Henrietta • Los Angeles, CA 90024 • AASL ALSC

Green Henrietta W. • Medical Library Technician • Beth Israel Hospital • Boston, MA 02215 • NMRT

Green Jacqueline H. • Reference Librarian • Harvard Public Library • Harvard, MA 01451 • ALSC

Green James F. • Student • University of Michigan School of Information and Library Studies • Ann Arbor, MI 48109-1092 • LITA

Green James N. • Curator of Printed Books • Library Company of Philadelphia • Philadelphia, PA 19107 • ACRL

Green Janice • Librarian • Poplar Tree Elementary School • Chantilly, VA 22021 • AASL

Green Janice D. • Tulsa, OK 74114 • AASL

Green Jeanne B. Mrs. • Southern University in New Orleans Leonard S. Washington Library • New Orleans, LA 70126 • GODORT

Green Jeannine Marie • Asst. Special Collections Ln. • University of Alberta Library • Edmonton AB, T6G 2J8 Canada • ACRL

Green Jewell • Librarian • Marine City High School • Marine City, MI 48039 • AASL

Green Joan C. • Library Media Specialist • Webster Elementary School • Syracuse, NY 13208 • AASL

Green Joseph H. • Director • Nassau Library System • Uniondale, NY 11553 • LAMA PLA

Green Judith F. • Windermere, FL 34786 • PLA

Green Judy M. • Coordinator of Admin Services • Louisiana High School • Louisiana, MO 63353 • AASL

Green Julian W. • Dean of Library Services • University of South Carolina at Spartanburg-Library • Spartanburg, SC 29303 • ACRL LAMA

Green Laura E. • Lena, IL 61048

Green Leon C. • Iowa City, IA 52245-5825 • ALCTS LITA

Green Leta • Assistant Librarian • Fort Stockton Public Library • Fort Stockton, TX 79735

Green Louise K. • Assistant Director • Villanova University Falvey Memorial Library • Villanova, PA 19085-1699 • ACRL RASD LIRT

Green Margaret • Director • Limestone College Library • Gaffney, SC 29340-3799

Green Marilynn • Librarian • University of Houston Libraries • Houston, TX 77204-2091 • ACRL

Green Mary Beth • Assistant Professor • Troy State University Library • Troy, AL 36082

Green Marybeth • Margaret Wills Elementary School • Amarillo, TX 79106 • AASL ALCTS

Green Mirian D. • Director of Library • Coahoma Junior College • Clarksdale, MS 38614

Green Morgan K. • Reference Librarian • Solano County Library Vacaville Branch • Vacaville, CA 95688

Green Nancy C. • Texas Woman's University School of Library & Information Studies • Denton, TX 76204 • ALCTS

Green Paula O. • Assistant Collection Development • Seattle Public Library • Seattle, WA 98104-1193 • RASD

Green Phyllis C. • Librarian • Chandler High School Media Center • Chandler, AZ 85234

Green Rachael P. • Serials Librarian • Louisiana State University • Shreveport, LA 71115

Green Roger O. • Student • State University of New York at Albany School of Information Science & Policy • Albany, NY 12222

Green Romandie P. • School Librarian • Robert E. Lee Elementary School Orleans Parish Schools • New Orleans, LA 70118

Green Ruth • Cataloger • Monroe County Public Library • Bloomington, IN 47408

Green Ruth L. • Portland, OR 97206

Green Sharon E. • Children's Librarian • District of Columbia Public Library Anacostia Branch • Washington, DC 20020

Green Stephen W. • Coor., Ref. & Instr. Services • University of Colorado at Denver Auraria Library • Denver, CO 80204 • ACRL LITA

Green Thomas A. • Ohio Wesleyan University • Delaware, OH 43015 • ACRL RASD

Green Tim C. • London, OH 43140 • RASD IFRT ILERT SRRT

Green Vera A. • Senior Staff Librarian • Carnegie Library of Pittsburgh • Pittsburgh, PA 15213-4080 • PLA

Green Virginia • Bell County Public Library • Middlesboro, KY 40965 • PLA

Green Walter H. • Head of Music Library • Southwest Missouri State University Meyer Library • Springfield, MO 65804 • ACRL

Greenawalt Mary • Elgin, IL 60120

Greenawalt Mary K. • Indianapolis-Marion County Public Library Eagle Branch • Indianapolis, IN 46222-1240 • RASD

Greenberg Astaire R. • Massapequa Park, NY 11762 • RASD

Greenberg Barbara • Director • Freehold Public Library • Freehold, NJ 07728 • PLA

Greenberg Donna • Branch Coordinator • Alameda Free Library West End Branch • Alameda, CA 94501 • PLA

Greenberg Emily R. • Director • University of Baltimore Law Library • Baltimore, MD 21201 • ACRL LITA IFRT SRRT

Greenberg Esther S. • Cleveland, OH 44121 • ACRL LITA *Life*

Greenberg Eva M. • Adult Services Librarian • Oberlin Public Library • Oberlin, OH 44074-1626 • PLA RASD LIRT

Greenberg Evelyn • Information Services Libraian • Rutgers University Libraries Archibald Stevens Alexander Library • New Brunswick, NJ 08903 • ACRL LITA RASD

Greenberg Hinda F. • Director • Carnegie Foundation for the Advancement of Teaching • Princeton, NJ 08540

Greenberg Jane • Student • Columbia University Library Service Library • New York, NY 10027 • ALCTS

Greenberg Janice L. • Student • Rutgers University School of Communication Information & Library Studies • New Brunswick, NJ 08903 • ALSC PLA EMIERT NMRT

Greenberg JoAnn H. • Support Services Manager • Escondido Public Library • Escondido, CA 92025

Greenberg Linda • Manager,Technical Services • Merrill Lynch Capital Markets • New York, NY 10281 • LITA

Greenberg Mitchell M. • Long Valley, NJ 07853

Greenberg Ruth S. • Branch Head • Mercer County Library Washington Branch • Robbinsville, NJ 08691

Greenberg Stephen • Silver Spring, MD 20902 • ACRL

Greenberger Christine • Librarian • Santa Monica Public Library • Santa Monica, CA 90401

Greenblatt Melinda Dale • Field Librarian • American Reading Council • New York, NY 10016 • AASL ALSC EMIERT IRRT

Greenblatt Ruth E. • Volunteer • Beth Israel Congregation Library • Vineland, NJ 08360

Greenblatt Stella S. • Royal Palm Beach, FL 33411

Greenburg Alice • Greencastle, IN 46135 • PLA

Greene Andrew Jr. • Acting Senior Librarian • Georgia State Prison • Riedsville, GA 30453

Greene Araby Y. • University of North Carolina-Asheville D Hiden Ramsey Library • Asheville, NC 28804-3299 • GODORT

Greene Audrey N. • Regional Sales Manager • EBSCO Subscription Services • Shrewsbury, NJ 07702-4321 • ALCTS

Greene Brian A. • Automation Librarian • Wyoming State Library • Cheyenne, WY 82002-0650 • ASCLA LITA SRRT

Greene Carol M. • Director of Library Services • Ashland Community College • Ashland, KY 41101 • ACRL LAMA

Greene Carol S. • Librarian • Shawnee Mission School District • Shawnee Mission, KS 66106 • AASL

Greene Danielle L. • Librarian • Powell, Goldstein, Frazer & Murphy, Attorneys • Washington, DC 20004

Greene Deborah C. • Music Librarian • Cleveland State University Library • Cleveland, OH 44115 • ACRL LITA IRRT LRRT

Greene Ellin • Point Pleasant, NJ 08742 • ALSC *Continuing*

Greene Frances V. • Librarian • Free Library of New Hope & Solebury • New Hope, PA 18938

Greene Gladys M. • Daytona Beach, FL 32114 • Continuing

Greene Grace Worcester • Children's Services Consultant • Vermont Department of Libraries • Montpelier, VT 05609 • ALSC

Greene Hattie J. • Library Manager • Appalachian Regional Library • West Jefferson, NC 28694 • PLA

Greene Jane Hanley • Young Adult Selection Librarian • Prince George's County Memorial Library System • Hyattsville, MD 20782-2098 • YALSA

Greene Jean H. • Tamworth, NH 03886

Greene Jeremiah E. Jr. • Reference Librarian • Fitchburg State College Library • Fitchburg, MA 01420 • ACRL LIRT LRRT

Greene Katherine S. • Assistant Director • Open,Inc. • Dallas, TX 75356-6025

Greene Lillie C. • Media Coordinator • Myers Park Trad. Elementary School • Charlotte, NC 28207 • AASL EMIERT IRRT

Greene Lucy E. • Center for Early Education • Los Angeles, CA 90048 • IFRT NMRT

Greene Martha • Branch Manager • Washoe County Library • Reno, NV 89505 • PLA

Greene Mary Fisch • Librarian • MPR Associates, Inc. • Washington, DC 20036 • LITA

Greene Maryann • Memorial Junior School • Whippany, NJ 07981 • AASL

Greene Nancy K. • Library Director • Mahwah Free Public Library • Mahwah, NJ 07430 • PLA

Greene Nancy S. • Cataloger • University of Wisconsin Center for Health Sciences Library • Madison, WI 53706

Greene Pamela M. • Children's Librarian II • Beverly Hills Public Library • Beverly Hills, CA 90210

Greene Richard C. • Student • Mankato State University Library Media Education Department • Mankato, MN 56003 • AASL

Greene Richard O. • Director • Mid-Mississippi Regional Library System • Kosciusko, MS 39090 • PLA

Greene Richard O. • Database Specialist • Online Computer Library Center (OCLC) • Dublin, OH 43017-3395 • LITA

Greene Robert J. Dr • Science Librarian • Emory University Libraries Robert W. Woodruff Library • Atlanta, GA 30322-2870 • ACRL

Greene Roberta E. • Director • West Shore Public Library • Camp Hill, PA 17011 • PLA

Greene Tom R. • Alexandria, VA 22304 • LITA RASD *Life*

Greene Virginia D. • Student • Texas Woman's University School of Library & Information Studies • Denton, TX 76204

Greener Jean W. • Trustee • Minneapolis Public Library & Information Center • Minneapolis, MN 55401-1992 • ALTA PLA

Greeney Joan A. • Head Librarian • F.D. Roosevelt High School • Hyde Park, NY 12538

Greenfeldt Eric • Assistant Director • Princeton Public Library • Princeton, NJ 08542 • LAMA PLA

Greenfield Jane W. • Highland Park Public Library • Highland Park, IL 60035 • LAMA PLA EMIERT

Greenfield Judith C. • Children's Librarian • Rye Free Reading Room • Rye, NY 10580 • ALSC

Greenfield Judith M. • Spotsylvania, VA 22553-1933 • YALSA

Greenfield Louise W. • University of Arizona Library • Tucson, AZ 85721 • ACRL LAMA LIRT

Greenfield Melissa R. • Librarian • Saint Petersburg Junior College M.M. Bennett Library • Pinellas Park, FL 34665 • ACRL LAMA

Greenfield Richard • Consultant • Library of Congress • Washington, DC 20541 • ACRL LITA RASD EMIERT FLRT GODORT IFRT IRRT SRRT

Greenfieldt John W. • Associate Editor • H. W. Wilson Company • Bronx, NY 10452 • ACRL

Greengrass Linda C. • Coordinator of Children's Svs • Bank Street College of Education Library • New York, NY 10025

Greenhalgh-Villemaire Charlotte • Keene, NH 03431

Greenholz Carol • Head of Technical Services • State University of New York Agricultural & Technical College Library • Farmingdale, NY 11735 • ACRL ALCTS CLENE EMIERT SRRT

Greenhow Janelle D. • Director • Cameron Parish Library • Cameron, LA 70631

Greening Catherine • Palo Alto, CA 94301 • Life

Greening Monica • Library Director • Monrovia Public Library • Monrovia, CA 91016

Greenlaw Jane V. • Librarian • New York Public Library • New York, NY 10018-2788 • ACRL

Greenlaw M. Jean • Professor • University of North Texas • Denton, TX 76203 • AASL ALSC

Greenleaf Adele • Fine Arts Librarian • Weber County Library • Odgen, UT 84401

Greenleaf Rene L. • Librarian • William Blair & Company • Chicago, IL 60603

Greenlee Joanne E. • Regional Reference Specialist • Cuyahoga County Public Library Mayfield Regional Branch • Mayfield Village, OH 44143-2179 • PLA RASD

Greenlee Marcia McAdoo • Washington, DC 20009

Greenlund Robyn • Data Trek, Inc. • Carlsbad, CA 92008 • LITA

Greenman Barbara A. • Student • Emporia State University Emporia in the Rockies • Denver, CO 80204

Greenspan Vivi S. • Librarian • Montclair Kimberley Academy • Montclair, NJ 07402 • AASL YALSA

Greenspon Joanna B. • Indexer • H. W. Wilson Company • Bronx, NY 10452 • ACRL

Greenspun Joanne • Director • Vineland Free Public Library • Vineland, NJ 08360 • PLA RASD

Greenstreet Jennifer K. • Director • Ada Public Library • Ada, OK 74820

Greenup Nadine • Public Library Consultant • Annenberg/CPB Project • Santa Barbara, CA 93116-1922 • PLA VRT

Greenwald Diane M. • Danbury, CT 06810 • PLA

Greenwald Evelyn • Los Angeles Public Library • Los Angeles, CA 90071

Greenwood-Smail Marva • Library Chief • Detroit Public Library Richard Branch • Detroit, MI 48204

Greenwood Anna S. • Media Specialist • Montgomery County Public Schools • Rockville, MD 20850

Greenwood Mary Anne • Student • University of South Carolina College of Library & Information Science • Columbia, SC 29208 • AASL NMRT SRRT

Greer Barbara A. • Media Specialist • Brookwood Elementary • Snellville, GA 30278 • AASL

Greer Barbara F. • Regional Librarian • FIVCO Regional Library • Louisa, KY 41230 • PLA

Greer David N. • Student • University of Georgia Libraries • Athens, GA 30602 • AASL

Greer Doris L. • Reference Librarian • District of Columbia Public Library Martin Luther King Memorial Library • Washington, DC 20001

Greer Elizabeth S. • Georgetown, KY 40324 • Continuing

Greer James A. • Librarian • Draughons Junior College • Montgomery, AL 36104

Greer Joyce • Stanley Elementary School • Overland Park, KS 66223 • AASL

Greer Roger C. • Professor & Dean Emeritus • Emporia State University School of Library & Information Management • Emporia, KS 66801 • LRRT

Greer Tena M • Student • Southern College of Seventh-Day Adventists • Collegedale, TN 37315

Greever Barbara C. • Principal Cataloger • University of Idaho Library • Moscow, ID 83843 • ACRL ALCTS CLENE NMRT

Greever Ellen A. • Chapel Hill, NC 27514 • AASL ALSC YALSA

Greever Karen E. • Student • University of Kentucky College of Library & Information Science • Lexington, KY 40506-0391 • ACRL ALCTS

Grefe Richard F. • Reference/Public Service Ln. • Washington & Lee University • Lexington, VA 24450 • ACRL RASD GODORT

Grefrath Richard W. • Reference Librarian • University of Nevada-Reno • Reno, NV 89557 • RASD

Grefsheim Suzanne F. • Director, Medical Library • University of Michigan Libraries Alfred Taubman Medical Library • Ann Arbor, MI 48109-0726 • ACRL ALCTS LAMA LITA

Gregg Charles B. CSC Br. • Holy Cross High School • Louisville, KY 40216

Greggs Elizabeth M. • Renton, WA 98056 • ALSC

Gregoire Christopher P. • Assistant Director • Clarence Public Library • Clarence, NY 14031 • PLA

Gregor Dorothy D. • University Librarian • University California-Berkeley • Berkeley, CA 94720 • LAMA LITA

Gregorek Rita • Student • Kent State University School of Library & Information Science • Kent, OH 44242-0001 • RASD

Gregory David James • Head, Access Services Dept. • Iowa State University Library • Ames, IA 50011-2140 • ACRL LAMA

Gregory Gwen • Assistant Branch Librarian • United States Court of Appeals for the Ninth Circuit/Courts Library • Phoenix, AZ 85025 • FLRT SRRT

Gregory Helen Byrne • Grosse Pointe Public Library Central Branch • Grosse Pointe, MI 48236

Gregory Joan A. • Acquistions Librarian • Mesa Public Library • Mesa, AZ 85201-6768

Gregory Kathleen • Council Bluffs Free Public Library • Council Bluffs, IA 51503

Gregory Louise S. • Librarian • Orangeburg Preparatory School • Orangeburg, SC 29115 • AASL LIRT

Gregory Mae • Librarian • Chicago Public Library Whitney M Young Jr Branch • Chicago, IL 60619

Gregory Mary Lou • Library Media Specialist • Hoquiam High School • Hoquiam, WA 98550 • AASL

Gregory Nancy Mrs • Librarian • American Management Systems • Arlington, VA 22209 • LITA RASD

Gregory Patricia L. • Head Reference Librarian • Saint Louis University Pius XII Memorial Library • St. Louis, MO 63108 • ACRL

Gregory Roderick F. • Salt Lake City, UT 84108 • LITA

Gregory Ruth W. • Waukegan, IL 60087 • PLA

Gregory Sara M. • Convington, GA 30209

Gregory Shirley S. • Library Director • Barton College Library • Wilson, NC 27893 • LAMA

Gregory Timothy P. • Archivist • Pasadena Historical Society • Pasadena, CA 91103

Gregory Valeria • Santa Fe High School-LMC • Santa Fe, NM 87505 • AASL YALSA

Gregory Vicki Dr. • Assistant Professor • University of South Florida School of Library & Information Science • Tampa, FL 33620 • ACRL ALCTS LITA LRRT

Greif Frank • Seattle Public Library • Seattle, WA 98104-1193 • ALTA PLA

Greig Eugenie M. Mrs. • Assoc. Librarian, Cataloging • MacQuarie University Library • New South Wales, 2109 Australia • ALCTS LITA

Greig Karen L. • Assistant Librarian • Stanford University • Stanford, CA 94305-6011 • ACRL

Greiner Eileen L. • Librarian • Cary Public Library • Cary, IL 60013 • ALCTS LAMA PLA

Greiner Joy Marilyn • Associate Professor • University of Southern Mississippi School of Library Science • Hattiesburg, MS 39406-5146 • PLA

Greisler Rachel • Librarian • Disston School • Phildelphia, PA 19135 • AASL

Greiwe Hermina H. Mrs • Cincinnati, OH 45243-3303 • Continuing

Grele Gaile A • Assistant Director • Old Bridge Public Library • Old Bridge, NJ 08857-2498 • PLA EMIERT SRRT

Gremillion Virginia P. • Librarian • Tucson Public Library Columbus Branch • Tucson, AZ 85711 • PLA IRRT

Gremmels Gillian S. • Director • Monmouth College Library • Monmouth, IL 61462-9989 • ACRL LAMA RASD SRRT

Gremont Joan C. • Librarian • Solomon Schechter Academy • Dallas, TX 75252 • AASL

Grendler Marcella • University of North Carolina Wilson Library • Chapel Hill, NC 27599 • ACRL ALCTS

Grennan Jon G. • Student • Indiana University School of Library and Information Science • Bloomington, IN 47405

Grenville Sally M. • Chicago, IL 60657 • ACRL RASD

Gresh William • Media Director • Lowell High School Media Center • Lowell, IN 46356 • AASL

Gresham Keith E. • Student • University of Washington Graduate School of Library and Information Science • Seattle, WA 98195

Gresko Florence M. • Library Board-Board Member • Whiting Public Library • Whiting, IN 46394

Gress Barbara L. • Student • San Jose State University Division of Library & Information Science • San Jose, CA 95192-0029 • RASD

Gretchen Mark A. • Reference Services Manager • Corpus Christi Public Library • Corpus Christi, TX 78401 • PLA

Grether Barbara • Circulation Librarian • Danville Community College Learning Resource Center • Danville, VA 24541

Greulich Margaret A. • Green Valley School Library • Danville, CA 94526

Greunke Lowell R. • Branch Manager • Omaha Public Library Swanson Branch • Omaha, NE 68131

Grevera Dorothy M. • Cataloger • Intel Corporation Library Systems Group • Santa Clara, CA 95052 • ALCTS

Grewell Johanne F. • Librarian • Peoria High School Library • Peoria, IL 61604 • AASL

Grey Elizabeth B. • Chapel Hill, NC 27514-9779

Grey Wilma J. • Asst. Director/Community Serv. • Newark Public Library • Newark, NJ 07101-0630 • LAMA PLA EMIERT ILERT

Greybill Robert A. • Plymouth-Whitemarsh High School • Plymouth Meeting, PA 17551

Gribben Alan • Hd, English & Philosophy • Auburn University at Montgomery • Montgomery, AL 36117-3596 • LHRT

Grice Ila M. • University of Oklahoma Libraries Serials Department • Norman, OK 73019 • ACRL ALCTS NMRT

Grice Tina A. • Head Librarian • Waipahu Public Library • Waipahu, HI 96707 • PLA

Grider Marcella H. • Fayetteville, AR 72703 • Continuing

Grieb Debra L. • Student • Emporia State University Emporia in the Rockies • Denver, CO 80204

Grieb Sherry J. • Branch Manager • Dallas Public Library Renner-Frankford Branch • Dallas, TX 75252-5747

Griebel Karen V. • Chicago Public Library Harold Washington Library • Chicago, IL 60605 • PLA

Griebel Michael J. • New York Public Library Belmont Branch • Bronx, NY 14058

Grieco Lise F. • Highland Park, IL 60035

Grieder Hilda M. Miss • Denver, CO 80233 • Continuing

Grieger Sharon • Collection Development Librarian • Mount Prospect Public Library • Mount Prospect, IL 60056 • PLA RASD IFRT

Griego Adan • Asst. Head of Reference • University of California Library • Santa Barbara, CA 93106 • ACRL RASD

Griego F. S. • Student • University of Arizona Graduate Library School • Tucson, AZ 85721 • ACRL RASD

Griem Rowena L. • Student • Simmons College Graduate School of Library & Information Science • Boston, MA 02115

Griepenstroh Kathleen • Director • Morton-James Public Library • Nebraska City, NE 68410

Grier Anita K. • Guilderland, NY 12084

Grier Helen R. • Media Specialist • Miami Senior High School • Miami, FL 33135

Grierson Christopher N • Predicasts • Cleveland, OH 44106 • ALCTS LAMA LITA RASD

Grierson Sirpa T. • Student • Brigham Young University School of Library & Information Sciences • Provo, UT 84602 • ALSC

Griesbach Elizabeth • Head Reference Dept. • Somerset County Library • Bridgewater, NJ 08807

Griesemer Ellen M. • Reference Librarian • Brookfield Public Library • Brookfield, WI 53005

Griest Lisa • School Librarian • International School of Amsterdam • NL1008 AD Amsterdam, Netherlands • AASL

Grieswell Iris A. • Head of Technical Services • Muncie-Center Township Public Library • Muncie, IN 47305 • ALCTS

Grieve Keith B. • Assistant Librarian • United Kingdom Mission to the United Nations • New York, NY 10022 • NMRT

Griffay Teresa A. • Redondo Beach, CA 90278

Griffel Eugene B. • Flint, MI 48503 • LAMA PLA   *Life*

Griffen Agnes M. • Director • Montgomery County Department of Public Libraries • Rockville, MD 20850 • ALTA ASCLA LAMA LITA PLA IFRT

Griffin Andrea R. • Student • University of Kentucky College of Library & Information Science • Lexington, KY 40506-0391 • YALSA

Griffin Barbara T. • Southampton Middle School • Bel Air, MD 21014 • AASL

Griffin Carole C. • Hinckley, OH 44233

Griffin Carolene P. • Student • North Carolina Central University • Durham, NC 27707 • EMIERT SRRT

Griffin Cheryl C. • Danville Community College Learning Resource Center • Danville, VA 24541

Griffin Cheryl J. • Media Specialist • Rhein Main Elementary School • APO, AE 09057-0005 • AASL

Griffin David E. • Publications Coordinator • Western Library Network (WLN) • Lacey, WA 98503-0888 • ALCTS

Griffin Debbie • Librarian-Director • Schleicher County Independent School District • Eldorado, TX 76936 • AASL YALSA NMRT

Griffin Donnie C. • Branch Supervisor • Cobb County Public Library System • Marietta, GA 30060 • PLA

Griffin Doris B. • Eric Smith School Library • Ramsey, NJ 07446 • AASL

Griffin Evelyn • Poinsett County Adminstrator • Crowley Ridge Regional Library • Jonesboro, AR 72401

Griffin Fredericia Sr. • Boston Public Library • Boston, MA 02117

Griffin Hillis L. • Laboratory Librarian • Lawrence Berkeley Laboratory Library Building 50B-4206 • Berkeley, CA 94720 • ACRL LAMA LITA

Griffin Janette J. • Asst Librarian-Cataloging • University of New Orleans Earl K. Long Library • New Orleans, LA 70148

Griffin Kathryn A. • Library Director • American Institute of Business • Des Moines, IA 50321 • ACRL RASD

Griffin Kelly K. • Medical Librarian • Good Samaritan Hospital • Dayton, OH 45406

Griffin Larry W. • Director of Library Services • Indiana University-Purdue University Walter E. Helmke Library • Fort Wayne, IN 46805-6514 • ACRL

Griffin Linda • Marketing Director • Weston Woods Studios Inc • Weston, CT 06883 • AASL ALSC

Griffin Lynne • Librarian • Williamston Community School • Williamston, MI 48895

Griffin Marie L. • Coordinator Media Services • South Lakes High School • Reston, VA 22091 • AASL

Griffin Marie P. • Barre, VT 05641

Griffin Marion • Hinsdale, IL 60521 • AASL YALSA
Continuing

Griffin Mary Ann • Library Director • Villanova University Falvey Memorial Library • Villanova, PA 19085-1699 • ACRL LAMA LITA

Griffin Mary T. • Branch Manager • Omaha Public Library Milton R. Abrahams Branch • Omaha, NE 68134

Griffin Nancy A. • Idaho State University Eli M. Oboler Library • Pocatello, ID 83209-8089

Griffin Patricia M • University of Georgia Costal Plain Experiment Station Library • Tifton, GA 31793

Griffin Patrick J. • Librarian/Edu. Media Director • Reed High School • Sparks, NV 89431 • AASL

Griffin Richard W. • Library Automation Coordinator • Oregon State University William Jasper Kerr Library • Corvallis, OR 97331-4501 • LITA

Griffin Ruth E. • Director of Library Services • Indiana Wesleyan University • Marion, IN 46953

Griffin Sara L. • Library Relations Representative • H. W. Wilson Company • Bronx, NY 10452 • LITA

Griffin Thelma • Head Librarian • Hinsdale Township High School Library • Hinsdale, IL 60521 • AASL

Griffin Timothy D. • Milwaukee, WI 53233 • ACRL ALCTS
Life

Griffing Elizabeth A. • Fairfax, VA 22033

Griffis Joan E. • Supervisor, Educational Media • Portland Public Schools • Portland, OR 97208-3107 • AASL

Griffith Alice B. • Yorkville, NY 13495 • ACRL

Griffith Ann C. • Dallas, TX 75248

Griffith Carol • Head of Circulation • West Des Moines Public Library • West Des Moines, IA 50265

Griffith Claudia D. • Head Librarian • Summer Institute of Linguistics Dallas Library • Dallas, TX 75236 • ACRL ALSC

Griffith David W. • Director, Retired • Reuben McMillan Free Library Association Youngstown & Mahoning Cnty P L • Youngstown, OH 44503 • ALCTS RASD YALSA *Life*

Griffith Donna P. • Librarian • Trinity Lutheran School Library • Newport News, VA 23607 • AASL ALSC

Griffith Dorothy • Head, Interlibrary Loan Dept. • Montgomery County Norristown Public Library • Norristown, PA 19401

Griffith Gail L. • Assistant Director • Carroll County Public Library • Westminster, MD 21157 • LAMA

Griffith Gustin Virginia M. • Children's Librarian • Santa Monica Public Library • Santa Monica, CA 90401 • ALSC IFRT SRRT

Griffith Jo M. • Acquisitions Librarian • Richland County Public Library • Columbia, SC 29201

Griffith Joan C. • Asst. Serials Librarian • Dartmouth College • Hanover, NH 03755 • ACRL ALCTS LITA

Griffith Kathryn R. • Librarian • Shady Spring High School • Shady Spring, WV 25918 • AASL

Griffith Kelly • Asst. Librarian • Marian College Library • Indianapolis, IN 46222 • ACRL RASD

Griffith Leah M. • Newberg Public Library • Newberg, OR 97132 • PLA

Griffith Mary E. • Student • University of Wisconsin-Milwaukee School of Library & Information Science • Milwaukee, WI 53201

Griffith Mary Margaret • Branch Manager • Pasco County Library System Centennial Park Branch • Holiday, FL 34690

Griffith Robert C. • Student • University of South Carolina College of Library & Information Science • Columbia, SC 29208 • AASL IFRT NMRT SRRT

Griffith Susan C. • Head Librarian • Boston College Bapst Library • Chestnut Hill, MA 02167 • ALSC RASD SRRT VRT

Griffith William J. • Director • Anaheim Public Library • Anaheim, CA 92805 • ACRL ALCTS ALSC LAMA LITA PLA RASD YALSA

Griffith Yvette J. • Manager. Library & Info. Servs. • Dialog Information Services • Chicago, IL 60601 • LITA

Griffiths Barbara • De Kalb, IL 60115 • ACRL ALCTS

Griffiths Dara J. • Exhibits Manager • Publishers Book Exhibit Inc • Millwood, NY 10546 • ERT

Griffiths Hicks G. • Trustee • Library of Michigan • Lansing, MI 48909

Griffiths Jose M. • Prof & Collaborating Scientist • University of Tennessee-Knoxville Graduate School of Library & Information Science • Knoxville, TN 37996-4330 • LITA LRRT

Griffiths Suzanne N. • Asst. Prof. of Lib. Emerita • University of Illinois Library • Urbana, IL 61801 • ACRL LAMA

Griffitts Joan K. • Indianapolis, IN 46268

Griffler Carl W. • Reference & Interlibrary Loan • Norfolk Public Library Kirn Memorial Library • Norfolk, VA 23510

Griffy Kay • Library Media Director • Bolingbrook High School • Bolingbrook, IL 60440 • AASL

Grigg Karen • Media Specialist • Eastvalley Elementary School • Marietta, GA 30067

Grigg Virginia C. • Tallahassee, FL 32312

Grigsby Alice B. • Inglewood, CA 90303

Grigsby Mary • Journalism Librarian • University of Missouri Adminstrative Offices • Columbia, MO 65201 • IRRT

Grilli Lynn A. • East Walpole, MA 02032

Grillo Dominick J. • Student • Illinois Institute of Technology Chicago Kent College of Law Library • Chicago, IL 60661-3901 • LITA

Grills Eleanor H. • Librarian • McQuaid Jesuit High School • Rochester, NY 14618 • AASL

Grim Jessica • Assistant Librarian • Oberlin College Library • Oberlin, OH 44074 • ACRL

Grima Sunee • Librarian II • Weber County Library • Odgen, UT 84401 • ALCTS

Grimble Bonnie J. • Media Specialist • Warsaw Senior High School • Warsaw, IN 46580 • AASL

Grimes Betty J. • Lexington, KY 40508

Grimes Carol L. • Springfield-Greene County Library • Springfield, MO 65801 • PLA

Grimes Deborah J. • Shelton State Community College Junior College Division Library • Tusacaloosa, AL 35405 • ACRL LAMA LRRT

Grimes Doria Beachell • Chief, Contract Operation • National Oceanic & Atomospheric Administration (NOAA) Library & Information Servs. Div. • Rockville, MD 20852 • FLRT GODORT

Grimes Gloria • Deputy Director • Palos Verdes Library District • Pls Vrd Pnsla, CA 90274 • PLA

Grimes Hallie M. • Oak Harbor, OH 43449 • Continuing

Grimes Joanne K. • Student • New Haven Free Public Library • New Haven, CT 06510 • ALSC

Grimes Linda O. • Children's Librarisn • Flesh Public Library • Piqua, OH 45356 • ALSC

Grimes Marcia E. • Reference Librarian • Wheaton College Wallace Library • Norton, MA 02766 • RASD LIRT

Grimes Myra • Librarian • Buckley County Day School • Roslyn, NY 11576 • AASL

Grimes Sydney V. • Whitwell, TN 37397 • AASL

Grimes Theodore R. • Library Chair • Florida Community College at Jacksonville Learning Resource Center • Jacksonville, FL 32216-6624

Grimes Timothy P. • Adult Services Specialist • Ann Arbor Public Library Nellie S. Loving Branch • Ann Arbor, MI 48104 • RASD LIRT

Grimley Arlene M. • Mt. Pleasant, MI 48858 • Continuing

Grimley Susan M. • Extension Librarian • Spartanburg County Public Library • Spartanburg, SC 29304

Grimley Toni Ann F. • Library Media Specialist • Christopher Rhodes School • Warwick, RI 02886 • IFRT

Grimm Barbara • Librarian • Oakdale Elementary School • Normal, IL 61761 • AASL

Grimm Ben E. • Rapidan, VA 22733

Grimm Dorothy Jean • San Diego, CA 92109 • RASD

Grimsbo Elisabeth A. • Reference Librarian • Waterloo Public Library • Waterloo, IA 50701 • PLA

Grimshaw Polly Swift • Ln for Sociology Anthropology & • Indiana University at Bloomington University Libraries • Bloomington, IN 47405 • ACRL

Grimsley Dorothy L. • School Librarian • Daspit Elementary School • New Iberia, LA 70560 • AASL

Grinninger Cheryl L. • Student • University of Kentucky College of Library & Information Science • Lexington, KY 40506-0391

Grinspoon Ruth S. • Librarian • Washington Irving High School • New York, NY 10003

Grippo Christopher F. • Seattle, WA 98122 • ACRL RASD

Grisa Gregg R. • District of Columbia Public Librry Takoma Park Branch • Washington, DC 20012 • YALSA NMRT

Grise Carol B. • Durham, NC 27707

Grisell Barbara G. • Student • University of Illinois • Champaign, IL 61801 • ALSC PLA YALSA

Grishaber P. Elaine • Student • State University New York at Buffalo School of Inf. & Library Studies • Buffalo, NY 14260

Grisham Frank P. • Executive Director • Southeastern Library Network (SOLINET) • Atlanta, GA 30309-2955 • ACRL ASCLA LAMA

Grisso Karl • Hd,Clln Management Services • Eastern Illinois University Booth Library • Charleston, IL 61920-3099 • ACRL LAMA RASD IFRT

Grissom Elena • Trustee • Jefferson County Public Library • Lakewood, CO 80215 • ALTA

Grissom Joyce • Librarian • Van Buren Junior Senior High School • Spencer, TN 38585 • AASL

Griswold Ardyce • Media Specialist • Sligo Adventist School • Takoma Park, MD 20912 • AASL

Griswold Esther A. • Director • Franklin Pierce College Library • Rindge, NH 03461-0060 • ACRL LAMA IFRT

Grizzle Ronda A. • Student • University of North Carolina at Chapel Hill School of Information and Library Science • Chapel Hill, NC 27599-3360 • LITA

Groat Pamela • Librarian • Baldwin Community Schools • Baldwin, MI 49304 • AASL

Grochmal Helen M. • California, PA 15419-1424

Grochowski Allison M. • Clifton, NJ 07011 • PLA RASD YALSA

Grochowsky Steven M. • Student • Emporia State University School of Library & Information Management • Emporia, KS 66801 • PLA NMRT

Grodin Alan R. • Trustee • Shelter Rock Public Library • Albertson, NY 11507 • ALTA

Grodinsky Deborah • Reference Library • North Suburban Library System • Wheeling, IL 60090

Groeb Lee A. • Assistant Director • Lenawee County Library • Adrian, MI 49221 • ALSC

Groen Frances • Assoc. Director of Libraries • McGill University • Montreal PQ, H3A 1Y1 Canada • ACRL

Groeneveld Jake • Trustee • Owosso Public Library • Owosso, MI 48867

Groesbeck Margaret A. • Instr & Biblio Retrieval Libn • Amherst College Library • Amherst, MA 01002 • ACRL

Grof Andrew P. • Social Science Librarian • Florida International University • Miami, FL 33199

Groh Patricia • Coordinator, Community • Skokie Public Library • Skokie, IL 60077-3680 • RASD

Groh Robert T. • Justice of Supreme Court • Queens Borough Public Library • Jamaica, NY 11432 • ALTA PLA

Gronberg Lydia M. • Library Tech • Washington State University • Spokane, WA 99201

Gronquist Jeanne • Trustee • Arrowhead Library System • Virginia, MN 55792 • ALTA

Groome Linda E. • Penn Manor School Dist • Millersville, PA 17551 • AASL

Grooms Richard Owen • Birmingham, AL 35205-1756

Gropen Polly • Delafield Public Library • Delafield, WI 53018

Gropman Jacqueline R. • Burke, VA 22015 • ALSC

Gropp Arthur E. • Greenbelt, MD 20770 • ACRL ALCTS
Life

Grosch Audrey N. • Professor • University of Minnesota S-98 Meredith Wilson Library • Minneapolis, MN 55455-0414 • LITA

Grosch Mary F. • Senior Business Librarian • Northern Illinois University University Libraries • DeKalb, IL 60115-2868 • RASD

Grose B. Donald • Director of Libraries • University of North Texas • Denton, TX 76203 • ACRL LAMA

Grose Kimberly K. • Media Coordinator • Monticello Elementary School • Statesville, NC 28677 • AASL

Grose Rosemary Fullerton • Library Media Specialist • Strickland Junior High School Library • Denton, TX 76201 • AASL

Grosek Ed • Teaneck, NJ 07666

Grosh Myra S. Miss • Mt. Joy, PA 17552 • Continuing

Gross Barbara L. • Children's Consultant • Montgomery County Norristown Public Library • Norristown, PA 19401 • ALSC

Gross Dorothy-Ellen • Director of Libraries • North Park College & Theo Sem Consolidated Library • Chicago, IL 60625 • ACRL LAMA RASD

Gross Glenn • Trustee • Mesa Public Library • Mesa, AZ 85201-6768 • ALTA

Gross Iva Helen • A/V Librarian • Amarillo Public Library • Amarillo, TX 79189 • LITA

Gross John • Director • Salinas Public Library • Salinas, CA 93901 • LAMA PLA
Life

Gross June F. • Coor. Instructional Media • Independent School District #279 • Maple Grove, MN 55369-6605 • AASL

Gross Karen S. • Chief of Children's Services • East Central Georgia Regional Library Augusta-Richmond County • Augusta, GA 30901 • ALSC

Gross Kenneth L. • Librarian • Rolling Meadows Library • Rolling Meadows, IL 60008 • PLA RASD

Gross Leann S. • Woodlawn Elementary School • Lawrence, KS 66044 • AASL

Gross Linda P. • Country Music Foundation Library and Media Center • Nashville, TN 37203

Gross Marcia A. • Fontanelle, IA 50846 • AASL

Gross Melissa • Library Assistant • San Marino Public Library • San Marino, CA 91108

Gross Myra S. • Media Specialist Librarian • DeWitt Middle School • Ithaca, NY 14850 • ALSC

Gross Rosemarie • Blue Bell, PA 19422

Gross Sally L. • University of Texas at Arlington • Arlington, TX 76019-0497 • ACRL RASD MAGERT

Gross Sharon A. • Library Media Specialist • Pickney School • Lawrence, KS 66044 • AASL

Gross Valerie A. • Student • University of Pittsburgh School of Library and Information Science • Pittsburgh, PA 15260

Gross Viola Sister • Librarian • St Marys Academy Bayview • Riverside, RI 02915

Grossardt Sharon R. • Director • Saint Charles Public Library • St. Charles, MN 55972

Grossberg Aileen D. • Librarian • Demarest School • Bloomfield, NJ 07003 • AASL ALSC

Grossett Sharon J. • Federal Librarian • United States Army • Warren, MI 48090

Grosshans Merilyn L. • Librarian • Las Vegas High School • Las Vegas, NV 89101 • AASL YALSA

Grossman April • Student • Appalachian State University Department of Library Science & Educational Foundation • Boone, NC 28608

Grossman Holly D. • Streamwood, IL 60107 • RASD

Grossman Jacqueline • Assistant Librarian • Littler Mendelson Fastiff & Tichy • San Francisco, CA 94108 • ACRL RASD

Grossman Joanne F. • Librarian • Charles River School • Dover, MA 02030 • AASL YALSA

Grossman Marjorie • Reference Coordinator • Santa Rosa Junior College • Santa Rosa, CA 95401

Grossman Michael P. • Duluth, MN 55804 • IFRT

Grossman Ronald • Sr. Vice President • Freeport McMoran, Inc. • New Orleans, LA 70112 • ALTA

Grossman Susan • Corporate Library Director • Millard Fillmore Hospitals • Buffalo, NY 14209

Grosso Katherine T. • Olney, MD 20832

Grotevant Jennilou S. • Wilmington College Watson Library • Wilmington, OH 45177 • LAMA

Groth Robert E. • Director • Garner Public Library • Garner, IA 50438 • SRRT

Grotheer Ruth D. • Jericho, NY 11753 • ASCLA PLA *Life*

Grothey Mina Jane • Reference Librarian • University of New Mexico General Library • Albuquerque, NM 87131 • ACRL ALCTS RASD IRRT

Grott Joan • Director • Mamaroneck Free Library • Mamaroneck, NY 10543 • LAMA PLA YALSA IFRT

Grotzinger Laurel • Prof., University Libs • Western Michigan University • Kalamazoo, MI 49008 • ACRL ALTA RASD LHRT LRRT
Life

Grout Nancy E. • Branch Manager • Miami-Dade Public Library System • Miami, FL 33130-1504

Grout Ronald N. • Hemet, CA 92543

Grovdahl Elba Dr. • University of Central Florida • Orlando, FL 32816 • ACRL RASD

Grove Debra A. • Media Specialist • Wegner Middle School • Boys Town, NE 68010

Grove Helen H. • Wytheville, VA 24382

Grove Louise • Williamsport, MD 21795-1399 • Continuing

Grove Lynn A. • Ithaca, NY 14850-9435 • ACRL

Grove Marsha A. • Assistant Director • Cumberland County Public Library and Information Center • Fayetteville, NC 28301 • PLA

Grove Nancy E. • Media Specialist • Bayville Elementary School Library • Bayville, NJ 08721

Grove Pearce S. • Library Director • U.S. Marine Corps James Carson Breckinridge Library • Quantico, VA 22134-5050 • ACRL LAMA FLRT
Life

Grove R Genevieve • Seattle, WA 98103

Grove Shari T. • Sr. Ref. Librarian Bibliographer • Boston College • Chestnut Hill, MA 02167 • ACRL

Grove Steven J. • Reference Librarian • Medina County District Library Brunswick Branch • Brunswick, OH 44212 • PLA RASD

Grover Crystal J. • Librarian • Lehi City Library • Lehi, UT 84043 • ALSC

Grover Diane B. • University of Washington Suzzallo Library • Seattle, WA 98195 • ALCTS

Grover Robert J. • Professor • Emporia State University School of Library & Information Management • Emporia, KS 66801 • AASL CLENE LRRT

Grover Thelma I. • Iowa City, IA 52245 • LAMA PLA *Life*

Groves Anne G. • Technical Services Librarian • West Florida Regional Library • Pensacola, FL 32501

Groves Heather • Technical Library Asst. • Furash & Company • Washington, DC 20036 • AASL IRRT LRRT

Groves Jacalyn • Morrisville Eaton Elementary School • Morrisville, NY 13346 • AASL

Groves Laura E. • Technical Services Librarian • Western Oregon State College Library • Monmouth, OR 97361 • ACRL

Groves Nancy J. • Student • Wayne State University • Detroit, MI 48202 • PLA

Groves Nicholas T. • Librarian • Chicago Public Library Carl Roden Branch • Chicago, IL 60631

Groves Percilla E. • Head, Reference Division • Simon Fraser University Library • Burnaby BC, Canada • ACRL LAMA RASD SRRT

Grovesteen Georgia L. • Student • Novi Public Library • Novi, MI 48375

Grube Sandra V. • Southern State Community College Learning Resources Center • Wilmington, OH 45177 • ALCTS

Gruber Ada • Trustee • Ouachita Parish Public Library • Monroe, LA 71201 • ALTA

Gruber David • Trustee • Queens Borough Public Library • Jamaica, NY 11432 • ALTA PLA

Gruber Marcella • C.P. Nicholas School • Jersey City, NJ 07306

Gruber Nancy • DataCenter • Oakland, CA 94612 • ALCTS SRRT
Life

Gruber Ronald J. • Clinical Prof. Serv. Coor. • Sanofi Winthrop Pharmaceuticals • New York, NY 10016

Grubman Donna • Assoc Dir for Public Servs • Broward County Division of Libraries Broward County Library • Fort Lauderdale, FL 33301 • LAMA

Grucan Sally P. • Sys Planning & Hd Catlg Ln • Wesleyan University Olin Memorial Library • Middletown, CT 06459 • ACRL ALCTS LITA

Grudem Cheryl L. • Student • California State University • Fullerton, CA 92634

Grudin Daniel F. • Bothell, WA 98012

Grudzias Francine M. • Sch. Library Serv. Spec. III • Hawaii Department of Education Special Instructional Programs & Services Branch • Honolulu, HI 96816 • AASL

Grudzien Pamela A. • Access Services Librarian • Central Michigan University Charles V. Park Library 315 • Mount Pleasant, MI 48859 • LAMA

Gruenbeck Laurie • Branch Manager • San Antonio Public Library Bazan Branch • San Antonio, TX 78207 • PLA EMIERT

Gruerio Margaret M. • Head, Youth Services Div. • Delaware County Library System • Brookhaven, PA 19015 • ALSC

Gruhl Andrea M. • Librarian • United States Government Printing Office • Washington, DC 20401 • ALCTS FLRT GODORT IRRT

Grumet Elinor J. • Student • Queens College Graduate School of Library & Information Studies • Flushing, NY 11367

Grumling Dennis • Chicago, IL 60607 • ALCTS

Grumman George R. • Assistant Librarian • Forecast International/DMS • Newton, CT 06470 • RASD

Grumman Joanne Pereira • Children's Librarian • Bethel Public Library • Bethel, CT 06801 • ALSC

Grund Diane J. • Associate Dean/Learning Res • Moraine Valley Community College Library • Palos Hills, IL 60465 • ACRL LAMA

Grundset Eric G. • Library Director • Daughters of the American Revolution • Washington, DC 20006 • ACRL ALCTS LAMA LITA RASD

Grundt Leonard • Professor • Nassau Community College Library • Garden City, NY 11530 • ACRL LAMA RASD *Life*

Gruner Robin S. • Southern Methodist University • Dallas, TX 75275 • ACRL GODORT

Grunfeld Miriam S. • Student • University of California-Berkeley School of Library & Information Studies • Berkeley, CA 94720 • AASL

Grunfeld Robert H. • Great Neck, NY 11021 • AASL

Grush Marilyn • Center for Research Libraries • Chicago, IL 60637

Gruszczak Margaret E. • Children's Librarian • Rathbun Free Memorial Library • East Haddam, CT 06423 • YALSA

Gruszewski Karin B. • Oak Creek, WI 53154-3714

Grutzmacher-Mayer Katherine M. • Green Fields Country Day School • Tucson, AZ 85741 • AASL IFRT

Grycz Jan Czeslaw • Ch, Scholarship & Tech Study Dep • University of California Division of Library Automation • Oakland, CA 94612-3550 • LITA

Grygotis Julie C. • Ann Arbor, MI 48103 • ALCTS

Grypp Betty J. • Children's Librarian • Greendale Public Library • Greendale, WI 53129 • ALSC

Grzenda Fran • Instructional Media Specialist • Fort Lupton Middle School • Fort Lupton, CO 80621

Guadagno Joan W. • Assistant Director • Smithtown Library • Smithtown, NY 11787 • LAMA

Guagliardo Victoria E. • Children's Librarian • Los Angeles County Public Library San Gabriel Branch • San Gabriel, CA 91776

Gualtieri Robert • Assistant Director • Hamden Library • Hamden, CT 06518

Guard Anara • Circulation/Ill Librarian • Wenham Public Library • Wenham, MA 01984 • PLA

Guardado Anthony S. • Student • University of Michigan School of Information and Library Studies • Ann Arbor, MI 48109-1092

Guarello Ione E. • Trustee • McCook Public Library • McCook, IL 60525

Guarin Martha C. • Head Librarian • Illinois Math & Science Academy • Aurora, IL 60506-1039 • ACRL LAMA IRRT LIRT

Guarino John P. • Branch Floater • San Francisco Public Library • San Francisco, CA 94102 • PLA EMIERT SRRT

Guasco Jean A. • Pittsburgh, PA 15241 • ALCTS LITA *Life*

Guay Beth • U. S. General Accounting Office • Washington, DC 20548

Gubbin Barbara A.B. • Assistant Director • Houston Public Library • Houston, TX 77002 • LAMA PLA SRRT

Gubert Betty K. • New York, NY 10025

Gubits Helen Sequeira • Haverstraw Kings Daughters Public Library • Haverstraw, NY 10927 • LAMA PLA

Gubser Gina Sue • Student • Northwest Missouri State University • Maryville, MO 64468

Gudelis Louise M. • Head, Circulation • Greenwich Library • Greenwich, CT 06830

Gudelius Elfriede Miss • Tacoma, WA 98403 • Continuing

Gudgen Gretta H. • Pittsburg State University Leonard Axe Library • Pittsburg, KS 66762

Gudjonsson Oskar • Supervisory Librarian • Naval Air Station Keflavik Station Library • FPO, AE 09728-0343 • PLA AFLRT

Guebert Lois • Fort Wayne • Concordia College Library • Ann Arbor, MI 48105 • ACRL ALCTS

Guebert Tracy D. • Library Assistant • Patrick Henry Community College • Martinsville, VA 24115-5311

Guedea Elizabeth Lisa • Corporate Librarian • Highsmith Co., Inc. • Fort Atkinson, WI 53538-0800 • ACRL ASCLA LAMA LITA

Guendelsberger Marie T. • Assistant Librarian • Bowling Green State Univ Firelands Campus • Huron, OH 44839 • RASD

Guenter Helen G. • Assistant Librarian • University of Arkansas Monticello Library • Monticello, AR 71655 • ACRL

Guenther Anne • Reference & Public Services • Fresno Pacific College Hiebert Library • Fresno, CA 93702

Guenther James A. • Director of Public Library • Carbondale Public Library • Carbondale, IL 62901-2995

Guenther Rebecca S. • Librarian/MARC Standards Spec. • Library of Congress • Washington, DC 20541 • LITA

Guenther Theresa A. • School Library Media Specialist • Arkport Central School • Arkport, NY 14807

Guentner Geraldine C. • Burlington, MA 01803 • ALSC PLA *Life*

Guerena Salvador • Librarian • University of California UCSB Library • Santa Barbara, CA 93106-9010 • ACRL EMIERT

Guering Phyllis M. • Library Specialist • University of Pittsburgh School of Library and Information Science • Pittsburgh, PA 15260

Guerra Cara A. • High School Media Specialist • Bethel High School Library • Bethel, CT 06801

Guerreri Doris S. • Easley High School Library • Easley, SC 29641

Guerrero Gilbert • Trustee • Kansas City Public Library • Kansas City, MO 64106 • ALTA

Guerrero Margaret • Senior Librarian • Santa Barbara Public Library Eastside Branch • Santa Barbara, CA 93103

Guerrier Mary L. • Student • University of Arizona • Tucson, AZ 85721

Guerriero Donald A. • Library Director • Defense Information Systems Agency • Arlington, VA 22204-2199 • ACRL PLA

Guerrini Janet M. • Librarian II • Sonoma County Library • Santa Rosa, CA 95404

Guertin Marie • Librarian Grade 2 • Free Library of Philadelphia • Philadelphia, PA 19103 • ALSC

Guevara Anne Mrs. • Sacred Heart School • Medford, OR 97501

Guffey Crystal M. • Athens, TN 37303

Guffey Gloria P. • Waldorf, MD 20601

Gugino Janice • Madison, WI 53703-3754 • ALSC IFRT SRRT

Guhin Emily K. • Aberdeen, SD 57401-9545

Guia Celine T. • Elk Grove, IL 60007

Guidarelli Ngoc-My • Student • University of Pittsburgh School of Library and Information Science • Pittsburgh, PA 15260 • ACRL

Guider Geneva Miss • El Paso, TX 79930-2503 • AASL YALSA *Life*

Guidinger Delmar • Branch Manager • Sebastopol Regional Branch Library • Sebastopol, CA 95472 • PLA

Guido John F. • Hd Ms Archives & Spec Cllns • Washington State University Library • Pullman, WA 99164-5610 • ACRL

Guidry Nancy T. • Young Adult Librarian • Santa Monica Public Library • Santa Monica, CA 90401 • YALSA

Guiett Diana S. • Columbus, OH 43212

Guilbert N. P. • Director of Material Resources • River East School Division #9 • Winnipeg MB, R2K 2P7 Canada • AASL

Guild Donna H. • School Librarian • John Muir Middle School • San Leandro, CA 94577 • AASL

Guile Eleanor A. • Troy, NY 12180

Guiles Kay Dean • Off for Descriptive Catlg Policy • Library of Congress • Washington, DC 20541 • ACRL ALCTS LITA RASD *Life*

Guilford Diane E. • Head Librarian • Langston Hughes Intermediate Sch • Reston, VA 22091 • AASL

Guilfoyle M C. • Periodicals Librarian • University of Evansville • Evansville, IN 47722 • ACRL

Guilfucci Ileana • Student • Inter American University Library San German Campus • San German, PR 00753

Guillory David • Assistant Catalog Librarian • McNeese State University Lether E. Frazar Memorial Library • Lake Charles, LA 70609

Guinn Mary E. • Elizabethtown, IN 47232 • AASL YALSA *Life*

Guinyard Allene J. Mrs • Media Specialist • American Senior High School • Hialeah, FL 33015 • AASL YALSA

Guirlinger Annette Nunn • Raleigh, NC 27607

Guitron Linda L. • Student • International Studies Academy • San Francisco, CA 94116 • AASL

Gulati Arthur S. • Coordinator of Public Services • Lake Villa Public Library District • Lake Villa, IL 60046

Guldner Joel R. • Cornell College Library Russell D. Cole Library • Mount Vernon, IA 52314 • IFRT

Guldseth Elizabeth A • Arlington, VA 22207 • ALSC

Gulick James E. • Ref. Librarian/Bibliographer • Haverford College James P. Magill Library • Haverford, PA 19041

Gulino Donna • Brooklyn, NY 11222

Gull Cloyd Dake • Silver Spring, MD 20906-1421

Gullett Elisabeth L. • Student • Florida State University School of Library and Information Studies • Tallahassee, FL 32306-2048 • PLA

Gullette Irene • Pompano Beach, FL 33060 • Continuing

Gulley Bobbie J. • Computer Dept. Supervisor • Salt Lake City Public Library • Salt Lake City, UT 84111 • LITA

Gulley Rose-Marie • Branch Manager • Broward County Libraries Collier City Branch • Pompano Beach, FL 33069 • NMRT

Gullikson Douglas L. • Student • University of Missouri-Columbia School of Library & Informational Science • Columbia, MO 65211 • SRRT

Gullikson Jean K. • Senior Librarian Youth • Tyler Public Library • Tyler, TX 75702 • ALSC

Gullion Susan L. • Head,Catalog Division • University of California-Los Angeles Biomedical Library • Los Angeles, CA 90024-1798 • ALCTS LITA

Gullo Robert • Director • Saint John Fisher College • Rochester, NY 14618 • LAMA

Gully Katherine B. • Librarian • Denver Museum of Natural History • Denver, CO 80205 • ALCTS LITA

Gulstad Rita J. • Director • Central Methodist College Smiley Memorial Library • Fayette, MO 65248 • ACRL RASD

Guma Karen E. • Librarian • Oakland Public Library Latin American Branch • Oakland, CA 94601 • ALSC ASCLA EMIERT SRRT

Gumerson Frances • Media Professional • Indianapolis Public Schools School #67 • Indianapolis, IN 46222 • AASL

Gumm Bruce A. • Student • University of Missouri-Columbia School of Library & Informational Science • Columbia, MO 65211

Gummere Judith B • A-V Librarian • Lake Forest Library • Lake Forest, IL 60045

Gumprecht Blake W. • Los Angeles Public Library • Los Angeles, CA 90071 • GODORT MAGERT

Gumulauski Debra A. • Reference Librarian • Lake County Public Library • Merrillville, IN 46410-5382 • PLA VRT

Gunckel David • Library Administrator • Sierra Vista Public Library • Sierra Vista, AZ 85635 • PLA IFRT

Gundara Jaswinder • Manager • Metropolitan Toronto Reference Library • Toronto ON, M4W 2G8 Canada • PLA RASD EMIERT

Gunde Michael G. • Associate Library Director • Florida Division of Blind Services • Daytona Beach, FL 32114 • ASCLA IFRT SRRT

Gundel Lorraine • Cancryn Junior High School • St. Thomas, VI 00801

Gunderman Merle D. • Asst. Manager, Extension Serv. • Toledo-Lucas County Public Library • Toledo, OH 43624

Gunderson Rebecca A. • Duncan, OK 73533

Gundrum Patricia C • Head,Technical Services • Lake Forest Library • Lake Forest, IL 60045

Gundy Frances Darnell • Student • Wayne State University Library Science Program • Detroit, MI 48202 • LITA IFRT NMRT SRRT

Gunkel Glenda J. • Librarian • Bruni High School • Bruni, TX 78344

Gunn-Bradley Joyce A. • Senior Branch Librarian • San Ramon Library • San Ramon, CA 94583 • ALSC PLA

Gunn Arthur A. • Associate Dean • Clark-Atlanta University School of Library & Information Studies • Atlanta, GA 30314-4391 • ACRL LHRT

Gunn Sharon M. • Atlanta, GA 30345 • AASL ALSC

Gunn Thomas H. • Director • Jacksonville University Carl S. Swisher Library • Jacksonville, FL 32211 • Life

Gunn Wendell • Treasuer, Board of Trustees • Lexington Public Library • Lexington, KY 40507 • ALTA

Gunnar Helge Mr. • Student • Long Island University Library School Library • Greenvale, NY 11548 • AASL

Gunnarsson Ingemar • Librarian • Telub AB • SE-351 80 Vaxjo, Sweden • LITA

Gunning Kathleen • Asst. Dir./Pub. Serv. & Clln Dev • University of Houston Libraries • Houston, TX 77204-2091 • ACRL LAMA LITA RASD IRRT

Gunsaulis Judy K. • Director • Fayette County Public Libraries • Oak Hill, WV 25901 • LAMA PLA

Gunson Alison • Assistant Head of Cataloging • Millikan Library • Pasadena, CA 91125 • LITA

Gunter Gwen • Director • Highland Home School • Highland Home, AL 36041

Gunter Joe D. • Director • Eagle County Public Library • Eagle, CO 81631 • LAMA LITA PLA RASD CLENE IFRT

Gunter Linda B. • Reference Librarian • Claremont Colleges Libraries Honnold/Mudd Library • Claremont, CA 91711 • ACRL RASD

Gunter Margaret • Trustee • Kansas City Public Library • Kansas City, MO 64106 • ALTA

Gunter Verlinda R. • Media Specialist • M.C. Riley Elementary School • Bluffton, SC 29910 • AASL

Guo Kezhen • Piscataway, NJ 08855 • LITA

Guo Youren • Student • University of Illinois Graduate School of Library and Information Science • Urbana, IL 61801

Gupta Meena • Student • University of Michigan School of Information and Library Studies • Ann Arbor, MI 48109-1092

Gupta Usha • University of Arkansas Mullins Library • Fayetteville, AR 72701

Gurcsik Joseph • Joseph J. Gurcsik Studios, Inc. • Rockledge, PA 19111

Gurevich Konstantin G. • Cataloger for Slavic Materials • Ohio State University Libraries • Columbus, OH 43210-1286 • ACRL

Gurewitz Kathryn V. • Northridge, CA 91324

Gurira Josephine F. • Ciculation Librarian/Deputy Hd • Zimbabwe University • Harare, Zimbabwe • ACRL

Gurrola Rosemary • Community Library Manager • Los Angeles County Public Library Maywood Library 412 • Maywood, CA 90270 • PLA NMRT

Gurshman Sandra J. • Manager, Publisher Services • Readmore • New York, NY 10007 • ALCTS LITA

Gursky Cynthia • Student • State University of New York (SUNY) School of Information & Library Studies • Buffalo, NY 14260

Gursky Kathryn M. • Librarian • Los Alamos National Lab Lib • Los Alamos, NM 87545-0020

Guscio Elizabeth N. • Student • University of South Carolina College of Library & Information Science • Columbia, SC 29208

Gushue Rhoda M. • Director • Bedford Hills Free Library • Bedford Hills, NY 10507 • PLA

Guss Emily R. • Regional Library Director • Chicago Public Library Carter G. Woodson Regional Library • Chicago, IL 60628 • PLA

Guss Karen M. • Student • University of Arizona Graduate Library School • Tucson, AZ 85721 • PLA

Gussin Harriet S. • Children's Librarian • Schenectady County Public Library Duane Branch • Schenectady, NY 12304

Gust Regina F. • Lubbock City-County Library • Lubbock, TX 79401 • YALSA

Gustafson Diane S. • Librarian • Southwestern College • Chula Vista, CA 91910 • ACRL

Gustafson Eleanor A. • Shrewsbury, MA 01545 • ACRL ALCTS *Continuing*

Gustafson Gary L. • Northern Arizona University Cline Library • Flagstaff, AZ 86011-6022

Gustafson Julia C. • Ref Ln/Bibl Instr Coor • College of Wooster Andrews Library • Wooster, OH 44691 • ACRL ASCLA LITA

Gustafson Kathleen Y. • Student • University of Hawaii School of Library & Information Studies • Honolulu, HI 96822 • ACRL

Gustafson Linda W. • Director • Belfast Area High School • Belfast, ME 04915 • AASL

Gustafson Nancy M. • Principal Serials Cataloger • University of Wyoming • Laramie, WY 82071 • LITA

Gustafson Rick E. • Mead Public Library • Sheboygan, WI 53081

Gustafson Ruth • Librarian • Elizabeth Public Library • Elizabeth, NJ 07202 • LITA

Gustafson Ruth A. • San Diego, CA 92122 • ACRL RASD LIRT

Gustaveson Susan K. • DYNIX Inc. • Provo, UT 84606

Gustavson Muriel J. • Student • St. Cloud State University • Saint Cloud, MN 56301 • PLA

Gustely Margo M. • Law Librarian • Manatt, Phelps, Phillips & Kantor • Washington, DC 20036 • LAMA

Gusts Lilita V. • Reference Librarian • Columbia University Libraries • New York, NY 10027 • LITA IRRT

Gusukuma Sherie K. • Reference Librarian • University of Hawaii Sinclair Library • Honolulu, HI 96816 • LIRT

Gutek Marya M. • Branch Librarian • Forest Township Library • Otisville, MI 48463

Guth Grace • School Librarian • Immaculate Conception Cathedral School • Lake Charles, LA 70601 • AASL ALSC

Guthrie-McNaughton Isabella C. • Librarian • Royal Ontario Museum • Toronto, ON, M5S 2C6 Canada • ACRL ALCTS LAMA LITA

Guthrie Dale • University of Missouri-Columbia School of Library & Informational Science • Columbia, MO 65211 • AASL

Guthrie Donna • Trustee • Pikes Peak Library District • Colorado Springs, CO 80901 • ALTA

Guthrie Douglas J. • Saint Paul Public Library • St. Paul, MN 55102 • LAMA RASD

Guthrie Jan • Student • Indian Plains Elementary School • Aurora, IL 60504

Guthrie Virginia • Five Points West Library • Birmingham, AL 35208 • YALSA IFRT

Guthro Clem P. • Point Loma Nazarene College Ryan Library • San Diego, CA 92106

Gutierrez-Witt Laura • Head of Benson Collection • University of Texas Benson Latin American Collection • Austin, TX 78713-7330 • ACRL IRRT

Gutierrez Carolyn • Stockton State College • Pomona, NJ 08240 • ACRL RASD

Gutierrez H. John • Librarian • Ratcliff Architects • Emeryville, CA 94608 • PLA SRRT

Gutierrez Ruby • Student • University of California-Los Angeles (UCLA) • Los Angeles, CA 90024-1450

Gutschenritter Victoria M. • Head/Mags., Newspapers & Fiction • Saint Joseph County Public Library • South Bend, IN 46601 • PLA

Gutteridge Jane • U.S. Sales Manager • National Film Board of Canada • New York, NY 10020

Guy Patricia • Senior Reference Librarian • Bay Area Library & Information System • Oakland, CA 94607 • RASD

Guy Susan A. • Public Library of Nashville and Davidson County • Nashville, TN 37203-3585

Guy Wendell A. • Director of the Library • Saint Francis College McGarry Library • Brooklyn Heights, NY 11201 • ACRL

Guydon Janet Hawkins • Head Librarian/General • Gary Public Library Dubois Branch • Gary, IN 46407-2298 • PLA

Guyette Fred • Saint Andrew's-Sewanee School • St. Andrews, TN 37372 • ACRL

Guyette Kay K. • Director • Shiocton Public Library • Shiocton, WI 54170

Guynes Catherine D. • Asst. Reference Librarian • West Texas State University Cornette Library • Canyon, TX 79016-0748 • ACRL

Guyonneau Christine H. • Reference Librarian • University of Indianapolis Krannert Memorial Library • Indianapolis, IN 46227 • ACRL RASD IRRT

Guyton Andrew L. • Seaside, CA 93955

Guzi Gloria J. • Akron, OH 44313 • ALCTS IFRT

Guzman Isidro Jr. • Corpus Christi State University • Corpus Chrsti, TX 78412

Guzman Mario A. • Reference Librarian • San Francisco Public Library Mission Branch • San Francisco, CA 94110 • EMIERT

Guzniczak Vivian • President • Milwaukee County Federated Library System • Milwaukee, WI 53233 • ALTA

Guzzy Judith E. • Serials Librarian • McNeese State University Lether E. Frazar Memorial Library • Lake Charles, LA 70609

Gwaltney Dolores D. • Ln-media Spec • Lutheran High West School • Detroit, MI 48228

Gwiazdowski Theresa A. • Student • San Jose State University Division of Library & Information Science • San Jose, CA 95192-0029 • LITA IFRT

Gwin James E. • Director of Technical Servs. • University of Richmond • Richmond, VA 23173 • ACRL

Gwinn Nancy E. • Asst Dir Clln Mgt • Smithsonian Institution Libraries • Washington, DC 20560 • ACRL ALCTS LAMA LITA *Life*

Gwyn Ann S. • Assistant Director-Spec. Clln. • Johns Hopkins University Milton S. Eisenhower Library • Baltimore, MD 21218 • ACRL

Gwyn Elizabeth • Reference Librarian • Sonoma County Library • Santa Rosa, CA 95404 • PLA

Gwyn Trish • Director • Rockingham County Public Library • Eden, NC 27288 • PLA IFRT

Gwynn Jane • Librarian • Norfolk Christian Schools • Norfolk, VA 23505

Gwynne Vanessa V. • AV/Reference Librarian • Coronado Public Library • Coronado, CA 92118 • PLA NMRT

Gyeszly Suzanne D. • Social Sci & Preservation Libn • Texas A & M University Sterling C. Evans Library • College Station, TX 77843-5000 • ACRL RASD

Gylseth Doris Hanson • School Librarian • Willard School • Long Beach, CA 90804 • ALSC

Gyori Irene T. • Sr. Electronic Svs Rep. • Baker & Taylor Books • Bridgewater, NJ 08807 • LITA NMRT

Haack John O. • Trustee • Clinton Public Library • Clinton, IA 52732 • ALTA

Haack Robert • Student • Emporia State University School of Library & Information Management • Emporia, KS 66801 • SRRT

Haag Enid E. Mrs • Education Librarian • Western Washington University Wilson Library • Bellingham, WA 98225 • ACRL

Haag Mary A. • Torrance, CA 90505 • AASL

Haag Nancy R. • Reference Librarian • North Haven Memorial Library • North Haven, CT 06473

Haake Susan J. • Senior Librarian • Commission on Peace Officer Standards & Training Lib. • Sacramento, CA 95816 • LITA

Haaker-Aronson Mary J. • Librarian • Reingold Elementary School • Fitchburg, MA 01420 • AASL

Haan Ralph • Calvin Christian High School • Grandville, MI 48418

Haar Gail R. • Reference Librarian • Marin County Free Library • San Rafael, CA 94903

Haar John M. III • Head, Clln Mgt Ser Dept. • Virginia Commonwealth University • Richmond, VA 23284-2033 • ACRL ALCTS

Haas-Wolfson Jody • Resource Technology Associates, Inc. • Des Plaines, IL 60018

Haas Carolyn B. • East Hampton, NY 11937-6027

Haas Dorothy A. • Library Clerk • Port Jervis Free Library • Port Jervis, NY 12771 • NMRT

Haas Elaine S. • President • Technical Library Service, Inc. • New York, NY 10001 • ACRL ALCTS

Haas Eva L. • Headquarters United States Air Force Europe • APO, AE 09094 • PLA FLRT

Haas Hedy L. • Cataloger • Brandeis University Main Library • Waltham, MA 02254-9110 • ACRL ALCTS LITA EMIERT ILERT

Haas Henry • Trustee • Tacoma Public Library • Tacoma, WA 98402 • ALTA

Haas John A. • Reference Librarian • Acorn Public Library District • Oak Forest, IL 60452

Haas Karyn F. • DeSoto, TX 75115 • AASL

Haas Leslie M. • Business Reference Librarian • Kent State University Libraries • Kent, OH 44242 • RASD

Haas Marilyn L. • Reference & Collection Devel. • State University of New York (SUNY) at Buffalo • Buffalo, NY 14260 • ACRL RASD

Haas Nancy J. • Student • University of Wisconsin-Milwaukee School of Library & Information Science • Milwaukee, WI 53201

Haas Ruth S. • Chief Serials Cataloger/CONSER • Harvard University Library • Cambridge, MA 02138-2901 • ALCTS

Haas Susan B. • Plano Public Library System W.O. Haggard Library • Plano, TX 75075 • LAMA PLA

Haas Warren J. • Washington, DC 20003 • Continuing

Haase Patricia A. • Library Tech. • Pikes Peak Library District • Colorado Springs, CO 80901-1579

Haaser Marsha K. • Librarian • Incline Middle School Library • Incline Village, NV 89450

Haban Mary • Professor of Library Science • James Madison University • Harrisonburg, VA 22807 • AASL ACRL LITA

Habel Sue A. • Ln Services Manager/Operations • Volusia County Public Library • Daytona Beach, FL 32124 • LAMA PLA

Haber Amy C. Mrs. • Trustee • The Bryant Library • Roslyn, NY 11576

Haber Walter • Lebanon, PA 17042 • Continuing

Haberkern Patricia L. • Student • University of North Carolina at Chapel Hill School of Information and Library Science • Chapel Hill, NC 27599-3360 • ACRL NMRT

Haberland Gail M. • Student • Florida State University School of Library and Information Studies • Tallahassee, FL 32306-2048

Haberland Jody • Head Fiction Fine Arts Sections • Arlington County Department of Libraries • Arlington, VA 22201

Haberli Joann L. • Director • Tusten-Cochecton Library • Narrowsburg, NY 12764

Haberman Mary • Young Adult Librarian • Maude Shunk Public Library • Menomonee Falls, WI 53051 • YALSA

Habermann Sigrun • Student • State University of New York School of Information & Library Sci • Albany, NY 12203 • PLA

Habib Joan • Coordinator of Media Services • Peel Board of Education • Mississauga, ON, L5R 1C6 Canada • AASL ALCTS LITA

Habich Elizabeth C. • Adminstrative Services Officer • Northeastern University Libraries • Boston, MA 02115 • ACRL LAMA LITA

Habstritt Mary • University of Minnesota Meredith Wilson Library • Minneapolis, MN 55455

Hach Stacy E. • Systems Administrator • Moravian College & Theological Seminary Reeves Library • Bethlehem, PA 18018 • NMRT

Hachmeister Helen M. • Director • Saint Francis Public Library • Saint Francis, WI 53235 • PLA

Hack Leo M. • Librarian • Black & Veatch • Kansas City, MO 64112 • LAMA PLA RASD

Hack Rosalinda I. • Chief Visual & Performing Arts • Chicago Public Library Harold Washington Library • Chicago, IL 60605

Hacken Richard • Germanic Lang. Bibliographer • Brigham Young University Harold B. Lee Library • Provo, UT 84602 • ACRL

Hackenberg Michael • Turtle Island Booksellers • Berkeley, CA 94704 • ACRL LHRT

Hacker Betty L. • Ft Collins, CO 80524

Hacker Carol P. • Roselle Public Library • Roselle, IL 60172 • RASD

Hacker Harold S. • Rochester, NY 14607 • PLA *Continuing*

Hacker Lois • New York, NY 10023 • Continuing

Hacker Martha K. • Boulder City, NV 89005 • ASCLA PLA *Continuing*

Hacker Mary H. • Anchorage, AK 99517 • AASL

Hackett Annastacia T. • Student • University of Washington Graduate School of Library and Information Science • Seattle, WA 98195

Hackett Cynthia A. • Substitute Teacher/Media Spec. • Anne Arundel County Public Schools • Annapolis, MD 21401 • AASL

Hackett Dorothy A. • Saint Pius X High School • Pottstown, PA 19464-2899

Hackett Joan L. • Director of Children Library • Harmomy Library • Harmony, RI 02829

Hackett Marlyn M. • Cook Memorial Library • Libertyville, IL 60048

Hackett Nancy • Head Librarian Chairperson Libra • Fountaindale Public Library Dist • Romeoville, IL 60441 • ALSC LAMA PLA

Hackett Timothy P. • Assistant Professor-Reference • California State University Library Dominguez Hills • Carson, CA 94705 • GODORT IFRT NMRT

Hackleman Debra • Head Catalog Dept. • Oregon State University William Jasper Kerr Library • Corvallis, OR 97331-4501 • ALCTS LITA

Hackman Philip F. • Chillocothe, OH 45601-1893

Hackney Carrie M. • Librarian • Howard University Libraries Founders Library • Washington, DC 20059 • RASD LIRT

Hackney Nancy • Lake Jackson Library • Lake Jackson, TX 77566

Hackworth Carolyn M. • Librarian • American Community School • Washington, DC 20521-6010

Hackworth Joan • Library Media Specialist • Lake Oswego Junior High School • Lake Oswego, OR 97034

Hada Jerrianne • Kingman High School • Kingman, KS 67068 • AASL

Hadaway Glyndell C. Mrs. • Director • Pinellas County School Board • Clearwater, FL 34624

Haddad Ann • Director • Falmouth Public Library • Falmouth, MA 02540 • LITA PLA

Haddad Marjorie A. • Brooklyn, NY 11209

Haddad Rosemary M. • Associate Librarian • Canadian Center for Architecture Library • PQ H3H 2S6, Canada • ACRL ALCTS

Hadden Joan E. • Dartmouth Elementary School • Aurora, CO 80013 • LITA

Hadden John K. • Director • Jefferson County Public Library • Louisville, GA 30434 • PLA

Hadden Linda W. • Director • Duplin County Library Wightman Library • Kenansville, NC 28349 • PLA

Haddix Eileen • Director of Library Services • Hazard Community College • Hazard, KY 41701 • ACRL GODORT

Haddock Michael J. • Science Reference Librarian • Kansas State University Farrell Library • Manhattan, KS 66506-1200 • ACRL

Haddock Miranda H. • Batavia, IL 60510

Haddock Suzanne M. • Student • Nogales/Santa Cruz County Library • Nogales, AZ 85621

Hadeler G. Kurt • Pearl River, NY 10965

Hadjimitsos Laura M. • Ela Area Public Library District • Lake Zurich, IL 60047

Hadley-Banahene Sara S. • Jersey City, NJ 07305

Hadley Alice E. • Medical Librarian • United States Naval Hospital Guam • FPO San Francisco, CA 96630-1649 • Life

Hadley Cheryl B. • Woodinville, WA 98072 • ALSC

Hadley Diana L. • Adult Services Librarian • Douglas County Library System • Roseburg, OR 97470

Hadley Janet M. • Librarian • Chukchi Consortium Library • Kotzebue, AK 99752 • AASL YALSA

Hadley Mary K. • Acton, MA 01720 • ALSC YALSA
Continuing

Hadley Peter H. • Laboratory Librarian • University of California Los Angeles Graduate School of Library & Information Science • Los Angeles, CA 90024

Hadley Virginia C. • Library Assistant • Sonoma County Library Guerneville Branch Library • Guerneville, CA 95446 • NMRT

Hadlock Ruth C. • Librarian • Marin Country Day School • Corte Madera, CA 94925 • EMIERT

Hadlow Ruth M. • Head, Children's Literature Dept • Cleveland Public Library • Cleveland, OH 44114-1271 • AASL ALSC PLA

Haebich Gail • Public Services Librarian • Kent County Library System East Grand Rapids Branch • East Grand Rapids, MI 49506

Haefele Ann W. • Children's Program Coordinator • Janes Branch Library • East Rochester, NY 14445 • ALSC

Haeker Jane • St. Vrain Valley School District • Longmont, CO 80501 • LITA

Haemker Charles H. • Extension Services Manager • Grand Rapids Public Library • Grand Rapids, MI 49503-3093 • LAMA

Haeuser Michael • Head Librarian • Gustavus Adolphus College Folke Bernadotte Memorial Library • St Peter, MN 56082 • ACRL ALCTS LAMA RASD IFRT LIRT SORT

Hafeman Robert E. • Director • Stinson Memorial Library • Anna, IL 62906

Hafner Arthur W. PhD • Director • American Medical Association • Chicago, IL 60610

Hafner Clara B D • Lewiston, MN 55952-0726 • ALCTS PLA
Continuing

Hafner Joseph • Librarian • Indianapolis Marion County Public Library • Indianapolis, IN 46206

Hafner Ruth • Librarian • Northbrook Public Library • Northbrook, IL 60062

Hafner William • Western Carolina University Hunter Library • Cullowhee, NC 28723-9002 • ACRL ALCTS RASD LIRT LRRT

Hafter Ruth • Professor • San Jose State University Division of Library & Information Science • San Jose, CA 95192-0029 • ACRL LAMA LRRT

Hagan Dalia Lapatinskas • Library Director • Saint Martins College • Lacey, WA 98503 • AASL ACRL ALCTS LAMA LITA GODORT

Hagan Michael F. • Director • Perrot Memorial Library • Old Greenwich, CT 06870 • PLA

Hagan Timothy L. • Student • University of Illinois Graduate School of Library and Information Science • Urbana, IL 61801

Hagar Alice • La Crosse, WI 54601 • Continuing

Hagberg Dorothy F. • Detroit Public Library • Detroit, MI 48202 • Continuing

Hage Christine L. • Director • Rochester Hills Public Library • Rochester, MI 48307 • LAMA PLA

Hage Elizabeth A. • Minneapolis, MN 55406 • ILERT

Hagedorn Dorothy • New Orleans, LA 70125 • Continuing

Hagedorn Margaret J. • Reference Librarian • Skokie Public Library • Skokie, IL 60077-3680 • RASD

Hagedorn Susan • Librarian • Willow Crest Elementary School Library • Anchorage, AK 99503 • AASL

Hagedorn William R. • Coordinator • North Suburban Library System Central Serials Services • Morton Grove, IL 60053 • ALCTS

Hagel Margaret M. • Branch Manager • Norfolk Public Library Little Creek Branch • Norfolk, VA 23518 • PLA IFRT

Hagelin Daniel Warn • Cleveland, OH 44109 • Continuing

Hagelin J Lars • Special Projects Librarian • Mid-Continent Public Library • Independence, MO 64050

Hageman Ronald B. • Reference Supervisor • Michigan City Public Library • Michigan City, IN 46360

Hagemeier Deborah A. • Bibliographic Access Librarian • Augustana College Mikkelsen Library • Sioux Falls, SD 57197 • LITA

Hagemeyer Alice L. • Silver Spg, MD 20904-1816 • ALCTS ASCLA PLA

Hagen Ada Miss • Ames, IA 50010 • Continuing

Hagen Becky • Reference Librarian • University of Saint Thomas • St. Paul, MN 55105 • ACRL

Hagen Dennis D. • Bibliographic Systems Librarian • California State Library • Sacramento, CA 94237-0001 • ALCTS

Hagen Miriam D. • Elisha D Smith Public Library • Menasha, WI 54952-3143 • PLA

Hagensee Susan E. • District Librarian • Center Cass School District #66 • Downers Grove, IL 60516 • AASL

Hager Elizabeth A. • Assistant Director • High Plains Regional Library Service System • Greeley, CO 80631 • AASL

Hager H. Lucille • Austin, TX 78731 • Continuing

Hager John R. • Student • Florida State University School of Library and Information Studies • Tallahassee, FL 32306-2048 • AASL

Hagerman Dorothy Mrs • Fairfax, VA 22030 • Continuing

Hagerty Elizabeth Ann • Librarian • Saddleback College • Mission Viejo, CA 92692

Haggart Juna • Portland, OR 97220

Haggarty Patrick W. • Ln • Oakland Public Library • Oakland, CA 94612

Haggarty Penny • Manager, Curriculum Resources • Vancouver School Board • Vancouver BC, V5R 2Y7 Canada • ALCTS

Haggerty Gary W. • Assistant Librarian • Berklee College of Music • Boston, MA 02115 • ACRL LITA

Haggerty Janeann • Buffalo, NY 14214 • AASL

Haggerty Mary W. • Deerfield, IL 60015 • ALSC
Continuing

Haggerty Maxine R. • Librarian Document Division • University of Utah Marriott Library • Salt Lake City, UT 84112-1179 • ACRL RASD GODORT

Hagin Ida Mae • Statesboro, GA 30458-9715 • Continuing

Hagle Claudette S. • Director of Public Services • University of Dallas William A. Blakley Library • Irving, TX 75062 • ACRL RASD

Hagler Ronald • Professor • University of British Columbia School of Library, Archival & Information Studies • Vancouver BC, V6T 1Z1 Canada • ALCTS

Hagloch Susan B. • Director • Tuscarawas County Public Library • New Phila, OH 44663-2634 • LAMA

Haglund Karen M. • Library Media Specialist • Harrand Creek Elementary School • Enterprise, AL 36330 • AASL

Hagood John Lindsey • Student • Simmons College Graduate School of Library & Information Science • Boston, MA 02115

Hagood Patricia • President • Oxbridge Commun. Inc. • New York, NY 10011

Hagstrom Steven W. Dr. • Library Director • Tarrant County Junior College Northeast Campus • Hurst, TX 76054 • ACRL LAMA

Hague R Dale • Head, Technical Services • Miami University Edgar W. King Library • Oxford, OH 45056 • ALCTS

Hagyard Alan • Hamden, CT 06517 • ACRL LITA

Hahn Bessie K. • University Librarian • Brandeis University Goldfarb Library • Waltham, MA 02254-9110 • ACRL

Hahn Betty Jean • Minneapolis, MN 55416 • Life

Hahn Boksoon • Hd Catlg Ln East Asian Clln • Yale University Sterling Memorial Library • New Haven, CT 06520 • ALCTS

Hahn Doyne M. • Reference Librarian/Asst. Prof. • Ball State University Bracken Library • Muncie, IN 47306-0160 • ACRL RASD
Life

Hahn Ellen • Dir. Public Serv & Clln. Mgr. • Library of Congress • Washington, DC 20541

Hahn Harvey • Palatine Public Library • Palatine, IL 60067 • ALCTS

Hahn Joyce K. • Librarian • Southern Elementary School • Lexington, KY 40503 • AASL

Hahn Karla L. • Manager for Curriculum Support • Johns Hopkins University Libraries William H Welch Medical Library • Baltimore, MD 21205

Hahn Maureen • Adult Service Librarian • Township of Shaler North Hills Library • Glenshaw, PA 15116

Hahn Susan E. • Student • Indiana University School of Library and Information Science • Bloomington, IN 47405

Hahne Linda L. • Administrative Assistant • Norfolk Public Library • Norfolk, VA 23510-1776

Hahus Linda K. • Supervisor for Youth Services • San Diego Public Library • San Diego, CA 92101 • ALSC NMRT

Haidar Ali H. • Inspector General • Ministry of Education School Library Adminstration • Safat, Kuwait • AASL

Haider Ron • Davis Middle School • Evanston, WY 82731-6002 • AASL

Haight Ann K. • Bibliography • Kalamazoo College Library • Kalamazoo, MI 49007-3285 • ALCTS

Haight Audrey Jean • Documents Librarian • Montana State University • Bozeman, MT 59717-0332 • ACRL GODORT

Haight Toni K. • Chemeketa Community College • Salem, OR 97309

Haikalis Peter D. • Librarian • San Francisco State University J. Paul Leonard Library • San Francisco, CA 94132 • ACRL LAMA

Haikin Lauralie M.G. • Student • Alameda County Library System • Fremont, CA 94538

Haile Dorothy • Librarian • Sherman County Public Library • Stratford, TX 79084

Haile Judy B • Library Media Specialist • Searcy Public Schools Ahlf Junior High School • Searcy, AR 72143 • AASL

Haimes Anne T. • Unit Manager • Atlanta-Fulton Public Library Northside Branch • Atlanta, GA 30327

Hain Marcella A. • Salem, CT 06420-3917 • IFRT SRRT

Hain Muriel • Everett, WA 98201

Haines Eleanor M. • Librarian/Media Specialist • T. E. Harrington Middle School Library • Mt. Laurel, NJ 08054 • AASL

Haines Fran • Librarian • John Baptist High School • Bangor, ME 04401

Haines Nancy H. • Media Spec • Barron Collier High School • Naples, FL 33942 • AASL IFRT

Haines Sharon G. • Branch Librarian • Greenup County Public Library Flatwoods Branch • Flatwoods, KY 41139 • PLA

Haines Valerie A. • Head of Adult Service • New Haven Free Public Library • New Haven, CT 06510

Haines William L. • Documents/Reference Librarian • Sarah Lawrence College Esther Raushenbush Library • Bronxville, NY 10708 • ACRL GODORT

Haire Jennifer C. • Branch Manager • Baltimore County Public Library Woodlawn Branch • Baltimore, MD 21207 • PLA

Haire Paul • Librarian • Temple Junior College • Temple, TX 76504 • ACRL ALCTS LITA

Hairgrove Dorothy G. Miss • Sitka, AK 99835 • ALSC PLA
Continuing

Hairston Irene Mrs • Trustee • Forsyth County Public Library • Winston-Salem, NC 27101 • ALTA PLA

Haist Lillian M. • Media Specialist • Robert Smalls Middle School • Beaufort, SC 29902 • AASL

Hajjar Tania G. • Student • University of Kentucky College of Library & Information Science • Lexington, KY 40506-0391

Hajnal Peter I. • Government Publications Spec. • University of Toronto • Toronto ON, M5S 1A5 Canada • ACRL GODORT

Haka Clifford H. • Michigan State University Libraries • East Lansing, MI 48824-1048 • ACRL LAMA

Hakimi Sharon E. • Los Angeles, CA 90045

Halbeisen Johanna • Student • University of Rhode Island Graduate School of Library & Information Studies • Kingston, RI 02881-0815 • AASL

Halbert Barbara S. • Special Collections Assistant • Rice University Fondren Library • Houston, TX 77251-1892

Halbert Martin • Rice University Fondren Library • Houston, TX 77251-1892 • ACRL LITA RASD

Halbrook Anne-Mieke P. • Head,Research Svs. & Clln Mgmt • Getty Center Resources Collections • Santa Monica, CA 90401 • ALCTS LAMA LITA

Halcli Albert • Springfield, IL 62704

Halcrow Katherine O. • University of California-Berkeley School of Library & Information Studies • Berkeley, CA 94720

Haldane Mary K. • Russian Jack Elementary School • Anchorage, AK 99508 • AASL

Haldeman Alice B. • Edgewater, FL 32132 • LAMA PLA

Haldeman Glenna Ruth • Ann Arbor Public Library • Ann Arbor, MI 48104 • PLA RASD

Hale Barbara S. • University of Kentucky Libraries • Lexington, KY 40506-0039

Hale Carolyn Rowe • Area Adminstrator • Free Library of Philadelphia • Philadelphia, PA 19103 • LAMA PLA

Hale Charles E. • Library Director • Millikin University Staley Library • Decatur, IL 62522 • ACRL

Hale Dawn L. • Head Cataloging • Johns Hopkins University Milton S. Eisenhower Library • Baltimore, MD 21218 • ALCTS LITA

Hale Diane L. • Library Circulation Atten. III • Phoenix Public Library Cholla Branch • Phoenix, AZ 85051-1598 • PLA

Hale Elizabeth • Asst to the Dir for Automated Sv • District of Columbia Public Library Martin Luther King Memorial Library • Washington, DC 20001 • LAMA LITA IFRT

Hale James Dr. • Trustee • Deer Park Public Library • Deer Park, TX 77536 • ALTA PLA

Hale Kathleen R. • Student • Millersville University • Millersville, PA 17551

Hale Kay K. • Librarian • University of Miami Rosenstiel School • Miami, FL 33149

Hale Kaycee • Fashion Institute of Design & Merchandising • Los Angeles, CA 90015 • ACRL LAMA

Hale Kimberly A. • Acquisitions/Serials Librarian • Columbia College Library • Chicago, IL 60605 • ACRL ALCTS

Hale Martha L. • Faculty • Emporia State University School of Library & Information Management • Emporia, KS 66801 • ACRL PLA LRRT

Hale Paula L. • Phoenix, AZ 85051 • PLA IFRT SRRT

Hale Robert G. • Madison, CT 06443 • AASL

Hale Ruth C. • Archives/Records Management • Georgia Institute of Technology Price Gilbert Memorial Library • Atlanta, GA 30332-0900 • ACRL LAMA RASD

Hales-Mabry Celia • Reference/Instruction Librarian • University of Minnesota Meredith Wilson Library • Minneapolis, MN 55455 • ACRL RASD LIRT

Hales David A. • Professor of Library Science • University of Alaska Elmer E. Rasmuson Library • Fairbanks, AK 99775-1005

Hales Glen • Trustee • Las Vegas-Clark County Library District Flamingo Library • Las Vegas, NV 89119 • ALTA

Hales John D. Jr. • Director of Libraries • Suwannee River Regional Library • Live Oak, FL 32060 • LAMA PLA

Haley Alice S. • Librarian • Greendale Public Library • Greendale, WI 53129

Haley Anne E. • Director • Walla Walla Public Library • Walla Walla, WA 99362 • LAMA PLA IRRT

Haley Annette N. • Grosse Ile High School Library • Grosse Ile, MI 48138 • AASL IFRT

Haley Cynthia C. • Library Media Specialist • Rome Board of Education • Rome, NY 13440

Haley Jan L. • Librarian • Textron Aerostructures • Nashville, TN 37202

Haley Jean W. • Director of Library Service • University of Saint Thomas O'Shaughnessy-Frey Library • Saint Paul, MN 55105 • ACRL LAMA GODORT IFRT

Haley Susan M. • Student • University of Missouri-Columbia School of Library & Informational Science • Columbia, MO 65211 • ALSC PLA

Haley Velma J. • Children's Coordinator • Portsmouth Public Library • Portsmouth, VA 23704

Halford Gwendolyn N. • Manager • Toledo-Lucas County Public Library Mott Branch • Toledo, OH 43607

Halford Mary-Bess • Reference Librarian • Bethany College Phillips Memorial Library • Bethany, WV 26032

Halgren Joanne V. • Head, Interlibrary Loan Services • University of Oregon Library • Eugene, OR 97403-1299 • ACRL

Halgren Kathy M. • Student • University of Wisconsin School of Library & Information Studies • Madison, WI 53706 • ACRL PLA RASD IFRT SRRT

Halkett Patricia H. • Student • San Jose State University Division of Library & Information Science • San Jose, CA 95192-0029

Hall Alan C. • Director • Public Library of Steubenville & Jefferson County • Steubenville, OH 43952 • PLA

Hall Alice L. • Waukegan, IL 60085

Hall Ann E. • Children's Librarian • United States Navy Medical Library Naval Hospital • Camp Pendleton, CA 92055

Hall Barbara • Venus Elementary School • Venus, TX 76084

Hall Barbara G. • Young Adult Services Librarian • Los Altos Public Library • Los Altos, CA 94022 • YALSA NMRT

Hall Barbara R. • Newport Beach, CA 92660

Hall Barnabas Sr. • Librarian • Dominican College Library • Blauvelt, NY 10913 • ACRL ALCTS RASD

Hall Beverly M. • Dothan, AL 36301

Hall Blaine H. • Humanities Librarian • Brigham Young University Harold B. Lee Library • Provo, UT 84602 • ACRL RASD

Hall C. Dianne • Coos Bay, OR 97420

Hall Carol A. • Student • Rosary College Graduate School of Library & Information Science • River Forest, IL 60305 • ALTA PLA

Hall Carolyn L. • Children's Librarian • Carrollton Public Library • Carrollton, TX 75006 • ALSC PLA YALSA

Hall Clark • Non-Fiction Services Librarian • Joliet Public Library • Joliet, IL 60431

Hall Commie Jo • Media Specialist • Lincoln Elementary School • Franklin, KY 42134 • AASL

Hall Crystal D. • Student • Florida State University School of Library and Information Studies • Tallahassee, FL 32306-2048

Hall Cynthia A. • Assistant Head of Reference • Porter Public Library • Westlake, OH 44145 • RASD GODORT

Hall D. Susan • Student • University of Hawaii School of Library & Information Studies • Honolulu, HI 96822

Hall David H. • Librarian • Sunnyvale Public Library • Sunnyvale, CA 94088-3714 • PLA

Hall Debbie • Director • Art Circle Public Library • Crossville, TN 38555

Hall Diana E. • Information Services Librarian • University of Washington Health Science Library & Info Center • Seattle, WA 98195 • RASD

Hall Diane S. • W. W. Gordon Elementary School • Richmond, VA 23236 • AASL

Hall Dianne F. • Documents Librarian • East Brunswick Public Library • E. Brunswick, NJ 08816 • GODORT

Hall Edward J. Jr. • Associate Prof., Head Map Lib. • Kent State University Libraries • Kent, OH 44242 • ACRL RASD FLRT GODORT MAGERT

Hall Elaine N. • Manager, Collection Devel. • National Library of New Zealand • Wellington, 6001, New Zealand • ALCTS LAMA LITA

Hall Elede Toppy • Librarian • Addison-Wesley Publishing Company • Menlo Park, CA 94025 • RASD

Hall Ethyl • Trustee • Anderson County Library • Anderson, SC 29622-4047

Hall Evelyn E. • Branch Librarian • Queens Borough Public Library • Jamaica, NY 11432

Hall F. Ellen • Audiovisual Supervisor • Bay County High School • Panama City, FL 32401 • AASL

Hall Forrest A. • Educational Research Center • Library of Congress • Washington, DC 20541

Hall Gary W. • Administrator • American Library Consultants • Huntington, NY 11743 • LAMA

Hall Heidi J. • Elementary Librarian • Puyallup School District Brouillet Elementary School • Puyallup, WA 98373

Hall Henry P. Jr Dr • Library Director • St. Mary's University Academic Library • San Antonio, TX 78228

Hall Holly • Head of Special Collections • Washington University Libraries • Saint Louis, MO 63130-4899 • ACRL

Hall Howard L. • Librarian • Cypress High School Library • Cypress, CA 90630 • AASL YALSA

Hall J. Mark • Media Services Librarian • Trevecca Nazarene College • Nashville, TN 37210

Hall James C. • Student • University of Iowa School of Library & Information Science • Iowa City, IA 52242 • ACRL

Hall Janet O. • Leighton, PA 18235-9316

Hall Jeri Ann • Media Specialist • Chattahoochee High School • Alpharetta, GA 30202 • AASL

Hall Jo Ann • Southwest High School • Jacksonville, NC 28540

Hall Jo Anne • Ann Arbor, MI 48107 • ACRL LAMA RASD EMIERT ILERT LIRT

Hall John D. • Head Cataloging Services • University of Houston Libraries • Houston, TX 77204-2091 • ALCTS SRRT

Hall John P. • Librarian • Greater Lowell Regional Vocational-Technical High School Library • Tyngsboro, MA 01879 • AASL ACRL

Hall Joyce H. • Librarian II • San Joaquin Valley Library System • Fresno, CA 93721 • RASD

Hall Juanita J. • Head, Technical Service • Morehead State University Camden-Carroll Library • Morehead, KY 40351 • ACRL ALCTS

Hall Kathleen Frederick • Ft. Lauderdale, FL 33315

Hall Kenneth Dean • Asst. Director • Mc Millan Memorial Library • Wisc Rapids, WI 54494 • PLA

Hall Lawrence E. • Reference/Documents Librarian • Alma College • Alma, MI 48801 • ACRL

Hall Leilani A. • Assistant Librarian • Princeton University Engineering Library • Princeton, NJ 08540

Hall Linda W. • Project Coordinator • Free Library of Philadelphia • Philadelphia, PA 19103

Hall Lois J. • Minneapolis, MN 55417

Hall Margaret • Lincoln, NE 68505

Hall Margery B. • Ludington Library • Bryn Mawr, PA 19010 • ALSC

Hall Marion L S • Onondaga County Public Library at the Galleries • Syracuse, NY 13202-2494

Hall Martha G. Miss • Belmont, NC 28012 • ACRL ALCTS   *Continuing*

Hall Mary A. • Chief, Public Services Support • Prince George's County Memorial Library System • Hyattsville, MD 20782-2098

Hall Paula • Carnegie Library of Pittsburgh Squirrel Hill Branch • Pittsburgh, PA 15217

Hall Phyllis M. • Salt Lake City, UT 84117-7400

Hall Richard B. • Library Consultant • California State Library Library Development Services Bureau • Sacramento, CA 95814-3324 • LAMA PLA

Hall Rita M. • Student • State University of New York (SUNY) School of Information & Library Studies • Buffalo, NY 14260

Hall Sandra N. • Media Specialist • Gahanna Middle School West • Gahanna, OH 43230

Hall Susan L. • Mississippi State University Mitchell Memorial Library • Mississippi State, MS 39762

Hall Susan M. • Rochester, NY 14625 • ACRL

Hall Sylvia • Chief Librarian • Vaughan Public Libraries • Maple ON, L6A 1T1 Canada • LAMA LITA

Hall Sylvia D. • President • Blue Bear Group Inc • Central City, CO 80427

Hall Thelma W. • Reference Librarian • Bridgewater College Alexander Mack Memorial Library • Bridgewater, VA 22812 • ACRL

Hall Thomas • Trustee • Baldwin Public Library • Birmingham, MI 48012-3002

Hall Thomas W. • Student • University of Wisconsin-Milwaukee School of Library & Information Science • Milwaukee, WI 53201

Hall Wendy • Library Manager • Boulder Public Library Meadows Branch • Boulder, CO 80303

Hall Wendy D. • Columbia College Library • Chicago, IL 60605

Halla Jennifer A. • Children's Librarian • Saint Louis Public Library Carondelet Branch • St. Louis, MO 63108 • ALSC

Hallam Arlita • North Richland Hills Public Library • North Richland Hills, TX 76180 • LAMA PLA

Hallard Lynn B. • Student • Catholic University of America School of Library and Information Science • Washington, DC 20064 • NMRT

Hallaron Elizabeth M. • Youth Services Librarian • Waukegan Public Library • Waukegan, IL 60085 • ALSC

Hallaron Joan M. • Librarian • Hinckley Big Rock High School • Hinckley, IL 60520

Hallberg Sharon P. • Librarian • Davis Senior High School • Davis, CA 95616 • AASL YALSA

Hallblade Shirley • Associate Director of Libraries • Vanderbilt University Library Jean & Alexander Heard Library • Nashville, TN 37240-0007 • ACRL

Hallen Leo • President • Hallenbook • Chatham, NY 12037 • AASL ACRL

Haller Huddy B. • Technical Information Specialist • Defense Technical Information Center • Alexandria, VA 22304-6145 • FLRT

Hallewell Laurence • University of Minnesota O. Meredith Wilson Library • Minneapolis, MN 55455-0414 • IRRT

Hallgren Mary A. • Student • State University of New York at Albany School of Information Science & Policy • Albany, NY 12222 • AASL

Halliburton Linda K. • Rochester, NY 14612

Halliday John • Director • Whatcom County Library System • Bellingham, WA 98226-9092 • PLA

Halliday Karen • Student • University of Washington Graduate School of Library and Information Science • Seattle, WA 98195 • PLA

Halliday Meta • Media Specialist • Hanau Middle School Media Center • APO, AE 09165-0005 • AASL

Hallier Sara J. • Librarian • Kansas City Public Library • Kansas City, MO 64106

Hallingby Leigh • Psychology Librarian • Columbia University Libraries Butler Library • New York, NY 10027 • ACRL

Hallisey Margaret A. • Librarian • Burlington High School Library • Burlington, MA 01803 • AASL YALSA

Halliwell Dean W. • Victoria BC, V8R 5W1 Canada • Continuing

Hallman Philip A. • Student • University of Michigan 123 Undergraduate Library • Ann Arbor, MI 48109-1185

Hallock Nancy • Hispanic/Latin Amer. Cataloger • University of Pittsburgh Hillman Library • Pittsburgh, PA 15260 • ACRL

Halloran Judith Irene • Highland Township Public Library • Highland, MI 48031 • PLA SRRT

Hallquist Lynn • Elementary Librarian/Teacher • Klatt Elementary School • Anchorage, AK 99515 • AASL ALSC

Halls Catharine M. E. • Research Librarian • New York Public Library • New York, NY 10018-2788 • ACRL IRRT

Halls Gwendolyn F. • Atlanta, GA 30318

Halman Ruth B. • Reference Librarian • University of California Rivera Library • Riverside, CA 92517 • ACRL RASD IFRT SRRT
Halmi Suzanne • Student • Rutgers University School of Communication Information & Library Studies • New Brunswick, NJ 08903 • LITA
Halperin Philip M. • New York, NY 10025
Halpin James R. • Head of Reference Services • Newburgh Free Library • Newburgh, NY 12550 • RASD
Halpin Jerome H. • Director • Northwest College John Taggart Hinckley Library • Powell, WY 82435 • ACRL ALCTS
Halpin Lola A. • Atlanta, GA 30345 • ACRL IFRT
Halporn Barbara • Collection Development Dept. • Harvard University • Cambridge, MA 02138 • ACRL
Halsey Kathryn L. • Dayton, OH 45405 • AASL
Halsey Kathy F. • Reference Librarian • University of Wisconsin-Stevens Point Albertson Learning Resource Center • Stevens Point, WI 54481 • RASD
Halsey Richard S. • Dean • State University of New York at Albany School of Information Science & Policy • Albany, NY 12222 • LAMA LITA RASD
Halter Robert Rev • Elkhorn, NE 68022
Haltiwanger Anna • Librarian • Midlands Technical College • Columbia, SC 29202
Haltzel Helen H. • Library Director • Defense Systems Management College Library • Fort Belvoir, VA 22060-5426
Halverson Eric G. • Public Library Consultant • North Dakota State Library • Bismarck, ND 58505
Halverson Helen A. • Librarian • Hennepin County Library Saint Louis Park Library • Saint Louis Park, MN 55426
Halverson Jacquelyn A. • Instructor • Texas A & M University Sterling C. Evans Library • College Station, TX 77843-5000 • LAMA
Halverson Kathleen B. • Media Specialist • Wheelock Elementary School • Keene, NH 03431
Halverson Mary E. • Head of Children's Librarian • Geneva Public Library District • Geneva, IL 60134 • ALSC
Halvorsen Jan • Huntington Beach Library Info. & Cultural Resource Center • Huntington Beach, CA 92648 • PLA IFRT
Halvorsen Jan T. • Morgan Hill, CA 95037-6902
Halvorson Hjordis D. • Reader Services Librarian • Newberry Library • Chicago, IL 60610 • ACRL
Halvorson Marjorie H. • Media Specialist • Tavelli Elementary School • Ft Collins, CO 80524 • AASL
Ham Alyce M. • Media Specialist • Waterloo School System • Waterloo, IA 50702
Ham Cynthia • Children's Librarian • Los Angeles County Public Library Baldwin Park Library 803 • Baldwin Park, CA 91706 • ALSC
Ham Michael • Senior Marketing Manager • Columbia Library System (CTB) • Monterey, CA 93940 • AASL ASCLA LITA PLA
Ham Sandra A. • Cranston, RI 02905 • ACRL ALCTS LAMA LITA PLA RASD GODORT
Hamada Elaine • Los Alamitos Unified School District • Los Alamitos, CA 90720 • AASL
Hamaguchi Charlene K. • School Librarian • Kamehameha Elementary School • Kapalama Heights, HI 96817 • AASL
Hamaker Charles A. • Asst. Dean Clln Devel • Louisiana State University Libraries Troy H. Middleton Library • Baton Rouge, LA 70803-3342 • ALCTS
Hamaker Vicki Clark • University of Central Florida Library • Orlando, FL 32816-0666
Haman Nancy A. • Miller Place, NY 11764
Hamann Edmund G. • Director • Suffolk University Sawyer Library • Boston, MA 02108 • ACRL
Hamann Linda K. • Nekoosa, WI 54457
Hamblin Carol • Director • Guilderland Public Library • Albany, NY 12203
Hambric Jacqueline B. • Education Reference • Texas A & M University Sterling C. Evans Library • College Station, TX 77843-5000 • ACRL RASD
Hambridge Sally L. • Intel Corporation SC1-02 • Santa Clara, CA 95052-8126 • ALCTS LITA LRRT
Hamburger Roberta L. • Director of Library • Phillips Graduate Seminary • Enid, OK 73702 • ACRL ALCTS
Hamby Tracy A. • Head of Cataloging • Central Arkansas Library System • Little Rock, AR 72201-4698
Hamdy Mohamed Dr • Denver, CO 80222 • ACRL ALCTS LITA
Hamel Barbara J. • Reference Services Librarian • University of Wisconsin Steenbock Memorial Library • Madison, WI 53706
Hamel Louise E. • Reference Librarian • Wayne County Public Library • Wooster, OH 44691
Hamell Nancy M. • Coordinator Technical Services • Fullerton Public Library • Fullerton, CA 92632
Hamer Collin B. Jr. • Head-Louisiana Division • New Orleans Public Library • New Orleans, LA 70140
Hames Sandy L. • Children's Librarian • Harrison Memorial Library • Carmel By The Sea, CA 93921 • ALSC
Hamil Margaret M. • Director • Flossmoor Public Library • Flossmoor, IL 60422 • PLA
Hamill Martha L. • Washington, NH 03280
Hamilton-Selway Joanne • Scottsdale Public Library • Scottsdale, AZ 85251
Hamilton Ann • Assoc. Director of Library • Georgia Southern University Henderson Library • Statesboro, GA 30460 • ACRL LAMA
Hamilton Anna B. • Grove City, PA 16127 • AASL YALSA *Continuing*
Hamilton Arloene • Supervisor Technical Processing • Redwood City Public Library • Redwood City, CA 94063-1868 • ALCTS
Hamilton B. Parker • Branch Manager • Montgomery County Public Library Aspen Hill Community Library • Rockville, MD 20853
Hamilton Barbara R. • Library Director • Sierra Army Library SDSSI-CRB Post Library • Herlong, CA 96113-5166
Hamilton Beth A. • Glenview, IL 60025
Hamilton Bonita B. • Librarian • Monterey High School • Monterey, LA 71354
Hamilton C. Rebecca • Student • Yale University Kline Science Library • New Haven, CT 06511-8142 • CLENE
Hamilton Carl W. • Alameda, CA 94501 • PLA SRRT *Continuing*
Hamilton Carolyn • Linworth Publishing, Inc. • Worthington, OH 43085 • AASL
Hamilton Carolyn • Librarian (Cataloger) • Smithsonian Institution Libraries • Washington, DC 20560 • ALCTS
Hamilton Cynthia • Director • Jaffrey Public Library • Jaffrey, NH 03452-1196 • ALSC PLA
Hamilton Darlene • Genealogy Librarian • Seattle Public Library • Seattle, WA 98104-1193 • RASD
Hamilton David A. • De Kalb, IL 60115
Hamilton David Mike • President • The Live Oak Press • Palo Alto, CA 94306 • ACRL ERT ILERT LRRT
Hamilton Elizabeth • Director • Campbell County Public Library • Rustburg, VA 24588 • PLA
Hamilton Fae K. • Carlisle, MA 01741 • ALCTS LITA ILERT
Hamilton Frances S. • Library Media Specialist • Loxahatchee Groves Elem Sch • Loxahatchee, FL 33470 • AASL ALSC
Hamilton George H. • McLean, VA 22101 • RASD
Hamilton Judy R. • Director • La Porte County Public Library • La Porte, IN 46350 • PLA
Hamilton Lee Ann • Head Librarian • Atlanta Public Library • Atlanta, TX 75551
Hamilton Leo F. • Librarian/Cataloger • University of Texas Libraries General Libraries • Austin, TX 78713-7330 • ALCTS
Hamilton Linda C. • Dallas, TX 75238-2929 • ALSC
Hamilton Linda K. • Director, Index Products • Institute for Scientific Information • Philadelphia, PA 19104 • ERT
Hamilton Malcolm • Librarian • Harvard University JF Kennedy School of Government Library • Cambridge, MA 02138 • ACRL LAMA
Hamilton Margaret L. • Library Director • Greenwood Public Library • Greenwood, IN 46143
Hamilton Marsha • Head, Monograph Acq. Div. • Ohio State University Libraries • Columbus, OH 43210-1286 • ALCTS
Hamilton Palmer C. • Trustee • Mobile Public Library • Mobile, AL 36602 • ALTA
Hamilton Patricia A. • Director • Pontiac Public Library • Pontiac, IL 61764 • PLA
Hamilton Patricia J. • Director • Rapid City Regional Hospital Library • Rapid City, SD 57709 • LAMA
Hamilton Reatha B. • Fort Pierce, FL 34950
Hamilton Rita • Cataloging Manager • Public Library of Nashville and Davidson County • Nashville, TN 37203-3585
Hamilton Robert D. Jr. • Student • University of Western Ontario School of Library & Information Science • London ON, N6G 1H1 Canada
Hamilton Rosemary • University City, MO 63130 • IFRT
Hamilton Ruth H. • Co-Director • Career Development Project • Seattle, WA 98103 • PLA
Hamilton Susan S. • Librarian • St Thomas More High School • Lafayette, LA 70508 • AASL
Hamilton Ted M. • Houston, TX 77098-1503
Hamilton Virginia A. • Adult Reference Librarian • El Dorado County Library • Placerville, CA 95667 • IRRT
Hamlin Arthur T. • Wiscasset, ME 04578 • ACRL LAMA *Life*
Hamlin Eileen M. • Kirkwood, NY 13795 • ACRL LAMA
Hamlin Judi Olsen • Brunswick, GA 31520
Hamlin Lisa K. • Librarian • Brentwood Public Library • Brentwood, TN 37027 • ALCTS
Hamm Julia T. • Assistant to the Director • University of Delaware Library • Newark, DE 19717-5267 • LAMA
Hamm Leta E. • Fort Myers, FL 33919-3201
Hamm Peggy • Kleberg Elementary School • Kingsville, TX 78364 • AASL
Hammack Jeff C. • New Hanover County Library • Wilmington, NC 28401-3998 • RASD
Hammad Azza J. Ms. • Amman, Jordan
Hamman Frances Miss • Ann Arbor, MI 48104 • Continuing
Hamman Linda • Trustee • Glenview Public Library • Glenview, IL 60025
Hammann Jill E. • Tipp City, OH 45371 • PLA RASD
Hammaren Evelyn • Randolph High School Library • Randolph, NJ 07869 • AASL
Hammargren Betty Lou • St Paul, MN 55116
Hammarskjold Carolyn • Hickory Corners, MI 49060 • ACRL
Hammel Genie T. • Children's Librarian • Plano Public Library System • Plano, TX 75086-0356 • ALSC EMIERT IFRT
Hammer Donald P. • Wheeling, IL 60090 • LITA *Life*
Hammer Jeanne • University of Virginia Alderman Library • Charlottesville, VA 22903-2498
Hammer John C. • Student • Palo Alto College • San Antonio, TX 78224 • ACRL ALCTS LITA LHRT MAGERT
Hammer Kevin G. • Student • Kent State University School of Library & Information Science • Kent, OH 44242-0001
Hammer Leonard • Director • Royal Oak Public Library • Royal Oak, MI 48068
Hammer Michael L. • Library Director • Independence Free Public Library • Independence, IA 50644
Hammer Sharon A. • Regional Library Director • Fort Vancouver Regional Library • Vancouver, WA 98663 • AASL ALCTS ALSC ALTA ASCLA LAMA LITA PLA RASD YALSA CLENE EMIERT GODORT IFRT LIRT SRRT
Hammerick Lilias R. • Corpus Chrsti, TX 78412 • PLA
Hammerly Hernan D. • University of Michigan School of Information and Library Studies • Ann Arbor, MI 48109-1092 • ACRL
Hammerstrand Kristine J. • Associate Director • Illinois Library Computer System Office • Champaign, IL 61820 • ACRL LITA CLENE IFRT SRRT
Hammesfahr Judith A. • Librarian • Ely High School • Pompano, FL 33060
Hammett Paula C. • College Librarian • World College West • Petaluma, CA 94952 • ACRL
Hammett Susan A. • Modesto, CA 95350
Hammitt Margaret R. • Elementary Librarian • East Ward School • Chadron, NE 69337 • AASL ALSC
Hammock Janice D. • Manager of Cataloging • Washington State Library • Olympia, WA 98504 • ALCTS
Hammock Pamela Grooms • Lindley Middle School • Mableton, GA 30059 • AASL
Hammond Carol Burroughs • Head Res/Inf Access Service • Arizona State University-West Fletcher Library • Phoenix, AZ 85069-7100 • ACRL RASD
Hammond Elizabeth D. • Clln Devel Librarian • Mercer University Main Library • Macon, GA 31207 • ACRL ALCTS
Hammond Jane L. • Cornell University Law School Library • Ithaca, NY 14853-4901 • ACRL ALCTS LITA RASD GODORT *Life*
Hammond Jean K. • Director of Libraries • Norfolk Academy May Library • Norfolk, VA 23502 • AASL
Hammond Jeffrey R. • Catalog Librarian • College of William and Mary Earl Gregg Swem Library • Williamsburg, VA 23187-8794 • ALCTS
Hammond John J. • Executive Director • North Country Reference and Resources Council • Canton, NY 13617 • ACRL ASCLA
Hammond Margaret • Department Head • Detroit Public Library Acq Dept • Detroit, MI 48202-4093 • PLA RASD *Life*
Hammond Margaret A. • Associate Librarian • University of Regina Library • Regina SK, Canada • ACRL ALCTS RASD
Hammond Mary Lou • Versailles, KY 40383
Hammond Mary W. • Reference Librarian • Pierce College Library • Tacoma, WA 98498 • ACRL IFRT LIRT
Hammond Mary-Love L. Mrs. • Rock Hill, SC 29732
Hammond Mildred A. • Mattapoisett, MA 02739-0026 • PLA *Life*
Hammond Patience M. • Student • University of California-Berkeley School of Library & Information Studies • Berkeley, CA 94720 • PLA EMIERT SRRT
Hammond Patricia R. • Branch Librarian • Summerville Library • Summerville, SC 29485
Hammond Sandy Bell • Head of Technical Services • Farmers Branch Public Library • Farmers Branch, TX 75234

Hammond Tracy J. • Librarian • Burlingame Public Library • Burlingame, CA 94010

Hammons James W. • Student • Indiana University School of Library and Information Science • Bloomington, IN 47405 • EMIERT IFRT IRRT LHRT SRRT

Hamon Peter G. • System Administrator • South Central Library System • Madison, WI 53704 • PLA

Hampel Elisabeth M. • Cataloging Librarian • Universitaetsbibliothek of Regensburg • 8400 Regensburg, Germany • ACRL IRRT

Hampel Nanci N. • Student • Indiana University School of Library and Information Science • Bloomington, IN 47405 • AASL

Hampton Byron D. • Assistant Director • Pierce County Rural Library District • Tacoma, WA 98446

Hampton Dorothea A. • Willow Park, TX 76087

Hampton Karen E. • Student • Kent State University School of Library & Information Science • Kent, OH 44242-0001 • AASL

Hampton Marcia W. • APO, AE 09244 • PLA YALSA FLRT

Hampton Marian E. • Assistant Director • Texas Tech University Libraries • Lubbock, TX 79409-0002 • LAMA

Hamrell Larry G. Mr • AV/Youth Librarian • Clearwater Public Library • Clearwater, FL 34623 • LITA PLA *Life*

Hamrick Clifford C. • Chief Librarian • National Institute for Occupational Safety & Health, ALOSH Library • Morgantown, WV 26505 • ACRL

Hamrick Jean T. • Asst Dir Inf Sys Planning • University of Texas Libraries General Libraries • Austin, TX 78713-7330 • ALCTS LITA

Hamrick Sarah E. • Public Services Librarian • Gallaudet University Library • Washington, DC 20002 • ACRL ASCLA LAMA NMRT SRRT

Hamrick Susan J. • Branch Librarian • Public Library of Cincinnati and Hamilton County Delhi Hills Branch • Cincinnati, OH 45238

Hamsher Joy G. • Assistant Director • York County Library System • York, PA 17402-9004 • LAMA

Hamson Darryl • Health Sciences Librarian • Portsmouth Regional Hospital • Portsmouth, NH 03801

Hanawalt Victoria L. • College Librarian • Reed College E. V. Hauser Library • Portland, OR 97202 • ACRL ALCTS LAMA

Hanby Bernadine C. • Bryan, OH 43506 • ACRL ALCTS *Continuing*

Hanchett Catherine M. • Cortland, NY 13045

Hanchey Betty Paige • Director • Allen Parish Libraries • Oberlin, LA 70655 • ALTA PLA

Hancock Bonnie B. • Northside Middle School • West Columbia, SC 29169

Hancock Linda • Librarian • Midland Senior High School • Midland, TX 79701 • AASL

Hancox Terry • Director, Library LRC • Cuyahoga Community College Eastern Campus • Warrensville, OH 44122 • ACRL LAMA NMRT

Hand Annamarie L. • Associate Director • Florham Park Public Library • Florham Park, NJ 07932 • RASD

Hand Beth • Librarian • Frederick Douglass School • Dallas, TX 75217

Hand Carol M. • Middle School Librarian • Chartiers Valley Middle School • Pittsburgh, PA 15220 • AASL

Hand Jody P. • Branch Librarian • Oakland Public Library Rockridge Branch • Oakland, CA 94618

Hand M. Dorcas • Houston, TX 77009 • AASL ALSC YALSA

Hand Mary E. • Columbus, OH 43206 • Continuing

Handis Michael W. • Library Specialist III • University of Pittsburgh Hillman Library • Pittsburgh, PA 15260 • RASD

Handler Mark J. • Stanford University Law School • Stanford, CA 94305 • ACRL LITA

Handman Gary P. • Head, Media Resources Center • University of California-Berkeley Moffitt Undergraduate Library • Berkeley, CA 94720 • ACRL VRT

Handrick Dorothy • Library Director • Mount Horeb Public Library • Mt. Horeb, WI 53512

Hands Nancy S. • Young Services Consultant • Livingston & Wyoming County Library Systems • Avon, NY 14414 • ALSC YALSA

Handschin Luke P. • Librarian • Swiss Re Library • Zurich, Switzerland • ACRL LITA

Handshu Laurie C. • Student • University of Tennessee-Knoxville Graduate School of Library & Information Science • Knoxville, TN 37996-4330

Handshy Lynn E. • Pacific Grove, CA 93950 • ALSC

Handville Scott A. • Public Services Librarian • Gardiner Public Library • Gardiner, ME 04345

Handy Catherine H. • West Springfield, MA 01089 • Continuing

Handy Lynne C. • Special Services Consultant • Houston Area Library Automated Network • Houston, TX 77002 • PLA

Hane Paula J. • Editor, Database Magazine • Online Inc. • Amawalk, NY 10501 • LITA

Hanefeldt Judith R. • Head Adult Information Dept. • Evansville-Vanderburgh County Public Library • Evansville, IN 47708-1694

Hanel Mary A. • Reference Librarian • Santa Clara Public Library • Santa Clara, CA 95051

Hanes Ann G. • Student • Catholic University of America School of Library and Information Science • Washington, DC 20064 • LITA

Hanes Fred W. • Overton, TX 75684 • ACRL

Hanes Linda H. • Childrens Librarian • Sonoma County Library • Santa Rosa, CA 95404 • YALSA

Hanes Susan • Catalog Librarian • National Museum of Naval Aviation Emil Buehler Naval Aviation Library • NAS Pensacola, FL 32508

Haney Annette J. • Student • Kent State University School of Library & Information Science • Kent, OH 44242-0001 • PLA

Haney Carolyn • Media Specialist • Valley Park Elementary School Cedar Falls School District • Cedar Falls, IA 50613 • AASL

Haney Janice M. • Teacher/Naturalist • Delaware Nature Society • Hockessin, DE 19707 • AASL

Haney Lenore Newins • Burlington, NC 27215

Haney Maribeth • Manager Office Services • American Library Association • Chicago, IL 60611-2795

Hanff Peter E. • Coordinator Technical Servs. • University of California-Berkeley Bancroft Library • Berkeley, CA 94720 • ACRL

Hanford Patricia A. • Acquisitions/Periodicals • Union College Schaffer Library • Schenectady, NY 12308 • ACRL

Hanhan Lila Mirhij • Librarian • Phillips Junior College • Greensboro, NC 27401

Hanible Phelix B. • Head Original Cataloging • University of Michigan Libraries • Ann Arbor, MI 48109-1205 • ALCTS LAMA

Hanif Ibrahim • Collection Development Librarian • Wofford College • Spartanburg, SC 29303-3663

Hanin Ann B. • Teacher of Library • Hillcrest High School • Queens, NY 11432 • AASL YALSA

Hankamer Roberta • Sandusky, OH 44870

Hanke Maxine K. • Deputy Chief • National Institute of Health Library • Bethesda, MD 20892 • LITA FLRT

Hankel Marilyn L. • Business Reference Librarian • University of New Orleans Earl K. Long Library • New Orleans, LA 70148 • ACRL RASD

Hankinson Frances Ms • Staten Island, NY 10301 • Continuing

Hankinson Linda K. • Hockaday School Library • Dallas, TX 75229 • AASL

Hankom Leann • Student • University of Iowa School of Library & Information Science • Iowa City, IA 52242

Hanks Gardner C. • Continuing Education Consultant • Idaho State Library • Boise, ID 83702 • CLENE SRRT

Hanks Janice L. • University of Southern California Doheny Library • Los Angeles, CA 90089-0182 • ACRL

Hanks Nancy S. • Serials Librarian • Slippery Rock University of Pennsylvania • Slippery Rock, PA 16057 • ALCTS

Hanks Robert • University of California • Los Angeles, CA 90024-1573 • ACRL ALCTS RASD

Hanks Rubie M. Mrs • Winnfield, LA 71483-2827 • PLA YALSA *Continuing*

Hanley Deirdre • Director • Reading Public Library • Reading, MA 01867-2550

Hanley Keith Mr. • Trustee • Louisville Free Public Library • Louisville, KY 40203-2257 • ALTA

Hanley Patricia A. • Student • University of Rhode Island Graduate School of Library & Information Studies • Kingston, RI 02881-0815 • ALSC

Hanlon Carol A. • Acting Head Libraian • Kalihi Palama Library • Honolulu, HI 96819 • PLA SRRT

Hanlon Jean W. • Milton Village, MA 02187-0223 • ALSC PLA *Life*

Hanlon Sharon K. • Children's Services Librarian • Fauquier County Public Library • Warrenton, VA 22186 • ALSC

Hanna Alice M. • Sedalia, MO 65301 • Continuing

Hanna C. Philip • Student • University of Kentucky College of Library & Information Science • Lexington, KY 40506-0391

Hanna Kerry B. • Account Executive • INLEX, Inc. • Ridgefield, CT 06877 • LITA

Hanna Mary Ann • Sebring, FL 33872-3452 • LAMA PLA

Hanna Patricia B. • Director • Howland Public Library • Beacon, NY 12508 • PLA

Hanna Sybil Ann • Jackson, MS 39211 • ALSC YALSA

Hannaford Paula M. • Reference Librarian • University of Alberta Rutherford Library North • Edmonton AB, T6G 2J4 Canada • RASD

Hannaford William E. Jr. • Director • Champlain College Library • Burlington, VT 05401 • ACRL

Hannah Jerry Mrs. • Trustee • Topeka Public Library • Topeka, KS 66604-1374

Hannah Laurie • Santa Barbara, CA 93108

Hannah Manuela C. • Acting Base Librarian • Barksdale Air Force Base Library • Barksdale Afb, LA 71110-5000

Hannah Marcus • Trustee • Northbrook Public Library • Northbrook, IL 60062 • ALTA

Hannegan Lizette D. • Glencarlyn Elementary School Library • Arlington, VA 22204 • AASL ALSC

Hannenberg Nancy • Student • California State University-Los Angeles John F. Kennedy Memorial Library • Los Angeles, CA 90032-8300 • AASL

Hannesdottir Sigrun Klara • Associate Professor • University of Iceland Faculty of Social Science Library & Information Science Studies • Reykjavik, Iceland • AASL ACRL ALCTS LAMA LITA PLA RASD CLENE IFRT IRRT LIRT LRRT

Hannigan Jane A. • Neshanic, NJ 08853 • AASL ALSC

Hannigan Margaret C. • St Paul, MN 55116-2751 • Continuing

Hannigan Matthew • Reference Librarian • Indianapolis Marion County Public Library • Indianapolis, IN 46206 • RASD

Hannigan Sallie B. • Reference Librarian • Newark Public Library • Newark, NJ 07101-0630 • RASD

Hanning Ann W. • Ohio Educational Library Media Association (OELMA) • Columbus, OH 43215 • AASL

Hannon Christine G. • Smith College William Allan Neilson Library • Northampton, MA 01063 • ACRL LAMA RASD IFRT LIRT

Hannon John P. • Director Library Services • Bryant College Hodgson Memorial Library • Smithfield, RI 02917 • ACRL LITA

Hannon Patricia A • Administrative Assistant • Lake Forest Library • Lake Forest, IL 60045

Hannon Patricia Ann • Director • Emerson Public Library • Emerson, NJ 07630 • ALSC ALTA PLA

Hannsz Sandra Lee • APO, AE 09045 • AASL

Hannula Mia L. • Medical Librarian • VA Medical Center Library • Seattle, WA 98108

Hanrahan Kathleen E. • Student • Kent State University School of Library & Information Science • Kent, OH 44242-0001 • ASCLA LITA SRRT

Hanrath Richard A. • Arlington Heights Memorial Library • Arlington Heights, IL 60004-5966 • LAMA LITA PLA NMRT

Hanscom Martha • Monographic Catlgr • University of Wyoming Coe Library • Laramie, WY 82071-3334 • ALCTS

Hansel Patsy J. • Director • Williamsburg Regional Library • Williamsburg, VA 23185 • LAMA PLA

Hansell William S. • Trustee • Oregon State Library • Salem, OR 97310-0640 • ALTA

Hanselman Lisa D. • Ann Arbor, MI 48104

Hansen-Shaw Beth • Reference Librarian • Governors State University University Library • University Park, IL 60466 • ACRL LAMA

Hansen-Smith Karen • San Ramon Library • San Ramon, CA 94583

Hansen Andrew M. • RASD/ASCLA Executive Director • American Library Association • Chicago, IL 60611-2795 • ASCLA PLA RASD

Hansen Arthur R. • Chicago, IL 60643

Hansen Betty Jo • Peru, IL 61354

Hansen Carol • Director • Avondale Public Library • Avondale, AZ 85323

Hansen Carol • Asst. Professor of Lib Sci • Weber State University Stewart Library • Ogden, UT 84408-2901 • ACRL IRRT LIRT

Hansen Cathy A. • Mesa, AZ 85213

Hansen Charles A. • Flint Public Library • Flint, MI 48502 • LAMA PLA IRRT

Hansen Debra L. • Professor • California State University • Fullerton, CA 92634 • ACRL RASD

Hansen Don • Trustee • Stillwater Public Library • Stillwater, MN 55082

Hansen Dorothy • Tarzana, CA 91356 • ALSC *Continuing*

Hansen Eleanore E. • Music Librarian • Bradley University Cullom-Davis Library • Peoria, IL 61625

Hansen Helen M. Miss • Valley City, ND 58072 • Continuing

Hansen Irene • Urbana, IL 61801-6058

Hansen Janet M. • Literacy Coordinator • Broward County Library Von D. Mizell Branch • Ft. Lauderdale, FL 33311 • PLA

Hansen Joanna J. • Librarian • Brooks Air Force Base Library • Brooks AFB, TX 78235 • AFLRT

Hansen John M. • Student • Emporia State University Emporia in the Rockies • Denver, CO 80204 • LITA

Hansen Judith • North Kirkwood Middle School • Kirkwood, MO 63122

Hansen Julia P. • Reference Librarian • St Tammany Parish Library Slidell Branch • Slidell, LA 70458

Hansen Kathleen A. • Assoc Prof & Sevareid Librarian • University of Minnesota Eric Sevareid Library • Minneapolis, MN 55455 • ACRL

Hansen Kathleen L. • Inter-Librarian Loan Supervisor • Brigham Young University Harold B. Lee Library • Provo, UT 84602 • RASD

Hansen Kenneth H. • Ref Librarian/Clln Develp • Porter County Public Library • Valparaiso, IN 46383

Hansen L. Jean • Waterford Township Public Library • Waterford, MI 48329 • PLA

Hansen Linda • Fredericton NB, E3B 6H6 Canada

Hansen Linda I. • Branch Librarian • Baltimore County Public Library • Towson, MD 21204 • PLA

Hansen Linda L. • Technical Service • Professional Media Serv Corp • Gardena, CA 90248 • ALCTS LITA PLA

Hansen Lois N. • Boise, ID 83704 • Continuing

Hansen Mary J. • Oklahoma City, OK 73107 • Continuing

Hansen Miriam B. • Indianhead Library System • Eau Claire, WI 54701 • AASL ASCLA

Hansen Pirkko L. • Mc Lean, VA 22102

Hansen Ralph W. • Boise, ID 83706

Hansen Randa • Account Manager • Data Research Associates Inc. • Saint Louis, MO 63132 • LITA

Hansen Roland C. • Readers Service Librarian • School of the Art Institute • Chicago, IL 60603 • ACRL ALCTS SRRT

Hansen S. • Librarian • Sunrise Elementary School • Puyallup, WA 98374 • ASCLA

Hansen Sally Griswold • Librarian • Desert View High School Learning Resource Center • Tucson, AZ 85706 • AASL

Hansen Sandra L. • Librarian II • Alameda County Library System • Fremont, CA 94538 • ALCTS

Hansen Susan M. • Children Librarian • Edythe L. Dyer Community Library • Hampden, ME 04444

Hansen Voanne M. • Trustee • Marion Carnegie Library • Marion, IA 52302 • ALTA

Hansen William H. • Director • Armor School Library • Fort Knox, KY 40121

Hansford L. O. Mrs • Librarian • Spokane Public Library • Spokane, WA 99201

Hanson Agnes O. • Cleveland, OH 44106 • Continuing

Hanson Alison W. • Student • State University of New York at Albany School of Information Science & Policy • Albany, NY 12222 • ALSC NMRT

Hanson Ardis • Student • University of South Florida School of Library & Information Science • Tampa, FL 33620 • ALCTS LITA EMIERT SRRT

Hanson Audry J. • Cooper Middle School • Fresno, CA 93705 • AASL

Hanson Beth F. • Information Specialist • Virginia Tech Information Center • Blacksburg, VA 24073

Hanson Carl A. • Head Bibliographer • Trinity University • San Antonio, TX 78212 • ACRL RASD IFRT LHRT LIRT

Hanson Charles D. • Grosse Pointe Public Library Central Branch • Grosse Pointe, MI 48236 • AASL ACRL LAMA PLA IFRT LRRT

Hanson Christina M. • Head, Access Services • University of Texas at San Antonio-Library • San Antonio, TX 78249 • ACRL

Hanson Deanna M. • Champaign, IL 61820-5164 • PLA

Hanson Donna M. • Science Librarian • University of Idaho Library • Moscow, ID 83843 • ACRL RASD IRRT

Hanson Dorothy A. • Coordinator • DeKalb County School System • Atlanta, GA 30329 • AASL

Hanson Elizabeth I. • Student • Indiana University School of Library and Information Science • Bloomington, IN 47405 • ACRL ALCTS IRRT LHRT LRRT

Hanson Eugene R. Mr. • Carlisle, PA 17013 • AASL ACRL ALCTS LITA *Life*

Hanson George • Chicago, IL 60657

Hanson Gilberta • Library Director • Copper Valley Community Library Association • Glennallen, AK 99588

Hanson Gloria J. • Assistant Chief of Branches • San Francisco Public Library • San Francisco, CA 94102 • PLA

Hanson Gretchen M. • Reference Librarian • Salt Lake County Library Systems Sandy Library • Sandy, UT 84092 • PLA

Hanson Heidi • Asst. Head, Catalog Mgt. Dept. • University of Maryland College Park Theodore R. McKeldin Library • College Park, MD 20742-7011 • ACRL ALCTS LITA

Hanson Irene A. • Wauwatosa, WI 53213 • ACRL ALCTS *Continuing*

Hanson Jacqueline M. • Assistant Univ. Ln.- Personnel • University of California-San Diego Central University Library • La Jolla, CA 92093-0175 • ACRL

Hanson Jan E. V. W. • Grays Harbor College • Aberdeen, WA 98520 • YALSA

Hanson Jean W. • Supervisor Children's Services • Shaker Heights Public Library • Shaker Heights, OH 44120 • PLA IFRT SRRT

Hanson Jody K. • Media Specialist • Northglenn Junior High School • Northglenn, CO 80233 • AASL

Hanson Katherine • Library Media Teacher • South High School • Torrance, CA 90505

Hanson Kathy Helen • Conley Hills Elementary School • East Point, GA 30349 • AASL

Hanson Katrina M. • Student • University of Michigan School of Information and Library Studies • Ann Arbor, MI 48109-1092 • IFRT SRRT

Hanson Lynn M. • IRMS Research Associate • University of Illinois Graduate School of Library and Information Science • Urbana, IL 61801

Hanson Margaret • Librarian • Medill Bair High School Library • Fairless Hills, PA 19030 • AASL YALSA

Hanson Martha J. • Preservation Administrator • Syracuse University Library E. S. Bird Library • Syracuse, NY 13244-2010 • ACRL ALCTS LAMA

Hanson Mary A. • Reference Librarian • Rolling Meadows Library • Rolling Meadows, IL 60008

Hanson Mary Ellen • Education Coordinator • University of New Mexico General Library • Albuquerque, NM 87131 • ACRL ALCTS

Hanson Michael • Librarian • Kuwait Inst For Sci Res • Kuwait, Kuwait • ACRL RASD IFRT IRRT

Hanson Michele G. • Student • University of Arizona Graduate Library School • Tucson, AZ 85721 • RASD IFRT SRRT

Hanson Norma Sue • Special Collection Librarian • Case Western Reserve Univ Freiberger Library • Cleveland, OH 44106-7151 • ACRL

Hanson Patricia • Oxford, MI 48371 • RASD

Hanson Pauline • Library Director • Lummi Library • Bellingham, WA 98226 • LAMA CLENE FLRT IFRT

Hanson Robin • Director • Muskingum College Library • New Concord, OH 43762 • ACRL

Hanson Roger K. • Director of Libraries • University of Utah Marriott Library • Salt Lake City, UT 84112-1179 • ACRL LAMA *Life*

Hanson Stephen L. • Hd, USC Cinema-TV Library • University of Southern California Doheny Library • Los Angeles, CA 90089-0182

Hanson Virginia M. • Reference Librarian • Dayton & Montgomery County Public Library Kettering-Moraine Branch • Kettering, OH 45429

Hanthorn Ivan E. • Head, Preservation Dept. • Iowa State University Library • Ames, IA 50011-2140 • ALCTS

Hanus Donna M. • Director • Franklin-Essex-Hamilton BOCES School Library System • Malone, NY 12953 • AASL IFRT

Hanus Karen L. • Menomonee Falls, WI 53051-6636

Hanway Wayne E. • Director • Southeastern Public Library System of Oklahoma • McAlester, OK 74501 • PLA

Hanzas Barbara • Librarian • Woodruff Memorial Library City Library of La Junta • La Junta, CO 81050-0479 • ALCTS ALSC PLA

Haper Margaret E. • Student • University of Kentucky College of Library & Information Science • Lexington, KY 40506-0391 • AASL

Hapij Mary S. • Copley Real Estate Advisors Information Resource Center • Boston, MA 02116

Happ George J. • Director • Salem Public Library • Salem, OR 97309-5020 • ALCTS ALSC ALTA LAMA LITA PLA RASD YALSA

Haq S. Farid-Ul • Director of Instruction Resource • State University of New York College of Technology • Canton, NY 13617 • ACRL

Har-Nicolescu Suzine • Trustee • Brooklyn Public Library • Brooklyn, NY 11238 • ACRL ALTA EMIERT IRRT

Harada Ryukichi • Professor of Faculty of Letters • Tohoku Gakuin University • Sendai, Japan • ACRL

Harada Violet • School Library Specialist • Hawaii Department of Education Special Instructional Programs & Services Branch • Honolulu, HI 96816 • AASL ALSC EMIERT

Haraz Janice E. • Library Director • North Brunswick Free Public Library • North Brunswick, NJ 08902 • LAMA PLA YALSA EMIERT LIRT

Harbaugh Julia A. • University of Oklahoma School of Library & Information Studies • Norman, OK 73019

Harbaugh Susan E. • Children's Services Coordinator • Troy-Miami County Public Library • Troy, OH 45373 • ALSC PLA

Harber Opal M. • Paonia, CO 81428 • ALCTS RASD *Life*

Harber Patty S. • Head of Technical Services • Bartram Trail Regional Library • Washington, GA 30673 • LITA

Harber Sandra • Chino Hills, CA 91709

Harbridge Virida • Marina Vista • Marina, CA 93933

Harcourt Kathryn M. • Head, Database Maintenance • Columbia University Libraries • New York, NY 10027 • ACRL ALCTS

Hardaway Elliott • Clearwater, FL 34624 • PLA RASD *Life*

Hardcastle Gladys • Young Adult Librarian • Los Angeles Public Library Westchester Branch • Los Angeles, CA 90045 • YALSA

Hardcastle Joyce • Trustee • Loudoun County Public Library • Leesburg, VA 22075 • ALTA

Hardee David R. • Student • University of South Carolina College of Library & Information Science • Columbia, SC 29208 • IFRT SRRT

Hardee Linda • Trustee • Vermilion Parish Library • Abbeville, LA 70510

Hardee Mary C. • Trustee • Horry County Memorial Library • Conway, SC 29526 • ALTA

Harden Elizabeth G. • Reference Librarian • Spartanburg County Public Library • Spartanburg, SC 29304

Harden Gwendolyn • Indianapolis, IN 46260

Harden James G. • Systems Librarian • North Carolina State Library • Raleigh, NC 27601-2807

Harden Johanna L. • Library Conservation Specialist • Douglas Public Library District • Castle Rock, CO 80104 • ALCTS

Harden Wanda D. • Community Relations Coordinator • Mideastern Michigan Library Coop. • Flint, MI 48502 • LAMA PLA

Hardenbergh Gail • Ferndale, MI 48220

Harder D. Carl • Seattle Public Library West Seattle Branch • Seattle, WA 98116 • ALSC IFRT

Harder Elsie Ruth • Student • San Jose State University Division of Library & Information Science • San Jose, CA 95192-0029 • ACRL

Harder Kenette J. • Government Documents Librarian • William Jewell College Curry Library • Liberty, MO 64068 • GODORT

Harder Marsha D. • Student • Indiana State University Department of Library Science • Terre Haute, IN 47809

Harders Faith • Assoc. Dir. for Facilities • University of Kentucky Libraries • Lexington, KY 40506-0039 • LAMA

Hardesty Kay Sue • Bridgeville Junior/Senior High School • Bridgeville, DE 19933 • AASL

Hardesty Larry L. • Director • Eckerd College William Luther Cobb Library • Saint Petersburg, FL 33711 • ACRL LAMA *Life*

Hardesty Vicki H. • Librarian • Findlay City Schools • Findlay, OH 45840 • AASL YALSA IFRT LIRT

Hardgrove David J. • Head Technical Services • Saint Peter's College Theresa & Edward O'Toole Library • Jersey City, NJ 07306 • ALCTS

Hardie Judith • Librarian • C. F. Brown Elementary School Sylvan Union School District • Modesto, CA 95355 • AASL

Hardie Karen R. • Trinity, NC 27370 • RASD

Hardie Susan H. • Asst. Director, Public Services • Tacoma Public Library • Tacoma, WA 98402 • PLA

Hardiman Karen C. • Librarian • King County Library System • Seattle, WA 98109-5191 • IFRT

Hardiman Mary Ellen • Librarian • Mayor Salvatore Mancini Union Free Public Library • North Providence, RI 02904 • PLA

Hardin Esther • Coordination Supv of Media • Prince Georges County Public Schools • Landover, MD 20785 • AASL

Hardin Mary U. • Inter-L Loan Librarian • Oklahoma Department of Libraries • Oklahoma City, OK 73105-3298 • RASD

Hardin Phoebe M. • Periodicals Librarian • Lambuth University L.L. Gobbel Library • Jackson, TN 38301

Hardin Steven R. • Tech Services/Reference • Indiana State University Cunningham Memorial Library • Terre Haute, IN 47809 • ALCTS

Hardin William D. • Student • Clark-Atlanta University School of Library & Information Studies • Atlanta, GA 30314-4391

Hardin Willie • Director • University of Central Arkansas Torreyson Library • Conway, AR 72032 • ACRL

Harding Joseph J. • Trustee • Ocean County Public Library • Toms River, NJ 08753

Harding Lore • Belle Mead, NJ 08502

Harding Margaret • Director • Crete Public Library • Crete, NE 68333 • AASL PLA

Harding Thomas S. • Topeka, KS 66606 • Continuing

Hardison Meg D. • Media Coordinator • Wake County Public Schools Enloe High School • Raleigh, NC 27610 • AASL

Hardisty Nancy S. • Head of Technical Services • LaGrange Public Library • La Grange, IL 60525 • ALCTS PLA NMRT

Hardman Joye • Librarian • Calgary Public Library • Calgary AB, T2G 2M2 Canada • ALSC

Hardman Regina • Librarian • Webster College • Fairmont, WV 26554 • ACRL

Hardsog Ellen L. • Director • Exeter Public Library • Exeter, NH 03833

Hardt Jim • Acting Branch Head • Chicago Public Library Richard J Daley Branch • Chicago, IL 60608

Hardt Mary J. • Librarian • Saint Xavier High School Library • Louisville, KY 40217 • AASL
Hardwick Bonnie Dr • Head Manuscripts Division • University of California-Berkeley Bancroft Library • Berkeley, CA 94720 • ACRL
Hardwick Marian W. • Student • University of South Florida School of Library & Information Science • Tampa, FL 33620
Hardy Barbara • Glendover Elementary School • Lexington, KY 40503 • AASL
Hardy Barbara W. • Reference Librarian • Las Positas College • Livermore, CA 94550
Hardy Carla L. • Student • Emporia State University Emporia in the Rockies • Denver, CO 80204
Hardy Carolyn Louise • Vivian, LA 71082-2422 • AASL
Hardy Catherine • Golden Gate University • San Francisco, CA 94105 • GODORT
Hardy Cynthia • Trustee • Columbus Metropolitan Library • Columbus, OH 43215 • ALTA PLA
Hardy Eileen D. • Collection Management Officer • Wellesley College Library Margaret Clapp Library • Wellesley, MA 02181-8275 • ACRL ALCTS
Hardy Floyd C. • Director • North Carolina Central University James E. Shepard Memorial Library • Durham, NC 27707 • ACRL
Hardy Gayle J. • Reference Librarian • Lockwood Memorial Library • Buffalo, NY 14260 • ACRL RASD SRRT
Hardy Jane L. • Media Specialist • Albert Einstein High School • Kensington, MD 20895 • AASL YALSA IRRT
Hardy Janice V. • Library Media Specialist • Chapel Hill Middle School • Douglasville, GA 30135 • AASL
Hardy Jean • Learning Center Director • Stratford Junior High School • Bloomingdale, IL 60108 • AASL
Hardy Linda • Librarian • Douglas County School District • Minden, NV 89423 • AASL
Hardy May G. • Hyattsville, MD 20782 • ACRL ALCTS *Life*
Hardy Peggy A.S. • Media Specialist • East Wake High School • Wendell, NC 27591 • AASL
Hardy Shaun J. • Carnegie Institution of Washington • Washington, DC 20015 • ACRL
Hardy Susan B. • Asst. Regional Director • United States Census Bureau Atlanta Regional Office • Atlanta, GA 30303-2700 • ACRL
Hardy Theresa K. • Technical Services/Dept. Head • Neuse Regional Library System • Kinston, NC 28501
Hare Ann Tingle • Head Librarian • Lander College Jackson Library • Greenwood, SC 29649 • ACRL GODORT IFRT
Hare Christopher B. • Columbia, SC 29209
Hare Karen • Associate Director,Program Plan • North Country Library System • Watertown, NY 13601 • PLA
Hare Wm. John • Director of Learning Resources • New Hampshire Technical Institute • Concord, NH 03301-2039 • ACRL
Harer John B. • Head of Circulation • Texas A & M University Sterling C. Evans Library • College Station, TX 77843-5000 • LAMA IFRT
Harfst Linda L. • University of Wisconsin • Madison, WI 53706
Harger Bruce E. • Student • Rutgers University School of Communication Information & Library Studies • New Brunswick, NJ 08903 • ACRL RASD
Harger Elaine M. • Librarian • Empire State College (SUNY) School of Labor Studies • New York City, NY 10036 • ACRL RASD IFRT IRRT SRRT
Hargesheimer Agnes H. • Hamburg, NY 14075
Hargrave Victoria E. • Librarian Emerita • MacMurray College Henry Pfeiffer Library • Jacksonville, IL 62650 • ACRL RASD *Life*
Hargreaves Martine MT • New Bedford, MA 02740
Hargrove Marion H. • Young Adult Age Level Specialist • Prince George County Memorial Library System New Carrollton Branch • New Carrollton, MD 20784 • PLA YALSA
Hargrove Thomas • San Francisco, CA 94109
Harig Katherine J. • Branch Manager • Enoch Pratt Free Library Roland Park Branch • Baltimore, MD 21210 • PLA RASD
Haritatos Nancy J.P. • Librarian • Patriach Athenagoras Orthodox Institute • Berkeley, CA 94709 • ACRL LITA
Harju Vincent W. • Palo Alto, CA 94303
Harkavy Ira B. • Trustee • Brooklyn Public Library • Brooklyn, NY 11238 • ALTA PLA
Harkavy Simone • Trustee • West Islip Public Library • West Islip, NY 11795-3999 • ALCTS ALTA PLA
Harke Victor W. • Student • University of Hawaii School of Library & Information Studies • Honolulu, HI 96822
Harken Henry R. Jr. • Electronic Information Spec. • Arizona State University West Campus Fletcher Library • Phoenix, AZ 85069 • ACRL LITA
Harken Shelby E. • Head Cataloger/Database Coor. • University of North Dakota Chester Fritz Library • Grand Forks, ND 58202-0175 • ACRL ALCTS LITA
Harker Carol M. • Field Account Services Manager • EBSCO Subscription Services • Shrewsbury, NJ 07702-4321 • ACRL ALCTS RASD
Harker Lois • Library Consultant • Mississippi Bend Area Education Agency • Bettendorf, IA 52722 • AASL YALSA
Harkins Frances H. • Librarian/Media Specialist • Weston High School Library Media Center • Weston, MA 02193 • AASL
Harkness Angeline M. • Librarian I • Atlanta-Fulton Public Library Georgia Hill Branch • Atlanta, GA 30312 • ALSC
Harkness Mary Lou • Director Emeritus • University of South Florida Library • Tampa, FL 33620-5600 • ACRL ALCTS *Life*
Harkness Robert Alan • Public Services Librarian • Screven-Jenkins Regional Library • Sylvania, GA 30467 • PLA NMRT
Harlan David A. • Student • University of Arkansas Young Law Library • Fayetteville, AR 72701 • PLA
Harlan Donna B. • South Bend, IN 46615 • ACRL ALCTS *Life*
Harlan Irma • Director • Chatham-Effingham-Liberty Regional Library (CEL) • Savannah, GA 31499-4301 • PLA
Harlan James H. • Consultant • Library Consulting Incorporation • San Pedro, CA 90731
Harlan Mildred • Punxsutawney, PA 15767 • Continuing
Harless Carol Sue Dr. • Media Specialist • Hooper Alexander School • Decatur, GA 30033 • IFRT
Harless Melanie • Library Media Specialist • Linden School • Oak Ridge, TN 37830 • AASL
Harley Donna Dean • School Library Media Specialist • Sewanhaka Central High School District • Elmont, NY 11003 • AASL
Harley Janice • Chicago, IL 60617 • AASL
Harley Ronald G. • Trustee & Treasurer • Acorn Public Library District • Oak Forest, IL 60452 • ALTA
Harloe Bart M. • Asst. Dir for Clln Development • Claremont Colleges Libraries Honnold/Mudd Library • Claremont, CA 91711 • ACRL ALCTS RASD
Harloe Susan • Librarian • King County Library System • Seattle, WA 98109-5191
Harlow Jacquelyn • Minneapolis, MN 55428
Harlow Neal • Los Angeles, CA 90026 • Continuing
Harman Vern • Minneapolis, MN 55419
Harmeyer David A. • San Bernardino, CA 92405-2815
Harmon Adella • Media Specialist • Cheney Elementary School Cheney Unified School District • Cheney, KS 67025
Harmon Amanda L. • Acquistions Librarian • University of North Carolina at Charlotte J. Murrey Atkins Library • Charlotte, NC 28223 • ACRL ALCTS
Harmon Charles • Headquarters Librarian • American Library Association • Chicago, IL 60611-2795 • ALCTS YALSA IFRT LHRT
Harmon Dianne • Children's Librarian • Joliet Public Library • Joliet, IL 60431 • ALSC
Harmon Elaine M. • Tampa, FL 33629
Harmon Elva A. Mrs • Tulsa, OK 74114 • AASL YALSA *Life*
Harmon Flo M. • Trustee • Jackson-Hinds Library System • Jackson, MS 39201 • ALTA
Harmon Gayle L. • Head Librarian • Edgewater Public Library • Edgewater, FL 32132
Harmon George J. • Student • University of Illinois Graduate School of Library and Information Science • Urbana, IL 61801
Harmon Jacqueline B. • Kendall, MI 49062 • AASL
Harmon Janet L. • Manager Processing Operations • Columbus Metropolitan Library • Columbus, OH 43215
Harmon Joseph C. • Monographic Cataloger • Indiana University-Purdue University at Indianapolis Library (IUPUI) • Indianapolis, IN 46202
Harmon Julia K. • Baton Rouge, LA 70820 • PLA RASD
Harmon Robert B. • Reference Librarian • San Jose State University Clark Library • San Jose, CA 95192-0028 • ACRL RASD IRRT
Harmon Valisa R. • Children's Librarian • Atlanta-Fulton Public Library Hobgood-Palmer Branch • Fairburn, GA 30213 • ALSC SRRT
Harms Alan L. • Vancouver, WA 98664
Harms Janet K. • Elementary Librarian • MJ Kaufman School • Lake Charles, LA 70605 • AASL
Harms Marie T. • Clear Lake, IA 50428
Harms Mary L. • Patrick Henry Elementary School • APO, AE 09102-0005 • AASL
Harned John C. • President • Bedford Advisors, Inc. • Boston, MA 02110 • LAMA LITA
Harned Robert L. • Reference Librarian • Baruch College Library • New York, NY 10010
Harner Rebecca • Reference Librarian • Pacific Lutheran University Mortvedt Library • Tacoma, WA 98447
Harness Barbara J. • Reference Librarian • Central Maine Medical Center Gerrish-True Health Science Library • Lewiston, ME 04240
Harness Gregory C. • Head, Reference Librarian • United States Senate Library • Washington, DC 20510-7112
Harnett Nancy • East Waterboro, ME 04030 • SRRT
Harnly Caroline D. • Reference Librarian • San Francisco State University J. Paul Leonard Library • San Francisco, CA 94132 • ACRL IFRT SRRT
Harnsberger R. Scott • Collection Development Librarian • Sam Houston State University Newton Gresham Library • Huntsville, TX 77341-2281
Haroutunian Robert J. • Trustee • Presentation Planning Inc. • Bethesda, MD 20827-0974
Harpel-Burke Pamela K. • Jackson District Library • Jackson, MI 49201 • ALCTS LITA PLA
Harper Cynthia R. • Systems Librarian • Colgate University Everett Needham Case Library • Hamilton, NY 13346 • SRRT
Harper Eunice • Librarian I • Enoch Pratt Free Library • Baltimore, MD 21201-4484
Harper Helen • Adult Reference Librarian • Warrenville Public Library District • Warrenville, IL 60555
Harper Kenneth J. • Physics-Optics-Astronomy Libn • University of Rochester Library • Rochester, NY 14627 • ACRL
Harper Laura G. • Head Govt Pubn Dept • University of Mississippi John Davis Williams Library • University, MS 38677 • ACRL LITA GODORT
Harper Lucy Bjorklund • Librarian • University of Rochester Charlotte Whitney Allen Library • Rochester, NY 14627 • ACRL RASD
Harper Marie F. • Los Alamos National Lab Lib • Los Alamos, NM 87545-0020 • ACRL RASD
Harper Marjory B. • Tullahoma, TN 37388 • Continuing
Harper Marsha • Director • Abilene Christian University Margaret & Herman Brown Library • Abilene, TX 79699 • ACRL LAMA
Harper Michael A. • Librarian • Murray Wright High School • Detroit, MI 48208 • AASL
Harper Nancy L. • Librarian • E Jack Sharpe Public Library • White Cloud, MI 49349-0156
Harper Patricia A. • Reference Coordinator • North State Coop. Library System • Willows, CA 95988
Harper Phyllis A. • Hathaway Brown School • Shaker Heights, OH 44122 • AASL
Harper Rosalia Atilano • Escondido Public Library • Escondido, CA 92025 • ALTA
Harper Sarah • Student • Kent State University School of Library & Information Science • Kent, OH 44242-0001
Harper Sarah H. • Senior Librarian • Tyler Public Library • Tyler, TX 75702
Harper Shirley F. • Director • Cornell University Industrial and Labor Relations Library • Ithaca, NY 14853 • ACRL ALCTS LITA
Harple Eugene G. • Trustee • Alameda County Library Pleasanton Branch • Pleasanton, CA 94566 • ALTA PLA RASD
Harpool Lynn E. • Project Manager • National Emergency Training Center • Emmitsburg, MD 21727
Harrar Joanne • Director • University of Maryland College Park Theodore R. McKeldin Library • College Park, MD 20742-7011 • ACRL ALCTS LAMA LITA RASD *Life*
Harrell Carroll M. • Media Coordinator • Manteo High School • Manteo, NC 27954
Harrell Charles B. • Dir. of University Libraries • University of Texas at Tyler • Tyler, TX 75701 • ACRL ALCTS RASD EMIERT GODORT LRRT
Harrell E. Gail • Wake County Public Library North Regional Library • Raleigh, NC 27615
Harrell Elizabeth T. • Manning Middle School • Manning, SC 29150 • AASL YALSA
Harrell Janice B. • Student • Pratt Institute Graduate School of Library & Information Science • Brooklyn, NY 11205
Harrell Jeanne • Head Acquisition • Texas A & M University Sterling C. Evans Library • College Station, TX 77843-5000 • ALCTS LAMA
Harrell Toni • Student • Emporia State University School of Library & Information Management • Emporia, KS 66801 • AASL
Harrell William L. • Chatham-Effingham-Liberty Regional Library (CEL) • Savannah, GA 31499-4301 • LITA RASD
Harrer Gustave A. Dr. • Distinguished Service Professor • University of Florida Libraries • Gainesville, FL 32611-2047 • ACRL ALCTS *Life*
Harrick Rosemary • Head, Government Documents • Kent State University Libraries • Kent, OH 44242 • ACRL RASD GODORT
Harrigian Paddy • Children's Librarian • Las Vegas-Clark County Library District East Las Vegas Branch • Las Vegas, NV 89121

Harrill Maureen G. • Student • University of Texas at Austin Graduate School of Library & Information Sciences • Austin, TX 78712-1276

Harriman Joy H. • Director,Medical Library • Mobile Infirmary Medical Library • Mobile, AL 36652 • LITA

Harriman Robert B. Jr • Coordinator • Library of Congress United States Newspaper Program • Washington, DC 20540 • ALCTS

Harrington Charles W. • Natchitoches, LA 71457 • Continuing

Harrington Drew • Director of Library Services • Albuquerque Academy Library • Albuquerque, NM 87109 • AASL LAMA

Harrington James P. • Oviedo, FL 32765 • ACRL LITA

Harrington Jane E. • Student • University of Oklahoma School of Library & Information Studies • Norman, OK 73019 • ALSC

Harrington Janice N. • Head of Children's Services • Champaign Public Library & Information Center • Champaign, IL 61820-5193 • ALSC

Harrington Janice N. • Champaign, IL 61820-7143 • ALSC

Harrington Judith F. • Librarian • Leo Bernabi School Harrington Library • Spencerport, NY 14559 • AASL ALSC

Harrington Lucilia M. G. • Reference Librarian • Organization of American States (OAS) Columbus Memorial Library • Washington, DC 20006-4499

Harrington Marcia • Adult Basic Education Spec. • District of Columbia Public Library Martin Luther King Memorial Library • Washington, DC 20001 • PLA

Harrington Mary E. • Radcliffe College Schlesinger Library • Cambridge, MA 02138 • ALCTS LITA

Harrington Molly • Iowa Lutheran Hospital Levitt Health Science Library • Des Moines, IA 50316 • RASD

Harrington Pasty • Saint Louis County Library • St. Louis, MO 63131

Harrington Patricia G. • Reference Librarian • Phoenix Public Library Acacia Branch • Phoenix, AZ 85020 • ALSC

Harrington Susan F. • Librarian I • Northbrook Public Library • Northbrook, IL 60062 • PLA

Harrington Thomas R. • Media Librarian • Gallaudet University Library • Washington, DC 20002

Harris Andrea L. • Assistant Director-Support Servs • Dallas Public Library • Dallas, TX 75201 • LAMA PLA

Harris Anita Westall • Parkview Junior High School • Lawrenceville, IL 62439

Harris Ann • Librarian • Peoria Public Library • Peoria, AZ 85381

Harris Anne • Children's Services Librarian • Norman Public Library • Norman, OK 73069

Harris Annie B. • Clementon, NJ 08021

Harris Aphrodite • Public Service Librarian • Vancouver Community College • Vancouver BC, V5T 4N3 Canada • EMIERT SRRT

Harris Ava Nell • Cataloger • University of Texas at Arlington • Arlington, TX 76019-0497 • ALCTS

Harris Barbara A. • Library Supervisor I • Free Library of Philadelphia • Philadelphia, PA 19103

Harris Barbara G. • Adult Services Librarian • Roswell Public Library • Roswell, NM 88201 • RASD

Harris Betty Fiveash • Atlanta, GA 30316 • AASL ALSC

Harris Beverly • Chief of Technical Service • Westchester Library System • Elmsford, NY 10523 • ALCTS LITA

Harris Beverly P. • Hope Mills, NC 28348

Harris C. T. • Director of Library Services • Wingate College • Wingate, NC 28174 • ACRL ALCTS LAMA RASD IFRT LRRT

Harris Carol • Medical Librarian • Deborah Heart/Lung Center Library • Browns Mills, NJ 08015 • ASCLA

Harris Carolyn L. • School Library Service • University of Texas at Austin Graduate School of Library & Information Sciences • Austin, TX 78712-1276 • ACRL ALCTS

Harris Christine Lee • Metropolitan Transportation Commission Library • Oakland, CA 94607 • RASD NMRT

Harris Colleen A. • Branch Librarian • Cobb County Public Library System Merchant's Walk Branch • Marietta, GA 30068

Harris Consuelo • Head, Children's Dept. • Public Library of Cincinnati and Hamilton County • Cincinnati, OH 45202 • ALSC

Harris David L. • Adult Services Librarian • Toledo-Lucas County Public Library • Toledo, OH 43624 • PLA

Harris Deborah K. • Haslett, MI 48840 • ACRL RASD

Harris Diane • English/Latin Teacher • H M King High Sch Lib • Kingsville, TX 78363

Harris Dorothy • Millbrook, AL 36054

Harris Dorothy • Brooklyn, NY 11233

Harris Edward • Central Methodist College Smiley Memorial Library • Fayette, MO 65248

Harris Edwin R. Dr • Ferris State University • Big Rapids, MI 49307 • ACRL ALCTS LAMA LITA

Harris Eileen M. • Supv. Libn./Adult Lending Lib. • Donnell Library Center • New York, NY 10019 • ALCTS PLA LRRT

Harris Eleanor B. • Brigantine, NJ 08203 • YALSA

Harris Eleanor C. Mrs • Montgomery, NY 12549 • ALSC ALTA *Life*

Harris Emma B. • Branch Manager • Anaheim Public Library Canyon Hills Branch • Anaheim, CA 92807-4763

Harris George D. • Columbia, MO 65203

Harris Georgette • Library Inf. Research Analyst • Library of Congress • Washington, DC 20541

Harris Howard S. • Vice President • RMG Consultants Inc. • Bethesda, MD 20817 • ACRL ASCLA LITA

Harris Ira W. • Professor Emeritus • University of Hawaii School of Library & Information Studies • Honolulu, HI 96822 • ACRL RASD SRRT

Harris Jacquelyn B. • N Plainfield, NJ 07063 • PLA RASD *Life*

Harris Jane S. • Senior Librarian • Jacksonville Public Library System Mandarin Branch • Jacksonville, FL 32257

Harris Janie L. • Bibliographer • Cornell University • Ithaca, NY 14853-5301 • ACRL GODORT

Harris Jimmie L. • Information Technology Librarian • Texas Woman's University Mary Evelyn Blagg-Huey Library • Denton, TX 76204-1715 • LITA RASD LIRT NMRT

Harris Jo Ann • Wharton, TX 77488 • AASL ALSC

Harris John C. • Annandale, NJ 08801-9705 • LITA IFRT

Harris John Jr. • Morris College Learning Resources Center Library • Sumter, SC 29150 • ACRL

Harris Judith A. • El Camino College Library and Media Services • Torrance, CA 90506 • ACRL ALCTS RASD LIRT

Harris Karen H. • Professor • University of New Orleans College of Education-Program in Library Science • New Orleans, LA 70148 • ALSC YALSA

Harris Karen S. • Library Director • Mayville Public Library • Mayville, WI 53050 • LAMA PLA YALSA

Harris Kathleen Jones • Library Director • Roxbury Public Library • Succasunna, NJ 07876 • LAMA

Harris Kenneth • Free Library of Philadelphia • Philadelphia, PA 19103 • RASD

Harris Kenneth E. • Director for Preservation • Library of Congress Preservation Office • Washington, DC 20540 • ALCTS

Harris Lee • Selection Reference Librarian • Concordia University Libraries • Montreal PQ, H3G 1M8 Canada • ACRL RASD

Harris Lee O. • Systems Manager • Utah State University Merrill Library • Logan, UT 84322-3000

Harris Linda B. • Library Media Specialist • Hamilton School District • Sussex, WI 53089 • AASL

Harris Linda Suttle • Business & Engineering Ln • University of Alabama at Birmingham Mervyn H. Sterne Library • Birmingham, AL 35294-0014 • RASD EMIERT

Harris Lisa • Trustee • Birmingham Public Library • Birmingham, AL 35203 • ALTA

Harris Lisa M. • Albuquerque, NM 87112

Harris M. Donna • Chairperson Librarian • Bellwood Public Library • Bellwood, IL 60104 • LAMA PLA

Harris Margaret J. • Regional Branch Librarian • Cuyahoga County Public Library Maple Heights Regional Branch • Maple Heights, OH 44137 • LAMA PLA YALSA IFRT SRRT

Harris Margaret R. • Castleton, NY 12033 • PLA RASD

Harris Mark J. • Student • Texas Woman's University School of Library & Information Studies • Denton, TX 76204

Harris Martha Jane • Ft Pierce, FL 34945

Harris Martha R. • Cataloger • Armed Forces Radiobiology Research Institute (AFRRI) • Bethesda, MD 20889-5145

Harris Mary A. • Student • University of North Texas School of Library & Information Sciences • Denton, TX 76203

Harris Mary B. • Librarian • Fairfax County Public Schools System • Fairfax, VA 22003

Harris Maureen • Head Public Documents • Clemson University Robert Muldrow Cooper Library • Clemson, SC 29634-3001 • GODORT MAGERT

Harris Michael H. • Professor • University of Kentucky College of Library & Information Science • Lexington, KY 40506-0391 • ACRL RASD *Life*

Harris Michael L. • Branch Manager • Medina County District Library • Brunswick, OH 44212 • PLA LIRT

Harris Nellie E. • Librarian • M.U.L. Street Academy • Minneapolis, MN 55403 • AASL

Harris Norma J. • Mercy College Libraries • Dobbs Ferry, NY 10522 • ACRL

Harris Patricia L. • Director • Alabama Public Library Service • Montgomery, AL 36130 • AASL ACRL ALCTS ALSC ALTA ASCLA LAMA LITA PLA RASD YALSA CLENE EMIERT FLRT GODORT LHRT LRRT MAGERT SORT

Harris Patricia R. • NISO • Bethesda, MD 20827 • LITA IRRT

Harris Paula Jane • Houston, TX 77083

Harris Peggy A. • Santa Clara County Free Library Gilroy Public • Gilroy, CA 95020

Harris Robert Alvord • Helen M. Plum Memorial Library • Lombard, IL 60148 • LAMA PLA

Harris Robert L. • Head, Reference Librarian • Southwest Texas State University Learning Resource Center • San Marcos, TX 78666-4604

Harris Robert R. • Media Specialist • Therrell High School • Atlanta, GA 30311 • AASL EMIERT

Harris Robin R. • Asst Law Ln,Asst Prof Legal Bibl • Louisville University Law School Library • Louisville, KY 40292 • ACRL

Harris Rodger S. • Head of Catalog Department • University of North Carolina • Chapel Hill, NC 27599-3914 • ACRL LAMA

Harris Roger L. • Branch Manager • Sonoma Cnty Library Northwest Regional Branch • Santa Rosa, CA 95401

Harris Roma M. • Associate Professor, SLIS • University of Western Ontario • London ON, N6G 1H1 Canada • RASD LRRT

Harris Sandra R. • Librarian • Atlanta-Fulton Public Library • Atlanta, GA 30303 • ACRL ALCTS LITA PLA

Harris Sara • Trustee • Western Plains Library System • Clinton, OK 73601

Harris Steven R. • Humanities Reference Librarian • Texas A & M University Sterling C. Evans Library • College Station, TX 77843-5000 • ACRL IFRT SRRT

Harris Susan A. • Belmont, MA 02178

Harris Thelma E. • Corona, NY 11368 • IRRT SRRT

Harris Thomas Joe • Cumberland Trail Library System • Flora, IL 62839 • AASL ASCLA LITA

Harris Thomas R. • Assistant Reference Librarian • Mesa State College Library • Grand Junction, CO 81501 • RASD

Harris Vicki J. • Media Specialist • Grayson Elementary School • Grayson, GA 30092

Harris Willie Mae • Librarian • Atlanta-Fulton Public Library • Atlanta, GA 30303 • ALCTS LITA CLENE

Harris Winifred E. • Director, Learning Resources • Fraser Valley University College • Abbotsford BC, V2S 4N2 Canada • ACRL ALCTS ASCLA RASD LIRT MAGERT VRT

Harrison Ann • Peterbourough, NH 03458-2430 • LITA

Harrison Annie W. • Librarian • Saint Paul's College Library • Lawrenceville, VA 23868

Harrison Bonnie Baumann • Douglas School System Instructional Materials Center • Ellsworth AFB, SD 57706 • AASL

Harrison Carol I. • Coor Serv To Shut-ins & Retirees • Detroit Public Library Shut-ins & Retirees • Detroit, MI 48208 • PLA

Harrison Cheryl A. • City Board of Education • Columbus, OH 43211

Harrison Constance • Adult Services Librarian • Ida Public Library • Belvidere, IL 61008

Harrison Donna • Manager Technical Services • Douglas Public Library District • Castle Rock, CO 80104

Harrison Dorothy E. • Sr Asst Ln/Serials Catlgr • University of Wyoming Coe Library • Laramie, WY 82071-3334 • ALCTS

Harrison Edna B. • San Francisco, CA 94124

Harrison Elaine • Continuing Education Specialist • Library of Michigan • Lansing, MI 48909 • ASCLA CLENE

Harrison Giles V. • Young Peoples Librarian • London Borough of Tower Hamlets Fairfoot Library • London, E3 4EA, England • ALSC PLA

Harrison Harriet W. • Hd Proc Sect Motion Pict Broadcasting & Rec Div • Library of Congress • Washington, DC 20541

Harrison James O. Jr • Head Reference Librarian • Georgia Southern University Henderson Library • Statesboro, GA 30460 • ACRL RASD LIRT

Harrison John A. • University of Arkansas Libraries • Fayetteville, AR 72701-1201 • ACRL

Harrison John C. • Student • University of Texas at Austin Graduate School of Library & Information Sciences • Austin, TX 78712-1276 • LITA

Harrison John Philip • Head of Cataloging • Boston Athenaeum • Boston, MA 02108 • ACRL ALCTS LHRT

Harrison Jon J. • Law Librarian • Michigan State University Libraries • East Lansing, MI 48824-1048 • ACRL RASD GODORT

Harrison Judith • Coor. of Instructional Material • Hayward Unified School District • Hayward, CA 94540 5000 • AASL

Harrison Kathryn B. • Librarian • Randolph School • Huntsville, AL 35802

Harrison Kathy • Director of L/Instr. Media Servs • Amarillo Independent School Education Support Center • Amarillo, TX 79109 • AASL LIRT

Harrison Laura • Librarian for the Blind • Southwest Georgia Regional Library Gilbert H Gragg Library • Bainbridge, GA 31717

Harrison Linda O. • High School Librarian • Kettering Fairmont High School • Kettering, OH 45429 • AASL

Harrison Lynn • Pikes Peak Library District • Colorado Springs, CO 80901

Harrison Margaret J. • Student • University of Hawaii School of Library & Information Studies • Honolulu, HI 96822

Harrison Marsha • Library Technician II • East Baton Rouge Parish Library Scotlandville Branch • Baton Rouge, LA 70807

Harrison Mary M. • Head of Reference Library • University of Nevada-Las Vegas James R. Dickinson Library • Las Vegas, NV 89154 • ACRL LAMA RASD

Harrison Nancy • Librarian/Documentation • The Library Corporation • Inwood, WV 25428-9733 • LITA

Harrison Richard Henry II • General Reference Librarian • University of Alabama at Birmingham Mervyn H. Sterne Library • Birmingham, AL 35294-0014

Harrison Robert E. • Student • Clarion University of Pennsylvania College of Library Science • Clarion, PA 16214 • PLA

Harrison Sandra J. • Media Specialist • Saint Dunstan Library • Arden, NC 28704

Harrison Scott E. • Bibliographer for East Asian Law • Harvard Law School Library • Cambridge, MA 02138 • ACRL

Harrison Susan B. • Assoc Dir Tech & Computer Serv • The New York Public Library • New York, NY 10016 • LITA PLA

Harrison Walter G. • Director of Library Services • Killeen Public Library • Killeen, TX 76541

Harrison William N. • Reference Librarian • Parsippany-Troy Hills Public Library Parsippany Branch • Parsippany, NJ 07054-4036

Harrison William T. • Alabama Public Library Service • Montgomery, AL 36130 • ALTA

Harrod Valerie J. • Director • Durham Public Library • Durham, CT 06422 • LAMA PLA

Harry Carolyn R. • Library Director • Platteville Public Library • Platteville, WI 53818

Harshberger Kathleen • New York, NY 10028 • ALSC

Harshe Florence E. • Saratoga Spg, NY 12866 • Continuing

Harsin Steven D. • Extension Librarian • Arrowhead Library System • Virginia, MN 55792

Hart Alice M. • Student • Emporia State University School of Library & Information Management • Emporia, KS 66801

Hart Andrew S. • Student • University of Pittsburgh School of Library and Information Science • Pittsburgh, PA 15260

Hart Carol Ann • McDonald High School • McDonald, OH 44437

Hart David J. • Associate Librarian • University of Michigan • Flint, MI 48502-2186

Hart Earl D. • Associate Professor of Ln Sci. • University of New Orleans College of Education-Program in Library Science • New Orleans, LA 70148 • AASL

Hart Eldon Charles • Rexburg, ID 83440 • ALSC PLA *Life*

Hart Geraldine J. • Librarian • District of Columbia Public Schools • Washington, DC 20020 • AASL

Hart James W. • Head of Public Services • University of Cincinnati • Cincinnati, OH 45221-0033 • ACRL

Hart Joan • Macungie, PA 18062

Hart John C. Dr. • Trustee • Peoria Public Library • Peoria, IL 61602 • ALTA

Hart Joseph T. Dr • New York University Elmer Holmes Bobst Library • New York, NY 10012 • ACRL ALCTS *Life*

Hart Julie C. • Consultant • Arkansas State Library • Little Rock, AR 72201 • LAMA

Hart Karen • Canon City, CO 81212 • AASL YALSA

Hart Katherine • Texas A & M University Sterling C. Evans Library • College Station, TX 77843-5000 • ALCTS

Hart Lea R. • Mead, CO 80542

Hart Lillie M. • Norman, OK 73069-4317 • IFRT

Hart Lorraine K. • Media Specialist • Franklin Monroe High School • Pitsburg, OH 45358 • AASL

Hart Margo W. • Director of Marketing • Neal-Schuman Publishers, Inc. • New York, NY 10013

Hart Mary A. • Law Librarian • Corvallis-Benton County Public Library • Corvallis, OR 97330-4728 • ASCLA

Hart Mary Lynn • Overton, TX 75684

Hart Merrily F. • Cleveland College of Jewish Studies Library • Beachwood, OH 44122

Hart Mildred • Branch Head Librarian • East Cleveland Public Library • East Cleveland, OH 44112

Hart Milly • Librarian • Heathwood Hall Episcopal School • Columbia, SC 29201 • AASL

Hart Minda N. • Student • Swarthmore College • Swarthmore, PA 19081

Hart Patricia L. • Assistant Librarian • University of Washington Suzzallo Library • Seattle, WA 98195 • ACRL ALCTS

Hart Richard L. • Associate Librarian • State University of New York College Daniel A. Reed Library • Fredonia, NY 14063

Hart Richard S. III • Librarian • Greenwich Library • Greenwich, CT 06830 • RASD

Hart Thomas L. • Professor • Florida State University School of Library and Information Studies • Tallahassee, FL 32306-2048 • AASL

Hart Winifred M. • Arlington, VA 22201 • FLRT

Hart-Hults Ronald L. • Reference Librarian • Indiana University-Purdue University at Indianapolis Library (IUPUI) • Indianapolis, IN 46202 • GODORT

Harte Julie A. • Library Director • Somonauk Public Library • Somonauk, IL 60552 • PLA NMRT

Hartel Mary Jean • YA/AV Librarian • Athens Regional Library • Athens, GA 30606 • YALSA VRT

Harter Bonnie • Librarian • Smithfield Middle School Library • Fort Worth, TX 76180

Harter Elizabeth W. • Coordinator, Ref Desk Services • George Washington University Gelman Library • Washington, DC 20052 • ACRL RASD

Harter Ellen M. • Student • University of Arizona Graduate Library School • Tucson, AZ 85721 • SRRT

Harter Margaret H. • Assistant Librarian • Indiana University • Bloomington, IN 47405 • ACRL RASD IFRT SRRT

Harter Stephen Paul • Professor • Indiana University School of Library and Information Science • Bloomington, IN 47405 • LRRT

Hartford Peter J. • Business Reference Librarian • University of Iowa Libraries • Iowa City, IA 52242-1379 • RASD GODORT

Harthman Susan E. • Claremont, CA 91711

Hartigan Barry • Science Bibliographer • University of Florida Libraries • Gainesville, FL 32611 • ACRL ALCTS RASD

Hartigan Richard F. • Trustee • River Bluffs Regional Library • Saint Joseph, MO 64501

Hartje George N. • Director of Libraries • Northeast Missouri State University • Kirksville, MO 63501 • ACRL

Hartle Ann G. • Middle School Library Coor. • Cincinnati Country Day School • Cincinnati, OH 45243 • AASL

Hartley Frances V. • Reference Librarian • Tacoma Public Library • Tacoma, WA 98402 • PLA

Hartley Jannette S. • Washington College Clifton M. Miller Library • Chestertown, MD 21620 • ALCTS

Hartley Olive Miss • Oakland, CA 94619 • PLA YALSA *Continuing*

Hartley Patricia W. Mrs. • Student • University of South Carolina College of Library & Information Science • Columbia, SC 29208 • ALSC

Hartline Cecila E. • Oklahoma City, OK 73122 • PLA

Hartman Anne-Marie • Flushing, NY 11358 • ALCTS

Hartman Cathy N. • Asst. Libn./Asst. Professor • Austin College Abell Library • Sherman, TX 75090 • ACRL GODORT LIRT NMRT

Hartman David W. • Public Services Librarian • Harcourt Brace Jovanovich • Orlando, FL 32821

Hartman Donald K. • Reference Librarian • State University of New York Lockwood Library Building • Buffalo, NY 14260 • ACRL

Hartman Elaine • Networking Consultant • Virginia State Library & Archives • Richmond, VA 23219 • ACRL ALCTS ASCLA LITA RASD

Hartman Eleanor C. • Museum Librarian • Los Angeles County Museum of Art Art Research Library • Los Angeles, CA 90036 • LAMA

Hartman Elizabeth • St Petersburg, FL 33701 • LAMA PLA *Continuing*

Hartman Freda Z. Dr. • Trustee • Montgomery County Department of Public Libraries • Rockville, MD 20850 • ALTA PLA IFRT

Hartman Janet L. • Student • Continental Bank • Chicago, IL 60626

Hartman Joel L. • Assoc. Provost for Inf. Tech. • Bradley University Cullom-Davis Library • Peoria, IL 61625

Hartman Linda C. • Media Specialist • Truman Elementary School • Kansas City, MO 64134 • AASL

Hartman Nola • Bloomington, IN 47401 • PLA

Hartman Richard W. • Media Specialist • Eastern High School Media Center • Voorhees, NJ 08043-0915 • AASL

Hartman Ruth D. • Emeritus Professor of Lnship. • Central Washington University • Ellensburg, WA 98926 • Continuing

Hartman Ruth M. • Manager Adult Services • Ventura County Library Service Agency • Ventura, CA 93002 • PLA RASD

Hartman Sherry • Director/Librarian • Albany Medical College Schaffer Library of Health Sciences • Albany, NY 12208-3479 • ACRL

Hartmann M. Clare Sr. • Teacher-Librarian • Saint Paul Indian Mission Media Library • Hays, MT 59527-0030

Hartmann Mary K. • Zelienople, PA 16063

Hartmann Thomas R. • Adult Services Librarian • Three Rivers Public Library • Channahon, IL 60410-0300

Hartmetz Walter J. • Library Director • North Kansas City Public Library • North Kansas City, MO 64116-3399 • LAMA PLA

Hartnett Sharon • New Haven, CT 06510

Hartnoll Gillian A. • Head of Library & Information • British Film Institute • London W1P 1PL, England • ALCTS LITA

Harton Bonnie L. • Manager • Indianapolis-Marion County Public Library Nora Branch • Indianapolis, IN 46240-1835 • PLA

Hartse Merri A. • Circulation Librarian • University of Illinois Library • Urbana, IL 61801 • LAMA LITA

Hartsell Lynaire K. • Head of Circulation • Fayetteville Public Library • Fayetteville, AR 72701

Hartsell Valiery J. • Librarian/Media Specialist • Guam Department of Education • Agana, GU 96911 • AASL

Hartsfield Mary W. • Toledo, OH 43614 • Continuing

Hartstone Judith A. • Bainbridge Island, WA 98110

Hartung Frank E. • Board Chairman • Houston Public Library • Houston, TX 77002 • ALTA LAMA PLA

Hartung Gertrude Miss • Saint Paul, MN 55116 • AASL YALSA *Continuing*

Hartvigas Mary D. • Amsterdam, NY 12010-1217 • ACRL

Hartwell J. Glenn • Library Director • Kelso Public Library • Kelso, WA 98626 • PLA

Hartwell Robert • Trustee • Fairfax County Public Library • Fairfax, VA 22033-1909

Hartwig Douglas Dean • Student • San Jose State University Division of Library & Information Science • San Jose, CA 95192-0029 • SRRT

Hartwig Lois • Leavenworth, WA 98826-1054 • RASD

Harty Monica L. • Student • Kent State University School of Library & Information Science • Kent, OH 44242-0001

Harty Rose Marie • Albert Lea Public Library • Albert Lea, MN 56007 • PLA

Hartzell Fena M. • Claremore, OK 74017 • AASL

Hartzell Gail V. • Crown Point, IN 46307 • IFRT

Hartzler Ruth A. • Head/Technical Services • Newton Public Library • Newton, KS 67114 • SRRT

Harvard Susan B. • Director • Village Library • Morgantown, PA 19543

Harvath John Jr • Manager Fine Arts & Rec Dept. • Houston Public Library • Houston, TX 77002 • PLA

Harvell Tony • Head of Reference • University of San Diego Copley Library • San Diego, CA 92110 • ACRL

Harvey Beverly • Librarian • Royal Valley High School • Hoyt, KS 66440 • AASL YALSA

Harvey Elizabeth A. • Brooklyn, NY 11215 • SRRT

Harvey Holly A. • Dynix Incorporated • Provo, UT 84601 • LITA

Harvey John F. • New York, NY 10005-3682 • ACRL LAMA IRRT LRRT *Life*

Harvey Joyce E. • Coordinator/Adult Services • Fairfield County District Library • Lancaster, OH 43130

Harvey Julia L. • OCLC Services Coordinator • PALINET Library Network • Philadelphia, PA 19104

Harvey Karen L. • Children's Librarian • Chicago Public Library Sulzer Regional Library • Chicago, IL 60625 • ALSC EMIERT SRRT

Harvey Kay • Executive Director • Broward Public Library Foundation, Inc. • Fort Lauderdale, FL 33301 • LAMA

Harvey Kay E. • Pittsburgh, PA 15241 • ALCTS

Harvey Kris • San Francisco, CA 94122

Harvey L. Beth • Johnson Creek, WI 53038

Harvey Lois M. • Hollywood Beach, FL 33019 • Continuing

Harvey Mary Nic • Westview Elementary School • Richmond, IN 47374 • AASL

Harvey Pamela A. • Librarian • Hillside Junior High School • Manchester, NH 03104

Harvey Paul W. • Head Adult Services • Dedham Public Library • Dedham, MA 02026

Harvey Phyllis J. • Reference Librarian • Wright State University College of Education & Human Services • Dayton, OH 45435 • ALCTS

Harvey Sally A. • Student • University of Arizona Graduate Library School • Tucson, AZ 85721 • SRRT

Harvey Sara J. • User Education Librarian • Dallas Public Library • Dallas, TX 75201 • LIRT

Harvey Sharon M. • Media Specialist • Beaufort Elementary School • Beaufort, SC 29902 • AASL ALSC

Harvie Nan A. • Cataloging Librarian • University of Hawaii Thomas Hale Hamilton Library • Honolulu, HI 96822 • ACRL ALCTS LITA

Harvill F Susan • Librarian • Rutledge Middle School • Midfield, AL 35228

Harvill Melba S. • Iowa Park, TX 76367 • ACRL LAMA

Harville Martha M. • Librarian • Westview Elementary School • Petersburg, VA 23803

Harward Terry Ann • Trustee • Provo City Public Library • Provo, UT 84601 • ALTA

Harwell Richard • Washington, GA 30673 • ACRL RASD
Life

Harwood Doreen J. • Reference Librarian • Alverno College Library Media Center • Milwaukee, WI 53234-3922

Harwood Eleanor C. • Chester, CT 06412

Harwood Ellen G. • Trustee • Morse Inst Library • Natick, MA 01760

Harwood Judith A. • Librarian • Southern Illinois University Delyte W. Morris Library • Carbondale, IL 62901-6632 • ACRL

Harwood Karen • Associate Professor • College of Saint Catherine • Saint Paul, MN 55105 • ACRL ALCTS

Harwood Rachel J. • Santa Cruz, CA 95060 • EMIERT IFRT SRRT

Harwood Richard L. • Music/Nonbook Cataloger • Pennsylvania State University E506 Pattee Library • University Park, PA 16802 • ALCTS LAMA

Hary Francesca L. • Dayton & Montgomery County Public Library • Dayton, OH 45402-2103 • PLA EMIERT

Hary Nicoletta C. • Assistant Director • University of Dayton Roesch Library • Dayton, OH 45469 • ACRL LRRT

Harzbecker Joseph J. • Reference Librarian • Boston University Alumni Medical Library • Boston, MA 02118 • ACRL RASD IFRT

Hasbrouck Clara H. • Media Service Director • Sullivan County Depatment of Education • Blountville, TN 37617 • AASL

Haschak Paul G. • Night Reference Librarian • Southeastern Louisiana University Linus A. Sims Memorial Library • Hammond, LA 70402

Hase Vickie • Head, Technical Services • Chatham College • Pittsburgh, PA 15232 • ALCTS

Hasegawa Yoshino T. • Sanger, CA 93657

Haselden Clyde L. • Wilmington, NC 28401 • ACRL
Continuing

Haselden Marsha B. • Hornets Nest Elementary School • Charlotte, NC 28216 • AASL ALSC

Haselhuhn Ronald P. Mr • Assistant Professor of Science • Emporia State University School of Library & Information Management • Emporia, KS 66801 • ACRL RASD
Life

Haseltine Michael • Student • University of Arizona Graduate Library School • Tucson, AZ 85721 • ACRL LITA RASD

Haselwood Eldon La Verne • Professor • University of Nebraska at Omaha University Library • Omaha, NE 68182-0237 • AASL

Hasenmyer Margaret J. • University of Arkansas Mullins Library • Fayetteville, AR 72701

Hasenstein Virginia P. • Librarian II • Minneapolis Public Library & Information Center • Minneapolis, MN 55401-1992

Hasenwinkel Nancy • Director • Charles City Public Library • Charles City, IA 50616 • PLA

Hashim Elinor M. • Govt Relations Officer • Online Computer Library Center (OCLC) • Washington, DC 20037 • LAMA LITA GODORT IRRT

Hashmi Ali Syed • Chief Executive Officer • State Government of Andhra Pradesh District Central Library • Karimnagar AP 505002, India

Hashweh Maher Dr. • Library Director • Birzeit University • West Bank Via, Israel • ACRL

Haskell Diana C. • Curator • Newberry Library • Chicago, IL 60610 • ACRL

Haskell Inez • Portland, OR 97267 • Continuing

Haskell John D. Jr. • Associate University Librarian • College of William and Mary Earl Gregg Swem Library • Williamsburg, VA 23187-8794 • ACRL RASD

Haskell Lucy A. • Assistant Director • Fort Lee Public Library • Fort Lee, NJ 07024 • PLA

Haskell Lucy A. • Summit, NJ 07901

Haskell Mary B. • Technical Services Librarian • Colonial Williamsburg Foundation • Williamsburg, VA 23187 • ALCTS LITA

Haskell Peter C. • Rodas Haskell Associates Inc. • Houston, TX 77098-0306

Haskett Thomas E. • Librarian • Emporia Senior High School • Emporia, KS 66801 • AASL

Haskin Susan M. • San Diego, CA 92103 • ACRL ASCLA
Life

Haskins Natalie R. • Student • Clarion University of Pennsylvania College of Library Science • Clarion, PA 16214

Haskins Patricia A. • Librarian • IBM Corporation • Owego, NY 13827 • LITA

Haskins Susan M. Miss • Watertown, MA 02172 • ACRL ALCTS
Life

Haslam David C. • Principia College Marshall Brooks Library • Elsah, IL 62028 • ACRL ALCTS LITA

Hass Barbara • La Salle, CO 80645

Hass Louise S. • Librarian • Saint Vincent Hospital & Health Care Center Garceau Library • Indianapolis, IN 46260

Hass Virginia • Head of Cataloging • New York Society Library • New York, NY 10021 • ALCTS

Hassar Lauretta C. • So. San Francisco, CA 94080

Hassard Cathy Ann • Librarian • Sandown Public Library • Sandown, NH 03873

Hassebrock Erna • Tri-Lakes Regional Library • Hot Springs, AR 71913 • PLA

Hassell Alice L. • Librarian • Whitaker Library Chowan College • Murfreesboro, NC 27855

Hassell Hank • Reference Librarian • Northern Arizona University • Flagstaff, AZ 86011-6022

Hassibe Wendy R. • Chief • United States Geological Survey • Reston, VA 22092 • MAGERT

Hasskamp Karen L. • Perham, MN 56573 • AASL ALSC PLA

Hasskarl Mark P. • Director • Chappaqua Library • Chappaqua, NY 10514 • ALSC PLA

Hassler Ann Keiko • Librarian • Mililani Public Library • Mililani, HI 96789 • RASD EMIERT FLRT

Hassler Peggy M. • Carlsbad, CA 92009

Hassler William B. • Pearl City, HI 96782 • PLA AFLRT FLRT

Hassman Dotta J. • Iowa Braille & Sightsaving School • Vinton, IA 52349

Hassman Rebecca • Technical Services Coordinator • Rochester Public Library • Rochester, MN 55904-3777 • ALCTS

Hasso Amy M. • Student • Kent State University School of Library & Information Science • Kent, OH 44242-0001

Hasson Seana M. • Student • University of Pittsburgh School of Library and Information Science • Pittsburgh, PA 15260

Hasting Eleanor R. Miss • Pasadena, TX 77502 • ALCTS ASCLA
Continuing

Hastings Aleta R. • Oxford Schools Unified School District 358 • Oxford, KS 67119 • AASL ALSC

Hastings Carolyn W. • Stow, MA 01775

Hastings Diana • Head Librarian • Little Rock Township Public Library • Plano, IL 60545 • PLA

Hastings Jean W. • Reference Librarian • Fairfax County Public Library Administrative Offices • Fairfax, VA 22030

Hastings John E. • Chairman • Etobicoke Public Library Board • Etobicoke, ON, M9C 2Y2 Canada

Hastings Marilyn • Durham, NC 27701

Hastings Richard S. • County Librarian • Tulolumne County Library • Sonora, CA 95370

Hastings Samantha K. • Florida State University School of Library and Information Studies • Tallahassee, FL 32306-2048 • ACRL LITA LRRT

Hastings Wallace H. • Trustee • Elmhurst Public Library • Elmhurst, IL 60126 • ALTA PLA

Hasty Douglas F. • Interlibrary Loan Librarian • Florida International University • Miami, FL 33199

Haswell Hollee • Curator, Columbiana Collection • Columbia University Libraries • New York, NY 10027 • ACRL
Life

Haswell Martha M. • Student • University of North Carolina at Chapel Hill School of Information and Library Science • Chapel Hill, NC 27599-3360

Hatayama Neal M. • Librarian • Hawaii State Library • Honolulu, HI 96813

Hatch Bonnie S. • Las Vegas Medical Center • Las Vegas, NM 87701

Hatch Jane • Director • Dodge City Public Library • Dodge City, KS 67801 • ASCLA LAMA PLA

Hatch Julie A. • Dir. of Advancement Research • St. Mary's College • St. Mary's City, MD 20686

Hatch Lillian E. • Annadale, VA 22003 • ALCTS ILERT

Hatch Lucile • Denver, CO 80210 • AASL ALSC
Life

Hatch Nancy • Librarian • F.S. Barry Elementary School Library • Cortland, NY 13045

Hatch Tina L. • Adult Services Librarian • Milford Township Library • Milford, MI 48381

Hatcher April M. • Riverhead, NY 11901 • AASL ALSC PLA

Hatcher Karen A. • Dean of Library Services • University of Montana Library • Missoula, MT 59812 • ACRL LAMA LITA

Hatcher Linda W. • Rockingham, NC 28379 • AASL

Hatcher Marie T. • Wilmot, WI 53192

Hatcher Marihelen • Columbus Metropolitan Library • Columbus, OH 43215 • ALCTS SRRT

Hatcher Nancy F. • Media Librarian • Kentucky Country Day School • Louisville, KY 40207 • AASL

Hatfield Carolyn • Nashville, TN 37210

Hatfield Charlotte K. • Librarian • University of Alaska-Anchorage Carolyn Floyd Library • Kodiak, AK 99615 • ACRL

Hatfield Emma H. • Waterloo, IA 50701

Hatfield Jean A. • Youth Services Coordinator • Johnson County Library • Shawnee Mission, KS 66201 • ALSC

Hatfield Joe • Rice University Fondren Library • Houston, TX 77251-1892

Hatfield Kathryn A. • River Vale, NJ 07675

Hatfield Rex P. • Student • University of Iowa School of Library & Information Science • Iowa City, IA 52242 • IFRT SRRT

Hatfield Theda H. • Norfolk, VA 23507

Hatfield V. Sue • Asst. Dir. of Library Serv. • DeKalb College Central Campus Library • Clarkston, GA 30021-2396 • ACRL LAMA

Hathaway Deborah L. • Head of Technical Services • Elk Grove Village Public Library • Elk Grove Village, IL 60007 • ALCTS

Hathaway Elaine B. • Wayzata, MN 55391

Hathaway Milton G. • Assistant Professor • Appalachian State University Department of Library Science & Educational Foundation • Boone, NC 28608 • AASL ALSC LRRT MAGERT

Hathaway Richard J. • Coordinator, M-Link Project • University of Michigan Libraries • Ann Arbor, MI 48109-1205 • PLA

Hathaway Ruth H. • Brevard, NC 28712 • Life

Hathaway Teresa M. • United States Air Force Base Library • Hanscom AFB, MA 01731-5000 • PLA AFLRT

Hathcock Janice M. • Information Officer • Virginia State Library & Archives • Richmond, VA 23219

Hathman Laurie E. • Circulation/Periodicals Ln. • Rockhurst College Library • Kansas City, MO 64110-2508

Hathway Judy A. • Cataloging Unit Administrator • University of Wisconsin Center for Health Sciences Library • Madison, WI 53706 • ALCTS

Hatlen Patricia A. • File Coordinator • Community Information Program • Belmont, CA 94002 • PLA

Hatley Ken • Clermont, FL 34711 • ACRL AFLRT

Haton Gregory Karen L. • Childrens Librarian • Indianapolis-Marion County Public Library Broadway Branch • Indianapolis, IN 46205 • ALSC YALSA

Hattan Nancy L. • Librarian • Centennial Engineering,Inc. • Arvada, CO 80001

Hattasch Maureen • Head Technical Service • Greenwich Library • Greenwich, CT 06830

Hattendorf Lynn C. • Assistant Reference Librarian • University of Illinois at Chicago University Library • Chicago, IL 60680 • ACRL RASD

Hattery Martha R. • Reference Librarian • Skokie Public Library • Skokie, IL 60077-3680 • RASD

Hattler Patricia T. • Reference Librarian • Thomas Hackney Braswell Memorial Library • Rocky Mount, NC 27804 • RASD

Hatton Jackie L. • Chief Documents Branch • United States Air Force Air University Library • Maxwell AFB, AL 36112-5564 • LITA AFLRT

Hatton John W. • Student • Florida State University School of Library and Information Studies • Tallahassee, FL 32306-2048 • ACRL RASD LHRT NMRT SRRT

Hatvany Bela R. • Group Chairman • SilverPlatter Information Ltd. • London W4 4PH, United Kingdom • LITA

Hauck Helen • Sebring, OH 44672 • Continuing

Hauck Janet E. • Sparanburg, SC 29302

Hauck Linda M. • Referemce Librarian • Proskauer Rose Goetz and Mendelsohn Library • New York, NY 10036

Hauck Susan • Services Coordinator • Palinet & Union Library Catalogue of Pennsylvania • Philadelphia, PA 19104 • LITA

Haudricourt George J. Jr. • Trustee • Henrico Public Library • Richmond, VA 23223 • ALTA

Hauenstein Margaret L. • Wooster, OH 44691 • Continuing

Hauer Mary T. • Information & Referral Librarian • Frederick County Public Library C. Burr Artz Library • Frederick, MD 21701 • PLA

Hauer Susan • Director • Port Ewen Free Library • Port Ewen, NY 12466

Haug Helen • St Petersburg, FL 33710 • PLA   *Continuing*

Haug James D. • Student • North Carolina Central University • Durham, NC 27707 • RASD

Haug Kathy L. • Children's Librarian • Richmond Public Library • Richmond, CA 94804

Haug Pauline C. • Library Media Specialist • Sparta Middle School • Sparta, WI 54656 • AASL

Haugen Christina L. • Long Beach, CA 90805

Haugen Fyrne • Mankato, MN 56001 • AASL ALSC   *Life*

Hauger James S. • Director • Cal Info • Los Angeles, CA 90028

Haugh Judith A • Student • Mankato State University Library Media Education Department • Mankato, MN 56003 • AASL

Haughton Buzz • Science Catlgr/Ref Librarian • University of California Shields Library • Davis, CA 95616 • ACRL ALCTS RASD SRRT

Haule Laura • Saint Charles Public Library • St. Charles, IL 60174

Haun-Mohamed Robin • United States Government Printing Office Library Programs Service • Washington, DC 20401

Haun Sherry J. • Arlington, TX 76013 • AASL

Haury Gertrude • Newton, KS 67114 • YALSA *Continuing*

Hauselt Suzanne M. • Student • University of Kentucky College of Library & Information Science • Lexington, KY 40506-0391

Hauser Janet M. • Head, Children's Department • Glencoe Public Library • Glencoe, IL 60022-1597 • ALSC

Hausman Kathryn J. • Library Director • Nippersink District Library • Richmond, IL 60071

Hausman Patricia R. • College of William & Mary Earl Gregg Swem Library • Williamsburg, VA 23187-8794

Hausrath Donald C. • Chief • United States Information Agency Library Program (USIA) • Washington, DC 20547 • FLRT IRRT

Hauth Allan C. • Educational Coordinator • Medical College of Wiconsin Libraries • Milwaukee, WI 53226

Havas Marie L. • Assistant Administrator • Las Vegas-Clark County Library Spring Valley Library • Las Vegas, NV 89103

Havener William M. • Assistant Professor • University of Oklahoma School of Library & Information Studies • Norman, OK 73019 • ACRL RASD GODORT LIRT

Havens Carolyn C. • Serials Cataloger • Auburn University Ralph Brown Draughon Library • Auburn, AL 36849-5606 • ALCTS

Havens Christy J. • Publisher • Ypsilanti District Library • Ypsilanti, MI 48197

Havens Lee H. • Vero Beach, FL 32961-1173

Havens Marlene P. • Librarian II • Clearwater Public Library • Clearwater, FL 34623

Havens Shirley E. • Contributing Editor • Library Journal Cahners Publishing Company • New York, NY 10011 • ASCLA RASD IFRT

Havenstein-Coughlin R. • Dept. Head Adult Services • Canton Public Library • Canton, MI 48188 • LAMA

Haverkamp Leona J. • Plano, TX 75024-2523 • NMRT

Havernrich Diane F. • Ann Arbor, MI 48105

Haviland Leona • St Cloud, FL 34769 • Continuing

Haviland Morrison C. • Highland Park, NJ 08904-2515 • ACRL *Continuing*

Havist Marjorie V. • Dean of Library • Skagit Valley College • Mount Vernon, WA 98273 • ACRL ALCTS LAMA LITA RASD LIRT

Havlik Barbara J. • Student • State University of New York at Albany School of Information Science & Policy • Albany, NY 12222 • AASL ALSC

Havlik Robert J. • South Bend, IN 46635 • ACRL LITA *Life*

Havlovic Elaine • Trustee • Lyons Public Library • Lyons, IL 60534

Havris Kathryn L. • Young Adult Librarian • Mesa Public Library • Mesa, AZ 85201-6768 • YALSA

Hawbaker A. Craig • Head of Reference • University of the Pacific • Stockton, CA 95211 • RASD

Hawes Beverly D. • Children's Librarian • Atlanta-Fulton Public Library East Atlanta Branch • Atlanta, GA 30316 • ALSC PLA

Hawes Karrin M. • Reference Librarian • Tigard Public Library • Tigard, OR 97223 • RASD IFRT

Hawes Kimberly • Provo, UT 84604 • PLA SRRT

Hawk Barbara S. • Library Media Specialist • Sallie Zetterower Elementary • Statesboro, GA 30458 • AASL

Hawk Randall F. • University of South Carolina College of Library & Information Science • Columbia, SC 29208

Hawk Steven • Director • Akron-Summit County Public Library • Akron, OH 44326-0001 • LAMA LITA PLA IFRT

Hawkanson Jane F. • Takoma Park, MD 20912 • AASL

Hawke Laura B. Mrs • Ann Arbor, MI 48105 • ACRL ALCTS *Life*

Hawker John • Assoc Chief/Gen Research Div. • New York Public Library • New York, NY 10018-2788 • ACRL LITA

Hawkes Gail R. • Student • Louisiana State University School of Library & Information Science • Baton Rouge, LA 70803-3290 • IFRT

Hawkes Linda M. • Southington High School • Southington, CT 06489 • AASL

Hawkes Sally • Coor. of Library Network Serv. • Arkansas State Library • Little Rock, AR 72201

Hawkins Anne E. • Reference/Music Librarian • Washoe County Library • Reno, NV 89505 • IFRT

Hawkins Barbara R. • Librarian • West Potomac High School • Alexandria, VA 22307 • AASL YALSA

Hawkins Daniel • Fort Worth, TX 76108 • PLA

Hawkins Elinor D. • Director • Craven-Pamlico-Carteret Regional Library • New Bern, NC 28560

Hawkins Ernestine L. • Assistant Director • East Cleveland Public Library • East Cleveland, OH 44112 • LAMA PLA

Hawkins Hatsuyo • Tucson, AZ 85741-9526

Hawkins Helma R. • Student • Emporia State University Emporia in the Rockies • Denver, CO 80204 • ALSC

Hawkins Jo Anne W. • Asst. Director Public Services • University of Texas Libraries • Austin, TX 78713 • ACRL

Hawkins Karen • Library Media Specialist • Boise-Eliot School • Portland, OR 97227 • AASL

Hawkins Lawrence • Peninsula School District • Gig Harbor, WA 98329

Hawkins Leah M. • Assistant Director • Hurst Public Library • Hurst, TX 76053 • ALTA PLA YALSA IFRT

Hawkins Leslie E. • ISDS Cataloger • Library of Congress • Washington, DC 20541 • ALCTS

Hawkins Linda J. • Head of Circulation • Bloomington Public Library • Bloomington, IL 61702-3308 • PLA

Hawkins Lynne B. • Volunteer • Sedgwick Middle School • West Hartford, CT 06107 • AASL

Hawkins M Diane • Gig Harbor, WA 98329

Hawkins Margaret E. • Auburn Hills, MI 48329 • ACRL LITA

Hawkins Mary David Sr • Louisville, KY 40206

Hawkins Mary J. • Assistant Dean of Libraries • University of Kansas Library • Lawrence, KS 66045-2800 • ACRL LAMA

Hawkins Pat M. • Coordinator-Human Resources • Kansas City Public Library • Kansas City, MO 64106 • PLA CLENE

Hawkins Paul Joseph • Assistant Systems Director • South Central Kansas Library System • Hutchinson, KS 67501 • ASCLA CLENE

Hawkins Peggy B. • Trustee • White County Public Library System • Searcy, AR 72143

Hawkins Sherlene Z. • Microforms • University of Kansas Watson Library • Lawrence, KS 66045-2800 • ACRL

Hawks Carol Pitts • Head, Acquistions Department • Ohio State University Libraries • Columbus, OH 43210-1286 • ACRL ALCTS LITA

Hawks Robert • Silver Spring, MD 20910

Hawley Brenda G. • Associate Director • Pikes Peak Library District • Colorado Springs, CO 80901 • LITA

Hawley George S. • Supervising Ln., NJ Div. • Newark Public Library • Newark, NJ 07101-0630 • RASD GODORT

Hawley Marsha Shigeyo • Trustee • Lincolnwood Public Library District • Lincolnwood, IL 60646

Hawley Mary B. • Sitka, AK 99835 • ACRL IRRT

Hawley Suzanne W. • Media Specialist • Vineyards Elementay School • Naples, FL 33999 • AASL ALSC

Hawman Susan M. • Student • Emporia State University School of Library & Information Management • Emporia, KS 66801 • LITA IRRT

Hawn Elizabeth L. • Head of Adult Services • High Point Public Library • High Point, NC 27261 • PLA

Haworth Audrey V. • Noblesville, IN 46060 • Continuing

Hawrusik Susan C. • Sr. Reference Librarian • Plainfield Public Library • Plainfield, NJ 07060 • RASD

Hawthorne Frank W. • Reference Librarian • Rochester Public Library • Rochester, MN 55904-3777 • IFRT

Hawthorne June C. • Document Librarian • Michigan Technological University Library • Houghton, MI 49931 • ACRL RASD GODORT MAGERT

Hawthorne Pat • Administrative Projects Ln. • University of Texas Health Science Center Briscoe Library • San Antonio, TX 78284-7940 • LAMA RASD NMRT

Hay Fred J. Ph.D. • Reference & Acquisitions Libn • Harvard University Tozzer Library • Cambridge, MA 02138 • ACRL

Hay M Kathleen • Lib. Coordinator & High Sch Ln. • Milton School District • Milton, WI 53563 • AASL YALSA IFRT

Hay Patricia F. • Cataloger • Academy of the New Church • Bryn Athyn, PA 19009 • ALCTS

Hay Terry T • Westmoor High Sch Lib • Daly City, CA 94015 • AASL

Hay Vivian A. • Head, Technical Services Dept. • California Institute of Technology • Pasadena, CA 91125 • LITA

Hayashi Harvey R. • Library/Media Generalist • Londonderry Junior High Shcool Library Media Center • Londonderry, NH 03053 • AASL

Hayashikawa Doris S. • Head, Cataloging Dept • University of Pittsburgh Hillman Library • Pittsburgh, PA 15260 • ACRL ALCTS LRRT

Haycock Carol-Ann • Consultant • HRD Group • Vancouver BC, V5Z 4C9 Canada • AASL

Haycock Gina M. • Kern County Library System • Bakersfield, CA 93301 • ACRL

Haycock Ken Dr. • University of British Columbia School of Library, Archival & Information Studies • Vancouver BC, V6T 1Z1 Canada • AASL YALSA

Hayden Alice C. • Librarian • Lower Yukon School District • Mountain Village, AK 99632 • ALSC

Hayden Carla D. • Deputy Commissions/Chief Ln. • Chicago Public Library Harold Washington Library • Chicago, IL 60605 • ALSC PLA

Hayden Cathy O. • Student • Rosary College Graduate School of Library & Information Science • River Forest, IL 60305 • AASL

Hayden Elizabeth • Supervisor Public Services • Lansing Public Library • Lansing, MI 48933 • ALSC LAMA PLA

Hayden Erin • Library Media Specialist • Laurel High School Library • Laurel, MD 20707 • AASL

Hayden J. J. III • Southeastern Library Network (SOLINET) • Atlanta, GA 30309-2955 • LITA

Hayden Jim D. • Media/Library Specialists • Redmond School District • Redmond, OR 97756 • AASL

Hayden Katharine Alix • University of Alberta • Edmonton AB, T6G 2J4 Canada • ACRL

Hayden Lee R. • Assistant Librarian • Madison Area Technical College • Madison, WI 53704 • ACRL

Hayden Marie Dr • Professor of Library Science • Sam Houston State University Department of Library Science • Huntsville, TX 77341-2236 • LIRT

Hayden Ronald L. • Library Director • Huntington Beach Library Info. & Cultural Resource Center • Huntington Beach, CA 92648 • LAMA PLA

Hayden Wallace • Reference Librarian • Bacon Memorial Public Library • Wyandotte, MI 48192 • RASD

Hayduk Sarah H. • Mt. Vernon, WA 98273

Haye Paul A. • Data Coordinator • New York Blood Center • New York, NY 10021 • ALCTS ASCLA

Hayes-Bohanan Pamela A. • Student • University of Arizona Graduate Library School • Tucson, AZ 85721 • IFRT MAGERT

Hayes Allene V. • Copyright Specialist • Library of Congress • Washington, DC 20541

Hayes Carolyn S. • Librarian • Warren Central High School • Indianapolis, IN 46229 • AASL

Hayes David L. • Reference Librarian • Radford University John P. McConnell Library • Radford, VA 24142

Hayes Dawn M. • Elem. Library/Media Specialist • Central School • Hastings, MI 49058 • AASL

Hayes Debra A. • Omaha, NE 68164

Hayes Elizabeth Hope • Chief of the Main Library • San Francisco Public Library • San Francisco, CA 94102 • LAMA

Hayes Emmie S. • Sebring, FL 33872 • Continuing

Hayes Florence C. • Associate Serials Librarian • Cornell University Library • Ithaca, NY 14853 • ALCTS LITA

Hayes Glenda • Library Board Trustee • West Florida Regional Library • Pensacola, FL 32501 • ALTA PLA

Hayes Hazel • Park Forest, IL 60466 • Continuing

Hayes Janice • Director,Client Services • CNIB Library for the Blind • Toronto ON, M4G 3EB Canada

Hayes Joan W. • Head of Technical Services • Huron Valley Library System • Ann Arbor, MI 48107 • ALCTS

Hayes Kitty • Deerfield, IL 60015

Hayes Lorena G. • Librarian • Walter Williams High School • Burlington, NC 27217 • AASL

Hayes Margaret L. • Technical Reports/Patents Ln. • University of Wisconsin-Madison Kurt F. Wendt Engineering Library • Madison, WI 53706 • GODORT

Hayes Martha • Crossville, AL 35962

Hayes Melinda K. • Collection Dev & Cons Ln • University of Southern California Hancock Bio & Ocean Library • Los Angeles, CA 90089-0372 • ACRL ALCTS

Hayes Nancy K. • Supervisior of Technical Service • North Carolina University Ramsey Library • Asheville, NC 28804

Hayes Oliver R. • Eastern Connecticut State University J. Eugene Smith Library • Willimantic, CT 06226 • ACRL

Hayes Paula • Children's Librarian • Boston Public Library • Boston, MA 02117 • ALSC

Hayes Ramona L. • Urbana, IL 61801

Hayes Richard E. • Chief Librarian • Paul Pratt Memorial Library • Cohasset, MA 02025 • ALSC PLA

Hayes Robert Mayo • University of California Los Angeles Graduate School of Library & Information Science • Los Angeles, CA 90024

Hayes Sara V • Library Media Specialist • Derby Hills Elementary • Derby, KS 67037 • AASL

Hayes Sherman L. • Director • Bentley College Solomon R. Baker Library • Waltham, MA 02154-4705 • ACRL LAMA

Hayes Stephen M. • Reference Documents Librarian • University of Notre Dame Theodore M. Hesburgh Library • Notre Dame, IN 46556 • GODORT

Hayes Susan M. • Columbia University School of Library Service • New York, NY 10027 • ACRL ALCTS

Hayhurst Sondra T. • Page High School • Franklin, TN 37221 • YALSA

Hayland Theresa E. • Cataloger • San Jose State University Division of Library & Information Science • San Jose, CA 95192-0029 • ACRL ALCTS LITA

Hayles Susan J. • New Brighton, MN 55112

Haym Ilene B. • Librarian • Beasley, Casey, Colleran, Thistle, Erbstein, & Kline • Phildelphia, PA 19107

Hayman Lynne Meyers • Assistant Director • University of California • Riverside, CA 92517-5900 • ALCTS

Hayman Maude E. • Colorado Springs, CO 80917

Haymore Teresa P. • Mountain Regional Library • Young Harris, GA 30582

Hayne Penelope P. • Student • University of South Carolina College of Library & Information Science • Columbia, SC 29208 • AASL LRRT SRRT

Haynes Annabel M. • Hutchinson School • Memphis, TN 38119 • AASL

Haynes Barbara E. • Student • University of Wisconsin-Milwaukee School of Library & Information Science • Milwaukee, WI 53201

Haynes Cheryl W. • Bell Multicultutal High School • Washington, DC 20010 • AASL

Haynes Craig C. • University of California-San Diego Biomedical Library • La Jolla, CA 92093

Haynes Elizabeth • Library Media Specialist • Texas Education Agency • Austin, TX 78701-1494 • AASL

Haynes Evelyn B. • Colorado State University William E. Morgan Library • Fort Collins, CO 80523 • ACRL RASD LIRT

Haynes Frances F. Miss • Darien, GA 31305 • ACRL RASD *Continuing*

Haynes Jean • Film/Video Librarian • Chautauqua-Cattaraugus Library System • Jamestown, NY 14701

Haynes Kathleen J M • University of Oklahoma School of Library & Information Studies • Norman, OK 73019 • ALCTS LITA

Haynes Mary K. • Knoxville, TN 37919

Haynes Maryjane • Librarian • Charlottesville High School • Charlottesville, VA 22901

Haynes Sarah W. • Trustee • West Florida Regional Library • Pensacola, FL 32501

Haynes Susan S.P. • Associate Librarian-Clln Svs. • George Mason University Libraries • Fairfax, VA 22030 • ACRL

Haynes Suzanne • Student • University of Oklahoma School of Library & Information Studies • Norman, OK 73019

Haynes Theodora T. • Business Librarian • Rutgers University Paul Robeson Library • Camden, NJ 08101-3990 • ACRL LITA RASD

Haynworth Patrcia F. • Carbondale, IL 62901

Hays Audrey G. • Prin. Librarian • Norfolk Public Library • Norfolk, VA 23510-1776

Hays Carl H. • Assoc Dir For Tech & Auto Serv • University of Maryland College Park Theodore R. McKeldin Library • College Park, MD 20742-7011 • ACRL LAMA *Life*

Hays George • Director • Salem Public Library • Salem, OH 44460 • PLA

Hays Jane • Business Manager • University of Houston Libraries • Houston, TX 77204-2091

Hays Janet K. • Resources Devlp. Spec./CRS • Library of Congress • Washington, DC 20541 • FLRT GODORT

Hays Judith E. • Librarian • Avon High School • Indianapolis, IN 46234 • AASL

Hays Kathleen M. • Director of Library Services • Morningside College Library • Sioux City, IA 51106 • ACRL LITA

Hays Laura J. • Naperville, IL 60540

Hays Patricia L. • Director • Monroeville Public Library • Monroeville, PA 15146-3381 • LAMA PLA

Hays Patt A. • Head, Monographic Cataloging • Texas Christian University Mary Couts Burnett Library • Fort Worth, TX 76129 • ACRL ALCTS LITA

Hays Sue J. • Madison County Public Library • Richmond, KY 40475 • PLA

Hayslett Dawn C. • Assistant Director • Ames Public Library • Ames, IA 50010 • LAMA

Hayward Karen L. • Administrative Librarian • Marine Corps Air Station Library • Santa Ana, CA 92709-5007 • PLA AFLRT

Hayward Linda L. • Indianapolis, IN 46239 • AASL LITA

Hayward Marilyn • Librarian • Contra Costa Community College • San Pablo, CA 94806 • AASL ACRL RASD EMIERT NMRT SRRT

Haywood Anne T. • Senior Librarian • Quintilla Geer Bruton Memorial Library • Plant City, FL 33566 • PLA

Hazel Betty J. • County Librarian • Douglas County Library System • Roseburg, OR 97470 • PLA

Hazelbaker S. Gayle • Director • Swanton Public Library • Swanton, OH 43558 • PLA

Hazeltine Robert • Ashtabula, OH 44004 • Continuing

Hazelton George R. • Assistant Director • Hart County Library • Hartwell, GA 30643

Hazelton Janet M. • Asst. Dir. Mgt. Services • Tacoma Public Library • Tacoma, WA 98402 • PLA

Hazen Richard A. • Bloomfield, NJ 07003 • ACRL ALCTS LHRT *Life*

Hazlett Florence • Phoenix, AZ 85020 • Continuing

He Shaoyi S. • Student • University of North Carolina School of Library Science • Chapel Hill, NC 27599-3360

Heaberlin John Charles • Director of Library Svs. • Univ of Kentucky Southeast Cmnty College • Cumberland, KY 40823

Head Alison J. • Library Director • Press Democrat Newspaper • Santa Rosa, CA 95401

Head Janet Kaiser • Bartlett School • South Lyon, MI 48178 • AASL

Head John W. • Faculty • Clarion University of Pennsylvania College of Library Science • Clarion, PA 16214 • LITA

Head Patricia A. • Clarion, PA 16214

Headlee John H. • Director of Staff Development • Citrus County Schools • Lecanto, FL 32661 • AASL

Headly Jacqueline M. • Adult Program Coordinator • Newport Beach Public Library • Newport Beach, CA 92660 • PLA

Heady Donna M. • Acquisitions Librarian • Indiana University-Purdue University at Indianapolis Library (IUPUI) • Indianapolis, IN 46202 • ACRL NMRT

Heady Patricia M. • Children's Librarian • District of Columbia Public Library Tenley Friendship Branch • Washington, DC 20016 • ALSC

Heafner Barbara E. • Bessemer City, NC 28016 • Continuing

Heagney Eleanor Adele • Webster Groves, MO 63119

Heagy Phillip T. • Librarian • Menil Collection Library • Houston, TX 77006

Heald Donna H. • Media Specialist • Piper High School Library • Sunrise, FL 33351 • AASL

Heald Georgia L. • Student • Iowa City Public Library • Iowa City, IA 52240

Heald L. M. Mrs. • Tallahassee, FL 32302 • Continuing

Heald Leanne • Student • University of Washington Graduate School of Library and Information Science • Seattle, WA 98195

Healer Constance • Librarian • Bebensee Elementary School A.I.S.D. • Arlington, TX 76018 • AASL

Healey Edward H. • Library Technical • Brown Healey Stone & Sauer Architects • Cedar Rapids, IA 52402 • ALTA LAMA

Healey Edward L. • Roanoke, VA 24015

Healy Doris B. • Burnsville, MN 55337 • ALCTS LITA *Life*

Healy Helen J. • Asst. Dean for Automation & Tech • Western Michigan University Libraries Dwight B. Waldo Library • Kalamazoo, MI 49008 • ACRL ALCTS LITA

Healy Hope M. • Librarian • Leisure City Elementary School • Homestead, FL 33033 • AASL

Healy Joan F. • Reference Librarian (Adult) • Plymouth Public Library • Plymouth, MI 48170

Healy Linda • Hunt Elementary • Sioux City, IA 52001

Healy Nancy • Educational Media Specialist • Sacred Heart School Library • Mt. Holly, NJ 08060 • AASL

Healy Ronald • Lathrup Village, MI 48076

Heanue Anne A. • Associate Director • American Library Association Washington Office • Washington, DC 20002 • FLRT GODORT

Heap Lewis D. • Student • Southern Connecticut State University School of Libray Science & Instructional Technology • New Haven, CT 06515 • RASD

Heaphy Mary Anne • Director • Englewood Public Library • Englewood, NJ 07631 • LAMA

Heard Jeffrey L. • Catalog Maintenance • State Library of Ohio • Columbus, OH 43266-0334 • ACRL ALCTS LAMA LITA IFRT

Hearing Brenda • Student • Columbia University Library Service Library • New York, NY 10027 • ACRL LHRT

Hearn Emily R. • Student • University of Southern Mississippi School of Library Science • Hattiesburg, MS 39406-5146

Hearn Stephen S. • Authority Control Coordinator • University of Minnesota O. Meredith Wilson Library • Minneapolis, MN 55455-0414 • ALCTS LITA

Hearne Elizabeth G. • Ch Book Review Ed & Asst Prof • University of Chicago Graduate Library School • Chicago, IL 60637 • ALSC

Hearne Mary Glenn • Library Supervisor • Public Library of Nashville and Davidson County • Nashville, TN 37203-3585 • RASD LHRT

Hearth Fred E. • Director of Library • University of Redlands Armacost Library • Redlands, CA 92374-3758 • ACRL

Heartwell Alison D. • Assistant Director • Central Rappahannock Regional Library Wallace Memorial Library • Fredericksburg, VA 22401 • PLA RASD LIRT

Hearty John A. • Dir of References Services Div. • OCLC Online Computer Library Center • Dublin, OH 43017-3395

Heasley Leila L. • Cleveland, OH 44144 • ALSC PLA *Life*

Heath Barbara S. • Assistant Dir. for Tech. Serv. • Wayne State University Purdy Library • Detroit, MI 48202 • ACRL

Heath Claire M. • Asst. Head of Childrens Dept. • Atlanta-Fulton Public Library • Atlanta, GA 30303 • ALSC PLA

Heath Clark E. • Detroit, MI 48219 • AASL IFRT

Heath Elizabeth G. • Brown Library • Seabrook, NH 03874 • PLA

Heath Ellen M. • Ho-ho-kus Public School • Ho-ho-kus, NJ 07423 • AASL

Heath Fred M. • University Librarian • Texas Christian University Mary Couts Burnett Library • Fort Worth, TX 76129 • ACRL LAMA

Heath H. Harrison • Building Manager • Johns Hopkins University Milton S. Eisenhower Library • Baltimore, MD 21218 • LAMA

Heath James L. • IMC Director • Douglas Education Service District • Roseburg, OR 97470 • AASL

Heath Jean B. • Fort Worth Independent School District • Ft. Worth, TX 76107 • AASL ALSC IFRT

Heath Joan L. • University Librarian • Southwest Texas State University • San Marcos, TX 78666 • ACRL

Heath Marjorie • Librarian • Hallsville High School Library • Hallsville, TX 75650 • AASL LIRT

Heath Patrick • Mayor • Boerne Public Library • Boerne, TX 78006

Heath Patsy J. • Librarian II-Children's Unit • Durham County Library • Durham, NC 27702 • ALSC

Heath Rebekah H. • Technical Services Librarian • Jefferson Community College Library • Louisville, KY 40202 • ACRL

Heath Thomas W. • Head of Information Services • Lexington Public Library • Lexington, KY 40507

Heathcote Lesley Muriel • Director Emerita • Montana State University • Bozeman, MT 59717-0332 • ACRL *Life*

Heatherly Linda • Reference Librarian • Fairfax County Public Library Pohick Regional Branch • Burke, VA 22015

Heaton Beth D. • Librarian • Nicholas Murray Butler School #23 • Elizabeth, NJ 07208 • AASL

Heaton Gwynneth T. • Head Science & Media Library • University of Toronto • Toronto ON, Canada • ACRL LITA

Heaton Shelley J. • University of Nevada-Las Vegas James R. Dickinson Library • Las Vegas, NV 89154 • ACRL

Heavner Phillip M. • Librarian • Western Youth Institution • Morganton, NC 28655 • AASL ASCLA

Hebditch Suzan A. • Law Librarian • Canada Department of Justice • Edmonton AL, T5J 2F2 Canada • GODORT

Hebdon Floyd E. • Family History Library • Salt Lake City, UT 84150

Hebel John • Assistant Director • Danbury Public Library • Danbury, CT 06810

Hebert Anta Maria • Boone, NC 28607

Hebert Elaine • Librarian • Holy Infant Jesus School • Nashua, NH 03060

Hebert Marianne • Student • State University of New York College at Purchase Library (SUNY) • Purchase, NY 10577-2826

Hebert Patricia V. • Assistant Cataloger • Nicholls State University Allen J. Ellender Memorial Library • Thibodaux, LA 70310

Hechler Catherine M. • United States Institute of Peace • Washington, DC 20005-1708

Hecht Helene • Media Specialist • Independent School 73 Q • Maspeth, NY 11378

Hecht James M. • Director • Somerset County Library System • Bridgewater, NJ 08807 • PLA IFRT

Hecht Joseph A. • Predicasts • Cleveland, OH 44106 • RASD

Hecht Willard L. • Branch Librarian • Great River Regional Library Carnegie Library • Little Falls, MN 56345 • PLA

Heck-Howard Elizabeth A. • System Manager • Virginia Theological Seminary • Alexandria, VA 22304-5201

Heck Jeffrey J. • Knoxville, TN 37919 • GODORT

Heck Judith F. • Student • Emporia State University Emporia in the Rockies • Denver, CO 80204

Heck-Rabi Louise E. • Lincoln Park, MI 48146 • ACRL RASD *Life*

Heckart Ronald J. • Librarian • University of California-Berkeley Institute of Governmental Studies • Berkeley, CA 94720 • ACRL ALCTS GODORT

Hecke Susan E. • Librarian II • San Antonio Public Library Ed Cody Branch • San Antonio, TX 78230

Heckel F • Librarian • River Edge Public Library • River Edge, NJ 07661 • ALSC PLA RASD

Heckel James • Great Falls Public Library • Great Falls, MT 59401 • PLA

Heckelman Janice • Lexington, MA 02173 • ACRL

Hecker Elizabeth A. • Student • University of North Texas School of Library & Information Sciences • Denton, TX 76203

Hecker Margaret Prentice • Cataloger • Kentucky State University Blazer Library • Frankfort, KY 40601 • ACRL ALCTS ASCLA

Hecker Thomas E. • Reference Dept. • University of Kentucky Libraries • Lexington, KY 40506-0039 • ACRL ASCLA RASD

Heckford Ian • Oshawa Public Library • Oshawa ON, L1H 1N2 Canada • LITA

Heckler Kenneth • Reference Librarian • Atlanta-Fulton Public Library • Atlanta, GA 30303 • PLA IFRT SRRT

Hecklinger Ellen • Long Beach, CA 90814

Heckman Lucy T. • Reference Librarian • Saint John's University Library • Jamaica, NY 11439 • RASD

Heckman Marlin L. • University Librarian • University of La Verne • La Verne, CA 91750 • ACRL

Heckman Stephen P. • N Manchester, IN 46962 • ACRL ALCTS

Hedberg James D. Mrs • Cleveland, OH 44124 • Life

Hedberg Jane • Serials Librarian/Pres. Adminis. • Wellesley College • Wellesley, MA 02181 • ACRL ALCTS

Hedberg Phyllis S. • Co-Children's Librarian • Woodbridge Town Library • Woodbridge, CT 06525 • ALSC

Hedden Kathleen A. • Media Specialist • William Annin Middle School • Basking Ridge, NJ 07920 • AASL

Hedges Linda Lane • Director, AV & Media Services • Crown Point Cmnty School • Crown Pt, IN 46307 • AASL

Hedges Michael J. • Coor of Computer & AV Serv. • Pierce County Rural Library District • Tacoma, WA 98446

Hedin Bonnie J. • Head, Cataloging & Instruction • Saint Cloud State University Centennial Hall LRC • St. Cloud, MN 56301-4498 • ACRL LITA

Hedlund Betta E. • Mary Riley Styles Public Library • Falls Church, VA 22046 • ALSC

Hedlund Connie • Trustee • Indian Trails Public Library District • Wheeling, IL 60090 • ALTA

Hedman Kenneth W. • Librarian • United States Military Academy Library • West Point, NY 10996-1799 • ACRL AFLRT

Hedrich Anne E • Utah State University Merrill Library • Logan, UT 84322-3000 • ACRL MAGERT SRRT

Hedrick David T. • Special Collection Librarian • Gettysburg College Musselman Library • Gettysburg, PA 17325-1493 • ACRL IFRT MAGERT

Hedrick Donna M. • Library Mgr. Contract Services • NASA/Langley Research Center Technical Library • Hampton, VA 23665 • LAMA

Hedrick Mary • Mildred B. Harrison Regional Library • Columbiana, AL 35051

Hedstrom Jackie B. • Student • North Carolina Central University • Durham, NC 27707 • PLA NMRT

Heemstra Linda • Director • Bay County Library System • Bay City, MI 48708 • LAMA PLA

Heezen Ronald R. • Director • Longview Public Library • Longview, TX 75601 • LAMA PLA

Heffelfinger Ellen • San Francisco, CA 94127 • ACRL

Heffernan Dorothy M. • Substitute Reference Librarian • Bethlehem Public Library • Delmar, NY 12054 • PLA RASD

Heffernan Joan M. • Librarian • Bridge Street School • Suffield, CT 06078

Heffington Carl • Pine Bluff & Jefferson County Library System • Pine Bluff, AR 71601 • LAMA PLA

Heffner Vickie Rowe • Reference Librarian • University of Lowell O'Leary Library • Lowell, MA 01854

Hefling Deborah M. • Preservation Librarian • Cleveland Public Library • Cleveland, OH 44114-1271 • ALCTS

Hefling Helen • Overland Park, KS 66204 • ACRL PLA *Continuing*

Heft Faye H. • Children's Librarian • Long Beach Public Library • Long Beach, NY 11561

Heft Sandra M. • Head Cataloger Dept. Librarian • California Inst of Tech • Pasadena, CA 91125 • ALCTS

Hefter Susan G. • Student • Catholic University of America School of Library and Information Science • Washington, DC 20064

Heftmann Erica S. • Student • University of Washington Graduate School of Library and Information Science • Seattle, WA 98195

Hefty Sheila A. • Librarian • Sacramento Country Day School • Sacramento, CA 95864

Hefzallah Mona G. • Head Cataloger • Fairfield University Library • Fairfield, CT 06430

Hegarty Kathleen B. • Staff Offc for Spec Progs & Svs • Boston Public Library • Boston, MA 02117 • ASCLA PLA

Hegarty Kevin • Director • Tacoma Public Library • Tacoma, WA 98402 • AASL ACRL ALCTS ALSC ALTA ASCLA LAMA LITA PLA RASD YALSA

Hegarty Mary S. • Instruc Spec for Lib Tech Servs • Newport News Public Schools • Newport News, VA 23601 • AASL

Hegdale Mary J. • Branch Librarian • Long Beach Public Library Ruth Bach Branch • Long Beach, CA 90808 • LAMA PLA

Hegemann Denise A. • Public Services Librarian • Saint Vincent College & Archabbey Libraries • Latrobe, PA 15650-2690 • RASD

Heggem Nancy J. • Statistical Analyst • A. C. Neilsen • Northbrook, IL 60062-6288 • ALTA

Hegland Maxine • San Jose, CA 95130-1833 • Life

Hegmann Myra • Library Media Specialist • Akron Central School • Akron, NY 14001

Hegstrom Elizabeth L. • Barrington Public Library District • Barrington, IL 60010 • ALCTS

Hehman Thomas J. • Library Director • Meherrin Regional Library • Lawrenceville, VA 23868 • PLA

Heibeck Jean • Adminstrator • Somerset County Library System • Princess Anne, MD 21853 • PLA

Heid Gregory G. • Branch Services Administrator • Atlanta-Fulton Public Library • Atlanta, GA 30303 • LAMA PLA

Heid Martha A. • Microsoft Corporation • Redmond, WA 98079-9717

Heidenblad Carl S. • Director • Nesmith Library • Windham, NH 03087 • ALSC PLA

Heidkamp Pat L. • Reference Librarian • Boston Consulting Group Research Library • Chicago, IL 60606

Heidrick Dana J. • Collection Development Librarian • Oakland Public Library • Oakland, CA 94612 • RASD

Heidtmann Toby • Head, Collection Management • University of Cincinnati • Cincinnati, OH 45221-0033 • ACRL ALCTS

Heifert Samatha M. • Student • University of Maryland College of Library and Information Services • College Park, MD 20742-4345

Heigemeir Ray G. • Harvard Law School Library • Cambridge, MA 02138 • ACRL FLRT

Heiges Mary J. • Director • Carver County Library • Chaska, MN 55318 • PLA

Heighton Karen • North Elementary School • Marshall, IL 62441

Heighton Nancy E. • Dan Mills ON, M3A 1N1 Canada • LAMA PLA

Heikkila Margo • Antilles School, Inc. • St Thomas, VI 00801 • AASL

Heikkinen Philip L. • Library Systems Coordinator • Tucson-Pima Library • Tucson, AZ 85701 • LITA

Heil Becky • Director • Dubuque County Library • Farley, IA 52046 • PLA

Heil Diane L. • Reference Librarian • Richmond Public Library • Richmond, VA 23219

Heil Karen A. • Media Specialist • Maybrook Elementary School • Maybrook, NY 12543

Heil Kathleen A. • Librarian • Maryland University Chesapeake Biol Lab • Solomons, MD 20688 • ACRL

Heiliger Edward M. • Boca Raton, FL 33433 • ACRL LITA *Life*

Heilman Deborah L. • Pittsburgh, PA 15215

Heilos Lawrence J. Jr. • University Librarian • University of South Florida Library • Tampa, FL 33620-5600

Heim Fern V. • Lincoln, NE 68512 • ALTA

Heim Janis J. • Student • Emporia State University School of Library & Information Management • Emporia, KS 66801 • PLA IFRT LHRT NMRT

Heim John W. • Hd, Business & Science Dept. • Miami-Dade Public Library System • Miami, FL 33130-1504

Heim Margaret M. • Baton Rouge, LA 70806

Heim Phyllis J. • Student • Rutgers University School of Communication Information & Library Studies • New Brunswick, NJ 08903 • ALSC

Heim Richard A. Mrs. • Lincoln, NE 68512

Heiman Larry W. • New York University Elmer Holmes Bobst Library • New York, NY 10012 • ALCTS SRRT

Heiman Paula • Librarian • Mechanicsburg Area Public Library • Mechanicsburg, PA 17055

Heimburger Bruce R. • Librarian • Abbeville-Greenwood Regional Library • Greenwood, SC 29646 • ALSC PLA

Heimlich Fannie W. • Media Librarian • Seneca East Local Schs • Attica, OH 44807 • AASL

Hein John M. • Head Technical Services • University of North Florida Thomas G. Carpenter Library • Jacksonville, FL 32245-7605 • Life

Hein Ruth B. • Pt Orchard, WA 98366

Heinan Kathleen K. • Assistant Director • Upper Saddle River Public Library • Upper Saddle River, NJ 07458-1699 • ALCTS

Heinbokel Mary E. • Branch Manager • Saint Charles City County Library K. Linneman Branch • St. Charles, MO 63301 • PLA

Heindel Allan J. • Asst. City Manager Cmnty Servs • Hurst Public Library • Hurst, TX 76053

Heineman Stephanie • Director • Northport-East Northport Public Library • Northport, NY 11768 • PLA

Heinemann Linda E. • Assistant Director • Four County Library System • Vestal, NY 13850

Heinemann Luba • Senior Information Specialist • Predicasts • Cleveland, OH 44106 • ACRL RASD

Heinemann Sandra W. • Hampden-Sydney, VA 23943

Heinen Toni A. • Minneapolis, MN 55426 • AASL

Heinen Ursula • Reference Ln/Foreign Lang Bibl • University of Rochester Rush Rhees Library • Rochester, NY 14627-0055 • ACRL

Heinlein Alan R. • Director • Neptune Township Public Library • Neptune, NJ 07753 • LAMA LITA PLA

Heinlein Lucinda • Childrens's Librarian • Lakewood Public Library • Lakewood, NJ 08701 • ALSC PLA

Heino Dan Robert • General Librarian • University of British Columbia Library • Vancouver BC, V6T 1Z3 Canada • ACRL

Heinrich Amy V. • East Asian Librarian • Columbia University East Asian Library • New York, NY 10027 • ACRL

Heinrich Kathy J. • Children's Librarian • Cuyahoga County Public Library Strongsville Branch • Strongsville, OH 44136-3495 • ALSC

Heinrich Lois M. • Baltimore, MD 21234 • AASL ALSC

Heinrichs Jean S. • • Fairfax County Public Library Sherwood Regional Branch • Alexandria, VA 22306

Heinritz Fred Dr • Professor • Southern Connecticut State University School of Libray Science & Instructional Technology • New Haven, CT 06515 • ACRL ALCTS LAMA LITA PLA RASD *Life*

Heins Ethel L. • Auburndale, MA 02166 • ALSC *Continuing*

Heinsdorf Carol W. • Librarian • John F. McCloskey School • Philidelphia, PA 19150

Heintz Robert L. • Media Director • Spencer Community Schools • Spencer, IA 51301 • AASL

Heintzelman Susan K. • Heintzelman's Bookstore • Los Altos, CA 94022

Heinz Catharine • Director • Broadcast Pioneers Library • Washington, DC 20036 • ACRL

Heinz Diane S. • Park View School • Morton Grove, IL 60053 • AASL

Heinz Roy R. • Washington Research Library Consortium • Lanham, MD 20706

Heinzinger Peggy • Trustee • Hillside Public Library • Hillside, IL 60162

Heinzkill J. Richard • Reference Librarian • University of Oregon Library • Eugene, OR 97403-1299 • ACRL RASD

Heinzl Gloria M. • Senior Librarian • San Jose Public Library Pearl Avenue Branch • San Jose, CA 95136

Heinzman Mary B. • Milan, IL 61264 • ALSC

Heise Donald E. • Student • University of Arizona Graduate Library School • Tucson, AZ 85721

Heise Dorothy A. • National Agricultural Library Rural Information Center • Beltsville, MD 20705 • PLA

Heise George F. • Chair,Budget & Systems/Library • Ramapo College of New Jersey Library • Mahwah, NJ 07430 • LITA

Heise Lynn M. • Manitowoc, WI 54220 • PLA

Heise Mary Lee • Omaha, NE 68132 • AASL ALSC

Heisel Adelaide J. • Atlanta-Fulton Public Library Alpharetta Branch • Alpharetta, GA 30201 • ALSC

Heiser Jane C. • Severna Park, MD 21146 • PLA

Heiser Nancy E. • Brunswick, ME 04011

Heisey Beth A. • Student • Norris School • Bakersfield, CA 93304 • AASL

Heisey Terry M. • Librarian • Evangelical School of Theology • Myerstown, PA 17067 • ACRL

Heishman Eleanor L. • Director of Libraries • State University of New York at Binghamton Libraries (SUNY) • Binghamton, NY 13902-6012 • ACRL ALCTS LITA *Life*

Heisinger Barbara B. • Student • University of South Dakota • Vermillion, SD 57069 • ACRL

Heisser David C. R. • Hd, Govt. Pubs & Maps Dept. • University of Miami Libraries Richter Library • Coral Gables, FL 33124 • ACRL GODORT MAGERT

Heitman Herrick • Seattle, WA 98105

Heitman Lynn • Young Peoples Librarian • Wauconda Area Library • Wauconda, IL 60084

Heitshu Sara C. • Asst Univ Ln For Tech Serv • University of Arizona Library • Tucson, AZ 85721 • ALCTS LITA

Heitz Sue A. • Albuquerque Public Library • Albuquerque, NM 87102

Heitz Thomas R. • Librarian • National Baseball Hall of Fame • Cooperstown, NY 13326 • LITA

Heitzig Carol C. • Librarian • Watsonville Public Library • Watsonville, CA 95076-4695 • YALSA

Heitzman Janet • Independence, MO 64050 • PLA SRRT

Heitzmann Brandon • Trustee • Grand Rapids Public Library • Grand Rapids, MI 49503-3093

Heizer Carolyn H. • Reference Librarian • Southern Methodist University • Dallas, TX 75275

Helbig Dagmar • Tucson, AZ 85718

Held Charles H. • Albion, MI 49224 • ACRL RASD   *Life*

Held Lila • Senior Librarian-In-Charge • Los Angeles County Library Manhattan Beach Branch • Manhattan Beach, CA 90266 • PLA

Held Ruth A. • University of South Carolina College of Library & Information Science • Columbia, SC 29208 • PLA

Helenita S. Mary • Librarian • Mary Louis Academy • Jamaica, NY 11432

Helfand Esther • Walnut Creek, CA 94596 • LAMA YALSA   *Life*

Helfeld Dorothy G. • Los Angeles, CA 90027 • ALSC RASD IFRT

Helfer Doris Small • Head, Special Projects • Rand Corporation Library • Santa Monica, CA 90406-2138

Helfer Robert S. • Automated Systems Administration • Texas State Library • Austin, TX 78711 • ALCTS ASCLA LITA LRRT

Helff Frances • Raymore, MO 64083-9157 • Continuing

Helfman Alyce • Demarest Public School • Demarest, NJ 07645 • AASL PLA

Helfrich Gair • Branch Librarian • Atlantic County Public Pleasantville Branch • Pleasantville, NJ 08232 • PLA

Helfrich Shirley L. • Consultant • Southern Maine Library District • Portland, ME 04101 • LAMA

Helgerson Patricia L. • Student • University of Wisconsin-Madison School of Library & Information Studies • Madison, WI 53706

Helgesen Anne • Byron, CA 94514 • ALCTS PLA

Helicher Karl • Director • Upper Merion Township Library • King of Prussia, PA 19406 • ALSC LAMA PLA RASD

Helin Sandra • Mount Senario College Library • Ladysmith, WI 54848

Hell Kelly J. • Student • Emporia State University School of Library & Information Management • Emporia, KS 66801 • ACRL IFRT NMRT

Hellams Pierce • Extension Coordinator • Pickens County Library • Easley, SC 29640

Hellard Ellen G. • Director of Field Service Div. • Kentucky Department for Libraries & Archives • Frankfort, KY 40602-0537 • ASCLA PLA IFRT

Helldorfer Ann Marie L. • Smithtown Library Nesconset Branch • Nesconset, NY 11767 • ALSC IFRT

Heller Dawn H. • La Grange, IL 60525 • AASL LAMA

Heller Dulcey L. • Student • University of Iowa School of Library & Information Science • Iowa City, IA 52242

Heller George F. Jr. • East Palestine, OH 44413 • AASL LITA PLA RASD

Heller Gretchen A. • Student • University of Maryland College of Library and Information Services • College Park, MD 20742-4345 • LITA AFLRT

Heller Linda H. Dr. • Media Specialist • Oak Ridge Elementary • Tallahassee, FL 32304 • AASL ALSC YALSA

Heller Lynda R. • Milford, MA 01757 • PLA IFRT   *Life*

Heller M. Kay • Director • Shippensburg Public Library • Shippensburg, PA 17257 • PLA

Heller Nancy M. • Director of Library Services • Schenectady County Community College Library Resources Center • Schenectady, NY 12305 • ACRL EMIERT

Heller Paul C. • Public Services Librarian • Norwich University Library • Northfield, VT 05663 • ACRL LAMA

Hellerich Janet L. • Supv. Children's Librarian • Richmond Public Library • Richmond, CA 94804 • ALSC

Helling Madelyn • Librarian • Nevada County Library • Nevada City, CA 95959 • PLA

Hellman David S. • Librarian • Brooklyn Public Library • Brooklyn, NY 11238 • ACRL IFRT

Hellmann George Rev. • Fairfield, OH 45014 • Continuing

Hellmer Rosetta K. • Trustee • Steger-South Chicago Heights Public Library District • Steger, IL 60475

Hellmuth Frances R. • Assistant Professor/Librarian • Longwood College Library Dabney S Lancaster Library • Farmville, VA 23901 • AASL

Hellum-Berman Bertha D. • Walnut Creek, CA 94595 • ALSC LAMA   *Life*

Hellwig Carla L. • Washington, DC 20037 • ACRL ASCLA RASD IFRT LHRT

Helm Margie M. • Glasgow, KY 42141-2086 • Continuing

Helm Steven P. • Computer Specialist • Montgomery-Floyd Regional Library • Christiansburg, VA 24073 • LITA IFRT

Helm William • Bronx, NY 10466

Helmbrecht Janice L. • Zanesville, OH 43701 • AASL

Helmeci Hollis E. • Student • University of Illinois Graduate School of Library and Information Science • Urbana, IL 61801 • YALSA

Helmer Dona • Director of Libraries • A.C. Stevens Elementary School • FPO, AP 96506-1240 • AASL ALSC PLA YALSA

Helmer John F. • University of Oregon Library • Eugene, OR 97403-1299

Helmick Aileen • Associate Professor/Dept. Chair. • Central Missouri State University Ward Edwards Library • Warrensburg, MO 64093 • AASL IFRT

Helmick Catherine • Branch Coordinator • Santa Fe Public Library Oliver LaFarge Branch • Santa Fe, NM 87505 • LITA

Helmke Elsie • Librarian • Merrick Public Library • Merrick, NY 11566

Helms Cynthia M. • Associate Reference Librarian • Andrews University James White Library • Berrien Springs, MI 49104-1400

Helms Frank Q. • Director of Library Services • West Chester University Francis Harvey Green Library • West Chester, PA 19383 • ACRL

Helms Joseph H. • Acquisitions/Reference Librarian • Vincennes University Shake Learning Resources Library • Vincennes, IN 47591

Helms Mary E. • Assoc. Dir. of Tech. Servs. • University of Nebraska Medical Ctr McGoogan Library of Medicine • Omaha, NE 68198-6705 • ACRL

Helmstadter Daniel C. • President • Scholarly Resources Inc • Wilmington, DE 19805

Helmstadter Rebecca • Media Specialist • Grady Elementary School • Tampa, FL 33629

Helsel Beth W. • Systems Librarian • Clemson University Robert Muldrow Cooper Library • Clemson, SC 29634-3001 • LITA

Helser Bettie R. Dr. • Professor Emeritus • University of Colorado at Denver Auraria Library • Denver, CO 80204

Helstien Brian A. • University of California-Los Angeles (UCLA) • Los Angeles, CA 90024-1450 • LITA

Helton Raefette B. • Communications Manager • UMI Data Courier Inc. • Louisville, KY 40202 • LITA

Heltsley Mary K. • Librarian • Faribault Regional Center Library • Faribault, MN 55021

Helwege Ruth M. • Student • East Baton Rouge Parish Library • Baton Rouge, LA 70806-7699

Helwig Karen A. • Reference Librarian • Janesville Public Library • Janesville, WI 53545-3971 • GODORT

Helwig Lily J. • Librarian II • Phoenix Public Library Century Branch • Phoenix, AZ 85016 • YALSA

Hembree Joy Mrs. • Board Member • Lexington Public Library • Lexington, KY 40507 • ALTA

Hemesath James B. • Director • Adams State College Library • Alamosa, CO 81102 • ACRL LAMA

Hemingson Ruth T. • Business Research Librarian • Hallmark Cards Res Lib-203 • Kansas City, MO 64141-6580 • RASD

Hemming Laura K • Inter Loan Librarian • University of Wisconsin-Green Bay Cofrin Library • Green Bay, WI 54311

Hemming Linda E. • Media Specialist • Burrows Elementary School • Quantico, VA 22134 • AASL

Hemmingson Robert • Director • Fergus Falls Public Library • Fergus Falls, MN 56537 • PLA

Hemond JoAnn M. • Charleston County Library • Charleston, SC 29403

Hemond Robyn M. • Student • Florida State University School of Library and Information Studies • Tallahassee, FL 32306-2048 • ALSC

Hemphill B. Frank • Woodbine, MD 21797 • LAMA

Hemphill Frank A. Jr. • Portage Public Library • Portage, MI 49002 • LAMA PLA

Hemphill Jean F. • Associate Director • University of Colorado at Denver Auraria Library • Denver, CO 80204 • ACRL

Hemphill Ruth A. • Wolfner Library for the Blind & Physically Handicapped • Jefferson City, MO 65109 • ASCLA

Hempstead John • Viterbo College Library • La Crosse, WI 54601

Hemrick Robin D. • Head of Adult Services • Wake County Public Library North Regional Library • Raleigh, NC 27615 • PLA RASD

Hench Joan M. • Harrisburg, PA 17103 • ACRL RASD

Hendelman Judith • Forest Hills, NY 11375 • AASL

Henderickson Karen J. • Elementary Teacher • Gibraltar School District Parsons Elementary School • Gibraltar, MI 48173 • AASL IFRT NMRT

Henders Rosemary A. • Student • Northern Illinois University Department of Library & Information Studies • DeKalb, IL 60115

Hendershot Jean • Branch Librarian • Mid-Continent Public Library Blue Ridge Branch • Kansas City, MO 64138

Hendershot Robin P. • Librarian • George Early Childhood Center • Idabel, OK 74745 • AASL

Henderson Bobbie J. • Library Media Specialist • Marrcus Foster Middle School • Oakland, CA 94608-4536

Henderson Bobby R. • Director • Bethune-Cookman College Swisher Library • Daytona Beach, FL 32115 • ACRL IRRT

Henderson Carol C. • Deputy Director • American Library Association Washington Office • Washington, DC 20002 • ACRL LITA GODORT

Henderson Carol G. • Faculty Librarian • Central Oregon Community College • Bend, OR 97701 • ACRL

Henderson Carolyn J. • Asst. Director, Support Services • University of Florida Libraries • Gainesville, FL 32611 • ACRL LAMA

Henderson Cathy • Librarian • University of Texas Ransom Humanities Research Center • Austin, TX 78713 • ACRL

Henderson Cynthia L. • Special Collections Librarian • Iowa State University Library • Ames, IA 50011-2140 • ACRL NMRT

Henderson Dan W. • Librarian • Brevard Cmnty Coll Learning Resources Center • Titusville, FL 32796

Henderson David W. • Instructional Services • Eckerd College William Luther Cobb Library • Saint Petersburg, FL 33711 • ACRL

Henderson Deneene Williams Mrs. • Resource Teacher • Dallas Independent School District Accounts Payable • Dallas, TX 75204

Henderson Donald L. • Trustee • Elk Grove Village Public Library • Elk Grove Village, IL 60007 • ALTA

Henderson Douglas A. • Administrator • Las Vegas-Clark County Library District Flamingo Library • Las Vegas, NV 89119

Henderson Elaine C. • Huber Heights, OH 45424-7072 • AASL ALSC YALSA IFRT

Henderson Elizabeth F. • Lynchburg College • Lynchburg, VA 24501 • ACRL

Henderson Eric T. • Abstractor/Indexer • Congressional Information Service Inc. • Bethesda, MD 20814

Henderson Geraldine J. • Ballwin, MO 63011

Henderson Gwendolyn E. • Technical Services Assistant • Pikes Peak Library District • Colorado Springs, CO 80901-1579

Henderson Harriet • Director • Louisville Free Public Library • Louisville, KY 40203-2257 • LAMA PLA

Henderson James W. • New York, NY 10011 • ACRL ALCTS   *Life*

Henderson Jane L. • School Media Specialist • Gateway Elementary School • Van Buren, ME 04785 • AASL

Henderson Janet K. • Disney Elementary School • Tulsa, OK 74129 • AASL IRRT NMRT

Henderson Kathryn Luther • Professor • University of Illinois Graduate School of Library and Information Science • Urbana, IL 61801 • ACRL ALCTS   *Life*

Henderson Lennijo • Circulation/Serials Librarian • Richland College • Dallas, TX 75243-2199

Henderson Linda F. • Junior High School Librarian • Junior High School • Wellington, KS 67152

Henderson Marguerite G. • Dallas, TX 75243

Henderson Martha C. • Government Documents Unit • Temple University Paley Library • Philadelphia, PA 19122 • RASD GODORT

Henderson Mary L. • Rockford, IL 61103 • Continuing

Henderson Pat • Valencia Community College East Campus • Orlando, FL 32825 • ACRL

Henderson Patricia S. • Student • University of Alabama School of Library & Information Studies • Tuscaloosa, AL 35487-0252

Henderson Roberta M. • Instructor • Northern Michigan University Lydia M. Olson Library • Marquette, MI 49855 • LIRT

Henderson Rosemary • Director Learning Resources • Coffeyville Community College • Coffeyville, KS 67337 • ACRL

Henderson S. Diane • Chief Librarian • University of Toronto Faculty of Library & Information Science • Toronto ON, M5S 1A1 Canada • ACRL

Henderson Sam Mrs. • Senior Library Assistant • Mercer County Library Hickory Corner Branch • East Windsor, NJ 08520

Henderson Sherry S. • Media Specialist • Macon Middle Scchool Macon County School System • Franklin, NC 28734 • AASL NMRT

Henderson Shirley A. • Manager,Information Services • Lakewood Public Library • Lakewood, OH 44107

Henderson Susan E. • Sacred Heart Preporatory • Atherton, CA 94027 • AASL

Henderson Susanne • Manager Library Services • General Electric Company • Rockville, MD 20855 • ALCTS LAMA LITA RASD FLRT   *Life*

Henderson Tona A. • Student • University of Missouri-Columbia School of Library & Informational Science • Columbia, MO 65211

Henderson Virginia • Osterville, MA 02655

Henderson William T. • Preservation Librarian • University of Illinois Library • Urbana, IL 61801 • ALCTS LITA   *Life*

Hendley Virginia D. • Santa Fe, NM 87501

Hendon Alison M. • Senior Librarian • Northern California Womens Facility • Stockton, CA 95213-9006 • ASCLA

Hendon Linda J. • Technical Services • Ramapo Catskill Library System • Middletown, NY 10940 • ALCTS
Hendrick Constance M. • Asst to Dir Ctrl Tech Serv • University of Minnesota O. Meredith Wilson Library • Minneapolis, MN 55455-0414 • ALCTS LITA
Hendrick Karen N. • Public Services Librarian • Abilene Christian University Margaret & Herman Brown Library • Abilene, TX 79699 • ACRL RASD GODORT IFRT LIRT
Hendrick Linda F. • Reference Librarian • Skagit Valley College • Mount Vernon, WA 98273 • ASCLA
Hendricks Dawn • OCLC Incorporation • Dublin, OH 43017
Hendricks Donald D. • Social Science Reference Ln. • University of New Orleans Earl K. Long Library • New Orleans, LA 70148 • ACRL ALCTS *Life*
Hendricks Elaine M. • Hudson, NY 12534 • AASL
Hendricks Epsy Y. Dr • Director of Library • Alcorn State University Library • Lorman, MS 39096 • ACRL LAMA
Hendricks Leta • Head, Human Ecology Library • Ohio State University Libraries • Columbus, OH 43210-1286 • ACRL
Hendricks Marlene • Adminstrative Assistant • Enid M Baa Library & Archives • Charlotte Amalie, VI 00802
Hendricks Thom • Director • Mandan Public Library • Mandan, ND 58554 • PLA
Hendricks Yoshi • Head, Bibliographic Control • University of Nevada-Reno • Reno, NV 89557
Hendrickson Betty T. • Peoria, IL 61615
Hendrickson Doris • Assistant University Librarian • Radford University John P. McConnell Library • Radford, VA 24142 • ACRL LITA EMIERT SRRT
Hendrickson Jan • Director • McLean-Mercer Regional Library Hazen Branch • Hazen, ND 58545
Hendrickson Kent H. • Dean of Libraries • University of Nebraska-Lincoln University Libraries • Lincoln, NE 68588-0410 • ACRL
Hendrickson Linda B. • Elementary School Librarian • Ford Elementary School • Dunbar, WV 25064 • AASL
Hendrickson Linnea M. • Albuquerque, NM 87107 • ALSC
Hendrickson Norma K. • Head, Micoform Cataloging Sec. • Library of Congress • Washington, DC 20541 • ALCTS
Hendrickson Susan Marie • Walt Disney Imagineering • Glendale, CA 91221
Hendrix Carla A. • Head of Access Services • State University of New York at Plattsburgh (SUNY) • Plattsburgh, NY 12901 • ACRL LAMA LITA
Hendrix Gayla C. • Smithville, TN 37166
Hendrix Linda • Marietta, GA 30067
Hendrix Madeline • Library Coordinator • Sawanhaka Central High School District H. Frank Carey High School • Franklin Square, NY 11010 • ALTA LRRT
Hendrix Mike L. • Librarian • Wilson High School • Tacoma, WA 98406
Hendry Leona A. • Chief Librarian • Belleville Public Library • Belleville ON, K8N 3A7 Canada
Henebry Carolyn L. • Reference Librarian • University of Texas at Dallas University Library • Richardson, TX 75083-0643 • ACRL
Heneghan Mary Ann • Cambridge, MA 02138-2910 • LAMA PLA *Life*
Heneisen Jane F. • Trustee • Evansville-Vanderburgh County Public Library • Evansville, IN 47708-1694 • ALTA
Hengel Susan L. • Wilmington, DE 19802
Hengen-Swan Jamie L. • Baton Rouge, LA 70821
Henigman Barbara D. • Librarian • University of Illinois Library • Urbana, IL 61801 • ALCTS LITA
Henington David M. • Houston Public Library • Houston, TX 77002 • LAMA PLA
Henjum Elaine M. • Associate University Librarian • Florida Center for Library Automation • Gainesville, FL 32609 • ACRL ALCTS LITA
Henke Christine M. • Austin, TX 78748 • LITA RASD
Henke Dan F. Prof • Librarian & Professor • University of California Hastings College of the Law Library • San Francisco, CA 94102 • ACRL LITA *Life*
Henke Esther Mae • Oklahoma Cty, OK 73105 • Continuing
Henkel Carol Lynn • Technical Services Librarian • Cranberry Public Library • Mars, PA 16046
Henkel Grace E. • Librarian • VGS, Incorporation • McLean, VA 22102
Henkle Herman H. • Mishawaka, IN 46544-5734 • Continuing
Henkle John W. • Librarian • Orange County Library System Orlando Public Library • Orlando, FL 32801-2471 • VRT
Henn Barbara • Head, Acquisitions • Indiana University • Bloomington, IN 47405 • ACRL ALCTS LAMA
Henne Frances • Greenfield, MA 01301 • AASL YALSA *Life*
Henneman John Bell Jr. • History Bibliographer • Princeton University • Princeton, NJ 08544-2098 • ACRL
Hennen Rita • Librarian • Worthington Elementary School • Parkersburg, WV 26104 • AASL
Hennessey Dennis A. • Community College of Allegheny County Allegheny Campus Library • Pittsburgh, PA 15212
Hennessey Gilbert • American Foundation for the Blind • New York, NY 10011
Hennessey Mary S. • Reference Librarian • East Lansing Public Library • East Lansing, MI 48823 • YALSA
Hennessy Charlene C. • Director • Harcum Junior College Library • Byrn Mawr, PA 19010-3476 • ACRL
Hennessy Mildred • Sun City, AZ 85351 • Continuing
Hennessy Rebecca M.D. • Atlanta-Fulton Public Library Roswell Branch • Roswell, GA 30075
Hennessy Roseann • Syosset, NY 11791
Hennig Karen L. • K-12 School Library/Media • Craftsbury Schools • Craftsbury Common, VT 05827 • AASL
Hennigan Millicent • Baton Rouge, LA 70808 • Life
Henning Arland B. • Catalog Librarian • Jacksonville State University Library • Jacksonville, AL 36265 • ACRL
Henning Betty • Manager, Young Adult Services • Allen County Public Library • Fort Wayne, IN 46801-2270
Hennings LeRoy Jr. • Director • Martin County Public Library • Stuart, FL 33494-2374 • LAMA
Hennington Betty • Trinidad, TX 75163
Henri Janine J. • Art Librarian • University of Texas • Austin, TX 78712-1276 • ACRL
Henrichs Virginia A. • Glencoe, IL 60022
Henricks Allen D. • Associate Dean, LCR • North Central Technical College • Wausau, WI 54401 • ALCTS LAMA *Life*
Henrickson Sally • Librarian • Tandem School Library • Charlottesville, VA 22902
Henriksen Mary J. • Student • Emporia State University School of Library & Information Management • Emporia, KS 66801 • PLA NMRT
Henriksson Ann W. • Shepherd College Ruth Scarborough Library • Shepherdstown, WV 25443-1568 • GODORT
Henry-Croom Martha L. • Assistant Librarian/Public Serv. • Kennesaw State College • Marietta, GA 30061
Henry Charles J. Dr. • Director of Libraries • Vassar College Library • Poughkeepsie, NY 12601 • ACRL LITA
Henry Elizabeth A. • Children's Librarian • Suffern Free Library • Suffern, NY 10901-5694
Henry Elizabeth C. • Serials • Auburn University • Auburn, AL 36849 • ALCTS
Henry Ellen W. • Librarian • Loudoun County Public Library Thomas Balch Library • Leesburg, VA 22075-2798 • PLA
Henry Eugene B. Jr • Head Librarian • Newport Public Library • Newport, RI 02840 • PLA
Henry Helen K. • Automation Coordinator • San Diego State University Library • San Diego, CA 92119-2120 • LITA
Henry Janet E. • Youngsville, PA 16371 • Continuing
Henry Jean B. • Juneau, AK 99801 • ALCTS
Henry Karen S. • Asst. Mgr., Business Sci Dept. • Houston Public Library • Houston, TX 77002
Henry Linda • St. Augustines College • Raleigh, NC 27611
Henry Lisa • Trustee • Clark County Public Library • Springfield, OH 45501-1080 • ALTA
Henry Lorrelle • Supervisor of Library Media • New York City Board of Education • Brooklyn, NY 11201 • AASL ALSC YALSA EMIERT SRRT
Henry Margaret Z. • Davenport Public Library • Davenport, IA 52801
Henry Marilyn Y. • Vanderbilt University Library Jean & Alexander Heard Library • Nashville, TN 37240-0007
Henry Mary K. • Short Hills, NJ 07078 • ACRL ALCTS
Henry Nancy L. • Librarian • Ephrata Middle School • Ephrata, PA 17522 • AASL
Henry Paula M. • Head, Acquisition Department • New York State University Geneseo College • Geneseo, NY 14454 • EMIERT SRRT
Henry Peggy L. • Branch Librarian • Mid-Continent Public Library • Independence, MO 64050
Henry Sandra M. • Austin, TX 78711
Henry Susan G. • Librarian I • Saint Paul Public Library • St. Paul, MN 55102 • ALCTS
Henschel Susan • Library Media Specialist • Saint Rose High School Library • Belmar, NJ 07719 • AASL YALSA LIRT NMRT
Henschke David • Media Specialist • Brainerd Senior High School • Brainerd, MN 56401 • AASL
Henshaw Rod • Director of Public Services • Emory University Libraries Robert W. Woodruff Library • Atlanta, GA 30322-2870 • ACRL LAMA
Hensinger James Speed • Mgr. MicroSYSTEMS & Services • Bibliographical Center for Research • Denver, CO 80222 • LITA
Hensler Anna M. • Huntingdon Valley Library • Huntingdon Valley, PA 19006 • ALSC
Hensler Beverley Irene • Librarian • Roy J. Wollam Elementary School Library Santa Fe Independent School District • Santa Fe, TX 77510 • AASL NMRT
Hensley Charlotta C. • Assoc Dir for Planning & Devel • University of Colorado at Boulder Libraries • Boulder, CO 80309 • ACRL ALCTS ALSC LAMA IFRT IRRT LRRT SRRT
Hensley Randall B. • Ass Head, Undergrad Library • University of Washington Libraries Odegaard Undergraduate Library • Seattle, WA 98195 • ACRL LIRT SRRT
Hensley Susan E. • Oakland, CA 94610
Hensman Kathleen M. • Woodhaven, MI 48183
Henson-Hunt Helen D. • Librarian • Loretto High School Library • Loretto, TN 38469 • AASL NMRT
Henson Debbie A. • Librarian • Taylor, Porter, Brooks & Phillips • Baton Rouge, LA 70821
Henson L L. • Director • Florida Institute of Technology Library • Melbourne, FL 32901 • ACRL ALCTS LAMA LITA RASD GODORT
Henson Ruby P. • Director • East Morgan County Library District • Brush, CO 80723 • PLA
Henstock Marilyn • Audiovisual Librarian • Kanawha County Public Library • Charleston, WV 25301
Henthorn Susan K. • Berea College Hutchins Library • Berea, KY 40404 • ACRL RASD LIRT
Henthorne Eileen M. • Senior Technical Staff I • Princeton University Library • Princeton, NJ 08544
Hentrich Ann C. • Children's Librarian • Dayton & Montgomery County Public Library Belmont Branch • Dayton, OH 45420
Hepburn-Ballou Rose • Miami-Dade Public Library System • Miami, FL 33130-1504
Hepfer Cynthia K. • Head of Serials • State University of New York (SUNY) Health Sciences Library • Buffalo, NY 14214 • ALCTS
Hepner John C. • Reference Librarian • Texas Woman's University Mary Evelyn Blagg-Huey Library • Denton, TX 76204-1715 • ACRL RASD GODORT IFRT SRRT
Hepp Thomas A. Mr • Librarian • Grossmont College Library • El Cajon, CA 92020 • ACRL *Life*
Heppner Cheryl • Director • Northern Virginia Resource Center for Deaf & Hard of Hearing • Fairfax, VA 22031
Hepting Edward M. • Librarian • Rhodes Middle School • Philadelphia, PA 19132 • AASL ALSC
Herald Di • Librarian • Mesa County Public Library • Grand Junction, CO 81502 • YALSA
Herald Susan M. • Children's Librarian • Lauri Ann West Memorial Library • Pittsburgh, PA 15238
Heraman Suresh • Teacher • New York City Board of Education • Brooklyn, NY 11201
Herb Betty D. • Librarian • West High School • Columbus, OH 43204
Herb Steven L. • Pennsylvania State University E506 Pattee Library • University Park, PA 16802 • AASL ACRL ALSC LITA
Herb Tina M. • Technical Services Librarian • Kirkwood College Library • Cedar Rapids, IA 52406
Herberg Robert G. • Alhambra, CA 91801
Herbert Diane M. • Children's Librarian • Hillsboro Public Library • Neshanic, NJ 08853 • PLA YALSA
Herbert Dorothy C. • Champlin, MN 55316 • ACRL PLA RASD LIRT
Herbert Ida L • Library Media Assistant • Wright State University Library • Dayton, OH 45435
Herbert Jennifer A. • Instructor-Adjunct Faculty • San Jose State University Clark Library • San Jose, CA 95192-0028
Herbert Jennifer L. • Forest Park, IL 60130
Herbert Karen G. • Gulfport, MS 39503 • AASL NMRT
Herbert Lynn M. • Student • University of Western Ontario School of Library & Information Science • London ON, N6G 1H1 Canada
Herbert Rue M. • Assistant Librarian • University of South Florida Library • Tampa, FL 33620-5600
Herbert Ruth E. • Media Specialist • Glide High School • Glide, OR 97443-9744 • AASL
Herbison Michael • Director • University of Alaska Juneau Library • Juneau, AK 99801-9977 • ACRL IFRT
Herbsman Yael • Cataloger • University of Florida Libraries • Gainesville, FL 32611-2047 • ACRL
Herbst Jay • Bloomfield Township Public Library • Bloomfield Hills, MI 48302-2437 • ALTA
Herbst Linda • Head, Reference Dept. • Bloomfield Township Public Library • Bloomfield Hills, MI 48302-2437
Herdklotz Cheryl A. Dr. • Assistant Director AV Services • Rochester Institute of Technology • Rochester, NY 14623
Herens Arlene G. • Student • Southern Connecticut State University School of Libray Science & Instructional Technology • New Haven, CT 06515 • AASL

Heriard Robert • Reference • University of New Orleans Earl K. Long Library • New Orleans, LA 70148 • ACRL RASD

Hering Paula E. • Warren County Community College • Washington, NJ 07882-9605 • ACRL RASD NMRT

Heringer Patricia G. • Director • Driftwood Library • Lincoln City, OR 97367 • ALSC PLA IFRT

Herington Nancy • Pikes Peak Library District • Colorado Springs, CO 80901

Heriot Angus M. • Portland, OR 97201

Heriot Jean • Washington State University • Vancouver, WA 98663

Herlihy Catherine S. • Catalog Librarian • California State University San Marcos • San Marcos, CA 92096 • ALCTS

Herlinger Peggy • Coordinator Resource Center • Champlain Regional College • St Lambert PQ, J4P 3P2 Canada • ACRL ALCTS RASD LIRT

Herlitz Barbara W. • Library Media Specialist • Anahuac High School Library Media Center • Baytown, TX 77521 • AASL

Herman Deirdre Ann • Student • University of Maryland College of Library and Information Services • College Park, MD 20742-4345

Herman Douglas C. • Brandeis University Main Library • Waltham, MA 02254-9110 • ACRL LITA RASD

Herman Edward P. • State University of New York Lockwood Library Building • Buffalo, NY 14260 • RASD GODORT

Herman Elizabeth • Los Angeles, CA 90049 • ACRL ALCTS LITA

Herman Gertrude B. • University of Wisconsin School of Library & Information Studies • Madison, WI 53706 • AASL ALSC *Continuing*

Herman Judith B. • Librarian III • Los Angeles Public Library • Los Angeles, CA 90071 • RASD

Herman Larry • Librarian • Wayne Public Library • Wayne, NJ 07470 • AASL

Herman Margaret O. • Reference Librarian • El Paso Public Library • El Paso, TX 79901 • LAMA PLA RASD CLENE IFRT LIRT SORT SRRT

Herman Marsha A. • Information Coordinator • Parsons Brinckerhoff Corporate Library • New York, NY 10119 • LITA NMRT

Herman Mary Lou • Assistant Librarian • University of Wisconsin Physics Library • Madison, WI 53706

Herman Michael L. • Seattle Public Library Mobile Services • Seattle, WA 98102

Herman Pamela C. • District Media Coordinator • Marsing School District • Marsing, ID 83639 • NMRT

Herman Rebecca G. • Berkeley, CA 94710 • PLA EMIERT IFRT SRRT

Herman Rhonda • Vice President • McFarland & Co Inc Publishers • Jefferson, NC 28640 • AASL ACRL RASD IFRT SRRT

Herman Steven J. • Library of Congress • Washington, DC 20541 • ACRL LAMA RASD FLRT

Herman Tina L. • Pittsburgh, PA 15213

Hermance-Moore Laurie K. • Librarian II • Columbus Metropolitan Library Main Library Branch • Columbus, OH 43215

Hermann Karen A. • Waupun, WI 53963-9561 • AASL

Hermann Sarah A. • Buffalo, NY 14213

Hermanson Robert B. • Student • University of Washington Graduate School of Library and Information Science • Seattle, WA 98195 • ACRL

Hermens Dorothy M. • Hillsboro, OR 97124 • Continuing

Hermsen Lesal L. • Student • Portland State University School of Education • Portland, OR 97207

Hernandez-Alaras Elizabeth • Asst Head Foreign Lang. Info.Cnt • Chicago Public Library Harold Washington Library • Chicago, IL 60605

Hernandez Carolina M. • Head, Cataloging Dept. • University of New Orleans Earl K. Long Library • New Orleans, LA 70148 • ALCTS

Hernandez Cynthia A. • Miami-Dade Public Library System South Dade Regional Branch • Miami, FL 33189

Hernandez Evelyn V. • Langhorne, PA 19047 • AASL

Hernandez Hector R. • Head Librarian • Chicago Public Library Rudy Lozano Branch • Chicago, IL 60608 • PLA RASD EMIERT

Hernandez Jane • Library Assistant I • Saint Joseph County Public Library • South Bend, IN 46601 • ALSC

Hernandez Ramon R. • Director • Ann Arbor Public Library • Ann Arbor, MI 48104 • PLA

Hernandez Yolanda G. • Mesa, AZ 85204

Hernandez Yolanda Quela • Burbank, IL 60459 • RASD

Herndon Debra H. • Librarian • Lowe Public Library • Shinnston, WV 26431

Herndon Dorothy J. • Assistant Librarian • North Lake College Library • Irving, TX 75038-3899 • RASD

Herndon Kimmetha H. • Serials/AV/Ill • Shorter College Livingston Library • Rome, GA 30165

Herndon Leon • Charlotte, NC 28210 • SRRT

Herndon Mary Ann • Coor. Library Media Servs. • Spring Branch School District • Houston, TX 77024 • AASL

Herner Saul • Chairman • Herner and Company • Arlington, VA 22201 • ACRL ALCTS LITA

Hernon Peter • Framingham, MA 01701 • ACRL LRRT

Herold Andrew • Director • Logan Hocking County Districk Library • Logan, OH 43138

Herold Irene M.H. • Student • University of Washington Graduate School of Library and Information Science • Seattle, WA 98195 • ACRL IFRT SRRT

Herold Jeffrey R Dr. • Director • Bucyrus Public Library • Bucyrus, OH 44820 • PLA

Heron David W. • Aptos, CA 95003 • ACRL ALCTS *Life*

Heron Susan J. • Tampa, FL 33620 • ALCTS LITA

Heroux Marlene S. • Manager Information Center • Rolls-Royce Inc. • Atlanta, GA 30339 • RASD

Heroy Phyllis B. • Supervisor of Libraries • East Baton Rouge Parish Sch Bd • Baton Rouge, LA 70821 • AASL YALSA

Herpich Cathy M. • San Antonio, TX 78217 • ALCTS LITA

Herr Mary • Student • Wayne State University Library Science Program • Detroit, MI 48202

Herr Sharon M. • Cataloger • Ohio Northern University Heterick Memorial Library • Ada, OH 45810 • ACRL ALCTS

Herr T. A J • Senior Lecturer • Univ of Tasmania Sch of Lnship • Tasmania 7001, Australia • AASL ACRL ALCTS ALSC LAMA LITA PLA RASD CLENE LRRT

Herr-Hoyman Susan M. • Madison, WI 53714

Herraghty Maureen E. • St. Louis, MO 63123

Herreid Walt • Student • University of Iowa School of Library & Information Science • Iowa City, IA 52242 • ACRL

Herreman Linda J. • Reference Librarian • Indianapolis-Marion County Pubilc Library • Indianapolis, IN 46202 • MAGERT

Herren Annette • Trustee • Western Plains Library System • Clinton, OK 73601

Herrera Deborah D. • Director • Seton Hall University Law Library • Newark, NJ 07102 • LAMA

Herrera Eleanor H. • Denver, CO 80210 • AASL

Herrera Luis • Deputy Director • San Diego Public Library • San Diego, CA 92101 • PLA EMIERT

Herrera Mariana G. • Head/Circulation/Reserv Dept • Chicago State University Paul & Emily Douglas Library • Chicago, IL 60628 • ACRL

Herrick Alida M. • Lexington, KY 40502 • ACRL IFRT LIRT

Herrick Elizabeth A. • Librarian • West High School • Painted Post, NY 14840 • AASL

Herrick Johanna W. • School Librarian • University of Hawaii Hilo Library • Hilo, HI 96720

Herrick Judith Matheny • Hd,Serial Catlg Section III • Library of Congress • Washington, DC 20541 • ALCTS LITA FLRT

Herrick Kenneth • Director of Library • University of Hawaii Hilo Library • Hilo, HI 96720 • ACRL

Herrick Mildred Miss • Bellingham, WA 98225 • Life

Herrick Patricia D. • Student • University of South Florida School of Library & Information Science • Tampa, FL 33620

Herrick Roxanna • Washington University Olin Library • Saint Louis, MO 63130 • ALCTS

Herrin Barbara R. • Deputy Exec. Dir. AASL • American Library Association • Chicago, IL 60611-2795 • AASL

Herrin Julie • Associate Executive Director • Michigan Library Consortium • Lansing, MI 48911 • ASCLA

Herring Beverly Z. • Director • Madison County-Canton Public Library • Canton, MS 39046 • PLA

Herring Billie G. • Professor • University of Texas at Austin Graduate School of Library & Information Sciences • Austin, TX 78712-1276 • AASL ALCTS LITA

Herring Eileen C. • Student • University of Hawaii School of Library & Information Studies • Honolulu, HI 96822 • LITA

Herring Gary L. • Jones County Junior College • Ellisville, MS 39437

Herring Peggie • Librarian • Western Hills High School Library • Fort Worth, TX 76116 • AASL

Herring Phyllis P. • Media Coordinator • Winston-Salem Forsyth County Schools • Winston-Salem, NC 27103 • AASL

Herring Susan D. • Engineering Reference Librarian • University of Alabama in Huntsville Library • Huntsville, AL 35899

Herring Susan K. • Assistant Director • Peoria Public Library • Peoria, IL 61602 • PLA

Herrington Nancy J. • Science Librarian • Syracuse University Library E. S. Bird Library • Syracuse, NY 13244-2010 • ACRL

Herrington Verlene J. • Phoenix, AZ 85044

Herrman Jeannette • Honesdale, PA 18431

Herrmann Edith A. • Reference Services Librarian • Ambassador College Library Roy Hammer Library Building • Big Sandy, TX 75755 • RASD

Herrmann Ellen L. • Reference Librarian • Crete Public Library District • Crete, IL 60417 • PLA RASD

Herrmann J. Lani • Student • University of California-Berkeley School of Library & Information Studies • Berkeley, CA 94720 • IFRT

Herrmann John F. • Whole Book Cataloger • Library of Congress • Washington, DC 20541 • ALCTS

Herrmann Lawrence • Trustee • Wright Memorial Public Library • Oakwood, OH 45419-2598

Herrmann Sara E. • Paideia School Library • Atlanta, GA 30307 • AASL

Herro Joseph K. • Stanford University Libraries Branner Earth Sciences Library • Stanford, CA 94305-2174 • MAGERT

Herrold Charles M. Jr • Senior Catalog Librarian • Carnegie Library of Pittsburgh • Pittsburgh, PA 15213-4080 • ALCTS

Herron Elizabeth K. • Circulation Services Manager • Spokane Public Library Comstock Building Library • Spokane, WA 99201-0976

Herron Joan E. • Librarian • Eureka High School • Eureka, IL 61530 • AASL

Herron Margie E. • Director Library Development • South Carolina State Library • Columbia, SC 29211 • ASCLA LAMA PLA

Herron Miriam E. • Shelbyville, IL 62565 • AASL ALSC *Continuing*

Herron Nancy L. • Dir. of Acdemic Affairs • Pennsylvania State Univ Ls McKeesport Campus Kelly Library • Mc Keesport, PA 15132 • ACRL LAMA LITA

Herroon Elaine A. • Student • Kent State University School of Library & Information Science • Kent, OH 44242-0001

Hersberger Julie A. • Student • Indiana University School of Library and Information Science • Bloomington, IN 47405 • PLA IFRT

Hersberger Rodney M. • Director • California State University • Bakersfield, CA 93311 • ACRL LAMA

Herschberg Jacqueline Golland • School Librarian • University Child Development School • Seattle, WA 98105 • AASL ALSC

Herschel Harriet • Children's Librarian • King County Library System Fairwood Library • Renton, WA 98058 • ALSC

Herschenfeld Larry P. • State University of New York (SUNY) • Stony Brook, NY 11794-2225

Hersey Ruth E. • Bloomington, MN 55438

Hersh Carole • Jericho, NY 11753

Hersh Daniel • Contra Costa County Library • Pleasant Hill, CA 94523 • SRRT

Hersh Marlene H. • Librarian • Arcola Elementary School Library • Arcola, VA 22010 • AASL

Hershbarger Elaine • Reference Librarian • Urbana Free Library • Urbana, IL 61801-3283 • ALCTS

Hershberger Helen • Information Services Librarian • Fountaindale Public Library Dist • Romeoville, IL 60441

Hershberger Sandra S. • Student • University of Washington Graduate School of Library and Information Science • Seattle, WA 98195

Hershenson Mimi • Broward County Library Coral Springs Library • Coral Springs, FL 33065

Hershey Fred E. Dr • Lima, OH 45805 • ACRL ALCTS *Life*

Hershey Johanna • Assoc Dir For Tech Serv • Johns Hopkins University Milton S. Eisenhower Library • Baltimore, MD 21218 • ACRL ALCTS LAMA

Hershey Kathryn E. • Technical Services Librarian • Metropolitan Community College • Omaha, NE 68103 • ACRL ALSC LAMA

Hershoff Nancy S. • Librarian • Florida International University North Miami Campus • North Miami, FL 33181 • ALCTS LAMA EMIERT

Hersom Cheryl A. • Vacaville, CA 95687 • RASD

Herstand Jo Ellen • Chief of Materials Selection • Metropolitan Library System • Oklahoma City, OK 73102 • PLA

Hert Carol A. • Student • Syracuse University School of Information Studies • Syracuse, NY 13244-4100 • LITA LRRT

Herther Nancy K. • St. Paul, MN 55117 • LITA

Hertsgaard Gudrun Miss • Librarian Literature Department • Minneapolis Public Library & Information Center • Minneapolis, MN 55401-1992 • RASD *Life*

Hertz Cynthia L. • Director, Learning Resources • SAR Academy Learning Resources Center • Riverdale, NY 10471 • AASL

Hertzoff Hilary L. • Student • Indiana University School of Library and Information Science • Bloomington, IN 47405 • ALSC

Hervey Norma J. • Head Librarian • Luther College • Decorah, IA 52101 • ACRL LAMA LITA
Herward Linda C. • University of Pittsburgh • Pittsburgh, PA 15260
Herwig Donna • Ashlawn Elementary School • Arlington, VA 22205
Herz Helga • Detroit, MI 48202 • ACRL ALCTS RASD GODORT IFRT IRRT LIRT SRRT *Continuing*
Herz Michael John • Tallahassee, FL 32312
Herzberg Lois • Branch Administrator • Yonkers Public Library • Yonkers, NY 10701 • PLA SRRT
Herzinger Mark • Sale Representative • Quality Books Inc. • Lake Bluff, IL 60044-2204
Herzinger Norm • Sales Representative • Quality Books Inc. • Lake Bluff, IL 60044-2204
Herzinger Sandra S. • Chair, Cataloging Department • University of Nebraska-Lincoln Libraries • Lincoln, NE 68588 • ALCTS LAMA
Herzog Barbara S. • Library Relations Rep. • H. W. Wilson Company • Bronx, NY 10452 • AASL LITA RASD
Herzog Kate S. • Director • State University of New York (SUNY) at Buffalo • Buffalo, NY 14260 • ACRL ALCTS
Hesch Nancy L. • Reference Librarian • Anchorage Municipal Libraries Z. J. Loussac Library • Anchorage, AK 99503 • PLA
Hesler Carolyn • Southern Methodist University Fondren Library • Dallas, TX 75275-0135
Hesler June • Reference Librarian • Larchmont Public Library • Larchmont, NY 10538
Hesler Raymond F. Rev • Baltimore, MD 21228 • Continuing
Hess Catherine W. • E Brunswick, NJ 08816
Hess David S. • Student • Indiana University School of Library and Information Science • Bloomington, IN 47405
Hess Elmer Beall • Document/Map Librarian • Valparaiso University Moellering Memorial Library • Valparaiso, IN 46383 • MAGERT
Hess James A. • Trustee • East Brunswick Public Library • E. Brunswick, NJ 08816 • ALTA
Hess Janet M. • Assistant Director • Acton Public Library • Old Saybrook, CT 06475
Hess Jayne L. Miss • Director • Phillipsburg Free Public Library • Phillipsburg, NJ 08865 • LAMA PLA *Life*
Hess M. Charlotte • Librarian • Workshop in Political Theory Policy Analysis • Bloomington, IN 47405 • ACRL IFRT LRRT
Hess Marjorie • Head Catalog Section • Amherst College Library • Amherst, MA 01002 • ALCTS
Hess Martha J. • Reference Librarian • East Brunswick Public Library • E. Brunswick, NJ 08816
Hess Sandra K. • Reference Librarian • Wartburg Theological Seminary Reu Memorial Library • Dubuque, IA 52003-7797 • ACRL
Hess Suzanne • Communities Library Director • San Diego County Library • San Diego, CA 92123 • PLA
Hess Tamra J. • Student • Kent State University School of Library & Information Science • Kent, OH 44242-0001 • PLA
Hess Vineca Lou • Librarian Assistant III • Mono County Library • Bridgeport, CA 93517 • AASL
Hesser Elizabeth • Roanoke, VA 24017 • Continuing
Hessler Nancy R. • Librarian • Moraine Valley Community College Library • Palos Hills, IL 60465
Hester Benjie • Childrens Librarian • Cameron Village Library • Raleigh, NC 27605 • ALSC
Hester Denia • Chicago, IL 60610 • AASL ASCLA
Hester Irene • Greensboro, NC 27410 • PLA RASD *Continuing*
Hester Mary • Librarian • Lyons Elementary Schools • Lyons, KS 67554 • AASL
Hester Rebecca C. • Coor Tech Serv • Pierce County Rural Library District • Tacoma, WA 98446
Hesting Joseph • Student • Indiana University School of Library and Information Science • Bloomington, IN 47405
Hetrick Sandra K. • Library Media Specialist • Lee Senior High School • Midland, TX 79707 • AASL
Hettel Lois A. • New York, NY 10023
Hettich Helen S. • Chair, Special Formats • Meadowood Library • Landsale, PA 19446 • ASCLA
Hettwer Margaret M. • Burbank, IL 60459 • ALTA
Hetzel Patricia A. • Librarian • Beckman Center for History of Chemistry • Philadelphia, PA 19104 • ALCTS
Hetzner Bernice M. • Omaha, NE 68114 • Continuing
Heuberger Karen W. • Reference Librarian • Public Library of Charlotte & Mecklenburg County • Charlotte, NC 28202 • RASD
Heuer Barbara P. • Savannah, GA 31405 • PLA
Heuer Judith B. • Librarian II • Phoenix Public Library Saguaro Branch • Phoenix, AZ 85008 • ALSC PLA YALSA
Heuer Kathryn A. • North Oaks, MN 55127
Heuertz Linda • Student • University of Washington Graduate School of Library and Information Science • Seattle, WA 98195 • IFRT SRRT
Heuman Fred S. Rabbi • Rabbi • American Congregation Of Jews From Austria • New York, NY 10025
Heuring Ruth A. • St. Peters, MO 63376 • AASL
Heus Kathleen • Librarian • Kenai Middle School Library • Kenai, AK 99611 • AASL
Heuser Lorraine Baggett • Periodicals/Reference Specialist • Camden County College • Blackwood, NJ 08012
Heusinkveld Judith A. • Media Specialist • Arrowhead AEA 5-Media Center • Fort Dodge, IA 50501 • AASL
Heussman John W. • Director • Pacific Lutheran University Mortvedt Library • Tacoma, WA 98447 • ACRL RASD *Life*
Hevelone Dorothy G. • Foundation Member • Beatrice Public Library • Beatrice, NE 68310 • ALTA
Heverly W. Gerald • University of Pittsburgh Hillman Library • Pittsburgh, PA 15260 • SRRT
Hewer Christine • Student • University of British Columbia School of Library, Archival & Information Studies • Vancouver BC, V6T 1Z1 Canada
Hewitt Carolyn C. • Librarian I • Aurora Public Library • Aurora, IL 60505-4299 • ALSC
Hewitt Debra D. • Paul Hadley Junior High School • Mooresville, IN 46158 • AASL YALSA
Hewitt James E. • Bibliographic Instr./Ref. Libn. • Concordia College Carl B. Ylvisaker Library • Moorhead, MN 56562 • ACRL LAMA LIRT
Hewitt Joan Lee • Librarian, Messing Library • Mary Institute & Saint Louis Country Day School • Saint Louis, MO 63124 • ACRL
Hewitt Joe A. • Assoc Univ Ln For Tech Servs • University of North Carolina Walter Royal Davis Library • Chapel Hill, NC 27599-3924 • ACRL ALCTS LAMA LRRT
Hewitt Marylouise • Free Lance Indexer • H. W. Wilson Company • Bronx, NY 10452 • ACRL
Hewitt Patricia A. • Loretto High School • Sacramento, CA 95821 • AASL
Hewitt Ruth P. • Mauldin, SC 29662
Hewitt Sharon M. • Baltimore, MD 21212
Hewitt Thomas B. • Skyline College Library • San Bruno, CA 94066
Hewitt Vivian D. • New York, NY 10025 • IRRT
Hewlett Carol C. • Sr. Information Resource Consult • University of Tennessee MTAS Library • Knoxville, TN 37996-4105
Hewlett Norma Jean • Student • University of California-Berkeley School of Library & Information Studies • Berkeley, CA 94720 • ACRL LITA
Hext Sharon J. • Anchorage, AK 99516 • AASL
Hexter Carolyn M. • Greenwood, VA 22943
Heydenryk Margit R. • Stonington, CT 06378
Heydorn Hella • Albany, CA 94710
Heydweiller Patricia B. • Syracuse, NY 13210-2936
Heyer Anna Harriet • Fort Worth, TX 76132 • Continuing
Heyer Robert A. • Student • University of California-Berkeley School of Library & Information Studies • Berkeley, CA 94720
Heyl Cynthia A. • Leal School • Mission, TX 78572 • AASL
Heylman Katherine M. • Cleveland, OH 44118 • ALSC IFRT
Heyman Berna L. • Asst. Univ Ln for Automation • College of William and Mary Earl Gregg Swem Library • Williamsburg, VA 23187-8794 • ACRL LITA
Heymoss Jennifer M. • Librarian • Henry Ford Museum & Greenfield Village • Dearborn, MI 48121-1970
Heyneman Alan L. Mr. • Rochester, NY 14618 • ACRL LAMA *Life*
Heynen Jeffrey W. • Chief, Hist. & Lit. Catlg. Div • Library of Congress • Washington, DC 20541
Heyns Erla P. • Indiana University Lilly Library • Bloomington, IN 47405 • LAMA
Heyser Teresa Poston Dr. • Trimble Technical High School • Fort Worth, TX 76104 • ALSC
Heyson Dawn L. • Student • Rutgers University School of Communication Information & Library Studies • New Brunswick, NJ 08903 • PLA
Heystek Kristen • Jonesboro, GA 30236 • PLA FLRT
Heyward Constance H. • Librarian • Wheeler High School • Marietta, GA 30067 • AASL
Hiatt Linda Rae • Seattle, WA 98177 • ACRL ALCTS ALSC *Life*
Hiatt Peter • University of Washington Graduate School of Library and Information Science • Seattle, WA 98195 • ALTA ASCLA LAMA PLA RASD *Life*
Hiatt Robert • Assistant To Director Catalog • Library of Congress • Washington, DC 20541 • ALCTS
Hibbard James B. • Student • Indiana University School of Library and Information Science • Bloomington, IN 47405
Hibbard Linda • Assistant Librarian • Burkburnett Library • Burkburnett, TX 76354
Hibbard Rosemary • Junior High School Librarian • Gaskill Middle School • Niagara Falls, NY 14301 • AASL ALSC
Hibbert Vicki • Assistant Adminstrator • Southeastern Library Services • Davenport, IA 52804-3026 • ALSC YALSA
Hibbet Scott A. • Young Adult Librarian • King County Library System • Seattle, WA 98109 • YALSA
Hibbs Hallie A. • Spokane Public Library Comstock Building Library • Spokane, WA 99201-0976 • PLA
Hibbs Jack E. • Head of Collection • University of Akron University Library & Learning Resource • Akron, OH 44325-1707 • ACRL
Hibbs Julie R. • Burbank, CA 91501
Hiber Virginia L. • Student • Wayne State University Library Science Program • Detroit, MI 48202
Hibler James P. • Clarkston, MI 48346
Hickerson H. Thomas • Dir of Rare & Mss. Clln. • Cornell University Library • Ithaca, NY 14853 • ACRL LAMA
Hickerson Joseph C. • Head, Archive of Folk Culture • Library of Congress • Washington, DC 20541
Hickey Cynthia L. • Student • Emporia State University School of Library & Information Management • Emporia, KS 66801
Hickey Damon D. • Director of the Library • College of Wooster Andrews Library • Wooster, OH 44691 • ACRL LAMA
Hickey Doralyn T. • Student • University of North Carolina at Chapel Hill School of Information and Library Science • Chapel Hill, NC 27599-3360 • LITA RASD NMRT SRRT
Hickey James E. • President • Quality Books Inc. • Lake Bluff, IL 60044-2204 • LAMA LITA PLA NMRT
Hickey John T. • Catalog Librarian • Ithaca College Library • Ithaca, NY 14850 • ALCTS SRRT
Hickey Kate D. • Director of the College Library • Pennsylvania College of Technology Learning Resources Center • Williamsport, PA 17701 • ACRL LAMA
Hickey Kathleen I. • Bethesda, MD 20814 • Life
Hickey Shirley K. • Associate Librarian • Margaret R. Grundy Memorial Library • Bristol, PA 19007 • ALSC PLA
Hickey Thomas B. • Consulting Research Scientist • Online Computer Library Center (OCLC) • Dublin, OH 43017-3395 • LITA
Hicklin Karen L. • Director • Livingston County Library • Chillicothe, MO 64601-2597 • PLA
Hickman Gerald W. • Assistant Librarian • Seminole Junior College Boren Library • Seminole, OK 74818 • ACRL NMRT
Hickman L. Karen • Librarian • Sabinal Independent School District • Sabinal, TX 78881
Hickman Michael L. • Librarian II • Atlanta-Fulton Public Library Sandy Springs Branch • Sandy Springs, GA 30328 • PLA SRRT
Hickman Theodore M. • Kutztown University Rohrbach Library • Kutztown, PA 19530-0721 • AASL
Hickman Traphene P. • Director • Dallas County Public Library • Dallas, TX 75202 • ALCTS LAMA PLA YALSA IFRT
Hickox Kaye • Forth Worth Indpendent School District • Fort Worth, TX 76106
Hicks Alyce J. • Davies County High School • Owensboro, KY 42303 • AASL
Hicks Athena A. • Coord. of Interlibrary Svcs • University of Tennessee T Carter & M Rawlings Lupton Lib • Chattanooga, TN 37403
Hicks Charles T. • Director • Logan County Public Library • Russellville, KY 42276
Hicks Cynthia S. • Senior Librarian • Los Angeles Public Library Systems Eagle Rock Branch • Los Angeles, CA 90041
Hicks Donna M. • Head Reader Services • Northbrook Public Library • Northbrook, IL 60062 • PLA
Hicks Doris A. • Mitchellville, MD 20721 • AASL
Hicks Emily A. • Lexington, KY 40508
Hicks Frederick M. • Library Consultant • Rolling Prairie Library System • Decatur, IL 62522
Hicks Jack Alan • Director • Deerfield Public Library • Deerfield, IL 60015
Hicks Janice P. • Student • Forbush Elementary School • East Bend, NC 27018 • LITA
Hicks Jim • Mgr. Technical Services • Quality Books Inc. • Lake Bluff, IL 60044-2204 • LITA
Hicks Kathleen • Director Media Service & Tech. • Maine Township High School • Park Ridge, IL 60068
Hicks Lisa S. • Student • Kent State University School of Library & Information Science • Kent, OH 44242-0001

Hicks Liz A. • Library Media Specialist • Rushton Elementary Library • Mission, KS 66202 • AASL

Hicks Marilyn A. • Bibliographer • University of Wisconsin • Madison, WI 53706 • ACRL

Hicks Mary Ellen • Raleigh, NC 27604 • AASL *Continuing*

Hicks Mary F. • Librarian • California Employment Development Department Labor Market • Sacramento, CA 95823 • RASD

Hicks Richard H. • Head of Technical Services • Drake University Cowles Library • Des Moines, IA 50311 • ACRL LITA

Hicks Robert L. • Librarian • Arkansas High School • Arkansas City, KS 67005 • AASL YALSA

Hidalgo Nilda R. • Santurce, PR 00909 • ACRL LRRT

Hidey Janice M. • Media Specialist • Liberty Christian School • Owings Mills, MD 21117-4605 • AASL

Hieb Louis A. • Head Librarian Special Clln. • University of Arizona Library • Tucson, AZ 85721 • ACRL

Hieber Barbara A. • Systems Analyst/Programmer • University of Pittsburgh • Pittsburgh, PA 15260 • LITA

Hieber Douglas M. • Head of Circulation Department • University of Northern Iowa Donald O. Rod Library • Cedar Falls, IA 50613-3675 • ACRL LAMA *Life*

Hieber Martha L. • Director • East Rochester Public Library • East Rochester, NY 14445 • ALSC PLA

Hiebert Harvey • Librarian • Bluffton College Musselman Library • Bluffton, OH 45817-1195 • ACRL ALCTS RASD

Hiebing Dottie R. • Director • Regional Library Cooperative V • Freehold, NJ 07728 • AASL ASCLA LAMA PLA CLENE

Hiebsch Helen J. • Columbus, IN 47203

Hielkema Arthur G. • Director Library/LRC • Northwestern College • Orange City, IA 51041

Hierholzer Bente • Librarian • Lyme Academy • Old Lyme, CT 06371

Hiett John H. • Librarian II • Iowa City Public Library • Iowa City, IA 52240 • RASD IFRT

Higa Mori Lou • Cypress, CA 90630

Higaki Steven Y. • Library Assistant • San Jose State University Clark Library • San Jose, CA 95192-0028 • GODORT

Higbee Florence • Arlington, VA 22201

Higbee Joan F. • Reference Specialist • Library of Congress • Washington, DC 20541 • ACRL SRRT

Higbie Elizabeth R. • Director of Technical Services • Los Angeles Public Library • Los Angeles, CA 90071 • ALCTS LAMA LITA

Higby Helen E. • Director • Sweetwater County Library Systems • Green River, WY 82935 • PLA

Higdon Mary Ann • Head of Reference Services • Texas Tech University Libraries • Lubbock, TX 79409-0002 • ACRL RASD GODORT

Higel Sandra T. • Reference Librarian • United States Air Force Academy Academy Library (DFSEL) • USAF Academy, CO 80840 • AFLRT FLRT

Higginbotham Barbra B. • Chief Librarian • Brooklyn College Library • Brooklyn, NY 11210 • ACRL LAMA LITA LHRT

Higginbotham Shirley • Director • Minnesota Valley Regional Library • Mankato, MN 56002-3446 • LAMA

Higgins Angie C. • Media Specialist • Gadsden City Schools • Gadsden, AL 35999 • AASL

Higgins Barbara J. • Library Media Specialist • Aurora South Middle School • Aurora, CO 80011 • AASL

Higgins Catherine M. • Albuquerque, NM 87105

Higgins Charles A. • Piscataway, NJ 08854

Higgins Elaine • Asst Catlg Ln • University of Montana Library • Missoula, MT 59812

Higgins Elaine I. Dr. • President • Friends of the Library of Palm Bay Inc. • Palm Bay, FL 32905

Higgins Gwen • Librarian • Quitman Independent School District • Quitman, TX 75783-1640

Higgins Janet L. • D P Production Specialist • Idaho State University Eli M. Oboler Library • Pocatello, ID 83209-8089 • LITA

Higgins John • Sales Representative • Quality Books Inc. • Lake Bluff, IL 60044-2204

Higgins Judith H. • Director of LRC • Valhalla Middle/High School Library • Valhalla, NY 10595 • AASL ACRL RASD LIRT

Higgins Mary Beth • Eastern Hancock Junior Senior High School • Charlottesville, IN 46117 • AASL

Higgins Matthew J. • Adm. of Library Operations • New Hampshire State Library • Concord, NH 03301 • ACRL

Higgins Paula • Newark, DE 19713

Higgins Renee S. • Chicago, IL 60622

Higgins Steven • New York University Elmer Holmes Bobst Library • New York, NY 10012 • ACRL RASD

Higgins Susan E. • Student • Florida State University Library Science Library • Tallahassee, FL 32306-2047

Higgins Wendy • Market Research Librarian • Wisconsin Power & Light Company • Madison, WI 53701

Higgs Kimball E. • Cataloger • The Grolier Club Library • New York, NY 10022 • ACRL

Higgs Nancy A. • Evansville-Vanderburgh County Public Library • Evansville, IN 47708-1694 • PLA SRRT

High Karen • Librarian • Glenwood High School • Chatham, IL 62629 • AASL

High Karen P. • Library Technical Assistant II • University of North Carolina • Chapel Hill, NC 27599-3902

High Walter M. • Head Cataloging • North Carolina State University • Raleigh, NC 27695 • ALCTS LAMA

Highfield Elizabeth Jane • Northbrook, IL 60062 • ACRL RASD *Life*

Highfill William C. • University Librarian • Auburn University Ralph Brown Draughon Library • Auburn, AL 36849-5606 • ACRL LAMA

Highiet Nancy • Librarian • Northwest School • Seattle, WA 98122 • AASL

Highsmith Anne L. • Head,Systems Office • Texas A & M University Sterling C. Evans Library • College Station, TX 77843-5000 • LITA RASD

Highsmith Douglas B. • Chair Dept of Public Services • California State University • Fullerton, CA 92634 • ACRL RASD

Highsmith Duncan • Highsmith Co., Inc. • Fort Atkinson, WI 53538-0800 • LITA IFRT

Highsmith June E. • Library Director • Philo Public Library District • Philo, IL 61864

Hight Mary Kay • Librarian • Christchurch School Library • Christchurch, VA 23031 • AASL

Hightower Gladys • Trustee • West Baton Rouge Parish Library • Port Allen, LA 70767

Hightower Monteria • Assoc Comm for Libs & State Ln • Missouri State Library • Jefferson City, MO 65102 • LAMA PLA

Highum Clayton • Illinois Wesleyan University Sheean Library • Bloomington, IL 61702 • ACRL

Highum Karen S. • Hd Barcoding/Monograph Recon. • University of Washington Suzzallo Library • Seattle, WA 98195 • ALCTS LITA

Higley Georgia M. • Fairfax, VA 22030 • ACRL GODORT LHRT LRRT

Higley Luella • Ft Worth, TX 76107 • AASL YALSA *Life*

Hiland Leah F. • Assistant Professor • University of Northern Iowa Department of Library Science • Cedar Falls, IA 50613-0462 • AASL LITA YALSA

Hilbert Rita L. • Maplewood, NJ 07040 • ALSC PLA RASD SORT

Hilbrink Diane L. • Librarian • Saint Joseph High School • Kenosha, WI 53140 • AASL

Hilburger Mary M. • Chicago, IL 60625 • RASD

Hilburn Maxine I. • Beaumont, TX 77713 • PLA EMIERT

Hildebrand Anna B. • Librarian • PS 197 John B. Russworm School • New York, NY 10037

Hildebrand Carol I. • Acting City Librarian • Eugene Public Library • Eugene, OR 97401 • LAMA PLA

Hildebrand Carolyn A. • Children's Librarian • Rochester Hills Public Library • Rochester, MI 48307 • ALSC

Hildebrand Jane L. • Brunswick-Glynn County Regional Library • Brunswick, GA 31523-0901

Hildebrand Janet • Youth Services Manager • Contra Costa County Library • Pleasant Hill, CA 94523 • ALSC PLA IFRT

Hildebrand Linda L. • Coor of Bibliographic Instr. • Oakland University • Rochester, MI 48309-4401 • Life

Hildebrandt Darlene Myers • Washington State University Owen Science & Engineering Library • Pullman, WA 99164-3200 • ACRL LAMA LITA

Hildebrandt Irene • Staff Specialist • Anne Arundel County Public School Library Media Services • Annapolis, MD 21401 • AASL YALSA

Hildebrandt Judith M. • Coor. Learning Resouces Ctr. • Keene State College Mason Library • Keene, NH 03431

Hildenbrand Suzanne • Associate Professor • State University of New York (SUNY) at Buffalo • Buffalo, NY 14260 • ACRL ALCTS RASD LHRT LRRT SRRT

Hildreth Charles Ray • Chief Consulting Scientist • READ Ltd. • Springfield, IL 62702 • LITA

Hildreth Susan H. • Deputy Library Director • Sacramento Public Library • Sacramento, CA 95814 • PLA

Hildum Priscilla • Trustee • Rochester Hills Public Library • Rochester, MI 48307 • ALTA

Hile Mary A. • Collections Manager • Johnson County Library • Shawnee Mission, KS 66201 • ALCTS PLA

Hilfiger Karen B. • Fond du Lac, WI 54935

Hilinski John M. • Librarian • Atlanta-Fulton Public Library • Atlanta, GA 30303 • ALCTS LAMA LITA PLA LRRT SRRT

Hilker Emerson • Head Sci & Tech Library • University of Texas at Arlington • Arlington, TX 76019-0497 • ACRL

Hill-Kipp Janette R. • Instructor of Library Services • Florida State University School of Library and Information Studies • Tallahassee, FL 32306-2048 • NMRT

Hill-Mitchell Audria D. • Student • Rosary College Graduate School of Library & Information Science • River Forest, IL 60305

Hill-Molock Eliane • Vice-President,Bd of Trustees • Atlantic City Free Public Library • Atlantic City, NJ 08401 • PLA

Hill Ann M. • Seattle, WA 98115

Hill Beverly K. • Suffolk Public Library • Suffolk, VA 23434

Hill Bonnie Naifeh • Asst Dir for Clln & Tech Serv • Tufts University Arts & Sciences Library • Medford, MA 02155

Hill Charles E. • President • Schwartz-Hill Book Company • Bethel, CT 06801

Hill Charlotte R. • Elementary Library Coordinator • Bismarck School District • Bismarck, ND 58501 • AASL

Hill Cindy • Manager • Failure Analysis Associates • Menlo Park, CA 94025 • LAMA LITA LIRT

Hill Constance • Community Librarian • Minneapolis Public Library & Information Center • Minneapolis, MN 55401-1992 • ALCTS LITA

Hill David K. • Student • State University of New York at Albany School of Information Science & Policy • Albany, NY 12222

Hill Diana J. • District Media Specialist • O'Fallon 90 School District • O'Fallon, IL 62269 • AASL

Hill Diane • Head of Educ Res Tech Services • Ball State University Bracken Library • Muncie, IN 47306-0160 • ALCTS

Hill Diane • Johnson County Public Library White River Branch • Greenwood, IN 46142 • PLA

Hill Edith A. • Arcade, NY 14009

Hill Ellyn A. • Las Vegas, NV 89128

Hill Elsie Isabel • Chula Vista, CA 92010 • ALSC *Continuing*

Hill Emily • Coor. of Library Media Center • Northern Arizona University • Flagstaff, AZ 86011-6022 • IRRT LIRT VRT

Hill Fay • Reference Librarian • Central Iowa Regional Library • Des Moines, IA 50312 • RASD

Hill George R. • Assoc Prof Music & Music Bibl • Baruch College • New York, NY 10010 • ACRL

Hill Harry M. • Librarian • Fort Worth Public Library • Fort Worth, TX 76102

Hill Helen K. • United States Court of Appeals • San Francisco, CA 94119-3939

Hill Helen Katherine • Northeastern Oklahoma State University John Vaughan Library-LRC • Tahlequah, OK 74464 • ACRL LAMA SRRT *Life*

Hill Holly K. • Librarian • United States Army • Fort Belvoir, VA 22060-5028 • AFLRT

Hill J. B. • Cuyahoga Falls, OH 44221

Hill Jane • Wellington Public Library • Wellington, New Zealand • PLA

Hill Janet A. • San Diego, CA 92130

Hill Janet B. • Librarian • Brandywine High School • Wilmington, DE 19803

Hill Janet Swan • Assistant Director of Tech. Serv • University of Colorado at Boulder Libraries • Boulder, CO 80309 • ACRL ALCTS LAMA LITA MAGERT

Hill Joanne M. • Student • University Center at Tulsa • Tulsa, OK 74106

Hill Joanne Schneider • Head, Collection Development • Middlebury College Egbert Starr Library • Middlebury, VT 05753-6007 • ACRL ALCTS

Hill John F. • Reference Librarian • Crystal Lake Public Library • Crystal Lake, IL 60014 • RASD

Hill John R. • Cataloger • Southern Connecticut State University Hilton C. Buley Library • New Haven, CT 06515 • ACRL ALCTS RASD

Hill Judith L. • Bryn Mawr, PA 19010 • ACRL

Hill Katherine H. • Getzville, NY 14068-1415 • ACRL

Hill Levirn • Assistant Librarian • State University of New York College at Buffalo, E. H. Butler Library • Buffalo, NY 14222-1095

Hill Linda Marshall • Xavier University • New Orleans, LA 70125 • GODORT

Hill Malcolm K. • Director • Mid-York Library System • Utica, NY 13502 • LAMA PLA

Hill Marian W. • Naples, FL 33962-5323

Hill Marilyn M. • Cataloger • Louisiana State University Noel Library • Shreveport, LA 71115 • ALCTS

Hill Martha J. • Palo Alto, CA 94304

Hill Martha J. • Serials Cataloger • Georgia Institute of Technology Price Gilbert Memorial Library • Atlanta, GA 30332-0900 • NMRT

Hill Mary C. • Student • State University New York at Buffalo School of Inf. & Library Studies • Buffalo, NY 14260 • AASL

Hill Mary Jane M. • Student • University of North Carolina at Chapel Hill School of Information and Library Science • Chapel Hill, NC 27599-3360 • PLA SRRT

Hill Michael John • Director Media Services • Saint Charles School District 303 • Saint Charles, IL 60174 • AASL

Hill Michael T. • Reference Librarian II • Ogelthrope Mall Library • Savannah, GA 31406 • PLA

Hill Naomi R. • Librarian • Compton Unified Sch Dist • Compton, CA 90220

Hill Norma L. • Assistant Director • Howard County Library • Columbia, MD 21044 • PLA

Hill Pamela • IMC Director • Lincoln High School • Wisconsin Rapids, WI 54494 • AASL

Hill Patricia A. • Youngstown, OH 44510 • PLA

Hill Patricia A. • School Library Media Specialist • Menomonee Fallls School District • Menomonee Falls, WI 53051 • AASL ALSC

Hill Rebecca A. • Librarian • West Millbrook Middle School • Raleigh, NC 27615 • AASL

Hill Richard C. • Reference Librarian • Richmond Public Library • Richmond, CA 94804 • EMIERT IFRT SRRT

Hill Ronni • Student • University of Arizona Graduate Library School • Tucson, AZ 85721 • EMIERT LHRT SRRT

Hill Sandra D. • Student • Villa Park Public Library • Villa Park, IL 60181 • ALCTS

Hill Sharon • Director of Public Relations • Birmingham Public Library • Birmingham, AL 35203 • LAMA

Hill Sherry R. • Student • Drexel University College of Information Studies • Philadelphia, PA 19104-2875

Hill Steven D. • Student • North Carolina Central University • Durham, NC 27707 • IFRT

Hill Sue A. • Baton Rouge, LA 70805 • AASL

Hill Susan H. • Director • Brigham City Library • Brigham City, UT 84302 • PLA

Hill Susan J. • Director • White Pine Library Cooperative • Saginaw, MI 48602-5590 • ASCLA LAMA PLA

Hill Susan L. • Student • University of North Carolina at Chapel Hill School of Information and Library Science • Chapel Hill, NC 27599-3360

Hill Susan M. • Vice-President • National Association of Broadcasters • Washington, DC 20036 • LITA

Hill Susan P. • Librarian III, Supervisor • Fresno County Free Library • Fresno, CA 93721-2285 • ALSC YALSA

Hill Suzanne P. • Librarian • Catonsville Community College • Baltimore, MD 21228 • ACRL

Hill Thomas E. • Art Librarian • Vassar College Library • Poughkeepsie, NY 12601 • ACRL IFRT LHRT

Hill Thomas W. • Librarian • Upper Savannah AHEC Self Memorial Hospital • Greenwood, SC 29646

Hill Victoria C. • General Reading Rooms Division • Library of Congress • Washington, DC 20541 • ACRL ALCTS LITA RASD GODORT LRRT

Hill Wendy Sayles • Librarian • United States Army • Fort Belvoir, VA 22060-5028 • ALCTS LITA PLA AFLRT FLRT *Life*

Hill William M. • Branch Head • Norfolk Public Library • Norfolk, VA 23510-1776 • PLA

Hillaire Pamela N. • Yng Adult Library Specialist • Lummi Library • Bellingham, WA 98226 • ACRL ALCTS EMIERT NMRT VRT

Hillcoat Donna S. • Data Research Associates Inc. • Saint Louis, MO 63132

Hillemann Beth C. • Ref Librarian-Asst Professor • University of Wisconsin-Whitewater Harold Andersen Library • Whitewater, WI 53190 • RASD

Hiller Ann M. • Seattle, WA 98116 • ACRL

Hiller Louise L. • Sandy, UT 84093-1630 • AASL ALCTS *Continuing*

Hiller Steven Z. • University of Washington • Seattle, WA 98195 • ACRL MAGERT

Hilles-Pilant Carolyn • Library Director • Wheeler School • Providence, RI 02906 • AASL

Hilliard Mary F. Mrs. • Trustee • Birmingham Public Library • Birmingham, AL 35203 • ALTA

Hilliard Thomas H. • Director • Pendleton Public Library • Pendleton, OR 97801

Hilligas Jean B. • Project Specialist • Sacramento County Office of Education • Sacramento, CA 95827

Hillis Patricia K. • Librarian • Palisades High School • Pacific Palisades, CA 90272 • AASL

Hillman Barbara • Preservation Asst. Librarian • New York State Library State Education Department • Albany, NY 12230

Hillman Kathy R. • Acquisitions Librarian • Baylor University Library • Waco, TX 76798-7026 • ACRL

Hillman Robert V. • University Archivist/Reference • Eastern Illinois University Booth Library • Charleston, IL 61920-3099 • ACRL

Hillman Stephanie • Associate Dean of Library Serv. • California State University,Fresno Henry Madden Library • Fresno, CA 93740-0034 • ACRL ALCTS LAMA LIRT

Hillman Victor L. • Trustee • Richmond Public Library • Richmond BC, V6X 2E3 Canada

Hillmann Diane I. • Librarian • Cornell University Law School Library • Ithaca, NY 14853-4901 • ALCTS LAMA LITA

Hillmer Cheryl • Arizona State Library Department of Library Archives & Public Records • Phoenix, AZ 85007 • ALCTS

Hillmer Jeanne C. • Dearborn, MI 48124

Hillmer Patricia • Director • Tiffin-Seneca Public Library • Tiffin, OH 44883 • PLA

Hills-Nova Clare E. • Riverdale, NY 10463 • ACRL GODORT

Hills Beverly D. • Library Assistant • Tidewater Community College Virginia Beach Campus Library • Virginia Beach, VA 23456

Hills Theodore S. Mr. • Cleveland, OH 44144 • LAMA PLA *Life*

Hillsamer Mark O. • Saint Albans School • Washington, DC 20016 • AASL

Hillsman Edgar L. • Atlanta, GA 30308-1129 • LAMA

Hillyard Susan E. • ETR Associates • Santa Cruz, CA 95061-1830 • LITA

Hils Cheryl L. • Student • State University of New York (SUNY) School of Information & Library Studies • Buffalo, NY 14260 • PLA

Hilt Elizabeth M. • Director of Student Services • Pacific Graduate School of Psychology Library • Palo Alto, CA 94303

Hilton Joseph M. Jr • Library Supervisor • Free Library of Philadelphia West Philadelphia Regional • Philadelphia, PA 19139 • NMRT

Hilton Linda D. • Director of the Libraries • Haverford School • Haverford, PA 19041

Hilton Margaret Lewis • Librarian • Gleason Public Library • Carlisle, MA 01741

Hilton Marjorie • Volunteer Coordinator • Weber County Library • Odgen, UT 84401

Hilton Robert B. • Director • Lees College • Jackson, KY 41339 • ACRL

Hilton Robert C. • Director • Cary Memorial Library • Lexington, MA 02173 • ALCTS ALSC PLA RASD

Hilton Sylvia C. • Lakewood, NJ 08701 • Continuing

Hilton Victoria K. • Librarian • Harper Woods Public Library • Harper Woods, MI 48225

Hilyard Lorna C. • Children's Librarian • Park Ridge Public Library • Park Ridge, IL 60068-4188 • ALSC

Hilyard Nann Blaine • Library Director • Auburn Public Library • Auburn, ME 04210 • PLA

Himan Douglas E. • Student • University of Rhode Island Graduate School of Library & Information Studies • Kingston, RI 02881-0815

Himber Lorraine L. • Director • Butler County Traveling Library • Butler, PA 16001

Hime Laurie H. • Librarian • Miami Dade Community College • Miami, FL 33176 • ACRL

Himel Sandra M. • University of Southwestern Louisiana Libraries • Lafayette, LA 70503 • GODORT SRRT

Himelfarb Irene • Librarian Media Specialist • Maryvale Prep School • Brooklandville, MD 21022 • AASL YALSA

Himes Dana M. • Student • University of Wisconsin-Milwaukee School of Library & Information Science • Milwaukee, WI 53201 • ACRL

Himes Nancy • Newport, VA 23606 • Continuing

Himmel Ethel E. • Himmel & Wilson • Milwaukee, WI 53201-1413 • ASCLA PLA

Himmel Ned A. • Head Reference & Adult Services • Redwood City Public Library • Redwood City, CA 94063-1868

Himmelberg Frances E. • Madison, CT 06443

Hinaber Jacqueline • Trustee • Mount Prospect Public Library • Mount Prospect, IL 60056 • PLA

Hinchcliff Marilou Z. • Catalog Librarian • Bloomsburg University Harvey A. Andruss Library • Bloomsburg, PA 17815 • ALCTS

Hinchliff Constance G. • California State University San Marcos • San Marcos, CA 92069-0001 • IFRT NMRT SRRT

Hinchliff Mary W. • Branch Manager Librarian • Santa Cruz City-County Library System • Santa Cruz, CA 95060

Hinckley Steven D. • Director of the Law Library • University of Richmond • Richmond, VA 23173 • ASCLA

Hinderliter Alison A. • Archival Technician • Newberry Library • Chicago, IL 60610

Hindes Debra L. • Reading, MA 01867 • RASD SRRT

Hindman Pamela J. • Arlington County Department of Libraries • Arlington, VA 22201

Hindmarsh Douglas P. • Grants Coor./Library Consultant • Utah State Library • Salt Lake City, UT 84115-2579 • ASCLA LAMA PLA RASD

Hinds Sharon M. • Brooklyn, NY 11218

Hinds Vira C. Dr. • Somers, NY 10589

Hine Betsy N. • Head, Monographic Cataloging • Indiana State University Cunningham Memorial Library • Terre Haute, IN 47809 • ACRL ALCTS

Hine Janet D. • Mosman NSW 2088, Australia • ALCTS *Continuing*

Hines Cordie R. • Branch Manager • Dallas Public Library Walnut Hill Branch • Dallas, TX 75220-4496

Hines Dana L. • Director • Lyon County Library • Yerington, NV 89447 • LAMA PLA

Hines Ellen K. • Assistant Dept. Head, Tech Serv. • Arlington Heights Memorial Library • Arlington Heights, IL 60004-5966 • ALCTS

Hines George • Trustee • Nantahala Regional Library • Murphy, NC 28906 • ALTA

Hines Julie K. • Children's Librarian • El Paso Public Library Westside Branch • El Paso, TX 79912

Hines Lisa • Library Assistant III • Rice University Fondren Library • Houston, TX 77251-1892

Hines Lori A. • Student • Saint John's University Division of Library & Information Science • Jamaica, NY 11439

Hines Patricia S. • Asst Chief Spec Materials Catlg Div • Library of Congress • Washington, DC 20541 • ALCTS ALSC *Life*

Hines Richard W. • Consulting Librarian • Duke University • Durham, NC 27708

Hinkle E. Douglas • Wheatland High School • Wheatland, WY 82201 • ACRL

Hinkle Kristina • Kodiak, AK 99615

Hinkle Sharon L. • Adult Services Librarian • Long Branch Public Library • Long Branch, NJ 07740 • YALSA

Hinkle Terri-Leigh • Acquisitions Librarian • University of New Hampshire Library • Durham, NH 03824

Hinkle Vivian L. • Pittsburgh, PA 15213

Hinkley Eve • Student • California State University • Fullerton, CA 92634 • PLA EMIERT IFRT SRRT

Hinkley William A. • Serials Cataloger • Library of Congress • Washington, DC 20541

Hinks Yvonne R. • Hd., Hum., Arts, Social Sci. • University of Calgary Libraries • Calgary AB, T2N 1N4 Canada • ACRL

Hinman Barry E. • Assistant Librarian • Stanford University Libraries Cecil H. Green Library • Stanford, CA 94305-6004 • ACRL ALCTS

Hinnebusch Mark T. • Assistant Director • Florida Center for Library Automation • Gainesville, FL 32609 • LITA NMRT

Hinogosh Monica • Corpus Christi, TX 78412

Hinojosa Susana A. • Librarian III • University of California-Berkeley University Library • Berkeley, CA 94720 • ACRL EMIERT

Hinrichs Frieda A. • East Lansing, MI 48823 • ACRL ALCTS *Continuing*

Hinrichs M. Margaret • Bryan, TX 77802

Hinrichs Pauline E. • Livonia, MI 48150

Hinsdale Karen • Trustee • Multnomah County Library • Portland, OR 97212 • ALTA

Hinshaw Carole S. • Reference Librarian • University of Central Florida • Orlando, FL 32816 • ACRL IFRT LIRT

Hinshaw Kevin L. • Librarian • Sedgwick County Law Library • Wichita, KS 67202

Hinshaw Marilyn L. • Director • Eastern Oklahoma District Library System • Muskogee, OK 74401 • LAMA PLA

Hinson Claudia J. • Librarian • Joseph Zito Elementary School • Phoenix, AZ 85035 • AASL

Hinson Lucalia A. • Oklahoma City, OK 73107 • AASL ALSC

Hinson Susan • Librarian • Graham Independent School District • Graham, TX 76046 • AASL YALSA

Hintereder Helen • Cotati, CA 94931

Hinton Frances • Philedelphia, PA 19144 • ALCTS LITA IRRT

Hinton Kathleen M. • Library Media Specialist • Denver Public Schools • Denver, CO 80220 • LITA EMIERT

Hinton Patricia G. • Student • North Carolina Central University School of Library & Information Science • Durham, NC 27707 • YALSA

Hinton Paula P. • BA/SS Reference Dept. • University of North Carolina Walter Royal Davis Library • Chapel Hill, NC 27599-3924 • ACRL RASD

Hinton Robert A. • Acting Head, Gov. Documents • Miami University Edgar W. King Library • Oxford, OH 45056

Hinton Susan R. • Student • University of Michigan School of Information and Library Studies • Ann Arbor, MI 48109-1092 • SRRT

Hintz Carl W. • Librarian Emeritus • University of Oregon Library • Eugene, OR 97403-1299 • Continuing

Hintz Jeanne E. • Director • Geneva Public Library District • Geneva, IL 60134 • PLA

Hintzman Christine Kay • Student • University of Illinois Graduate School of Library and Information Science • Urbana, IL 61801

Hintzman Douglas M. • Student • University of Wisconsin-Milwaukee School of Library & Information Science • Milwaukee, WI 53201 • NMRT SRRT

Hinz Julianne P. • Assistant Director for Pub Serv • University of Utah Marriott Library • Salt Lake City, UT 84112-1179 • ACRL LAMA RASD GODORT

Hiott Judith H. • Librarian, Humanities Dept. • Houston Public Library • Houston, TX 77002 • PLA RASD

Hiott Suzanne • Wilson Hall • Sumter, SC 29150 • AASL

Hipke Karen • Whole Language Workshop • Pasco, WA 99302

Hipkens Sue • Librarian • Trinity School Upper School Library • New York, NY 10024

Hipp Caroline L. • Dublin, GA 31021

Hippenhammer Craighton • Reference Librarian • Olivet Nazarene University Benner Library & Resource Center • Kankakee, IL 60901-0592 • ACRL LITA IFRT

Hipps Julie • Librarian • Hale High School Library • Raleigh, NC 27619

Hipsher Jo • Librarian • Brunswick High School • Brunswick, ME 04011 • AASL

Hirabayashi Joanne V. • Coordinator • Novato Unified School District • Novato, CA 94945 • ALSC

Hirata Yasuko • Student • Columbia University Libraries Butler Library • New York, NY 10027 • LITA IFRT IRRT

Hird John • Red Bank Regional High School • Little Silver, NJ 07739 • AASL LITA

Hirko Bobbie • Word Merchant • Gig Harbor, WA 98335 • LAMA PLA CLENE

Hiron Barbara A. • Beaconsfield Public Library • Beaconsfield PQ, H9W 4A7 Canada • ALSC YALSA

Hirons Jean L. • Supervisory Librarian • Library of Congress • Washington, DC 20541 • ALCTS LIRT

Hirooka Kathleen • Albany, CA 94706

Hirose Peter I. • Institute of Transpersonal Psychology Library • Menlo Park, CA 94025

Hirosmi Iwamoto • Director of Library Services • Osaka International University Library • Osaka-fu 573-01, Japan • ACRL ALCTS LITA RASD

Hirsch Beverly J. • Librarian • Heritage School of Kendall • Miami, FL 33186

Hirsch David G. • Jewish Studies Bibliographer • UCLA Library University Research Library • Los Angeles, CA 90024-1575 • ACRL IRRT

Hirsch Jane K. • Rockville, MD 20852 • IFRT

Hirsch Marie H. • Student • Saint John's University Division of Library & Information Science • Jamaica, NY 11439

Hirsch Peter J. • Supervisor • Muze, Inc. • Brooklyn, NY 11211

Hirsch Sol M. • Trustee • Metro Dade County Office of Management and Budget • Miami, FL 33128 • LAMA PLA

Hirsch Steven P. • MayaTech Corporation • Silver Spring, MD 20902 • ILERT

Hirschberg Carol T. • Oceanside, NY 11572

Hirschberg Jeanne • Trustee • Topeka Public Library • Topeka, KS 66604-1374

Hirschi Cheryl E. • Adult Services Coordinator • Peter White Public Library • Marquette, MI 49855

Hirschi Michael J. • Library Media Teacher • Roy High Library • Roy, UT 84067 • AASL

Hirschi Virginia • Reference Librarian • Central Michigan University Charles V. Park Library 315 • Mount Pleasant, MI 48859 • ACRL LITA

Hirschman Rita J. • Student • University of Iowa School of Library & Information Science • Iowa City, IA 52242 • ALSC PLA LHRT

Hirschman Susan • Editor-In-Chief • Greenwillow Books • New York, NY 10016 • ALSC YALSA

Hirshberg Ann B. • Tampa, FL 33618

Hirshfield Laura • Audiovisual Librarian • Evanston Public Library • Evanston, IL 60201

Hirshon Arnold • Director • Wright State University • Dayton, OH 45435 • ACRL ALCTS LAMA LITA

Hirst Donna L. • Manager of Library Automation • University of Iowa Libraries • Iowa City, IA 52242-1379 • LAMA LITA

Hirst Ella J. • Student • University of California-Berkeley School of Library & Information Studies • Berkeley, CA 94720 • RASD

Hirst Jane E. • Children's Librarian • Thomas Hackney Braswell Memorial Library • Rocky Mount, NC 27804 • ALSC

Hirt Janet R. • Associate Director • Widener University School of Law • Harrisburg, PA 17110-9450 • ACRL LAMA GODORT

Hirt Terri A. • Adult Program Librarian • Los Altos Public Library • Los Altos, CA 94022

Hisatsune Kimi • San Francisco, CA 94109 • ALCTS *Continuing*

Hiseley Rick • Sacramento Public Library • Sacramento, CA 95814 • LAMA

Hisle W. Lee • Dir., Learning Resource Services • Austin Community College Learning Resource Services • Austin, TX 78701 • ACRL

Hisrich Jennifer D. • Fort Collins, CO 80526-3605

Hiss Sheila M. • Director of Library Services • North Florida Junior College Library • Madison, FL 32340 • ACRL

Histand Willard G. Mr. • President Board of Directors • Bucks County Free Library • Doylestown, PA 18901 • ALTA

Hisz Evelyn • Associate Professor • Borough of Manhattan Community College Randolph Memorial Library • New York, NY 10007

Hitchcock-Mort Karen A. • Acquisitions Librarian • Orange County Public Library • Santa Ana, CA 92705 • ALCTS

Hitchcock Charlene R. • Pennsylvania State University Pattee Library • University Park, PA 16802

Hitchcock Constance A. • Educational Media Specialist • Clark Mills School • Englishtown, NJ 07726 • AASL

Hitchcock Eloise R. • Tennessee Technological University • Cookeville, TN 38505 • IFRT

Hitchcock Gail A. • Cataloging Librarian • Occidental College Library • Los Angeles, CA 90041 • ALCTS

Hitchcock John • Tennessee Technological University University Library • Cookeville, TN 38505 • ALCTS

Hitchcock Leonard A. • Head, Collection Development • Idaho State University Eli M. Oboler Library • Pocatello, ID 83209-8089 • ACRL

Hitchens Susan H. • Lawrence, KS 66046-5043 • ACRL

Hitchingham Eileen E. • Dean of Library Services • Drexel University W. W. Hagerty Library • Philadelphia, PA 19104 • ACRL LAMA

Hitchings Donna P. • Carolina Power & Light • Raleigh, NC 27602 • LAMA RASD VRT

Hite Debby S. • Greenville Street Elementary School • Abbeville, SC 29620 • AASL ALSC

Hitt Charles J. • Reference Librarian • Mankato State University Memorial Library • Mankato, MN 56001 • ACRL LITA

Hitt Gail • Fordham University • Bronx, NY 10458 • ACRL

Hitt Raymond W. • Assistant Director • Texas State Library • Austin, TX 78711

Hitt Samuel • Chapel Hill, NC 27516 • ACRL LAMA *Continuing*

Hittle Barbara K. • Librarian • Indianapolis Marion County Public Library • Indianapolis, IN 46206

Hitzfelder Lucy M. • Southside High School • San Antonio, TX 78221 • AASL

Hixon Cecil • Adult Services • The New York Public Library • New York, NY 10016 • PLA EMIERT

Hixon Jeff • System Consultant • North Central Kansas Ls • Manhattan, KS 66502 • PLA

Hixson Charles R. III • History Selector/Clln. Devel. • University of Florida Libraries • Gainesville, FL 32611-2047

Hizer Marlene • Nevada Public Library • Nevada, MO 64772 • PLA

Hjelmeland Margaret M. • Clln Development Specialist • Lake Lanier Regional Library Lawrenceville Branch • Lawrenceville, GA 30245-4707

Hjemboe Philip J. • Student • University of Iowa School of Library & Information Science • Iowa City, IA 52242 • LITA PLA

Hjort Illah D. • Carmel Valley, CA 93924 • AASL YALSA *Life*

Hladky Beverly P. • Librarian/Youth Services • Tampa-Hillsborough County Public Library • Tampa, FL 33602

Hlavaty Anna M. • Librarian • Passmore Elementary School • San Antonio, TX 78227 • Life

Hlinak Susan J. • Library Media Special • Senior High School • New London, WI 54961 • AASL

Hnateyko-Charkewycz Roxana • Chicago, IL 60622 • ACRL

Ho Agnes W. • Associate Director • Neuse Regional Library System • Kinston, NC 28501 • PLA

Ho Birong A. • Tech Services Librarian II • Wayne State University • Detroit, MI 48202 • ALCTS LITA

Ho Clare • Librarian • Midkiff Learning Center Kamehameha Schools • Honolulu, HI 96817

Ho Dora • San Grabriel, CA 91776-4248 • NMRT

Ho Gene Y. I. • Assistant Librarian II • Hong Kong University of Science & Technology University Library • Kowloon, Hong Kong

Ho James • Assistant Director • Howard University Libraries Founders Library • Washington, DC 20059

Ho Maria M.L. • London ON, N6G 2H1 Canada

Ho Pao-Fen • East Texas State University Library • Commerce, TX 75428

Ho Sheila K. • Librarian • Santa Clara County Free Library Milpitas Community Library • Milpitas, CA 95035

Ho Virginia M. Y. • Dow Chemical Canada, Inc Modeland Centre Library • Sarnia, ON, N7T 7K7 Canada

Ho Yan-Sheung • Student • University of Kentucky College of Library & Information Science • Lexington, KY 40506-0391

Hoadley Irene B. • Director • Texas A & M University Sterling C. Evans Library • College Station, TX 77843-5000 • ACRL ALCTS LAMA LRRT *Life*

Hoag Edward A. • West Trenton, NJ 08628 • YALSA

Hoag Robert Edward • St Paul, MN 55101

Hoage Elizabeth A. • Los Angeles Public Library Expositition Park Branch • Los Angeles, CA 90007 • ALSC PLA

Hoagland Antoinette • Library Supervisor I • Free Library of Philadelphia • Philadelphia, PA 19103

Hoagland Monica M. • Student • Black Hills State University • Spearfish, SD 57799-9548 • AASL IFRT LHRT

Hoar Luva Mead • Chairman, Board of Directors • Portland Public Library • Portland, CT 06480 • ALTA

Hoard Kimberly • St. Louis, MO 63121

Hoban Michele E. • Assistant Reference Librarian • Jersey City State College Forrest A Irwin Library • Jersey City, NJ 07305-1597 • ACRL GODORT

Hoban Michi S. • Dartmouth College Library Baker Memorial Library • Hanover, NH 03755-3525 • ACRL ALCTS

Hobbs Brian E. • Acquisitions • University of Alberta • Edmonton AB, T6G 2J8 Canada

Hobbs Ellen • Dallas, TX 75248 • PLA

Hobbs Harriett • Librarian Serials Department • Northeastern Oklahoma State University John Vaughan Library-LRC • Tahlequah, OK 74464 • ACRL ALCTS LITA

Hobbs Jim • Reference Librarian • Loyola University Library • New Orleans, LA 70118

Hobbs Marilyn J. • Library Manager • Arapahoe Library District • Littleton, CO 80121 • LAMA PLA

Hobbs Thomas C. • Head of Public Services • University of South Carolina at Aiken Gregg-Graniteville Library • Aiken, SC 29801

Hobday Barbara F. • Assistant Director • Frederick County Public Library C. Burr Artz Library • Frederick, MD 21701 • PLA YALSA SORT

Hobeika George L. • TSD Librarian • Florence County Library • Florence, SC 29501

Hobert Collin B. • Iowa State University Library • Ames, IA 50011-2140 • ALCTS LITA

Hobrock Brice G. • Dean of Libraries • Kansas State University Farrell Library • Manhattan, KS 66506-1200 • ACRL

Hobson Jane G. • Georgia State University Pullen Library • Atlanta, GA 30303-3081 • RASD

Hobson Mary A. • Principal Librarian • San Diego County Library • San Diego, CA 92123

Hobson Mary K. • Librarian • Vermillion Primary • Maize, KS 67101 • AASL ALSC

Hobson Sara J. • Media Specialist • Heritage Junior Senior High School • Monroeville, IN 46773 • AASL

Hocevar Ann • Gainesville, FL 32607

Hoch Kenneth M. • Vice President • Jerry Alper Inc • Eastchester, NY 10707

Hochberg Carol R. • Librarian • Long Island Library Resources Council, Inc. • Stony Brook, NY 11794 • RASD

Hochberg Jean B. • Young Adult Librarian • Fairfax County Public Schools Beech Tree Elementary Sch • Falls Church, VA 22042 • AASL

Hochman Mary A. • San Pedro, CA 90732 • LITA

Hochstein Nancy M. • Media Specialist • Clinton Middle School • Clinton, MA 01510 • AASL ALSC

Hochstetler Donald D. • Director • Marian College Library • Indianapolis, IN 46222 • ACRL RASD

Hochstetler Ralph E. • Media Specialist • High School • Batesville, IN 47006 • AASL

Hock Paula C. • Reference Librarian • County of Los Angeles Public Library Lancaster Library 101 • Lancaster, CA 93534 • ACRL IFRT IRRT SRRT

Hockel Kathleen L. • Thousand Oaks Library • Thousand Oaks, CA 91362 • PLA

Hocker Justine L. • Director Emeritus • Haverford Township Free Library • Havertown, PA 19083 • ALSC RASD

Hocker Margaret L. • La Crosse, WI 54601 • Continuing

Hocker Susan E. • Head Science Librarian • Miami University Brill Science Library • Oxford, OH 45056 • ACRL LITA RASD

Hocker Vickie • Library Director • Dittlinger Memorial Library • New Braunfels, TX 78130 • PLA

Hockett Joanne N. • Branch Manager • Sonoma County Library • Santa Rosa, CA 95404

Hockstad Catherine C. • Reference Librarian • Escanaba Public Library • Escanaba, MI 49829 • PLA

Hodapp Patricia Conor • Director of Marketing • Denver Public Library • Denver, CO 80204-2602 • LAMA PLA

Hodczak Rose M. • Head, Adult Services • Barrington Area Library • Barrington, IL 60010

Hodd Rebecca A. • Student • Clarion University of Pennsylvania • Clarion, PA 16214 • LITA

Hodell Jack E. • Library Planner& Consultant • Jack E. Hodell Consultants • Cincinnati, OH 45227

Hodes Charlotte • Assistant Librarian • Monona Public Library • Monona, WI 53716

Hodes Jacqueline B. • New York, NY 10009

Hodge Blanca I.Th.M. • Librarian • Philipsburg Jubilee Library • Antilles, Netherlands
Hodge Daniel H. • Librarian • Data Center • Oakland, CA 94612-2294 • IFRT SRRT
Hodge Gail L. • Mac Cmd Librarian • United States Air Force Air Weather Service Technical Library • Scott AFB, IL 62225-5458 • AFLRT FLRT
Hodge Jonathan R. • Trumbull, CT 06611 • ACRL ALCTS LITA
Hodge Peggye D. • Easley, SC 29641
Hodge Stanley P. • Director of Collection Devel. • Ball State University Bracken Library • Muncie, IN 47306-0160 • ACRL ALCTS
Hodge Thomas A. • Director • Fort Dodge Public Library • Ft. Dodge, IA 50501 • PLA RASD
Hodges Anita • Librarian • Forrest City High School • Forrest City, AR 72335
Hodges Bonnie A. • Access Servs. Coordinator • Centenary College of Louisiana • Shreveport, LA 71134-1188 • ACRL
Hodges Celeste J. • Student • Rutgers University School of Communication Information & Library Studies • New Brunswick, NJ 08903
Hodges Doreen • Assistant Director • Valdez Consortium L • Valdez, AK 99686
Hodges Eleanor A. • Librarian • Saint Louis Special School District • St. Louis, MO 63131 • AASL
Hodges Elizabeth J. • Cambridge, MA 02138 • Continuing
Hodges F. Holly • Reference Librarian • South Norfolk Memorial Library • Chesapeake, VA 23324
Hodges Gerald G. • Dir. Membership Services/CR • American Library Association • Chicago, IL 60611-2795 • YALSA IFRT
Hodges Katherine A. • Real Estate Broker • Bristolecone Real Estate • Alma, CO 80420
Hodges Laura J. • Library Program Administrator • State Library of Florida Division of Library & Information Services • Tallahassee, FL 32399-0250 • ASCLA
Hodges Lois I. • Esperance, NY 12066 • ALSC
Hodges Mari Katherine • Head of Library Automation & Sys • Marymount University Reinsch Library • Arlington, VA 22207-4299 • ALCTS
Hodges Regina M. Ms. • Librarian/Media Specialist • North Drive Middle School • Hopkinsville, KY 42240 • ALSC
Hodges Rose M. • Roslindle, MA 02131
Hodges Ruth A. • Reference Librarian • Howard University Libraries Founders Library • Washington, DC 20059
Hodges Theodora L. • Berkeley, CA 94708 • ACRL LITA
Hodges Valerie C. • Reference Librarian • Olathe Public Library • Olathe, KS 66061
Hodgkins Mary O. • Morehouse Parish Library • Bastrop, LA 71220 • PLA
Hodgson Clarice • Librarian • Brooklyn Public Library • Brooklyn, NY 11238 • PLA
Hodgson Elizabeth A. • Niagara County Community College Faculty Resource Center • Sanborn, NY 14132
Hodgson Michael • Director • Merrick Public Library • Merrick, NY 11566 • PLA
Hodis Haydee C. • Springfield Library/Museums Association • Springfield, MA 01103 • EMIERT
Hodkin Katherine • Library Media Specialist • Salt Lake City Public Schools • Salt Lake City, UT 84103 • AASL
Hodlofski Carol • Librarian • Cape May County Library • Cape May, NJ 08204 • AASL PLA
Hodock Irene H. • Byesville, OH 43723 • ASCLA *Continuing*
Hodos Susan G. • Librarian III-Branch Librarian • Broward County Public Library Margate Branch • Margate, FL 33063 • LAMA PLA
Hodosy Kenneth G. Jr. • Director • Roswell P. Flower Memorial Library • Watertown, NY 13601 • PLA
Hodowanec George V. • University of Akron University Library & Learning Resource • Akron, OH 44325-1707 • ACRL ALCTS LAMA
Hodson James L. • University of Minnesota Walter Library • Minneapolis, MN 55455 • ACRL LITA RASD
Hodson Kay E. • Assistand Head, Adult Services • Dayton & Montgomery County Public Library • Dayton, OH 45402-2103 • LITA PLA RASD *Life*
Hodson Sara S. • Curator, Lit MSS • Huntington Library • San Marino, CA 91108 • ACRL
Hoduski Bernadine Abbott • Professional Staff Member • United States Congress Joint Committee on Printing • Washington, DC 20510 • ALCTS LITA EMIERT FLRT GODORT IRRT MAGERT SRRT
Hoecker Heidi A. • Escondido, CA 92027 • AASL
Hoef Gail L. • Downers Grove, IL 60516
Hoefer Christine A. • Media Specialist • Richfield School District • Richfield, WI 53076
Hoegh Gloria • Winnefox Library System • Oshkosh, WI 54901-4985 • ASCLA LAMA PLA
Hoehn Ann I. • Student • Pratt Institute Graduate School of Library & Information Science • Brooklyn, NY 11205
Hoehn Diana L. • Student • Wayne State University Library Science Program • Detroit, MI 48202 • RASD
Hoehn Eleanor • Milwaukee, WI 53222 • Continuing
Hoehn Philip • Map Librarian • University of California-Berkeley University Library • Berkeley, CA 94720 • ACRL GODORT MAGERT
Hoehne Audrey C.G. • Student • University of Arizona Graduate Library School • Tucson, AZ 85721
Hoehne Marilyn E. • Marietta, GA 30062 • AASL
Hoekzema Leslie G. • Cataloging Librarian • Kenton County Public Library • Covington, KY 41011 • ALCTS LITA
Hoel Linda Jeanette • Assistant Command Librarian • Langley Air Force Base • Langley AFB, VA 23665 • AFLRT
Hoelle Dolores M. • Engineering Librarian • Princeton University • Princeton, NJ 08544-2098 • ACRL RASD
Hoelle Robin • Cincinnati, OH 45218
Hoelzen Randall W. • Reference/Bibliographic Instr Ln • University of Wisconsin Murphy Library • La Crosse, WI 54601 • RASD IFRT LIRT
Hoemann Cheryl Ann • High School Librarian • Montgomery County R-II Schools • Montgomery City, MO 63361 • AASL YALSA
Hoeppner Christopher J. • Student • University of Wisconsin-Madison School of Library & Information Studies • Madison, WI 53706 • RASD
Hoerle Darrel D. • Librarian • United States Army Fort Riley Post Library • Fort Riley, KS 66442 • PLA AFLRT
Hoerman Heidi L. • Student • Indiana University School of Library and Information Science • Bloomington, IN 47405 • ACRL ALCTS LRRT
Hoermann Colene D. • Librarian & Instructor • Our Lady of the Lake University • San Antonio, TX 78207-4666 • AASL ALSC
Hoey Anita B. • Sr. Librarian • Fullerton Public Library Hunt Branch • Fullerton, CA 92633 • ALSC
Hofer James D. • Archivist • San Bernardino County Library • San Bernardino, CA 92415-0795 • RASD
Hoff Jennifer C. • Serials Acquisitionist • Emerson College Library • Boston, MA 02116
Hoff Julie A. • Asst. Documents & Map Librarian • University of Kansas Library • Lawrence, KS 66045-2800 • ACRL GODORT MAGERT
Hoff Vickie • Media Specialist • Rawlins High School • Rawlins, WY 82301 • AASL
Hoffberg Judith A. • Director • Umbrella Assoc • Pasadena, CA 91114
Hoffer Beth • Reference Librarian • Bradford College Hemingway Library • Haverhill, MA 01835 • ACRL
Hoffert Barbara • Senior Editor, Book Review • Library Journal Cahners Publishing Company • New York, NY 10011
Hoffman Andrea C. • Library Director • Wheelock College Library • Boston, MA 02215 • ACRL
Hoffman Anne • Appleton Public Library • Appleton, WI 54911-4780 • ALSC
Hoffman Carol • Jerusalem 94103, Israel • ACRL ASCLA LAMA LITA PLA RASD CLENE IRRT LRRT
Hoffman David R. • Director Library Services Div. • State Library of Pennsylvania Department of Education • Harrisburg, PA 17105 • ACRL LITA *Life*
Hoffman Douglas S. • Tyrrell County Public Library • Columbia, NC 27925
Hoffman E. P. • Director • Haverford Township Free Library • Havertown, PA 19083 • PLA
Hoffman Elaine R. • Asst. Librarian Serials • State University of New York (SUNY) Frank Melville Jr. Memorial Library • Stony Brook, NY 11794-3300 • ACRL EMIERT NMRT
Hoffman Frances F. • Reference Librarian • Wyckoff Public Library • Wyckoff, NJ 07481
Hoffman Irene M. • Sales Manager • Online Computer Library Center (OCLC) Pacific Network • Rancho Cucamonga, CA 91730 • ACRL
Hoffman Jay J. • Ref. Doucments/Gov't Lib • Kentucky State University Blazer Library • Frankfort, KY 40601
Hoffman Jeffrey R. • Student • Indiana University School of Library and Information Science • Bloomington, IN 47405
Hoffman Jennifer M. • Assistant Librarian • Lackawanna Public Library • Lackawanna, NY 14218
Hoffman Kathryn J. • Director • University of Texas Southwestern Medical Center at Dallas Library • Dallas, TX 75235-9049 • ACRL LAMA
Hoffman Lavinia J. • Cleveland, OH 44143 • ALSC *Continuing*
Hoffman Louise J. • Assoc. Ed., Social Sci. Index • H. W. Wilson Company • Bronx, NY 10452 • RASD
Hoffman Maria T. • Branch Supervisor • Wake County Public Library System Wendell Branch • Wendell, NC 27591
Hoffman Pamela • Montreal PQ, H4W 1V5 Canada • PLA
Hoffman Paul S. • OCLC Network Coodinator • Nebraska Library Commission • Lincoln, NE 68508 • LITA
Hoffman Preston J. • Valdese Public Library • Valdese, NC 28690 • PLA
Hoffman Sandra D. • Reference/Selection Libn-Comm. • Concordia University Libraries • Montreal PQ, H3G 1M8 Canada • ACRL RASD
Hoffman Sharon L. • Administrative Librarian • Addison Public Library • Addison, IL 60101-2499 • LAMA PLA
Hoffman Susan J. • Reference & Instruction Ln. • University of Minnesota • Minneapolis, MN 55455 • ACRL
Hoffman William H. • Librarian • Lee County Library System • Fort Myers, FL 33901
Hoffmann Artis Ann • McCulloch Middle School • Marion, IN 46953 • AASL
Hoffmann Beth A. • San Francisco, CA 94131
Hoffmann Christa • Head Catalog Section • National Library of Medicine • Bethesda, MD 20894 • ACRL ALCTS LITA FLRT
Hoffmann Ellen • University Librarian • York University Libraries • North York ON, M3J 1P3 Canada • ACRL ALCTS LAMA LITA RASD
Hoffmann Frances P. • Librarian • Palo Alto College • San Antonio, TX 78224 • ACRL
Hoffmann Ginny • Librarian • Saint Martin's Episcopal School Library Martin Family Library • Metairie, LA 70003
Hoffmann John • Facilities Planner • Cornell University 213 Olin Library • Ithaca, NY 14853-5301 • LAMA
Hoffmann Lois K. • Branch Head • Rochester Public Library Winton Branch • Rochester, NY 14609 • ALSC
Hoffmann Paul E. • Petaluma, CA 94954 • Continuing
Hoffmann Rita J. • Chairperson Librarian • Chicago Public Library Sulzer Regional Library • Chicago, IL 60625 • ALSC PLA IFRT
Hoffmann Walter • Houston, TX 77006-5816
Hoffpauir Dian • Director • Ada County District Library • Boise, ID 83709
Hofland Freda B. • Ref. Serv. Program Manager • San Mateo County Library • San Mateo, CA 94402
Hofmann Anne J. • 2 • New York Public Library Donnell Library Center • New York, NY 10019 • PLA IFRT
Hofmann Judith M • Library/Media Specialist • Mowrey Elememtary School • Quincy, PA 17247 • AASL
Hofmann Patricia • Librarian • Calvert County Public Library • Prince Frederick, MD 20678 • PLA
Hofmann Roger M. • Assistant Editor • H. W. Wilson Company • Bronx, NY 10452 • ACRL
Hofsas Elizabeth • Hamden, CT 06514 • ACRL ALCTS LITA *Life*
Hofschield Kathleen S. • Mead Public Library • Sheboygan, WI 53081 • ALSC
Hofstede Diane • Trustee • Minneapolis Public Library & Information Center • Minneapolis, MN 55401-1992 • ALTA PLA
Hofstetter Eleanore O. • Associate Director • Towson State University • Towson, MD 21204
Hogan Alan D. • Dir. of Library Sys & Processing • University of Toledo William S. Carlson Library • Toledo, OH 43606-3399 • ACRL
Hogan Donna R. • Metropolitan Library System in Oklahoma Southern Oaks Branch • Oklahoma City, OK 73139-7299 • RASD NMRT
Hogan Eddy • California State University-Sacramento Library • Sacramento, CA 95819-6039 • ACRL RASD
Hogan Gerard P. • Document Librarian • Central Washington University • Ellensburg, WA 98926 • MAGERT
Hogan James E. • College of the Holy Cross Dinand Library • Worcester, MA 01610 • ACRL ALCTS LAMA LITA
Hogan Janice A. • Library Assistant • Washburn University of Topeka Mabee Library • Topeka, KS 66621 • YALSA
Hogan Lisa A. • Referene Librarian • Palm Beach Community College -E • Palm Beach Gardens, FL 33410 • RASD
Hogan Louise G. • Director • Seneca Public Library • Seneca, IL 61360 • PLA
Hogan Nell Paige • Reference Librarian • Sholas Community College • Muscle Shoals, AL 35662
Hogan Patricia M. • Administrative Librarian • Poplar Creek Public Library Dist • Streamwood, IL 60107 • LAMA PLA RASD
Hogan Peggy • Promotion Dir Ch Trade Div L Serv • Houghton Mifflin Company Library • Boston, MA 02108 • AASL
Hogan Sarah T. • Head Bibliographic Control • University of North Texas • Denton, TX 76203 • ACRL ALCTS LITA
Hogan Sharon A. • University Librarian • University of Illinois at Chicago • Chicago, IL 60680 • ACRL RASD IFRT LIRT SRRT *Life*

Hogan Suzanne Hess • Childrens Young Adult Librarian • Weber Conty Library Southwest Branch • Roy, UT 84067

Hogan Thomas J. • Reference Librarian • Chicago Public Library Harold Washington Library • Chicago, IL 60605

Hogge Karin Waters • Newport News, VA 23602 • AASL

Hoggs Marie • Gary Public Library • Gary, IN 46402

Hogue Elizabeth M. • San Jose State University Clark Library • San Jose, CA 95192-0028 • SORT

Hogue Margaret • Florida Center for Library Automation • Gainesville, FL 32609 • LAMA

Hoh Jennifer L. • Student • University of Texas at Austin Graduate School of Library & Information Sciences • Austin, TX 78712-1276

Hohe Mary J. • Professor • Kutztown University Rohrbach Library • Kutztown, PA 19530-0721 • ACRL

Hohl Robert Joseph • Reference & Instruction Ln • Saint Mary's College Cushwa-Leighton Library • Notre Dame, IN 46556 • SRRT *Life*

Hohman Heidi H. • Elk Grove Village Public Library • Elk Grove Village, IL 60007 • ALSC

Hohmeister Catharine G. • Tallahassee, FL 32303

Hohn Jane T. • Library Media Specialist • Nottoway High School • Nottoway, VA 23955 • AASL

Hoitt Marilyn • Media Specialist • Forbes Elementary School • Torrington, CT 06790 • AASL

Hojilla Azucena A. • Somerset County Library System • Bridgewater, NJ 08807

Hokanson Naomi E. • Stillwater, MN 55082 • AASL YALSA *Life*

Hoke Elizabeth C. • Bethesda, MD 20816 • ALSC

Hoke Joy • Media Coordinator • Northwest Middle School • Greensboro, NC 27409 • AASL

Hoke Sheila Wilder • Library Director • Southwestern Oklahoma State University Al Harris Library • Weatherford, OK 73096

Hokkanen Karen • Palmer Lake Elementary School Palmer Lake Library/Media Center • Brooklyn Park, MN 55429-3599 • AASL

Holahan Paulette H. • Trustee • State Library of Louisiana • Baton Rouge, LA 70821-0131 • ALTA

Holba Carrie A. • Public Services Librarian • Oil Spill Public Information Center • Anchorage, AK 99501 • ACRL ERT FLRT

Holberg Constance A • Manuscripts Cataloger • Illinois State Historical Library • Springfield, IL 62701

Holbert Sandra S. • Librarian • Lancaster City Schools-Sanderson • Lancaster, OH 43130 • ALSC RASD

Holbrook Betty J. • Ch Ln • Pocatello Public Library • Pocatello, ID 83201 • ALSC PLA

Holbrook Rhonda J. • Archdale, NC 27263 • AASL

Holch Ellen C. • Coor of Bus Inf & Computer Serv • Greenwich Library • Greenwich, CT 06830

Holcomb Mary L. • Catalog Librarian • University of Arizona Library • Tucson, AZ 85721 • IRRT

Holcomb N. Kay • Director • New Madison Public Library • New Madison, OH 45346 • LAMA

Holcomb Nancy H. • Science-Technology Cataloger • Cornell University Library • Ithaca, NY 14853 • ACRL ALCTS MAGERT

Holcomb Sherri R. • Student • University of Georgia Department of Instructional Technolgy • Athens, GA 30602 • AASL

Holden Douglas H. • Reference Librarian • Prairie Search & Information Services • Drayton, ND 58225 • RASD IFRT ILERT SRRT

Holden Kathryn A. • Information Database Consultant • Rider College • Lawrenceville, NJ 08648-3099 • ACRL LAMA RASD LIRT

Holden Marsha S. • Evanston, IL 60201 • ACRL

Holden Myretta • Director • Chattahoochee Valley Regional Library • Columbus, GA 31995

Holden Opal R. • Austin, TX 78746 • Continuing

Holder Ann H. • Head User Services • Sam Houston State University Newton Gresham Library • Huntsville, TX 77341-2281

Holder Jenny K • Student • University of Washington Graduate School of Library and Information Science • Seattle, WA 98195 • AASL ALSC YALSA

Holder Mary Grace • Lilburn, GA 30247

Holderfield Linda H. • ILL/Reference Librarian • University of South Carolina • Columbia, SC 29208 • RASD

Holdredge Faith A. • Regional Director • Caney Fork Regional Library • Sparta, TN 38583 • PLA IFRT

Hole Carol C. • Community Services Coordinator • Alachua County Library District • Gainesville, FL 32601 • PLA

Holewinski Lori G. • Reference Librarian • DePauw University Roy O. West Library • Greencastle, IN 46135-0037

Holibaugh Ralph W. • Director of Library Services • Western Connecticut State University • Danbury, CT 06810 • ACRL LAMA

Holicky Bernard H. • Director & Professor Library Sci • Purdue University Calumet The Library • Hammond, IN 46323-2094 • ACRL ALCTS

Holifield Betty L. • Librarian, Tech Service • G M I Engineering & Management Inst. Library • Flint, MI 48504-4898

Holifield David A. • Reference Assistant • Fuller Theological Seminary • Pasadena, CA 91182

Holl Deborah G. • Head of Technical Services • Widener University Wolfgram Library • Chester, PA 19013 • ACRL LAMA LITA

Holladay Andrea C. • High Bridge, NJ 08829-1213

Holland Agnes F. • Indexer • H. W. Wilson Company • Bronx, NY 10452 • LITA

Holland Ann H. • Washington, DC 20521-8300 • ALCTS LAMA

Holland Carl B. • Hood River, OR 97031

Holland Cheryl D. • Conservation Librarian • Washington University Libraries • Saint Louis, MO 63130

Holland Deborah K. • Corvallis, OR 97339 • AASL

Holland Edna • Elgin, IL 60123 • PLA IFRT

Holland F. Alleene • Columbia, SC 29210 • AASL

Holland Gloria • Librarian • Defense Systems Management College Library • Fort Belvoir, VA 22060-5426

Holland Harold E. • Malibu, CA 90265-4744 • Continuing

Holland Jeffrey F. • Serials Cataloger • Bates College George & Helen Ladd Library • Lewiston, ME 04240

Holland John R. • Student • Rosary College Graduate School of Library & Information Science • River Forest, IL 60305

Holland Judith • Student • Emporia State University School of Library & Information Management • Emporia, KS 66801 • SRRT

Holland Laura L. • Master Builders, Inc. • Cleveland, OH 44122-5554 • ACRL RASD

Holland Linda J. • Manager • Dallas Public Library Lancaster-Kiest Branch • Dallas, TX 75216-4448

Holland M. V. • Marketing Director • Research Publications Ltd. • Reading RG1 8LJ, England • ACRL

Holland Mary Kathryn • Chair, Dept. of Library Serv. • Kutztown University Library Science Department • Kutztown, PA 19530 • AASL

Holland Mitchell Jr. • School Media Specialist • Twiggs County Board of Education Jeffersonville Elementary School • Jeffersonville, GA 31044 • AASL YALSA LIRT

Holland Molly C. • Murfreesboro, TN 37130

Holland Nancy J. • Manager • KPMG Peat Marwick • Washington, DC 20036 • ACRL

Holland Paul E. Jr. • Idaho Falls Public Library • Idaho Falls, ID 83401 • PLA

Hollander Barbara • University of Maryland College of Library and Information Services • College Park, MD 20742-4345 • ASCLA

Hollander Deborah L. • Chicago, IL 60657 • ALCTS NMRT SRRT

Hollander Sue M. • Student • University of Illinois College of Medicine • Rockford, IL 61107 • SRRT

Hollander Terri K. • Student • University of North Texas School of Library & Information Sciences • Denton, TX 76203 • ALSC

Hollands William D. • Student • University of Michigan School of Information and Library Studies • Ann Arbor, MI 48109-1092 • RASD EMIERT IFRT NMRT SRRT

Hollar Rosita H. • Comfort, TX 78013 • ALSC RASD *Life*

Holle Arthur J. • Librarian/AV Coordinator • Rice Lake High School • Rice Lake, WI 54868 • AASL

Holleman Curt P. • Assoc Dir Ctrl Univ Libs • Southern Methodist University • Dallas, TX 75275 • ACRL ALCTS

Holleman Margaret A. • Director of Library Services • Pima Community College West Campus LRC • Tucson, AZ 85709 • ACRL

Hollenbeck Anne M. • Student • Texas Woman's University School of Library & Information Studies • Denton, TX 76204

Hollenhorst M. Bernice Sr • Director • Saint Mary's College Cushwa-Leighton Library • Notre Dame, IN 46556 • ACRL SRRT

Hollens Deborah • Government Documents Librarian • Southern Oregon State Coll Library • Ashland, OR 97520 • ACRL GODORT

Hollenshead Karen L. • Librarian • Bleyl Junior High School • Houston, TX 77070 • AASL

Holler Suzanne E. • University of Central Florida Library • Orlando, FL 32816-0666 • ACRL RASD LIRT

Hollerich Mary A. • Assistant Head of Access Svs. • University of Southern California Doheny Library • Los Angeles, CA 90089-0182 • ACRL RASD

Holles Melanie J. • Student • Emporia State University School of Library & Information Management • Emporia, KS 66801 • ACRL

Holley E. Jens • Interlibrary Loan Librarian • University of South Carolina • Columbia, SC 29208 • ACRL RASD

Holley Edward G. • Kenan Professor • University of North Carolina at Chapel Hill School of Information and Library Science • Chapel Hill, NC 27599-3360 • ACRL ALCTS LAMA RASD IFRT IRRT LHRT LRRT *Life*

Holley Geneva A. • Louisville, KY 40220

Holley James L. • Director • Vestal Public Library • Vestal, NY 13850

Holley Leslie F. • Librarian • Arabian Horse Trust • Westminster, CO 80234

Holley Robert P. • Associate Dean of Libraries • Wayne State University • Detroit, MI 48202 • ACRL ALCTS LAMA LITA RASD IRRT *Life*

Holliday Barbara • Assistant Reference Librarian • Texas Southern University • Houston, TX 77004

Holliday Christine A. • Toledo, OH 43613

Holliday Geneva R. • Collection Development Librarian • Columbia University Health Sciences Library • New York, NY 10032

Holliday Judy L. • Trustee • Jefferson County Public Library • Lakewood, CO 80215 • ALTA

Holliday Karen • Librarian • Lawrence Cnty Library • Walnut Ridge, AR 72476

Holliday Paul • Technical Services/System Coor. • Cranston Public Library • Cranston, RI 02920

Holliday Shirley J. • Scarsdale, NY 10583 • AASL

Hollier Joan J. • Detroit, MI 48235

Hollifield Hannah • Central Davidson High School • Lexington, NC 27292

Hollinger Barbara W. • Miami, FL 33175 • ACRL LITA LRRT

Hollinger James L. • District Consultant • Dauphin County Library System • Harrisburg, PA 17101 • PLA

Hollinger Susan • Galesburg, IL 61401

Hollingsworth Gretchen H. • Technical Services Libraian • Corona Public Library • Corona, CA 91720 • ALCTS

Hollingsworth Rebecca M. • Student • University of North Carolina Wilson Library • Chapel Hill, NC 27599 • PLA

Hollinrake Mary H. • Branch Manager • Wyoming Public Library • Wyoming, MI 49509

Hollinshead Marilyn P. • Pinocchio Bookstore • Pittsburgh, PA 15232 • ALSC

Hollis Deborah R. • Minority Librarian Intern • Ohio State University Libraries • Columbus, OH 43210-1286

Hollis Fran • Okalhoma City, OK 73127

Hollis Jean A. • Media Specialist • Stevens Creek Elementary School • Martinee, GA 30907 • AASL

Hollister Todd B. • University of New Mexico General Library • Albuquerque, NM 87131

Hollmann Pauline V. • Science Bibliographer • Georgia State University Pullen Library • Atlanta, GA 30303-3081 • ALCTS

Holloway Amy E. • Student • Clark University School of Library & Info Science • Atlanta, GA 30314 • PLA EMIERT

Holloway Carson G. • Sales Representative • EBSCO Subscription Services • Springfield, VA 22151 • ACRL ALCTS LITA RASD

Holloway Donald • Akron, OH 44320 • ACRL

Holloway Geraldine B. • San Antonio, TX 78227 • ACRL

Holloway Jean C. • Director • South Yarmouth Library • South Yarmouth, MA 02664 • PLA IFRT

Holloway Johnna H. • Whitmore, MI 48189

Holloway Kay • Librarian • Duval High School Media Center • Lanham-Seabrook, MD 20706

Holloway Marigay • Copyright Cataloger • Library of Congress • Washington, DC 20541

Holloway Patricia W. • Director • Southeastern Connecticut Library Association • Groton, CT 06340-6097 • LAMA PLA

Holloway Robin L. • Naval Air Station Library Sigonella Sicily • FPO, AE 09627-0824 • PLA AFLRT

Holloway Sara L. • The Library Corporation • Inwood, WV 25428-9733 • ACRL

Hollowell Luther S. • Librarian • Burleson Elementary School • Odessa, TX 79761 • AASL ACRL RASD YALSA

Holltorf Connie S. • Librarian • Yankton Community Library • Yankton, SD 57078-4042

Holly James F. • Shelton, WA 98584 • ACRL ALCTS IFRT SRRT *Life*

Holly Janet S. • Assistant Reference Librarian • Virginia Military Institute J.T.L. Preston Library • Lexington, VA 24450 • ACRL RASD GODORT LIRT

Hollyfield Diane S. • Burke, VA 22015 • ACRL

Holm Blair I. • Princial Librarian • Colton Public Library • Colton, CA 92324 • ALSC PLA

Holm Celia • New York Public Library Washington Heights Branch • New York, NY 10036 • ALSC NMRT

Holm Edla K. • Head Inter-Library Loan • University of Massachusetts Library • Amherst, MA 01003

Holm Eleanor M. • Victoria, TX 77901

Holm Peter J. • Watford City, ND 58854

Holman Emily C. • Chairperson Coordinator • Ocean County Public Library • Toms River, NJ 08753 • ALSC PLA

Holman Jill A. • Student • University of Michigan Libraries Information and Library Studies • Ann Arbor, MI 48109

Holman Jos N. • Cleveland Heights-University Heights Public Library • Cleveland Heights, OH 44118

Holman Norman D. • Deputy Director • Cleveland Public Library • Cleveland, OH 44114-1271 • LAMA

Holman William R. Mr • Austin, TX 78731 • ACRL PLA *Life*

Holmberg Jeanette L. • Reference Librarian • Lincoln Library • Springfield, IL 62701 • PLA RASD

Holmberg Olga S. • Director • Palmer Public Library • Palmer, MA 01069

Holmberg Thomas G. • Reference Librarian • Schaumburg Township District Library • Schaumburg, IL 60194 • RASD

Holmer Paul L. • Hamden, CT 06518 • ACRL LAMA

Holmer Susan E. • Asst Dir/Ref Coordinator • South Bay Cooperative Library System • San Jose, CA 95113

Holmes Alma • Quitman, TX 75783

Holmes Anne W. • Student • Queens College Graduate School of Library & Information Studies • Flushing, NY 11367 • ACRL LITA

Holmes Beverly • Director of Library Services • El Centro College • Dallas, TX 75202

Holmes Christian • Librarian • Bay De Noc Community College Learning Resources Center • Escanaba, MI 49829 • ACRL

Holmes Colette O. • Instruction Librarian • Rensselaer Polytechnic Institute • Troy, NY 12180 • ACRL LIRT

Holmes Daniel O. • Orinda, CA 94563 • ACRL MAGERT

Holmes Dorris D. • Trustee • DeKalb County Public Library • Decatur, GA 30030 • ALTA

Holmes Eliana P. • Chevy Chase, MD 20815-4506 • ACRL

Holmes Elizabeth • Library Media Specialist • Poland Community School • Poland, ME 04273 • AASL

Holmes Elizabeth A. • Librarian • St. Andrews Presbyterian College DeTamble Library • Laurinburg, NC 28352-5598 • ACRL ALCTS RASD

Holmes Elizabeth G. • Student • University of Rhode Island Graduate School of Library & Information Studies • Kingston, RI 02881-0815 • RASD

Holmes Elizabeth H. • Senior Librarian • Richmond Public Library East End Branch • Richmond, VA 23223-5299

Holmes Fontayne B. • Assistant Director of Branches • Los Angeles Public Library • Los Angeles, CA 90071 • LAMA PLA IFRT

Holmes Gerald V. • Reference Libararian • Kent State University Library • Kent, OH 44242 • ACRL NMRT

Holmes Grace H. • Librarian • Division of Legislative Services • Richmond, VA 23219 • LITA NMRT

Holmes Jill M. • Assistant Social Science Ln. • Oklahoma State University Library • Stillwater, OK 74078-0375 • AASL PLA *Life*

Holmes Jo Ann • Trustee • Springfield Free Public Library • Springfield, NJ 07081

Holmes John L. • Bellevue, WA 98005 • LAMA PLA *Life*

Holmes Joyce • Trustee • Prince William Public Library System Administrative Support Center • Prince William, VA 22192-5073

Holmes Karen-Denise • Children's Librarian • County of Los Angeles Public Library Huntington Park Library 633 • Huntington Park, CA 90255 • YALSA

Holmes Katherine E. • Instruction Librarian • Rider College • Lawrenceville, NJ 08648-3099 • ACRL IFRT

Holmes Marion • Director • Lady Lake Public Library • Lady Lake, FL 32159 • PLA

Holmes Mary • School Librarian • Union County Schools • Union, SC 29379 • AASL ALSC

Holmes Mary • Assistant Director • Greenfield Public Library • Greenfield, MA 01301

Holmes Mary Ann • Library Media Specialist • Park Hill Senior High School • Kansas City, MO 64152 • AASL

Holmes Melvin • Norcross, GA 30093

Holmes Melvin L. • Trustee • Saint Joseph County Public Library • South Bend, IN 46601 • ALTA

Holmes Nancy Moore • Bookmobile Librarian • Piedmont Regional Library • Winder, GA 30680

Holmes Norman W. Jr. • Austin, TX 78758-3706

Holmes Pamela V. • Irvington, NJ 07111 • ALCTS

Holmes Robert R. • Fort Lauderdale, FL 33308 • ACRL ALCTS *Life*

Holmes Sandra • Public Services Ln/ Asst. Dir • Texarkana Public Library • Texarkana, TX 75501 • RASD

Holmes Sue Ellen • Director • Stevens Memorial Library • North Andover, MA 01845 • PLA

Holmes Susan F. • Assistant Department Head • Carnegie Library of Pittsburgh Allegheny Regional Branch • Pittsburgh, PA 15212

Holmes Vivian T. • Graduate Student • University of Michigan Libraries Information and Library Studies • Ann Arbor, MI 48109 • LITA IFRT NMRT

Holmgren Edwin S. • Sr. Vice-Pres./Dir. Branch Libs. • The New York Public Library • New York, NY 10016 • LAMA PLA IFRT IRRT

Holmgren Everett C. • Trustee • Saint Joseph County Public Library • South Bend, IN 46601 • ALTA

Holmgren Lynn R. • Manager,Cataloging Services • Baker & Taylor Books • Bridgewater, NJ 08807 • ALCTS LITA

Holobeck Noel C. • Area Studies Center, Libraian • Saint Louis Public Library • St. Louis, MO 63103-2389 • PLA

Holowka Olia • Student • University of Saint Thomas • Houston, TX 77006

Holst C. Kathryn • Director • Huntington City Township Public Library • Huntington, IN 46750 • YALSA

Holst Ruth • Director • Columbia Hospital Library • Milwaukee, WI 53211

Holsted Carolyn • Little Rock, AR 72207

Holsten Virginia K. • Director • Vinton Public Library • Vinton, IA 52349

Holster Debra L. • Consultant • North Texas Library System • Fort Worth, TX 76107-2921

Holsworth Patricia L. • Director • Oberlin Public Library • Oberlin, OH 44074-1626 • LAMA PLA

Holt-Zimmerman Gloria A. • Student • Miami High School • Miami, OK 74354 • AASL RASD YALSA IFRT

Holt Aina Mae • Media Specialist • Washington County School District #15 • Forest Grove, OR 97116-2296 • AASL ALSC IFRT LIRT SRRT

Holt Alison • Catalog Librarian • Art Center College of Design • Pasadena, CA 91103 • ACRL SRRT

Holt Ann C. • Regional Librarian • Jackson District Library Eastern Branch • Jackson, MI 49202 • RASD

Holt Carol F. • Librarian • Henry J. Kaiser Family Foundation • Menlo Park, CA 94025

Holt Constance W. • Minneapolis, MN 55427 • ACRL

Holt Cynthia R. • Special Needs Center Supervisor • Phoenix Public Library • Phoenix, AZ 85004 • ASCLA LITA

Holt David A. • Medical Librarian • Hardin Memorial Hospital • Elizabethtown, KY 42701

Holt Dianne E. • Veterans Memorial Library • Mt. Pleasant, MI 48858 • ALCTS

Holt Ethel F. • Sarasota, FL 34235

Holt Fianna D. • Head of Cataloging & Special Col • Albright College • Reading, PA 19612-5234 • ALCTS

Holt Glen E. • Executive Director • Saint Louis Public Library • St. Louis, MO 63103-2389 • LAMA LITA PLA

Holt Jeri Ann • Library Media Specialist • Erskine Academy • Augusta, ME 04330

Holt Laura Maness • Library Media Director • Cherokee Heights Middle School • Madison, WI 53711

Holt Raymond M. • Del Mar, CA 92014 • ACRL LAMA LITA PLA

Holt Ross A. • Asheboro, NC 27203

Holt Sarah V. • Library Consultant • Raymond M Holt & Assoc • Del Mar, CA 92014 • LAMA

Holt Susan S. • Cataloger • University of Alabama at Birmingham Mervyn H. Sterne Library • Birmingham, AL 35294-0014 • ACRL ALCTS LITA

Holt Thomas J. Jr. • Stanford University • Stanford, CA 94305-6011 • ACRL ALCTS IFRT SRRT

Holtcamp Virginia M. • Director • Oktibbeha County Library • Starkville, MS 39759-1406

Holten Gretchen E. • Asst. Prof, Ref. Lbrn./Bibl. • University of Nebraska Love Library • Lincoln, NE 68588-0410 • ACRL

Holtkamp Irma S. • Cataloging Coordinator • Los Alamos National Lab Lib • Los Alamos, NM 87545-0020 • ALCTS LITA GODORT

Holton Barbara Anne • Washington, DC 20024 • ALSC

Holton M L. Mrs • Rancho Pablos Verdes, CA 90274 • Continuing

Holtslander Linda • Library Program Coordinator • Loudoun County Public Library • Leesburg, VA 22075 • ALSC IFRT

Holtz John W. • Instructional Svs Librarian • Sangamon State University Norris L. Brookens Library • Springfield, IL 62794-9243 • ACRL

Holtz Randall J. • Trustee • Lyons Public Library • Lyons, IL 60534

Holtz Virginia • Director • University of Wisconsin Center for Health Sciences Library • Madison, WI 53706 • LAMA LITA

Holtzclaw John W. • Librarian • Columbus Metropolitan Library • Columbus, OH 43215 • RASD

Holtze Sally Holmes • New York, NY 10010

Holtzman Angela I. • Chicago, IL 60626

Holtzman Douglas • Reference Librarian • Richmond Public Library • Richmond, CA 94804 • ALCTS PLA RASD IFRT SRRT

Holverson Mary Lou • Trustee • Zion-Benton Public Library District • Zion, IL 60099

Holwick Diane R. • Student • University of Illinois Graduate School of Library and Information Science • Urbana, IL 61801 • ALSC

Holzapfel Mary L. • Fairfax, VA 22031 • ACRL ALCTS *Life*

Holzbaur Johanna E. • Children's Librarian • Southbury Public Library • Southbury, CT 06488

Holzberlein Deanne Dr • Northern Illinois University Department of Library & Information Studies • DeKalb, IL 60115 • ACRL ALCTS LITA GODORT *Life*

Holzenberg Eric • Student • Loyola University E.M. Cudahy Memorial Library • Chicago, IL 60626 • ACRL NMRT

Holzenberg Phyllis E. • University of Colorado Norlin Library • Boulder, CO 80309-0184 • ACRL ALCTS LRRT

Holzer Anna R. • Assistant Director Library Serv. • Tarrant County Jr College Library NW Campus • Fort Worth, TX 76179 • ACRL

Holzer Joann • Librarian • Sacred Heart Cathedral School • Knoxville, TN 37919

Holzhauer SarahJane • Librarian • Clay Senior High School Library • Oregon, OH 43616 • AASL YALSA

Holzheimer Diane F. • Librarian • Tenacre Country Day School Library • Wellesley, MA 02181 • AASL ALSC YALSA SRRT

Holzle Amy M. • Librarian • 3M Center • Saint Paul, MN 55144-1000 • ACRL

Holzman Daphne T. • Student • Princeton University Firestone Library • Princeton, NJ 08544 • ALSC

Hom Mee-Len • Student • Queens College Grad Sch of Lib & Inf Studies • Flushing, NY 11367 • ACRL

Hom Sharon L. • Nashville, TN 37221-2113

Homa Linda L. • Head, Children's Services • Jefferson-Madison Regional Library • Charlottesville, VA 22901-5287

Homan J. Michael • Assistant University Librarian • University of California-Irvine Library • Irvine, CA 92713 • ACRL LAMA

Homan Mary E. • President • Patrick Henry Middle School • Sioux Falls, SD 57105 • AASL YALSA

Homans Phoebe B. • Head of Reference • Wayland Free Public Library • Wayland, MA 01778-1999

Homblette Kathryn M. • Dr. Phillips Elementary School • Orlando, FL 32819 • ALSC

Homburger Louise • Glencoe, IL 60022

Homer Ruth • Librarian • Fanny Rittenberg School Doernbach Library • Egg Harbor City, NJ 08215 • AASL

Homes Nellie M. • Nevada, MO 64772 • ACRL RASD *Continuing*

Homeyard Marjorie A. • Naval Gen. Lib. Serv. Staff • Naval Education & Training Progam Management • Pensacola, FL 32509-5100 • PLA AFLRT FLRT

Homick Ronald J. • Coordinator of Public Services • Houston Community College • Houston, TX 77004 • ACRL

Homola Barbara • Head, Children's Services • The Bryant Library • Roslyn, NY 11576 • ALSC

Honaker Linda L. • Media Coordinator • Hurst-Euless-Bedford Independent School District • Bedford, TX 76022 • AASL

Honeyman Justine P. • Government Documents • University of Massachusetts Medical School Medical Center Library • Worcester, MA 01655 • GODORT MAGERT

Honkisz Robert E. • Trustee • Oak Lawn Public Library • Oak Lawn, IL 60453 • ALTA

Honor Naomi Goldberg • New City Library • New City, NY 10956

Honor-Forte Mollyne • Columbia, MD 21045

Honsa Vlasta • Asst. Administrator • Las Vegas-Clark County Library District Flamingo Library • Las Vegas, NV 89119

Honza Julian C D P Sr • Librarian • Our Lady of the Lake University • San Antonio, TX 78207-4666 • AASL ALCTS LAMA LITA RASD YALSA

Hood Ben R. • Clln Devel Librarian • Stonehill College Cushing-Martin Library • North Easton, MA 02357 • ACRL

Hood Catherine E. • Student • Texas Woman's University School of Library & Information Studies • Denton, TX 76204 • NMRT

Hood Elizabeth • University of California-Los Angeles University Research Library • Los Angeles, CA 90024 • ALCTS MAGERT

Hood Joan • Sarasota, FL 34238 • LITA

Hood Joan M. • Dir of Devel & Pub Affairs Lib • University of Illinois Library • Urbana, IL 61801

Hood Karye K. • Student • California State University • Fullerton, CA 92634

Hood Kenneth E. • Personnel & Staff Devl Officer • State University of New York (SUNY) at Buffalo • Buffalo, NY 14260

Hood Martha W. • Technical Information Spec. • United States Department of Agriculture National Agricultural Library • Beltsville, MD 20705-2351

Hood Mary Eliza • Cataloger • North Georgia College Stewart Library • Dahlonega, GA 30597-3001 • Continuing

Hood Mary Neville • Librarian • Stowe Middle/High School • Stowe, VT 05672 • AASL

Hood Sandra D. • Cataloger • Palo Alto College • San Antonio, TX 78224 • ACRL ALCTS

Hood Sharon L. • Yorkton, SK, S3N 2G6 Canada • ACRL LITA

Hoogcarspel Annelies • Cataloger/Research Assisant • Center for Electronic Texts in the Humanities • New Brunswick, NJ 08903 • ALCTS IRRT SRRT

Hoogenboom Dennis R. • Glendale, AZ 85302

Hoogstra James W. • Chief Librarian • Detroit Public Library Jefferson Branch • Detroit, MI 48224 • PLA SRRT

Hook Alexandra M. • Winnipeg MB, R3J 3N9 Canada

Hook Alice Palo • Cincinnati, OH 45220 • Continuing

Hook Carolyn D. • Naval Explosive Ordnance Disposal Technical Center • Indian Head, MD 20640-5070 • AFLRT

Hook Carolyn J. • Technical Service Librarian • Dearborn Department of Libraries Henry Ford Centennial Library • Dearborn, MI 48126 • LITA PLA

Hook Harriett B. Mrs. • Bloomfield Junior High School • Bloomfield, CT 06002 • AASL LAMA

Hook Margaret M. • Librarian • Annadale High School • Annadale, VA 22003 • AASL

Hook Marilyn • Director • Midlands Technical College • Columbia, SC 29202

Hook Mary Barton • Branch Manager • Atlanta-Fulton Public Library Georgia Hill Branch • Atlanta, GA 30312 • ALSC

Hook Robert D. • University of Idaho Library • Moscow, ID 83843 • ACRL *Life*

Hooks James D. Dr. • Librarian • Indiana Univ of Pennsylvania • Indiana, PA 15705

Hooks Vernon G. • Librarian • Miami-Dade Community College • Miami, FL 33176

Hooper Anthony O. • Honolulu, HI 96813 • IRRT

Hooper Barbara • Media Servs/AV/Library Supv. • Timpson Independent School District Libraries • Timpson, TX 75975

Hooper Britta B. • Student • University of Washington Graduate School of Library and Information Science • Seattle, WA 98195

Hooper James E. • Librarian • Baylor School Library • Chattanooga, TN 37401 • AASL ACRL LITA RASD YALSA IFRT

Hooper Jane F. • Librarian • Corona Delmar High School Library • Newport Beach, CA 92660 • YALSA

Hooper Jessie R. • Fort Myers, FL 33919 • PLA RASD AFLRT *Continuing*

Hooper John • Boston Public Library • Boston, MA 02117 • ACRL

Hooper Martha S. • Librarian • University School of Nashville • Nashville, TN 37212 • AASL

Hooper Mary G. • Washington, DC 20018

Hooper Mary Janis • College Station, TX 77845

Hooper Susan M. • Librarian • Lovett School • Atlanta, GA 30327 • AASL

Hoopes Maria Segura • Reference Librarian • University of Arizona Library • Tucson, AZ 85721 • RASD

Hoornbeek Lynda C. • Glen Ellyn, IL 60137

Hoose Beverly D. • Librarian/Instrustion Coord. • Eastern Montana College Library • Billings, MT 59101-0298 • ACRL

Hooten Patricia A. • Student • Indiana University School of Library and Information Science • Bloomington, IN 47405

Hooten Ruth • Bradford College Hemingway Library • Haverhill, MA 01835

Hoover A.L.A M. Rosalind • Libertyville, IL 60048

Hoover Austin • Archivist • New Mexico State University Library • Las Cruces, NM 88003-0006 • ACRL

Hoover Clara G. • Librarian • Millard South High School Library • Omaha, NE 68137 • AASL YALSA IFRT LIRT

Hoover Danise Gianneschi • Coor. Reference Technologies • Hunter College Library • New York, NY 10021 • RASD GODORT

Hoover Denise A. • Sterling Morton Elementary School • Mentor, OH 44060 • AASL

Hoover Gloria E. • Librarian • Forest Trail Elementary School Library • Austin, TX 78746 • AASL

Hoover Grace V. • Associate Science Librarian • San Diego State University Love Library • San Diego, CA 92182-0511 • ACRL *Continuing*

Hoover James L. • Law Librarian • Columbia University • New York, NY 10027-7297 • LITA

Hoover Jimmie H. • Baton Rouge, LA 70808

Hoover John N. • Hd. Special Cllns./Rare Bk. Ln. • Saint Louis Mercantile Library Association • Saint Louis, MO 63101 • ACRL

Hoover Lona L. • Student • University of Alabama School of Library & Information Studies • Tuscaloosa, AL 35487-0252

Hoover Louise H. • Librarian • George Junior/Senior High School McFeely Library • Newton, PA 18940 • AASL

Hoover Nancy • Technical Services Librarian • Marylhurst College Shoen Library • Marylhurst, OR 97036

Hoover Pauline • Johnstown, OH 43031 • Continuing

Hoover Terry L. • Student • University of Michigan School of Information and Library Studies • Ann Arbor, MI 48109-1092

Hope-Balcerzak Marilyn • Reference Librarian • University of Arizona Arizona Health Sciences Center Library • Tucson, AZ 85724

Hope Ann J. • Asst Hd Catlg and Hd Mono Catlg • University of Georgia Libraries • Athens, GA 30602 • ACRL ALCTS LITA

Hope Anne S. • Student • Brigham Young University Harold B. Lee Library • Provo, UT 84602

Hope Dorothy H. • Asst Chair-Hd of Monograph Catlg • University of Florida Libraries • Gainesville, FL 32611-2047 • ACRL ALCTS

Hope Laurie • Reference Librarian • Escondido Public Library • Escondido, CA 92025 • RASD

Hopkins-Carroll Carolyn E. • Reference Librarian • University of South Dakota • Vermillion, SD 57069 • LIRT

Hopkins Barbara A. • Director • Baldwin Public Library • Baldwin, NY 11510 • LAMA IFRT

Hopkins Beatrice • Librarian • Maplewood Middle School • Sulphur, LA 70663 • AASL

Hopkins Betty J. • Detroit, MI 48202 • ACRL RASD *Life*

Hopkins Dianne McAfee • Assistant Professor • University of Wisconsin • Madison, WI 53706 • AASL YALSA IFRT LRRT

Hopkins Donna K. • Student • State University of New York (SUNY) School of Information & Library Studies • Buffalo, NY 14260

Hopkins Edith I. • Deputy Director • Oakville Public Library • Oakville ON, L6J 2Z4 Canada • PLA

Hopkins Frances L. • Assoc Dir Coll Devel & P Serv • Temple University Paley Library • Philadelphia, PA 19122 • ACRL ALCTS

Hopkins Helen G. • New York, NY 10001

Hopkins James W. • Director • United States Air Force Academy Academy Library (DFSEL) • USAF Academy, CO 80840

Hopkins Jane L. • Greenville College Ruby E. Dare Library • Greenville, IL 62246 • ACRL

Hopkins Joan • Dir of Sarasota Co Pub Lib Sys. • Selby Public Library • Sarasota, FL 34236 • LAMA

Hopkins Joseph S. • Saline, MI 48176

Hopkins Judith • Tech Serv Res & Analysis Offr. • State University of New York (SUNY) Central Technical Services • Buffalo, NY 14260 • ACRL ALCTS LAMA LITA LHRT LRRT *Life*

Hopkins Karen L. • Humanities Catalog Librarian • University of Texas at Arlington • Arlington, TX 76019-0497 • ACRL ALCTS

Hopkins Lee Bennett • Scarborough, NY 10510 • YALSA

Hopkins Linda A. • Student • Emporia State University School of Library & Information Management • Emporia, KS 66801 • PLA

Hopkins Lola R. • Preservation Specialist • Stanford University J. Henry Meyer Memorial Library • Stanford, CA 94303

Hopkins Margaret Mrs. • Library Media Specialist • Court Street Elementary School • Lancaster, NY 14086 • AASL

Hopkins Richard L. • Assistant Professor • University of British Columbia School of Library, Archival & Information Studies • Vancouver BC, V6T 1Z1 Canada • ACRL RASD

Hopkins Susan S. • Student • North Carolina Central University School of Library & Information Science • Durham, NC 27707 • AASL

Hopkinson Shirley L. • San Jose, CA 95112 • ALCTS MAGERT

Hopp Ralph H. • St Paul, MN 55108 • ACRL LAMA *Life*

Hoppe Barbara J. • Technical Library Asst. • University of Michigan 123 Undergraduate Library • Ann Arbor, MI 48109-1185

Hopper Hazel W. • Fishers, IN 46038 • Continuing

Hopper James N. • Student • Florida State University School of Library and Information Studies • Tallahassee, FL 32306-2048

Hopper Jean G. • Philadelphia, PA 19103 • Continuing

Hopper Laura • Reference Librarian • Northland Public Library • Pittsburgh, PA 15237 • PLA IFRT

Hopper Lorraine E. • York, PA 17402

Hopper Lyn W. • Assistant Director • Troup Harris Coweta Rgnl • Lagrange, GA 30240 • PLA

Hopper Michael E. • Islamic Studies Librarian • University of California Library • Santa Barbara, CA 93106 • ACRL ALCTS

Hopper Mildry S. • Washington, DC 20016

Hopper Rosita E. • Cataloging Librarian • Johnson & Wales University • Providence, RI 02912

Hopper Toni S. • Librarian • MacDougall Youth Correction Center • Ridgeville, SC 29472 • ASCLA

Hopson Jean B. Dr. • Assistant Dean and Librarian • Wake Forest University Charles H. Babcock Graduate School Management • Winston-Salem, NC 27109 • ACRL

Hopwood Susan H. • Head Reference • Marquette University Memorial Library • Milwaukee, WI 53233 • ACRL

Hor Annie Y. • Technical Services Dept. • Williams College Sawyer Library • Williamstown, MA 01267 • ACRL

Horacek John I. • Assistant • La Trobe University Library • Bundoora Victoria, Australia • ACRL ALCTS

Horak Janice J. • Swisher, IA 52338-9590

Horal Stephanie • Madera County Library • Madera, CA 93637

Horalek Joan M. • Chicago, IL 60652 • SRRT

Horan Ada L. • Student • University of South Florida School of Library & Information Science • Tampa, FL 33620

Horan Meredith Louise • Librarian • National Library of Medicine • Bethesda, MD 20894

Horchler Eleanor • Director • River Vale Public Library • River Vale, NJ 07675 • PLA

Hord Bill G. • Campus Services Librarian • Houston Community College • Houston, TX 77004 • ACRL LAMA LRRT

Hord Leveta J. • Serial Cataloger • University of Texas at Arlington • Arlington, TX 76019-0497 • ALCTS

Hordusky Clyde W. • Document Librarian • State Library of Ohio • Columbus, OH 43266-0334 • GODORT MAGERT

Horenstein Tova • Librarian • Harold W. Smith Elementary School • Glendale, AZ 85301

Horgen Judith E. • Director • New Milford Public Library • New Milford, CT 06776 • PLA

Hori Joan M. T. • Reference Librarian • University of Hawaii Sinclair Library • Honolulu, HI 96816 • LIRT

Hori Ruby M. • Los Angeles, CA 90019 • ALCTS

Horie Ruth H. • Honolulu, HI 96823-2632

Horigan Evelyn • Art Librarian • California Institute of the Arts • Valencia, CA 91355 • ACRL EMIERT NMRT

Horikawa Teruyo • Librarian • Shimane Women's Junior College • Shimane-ken 690, Japan • AASL ALSC

Horio Nina D.P. • Science/Technology Reference • University of Hawaii Thomas Hale Hamilton Library • Honolulu, HI 96822 • ACRL RASD SORT

Horiuchi Linda M. • Student • University of Washington Graduate School of Library and Information Science • Seattle, WA 98195

Horiuchi Susan K. • Head Librarian • Aina Haina Public Library • Honolulu, HI 96821 • YALSA

Horlbeck Christine • Blanding Public Library • Rehoboth, MA 02769

Hormel Mary M. • Denver, CO 80221 • AASL ALSC *Continuing*

Horn Anna • Associate Dir for MAin Lib • Kansas City Public Library • Kansas City, MO 64106 • LAMA PLA RASD *Life*

Horn Catherine S. • Cambridge, MA 02138

Horn Claudia B. • Reference Librarian • Chapman University Thurman Clarke Memorial Library • Orange, CA 92666

Horn Eileen M. • School Librarian • Elaine Winn Elementary School • Las Vegas, NV 89102 • ALSC

Horn Elizabeth J. • Student • Indiana University School of Library and Information Science • Bloomington, IN 47405

Horn Janice H. • Technical Service Coordinator • Clarion University of Pennsylvania Rena M. Carlson Library • Clarion, PA 16214 • ACRL ALCTS GODORT

Horn Jerry • Medford, NY 11763 • AFLRT

Horn Judith G. • Market Development Manager • Information Access Company • Foster City, CA 94404 • ACRL PLA RASD

Horn Judy K. • Head Government Document Dept • University of California-Irvine Library • Irvine, CA 92713 • ACRL GODORT

Horn Linda D. • Madison Heights Public Library • Madison Heights, MI 48071

Horn Lisa M. • Student • Drexel University W. W. Hagerty Library • Philadelphia, PA 19104 • IFRT

Horn Marguerite E. • Serials Catalog Librarian • University of California Shields Library • Davis, CA 95616 • ALCTS LAMA

Horn Polly • Library Director • Community Library • Sunbury, OH 43074 • IFRT

Horn Sarah C. • Riverside Public Library • Riverside, IL 60546

Hovatter Charlene E. • Student • University of Kentucky College of Library & Information Science • Lexington, KY 40506-0391 • ACRL EMIERT SRRT

Hovde David M. • Social Sciences Librarian • Purdue University Libraries • West Lafayette, IN 47907-1530 • ACRL RASD LHRT

Hovden Norma L. • Minneapolis, MN 55406 • ACRL RASD *Life*

Hover Katherine A. • Student • University of Hawaii School of Library & Information Studies • Honolulu, HI 96822 • LITA PLA RASD

Hoverson Martha • Section Head • Hawaii State Public Library System Office of the State Librarian • Honolulu, HI 96813 • LITA

Hoverson Mary V. • Media Spec • Coppell Middle School • Coppell, TX 75019

Hovish Joseph J. • American Legion Library • Indianapolis, IN 46206

Hovorka Marjorie J. • Milton, MA 02186

How Sarah E. • Cornell University Library • Ithaca, NY 14853-5301 • ACRL ALCTS

Howard-Reguindin Pamela F. • Arlington, VA 22209 • IRRT

Howard Ada M. • Director • Seguin-Guadalupe County Public Library • Seguin, TX 78155 • PLA

Howard Carol Sergel • Orchard Park, NY 14127 • AASL

Howard Catherine • Coordinator of Children's Servs. • Carnegie-Stout Public Library • Dubuque, IA 52001 • ALSC

Howard Cecelia R. • Reference & Young Adult Libn. • Muncie-Center Township Public Library • Muncie, IN 47305

Howard Clinton N. • Asst. Univ. Ln./Collections • University of California-Davis Library • Davis, CA 95616 • ACRL ALCTS

Howard Cordelia • Director • Long Beach Public Library • Long Beach, CA 90802-4482 • LAMA PLA IFRT

Howard Dara Lee • Doctoral Student • University of Hawaii School of Library & Information Studies • Honolulu, HI 96822 • ACRL LITA

Howard David • David Lipscomb University University Library • Nashville, TN 37204-3951

Howard Debbie A. • Children's Librarian • Seattle Public Library Southwest Branch • Seattle, WA 98126 • ALSC

Howard Donald H. • Reference Coordinator • Brigham Young University Harold B. Lee Library • Provo, UT 84602 • ACRL RASD

Howard Dorothy F. • Keene, NH 03431 • PLA

Howard Edward A. • Director • Evansville-Vanderburgh County Public Library • Evansville, IN 47708-1694 • PLA

Howard Elizabeth F. • Professor • West Virginia University Department of Library Science • Morgantown, WV 26506-6069 • AASL ALSC

Howard Ella Mae • Chatham ON, N7L 4X9 Canada

Howard Evelyn E. • Techincal Service Supervisor • Santa Clara County Free Library • San Jose, CA 95112-4446

Howard Helen A. • Associate Professor • McGill University Graduate School of Library & Information Studies • Montreal PQ, H3A 1Y1 Canada • ACRL LAMA

Howard Jeanne G. • Assoc Prof./Hd Clln Mgt • New Mexico State University Library • Las Cruces, NM 88003-0006 • ACRL

Howard Joseph H. • Librarian • United States Department of Agriculture National Agricultural Library • Beltsville, MD 20705-2351 • ACRL ALCTS

Howard Joyce M. • Editor • H. W. Wilson Company • Bronx, NY 10452 • ACRL

Howard Judith T. • Media Specialist • Beverly City School • Beverly, NJ 08010

Howard Judy T. • Student • Florida State University School of Library and Information Studies • Tallahassee, FL 32306-2048

Howard Lisa M. • Student • University of Illinois Graduate School of Library and Information Science • Urbana, IL 61801 • IFRT SRRT

Howard Louise M. • Reference Librarian • Chicago Public Library Wrightwood Branch • Chicago, IL 60652 • LITA PLA RASD

Howard Mary • Director of Univ. Libs. • Mercer University Main Library • Macon, GA 31207 • ACRL ALCTS LAMA LITA RASD

Howard Mary Jo • Reference Librarian • Georgia State University Pullen Library • Atlanta, GA 30303-3081 • ACRL IFRT LIRT NMRT

Howard Molly B. • Humanities Librarian • University of Georgia Libraries • Athens, GA 30602

Howard Pamela A. • Librarian • El Capitan High School Grossmont Union High School • Lakeside, CA 92040 • AASL LITA

Howard Paul • Chevy Chase, MD 20815 • ACRL LAMA *Continuing*

Howard Romona Mrs. • Trustee • Gary Public Library • Gary, IN 46402 • ALTA

Howard Sandra L. • Pittsburgh, PA 15215

Howard Sara-Catherine • Librarian • Spring Independent School District Wells Middle School • Houston, TX 77068 • AASL

Howard Sarah J. • Children's Librarian • Daniel Boone Regional Library • Columbia, MO 65205-1267 • ALSC PLA

Howard Sharon L. • Library Director • Scottsdale Community College Library • Scottsdale, AZ 85256 • ACRL

Howard Susan E. • Burgaw, NC 28425 • ALCTS ASCLA LITA PLA NMRT

Howard Tammy E. • Cooperstown, NY 13326

Howarth Lynne C. • Assistant Professor • University of Toronto Faculty of Library & Information Science • Toronto ON, M5S 1A1 Canada • ALCTS LAMA LRRT

Howatt Helen Sr • Library Director • Holy Names College • Oakland, CA 94619 • ACRL

Howd David • Berkeley Public Library North Branch • Berkeley, CA 94707

Howden Norman • Assistant Professor • University of North Texas School of Library & Information Sciences • Denton, TX 76203 • RASD

Howden Regis • Edgewood High School • Madison, WI 53711

Howder Murray L. • V S E Corporation • Alexandria, VA 22303

Howe Andrea M. • Albuquerque Academy Library • Albuquerque, NM 87109 • AASL ALSC YALSA

Howe Anne E. • Student • University of South Florida School of Library & Information Science • Tampa, FL 33620 • AASL

Howe Dicksy June • Librarian • Southwest State University • Marshall, MN 56258 • ACRL GODORT

Howe Eleanor B. • Lancaster, PA 17603 • AASL

Howe Ernest A. • Edmonton AB, T6C 3T2 Canada

Howe Judith D. • Student • San Jose State University Division of Library & Information Science • San Jose, CA 95192-0029

Howe Marilyn J. • Librarian • Houston Northwest Medical Center • Houston, TX 77090

Howe Priscilla P. • Children's Librarian • Russell Library • Middletown, CT 06457

Howe Rose M. • Student • Louisiana State University School of Library & Information Science • Baton Rouge, LA 70803-3290 • RASD

Howe Susan • Children's Librarian • Bozeman Public Library • Bozeman, MT 59715

Howell Charles • Librarian • Millinocket Memorial Library • Millinocket, ME 04462

Howell Clare • Trustee • Livonia Public Library • Livonia, MI 48154-3045 • ALTA

Howell David B. • Librarian • Nicholls State University Allen J. Ellender Memorial Library • Thibodaux, LA 70310 • ACRL RASD

Howell Donna W. • Assistant Director • Mountain Regional Library • Young Harris, GA 30582 • PLA

Howell Dylan • Student • State University of New York School of Information & Library Sci • Albany, NY 12203

Howell Jane L. • Director • Eastern Montana College Library • Billings, MT 59101-0298 • ACRL

Howell Karen M G • Los Angeles, CA 90035-1815 • ACRL LITA NMRT

Howell Linda J. • Student • Texas Woman's University School of Library & Information Studies • Denton, TX 76204

Howell Margaret A. • Special Collection Librarian • University of Missouri Libraries-Columbia Elmer Ellis Library • Columbia, MO 65201-5149 • ACRL

Howell Margaret C. • Librarian • West Springfield Elementary School • Springfield, VA 22152 • AASL ALSC

Howell Marvin • Librarian • Sacramento City College Library • Sacramento, CA 95822 • AASL ACRL *Life*

Howells James M • Deputy Director- Public Ser. • Salt Lake County Library System • Salt Lake City, UT 84121-3188 • PLA

Howells Joyce W. • Head of Cataloging Department • Southwest Missouri State University Library • Springfield, MO 65804-0095 • ALCTS

Howes Bernard R. • Partner • Lindsay & Howes Booksellers • Surrey GU8 5TU, England • ERT

Howestine Alan • Trustee • Michigan City Public Library • Michigan City, IN 46360 • ALTA

Howey Rebecca L. • Rochester Hills, MI 48309 • IFRT

Howington Lee R. • Library Director • Bartow County Public Library • Cartersville, GA 30120

Howitson Brenda • Chief of Special Collections • State Library of Massachusetts • Boston, MA 02133 • ALCTS MAGERT

Howland Eleanor J. • Director • Temple Terrace Public Library • Temple Terrace, FL 33617

Howland Joan S. • Director & Prof of Law • University of Minnesota • Minneapolis, MN 55455 • ACRL LAMA

Howland Nancy K. • Student • Texas Woman's University School of Library & Information Studies • Denton, TX 76204 • ALSC

Howlett Dianne • Technical Services Librarian • Saint Mary's College of California • Moraga, CA 94575 • LITA

Howley Louis C • Library Assistant II • Maricopa County Library District • Phoenix, AZ 85032 • PLA

Howley Richard M. • Library Aide I, Cataloger • Tempe Public Library • Tempe, AZ 85282

Howling Bernice • Somers, NY 10589 • ALSC IFRT

Howrey Mary M. • Media Specialist • Mercy Center for Health Care Services • Aurora, IL 60506 • LITA

Howser Ray E. • Director • Illinois Valley Library System • Peoria, IL 61602

Howton Louise • Director, Ch. Book Div. • Harcourt Brace Jovanovich Publishers • San Diego, CA 92101 • ALSC

Howze Philip C. • Asst. Prof./Bibl Inst Librarian • Iowa State University Library • Ames, IA 50011-2140 • ACRL NMRT

Hoxie David • Director of Library • Alderson-Broaddus College • Philippi, WV 26416 • ACRL PLA

Hoxsey Judy A. • Director • Estes Park Public Library District • Estes Park, CO 80517 • LAMA PLA IFRT SRRT

Hoy Catherine J. • Dir of Dist Learning & Cont Ed • Emporia State University School of Library & Information Management • Emporia, KS 66801 • CLENE

Hoy Chris J. • Munster, IN 46321 • Continuing

Hoy Isabel M. • Goshen County Library • Torrington, WY 82240

Hoyer Fred B. • Staten Island, NY 10310

Hoyle Karen Nelson • Librarian • University of Minnesota Walter Library • Minneapolis, MN 55455 • ACRL ALSC

Hoyle Louise M. • Raleigh County Public Library • Beckley, WV 25802-1876

Hoyle Ruth A. • Director • Davie County Public Library • Mocksville, NC 27028-2115 • PLA

Hoyle Zoe A. • Knoxville, TN 37916

Hoylo Katherine J. • Student • Northern Illinois University Department of Library & Information Studies • DeKalb, IL 60115 • PLA SRRT

Hoyman Lisa M. • Director • Watertown Public Library • Watertown, WI 53094 • PLA

Hoyt Beryl E. • So Sioux City, NE 68776 • Life

Hoyt Dolores J. • Head of Technical Services • Indiana University-Purdue University at Indianapolis Library (IUPUI) • Indianapolis, IN 46202 • ALCTS

Hoyt F. Sherman Mrs • Hollis Social Library • Hollis, NH 03049

Hoyt Helen • Library Director • Rapid City Public Library • Rapid City, SD 57701-3630 • Continuing

Hoyt Mary Ann • Reference Librarian • Akron-Summit County Public Library • Akron, OH 44326-0001

Hoyt Ruth B. • Pennsbury School District • Fallsington, PA 19054 • AASL

Hrabak Robert J. • Twinsburg, OH 44087

Hren Richard G. • Library Assistant • Milwaukee Public Museum • Milwaukee, WI 53233

Hresko-Altadonna Carol • Librarian • Abington School District • Abington, PA 19001 • AASL

Hronek Beth C. • Henderson, KY 42420

Hruska Martha • Acting Asst Dir for Tech Servs • University of Florida Libraries • Gainesville, FL 32611-2047 • ALCTS LITA

Hryciw-Wing Carol A. • Rhode Island College James P. Adams Library • Providence, RI 02908 • ACRL ALCTS

Hrzina Josephine T. • Thomas Brothers Maps • Los Angeles, CA 90017 • MAGERT

Hsia Ting-Mei • Serials Catalog Librarian • California State Polytech University • Pomona, CA 91768

Hsiao Hwa-Chun S. • Student • University of Washington Suzzallo Library • Seattle, WA 98195

Hsiao Karin P. • Student • University of California Los Angeles Graduate School of Library & Information Science • Los Angeles, CA 90024 • NMRT SRRT

Hsiao Shu-yi • Assistant Editor • H. W. Wilson Company • Bronx, NY 10452 • ALSC

Hsieh-Yee Ingrid P Y • Catholic University of America School of Library and Information Science • Washington, DC 20064 • ACRL ALCTS

Hsieh Cynthia C. • Columbia College Library • Chicago, IL 60605 • ACRL LITA

Hsieh Fanny H. • Processing Services • Yale University Sterling Memorial Library • New Haven, CT 06520 • ALCTS

Hsieh Kuo-ping • Librarian • Columbia University • New York, NY 10027-7297 • ALCTS

Hsin Chin-Luen • American Jewish Historical Society Lee M Friedman Memorial Library • Waltham, MA 02154 • ACRL LITA

Hsiu-Mei Chen Liu • System Coordinator • Cigna Corporation • Los Angeles, CA 90010

Hsu Bonnie C. • N Dartmouth, MA 02747

Hsu Chi-ya • Student • University of South Carolina College of Library & Information Science • Columbia, SC 29208 • SRRT

Hsu Elizabeth • Fresh Meadows, NY 11365-1619

Hsu Karen M. • Assistant Director,Cataloging • New York Public Library • New York, NY 10018-2788 • ALCTS LITA

Hsu Marilyn • Librarian • California State University,Fresno Henry Madden Library • Fresno, CA 93740-0034

Hsu Martha R. • N. European Studies Bibl. • Cornell University • Ithaca, NY 14853-5301 • ACRL ALCTS

Hsu Patrick K. • College Librarian • Texas Lutheran College Blumberg Memorial Library • Seguin, TX 78155

Hsu Rosa C. • Acquisition Librarian • Houston Community College • Houston, TX 77004

Hsu Ya-Huei • Student • University of Texas at Austin Graduate School of Library & Information Sciences • Austin, TX 78712-1276 • PLA

Hsueh Daphne C. • Retrospective Conversion • Ohio State University Libraries • Columbus, OH 43210-1286 • ALCTS LITA

Hu Ben G. • Student • Kent State University School of Library & Information Science • Kent, OH 44242-0001

Hu Estelle M.H. • Cataloger • H.W. Wilson Company • Bronx, NY 10452 • LITA

Hu James S C • Dean & Professor • Natl Taiwan University • Taipei 10764 ROC, Taiwan

Hu Jane C. • Reference Librarian • North Brunswick Free Public Library • North Brunswick, NJ 08902

Hu May M. • Murray, KY 42071

Hu Mei X. • Cataloging Librarian • Tennessee Technological University • Cookeville, TN 38505

Hu Rachel J. • Student • University of Hawaii • Manoa, HI 96789

Hu Shih-Sheng • Chief Provincial Law Librarian • Law Library Division Department of the Attorney General • Edmonton AB, Canada • LAMA

Hu Wendy • New York, NY 10024

Hu Zhi J. • Student • Queens College Graduate School of Library & Information Studies • Flushing, NY 11367

Huang Becky • Adult Services Librarian • Livonia Public Library • Livonia, MI 48154-3045

Huang Chuan Hui • Student • Indiana University School of Library and Information Science • Bloomington, IN 47405

Huang Felicia S. • Director • Middletown Township Free Public Library • Middletown, NJ 07748

Huang George W. Dr • Professor Of Education • California State University-Chico Department of Education-Librarianship Program • Chico, CA 95929-0222 • AASL LITA

Huang Hui-Lan • Student • University of California-Berkeley University Library • Berkeley, CA 94720 • LITA

Huang Hui-Yen • Student • University of Wisconsin-Madison Memorial Library • Madison, WI 53706

Huang Hui-yu • Catalog Librarian • Western State University College of Law • Irvine, CA 92718 • ALCTS

Huang Irene C. • Branch Head • Chicago Public Library Chinatown Branch • Chicago, IL 60616

Huang Joyce L. • Head Collection Mgt. • University of Wisconsin Library and Learning Resources • Whitewater, WI 53190 • ACRL ALCTS

Huang Mary J. • Student • Brown University Rockefeller Library • Providence, RI 02912

Huang Samuel T. • Northern Illinois University University Libraries • DeKalb, IL 60115-2868 • ACRL ASCLA RASD

Huang Shih-Hsion • Director • Tamkang University Chueh-Sheng Memorial Library • Tamsui Taipei 25137, Taiwan • ACRL ALCTS LITA PLA RASD

Huang Shu • London, ON, N6G 2J7 Canada

Huang Theodore S. Dr. • Teaneck, NJ 07666 • AASL ACRL ALCTS ASCLA LAMA LITA RASD   *Life*

Huang Theresa C. • Brooklyn Public Library New Utrecht Branch • Brooklyn, NY 11214 • ALSC PLA IRRT

Huang Yahui • Concordia College • Bronxville, NY 10708

Huang Yiajung • Student • University of North Texas School of Library & Information Sciences • Denton, TX 76203

Huang Zhonghe • Saint Louis University Pius XII Memorial Library • St. Louis, MO 63108

Hubbard Elizabeth A. • Carnegie Library of Pittsburgh • Pittsburgh, PA 15213-4080

Hubbard Howard W. • Baltimore, MD 21212 • Continuing

Hubbard Joan • Director • Weber State University Stewart Library • Ogden, UT 84408-2901 • ACRL ALCTS RASD LRRT

Hubbard Mary • Serials Librarian • University of Iowa Libraries • Iowa City, IA 52242-1379 • ACRL

Hubbard Mary Kathryn • Library Manager • Brown & Root Inc., Information Resource Center • Houston, TX 77020 • ALCTS LAMA LITA RASD

Hubbard Rebecca L. • Librarian • Dallas Public Library North Oak Cliff Branch • Dallas, TX 75208-4617

Hubbard Terry E. • Reference/Member of the Faculty • Evergreen State College • Olympia, WA 98505 • ACRL RASD EMIERT GODORT

Hubbard Virginia F. • Branch Librarian • Greenhaven Library • Tonawanda, NY 14150

Hubbard Wendy M. • Student • Syracuse University School of Information Studies • Syracuse, NY 13244-4100 • LITA

Hubbard William J. • University Librarian • Jacksonville State University Library • Jacksonville, AL 36265 • LAMA

Hubbard Willis M. • Librarian • Gettysburg College Musselman Library • Gettysburg, PA 17325-1493 • ACRL LITA   *Life*

Hubbell Jill J. • Haymarket, VA 22069

Hubbell John T. • Asheville, NC 28804-1854

Hubbell Lillian L. • Greenville, IL 62246 • Continuing

Hubble Gerald B. • Director • Rockhurst College Library • Kansas City, MO 64110-2508 • ACRL LAMA   *Life*

Hubbs Catherine S. • Austin, TX 78731-4420

Hubbs Linda • Student • Rosary College Graduate School of Library & Information Science • River Forest, IL 60305 • SRRT

Hubbs Preston E. • Trustee • Las Vegas-Clark County Library District Flamingo Library • Las Vegas, NV 89119 • ALTA

Hubbs Ronald B. • Librarian • Windsor Locks Public Library • Windsor Locks, CT 06096

Hubener Hal H. • Special Collection • Lakeland Public Library • Lakeland, FL 33801

Huber Charles • University of California Science and Engineering Library • Santa Barbara, CA 93106 • ACRL LITA RASD

Huber Dale R. • Librarian • Kapaa Public Library • Kapaa, HI 96746 • PLA

Huber David G. • Student • University of Michigan School of Information and Library Studies • Ann Arbor, MI 48109-1092

Huber Ella Mae • Supv Instructional Materials • Alachua County School Board • Gainesville, FL 32601 • AASL

Huber Grace M. • Librarian • Hamilton Elementary School • Carlisle, PA 17013 • AASL

Huber Janet B. • Librarian • Isle of Wight Academy Library • Isle of Wight, VA 23397 • AASL

Huber Jean Sample • Mechanicsburg, PA 17055 • PLA YALSA   *Continuing*

Huber Jeffrey T. • University of Pittsburgh • Pittsburgh, PA 15260 • SRRT

Huber Katherine B. • Librarian • King County Library System • Seattle, WA 98109-5191 • ALSC

Huber Kathy J. • Geneology Librarian • Rudisill North Regional Library (Tulsa City-County Library) • Tulsa, OK 74106 • IFRT NMRT

Huber Kristina R. • Reference Librarian • Saint Olaf College Rolvaag Memorial Library • Northfield, MN 55057-1097 • ACRL LIRT

Huber Mary L. • Sante Fe, NM 87501 • Continuing

Huberman Anne E. • Canisius College Andrew L. Bouwhuis Library • Buffalo, NY 14208-1098 • IFRT

Huberman Debbie H. • Youngstown, OH 44512

Hubert Athena J. • Downers Grove Public Library • Downers Grove, IL 60515 • ALSC

Hubert Carol • Cook Memorial Library • Libertyville, IL 60048

Hubert Gail C. • Student • Texas Woman's University School of Library & Information Studies • Denton, TX 76204

Hubert Rebecca L. • Houston Public Library Alief Branch • Houston, TX 77072 • PLA IFRT

Huch Cathryn R. • Children's Librarian • Livonia Public Library Alfred Noble Branch • Livonia, MI 48150 • ALSC

Huck Amy K. • Adult Services Librarian • Vernon Area Public Library • Prairie View, IL 60069 • NMRT

Huck Charlotte S. Dr. • Redlands, CA 92373 • ALSC   *Continuing*

Huckleby Melissa M. • Student • University of Kentucky College of Library & Information Science • Lexington, KY 40506-0391

Hucks Herbert Jr. • Archivist • Wofford College Sandor Teszler Library • Spartanburg, SC 29303-3663 • ACRL   *Continuing*

Hudak Ann L. • Reference/Documents Librarian • University of Maryland College Park Theodore R. McKeldin Library • College Park, MD 20742-7011 • RASD GODORT

Hudak Margaret B. • Trustee • Lorain Public Library • Lorain, OH 44052 • ALTA IFRT SORT

Hudak Melissa A. • Student • University of Illinois Graduate School of Library and Information Science • Urbana, IL 61801 • ALSC PLA

Hudders Marion L. • Manitowoc, WI 54220 • Continuing

Huddle Annette W. • Head of Reference Services • Mobile Public Library • Mobile, AL 36602

Huddleston Jackson N. Mrs. • Trustee • Cabell County Public Library • Huntington, WV 25701 • ALTA PLA

Hudgens Ann Y. Dr. • Librarian • David Lipscomb Middle School • Nashville, TN 37203 • AASL

Hudgens Yvonne Thomas • Student • University of South Carolina College of Library & Information Science • Columbia, SC 29208

Hudgins Catherine R • Student • University of Toronto Faculty of Library & Information Science • Toronto ON, M5S 1A1 Canada

Hudgins R Jean • Head Monographic Cataloging • Georgia Institute of Technology • Atlanta, GA 30332 • ALCTS LAMA

Hudgins Rena • Head Librarian • Chrysler Museum Library • Norfolk, VA 23510-1587 • ACRL ALCTS LITA

Hudiburgh Audrey H. • Librarian • Aspen Publishers • Gaithersburg, MD 20878

Hudson Alice C. • Chief Map Division • New York Public Library • New York, NY 10018-2788 • ACRL LAMA IFRT MAGERT SRRT

Hudson Anne • Trustee • East Saint Louis Public Library • East St. Louis, IL 62201 • ALTA

Hudson Anne M. • Student • University of Maryland College of Library and Information Services • College Park, MD 20742-4345

Hudson Anne S. • Assoc. Dir. Syst. & Access Serv • DePaul University Libraries • Chicago, IL 60614 • ACRL ALCTS LAMA LITA

Hudson Beth H. • Graduate Student • University of Washington Graduate School of Library and Information Science • Seattle, WA 98195 • RASD

Hudson Carol • Cincinnati, OH 45238 • ALCTS NMRT

Hudson Corey R • Director • Midwest Library Service • Bridgeton, MO 63044 • LITA

Hudson Diane E • Central Arkansas Library System Jacksonville Branch Library • Jacksonville, AR 72076

Hudson Diane J. • Student • University of Texas Southwestern Medical Center Library • Dallas, TX 75235-9049 • LITA

Hudson Donna T. • Head Chemistry Library • Emory University • Atlanta, GA 30329 • ACRL LRRT

Hudson Gary A. • Acquisitions Librarian • Mankato State University Memorial Library • Mankato, MN 56002-8400

Hudson Jane • Oakland, CA 94618

Hudson Jeannette M. • Student • University of Rhode Island Graduate School of Library & Information Studies • Kingston, RI 02881-0815 • SRRT

Hudson Judith A. • Head,Cataloging Department • State University of New York (SUNY) University Libraries • Albany, NY 12222 • ACRL ALCTS LITA

Hudson Julie • Wiscasset, ME 04578-0533 • Continuing

Hudson Julie Robinson • Clearwater, FL 34624 • ALSC

Hudson Kathy A. • California State Library • Sacramento, CA 94237-0001 • LAMA LITA

Hudson Leslie T. • Smyma, GA 30080 • NMRT

Hudson M. Janet • Ligonier Valley Library Association Inc • Ligonier, PA 15658

Hudson Margaret E. • Children's Librarian • Fort Worth Public Library East Berry Branch • Fort Worth, TX 76105 • ALSC ASCLA

Hudson Myrna • Coordinator of Adult Services • Wichita Public Library • Wichita, KS 67202 • LAMA PLA RASD

Hudson Nancy L. • Assistant Director • Las Vegas-Clark County Library District Flamingo Library • Las Vegas, NV 89119 • LAMA LITA

Hudson Patricia A. • Head Librarian • East Moline Public Library • East Moline, IL 61244 • LAMA PLA

Hudson Phyllis J. • Librarian • University of Central Florida Library • Orlando, FL 32816-0666 • LIRT SRRT

Hudson Shirley D. Mrs. • Library Specialist/Reference • Jarvis Christian College Olin Library & Communication Center • Hawkins, TX 75765

Hudson Teresa W. • St. Charles, MO 63303 • ALCTS PLA RASD

Hudspeth Deborah A. • Student • Columbia University Library Service Library • New York, NY 10027 • ACRL PLA RASD SRRT

Hudspeth Sally S. • Student • University of South Florida School of Library & Information Science • Tampa, FL 33620

Huebner Joseph H. • Collection Development Dept. • Hesburgh Library • Notre Dame, IN 46556 • ACRL

Huebner Orma • Shelby, OH 44875 • Continuing

Huebscher Mary • Cuyahoga County Public Library Parma Regional • Parma, OH 44129-3199 • YALSA

Huecker Celeste • Librarian • Social Security Administration Library • Baltimore, MD 21235 • ALCTS LITA FLRT SRRT

Huelsenbeck Susan F • Jennie E. Smith Elementary School • Newark, DE 19713 • ALSC

Huemer Christina G. • 00152 Roma, Italy

Huene Glendy • Sarasota, FL 34234 • AASL

Huerta Lilia • Trustee • San Antonio Public Library • San Antonio, TX 78205

Huerta Raul A. • Librarian • Mohawk Valley Community College Library • Utica, NY 13501 • ACRL LAMA

Huesmann James L. • Librarian for Automated Sys. • Linda Hall Library • Kansas City, MO 64110 • ACRL LITA IRRT
Huestis Jeffrey C. • Head, Library Systems • Washington University Libraries • Saint Louis, MO 63130-4899 • LITA
Hueter Eike • Director • Richard Bland College Library • Petersburg, VA 23805 • ACRL RASD *Life*
Hueting Gail P. • Modern Languages Librarian • University of Illinois Library • Urbana, IL 61801 • ACRL ALCTS *Life*
Huey Charles P. • Student • Northern Illinois University Department of Library & Information Studies • DeKalb, IL 60115 • SRRT
Huey Talbott W. • Bibliographer & Coordinator • Michigan State University Libraries • East Lansing, MI 48824-1048 • ACRL
Huff Edward • University of Notre Dame Kresge Law Library • Notre Dame, IN 46556
Huff James Ellen Sr. • Rare Books Librarian • Spalding University • Louisville, KY 40203
Huff Miriam M. • Mishawaka, IN 46544
Huff William H. • Dir Collection Devel., Emeritus • University of Illinois Graduate School of Library and Information Science • Urbana, IL 61801 • ACRL ALCTS *Life*
Huffer Mary A. • Lanham, MD 20706 • FLRT *Continuing*
Huffman Carol P. • Technical Services Librarian • Bloomington Public Library • Bloomington, IL 61702-3308
Huffman Claudia S. • Installation Specialist • Data Research Associates Inc. • Saint Louis, MO 63132 • LAMA
Huffman Jean S. • Manitou Springs, CO 80829
Huffman Margie B. • Director • Auburn Public Library • Auburn, AL 36830
Huffman Melissa L. • Reference/Special Projects Ln. • Rose State College Learning Resources Center • Midwest City, OK 73110 • ACRL RASD NMRT
Huffman Nell H. • Conway Primary School • Conway, SC 29526 • AASL
Huffman Richard S. • Student • University of Maryland College of Library and Information Services • College Park, MD 20742-4345 • AASL
Huffman Sharon • Head Librarian • Reginald J P Dawson Library • Montreal PQ, H3R 1G9 Canada • ALSC PLA RASD
Hufford Gordon Lynn • Director • Indiana University East Library Learning Resources Center • Richmond, IN 47374-1289 • ACRL LAMA
Hufford Jon R. • Reference Dept. • State University of New York (SUNY) Frank Melville Jr. Memorial Library • Stony Brook, NY 11794-3300 • ACRL
Hug Rita • Fort Smith, AR 72901 • ACRL ALCTS LAMA LITA
Huge Carol R. • Cleveland Public Library South Brooklyn Branch • Cleveland, OH 44109
Huge Sharon A. • Reference Librarian • Ohio University Vernon R. Alden Library • Athens, OH 45701-2978 • ACRL
Huges-Brown JoAnn C. • Media Specialist/Teacher • Springbrook Elementary School Kent School District • Kent, WA 98031
Huget Charlene D. • Student • University of Michigan School of Information and Library Studies • Ann Arbor, MI 48109-1092
Huggens Gary D. • Automated Operations Coordinator • Library of Congress • Washington, DC 20541
Huggins Heather S. • Portsmouth, RI 02871
Huggler Joan S. • Great Falls, VA 22066
Hughes-Nelson Tina C. • Student • San Jose State University Division of Library & Information Science • San Jose, CA 95192-0029 • ALSC
Hughes-Oldenburg D. K. • Librarian • University of San Francisco School of Law Library • San Francisco, CA 94117-1080 • ACRL LRRT SRRT
Hughes Almina J. • Fairfield Unified School District #310 • Langdon, KS 67583 • AASL
Hughes Barbara Mrs • Trustee • Anoka County Library • Blaine, MN 55434 • ALTA PLA *Life*
Hughes Barbara W. • Administrative Librarian • Marin County Free Library • San Rafael, CA 94903 • RASD
Hughes Carol A. • Student • University of Michigan • Ann Arbor, MI 48109-1205 • ACRL LAMA
Hughes Carole G. • Student • Kent State University School of Library & Information Science • Kent, OH 44242-0001
Hughes Clare Marie • Children's Librarian • Atlantic County Library Egg Harbor Township • Pleasantville, NJ 08232
Hughes D. Linda • Wichita Falls, TX 76301
Hughes Dean • Trustee • Provo City Public Library • Provo, UT 84601 • ALTA
Hughes Diane M • Student • San Jose State University Clark Library • San Jose, CA 95192-0028
Hughes Doris C. • Director of Elementary L. Serv. • Unified Sch Dist-480 • Liberal, KS 67901 • AASL
Hughes Edwin J. • Oxnard, CA 93030
Hughes Elizabeth S. • Director • Glen Ellyn Public Library • Glen Ellyn, IL 60137 • LAMA PLA IFRT
Hughes Frances • Student • Northern Illinois University Department of Library & Information Studies • DeKalb, Il 60115 • AASL
Hughes Frances M. • Microforms Librarian • Southern Connecticut State University Hilton C. Buley Library • New Haven, CT 06515 • ACRL ALCTS
Hughes Glenda J. • Map Librarian • Georgia State University Pullen Library • Atlanta, GA 30303-3081 • ACRL RASD LIRT MAGERT
Hughes Janet M. • Porter County Public Library • Valparaiso, IN 46383
Hughes Jean C. • Social Sciences Section • San Diego Public Library • San Diego, CA 92101
Hughes Kathleen A. • Head Cataloger • Montclair State College Harry Sprague Library • Upper Montclair, NJ 07043 • ACRL ALCTS
Hughes Kenneth G. • North Platte Public Schools • North Platte, NE 69101 • AASL
Hughes Leslie I. • Library Director • Kemper-Newton Regional Library System • Union, MS 39365
Hughes Lisa Mead • Children's Librarian II • Santa Clara County Free Library Saratoga Commmunity Library • Saratoga, CA 95070
Hughes Lorna H. • Database Maintenance Manager • University of Houston Libraries • Houston, TX 77204-2091
Hughes Marcelle Elaine • Associate Librarian • University of Cincinnati Langsam Library • Cincinnati, OH 45221-0033 • ACRL RASD
Hughes Margaret E. • Portland, OR 97201 • Continuing
Hughes Margaret J. • Student • State University of New York at Albany School of Information Science & Policy • Albany, NY 12222 • AASL
Hughes Margaret Nan A. • Student • University of Washington Graduate School of Library and Information Science • Seattle, WA 98195 • IFRT SRRT
Hughes Marilyn • Vice President Cust. Relations • News Net Incorporation • Bryn Mawr, PA 19010 • AFLRT
Hughes Martha Tanner • Head, Records Maintenance • University of Georgia Libraries • Athens, GA 30602 • ACRL ALCTS
Hughes Melissa • Director • Wyckoff Public Library • Wyckoff, NJ 07481 • LAMA PLA RASD
Hughes Nancy B. • Btranch Supervisor • Kern County Library Rathbun Branch • Bakersfield, CA 93308
Hughes Nancy J. • American Embassy Moscow MSG • APO, AE 09721
Hughes Patrice L. • Student • Hastings College Perkins Library • Hastings, NE 68901 • ACRL
Hughes Raylynn M. • Info-Motion • Atlanta, GA 30307
Hughes Robbie • Librarian • Montezuma Public Library • Montezuma, GA 31063
Hughes Ruth • Librarian • Bonita Springs Public Library • Bonita Springs, FL 33923
Hughes Ruth I. • Rare Book Librarian • Saint Charles Borromeo Seminary Ryan Memorial Library • Overbrook, PA 19096-3012 • ACRL
Hughes Sandra • Brant County Board of Education • Brantford ON, N3R 4Z6 Canada • AASL ALSC LITA RASD YALSA
Hughes Sandra H. • Reference Librarian • Charleston Southern University L Mendel Rivers Library • Charleston, SC 29411
Hughes Sandra M • Student • University of North Carolina at Chapel Hill School of Information and Library Science • Chapel Hill, NC 27599-3360 • AASL
Hughes Sondra K. • Librarian/Media Specialist • University of Northern Colorado James A. Michener Library • Greeley, CO 80639 • AASL
Hughes Sue M. • Special Materials Consultant • Baylor University Moody Memorial Library • Waco, TX 76798-7148 • ACRL ALCTS LAMA LITA RASD GODORT LHRT
Hughes Suzanne M. • Portland, OR 97223
Hughes Tandy L • Community Relations Librarian • Stockton-San Joaquin County Public Library • Stockton, CA 95202
Hughey Elizabeth H. • Springfield, VA 22152-3038 • ASCLA *Continuing*
Hughey Sandra L. • Information Specialist • Program Resources, Inc. • Research Triangle Pk, NC 27709
Hugo Terri R. • Student • Texas Woman's University School of Library & Information Studies • Denton, TX 76204 • IFRT
Huguelet Eugene W. • Director • University of North Carolina At Wilmington Randall Library • Wilmington, NC 28403-3297 • ACRL
Hugus Susan E. • Branch Librarian • Jones Library • Amherst, MA 01002
Hui Frances M. • West Los Angeles, CA 90025 • YALSA
Huiskamp Juliana G. • Director • Cresco Public Library • Cresco, IA 52136 • PLA
Huisman Gary B. • Librarian • Covenant College Kresge Memorial Library • Lookout Mountain, GA 30750 • ACRL
Hukill Jane E. • Worton, MD 21678
Hulbert Doris J. • Director • University of North Carolina Walter Clinton Jackson Library • Greensboro, NC 27412-5201 • ACRL
Huling Nancy • Head Public Service • University of California Rivera Library • Riverside, CA 92517 • ACRL RASD
Huling Sharron • University of California-Los Angeles (UCLA) • Los Angeles, CA 90024-1450
Huling Willadean • Librarian • Vale Elementary & Middle Schools Libraries • Vale, OR 97914 • AASL
Hull Barbara • Library Media Specialist • Jamaica High School Library • Jamaica, NY 11432 • AASL RASD YALSA
Hull Charlotte • Trustee • Gary Public Library • Gary, IN 46402 • ALTA
Hull Donald R. Mrs • Wilmington, DE 19807
Hull Elizabeth M. • Librarian • McKinley Elementary School • Long Beach, CA 90805 • AASL
Hull Emily E. • Student • University of Washington Graduate School of Library and Information Science • Seattle, WA 98195 • IFRT LIRT SRRT
Hull Jennifer L. • Student • Brigham Young University School of Library & Information Sciences • Provo, UT 84602 • PLA
Hull Lois J. • Tulsa, OK 74127
Hull Nola • Indianapolis, IN 46220
Hull Sharon M. • Colonial High School • Orlando, FL 32807 • AASL
Hull Sondra • Librarian • Raytown South High School • Raytown, MO 64138 • AASL
Huls Mary E. • Head, Information Services Dept. • College of Saint Catherine • Saint Paul, MN 55105 • ACRL RASD *Life*
Hulse Bruce M. • Associate Project Manager • Washington Research Library Consortium • Lanham, MD 20706 • ACRL LAMA
Hulser Richard P. • Advisory Industry Representive • IBM ACIS • Milford, CT 06460 • ACRL LITA
Hulsey Richard A. • Director • Willard Public Library • Battle Creek, MI 49017 • LITA
Hulshof Robert B. • Student • University of Washington Graduate School of Library and Information Science • Seattle, WA 98195 • ALCTS
Hulstedt Rita A. • Student • University of Wisconsin-Milwaukee School of Library & Information Science • Milwaukee, WI 53201
Hults Patricia A. • State University of New York Agricultural & Technical College • Cobleskill, NY 12043 • LAMA SRRT
Hultz Karen W. • Young Adult Librarian • Irondequoit Public Library Helen McGraw Branch • Rochester, NY 14622
Hulverson Ellen M. • Wayne State University Library Science Program • Detroit, MI 48202
Hulyk Barbara R. • Longboat Key, FL 34228 • GODORT
Humbertson Jane V. • Librarian • Hagerstown Junior College Library • Hagerstown, MD 21742-6590 • ACRL
Humble Jane • Media Sepcialist • Grand Haven Public Schools • Grand Haven, MI 49417 • AASL
Humble Leslie Trich • Silver City, NM 88062
Hume Margaret A. • Cataloguing Librarian • Concordia University Libraries • Montreal PQ, H3G 1M8 Canada
Humel Joyce A. • Associate Director • River Bluffs Regional Library • Saint Joseph, MO 64501 • PLA
Humerickhouse-Lepore Susan • Warwick Public Library • Warwick, RI 02886 • ALSC
Humes Dorothy T. • Rochester, NY 14620 • Continuing
Humeston Dale K. • Student • Wayne State University Library Science Program • Detroit, MI 48202 • AASL
Humiston Alice M. Miss • Whittier, CA 90602 • ACRL ALCTS *Continuing*
Humlicek Barbara • USAA Corporate Library • San Antonio, TX 78288
Hummel Kathryn A. • Student • University of California Los Angeles Graduate School of Library & Information Science • Los Angeles, CA 90024 • LITA EMIERT IRRT NMRT SRRT
Hummel Miriam E. • Davis, CA 95616 • ACRL ALCTS LITA *Life*
Hummel Ray O. Jr • Scholar In Residence • Virginia Commonwealth University James Branch Cabell Library • Richmond, VA 23284-2033 • ALCTS RASD *Life*
Hummer Ann L. • Library Media Supervisor • Frederick County Public Schools • Frederick, MD 21701 • AASL LITA
Humphrey Elizabeth • Library Assistant II • Texas Department of Human Services Library • Austin, TX 78704 • IFRT

Humphrey Graham H. Jr • Escondido, CA 92033-0308
Humphrey Guy W. • Preble County District Library • Eaton, OH 45320
Humphrey Linda K. • Librarian II • San Bernardino County Library Montclair Branch • Montclair, CA 91763
Humphrey Martha M. • Fredericksburg, VA 22401
Humphrey Norma V. • Reference/Serials Lib • Yonkers Public Library • Yonkers, NY 10701
Humphrey Richard • Director Library Division • The Bookmen Inc • Minneapolis, MN 55401 • PLA ERT
Humphrey Susanne M. • Wheaton, MD 20902
Humphrey Thomas W. • Ayers State Technical College • Anniston, AL 36202-1647
Humphrey Virginia Shea • Ballston Spa Public Library • Ballston Spa, NY 12020
Humphreys Anne C. • Asst. Hd. of Materials • Free Library of Philadelphia • Philadelphia, PA 19103 • ALSC
Humphreys Betsy L. • Dep Assoc Dir L Ops • National Library of Medicine • Bethesda, MD 20894 • Life
Humphreys Glenn S. • Librarian • Chicago Public Library Harold Washington Library • Chicago, IL 60605 • ACRL ALCTS
Humphreys Judy F. • Supervising Librarian • Mountain View Public Library • Mountain View, CA 94041 • LITA
Humphreys Maris S. • Cataloger • Redwood Library & Athenaeum • Newport, RI 02840-3292
Humphreys Peggy F. • New York, NY 10027-4708
Humphreys Susan W. • School Library Media Spec. • LBC Middle School • Langley, SC 29834 • AASL
Humphries Lajean • Librarian • Schwabe, Williamson & Wyatt • Portland, OR 97204-3795 • LAMA LITA
Humphris Jeannine • Assistant Library Administrator • Kemp Public Library • Wichita Falls, TX 76301
Humphry James III • New Rochelle, NY 10804 • ACRL LAMA *Life*
Hund Carole • Adult Service Librarian • Farmington Community Library • Farmington Hills, MI 48334 • ASCLA PLA
Hund June C. • Reference Librarian • Case Western Reserve University • Cleveland, OH 44106-7151
Hunenko Maria P. • Prin Catlgr • Yale University Sterling Memorial Library • New Haven, CT 06520
Hung Elaine • Supervising Library • Alameda Free Library • Alameda, CA 94501
Hung Howard K. Dr. • Trustee • Montgomery County Department of Public Libraries • Rockville, MD 20850 • ALTA
Hung Mei • Librarian • Lincoln University • San Francisco, CA 94118 • ACRL
Hung Shang-wen • Pasadena Public Library • Pasadena, CA 91101
Hung Winifred • Cataloging Services Supervisor • Appleton Public Library • Appleton, WI 54911-4780 • ALCTS
Hung Yu-Chu • Panchiao Taipei, Taiwan • RASD
Hunker Paula L. • Elementary Librarian • Southside Elementary School • Lander, WY 82520 • AASL
Hunley Mary L. • Student • University of South Carolina College of Library & Information Science • Columbia, SC 29208
Hunsberger Barbara B. • Acquisitions Librarian • Millersville University of Pennsylvania • Millersville, PA 17551-0302 • ACRL
Hunsberger Charles W. • Director • Las Vegas-Clark County Library District Flamingo Library • Las Vegas, NV 89119 • LAMA LITA PLA
Hunsberger Willard • Fort Wayne, IN 46815 • Continuing
Hunsicker Jennifer L. • Student • University of Tennessee-Knoxville Graduate School of Library & Information Science • Knoxville, TN 37996-4330 • LITA SRRT
Hunsucker Coy K. • Head Exceptional Children's Div. • Public Library of Cincinnati and Hamilton County • Cincinnati, OH 45202 • ALSC ASCLA
Hunt-Patterson Marilyn L. • Youth Services Librarian • Ashland Public Library • Ashland, OH 44805
Hunt Becky • Oak Hill School • Nashville, TN 37220 • AASL ALSC
Hunt C. Amoes • Branch Librarian • Stockton-San Joaquin County Public Library Manteca Branch • Manteca, CA 95336 • PLA SRRT
Hunt Caroline C. • College of Charleston Robert Scott Small Library • Charleston, SC 29424 • YALSA
Hunt Chance A. • Student • University of Washington Graduate School of Library and Information Science • Seattle, WA 98195
Hunt Debra M. • School Librarian • Aylett B. Cotton Library • Hillsborough, CA 94010
Hunt Diana C. • Extension Librarian • Briggs Lawrence County Public Library • Ironton, OH 45638
Hunt Diane Mrs. • Head Librarian • Avon Park Public Library • Avon Park, FL 33825
Hunt Gary A. • Associate Dean • Ohio University Vernon R. Alden Library • Athens, OH 45701-2978 • ACRL LAMA
Hunt James F. • San Pedro, CA 90732 • ACRL LIRT
Hunt James Robert • Librarian • Public Library of Cincinnati and Hamilton County • Cincinnati, OH 45202 • LAMA PLA *Life*
Hunt Janet W. • Branch Librarian • Santa Monica Public Library Montana Avenue Branch • Santa Monica, CA 90403
Hunt Judith L. • University Librarian • University of Richmond Boatwright Library • Richmond, VA 23173 • ACRL LAMA
Hunt Karen • Reference Librarian • University of Manitoba Elizabeth Dafoe Library • Winnipeg MB, R3T 2N2 Canada • LITA
Hunt Katye • Director Angel Processing Center • Southern Missionary College McKee Library • Collegedale, TN 37315 • YALSA
Hunt Linda A. • Director • Fairfax County Public Schools System • Fairfax, VA 22003 • AASL LITA
Hunt Linda L. • Library Resource Center Director • DeVry Institute of Technology • City of Industry, CA 91746-3495 • ALCTS
Hunt Margaret M. • Trustee • Lake County Public Library • Merrillville, IN 46410-5382 • AASL ALTA YALSA
Hunt Margaret Rogers • Hd of Clln Management • North Carolina State University • Raleigh, NC 27695 • ACRL ALCTS
Hunt Marjorie C. Mrs • Newtonville, MA 02160 • ACRL *Life*
Hunt Marsha A. • Delaware, OH 43015 • ALCTS LITA IFRT
Hunt Mary Alice • Professor • Florida State University School of Library and Information Studies • Tallahassee, FL 32306-2048 • AASL ALSC
Hunt Nancy • New Technologies Coordinator • Indianhead Library System • Eau Claire, WI 54701 • LITA
Hunt Ruby • Program Specialist Media • Winston Salem/Forsythe County School • Winston Salem, NC 27102 • AASL
Hunt Sally • Director • Loudoun County Public Library • Leesburg, VA 22075 • ALCTS ALSC LAMA LITA PLA RASD YALSA IFRT IRRT
Hunt Suellyn • Central Library Development • Rochester Public Library • Rochester, NY 14604 • LAMA PLA CLENE
Hunt Vance • President • Library Bureau • Dallas, TX 75229
Hunter Andrew W. • Youth Services Librarian • Public Library of Charlotte & Mecklenburg County • Charlotte, NC 28202 • ALSC YALSA SRRT
Hunter Brenda M. • Branch Librarian • Atlanta-Fulton Public Library West End Branch • Atlanta, GA 30310 • PLA RASD YALSA
Hunter Clarence • Cataloger • Coleman Library • Tougaloo, MS 39174
Hunter Cynthia • Norcross Public Library • Norcross, GA 30071
Hunter David C. • University of Texas Libraries General Libraries • Austin, TX 78713-7330 • ACRL
Hunter Diana • Trustee • Skokie Public Library • Skokie, IL 60077-3680 • ALTA PLA
Hunter Diane • Head of Reference Services • Ball State University Bracken Library • Muncie, IN 47306-0160 • ACRL RASD
Hunter Dorothea A. • Librarian • Berry School Library • Detroit, MI 48207 • AASL ALSC
Hunter Dorothy M. • Our Lady of the Elms High School • Akron, OH 44313 • AASL PLA *Life*
Hunter Elaine H. • Phoenix, AZ 85033
Hunter Elinor Green • Chair, Advisory Board • Phoenix Public Library • Phoenix, AZ 85004 • ALTA PLA
Hunter Eric T. • West Palm Beach, FL 33415
Hunter Frances • Trustee • Cleveland Public Library • Cleveland, OH 44114-1271 • ALTA
Hunter Grant W. • Greensburg, PA 15601
Hunter Gregory S. • Assoc. Prof. • Long Island University Palmer School of Library & Info. Sci. • Brookville, NY 11548 • ALCTS LIRT
Hunter J. Michael • Student • Brigham Young University School of Library & Information Sciences • Provo, UT 84602
Hunter Jean • Cary Junior High School • Cary, IL 60013 • AASL YALSA
Hunter Jean B. Miss • Battle Creek, MI 49017 • Continuing
Hunter John H. • Ref. Coll. Development Librarian • Rice University Fondren Library • Houston, TX 77251-1892 • ACRL RASD
Hunter Judy • Librarian • Huntsville Public Library • Huntsville, TX 77340 • ALCTS ALSC LAMA LITA PLA RASD
Hunter Julie V. • Assistant Director • DeKalb County Public Library Adminstration Building • Decatur, GA 30030 • LAMA PLA
Hunter Lora C. • Librarian • Saint Petersburg Junior College Library Processing Center • St. Petersburg, FL 33733 • ACRL ALCTS LITA *Life*
Hunter Lynn • Director • Piscataway Township Free Public Library John F. Kennedy Memorial Library • Piscataway, NJ 08854 • LAMA PLA
Hunter Mark I. • Student • Rutgers University School of Communication Information & Library Studies • New Brunswick, NJ 08903 • IFRT SRRT
Hunter Mary C. • Farmington Hls., MI 48336 • Continuing
Hunter Patricia H. • Coordinator • Virginia Highlands Community College Library • Abingdon, VA 24210
Hunter Patricia Kuhn • Student • Gaylord Brothers • Syracuse, NY 13221 • LITA
Hunter Patricia S. • Librarian • North River Elementary School • Mt Solon, VA 22843
Hunter Peggy • Media Specialist • Sapulpa Middle School • Sapulpa, OK 74066 • AASL
Hunter Rhonda N. • Charleston, SC 29414 • RASD LIRT
Hunter Robert D. • Architect • O'Donnell Wicklund Pigozzi & Peterson, Architects Inc. • Deerfield, IL 60015
Hunter Ruby B. • Branch Manager • Public Library of Annapolis & Anne Arundel County Severna Park Branch • Severna Park, MD 21146 • LAMA PLA RASD
Hunter Ruby J. • Adult Librarian • Dallas Public Library • Dallas, TX 75201
Hunter Steven B. • Circulation Assistant • Morgan Stanley & Co Inc • New York, NY 10020
Hunter Susan W. • Riverside Junior High School • Springfield, VT 05156 • AASL ALSC YALSA
Hunter Tracey J. • Special Collections Libn • Lincoln University Langston Hughes Memorial Library • Lincoln University, PA 19352 • LAMA EMIERT IRRT SRRT
Hunter V. S. Mrs • S. Burlington, VT 05403 • AASL *Continuing*
Hunter Vera G. • Librarian • Dunbar High School Library • Washington, DC 20001 • AASL
Hunting Susan K. • Head of Information Services • Sioux City Public Library • Sioux City, IA 51101-1203 • RASD
Huntington Deborah S. • Student • University of Southern Mississippi School of Library Science • Hattiesburg, MS 39406-5146
Huntington Joan L. • Media Center • Kent County High School • Worton, MD 21678 • AASL YALSA
Huntley George W. III • Student • Florida State University School of Library and Information Studies • Tallahassee, FL 32306-2048
Huntley Nancy J. • Assistant Director • Lincoln Library • Springfield, IL 62701 • PLA
Huntoon Elizabeth • Librarian • Chicago Public Library Harold Washington Library • Chicago, IL 60605
Huntting Ann L. • Librarian • Chicago Public Library Humboldt Branch • Chicago, IL 60647
Huntzinger Ralph E. • Coordinator Media Service • King County Library System • Seattle, WA 98109-5191 • PLA YALSA IFRT VRT
Hupp Sherry W. • Director • Hamden Library • Hamden, CT 06518 • ALCTS LITA PLA RASD
Hupp Stephen L. • Public Service Librarian • Capital University Library • Columbus, OH 43209 • ACRL RASD IFRT LHRT SRRT
Huq A Abdul Dr • Head, Cataloging Dept. • Saint John's University Library • Jamaica, NY 11439 • ALCTS IRRT
Hurd Albert E. • Executive Director • American Theological Library Association • Evanston, IL 60201 • ALCTS
Hurd Elizabeth B. • Children's Librarian II • Greensboro Public Library • Greensboro, NC 27402 • ALSC
Hurd Julie M. • Science Librarian • University of Illinois at Chicago University Library • Chicago, IL 60680 • ACRL
Hurd Patricia M. • Medina County District Library • Medina, OH 44256 • RASD
Hurd Sandra H. • Acton, MA 01718-1007 • LAMA LITA
Hurlbert Bruce M. • Director of Library Services • Lycoming College Library • Williamsport, PA 17701-5192 • ACRL LAMA
Hurlbert Irene W. • Librarian • University of California-San Diego Central University Library • La Jolla, CA 92093-0175 • ACRL RASD
Hurlbert Terry A. • Carnegie-Mellon University Libraries Hunt Library • Pittsburgh, PA 15213 • ALCTS
Hurley Bernard J. • Head Library System • University of California-Berkeley University Library • Berkeley, CA 94720 • LITA
Hurley Doreen S. • Mount Lebannon Public Library • Pittsburgh, PA 15228
Hurley Dorothy E. • Children's Librarian • Westborough Public Library • Westborough, MA 01581
Hurley Geraldine C. • Training Program • Silver Platter Information • Norwood, MA 02062-5026 • LITA RASD
Hurley Jamie K. • Innovative Interfaces, Inc. • Berkeley, CA 94710

Hurley John • Assistant Director • Somerset County Library Bridgewater Branch • Bridgewater, NJ 08807 • LAMA PLA

Hurley Marie V. • Stamford, CT 06905

Hurley Marlene M. • Science Librarian • University of the Pacific • Stockton, CA 95211

Hurley Robert E. • Lake Worth, FL 33463-2029 • PLA

Hurley Trudy M. • Documents/Public Service Ln. • Western Connecticut State University • Danbury, CT 06810 • ACRL GODORT

Hurley Vivian • Librarian • Watsonville Public Library • Watsonville, CA 95076-4695

Hurowitz Robert I. • Librarian • Stanford University • Stanford, CA 94305-6011 • ALCTS

Hurr Barbara B. • Rockville, MD 20850 • AASL ACRL ALCTS PLA

Hurr Doris S. • Charlotte, NC 28209 • PLA

Hurrey Katharine C. • Director • Southern Maryland Regional Library Association • Charlotte Hall, MD 20622 • ASCLA LAMA PLA

Hurst Anne S. • Reference Librarian • University of Georgia Libraries • Athens, GA 30602 • ACRL

Hurst Billie K. Miss • Bibliographer • Southwest Missouri State University Meyer Library • Springfield, MO 65804 • ALCTS RASD *Life*

Hurst Brenda • Ottawa ON, K1K 3Y3 Canada • ALCTS

Hurst Eleanor A. • Americus, GA 31709 • Continuing

Hurst Ettie F. • Librarian • Crosby High School • Crosby, TX 77532 • AASL YALSA

Hurst Kimberly A. • Grandville, MI 49418 • ACRL

Hurst Vivian Wylene • Librarian • Louisiana State University Laboratory School Library • Baton Rouge, LA 70803 • AASL PLA

Hurt Charlene S. • University Librarian • George Mason University Libraries • Fairfax, VA 22030 • ACRL LAMA SRRT

Hurt Charlie D. • Director • University of Arizona Graduate Library School • Tucson, AZ 85721 • LRRT

Hurt Geraldine L. • Dept. Head,Clln Mgmt Services • Ferris State University • Big Rapids, MI 49307

Hurt Marion J. • Librarian • Pine Spring Elementary School • Falls Church, VA 22042 • AASL ALSC

Hurt Mary Ellen • Reference Librarian/ Selector • Iowa State University Library • Ames, IA 50011-2140 • ACRL RASD

Hurt Nancy S. • Head Librarian • McCamish Ingram Martin & Brown • San Antonio, TX 78216

Hurt Patricia M. • Chambersburg, PA 17201

Hurt Susan • Assistant to the Director • University of Arizona • Tucson, AZ 85721

Hurwitz Jack D. • Library Director • Hinsdale Public Library • Hinsdale, IL 60521 • PLA IFRT

Hurwitz Johanna • Librarian • Great Neck Library • Great Neck, NY 11024

Hurwitz K. Sue • Vienna, VA 22182 • AASL ALSC

Hurwitz Michael D. • Greenfield, MA 01301-9609

Hurwood Gilbert A. • Librarian • London Correctional Institute • London, OH 43140 • ASCLA NMRT

Hurych Jitka • Head Science & Engineering Dept. • Northern Illinois University University Libraries • DeKalb, IL 60115-2868 • ACRL

Husband Janet G. • Director • Rockland Memorial Library • Rockland, MA 02370

Husband Jonathan F. • Braintree, MA 02184

Husband Susan M. • Tucson, AZ 85716

Husbands Charles W. • Senior Systems Librarian • Harvard University • Cambridge, MA 02138 • ACRL ALCTS LITA *Life*

Huseman Dwight A. Rev. • Sipesville, PA 15561

Huser Agnes Irene Sr • Assistant Librarian • Conception Seminary College Library • Conception, MO 64433

Husfeldt Jerry J. • Librarian I • Chicago Public Library • Chicago, IL 60605

Huskey Jerry • Trustee • Jackson-Hinds Library System • Jackson, MS 39201 • ALTA

Huskey JoAnn • Librarian • Dellview Elementary School • San Antonio, TX 78213 • ALSC

Huskey Julia • Macon, GA 31210 • MAGERT

Huslig Dennis M. • Assistant Director • Suburban Audio-Visual Service • La Grange Park, IL 60525-1698 • LAMA PLA

Husman Susan E. • Librarian • Attorney General's Office • Columbia, SC 29211

Huso Charlene • President Board Of Trustees • Stockton Township Public Library • Stockton, IL 61085

Huso Debra A. • Librarian • Stockton Community Unit District 206 • Stockton, IL 61085 • AASL

Husom Elsie C. • Media/Technolgy Director • Brainerd Senior High School • Brainerd, MN 56401 • AASL

Huss Lawrence • Director • Dover Free Public Library • Dover, NJ 07801

Hussain Mohammad R. • Technical University of Nova Scotia Library • Halifax NS, B3J 2X4 Canada • ACRL

Hussey Jolee • Oxford, MS 38655-9771

Hussey Sandra Ruppert • Bibliogrpahic Instruction Coor. • Georgetown University Joseph Mark Lauinger Library • Washington, DC 20057-1006 • ACRL RASD NMRT

Hussin Donna J. • Member Services Librarian • NELINET Inc. • Newton, MA 02162 • LITA CLENE LIRT

Hustad Saundra S. • St Paul, MN 55126

Husted Caroline E. • Ann Arbor, MI 48105-2771 • AASL ALSC *Continuing*

Husted Deborah J. • Associate Librarian • State University of New York (SUNY) Central Technical Services • Buffalo, NY 14260 • ALCTS LITA

Husted Grace S. • Director • New Castle County Department of Libraries Administrative Offices • New Castle, DE 19720 • LAMA PLA

Husted Margery • School Library Media Specialist • Bloomfield-Mespo Local Schools • North Bloomfield, OH 44450 • AASL

Husted Ruth E. • Rolla, MO 65401

Huston Esther L. • Senior Librarian • California State Library • Sacramento, CA 94237-0001

Huston Evelyn E. • Claremont, CA 91711 • ACRL *Continuing*

Huston Kathleen M. • City Librarian • Milwaukee Public Library • Milwaukee, WI 53233 • PLA

Huston Mary M. • Associate Professor • Texas Woman's University School of Library & Information Studies • Denton, TX 76204 • IRRT

Huston Susan S. • Missouri Southern State College Library • Joplin, MO 64801 • ACRL

Hustuft Carol A. • Serials/Systems Librarian • Concordia College Carl B. Ylvisaker Library • Moorhead, MN 56562 • ACRL ALCTS LITA

Hutchens Dee Ann • Nedford, NJ 08055 • AASL

Hutcheson Stephanie • Assistant Chief Librarian • Toronto Public Library • Toronto ON, M5A 4L2 Canada • LAMA PLA EMIERT

Hutchings Anne E.M. • Teacher/Librarian • Bellwood Public School • Whitby ON, L1N 8M4 Canada • AASL

Hutchins Geraldine L. • Reference Librarian • AMIGOS Bibliographic Council,Inc. • Dallas, TX 75251-2104 • ASCLA LITA

Hutchins Kathleen D. • Head of Youth Services • Haverhill Public Library • Haverhill, MA 01830 • ALSC

Hutchins Mary J. • St. Johns, MI 48879 • PLA

Hutchins Paul R. • Director • Gladwin County Library • Gladwin, MI 48624-2096 • PLA

Hutchins Thelma J. • Library Director • Emory & Henry College • Emory, VA 24327 • ACRL IFRT

Hutchinson Barbara G. • Jacksonville Beach, FL 32250

Hutchinson Barbara J. • Director • Georgian Court College Farley Memorial Library • Lakewood, NJ 08701 • LITA MAGERT

Hutchinson Gregory A. • Student • University of Pittsburgh School of Library and Information Science • Pittsburgh, PA 15260

Hutchinson Heidi Lou • Cataloging • University of California Rivera Library • Riverside, CA 92517 • ACRL ALCTS IRRT

Hutchinson Joan D. • Media Specialist • Mary McLeod Bethune Elementary School • Jacksonville, FL 32209 • ALSC

Hutchinson Margaret • Charlottsvle, VA 22901 • ALSC

Hutchinson Margaret B. • Librarian • Holland Society of New York • New York, NY 10022

Hutchinson Mary Claire • Business Librarian • Washoe County Library • Reno, NV 89505 • PLA

Hutchinson Ramona • Mesa Verde Research Library • Mesa Verde, CO 81330

Hutchinson Virginia N. • Librarian • Government Employees Companies • Washington, DC 20076 • ALCTS

Hutchison Lucinda L. • Comstow Information Services • Harvard, MA 01451 • ALCTS LITA

Huth Geoffrey A. • New York State Archives & Records • Albany, NY 12230

Hutsler Betty A. • Library Coordinator • Frederick County Public Schools • Winchester, VA 22601 • AASL

Hutt Karen J. • American Library Association • Chicago, IL 60611-2795 • AASL EMIERT IFRT

Hutter Helmut • Assistant Architect • Brooklyn Public Library • Brooklyn, NY 11238 • LAMA

Huttner Marian • Bloomington, MN 55438 • LAMA PLA *Life*

Huttner Sidney F. • University of Tulsa Ls • Tulsa, OK 74104 • ACRL

Hutto Dena M. • Pennsylvania State University E506 Pattee Library • University Park, PA 16802 • ACRL ALCTS GODORT

Hutton Ann Barnett • Assistant Executive Director • Southeastern Libraries Cooperating (SELCO) • Rochester, MN 55901 • PLA

Hutton Catherine L. • Alcohol Research Group Library • Berkeley, CA 94709-2176 • ACRL LITA

Hutton Emily • Head of Acquisitions • Colgate University Everett Needham Case Library • Hamilton, NY 13346

Hutton Emily Admas • Vancouver, WA 98661

Hutton Jean R. • Director • Warren Wilson College Martha Ellison Library • Swannanoa, NC 28778 • ACRL LAMA LITA

Hutton Kathleen P. • Student • University of Maryland College of Library and Information Services • College Park, MD 20742-4345

Hutton Marilyn • Librarian • Frederick Public Schools • Frederick, OK 73542 • AASL

Hutton Paula Larkin • Student • San Jose State University Division of Library & Information Science • San Jose, CA 95192-0029

Hutton Todd S. • Vice Pres. for Acad. Adm. • Willamette University Mark O Hatfield Library • Salem, OR 97301 • ACRL LITA

Huwe Terence Keith • Head Librarian • University of California Berkeley Institute of Industrial Relations Library • Berkeley, CA 94720 • ACRL

Hux Roger K. • Reference Librarian • Francis Marion College Library • Florence, SC 29501 • LHRT

Huxhold Margaret • St Louis, MO 63122

Huxtable Michael J. • Librarian • Portsmouth Public Library • Portsmouth, NH 03801 • PLA RASD

Huygen Eva • Transcriptionist • Columbia Periodontal Associates • Columbia, SC 29201

Huygen Michaele Lee • Pacifica, CA 94044 • ACRL

Hveem Michael W. • Student • University of Connecticut Health Center Lyman Maynard Stowe Library • Farmington, CT 06032 • RASD

Hyatt Ruth • Vineyard Hvn, MA 02568-9715 • Continuing

Hyatt Sue Y. • Dir., Alternative Delivery Sys. • Chattanooga State Technical Community College Library • Chattanooga, TN 37406 • PLA NMRT

Hyatt Wendy J. • Director of Outreach • ACCESS : A Security Information Service • Washington, DC 20036 • ACRL RASD SRRT

Hycnar Barbara J. • Assoc. Dir./Hd. of Tech. Serv. • Northwestern University Law School Library • Chicago, IL 60611 • ALCTS LITA

Hyde Ann • Manuscripts Librarian Spec Clln. • University of Kansas Spencer Research Library • Lawrence, KS 66045-2800 • ACRL LITA *Life*

Hyde Dorothy V. • Director • Verona High School • Verona, WI 53593

Hyde E Clarendon Rev • Columbia, MO 65203 • Continuing

Hyde J Dennis • Collection Development • Pennsylvania University • Philadelphia, PA 19104 • ACRL

Hyde Jane L. • Student • University of North Carolina at Chapel Hill School of Information and Library Science • Chapel Hill, NC 27599-3360 • IFRT

Hyde Linda D. • Branch Head • Clemmons Branch Library • Clemmons, NC 27012

Hyde Mary A. • Winchester Medical Center Health Sciences Library • Winchester, VA 22601

Hyde Peggy • Public Relations Specialist • Howe Public Library • Hanover, NH 03755 • PLA

Hyde Rebecca E. • Librarian • Rowan-Cabarnes Community College • Salisbury, NC 28144 • ALCTS

Hyde Rhoda P. • Head, Cataloging Dept. • University of Maryland College Park Theodore R. McKeldin Library • College Park, MD 20742-7011 • ALCTS LITA

Hyde William H. Jr • La Jolla, CA 92037 • ACRL LAMA *Continuing*

Hyde William W. • Edison Electric Institute • Washington, DC 20004

Hylen Elizabeth J. • Acquisitions • Corning Museum of Glass • Corning, NY 14830

Hylen Jan • Merrimack, NH 03054 • AASL IFRT

Hylton Sharon F. • Tustin Unified School • Tustin, CA 92680 • AASL

Hyman Arnold S. • Supv. Asst. Branch Libn • New York Public Library Kingsbridge Branch • New York, NY 10463 • YALSA

Hyman Debra F. • Executive Assistant • DnA Enterprises • Fort Lauderdale, FL 33311 • RASD

Hyman Elaine Kelly • Head Systems Dept. • Florida Atlantic University Library • Boca Raton, FL 33431 • LITA

Hyman Ferne B. • Assistant University Librarian • Rice University Fondren Library • Houston, TX 77251-1892 • ACRL LAMA RASD

Hyman Karen • Executive Director • South Jersey Regional Library Midway Professional Center • Hammonton, NJ 08037 • ACRL ASCLA LAMA LITA PLA RASD

Hyman Richard J. Dr. • New York, NY 10025 • ALCTS LITA

Hyman Toby A. • Director • Bethpage Public Library • Bethpage, NY 11714 • LAMA PLA RASD IFRT

Hyman Wendy • Berkeley Public Library West Branch • Berkeley, CA 94702 • PLA RASD
Hymes Judith I. • Asst. Librarian Dir. Tech. Serv. • Washington College Clifton M. Miller Library • Chestertown, MD 21620
Hynes Edward J. • Director • Stonehill College Cushing-Martin Library • North Easton, MA 02357 • ACRL ALCTS LAMA RASD
Hypio Mike • Librarian • West Shore Community College • Scottville, MI 49454 • ACRL
Hyslop Colleen F. • Head,Technical Services • Michigan State University Libraries • East Lansing, MI 48824-1048 • ACRL ALCTS LAMA
Hyslop Gary L. • Indiana University School of Library and Information Science • Bloomington, IN 47405 • LIRT
Hyslop Grace • Sheridan Elementary School • Washington, DC 20008 • AASL
Hyzak Casilda Sister • Reference Librarian • Our Lady of the Lake University • San Antonio, TX 78207-4666 • RASD
Iacobucci Marisa T. • Hamilton, NY 13346-1320
Iacone Audrey • Librarian • Historical Society of Western Pennsylvania Library • Pittsburgh, PA 15213 • ALCTS RASD
Iacullo Josephine • Young Adult Librarian • New York Public Library Yorkville Branch • New York, NY 10021 • YALSA
Iadovito Carolyn • Williamsville, NY 14221
Ianni Madeline Z. • Library Media Specialist • Eastern High School Media Center • Voorhees, NJ 08043-0915 • AASL
Iannitto Deborah D. • Assistant to Director • Henrico Public Library • Richmond, VA 23223
Iannucci Patricia A. • Livermore Public Library • Livermore, CA 94550 • ALSC PLA RASD
Iannuzzi June H. • Media Specialist • Lafayette High School • Williamsburg, VA 23188
Iannuzzi Patricia • Head of Reference • Florida International University • Miami, FL 33199 • LAMA RASD
Iarusso Marilyn Berg • Asst. Coordinator Childrens Serv • The New York Public Library • New York, NY 10016 • ALSC
Iasso Gloria • Bookseller • Waldenbooks Freehold Raceway Mall • Freehold, NJ 07728
Iavicoli Sharon • Covina, CA 91723
Ibach Robert D. • Director • Dallas Theological Seminary Turpin Library • Dallas, TX 75204-6411 • ACRL ALCTS LITA RASD
Ice Priscilla T. • Librarian • Spokane County Library District Valley Branch • Spokane, WA 99206
Icenhower Della D. • Mansfield, TX 76063
Icenhower Elizabeth G. • University of Chicago Library • Chicago, IL 60637-1502 • LITA
Ichihana Anne • Part-time Reference Librarian • Herkimer Cnty Cmnty Coll • Herkimer, NY 13350
Ichino Estelle • Children's Librarian • Los Angeles Public Library Angeles Mesa Branch • Los Angeles, CA 90043 • ALSC PLA
Ichinose Mitsuko • Cataloger/Ref, East Asian Coll'n • Yale University Sterling Memorial Library • New Haven, CT 06520 • ACRL
Ickes Barbara J. • Asst. Chief, Central Public Serv • Free Library of Philadelphia • Philadelphia, PA 19103 • LAMA PLA
Iconis Kim • Cataloger • United States Air Force • Wright Patterson AFB, OH 45433
Iddings Daniel H. • Chicago, IL 60660-3326 • ALCTS LITA
Iddings Mary Sue • Loyola University E.M. Cudahy Memorial Library • Chicago, IL 60626 • ALCTS LITA
Idelberger Linda R. • Venice, FL 34292
Iden Stephen D. • Librarian • Springfield College in Illinois Charles E. Becker Library • Springfield, IL 62702 • ACRL LITA RASD NMRT
Idleman Rhonda • Farmington, CT 06085-1569 • AASL
Ifshin Steven L. • Associate Librarian for Systems • C.D. Plus • New York, NY 10001 • LITA
Igklegibe Ngozika I. • Baton Rouge, LA 70803
Iglehart Toma M. • Reference Librarian • Austin Community College Learning Resource Services • Austin, TX 78701 • ACRL
Iglesias Estrella M. • Chair Person of Circulation • Florida International University • Miami, FL 33199 • LAMA
Iglesias Judith T. • Reference Librarian • Tampa-Hillsborough County Public Library • Tampa, FL 33602
Igoe James Gerard • Director • Ypsilanti District Library • Ypsilanti, MI 48197 • LAMA PLA *Life*
Igwe Ben O. Dr. • Regional Librarian • District of Columbia Public Library Francis Gregory Regional Branch • Washington, DC 20020 • PLA IFRT IRRT
Igyarto Cynthia L. • Trustee • Stickney-Forest View Library • Stickney, IL 60402 • ALTA
Iha Linnel M. • Hawaii State Public Lib System McCully-Moiliili Branch • Honolulu, HI 96826
Ihde Linda M. • APO, NY 09178 • PLA AFLRT FLRT
Iheanacho Morris A. • Catalog Librarian • Oakwood College Eva B. Dykes Library • Huntsville, AL 35896 • ACRL ALCTS
Iheanacho Paulinus C. • Pennsylvania State University Behrend College Library • Erie, PA 16563-0902 • RASD
Ihle Trina K. • Student • University of Michigan School of Information and Library Studies • Ann Arbor, MI 48109-1092 • RASD
Ihlenfeldt Kay M. • Department of Public Instruction Division for Library Services • Madison, WI 53707
Ihrig Alice • Volunteer Coordinator • Oak Lawn Public Library • Oak Lawn, IL 60453 • ALTA PLA IFRT SRRT
Ihrig Elizabeth A. • Curator,Books & Manuscripts • Bakken Library • Minneapolis, MN 55416 • ACRL
Ihrig Marjorie L. • Secretary • Archdiocese of New York Manhattan Catholic School Office • New York, NY 10014
Ihrig Robert K. • Head, Catalog Department • Rochester Public Library • Rochester, NY 14604 • ACRL ALCTS LAMA LITA PLA RASD GODORT MAGERT
Ijeoma Celestine C. • Harmony Library • Owerrio Imo, Nigeria W. Africa
Ijeoma Victor O. • Library Officer • Imo State University College of Legal Studies • Okigwe, Imo State, Nigeria W. Africa • IRRT
Ike Adebimpe Olurinsola Mrs. • University Librarian • Federal University of Technology • Bauchi, Nigeria W. Africa • ACRL
Ikeda Naomi R. • Yale University Medical Library • New Haven, CT 06510
Ikehara Claire Y. • Librarian • Waianae Public Library • Waianae, HI 96792 • PLA YALSA IFRT SRRT
Ikehara Hide • Ann Arbor, MI 48105-2768
Ikushima Keiko • Kyoto, 619-02, Japan • ACRL
Ikuta Kay K. • Librarian • City of Inglewood Public Library • Inglewood, CA 90301-1771 • RASD MAGERT SORT
Ilacqua Anne Kennedy • Head Educational Resources • Boston University • Boston, MA 02215 • ACRL
Iliff John K. • Reference Librarian • Pinellas Park Public Library • Pinellas Park, FL 34665
Illback Lynn • Children's Librarian • Greenbelt Branch PGCMLS • Greenbelt, MD 20770
Illes Doris • Regional Manager • Riverside City & County Public Library Central Branch • Riverside, CA 92502
Illian Barbara E. • Trustee • Palatine Public Library • Palatine, IL 60067 • ALTA
Ilmer Constance W. • Farmington Hills, MI 48336-1206
Iltis Deanna W. • Head,Catalog Section • Oregon State Library • Salem, OR 97310-0640
Im Kui-Bin C. • Assistant Librarian • University of Michigan • Flint, MI 48502-2186 • LITA
Imamura Hiroshi • President • Kaisei-Sha Publishing Co. • Tokyo, Japan
Imber Jane H. • Quail Run Elementary School • Lawrence, KS 66049 • AASL ALSC
Imboden Chris • Trustee • East Central Arkansas Regional Library • Wynne, AR 72396
Imhoff Kathleen R. • Director • Mildred B. Harrison Regional Library • Columbiana, AL 35051 • LAMA PLA
Imholtz August A. Jr. • Executive Editor • Congressional Information Service • Bethesda, MD 20814-3389 • ALCTS
Imler Bonnie B. • Student • University of Pittsburgh School of Library and Information Science • Pittsburgh, PA 15260
Imler Charles Leroy • Marion High School • Marion, IN 46953 • AASL
Immaculata Sister • Librarian • Bethlehem Catholic High School • Bethlehem, PA 18017-4699
Immisch Diana E. • Librarian • Chabot College • Hayward, CA 94545 • ACRL
Immler Frank • Hd. Hum./Soc Sci. Libs Coll Dev. • University of Minnesota O. Meredith Wilson Library • Minneapolis, MN 55455-0414 • ALCTS LAMA
Immroth Barbara F. • University of Texas at Austin Graduate School of Library & Information Sciences • Austin, TX 78712-1276 • AASL ALSC ASCLA IFRT LRRT
Imoisi Ann U. • Benin City Bendel, Nigeria W. Africa
Imon Keith • Greece Central School District • Rochester, NY 14615 • AASL
Inabnett Nancy • Trustee • Ouachita Parish Public Library • Monroe, LA 71201 • ALTA
Inagaki Miki • University Heights, OH 44118-2638
Inbody Barbara G. • Head Librarian • Adlai E. Stevenson High School Library • Lincolnshire, IL 60069 • AASL
Indresano Rita J. • Library Media Specialist • Torrejon High School • APO, AE 09641-0005
Infanti Cathleen M. • Librarian • Bishop Ludden High School • Syracuse, NY 13219 • AASL
Infantino Cynthia P. • Adult Services Coordinator • Lake Forest Library • Lake Forest, IL 60045
Ingalls Carol A. • Regional Sales Mgr. • R.R. Bowker/ Martindale Hubbell • San Antonio, TX 78238 • ACRL
Inge Linda • Sales Representative • Quality Books Inc. • Lake Bluff, IL 60044-2204
Ingeman Karen M. • Maps & Government Information • Syracuse University Library E. S. Bird Library • Syracuse, NY 13244-2010 • ACRL
Ingersoll Diane S. • Hastings, MN 55033
Ingersoll Helen F. Miss • Denver, CO 80202 • Continuing
Ingersoll Jared Swift • Program Officer • International Research & Exchanges Board • Princeton, NJ 08540 • IRRT
Ingersoll Julie Narvell • Student • Indiana University School of Library and Information Science • Bloomington, IN 47405
Ingersoll Lynne S. • Student • Rosary College Graduate School of Library & Information Science • River Forest, IL 60305 • ALSC PLA IFRT SRRT
Ingersoll U. B. • Library Supervisor • Savannah-Chatham County Board of Education • Savannah, GA 31401
Ingersoll Vivien W. • Librarian I • Clearwater Public Library East Branch • Clearwater, FL 34625
Ingerson Myrtle L. • Technical Research Librarian • Phillips Petroleum Company Research & Development Library • Bartlesville, OK 74004 • LITA
Ingibergsson Asgeir • Augustana University College • Camrose AB, T4V 2R3 Canada • ACRL
Ingish Karen S. • Manager-Library & Inf. Services • Ameritech Services • Hoffman Estates, IL 60196-1025 • ACRL LAMA
Ingles Ernie B. • Director of Libraries • University of Alberta Library • Edmonton AB, T6G 2J8 Canada • ACRL LAMA
Inglett Betty L. • Richmond County School District • Augusta, GA 30904 • AASL
Inglin Jill A. • Shorewood, WI 53211 • PLA
Inglis Jennifer R. • Librarian I • Free Library of Philadelphia West Oak Lane Branch Library • Philadelphia, PA 19138 • PLA
Inglis Kari F. • Media Coordinator • Bishop Watterson High School • Columbus, OH 43214 • AASL
Ingold Marion B. • Children's Librarian • La Grange Park Public Library • La Grange Park, IL 60525 • ALSC PLA
Ingolfsland Dennis • Reference Librarian • George Fox College • Newberg, OR 97132 • ACRL
Ingraham-Swets Leonoor • Library & Media Services Dir. • Clark College Lewis D Cannell Library • Vancouver, WA 98663
Ingraham Janet A. • Reference Librarian • Worthington Public Library • Worthington, OH 43085 • SRRT
Ingram Jamie J. • Automation Project Manager • Wentworth Institute of Technology • Boston, MA 02115 • LITA
Ingram John E. • S.E.I.-Curator, Spec Coll • Colonial Williamsburg Foundation • Williamsburg, VA 23187 • ACRL LAMA
Ingram John J. • President • Ingram Industrial, Inc. • Jacksonville, FL 32217
Ingram Ricarda L. • Hyattsville, MD 20782
Ingrassia Barbara C. • Cataloger • Clark University Robert Hutchings Goddard Library • Worcester, MA 01610
Ingrim Sharon K. • Westmoreland, KS 66549
Ink Gary Louis • Research Librarian • Publishers Weekly • New York City, NY 10011
Inks Cordelia R. • Technical Services Librarian • Lee College Learning Resources Center • Baytown, TX 77520-4703 • ACRL ALCTS
Inkster Christine D. • Saint Cloud State University Centennial Hall LRC • St. Cloud, MN 56301-4498 • LITA
Inman Gail E. • Adult Services Coordinator • Lincolnwood Public Library District • Lincolnwood, IL 60646
Inman Harvey J. • Cataloger • Eden Webster Libraries • Saint Louis, MO 63119-9957 • ALCTS
Inman Rhonda K. • Engineering Librarian • Cessna Aircraft Co. • Wichita, KS 67215
Inman Ruth A. • Music Cataloger • University of Illinois at Chicago University Library • Chicago, IL 60680
Inmon Katie B. • Collection Development Librarien • University of the District of Columbia Learning Resources Division • Washington, DC 20008 • ACRL RASD
Inness Virginia J. • Catalog Librarian • University of Missouri-Kansas City Library • Kansas City, MO 64110-2499 • ALCTS LAMA
Innis Bertha J. Mrs. • Media Center Director • Medford Public School Library K-12 • Medford, OK 73759 • AASL
Inoue Yasuyo • Kyoto University of Foreign Studies • Kyoto, 617, Japan • ALSC PLA
Inouye Patricia C. • Technical Processing Supv. • University of California Shields Library • Davis, CA 95616 • GODORT
Inslee Frances S. • Adult Literacy Assistant • Chester County Library & District Center • Exton, PA 19341-2496 • IRRT

Intner Sheila S. • Professor • Simmons College Graduate School of Library & Information Science • Boston, MA 02115 • ACRL ALCTS LITA RASD LRRT

Inui Tonau • Student • Arizona State University Department of Education Library Science • Tempe, AZ 85287

Inwood Judy E. • Public Library of Cincinnati and Hamilton County • Cincinnati, OH 45202

Inzer Angela J. • Athens, TN 37303

Ipema Tina Van Staalduinen • Grand Rapids, MI 49509

Ippolito Andrew V. • Bayside, NY 11361

Ipsen Patricia • Director • New Hampton Public Library • New Hampton, IA 50569 • PLA

Iraci Barbara Mrs. • Librarian • East Hill Elementary School • Canajoharie, NY 13317

Irby Jacquelin T. • Elementary Library Coordinator • Lewisville Independent School District • Lewisville, TX 75057 • AASL

Ireland Judith F. • Librarian • Salt Lake City Public Library Rose Park Branch • Salt Lake City, UT 84116

Ireland Judith G. • Reference Librarian • Takoma Park Maryland Library • Takoma Park, MD 20912

Ireland Laverne H. • Librarian • Live Oak High School • Morgan Hill, CA 95038 • AASL

Ireland Leland R. • Marketing Director • AMIGOS Bibliographic Council,Inc. • Dallas, TX 75251-2104

Ireland Mary R. • Librarian • Public Schools • Roseau, MN 56751 • AASL

Irish Elizabeth D. • Engineering Librarian • Rensselaer Polytechnic Institute • Troy, NY 12180 • ACRL

Irish Elizabeth F. • Children's Librarian • Orange Public Library • Orange, CA 92666 • ALSC PLA

Irons Florence K. • Goshen, NY 10924

Irvin Marcia A. • Library Director • Geological Survey of Alabama • Tuscaloosa, AL 35486

Irvin Sheri D. • Head Circulation • Claremont Colleges Libraries Honnold/Mudd Library • Claremont, CA 91711 • ACRL LAMA IFRT

Irvine Ann E. • Community Librarian • Montgomery County Department of Public Libraries Kensington Branch • Kensington, MD 20895 • PLA RASD

Irvine Betty Jo • Librarian • Indiana University • Bloomington, IN 47405 • ACRL

Irvine Cynthia R. • Student • Simmons College Graduate School of Library & Information Science • Boston, MA 02115 • ACRL SRRT

Irvine Jayne M. • Ft. Lewis, WA 98433 • AFLRT LHRT

Irvine Kay M. • Librarian • Western States Chiropractic College • Portland, OR 97230 • ACRL

Irving Jane A. • Reference-Circuit • Delaware Academy of Medicine Lewis B. Flinn Library • Wilmington, DE 19806 • ASCLA

Irving Janet K. • State Library of Iowa • Des Moines, IA 50319 • ALSC

Irving M. Suzanne • Head, Interlibrary Loan Dept. • State University of New York (SUNY) University Libraries • Albany, NY 12222 • RASD IFRT

Irving Mary Lou • Maui High School • Kahului, HI 96732

Irving Ophelia M. • Assistant Chief, Info Services • North Carolina Department of Cultural Resources State Library • Raleigh, NC 27601-2807

Irving Richard • Albany, NY 12203-4113 • ACRL IFRT

Irwin B. Dale • Head of Bibliographic Services • York University Libraries • North York ON, M3J 1P3 Canada • LITA

Irwin Bonnie J. • University of Illinois Urbana Engineering Publications • Urbana, IL 61801

Irwin Denise M. • Student • Emporia State University School of Library & Information Management • Emporia, KS 66801 • AASL ASCLA

Irwin Elaine D. • Cataloger • Upper Darby Township & Sellers Free Public Library • Upper Darby, PA 19082

Irwin Iris • Ref. Librarian-Govt. Documents • CW Post Palmer Grad L Sch • Brookville, NY 11548 • ACRL GODORT

Irwin Joan M. • Director of Publications • International Reading Association • Newark, DE 19714-8139 • IFRT

Irwin John W. • Associate Director, Pub Servs. • Flagstaff City-Coconino County Public Library • Flagstaff, AZ 86001

Irwin Kyle S. • Student • Westrn Michigan University • Kalamazoo, MI 49008

Irwin Larry • Librarian • Cleary College Library • Howell, MI 48843 • ACRL

Irwin Margaret A. • Houston Academy of Medicine Texas Medical Center Library • Houston, TX 77030 • ACRL

Irwin Marilyn M. • Director/Office of Dissemination • Institute for the Study of Developmental Disabilities • Bloomington, IN 47405 • ALSC ASCLA YALSA

Irwin Ned L. • Chattanooga-Hamilton County Bicentennial Library • Chattanooga, TN 37402

Irwin Patricia C. • Dexter Consolidated Schools • Dexter, NM 88230 • AASL IFRT

Irwin Richard G. • Student • Kent State University School of Library & Information Science • Kent, OH 44242-0001 • ALCTS RASD

Irwin Susan E. • Student • University of Hawaii School of Library & Information Studies • Honolulu, HI 96822 • ALSC PLA

Irwin Tye • Designer • INTRAX • Port Stanley, ON, N0L 2A0 Canada

Isaac Fredrick J. • Head, Librarian • Jewish Community Library • San Francisco, CA 94118 • ACRL LAMA IFRT LRRT

Isaac Stephen J. • Library Technician • Enid M. Baa Library • Saint Thomas, VI 00802 • ACRL PLA CLENE

Isaacs Minnie Miss • Fort Lauderdale, FL 33308 • AASL YALSA   *Continuing*

Isaacs Nancy B. • Librarian • Lesley College Library • Cambridge, MA 02138 • LITA

Isaacs Suzanne T. • Society for Visual Education, Inc. • Chicago, IL 60614

Isaacs Winnie K. • Librarian/Information Associate • Access Information Associates Inc. • Bellaire, TX 77401

Isaacson David K. • Assistant Head of Reference • Western Michigan University Libraries Dwight B. Waldo Library • Kalamazoo, MI 49008 • RASD

Isaacson Kathy • Ref Ln & Lib Sys Coordinator • Lawrence University Seeley G. Mudd Library • Appleton, WI 54911 • ACRL

Isaacson Melvin S. • Library Director • Pace University Library New York Civic Center • New York, NY 10038 • ACRL

Isaacson Richard H. • Indexer • H. W. Wilson Company • Bronx, NY 10452 • RASD

Isaacson Sandra A. • Duluth, MN 55811

Isaacson Sarabell • Educational Media Specialist • Elizabeth Avenue School • Somerset, NJ 08873 • AASL

Isacco Jeanne M. • Greensboro, NC 27410 • GODORT

Isackes Beverly A. • Austin, TX 78734

Isarin W. J. • Librarian • University of Manitoba • Winnipeg MB, Canada • ACRL ALCTS

Isbell Dennis H. • Assistant Reference Librarian • Arizona State University-West Fletcher Library • Phoenix, AZ 85069-7100 • ACRL RASD LIRT

Isely Megan M. • Aurora Public Library • Aurora, IL 60505-4299 • RASD

Isensee Karen P. • Petrified Forest NP, AZ 86028

Isenstein Laura J. • Baltimore County Public Library • Towson, MD 21204 • LAMA PLA RASD

Isgro Carol A. • Berea, OH 44017

Ishibashi Jane M. • Director • Library of the Institute for North American Studies • Barcelona, Spain

Ishibashi Joan C. • Director, Resource Center • Hawaii Conference UCC • Honolulu, HI 96817

Ishihara Faith E. • Honolulu, HI 96813

Ishihara Fay K. • Waimea, HI 96796

Ishimaru Coreen E. • Catalog Librarian • University of Hawaii Hilo Library • Hilo, HI 96720 • ALCTS

Ishimoto Carol F. • Cambridge, MA 02138 • ACRL ALCTS LAMA LITA   *Life*

Ishler Beatrice D. • Alba High School • Bayou La Batre, AL 36509 • AASL

Ismail Noha S. • Reference Librarian • Hennepin County Library Penn Lake Branch Library • Bloomington, MN 55431 • SRRT

Isman Bonnie J. • Director • Jones Library • Amherst, MA 01002 • ALSC PLA RASD

Isobe Shigeharu • Okura Institute of Spiritual Culture • Yokohama, 222, Japan • ACRL

Isom Angela G. • Media Specialist • Stone Mountain High School • Stone Mountain, GA 30083 • AASL YALSA

Isom Cheryl Nordlund • Head Librarian • Zion-Benton Public Library District • Zion, IL 60099 • LAMA PLA

Ison Betty S. • Saint Claire Medical Center Medical Library • Morehead, KY 40351 • ACRL ASCLA LITA

Ison Janice Beck • Executive Director • Lincoln Trail Libraries System • Champaign, IL 61821-1068 • ASCLA LAMA PLA

Ison John E. • Urbana, IL 61801 • ERT

Israel Elaine • Student • University of Pittsburgh School of Library and Information Science • Pittsburgh, PA 15260 • AASL ALSC

Israel Girgis Z. • Cataloger Assistant • Denver Public Library • Denver, CO 80204-2602 • LITA

Israel Jodi L. • Faxon Company Inc. • Westwood, MA 02090 • LITA RASD IFRT NMRT

Israelson Dara J. • Student • University of Michigan School of Information and Library Studies • Ann Arbor, MI 48109-1092 • ALSC

Italie Barbara S. • Collection Development Manager • Mount Vernon Public Library • Mount Vernon, NY 10550

Itina Irene • Yonkers, NY 10703 • GODORT

Itnyre Jacqueline H. • Stanford University • Stanford, CA 94305-6011

Ito Mary E. • Winona, MN 55987

Ito Shirley • Amateur Athletic Foundation • Los Angeles, CA 90018 • LITA

Itoga Mary Ann T. • Prin Cataloger, Catlgr Sect. • Washington State University Library • Pullman, WA 99164-5610 • ALCTS

Itoga Masaru • Visiting Scholar • Keio University School School of Library & Information Science • Tokyo, 108, Japan • PLA LRRT

Ittner Dwight R. • BioSciences Librarian • University of Alaska • Fairbanks, AK 99775 • ACRL ALCTS LITA

Ivaldi Janet L. • Bridgeport, CT 06604 • SRRT

Iversen David S. • Catalog/Serials Librarian • Rider College • Lawrenceville, NJ 08648-3099 • ACRL ALCTS

Iversen Dian • Santa Teresa High School Library • San Jose, CA 95123

Iversen Teresa L. • Student • University of Tennessee-Knoxville Graduate School of Library & Information Science • Knoxville, TN 37996-4330 • ASCLA IFRT SRRT

Iverson Deborah P. • Director • Sheridan College Instructional Resource Center • Sheridan, WY 82801

Iverson Edwin • District Library Coordinator • Churchill County School District • Fallon, NV 89406 • AASL

Iverson Terri E. • Director of Media Services • Cooperative Educational Services Agency #3 • Ferrimore, WI 53809 • AASL

Iverson Yvonne M. • Librarian • Fort Vancouver Regional Library • Vancouver, WA 98663

Ives Alan • University Archivist • Charles Sturt University Riverina • Wagga Wagga NSW 2650, Australia • ACRL LAMA LITA RASD CLENE ERT IRRT LHRT LIRT MAGERT

Ives Cornelia M. • Librarian • Baltimore County Public Library • Towson, MD 21204 • PLA

Ives Elizabeth N. Miss • Hamden, CT 06517 • Continuing

Ives Gary W. • Head, Access Services • University of Texas at El Paso Library • El Paso, TX 79968-0582 • ACRL LAMA

Ives Helen E. • Reference Librarian • The American University Library • Washington, DC 20016-8046 • ACRL RASD GODORT

Ives Peter B. • University of New Mexico • Albuquerque, NM 87131 • RASD MAGERT

Ivey Barbara M. • Colorado Springs, CO 80917

Ivey David M. • Librarian • Allen County Public Library • Fort Wayne, IN 46801 • PLA

Ivey Robert T. Dr. • Assistant Director, Cataloging • Memphis State University Libraries • Memphis, TN 38152 • ACRL ALCTS

Ivins October R. • Head, Serials Services • Louisiana State University Libraries Troy H. Middleton Library • Baton Rouge, LA 70803-3342 • ACRL ALCTS LITA

Ivliano Russell • Auburndale, MA 02166 • LITA

Ivory Edrice G. • Columbia, MD 21044 • LAMA PLA

Ivory Paula R. • Student • University of Kentucky College of Library & Information Science • Lexington, KY 40506-0391

Ivy Barbara A. • Ada, OK 74820 • LAMA PLA LRRT SRRT

Iwabuchi Yasuo • Professor • Toyo University • Tokyo 112, Japan • ACRL ALCTS LITA RASD

Iwanter Sidney E. • Director • Fox Broadcasting Company • Los Angeles, CA 90028 • IFRT

Iyer Thangam R. • Cataloger • Library of Congress • Washington, DC 20541 • ALCTS FLRT IRRT SRRT

Izbicki Thomas M. • Resource Services • Johns Hopkins University Milton S. Eisenhower Library • Baltimore, MD 21218 • ACRL

Izumo Patsy M. Dr. • Director • Hawaii Department of Education Special Instructional Programs & Services Branch • Honolulu, HI 96816 • AASL LITA

Izzo Cheryl R. • Librarian/Media Specialist • Stillmeadow Elementary School • Stamford, CT 06902

Jaacks Carole • High School Librarian • Maine Township High School East • Park Ridge, IL 60068 • AASL

Jaap Karilyn B. • Director • Gulf Beaches Public Library • Madeira Beach, FL 33708 • PLA

Jabido Penelope B. • Cataloger • Newark Public Library • Newark, NJ 07101-0630

Jabloner Paula R. • Student • University of Michigan School of Information and Library Studies • Ann Arbor, MI 48109-1092

Jacak Wanda • Sr. Foreign Lang Specialist • Emory University • Atlanta, GA 30329

Jacaruso Beth A. • Student • Simmons College Graduate School of Library & Information Science • Boston, MA 02115

Jack Alison L. • University of Oklahoma Libraries University Libraries • Norman, OK 73019

Jack Joyce H. • Averill Park, NY 12018-9621 • AASL ALSC

Jackanicz Donald W. • Chicago, IL 60641

Jackman Mabel E. • Rochester, MN 55901 • AASL YALSA   *Continuing*

Jackson-Beck Lauren A. • Cloisters Library Fort Tryon Park • New York, NY 10040 • ACRL ALCTS

Jackson-Brown Grace • Reference Librarian • Indiana University • Bloomington, IN 47405 • ACRL LIRT

Jackson Ada E. • Community Affairs Liaison • The New York Public Library • New York, NY 10016 • PLA

Jackson Alice A. • Petersburg, VA 23803 • Continuing

Jackson Alison K. • Children's Librarian • Fullerton Public Library • Fullerton, CA 92632

Jackson Althea H. Sr. • Saint Augustine, FL 32095 • Life

Jackson Arden Marie • Seattle, WA 98115 • AASL ALSC

Jackson Arlyne A. • Librarian,Littauer Library • Harvard University • Cambridge, MA 02138 • ACRL LAMA LITA

Jackson Aubrey A. • Duke University William R. Perkins Library • Durham, NC 27706

Jackson Audrey N. • Zachary, LA 70791-9422 • Continuing

Jackson Barbara A. • Asst. Dir., Circulation Services • University of Virginia Alderman Library • Charlottesville, VA 22903-2498

Jackson Betty Baucum • Administrative Director • Franklin Parish Library • Winnsboro, LA 71295

Jackson Brenda G. • Circulation Supervisor • Shreve Memorial Library • Shreveport, LA 71120-1523 • PLA

Jackson C. Bennett • Trustee • Newport Beach Public Library • Newport Beach, CA 92660 • ALTA

Jackson Carleton L. • University of Maryland Hornbake Library • College Park, MD 20742 • ACRL LITA LIRT VRT

Jackson Carol Ms. • Librarian • Socorro High School Bill Sybert Library • El Paso, TX 79927 • AASL LITA YALSA

Jackson Caroline J. • President • The Belvedere Press • Arlington, VA 22205 • AASL ALSC PLA IRRT

Jackson Catherine A. • St. Louis, MO 63129 • IFRT SRRT

Jackson Christine A. • Librarian • Narberth Community Library • Narberth, PA 19072 • ALSC LAMA LITA PLA YALSA ERT LRRT SORT

Jackson Claudine M. • Young Adult Specialist • Kansas City Public Library • Kansas City, MO 64106 • YALSA

Jackson Colleen F. • Student • University of North Carolina Department of Library & Information Studies • Greensboro, NC 27412-5001 • AASL EMIERT IFRT LHRT

Jackson Debra Brunberg • Supervisor-Children's Services • Lorain Public Library • Lorain, OH 44052 • ALSC PLA

Jackson Donna • University of North Texas School of Library & Information Sciences • Denton, TX 76203

Jackson Donna E. • Radiology Librarian • Carolinas Medical Center Department of Radiology • Charlotte, NC 28232-2861

Jackson Doris C. • Librarian • Atlanta-Fulton Public Library • Atlanta, GA 30303 • ALSC PLA CLENE

Jackson Dorothy • Electronic Services Analyst • AT&T Bell Laboratories • Murray Hill, NJ 07974 • LITA

Jackson Eddie • Trustee • East Saint Louis Public Library • East St. Louis, IL 62201 • ALTA

Jackson Edgar N. • Trustee • William Leonard Public Library District • Robbins, IL 60472 • ALTA

Jackson Edna • Trustee • East Saint Louis Public Library • East St. Louis, IL 62201 • ALTA

Jackson Edwin G. • Chapel Hill, NC 27514 • LAMA PLA   *Life*

Jackson Elizabeth C. • Associate Director • Mercer University in Altanta School of Pharmacy • Altanta, GA 30312 • ACRL LAMA LHRT

Jackson Emily • Programs Administrator • Orange County Public Library • Irvine, CA 92714 • LAMA PLA

Jackson Frances P. • Media Specialist • Elm Grove Elementary School • Kingwood, TX 77319 • AASL ALCTS LIRT

Jackson Gloria D. • Sacramento, CA 95831

Jackson Gwendolyn G. • Southeast Technical Assistance Center • Jacksonville, NC 28540 • AASL

Jackson Harriett D. • Librarian • Memphis-Shelby County Public Library Parkway Village Branch • Memphis, TN 38118

Jackson Jane E. • Director • Escambia County Cooperative Library System • Atmore, AL 36502

Jackson Jean • Saint Augustine, FL 32095

Jackson Jean E. • Librarian • Jackson Library Services • LaVerne, CA 91750 • ILERT

Jackson Jennifer • Campus Librarian • University of the Virgin Islands Saint Croix Campus • St. Croix, VI 00850 • ACRL

Jackson Joan • Branch Head • San Francisco Public Library Western Addition Branch • San Francisco, CA 94115 • PLA EMIERT SRRT

Jackson Johnny W. • Assistant University Librarian • Central State University Hallie Q Brown Memorial Library • Wilberforce, OH 45384

Jackson Joseph A. • Dean of Libraries • University of Tennessee T Carter & M Rawlings Lupton Lib • Chattanooga, TN 37403 • ACRL

Jackson Julia A. • Chicago, IL 60613

Jackson Kathryn M. • Liberty, MO 64068 • GODORT

Jackson Lila E. • Oak Lawn, IL 60453 • Continuing

Jackson Linda Guardia • Librarian • Judson Montessori School • San Antonio, TX 78216 • AASL ALSC

Jackson Lorraine A. • Student • County of Los Angeles Public Library Hacienda Heights Library 815 • Hacienda Heights, CA 91745

Jackson Lorraine Sano • Director • South Brunswick Public Library • Monmouth Junction, NJ 08852 • LAMA PLA

Jackson Lynne • Library/Media Generalist • Londonderry High School Library/Media Center • Londonderry, NH 03053 • AASL

Jackson Lynne-Marie • Head Librarian • American Academy of Dramatic Arts • New York, NY 10016

Jackson Margaret W. • Eastern Loudon Regional Library • Sterling, VA 22170 • RASD

Jackson Marian Dee • Asst Librarian Ref/Pub Servs • Tyler Junior College Vaughn Library & Learning Res Ctr • Tyler, TX 75711-9020 • RASD LRRT

Jackson Marie V. • Student • Drexel University College of Information Studies • Philadelphia, PA 19104-2875 • EMIERT

Jackson Martha • Chidlren's Book Specialist • A Clean Well-Lighted Place for Books • Larkspur, CA 94939 • ALSC

Jackson Mary • Children's Coodinator • Nebraska Library Commission • Lincoln, NE 68508 • ALSC PLA

Jackson Mary E. • Head, Interlibrary Loan • University of Pennsylvania Library Van Pelt-Dietrich Library Center • Philadelphia, PA 19104-6206 • ACRL LITA RASD

Jackson Mary F. • Bronx, NY 10468

Jackson Mary M. • Indiana University School of Library and Information Science • Bloomington, IN 47405 • AASL LIRT

Jackson Mattie M. • Director • Miles College Learning Resources Center • Birmingham, AL 35208

Jackson Maxine • School Librarian • Williams Elementary School • Pasadnea, TX 77502

Jackson Melinda I. • Branch Head • Central Arkansas Library System Fletcher Branch • Little Rock, AR 72205 • PLA

Jackson Miles M. • Dean • University of Hawaii School of Library & Information Studies • Honolulu, HI 96822 • ACRL IRRT

Jackson Nancy G. • Head, Post Cataloging Section • Library of Congress • Washington, DC 20541

Jackson Nancy I. • School Media Specialist • Broward County Schools • Fort Lauderdale, FL 33325 • AASL

Jackson P. Jean • Maryville, TN 37801

Jackson Pamela A. • Fayetteville, NC 28304

Jackson Patience K. • Library Building Consultant • Massachusetts Board of Library Commissioners • Boston, MA 02215-2070 • LAMA

Jackson Patricia A. • Coor. for Collection Devel. • Texas Woman's University Mary Evelyn Blagg-Huey Library • Denton, TX 76204-1715 • LAMA LITA

Jackson Patricia Lee • Barstow, CA 92311

Jackson Paulette E. • Library Media Specialist • Columbia Adventist Academy • Battle Ground, WA 98604 • AASL

Jackson Queen E. • Teacher-Librarian • Steinmetz High School • Chicago, IL 60634

Jackson Reba J. • Librarian • Perry County Public Lib • Hazard, KY 41701

Jackson Rebecca • Coor. of Instructional Services • University of Maryland Hornbake Library • College Park, MD 20742 • ACRL RASD LIRT

Jackson Rosalind F. • Head, Interlibrary Loan Dept • Cleveland Public Library • Cleveland, OH 44114-1271

Jackson Ruth L. • Austin, TX 78759 • Continuing

Jackson Sharon T. • Lake Lanier Regional Library • Duluth, GA 30245 • PLA RASD

Jackson Sheila T. • Dept. Head, Social Science • Carnegie Library of Pittsburgh • Pittsburgh, PA 15213-4080 • PLA

Jackson Susan B. • Huntington Beach, CA 92646

Jackson T. Haller III • Tucker, Jetter, Jackson and Hickman • Shreveport, LA 71101-3146 • PLA

Jackson Theresa R. • Library Media Specialist • Wilson Magnet High School • Rochester, NY 14611 • AASL

Jackson Therese A. • City Librarian • San Bruno Public Library • San Bruno, CA 94066 • LAMA PLA RASD

Jackson Theria M. • Martin Luther King Jr. High School • Centerville, IL 62203 • AASL

Jackson William H. • Department Director • Iowa Department of Cultural Affairs • Des Moines, IA 50319

Jackson William V. • Professor • University of Texas • Austin, TX 78712-1276 • ACRL ALCTS RASD IRRT   *Life*

Jackson Willie E. • Supervisior Law Librarian • Connecticut State Library Law Library at Bridgeport • Bridgeport, CT 06604

Jacob Anita • Secondary Libn./Media Specialist • Iowa Valley Junior-Senior High School • Marengo, IA 52301 • AASL

Jacob Helen • Schaumburg, IL 60194 • ALSC ALTA   *Life*

Jacob Marc G. • Vice President, Cont. Lib. Subs. • Bantam, Doubleday, Dell Publishing Group • New York, NY 10103

Jacob Mary Ellen L • Columbus, OH 43220 • ACRL ALCTS LAMA LITA

Jacob Merle L. • Adult Materials Specialist • Chicago Public Library Harold Washington Library • Chicago, IL 60605 • ALCTS RASD

Jacob Nora B. • Executive Director • Orange County Public Library • Santa Ana, CA 92705 • LAMA PLA

Jacob Norman P. • Branch Librarian • Prince George's County Memorial Library Bowie Branch • Bowie, MD 20715 • PLA

Jacob Rosamond T. • Document Librarian • Saint Paul Public Library • St. Paul, MN 55102 • GODORT

Jacobe Angela C. • Head, Business & Science Dept. • Orange County Library System Orlando Public Library • Orlando, FL 32801-2471 • PLA

Jacobek Phyllis Ann • President, Board of Trustees • Mokena Community Public Library District • Mokena, IL 60448 • ALTA

Jacober Sheryl A. • Assistant Director • Shaker Heights Public Library • Shaker Heights, OH 44120 • LAMA PLA

Jacobi Monica T. • Student • National University Library • San Diego, CA 92108 • LITA RASD

Jacobowitz Neil A. • Cataloger • City College of New York (CUNY) • New York, NY 10031 • ACRL IRRT

Jacobs Alice E. • Assistant Head Cataloging • National Library of Medicine • Bethesda, MD 20894 • ALCTS

Jacobs Alice Fontenot • San Francisco, CA 94127 • ALSC EMIERT SRRT

Jacobs Barbara • Librarian • San Anselmo Public Library • San Anselmo, CA 94960 • LAMA PLA

Jacobs Carol S. • Archivist • Cleveland Orchestra • Cleveland, OH 44106

Jacobs Deborah • Director • Corvallis-Benton County Public Library • Corvallis, OR 97330-4728 • ALTA ASCLA LAMA PLA SRRT

Jacobs Donna K. • Science/Reference Librarian • College of Wooster Andrews Library • Wooster, OH 44691 • ACRL

Jacobs Gloria • Somerville, MA 02144

Jacobs Jane W. • Senior Cataloger • Benjamin N. Cardozo School of Law • New York, NY 10003 • ALCTS

Jacobs Leona • Systems Librarian • University of Lethbridge Library • Lethbridge AB, T1K 3M4 Canada • LITA

Jacobs Lois S. • Media Specialist • Tenney Middle School • Methuen, MA 01844

Jacobs Marianne • Board of Trustees Member • Pierce County Rural Library District • Tacoma, WA 98446 • ALTA PLA

Jacobs Marilyn B. • Librarian • Mattison Avenue Elementary School • Ambler, PA 19002-4798

Jacobs Mark D. • Reference & Information Services • Georgetown University Joseph Mark Lauinger Library • Washington, DC 20057-1006 • ACRL RASD

Jacobs Mildred H. • Librarian • Windermere High School • Eleuthera, Bahamas • AASL

Jacobs Nina F. • Librarian • U S Air Force Base Library Mitchell Memorial Library • Travis AFB, CA 94535-5000 • AFLRT FLRT

Jacobs Olivia • Library Media Specialist • Wichita High School Heights • Wichita, KS 67219 • AASL

Jacobs Peter • Professional Media Services • Gardena, CA 90248 • ALCTS LITA PLA

Jacobs Roger F. • Director • University of Notre Dame Kresge Law Library • Notre Dame, IN 46556 • ACRL LITA

Jacobs Sally J. • Reference Services • Virginia Commonwealth University Library Media & Educational Media • Richmond, VA 23284 • ACRL LIRT

Jacobs Susan K. • Student • Saint John's University Division of Library & Information Science • Jamaica, NY 11439 • RASD IFRT

Jacobs Susan Logue • Head,Preservation Section • Southern Illinois University Delyte W. Morris Library • Carbondale, IL 62901-6632 • ALCTS

Jacobs Terri C. • Chicago, IL 60610 • ALTA PLA IFRT

Jacobs Veronica J. • Student • State University of New York (SUNY) School of Information & Library Studies • Buffalo, NY 14260

Jacobsen Bruce F. • Vice President • Bridgeport National Bindery • Agawam, MA 01001 • ALCTS LITA

Jacobsen Donald W. • Assistant Director • American Museum of Natural History Library • New York, NY 10024 • MAGERT

Jacobsen Kristin E. • Clln Develp/Reference Librarian • Southern Methodist University DeGolyer Library & Fikes Hall • Dallas, TX 75275-0396 • ACRL ERT

Jacobsen Lavonne • Reader's Services Librarian • San Francisco State University J. Paul Leonard Library • San Francisco, CA 94132 • RASD GODORT MAGERT SRRT

Jacobsen Lynne A. • Student • Cook Memorial Library • Libertyville, IL 60048

Jacobsen Teresa L. • Santa Monica Public Library • Santa Monica, CA 90401 • RASD

Jacobsma Kelly L. • Head of Public Services • Hope College Van Wylen Library • Holland, MI 49423 • ACRL LAMA

Jacobson Avery H. • Library Assistant • Phoenix Public Library Century Branch • Phoenix, AZ 85016

Jacobson Beyer Harry E. • Coordinator of Children's Serv. • Louisville Free Public Library • Louisville, KY 40203-2257 • ALSC YALSA

Jacobson Donna Breen • Teacher-Librarian • Disney Magnet Elementary School • Chicago, IL 60613

Jacobson Frances F. • University High School Library • Urbana, IL 61801 • AASL ACRL YALSA

Jacobson Gerald J. • Librarian • Dr. Martin Luther College • New Ulm, MN 56073 • AASL ACRL ALCTS ALSC RASD YALSA LIRT

Jacobson L. L. Mrs • Valley City, ND 58072 • Continuing

Jacobson Lynn M. • Stoughton, WI 53589 • RASD

Jacobson Margaret R. • Exton, PA 19341

Jacobson Michele A. • Librarian I • Bridgeport Public Library • Bridgeport, CT 06604 • ALSC

Jacobson Nancy L. • Oak Park, MI 48237

Jacobson Nancy L. • Cambridge, MA 02139

Jacobson Sandra K. • Research Librarian • Jenner & Block • Chicago, IL 60611

Jacobson Shari L. • Student • Rutgers University School of Communication Information & Library Studies • New Brunswick, NJ 08903

Jacobson Susan • Westfield, NJ 07090 • AASL

Jacobson Susan I. • Asst Ln for Access & Tech Serv • Columbia University Health Sciences Library • New York, NY 10032 • ACRL ALCTS LITA

Jacobson Trudi E. • Bibl Instr Coor • State University of New York (SUNY) University Libraries • Albany, NY 12222 • ACRL RASD

Jacobus Catherine H. • Student • University of Arizona Graduate Library School • Tucson, AZ 85721

Jacoby Beth E. • University of Delaware Library • Newark, DE 19717-5267 • ALCTS NMRT

Jacoby Denise L. • Student • San Jose State University Division of Library & Information Science • San Jose, CA 95192-0029 • RASD EMIERT IFRT

Jacoby Marcia • Reference Librarian • Hagaman Memorial Library • East Haven, CT 06512-3098 • RASD

Jacocks Jean P. • Head, Fiction Dept. • Enoch Pratt Free Library • Baltimore, MD 21201-4484 • RASD

Jacocks Marcia W. • Librarian • Hammond Lower School • Columbia, SC 29209 • AASL

Jacox Corinne C. • Student • University of Nebraska-Lincoln College of Law Library • Lincoln, NE 68583-0902 • NMRT

Jacque Zella B. Mrs • New London, OH 44851-1125 • LAMA PLA *Continuing*

Jacques Donna M. • Reference Librarian Coordinator • Tufts University • Medford, MA 02155 • ACRL

Jaderborg Jean A. • Head of West Branch Library • Lincoln Library • Springfield, IL 62701 • ALSC PLA

Jadlos Melissa • Catalog/Reference Librarian • Saint Lawrence University Owen D. Young Library • Canton, NY 13617 • ALCTS

Jaech Carol • Adult Services • Santa Clara County Free Library • San Jose, CA 95112-4446

Jaeger Bret K. • Director • Meeker Regional Library District • Meeker, CO 81641

Jaeger James P. • Student • University of Missouri-Columbia School of Library & Informational Science • Columbia, MO 65211 • LITA PLA

Jaeger Kristin A. • South Holland, IL 60473

Jaeger Lucja • Reference Librarian • Boston Public Library • Boston, MA 02117 • ACRL

Jaeger Nancy • Assistant to the Dean • University of Kansas Watson Library • Lawrence, KS 66045-2800 • LAMA

Jafari May • Indiana University-Purdue University at Indianapolis Library (IUPUI) • Indianapolis, IN 46202 • ACRL

Jaffarian Sara • Haverhill, MA 01830 • Continuing

Jaffe Howard • Cataloger • Library of Congress • Washington, DC 20541 • ALCTS SRRT

Jaffe John G. • Dir of Libraries & Media Servs • Sweet Briar College Library • Sweet Briar, VA 24595 • ACRL LAMA

Jaffe Lawrence L. • Librarian • Lionville Junior High School Library • Downingtown, PA 19335 • AASL ALSC LIRT LRRT

Jaffe Lee D. • University of California McHenry Library • Santa Cruz, CA 95064 • ACRL

Jaffe Lucy A. • Reference Librarian • Garden City Public Library • Garden City, NY 11530

Jaffe Peter S. • Reference/Interlibrary Loan • Reading Public Library • Reading, PA 19602 • ACRL LITA RASD LRRT

Jaffe Walter • Vice President • K G Saur/R R Bowker • New York, NY 10011 • ACRL

Jaffray Carol A. • Bibliographic Controller • University of Toronto Library System • Toronto ON, M5S 1A5 Canada • ALCTS

Jagels Suellen T. • Director • Eastern Maine Medical Center • Bangor, ME 04401

Jagelski Kristin A. • Student • University of Washington Graduate School of Library and Information Science • Seattle, WA 98195

Jager Shannon J. • Westminister, CA 92683 • LITA

Jagodzinski Cecile M. • Hd Catlg & Records Maintenance • Illinois State University Milner Library • Normal, IL 61761-0900 • ACRL ALCTS

Jagusch Sybille A. • Childrens Literature Spec. • Library of Congress • Washington, DC 20541 • ALSC

Jahnke Chris J. • Library Assistant • Getty Center Resources Collections • Santa Monica, CA 90401 • ALSC

Jahnke Elizabeth • Librarian • Columbia Basin College • Pasco, WA 99301

Jahnke Kenneth • Driver • Fitz Freight • Des Plaines, IL 60018

Jahns Cynthia T. • Public Services Librarian • University of California-San Diego • La Jolla, CA 92093-0175 • ACRL RASD LIRT

Jahoda Gerald Dr • Professor Emeritus • Florida State University School of Library and Information Studies • Tallahassee, FL 32306-2048 • ASCLA RASD *Life*

Jaime Mary H. • Assistant Social Science Librari • New Mexico State University Library • Las Cruces, NM 88003-0006

Jain Nirmal K. Dr. • Head Public Services • Acadia University Library • Wolfville NS, B0P 1X0 Canada

Jain Raj K. • Asst. Head, Cataloging Dept. • University of Western Ontario Allyn & Betty Taylor Library • London ON, N6A 3K7 Canada

Jaker Dorothy S. • Maplewood, NJ 07040

Jakes Jean T. • School Media specialist • Fairfax County Belvedere Elementary School • Falls Church, VA 22041

Jakes John • Hilton Head Island, SC 29926

Jakle Cynthia A. • Librarian • Central High School • Champaign, IL 61820

Jakubawski Mary Jean • Buffalo & Erie County Public Library • Buffalo, NY 14203 • PLA

Jakubcin Margaret D. • Student • University of Washington Graduate School of Library and Information Science • Seattle, WA 98195 • IFRT SRRT

Jakubiak Victoria M. • Librarian • Newark Public Schools • Newark, NJ 07104

Jakubowski Kathi L. • Head Serials Cataloger • University of Wisconsin-Milwaukee Golda Meir Library • Milwaukee, WI 53201 • ALCTS

Jambor-Smith Carol • Trustee • Rockford Public Library • Rockford, IL 61101-1061 • ALTA

Jambrek William L. • Head of Acquistions & Clln Devel • Kenosha Public Library • Kenosha, WI 53142-5799 • PLA

Jamerson Ginnette M. • Lexington, KY 40508 • IFRT SRRT

James Alice E. • Branch Library Manager • Detroit Public Library Wilder Branch • Detroit, MI 48234 • PLA

James Anne Snd Sr. • Librarian • Northeast Catholic High School • Philadelphia, PA 19124

James Antoinette • Director • Pike-Amite-Walthall Library System • McComb, MS 39648

James Barbara Buffett • Leavenworth, KS 66048 • Continuing

James Beatrice • Bergenfield, NJ 07621 • SRRT *Continuing*

James Beverly A. • Roanoke City Public Library • Roanoke, VA 24016 • LAMA PLA

James Bonnie B. • Senior Managing Editor • UMI Data Courier Inc. • Louisville, KY 40202 • RASD

James Clyde • Trustee • Farmers Branch Public Library • Farmers Branch, TX 75234 • ALTA

James Darryl D. • Houston, TX 77081 • LITA

James David W. • Head, Acquistions Department • Johns Hopkins University Milton S. Eisenhower Library • Baltimore, MD 21218 • ACRL ALCTS LITA

James Denise Taylor • Assistant Director • Darlington County Library • Darlington, SC 29532

James Eleanor • Director • Oakville Public Library • Oakville ON, L6J 2Z4 Canada

James Elizabeth A. • Student • University of Michigan School of Information and Library Studies • Ann Arbor, MI 48109-1092 • ALSC PLA EMIERT LRRT SRRT

James Elizabeth S. • School Librarian • Wilder Elementary School • Sumter, SC 29150

James Elvira J. • LAI-Superfund Records Center • Labat-Anderson Inc. • San Francisco, CA 94105

James Fritz C. • President • Library Binding Service Archival Products • Des Moines, IA 50305 • ACRL

James Henry Jr. Mr. • New Haven, CT 06515 • ACRL ALCTS *Life*

James Jane W. • Supervisior • Roanoke County Public Schools • Salem, VA 24153 • AASL

James Jean H. • East Orange High School • East Orange, NJ 07017 • AASL

James Joey • Sales Representative • Quality Books Inc. • Lake Bluff, IL 60044-2204

James John R. • Dir for Clln Devel & Bibl Contro • Dartmouth College Library Baker Memorial Library • Hanover, NH 03755-3525 • ACRL ALCTS LAMA

James Judith A. • Reference Librarian • United States Navy NSWC • Dahlgren, VA 22448-5020 • RASD FLRT

James Karen G. • Manager, Children's Serv. • Louisville Free Public Library • Louisville, KY 40203-2257 • ALSC

James Lillie B. • Media Specialist • Prince George Public Schools • Upper Marlboro, MD 20870

James Linda • Head Librarian • Saint Paul Pioneer Press Dispatch • St. Paul, MN 55101 • EMIERT IRRT

James Margaret • Arlington, WA 98223 • AASL IFRT

James Martha W. • Austin, TX 78731 • Continuing

James Maybelle V. • Knoxville, TN 37920

James Olive C. • San Francisco State University J. Paul Leonard Library • San Francisco, CA 94132 • ACRL LAMA LITA

James Patricia M. • Department Head • Carnegie Library of Pittsburgh Squirrel Hill Branch • Pittsburgh, PA 15217

James Paul M. • Waterbury, CT 06708

James Robert B. • Trustee • Memphis-Shelby County Public Library and Information Center • Memphis, TN 38104-4025

James Stephen E. Ph.D. • Assistant Chief • Library of Congress Library for the Blind & Physically Handicapped • Washington, DC 20542

Jameson Andrew G. Dr. • Librarian • Bohemian Club Library • San Francisco, CA 94102

Jameson Barbara E. • Director of Library Services • Tampa Technical Institute • Tampa, FL 33612

Jameson Harriet C. • Ann Arbor, MI 48105 • Continuing

Jameson Patricia • Milwaukee, WI 53222-1150 • ACRL RASD

Jamieson Jody • Children's Librarian • Wakarusa Public Library • Wakarusa, IN 46573 • ALSC

Jamieson Rosemary • Santa Monica, CA 90403 • Continuing

Jamison Charles A. • Director • Ursinus College Library • Collegeville, PA 19426 • ACRL

Jamison Irish V. • Branch Manager • Public Library of Charlotte & Mecklenburg County North Branch • Charlotte, NC 28216 • EMIERT

Jamison Martin P. • Columbus, OH 43204-2180 • ACRL RASD LHRT

Jamison Sandra • Researcher/Librarian • New York Times • New York, NY 10036 • RASD EMIERT ILERT

Jamison Susan C. • Director • Corbit-Calloway Memorial Library • Odessa, DE 19730

Jamison Tanya • Manager, AV Services • Westerville Public Library • Westerville, OH 43081 • PLA VRT

Janac Anne Riordan • Arnold, MD 21012 • RASD FLRT

Janakiev Elisabeth • Head, Catalog Department • Northwestern University Library • Evanston, IL 60208-2300 • ALCTS

Janbazian Hoku • Student • University of California Los Angeles Graduate School of Library & Information Science • Los Angeles, CA 90024

Janda Linda D. • APO, AP 96205-0017 • PLA

Janders Ann Marie • Coordinator, Information Service • Northampton County Area Community College-LRC • Bethlehem, PA 19103

Jandrisevits Anne M. • Cataloger • H. W. Wilson Company • Bronx, NY 10452 • ACRL

Jane Mary CFSN Sr. • 00166 Roma, Italy • Continuing

Jane Sarah Sartain • Reference Librarian • Lee County Library System • Fort Myers, FL 33901 • RASD

Janecek Blanche E. • High School Librarian • University of Chicago Lab School Library • Chicago, IL 60637 • Continuing

Janes Patricia J. • Library Media Coordinator • Meeker School District • Meeker, CO 81641 • AASL

Janes Phoebe • Reference Librarian • University of California-Berkeley Moffitt Undergraduate Library • Berkeley, CA 94720 • ACRL

Janeway Mary • Trustee • Bridgeview Public Library • Bridgeview, IL 60455 • LITA

Jang Hwa-Bin • User Services Librarian • H. W. Wilson Company • Bronx, NY 10452

Janiak Jane M. • Port Authority of NY & NJ Library • New York, NY 10048 • ALCTS LAMA LITA RASD

Janicki Sandra L. • Librarian • Patrick J. Stapleton Library Indiana University of Pennsylvania • Indiana, PA 15705

Janifer Josephine B. • Trustee • Newark Public Library • Newark, NJ 07101-0630 • ALTA PLA

Janiszewski Cynthia A. • Student • Wayne State University Library Science Program • Detroit, MI 48202

Jank David A. • FIND/SVP • New York, NY 10011 • LITA

Janke Leslie H. • San Jose, CA 95123 • Continuing

Jankolovits Judith • Head, Reference • North Merrick Public Library • North Merrick, NY 11566

Jankowska Maria A. • Cataloger • University of Idaho Library • Moscow, ID 83843 • IRRT SRRT

Jankowski Michael A. • Austin, TX 78713

Jankowski Terry Ann • Info Retrieval & Mgt Ln • University of Washington Health Science Library & Info Center • Seattle, WA 98195 • ACRL LITA RASD CLENE LIRT

Janky Donna L. • George W. Armstrong Library • Natchez, MS 39120 • LAMA PLA

Jann Adele L. • Technical Services Librarian • Pace University Library New York Civic Center • New York, NY 10038

Janner Linda • Goldthwaite Independent School District • Goldthwaite, TX 76844

Janney Kody • Interactive Home Systems • Redmond, WA 98052 • ALCTS LITA

Jannink Regina A. • Overdues Clerk • Richland Community College • Decatur, IL 62521

Janoch Evelyn F. • Streetsboro, OH 44241 • PLA IFRT

Janousek Kelly • Reference Librarian • California State University-Long Beach University Library & Learning Resources • Long Beach, CA 90840-1901 • RASD GODORT LIRT

Janovicz Juliann M. • Winnetka Public Library District • Winnetka, IL 60093

Janowski Adam G. Jr. • Library Media Specialist • Kinnick High School • FOP Seattle, WA 98762 • AASL

Janowski Bronislaw • Oakdale, LA 71463 • Continuing

Janowski Mary T. • Oakdale, LA 71463 • Continuing

Jansen Barbara A. • Live Oak Library Media Center • Austin, TX 78729-4706 • AASL

Jansen Guenter A. Mr. • General Manager • Viva Tours USA • Bellport, NY 11713 • ASCLA PLA   *Life*

Jansen Lloyd M. • Student • University of California-Los Angeles (UCLA) • Los Angeles, CA 90024-1450 • IFRT

Jansen Raymond J. • Reference Librarian • Cuyahoga Community College Western Campus Library • Parma, OH 44130

Jansen Robert N. • Head Librarian • Minneapolis Star & Tribune Library • Minneapolis, MN 55488 • RASD

Jansens Gertrude • San Jose, CA 95112 • Continuing

Janson Brenda L. • Provo, UT 84604

Janssen Barbara J. • Elementary Media Specialist • Norfolk Public Schools • Norfolk, NE 68701 • AASL

Janssen Bonnie J. • Supervisory Librarian I • Alameda County Library System • Fremont, CA 94538 • ALSC LAMA PLA

Janssen Horst F. • Manager,Book & Periodical Export • Stern-Verlag Janssen & Company • Duesseldorf, Germany • ACRL

Jantz Cynthia M. • Librarian • T.W. Hunter Middle School • Hendersonville, TN 37075 • AASL NMRT

Janzen Deborah K. • Moorhead, MN 56560

Janzen Deborah M. • Librarian • Fresno County Free Library Blind & Handicapped Services • Fresno, CA 93728

Janzer Lisa M. • Student • University of Arizona Graduate Library School • Tucson, AZ 85721

Jaquay Robert L. • Director • William K. Sanford Town Library • Loudonville, NY 12211 • PLA IFRT SRRT

Jaques Barbara L. • District Librarian • Bayfield School District • Bayfield, CO 81122-0258

Jaques Thomas Francis • State Librarian • State Library of Louisiana • Baton Rouge, LA 70821

Jaques Trudy Seidel • Assistant Director • East Baton Rouge Parish Library • Baton Rouge, LA 70806-7699 • PLA

Jaquith F. Luree Ms • Joseph Estabrook Elementary School • Lexington, MA 02173 • AASL ALSC   *Life*

Jarabek Leona T. • Middleburg Ht, OH 44130 • ACRL LITA FLRT

Jaramillo Carmen M. • Librarian • Los Lunas Community Library • Los Lunas, NM 87031

Jaramillo Ellen M. • Principal Catalog Librarian • Yale University Sterling Memorial Library • New Haven, CT 06520

Jaramillo George R. • Director of Public Services • University of Northern Colorado James A. Michener Library • Greeley, CO 80639 • ACRL ALCTS LAMA

Jaramillo Juana S. • Library Director • University of Puerto Rico Aguadilla Regional College • Aguadilla, PR 00604 • ACRL

Jarboe Betty M. • Tyler, TX 75703 • Continuing

Jarchow Patricia • Trustee • Euclid Public Library • Euclid, OH 44123-2091 • ALTA

Jardine Carolyn W. • Student • State University of New York at Albany School of Information Science & Policy • Albany, NY 12222 • RASD

Jarez Teresa • Trustee • Alhambra Public Library • Alhambra, CA 91801

Jargo Lori E. • Iowa City, IA 52246 • PLA

Jaric Robert R. • Vice President, Sales • CBIS • Norcross, GA 30092

Jarmak Sandra B. • Student • University of Rhode Island Graduate School of Library & Information Studies • Kingston, RI 02881-0815

Jarmon Rodney K. • East Point, GA 30344 • SRRT

Jarmusz Ruth M. • Librarian • San Bernardino County Library • San Bernardino, CA 92415

Jarodsky Deborah • Student • University of South Florida School of Library & Information Science • Tampa, FL 33620 • YALSA

Jaros Oliver J. • Computer Systems Manager • Texas A & M University Sterling C. Evans Library • College Station, TX 77843-5000 • ACRL

Jaros Rod • Library Coordinator • Horace Greeley High School Library • Chappaqua, NY 10514 • AASL

Jarosh Harriet S. • Director • Malvern Public Library • Malvern, PA 19355 • LAMA PLA

Jarpe Jack D. • Librarian • New Richmond Public Schools • New Richmond, WI 54017 • AASL

Jarred Ada D. • Director • Northwestern State University Watson Memorial Library • Natchitoches, LA 71497 • ACRL

Jarrell Ann S. • Reference/Documents Librarian • Clark County Law Library • Las Vegas, NV 89101 • GODORT

Jarrell Doris J. • Port Richey, FL 34668 • IFRT SRRT

Jarrell James R. • Greensboro, NC 27401 • ACRL

Jarrell Judith B. • Media Coordinator • Ragsdale High School • Jamestown, NC 27407 • AASL

Jarrett Mitzi M. • Library Director • Virginia Theological Seminary • Alexandria, VA 22304-5201 • ACRL ALCTS LITA

Jarrette Margaret M. • Catalog Librarian • Temple University Paley Library • Philadelphia, PA 19122 • ALCTS

Jarvella Shirley M. • Belfast, ME 04915 • AASL

Jarvi Edith • Toronto ON, M6C 3Z5 Canada • GODORT
                                                    Continuing

Jarvis Carol L. • Student • University of South Carolina College of Library & Information Science • Columbia, SC 29208 • ACRL

Jarvis Katherine S. • Technical Information Specialist • Xerox Corporation PARC • Palo Alto, CA 94304 • ACRL ALCTS

Jarvis Mary J. • Medical Librarian • Methodist Hopsital Medical Library • Lubbock, TX 79410

Jarvis Mary Lynne • Librarian • Ozark South Elementary School Library • Ozark, MO 65721 • AASL

Jarvis William E. • Head, Acquisitions/Serials • Washington State University Library • Pullman, WA 99164-5610 • ALCTS LAMA RASD

Jarzemsky Timothy P. • Student • Northern Illinois University Department of Library & Information Studies • DeKalb, IL 60115

Jascha Jill M. • Student • University of Oklahoma School of Library & Information Studies • Norman, OK 73019 • NMRT SRRT

Jasek Elaine I. • Manning, SC 29102 • AASL

Jasin Betty C. • Santa Rosa Beach, FL 32459

Jasinski Margaret S. • Arlington Heights Memorial Library • Arlington Heights, IL 60004-5966 • ALCTS

Jasinski Nancy J. • Head Librarian • Crestwood Public Library District • Crestwood, IL 60445 • PLA

Jasko Agnese Sr. • Director of Library • Sacred Heart School of Theology Leo Dehon Library • Hales Corners, WI 53130 • ACRL

Jaskowski Selma K. • Director • Panhandle Library Access Network • Panama City, FL 32401 • ASCLA

Jason Annemarie • Buffalo School #17 ECC Library • Buffalo, NY 14209

Jason Lynne A. • Librarian • The Williams School • New London, CT 06320 • AASL

Jaspan Sharon Z. • Student • Rutgers University School of Communication Information & Library Studies • New Brunswick, NJ 08903

Jasper Richard P. • Head, Acquisitions Dept. • Emory University Libraries Robert W. Woodruff Library • Atlanta, GA 30322-2870 • ACRL ALCTS

Jaster Herbert A. • Librarian • Martin Luther Prep School • Prairie du Chien, WI 53821 • YALSA

Jastrzebski Luke • Head, Reference/Documents • University of Texas at El Paso Library • El Paso, TX 79968-0582 • ACRL

Jaszcar Deborah A. • Port Washington Public Library • Port Washington, NY 11050

Jaugstetter Michael A. • North Dakota State Library • Bismarck, ND 58505 • PLA

Jauquet-Kalinoski Barbara J. • Director • Northwest Regional Library • Thief River Falls, MN 56701 • PLA

Javaher Patricia J. • Library Director • United States Army Libraries • Seoul, South Korea • AFLRT

Javelin Muriel C. Mrs • Southbury, CT 06488 • Continuing

Javer Sharon A. • Student • Rutgers University School of Communication Information & Library Studies • New Brunswick, NJ 08903

Javier Victoria-Linda B. • Kitchener ON, N2A 4A6 Canada

Javitz Naomi B. • Librarian • Harvard School • North Hollywood, CA 91604 • AASL

Javonovich Kenneth L. • Librarian III • Chicago Public Library • Chicago, IL 60607 • ALCTS

Javorski Susanne M. • Art Librarian • Wesleyan University • Middletown, CT 06457 • ACRL

Jawitz Marilyn C. • El Sobrante, CA 94803

Jax John J. • Director • University of Wisconsin-Stout Library Learning Center • Menomonie, WI 54751 • ACRL

Jax John N. • East Central University Linscheid Library • Ada, OK 74820-6899 • ACRL

Jay Donald F. • Lancaster, PA 17603 • ACRL RASD   *Life*

Jay Hilda L. • Bowie, MD 20721 • AASL RASD

Jay Joan H. • Head Media Specialist • Dade County Public Schools Homestead Senior High School • Homestead, FL 33035

Jay Jonathan H. • Student • Clark-Atlanta University School of Library & Information Studies • Atlanta, GA 30314-4391 • ACRL NMRT

Jay M. Ellen • Media Specialist • Page Elementary School • Silver Spring, MD 20904 • AASL   *Life*

Jaye-Aiken Herma • Saint John's University Division of Library & Information Science • Jamaica, NY 11439

Jayes Linda D. • Serials Librarian • University of Chicago Library • Chicago, IL 60637-1502

Jayne Elaine A. • Student • University of Michigan School of Information and Library Studies • Ann Arbor, MI 48109-1092

Jaynes Phyllis E. • Director, User Services • Dartmouth College Library Baker Memorial Library • Hanover, NH 03755-3525 • ACRL LAMA

Jean Jill K. • Children's Services Coor. • Seattle Public Library • Seattle, WA 98104-1193 • PLA

Jean Lorraine A. • Essex Junction, VT 05452 • ACRL RASD

Jeanneney Mary L. • Reference Librarian/Head Circ. • Vassar College • Poughkeepsie, NY 12601 • ACRL

Jeannet Paula • Durham, NC 27701

Jebb Marcia • Bibliographer • Cornell University Library • Ithaca, NY 14853-5301 • ACRL

Jedlicka Elizabeth L. • Catalog Librarian • Goucher College Julia Rogers Library • Towson, MD 21204 • ALCTS LITA

Jedzinek Mary C. • Elk Grove Village, IL 60007

Jeffcoat Pamela H. • Systems Librarian • John Hopkins University • Baltimore, MD 21218 • LITA

Jeffers Dorothy W. • School Librarian • Madison Elementary School • Norman, OK 73072 • AASL

Jeffers Lori A. • Willimantic, CT 06226

Jefferson Anne Mason • Elkhart Public Library • Elkhart, IN 46516-3184 • PLA

Jefferson Gwendolyn W. • School Librarian • Ballou Senior High School • Washington, DC 20032 • AASL

Jefferson Joyce B. • Library Principal Associate • Atlanta-Fulton Public Library • Atlanta, GA 30303

Jefferson Patricia • Carroll Elementary School • Southlake, TX 76092 • AASL ALSC

Jefferson Robert M. • Florissant, MO 63033

Jefferson Suzette B. • J.V. Fletcher Library • Westford, MA 01886 • ALCTS RASD

Jeffery Debby A. • Children's Librarian/Branch Mgr • San Francisco Public Library Potrero Branch • San Francisco, CA 94107 • ALSC

Jeffery E. Lorraine • Student • Brigham Young University School of Library & Information Sciences • Provo, UT 84602 • IFRT SRRT

Jeffery Jonathan B. • Associate Reference Librarian • University of Delaware Morris Library • Newark, DE 19717-5267

Jeffery Katherine • North Easton, MA 02356 • YALSA

Jeffery Kathryn Fagan • LRC Director • Jefferson Junior High School • Naperville, IL 60540

Jeffery Phyllis D. • Supervisor of Branches • Mobile Public Library • Mobile, AL 36602 • PLA

Jeffords Margaret • Fayetteville, NY 13066-2037 • Continuing

Jeffrey Beryl • Richmond Public Library • Richmond BC, V6X 2E3 Canada

Jeffrey Penelope S. • Materials Selection Manager • Cuyahoga County Public Library Administration Building • Parma, OH 44134-2792 • PLA YALSA IFRT

Jeffries Carolyn M. • Assistant Director • Winter Park Public Library • Winter Park, FL 32789 • PLA

Jeffries Emily S. • Bloomington, IN 47404-2157

Jeffries Michelle M. • Student • University of Washington Graduate School of Library and Information Science • Seattle, WA 98195 • IFRT SRRT

Jeffus Barbara • Director, Support Services • Clovis Unified School District • Clovis, CA 93612 • AASL LAMA

Jehlik Theresa A. • Omaha Public Library • Omaha, NE 68102

Jelinek Janet • Librarian • Rocky Mountain College • Billings, MT 59101

Jelks Joyce E. • Mgr. Acquisitions Dept. • Atlanta-Fulton Public Library • Atlanta, GA 30303 • ACRL ALCTS PLA RASD LHRT LRRT SORT

Jemison Keith • Tulsa, OK 74127 • EMIERT

Jen Pingchih Esther • Reference Librarian • Lake Forest College Donnelley Library • Lake Forest, IL 60045 • RASD

Jeney Judith E. • Chair,Div. of Clln. Mgmt. • Ramapo College of New Jersey Library • Mahwah, NJ 07430 • ACRL

Jenft Sharon • Presidents Elementary School • Arlington, WA 98223

Jeng-Chu Wei • Indian Trails Public Library District • Wheeling, IL 60090 • ALCTS

Jeng Judy • Rutgers University John Cotton Dana Library • Newark, NJ 07102 • ACRL ALCTS LAMA LITA LRRT

Jeng Ling-Hwey • University of California-Los Angeles Graduate School of Library & Information Science • Los Angeles, CA 90024-1520 • ALCTS LITA

Jenicke Alice • Librarian • Veterans Memorial Library City of Mount Pleasant Library • Mount Pleasant, MI 48858 • PLA RASD

Jenkins-Wright Angela • Southern Company Services • Birmingham, AL 35209

Jenkins Abby A. • Senior Librarian • Los Angeles Public Library Loyola Village Branch • Los Angeles, CA 90045 • PLA

Jenkins Althea H. • ACRL Exective Director • American Library Association • Chicago, IL 60611-2795 • ACRL

Jenkins Barbara Baxter • Head, Reference Dept. • University of Oregon Library • Eugene, OR 97403-1299 • LAMA LITA RASD

Jenkins Beverly W. • Account Executive • Dean Witter Reynolds Inc • Tucson, AZ 85712

Jenkins Bridgetta C. • Supervisory Librarian • Library of Congress • Washington, DC 20541 • ALCTS LITA

Jenkins Carol A. • Hawaii State Library • Honolulu, HI 96813

Jenkins Carolyn M. • Librarian • Bethune Junior High School • Los Angeles, CA 90035 • AASL

Jenkins Christine • Librarian • University of Wisconsin School of Library & Information Studies • Madison, WI 53706 • AASL ALSC YALSA EMIERT IFRT LHRT SRRT

Jenkins Craig L. • Teacher • Rockingham County Senior High Media Center • Wentworth, NC 27375

Jenkins Darrell L. • Director of Library Service • Southern Illinois University Delyte W. Morris Library • Carbondale, IL 62901-6632 • ACRL LAMA LITA LRRT

Jenkins Diana • Director • James Memorial Library • Saint James, MO 65559

Jenkins Diane G. • Reference Librarian • Long Island University B. Davis Schwartz Memorial Library • Greenvale, NY 11548 • ACRL

Jenkins Florence E. • Belmont Technical College • Saint Clairsville, OH 43950

Jenkins Frances B. • Creve Coeur, IL 61611 • ACRL RASD *Life*

Jenkins Fred W. • Catalog Specialist • University of Dayton Roesch Library • Dayton, OH 45469 • ACRL

Jenkins Georgann Klaus • School Librarian • Whitehall Elementary School • Pittsburgh, PA 15236 • AASL

Jenkins Gina • Librarian • Dekalb County Public Library • Decatur, GA 30032

Jenkins Gordon W. • Trustee • Forsyth County Public Library • Winston-Salem, NC 27101 • ALTA

Jenkins Joyce • City Librarian • Petersburg Public Library • Petersburg, AK 99833

Jenkins Judith G. • Misson Viejo, CA 92675

Jenkins Laura M. • San Pedro, CA 90732 • ALSC YALSA

Jenkins Lydia E. • Librarian • Alice Deal Junior High School • Washington, DC 20016 • AASL

Jenkins Marjorie • Media Generalist • Saint James High School • St. James, MN 56081-0509 • AASL

Jenkins Martin D. II • Student • University of Illinois Graduate School of Library and Information Science • Urbana, IL 61801

Jenkins Mary C. • Hurst, TX 76053 • AASL LAMA YALSA IFRT

Jenkins Pamela A. • Lower School Librarian • Moses Brown School Walter Jones Library • Providence, RI 02906 • AASL

Jenkins Regina J. • Media Specialist • Western Reserve High School • Berlin Center, OH 44401 • AASL

Jenkins Ronald K. • Director • Logan Library • Logan, UT 84321-3914 • ALSC PLA

Jenkins Sharon D. • Student • University of Missouri-Columbia School of Library & Informational Science • Columbia, MO 65211 • LITA EMIERT

Jenkins Sylvia M. • Librarian • Moraine Valley Community College Library • Palos Hills, IL 60465

Jenkins Valerie • Coordinator • Amherst Public Schools Libraries • Amherst, OH 44001 • ALTA LAMA *Life*

Jenkins Victoria L. • Downey City Library • Downey, CA 90241 • PLA

Jenkinson Judith • Librarian • White Cliff Elementary School • Ketchikan, AK 99901 • AASL IFRT *Life*

Jenks George M. • Collection Development Librarian • Bucknell University Bertrand Library • Lewisburg, PA 17837-2086

Jenks Janet C. • Head, Humanities & Social Sci. • Caltech Libraries I-32 • Pasadena, CA 91125 • ACRL ALCTS GODORT IFRT SRRT

Jenks Zoya E. • Lewisburg, PA 17837 • ACRL

Jenner Lois P. • Media Specialist • Governor Livingston High School Union County Regional School • Berkeley Heights, NJ 07922

Jenner Ruby M. Miss • Wichita, KS 67203 • Continuing

Jennerich Elaine Z. Dr. • Acting Staff Devel. Coor. • University of Washington Suzzallo Library • Seattle, WA 98195 • ACRL LAMA RASD

Jennings Diane Richmond • Manager • Palo Alto City Library • Palo Alto, CA 94303 • LAMA LITA PLA RASD

Jennings Kathryn A. • Lake Forest Country Day School • Lake Forest, IL 60045 • AASL ALSC

Jennings Kelly • Spvr Ln/Central Children's Dept • Tulsa City-County Library System • Tulsa, OK 74103 • ALSC

Jennings Kriza A. • Diversity Consultant • Association of Research Libraries (ARL) • Washington, DC 20036 • ACRL LAMA LITA

Jennings Margareta R. • Needles, CA 92363 • NMRT

Jennings Maria • Librarian • Carollton School Library • Oak Creek, WI 53154 • AASL

Jennings Mary • Librarian • Alasak State Library Services for the Blind & Physically Handicapped • Anchorage, AK 99501 • LAMA

Jennings Pauline W. • Chevy Chase, MD 20815 • ACRL ALCTS *Life*

Jennings Vincent J. • Documents & Map Librarian • Hofstra University Axinn Library • Hempstead, NY 11550 • ACRL GODORT MAGERT SRRT *Life*

Jennison Elizabeth M. • Student • University of South Florida School of Library & Information Science • Tampa, FL 33620 • AASL

Jenny Judith B. • Lower School Librarian • Louise S. McGehee School • New Orleans, LA 70130 • AASL

Jenny Mary • Economic Development Librarian • Oregon State University William Jasper Kerr Library • Corvallis, OR 97331-4501

Jensen Ann • Reference Libn./Asst. Head • University California-Berkeley • Berkeley, CA 94720 • ACRL RASD

Jensen Carolyn P. • Administrative Librarian • Quincy Public Library • Quincy, IL 62301 • LAMA PLA

Jensen Catherine V. • Youth Services Librarian • Dallas Public Library Park Forest Branch • Dallas, TX 75234

Jensen Claudia R. • Supervisor, Technical Services • Falmouth Public Library • Falmouth, MA 02540 • ALCTS LITA

Jensen Craig W. • President • Booklab • Austin, TX 78754 • ALCTS LITA

Jensen David P. • Director of Library • Hope College Van Wylen Library • Holland, MI 49423 • ACRL LAMA

Jensen Deborah K. • New England Rgnl Representative • Faxon Company Inc. • Westwood, MA 02090 • ACRL ALCTS LITA

Jensen Dennis F. • Syosse, NY 11791 • ACRL RASD

Jensen Dorothy L. • Los Altos High School • Los Altos, CA 94022 • AASL

Jensen Gary D. • Library Director • Western Oregon State College Library • Monmouth, OR 97361 • ACRL

Jensen Hans W. • Director • Portage Public Library • Portage, WI 53901

Jensen Janet M. • Trustee • Copiague Memorial Public Library • Copiague, NY 11726 • ALTA

Jensen Jean C. • Utah State University Merrill Library • Logan, UT 84322-3000

Jensen Joyce • Librarian • Viborg Public Library • Viborg, SD 57070

Jensen Judith Bourgeois • Librarian • Agnes Scott College • Decatur, GA 30030

Jensen Judy K. • Manhattan Public Library • Manhattan, KS 66502 • ALSC

Jensen Karen M. • Juv. Librarian • Monroe County Public Library • Key West, FL 33040 • ALSC

Jensen Katherine A. • Elementary School Librarian • Sandy Elementary School District Firwood Elementary School • Sandy, OR 97055

Jensen Kenneth O. • Director, Collection Development • University of Virginia Library • Charlottesville, VA 22903 • ACRL

Jensen Laura W. • Student • Northern Illinois University Department of Library & Information Studies • DeKalb, IL 60115

Jensen Linda • Librarian • Desert Foothills School Library • Phoenix, AZ 85023 • AASL YALSA

Jensen Lisa • SRI International Research Information Services • Menlo Park, CA 94025

Jensen Margaret K. • Teacher • Huegel Elementary School • Madison, WI 53711 • ALSC

Jensen Mary L. • Consultant • Connecticut State Library • Hartford, CT 06106 • LAMA

Jensen Nancy S. • Student • University of Washington Graduate School of Library and Information Science • Seattle, WA 98195

Jensen Niki L. • Library Tech • Douglas Junior High School Woodland Joint Unified School Dist • Woodland, CA 95695

Jensen Paul E. • Reference Librarian • King County Library System Des Moines Library • Des Moines, WA 98198 • PLA RASD

Jensen Sandy • University California Lawrence Livermore National Laboratory Library • Livermore, CA 94550

Jensen Wilma W. • Volunteer Consultant • Lutheran Church Library Association • Minneapolis, MN 55404 • ALSC *Continuing*

Jenson Gloria D. • Head Cataloging • Brigham Young University Harold B. Lee Library • Provo, UT 84602 • ALCTS

Jenson John R. • Asst.Curator Specl Coll/Rare Bks • University of Minnesota O. Meredith Wilson Library • Minneapolis, MN 55455-0414 • ACRL ALCTS

Jenson Melenie S. • MLS Teacher/Librarian • Elsinore High School • Lake Elsinore, CA 92330 • AASL LIRT

Jenson Norma B. • APO, AE 09213-5010 • ALCTS LAMA LITA

Jeong Dong-Youl • Assistant Professor • Ewha Womans University • Seoul, 120-750, South Korea • LRRT

Jeppesen Bruce • Stow Public Library • Stow, OH 44224 • PLA

Jerabek Judy Ann • Sam Houston State University Newton Gresham Library • Huntsville, TX 77341-2281 • ACRL

Jerauld Janet A. • Branch Manager • Cuyahoga County Public Library Middleburg Heights Branch • Middleburg Heights, OH 44130 • ALSC

Jerkich Louis J. • Reference & Adult Services Librn • Geauga County Public Library Chardon Library • Chardon, OH 44024

Jerles Julia H. • High School Medai Specialist • Jay County High School • Portland, IN 47371 • AASL

Jerme Martha G. • Cardinal Stritch College • Milwaukee, WI 53217

Jerolleman Lois J. • Children's Librarian • Houston Public Library Alief Branch • Houston, TX 77072 • ALSC CLENE ILERT

Jerome Amy G. • Student • Syracuse University School of Information Studies • Syracuse, NY 13244-4100 • AASL

Jerome Anne E. • Librarian • Dixon Schools • Dixon, MO 65459 • AASL

Jerome Daurene A. • Head Librarian • Julia A. Morse Memorial Library • Greene, ME 04236

Jerousek William R. • Local History Librarian • Oak Park Public Library • Oak Park, IL 60301 • PLA

Jersey Patricia • Reference/Public Service Librarn • East Stroudsburg University Kemp Library • East Stroudsburg, PA 18301 • ACRL RASD LIRT

Jesberg Michelle M. • San Jose State University Division of Library & Information Science • San Jose, CA 95192-0029

Jesby Peg Holland • Librarian • Carro, Spanbock, Kaster & Cuiffo • New York, NY 10105

Jeser-Skaggs Sharlee • Libr Instructor/Reference Librn • Richland College • Dallas, TX 75243-2199 • RASD LIRT

Jeske James T. • Children's Librarian I • Chicago Public Library Marshall Square Branch • Chicago, IL 60608

Jeske Michelle R. • Student • University of Washington Graduate School of Library and Information Science • Seattle, WA 98195

Jessee Frances E. • Head Librarian • Chancellor High School • Fredericksburg, VA 22407 • AASL

Jessee Gordon E. • Roanoke, VA 24015

Jessee Jill • Director • Smyth-Bland Regional Library • Marion, VA 24354

Jessee John M. • Washington County Public Library • Chatom, AL 36518

Jessee Karen D. • Library Director • Washington County Public Library • Chatom, AL 36518 • LAMA PLA RASD NMRT

Jessie Judy Carol • Pleasant Garden Elementary School • Pleasant Garden, NC 27313 • AASL

Jessop Nancy A. • Librarian • Toronto Public Library Danforth & Coxwell Branch • Toronto ON, M4C 1H7 Canada • RASD

Jessup Margaret Ross • Student • Simmons College Graduate School of Library & Information Science • Boston, MA 02115

Jessup Nancy L. • Carnegie Library of Pittsburgh Mount Washington Branch • Pittsburgh, PA 15211

Jestat William T. • Los Angeles Public Library Pio Pico Korea Town Branch • Los Angeles, CA 90006 • YALSA SRRT

Jestel Joan • Librarian • Souers Junior High School • Canton, OH 44710 • AASL

Jester Joan E. • Business Manager • Metropolitan Library System • Oklahoma City, OK 73102 • LAMA

Jester Valerie J. • Community Librarian • Timberland Regional Library W.H. Abel Memorial Library • Montesano, WA 98563

Jesus Marcello • Trustee • Nieves M. Flores Memorial Library • Agana, GU 96910 • ALTA

Jeter Chrystal C. • Head, Youth Services • Anchorage Municipal Libraries Z. J. Loussac Library • Anchorage, AK 99503 • ALSC LAMA PLA

Jeter Hattie Bell • Media Specialist • Druid Hills High School DeKalb County Board of Education • Atlanta, GA 30307

Jette Karen D. • Circulation Librarian • Purdue University • West Lafayette, IN 47907 • LAMA

Jetter Margaret A. Dr. • Associate Professor • Clarion University of Pennsylvania • Clarion, PA 16214 • AASL ALSC

Jetton Marcia • Reference Librarian • Peoria Public Library • Peoria, IL 61602

Jevec Thomas E. • Lexington, KY 40508 • ACRL

Jewell Debra • Director • Mickey Reily Public Library • Corrigan, TX 75939

Jewell Jeanne • School Librarian • M.U. Lujan Elementary School • Agana, GU 96910 • AASL

Jewell John H. • Hd, State Inf & Ref Center • California State Library • Sacramento, CA 94237-0001 • ACRL ASCLA LITA PLA RASD

Jewell Therese W. • Senior Librarian • California Department of Corrections Pelican Bay State Prison • Crescent City, CA 95531-7000 • ASCLA

Jewell Timothy D. • Acting Head of Reference • University of Washington Suzzallo Library • Seattle, WA 98195 • ACRL LITA RASD

Jewett Kendra L. • Cedar City, UT 84720

Jewett Lillian C. • School Library Media Specialist • J A F Middle School • Stony Point, NY 10980

Jewett Linda • District Librarian • Sacramento City Unified School District Professional Library • Sacramento, CA 95822 • AASL

Ji Dorothy • Union Township Public Library • Union, NJ 07083 • RASD

Jia Ying • Student • Rosary College Graduate School of Library & Information Science • River Forest, IL 60305

Jiang Diana Y. • Technical Services Librarian • Delta State University • Cleveland, MS 38733 • ALCTS

Jiang Yishu • St. Louis, MO 63112-3105

Jiannacopoulos Krista M. • Head of Circulation • Thomas Ford Memorial Library • Western Springs, IL 60558

Jiga Ela M. • Detroit, MI 48228 • PLA

Jimenez Ivonne R. • Extension Services Adm. • El Paso Public Library • El Paso, TX 79901

Jimenez Ralph M. • Head Library Media Specialist • Wichita High School Heights • Wichita, KS 67219 • AASL YALSA EMIERT

Jin Qiang • Part-Time Cataloger • Colgate University Everett Needham Case Library • Hamilton, NY 13346

Jinks William Paul • Director od Support Services • Saint Louis Public Library • St. Louis, MO 63103-2389 • PLA

Jinnette Isabella • Cockeysville, MD 21030 • ALSC *Continuing*

Jiuliano Margaret C. • Director • Bernards Township Library • Basking Ridge, NJ 07920 • PLA IFRT

Jizba Laurel • Principal Cataloger • Michigan State University Libraries • East Lansing, MI 48824-1048 • ALCTS

Joa Seung Heui • Student • Brigham Young University School of Library & Information Sciences • Provo, UT 84602 • LITA

Joachim Linda UmBayemake • Frankfort, KY 40601

Joachim Martin • Cataloger • Indiana University at Bloomington University Libraries • Bloomington, IN 47405 • ACRL ALCTS LITA LHRT

Job Amy G. • Librarian I • William Paterson College • Wayne, NJ 07470 • ACRL *Life*

Job AnnaMarie • Librarian • Atlantic County Library • Mays Landing, NJ 08336

Job Sue • Technical Services Manager • Johnson County Library • Shawnee Mission, KS 66201 • LAMA PLA

Jobe Janita A. • Government Publications Libn. • University of Nevada-Reno Noble H. Getchell Library • Reno, NV 89557 • ACRL GODORT

Jobe Margaret M. • Central Colorado Library System • Wheat Ridge, CO 80033 • RASD

Jobe Ronald A. • Dept. of Language Education • University of British Columbia Department of Language Education • Vancouver BC, V6T 1Y3 Canada • AASL ALSC

Jobrack Avis J. • Children's Librarian • King County Library System • Seattle, WA 98109-5191

Jobson Betty S. • Assoc. Dir./Head of Tech. Svcs. • West Georgia College Irvine Sullivan Ingram Library • Carrollton, GA 30118 • ACRL

Jocius Christopher R. • Reference Librarian • Illinois Math & Science Academy • Aurora, IL 60506-1039 • ACRL ALCTS RASD

Jocson Rebecca M. • Chief Librarian • Pamantasan Ng Lungsod • Manila, Philippines

Jocz Elisabeth A. • Rare Book Librarian • University of Toronto • Toronto ON, Canada • ACRL

Jodrey Micheline E. • College Librarian • Wellesley College • Wellesley, MA 02181 • ACRL ALCTS LAMA

Johannessen Dorothy • Greenwich Library • Greenwich, CT 06830

Johansen Marjorie H. • Sr. Librarian-Ref. Services • San Mateo Public Library • San Mateo, CA 94402

Johanson Cynthia J. • Asst. Chief,Marc Ed Division • Library of Congress • Washington, DC 20541 • SRRT

Johanson Dawn E. • Adult Services Librarian • Bartlett Public Library District • Bartlett, IL 60103

Johanson Ellen M. • Student • Long Island University Palmer School of Library & Information Science • Greenvale, NY 11548 • AASL

Johanson Nancy L. • Washington, DC 20037

Johansson David • Student • University of North Texas School of Library & Information Sciences • Denton, TX 76203

Johmann Nancy • Assistant Director • Bridgeport Public Library • Bridgeport, CT 06604

John Nancy R. • Assistant University Librarian • University of Illinois at Chicago University Library • Chicago, IL 60680 • ACRL ALCTS LITA IRRT

John Patricia La Caille • Head, Rural Information Center • United States Department of Agriculture National Agricultural Library • Beltsville, MD 20705-2351 • PLA RASD

Johnas Julia A. • Director of Adult Services • Highland Park Public Library • Highland Park, IL 60035

Johner Patricia E. • Reference Librarian • Pennsylvania State University Heindel Library • Middletown, PA 17057 • ACRL RASD

Johner Paul E. • Indiana, PA 15701 • ACRL

Johnroe Crystal • Media Specialist • Parkdale Elementary School • Midland, MI 48640 • AASL

Johns Cecily A. • Associate University Librarian • University of California UCSB Library • Santa Barbara, CA 93106-9010 • ACRL ALCTS LITA IRRT

Johns David L. • Student • Malone College • Canton, OH 44709

Johns Elizabeth A. • Principal Librarian • Abilene Public Library • Abilene, TX 79601-5793 • ALCTS

Johns F. A. Mr. • Professor Emeritus • Rutgers University Libraries • New Brunswick, NJ 08903 • ACRL ALCTS *Life*

Johns Jane D. • Student • University of Wisconsin Library and Learning Resources • Whitewater, WI 53190 • AASL

Johns Jean B. • Cincinnati, OH 45231

Johns Lucy Rose • Library Media Specialist • Humke Elementary School • Nekoosa, WI 54457 • AASL

Johns Mary E. • Librarian • Morristown Hamblen East School • Morristown, TN 37813

Johns Mary M. • Department Manager • Salt Lake City Public Library • Salt Lake City, UT 84111

Johns Michelle • Technical Services Assistant • Dorsey & Whitney Law Library • Minneapolis, MN 55402 • ALCTS LITA RASD

Johns Sara Kelly • Library Media Specialist • Beekmantown Junior-Senior High School • Plattsburgh, NY 12901 • AASL

Johns Susan M. • Systems Circulation Librarian • Pittsburg State University Leonard Axe Library • Pittsburg, KS 66762

Johnsen Mary Catharine • Carnegie-Mellon University Libraries Hunt Library • Pittsburgh, PA 15213 • ACRL

Johnson-Blount Theresa • Student • Louisiana State University School of Library & Information Science • Baton Rouge, LA 70803-3290 • GODORT

Johnson-Corcoran Lynn M. • Automation Librarian • Central Connecticut State University Elihu Burritt Library • New Britain, CT 06050 • LITA

Johnson-Houston Debbie L. • Branch Head Librarian • Broward County Library Northwest Branch • Pompano Beach, FL 33060 • EMIERT IFRT

Johnson Adele Dell J. • Brown & Root, Inc. • Houston, TX 77072

Johnson Aileen A. • Head Librarian • East Cheltenham Free Library • Cheltenham, PA 19012 • LAMA

Johnson Albert W. • Young Adult Librarian • Los Angeles Public Library North Hollywood Regional Branch • North Hollywood, CA 91601

Johnson Albertine C. • Reference Librarian, Dept. Chair • University of the District of Columbia Learning Resources Division • Washington, DC 20008 • ACRL

Johnson Alice E. • Evanston, IL 60201

Johnson Alice J. • LRC Director • San Antonio College Library • San Antonio, TX 78212 • ACRL LAMA

Johnson Amy L. • Cataloger • Clinton Public Library • Clinton, IA 52732 • ALCTS

Johnson Amy L. • Assistant Librarian Cataloging • North Florida Junior College Library • Madison, FL 32340 • ALCTS

Johnson Andrea R. • Innovative Interfaces, Inc. • Berkeley, CA 94710 • LITA EMIERT IFRT SRRT

Johnson Andrew F. • State & Local Documents Libn. • University of Washington Suzzallo Library • Seattle, WA 98195 • ACRL GODORT

Johnson Anita D. • Librarian • Carle Foundation Hospital • Urbana, IL 61801 • ACRL

Johnson Anita K. • Ref./Govt. Doc. Librarian • University of Dayton Roesch Library • Dayton, OH 45469 • ACRL

Johnson Anne C. • Director • Scott County Library System • Eldridge, IA 52748 • PLA NMRT

Johnson Anne M. • Technical Services Librarian • Eagle County Public Library • Eagle, CO 81631 • ALCTS

Johnson Arlene L. • Student • Pratt Institute Graduate School of Library & Information Science • Brooklyn, NY 11205 • IFRT

Johnson B. Lamar Dr. • Prof. Emeritus of Higher Educ. • University of California & Pepperdine University • Los Angeles, CA 90049 • ACRL PLA *Life*

Johnson Barbara • Redondo Beach, CA 90278

Johnson Bary L. • Rare Materials Cataloger • Duke University William R. Perkins Library • Durham, NC 27706

Johnson Bennett J. • Path Press, Inc. • Chicago, IL 60604

Johnson Betty D. • Associate Director Technical Ser • Stetson University DuPont-Ball Library • De Land, FL 32720-3769 • ACRL ALCTS LAMA

Johnson Betty J. • Library Media Specialist • Mary Lin Elementary School • Atlanta, GA 30307

Johnson Betty L. • Branch Librarian • Mid-Continent Public Library Gladstone Branch • Kansas City, MO 64155 • PLA

Johnson Blanche Battin • Huron, SD 57350 • Continuing

Johnson Bobbie R. • Mattawa, WA 99344

Johnson Bonnie E. • Cataloger • Montana State University • Bozeman, MT 59717-0332 • ACRL

Johnson Brenda • Assistant Director • District of Columbia Public Library Martin Luther King Memorial Library • Washington, DC 20001 • LAMA PLA IFRT

Johnson Brenda A. • Student • University of South Carolina College of Library & Information Science • Columbia, SC 29208 • AASL ALSC

Johnson Brenda J. • Circleville, OH 43113

Johnson Brenda L. • Coordinator, Public Services • University of Michigan Libraries • Ann Arbor, MI 48109-1205 • ACRL

Johnson Bruce Chr. • Senior Analyst • Library of Congress • Washington, DC 20541 • ALCTS

Johnson Bruce L. • Director • Indiana Historical Society Library • Indianapolis, IN 46202 • ACRL

Johnson C E. Mrs • Saint Paul, MN 55104-6648 • AASL PLA *Continuing*

Johnson C. • Student • Drexel University College of Information Studies • Philadelphia, PA 19104-2875

Johnson Carol • Senior Cataloger-Acquisitions • Church of Jesus Christ of Latter-Day Saints • Salt Lake City, UT 84150 • ALCTS

Johnson Carol A. • Chief Social Science Cataloger • University of Minnesota O. Meredith Wilson Library • Minneapolis, MN 55455-0414 • ACRL ALCTS LHRT

Johnson Carol A. • Director • Dewitt Community Library • Dewitt, NY 13214

Johnson Carol French • Director • Cedar Falls Public Library • Cedar Falls, IA 50613 • LAMA PLA

Johnson Carol M. • Manager,Texas & Local History • Houston Public Library • Houston, TX 77002 • PLA

Johnson Carol P. • Associate Director • Saint Johns University Alcuin Library • Collegeville, MN 56321-7155 • ACRL LAMA

Johnson Carole • Berkeley, CA 94710 • AASL

Johnson Carole • Director of Library Services • Richland College • Dallas, TX 75243-2199

Johnson Carolyn A. • Music Librarian • Connecticut College • New London, CT 06320-4196 • ACRL

Johnson Carolyn E. • Director • Pearl River Public Library • Pearl River, NY 10965 • ALSC ALTA LAMA PLA RASD YALSA IFRT

Johnson Carolyn E. • Fullerton, CA 92631 • ALSC PLA

Johnson Carolyn R. • Librarian • Arizona State University Hayden Library • Tempe, AZ 85287-1006 • ACRL LIRT

Johnson Carolyn V. • Science Librarian • Northwest Missouri State University Owens Library • Maryville, MO 64468 • ACRL

Johnson Carolynn K. • Deputy Librarian Facilities Devp • King County Library System • Seattle, WA 98109-5191 • LAMA PLA

Johnson Catherine J. • Assistant Curator • Harvard College Library Harvard Theatre Collection • Cambridge, MA 02138 • ACRL

Johnson Charles • Library Assistant • University of South Carolina • Columbia, SC 29208 • ACRL NMRT

Johnson Charlotte L. • Edwardsville, IL 62025-1124 • ACRL LITA

Johnson Clare W. • Media Specialist • Henderson Elementary School • McDonough, GA 30253 • AASL

Johnson Coburn R. • Asst. Catalog Librarian • University of Montana Library • Missoula, MT 59812 • ACRL ALCTS LITA

Johnson Connelly J. • Seattle, WA 98199 • SRRT

Johnson Constance • Librarian • U.S. Air Force Base Library • Plattsburgh, NY 12903

Johnson Constance A. • Librarian • Earl Warren Jr. High School • Solana Beach, CA 92075 • AASL YALSA VRT

Johnson Corinne • Director • Southwest Ohio Regional Library System SWORL • Wilmington, OH 45177 • ASCLA PLA

Johnson Cynthia A. • Public Services Librarian • Pratt Institute Library • Brooklyn, NY 11205 • ACRL

Johnson Cynthia L. • Chicago, IL 60626

Johnson Dana H. • Student • University of Illinois School of Library Information Science • Champaign, IL 61820 • ACRL IRRT

Johnson Daniel J. • Hull Public Library • Hull, MA 02045

Johnson Danita • Trustee • Gary Public Library • Gary, IN 46402 • ALTA

Johnson Darlene M. • Student • Wayne State University Library Science Program • Detroit, MI 48202

Johnson Deborah S. • Branch Head • Clemson University Gunnin Architectural Library • Clemson, SC 29634

Johnson Deborah S. • University of Minnesota-Duluth Library • Duluth, MN 55812-2495

Johnson Debra W. • University of Wisconsin School of Library & Information Studies • Madison, WI 53706

Johnson Diane E. • Continuing Educ Prog Director • University of Missouri-Columbia School of Library & Informational Science • Columbia, MO 65211 • ASCLA LAMA PLA CLENE

Johnson Diane L. • Head, Serials Department • New York State University Geneseo College • Geneseo, NY 14454 • ALCTS LITA

Johnson Diane M. • Media Specialist • Hamilton Disston School • Gulfport, FL 33707 • AASL

Johnson Dianne • Assistant Professor • University of South Carolina • Columbia, SC 29208 • ALSC EMIERT NMRT

Johnson Don • Director • Porter County Public Library • Valparaiso, IN 46383

Johnson Donald Clay • Librarian • University of Minnesota Meredith Wilson Library • Minneapolis, MN 55455 • ACRL RASD IRRT LHRT *Life*

Johnson Donna S. • Park Tudor Lower School Library • Indianapolis, IN 46240 • AASL

Johnson Dorothy E. • Director • Bloomfield Public Library • Bloomfield, NJ 07003 • ALCTS ALSC ALTA ASCLA LAMA LITA PLA RASD YALSA IFRT

Johnson Dorothy T. • Orlando, FL 32819-5018

Johnson Duane A. • San Antonio, TX 78217-4004

Johnson Duane F. • State Librarian • Kansas State Library • Topeka, KS 66612-1593 • ASCLA PLA

Johnson Edna P. • Children's Librarian • Madison County-Canton Public Library • Canton, MS 39046

Johnson Edward R. • Director of Libraries • Oklahoma State University Library • Stillwater, OK 74078-0375 • ACRL LAMA *Life*

Johnson Edwin A. • Director of Libraries • Valparaiso University Moellering Memorial Library • Valparaiso, IN 46383

Johnson Elaine D. • Evergreen Park Public Library • Chicago, IL 60642

Johnson Elaine Denise • Director • Danville Public Library • Danville, VA 24541 • Life

Johnson Eleanor S. • Automated Systems Librarian • Knox County Public Library System • Knoxville, TN 37902

Johnson Elizabeth A. • Student • San Jose State University Division of Library & Information Science • San Jose, CA 95192-0029 • IFRT SRRT

Johnson Elizabeth Benson • University of Minnesota-Duluth Library • Duluth, MN 55812-2495

Johnson Elizabeth L. • Associate Librarian • Indiana University Lilly Library • Bloomington, IN 47405 • ACRL ALCTS

Johnson Ellen • University of Central Arkansas Torreyson Library • Conway, AR 72032 • ACRL

Johnson Elvernoy H. • Emmanuel College Library • Boston, MA 02115

Johnson Emily C. • Administrative Officer • West Florida Regional Library • Pensacola, FL 32501

Johnson Eric A. • European Exchange Specialist • Library of Congress • Washington, DC 20541

Johnson Eric W. • Head of Reference Dept. • University of Bridgeport Magnus Wahlstrom Library • Bridgeport, CT 06601 • ACRL

Johnson Erna F. • Amherst Town Library • Amherst, NH 03031 • ALSC YALSA

Johnson Esther Khoo • Librarian • NASA/Ames Research Center • Moffett Field, CA 94035-1000 • ACRL

Johnson Evelyn E. • Director • American Postal Workers Union Library Information Center • Washington, DC 20005

Johnson Floy Mrs. • Trustee • Dayton & Montgomery County Public Library • Dayton, OH 45402-2103 • ALTA

Johnson G. Victor • Trustee • Arlington Heights Memorial Library • Arlington Heights, IL 60004-5966 • ALTA PLA

Johnson Gary A. • Data Processing Consultant • Unisys Corporation • Norcross, GA 30092 • LITA

Johnson Gary L. • Librarian • Birmingham Public & Jefferson County Free Library • Birmingham, AL 35203 • PLA

Johnson George T. • Director • Central State University Hallie Q Brown Memorial Library • Wilberforce, OH 45384 • ACRL

Johnson Glenn • Library Media Specialist • State College Area Junior High • State College, PA 16828 • AASL

Johnson Glenn H. Jr • Western New England College • Springfield, MA 01119 • ACRL LITA *Life*

Johnson Godlind • Head, Engineering Library • State University of New York (SUNY) • Stony Brook, NY 11794-2225 • ACRL

Johnson Gretchen J. • Associate Director/Information • California State University-Long Beach University Library & Learning Resources • Long Beach, CA 90840-1901 • ACRL LAMA RASD

Johnson Guy M. • Director • Nichols School Libraries • Buffalo, NY 14216 • AASL

Johnson H. Joan • Director • Liberal Memorial Library • Liberal, KS 67901 • PLA

Johnson Harlan R. • Professor of Library Science • Northern Arizona University • Flagstaff, AZ 86011-6022

Johnson Hazel • Pittsburgh, PA 15213 • Continuing

Johnson Hazel A. • Milwaukie, OR 97222 • ACRL LAMA *Life*

Johnson Hazel S Jones • Director Emeritus • Grambling State University A. C. Lewis Memorial Library • Grambling, LA 71245

Johnson Helen W. • Mechanicsburg, PA 17055 • Continuing

Johnson Herbert F. • Emory University Libraries Robert W. Woodruff Library • Atlanta, GA 30322-2870 • ACRL

Johnson Holly A. • Head of Technical Services • Howard County Library • Columbia, MD 21044 • ALCTS

Johnson J. Sigrid • Head, The Icelandic Collection • University of Manitoba • Winnipeg MB, R3T 2N2 Canada • ACRL

Johnson Jacqueline M. • Student • University of Wisconsin School of Library & Information Studies • Madison, WI 53706 • AASL

Johnson James B. Jr. • Director • South Carolina State Library • Columbia, SC 29211 • ASCLA PLA

Johnson James G. Bro. • Director • Passionist Monastic Library • Jamaica, NY 11432-0024

Johnson James H. • Trustee • East Orange Public Library • East Orange, NJ 07018 • ALTA

Johnson James R. • Pittsburgh, PA 15227

Johnson James R. • Reference Librarian • Memphis-Shelby County Public Library and Information Center • Memphis, TN 38104-4025 • PLA IFRT

Johnson Jan • Head Librarian • McKinney High School • McKinney, TX 75069

Johnson Jane • Waterford Schools • Waterford, MI 48327

Johnson Jane A. • Humanities, Project Director • New England Foundation for Humanities • Boston, MA 02116-4802

Johnson Jane G. • Head, Acquisitions Department • Georgia Southern University Henderson Library • Statesboro, GA 30460 • LAMA

Johnson Jane S. • Tucson, AZ 85715 • LITA ILERT

Johnson Jane W. • Collection Mgmt./Library Service • Virginia Commonwealth University • Richmond, VA 23284 • ACRL ALCTS

Johnson Janet • Breidablik Elementary School • Poulsbo, WA 98370

Johnson Janet M. • Librarian II • Los Angeles Public Library Loyola Village Branch • Los Angeles, CA 90045

Johnson Janine M. • LRC Director • Cloud County Community College • Concordia, KS 66901 • ACRL LHRT LIRT

Johnson Jean E. • Student • University of Illinois Graduate School of Library and Information Science • Urbana, IL 61801 • PLA

Johnson Jean M. • Manager,Information Service • Lehigh University Mountaintop Library • Bethlehem, PA 18015-4732 • ACRL ILERT

Johnson Jean T. • Director of Media Services • Wake County Public School System • Raleigh, NC 27611 • AASL ALCTS YALSA

Johnson Jeanne S. • Branch Librarian • Fresno County Free Library Leo Politi Branch • Fresno, CA 93710

Johnson Jeannie W. • Tech Serv Ln • Mesquite Public Library • Mesquite, TX 75149 • ALCTS

Johnson Jeffrey P. • Haslett, MI 48840 • ASCLA LAMA PLA

Johnson Jennie S. • Reference Librarian • University of Toledo William S. Carlson Library • Toledo, OH 43606-3399 • ACRL ALSC RASD

Johnson Jenny • Student • State University of New York at Albany School of Information Science & Policy • Albany, NY 12222 • AASL IFRT SRRT

Johnson Jenny M. • University of Washington Suzzallo Library • Seattle, WA 98195 • ACRL GODORT MAGERT

Johnson Jerry D. • Children's Librarian • Rapid City Public Library • Rapid City, SD 57701-3630 • ALSC PLA SORT

Johnson JoAnn K. • Burnsville, MN 55337 • AASL

Johnson JoAnna • Asst. Director Tech Services • Los Angeles Public Library • Los Angeles, CA 90071 • LITA PLA

Johnson Joan Ellen • Acquisitions Librarian • Community College of Philadelphia Educational Resource Center • Philadelphia, PA 19130 • ACRL

Johnson Joanne M. • First Assistant • Detroit Public Library Hubbard Branch • Detroit, MI 48235 • YALSA

Johnson Johanna H. • Patent Librn., Gvmt. Pubs. Div. • Dallas Public Library • Dallas, TX 75201

Johnson Johnny L. • Science & Engineering Librarian • Oklahoma State University Library • Stillwater, OK 74078-0375 • ACRL

Johnson Joseph J. • Senior Reference Librarian • Monterey Public Library • Monterey, CA 93940 • Life

Johnson Joy A. • Director • Community Public Library • St. Marys, OH 45885 • PLA

Johnson Joy J • Student • Los Angeles Public Library West Valley Regional Library • Reseda, CA 91335

Johnson Joyce M. • Rare Bks Libn in Charge of Convs • Peoria Public Library • Peoria, IL 61602 • ACRL ALCTS PLA RASD

Johnson Judith A. • Librarian • Rapid City Central High School Library • Rapid City, SD 57701 • AASL

Johnson Judith R. J. • Logan, UT 84321 • ACRL RASD IFRT

Johnson Judy • Overton Public School • Overton, NE 68863 • AASL

Johnson Judy L. • Chair Acquisitions Department • University of Nebraska Love Library • Lincoln, NE 68588-0410 • ALCTS LAMA

Johnson Julia C. • Catholic University of America School of Library and Information Science • Washington, DC 20064

Johnson Julia M. • Head Government Documents Dept. • University of Southern California Doheny Library • Los Angeles, CA 90089-0182 • GODORT

Johnson June R. • AV Cataloger • Durham County Library • Durham, NC 27702

Johnson Karen • Assistant Agency Head • Salt Lake City Public Library Sprauge Branch • Salt Lake City, UT 84106

Johnson Karen A. • Assistant Librarian • University of San Francisco Richard A. Gleeson Library • San Francisco, CA 94117 • LITA

Johnson Karen M. • St. Charles, IL 60174 • AASL

Johnson Karl B. • Director of Library Services • Pima Community College East Campus • Tucson, AZ 85730 • ACRL

Johnson Katharine S. • Associate Director • Ingham County Library • Mason, MI 48854

Johnson Kathleen A. • Associate Professor • University of Nebraska Love Library • Lincoln, NE 68588-0410 • ACRL SRRT

Johnson Kathleen S. • Head, Childrens Service Dept. • Minneapolis Public Library & Information Center • Minneapolis, MN 55401-1992 • ALSC PLA

Johnson Kathryn • Trustee • Rapid City Public Library • Rapid City, SD 57701-3630

Johnson Kathryn W. • Collection Development Librarian • Southern University John B. Cade Library • Baton Rouge, LA 70813 • RASD

Johnson Kathy L. • Media Coordinator • Kirkman Park School • High Point, NC 27262 • AASL

Johnson Kenneth E. • Director, Instruc'l Mater'l Ctr. • Bloomington Public Schools • Bloomington, MN 55420 • AASL

Johnson Kirby • Student • University of Iowa School of Library & Information Science • Iowa City, IA 52242 • LITA RASD

Johnson Kirsten A. • Student • Indiana University School of Library and Information Science • Bloomington, IN 47405

Johnson Kristin M. • Harvard College Library Widener Memorial Library • Cambridge, MA 02138 • ACRL

Johnson L. Rebecca • University of Delaware Library • Newark, DE 19717-5267 • ACRL

Johnson LaVonne M. • Librarian • Parkway Elementary School • Fort Lewis, WA 98433

Johnson Larry • Trustee • Alpha Park Public Library District • Bartonville, IL 61607 • ALTA

Johnson Larry G. • Student • University of Oklahoma School of Library & Information Studies • Norman, OK 73019 • RASD

Johnson Laura G. • Associate Director Public Serv. • Indianapolis Marion County Public Library • Indianapolis, IN 46206 • PLA

Johnson Lavinia L. • Detroit, MI 48217

Johnson Lavonne M. • Director of Library Services • Bryan College Ironside Memorial Library • Dayton, TN 37321 • ACRL ALCTS RASD

Johnson Lazelle S. • Trustee • Seattle Public Library • Seattle, WA 98104-1193 • ALTA PLA

Johnson Leila • Minneapolis, MN 55410 • RASD

Johnson Lenore J. • Head, Public Services • Tangipahoa Parish Library • Amite, LA 70422 • PLA

Johnson Les • Librarian II • San Bernardino County Library • San Bernardino, CA 92415 • PLA

Johnson Linda • Folsom High School • Folsom, CA 95630 • AASL

Johnson Linda • Beaumont District Library • Beaumont, CA 92223

Johnson Linda B. • Hd Government Publications Dept • San Jose State University Clark Library • San Jose, CA 95192-0028 • ACRL LAMA GODORT MAGERT

Johnson Lisa H. • Kent, OH 44240 • ACRL

Johnson Lois • System Advisory Board Member • Alhambra Public Library • Alhambra, CA 91801

Johnson Lorrie Apple • Knoxville, TN 37922

Johnson Louise M. • Student • Emporia State University School of Library & Information Management • Emporia, KS 66801 • AASL

Johnson Lucy C Trent • Washington, DC 20010 • Continuing

Johnson Lynda Mrs. • Carthage Junior High School • Carthage, TX 75633 • AASL

Johnson Lynn M. • Head of Children's Services • Carol Stream Public Library • Carol Stream, IL 60188 • ALSC IRRT

Johnson Lynn R. • Student • James Madison University • Harrisonburg, VA 22807

Johnson Madeleine M. • Head, Cataloging Dept. • California Polytechnic State University Robert E. Kennedy Library • San Luis Obispo, CA 93407 • ACRL ALCTS LAMA LITA

Johnson Marda L. • Mgr. OLUC Database Serv. • Online Computer Library Center (OCLC) • Dublin, OH 43017-3395

Johnson Margaret • Carson City, NV 89701

Johnson Margaret A. • Director • National Museum of Naval Aviation Emil Buehler Naval Aviation Library • NAS Pensacola, FL 32508

Johnson Margaret E. • Children's Coordinator • Seminole County Library System Central Branch • Casselberry, FL 32707

Johnson Margaret H. • Albany, NY 12202 • AASL

Johnson Margaret L. • Director • University of Minnesota-Duluth Library • Duluth, MN 55812-2495 • ACRL ALCTS LITA

Johnson Margie M. • Systems Specialist • Hewlett-Packard Company • Corvallis, OR 97330 • ACRL

Johnson Maria S. • Director • Nebraska Christian College • Norfolk, NE 68701-2458 • ACRL ALCTS

Johnson Marietta W. • Executive Director • Eastern Connecticut Library Association • Willimantic, CT 06226

Johnson Marilyn S. • Florence, AL 35630

Johnson Marilyn Tamura • Los Angeles, CA 90064

Johnson Marjorie • Librarian Emerita • New York Public School 194 • New York, NY 10030 • AASL

Johnson Marjory F. • San Luis Obispo, CA 93401

Johnson Martha • Moses Brown School Walter Jones Library • Providence, RI 02906 • ACRL

Johnson Martha L. • Elementary Librarian • St. Maur International School • Yokohama, 231, Japan • AASL ALSC

Johnson Mary • Library Specialist • Orange County Public Library • Santa Ana, CA 92705

Johnson Mary Ann • Trustee • Mid-Continent Public Library • Independence, MO 64050 • ALTA

Johnson Mary Ann E. • Student • University of Wisconsin-Milwaukee School of Library & Information Science • Milwaukee, WI 53201

Johnson Mary E. • Librarian Specialist • Kent County Library System Plainfield Branch • Grand Rapids, MI 49505

Johnson Mary E. • Muncie, IN 47303-4708 • Continuing

Johnson Mary E. • Library Director • Missouri Institute of Mental Health • Saint Louis, MO 63139 • ACRL

Johnson Mary Ellen • Reference Librarian • Windsor Public Library • Windsor, CT 06095 • RASD

Johnson Mary J. • Colorado Springs, CO 80919

Johnson Mary Jean • Champaign, IL 61821

Johnson Mary K. • Colorado Springs, CO 80920

Johnson Mary V. • East Central Regional Library • Cambridge, MN 55008

Johnson Max Cody Jr. • Librarian IV, Asst. Director • Hancock County Library System Headquarters • Bay Saint Louis, MS 39520

Johnson Megan • Dothan, AL 36303

Johnson Merrill • George Fox College • Newberg, OR 97132 • ACRL

Johnson Minnie R. • Chicago, IL 60616

Johnson Miriam H. • Batavia, IL 60510 • Continuing

Johnson Myrna Rae • Senior Analyst • American Express • Phoenix, AZ 85018 • LITA

Johnson Nancy Becker • Assistant Professor • University of Arizona Graduate Library School • Tucson, AZ 85721 • LHRT LRRT

Johnson Nancy E. • Des Moines, IA 50317

Johnson Nancy Lynn • Riverside, CA 92501

Johnson Nellie B. • School Librarian • Charlestown High School • Charlestown, MA 02125

Johnson O. B. • Vice-President, General Manager • EBSCO Subscription Services • San Mateo, CA 94403

Johnson Olivia Miss • R. P. Heffernan-Attorney • West Hartford, CT 06107 • PLA RASD *Continuing*

Johnson Pamela A. • Vienna, VA 22181

Johnson Pamela M. • Substitute Teacher • City School District of Albany • Albany, NY 12207 • AASL

Johnson Pat • Trustee • Western Plains Library System • Clinton, OK 73601

Johnson Patrelle E. • Senior Young Adult Librarian • New York Public Library Todt Hill-Westerleigh Branch • Staten Island, NY 10314 • PLA YALSA NMRT

Johnson Patricia • Network Administrator • Old Colony Library Network • Canton, MA 02021 • ALCTS LITA

Johnson Patricia • District Librarian • Weslaco High School • Weslaco, TX 78596 • AASL YALSA

Johnson Patricia A. • Librarian • Hillside Public Library • Hillside, IL 60162 • YALSA

Johnson Patricia B. • Tritt Elementary School • Marietta, GA 30062 • AASL

Johnson Patricia C. • Reference Librarian • Wallingford Public Library • Wallingford, CT 06492

Johnson Patricia L. • Arcadia Public Library • Arcadia, CA 91007 • PLA

Johnson Patricia M. • APO New York, NY 09406 • AFLRT

Johnson Patrick J. • Trustee • Macomb County Library • Mount Clemens, MI 48044 • ALTA

Johnson Paul A. • Adult Services Librarian • Ontario City Library • Ontario, CA 91764

Johnson Paulette • Media Specialist • Boulder High School Lib • Boulder, CO 80302 • AASL

Johnson Peg • Director • Sioux Center Public Library • Sioux Center, IA 51250 • LAMA PLA

Johnson Peggy • Assistant Director • University of Minnesota Saint Paul Campus Libraries • Saint Paul, MN 55108 • ACRL ALCTS LAMA LITA

Johnson Penelope B. • Head Librarian • Worcester Public Library • Worcester, MA 01608 • ALTA LAMA PLA IFRT

Johnson Penny L. • Oil City Elementary/Middle School • Oli City, LA 71061

Johnson Peter • Librarian • Stanford University J. Henry Meyer Memorial Library • Stanford, CA 94305 • ACRL

Johnson Phyllis Ann • Media Specialist • MSD Washington Township Nora School • Indianapolis, IN 46240 • AASL

Johnson Phyllis H. • Director • Michigan Technological University J. R. Van Pelt Library • Houghton, MI 49931-1295 • ALCTS LITA

Johnson Rafe A. • Assistant Director • Jefferson Community College-SW Campus • Louisville, KY 40272

Johnson Ralph J. • Head Librarian • Fountaindale Public Library District • Bolingbrook, IL 60440 • PLA

Johnson Ralph W. • Los Angeles, CA 90019 • AASL ALSC *Continuing*

Johnson Rebecca L. • Reference Librarian • University of Iowa Libraries • Iowa City, IA 52242-1379 • ACRL RASD IFRT

Johnson Richard D. • Director of Libraries • State University of New York College at Oneonta-Library • Oneonta, NY 13820-4014 • ACRL ALCTS *Life*

Johnson Richardia S. • Director • Lonesome Pine Regional Library • Wise, VA 24293 • LAMA PLA

Johnson Rita M. • Librarian/Media Specialist • Riverdahl Elementary School • Rockford, IL 61109 • AASL

Johnson Robert D. • Librarian • Tumwater High School • Tumwater, WA 98501 • AASL

Johnson Robin A. • Director • Idaho Springs Public Library • Idaho Springs, CO 80452 • PLA

Johnson Rochelle H. • Librarian/Media Specialist • Gilbert Linkous Elementary School • Blacksburg, VA 24060 • AASL

Johnson Ross G. • Information Adminstrator • N.C.R. Comten Inc. • Saint Paul, MN 55113

Johnson Roxanne E. • Media Specialist • Little River Elementary School • Woodstock, GA 30188

Johnson Russell A. • Student • University of California Los Angeles Graduate School of Library & Information Science • Los Angeles, CA 90024 • ALCTS NMRT

Johnson Ruth C. • Minneapolis, MN 55410 • LAMA PLA *Life*

Johnson Ruth R. • Rancocas, NJ 08073 • ALSC *Continuing*

Johnson S. M. • Cataloging • Clarion University of Pennsylvania Rena M. Carlson Library • Clarion, PA 16214 • LAMA

Johnson Sallie • Deputy Director • Memphis-Shelby County Public Library and Information Center • Memphis, TN 38104-4025 • LAMA PLA

Johnson Sally K. • Library Media Specialist • Hawthorne & Oak Heights Schools Sweet Home School District • Sweet Home, OR 97386 • AASL

Johnson Sam • Student • University of North Dakota Department of Library Science & Audiovisual Instruction • Grand Forks, ND 58202 • AASL

Johnson Sandra R. • Branch Librarian • Mercer County Library Hightstown Branch • Hightstown, NJ 08520 • PLA SRRT

Johnson Sara H. • Product Manager • CLSI, Inc. • Newtonville, MA 02160 • LITA PLA

Johnson Sharon C. • Fullerton, CA 92633 • ALSC SRRT

Johnson Sharon E. • Student • Emporia State University Emporia in the Rockies • Denver, CO 80204

Johnson Sharon M. • Maine University Blake Library • Fort Kent, ME 04743 • ACRL LITA

Johnson Sheila • Reference Services Head • University of Southern Maine • Portland, ME 04103 • ACRL

Johnson Sheila A. • Division Chief • Brooklyn Public Library • Brooklyn, NY 11238

Johnson Sheila G. • Asst. Ln. Ref., Instr. & Cllns. • Oklahoma State University Library • Stillwater, OK 74078-0375 • ACRL LAMA

Johnson Sheila M. • Librarian III • Forsyth County Public Library • Winston-Salem, NC 27101 • NMRT

Johnson Shirley • Librarian • Bellevue Community College • Bellevue, WA 98007 • ACRL

Johnson Shirley E. • Librarian/Branches • Enoch Pratt Free Library • Baltimore, MD 21201-4484

Johnson Shirley K. • Asst. Head Tech. Services • Gettysburg College Musselman Library • Gettysburg, PA 17325-1493 • ACRL ALCTS

Johnson Stephen C. • Research Manager • National Association of College Stores • Oberlin, OH 44074 • LAMA

Johnson Stephen K. • Student • University of Iowa School of Library & Information Science • Iowa City, IA 52242 • LITA RASD

Johnson Steven D. • Asst. Acquisitions Librarian • Clemson University Robert Muldrow Cooper Library • Clemson, SC 29634-3001

Johnson Susan Amber • Student • University of Wisconsin School of Library & Information Studies • Madison, WI 53706 • ALSC RASD NMRT

Johnson Susan G. • Advisory Commission • Newark City Council • Newark, CA 94560

Johnson Susan Massie • Children' Librarian (Part-time) • Massanutten Military Academy • Woodstock, VA 22664 • YALSA

Johnson Tara Kay • Rockford, IL 61104 • PLA SRRT

Johnson Theresa Preuit • Humanities Reference Librarian • University of West Florida John C. Pace Library • Pensacola, FL 32514 • ACRL

Johnson Thomas L. • Assistant City Librarian • Newport Beach Public Library • Newport Beach, CA 92660 • PLA RASD

Johnson Timothy J. • Director of Archives • North Park College & Theo Sem Consolidated Library • Chicago, IL 60625 • ACRL

Johnson Tucker Nancy Ellen • Library Services Manager • Westminster Public Library • Westminster, CO 80030 • LAMA PLA

Johnson Veronica A. • Chief Legislative Aide & Cons. • Michigan House of Representatives • Lansing, MI 48913

Johnson Victoria L. • Reference Services • Pasadena Public Library • Pasadena, CA 91101 • PLA

Johnson Virginia K. • Student • Simmons College Graduate School of Library & Information Science • Boston, MA 02115 • ALCTS

Johnson Virginia L. • Director • Morton County Public Library • Elkhart, KS 67950

Johnson W. Duane • Indianapolis, IN 46220 • Continuing

Johnson Walt A. • Minneapolis Public Library & Information Center • Minneapolis, MN 55401-1992 • SRRT

Johnson Walter • President • Walter J. Johnson, Inc. • Norwood, NJ 07648

Johnson Wendell G. • Student • Northern Illinois University Department of Library & Information Studies • DeKalb, IL 60115

Johnson William B. • Branch Manager • First Regional Library M R Davis Public Library • Southavon, MS 38671

Johnson William W. • Assistant Director • Chatham-Effingham-Liberty Regional Library (CEL) • Savannah, GA 31499-4301

Johnson Wilma Jean • Choctaw High School • Choctaw, OK 73020 • AASL

Johnson Winifred • Washington, DC 20015 • ACRL ALCTS   *Continuing*

Johnson Yvette Tetrault • Childrens Librarian • Glenview Public Library • Glenview, IL 60025 • ALSC

Johnsson Gilford • Library Director • Cozard Memorial Library • Chamberlain, SD 57325 • PLA

Johnston Ann T. • Technical Services Librarian • North Idaho College Library • Coeur d'Alene, ID 83814

Johnston B. J. • Head of Collection Development • Washington University Libraries • Saint Louis, MO 63130-4899 • ACRL ALCTS

Johnston Caroline F. • Librarian, Lower School • Saint Agnes Saint Stephen's School • Alexandria, VA 22302 • AASL

Johnston Carolyn S. • Student • Texas Woman's University School of Library & Information Studies • Denton, TX 76204 • AASL

Johnston Christine • Georgetown University Joseph Mark Lauinger Library • Washington, DC 20057-1006

Johnston Cynthia J. • Librarian • Saint Mary's Episcopal Day School • Tampa, FL 33629 • AASL

Johnston Dolores C. • L Media Spec 6-8 • Bolton School • West Linn, OR 97068

Johnston Francena M. • Medical Librarian • San Antonio Community Hospital • Upland, CA 91786 • ASCLA

Johnston George F. • Cataloger • University of Cincinnati Langsam Library • Cincinnati, OH 45221-0033 • ACRL ALCTS

Johnston James G. • Director • Enfield Public Library • Enfield, CT 06082

Johnston James R. • Director • Joliet Public Library • Joliet, IL 60431 • ALCTS LAMA LITA PLA RASD YALSA

Johnston Janet L. • Manager • Flowers By Posie Post • Scottsdale, AZ 85251

Johnston Janet R. • Asst. Library Director • Oceanside Public Library • Oceanside, CA 92054 • PLA

Johnston Janis L. • Assoc Director of Tech Serv • University of Notre Dame Kresge Law Library • Notre Dame, IN 46556 • ALCTS

Johnston Joyce E.M. • Student • University of South Carolina College of Library & Information Science • Columbia, SC 29208 • ACRL

Johnston Judy A. • Assistant Catalog Librarian Ser. • North Texas State University Willis Library • Denton, TX 76203 • ALCTS

Johnston Julie M. • Student • Florida State University School of Library and Information Studies • Tallahassee, FL 32306-2048 • PLA IFRT SRRT

Johnston Kathryn A. • Instructional Services Ln. • Eckerd College William Luther Cobb Library • Saint Petersburg, FL 33711

Johnston Lisa N. • Reference Librarian • Sweet Briar College Library • Sweet Briar, VA 24595 • ACRL SRRT

Johnston Loranne H. • Marietta, GA 30064 • AASL

Johnston Lynwood • Waterbury, VT 05676 • ACRL RASD   *Life*

Johnston Margaret • Buffalo, NY 14221 • Continuing

Johnston Marjory A. • Michigan Technological University Library • Houghton, MI 49931

Johnston Maxine • Batson, TX 77519 • Continuing

Johnston Raymond S. • Seattle, WA 98115

Johnston Robert C. • Reader Services/Automation Ln. • Pennsylvania College of Technology Learning Resources Center • Williamsport, PA 17701

Johnston Sarah Hager • Director, Tech. Research Serv. • ITT Hartford Insurance Group • Hartford, CT 06115 • ALCTS LAMA LITA RASD

Johnston Stanley H. • Curator of Rare Books • Holden Arboretum Lib • Mentor, OH 44060 • ACRL

Johnston Susan E. • Livermore Public Library • Livermore, CA 94550

Johnston Susan E. • Head of Children's Dept. • Ben West Public Library • Nashville, TN 37203

Johnston Tony • San Marino, CA 91108 • ALSC

Johnston Wanda K. • Director of Library Resources • Broome Community College • Binghamton, NY 13902 • ACRL LAMA

Johnstone Jay • Regional Librarian • Yolo County Library Arthur F. Turner Branch • West Sacramento, CA 95691

Johnstone Jennifer • Summit Public Library District • Summit, IL 60501

Joiner Carol • Reference Librarian • University of New Mexico General Library • Albuquerque, NM 87131 • ACRL IFRT

Joiner Mary Jo • Head Librarian • West Tisbury Free Public Library • West Tisbury, MA 02575

Joines Alyce B. • Media Coordinator • Fairview Elementary School • High Point, NC 27260 • AASL YALSA

Jolivet Anna Dr. • Superintendent TUSD • Tucson Pima Library • Tucson, AZ 85726 • ALTA

Jolivet Linda C. • Frankfort, KY 40601 • SRRT

Jolley Lora Ann • Cody High School Library • Cody, WY 82414 • AASL

Jondrow James F. • Director • Glasgow City-County Library • Glasgow, MT 59330 • LAMA

Jonen Ruth • Trustee • Schaumburg Township District Library • Schaumburg, IL 60194

Jones-Eddy Julie • Government Documents Librarian • Colorado College Tutt Library • Colorado Springs, CO 80903 • ACRL GODORT

Jones-Fuller Paula J. • APO New York, NY 09178

Jones-Hayes Judith C. • Old Washington, OH 43768

Jones-Litteer Corene A. • Timberland Regional Library Chehalis Branch • Chehalis, WA 98532 • LAMA PLA

Jones-Trent Bernice R. • Director, Library Services • Montclair State College Harry Sprague Library • Upper Montclair, NJ 07043 • ACRL LAMA

Jones-Warren Sandra • Manager Corp. Info. • First Card Inc Computer Services Library • Elgin, IL 60121-2019 • LAMA

Jones Adrian Mr. • Director • Roosevelt University Library • Chicago, IL 60605 • ACRL ALCTS LAMA LITA RASD EMIERT GODORT IRRT LIRT LRRT

Jones Agnes B. • Richmond, VA 23221 • YALSA   *Continuing*

Jones Alicia • High School Librarian • San Ramon Valley High School • Danville, CA 94526 • AASL

Jones Angela R. • Reference Librarian/Cataloger • University of Southern Mississippi McCain Library & Archives • Hattiesburg, MS 39406-5148 • ACRL ALCTS NMRT

Jones Anita L. • Hagerstown, MD 21740-6783

Jones Ann L. • Serials Librarian • Art Institute of Chicago Ryerson & Burnham Library • Chicago, IL 60603 • ACRL ALCTS LITA

Jones Ann L. • Library Media Specialist • Jefferson County Public Schools North Arvada Junior High • Arvada, CO 80003 • AASL

Jones Ann-K. • Student • University of Washington Graduate School of Library and Information Science • Seattle, WA 98195 • ACRL LITA

Jones Anna E. • Burlington, NJ 08016 • Continuing

Jones Anne B. • Adult Services Librarian • Vernon Area Public Library • Prairie View, IL 60069 • PLA

Jones Anne Goddard • Librarian • White Pine School Library • White Pine, TN 37890

Jones Annease • Atlanta, GA 30331

Jones Ardele C. • Reference Librarian • Clinton Community College • Plattsburgh, NY 12901

Jones Arla D. • Librarian • Fieldston School Tate Library • Bronx, NY 10471

Jones Arthur E. Jr Dr • Davidson, NC 28036 • ACRL   *Continuing*

Jones Barbara A. • Haddonfield, NJ 08033

Jones Barbara A. • Palm Harbor, FL 34684

Jones Barbara J. • Detroit, MI 48227 • AASL SRRT

Jones Barbara L. • Media Specialist • Hohokam Elementary School • Scottsdale, AZ 85257

Jones Barbara M. • Library Director • Union College Schaffer Library • Schenectady, NY 12308 • ACRL PLA RASD IFRT ILERT IRRT LHRT

Jones Barbara P. • Librarian • East Lake High School • Chula Vista, CA 91915 • AASL

Jones Barbara S. • Finger Lake Elementary School • Wasilla, AK 99687 • AASL

Jones Bea • Owner • BNI • Gunnison, CO 81230 • LITA

Jones Billie J. • Library Manager • Salt Lake County Library Systems Calvin Smith Library • Salt Lake City, UT 84106 • PLA

Jones Brenda L. • Student • Glendale Community College Library • Glendale, CA 91208

Jones C. Lee • Consultant • CBR Consulting Services • Bethlehem, PA 18017 • ACRL LITA   *Life*

Jones Carol L. • Technical Services Librarian • Yale University Kline Science Library • New Haven, CT 06511-8142 • ACRL ALCTS LITA GODORT IRRT

Jones Carolyn J. • Lake Orion, MI 48360 • RASD

Jones Carolyn Thomas • Librarian • Chappaqua Library • Chappaqua, NY 10514

Jones Carrie E. • Media Specialist • Culver Community Junior-Senior High School • Culver, IN 46511

Jones Cassandra • YA Librarian • Broward County Library Fort Lauderdale Branch • Ft. Lauderdale, FL 33304 • YALSA

Jones Catherine E. • Lexington, MA 02173 • AASL

Jones Celia B. • Deland, FL 32724

Jones Charles E. • Chicago, IL 60613

Jones Charles F. Dr. • LRC Director • North Harris College • Houston, TX 77073

Jones Charlotte W. • Mgr Planning & Research • Spokane Public Library Comstock Building Library • Spokane, WA 99201-0976 • LAMA PLA

Jones Cindy • Catalog Librarian • Boston State College • Boston, MA 02115 • SRRT

Jones Clara S. • Oakland, CA 94610 • AASL ACRL ALCTS ALSC ALTA ASCLA LAMA LITA RASD YALSA   *Honorary*

Jones Clifton H. • Dean of Libraries • Idaho State University Eli M. Oboler Library • Pocatello, ID 83209-8089 • ACRL LAMA

Jones Constance R. • Department Director • Municipality of Anchorage Cultural & Recreational Services • Anchorage, AK 99519-6650

Jones Curley C. • Salt Lake City, UT 84111 • ACRL LAMA RASD EMIERT LRRT   *Life*

Jones Cynthia • Young Adult/Audio-Visual Spec. • Howard County Library • Columbia, MD 21044 • ALCTS RASD YALSA

Jones Daniel S. • President • NewsBank, Inc. • New Canaan, CT 06840 • AASL ACRL ALTA LITA PLA RASD AFLRT ERT FLRT GODORT

Jones David M. • Harris County Public Library • Houston, TX 77054 • ALCTS LITA

Jones Deborah A. • Indianapolis, IN 46208 • ACRL RASD

Jones Dolores Blythe • Curator, De Grummond Collection • University of Southern Mississippi McCain Library & Archives • Hattiesburg, MS 39406-5148 • ACRL ALSC

Jones Donald E. • Director • Community College of Philadelphia • Philadelphia, PA 19130

Jones Donald W. • Catalog Librarian • Vanderbilt University Library Jean & Alexander Heard Library • Nashville, TN 37240-0007 • ALCTS IRRT

Jones Donna R. • Director • Arkansas Valley Regional Library Service System • Pueblo, CO 81004 • ASCLA LAMA LITA PLA CLENE IFRT LIRT

Jones Donna R. • Student • Northwestern School of Law Boley Library • Portland, OR 97219

Jones Dora Ann • Special Collection Librarian • Black Hills State University • Spearfish, SD 57799-9548 • ACRL

Jones Dorothy • East Orange, NJ 07018 • LAMA PLA YALSA   *Continuing*

Jones Dorothy C. • Librarian • Plainfield High School Library • Plainfield, NJ 07060 • Continuing

Jones Dorothy E. • Ref & Serv Persons Disabilities • Northern Illinois University University Libraries • DeKalb, IL 60115-2868 • ASCLA

Jones Douglas E. • Coordinator, Collection Devel. • University of Arizona Library • Tucson, AZ 85721 • ACRL GODORT

Jones Ed Sully • Trustee • Fairfax County Public Library • Fairfax, VA 22033-1907

Jones Edgar A. • Student • University of Illinois at Urbana Champaign • Urbana, IL 61801 • ALCTS

Jones Edith C. Miss • Classics Librarian Emerita • University of Illinois Library • Urbana, IL 61801 • Continuing

Jones Edward • Order Librarian • Fairfax County Public Library • Fairfax, VA 22033-1909

Jones Eleanor R. • Director • Western Reserve Acad • Hudson, OH 44236 • AASL LITA IFRT

Jones Elizabeth A. • San Antonio, TX 78209

Jones Elizabeth E. • Indexing Editor • Spring Independent School District Salyers Elementary • Spring, TX 77373

Jones Ellen R. • Cataloger • Saint Xavier University • Chicago, IL 60655 • ALCTS

Jones Evelyn R. • Trustee • East Cleveland Public Library • East Cleveland, OH 44112 • ALTA

Jones Florence K. Mrs. • Lakewood, OH 44107 • Continuing

Jones Florence W. • University of Colorado at Denver Auraria Library • Denver, CO 80204 • IFRT SRRT

Jones Frances M. • University Librarian • West Texas State University Cornette Library • Canyon, TX 79016-0748 • ACRL LAMA

Jones Frank N. • Dallas, TX 75243 • ACRL ALCTS
Continuing

Jones Frederick S. II • Associate Librarian • Tufts University Nils Yngve Wessell Library • Medford, MA 02155 • ACRL RASD

Jones Gary H. • Syracuse, NY 13207 • ALCTS

Jones Gina E. • Burroughs Wellcome Company • Research Triangle Pk, NC 27709 • ACRL ALCTS LAMA LITA

Jones Glenda Sue • Hoxie Elementary School • Hoxie, AR 72433 • AASL

Jones Harold D. Prof. • Brooklyn, NY 11201 • ACRL LAMA IFRT
Life

Jones Helen Carol • Asst. Professor/Reference Librn. • Georgia State University Pullen Library • Atlanta, GA 30303-3081 • RASD

Jones Herbert U. • Purchasing Officer • University of California Res Lib • Los Angeles, CA 90024 • LAMA LITA IFRT

Jones Jacqueline F. • Lebanon, NJ 08833

Jones Jacqueline M. • Assistant Librarian • Oakville Senior High School • Saint Louis, MO 63129 • AASL

Jones Jan Jordan • Student • Texas Woman's University School of Library & Information Studies • Denton, TX 76204 • LITA RASD EMIERT IFRT LHRT NMRT SRRT

Jones Jane A. • Beaufort, SC 29902

Jones Janet Eakins • Coordinator-Youth Services • Belleville Public Library • Belleville, IL 62220 • PLA

Jones Jean • South Pasadena, CA 91030

Jones Jean M. • Supervisor, Circulation Serv. • University of Michigan Natural Science Library • Ann Arbor, MI 48109

Jones Jean M. • Reference Librarian • New Orleans Public Library • New Orleans, LA 70140 • PLA GODORT

Jones Jean R. • Librarian • E. J. Russell Elementary School Library • Pine Bush, NY 12566

Jones Jeannette M. • Medford, NJ 08055

Jones Jerry E. • Trustee • Fairfax County Public Library • Fairfax, VA 22033-1909

Jones Jesse R. • Social Science Bibliographer • University of Florida Libraries • Gainesville, FL 32611-2047 • ACRL ALCTS RASD

Jones Jill F. Mrs. • Student • University of Alabama School of Library & Information Studies • Tuscaloosa, AL 35487-0252

Jones Jody • Pikes Peak Library District • Colorado Springs, CO 80901

Jones Joel L. • Student • Jefferson County Public Library Arvada Branch • Arvada, CO 80002

Jones John W. • Director • Neuse Regional Library System • Kinston, NC 28501 • PLA

Jones Joseph W. Col. • President • Tennessee Library Association • Nashville, TN 37215-8417

Jones Josephine Neil • Charleston, SC 29401 • Continuing

Jones Joyce • Library Board of Trustee • Spokane Public Library Comstock Building Library • Spokane, WA 99201-0976 • ALTA

Jones Judith • Head Librarian • Mill Memorial Library • Nanticoke, PA 18634 • PLA

Jones Judith A. • Hana, HI 96713 • PLA

Jones Judith T. • Packer Collegiate Institute Main Library • Brooklyn, NY 11201

Jones Judy • Bear River High School • Glass Valley, CA 95949

Jones Kathleen M. • Glen Carbon Reading Center • Glen Carbon, IL 62034

Jones Kathryn E. • Media Specialist • Chamberlain High School • Tampa, FL 33612

Jones Kathryn L. • Reference • University of South Alabama Library • Mobile, AL 36688

Jones Kay F. • Assistant University Librarian • California State University-Sacramento Library • Sacramento, CA 95819-6039 • ACRL SRRT

Jones Ken • Head, Support Services • Josephine County Library System • Grants Pass, OR 97526

Jones Kevin R. • Head Reference/Research Services • Kansas State University Farrell Library • Manhattan, KS 66506-1200 • ACRL RASD LRRT

Jones Kyle S. • Cary, NC 27511

Jones L. Frances Mrs. • Riverdale, MD 20737-1137

Jones Linda C. • Elementary Librarian • Columbia Public Schools • Columbia, MO 65201 • AASL

Jones Linda L. • Library Director • Southeastern College The Assemblies of God • Lakeland, FL 33801 • ACRL LIRT

Jones Linda L. • Library Consultant • Waverly-Belmont Building • Nashville, TN 37204 • AASL

Jones Linda M. • Cataloger/Bibliographer • International Council for Canadian Studies • Ottawa ON, K1N 6E2 Canada • ACRL ALCTS

Jones Lois M. • Head of Cataloging • University of Denver Penrose Library • Denver, CO 80208 • LITA

Jones Maralyn • University of California-Berkeley Conservation Department • Berkeley, CA 94720 • ALCTS

Jones Margaret E. • Librarian • South Carolina Criminal Justice Academy • Columbia, SC 29210-4088 • NMRT

Jones Marie F. • Ref & Bibliographic Instr Ln. • Muskingum College Library • New Concord, OH 43762 • ACRL LIRT

Jones Marilyn K • Children's Librarian I • Memphis-Shelby County Public Library Collierville Branch • Collierville, TN 38017 • ALSC

Jones Marjorie • Editorial Director • The Junior Library Guild • New York, NY 10103 • AASL ALSC YALSA

Jones Mary A. • Ramsey County Public Library Adminstrative Offices • Shoreview, MN 55126-5800

Jones Mary Chambers • Portland, OR 97221 • AASL ALSC

Jones Mary E. • Library-Staff Assistant • Computer Services Division of Glendale/Pasadena Public Library • Pasadena, CA 91101

Jones Mary Elizabeth • Head, Technical Services • Williams College Sawyer Library • Williamstown, MA 01267

Jones Mary Jane • Media Specialist • Smoky Row Elementary • Carmel, IN 46032

Jones Mary K. • Media Specialist • Montgomery County Public Schools Flower Valley Elementary School • Rockville, MD 20850 • AASL

Jones Mary V. • Librarian • West High School Library • Waterloo, IA 50702 • YALSA
Life

Jones Mattie L. • Team Leader, Pub. Servs. Lbrn. • U S Army Aviation Systems Command Library & Information Center • St Louis, MO 63120 • FLRT

Jones Michael D. • Senior Librarian • California State Department of Justice • San Francisco, CA 94102

Jones Milbrey L. • Chief, Library Unit • United States Department of Education Office of Educational Res & Improvement • Washington, DC 20208-5571 • AASL ACRL FLRT

Jones Myrtle C. • Palm Bay, FL 32907 • Continuing

Jones Nancy • Librarian • Camargo Township Public Library • Villa Grove, IL 61956

Jones Norah E. • Librarian • University of California Library • Los Angeles, CA 90024 • Continuing

Jones Norma L. • Acting Executive Director • University of Wisconsin-Oshkosh • Oshkosh, WI 54901 • AASL ACRL ALCTS ALSC LAMA LITA RASD YALSA

Jones Owen T. • Researcher • Hill & Knowlton • New York, NY 10017 • ACRL

Jones Pamela R. • Cheektowaga, NY 14225

Jones Patricia • Genesee Community College Alfred O'Connell Library • Batavia, NY 14020

Jones Patricia A. • Senior Librarian • New York Public Library Public Relations Office • New York, NY 10018 • RASD

Jones Patricia R. • Student • University of South Carolina College of Library & Information Science • Columbia, SC 29208

Jones Patrick Scott • Manager • Allen County Public Library Tecumseh Branch • Fort Wayne, IN 46805 • PLA YALSA

Jones Penelope L. • Lexington, KY 40517

Jones Philip L. • Central Arkansas Library System • Little Rock, AR 72201-4698 • RASD

Jones Phyllis B. • Audio Visual Librarian • Montgomery City-County Library Lawrence Street Branch • Montgomery, AL 36104 • RASD

Jones Plummer A. Jr. • Head Librarian/Dir. Learning Res • Elon College Iris Holt McEwen Library • Elon College, NC 27244-0187 • ACRL LAMA EMIERT LHRT

Jones Pyddney K. • Librarian • Breckenridge Elementary School • Lexington, KY 40502 • AASL LAMA

Jones Rhonda • Student • University of Oklahoma Libraries University Libraries • Norman, OK 73019 • LITA

Jones Rita Anne • Chief Cataloging Branch • United States Air Force Academy Academy Library (DFSEL) • USAF Academy, CO 80840 • ALCTS AFLRT FLRT

Jones Rita J • Dean of Library Services • City College of San Francisco • San Francisco, CA 94112 • ACRL

Jones Robert A. • Library Director • Milton-Freewater Public Library • Milton-Freewater, OR 97862

Jones Robert M. • Director • Putnam County District Library • Ottawa, OH 45875 • PLA

Jones Robert P. • Head, Public Services Division • University of North Florida Thomas G. Carpenter Library • Jacksonville, FL 32245-7605 • LAMA

Jones Roger Dr. • Salt Lake City Public Library • Salt Lake City, UT 84111 • ALTA

Jones Roger G. • Head/Collections Coordinator • Tennessee Technological University University Library • Cookeville, TN 38505 • AASL ACRL ALCTS LAMA LITA RASD YALSA GODORT IFRT MAGERT

Jones Ron I. • Wake County Public Library System • Raleigh, NC 27610

Jones Rose M. • Library Media Specialist • Chillum Elementary School • Hyattsville, MD 20782 • AASL

Jones Rosemary E. • Editor & Publicist • Omnigraphics Inc. • Fort Lauderdale, FL 33301

Jones Ruby L. • Head of Catalog Department • Atlanta-Fulton Public Library • Atlanta, GA 30303 • ALCTS LITA

Jones Russell G. • Trustee • Mid-Continent Public Library • Independence, MO 64050 • ALTA

Jones Ruth Ann • Haslett, MI 48840

Jones Sally C. • Librarian • Mount Saint Dominic Academy School • Caldwell, NJ 07006 • AASL

Jones Sandra • Librarian • Seymour High School • Seymour, TX 76380 • AASL

Jones Sandra K. • Library Director • Clark Public Library • Clark, NJ 07066 • PLA

Jones Sandra M. • Children's Librarian • Carmody Hills Elementary School • Capitol Heights, MD 20743

Jones Sarah D. • Cockeysville, MD 21030 • ACRL
Life

Jones Sheila • Maywood Public Library • Maywood, IL 60153 • ALSC

Jones Shirley A. • Head Acquisitions Serials Dept. • Washington University Libraries • Saint Louis, MO 63130-4899 • ALCTS LITA

Jones Stephanie N. • Assistant Professor • San Jose State University Division of Library & Information Science • San Jose, CA 95192-0029 • AASL

Jones Stephanie P. • Belvidere, IL 61008-3053 • AASL

Jones Susan A. • Librarian • American States Insurance Co. • Indianapolis, IN 46204

Jones Susan D. • Librarian • Phoenix Public Library • Phoenix, AZ 85004 • PLA

Jones Terry L. • Student • State Farm Insurance Company • Dallas, TX 75078

Jones Thea J. • Library and Media Services • Baltimore County Public Schools • Towson, MD 21204 • AASL

Jones Thomas T. • Director • Bismarck Veterans Memorial Public Library • Bismarck, ND 58501 • LAMA PLA RASD IFRT

Jones Trevelyn • Book Review Editor • School Library Journal • New York, NY 10011 • ALSC YALSA

Jones Trudy (Gertrude) • Childrens Librarian III • Evanston Public Library • Evanston, IL 60201 • ALSC PLA

Jones Victoria A. • Manuscripts Curator • University of Oregon Library • Eugene, OR 97403-1299 • ACRL

Jones Viola E. • Regional Librarian • Free Library of Philadelphia Northwest Regional Branch • Philadelphia, PA 19144 • PLA

Jones Virginia C. • Madisonville, KY 42431 • ALSC PLA
Life

Jones Vivian C. • Lake Ridge, VA 22912 • RASD FLRT SRRT

Jones Vivian T. • Altoona, FL 32702 • PLA

Jones William D. • Reference Librarian • Dawson College • Westmount, PQ, H3Z 1A4 Canada

Jones William G. • Assistant University Librarian • University of Illinois at Chicago University Library • Chicago, IL 60680 • ACRL LAMA

Jones William W. Jr. • Catalog Maintenance Librarian • New York University Elmer Holmes Bobst Library • New York, NY 10012 • ALCTS LITA

Jones Winnifred • Maple Plain, MN 55359-9415 • Continuing

Jones Winona • Librarian • East Lake High School • Tarpon Springs, FL 34689 • AASL YALSA

Jones Yolanda P. • Ann Arbor, MI 48105

Joniec Allathea M. • Head of Acquisitions • Free Library of Philadelphia • Philadelphia, PA 19103 • ALCTS LITA

Jonke Grace M. • Branch Manager • Baltimore County Public Library Parkville-Carney Branch • Baltimore, MD 21234 • PLA IRRT

Joramo Marjorie K. • San Diego, CA 92129-2354 • YALSA SRRT

Jordahl Ronald T. • Library Director • Prairie Bible Institute • Three Hills AB, T0M 2A0 Canada • ACRL

Jordan Alma Dr • Valsayn Park, Trinidad

Jordan Caroline • Reference Librarian • Williamsburg Regional Library • Williamsburg, VA 23185 • PLA

Jordan Casper Leroy • Atlanta, GA 30331

Jump Eric T. • Student • Northern Kentucky University • Highland Heights, KY 41099-6101

Juneja Derry C. • Head, Technical Services • Riverside City & County Public Library-Central • Riverside, CA 92502 • ALCTS LAMA LITA PLA

Jung Norman O. • Director • State University of New York (SUNY) College at Old Westbury Library • Old Westbury, NY 11568 • ACRL LAMA RASD

Jung Soon • Head Cataloger • Newport Beach Public Library • Newport Beach, CA 92660 • PLA

Jung Suzanne J. • Librarian, Childrens Services • Chula Vista Public Library • Chula Vista, CA 91910 • ALSC PLA

Junge Marian S. • Library Media Specialist • Hixson Junior High School School District • Webster Groves, MO 63119 • AASL YALSA

Jungerberg Pamela S. • Reference Librarian • Harrison Memorial Library • Carmel By The Sea, CA 93921 • RASD

Jungkuntz Andrea R. • Tacoma, WA 98499 • RASD

Junion-Metz Gail • Head, Bibliographic Services • Cleveland State University Library • Cleveland, OH 44115 • ACRL ALCTS

Jurale Joan T. • Head Reference Librarian • Wesleyan University Olin Memorial Library • Middletown, CT 06459 • ACRL

Jurden Johnetta E. • Trustee • Jackson-Hinds Library System • Jackson, MS 39201 • ALTA

Jurena Donna J. • Assistant Director • Doane College Perkins Library • Crete, NE 68333 • ACRL LITA IFRT NMRT

Jurich Diane K. • Librarian • Holy Redeemer High School Library • Detroit, MI 48209 • AASL

Jurin Carol A. • Holicong Middle School • Buckingham, PA 18912 • AASL

Jurist Susan • Visual Arts Librarian • University of California-San Diego • La Jolla, CA 92093-0175 • ALCTS LITA

Jurney Nancy H. • Oklahoma State University Edmon Low Library • Stillwater, OK 74078-0375 • VRT

Jurow Susan R. • Director • Association of Res Libraries Office of Management Services • Washington, DC 20036 • ACRL LAMA RASD ILERT LRRT

Jurries Elaine F. • Fort Lupton, CO 80621 • ACRL ALCTS LAMA LITA RASD GODORT

Jursted Sandra D. • Attica High School • Attica, NY 14011 • AASL

Jushchyshyn Caroline B. • Librarian • Upper Darby Township & Sellers Memorial Library • Upper Darby, PA 19082

Justen Nancy E. • Elmhurst Public Library • Elmhurst, IL 60126 • RASD

Justice Hermia • Los Angeles, CA 90016

Justice Kim B. • Cataloger • Southeastern Louisiana University Linus A. Sims Memorial Library • Hammond, LA 70402 • ALCTS

Justice LaDonna H. • Administrative Librarian • Daniel Boone Regional Library Callaway Co. Service Center • Fulton, MO 65251 • LAMA

Justice Sharon • Interlibrary Loan Librarian • Central Texas Library System • Austin, TX 78768-2287 • PLA

Justie Kevin M. • Coordinator of Automated Serv • Morton Grove Public Library • Morton Grove, IL 60053

Justin Robert M. • Trustee • Rochester Hills Public Library • Rochester, MI 48307 • ALTA

Justis Janet L. • Student • University of North Carolina at Chapel Hill School of Information and Library Science • Chapel Hill, NC 27599-3360 • PLA

Justiss Larry D. • Director • Tom Green County Library • San Angelo, TX 76903-5834

Justus Meg • Nelsonville Public Library • Nelsonville, OH 45764

Kaag Cynthia S. • Head, Collection Development • Washington State University Owen Science & Engineering Library • Pullman, WA 99164-3200 • ACRL RASD

Kaaina Jean F. • Library Technician VI • Waimanalo Public & School Library • Waimanalo, HI 96795

Kaaret Meeri H. • Cataloging Librarian • Cornell University Albert R. Mann Library • Ithaca, NY 14853-4301 • ALCTS

Kaatrude Peter B. • Dean of Library Services • Lamar University-Port Arthur Gates Library • Port Arthur, TX 77640 • ACRL LAMA LRRT

Kabat Diane R. • Head Librarian • Santa Catalina School Library • Monterey, CA 93940 • ALCTS

Kabel Carole J. • Librarian • National-Louis University • Chicago, IL 60603 • ACRL

Kabel Jody B. • Music & Fine Arts Librarian • Jacksonville University Carl S. Swisher Library • Jacksonville, FL 32211 • ACRL

Kabelac Karl • Mss. Librarian • University of Rochester Rush Rhees Library • Rochester, NY 14627-0055 • ACRL

Kabir Abulfazal M. Fazle • Assistant Professor • Clark-Atlanta University School of Library & Information Studies • Atlanta, GA 30314-4391 • LHRT LRRT

Kabler Deborah Z. • Madison, WI 53713-3955

Kacena Carolyn • Director of Academic Supp. Autom • Southern Methodist University • Dallas, TX 75275 • ACRL ALCTS LAMA LITA

Kachel Debra E. • Library Media Specialist • Ephrata Senior High School Media Center • Ephrata, PA 17522 • AASL

Kachmar Diane C. • Monographic Acquisitions Libn • Florida Atlantic University S.E. Wimberly Library • Boca Raton, FL 33431 • ALCTS NMRT

Kackley Robert A. • Reference Librarian • U S Dept of Energy Library • Washington, DC 20585

Kaczmarek Paula • Chief Sociology & Economics Dept • Detroit Public Library Acq Dept • Detroit, MI 48202-4093 • ACRL LAMA PLA RASD GODORT *Life*

Kaczmarek Susan L. • Franklin, WI 53132

Kaczor Sue A. • Librarian • Hillsborough Community College Dale Mabry Campus • Tampa, FL 33630

Kadamus Carol A. • Voorheesville Elementary School • Voorheesville, NY 12186 • AASL

Kadanoff Diane Gordon • Director • Norwell Public Library • Norwell, MA 02061 • PLA RASD SRRT

Kadhum Ana • Reference • Uncle Remus Regional Library System • Madison, GA 30650

Kadis Averil J. • Public Relations Director • Enoch Pratt Free Library • Baltimore, MD 21201-4484 • PLA

Kadus John J. • Skokie Public Library • Skokie, IL 60077-3680 • PLA

Kaempfe Jennifer L. • Student • Rosary College Graduate School of Library & Information Science • River Forest, IL 60305

Kaempfer Edna B. • Adult Services Librarian • Addison Public Library • Addison, IL 60101-2499 • PLA RASD

Kafes Joan • Head of Reference Services • Fort Lee Public Library • Fort Lee, NJ 07024

Kafin Carol F. • Student • CW Post Palmer Grad L Sch • Brookville, NY 11548

Kafton-Minkel Walter • Youth Librarian • Multnomah County Library Gresham Branch • Gresham, OR 97030 • ALSC

Kagan Alfred • Res & Info Services Dept. • University of Connecticut Homer Babbidge Library • Storrs, CT 06269-1005 • GODORT IRRT SRRT

Kagemoto Raymond Y. • Librarian • Waipahu High School • Waipahu, HI 96797 • AASL

Kager Marguerite M. • Tuckahoe, NY 10707 • AASL

Kagermeier Janice C. • Cincinnati, OH 45206 • PLA

Kahil Liliane • Teaching & Research Assistant • University of Montreal Ecole de Bibliotheconomie • Montreal PQ, H3C 3J7 Canada • RASD

Kahkonen Laura • Director • Windsor Public Library • Windsor, CT 06095 • LAMA PLA

Kahl Barbara J. • Periodical Section Manager • Multnomah County Library Holgate Branch Library • Portland, OR 97205 • ALCTS RASD MAGERT

Kahler George W. • Falls Church, VA 22041 • ACRL LITA *Life*

Kahler June • Director, Lib/Media Programs • Texas Education Agency • Austin, TX 78701-1494 • AASL ALSC

Kahler Karl K. • East Asian Bibliographer • University of Pennsylvania Library Van Pelt-Dietrich Library Center • Philadelphia, PA 19104-6206 • ACRL ALCTS IRRT

Kahles William R. • Library Services Director • Northwest Municipal Conference • Des Plaines, IL 60016 • GODORT

Kahn Dency B. • Sci/Eng Librarian • Washington University Libraries • Saint Louis, MO 63130-4899 • ACRL RASD

Kahn Evelyn S. • Children's Librarian • Monmouth County Library Colts Neck Branch • Colts Neck, NJ 07722

Kahn Gerda M. • Chief Extension Services • Richland County Public Library • Columbia, SC 29201

Kahn Helen • Program Coordinator • Maui Library District Kahului Library • Kahului, HI 96732

Kahn Leslie • Supervising Librarian • Newark Public Library • Newark, NJ 07101-0630 • RASD SRRT

Kahn Marion Clare • Referecne Librarian • Fort Lee Public Library • Fort Lee, NJ 07024 • IFRT

Kahn Maureen L. • Wooster School Library • Danbury, CT 06810 • AASL

Kahn Merry • Library Media Specialist • Maquoketa Community Schools • Maquoketa, IA 52060 • AASL ALSC

Kahn Miriam B. • Preservation Consultant • MBK Consulting • Columbus, OH 43202 • ALCTS

Kai Miwa • Columbia University Libraries • New York, NY 10027 • ACRL *Continuing*

Kaihara Yasuto • Honolulu, HI 96816 • ACRL ALCTS LITA RASD *Life*

Kaikow Rita E. • Librarian • Oceanside High School Library • Oceanside, NY 11572 • Life

Kaimowitz Jeffrey H. • Curator • Trinity College Library • Hartford, CT 06106 • ACRL

Kain-Breese April • University of Wisconsin Center-Fox Valley Library • Menasha, WI 54952 • ACRL

Kaiser Alvira A. • Trustee • Crestwood Public Library District • Crestwood, IL 60445

Kaiser Donald W. • Colorado Alliance of Research Libraries • Denver, CO 80210 • LAMA LITA

Kaiser John R. • Chief, Commonwealth Campus Ln. • Pennsylvania State University Libraries • University Park, PA 16802 • ACRL ALCTS

Kaiser Roberta S. • Library Media Specialist • Nautilus Middle School • Miami Beach, FL 33140 • AASL

Kajee Yasmin • Library Specifications Spec. • H. W. Wilson Company • Bronx, NY 10452 • LITA

Kajiwara Sandra H. • Reference Librarian • San Jose State University Clark Library • San Jose, CA 95192-0028 • ACRL

Kajlik Vladimir • Librarian • Wayne State University Science & Engineering Library • Detroit, MI 48202 • ACRL

Kakinohana Yuko • Okinawa 903, Japan

Kakinuma Takashi • Professor • Daito Bunka University • Tokyo, Japan • AASL ACRL ALCTS PLA RASD

Kalabus Robert L. • Acting Director • Western Wyoming Community College • Rock Springs, WY 82902

Kalaj Robert • Exhibit Coordinator • H.W. Wilson Company • Bronx, NY 10452 • ERT

Kalal Robert J. • Trustee • Ohio State University • Columbus, OH 43210

Kalaminsky Janet L. • Branch Librarian • Free Library of Philadelphia Wadsworth Avenue Branch • Philadelphia, PA 19150 • PLA YALSA

Kalay Rachel R. • Research Librarian • State University of New York (SUNY) at Buffalo • Buffalo, NY 14260 • LITA

Kalb Virginia G. • Coordinator of Media Services • Montebello Unified School District • Montebello, CA 90640 • AASL

Kalbfleisch John B. • Manager, Adult Materials Dept. • Lexington Public Library Eastland Branch • Lexington, KY 40505

Kaldenberg Katherine A. • Reference Librarian • Mountain View Public Library • Mountain View, CA 94041 • LAMA PLA

Kaleda Jean M. • Reference Librarian • Riverhead Free Library • Riverhead, NY 11901

Kaler Susan J. • Reference Services Librarian • Wheelock College Library • Boston, MA 02215 • ACRL

Kalfatovic Martin R. • Smithsonian Institution Libraries • Washington, DC 20540

Kalfatovic Mary C. • TeleSecLibrary Services • Kensington, MD 20895

Kali Lalitha • Indexer Applied Sci & Tech • H. W. Wilson Company • Bronx, NY 10452 • ACRL

Kalick Rosanne • Chairperson, Library Dept. • Westchester Community College • Valhalla, NY 10595 • ACRL

Kalif Alexander J. • Shippensburg, PA 17257

Kalin Sally Wayman • Computer Based Res. & Servs Team • Pennsylvania State University Pattee Library • University Park, PA 16802 • ACRL LITA RASD

Kalina Kamile • Dir of Edu Psycho-Social Rehab. • Department of Mental Health John J. Madden Mental Health Center • Hines, IL 60141

Kalinsky Karen I. • Asst Chief of Catlg Dept • Stanford University • Stanford, CA 94305-6011

Kalinsky Rose L. • Media Specialist • Public Schools • Brooklyn, NY 11202

Kalis M. B. • Pasadena, CA 91104

Kalison Mildred K. Mrs. • Senior Librarian • West Haven High School Library • West Haven, CT 06516 • AASL IFRT

Kalkhoff Ann L. • Branch-Children's Librarian • Brooklyn Public Library Park Slope Branch • Brooklyn, NY 11215 • ALSC

Kalkus Stanley • Arlington, VA 22209-3713 • AFLRT

Kallas Eric • Reference Librarian • University of Saint Thomas • St. Paul, MN 55105 • LITA

Kallay Ernest R. Jr • Director • Clarksburg-Harrison Public Library • Clarksburg, WV 26301 • PLA

Kallberg Judy E. • Student • University of Wisconsin School of Library & Information Studies • Madison, WI 53706 • SRRT

Kallen Arlene • Reference Librarian • Sonoma County Library Rohnert Park-Cotati Branch • Rohnert Park, CA 94928 • PLA ERT IFRT SRRT

Kallenberg John K. • County Librarian • Fresno County Free Library • Fresno, CA 93721-2285 • ACRL LAMA PLA *Life*

Kallenberg Mary E. • Chugiak, AK 99567

Kallenberg Ruth B. • Acquisitions • California State University,Fresno Henry Madden Library • Fresno, CA 93740-0034 • ALCTS

Kallok Susan • Marymount High School Library • Los Angeles, CA 90077 • AASL

Kallunki Sandra • Brown County Library • Green Bay, WI 54301 • SRRT

Kalmanek Dorothy • Trustee • Acorn Public Library District • Oak Forest, IL 60452 • ALTA

Kalra Bhupinder S. • Reference Librarian • Niles Public Library • Niles, IL 60648 • PLA RASD

Kalstein Ali Patricia • Tech Serv & Automated Sys Head • Flint Public Library • Flint, MI 48502 • ALCTS LITA

Kaltenborn Helen P. • Baltimore, MD 21204

Kaltwasser Patricia F. • Librarian • Troy Public Library • Troy, MI 48084 • PLA

Kalvee Debbie H.E. • Head, Documents Collection • University of Alaska Elmer E. Rasmuson Library • Fairbanks, AK 99775-1005 • GODORT

Kalvonjian Araxie • Head Librarian • Gateway Technical Institute • Kenosha, WI 53141 • ACRL ALCTS

Kalyoncu Aydan A. • Fairfax, VA 22030-7721 • ACRL GODORT

Kam Thomas • Subject Specialist • Redwood City Public Library • Redwood City, CA 94063-1868

Kambitsch Timothy G. • Associate Director for Systems • Butler University Irwin Library • Indianapolis, IN 46208 • LITA

Kamens Harry H. • Kent State University Libraries • Kent, OH 44242 • ACRL

Kameo Rosella • Library Director • Satya Wacana University • Saltiga,Jateng 50711, Indonesia • ACRL LAMA PLA IRRT

Kamerman Jeannie • Catalog Librarian • University of West Florida John C. Pace Library • Pensacola, FL 32514 • ALCTS

Kamin Linda • Youth Services • Broward County Public Library Margate Branch • Margate, FL 33063 • ALSC

Kaminer Noam • Student • University of California-Berkeley School of Library & Information Studies • Berkeley, CA 94720 • LRRT

Kaminow Susan • Branch Manager • Arlington County Department of Libraries Cherrydale Branch • Arlington, VA 22207 • ALSC LAMA PLA IFRT

Kaminsky Ann M. • Library Board Treasurer • Whiting Public Library • Whiting, IN 46394

Kamisato Mary M. • Children's Librarian • Liliha Public Library • Honolulu, HI 96817

Kamm Sue • City of Inglewood Public Library • Inglewood, CA 90301-1771 • LAMA PLA IFRT VRT

Kammerer Catherine N. • Librarian • Woodrow Wilson High School • Portsmouth, VA 23704 • AASL

Kammerer Tom • Sales Representative • Quality Books Inc. • Lake Bluff, IL 60044-2204

Kammerlocher Lisa • Information & Res. Librarian • Arizona State University-West Fletcher Library • Phoenix, AZ 85069-7100 • ACRL LIRT

Kammermeyer Janet C. • Morgan Hill, CA 95037 • YALSA

Kammeyer Connie J. • Media Coordinator • Western Guilford High School • Greensboro, NC 27410 • AASL

Kammradt Doris • Trinity College Library • Hartford, CT 06106

Kampa Ruth A. • San Jose Public Library • San Jose, CA 95113 • ALTA

Kampen Jeanette L. • Granite City Public Library District • Granite City, IL 62040 • RASD

Kampenga Nelis R. • Stevens Point, WI 54481 • Continuing

Kampmeier Caroline • Redlands, CA 92373 • ASCLA YALSA *Continuing*

Kamras Elizabeth L. • Student • University of South Florida School of Library & Information Science • Tampa, FL 33620 • PLA

Kamsar Rochelle • Sr. Librarian-Information Servs • Ocean County Library • Toms River, NJ 08753 • RASD

Kamykoski David • Library Director • Waldwick Public Library • Waldwick, NJ 07463

Kan Katharine Louise • Young Adult Librarian • Aiea Public Library • Aiea, HI 96782 • YALSA

Kanady Cathy A. • Assistant Director for P. Serv. • Northeast Regional Library • Corinth, MS 38834

Kanaley Daniel L. • Acting Director • New York Chiropractic College Library • Seneca Falls, NY 13148-0800 • ALCTS LITA

Kanaley Louise A. • Media Specialist • Brighton Central Schools French Road Elementary School • Rochester, NY 14618 • AASL ALSC

Kanalley William J. • Assistant Librarian • Siena College • Loudonville, NY 12211-1462 • ACRL

Kanapes Donna • Branch Librarian • Chicago Public Library Austin Branch • Chicago, IL 60644 • PLA LIRT

Kanarski Kathleen A. • Children's Librarian • Austin Public Library Manchaca Road Branch • Austin, TX 78745 • ALSC RASD IFRT

Kanavel Lori A. • Student • Kent State University School of Library & Information Science • Kent, OH 44242-0001

Kandel Krystyna J. • Dearborn Heights, MI 48127 • ACRL NMRT SRRT

Kandoian Nancy A. • Map Cataloger • New York Public Library • New York, NY 10018-2788 • ALCTS MAGERT

Kane Bart • State Librarian • Hawaii State Public Library System Office of the State Librarian • Honolulu, HI 96813

Kane Beverly • Student • State University of New York at Albany School of Information Science & Policy • Albany, NY 12222

Kane Carol J. • Head Technical & Reference Svs • Northern Waters Library Service • Ashland, WI 54806 • ACRL PLA RASD

Kane Deborah A. • Baltimore, MD 21209 • ACRL

Kane Dennis M. • Minneapolis Public Library & Information Center • Minneapolis, MN 55401-1992

Kane Jane A. • Belleville Area College Library • Belleville, IL 62221

Kane Joseph P. • Geneseo, NY 14454 • ACRL ALCTS LAMA RASD *Life*

Kane Kay • University of Minnesota O. Meredith Wilson Library • Minneapolis, MN 55455-0414

Kane Lois B. • Director • Fall River Law Library • Fall River, MA 02720 • ASCLA

Kane Matthew J. • Altoona Area Public Library • Altoona, PA 16602-3693

Kane Susan J. • Student • Drexel University College of Information Studies • Philadelphia, PA 19104-2875 • RASD IFRT

Kane Susan M. • Phoenix, AZ 85029 • SRRT

Kane William P. • Librarian II • Wayne State University • Detroit, MI 48202 • ACRL LITA

Kaneko Hideo • Cura. East Asian Clln. • Yale University Sterling Memorial Library • New Haven, CT 06520 • ACRL IRRT

Kaneko Marie A. • Senior Reference Librarian • City of Commerce Public Library • Commerce, CA 90040

Kanemura Marilyn May • Special Projects Librarian • Monterey County Free Libraries • Salinas, CA 93901 • PLA

Kanenaga Etsuko • Children Librarian • Yolo County Library • Woodland, CA 95695

Kaneps Gundars • Principal • Gundars Kaneps Architects • Forest Grove, OR 97116 • LAMA

Kaneshiro Anthony D. • Cataloger • Pasadena Public Library • Pasadena, CA 91101

Kaneshiro Roberta L. • School Librarian • Department of Kalani High School • Honolulu, HI 96821

Kanfman Charles B. • Community Library Manager • County of Los Angeles Public Library Hacienda Heights Library 815 • Hacienda Heights, CA 91745 • PLA

Kang Byung I. • Cataloging Librarian • Palomar Community College Library • San Marcos, CA 92069 • ALCTS EMIERT

Kang Hsiu-wei Silvia • Librarian • San Jose Public Library East San Jose Carnegie Library • San Jose, CA 95112

Kang Mia H. • Duksung Women's University Library • Seoul 132-130, South Korea • ACRL LAMA LITA

Kangro Aime • Somerset, NJ 08873 • Continuing

Kania Antoinette M. • Dean of Libraries • Suffolk Community College Selden Campus Library • Selden, NY 11784-2899 • ACRL IRRT

Kania Eileen Q. • Hauula, HI 96717

Kanies Mary K. • Head Librarian • Saint Edward High School • Elgin, IL 60123 • AASL

Kanipe Deborah M. • School Media Specialist • Military Road School • Niagara Falls, NY 14305

Kanis James A. • Operations Manager • American Library Association • Chicago, IL 60611-2795 • Life

Kankus Stephen R. • Student • Syracuse University School of Information Studies • Syracuse, NY 13244-4100

Kann Mary J. • Pittsburgh, PA 15213

Kanner Elliott E. Dr. • Deerfield, IL 60015 • ASCLA PLA RASD IFRT

Kanning Anna Rose • Serials/Reference Librarian • Our Lady of the Lake University • San Antonio, TX 78207-4666

Kanno Faith C. • Student • University of Hawaii School of Library & Information Studies • Honolulu, HI 96822

Kanouse Elizabeth L. • Children's/Reference Librarian • Parsippany-Troy Hills Public Library Lake Hiawatha Branch • Lake Hiawatha, NJ 07034

Kansas B. Gordon • Bernardsville, NJ 07924

Kansfield Norman J. • Director of Library Service • Ambrose Swasey Library • Rochester, NY 14620 • ACRL LAMA

Kansier Earl F. • Harper Woods, MI 48225 • LITA PLA NMRT SRRT

Kant Louise H. • Media Specialist • Carmel High School • Carmel, IN 46032 • AASL

Kantar Nancy • Bow School District • Bow, NH 03304 • AASL

Kanter Dorothy A. • Clln. Development Librarian • University of Wisconsin Center for Health Sciences Library • Madison, WI 53706 • ALCTS

Kanter Elliot J. • Reference Librarian-Bibliographi • University of California-San Diego Central University Library • La Jolla, CA 92093-0175 • ACRL LITA RASD

Kantner Patricia • Head, Technical Services • Purdue University • West Lafayette, IN 47907 • ACRL ALCTS LAMA

Kantor Judith Ann • Librarian • University Elementary School Library • Los Angeles, CA 90024 • ALSC IFRT

Kantor Paul B. • Rutgers University School of Communication Information & Library Studies • New Brunswick, NJ 08903

Kantor Scott L. • Public Services Librarian • Texas State Technical College Library • Waco, TX 76705

Kanzler Diane • Trustee • Manatee County Public Library System • Bradenton, FL 34205

Kao Anita S. • Head Cataloger • Capital University Library • Columbus, OH 43209 • ALCTS

Kao Bernice C. • Reference Librarian • Rolling Meadows Library • Rolling Meadows, IL 60008 • IRRT SRRT

Kao Winnie C. • Principal Cataloger • National Library of Medicine • Bethesda, MD 20894 • ALCTS

Kao Yasuko W. • Director • Teikyo Loretto Heights University Library • Denver, CO 80236

Kaper Hillegonde J. • Trustee • Downers Grove Public Library • Downers Grove, IL 60515 • ALTA

Kapila Alexandria S. • Wenonah, NJ 08090 • ALSC

Kaplan Allison • University of Delaware Education Resource Center • Newark, DE 19716-2901 • ACRL ALCTS

Kaplan Amy M. • Congregation Librarian • Congregation Beth El • Cherry Hill, NJ 08002 • ILERT

Kaplan Denise P. • Assistant Director • Lincoln Library • Springfield, IL 62701

Kaplan Elise M. • Student • University of Maryland College of Library and Information Services • College Park, MD 20742-4345

Kaplan Gail C. • Executive Director • Broward Public Library Foundation, Inc. • Fort Lauderdale, FL 33301 • LAMA

Kaplan George R. • New York, NY 10011

Kaplan Gloria • Trustee • Commack Public Library District • Commack, NY 11725 • ALTA

Kaplan Gordon • Librarian/Cataloger • Black Gold Cooperative Library System • Ventura, CA 93003 • ALCTS PLA RASD IFRT

Kaplan Isabel • Engineering Librarian • University of Rochester Carlson Library • Rochester, NY 14627 • MAGERT

Kaplan Judith • Library Media Specialist • Founders Memorial School Learning Center Director • Essex Juction, VT 05452 • AASL

Kaplan Kristine D. • Aspen Systems Corporation • Rockville, MD 20850-3172

Kaplan Leslie R. • Babylon Public Library • Babylon, NY 11702 • ALSC

Kaplan Lesly A. • Librarian • Sno-Isle Regional Library Lynnwood Branch • Lynnwood, WA 98036 • ALSC IFRT

Kaplan Lois J. • High Librarian • Shaker Heights City School • Shaker Hts, OH 44120 • AASL

Kaplan Louis • Professor • University of Wisconsin School of Library & Information Studies • Madison, WI 53706 • Life

Kaplan Michael Dr • Head of Catalog Support Services • Harvard College Library Widener Memorial Library • Cambridge, MA 02138 • ALCTS MAGERT

Kaplan Patricia R. • Metz Elementary School • Austin, TX 78752 • ALSC

Kaplan Penelope • Maurice M. Pine Free Public Library • Fair Lawn, NJ 07410

Kaplan Renee E. • Bayside, NY 11364

Kaplan Richard M. • Pittsburgh, PA 15218-1016 • RASD

Kaplan Robert • Shoreham-Wading River Middle School • Shoreham, NY 11786 • AASL

Kaplan Sandi L. • Librarian III • Ventura County Library Services Agency Camarillo Library • Camarillo, CA 93010 • IFRT

Kaplowitz Joan • University of California Los Angeles Biomedical Library (UCLA) • Los Angeles, CA 90024 • ACRL RASD LIRT NMRT SRRT

Kapnick Laura B. • Director, Reference Library • C.B.S. News • New York, NY 10019 • LITA

Kapoun Jim M. • Pennsylvania State University Behrend College Library • Erie, PA 16563-0902 • ACRL

Kapp David • Associate Director • University of Connecticut Homer Babbidge Library • Storrs, CT 06269-1005

Kappler Andrea C. • Technical Services Librarian • Ohio Township Public Library System • Newburgh, IN 47630 • ALCTS

Kapstein Joan • Rockford, IL 61107

Kapur Geraldine P. • Norman, OK 73072 • LITA

Karadsheh Deena • Student • University of Wisconsin School of Library & Information Studies • Madison, WI 53706 • LRRT NMRT

Karafotias Evelyn S. • Cataloger Trainee • Brevard County Library Library Administrative Services Division • Cocao, FL 32922
Karaim Betty J. • Director of Library Services • Mayville State University Library • Mayville, ND 58257 • ACRL
Karam Marilyn R. • School Librarian • Welch Junior High School • Houston, TX 77036 • Life
Karamcheti Rama • Reference Librarian • Ohio County Public Library • Wheeling, WV 26003 • RASD
Karas Alice M. • Carmel High School • Mundelein, IL 60060 • AASL YALSA
Karash Olga S. Mrs. • New Paltz, NY 12561 • Continuing
Karatjas Susan • Non-Salaried Librarian • Indiana Free Library • Indiana, PA 15701
Karbach Lois L. • Aurora, CO 80012-145 • ALSC YALSA
Kardaleff Patricia • Lincoln Elementary School • Lawton, OK 73505 • AASL
Kardokas Christine C. • Head of Public Services • Worcester Public Library • Worcester, MA 01608 • ALSC ASCLA PLA
Kardon Beth A. • West Nyack, NY 10994 • AASL
Kardon Cynthia L. • Student • Drexel University College of Information Studies • Philadelphia, PA 19104-2875
Kardy Elizabeth W. • Kensington, MD 20895
Kardy Ellen E. • Reference Librarian • District of Columbia Public Library Northeast Branch • Washington, DC 20002
Karel Thomas A. • Assoc. Director for Public Serv. • Franklin & Marshall College Library • Lancaster, PA 17604-3003 • ACRL
Karen Lynne M. • Librarian • Westchester Community College • Valhalla, NY 10595 • ACRL LITA LIRT
Kares Artemis C. • Clln Devel/Reference Serv. • East Carolina University Joyner Library • Greenville, NC 27858-4353 • ACRL LAMA RASD
Kares Joanne • Supervising Libn/Reference • Morris County Free Library • Whippany, NJ 07981 • RASD
Kargacin Cathy A. • Puyallup, WA 98731-5754 • ALCTS LAMA PLA AFLRT FLRT
Karis Carolyn • San Francisco, CA 94127 • AASL
Karkhanis Sharad • Kingsborough Community College Library • Brooklyn, NY 11235 • ACRL EMIERT IRRT
Karklins Vija L. • Deputy Director • Smithsonian Institution Libraries • Washington, DC 20560 • ALCTS
Karl Gretchen F. • Getty Center Resources Collections • Santa Monica, CA 90401 • ALCTS
Karl Jean • Lancaster, PA 17602 • ALSC
Karl Maureen • Danbury Public Library • Danbury, CT 06810 • ALCTS PLA
Karl Roger M. • Director • Cumberland University Vise Library • Lebanon, TN 37087
Karlinchak Stephen M. • Information Specialist • Pittsburgh Post-Gazette • Pittsburgh, PA 15222
Karloski Ruth • Librarian K-8 • Carlinville Community School District Library Service Unit • Carlinville, IL 62626 • AASL YALSA
Karmazin Sharon M. • Director • East Brunswick Public Library • E. Brunswick, NJ 08816 • LAMA PLA
Karmiole Kenneth • Santa Monica, CA 90402 • ACRL
Karnes Patricia • Librarian II • San Diego Public Library University Community Branch • San Diego, CA 92122 • ALSC PLA
Karney James A. • Public Service Librarian • Irving Public Library System • Irving, TX 75015-2288
Karnoscak William F. • AV Acquisitions Coordinator • Rush University Library • Chicago, IL 60612 • IFRT
Karoblis Dalija P. • Assistant Town Librarian • Brookline Public Library • Brookline, MA 02146
Karon Bernard L. • Chief Sci Catlgr & Asst Prof • University of Minnesota O. Meredith Wilson Library • Minneapolis, MN 55455-0414 • ALCTS
Karon Joyce E. • Coordiantor of Media Services • Community Unit School District-#220 Barrington High School • Barrington, IL 60010 • AASL
Karotkin Charlotte S. • Librarian • Lawrence Cook Junior High School • Santa Rosa, CA 95407
Karow Sara E. • Houston Public Library Carnegie Branch • Houston, TX 77009 • PLA
Karp Hazel B. • Elem Sch Media Spec • Greenfield Hebrew Academy • Atlanta, GA 30342 • AASL ALSC
Karp Lenore • Ln Lit Phil & Religion Dept • San Antonio Public Library • San Antonio, TX 78205 • ACRL EMIERT IFRT
Karp Rashelle S. • Associate Professor • Clarion University of Pennsylvania • Clarion, PA 16214 • ASCLA LAMA RASD
Karp Steven G • Berkkeley, CA 94704
Karpe Margaret • Modesto, CA 95350-4969 • AASL ACRL PLA YALSA
Karpen Leah • Media Specialist • Charles Dewolf School Library • Old Tappan, NJ 07675 • AASL ALSC
Karpf Pamela Monaster • Reference Librarian • Beverly Hills Public Library • Beverly Hills, CA 90210 • NMRT
Karpiel Sharon • Adult Services Librarian • Elmhurst Public Library • Elmhurst, IL 60126
Karpin Molly K. • Brentwood Public Library • Brentwood, NY 11717
Karpinski Mary Helen • Memphis, TN 38107
Karpisek Marian E. • Library Media Supervisor • Salt Lake City School District • Salt Lake City, UT 84104 • AASL LAMA
Karplus Rosemary H. • Emeryville, CA 94608-1944
Karpowicz Mary • Librarian • Hartford Union High School • Hartford, WI 53027 • AASL
Karpuk Deborah J. • Denton, TX 76202-1509 • ACRL ALCTS LITA
Karr Cheryl A. • Student • University of North Carolina at Chapel Hill School of Information and Library Science • Chapel Hill, NC 27599-3360
Karr Juanita P. • Director • Northern Nevada Community College • Elko, NV 89801 • ACRL LAMA LITA
Karre David J. • Executive Director • Four County Library System • Vestal, NY 13850 • ASCLA LAMA PLA
Karrenbrock Marilyn • Associate Professor • University of Tennessee-Knoxville Graduate School of Library & Information Science • Knoxville, TN 37996-4330 • AASL ALSC ASCLA
Karrow Robert W. Jr • Curator of Special Collections • Newberry Library • Chicago, IL 60610 • ACRL MAGERT
Karsten Eileen S. • Head of Technical Services • North Park College & Theo Sem Consolidated Library • Chicago, IL 60625 • ACRL ALCTS LITA
Kart Maria M. • Student • Long Island University Palmer School of Library & Information Science • Greenvale, NY 11548
Kartman Edwin A. • Oakland, CA 94602
Karukin Mildren • Manager, Medical Library • Mount Sinai Medical Center Library • Miami Beach, FL 33140
Karwoski Grace A. • Montague, CA 96064
Kasai Masako • Library Assistant IV • University California-Berkeley • Berkeley, CA 94720 • LITA NMRT
Kasalka Gale L. • Ralston, NE 68127 • ALTA
Kasang John • Trustee • Acorn Public Library District • Oak Forest, IL 60452 • ALTA
Kaschins Elizabeth W. • Reference Librarian • Luther College • Decorah, IA 52101 • ACRL RASD
Kascus Marie A. • Central Connecticut State University Elihu Burritt Library • New Britain, CT 06050 • ACRL ALCTS LRRT
Kase Diana C. • Pensacola, FL 32504-6635 • AASL ALSC
Kase Janet A. • System Director • 49-99 Cooperative Library System Central Association of Libraries • Stockton, CA 95202
Kaser David • Indiana University School of Library and Information Science • Bloomington, IN 47405 • ACRL LAMA *Life*
Kaser James A. • Washington, DC 20007
Kaser John A. • Monroe County Public Library • Bloomington, IN 47408 • ACRL
Kaser Linda R. Miss • Pines Lake School • Wayne, NJ 07470 • AASL
Kaser Peggy J. • Children's Librarian • Indianapolis-Marion County Public Library Prospect Branch • Indianapolis, IN 46203-2088
Kash Denise • Spotsylvania, VA 22553
Kashap Nancy • Cataloger • County of Santa Clara Free Library • San Jose, CA 95112 • PLA IRRT
Kashihara Lillian • Gaithersburgh, MD 20882
Kasica Marianne • Head, Serials Cataloging • University of Pittsburgh Hillman Library • Pittsburgh, PA 15260 • ALCTS
Kaske Neal K. • United States Department of Education Office of Educational Res & Improvement • Washington, DC 20208-5571 • LITA LRRT
Kasker Marian • Free Library of Philadelphia • Philadelphia, PA 19103
Kaskey Sid • University of Miami Law Library • Coral Gables, FL 33124
Kasling Theresa L. • Head,Tech Serv/Music Librarian • College of Saint Benedict & Saint John's University • Collegeville, MN 56321 • ACRL ALCTS
Kasner Merrialyce K. • Admin. for Technical Services • Salem State Library • Salem, OR 97310
Kasofsky Anna D.B. • Hd of Pub Servs • Sanad Support Tech. • Rockville, MD 20852 • ACRL ALCTS LITA RASD
Kasow Harriet • Jerusalem, Israel
Kaspar Reta S. • Branch Supervisor • Calcasieu Parish Public Library • Lake Charles, LA 70601
Kasper Barbara • Moosup, CT 06354
Kasper Pauline E. • APO New York, NY 09139 • FLRT
Kasper Ruth M. • Children's Librarian • Bucks County Free Library James A Michener Branch • Quakertown, PA 18951 • ALSC
Kasperski Anna S. • Library Trustee • Hillside Public Library • Hillside, IL 60162
Kasperson Jeanne X. • Woodsotck, CT 06281 • ACRL ALCTS GODORT IRRT
Kaspik Arlene M. • Executive Director • McHenry Public Library District • McHenry, IL 60050-5796 • ALSC LAMA PLA
Kass B J. • Children's Buyer • Bookstall at Chestnut Court • Winnetka, IL 60093
Kass Eric A. • Adult Services Librarian • Albany Public Library Delaware Branch • Albany, NY 12209
Kassanoff Mady G. • Denver, CO 80204-3555 • RASD
Kassinger Tim • Collection Development Coor. • Geauga County Public Library • Chardon, OH 44024 • RASD
Kassir Kay • Library Media Specialist • Creeds Elementary School • Virginia Beach, VA 23451 • CLENE IFRT LRRT
Kast Gloria E. • Sacramento, CA 95821
Kastanis Penny G. • Coor. Libary/Technology Services • Sacramento County Office of Education • Sacramento, CA 95827 • AASL
Kastanis Terry I. • Sacramento, CA 95823 • LITA
Kastanotis William C. • Branch Librarian • Ocean County Library • Toms River, NJ 08753
Kastelle Arlene J. • Head Librarian • Kellogg Public Library • Kellogg, ID 83837
Kasten Seth E. • Hd of User Serv & Ref Ln • Union Theological Seminary Library The Burke Library • New York, NY 10027 • ACRL
Kastin Shelli M. • University, MO 63130 • ALCTS
Kastner Arno A. • Head of Catalog • New York University Elmer Holmes Bobst Library • New York, NY 10012 • ALCTS
Kasuboski Anne M. • Government Document Librarian • University of Wisconsin-Green Bay Library Learning Center • Green Bay, WI 54311 • GODORT
Kaszar Stephen T. • Circulation Staff • University of Akron Bierce Library • Akron, OH 44325-1706
Kaszczynec Jane Mrs. • Savona Central School • Savona, NY 14879 • AASL
Katchen Rosalie E. • Hebraica Librarian • Brandeis University Main Library • Waltham, MA 02254-9110 • ACRL LITA
Katebi-Sarmadi Shamsi • Claremont, CA 91711 • AASL EMIERT IFRT IRRT
Kathman Michael D. • Director • Saint Johns University Alcuin Library • Collegeville, MN 56321-7155 • ACRL ALCTS LAMA GODORT *Life*
Katka Patricia • Branch Librarian • San Diego Public Library Point Loma Branch • San Diego, CA 92107
Kato Hisae • Catalog Librarian • Tsuda College • Tokyo 187, Japan
Katona Florence C. • Maple Hts, OH 44137 • Continuing
Kats Amy L. • Warwick Public Library • Warwick, RI 02886
Katsh Sara • Librarian • Association of Operating Room Nurses Library • Denver, CO 80231 • LAMA
Katsouleas Linda L. • System Director • Metropolitan Cooperative Library System • Altadena, CA 91001 • PLA
Katsufrakis Martha D. • Los Angeles Public Library • Los Angeles, CA 90071 • ALTA
Katsui Irene A. • Librarian • Orange Coast College • Costa Mesa, CA 92628-5005 • ACRL ALCTS LIRT
Katsune Joanna • Bibliographic Control Coor. • Brown University Rockefeller Library • Providence, RI 02912 • ACRL ALCTS
Kattenhorn Donna S. • Reference Librarian • Shasta County Library • Redding, CA 96001
Katterjohn Patricia L • School Librarian • Warren Central High School • Indianapolis, IN 46229 • AASL
Katz Barbra N. • Director • Ames Free Library • North Easton, MA 02356 • PLA IFRT
Katz Beth A. • Student • University of Michigan School of Information and Library Studies • Ann Arbor, MI 48109-1092 • SRRT
Katz Bill • Forest Hills, NY 11375
Katz Bonnie A. • Senior Staff Analyst • Solano County Library • Fairfield, CA 94533 • PLA
Katz Carol S. • Student • Texas Woman's University School of Library & Information Studies • Denton, TX 76204
Katz David • Trustee • Silver Moon Press • New York, NY 10011
Katz Jacqueline E. • Librarian • Rochester Public Library • Rochester, NY 14604
Katz Jeffrey • Director • Bard College Library • Annandale-on-Hudson, NY 12504
Katz Jeffrey • Queens Borough Public Library • Jamaica, NY 11432
Katz Jeffrey P. • Rutgers University Libraries • New Brunswick, NJ 08903 • LITA
Katz Judith • Head of Reference • Fairleigh Dickinson University Weiner Library • Teaneck, NJ 07666 • RASD
Katz Judith P. • Sr Ln • Los Angeles Public Library John C. Fremont Branch • Los Angeles, CA 90038-3339 • RASD

Katz Lillian R. • Director/Media Services • Port Washington Public Library • Port Washington, NY 11050 • VRT

Katz Lorraine F. • Head of Adult Services • Shelter Rock Public Library • Albertson, NY 11507

Katz Ruth M. • Weaverville, NC 28787 • ACRL ASCLA LAMA RASD LRRT

Katz Sharon F. • Indexer • H. W. Wilson Company • Bronx, NY 10452 • LITA

Katz Sue • Trustee • Silver Moon Press • New York, NY 10011

Katz Suzanne • ILL Librarian • Queens College Benjamin S. Rosenthal Library • Flushing, NY 11367-0904 • ACRL RASD

Katz Vicki • Trustee • Northbrook Public Library • Northbrook, IL 60062 • ALTA

Katzen Barry • Director • Kraus International Publications • Millwood, NY 10546 • ACRL RASD GODORT

Katzenstein Lisa B. • Librarian I • New Orleans Public Library • New Orleans, LA 70140

Katzer Audrey • Librarian • F. M. Hillers School • Hackensack, NJ 07601 • ALSC

Katzin Robbin R. • Chicago, IL 60645

Katzman Dexter N. • Austin, TX 78757

Katzman Hester P. • Las Vegas-Clark County Library District Flamingo Library • Las Vegas, NV 89119

Katzmann Betty S. • Orange County Public Library Mary Wilson Branch • Seal Beach, CA 90740 • ALSC

Katzmann Deborah L. • Media Specialist • High Point Elemantary School • Orland Park, IL 60462

Kauffelt T. D. • Trustee • Kanawha County Public Library • Charleston, WV 25301 • ALTA

Kauffman Bruce R. • Director • Boca Raton Public Library • Boca Raton, FL 33432-3798 • ACRL ALCTS ALSC LAMA LITA PLA RASD *Life*

Kauffman Ingrid • Library Assistant • Arlington County Department of Libraries Westover Branch • Arlington, VA 22205

Kauffman Kathy A. • Technical Services Librarian • Goshen College • Goshen, IN 46526

Kauffman Linda • Trustee • Metropolitan Library System • Oklahoma City, OK 73102 • ALTA PLA

Kauffman Lynn C. • Washington, DC 20016

Kauffman Patricia J. • Media Specialist • Springville High School • Springville, UT 84663 • AASL

Kauffman Phyllis • Librarain • Free Library of Philadelphia Northeast Regional Library • Philadelphia, PA 19149 • PLA

Kauffman S. Blair • Law Library Director • Universary of Wisconsin-Madison Law Library • Madison, WI 53706 • ACRL

Kauffman Susan J. • Student • Northern Illinois University Department of Library & Information Studies • DeKalb, IL 60115

Kauffmann Mary E. Miss • Dorchester, MA 02124-4742 • ACRL ALCTS *Continuing*

Kaufman Cheryl T • Student • Abilene Public Library • Abilene, TX 79601-5793 • RASD

Kaufman Ellen • Dewey, Ballantine • New York, NY 10019

Kaufman Judith • Personnel & Development Ln. • State University of New York (SUNY) Frank Melville Jr. Memorial Library • Stony Brook, NY 11794-3300 • ACRL LAMA SRRT

Kaufman Marguerite Sara • Woodstock, IL 60098

Kaufman Marianna B. • Board of Commissioners • Atlanta-Fulton Public Library • Atlanta, GA 30303 • ACRL

Kaufman Michelle I. • Student • University of California-Berkeley University Library • Berkeley, CA 94720

Kaufman Oxanna S. • Head,Preservation Dept. • University of Pittsburgh Hillman Library • Pittsburgh, PA 15260 • ACRL ALCTS

Kaufman Paula T. • Dean of Libraries • University of Tennessee John C. Hodges Library • Knoxville, TN 37996-1000 • ACRL LAMA LITA

Kaufmann Frances G. • Glen Rock, NJ 07452 • ACRL

Kaufmann Linda M. • Student • State University of New York at Albany School of Information Science & Policy • Albany, NY 12222

Kaufmann Lois W. • Warren Public Library • Warren, VT 05674

Kaufmann Paulette Clark • Vice-Pres./Editor-in-Chief • William Morrow & Company,Inc. • New York, NY 10019 • AASL ALSC YALSA ERT SRRT

Kaul Nancy J. • HD, Collection Management • University of Southern Mississippi Cook Memorial Library • Hattiesburg, MS 39406-5053 • ALCTS LAMA IFRT

Kaup Jermain A. • Director • Minot Public Library • Minot, ND 58701 • LAMA PLA

Kaus Margaret A. • Jacksonville, FL 32256

Kaus Toni • Assistant Library Director • Prescott Public Library • Prescott, AZ 86303

Kauskay Roberta B. • Supv Microform Area • University of Oklahoma Libraries University Libraries • Norman, OK 73019

Kautzman Amy M. • Northeastern University • Boston, MA 02115 • ACRL

Kavanagh Eileen M. • New York, NY 10021

Kavanagh Margaret • Head of Extension Services • Contra Costa County Library • Pleasant Hill, CA 94523 • LAMA PLA

Kavanagh R. • CNIB Library for the Blind • Toronto ON, M4G 3EB Canada

Kavanaugh Karalyn F. • Student • EBSCO Subscription Service • Birmingham, AL 35201 • ACRL

Kavin Mel • President • Kater-Crafts Bookbinders • Pico Rivera, CA 90660 • ALCTS

Kawachi Kikuko M. • Assistant Librarian • Ohio State University Libraries • Columbus, OH 43210-1286 • ALCTS

Kawaguchi Ai M K • Cataloger • Library of Congress • Washington, DC 20541 • ACRL ALCTS *Life*

Kawaguchi Miyako Dr. • Library Director • Pensacola Christian College Library • Pensacola, FL 32523 • ACRL

Kawakami Alice K. • A-V Reference Librarian • Los Angeles County Public Library Marina Del Rey Branch • Marina del Rey, CA 90292

Kawakami Toyo Mrs • Columbus, OH 43214 • ACRL

Kawano Brenda S. • Library Media Specialist • Western Springs School District #101 • Western Springs, IL 62558

Kawano Kei • Reference & Cataloging Ln • Cherry Hill Free Public Library • Cherry Hill, NJ 08034 • ALCTS

Kawata Jean M. • Librarian • Honigman Miller Schwartz & Cohn • Detroit, MI 48226 • ALCTS LAMA

Kawatachi Myrna • Librarian • Highlands Elementary School Library • Pearl City, HI 96782

Kay Amanda J. • Lacey's Spring, AL 35754 • IFRT

Kay Debra A. • Library Director • Spartanburg Technical College • Spartanburg, SC 29305 • ACRL LAMA LITA

Kay Marjorie A. • Montclair, NJ 07042 • AASL YALSA *Life*

Kay Patricia • Librarian • Morrice High School • Morrice, MI 48857 • AASL

Kay Patricia P. • Librarian • Embassy of Australia Library • Washington, DC 20036-2273

Kaya Kathryn K. • Montana State University • Bozeman, MT 59717-0332 • ACRL RASD

Kaya Mariko • Head, Management Service • Los Angeles County Treasurer & Tax Collector • Los Angeles, CA 90012 • LITA

Kayaian Mary • Wilmette, IL 60091 • AASL

Kayden Mimi • Children's Marketing • Dutton Children's Books Penguin USA • New York, NY 10014 • AASL ALSC YALSA

Kaye Alan L. • Associate Director • Chestatee Regional Library • Gainesville, GA 30505-2399 • LAMA

Kaye Dina L. • Student • University of Wisconsin-Milwaukee School of Library & Information Science • Milwaukee, WI 53201

Kaye Sheldon B. • Director • Portland Public Library • Portland, ME 04101 • PLA

Kayler Grant R. • Head, Adm and Access Services • Univ of Alberta Herbert T. Coutts Library • Edmonton AB, T6G 2G5 Canada • ACRL LAMA LITA

Kaze Kathleen A. • Henderson District Public Library • Henderson, NV 89015 • RASD

Kazell Doris L. • Kenosha, WI 53142 • ALSC

Kazelunas Sara • New York, NY 10150 • IFRT

Kazilsky Amy B. • Special Sales Manager • Sage Publications, Inc. • Newbury Park, CA 91320

Kazlauskas Diane • Head Media Resources Dept. • University of North Florida Thomas G. Carpenter Library • Jacksonville, FL 32245-7605

Kazlauskas Edward J. Dr • Associate Professor • University of Southern California • Los Angeles, CA 90033

Kazlo Susan A. • Reference Librarian • Arlington Heights Memorial Library • Arlington Heights, IL 60004-5966 • RASD

Kazmer Margaret M. • Supv. Literature & Language • San Diego Public Library • San Diego, CA 92101 • PLA

Kea Sandra T. • Cedar Grove Elementary School Library • Nashville, NC 27856 • AASL

Keable Doreen M. Dr. • Associate Professor • Saint Cloud State University Centennial Hall LRC • St. Cloud, MN 56301-4498 • AASL

Kealey Marguerite B. • Oceanside High School • Oceanside, CA 92054 • AASL

Kean Lisa M. • Children's Librarian • Mitchell Library • New Haven, CT 06515 • ALSC EMIERT

Keane John J. Jr. • Manager Administration & Finance • University of Pennsylvania Library Van Pelt-Dietrich Library Center • Philadelphia, PA 19104-6206

Keane Mary Michaeleen Sr. • McAuley High School • Cincinnati, OH 45224

Keane Nancy J. • Director of Library & Learning • Trinity College • Burlington, VT 05401 • ACRL IRRT

Keane Yvette M. • St. Vincent, West Indies

Keaney Mary Beth • Librarian • Forestville Elementary School • Great Falls, VA 22066 • AASL

Kearley David A. • University Librarian • University of the South Jessie Ball duPont Library • Sewanee, TN 37375-4005 • ACRL LAMA RASD

Kearney Carol A. • Director • Public Schools • Buffalo, NY 14202 • AASL

Kearney Judith A. • Student • University of Hawaii • Manoa, HI 96789

Kearns Ellen • Trustee • Willingboro Public Library • Willingboro, NJ 08046 • ALTA

Kearns Karen M. • Marietta, GA 30064-1298

Kearns Patricia M. • Catalog Librarian • Christopher Newport College Captain John Smith Library • Newport News, VA 23606

Kearns Tricia • Librarian • John Thomas Dye Sch • Los Angeles, CA 90049 • AASL

Keaschuk Michael J. • Director • Chinook Regional Library • Swift Current SK, Canada • PLA

Keate Heather • Asst. Univ. Ln. Pub. Serv. • University of British Columbia • Vancouver BC, V6T 1Z1 Canada • LAMA

Keath Mary Lee Miss • Denver, CO 80013 • AASL ALSC *Life*

Keating Clare M. • Student • State University New York at Buffalo School of Inf. & Library Studies • Buffalo, NY 14260 • AASL ALSC

Keating Dorothy • Librarian • South Windsor Elementary Schools • South Windsor, CT 06074

Keating Faith • West Islip, NY 11795

Keating Kathleen • Albuquerque, NM 87110 • GODORT

Keating Lawrence R. II • Head Serials Department • University of Houston Libraries • Houston, TX 77204-2091

Keating Linda • Library Assistant • Alameda County Library Fremont Branch • Fremont, CA 94536 • ALSC

Keating Linda C. • Head, Serials Cataloging Dept. • Rice University Fondren Library • Houston, TX 77251-1892 • ALCTS

Keating Michael F. • Lakewood, OH 44107

Keating Robert D. • Student • University of Michigan School of Information and Library Studies • Ann Arbor, MI 48109-1092

Keating Sue • Media Specialist • Eagleview Middle School • Colorado Springs, CO 80919 • AASL

Keator Carol L. • Santa Barbara, CA 93101 • PLA

Keaveney Sydney Starr • Asst. Dean of Libraries • Pratt Institute • Brooklyn, NY 11205 • ACRL

Kebabian Ann K. • Colgate University Everett Needham Case Library • Hamilton, NY 13346 • ALCTS

Kebabian Paul B. • South Burlington, VT 05403 • ACRL ALCTS *Life*

Keck Bruce L. • Assistant Director • United States Geological Survey • Reston, VA 22092 • RASD FLRT

Keck Carol A. • Student • Center for Creative Leadership Library • Greensboro, NC 27438-6300 • LITA RASD

Keck Kerry A. • Coord for Clln & Info Res • Rice University Fondren Library • Houston, TX 77251-1892 • ACRL ALCTS GODORT MAGERT

Keck Mary E. • Management Analyst • United States Department of the Interior • Washington, DC 20420

Keckley Mary W. • Associate University Librarian • University of Texas at El Paso Library • El Paso, TX 79968-0582 • ACRL ALCTS

Keddle David G. • Director • John W. Chi Memorial Medical Library • Lansing, MI 48910 • ASCLA

Keder Jan • Science Librarian • Colorado College Tutt Library • Colorado Springs, CO 80903 • ACRL

Kedley Jane • Director • Frances Banta Waggoner Cmnty Library • DeWitt, IA 52742

Kee Leslie L. • Assistant Director • Spokane Public Library Comstock Building Library • Spokane, WA 99201-0976 • LAMA

Kee S Janice • Library Service Program Officer • United States Office of Education • Dallas, TX 75202 • Continuing

Keeble Katherine B. • Volunteer Support Staff • Bloomfield Hills Middle School • Bloomfield Hills, MI 48302 • AASL

Keefe Brian E. • Loyola Marymount University William M. Rains Library • Los Angeles, CA 90015-1295

Keefe Elizabeth J. • Bellevue Public School Leonard Lawrence School • Bellevue, NE 68123 • AASL

Keefe Janis D. • School Librarian • Mother of Good Cousel Library • Louisville, KY 40242 • AASL

Keefe John J. • Executive Director • Massachusetts L Staff Assn • Quincy, MA 02169 • SORT

Keefe Margaret J. • Oak Park, IL 60302 • RASD *Continuing*

Keefe Margaret Johnson • Assoc. Prof. Reference • University of Rhode Island Library • Kingston, RI 02881-0803 • ACRL

Keefer Alice C. • 08028 Barcelona, Spain • LITA

Keefer Daniel J. • Head of Systems Automation • Old Dominion University Library • Norfolk, VA 23529-0256
Keefer Jane A. • Eastern Michigan Univ • Ypsilanti, MI 48197 • ACRL
Keefer Mary L. • Reference Librarian • Outagamie Waupaca Library System • Appleton, WI 54911 • RASD YALSA
Keel Linda K. • Reference Librarian • Evergreen Park Public Library • Chicago, IL 60642
Keelan Mary A. • Head of AV, Manager of NYSCAT • Mid-Hudson Library System • Poughkeepsie, NY 12601 • PLA IFRT VRT
Keeler Deborah J. • Miami, FL 33196
Keeley Barbara P. • Professor • Oakton Community College Library • Des Plaines, IL 60016 • ACRL
Keeling Betty Ms • Director • Kingston City Library • Kingston, TN 37763-0057
Keeling Mary Ann • Baltimore, MD 21228
Keely Alan • Principal Catalog Librarian • University of North Carolina at Charlotte J. Murrey Atkins Library • Charlotte, NC 28223 • ALCTS
Keem Lida • Technical Services Librarian • University of Detroit Law Library • Detroit, MI 48226 • ALCTS *Life*
Keen Denise L. • Student • Millersville University of Pennsylvania • Millersville, PA 17551-0302 • AASL IFRT SRRT
Keen Eunice E. • Lakeland, FL 33803 • AASL ALCTS *Continuing*
Keen Kaylene S. • Media Specialist • Deyton Primary School • Spruce Pine, NC 28777 • AASL
Keen Sherry • Head Acquisitions/Serials • Brandeis University Goldfarb Library • Waltham, MA 02254-9110 • ACRL ALCTS
Keenan Barbara L. • Voorhees Township Schools • Voorhees, NJ 08043
Keenan Eileen F. • Montclair Kimberley Academy • Montclair, NJ 07402 • AASL
Keenan Eleanor M. • Saint Albans, WV 25177 • Continuing
Keenan Elizabeth L. • Director of the Library • Regis College Library • Weston, MA 02193 • ACRL
Keenan Joseph J. Jr. • Assistant Library Director • Elizabeth Public Library • Elizabeth, NJ 07202 • PLA
Keenan Lori • Director • Moscow-Latah County Library • Moscow, ID 83843 • PLA
Keenan Marguerite Donnellan • Director • Pickens County Library • Easley, SC 29640
Keenan Nancy N. • Librarian • Glenva High School Library • Salem, VA 24153 • AASL
Keenan Susan S. • Aspen, CO 81612
Keene Deborah Mann • Associate Law Librarian • Emory University Law Library • Atlanta, GA 30322
Keene Gloria J R • Acting Children's Services Mgr. • Anaheim Public Library • Anaheim, CA 92805
Keene Janis C. • Assistant Director • Tulsa City-County Library System • Tulsa, OK 74103 • LAMA PLA
Keene Jean M. • Media Generalist • Bernice A. Ray School • Hanover, NH 03755 • AASL
Keene Maxine • Beloit Public Library • Beloit, WI 53511
Keene Susie H. Mrs. • George F. Johnson Elementary School • Virgie, KY 41572 • AASL
Keeney Donald E. • Library Director • Nyack College and Alliance Theological Seminary • Nyack, NY 10960-4203 • ACRL
Keeney Kathy W. • School Librarian • Accomac Primary School • Accomac, VA 23301 • AASL ALSC
Keeney Nancy G. • Non-Salaried Librarian • State University of New York at Albany School of Information Science & Policy • Albany, NY 12222
Keeney Robert • Director • Eastern Shore Public Library • Accomac, VA 23301-0360 • LAMA PLA
Keenon Una H R • Trustee • Cuyahoga County Public Library • Cleveland, OH 44134-2792
Keeran Peggy A. • Librarian • University of Denver Penrose Library • Denver, CO 80208
Keese Rebecca T. • Charlottesville, VA 22901 • AASL
Keesing Linda F. • School Libraian • Gibbs School • New Milford, NJ 07646 • AASL
Keeth John Earl • Acquistion Librarian • University of South Florida Library • Tampa, FL 33620-5600 • ALCTS
Keeton Jane E. • Department Head • Birmingham Public & Jefferson County Free Library • Birmingham, AL 35203 • PLA
Keeton Mary Ellen • Library Media Specialist • Ruidoso Middle School • Ruidoso, NM 88345 • AASL
Keever Beverly Ann • Student • University of Hawaii at Manoa Catalog Dept. • Honolulu, HI 96822 • LITA
Keffer Kathleen L. • Columbine High School • Littleton, CO 80123 • LITA
Keffer Theodore • Trustee • Warren Public Library • Warren, MI 48092
Kegan Elizabeth H. • Assistant Librarian • Library of Congress • Washington, DC 20541 • ACRL RASD *Life*
Kehl M Margaret • Fort Washington, PA 19034 • Continuing
Kehler William L. • Student • Eastern Montana College Library • Billings, MT 59101-0298
Kehnast Annamarie • Reader Services Tech. • Gloucester County College Library Media Center • Sewell, NJ 08080 • ASCLA CLENE SORT
Kehner Robert • Librarian • Massachusetts Institute of Technology Libraries (MIT) • Cambridge, MA 02139
Kehoe Kathleen M. • Physics, Astronomy & Biology Ref • Columbia University Biological Sciences Library • New York, NY 10027 • ACRL
Kehr Alicia • Student • Long Island University Palmer School of Library & Information Science • Greenvale, NY 11548 • AASL PLA RASD
Keil Jayne • Media Technology Director • Springville Elementary School • Omaha, NE 68152 • AASL
Keil Mary • Trustee • Fondulac District Library • East Peoria, IL 61611 • ALTA
Keil Wayne • Head of Circulation • Fountaindale Public Library District • Bolingbrook, IL 60440 • PLA
Keim Catharine K. • Librarian • Meadowbrook School Library • Meadowbrook, PA 19046 • AASL ALSC
Keim Eileen • Director of Handicapped Servs • New Hampshire State Library Services to the Handicapped Section • Concord, NH 03301 • ASCLA
Keinath Janet S. • Librarian III • Detroit Public Library • Detroit, MI 48202
Keiser Barbara J. • Adult Services Librarian • Monroe County Public Library • Stroudsburg, PA 18360-1698 • PLA RASD
Keiser Helen • Bibliographic Products Lbrn. • Western Library Network (WLN) • Lacey, WA 98503 • LITA
Keiser Mary E. • Fort Myers, FL 33908
Keisler Martha • Stow, OH 44224 • Continuing
Keisling Sarah M. • New York Public Library Schomburg Center for Research in Black Culture • New York, NY 10037 • ALCTS
Keist Sandra H. • Kansas Wesleyan University Memorial Library • Salina, KS 67401 • ACRL
Keitel Susan Lehman • Executive Director • New York Library Association • Albany, NY 12210-1802 • PLA IFRT IRRT SRRT
Keiter Linda S. • Asst. to the Dean of Arts & Sci • University of Wyoming • Laramie, WY 82071 • ACRL
Keith Deborah F. • Student • University of Texas at Austin Graduate School of Library & Information Sciences • Austin, TX 78712-1276 • ALSC
Keith Linda Sue • Base Librarian • Wurtsmith Air Force Base • Oscoda, MI 48753 • AFLRT
Keith Marjorie A. • Head Librarian • Phillips Junior College • Raleigh, NC 27604
Keith Sandra J. • Librarian • Pima Community College Downtown Campus • Tucson, AZ 85703-0027 • RASD
Kejecuas Anne S. • Student • Catholic University of America School of Library and Information Science • Washington, DC 20064 • ALCTS IFRT SRRT
Kelchner Kathryn Anne • Library Media Specialist • Severn River Junior High School • Arnold, MD 21012 • AASL
Keleher Carolyn • Public Services Coordinator • Wellesley Free Library • Wellesley, MA 02181-5989 • LITA
Keleher Jean P. • Librarian • Wally Findley Galleries, Inc. • Chicago, IL 60611
Keleher Jean S. • Silver Spring, MD 20902 • IRRT
Kelinson Norman • President, Board of Trustees • Bettendorf Public Library • Bettendorf, IA 52722 • ALTA
Kelker Pat C. • Library Coordinator I • Free Library of Philadelphia • Philadelphia, PA 19103 • PLA EMIERT
Kelker Signe J. • Shippensburg University Lehman Memorial Library • Shippensburg, PA 17257-2299 • ACRL RASD
Kelkres Eileen • Student • Southern Connecticut State University School of Libray Science & Instructional Technology • New Haven, CT 06515 • ALCTS LITA SRRT
Kell Kathleen Vick • Executive Director • Consortium for Health Information & Library Services (CHI) • Upland, PA 19013 • ASCLA
Kellaher Sandra M. • Attorney • Law office of Sandra Kellaher • Brandon, FL 33511
Kellam W P. • Nokomis, FL 34275 • Continuing
Kelland John L. • Wakefield, RI 02879 • ACRL
Kellar James L. • Assistant Curator/Cllns. Catlgr. • Colorado Historical Society • Denver, CO 80203
Kelleher Genevieve Marie SSND Sr. • Librarian • Academy of the Holy Angels Library • Demarest, NJ 07627 • AASL
Kellems Gretchen H. • Branch Librarian-Librarian I • Dakota County Library System Galaxie Library • Apple Valley, MN 55124
Kellen Ethel N. • Branch Librarian • Toronto Public Library City Hall Branch • Toronto ON, Canada • LAMA PLA
Keller Arlene R. • Head Dept of Information Service • Edison Community College Univ. of S Florida Learning Resources Center • Fort Myers, FL 33906-6210 • ACRL
Keller Barbara J. • Catalog Librarian • Indiana State University Cunningham Memorial Library • Terre Haute, IN 47809 • ACRL ALCTS
Keller Cecy • Executive Director • Cooperating Libraries of Central Maryland (CLCM) • Baltimore, MD 21401 • ASCLA LAMA PLA CLENE
Keller Clara D. • Salinas, CA 93908 • ACRL ALCTS
Keller Connie • Technical Services Librarian • Elon College Iris Holt McEwen Library • Elon College, NC 27244-0187 • ACRL LAMA
Keller Elizabeth P. • Student • Loudoun County Public Library Rust Library of Leesburg • Leesburg, VA 22075 • PLA YALSA
Keller Genevieve Ann • Gilpin School District • Black Hawk, CO 80422 • AASL YALSA
Keller Jan K. • Asst Dean Learning Resources • College of the Canyons • Santa Clarita, CA 91355 • ACRL
Keller Joan R. • San Francisco, CA 94121 • ALSC PLA *Life*
Keller John G. • Boston, MA 02108 • AASL ALSC YALSA
Keller Kathleen M. • West Chester, PA 19341 • RASD
Keller Kirk • Student • Brigham Young University School of Library & Information Sciences • Provo, UT 84602
Keller Louise • San Jose, CA 95123 • Continuing
Keller Michael A. • Yale University Sterling Memorial Library • New Haven, CT 06520 • ACRL
Keller Nancy O. • Greenville, SC 29609 • IRRT
Keller Shelly G. • Shelly G. Keller Marketing • Sacramento, CA 95818 • PLA
Keller Susan J. • Library Administrator • Newport News Public Library System • Newport News, VA 23607 • PLA SORT
Keller William B. • Resource Services Devplmt • John Hopkins University • Baltimore, MD 21218 • ACRL ALCTS MAGERT
Kellerman Carol • Library Media Specialist • Santa Fe High School-LMC • Santa Fe, NM 87505 • AASL IFRT
Kellerman Lydia Suzanne • Pennsylvania State University Pattee Library • University Park, PA 16802 • ACRL ALCTS
Kellerstrass Amy L. • LSCA Coordinator • Illinois State Library • Springfield, IL 62701-1796 • ASCLA
Kelley Ann C. • Library Special Clln Cataloger • University of Texas at Arlington • Arlington, TX 76019-0497 • ALCTS
Kelley Betty H. • Garland, TX 75041
Kelley Brian C. • Dist Dir of Library Services • Palm Beach Junior College Library Learning Resource Center • Lake Worth, FL 33461 • ACRL CLENE IFRT
Kelley C. M. • Technical Services Librarian • University of the Health Sciences Learning Resources Center • Bethesda, MD 20874 • LITA
Kelley Carol M. • Asst. Univ. Ln. Clln. Devel. • University of Texas at El Paso Library • El Paso, TX 79968-0582 • ACRL ALCTS LAMA RASD
Kelley Carrie J. • Salt Lake City, UT 84121 • ALSC
Kelley Colleen L. • Authority Cntrl.Databse Maint.Ln • Ball State University Bracken Library • Muncie, IN 47306-0160 • ACRL ALCTS
Kelley David Otis Mr • Librarian Emeritus • University of New Mexico General Library • Albuquerque, NM 87131 • ACRL LAMA *Life*
Kelley Dennis J. • Director • Melrose Public Library • Melrose, MA 02176
Kelley H. Neil • Specialized Services Consultant • Illinois State Library • Springfield, IL 62701-1796 • ASCLA
Kelley Helen G. • Media Specialist • Cloonan Middle School • Stamford, CT 06902
Kelley Irene W. • Student • Boston University • Boston, MA 02215 • AASL LRRT
Kelley Judith Ann • Children's Service Coordinator • Newport Beach Public Library • Newport Beach, CA 92660 • ALSC PLA
Kelley Karen • Senior Librarian • Denver Public Library Field Branch • Denver, CO 80209 • RASD
Kelley Karen G. • Supv., Library Operations • Bristol-Myers Squibb • Evansville, IN 47721 • ALCTS LAMA
Kelley Kendi L. • Administrative Librarian • C E Brehm Mem L • Mt Vernon, IL 62864
Kelley Kimberly B. • Director of Library Services • University of Maryland University College • Hyattsville, MD 20742 • ACRL LAMA LITA
Kelley Lois I. • Middle School Librarian • Fort Worth Independent School District • Ft. Worth, TX 76107 • AASL
Kelley Marilyn A. • Media Specialist/Librarian • Indiana Creek School • Crownsville, MD 21032 • YALSA
Kelley Mary Ann • Elementary Media Coordinator • Gibsonville Elemantary School • Gibsonville, NC 27249 • AASL

Kelley Maureen K. • Student • San Jose State University Division of Library & Information Science • San Jose, CA 95192-0029 • RASD

Kelley Nancy J. • Director • Way Public Library • Perrysburg, OH 43551 • ALSC ALTA LAMA PLA

Kelley Norma S. • Librarian • Whittle Springs Middle School • Knoxville, TN 37917 • AASL

Kelley Patricia M. • Assoc. Univ. Librarian • George Washington University Gelman Library • Washington, DC 20052 • ACRL LAMA RASD

Kelley Robert E. • Librarian • Houston Public Library Hillendahl Branch • Houston, TX 77080 • ACRL LITA RASD LRRT VRT

Kelley Robin L. • Student • Indiana University School of Library and Information Science • Bloomington, IN 47405 • LITA PLA SRRT

Kelley Sally J. • Agricultural Law Librarian • University of Arkansas Libraries • Fayetteville, AR 72701-1201 • ACRL ALCTS LITA RASD GODORT LIRT

Kelley Sarah K. • Extension Librarian • Kentucky Department for Libraries & Archives • Frankfort, KY 40602-0537 • LAMA PLA

Kelley Sheila • Media Specialist • Sarasota Middle School • Sarasota, FL 34237 • AASL ALSC

Kelley Shirley A. • Winston-Salem, NC 27105

Kelley Susan A. • Coordinator of Library • Cypress-Fairbanks ISD • Houston, TX 77084 • AASL IFRT

Kelley Todd • Reference Librarian • Saint Mary's College of Maryland Library • St. Mary's City, MD 20686 • ACRL LIRT

Kellman Amy • Coordinator of Children's Servs. • Carnegie Library of Pittsburgh • Pittsburgh, PA 15213-4080 • ALSC PLA

Kellogg Betty • Student • University of Maryland • College Park, MD 20742-2411

Kellogg Jean E. • Elementary School Librarian • Jennie Reed Elementary School Tacoma School District • Tacoma, WA 98403

Kellogg Joanne T. • Director • Windham Public Library • Windham, ME 04062

Kellogg Martha H. • Assistant Acquistion Librarian • University of Rhode Island Library • Kingston, RI 02881-0803 • ACRL ALCTS

Kellogg Marya S. • Middlebury, VT 05753-1005

Kellow Ethel Miss • Allen Park, MI 48101 • Continuing

Kellstedt Jenny • Peoria Heights, IL 61614

Kellum-Rose Nancy P. • Chicago, IL 60640

Kellum Cathy • Tec-Masters, Inc. • Huntsville, AL 35806 • ALCTS LAMA LITA

Kelly-Keightley Jane Y. • West Midlands, England • LITA

Kelly Andrea L. • Grant Elementary School • Waterloo, IA 50703 • AASL

Kelly Anna Marie • Librarian • Libertyville High School Library • Libertyville, IL 60048 • AASL

Kelly Anne • Associate Professor • Pratt Institute Library • Brooklyn, NY 11205 • RASD GODORT

Kelly Anthony H. Dr. • Trustee • Sioux City Public Library • Sioux City, IA 51101-1203 • ALTA

Kelly Arthe B. • Student • Pace University Library New York Civic Center • New York, NY 10038 • ACRL

Kelly Barbara • Green Valley, AZ 85614 • Continuing

Kelly Barbara J. • Appleton Public Library • Appleton, WI 54911-4780 • PLA RASD

Kelly Beth • Head of Adult Services • Duluth Public Library • Duluth, MN 55802 • PLA

Kelly Bonnie J. • Student • Kent State University School of Library & Information Science • Kent, OH 44242-0001 • ALSC YALSA

Kelly Carol A. • Cataloger • Baldwin Public Library • Baldwin, NY 11510

Kelly Carol N. • Librarian • Saint Paul's School for Girls • Brooklandville, MD 21022 • AASL

Kelly Carroll • Director • Huntington Public Library • Huntington, NY 11743 • LAMA PLA

Kelly Celine Sr • Librarian/Media Specialist • Holy Trinity Diocesan High School • Hicksville, NY 11801 • AASL

Kelly Cheryl E. • Children's Librarian • Wayne County Public Library • Wooster, OH 44691

Kelly Cleo B. • Nacogdoches, TX 75961 • Continuing

Kelly Cleo B. • Student • Seattle Public Library • Seattle, WA 98104-1193

Kelly Cynthia M. • Chicago, IL 60453

Kelly Donald V. L. • Asst. to Dean for Clln. Devel. • Adelphi University Swirbul Library • Garden City, NY 11530 • ACRL ALCTS *Life*

Kelly Dorothy R. • Librarian • Sun Coast Medical Library • Largo, FL 34644 • CLENE NMRT VRT

Kelly E. Anne • Student • University of Western Ontario School of Library & Information Science • London ON, N6G 1H1 Canada • LITA

Kelly Elizabeth • Library Director • Mary Vinson Memorial Library Baldwin/Milledgeville Pub Lib • Milledgeville, GA 31061 • ALSC LAMA

Kelly Elizabeth W. • Reference Librarian • Plano Public Library System • Plano, TX 75086-0356

Kelly Esther • Dayton, OH 45426 • Continuing

Kelly Florence • Indian Crest School • Souderton, PA 18964 • IFRT

Kelly Glen J. • Laurentian University • Sudbury ON, P3E 2C6 Canada • ACRL ALCTS LAMA LITA

Kelly Gregory J. • Bronx, NY 10461

Kelly Janice E. • Deputy Director • Suburban Library System • Burr Ridge, IL 60521 • ASCLA

Kelly Jim • Dir. of Sales & Marketing • Lerner Publications • Minneapolis, MN 55401 • ALSC

Kelly Joanne W. • Coordinator of Libraries • Urbana School District #116 • Urbana, IL 61801 • AASL

Kelly John A. • Cincinnati, OH 45208

Kelly John M. • Chief Bibliographer • University of Alabama Amelia Gayle Gorgas Library • Tuscaloosa, AL 35487-0266 • ACRL ALCTS

Kelly Joyce P. • Media Coor • Murray Elementary School • Fort Bragg, NC 28703 • AASL

Kelly Judith J. • Asst Hd of Ref Dept • University of Georgia Libraries • Athens, GA 30602 • ACRL LITA RASD LIRT

Kelly Judy • Library Director • Hubbard Memorial Library • Ludlow, MA 01056

Kelly Julia A. • University of Minnesota Bio-Medical Library • Minneapolis, MN 55455 • ACRL

Kelly Kathleen • Associate Librarian & Info. Svcs • Ameritech Services • Hoffman Estates, IL 60196-1025 • ALCTS LITA

Kelly Kathleen A. • Kensington, MD 20895

Kelly Kathleen W. • Reference Librarian • Lake Forest Library • Lake Forest, IL 60045

Kelly Kathy L. • Promotional Services Coordinator • Sioux City Public Library • Sioux City, IA 51101-1203

Kelly Liam M. • Associate Director • Boston Public Library • Boston, MA 02117 • LITA PLA

Kelly Lianna • Library Assistant • The College Board • New York, NY 10023 • ACRL

Kelly Lori • Student • University of California-Berkeley School of Library & Information Studies • Berkeley, CA 94720 • ALSC

Kelly Margaret I. • Garden City, NY 11530

Kelly Mark • Information Services Spec. • Defense Intelligence Agency • Washington, DC 20340-3341 • ALCTS LITA

Kelly Mary B. • Supervisory Librarian • Scranton School District • Scranton, PA 18503 • AASL YALSA

Kelly Mary E. • Manager-Popular Library Division • Columbus Metropolitan Library • Columbus, OH 43215 • PLA

Kelly Maureen A. • Sherrod Elementary School • Palmer, AK 99645 • AASL

Kelly Maureen A. • University of Puget Sound Collins Memorial Library • Tacoma, WA 98416

Kelly Mavis M. • School Librarian • D H Robinson Junior High School • Las Vegas, NV 89110

Kelly Michael F. • Library Director • University of Texas at San Antonio-Library • San Antonio, TX 78249

Kelly Patricia B. • New Georgia Elementary School • Villa Rica, GA 30180 • AASL

Kelly Patricia M. • Catalog & Systems Librarian • Deerfield Academy • Deerfield, MA 01342 • AASL ALCTS

Kelly Phyllis • Librarian • Locust Valley Library • Locust Valley, NY 11560 • LITA

Kelly Raymond T. Dr. • Head Librarian • Calumet High School • Chicago, IL 60620 • AASL

Kelly Richard J. • Bibliographer • University of Minnesota Meredith Wilson Library • Minneapolis, MN 55455 • ACRL

Kelly Rita P. • Librarian • Catoctin School Library • Leesburg, VA 22075 • AASL

Kelly Robert • Head of Information Services • University of Michigan-Dearborn Mardigian Library • Dearborn, MI 48128-1491 • ACRL LITA

Kelly Robert E. IV • Ref. Librarian & Team Leader • Adams State College Library • Alamosa, CO 81102 • ACRL

Kelly Robert M. • Executive Director • Margaret R. Grundy Memorial Library • Bristol, PA 19007

Kelly Roger • Youth Services Librarian • El Segundo Public Library • El Segundo, CA 90245

Kelly Roger J. • Student • Queens College Graduate School of Library & Information Studies • Flushing, NY 11367 • LITA

Kelly Sandra N. • Bookmobile Librarian • Durham County Library • Durham, NC 27701

Kelly Sarah A. • Assistant Life Sciences Ln. • Purdue University Libraries Life Sciences Library • West Lafayette, IN 47907-1323 • ACRL

Kelly Sarah A. • Media Librarian • Kammerer Middle School • Louisville, KY 40222 • AASL

Kelly Susan A. • Connecticut Savings Bank Mortgage Savings Bank • New Haven, CT 06510

Kelly Trudy A. • Student • Kent State University School of Library & Information Science • Kent, OH 44242-0001

Kelm Carol R. • Oak Park, IL 60302 • ALCTS *Continuing*

Kelm Rebecca Sturm • Head of Public Services • Northern Kentucky University Steely Library • Highland Heights, KY 41099-6101 • ACRL

Kelsey Ann L. • Assoc Dir P & Tech Serv • County College of Morris Masten Learning Resource Center • Randolph, NJ 07869-2086 • ACRL LAMA LITA ILERT

Kelsey Betsy R. • Temple, TX 76502-1527

Kelsey Donald G. • Library Space & Preservation • University of Minnesota • Minneapolis, MN 55455 • ACRL ALCTS LAMA *Life*

Kelsey Rose Marie • Indianapolis, IN 46260-2953 • AASL LAMA PLA EMIERT

Kelson Selma • Reference Services Librarian • Patchogue-Medford Library • Patchogue, NY 11772 • PLA

Keltner Linda • Reference Librarian • Winthrop College Ida Jane Dacus Library • Rock Hill, SC 29733 • RASD LIRT

Kelton Jon D. • Asst Dir for Support Services • Greene County Public Library • Xenia, OH 45385 • ALCTS LITA PLA RASD

Kelton Kate A. • Media Specialist • Borger Middle School • Borger, TX 79007 • AASL

Kelver Ann E. • Brighton, CO 80601

Kem Carol Ritzen • Assoc Univ Librarian • University of Florida • Gainesville, FL 32605 • ACRL NMRT

Kemble Jean E. • Student • State University of New York at Albany School of Information Science & Policy • Albany, NY 12222 • ACRL LIRT SRRT

Kemble Marcia J. • Student • University of Hawaii School of Library & Information Studies • Honolulu, HI 96822 • AASL

Kemmerling Roberta M. • Hanover, PA 17331

Kemp Barbara • Darnestown, MD 20878 • ACRL LAMA RASD *Life*

Kemp Betty • Director • Lee-Itawamba Library System Lee County Library • Tupelo, MS 38801-3899 • LAMA PLA

Kemp Charles H. • Head Librarian • Missouri Southern State College Library • Joplin, MO 64801 • ACRL LAMA LITA

Kemp Cheryl A. • Librarian • Green City RSD • Green City, MO 63545 • AASL

Kemp Dana • Head Cataloger • Mercer University Main Library • Macon, GA 31207 • ALCTS

Kemp E. Ann • Librarian • Dawson Springs Schools • Dawson Springs, KY 42431

Kemp Frank A. • University of Regina • Regina SK, S4S 0A2 Canada • ACRL ALCTS IFRT LHRT

Kemp Henrietta J. • Circulation Reference Librarian • Luther College • Decorah, IA 52101 • ACRL

Kemp Jan H. • Head, Aquisition Dept. • Texas Tech University Libraries • Lubbock, TX 79409-0002 • ACRL

Kemp Janice C. • Librarian • United States Department of Agriculture National Agricultural Library • Beltsville, MD 20705-2351 • ACRL FLRT IFRT SRRT

Kemp Mary Ellen • Arlington, VA 22201

Kemp Thomas J. • Director • University of South Florida Library • Tampa, FL 33620-5600 • ACRL RASD IRRT LHRT

Kempcke Ken R. • Administrative Aide • Tippecanoe County Public Library • Lafayette, IN 47901

Kempe M. Rosalie • Chicago, IL 60640 • Continuing

Kemper Ann Louise • Columbus, OH 43220

Kemper Brett E. • Head, Automated Systems Unit • Broward County Library Florida Center for the Book • Fort Lauderdale, FL 33301

Kempf Andrea C. • Reference Services Librarian • Johnson County Community College Library • Overland Park, KS 66210

Kempf Trudy M. • Library Assistant • Ashland Chemical, Inc. Library & Information Services • Dublin, OH 43017 • LITA

Kemps Colleen • Librarian K-6 • Alburnett School • Alburnett, IA 52202 • AASL

Kenady Carolyn • Consultant • Towers Perrin • Los Angeles, CA 90067

Kenagy Charles Roy • Deputy County Librarian • Johnson County Library • Shawnee Mission, KS 66201 • LAMA PLA RASD IFRT

Kenan Sharon K. • Reference Librarian • McLennan Community College Library • Waco, TX 76708

Kendall Harry • Trustee • Willingboro Public Library • Willingboro, NJ 08046 • ALTA

Kendall John D. • Kensington PE, C0B 1M0 Canada • MAGERT

Kendall Joyce M. • Librarian/Media Specialist • Fall Mountain High School • Alstead, NH 03602 • AASL

Kendall Kathleen M. • Glendale, AZ 85302
Kendall Lubell G. • St Cloud, MN 56304 • AASL
Kendall Nancy J. • Specialist for the Sciences • Seattle Pacific University Weter Memorial Library • Seattle, WA 98119 • ACRL IFRT LIRT
Kendall Nellie D. • Dallas Public Library • Dallas, TX 75201
Kendall Stephen K. • Manager, Library Operations • Family History Library • Salt Lake City, UT 84150
Kendall Susan H. • Director • Preble County District Library • Eaton, OH 45320 • LAMA LITA PLA RASD
Kendall Susan L. • Reference Librarian • University of Dallas William A. Blakley Library • Irving, TX 75062 • ACRL RASD
Kendig Gayle • Library Media Specialist • Rochester #14 School Library • Rochester, NY 14605 • AASL IFRT LIRT
Kendra William E. • Library Director • U S Air Force Base L • Minot Afb, ND 58705 • FLRT
Kendrick Aubrey W. • Huntsville, AL 35816-2614 • ACRL LAMA RASD
Kendrick Cherie • Weatherford, TX 76087 • PLA
Kendrick Curtis L. • Decatur, GA 30030 • ACRL LAMA LITA
Kendrick Joan M. • Nashua, NH 03060
Kendrick Sherri L. • Reference • Englewood Library • Englewood, NJ 07631 • ACRL RASD EMIERT IFRT IRRT
Kendzierski Sonia • Library Media Specialist • Chain O' Lakes School • Waupaca, WI 54981 • AASL
Kenefick J Gordon • Associate Library Emeritus • Yale University Sterling Memorial Library • New Haven, CT 06520 • ACRL ALCTS *Life*
Keniston Roberta • Boston, MA 02114-4002 • Continuing
Kenly Patricia E. • Business Reference Librarian • University of Central Florida Library • Orlando, FL 32816-0666 • ACRL RASD
Kenne Ann M. • Iowa State University Library • Ames, IA 50011-2140
Kennedy-Olsen Jan R. • Cornell University Albert R. Mann Library • Ithaca, NY 14853-4301 • ACRL
Kennedy Ann L. • Head of Adult Servs/Reference • Carol Stream Public Library • Carol Stream, IL 60188 • PLA
Kennedy Anne M. • Senior Clerk • Albert Wisner Public Library • Warwick, NY 10990 • PLA
Kennedy Beverly K. • Student • University of Hawaii School of Library & Information Studies • Honolulu, HI 96822
Kennedy Charlene F. • Head of Reference Services • Carlsbad City Library • Carlsbad, CA 92008 • ACRL
Kennedy D. Sue • Librarian • Arab Junior High School • Arab, AL 35016
Kennedy Donna G. • Head Librarian • Northeastern University • Burlington, MA 01803 • ACRL
Kennedy Frances • Oklahoma City, OK 73112 • Life
Kennedy Francine C. • Homewood, IL 60430
Kennedy Gail A. • Assoc Director of Libraries • University of Kentucky Libraries • Lexington, KY 40506-0039 • ALCTS LAMA
Kennedy James R. • Director • Buena Vista College Ballou Libray • Storm Lake, IA 50588 • ACRL ASCLA LAMA ILERT LRRT
Kennedy James W. • Head Librarian • Murray State College Library • Tishomingo, OK 73460 • ACRL
Kennedy Joseph M. • Chief of Mobile Library Serv. • Boston Public Library • Charlestown, MA 02129
Kennedy Joy C. • Director • American Hospital Association Resource Center • Chicago, IL 60611 • ALCTS LITA
Kennedy Kathleen • Academic Specialist • Readmore • New York, NY 10007 • ACRL ALCTS LAMA LITA
Kennedy Kathleen A. • Assistant Director Public Serv • Glassboro State College • Glassboro, NJ 08028 • ACRL
Kennedy Kathy K. • Assistant Director • Monroeville Public Library • Monroeville, PA 15146-3381 • PLA
Kennedy Leanna J. • APO, AA 34020
Kennedy Linda M. • Head of Govt. Documents Dept. • University of California-Davis Library • Davis, CA 95616 • ACRL RASD GODORT
Kennedy Linda M. • Snyder, NY 14226 • LHRT
Kennedy Madonna Davis • Reference/Humanitess Librarian • Northwest Missouri State University Owens Library • Maryville, MO 64468
Kennedy Monika M. • Head School Librarian • Newburyport High School Library • Newburyport, MA 01950 • AASL
Kennedy Patricia A. • Children Librarian • Milwaukee Public Library • Milwaukee, WI 53233 • ALSC
Kennedy Patricia A. • Director of Medical Records • Bridgeport Health Care Center Incorporation • Bridgeport, CT 06610
Kennedy Phyllis J. • Librarian/Media Specialist • Jennings Middle School • Akron, OH 44310 • AASL
Kennedy Rose Marie • Deputy County Librarian • Contra Costa County Library • Pleasant Hill, CA 94523 • PLA EMIERT
Kennedy Scott E. • Bibliographer Reference Clln • University of Connecticut Homer Babbidge Library • Storrs, CT 06269-1005 • RASD
Kennedy Shirley Duglin • Clearwater, FL 34624
Kennedy Shirley F. • Academy Archivist • Atas-Emmy Awards • Burbank, CA 91505
Kennedy Terry L. • Librarian • Eastern Pentecostal Bible Coll • Peterborough ON, K9H 5T2 Canada • ACRL
Kennedy Thomas R. • Supervisor Library/Media • School District of Beloit • Beloit, WI 53511 • AASL IFRT
Kennelly Tamara J. • Student • University of Kentucky College of Library & Information Science • Lexington, KY 40506-0391
Kennemer Phyllis K. • Library Media Specialist • Green Mountain Elementary School Library • Lakewood, CO 80228 • AASL ALSC
Kennerly Sarah L. • Denton, TX 76205-5559 • AASL ALSC *Life*
Kenney Andrea F. • Reference Librarian • Edgewood College Oscar Kennebohm Library • Madison, WI 53711 • ACRL
Kenney Ann J. • Middle School Librarian • Catlin Gabel School • Portland, OR 97225 • AASL YALSA
Kenney Anne R. • Asst. Director, Dept of Presv. • Cornell University Library • Ithaca, NY 14853 • ALCTS
Kenney Brigitte L. • Golden, CO 80403 • Continuing
Kenney Donald J. • Asst. to the Univ. Librarian • Virginia Polytechnic Institute and State University, Newman Library • Blacksburg, VA 24061-0434 • ACRL ALSC RASD YALSA
Kenney Elizabeth Mary • Arcadia, FL 33821 • LIRT
Kenney Jo Ellen • Director • Carnegie Free Library • McKeesport, PA 15132
Kennish Patricia • Librarian • St. Elizabeth Ann Seton School • Anchorage, AK 99516 • AASL
Kennon Patrick Mrs. • Dallas, TX 75205 • ALSC YALSA *Continuing*
Kennson Brian • Student • Florida State University School of Library and Information Studies • Tallahassee, FL 32306-2048
Kenny Brenda Gail • Graduate Student • Riverside City & County Public Library • Riverside, CA 92502-0468
Kenny Kathleen E. • Bowdoin College Library • Brunswick, ME 04011 • ACRL LITA
Kenny Margaret E. • Ossining, NY 10562
Kenny Theresa M. • Library Technical Assistant • University of Illinois Library • Urbana, IL 61801
Kenreich Mary Ellen • Albuquerque, NM 87112
Kenselaar Robert W. • New York Public Library • New York, NY 10018-2788 • ALCTS
Kent Ada G. • Columbus, OH 43206 • AASL VRT
Kent Allen • Pittsburgh, PA 15243
Kent Candace D. • Assistant Director • Brunswick-Glynn County Regional Library • Brunswick, GA 31523-0901
Kent Carl • School Library Director • Unified School District 500 • Kansas City, KS 66101 • AASL
Kent Caroline M. • Head, Research Services • Harvard College Library Widener Memorial Library • Cambridge, MA 02138 • ACRL LITA RASD LIRT
Kent Charles D. Mr • Gloucester ON, K1B 5G2 Canada • Continuing
Kent David • Head Librarian • Kent Place School • Summit, NJ 07902-0308 • AASL
Kent David I. • Cooperstown, NY 13326
Kent Iris J. • Kadena Elementary School • APO, AP 96367-5064 • AASL
Kent Jeffrey A. • Coor Library Media Srvs, K-6 • Broken Ground School Library Media Services Office • Concord, NH 03301 • AASL
Kent Joyceanne • Librarian • Seattle Public Library • Seattle, WA 98104-1193
Kent Mary E. • Acquisition/Technical Supervisor • Tulsa Junior College • Tulsa, OK 74115
Kent Rick C. • Asst. Superintendent • Grand Haven Area Public Schools • Grand Haven, MI 49417 • AASL YALSA
Kent Virginia P. • Newton, MA 02158 • PLA YALSA *Continuing*
Kentgen Carol Jean • Librarian I/Inf. Center • Chicago Public Library • Chicago, IL 60605 • ASCLA PLA RASD LIRT
Kentner Kathleen M. • Oyster River High School Library • Durham, NH 03824 • AASL IFRT
Kenyon Elizabeth A. • Library Director • Chisholm Public Library • Chisholm, MN 55719 • PLA
Kenyon Sharmon H. • Associate Librarian • Humboldt State University Library • Arcata, CA 95521 • ACRL LITA RASD LIRT
Keogh Judith L. • Consultant Librarian • Chester County Library & District Center • Exton, PA 19341-2496 • PLA
Keough Anne • Chicago Public Library • Chicago, IL 60605
Keough Francis P. • Springfield, MA 01108 • Continuing
Keough Joseph A. Bro • Librarian • La Salle College High School • Wyndmoor, PA 19118-1199 • AASL
Kepics Joanne M. • Sr. OCLC Servs. Marketing Rep. • Southeastern Library Network (SOLINET) • Atlanta, GA 30309-2955 • ASCLA CLENE
Kepley Cyndi • Head of Technical Services • New Albany-Floyd County Public Library • New Albany, IN 47150
Keplinger JoAnn M. • Coor Instr Media Serv • Lodi Unified School District • Lodi, CA 95240 • AASL
Kepner Frances R. • Terre Haute, IN 47802 • Continuing
Kepner Linda Tiernan • Assistant Director/Cataloger • Peterborough Town Library • Peterborough, NH 03458
Kepner Mary Jane • Library Services Consultant • Suburban Library System • Burr Ridge, IL 60521 • PLA
Keppel Margery A. • Student • University of Washington Graduate School of Library and Information Science • Seattle, WA 98195 • LITA
Kerbel Sandra S. • Head Ln. Bevier Engr. Library • University of Pittsburgh • Pittsburgh, PA 15260 • ACRL LAMA
Kerber Stephen • Edwardsville, IL 62025 • ACRL
Kerby Mona • Little Elementary School Arlington Independent School District • Arlington, TX 76016 • AASL ALSC
Kercher Marilyn L. • Ohio State University • Columbus, OH 43210
Kerchoff Steven P. • Network Librarian • Federal Library & Information Network (FEDLINK) • Washington, DC 20540 • RASD IRRT NMRT
Kerdolff Kathryn E. • Reference Librarian • Louisiana State University Medical Center Library • New Orleans, LA 70112-2223
Keresey Gayle • Media Coordinator • East Arcadia School Media Center • Riegelwood, NC 28456 • AASL YALSA IFRT SRRT
Kerhoulas Barbara • Reference Supervisor • Fair Oaks/ Orangevale Community Library • Fair Oaks, CA 95826 • RASD
Kerin David • General Manager • EBSCO Subscription Services • Los Angeles, CA 90009 • ACRL *Subscribing*
Kerley Izoro D. • Director of the Library • Connors State College • Warner, OK 74469 • ACRL ALCTS LAMA RASD
Kerlin Diane • Library Director • Milton Memorial Library • Milton, WA 98354 • ALSC PLA
Kerman Edwin • The Meeting School • Rindge, NH 03461 • ALSC IRRT SRRT
Kern-Simirenko Cheryl A. • Asst Univ Libn/Clln Devel/ Res Sv • University of Oregon Library • Eugene, OR 97403-1299 • ACRL ALCTS LAMA LITA
Kern Anne Merdinger • Cataloger • Harvard University • Cambridge, MA 02138 • ALCTS
Kern Eileen F. • Librarian • Parkland School District Katzer Elementary School Library • Allentown, PA 18104 • AASL
Kern Jean • Linden West Elementary School Library • Gladstone, MO 64118 • AASL IFRT
Kern Jeanne M. • Phillips,Lytle,Hitchcock,Blaine & Huber Library • Buffalo, NY 14203 • LAMA
Kern Jewel • Trustee • Mount Prospect Public Library • Mount Prospect, IL 60056 • PLA
Kern Joanne F. • Librarian/ Head of Media Dept • Riverdale High School • Fort Myers, FL 33905
Kern John D. • Sales • Holliston Mills • Kingsport, TN 37662
Kern Louise • Librarian • Madison Public Library • Madison, IL 62060
Kern Marjorie M. • Student • Wayne State University Library Science Program • Detroit, MI 48202 • IFRT SRRT
Kern Shirley • FPO, AP 96372-0445 • AASL YALSA *Life*
Kern Stella V. • Public Relations Librarian • Ocean County Public Library • Toms River, NJ 08753 • LAMA PLA
Kern Susan K. • Uniondale Public Library • Uniondale, NY 11553-1995 • ALSC PLA RASD IFRT
Kernan John W. • Representative • Kernan Library Office Group Inc. • New Hartford, NY 13413 • ACRL
Kernan Timothy S. • Student • University of Pittsburgh School of Library and Information Science • Pittsburgh, PA 15260 • ACRL
Kerndt Miriam E. • Geography Librarian • University of Wisconsin-Madison Geography Library • Madison, WI 53706 • ACRL MAGERT
Kerner Cora A. • Volunteer Librarian • Hellertown Area Library • Hellertown, PA 18055
Kernerman Vladimir Y. • Student • Rosary College Graduate School of Library & Information Science • River Forest, IL 60305
Kerns Bettye Fowler • Youth Services Librarian • Central Arkansas Library System • Little Rock, AR 72201-4698 • AASL PLA IFRT

Kerns Kathryn M. • Feminist Studies Librarian • Stanford University J. Henry Meyer Memorial Library • Stanford, CA 94305 • ACRL

Kerns Mary E. • Director, Instructional Services • Yamhill Cnty Edu Serv Dist • Mcminnville, OR 97128 • AASL

Kerper Richard M. • Columbus, OH 43229-9116 • ALSC

Kerr Derek N. • Vancouver, BC, V5T 1L7 Canada

Kerr Donna S. • Librarian • Mendocino County Library • Ukiah, CA 95482 • EMIERT

Kerr Laura S. • Librarian • Amsdell Heights Jr High School • Hamburg, NY 14075

Kerr Loralee V. • Reference Librarian • University of Minnesota Library • St Paul, MN 55108 • ACRL RASD GODORT LIRT

Kerr Paula M. • Student • University of Maryland College of Library and Information Services • College Park, MD 20742-4345

Kerr Sharon Hybki • Academic Centers Librarian • Chapman College Clarke Memorial Library • Orange, CA 92666 • ACRL RASD

Kerr Sharon W. • Student • San Jose State University Division of Library & Information Science • San Jose, CA 95192-0029

Kerschner Joan G. • State Librarian • Nevada State Library & Archives • Carson City, NV 89710

Kersey Harriet F. • Head, Serials Cataloging Dept. • Georgia Institute of Technology Price Gilbert Memorial Library • Atlanta, GA 30332-0900 • ALCTS LITA NMRT

Kershaw Kathleen W. • Librarian • Hargrave High School • Huffman, TX 77336

Kershaw William B. Mr • Traverse City, MI 49684 • AASL ALSC *Life*

Kershner Bruce S. • Librarian • Fairfield Public Library • Fairfield, CT 06430 • LAMA PLA

Kershner Lois M. • Director • Peninsula Library Automation Network • San Mateo, CA 94402 • LAMA LITA

Kershner Stephen A. • Director • Baldwin Public Library • Birmingham, MI 48012-3002 • LAMA PLA

Kerski Janell D. • Lakewood, CO 80228-4322 • IFRT

Kersley Sandra L. • Community Library Coordinator • Timberland Regional Library Centralia Branch • Centralia, WA 98531 • LAMA

Kersten Nancy D. • Green Hills Public Library • Palos Hills, IL 60465 • ALCTS IFRT SRRT

Kerstetter Judith A. • Sachem Public Library • Holbrook, NY 11741

Kerszke-Paronto Linda • Trustee • University of New Mexico General Library • Albuquerque, NM 87131

Kertman Lois P. • Library Media Specialist • Waterfront Elem Sch • Buffalo, NY 14202 • AASL

Kerze Naomi V. • Loyola Marymount University Charles Von Der Ahe Library • Los Angeles, CA 90045

Kesel Barbara A. • Student • University of Arizona Graduate Library School • Tucson, AZ 85721

Keshkekian Shake • Librarian • Stanford University • Stanford, CA 94305-6011

Kesler Jean Ann • Library Media Specialist • R-I-C-A School • Rockville, MD 20850 • AASL

Kesner Susan • Silver Platter Information • Norwood, MA 02062-5026 • ACRL

Kesse Erich J. • Preservation Librarian • University of Florida Libraries • Gainesville, FL 32611-2047 • ACRL ALCTS

Kesselman Martin A. • Hd, Ref, & Instr. Serv. • Rutgers University Libraries Library of Science & Medicine • Piscataway, NJ 08855-1029 • ACRL LITA RASD IRRT

Kessenich Judy H. • Cataloger, Library • Walter Reed Army Institute of Research • Washington, DC 20307-5100 • LITA

Kessinger David Rev. • Belmont Abbey College Library • Belmont, NC 28012 • ACRL

Kessinger Judith A. • Mill Creek, WA 98012

Kessler Barbara • Jericho Public Library • Jericho, NY 11753 • RASD YALSA

Kessler Charlotte P. • Trustee • Columbus Metropolitan Library • Columbus, OH 43215 • LAMA PLA

Kessler Ellen L. • Student • Indiana University School of Library and Information Science • Bloomington, IN 47405 • PLA SRRT

Kessler Howard • Trustee • Glenview Public Library • Glenview, IL 60025

Kessler Jack • San Francisco, CA 94146 • ACRL ALCTS LITA IRRT LIRT

Kessler Janis • Director, IMC • Bakersfield City Schools • Bakersfield, CA 93305 • AASL

Kessler Katheryn M. • Librarian • Patrick Air Force Base Library • Patrick AFB, FL 32925 • AFLRT FLRT

Kessler Libbie Miss • Saginaw, MI 48603 • AASL YALSA *Life*

Kessler Ridley R. • Federal Documents Librarian • University of North Carolina Walter Royal Davis Library • Chapel Hill, NC 27599-3924 • GODORT

Kessler Selma P. • Moorestown, NJ 08057

Kessler Thomas L. • Order Librarian • University of Northern Iowa Donald O. Rod Library • Cedar Falls, IA 50613-3675 • ACRL

Kestell John R. • Student • Contra Costa County Library • Pleasant Hill, CA 94523 • ACRL SRRT

Kester Diane D. • Assistant Professor • East Carolina University Department of Library & Information Studies • Greenville, NC 27858-4353 • AASL ASCLA LITA LRRT

Kester John E. • Rochester Institute of Technology Wallace Memorial Library • Rochester, NY 14623-0887

Kester Martha • Assistant Cataloging Librarian • University of Illinois at Chicago University Library • Chicago, IL 60680 • ACRL ALCTS *Life*

Kester Tara B. • Librarian • Allen-Stevenson School • New York, NY 10021 • AASL

Ketcham Lee C. Ms. • Director of Libraries • Montevallo University Carmichael Library • Montevallo, AL 35115 • ACRL ALCTS LAMA LITA RASD

Ketchell Debra • Acting Associate Director • University of Washington Health Science Library & Info Center • Seattle, WA 98195 • LITA

Ketchersid Arthur • Associate Director Tech. Servs • University of South Florida Library • Tampa, FL 33620-5600 • ALCTS LITA

Ketchner Kevin G. • Student • University of Arizona Graduate Library School • Tucson, AZ 85721 • ACRL

Ketchum Alice B. • Saint Clair County Community College • Port Huron, MI 48061-6015 • ACRL

Ketchum Irene F. • Trustee • Lake County Public Library • Merrillville, IN 46410-5382 • ALTA

Ketrick Margot • Librarian • Whitney Point Senior High School • Whitney Point, NY 13862

Ketterer Barbara A. • Piscataway, NJ 08854 • LITA PLA

Kettler Roberta Feier • Hebrew Academy of San Francisco • San Francisco, CA 94118 • AASL

Kettling Elys L. • Student • University of Wisconsin-Milwaukee School of Library & Information Science • Milwaukee, WI 53201 • RASD IFRT

Keuck Louise F. • Franklin Pk, IL 60131 • Continuing

Keuneke Beth A. • Technical Processing Assistant • Brumback Library • Van Wert, OH 45891

Keuper Deborah S. • Student • Rosary College Graduate School of Library & Information Science • River Forest, IL 60305

Kevil L. Hunter • Product Specialist • Data Research Associates Inc. • Saint Louis, MO 63132 • ACRL

Kevin Doris J. • Library Director • Gulfport Public Library • Gulfport, FL 33707 • LAMA PLA

Key Ann C. • Library Trustee • West Florida Regional Library • Pensacola, FL 32501

Key Hazel • Charlottesville, VA 22903 • Continuing

Key Janet S. • Public Services Librarian • Tarrant County Junior College Northeast Campus • Hurst, TX 76054 • ACRL

Key Kathleen M. • Reference Librarian • West Virginia University Evansdale Library • Morgantown, WV 26506-6105 • LIRT

Key Leslie • Media Coordinator • Long Creek-Grady Elementary School • Rocky Point, NC 28457 • AASL

Key Ruth B. • Neal Middle School • Durham, NC 27704

Keyes Clara B. • Special Collections • Morehead State University Camden-Carroll Library • Morehead, KY 40351 • ALCTS

Keyes David L. • Ln • Indian Hills Elementary • Salt Lake Cty, UT 84108

Keyes Edna • Art Librarian • Portland School of Art Library • Portland, ME 04101

Keyhani Andrea • Mgr. of Database Acq. • Online Computer Library Center (OCLC) • Dublin, OH 43017-3395 • RASD

Keys Charlotte • Reference Librarian • Brandeis University Main Library • Waltham, MA 02254-9110 • ACRL LITA

Keys Marshall • NELINET Inc. • Newton, MA 02162 • ACRL ALCTS LITA

Keyser Meredith J. • Technical Librarian • Martin Marietta Energy Systems Library Oak Ridge National Laboratory • Oak Ridge, TN 37831-6208 • LITA

Keyser Sue C. • Albemarle High School • Charlottesville, VA 22901 • AASL

Kfoury Jennifer F. • Chicago, IL 60611

Khader Majed J. • Huntington, WV 25729-4124

Khalil Mounir A. • Systems Librarian • City College of New York (CUNY) • New York, NY 10031 • LITA

Khan Karen P. • Director • Mooresville Public Library • Mooresville, NC 28115 • ALSC LAMA PLA

Khan Mohammed A. S. • Information Specilaist • Automobile Club of Southern California Technical Information Center H207 • Los Angeles, CA 90051-0890 • ACRL IRRT

Khan Munawwar J. Mrs • Head of Information Services • University of Toledo • Toledo, OH 43606 • ACRL

Khan Nafis A. • Chicago, IL 60615

Khan Syed M A • Boston College O'Neill Library • Chestnut Hill, MA 02167 • ACRL

Kharbas Judith N. • Asst. Dir for Tech. Serv. • University of Rochester Rush Rhees Library • Rochester, NY 14627-0055 • ACRL ALCTS

Kharfen Stephen • Moving-image Cataloger • Library of Congress, Motion Picture Broadcast & Recorded Sound Division • Washington, DC 20541 • SRRT

Khattab Hosneya • Young Adult Librarian • Los Angeles Public Library Robertson Branch • Los Angeles, CA 90035 • ACRL IRRT

Khatun Halima • Dhaka, Bangladesh • ALCTS LRRT

Khawam Yves J. • Professor • Ecole de Bibliotheconomie Universite de Montreal • Montreal PQ, H3C 3J7 Canada • ACRL

Khayutin Mila • Library Assistant/Acquisitions • McMaster University Health Sciences Library • Hamilton ON, L8N 3Z5 Canada

Kheel Susan T. • Head of Reference Services • East Brunswick Public Library • E. Brunswick, NJ 08816 • PLA RASD

Kho Lian Tie • Ln Southeast Asia Clln • Yale University Sterling Memorial Library • New Haven, CT 06520 • ALCTS IRRT

Khoodikians-Guillette Elizabeth • Watertown, MA 02172 • ACRL

Khoury Nancy L. • Director • McNeese State University Lether E. Frazar Memorial Library • Lake Charles, LA 70609

Khovry Alissar • Student • Columbia University Library Service Library • New York, NY 10027

Kiah Rosalie Black • Norfolk State University • Norfolk, VA 23504 • ALSC

Kiang John C. • South Bend, IN 46637 • Continuing

Kiang Li-Du • Vernon, CT 06066

Kianovsky Rochelle • Adult Services Librarian • Milwaukee Public Library Atkinson Branch • Milwaukee, WI 53209 • PLA

Kibbe Lucena J. • Yorkville, NY 13495 • Continuing

Kibbee Josephine Z. • Head of Reference • University of Illinois Library • Urbana, IL 61801 • RASD

Kibbey Mark H. • Assoc. Director, Libr Systems • University of Washington Suzzallo Library • Seattle, WA 98195 • LITA

Kibreah Golam • Children's Libraian/Asst. Dir. • Danville Public Library • Danville, IN 46122

Kice Carmella M. • Student • Kutztown University Library Science Department • Kutztown, PA 19530

Kicinski Judith • Assistant Director • Sarah Lawrence College Esther Raushenbush Library • Bronxville, NY 10708

Kickel Sally A. • Cleveland, OH 44102

Kickingbird Robin • El Reno, OK 73036 • EMIERT ILERT SRRT

Kidder Audrey J. • Coordinator of Information • Pepperdine University Payson Library • Malibu, CA 90263 • ACRL LAMA LITA PLA RASD LIRT LRRT

Kidder Frederick E. Dr • Guaynabo, PR 00657 • Continuing

Kidder Robert W. • Urbana, IL 61801 • ACRL ALCTS *Life*

Kidman Roy L. • University Librarian • University of Southern California Doheny Library • Los Angeles, CA 90089-0182 • Continuing

Kidwell Eric A. • Director of the Library • Huntingdon College Houghton Memorial Library • Montgomery, AL 36106 • ACRL

Kie Kathleen M. • Support & Training Specialist • Online Computer Library Center (OCLC) • Dublin, OH 43017-3395 • ALCTS LITA LIRT NMRT

Kieczykowski Edward M. • Director • Solano County Library • Fairfield, CA 94533 • PLA

Kieda Sue A. • International Association of Machinists • Washington, DC 20036

Kiedaisch Karl Jr • Keokuk, IA 52632-2360

Kiefer Barbara Z. Dr. • Teachers College-Columbia University Millbank Memorial Library • New York, NY 10027 • ALSC

Kiefer Cynthia • Tucson, AZ 85712

Kiefer Gilbert V. • Librarian • Kratz Elementary School Library • Berkeley, MO 63134 • AASL RASD YALSA *Life*

Kiefer Marilyn V. • Librarian • Novi High School • Novi, MI 48375 • AASL YALSA

Kiefer Patricia M. • Senior Librarian • Los Angeles Public Library • Los Angeles, CA 90071

Kiefer Thomas A. • Library Assistant • University of Iowa Libraries • Iowa City, IA 52242-1379

Kieffer Lawrence W. • Reader's Services Librarian • University of Northern Iowa Donald O. Rod Library • Cedar Falls, IA 50613-3675 • ACRL RASD IFRT

Kieft Robert K. • Reference Librarian • Haverford College James P. Magill Library • Haverford, PA 19041 • ACRL

Kiegel Joseph A. • Asst. Head, Cataloging Division • University of Washington Suzzallo Library • Seattle, WA 98195 • ALCTS LITA
Kiel Rebecca • Reference Librarian • Cottey College • Nevada, MO 64772 • ACRL
Kielbowicz Joyce • Children's Librarian • Hammond Public Library • Hammond, IN 46319
Kielpsz Eryk Talat • Cataloger • Ohio State University • Columbus, OH 43210 • ACRL ALCTS LITA RASD *Life*
Kiely Theresa • Librarian • Kroll Associates Inc • New York, NY 10022
Kienberger Alice J. • Head Librarian • Warner Pacific College Otto F. Linn Library • Portland, OR 97215 • ACRL
Kiener Maureen S. • Trustee • Lyons Public Library • Lyons, IL 60534 • ALTA
Kienitz LaDonna T. • City Librarian • Newport Beach Public Library • Newport Beach, CA 92660 • ALTA LAMA PLA IFRT
Kieran Barbara • Media Center Director • Mary Hogan Public School • Midddlebury, VT 05753 • AASL
Kiernan Katharine • Assistant Director • Vermont State Colleges • Waterbury, VT 05676 • LITA
Kierstead Marilyn J. • Reader Services Librarian • Reed College E. V. Hauser Library • Portland, OR 97202 • ACRL RASD IFRT
Kies Cosette • Chair • Northern Illinois University Department of Library & Information Studies • DeKalb, IL 60115 • PLA YALSA *Life*
Kiesel Jean Schmidt • Louisiana Room Librarian • University of Southwestern Louisiana Libraries • Lafayette, LA 70503 • ACRL RASD
Kiesling Kristi L. • Head, Manuscripts & Archives • University of Texas • Austin, TX 78712-1276 • ACRL
Kiessel-Brandt Ingeborg • Newmarket, NH 03857
Kietzman Ann R. • Cataloging Manager • Harford County Library • Belcamp, MD 21017 • ALCTS
Kiewitt Eva L. • Associate Dean • Regent University • Virginia Beach, VA 23464-9875 • ACRL LAMA RASD
Kiffmeyer Barbara B. • Children's Librarian • Indianapolis-Marion County Public Library Broad Ripple Branch • Indianapolis, IN 46220 • ALSC PLA YALSA IFRT *Life*
Kiger Janeane Dominey • Student • University of North Carolina at Chapel Hill School of Information and Library Science • Chapel Hill, NC 27599-3360
Kiger Jean • Media Specialist • Thomasville High School • Thomasville, NC 27360 • AASL
Kight Lori Ann • McLean, VA 22101
Kihara Michio • Professor of Library Science • Sugiyama Jogakuen University • Nayoya, Japan • ALCTS LITA
Kijanka Dorothy M. • University Librarian • Sacred Heart University Library • Fairfield, CT 06432-1023 • ACRL ALCTS LAMA LITA RASD IRRT
Kiker Suzanne B. • University of Florida Libraries • Gainesville, FL 32611 • ALCTS
Kilander Ann H. • Librarian • Oconomowoc High School Library • Oconomowoc, WI 53066 • AASL YALSA
Kilberg Jacqueline L. • Coopers & Lybrand • New York, NY 10020
Kilbert Linda S. • Reference Associate • Indiana University School of Medicine Ruth Lilly Medical Library • Indianapolis, IN 46220
Kilbridge Rosemary J. • Library Director • Chippewa Falls Public Library • Chippewa Falls, WI 54729 • PLA
Kilcommons Christopher • Director of Personnel • Brooklyn Public Library • Brooklyn, NY 11238 • LAMA IRRT
Kile Barbara • Assistant to the University Ln • Rice University Fondren Library • Houston, TX 77251-1892 • ACRL LAMA GODORT IRRT
Kiley G David Mr • Library Coordinator • Santa Barbara City College • Santa Barbara, CA 93109
Kilgen Kathleen M. • Director • Lafourche Parish Public Library • Thibodaux, LA 70301 • PLA IFRT IRRT VRT
Kilgo Kerstin D. • Knoxville, TN 37922
Kilgore Darlene Carol • Tampa, FL 33612
Kilgour Frederick • Distinguished Research Prof. • University of North Carolina at Chapel Hill School of Information and Library Science • Chapel Hill, NC 27599-3360 • AASL ACRL ALCTS ASCLA LAMA LITA PLA RASD YALSA *Honorary*
Kilianski Brenda J • Sales Representative • J. A. Majors Company • Compton, CA 90220
Kilkka Lois A. • Director • Scotland County Memorial Library • Laurinburg, NC 28352
Killam Lane • Division Librarian • United States Army Corps of Engineers • Norfolk, VA 23510-1096 • AFLRT
Killeen Erlene Bishop • K-12 Coordinator • Stoughton Area Schools • Stoughton, WI 53589 • AASL ALSC LAMA
Killen Rosemary M. • Trustee • American School Publishers • New York, NY 10011
Killens Caroline A. • Head Acquisitions Department • University of Georgia Libraries • Athens, GA 30602 • ACRL ALCTS LAMA
Killian Barbara G. • Washington, DC 20008
Killian Daniel R. • Library Director • North Tonawanda Public Library • North Tonawanda, NY 14120
Killian J. A. • Trustee • Sandhill Regional Library System • Rockingham, NC 28379-4995 • ALTA
Killian Richard M. • Library Director • Sacramento Public Library • Sacramento, CA 95814 • PLA
Killian Tessa E. • Antioch College • Yellow Spring, OH 45387 • IFRT
Killings Allen F. Dr • Trustee • Akron-Summit County Public Library • Akron, OH 44326-0001 • ALTA
Killion John M. • Davenport, IA 52803 • Continuing
Killoran Katherine B. • Asst. Professor/Librarian • John Jay College of Criminal Justice • New York, NY 10019 • ACRL RASD
Kilman Leigh Ann • Wimberley, TX 78676-2230
Kilmer Brenda S. • Media Specialist • South Miami Middle School • Miami, FL 33143 • AASL YALSA
Kilmer M. Sue • Mabel C. Fry Public Library • Yukon, OK 73099
Kilmer Ruth K. • Brevard, NC 28712 • Continuing
Kilmer Susan Broom • Director • Saint Lucie County Library Systems • Fort Pierce, FL 34950 • LAMA
Kilpatrick Barbara A. Sr. • Media Specialist • Saint Bernard Academy • Nashville, TN 37212 • AASL
Kilpatrick Carlton E. Jr. • Tavares High School • Tavares, FL 32778 • AASL
Kilpatrick Janet L. • Periodicals Librarian • East Carolina University Joyner Library • Greenville, NC 27858-4353 • ALCTS
Kilpatrick Karen • Roebling, NJ 08554 • PLA
Kilpatrick Thomas L. • Interlibrary Loan Librarian • Southern Illinois University Delyte W. Morris Library • Carbondale, IL 62901-6632 • ACRL RASD
Kilrain Eileen P. • Head Reference & Adult Services • Bethlehem Public Library • Delmar, NY 12054 • PLA RASD
Kilroy Barbe • Library Media Specialist • Lomond Elementary School Shaker Heights Board of Education • Shaker Heights, OH 44122
Kilroy Edward • Assistant Dir./Operations • Lee County Library System • Fort Myers, FL 33901 • LAMA PLA
Kilton Tom D. • Asst Modern Lang Ln • University of Illinois Library • Urbana, IL 61801 • ACRL
Kim-Prelutsky Carolynn • Mercer Island, WA 98040 • ALCTS LITA EMIERT
Kim B.J. Mrs. • Head of Catalog Department • South Dakota State University Briggs Library • Brookings, SD 57007 • ACRL LITA
Kim Catherine • Library Media Specialist • Richard E. Miller School • Phoenix, AZ 85021 • AASL
Kim Chang K. • Head Librarian • Korea Advanced Institute of Science and Technology • Teajon-shi 305-701, South Korea • ACRL ALCTS LAMA
Kim Chung N. • Catalog Librarian • Cornell University Industrial and Labor Relations Library • Ithaca, NY 14853 • ALCTS
Kim Chung-Sook Charlotte • Asst. Commissioner Neighborhoods • Chicago Public Library Harold Washington Library • Chicago, IL 60605 • PLA EMIERT
Kim David U. • Director of Library • Salve Regina University Library • Newport, RI 02840 • ACRL LITA
Kim Grace S. • Volunteer Librarian • Oriental Mission Church Library • Los Angeles, CA 90004
Kim Imsoon • Librarian • United States Air Force FL5294 Base Library • APO, AP 96278-5280
Kim Inja H. • Dean of Learning Resources • Lake Michigan College Library • Benton Harbor, MI 49022
Kim Joanne Y. • Acquisitions Librarian • Pasadena City College • Pasadena, CA 91106 • ACRL
Kim Jung A. • Librarian • Base Library • APO, AP 96278 • AFLRT
Kim Kumsum • Original Cataloger • California State University • Fullerton, CA 92634 • ALCTS
Kim Kyung Joo • Assistant Director/Pub Serv • Widener University Wolfgram Library • Chester, PA 19013 • ACRL RASD
Kim Linda • Librarian • York Suburban School District • York, PA 17403 • AASL
Kim Linda T. • Librarian • Mililani Waena Elementary School • Mililani, HI 96789 • AASL
Kim Mary T. • Assistant Professor & Coor. • Kent State University School of Library Science/Columbus Program • Columbus, OH 43210 • ACRL LRRT
Kim Mi-Hyeon • Student • Indiana University School of Library and Information Science • Bloomington, IN 47405 • LITA
Kim Moon Ok • Assistant Professor • North Carolina Agricultural & Technical State University • Greensboro, NC 27411 • ALCTS
Kim San-Oak • Huntington Beach, CA 92646
Kim Sanok Peggy • Librarian Supervisor • Washington University Olin Library • Saint Louis, MO 63130 • ALCTS
Kim Sook-Hyun • Associate Professor • University of Tennessee Library • Knoxville, TN 37996-1000 • LITA
Kim Soonja Lee • Professor • Sook-Myung Women's University • Seoul, South Korea • LAMA RASD
Kim Sung Ai • Bangor, ME 04401
Kim Tae-Ock • Associate University Librarian • Santa Clara University Michel Orradre Library • Santa Clara, CA 95053 • ACRL
Kim Vanessa S.H. • Studery • McGill University Graduate School of Library & Information Studies • Montreal PQ, H3A 1Y1 Canada • LAMA
Kim Young A. • Systems Librarian • University of Maryland College Park Theodore R. McKeldin Library • College Park, MD 20742-7011 • LITA
Kimball Cynthia K. • Laughlin, NV 89028
Kimball Dianne D. • Wallingford Public Library • Wallingford, CT 06492 • ALSC
Kimball James P. • Lib. Info. Systems Specialist • Library of Congress • Washington, DC 20541 • LITA
Kimball Jane A. • Social Sciences Clln Devel Coor. • University of California-Davis Library • Davis, CA 95616 • ACRL
Kimball Judith A. • New Hampshire State Library • Concord, NH 03301 • LAMA
Kimball Margaret J. • Head, Special Collecttions • Stanford University • Stanford, CA 94305-6011 • ACRL
Kimball Tracey • Circulation Supervisor • College of Santa Fe Library • Santa Fe, NM 87501 • ACRL
Kimber Karen L. • Documents Librarian • Wright State University University Library • Dayton, OH 45435 • GODORT MAGERT
Kimberly Laura • AMIGOS Bibliographic Council,Inc. • Dallas, TX 75251-2104 • LITA CLENE
Kimble Alvin • President • JOAT Information • New York, NY 10017 • LITA
Kimble Valerie F. • Librarian • Mental Health Service of South Oklahoma • Ardmore, OK 73401
Kimbro Jo R. • Leander, TX 78641 • ACRL ALCTS LHRT LRRT MAGERT *Life*
Kimbrough Ginger C. • Grapeuine, TX 76051 • SRRT
Kimbrough W. J. • Edina, MN 55435
Kime Brigitte L. • Alexandria, LA 71303 • AASL
Kimmage Dennis A. • Librarian,Head of Reference • State University of New York at Plattsburgh (SUNY) • Plattsburgh, NY 12901 • ACRL
Kimmel Beth E. • Chicago, IL 60645-4303
Kimmel DeeAnne M. • Elementary School Librarian • Frankfort International School • Oberursel 1, Germany • AASL
Kimmel Emily R. • Head/Information Processing • University of Massachusetts Library • Amherst, MA 01003 • ACRL LAMA
Kimmel Lynn A. • Stevens T. Mason Middle School • Waterford, MI 48329 • AASL
Kimmel Margaret M. • Professor • University of Pittsburgh School of Library and Information Science • Pittsburgh, PA 15260 • AASL ALSC
Kimmel Sue C. • Greensboro, NC 27408 • AASL ALSC
Kimmel Terry L. • Roslyn, NY 11576
Kimmich Rosalind • Auburn, NY 13021 • ALTA
Kimsey Linda J. • Head,Cataloging Dept. • West Texas State University Cornette Library • Canyon, TX 79016-0748
Kimzey Ann C. • Associate Dean Technical Serv. • University of Houston Clear Lake Neumann Library • Houston, TX 77058
Kinard Amy Ellen • Reference Librarian • Jackson County Library System • Medford, OR 97501
Kincaid Anne • San Francisco Public Library • San Francisco, CA 94102 • RASD
Kinch Michael P. • Head,Reference Services • Oregon State University William Jasper Kerr Library • Corvallis, OR 97331-4501 • ACRL LAMA
Kinchla Julie A. • Reference/ILL • Winchester Public Library • Winchester, MA 01890
Kind Jule L • Indianpolis, IN 46256
Kindall Max R. • Librarian • Sparks High School Library • Sparks, NV 89431 • AASL
Kinder Jackie S. • Student • University of South Carolina College of Library & Information Science • Columbia, SC 29208 • ACRL
Kinder Katharine Miss • Littleton, CO 80123 • Continuing
Kinder Robin C. • Smith College William Allan Neilson Library • Northampton, MA 01063
Kindilien Maureen • Reference Librarian • Fairfield University Gustav & Dagmar Nyselius Library • Fairfield, CT 06430-7524 • RASD
Kindle Thomas G. • Student • San Jose State University Division of Library & Information Science • San Jose, CA 95192-0029
Kindraka Monica F. • Library Marketing Director • Nolo Press • Berkeley, CA 94710

Kindred Lou Mrs • Trustee • Mid-Continent Public Library • Independence, MO 64050 • ALTA

Kindrick Carolyn J. • Elementary Principal • Washington School • Mattoon, IL 61938 • AASL

Kindrick Lisa K. • Automation & Systems Librarian • University of New Mexico Medical Center Library • Albuquerque, NM 87131 • LITA

Kindschi Margaret L. • Librarian • Colona Grade School • Colona, IL 61241 • AASL

Kineen James P. • Trustee • Omaha Public Library • Omaha, NE 68102 • ALTA

King Alan S. • Corporate Librarian • Central Maine Power Corporation • Augusta, ME 04336 • LAMA LITA RASD

King Alma M. • Student • Wayne State University Library Science Program • Detroit, MI 48202 • AASL

King Amy A. • Athens, OH 45701

King Anita F. • Jacksonville, NC 28540 • AASL YALSA

King Ann Ivy • Branch Head • Jess Yancy Memorial Public Library • Bruce, MS 38915

King Beth F. • Coordinator of Clearinghouse • University of Mississippi • University, MS 38677 • ASCLA LITA

King Carol L. • Mamager, Collection Devlp • Denver Public Library • Denver, CO 80203-2165 • ALCTS

King Carol M. • Student • University of North Carolina Department of Library & Information Studies • Greensboro, NC 27412-5001

King Caroline • Kenneth Hall Elementary School • Spring Lake Park, MN 55432 • AASL ALSC

King Catharine • Director • Curry College Library • Milton, MA 02186 • ACRL ALCTS RASD

King Charles D. • Librarian • Kenton County Public Library • Covington, KY 41011 • RASD SORT

King Charles L. • Student • University of Hawaii School of Library & Information Studies • Honolulu, HI 96822 • AASL RASD CLENE NMRT SRRT

King Chris C. Ms. • Allen High School Library • Allen, TX 75002 • AASL

King Christine E. • Associate Librarian • State University of New York (SUNY) Frank Melville Jr. Memorial Library • Stony Brook, NY 11794-3300 • ACRL

King Christine H. • Assistant Director • Atlantic City Free Public Library • Atlantic City, NJ 08401 • LAMA PLA

King Claire A. • Davis, CA 95616

King Cornelia S. • Rare Book Cataloger • Free Library of Philadelphia • Philadelphia, PA 19103 • ACRL ALCTS

King Cynthia • Fresno, CA 93705 • ALSC

King Dana L. • Niles Community Library • Niles, MI 49120

King David E. • Librarian • Standard Education Corp. • Chicago, IL 60606

King Diane M. • Ft. Lauderdale, FL 33312 • ACRL IFRT SRRT

King Dixie L. • Bartlesville, OK 74006

King Donald E. • Student • University of Iowa School of Library & Information Science • Iowa City, IA 52242

King Donald R. • Associate Professor • Rutgers University School of Commun Info & Library Studies • New Brunswick, NJ 08903 • LITA

King Donald W. • Student • University of Pittsburgh School of Library and Information Science • Pittsburgh, PA 15260 • AASL IFRT SRRT

King Dorothy T. • Librarian/ Special Collector • East Hampton Library • East Hampton, NY 11937

King Ebba Kraar • Reference Librarian • Melbourne Public Library • Melbourne, FL 32901 • PLA RASD GODORT

King Eileen F. • West Hartford Public Library Julia Faxon Branch • West Hartford, CT 06110

King Elizabeth L. • Greene, NY 13778 • AASL ALSC *Continuing*

King Emily • News • Pointe Coupee Parish Library • New Road, LA 70760 • ALTA

King Evelyn M. • College Station, TX 77842 • ACRL IFRT

King Florence L. Miss • Horseheads, NY 14845 • Continuing

King Frederick D. • American Library Association Washington Office • Washington, DC 20002 • LITA

King Gail O. • Asian Studies Bibl/Cura Asian Cl • Brigham Young University Harold B. Lee Library • Provo, UT 84602 • ACRL

King Geffry B. • Acquistions Librarian • Labat-Anderson Incorporated EPA/OTS Chemical Library • Washington, DC 20460 • ALCTS RASD FLRT

King Gennice W. • School Librarian • L.B. Landry Junior-Senior High School Library • New Orleans, LA 70114 • AASL ACRL

King Geraldine Dr. • Associate Director • Ramsey County Public Library • Shoreview, MN 55126 • RASD

King Hannah M. • F-T, Assistant • State University of New York Health Science Center Library • Syracuse, NY 13210 • ALCTS LITA GODORT

King Jack • University Librarian • Hamline University Bush Memorial Library • Saint Paul, MN 55104 • ACRL LAMA

King Jae Luree • Librarian • Mother Whiteside Memorial Library • Grants, NM 87020

King James L. • Managing Librarian • King County Library System • Seattle, WA 98109-5191

King JoAnn C. • Carleton Washburne School • Winnetka, IL 60093 • AASL ALCTS YALSA

King John W. • Associate Librarian • University of Maryland Hornbake Library • College Park, MD 20742 • ASCLA

King Joseph T. • Community College Librarian • San Jose City College • San Jose, CA 95128 • ACRL

King Josephine S. • Dir. of Inf. & Access Servs. • University of South Florida Library • Sarasota, FL 34243-2197 • ACRL

King Judith D. • Reference Librarian • Hartford Public Library • Hartford, CT 06103-3003 • SRRT

King Judith L. • School Librarian • Galena Park Middle Street • Galena Park, TX 77547 • AASL LIRT

King Judith M. • Library Media Specialist • Martin L. King Jr. Intermediate School • Germantown, MD 20876 • AASL

King Kamla J. • Corporate Librarian • Bureau of National Affairs Inc. • Washington, DC 20037 • ACRL ALCTS LITA RASD FLRT GODORT

King Kenneth • Farmington Hills, MI 48331 • PLA

King Kenneth E. Jr. • Coor., Bibliographic Control • University Microfilms International • Ann Arbor, MI 48106-1346 • ALCTS LITA

King Ladonis J. • Redington Shores, FL 33708 • PLA RASD *Life*

King Linda D. • Chicago, IL 60649

King Lucinda • Honolulu, HI 96822 • Continuing

King Marcia • Director • Kings Associates • Tucson, AZ 85743 • LAMA PLA

King Marion May • Elyria, OH 44035 • LAMA PLA *Continuing*

King Martha L. • Head, Technical Services • Plainfield Public Library • Plainfield, NJ 07060 • LITA

King Martha W. • Media Specialist • Parchment School District Kalamazoo County • Parchment, MI 49004 • AASL

King Mary K. • Regional Librarian • Western Massachusetts Regional Library System • Hatfield, MA 01038

King Mary M. • Atlantic Beach, FL 32233

King Mathew G. • Director, Books ofr Asia • Asia Foundation • San Francisco, CA 94103

King Mimi • Head of Reference • University of Wisconsin-Eau Claire William D. McIntyre Library • Eau Claire, WI 54702 • ACRL LITA LIRT

King Monique A. • Children's Librarian • Solano County Library John F. Kennedy Branch • Vallejo, CA 94590 • ALSC

King Muriel Y. • Honolulu, HI 96825

King Naomi • Librarian • Lathrop High School • Fairbanks, AK 99701 • AASL

King Natalie S. • Wayne State University Vera P. Shiffman Medical Library • Detroit, MI 48201 • ACRL ALCTS

King Peggy L. • Adult Reference Librarian • Chula Vista Public Library • Chula Vista, CA 91910 • RASD

King Rhonda • Library Media Specialist • Cherry Valley-Springfield Central School • Cherry Valley, NY 13320 • AASL NMRT

King Rhonda A. • Librarian • Charles W. Longer Elementary School • Hollidaysburg, PA 16648 • AASL

King Richard L. • Reference Librarian • Vincennes University Shake Learning Resources Library • Vincennes, IN 47591 • ACRL

King Robert B. • Coordinator Library • Albany Memorial School of Nsq. • Albany, NY 12204 • ASCLA

King Robert J. • Librarian • La Salle High School • Cedar Rapids, IA 52405 • AASL LITA

King Ruth C. • Librarian • Howard Elementary School • APO Miami, FL 34001 • AASL

King Ruth Sanborn • Henniker, NH 03242 • Continuing

King Susan T. • Children's Librarian • Harris County Public Library Bear Creek Branch • Houston, TX 77084 • ALSC

King Suzanne P. • Uncle Remus Regional Library System • Madison, GA 30650

King Terence K. • State University of New York College at New Paltz Sojourner Truth Library • New Paltz, NY 12561 • ACRL ALCTS LITA

King Thelma R. • Elmira, NY 14904 • Continuing

King Thomas L. • Science Library • State University of New York at Binghamton Libraries (SUNY) • Binghamton, NY 13902-6012 • ACRL MAGERT

King Trina E. • Indexer • H. W. Wilson Company • Bronx, NY 10452 • ALCTS ILERT

King Valery G. • Oregon State University William Jasper Kerr Library • Corvallis, OR 97331-4501

King Willard B. Mrs • Reidsville, NC 27323 • SRRT *Continuing*

King William H. • Information Specialist • North Carolina Department of Cultural Resources State Library • Raleigh, NC 27601-2807

Kingery Victor Rev • Librarian • Quincy College Brenner Library • Quincy, IL 62301-2699 • AASL ACRL ALCTS ALSC RASD IFRT

Kingsbery Evelyn B. • Library Director • Southwest Texas Junior College Will C Miller Memorial Library • Uvalde, TX 78801-6297

Kingsbury Mary E. • Professor • University of North Carolina at Chapel Hill School of Information and Library Science • Chapel Hill, NC 27599-3360 • ALSC

Kingsbury Patrick • Library Automation Analyst • University of Kansas • Lawrence, KS 66045-2121

Kingsley Diane A. • Librarian • Kenneth C. Coombs School • Mashpee, MA 02649

Kingsley Eleanor V. • President • Jackson Manufacturers Company Inc. Kingsley Library Equipment Co. • Pomona, CA 91769

Kingsley Marcia S. • Head of Acquisitions/Serials • Western Michigan University Libraries Dwight B. Waldo Library • Kalamazoo, MI 49008 • ALCTS

Kingston Jo Ann • Grand Blanc, MI 48439 • YALSA

Kingston Mary Lynn • Pittsburgh Regional Library Center • Pittsburgh, PA 15221 • ALCTS

Kingston MaryAnn • School Library Media Specalist • Abbott Union Free School District • Irvington, NY 10533 • AASL

Kinley Sharon • Research Specialist • Lummi Library • Bellingham, WA 98226 • ACRL EMIERT IFRT LRRT

Kinne Karla M. • Library Media Specialist • Schweinfurt American School • APO, AE 09033 • AASL ALSC LIRT

Kinne Linda E. • Librarian • School District #25 High School Media Center • Riverton, WY 82501 • AASL *Life*

Kinne Martha B. • Student • San Jose State University Division of Library & Information Science • San Jose, CA 95192-0029 • RASD

Kinneary Marie K. • Student • Queens College Graduate School of Library & Information Studies • Flushing, NY 11367 • AASL ALSC LITA RASD IFRT LRRT SRRT

Kinnebrew Rick • Children's Librarian • Niles Public Library • Niles, IL 60648

Kinnersley Ruth T. • ILL Librarian • Lubbock City-County Library • Lubbock, TX 79401

Kinney Daniel W. • Assistant Head, Cataloging Dept. • State University of New York (SUNY) Frank Melville Jr. Memorial Library • Stony Brook, NY 11794-3300 • ACRL ALCTS LHRT

Kinney Janet S. • Director • College of Saint Catherine • Saint Paul, MN 55105 • ACRL LAMA

Kinney Karen • Asst Univ Ln, Public Serv. • San Diego State University Library • San Diego, CA 92119-2120 • ACRL LAMA RASD

Kinney Margaret M. • Chief Librarian • U S Veterans Affairs Medical Center Library • Bronx, NY 10468 • ASCLA

Kinney Michael F. • Milwaukee Public Library Llewellyn Branch • Milwaukee, WI 53207 • PLA

Kinney Molly • Doctural Student • University of Pittsburgh School of Library and Information Science • Pittsburgh, PA 15260 • ALSC

Kinney Ruth • Monmouth, IL 61462 • Continuing

Kinney Thomas E. • Gainesville, FL 32611 • ACRL LAMA LITA GODORT LRRT

Kinnison Luella • Director • Weld County Library District • Greeley, CO 80631 • LAMA PLA

Kinsey Frank E. Jr • Chatham, MA 02633 • AASL ALCTS *Life*

Kinsey Jacqueline A. • Rosenberg Library Adult Services • Galveston, TX 77550

Kinsinger Patti L. • Library Coordinator • Wilmington College Watson Library • Wilmington, OH 45177 • ASCLA EMIERT

Kinsler Don • Manager • Grandma's Bookshelf • Dayton, OH 45415

Kintz Robert L. • Brighton, MA 02135 • ACRL

Kinyon William R. • Assistant Department Head • Georgia State University Pullen Library • Atlanta, GA 30303-3081 • ACRL RASD

Kinzer Kathryn P. • Librarian • Saint John's College Library • Annapolis, MD 21404

Kinzey Trilby Taylor • Reference Librarian • Bergen Community Coll • Paramus, NJ 07652

Kinzler Cathy • William Fox Elementary School • Richmond, VA 23220-3497 • AASL

Kipp Laurence J. • Librarian • Harvard University Library Baker Library • Boston, MA 02163 • Continuing

Kirbawy Barbara L. • Director • Barberton Public Library • Barberton, OH 44203-2458

Kirby Barbara R. • Asst. Tech. Servs. Adm. • Miami-Dade Public Library System • Miami, FL 33130-1504 • PLA

Kirby Colleen M. • Technical Services Librarian • South Dakota State Library • Pierre, SD 57501-2294

Kirby Connie A. • Assistant Documents Librarian • Oklahoma State University Library • Stillwater, OK 74078-0375

Kirby Frederick John • Director • Benton Harbor Public Library • Benton Harbor, MI 49022 • LAMA PLA

Kirby Sharon R. • Knox College Henry W. Seymour Library • Galesburg, IL 61402 • ACRL

Kirch Kathy • Circulation Librarian • Cadillac-Wexford Public Library • Cadillac, MI 49601-0700 • PLA

Kircheis Erma N. • Reference Librarian • Kent County Library System • Grand Rapids, MI 49503 • RASD

Kircher Clara J. • Hyattsville, MD 20782 • AASL YALSA
Continuing

Kircher Pamela • Online Computer Library Center (OCLC) • Dublin, OH 43017-3395

Kircher Rene Cox • Urbana Free Library • Urbana, IL 61801-3283

Kirchgraber Nancy B. • Belleville, IL 62220

Kirchhof Ann • Trustee • Denver Public Library • Denver, CO 80203-2165 • ALTA PLA

Kirchner Bette L. • Information Officer • South Pacific Forum Fisheries Agency • Honiara, Solomon Islands

Kirchner James R. • Student • University of Maryland College of Library and Information Services • College Park, MD 20742-4345 • ACRL

Kirchner Mandy L. • Librarian • Iowa Department of Commerce • Des Moines, IA 50319

Kire Kathy J. • Allston, MA 02134 • ACRL ERT LIRT

Kirk-Thornton M. Hope • Student • University of Southern Mississippi School of Library Science • Hattiesburg, MS 39406-5146

Kirk Artemis M. G. • Director • Simmons College Beatley Library • Boston, MA 02115 • ACRL LAMA

Kirk David D. • Student • San Jose State University Division of Library & Information Science • San Jose, CA 95192-0029

Kirk Deborah • Library Media Coordinator • Weld County School District 6 • Greeley, CO 80631 • AASL

Kirk Elizabeth E. • Student • Brown University John Hay Library, Box A • Providence, RI 02912

Kirk Jay H. • Head of Science Library • Marquette University • Milwaukee, WI 53233 • ACRL ALCTS

Kirk Karen E. • Des Plaines, IL 60016-6536

Kirk Peggy • Utica, KS 67584

Kirk Ruth M. • Seattle, WA 98125 • ACRL RASD IFRT
Continuing

Kirk Sarah F. • Oak Knoll Elementary School • East Point, GA 30344 • AASL ALSC

Kirk Sherwood • Executive Director • Western Illinois Library System • Galesburg, IL 61401 • ASCLA LAMA PLA GODORT SRRT

Kirk Thomas • College Librarian • Berea College Hutchins Library • Berea, KY 40404 • ACRL

Kirkby Arthur M. • Norfolk, VA 23507 • Continuing

Kirkegard Mary Joan • Student • Saint John's University Division of Library & Information Science • Jamaica, NY 11439

Kirkendall H R. • Cataloger • Genealogical Society of Utah • Salt Lake City, UT 84150 • ACRL ALCTS LAMA LITA RASD

Kirkham Phebe • Hd, Inf & Readers' Services • New Canaan Library • New Canaan, CT 06840 • RASD

Kirking Clayton • Director of Librarian • Phoenix Art Museum • Phoenix, AZ 85004-1685

Kirkland Janice J. • Coor. of Bibliographic Control • California State University • Bakersfield, CA 93311 • ACRL

Kirkland Jean • Head Dept of Microforms • Georgia Institute of Technology • Atlanta, GA 30332 • ACRL RASD

Kirkland Kenneth L. • Collection Development Coor. • DePaul University • Chicago, IL 60614 • ACRL ALCTS GODORT

Kirkland Ruth • Reference Librarian • Hackley Public Library • Muskegon, MI 49440

Kirkpatrick Brett A. • Director of Library Services • University of Texas Medical Branch Moody Medical Library • Galveston, TX 77555-1035 • ACRL ALCTS LITA

Kirkpatrick Elizabeth M. • Assistant Librarian • Wethersfield Public Library • Wethersfield, CT 06109

Kirkpatrick Jane E. • Chief Executive Officer • Stratford Public Library • Stratford ON, N5A 1A2 Canada • LAMA PLA

Kirkpatrick Linda J. • Media Specialist • Lakeside Junior High School • Orange Park, FL 32073

Kirkpatrick Margaret L. • Elementary Librarian • Unified School District 259 • Wichita, KS 67204 • AASL ALSC YALSA

Kirkpatrick Melba L. • Library Head • Metropolitan Library System in Oklahoma Southern Oaks Branch • Oklahoma City, OK 73139-7299

Kirkpatrick Sandy • Benicia, CA 94510 • ALSC

Kirkpatrick Stephen H. • Head Reference Librarian • State University of New York (SUNY) College at Old Westbury Library • Old Westbury, NY 11568 • ACRL IFRT

Kirkpatrick Teresa E. • Student • University of Washington Graduate School of Library and Information Science • Seattle, WA 98195 • ALCTS

Kirks James H. Jr. • Coordinator • North State Coop. Library System • Willows, CA 95988 • LITA PLA

Kirkwood Sonya A. • Reference Librarian • Sinclair Community College Learning Resource Center • Dayton, OH 45402-1421 • LAMA LITA RASD LIRT

Kirley Michael D. • Librarian III • Los Angeles Public Library • Los Angeles, CA 90071 • RASD

Kirsch Gerald P. • Senior Assistant Librarian • State University of New York Agricultural & Technical College • Cobleskill, NY 12043 • RASD ILERT

Kirsch Judith L. • Wyandotte, MI 48192

Kirsch Robert • Library Director • Lake Forest High School • Lake Forest, IL 60045 • AASL

Kirschbaum Doris • Branch Manager • Prince George's County Memorial Library System Beltsville Branch • Beltsville, MD 20705 • SRRT

Kirschenbaum Arthur S. • Edmonds, WA 98020 • ALTA

Kirschenbaum Athalie • Edmonds, WA 98020 • ALTA

Kirschenheiter Frank • General Manager • K B I Enterprises • Antioch, IL 60002 • LITA

Kirschner Sue Ellen • Roseville, MN 55113

Kirschner Susan M • Reference Department • Miami-Dade Public Library System West Dade Regional Library • Miami, FL 33165 • PLA

Kirven Talma Sheila D. • School Librarian • Shaker Junior High School • Latham, NY 12110

Kirwan William J. • University Librarian • Western Carolina University Hunter Library • Cullowhee, NC 28723-9002 • ACRL LAMA

Kirwin Kathy A. • Forest Preserve District of Du Page County • Glen Ellyn, IL 60138 • ALCTS ILERT NMRT

Kisby Cynthia M. • Librarian • Morton Plant Hospital • Clearwater, FL 34617

Kisch Nora F. • Greenwood Publishing Group • Westport, CT 06881 • ACRL ERT

Kiser Betsy N. • Users Council Coordinator • OCLC Online Computer Library Center • Dublin, OH 43017-3395

Kiser Edwin L. • Denton, TX 76201

Kiser Nagiko Sato • Senior Librarian Prof. Library • Camarillo State Hospital & Developmental Center • Camarillo, CA 93011-6022

Kiser Sharon S. • Media Specialist • Osterholz High School • APO, AE 09272-0005 • AASL

Kish Andrea J. • Community Library Manager • Los Angeles County Library Canyon Country Branch • Canyon Country, CA 91351 • ALSC

Kish Mary C. • Reference Circulation Librarian • Monroe County Community College Library • Monroe, MI 48161 • ACRL RASD
Life

Kishibe Kaye • Head of Technical Services • Toronto Public Library • Toronto ON, Canada

Kislitzin Elizabeth • Librarian • University of California-Berkeley University Library • Berkeley, CA 94720 • ACRL RASD

Kisor Deborah A. • Haven Middle School • Evanston, IL 60201 • AASL

Kiss Helen T. • Chief Librarian • Fort McPherson Library • Ft. McPherson, GA 30330

Kiss Marian S. • Melbourne, FL 32940

Kissane Emily C. • Student • Gustavus Adolphus College Folke Bernadotte Memorial Library • St Peter, MN 56082

Kissel Elaine L. • Librarian • Saint Joseph Mercy Hospital • Pontiac, MI 48341-2985 • ASCLA

Kissel Francis Rev. • Marist School • Atlanta, GA 30319

Kissinger Patricia M. • Warrenville, IL 60555 • ACRL RASD

Kissner Ellen L. • Hamden, CT 06517 • ACRL ALCTS LITA LIRT

Kistenmacher Pat Dr. • Saint Thomas Aquinas High School • Ft. Lauderdale, FL 33310 • AASL

Kister Mark A. • Student • Kent State University School of Library & Information Science • Kent, OH 44242-0001 • ACRL SRRT

Kistner Glen A. • Reference Librarian • Northeastern Illinois University Library • Chicago, IL 60625 • ACRL ALTA PLA

Kitch Richard D. • Librarian • Joslin Diabetes Center,Inc. Medical Library • Boston, MA 02115 • ACRL

Kitchens Christine • Evergreen, CO 80439

Kitchens Larry E. • Dir of Instructional Serivces • Texas Christian University Center for Instructional Services • Fort Worth, TX 76129 • AASL

Kitchens Rhonda K. • Dover, FL 33527 • PLA IFRT SRRT

Kitover Jordan C. • Lincolnwood, IL 60645

Kitrosser Joan Tinley • School Library Media Spec. • Alexandria City School District • Alexandria, VA 22302 • AASL

Kittel Dorothy Ann • Librarian Extension Specialist • United States Department of Education Office of Educational Res & Improvement • Washington, DC 20208-5571 • Life

Kitterer Carolyn A. • Media Specialist • American Cooperative School • La Paz, Bolivia • AASL

Kittilson Bruce J. Dr • Hosterman Middle School • New Hope, MN 55428 • AASL LITA
Life

Kitts Murray • Orleans ON, K1C 4P1 Canada • AASL

Kjeldsen Nancy • Library Media Teacher • Sierra/Pacific Library • Stockton, CA 95207 • AASL

Klaas Janet E. • Reference Librarian • Ames Public Library • Ames, IA 50010 • GODORT

Kladder Jerianne S. • Columbus, OH 43206 • ALSC

Klaessig Janet • Reference Librarian • Delaware Valley College Sci & Agr Krauskopf Memorial Library • Doylestown, PA 18901

Klaiber David J. • Head Catalog Dept • Minneapolis Public Library & Information Center • Minneapolis, MN 55401-1992 • ALCTS LITA

Klaiber Diane Reed • Lebanon, NJ 08833-9307

Klair Arlene • Head, Catalog Management Dept. • University of Maryland College Park Theodore R. McKeldin Library • College Park, MD 20742-7011 • ALCTS LITA

Klais Madge • Sherman Middle School • Madison, WI 53704 • AASL

Klamm Judith E. • Kansas City Public Library • Kansas City, MO 64106

Klamroth Susan H. • Student • Florida State University School of Library and Information Studies • Tallahassee, FL 32306-2048

Klansky Coleen E. • Hamden, CT 06514

Klappersack Dennis • Director of Libraries • Houston Community College • Houston, TX 77004 • ACRL

Klapthor Robert W. • Science Librarian • Wittenberg University Thomas Library • Springfield, OH 45501 • ACRL RASD LIRT

Klasing Jane P. • Director • School Board of Broward County Learning Resources Department • Fort Lauderdale, FL 33312-7533 • AASL

Klassen JoAnn E. • Library/Media Specialist • Cedaroak Elementary School • West Linn, OR 97068-0100 • AASL ALSC

Klassen Robert • Dir. Public Library Supp. Staff • United States Department of Education Office of Educational Res & Improvement • Washington, DC 20208-5571 • ACRL ASCLA LAMA

Klath Nancy S. • Princeton, NJ 08540 • ACRL LAMA LITA

Klatt Melvin J. • Librarian • Elmhurst College A. C. Buehler Library • Elmhurst, IL 60126 • ACRL LAMA ERT

Klatzkin Elizabeth Mrs • Trustee • Bucks County Free Library • Doylestown, PA 18901 • ALTA

Klauber Julie B. • Administrator-Outreach Services • Suffolk Cooperative Library System • Bellport, NY 11713 • ASCLA

Klaus Fred • Trustee • Elk Grove Village Public Library • Elk Grove Village, IL 60007

Klaus Jo Anne • Library Media Specialist • Mount Scott Elementary School • Portland, OR 97266 • AASL

Klause Annette Curtis • Head, Children's Services • Montgomery County Public Library Kensington Park • Kensington, MD 20895 • ALSC YALSA

Klausmeier Arno M. • Milwaukee, WI 53213-2741

Klauss Rainer • Lake Lanier Regional Library Lawrenceville Branch • Lawrenceville, GA 30245-4707

Klavano Ann M. • Reference Librarian • Mercy College Libraries • Dobbs Ferry, NY 10522 • SRRT

Klawitter Michael J. • Student • University of Wisconsin-Milwaukee School of Library & Information Science • Milwaukee, WI 53201

Klebs Elmer A. • Library of Congress • Washington, DC 20541 • ALCTS ALSC IFRT

Klecka Florence • Cataloger • University of Notre Dame Kresge Law Library • Notre Dame, IN 46556

Klecker Anita N. • Medical Librarian • Torrance Memorial Medical Center • Torrance, CA 90505

Klee Edward Lee • Training Consultant • Kentucky State University Governmental Services Center • Frankfort, KY 40601 • ASCLA LAMA PLA

Klehn Victoria L. • Coordinating Librarian • Sterling Municipal Library • Baytown, TX 77520 • RASD

Kleiman Allan M. • Chief Servs to the Aging • Brooklyn Public Library Service to the Aging (SAGE) • Brooklyn, NY 11229 • ALSC ASCLA PLA RASD EMIERT IRRT SRRT

Kleiman Rhoda E. Dr. • Staff Developer-Library Media • Office of Manhattan Superintendent of High Schools • New York, NY 10023 • AASL IFRT

Klein Agatha L. • San Diego, CA 92128 • PLA IFRT   Life

Klein Barbara • Director, Mkt Research Ctr • Digital Equipment Corporation • Marlboro, MA 01752 • ACRL

Klein Barbara H. • Corona Del Mar, CA 92625

Klein Cheryl S. • Student • University of North Carolina at Chapel Hill School of Information and Library Science • Chapel Hill, NC 27599-3360 • AASL

Klein Deborah S. • Pomona Valley Hospital Medical Center Library • Pomona, CA 91767

Klein Denise • Student • University of Oklahoma School of Library & Information Studies • Norman, OK 73019 • ALSC

Klein Gary M. • Librarian • University of Toledo William S. Carlson Library • Toledo, OH 43606-3399 • ACRL RASD LIRT SRRT

Klein Kay • Media Specialist • Bedford Memorial School • Bedford, NH 03102 • AASL

Klein Leah • Chicago, IL 60640 • Continuing

Klein Lori J. • Reference Librarian • National Library of Medicine • Bethesda, MD 20894 • RASD FLRT

Klein Mary E. • Oshkosh, WI 54904 • AASL

Klein Mindy F. • Consultant • Klein Information Management • Houston, TX 77096 • ILERT

Klein Miriam B. • Cleveland Heights, OH 44118

Klein Pamela P. • Business Inf. Center Manager • Senco Products Inc. Business Development • Cincinnati, OH 45244 • LITA

Klein Pamela S. • Student • San Jose State University Division of Library & Information Science • San Jose, CA 95192-0029

Klein Pauline • DeKalb County Public Library Wesley Chapel Branch • Decatur, GA 30034 • ACRL SRRT

Klein Phyllis H. • Technical Service Librarian • Skagit Valley College • Mount Vernon, WA 98273 • ACRL

Klein Rhona • Librarian • Portland State University Library • Portland, OR 97207 • ACRL

Klein Robert • Trustee • Elmhurst Public Library • Elmhurst, IL 60126 • ALTA PLA

Klein Ronnie • Assistant Reference Librarian • Framingham State College Henry Whittemore Library • Framingham, MA 01701 • ACRL

Klein Sami W. • Chief Research Inf Serv • National Institute of Standards & Technology • Gaithersburg, MD 20899 • LITA FLRT

Klein Stephen C. • Assistant Library Adminstrator • County of Los Angeles Public Library South County Region 500 • Norwalk, CA 90650 • PLA SRRT

Klein Susan R. • Chief Librarian • Sturgis Library • Barnstable, MA 02630 • ALCTS LAMA PLA RASD

Kleinberg Deborah H. • Student • Long Island University Palmer School of Library & Information Science • Greenvale, NY 11548 • AASL IFRT SRRT

Kleinburd Freda • Riverdale, NY 10471 • ALSC

Kleindienst Juedi S. • North Carolina State University • Raleigh, NC 27695

Kleiner Jane P. • Head, Reference Services • Louisiana State University Libraries • Baton Rouge, LA 70803 • ACRL RASD

Kleinman Eve R. • Student • University of Texas at Austin Graduate School of Library & Information Sciences • Austin, TX 78712-1276 • ACRL

Kleinschmidt Bruce L. • Reference Librarian • University of Texas Tarlton Law Library • Austin, TX 78705-5799

Kleinschmidt Lynnea • Supervising Librarian • Richmond Public Library • Richmond, CA 94804 • ALCTS

Klekowski Lynn M. • Coor. of Suburban Campus Libs. • DePaul University Suburban Campus Libraries • Westchester, IL 60154 • ACRL

Klement Judith A. • School Librarian • East Dover School • Dover, NJ 07801 • AASL

Klement Susan P. • Tucson, AZ 85751 • ILERT

Klemperer Katharina E. • Director of Library Automation • Dartmouth College Library Baker Memorial Library • Hanover, NH 03755-3525 • LITA

Klene Joanne M. • Willowbrook, IL 60514

Klenk Anne S. • Denver, CO 80220

Klenk Dolores R. • Student • State University of New York (SUNY) School of Information & Library Studies • Buffalo, NY 14260

Klenklen Jonathan A. • Acquisitions Specialist • Catholic University of America John K. Mullen of Denver Memorial Library • Washington, DC 20064 • ALCTS NMRT

Klepper Miriam J. • Librarian II • North Babylon Public Library • North Babylon, NY 11703

Kleptach Sharon M. • Technical Services • Jefferson County Public Library Library Service Center • Wheat Ridge, CO 80033 • ACRL ALCTS

Klett Rex E. • Library Director • Hampton B. Allen Library • Wadesboro, NC 28170

Kleven Lillie M. • Walnut Creek, CA 94595 • IRRT

Klevorn Thomas G. • Manager of Conversion Serv. • Data Research Associates Inc. • Saint Louis, MO 63132 • LITA

Klimek Robert F. • Managing Attorney • Klimek & Richiardi, Ltd. • Arlington Heights, IL 60005 • ACRL

Klimley S. • Geology Librarian • Lamont Doherty Geological Observatory • Palisades, NY 10964 • ACRL MAGERT

Klimowicz Judith A. • Assistant Director • Cranford Public Library • Cranford, NJ 07016 • ALSC

Klinck Cynthia A. • Director • Washington Township Public Library • Centerville, OH 45459 • LAMA PLA

Klinck Patricia E. • State Librarian • Vermont Department of Libraries • Montpelier, VT 05609 • ASCLA LAMA LITA PLA

Kline Candace W. • Library Assistant/Reference • Hutchinson Public Library • Hutchinson, KS 67501 • RASD NMRT

Kline Eve • Friedens, PA 15541

Kline George A. • Documents Specialist • Toledo-Lucas County Public Library • Toledo, OH 43624 • PLA GODORT

Kline Gerald M. • President • Innovative Interfaces, Inc. • Berkeley, CA 94710 • LITA

Kline Linda L. • Childern's Librarian • Newport Beach Public Library • Newport Beach, CA 92660 • ALSC YALSA

Kline Mary Alice • Children's Librarian • Rogers-Hough Memorial Library • Rogers, AR 72756 • ALSC

Kline Nancy M. • Research & Info. Services Dept. • University of Connecticut Homer Babbidge Library • Storrs, CT 06269-1005 • ACRL LITA RASD

Kline Norman C. • President • CASPR, Inc • Cupertino, CA 95014 • LITA

Kline Peggy S. • Decatur, GA 30030 • ALCTS

Kline Sandra A. • Media Specialist • Union Academy • Bartow, FL 33830 • AASL

Kline Vickie L. • Head of Technical Services • York College of Pennsylvania Schmidt Library • York, PA 17403 • ALCTS LITA

Kline Victoria E. • Pasadena, CA 91106-3843

Klinefelter P. Anne • Law Student • University of Alabama • Tuscaloosa, AL 35487-0266

Kling Lisa L. • Associate Director • Union County Public Library • Monroe, NC 28110

Kling Susan • Director • Marion Carnegie Library • Marion, IA 52302 • PLA

Klingberg Susan • Librarian • San Jose State University Clark Library • San Jose, CA 95192-0028 • ACRL LAMA RASD

Klingeman David J. • Librarian • Saint Johns University Alcuin Library • Collegeville, MN 56321-7155 • GODORT

Klinger Marvin J. • Student • University of Wisconsin School of Library & Information Studies • Madison, WI 53706

Klingerman Ethel • Director • Moorestown Library • Moorestown, NJ 08057 • LAMA PLA   Life

Klingle Philip • Senior Law Librarian • Supreme Court Library Richmond County Court House • Staten Island, NY 10301

Klingler Catherine • Edison, NJ 08817 • Continuing

Klingler Thomas E. • Head, Reference Dept. • University of Akron • Akron, OH 44325-1707 • ACRL LAMA LITA RASD GODORT IFRT

Klink LaRene • Genesee Schools • Genesee, MI 48437 • AASL

Klinkow Margaret G. • Director of Research Center • F.L. Wright Home & Studio Foundation • Oak Park, IL 60302 • ACRL LAMA LRRT

Klionsky Martha K. • Asst to Dir for Facilties Serv • State University of New York at Binghamton Libraries (SUNY) • Binghamton, NY 13902-6012 • LAMA

Klipsch Pamela R. • Youth Services Librarian • Hayner Public Library District • Alton, IL 62002 • PLA YALSA IFRT

Klipsch Sue A. • Technical Services Librarian • Knox County Public Library System • Knoxville, TN 37902-2505 • ALCTS

Klitzkie Ron • Random Lake High School • Random Lake, WI 53075 • AASL

Klob Priscilla • Student • University of Texas at Austin Graduate School of Library & Information Sciences • Austin, TX 78712-1276

Kloberdanz Eileen C. • Adult Services Librarian • Cook Memorial Library • Libertyville, IL 60048

Klobucar Christine K. • Chicago, IL 60633 • RASD

Klockenga Gary R. • Reference Coordinator • San Diego County Library Vista Branch • Vista, CA 92083-6686 • GODORT SRRT

Kloepper Daniel C. • Tech Svs. Libn/Automation • Starved Rock Library System • Ottawa, IL 61350 • LITA

Klofas-Hinger Ann Marie H. • Cataloger • Environmental Protection Agency EPA Region 10 Library • Seattle, WA 98101 • ALCTS

Klopfer Jerome J. • Library Media Specialist • New Mexico Military Inst • Roswell, NM 88201 • AASL LITA

Klor Ellin B. • Supervisor of Children's Servs. • Santa Clara Public Library • Santa Clara, CA 95051 • ALSC

Klos Patricia • Librarian Media Specialist • Robert McQueen High School • Reno, NV 89503 • AASL

Klos Shelia M. • Hd., Arch. & Allied Arts Lib. • University of Oregon • Eugene, OR 97403

Klossner Michael J. • Cataloger • Arkansas State Library • Little Rock, AR 72201 • ALCTS GODORT

Klostermann Helen • Head of Technical Services • Emporia State University William Allen White Library • Emporia, KS 66801 • ACRL ALCTS LITA GODORT

Kloswick John • Original Cataloging-Monographs • Michigan State University Libraries • East Lansing, MI 48824-1048 • ACRL ALCTS

Klotzberger Vera B. • Librarian • Page-Jackson Solar School • Charles Town, WV 25414 • AASL

Klotzbucher Enza I. • Ill Librarian • Widener University School of Law Library • Wilmington, DE 19803-0475 • ACRL

Klowden Molly A. • Elmhurst, IL 60126

Klucevsek Janet L. • Senior Adult Librarian • New York Public Library Branches Staten Island Borough Office • Staten Island, NY 10301 • RASD

Kluegel Kathleen • Reference Librarian • University of Illinois Library • Urbana, IL 61801 • ACRL RASD

Kluesner Marvin P. • Laurel, MD 20707

Klug Sharon A. • Student • State University of New York (SUNY) School of Information & Library Studies • Buffalo, NY 14260 • PLA SRRT

Klugkist A. C. • University Librarian • Bibliotheek Rijksuniversiteit • 9700 AN, Groningen, Netherlands • ACRL ALCTS LAMA LITA

Klumpp Geraldine • Student • Rutgers University School of Communication Information & Library Studies • New Brunswick, NJ 08903

Kluver Mary L. • King Science Center • Omaha, NE 68110 • AASL

Kmetz Brian P. • Trustee • Streator Public Library • Streator, IL 61364

Knab Sheryl L. • Student • State University of New York (SUNY) School of Information & Library Studies • Buffalo, NY 14260 • ACRL

Knachel Philip A. • Associate Director • Folger Shakespeare Library • Washington, DC 20003-1094 • ACRL ALCTS LAMA LITA RASD

Knape Anne S. • Tyler, TX 75701 • Continuing

Knapp Alice S. • Director • Canastota Public Library • Canastota, NY 13032 • PLA

Knapp Carolyn S. • Oakland, CA 94611

Knapp Caron E. • Student • John Carroll University Grasselli Library • University Heights, OH 44118

Knapp Karen M. • Student • State University of New York (SUNY) School of Information & Library Studies • Buffalo, NY 14260 • PLA

Knapp Leslie C. • Field Account Services Manager • EBSCO Subscription Services • Shrewsbury, NJ 07702-4321 • ACRL ALCTS

Knapp Mabel Jean • Librarian • Bala-Cynwyd Library • Bala Cynwyd, PA 19004-3095 • PLA RASD

Knapp Marilyn S. • Annandale, VA 22003 • AASL

Knapp Mary C. • Librarian I • Madison Public Library • Madison, WI 53703 • RASD SRRT

Knapp Peter J. • Hd, Ref & Instr Servs & Archv • Trinity College Library • Hartford, CT 06106 • ACRL RASD

Knapp Sara D. • Computer Search Service Coor • State University of New York (SUNY) University Libraries • Albany, NY 12222 • ACRL RASD IFRT

Knappman Edward W. • New England Publishing Associates • Chester, CT 06412 • RASD

Knaster Nanette • Putnam & Grosset Group • New York, NY 10016 • AASL ALSC YALSA

Knauer Kay L. • Assistant Director • Mead Public Library • Sheboygan, WI 53081

Knauer Wanda • Media Specialist • O'Dea Elementary School Media Center • Fort Collins, CO 80525

Knauff Elisabeth S. • Circuit Librarian • United States Court of Appeals Ninth Circuit Library • San Francisco, CA 94119-3939 • ALCTS RASD FLRT GODORT

Knauss Bonnie • William Jewell College Curry Library • Liberty, MO 64068

Knavel Brenda S. • Coordinator, Technical Services • University of Alaska Elmer E. Rasmuson Library • Fairbanks, AK 99775-1005 • ALCTS

Kneale Rosemary • Branch Manager • Cuyahoga County Public Library South Euclid-Lyndhurst Branch • South Euclid, OH 44121-4087 • LAMA PLA YALSA IFRT

Knecht Lou Wave S. • Librarian • National Library of Medicine • Bethesda, MD 20894 • Life

Knecht Margaret B. • Kansas State Historical Society Library • Topeka, KS 66612

Knecht Michael W. • Student • Emporia State University School of Library & Information Management • Emporia, KS 66801 • LAMA FLRT SRRT

Knee Millie • Trustee • West Des Moines Public Library • West Des Moines, IA 50265

Kneedler Carolyn W. • Librarian HS & Jr. H. • Washington Unified School District • West Sacramento, CA 95691

Kneedler William H. • Library Automation Coordinator • Phoenix Public Library • Phoenix, AZ 85004 • ALCTS LITA PLA

Knepel Nancy P. • Director • High Plains Regional Library Service System • Greeley, CO 80631 • ASCLA LAMA PLA YALSA

Knetzer Leean • Librarian • San Diego Jewish Academy • La Jolla, CA 96037

Knezek Kay N. • Librarian • Victoria High School • Victoria, TX 77901 • AASL YALSA

Knibbs Barbara L. • Unionville, CT 06085 • LITA

Knickerbocker Anne T. • University of Texas at Austin Graduate School of Library & Information Sciences • Austin, TX 78712-1276 • AASL ALSC

Knickerbocker Wendy • Rhode Island College James P. Adams Library • Providence, RI 02908 • ACRL ALCTS

Knieriem Kathryn L. • Student • Lane Public Library Fairfield Branch • Fairfield, OH 45014 • PLA RASD YALSA

Knierim Mark R. • Student • University of California-Berkeley School of Library & Information Studies • Berkeley, CA 94720

Knifer Kay L. • Librarian • Boulder Public Library • Boulder, CO 80306 • ALCTS

Kniffel Leonard • Managing Editor • American Library Association • Chicago, IL 60611-2795

Kniffin Lisa A. • Student • University of Arizona • Tucson, AZ 85721 • PLA IFRT SRRT

Kniffin Nancy I. • Assistant Library Director • Asheville-Buncombe Library System • Asheville, NC 28801

Knight Anna M. • Librarian • Louis Pizitz Middle School • Vestavia Hills, AL 35216

Knight Anne F. • Coordinator for Research Svs • Birmingham Public Library • Birmingham, AL 35203 • PLA

Knight C J. • Roundlake, IL 60073 • Continuing

Knight Diane M. • Librarian • Carl Sundahl School • Folsom, CA 95630

Knight Frances Y. • Burbank Elementary School • Belmont, MA 02178 • AASL ALSC

Knight Janice R. • Branch Library • Boston Public Library Codman Square Branch • Dorchester, MA 02124-3598 • ALSC

Knight Joan • Regional Librarian • Vermont Department of Libraries SE Regional Library-R D 1 • Brattleboro, VT 05301 • PLA

Knight Joanne E. • San Bernardino County Library Barstow Branch • Barstow, CA 92311 • PLA

Knight Judy N. • Media Specialist • Culbreth Junior High School • Chapel Hill, NC 27514 • AASL YALSA

Knight Julie L. • Media Specialist • Fairington Elementary School • Decatur, GA 30038

Knight Linda • Unionville ON, L3R 2P9 Canada • AASL

Knight Lorrie A. • Norwich, CT 06360

Knight Margaret L. • Lindenwood, IL 61049 • AASL
Continuing

Knight Nancy • Toronto ON, M4W 1V5 Canada • Continuing

Knight Nancy Hoyt • Dir of Product Mgmt • Silver Platter Information • Arlington, VA 22201 • ACRL LITA   *Life*

Knight Rebecca C. • University of Delaware Library • Newark, DE 19717-5267 • GODORT

Knight Rita Cecilia • Principal Catalog Librarian • University of Arizona Library • Tucson, AZ 85721 • ALCTS

Knight Susan J. • Media Resource Teacher • Northeast High School • Kansas City, MO 64124 • AASL

Knight Wanda • Systems Manager • Claremont Colleges Libraries Honnold/Mudd Library • Claremont, CA 91711

Knightly John J. • Records Management Specialist • Performance Development Corporation • Oak Ridge, TN 37830 • ACRL RASD   *Life*

Knights Sheila • Librarian • San Francisco State University J. Paul Leonard Library • San Francisco, CA 94132

Knipe Nancy N. • Head of Technical Services • Colorado College Tutt Library • Colorado Springs, CO 80903 • ACRL

Knipe Susan M. • Camano Island, WA 98292 • ALSC

Knippel Ronald R. • Librarian • Brookfield Public Library • Brookfield, WI 53005

Kniss Bonnie Miss • APO San Francisco, CA 96343 • PLA RASD   *Continuing*

Knoblauch Carol J. • Library Applications Analyst • Information Dimensions Inc. • Dublin, OH 43017 • LITA

Knoblauch Mark G. • Coordinator, Clln Management • Chicago Public Library Harold Washington Library • Chicago, IL 60605 • ALCTS LITA IFRT

Knoch Gene E. • Director • Indiana Institute of Technology McMillen Library • Fort Wayne, IN 46803 • ACRL

Knodel Donna M. • Quincy, IL 62301 • PLA

Knoebel Laurie G. • Elysburg, PA 17824

Knoedel Margie A. • Librarian • Hennepin County Library • Minnetonka, MN 55343 • ALSC PLA

Knoles Gail W. • Branch Librarian • Monterey County Free Libraries • Salinas, CA 93901 • ALSC NMRT

Knop Judy A. • Head of Technical Services • American Theological Library Association Preservation Board • Evanston, IL 60201 • ALCTS

Knopp Judy • Eisenhower Middle School • San Antonio, TX 78216 • AASL

Knopp Marie-Louise M. • Library Media Specialist • Brien McMahon High School • Norwalk, CT 06854 • AASL

Knorr Martin R. • Director of Library Service • Harris-Stowe State College • Saint Louis, MO 63103 • ACRL

Knorr Susan • Children's Librarian • Milwaukee Public Library Finney Branch • Milwaukee, WI 53208 • ALSC

Knott Deborah L. • Branch Head • Charles County Public Library • La Plata, MD 20646

Knott E. Joseph Dr. • Trustee • Syosset Public Library • Syosset, NY 11791 • ALTA

Knott Martha E. • Media Automation Consultant • San Antonio Area Library System • San Antonio, TX 78205 • PLA

Knott Mary Read • Head of Reference • Wake Forest University Z Smith Reynolds Library • Winston Salem, NC 27109-7777 • ACRL

Knott William A. • Director • Jefferson County Public Library • Lakewood, CO 80215 • LAMA PLA

Knotts Barbara A. • Manager of Acquisitions • Saint Louis Public Library • St. Louis, MO 63103-2389

Knower Lynn C. • Student • University of Maryland College of Library and Information Services • College Park, MD 20742-4345

Knowles Bernice • Branch Manager • Houston Public Library • Houston, TX 77002 • PLA

Knowles Cynthia R. • Austin, TX 78751 • SRRT

Knowles Ellen F. • Ames, IA 50010

Knowles Em Claire • Assistant Dean/Library Sch • Simmons College Graduate School of Library & Information Science • Boston, MA 02115 • ACRL LAMA
Life

Knowles Lorelette M. • 3G Graphics • Kirland, WA 98034

Knowles Ruth E. • Media Services Director • Hooksett School District c/o Hooksett Memorial School • Hooksett, NH 03106 • AASL

Knowles Sadie A. Miss • Sarnia ON, CANADA Canada • Continuing

Knowles W. Reginald • Trustee • Deer Park Public Library • Deer Park, TX 77536 • ALTA PLA

Knowlton Ginger T. • Literary Agent • Curtis Brown Ltd • New York, NY 10003

Knowlton John D. • Specialist • Library of Congress • Washington, DC 20541

Knowlton Suzanne L. • Associate University Librarian • University of Southern Maine • Portland, ME 04103 • ACRL

Knox Jo Emily Ms • Media Specialist • Magruder High School • Rockville, MD 20850

Knox Kathy M. • Pueblo, CO 81004

Knox Linda • Middle School Librarian • St. Paul's School • Brooklandville, MD 21022

Knox Lorraine J. • Assistant Science Librarian • University of Kansas Anschutz Science Library • Lawrence, KS 66045-2800 • ACRL LRRT

Knox Luanne B. • Williamsburg, MA 01096-0911 • RASD

Knox Mark R. • Student • Wayne State University Library Science Program • Detroit, MI 48202 • ACRL

Knox Mary Anne • Teacher • Spring View Middle School • Rocklin, CA 95677 • AASL

Knox Richard R. • Library Marketing Director • NTC Publishing Group • Lincolnwood, IL 60646 • AASL ACRL PLA RASD ERT NMRT

Knudsen Carmelle • Head Librarian • Bishop O'Dowd High School Library • Oakland, CA 94605 • AASL

Knudsen Judith A. • Arlington, VA 22205

Knudson June M. • Director • Hood River County Library • Hood River, OR 97031 • PLA

Knull Susan N. • Student • State University of New York School of Information & Library Sci • Albany, NY 12203 • AASL

Knupp Blaine E. • Library Assistant II • Patrick J. Stapleton Library Indiana University of Pennsylvania • Indiana, PA 15705 • ACRL

Knuth Rebecca • School Librarian • Indiana University School of Library and Information Science • Bloomington, IN 47405 • AASL

Knutson Gunnar S. • Cataloger • Newberry Library • Chicago, IL 60610 • ACRL ALCTS IFRT LRRT

Knutson Kandace L. • Lawtey Correctional Institution • Lawtey, FL 32058 • ASCLA

Knutson Kristine A. • Student • University of Washington Graduate School of Library and Information Science • Seattle, WA 98195 • EMIERT IFRT

Knutson Lee M. • Reference Services Specialist • Wausau Insurance Companies • Wausau, WI 54502-8017

Knutson Linda J. • LITA Executive Director • American Library Association • Chicago, IL 60611-2795 • LITA

Knutson Lois E. • Roland-Story Middle School • Roland, IA 50236

Ko Lihsueh Lin • Student • University of South Carolina College of Library & Information Science • Columbia, SC 29208

Kobasa Paul A. • Manager, Product Development • World Book Inc. • Evanston, IL 60201

Kobayashi Carolyn Y. • I & R Director • Municipal Reference-MUN County of Los Angeles Public Library • Hawthorne, CA 90250 • RASD

Kobayashi Deanna H. • Public Services Librarian • Merced County Library • Merced, CA 95340

Kobayashi Fujiko • Student • Indiana University School of Library and Information Science • Bloomington, IN 47405

Kobayashi Gloria R. • Librarian • Waiakea High School • Hilo, HI 96720 • AASL

Kobayashi Lee P. • Houston, TX 77024 • AASL ALSC IFRT

Kobayashi Lynne M. • Librarian • East Oahu Library District Waikiki-Kapahulu Public Lib • Honolulu, HI 96815 • RASD

Kobayashi Noriko • Musashino Womens College • Tokyo 202, Japan • ACRL ALCTS ALSC LIRT

Kobayashi Vivian N. • Sr. Information Specialist • Dialog Information Service Inc. • Palo Alto, CA 94304 • ACRL

Kobe Elizabeth E. • Senior Librarian • Oak Lawn Public Library • Oak Lawn, IL 60453 • PLA YALSA

Kobersy Krystyna I. • Reference Librarian-Subscription • Sterling Heights Public Library • Sterling Heights, MI 48313

Kobrin Lisa Brantley • Central North Carolina Regional Library • Burlington, NC 27215

Kobrin Marjory R. • Student • Long Island University Palmer School of Library & Info. Sci. • Brookville, NY 11548 • RASD

Kobulnicky Michael • Library Director • Kent State University Tuscarawas Campus Library • New Philadelphia, OH 44663 • ACRL

Kobulnicky Paul J. • University of Pittsburgh Hillman Library • Pittsburgh, PA 15260 • ACRL ALCTS

Kobus Julie A. • Collection Development Ln • Southern Connecticut State University Hilton C. Buley Library • New Haven, CT 06515

Kobzina Norma G. • Librarian • University of California-Berkeley Biosciences Library • Berkeley, CA 94720 • ACRL

Kocak Anna M. • Librarian • Neil Armstrong School • Bethel Park, PA 15102 • AASL

Kocevar-Weidinger Elizabeth A. • Student • University of Texas at Austin Graduate School of Library & Information Sciences • Austin, TX 78712-1276 • ACRL

Koch Ann L. • Library Development Officer • University of Chicago • Chicago, IL 60637 • LAMA

Koch Charles W. Dr • Nashville, IL 62263 • ACRL
Continuing

Koch David V. • Dir. of Spec. Clln & Develp • Southern Illinois University Delyte W. Morris Library • Carbondale, IL 62901-6632 • ACRL LAMA IFRT

Koch Esther D. • Oakland, CA 94612 • Continuing

Koch Henry C. • Okemos, MI 48864 • ACRL   *Life*

Koch Janet L. • Director • Montpelier Public Library • Montpelier, OH 43543

Koch John N. • Ref Librarian/Documents Coor. • University of Wisconsin Steenbock Memorial Library • Madison, WI 53706 • RASD GODORT

Koch Loretta P. • Asst. Humanities Librarian • Southern Illinois University Delyte W. Morris Library • Carbondale, IL 62901-6632 • ACRL

Koch Suzanne L. • Library Director • Oyster Bay-East Norwich Public Library • Oyster Bay, NY 11771 • LAMA

Koch Vickie Mrs. • Trustee • Pekin Public Library • Pekin, IL 61554

Kochan Carol A. • Student • University of Arizona Graduate Library School • Tucson, AZ 85721 • SRRT

Kocher Eileen R. • Bloomsburg, PA 17815

Kocher Evelyn M. • Chief Cataloger • West Virginia University Charles C. Wise Jr. Library • Morgantown, WV 26506 • ALCTS LITA

Kocher Karl A. • Systems Department • University of California Shields Library • Davis, CA 95616 • LITA

Kochik Mary Lisa • Highland, NY 12528 • ACRL LITA

Kochis Kelly L. • Student • University of Rhode Island Graduate School of Library & Information Studies • Kingston, RI 02881-0815 • ALSC

Kovacic Mark • Asst. Hd,Coll. Mgmt. Dept. • University of Cincinnati Libraries • Cincinnati, OH 45221-0033 • ALCTS

Kovack Zena • Associate State Librarian • Connecticut State Library • Hartford, CT 06106 • ASCLA LAMA PLA

Kovacs Beatrice D L S • University of North Carolina • Greensboro, NC 27412-5001 • ACRL ALCTS

Kovacs Gabor • Greeley, CO 80631

Kovacs Laszlo L. • Library Director • Saint Olaf College Rolvaag Memorial Library • Northfield, MN 55057-1097 • ACRL

Kovacs Sue • Buffalo Grove, IL 60089 • RASD

Kovanda Emilie E. Miss • Media Administrator • Senior High School Library • White Bear Lake, MN 55110 • AASL YALSA *Life*

Kovic Annette E. • Director • Upper St. Clair Township Library • Upper St. Clair, PA 15241 • LAMA PLA

Kovitz Nancy R. • Manager/Information Center • Frankel & Co • Chicago, IL 60601 • RASD

Kovitz Roberta L. • Curatorial Assoc for Bibl Svs • Harvard University Archives • Cambridge, MA 02138 • ACRL

Kovitz Selma • Reference Librarian • Union City Free Public Library • Union City, NJ 07087

Kovnat Stephen • Library Media Specialist • Martha Lake School • Lynnwood, WA 98037

Kowal Dennis J. AIA • Somerville, NJ 08876

Kowal Janet P. • Children's & YA Librarian • Durham Public Library • Durham, CT 06422 • YALSA

Kowal Ruth Chamberlain • Regional Administrator • Eastern Massachusetts Regional Library System • Boston, MA 02117 • ASCLA LAMA LITA PLA

Kowalczyk Helen V. • Head Librarian • Winnetka Public Library Northfield Branch • Winnetka, IL 62094 • ALSC LAMA

Kowaleski Elizabeth • Reference Librarian • Bacon Memorial Public Library • Wyandotte, MI 48192 • PLA

Kowalewski Donna • Galesburg Memorial Library • Galesburg, MI 49053-9501

Kowalski Amy B. • Student • Kent State University School of Library & Information Science • Kent, OH 44242-0001 • ALSC

Kowalski Ann M. • Cataloger • Salve Regina University Library • Newport, RI 02840 • ALCTS LITA

Kowalski Mary Anne • Muncie, IN 47304

Kowalski Rosalie • Student • Wayne State University Library Science Program • Detroit, MI 48202 • PLA SRRT

Kox Christopher J. • Student • University of California-Berkeley School of Library & Information Studies • Berkeley, CA 94720 • IFRT LRRT SRRT

Koyama Janice T. • Asst. Librarian of Public Serv. • University of California Res Lib • Los Angeles, CA 90024 • ACRL LAMA

Kozak Anne M. • Director • Thomas Ford Memorial Library • Western Springs, IL 60558 • PLA

Kozak Carla J. • Librarian II • San Francisco Public Library Chinatown Branch • San Francisco, CA 94108 • ALSC

Kozar John J. • Supervisory Librarian • Library of Congress • Washington, DC 20541

Kozel-Emmendorfer Bethany A. • Marietta, GA 30067-6272

Kozel-La Ha Sheree • Library Director • Bedford Park Public Library District • Bedford Park, IL 60501 • ALSC

Kozelka Marcia Lee • Childrens Dept. • Park Ridge Public Library • Park Ridge, IL 60068-4188

Koziol Scott D. • Temporary Serials/Microforms Cat • University of Pittsburgh Hillman Library • Pittsburgh, PA 15260 • ACRL ALCTS

Kozlovsky Sonia • Solomon Schechter Day School • Baltimore, MD 21208 • AASL

Kozlowski Ronald S. • Executive Director • Miami-Dade Public Library System • Miami, FL 33130-1504 • ASCLA LAMA PLA

Kozlowski Yvonne • Head of Social Science Dept • Auburn University Ralph Brown Draughon Library • Auburn, AL 36849-5606 • ACRL RASD

Kozsely Marianne G. • Student • Kent State University School of Library & Information Science • Kent, OH 44242-0001 • EMIERT IFRT IRRT SORT SRRT

Kozuboski Linda • Student • State University of New York at Albany School of Information Science & Policy • Albany, NY 12222 • AASL

Kozup Peter C. • Warren, OH 44481 • ASCLA

Kraakevik Robert L. • Student • Texas Woman's University School of Library & Information Studies • Denton, TX 76204

Krabbe Gordon E. • Dir. Administrative Services • Enoch Pratt Free Library • Baltimore, MD 21201-4484

Kracke Laura H. • Student • Rosary College Graduate School of Library & Information Science • River Forest, IL 60305 • AASL

Kraehe Mary A. • Charlottesvl, VA 22901 • ACRL

Kraemer Alfred B. • Milwaukee, WI 53223 • IRRT

Kraemer Mary Pat • Director • Los Alamos County Library • Los Alamos, NM 87544 • PLA

Kraemer Ruth F. • Lincoln, NE 68504 • Continuing

Kraft Betty Diane • Apopka, FL 32712 • AASL

Kraft Dorothy H. • Librarian • Haycock Elementary School Library • Falls Church, VA 22180 • AASL

Kraft Elizabeth L. • New York, NY 10009 • PLA

Kraft Kelly • Library Media Specialist • Sheridan High School • Sheridan, WY 82801 • AASL

Kraft Linda G. • Automation Coordinator • East Baton Rouge Parish Library • Baton Rouge, LA 70806-7699

Kraft Mary H. • Coordinator of Media Services • Noblesville School Corp. • Noblesville, IN 46060 • AASL

Kragh Linda J. • Miami, FL 33157

Krahling Charlene C. • Librarian • Sioux Center Community School • Sioux Center, IA 51250 • AASL

Krahnke Kathleen A. • Children's Librarian • Northland Public Library • Pittsburgh, PA 15237 • ALSC YALSA

Krajnak Pat • Assistant Director • International Foundation of Employee Benefit Plans • Brookfield, WI 53008-0069 • RASD

Krakora Ed M. • Director • Heidelberg College • Tiffin, OH 44883

Krakowiak Philip • Buffalo, NY 14222 • IFRT

Kral Karen S. • Mgr, Information & Resources • Career Development Services • Rochester, NY 14604 • RASD

Kralick Ann G. • Telebase Systems, Inc. • Wayne, PA 19087-1992

Kralisz Victor Frank • Manager • Dallas Public Library Preston Royal Branch • Dallas, TX 75229-5599 • PLA

Kraljic Mary B. • Reference Librarian • South Dakota State University Briggs Library • Brookings, SD 57007

Krall Diane Schweier • Adult Services Librarian • Elm Grove Public Library • Elm Grove, WI 53122-0906 • ASCLA RASD

Kram Lorraine M. • Head of Public Affair Services • University of California-Los Angeles (UCLA) • Los Angeles, CA 90024-1450 • GODORT

Kramarczyk June F. • Library Media Supervisor • Elm Street Junior High School • Nashua, NH 03060 • AASL

Kramer-Greene Judith • Editor • Forest Press/OCLC • Albany, NY 12206-2082

Kramer Anne E. • East Detroit Memorial Library • East Detroit, MI 48021-2390

Kramer Arlene H. • Media Specialist • Portage High School East • Portage, IN 46368 • AASL

Kramer Carol • University of California-Berkeley School of Library & Information Studies • Berkeley, CA 94720 • ALSC LITA PLA RASD

Kramer Christine M. • The Boeing Company Shea Technical Library • Seattle, WA 98124

Kramer Deborah J. • Head of Acquistions/Audiovisual • Southwestern University • Georgetown, TX 78628

Kramer Dorothy • YA Librarian • Cuyahoga County Public Library Beachwood Branch • Beachwood, OH 44122

Kramer Dorothy A. Dr. • Estee Lauder Inc. • Melville, NY 11747

Kramer Dorothy J. • Student • Robeson County Public Library • Lumberton, NC 28358 • ALSC

Kramer Gretl L. • Public Service Librarian • Elgin Community College • Elgin, IL 60123 • ACRL RASD

Kramer Hannah K. • Librarian II • Los Angeles Public Library • Los Angeles, CA 90071 • PLA

Kramer Helen A. • Brown & Root Braun Reference Library • Alhambra, CA 91803-1300

Kramer Janice H. • Technical Services Libraian • Belleville Area College Library • Belleville, IL 62221

Kramer Joseph • Librarian • California State University-Sacramento Library • Sacramento, CA 95819-6039 • ACRL

Kramer Karen A. • Salt Lake City, UT 84124

Kramer Karen M. • Young Adults Librarian • Somerville Public Library • Somerville, MA 02143 • PLA

Kramer Linda • Director, Library & Book Prog. • English-Speaking Union • New York, NY 10021

Kramer Linda N. • Morrisville, VT 05661 • ACRL RASD

Kramer Loren W. • Children's Services • Oxnard Public Library • Oxnard, CA 93030 • PLA EMIERT

Kramer Margy • Director • Hocking Technical College Library • Nelsonville, OH 45764 • ACRL

Kramer Marilyn • Head of Catalog Department • State University of New York (SUNY) Central Technical Services • Buffalo, NY 14260 • ACRL ALCTS LITA

Kramer Mollie W. • Bronx, NY 10471 • ASCLA PLA

Kramer Moshe Y. • Librarian/Library Teacher • Magen David Yeshivah • Brooklyn, NY 11204

Kramer Pamela • Youth Service Consultant • Libertyville High School Library • Libertyville, IL 60048 • AASL

Kramer Roberta J. • Media Ref Ln/Assoc Prof of L Sci • Purdue University Libraries • West Lafayette, IN 47907 • ACRL LIRT

Kramer Ruth M. • Reference Librarian • Orland Park Public Library • Orland Park, IL 60462 • RASD

Kramer Stefan • Student • University of Washington Graduate School of Library and Information Science • Seattle, WA 98195

Kramer Thomas F. Mrs. • Trustee • Saint Mary Parish Library • Franklin, LA 70538 • ALTA IFRT

Kranch Douglas A. • Associate Library Director • Ambassador College Library Roy Hammer Library Building • Big Sandy, TX 75755 • LITA

Kraner Debra • Head of A-V/Outreach • Manatee County Public Library System • Bradenton, FL 34205

Kranich Nancy C. • Director, Public Service • New York University Elmer Holmes Bobst Library • New York, NY 10012 • ACRL LAMA LITA RASD FLRT GODORT IFRT SRRT

Kranis Emily S. • Student • Pratt Institute Library • Brooklyn, NY 11205

Kranodebski Renita M. • Student • Rutgers University School of Communication Information & Library Studies • New Brunswick, NJ 08903

Kranovich Patricia A. • Clinton, IA 52733

Krantz Linda L. • Director • Rockbridge Regional Library • Lexington, VA 24450 • PLA

Krantz Marcia • Student • State University of New York at Albany School of Information Science & Policy • Albany, NY 12222 • AASL

Kranz Ralph E. • Audio-Visual Division Librarian • University of Utah Marriott Library • Salt Lake City, UT 84112-1179 • ACRL IFRT

Krarup Agnes • Pittsburgh, PA 15213 • AASL ALSC *Life*

Krarup Karl • Royal Library • Copenhagen, Denmark • LITA

Krasner Joan K. • Chief Access Serv • Stanford University • Stanford, CA 94305-6011 • ACRL

Kratochvil Ruth • Tualatin Public Library • Tualatin, OR 97062 • LAMA

Kratz Abby R. • Assoc Director for Library Serv. • University of Texas at Dallas University Library • Richardson, TX 75083-0643 • ACRL LAMA RASD

Kratz Ann. B. • Indianapolis, IN 46229 • LITA NMRT

Kratz Charles E. Jr. • Library Director • University of Scranton Harry & Jeanette Weinberg Memorial • Scranton, PA 18510-4700 • ACRL LAMA

Kratzert Mona Y. • Reference Coordinator • California State University • Fullerton, CA 92634 • ACRL RASD

Kraus Anne • Director • Nolichucky Regional Library • Morristown, TN 37814 • ALSC PLA *Life*

Kraus Betsy J. • Environmental Evaluation Group • Albuquerque, NM 87109 • ACRL

Kraus Jan A. • Stevens Point, WI 54481

Kraus Joe W. • Bloomington, IL 61701 • Continuing

Kraus Lynne C. • Cataloging Librarian • Solano County Library • Fairfield, CA 94533 • ACRL ALCTS LITA

Kraus Richard S. • Los Angeles Public Library West L.A. Rgnl. Branch • Los Angeles, CA 90025 • Life

Kraus Rose Marie • Daly City, CA 94016 • ACRL ALCTS ALSC RASD *Continuing*

Krause Alana M. • Westminster, CA 92683-2106 • PLA

Krause Dorothea M. • Redlands, CA 92373 • RASD YALSA *Life*

Krause John J. • Student • Rosary College Graduate School of Library & Information Science • River Forest, IL 60305

Krause Melanie C. • Librarian I Media • Maricopa County Library District • Phoenix, AZ 85032

Krauss Susan • Senior Reference Librarian • Dillon Read & Co Inc • New York, NY 10022 • SRRT

Krausse Sylvia C. • Ref. Librarian Bibliographer • University of Rhode Island Library • Kingston, RI 02881-0803 • ACRL RASD IRRT

Krauter Barbara J. • New York, NY 10023 • RASD

Krautheim Joan A. • Director • Dwight D. Eisenhower Library • Totowa Borough, NJ 07512

Kravetz-Cronizer Susan R. • General Foods USA • White Plains, NY 10625

Kravetz Mary Lou • Santa Monica, CA 90402

Kravitz David P. • Reference Librarian • San Jose Public Library • San Jose, CA 95113

Kravitz Rhonda A. Rios • Access Services Librarian • California State University-Sacramento Library • Sacramento, CA 95819-6039 • ACRL EMIERT SRRT

Krawec Randy W. • Student • McGill University Graduate School of Library & Information Studies • Montreal PQ, H3A 1Y1 Canada • RASD

Krayer Christina A. • Varsity Reading Services • Clearwater, FL 34625

Krchmar Sandra L. • Reference Librarian • Journal/Sentinel Inc. News Information Center • Milwaukee, WI 53201

Krcmar Gregory • Trustee • Stickney-Forest View Library • Stickney, IL 60402 • ALTA

Kreager Susan • Reference • Ball State University Bracken Library • Muncie, IN 47306-0160 • ACRL

Kreamer Jean T. • Lafayette, LA 70504 • ALTA VRT

Krebs Raymond L. • Cataloging Librarian • Coeur d' Alene Public Library • Coeur d' Alene, ID 83814 • ALCTS
Life

Krecidlo Janine • Library Director • Dunham Public Library • Whitesboro, NY 13492 • LAMA PLA IFRT

Kreckman Ellen E. • Cataloger • Houghton College Willard J Houghton Library • Houghton, NY 14744 • ALCTS

Kreczmer Nancy J. • Jacksonville, IL 62651 • LAMA

Kredel Stephen F. • Greensburg, PA 15601 • Continuing

Kreh Susan E. • Baltimore County Public Library Cockeysville Branch • Cockeysville, MD 21030 • ALSC

Krehbiel John D. Jr. • Ann Arbor, MI 48103 • ALSC

Krehbiel Kay P. • Public Services Librarian • New Mexico Institute of Mining & Technology Library • Socorro, NM 87801 • ACRL GODORT

Krehbiel Leona • North Newton, KS 67117 • ACRL LAMA
Continuing

Krei Nancy A. • Library Director • Marinette County Consolidated Public Library Services • Marinette, WI 54143 • LAMA PLA IFRT

Kreibich Diane J. • Hudson, OH 44236

Kreimeier Danis E. • Student • San Jose State University Division of Library & Information Science • San Jose, CA 95192-0029 • ALSC PLA

Kreimeyer-Brown Vicki R. • Boise, ID 83712-7718 • ACRL LAMA

Kreiner Mary B. • Student • Wayne State University Library Science Program • Detroit, MI 48202

Kreis Jill K. • King County Library System • Seattle, WA 98109

Kreischer Patricia A • Graphic Artist-Head Art Dept. • Lake Forest Library • Lake Forest, IL 60045

Kreiser Bonnielynn C. • Department Chair • Glenbard East High School • Lombard, IL 60148 • AASL

Kreiser Latane C. • Media Specialist • Washington School • Junction City, KS 66441 • AASL

Kreisler Helen A. • Cambridge, MA 02140 • PLA

Kreissman Bernard • Davis, CA 95616 • Continuing

Kreitz Patricia A. • Manager,Library Services • Superconducting Super Collider • Dallas, TX 75237-3946 • ACRL ALCTS LAMA LITA RASD

Kreitzburg M. J. • Ref & Hd of Instruction Servs • University of Pittsburgh Johnstown Campus Library • Johnstown, PA 15904 • ACRL

Krell Denise L. • New York Public Library Woodstock Branch • Bronx, NY 10456 • ALSC PLA NMRT SRRT

Krell Elaine W. • Media Specialist • North Charleston High School • North Charleston, SC 29407

Krema Martha L. • Assistant Librarian • Glenbard South High School Library • Glen Ellyn, IL 60137 • AASL

Kremer Beth A. • Govt. Publications Ref. Libn. • Johns Hopkins University Milton S. Eisenhower Library • Baltimore, MD 21218 • ACRL GODORT

Krenitsky M. V. • Houghton, MI 49931 • Continuing

Krenn Sue • School Librarian • Glenfield Middle School • Montclair, NJ 07042 • AASL

Krentz Roger F. Dr. • Hd Learning Materials Center • University of Wisconsin Library and Learning Resources • Whitewater, WI 53190 • AASL

Krentzin Alexander • Children's Librarian • Berkley Public Library • Berkley, MI 48072 • ALSC

Kreps Stephanie A. • St Charles, IL 60175

Kresh Diane N. • Acting Director Pscm I • Library of Congress • Washington, DC 20541 • ALCTS RASD

Kresnoff Bruce J. • Student • Rosary College Graduate School of Library & Information Science • River Forest, IL 60305 • SRRT

Krettek Germaine Miss • Council Bluffs, IA 51503 • LAMA
Honorary

Kreunen Julie A. • Superconducting Super Collider Laboratory-SSC Library • Dallas, TX 75237-3946 • LITA

Krevit Leah • Director • University of Texas Health Science Center Dental Branch Library • Houston, TX 77225

Kreyche Michael R. • Kent State University Library • Kent, OH 44242 • LITA IRRT

Kridler Virginia R. • Prison Librarian • Mid-Michigan Correctional Facility • St. Louis, MI 48880 • ASCLA

Kriebel Gail I. • Library Mgr.-Circulation Serv. • Lehigh University Libraries Fairchild-Martindale Library • Bethlehem, PA 18015 • ACRL

Krieg-Sigman Kelly M. • Director • Duerrwaechter Memorial Library • Germantown, WI 53022

Krieg Amelia • Eugene, OR 97405-3361 • ALCTS

Krieg Clarice E. • Eugene, OR 97405-3361 • Continuing

Krieger Michael T. • Librarian Tech. Serv. • University of Dayton Roesch Library • Dayton, OH 45469 • ACRL ALCTS LITA EMIERT SRRT

Krieger R. E. • Robert E. Krieger Publishing Company Inc. • Melbourne, FL 32901

Krieger Susan M. • Director • Edison Free Public Library • Edison, NJ 08817 • PLA

Krieger Tillie • Eugene, OR 97405 • Continuing

Kriesel Ronald W. • Director • Mid-America Bible College Charles Ewing Brown Library • Oklahoma City, OK 73170-9797 • ACRL LITA

Kriewall Gloria • Madison, WI 53704 • ACRL

Krigas Mary S. • Arlington Heights, IL 60005

Kriigel Barbara J. • University of Michigan-Dearborn Mardigian Library • Dearborn, MI 48128-1491

Krikos Linda A. • Head, Women's Studies Library • Ohio State University Libraries • Columbus, OH 43210-1286 • ACRL

Krinsky Joan L. • Irvine, CA 92714

Krinsky Sharon F. • Student • Pratt Institute Graduate School of Library & Information Science • Brooklyn, NY 11205

Krishan Kewal • Serials Cagalogue Librarian IV • University of Saskatchewan Library • Saskatoon SK, S7N 0W0 Canada • ALCTS

Krishnan Sujata • Student • San Jose State University Division of Library & Information Science • San Jose, CA 95192-0029 • LITA

Krismann Carol H. • Business Librarian • University of Colorado-Boulder University Libraries • Boulder, CO 80309 • RASD

Krissiep Margot S. • Pullman, WA 99165-2683 • ACRL ALCTS GODORT

Kristian Alice • Ref Ln & Hd of Ref Dept • Syosset Public Library • Syosset, NY 11791

Kristie William • California State University-Sacramento Library • Sacramento, CA 95819-6039 • ACRL RASD LIRT MAGERT

Kristinik P. Jean • Library Media Specialist • Lyman Elementary School Library • Lyman, SC 29365

Kristy Cynthia LaNa • Librarian II • Phoenix Public Library • Phoenix, AZ 85004 • PLA

Kritzer Hyman W. • Director of Libraries • Kent State University Libraries • Kent, OH 44242

Kriz Harry M. • Automation Librarian • Virginia Polytechnic Inst & State Univ University Libraries • Blacksburg, VA 24062-9001 • ACRL

Kriz Leo V. • Head of Technical Services • Sioux City Public Library • Sioux City, IA 51101-1203 • ALCTS SRRT

Krizanic Arlene A. • Assistant Librarian • CNA Insurance Corporate Library • Chicago, IL 60685 • ALCTS

Krizek Kathleen A. • Student • University of North Carolina at Chapel Hill School of Information and Library Science • Chapel Hill, NC 27599-3360 • ALSC PLA

Krizmis William J. • Trustee • East Chicago Public Library • E. Chicago, IN 46312 • PLA

Kroah Larry A. • Dir of Ls & Media Resources • Indiana Univ of Pennsylvania • Indiana, PA 15705 • ACRL ALCTS LAMA LITA RASD LRRT

Krober Alfred C. • Director • Roberts Wesleyan College Kenneth B. Keating Lib. • Rochester, NY 14624 • ACRL ALCTS LITA RASD

Kroehler Beth A. • Special Projects Librarian • Muncie-Center Township Public Library • Muncie, IN 47305 • PLA

Kroeker Lois M. • Librarian • Levelland Independent School District • Leveland, TX 79336 • AASL

Krohn Marilyn • Hastings, NY 10706

Krois Jerome W. • Deputy State Librarian • Wyoming State Library • Cheyenne, WY 82002-0650 • ASCLA PLA

Kroll Carol • Director • Nassau School Library System • Carle Place, NY 11514 • AASL ALSC

Kroll Gail K. • Circulation Clerk • Northbrook Public Library • Northbrook, IL 60062

Kroll H. Rebecca • Asst Prof/Reference Librarian • Lorain County Community College Library • Elyria, OH 44035 • ACRL LAMA RASD

Kroll James X. • Manager,Humanities Dept • Denver Public Library • Denver, CO 80203-2165

Kroll Kathleen M. • Mercer University Monroe F. Swilley Jr Library • Atlanta, GA 30341 • IFRT

Kroll Kim Adele • Graduate Student • University of Hawaii School of Library & Information Studies • Honolulu, HI 96822 • ACRL

Kroll Margaret A. • Belcourt, ND 58316 • ACRL

Kroll Susan M. • Director • Ohio State University Health Sciences Library • Columbus, OH 43210 • ACRL LAMA

Kromann Sonja E. • National Marine Mammal Laboratory • Seattle, WA 98115-0070

Krompart Janet A. • Professor • Oakland University • Rochester, MI 48309-4401 • ACRL

Kronstedt Richard H. • Serials Librarian • Cleveland Museum of Art • Cleveland, OH 44106 • ACRL

Krontiras John • Manager • JK Consultants • Birmingham, AL 35238

Krook Tina S. • Librarian • Our Lady of Mount Carmel School • Asbury Park, NJ 07712 • AASL

Krooks David A. • Student • University of Illinois Graduate School of Library and Information Science • Urbana, IL 61801 • SRRT

Kropog Alex • Librarian • Springfield High School • Springfield, LA 70462 • AASL

Kropp Anthony R. • A. R. Kropp Co. • Huntington, NY 11743

Kroshus Mary C. • Trustee • North Dakota State School of Science Mildred Johnson Library • Wahpeton, ND 58075

Krotz-Oxby Shirley • Mobile, AL 36609

Krub-Nelles Barbara Ms. • Conway, WA 98238

Kruck Thomas E. • Library Clerk • Arizona State University F.I.R.S.T. • Tempe, AZ 85287

Krueger Amy J. • Pt. Charlotte, FL 33952

Krueger Bonnie • Cataloging-Reference Librarian • Owatonna Public Library • Owatonna, MN 55060

Krueger Carol A. • Journal Selector/Doct. Librarian • National Library of Medicine • Bethesda, MD 20894 • GODORT

Krueger Diane L. • School Library Media Specialist • Saint John Lutheran School • Rochester, MI 48307 • AASL

Krueger Gerald J. • Documents Librarian • University of Wisconsin at Oshkosh Polk Library • Oshkosh, WI 54901 • GODORT

Krueger Hanna E. • Lacey, WA 98503 • Continuing

Krueger Karen J. • Director • Janesville Public Library • Janesville, WI 53545-3971 • LAMA PLA

Krueger Rita • Librarian • Seattle Public Library Southwest Branch • Seattle, WA 98126

Krueger Sharon B. • Reference Librarian • Stevenson High School • Prairie View, IL 60069 • AASL

Krug Judith F. • OIF Director • American Library Association • Chicago, IL 60611-2795 • ALCTS ALSC LAMA PLA RASD YALSA IFRT

Krug Patricia A. • Reference • United States Department of Agriculture National Agricultural Library • Beltsville, MD 20705-2351 • ACRL LITA RASD FLRT

Krug Ruth A. • Cataloging/Reference Librarian • Albuquerque Technical Vocational Institute • Albuquerque, NM 87106

Kruger Betsy • Assistant Acquisitions Librarian • University of Illinois Library • Urbana, IL 61801 • ALCTS VRT

Kruger Joan • Media Specialist • Dutch Fork Elementary School • Irmo, SC 29063 • AASL

Kruger Kathleen Joyce • Catalog Librarian • Colorado State University William E. Morgan Library • Fort Collins, CO 80523 • ALCTS LAMA

Kruger Linda M. • Rare Books Cataloger • Columbia University Libraries Butler Library • New York, NY 10027 • ACRL ALCTS LHRT

Kruger Martha Harton • YA/Librarian I • Santa Clara County Free Library Milpitas Community Library • Milpitas, CA 95035 • YALSA EMIERT

Kruger Sy • Monsey, NY 10952 • LAMA PLA RASD

Kruise Carol Sue • School/Library Media Specialist • Littleton School District #6 Mary Hopkins Elementary School • Littleton, CO 80122 • AASL

Krukonis Perkunas P. • Roxbury Community College Learning Resource Center • Boston, MA 02120 • IFRT

Krull Jeffrey R. • Director • Allen County Public Library • Fort Wayne, IN 46801-2270 • LAMA PLA

Krumholtz Nancy • Chief Corp. Services • New York Public Library • New York, NY 10018-2788

Krumm Carol R. • Columbus, OH 43229 • Continuing

Krummel D. W. Prof. • Prof. of Library Science • University of Illinois Graduate School of Library and Information Science • Urbana, IL 61801 • ACRL RASD LHRT
Life

Krummel Sonja B. • Vaud, Switzerland

Krumwiede Richard W. • Director • Outagamie Waupaca Library System • Appleton, WI 54911 • ASCLA LAMA LITA PLA

Krupa Lee • Trustee • East Chicago Public Library • E. Chicago, IN 46312 • PLA

Krupczak Maribeth • Collection Development Librarian • Union College Schaffer Library • Schenectady, NY 12308 • ACRL ALCTS LAMA

Krupp Peggy • Library Media Specialist • Sayreville W. M. High School • Parlin, NJ 08859 • AASL

Krupp Robert A. • Library Director • Western Conservative Baptist Seminary Cline-Tunnell Library • Portland, OR 97215-3399

Kruse Carolyn J. • Reserves/Acquisitions/Asst 4 • University of Wisconsin • Madison, WI 53706 • IFRT SRRT

Kruse Claire M. • Student • Wayne State University • Detroit, MI 48202 • AASL

Kruse Ginny Moore • Director • Cooperative Children's Book Center University of Wisconsin-Madison • Madison, WI 53706 • AASL ALSC YALSA EMIERT IFRT SRRT

Kruse Holly • Plainfield, VT 05667 • AASL IFRT

Kruse Janice L. • Media Specialist • Fremont Public Schools • Fremont, NE 68025 • AASL
Kruse Marina • Director • Romeo District Library • Romeo, MI 48065 • LAMA PLA
Kruse Michael J. • Student • State University New York at Buffalo School of Inf. & Library Studies • Buffalo, NY 14260 • AASL IFRT SRRT
Kruse Nancy F. • Student • University of Illinois Graduate School of Library and Information Science • Urbana, IL 61801 • ALSC
Kruse Paul Dr • Seattle, WA 98109-2269
Kruse Sue H. • Elementary Media Specialist • Hermosa Vista Public School • Mesa, AZ 85201 • AASL
Kruse Thelma M. • Director • Plymouth Public Library • Plymouth, MA 02360 • IFRT
Kruse Theodore H. • Tech Serv Ln • University of Baltimore Langsdale Library • Baltimore, MD 21201
Kruser Barbara A. • Adult Reference Libraran • Niles Public Library • Niles, IL 60648
Krusko Vilma • Bay Village, OH 44140
Krusor Sara J. • Cupertino, CA 95014
Kruthoffer Robert E. III • Student • University of Kentucky College of Library & Information Science • Lexington, KY 40506-0391 • PLA RASD SRRT
Krutulis Mary E. • Indiana University School of Library and Information Science • Bloomington, IN 47405 • GODORT
Krych Nobuko • Lakewood, CA 90711-3633 • RASD
Krygsman Nancy Tudor • Assistant Chief Librarian • Toronto Public Library • Toronto ON, M5A 4L2 Canada • LAMA
Kryszak Wayne D. • Mithcellville, MD 20716
Krzak Alice J. • Palos Heights, IL 60463 • ALSC
Kuan Chi-ming • Pittsburgh, PA 15213
Kuan David A. • Head Cataloger • Morgan State University Soper Library • Baltimore, MD 21239-4098 • ALCTS
Kuan Jenny • Reference Librarian • Cherry Hill Free Public Library • Cherry Hill, NJ 08034 • RASD
Kubal Gene J. • Lexington, VA 24450 • ACRL RASD *Life*
Kubasta Brent W. • Student • Kent State University School of Library & Information Science • Kent, OH 44242-0001
Kubat Margaret M. • Andersen Middle School • Omaha, NE 68137 • AASL
Kube Kathryn J. • Reference Librarian • Madison Public Library • Madison, WI 53703 • RASD
Kubena Pamela D. • Staff Librarian • Rufus Young King Library • Giddings, TX 78942
Kubenka Jennifer D. • Student • Texas Woman's University School of Library & Information Studies • Denton, TX 76204 • IFRT
Kubiak Matthew C. • Bloomington Public Library • Bloomington, IL 61702-3308 • LAMA PLA IFRT
Kubic Joseph Craig Rev. • Librarian • Midwestern Baptist Theological Seminary Library • Kansas City, MO 64118 • ACRL ALCTS LITA RASD
Kubis Mary Ellen • Media Specialist • Sprayberry High School • Marietta, GA 30066 • AASL
Kubli Barbara B. • Ref. & Instruction Librarian • North Adams State College • North Adams, MA 01247 • ACRL
Kucera Barbara M. • K-12 Librarian • Verdigre Public School Library • Verdigre, NE 68783 • AASL
Kucera Kathleen A. • Children's Librarian • Jefferson County Public Library Villa Regional Branch • Lakewood, CO 80226
Kucera Nadia R. • Student • University of Hawaii School of Library & Information Studies • Honolulu, HI 96822 • ALSC
Kuchenbrod Susanah E. • Dept Head Circulation • Syosset Public Library • Syosset, NY 11791
Kuchta Carol S. • Reference Librarian • Canton Public Library • Canton, MI 48188
Kudryk Oleg Dr. • Librarian Emeritus & Consultant • Indiana University at Bloomington University Libraries • Bloomington, IN 47405 • Continuing
Kuebler David F.S.C. Bro. • Christian Brothers High School Library • Memphis, TN 38120
Kuebler Janice R. • Assistant Children's Librarian • Fulton High School • Middleton, MI 48856 • AASL
Kuechmann Christopher R. • Director of Library Service • Starr County Public Library • Rio Grande City, TX 78582 • PLA SRRT
Kuehl Linda L. • Streamwood High School • Streamwood, IL 60107 • AASL YALSA
Kuehl Nancy J. • Children's Librarian • Indianapolis Marion County Public Library • Indianapolis, IN 46206
Kuehl Sylvia • Middletown, NY 10940
Kuehler Stephen G. • Berkeley, CA 94704
Kuehn Claire R. • Archivist • Panhandle-Plains Historical Museum Library • Canyon, TX 79016
Kuehn V. R. • University Librarian • Florida State University Robert M. Strozier Library • Tallahassee, FL 32306-2047 • ALCTS
Kuehster Susan E. • Palmer Lake, CO 80133 • LITA
Kuenstler Rita • Branch Librarian • Brooklyn Public Library Flatbush Branch • Brooklyn, NY 11226
Kueppers Brigitte J. • Head of Theater Arts Library • University of California-Los Angeles Institute for Social Science Reserch • Los Angeles, CA 90024 • ACRL
Kuertz Ruth • Librarian • William Mason High School • Mason, OH 45040 • AASL
Kueter Andrea J. • Saint Martins College • Lacey, WA 98503 • IFRT SRRT
Kuffuor-Berko Kwame • Bronx, NY 10469 • LHRT
Kugle Paula T • Clln Develp. Librarian • Houston Public Library • Houston, TX 77002
Kugler Cheryl C. • Head of Monograph Services • Vanderbilt University Library Jean & Alexander Heard Library • Nashville, TN 37240-0007 • ACRL ALCTS
Kugler Kathleen M. • Foster High School • Seattle, WA 98168 • AASL YALSA
Kuhagen Judith A. • Sr. Descriptive Catlg Spec. • Library of Congress • Washington, DC 20541 • ALCTS
Kuhl-Yamashita Sylvia • Mansfield, PA 16933
Kuhl Corrine M. • Denver, CO 80203
Kuhl Marlene • Branch Manager • Reisterstown Library • Reisterstown, MD 21136 • PLA RASD
Kuhlthau Carol C. • Associate Professor • Rutgers University School of Communication Information & Library Studies • New Brunswick, NJ 08903 • AASL ACRL ALSC LIRT LRRT
Kuhn David J. • Trustee • Plainfield Public Library District • Plainfield, IL 60544 • ALTA
Kuhn Joanne • University of Waterloo • Waterloo ON, N2L 3G1 Canada
Kuhn Kendrick Charmette S. • Student • University of Alabama School of Library & Information Studies • Tuscaloosa, AL 35487-0252
Kuhn Martin A. • Lakehurst, NJ 08733 • Continuing
Kuhn Philip J. • Student • Indiana University School of Library and Information Science • Bloomington, IN 47405
Kuhn Tamara J. • Bloomington, IN 47408 • PLA
Kuhn Warren B. • Dean of Library Services, Emer. • Iowa State University Library • Ames, IA 50011-2140 • ACRL LAMA *Life*
Kuhner Robert A. • Library Planning Officer • City College of New York (CUNY) • New York, NY 10031 • LAMA LIRT
Kuhns Barbara J. • Dayton & Montgomery County Public Library • Dayton, OH 45402-2103
Kuhns Louetta M. • Librarian • Kauluwela Elementary School • Honolulu, HI 96817 • AASL ALSC *Life*
Kuhns Myrle R. • Allentown, PA 18104 • AASL
Kuhr Joann • Data Entry Manager • Suburban Library System • Burr Ridge, IL 60521 • ALCTS
Kuhr Patricia S. • Editor, Subject Files • H. W. Wilson Company • Bronx, NY 10452 • ALCTS LITA
Kuhta Richard J. • University Librarian • Saint Lawrence University Owen D. Young Library • Canton, NY 13617 • ACRL
Kujansuu Asko J. • Cataloger • University of Alberta Library • Edmonton AB, Canada
Kujawa Kathryn G. • Prescott, AZ 86302
Kujoory Parvin Ph. D. • Asst Prof of Media & Technology • University of the District of Columbia Learning Resources Division • Washington, DC 20008
Kukainis Beate N. • Acquisitions/Serials Dept. • University of Southwestern Louisiana Libraries • Lafayette, LA 70503 • ACRL ALCTS
Kukil Karen V. • Assistant Curator of Rare Books • Smith College William Allan Neilson Library • Northampton, MA 01063 • ACRL
Kukla Edward R. • Department Head Special Clln. • Minneapolis Public Library & Information Center • Minneapolis, MN 55401-1992 • ACRL ALCTS
Kuklewski Virginia • Librarian • Pequea Valley High School • Kinzer, PA 17532 • AASL
Kuklinski Joan L. • Executive Director • Minuteman Library Network • Framingham, MA 01701 • LITA
Kulak Debra S. • Manager • Dun's Marketing Services • Parsippany, NJ 07054 • ACRL LITA PLA RASD ERT
Kulasekara Susan L. • Adult Services Librarian • Hayner Public Library District • Alton, IL 62002
Kulaski Monica F. • Head,Library Systems Office • Temple University Paley Library • Philadelphia, PA 19122 • ACRL ALCTS LITA
Kulberg Raoul F. Mr • Washington, DC 20015 • ACRL ALCTS LITA RASD EMIERT IFRT IRRT *Life*
Kulessa Ruth M. • Librarian • Garden Park Elementary School • Brownsville, TX 78520
Kulick Jan • Teacher-Librarian • Arbor School Library • Piscataway, NJ 08854 • AASL
Kulig Yvonne L. • Elementary School Librarian • Rockaway Public Schools • Rockaway, NJ 07866 • AASL
Kulik Laura J. • Head of Technical Services • Chelmsford Public Library • Chelmsford, MA 01824-3088 • ALCTS
Kulis Margaret M. • Reference Specialist • Newberry Library • Chicago, IL 60610 • NMRT
Kulka Lisa G. • Student • Wayne State University • Detroit, MI 48202 • AASL
Kulleseid Eleanor R. • Director • Bank Street College of Education Library • New York, NY 10025 • AASL ACRL LRRT
Kulp Arthur C. • Ithaca, NY 14850-4712 • ACRL
Kulp Leslie A. • Head Ref. & User Services • National Agricultural L • Beltsville, MD 20705 • RASD
Kulp William A. • Baltimore, MD 21229 • ACRL
Kulpa Kathryn A. • Student • University of Rhode Island Graduate School of Library & Information Studies • Kingston, RI 02881-0815 • NMRT SRRT
Kulzy MaryEllen P. • Lyndhurst High School • Lyndhurst, NJ 07071
Kumaar Kundan L. • Library Assistant • Advance Information Management • Mountain Veiw, CA 94041
Kumar C. Shireen • Director Library • Shea & Gould • New York, NY 10020 • LAMA LITA RASD
Kumar Rakesh • Trustee • Multi-Cultural Audio Video Systems • Southfield, MI 48076 • ASCLA EMIERT IRRT
Kumble Stephanie A. • Trustee • Rockport Public Library • Rockport, ME 04856
Kumler Sherrill A. • Children Librarian • Hayward Public Library • Hayward, CA 94541 • ALSC
Kundert Lorna J. • Alexandria, VA 22302
Kundla Linda Y. • Trustee • Huntington Public Library • Huntington, NY 11743 • ALTA LAMA
Kunes Betty J. • Student • Kent State University School of Library & Information Science • Kent, OH 44242-0001
Kung Mei-Lin • Reference Librarian • Huntsville-Madison County Public Library • Huntsville, AL 35804
Kunimura Joan M. • Librarian • High & Intermediate Sch • Kapaa, HI 96756 • AASL YALSA
Kunitz Isadora D. • Adult Service Librarian • Brighton Memorial Library • Rochester, NY 14618 • IFRT
Kunkel Leslie Kent • Librarian • Fielding Institute • Santa Barbara, CA 93105 • ACRL
Kunkel Lilith R. • Library Director • Kent State University Geauga Campus Library • Burton, OH 44021 • ACRL LIRT
Kunselman JoAn D. • University Librarian • California State University-Los Angeles John F. Kennedy Memorial Library • Los Angeles, CA 90032-8300 • ACRL LITA
Kunstler Jane • Circulation System Coordinator • The New York Public Library • New York, NY 10016 • ALSC LITA PLA
Kuntz-Thorsen Connie S. • Head Librarian/IMC • Saint John's University Division of Library & Information Science • Jamaica, NY 11439 • ACRL
Kuntz Ann E. • South Bend, IN 46614
Kuntz Leigh • Reference Librarian • Pikes Peak Library District • Colorado Springs, CO 80901
Kuntz Robert A. • Edinboro University of Pennsylvania Baron-Forness Library • Edinboro, PA 16444
Kuntzelman Carol A. • Roscoe, IL 61073 • RASD
Kuntzman Ann • Phoenix, AZ 85020-3636 • GODORT
Kunz Margarett N. • Head of Acquisitions • National Institutes of Health Clinic Center Library • Bethesda, MD 20892 • ALCTS LITA IFRT
Kunz Robin • Associate Interiors • Hardy Holzman Pfeiffer • New York, NY 10010 • PLA
Kunzel Bonnie • Franklin Township Public Library • Somerset, NJ 08873 • YALSA
Kuo Evelyn C. • Asst. Dir. Automation & Tech. • Merrimack Valley Library Consortium Memorial Hall Library • Andover, MA 01810 • ALCTS
Kuo Huimin L. • Technical Services Librarian • Albany Medical College Schaffer Library of Health Sciences • Albany, NY 12208-3479
Kuo Jiun-Huei C. • Cataloging Librarian • Rice University Fondren Library • Houston, TX 77251-1892
Kuo Margaret P. • Engineering Librarian • Schlumberger Well Services • Houston, TX 77252
Kuo Ming-Ming S. • Clln Dev Librn & Asst Prof • Ball State University Bracken Library • Muncie, IN 47306-0160 • ACRL ALCTS
Kupchella R. Adele • Univ Libs Development Officer • Western Kentucky University Helm-Cravens Library • Bowling Green, KY 42101
Kupelian Carole • Library Media Specialist • Stockville Valley CS • Munnsville, NY 13409 • AASL
Kuperman Aaron W. • Subject Cataloging Librarian • Library of Congress • Washington, DC 20541 • ALCTS EMIERT
Kupersmith Peter A. • Juniata College L A Beeghly Library • Huntingdon, PA 16652 • ACRL
Kupferberg Natalie • Reference Librarian • Montana State University • Bozeman, MT 59717-0332 • ACRL

Kupferman Norman • Assistant Director • Brentwood Public Library • Brentwood, NY 11717 • PLA

Kupidura Peter • Toronto, ON, M6K 2E4 Canada

Kupitz Carla • German Language Cataloger • Brigham Young University • Provo, UT 84602

Kupitz Gabriele I. • Brigham Young University School of Library & Information Sciences • Provo, UT 84602

Kupper Ronald J. • Assoc. Dean-Learning Resources • Northland Pioneer College Department of Library Technology • Holbrook, AZ 86025 • ACRL

Kupperle Helen A. • Thirty-Eight Street Elementary School Media Center • Milwaukee, WI 53210 • AASL

Kurahara Jane M. • Honolulu, HI 96822 • AASL

Kuriger Linda L. • Energy Librarian • U S Department of Energy Bonneville Power Administrative Library • Portland, OR 97208

Kurihara Hitoshi • Japan Library Association • Tokyo, 154 Japan • LAMA PLA

Kurina Nancy • Media Specialist • Palm View Elementary School • Palmetto, FL 34221 • AASL

Kurklen William • Trustee • North Bellmore Public Library • N. Bellmore, NY 11710 • ALTA

Kurland Roslyn S. • Head Librarian • Temple Beth El Library • Hollywood, FL 33020 • ALTA PLA

Kurman Tiina A. • Reference Librarian • Western Illinois University Libraries • Macomb, IL 61455

Kurnos Shirley • Trustee • Springfield Free Public Library • Springfield, NJ 07081

Kuroiwa-Green Nahoko • Evanston, IL 60202

Kuroki Violet H. • Sr Ln/Catlg Dept • Los Angeles Public Library • Los Angeles, CA 90071 • LITA PLA

Kurt Charles M. • Vice President • The Durrant Architects,Inc. • Dubuque, IA 52001 • LAMA

Kurth Galen R. • Student • University of Oklahoma School of Library & Information Studies • Norman, OK 73019

Kurth Martin M. • Head Serials Librarian • Eastern Washington University • Cheney, WA 99004 • ALCTS LITA LRRT

Kurtz Bonnie • Trustee • Long Beach Public Library • Long Beach, NY 11561 • ALSC ALTA

Kurtz Grace J. • Librarian • Frost Lake School Library • Saint Paul, MN 55106 • AASL

Kurtz Linda M. • Mount Kisco Public Library • Mount Kisco, NY 10549 • AASL

Kurtz M. Charlene • Student • Sam Houston State University Department of Library Science • Huntsville, TX 77341-2236 • AASL EMIERT IFRT SRRT

Kurtz Royce D. • Librarian • University of Mississippi John Davis Williams Library • University, MS 38677 • ACRL

Kurtz Winifred M. • Youth Services Librarian • Thomas Ford Memorial Library • Western Springs, IL 60558 • ALSC

Kurutz Gary • Special Collections Librarian • California State Library • Sacramento, CA 94237-0001 • ACRL ALCTS

Kurz David • Director • Herbert Wescoat Memorial Library • McArthur, OH 45651

Kurz Susan Martha • Anne Arundel County Library Linthicum Branch • Linthicum, MD 21090 • PLA

Kurzban Nina L. • Chappagua, NY 10514 • AASL

Kusack James M. • Associate Professor • South Connecticut State University • New Haven, CT 06515 • ACRL LAMA LRRT

Kusch Maria C. • Student • University of Texas at Austin Graduate School of Library & Information Sciences • Austin, TX 78712-1276

Kuselias Christopher J. • President • Kuselias Enterprises Inc. • New Haven, CT 06510 • PLA

Kuser Charlotte C. • Student • University of North Texas School of Library & Information Sciences • Denton, TX 76203 • PLA NMRT

Kushner Scott R. • Librarian III/Ext Services • South Brunswick Public Library • Monmouth Junction, NJ 08852

Kusik James P. • Student • University of Wisconsin-Milwaukee Golda Meir Library • Milwaukee, WI 53201

Kuss Martha A. • Library/Media Specialist • Crawford High School • San Diego, CA 92115 • AASL YALSA

Kussey Christine M. • Student • State University of New York (SUNY) School of Information & Library Studies • Buffalo, NY 14260

Kuszczak Marta H. • Librarian • University of Illinois at Chicago University Library • Chicago, IL 60680 • GODORT IRRT

Kuszmaul Marcia J. • Dir. of Mkt.,ALA Communications • American Library Association • Chicago, IL 60611-2795

Kutchera Thomas G. • Trustee • Milwaukee County Federated Library System • Milwaukee, WI 53233 • ALTA

Kutchukians Winifred H. • Evening/Weekend Spvr. • State University of New York (SUNY) University Libraries • Albany, NY 12222 • ACRL NMRT

Kutler Emily H. • Children's Librarian • Summit Public Library • Summit, NJ 07901 • ALSC

Kutter Marti • Head Librarian • Aloha High School • Beaverton, OR 97075

Kutteroff Ethel C. • Richmond, VA 23221 • AASL *Continuing*

Kuttler Barbara J. • Davenport, IA 52804 • YALSA

Kuttler Eugenia • Berkeley, CA 94709 • PLA

Kutulas Nancy Louise • Reference Librarian • United States Army L • Fort Bragg, NC 28307 • RASD

Kutz Edward F. • Student • Emporia State University William Allen White Library • Emporia, KS 66801

Kutzik Jennifer S. • Colorado State University William E. Morgan Library • Fort Collins, CO 80523 • LITA

Kuykendall Judith • Director • Corsicana Public Library • Corsicana, TX 75110-5296 • PLA RASD YALSA

Kuykendall William J. • Library Specialist III • Jarvis Christian College Olin Library & Communication Center • Hawkins, TX 75765 • IFRT

Kuzel Judith F. • Administrative Librarian • Aurora Public Library • Aurora, IL 60505-4299 • ALCTS PLA

Kuzen Theodore Jr. • Preservation Librarian • University of Virginia Alderman Library • Charlottesville, VA 22903-2498 • ACRL ALCTS

Kverno Ellen M. • Monterey Park, CA 91754 • Continuing

Kviklys Danguole • Reference Librarian • DePaul University Library • Chicago, IL 60604-2287

Kwack Dong Chul • Acquisitions Librarian • Korea Atomic Enegery Research Institute • Dae Jeon City, South Korea • ASCLA LAMA LITA RASD IFRT IRRT LIRT

Kwajewski Ken A. • Technology/Media Director • Doherty Middle School • Andover, MA 01810 • AASL LAMA

Kwakye-Berko Abena • Bronx, NY 10453

Kwan Barbara P. • Head of Reference Department • California State University Hayward Library • Hayward, CA 94542 • ACRL

Kwan Cecilia • Head Cataloger • University of California-Davis Library • Davis, CA 95616 • ALCTS LITA

Kwan Julie K. • Science & Engineering Libraian • University of Southern California • Los Angeles, CA 90033 • ACRL RASD

Kwan Laisheung • Senior Library Assistant • Hong Kong Polytech Library • Kowloon, Hong Kong

Kwan Y. Kathy • Reference Librarian • Winthrop University Hospital Health Sciences Library • Mineola, NY 11501 • LITA

Kwidzinski Irene • New Milford, CT 06776 • AASL

Kwik Marilyn S. • Hamtramck, MI 48212

Kwok Louisa W. Y. • Assistant Librarian II • Hong Kong University of Science & Technology University Library • Kowloon, Hong Kong

Kwok Maureen • Sr Ln • San Jose Public Library • San Jose, CA 95113

Kwok Rosita C. • Technical Services Librarian • Pepperdine University Payson Library • Malibu, CA 90263 • ACRL

Kwon Myoungja L. • Systems & Budget Librarian • University of Nevada-Las Vegas James R. Dickinson Library • Las Vegas, NV 89154 • ACRL LAMA LITA

Kwon Veong S. • Libray/Information Services Dept • Sandoz Pharmaceutical Corp. • East Hanover, NJ 07936 • ALCTS LAMA LITA

Kwong Marsha J. • Odenton, MD 21113

Kylander RuDell • Librarian • The Fay School • Southboro, MA 01772-9106

Kyles Rubye R. • Assistant Executive Director • Columbus Metropolitan Library • Columbus, OH 43215 • PLA

Kynast Mary • Fond du Lac, WI 54935

Kypros Cally • Librarian II First Assistant • Detroit Public Library Acq Dept • Detroit, MI 48202-4093 • ALSC YALSA

Kyrillidou Martha • Student • University of Illinois Graduate School of Library and Information Science • Urbana, IL 61801 • ACRL LAMA IFRT

Kyropoulos Mary S. • Librarian • Oakwood Secondary High School • North Hollywood, CA 91601 • AASL

Kysely Elizabeth Coxe • Colorado Spgs, CO 80906

Kyte Craig D. • Coor.,Gen Info & Ref Services • Seattle Public Library • Seattle, WA 98104-1193 • PLA

La Cava Lydia R. • Director • Broward Community College • Fort Lauderdale, FL 33314 • ACRL

La Clair Carol A. • Librarian • Wayne Oakland Library Federation • Wayne, MI 48184 • ALSC PLA CLENE NMRT

La Croix Carla E. • Asst. Mgr., Bus. & Tech Div. • Dallas Public Library • Dallas, TX 75201 • PLA RASD

La Moy William T. • Director of the Library • Essex Institute Library • Salem, MA 01970 • ACRL

La Perriere Renee J. • Portales, NM 88130

La Pierre Kay • Student • University of North Texas School of Library & Information Sciences • Denton, TX 76203 • ALSC PLA

La Polt Margaret B. • Norwalk, CT 06851 • AASL

La Porte Toni • Youth Services Librarian • Pierce Jr High Sch Lib • Grosse Pointe, MI 48230

La Russa Carol J. • Associate Librarian • University of California Physical Sciences Library • Davis, CA 95616 • ACRL MAGERT

La Stella Sharon Y. • Little Silver, NJ 07739

La Vallee Katherine M. • Librarian • TASC • Arlington, VA 22209

LaBarbera Diane M. • Student • University of Illinois Graduate School of Library and Information Science • Urbana, IL 61801

LaBorde Pamela • Children's Librarian • Seattle Public Library High Point Branch • Seattle, WA 98126

LaBorie Tim • System Librarian • Saint Josephs University Drexel Library • Philadelphia, PA 19131-1395 • ACRL

LaBossiere Holly A. • Madison, WI 53703

LaBrake Lynn B. • Associate Director • University of Central Florida Library • Orlando, FL 32816-0666 • ACRL

LaBreche Janet K. • Librarian • Alger Maximum Correctional Facility • Munising, MI 49862 • ASCLA

LaBrecque Jean R. • High School Librarian • Bonny Eagle High School • West Buxton, ME 04093 • AASL YALSA

LaBudde Kenneth J. • Kansas City, MO 64112 • ACRL RASD LRRT *Life*

LaCaff Lena B. • Coordinator • San Antonio Area Library System • San Antonio, TX 78205 • PLA

LaChapelle Catherine I. • Bardonia, NY 10954

LaCharite Paul A.L. • Boston, MA 02108-1412

LaCroix Michael J. • Director of Libary Services • Albright College • Reading, PA 19612-5234 • ACRL ALCTS LAMA LITA

LaCroix Mina B. • Humanities Bibliographer • State University of New York (SUNY) University Libraries • Albany, NY 12222 • ACRL

LaDue Annette Schwartz • New York Public Library Van-Nest Pelham Branch • Bronx, NY 10462 • ALSC

LaDue William • Trustee • Tucson Pima Library • Tucson, AZ 85726 • ALTA

LaFaille Eugene E. • Library Director • Brunswick School • Greenwich, CT 06830 • YALSA

LaFantasie Susan L. • Student • University of Washington Graduate School of Library and Information Science • Seattle, WA 98195

LaFaro Lydia E. • Arizona State University Hayden Library • Tempe, AZ 85287-1006 • ACRL RASD

LaFever Susan • Coordinator of Bibl Control • Tennessee Technological University University Library • Cookeville, TN 38505 • ALCTS

LaFlam Edela • Director • Ashland Public Library • Ashland, MA 01721

LaFlamme Simonne C. Sr. • Catherine McAuley High School Library • Portland, ME 04103

LaFond Deborah M. • Student • University of California-Berkeley School of Library & Information Studies • Berkeley, CA 94720

LaForce Gina • Head of Technical Support Serv. • Hamilton Public Library • Hamilton ON, L8N 4E4 Canada • ALCTS LAMA LITA PLA

LaFrance Cynthia • Assistant Librarian • Gray North Gloucester Middle School • Gray, ME 04039

LaFrance Dorothy R. • Director • Newburyport Public Library • Newburyport, MA 01950

LaGasse G. Paulette • Elem Library Media Specialist • Broken Bow Public Schools • Broken Bow, OK 74728

LaGodna Barbara E. • Belcamp, MD 21017

LaGrange Johanne L. • A/V Cataloger • Columbia University Health Sciences Library • New York, NY 10032 • ALCTS NMRT

LaGrutta Charles J. • Chicago Board Options Exchange • Chicago, IL 60605

LaGuardia Cheryl M. • Libray Coor. of Computerizes • University of California UCSB Library • Santa Barbara, CA 93106-9010 • ACRL LITA LIRT

LaHood Charles G. Jr. • Port Tobacco, MD 20677 • ACRL ALCTS *Life*

LaLuzerne Anthony J. • Head of Technical Services • Saint Norbert College Todd Wehr Library • De Pere, WI 54115

LaManna Jean D. • Ludlum Elementary School • Hempstead, NY 11550 • AASL

LaMantia Birgit N. • Palos Heights Public Library • Palos Heights, IL 60463

LaMarca Christine L. • Student • Catholic University of America School of Library and Information Science • Washington, DC 20064 • ASCLA

LaPenna Patricia Mrs. • West Islip, NY 11795 • ALTA PLA YALSA

LaPierre Barbe • Supervisor/Periodicals • Springfield City Library • Springfield, MA 01103

laPlante Jane M. • Minot State University Memorial Library • Minot, ND 58701

LaPolt Lisa A. • Student • State University of New York at Albany School of Information Science & Policy • Albany, NY 12222

LaPorte Terry • Library Media Specialist • North Hartford Middle School • Pylesville, MD 21132 • AASL

LaReau Rebecca • Cataloger • Simpson Thacher & Bartlett • New York, NY 10017-3909 • ALCTS LAMA LITA

LaRiviere Gladys M. • Core Teacher • University of Hawaii School of Library & Information Studies • Honolulu, HI 96822 • AASL IRRT SRRT

LaRose Patricia • Head Adult Serivces/Reference • Newport Public Library • Newport, RI 02840

LaRossa Daniel • Trustee • Suffolk Cooperative Library System • Bellport, NY 11713 • AASL ACRL ALCTS ALSC ALTA ASCLA LAMA LITA PLA RASD GODORT IFRT LHRT

LaRue James • Library Director • Douglas Public Library District • Castle Rock, CO 80104 • PLA

LaRue Paula J. • Lincoln Jr. High School • Van Wert, OH 45891 • AASL

LaRue Rosemary • Kalamazoo Central High School • Kalamazoo, MI 49007 • AASL

LaTronica Marina Starr • Senior Librarian • Berkeley Public Library • Berkeley, CA 94704 • ALSC PLA

LaViolette Pat • Director • Brown County Library • Green Bay, WI 54301 • LAMA LITA PLA CLENE

Laakso Mary Jo. • Reference Librarian • College of St. Catherine Library • St. Paul, MN 55105 • ACRL

Lab Margaret W. • Assistant Librarian • Billings Senior High School • Billings, MT 59102 • AASL

Labaree Robert V. • Reference/Acquisitions Librarian • The American University Library • Washington, DC 20016-8046 • ACRL RASD

Labash Stephen Peter • University of Baltimore Langsdale Library • Baltimore, MD 21201 • ACRL RASD IFRT SRRT

Labatut Julia A. • Student • Louisiana State University School of Library & Information Science • Baton Rouge, LA 70803-3290 • PLA RASD

Labdon Mark A. • Kansas City, MO 64114-2906

Labodda Marsha J. • Librarian • Del Valle High School Library • El Paso, TX 79907 • AASL YALSA EMIERT IFRT VRT

Laborde Andrea M. • Coor of LRC • Southeastern Louisiana University • Hammond, LA 70402 • AASL

Labory Louise • Director • Anjou Municipal Library • Anjou, PQ, H1K 3X9 Canada • PLA

Labosky Theodore P. • Forsyth County Public Library • Winston-Salem, NC 27101 • PLA

Labounty Maxine • Chevy Chase, MD 20815 • Continuing

Labrecque Julie • Trustee • Pierce County Rural Library District • Tacoma, WA 98446 • ALTA PLA

Labrie O Muriel • Keene, NH 03431

Labuda Gloria • Media Specialist • Chippewa Valley High School • Mount Clemens, MI 480414 • AASL

Labuda Joseph • Librarian • Pima Community College West Campus LRC • Tucson, AZ 85709

Labuda Kathy D. • Library Director • Antioch Public Library District • Antioch, IL 60002 • PLA

Lacerba Francesca • Librarian • Good Counsel High School • Chicago, IL 60659

Lachance Barbara • Sandown, NH 03873

Lachance Frances E. • Librarian • Bliss Elementary School • El Paso, TX 79906 • AASL

Lachendro Leonard L. • Lodi, CA 95240 • Continuing

Lachowicz Constance • Library Director • South Kingstown Public Library • Peace Dale, RI 02883-0037 • ALSC PLA

Lackey Ann F. • Librarian • Phineas Banning High School • Wilmington, CA 90744 • AASL LAMA EMIERT

Lackey Charlie S. Mrs. • Frostburg, MD 21532

Lackey Michael M. • Public Services Librarian • University of South Carolina Coastal Carolina College Kimbel Library • Conway, SC 29526

Lackmann Jennifer G. • Student • State University of New York at Albany School of Information Science & Policy • Albany, NY 12222 • LITA

Lackore Lois • Groton, CT 06340 • AASL YALSA

Lacks Bernice K. • Head of Reference • California State University,Fresno Henry Madden Library • Fresno, CA 93740-0034 • ACRL RASD

Lacook Nancy C. • Branch Manager • Memphis-Shelby County Public Library Collierville Branch • Collierville, TN 38017

Lacroix Phyllis Dr. • Head/Information Media • Saint Cloud State University Centennial Hall LRC • St. Cloud, MN 56301-4498 • AASL

Lacroix Yvon-Andre • Director • Bibliotheque Municipale de Brossard • Brossard, PQ, J4Z 2B4 Canada • PLA

Lacy Emilia • Director • Centenary College Taylor Memorial Library • Hackettstown, NJ 07840 • ACRL

Lacy Mary A. • Rare Book & Spec Collection Div. • Library of Congress • Washington, DC 20541 • ACRL ALCTS

Laczko Ethel • California Association for Bilingual Education • Ontario, CA 91762

Lada Lynn M. • Head of Youth Services • Michigan City Public Library • Michigan City, IN 46360 • ALSC

Ladd Dennis W. • University of Hawaii William S. Richardson • Honolulu, HI 96822

Ladd Dorothy P. • Warsaw, VA 22572 • ACRL ALCTS IFRT   *Continuing*

Ladd Frances R. • Rochester, NY 14618 • Continuing

Ladd Jay L. • Assistant Director • Ohio State University Libraries • Columbus, OH 43210-1286 • ACRL RASD *Life*

Laderman Anne B. • Glen Rock, NJ 07452 • AASL   *Continuing*

Ladley Winifred C. • Edmonds, WA 98020 • AASL ALSC   *Life*

Ladner Sharyn J. • Assistant Professor • University of Miami Libraries Richter Library • Coral Gables, FL 33124 • ACRL LITA

Ladof Nina Sydney • Librarian • Camden County Library Echelon Urban Center • Voorhees, NJ 08043 • PLA

Ladzick Margie • Library Media Specialist • Allen Elementary School • Plymouth, MI 48170 • AASL ALSC

Laesch Steven P. • Consultant • Amaranth Consultants • Canton, NY 13617 • LITA

Lafaye Cary DuPre • Reference & Periodicals Libn. • Midlands Technical College • Columbia, SC 29202

Lafayette Patricia E. • Director • Trenton Public Library • Trenton, MI 48183

Lafferty-Cohen Kimberly A. • Seattle, WA 98119 • PLA YALSA IFRT

Lafferty Robert • Technical Services Librarian • Broadview Public Library District • Broadview, IL 60153

Laffrey Laurel W S • Edmonton, AB, T5W 1W9 Canada

Lafleur Bruce • Columbia, SC 29205-2366

Laframboise Joseph • Data Archivist/Asst. Librarian • Pennsylvania State University Pattee Library • University Park, PA 16802

Lafranchi William E. Mr. • Patrick J. Stapleton Library Indiana University of Pennsylvania • Indiana, PA 15705 • ACRL LAMA   *Life*

Lagana Gretchen L. • Special Collections Librarian • University of Illinois at Chicago University Library • Chicago, IL 60680 • ACRL

Lagasse Carol T. • Scotia, NY 12302

Lage Alice M. • Alexandria, VA 22302 • Life

Lager Mark A. • Director • St. Johns Seminary Edward Laurence Doheny Memorial Library • Camarillo, CA 93012 • ACRL SRRT

Lageschulte Judith M. • Librarian • Los Altos Christian School • Los Altos, CA 94086-7025

Lagrave Virginia Z. • Oklahoma City, OK 73120-1789 • PLA   *Continuing*

Lagree Enid S. • APO New York, AE 09220-5000

Lahann Julie L. • Industry Representative • IBM Corporation • Manassas, VA 22110 • ACRL PLA ERT

Lahey Cynthia B. • Head of Technical Services • New Canaan Library • New Canaan, CT 06840

Lahey Kate • Trustee • Salt Lake City Public Library • Salt Lake City, UT 84111 • ALTA

Lahiri Amar K. • Professor • University of Rhode Island Library • Kingston, RI 02881-0803 • ALCTS

Lahlum K. M. • U.S. Fish & Wildlife Service Northern Praire Wildlife Res Ctr • Jamestown, ND 58402

Lahman Katherine B. • Librarian • Robious Middle School • Midlothian, VA 23113 • AASL

Lahtinen Sandra C. • Wilton, CT 06897-3508 • ACRL RASD NMRT

Lahue Dena C. • Student • University of Southern Mississippi School of Library Science • Hattiesburg, MS 39406-5146

Lai Diane Z. • Port Hueneme, CA 93041-3061

Lai Francesco A. • London ON, N5W 1A2 Canada • ACRL RASD

Lai Hui-Lan • Student • University of South Carolina College of Library & Information Science • Columbia, SC 29208

Lai Libby • Trustee • Santa Clara County Free Library • San Jose, CA 95112-4446 • ALTA

Lai Mayling • Lecturer • National Open University • Taipei County 24702, Taiwan • LITA

Lai Sheila S. • Reference Librarian • California State University-Sacramento Library • Sacramento, CA 95819-6039 • ACRL

Lai Winnie W. • Sir Speedy Printing • Seattle, WA 98125

Laibach John H. • Trustee • Massepequa Public Library • Massapequa, NY 11758 • ALTA PLA

Laich Katherine • North Hollywood, CA 91601

Laidlaw Sheila M. • Fredericton NB, E3B 4N1 Canada • ACRL LAMA LITA CLENE LIRT   *Continuing*

Lain Christine R. • Ft. Worth, TX 76107 • Continuing

Laine Rebecca R. • Hampden-Sydney, VA 23943

Laing Sally • Trustee • Mid-Hudson Library System • Poughkeepsie, NY 12601

Laird Bruce A. • Trustee • Elk Grove Village Public Library • Elk Grove Village, IL 60007 • ALTA

Laird Cathryn • Librarian • Safety Harbor Public Library • Safety Harbor, FL 34695 • LITA

Laird Nancy M. • Student • University of Missouri-Columbia School of Library & Informational Science • Columbia, MO 65211

Laird Suzanne T. • Librarian • Wilson Hill Elementary School • Worthington, OH 43085

Laird W. David Jr. • Tucson, AZ 85716

Laite Berkley H. • Reference Coordinator • Shippensburg University Lehman Memorial Library • Shippensburg, PA 17257-2299

Laite Carol • Librarian • Hagerstown Business College • Hagerstown, MD 21742

Lajara Migdalia • MS/US Librarian • Baldwin School of Puerto Rico • Guaynalbo, PR 00657

Lajewski Catherine M. • Assoc. Dir., Young People's Svs. • Elkhart Public Library • Elkhart, IN 46516-3184 • ALSC

Lakatos Rhonda L. • Branch Supervisor • San Jose Public Library Evergreen Branch • San Jose, CA 95121 • PLA

Lake Brenda B. • Graduate Student • University of Rhode Island Graduate School of Library & Information Studies • Kingston, RI 02881-0815

Lake Carole S. • Media Specialist • Philander Lee Sch • Canby, OR 97013 • AASL

Lake Gretchen L. • Assistant Archivist • University of Alaska Elmer E. Rasmuson Library • Fairbanks, AK 99775-1005 • ACRL RASD CLENE LHRT LIRT MAGERT   *Life*

Lake Kathy • Westside High School Library • Omaha, NE 68114 • AASL

Lake Lin C. • Columbia College J. Drake Edens Library • Columbia, SC 29203

Lake Patricia B. • Library Director • Fayette County Public Library • Connersville, IN 47331 • PLA

Lakhanpal Sarv K. • Head of Gifts Section • University of Saskatchewan Library • Saskatoon SK, S7N 0W0 Canada

Lakin Paula M. • Librarian • Flagstaff High School • Flagstaff, AZ 86001 • AASL YALSA VRT

Lakus Priscilla • Youth Services Librarian • Tampa-Hillsborough County Public Library • Tampa, FL 33602 • ALSC

Laliberte Madeleine A. • Librarian • Universite Laval Bibliotheque Cite Universitaire • Quebec PQ, G1K 7P4 Canada

Lalime-Mowry Laura J. • Student • University of Rhode Island Graduate School of Library & Information Studies • Kingston, RI 02881-0815

Lallier Betty • Essex Junction, VT 05452 • AASL

Lally Ann M. • Student • University of Missouri-Columbia School of Library & Informational Science • Columbia, MO 65211 • SRRT

Lalwani Leena • South Lyon, MI 48178

Lam Helen Shui-Ching • Toronto ON, M4M 1Y3 Canada

Lam Janet • Librarian • Thelma Parker Memorial City State Library • Kamuela, HI 96743 • PLA

Lam Kwan-Yau • Student • Indiana University School of Library and Information Science • Bloomington, IN 47405

Lamarque Joan E. • Outreach/Reference Librarian • Rolling Meadows Library • Rolling Meadows, IL 60008 • ASCLA

Lamb-Deans Debra S. • Public Service Librarian • Ithaca College Library • Ithaca, NY 14850 • ACRL LITA

Lamb Annette C. • Associate Professor • University of Toledo • Toledo, OH 43606 • AASL

Lamb Connie • Reference Librarian • Brigham Young University Harold B. Lee Library • Provo, UT 84602 • ACRL RASD CLENE

Lamb Donald K. • Consultant • Wisconsin Division for Library Services • Madison, WI 53707

Lamb Edna C. • Branch Librarian • Free Library of Philadelphia Tacony Branch • Philadelphia, PA 19135 • PLA RASD

Lamb Heather A. • Children's Services • San Anselmo Public Library • San Anselmo, CA 94960 • ALSC LITA

Lamb Jay A. • Librarian/Computers/Teacher • Peach Springs School • Peach Springs, AZ 86434 • AASL

Lamb Joan B. • Director • Howard Whittemore Memorial Library • Naugatuck, CT 06770

Lamb Jolaine B. • Reference Librarian • United States Air Force Flight Test Center • Edwards AFB, CA 93523-5000 • AFLRT FLRT

Lamb June Louise • Library Director • North West Arkansas Community College • Bentonville, AR 72712 • ACRL

Lamb Kurt H. • Director • Mexico-Audrain County Library • Mexico, MO 65265 • PLA

Lamb Michael J. • Student • Wayne State University Library Science Program • Detroit, MI 48202 • ACRL PLA RASD

Lamb Robert Scott II • Presv and Consv Librarian • Indiana State University Cunningham Memorial Library • Terre Haute, IN 47809 • ACRL ALCTS

Lamb Ruth • University of Waterloo • Waterloo ON, N2L 3G1 Canada

Lamb Sara E. • Head Librarian • Lake Bluff Public Library • Lake Bluff, IL 60044 • LAMA PLA

Lamb Sheila K. • Technical Services Librarian • United States Coast Guard Academy Library (d1) • New London, CT 06320-4195 • AFLRT

Lamb Susan D. • Balboa, CA 92661 • PLA

Lamb Therese M. • Assistant Prof. of Library Svs. • University of Southern Colorado • Pueblo, CO 81001 • LITA

Lambe Jennifer J. • Port Huron, MI 48060

Lambelet Jennifer S. • Adult Services Coordinator • Los Angeles Public Library • Los Angeles, CA 90071 • PLA IFRT

Lambert Adrienne C. • Trustee • Villa Park Public Library • Villa Park, IL 60181 • ALTA

Lambert Bess Mrs. • Student • Indiana University School of Library and Information Science • Bloomington, IN 47405

Lambert Beverly • Edythe L. Dyer Community Library • Hampden, ME 04444 • PLA

Lambert Deborah Nolan • Librarian Media Specialist • Montgomery County Public Schools Diamond Elementary School • Gaithersburg, MD 20878 • AASL ACRL

Lambert Debra Anne • Student • Wayne State University Library Science Program • Detroit, MI 48202 • LITA

Lambert Dennis K. • Head, Collection Management • Villanova University Falvey Memorial Library • Villanova, PA 19085-1699 • ACRL ALCTS

Lambert H. Jeanette • Waco, TX 76712 • ALSC

Lambert Karen A. • Kansas City, MO 64114

Lambert Linda • Trustee • Bellingham Public Library • Bellingham, WA 98227 • ALTA

Lambert Linda J. • Librarian • George Fox College • Newberg, OR 97132 • RASD

Lambert Lyn D. • Law Librarian • Massachusetts Trial Court Fitchburg Law Library • Fitchburg, MA 01420

Lambert Marsha L. • Media Director,L.R.C. • Marshall Public Schools • Marshall, MI 49068 • AASL ALSC

Lambert Pat • Upland Public Library • Upland, CA 91786

Lambert Sandra L. • Assistant Children's Librarian • Cook Memorial Library • Libertyville, IL 60048

Lambert Sarah E. • Girls Preparatory School • Chattanooga, TN 37405 • AASL

Lambert Sharon A. • Vero Beach, FL 32960

Lambert Toni L. • Chief of Automation/HALAN • Houston Public Library • Houston, TX 77002 • LITA PLA

Lamberta Joseph • Trustee • Babylon Public Library • Babylon, NY 11702 • ALTA

Lambeth V • Librarian • De Witt Road School • Webster, NY 14580 • AASL

Lamborn Joan G. • Acquisitions/Serials Librarian • University of Northern Colorado James A. Michener Library • Greeley, CO 80639

Lambrecht Jay H. • University of Illinois at Chicago University Library • Chicago, IL 60680 • ALCTS

Lambrecht Jeanette M. • Children's Bookstore Manager • Family After School Program • Milwaukee, WI 53211

Lambrecht Melissa Mahood • Chicago, IL 60646-6103 • ACRL

Lambrev Garrett I. • Oakland Public Library Martin Luther King Branch • Oakland, CA 94621 • PLA EMIERT IFRT

Lamer Pamela R. • Bloomington, IN 47408 • ALSC

Lamere Sheena G. • Inst Cons • Maryland State Department of Environment • Baltimore, MD 21224-6612

Lamey Diana • Media Specialist • Wyncote School Library • Wyncote, PA 19095 • AASL EMIERT

Lamkin Bernice M. • Director of REMC 7 • Ottawa Area Intermediate School District • Holland, MI 49424 • AASL ALSC YALSA

Lamm Sylvia L. • School Librarian • Durham City Schools Fayetteville St School • Durham, NC 27705 • AASL

Lammers Barbara J. • University of South Carolina • Columbia, SC 29208 • ACRL

Lammers Keith S. • Student • Drexel University College of Information Studies • Philadelphia, PA 19104-2875

Lamon Sara Louise • Macon, GA 31211 • Continuing

Lamond Joanne J. • Library Media Specialist • Barnum Woods Elementary • East Meadow, NY 11554

Lamont Bridget Later • Director • Illinois State Library • Springfield, IL 62701-1796 • ASCLA LAMA PLA

Lamont Melissa • Government Documents • University of Virginia Alderman Library • Charlottesville, VA 22903-2498 • GODORT MAGERT

Lamorte Laura • New York, NY 10033 • LITA RASD IFRT

Lamoureux Theresa A. • Student • University of North Carolina at Chapel Hill School of Information and Library Science • Chapel Hill, NC 27599-3360

Lamp Deborah P. • Librarian • Blennerhassett Elementary School • Parkersburg, WV 26101 • AASL

Lamphere Ginni S. • Student • University of Michigan School of Information and Library Studies • Ann Arbor, MI 48109-1092 • PLA

Lampkins Donna L. • Fayetteville, NC 28303 • SORT

Lampman Sherry • Saint Paul, MN 55103

Lamprey Patricia M. • Head,Reference & Adult Services • Jefferson County Public Library • Lakewood, CO 80215

Lan Wen-Chin • Student • University of North Carolina at Chapel Hill School of Information and Library Science • Chapel Hill, NC 27599-3360

Lancaster Adrianna • Student • Texas Woman's University School of Library & Information Studies • Denton, TX 76204

Lancaster Barbara G. • Arlington, TX 76006 • AASL

Lancaster Elizabeth • Branch Librarian • Howard County Library • Columbia, MD 21044

Lancaster Frederick W. • Professor • University of Illinois Graduate School of Library and Information Science • Urbana, IL 61801

Lancaster Joann • Tech Serv • Monument Mountain Regional High School • Great Barrington, MA 02130

Lancaster John • Curator of Special Collections • Amherst College Library • Amherst, MA 01002 • ACRL

Lancaster Ruth • Grande Prairie Public Library District • Hazel Crest, IL 60429 • PLA

Lance Kathleen A. • Head of Public Services • Sweet Briar College Library • Sweet Briar, VA 24595 • ACRL LITA RASD LIRT

Lance Keith Curry • Dir. Library Research Service • Colorado State Library and Adult Education Office • Denver, CO 80203 • ASCLA LAMA PLA LRRT

Lance Marguerita M. • Library Trustee • DeKalb County Public Library • Decatur, GA 30030 • ALTA

Lance Susan Cardot • Lakewood, CA 90713

Lance Tim • Student • University of Texas at Austin Graduate School of Library & Information Sciences • Austin, TX 78712-1276 • ALSC

Land Barbara • San Francisco, CA 94121 • ACRL RASD ILERT

Land Jamie E. • Student • Shippensburg University Lehman Memorial Library • Shippensburg, PA 17257-2299

Land Patricia • Trustee • Palos Heights Public Library • Palos Heights, IL 60463

Land Reginald Brian • Executive Director • Ontario Legislative Library • Toronto ON, M7A 1A9 Canada

Land Roy • Charlottesville, VA 22903 • Continuing

Land Susan Hagen • Head of Adult Serivces • Skokie Public Library • Skokie, IL 60077-3680 • ALSC LAMA PLA RASD IFRT

Landau Edith • Director of Libraries • Navajo Community College Naaltsoos Ba'Hooghan Library • Tsaile, AZ 86556 • ACRL ALCTS LAMA LITA RASD

Landau Elaine • Sparta, NJ 07871

Landau Elvita A. • Director • Brookings Public Library • Brookings, SD 57006-2077 • PLA

Landau Herbert B. • Westport, CT 06880 • ILERT

Landauer Anne M. • Bigleville, PA 17307

Landazuri Roberto D. • Student • University of California-Berkeley University Library • Berkeley, CA 94720

Lande Dilys E. • Banneker High School • Washington, DC 20001 • AASL

Landeck Mary E. • Assistant Ln, Reference & Circ. • Milwaukee Area Technical College Rasche Memorial Library • Milwaukee, WI 53233 • ACRL LITA

Landenwitsch Margaret J. • Cincinnati, OH 45211 • ASCLA LITA *Continuing*

Lander Dorothy • Armonk, NY 10504 • Continuing

Lander Faye A. • Educational Media Specialist • Cleveland Public Schools • Cleveland, OH 44114 • ALSC SRRT

Landergan Kathe • Marblehead, MA 01945

Landers Alison B. • Supervising Librarian • San Jose Public Library • San Jose, CA 95113 • LAMA PLA

Landers Lora • Northfield, MN 55057 • RASD YALSA *Life*

Landers Patricia A. • Vancouver, WA 98662

Landers Teresa P. • Head Business & Science • Phoenix Public Library • Phoenix, AZ 85004 • PLA RASD

Landes Edythe M. • Director • Stratford Library Association • Stratford, CT 06497 • ALCTS ALSC ALTA LAMA LITA PLA RASD

Landes Jan • Library Media Specialist • Hinkletown Mennonite School • Ephrata, PA 17522 • AASL

Landes Sonja • Student • State University of New York (SUNY) School of Information & Library Studies • Buffalo, NY 14260

Landesman Betty • Coordinator for Systems Planning • George Washington University Gelman Library • Washington, DC 20052 • ACRL ALCTS LAMA LITA

Landesman Margaret M. • Acquisitions Librarian • University of Utah Marriott Library • Salt Lake City, UT 84112-1179 • ALCTS

Landfried Tracy A. • Librarian • United States Army APG Post Library • ABRDN PRV GRD, MD 21005-5001 • PLA AFLRT FLRT

Landgraf Mary N. • Asst. Chief of Tech Services • San Francisco Public Library • San Francisco, CA 94102 • LAMA

Landgren Barbara R. • Longmont, CO 80501 • LITA

Landi Regina D. • Pittsburgh, PA 15206

Landingham Alpha Mark • Reference Librarian • University of Saint Thomas • Houston, TX 77006 • RASD

Landis Dennis C. • Editor European Americana • John Carter Brown Library • Providence, RI 02912 • ACRL

Landis Eve M. • Santa Barbara, CA 93105 • PLA RASD *Continuing*

Landis Kathryn T. • Reference Librarian • North Arlington Public Library • North Arlington, NJ 07032

Landis Martha • Senior Spec. Collection Bibl. • University of Illinois Library • Urbana, IL 61801 • ACRL ALCTS RASD *Life*

Landis Sharon M. • Kalamazoo, MI 49009

Landman Libby Geller Lynch • Reference Librarian • Larchmont Public Library • Larchmont, NY 10538

Landon Betty B. • Collection Development Librarian • Northeast Texas Library System • Garland, TX 75040-6304

Landon Chris R. • Trustee • Multnomah County Library • Portland, OR 97212 • ALTA

Landon Florence • Associate Librarian • Mesa Community College Library Technician Program • Mesa, AZ 85202 • LIRT

Landon Mary • Librarian • Larmar Junior High School • Irving, TX 75060 • AASL

Landor Blake • Humanities Selector • University of Florida Libraries • Gainesville, FL 32611-2047 • ACRL

Landow Janet G. • North Tarrytown, NY 10591 • PLA RASD IFRT

Landquist Audrey Dolores • Minneapolis, MN 55422 • Continuing

Landram Christina • Head, Cataloging Department • Georgia State University Pullen Library • Atlanta, GA 30303-3081 • ACRL ALCTS LITA *Life*

Landrum Joe • Library Consultant • State Library of Louisiana • Baton Rouge, LA 70821

Landrum Margaret C. • Dean • Everett Community College Library Media Center • Everett, WA 98201-1327 • ACRL LAMA

Landrum Susan A. • Student • Louisiana State University School of Library & Information Science • Baton Rouge, LA 70803-3290

Landry Abbie V. • Ln, Head of Ref., Asst Professor • Northwestern State University Watson Memorial Library • Natchitoches, LA 71497

Landry Carole T. • Media Specialist • South Central Services Co-Op • Camden, AR 71701 • AASL VRT

Landry Denise C. • Librarian • Southeastern Louisiana University Linus A. Sims Memorial Library • Hammond, LA 70402 • ACRL

Landry Mary E. • Director of Library Services • Dundalk Community College • Baltimore, MD 21222 • ACRL LAMA LITA PLA RASD *Life*

Landry Paul B. • Trustee • West Baton Rouge Parish Library • Port Allen, LA 70767

Landry Pauline • Saint Bernard School • Breaux Bridge, LA 70517

Landry Ted L. • Assistant Director • Iberville Parish Library • Plaquemine, LA 70764

Landsberg Janet • Librarian • Thurston High School Library • Redford, MI 48239 • AASL

Landsburg Ellen P. • Librarian/Research Assistant • Pew Charitable Trusts One Commerce Square • Philadelphia, PA 19103-7017

Landset Nancy H. • Library Media Specialist • Camden High School • Camden, NY 13316 • AASL

Landtroop Ann F. • Houston, TX 77007 • PLA

Lane Alfred H. • New York, NY 10014 • ACRL ALCTS *Life*

Lane Anne M. • Boonville, MO 65233

Lane Betty M. • Wickliffe, KY 42087

Lane Beverly S. • Assistant Librarian • Pontifical Coll Josephinum A.T. Wehrle Memorial Library • Columbus, OH 43235 • ACRL ILERT

Lane Carol • Youth Specialist • Quintilla Geer Bruton Memorial Library • Plant City, FL 33566 • ALSC

Lane Carolyn D. • APO New York, NY 09132 • AASL ALSC *Life*

Lane Constance V. • Trustee • Rockford Public Library • Rockford, IL 61101-1061 • ALTA

Lane David M. • Librarian • University of New Hampshire Biological Sciences Library • Durham, NH 03824 • ACRL

Lane David O. • Somers, NY 10589 • ACRL LAMA   *Life*

Lane Elizabeth S. • Congressional Information Service Inc. • Bethesda, MD 20814 • LITA

Lane James A. • Preservation Librarian • New York State Library State Education Department • Albany, NY 12230 • ALCTS

Lane James H. • Reference/Catalog Librarian • Allegheny College Pelletier Library • Meadville, PA 16335

Lane Janeane • Program Director • Crestview Professional Library • Crestview, FL 32536

Lane Judith L. • Reference Coordinator • Mountain Valley Library System • Sacramento, CA 95814 • RASD

Lane Keith • Trustee • Western Plains Library System • Clinton, OK 73601

Lane Laura • Science Bibliographer • Temple University Paley Library • Philadelphia, PA 19122 • ACRL RASD

Lane Linda A. • Children's Librarian • Atlanta-Fulton Public Library Cleveland Avenue Branch • Atlanta, GA 30315 • ALSC PLA IFRT NMRT

Lane Liz A. • Principal Librarian • New York State Library State Education Department • Albany, NY 12230 • ASCLA LITA

Lane Margaret • Archivist • Boxford Historical Document Center • Boxford, MA 01921 • Continuing

Lane Margaret T. • Baton Rouge, LA 70821 • GODORT
Continuing

Lane Mary Jane • Associate Librarian • Louisiana State University Libraries Troy H. Middleton Library • Baton Rouge, LA 70803-3342 • ACRL ALCTS

Lane Mary Seminara • Ashland, MA 01721

Lane Michael J. • Avon Middle-High School • Avon, MA 02322 • AASL

Lane Molly • Trustee • Tacoma Public Library • Tacoma, WA 98402 • ALTA

Lane Rae Gordeane • Taku Elementary Library • Anchorage, AK 99507

Lane Renita K. • Reference Specialist • Mississippi Library Commission • Jackson, MS 39209 • ASCLA

Lane Robert B. • Director • United States Air Force Air University Library • Maxwell AFB, AL 36112-5564 • ACRL AFLRT

Lane Rochelle B. • Trustee • Lincolnwood Public Library District • Lincolnwood, IL 60646 • ALTA

Lane Rosemary • Director • Chula Vista Public Library • Chula Vista, CA 91910 • LAMA PLA

Lane Sharon Miss • Librarian • Akron-Summit County Public Library • Akron, OH 44326-0001 • YALSA

Lane Steven P. • Library Manager • Army Tactical Command & Control System Experimentation Site • Fort Lewis, WA 98433 • ALCTS PLA FLRT SRRT

Lane Virginia H. • Aurora, CO 80013-2007

Laney Elizabeth J. • Spring Hope, NC 27882

Laney Thomas H. • Book House • Jonesville, MI 49250 • ACRL ALCTS

Lang Anita E. • Director of Information Science • Design Execellence Inc • San Antonio, TX 78229 • LAMA IFRT

Lang Anna Mary • Librarian • Paoli Library • Paoli, PA 19301

Lang Carol J. • Student • Temple University Paley Library • Philadelphia, PA 19122

Lang David W. • Venable, Baetjer, Howard & Civiletti Law Library • Washington, DC 20005

Lang Gerald A. • Director R E M C 15 • Jackson County Independent School District • Jackson, MI 49204 • AASL

Lang Janice N. • Sun Prairie, WI 53590

Lang John R. • Lake Orion, MI 48035

Lang Jovian Rev • Professor • University of South Florida School of Library & Information Science • Tampa, FL 33620 • ACRL RASD

Lang Michelle A. • Reference Librarian • Chatham College • Pittsburgh, PA 15232 • ACRL

Lang Patti J. • Adult Service Librarian • Suburban Audio-Visual Service • La Grange Park, IL 60525-1698

Lang Sally L. • Martinsburg, WV 25401-3124

Lang Shannon S. • Mansfield-Richland County Public Library • Mansfield, OH 44902-1295 • ALSC IFRT

Lang Shirley • Trustee • Syosset Public Library • Syosset, NY 11791 • ALTA PLA

Lang Valerie A. • Averrill Park, NY 12018 • AASL SRRT

Langa Patricia A. • District Librarian • Krum Independent School District • Krum, TX 76249

Langan Kerry M. • Reference Librarian • Oberlin College Library • Oberlin, OH 44074 • ACRL

Langdoc Thomas R. • Media Specialist • Metropolitan School District Wayne Township • Indianapolis, IN 46241 • AASL

Lange Clifford E. • Director • Carlsbad City Library • Carlsbad, CA 92008 • ALCTS ALSC ALTA ASCLA LAMA LITA PLA RASD YALSA

Lange Elizabeth Ann • Dean of Library • Winona State University • Winona, MN 55987 • ACRL LAMA

Lange Emily C. • Resource Center Coordinator • Milwaukee AIDS Project • Milwaukee, WI 53202 • ASCLA

Lange Holley R. • Colorado State University William E. Morgan Library • Fort Collins, CO 80523 • ACRL ALCTS LITA LHRT

Lange Janet M. • Oceanside, CA 92056

Lange Janice P. • Head of Tech Servs & Asst Dir. • Sam Houston State University Newton Gresham Library • Huntsville, TX 77341-2281 • ALCTS

Lange Linda • Technical Service Coordinator • Clearwater Public Library • Clearwater, FL 34623 • PLA

Lange Margarete • Head of Information Services • Wheeler Basin Regional Library • Decatur, AL 35602

Lange Torrey B. • Student • University of Arizona Graduate Library School • Tucson, AZ 85721

Langel Lynn Ann • School Librarian • Harford Public Schools • Bel Air, MD 21014 • AASL

Langelier Patricia A. • Institute of Govt. Librarian • University of North Carolina • Chapel Hill, NC 27599

Langemack S Chapple • King County Library System Issaquah Branch • Issaquah, WA 98027 • PLA YALSA

Langenberg David L. • Assoc. Ln. Reference Department • University of Delaware Library • Newark, DE 19717-5267 • LITA RASD

Langenwalter Laurel B. • Tillamook, OR 97141 • PLA

Langer Frank A. • Director • Front Free Library • Salem, WV 26426

Langer Mark P. • Acquisitions Librarian • Marquette University Memorial Library • Milwaukee, WI 53233 • ALCTS

Langer Mary C. • Royal Oak, MI 48067 • AASL

Langerman Deborah J. • Champaign, IL 61820 • ALSC IFRT SRRT

Langevin Ann • Administrator • Las Vegas-Clark County Library District • Las Vegas, NV 89101 • LITA

Langfield Toni • Librarian • Town School for Boys Library • San Francisco, CA 94115 • AASL

Langford Joel C. • Director • Reinhardt College Hill Freeman Library • Waleska, GA 30183-0068 • ACRL

Langholz Lois E. • Student • Pratt Institute Graduate School of Library & Information Science • Brooklyn, NY 11205 • AASL SRRT

Langhorne Mary Jo • Library Media Director • Iowa City High School • Iowa City, IA 52240 • AASL

Langley Jean • Library Director • Northborough Free Library • Northborough, MA 01532-1997 • ALSC LAMA PLA RASD

Langley Linda E. • Librarian • Chesaning Union School • Chesaning, MI 48616 • Life

Langlinais Carolyn • Metairie, LA 70003

Langlois Dianne C. • Director • Andrew Mellon Library • Wallingford, CT 06492 • LIRT

Langmo James O. • Library Director • East Lansing Public Library • East Lansing, MI 48823 • PLA RASD

Langsam Christine • Kalamazoo, MI 49001-4204 • AASL

Langstaff Eleanor M. • Head, Library Instruction • Bernard M. Baruch College • New York, NY 10010 • ACRL LIRT

Langston Diane R. • Librarian • Amelia County Elementary School • Amelia, VA 23002 • AASL

Langston Joanne E. • Librarian • United States Fish & Wildlife Service National Wetlands Research Center • Lafayette, LA 70506 • ACRL FLRT IRRT

Langstraat Donald H. • Technical Services Librarian • Peoria Public Library • Peoria, IL 61602 • PLA

Langton Mary V. • Trainee • Queens Borough Public Library Peninsula Branch • Rockaway Beach, NY 11693

Langville Alan R. • Supervising Librarian • Ventura County Library Services Agency • Ventura, CA 93003

Lanham Allen K. • Eastern Illinois University Booth Library • Charleston, IL 61920-3099 • ACRL ALCTS LAMA LITA RASD IFRT

Lanham Brenda • Newport High School • Newport, KY 41073

Lanier Delores Ann • Colorado Legislative Council Joint Legislative Library • Denver, CO 80203 • LITA

Lanier Donald L. • Health Sciences Librarian • University of Illinois College of Medicine • Rockford, IL 61107 • ACRL ALCTS

Lanier Gene D. • Director of Graduate Studies • East Carolina University Department of Library & Information Studies • Greenville, NC 27858-4353 • AASL IFRT

Lanigan Barbara Ann • Media Specialist • Beechview Elementary School Media Center • Farmington Hills, MI 48018 • AASL

Laning Melissa A. • University of Louisville Ekstrom Library • Louisville, KY 40292 • ACRL ALCTS LAMA LITA NMRT

Lankelin Armi Anna E. • Chief Librarian • Finnish Centre for Radiation & Nuclear Safty Library • Helsinki 00101, Finland • LAMA

Lankford Mary D. • Director, Library Media Services • Irving Independent School District Instructional Center • Irving, TX 75061 • AASL ALSC

Lankin Marc • Student • Drexel University W. W. Hagerty Library • Philadelphia, PA 19104

Lanning Dixie M. • Director • Bethany College Wallerstedt Library • Lindsborg, KS 67456-1896 • ACRL LAMA LIRT

Lanning Mary A. • Assistant Professor/Reference Ln • Ball State University Bracken Library • Muncie, IN 47306-0160 • ACRL

Lanning Scott W. • Reference Librarian • DePaul University Library • Chicago, IL 60604-2287 • LITA

Lannom Barbara Ms. • Trustee • Summit Public Library District • Summit, IL 60501

Lanoue Margaret A. • Student • State University of New York at Albany School of Information Science & Policy • Albany, NY 12222 • RASD EMIERT SRRT

Lanphier Margaret C. • Media Librarian • City College of San Francisco • San Francisco, CA 94112 • LITA

Lansing Susan H. • Student • State University of New York at Albany School of Information Science & Policy • Albany, NY 12222 • RASD

Lanto Ellen R. • Senior Librarian • San Bernardino Public Library • San Bernardino, CA 92410

Lantvit Mary Louise • Trustee • Lyons Public Library • Lyons, IL 60534

Lantz Laura A. • Euclid, OH 44123

Lantz Patricia • Pierce County Rural Library District • Tacoma, WA 98446 • ALTA PLA

Lantzy M. Louise • Director Barclay Law Library • Syracuse University • Syracuse, NY 13244 • ACRL

Lanz Jeffrey B. • Assistant Director • Hardin County Public Library • Elizabethtown, KY 42701 • ALCTS LIRT

Lanzalotto Stephanie • Mgr. Vendor Elect. Interface • Baker & Taylor Books • Bridgewater, NJ 08807-0920 • ALCTS LITA ERT

Lanzeritsch Maria • Herndon, VA 22070

Lanzim Kathy M. • Ocean County Library Lacey Township Branch • Forked River, NJ 08731

Lanzim Marc J. • Coordinator-Technical Services • Ocean County Library System • Toms River, NJ 08753 • PLA

Lapachet Jaye A.H. • Librarian • Folger & Levin • San Francisco, CA 94111 • IFRT

Lapas Martha E. • East Carolina University Joyner Library • Greenville, NC 27858-4353

Lapenotiere Mary E. • Carney, MD 21234 • PLA

Lapides Linda F. • Baltimore, MD 21217 • Continuing

Lapidow Amy R. • Cambridge, MA 02140

Lapidus Lois E. • Port Washington, NY 11050

Lapierre Maurice E. • Sterling, VA 22170 • ACRL ALCTS
Life

Laplante Effie N. Mrs • Evanston, IL 60201 • AASL ALSC
Life

Lapointe Harriet • Project Director • Library Power/Providence • Providence, RI 02903 • AASL YALSA

Lapointe Michael L. • San Francisco, CA 94107

Lapp Natalie • Director • Lynbrook Public Library • Lynbrook, NY 11563 • PLA

Lapsley Andrea • Director, Marketing & Devel. • Houston Public Library • Houston, TX 77002 • LAMA PLA

Laquatra Marilyn J. • Part-time para-professional • Lakewood Public Library • Lakewood, OH 44107

Laramie Mary • Librarian • Floyd M. Stork Elementary School • Alta Loma, CA 91701

Larew Christian K. • Director,Customer Electronics • Baker & Taylor Books • Bridgewater, NJ 08807-0920 • ALCTS LITA

Large Alfred P. • Administrator • South Bend Community School Corporation • South Bend, IN 46601 • AASL

Large Deborah S. • Head of Cataloging • San Antonio Public Library • San Antonio, TX 78205

Large Helen M. • Language Services Div Librarian • World Bank • Washington, DC 20433

Large J. Andrew • Director • McGill University Libraries • Montreal PQ, H3A 1Y1 Canada

Larimer Hugh C. • Reference Librarian • University of Manitoba Libraries Elizabeth Dafoe Library • Winnipeg MB, R3T 2N2 Canada • ACRL MAGERT

Larkin Alice J. • Reference Assistant • Evansville-Vanderburgh County Public Library • Evansville, IN 47708-1694 • PLA

Larkin David H. • Head, Government Documents • University of Texas at El Paso Library • El Paso, TX 79968-0582 • ACRL GODORT

Larkin Patrick J. • Chief Librarian • Iona College Ryan Library • New Rochelle, NY 10801

Larkin Sally S. • Reference Librarian • Contra Costa County Library • Pleasant Hill, CA 94523

Larm Carol M. • Hawaii State Public Library System Office of the State Librarian • Honolulu, HI 96813

Larose Albert J. • North Carolina Wesleyan College Elizabeth Braswell Pearsall Library • Rocky Mount, NC 27804 • ACRL LAMA RASD

Larose Joseph A • Reference Librarian • University of Akron • Akron, OH 44325-1707 • RASD

Larque Delores • Institutional Technologist • Needham Public Schools • Needham, MA 02192 • AASL

Larrabee Betty • Librarian • Saint Julianas School • West Palm Beach, FL 33405 • AASL

Larremore Lynda R. • Murray, KY 42071

Larrick Nancy • Winchester, VA 22601 • ALSC

Larry Charles E. • Arts Librarian • Northern Illinois University University Libraries • DeKalb, IL 60115-2868 • ACRL ALSC

Larsen A. Dean • Associate University Librarian • Brigham Young University Harold B. Lee Library • Provo, UT 84602 • ACRL

Larsen Anne M. • Reference Librarian • Sullivan County Cmnty College • Loch Sheldrake, NY 12759

Larsen Dee A. • Salt Lake City, UT 84108

Larsen Erik D. • Student • University of Michigan School of Information and Library Studies • Ann Arbor, MI 48109-1092 • ACRL RASD IFRT NMRT

Larsen Hans L. • Asst Dean,Learning Resources • Ohlone College Blanchard Learning Resources Center • Fremont, CA 94539

Larsen James M. • President • Bridgeport National Bindery • Agawam, MA 01001 • ALCTS

Larsen Joan A. • Head of Reference & Instr. Serv. • Saint Lawrence University Owen D. Young Library • Canton, NY 13617 • GODORT

Larsen Joanne • Roselle Public Library • Roselle, IL 60172 • ALSC

Larsen John C. Dr. • Baltimore, MD 21218 • ACRL RASD
Life

Larsen Lida L. • Asst. Manager, Workstations • University of Maryland • College Park, MD 20742-2411

Larsen Linda • County of Los Angeles Public Library • Downey, CA 90241-7400

Larsen Lotte • Hd of Reference & Archives • Western Oregon State College Library • Monmouth, OR 97361 • ACRL LIRT

Larsen Nancy E. • Managing Editor, Landmarks • University of Oklahoma Libraries University Libraries • Norman, OK 73019 • ALCTS

Larsen Patricia M. • Asst. Director Access Service • University of Northern Iowa Donald O. Rod Library • Cedar Falls, IA 50613-3675 • ACRL ALCTS LAMA LITA

Larsen Richard • Production Manager • Cargill Hybrid Seeds • Minneapolis, MN 55440

Larsen Ronald L. • Assoc. Director for Info. Tech. • University of Maryland College Park Theodore R. McKeldin Library • College Park, MD 20742-7011 • LITA

Larsen Sandra C. • Tiffin, OH 44883

Larsen Steen Bille • Royal Library • 1016 Copenhage K, Denmark • LITA

Larsgaard Mary L. • Asst. Head, Map & Imagery Lab. • University of California UCSB Library • Santa Barbara, CA 93106-9010 • ALCTS GODORT MAGERT

Larson-Makar Susan M. • Reference Librarian • Georgetown University • Washington, DC 20013 • ACRL LITA RASD NMRT

Larson Amy L. • Student • University of Wisconsin-Milwaukee School of Library & Information Science • Milwaukee, WI 53201

Larson Berkley • Director • College of Saint Scholastica Library • Duluth, MN 55811

Larson Beulah M. • Stevens Point, WI 54481-5246 • Continuing

Larson Carol J. • Director • Ela Area Public Library District • Lake Zurich, IL 60047 • LAMA PLA

Larson Carole A. • Reference Librarian • University of Nebraska at Omaha University Library • Omaha, NE 68182-0237 • ACRL

Larson Catherine A. • Kalamazoo Public Library • Kalamazoo, MI 49007-5270 • RASD SRRT

Larson Catherine A. • Preservation Librarian • University of Iowa Libraries • Iowa City, IA 52242-1379 • ALCTS SRRT

Larson Christine M. • Student • University of Illinois Graduate School of Library and Information Science • Urbana, IL 61801 • ACRL IFRT

Larson D. A. • Northside High School • Fort Smith, AR 72901 • AASL

Larson Darlene • School District of Beloit-Turner • Beloit, WI 53511 • AASL

Larson Ednor E. • Cranston, RI 02910 • AASL YALSA NMRT

Larson Elaine M. S. • Rossman Elementary School • Saint Louis, MO 63141 • AASL

Larson Elizabeth Ann • Assistant Librarian • Children's Memorial Hospital Brennemann Library • Chicago, IL 60614

Larson Evva L. • Boise, ID 83706

Larson Harriet • Trustee • Livonia Public Library • Livonia, MI 48154-3045 • ALTA

Larson Jane A. • Director • Vermillion Public Library • Vermillion, SD 57069 • PLA

Larson Janet E. • Librarian • Sacramento Public Library • Sacramento, CA 95814 • PLA

Larson Jay B. • Assistant Director • Bur Oak Library System • Shorewood, IL 60436

Larson Jeanette C. • Manager, Continuing Education • Texas State Library • Austin, TX 78711 • ALSC ASCLA CLENE

Larson Jeffery K. • Humanities Bibliographer • Yale University Sterling Memorial Library • New Haven, CT 06520 • ACRL

Larson Joan B. • Director • Northern Lights Library Network • Alexandria, MN 56308 • ASCLA PLA

Larson Judith W. • School Library Media Teacher • Bountiful Junior High School • Bountiful, UT 84010

Larson Judy • Librarian • Roswell High School Library • Roswell, NM 88201 • AASL

Larson Larry • Director/Librarian • Fort Smith Public Library • Fort Smith, AR 72901 • LITA PLA

Larson M. Kathleen • Extension Coordinator • Cabell County Public Library • Huntington, WV 25701 • PLA

Larson Marilyn Heers • Children's Librarian • West Branch Library • Ann Arbor, MI 48103 • ALSC PLA

Larson Marilyn J. • Long Beach Office of Library Services • Long Beach, CA 90805 • AASL

Larson Mary E. • Reference Librarian • Concordia College Carl B. Ylvisaker Library • Moorhead, MN 56562 • ACRL RASD

Larson Mildred N. • Associate Director • L.E. Phillips Memorial Public Library • Eau Claire, WI 54701 • PLA IFRT

Larson Peggy A. • Assistant Director • Educational Enrichment Foundation • Tucson, AZ 85712 • AASL EMIERT

Larson Phyllis S. • Delaware County Library System • Brookhaven, PA 19015

Larson Ray R. • Associate Professor • University of California-Berkeley School of Library & Information Studies • Berkeley, CA 94720 • ACRL ALCTS LITA LRRT

Larson Roberta M. • Librarian • Sherman Elementary School • Tacoma, WA 98407 • AASL

Larson Ruth A. • Librarian • Emporia State University School of Library & Information Management • Emporia, KS 66801

Larson Sandra M. • Monterey, CA 93940

Larson Signe E. • Chief Research Librarian • Information Masters • Manzanita, OR 97130 • ACRL RASD

Larson Stephen A. • Student • Rutgers University School of Communication Information & Library Studies • New Brunswick, NJ 08903 • AASL

Larson Suzanne R. • Children's Librarian • Carnegie-Viersen Public Library • Pella, IA 50219 • ALSC

Larson Teresa B. • Audiovisual Department Head • Ames Public Library • Ames, IA 50010 • LITA

Larson Timothy M. • Slavic Cataloger • Indiana University • Bloomington, IN 47405 • ACRL

Larson-Aligne Elizabeth A. • Student • University of California-Los Angeles (UCLA) • Los Angeles, CA 90024-1450 • EMIERT IFRT SRRT

Lasater Mary C. • Authorities Coordinator • Vanderbilt University Library Jean & Alexander Heard Library • Nashville, TN 37240-0007 • ACRL ALCTS LITA GODORT

Laseter Ernest P. • Technical Librarian • Air Force Logistics Mgmt Ctr Gunter Air Force Base • Gunter AFB, AL 36014-6693 • LITA AFLRT

Laseter Shirley B. • Chief, Reference Branch • United States Air Force Air University Library • Maxwell AFB, AL 36112-5564 • LITA

Lash Elayne • Head Media Specialist • Hallandale High School • Hallandale, FL 33009 • AASL

Lash MaryAnn • President • Peter Smith Publisher Inc. • Magnolia, MA 01930

Lasha Laurian Sister • Director • Crookston Public Library • Crookston, MN 56716

Lashbrook John E. • Automation Services Consultant • Wright State University University Library • Dayton, OH 45435

Lashbrook Sarah E. • Librarian • Benjamin Syms Middle School • Hampton, VA 23669 • AASL

Lasher-Tidwell Judith C. • Bradenton, FL 34207-4508 • RASD

Lashua Helen M. • Librarian • Atkinson Middle School • Atkinson, NC 28403 • AASL

Laskaris Lisa A. • Student • University of Arizona Graduate Library School • Tucson, AZ 85721 • IFRT SRRT

Lasko Kim Lombard • Memphis, TN 38120-2543 • ALSC

Laskow Mary M. • Birmingham, AL 35243 • ACRL

Laskowski Nancy M. • Adult Area Specialist • Free Library of Philadelphia Northeast Regional Library • Philadelphia, PA 19149 • PLA RASD

Laskowski Seno • Head of Cataloging Department • University of Alberta • Edmonton AB, T6G 2J8 Canada • ACRL ALCTS

Lasky Lynnette Jane • Head Circulation/ILL • Eastern Illinois University Booth Library • Charleston, IL 61920-3099 • IFRT

Lasley Norma J. • Head of Adult Services • Muncie-Center Township Public Library • Muncie, IN 47305

Laslo Lili B. • Student • University of Hawaii School of Library & Information Studies • Honolulu, HI 96822

Lason Terry L. • Head of Extension Services • Kalamazoo Public Library • Kalamazoo, MI 49007-5270 • PLA

Lasslo Andrew Dr. • Emeritus Professor • University of Tennessee Health Science Center • Memphis, TN 38163 • ACRL ALCTS   *Life*

Last Kimberly L. • Triodyne Inc. Information Center • Niles, IL 60648

Last Lydia E. • Student • Brooklyn Public Library • Brooklyn, NY 11238

Lastrapes Blanca J. • Librarian • State Library of Louisiana • Baton Rouge, LA 70821 • ASCLA

Lastres Steven A. • Arnold & Porter • New York, NY 10022-4690

Laszuk Renata S. • Librarian/Editorial Assistant • Morning Star, Inc. • Chicago, IL 60604 • LAMA

Latalladi Beverly E. • Media Spec • Prince William County Schools Beville Middle School • Woodbridge, VA 22193 • AASL IFRT

Latch Patricia • Youth Services Coordinator • Cobb County Public Library System • Marietta, GA 30060 • ALSC PLA IFRT

Later Sarah L. • Student • Indiana University School of Library and Information Science • Bloomington, IN 47405 • PLA SRRT

Latham Candace • Media Spec • Ira W Travell School Ridgewood Public Schools • Ridgewood, NJ 07450 • AASL

Latham Marian Gayle • Media Specialist • Hunters Lane High School • Nashville, TN 37207 • AASL

Latham Martha Ann • Librarian • Southeastern Oklahoma State University • Durant, OK 74701

Latham Ronald B. • Director • Bershire Athenaeum Pittsfield Public Library • Pittsfield, MA 01201 • PLA

Lathrom Teresa J. • Librarian • Cobb County Public Library System Sibley Branch • Marietta, GA 30060

Lathrop Ann • Associate Professor • California State University-Long Beach Instructional Systems Technology Dept. • Long Beach, CA 90840-1901 • AASL YALSA

Lathrop Carolynne S. • Curriculum Lab. Director • University of Dubuque • Dubuque, IA 52001 • ALSC

Lathrop Gael • New London Public Library • New London, WI 54961

Lathrop Muriel C. • Business Manager • Calumet City Public Library • Calumet City, IL 60409-4003 • LAMA PLA

Lathrope Mary • Downers Grove, IL 60515 • AASL
Continuing

Latiak Dorothy V. • Chicago, IL 60649 • PLA YALSA *Life*

Latini Joseph J. • Assistant Director • Great Neck Library • Great Neck, NY 11024

Latour Suzanne C. • Asst. Documents Librarian • Oklahoma State University Library • Stillwater, OK 74078-0375 • GODORT

Latour Terry S. • Hattiesburg, MS 39406-5148 • ACRL LAMA

Latrobe Kathy H. • Norman, OK 73072 • AASL ALSC YALSA

Latshaw Patricia H. • Director of Community Relations • Akron-Summit County Public Library • Akron, OH 44326-0001 • LAMA IFRT

Latta Ann W. • Assistant Head • Stanford University • Stanford, CA 94305-6011 • ACRL

Latta Gail F. • University of Nebraska Love Library • Lincoln, NE 68588-0410 • ACRL LITA RASD LRRT

Latta Joye M. • Director of Media • Reidsville Senior High School Lib • Reidsville, NC 27320-6899 • AASL

Lattimer Barbara A. • Twentynine Palms, CA 92277-2156 • ALSC PLA

Lattimore Clare I. • Head of Serials Department • Southern Methodist University Fondren Library • Dallas, TX 75275-0135 • ALCTS

Latture Betty J. • Director Library Services • Department of Education • Nashville, TN 37219 • AASL

Latzer Sandra A. • Head Librarian • Dwight-Englewood School • Englewood, NJ 07631 • AASL

Latzke Henry R. • Director of Library Services • Concordia University Klinck Memorial Library • River Forest, IL 60305-1499 • AASL ACRL ALCTS LITA RASD

Lau Chu Sing • Student • Trinity College Library • Washington, DC 20017

Lau Eloise • Mission Viejo, CA 92691

Lau Eppie Y. • Student • Louisiana State University School of Library & Information Science • Baton Rouge, LA 70803-3290

Lau Jesus PhD • 34200 Durango DGO, Mexico • IRRT

Lau Lily H. • Administrator Supervisor • East Central Regional Library • Cedar Rapids, IA 52401 • PLA

Lau Mildred R. • Honolulu, HI 96816 • Life

Lau Nora E. • Librarian • Burrus Elementary School Independent School District • Houston, TX 77022 • AASL

Lau Shuk-Fong • Memphis State University Libraries • Memphis, TN 38152

Lau Tammy L. • Student • University of Michigan School of Information and Library Studies • Ann Arbor, MI 48109-1092

Lau Wing M. • Business Periodical Indexer • H. W. Wilson Company • Bronx, NY 10452 • ALCTS

Lau Yvonne S. • Mililani, HI 96789 • AASL

Laub Mary • Trustee • Las Vegas-Clark County Library District Flamingo Library • Las Vegas, NV 89119 • ALTA

Laubacher Marilyn R. • Director • Baldwinsville Public Library • Baldwinsville, NY 13027-2485 • PLA

Laubacker Ann M. • Library Director • Orchard Park Public Library • Orchard Park, NY 14127 • PLA

Laube Lois R. • Mgr, Social Sciences Division • Indianapolis Marion County Public Library • Indianapolis, IN 46206

Lauber Alexander • Trustee • Shelter Rock Public Library • Albertson, NY 11507 • ALTA

Lauch Mike M. • El Paso, TX 79912

Laucus John P. • Director • Boston University Mugar Memorial Library • Boston, MA 02215 • ACRL LITA

Laude Maria E. • Automated Sys/Reference Libn • University of Maryland • Baltimore, MD 21228 • NMRT

Lauderdale Kevin R. • Student • San Francisco State University • San Francisco, CA 94132

Laudicina Sal Mr. • Vice-President • Motion Picture Licensing Corp. • Los Angeles, CA 90066

Lauer Jonathan D. • Director • Messiah College Murray Learning Resources Center • Grantham, PA 17027 • ACRL

Lauer Joseph J. • Michigan State University Libraries • East Lansing, MI 48824-1048 • ACRL

Lauer Judy A. • Law Librarian • New York State Supreme Court Library Broome County Courthouse • Binghamton, NY 13901

Lauffer Donna • Deputy County Librarian • Johnson County Library • Shawnee Mission, KS 66201 • LAMA

Laughlin-Porter Jeannine L. • Associate Professor • University of Southern Mississippi School of Library Science • Hattiesburg, MS 39406-5146 • AASL

Laughlin Beverly E. • Director • Bayouland Library System • Lafayette, LA 70501 • ACRL ASCLA LAMA PLA

Laughlin Carolyn H. • Head Librarian • United States Naval Hospital • San Diego, CA 92135 • AFLRT FLRT

Laughlin Mary L. • Main Library Supervisor • Mobile Public Library • Mobile, AL 36602 • PLA

Laughlin Mildred • Professor Emeritus • University of Oklahoma School of Library & Information Studies • Norman, OK 73019

Laughlin Sara G. • Coordinator • Stone Hills Library Network • Bloomington, IN 47408 • ASCLA

Laughlin Sherry • Head of Reference • University of Southern Mississippi Cook Memorial Library • Hattiesburg, MS 39406-5053 • ACRL

Laughlin Steven G. • Head, Administrative Services • University of Alabama at Birmingham Mervyn H. Sterne Library • Birmingham, AL 35294-0014 • ACRL

Laughrey Edna C. • Service Quality Consultant • Faxon Company Inc. • Westwood, MA 02090 • ACRL ALCTS LAMA   Life

Laumeister Virginia • Outreach Librarian • William K. Sanford Town Library • Loudonville, NY 12211

Launay Catherine L. • Evanston, IL 60202

Laundry Suzanne M. • Lake Forest, IL 60045

Laurence Helen • Reference Librarian • Florida Atlantic University Library • Boca Raton, FL 33431

Laurence Katherine S. • Library Director • Cornell University School of Hotel Administration Library • Ithaca, NY 14853-6902 • ACRL LAMA RASD

Laurent Raymond A. • Media Specialist • Village Oaks Elementary • Immokalee, FL 33934

Laurich Robert A. • Instructor Acquisitions Mgr. • Hunter College Library • New York, NY 10021

Laurion Brenda J. • Albuquerque, NM 87123

Laurito Gerard P. • Gannon University Nash Library • Erie, PA 16541 • ACRL

Lauritsen James H. • Librarian • Gettysburg High School • Gettysburg, PA 17325 • AASL

Lauritzen Heidi A. • Director • Coralville Public Library • Coralville, IA 52241

Laursen Allan R. • Stockton, CA 95204 • Continuing

Lauscher Alveeda • Salt Lake City Public Library • Salt Lake City, UT 84111 • AASL ALSC PLA YALSA IFRT

Lauster Kristen E. • Student • State University of New York (SUNY) School of Information & Library Studies • Buffalo, NY 14260

Lautemann Eva • Systems Librarian • DeKalb College Central Campus Library • Clarkston, GA 30021-2396

Lauterbach Diana M. • Student • Syracuse University School of Information Studies • Syracuse, NY 13244-4100

Lauterbach Rowena L. • Librarian • Carver County Library • Chaska, MN 55318

Lauterwasser Nancy • Children's Librarian • Public Library of Cincinnati and Hamilton County • Cincinnati, OH 45202 • ALSC

Lauth Barbara • Librarian • Maywood Public Library • Maywood, IL 60153 • ALTA

Lauver Joan • Librarian • Unified School District • Tucson, AZ 85717-0400 • ACRL IRRT

Lavagnino Merri Beth • University of Vermont Bailey Howe Library • Burlington, VT 05405-0036 • ACRL LAMA LITA

Lavanhar Caroline M. • L Media Spec • Tisdale Elem Sch • Ramsey, NJ 07446 • AASL

Lavender Kenneth Dr. • Curator,Rare Bk & Texana Cllns • University of North Texas • Denton, TX 76203 • ACRL ALCTS

Lavender Sharon M. • Librarian • Lafayette Parish Public Library • Lafayette, LA 70502-3427

Laverdi Adelaide • Leicester, NY 14481 • ACRL ALCTS LITA

Laverty Mary P. • Student • Cooper High School Library • Abilene, TX 79605 • ACRL ALCTS NMRT

Lavery Janice L. • Head Multicultural Services Dept • Toronto Public Library • Toronto ON, M5A 4L2 Canada • PLA EMIERT

Lavine Frank • Medford, MA 02155 • Continuing

Lavoie Gaston J F • Director of Exploitation • Universite Du Quebec A Rimouski • Rimouski PQ, Canada • ALCTS

Lavorgna Lois • Trustee • Wayne Public Library • Wayne, NJ 07470 • ALTA

Law Aileen P. • Director of Administrative Servs • South Carolina State Library • Columbia, SC 29211 • ASCLA PLA

Law Birdie L. • Suitland, MD 20746

Law Gordon T. Jr. • Head of Mgt. & Econ. Library • Purdue University Krannert Management & Economics Library • West Lafayette, IN 47907 • ACRL LAMA

Law Sharon E. • Student • Louisiana State University School of Library & Information Science • Baton Rouge, LA 70803-3290

Lawal Ibironke O. • Physical Science Ref. Librarian • Dartmouth College • Hanover, NH 03755 • LAMA

Lawal Linda D. • Librarian • Gracewood State School and Hospital • Gracewood, GA 30812

Lawall Richard W. • Tuckerton, NJ 08087

Lawhorn James S. • Librarian I • Dearborn Department of Libraries Henry Ford Centennial Library • Dearborn, MI 48126

Lawhorne Anne R. • Data Archive/Reference Libn. • University of Missouri-Columbia Ellis Library • Columbia, MO 65201 • ACRL RASD

Lawler Jeanne L. • Head, Adult Services Dept. • Kalamazoo Public Library • Kalamazoo, MI 49007-5270 • LAMA PLA RASD

Lawler Martha M. • Reference Librarian • Bossier Parish Library • Bossier City, LA 71111

Lawler Sally H. • Librarian • Wayne State University Purdy-Kresge Library • Detroit, MI 48202

Lawless Donna • Branch Assistant/Children Ln. • Kansas City Public Library South Branch • Kansas City, MO 64114 • ALSC

Lawrence A. Ms. • York House Senior Library • Vancouver BC, V6J 2V6 Canada

Lawrence Anitha • Librarian • Woodstock School • Mussoorie UP 248 179, India

Lawrence Betty A. • Assistant Head, Central Library • Rochester Public Library • Rochester, NY 14604 • ALCTS PLA RASD

Lawrence Brenda A. • Salem Public Library • Salem, OR 97309-5020

Lawrence Eileen M. • Marketing • Turner Subscriptions • New York, NY 10003

Lawrence Gary S. • Coordinator of Library Affairs • University of California • Oakland, CA 94612-3550 • ACRL LITA

Lawrence Gayle L. • Sand Springs, OK 74063 • AASL

Lawrence Gregory W. • Student • State University of New York (SUNY) University Libraries • Albany, NY 12222

Lawrence Huston S. • Library/Bookstore Manager • East-West University • Chicago, IL 60605

Lawrence Janet K. • Curriculum Materials Librarian • University of Georgia Libraries • Athens, GA 30602 • ACRL

Lawrence John R. M. • Inter-l Loan-Reference Librarian • College of William and Mary Earl Gregg Swem Library • Williamsburg, VA 23187-8794 • ACRL RASD

Lawrence Karen C. • Montvale, NJ 07645

Lawrence Kelly • Salem Public Library • Salem, OR 97309-5020

Lawrence Linda C. • Head Librarian • Reading Area Community College • Reading, PA 19603

Lawrence Margaret • Glen Loch Elementary School • The Woodlands, TX 77381

Lawrence Margaret D. • James Madison Middle • Upper Marlboro, MD 20772

Lawrence Marie K. Miss • South Bend, IN 46637 • Continuing

Lawrence Patricia A. • Director • Pacific Gas, Electric Pacific Energy Center • San Francisco, CA 94103 • LAMA

Lawrence Purnell W. Mrs • Mt Rainier, MD 20712

Lawrence Rhonda K. • Bibliographic Access Librarian • University of California L.A. Library Law Library • Los Angeles, CA 90024-1302 • ALCTS

Lawrence Susan B. • Director • Withers Memorial Public Library • Nicholasville, KY 40356 • PLA

Lawrence Thomas A. • Regional Coordinator • Region One Cooperating Library Service • Waterbury, CT 06702 • LAMA

Lawrence Thomas E. • Librarian • Ogdensburg Correctional Facility General Library • Ogdensburg, NY 13669

Lawrence William • Trustee • Timberland Regional Library • Olympia, WA 98501 • ALTA

Lawryk Judith A. • New Brunswick, NJ 08901

Laws Melzetta P. • Branch Manager • Atlanta-Fulton Public Library Dogwood Branch • Atlanta, GA 30318 • PLA

Laws Naomi C. • Middle Librarian • Dan River Middle School Pittsylvania County School Board • Ringgold, VA 24586

Lawsine Mary • Administrative Librarian • Association for Research and Enlightenment, Cayce Memorial Library • Virginia Beach, VA 23451

Lawson A Venable • Atlanta, GA 30306 • IFRT

Lawson Ann P. • Slaes Representative • Quality Books Inc. • Lake Bluff, IL 60044-2204

Lawson Connie H. • Media Technologist • W.B. Patterson Public School • Washington, DC 20011

Lawson Constance P. • Regional Young Adult Serv Mgr • Cuyahoga County Public Library Maple Heights Regional Branch • Maple Heights, OH 44137 • AASL YALSA

Lawson Dennis C. • Administrator • Wabash Valley Library Network • Lafayette, IN 47901-1470

Lawson George T. • Director • Ames Public Library • Ames, IA 50010 • LAMA PLA

Lawson Judith • Southfield, MI 48034

Lawson Lorinda L. • Student • Texas Woman's University School of Library & Information Studies • Denton, TX 76204 • AASL NMRT

Lawson Martha G. • Director • Southeast Arkansas Regional Library • Monticello, AR 71655 • LAMA LITA PLA RASD CLENE GODORT LRRT

Lawson Mary L. • Chief of Community Libraries • Minneapolis Public Library & Information Center • Minneapolis, MN 55401-1992 • LAMA PLA IFRT

Lawson Mary Lou • K-8 School Librarian • Normal Public Library • Normal, IL 61761

Lawson Mary Rosen • Member, Broward Advisory Board • Broward County Library Fort Lauderdale Branch • Ft. Lauderdale, FL 33304 • ALTA SRRT

Lawson Pat N. • Teacher • Bradford County School Board Bradford County High School • Starke, FL 32091

Lawson Rhea B. • Literacy Resources Librarian • Enoch Pratt Free Library Broadway Branch • Baltimore, MD 21224 • PLA

Lawson Sheila M. • Lenexa, KS 66219 • PLA

Lawson V. Lonnie • Central Missouri State University Ward Edwards Library • Warrensburg, MO 64093 • ACRL NMRT

Lawton Bethany L. • Chatham, NY 12037 • SRRT

Lawton Kelley Ann • Student • University of North Carolina School of Library Science • Chapel Hill, NC 27599-3360

Lawton LaRoi M. Mr. • Brooklyn Public Library • Brooklyn, NY 11238

Lawton Patricia A. • Head, Reference Services • Saint Joseph County Public Library • South Bend, IN 46601 • RASD

Lawton Wesley • Manager • CRC Press, Incorporation • Boca Raton, FL 33431 • ALCTS

Laxton Matthew B. • Sno-Isle Regional Library • Marysville, WA 98271-9164 • PLA YALSA

Lay Marion S. • East Lansing, MI 48823 • LAMA PLA Life

Lay Shirley S. • Medical Librarian • Harbor Hospital Center • Baltimore, MD 21230

Laybold Lillian V. • Terre Haute, IN 47802-4066

Layman Ellen M. • Asst. Ref Librarian, ILL Coor. • University of Maryland-Eastern Shore Frederick Douglass Library • Princess Anne, MD 21853

Layman Marla M. • Clovis, NM 88101

Layman Mary F. • University of California-San Diego • La Jolla, CA 92093-0175 • ACRL IRRT

Laymon Diane Locke • Branch Manager • Pasadena Public Library • Pasadena, TX 77506-4895 • PLA

Layne Margaret H. • Speedway, IN 46224
Layne Sara Shatford • Cataloging, Physical Sci & Tech • University of California (UCLA) Physical Sciences & Technology Libraries • Los Angeles, CA 90024-1598 • ACRL ALCTS LITA RASD MAGERT
Layne Sherry E. • Trustee • Las Vegas-Clark County Library District Flamingo Library • Las Vegas, NV 89119 • ALTA
Layton Colleen • Michigan Municipal League • Ann Arbor, MI 48106-1487
Layton Jeanne • Kaysville, UT 84037 • IFRT
Layton Lynn Y. • Reference Librarian • Adams State College Library • Alamosa, CO 81102 • ACRL
Layton Patricia C. • Cataloger • Wicomico County Free Library • Salisbury, MD 21801
Layton Pauline • Atlanta, GA 30319
Lazar Jon H. • Supervisor of Technical Services • Rochester Public Library • Rochester, NY 14604 • ALCTS LAMA
Lazar Kathleen D. • Library Director • Strong Museum • Rochester, NY 14607
Lazar Laura R. • Assistant Prossor of Accounting • Valparaiso University Moellering Memorial Library • Valparaiso, IN 46383
Lazar Nancy P. • Librarian • United States Court House Court of Appeals • Washington, DC 20001 • ALCTS LITA FLRT
Lazaron Ed • Design Collaborative • Virginia Beach, VA 23452
Lazarus Betty B. • Librarian • Ridgewood Prep School • Metairie, LA 70001 • AASL YALSA
Lazarus Josephine G. • Colorado Springs, CO 80907 • RASD ILERT
Lazenby Gail R. • Director • Cobb County Public Library System • Marietta, GA 30060 • LAMA PLA
Lazouskas Lorraine M. • Chicago, IL 60638
Le Beau Renee • Head of Circulation/Serials • Chapman University Thurman Clarke Memorial Library • Orange, CA 92666
Le Ber Jeanne Marie • Salt Lake City, UT 84102
Le Brun Marlene May • Finance Manager • Harford County Library • Belcamp, MD 21017
Le Duc Carol A. • Librarian • Hennepin County Library Penn Lake Branch Library • Bloomington, MN 55431
Le Khac Thanh-Chan • Honolulu, HI 96825
Le May Neil Curtis • Collection Development Librarian • University of Wisconsin-River Falls Chalmer Davee Library • River Falls, WI 54022 • ACRL
Le Pors Teresa W. • Reference/Public Service Ln • Elon College Iris Holt McEwen Library • Elon College, NC 27244-0187 • RASD LRRT
LeBaron Melanie G. • O'Fallon, MO 63366
LeBarron Suzanne J. • Wyoming State Library • Cheyenne, WY 82002-0650 • ASCLA SRRT
LeBel Debra M. • Student • Dalhousie University School of Library & Inf. Studies • Halifax NS, B3H 4H8 Canada
LeBel J. • Director • New Brunswick Library Service • Fredericton NB, E3B 5C3 Canada • ALCTS ALTA LAMA LITA PLA RASD
LeBelle Darlene M. • Student • University of Western Ontario School of Library & Information Science • London ON, N6G 1H1 Canada
LeBlanc Anne • Student • University of California-Berkeley School of Library & Information Studies • Berkeley, CA 94720
LeBlanc Charles A. • Network Services • New Hampshire State Library • Concord, NH 03301 • LITA
LeBlanc Diana • Librarian • Caseyville Public Library • Caseyville, IL 62232
LeBlanc James D. • Cornell University Library • Ithaca, NY 14853 • ACRL ALCTS
LeBreton Jonathan A. • Assistant Director, Admin Serv • University of Maryland Baltimore County Kuhn Library • Catonsville, MD 21228 • ACRL
LeBris Elisabeth • Director of Media Services • Joseph Sears School-District 38 • Kenilworth, IL 60043 • AASL ALSC
LeCroy Judy • Davidson County Schools • Lexington, NC 27292
LeDonne Claire • Information Services Manager • University California-Berkeley • Berkeley, CA 94720 • LITA IFRT
LeDonne Marjorie E. • Senior Librarian • Correctional Training Facility North Library • Soledad, CA 93960 • ASCLA IFRT SRRT
LeFevre William W. • Archivist • Wayne State University Purdy Library • Detroit, MI 48202
LeJeune Kay • Jefferson Parish Library Department • Metairie, LA 70010
LeKernec William J. • Middletown, NJ 07748
LeLoup Dennis J. • Consultant • Indiana Department of Education Ctr for Sch Impro & Performance • Indianapolis, IN 46204 • AASL
LeMay Geraldine • Macon, GA 31204 • LAMA PLA *Continuing*
LeMay Jill • New Searles School • Nashau, NH 03062
LeMond Elizabeth A. • Student • Indiana University School of Library and Information Science • Bloomington, IN 47405 • ALCTS LITA RASD IFRT
LeSueur Richard • Head, Technical Svs Dept • Ann Arbor Public Library • Ann Arbor, MI 48104 • ALCTS
LeValley Beatrice K. • Cataloging Librarian • Northwestern Oklahoma State University J. W. Martin Library • Alva, OK 73717
LeVeque Anne • Student • University of Texas at Austin Graduate School of Library & Information Sciences • Austin, TX 78712-1276 • IFRT SRRT
LeVine Fay • Head of Cataloging • Memphis-Shelby County Public Library and Information Center • Memphis, TN 38104-4025 • ALCTS
Lea Lorri • Information Specialist • Saginaw News • Saginaw, MI 48607-1283
Lea Marcia • R.H. Johnson Library • Sun City West, AZ 85375
Leab Katharine Kyes • Ed-Publisher • American Book Prices Current • Washington, CT 06793 • ACRL LITA
Leach Alexandra N. • Saint Francis College • Fort Wayne, IN 46808
Leach Bruce A. • Hd. Biological Sciences Library • Ohio State University • Columbus, OH 43210
Leach Catherine S. • Librarian I • Vancouver Public Library • Vancouver BC, Canada
Leach Joan E. • Program Dir. Library Media Serv. • Fort Worth Independent School District • Ft. Worth, TX 76107 • AASL
Leach Lynda Nash • Resource Libr/Info. Specialist • University of Illinois Transition Institute • Champaign, IL 61821
Leach Patrica J. • Lincoln City Libraries South Branch • Lincoln, NE 68502-3099 • PLA
Leach Richard G. • Assistant Director • East Central Georgia Regional Library Augusta-Richmond County • Augusta, GA 30901 • PLA
Leach Ronald G. • Dean of the Libraries • Indiana State University Cunningham Memorial Library • Terre Haute, IN 47809 • ACRL LAMA LITA *Life*
Leach Sally Ann • Owatonna, MN 55060 • ALCTS PLA *Life*
Leach Sally S. • Associate Director • University of Texas Ransom Humanities Research Center • Austin, TX 78713 • ACRL
Leach Sandra S. • Database Searching Coordinator • University of Tennessee John C. Hodges Library • Knoxville, TN 37996-1000 • RASD IRRT
Leachman Charles L. • Sales Manager • Ebsco Subscription Services • Birmingham, AL 35202 • PLA
Leachman Nancy Jo • Extension Librarian • Rochester Public Library • Rochester, MN 55904-3777 • ASCLA EMIERT
Leachman Roger M. • Multitype Librarian • Southeastern Libraries Cooperating (SELCO) • Rochester, MN 55901 • ASCLA
Leacy Richard • Head of Government Doc/Maps • Georgia Institute of Technology Price Gilbert Memorial Library • Atlanta, GA 30332-0900 • GODORT
Leadbetter Laurie T. • Reference Librarian • University of North Carolina • Chapel Hill, NC 27599-3902
Leader Shelley E. Allen • Automation Librarian • Moore Memorial Public Library • Texas City, TX 77590 • PLA
Leadley Sarah P. • Student • University of Washington Graduate School of Library and Information Science • Seattle, WA 98195
Leahy Lynda C. • Associate Dean • Northeastern University Libraries • Boston, MA 02115 • ACRL LAMA RASD
Leahy Mary S. • Head of Rare Books Collection • Bryn Mawr College Canaday Library • Bryn Mawr, PA 19010 • ACRL
Leahy Michael D. Dr • Library Media Specialist • Bristol Eastern High School • Bristol, CT 06010 • AASL ALCTS RASD YALSA
Leahy Phillip • Trustee • Ramapo Catskill Library System • Middletown, NY 10940
Leahy Sheila • Head, Catalog Department • University of Southwestern Louisiana Libraries • Lafayette, LA 70503 • LRRT
Leamon David L. • Director • San Antonio Public Library • San Antonio, TX 78205 • LAMA LITA PLA
Leanza Elizabeth J. • Saratoga Springs Public Library • Saratoga Springs, NY 12861 • PLA
Lear Brett W. • Student • Florida State University School of Library and Information Studies • Tallahassee, FL 32306-2048
Lear Ellen H. • Tampa, FL 33617
Lear Martha A. • Reference Specialist • Mid-Continent Public Library • Independence, MO 64050 • RASD
Lear Winston R. • Librarian • Western Piedmont Community College Phifer LRC • Morganton, NC 28655 • ACRL LAMA
Learmont Carol L. • Assoc Dean • Columbia University School of Library Service • New York, NY 10027 • ACRL
Learned-Au Marcia • Assistant Director • Evansville-Vanderburgh County Public Library • Evansville, IN 47708-1694 • LAMA PLA IFRT
Learon Joy M. • Fairfax, VT 05454 • AASL
Leary Barbara • Bedford, MA 01730
Leary II Bayard • Willingboro Public Library • Willingboro, NJ 08046 • ALTA
Leary Margaret A. • Director • University of Michigan Law Library • Ann Arbor, MI 48109-1210 • ACRL ALCTS LAMA LITA GODORT
Leary Nancy Noon • Clarion, PA 16214
Leary Stephen D. • Reference Librarian • University of San Francisco Richard A. Gleeson Library • San Francisco, CA 94117 • ACRL
Leasher Evelyn M. • Librarian • Central Michigan University Charles V. Park Library 315 • Mount Pleasant, MI 48859
Leath Janis H. • Reference Librarian • University of Wyoming • Laramie, WY 82071 • RASD
Leather Deborah J. • Director of the Library • Towson State University • Towson, MD 21204 • ACRL LAMA
Leather Victoria P. • Director • Chattanooga State Technical Community College Library • Chattanooga, TN 37406
Leatherbury Maurice C. • President • University of Missouri-Columbia School of Library & Informational Science • Columbia, MO 65211 • LAMA LITA
Leatherman Candace M. • Research Associate • University of Illinois Library • Urbana, IL 61801 • ALSC LAMA IFRT
Leatherman Donald • Educ & Soc Sci Reference Ln • Arlington Public Library • Arlington, TX 76010
Leaver Rose Mary • Arrowhead Library System • Janesville, WI 53545 • ASCLA PLA CLENE
Leavitt Janice U. • Asst. Dit Dev. & PD • Rutgers University Libraries Archibald Stevens Alexander Library • New Brunswick, NJ 08903
Leavitt Melanie A. • Troy Public Library • Troy, NY 12180 • ALSC
Leavy Joy A. • Stacks Supervisor • Kent State University Libraries • Kent, OH 44242 • ACRL IFRT LHRT
Leavy Marvin D. • Western Kentucky University Helm-Cravens Library • Bowling Green, KY 42101-3576 • ACRL LHRT LRRT
Leazer Gregory H. • Student • Columbia University School of Library Service • New York, NY 10027 • ALCTS LITA LRRT
Leb Joan P. • Research Librarian • W.B. Doner & Company Advertising Research Library • Southfield, MI 48075
Lebbin Lee J. • Director • Grand Valley State University Zumberge Library • Allendale, MI 49401-9403 • ACRL
Lebbin Vickery K. • Student • University of Michigan School of Information and Library Studies • Ann Arbor, MI 48109-1092
Lebeau Chris • Ref Libn/Comp Servs Libn • Creighton University Reinert-Alumni Memorial Library • Omaha, NE 68178 • ACRL
Lebeau Marcia M. • Naperville Public Libraries • Naperville, IL 60540 • LAMA
Lebeau Zelia G. • Student • University of Illinois Graduate School of Library and Information Science • Urbana, IL 61801
Lebel Louise • South Aroostook County School District • Island Falls, ME 04747 • AASL
Leber Michele M. • Asst. Coor., Collection Devel. • Fairfax County Public Library • Fairfax, VA 22033-1909 • ALCTS LAMA PLA RASD IFRT SRRT
Lebish Alan R. • Coordinator of Technical Serv. • Horace W. Sturgis Library • Marietta, GA 30061
Leblanc Donna P. • Rapides Parish Library • Alexandria, LA 71301
Lebo Marjorie S. • Cambridge, MA 02140
Lebo Martha M. • Librarian • Miller's Point Elementary School • Converse, TX 78109
Lebo Shirley B. • Washington, DC 20003 • ACRL ALCTS *Life*
Lebowitz Gloria • University of Northern Colorado James A. Michener Library • Greeley, CO 80639 • ACRL LIRT
Lebrenz Jody E. • Student • State University of New York (SUNY) School of Information & Library Studies • Buffalo, NY 14260 • ACRL PLA RASD
Lech Daniel C. • Telesec Library Services • National Agricultural Library • Beltsville, MD 20705-2351 • ACRL ALCTS RASD
Lechert Karen R. • Boyle County Public Library • Danville, KY 40422
Lechner Judith V. • Dept. of Educational Technology • Auburn University • Auburn, AL 36849 • AASL ALSC

Lechowicz Mary Ann • Librarian • Lansdowne High School • Baltimore, MD 21227 • AASL LIRT
Lechtenberger John • Morenci Public School Libraries • Morenci, AZ 85540
Leckbee Robin C. • Special Collections Librarian • Lake Forest College Donnelley Library • Lake Forest, IL 60045 • ACRL
Leckie Dorothy • Trustee • Farmers Branch Public Library • Farmers Branch, TX 75234 • ALTA
Leckrone Dian L. • Media Specialist • Halvorsen Elementary School • APO AE, NY 09057 • AASL
Leclair-Marzolf Marsha M. • Deputy Director • Salt Lake County Library System • Salt Lake City, UT 84121-3188 • PLA
Lecznar Margaret • Trustee • San Antonio Public Library • San Antonio, TX 78205
Ledbetter Janet A.H. • Waterbury, CT 06706 • AASL
Ledbetter Sherry H. • Hd Bus Sci & Tech Dept • Enoch Pratt Free Library • Baltimore, MD 21201-4484
Leddon Sylvia A. • Head, Lang, Lit, & Hist Division • Akron-Summit County Public Library • Akron, OH 44326-0001 • PLA
Leddy Mariene • Trustee • Western Plains Library System • Clinton, OK 73601
Ledeboer Nancy R. • Librarian I • Contra Costa County Library • Pleasant Hill, CA 94523
Lederer Naomi J. • Arizona State University Hayden Library • Tempe, AZ 85287-1006 • ACRL RASD LIRT
Lederhouse Susan M. • Eastham Public Library • Eastham, MA 02642 • PLA
Lederman Jan E. • Plainview, NY 11803 • ALSC
Ledet Henry J. III • Director • Lincoln-Lawrence-Franklin Regional Library • Brookhaven, MS 39601
Ledford Carole L. • Griffin, GA 30223
Ledford Mary T. • Altamonte Springs, FL 32701 • AASL
Ledig Ruth • Trustee • West Baton Rouge Parish Library • Port Allen, LA 70767
Ledington Tammy A. • Gilbert, AZ 85234 • ACRL IFRT IRRT SRRT
Ledlie Mary E. • Trustee • West Des Moines Public Library • West Des Moines, IA 50265 • Continuing
Ledlie Mary Elizabeth • Trustee • West Des Moines Public Library • West Des Moines, IA 50265
Ledlow Elaine A. • Denton, TX 76201 • Continuing
Ledoux Louise P. • County Librarian • Crockett County Public Library • Ozona, TX 76943
Ledoux Mary E. • Circulation Librarian • Franklin Pierce College Library • Rindge, NH 03461-0060 • ACRL
Lee-Smeltzer Kuang-Hwei • Student • University of Illinois Graduate School of Library and Information Science • Urbana, IL 61801
Lee-Wolfe Yee Sen • Reference Librarian • Contra Costa County Library • Pleasant Hill, CA 94523 • RASD
Lee Alice I. • Elementary Media Specialist • Casey Westfield Schools • Casey, IL 62421 • AASL
Lee Amy C. • Bethesda, MD 20817
Lee Angela S. W. • Reference Librarian • Washington State University Library • Pullman, WA 99164-5610 • ACRL
Lee Anne S. • County Administrator • San Diego County Library • San Diego, CA 92123 • PLA
Lee BangSook M. • Student • Columbia University Music Library • New York, NY 10027
Lee Barbara • Library Director • Worcester Foundation for Experimental Biology • Shrewsbury, MA 01545 • ACRL LITA
Lee Barbara A. • Librarian III • Milwaukee Public Library • Milwaukee, WI 53233 • ALCTS
Lee Barbara A. • Senior Editor/Production Mgr. • Scarecrow Press, Inc. • Metuchen, NJ 08840 • SRRT
Lee Barbara M. • Youth Services Librarian • McTigue Junior High School • Toledo, OH 43615 • AASL
Lee Ben • Library Director • Armstrong State College Lane Library • Savannah, GA 31419-1997
Lee Betty W. Mrs. • Librarian • University of Hong Kong Main Library • Hong Kong, Hong Kong • ACRL ALCTS LITA
Lee Beverly A. • Young Adult • Douglas County Library System • Roseburg, OR 97470 • YALSA SORT
Lee Bobbie H. • Atlanta-Fulton Public Library • Atlanta, GA 30303
Lee Carl R. • Assoc. Dir. Systems & Access • Michigan State University Libraries • East Lansing, MI 48824-1048 • LITA
Lee Carol E. • Harris County Public Library Crosby Branch • Crosby, TX 77532
Lee Catherine A. • Reference Librarian • Eastern Kentucky University John Grant Crabbe Library • Richmond, KY 40475-3121
Lee Catherine A. • Student • University of Pittsburgh School of Library and Information Science • Pittsburgh, PA 15260
Lee Catherine Y. • Reference Librarian • Santa Monica Public Library • Santa Monica, CA 90401 • ACRL
Lee Chang C. • University Librarian • University of Central Florida Library • Orlando, FL 32816-0666
Lee Che-jung • Student • University of Pittsburgh School of Library and Information Science • Pittsburgh, PA 15260 • RASD
Lee Choon S. • Pusan 612-022, South Korea • ACRL LITA
Lee Christina Sr • Librarian • Our Lady of Mercy School • Daly City, CA 94015 • AASL
Lee Chui-Chun • Associate Dir. of the Library • State University of New York College at New Paltz Sojourner Truth Library • New Paltz, NY 12561 • ACRL LAMA LITA
Lee Clark • Las Vegas-Clark County Library District Flamingo Library • Las Vegas, NV 89119 • ALTA
Lee Corliss S. • American Cultures Librarian • University of California-Berkeley Moffitt Undergraduate Library • Berkeley, CA 94720 • ACRL EMIERT
Lee Dan R. • Librarian • Lander College Jackson Library • Greenwood, SC 29649 • LHRT
Lee Daniel E. • Student • University of Wisconsin-Milwaukee School of Library & Information Science • Milwaukee, WI 53201
Lee Daniel R. • Asst. Circulation Librarian • Yale University Sterling Memorial Library • New Haven, CT 06520 • ACRL LAMA IFRT
Lee Danny • Trustee • Las Vegas-Clark County Library District Flamingo Library • Las Vegas, NV 89119 • ALTA
Lee David J. • APO, AP 96337-0001 • ACRL ALCTS *Life*
Lee Deborah O • Millsaps College Millsaps-Wilson Library • Jackson, MS 39210 • ACRL ALCTS
Lee Earl W. • Collection Development Libn • Pittsburg State University Leonard Axe Library • Pittsburg, KS 66762 • IFRT
Lee Elizabeth B. • Secretary • Richland Northeast High School • Columbia, SC 29223 • AASL
Lee Elizabeth J. Mrs • Emeritus Cataloging Librarian • University of Wisconsin-Milwaukee Golda Meir Library • Milwaukee, WI 53201 • ACRL ALCTS *Continuing*
Lee Ella Jean Mrs. • Librarian • Robert E. Lee High School • Baytown, TX 77520
Lee Ethel M. • Smithfield, RI 02917 • GODORT
Lee Frances C. • Director • Somers Public Library • Somers, NY 10589 • LITA
Lee Frank Stanger • Director of Information Services • Latham & Watkins • Los Angeles, CA 90071 • ACRL RASD
Lee Heung-Kyu • Taejon, 302-350, South Korea • ACRL ALCTS ASCLA LITA LRRT
Lee Hsiang C. • Chappaqua, NY 10514
Lee Hsiao-Hung • Student • Rutgers University School of Communication Information & Library Studies • New Brunswick, NJ 08903
Lee Hwa-Wei • Dean of University Libraries • Ohio University Vernon R. Alden Library • Athens, OH 45701-2978 • ACRL IRRT
Lee Hyun Kee K • Seoul 138-071, South Korea • LITA IRRT
Lee I Wen Yen • Princeton, NJ 08540-5416
Lee James E. Jr. • Trustee • Lexington Public Library • Lexington, KY 40507 • ALTA
Lee Janelle • Library Media Servs. Director • Putnam City School • Oklahoma City, OK 73122 • AASL
Lee Janet • Technical Services Librarian • Regis University Dayton Memorial Library • Denver, CO 80221-1099 • ACRL
Lee Janet W. • Media Specialist • Woodland Middle School • East Point, GA 30344 • AASL
Lee Janis M. • Pepper, Hamilton, & Scheetz • Philadelphia, PA 19103 • IFRT
Lee Joann • Supervisor • Detroit Board of Education • Detroit, MI 48227 • AASL
Lee Joann H. • Bainbridge Island, WA 98110
Lee Joel M. • Marketing Manager • Auto-Graphics Inc. • Pomona, CA 91768
Lee John M. • Information Access Company • Foster City, CA 94404 • ALCTS
Lee Jounghyoun K. • Assistant Engineering Librarian • University of Illinois • Urbana, IL 61801 • ACRL
Lee Joyce C. • Assistant Director • Nevada State Library & Archives • Carson City, NV 89710 • ASCLA PLA
Lee Judy A. • Manager,Information Services • RWR Advertising • New York, NY 10010
Lee Karen S. • Houston, TX 77062-2231 • LITA
Lee Katherine T. • Flushing, NY 11358
Lee Kim • Nuclear Assurance Corporation • Norcross, GA 30092
Lee Kristy P. Y. • Associate Editor • H.W. Wilson Company • Bronx, NY 10452 • LITA
Lee Lai F. • Student • University of Hawaii School of Library & Information Studies • Honolulu, HI 96822 • ASCLA PLA
Lee Lauren K. • Manager, Collection Development • Brodart Company • Williamsport, PA 17705 • ALCTS ALSC PLA
Lee Linda T. • Head of Circulation • Hong Kong University of Science & Technology University Library • Kowloon, Hong Kong • ACRL
Lee Lucy Te-Chu • Natl Taiwan University • Taipei 10764 ROC, Taiwan • LITA
Lee Lydia Rong-Jang • Librarian II Children Services • Los Angeles Public Library Valley Plaza Library • Los Angeles, CA 90071
Lee Lynda M. • Director • Calcasieu Parish Public Library • Lake Charles, LA 70601 • LAMA
Lee Lynda P. • Librarian • Alcolu Elementary School • Alcolu, SC 29001 • AASL
Lee Margaret I. Miss • New York, NY 10027 • ACRL YALSA *Continuing*
Lee Marianne M. • Student • El Segundo Public Library • El Segundo, CA 90245
Lee Marie B. • Head, Business Office • Atlanta-Fulton Public Library • Atlanta, GA 30303 • CLENE
Lee Marina E. • Student • University of Maryland College of Library and Information Services • College Park, MD 20742-4345 • LITA IFRT
Lee Marlene K. • Youth Services Coordinator • Broward County Division of Libraries Broward County Library • Fort Lauderdale, FL 33301 • ALSC PLA
Lee Mary Ann • Woodruff, SC 29388 • AASL
Lee Mei-Yun • Student • University of South Carolina College of Library & Information Science • Columbia, SC 29208
Lee Michael M. • Dean of Lib & Learning Res. • University of Houston Clear Lake Neumann Library • Houston, TX 77058
Lee Michele • Studio Museum • New York, NY 10027
Lee Mildred C. • Santa Rosa, CA 95409 • AASL ALSC
Lee Myung J. • Youngsan Library • APO San Francisco, CA 96301-0074
Lee Nancy C. • Librarian • State Library of Iowa • Des Moines, IA 50319
Lee Ocine • Librarian • Killough Middle School • Houston, TX 77083
Lee Paul Tak Po • Honolulu, HI 96828-1242 • RASD
Lee Pauline W. • Director • Grambling State University A. C. Lewis Memorial Library • Grambling, LA 71245 • ACRL LAMA
Lee Pier M. • Head Librarian • Peters Township Library • McMurry, PA 15317
Lee Regina H. • Reference Librarian • Texas College of Osteopathic Medicine • Fort Worth, TX 76107 • LAMA CLENE
Lee Richard C. • Las Vegas-Clark County Library District • Las Vegas, NV 89101
Lee Rolly J. Jr. • Director • Roosevelt Public Library • Roosevelt, NY 11575
Lee Ronald A. • Knoxville, TN 37922
Lee Sheila Y. • Serial Cataloger • Louisiana State University Libraries Troy H. Middleton Library • Baton Rouge, LA 70803-3342 • ALCTS
Lee Silva • Library Director • South Huntington Public Library • Huntington Station, NY 11746
Lee Soo Kyung • Chief of Technical Services • Messiah College Murray Learning Resources Center • Grantham, PA 17027 • ACRL LAMA
Lee Soancha • Head, Serials Department • Public Library of Cincinnati and Hamilton County • Cincinnati, OH 45202 • ALCTS
Lee Stella Liu • St. Louis, MO 63108
Lee Sul H. • Dean • University of Oklahoma Libraries University Libraries • Norman, OK 73019 • ACRL ALCTS LAMA LITA *Life*
Lee Susan A. • Assoc. Dir., Adm. Services • Harvard College Library Widener Memorial Library • Cambridge, MA 02138 • ACRL LAMA
Lee Sylvia J. • Automation/Technical Serv Coor • Chautauqua-Cattaraugus Library System • Jamestown, NY 14701 • ALCTS LAMA LITA
Lee T. M. • Director • Korea Social Science Library • Seoul 100-666, South Korea • ACRL RASD
Lee Tae Moon • Professor • Kun-kuk University Department of Library Science • Seoul, South Korea • ACRL GODORT IRRT
Lee Tamera Nell • Head of Veterinary Medical Lib. • Auburn University Veterinary Medicine Library • Auburn University, AL 36849-5606 • LAMA
Lee Thomas H. • East Asian Librarian • Indiana University at Bloomington University Libraries • Bloomington, IN 47405
Lee Tsaiyu • Cataloger • Santa Clara County Free Library • San Jose, CA 95112-4446 • PLA
Lee Tung-fen • Student • University of North Carolina at Chapel Hill School of Information and Library Science • Chapel Hill, NC 27599-3360

Lee Valerie L. Hopkins • Children's Librarian • Gary Public Library Tolleston Branch • Gary, IN 46404-2297

Lee Wai Yan • Student • University of Pittsburgh School of Library and Information Science • Pittsburgh, PA 15260

Lee William M. • University of West Florida John C. Pace Library • Pensacola, FL 32514 • ACRL RASD *Life*

Lee Wol Sue C. • Principal Librarian • Brooklyn Public Library New Lots Branch • Brooklyn, NY 11238

Lee Youngsil • Student • Louisiana State University School of Library & Information Science • Baton Rouge, LA 70803-3290

Lee Yvonne L. • Head, Science Dept. • University of Wisconsin-Madison Memorial Library • Madison, WI 53706 • ALCTS

Leech Charles • Trustee • Waukegan Public Library • Waukegan, IL 60085

Leedom Kathryn • Marshall Public Schools • Marshall, MN 56258 • AASL ALSC

Leek Cary L. • Teacher • Sacramento Country Day School • Sacramento, CA 95864

Leek Max • Director • Pocatello Public Library • Pocatello, ID 83201 • LAMA PLA

Leeper Dennis P. Dr • Audiovisual Services • Temple Univ • Philadelphia, PA 19122 • PLA

Leerhoff Ruth E. • Special Coll. Lib.-Retired • San Diego State University Library • San Diego, CA 92119-2120

Lees John • School Librarian • Washington Elementary School • Auburn, WA 98002 • AASL

Lees Peggy • Librarian • Richmond Public Library • Richmond BC, V6X 2E3 Canada

Leeseberg Karen A. • Student • Louisiana State University School of Library & Information Science • Baton Rouge, LA 70803-3290

Leeson Karen A. • Eugene, OR 97405

Leeson Rosanne D. • Los Altos, CA 94024

Leety Christine M. • Reference Librarian • Scranton Public Library Albright Memorial Library • Scranton, PA 18509-3248

Lefebvre Veronica A. • Librarian • United States Department of Agriculture National Agricultural Library • Beltsville, MD 20705-2351 • ALCTS

Lefever Margaret B. • Media Specialist • Montgomery County Public Schools • Rockville, MD 20850

Leff Barbara • Library Director • Stephen S Wise Temple Library • Los Angeles, CA 90077

Leff Judith A. • Tampa, FL 33624 • PLA RASD

Leffler Laurel K. • Marion, OH 43302 • Continuing

Lefkofsky Anne E. • Richmond, TX 77469 • PLA

Lefkowitz Mona • Librarian • Bronxville Public Library • Bronxville, NY 10708

Lefkowitz Paula • Children's Librarian • Parsippany-Troy Hills Public Library Parsippany Branch • Parsippany, NJ 07054-4036 • ALSC

Legear Russell Mr • Washington, DC 20008 • Life

Legel David L. • Reference Bibliographer • University of Rochester Rush Rhees Library • Rochester, NY 14627 • ACRL IFRT

Leger-Hornby Tracey • Coordinator of Reader Services • Simmons College Beatley Library • Boston, MA 02115 • LITA

Leget Max • Reference Librarian • University of South Dakota I.D. Weeks Library • Vermillion, SD 57069-2390 • ACRL

Legg Dianne C. • Reference Librarian • University of Minnesota O. Meredith Wilson Library • Minneapolis, MN 55455-0414 • ACRL LAMA RASD

Legg Jeannette • Technical Serv./Supv. Libn. Asst • Plumas County Library • Quincy, CA 95971 • ALCTS LITA

Legge Christopher A. • Base Librarian • United States Air Force Headquarters 81st Combat Support Group • APO New York, NY 09755 • LAMA PLA *Life*

Leggett Deborah H. • Faxon Company,Inc. • Westwood, MA 02090 • ACRL ALCTS

Leggett Elaine B. • Library Coordinator • Eanes Independent School District Westlake High School • Austin, TX 78746 • AASL LAMA LIRT LRRT

Leggett Kim E. • Reference Librarian • Worthington Public Library • Worthington, OH 43085

Leggett Lois D. • Librarian • Forsyth County Public Library • Winston-Salem, NC 27101

Leggett Mark • Manager, Bus., Sci & Tech Div. • Indianapolis Marion County Public Library • Indianapolis, IN 46206 • PLA RASD SRRT

Lego Jane B. • Norfolk, VA 23502 • PLA

Lehan Terri • Community Library Supervisor • Santa Clara County Free Library Campbell Public • Campbell, CA 95008 • PLA

Lehlbach Anna T. • Maplewood, NJ 07040 • Continuing

Lehman Carol B. • Associate Director for Tech Serv • Jefferson County Public Library Library Service Center • Wheat Ridge, CO 80033 • ALCTS PLA

Lehman Charlene S. • Serials Cataloger • University of Iowa Libraries • Iowa City, IA 52242-1379 • ACRL ALCTS LITA GODORT IFRT IRRT

Lehman Diane Larson • Kingston, NY 12401

Lehman Douglas K. • Director, Library Technical Svs • Miami-Dade Community College North Campus Library • Miami, FL 33167 • ACRL LITA

Lehman James O. • Eastern Mennonite Coll • Harrisonburg, VA 22801 • ACRL

Lehman Lois J. • Dean • Regent University • Virginia Beach, VA 23464-9875 • ACRL ALCTS LAMA LITA

Lehmann Ann C. • Ballston Spa, NY 12020 • RASD

Lehmann Candee S. • Mary Cotton Public Library • Sabetha, KS 66534

Lehmann Karen Shostrom • Media Specialist • Hampton Community High School • Hampton, IA 50441 • AASL

Lehmann Kathleen A. • Adult Services Librarian • Louis Bay Second Library • Hawthorne, NJ 07506

Lehmann Nieves K. • Student • University of South Carolina College of Library & Information Science • Columbia, SC 29208

Lehmann Stephen R. • Humanities Bibliographer • University of Pennsylvania Library Van Pelt-Dietrich Library Center • Philadelphia, PA 19104-6206 • ACRL ALCTS

Lehmann Vibeke • Library Director • Wisconsin Department of Corrections • Madison, WI 53707-7925 • ASCLA

Lehmkuhl Ruth E. • Media Specialist • Monroe Elementary School • Davenport, IA 52802 • AASL

Lehn Laura P. • Annadale, VA 22003 • LITA

Lehocky Barbara • Director of Research/Development • Optimist International • St. Louis, MO 63108 • ACRL LAMA

Lehr Daniel S. • Greenbelt, MD 20770 • AASL IFRT

Lehrer Beverly S. • Silver Spring, MD 20910

Lehrmann Glenda M. • Reference Librarian • Texas Woman's University Mary Evelyn Blagg-Huey Library • Denton, TX 76204-1715

Lehto Anita L. • Reference/Adult Services Libn. • Stoughton Public Library • Stoughton, MA 02072

Leibee Nancye J. • Student • Louisiana State University School of Library & Information Science • Baton Rouge, LA 70803-3290

Leibiger Carol A. • University of South Dakota • Vermillion, SD 57069 • LHRT

Leibik Leonora • Head of Reference • Eisenhower Public Library District • Harwood Heights, IL 60656 • PLA RASD IFRT SRRT

Leibman Valentina G. • Student • Southern Connecticut State University School of Libray Science & Instructional Technology • New Haven, CT 06515 • LITA IFRT

Leibold Mary L. • San Antonio, TX 78212

Leibow-Gigerich Nicole • Student • Columbia University Library Service Library • New York, NY 10027 • ACRL

Leibowitz Faye R. • Serials/Microforms Cataloger • University of Pittsburgh • Pittsburgh, PA 15260 • ALCTS EMIERT

Leibowitz Margaret • Juneau, AK 99802

Leibowitz Roselyn • Librarian • Queens Borough Public Library • Jamaica, NY 11432 • PLA

Leich Harold M. • Russian Area Specialist • Library of Congress • Washington, DC 20541 • ACRL ALCTS LITA

Leicht Donna R. • Appleton, WI 54915-6120

Leide John E. • McGill University Graduate School of Library & Information Studies • Montreal PQ, H3A 1Y1 Canada • Life

Leider Karen • Alexandria, VA 22302 • ACRL ALCTS LAMA

Leiding Reba M. • Elk Rapids, MI 49629 • PLA

Leigh Carma • San Diego, CA 92115 • ASCLA PLA *Life*

Leigh Slavka • Director • South Country Library • Bellport, NY 11713 • LAMA PLA

Leighton Ann V. • Librarian III • Hawaii State Public Library System Office of the State Librarian • Honolulu, HI 96813 • ALSC

Leighton Herbert V. • Winona State University • Winona, MN 55987 • ACRL GODORT

Leighton Lee W. • Head, Catalog Dept. • University of California-Berkeley University Library • Berkeley, CA 94720 • ACRL ALCTS

Leighton Vera • Director • Quoque Library Inc • Quoque, NY 11959

Leighty Linda C. • Dir. of A/V & Media Prod. Servs. • Pitt Community College • Greenville, NC 27835-7007 • ACRL LITA

Leinbach Philip E. • Librarian • Tulane University Howard-Tilton Memorial Library • New Orleans, LA 70118 • ACRL *Life*

Leiner Paul C. • Goldhaber Research Associates • Amherst, NY 14228

Leiner Paula A. • Student • University of Pittsburgh School of Library and Information Science • Pittsburgh, PA 15260 • ALCTS

Leipold Lance J. • Reference Librarian • Mankato State University Memorial Library • Mankato, MN 56002-8400 • ACRL

Leirdahl Lori • Preservation Outreach Rep. • Minnesota Historical Society • Saint Paul, MN 55102 • ACRL ALCTS

Leise J. • Librarian • Lincoln High School Library • Des Moines, IA 50315 • AASL

Leisner Anthony B. • Special Assistant to the CEO • Dawson Group, The • Lake Bluff, IL 60044-2204 • PLA ERT NMRT

Leisner Edward J. • Tonawanda, NY 14150

Leister Carol • Supervisor of Library Media Serv • Longwood Senior High School • Middle Island, NY 11953 • AASL

Leister Janet K. • Information Specialist • Info To Go • Portland, OR 97213 • ACRL

Leister Susan E. • Catalog Librarian • George Washington University Himmelfarb Health Sciences Library • Washington, DC 20037

Leisz Sterling • Davis, CA 95617

Leita Carole • Reference Librarian • Berkeley Public Library • Berkeley, CA 94704 • SRRT

Leiter Richard A. • Director • Regent University • Virginia Beach, VA 23464-9875 • ACRL LAMA LITA RASD ERT GODORT IFRT LHRT LRRT

Leith Barbara R. • Reference • Manhattan Public Library • Manhattan, KS 66502

Leithauser Jackie L. • Director • Silverton Public Library • Silverton, CO 81433

Leitle B. Kathy • East Regional Branch Coordinator • Saint Louis Public Library Carpenter Branch • St. Louis, MO 63118 • ALSC PLA

Leitzke Nowell D. • Minnesota Department of Education • Saint Paul, MN 55101

Lekus Diana R. • Librarian • Kleid Company • New York, NY 10036 • IFRT NMRT

Lelansky Craig D. • Student • Catholic University of America School of Library and Information Science • Washington, DC 20064

Lele Pradeep • Student • University of Missouri-Columbia School of Library & Informational Science • Columbia, MO 65211

Lellinger Linda K. • Librarian • Silverbrook Elementary School • Fairfax Station, VA 22039 • AASL

Lemann Catherine • Reference Librarian • Law Library of Louisiana • New Orleans, LA 70112

Lemberg W. Richard Bro • Faculty Community • Saint Mary's College of California • Moraga, CA 94575 • ACRL ALCTS LITA LRRT

Lembersky Galina F. • Student • Massachusetts Institute of Technology Libraries (MIT) • Cambridge, MA 02139

Lembke Melody • Los Angeles County Law Library • Los Angeles, CA 90012

Lemke Darrell H. • University of the District of Columbia Learning Resources Division • Washington, DC 20008 • ACRL ALCTS LAMA RASD *Life*

Lemke Marcia A. • Media Specialist/Media Coord. • Heartland Area Education Agency • Johnston, IA 50131-1603 • AASL YALSA

Lemmer Lois Marie • Student • Syracuse University School of Information Studies • Syracuse, NY 13244-4100 • ALSC PLA

Lemmon Anne B. • Information Specialist • Ethyl Corporation • Baton Rouge, LA 70801

Lemmon Cynthia E. • Holy Cross High School • New Orleans, LA 70117 • AASL

Lemmons Judy • Media Specialist • Beck Middle School • Greenville, SC 29607

Lemon Tracey E. • Syracuse, NY 13210-2235 • ALCTS

Lemp Vicki E. • Museum of Television and Radio • New York, NY 10019

Lempinen Nance A. • Farmington Hills, MI 48823 • IFRT SRRT

Lemunyon Karen E. • Reference/Instruction Librarian • University of Texas Libraries General Libraries • Austin, TX 78713-7330 • ACRL RASD LIRT

Lenahan Linda A. • Louisville, KY 40207

Lenart Lynn M. • Hartville, OH 44632 • GODORT IFRT

Lener Edward F. • Student • Virginia Polytechnic Institute and State University, Newman Library • Blacksburg, VA 24061-0434 • ACRL

Lenius Sharon A. • Director • United States Army Reserve Component Automation System • Newington, VA 22122-8510 • AFLRT FLRT GODORT

Lenkowski Patricia • Reference Librarian • Widener University Wolfgram Library • Chester, PA 19013 • ACRL LIRT

Lenn Kathy • Librarian • University of Oregon Library • Eugene, OR 97403-1299 • ACRL

Lennartson Cynthia K. • Student • University of Texas at Austin Graduate School of Library & Information Sciences • Austin, TX 78712-1276

Lennartz Mary Frances O.P. Sr. • Librarian • Saint Rita High School • Chicago, IL 60620 • AASL

Lennertz Lora L. • Head, Circulation/Access Serv. • University of Arkansas Mullins Library • Fayetteville, AR 72701 • ALCTS LAMA NMRT

Lennig Carol L. • Librarian • West Hartford Public Library Julia Faxon Branch • West Hartford, CT 06110

Lennon Robert H. • Rancho Palo Verdes, CA 90732 • PLA RASD *Life*

Lennon Suzanne L. • Scottsdale, AZ 85250

Lennox Claire H. • Princeton, NJ 08540-3049 • ALSC

Lennox Janice C. • Supervisory Librarian • National Library of Medicine • Bethesda, MD 20894

Lennox Valerie A. • Student • University of Pittsburgh School of Library and Information Science • Pittsburgh, PA 15260 • ALSC

Lenobel Abraham M. MD • President • Port Jefferson Free Library • Pt. Jefferson, NY 11777-1897

Lenoir Joyce E. • Library Director • San Bernardino County Library • San Bernardino, CA 92415 • YALSA EMIERT

Lenox Mary F. • Dean • University of Missouri-Columbia School of Library & Informational Science • Columbia, MO 65211 • AASL

Lenser Jane L. • Program Coordinator • Indian Trails Public Library District • Wheeling, IL 60090

Lent Emily I. • Highland, NY 12528

Lent Laura J. • San Francisco Public Library Richmond Branch • San Francisco, CA 94118

Lentini Rosemarie • Librarian • Norfeldt Elementary School • West Hartford, CT 06117 • AASL

Lentz Christie • Columbia Central High School • Columbia, TN 38401 • AASL

Lentz J. Michael Dr. • Trustee • West Florida Regional Library • Pensacola, FL 32501

Lentz Janice Q. • Media Coordinator • Alexander Central High School • Taylorsville, NC 28681 • AASL

Lentz Mary H. • Law Librarian • Lincoln County Law Library • Newport, OR 97365 • NMRT

Lentz Robert L. • Wenonah, NJ 08090

Lentz Shirley V. • Associate Librarian • Carlton Fields Law Firm Library • Tampa, FL 33601

Lentz Susan A. • Associate Librarian • University of California UCSB Library • Santa Barbara, CA 93106-9010 • ALCTS

Lenz Millicent A. Dr • Assistant Professor • State University of New York at Albany School of Information Science & Policy • Albany, NY 12222 • ASCLA YALSA

Lenze James B. • Student • Roseville Public Library • Roseville, MI 48066 • RASD

Lenzini Rebecca T. • Denver, CO 80218-3513 • LITA

Leo Karen Ann • Director • Corona Public Library • Corona, CA 91720 • ALCTS ALSC LAMA LITA PLA RASD EMIERT IFRT

Leo Susan L. • Student • University of Iowa School of Library & Information Science • Iowa City, IA 52242 • IFRT

Leo William G. • The Bryant Library • Roslyn, NY 11576

Leon Carmencita • Guaynabo, PR 00966 • AASL

Leon Louise Bondow • Technical Processes Director • Western New Mexico University • Silver City, NM 88062

Leon Margareta • Librarian IV • New York Public Library • New York, NY 10018-2788 • ALCTS

Leonard-Malis Helen • Grosse Pointe, MI 48230 • PLA

Leonard Angela M. • Dickinson College Denny Hall • Carlisle, PA 17013

Leonard Barbara • Coor. of Cllns/Fiscal Planning • San Jose State University Clark Library • San Jose, CA 95192-0028 • ACRL ALCTS LAMA

Leonard Betty Jane • Chicago Public Library McKinley Park Branch • Chicago, IL 60609

Leonard Carolyn • Greenland High School • Greenland, AR 72737 • AASL

Leonard Carolyn Snidow • Librarian • State University of New York at Plattsburgh (SUNY) • Plattsburgh, NY 12901

Leonard Charlotte • Dayton, OH 45409 • Continuing

Leonard E. Doris • Assistant Librarian • Becker Junior College at Leicester Paul Swan Library • Leicester, MA 01524

Leonard Gloria J. • Administrator • Seattle Public Library • Seattle, WA 98104-1193 • PLA RASD

Leonard June R. • Reference Librarian • Thomas Jefferson Library • Jefferson City, MO 65101

Leonard Kathleen P. • Pawtucket School Department Henry J. Winters School • Pawtucket, RI 02860 • AASL ASCLA

Leonard Kathryn H. • Student • Texas Woman's University School of Library & Information Studies • Denton, TX 76204

Leonard Lawrence E. Dr • Chief Library • U.S. Department of Transportation Library • Washington, DC 20590 • ACRL LITA FLRT *Life*

Leonard Lucinda E. • President • Trileon, Inc. • Potomac, MD 20854

Leonard Patricia Jeanne • Student • University of Illinois Graduate School of Library and Information Science • Urbana, IL 61801

Leonard Peter C. • Director • Mount Lebannon Public Library • Pittsburgh, PA 15228 • LAMA PLA

Leonard Ronald P. • Student • University of Kentucky College of Library & Information Science • Lexington, KY 40506-0391

Leonard Ruth • Librarian • Thousand Oaks Library • Thousand Oaks, CA 91362 • LAMA

Leonard Ruth S. • Boston, MA 02215 • ACRL ALCTS *Life*

Leonardi Catherine F. • Duke University William R. Perkins Library • Durham, NC 27706 • MAGERT

Leonberger Janet • Librarian • Glastonbury High School Library • Glastonbury, CT 06033 • AASL

Leonchik Natalie • Trustee • Bedford Park Public Library District • Bedford Park, IL 60501 • ALTA PLA

Leondar Judith • Kingston, NJ 08528 • ACRL LAMA *Continuing*

Leone Donna R. • Librarian/Director • University of South Florida Library • Tampa, FL 33620-5600 • ACRL

Leone Dorothy M. • La Grange, IL 60525 • Continuing

Leone Lucille P. • S. Glastonbury, CT 06073 • AASL NMRT

Leone Mary C. • Librarian • Franklin Music Magnet School • St Paul, MN 55101 • AASL

Leone RoseMarie G. • Director • Providence Hospital Health Sciences Library • Washington, DC 20017

Leong-Kurio Nadine R. • Librarian • Honolulu Community College Library • Honolulu, HI 96817-4598 • ALCTS ERT

Leong Carol L.H. • Hd, Cataloging Dept. • Hong Kong University of Science & Technology • Kowloon, Hong Kong

Leong Joan C. • District Librarian • Brisbane School District • Burlingame, CA 94010

Leong Patrick L. • Hayward, CA 94544-6775 • EMIERT

Leonhardt Thomas W. • Dean of Libraries • University of the Pacific • Stockton, CA 95211 • ACRL ALCTS LAMA LITA

Leopold Alan J. • Rare Book Cataloger • Newberry Library • Chicago, IL 60610 • ACRL

Lepage Mary K. • Branch Manager • Baltimore County Public Library Cockeysville Branch • Cockeysville, MD 21030 • PLA

Leporati Elizabeth T. • Student • Florida State University School of Library and Information Studies • Tallahassee, FL 32306-2048

Lepore Wilma J. • Director • Newark Public Library • Newark, OH 43055 • ALCTS ALSC LAMA PLA RASD

Leppe Jan • Librarian • K.I. Jones Elementary School & Oakbrook Elementary School • Fairfield, CA 94533 • AASL

Leppert Elaine C. • Library Director • Caldwell Public Library • Caldwell, ID 83605 • PLA RASD YALSA

Lepsig Robert • Trustee • Monroe County Library System • Monroe, MI 48161 • ALTA

Lercangee Francine • 1000 Brussels, Belgium

Lerch Barbara A. • Loan Librarian • University of New Hampshire Library • Durham, NH 03824 • ACRL LAMA LITA

Lerch Jennifer A. • Massillon, OH 44646

Lerdahl Audrey • Ramsey County Public Library Adminstrative Offices • Shoreview, MN 55126-5800

Lerman Linda P. • Judacia Curator • Yale University Sterling Memorial Library • New Haven, CT 06520 • ACRL EMIERT SRRT

Lerman Rob C. • Woburn Public Library • Woburn, MA 01801 • SRRT

Lerner Arthur • Trustee • Great Neck Library • Great Neck, NY 11024

Lerner Bobette S. Ms. • Trustee • Omaha Public Library • Omaha, NE 68102 • ALTA

Lerner David • New York, NY 10011 • LITA

Lerner Esther T. • Toledo, OH 43606 • SRRT *Continuing*

Lerner Harry J. • Minneapolis, MN 55401 • ALSC

Lerner Terez • Adult Services Librarian • Flemington Free Public Library • Flemington, NJ 08822 • ALCTS

Leroy Louise S. • Woodland Pk, CO 80866 • PLA RASD *Continuing*

Lerud Joanne V. • Director of the Library • Colorado School of Mines Arthur Lakes Library • Golden, CO 80401 • ACRL LAMA

Les Catherine A. • Adult Services Librarian • Solano County Library Vacaville Branch • Vacaville, CA 95688

Lescroart Joanna M. • Olinda Elementary School • Miami, FL 33142-3099

Lescue Kathleen M. • Children's Librarian • Prosser Public Library • Bloomfield, CT 06002

Lesesne Teri S. • Assistant Professor • Sam Houston State University Department of Library Science • Huntsville, TX 77341-2236 • AASL YALSA

Lesh Jane G. Mrs • Librarian • Schools of the Sacred Heart High School Library • San Francisco, CA 94115 • AASL

Lesh Nancy L. • Librarian • University of Alaska • Anchorage, AK 99508

Lesh Robert W. • Cataloger • Northwestern University Library • Evanston, IL 60208-2300

Lesher Marcella C. • San Antonio, TX 78253 • NMRT

Lesieur Denis J. • Director • Lenox Library • Lenox, MA 01240 • PLA

Lesley J. Ingrid • Chief, Arts and Letters Division • Harold Washington Library Center Chicago Public Library • Chicago, IL 60605 • PLA RASD

Leslie Camille J. • Director • Massillon Public Library • Massillon, OH 44646 • LAMA PLA RASD YALSA IFRT

Leslie Deborah J. • Rare Book Cataloguer • Library Company of Philadelphia • Philadelphia, PA 19107 • ACRL

Leslie Donald S. • Marketing Supervisor • 3M Safety Security Systems • Saint Paul, MN 55144 • AASL ACRL ALCTS LITA PLA AFLRT

Leslie John F. • Grand Rapids, MI 49506

Leslie Kay V. • Director • Guthrie Public Library • Guthrie, OK 73044 • LAMA PLA NMRT

Lesnak Stephen R. • Director of Branch Libraries • Rochester Public Library • Rochester, NY 14604 • LAMA PLA IRRT

Lessard V Cheponis • La Grange School District 102 • La Grange, IL 60525 • AASL ALSC

Lessek Miriam T. • Librarian • Naperville Public Libraries • Naperville, IL 60540

Lessel Alan • Director • Apache County Library • St. Johns, AZ 85936 • PLA IFRT

Lesser Arlene • Young Adult Librarian • Smithtown Library Commack Branch • Commack, NY 11725

Lesser Barbara • Chief, User Liaison Division • Defense Technical Information Center • Alexandria, VA 22304-6145 • AFLRT FLRT

Lesser Charlotte B. • Keene, NH 03431-3308 • ALSC

Lesser Frances • Electrum Library • S164 40 Kista, Sweden

Lesser Susan • Librarian • American Kennel Club Inc Library • New York, NY 10010 • LAMA LITA

Lessey Lorraine M. • Branch Librarian • Fort Bend County Library System Mamie George Branch • Stafford, TX 77477 • PLA

Lessin Barton M. • Assistant Dean of Univ Libs • Wayne State University • Detroit, MI 48202 • ACRL LAMA

Lesslie Kathleen A. • Haysville, KS 67060 • AASL YALSA SRRT

Lesso Judith L. • Staff Librarian • West Virginia University Health Sciences Center Library • Morgantown, WV 26506

Lessun Walter • Public Services Librarian • University of Findlay Shafer Library • Findlay, OH 45840

Lester Daniel W. • Associate University Librarian • Boise State University Library • Boise, ID 83725 • ACRL LAMA LITA

Lester David F. • Southern Connecticut State University School of Libray Science & Instructional Technology • New Haven, CT 06515 • ACRL

Lester Donna L. • Professional • Cornell University Library • Ithaca, NY 14853

Lester June • Associate Dean • University of North Texas School of Library & Information Sciences • Denton, TX 76203 • PLA LRRT

Lester Karen J. • Chugiak, AK 99567

Lester Linda L. • Director, Reference Service • University of Virginia Alderman Library • Charlottesville, VA 22903-2498 • ACRL RASD

Lester Marilyn A. • Dean of Instr. Res./Librarian • National-Louis University • Evanston, IL 60201-1796 • ACRL

Lester Mark R. • San Diego State University Library • San Diego, CA 92182-0511

Lester Mary P. • Wyoming, NY 14591 • Continuing

Lester Noland D. • Branch Manager • Dayton & Montgomery County Public Library-Westwood Branch • Dayton, OH 45417

Lester Pam • Media Specialist • Richlands Elementary School • Richlands, VA 24641 • AASL

Lester Penny S. • Assistant Director • Erie 2 Chautauqua Cattaraugus BOCES • Fredonia, NY 14063 • AASL

Letcher Phillip M. • Student • San Jose State University Division of Library & Information Science • San Jose, CA 95192-0029

Lethbridge Jackson • State College, PA 16801-6211 • ACRL ALCTS RASD *Life*

Letourneau Marlene • Quebec PQ, G1N 2H4 Canada

Letowski Anna Z. • Assistant Cataloger • Bucknell University Bertrand Library • Lewisburg, PA 17837-2086
Lettieri Claire • Dunmore, PA 18512 • Continuing
Lettieri Diane M. • Student • Saint John's University Division of Library & Information Science • Jamaica, NY 11439 • YALSA
Lettieri Robin Mendel • Director • Port Chester Public Library • Port Chester, NY 10573 • PLA YALSA
Lettow Lucille J. • Youth Librarian • University of Northern Iowa Donald O. Rod Library • Cedar Falls, IA 50613-3675 • AASL
Lettus Dorothy M. • Branch Manager • Cuyahoga County Public Library Brook Park Branch • Brook Park, OH 44142-2198 • PLA
Letzring Bryndis A. • Student • University of Missouri-Columbia School of Library & Informational Science • Columbia, MO 65211 • LITA IFRT
Leu Brian Y. N. • Leeward Community College Library • Pearl City, HI 96782
Leung Kai-Chung • Systems • Youngstown State University William F. Maag Library • Youngstown, OH 44555
Leung Polly • Riverside City & County Public Lib Moreno Valley Branch Library • Moreno Valley, CA 92553
Leung Shirley W. • Asst. Univ. Libn. for Tech. Serv • University of California-Irvine Library • Irvine, CA 92713 • ACRL ALCTS LAMA LITA
Leung Terry S. • Sub-Librarian • Hong Kong University of Science & Technology • Kowloon, Hong Kong • ACRL
Leupold Diane A. • Coordinator of Tech. Service • Topeka Public Schools • Topeka, KS 66605 • AASL
Lev Lenore • Newport Beach, CA 92660 • RASD GODORT
Lev Yvonne T. • Serials Librarian • Towson State University • Towson, MD 21204 • ACRL ALCTS LITA
Levas Andrew • Director • Easton Area Public Library • Easton, PA 18042 • YALSA IFRT
Leveille Linda L. • Head Librarian • Allen-Bradley Company • Milwaukee, WI 53204
Level Allison V. • Science Reference Librarian • Library of Congress • Washington, DC 20541 • ACRL RASD LIRT LRRT
Level June S. • Children's Consultant • Martin County Public Library • Stuart, FL 33494-2374 • AASL ALSC
Levell-Braggs Marsha J. • Exhibit Marketing Manager • Association of American University Presses • New York, NY 10012 • ERT
Levendosky Susan E. • Student • University of North Carolina at Chapel Hill School of Information and Library Science • Chapel Hill, NC 27599-3360 • PLA
Levene Donna B. • Library Media Specialist • Homestead Elementary School • Englewood, CO 80112 • AASL
Leverence Mari Ellen • Reference Librarian • Governors State University University Library • University Park, IL 60466 • ACRL
Leverett Gladys M. • San Antonio, TX 78232
Levering Mary Berghaus • Exec Dir Fed Lib & Inf Ct Comm • Library of Congress • Washington, DC 20541 • ASCLA FLRT
Levesque Ellen B. • Tacoma, WA 98406
Levesque Janet A. • Director • Cumberland Public Library Edward J. Hayden Library • Cumberland, RI 02864 • LAMA
Levey Carol • Trustee • Niles Public Library • Niles, IL 60648 • ALTA
Levi Annalina • New York, NY 10023
Levi Preston H. • Dir. of Research Services • International Swimming Hall of Fame • Ft. Lauderdale, FL 33316
Levi Selma K. • Childrens Librarian • Enoch Pratt Free Library • Baltimore, MD 21201-4484 • ALSC
Levie Andre P. • Student • University of Texas at Austin Graduate School of Library & Information Sciences • Austin, TX 78712-1276 • PLA
Levin Amy E. • Assistant Chief, Access Services • Smithsonian Institution Libraries National Air & Space Museum Library • Washington, DC 20560 • RASD
Levin Carol Simon • Somerset, NJ 08873
Levin Doris • Saddle Brook, NJ 07662
Levin Elizabeth A. • Director • Blair Memorial Library • Clawson, MI 48017 • PLA
Levin Fran • Serials Librarian • Houston Public Library • Houston, TX 77002 • ALCTS LITA
Levin Frances W. • Reference Librarian/Literacy • Rogers-Hough Memorial Library • Rogers, AR 72756 • RASD
Levin Joan • Chicago, IL 60611
Levin Joan • Trustee/Secretary • Jacksonville Public Libraries Main Library • Jacksonville, FL 32202
Levin Kathleen Mehring • Baltimore County Public Library • Towson, MD 21204 • ALTA PLA
Levin Martin S. • San Jose State University Division of Library & Information Science • San Jose, CA 95192-0029 • PLA RASD
Levin Seth • President • Gessler Publishing Company • New York, NY 10011 • AASL
Levine Adeline L. • Media Specialist • Farmington City Public Schools Woodcreek Elementary School • Farmington, MI 48334 • AASL ALSC
Levine Amy M. • Montclair Free Public Library • Montclair, NJ 07042 • PLA
Levine Amy M. • Librarian • Saint Michael's Montessori School • New York, NY 10025 • AASL
Levine Cynthia R. • Reference Librarian • North Carolina State University D. H. Hill Library • Raleigh, NC 27695-7111 • ACRL
Levine Ethan • Trustee • Laramie County Library System • Cheyenne, WY 82001-2799
Levine Harriet L. • Information Services Librarian • Irving Public Library System • Irving, TX 75015-2288
Levine Jacalyn R. • Student • Simmons College Graduate School of Library & Information Science • Boston, MA 02115 • ACRL IFRT SRRT
Levine Jack W. • Acquisitions Librarian • Reed College E. V. Hauser Library • Portland, OR 97202 • ACRL ALCTS RASD
Levine Jane • Head of Technical Services • Winnetka Public Library District • Winnetka, IL 60093
Levine Jennifer I. • Student • University of Illinois Graduate School of Library and Information Science • Urbana, IL 61801
Levine Judith L. • Library Development Spec • New York State Library State Education Department • Albany, NY 12230 • ASCLA LAMA PLA
Levine Lesley B. • County Librarian • Lincoln County Public Library • Lincolnton, NC 28092
Levine Marjorie Paris • Marietta, GA 30068
Levine Mark • Librarian • Brooklyn Public Library • Brooklyn, NY 11238 • PLA RASD IRRT
Levine Stephanie D. • Sunnyvale Public Library • Sunnyvale, CA 94088-3714
Levine Susan H. • Silver Spring, MD 20903 • PLA YALSA
Levins Betsy • Elmhurst Public Library • Elmhurst, IL 60126
Levinson Barbara • Administrator of Sch. Lib. Sys. • Rockland BOCES Sch. Lib. Sys. • West Haverstraw, NY 10993 • AASL YALSA
Levinson David E. • Student • University of Illinois Graduate School of Library and Information Science • Urbana, IL 61801 • LITA NMRT
Levinson Marilyn I. • Curator of Manuscripts • Bowling Green State University William Jerome Library • Bowling Green, OH 43403-0175
Levinson Michael H. • Student • University of Maryland College of Library and Information Services • College Park, MD 20742-4345 • LITA
Levinson Riki • New York, NY 10022 • ALSC
Levis Joel • County Librarian • Haliburton County Public Library • Haliburton, ON, K0M 1S0 Canada • LAMA PLA RASD YALSA
Levitan Shelia • Student • Simmons College Graduate School of Library & Information Science • Boston, MA 02115 • PLA
Levitov Deborah D. • Library Media Specialist • Park Elementary School • Lincoln, NE 68508 • AASL
Levitt Irene S. • Head, Admin/Support Services • Massachusetts Board of Library Commissioners • Boston, MA 02215-2070
Levitt Janet G. • Librarian • Temple Sholom of West Essex • Cedar Grove, NJ 07009 • AASL
Levitt Judith E. • University of California-Davis Carlson Health Sciences Library • Davis, CA 95616-5291 • ACRL
Levitt Martin L. Dr. • American Philosophical Society Library • Philadelphia, PA 19106 • ACRL
Levitt Wendy S. • Perrysburg, OH 43551 • PLA
Levkovitz Susan • Chief Cataloging Librarian • City College of New York (CUNY) Graduate School • New York, NY 10036 • ALCTS
Levy Barbara J. • Reference Librarian • University of North Texas • Denton, TX 76203 • ACRL NMRT
Levy Billie M. • W. Hartford, CT 06107 • ALSC
Levy Debbie E. • Librarian • Atlanta-Fulton Public Library • Atlanta, GA 30303 • YALSA
Levy Elizabeth • Associate Librarian, Ref Srvs • Cambridge Public Library • Cambridge, MA 02138
Levy Elyse • Branch Librarian • Miami-Dade Public Library System South Dade Regional Branch • Miami, FL 33189
Levy Janice • Assistant Director • Onondaga Free Library • Syracuse, NY 13215 • PLA
Levy Jeffrey Bryan • University of North Texas • Denton, TX 76203 • ACRL RASD NMRT
Levy John Dana • Serial Record Division • Library of Congress • Washington, DC 20541 • ALCTS LITA FLRT
Levy Judith B. • Branch Manager • San Mateo County Free Library System Sanchez Branch • Pacifica, CA 94044
Levy Mary Jo • Director • Palo Alto City Library Downtown Branch • Palo Alto, CA 94301 • ALSC LAMA PLA IFRT
Levy Norma • Tech. Services Coordinator • Azusa City Library • Azusa, CA 91702 • ALCTS EMIERT IFRT
Levy Norma E. • Ridgewood, NJ 07450 • ACRL
Levy Phyllis • Branch Manager • Miami-Dade Public Library System Kendall Branch Library • Miami, FL 33176-1985
Levy Richard J. • Senior Systems Analyst • West Chester County Information Systems • White Plains, NY 10601 • LITA
Levy Sandra L. • Assistant Slavic Librarian • University of Chicago Library • Chicago, IL 60637-1502 • ACRL
Levy Sharon L. • Librarian • National Wildlife Federation • Vienna, VA 22180
Levy Susan L. • Director of Marketing • Ameritech Information Systems Information Resource Center • Chicago, IL 60606 • LITA
Levy Susan N. • Asst. Div. Chief Telephone Ref. • Brooklyn Public Library • Brooklyn, NY 11238 • SRRT
Levy Suzanne S. • Virginia Room Librarian • Fairfax County Public Library Fairfax City Regional Branch • Fairfax, VA 22030 • GODORT
Lew Bonnie C. • Supervising Librarian • Stockton-San Joaquin County Public Library • Stockton, CA 95202
Lew Cindy D. • University of Wisconsin • Madison, WI 53706
Lew Susan • Head, Technical Services • Greenburgh Public Library • Elmsford, NY 10523
Lewandowski Sue Ann • Buffalo, NY 14215
Lewark Kathryn Warren • Manager, Information Resources • SynOptics Communications, Inc. • Santa Clara, CA 95052-8185 • IFRT
Lewicky George I. • Vice Pres/Dir of Indexing Serv • H. W. Wilson Company • Bronx, NY 10452 • AASL ACRL ALCTS ALSC LAMA LITA PLA RASD YALSA
Lewicky Martha K. • Technical Services Librarian • Bergen Community College Library & Learning Resource Center • Paramus, NJ 07652-1595
Lewicky Sally S. Mrs. • Librarian • Franklin Avenue Middle School • Franklin Lakes, NJ 07417 • AASL
Lewin June E. • Reference Librarian • Beverly Hills Public Library • Beverly Hills, CA 90210
Lewin Martin • Kenmore, NY 14223 • Continuing
Lewis-Frazier Monta R. • Student • University of Illinois Graduate School of Library and Information Science • Urbana, IL 61801 • ALSC PLA
Lewis-Heise Elsa M. • Martinsville, IN 46151
Lewis Alan D. • Assistant Director • Office of Library Development & Services • Saint Paul, MN 55101 • ASCLA
Lewis Alice G. • Librarian • Owensboro-Daviess County Public Library • Owensboro, KY 42301
Lewis Alison S. • Trustee • Hayward Public Library • Hayward, CA 94541 • ALTA
Lewis Andrea S. • Cable Elementary School • San Antonio, TX 78227 • AASL
Lewis Ann Marie • Director • Fairmont Cmnty Lib Sys • Syracuse, NY 13219 • PLA
Lewis Barbara A. • Livonia Civic Center Library • Livonia, MI 48154 • ALSC
Lewis Barbara B. • Gary, IN 46402 • AASL
Lewis Bernice F. • Librarian • Midlothian Middle School • Midlothian, VA 23113 • AASL
Lewis Betty Jane • Cincinnati, OH 45236-2286 • PLA RASD *Life*
Lewis Beverly Ann • Library Director • Paris Public Library • Paris, TX 75460 • PLA
Lewis Brian G. • County Ln • Tulare County Library System • Visalia, CA 93277 • LAMA PLA
Lewis Carol F. • Library Media Specialist • Thompson Elementary School Intermediate Library • Alabaster, AL 35007
Lewis Carol G. • Director, School Media Prog Div • North Carolina State Department of Public Instruction • Raleigh, NC 27603-1712 • AASL
Lewis Charles S. • Media Processing Center Coor. • J. Sargeant Reynolds Community College Library • Richmond, VA 23261-2040 • ACRL
Lewis Charlotte O. • Library Media Specialist • H. D. Woodson Senior High School • Washington, DC 20019 • AASL
Lewis Charlotte P. • Director • Russell County Public Library • Lebanon, VA 24266
Lewis Christopher G. • Media Reference Librarian • The American University Library • Washington, DC 20016-8046 • LITA VRT
Lewis Cynthia K. • Independent Consultant • Berkeley, CA 94702
Lewis David G. • Cortland, NY 13045 • ACRL RASD
Lewis David W. • University of Connecticut Homer Babbidge Library • Storrs, CT 06269-1005 • ACRL LITA

Lewis Deanna L. • Access Control Librarian • Winthrop College Ida Jane Dacus Library • Rock Hill, SC 29733 • ACRL LITA

Lewis Del Marie • Library Media Specialist • Pinellas County Schools Shore Acres Elementary School • St. Petersburg, FL 33702 • AASL

Lewis Donna H. • Librarian • Carmel High School • Carmel, CA 93922

Lewis Dorothy G. • Librarian • Carlisle School • Martinsville, VA 24112 • AASL YALSA

Lewis Dorothy J. • Media Specialist • Stillwater Elementary School • Carnation, WA 98014

Lewis E. Brien • Vice-President • Electronic Information System Group • Bethesda, MD 20817 • LITA FLRT GODORT

Lewis Elizabeth S. • Gwynedd, PA 19436 • Continuing

Lewis Eva B. • Librarian • Proviso East High School Library • Maywood, IL 60153

Lewis G. Gordon • Director • Metropolitan Library System • Oklahoma City, OK 73102 • Life

Lewis Gabrielle A. • Oak Park, IL 60302 • SRRT

Lewis George R. • Starkville, MS 39759 • Continuing

Lewis Georgina M. • Coordinator, Preservation • University of Manitoba • Winnipeg MB, R3T 2N2 Canada • ACRL ALCTS

Lewis Gillian H. • Associate Editor • BHA-Getty Art History Information Program • Williamstown, MA 01267

Lewis Gregory J. • Student • Queens College Grad Sch of Lib & Inf Studies • Flushing, NY 11367 • ALCTS LITA

Lewis Gwen • Library Media Specialist • West Junior High School • Tiffin, OH 44883 • AASL

Lewis Heidi • School Library Media Specialist • Guinyard-Butler Middle School • Barnwell, SC 29812 • AASL

Lewis Helen • Reference Librarian • University of Connecticut Homer Babbidge Library • Storrs, CT 06269-1005 • LITA SRRT

Lewis Helena H. • Documents Librarian • Tuskegee University • Tuskegee Institute, AL 36088 • GODORT

Lewis Jacqueline S. • Library Supervisor • Virginia Beach Public Library Great Neck Area Library • Virginia Beach, VA 23454

Lewis Janet M. • Newnan-Coweta Public Library • Newnan, GA 30263 • ALSC YALSA

Lewis Janice B. • Sullivan High School • Chicago, IL 60626 • AASL

Lewis Jannith • Librarian • Oakwood College Eva B. Dykes Library • Huntsville, AL 35896 • ACRL

Lewis Joan W. • Library Media Specialist • Fairfax County Public Schools Area II Office • Alexandria, VA 22312 • AASL

Lewis Joe N. • Readers Advisor • District of Columbia Public Library Martin Luther King Memorial Library • Washington, DC 20001

Lewis Joseph R. • Bronx, NY 10466

Lewis Joy L. • Librarian • Wakulla Middle School • Crawfordville, FL 32327 • AASL YALSA IFRT VRT

Lewis Judith B. • Director of Library Services • Moses Brown School Walter Jones Library • Providence, RI 02906 • AASL

Lewis Julia A. • Special Service Librarian • Millsaps College Millsaps-Wilson Library • Jackson, MS 39210 • ACRL

Lewis Julia C. • Morehead, KY 40351 • LITA

Lewis Junko Yokota • University of Northern Iowa Purchasing Off • Cedar Falls, IA 50614 • ALSC

Lewis Karen J. • Young Adult Librarian • Mililani Public Library • Mililani, HI 96789

Lewis Kathleen M. • Student • University of Maryland College of Library and Information Services • College Park, MD 20742-4345

Lewis Kathryn Roots • Student • West Mid High School • Norman, OK 73069

Lewis Lenore • Salt Lake City Public Library • Salt Lake City, UT 84111 • ALCTS PLA YALSA IFRT

Lewis Linda K. • Collection Development Officer • University of New Mexico General Library • Albuquerque, NM 87131 • ACRL ALCTS LAMA RASD

Lewis Marcia • Co-Director • Springfield Library/Museums Association • Springfield, MA 01103

Lewis Marcia M. • Assistant Librarian • Loveland Public Library • Loveland, CO 80537 • PLA

Lewis Margaret A. • Documents Librarian • Miami University Edgar W. King Library • Oxford, OH 45056 • GODORT

Lewis Margaret E. • Hyde Park, MA 02136 • ALSC
Continuing

Lewis Marguerite D. • Bethlehem Public Library • Delmar, NY 12054 • ALSC

Lewis Marilyn • Alachua County Library District • Gainesville, FL 32601 • ALCTS LAMA LITA PLA

Lewis Marjorie • Librarian • Scarsdale Heathcote School • Scarsdale, NY 10583 • YALSA IFRT

Lewis Mark E. • Student • University of Arizona Graduate Library School • Tucson, AZ 85721 • PLA

Lewis Mary Ellen • Lewisville, MN 56060 • AASL YALSA
Life

Lewis Mary L. • Librarian • Robin Hill School • Norman, OK 73071 • AASL

Lewis Nancy L. • San Mateo County Library • San Mateo, CA 94402 • LAMA PLA

Lewis Norma J. • Project Manager • University of Toronto John Robarts Library • Toronto ON, M5S 1A5 Canada • LAMA LITA

Lewis Patricia J. • Childrens Librarian • Sonoma County Library • Santa Rosa, CA 95404 • ALSC

Lewis Patricia M. • Mary Cook Public Library • Waynesville, OH 45068

Lewis Paul H. • Gov't. Documents Librarian • University of South Carolina at Aiken Gregg-Graniteville Library • Aiken, SC 29801 • GODORT

Lewis Paula Miriam • Reference Librarian • Montgomery County Public Library Wheaton Regional Branch • Wheaton, MD 20902-1997 • YALSA

Lewis Phyllis N. • Administrative Librarian • Los Angeles Public Library Canoga Park Branch • Canoga Park, CA 91303

Lewis Priscilla A. • Circulation Manager • Durham County Library • Durham, NC 27702

Lewis Riva • Thornton, CO 80241 • ASCLA PLA

Lewis Robert M. • Media Specialist • Yokota West Elementary School • APO San Francisco, CA 96328 • LITA

Lewis Roberta W. • Library/Media Specialist • Mitchell & Shaplegh Libraries • Kittery Point, ME 03905

Lewis Robin D. • Marking Research & Planning • American Compensation Association • Scottsdale, AZ 85260

Lewis Rodger C. • Gainesville, FL 32607

Lewis Rosalyn • Librarian • United Methodist Publishing House L • Nashville, TN 37202 • LAMA

Lewis Ruth E. • Biology Librarian • Washington University Libraries • Saint Louis, MO 63130-4899 • ACRL

Lewis Sherril • Reference Coordinator • River Bluffs Regional Library • Saint Joseph, MO 64501 • RASD

Lewis Shirley A. • Consultant • Washington State Library • Olympia, WA 98504-2470 • RASD SRRT

Lewis Sonia • Assistant Director • Burlington Public Library • Burlington ON, L7R 1J4 Canada

Lewis Susan F. • Miami, FL 33157 • AASL

Lewis Susan W. • User Services Librarian • Missouri Library Network Corp. • Saint Louis, MO 63141

Lewis Tara T. • Circulation Librarian • Hardin County Public Library • Elizabethtown, KY 42701 • IFRT

Lewis Terri L. • Technical Services Center • Jefferson County Public Library Library Service Center • Wheat Ridge, CO 80033

Lewis Thomas F. • President • Informed Libraries • Uxbridge, MA 01569 • ACRL

Lewis Valerie V. • Bookstore Owner • Hicklebee's • San Jose, CA 95125 • ALSC

Lewis Willie Mae • Julia C. Frazier Elementary School • Dallas, TX 75224

Lewis Yale O. Jr. • Trustee • Seattle Public Library • Seattle, WA 98104-1193 • ALTA PLA

Lewitzky Beth L. • Student • State University of New York (SUNY) School of Information & Library Studies • Buffalo, NY 14260 • PLA IFRT

Lewkovich Pamela • Trustee • Glenview Public Library • Glenview, IL 60025

Lewontin Amy • Reference Librarian • Bentley College Solomon R. Baker Library • Waltham, MA 02154-4705 • ACRL

Ley Elaine C. • Media Specialist • Carmel High School • Carmel, IN 46032 • AASL YALSA

Ley Pamela S. • Branch Manager • Columbus Metropolitan Library Whetstone Branch Library • Columbus, OH 43214 • PLA

Leyden Susan L. • Holmes Middle School Library • Alexandria, VA 22312 • AASL

Leydon William • Sales Representative • New England Mobile Book Fair • Newton Highlands, MA 02161 • PLA

Leyko Andrea K. • Training Specialist • Pittsburgh Regional Library Center • Pittsburgh, PA 15221 • CLENE

Leysen Joan M. • Librarian • Iowa State University Library • Ames, IA 50011-2140 • ACRL ALCTS

Leyva Florence R. • Monterey Park, CA 91754 • AASL

Lezotte Alice K. • Dearborn, MI 48128 • AASL

Lhotka Dan • AV Librarian • State Library of Florida Division of Library & Information Services • Tallahassee, FL 32399-0250

Li Alec • Mont Dora, FL 32757

Li Dai • Chesapeake Public Library Russell Memorial Branch • Chesapeake, VA 23321 • SRRT

Li Grace Y. • Assistant Director Support Serv. • Waukegan Public Library • Waukegan, IL 60085 • ALCTS

Li Haipeng • Student • University of Arizona Graduate Library School • Tucson, AZ 85721

Li Hong-Chan • Librarian • Child and Family Services, Inc. • Hartford, CT 06105

Li Jian Ping D. • San Diego, CA 92104

Li Lai Lee • Student • Clarion University of Pennsylvania College of Library Science • Clarion, PA 16214

Li Li-Li L. • Student • University of Southern Mississippi • Hattiesburg, MS 39406-5053

Li Lisa Q. • Student • State University of New York (SUNY) at Buffalo • Buffalo, NY 14260

Li Marjorie H. • CJK Liason-RLIN • Rutgers University Libraries Technical & Automated Services • Piscataway, NJ 08855 • LAMA IRRT

Li Ming • Eastern Asian Cataloging Ln. • Purdue University Libraries • West Lafayette, IN 47907-1530

Li Nan • Student • University of Pittsburgh School of Library and Information Science • Pittsburgh, PA 15260 • LITA

Li Pei-Tzu • Milwaukee, WI 53211 • LITA

Li Qiutong • GOAL/QPC • Methuen, MA 01844

Li Tze-Chung • Professor • Rosary College Graduate School of Library & Information Science • River Forest, IL 60305 • ACRL RASD IRRT

Li Xia • Library Instructor • University of Vermont Bailey Howe Library • Burlington, VT 05405-0036 • RASD

LiCausi Dom • Library Media Specialist • Gatelot School Library • Lake Ronkonkoma, NY 11779

Liacouras Sandra P. • Swarthmore, PA 19081 • AASL YALSA

Lian Xiao-Bu • Systems Librarian • Saint John Fisher College • Rochester, NY 14618

Liang Marie • Assistant Library Director • Paducah Public Library • Paducah, KY 42001 • ALCTS LITA

Liang Rachel L. • Head, Humanities/Social Science • University of Hawaii Thomas Hale Hamilton Library • Honolulu, HI 96822

Liang Sailan • Wayne State University • Detroit, MI 48202

Liangu Anna U. • Head Librarian • University of Toronto • Toronto ON, Canada • ACRL

Liaw Barbara C. • Huntsville, AL 35803 • PLA

Libberton Gayle B. • Charlotte, NC 28270-2558 • ALSC

Libbey George H. • Assistant Director, Admin Serv • University of Georgia Libraries • Athens, GA 30602 • ACRL ALCTS LAMA LRRT

Libbey Maurice C. • Head, Aquisitions/Library Serv • Eastern Illinois University Booth Library • Charleston, IL 61920-3099

Libby Edith M. • Holyoke, MA 01040 • Continuing

Libby Jean • Library Researcher • University of California San Francisco Library • San Francisco, CA 94143-0840

Liberace Robert • Trustee • Finkelstein Memorial Library • Spring Valley, NY 10977

Liberman Kristen • Lotus Development Corporation Information Resources Group • Cambridge, MA 02142

Libretto Ellen V. • Young Adult Consultant • Queens Borough Public Library • Jamaica, NY 11432 • PLA YALSA

Libutti Patricia E. • Education Subject Specialist • Fordham University Library at Lincoln Center • New York, NY 10023-7480 • ACRL LITA LIRT

Licalzi Jacqueline M. • Student • University of Michigan School of Information and Library Studies • Ann Arbor, MI 48109-1092 • LITA

Lichenstein Phyllis • Oregon State Library • Salem, OR 97310-0640 • ALTA

Lichtenberg Elsa R. • Director • Swarthmore Public Library • Swarthmore, PA 19081 • PLA

Lichtenberger Lynn • Western Library Network • Western Library Network (WLN) • Lacey, WA 98503 • ALCTS

Lichtenfels Dave • Saint Petersburg Junior College Clearwater Campus Library • Clearwater, FL 34625

Lichtenstein Arthur A. • University of Central Arkansas Torreyson Library • Conway, AR 72032 • ACRL

Lichtenwalter W. A. • Leavenworth Public Library • Leavenworth, KS 66048 • PLA

Lichter Patricia C. • Supervising Librarian • Alameda County Library Centerville Branch • Fremont, CA 94536 • PLA NMRT

Lichtman Catherine S. • Student • Oakland University • Rochester, MI 48309-4401 • ACRL RASD

Lichtman Jacqueline • Law Librarian • University of Virginia • Charlottesville, VA 22901 • AASL

Lichtman Jules Mrs • West Orange, NJ 07052 • AASL

Lichtman Marie D. • Birmingham, AL 35213 • ACRL LRRT NMRT

Lickteig Jo A. • North Texas State University Willis Library • Denton, TX 76203

Licona Ruby A • Asst. Professor Lib Sci • Weber State University Stewart Library • Ogden, UT 84408-2901 • ACRL

Lidawer Ruth Carter • Reference Ln, Head Audio-Visual • Euclid Public Library • Euclid, OH 44123-2091

Liddell Margaret A. • William R. De Avila Elementary School • San Francisco, CA 94117 • AASL

Liddle Glenda T. • Media Specialist • B.B. Harris Elementary School • Duluth, GA 30136

Liddon Gabrielle G. • International Media Coordinator • Huntsville-Madison County Public Library • Huntsville, AL 35804

Liddy Martin J. • Student • University of Wisconsin-Milwaukee School of Library & Information Science • Milwaukee, WI 53201

Lidman Ruthanne • Waldport, OR 97394

Lidz Richard • Publisher • Visual Education Corporation • Princeton, NJ 08543

Lieb Lucy J. • Student • Drexel University College of Information Studies • Philadelphia, PA 19104-2875 • ALCTS

Liebaers Herman Dr. • President • European Foundation for Library Cooperation • B-1040 Brussels, Belgium • AASL ACRL ALCTS ALSC ALTA ASCLA LAMA LITA PLA RASD YALSA *Honorary*

Liebenberg Irene • Regional Manager • Riverside City & County Public Library • Riverside, CA 92502-0468 • LAMA PLA

Lieber-Mackay Gerry • Dean • College of the Redwoods • Eureka, CA 95501

Lieberenz Pamela J. • Librarian I Readers Advisor • Erie County Library System • Erie, PA 16501

Lieberman Barbara S. • Senior Librarian • Morris County Free Library • Whippany, NJ 07981 • RASD NMRT

Lieberman Irving • Bellevue, WA 98004 • Continuing

Lieberman Janice A. • Santa Clara, CA 95051 • ALSC

Lieberman Murray S. • Delray Beach, FL 33445 • Continuing

Lieberman Ronald • Glen Rock, PA 17327

Liebeskind Eileen G. • Information Specialist • Moore Business Forms • Lake Forest, IL 60045 • LITA

Liebhaber Arthur L. • Branch Librarian • Miami-Dade Public Library System Miami Lakes Branch • Miami Lakes, FL 33014

Liebman Anne Beth • Technical Services Librarian • Central North Carolina Regional Library • Burlington, NC 27215

Liebman Gayl A. • Evanston, IL 60203

Liebson Donald C. • President • Oil Pipeline Research Institute • Redondo Beach, CA 90277

Liebst C. Anne • Govt Doc/Periodicals Librarian • Baker University Library • Baldwin, KS 66006 • GODORT NMRT

Liebtag Daniel • Coor. Technical Services • Fairfield County District Library • Lancaster, OH 43130

Liedtka Jeanne • Trustee • Franklin Park Public Library District • Franklin Park, IL 60131

Liefeld Walter L. • Audiovisual Director • Saint Andrews School Irene Dupont Library • Middletown, DE 19709 • AASL

Lieffers Roxanne F. • Librarian II • Atlanta-Fulton Public Library • Atlanta, GA 30303 • PLA

Lieffort Nancy • Librarian • Patient Library • Newtown, CT 06470

Liegl Beryl R. • Emporia, KS 66801

Liegl Dorothy M. • Deputy State Librarian • South Dakota State Library • Pierre, SD 57501-2294 • ASCLA PLA IFRT VRT

Lien Lester G. • Reference Librarian • County of Los Angeles Public Library Clifton M. Brakensiek Library 505 • Bellflower, CA 90706 • LAMA PLA *Life*

Lienemann Joan E. • Student • San Jose State University Division of Library & Information Science • San Jose, CA 95192-0029

Liening Patricia A. • Director • Tipp City Public Library • Tipp City, OH 45371 • PLA

Liesenbein Barbara • Student • State University of New York (SUNY) University Libraries • Albany, NY 12222 • SRRT

Liesener James W. • Professor • University of Maryland College of Library and Information Services • College Park, MD 20742-4345 • AASL YALSA

Liesse Melanie J. • Whiting, IN 46394 • AASL

Liestman Daniel D. • Bibl Spec for the Soc Sciences • Seattle Pacific University Weter Memorial Library • Seattle, WA 98119

Liette Mary Ann • Coordinator • Riverside County Office of Education • Riverside, CA 92502 • AASL

Lietz Kirsten D. • Reference Librarian • Library of Michigan • Lansing, MI 48909 • GODORT

Lietzan Caitlin S. • Chapel Hill, NC 27514

Life Elaine • Director of Media & Technology • Warren Central High School • Indianapolis, IN 46229 • AASL

Liff Judy • Trustee • Public Library of Nashville and Davidson County • Nashville, TN 37203-3585

Lifshin Arthur • Bangor, ME 04401 • ACRL

Lifson Delores Sue • Reference Librarian • Cornell College Library Russell D. Cole Library • Mount Vernon, IA 52314 • ACRL

Liggett Jane Ann • Librarian • Lawrence High School • Lawrence, KS 66046 • YALSA

Liggett Joanna • Tri-County Joint Vocational School • Nelsonville, OH 45764 • AASL

Liggett Suzanne L. • Coor of Nat'l Coop Catlg Projs. • Library of Congress • Washington, DC 20541 • ALCTS GODORT *Life*

Liggin Nancy J. • Readers Services Librarian • Park Ridge Public Library • Park Ridge, IL 60068-4188 • PLA

Lighfoot Ed • University of Washington Information Systems • Seattle, WA 98105 • LITA

Light Barbara • Branch Librarian • Fresno County Free Library Sanger Branch • Sanger, CA 93657

Light Jane • Library Director • Redwood City Public Library • Redwood City, CA 94063-1868 • ALSC LAMA PLA RASD

Light Karen • Head, Technical Services • Westerly Public Library • Westerly, RI 02891

Light Lin • Head, Technical Services • Herrick Public Library • Holland, MI 49423 • ALCTS LAMA

Light Marvin J. • Head Librarian • University of South Carolina Salkehatchie Campus Library • Allendale, SC 29810 • ACRL

Lightbody Melanie W. • King County Library System Kent Branch • Kent, WA 98031 • PLA YALSA GODORT

Lighthall Lynne J. • Instructor II • University of British Columbia Library • Vancouver BC, V6T 1Z1 Canada

Lightman Benjamin • Chief Librarian • Time Warner Inc • New York, NY 10020 • IFRT SRRT

Lightner Karen J. • Free Library of Philadelphia • Philadelphia, PA 19103-1189 • ACRL

Lightner Richard T. • Student • University of Hawaii School of Library & Information Studies • Honolulu, HI 96822 • IFRT

Lightsey Virginia Ann • Trustee • Pine Bluff & Jefferson County Library System • Pine Bluff, AR 71601 • ALSC PLA

Lignell Ellen W. • Albuquerque, NM 87196

Ligon Julie Ann • College Librarian • Western Oklahoma State College W.C. Burris LRC • Altus, OK 73521

Ligon Linda • Librarian • Traverse City Senior High School • Traverse City, MI 49685 • AASL

Likness Craig S. • Humanities Reference Librarian • Trinity University • San Antonio, TX 78212 • ACRL ALCTS

Liles Martha A. • Librarian • ESCA Genetics Corporation Technical Library • San Carlos, CA 94070 • ACRL

Lilienthal Mary E. • Readers Services Librarian • Suffolk Community College Selden Campus Library • Selden, NY 11784-2899

Lilja Linnea D. • Associate Professor • University of Missouri-Columbia College of Education • Columbia, MO 65211 • ALSC

Lillard Martha • Centralized Library Tech Serv • Jefferson County Public School • Louisville, KY 40209 • AASL

Lilleston Ruth Elizabeth • School Librarian • Clinton Middle School • Clinton, MO 64735 • AASL IFRT

Lilley Barbara A. • Columbia University Libraries Butler Library • New York, NY 10027 • ALCTS

Lillibridge Janet R. • Library Media Specialist • Greenwich Central School • Greenwich, NY 12834 • AASL

Lillie Elizabeth L. • Children's Librarian • Free Pub Lib Of Monroe • Williamstown, NJ 08094

Lillie Milton G. III • Librarian • Kenwood Academy • Chicago, IL 60615 • AASL

Lillig Margaret L. • Student • Rosary College Graduate School of Library & Information Science • River Forest, IL 60305

Lillis John G. • University of Nebraska at Kearney Library • Kearney, NE 68849

Lilly Anne Marie • Librarian • Newhall Junior High School Library • Wyoming, MI 49509

Lilly Brian J. • Houston Public Library • Houston, TX 77002 • RASD

Lilly Catherine C. • Technical Services Librarian • Burke County Public Library • Morganton, NC 28655 • ALCTS

Lilly Donna Jean • Children's Department • Rosenberg Library Adult Services • Galveston, TX 77550 • ALSC YALSA

Lilly Dorothy L. • Librarian • Grosse Pointe North High School • Grosse Pointe Woods, MI 48236 • AASL

Lilly Erica B. • Science Librarian • Miami University Brill Science Library • Oxford, OH 45056 • ACRL LITA

Lilly George D. • Reference Librarian • Huntsville-Madison County Public Library • Huntsville, AL 35804 • RASD

Lilly Jane L. • Branch Manager • Pioneer Library System Moore Public Library Branch • Moore, OK 73160 • PLA

Lilly Joyce S. • Director • Bienville Parish Library • Arcadia, LA 71001

Lilly May Miss • Philadelphia, PA 19151 • ALSC PLA *Continuing*

Lilly Paige • Penobscot Marine Museum Stephen Phillips Memorial Library • Searsport, ME 04974

Lilly Patricia • Librarian • Holub Middle School • Houston, TX 77099

Lim C. H. • Librarian • Universiti Sains Malaysia Library • 11800 Penang, Malaysia • AASL ACRL ALCTS LITA RASD

Lim Chen Cheng • Singapore 2365, Singapore

Lim Coralie Wolf • Northland Pioneer College • Holbrook, AZ 86025 • LAMA PLA LIRT

Lim Lois Y. • School Librarian • Kipapa Elementary School • Mililani, HI 96789 • AASL

Lim Poh Kim • Student • University of California Los Angeles Graduate School of Library & Information Science • Los Angeles, CA 90024

Lim Sue C. • California State Polytech University • Pomona, CA 91768 • ACRL

Lima Carolyn W. • Chief Librarian • San Diego Public Library Pacific Beach Branch • San Diego, CA 92109 • ALSC LITA IFRT

Lima Gercina Angela Borem • Student • Clark-Atlanta University School of Library & Information Studies • Atlanta, GA 30314-4391

Lima Jeffrey S. • Parker, TX 75002 • PLA NMRT SRRT

Lima John A. • San Diego, CA 92111 • LITA IFRT

Lima Sharon L. • W. Columbia, TX 77486 • ALSC EMIERT LIRT

Limanni Theresa A. • Head Technical Services • Russell Library • Middletown, CT 06457

Limbach Linda • Moreland Hills Elementary Library • Pepper Pike, OH 44124 • ALSC

Limon Judith S. • Reference Librarian • Bartlett Public Library District • Bartlett, IL 60103 • RASD

Limper Hilda K. • Louisville, KY 40218 • Continuing

Limpert Lynda W. • Media Specialist • Elizabethtown Area High School • Elizabeth, PA 17022 • AASL

Lin Bin • Student • University of South Carolina College of Library & Information Science • Columbia, SC 29208 • ACRL

Lin James J. • Belleville, IL 62221

Lin Joseph C. • Science Cataloger • Indiana University at Bloomington University Libraries • Bloomington, IN 47405-9998 • ACRL ALCTS LITA MAGERT

Lin Katy C. • Periodicals/Documents Librarian • Capital University Library • Columbus, OH 43209 • ACRL

Lin Linda L. • Schaumburg, IL 60195-3619 • ALCTS LITA

Lin Mei-Yun Annie • Librarian • University of Wisconsin-Madison Memorial Library • Madison, WI 53706

Lin Na • New Brunswick, NJ 08901

Lin Nancy • Prod. Develp. Mgr., • Muze, Inc. • Brooklyn, NY 11211

Lin Poping • Reference/Instruction Librarian • Purdue University Libraries • West Lafayette, IN 47907 • ACRL LITA

Lin Selina S. • Serials Librarian • University of Iowa Libraries • Iowa City, IA 52242-1379 • ACRL

Lin Shao-Chen • Cataloger • Palatine Public Library • Palatine, IL 60067

Lin Shiou-Chii Rosa • Data Base Administrator • Houston Area Library Automated Network • Houston, TX 77002 • LITA PLA

Lin Steven • Garland, TX 75040 • PLA IFRT LRRT SRRT

Lin Yi-Ju S. • Taipei Municipal Library • Taipei, Taiwan

Lin Yin • Student • University of Alabama School of Library and Information Studies • Tuscaloosa, AL 35487 • LITA

Lin Zhi • Student • Wayne State University • Detroit, MI 48202

Linbeck Sharon E. • System Analyst III • Houston Public Library • Houston, TX 77002 • LITA

Linberger Peter • University of Akron University Library & Learning Resource • Akron, OH 44325-1707

Linck Rita C. • Library Media Specialist • Parkway South Senior High School • Manchester, MO 63021 • AASL

Lincoln Chris • Northrop Corporation • Los Angeles, CA 90067 • LAMA LITA

Lincoln Joanne • Librarian • Atlanta Public Schools Professional Library • Atlanta, GA 30315 • AASL

Lincoln John R. • Reference Librarian • Lakeland Community College Library • Mentor, OH 44060-7594 • ACRL LITA RASD LIRT

Lincoln Lynda K. • School Library Teacher • Jedediah Smith Academy of Literary Arts Through Technology • Sacramento, CA 95818 • AASL

Lincoln Sharon A. • Arlington, VA 22201 • ACRL LAMA

Lincoln Timothy D. • Student • Maryknoll School Theology Library • Maryknoll, NY 10545-0305 • ACRL

Lincove David A. • Coordinator, Online Reference • Ohio State University Libraries • Columbus, OH 43210-1286 • RASD LHRT

Lind Anda S. • Adult Services Librarian • Prince William Public Library System Central Branch • Manassas, VA 22111

Lind Beverly F. • Librarian • Waterloo Public Library • Waterloo, IA 50701 • ALTA LAMA PLA

Lind Harold J. Jr. • Alexandria, VA 22307

Lind Judith Yankielun • Roseland Free Public Library • Roseland, NJ 07068

Lindahl Susan E. • Student • University of Tennessee-Knoxville Graduate School of Library & Information Science • Knoxville, TN 37996-4330

Lindauer Dinah E. • Merrick, NY 11566

Lindberg Carolyn H. • Student • University of Pittsburgh School of Library and Information Science • Pittsburgh, PA 15260

Lindberg Sandra • Head of Technical Services • Xavier University McDonald Memorial Library • Cincinnati, OH 45207 • ACRL ALCTS LITA

Lindberg Susan J. • Seabrook, TX 77586

Lindemann Richard H.F. • Special Collections Librarian • University of California-San Diego • La Jolla, CA 92093-0175 • ACRL

Linden Jack • Director • Orangeburg Library • Orangeburg, NY 10962

Linden Nancy • Shell Oil Library • Houston, TX 77210-4302

Linden Sally B. • Research Librarian • Wellesley College Library Margaret Clapp Library • Wellesley, MA 02181-8275 • ACRL RASD

Lindenbaum Ellen T. • Baldwin, MD 21013

Lindenfeld Ellen L. • Reference Librarian • Broward County Division of Libraries West Regional Branch • Plantation, FL 33324

Lindenfeld Joseph F. • Reference Librarian • Memphis-Shelby County Public Library and Information Center • Memphis, TN 38104-4025 • ACRL LITA PLA RASD LIRT

Lindenmuth Janet S. • Widener University School of Law Library • Wilmington, DE 19803-0475 • ALCTS

Linder George R. • Ponte Vedra Beach, FL 32082 • Continuing

Linder Sarah C. • Chief Adult Services • Richland County Public Library • Columbia, SC 29201 • PLA RASD

Linderman Mary Ellen • Naubuc School Library • Glastonbury, CT 06033 • AASL EMIERT

Linderman Winifred • Professor Emeritus • Columbia University Library Service Library • New York, NY 10027 • ACRL RASD *Continuing*

Lindgren Beverly P. • Ln Dept Hd • Guilford High School • Rockford, IL 61111 • AASL IFRT SRRT

Lindgren Jon T. • University Librarian • Wilkes University • Wilkes-Barre, PA 18766 • ACRL LIRT

Lindgren Merri V. • Librarian • Cooperative Children's Book Center University of Wisconsin-Madison • Madison, WI 53706 • ALSC

Lindgren William D. • Director • Illinois Central College Learning Resources Center • East Peoria, IL 61635-0001 • ACRL ALCTS

Lindgren William F. • Fort Collins, CO 80526 • ACRL ALCTS *Life*

Lindheimer Sandra K. • Trustee • Sharon Public Library • Sharon, MA 02067

Lindlan Kristin L. • Head,Serials Cataloging Section • University of Washington Suzzallo Library • Seattle, WA 98195 • ALCTS LITA

Lindley-Meek Bettie Gail • Learning Resources Specialist • Fossil Hill Middle School • Ft. Worth, TX 76248 • AASL

Lindley Angela • Collection Development Librarian • Bowling Green State University William Jerome Library • Bowling Green, OH 43403-0175 • ALCTS

Lindley Ardis Dee • Librarian • Lower Elementary School • Vidalia, LA 71373 • AASL

Lindley Patricia J. • Director • Herrick Memorial Library Wellington Public Library • Wellington, OH 44090 • PLA

Lindner Anne H. • Elementary School Librarian • West Irondequoit School District • West Irondequoit, NY 14617 • AASL ALSC

Lindner Charles C. • Director • Immaculate Conception Center Library • Douglaston, NY 11362 • LITA

Lindquist Christopher • Reference Librarian • Windsor Public Library • Windsor, CT 06095

Lindquist Janice • University of Missouri-Kansas City Library • Kansas City, MO 64110-2499 • ACRL

Lindquist Karen E. • Director • Lenawee County Library • Adrian, MI 49221 • PLA RASD

Lindsay Jane A. • Media Specialist • Gompers Elementary LMC • Madison, WI 53704 • AASL

Lindsay Jean S. • Wayne, PA 19087-1537 • ACRL

Lindsay Linda J. • Librarian • Seabury Hall • Makawao, HI 96768 • AASL YALSA

Lindsay Miriam R. • Partner • Lindsay & Howes Booksellers • Surrey GU8 5TU, England

Lindsay Opal B. • Asst Div Chief of Soc Sci/Phil • Brooklyn Public Library • Brooklyn, NY 11238

Lindsey Harriet W. • Hall Fletcher Middle School • Asheville, NC 28806 • AASL

Lindsey Jonathan A. • Dir. Corp. & Fdn Development • Baylor University Library • Waco, TX 76798-7026 • ACRL

Lindsey Lowell L. • Director • Nicholson Memorial Library • Garland, TX 75040-6365 • ALTA LAMA LITA PLA YALSA

Lindsey Nancy L. • Jefferson City, TN 37760 • AASL

Lindsey Sally A. • Assistant Librarian • El Paso Cnty Library • Fabens, TX 79838

Lindsey Susan B. • Swarthmore, PA 19081

Lindsey Thomas K. • Pub. Svc. Libn./Bibliographer • University of Texas at Arlington • Arlington, TX 76019-0497

Lindsey Trudy • Branch Head • Champaign Public Library Douglass Branch • Champaign, IL 61820

Lindsley Alice L. Miss • Sheridan, WY 82801 • Continuing

Lindsley Elizabeth M. • Librarian • Santa Monica Public Library • Santa Monica, CA 90401 • RASD

Lindstrom Daryl M. • Middletown, MD 21769 • AASL

Lindstrom Elaine C. • Branch Manager • Dayton & Montgomery County Public Library Brookville Branch Library • Brookville, OH 45309 • RASD

Lindstrom Kevin • Edmonton AB, T6T 1H1 Canada • ACRL LITA

Lindvall Robert J. • Rockford, IL 61103

Line Faith A. • Director • Sumter County Library • Sumter, SC 29150 • PLA

Line Joanne • University of Minnesota-Duluth Library • Duluth, MN 55812-2495 • LAMA

Line Maurice B. • N. Yorks, HG3 1NZ, United Kingdom • ACRL ALCTS LAMA

Linehan Eileen C. • Library Media Specialist • West Orange High School Library • West Orange, NJ 07052 • AASL

Liner Devon S. Ms. • Special Needs Library • Montgomery County Dept of Pub Lib Davis Community Library • Bethesda, MD 20817-1699 • ASCLA

Lines Adelia • Library Director • Richmond Public Library • Richmond, CA 94804 • PLA EMIERT

Lingelbach Clyde • Christ the King School Library • Kansas City, KS 66104 • AASL

Lingeman Carol L. • Sterling Heights Public Library • Sterling Heights, MI 48313 • ALSC LAMA PLA RASD

Linger Melody S. • Architect • Sverdrup Corporation • Jacksonville, FL 32247-5600 • LAMA PLA

Linger Neil B. • Reference Librarian • Broward Community College • Fort Lauderdale, FL 33314 • ACRL LAMA

Lingle Ronald M. • Librarian • Mann Middle School • San Diego, CA 92115

Link Claudia Gilcreast • East Brunswick Public Library • E. Brunswick, NJ 08816

Link Elizabeth M. • Director • Riverside Regional Library • Jackson, MO 63755 • PLA

Link Mary B. • Branch Manager • Milwaukee Public Library Center Street Branch • Milwaukee, WI 53210 • PLA

Link Terry P. Mr • Reference Librarian • Michigan State University Libraries • East Lansing, MI 48824-1048 • ACRL SRRT

Linke Erika C. • Hd. Collections and Access • Carnegie Mellon University Libraries • Pittsburgh, PA 15213 • ACRL ALCTS LAMA LITA RASD

Linkhart Edward G. • Lewiston, ID 83501 • Continuing

Linkins Germaine C. • Director of Libraries • State Univ of NY Coll at Potsdam Frederick W. Crumb Memorial Library • Potsdam, NY 13676 • ACRL LAMA

Linn Carol • Staff Analyst/Lib Info Systems • Brooklyn Public Library • Brooklyn, NY 11238

Linn Mary • Branch Librarian • Boston Public Library East Boston Branch • Boston, MA 02128 • PLA

Linn Mary Jane H. • Head of Catalog Department • Smithsonian Institution Libraries • Washington, DC 20560

Linn Sheila D. • School Librarian • Hunter Lake Elementary School • Reno, NV 89509

Linnavuori Julie • Director • Park Ridge Public Library • Park Ridge, NJ 07656

Linnemeyer Mary A. • Director • Springfield-Greene County Library • Springfield, MO 65801 • PLA

Linnenbruegge Gertrude R. • Lacy, WA 98503-9990 • ALSC *Continuing*

Linner Rachelle • Student • Simmons College Graduate School of Library & Information Science • Boston, MA 02115

Linos Barbara • Trustee • Hammond Public Library • Hammond, IN 46320 • ALTA

Linse Mary M. • Supervisor of Support Services • Olathe Public Library • Olathe, KS 66061 • PLA

Linsky Leonore K. • Data Base Manager • Minuteman Library Network • Framingham, MA 01701 • LITA

Linsley Laurie S. • Head, Cataloging Dept. • Seminole Community College Library • Sanford, FL 32773 • ACRL

Lintner Barbara • Director of Childrens Services • Urbana Free Library • Urbana, IL 61801-3283 • ALSC

Linton Helen • Librarian • Austen Riggs Center, Inc. Austen Fox Riggs Library • Stockbridge, MA 01262 • ASCLA

Linton Linda • Adult Services Coordinator • Town of Pickering Public Library • Pickering ON, L1V 2R6 Canada

Linton Linda A. • Children's Librarian • Montgomery County Department of Public Libraries Long Branch Community • Silver Springs, MD 20901-3898

Linton Teresa D. • Information Services Librarian • United States Nuclear Regulatory Commission • Washington, DC 20555 • FLRT GODORT

Lintz Rebecca R. • Asst. Dir. of Clln Services • Colorado Historical Society • Denver, CO 80203

Linville Herbert • Santa Barbara, CA 93103 • ACRL *Continuing*

Linville J. Harmon • Trustee • Forsyth County Public Library • Winston-Salem, NC 27101 • ALTA

Linz Christina S. • Student • Florida State University School of Library and Information Studies • Tallahassee, FL 32306-2048

Liou Bao-Jiun A. • Fort Lee, NJ 07024

Liou Fen-yin • Research Worker • Taipei Municipal Library • Taipei, Taiwan • ALSC

Lipetz Ben-Ami Dr. • Professor • State University of New York at Albany School of Information Science & Policy • Albany, NY 12222 • ACRL ALCTS LITA LRRT *Life*

Lipinski Barry V. • Acting Head, Circulation • Rutgers University Libraries Archibald Stevens Alexander Library • New Brunswick, NJ 08903 • LRRT NMRT

Lipkis Rita M. • Los Angeles, CA 90036 • ALSC

Lipman Lucile M. • Altadena, CA 91001

Lipnik Ruth A. • Reference Librarian • Roanoke County Public Library • Roanoke, VA 24018 • RASD

Lipoma Debbie • Librarian • Watsonville Public Library • Watsonville, CA 95076-4695

Lipow Anne Grodzins • Berkeley, CA 94705 • ACRL LAMA LITA RASD

Lipow Stephanie S. • Student • University of California-Berkeley School of Library & Information Studies • Berkeley, CA 94720 • LITA

Lippencott Suzanne H. • Children's Librarian • Naperville Public Libraries Nichols Library • Naperville, IL 60540-5351 • ALSC

Lipper Lucretia A. • Youth Services Librarian • East Brunswick Public Library • E. Brunswick, NJ 08816 • YALSA

Lippert Flora R. • Reference Librarian • Portland Community College Library • Portland, OR 97219

Lippert Harriet A. • Librarian • Brittany Woods Middle School • University City, MO 63130 • AASL

Lippert Margret G. • Head Chemistry-Biology Library • University of Cincinnati Chemistry-Biology Library • Cincinnati, OH 45221-0151 • ACRL LITA

Lippert Theresa J. • Sr. Editor Legal Publications • West Publishing Company • Eagan, MN 55123

Lippincott J. W. Jr. • Nokomis, FL 34275 • ALTA

Lippincott Joan K. • Coalition for Networked Information • Washington, DC 20036 • ACRL LITA

Lippincott Teresa H. • Librarian • Blessed Sacrament School • Fort Mitchell, KY 41017 • AASL

Lipschultz Rose S. Miss • Chicago, IL 60657 • PLA RASD *Continuing*

Lipscomb-Davis Pamela • Library Media Specialist • Richardson Elementary School • Washington, DC 20011 • AASL

Lipscomb Jean M. • Board Member • Lake Lanier Regional Library System Forsyth County Branch • Cumming, GA 30130

Lipscomb Robert M. • Director • Central Florida Regional Library • Ocala, FL 32671

Lipshie Mary J. • Mesa, AZ 85202

Lipsitz Vivienne L. • Asst. Dir. Media Service • Port Washington Public Library • Port Washington, NY 11050 • IFRT VRT

Lipski Alison J. • Head of Reference • University of New Haven Marvin K Peterson Library • West Haven, CT 06516

Lipski Victor • New Haven, CT 06511

Lipsky Orah • Solomon Schecter Day School • West Orange, NJ 07052 • AASL

Liptak Catherine S. • Director • Virginia Public Library • Virginia, MN 55792 • LAMA PLA *Life*

Liptak Deborah A. • Fort Worth, TX 76137

Liptak Stephany • Library Assistant • University of Southern Colorado • Pueblo, CO 81001

Lira Judith A. • Media Specialist • Rocky Mountain High School • Fort Collins, CO 80526 • AASL

Liriano Maira I. • Reference Librarian • George Washington University Gelman Library • Washington, DC 20052 • ACRL RASD

Lisbon Peter W. • Chief Subject Cataloger • Harvard College Library Widener Memorial Library • Cambridge, MA 02138 • ACRL ALCTS LITA

Lloyd Rollin • State College, PA 16801 • ACRL LAMA *Life*

Llull-Kaczor Lynn M. • Albuquerque, NM 87112 • ACRL RASD AFLRT IFRT

Llull Harry P. • Director • University of New Mexico Centennial Science & Engineering Library • Albuquerque, NM 87131 • ACRL LAMA LITA

Lo Catherine P. • Koloa, HI 96756 • ACRL

Lo Chou Vivian Mei-Sheng • Head, Monographic Cataloging • Temple University Paley Library • Philadelphia, PA 19122 • ACRL ALCTS

Lo Gloria • Monterey Park, CA 91754

Lo Henrietta • Librarian • California State University-Chico Meriam Library • Chico, CA 92929-0295

Lo Henry • Coram, NY 11727

Lo Howard • Cataloger • Brigham Young University Hall Library • Provo, UT 84602

Lo Jing • Student • University of Wisconsin School of Library & Information Studies • Madison, WI 53706

Lo Karl K. • Hd, Intl Relations & Pacific • University of California-San Diego Library 0175A • La Jolla, CA 92093-0175 • IRRT

Lo Lisa Mrs. • Chief Executive Officer • Newmarket Public Library • Newmarket, ON, L3Y 1W1 Canada • PLA

Lo May • Childrens Librarian • Boston Public Library • Boston, MA 02117

Lo Mei-Ling • Student • Columbia University Library Service Library • New York, NY 10027

Lo Suzanne • Branch Librarian • Oakland Public Library Asian Branch • Oakland, CA 94607 • ALSC PLA

Lo Szu-chia S. • Student • Indiana University School of Library and Information Science • Bloomington, IN 47405 • LITA

LoDolce Nanette L. • Librarian • Dechert Price & Rhoads • New York, NY 10022

Loader M. Rebecca • Director • Columbia Heights Public Library • Columbia Heights, MN 55421-2996 • LAMA

Loafman Kathryn A. • Head Serials Cataloger • University of North Texas • Denton, TX 76203 • ALCTS LITA

Loaiza Bibiana • Chesterfield, MO 63017 • LITA

Loarridge Carol • Easley, SC 29640 • LITA

Lobaza Cynthia • Library Associate • Fox Lake District Library • Fox Lake, IL 60020

Lobdell Patsy A. • Head of Technical Services • El Paso Community College • El Paso, TX 79998

Lobeck Sandy • Yuma School District #1 • Yuma, AZ 85366 • AASL

Lober Robin L. • Catalog Librarian • San Bernardino County Library • San Bernardino, CA 92415 • ALCTS

Loberg Margery K. • Children's Librarian • Queens Anne's County Free Library Kent Island Branch • Stevenville, MD 21666 • ALSC

Lobianco Carol R. • Senior Principal/Regional Ln • New York Public Library Todt Hill-Westerleigh Branch • Staten Island, NY 10314 • PLA

Lobsenz Shelia M. • Student • Southern Connecticut State University Hilton C. Buley Library • New Haven, CT 06515

Lobyr Elena • Staff Librarian • Hemet Public Library • Hemet, CA 92543

Locascio Aline M. • Assistant Dean of Libraries • Polytechnic University • Brooklyn, NY 11201

Locascio John F. • Librarian • Freeport Public Library • Freeport, IL 61032 • LAMA PLA

Locatelli Janet A. • Cataloging Librarian • Michigan Technological University Library • Houghton, MI 49931 • ACRL ALCTS

Loch-Wouters Marge • Childrens Librarian • Menasha Public Library • Menasha, WI 54952 • ALSC IFRT SRRT

Lochard Josephine F. • St. Petersburg, FL 33710

Locher Sylvia L. • Student • Kent State University School of Library & Information Science • Kent, OH 44242-0001 • ALCTS RASD

Lochhead Sara L. • Manager, Learning Resources Cntr • East Kootenay Community College • Cranbrook BC, V1C 5L7 Canada • ACRL

Lochhead Shelley • Hopkinton High School Library • Contoocook, NH 03229 • AASL LITA

Locke Claire M. • Science Reference Librarian • North Carolina State University • Raleigh, NC 27695 • LITA

Locke Jill L. • University of North Carolina • Greensboro, NC 27412-5001 • ALSC PLA

Locke Jo Ellen • Reference & Bibliography Instr • Capital University Library • Columbus, OH 43209 • ACRL

Locke John W. • Head Librarian • Harold Washington College Library • Chicago, IL 60601-2449 • ACRL

Locke Lauren Lukasik • Arlington Heights, IL 60005

Locke Lynda L. • Head Librarian • King County Library System Shoreline Branch • Seattle, WA 98155

Locke Richard M. • Shelver II/Circulation Dept. • Evanston Public Library • Evanston, IL 60201

Locker Angie M. • Florence, AL 35630 • SRRT

Locker Frank J. • Silver Spring, MD 20902

Locker Pamela Scott • Branch Librarian • Evansville-Vanderburgh County Public Library • Evansville, IN 47708-1694 • PLA

Lockett Barbara A. • Director of Libraries • Rensselaer Polytechnic Institute • Troy, NY 12180 • ACRL LITA

Lockett E. M. Mrs • Toronto ONT, M4Y 2T6 Canada • AASL YALSA

Lockett Lenora C. • Library Director • Delgado Community College Moss Memorial Library • New Orleans, LA 70119 • ACRL

Lockett Mary • Reference Librarian • Kinderhook Regional Library • Lebanon, MO 65536 • PLA RASD

Lockett Sandra B. • Assistant City Librarian • Milwaukee Public Library • Milwaukee, WI 53233 • PLA

Lockhart Carol A. • Reference Librarian • Northeast Missouri State University • Kirksville, MO 63501

Lockhart Helen D. • Memphis, TN 38122 • Continuing

Lockhart Janet K. • Cary, NC 27513-2834

Lockhart Vickie • California State Library Foundation • Sacramento, CA 94237-0001

Lockhart William S. • Children Librarian • El Paso Public Library Clardy Fox Branch • El Paso, TX 79905 • ALSC PLA RASD YALSA IFRT LIRT SRRT

Lockley Lucy M. • Reference Librarian • Saint Charles City-County Library System Kisker Road Branch Library • Saint Charles, MO 63303 • RASD VRT

Lockman Edward J. • Faxon Fulfillment Center • Ann Arbor, MI 48103 • ACRL ALCTS

Lockman Gail E. • Head of Reference • San Rafael Public Library • San Rafael, CA 94901 • RASD IRRT

Lockrem E. Jane • San Jose, CA 95127

Lockridge Eunice A. • Childrens Librarian • Chicago Public Library Hiram Kelly Branch • Chicago, IL 60621 • ALSC

Lockwood James T. Jr. • Indiana University-Purdue University at Indianapolis Library (IUPUI) • Indianapolis, IN 46202

Lockwood Juliet • Br Hd • Chicago Public Library Marshall Square Branch • Chicago, IL 60608 • PLA EMIERT

Lockwood Lynn • Library Associate • Baltimore County Public Library • Towson, MD 21204 • PLA

Lockwood Marsha D. • Branch Manager • Dallas Public Library Park Forest Branch • Dallas, TX 75234

Locy Steven M. • Ponca City, OK 74604 • ACRL

Loder Michael Wescott • Campus Librarian • Pennsylvania State University Schuykill Campus Library • Schuylkill Haven, PA 17972 • ACRL

Lodge Ardis • Pasadena, CA 91104-2665 • ACRL RASD
Continuing

Lodge Constance Miss • Pasadena, CA 91101-1259 • Continuing

Lodish Erica Kessler • School Library Media Specialist • Montgomery Blair High School • Silver Spring, MD 20910 • AASL LITA YALSA

Loe Mary K. H. • Associate Librarian • State University of New York (SUNY) Penfield Library • Oswego, NY 13126-3514 • ACRL

Loe Sharon L. • Assistant Director • Northern Illinois Library System • Rockford, IL 61108 • PLA

Loeb Linda I. • Program Officer/Admin. Librarian • United States Department of Education Office of Educational Res & Improvement • Washington, DC 20208-5571 • ACRL

Loebel Janet L. • Kansas State Dept of Education • Topeka, KS 66612

Loechner Catherine • N. Merrick, NY 11566

Loeding Deborah • Manager, Library Relations • H. W. Wilson Company • Bronx, NY 10452 • AASL ACRL LITA RASD

Loeffler Marilyn Y. • Librarian • Instructional Materials Center • Newton, KS 67114 • AASL

Loeffler Mildred • Manhattan, KS 66502 • ALTA
Continuing

Loehr Eric R. • Reference Librarian • Oberlin College Library • Oberlin, OH 44074 • ACRL RASD GODORT IFRT

Loeivanichjaroen Laddawan • Student • University of Missouri-Columbia School of Library & Informational Science • Columbia, MO 65211

Loer Stephanie J.H. • Children's Book Editor • Boston Globe Newspaper • Boston, MA 02107

Loertscher David V. • Libraries Unlimited Inc • Englewood, CO 80112 • AASL YALSA

Loesch Gay Ann • Media Specialist • Sterling Elementary School • Pineville, NC 28134 • AASL

Loesch Marilyn N. • Reference Librarian • Hampton University Collis P. Huntington Memorial Library • Hampton, VA 23668 • ACRL LAMA RASD

Loesing Cathie • K-6 Media Specialist • Columbia Public Schools • Columbia, MO 65201 • AASL

Loevy Robert L. • Skokie, IL 60076 • RASD

Loew Janet S. • Public Information Manager • Reuben McMillan Free Library Association Youngstown & Mahoning Cnty P L • Youngstown, OH 44503 • LAMA

Loewe Patricia A. • Trustee • Chicago Ridge Public Lib • Chicago Ridge, IL 60415 • ALTA PLA

Loewen Martha A. • San Antonio Public Library • San Antonio, TX 78205 • IFRT

Lofgren Gail M. • Head of Reference • Berwyn Public Library System • Berwyn, IL 60402 • RASD

Lofgren Lauran K. • Reference Librarian • Saint Mary of the Plains College Library Science Program • Dodge City, KS 67801

Loftis Deborah C. • Student • University of Alabama School of Library & Information Studies • Tuscaloosa, AL 35487-0252 • RASD SRRT

Loftis Susanna S. • Hanahauoli School • Honolulu, HI 96822 • AASL ALSC

Logan Betty C. • Student • State University New York at Buffalo School of Inf. & Library Studies • Buffalo, NY 14260

Logan Carolyn • Trustee • Bossier Parish Library • Bossier City, LA 71111

Logan Elaine M. • Parke-Davis Pharmaceutical Research Library • Ann Arbor, MI 48105 • ALCTS LITA

Logan Elisabeth L. • Assoc. Professor • Florida State University School of Library and Information Studies • Tallahassee, FL 32306-2048 • LITA LRRT

Logan J. C.M. Mrs. • Librarian • Chamberlain Career Development Center • Washington, DC 20003

Logan Kenneth R. • Librarian • Colegio Americano De Quito • Quito, Ecuador • AASL

Logan Robert B • Columbia, MD 21045

Logan Susan J. • Coordinator of Automation • Ohio State University Libraries • Columbus, OH 43210-1286 • ACRL LAMA LITA

Logan Thama • Librarian • Mifflin Middle School • Columbus, OH 43219

Logan Virginia • Santurce, PR 00907 • Continuing

Loggins Doris Ann • Consultant • North Texas Library System • Fort Worth, TX 76107-2921

Loghry Margaret • Coordinating Librarian • Tucson Unified School District • Tucson, AZ 85719 • AASL

Loghry Patricia A. • University of Wisconsin-Madison Memorial Library • Madison, WI 53706 • IFRT

Logsden Kara A. • Student • University of Iowa School of Library & Information Science • Iowa City, IA 52242 • ALSC PLA

Logsdon Janis • Brea, CA 92621 • ALCTS NMRT SRRT

Logsdon Mary F. • Fort Benning, GA 31905-5122 • AASL AFLRT

Logsdon Patricia A. • Catalog Librarian • Washington University Olin Library • Saint Louis, MO 63130 • ACRL

Logsdon Paul M. • Director • Ohio Northern University Heterick Memorial Library • Ada, OH 45810 • LAMA

Logsdon Richard H. • New York, NY 10025 • ACRL LAMA
Life

Logue Carol • Head Librarian • Sycamore Public Library • Sycamore, IL 60178-1440 • PLA

Loh Eudora Isabel • Foreign Document Librarian • University of California-Los Angeles (UCLA) • Los Angeles, CA 90024-1450 • ACRL GODORT

Loh Wallace • Dean • Seattle Public Library • Seattle, WA 98104-1193 • ALTA PLA

Lohman Barbara T. • Geneseo, IL 61254 • NMRT

Lohman Toni A. • Collection Management Librarian • Virginia Beach Public Library Central Library • Virginia Beach, VA 23452 • RASD

Lohmann Gwendolyn K. • Claremont, CA 91711

Lohmeier Mary M • Graduate Student • University of Wisconsin-Milwaukee School of Library & Information Science • Milwaukee, WI 53201 • IRRT

Lohr Neah J. • Department of Public Instruction Division for Library Services • Madison, WI 53707 • AASL LITA

Lohr Susan J. • Carroll County Public Library Eldersburg Branch • Eldersburg, MD 21784

Lohrer Alice • Professor Emeritus • University of Illinois Graduate School of Library and Information Science • Urbana, IL 61801 • AASL ALSC
Life

Loiselle Susan M. • Media Serv./AV/Library Supv. • Lansing High School Library • Lansing, NY 14882

Loizeaux Marie D. • Lancaster, PA 17602-4890 • LAMA PLA
Continuing

Loizzo Anthony F. • Melrose Park Public Library • Melrose Park, IL 60160

Lokanis Patricia • Children's Librarian • Romeo District Library • Romeo, MI 48065

Loke Lesley C. • Assistant Director, Comm. Serv. • Boston Public Library • Boston, MA 02117 • ASCLA LAMA PLA

Loken Sarah F. • Olympia, WA 98503

Lokey Patricia • Public Services Librarian • Scottsdale Community College Library • Scottsdale, AZ 85256

Lokke Jean • Urbana, IL 61801 • ACRL RASD
Life

Lollis William F. • Director • Westbury Memorial Public Library • Westbury, NY 11590

Lom Jerome A. • Librarian • Saint Norbert College Todd Wehr Library • De Pere, WI 54115 • ACRL LAMA

Lomax Debbie • Librarian • Bearden High School • Knoxville, TN 37919

Lomax Edward C. • Student • University of Pittsburgh School of Library and Information Science • Pittsburgh, PA 15260 • LITA

Lomax Eleanor L. • Student • University of Rhode Island Graduate School of Library & Information Studies • Kingston, RI 02881-0815

Lomax Georgia L. • Director • Flathead County Library • Kalispell, MT 59901

Lomax Michael L. • Trustee • Atlanta-Fulton Public Library • Atlanta, GA 30303 • PLA

Lombard Ga • Bookshop Santa Cruz • Santa Cruz, CA 95060

Lombardo Cindy A. • Children's Librarian • Medina County District Library • Medina, OH 44256 • ALSC

Lombardo Nancy T. • Librarian • Denver Public Library • Denver, CO 80203-2165 • LITA

Lomen Nancy L. • Camden, DE 19934-1642 • AFLRT

Lomicka Janet • Librarian III • Onondaga County Public Library at the Galleries • Syracuse, NY 13202-2494

Lomker Linda Haack • Humanities/Soc. Sci. Cataloger • University of Minnesota • Minneapolis, MN 55455 • ACRL ALCTS SRRT

Lonberger Jana L. • Head, Serials Control • Georgia Institute of Technology • Atlanta, GA 30332 • ACRL ALCTS NMRT

London Ellen J. • Librarian • Rabat American School • Rabat, Morocco • AASL YALSA IRRT LIRT

London Kaisa M. • Temporary Beg. Libr/Part-time • Seattle Public Library • Seattle, WA 98104-1193

London Sarah F. • Brooklyn, NY 11201

London Stephanie R. Mrs. • Jacksonville Public Library System Mandarin Branch • Jacksonville, FL 32257 • ALSC

London Susan • Media Specialist • Red Bud High School • Red Bud, IL 62278

Londono Lia • Spanish Information Services • Chicago Public Library Harold Washington Library • Chicago, IL 60605 • CLENE LRRT

Lonergan David • Reference Librarian • Northern Illinois University University Libraries • DeKalb, IL 60115-2868 • ACRL

Lonergan Edmond P. • Librarian • Springfield City Library • Springfield, MA 01103 • GODORT MAGERT

Lonergan Lynn A. • Craven Community College Godwin Library • New Bern, NC 28563

Lonergan Penelope A. • Library Director • Saint Mary College DePaul Library • Leavenworth, KS 66048 • ACRL LITA IFRT

Lonergan Susan M. • Whitesboro, NY 13492

Loney Al C. • Chairman of Board of Trustees • Nepean Public Library • Nepean ON, K2G 5K7 Canada

Long Abbie S. • Clarksville, IN 47129 • AASL

Long Betty J. • Director • Roswell Public Library • Roswell, NM 88201 • PLA

Long Bobbie G. • Head Librarian • Art Institute of Dallas Learning Resource Center • Dallas, TX 75231 • ACRL

Long Caroline C. • Reference Librarian • George Washington University Gelman Library • Washington, DC 20052 • ACRL RASD

Long Carolyn W. • Director, Learning Resource Ctr. • Williamsburg Technical • Kingstree, SC 29556 • ACRL

Long Christine A. • Student • San Jose State University Division of Library & Information Science • San Jose, CA 95192-0029 • PLA

Long Clay • Trustee • Atlanta-Fulton Public Library • Atlanta, GA 30303 • PLA

Long Donna L. • Children's Librarian • Free Library of Philadelphia Oak Lane Branch • Philadelphia, PA 19126

Long Elizabeth A. • Senior Childrens Librarian • New York Public Library For the Performing Arts • New York, NY 10023 • ALSC

Long Elizabeth L. • Chief Librarian • Lithgow Public Library • Augusta, ME 04330

Long Elizabeth R. • Assistant Librarian • Severn School • Severna Park, MD 21146 • AASL

Long Hank • Library Director • Englewood Public Library • Englewood, CO 80110 • LAMA LITA PLA IFRT SRRT

Long Harriet G. • Oberlin, OH 44074 • Continuing

Long Harvey S. • Education Industry Consultant • IBM Corporation • Bethesda, MD 20817 • AASL LITA

Long Henry C. • Baltimore, MD 21216

Long Jeanne S. • Acquisitions Librarian • C I S Inc • Bethesda, MD 21204 • RASD GODORT

Long Jennifer A. • Ventura, CA 93004 • ALSC NMRT

Long Joan Y. • Murrysville, PA 15668-9539 • Continuing

Long Joanna R. • The Kirkus Service Inc. • New York, NY 10003 • ALSC SRRT

Long Jude Sanner • Librarian • Morro Bay Library • Morro Bay, CA 93442

Long Judith N. • Rockford Public Library • Rockford, IL 61101-1061 • LAMA PLA

Long Karen Draut • Shaker Hts, OH 44122

Long Katherine C. • Bethesda, MD 20814 • Life

Long Kathryn E. • Reference Librarian • Prince William Public Library Chinn Park Regional Library • Prince William, VA 22192

Long Laurette H. Mrs. • Assistant Librarian • Troy State University Dothan Library • Dothan, AL 36303 • ACRL

Long Lora A. • Hattiesburg, MS 39402

Long Marianna • Durham, NC 27705 • ALSC *Continuing*

Long Marilyn L. • Library Media Teacher • Palma High School • Salinas, CA 93901 • AASL YALSA

Long Mary Belle • Frankenmuth, MI 48734 • ALSC PLA *Continuing*

Long Mary J. • Director of Library Services • Massachusetts Board of Library Commissioners • Boston, MA 02215-2070

Long Melanie C. • Library Supervisor • NASA Lewis Research Center Library • Cleveland, OH 44135 • LITA NMRT

Long Patricia A. • Senior Librarian • New York Public Library Tremont Branch • Bronx, NY 10457

Long Paula L. • Lafayette, LA 70501

Long Roger J. • Vice President of Marketing • Nichols Advanced Technologies Inc. • LaCrosse, WI 54601 • ERT

Long Russell • Director • Sidney Public Library • Sidney, NE 69162-2008 • PLA RASD

Long Sandra K. • Coor. of Library Mgr. Info. • Utah State Library • Salt Lake City, UT 84115-2579 • ASCLA LAMA LITA PLA IFRT

Long Sarah Ann • Director • North Suburban Library System • Wheeling, IL 60090 • ALTA ASCLA PLA

Long Sarah P. • Mobile, AL 36618

Long Shushano • Branch Librarian • Cleveland Heights-Univ Hts Pub Lib Coventry Branch • Cleveland Heights, OH 44118 • PLA

Long Sonia K. • Director • Amsterdam Free Library • Amsterdam, NY 12010 • PLA

Long Sue • Hamilton Public Library • Hamilton, New Zealand • PLA

Long Susan A. • Director Library/Media Services • Akron Public Schools • Akron, OH 44301 • AASL ALSC

Long Zelda • Baton Rouge, LA 70806-7436

Longacher Joseph L. Dr. • Trustee • Henrico Public Library • Richmond, VA 23223 • ALTA

Longaker Judy • Librarian • National Business College • Roanoke, VA 24017 • ACRL

Longfellow Charles A. • Port Penn, DE 19731-0039 • AASL AFLRT SRRT

Longfellow Harry E. • Trustee • Livingston & Wyoming County Library Systems • Avon, NY 14414

Longmire Leslie A. • Children's Librarian I • Sno-Isle Regional Library • Marysville, WA 98271-9164

Longmoor Caroline G. • Head, Clln Development Section • National Library Service for the Blind & Physically Handicapped • Washington, DC 20542 • ASCLA

Longo John • Assoc Head Libn Technical Servs • Suffolk Community College Selden Campus Library • Selden, NY 11784-2899 • ACRL ALCTS LAMA LITA

Longoria Pamela J. • San Antonio Public Library Thousand Oaks Branch • San Antonio, TX 78233

Longstreet Christine R. • Delray Beach, FL 33483 • Continuing

Longstreet Donna M. • Longstreet Research Associates • Garden Grove, CA 92645 • ACRL GODORT IRRT

Longstreth Judith A. • St. Louis, MO 63108-2340

Longstreth Karl Eric • Map Librarian • University of Michigan • Ann Arbor, MI 48109-1205 • ACRL ALCTS MAGERT

Longsworth Eileen B. • Director • Salt Lake County Library System • Salt Lake City, UT 84121-3188 • LAMA PLA

Longworth Ruth O. • Santa Barbara, CA 93101 • Continuing

Lonning Roger D. • Albert Lea, MN 56007 • AASL YALSA *Life*

Lonsak John A. • Regional Librarian • Cuyahoga County Public Library • Cleveland, OH 44134-2792 • LAMA PLA

Loo Lilly C. • County of Los Angeles Public Library South County Region 500 • Norwalk, CA 90650

Loo Shirley • Specialist, Info. Control & AS • Library of Congress • Washington, DC 20541 • LAMA LITA FLRT SORT

Look Lin • Librarian • Contra Costa County Library Concord Branch • Concord, CA 94519 • ALSC EMIERT SRRT VRT

Loomba Mary A. • Inst. Serv./Reference Librarian • Westchester Community College • Valhalla, NY 10595 • ACRL

Loomis Abigail A. • Coor. of Library User Educ. • University of Wisconsin-Madison Memorial Library • Madison, WI 53706 • ACRL LHRT LIRT

Loomis Barbara • Assistant Engineering Librarian • University of Illinois • Urbana, IL 61801 • ACRL ALCTS LITA IFRT

Loomis Barbara L. • Asst. City Librarian • Escondido Public Library • Escondido, CA 92025 • PLA

Loomis Elena R. • Student • San Jose State University Clark Library • San Jose, CA 95192-0028

Loomis Lynn A. • Librarian • Loudoun County Public Library Rust Library of Leesburg • Leesburg, VA 22075 • ALSC YALSA

Loomis Mary Kay • Redding, CT 06896 • ACRL

Looney JoAnn L. • Reference Librarian • Louisiana State University Libraries Troy H. Middleton Library • Baton Rouge, LA 70803-3342 • ACRL LIRT NMRT

Looney Robert J. • Assistant Director, Central Srvs • Burnaby Library Services Branch • Burnaby BC, V5G 4H7 Canada

Loorie Nancy Slater • Reference Librarian • Atlantic City Free Public Library • Atlantic City, NJ 08401

Loos Jean E. D. • Director • Glen Ridge Public Library • Glen Ridge, NJ 07028 • PLA

Loos Joann • Okeana, OH 45053 • AASL

Loos Norma Ende Mrs • Sanibel, FL 33957 • Life

Loos William H. • Curator, Rare Book Room • Buffalo & Erie County Public Library • Buffalo, NY 14203 • ACRL

Lootens Bernard • Trustee • Michigan City Public Library • Michigan City, IN 46360 • ALTA

Lopatic Paula J. • Children's Librarian • Vespasian Warner Public Library • Clinton, IL 61727

Lopatin Edith K. • Plainview, NY 11803

Lopatin Laurie J. • Bellmore, NY 11710 • ALCTS

Lopato Esther W. Dr. • Trustee • Brooklyn Public Library • Brooklyn, NY 11238 • ALTA PLA

Loper John R. • Cristobal, Panama • ACRL RASD

Loper Linda Sue • Director of LRC • Columbia State Community College • Columbia, TN 38402-1315 • LAMA NMRT

Lopes Marlene L. • Rhode Island College James P. Adams Library • Providence, RI 02908 • ACRL

Lopez-Elzo Angelica • Library Specialist • Stanford University J. Henry Meyer Memorial Library • Stanford, CA 94305

Lopez Andres • Librarian • Escuela Hotelera de Puerto Rico • Isla Verde, PR 00937

Lopez Angel • Partner • Squires & Lopez Attorneys at Law • Portland, OR 97205

Lopez Crystal T. • Boulder, CO 80303

Lopez Deborah A. • Librarian • Christ The King School • Tampa, FL 33629 • AASL

Lopez Irma • Student • University of Texas at Austin Graduate School of Library & Information Sciences • Austin, TX 78712-1276

Lopez Kathleen R. • Adult/Reference Librarian • New City Library • New City, NY 10956 • PLA SORT

Lopez Kathryn P. • Media Specialist • Alameda Junior High School Library • Santa Fe, NM 87501 • AASL LIRT

Lopez Michael A. • Fort Salonga, NY 11768

Lopiano Sarah E. • North Raleigh, NC 27614

Lopresti Robert J. • Documents Librarian • Western Washington University Wilson Library • Bellingham, WA 98225

Lora Mary Patricia • Head, Visual Service • Toledo-Lucas County Public Library • Toledo, OH 43624 • IFRT VRT

Lorance Jane • Adminstrator • Las Vegas-Clark County Library District Flamingo Library • Las Vegas, NV 89119

Loranth Alice N. • Head, Fine Arts/Special Colls. • Cleveland Public Library • Cleveland, OH 44114-1271 • ACRL ALCTS

Lorber Carl L. • Serials Librarian • Eastern Illinois University Booth Library • Charleston, IL 61920-3099 • ACRL RASD

Lord Judy B. • Salt Lake City, UT 84105 • PLA

Lord Mary E. • Executive Director • ACCESS : A Security Information Service • Washington, DC 20036 • LITA

Lordi Joseph A. • Director • Bayard Taylor Memorial Library • Kennett Square, PA 19348

Lords Debra D. • Student • University of Utah Marriott Library • Salt Lake City, UT 84112-1179 • LITA LRRT MAGERT

Lorentowicz Genia • Director, Technical Services • Mississauga Public Library System • Mississauga ON, L5B 3Y3 Canada • ALCTS LITA

Lorenz Denis • Director • West Hartford Public Library • W. Hartford, CT 06107 • LAMA PLA

Lorenz Elizabeth W. Mrs • St. Petersburg, FL 33707-2037 • PLA YALSA *Continuing*

Lorenz Harriet F. • Assistant Director • Bristol Public Library • Bristol, CT 06010 • PLA

Lorenz Janice C. • Cataloging Technician • Indiana University Libraries Monographic Proc Serv Dept • Bloomington, IN 47405 • ALCTS

Lorenz John G. • Bethesda, MD 20816 • ACRL LAMA *Life*

Lorenzen Michael G. • Serials • Bowling Green State University William Jerome Library • Bowling Green, OH 43403-0175

Lorenzo Janet B. • Ln/ A-YA Serivces Coordinator • Tampa-Hillsborough County Public Library • Tampa, FL 33602

Lorenzo Susan Brune • Student • Rutgers University School of Communication Information & Library Studies • New Brunswick, NJ 08903

Lorimer Suzanne K. • Assistant Head, Reference Dept. • Yale University Sterling Memorial Library • New Haven, CT 06520 • ACRL ALCTS RASD

Loring Christopher B. • Access Servs. Linn-H/SS Libs • University of Minnesota • Minneapolis, MN 55455 • LAMA RASD

Lorio Mary Lee • Pointe Coupee Parish Library • New Road, LA 70760 • ALTA

Lorish Ann D. • Allentown College of St. Francis De Sales • Center Valley, PA 18034 • ACRL LIRT

Lorkovic Tatjana • Yale University Sterling Memorial Library • New Haven, CT 06520 • ACRL ALCTS IRRT

Lorona Lionel V. • New York, NY 10014

Lorriman Alice R. • Assistant Chief Librarian • East York Public Library • Toronto ON, M4H 1H2 Canada • PLA

Lortie Tina M. • Technical Librarian • Metters Industries, Inc. • Camarillo, CA 93010 • ALCTS LAMA LITA PLA CLENE GODORT

Lorz Marie L. • Director • London Public Library • London, OH 43140

Los Margaret • Trustee • Elmhurst Public Library • Elmhurst, IL 60126 • ALTA PLA

Losey Betsy • Media Specialist • Roosevelt Elementary School • Hays, KS 67601 • AASL

Losey Doris C. • Youth Specialist • Brandon Regional Library • Brandon, FL 33511 • YALSA

Losey Eileen • Royal Oak, MI 48703

Losick Merill B. • Reference Librarian • Dean Witter Reynolds Inc • New York, NY 10048 • LITA RASD

Losinski Julia • Baltimore, MD 21212 • Continuing

Losinski Patrick A. • Director • Warren-Newport Public Library District • Gurnee, IL 60031

Loslo Joan K. • Serials Librarian • University of Northern Iowa Donald O. Rod Library • Cedar Falls, IA 50613-3675 • ACRL ALCTS

Loss Joan E. • Baltimore, MD 21234 • AASL ALSC *Life*

Losse Arlyle M. • Milwaukee, WI 53210-1185 • ACRL RASD *Life*

Losse Carl H. • Milwaukee, WI 53210-1185 • ALCTS PLA *Life*

Loth Sandra • Mead Public Library • Sheboygan, WI 53081

Lothrop Jean • Director • Burton L. Wales Public Library • Abington, MA 02351

Lotlikar S. D. • Librarian • Millersville University of Pennsylvania • Millersville, PA 17551-0302

Lotman Orrell • Pampa, TX 79065-3022 • AASL ALSC YALSA

Lotos Helen L. • Community Relations Manager • Orange County Public Library • Santa Ana, CA 92705 • LAMA PLA

Lotreck Annelaine • Willoughby Wallace Memorial Library • Stony Creek, CT 06405

Lott Barbara F. • Coodinator, Servs for Disabled • University of Connecticut Homer Babbidge Library • Storrs, CT 06269-1005 • ACRL ASCLA RASD IFRT LIRT

Lott Diana L. • Trustee • Pine Bluff & Jefferson County Library System • Pine Bluff, AR 71601

Lott Kristin R. • Student • East Brunswick Public Library • E. Brunswick, NJ 08816

Lotz Marilyn R. • Burlington County Library • Mount Holly, NJ 08060-1394

Lotz Marsha A. • Reference/Adult Services Ln. • Matteson Public Library • Matteson, IL 60443 • RASD

Lotz Wendell • Baker & Taylor Books • Bridgewater, NJ 08807-0920 • AASL ALCTS LITA

Louch Janet K. • Assistant Director-Reference • Douglas County Library • Minden, NV 89423

Louden William F. • Asst Univ Ln/Planning & Budget • University of Cincinnati Libraries • Cincinnati, OH 45221-0033 • ACRL LAMA LITA

Louderback Clyde Arthur • Librarian • Historical Society of Western Pennsylvania Library • Pittsburgh, PA 15213 • ALCTS

Louderback Mary A. • Circulation Librarian • University of Washington Gallagher Law Library • Seattle, WA 98105

Lougee Wendy Pradt • Ann Arbor, MI 48105-3037 • ACRL ALCTS LAMA LITA PLA RASD *Life*

Lough Margaret E. • Frederick, MD 21701 • ACRL RASD *Continuing*

Lough Mary M. • Librarian/Media Specialist • Beeks Elementary School • Blacksburg, VA 24060 • AASL ALSC

Loughlin Beverly A. • Asst. Hd Ref & Curator Clln • Hartford Public Library • Hartford, CT 06103-3003

Loughlin Ellen B. • Reference Librarian • Sibson & Company • Princeton, NJ 08543-5323

Loughner William • University of Georgia Libraries • Athens, GA 30602 • LITA

Loughney Katharine L. • Reference Librarian • United States International Trade Commission • Washington, DC 20436

Loughran Ellen • Coor. Public Service Support • Brooklyn Public Library • Brooklyn, NY 11238 • ALSC PLA RASD YALSA IFRT

Loughran Helen M. • Director • Gogebic Community College Learning Resource Center • Ironwood, MI 49938 • ACRL ERT

Loughridge John J. • Frederick, MD 21701 • ACRL ALCTS

Louhier Barbara • Media Specialist • Burlington Road School • Freehold, NJ 07762 • AASL

Loui Pamela S. • Director • Apache Junction Public Library • Apache Junction, AZ 85219 • ALSC PLA

Louie Ruby Ling Phd • Librarian, LAUSD • South Gate Junior High School • South Gate, CA 90280 • Continuing

Louis-Jacques Lyonette • Associate Librarian • University of Minnesota Law Library • Minneapolis, MN 55455 • ACRL RASD GODORT IFRT IRRT SRRT

Louis Dorothy M. • Student • Kent State University School of Library & Information Science • Kent, OH 44242-0001 • PLA

Louis Patricia A.L. • Native Hawaiian Library Project • Honolulu, HI 96819-4429

Louistall-Monroe Victorine • Clarksburg-Harrison Public Library • Clarksburg, WV 26301 • ALTA *Continuing*

Loulousis Penelope • Brookfield, IL 60513 • AASL

Lounsberry Laurie • Student • State University of New York (SUNY) School of Information & Library Studies • Buffalo, NY 14260

Loup Jean L. • University of Michigan Libraries • Ann Arbor, MI 48109-1205 • ACRL

Loupe Mary Edward • Administrative Librarian • Pointe Coupee Parish Library • New Road, LA 70760 • AASL ALSC ALTA LAMA PLA RASD YALSA

Lourdou Dorothy A. • Librarian III • New York Public Library Performing Arts • New York, NY 10023 • ACRL

Lourie Margaret A. • Cambridge, MA 02140 • ACRL ALCTS LITA

Loux Janice K. • Librarian • Bellevue Public Schools • Bellevue, WA 98009-9010

Loux Mary Curtin • D/IRM-Mgmt Prog Mgr • Analysis & Technology Inc. • New London, CT 06320 • LITA AFLRT

Lovato Renee M. • Director of Branch • San Bernardino County Library Bloomington Branch • Bloomington, CA 92316

Love Cynthia • Divisional Librarian • CSIRO Division of Human Nutrition • Adelaide 5000, Australia

Love Martha • Springfield-Greene County Library Brentwood Branch Library • Springfield, MO 65804

Love Mary E. Mrs. • Trustee • T.L.L. Temple Memorial Library • Diboll, TX 75941 • PLA

Love Pauline J. • Topeka, KS 66614 • AASL ALSC *Life*

Love Phyllis S. • Student • Florida State University School of Library and Information Studies • Tallahassee, FL 32306-2048

Love Terry A. • Student • Catholic University of America School of Library and Information Science • Washington, DC 20064 • AASL

Lovegren Joseph • President • Maine Library Funiture Inc • Portland, ME 04104-3114

Lovejoy Janet M. • Librarian • Wilson Junior High School Library • Glendale, CA 91206 • AASL ALSC

Lovelace Frances P. • Youth Special/Services Cons. • DuPage Library System • Geneva, IL 60134 • AASL ALSC

Lovelace Hazel M. • Media Specialist • Gaffney Senior High School Library • Gaffney, SC 29342 • AASL

Lovelace Julianne • Richardson Public Library • Richardson, TX 75080 • ALSC LAMA PLA RASD IFRT

Lovelace Rebecca • Trustee • Horry County Memorial Library • Conway, SC 29526 • ALTA

Loveland Catherine R. • Media Specialist • Sells Middle School • Dublin, OH 43017 • AASL

Loveland Erma J. • Librarian for Special Services • Abilene Christian University Margaret & Herman Brown Library • Abilene, TX 79699 • ACRL ERT

Loveless Helene B. • Cromwell, CT 06416 • YALSA

Lovell Clark P. • Cataloger • Library of Congress • Washington, DC 20541 • ALCTS

Lovell Mary • Assistant Librarian • Golden Valley County Library • Beach, ND 58621

Lovell Susan A. • Teacher • Bridgeport Middle School • Bridgeport, TX 76426 • AASL

Lovely Victoria Teal • Database Coordinator • South Central Library System • Madison, WI 53703 • ALCTS

Lovenburg Susan L. • Library Consultant (Freelance) • Fredericton, E3B 3K3

Lovering Virginia E. • De Kalb, IL 60115 • Continuing

Lovetere John P. • Trustee • Indian Trails Public Library District • Wheeling, IL 60090 • ALTA

Lovett John R. • Librarian • University of Oklahoma Western History Collection • Norman, OK 73019

Lovett Joy K. • School Librarian • Lopez-Riggins Elementary School • Los Fresnos, TX 78566 • AASL

Lovett Margie E. • Tomball, TX 77375

Lovett Patricia K. • University of California-Irvine Library • Irvine, CA 92713 • ACRL

Lovett Valerie W. • Assistant Director • Wake County Public Library System • Raleigh, NC 27610 • LAMA PLA SRRT

Lovin Jane • Media Specialist • Central Gwinnett High School • Lawrenceville, GA 30245

Loving Joyce R. • Maryland Heights, MO 63043

Loving Kathleen B. • Librarian • Langley High School • McLean, VA 22101 • AASL ALSC

Low D Lynette • Assistant City Librarian • Whittier Public Library • Whittier, CA 90602

Low Frederick E. • Coordinator Technical Services • LaGuardia Community College • Long Island City, NY 11101 • ACRL

Low Janet • Children's/YA Librarian • Orem Public Library • Orem, UT 84058 • ALSC

Low Kathleen • California State Library • Sacramento, CA 94237-0001

Low Tammy • Student • University of Wisconsin-Milwaukee School of Library & Information Science • Milwaukee, WI 53201 • AASL

Low Yuen-Man • Student • University of Illinois School of Library Information Science • Champaign, IL 61820 • ALCTS RASD

Lowchy Gregory P. • Student • University of North Carolina at Chapel Hill School of Information and Library Science • Chapel Hill, NC 27599-3360

Lowd Monique F. • Head Librarian-Edu. Res. Ctr. • Boston College Libraries • Chestnut Hill, MA 02167

Lowe Areena J. • Chespeake, VA 23325 • AFLRT

Lowe Avis T • Northville, MI 48167 • AASL

Lowe Carolyn E. • Graduate Student • Johnson Bible College Glass Memorial Library • Knoxville, TN 37998

Lowe Carrie A. • Student • University of California-Berkeley School of Library & Information Studies • Berkeley, CA 94720

Lowe Dawn E. • Milwaukie, OR 97267

Lowe Elizabeth A. • Librarian • Thomas J. Lahey School • Greenlawn, NY 11740 • AASL

Lowe Flora S. • Library Director • Mount Saint Clare College • Clinton, IA 52732 • ACRL ALCTS LITA

Lowe Jennie • Librarian • Waukegan East High School Library • Waukegan, IL 60085 • AASL

Lowe Joy L. • Associate Professor of Lib Sci • Louisiana Tech University Teacher Education-Library Science • Ruston, LA 71272 • AASL ALSC YALSA

Lowe Katherine E. • Librarian/Media Specialist • Lunenburg Public Schools • Lunenburg, MA 01462 • AASL

Lowe Mary E. • Library Director • Shamokin-Coal Township Public Library • Shamokin, PA 17872

Lowe Ruthanne • Campbell, CA 95009 • ALCTS

Lowe Susan S. • Coordinator Off-Campus Lib. Serv • University of Maine at Augusta Learning Resources Center • Augusta, ME 04330 • ACRL

Lowe William B. • Student • San Jose State University Division of Library & Information Science • San Jose, CA 95192-0029

Lowell Charlesa A. • Director • State Librarian Delaware Division of Libraries • Dover, DE 19901 • PLA

Lowell Dawn E. • Librarian • W. Walworth Harrison Public Library • Greenville, TX 75401-3999 • PLA

Lowell Gerald R. • Assoc Univ Ln for Tech Serv • Yale University Sterling Memorial Library • New Haven, CT 06520 • ACRL ALCTS LITA

Lowell Kay E. • Buffalo, NY 14223-1630 • ALCTS

Lowell Virginia L. • Director • Jackson District Library • Jackson, MI 49201 • LAMA LITA PLA

Lowenberg Susan • University of Colorado-Boulder University Libraries • Boulder, CO 80309 • ACRL

Lowenburg Deborah P. • Librarian • Pleasant Valley Middle School Pleasant Valley School District • Brodheadsville, PA 18322 • AASL

Lowenfels Doris B. • Thornwood, NY 10594

Lowenthal Ralph A. • Head, Education Library • Washington State University • Pullman, WA 99164-2112 • ACRL RASD

Lower Jacquelyn D. Mrs. • Librarian • Mary Hoge Junior High School Library • Weslaco, TX 78596

Lowery Clorene Miss • Librarian • Southwest Middle School Library • Little Rock, AR 72201 • AASL YALSA *Life*

Lowery Merry E. • Dallas Public Library • Dallas, TX 75201 • ALCTS

Lowman Judith T. • Personnel Librarian • Northwestern University Library • Evanston, IL 60208-2300 • ACRL LAMA SORT

Lowman Sara A. • Coor. of Collection Development • Rice University Fondren Library • Houston, TX 77251-1892 • ACRL

Lowrey Anna Mary • East Amherst, NY 14051

Lowrey Jane • Community Relations Librarian • Bellingham Public Library • Bellingham, WA 98227 • SRRT

Lowrey Mary L. • LaGrange, IL 60525 • LAMA LITA PLA

Lowrie Jean E. • Kalamazoo, MI 49006 • AASL ALSC IRRT *Continuing*

Lowry Charles B. • University Librarian • Carnegie-Mellon University Libraries Hunt Library • Pittsburgh, PA 15213 • ACRL LAMA LITA

Lowry Clarissa S. • Franklin Middle School (LLC) • Wheaton, IL 60187 • AASL

Lowry H. Maynard • Library Director • La Sierra University Library • Riverside, CA 92515 • ACRL LITA

Lowry Lina M. • Chief Librarian • Borough of Manhattan Community College Randolph Memorial Library • New York, NY 10007 • ACRL

Lowry Lucy J. • Director • SMILE • Mankato, MN 56001 • ASCLA PLA

Lowry Suzanne R. • Media Specialist • Cache School District Millville Elementary School • Millville, UT 84326 • AASL

Lowry Sydney P. • Student • University of Georgia Department of Instructional Technolgy • Athens, GA 30602

Lowry Timothy R. • B. F. Stevens and Brown Ltd. • Surrey GU7 3HT, England

Lowry William H. • Pioneer Library System • Norman, OK 73069

Lowy Beverly R. • Director • North Bellmore Public Library • N. Bellmore, NY 11710 • PLA

Lowy Gerhard • Cataloger • Columbia University Libraries Butler Library • New York, NY 10027

Loy Dale • Trustee • Cabell County Public Library • Huntington, WV 25701 • ALTA PLA

Loyd Marie S. • Book Selection Supervisor • Amarillo Public Library • Amarillo, TX 79189

Loyd Marjorie M. • Jefferson West Elementary Middle Schools • Meriden, KS 66512

Loyster Sara J. • Branch Librarian • Contra Costa County Library Pinole Branch • Pinole, CA 94564

Lozel Stephanie O. • East Point Public Library • East Point, GA 30344

Lozoski Laurene E. • St. Paul, MN 55116-3808 • ACRL

Lswry Patricia B. • Librarian • National Fed of Ind Bus • Washington, DC 20024 • LAMA

Lu Janet C. • Public Service Librarian • Nebraska Wesleyan University Cochrane-Woods Library • Lincoln, NE 68504

Lu Min-Heui • Assistant Acquisitions Librarian • State University of New York (SUNY) Frank Melville Jr. Memorial Library • Stony Brook, NY 11794-3300 • NMRT

Lu Ming-hsiang • Pittsburgh, PA 15213

Lu Xuehong • Student • Brigham Young University School of Library & Information Sciences • Provo, UT 84602

Lubans John Jr. • Deputy University Librarian • Duke University William R. Perkins Library • Durham, NC 27706 • LAMA

Lubansky Marcia A. • Technical Services • Somerville Public Library • Somerville, NJ 08876

Lubell Leonore • Librarian • Elmont Public Library • Elmont, NY 11003

Lubelski Gregory • Geauga County Public Library • Chardon, OH 44024 • LAMA

Lubetski Edith • Librarian • Stern College • New York, NY 10022 • ACRL RASD

Lubin Lloyd G. • Senior Cataloging Librarian • Free Public Library of Woodbridge • Woodbridge, NJ 07095 • ALCTS LITA RASD

Lubin Marilyn • Adult Services Coordinator • Queens Borough Public Library • Jamaica, NY 11432 • PLA RASD

Lubovich Linda M. • Reference Coordinator • Santa Clara County Free Library Cupertino Public Library • Cupertino, CA 95014 • PLA

Lubow Dana N. • Librarian • Bruggemeyer Memorial Library City of Monterey Park • Monterey Park, CA 91754 • LAMA SRRT

Lubrecht Alice L. • Assistant Director Pub. Servs. • State Library of Pennsylvania Department of Education • Harrisburg, PA 17105 • LAMA RASD

Lucas A Lynne • Indiana, PA 15701 • ALSC

Lucas Aileen • Bridgeport, WV 26330 • AASL YALSA *Continuing*

Lucas Amanda C. • Library Media Specialist • Foster Village Elementary Birdville Schools • Ft. Worth, TX 76180 • AASL ALSC LRRT NMRT

Lucas Annie M. • Director • Macon County-Tuskegee Public Library • Tuskegee, AL 36083 • LAMA PLA YALSA

Lucas Catherine E. • County Librarian • San Diego County Library • San Diego, CA 92123 • ALSC LAMA LITA PLA RASD YALSA EMIERT GODORT IFRT IRRT

Lucas Cynthia S. • Systems Librarian • University of North Carolina Wilson Library • Chapel Hill, NC 27599 • ACRL LITA

Lucas Diane E. • University of Pittsburgh Hillman Library • Pittsburgh, PA 15260 • ALCTS

Lucas Elaine M. • Student • Indiana University School of Library and Information Science • Bloomington, IN 47405

Lucas Jean F. • Student • San Jose State University Division of Library & Information Science • San Jose, CA 95192-0029 • RASD

Lucas John • Trustee • Schaumburg Township District Library • Schaumburg, IL 60194

Lucas Karen G. • Student • University of Wisconsin-Madison School of Library & Information Studies • Madison, WI 53706

Lucas Kari M. • Head of Undergrad. Library • University of California-San Diego • La Jolla, CA 92093-0175 • LIRT

Lucas Linda • Associate Dean of Instruction • Las Positas College • Livermore, CA 94550 • ACRL LAMA

Lucas Maxine C. • Student • University of California • Los Angeles, CA 90024-1573 • AASL ALSC

Lucas Michael J. • Student • University of Wisconsin School of Library & Information Studies • Madison, WI 53706 • PLA

Lucas Pamela D. • Reference Librarian • Library of Michigan • Lansing, MI 48909

Lucas Prudence W. • Irving, TX 75063 • ACRL ALCTS

Lucas Thomas A. • Asst Libn for Clln Devlp. • New York Public Library • New York, NY 10018-2788 • ACRL ALCTS

Lucchesi Jane C. Mrs. • Librarian • Jefferson High School Library • Painesdale, MI 48106

Lucchino Linda A. • Librarian • Apoll/-Ridge Sch Dist/ Elders Ridge Elem School • Saltsburg, PA 15656

Lucco Susan • Librarian • Edwardsville Public Library • Edwardsville, IL 62025

Luccy Diane Maria • Student • University of Texas at Austin Graduate School of Library & Information Sciences • Austin, TX 78712-1276

Luce Ann • Librarian • Lake Country School Resource Center • Minneapolis, MN 55409

Luce Clarice • Asst Acquisitions Librarian • University of North Texas • Denton, TX 76203 • ALCTS

Luce John A. • Teacher • Mount Vernon Junior High School • Los Angeles, CA 90019

Luce Louise B Wenberg • Issaquah, WA 98027-9231 • Continuing

Luce Margaret M. • Carmel, CA 93921 • Continuing

Luce Mary Ann • Santa Rosa, CA 95403

Luce Richard • Library Director • Los Alamos National Lab Lib • Los Alamos, NM 87545-0020 • ASCLA LAMA LITA PLA

Luce Sue Jackson • Director • Ontario City Library • Ontario, CA 91764 • LAMA PLA IFRT

Lucero Mary Ellen K. • Student • San Jose State University Division of Library & Information Science • San Jose, CA 95192-0029 • YALSA

Lucey Lucinda M. • Librarian I • University of Massachusetts Library • Amherst, MA 01003

Luchinsky Ellen A. • Librarian • Enoch Pratt Free Library • Baltimore, MD 21201-4484 • PLA IFRT

Luchsinger Arlene E. • Science Librarian • University of Georgia Libraries • Athens, GA 30602 • ACRL LAMA

Luchsinger Caroline L. • Stack Supervisor • Wake Forest University Z Smith Reynolds Library • Winston Salem, NC 27109-7777 • NMRT

Luchsinger Dale F. • Director, Library & Media Servs • Athens Area Technical Institute • Athens, GA 30610-0399 • ACRL ALCTS RASD *Life*

Luchsinger Wilma J. • Librarian • Blairsville Senior High School • Blairsville, PA 15717 • AASL

Lucht Bonghee K. • Pittsburgh, PA 15217

Lucht Irma M. • Chicago, IL 60610

Lucia Joseph P. • Library Systems Manager • Lehigh University Libraries Fairchild-Martindale Library • Bethlehem, PA 18015 • LITA

Lucianna Roy M. • Assistant Editor • H. W. Wilson Company • Bronx, NY 10452 • ACRL

Luciano Tulay • Student • Southern Connecticut State University School of Libray Science & Instructional Technology • New Haven, CT 06515

Lucier Donna G. • Fairfield, CT 06430

Lucioli Clara E. • Cleveland Public Library • Cleveland, OH 44114-1271 • ASCLA *Continuing*

Luck Beverly • Monmouth County Library • Manalapan, NJ 07726

Luck DeAnne L. • Student • University of Illinois Graduate School of Library and Information Science • Urbana, IL 61801 • IFRT SRRT

Lucke Linda H. • LC Director • Butterfield School • Libertyville, IL 60048 • AASL

Lucke Louise Z. • Student • Emporia State University School of Library & Information Management • Emporia, KS 66801

Luckenbach Martha O. • Bethlehem, PA 18018-5702 • AASL YALSA *Continuing*

Lucker Jay K. • Director of Libraries • Massachusetts Institute of Technology Libraries (MIT) • Cambridge, MA 02139 • ACRL LAMA LITA

Luckert Yelena • Student • State University of New York at Albany School of Information Science & Policy • Albany, NY 12222 • ACRL

Luckett Lynne C. • Librarian I • Atlanta-Fulton Public Library • Atlanta, GA 30303 • PLA RASD

Luckett Richard A. • Student • Texas Woman's University School of Library & Information Studies • Denton, TX 76204 • LITA

Luckinbill Eva L. • Assistant Director • Lisle Library District • Lisle, IL 60532

Lucoff Margot B. • Berkeley Public Library • Berkeley, CA 94704 • ALCTS

Lucs Daina M. • North Brunswick, NJ 08902 • ALSC PLA

Ludemann Robert E. • Reference Librarian • Merrick Public Library • Merrick, NY 11566 • PLA

Luderitz Mary Ellin • CLSI, Inc. • Newtonville, MA 02160

Ludgin Marilyn • Hemlock, MI 48626 • AASL YALSA

Ludington Ivan Jr. • Library Commissioner • Detroit Public Library • Detroit, MI 48202 • ALTA

Ludlum James C. Mr. • Trustee • Montgomery County Department of Public Libraries • Rockville, MD 20850 • ALTA

Ludlum Mary E. • Assistant Director • Grandview Heights Public Library • Columbus, OH 43212 • PLA

Ludmer Joyce Pellerano • Humanities Bibliographer • UCLA Library University Research Library • Los Angeles, CA 90024-1575 • ACRL

Ludwig Barbara K. • Pembroke Pine, FL 33024 • YALSA

Ludwig Deborah L. • Reference Librarian • Porter Public Library • Westlake, OH 44145

Ludwig Deborah M. • Coor. for Technical Services • Kansas City Kansas Public Library • Kansas City, KS 66101 • LITA

Ludwig Fruma D. • Philadlphia, PA 19103

Ludwig Louise T. • Librarian • East Liverpool Public Schools Library • East Liverpool, OH 43920 • AASL YALSA

Ludwig Mary Beth • Technical Services Librarian • Maitland Public Library • Maitland, FL 32751

Ludwig Paul G. • Vice President • Priegel & Ludwig Inc. • Roshell, GA 30076 • LAMA

Ludwig Stephen M. • Main Library Supervisor • Jacksonville Public Libraries Main Library • Jacksonville, FL 32202 • LAMA PLA

Ludwig Sylvia A. • Library Assistant • Chemeketa Community College • Salem, OR 97309

Ludwig Zora V. • Director • Capes House Family Emergency Shelter • Hammond, IN 46320

Ludwigsen Vera • Coordinator of Libraries • Public School • Oconomowoc, WI 53066 • AASL

Ludwikowski Stella E. • Colorado Springs, CO 80904

Lue Mona H. C. • Elizabeth Public Library • Elizabeth, NJ 07202 • Continuing

Lueb Darla D. • Student • Valley City State University • Valley City, ND 58072

Luebbert Karen • Library Director • Eden Webster Libraries • Saint Louis, MO 63119-9957

Lueck Brenda J. • Adminstrative Librarian • Fox River Grove Public Library District • Fox River Grove, IL 60021 • LAMA

Lueck Lorna M. • Reference Dept. • University of California Library • Santa Barbara, CA 93106 • ACRL RASD LIRT NMRT

Lueck Peri I. • Administrative Assistant • Enem Systems Inc. • Waunakee, WI 53597-9586

Lueder Dianne Bertelsen • Wauconda, IL 60084 • LAMA PLA

Luedtke Cherry Beth • Reference Librarian • Austin Community College Rio Grande Campus • Austin, TX 78701 • ACRL LIRT

Luehs Jeanne • Director • Cedar Grove Public Library • Cedar Grove, NJ 07009

Lueptow Margaret B. • Orange Prk, FL 32065-7201

Luesing Lois L. • Director of Library Services • Asbury College • Wilmore, KY 40390 • ACRL

Luetkehans Lara M. • Schaumburg, IL 60194

Luetkehoelter Mark T. • Student • University of Wisconsin-Madison School of Library & Information Studies • Madison, WI 53706

Luetkemeyer Mark D. • Serials Cataloger • Saint Louis University Pius XII Memorial Library • St. Louis, MO 63108

Luevano Susan C. • Rancho Santiago College Nealley Library • Santa Ana, CA 92706 • ACRL EMIERT SRRT

Lufkin Beatrice A. • Vice President • Dynix Inc • Provo, UT 84606 • LITA

Luftig Merle • Teacher-Librarian • Hamilton Elementary School • Chicago, IL 60657 • AASL LIRT

Lugar Gary Lance • Student • University of Pittsburgh School of Library and Information Science • Pittsburgh, PA 15260

Luger Mary Jeanine Sr • Cataloging Librarian • Viterbo College Library • La Crosse, WI 54601 • ALCTS

Lugg Richard • Manager, Approval Plan Services • Yankee Book Peddler • Contoocook, NH 03229 • ALCTS LITA

Luh Beatrice K. • Orange, CT 06477

Luikart Nancy Bird • Librarian • Texas Tech University Libraries • Lubbock, TX 79409-0002 • ACRL

Luizzi Jacqueline M. • Hudson, OH 44236

Lukacovic Gloria A. • Notre Dame Academy for Girls • Los Angeles, CA 90064

Lukacs Mary M. • Reference Librarian • Exxon Biomedical Sciences Library • East Millstone, NJ 08875

Lukas Jennifer J. • Stockton-San Joaquin County Public Library • Stockton, CA 95202

Lukas Vicki A. • Head Technical Services • New Bedford Free Public Library • New Bedford, MA 02740

Lukasiewicz Barbara J. • Director • Henry Ford Community College • Dearborn, MI 48128-1495

Luke Edith J. • Librarian • Holbrook High School Library • Holbrook, AZ 86025 • AASL

Luke Joyce P. • Student • University of Southern Mississippi School of Library Science • Hattiesburg, MS 39406-5146

Luke Linda S. • Gainesville, FL 32605 • ALSC

Luke Terri Michele • Head of Adult Services • Cary Public Library • Cary, NC 27511 • PLA

Lukehart Wendy Bauder • Children's Librarian • District of Columbia Public Library • Washington, DC 20016 • ALSC

Luker Kenneth • Assistant Director • University of Utah Marriott Library • Salt Lake City, UT 84112-1179 • ACRL

Luks Lewis F. • Summerland Key, FL 33042

Lum Frances M. • Librarian • Chicksands Air Force Base • Chicksands, England

Lumaree Phoebe Miss • Fort Wayne, IN 46804 • ACRL ALCTS *Continuing*

Lumetta Joanne J. • Chief • Detroit Public Library Conely Branch • Detroit, MI 48210-2343

Lumley Arvina M. • Librarian • Kansas Talking Books Regional • Emporia, KS 66801 • AASL LITA LIRT LRRT

Lumley Helen R. • New Concord, OH 43762-1207 • AASL YALSA *Continuing*

Lumpkins Charles • Reference/Cataloging Librarian • Bloomsburg University Harvey A. Andruss Library • Bloomsburg, PA 17815 • ACRL ALCTS LAMA RASD

Lunas Susan • Conservator • Ohio University Vernon R. Alden Library • Athens, OH 45701-2978 • ALCTS

Lunce Carol S. • Bibl. Instr./Reference Ln. • University of Evansville • Evansville, IN 47722 • ACRL RASD NMRT

Lund Anne G. • Burke, VA 22015

Lund Barbara S. • Media Center Director • Lisle Senior High School • Lisle, IL 60532 • AASL YALSA

Lund Bernard A. • St. Paul, MN 55103 • ALCTS *Life*

Lund Ethel Beeler • Des Moines, IA 50311 • Continuing

Lund George H. • Project Librarian • University of Texas Ransom Humanities Research Center • Austin, TX 78713 • ACRL LHRT

Lund Katharine L. Miss • Santa Barbara, CA 93102 • Continuing

Lund Pat • Stoughton, WI 53589 • RASD

Lund Robert C. • Trustee • Kansas City Public Library • Kansas City, MO 64106 • ALTA

Lund Valerie M. • Trustee • Nieves M. Flores Memorial Library • Agana, GU 96910 • ALTA

Lundahl Margaret A. • Librarian • Lundahl Enterprises • Chicago, IL 60617 • ALCTS LITA ILERT

Lunde Diane B. • Conservation Librarian • Colorado State University William E. Morgan Library • Fort Collins, CO 80523 • ALCTS

Lunde Joyce E. • Assistant Librarian, Ref Serv • Northeastern University Dodge Library • Boston, MA 02115 • ACRL LAMA RASD GODORT

Lunden Elizabeth A. • Spring, TX 77373 • ACRL

Lundgard Joan • Library-Media Teacher • Bellarmine College Preparatory School • San Jose, CA 95126 • AASL YALSA

Lundgren Jimmie H. • Student • Florida State University School of Library and Information Studies • Tallahassee, FL 32306-2048 • SRRT

Lundgren Mary Em • Trustee • Kitchigami Regional Library • Pine River, MN 56474-0084

Lundgrin Karen • Librarian • Indian Woods Middle School • Shawnee Mission, KS 66207 • AASL

Lundin Anne • University of Southern Mississippi McCain Library & Archives • Hattiesburg, MS 39406-5148 • ALSC

Lundin Jane E. • Seattle, WA 98102 • AASL

Lundin Joan A. • Dept. Chair • West High School • Madison, WI 53705 • AASL

Lundin Marcia M. • Librarian • Cretin-Derham Hall High School Library • St Paul, MN 55116 • AASL

Lundquist Carmella R. • Librarian • Chicago Public Library Harold Washington Library • Chicago, IL 60605

Lundquist Cindy • Associate Librarian • Pepperdine University Plaza Library • Culver City, CA 90230 • ACRL

Lundquist Mitchell E. • Student • University of Wisconsin-Madison Memorial Library • Madison, WI 53706

Lundstrom Dave Dr. • Weber School District Office • Ogden, UT 84405 • AASL

Lundstrom Marie • Student • University of Wisconsin School of Library & Information Studies • Madison, WI 53706 • AASL IFRT NMRT

Lundstrom Thomas E. • Assistant Librarian • State University of New York (SUNY) Penfield Library • Oswego, NY 13126-3514

Lundy Christine • Montgomery County Department of Public Libraries Gaithersburg Regional Library • Gaithersburg, MD 20879

Lundy Kathryn R. • Lincoln, NE 68506 • ACRL *Continuing*

Lundy Linda R. • West Columbus High School • Cerro Gordo, NC 28430 • AASL

Lundy Winslow • Rare Book Cataloger • Bryn Mawr College Canaday Library • Bryn Mawr, PA 19010 • ACRL ALCTS MAGERT

Lungren John E. • Associate Librarian • Edgewood College Library • Madison, WI 53711

Lungren Millie L. • Director • Evangelical Covenant Church Resource Center • Chicago, IL 60625 • ALSC

Lunnon Elizabeth S. • Dunnellon, FL 32630 • AASL *Continuing*

Lunnon Rita A. • Associate Librarian • Stanford University Libraries Cecil H. Green Library • Stanford, CA 94305-6004 • ACRL

Lunsford Adrianne • Roswell, GA 30075 • Continuing

Lunsford Alice J. • Media Coordinator • Orange County Schools • Hillsborough, NC 27278

Lunsford Judith T. • Public Relations Officer • Atlanta-Fulton Public Library • Atlanta, GA 30303

Lunskis Michael J. • Clln Development Manager • Manatee County Public Library System • Bradenton, FL 34205 • YALSA

Lunt Ruth B. • Reference Librarian • Rochester Institute of Technology Wallace Memorial Library • Rochester, NY 14623-0887 • ACRL

Luoma G. Robert • Librarian • United States Government Printing Office • Washington, DC 20401

Lupa Robyn M. • Student • Gale Research, Inc. • Detroit, MI 48226 • IFRT NMRT

Lupia John N. • Student • Rutgers University School of Communication Information & Library Studies • New Brunswick, NJ 08903 • ACRL

Lupo Lawrence Dr. • Trustee • North Bellmore Public Library • N. Bellmore, NY 11710 • ALTA

Lupoletti Richard M. • Floral Park, NY 11001

Lupone George • Cleveland State University Library • Cleveland, OH 44115 • ACRL LAMA

Luquire Shari E. • Librarian • Alameda County Library Dublin Branch • Dublin, CA 94568 • YALSA

Lurie Debra • Librarian II • San Jose Public Library Seventrees Branch • San Jose, CA 95111

Lurie Syrul F. • Librarian • Brookline High School Burack Library • Brookline, MA 02146 • AASL YALSA

Luscomb Marilyn J. • Student • Wayne State University • Detroit, MI 48202 • AASL

Luse Nancy H. • Librarian • Buena High School • Sierra Vista, AZ 85635 • AASL LIRT

Lusey Beverly A. • Assistant Director • Bellevue Public Library • Bellevue, NE 68005 • RASD

Lushington Nolan • Assistant Professor • Southern Connecticut State University School of Libray Science & Instructional Technology • New Haven, CT 06515 • LAMA PLA

Lusk Eva-Maria • Children's Services Coordinator • Spokane Public Library Comstock Building Library • Spokane, WA 99201-0976 • ALSC YALSA

Lusk Marie N. • El Paso, TX 79930 • Continuing

Lusk Shirley S. • Librarian • Oxford Academy • Westbrook, CT 06498

Lusko Marjorie M. • Student • Wayne State University Library Science Program • Detroit, MI 48202 • ALSC SRRT

Lusnia Albert J. • Student • University of Cincinnati • Cincinnati, OH 45221-0033

Lussier Christine • Fort Wayne, IN 46807

Lussky Joan P. • Catlgr. of Sci & Tech Materials • University of Pennsylvania Library Van Pelt-Dietrich Library Center • Philadelphia, PA 19104-6206 • ACRL ALCTS SRRT

Lust Darlene F. • Yakima, WA 98902

Lust Vernon G. • Davis, CA 95616 • ACRL ALCTS

Luster Arlene L. • Command Librarian/Library Dir. • United States Air Force HQ PACAF/MWOL • Hickam AFB, HI 96853-5001 • LAMA AFLRT FLRT

Luster Louveller M. • Virginia Commonwealth University • Richmond, VA 23284-2033 • ACRL EMIERT SRRT

Lustig Joy G. • Student • State University of New York at Albany School of Information Science & Policy • Albany, NY 12222 • AASL

Lute Harriet • Denver, CO 80231 • LAMA PLA *Continuing*

Lutenske Paul S. • Branch Librarian • Bay County Library System • Bay City, MI 48708 • PLA

Luteri Laura • Mount Prospect Public Library • Mount Prospect, IL 60056 • PLA

Luters Aina • San Francisco, CA 94118

Lutes Judith H. • Student • State University of New York at Albany School of Information Science & Policy • Albany, NY 12222 • AASL YALSA

Lutes Lisa M. • Student • Wayne State University Library Science Program • Detroit, MI 48202 • PLA AFLRT IFRT SRRT

Lutes Michael A • Reference Librarian • University of Notre Dame Libraries • Notre Dame, IN 46556 • RASD GODORT MAGERT SRRT

Lutes Virgil C. • Director • Eastchester Public Library • Eastchester, NY 10709

Lutgens Carol J. • Linden High School • Linden, MI 48451 • AASL

Luther Judy • Faxon Company Inc. • Westwood, MA 02090 • ACRL LITA

Luthy Jean M. • Librarian • Canmore Public Library • Canmore AB, Canada • PLA

Luton Barbara C. • Director • Shaker Heights Public Library • Shaker Heights, OH 44120 • PLA

Lutovsky Margaret • Milwaukee, WI 53223 • Continuing

Lutton Helen M. • Gibsonia, PA 15044 • AASL YALSA *Continuing*

Lutz Alexandra • History & Social Science • New York Public Library Mid-Manhattan Branch • New York, NY 10016 • ACRL RASD GODORT IRRT

Lutz George J. • Hempstead, NY 11550 • PLA

Lutz Janet M. • Sequim, WA 98382-9205

Lutz Judith A. • Audio-Visual Services Librarian • Compaq Computer Corp. • Houston, TX 77269-2000 • LITA

Lutz Maija M. • Hd of Tech Serv & Clln Devel Ln. • Harvard University Tozzer Library • Cambridge, MA 02138 • ACRL ALCTS

Lutz Marilyn • Systems Librarian • University of Maine Raymond H. Fogler Library • Orono, ME 04469 • LITA

Lutzker Marilyn • Chief Librarian • John Jay College of Criminal Justice • New York, NY 10019 • ACRL LAMA EMIERT

Lux Catherine • Director, L.R.C. • University of Arkansas Libraries • Fayetteville, AR 72701-1201

Lux Martha W. • Oak Ridge, TN 37830

Luxner Ann F. • Clarks Summit, PA 18411-1431 • LITA

Lybecker Linda • Reference Librarian • Washington County Cooperative Library Service • Aloha, OR 97006 • RASD

Lyday Donna J • Student • Texas Woman's University School of Library & Information Studies • Denton, TX 76204

Lyddy Ruth R. • Arlington, MA 02174 • IFRT SRRT

Lyders Josette A. • Houston, TX 77035 • AASL YALSA

Lyders Richard • Executive Director • Houston Academy of Medicine Texas Medical Center Library • Houston, TX 77030 • ACRL LAMA

Lydia Mary Sr • Library Director • Madonna University Library • Livonia, MI 48150 • ACRL

Lydick Karen R. • Media Spec • Fulton Junior High School • Indianapolis, IN 46214 • AASL

Lydy Jane E. • Reference/Technical Services • West Bend Community Memorial Library • West Bend, WI 53095

Lyle Jack Ward • Documents Librarian • Indiana State University • Terre Haute, IN 47809 • GODORT

Lyle Martha E. • Engineering Ref. Librarian • Clemson University Robert Muldrow Cooper Library • Clemson, SC 29634-3001 • ACRL

Lyle Stanley P. • Reference Librarian • University of Northern Iowa Donald O. Rod Library • Cedar Falls, IA 50613-3675 • RASD

Lyles Laura • Assistant Reference • Michigan City Public Library • Michigan City, IN 46360

Lyles Sandra H. • Hope Valley Elementary School • Durham, NC 27704 • AASL NMRT

Lyman Helen H. • Orchard Pk, NY 14127 • PLA RASD *Life*

Lyman Sylvia L. • Librarian-Cataloger • East Los Angeles Community College • Monterey Park, CA 91754 • ACRL EMIERT ILERT IRRT

Lynam Les • Warrensburg, MO 64093 • LITA NMRT

Lynaugh Ethel M. • Sun City Center, FL 33573 • Continuing

Lynch-Brown Carol • Professor • Florida State University Department of Childhood Education • Tallahassee, FL 32306-2047 • ALSC

Lynch Anne L. • Librarian • University of Southern California Doheny Library • Los Angeles, CA 90089-0182 • ACRL LITA RASD LIRT

Lynch Beverly P. • Dean, Grad Sch of Inf Sci • University of California-Los Angeles (UCLA) • Los Angeles, CA 90024-1450 • ACRL ALCTS LITA RASD IRRT   *Life*

Lynch Candace • Assistant Librarian • Clairbourn School • San Gabriel, CA 91775 • ALSC

Lynch Catherine E. • Elementary School Librarian • Monroe County Community Schools • Bloomington, IN 47401 • AASL ALSC

Lynch Clifford A. • Director, DLA • University of California • Oakland, CA 94612-3550 • LITA

Lynch D'Nis L. • Library Department Head • Upper St. Clair High School School District • Upper St. Clair, PA 15241 • AASL YALSA

Lynch Divina M. • San Jose, CA 95120

Lynch Eugene A. • Director of Media Services • Groton Public Schools • Mystic, CT 06355 • AASL LITA IFRT MAGERT

Lynch Isabelle C. • North East, MD 21901 • PLA

Lynch Karen A. • Redford, MI 48239

Lynch Kathy A. • Coor. Library Technical Services • Maricopa County Community Colleges • Tempe, AZ 85281-6941 • ACRL ALCTS LAMA LITA CLENE

Lynch M Frances • Granite City, IL 62040 • AASL YALSA   *Life*

Lynch Margaret • Assistant Deputy Director • Buffalo & Erie County Public Library • Buffalo, NY 14203

Lynch Margie R. • Hattiesburg, MS 39401 • Continuing

Lynch Mary C. • Reference Librarian • Georgia Institute of Technology Price Gilbert Memorial Library • Atlanta, GA 30332-0900 • RASD

Lynch Mary Carole • Danville Community College Learning Resource Center • Danville, VA 24541 • ACRL ALCTS RASD

Lynch Mary Jo • Director, Office for Research • American Library Association • Chicago, IL 60611-2795 • ACRL PLA RASD LRRT   *Life*

Lynch Mary-Alice • Hd,Technical Services • Schenectady County Community College Library Resources Center • Schenectady, NY 12305 • ACRL

Lynch Maureen M. • Student • University of Pittsburgh School of Library and Information Science • Pittsburgh, PA 15260

Lynch Michael S. • Systems Librarian • Bucknell University Bertrand Library • Lewisburg, PA 17837-2086 • LITA

Lynch Minnie-Lou • Trustee • Allen Parish Libraries • Oakdale, LA 71463 • ALTA PLA

Lynch Mollie S. • Director • Independence Township Library • Clarkston, MI 48346 • LAMA LITA PLA

Lynch Paula M. • Student • University of Hartford Mortensen Library • West Hartford, CT 06117 • ALSC EMIERT IFRT NMRT SRRT

Lynch Robert J. • Assoc Dir, Technical Service • University of Massachusetts University Library • Amherst, MA 01003

Lynch Rosemary C. • Librarian • Rochester Hills Public Library • Rochester, MI 48307 • ALSC

Lynch Sherry • Asst. Dir. for Admin. Services • Broward County Division of Libraries Broward County Library • Fort Lauderdale, FL 33301

Lynch Terence R. • Sales Representative • Library Interiors, Inc. • Mataire, LA 70002

Lynch Timothy P. • Coordinator of Continuing Educ. • Nebraska Library Commission • Lincoln, NE 68508 • ASCLA PLA SRRT

Lynch Vivian L. • Librarian • Hill Central School Library • New Haven, CT 06519 • AASL

Lynden Frederick C. • Asst Univ Ln for Tech Services • Brown University Rockefeller Library • Providence, RI 02912 • ACRL ALCTS

Lyndes Lynn • Student • Clarion University of Pennsylvania College of Library Science • Clarion, PA 16214 • AASL

Lynds Katherine H. • Mill Valley, CA 94941 • ALSC

Lyngholm Miriam I. • Kalispell, MT 59901

Lyngholm Nancy A. • Reference Librarian • Moline Public Library • Moline, IL 61265

Lynk Kelly • Unisys Corporation • Eagan, MN 55164-0663

Lynn Ann D. • Y/A Reference Librarian • Berkeley Public Library Claremont Branch • Berkeley, CA 94705

Lynn Barbara A. • Librarian • The American Companies • Topeka, KS 66601 • AASL ALSC YALSA ERT IFRT

Lynn Brian E. • Trustee • Elmont Public Library • Elmont, NY 11003 • ALTA

Lynn Kathleen L. • Louisville, KY 40241

Lynn Michael • Palos Heights Public Library • Palos Heights, IL 60463

Lynn Patricia D. • Haverford College James P. Magill Library • Haverford, PA 19041 • ACRL RASD GODORT

Lyon Bruce C. • Assistant Reference Librarian • Miami-Dade Public Library System • Miami, FL 33130-1504

Lyon Charlotte G. • La Jolla, CA 92037 • Continuing

Lyon David A. IV • Director • York County Library • Rock Hill, SC 29730 • PLA

Lyon Elaine R. • Head, Adult Services • Liverpool Public Library • Liverpool, NY 13088 • PLA RASD

Lyon George P. Mr. • Bucks County Free Library • Doylestown, PA 18901 • ALTA

Lyon Katherine W. • Branch Manager • Tucson Public Library Wilmot Branch • Tucson, AZ 85710 • PLA IFRT

Lyon Lucy M. • Coordinator of Library Services • Little Rock School District • Little Rock, AR 72201 • AASL

Lyon Martha V. • Adult Services Librarian • Oswego City Library • Oswego, NY 13126

Lyon Nina • Dir., of Main Library Service • Public Library of Charlotte & Mecklenburg County • Charlotte, NC 28202 • PLA

Lyon Peggy • Library Media Specialist • Abraham Lincoln High School • Denver, CO 80219 • AASL

Lyon Richard M. • Chicago, IL 60603

Lyon Sara Jane • Chief Reference Division • City College of New York (CUNY) • New York, NY 10031 • ACRL RASD LIRT

Lyon Susan T. • Head, Health Science Library • University of North Carolina • Chapel Hill, NC 27599-3902 • RASD

Lyons Agatha A. • Richmond, VA 23225 • LAMA PLA

Lyons Amy G. • Williamsville, NY 14221 • ACRL LAMA LITA

Lyons Anita Z. • Media Specialist • Birches School • Turnersville, NJ 08012 • AASL

Lyons Anne WN • Assistant • Auerbach Art Library Wadsworth Atheneum • Hartford, CT 06103

Lyons Carol C. • Education Program Specialist • United States Department of Education • Washington, DC 20208

Lyons Cynthia J. • Community Librarian • Sno-Isle Regional Library Marysville Branch • Marysville, WA 98270 • PLA

Lyons Diana • Branch Librarian • Maui Library District • Wailuku, HI 96793 • PLA

Lyons Evelyn • Millersville University of Pennsylvania • Millersville, PA 17551-0302 • ACRL LITA

Lyons Grace Jean • Librarian • District of Columbia Public Library Martin Luther King Memorial Library • Washington, DC 20001 • ASCLA IFRT

Lyons James • Manager of Adult Education • Saint Louis Public Library • St. Louis, MO 63103-2389 • PLA

Lyons Jennifer M. • Oswego, NY 13126 • AASL

Lyons Margaret J. Mrs. • Holmes Beach, FL 34218

Lyons Marian • Trustee • Jackson-Hinds Library System • Jackson, MS 39201 • ALTA

Lyons Marlene M. • Learning Resource Specialist • Cedarcrest Junior High School • Spanaway, WA 98387 • AASL

Lyons Melinda L. • Bangkok 10400, Thailand • ACRL IRRT

Lyons Molly M. • Cataloger • Saint Patrick's Seminary • Menlo Park, CA 94025

Lyons Pamela O. • Coordinator • Birmingham Public & Jefferson County Free Library Avondale Branch • Birmingham, AL 35222 • RASD SRRT

Lyons Phyllis R. • Librarian • Gannett Foundation • Arlington, VA 22209

Lyons Robert B. • Trustee • Schaumburg Township District Library • Schaumburg, IL 60194

Lyons Susan • Head, Reference • Cherry Hill Free Public Library • Cherry Hill, NJ 08034 • LITA

Lyons Sylvia C. • Gainesville Middle School • Gainesville, TX 76240 • AASL

Lyons Virginia M. • Adults Librarian • Boston Public Library Hyde Park Branch • Hyde Park, MA 02136

Lyons Wendy • Manager Tape/Online Services • R. R. Bowker • New Providence, NJ 07974 • LITA

Lysiak Lynne D. • Automation Librarian • Appalachian State University Carol Grotnes Belk Library • Boone, NC 28608 • LITA

Lytinen Susan L. • Assistant Head of Technical • Gail Borden Public Library • Elgin, IL 60120

Lytle Charlotte W. • Springfield, OH 45502-1323 • ALCTS ASCLA   *Continuing*

Lytle Marguerite S. • Rydal, PA 19046-1628 • Continuing

Lytle Penny W. • Automated Services • New Orleans Public Library • New Orleans, LA 70140

Ma Evelyn L. • Fordham University School of Law Library • New York, NY 10023

Ma Helen Y. • Automation Implementation Coor • Detroit Public Library • Detroit, MI 48202 • LITA

Ma Margaret • Branch Librarian • New York Public Library West New Brighton Branch • Staten Island, NY 10310

Ma Marlene S. • Student • University of California-Berkeley School of Library & Information Studies • Berkeley, CA 94720

Ma Susan Y. • Senior Librarian • San Jose Public Library Rosegarden Branch • San Jose, CA 95126 • EMIERT

Ma Tai-Loi • Curator • University of Chicago East Asian Library • Chicago, IL 60637 • ACRL ALCTS

Ma Yongli • Student • University of South Carolina College of Library & Information Science • Columbia, SC 29208

MaLamut Harriet • Marley Elementary School • Glen Burnie, MD 21061 • AASL

Maack David J. • Librarian • University of Washington Suzzallo Library • Seattle, WA 98195 • GODORT

Maack Mary Niles • Associate Professor • University of California Los Angeles Graduate School of Library & Information Science • Los Angeles, CA 90024 • PLA RASD IRRT LHRT

Maag Albert F. • Librarian • Capital University Library • Columbus, OH 43209 • ACRL

Maas Dorothy Wichmann • Children's Librarian • Lodi Public Library • Lodi, CA 95240 • ALSC

Maas Norman L. • Director • Public Libraries of Saginaw • Saginaw, MI 48605 • PLA SRRT

Maas Patricia A. • Librarian • Washington School District School Moon Mountain School • Phoenix, AZ 85029 • AASL

Maaskant Simona • Librarian • The Kings College • Edmonton AB, T5H 2M1 Canada • ACRL

Mabe Michael R. • Salt Lake City Public Library • Salt Lake City, UT 84111

Maberry Carolyn Sue • Director Otis/Parsons Art Lib • Otis Parsons School of Design Library • Los Angeles, CA 90057 • ACRL IFRT SRRT VRT

Mabomba R. S. • National Librarian • National Library Service • Lilongwe 3, Malawi

Mabry Mariana G. • Deputy Clerk • United States District Court • Dallas, TX 75242 • PLA

Mabson Robert L. Rev. • Mt. Holly, AR 71758 • ACRL ALCTS LITA RASD   *Continuing*

Mabwa Rose N. • Student • Illinois State Psychiatric Institute • Chicago, IL 60612 • IFRT

Mac Kinnon Janice E. • Librarian • Stuart-Hobson Middle School • Washington, DC 20002 • AASL

Mac Leod June F. • Manager of Library Services • Gray Cary Ames & Frye Law Library • San Diego, CA 92101

Mac Leod Valerie • Mgr, Online Database Licensing • UMI Data Courier Inc. • Louisville, KY 40202 • LITA

MacAdam Barbara A. • Head, Undergraduate Library • University of Michigan Libraries • Ann Arbor, MI 48109-1205 • ACRL LRRT

MacAdam Barbara L. • Student • Kent State University School of Library & Information Science • Kent, OH 44242-0001 • LITA FLRT NMRT

MacAdam Muriel F. • Rochester, NY 14626 • Continuing

MacArthur Marit S. • Serials Catlgr/Automation Spec. • University of Colorado at Denver Auraria Library • Denver, CO 80204 • ACRL ALCTS LITA

MacBeth In-Cheung • Murfreesboro, TN 37129

MacCallum Martha B. • Coordinator,Young Peoples • Lincoln City Libraries • Lincoln, NE 68508

MacCann Donnarae • Iowa City, IA 52246 • EMIERT SRRT

MacConomy Edward N. Dr. • National Referral Center-Chief • Library of Congress • Washington, DC 20541 • ACRL RASD   *Life*

MacCormick Kristina • Delmar, NY 12054

MacCusworth Frances • Dir of Division Programs • Ontario Library Association • Toronto ON, M5C 1M3 Canada

MacDonald Ann • Middlesex County College Library • Edison, NJ 08818-3050 • LITA

MacDonald Barbara B. • Lakewood, CO 80228 • LITA

MacDonald Bernice • Deputy Director • New York Public Library • New York, NY 10018-2788 • PLA

MacDonald Brad S. • Student • Clarion University of Pennsylvania Rena M. Carlson Library • Clarion, PA 16214 • SRRT

MacDonald Carol M. • Library Systems Manager • University of Regina • Regina SK, S4S 0A2 Canada • LITA

MacDonald Christine S. • Planning Officer • Metropolitan Toronto Library Board • Toronto ON, M4W 2G8 Canada • LAMA PLA

MacDonald Cynthia R. • Children's Services Coordinator • Fresno County Free Library • Fresno, CA 93721-2285

MacDonald Eleanor K. • Librarian II • Beverly Hills Public Library • Beverly Hills, CA 90210

MacDonald Elsie Sinclair • Riverside, RI 02915-4824 • Continuing

MacDonald Eric C. • Preservation Librarian • University of California General Library • Irvine, CA 92713 • ACRL ALCTS

MacDonald Gerald J. • Curator of the Modern Library • Hispanic Society of America • New York, NY 10032 • ACRL

MacDonald Harriet P. • New Smyrna, FL 32168 • AASL YALSA *Life*

MacDonald Hugh • Coordinator for Public Services • Texas Christian University Mary Couts Burnett Library • Fort Worth, TX 76129 • ACRL

MacDonald Judy • Poudre School District R-1 • Fort Collins, CO 80521 • AASL

MacDonald Linda B. • Curriculum Material Ctr Coor. • University of Vermont Bailey Howe Library • Burlington, VT 05405-0036

MacDonald Margaret Read • Children's Librarian • King County Library System Bothell Branch • Bothell, WA 98011 • ALSC

MacDonald Margot B. • Claremont, CA 91711 • Continuing

MacDonald Roderick • Director • Dakota County Library • Eagan, MN 55123 • RASD YALSA

MacDougall Frank C. • Office of the Asst. Provost • Michigan State University Lifelong Education Library • East Lansing, MI 48824 • ACRL LITA *Life*

MacEachron Lyn L. • Reference Librarian • Pontiac Public Library • Pontiac, MI 48058 • RASD IFRT

MacEwan Bonnie • Coor. of Collection Development • Pennsylvania State University Libraries • University Park, PA 16802 • ACRL ALCTS RASD

MacEwen Virginia B. • George Washington University Gelman Library • Washington, DC 20052 • ACRL RASD

MacFarland Janet • Librarian • Newman Smith High School • Carrollton, TX 75006 • AASL IFRT

MacFarland Scott D. • President • Turner Subscriptions • New York, NY 10003 • ACRL ALCTS LITA PLA

MacFarlane Francis X. • Director • Washington Parish Library • Franklinton, LA 70438

MacGahan Carroll • Trustee • Mid-Hudson Library System • Poughkeepsie, NY 12601

MacGibeny Robert R. • Student • Rutgers University School of Communication Information & Library Studies • New Brunswick, NJ 08903

MacGown Madge • University of Windsor Leddy Library • Windsor ON, N9B 3P4 Canada • ACRL LAMA

MacIntosh Alison J. • Marketing Manager • Canadian Standards Association Electronic Publishing • Rexdale, ON, Canada

MacIntosh Helen A. • Mississauga ON, L5G 2G9 Canada

MacKay Lynn P. • Knowledge Link Services, Inc. • Nepean, ON, K2G 0T3 Canada • LITA

MacKechnie Nancy S. • Cura/Rare Bks & Manuscripts • Vassar College Library • Poughkeepsie, NY 12601 • ACRL

MacKeever V. Kay • Glendale, AZ 85302 • ACRL RASD LIRT

MacKellar Dare C. • Senior Library Technical Asst. • University of West Florida John C. Pace Library • Pensacola, FL 32514

MacKellar Pamela • Albuquerque Technical Vocational Institute • Albuquerque, NM 87106 • LAMA

MacKenzie Catherine M. • Student • Louisiana State University School of Library & Information Science • Baton Rouge, LA 70803-3290

MacKenzie Linda • Director of Public Services • North York Public Library • North York ON, M2N 5N9 Canada • LAMA PLA

MacKenzie Marjorie F. • Librarian II • Washington State University Library • Pullman, WA 99164-5610 • ACRL LIRT

MacKinney Ellie • Elgin Unit School District 46 Adminstration Office • Elgin, IL 60120 • AASL YALSA

MacKinnon Dennis A. • Director, Communication Cons. • Software Kinetics, Ltd. • Stittsville, ON, K2S 1E7 Canada • LITA

MacKinnon Joan G. • Head of Technical Services • Piscataway Public Library Westergard Branch • Piscataway, NJ 08854 • ALCTS

MacKintosh Pamela J. • University of Michigan Libraries • Ann Arbor, MI 48109-1205 • ACRL

MacLaren Brinley M. • Neosho, MO 64850

MacLaughlin Elissa V. • Librarian • Doherty School • Cincinnati, OH 45206 • AASL

MacLean Dougald L. • Trustee • Queens Borough Public Library • Jamaica, NY 11432 • ALTA PLA

MacLean Eleanor Anne • Librarian • McGill University Library • Montreal PQ, Canada • ACRL RASD

MacLean Ellen G. • Librarian • Department of Education • St. Thomas, VI 00801 • AASL EMIERT

MacLean Paul D. Jr. • Government Documents Librarian • State University of New York (SUNY) College at Geneseo Milne Library • Geneseo, NY 14454-1498 • GODORT

MacLean Susan E. • Library Director • Cheboygan Area Public Library • Cheboygan, MI 49721 • PLA

MacLeish Kay J. • Librarian • Denmark Schools • Denmark, WI 54208

MacLeish Margaret A. • Tucson Public Library Marana Branch Library • Marana, AZ 85653 • LITA PLA

MacLennan Birdie • Serials Cataloger • University of Vermont Bailey Howe Library • Burlington, VT 05405-0036 • ALCTS LITA SRRT

MacLeod James M. • Library of Congress • Washington, DC 20541

MacLeod Judith M. • Music & Humanities Cataloger • Southern Illinois University Delyte W. Morris Library • Carbondale, IL 62901-6632

MacLeod Margaret • Baltimore County Public Library • Towson, MD 21204 • ALSC

MacLeod Mary L. • Arts Cataloguer • Acadia University Library • Wolfville NS, B0P 1X0 Canada • ACRL ALCTS LAMA LITA

MacLeod Stephen E. • Head of Reference Department • University of California-Irvine Library • Irvine, CA 92713 • ACRL LAMA RASD

MacMillan Gary D. • Associate University Librarian • University of Hawaii Library • Honolulu, HI 96822 • ALCTS LITA

MacMorris Lee M. • Laguna Niguel, CA 92677 • PLA

MacMurdy Laura L. • Student • Texas Woman's University School of Library & Information Studies • Denton, TX 76204

MacNaughton M. H. Mrs. • South Euclid, OH 44121

MacNeil Roderick • Senior Business Analyst • TMF Inc. • Princeton, NJ 08540 • LAMA SRRT

MacNeil Stephen • Systems Analyst • Acadia Univeraity • Wolfville NS, B0P 1X0 Canada • LITA

MacNeill Daniel S. • Director • Union County Public Library • Monroe, NC 28110

MacNeish Judith J. • Student • Rosary College Graduate School of Library & Information Science • River Forest, IL 60305

MacPhail Jessica • Director • Northwestern Regional Library • Elkin, NC 28621 • LAMA PLA

MacPherson Jean • Mayslanding, NJ 08330

MacRae Catherine M.G. • Young Adult Librarian • Boulder Public Library • Boulder, CO 80306 • YALSA

MacRae Jean M. • Duluth, MN 55803 • AASL YALSA *Continuing*

MacRitchie Andrea E. • Westfield, NJ 07090 • ACRL PLA RASD

MacVicar Suzanne M. • Library Media Specialist • Burcham Elementary School • Lake Wood, CA 90712-3009

MacWilliam Mary • Associate Director • San Francisco State University J. Paul Leonard Library • San Francisco, CA 94132

MacWilliams Sylvia E. • Director Library Services • Southwest Washington Medical Center Library Services • Vancouver, WA 98668

MacWithey Mary E. • University of Texas at Dallas University Library • Richardson, TX 75083-0643 • NMRT

Macari Joy L. • Senior Librarian/Acquisitions • San Jose Public Library • San Jose, CA 95113 • ALCTS PLA

Macaulay Joanna L. • Student • Drexel University College of Information Studies • Philadelphia, PA 19104-2875 • AASL

Macbeth Melora A. • Director • Salina Free Library • Syracuse, NY 13211 • LAMA PLA

Maccaferri James T. • Clarion University of Pennsylvania • Clarion, PA 16214 • ACRL ALCTS LITA

Maccarone Barbara A. • Student • University of Rhode Island Graduate School of Library & Information Studies • Kingston, RI 02881-0815 • ALTA PLA

Macchietto Donna D. • Librarian • Tarleton State University • Stephenville, TX 76402

Macdonald Maggie • ChinookArch Library Project • Lethbridge, AB, T1H 0H5 Canada • LAMA

Macek Carol • Central Librarian • Dearborn Department of Libraries Henry Ford Centennial Library • Dearborn, MI 48126 • PLA RASD EMIERT

Macek Rosanne M. • Manager, Library Operations • Apple Computer, Inc. Library • Cupertino, CA 95014 • LAMA LITA

Macer Robert J. • Albuquerque, NM 87108

Machado Dianne L. • Acquistions Librarian • Adams State College Library • Alamosa, CO 81102

Machado Lori A. • Library Technician • Orestimba High School • Newman, CA 95360

Machael Carol • Trustee • Clinton Public Library • Clinton, IA 52732 • ALTA

Machak Patricia • Supervisory • Waukegan Public Library • Waukegan, IL 60085 • ALCTS

Machan Winifred E. • Cleveland Heights, OH 44118 • ALSC

Machin Mary S. • Doctoral Student • Texas Woman's University School of Library & Information Studies • Denton, TX 76204 • RASD LRRT SRRT

Machovec George S. • Library Technology & Systems • Arizona State University Library Technology & Systems • Tempe, AZ 85287 • ACRL LITA

Machules Regina B • Senior Librarian • New York Public Library West New Brighton Branch • Staten Island, NY 10310 • ALSC

Maciejak Lisa Richland • Director • Floyd Memorial Library • Greenport, NY 11944 • PLA IFRT

Maciejewski Felice E. • HSSE Circulation Librarian • Tulane University Howard-Tilton Memorial Library • New Orleans, LA 70118 • ACRL

Macin Colette P. • Librarian • Commonwealth College • Norfolk, VA 23510 • ACRL

Maciolek Penny • Student • San Jose State University Division of Library & Information Science • San Jose, CA 95192-0029

Maciuszko Jerzy J. Dr • Berea, OH 44017 • ACRL *Continuing*

Mack Edna Ballard • Geneseo, NY 14454-1105 • Continuing

Mack Helen P. • Manager, Acquisitions Dept. • Lehigh University Libraries Linderman Library 30 • Bethlehem, PA 18015-3067 • ALCTS

Mack Perry Anne • Cataloger • Loudoun County Public Library • Leesburg, VA 22075 • ALCTS LITA PLA

Mack Phyllis G. • Regional Librarian • New York Public Library Countee Cullen Regional Library • New York, NY 10030

Mack Sara R. • Kutztown, PA 19530 • Continuing

Mack Theodore D. • Director • Paul Smiths College Frank L. Cubley Library • Paul Smiths, NY 12970

Mack Wilmetta S. • Arlington, VA 22207

Mackay Shelagh M. • Head of Technical Services • University of California-Davis Institute of Governmental Affairs • Davis, CA 95616-8617 • ALCTS LITA

Macke Barbara M. • Ln. Physical Sciences & Engineer • United States Air Force Academic Library Institute of Technology • Wright-Patterson AFB, OH 45433 • FLRT

Mackellar Laurie A. • Student • University of Kentucky College of Library & Information Science • Lexington, KY 40506-0391

Mackevicius Aldona • Kew Garden Hills, NY 11435 • Continuing

Mackey Arthur Jr. • Roosevelt Public Library • Roosevelt, NY 11575 • ALTA

Mackey Ellen J. • Denver Botanic Gardens • Denver, CO 80206 • AASL

Mackey Jean P. • Head Cataloger • University of Tulsa McFarlin Library • Tulsa, OK 74104-3189 • ACRL ALCTS LITA

Mackey Kitty J. • Reference Librarian • Converse College Mickel Library • Spartanburg, SC 29302-0006

Mackey Laure M. • Student • Syracuse University School of Information Studies • Syracuse, NY 13244-4100 • LITA SRRT

Mackey Lyla T. Mrs. • Nashville, TN 37210 • ACRL RASD *Continuing*

Mackey Margaret • Media Specialist • Andrew Jackson High School • Kershaw, SC 29067 • AASL YALSA

Mackey Neosha A. • Associate Dean • Southwest Missouri State University Library • Springfield, MO 65804-0095 • ACRL LAMA

Mackey Patricia E. • Librarian • Rockefeller University Library • New York, NY 10021 • ACRL LAMA

Mackey Sandra L. • Pueblo, CO 81001

Mackey Susan A. • Media Specialist • Montgomery County Public Schools • Rockville, MD 20850 • AASL YALSA

Mackey Terry K. • Librarian • University of South Carolina at Spartanburg-Library • Spartanburg, SC 29303

Mackler Mark E. • Bancroft Avery & McAlister Attorneys at Law • San Francisco, CA 94111

Macklin Colleen • Librarian • Charles D. Owen High School • Black Mountain, NC 28711 • YALSA

Macklin James R. • Director of Library • Macon College Library • Macon, GA 31297

Macksam David • Director • Clermont County Public Library • Batavia, OH 45103-3192 • LAMA PLA

Mackzum Mary F. • Head Librarian • Toledo Blade • Toledo, OH 43660

Maclachlan Rachel C. • Director of Security • San Francisco Public Library • San Francisco, CA 94102 • LAMA IFRT SRRT

MacIver Bonnie • Director • Leach Public Library • Wahpeton, ND 58075

Macomber Jean L. • Riverside City & County Public Library • Riverside, CA 92502-0468 • LITA

Macomber Nancy • Documents/Reference Librarian • Queens College Benjamin S. Rosenthal Library • Flushing, NY 11367-0904 • GODORT

Macon Myra • Director of Libraries • Delta State University • Cleveland, MS 38733 • ACRL
Macoy Gladys M. • Rochester, MN 55901
Macrae Denise C. • Port Washington, NY 11050 • ALSC
Macy Brenda G. • Director • Hardin County Public Library • Elizabethtown, KY 42701 • PLA
Maczuga Ann • Phoenix Public Library Ironwood Branch • Phoenix, AZ 85041 • ALSC PLA
Madacsi Nancy W. • Basking Ridge, NJ 07920 • RASD
Madak Gail I. • Student • Rutgers University School of Communication Information & Library Studies • New Brunswick, NJ 08903
Madan Raj Mrs. • State University of New York Drake Memorial Library • Brockport, NY 14420 • ACRL
Madara Bella J. • Librarian • Oakland Public Library Golden Gate Branch • Oakland, CA 94608
Madarash-Hill Cherie • Cuyahoga Fall, OH 44221
Madatian George A. • Librarian • La Canada High School • La Canada, CA 91011 • AASL
Madaus J. Richard Dr. • Director • College Center for Library Automation • Tallahassee, FL 32304 • ACRL LITA
Maddalena Elisa M. • Childrens Librarian • Pacific Grove Public Library • Pacific Grove, CA 93950 • ALSC
Madden Irene Dasco • Librarian • MacDuffie School • Springfield, MA 01105 • AASL
Madden Mary K. • Catgr • University Microfilms International • Ann Arbor, MI 48106-1346 • LITA
Madden Michael J. • Director • Schaumburg Township District Library • Schaumburg, IL 60194 • PLA
Madden Robert J. • Special Collection Librarian • Keene State College Mason Library • Keene, NH 03431 • ACRL
Madden Sallyann • Northampton Senior High School Library • Northampton, PA 18067 • AASL
Madden Serena L. • Student • Long Island University Palmer School of Library & Information Science • Greenvale, NY 11548
Madden Susan B. • Literacy & Young Adult Serv Coor • King County Library System • Seattle, WA 98109-5191 • ASCLA PLA YALSA CLENE IFRT
Madden Terry Jo • Reference Librarian • Boise State University Library • Boise, ID 83725
Maddox Aileen F. • Sioux Falls, SD 57105
Maddox Barbara J. • Sarah Lawrence College Esther Raushenbush Library • Bronxville, NY 10708
Maddox Cindy S. • Student • Emporia State University Emporia in the Rockies • Denver, CO 80204
Maddox Connie W. • Student • University of Kentucky College of Library & Information Science • Lexington, KY 40506-0391 • AASL ALSC
Maddox Deborah G. • Student • University of South Carolina College of Library & Information Science • Columbia, SC 29208
Maddox Eugenia • Tulsa, OK 74114 • ACRL ALCTS *Continuing*
Maddox Jim F. • Trustee • Atlanta-Fulton Public Library • Atlanta, GA 30303 • PLA
Maddox Kelly A. • Fort Worth, TX 76133
Maddox Margaret E. • Student • Kent State University School of Library & Information Science • Kent, OH 44242-0001
Maddox Maria C. • Cambridge, MA 02138
Maddox Nova C. • Base Librarian • U S Air Force Base Library • APO San Francisco, CA 96239 • PLA AFLRT
Maddox Trean A. • Tulsa, OK 74114 • AASL YALSA *Continuing*
Maddox Vivian • Jonesboro, AR 72401 • Continuing
Maddox W. Jane • President • Library Consultants Inc • Columbia, MD 21045 • ACRL ALCTS LITA
Maddux Bonnie M. • Student • University of Tennessee-Knoxville Graduate School of Library & Information Science • Knoxville, TN 37996-4330 • ALSC
Maddux Linda B. • Student • University of Alabama School of Library & Information Studies • Tuscaloosa, AL 35487-0252
Maddux Michael D. • Portland, OR 97201
Madell Phillip • Topeka Public Library • Topeka, KS 66604-1374
Mader Marion C. • Philadelphia, PA 19111 • ACRL *Continuing*
Mader Sharon B. • Associate Director • DePaul University Libraries • Chicago, IL 60614 • ACRL
Madere Sue Ellen • Shorewood, WI 53211
Madero Elizabeth • Branch Librarian • District of Columbia Public Librry Takoma Park Branch • Washington, DC 20012
Madewell Ramona J. • Automation Project Librarian • Vanderbilt University Library • Nashville, TN 37240-0007
Madigan C. Ann • Media Specialist • West Grade School Library • Stanfield, OR 97875 • AASL
Madigan Ellen E. • Student • University of Alabama School of Library and Information Studies • Tuscaloosa, AL 35487
Madisen Randi L. • Minnesota Legislative Reference Library • Saint Paul, MN 55155
Madison Irma J. • Librarian • Calloway Elementary School • Birmingham, AL 35207 • AASL NMRT
Madison Olivia M. A. • Asst. Dir. for Public Svs. • Iowa State University Library • Ames, IA 50011-2140 • ACRL ALCTS RASD
Madonna Diana R. • Metairie, LA 70001
Mador Harriet S. • Garland, TX 75043 • LAMA PLA
Madore Anne • Head Children's Services • Bangor Public Library • Bangor, ME 04401 • ALSC
Madorin Susan C. • Oak Brook, IL 60521 • AASL ALSC
Madsen Anne J. • Coordinator of Media Services • Norfolk Public Schools • Norfolk, VA 23510 • AASL
Madsen Carol R. • Microcomputer Specialist • Nevada State Library & Archives • Carson City, NV 89710
Madsen Debora L. • Head, Acquisitions Department • Kansas State University Farrell Library • Manhattan, KS 66506-1200 • ACRL ALCTS
Madsen Elizabeth K. • Palmer, AK 99645 • ACRL LAMA
Madsen Jean E. • Denver, CO 80203 • LITA
Madsen Marci • Branch Support Assistant • Monterey County Free Libraries • Salinas, CA 93901
Madsen Niles J. • Student • University of Rhode Island Graduate School of Library & Information Studies • Kingston, RI 02881-0815
Madsen Winifred B. • Detroit, MI 48215 • AASL ALSC IFRT
Madson Patricia L. • Student • University of Washington Graduate School of Library and Information Science • Seattle, WA 98195
Maeda Karen H.K. • Librarian • Laie Elementary School • Laie, HI 96762 • AASL ALSC LITA
Maes William R. • University Librarian • University of Regina • Regina SK, S4S 0A2 Canada • ACRL LAMA IFRT
Maese Lucy • Library Commissioner • City of Commerce Public Library • Commerce, CA 90040 • ALTA
Maeser Vera M. • Data Research Associates Inc. • Saint Louis, MO 63132
Maffei Gloria J. • Librarian • Saint Sylvester School Library • Pittsburgh, PA 15227
Magagnosc Jacqueline K. • Student • Drexel University College of Information Studies • Philadelphia, PA 19104-2875
Magal Ethel R. • Cataloger • University of Tel Aviv • Tel Aviv Israel, Israel • SRRT
Magane Martha R. • Student • Simmons College Graduate School of Library & Information Science • Boston, MA 02115
Magdal Samuel • Des Plaines, IL 60016
Magdalene M. D.M. Sr. • Librarian • Bishop O'Reilly High School • Kingston, PA 18704
Magee Dottie Erb • Sacramento, CA 95819
Magee Elizabeth • Acquisitions Services Manager • University of Regina • Regina SK, S4S 0A2 Canada • LITA
Magee Jo Ann • Fitchburg Public Library • Fitchburg, MA 01420 • ALSC
Magee John • Los Angeles, CA 90039
Magee Laurie A. • Outreach Librarian • Oshkosh Public Library • Oshkosh, WI 54901 • ASCLA PLA
Magee Robin L. • Assistant Director • Wilkinson Library • Telluride, CO 81435
Magenau Carol • Serials Librarian • Dartmouth College Library Baker Memorial Library • Hanover, NH 03755-3525 • ACRL ALCTS LAMA LITA
Maggio Drexel E. • Student • University of Hawaii School of Library & Information Studies • Honolulu, HI 96822
Maggio Teri • Head Reference & Tech Servs • Southwest Georgia Regional Library Gilbert H Gragg Library • Bainbridge, GA 31717 • PLA RASD
Maghsoudi Paymaneh • Assistant City Librarian • Azusa City Library • Azusa, CA 91702
Maginnis Holly A. • Eugene, OR 97404-3268
Maginnity Gerald • Coordinator • Mountain Valley Library System • Sacramento, CA 95814 • PLA IRRT
Maglinger Cindy • Children's Librarian • Briggs Lawrence County Public Library • Ironton, OH 45638 • ALSC
Magner Mary Jo • Head Librarian • Lakeland Community College Library • Mentor, OH 44060-7594 • LAMA
Magnoni Dianna • Student • State University of New York at Albany School of Information Science & Policy • Albany, NY 12222 • ACRL LITA IFRT LHRT NMRT SRRT
Magnuson Mary F. • Tucson, AZ 85710 • Continuing
Magnuson Nancy L. • Director • Goucher College Julia Rogers Library • Towson, MD 21204 • ACRL LAMA SRRT
Magnussen Ruth A. • Branch Librarian • Palatine Public Library • Palatine, IL 60067 • ALSC LAMA PLA
Magpantay J. Andrew • College of William and Mary Earl Gregg Swem Library • Williamsburg, VA 23187-8794 • ACRL LITA NMRT
Magrath Lynn L. • Alexandria, VA 22310 • LAMA
Magraw Katherine L. • Alexandria, VA 22314
Magree Jane Dunbar • University of California Los Angeles Film & Television Archive (UCLA) • Los Angeles, CA 90038 • ALCTS LITA VRT
Magrill Rose Mary • Director of the Library • East Texas Baptist University • Marshall, TX 75670 • ACRL ALCTS RASD LRRT *Life*
Magro Emanuel P. • Washington, DC 20015 • ACRL
Magua Leah N. • Children's Book Evaluator • Los Angeles County Public Library • Downey, CA 90242 • EMIERT SRRT
Maguda Joyce M. • Orchard Park Public Library • Orchard Park, NY 14127
Mague Kathleen R. • Londonderry, NH 03053
Maguire Beatrice K. • School Library Media Specialist • Fox Lane Middle School Bedford Central Schools • Bedford, NY 10506 • AASL
Maguire Carmel J. • Associate Professor • University of New South Wales School of Librarianship • Kensington, Australia • ACRL LITA LRRT
Maguire Cynthia J. • Student • State University of New York at Albany School of Information Science & Policy • Albany, NY 12222
Maguire Mary M. • Director • J. Lewis Crozer Library • Chester, PA 19013 • LAMA PLA EMIERT SORT
Maguire Patricia V. • Assistant Director • Babson College Horn Library • Babson Park, MA 02157-0901 • ACRL
Maguire Theresa • Adult Services Coordinator • Palmdale City Library • Palmdale, CA 93550 • PLA
Magyar Diane E. • Student • Kent State University School of Library & Information Science • Kent, OH 44242-0001 • ALSC
Mah Jeffery • Chief Librarian • Bechtel Corporation Central Library • San Francisco, CA 94119 • LAMA
Mahaffey Susan M. • Santa Barbara, CA 93107
Mahalov Jean L. • Student • State University of New York at Albany School of Information Science & Policy • Albany, NY 12222
Mahamedi Hamid • Librarian • University of California-Berkeley School of Library & Information Studies • Berkeley, CA 94720
Mahan Joan Blessum • Librarian • Archbishop Chapelle High School • Metairie, LA 70003 • AASL EMIERT
Mahan Peggy J. • Head of Technical Services • Jenkins Memorial Law Library • Phildelphia, PA 19107 • ALCTS LAMA
Mahaney Ruth • Reference Librarian/Cataloger • Estes Park Public Library District • Estes Park, CO 80517 • PLA
Maher Diana • West Tisbury School • West Tisbury, MA 02575 • AASL ALSC YALSA
Maher Javad • Student • University of Texas at Austin Graduate School of Library & Information Sciences • Austin, TX 78712-1276
Maher John G. • Indiana Wesleyan University • Marion, IN 46953 • ALCTS
Maher Patricia M. • Student • Northwestern University Library • Evanston, IL 60208-2300 • SRRT
Maher Veronica T. • Roger Williams College Library • Bristol, RI 02809-2921 • ACRL
Mahfuez Suheir A. • Teacher • American University in Cairo Library • Cairo, Egypt • ALSC
Mahler Jeanne H. Mrs • Philadelphia, PA 19107 • ALCTS RASD *Life*
Mahler Mary Nell • Beaverton, OR 97005 • AASL
Mahmoodi Suzanne H. • CE & Library Research Consultant • Office of Library Development & Services • Saint Paul, MN 55101 • LAMA PLA CLENE
Mahmoud Amatullah L. Ms. • Manager, Donor Research • Wayne State University • Detroit, MI 48202 • ACRL LRRT
Mahnke Billy A. • Omaha, NE 68106 • AASL
Mahon Carol Ann • Library/Media Coordinator • Riverside Brookfield High School Media Services • Riverside, IL 60546 • AASL
Mahon Margaret Miss • Greenville, SC 29605 • ALSC PLA *Continuing*
Mahon Maureen • Student • Rutgers University School of Communication Information & Library Studies • New Brunswick, NJ 08903 • RASD
Mahone Darlene A. • Director • Chesterfield County Library • Chesterfield, SC 29709 • LAMA PLA
Mahoney Carol A. • Director • Lynnfield Public Library • Lynnfield, MA 01940
Mahoney Carol A. • Technical Information Specialist • National Archives & Records Administration • Washington, DC 20408 • GODORT
Mahoney Cathy L. • Head Librarian • Fruitland Park Library • Fruitland Park, FL 34731 • PLA
Mahoney Elizabeth Tillapaugh • Head,SLIS Library • University of Pittsburgh School of Library and Information Science • Pittsburgh, PA 15260 • ACRL ALSC
Mahoney Janice P. • Camden, SC 29020 • AASL

Mahoney Joan M. • Coconut Creek, FL 33063

Mahoney John J • Trustee • Lackawanna County Library System • Scranton, PA 18503

Mahoney Josephine • Educational Media Specialist • Township of Ocean Intermediate School • Ocean, NJ 07712 • AASL

Mahoney Judith J. • Librarian • Fox Hill School Library • Kansas City, MO 64118 • AASL

Mahoney Mary E. • Director • Chelmsford Public Library • Chelmsford, MA 01824-3088 • PLA

Mahony Molly C. • Ann Arbor, MI 48103 • RASD IRRT

Mahood Kristine • Rowan Public Library • Salisbury, NC 28144 • PLA YALSA IFRT

Mahood Mary Louise K. • Librarian I • Henrico County Public Library Tuckahoe Area Library • Richmond, VA 23229 • PLA

Mahood Ramona M. • Library Education • Memphis State University Libraries • Memphis, TN 38152 • AASL

Mahound M. Zahir • Assistant Director • Waynesboro Public Library • Waynesboro, VA 22980

Mahr Nancy • Palos Verdes Library District • Pls Vrd Pnsla, CA 90274

Mai Brent Alan • Reference/Research Librarian • Brown & Root Inc., Information Resource Center • Houston, TX 77020

Mai Jens-Erik • 9000 Aalborg, Denmark • ACRL

Maiara Ann L. • Librarian • River Dell Junior High School • River Edge, NJ 07661 • AASL

Maiden Vicki S. • Director, LRC • Community Unit School Dist. #303 Munhall School • Saint Charles, IL 60174 • AASL

Maier Catherine A. • County Librarian • Glacier County Library • Cut Bank, MT 59427 • PLA

Maier Judith • Librarian • Lakeland School District • Shrub Oak, NY 10588 • AASL

Maier Martha S. • Reference Librarian • Providence Public Library • Providence, RI 02903-3283

Maier Robert C. • Director • Massachusetts Board of Library Commissioners • Boston, MA 02215-2070 • ASCLA LITA

Maiers Michael A. • Warren, MI 48093 • RASD

Maiken Margaret M. • Beloit, WI 53511-6439 • LITA

Maillet Lucienne • Professor of Lib & Inf Sci • Long Island University Palmer School of Library & Info. Sci. • Brookville, NY 11548 • ACRL

Main Annette Zamberlin • Designs for the Library & Office • Round Rock, TX 78680 • ACRL ALCTS LAMA LITA RASD CLENE ILERT LHRT

Main Isabelle G. • Librarian • Red Mountain High School • Mesa, AZ 85207 • AASL

Main Steven B. • Librarian • Big Valley High School • Bieber, CA 96009 • ALSC

Maina William E. • Collection Development Librarian • University of Texas Southwestern Medical Center Library • Dallas, TX 75235-9049 • ACRL

Maine John S. • Millersville, PA 17551 • Continuing

Maine Valerie A. • Vernon Area Public Library • Prairie View, IL 60069

Mainelli Helen Kenik Ph.D. • Library Director • The Seminary Library • Oak Brook, IL 60521 • ACRL LAMA

Mainiero Elizabeth T. • Library Director • Greenwich Library • Greenwich, CT 06830 • LITA PLA

Mainwood E. G. Mrs. • St. Petersburg, FL 33701 • Life

Maiorano Carol L. • Reference Supervisor • Clark County Public Library • Springfield, OH 45501-1080 • PLA

Maiorano Isabelle J. • Staten Island, NY 10314-2738

Maisel Mary S. • Assistant Director • Jackson-Hinds Library System • Jackson, MS 39201 • PLA

Maitland Douglas B. Mr. • Librarian/Media Specialist • Swampscott High School Jennie M. McVey Memorial Library • Swampscott, MA 01907-2293 • AASL

Maitland Ellen H. • Little Lake, MI 49833 • Continuing

Maiullo Michele M. • Director • Free Public Library • Hasbrouck Hts, NJ 07604 • PLA

Maj Karen J. • Student • Wayne State University Library Science Program • Detroit, MI 48202 • PLA

Majanja Mabel K. • Student • University of Pittsburgh School of Library and Information Science • Pittsburgh, PA 15260

Majcharzak Donna M. • Student • State University of New York (SUNY) School of Information & Library Studies • Buffalo, NY 14260 • PLA

Majeau Alison K. • Editor • Boston Library Consortium • Boston, MA 02117 • ALCTS LITA

Majilton Janet W. • Collection Development Officer • Memphis-Shelby County Public Library and Information Center • Memphis, TN 38104-4025 • ALCTS PLA RASD

Majka Annette E. • Student • Wayne State University • Detroit, MI 48202

Majka Sally L. • Student • Flint Hill Elementary School • Vienna, VA 22181

Major Carol • School Librarian • Bryson Elementary School • Fort Worth, TX 76179 • AASL

Major Caryl M. • Media Director • Moon Valley High School • Phoenix, AZ 85029 • AASL

Major Edna T. • Library Media Specialist • Black Fox Elementary School • Murfreesboro, TN 37130 • AASL

Major Hannelore Sorg • Librarian • Ogelthrope Mall Library • Savannah, GA 31406 • AASL ALSC PLA

Major Jean A. • Old Dominion University Library • Norfolk, VA 23529-0256 • ACRL

Majors Kern T. • Documents Librarian • California State University,Fresno Henry Madden Library • Fresno, CA 93740-0034 • ACRL GODORT

Majure Stephen L. • Assistant Head Librarian • Savannah College of Art & Design • Savannah, GA 31401 • ALCTS

Mak Collette G. • Document Development Specialist • Online Computer Library Center (OCLC) • Dublin, OH 43017-3395 • ALCTS RASD

Mak Kevin • Student • Southern Connecticut State University School of Libray Science & Instructional Technology • New Haven, CT 06515 • ACRL

Maki Heather • Teacher-Librarian • Dr. Ep. Scarlett High School • Calgary AB, T2W 2J2 Canada • AASL

Maki Karen E. • Adult Services Librarian • Gail Borden Public Library • Elgin, IL 60120 • PLA RASD GODORT IFRT

Makinen Barbara • Saint Clement School • Chicago, IL 60614

Makino Yasuko • Japanese Cataloger • Columbia University • New York, NY 10027-7297 • ACRL ALCTS

Makosky Martha M. • Director • Carroll County Public Library • Westminster, MD 21157 • ASCLA LAMA LITA PLA IFRT

Makow Berta • Reference Librarian • County of Los Angeles Public Library West Covina Library 801 • West Covina, CA 91790

Makowski Marilyn S. • Media Specialist • Greenwood High School • Greenwood, SC 29646 • AASL IFRT

Makowski Silvia A. • Childrens & Young Adult Coor. • Wayne Oakland Library Federation • Wayne, MI 48184 • ALSC PLA YALSA

Makuch Andrew L. • Bibliographer, Collection Devel. • University of Arizona Library • Tucson, AZ 85721 • ACRL ALCTS

Malague Mary Ellen • Library Director • Milltown Public Library • Milltowm, NJ 08850 • PLA

Malakoff Dina • Student • San Jose State University Division of Library & Information Science • San Jose, CA 95192-0029 • ALSC

Malamud Judie • Director • Albert Einstein College of Medicine Gottesman Library • Bronx, NY 10461 • ACRL

Malanchuk Iona R. • Head Mead Library • University of Florida Libraries • Gainesville, FL 32611-2047 • AASL ACRL

Malanchuk Peter P. • Africana & Political Sci Bibl Gr • University of Florida Libraries • Gainesville, FL 32611-2047 • ACRL RASD IRRT

Malane Charles E. • Student • Rosary College Graduate School of Library & Information Science • River Forest, IL 60305 • RASD

Malanga Kathleen • Head of Reference • William Paterson College • Wayne, NJ 07470 • ACRL RASD

Malar John • Cranford Public Library • Cranford, NJ 07016 • PLA

Malatesta William J. • Albany High School Library Media Center • Albany, NY 12203 • AASL

Malcolm J. Parke • Senior Vice President • University Microfilms International • Ann Arbor, MI 48106-1346

Malcolm Linda M. • Vice President • RII • Silver Spring, MD 20910 • ALCTS ASCLA LITA PLA

Malcolm Melissa A. • Mount Abraham Union High School John D. Connolly Library • Bristol, VT 05443 • AASL IFRT VRT

Malcomb J. Louise • Head, Undergrad Library Serv. • Indiana University • Bloomington, IN 47405 • ACRL GODORT LIRT

Malecki Paul M. • Director • Southern Tier Library System • Corning, NY 14830-2898 • PLA CLENE

Malefatfo Thomas J. • Student • Indiana University School of Library and Information Science • Bloomington, IN 47405

Malek-Wiley Rebecca R. • Tulane University Howard-Tilton Memorial Library • New Orleans, LA 70118 • ACRL ALCTS IRRT

Maletta Angela M. • Roslyn Heights, NY 11577 • AASL

Malette Joan M. • Concord, CA 94524-5638

Malette Phyllis L. • Librarian • Toronto Public Library • Toronto ON, M5A 4L2 Canada • PLA

Malewitz Joan • School Librarian • Public School 160 Q • Jamaica, NY 11435 • AASL

Maley Desmond • Librarian • Huntington College J. W. Tate Library • Sudbury, ON, P3E 2C6 Canada • RASD

Malgeri Dina G. • Director • Malden Public Library • Malden, MA 02148-5291

Malik Abdul Mr. • Assistant Personal Director • Queens Borough Public Library • Jamaica, NY 11432 • ACRL RASD *Life*

Malin Margery • District Librarian • Riviera Independent School District • Riviera, TX 78379 • AASL YALSA

Malinconico S. Michael • EBSCO Professor • University of Alabama School of Library & Information Studies • Tuscaloosa, AL 35487-0252 • ACRL ALCTS LITA PLA

Malinowski Marianne T. • Ames Public Library • Ames, IA 50010 • ALCTS

Malinowski Teresa M. • Serials Coordinator • California State University • Fullerton, CA 92634 • ALCTS

Malinowsky H Robert • Science & Engineering Bibliogr. • University of Illinois at Chicago University Library • Chicago, IL 60680 • ACRL SRRT

Malinski Richard • Chief Librarian • Ryerson Polytech Institute • Toronto ON, M5B 2K3 Canada • ACRL ALCTS

Malish Basil • Sr. Hispanic Acquisitions Ln. • Library of Congress • Washington, DC 20541 • FLRT IRRT

Malkin M. A. O'Brian • Hotel Olcott #1415 • New York, NY 10023 • ACRL

Malkmus Bernard R. • Trustee • Alabama Public Library Service • Montgomery, AL 36130 • ALTA PLA

Malkoff-Moon Susan • Associate Librarian • Nelson-Atkins Museum of Art • Kansas City, MO 64111 • ALCTS LITA

Mall Barbara S. • Columbia, MD 21044

Mall Bettina • Learning Center Director • Twin Groves Middle School • Buffalo Grove, IL 60089

Mallalieu Robert K. • Head Librarian • Newark Acasemy • Livingston, NJ 07039 • AASL

Mallard Ann H. • Librarian II • Evanston Public Library • Evanston, IL 60201 • PLA

Maller Alma L. • Reference Ln/Special Projects • Shipley School, The • Bryn Mawr, PA 19010-3598

Mallery Mary S. • Regional Librarian • Western Maryland Public Libraries • Hagerstown, MD 21740

Malles Evelyn M. • Ferndale, MI 48220 • SRRT

Mallett Stephen N. • Cleveland, OH 44121-3359 • RASD

Mallinger Stephen M. • Library Development Adviser • State Library of Pennsylvania Department of Education • Harrisburg, PA 17105 • ASCLA EMIERT

Mallis Sophia • Trustee • Bedford Park Public Library District • Bedford Park, IL 60501 • PLA

Mallon Patricia • Associate in Library Services • New York State Library Division 10C50 Cultural Education Center • Albany, NY 12230 • ASCLA *Life*

Mallon Patricia R. • Vice President,Bus Reference • Dun's Marketing Services • Parsippany, NJ 07054 • ACRL PLA RASD ERT

Mallonee Mary Jane • Widener University School of Law Library • Wilmington, DE 19803-0475 • ACRL GODORT

Mallory Carlyle • Librarian • Scioto Memorial Hospital • Portsmouth, OH 45662

Mallory Elizabeth J. • Reference Librarian • El Paso Community College • El Paso, TX 79998 • ACRL NMRT

Mallory Joyce Mrs. • Trustee • Milwaukee Public Library • Milwaukee, WI 53233 • ALTA

Mallory Kevin • Student • University of Tennessee-Knoxville Graduate School of Library & Information Science • Knoxville, TN 37996-4330 • IFRT SRRT

Mallory Langhorne C. • Information Manager • University of Georgia SBDC Connection • Athens, GA 30602 • RASD

Mallory Mary L. • Documents Librarian • University of Illinois Library • Urbana, IL 61801 • GODORT LHRT LRRT SRRT

Mallory Tim • Librarian • Shasta County Library • Redding, CA 96001

Mallory Yvonne F. • Library Director • Tama Public Library • Tama, IA 52339

Mallos Diane E. • Library Coordinator • National Park Service Information & Telecommunications Div • Washington, DC 20013-7127 • LAMA LITA FLRT GODORT NMRT

Mallow Marilyn • Alhambra High School • Alhambra, CA 91801 • AASL YALSA

Malloy Caroline B. • Baker & Hostetler • Washington, DC 20036

Malloy Catherine M. • Chicago, IL 60646

Malloy Luke J. • Librarian • Southern Seminary College Von Canon Library • Buena Vista, VA 24416

Malloy Susan D. • Manager Humanities & Fine Arts • Columbus Metropolitan Library Main Library Branch • Columbus, OH 43215 • RASD

Malloy Verna • Tenafly, NJ 07670 • Continuing

Malmud Maureen S. • Toronto, ON, M4Y 1R7 Canada

Malnar Mary S. • Oshkosh, WI 54901 • ALSC PLA *Life*

Malone David P. • Saint Johns University Alcuin Library • Collegeville, MN 56321-7155 • ACRL

Malone Debbie • Ursinus College Library • Collegeville, PA 19426 • ACRL

Malone Dixie • Denver, CO 80223

Malone Donna • Director • Clayville Library Association • Clayville, NY 13322

Malone Jacqueline • Director • Island Park Public Library • Island Park, NY 11558 • PLA

Malone Marie A. • Director • Notre Dame College Paul Harvey Library • Manchester, NH 03104 • ACRL

Malone Nancy J. • Library Director • Central College Briner Library • McPherson, KS 67460 • ACRL

Malone Noreen R. • Montini High School • Lombard, IL 60148

Maloney Ann K. • Middletown, RI 02840-0498

Maloney Bridget J. • Student • University of Illinois Graduate School of Library and Information Science • Urbana, IL 61801

Maloney Charlotte A. • Personnel Assistant • Salt Lake City Public Library • Salt Lake City, UT 84111

Maloney Clare J. • Branch Director • Greece Public Library Paddy Hill Branch • Rochester, NY 14612 • PLA

Maloney James J. • Contra Costa County Library • Pleasant Hill, CA 94523 • LITA RASD

Maloney Lena P. • Head Librarian • Wilmington Friends School • Wilmington, DE 19803 • AASL

Maloney Margaret Crawford • Head, Osborne Collection • Toronto Public Library • Toronto ON, M5S 2E4 Canada • ACRL ALSC

Maloney Sean P. • Reference Services Coordinator • Siena College • Loudonville, NY 12211-1462 • ACRL RASD

Malonis Jane A. • Birmingham, MI 48009 • LRRT SRRT

Malott Judith C. • Gilsum Public Library • Gilsum, NH 03448

Maloy Frances J. • Director, Public Services • Hamilton College Library • Clinton, NY 13323 • ACRL LAMA

Malsawma Lallianzuali H. • College Park, MD 20740 • RASD EMIERT IRRT

Maltby Florence H. • Associate Professor, Library Sci • Southwest Missouri State University Library • Springfield, MO 65804-0095 • AASL

Maltese Susan M. • Cataloging Librarian • Oakton Community College Library • Des Plaines, IL 60016 • ACRL ALCTS

Maltz Nanette W. • Student • Wayne State University Library Science Program • Detroit, MI 48202 • AASL ALSC

Malufka Charles • Trustee • Calumet City Public Library • Calumet City, IL 60409-4003 • ALTA

Malumphy Sharon M. • Corporate Librarian • Ohio Edison Company • Akron, OH 44308-1890

Malyshev Nina A. • Head of Library Services • Alaska State Library • Juneau, AK 99811-571

Maman Marie • Circulation Librarian • Rutgers University Libraries Mabel Smith Douglass Library • New Brunswick, NJ 08903-0270 • ACRL IRRT LIRT

Mambi Nancy E. • Librarian • Groveland Park • St. Paul, MN 55105 • AASL

Mambu Barbara J. • Hawthorne School • Wheaton, IL 60187 • AASL

Maminski Dolores • Branch Librarian • Carroll County Public Library Westminster Branch • Westminster, MD 21157 • YALSA

Man David G. • Reference Librarian • New York Academy of Medicine Library • New York, NY 10029 • ASCLA

Man May L. • Student • University of Kentucky College of Library & Information Science • Lexington, KY 40506-0391

Manacop Irene E. • Librarian Tech. Servs. • Atlanta-Fulton Public Library • Atlanta, GA 30303 • ALCTS LITA PLA

Manahan Martin • Legal Librarian • Washington State Penitentiary • Walla Walla, WA 99362 • ASCLA

Manaka Pauline D. • Social Sciences Librarian • University of California General Library • Irvine, CA 92713 • ACRL

Manbeck Virginia B. • Assistant Dir.,Hospital Services • New York Metropolitan Reference & Research Library Agency (METRO) • New York, NY 10003 • ASCLA

Mancall Jacqueline C. • Professor • Drexel University College of Information Studies • Philadelphia, PA 19104-2875 • AASL ALCTS ALSC

Mancini Donna • Director • DeKalb County Public Library Adminstration Building • Decatur, GA 30030 • LAMA PLA

Mancini Mary L. • Chula Vista, CA 91910

Mancuyas N D. • Ormond Beach, FL 32176

Manczuk Suzanne • Pennington, NJ 08534 • AASL ALSC YALSA

Mandal Mina R. • Rancho Palos Verdes, CA 90274

Mandel Carol A. • Director, Technical Services • Columbia University Libraries Butler Library • New York, NY 10027 • ALCTS LITA

Mandel Debra H. • Head, Media Center • Northeastern University Libraries • Boston, MA 02115 • ACRL

Mandel Lawrence G. • University Heights, OH 44118

Mandel Rene S. • Framingham, MA 01701

Mandelbaum Jane B. • Washington, DC 20016-2248 • LITA FLRT

Mandell Edward • Libray Director • Penn Hills Library • Pittsburgh, PA 15235-2099 • LAMA PLA

Mandell Gail M. • Librarian • Ramora Elementary School • Bellflower, CA 90706

Manderen Elizabeth S. • Public Service Coordinator • Akron-Summit County Public Library • Akron, OH 44326-0001 • LAMA PLA

Mandernack Scott B. • Reference & Instruction Ln. • Purdue University Libraries • West Lafayette, IN 47907 • ACRL IFRT LIRT LRRT

Manderscheid Dorothy H. • Michigan State University Libraries • East Lansing, MI 48824-1048 • ACRL

Mandes Louis C. Jr. • Director • Irene duPont Library Saint Andrew's School • Middletown, DE 19709 • AASL

Mandler Sally A. • Anoka County Library Systems Mississippi Branch Library • Fridley, MN 55432-4498

Mandour Cecile A. • Principal Catalog Librarian • Yale University Sterling Memorial Library • New Haven, CT 06520 • ALCTS

Mandresh Gladys • Trustee • Syosset Public Library • Syosset, NY 11791 • ALTA

Manduley Beatriz Mrs. • Trustee • Greensboro Public Library • Greensboro, NC 27402 • ALTA

Mandziara Penny M. • Bensenville, IL 60106 • YALSA

Manely Frances • Trustee • Memphis-Shelby County Public Library and Information Center • Memphis, TN 38104-4025

Manes Esther S. • Librarian • The Bearley School • New York, NY 10028 • AASL IFRT

Maness L. George • Metairie, LA 70001

Mangan Elizabeth U. • Head Data Prep,Geography & Maps • Library of Congress • Washington, DC 20541 • ALCTS MAGERT

Mangan Jean M. • Reference Librarian • Rockford Public Library • Rockford, IL 61101-1061

Manger Ronelle M. • Student • University of South Carolina College of Library & Information Science • Columbia, SC 29208 • EMIERT IFRT SRRT

Manges Donna M. • N. E. Regional Sales Manager • Sirs, Incorporated • Boca Raton, FL 33427 • AASL ERT IFRT

Manget Deborah S. • Director • Conyer-Rockdale Library Systems • Conyers, GA 30207

Mangieri Jill • Walsingham Academy Upper School • Williamsburg, VA 23187-8702

Mangin Julianne • Librarian • United States Department of Agriculture National Agricultural Library • Beltsville, MD 20705-2351

Mangino Terri C. • Trustee • Queens Borough Public Library • Jamaica, NY 11432 • ALTA PLA

Mangold Patricia • Business Manager • Yonkers Public Library • Yonkers, NY 10701 • LAMA

Mangum Sheila A. • Head of Acquisition Department • University of North Florida Thomas G. Carpenter Library • Jacksonville, FL 32245-7605 • ALCTS

Mangus Florence L. • Boca Raton, FL 33431

Manheim Ted • Plymouth, MI 48170

Manheimer Caroline E. • Librarian • Carolina Day School • Asheville, NC 28803 • AASL

Manhein Louise McAnulty • Bolivar, TN 38008

Manila Estela L. • Bilingual Lib. Asst. • Contra Costa County Library Pinole Branch • Pinole, CA 94564

Manini Joan R. • Librarian III • Burlingame Public Library • Burlingame, CA 94010

Manion Elizabeth S. • Director • Marlboro Free Library • Marlboro, NY 12542-0780 • PLA

Manion Margaret A. • Librarian II • University of Lowell Lydon Library • Lowell, MA 01854 • ACRL

Manis Cathy M. • Librarian • Vestavia Hills High School • Vestavia Hills, AL 35216 • AASL

Manke Merrill E. • Librarian • Monterey Bay Aquarium • Monterey, CA 93940-1085 • ALCTS

Mankin Donald R. • Helena, AR 72342 • IFRT

Manley Charles W. • Associate Director • Washoe County Library • Reno, NV 89505 • PLA

Manley Cynthia G. • Head of Acquisitions • Martin Marietta Energy Systems Library Oak Ridge National Laboratory • Oak Ridge, TN 37831-6208 • LITA

Manley Karin P. • Director of Library Services • Waterloo Regional Library • Waterloo ON, N2J 4G7 Canada • LAMA PLA

Manley Phyllis • American International School • Vienna II90, Austria

Manley Robin • Hobart & William Smith Colleges Warren H. Smith Library • Geneva, NY 14456

Manley Will • Asst. Dir.-Community Services • Tempe Public Library • Tempe, AZ 85282 • ALTA PLA IFRT SRRT

Manly Virginia • Philadelphia, PA 19128 • ACRL ALCTS   *Life*

Mann Caroline E. • Health Inf Network Coordinator • University of New Mexico Medical Center Library • Albuquerque, NM 87131 • ALCTS

Mann Charles R. • Media Specialist • Lincoln Elementary School • Elk River, MN 55330 • AASL

Mann Curtis R. • Research Librarian • University of Illinois School of Library Information Science • Champaign, IL 61820

Mann Cynthia • Atlanta Public Schools Media Processing Center • Atlanta, GA 30307

Mann Loisteen J. • Librarian • Atlanta Area School for the Deaf • Clarkston, GA 30021

Mann Marcia M. • Student • Kent State University School of Library Science/Columbus Program • Columbus, OH 43210

Mann Olive E. • Plymouth, MI 48170-4739

Mann Peggy K. • Librarian • United States Marine Corps Air Station Library • Cherry Point, NC 28533 • AFLRT FLRT

Mann Sally F. Mrs. • Charleston, WV 25302

Mann Thomas • National League of Cities • Washington, DC 20004 • ACRL ALCTS

Mann Thomas J. • Reference Librarian • Library of Congress • Washington, DC 20541 • RASD

Mann Vijai S. • Law Librarian • Cook County Law Library • Chicago, IL 60602 • ALCTS

Mann Wendy S. • Pittsburgh, PA 15204

Mannan Susan • LRC Coordinator • Indiana Vocational Technical College Learning Resource Centerc Coord. • Indianapolis, IN 46206 • ACRL

Mannarino Elizabeth Rose • Reference Librarian • Corvallis-Benton County Public Library • Corvallis, OR 97330-4728 • PLA

Manners Katherine E. • Librarian II • State Correctional Institution at Pittsburgh • Pittsburgh, PA 15233 • ASCLA IFRT

Mannherz Mary Jane • Library Director • Margaret R. Grundy Memorial Library • Bristol, PA 19007 • LAMA LITA PLA

Manni Jacqueline E. • Student • Drexel University College of Information Studies • Philadelphia, PA 19104-2875

Manning Beverley J. • University Librarian III • University of Connecticut H. B. Trecker Library • West Hartford, CT 06117 • ACRL ALCTS

Manning Dale • English Bibliographer • Vanderbilt University Central Library • Nashville, TN 37240-0007 • ACRL ALCTS IFRT

Manning Jennifer E. • Congressional Ref. Librarian • Library of Congress • Washington, DC 20541 • IFRT

Manning Leslie A. • Library Director • University of Colorado At Colorado Springs Library • Colorado Springs, CO 80933-7150 • ACRL LAMA LITA   *Life*

Manning Mary • Library Director • Minneapolis Coll of Art & Design Library • Minneapolis, MN 55404-3593 • ACRL ALCTS

Manning Matthew D. • Student • Florida State University School of Library and Information Studies • Tallahassee, FL 32306-2048

Manning Maureen • Rockefeller Foundation • New York, NY 10036

Manning Maureen F. • Manager of Children Dept. • Corvallis-Benton County Public Library • Corvallis, OR 97330-4728

Manning Ralph W. • Senior Coordinator for Standards • National Library of Canada • Ottawa, ON, K1A 0N4 Canada • ALCTS

Manning Susan E. • Reference/AV Librarian • Merced County Library • Merced, CA 95340

Manns Elizabeth A. • Student • North Adams State College • North Adams, MA 01247 • RASD

Manojlovich Slavko • Systems Librarian • Memorial University Queen Elizabeth II Library • St Johns NF, A1B 3Y1 Canada • LITA

Manoogian Sylva N. • Los Angeles Public Library • Los Angeles, CA 90071 • PLA RASD EMIERT IRRT

Manor LaWanda • Library Media Specialist • Lincoln Junior High School Media Center • Washington, DC 20019

Manos John W. • Director of Development • Denver Public Library • Denver, CO 80204-2602

Manry Edna L. • Student • University of Texas at Austin Graduate School of Library & Information Sciences • Austin, TX 78712-1276 • PLA

Manry Helen H. • Librarian • Kinchafoonee Regional Library • Dawson, GA 31742

Mansbach Judith E. • Children's Librarian • Edison Free Public Library • Edison, NJ 08817

Mansfield Diane J. • Ossining, NY 10562

Mansfield Jerry W. • Sr. Reference Librarian • United States Postal Services Library • Washington, DC 20260-1641 • ACRL LAMA   *Life*

Mansfield John S. • Saint Florian High School • Hamtramck, MI 48212 • AASL

Mansfield Meribah H. • Director of Main Library • Worthington Public Library • Worthington, OH 43085 • PLA

Mansheim Renee E. • Norfolk, VA 23507

Manson Clara S. • Portola Valley, CA 94028 • ACRL ASCLA *Life*

Mansour Zeinab A. • Student • Catholic University of America Library School Library • Washington, DC 20064 • IRRT SRRT

Mansson Joan • Public Services Librarian • Maitland Public Library • Maitland, FL 32751

Manstein Robert A. • Library Assistant • Gratz College Tuttleman Library • Melrose Park, PA 19126

Mantarro Yolanda • Branch Librarian • Broward County Library Deerfield Beach Branch • Deerfield Beach, FL 33441

Mantei G. Shirlene • Library Assistant • Shasta County Library • Redding, CA 96001

Mantel Melissa A. • Assistant Librarian • Houston Chronicle • Houston, TX 77210 • IFRT

Manthey Teresa M. • Reference Librarian • University of Southern California Norris Medical Library • Los Angeles, CA 90033-4582 • AASL

Mantilla Mercedes • Director of Technical Services • Highland Park Public Library • Highland Park, IL 60035

Manuszak John • Trustee • Calumet City Public Library • Calumet City, IL 60409-4003 • ALTA

Manvel Barbara • Reference Librarian • United States Naval Academy Nimitz Library • Annapolis, MD 21402-5029 • ACRL RASD

Manwaring Sarah S. • Govt. Publication Ln Head • University of Alberta • Edmonton AB, T6G 2J8 Canada • GODORT

Manwell Constance E. • Silver Spring, MD 20902

Many Florence L. • Chester, NJ 07930

Manzari Laura Slepetis • Long Island University B. Davis Schwartz Memorial Library • Greenvale, NY 11548 • ACRL

Mao Agnes Liu • George Mason University Libraries • Fairfax, VA 22030

Maple Amanda L. • Astoria, NY 11103

Maples Marjorie J. • Library Services Coordinator • Washoe County School District • Reno, NV 89520 • AASL YALSA

Maples Mary L. • Student • University of Alabama School of Library & Information Studies • Tuscaloosa, AL 35487-0252

Mapp Erwin E. Jr. • Tallahassee, FL 32304 • Continuing

Mar Dennis R. • Statistician • Pacific Grove Public Library • Pacific Grove, CA 93950 • PLA IFRT

Mara Heather Hull • Student • University of Arizona Graduate Library School • Tucson, AZ 85721

Maraist Barbara G. • Student • University of Hawaii School of Library & Information Studies • Honolulu, HI 96822 • ALSC PLA

Maramaldi Paul • Trustee • Paramus Public Library • Paramus, NJ 07652 • ALTA PLA

Marangoni Eugene Garver • Information Specialist • Dialog Information Service Inc. • Palo Alto, CA 94304 • LITA

Marano Vera A. • Head, Ref. & Info Serv Div • Delaware County Library System • Brookhaven, PA 19015 • RASD

Marantz Kenneth A. • Professor, Art Edu Dept. • Ohio State University • Columbus, OH 43210 • ALSC

Marantz Sylvia S. • Librarian • Saint Michael School • Worthington, OH 43085 • AASL

Marble Beatrice • Syracuse, NY 13205-2918

Marble Lawrence W. • Reference Librarian • Temple University Paley Library • Philadelphia, PA 19122 • ACRL

Marbois Patricia D. • Asheboro, NC 27203 • AASL

Marcantonio Columbia P. • Head Librarian • Horace Mann School • Bronx, NY 10471 • AASL

Marcato Carolyn K. • Librarian/Media Specialist • Dwight Elementary School • Fairfield, CT 06897 • AASL

Marcell Katherine • Sr. Library Assistant • Newport Beach Public Library Mariners Branch • Newport Beach, CA 92660 • ALSC

March Donna Rae • E.C. Best Middle School • Fallon, NV 89407

March Susan F. • Student • University of California Los Angeles Graduate School of Library & Information Science • Los Angeles, CA 90024

Marchand Janet H. • Greenwich High School • Greenwich, CT 06830 • AASL LIRT

Marchand Paul • Ecole De Technolgie Superieure Library • Montreal, PQ, H2T 2C8 Canada • ACRL

Marchant Cathy • Salt Lake County Library System • Salt Lake City, UT 84121-3188

Marchant Cynthia • Lawrenceville, NJ 08648

Marchant Hilda • Head of Technical Services • Chicago Municipal Reference Library • Chicago, IL 60602 • LITA MAGERT

Marchant Mary S. • Assistant Librarian • East Central Oklahoma State University • Ada, OK 74820 • ACRL ALCTS RASD NMRT

Marchant Maurice P. • Professor, Library School • Brigham Young University School of Library & Information Sciences • Provo, UT 84602 • ACRL LAMA PLA CLENE LRRT

Marchant Nancy H. • Branch Librarian • Weber County Library North Branch • Ogden, UT 84414

Marchbanks Rose • III Librarian II • La Canada Elementary School Computer Lab. • Lompoc, CA 93436

Marchese Marie-Ann • Director of Library Services • Lexington School for the Deaf • Jackson Heights, NY 11370 • AASL

Marchesse Michelle A. • Adult Services Librarian • Anderson County Library • Anderson, SC 29622-4047 • PLA RASD

Marchesseault Madeleine • Dayton, OH 45406 • ALCTS

Marchiafava Anna G. • Assistant Librarian • West Baton Rouge Parish Library • Port Allen, LA 70767

Marchio Mary S. • Omaha, NE 68102

Marciarille Kathy A. • Head Librarian • C M Bailey Library • Winthrop, ME 04364 • PLA

Marcil Thomas A. • Head, Circulation Department • University of South Carolina College of Library & Information Science • Columbia, SC 29208

Marcinko Dorothy K. • Head of Acquisitions • Auburn University Ralph Brown Draughon Library • Auburn, AL 36849-5606 • ACRL ALCTS IRRT

Marcinko Sarabeth • Turkey Run Elementary School • Marshall, IN 47859 • AASL

Marckwardt Marilyn • Manhattan Beach, CA 90266 • AASL YALSA   *Life*

Marco Guy A. • Chicago, IL 60657 • IRRT

Marconi Joseph V. • Director • Wayne County Public Library • Wooster, OH 44691

Marcotte Frederick • Librarian • Clermont College Library • Batavia, OH 45103 • ACRL RASD

Marcoux Elizabeth L. • Head Librarian • Rincon University High School Library • Tucson, AZ 85710 • AASL

Marcum Deanna B. • Dean • Catholic University of America School of Library and Information Science • Washington, DC 20064 • ACRL LAMA PLA LHRT

Marcum James W. • Director of Library Services • Centenary College of Louisiana • Shreveport, LA 71134-1188

Marcum Thomas P. • Librarian • Catholic University of America Libraries • Washington, DC 20064 • ACRL ALCTS LITA

Marcus Ari • Principal • Ari Marcus & Company • San Francisco, CA 94114 • LITA

Marcus Barbara A. • Scholastic Inc. • New York, NY 10003 • YALSA

Marcus Pat • Trustee • West Florida Regional Library • Pensacola, FL 32501

Marcus Philip N. • Boca Raton, FL 33433-1930

Marcus Shelley • Claremont, CA 91711 • RASD IFRT SRRT

Marcus Terry C. • Milwaukee, WI 53209 • ACRL

Marcy Henry O. IV • Deputy Commissioner • Massachusetts Department of Employment & Training • Boston, MA 02114

Marden William • Sutton Place Foundation • New York, NY 10021 • ACRL

Marder Kenneth C • New Haven, CT 06515

Mardeusz Patricia E. • Head, Interlibrary Loan • University of Vermont Bailey Howe Library • Burlington, VT 05405-0036 • IRRT

Mardiguian Mary T. • Alexandria, VA 22306

Mardorf Helen • St Louis, MO 63104 • ALSC   *Continuing*

Marek Kate • Administrator • Southeast Library System • Lincoln, NE 68506 • PLA

Mares Rosie • San Benito Public Library • San Benito, TX 78586

Marfell Ruth A. • Minneapolis, MN 55435 • Continuing

Margalith Helen M. • New York, NY 10023

Marger Deborah J. • Line Mountain Senior High School • Herndon, PA 17830 • AASL   *Life*

Margeson Deborah M. • Peter White Public Library • Marquette, MI 49855

Margis Robert J. • Student • University of Wisconsin-Milwaukee School of Library & Information Science • Milwaukee, WI 53201

Margolin Nancy • Hilclaire Information Services • Chicago, IL 60626-2322

Margolis Bernard A. • Director • Pikes Peak Library District • Colorado Springs, CO 80901 • ACRL ALCTS LAMA LITA PLA RASD GODORT IFRT NMRT SRRT

Margolis Patricia • Librarian • Solomon Schechter Day School • Newton Center, MA 02159

Margolis Sally T. • Deerfield Public Library • Deerfield, IL 60015 • ALSC

Marguerite Mary Sr. • Librarian • Dominican College of San Rafael Archbishop Alemany Library • San Rafael, CA 94901 • ACRL ALCTS

Marguglio C. A. Mrs • Fayetteville, NC 28304 • ALSC

Margutti Elizabeth A. • Public Services Librarian • University of Virginia Clemons Library • Charlottesville, VA 22904-0100 • ACRL LIRT

Marhanka Jane • Oakland, CA 94606

Marhenke Chris E. • Government Documents Librarian • Broward County Division of Libraries Broward County Library • Fort Lauderdale, FL 33301

Marhoul Thea C. • Riverside, IL 60546 • AASL

Mariconda Richard L. • Children's Services Librarian • Tenafly Public Library • Tenafly, NJ 07670-2087

Marics Joseph F. Jr. • Head Librarian • Assemblies of God Theological Seminary Library • Springfield, MO 65803 • LITA

Marie Jacquelyn • Women's Studies Librarian • University of California • Santa Cruz, CA 95064 • ACRL

Marie Paula Sister • Camp Hill, PA 17011

Marill Jennifer L. • Automation Planning Analyst • Library of Congress Automation Planning & Liaison • Washington, DC 20540 • ALCTS LITA

Marine Barbara A. • Director • Washington Township Library • Washington, IL 61571 • PLA

Marine Stephen A. • Head, Clln. Mgt.& Proc. Serv Div • University of Cincinnati • Cincinnati, OH 45221-0033 • ALCTS LAMA LITA

Marinelli Anne V. • Hibbing, MN 55746 • Continuing

Marino Fonseca Yolanda C. • Evanston, IL 60201

Marino Hector A. • Document Supervisor • World Bank • Washington, DC 20433

Marino Jacqueline • Librarian • Waverly Park Elementary School • E. Rockaway, NY 11423 • ALSC

Marino Jane B. • Children's Librarian • White Plains Public Library • White Plains, NY 10601 • ALSC

Marino John J. • Trustee • Lincolnwood Public Library District • Lincolnwood, IL 60646 • ALTA

Marino Lucia A. • Reference Librarian • University of Iowa Libraries • Iowa City, IA 52242-1379 • ACRL

Marino Samuel J. • Denton, TX 76205 • ACRL ALCTS*Life*

Marinsky Deborah • Librarian • Frenchtown Elementary School • Frenchtown, NJ 08825 • AASL

Marinuzzi Karen-Lynn M. • Rare Book & Manuscript Library • Yale University • New Haven, CT 06520 • ACRL

Mario Crystal • Xerox Imaging Systems • Peabody, MA 01960

Marion Gail E. • Librarian • Jacksonville Public Libraries Main Library • Jacksonville, FL 32202

Marion Mary • Assistant Reference Librarian • Jefferson Parish Library • Metairie, LA 70010

Marion Michael B. • Customer Support Representative • IBM Corporation • Oakland, CA 94607

Marion Yvonne N. • Librarian Assistant • Virginia Commonwealth University Tompkins-McCaw Library • Richmond, VA 23298-0001

Marish Thelma J. • Grambling State University A. C. Lewis Memorial Library • Grambling, LA 71245

Marix Mary L. • Louisiana State University Medical Center Library • New Orleans, LA 70112-2223 • ACRL RASD LIRT

Mark Beth L. • Messiah College Murray Learning Resources Center • Grantham, PA 17027 • ACRL

Mark Janice V. • Elementary School Librarian • Garfield Heights Board of Education William Foster School • Garfield Heights, OH 44125

Mark Kathleen D. Gibb • Librarian • Harrodsburg High School • Harrodsburg, KY 40330 • AASL

Mark Linda R. • Assoc. Ed., Wilson Lib. Bulletin • H. W. Wilson Company • Bronx, NY 10452 • ACRL

Mark Paul • Information Specialist III • Hawaii State Public Library System • Honolulu, HI 96813

Mark Paula F. • Instructional Services Librarian • University of Massachusetts Library • Amherst, MA 01003 • ACRL

Markarian Linda • Longmeadow, MA 01106

Markel Bonnie • Head of Children's Services • Merrick Public Library • Merrick, NY 11566

Markel J. Louise • Oak Ridge, TN 37830 • ACRL RASD
                                                           Life

Markell Barbara J. • Head Circulation Services • Sno-Isle Regional Library • Marysville, WA 98271-9164

Marker Rhonda J. • Hd,Orig Mono Catlg & Prin Catlgr • Rutgers University Libraries Technical & Automated Services • Piscataway, NJ 08855 • ALCTS LITA GODORT

Markette Marilyn • Director • Huntingdon Valley Library • Huntingdon Valley, PA 19006

Markevich Beverly J. • Trustee • Schwartz-Hill Book Company • Southbury, CT 06488

Markey Kate L. • Solano County Library • Fairfield, CA 94533

Markey Leslie A. • Technical Services Librarian • Brooks Memorial Library • Brattleboro, VT 05301

Markey Lois R. • Woburn, MA 01801 • ALSC

Markey Penny S. • Asst. Library Administrator • County of Los Angeles Public Library • Downey, CA 90241-7400 • ALSC PLA

Markey Raymond H. • President • New York Public Library • New York, NY 10018 • PLA RASD IFRT SORT SRRT

Markgraf Jill S. • University of Mississippi Medical Center • Jackson, MS 39216-4505

Markham-Smith Sally • Marshall, VA 22115

Markham James W. • University of California UCSB Library • Santa Barbara, CA 93106-9010 • ACRL ALCTS

Markham Scott C. • Cataloger • Minneapolis Public Library & Information Center • Minneapolis, MN 55401-1992 • ALCTS PLA SRRT

Markham Susan D. • Head, Branch Operations • Huntsville-Madison County Public Library • Huntsville, AL 35804 • PLA

Markiewicz Sally H. • Children's Librarian • Plumb Memorial Library Huntington Branch • Shelton, CT 06484

Markinson Andrea B. • Valley Stream, NY 11581

Markiw Michael • Slavic Studies Librarian • Arizona State University Libraries • Tempe, AZ 85287-1006 • ACRL

Markland Mary J. • Physical Sciences Librarian • North Dakota State University Library • Fargo, ND 58105-5599 • ACRL SRRT

Markle Aldeen B. • Newlington, VA 22122

Markley Beth A. • School Library Media Specialist • West Antioch Elementary School • Shawnee Mission, KS 66203 • AASL

Markley E. Elaine • Children's Librarian • Irving Public Library • Irving, TX 75060 • ALSC

Markley Susan B. • Villanova University Falvey Memorial Library • Villanova, PA 19085-1699 • ACRL

Markowetz Marianna • Milwaukee, WI 53214 • CLENE *Continuing*

Markowitz Lois • Head, Technical Services • Touro College Law School Library • Huntington, NY 11743 • ACRL IFRT

Marks Betty L. • Faxon Company • Los Gatos, CA 95030

Marks Carol Satin • Highland Pk, IL 60035

Marks Cicely P. • Sr. Technical Service Specialist • American Overseas Book Company • Norwood, NJ 07648 • ALCTS AFLRT

Marks Cynthia J. • Assistant Librarian • University of Massachusetts-Dartmouth Library • North Dartmouth, MA 02747 • ACRL ALCTS

Marks Jane A. • Information Services Librarian • Alabama Public Library Service • Montgomery, AL 36130

Marks Janice S. • Sales Manager • IME • Dedham, MA 02026-6790

Marks Joy W. • Librarian • Wylie Middle School • Wylie, TX 75098 • AASL

Marks Kenneth E. • Director Academic Library Svs. • East Carolina University Joyner Library • Greenville, NC 27858-4353 • ACRL LAMA LITA

Marks Lucy K. • Assistant Methodist Cataloger • Drew University • Madison, NJ 07940-4007 • ACRL

Marks Mary L. • Belton, TX 76513

Marks Mary T. • Library Director • Daniel Webster College • Nashua, NH 03060 • ACRL

Marks Roland P. • Reference Librarian • Houston Public Library Carnegie Branch • Houston, TX 77009

Marks Samuel M. III • Trustee • Memphis-Shelby County Public Library and Information Center • Memphis, TN 38104-4025 • ALTA PLA

Marks Susan • Coordinator Access Services • University of Iowa Libraries • Iowa City, IA 52242-1379 • ACRL LAMA

Markus Florence • Santa Barbara, CA 93105 • Continuing

Markus Jacqueline P. • Toledo, OH 43620

Markus Timothy J. • Technical Servs./Systems Lbrn. • Oklahoma City Community College Learning Resources Center • Oklahoma City, OK 73159

Markuson Barbara E. • Executive Director • Indiana Cooperative Library Services Authority (INCOLSA) • Indianapolis, IN 46278 • ACRL ALCTS LITA IFRT LRRT

Markuson Carolyn • Sudbury, MA 01776 • AASL RASD

Markuson Jayne L. • Pt. Angeles, WA 98362

Markwiese Catherine M. • Reference Librarian • Milwaukee Public Library • Milwaukee, WI 53233 • ACRL PLA RASD *Life*

Markwith Michael W. • Richmond, VA 23225 • ACRL ALCTS LITA

Markworth Lawrence L. • Supervisor Technical Library • Hughes Research Labs, RL84 • Malibu, CA 90265

Marlatt Greta E. • Librarian • San Diego State University Love Library • San Diego, CA 92182-0511 • ACRL AFLRT GODORT

Marley Janis E. • Librarian • Truman College, LRC • Chicago, IL 60640

Marley Susan L. • Media Specialist • Washington Elementary School • Westfield, IN 46074 • AASL

Marlin Joyce • Senior Branch Librarian • Contra Costa County Library Concord Branch • Concord, CA 94519

Marlin Michael L. • Student • University of Washington Graduate School of Library and Information Science • Seattle, WA 98195 • LITA EMIERT IFRT SRRT

Marlow Julie C. • Reference Librarian • Gainesville College John Harrison Hosch Library • Gainesville, GA 30503 • ACRL

Marlow Marilyn E. • Literary Agent/Exec Vice Pres • Curtis Brown Ltd • New York, NY 10003

Marlow Sandra K • Institutional Librarian • Fernald State School Library Services • Belmont, MA 02178 • ASCLA IFRT

Marlowe-Dziuk Rosemary C. • Lead Reference Librarian • National Defense University • Washington, DC 20319 • AFLRT

Marlowe Carol I. • Adult Service Librarian • Rahway Free Public Library • Rahway, NJ 07065 • PLA YALSA *Life*

Marman Edward D. • Librarian • Franklin Junior High School Wayne-Westland Schools • Wayne, MI 48184 • ALTA

Marmion Dan K. • Head, Library System • Oklahoma State University Edmon Low Library • Stillwater, OK 74078-0375 • LITA

Marmozewicz Phyllis M. • Secretary • Suburban Library System • Burr Ridge, IL 60521

Marner Jonathan C. • Database Management Division • Texas A & M University Sterling C. Evans Library • College Station, TX 77843-5000 • ACRL ALCTS LITA NMRT

Maroney Daryle • Librarian • Georgia State University Pullen Library • Atlanta, GA 30303-3081

Maroney Diane E. • Vienna, VA 22180

Maroney Patricia J. • Chattanooga-Hamilton County Bicentennial Library • Chattanooga, TN 37402

Maroon Lois K. • Librarian II • Clearwater Countryside Library • Clearwater, FL 34621

Maroscher Betty J. • Learning Resource Center Coor. • Saint Philip's College LRC • San Antonio, TX 78203 • ACRL LAMA

Maroscia Marie F. • Serials Librarian • Brooklyn College Library • Brooklyn, NY 11210 • ALCTS LITA

Marose Georganna • Co-Librarian • Hometown Public Library • Oak Lawn, IL 60456

Marotti Frank Jr. • Instructor • Sam Houston State University Newton Gresham Library • Huntsville, TX 77341-2281

Marovich Isabel • Library Trustee • Kalamazoo Public Library • Kalamazoo, MI 49007-5270 • ALTA PLA

Marple Rebbecca Jane • Librarian • Window Rock High School • Fort Defiance, AZ 86504

Marples Sarah T. • Librarian • Marshfield High School • Marshfield, MA 02050 • AASL IFRT LIRT LRRT

Marquand Fanny E. Miss • Hastings-Hudson, NY 10706 • Continuing

Marquardt Larry Dean • University of Osteopathic Medicine and Health Sciences Library • Des Moines, IA 50312 • ACRL

Marquardt Steve R. • Director • University of Wisconsin-Eau Claire William D. McIntyre Library • Eau Claire, WI 54702 • ACRL ALCTS LAMA LITA RASD GODORT LIRT LRRT

Marquart Phyllis J. • Oyster Bay, NY 11771 • ACRL EMIERT SRRT

Marques Audrey J. • Eastampton, NJ 08060 • AFLRT FLRT

Marquette Carl G. Jr • Department Head • Public Library of Cincinnati and Hamilton County • Cincinnati, OH 45202

Marquez Teresa C. • Student • East Carolina University Department of Library & Information Studies • Greenville, NC 27858-4353

Marquis Daniel • College of Granby Bibliotheque • Granby, PQ, J2G 9H7 Canada • ACRL

Marquis Kathleen A. • Director • Baxter Memorial Library • Gorham, ME 04038 • PLA

Marquis Rollin P. • Dearborn, MI 48124

Marr Eloise • Librarian • Webling Elementary School • Honolulu, HI 96822 • AASL

Marr Miriam • Librarian II • Los Altos Public Library • Los Altos, CA 94022

Marr Rhonda A. • Cataloger/Automation Manager • Burton Public Library • Burton, OH 44021

Marra Jean • Editor • H. W. Wilson Company • Bronx, NY 10452 • ALCTS RASD

Marrazzo William J. • Trustee • Free Library of Philadelphia • Philadelphia, PA 19103 • ALTA

Marredeth Gail E. • Health Sciences Librarian • Cleveland State University Library • Cleveland, OH 44115 • ACRL LIRT

Marren Patricia P. • Media Specialist • Ramsey Junior High Library • Saint Paul, MN 55105 • AASL

Marrero Carmen A. • Student • Florida State University School of Library and Information Studies • Tallahassee, FL 32306-2048 • ACRL ALCTS LITA PLA RASD EMIERT NMRT

Marrero Marilee • Community Library Manager • County of Los Angeles Public Library Norwalk Library 501 • Norwalk, CA 90650

Marrical Beverly • Watseka Community High School • Watseka, IL 60970 • AASL YALSA

Marriott Catherine E. • Coor. of Computer Library Serv. • Orchard Park Central Schools • Orchard Park, NY 14127 • AASL

Marriott Lois I. • Asst. Dean, Instructional Resour • Southwestern College • Chula Vista, CA 91910 • ACRL

Marritt Isabel A. • Media Specialist • Chatham High School • Chatham, NJ 07928 • AASL

Marrs Sharon • Librarian • Keystone Oaks School District • Castle Shannon, PA 15234 • AASL

Marsales Rita • Data Base Management Librarian • Rice University Fondren Library • Houston, TX 77251-1892 • LITA

Marschall Katherine T. • Cataloging Clerk • University of Notre Dame Libraries • Notre Dame, IN 46556 • ALCTS IFRT

Marsden Mary T. • East Hanover Township Library • East Hanover, NJ 07936

Marsen Louise • Media Specialist • Brookdale Community College • Lincroft, NJ 07738

Marsh Ann K. • Merriam, KS 66202

Marsh Carrie L. • Reference Librarian • Claremont Colleges Scripps College • Claremont, CA 91711 • ACRL

Marsh Corrie V. • Head of Acquisitions Services • Notis Systems Inc. • Evanston, IL 60201-3622 • ALCTS LITA

Marsh Elizabeth C. • Dublin, OH 43017

Marsh Ellie E. • Social Science Reference Ln. • Kansas State University Libraries • Manhattan, KS 66506-7166 • ACRL

Marsh Frieda L. • Acquisitions Supervisor • Lake Lanier Regional Library Lawrenceville Branch • Lawrenceville, GA 30245-4707

Marsh Martha Mae • Salina, KS 67401 • AASL YALSA *Continuing*

Marsh Paul L. • Metropolitan Community College • Omaha, NE 68103 • LITA

Marsh Sharon A. • School Library Media Specialist • Horace Mann School • Springfield, MO 65807 • AASL IFRT

Marsh Sharon L. • Documents Section Chief • Eastern Kentucky University John Grant Crabbe Library • Richmond, KY 40475-3121 • GODORT

Marsh Steven D. • Seattle, WA 98133 • EMIERT IFRT

Marsh Sue C. • Director, Current Collections • Harvard University Library Baker Library • Boston, MA 02163 • ACRL LAMA RASD

Marsh Valerie H. • Fort Myers, FL 33901-8654

Marshalek Anthony C. • Director • North East Ohio Instructional Media Center • Warren, OH 44481 • AASL

Marshalek Sonja E. • Indiana University at South Bend Franklin D. Schurz Library • South Bend, IN 46634 • LITA

Marshall Albert P. • Ypsilanti, MI 48197 • ACRL *Continuing*

Marshall Anita • Bibliographer/Clln. Management • Michigan State University Libraries • East Lansing, MI 48824-1048 • ALCTS EMIERT

Marshall Ann L. • Librarian • Intelsat Library • Washington, DC 20008 • LITA

Marshall Calvin B. III Dr. • Trustee • Brooklyn Public Library • Brooklyn, NY 11238 • ALTA

Marshall Charlotte • Wilton, CT 06897 • Life

Marshall Charlotte C. • Cataloger • University of South Carolina Libraries • Columbia, SC 29208

Marshall Christine • Poplar Creek Public Library Dist • Streamwood, IL 60107 • ALTA

Marshall Clyde V. • Reference Librarian • Multnomah County Library Central Branch • Portland, OR 97205 • PLA

Marshall David L. • Assistant Head of Acquisitions • Georgetown University Joseph Mark Lauinger Library • Washington, DC 20057-1006 • ACRL ALCTS

Marshall Debra H. • Associate Consultant • H.B.W. Associates, Inc. • Denton, TX 76201

Marshall Ellen • Hingham, MA 02043

Marshall Eunice Anne • Student • University of North Texas School of Library & Information Sciences • Denton, TX 76203

Marshall Glenda R. • Student • University of North Texas School of Library & Information Sciences • Denton, TX 76203 • AASL

Marshall Jane C. • Norfolk Public Library • Norfolk, VA 23510-1776 • LITA PLA

Marshall Jane R. • Head Cataloger • Hamilton College Burke Library • Clinton, NY 13323 • ALCTS LITA

Marshall Jerilyn A. • Assistant Librarian • Northwestern University Joseph Schaffner Library • Chicago, IL 60611 • ACRL IRRT

Marshall Jessica A. • Assoc. Dean of Technical Servs. • Slippery Rock University of Pennsylvania • Slippery Rock, PA 16057 • ACRL ALCTS LAMA LITA

Marshall Joan • Non-Salaried Librarian • Brooklyn College Library • Brooklyn, NY 11210 • ALCTS IFRT SRRT

Marshall John David • Professor • Middle Tennessee State University Library • Murfreesboro, TN 37132 • ACRL RASD   *Life*

Marshall Julie C. • Student • University of Michigan School of Information and Library Studies • Ann Arbor, MI 48109-1092

Marshall Karen Kates • Instructional Services Librarian • University of Virginia Alderman Library • Charlottesville, VA 22903-2498 • ACRL RASD LIRT

Marshall Kathryn E. • Librarian • United States Air Force Air Weather Service Technical Library • Scott AFB, IL 62225-5458 • FLRT

Marshall Linnea D. • Assistant Librarian • Western Montana College Lucy Carson Library • Dillon, MT 59725 • ACRL ALCTS

Marshall Margaret A. • Reference Librarian • Allen Public Library • Allen, TX 75002

Marshall Margaret E. • Director • Merrimack Public Library • Merrimack, NH 03054 • PLA

Marshall Mary E. • Dayton, OH 45402 • LITA RASD

Marshall Michele R. • Director • Cora J Belden Library • Rocky Hill, CT 06067 • Life

Marshall Nancy H. • University Librarian • College of William & Mary Earl Gregg Swem Library • Williamsburg, VA 23187-8794 • ACRL RASD

Marshall Norma E. • Bellevue, WA 98004

Marshall Paula R. • A-V Librarian • Manchester High School • Richmond, VA 23235

Marshall Peter J. • New Berlin, WI 53151

Marshall Robert A. Mrs. • Hendersonville, NC 28739 • Continuing

Marshall Ruth Ann • Pittsburgh, PA 15232 • Continuing

Marshall Sharan D. • Assistant Director • Washington County Free Library • Hagerstown, MD 21740 • PLA

Marshall Stephanie D. • Student • State University of New York (SUNY) School of Information & Library Studies • Buffalo, NY 14260 • PLA

Marshall Susan K. • Wenatchee, WA 98801

Marshall Susan O. • Reference Librarian • University of Southwestern Louisiana Libraries • Lafayette, LA 70503

Marshall Thomas H. • Catalog Librarian • University of Arizona Library • Tucson, AZ 85721 • ALCTS LITA

Marson Joyce • Librarian • White Memorial Medical Center Courville-Abbott Memorial Library • Los Angeles, CA 90033

Marsteller Matthew R. • Information Specialist II • EG & G Washington Analytical Services Center, Inc. • Morgantown, WV 26507-0880 • ACRL

Marstiller Joan M. • Student • University of Pittsburgh School of Library and Information Science • Pittsburgh, PA 15260

Marston Hope Irvin • Blackriver, NY 13612 • AASL

Mart Jackie E. • Head of Inf. & Reference • Pikes Peak Library District • Colorado Springs, CO 80901

Martel Michelle • Arlington Heights, IL 60004 • ACRL

Martell Charles • Dean & University Librarian • California State University-Sacramento Library • Sacramento, CA 95819-6039 • ACRL LITA

Martell Joyce • Librarian II • San Bernardino County Library Rialto Branch • Rialto, CA 92376 • PLA

Martell Sheila H. • Librarian • Blue Ridge Community College • Weyers Cove, VA 24486

Martelle Harold D. Jr. • Sacramento, CA 95833 • LAMA PLA   *Life*

Marten Kathleen E. • Children's Librarian II • Akron-Summit County Public Library Maple Valley Branch • Akron, OH 44320 • ALSC

Marten Ramona S. • Librarian • Harding School • Santa Barbara, CA 93101

Martens Kathryn I. • Administrative Librarian • Crystal Lake Public Library • Crystal Lake, IL 60014 • LAMA PLA

Martens Margaret B. Miss • Librarian • Pilot Butte Junior High School Library • Bend, OR 97701 • ALCTS RASD   *Continuing*

Martens Shirleen R. • Argos, IN 46501 • PLA

Marthaler Margaret Sr • Director • Saint Francis Convent • Little Falls, MN 56345

Marthey Rebecca J. • Assistance Administrator • Wabash Valley Library Network • Lafayette, IN 47901-1470

Marthinson Normakay Miss • Community Librarian • Minneapolis Public Library Roosevelt Community Branch • Minneapolis, MN 55406

Marti Gail • Assistant Director • Mishawaka-Penn Public Library • Mishawaka, IN 46544

Martin-Diaz Pamela A. • Librarian • Chicago Public Library Logan Square Branch • Chicago, IL 60647 • ALSC PLA EMIERT SRRT

Martin-Lee Valerie A. • Media Specialist • Department of Defense-Bermuda Chaffee High School • NAS Bermuda FPO, NY 09560 • AASL EMIERT LIRT

Martin Alphonse Jr. • Trustee • New Orleans Public Library • New Orleans, LA 70140 • ALTA

Martin Ann F. • City Librarian • Paso Robles Public Library • Paso Robles, CA 93446 • LAMA PLA

Martin Ann Jeryl • Academic Exchange Progam Div. • United States Information Agency (USIA) • Washington, DC 20547

Martin Ann M. • Library Assistant • Holiday Heights Elementary School • North Richland Hills, TX 76180 • ALSC

Martin Ann M. • Head Librarian • Chesterfield County Public Schools Bailey Bridge Middle School • Midlothian, VA 23112

Martin Anna L. • Literacy Coordinator • Yuma County Library District • Yuma, AZ 85364 • PLA

Martin Barbara K. • Media Specialist • Cotton Joint Unified School District • Bloomington, CA 92316 • NMRT

Martin Basil D. • Student • Clarion University of Pennsylvania College of Library Science • Clarion, PA 16214 • IFRT SRRT

Martin Betty • Denver, CO 80222 • AASL ALCTS ALSC ASCLA LAMA LITA PLA RASD YALSA ERT LIRT LRRT NMRT SRRT

Martin Betty C. • Director • Vigo County Public Library • Terre Haute, IN 47807 • LAMA PLA

Martin Betty Ruth • Northwood Elementary School • Baltimore, MD 21239 • AASL

Martin Beverly A. • Director • Johnson County Public Library • Franklin, IN 46131 • LAMA PLA IFRT

Martin Bradford L. • Student • University of Washington Graduate School of Library and Information Science • Seattle, WA 98195

Martin Candace L. • Bay City, MI 48706 • AASL ALSC YALSA

Martin Cheryl M. • Student • University of North Texas School of Library & Information Sciences • Denton, TX 76203

Martin D. Lindsey • Tazewell County Public Library • Tazewell, VA 24651

Martin David R. • Branford, CT 06405

Martin Dawn • Student • Indiana University School of Library and Information Science • Bloomington, IN 47405 • ALSC PLA

Martin Dean • Trustee • Tacoma Public Library • Tacoma, WA 98402 • ALTA

Martin Deesha R. • Children's Librarian • Milford Public Library • Milford, CT 06460 • ALSC

Martin Dena Z. • Student • University of Pittsburgh School of Library and Information Science • Pittsburgh, PA 15260 • ACRL

Martin Diane C. • River Oaks High School • Monroe, LA 71203

Martin Diane L. • Student • University of Michigan 123 Undergraduate Library • Ann Arbor, MI 48109-1185

Martin Dolores L. • Hot Springs, AR 71913

Martin Elizabeth • Cedar Falls, IA 50613 • AASL   *Continuing*

Martin Elizabeth M. • Adult Services Librarian • Romeo District Library • Romeo, MI 48065

Martin Ernest • Associate Executive Director • American Library Association • Chicago, IL 60611-2795

Martin Fenton S. • Librarian • Indiana University-Research Collection Department of Political Science • Bloomington, IN 47401

Martin Fowler C. • Denver, CO 80231 • Continuing

Martin Fred • Trustee • Detroit Public Library • Detroit, MI 48202 • ALTA

Martin George McKinley • Silver Spring, MD 20910 • ACRL

Martin Geraldine • Pointe Coupee Parish Library • New Road, LA 70760 • ALTA

Martin Gilbert D. • Student • Drexel University College of Information Studies • Philadelphia, PA 19104-2875

Martin Harriet Z. • Brookhaven National Lab Research Library Building 477 • Upton, NY 11973

Martin Harry S. III • Director • Harvard Law School Library • Cambridge, MA 02138 • ACRL LITA GODORT IFRT IRRT

Martin Hazel L. • Library Director • Stevens County Library • Hugoton, KS 67951

Martin Heather • Graduate Student • University of South Carolina College of Library & Information Science • Columbia, SC 29208 • RASD SRRT

Martin Heidi K. • Indianapolis, IN 46227

Martin Helen Sr. • Library Director • Canton Free Library • Canton, NY 13617 • ACRL

Martin Helen T. • Mamie Doud Eisenhower Pub. Lib. • Broomfield, CO 80020 • LAMA PLA YALSA GODORT

Martin Iva R. • Manchester, MD 21102 • AASL EMIERT IFRT SRRT

Martin J. David • Business Librarian • University of Iowa Libraries • Iowa City, IA 52242-1379 • ACRL LITA RASD IRRT

Martin James R. Dr. • Director, Libraries • University of Southern Mississippi • Hattiesburg, MS 39406-5053 • ACRL LAMA

Martin Janet • Student • University of Texas at Austin Graduate School of Library & Information Sciences • Austin, TX 78712-1276

Martin Janet L. • Bloomfield, KY 40008

Martin Jean Gregory • S.P. Morton Middle School • Franklin, VA 23851

Martin Jeannette • Tampa-Hillsborough County Public Library • Tampa, FL 33602 • PLA

Martin John B. • Kentucky State University Blazer Library • Frankfort, KY 40601 • ALCTS

Martin John E. • Director • Oak Park Public Library • Oak Park, MI 48237 • ALSC LAMA PLA

Martin John H. • Corning, NY 14830

Martin John H. Jr. • Head, Division of Branches • Orange County Library System Orlando Public Library • Orlando, FL 32801-2471 • LAMA PLA   *Life*

Martin Jolene P. • Student • University of South Carolina College of Library & Information Science • Columbia, SC 29200 • AASL

Martin Judith D. • Williamsville, NY 14221

Martin Judith L. • Dan O. Root Elementary School • Suisun, CA 94585 • AASL

Martin Judith R. • Cataloger • West Virginia Wesleyan College Annie Merner Pfeiffer Library • Buckhannon, WV 26201-2998 • ALCTS

Martin Judy • Tempe Public Library • Tempe, AZ 85282

Martin Julia A. • Student • Kent State University School of Library & Information Science • Kent, OH 44242-0001 • PLA

Martin June • Trustee • Anderson County Library • Anderson, SC 29622-4047

Martin June R. • Charleston, WV 25311 • Continuing

Martin Katherine F. • Head, Collection Management • University of Northern Iowa Donald O. Rod Library • Cedar Falls, IA 50613-3675 • ALCTS LAMA RASD

Martin Kathleen A. • Rockford, IL 61108-2326

Martin Kathleen E. • Catalog Librarian • Huntington Library • San Marino, CA 91108

Martin Kathleen J. • University of North Carolina Walter Clinton Jackson Library • Greensboro, NC 27412-5201 • ACRL RASD

Martin Kimberly A. • Assistant Librarian-Cataloging • Washington University Libraries • Saint Louis, MO 63130 • ALCTS

Martin Kimberly W. • Catalog Librarian • Stetson University DuPont-Ball Library • De Land, FL 32720-3769 • ACRL

Martin Kye • School Librarian • Lew Muckle School • St. Croix, VI 00820

Martin Laurelle • Supervising Librarian • Solano County Library Springstowne Branch • Vallejo, CA 94590

Martin Linda R. • Library Assistant • Ursuline Academy High School • Wilmington, DE 19806 • AASL

Martin Lori • Library Director • Bradley, Arant, Rose, & White Attorneys • Birmingham, AL 35203

Martin Louis E. • Director • Linda Hall Library • Kansas City, MO 64110 • ACRL

Martin Lowell A. Dr. • Ticonderoga, NY 12883 • Honorary

Martin Lyn M. • State University of New York (SUNY) University Libraries • Albany, NY 12222 • ACRL ALCTS

Martin M. Marlene • Human Relations Area Files, Inc. • New Haven, CT 06511 • LITA

Martin Marcia J. • Bibl. Instr. and Ref. Librarian • University of Cincinnati • Cincinnati, OH 45221-0033 • ACRL LITA RASD

Martin Margaret • Librarian • Holston Middle School • Blountville, TN 37617 • AASL

Martin Margaret E. • Ellensburg Public Library • Ellensburg, WA 98926

Martin Margaret N. • Columbia, MO 65203 • Life

Martin Marilyn • Library Administrator • Henderson State University • Arkadelphia, AR 71999-0001 • ACRL

Martin Marilyn K. • Branch Librarian • Lynchburg Public Library • Lynchburg, VA 24504

Martin Marjorie Anne • Head of Technical Processing • Bettendorf Public Library • Bettendorf, IA 52722 • ALCTS

Martin Mark E. • Director of Archives • T.L.L. Temple Memorial Library • Diboll, TX 75941 • SRRT

Martin Mary A • Claremont Colleges Libraries Honnold/Mudd Library • Claremont, CA 91711 • GODORT

Martin Mary A. • Washington, DC 20017

Martin Mary E. • Director • University of Saint Thomas, Divinity Archbishop Ireland Memorial Library • Saint Paul, MN 55105

Martin Mary I. • Long Beach, CA 90808 • AASL
Martin Mary O. • Powell Elementary School • Birmingham, AL 35203 • AASL
Martin Melissa S. • Head Adult Services • Albany County Public Library • Laramie, WY 82070 • RASD
Martin Moxie • Branch Manager • Houston Public Library Carnegie Branch • Houston, TX 77009
Martin Murray S. • Windsor, CT 06095 • ACRL ALCTS LAMA LITA ILERT
Martin Nadia J • Reference Info. Services • University of Michigan Libraries Alfred Taubman Medical Library • Ann Arbor, MI 48109-0726
Martin Nannete • Silver Spring, MD 20910
Martin Nannette • Silver Spring, MD 20910 • GODORT
Martin Natalie K. • Assistant Branch Manager • Charlotte & Mecklenburg Public Library Morrison Regional Library • Charlotte, NC 28211 • RASD
Martin Noelene P. • Interlibrary Loan Librarian • Pennsylvania State University Pattee Library • University Park, PA 16802 • ACRL LAMA RASD
Martin Norma H. • Head, Catalog Dept. • Louisiana State University Libraries Troy H. Middleton Library • Baton Rouge, LA 70803-3342 • ACRL ALCTS LAMA
Martin Patricia • Young Adult Librarian • Indian River County Library • Vero Beach, FL 32960 • YALSA
Martin Patricia • Tulsrosa, NM 88352
Martin Paula L. • Sandy, UT 84092
Martin Philip • Library Trustee • Hammond Public Library • Hammond, IN 46320 • ALTA
Martin Phyllis J. • Head,Community Services • Cleveland Public Library • Cleveland, OH 44114-1271 • LAMA PLA
Martin Phyllis R. • K-12 Library Dept. Chair • Manheim Township School District • Lancaster, PA 17601 • AASL
Martin Rebecca R. • Director of Libraries • University of Vermont Bailey Howe Library • Burlington, VT 05405-0036 • ACRL LAMA
Martin Robert A. • Librarian II • Brevard Correctional Institution Library • Sharpes, FL 32959
Martin Robert J. • Product Manager • Broderbund Software • San Rafael, CA 94941
Martin Robert S. • Asst Dir of Ln for Spec Clln • Louisiana State University Libraries • Baton Rouge, LA 70803 • ACRL LAMA LHRT LRRT MAGERT
Martin Robin E. • Director • Central College Library • Pella, IA 50219 • ACRL
Martin Roger M. • Monterey, CA 93943 • ACRL RASD *Life*
Martin Ron G. • Assoc Dean for Public Services • Indiana State University Cunningham Memorial Library • Terre Haute, IN 47809 • LAMA
Martin Rosa Maria • Pasadena Public Library • Pasadena, CA 91101
Martin Rose Marie Sr. • Librarian • Aquinas College Learning Resource Center • Grand Rapids, MI 49506-1799
Martin Rosemary S. • Director • Fairfield County District Library • Lancaster, OH 43130 • PLA
Martin Ruth A. Harrison • Reference Librarian • Sonnenschein Nath & Rosenthal • Chicago, IL 60606 • ALCTS RASD
Martin Ruth E. • Reference Librarian • Cedarville College Centennial Library • Cedarville, OH 45314
Martin Salley B. • Director • Marion County Library • Marion, SC 29571 • LAMA PLA
Martin Sally J. • Eanes Independent School District Westlake High School • Austin, TX 78746 • AASL YALSA
Martin Sandra A. • Head, Reference Services • University of Oklahoma Robert M Bird Health Sciences Library • Oklahoma City, OK 73190 • ACRL LITA LRRT
Martin Sara E. • Natl Oceanic & Atmospheic Adm. MASC Library,MC5 • Boulder, CO 80303
Martin Sara J.K. • Lincoln, NE 68502 • LITA
Martin Sharon K. • Longwood, FL 32779
Martin Shelby • Head Cataloger • Montgomery County Community College Learning Resource Center • Blue Bell, PA 19422-0758 • ALCTS
Martin Stephanie • Northeastern University • Boston, MA 02115 • ACRL
Martin Stephen H. • Director • North Madison County Public Library System • Elwood, IN 46036-1598 • PLA
Martin Susan J. • Library/Media Specialist • Garrison Union Free School District • Garrison, NY 10524 • AASL ALSC
Martin Susan K. • University Librarian • Georgetown University Joseph Mark Lauinger Library • Washington, DC 20057-1006 • ACRL LAMA LITA *Life*
Martin Sylvia O. • Coor. of Resource Services • Vanderbilt University Library Jean & Alexander Heard Library • Nashville, TN 37240-0007 • ALCTS
Martin Terry L. • Library Acquisitions • Upjohn Medical Library • Kalamazoo, MI 49001
Martin Tina • Mount Prospect, IL 60056 • YALSA
Martin Virginia A. • Head of Circulation • Rice University Fondren Library • Houston, TX 77251-1892
Martin Walter F. III • Clerk • Yale-New Haven Hospital • New Haven, CT 06481 • PLA
Martin William G. • Library Director • Neshoba County Public Library • Philadelphia, MS 39350 • LAMA PLA
Martindale James A. • Greencastle, IN 46135 • ACRL LAMA *Life*
Martinek Josephine A. • Science Libn/Bibliographer • University of Texas at Arlington • Arlington, TX 76019-0497
Martinez-Nazario Ronaldo • Head Engineering Librarian • University of Puerto Rico • Mayaguez, PR 00708
Martinez-Vidal Vivian D. • Library Director • Bishop Eustace Prep Sch Library • Pennsauken, NJ 08110 • AASL LAMA
Martinez Anna M. • Assistant City Librarian • San Diego Public Library • San Diego, CA 92101 • LAMA PLA
Martinez Antonio • Assistant Director • Victoria Public Library • Victoria, TX 77901 • PLA
Martinez Barbara A. • Senior Librarian • California Department of Housing and Community Development • Sacramento, CA 94252-2055 • LAMA LITA GODORT
Martinez Carmen L. • Assistant County Librarian • Los Angeles Public Library • Los Angeles, CA 90071 • PLA
Martinez Carol M. • Student • Rosary College Graduate School of Library & Information Science • River Forest, IL 60305 • RASD
Martinez Christina M. • Head of User Services • University of Colorado At Colorado Springs Library • Colorado Springs, CO 80933-7150 • ACRL EMIERT
Martinez Dorothy M. • Milwaukee, WI 53214-2842
Martinez Edward B. • Public Access Librarian • El Camino College Library and Media Services • Torrance, CA 90506
Martinez Gena K. • Chicago, IL 60645
Martinez Jane A. • Library Coordinator • Summit Public Schools • Summit, NJ 07901 • AASL LITA
Martinez Jeanne Franco • Librarian • Education Service Center, Region 20 • San Antonio, TX 78208-1899
Martinez Karen Lee • Northwest Area Health Education Center Library • Hickory, NC 28602-9643 • LITA GODORT IFRT MAGERT SRRT
Martinez Kari S. • Head, Tech Services • Salem Public Library • Salem, OR 97309-5020
Martinez Maria E. • Prince George's County Memorial Library System • Hyattsville, MD 20782-2098 • PLA RASD
Martinez Marjorie • Librarian • Buda Public Library • Buda, TX 78610
Martinez Olga Lydia MacNamara • Sunset High School • Dallas, TX 78225 • AASL YALSA
Martinez Rafael A. • Horseheads, NY 14845 • ACRL
Martinez Robert O. • Librarian • Albuquerque Public Library • Albuquerque, NM 87102
Martinez Sahyly • Branch Manager • El Paso Public Library Ysleta Branch Library • El Paso, TX 79907 • RASD
Martini M. Robert • Supervisor/Information Specialist • Baltimore County Public Library • Towson, MD 21204
Martins Sophia J. • Director • Mineola Memorial Library • Mineola, NY 11501 • ALSC RASD
Martinson Carol E. • Librarian II • Saint Paul Public Library • St. Paul, MN 55102 • PLA RASD
Martinson Kathy L. • Student • University of Texas at Austin Graduate School of Library & Information Sciences • Austin, TX 78712-1276
Marton Diane S. • Children's Librarian • Arlington County Department of Libraries • Arlington, VA 22201 • ALSC
Marton Jane E. • Subject Cataloger/Childrens Lit. • Library of Congress • Washington, DC 20541 • ALCTS ALSC
Martorana Janet V. • Documents Librarian • University of California UCSB Library • Santa Barbara, CA 93106-9010 • ACRL LIRT
Martorelli Karen • Librarian • Viola Elementary School • Suffern, NY 10901
Marts Thomas D. • Trustee • Pikes Peak Library District • Pikes Peak, CO 80901 • ALTA
Martyn Beverly A. • San Diego, CA 92115 • ILERT
Martz Frederick M. • Head,Database Mamagement • Yale University Sterling Memorial Library • New Haven, CT 06520 • LITA
Martz Janice L • Midland, MI 48642 • ACRL
Maruca Pat • Cathedral School Library • Raleigh, NC 27603
Marumoto Ikuko • Professor • Osaka Jogakuin Junior College • Chuoku Osaka 540, Japan • AASL ACRL ALSC RASD IFRT LIRT
Maruyama Lenore S. • President • Maruyama Assoc. Inc. • Arlington, VA 22209 • ALCTS RASD *Life*
Marvel Joyce A.K. • Trustee • William Leonard Public Library District • Robbins, IL 60472 • ALTA
Marvin Carolyn • Librarian • Newmarket Elementary School • Newmarket, NH 03857 • AASL
Marvin James C. • Director • Topeka Public Library • Topeka, KS 66604-1374 • ACRL ALTA PLA *Life*
Marvin Kathleen • Systems Analyst • West Chester University Francis Harvey Green Library • West Chester, PA 19383
Marvin Rebecca R. • Aiken Technical College • Aiken, SC 29802 • ACRL
Marx Charles H. • Catalog Librarian • University of Wisconsin Murphy Library • La Crosse, WI 54601 • ACRL ALCTS
Marx Dolores • Assistant Catalog Librarian • Grossmont Union High School District • La Mesa, CA 92044 • AASL YALSA *Life*
Marx Lucy C. • Childrens Librn/Young Adult Spec • Louisville Free Public Library • Louisville, KY 40203-2257 • ALSC YALSA
Marx Victor F. • Reference Librarian/Assoc. Prof. • Central Washington University • Ellensburg, WA 98926 • ACRL
Marxsen Sarah L. • Carrabelle, FL 32322
Marynowych Roman V. • Washington, DC 20017
Marzalado Josephine J. • Quezon City, Philippines
Marzec Kathleen C. • Children's Librarian • Contra Costa County Library • Pleasant Hill, CA 94523
Marzolla Mary K. • Reference Librarian • Widener University School of Law Library • Wilmington, DE 19803-0475
Mascari Walter C. • Head Acquisitions • New Orleans Public Library • New Orleans, LA 70140
Mascia Regina B. • Student • Queens College Graduate School of Library & Information Studies • Flushing, NY 11367
Masck M. Beth A. • Marketing Specialist • University Microfilms International • Ann Arbor, MI 48106-1346 • LITA RASD SRRT
Mase-Brookens Sheryl L. • Head of Technical Services • Kent County Library System • Grand Rapids, MI 49503
Mase Stefanie • Tucson, AZ 85716
Maseda Maria M. • Librarian • Miami Dade Community College • Miami, FL 33176
Masek Doris • Las Vegas, NV 89128 • AASL
Masengill Shirley M. • Children's Book Buyer • The Storyteller • Lafayette, CA 94549 • ALSC
Mash S. David • Director • Columbia Bible College • Columbia, SC 29230-3122 • ACRL ALCTS
Masin Anton C. • South Bend, IN 46615
Masirovits Susan • Director • Henderson Memorial Public Library • Jefferson, OH 44047-1198 • LAMA PLA
Masket Meta M. • Fargo, ND 58103
Maslekoff Barbara • Ohioana Library Association • Columbus, OH 43266-0334
Masley Betty A. • Librarian • Saint Eugene School • Chicago, IL 60656
Masliah Michael L. • Government Publications Ref Ln • County of Los Angeles Public Library Culver City Library 330 • Culver City, CA 90230 • ACRL GODORT
Maslyk Karen L. • Reference Librarian • Rocky River Public Library • Rocky River, OH 44116-2699
Masnik Ann S. • University of Maryland Hornbake Library • College Park, MD 20742 • ACRL
Maso Lawrence A. • Student • Pennsylvania State University Heindel Library • Middletown, PA 17057
Mason-Robinson Sally E. • Chicago, IL 60657 • ILERT VRT
Mason Aileen J. • Student • University of Texas at Austin Graduate School of Library & Information Sciences • Austin, TX 78712-1276 • PLA NMRT
Mason Alexandra • Spencer Librarian • University of Kansas Spencer Research Library • Lawrence, KS 66045-2800 • ACRL ALCTS *Life*
Mason Carol L. • Patapsco High School • Baltimore, MD 21222
Mason Catherine G. • Spokane Public Library Comstock Building Library • Spokane, WA 99201-0976 • RASD
Mason Charlene • Asst Univ Ln for Automated Sys • University of Minnesota Meredith Wilson Library • Minneapolis, MN 55455 • ACRL LAMA LITA
Mason Cheryl J. • Media Specialist • Munster High School • Munster, IN 46321 • AASL
Mason Deborah J. • Librarian II • Chicago Public Library • Chicago, IL 60605 • RASD
Mason Elisa E. • Washington, DC 20007 • IRRT
Mason Elizabeth A. • Medical Librarian • San Jose State University Clark Library • San Jose, CA 95192-0028 • LITA
Mason Ellsworth G. • Lexington, KY 40502 • ACRL LAMA *Life*
Mason Florence M. • Durango, CO 81301 • ACRL LAMA LITA PLA
Mason Gary Stephen Mr. • Librarian • Patten Free Library • Bath, ME 04530 • PLA YALSA
Mason Helen H. • Knoxville, TN 37921 • ACRL PLA *Life*
Mason Helen R. • Chicago, IL 60645

Mason James W. • Preservation Libn/Clln Devlp Ast • Kansas State University Farrell Library • Manhattan, KS 66506-1200 • ACRL ALCTS SRRT

Mason Janice L. • Owings Mills, MD 21117 • IFRT NMRT

Mason John • Marketing Manager, Trade Books • Scholastic Inc. • New York, NY 10003 • ALSC YALSA

Mason John A. Jr. • Wyoming Seminary College Preparatory School • Kingston, PA 18704-3593 • AASL *Life*

Mason Katherine M. • South Milwaukee, WI 53172

Mason Laura L. • Shelbyville, MO 63469

Mason Lida • Serials Librarian • Thiel College • Greenville, PA 16125 • LAMA

Mason Marilyn Gell • Director • Cleveland Public Library • Cleveland, OH 44114-1271 • PLA IRRT

Mason Martha A. • Senior Librarian • Binghamton Psychiatric Center Professional Library • Binghamton, NY 13904 • ASCLA

Mason Martha D. • Assistant Head, Cataloging Dept. • University of South Carolina • Columbia, SC 29208 • ALCTS

Mason Mary Brook • Childrens Librarian • Multnomah County Library Capitol Hill Branch • Portland, OR 97219 • Continuing

Mason Michael Lamott • Library Director • Ocean City Free Public Library • Ocean City, NJ 08226-3071 • ACRL LITA RASD IFRT LRRT NMRT

Mason Monique V. • AVS Librarian • Akron-Summit County Public Library • Akron, OH 44326-0001 • IFRT

Mason Nancy M. • Kingston, NJ 08528

Mason Orpha S. • Tucson, AZ 85741 • Continuing

Mason Pamela R. • United States Department of Agriculture National Agricultural Library • Beltsville, MD 20705-2351 • LITA FLRT

Mason Randall J. • Plymouth, MA 02360

Mason Sharon G. • Reference Librarian • Sunnyvale Public Library • Sunnyvale, CA 94088-3714

Mason Sharon L. • Head Catloging • University of Nebraska at Kearney Library • Kearney, NE 68849 • ALCTS *Life*

Mason Shirley A. • Librarian • Philomath Middle School • Philomath, OR 97370 • AASL ALSC

Mason Theodore D. • Director • East Chicago Public Library • E. Chicago, IN 46312 • AASL PLA

Masone Marsha • Clifton, VA 22024 • AASL

Masoni Daniel • Director • Emporia Public Library • Emporia, KS 66801

Massar Phyllis Y. • Arts & Media Serv Supervisor • Ferguson Library • Stamford, CT 06904 • PLA RASD VRT

Massarelli Mary Pat • Trustee • Harford County Library • Belcamp, MD 21017 • ALTA

Masselink Linda R. • Assistant Director • Davenport College of Business Library • Grand Rapids, MI 49502 • ACRL

Massengill Ellen Webb • Learning Resources Specialist • Littlefield High School • Littlefield, TX 79339 • AASL YALSA

Massengill Tom • Trustee • San Antonio Public Library • San Antonio, TX 78205

Massey-Burzio Virginia • Head, Resource Services • Johns Hopkins University Milton S. Eisenhower Library • Baltimore, MD 21218 • ACRL RASD

Massey Catherine M. • Media Specialist • Northwestern Middle School • Jacksonville, FL 32209 • AASL

Massey Connie H. • Assoc. Dir. Abstracting Services • H. W. Wilson Company • Cambridge, MA 02138 • RASD

Massey Eleanor Nelson • Media Specialist • Campbell Elementary School Library • Metuchen, NJ 08840 • AASL

Massey James E. • Coor. of Admin. Servs. • Harford County Library • Belcamp, MD 21017 • ALSC PLA VRT

Massey Katha D. • Head Catalog Department • University of Georgia Libraries • Athens, GA 30602 • ACRL ALCTS LAMA LITA LHRT

Massey Katherine Jagoe • Director Library Prog & Services • Asssociation For Higher Education of North Texas • Dallas, TX 75248 • ACRL ALCTS ASCLA LAMA LITA PLA RASD CLENE IRRT

Massey Kendra J. • Glenbrook South High School • Glenview, IL 60025 • ACRL ALCTS IFRT

Massey Lorna M. • Durham, NC 27704 • PLA IFRT SRRT

Massey Susan A. • The Historic New Orleans Collection • New Orleans, LA 70130-2179

Massie Dennis R. • Student • Queens College Graduate School of Library & Information Studies • Flushing, NY 11367

Massie Sherry C. • Student • Catholic University of America School of Library and Information Science • Washington, DC 20064

Massin Susan M. • Library Director • Fitzwilliam Town Library • Fitzwilliam, NH 03447

Massingill Alberta R. • Grand Rapids, MI 49546 • Continuing

Massingill Carol S. • Media Specialist • Mt. Hope/ Nanjemoy Elementary • Nanjemoy, MD 20662 • AASL ALSC

Massingill Margie B. • Librarian/Media Specialist • Liberty Middle School • Liberty, SC 29657 • AASL

Massis Bruce E. • Library Director • Jewish Guild for the Blind JGB Cassette Library International • New York, NY 10023

Massman Virgil F. • St. Paul, MN 55113 • ACRL LAMA *Life*

Masson Patricia J. • Head, Collection Development • The American University Library • Washington, DC 20016-8046 • ACRL ALCTS LAMA IFRT IRRT

Massonneau Suzanne • Shelburne, VT 05482 • Continuing

Mast Cynda O. • Assistant Professor • Texas Wesleyan University West Library • Fort Worth, TX 76105

Mast Ruth E. • Dublin, OH 43017

Mast Susan • Children's Librarian • Mount Pleasant Public Library • Mt. Pleasant, IA 52641 • ALSC

Mastalir Janet • Community College of Southern Nevada Library • Las Vegas, NV 89030 • ACRL

Mastalski Wayne • Trustee • Schiller Park Public Library • Schiller Park, IL 60176-1699 • ALTA

Mastel Bonnie M. • Portland, OR 97215

Master Christine • Supervisor • Dade County Public School Library Media Services • Miami, FL 33132 • AASL

Master Lawrence S. • Librarian • Ira Earl Elementary School • Las Vegas, NV 89110

Master Mary R. • Newtown, PA 18940

Masters Anne • Dor. of Media Svs/Technology • Norman Public Schools Indp Sch Dist No. 29 • Norman, OK 73069 • AASL ALSC LAMA LITA YALSA

Masters Deborah C. • George Washington University Gelman Library • Washington, DC 20052 • ACRL LAMA LITA RASD GODORT

Masters Douglas D. • Media Services Administrator • Portage Public Schools Audio-Visual & Library • Portage, MI 49002 • AASL

Masters Karen R. • Clerk • Small Business Administration • Atlanta, GA 30309 • ALSC PLA

Masterson Delta B. • Belleville, IL 62223

Masterson Roann D. • AV Coordinator • University of Mary Library • Bismarck, ND 58504 • ACRL LITA

Masterton George A. Mr • Windsor ON, NGA 6Y6 Canada • ACRL ALCTS *Life*

Mastin Charles D. • San Anselmo, CA 94960

Mastrangelo Paul J. • Flushing, NY 11358

Mastroianni Carolyn Lee • Librarian • F. W. Traner Middle School • Reno, NV 89503

Masuchika Glenn • Technical Services Librarian • Chaminade University • Honolulu, HI 96816

Masud Janice Harding • Hickory Hills, IL 60457 • ACRL LITA RASD

Masumoto Lynn A. • Statewide Children's Serv. Coor. • Hawaii State Public Library System Office of the State Librarian • Honolulu, HI 96813 • ALCTS ALSC

Masura Andrew G. • Orland Park Public Library • Orland Park, IL 60462

Masutani Caroline N. • Librarian • Hawaii State Public Library System Centralized Processing Center • Honolulu, HI 96813 • ALCTS

Mata Vicki • Children's Librarian • Bibliotech Latino Americana • San Jose, CA 95110

Matarazzo James M. • Professor • Simmons College Graduate School of Library & Information Science • Boston, MA 02115

Matazzoni S. F. • Tempe, AZ 85284

Matcham Richard W. • Student • San Jose State University Division of Library & Information Science • San Jose, CA 95192-0029 • RASD SRRT

Mate Albert V. • London ON, N6B 3N8 Canada • ACRL ALCTS LAMA LITA RASD

Matecun Marilyn • Chippewa Valley Schools • Mt Clemens, MI 48043 • AASL

Mateer Jeanette • Media Specialist • Willow Woods Elementary School • Sterling Hts, MI 48312 • AASL

Mateer Karen M. • Catalog Librarian • Augsburg College George Sverdrup Library • Minneapolis, MN 55454 • ALCTS LITA

Mater Dee A. • Skokie, IL 60077

Mates Barbara T. • Regional Libn.,Blind/Phys. Hdcp. • Cleveland Public Library • Cleveland, OH 44114-1271 • ASCLA IFRT

Matheny-White Pat • Librarian • Evergreen State College • Olympia, WA 98505 • EMIERT

Mather Becky R. • Media Specialist • Muscatine High School • Muscatine, IA 52761 • AASL EMIERT

Mathers Janet C. • University of Pittsburgh Libraries Falk Library of the Health Sciences • Pittsburgh, PA 15261 • ACRL RASD

Mathes Jacqueline W. • Librarian • Beyond War Foundation • Palo Alto, CA 94301 • SRRT

Mathes Miriam Snow • Lacey, WA 98503 • AASL ALSC *Continuing*

Matheson Iver A. • Hoquiam, WA 98550 • ACRL

Matheson John William • Baltimore, MD 21201 • ACRL *Continuing*

Matheson Marcia K. • Director • La Crosse County Library • Holmen, WI 54636 • PLA

Matheson Nina W. • Director • Johns Hopkins University Libraries William H Welch Medical Library • Baltimore, MD 21205

Matheson Tim • Attorney • Legal Services of Upper Tennessee • Johnson City, TN 37604

Mathews Anne J. • Director, Education Research L. • United States Department of Education • Washington, DC 20208

Mathews Barbara L. • Director • Churchill County Library • Fallon, NV 89406 • PLA

Mathews Eleanor R. • Head,Reference Dept. • Iowa State University Library • Ames, IA 50011-2140 • ACRL LAMA RASD LIRT LRRT

Mathews Fred L. • Huntsville, AL 35803-1762

Mathews Jane L. • Software Specialist • Data Research Associates Inc. • Saint Louis, MO 63132

Mathews Janice L. • Student • Indiana University School of Library and Information Science • Bloomington, IN 47405 • LHRT

Mathews Karlotta • Librarian • Glenview Public Library • Glenview, IL 60025 • PLA RASD EMIERT

Mathews M Susan • Library Director • Helen Hall Public Library • League City, TX 77573 • LAMA LITA PLA

Mathews Mary C. • Director of Grants Management • Chicago Public Library Harold Washington Library • Chicago, IL 60605 • LAMA PLA

Mathews Mary P. • Acquisitions Librarian • ERIC Processing & Reference Facility • Rockville, MD 20850 • AASL

Mathews Susan C. • Information Services Librarian • Mead Public Library • Sheboygan, WI 53081

Mathews Tressa H. • Milkovich Middle School Library Media Center • Maple Heights, OH 44137

Mathews Virginia H. • Madison, CT 06443 • AASL ALSC *Continuing*

Mathias Christopher R. • Massachusetts Supreme Judicial Court Archives & Records Preser • Boston, MA 02108 • ALCTS

Mathies Bonnie K. • Wright State University • Dayton, OH 45435 • AASL ACRL

Mathies Lorraine Dr. • Librarian Emeritus • University of California Education & Psychology Library • Los Angeles, CA 90024 • ACRL

Mathiesen Penelope P. • Student • Indiana University School of Library and Information Science • Bloomington, IN 47405

Mathieu Lynn • Librarian • Johnnycake Middle School • Baltimore, MD 21207 • AASL

Mathis Barbara B. • Norman, OK 73069

Mathis Barbara E. • Leavenworth, KS 66048 • ASCLA LITA AFLRT FLRT LIRT MAGERT

Mathis Marie V. • Senior Librarian • Los Angeles Public Library Benjamin Franklin Library • Los Angeles, CA 900303

Mathis Mary L. • Norman, OK 73072-3130 • Life

Mathis Rama F. • Acquisitions Supervisor • Texas State Library • Austin, TX 78711 • ALCTS

Mathis Sharon Bell • Ft Washington, MD 20744 • PLA RASD

Mathison Arlene M. • Bismarck, ND 58501-2878

Matisoff Susan I. • Librarian I • Cleveland Heights-University Heights Public Library University Heights Branch • University Heights, OH 44118 • PLA RASD

Matjeka Anne L. • Curriculum Resource Librarian • Boise State University Library • Boise, ID 83725 • ACRL

Matlaw Julia M. • School Librarian • P.S. 84 Manhattan • New York, NY 10025 • AASL EMIERT

Matlock Elizabeth M. • Librarian • Bearden Middle School Knox County School • Knoxville, TN 37909 • AASL

Matlow Randall J. • Director • Ridgway Memorial Library Bullitt County Library • Shepherdsville, KY 40165 • PLA

Matochik Michael J. • Lee County Library System • Sanford, NC 27330

Matonti Emily J. • Caldwell, NJ 07006

Matsco Sandra L. • Head/Adult Services • Rochester Hills Public Library • Rochester, MI 48307 • PLA RASD

Matson Linda R. • President • New Hampshire Library Trustee's Association • Brentwood, NH 03833 • AASL ALTA PLA

Matson Malinda • Northern Marianas College • Saipan, MP 96950 • ACRL ALCTS LAMA

Matson Susan A. • Assistant Serials Librarian • Southern Illinois University Delyte W. Morris Library • Carbondale, IL 62901-6632

Matson Virginia D. • Sherwood, AR 72116-6433

Matsu Dorathy • Everett Public Library • Everett, WA 98201

Matsudo Yasuko • Curator • University of Michigan Libraries • Ann Arbor, MI 48109-1205

Matsui Sachiko • Professor • University of Library & Information Science • Tsukuba-shi, 305, Japan • ACRL ALCTS LITA

Matsumori Donald M. • Honolulu, HI 96816

Matsumoto Iku Mrs. • Trustee • Spokane Public Library Comstock Building Library • Spokane, WA 99201-0976 • ALTA

Matsumura Wilma • Branch Head • Hilo Public Library • Hilo, HI 96720 • PLA

Matsunaga Fay L. • Primary/Elementary Librarian • Twombly Primary School • Fort Lupton, CO 80621 • AASL ALSC

Matsuoka Diane H. • Vice-Principal • Pearl City High School • Pear City, HI 96782 • AASL

Matta Aldor L. • Librarian/Media Specialist • Sarah T. Reed Senior High School • New Orleans, LA 70129 • LITA

Matta Seoud M. • Professor • Pratt Institute Graduate School of Library & Information Science • Brooklyn, NY 11205 • LITA IRRT

Matteo Christine E. • Chief of Public Services • Ocean County Library • Toms River, NJ 08753 • PLA

Matteou Antonia S. • Flushing, NY 11366 • EMIERT IRRT LRRT SRRT

Matter Jane M. • Tucson, AZ 85711

Matter Loretta L. • Library Assistant II • Sierra Madre Public Library • Sierra Madre, CA 91024

Mattern Carolyn • School Library Media Spec. • Glenwood Elementary School • Vestal, NY 13850 • AASL

Mattern Penny G. • Member Serv Ln • Online Computer Library Center (OCLC) • Dublin, OH 43017-3395 • ALCTS LIRT

Mattern Susan P. • Schnecksville, PA 18078

Matters Marion • St. Paul, MN 55105 • ALCTS LITA

Mattes Durrett Daniel • Universidad Anahuac Biblioteca • Mexico 11000, Mexico

Matteson James S. • Branch Librarian • Grand Rapids Public Library • Grand Rapids, MI 49503-3093

Matteucci Emily P. • Librarian • Latham & Watkins • San Francisco, CA 94111 • RASD MAGERT

Matthew Judith A. • Pleasanton, CA 94566 • AASL

Matthews Ann E. • Oxford College O'Kelley Memorial Library • Oxford, GA 30267 • ACRL

Matthews Eleanor • Normal, IL 61761 • Continuing

Matthews Geoffrey Mrs • Medina, OH 44256 • ALSC ASCLA   *Life*

Matthews Geraldine M. • Director • Central Wisconsin Center • Madisn, WI 53713 • PLA

Matthews Geraldine O. • Alcorn State University • Lorman, MS 39096

Matthews Joseph R. • Vice Pres. Intl Business • Data Research Associates Inc. • Saint Louis, MO 63132 • ACRL ALCTS LAMA LITA PLA RASD

Matthews Karen • Emporia, KS 66801 • ACRL ALCTS LITA

Matthews Linda M. • Head,Special Collection Departm. • Emory University Libraries Robert W. Woodruff Library • Atlanta, GA 30322-2870 • ACRL

Matthews Lynn I. Mr. • Chief Librarian • Kitchener Public Library • Kitchener ON, N2H 2H1 Canada • ALSC LAMA RASD

Matthews Melinda F. • Interlibrary Loan Librarian • Northeast Louisiana University Sandel Library • Monroe, LA 71209-0720

Matthews Miriam • Los Angeles, CA 90019 • ACRL PLA EMIERT   *Continuing*

Matthews Pamela A. • Student • Reading Public Library • Reading, PA 19602 • PLA IFRT

Matthews Paula D. • Assistant Librarian • Bates College George & Helen Ladd Library • Lewiston, ME 04240 • ACRL

Matthews Priscilla J. • Catalog Librarian • Illinois State University • Normal, IL 61761 • ACRL ALCTS LITA LHRT

Matthews Rita A. • Library Director • Copperas Cove Public Library • Copperas Cove, TX 76522 • PLA

Matthews Sidney 11426 • Associate Director,Library Serv. • Southern Illinois University Delyte W. Morris Library • Carbondale, IL 62901-6632 • ACRL ALCTS *Life*

Matthews Stephen L. • Foxcroft School Currier Library • Middleburg, VA 22117 • AASL ACRL IFRT LIRT

Matthews Suzanne W. • Public Relations Director • Huntsville-Madison County Public Library • Huntsville, AL 35804

Matthews Virginia M. • Chapin, SC 29036

Matthews Winton E. Jr. • Library of Congress • Washington, DC 20541 • ALCTS

Matthias A. Marion Mrs • Thornhill ON, L3T 1Z4 Canada • LITA

Matthias Jeffrey C. • Librarian • Jefferson Community College Library • Louisville, KY 40202 • NMRT

Matthies Donna K. • Woodland, CA 95695

Matthies Eileen F. • Children's Librarian • Elmhurst Public Library • Elmhurst, IL 60126 • ALSC

Matthiesen Janice E. • Rarebook Cataloger • University of California-Los Angeles University Research Library • Los Angeles, CA 90024 • ACRL ALCTS

Matthis Della A. • Librarian • Gruening Middle School • Eagle River, AK 99577 • AASL ALSC

Mattie Joseph J. • Developmemt Specialist II • New York State Library State Education Department • Albany, NY 12230 • AASL

Mattill Phyllis • Children's Services Librarian • Hennepin County Library Penn Lake Branch Library • Bloomington, MN 55431 • ALSC

Mattis George E. Jr. • Assistant Librarian • Wytheville Community College • Wytheville, VA 24382

Mattison Leona • Richland, WA 99352 • Continuing

Mattison Lester Mr. • Director • Bemidji State University A. C. Clark Library • Bemidji, MN 56601-2699 • ACRL ALCTS   *Life*

Mattlage Parilee Ann • Media Specialist • Soda Creek Elementary • Steamboat Springs, CO 80477

Mattleman Marciene Dr. • Director • Free Library of Philadelphia • Philadelphia, PA 19103 • ALTA

Mattox Sherie • Alabama Power Company Corporate Library • Birmingham, AL 35291-0251

Mattrey Deborah Cochran • San Diego, CA 92103

Mattsen Stephan M. • Student • University of Wisconsin-Milwaukee School of Library & Information Science • Milwaukee, WI 53201

Mattson Francis O. • Hd.,Spec. Clln. Catlg./Curator • New York Public Library Berg Collection • New York, NY 10018 • ACRL

Mattson Mary Ellen • Trustee • Indian Trails Public Library District • Wheeling, IL 60090 • ALTA

Mattson Merry • Technology Specialist • Minnehaha Academy • Minneapolis, MN 55406 • AASL

Mattson Virginia R. • Reference Department • Duke University Medical Center Library • Durham, NC 27710 • ACRL

Matturro Richard C. • Librarian • Captital Newspapers Library • Albany, NY 12212 • LAMA

Matujec Patrice K. • Royal Oak, MI 48067

Matulionis Susan • Media Services • Cicero School District #99 • Cicero, IL 60650

Matusiewicz Cornelia J. • Adriance Memorial Library • Poughkeepsie, NY 12601 • ASCLA GODORT

Matyas Catherine • Manager, Information Services • Kitchener Public Library • Kitchener ON, N2H 2H1 Canada • PLA

Matyi Stephen G. • Cleveland, OH 44122

Matyskella Jane • Librarian I • Columbus & Franklin County Public L Reynoldsburg Branch • Reynoldsburg, OH 43068

Matzek Richard A. • Librarian • Nazareth College of Rochester • Rochester, NY 14610-8950 • ACRL LAMA LITA

Matzen Caroline B. • Director • Kingston Area Library • Kingston, NY 12401 • LAMA PLA RASD

Matzen Nita J. • Media Coordinator • Hendersonville Junior High School • Hendersonville, NC 28739 • AASL

Matzke Patricia • California State University-Long Beach Instructional Systems Technology Dept. • Long Beach, CA 90840-1901

Matzner Rosalind F. • Librarian • Queens Borough Public Library • Jamaica, NY 11432 • PLA EMIERT

Mau Catherine E. • Student • University of Illinois Graduate School of Library and Information Science • Urbana, IL 61801

Mauch Ruby H. Miss • Librarian Emerita • State School of Mines & Technology-Library • Huron, SD 57350 • ACRL   *Continuing*

Mauck Virginia L. • Bloomington, IN 47408 • Continuing

Maud Pamela S. • Branch Supv • Lake County Public Library • Merrillville, IN 46410-5382 • PLA

Maudslien Clifton • Librarian • Mount Rainier High School • Des Moines, WA 98198 • YALSA

Maughan Laurel S. • Reference Librarian • Oregon State University William Jasper Kerr Library • Corvallis, OR 97331-4501 • ACRL LIRT

Maughan Patricia Davitt • Head of the Science Libraries • University of California-Berkeley University Library • Berkeley, CA 94720 • ACRL

Maul Helen G. • Director • Nogales/Santa Cruz County Library • Nogales, AZ 85621 • ALCTS LAMA LITA PLA RASD EMIERT IFRT IRRT

Maul Katherine M. • Student • University of Wisconsin-Milwaukee School of Library & Information Science • Milwaukee, WI 53201

Maul Shirley A. • Head of Reader Services • Vassar College Library • Poughkeepsie, NY 12601 • ACRL LAMA RASD IRRT

Mauldin Ellen D. • Head, Serials Processing • Mississippi State University Mitchell Memorial Library • Mississippi State, MS 39762 • ALCTS

Maulding Virginia F. • Trustee • Centralia Public Library • Centralia, IL 62801 • ALTA

Mault Cindy • Librarian • Good Hope School • Saint Croix, VI 00841

Maunu Helen J. • Cleveland, OH 44106 • Continuing

Maupin Rita M. • Library Director • Calhoun County Public Library System • Blountstown, FL 32424

Maurantonio Joe • Librarian Tech Asst • Yonkers Public Library Will Branch • Yonkers, NY 10708

Maurath Elizabeth B. • Columbus, OH 43221 • AASL

Maurer Bradley G. • Branch Librarian • Davis County Library South Branch • Bountiful, UT 84010

Maurer Cecile P. Mrs • McConnells, SC 29726 • ACRL ALCTS   *Continuing*

Maurer Charles B. • Granville, OH 43023

Maurer Eric • Catskill Supreme Court Library • Catskill, NY 12414 • ACRL GODORT

Maurer Karen • Children's Librarian • Parkland Community Library • Allentown, PA 18104 • ALSC

Maurer Laura H. • Library Development Officer • Virginia Commonwealth University • Richmond, VA 23284 • LAMA

Maurer Lewis R. • Product Specialist • Online Computer Library Center (OCLC) • Dublin, OH 43017-3395 • LITA SRRT

Mauricio Christine A. • Grosse Pointe Woods, MI 48236 • ALSC PLA

Mauriello Jeanne • Baker & Taylor Books • Bridgewater, NJ 08807

Maurins Arnold • Reference & Serials Librarian • San Leandro Library • San Leandro, CA 94577

Mauro Deborah A. • Student • University of Maryland College of Library and Information Services • College Park, MD 20742-4345

Mauro Eleanor • Reference Librarian • College of the Siskiyous Library • Weed, CA 96094

Maury Alfred B. • Branch Librarian • District of Columbia Public Library Northeast Branch • Washington, DC 20002

Mauseth Barbara J. • Florence, OR 97439

Maushay Jane A. • Silas Wood Early Childhood Center • Huntington Station, NY 11746 • ALSC

Maust Sara H. • Santa Barbara, CA 93108 • Continuing

Mautino Patricia H. • Director • Oswego County BOCES • Mexico, NY 13114 • AASL ALTA

Mavoides Alicia • Trustee • Huntington Public Library • Huntington, NY 11743 • ALTA

Mavrogenes Sylvia A. • Youth Services Adminstrator • Miami-Dade Public Library System • Miami, FL 33130-1504 • ALSC

Mavromatis Lisa • Head of Monographic Services • University of Rochester Edward G Miner Library • Rochester, NY 14642 • ALCTS

Maw Toria • University of California Shields Library • Davis, CA 95616

Mawdsley Katherine F. • Assoc. Univ. Ln./Public Serv. • University of California Shields Library • Davis, CA 95616 • ACRL LAMA RASD GODORT

Mawhinney Paul C. • Record-Rama Sound Archives • Pittsburgh, PA 15237 • LITA

Mawson Diane M. • Trustee • Rochester Hills Public Library • Rochester, MI 48307 • ALTA

Max Patrick J. • Director • Castleton State College Calvin Coolidge Library • Castleton, VT 05735 • ACRL IFRT

Maxey Constance • Gotha, FL 34734 • AASL

Maxfield David K. • Ann Arbor, MI 48104-4970 • ACRL   *Life*

Maxfield Grace • Ann Arbor, MI 48104-4970 • ALCTS   *Continuing*

Maxfield Sandy • Head of Reference • James Madison University Carrier Library • Harrisonburg, VA 22807 • ACRL LAMA LITA RASD

Maxie Linda F. • Librarian • Henry Elementary School • Henry, VA 24102 • AASL

Maxim Bradley C. • Austin, TX 78753 • Continuing

Maxon Lou B. • Library Media Specialist • Hayward Smith Elementary School • Owasso, OK 74055 • AASL

Maxson Andrew A. • Student • Indiana University School of Library and Information Science • Bloomington, IN 47405 • ALCTS SRRT

Maxson Charles M. • Whittier, CA 90605

Maxson Wayne C. • Sewanee, TN 37375 • RASD

Maxton Pauline • Birdsboro, PA 19508 • PLA *Continuing*

Maxwell Barbara • Trustee • Thomas Jefferson Library System • Jefferson Cty, MO 65102 • ALTA

Maxwell Barbara A. • Assistant Librarian • Shepherd College Ruth Scarborough Library • Shepherdstown, WV 25443-1568 • ACRL ALCTS LAMA

Maxwell Barbara A. • South Area Children Specialist • Free Library of Philadelphia • Philadelphia, PA 19103 • ALSC IRRT

Maxwell Bonnie J. • Georgetown, IN 47122 • ACRL ALCTS LITA RASD

Maxwell Donald W. • Reference Librarian • Stone Hills Library Network • Bloomington, IN 47408 • RASD

Maxwell Florenz W. • Librarian • Bermuda Youth Library • Hamilton HM 12, Bermuda • ALCTS ALSC LAMA PLA YALSA SRRT

Maxwell James D. • Student • Kent State University Geauga Campus Library • Burton, OH 44021

Maxwell James G. • Superintendent • Lane Education Service District • Eugene, OR 97402

Maxwell Jan C. • Head of Acquisitions • University of Oregon Library • Eugene, OR 97403-1299 • ALCTS LAMA

Maxwell M. F. Mrs • Tucson, AZ 85716 • ALCTS

Maxwell Martha A. • Director • Jefferson County Library • High Ridge, MO 63049 • ALCTS LAMA PLA IFRT

Maxwell Mary C. • Casady School • Oklahoma City, OK 73156 • AASL

Maxwell Nancy • Student • Catholic University of America School of Library and Information Science • Washington, DC 20064

Maxwell Nancy J. • Public Library Consultant • North Dakota State Library • Bismarck, ND 58505 • ALSC PLA

Maxwell Nancy L. • Corona Public Library • Corona, CA 91720 • RASD

Maxwell Nicola R. • Media Specialist • Crest Drive Elementary • Eugene, OR 97405 • AASL

Maxwell Norris K. • Reference Librarian • Tom Green County Library • San Angelo, TX 76903-5834

Maxwell Robert L. • Toronto ON, M4Y 1R6 Canada • ACRL

Maxwell Susan • Director • Nichols P. Sims Library • Waxahachie, TX 75165 • PLA

Maxymuk John • Rutgers University • Camden, NJ 08102

May Ann M. • Documents Genealogy Librarian • El Paso Public Library • El Paso, TX 79901 • LITA PLA RASD GODORT

May Barbara N. • Head Librarian • Woodberry Forest School William White Library • Woodberry Forest, VA 22989 • AASL

May David G. • Library Director • Los Angeles Valley College • Van Nuys, CA 91401 • ACRL ALCTS LITA

May Diane L. • Senior Library Associate • Kent State University Libraries • Kent, OH 44242

May Eleanor T. • Student • Rockingham County Tax Department • Wentworth, NC 27288

May F. Curtis • Woodside, CA 94062 • AASL YALSA *Life*

May Frances G. • Director of Library Services • American College for the Applied Arts Library • Los Angeles, CA 90024 • ACRL LAMA

May Holly L. • Librarian I • Clearwater Public Library • Clearwater, FL 34623

May James H. • Vice Provost for Information Res • California State University-Chico Meriam Library • Chico, CA 92929-0295

May John R. • Danville, KY 40422 • Continuing

May Kathrine • Media Specialist • Archdale-Trinity Middle School • Trinity, NC 27370 • AASL

May Lesa A. • Student • University of Washington Graduate School of Library and Information Science • Seattle, WA 98195 • ACRL

May Linda L. • Director Marketing & Sales • ABC-CLIO Inc. • Santa Barbara, CA 93116-1911 • AASL LAMA PLA RASD

May Pamela • Rockford, IL 61103

May Philip S. Jr. • Board Member • Jacksonville Public Libraries Main Library • Jacksonville, FL 32202

May Robert • President • Library Equipment Space Design • Summerville, SC 29483

May Robert H. • Executive Officer • Seattle Public Library • Seattle, WA 98104-1193 • LAMA PLA

May Roberta J. • Reference Librarian • Mead Public Library • Sheboygan, WI 53081 • RASD

May Ruth • Shorewood, WI 53211

May Vicki • Student • Central Missouri State University Library Science & Information Services • Warrensburg, MO 64093 • AASL IFRT

Mayberry Carol G. • Media Specialist • East Wake High School • Wendell, NC 27591 • AASL

Mayberry Julia L. • Librarian • Woodside School • Woodside, CA 94062

Mayberry Katherine A. • Student • University of South Carolina College of Library & Information Science • Columbia, SC 29208 • AASL IFRT

Mayden Priscilla M. • Trustee • Salt Lake City Public Library • Salt Lake City, UT 84111 • ALTA

Maye Letita T. • Cataloger • Madison County-Canton Public Library • Canton, MS 39046 • ALCTS NMRT

Mayeaux Thurlow M. Mrs • Northwestern State University Watson Memorial Library • Natchitoches, LA 71497

Mayer-Hennelly Mary • Assistant Director • Norfolk Public Library • Norfolk, VA 23510-1776 • LAMA PLA

Mayer Albert I. • Trustee • Ocean County Public Library • Toms River, NJ 08753 • ALTA

Mayer Clara • Librarian • Brooklyn Public Library Flatlands Branch • Brooklyn, NY 11234 • LAMA PLA

Mayer Debra H. • Librarian • Bethlehem High School • Bardstown, KY 40121 • AASL

Mayer Lauren L. • Senior Children's Librarian • New York Public Library Aguilar Branch • New York, NY 10029 • ALSC

Mayer Mary C. • Supervisor,K-12 • Akron Public Schools • Akron, OH 44301 • AASL YALSA

Mayer Mary Jane • Birmingham, MI 48009

Mayer Pamela A. • Librarian • SMSU Fruit Experiment Station • Mountain Grove, MO 65711 • NMRT

Mayer Robert E. • Public Services Librarian • Stanford University • Stanford, CA 94305-6011 • ALCTS RASD

Mayer Thomas J. • Trustee • River Grove Public Library District • River Grove, IL 60171

Mayer Thomas R. • Director • Sno-Isle Regional Library • Marysville, WA 98271-9164

Mayeres Mary V. • Librarian I • Columbus Metropolitan Library Whetstone Branch Library • Columbus, OH 43214

Mayes Susan E. • Cataloger • Belmont Abbey College Library • Belmont, NC 28012

Mayeski John K. • Director • University of Nebraska at Kearney Library • Kearney, NE 68849 • ACRL LAMA

Mayfield David M. • Director • Family History Library • Salt Lake City, UT 84150 • LITA

Mayfield Gail J. • Student • University of Washington Graduate School of Library and Information Science • Seattle, WA 98195 • AASL

Mayfield Gayle R. • Librarian • Nevada County Library • Nevada City, CA 95959

Mayfield Lee S. • Student • North Carolina Central University • Durham, NC 27707 • AASL SRRT

Mayhood Gary W. • New Mexico State University Library • Las Cruces, NM 88003-0006 • ACRL ALCTS

Maymi-Sugranes Hector J. • Madison, WI 53705 • IFRT LHRT LRRT SRRT

Maynard Almeda G. • Librarian • Chicago Public Library Edgebrook Branch • Chicago, IL 60646 • PLA

Maynard Antoinette L. • Librarian • Library of Congress • Washington, DC 20541

Maynard J. Edmund • Daniel Library The Citadel • Charleston, SC 29409 • LITA

Maynard James W. • Head of Adult Services • Pasadena Public Library • Pasadena, TX 77506-4895

Maynard Janet M. • Circulation Librarian • Hershey Public Library • Hershey, PA 17033 • PLA

Maynard Joan • Administrator • Saint Catherines Montessori • Houston, TX 77225-0728

Maynard Joanne • Librarian • Interboro Institute • New York, NY 10019 • ACRL

Maynard Kathy M. • San Francisco, CA 94118

Maynard Kay • Learning Center Director • Cumberland Trail Library System • Flora, IL 62839 • AASL YALSA

Maynard Linda S. • Student • Middle Tennessee State University Library • Murfreesboro, TN 37132 • ALSC

Maynard Mary P. • Westinghouse Electric Corporation Library • Orlando, FL 32826

Maynard Michael • Tempe, AZ 85281

Maynard Nancy R. • High School Librarian • Lucia Mar Unified School District • Arroyo Grande, CA 93420 • YALSA

Maynard Richard H. • Supervising Librarian • E. P. Foster Library • Ventura, CA 93001 • LAMA PLA

Maynes Kathleen • Librarian • Dumont High School • Dumont, NJ 07628 • AASL

Maynor-Mitchell Karen V. • Technical Serivce Clerk • Carlsbad City Library • Carlsbad, CA 92008

Mayo Harriet E. • Head Librarian • Abraham Baldwin Agricultural College Baldwin Library • Tifton, GA 31793-4401 • ACRL

Mayo Hope • Pierpont Morgan Library • New York, NY 10016 • ACRL ALCTS LHRT

Mayo Janet L. • Monographs Department • University of Louisville Ekstrom Library • Louisville, KY 40292 • ACRL ALCTS

Mayo Kathleen O. • Special Services Coordinator • Lee County Library System • Fort Myers, FL 33901 • ASCLA PLA

Mayo Wayne • Library Director • Lawrence Public Library • Lawrence, KS 66044

Mayol Josefina • Clearwater, FL 33516

Mayover Steven J. • Chief Central Public Serv. Div. • Free Library of Philadelphia • Philadelphia, PA 19103 • LAMA PLA

Mayreis Rex • Los Angeles Public Library • Los Angeles, CA 90071

Mays Antje • Student • University of South Carolina College of Library & Information Science • Columbia, SC 29208 • ACRL

Mays Charlotte K. • Riverdale, GA 30274

Mays Louis E. • LRC Coordinator • Southern State Community College • Hillsboro, OH 45133 • ACRL LIRT

Mayton Regina A. • Chief of Systems • Air University Library • Maxwell AFB, AL 36112 • ALCTS

Mayzel Judith E. • Reference Librarian • Oakton Community College Library • Des Plaines, IL 60016 • ACRL

Mazeau Mary I. • Deer Park, NY 11729 • LITA PLA *Life*

Mazefsky William Mrs. • Pittsburgh, PA 15206-3724 • Continuing

Mazerov Louise S. • Department Librarian II • Long Beach Public Library • Long Beach, CA 90802-4482 • PLA IFRT

Mazur Emily • Tucson, AZ 85712

Mazur Myles A. • Student • University of Arizona Graduate Library School • Tucson, AZ 85721

Mazur Victoria Parr • State College, PA 16801

Mazurek Adam P. Jr. • Anne Arundel County Library Linthicum Branch • Linthicum, MD 21090 • PLA

Mazurek Laura A. • Chicago, IL 60618

Mazza Dorothy E. • Library Associate • Kansas City Public Library Plaza Branch • Kansas City, MO 64112 • PLA IFRT SRRT

Mazza Janice M. • Tallahassee, FL 32308 • AASL

Mazzocchi Brenda W. • Decatur, GA 30033

Mazzolini Deborah D. • Director • Belmont Public Library • Belmont, MA 02178 • ALCTS ALSC LAMA LITA PLA RASD IRRT

Mazzuca Michelle M. • Student • Texas Woman's University School of Library & Information Studies • Denton, TX 76204

Mc Culloch Linda H. • Media Servs/AV/Library Supv. • Bonner School Library • Bonner, MT 59823 • AASL

Mc Guire Waller E. • St. Louis, MO 63112-1843 • PLA

McAdam Cynthia L. • Reference Librarian • Olathe Public Library • Olathe, KS 66061

McAdam Paul E. • Director of Lib & Media Services • Carroll Community College • Westminster, MD 21157 • ACRL LAMA LIRT

McAdam Tim • University of California-Irvine Library • Irvine, CA 92713 • ACRL ALCTS LAMA

McAdams Cecilia D. • Branch Manager/Adult Services • Columbus Metropolitan Library • Columbus, OH 43215 • PLA

McAdams Nancy R. • McAdams Planning Consultants Inc. • Austin, TX 78755-0805 • ACRL ALCTS LAMA RASD ILERT

McAdoo Jannifer • New Jersey Department of Labor Library • Trenton, NJ 08625-0943

McAfee Alberta M. • IMC Librarian • West Chester University Francis Harvey Green Library • West Chester, PA 19383 • ACRL

McAfee Mary • Asst. Director-Extension Div. • Forsyth County Public Library • Winston-Salem, NC 27101 • LAMA PLA

McAfee Mary • Trustee • San Antonio Public Library • San Antonio, TX 78205

McAfee Mary L. • Coordinating Media Specialist • Richland County School District One Media Service Department • Columbia, SC 29204 • AASL

McAfoos Lou A. • Media Coordinator • Enka High School • Enka, NC 28728 • AASL

McAleese James • Garden City High School • Garden City, NY 11530 • AASL

McAllister Carol A. • Bibliographer/Inf Serv Ln. • College of William & Mary Earl Gregg Swem Library • Williamsburg, VA 23187-8794 • ACRL ALCTS RASD

McAloon Judith • Springfield, VA 22150

McAna Margaret G. • Philadelphia, PA 19111-4327

McAnallen Deborah K. • Greenwood, IN 46143 • ACRL ALCTS

McAnally Charlotte L. • Coordinator • Metro-Nashville-Davidson County Public Schools • Nashville, TN 37204 • AASL

McAndrew-Taylor Marie • Simmons College Graduate School of Library & Information Science • Boston, MA 02115

McAndrew Rosemary • Technical Services Librarian • Wolf, Block, Schorr Solis & Cohen • Philadelphia, PA 19103 • ACRL ALCTS NMRT

McAndrews Kim T. • Reference • Clinton Public Library • Clinton, IA 52732 • RASD

McAnelly Debra D. • Media Specialist • Fort Pierce Central High School • Fort Pierce, FL 34982 • AASL

McAninch Sandra L. • Hd,Govt Pubns/Maps Dept. • University of Kentucky Libraries • Lexington, KY 40506-0039 • GODORT

McAnna Suzanne K. • Hd. Libn., Circulation Servs. • University of Texas Libraries • Austin, TX 78713

McAnulty Sharon K. • Director/Children's Librarian • La Vista Public Library • La Vista, NE 68128 • ALSC PLA

McArdell Carol E. • El Jebel, CO 81628

McArdle Eileen F. • Cataloger • Fordham University Libraries • Bronx, NY 10458 • ACRL ALCTS

McArdle Kathleen A. Ms. • Librarian • Westlake High School • Thornwood, NY 10594 • AASL YALSA

McArdle Mary Lou • Phoenix Academy • Shrub Oak, NY 10588

McArthur Patricia • Orland Park, IL 60462 • PLA

McArthur William Neil • Student • Florida State University School of Library and Information Studies • Tallahassee, FL 32306-2048 • ACRL

McAskill John K. • La Salle University Connelly Library • Philadelphia, PA 19141 • ACRL ALCTS

McAulay Louise S. • Director • Aiken-Bamberg-Barnwell-Edgefield Regional Library System (ABBE) • Aiken, SC 29802 • LAMA PLA

McAulay T. L. Mrs. • Cos Cob, CT 06807 • ALCTS PLA *Continuing*

McBane Gean I. • Snow Camp, NC 27349

McBrian Judith • Boonvile-Warrick County Public Library • Boonville, IN 47601 • LITA

McBride-Brown Sherry L. • Interlibrary Loan Librarian • Daniel Boone Regional Library • Columbia, MO 65205-1267

McBride Cheryl • East Brunswick Public Library • E. Brunswick, NJ 08816 • RASD

McBride Diantha • Youth Services Coordinator • Grand Rapids Public Library • Grand Rapids, MI 49503-3093

McBride Jerry • Middlebury College Egbert Starr Library • Middlebury, VT 05753-6007

McBride John • Student • Rutgers University School of Communication Information & Library Studies • New Brunswick, NJ 08903

McBride Kelly R. • Director, Public Services • Mars Hill College Memorial Library • Mars Hill, NC 28754 • ACRL

McBride Patricia A. • School Librarian • Salpointe Catholic High School • Tucson, AZ 85719

McBride Patricia E. • Longview, TX 75604

McBride Ruth B. • Champaign, IL 61820

McBride Suzan • Interlibrary Loan Head • Utah State University Merrill Library • Logan, UT 84322-3000 • ACRL

McBroom Kathleen Morrissey • Media Specialist • Fordson High School • Dearborn, MI 48126

McBryde Susan R. • Media Coordinator • W.R. Odell Elementary School • Concord, NC 28025 • AASL

McBurney Melissa K. • Student • University of North Carolina at Chapel Hill School of Information and Library Science • Chapel Hill, NC 27599-3360 • SRRT

McCabe-Power Maureen M. • President • Human Systems Development Group • East Lansing, MI 48826-4234 • LAMA PLA

McCabe Deborah M. • Wisconsin Rapids, WI 54494 • PLA

McCabe Dorothy A. • Librarian • William Rainey Harper College Learning Resources Center • Palatine, IL 60067 • ACRL

McCabe Ellen T. • Adjunct Assistant Librarian • State University of New York Bartle Library • Binghamton, NY 13902-6012 • NMRT

McCabe Emma R. • Director • Millsboro Public Library • Millsboro, DE 19966

McCabe Gerard B. • Director of Libraries • Clarion University of Pennsylvania Rena M. Carlson Library • Clarion, PA 16214 • ACRL ALCTS LAMA *Life*

McCabe James • University Librarian • Fordham University Libraries • Bronx, NY 10458 • ACRL

McCabe Jeffery C. • Port Huron High School • Port Huron, MI 48060 • LITA SRRT

McCabe Kathleen H. • Children's Librarian • East Meadow Public Library • East Meadow, NY 11554-1700

McCabe Margaret • Reference Librarian • Clearwater Public Library East Branch • Clearwater, FL 34625 • PLA

McCabe Michael M. • Library Director • Brevard College James A. Jones Library • Brevard, NC 28712

McCabe Rebecca M. • Young Adult Librarian • Enoch Pratt Free Library Hamilton Branch • Baltimore, MD 21214 • IFRT

McCabe Robert E. Jr. • Student • Wayne State University • Detroit, MI 48202 • AASL ACRL ALCTS LITA PLA EMIERT IFRT NMRT SRRT VRT

McCabe Ronald B. • Director • McMillan Memorial Library • Wisconsin Rapids, WI 54494 • LAMA PLA IFRT LIRT SRRT

McCafferty Brian • Wabash College • Crawfordsville, IN 47933 • ALCTS

McCafferty Carol • Head of Technical Services • Morrisson-Reeves Library • Richmond, IN 47374 • PLA

McCafferty Caroline M. • Student • University of Oklahoma School of Library & Information Studies • Norman, OK 73019

McCaffery Laurabelle • Librarian,Reader Service Dept. • Allen County Public Library • Fort Wayne, IN 46801 • PLA RASD IFRT

McCaffery Susanne L. • Pacific Grove, CA 93950 • ACRL

McCaffrey Erika M. • Head, Reference Department • Harvard Business School Baker Library • Boston, MA 02163

McCaffrey Martha S. • Librarian • Mandeville High School • Mandeville, LA 70448 • AASL

McCain Claudia J. • Director • Bellingham Public Library • Bellingham, WA 98227 • PLA

McCain Mary Maude • Library Media Specialist • Mountain Brook Elementary School • Mt. Brook, AL 35223 • AASL

McCain Nancy • Student • Emporia State University Emporia in the Rockies • Denver, CO 80204

McCaleb Penny • Trustee • Metropolitan Library System • Oklahoma City, OK 73102 • ALTA PLA

McCall Kathryn B. • Winchester, VA 22601 • PLA RASD

McCall Leslie C. • Wake Forest University Z Smith Reynolds Library • Winston Salem, NC 27109-7777 • ACRL ALCTS

McCall Margaret Ruth • Maryville, TN 37801 • AASL ALSC *Life*

McCall Patricia • Coordinator of LRC • Tulsa Junior College Southeast Campus • Tulsa, OK 74133 • ACRL

McCall Sandra C. • Claxton Elementary School • Greensboro, NC 27410 • AASL

McCall Vicki L. • Anchorage, AK 99508 • AASL IFRT

McCallion Peter • Head of Acquisitions • New York Public Library • New York, NY 10016 • ALCTS PLA RASD IFRT

McCallister Myrna Joy • Associate Librarian Tech. Serv. • Appalachian State University Carol Grotnes Belk Library • Boone, NC 28608 • ALCTS LAMA

McCallon Kaye • Denton Senior High School Ryan Campus • Denton, TX 76201 • AASL

McCallum Amanda M. • Library Assistant 1 • University of Texas Libraries General Libraries • Austin, TX 78713-7330

McCallum Edna C. • Jackson, MS 39206 • NMRT SRRT

McCallum Eleanor • Librarian • Jesuit High School • Tampa, FL 33614

McCallum Jeanne R. • Librarian • East Middle School • Sioux City, IA 51106 • AASL

McCallum John • Reference/Collections Librarians • Wilfrid Laurier University Library • Waterloo ON, N2L 3C5 Canada • ACRL IFRT LIRT

McCallum Sally H. • Chief Network Development & Marc • Library of Congress • Washington, DC 20541 • ACRL ALCTS LITA IRRT LRRT

McCalmont Charlyn L. • Student • University of South Florida School of Library & Information Science • Tampa, FL 33620 • AASL LRRT SRRT

McCambridge Charles • Director,Instruc'l Materls. Serv • Niskayuna Central School District • Schenectady, NY 12309 • AASL ALCTS LITA YALSA

McCammon Carol G. • Librarian • Berkeley Prep School • Tampa, FL 33615 • AASL YALSA

McCammon Dorothy V. • Boulder, CO 80303 • Continuing

McCammon Leslie V. • Head-Technical Services • Florida International University North Miami Campus • North Miami, FL 33181

McCandless Patricia A. • Assistant Director Public Serv. • Ohio State University Libraries • Columbus, OH 43210-1286 • ACRL LAMA LITA RASD GODORT

McCanless Alice Murphy • Reference Librarian/Part-time • Clayton State College • Morrow, GA 30260

McCann Eleanor • Pittsburgh, PA 15201 • ACRL RASD *Continuing*

McCann Helga F. • Birmingham, MI 48009-1860

McCann Jesweida • Jefferson County Committee for Economic Opportunity • Birmingham, AL 35214

McCann Katharine T. • Automation Librarian • Case Western Reserve University Sears Library • Cleveland, OH 44106 • ACRL

McCann Linda J. • Info & Records Manager • Armand Hammer Museum of Art and Cultural Center • Los Angeles, CA 90024

McCann Paul T. • Student • University of Michigan School of Information and Library Studies • Ann Arbor, MI 48109-1092 • PLA EMIERT IFRT SRRT

McCann Susan F. • Assistant Director • Portsmouth Public Library • Portsmouth, NH 03801 • LITA

McCann Suzanne S. • Shawnee Mission, KS 66208 • YALSA

McCann Teresa B. • San Francisco, CA 94115

McCann Tracy • Ross-McCann Research & Information Service • Chicago, IL 60601 • ILERT

McCanna Timothy J. • Pacifica, CA 94044

McCanne Barbara L. • Sno-Isle Regional Library System Snohomish Public Library • Snohomish, WA 98290

McCargar Susan E. • El Paso, TX 79936 • PLA RASD

McCarl Mary Rhinelander • Birmingham, AL 35216-2229 • ACRL LHRT

McCarn Davis B. Mr • Board Member • Montgomery County Department of Public Libraries • Rockville, MD 20850 • ALTA PLA

McCarrell Sharon L. • Branch Librarian • Fowler Memorial Branch • Concord, MA 01742 • IFRT

McCarren Angela C. • Librarian • San Jose Public Library • San Jose, CA 95113 • PLA RASD MAGERT

McCarroll Norma • Trustee • Mid-Continent Public Library • Independence, MO 64050 • ALTA

McCarter Bobbye L. • Serials Librarian • Georgia Southwestern College James Earl Carter Library • Americus, GA 31709 • ACRL

McCarthy Carrol B. • Librarian • Tower Hill School • Wilmington, DE 19806 • AASL

McCarthy Cecelia • Champaign, IL 61820 • ACRL RASD *Continuing*

McCarthy Connie K. • Associate University Librarian • Duke University William R. Perkins Library • Durham, NC 27706 • ACRL ALCTS LAMA RASD

McCarthy Deborah A. • Xavier University McDonald Memorial Library • Cincinnati, OH 45207

McCarthy John J. • Trustee • Cuyahoga County Public Library • Cleveland, OH 44134-2792 • ALTA

McCarthy Julia A. • Student • University of Texas at Austin Graduate School of Library & Information Sciences • Austin, TX 78712-1276

McCarthy Kathleen J. • Reference/Clln Maintenance • Seton Hall University Law Library • Newark, NJ 07102

McCarthy Laine H. • Technical Writer • Oklahoma University Health Science Ct Family Medicine Department • Oklahoma City, OK 73104

McCarthy Linda S. • Leon County Public Library System • Tallahassee, FL 32301-7720

McCarthy Malachy R. Bro. • Archivist • Saint Anselm College Geisel Library • Manchester, NH 03102-1310 • ALCTS LITA RASD

McCarthy Marcia O. • Student • State University of New York (SUNY) School of Information & Library Studies • Buffalo, NY 14260 • AASL YALSA

McCarthy Margaret A. • Rutgers University School of Communication Information & Library Studies • New Brunswick, NJ 08903 • ACRL

McCarthy Margaret A. • Commack, NY 11725 • AASL

McCarthy Mary Constance • Assistant Head of Reference Dept • Northwestern University Library • Evanston, IL 60208-2300 • ACRL RASD

McCarthy Mary Louise • Northville, MI 48167 • SRRT

McCarthy Maryellen P. • Harvard University Littauer Library • Cambridge, MA 02138

McCarthy Michael T. • Student • Queens College Grad Sch of Lib & Inf Studies • Flushing, NY 11367 • ACRL

McCarthy Patricia E. • Student • University of Rhode Island Graduate School of Library & Information Studies • Kingston, RI 02881-0815

McCarthy Patrick G. • Assistant Head, Acquisitions • Saint Louis University Pius XII Memorial Library • St. Louis, MO 63108 • ALCTS

McCarthy Paul H. Jr. • Director • University of Alaska Elmer E. Rasmuson Library • Fairbanks, AK 99775-1005 • ACRL LAMA IFRT

McCarthy Ruth P. • Director • Upper Dublin Public Library • Dresher, PA 19025 • PLA

McCarthy Susan A. • Librarian Supervisor • Arlington County Dept of Libraries Shirlington Branch • Arlington, VA 22206 • ALSC PLA

McCarthy Terry F. • Head Librarian • University of Bridgeport • Bridgeport, CT 06601 • ACRL LAMA NMRT

McCarthy Theresa E. • Librarian • The Hewitt School • New York, NY 10021

McCarthy Tricia • Mountain View, CA 94040

McCartney Betty S. • Head Librarian • Grant County Public Library • Petersburg, WV 26847

McCartney D. Steven • Library Director • Meridian Public Library • Meridian, MS 39301 • ALSC PLA

McCartney Elizabeth • NOTIS Systems, Inc. • Evanston, IL 60201-3622 • ACRL LAMA RASD

McCartney Elizabeth J. • Lakewood, CO 80226-1314 • MAGERT

McCartney Ellen D. • Long Island University Brentwood Campus Library • Brentwood, NY 11717

McCartney Jean Ann • Executive Director • Missouri Library Association • Columbia, MO 65201 • ERT

McCartney Margaret W. • Trustee • East Meadow Public Library • East Meadow, NY 11554-1700 • ALTA

McCarty Adelle • Head Librarian • Riverdale Public Library • Riverdale, IL 60627 • LAMA PLA

McCarty Judy • Trustee • San Diego City • San Diego, CA 92101

McCarty Mary L. • Kelly Air Force Base • San Antonio, TX 78213 • AFLRT

McCarty Melissa P. • Administrative Assistant • University of Southern Mississippi School of Library Science • Hattiesburg, MS 39406-5146 • ALCTS

McCarty Trudy E. • Virginia State Library & Archives • Richmond, VA 23219

McCarver Paul S. • University of Southern Mississippi Cook Memorial Library • Hattiesburg, MS 39406-5053 • ACRL

McCarville Sarah M. • Head of Youth Services • Oshkosh Public Library • Oshkosh, WI 54901 • ALSC PLA

McCarville Susan • Media Specialist • Harrison Elementary School • Janesville, WI 53546 • AASL

McCary Margaret L. • Pensacola, FL 32503

McCary Sharon L. • Cataloger • Library of Congress • Washington, DC 20541 • ALCTS LITA

McCaskey Margaret T. • Librarian • Upper Merion School District • King of Prussia, PA 19406 • AASL

McCaslin Chris L. • Trustee • Suffolk Cooperative Library System • Bellport, NY 11713 • ALTA

McCaslin Sharon • Assistant Librarian • Peru State College Library • Peru, NE 68421 • ACRL IFRT

McCaul Isabel • Elementary Librarian • University of Chicago Lab School Library • Chicago, IL 60637 • ALSC

McCauley Diantha G. • Asst. Director • Augusta County Library • Fishersville, VA 22939 • ALSC

McCauley Elfrieda B • Riverside, CT 06878 • LHRT

McCauley Hannah V. • Director • Ohio University-Lancaster Library • Lancaster, OH 43130 • ACRL

McCauley Joan E. • Librarian • California State University-Long Beach University Library & Learning Resources • Long Beach, CA 90840-1901 • ACRL ALCTS RASD

McCaulley Marion • Austin, TX 78764 • Continuing

McCausland Linda • Kingsley Elementary School • Waterloo, IA 50701 • AASL

McCawley Christina W. • Serials & Acquisitions Librarian • West Chester University Francis Harvey Green Library • West Chester, PA 19383 • ACRL ALCTS

McCay Karen S. • Student • Kutztown University Library Science Department • Kutztown, PA 19530

McClain Alice • Bozeman, MT 59715 • Continuing

McClain Carol • Media Specialist • Atlantic County Vocational School Media Center • Mays Landing, NJ 08330

McClain Edith T. • Prichard, AL 36612 • Continuing

McClain Gabriel Sr. • Sacred Heart Academy • Hamden, CT 06514

McClain Gail A. • Ambrose Swasey Library • Rochester, NY 14620

McClain Lucinda R. • Librarian • Chevron Chemical Company • Houston, TX 77010 • ACRL RASD MAGERT

McClain Susan W. • Student • University of South Carolina College of Library & Information Science • Columbia, SC 29208

McClamroch Jo Ellen • Rochester, NY 14626

McClanahan Gloria A. • Librarian • Round Rock Independent School District Westwood 9th Grade Annex • Austin, TX 78729 • AASL LITA

McClanahan Patricia • Senior Programmer Analyst • Tarleton State University • Stephenville, TX 76402

McClane Joseph C. • Chief Depository Services • U.S. Government Printing Office Library Program Service • Washington, DC 20401 • GODORT

McClarren Robert R. • Deerfield, IL 60015 • Continuing

McClary Maryon L. • University of Alberta Library Periodicals & Microform Center • Edmonton AB, T6G 2T8 Canada • ACRL ALCTS LAMA IRRT

McClary Nancy • Public Services Librarian II • Baltimore County Public Library • Towson, MD 21204 • PLA

McClaskey Marilyn H. • Head of Cataloging • University of Minnesota Saint Paul Campus Libraries • Saint Paul, MN 55108 • ALCTS

McClatchey Janice D. • Director • Oradell Public Library • Oradell, NJ 07649 • PLA

McClatchey Sally B. • Atlanta, GA 30327 • Continuing

McClaughry Helen • Base Librarian • Lowry Air Force Base Base Library • Lowry AFB, CO 80230-5000 • FLRT

McCleary George F. Jr. • Associate Professor • University of Kansas • Lawrence, KS 66045-2121 • MAGERT

McCleary Linda Sue • Hd, Reference/Doc. Section • Arizona State Library Department of Library Archives & Public Records • Phoenix, AZ 85007 • RASD

McClellan Cynthia S. • Law Librarian • Cartwright, Slobodin • San Fracisco, CA 94111

McClellan Edna S. • Winter Park, FL 32790 • ACRL ALCTS

McClellan Norris • Baton Rouge, LA 70806 • ALSC YALSA *Life*

McClelland Catherine A. • Librarian • Eureka City Schools Winship Junior High School • Eureka, CA 95501

McClelland Joan Mrs. • West Shore Elementary School • Tampa, FL 33616 • AASL

McClelland Katherine L. • Librarian • The Westminster Schools • Atlanta, GA 30327 • AASL YALSA

McClelland Kathryn • Asst Dir/Hd of Ch Serv • Perrot Memorial Library • Old Greenwich, CT 06870 • ALSC YALSA

McClendon Juliet R. • Richland County Public Library • Columbia, SC 29201 • LAMA

McClintock Deanne H. • Scarsdale, NY 10583 • ACRL RASD

McClintock Mary • Librarian • Roseburg Senior High School Library • Roseburg, OR 97470 • AASL

McClintock Patrick J. • Consultant • RMG Consultants Inc. • Chicago, IL 60610 • LITA PLA

McClish Lois E. • Long Beach, CA 90814

McCloat Elizabeth A. • Director • The Bryant Library • Roslyn, NY 11576 • LAMA LITA PLA

McCloskey Donna M. • Adults Services Librarian • Margaret R. Grundy Memorial Library • Bristol, PA 19007

McCloud Brenda R. • Director • Bowerston Public Library • Bowerston, OH 44695 • PLA

McCloud Earnestine T. Dr. • Library Media Specialist • Edmondson-Westside Senior High School • Baltimore, MD 21229-2740 • AASL

McCluer Molly • Asst. Libn. for Public Svs. • University of Washington Gallagher Law Library • Seattle, WA 98105 • IFRT

McClung Andrew C. • Spokane Public Library Comstock Building Library • Spokane, WA 99201-0976

McClung Patricia A. • Associate Director • Research Libraries Group Inc. (RLG) • Mountain View, CA 94041-1100 • ACRL ALCTS

McClung Susan • Administrator, Librarian • Naval Air Station Whidbey Island • Oak Harbor, WA 98278-2200 • AFLRT

McClure Bob • Trustee • Post Falls Public Library • Post Falls, ID 83854 • ALTA PLA

McClure Charles R. • Professor • Syracuse University School of Information Studies • Syracuse, NY 13244-4100 • ACRL PLA GODORT LRRT

McClure Frances L. • Chief, Library Tech Operations • Montgomery County Department of Public Libraries • Rockville, MD 20850 • ALCTS LAMA LITA PLA

McClure Jane Scott • Newtown, PA 18940 • Continuing

McClure Joann M. • Head of Collection Development • Saint Joseph County Public Library • South Bend, IN 46601 • PLA

McClure Kathleen E. • Kansas City, MO 64123 • IFRT

McClure Marguerite • Teacher • Mount Pleasant School District Fred Marten School • San Jose, CA 95112

McClure Mary L. • Director • Decatur Public Library • Decatur, TX 76234-0141

McClure Patricia M. • Associate Director, Adult Serv. • Elkhart Public Library • Elkhart, IN 46516-3184 • PLA

McClure Ruth K. • Acquisitions Librarian • Atlanta University Center Robert W. Woodruff Library • Atlanta, GA 30314 • ACRL

McClurg Roger A. • Librarian • Oregon City Public Library • Oregon City, OR 97045 • PLA

McClurkin Brenda S. • Arizona State Library Department of Library Archives & Public Records • Phoenix, AZ 85007 • ACRL

McCluskey Eileen T. • Student • Rutgers University School of Communication Information & Library Studies • New Brunswick, NJ 08903 • AFLRT

McCluskey Elizabeth B. • Marin Academy • San Rafael, CA 94901-1859 • AASL

McCluskey Marianne • Student • Texas Woman's University School of Library & Information Studies • Denton, TX 76204

McCluski Mark • Branch Librarian • New York Public Library Washington Heights Branch • New York, NY 10036

McClusky Duncan K. • Auburn University Ralph Brown Draughon Library • Auburn, AL 36849-5606 • ACRL

McCoart Patrica • Trustee • Prince William Public Library System Administrative Support Center • Prince William, VA 22192-5073

McColl Margaret C. • Media, PA 19063 • Life

McCollister Jean M. • Athens, OH 45701

McCollough Carole J. • Asst. Professor Library Science • Wayne State University Library Science Program • Detroit, MI 48202 • AASL ALSC PLA YALSA SRRT

McCollum Jamie P. • Library Assistant • Elkin Public Library • Elkin, NC 28621

McComas Jill P. • Raytown, MO 64138 • AASL

McComb Ralph W. • State College, PA 16801 • ACRL

McCombs Gillian M. • Assistant Director, Tech. Serv. • State University of New York (SUNY) University Libraries • Albany, NY 12222 • ACRL ALCTS LAMA

McConagha John M • Library Director • Greenfield Public Library • Greenfield, IN 46140

McConaghy Adele • Student • Simmons College Graduate School of Library & Information Science • Boston, MA 02115

McConaghy Timothy O. • U.S. Army Officer • First Special Warfare Training Group • Ft. Bragg, NC 28314

McCone Gary K. • National Agricultural Library • Beltsville, MD 20705 • LITA

McConkey Joan S. • Assoc Dir. for Admin Svs. • University of Colorado-Boulder University Libraries • Boulder, CO 80309 • ACRL LAMA

McConnell Barbarly K. • Madison, WI 53705

McConnell Elaine H. • Director • Ocean County Library System • Toms River, NJ 08753 • LAMA LITA PLA RASD

McConnell J. Christopher • Arizona State University Hayden Library • Tempe, AZ 85287-1006

McConnell Lorelei C. • Director • Irvington Public Library • Irvington, NJ 07111 • LAMA

McConnell Mary Faye • Library Cataloger • Judson College • Marion, AL 36756 • ACRL ALCTS

McConnell Molly K. • Student • University of Kentucky College of Library & Information Science • Lexington, KY 40506-0391

McConnell Pamela Jean • Organzied to Succeed • Shaker Heights, OH 44122

McConnell Ruth M. • Children's Librarian • San Antonio Public Library Westfall Branch • San Antonio, TX 78201 • ALSC IRRT

McConnell Trist B. • Williamsburg, VA 23185

McConville Barbara M. • Florham Park Public Library • Florham Park, NJ 07932 • PLA

McCook Kathleen de la Pena • Professor • Louisiana State University School of Library & Information Science • Baton Rouge, LA 70803-3290 • RASD LRRT SRRT

McCook William W. • Marathon, FL 33050

McCool Donna L. • Acting Director • Washington State University • Pullman, WA 99164-2112 • ACRL LAMA LITA IRRT

McCord Gretchen M. • Student • University of North Texas School of Library & Information Sciences • Denton, TX 76203 • IFRT NMRT SRRT

McCord Kathy • Librarian • Richard Rundle School • Las Vegas, NV 89110 • AASL

McCord Maury K. • Downey City Library • Downey, CA 90241

McCord S. Joe • Director of Library Services • Lamar University Gray Library • Beaumont, TX 77710 • ACRL

McCorison Marcus A. • President Emeritus • American Antiquarian Society • Worcester, MA 01609-1634 • ACRL

McCorkle Barbara B. • Hamden, CT 06517 • ACRL MAGERT

McCormack-Dunfee Barbara J. • Information Services Tech • South Dakota School of Mines & Technology • Rapid City, SD 57701 • SRRT

McCormack Anne V. • Librarian • Baldwin County Library System • Robertsdale, AL 36567 • PLA

McCormack Edward G. • Associate Professor • College of New Rochelle Gill Library • New Rochelle, NY 10805

McCormack Mary C. • Trustee • Baldwin Public Library • Birmingham, MI 48012-3002

McCormick Ann B. • Harnett County Schools • Lillington, NC 27546 • AASL

McCormick Edith J. • Senior Editor Production • American Library Association • Chicago, IL 60611-2795 • ALSC

McCormick Emily S. • Adult Services Librarian • Public Library of Charlotte & Mecklenburg County • Charlotte, NC 28202

McCormick Leo M. • Student • Texas Woman's University School of Library & Information Studies • Denton, TX 76204

McCormick Margaret W. • Dist. Coor. of Libraries/Ln • Clayton High School Library • St Louis, MO 63105 • AASL

McCormick Mary C. • Student • Louisiana State University School of Library & Information Science • Baton Rouge, LA 70803-3290 • SRRT

McCosh Roberta A. • Library Relations Rep • H. W. Wilson Co. • Evanston, IL 60201

McCourt Ellen J. • Library Media Specialist • Wildwood School • Mt. Lakes, NJ 07046 • AASL

McCowan Glenna R. • Librarian • Department of Veterans Affairs Medical Center North Little Rock Division • North Little Rock, AR 72114-1706

McCowan Tray K. • Community Services Librarian • Anderson County Library • Anderson, SC 29622-4047

McCown Alice A. • Librarian • Columbus Technical Institute • Columbus, GA 31995

McCown Leonard Joe • Librarian • Nimitz High School • Irving, TX 75060 • AASL YALSA *Life*

McCown Nall Douglas • Atlanta-Fulton Public Library • Atlanta, GA 30303

McCoy Cheryl S. • Instructor Librarian • University of South Florida Library • Tampa, FL 33620-5600 • ACRL

McCoy Jacquelyn A. • Director • Occidental College Library • Los Angeles, CA 90041 • ACRL LAMA CLENE IFRT IRRT SRRT

McCoy James F. • Philadelphia, PA 19115 • ACRL RASD IFRT SRRT *Continuing*

McCoy Jan N. • Media Specialist • Willamette High School • Eugene, OR 97402 • AASL

McCoy Jody • Crabtree Library Director • Casady School • Oklahoma City, OK 73156 • AASL

McCoy Judy I. • Fort Worth Public Library Seminary South Branch • Ft. Worth, TX 76110

McCoy Lyn L. • Reference Librarian • United States Enviromental Protection Agency Region I • Boston, MA 02203

McCoy Mary Ellen • Branches & Clln. Devel. Coor. • Anchorage Municipal Libraries Z. J. Loussac Library • Anchorage, AK 99503 • PLA

McCoy Mary Watson • Gainesville, FL 32607 • Continuing

McCoy Michael A. • Director • Dobbs Ferry Public Library • Dobbs Ferry, NY 10522 • PLA

McCoy Nanette M. • Student • Emporia State University Emporia in the Rockies • Denver, CO 80204

McCoy Ralph E. • Carbondale, IL 62901 • ACRL ALCTS *Life*

McCoy Sharron L. • Director • Morton Grove Public Library • Morton Grove, IL 60053 • PLA

McCoy Virginia R. • Director • Eureka College Melick Library • Eureka, IL 61530 • LAMA

McCoy W. Keith • Director • Dowdell Library of South Amboy • South Amboy, NJ 08879 • PLA SRRT

McCracken John R. • Texas Woman's University School of Library & Information Studies • Denton, TX 76204

McCracken Linda • Yakima Valley Regional Library • Yakima, WA 98901 • PLA

McCrackin Olympia Foster • Librarian • Bryce Hospital Patients Library • Tuscaloosa, AL 35401

McCrady Ellen R. • Editor • Abbey Publications Inc. • Provo, UT 84606

McCrady Jacqueline C. • Director • Mount Hood Community College • Gresham, OR 97030 • ACRL

McCrank Lawrence J. • Dean Library & Instructional Ser • Ferris State University • Big Rapids, MI 49307 • ACRL LAMA LHRT LRRT

McCrank Ruth D. • Deputy Director • Kent County Library System • Grand Rapids, MI 49503 • ALSC LAMA

McCrate Bridget C. • Student • Kent State University School of Library & Information Science • Kent, OH 44242-0001 • ACRL

McCrave Kate G. • Naval Postgraduate School Dudley Knox Library • Monterey, CA 93943-5002

McCraw Virginia F. • McColl Elementary School • McColl, SC 29570

McCray Evelina W. • Palqwemine, LA 70764

McCray Helen A. • Miami, FL 33176

McCray Jeanette C. • Associate Director • University of Arizona Arizona Health Sciences Center Library • Tucson, AZ 85724 • LAMA LITA

McCray Marilyn J. • Branch Librarian • Barboursville Public Library • Barboursville, WV 25504 • PLA YALSA

McCray Nancy H. • Assistant Editor, Booklist Nonpr • American Library Association • Chicago, IL 60611-2795

McCray Thomas G. • Documents Librarian • United States Senate Library • Washington, DC 20510-7112 • LITA

McCreary Alice E. • McCarter & English • Cherry Hill, NJ 08002 • RASD

McCreight Brian W. • Student • College Of Charleston • Charleston, SC 29401 • ALCTS ALSC EMIERT

McCreight Elaine J. • Student • State University of New York (SUNY) School of Information & Library Studies • Buffalo, NY 14260 • ALSC PLA

McCreight JoAnn O. • Head Librarian • Fulton-Montgomery Community College Library • Johnstown, NY 12095

McCreight Penny • Library Director • University Park Public Library District • University Pk, IL 60466 • LAMA PLA

McCreless Susan • Head of Cataloging • University of Alabama in Huntsville Library • Huntsville, AL 35899 • ACRL ALCTS

McCrimmon Barbara • Tallahassee, FL 32301

McCrory Kathleen B. • Children's Hospital & Medical Center • Seattle, WA 98105

McCroskey Marilyn J. • Asst. Prof. of Lib. Sci. • Southwest Missouri State University Library • Springfield, MO 65804-0095 • AASL

McCrosky Janet Ellen • Order Librarian/Asst. Cataloger • Clark County Public Library • Springfield, OH 45501-1080 • ALCTS RASD

McCrossan John A. • Director • University of South Florida School of Library & Information Science • Tampa, FL 33620 • PLA SRRT

McCue Janet A. • Head Technical Services Division • Cornell University Library • Ithaca, NY 14853-5301 • ALCTS LITA

McCue Mary Ann E • High School Librarian • Unified School District 500 • Kansas City, KS 66101

McCue Michael D. • Director • Teaneck Public Library • Teaneck, NJ 07666 • PLA

McCue Nancy • New England College • Henniker, NH 03242

McCuen Kelley Jo • Automation Librarian • Peoria Public Library • Peoria, IL 61602 • PLA LHRT LRRT NMRT

McCuistion Thomas M. • Trustee • Clark County Public Library • Springfield, OH 45501-1080 • ALTA

McCulley Lucretia G. • Director of Public Services • University of Richmond • Richmond, VA 23173 • ACRL

McCulley Nettie J. • Media Specialist • Brownsville Middle School • Pensacola, FL 32505

McCulloch Marilyn • Young Adult Specialist • Ottawa Public Library • Ottawa ON, K1P 5M2 Canada • AASL ALSC YALSA

McCulloch Meredith • Director • Bedford Public Library • Bedford, MA 01730 • ALCTS LITA PLA RASD YALSA

McCullough Barbara S. • Assistant Director • Lee College Church of God School of Theology • Cleveland, TN 37311

McCullough David A. • Ferndale, MI 48220 • ACRL

McCullough Doreen J. • Proctor, VT 05765 • ACRL

McCullough Jan A. • O'Fallon, IL 62269 • AFLRT FLRT

McCullough Jane M. • Administrative Assistant • Raytest U.S.A., Inc. • Pittsburgh, PA 15241 • AASL

McCullough Mary T. • Arlington, VA 22207-4438

McCullough Peg • Tucson, AZ 85718

McCullough Rhea K • Columbia, MD 21045 • AASL

McCully June J. • Librarian • North Richland Junior High School • Ft. Worth, TX 76180

McCully Sarajane • Librarian • Hyde Magnet School • Wichita, KS 67208 • AASL

McCully William C. Jr. • Park Ridge Public Library • Park Ridge, IL 60068-4188 • LAMA PLA

McCune Donna K. • Riverside City & County Public Library Palm Desert Country Branch • Palm Desert, CA 92260 • RASD

McCune Lois M. • Assistant Head • Indiana University Libraries Monographic Proc Serv Dept • Bloomington, IN 47405

McCune Patricia A. • Librarian • Academy Central School • Tulsa, OK 74127

McCurdy-Crescimanno P. A. • New Britain, CT 06053

McCurdy Frances J. • Children's Librarian • Pittsburg Public Library • Pittsburg, KS 66762 • ALSC

McCurdy Virginia M. • Trustee • DeKalb County Public Library Adminstration Building • Decatur, GA 30030 • ALTA

McCurley Donna S. • Social Sci. Monographic Catlgr. • Auburn University Ralph Brown Draughon Library • Auburn, AL 36849-5606 • ACRL ALCTS

McCurley Henry H. Jr. • Serials Cataloger • Auburn University Ralph Brown Draughon Library • Auburn, AL 36849-5606

McCurley Marsha J. • Head of Cataloging • Clemson University R. M. Cooper Library • Clemson, SC 29634-3001 • ALCTS LITA GODORT

McCurry Alan P. • District Librarian • Yukon-Koyukuk School District • Nenana, AK 99760 • AASL ALCTS LITA

McCusker Joseph H. Mrs. • Trustee • New Orleans Public Library • New Orleans, LA 70140

McCusker M. Lauretta Sr. • Professor Emeritus • Rosary College Graduate School of Library & Information Science • River Forest, IL 60305

McCuskey Jean • Canton, OH 44708 • AASL ALSC *Continuing*

McCutchen Peggy • Director • Scottsboro Public Library • Scottsboro, AL 35768 • PLA

McCutcheon Dorothy A. • Kansas City, MO 64110 • AASL ALSC *Continuing*

McCutcheon Margo • Student • University of British Columbia School of Library, Archival & Information Studies • Vancouver BC, V6T 1Z1 Canada

McDace Arlene • Pine Crest Upper School Library • Ft Lauderdale, FL 33308

McDade Darlene Y. • Reference • Atlanta-Fulton Public Library Southwest Regional Library • Atlanta, GA 30331 • PLA RASD

McDade Juanita • Librarian • Moon Middle School • Oklahoma City, OK 73136 • NMRT

McDanel Diana M. • Norman, OK 73072 • YALSA

McDaniel Amanda R. • Reference Adult Service • Edgecombe County Memorial Library • Tarboro, NC 27886

McDaniel Angela M. • Atlanta, GA 30305-1417

McDaniel Carse • Media Librarian • San Francisco Public Library • San Francisco, CA 94102

McDaniel Charles J. • Administrator Services Coor. • Lake Lanier Regional Library Lawrenceville Branch • Lawrenceville, GA 30245 • PLA

McDaniel Deanna J. • Librarian • Elmwood Elementary School • Lima, OH 45806 • AASL ALSC

McDaniel Donna W. • Colorado Springs, CO 80920 • IFRT SRRT

McDaniel Julie A. • Public Services Librarian • Ohio Wesleyan University • Delaware, OH 43015 • RASD

McDaniel Karen C. • Director • Kentucky State University Blazer Library • Frankfort, KY 40601 • ACRL

McDaniel Paula • Media Specialist • Waldron Junior-Senior High School Library • Waldron, IN 46182

McDavid Lisa • Cataloger • University of South Carolina • Columbia, SC 29208 • ALCTS

McDermand Robert • Head of Serials Department • San Jose State University Clark Library • San Jose, CA 95192-0028 • ALCTS

McDermot Terri • Dir. of Lib Pub Relations Dept. • University of Nevada-Reno • Reno, NV 89557-0020 • ACRL LAMA

McDermott Ellen • Manager • Nynex Corporation • White Plains, NY 10604

McDermott Francis X. • Emeritus • Immaculate Conception Center Library • Douglaston, NY 11362 • Continuing

McDermott Laura J. • Student • Hamline University Bush Memorial Library • Saint Paul, MN 55104 • RASD

McDermott Leone M. • Audiovisual Librarian • Truman College, LRC • Chicago, IL 60640

McDermott Lucille • Student • Queens College Graduate School of Library & Information Studies • Flushing, NY 11367 • LITA EMIERT NMRT

McDermott Margaret A. • Librarian/Director • Dumbomce Public Library • Duncombe, IA 50532

McDermott Margaret H. • Reference Librarian • Washington University Libraries Freund Law Library • St. Louis, MO 63130 • ACRL RASD

McDermott Marjorie • Belmont Abbey College Library • Belmont, NC 28012

McDermott Molly Ms • Assistant Director • Sonoma County Library • Santa Rosa, CA 95404 • LAMA

McDiarmid Errett W. • St. Paul, MN 55108

McDonald Alison D. • Librarian Yourh Services Dept • Hackley Public Library • Muskegon, MI 49440 • ALSC

McDonald Anne • Law Library Coordinator • Rhode Island Dept of Attorney General, Library • Providence, RI 02903 • ASCLA LAMA

McDonald Beverly I. • Cataloger • Ohio State University Libraries • Columbus, OH 43210-1286 • ACRL ALCTS LITA

McDonald Brenda D. • Coordinator of Information Svs. • Saint Louis Public Library • Saint Louis, MO 63103-2389 • PLA RASD GODORT

McDonald Carrie S. • Branch Librarian • Kansas City Public Library Landing Kiosk • Kansas City, MO 64132

McDonald Christine M. • Moore, SC 29369-9722 • ALSC

McDonald Christine Ms. • Director • Crandall Library • Glen Falls, NY 12801 • PLA

McDonald David • CLSI INC. • Richmond, VA 23230 • LITA

McDonald David R. • Director • Tufts University • Medford, MA 02155 • ACRL LITA

McDonald Donna M. • Commack, NY 11725 • PLA

McDonald Ellen J. • Lexington, MA 02173

McDonald Frances M. • Professor • Mankato State University Library Media Education Department • Mankato, MN 56003 • AASL YALSA IFRT

McDonald Gail E. • Bryn Mawr, PA 19010

McDonald Gillian A. • Reader Services Librarian • Heriot-Watt University Library • Edinburgh EH14 4AS, Scotland

McDonald Isabel • Portland, OR 97225

McDonald Janice • Student • Ohio State University • Columbus, OH 43210 • AASL

McDonald John P. • Director Emeritus • University of Connecticut Homer Babbidge Library • Storrs, CT 06269-1005 • ACRL LAMA *Life*

McDonald Joseph • Vice President Inf. Services • Dordt College Library • Sioux Center, IA 51250 • ACRL LAMA RASD LIRT *Life*

McDonald June E. • Practising Law Institute • New York, NY 10019

McDonald Kathleen W. • Student • State University of New York (SUNY) School of Information & Library Studies • Buffalo, NY 14260 • AASL

McDonald Larry G. • Reference Librarian • University of Regina • Regina SK, S4S 0A2 Canada • ACRL ALCTS

McDonald Laurie M. • Student • Florida State University School of Library and Information Studies • Tallahassee, FL 32306-2048

McDonald Linda J. • High School Librarian • Tri-Valley High School • Hegins, PA 17961 • AASL ALSC LIRT

McDonald Maguerita • Corvallis, OR 97330 • ACRL RASD *Continuing*

McDonald Marilyn M. • Dean of Instr. Servs. & Libs. • Foothill College Library • Los Altos Hills, CA 94022-4599 • ACRL

McDonald Martha J. • Executive Director • Greater Cincinnati Library Consortium • Cincinnati, OH 45220 • ASCLA

McDonald Murray F. • Director • Dedham Public Library • Dedham, MA 02026 • ALSC

McDonald Nancy L. • Student • University of Michigan School of Information and Library Studies • Ann Arbor, MI 48109-1092

McDonald Pamela J. • Media Specialist • Max Bruner Junior Middle School Library • Fort Walton Beach, FL 32548

McDonald Patricia S. • Wood Elementary School • Tempe, AZ 85283 • ALSC

McDonald Paula J. • District Elementary Librarian • Neal Dow Library • Chico, CA 95926

McDonald Richard L. • Children's Librarian • Champaign Public Library & Information Center • Champaign, IL 61820-5193 • ALSC

McDonald Robert • Head, Technical Services • Columbia University Health Sciences Library • New York, NY 10032 • ALCTS

McDonald Rose-Naree • Librarian • Black Gold Coop Library System • San Luis Obispo, CA 93403

McDonald Ruby K. • Trustee • Yakima Valley Regional Library • Yakima, WA 98901

McDonald S. Lynn • Network Librarian Flc/Fedlink • Library of Congress • Washington, DC 20541 • ALCTS LITA CLENE FLRT

McDonald Sekiko K. • East Asian Librarian • Yale University Sterling Memorial Library • New Haven, CT 06520

McDonald Sharon • Librarian • Newport Harbor High School • Newport Beach, CA 92663 • AASL

McDonald Stanley M. Jr. • Framingham State College Henry Whittemore Library • Framingham, MA 01701 • AASL ACRL ALCTS ALSC LAMA LITA RASD

McDonald Susan J. • Supervisor of Reference Services • Pacific Lutheran University Mortvedt Library • Tacoma, WA 98447 • ACRL RASD

McDonald Timothea • Branch Librarian • Boston Public Library South End Branch • Boston, MA 02118 • YALSA

McDonnell Diana M. • Director • Delmar Public Library • Delmar, DE 19940 • PLA

McDonnell Eileen D. • Sno-Isle Regional Library Edmonds Branch • Edmonds, WA 98020

McDonnell Frances • Arlington, VA 22205 • ACRL

McDonnell M. Jeanne U. Sr. • Fontbonne Hall Academy Library • Brooklyn, NY 11209

McDonnell Michael P. • Documents Librarian • Western Michigan University Libraries Dwight B. Waldo Library • Kalamazoo, MI 49008 • ACRL RASD GODORT MAGERT

McDonnell Richard H. • Ref. Librarian/Science Bibliogr. • University of Texas at San Antonio-Library • San Antonio, TX 78249 • ACRL RASD

McDonnell Virginia M. • Student • Rutgers University School of Communication Information & Library Studies • New Brunswick, NJ 08903 • AASL

McDonough Betsy • Brookfield, CT 06804 • PLA

McDonough Douglas M. • Director • Manchester Public Library • Manchester, CT 06040 • PLA

McDonough Garnett • Trustee • Clark County Public Library • Springfield, OH 45501-1080 • ALTA

McDonough Jean R. • Princeton, NJ 08540 • AASL ALSC *Life*

McDonough Jerome P. • Student • University of California-Berkeley School of Library & Information Studies • Berkeley, CA 94720 • LITA IFRT SRRT

McDonough Joyce G. • Assistant Director, Tech. • Columbia University Libraries Butler Library • New York, NY 10027 • ACRL ALCTS LITA IFRT LRRT

McDonough Kathleen Celia • Library Consultant • UpCountry Consultants • Twin Mountain, NH 03545 • LAMA PLA

McDonough Kristin A. • Library Director • Baruch College Library • New York, NY 10010 • ACRL LAMA

McDonough Marita E. • Camdridge, MA 02142

McDonough Mary • Student • University of South Carolina College of Library & Information Science • Columbia, SC 29208

McDonough Pat • Trustee • Salisbury Free Library • Salisbury, NH 03268

McDonough Roger H. Mr. • Princeton, NJ 08540 • Life

McDonough Terrence R. • Technical Services Associate • Salomon Brothers Inc. Investment Banking Library • New York, NY 10048 • ACRL ALCTS LAMA LITA

McDougal Sarah H. • Student • University of Illinois Graduate School of Library and Information Science • Urbana, IL 61801 • ACRL

McDougal Terri L. • Head of Children's Services • Kanawha County Public Library • Charleston, WV 25301 • ALSC NMRT

McDowell Bernadette B. • Ventura County Library Service Agency • Port Hueneme, CA 93041

McDowell C. Blake Jr. • Trustee • Akron-Summit County Public Library • Akron, OH 44326-0001 • ALTA

McDowell Carole L. • Public Service Librarian • Bessemer Public Library • Bessemer, AL 35020

McDowell Catherine L. • Assistant Director • Greenburgh Public Library • Elmsford, NY 10523

McDowell Gayla K. • Library Director • S California Coll of Chiropractic • Pico Rivera, CA 90660 • ALCTS IFRT

McDowell Ida L. • Director • Four Rivers ALSA • Evansville, IN 47708

McDowell Jessie C. • Librarian • Stephen Decatur Elementary School • Philadelphia, PA 19154

McDowell Josephine E. • Lexington, KY 40503

McDowell Mary-Louise • Elementary Library Supervisor • Lower Dauphin School District • Hummelstown, PA 17036 • AASL

McDowell Noel A. Dr. • Elem. Libraries/Media Coor. • Wooster City Schools • Wooster, OH 44691 • AASL

McDuff Rebecca L. • Head of Information Services • San Francisco Public Library • San Francisco, CA 94102

McEachern Virginia S. • St Augustine, FL 32084 • Continuing

McElderry Margaret Knox • Vice President & Publisher • Margaret K. McElderry Books • New York, NY 10022 • ALSC

McEldowney Patricia J. • Grande Prairie Public Library District • Hazel Crest, IL 60429 • AASL PLA YALSA

McElfresh Rose Marie • Marketing Representative • Marcive, Inc. • San Antonio, TX 78265 • ERT

McElhatton John F. • Librarian • New York Public Library • Bronx, NY 10458 • PLA

McElmeel Sharron • Marion, IA 52302

McElmurry-Reich Lynn M. • Fitchburg, WI 53711

McElroy Anna Y. • Head of Children's Services • San Diego County Library • San Diego, CA 92123

McElroy Joseph • Executive Director • Bur Oak Library System • Shorewood, IL 60436

McElroy Neil J. • Director of Libraries • Lafayette College Skillman Library • Easton, PA 18042-1797 • ACRL

McElroy Robert A. • Monterey County Free Libraries • Salinas, CA 93901

McElroy Stewart J. • Student • University of Michigan Libraries Music Library School of Music • Ann Arbor, MI 48109

McElveen Paul A. • Children's Librarian • Public Library of Cincinnati and Hamilton County • Cincinnati, OH 45202 • ALSC

McElwain Connie L. • Librarian • Marshall County Board of Education High School Library • Benton, KY 42025 • AASL

McElwain Maryhardy • Director • Elizabeth Jones Library • Grenada, MS 38901

McElwain Michael F. • Student • University of Texas at Austin Graduate School of Library & Information Sciences • Austin, TX 78712-1276

McElwain William E. • Librarian • Chicago Public Library Harold Washington Library • Chicago, IL 60605

McEnaney Barbara Sr. • Saint Mary's Hospital • Troy, NY 12180-1613

McEneaney Regina G. • Sayville, NY 11782 • ALCTS

McEntee Mary F. • Librarian • Dittlinger Memorial Library • New Braunfels, TX 78130 • PLA

McEntyre Judith S. • Library Media • Harborside Elementary School • Chula Vista, CA 92011 • AASL

McErlean Catherine • Director • Passaic Township Public Library • Stirling, NJ 07980 • PLA

McEuen Joddy R. • Librarian • Pinal County Library District • Florence, AZ 85232 • PLA

McEvoy Courtney A. • Wilkes Barre, PA 18702 • ACRL EMIERT SRRT

McEvoy Ruth M. • Batavia, NY 14020

McEwan Jodie • Carleton, MI 48117

McEwan Linda L. • Elgin Community College • Elgin, IL 60123 • ACRL ALCTS LITA ILERT SRRT

McEwen Margie • Rpt. Coffin Elementary School • Brunswick, ME 04011 • AASL ALSC

McEwen Mary • Librarian • James E. Wickson Memorial Library • Frankenmuth, MI 48734

McFadden David L. • Reference Librarian • Southwestern University Law Library • Los Angeles, CA 90005 • GODORT

McFadden Evelyn G. • Bloomfield Hills, MI 48302

McFadden Linda • Manager, Business Communications • Herman Miller Research Corp • Zeeland, MI 49464 • LITA

McFadden Molly C. • Gonzaga University Crosby Library • Spokane, WA 99258

McFadden Thomas G. • Head, Humanities/Social Sciences • University of California-Davis Library • Davis, CA 95616 • ACRL LITA RASD

McFall Betty N. • User Services Librarian • Middle Tennessee State University Andrew L. Todd Library • Murfreesboro, TN 37132

McFarland Anne L. • Student • University of North Carolina at Chapel Hill School of Information and Library Science • Chapel Hill, NC 27599-3360 • ALCTS

McFarland Betty J. • Librarian • University of Kentucky • Elizabethtwn, KY 42701 • ACRL

McFarland Carolyn • Document Librarian • Rollins College Olin Library • Winter Park, FL 32789-4499 • RASD GODORT

McFarland Jane E. • Director • Chattanooga-Hamilton County Bicentennial Library • Chattanooga, TN 37402 • LAMA PLA IFRT SRRT

McFarland Marilyn Jean • Cataloging Library Associate • Palo Alto City Library • Palo Alto, CA 94303

McFarland Mary Ann • Science and Nursing Librarian • Southern Illinois University • Edwardsville, IL 62026 • ACRL

McFarland Sharron D. • Maryland State Department of Education Division of Library Development & Services • Baltimore, MD 21201 • ASCLA PLA

McFarland Thomas • Head of Technical Services • Florida Institute of Technology Library • Melbourne, FL 32901 • ACRL

McFarland Trudy • New Orleans, LA 70124

McFarling Patricia • Technical Services • Owensboro Community College • Owensboro, KY 42303 • ACRL IFRT LIRT

McFatridge Todd R. • Adult Services Librarian • Mount Prospect Public Library • Mount Prospect, IL 60056

McFerran Warren • N Muskegon, MI 49445 • PLA *Continuing*

McFerren Priscilla Greco • Director • Hanover Public Library • Hanover, PA 17331 • PLA

McFerrin James B. • Librarian • Union College Abigail E. Weeks Memorial Library • Barbourville, KY 40906-1499 • Continuing

McFerson Shirley • Director • Caldwell-Lake George Library • Lake George, NY 12845

McGalliard Mary L. • Deputy Director • Yakima Valley Regional Library • Yakima, WA 98901 • LITA PLA

McGann Kate E. • Bus Librarian • Jackson County Library System • Medford, OR 97501

McGarigle Diane • Head Technical Services • Sarasota County Library System • Sarasota, FL 34236 • ALCTS

McGarity Mary Sue Dr. • Birmingham, AL 35209 • AASL ALCTS

McGarr Sheila M. • Chief Depository Adm. Branch • U.S. Government Printing Office Library Program Service • Washington, DC 20401 • GODORT

McGarrell Andrew R. • Cataloging Librarian • Missouri Western State College Hearnes Learning Resources Center • Saint Joseph, MO 64507 • ACRL

McGarry Dorothy • University of California (UCLA) Physical Sciences & Technology Libraries • Los Angeles, CA 90024-1598 • ACRL ALCTS LITA RASD GODORT IRRT LRRT MAGERT

McGarry Jane A. • Head of Acquisition Division • Bryn Mawr College Canaday Library • Bryn Mawr, PA 19010 • ALCTS

McGarry Sarah • Librarian IV • Phoenix Public Library • Phoenix, AZ 85004 • PLA IFRT

McGavick Mary H. • Reference Librarian • Public Library of Mont Vernon & Knox County • Mt Vernon, OH 43050 • RASD

McGaw Howard F. Dr. • Professor Emeritus, Library Sci. • Western Washington University Wilson Library • Bellingham, WA 98225 • ACRL RASD *Life*

McGeachin Robert B. • Student • University of Texas at Austin Graduate School of Library & Information Sciences • Austin, TX 78712-1276 • ACRL LITA RASD

McGeachy John A. III • Documents Librarian • North Carolina State University D. H. Hill Library • Raleigh, NC 27695-7111 • ACRL GODORT

McGeath Kerry • Corporate Buyer • Great Train Store • Dallas, TX 75248 • PLA

McGee Alvin • Trustee • Jackson-Hinds Library System • Jackson, MS 39201 • ALTA

McGee Leigh • Librarian • Blewett Middle School • St. Louis, MO 63106 • AASL

McGee Leora R. • School Media Supervisor • Milwaukee Public Schools Media Center • Milwaukee, WI 53208 • AASL

McGee Mary Ann • Oakland Community College • Farmington Hills, MI 48334-4579

McGee Mary H. • Director • Oil Spill Public Information Center • Anchorage, AK 99501

McGee Rob • Consultant • RMG Consultants Inc. • Chicago, IL 60610

McGee William H.J. • Coordinator • Hidalgo County Library System • McAllen, TX 78501 • PLA

McGeehon Carol L. • Sr. Librarian, Tech. Servs. • Douglas County Library System • Roseburg, OR 97470 • LITA

McGhee Marian H. • Dallas, TX 75230

McGiffin Patricia • Unified Media Specialist • Fort River School • Amherst, MA 01002

McGill-Ondrejko Sara L. • Guernsey County District Public Library • Cambridge, OH 43725 • PLA

McGill Evelyn A. • Children's Librarian • Lexington Public Library Northside Branch • Lexington, KY 40505

McGill Nancy L. • King County Library System • Seattle, WA 98109-5191 • PLA

McGill Sylvia • Media Specialist • Mill Creek Elementary School • Columbia, MO 65203 • AASL

McGill Wilbur • Enoch Pratt Free Library • Baltimore, MD 21201-4484 • RASD

McGinley Ann M. • Librarian • Shamokin Area Middle School • Shamokin, PA 17872

McGinn Barbara S. • Media Specialist • Anne Arundel County Public School Oak Hill Elementary School • Severna Park, MD 21146 • AASL

McGinn Howard F. • State Librarian • North Carolina Department of Cultural Resources State Library • Raleigh, NC 27601-2807 • ASCLA

McGinn Thomas P. Dr. • Wayne State University Library Science Program • Detroit, MI 48202 • LITA IRRT

McGinnies Nancy • Assistant Director • Tompkins County Public Library • Ithaca, NY 14850

McGinnis Alma K. • Library Media Specialist • T. Eugene Crocker Primary School • Hogansville, GA 30230 • AASL

McGinnis Deborah K. • Librarian • United States Office of Surface Mining • Denver, CO 80202 • FLRT

McGinnis John J. • Director of the Library • Cerritos College Library • Norwalk, CA 90650 • AASL ACRL LAMA

McGinnis Julia F. • Student • University of Michigan School of Information and Library Studies • Ann Arbor, MI 48109-1092 • ALCTS LAMA

McGinnis Leslie • Literacy Coordinator • Oakland Public Library • Oakland, CA 94612

McGinnis Margaret M. • Student • Drexel University College of Information Studies • Philadelphia, PA 19104-2875 • AASL

McGinnis Michael M. • Student • University of Hawaii School of Library & Information Studies • Honolulu, HI 96822

McGinnis Mildred M. • Acquistion Search & Order Ln. • Ball State University Library Department of Library Services • Muncie, IN 47306 • ACRL ALCTS

McGinniss Daniel D. • Student • University of Pittsburgh School of Library and Information Science • Pittsburgh, PA 15260

McGinty Stephen P. • Head of Acquisitions • Harvard University Littauer Library • Cambridge, MA 02138 • ACRL LITA

McGiverin Rolland H. • Teaching Materials & Spec Serv Ln • Indiana State University Cunningham Memorial Library • Terre Haute, IN 47809 • ACRL

McGivern Katherine B. • Student • Rutgers University School of Communication Information & Library Studies • New Brunswick, NJ 08903

McGlamery Thornton P. • Map Librarian-University Lbn III • University of Connecticut Homer Babbidge Library • Storrs, CT 06269-1005 • LITA MAGERT

McGlasson Laura M. • Student • University of North Texas School of Library & Information Sciences • Denton, TX 76203 • ACRL

McGlinchey Andrea • McLean, VA 22102-2915 • RASD FLRT GODORT IRRT

McGlinn Sharon Hilts • The American University Library • Washington, DC 20016-8046

McGlohon Leah L. • Reference Librarian • East Carolina University Joyner Library • Greenville, NC 27858-4353

McGlone Jamie A. • Staff Officer for Special Proj. • Boston Public Library • Boston, MA 02117

McGlynn Ed • Trustee • Hennepin County Library • Minnetonka, MN 55343 • ALTA

McGlynn Eileen Ann • Madison, WI 53703-3810 • AASL ALSC RASD

McGoldrick Kathleen A. • Student • Saint John's University Division of Library & Information Science • Jamaica, NY 11439

McGonigle Karla • MEDIA, PA 19063 • AASL

McGonigle Marlene F. • Director • Kinnelon Public Library • Kinnelon, NJ 07405 • PLA

McGorey Timothy E. • Community Services Coordinator • Monroe County Library System • Monroe, MI 48161

McGovern Alice M. • Cataloger • Dutchess Community College Library • Poughkeepsie, NY 12601

McGovern Gail J. • Library Consultant • California State Library Library Development Services Bureau • Sacramento, CA 95814-3324 • ASCLA PLA CLENE ILERT

McGovern Kathryn S. • Library Media Specialist • Oxford Middle School • Overland Park, KS 66213 • AASL

McGovern Timothy J. • Manager,Distributed Applications • Massachusetts Institute of Technology Libraries (MIT) • Cambridge, MA 02139 • LITA

McGovney Beth A. • Horseshoe Bend School District No 73 • Horseshoe Bend, ID 83629

McGowan Frank M. • Director Acquis. Overseas Oper. • Library of Congress • Washington, DC 20541 • ACRL ALCTS *Life*

McGowan Margaret J. • Director • Wauwatosa Public Library • Wauwatosa, WI 53213 • ALCTS ALSC LAMA LITA PLA RASD YALSA

McGowan Margaret M. • Library Director • Alameda Free Library • Alameda, CA 94501 • LAMA PLA IFRT

McGowan Owen T. P. • Fall River, MA 02720

McGowan Sarah M. • Director • Ripon College Library • Ripon, WI 54971 • ACRL LITA RASD GODORT SRRT

McGowan Susan M. • Librarian • Saint Bartholomew School • Chicago, IL 60641 • NMRT

McGowan Timothy • Head, Reference & Adult Servs. • Schenectady County Public Library • Schenectady, NY 12305-2083

McGowen Mercedes A. • Trustee • Poplar Creek Public Library Dist • Streamwood, IL 60107 • ALTA

McGown Sue W. • Librarian Lower School • St. John's School • Houston, TX 77019 • AASL

McGrady Amanda B. • Wilmington, DE 19806 • PLA

McGrady Theresa • Librarian • C.E.S. 63 • Bronx, NY 10456

McGrath Catherine C. • Laguna Beach, CA 92651

McGrath Charlene K. • Southeast Area Health Education Center • Hazard, KY 41701

McGrath Eileen L. • Cataloger • University of North Carolina • Chapel Hill, NC 27599-3902 • ACRL LHRT

McGrath Ellen T. • State University of New York (SUNY) Charles B. Sears Law Library • Buffalo, NY 14260 • ALCTS

McGrath Judith A. • Middletown Psychiatric Center • Middletown, NY 10940

McGrath Karen E. • Branch Librarian • Cranston Public Library Auburn Branch Library • Cranston, RI 02910

McGrath Marsha Burge • Youth Division Manager • Clearwater Public Library • Clearwater, FL 34623 • PLA

McGrath Martha • Principal Catalogue Librarian • Yale University Sterling Memorial Library • New Haven, CT 06520 • LAMA LITA

McGrath Murel J. • Dallas Public Library • Dallas, TX 75201 • RASD MAGERT

McGrath Robert E. • President • Robert E. McGrath & Associates • Stamford, CT 06902 • RASD

McGrath Shirley H. • Assistant Director,Public Serv. • Memorial Hall Library • Andover, MA 01810

McGrath William E. • Amherst, NY 14228 • ACRL ALCTS LAMA LITA LRRT *Continuing*

McGrath William T. • Trustee • Willingboro Public Library • Willingboro, NJ 08046 • ALTA

McGrattan Alana E. • Santa Fe Indian School • Santa Fe, NM 87501 • AASL

McGraw-Allen Nancy • Seattle Community College District • Seattle, WA 98101 • ALCTS

McGraw-Wagner Elizabeth • Public Services Librarian III • Baltimore County Public Library • Towson, MD 21204 • ALSC PLA

McGraw Jane H. • Director • East Detroit Memorial Library • East Detroit, MI 48021-2390 • PLA

McGreal Patricia • Resource Center Director • Mother McAuley Liberal Arts High School Library • Chicago, IL 60642

McGreer Anne J. • Associate Librarian • Indiana University Libraries Monographic Proc Serv Dept • Bloomington, IN 47405 • ALCTS LITA

McGreer Dennis M. • Asst. Lib Automation Officer • Indiana University • Bloomington, IN 47405 • LITA

McGreer Pamela K. • Assistant Children's Librarian • Saint Charles Public Library • St. Charles, IL 60174

McGreevy Kathleen T. • Santa Rosa Junior College • Santa Rosa, CA 95401 • ACRL LITA RASD LIRT

McGregor Ann L. • Asst. Library Director • Watauga Hospital Inc. • Boone, NC 28607

McGregor Colleen • Director • Buena Park Library District • Buena Park, CA 90620-6270 • PLA

McGregor James Wilson • Chicago, IL 60625

McGregor Jane Ann • Children's Services Consultant • South Carolina State Library • Columbia, SC 29211 • ALSC PLA IFRT

McGregor Joy H. • Student • Florida State University School of Library and Information Studies • Tallahassee, FL 32306-2048 • AASL IFRT

McGregor R. Bruce • Information Specialist • IIT Research Institute Manufacturing Tech Info Anly Ctr • Chicago, IL 60616 • ACRL

McGrew Kevin W. • Duluth, MN 55811-2905

McGrew Linda L. • Library Media Specialist • Wright Elementary School • Cedar Rapids, IA 52402 • AASL

McGrew Mary Lou • Cedar Rapids, IA 52402 • AASL

McGriff Mary E. • Indianapolis-Marion County Public Library Lawrence Branch • Indianapolis, IN 46256-1754 • PLA

McGriff Ronald I. • Braham, MN 55006 • PLA

McGuane James L. Jr • Head of Cataloging Libraries • State University of New York at Binghamton Libraries (SUNY) • Binghamton, NY 13902-6012 • ACRL ALCTS LITA

McGuff Joseph T. • Trustee • Johnson County Library • Shawnee Mission, KS 66201 • ALTA

McGugan Debbie A. • Head, Education Library • University of Saskatchewan Library • Saskatoon SK, S7N 0W0 Canada • ACRL

McGuire Bernadette Marie Sr. • Librarian • Sacred Heart-Griffin Library • Springfield, IL 62704 • YALSA

McGuire Brenda • Scott Elementary School • Temple, TX 76504-6552 • AASL

McGuire Edith S. • Wyalusing Elementary School Library • Wyalusing, PA 18853 • AASL

McGuire Elaine M. • Student • Findlay-Hancock County Public Library • Findlay, OH 45840 • AASL YALSA

McGuire Eva H. • Lexington, KY 40508-3424 • PLA

McGuire John E. • Director of Library Service • Jefferson Technical College • Steubenville, OH 43952

McGuire Laura H. • Portales, NM 88130

McGuire Michael C. • Student • Syracuse University School of Information Studies • Syracuse, NY 13244-4100 • LITA

McGuire Michael L. • Director • Traverse Area District Library • Traverse City, MI 49684

McGuire Nancy B. • Student • University of Wyoming • Laramie, WY 82071 • LITA IFRT SRRT

McGuire Paula • Editor • Visual Education Corporation • Princeton, NJ 08543

McGuire Serena E. • Student • University of North Carolina at Chapel Hill School of Information and Library Science • Chapel Hill, NC 27599-3360 • PLA CLENE

McGuire Susan J. • Iowa City, IA 52245 • CLENE ILERT

McGurk Patricia H. • Fishkill, NY 12524 • Continuing

McHale Joseph • Vice President • Janes Publishing Inc • Alexandria, VA 22313-2036 • PLA AFLRT ERT FLRT

McHarg Kathleen M. • Library Director • San Juan Island Public Library • Friday Harbor, WA 98250 • PLA

McHarg Kristine L. • Library Media Specialist • Peck Place School • Orange, CT 06477 • AASL

McHenry-Hepner Virginia M. • Ext. Servs. Mgr. • Lexington Public Library • Lexington, KY 40507

McHenry Cheryl • Elementary Librarian • Northern Lebanon School District • Fredericksburg, PA 17026 • AASL

McHenry Cheryl A. Dr. • Assistant Professor • University of Rhode Island Library • Kingston, RI 02881-0803 • AASL IFRT

McHenry Kelley E. • Refernece Librarian/Instructor • Seattle Central Community College • Seattle, WA 98122 • ACRL EMIERT LIRT

McHorney Brenda W. • Williamsburg, VA 23188

McHugh Alicia • Library Director • Oakland Park City Library • Oakland, FL 33334

McHugh Christine M. • Greensburg, PA 15601 • AASL

McHugh Robert S. • Northridge, CA 91324

McHugh William A. • Reference Librarian • Northwestern University Library • Evanston, IL 60208-2300 • ACRL RASD LHRT

McHugo Ann Y. • Assistant Catalog Librarian • Dartmouth College Library Baker Memorial Library • Hanover, NH 03755-3525 • ACRL ALCTS

McIlroy William R. • Summit, NJ 07901

McIlvain Leah G. • School Media Specialist • Eastern Kentucky University • Richmond, KY 40475 • AASL

McIlvaine Eileen • Head of Reference Department • Columbia University Libraries Butler Library • New York, NY 10027 • LITA RASD

McIlwain Anna K. • Talladega, AL 35160 • AASL

McIndoo Larry R. • Senior Personnel Analyst • City of Los Angeles • Los Angeles, CA 90012 • SRRT *Life*

McInerney Claire R. • Associate Professor • College of Saint Catherine • Saint Paul, MN 55105 • IFRT SRRT

McInerney Melanie • Reference Librarian • Santa Clara County Free Library Milpitas Community Library • Milpitas, CA 95035

McInnis Raymond G. • Social Science Librarian • Western Washington University Wilson Library • Bellingham, WA 98225 • ACRL RASD

McInroy Mary • Documents Librarian • University of Iowa Libraries • Iowa City, IA 52242-1379 • ACRL GODORT

McIntire Ann B. • Oakland, NJ 07436

McIntire Ann K.R. • Student • San Jose State University Division of Library & Information Science • San Jose, CA 95192-0029

McIntosh Ann R. • Childs Elementary School • Bloomington, IN 47401 • AASL ALSC

McIntosh Binnie B. • Library Media Specialist • Newark Board of Education • Newark, NJ 07102

McIntosh Carolyn Y. • Reference Librarian • California State University-Los Angeles John F. Kennedy Memorial Library • Los Angeles, CA 90032-8300 • ACRL EMIERT

McIntosh James G. • Milwaukee, WI 53211 • NMRT

McIntosh Jean P. • Honolulu, HI 96825

McIntosh Marilyn J. • Assistant Director • Monroe Free Library • Monroe, NY 10950

McIntosh Nadia • Catalog Librarian • University of Massachusetts University Library • Amherst, MA 01003 • ACRL ALCTS

McIntosh Patricia S. • Student • University of Rhode Island Graduate School of Library & Information Studies • Kingston, RI 02881-0815

McIntyre B. • Senior Lecturer • Royal Melbourne Institute of Technology • Melbourne, 3000 Australia • ACRL LITA PLA

McIntyre Barbara W. • Student • Rutgers University School of Communication Information & Library Studies • New Brunswick, NJ 08903 • AASL

McIntyre Helen • Albuquerque, NM 87108 • ACRL ALCTS *Life*

McIntyre Jacalynn Diane • Branch Librarian • Romeo District Library Washington Branch • Washington, MI 48094 • PLA

McIntyre Joan • Children's Librarian • Phoenixville Public Library • Phoenixville, PA 19460 • ALSC

McIntyre Joan M. • Library Director • Allentown College of St. Francis De Sales • Center Valley, PA 18034 • ACRL

McIntyre Joy • Student • University of Maryland College of Library and Information Services • College Park, MD 20742-4345 • ALSC

McIntyre Pattie B. • Chapel Hill, NC 27515

McInvaill Dwight E. H. • Head of Reference Department • Neuse Regional Library System • Kinston, NC 28501

McIver Minna H. • Gaithersburg, MD 20877-0962 • ACRL ALCTS LITA

McIver Stephanie P. • Division Manager • Atlanta-Fulton Public Library • Atlanta, GA 30303 • PLA

McKann Helen H. • Branch Librarian • Henrico County Public Library Gayton Branch • Richmond, VA 23233

McKann Michael R. • Deputy State Librarian • State Library of Louisiana • Baton Rouge, LA 70821-0131

McKay Beatrice L. • Catalog Librarian/Serials • Trinity University • San Antonio, TX 78212 • ALCTS NMRT

McKay Curt B. • University of Illinois Graduate School of Library and Information Science • Urbana, IL 61801 • SRRT

McKay James • Columbia, MD 21045 • ALSC RASD

McKay Mary F. • Library-Media Director • Henrietta ISD • Henrietta, TX 76365 • AASL

McKay Mary Helen • Fresno, CA 93710

McKay Michael W. • Director of Accounting • American Craft Information Center • New York, NY 10012 • ACRL

McKay Pamela R. • Reference Librarian • Worcester State College • Worcester, MA 01602 • ACRL

McKay Peter Zachary • Business Librarian • University of Florida Libraries • Gainesville, FL 32611-2047 • RASD

McKay Rebecca L. • Student • Louisiana State University School of Library & Information Science • Baton Rouge, LA 70803-3290

McKay Robert D. • Lindale, TX 75771

McKay Robert W. • Director • River Bend Library System • Coal Valley, IL 61240

McKay Sharon C. • Vice President of Marketing • CASPR, Inc • Cupertino, CA 95014 • ALCTS LITA RASD ILERT

McKean Gregory • Alameda County Library System • Fremont, CA 94538 • NMRT

McKean Janet E. • University of Missouri-Rolla Curtis Laws Wilson Library • Rolla, MO 65401

McKean Joan Maier • Supervisory Librarian • National Oceanic & Atomospheric Administration (NOAA) Library & Information Servs. Div. • Rockville, MD 20852 • AASL LITA FLRT

McKee Anne E. • Bibliographic Servs. Librarian • Arizona State University-West Fletcher Library • Phoenix, AZ 85069-7100 • ACRL ALCTS

McKee Barbara Jo • Librarian & Media Director • Streetsboro Senior High School • Streetsboro, OH 44241 • AASL

McKee Bette J. • Library Tech • East Carolina University • Greenville, NC 27834

McKee Cheryl Spiese • Biblio for Comparative Lit/ Germn • State University of New York at Binghamton Libraries (SUNY) • Binghamton, NY 13902-6012 • ACRL

McKee Chris F. • Patent Librarian • New York Public Library Annex • New York, NY 10036-4396 • ACRL

McKee Elizabeth C. • Associate Reference Librarian • University of Arkansas Mullins Library • Fayetteville, AR 72701 • ACRL RASD

McKee Genie • Head of Technical Services • Maryville University • St. Louis, MO 63141 • ACRL ALCTS RASD

McKee Jennie L. • Technical Services & Systems Ln • Reed College E. V. Hauser Library • Portland, OR 97202 • LITA

McKee Jim • Director • Caldwell County Public Library • Lenoir, NC 28645 • LAMA LITA PLA

McKee Ruth • Media Specialist • Sanchez Elementary School • Lafayette, CO 80026 • AASL EMIERT

McKee Sarah Ann • Bloomington, IN 47424-9803

McKee Virginia • Chief of Children's Services • Providence Public Library • Providence, RI 02903-3283 • ALSC PLA YALSA *Life*

McKeeth Mari J. • Public Relations/Adult Services • Normal Public Library • Normal, IL 61761

McKellar Caryl • Librarian • Alachua County Library District • Gainesville, FL 32601

McKellar Martha S. • Learning Center Director • Heritage Lakes School Library Learning Center • Carol Stream, IL 60188 • AASL

McKelvey Betsy • West Newton, MA 02165 • ACRL RASD GODORT

McKelvey Josephine Faulkner Mrs. • Richfield Spg, NY 13439

McKendree Mary E. • Trustee • Alsip-Merrionette Park Library District • Alsip, IL 60658

McKenna Anne E. • Student • University of Hawaii School of Library & Information Studies • Honolulu, HI 96822 • AASL

McKenna Charles Raymond • Director • Oconomowoc Public Library • Oconomowoc, WI 53066-5299 • LAMA PLA

McKenna Dee J. • Head Librarian • Kegoayah Kozga Library • Nome, AK 99762

McKenna Florence M. • Hd., GSPIA/Economics Library • University of Pittsburgh • Pittsburgh, PA 15260 • ACRL ALCTS

McKenna Francis J. • Student • Queens College Graduate School of Library & Information Studies • Flushing, NY 11367

McKenna Gerald M. • Library Director • Pasco County Library System • Hudson, FL 34667 • LAMA PLA IFRT NMRT

McKenna Janet • Adult Services Librarian • North Tonawanda Public Library • North Tonawanda, NY 14120 • PLA

McKenna Marianne C. • Elementary School Librarian • F.S. Key Elementary School • Philadelphia, PA 19139

McKenna Melissa A. • Clarion, PA 16214 • RASD LHRT SRRT

McKenna Patricia A. • Charlotte, NC 28210

McKenna Patricia R. • Library Technician • Milton Memorial Library • Milton, WA 98354

McKenna Virginia • Saint Anne Community High School District #302 • Saint Anne, IL 60964 • AASL YALSA

McKenna Virginia M. RSHM Sr. • Director • Marymount College Gloria Gaines Memorial Library • Tarrytown, NY 10591

McKenney Deborah D. • Executive Director • Pacific NW Booksellers Association • Banks, OR 97106 • IFRT

McKenty Elizabeth J. • Coor. of Cooperating Collections • Foundation Center • New York, NY 10003

McKenzie Chandra V. • Asst. Dir.-Access Services • Rochester Institute of Technology Wallace Memorial Library • Rochester, NY 14623-0887 • ACRL

McKenzie Doyne M. • Public Services Librarian • Daniel Boone Regional Library • Columbia, MO 65205-1267 • PLA

McKenzie Duncan J. • Manager • Quaker Oats Co. • Chicago, IL 60604-9001

McKenzie Eugenie • Acquisitions Librarian • Portland State University Library • Portland, OR 97207 • ALCTS LRRT NMRT

McKenzie Gail • Indiana University School of Library and Information Science • Bloomington, IN 47405 • ACRL LAMA LITA LRRT

McKenzie Jennifer Bass • Clearlake, CA 95422-1921

McKenzie Joe • Director • Salina Public Library • Salina, KS 67401 • LAMA PLA IFRT

McKenzie Katherine F. • Reference Librarian • College of William & Mary Earl Gregg Swem Library • Williamsburg, VA 23187-8794 • NMRT

McKenzie Mary A. • Essex, CT 06426 • Life

McKenzie Mattie Foster • Supervicer of Media Services • Chattanooga Public Schools • Chattanooga, TN 37421 • AASL

McKenzie Monica R. • Supv. Library Technical Servs. • Schering-Plough Research Institute • Bloomfield, NJ 07003 • ALCTS RASD NMRT

McKenzie Rolaant L. • Student • University of Michigan School of Information and Library Studies • Ann Arbor, MI 48109-1092

McKeon Newton F. • Simsbury, CT 06070-1729 • ACRL ALCTS *Continuing*

McKeown Deb C. • Denison, IA 51442 • AASL PLA IFRT

McKeown Jonathan O. • Librarian I • Cobb County Public Librray System Acworth Branch • Acworth, GA 30101 • NMRT SRRT

McKeown Mary A. • Dayton, OH 45449-2344 • Continuing

McKern Debra • Librarian, Preservation Office • Emory University Libraries Robert W. Woodruff Library • Atlanta, GA 30322-2870 • ALCTS

McKerrow Edith • Boulder, CO 80302 • Continuing

McKever Jane L. • Chicago, IL 60649 • ACRL ASCLA RASD

McKibben Margaret C. • Seattle, WA 98103

McKibben Mary Ann • Librarian • Douglas High School • Minden, NV 89423

McKie Donald S. • Document Librarian • University of California-San Diego Library 0175A • La Jolla, CA 92093-0175 • ACRL RASD *Life*

McKie Michael Tarrant • Reference Librarian • Neuse Regional Library System • Kinston, NC 28501

McKiernan Gerard • Reference Librarian • Iowa State University Library • Ames, IA 50011-2140 • ACRL

McKiernan Lester I. • Coordinator • North Texas Library System • Fort Worth, TX 76107-2921

McKiernan Marianne Sackett • Assoc Dir of Financial Aid • University of South Dakota • Vermillion, SD 57069

McKillip Barbara J. • Senior Project Manager • Saztec International • Eugene, OR 97401 • ALCTS ALSC

McKillip Rita J. • Garden Homes Elementary School Milwaukee Public Schools • Milwaukee, WI 53209 • AASL

McKillop Barbara • Executive Assistant • Calgary Public Library • Calgary AB, T2G 2M2 Canada • LAMA PLA

McKim Robb • Vice-President • Peckham Guyton Albers & Viets Architects & Planners • Shawnee Mission, KS 66205-1801 • LAMA

McKimm Janet • Littleton, CO 80124

McKimm Susan V. • Business Reference Specialist • Cuyahoga County Public Library Maple Heights Regional Branch • Maple Heights, OH 44137 • PLA RASD

McKimmie Timothy I. • Reference Librarian • New Mexico State University Library • Las Cruces, NM 88003-0006 • ACRL

McKinin Emma Jean • Assistant Professor • University of Missouri-Columbia School of Library & Informational Science • Columbia, MO 65211 • ACRL RASD GODORT LIRT

McKinlay Jennifer A. • Adult Services Librarian • Cromwell Belden Public Library • Cromwell, CT 06416

McKinley Alice E. • Lakeland, FL 33801 • ASCLA LAMA LITA *Life*

McKinley Beebe M. • Cataloger • Tuscaloosa Public Library • Tuscaloosa, AL 35401 • ALCTS

McKinley Brenda J. • New Fairfield, CT 06812

McKinley Celia J. • Student • San Jose State University Division of Library & Information Science • San Jose, CA 95192-0029 • PLA

McKinley Jimmie J. • Longview, TX 75606

McKinley Judith • Youth Services Librarian • Glendale Public Library • Glendale, AZ 85302

McKinley Margaret M. • Head of Serial Department • University of California Res Lib • Los Angeles, CA 90024 • ALCTS LITA LRRT

McKinley Nancy P. • Washington, DC 20015

McKinney Agnes M. • Tallahassee, FL 32304-1257

McKinney Alice L. • Technical Services • Fort Lewis College Library • Durango, CO 81301

McKinney Annabel • San Diego, CA 92103 • Life

McKinney Billie S. • Knoxville, TN 37918

McKinney Ceola S. • Head Librarian • Ecorse High School • Ecorse, MI 48229 • AASL

McKinney Eleanor Ruth • Kalamazoo, MI 49008 • Continuing

McKinney Gayle • Lake Lanier Regional Library Lawrenceville Branch • Lawrenceville, GA 30245

McKinney Janet • University of Missouri-Kansas City Library • Kansas City, MO 64110-2499 • ALCTS

McKinney Kevin M. • Hance Elementary School • Gibsonia, PA 15044

McKinney Loretta M. • Community Libraries Director • San Diego County Library • San Diego, CA 92123 • LAMA NMRT

McKinney Rose • Colorado Springs, CO 80901

McKinney Susan D. • Librarian • St. Joseph Township Library • St. Joseph, IL 61873

McKinney Venora • Deputy City Librarian • Milwaukee Public Library • Milwaukee, WI 53233 • PLA

McKinnie Joan Marie • Assistant Librarian • Weber County Library • Odgen, UT 84401

McKinstry Jill M. • University of Washington • Seattle, WA 98195 • ACRL LAMA

McKinstry Leslie E. • Supervisor Children's Services • Findlay-Hancock County Public Library • Findlay, OH 45840 • ALSC

McKinstry Mark • Westlake, OH 44145 • PLA

McKinzie Birt • Librarian • Chowchilla Union High School • Chowchilla, CA 93610 • AASL

McKirdy Colin • Greensboro, NC 27410 • ACRL LITA *Life*

McKirdy Pamela Reekes • Burlington, NC 27215-4843 • ALCTS LITA *Life*

McKissick Gail S. • Librarian I-YA • Los Angeles Public Library West L.A. Rgnl. Branch • Los Angeles, CA 90025 • ACRL PLA IFRT IRRT

McKissick Mabel R. • New London, CT 06320 • AASL SRRT

McKnelly Michele T. • Documents/Reference Librarian • University of Wisconsin-River Falls Chalmer Davee Library • River Falls, WI 54022 • RASD GODORT IFRT

McKnight Connie A. • Brookings, SD 57006

McKnight Cynthia L. • Media Specialist • Estill Middle School • Estill, SC 29918 • AASL LIRT

McKnight Joyce A. • Division Head • Akron-Summit County Public Library • Akron, OH 44326-0001 • RASD

McKnight Mark C. • University of North Texas • Denton, TX 76203 • ACRL ALCTS

McKnight Melanie F. • Harvey, IL 60426 • ACRL EMIERT IFRT SRRT

McKnight Sharon A. • Technical Services • New Jersey State Library Library for the Blind & Handicapped • Trenton, NJ 08618

McKnight Susan T. • Center for the Future of Children • Los Altos, CA 94022

McKowen Dorothy Keeton • Cataloger/Network Librarian • Indiana Cooperative Library Services Authority (INCOLSA) • Indianapolis, IN 46278 • ALCTS

McKown Cornelius J. • Pennsylvania State University Libraries • University Park, PA 16802

McLachlan Ross W. • Technical Services Adm. • Phoenix Public Library • Phoenix, AZ 85004 • LAMA LITA PLA

McLain Ilene Rewerts • Coor of Inst.,Media Technology • Davenport Schools • Davenport, IA 52806 • AASL

McLain Swan M. • Augusta, GA 30909-3323 • ACRL PLA *Continuing*

McLane Eugene G. • Director • Fond du Lac Public Library • Fond du Lac, WI 54935 • LAMA PLA

McLane Maria L. • Akron, OH 44305

McLane Michael J. • Dir of Libraries & Learning Res. • State University of New York (SUNY) Penfield Library • Oswego, NY 13126-3514 • ACRL

McLaren Duncan • Director • McLaren Micropublishing Ltd. • Toronto ON, M4Y 2N9 Canada • EMIERT

McLaren Juliet • Bibliographer/Cataloger • University of California Rivera Library • Riverside, CA 92517 • ACRL

McLaren Margot A. • Catalog Librarian • Rhode Island State Library • Providence, RI 02903

McLaren Mary K. • Head of Acquisitions • University of Kentucky Libraries • Lexington, KY 40506-0039 • ALCTS

McLaren Thomas M. • Trustee • McLaren Resources,Inc. • Tyler, TX 75702 • ALTA

McLaren Virginia S. • Branch Manager • Healdsburg Regional Library • Healdsburg, CA 95448 • PLA

McLaughlin Ann E. • Assistant Director • Crane Public Library • Quincy, MA 02169

McLaughlin Ann F. • North Reading, MA 01864-2421 • IFRT

McLaughlin Claire S. • Librarian • Canton Public Library • Canton, MI 48188

McLaughlin Colleen M. • Community Relations Director • Salt Lake City Public Library • Salt Lake City, UT 84111 • PLA

McLaughlin Dona • Director • Starr Library • Rhinebeck, NY 12572

McLaughlin Douglas F. • Information/Reference Supv. • Oxnard Public Library • Oxnard, CA 93030

McLaughlin Eleanor C. • Miami, FL 33138 • LAMA

McLaughlin Hilda • Librarian • Thomas Jefferson High School • Dallas, TX 75229 • AASL

McLaughlin Jaye R. • Librarian III • Fort Worth Public Library • Fort Worth, TX 76102 • ALSC

McLaughlin Laverne L. • Asst. Prof./Ln./Hd of Tech. Serv • Georgia Southwestern College James Earl Carter Library • Americus, GA 31709

McLaughlin Lee R. • Phillips Laboratory Kirkland Technical Library • Kirkland AFB, NM 87117 • AFLRT FLRT

McLaughlin Lois A. • Librarian • Cameron County Public Library • Emporium, PA 15834

McLaughlin Mary L. Sr. • Librarian • CMC School of Nursing-Library • Woodhaven, NY 11421

McLaughlin Mary Pat • Director • Georgetown Public Library • Georgetown, TX 78626 • PLA

McLaughlin Mary W. • Library Media Teacher • Middle County School District Centereach High School • Centereach, NY 11720 • IFRT

McLaughlin Maureen E. • Student • State University of New York (SUNY) School of Information & Library Studies • Buffalo, NY 14260

McLaughlin Patricia A. • Free Library of Philadelphia Walnut Street West Branch • Philadelphia, PA 19104 • ALSC

McLaughlin Phyllis • Librarian II • Morgan Hill Public Library • Morgan Hill, CA 95037 • ALSC

McLaughlin Robert B. • Finger Lakes Library System • Ithaca, NY 14850 • ALCTS

McLaughlin Sandra • Librarian • Octorara Area Elem Sch • Atglen, PA 19365 • AASL ALSC

McLaughlin Shirley B. • Director • Asheville-Bucombe Technical College • Asheville, NC 28801

McLaughlin Terry • City Librarian • Ashland Public Library • Ashland, OH 44805 • PLA

McLaurin Genette • Student • University of Michigan School of Information and Library Studies • Ann Arbor, MI 48109-1092

McLawhorn Marian N. • D.H. Conley High School • Greenville, NC 27858 • AASL

McLean Bessie Norton • Lakewood, NJ 08701 • Continuing

McLean Carla B. • Dallas, TX 75287

McLean Cheryl D. • Tucson, AZ 85737 • IFRT

McLean Clark E. • Library Specialist III • University of New Mexico General Library • Albuquerque, NM 87131 • LITA GODORT

McLean Elaine P. • Branch Librarian • Boston Public Library Uphams Corner Branch • Dorchester, MA 02125-2389

McLean Elfriede H. • Augusta College Reese Library • Augusta, GA 30910

McLean Joan M. • Watkinson School • Hartford, CT 06105

McLean Loche A. • Library Systems Specialist • Library of Congress • Washington, DC 20541

McLean Marie-Grace M. • Bronx, NY 10451 • ALSC

McLean Mavis • Director of Library • Alliance Public Library • Alliance, NE 69301

McLean R. Blanton • Library Director • Eastern State Hospital • Williamsburg, VA 23187-3701 • ASCLA

McLean Robert M. • Student • University of South Carolina College of Library & Information Science • Columbia, SC 29208 • PLA

McLean Yvonne A. • Student • University of Illinois-Chicago • Chicago, IL 60680 • ALCTS

McLear Pat A. • Juneau School District Glacier Valley Elementary School • Juneau, AK 99801 • AASL

McLees Nancy F. • Dauphin County Library System • Harrisburg, PA 17101

McLellan Bonnie • Assistant Director • Dakota County Library • Eagan, MN 55123 • PLA

McLelland Richard J. • Reference Librarian • Chicago Public Library • Chicago, IL 60605 • ACRL PLA RASD

McLemore Barbara G. • Student • University of Alabama School of Library & Information Studies • Tuscaloosa, AL 35487-0252

McLemore Janice • Librarian • Crownhill Elementary • Bremerton, WA 98312 • AASL

McLeod Ann • Unit Head, Circulation • University of Pittsburgh Hillman Library • Pittsburgh, PA 15260

McLeod Clara P. • Washington University Libraries • Saint Louis, MO 63130-4899 • ACRL MAGERT

McLeod Debra A. • Youth Collections Librarian • Johnson County Library • Shawnee Mission, KS 66201 • ALSC

McLeod Gillisn M. • Student • University of Western Ontario School of Library & Information Science • London ON, N6G 1H1 Canada • RASD

McLeod Grace E. • Head Technical Systems • Dekalb County Public Library • Decatur, GA 30032

McLeod H. Eugene Dr. • Librarian • Southeastern Baptist Theological Seminary Library • Wake Forest, NC 27588-1499 • ACRL ALCTS RASD

McLeod Julianne Babbitt • Childrens & Young Adult • Alameda County Library Irvington Branch • Fremont, CA 94538 • ALSC

McLeod Krista I. • Pollard Memorial Library • Lowell, MA 01852

McLeod Marilyn A. • Head of Reference • Daniel Boone Regional Library • Columbia, MO 65205-1267 • RASD IFRT

McLeod Martha • Silver Spg, MD 20902

McLeod Patricia A. • Film Librarian • Somerset County Library • Bridgewater, NJ 08807

McLeroy Sandra • High School Ln/Dist Coordinator • Leander Independent School District c/o Leander High School • Leander, TX 78641 • AASL

McLoone Mary F. • Student • San Jose State University Division of Library & Information Science • San Jose, CA 95192-0029

McMahon Christine M. • Information Consultant • Christine M. McMahon Inc • Palm City, FL 34990 • ASCLA LITA ILERT

McMahon Edmund A. • Willowdale ON, M2M 4B9 Canada

McMahon Geraldine • Children's Librarian • Franklin Lakes Public Library • Franklin Lakes, NJ 07417 • ALSC PLA

McMahon Janet E. • Student • University of South Florida School of Library & Information Science • Tampa, FL 33620

McMahon Judith L. • Children's Librarian • Oak Lawn Public Library • Oak Lawn, IL 60453 • ALSC PLA

McMahon Kathleen A. • Student • University of Maryland College of Library and Information Services • College Park, MD 20742-4345 • LITA

McMahon Patricia K. • Media Specialist • Kendrick High School • Columbus, GA 31907 • AASL

McMahon Robert A. • South Park Middle School • Oshkosh, WI 54901

McMahon Robert A. • Student • Long Island University Palmer School of Library & Information Science • Greenvale, NY 11548

McMahon Susan K. • Director • Bedford Free Library • Bedford, NY 10506

McMahon Suzanne • Serials Cataloger • Stanford University Libraries Cecil H. Green Library • Stanford, CA 94305-6004 • ACRL ALCTS LITA NMRT

McMahon Thomas P. • Trustee • Euclid Public Library • Euclid, OH 44123-2091 • ALTA

McManus Alesia • Student • University of California Los Angeles Graduate School of Library & Information Science • Los Angeles, CA 90024 • IFRT IRRT

McManus Blanche C. • Staff Librarian • Carnegie Library of Pittsburgh • Pittsburgh, PA 15213-4080 • RASD

McManus Jan H. • EM Graphics • Greenville, NC 27835-8233

McManus Jean C. • Resident Librarian • University of Illinois at Chicago • Chicago, IL 60680 • ACRL RASD

McManus Marilyn C. • Annapolis, MD 21403

McManus Mark G. R. • Systems Librarian • Mary Washington College Library Simpson Library • Fredericksburg, VA 22401-4664 • ACRL ALCTS LITA LHRT

McManus MaryAnn Sr. • Saint Francis College • Fort Wayne, IN 46808 • ACRL

McMartin Ruth C. • Minneapolis, MN 55406 • AASL *Continuing*

McMaster Sarah D. • Director • Fairfield County Library • Winsboro, SC 29180 • PLA

McMillan Barbara A. • Mount Vernon Ladies' Association of The Union Res & Ref Library • Mt Vernon, VA 22121 • ACRL RASD LHRT

McMillan Gail • Serials Team Leader • Virginia Polytechnic Inst & State Univ University Libraries • Blacksburg, VA 24062-9001 • ALCTS LITA

McMillan Gary A. • University of Maryland College Park Theodore R. McKeldin Library • College Park, MD 20742-7011 • ACRL

McMillan Mary M. • Plainfield, IN 46168

McMillan Susan R. • Reference Librarian • York College of Pennsylvania Schmidt Library • York, PA 17403 • ACRL RASD LIRT

McMillen Donna K. • Librarian • King County Library System Fairwood Library • Renton, WA 98058 • YALSA NMRT

McMillen Sophia A. • Cataloger • University of Hawaii at Manoa Catalog Dept. • Honolulu, HI 96822 • ACRL ALCTS *Life*

McMillian-Nelson Sharyl A. • Ref/Bibliographic Instr. Libn. • Lamar University Gray Library • Beaumont, TX 77710 • ACRL

McMinn-Omberg Mari • Librarian • Spengler,Carlson,Gubar et al • New York, NY 10022

McMorland Irene • Emory University Libraries Robert W. Woodruff Library • Atlanta, GA 30322-2870 • ACRL ALCTS ILERT

McMorran Charles E. • Chief, Technical Services Dept. • Queens Borough Public Library • Jamaica, NY 11432

McMorran Monica A. • Library Media • Ridgefield High School Library • Ridgefield, CT 06877 • AASL

McMorries Kathy R. • Student • University of Texas at Austin Graduate School of Library & Information Sciences • Austin, TX 78712-1276

McMullan T N. • Ft Pierce, FL 33450

McMullen Dennis K. • Student • University of Michigan School of Information and Library Studies • Ann Arbor, MI 48109-1092

McMullen Glenn L. • Special Collections Librarian • Virginia Polytechnic Inst & State Univ University Libraries • Blacksburg, VA 24062-9001 • ACRL

McMullen Haynes • Hampton, VA 23661 • LHRT *Life*

McMullen Marilee • Librarian • West Allis Public Schools • West Allis, WI 53227 • Continuing

McMullen Peggy L. • University Archivist • Saint John's University Division of Library & Information Science • Jamaica, NY 11439 • ACRL ALCTS

McMullin Joyce A. • APO New York, NY 09173 • PLA

McMullin William • Collection Development Librarian • Northeast Regional Library • Corinth, MS 38834

McMurrin David G. • Student • University of Rhode Island Graduate School of Library & Information Studies • Kingston, RI 02881-0815 • ACRL RASD

McMurrin Jean Ann • Non-Fiction Librarian • Weber County Library • Odgen, UT 84401 • RASD

McMurry Nan • History Bibliographer • University of Georgia Libraries • Athens, GA 30602 • ACRL ALCTS

McNabb Carolyn J. • Librarian • St. Mary's Ryken High School • Leonardtown, MD 20650

McNabb Corrine R. • Librarian • Community Medical Center Doctors Library • Scranton, PA 18510

McNabb Katherine C. • Associate Univ Ln Emeritus • University of California UCSB Library • Santa Barbara, CA 93106-9010 • ACRL   Continuing

McNabb Mary C. • Cary Public Library • Cary, NC 27511 • PLA RASD

McNabb Michele C. • Urbana Free Library • Urbana, IL 61801-3283 • RASD IRRT

McNair Jane • Manager Central Children's Room • Houston Public Library • Houston, TX 77002 • ALSC

McNair Jeanene • Human Resources Librarian • University of South Florida Library • Tampa, FL 33620-5600 • ACRL ALCTS LAMA SRRT

McNair Marian B. • Supervisor of School Libraries • Cincinnati Public Schools • Cincinnati, OH 45202

McNally Barbara J. • Director • Resource Sharing Alliance • East Peoria, IL 61635-0001 • LITA

McNally Crystal Elaine • Wichita, KS 67211-2006 • AASL ALSC IFRT   Life

McNally Mary Jane • Librarian • Ridge High School • Basking Ridge, NJ 07920 • AASL LRRT

McNally Miriam E. Miss • Denver, CO 80218 • LAMA PLA   Life

McNally Ruth C. • Oak Harbor, WA 98277

McNally Thomas F. • Chicago, IL 60626 • ACRL

McNamara A. Jeanie • University of South Carolina College of Library & Information Science • Columbia, SC 29208 • AASL ALSC YALSA IFRT

McNamara Barbara • Mount Ida College Learning Resouce Center • Newton Centre, MA 02159

McNamara Charles B. • Curator of Rare Books • University of North Carolina Wilson Library • Chapel Hill, NC 27599 • ACRL

McNamara Emma J. • Environmental Protection Agency Headquarters Library • Washington, DC 20460 • RASD

McNamara Frances D. • Project Manager • Ameritech Information Systems • Dublin, OH 43017 • LITA

McNamara Jay • Reference Librarian • University of Alabama in Huntsville Library • Huntsville, AL 35899 • RASD GODORT LRRT

McNamara Karen S. • Library Media Specialist • Altmar Elementary School • Altmar, NY 13302 • AASL

McNamara Kimberly A. • Technical Librarian • SPS Technologies • Jenkintown, PA 19046

McNamara Michael A. • Managing Librarian • King County Library System Des Moines Library • Des Moines, WA 98198 • PLA

McNamara Nancy A. • Student • Rutgers University School of Communication Information & Library Studies • New Brunswick, NJ 08903 • LITA LRRT

McNamara Pearl E. • Librarian • Friends School Baltimore Middle School Resource Center • Baltimore, MD 21210 • AASL

McNamara Shelley G. • Professor of Children & YA Servs • Drexel University College of Information Studies • Philadelphia, PA 19104-2875 • ALSC

McNamara Valerie E. • Student • Bridgewater State College Clement C. Maxwell Library • Bridgewater, MA 02325

McNamee Alice M. • Assistan County Librarian • Marin County Free Library • San Rafael, CA 94903 • LITA

McNamee Gilbert W. • San Francisco, CA 94123

McNamee Phyllis G. • Trustee • Prince George's County Memorial Library System • Hyattsville, MD 20782-2098 • ALTA

McNatt Susanne • Inter-L Service Librarian • Princeton University Library • Princeton, NJ 08544 • RASD

McNaught Lori A. • Lincoln, RI 02865

McNaughton Sue • Publisher • Ashgate Publishing Limited • Hants, GU11 3HR, England • RASD

McNeal Anita S. • Branch Manager • Cuyahoga County Public Library Berea Branch • Berea, OH 44017-2524

McNeal Archie L. • Miami, FL 33156 • ACRL LAMA   Life

McNeal Mary C. • Librarian • Huntsville High School • Huntsville, AL 35801

McNeal Tyrone M. • Reference Librarian • District of Columbia Public Library Martin Luther King Memorial Library • Washington, DC 20001

McNee John • Trustee • Central Arkansas Library System • Little Rock, AR 72201-4698 • ALTA

McNee John C. • Ames, IA 50010 • ACRL RASD   Life

McNeece Judy M. • Greenwood, MS 38930

McNeely Bonnie Michaels • Texas Woman's University Mary Evelyn Blagg-Huey Library • Denton, TX 76204-1715 • LITA

McNeely Cate • Hd, Youth Svs & Pub. Relations • Richmond Public Library • Richmond BC, V6X 2E3 Canada • PLA

McNeer Elizabeth J. • McNeer Associates • Miami, FL 33175 • RASD

McNeil-Marshall Susan • Head of Ref & Info Svs • Hinsdale Public Library • Hinsdale, IL 60521 • PLA RASD

McNeil Charles A. • Associate Librarian • University of Massachusetts-Dartmouth Library • North Dartmouth, MA 02747 • LITA

McNeil Deborah W. • Seattle, WA 98103 • PLA   Life

McNeil Mary Elizabeth • Collections Mgt & Serials Libr. • Bradley University Cullom-Davis Library • Peoria, IL 61625 • ACRL

McNeil Nicholas J. Rev. • Worcester, MA 01610-2395 • Continuing

McNeill Dale K. • Branch Librarian • Harris County Public Library Octavia Fields Branch • Humble, TX 77338 • SRRT

McNeill Ginger • McDonald Road Elementary School • Georgetown, SC 29440 • AASL

McNeill Janice • Chicago Historical Society Library • Chicago, IL 60614 • ACRL ALCTS LAMA RASD

McNeill John J. • Student • Florida Atlantic University Library • Boca Raton, FL 33431 • IFRT

McNeill Joseph P. Jr. • Head of Technical Services • McNeese State University Lether E. Frazar Memorial Library • Lake Charles, LA 70609

McNeill Katharine N. • Director • Floral Park Public Library • Floral Park, NY 11001 • LAMA PLA

McNeill Margaret M. • Medical Librarian • Elkhart General Hospital • Elkhart, IN 46515

McNeill Mary • Librarian • Oxford College O'Kelley Memorial Library • Oxford, GA 30267 • ACRL LAMA

McNeill Mona L. • Student • Long Island University Library School Library • Greenvale, NY 11458

McNellis Claudia • Systems Info Tech Services • Library of Congress • Washington, DC 20541 • LITA

McNerney James • Hopewell Junction, NY 12533 • IFRT   Continuing

McNew Christine E. • Student • Harris County Public Library Spring Memorial Branch • Houston, TX 77024

McNicol Lois E. • Prospect Park K-8 School • Prospect Park, PA 19036 • AASL

McNicol Nancy • Assistant Director • Hagaman Memorial Library • East Haven, CT 06512-3098 • LAMA RASD

McNiff Philip J. • Chestnut Hill, MA 02167 • Continuing

McNiff Valerie Anne • Personnel Manager • Genesee District Library • Flint, MI 48504

McNinch Eleanor • St Petersburg, FL 33705 • Continuing

McNitt Evelyn B. • Children's Librarian • Brunswick Community Library • Brunswick, OH 44212-0430 • ALSC

McNulty Diane R. • Head of Technical Serv • Barrington Public Library District • Barrington, IL 60010

McNulty Helen R. • Librarian • Hennepin County Library Edina Library • Edina, MN 55424

McNulty Philip • Director • Medway Public Library • Medway, MA 02053 • PLA

McNulty Tom • Student • New York University Elmer Holmes Bobst Library • New York, NY 10012 • EMIERT SRRT

McNutt Dorothy C. • Public Library of Cincinnati and Hamilton County • Cincinnati, OH 45202 • ACRL LAMA   Continuing

McNutt Esther Marian • Rock Island, IL 61201 • AASL YALSA   Continuing

McOmber Virginia G. • Associate Librarian • Salt Lake City Public Library Avenues Branch • Salt Lake City, UT 84103 • PLA

McOuat Janet D. • Librarian • Alexander Fleming Jr High Sch • Lomita, CA 90717 • ALSC YALSA

McPartland Gail R. • South Pasadena, CA 91030 • ACRL

McPeak James J. • Library Director • Lepper Public Library • Lisbon, OH 44432 • LAMA PLA YALSA IFRT SRRT

McPeak Joseph E. • Reference & Inf. Librarian • Free Library of Philadelphia • Philadelphia, PA 19103 • LAMA PLA

McPeters Inman J. • Albany, NY 12203-3003 • IFRT

McPhail Martha • Special Collections Librarian • San Diego State University Library • San Diego, CA 92119-2120 • ACRL IRRT SRRT

McPhee James S. • University of Nevada-Las Vegas James R. Dickinson Library • Las Vegas, NV 89154 • ACRL RASD IFRT LHRT LIRT LRRT

McPhee Jan D. • Carrollton, TX 75006

McPheeters Annie L. • Atlanta, GA 30314

McPheeters Roger A. • Dept Head Inf. Serv. • Ricks College McKay Learning Resource Center • Rexburg, ID 83440 • ACRL LAMA LITA RASD

McPherson Carolyn S. • Coor. of Information Services • Valdosta State College Library • Valdosta, GA 31698-0001 • RASD

McPherson Donna F. • Champaign, IL 61821 • ASCLA RASD   Continuing

McPherson Dorothy • El Cerrito, CA 94530 • LITA IRRT

McPherson James A. Mr. • Trustee • Mid-Continent Public Library • Independence, MO 64050 • ALTA

McPherson Kay • Librarian I • Atlanta-Fulton Public Library • Atlanta, GA 30303 • ALSC PLA

McPherson Kenneth F. • Library Consultant • Morris County Free Library • Whippany, NJ 07981 • LAMA PLA   Continuing

McPherson Margaret L. • Elkhart, IN 46514

McPherson Mary W. • Durham, NC 27707 • AFLRT

McPike Katharine • Mason County Eastern Schools • Custer, MI 49405

McQuade Jayne W. • Head of Central Library • Arlington County Department of Libraries • Arlington, VA 22201

McQuaid Mary C. Miss • Oakland, CA 94601-1818 • Continuing

McQuaide Esther • Teacher/Librarian • West Long Branch Public Schools • West Long Branch, NJ 07764

McQuail Edward J. III • Bluefield, WV 24701 • RASD Life

McQuarrie Susan L. • Librarian-Public Services • King County Library System • Seattle, WA 98109-5191

McQueen Ann E. • Menlo Park, CA 94025

McQueen Howard Jr. • President • CD Consultants, Inc. • Baltimore, MD 21210 • LITA

McQueen Judith D. • Chicago, IL 60611

McQuillan Dorothy K. • Librarian • Sharon Senior High School Library • Sharon, MA 02067 • AASL

McQuillan Nancy • Branch Manger • Orange County Public Library Dana Niguel Branch • Monarch Beach, CA 92677 • LAMA

McQuinn James • Adrian, MI 49221-2902

McQuitty Jeanette • User Services Director • Northeastern Oklahoma State University John Vaughan Library-LRC • Tahlequah, OK 74464 • ACRL

McQuown Eloise • San Francisco, CA 94132 • ACRL LAMA

McRae Alexander D. • Director of Research • Congressional Information Service Inc. • Bethesda, MD 20814 • AASL ACRL

McRae Sami • Kimball Public Library • Randolph, VT 05060 • PLA

McRae Woodburn • Cataloger • Ministry of the Solicitor General Library & Reference Centre • Ottawa, ON, K1A 0P8 Canada • ACRL ALCTS

McRee John W. • Librarian • Greenville County Library • Greenville, SC 29601

McReynolds Mary R. • Librarian-Childrens Specialist • DeKalb County Public Library Adminstration Building • Decatur, GA 30030 • ALSC PLA

McReynolds Rosalee • Serials Librarian • Loyola University Library • New Orleans, LA 70118 • LHRT

McRowe Patricia T. • YA Librarian • Cuyahoga County Public Library Brecksville Branch • Brecksville, OH 44141-2499 • YALSA

McShane James J. • Librarian • Queens Borough Public Library • Jamaica, NY 11432 • ACRL

McShane Rose Marie • Librarian • Turner Elementary School • Wilkinsburg, PA 15221

McSparren Christine • Regional Manager • Orange County Public Library • Santa Ana, CA 92705

McSwain Kathleen M. • Youth Services Librarian • Chicago Ridge Public Lib • Chicago Ridge, IL 60415 • ALSC PLA

McSwain Mary B. • San Marcos, TX 78666

McSween Michele A. • District of Columbia Libraries Watha T. Daniel Branch • Washington, DC 20001 • RASD CLENE

McSween Thelma Gales • Cast Brunswick, NJ 08816

McSweeney Josephine • Reference Librarian & Professor • Pratt Institute Library • Brooklyn, NY 11205 • ACRL RASD GODORT   Life

McSweeney Linda • Director • Vermont Technical Coll • Randolph Ctr, VT 05061

McSweeney Marilyn G. • Head, Serials & Acq. Services • Massachusetts Institute of Technology Libraries (MIT) • Cambridge, MA 02139 • ALCTS

McSweeny Marilee E. • Manager • Toledo-Lucas County Public Library Reynolds Corner Branch • Toledo, OH 43615

McTamaney Mary R. • Director • Mount Saint Mary College Curtin Memorial Library • Newburgh, NY 12550-3598 • ACRL ALCTS RASD

McTavish Isabel G. Miss • Vancouver BC, Canada • ALSC PLA *Continuing*

McTavish Mary L. • Librarian Reference Department • University of Toronto Library • Toronto ON, M5S 1A5 Canada • ACRL RASD

McVey Karen R. • Student • University of California-Los Angeles (UCLA) • Los Angeles, CA 90024-1450

McVey Marolyn • Librarian K-12 • Chico Independent School District • Chico, TX 76030 • AASL

McWhirter Craig A. • Automation Mgr/Info Proc Spec. • University of Northern Colorado James A. Michener Library • Greeley, CO 80639 • LITA

McWhorter Betty • Trustee • Michigan City Public Library • Michigan City, IN 46360 • ALTA

McWhorter Jimmie M. • Mobile, AL 36608

McWhorter Mildred • Mauldin, SC 29662 • ASCLA RASD *Continuing*

McWilliam Deb A. • Director, Main Library • Columbus Metropolitan Library • Columbus, OH 43215 • PLA

McWilliams Betsy • Bibliotecas Inc. • Cleveland, OH 44122

McWilliams Linda • Trustee • West Florida Regional Library • Pensacola, FL 32501

Mdaba Sibusico Victor • Umlazi 4031, South Africa • LITA

Meacham Jane C. • Librarian • Abbott Loop Elementary School Library • Anchorage, AK 99504 • AASL

Meacham Mary • Librarian • National Severe Storms Lab • Norman, OK 73069

Meachen Edward W. • Union Grove, WI 53182 • ACRL

Mead-Donaldson Susan L. • Miami-Dade Public Library System • Miami, FL 33130-1504 • ALCTS LAMA LITA

Mead Catherine S. • Head Reference • State Library of Ohio • Columbus, OH 43266-0334 • ASCLA

Mead Clifford S. • Special Collection Librarian • Oregon State University William Jasper Kerr Library • Corvallis, OR 97331-4501 • ACRL

Mead Dale C. • Senior Information Specialist • Apple Computer, Inc. Library • Cupertino, CA 95014 • RASD

Mead Elizabeth A. • Children's Librarian • Klamath County Public Library System • Klamath Falls, OR 97603

Mead John R. • Librarian • Chicago Public Library • Chicago, IL 60605 • LAMA LITA

Mead Katherine G. • District Librarian • Fredonia Central School Library • Fredonia, NY 14063 • AASL

Mead Margo B. • Reference Librarian • University of Alabama in Huntsville Library • Huntsville, AL 35899 • ACRL LIRT

Mead Sean M. • Student • Indiana University School of Library and Information Science • Bloomington, IN 47405 • ACRL AFLRT EMIERT FLRT IRRT SRRT

Meade Barbara J. • Head of Technical Services • Seton Hall University Law Library • Newark, NJ 07102 • ACRL

Meade Donaldlene M. • Library Assistant • Hennepin County Library • Minnetonka, MN 55343

Meade Gail Mrs • Detroit, MI 48219 • Continuing

Meade Jennie C. • George Washington University Jacob Burns Law Library • Washington, DC 20052 • LAMA

Meade Kathryne A. • AT&T Bell Laboratories • Murray Hill, NJ 07974 • LITA

Meade Louise L. • Trustee • Fairfax County Public Library • Fairfax, VA 22033-1909 • ALTA

Meade Renee • Reference Librarian • Kingston Area Library • Kingston, NY 12401 • NMRT

Meader Lauren R. • Arlington, VA 22201 • RASD

Meador Cornie • Learning Resources Spec • Stratford High School • Houston, TX 77079 • AASL

Meador Joan S. • Head of Reference Department • Tulsa City-County Library System • Tulsa, OK 74103 • RASD

Meador John M. Jr • Dean of Library Services • Southwest Missouri State University Library • Springfield, MO 65804-0095 • ACRL LAMA LITA

Meador Karen M. • Fairport, NY 14450 • AASL

Meador Lottie Simpkins • San Angelo, TX 76904-4612 • LITA

Meadors Gary K. • Librarian, Cataloging Dept. • University of Texas • Austin, TX 78712-1276 • ALCTS SRRT

Meadors Jean • Northwest Branch Library • Corpus Christi, TX 78410 • ALSC

Meadors Margaret S. • H.F. Schricker-Edgewood High School • Ellettsville, IN 47429

Meadors William A. • High School Librarian • Lubbock High School • Lubbock, TX 79401 • YALSA

Meadows Brenda L. • Grand Blanc, MI 48439 • LAMA SORT

Meadows J. J. • Newport News, VA 23604 • AASL

Meadows Meralyn • Stanly County Public Library • Albemarle, NC 28001

Meagher Agnes Sr. • Library Director • Saint Joseph's College Callahan Library • Patchogue, NY 11772 • ACRL

Meahl D. Darren • Michigan State University Libraries • East Lansing, MI 48824-1048 • ACRL LAMA LITA

Mealmaker John D. • Haddonfield, NJ 08033

Meanley Carolyn A. • Coordinator, Government Document • University of Houston Libraries • Houston, TX 77204-2091 • ACRL LAMA RASD GODORT IRRT NMRT

Means Raymond B. • Director • Creighton University Reinert-Alumni Memorial Library • Omaha, NE 68178 • ACRL LAMA

Means Robert S. • Student • Brigham Young University School of Library & Information Sciences • Provo, UT 84602

Meany Anne M. • Library Director • Somerville Public Library • Somerville, NJ 08876 • LAMA PLA

Meany Philip • Director • Centralia College • Centralia, WA 98531

Mearns Barbara A. • Ho Ho Kus, NJ 07423 • PLA *Continuing*

Mears-Haskell Mary • Student • Portland State University School of Education • Portland, OR 97207

Mears Michelle M. • University of Texas at Austin Graduate School of Library & Information Sciences • Austin, TX 78712-1276

Mech Terrence F. • Library Director • King's College • Wilkes Barre, PA 18711 • ACRL

Mecha Michele L. • Ann Arbor, MI 48104

Mechanic Margaret A. • Head, Technical Library Serv. • Naval Maritime Intelligence Center • Washington, DC 20395-5020 • LAMA LITA AFLRT FLRT

Meche A. Bob • Trustee • Ascension Parish Library • Donaldsonville, LA 70346-2535 • ALTA PLA

Mechtenberg Paul • Head Librarian • Dundee Township Library • Dundee, IL 60118 • PLA

Meck Susan • Librarian • Rochester School for The Deaf • Rochester, NY 14621 • ALSC ASCLA YALSA

Meck Wanda L. • Connecticut State Library • Hartford, CT 06106 • ALCTS

Meckler Alan • Westport, CT 06880 • ACRL ALCTS LITA RASD

Medaglia Victoria J. • Serials Librarian • Bates College George & Helen Ladd Library • Lewiston, ME 04240 • ALCTS

Medal Carole A. • Executive Director • Rolling Meadows Library • Rolling Meadows, IL 60008

Medaris Linda L. • Central Missouri State University Ward Edwards Library • Warrensburg, MO 64093

Meddings Nancy • Santa Maria Public Library • Santa Maria, CA 93454

Medeiros Borden Robin A. • Albuquerque, NM 87106-5237

Medeiros Hayley M. • Scottsdale, AZ 85251 • AASL ALSC YALSA

Meder Marylouise • Emporia, KS 66801 • ACRL LHRT *Continuing*

Meder Stephen A. Rev • Librarian • Colombiere Center Dinan Library • Clarkston, MI 48347

Mediatore Kaite • Student • Emporia State University School of Library & Information Management • Emporia, KS 66801 • YALSA

Mediavilla Cindy • Orange Public Library • Orange, CA 92666 • PLA CLENE

Medin Alice L. • Director • Rogers-Hough Memorial Library • Rogers, AR 72756 • LAMA PLA

Medina Carolyn C. • Student • University of Texas at Austin Graduate School of Library & Information Sciences • Austin, TX 78712-1276

Medina Julio D. • San Francisco, CA 94114 • ALSC PLA

Medina Kay A. • Asst Head/Fine Arts-AV • Broward County Division of Libraries Broward County Library • Fort Lauderdale, FL 33301 • LAMA

Medina Martha H. • El Paso Community College • El Paso, TX 79998

Medina Sue O. • Director • Network of Alabama Academic Libraries • Montgomery, AL 36104-3584 • ACRL ALCTS

Medley-Weeks Clarice • South Ozone Park, NY 11420

Medley Liz • Tulsa, OK 74112

Medley Sherry L. • West Chester, OH 45069 • IFRT

Medvidovich Joel • Dauphin, PA 17018 • PLA

Medwedeff Joan K. • Librarian • Harding Academy • Nashville, TN 37205 • AASL

Medzie Deena M. • Acquisition & Business & Econs. • Widener University Wolfgram Library • Chester, PA 19013 • ACRL

Meece June G. • Librarian I • Jacksonville Correctional Center • Jacksonville, IL 62650

Meehan-Black Elizabeth C. • Head, Bibliographic Searching • University of North Carolina • Chapel Hill, NC 27599-3902

Meehan Emily • Chicago Ridge Public Lib • Chicago Ridge, IL 60415

Meek Carol Lyn • Director • Cambria County Library System Glosser Memorial Library Building • Johnstown, PA 15901 • PLA

Meek Sammie J. • School Librarian • Falfurrias Junior School Brooks County ISD • Falfurrias, TX 78355 • AASL

Meeker Kathleen • Scituate Town Library • Scituate, MA 02066

Meeker Richard • Juneau, AK 99802-1344 • LITA IFRT ILERT IRRT LHRT

Meeker Robert B. • Head Reference Librarian • Chicago State University Paul & Emily Douglas Library • Chicago, IL 60628 • RASD

Meeks Elizabeth • Redwood City Public Library • Redwood City, CA 94063-1868

Meeks Selene • Library Administrator • Lake Forest Academy Library • Lake Forest, IL 60045 • AASL

Meer Muhammad P. • Student • University of Hawaii School of Library & Information Studies • Honolulu, HI 96822 • LRRT SRRT

Meerdink Richard E. • Librarian • Milwaukee Area Technical College Rasche Memorial Library • Milwaukee, WI 53233 • ACRL LITA

Meernik Mary A. • Cataloging Librarian • Eastern Michigan University Library Center of Educational Resources • Ypsilanti, MI 48197 • ACRL ALCTS

Meese Jane E. • Librarian • Ashton Middle School • Reynoldsburg, OH 43068 • AASL

Meeske Susan • Student • Rutgers University School of Communication Information & Library Studies • New Brunswick, NJ 08903

Meeson Deborah M. • Librarian • William Fleming High School • Roanoke, VA 24017 • LAMA

Megargee Ann P. • Media Specialist • Trinity Catholic School • Tallahassee, FL 32308

Megariz Carolyn S. • Extension Librarian • Nogales/Santa Cruz County Library • Nogales, AZ 85621

Megarry Susan M. • Student • University of Pittsburgh School of Library and Information Science • Pittsburgh, PA 15260

Megas Melissa • Trustee • Daniel Boone Regional Library • Columbia, MO 65205-1267 • ALTA

Megaw Karen A. • First Lutheran Church & School • Torrance, CA 90503 • AASL ALSC

Megehee Josephine Z. • Pearl River County Library System • Picayune, MS 39466

Meghabghab Dania Bilal • Valdosta, GA 31602

Meghreblian Caren A. • Art Institute of Seattle • Seattle, WA 98121 • ACRL

Megill Kenneth A. • Records Manager-IRM • United States Department of the Treasury Comptroller of the Currency Library • Washington, DC 20219 • IFRT SRRT

Meglio Delores D. • Vice President-Publisher • Information Access Company • Foster City, CA 94404 • LITA RASD

Mehaffey Karen Rae • Assistant Librarian • Sacred Heart Major Seminary • Detroit, MI 48206

Mehal Steven • Baylor Health Sciences Library • Dallas, TX 75246 • ACRL LITA RASD IFRT SRRT

Mehlhaff Bruce G. • Librarian/Archivist • South Dakota School of Mines & Technology • Rapid City, SD 57701

Mehne Richard G. Jr. • Student • University of Arizona Graduate Library School • Tucson, AZ 85721 • LITA

Mehrad Jafar • Associate Professor • University of Shiraz College of Literature • Shiraz, Iran

Mei Angela L. • Portland, OR 97229

Mei Ciming • Serials/Non Print Mats. Catlgr. • Northeastern University Libraries • Boston, MA 02115

Meier Carey B. • Librarian • Poway Unified School District Mount Carmel High School • San Diego, CA 92129 • AASL

Meier Julie • Director • Coeur d' Alene Public Library • Coeur d' Alene, ID 83814

Meier Margaret O. • Schenectady, NY 12308 • Continuing

Meier Marjorie A. • Librarian • Concordia Teachers College Link Library • Seward, NE 68434

Meier Patricia L. • School Library Media Specialist • Paul Norton School • Bettendorf, IA 52722 • AASL

Meier Rick • Trustee • Sioux Falls Public Library • Sioux Falls, SD 57102

Meierhoffer John C. • Computer System Analyst • New York State Library State Education Department • Albany, NY 12230 • LITA MAGERT

Meighen Martin L. • Reference Librarian • Public Library of Cincinnati and Hamilton County • Cincinnati, OH 45202 • ALSC YALSA

Meigs Carolyn R. • Giessen American High School • APO, AE 09169 • AASL

Meikle Teresa C. • Library of Congress • Washington, DC 20541 • ACRL

Meillon Eileen • Librarian • The David M. Stewart Museum • Montreal PQ, H3C 3P3 Canada • ACRL

Meinel Nancy Thomas • Librarian • Minnie Ruffin Elementary School • Monroe, LA 71202 • AASL *Life*

Meinersmann Rosali • Athens, GA 30605 • Continuing

Meinert Walter F. • Trustee • Aurora Public Library • Aurora, IL 60505-4299 • ALTA

Meinhardt Lucile P. • Antioch Library • Antioch, CA 94509 • ACRL ALCTS LITA PLA RASD EMIERT NMRT

Meinhold Janet R. • Chief of Technical Services • East Central Georgia Regional Library Augusta-Richmond County • Augusta, GA 30901

Meinhold Leonard J. • Director • North Country Library System • Watertown, NY 13601 • ALCTS LAMA LITA PLA RASD *Life*

Meinke Darrel M. • Dean of Instructional Resources • Moorhead State University Livingston Lord Library • Moorhead, MN 56563-2989 • ACRL

Meirose Judy K. • Clermont County Public Library New Richmond Branch • New Richmond, OH 45157

Meisart Michele F. • 86280 St. Benoit, France

Meisel Gloria B. • Assistant Professor/Librarian • Westchester Community College • Valhalla, NY 10595 • ACRL IFRT LIRT

Meisels Henry R. • Normal, IL 61761

Meisels Sarah • Library Director • Wheaton Public Library • Wheaton, IL 60187-5376 • LAMA PLA

Meisenheimer Barbra L. • Student • University of California Los Angeles Graduate School of Library & Information Science • Los Angeles, CA 90024

Meisner Elizabeth • Trustee • York Public Library • Yorktown, VA 23692

Meisner Erna E. • Department Head • Soreq Nuclear Research Center Library & Technical Information Dept. • Yavne 70600, Israel

Meiss Linda Paulo • Online Reference Services • San Jose Public Library • San Jose, CA 95113 • RASD LIRT

Meissner Lana • Librarian • Alfred University Herrick Memorial Library • Alfred, NY 14802 • ACRL LAMA

Meister Alice M. • Library Director • Sheridan County Fulmer Public Library • Sheridan, WY 82801 • PLA

Meister Bertha • Media Specialist Librarian • Montgomery County Public Schools • Rockville, MD 20850

Meister Marcia • Documents Librarian • University of California-Davis Library • Davis, CA 95616 • GODORT

Meizner Karen L. • Ona, WV 25545-9757 • ACRL ALCTS IFRT

Meizner Kathie L. • Head of Children's Services • Montgomery County Department of Public Library/ Bethesda Regional Library • Bethesda, MD 20814 • ALSC PLA IFRT

Melancon Rebecca A. • Charleston County Library • Charleston, SC 29403

Melanson Holly F. • Asst. University Librarian • Dalhousie University Library • Halifax NS, B3H 4H8 Canada • ALCTS LAMA

Melanson Lloyd J. • Halifax NS, B3N 2V1 Canada • ACRL ALCTS

Melanson Robert G. • Director • Winter Park Public Library • Winter Park, FL 32789 • ALTA

Melbinger Joyce A. • Placentia, CA 92670 • LAMA PLA RASD IFRT

Melcher Margaret • Publisher • Melcher Ediciones • San Juan, 000906 Puerto Rico • ACRL RASD EMIERT IRRT

Melcher Susan Z. • Librarian • Hawthorne Elementary School • Louisville, KY 40205 • AASL ALSC

Meldrem Joyce A. • Social Science Librarian • Northwest Missouri State University Owens Library • Maryville, MO 64468 • ACRL LAMA

Meldrum Dennis L. • User Specialist • Family History Service Centers • Salt Lake City, UT 84150

Meldrum Janifer • Director of Marketing • Marcive, Inc. • San Antonio, TX 78265 • ACRL LITA PLA

Melendez Araceli • El Paso, TX 79915 • EMIERT IFRT NMRT SRRT

Melendez Carmen M. • Student • Syracuse University School of Information Studies • Syracuse, NY 13244-4100

Melendez Lisa • University of California UCSB Library • Santa Barbara, CA 93106-9010 • ACRL

Melican Regina Anne Sr • Director • Saint Josephs Seminary Corrigan Memorial Library • Yonkers, NY 10704 • ACRL ALCTS

Melick Cal G. • Washburn University Library • Topeka, KS 66621 • ACRL ALCTS

Melik Ella M. • Assistant Humanities Librarian • Oklahoma State University Library • Stillwater, OK 74078-0375 • ACRL LAMA

Melin Helen Widdis • Catalog Librarian • Champaign Public Library & Information Center • Champaign, IL 61820-5193 • ALCTS

Melin Henry Jr. • Chicago, IL 60643

Melkin Audrey D. • Director of Marketing • Henry Holt and Company • New York, NY 10011 • ALCTS RASD

Melkonian Esther A. • Warwick, RI 02886

Mellby Julie L. • Whitney Museum of American Art Library • New York, NY 10021

Mellen Ellen B. • Elementary Librarian • Chelmsford High School Library • North Chelmsford, MA 01863 • AASL ALSC

Mellen Georganne • Librarian-Cataloger • Albuquerque Public Schools • Albuquerque, NM 87125-0704

Mellendorf Naomi R. • Student • Olivet Nazarene University Benner Library & Resource Center • Kankakee, IL 60901-0592 • ALCTS LITA IFRT NMRT SRRT

Mellendorf Scott A. • Student • Saginaw Valley State University Melvin J. Zahnow Library • University Center, MI 48710 • NMRT SRRT

Melleno Robin L. • Librarian • Hillside Avenue School • Cranford, NJ 07016 • AASL

Mellett Mary H. • Student • University of Alabama School of Library & Information Studies • Tuscaloosa, AL 35487-0252 • ACRL SRRT

Melley Jean • Lead Reference • County of Los Angeles Public Library Valencia Library 113 • Valenica, CA 91355

Mellican Nancy J. • Library Director • Oldsmar Public Library • Oldsmar, FL 34677 • LAMA PLA

Mellon Constance A • East Carolina University Department of Library & Information Studies • Greenville, NC 27858-4353 • AASL YALSA

Mellor Laura B. • Children's Librarian • Hillsboro Public Library • Neshanic, NJ 08853 • ALSC

Mellott Constance • Assistant Professor • Kent State University School of Library & Information Science • Kent, OH 44242-0001 • LITA

Mellown Richard H. • Social Sciences Bibliographer • University of Georgia Libraries • Athens, GA 30602

Melman Amy S. • Student • Queens College Grad Sch of Lib & Inf Studies • Flushing, NY 11367 • PLA RASD

Melnick Ralph • Head Librarian • Williston Northampton School • Easthampton, MA 01027 • AASL

Melnychuk Dianne K. • Head Acquistion Services • Muhlenberg College Trexler Library • Allentown, PA 18104-5586 • ACRL GODORT

Melom Connie J. • Marymount College Library • Rancho Palos Verdes, CA 90274 • ACRL RASD

Melson Doris I. • Hunter School • Greensboro, NC 27407 • AASL

Melston Kathleen F. • Director • Rockwall County Public Library • Rockwall, TX 75087 • PLA

Melton Diana S. • Evansville-Vanderburgh County Public Library Red Bank Branch • Evansville, IN 47712 • ALSC SORT

Melton Emily I. • Executive Board Secretariat • American Library Association • Chicago, IL 60611-2795

Melton Lynn • Director • Boise Public Library • Boise, ID 83702-0715 • LAMA PLA

Melton Marie F. Sr. • Dean of University Libraries • Saint John's University Library • Jamaica, NY 11439 • ACRL LAMA

Melton Robert W. • Humanities Bibliographer • University of Kansas Library • Lawrence, KS 66045-2800 • ACRL RASD

Meltzer Ellen J. • Librarian • University of California-Berkeley Moffitt Undergraduate Library • Berkeley, CA 94720 • ACRL LAMA RASD LIRT

Meltzer Yvonne • Library Media Center Director • Washington School • Mundelein, IL 60060 • AASL

Melville Annette • Student • University of California-Berkeley School of Library & Information Studies • Berkeley, CA 94720

Melville Joan R. • Media Specialist • Landsdowne Elementary School • Charlotte, NC 28226 • AASL

Melville Karen E. • Dir of Placement & Public Rel • University of Toronto Faculty of Library & Information Science • Toronto ON, M5S 1A1 Canada

Melvin Linda S. • Rose Hill Elementary School • Alexandria, VA 22310 • AASL

Melvin Thomas C. • Senior Assistant Librarian • University of Delaware Morris Library • Newark, DE 19717-5267 • ACRL

Melyon Ellen J. • Head of Cataloging & Automation • Kenosha Public Library • Kenosha, WI 53142-5799

Melz-Trussler Christine • Librarian • Castillero Middle School • San Jose, CA 95120 • AASL

Memberg Samuel V. • Donnell Library Center • New York, NY 10019 • LITA

Memhard Charles • Trustee • Mid-Hudson Library System • Poughkeepsie, NY 12601

Memmott Sara A. • Graduate Student • University of North Dakota Chester Fritz Library • Grand Forks, ND 58202-0175 • ACRL MAGERT

Men Jo Yen T. • Engineering & Comp. Science Ln. • North Dakota State University Library • Fargo, ND 58105-5599 • ACRL GODORT

Menahan Ellen L. • Student • Brigham Young University School of Library & Information Sciences • Provo, UT 84602 • PLA RASD EMIERT

Menanteaux Kathleen A. • Director, Technical Services • Library of Michigan • Lansing, MI 48909

Menard Margaret M. • Student • Southern Connecticut State University School of Libray Science & Instructional Technology • New Haven, CT 06515 • SRRT

Menc William E. III • Erie, PA 16508

Mendel Roger • Director • Alpena County Library • Alpena, MI 49707

Mendelsohn Henry N. • Bibliographer & Reference Libn • State University of New York (SUNY) Thomas E. Dewey Graduate Library • Albany, NY 12222 • ACRL

Mendelsohn Jennifer • Head Librarian • University of Toronto • Toronto ON, M5S 1A5 Canada • LITA RASD NMRT

Mendelson Rita E. • Elementary School Librarian • Carman Trails School • Manchester, MO 63021 • AASL

Mendenhall Bethany R. • Head, Technical Services • Getty Center Resources Collections • Santa Monica, CA 90401 • ALCTS LITA

Mendenhall Kathryn M. • Sr. Lib Info Syst. Specialist • Library of Congress • Washington, DC 20541

Menditto Michele C. • Edison, NJ 08817 • ALCTS SRRT

Mendle Gillian F. • Reference Librarian • University of Alabama Amelia Gayle Gorgas Library • Tuscaloosa, AL 35487-0266 • ACRL RASD

Mendoza Tracey E. • Student • University of North Texas School of Library & Information Sciences • Denton, TX 76203 • NMRT

Mendrinos Roxanne B. Dr. • Head of Library Services • Foothill College Library • Los Altos Hills, CA 94022-4599 • ACRL LITA LRRT

Menear William H. Mr • Director • Hewlett Woodmere Public Library • Hewlett, NY 11557-2301 • ACRL LAMA *Life*

Meneely William E. • Head, Collection Development • Georgia State University Pullen Library • Atlanta, GA 30303-3081 • ACRL ALCTS LAMA

Menefee William D. Jr. • Columbus, OH 43206 • ACRL RASD

Meneray Wilbur E. • Asst Librarian Special Clln • Tulane University Howard-Tilton Memorial Library • New Orleans, LA 70118 • ACRL

Menet Margaret • Trustee • Franklin Park Public Library District • Franklin Park, IL 60131 • ALTA PLA

Mengeling Kristina M. • Reference Librarian • Mc Henry County College • Crystal Lake, IL 60014 • IRRT

Menger Thomas C. • Trustee • Peoria Public Library • Peoria, IL 61602 • ALTA

Mengers Frederick M. • Dept. Chairman Lib & Media Svs. • Milford Mill High School Baltimore County Board of Education • Baltimore, MD 21202 • AASL

Mengers Sharon L. • Eldersburg, MD 21784 • AASL

Mengers Susan • Director of Children's Services • River Edge Public Library • River Edge, NJ 07661

Menges Gary L. • Hd,Spec. Collections & Preser. • University of Washington • Seattle, WA 98195 • ACRL ALCTS LAMA RASD

Meningall Evelyn L. • E Brunswick, NJ 08816 • AASL

Menk Ellen F. • Library Assistant I • Alexandria Public Library Ellen Coolidge Burke Branch • Alexandria, VA 22304

Menke Mary V. • Bibliographic Maintenance Ln • Northeastern University Libraries • Boston, MA 02115 • ACRL

Menke Merna R. • Director • Hartley Public Library • Hartley, IA 51346

Menna Elizabeth Bentley • Chief, Sci. & Tech. Res. Ctr. • New York Public Library • New York, NY 10018-2788 • ACRL LAMA

Mennella Mary Helen • Lansing, IL 60438

Menoche Patricia • School Librarian • Tiverton Middle School • Tiverton, RI 02878 • AASL

Menoher Violet I. • Librarian • University of California UCSB Library • Santa Barbara, CA 93106-9010

Menon Rani • Student • University of Michigan Libraries Information and Library Studies • Ann Arbor, MI 48109

Menon Vanaja S. • Gurnee, IL 60031 • ACRL

Mentzel Nina C. • Student • Syracuse University School of Information Studies • Syracuse, NY 13244-4100

Menzel Heidi A. • Student • Indiana University School of Library and Information Science • Bloomington, IN 47405

Menzel John P. • Supervisior of Reader's Services • Morris County Free Library • Whippany, NJ 07981 • RASD

Menzel William H. • Student • Seton Hall University Law Library • Newark, NJ 07102 • AASL

Menzer Karin Garlieb • Assistant Children's Librarian • Mead Public Library • Sheboygan, WI 53081

Menzies Annelie W. • Salt Lake City Public Library • Salt Lake City, UT 84111 • LAMA PLA

Menzies Teresa E. • Brooklyn, NY 11210 • ASCLA

Meola Mary B. • Reference Librarian • Georgian Court College Farley Memorial Library • Lakewood, NJ 08701

Meola-Librizzi Rose Marie • Director • Jersey City Public Library • Jersey City, NJ 07302-3499 • LAMA

Mepham Wendy Ruth • Student • San Jose State University Division of Library & Information Science • San Jose, CA 95192-0029 • PLA YALSA NMRT SRRT

Mercado Elnora M. • Denver, CO 80221

Mercado Marilyn J. • Head of Cataloging Dept. • University of Northern Iowa Donald O. Rod Library • Cedar Falls, IA 50613-3675 • ALCTS

Mercer Bernard A. • Acquisitions Searcher II • The American University Library • Washington, DC 20016-8046

Mercer Beth A. • Director • E.G. Fisher Public Library • Athens, TN 37303 • PLA

Mercer Deborah • Student • Rutgers University School of Communication Information & Library Studies • New Brunswick, NJ 08903 • EMIERT SRRT

Mercer Gloritha L. • Supervising Librarian • United States Army L • Fort Bragg, NC 28307 • AFLRT FLRT

Mercer Kent • Librarian • Schlumberger Well Services • Austin, TX 78726

Mercer Yvonne L.R. • Library Media Specialist • Barclay School-54 Baltimore City Public School • Baltimore, MD 21218 • AASL

Merchant Jacqueline M. • School Librarian • Baltimore City Dapartment of Education • Baltimore, MD 21215 • AASL

Merchant Thomas L. • Director • Milton Public Library • Milton, WI 53563 • PLA

Mercier Cathryn M. • Childrens Literature • Simmons College Center for the Study of Children's Literature • Boston, MA 02115 • ALSC

Mercier Mellanie A. • Student • University of Wisconsin-Madison School of Library & Information Studies • Madison, WI 53706

Mercier Patricia S. • Children's Librarian • Palm Beach County Public Library System Greenacres City Branch • Greenacres City, FL 33463 • EMIERT

Mercier Sylvia A. • Coor., Reference/Clln. Devel. • Community College of Rhode Island • Warwick, RI 02886 • ACRL

Meredith Barbara A. • Boca Raton, FL 33432 • RASD

Meredith Deborah J. • Head, Reference • Chattanooga-Hamilton County Bicentennial Library • Chattanooga, TN 37402 • ACRL

Meredith Dorothy • Library Director • Armand Hammer United World College Library • Montezuma, NM 87731 • ACRL IRRT

Meredith Mairi • Technical Services Librarian • University of Findlay Shafer Library • Findlay, OH 45840 • ALCTS

Meredith William G. • Denver, CO 80220

Meredith Willis C. • Preservation Librarian • Harvard Law School Library • Cambridge, MA 02138 • ALCTS

Merguerian Gayane K. • Seton Hall University • South Orange, NJ 07079-2690

Merich Lillian • Library Director • Three Oaks Twp Library • Three Oaks, MI 49128

Meridian Anne • Children's Librarian • King County Library System • Seattle, WA 98109-5191 • ALSC

Meridith Shirley A. • Victor R. Marshall & Associates • Albuquerque, NM 87102 • GODORT

Merilees Bobbie • Vancouver BC, V6J 1B7 Canada • LITA

Mering Margaret • Principal Serials Cataloger • University of Nebraska Love Library • Lincoln, NE 68588-0410 • ALCTS LITA

Meringolo Anne • Brooklyn, NY 11234

Meringolo Salvatore M. • Asst. Dean, Clln & Ref. Services • Pennsylvania State University E506 Pattee Library • University Park, PA 16802 • ACRL LAMA RASD

Merk P. Evelyn • Librarian • Nola Brantley Memorial Library • Warner Robins, GA 31093 • PLA

Merkl Anthony E. • So Orange, NJ 07079

Merrell Rebecca J. • Student • Elkhart Baptist Christian School • Elkhart, IN 46517 • AASL

Merrell Sheila J. • St Louis, MO 63124 • AASL

Merriam Doris E. • Supervisor Lib. Media Services • Hempfield School District • Landisville, PA 17538 • AASL

Merriam Joyce • Assistant Head of Reference • University of Massachusetts Library • Amherst, MA 01003 • ACRL RASD LIRT

Merriam Louise A. • Eau Claire, WI 54701 • ACRL

Merrick D. Cynthia • Trustee • Copiague Memorial Public Library • Copiague, NY 11726 • ALTA

Merrick Jerald A. • Head of Reference • Decatur Public Library • Decatur, IL 62523 • Life

Merrifield Mark D. • Director • Adams County Library • Gettysburg, PA 17325-2311 • LAMA PLA NMRT

Merrigan Helen T. • Cape Coral, FL 33904 • Continuing

Merrigan Paul G. • Cape Coral, FL 33904 • Continuing

Merrill-Oldham Jan • Head of Preservation Department • University of Connecticut Homer Babbidge Library • Storrs, CT 06269-1005 • ALCTS

Merrill Anne Cecile Sr. • Dominican College Library • Blauvelt, NY 10913

Merrill Barbara P. • Albion, NY 14411

Merrill Beverly A. • Manchester, NH 03102

Merrill George P. Jr • Librarian • Montgomery High School Library • Santa Rosa, CA 95405 • AASL

Merrill Marie • Laguna Hills, CA 92653 • Continuing

Merrill Martha • Professor of Inst Media • Jacksonville State University Library • Jacksonville, AL 36265 • AASL *Life*

Merriman Faith A. • Central Connecticut State University Elihu Burritt Library • New Britain, CT 06050 • ACRL

Merriman Maxine M. PhD • Chief Librarian • General Dynamics Division Research Library • Ft Worth, TX 76101

Merriss Eunice • State College, PA 16801 • Continuing

Merritt Dee Anne • Assistant Director • Helen Hoffman Plantation Library • Plantation, FL 33317

Merritt Floyd S. • Reference Librarian • Amherst College Library • Amherst, MA 01002 • ACRL RASD GODORT *Life*

Merritt Gertrude • Durham, NC 27701 • Continuing

Merritt Marjorie L. • Documents Librarian • San Bernardino County Law Library • San Bernardino, CA 92415-0015 • GODORT

Merritt Nina T. Ms. • Student • Syracuse University School of Information Studies • Syracuse, NY 13244-4100

Merritt Nisa K. • Staff Specialist • Maryland State Department of Education Division of Library Development & Services • Baltimore, MD 21201 • PLA CLENE

Merritt Patrice R. • Wayne State University Purdy Library • Detroit, MI 48202

Merry Allen D. • Student • University of Illinois Graduate School of Library and Information Science • Urbana, IL 61801

Merry Lois K. • Keene State College Mason Library • Keene, NH 03431 • ACRL

Merryweather J. Mark Dr. • Mississauga, ON, L5L 2Z4 Canada

Mersereau Kent W. • Marketing Research Interviewer • Fenton Swanger Consumer Research, Inc. • Dallas, TX 75240 • NMRT

Mershon J. Lee • Saratoga, CA 95070

Mershon Loretta K. • Librarian • North Carolina State University D. H. Hill Library • Raleigh, NC 27695-7111

Merskey Marie G. • Trustee • Mamaroneck Free Library • Mamaroneck, NY 10543

Mersky Roy M. • Law Librarian • University of Texas Tarlton Law Library • Austin, TX 78705-5799 • ACRL ALCTS ASCLA LAMA LITA RASD ERT GODORT IFRT IRRT LHRT LRRT SORT SRRT

Mersmann Patti J. • Student • Emporia State University School of Library & Information Management • Emporia, KS 66801

Mertens Sushila • Twin Ridges Elementary School District • North San Juan, CA 95960

Mertes Susan • Memorial Hospital of Southern Oklahoma • Ardmore, OK 73403

Mertins Barbara J. • Assistant Professor • West Virginia University Department of Library Science • Morgantown, WV 26506-6069 • AASL

Mertins Lynn A. • Student • University of South Carolina College of Library & Information Science • Columbia, SC 29208

Mertz Dee J. • Library Media Specialist • Denn John Middle School • Kissimmee, FL 34744 • AASL

Mery Michael J. • Student • Columbia University School of Library Service • New York, NY 10027

Merz Lawrie H. • Reference & Music Librarian • Houghton College Willard J Houghton Library • Houghton, NY 14744 • ACRL

Merz Mildred H. • Collection Development Librarian • Oakland University • Rochester, MI 48309-4401 • ACRL ALCTS

Meserve Harry • Felton, CA 95018 • PLA

Meshot Genevieve • Hubbard, OH 44425 • Continuing

Mesina Irene M. • Librarian • Honolulu Community College Library • Honolulu, HI 96817-4598

Meskauskas Debora • Public Information Officer • Arlington Heights Memorial Library • Arlington Heights, IL 60004-5966 • LAMA

Mesner Lillian R. • Technical Services Librarian • University of Kentucky Libraries Agriculture Department • Lexington, KY 40546-0091 • ACRL ALCTS

Messenger Nancy • Sno-Isle Regional Library • Marysville, WA 98271-9164 • PLA

Messer Barbara • Genentech Inc • So. San Francisco, CA 94080 • LITA

Messer Frances P. • Librarian • Kinchafoonee Regional Library • Dawson, GA 31742

Messer Katharine Holden • Hartford, CT 06106 • LAMA PLA *Continuing*

Messerchmitt Carol L. • School Librarian • Reid Middle School • Pittsfield, MA 01201 • AASL EMIERT

Messerle Judith • Director • Harvard University Countway Library of Medicine • Boston, MA 02115 • LAMA LITA

Messersmith Susan • Lebanon Public Library • Lebanon, OR 97355

Messick Holly • Librarian • Perry Middle School • Worthington, OH 43085

Messick Karen J. • Hd, Children & Yng. Adult Serv • New Jersey State Library Library for the Blind & Handicapped • Trenton, NJ 08618 • ASCLA

Messick Steve • Director • Dorchester County Library • Saint George, SC 29477 • PLA

Messier Real C. • General Director • Bibliotheque Centrale De Pret- Regions de Quebec • Charny PQ, G6X 3A1 Canada • PLA

Messineo Anthony • Director • Greenville County Library • Greenville, SC 29601 • ALTA LAMA LITA PLA IFRT

Messineo Nancy A. • Youth Services Officer • Long Beach Public Library • Long Beach, CA 90802-4482 • PLA

Messing Lizbeth • Traverse City Senior High School • Traverse City, MI 49685 • AASL

Messman-Mandicott Eleanor • Reference Librarian • Frostburg State University Lewis J. Ort Library • Frostburg, MD 21532 • ACRL

Mestas-Holm Cecelia A. • Reference Librarian • Inland Library System Reference Center • Riverside, CA 92502 • RASD

Mestas Marie D. • Reference Libraian • San Bernardino Valley College Library • San Bernardino, CA 92410

Mester Jeannette • New York, NY 10025

Mestre Lori S. • Graves Memorial Library • Sunderland, MA 01375 • PLA

Meszaros Imre • Director of Libraries • University of South Dakota I.D. Weeks Library • Vermillion, SD 57069-2390 • ACRL

Meszaros Rosemary L. • U.S. Documents Librarian • University of California UCSB Library • Santa Barbara, CA 93106-9010 • GODORT

Metallo Charmaine M. • Assistant Librarian • United States Courts Library • Baltimore, MD 21201

Metcalf Davinci C. • Jacksonville Public Libraries Main Library • Jacksonville, FL 32202

Metcalf Roger W. • Derwood, MD 20855

Metcalf Ruth A. • Children's Librarian • State Library of Ohio • Columbus, OH 43266-0334 • ALSC

Metcalf Ruth B. • Circulation Librarian • University of Texas at Arlington • Arlington, TX 76019-0497

Metcalf Steven A. • System Manager • Evergreen State College Consortium for Automated Library Systems • Olympia, WA 98505 • LITA

Metcalfe Christine M. • Director • Mechanicsburg Area Public Library • Mechanicsburg, PA 17055

Metheny Cheryl • Lake Lanier Regional Library Lawrenceville Branch • Lawrenceville, GA 30245-4707

Metier Ellen • Trustee • West Des Moines Public Library • West Des Moines, IA 50265

Metro Christine A. • Los Angeles Public Library Felipe de Neve Branch • Los Angeles, CA 90057

Metros Teri • Library Administrator • Tempe Public Library • Tempe, AZ 85282 • LAMA PLA

Metson Sigrid • Dir. of Publisher Relations • Reference Software • San Francisco, CA 94107 • ACRL

Metternich Viola B. Miss • Cincinnati, OH 45238-3509 • Continuing

Metz Arlene • Wapakoneta, OH 45895 • AASL YALSA

Metz Carolyn E. • Branch Manager • Orange County Library System Edgewater Branch • Orlando, FL 32810

Metz Jane F. • San Jose Mercury News Library • San Jose, CA 95091

Metz Paul • Principal Bibliographer • Virginia Polytechnic Inst & State Univ University Libraries • Blacksburg, VA 24062-9001 • ACRL LRRT

Metz Ray E. • Director of Lib Inf Tech • Case Western Reserve University • Cleveland, OH 44106-7151 • ACRL LITA

Metz Ruth Foley • System Coordinator • Bay Area Library & Information System • Oakland, CA 94607 • PLA

Metz T. John • Carleton College Library • Northfield, MN 55057-4097 • ACRL

Metz Terrance J. • Systems Support & Instruction Ln • Carleton College Library • Northfield, MN 55057-4097 • ACRL LAMA LITA

Metzenbacher Gary W. • Milwaukie, OR 97267 • ACRL

Metzger Deborah A. • California State University-Sacramento Library • Sacramento, CA 95819-6039

Metzger Mary J. • Library Cataloger • Alton Community School District 11 • Alton, IL 62002

Metzger Philip A. • Curator of Special Collections • Lehigh University Libraries Linderman Library 30 • Bethlehem, PA 18015-3067 • ACRL LHRT

Metzger Stephen K. • Chicago Public Library • Chicago, IL 60605 • RASD

Metzler Kathleen L. • Tulsa City-County Library System • Tulsa, OK 74103

Metzler Laura J. • Albuquerque, NM 87111 • ALSC

Metzler Violet • Portland, OR 97229 • RASD

Metzner Nancy J. • Literacy Program & Homebound Svs • High Point Public Library • High Point, NC 27261

Meunier Judith C. • Cataloger • Bradford College Hemingway Library • Haverhill, MA 01835 • ALCTS

Meurer Tamsie • Director • Charlestown-Clark County Library • Charlestown, IN 47111 • PLA

Meuse Linda A. • Children's Librarian • Cherry Hill Free Public Library • Cherry Hill, NJ 08034 • ALSC

Mevis Susan Mary • Arabut Ludlow Memorial Library • Monroe, WI 53566 • PLA

Mevnier Suzanne J. • Aquisitions Librarian • Woburn Public Library • Woburn, MA 01801

Mewshaw Dorothy R. • Tallahassee, FL 32308-4510 • MAGERT

Meyer Albert • Librarian • Saint Bernards School • New York, NY 10029 • AASL

Meyer Allen • Administrative Librarian • Vernon Area Public Library • Prairie View, IL 60069 • LAMA PLA SRRT

Meyer Barbara G. • Reference Librarian • Chicago Public Library Rudy Lozano Branch • Chicago, IL 60608 • PLA RASD

Meyer Bettina S. • Asst. Dean for Resources • Western Michigan University Libraries Dwight B. Waldo Library • Kalamazoo, MI 49008 • ACRL ALCTS LAMA

Meyer Betty Jane • Worthington, OH 43085

Meyer Beverly R. • Materials Center Cataloger • Chicago State University Paul & Emily Douglas Library • Chicago, IL 60628 • ACRL ALCTS

Meyer Brian L. • Student • Rosary College Graduate School of Library & Information Science • River Forest, IL 60305 • IFRT

Meyer Christina P. • Librarian • University of Minnesota O. Meredith Wilson Library • Minneapolis, MN 55455-0414 • ALCTS LITA

Meyer Connie • Director • Dwight Foster Public Library • Fort Atkinson, WI 53538 • ALSC

Meyer Daniel • Associate Curator • University of Chicago Library • Chicago, IL 60637-1502 • ACRL

Meyer David R. • St. Louis, MO 63146

Meyer Debra S. • Saint Charles City-County Library • St. Peters, MO 63376-0529 • ALSC PLA

Meyer Diane • Media Specialist • East Syracuse-Minoa School District Adm Blvd. • E Syracuse, NY 13217 • AASL

Meyer Elaine • Circulation Librarian • Amery Public Library • Amery, WI 54001

Meyer Elaine E. • Vermillion, SD 57069 • Continuing

Meyer Ellen B. • Reference Librarian • Valparaiso University Moellering Memorial Library • Valparaiso, IN 46383 • ACRL

Meyer J. Patricia • Assist Librarian, Reference • American Institute of Certified Public Accountants • New York, NY 10036-8775 • RASD

Meyer Jane G. • Acquisitions Librarian • Ventura County Library Services Agency • Ventura, CA 93001 • ALCTS

Meyer Janet W. • Des Plaines, IL 60016

Meyer Jerry • Davis County Library Central Branch • Layton, UT 84041

Meyer Joan L. • Head of Technical Services • Springfield Free Public Library • Springfield, NJ 07081 • Life

Meyer Kathy • Longview, TX 75608 • LAMA

Meyer Kurt A. • Librarian II • Valley City State University • Valley City, ND 58072

Meyer Laura • Children's Librarian • Seattle Public Library Lake City Branch • Seattle, WA 98125 • ALSC

Meyer Margaret M. • Alton, IL 62002

Meyer Mary Louise • Chapel Hill, NC 27514

Meyer Mona L. • Reference Librarian • University of Southern Indiana • Evansville, IN 47712

Meyer Nadean J. • Spokane, WA 99204 • AASL ALSC

Meyer Nancy R. • Graduate Student • Emporia State University School of Library & Information Management • Emporia, KS 66801 • AASL

Meyer Rayme • Branch Manager • Alameda County Library Dublin Branch • Dublin, CA 94568

Meyer Richard W. • Director of the Library • Trinity University • San Antonio, TX 78212 • ACRL

Meyer Sally S. • Cedar Rapids, IA 52402

Meyer Sandra Kay • Andrew Carnegie Free Library • Carnegie, PA 15106

Meyer Sharon I. • Triodyne Inc., • Niles, IL 60648

Meyer Stephanie H. • Librarian • Campbell Hall School Library • North Hollywood, CA 91607 • ALSC

Meyer Terry • Reference Librarian • Pacific Lutheran University School of Education • Tacoma, WA 98447

Meyer Ursula • Director of Library Services • Stockton-San Joaquin County Public Library • Stockton, CA 95202 • LAMA PLA IFRT

Meyer Wayne H. • Architecture Librarian • Ball State University Bracken Library • Muncie, IN 47306-0160 • ACRL SRRT

Meyering Mary Anne • Eisenhower Public Library District • Harwood Heights, IL 60656 • RASD IFRT

Meyers Arthur S. • Director • Hammond Public Library • Hammond, IN 46320 • ASCLA LAMA PLA RASD EMIERT IFRT

Meyers Barbara J. • Director • Blue Island Public Library • Blue Island, IL 60406 • PLA

Meyers Darlene S. • Supervisor of School Lib Svs • Pinellas County School Board • Clearwater, FL 34624 • AASL IFRT

Meyers David K. • Student • University of North Texas School of Library & Information Sciences • Denton, TX 76203

Meyers Diane E. • Pasadena Public Library • Pasadena, CA 91101

Meyers Duane H. • Special Consultant • Metropolitan Library System • Oklahoma City, OK 73102 • PLA IFRT

Meyers Elaine E. • Head, Children's Dept. • Phoenix Public Library • Phoenix, AZ 85004 • ALSC PLA

Meyers Ellen S. • San Francisco, CA 94114-2347 • ACRL IFRT SRRT

Meyers Elsa M. • Cataloger • New Jersey Historical Society • Newark, NJ 07104 • IFRT

Meyers Helene R. • Broward County Division of Libraries Broward County Library • Fort Lauderdale, FL 33301 • GODORT

Meyers Judith K. • Palatine, IL 60074 • AASL ALSC YALSA   *Life*

Meyers Kathleen H. • Reference Librarian • Phoenix Public Library Yucca Branch • Phoenix, AZ 85015 • LITA PLA RASD CLENE IFRT VRT

Meyers Martha L. • Genealogy Reference Librarian • Mid-Continent Public Library • Independence, MO 64050 • RASD

Meyers Nancy J. • Student • Florida State University School of Library and Information Studies • Tallahassee, FL 32306-2048

Meyers Susan • Trustee • Downers Grove Public Library • Downers Grove, IL 60515 • ALTA

Meyers Susan M. • Macedon, NY 14502 • RASD

Meyerson Marilyn • Libraian • Key School Libraries • Annapolis, MD 21403

Meyerson Valerie Lee • Librarian • Wixom Public Library • Wixom, MI 48096 • LAMA PLA YALSA IFRT

MiKash Debbi K. • Colorado Springs, CO 80908 • SRRT

Miah Abdul J. • Director of LRC • J. Sargeant Reynolds Community College Library • Richmond, VA 23261-2040 • ACRL

Mianoor Razia • Librarian • Raynet Corporation • Menlo Park, CA 94025 • ACRL ALCTS LAMA LITA

Miasek Meryl A. • Corvallis-Benton County Public Library • Corvallis, OR 97330-4728 • ACRL LITA

Miatech Jill A. • Adult Services Librarian • Prescott Public Library • Prescott, AZ 86303

Michael Ann B. • Manager,Library Services • Gas Research Institute • Chicago, IL 60631 • ALCTS LAMA LITA RASD

Michael Delores • Whithall High School • Greenfield, WI 53228 • AASL

Michael Douglas O. • Director of Learning Resources • Cayuga Community College,Bourke Memorial Library Learning Resources Center • Auburn, NY 13021 • ACRL

Michael Gail M. • Louisville, KY 40205

Michael James • Data Research Associates Inc. • Saint Louis, MO 63132 • ACRL ALCTS LAMA LITA PLA RASD ERT

Michael Nancy B. • Reference Librarian • Foreign Mission Board,SBC Jenkins Research Library • Richmond, VA 23230 • RASD

Michael Nancy F. • Student • Northern Illinois University Department of Library & Information Studies • DeKalb, IL 60115 • LITA

Michael Roberta M. • District Library Coordinator • Unified School District # 464 • Tonganoxie, KS 66086 • AASL

Michael Thomas E. • Windsor Elementary School • Windsor, VA 23487 • AASL

Michaels Andrea A. • President • Michaels Associates • Alexandria, VA 22309 • ACRL LAMA

Michaels Barbara P. • Graduate Assistant • Mankato State University • Mankato, MN 56002

Michaels Carolyn Leopold • Consultant • Childhood Memories • Charleston, SC 29401 • RASD LIRT   *Continuing*

Michaels David L. • Vice President • Michaels Associates • Alexandria, VA 22309 • LAMA PLA

Michaels Jeffrey A • Student • Catholic University of America School of Library and Information Science • Washington, DC 20064

Michaels Judith Ann • Librarian • Lincoln, Washington, Harrison Elementary School • Roselle, NJ 07203

Michaels Virginia C. • Tallahassee, FL 32308

Michaelsen Karen L. • Reference Librarian • Seattle Central Community College • Seattle, WA 98122

Michaelson Judith A. • Dir., Marketing Communications • Online Computer Library Center (OCLC) • Dublin, OH 43017-3395 • LAMA

Michaelson Robert • Head Librarian • Northwestern University Library Mudd Library for Science & Engineering • Evanston, IL 60208 • ACRL

Michalak Jo-Ann • Asst. Dir. for Public Svs. • Tufts University Nils Yngve Wessell Library • Medford, MA 02155 • LITA

Michalak Sarah C. • Assistant Director • University of Washington Suzzallo Library • Seattle, WA 98195 • ACRL ALCTS LAMA LITA

Michalak Thomas J. • President & CEO • Faxon Research Services Inc • Cambridge, MA 02142 • ACRL ALCTS LAMA LITA RASD

Michalko James P. • President • Research Libraries Group Inc. (RLG) • Mountain View, CA 94041-1100

Michals Mary H. • Children's Librarian • Medford Public Library • Medford, MA 02155 • ALSC

Michalski Anne White • American Medical Association • Chicago, IL 60610 • RASD

Michalski Evelyn L. • Carrizo Springs, TX 78834

Michalski Maria G. • Cheektowaga, NY 14227

Michaud-Oystryk Nicole R. • Head, Dafoe Library • University of Manitoba • Winnipeg MB, R3T 2N2 Canada • ACRL LRRT

Michaud Charles • Director • Turner Free Library • Randolph, MA 02368

Michaud Jean-Paul • Reference Specialist • The New York Public Library • New York, NY 10016 • LITA PLA

Michaud Noreen R. • Director of Library/Media Servs. • Simsbury High School Library • Simsbury, CT 06070 • AASL

Michel William D. • Branch Reference Coordinator • Ramsey County Public Library Adminstrative Offices • Shoreview, MN 55126-5800 • RASD

Michels Fredrick A. • Library Media Director • Lake Superior State University Library • Sault Sainte Marie, MI 49783

Michels Mary Jane • Student • University of South Carolina College of Library & Information Science • Columbia, SC 29208

Michelson-Holland Enda M. • Librarian • Southern Regional Middle School • Manahawkin, NJ 08050

Michelson Beth N. • Stansberry Chiropractice • Gainesville, FL 32601

Michelson Theresa H. • Librarian/Media Specialist • Urbana High School • Urbana, IL 61801 • AASL

Michlich Sandra J. • Lakewood Public Library • Lakewood, NJ 08701

Michniewski Henry J. • Trenton, NJ 08618 • LAMA PLA   *Life*

Mick Vickie E. • Southern Connecticut State University Hilton C. Buley Library • New Haven, CT 06515 • ACRL

Mickel Mary G. • Librarian • Decorah School Library • West Bend, WI 53095 • AASL

Mickells Gregory • Student • Emporia State University School of Library & Information Management • Emporia, KS 66801

Mickey Melissa B. • Schiff Hardin & Waite • Chicago, IL 60606 • LITA RASD   *Life*

Micuda Vladimir • State College, PA 16801

Miczan Marie C. • Library Media Specialist • Solvay Elementary School • Solvay, NY 13209 • AASL

Midden Mary Ann • Student • University of Illinois Graduate School of Library and Information Science • Urbana, IL 61801 • PLA

Middendorf Jack L. • Director • Wayne State College U S Conn Library • Wayne, NE 68787

Middleswart Patricia A. • Elementary Media Specialist • Dike Community Schools • Dike, IA 50624 • AASL

Middleton Anne G. • Serials Librarian • New Orleans Public Library • New Orleans, LA 70140

Middleton Cheryl A. • Management Assistant • Oregon State University William Jasper Kerr Library • Corvallis, OR 97331-4501

Middleton Dori V. • Detroit, MI 48208

Middleton Francine K. • Microforms Librarian • Nicholls State University Allen J. Ellender Memorial Library • Thibodaux, LA 70310 • ACRL

Middleton Marcella • Aurora, CO 80010

Middleton Mary Ellen • Batavia Public Library • Batavia, IL 60510 • ALSC

Middleton Mary J. • Media Spec • TeWinkle Middle School • Costa Mesa, CA 92626 • AASL

Middleton Patricia • Public Services Reference Ln • Yale University Sterling Memorial Library • New Haven, CT 06520 • ACRL

Middleton R. Kent • Austin Public Library Little Walnut Creek • Austin, TX 78758

Middleton Susan M. • La Jolla Country Day School • La Jolla, CA 92037

Middleton William C. • Librarian • Columbia University Libraries • New York, NY 10027 • ACRL GODORT IRRT MAGERT

Midgorden Judith M. • Student • San Jose State University Division of Library & Information Science • San Jose, CA 95192-0029

Miehe Virginia M. • West Liberty Junior & Senior High School • West Liberty, IA 52776 • AASL YALSA

Miele Anthony W. • Arizona State Library Department of Library Archives & Public Records • Phoenix, AZ 85007 • ASCLA

Miele Joel A. • Trustee • Queens Borough Public Library • Jamaica, NY 11432 • ALTA PLA

Mielke Laurie • Community Librarian • Montgomery County Department of Public Libraries White Oak Community Branch • Silver Spring, MD 20904-2898 • LAMA PLA RASD EMIERT IFRT *Life*

Mielke Linda • Associate Administrator • Annapolis & Anne Arundel County Public Library • Annapolis, MD 21401-7042 • PLA

Mielke Nancy C. • Reference Librarian • Tennessee Technological University University Library • Cookeville, TN 38505 • ACRL RASD

Mielke Sally Jo • La Grande, OR 97850

Mier Guadalupe J. • Director • Bellevue Public Library • Bellevue, NE 68005 • PLA

Miericke Susan S. • Student • Texas Woman's University School of Library & Information Studies • Denton, TX 76204

Miesse Cathy C. • Head of Circulation • Loyola University E.M. Cudahy Memorial Library • Chicago, IL 60626 • ACRL LAMA RASD

Miesse James E. • Mgr. Release Integration & Distr • NOTIS Systems, Inc. • Evanston, IL 60201-3622 • ACRL LAMA LITA

Miethke Heidi • Student • University of California Los Angeles Graduate School of Library & Information Science • Los Angeles, CA 90024

Mifflin Ingrid • Head Bibliographic Control Unit. • Washington State University Library • Pullman, WA 99164-5610 • ALCTS LAMA LITA

Mignard Phyllis • Graphic Artist/Illustrator • Las Vegas-Clark County Library District Flamingo Library • Las Vegas, NV 89119

Migneault Robert L. • Dean of Library Services • University of New Mexico General Library • Albuquerque, NM 87131 • ACRL LAMA

Mignogna Jacalyn C. • Monroeville, PA 15146

Migut Teresa • Brooklyn, NY 11220

Mihalevich Norma L. • Trustee • Kinderhook Regional Library • Lebanon, MO 65536 • ALTA

Mihalic Sue A. • Student • Wayne State University Library Science Program • Detroit, MI 48202 • PLA

Mihalic Tom • Systems Officer • Pikes Peak Library District • Colorado Springs, CO 80901 • LITA

Mihm Peter M. • Student • University of Pittsburgh School of Library and Information Science • Pittsburgh, PA 15260 • SRRT

Mihovich Mary F. • Oak Park, MI 48237

Mihram Danielle • Western European Languages Ln • University of Southern California Doheny Library • Los Angeles, CA 90089-0182 • ACRL

Mika Joseph J. • Director • Wayne State University Library Science Program • Detroit, MI 48202 • ACRL

Mikel Sarah A. • Library Director • National Defense University • Washington, DC 20319 • AFLRT

Mikesell Gladys E. • Waynesboro, PA 17268

Miki Mihoko • Cataloger • University of California-Los Angeles (UCLA) • Los Angeles, CA 90024-1450 • ACRL ALCTS

Mikita Elizabeth G. • Bibliographic Management Libn. • Thomas Jefferson University Scott Memorial Library • Philadelphia, PA 19107 • LITA

Mikkelsen June L. • Central Library Director • Multnomah County Library Central Library • Portland, OR 97205 • LAMA PLA

Mikkola Elizabeth R. • Librarian • Oklahoma Med Res Fdn L • Oklahoma Cty, OK 73104

Miklas Josephine C. • Extended Day Librarian • Cypress College • Cypress, CA 90630 • ACRL

Miklitz Heide • Student • University of Maryland College of Library and Information Services • College Park, MD 20742-4345 • ACRL

Miklosvary Jozsef • Associate Librarian • University of California-Berkeley Law Library • Berkeley, CA 94720-2499

Mikrut Elsie • Director • Bridgeview Public Library • Bridgeview, IL 60455 • LAMA PLA

Miks Maureen • Learning Center Director • Monroe School • Hinsdale, IL 60521 • AASL

Miksa Francis • Professor • University of Texas at Austin Graduate School of Library & Information Sciences • Austin, TX 78712-1276 • ALCTS LITA LHRT LRRT

Mikulich Karin S. • Librarian • Independent School District 241 Media Services • Albert Lea, MN 56007 • AASL

Milam Sheila A. • Foreign, Languages Catatlog Ln • University of Nevada-Reno • Reno, NV 89557-0020 • ACRL ALCTS IRRT

Milberger Steven C. • Student • Emporia State University School of Library & Information Management • Emporia, KS 66801

Milburn Gina G. • Student • University of Missouri-Columbia School of Library & Informational Science • Columbia, MO 65211

Milbury Peter G. • Librarian Media Teacher • Pleasant Valley High School • Chico, CA 95926 • AASL

Milcetich Marybeth • Saint Mary's Elementary School • Laurel, MD 20707

Milde Marjorie H. • Litchfield, CT 06759

Milek Valerie A. • Assistant Professor/Cataloger • Black Hills State University E.Y. Berry Library-Learning Center • Spearfish, SD 57799-9549

Miles Barbara B. • Librarian • Portledge School Libraries • Locust Valley, NY 11560 • AASL

Miles Cynthia G. • Materials Selector • Multnomah County Library • Portland, OR 97212

Miles Dennis B. • Durant, OK 74701

Miles Georgianna S. • Broward County Division of Libraries Broward County Library • Fort Lauderdale, FL 33301 • ALCTS RASD IFRT

Miles Harriet • Palmdale City Library • Palmdale, CA 93550

Miles Linda • Sweeny Junior High School • Sweeny, TX 77480

Miles Linda J. • Student • University of Rhode Island Graduate School of Library & Information Studies • Kingston, RI 02881-0815 • AASL IFRT

Miles Lois E. • Coordinator of Junior Services • East Orange Public Library • East Orange, NJ 07018 • ALSC

Miles Margaret A. • New Hanover County Library • Wilmington, NC 28401-3998 • ALSC YALSA IFRT

Miles Ruby A. • School Librarian • Houston Indpendent School District • Houston, TX 77053 • YALSA

Miles Theodore • Palmdale, CA 93551

Miles William • Library Director • Madison Heights Public Library • Madison Heights, MI 48071 • LAMA

Miles William A. • Assistant Deputy Director • Buffalo & Erie County Public Library • Buffalo, NY 14203

Miletic Ivan • Branch Librarian • Cleveland Public Library Rice Branch • Cleveland, OH 44120 • ACRL EMIERT

Miletich John J. • Reference Librarian • University of Alberta • Edmonton AB, T6G 2J8 Canada • ACRL

Milevski Robert J. • Preservation Librarian • Princeton University Library • Princeton, NJ 08544 • ACRL ALCTS

Milevski Sandra N. • Research Associate • National Commission on Library & Information Science (NCLIS) • Washington, DC 20036

Miley David W. • Student • Kent State University School of Library & Information Science • Kent, OH 44242-0001

Miley James A. • Director • Troy-Miami County Public Library • Troy, OH 45373 • LAMA PLA IFRT

Milford Lila • Trustee • Marion Public Library • Marion, IN 46953 • ALTA PLA

Milichich James S. • Mgr., Technical Ref. Center • BDM International • McLean, VA 22102 • GODORT MAGERT

Milikien Norma L. • El Paso, TX 79912 • LAMA PLA RASD FLRT IRRT

Milinkovich Mary L. • Ready Reference Library • Milwaukee Public Library • Milwaukee, WI 53233

Milkoski Kathryn J. • Head, Document Delivery • Canada Institute for Scientific & Technical Information National Research Council • Ottawa ON, K1A 0S2 Canada • ACRL LAMA LITA RASD

Mill David H. • Reference Librarian • Ursinus College Library • Collegeville, PA 19426 • ACRL RASD

Mill David W. • Librarian • County of Los Angeles Public Library • Downey, CA 90241-7400 • ALCTS LITA PLA

Millard Holly • Burbank Public Library • Burbank, CA 91502 • LAMA PLA

Millea Megan F. • Student • University of Missouri-Columbia School of Library & Informational Science • Columbia, MO 65211 • PLA

Millen George A. • Central Missouri State University • Warrensburg, MO 64093 • ACRL ALCTS NMRT

Millen Jean • Librarian • Johnson County R-7 Schools • Centerview, MO 64019 • AASL

Millender Gwen W. • High School Librarian • Scotlandville Magnet High School • Baton Rouge, LA 70807

Millenson Roy H. • Bethesda, MD 20817

Miller-Deasy Diane A. • Student • Clark-Atlanta University School of Library & Information Studies • Atlanta, GA 30314-4391

Miller-Kummerfeld Elizabeth K. • Kummerfeld Associates, Inc. • New York, NY 10022 • ACRL LITA *Life*

Miller-Lachmann Lyn • Siena College • Loudonville, NY 12211-1462 • YALSA EMIERT IFRT

Miller A Carolyn • Assoicate Librarian • Pennsylvania State University Heindel Library • Middletown, PA 17057 • ACRL RASD LIRT LRRT

Miller A. Joann • Librarian • North Hagerstown High School • Hagerstown, MD 21740

Miller Alice W. • San Ramon, CA 94583 • AASL

Miller Amy • President • Yankee Book Peddler • Contoocook, NH 03229 • ALCTS LITA

Miller Andrea • Children's Librarian • Granite City Public Library District • Granite City, IL 62040 • ALSC

Miller Andrea L. • Clarion, PA 16214 • AASL LIRT

Miller Anita A. • School Librarian • Dodson Junior High School • San Pedro, CA 90732 • AASL

Miller Ann • Director • Coshocton Public Library • Coshocton, OH 43812 • PLA

Miller Ann Perry • Librarian • Clearwater Public Library • Clearwater, FL 34623 • PLA

Miller Ann S. • Branch Head Librarian • Broward County Division of Libraries Broward County Library • Fort Lauderdale, FL 33301 • PLA SRRT

Miller Anne M. • Reference Librarian • Bellevue Community College • Bellevue, WA 98007 • EMIERT SRRT

Miller Anne T. • Children's Librarian • Watertown Public Library • Watertown, WI 53094

Miller Annie D. • Librarian • Chicago Public Library • Chicago, IL 60605

Miller Anthony G. • Music Sub Spec/Librarian II • Atlanta-Fulton Public Library • Atlanta, GA 30303 • PLA

Miller Arthur H. • College Librarian • Lake Forest College Donnelley Library • Lake Forest, IL 60045 • ACRL ALCTS RASD GODORT

Miller Barbara • Trustee • Mid-Continent Public Library • Independence, MO 64050 • ALTA

Miller Barbara A. • Director of Library Services • Jennings, Strouss & Salmon • Phoenix, AZ 85004-2393 • AASL LAMA

Miller Barbara A. • Student • University of California Los Angeles Graduate School of Library & Information Science • Los Angeles, CA 90024 • ACRL IRRT

Miller Barbara J. • Keokuk, IA 52632

Miller Barbara S. • Deputy University Librarian • James Madison University Carrier Library • Harrisonburg, VA 22807 • ACRL LAMA

Miller Barbara S. Mrs. • Trustee • Louisville Free Public Library • Louisville, KY 40203-2257 • ALSC ALTA

Miller Bertha N. • Ormond Beach, FL 32174 • Continuing

Miller Betty D. • Tallahassee, FL 32312 • ALSC

Miller Betty S. • Albion, NY 14411

Miller Bonnie R. • Elementary Librarian • C-EB Upper Elementary School • Eagale Butte, SD 57625

Miller Bradford S. • Librarian • Thousand Oaks Library • Thousand Oaks, CA 91362 • ACRL

Miller Brita J. • AV Librarian • Canyon Del Oro High Sch • Tucson, AZ 85704

Miller Bruce • Huntington, NY 11743

Miller C. Martin Mr • Head, Special Clln & Archives. • Miami University Acq Dept. • Oxford, OH 45056 • ACRL RASD *Life*

Miller Candace Y. • Reference Librarian • James Madison University • Harrisonburg, VA 22807 • ACRL IFRT

Miller Caroline J. • Naval Postgraduate School Dudley Knox Library • Monterey, CA 93943-5002

Miller Carolyn • Librarian • Sahuarita Elementary School • Sahuarita, AZ 85629 • AASL

Miller Catherine L. • Librarian-Lower & Middle School • Princeton Day School • Princeton, NJ 08542 • AASL ALSC

Miller Cathleen E. • Graduate Student • University of Rhode Island Graduate School of Library & Information Studies • Kingston, RI 02881-0815 • LITA SRRT

Miller Charles E. • Director • Florida State University Robert M. Strozier Library • Tallahassee, FL 32306-2047 • ACRL

Miller Charlotte B. • Director • Mount Pleasant Public Library • Pleasantville, NY 10570 • LAMA PLA

Miller Christina W. • Prevention Research Center Library • Berkeley, CA 94704 • LITA

Miller Cynthia M. • Special Project Librarian • County of Los Angeles Public Library • Downey, CA 90241-7400 • PLA

Miller Daniel J. • Senior Account Manager • Blackwell North America • Lake Oswego, OR 97034 • ALCTS LITA

Miller David A • Ohio University Vernon R. Alden Library • Athens, OH 45701-2978 • ALCTS IRRT

Miller David P • Cataloging • Emerson College Library • Boston, MA 02116 • ALCTS LRRT

Miller Deborah • Trustee • Schaumburg Township District Library • Schaumburg, IL 60194 • ALTA ASCLA PLA

Miller Denise C. • Librarian • Thacher School • Ojai, CA 93023 • AASL
Miller Diane K. • Librarian III • Dayton & Montgomery County Public Library Wilmington-Stroop Branch • Kettering, OH 45429
Miller Donna L. • Librarian • Lebanon Valley College • Annville, PA 17003
Miller Donna P. • Coor. Lib./Media Services • Mesquite Independent School District • Mesquite, TX 75149
Miller Doris A. • Head of Reference • Northern Illinois University University Libraries • DeKalb, IL 60115-2868 • ACRL LAMA
Miller Dorothy R. • Newark, DE 19711
Miller Edna Miss • Indianapolis, IN 46234 • Continuing
Miller Edward P. • Payson Public Library • Payson, AZ 85541 • LAMA PLA RASD IFRT *Continuing*
Miller Elaine N. • Northampton, MA 01060 • ACRL ILERT
Miller Eleanor R. • Aiken, SC 29801
Miller Elissa R. • Adult Services Librarian • Oakland Public Library • Oakland, CA 94612 • PLA RASD EMIERT SRRT
Miller Elizabeth • Woodbury, CT 06798 • Continuing
Miller Ellen G. • Ellen Miller Group • Lenexa, KS 66215 • PLA
Miller Ellen L. • Managing Librarian • Spokane County Library District • Spokane, WA 99212-1853
Miller Elsa A. • Circulation Librarian • Southern Baptist Theological Seminary Library • Louisville, KY 40280
Miller Elyse D. • Student • University of Iowa School of Library & Information Science • Iowa City, IA 52242 • IFRT
Miller Emily G. • Public Services Libn. • Missouri Historical Society • Saint Louis, MO 63112-0040 • ACRL RASD
Miller Emma L. • Head of Public Services • Huntsville-Madison County Public Library • Huntsville, AL 35804 • PLA
Miller Eve-Marie • Student • Simmons College Graduate School of Library & Information Science • Boston, MA 02115 • ALSC
Miller Everett G. Sr. • President • McKendree School of Religion • Baltimore, MD 21215 • SRRT
Miller Faye M. • United States Air Force Libraries • Randolph AFB, TX 78150-6001 • AFLRT FLRT
Miller Floyd W. • Shepherdstown, WV 25443
Miller Fran • Student • Arkansas School for the Deaf • Little Rock, AR 72203
Miller Fran V. • Head of Circulation • Tippecanoe County Public Library • Lafayette, IN 47901
Miller Frances A. • Baton Rouge, LA 70808 • YALSA
Miller Frank W. • H. W. Wilson Company • Bronx, NY 10452 • AASL ACRL ALCTS ASCLA LAMA LITA PLA RASD ERT
Miller George Anne H. • Assistant Librarian • Tigard Public Library • Tigard, OR 97223 • PLA
Miller George M. • Director • Austin Preparatory School • Reading, MA 01867 • AASL YALSA IFRT
Miller Gina • Librarian • Valley Grove Elementary School • Charleston, WV 25302 • ALSC
Miller Glenn F. Mr • Director • Orange County Library System Orlando Public Library • Orlando, FL 32801-2471 • LAMA PLA *Life*
Miller Gloria • Media Supervisor • Charlotte-Mecklenburg Schools • Charlotte, NC 28205 • AASL
Miller Gloria A. • Librarian • Air Force Office of Scientific Research • Bolling AFB, DC 20332-6448 • AFLRT FLRT
Miller Gordon W. • Information Services Librarian • James Madison University Carrier Library • Harrisonburg, VA 22807 • ACRL RASD GODORT
Miller Gregory M. • Librarian II • Toledo-Lucas County Public Library • Toledo, OH 43624
Miller Harold E. • Trustee • Ramapo Catskill Library System • Middletown, NY 10940
Miller Heather S. • Librarian • University at Albany Libraries • Albany, NY 12222 • ACRL ALCTS
Miller Helen M. • Chief Extension Division • Free Library of Philadelphia • Philadelphia, PA 19103 • LAMA
Miller Helen M. • Boise, ID 83703 • ASCLA *Continuing*
Miller Helen R. • Assitant Head of Acquisitions • University of North Carolina • Chapel Hill, NC 27599-3902 • ACRL ALCTS
Miller Hester M. • Albuquerque, NM 87111 • Continuing
Miller Howard E. • Assistant Librarian • Blue Cross/Blue Shield of Missouri • St. Louis, MO 63108 • IFRT
Miller Inabeth • Executive Director • Massachusetts Corporation of Educational Telecommunication • Cambridge, MA 02139-4135
Miller Ingrid O. Miss • Library Consultant • Edina Public Schools • Edina, MN 55435 • AASL YALSA *Life*
Miller J. Gormly • Cornell University Industrial and Labor Relations Library • Ithaca, NY 14853 • ACRL
Miller Jack E. Dr. • Museum Librarian • High Museum of Art • Atlanta, GA 30309
Miller Jacqueline C. • Children's Librarian • Rockingham County Public Library • Eden, NC 27288 • ALSC PLA
Miller Jacqueline E. • Director • Yonkers Public Library • Yonkers, NY 10701 • PLA
Miller Jane • Student • Louisiana State University School of Library & Information Science • Baton Rouge, LA 70803-3290 • PLA
Miller Janet L. • Student • Utah Valley Community College • Orem, UT 84058 • ALCTS LITA
Miller Janice M. • Antioch College • Yellow Spring, OH 45387 • SRRT
Miller Jean Elizabeth • Director of Media Services • Western School Corporation • Russiaville, IN 46979 • AASL
Miller Jeannie Dr. • Science Reference Librarian • Texas A & M University Sterling C. Evans Library • College Station, TX 77843-5000 • ACRL
Miller Jerome K. • Friday Harbor, WA 98250
Miller Jessie D. • Student • University of Wisconsin-Milwaukee School of Library & Information Science • Milwaukee, WI 53201
Miller Jill C. • Director • Kirkwood College Library • Cedar Rapids, IA 52406 • ACRL LAMA LITA
Miller John Edward • Dir. of Tech. & Instr. Resources • City Schs Educational Tech Ctr • Troy, OH 45373 • AASL
Miller John S. • Automation Librarian • University of Kansas Watson Library • Lawrence, KS 66045-2800 • ACRL ALCTS LITA LRRT
Miller John V. • University of Akron Bierce Library • Akron, OH 44325-1706 • ACRL
Miller Johnnye M. • Librarian • Archbold Area Local School District • Archbold, OH 43502 • AASL
Miller Jonathan • Student • Rochester Institute of Technology Wallace Memorial Library • Rochester, NY 14623-0887 • ACRL RASD SRRT
Miller Joseph B. • Student • University of Kentucky College of Library & Information Science • Lexington, KY 40506-0391 • LITA
Miller Joseph R. • Cataloger • H.W. Wilson Company • Bronx, NY 10452 • ACRL
Miller Joyce • Librarian • Warrensburg High School Library • Warrensburg, MO 64093 • AASL
Miller Joyce A. • Public Services Librarian • Trinity College • Burlington, VT 05401
Miller Juanita F. • Librarian • Albany State College Margaret Rood Hazard Library • Albany, GA 31705 • ACRL
Miller Judith B. • New Rochelle, NY 10804
Miller Judith K. • Serials Librarian • Valparaiso University Moellering Memorial Library • Valparaiso, IN 46383 • ALCTS LITA
Miller Judy E. • Lawrence, KS 66046 • ACRL RASD *Life*
Miller Karen • Lawrence Junior High School • Falmouth, MA 02540 • AASL YALSA
Miller Karen L. • Head, Circulation Services • San Diego State University Library • San Diego, CA 92182-0511
Miller Karl F. • Librarian • University of Texas • Austin, TX 78712-1276 • ACRL LAMA
Miller Katherine E. • Asst Professor of Lib Science • Drury College Library • Springfield, MO 65802 • ACRL NMRT
Miller Kathy A. • Business Planner • IBM Corporation Dept. 53Q • Rochester, MN 55901 • LAMA LRRT
Miller Kay L. • Librarian • Sacred Heart School • Danville, VA 24541
Miller Kent E. • Serials Librarian • University of Kansas Library • Lawrence, KS 66045-2800
Miller L. H. • Media Specialist • Warner Middle School • Farmington Hills, MI 48334
Miller L. Nadene • Public Service Librarian • University of Portland Clark Memorial Library • Portland, OR 97203-5798 • ACRL
Miller Larry Alan Dr. • Director • Chandler-Gilbert College Learning Resource Center • Chandler, AZ 85225 • ACRL
Miller Laurence A. • University Director • Florida International University • Miami, FL 33199 • ACRL ASCLA LAMA IFRT
Miller Laurence H. Mr • Special Language Department Head • University of Illinois Graduate School of Library and Information Science • Urbana, IL 61801 • ACRL ALCTS *Life*
Miller Leslie C. • Coordinator, Library Media Prog. • Escambia County School District • Pensacola, FL 32503
Miller Lewis R. • Associate Director • Gonzaga University Crosby Library • Spokane, WA 99258 • ACRL LAMA LRRT
Miller Lillie B. • Associate Librarian • Arlington Public Library • Arlington, TX 76010 • ALCTS
Miller Linda C. • Reference Librarian • Kanawha County Public Library • Charleston, WV 25301 • RASD GODORT
Miller Linda D. • Library of Congress • Washington, DC 20541 • ALCTS LITA
Miller Linda K. • Rockford, IL 61107 • LITA
Miller Linda L • Lexington, NE 68850 • ALTA
Miller Linda L. • Librarian/Research Associate • University of Central Florida • Orlando, FL 32816 • LITA
Miller Linda R.H. • Technical Services Librarian • Cornell University Library • Ithaca, NY 14853-5301 • ALCTS NMRT
Miller Lisa K. • Computer Services/Ref. Libn • American Graduate School of International Management Barton K Yount Memorial Library • Glendale, AZ 85306 • LITA
Miller Liz R. • Deputy Director • Tucson Pima Library • Tucson, AZ 85726 • LAMA PLA
Miller Lois V. • St Charles, IL 60174
Miller Lola M. • Charlotte, TN 37036 • YALSA *Continuing*
Miller Lola R. • Branch Manager • Cabell County Public Library West Huntington Public Library • Huntington, WV 25704
Miller Lorraine K. • Owings Mills, MD 21117
Miller Louise B. • Library Media Specialist • Round Valley School • Lebanon, NJ 08833 • AASL LRRT
Miller Lucy F. • Council Bluff, IA 51503 • AASL YALSA *Continuing*
Miller Lynne K. • Assistant Director • Sachem Public Library • Holbrook, NY 11741
Miller M. Ann • Reference Librarian • College of The Mainland Learning Resources Center • Texas City, TX 77591 • ACRL RASD LIRT
Miller M. R. • Ft Lauderdale, FL 33317-1850 • NMRT
Miller Marcia I. Miss • Kinderhook, NY 12106 • ALCTS PLA *Continuing*
Miller Marcia J. • Chevy Chase, MD 20815 • ALCTS RASD
Miller Margaret • Rare Materials Catalog Libn • Duke University William R. Perkins Library • Durham, NC 27706 • ACRL
Miller Margaret • Birmingham, AL 35205 • Continuing
Miller Margaret H. • Sherman Oaks, CA 91423 • AASL ALSC YALSA EMIERT *Continuing*
Miller Margery • Eveleth-Gilbert Senior High School • Eveleth, MN 55734 • AASL
Miller Margo M. • Massachusetts Institute of Technology Libraries (MIT) • Cambridge, MA 02139 • ACRL
Miller Mari T. • Associate Librarian • University of California-Berkeley Moffitt Undergraduate Library • Berkeley, CA 94720 • ACRL LITA GODORT
Miller Maria S. • Student • University of North Carolina Department of Library & Information Studies • Greensboro, NC 27412-5001
Miller Marian I. • Reference Librarian • Augustana College Library • Rock Island, IL 61201 • ACRL RASD
Miller Marilyn • Library Director • Eastern Wyoming College • Torrington, WY 82240 • ACRL LAMA LIRT
Miller Marilyn E. • Lake Lanier Regional Library Lawrenceville Branch • Lawrenceville, GA 30245
Miller Marilyn L. • Professor & Chair • University of North Carolina Department of Library & Information Studies • Greensboro, NC 27412-5001 • AASL ALSC ALTA LAMA PLA YALSA LRRT
Miller Marilyn R. • Children's Librarian • Dallas Public Library Lakewood Branch • Dallas, TX 75216-4448 • ALSC
Miller Marjorie • Pittsburgh, PA 15238
Miller Marjorie E. • Trevor, WI 53179 • AASL YALSA *Life*
Miller Marlyn M. • Kranz Intermediate School • El Monte, CA 91732 • AASL YALSA
Miller Marsha A. • Instruction Librarian • Indiana State University Cunningham Memorial Library • Terre Haute, IN 47809 • ACRL LIRT
Miller Martha • Director • Carnegie Public Library District • La Harpe, IL 61450
Miller Martha Lou • Director • Delphi Public Library • Delphi, IN 46923 • PLA
Miller Mary Ann • Librarian • Suffolk Community College Eastern Campus Library • Riverhead, NY 11901-9990 • ACRL
Miller Mary Celine • Director • Robert Morris College Library • Coraopolis, PA 15108-1189 • ACRL ALCTS LAMA LITA RASD
Miller Mary D.S. • Lake Stevens Elementary School • Miami, FL 33055 • AASL
Miller Mary E. • University of Pittsburgh Hillman Library • Pittsburgh, PA 15260 • ACRL GODORT
Miller Mary F. • Library Specialist • Campus America, Inc. • Knoxville, TN 37915
Miller Mary J. • Branch Head Librarian • Akron-Summit County Public Library Green Branch • Greensburg, OH 44232 • PLA
Miller Mary Jo • Librarian • Otranto Road Regional Branch Library • North Charleston, SC 29418
Miller Mary Lou • Senior Automation Planning Spec. • Library of Congress • Washington, DC 20541 • ALCTS LITA
Miller Mary Lynn M. • Graduate Student • University of Washington Graduate School of Library and Information Science • Seattle, WA 98195 • ALSC IFRT SRRT

Miller Mary M. • Media Specialist/Librarian • Wachter School Media Center • Bismarck, ND 58504 • AASL

Miller Melanie A. • Director • Hays Public Library • Hays, KS 67601 • PLA

Miller Merlyn • Burr and Burton Seminary • Manchester, VT 05254

Miller Michael D. • Head Librarian • Stanford University J. Henry Meyer Memorial Library • Stanford, CA 94305 • ACRL LITA

Miller Michael J. • Bethlehem, PA 18015 • ACRL SRRT

Miller Michael K. • Walker Technical Institute • Rock Spring, GA 30739

Miller Michael M. • Bibliographer • North Dakota State University Library • Fargo, ND 58105-5599 • ACRL IRRT

Miller Mildred V. • Bridgewater, VA 22812-1325 • Continuing

Miller Nancy • Dallas, TX 75243

Miller Nancy G. • Library Assistant, Cataloger • Ashland High School • Ashland, OR 97520

Miller Nancy M. • Clln Management Bibliographer • Virginia Beach Public Library Central Library • Virginia Beach, VA 23452 • VRT

Miller Norma Burrus • Lexington Public Library Emrath Lansdowne Branch • Lexington, KY 40502 • PLA

Miller Opal • Librarian • Live Oak County Library • George West, TX 78022

Miller Patricia A • Head of Circulation Department • Lima Public Library • Lima, OH 45801 • PLA

Miller Patricia M. • Librarian • New York State School for the Deaf • Rome, NY 13440 • RASD

Miller Patti A. • Assistant Director • Colon Township Library • Colon, MI 49040

Miller Paulette S. • Librarian • Fairview Elementary School • Fairfax Station, VA 22039 • AASL

Miller Pearl A. • B C L Schools • Conrad, IA 50621

Miller Pearl Ann • Retirement Bureau • Lansing, MI 48909

Miller Phyllis K. • Branch Librarian • Monmouth County Library Holmdel Branch • Holmdel, NJ 07757 • IFRT

Miller R. Bruce • AUL-Technical Services • University of California-San Diego • La Jolla, CA 92093-0175 • ALCTS LAMA LITA

Miller Rachel B. • Head Acquisition Dept • University of Kansas Watson Library • Lawrence, KS 66045-2800 • ACRL ALCTS

Miller Rachel Dahmm • Boody, IL 62514

Miller Randy L. • Head Librarian • Pillsbury College Library • Owatonna, MN 55060 • ACRL

Miller Randy S. • York, PA 17403

Miller Rex F. • Director • Petoskey Public Library • Petoskey, MI 49770 • PLA

Miller Rhonda R. • New London, IA 52645 • ALSC PLA

Miller Richard A. • Technical Services Administrator • Dallas Public Library • Dallas, TX 75201 • PLA

Miller Richard F. • Director • AKZO Chemicals Inc. • Fairfield, CT 06430 • ALCTS

Miller Richard T. Jr. • State Librarian • Montana State Library • Helena, MT 59620 • ASCLA

Miller Robert • Curator,Harsh Research Clln • Chicago Public Library Carter G. Woodson Regional Library • Chicago, IL 60628 • ACRL

Miller Robert C. • Director of Libraries • University of Notre Dame Libraries • Notre Dame, IN 46556 • ACRL LAMA LITA

Miller Robert H. Dr • Sorrento, FL 32776 • AASL

Miller Ron • Library Board Chairman • Spokane Public Library Comstock Building Library • Spokane, WA 99201-0976 • ALTA

Miller Ronald F. • Executive Director • Western Library Network (WLN) • Lacey, WA 98503-0888 • LITA

Miller Rosa G. • Student • Broward County Division of Libraries Broward County Library • Fort Lauderdale, FL 33301 • PLA IFRT SRRT

Miller Rosalind E. • Professor • Georgia State University Pullen Library • Atlanta, GA 30303-3081 • AASL

Miller Rosanna • Head of Map Collection • Arizona State University Libraries • Tempe, AZ 85287-1006 • ACRL MAGERT

Miller Rosemary I. • Scottsdale, AZ 85251 • AASL

Miller Roy D. Jr • Assistant to The Director • Brooklyn Public Library • Brooklyn, NY 11238 • LAMA PLA

Miller Ruby E. • Assistant Director • Trinity University • San Antonio, TX 78212 • ALCTS LITA

Miller Rush G. • Dean of Libraries • Bowling Green State University William Jerome Library • Bowling Green, OH 43403-0175 • ACRL LAMA

Miller Ruth • Administrative Librarian • Murray State University • Murray, KY 42071-3309

Miller Ruth H. • Head, Clln Devlp Dept. • Hong Kong University of Science & Technology University Library • Kowloon, Hong Kong • ACRL ALCTS

Miller Ruth Miss • Rochester, NY 14610 • Continuing

Miller Sally Gray • Assistant Manager • Lexington Public Library • Lexington, KY 40507

Miller Sara L. • Young Adult Consultant • Nassau Library System • Uniondale, NY 11553 • ALSC

Miller Sarah Jordan • Professor Emerita • Rutgers University School of Communication Information & Library Studies • New Brunswick, NJ 08903 • ACRL GODORT

Miller Sheila D. • Librarian • Muskegon County Library Norton Shores Branch • Muskegon, MI 49441 • PLA

Miller Shelby M. • Jacksonville, FL 32211

Miller Shelley • University of Kansas Library • Lawrence, KS 66045-2800

Miller Shirley • Reference Librarian • Kalamazoo Public Library • Kalamazoo, MI 49007-5270 • PLA RASD *Life*

Miller Sondra J. • Librarian • Pleasant Plains Middle/ Senior High School • Pleasant Plains, IL 62677 • AASL

Miller Stephen G. • Fort Wayne, IN 46802 • SRRT

Miller Stephen R. • Assistant City Librarian • New Haven Free Public Library • New Haven, CT 06510

Miller Steve • Student • San Jose State University Division of Library & Information Science • San Jose, CA 95192-0029

Miller Steven R. • Law Librarian • Burke, Wilson & McIlvaine • Chicago, IL 60661-2511

Miller Stuart W. • Professional Services • NOTIS Systems, Inc. • Evanston, IL 60201-3622 • ACRL ALCTS LAMA LITA ERT

Miller Susan C. • Assistant Director • Brownell Library • Essex Junction, VT 05452

Miller Susan E. • Reference Librarian • Washington State Historical Society Henry Hewitt Research Library • Tacoma, WA 98403

Miller Susan G. • Coor. of Library Instruction • Illinois State University Milner Library • Normal, IL 61761-0900 • ACRL

Miller Susan M. • Student • Syracuse University Library E. S. Bird Library • Syracuse, NY 13244-2010 • ALCTS LITA

Miller Suzanne • Chula Vista Public Library • Chula Vista, CA 91910 • ALTA

Miller Sylvia G. • Kinston, NC 28501 • AASL

Miller Tamara J. • Head of Library Automation • University of Tennessee Library • Knoxville, TN 37996-1000 • LITA

Miller Thayer A. • Student, LMS • Appleby Elementary School • Marathon, NY 13803 • AASL

Miller Thomas B. • Senior Media Assistant • Austin Community College Rio Grande Campus • Austin, TX 78701

Miller Thurston D. • Kennewick, WA 99336 • ACRL

Miller Velda A. • Assistant Director • Indiana State University • Terre Haute, IN 47809 • LAMA

Miller Vicki Smith • Reference/Information • Winston-Salem State University • Winston-Salem, NC 27110 • LIRT

Miller Vickie • Librarian • Crystal City Elementary School Library • St. Louis, MO 63019

Miller Victoria B. • Pre School Teacher • AJCC Sunshine School • Marietta, GA 30062

Miller Vivian • Trustee • Millwood Elementary School • Oklahoma City, OK 73111 • ALTA PLA

Miller Wendy A. • Student • University of California Los Angeles Graduate School of Library & Information Science • Los Angeles, CA 90024 • IFRT IRRT

Miller Whitney • Student • University of South Carolina College of Library & Information Science • Columbia, SC 29208

Miller William • Director of Libraries • Florida Atlantic University S.E. Wimberly Library • Boca Raton, FL 33431 • ACRL ASCLA LAMA LITA RASD

Miller William C. • Librarian • Nazarene Theological Seminary • Kansas City, MO 64131

Millet Norris J. • Trustee • Saint John the Baptist Parish Library • LaPlace, LA 70068 • ALTA

Millette M. Elizabeth • Student • Catholic University of America School of Library and Information Science • Washington, DC 20064 • PLA

Millhouser Frances E. • Assistant Regional Librarian • Fairfax County Public Library Fairfax City Regional Branch • Fairfax, VA 22030 • LAMA PLA

Millican Annie Ruth • Baton Rouge, LA 70806

Milliken Linda A. • W. S. Mount School • Stony Brook, NY 11755

Milliken Ruth L. • Cocoa Beach, FL 32931-2605 • Continuing

Milling David C. • Culbertson Jacobs & Milling Architects • Ann Arbor, MI 48104 • LAMA

Milling Marian C. • Adult Services Librarian • Ela Area Public Library District • Lake Zurich, IL 60047 • PLA

Million Angela C. • Reference Librarian • University of Oklahoma Libraries University Libraries • Norman, OK 73019 • ACRL GODORT IFRT IRRT

Milliot Christy L. • Automation Consultant • Houston Area Library Automated Network • Houston, TX 77002 • LITA PLA IFRT SRRT

Milliron Annette M. • Administrator • North Bay Cooperative • Santa Rosa, CA 95404 • ASCLA LAMA PLA

Millis Jonathan • Student • Rochester Institute of Technology Wallace Memorial Library • Rochester, NY 14623-0887 • LITA

Millis Kathryn Courtland • Reference Librarian • DePauw University Roy O. West Library • Greencastle, IN 46135-0037 • LAMA

Millius Paul P. • Trustee • Paul Millius Associates • Portland, OR 97232 • ALTA

Millman Carolyn A. • Library Director • Strake Jesuit College Preparatory Moody Memorial Library • Houston, TX 77036

Millman Lorrie L. • New York, NY 10024

Millon-Levin Adrienne • Archivist • New York University Medical Library • New York, NY 10016 • ACRL NMRT

Millrod Leslie J. • Coram, NY 11727 • ALSC

Mills Barry P. • Librarian • Santa Clara County Free Library Saratoga Commmunity Library • Saratoga, CA 95070

Mills Bruce E. • Technical Svcs./Reference Libn. • Kellogg Community College Learning Resource Center • Battle Creek, MI 49017-3397 • ALCTS IFRT

Mills Cliff • Information Center Manager • Catalytica Inc • Mountain View, CA 94043

Mills Cynthia • Osterville Free Library • Osterville, MA 02655 • LAMA LITA PLA RASD

Mills David L. • Branch Librarian • Brooklyn Public Library • Brooklyn, NY 11238

Mills Denise Y. • School Librarian • Bloomington High School • Bloomington, CA 92316 • AASL

Mills Douglas E. • Missoula, MT 59801 • Continuing

Mills Elizabeth A. • Teacher-Librarian • Milton Elementary School • Milton, MA 02156 • AASL ALSC

Mills Grace M. • Professor • CUNY Law School • Flushing, NY 11367 • RASD

Mills Jane P. • Coordinator of Technical Servs. • University of Tulsa McFarlin Library • Tulsa, OK 74104-3189 • ACRL ALCTS

Mills Jean T. • Cataloger • Library of Congress • Washington, DC 20541 • FLRT

Mills Karen E. • Student • University of North Carolina at Chapel Hill School of Information and Library Science • Chapel Hill, NC 27599-3360 • AASL

Mills Linda • Media Specialist • Billings Elementary School • Greensburg, IN 47240 • AASL

Mills Lois P. • Macomb, IL 61455 • ACRL ALCTS GODORT IFRT SRRT *Life*

Mills Olga A. • Saint Clairsville, OH 43950 • RASD

Mills Peggy A. • Director,LRC • Truckee Meadows Community College Learning Resources Center • Reno, NV 89512 • ACRL

Mills Robin K. • Librarian • Emory University Law Library • Atlanta, GA 30322 • ACRL ALCTS LAMA LITA RASD

Mills Robin K. • IMC Director • Spash, IMC • Stevens Point, WI 54481 • AASL

Mills Rolland W. • Rio Piedras, PR 00923 • ALCTS

Mills Susan W. • A-V Librarian • Liverpool Public Library • Liverpool, NY 13088

Mills Victoria A. • University of Arizona Library • Tucson, AZ 85721 • ACRL ALCTS

Millsap Gina J. • Head, of Computer Services • Daniel Boone Regional Library • Columbia, MO 65205-1267 • LITA IFRT

Millsap Larry D. • Head of Bibliographic Records • University of California-Santa Cruz Library • Santa Cruz, CA 95064 • ALCTS LITA SRRT

Millson-Martula Christopher • Assistant Director • Arizona State University-West Fletcher Library • Phoenix, AZ 85069-7100 • ACRL LAMA

Millwood Kent • Director • Anderson College Library Johnston Memorial Library • Anderson, SC 29621

Milman Jackie A. • Librarian • Fairfield School • Van Nuys, CA 91406

Milnarich-Garett Sarah H. • Student • Florida State University School of Library and Information Studies • Tallahassee, FL 32306-2048 • EMIERT IFRT IRRT SRRT

Milne Elizabeth B. • Hilton Head Island, SC 29928

Milne Sally J. • Goshen College • Goshen, IN 46526 • ACRL LITA RASD LIRT

Milner Devin C. • Head,Reference Department • Mesa College Library • San Diego, CA 92111 • ACRL

Milner Gail L. • Branch Manager/Librarian • Public Library of Columbus and Franklin County Shepard Branch Lib. • Columbus, OH 43219 • PLA EMIERT

Milner Lesley A. • Head of Access Services • Ball State University Bracken Library • Muncie, IN 47306-0160 • LAMA RASD

Milner Olive W. • Elementary Media Specialist • Arkansas City U.S.D. #470 • Arkansas City, KS 67005 • AASL

Milnes Patricia C. • Director • Lindenhurst Memorial Library • Lindenhurst, NY 11757 • LAMA
Milnor Ann C. • Adult Librarian • Dallas Public Library Renner-Frankford Branch • Dallas, TX 75252-5747
Milo Albert J. • Fullerton Public Library • Fullerton, CA 92632 • LAMA PLA
Milszyn Natalia • Reference Librarian • Seton Hall University • South Orange, NJ 07079-2690
Milton A. Denise • Director • Demopolis Public Library • Demopolis, AL 36732
Milton April M. • Librarian • State Library of Louisiana • Baton Rouge, LA 70821-0131 • NMRT
Milton Betty L. • Head Librarian • Trinity Christian Academy • Addison, TX 75248 • AASL
Milton Donna R. • Farmers Branch Public Library • Farmers Branch, TX 75234 • ALTA
Milton Linda J. • Tucson, AZ 85730
Milum Betty L. • Reference Librarian • Ohio State University • Lima, OH 45807 • ACRL LHRT
Mims Gloria J. • African American Studies Spec. • Atlanta-Fulton Public Library • Atlanta, GA 30303 • ACRL EMIERT IRRT
Mims Judith • Caesar Rodney High School • Camden, DE 19934 • AASL
Minami Atsumi • San Francisco, CA 94131
Minar Kathryn Sr • Rochester, MN 55903
Mincey Cynthia C. • Media Specialist • Southwest High School • Macon, GA 31206 • YALSA
Minch-Kelly Valorie A. • Head of Cataloging • Westfield State College Ely Memorial Library • Westfield, MA 01086 • ALCTS
Minch Linda J. • Reference Librarian • Gilbert Public Library • Gilbert, AZ 85234 • PLA
Mindeman George A. • Library Director • John Brown University Library Arutunoff Learning Resource Center • Siloam Spring, AR 72761 • ACRL
Minehart Shirley H. • Alexandria, VA 22304 • ALCTS RASD
Minemier Betty M. • Dansville, NY 14437
Miner Afton M. • Education Librarian • Brigham Young University Harold B. Lee Library • Provo, UT 84602
Miner Deborah D. • Librarian • Stanford Gibson Elementary School LMC • Norwich, NY 13815 • AASL
Miner Fern P. • Director • Lebanon Public Library • Lebanon, IN 46052 • LAMA PLA
Miner Nancy W. • Data Research Associates Inc. • Saint Louis, MO 63132 • LITA
Minerva Jane R. • Director • Cutchogue Free Library • Cutchogue, NY 11935
Minervino Louise • New Jersey State Library Department of Education • Trenton, NJ 08625-0520 • ACRL ASCLA PLA IFRT
Minges James D. • Library Development Director • Nebraska Library Commission • Lincoln, NE 68508 • ASCLA
Minges M. Sue • Branch & Extension Assistant • Dayton & Montgomery County Public Library • Dayton, OH 45402-2103
Mingin Margaret Mary A. • Director of Media • School District of South Orange- Maplewood • Maplewood, NJ 07040 • AASL
Mingle Jeffrey W. • General Accident Insurance InformationServices Library • Philadelphia, PA 19105-1109 • LITA
Minick A Rachel • Chambersburg, PA 17201 • ACRL ALCTS *Continuing*
Minick Donna J. • Branch Manager • Santa Ana Public Library Newhope Branch • Santa Ana, CA 92703
Minick Evelyn C. • Director • Philadelphia College of Textiles & Science Senator John Pastore Library • Philadelphia, PA 19144 • ACRL LAMA PLA
Minick Mary Beth • Associate Librarian • Indiana University-Purdue University at Indianapolis Library (IUPUI) • Indianapolis, IN 46202 • ACRL RASD
Minihan Charles E. • DeKalb College Central Campus Library • Clarkston, GA 30021-2396
Minkel Lester M. • Newtown, PA 18940 • ACRL RASD *Continuing*
Minkler Leslie R. • Information Specialist/Editor • United Way of New York City • New York, NY 10016 • RASD SRRT
Minkow Mildred • Trustee • Bloomfield Township Public Library • Bloomfield Hills, MI 48302-2437 • ALTA
Minnich Conrad H. • Librarian • Exempted Village High School District Library • Versailles, OH 45380 • AASL LITA
Minnich Nancy P. • Tower Hill School Library • Wilmington, DE 19806
Minnick Nelle F. • Fresno, CA 93704 • Continuing
Minnick Roy • Sacramento, CA 95814 • MAGERT
Minnis Mary Lee • Head of Youth Services • Meadville Public Library • Meadville, PA 16335 • ALSC YALSA
Minniti Rosa A. • Student • Kent State University School of Library & Information Science • Kent, OH 44242-0001
Minor Jane C. • John F. Kennedy University • Walnut Creek, CA 94596
Minor Joyce A. • Technical Services Librarian • Thiel College • Greenville, PA 16125 • IFRT
Minor William M. • Student • North Carolina Central University School of Library & Information Science • Durham, NC 27707 • IFRT SRRT
Minott Laurel L. • Head, Govt. Documents • Michigan State University Libraries • East Lansing, MI 48824-1048 • ACRL LAMA GODORT LRRT SRRT
Minow Mary R. • Adult Services • Santa Clara County Free Library Cupertino Public Library • Cupertino, CA 95014 • Life
Minowitz A. Maria • Glendale, MO 63122
Minson Colleen • Trustee • Salt Lake City Public Library • Salt Lake City, UT 84111 • ALTA
Mintel Richard H. Rev. • Librarian • Trinity Lutheran Seminary Hamma Library • Columbus, OH 43209 • ACRL
Minter Elizabeth D. • Director • Placentia Library District • Placentia, CA 92670 • LAMA PLA
Minter Jennifer M. • Librarian • Dona Ana Community College • Las Cruces, NM 88003
Minto Mary L. • Librarian • Palo Alto City Library • Palo Alto, CA 94303 • ALCTS LITA
Mintz Ellen M. • Librarian • Westridge School for Girls Library • Pasadena, CA 91105 • AASL
Mintz Graham W. • Senior Librarian • Kentucky State Penitentiary • Eddyville, KY 42038-0128 • ASCLA
Mintz Kenneth A. • Cataloger • Hoboken Public Library • Hoboken, NJ 07030 • ACRL ALCTS PLA CLENE IFRT ILERT LHRT LIRT LRRT
Mintz Louis • Chief Stack Maintenance And Delivery Div • The New York Public Library • New York, NY 10016 • ACRL
Mintz Mary M. • Head, Reference • The American University Library • Washington, DC 20016-8046 • ACRL RASD
Mintz Walter M. • Trustee • Merrick Public Library • Merrick, NY 11566 • PLA IFRT
Minudri Regina U. • Director • Berkeley Public Library • Berkeley, CA 94704 • ALSC LAMA PLA YALSA *Life*
Minyard Beverly D. • Richardson, TX 75081 • ALSC PLA
Miotto Mary Ann • Cos Cob, CT 06807
Mirabella Charlene M • Reference Librarian • D'Youville College Library • Buffalo, NY 14201
Mirabile Jacqueline H. • Reference Librarian • Villanova University Falvey Memorial Library • Villanova, PA 19085-1699 • ACRL RASD GODORT
Miraldi Patricia A. • Tacoma, WA 98467-2958
Miranda Sandra C. • Director • White Plains Public Library • White Plains, NY 10601 • ALTA LAMA LITA PLA RASD
Mirisola Ann Marie • Director • Derby Neck Library • Derby, CT 06418 • LAMA ILERT
Mirkovich Thomas R. • Business Reference Librarian • University of Nevada-Las Vegas James R. Dickinson Library • Las Vegas, NV 89154 • RASD IRRT LRRT
Mirsky Phyllis S. • Associate University Librarian • University of California-San Diego Library 0175A • La Jolla, CA 92093-0175 • ACRL LAMA LITA
Mirus Pegge • Librarian • Moeller High School • Cincinnati, OH 45242 • AASL
Mirza Melora P. • Librarian • DeKalb College Library • Clarkston, GA 30021 • ACRL
Misakian Jo E. • Fresno, CA 93727
Misasi John F. • Trustee • Melrose Park Public Library • Melrose Park, IL 60160
Misawa Michiko • Instructor • Shinshu Honan Women's Junior College • Naganoken 399-04, Japan
Misch Mary G. • Assistant Librarian • National Cathedral School • Washington, DC 20016 • AASL
Mischnick Carol J. • Fort Collins, CO 80526 • ALCTS
Mischo Lawrence H. • Manager, Automation Systems • Tacoma Public Library • Tacoma, WA 98402 • ALCTS LITA
Mischo William H. • Engineering Librarian • University of Illinois Library • Urbana, IL 61801 • ACRL LITA
Mish Joan • Media Specialist • Dodgeville Middle School • Dodgeville, WI 53533 • AASL
Mishra Ruicha • Sunrise, FL 33322
Mishra Veena • Student • University of Western Ontario School of Library & Information Science • London ON, N6G 1H1 Canada
Misiano Margaret • Library Media Specialist • Shoreham-Wading Senior High School Library Media Center • Shoreham, NY 11786 • AASL
Misirliyan Ared • University of Pennsylvania Library Van Pelt-Dietrich Library Center • Philadelphia, PA 19104-6206 • ACRL
Miskell Elizabeth S. • Automated Circ Proj Ln • Public Library of Cincinnati and Hamilton County • Cincinnati, OH 45202 • ASCLA
Misko Elaine J. • Carlow College • Pittsburgh, PA 15213 • ACRL ALCTS LAMA LITA LIRT
Misner Joyce V. • Mgr., Reader's Servs. Dept. • Allen County Public Library • Fort Wayne, IN 46801 • PLA IFRT
Misner Sophie G. • Trustee • Lake County Public Library • Merrillville, IN 46410-5382 • ALTA
Misra Jayasri T. • Stone Mountain, GA 30083 • PLA RASD EMIERT
Missar Charles D. • Washington, DC 20015 • RASD
Missavage Leonard • Chief, Library Division • Defense Equal Opportunity Management Institute • Patrick AFB, FL 32925 • AFLRT FLRT
Missbach Marilla • Trustee • Bedford Park Public Library District • Bedford Park, IL 60501 • ALTA PLA
Missel Fred • Trustee • Mesa Public Library • Mesa, AZ 85201-6768 • ALTA
Missner Michele • Librarian • Appleton Public Schools McKinley Elementary School • Appleton, WI 54915 • AASL
Missonis George E. • Director of A-V Services • Albright College • Reading, PA 19612-5234
Mistaras Evangeline • Chicago, IL 60640 • RASD *Continuing*
Mistele Yolan • Media Specialist • Lake Mills High School • Lake Mills, WI 53551 • AASL
Mistlebauer Holly L. • Student • University of Wisconsin-Milwaukee School of Library & Information Science • Milwaukee, WI 53201 • AFLRT IFRT NMRT SRRT
Mitch Bonnie S. • Catalog Librarian • University of Iowa Libraries • Iowa City, IA 52242-1379 • ACRL ALCTS
Mitch Kathryn A. • New York, NY 10011 • IFRT
Mitchell-Powell Brenda M. • Orange Ball Corporation • Westport, CT 06880 • ACRL PLA EMIERT
Mitchell-Tapping Nancy A. • Dallas, TX 75206
Mitchell Ann M. • Rollng Hl Est, CA 90274
Mitchell AnnMarie D. • Librarian for Polish Collection • University of California-Berkeley University Library • Berkeley, CA 94720
Mitchell Anne M. • Macon, GA 31204 • Continuing
Mitchell Aubrey H. • Associate Dean for Public Serv. • University of Tennessee Library • Knoxville, TN 37996-1000 • ACRL
Mitchell Audrey E. • Detroit, MI 48221-2577
Mitchell Barbara A. • Head of Access Services • Harvard College Library Widener Memorial Library • Cambridge, MA 02138 • ACRL LAMA
Mitchell Beth H. • Student • University of Kentucky College of Library & Information Science • Lexington, KY 40506-0391 • PLA NMRT
Mitchell Beth M. • Adminstrative Librarian • Mokena Community Public Library District • Mokena, IL 60448
Mitchell Betty Jo • Tehachapi, CA 93561
Mitchell Bonnie Beth • Columbus, OH 43206 • ALTA ASCLA PLA
Mitchell Bonnie J. • Circulation Librarian • Mohawk Valley Community College Library • Utica, NY 13501 • ACRL
Mitchell Carol L. • Curator, Southeast Asia Clln • University of Wisconsin-Madison Memorial Library • Madison, WI 53706 • EMIERT IRRT SRRT
Mitchell Christine M. • Assistant Chief • Library of Congress • Washington, DC 20541 • ALCTS LAMA GODORT
Mitchell Colleen • California State University,Fresno Henry Madden Library • Fresno, CA 93740-0034 • ALCTS
Mitchell Connie Jo Mrs. • IMC Director • Perry Meridian High School IMC • Indianapolis, IN 46217 • AASL ASCLA YALSA IFRT LIRT SRRT
Mitchell Deborah S. • Director • Warren County-Vicksburg Public Library • Vicksburg, MS 39180 • PLA
Mitchell Doris F. • Collection Development Librarian • University of North Carolina • Greensboro, NC 27412-5001 • RASD
Mitchell Elaine C. • Bloomingdale, IL 60108 • Continuing
Mitchell Eleanor • Information Delivery Specialist • Arizona State University-West Fletcher Library • Phoenix, AZ 85069-7100 • RASD
Mitchell Elizabeth • Student • University of South Florida School of Library & Information Science • Tampa, FL 33620 • ALSC
Mitchell Elizabeth Boyd • Library Media Specialist • Acworth Elementary School Library • Acworth, GA 30101 • AASL
Mitchell Eugene S. • Associate Director for Clln. • William Paterson College Sarah Byrd Askew Library • Wayne, NJ 07470 • ACRL ALCTS LAMA LITA LRRT
Mitchell Florence • San Francisco, CA 94127 • SRRT
Mitchell Frances S. • Columbus, GA 31904
Mitchell George D. III • Media Library Director • North Texas State University Libraries • Denton, TX 76203 • ACRL
Mitchell Gregory A. • Winchester, KY 40391 • PLA

Mitchell Gretchen E. • Jacksonville Public Library System Mandarin Branch • Jacksonville, FL 32257
Mitchell Hannah S. • San Francisco Public Library • San Francisco, CA 94102
Mitchell James L. • Frederiction, NB, E3B 2A4 Canada
Mitchell Joan S. • Dir.,Acad. Comp & Inst. Tech • Carnegie-Mellon University • Pittsburgh, PA 15213 • ACRL ALCTS LITA
Mitchell John N. • Head of Cataloging • Library of Congress • Washington, DC 20541
Mitchell Joyce L. • Director • Public Library of Johnston County & Smithfield • Smithfield, NC 27577 • LAMA PLA
Mitchell Joyce P. • Systems Librarian • Joint Computer Program for Libraries • Skokie, IL 60077
Mitchell Julie M. • Student • University of Western Ontario School of Library & Information Science • London ON, N6G 1H1 Canada
Mitchell June L. • Media Specialist • Webster Hill School • W Hartford, CT 06107 • AASL
Mitchell Karen S. • Clln Manager/Adm. Librarian • United States Information Agency (USIA) • Washington, DC 20547
Mitchell Katherine • Trustee • Central Arkansas Library System • Little Rock, AR 72201-4698 • ALTA
Mitchell Katherine A. • Student • Indiana University School of Library and Information Science • Bloomington, IN 47405
Mitchell Kathryn E. • Tallahassee, FL 32303 • AASL
Mitchell Laura • Escondido Public Library • Escondido, CA 92025 • LAMA PLA
Mitchell Lisa A. • Children's Librarian • Walkertown Branch Library • Walkertown, NC 27051 • ALSC
Mitchell Lorna K. • Librarian • Westminster College Reeves Memorial Library • Fulton, MO 65251-1299 • ACRL LAMA LITA RASD LIRT
Mitchell Margaret L. • Library Media Specialist • Indian Hollow Elementary School Library • Winchester, VA 22601 • AASL LIRT
Mitchell Margaret M. • Lincoln, NE 68506 • ACRL RASD
Mitchell Marilyn J. • Director • University of Puget Sound Collins Memorial Library • Tacoma, WA 98416 • ACRL ALCTS LAMA LITA
Mitchell Martha M. • Kittanning, PA 16201
Mitchell Mary Geli • Librarian II • Phoenix Public Library • Phoenix, AZ 85004
Mitchell Mary Lu • Trustee • Atlanta-Fulton Public Library • Atlanta, GA 30303 • PLA
Mitchell Mattie • Harrisburg, NC 28075
Mitchell Megan S. • Student • Rutgers University School of Communication Information & Library Studies • New Brunswick, NJ 08903 • RASD
Mitchell Melissa C. • Eugene, OR 97401-3853 • SRRT
Mitchell Melissa D. • Colorado Springs, CO 80910 • SRRT
Mitchell Michael D. • Catalog Librarian • Spring Branch Independent School District Library Processing Center • Houston, TX 77055 • IFRT
Mitchell Michael L. • Head of Information Service • Alaska State Library • Juneau, AK 99811-571 • RASD
Mitchell Milton • Director • Indianhead Library System • Eau Claire, WI 54701 • LAMA
Mitchell Nancy S. • Librarian • Alconbury High School • Huntingdon, England • AASL
Mitchell Patricia • Sales Manager • University Microfilms International • Ann Arbor, MI 48106-1346 • AASL AFLRT
Mitchell Phyllis R. • Carrollton High School • Carrollton, GA 30117 • AASL
Mitchell Raineyl V. • AV/ILL Librarian • Eastern Shore Regional Library • Salisbury, MD 21801 • IFRT
Mitchell Robert P. • International Document Librarian • University of Arizona Library • Tucson, AZ 85721 • ACRL GODORT
Mitchell Ruth F. • Austin, MN 55912 • AASL YALSA *Life*
Mitchell Sandra • Document Librarian • Mankato State University Memorial Library • Mankato, MN 56002-8400 • GODORT
Mitchell Sarah • Hd, Bibliopraphic Access Servs. • Massachusetts Institute of Technology Libraries (MIT) • Cambridge, MA 02139 • ACRL LITA
Mitchell Sue S. • Reference Librarian • Huntsville-Madison County Public Library • Huntsville, AL 35804
Mitchell Sylvia C. • Branch Manager • Liliha Public Library • Honolulu, HI 96817 • PLA YALSA
Mitchell Thomas M. • Dir., Instructional Media Ctr. • O'Fallon Township High School • O'Fallon, IL 62269 • AASL LITA
Mitchell Valencia • Librarian • Cerritos College Library • Norwalk, CA 90650 • ACRL EMIERT
Mitchell Victoria S. • Science Librarian • Reed College E. V. Hauser Library • Portland, OR 97202 • ACRL
Mitchell W. Bede • Assoc. Ln. for Public Service • Appalachian State University Carol Grotnes Belk Library • Boone, NC 28608 • ACRL LAMA
Mitchell William F. • Student • University of California-Berkeley School of Library & Information Studies • Berkeley, CA 94720
Mitchell William J. • Chief, Field Support Svs. • United States Information Agency (USIA) • Washington, DC 20547 • ACRL
Mitchum David C. • Austin, TX 78705 • RASD
Mitlin Laurance R. • Associate Dean of Library Serv. • Winthrop College Ida Jane Dacus Library • Rock Hill, SC 29733
Mitnick Eva M. • Venice, CA 90291-2973 • ALSC
Mitoma Dona J. • Librarian, Bibliographic Inst. • Pasadena City College • Pasadena, CA 91106 • ACRL LIRT
Mitrevics Audrey • Portola Elementary School • Portola, CA 96122 • AASL
Mittag Carol A. • Grafton, WI 53024 • PLA
Mittelgluck Eugene L. • Director • Mount Vernon Public Library • Mount Vernon, NY 10550 • ALCTS ALSC ALTA LAMA LITA PLA RASD GODORT SRRT
Mittelstaedt Gerard E. • Library Director • McAllen Memorial Library • McAllen, TX 78501-4688 • LAMA PLA MAGERT
Mitten Lisa • University of Pittsburgh Hillman Library • Pittsburgh, PA 15260 • ACRL
Mittermeyer Diane H. • Faculty Member • McGill University Graduate School of Library & Information Studies • Montreal PQ, H3A 1Y1 Canada • ACRL PLA LRRT
Mittge Kevin K. • Student • University of Washington Graduate School of Library and Information Science • Seattle, WA 98195
Mittlestadt Linda L. • Appleton, WI 54915 • IFRT NMRT
Mitzel Gwendolyn A. • Student • Indiana University School of Library and Information Science • Bloomington, IN 47405
Miu Anna • Texas Southern University • Houston, TX 77004
Miura Itsuo • Associate Professor • University of Tokyo Faculty of Education • Tokyo 145, Japan • ACRL ALCTS LITA RASD
Mix Adeline H. • Stony Creek, CT 06405 • PLA RASD *Continuing*
Mix Wendy K. • Student • University of Wisconsin-Madison School of Library & Information Studies • Madison, WI 53706
Mixon Edgar A. • Student • Louisiana State University School of Library & Information Science • Baton Rouge, LA 70803-3290 • LITA
Miya Lucia J. • Rolling Meadows Library • Rolling Meadows, IL 60008 • ALSC YALSA
Miyabe Yoriko • Librarian • Keisen Jogakuen Junior College Library • Tokyo, 206, Japan • ACRL ALCTS RASD LIRT
Miyagawa Haruyo • Reference Librarian • Birmingham Public Library • Birmingham, AL 35203 • NMRT
Miyaji Yuriko • Librarian • Tokyo American Club Library • Minato-ku,Tokyo 106, Japan
Miyamoto Joyce • Librarian • Hawaii State Library • Honolulu, HI 96813 • PLA
Mizer June • Berea, OH 44017
Mizrahi Renee V. • Tilden High School Library • Brooklyn, NY 11203
Mizumoto Margaret M. • Federal Way, WA 98003
Mladinov Barbara P. • Director • Bethlehem Public Library • Delmar, NY 12054 • LAMA LITA PLA
Moak Thomas C. • Senior Librarian • Mid-Columbia Library Kennewick Branch • Kennewick, WA 99336
Moallendick Jeanne • Education Consultant • TI-IN Network Inc • San Antonio, TX 78216-1803 • AASL
Moazzami Michelle • Dallas, TX 75229 • FLRT
Moberg F Alden • Reference Consultant • Oregon State Library • Salem, OR 97310-0640 • ASCLA RASD MAGERT
Mobley Buford • Trustee • South Carolina State Library • Columbia, SC 29211 • ALTA
Mobley Caryl Jean E. • Adult Services • Arlington Heights Memorial Library • Arlington Heights, IL 60004-5966 • ASCLA PLA
Mobley Emily R. • Dean • Purdue University Libraries • West Lafayette, IN 47907-1530 • ACRL LAMA
Mobley Richard L. • Director • Orange Public Library • Orange, TX 77630 • ALCTS ALSC LAMA PLA
Moburg Judith A. • Bayside School • Milwaukee, WI 53217 • AASL
Moccero Lydia • Student • Villanova University School of Library Science • Villanova, PA 19083
Moch Mary Inez Sr • Director of Library Services • Montay College Library • Chicago, IL 60659-3115 • ACRL ALCTS
Mochedlover Helene G. • Pasadena, CA 91106
Mochida Paula L. T. • Coordinator of Public Services • University of Hawaii Thomas Hale Hamilton Library • Honolulu, HI 96822 • ACRL
Mock-Kooken Sue Gale • Reader Assistant Librarian • San Jacinto College Lee Davis Library • Pasadena, TX 77505-2007 • ACRL ALCTS LITA RASD MAGERT
Mock Marci Ann • Library Assistant • Sheridan County Fulmer Public Library • Sheridan, WY 82801
Mock Sara M. • Head Technical Services • Pikes Peak Community College • Colorado Springs, CO 80906
Mockett Sara H. • Librarian • Seattle Country Day Sch • Seattle, WA 98109
Modeste Judith M. • Student • Queens College Graduate School of Library & Information Studies • Flushing, NY 11367 • LRRT
Modig Zeau D. • Customer Service Manager • Elsevier Science Publishers North American Database Department • New York, NY 10010 • LITA RASD
Modisakeng Tiny J. • Flushing, NY 11366 • AASL
Moe Louise • Reference Librarian • Rochester Public Library • Rochester, MN 55904-3777 • RASD
Moe Sandra J. • Manager • Dakota County Library System Galaxie Library • Apple Valley, MN 55124
Moeckel Lisa E. • Assistant Head of Reference • Loyola University E.M. Cudahy Memorial Library • Chicago, IL 60626 • ACRL LAMA RASD GODORT
Moecker Roberta H. • School Librarian • Temple Independent School District • Temple, TX 76502 • AASL
Moehlman Lillian • Madison, WI 53703 • Continuing
Moehrke Deborah • Adm Ln Automation/Tech Servs • Solano County Library • Fairfield, CA 94533 • LAMA LITA
Moeller-Peiffer Kathleen • Systems Adminstrator • Durham County Library • Durham, NC 27702 • AASL LITA PLA NMRT
Moeller Carol C. • Reference Librarian • Elk Grove Village Public Library • Elk Grove Village, IL 60007
Moeller Helen Morgan • Director • Leon County Public Library System • Tallahassee, FL 32301-7720 • LAMA LITA RASD
Moeller Henry W. • Associate Director Finance • Brooklyn Public Library • Brooklyn, NY 11238 • PLA
Moeller James L • Trustee • Kansas City Public Library • Kansas City, MO 64106 • ALTA
Moeller Josephine F. • Librarian I • Park Ridge Public Library • Park Ridge, IL 60068-4188 • ALCTS
Moeller Paul D. • Library Assistant • University of Iowa Libraries • Iowa City, IA 52242-1379
Moeller Sheryl S. • Student • University of North Texas School of Library & Information Sciences • Denton, TX 76203
Moen Phyllis A. • Librarian • Notre Dame High School • Peoria, IL 61614
Moen William E. • Student • Syracuse University School of Information Studies • Syracuse, NY 13244-4100 • LITA SRRT
Moens Rebecca W. • Tucson, AZ 85716
Moeschl Sue H. • Media Spec • Lawrence Central High School • Indianapolis, IN 46226 • AASL
Moffat Edward S. Prof • Associate Professor • Long Island University Palmer School of Library & Information Science • Greenvale, NY 11548 • ACRL ALCTS LAMA PLA RASD *Life*
Moffat Riley M. • Reference Librarian • Brigham Young University Hawaii Campus • Laie, HI 96762 • MAGERT
Moffatt Leah N. • Bloomington, IN 47401
Moffeit Tony • Assistant Director • University of Southern Colorado • Pueblo, CO 81001 • ACRL LAMA
Moffet James W. • Head of Reference Department • Baldwin Public Library • Birmingham, MI 48012-3002
Moffett William A. • Director • Huntington Library • San Marino, CA 91108 • ACRL LAMA
Moffi Joan W. • Alexandria, VA 22307
Moffitt Sally M. • Bibliography & Reference Ln. • University of Cincinnati Central Library • Cincinnati, OH 45221-0033 • ACRL
Mofjeld Pamela A. • Head Librarian • University of Washington Fisher-Oceangraphy Library • Seattle, WA 98195
Moger Elizabeth H. • Roslyn, NY 11576
Mogge Dru W. • Adm Records Coordinator • University of California • Riverside, CA 92517-5900 • LITA IFRT NMRT SRRT
Moghtassed Shokoufeh • Los Angeles, CA 90024-4929
Mogle Ann Messick • Lafayette, CA 94549
Mogle Dawn E. • Head of A-V Services • Lake County Public Library • Merrillville, IN 46410-5382 • PLA VRT
Mogle Kristine K. • Librarian • Musser Public Library • Muscatine, IA 52761
Mogren Paul A. • Head, Reference Department • University of Utah Marriott Library • Salt Lake City, UT 84112-1179 • RASD
Mohalley Patricia • Haude Elementary School Klein Independent School District • Spring, TX 77373 • AASL
Mohamedali O N • Senior Lecturer • University of the West Indies-Mona Department of Library Studies • Kingston, Jamaica • AASL

Mohammed Selima • Music & Fine Arts Cataloger • McGill University Libraries • Montreal PQ, H3A 1Y1 Canada

Mohle Jacqueline C. • High School Librarian • Callaway High School • Jackson, MS 39206 • AASL YALSA IFRT

Mohler Dorothy C. • Librarian • Central Catholic High School • Toledo, OH 43608 • AASL

Mohler Harry L. • Architect • H. L. Mohler & Associates P.C. • Lafayette, IN 47901 • LAMA

Mohler Linda G. • Librarian • McKinsey & Company-Firm • New York, NY 10022

Mohlhenrich Janice • Preservation Librarian • Marquette University Memorial Library • Milwaukee, WI 53233 • ALCTS

Mohn Kari • District Media Coordinator • KPBSD School Media Center • Soldotna, AK 99669-7553

Mohn Marcia D. • Colorado Springs, CO 80919 • LAMA PLA AFLRT FLRT

Mohr Diane L. • Assistant Coordinator • District of Columbia Public Library Martin Luther King Memorial Library • Washington, DC 20001 • EMIERT

Mohr Lynn R. • Los Angeles County Public Library Manhattan Heights Branch • Manhattan Beach, CA 90266

Mohr Mary C. • Oregon State Library • Salem, OR 97310-0640

Mohr Nelda • Louisville Public Library • Louisville, CO 80027 • PLA

Mohrhardt Foster E. • Arlington, VA 22202

Mohrhardt Susan E. • Student • University of Texas at Austin Graduate School of Library & Information Sciences • Austin, TX 78712-1276 • ALSC PLA

Mohrmann Suzanne • Reference/Information • Leavenworth Public Library • Leavenworth, KS 66048 • RASD

Moinette David A. • Student • University of Oklahoma School of Library & Information Studies • Norman, OK 73019 • RASD AFLRT

Moini Massi • San Francisco, CA 94110 • LAMA

Moisan Bonnie • Orange County Public Library • Hillsborough, NC 27278

Mojo Anne Z. • Assistant Director • West Palm Beach Public Library • West Palm Beach, FL 33401

Mokrzycki Elaine P. • Staff-Circulation • Weber State University Stewart Library • Ogden, UT 84408-2901 • AASL ALSC

Mokrzycki Karen • Head of Acq/Preservation Officer • University of California-Santa Cruz Library • Santa Cruz, CA 95064 • ALCTS SRRT

Mole Deborah L. • Duluth Public Library • Duluth, MN 55802

Moler Dennis • Acquisitions Coordinator • Newport Public Library • Newport, OR 97365

Moles Jean A M • Serials Librarian • University of Arkansas for Medical Science Library • Little Rock, AR 72205-7186 • ACRL

Molholt Pat • Asst. Vice Pres. & Assoc. Dean • Columbia University Health Sciences Library • New York, NY 10032

Molin Karen Wells • Tucson, AZ 85741

Molinaro Michael J. • Vice-President • Frye Gillian Molinaro Architects • Chicago, IL 60610 • LAMA

Mollberg Amy A. • Librarian • American Capital Asset Management • Houston, TX 77253 • GODORT

Molle Wendy E. • Albany, NY 12203 • AASL IFRT SRRT

Mollenkamp James L. • Trustee • Mid-Continent Public Library • Independence, MO 64050 • ALTA

Mollenkopf Jacquelyn R. • San Anselmo, CA 94960 • IFRT

Mollica Gregory S. • Project Coordinator • Northern Michigan University Lydia M. Olson Library • Marquette, MI 49855

Mollica Kathleen • Assistant Director • Passaic Public Library • Passaic, NJ 07055 • PLA YALSA

Mollner Daniel J. • Government Documents/Ref. Librn • Gustavus Adolphus College Folke Bernadotte Memorial Library • St Peter, MN 56082 • GODORT

Molloy Molly E. • Humanities & Social Science Ref. • University of Florida Libraries • Gainesville, FL 32611-2047 • ACRL RASD IRRT LIRT SRRT

Molloy Molly F. • Slavic Reference Librarian • Hoover Institution on War, Revolution & Peace Library • Stanford, CA 94305-6010 • ACRL

Mollyneaux Jane A. • Library Relations Specialist • H. W. Wilson Company • Bronx, NY 10452 • LITA

Molnar Martin A. Dr. • 00136 Roma, Italy • LAMA *Continuing*

Moloney Genevieve A. • Director • Abbot Public Library • Marblehead, MA 01945 • LAMA PLA RASD YALSA SORT

Moloney Julia B. • Middleburg, FL 32068

Moloney Kevin F. Esquire • Commissioner • Massachusetts Board of Library Commissioners • Boston, MA 02215-2070 • ASCLA PLA

Mols Frank • Assistant Director Tech. Service • State University of New York at Binghamton Libraries (SUNY) • Binghamton, NY 13902-6012

Molson Gerda • Chief Executive Officer • Niagara-on-the-Lake Public Library • Niagara-on-the-Lk ON, L0S 1J0 Canada

Molto Mavis B. • Los Angeles, CA 90034

Moltzan Janet R. • Assistant Director of Pub Serv • Dallas Public Library • Dallas, TX 75201 • ALSC LAMA PLA

Molumby Lawrence • Deputy Director • District of Columbia Public Library Martin Luther King Memorial Library • Washington, DC 20001 • PLA

Molyneux Robert E. • Div. of Research Statistics • Federal Deposit Insurance Corp L • Washington, DC 20429 • ACRL

Molz J. Barry • Baltimore County Public Library • Towson, MD 21204 • LAMA LITA PLA RASD IFRT

Molz R. Kathleen • Professor • Columbia University Library Service Library • New York, NY 10027 • ACRL LAMA PLA LHRT LRRT

Moman Orthella Polk • Assistant Librarian • Tougaloo College • Tougaloo, MS 39174 • ACRL ALCTS RASD GODORT SRRT

Momenee Gary T. • Reference Librarian • University of North Carolina • Chapel Hill, NC 27599-3902 • ACRL

Momosor Stetson P. • Professional Librarian/Youth Ser • Anchorage Municipal Libraries Samson-Diamond Branch • Anchorage, AK 99515 • ALSC

Monaco Gay L. • Fairfax Station, VA 22039

Monaghan Elizabeth M. • Children's Librarian • Baldwin Public Library • Birmingham, MI 48012-3002

Monaghan Jennifer M. • Student • Simmons College Graduate School of Library & Information Science • Boston, MA 02115

Monaghan Mary E. • Student • University of Pittsburgh School of Library and Information Science • Pittsburgh, PA 15260

Monahan Diane • Foxborough, MA 02035

Monahan Elizabeth A. • Librarian • United States Navy Base Library • Groton, CT 06349-5015 • ALCTS LAMA PLA AFLRT

Monahan Elizabeth A. • Librarian • Bartram Trail Regional Library • Washington, GA 30673

Monahan Jennifer M. • Three Bridges, NJ 08887

Monahan John P. • Dist Dept Hd-L-Media & Instr • Wappingers Central School District Central Media • Wappingers Falls, NY 12590 • AASL

Monahan Mary Jane • Head Librarian • Naugatuck High School • Naugatuck, CT 06770 • AASL

Monahan Nancy E. • Gales Ferry, CT 06835-1944 • IFRT

Monajami Sirous • Berkeley, CA 94709-126

Monakes Minoo • Coker College J.L. Coker III Memorial Library • Hartsville, SC 29550

Monat Peter C. • University of Missouri-Saint Louis • St. Louis, MO 63121-4499

Monath Jennifer M. • Social Sci. & Humanities Lbrn. • Colorado State University William E. Morgan Library • Fort Collins, CO 80523 • ACRL

Moncla Carolyn S. • Director • Moore Memorial Public Library • Texas City, TX 77590 • ALSC RASD

Moncrief Charlotte J. • System Coordinator • Library Management Network • Huntsville, AL 35804 • LITA

Monders Carol J. • Roseburg, OR 97470-9462 • ALSC

Mondi Leonard • Melrose Park Public Library • Melrose Park, IL 60160

Mondowney JoAnn G. • Executive Asst. to Director • Enoch Pratt Free Library • Baltimore, MD 21201-4484 • LAMA PLA YALSA

Mondrus Maryann • Reference Librarian • Skokie Public Library • Skokie, IL 60077-3680 • PLA

Monell Christopher B. • Technical Services Librarian • H. W. Wilson Company • Bronx, NY 10452 • LITA

Monette Elizabeth H. • Bartholomew County Library Cleo Rogers Memorial Library • Columbus, IN 47201

Money Charlene B. • Albuquerque Public Schools Dist Lib Instr Tech Serv • Albuquerque, NM 87106 • AASL

Mongan Janet • Research Officer • Cleveland State University Library • Cleveland, OH 44115 • ACRL

Mongeau Alexandre • Student • University of Ottawa Libraries Morisset Library • Ottawa ON, K1N 9A5 Canada

Mongeau Deborah J. • Gov. Publications Librarian • University of Rhode Island Library • Kingston, RI 02881-0803 • ACRL GODORT

Monger Peggy • Librarian-Media Specialist • Farragut Middle School • Knoxville, TN 37922

Monheit Albert • Director • Wantagh Public Library • Wantagh, NY 11793 • PLA

Monhollon Kathy A. • Staff Association of the Dayton & Montgomery County Public Library • Dayton, OH 45402

Monica M. Sr • Librarian • Madonna High School • Chicago, IL 60641

Monical Ruth • Head of Reference • Southern Oregon State Coll Library • Ashland, OR 97520 • ACRL RASD MAGERT

Monk Virginia A. • Principal • Pointe Coupee Parish Library • New Road, LA 70760 • ALTA

Monke Arthur • Brunswick, ME 04011 • Continuing

Monlux Carole D. • Library Coordinator • Missoula School District No. 1 • Missoula, MT 59801 • AASL

Monner Rochelle V. • Librarian • Washington Hoyt Elementary School • Tacoma, WA 98407

Monnier Diane P. • Children's Librarian • Germantown Public Library • Germantown, MD 20874 • ALSC PLA YALSA

Monnig Ruth J. • Library Director • Herald-Sun Library • Durham, NC 27705

Monprode-Holt Lorrie M. • Library Media Specialist • Montana Office of Public Instruction Resource Center • Helena, MT 59602 • AASL LAMA YALSA

Monroe Judith F. • Librarian • Alaska State Library • Anchorage, AK 99503 • ASCLA PLA

Monroe Margaret E. • Professor Emeritus • University of Wisconsin • Madison, WI 53706 • RASD *Continuing*

Monroe William S. • Geneva, NY 14456 • ACRL

Monsma Marvin E. • Director • Calvin College & Seminary Library • Grand Rapids, MI 49546 • AASL ACRL ALCTS LAMA LITA RASD YALSA

Monson Dianne L. • Professor of Education • University of Minnesota • Minneapolis, MN 55414 • ALSC

Monson Gerald • Salt Lake County Library System • Salt Lake City, UT 84121-3188 • LAMA LITA PLA

Monson Mary H. • Coor. of Central Tech Serv. • University of Iowa Libraries • Iowa City, IA 52242-1379 • ALCTS LITA

Montag John J. • Director • Wittenberg University Thomas Library • Springfield, OH 45501 • ACRL LAMA LITA RASD IFRT

Montague Elizabeth • Flint, MI 48504 • ASCLA *Life*

Montague Nancy • Staff Artist • Burlingame Public Library • Burlingame, CA 94010 • ALSC

Montague Robert • Research Associate • University of Western Ontario School of Library & Information Science • London ON, N6G 1H1 Canada • ALCTS

Montague Winnell M. • Branch Librarian • Shepherd Park Library • Washington, DC 20012

Montalvo Marilyn • Head Catloger • University of Puerto Rico • Rio Piedras, PR 00931 • IFRT IRRT

Montalvo Rene J. • Indexer • H. W. Wilson Company • Bronx, NY 10452 • LITA

Montana Edward J. Jr • Assistant Regional Administrator • Eastern Massachusetts Regional Library System • Boston, MA 02117 • LAMA PLA

Montanaro Ann R. • Head Systems Dept. • Rutgers University Libraries Technical & Automated Services • Piscataway, NJ 08855 • LITA

Montanelli Dale S. • Director of Administrative Serv • University of Illinois Library • Urbana, IL 61801 • ACRL LAMA

Montavon Victoria A. • Director of the Library • Saint Josephs University Drexel Library • Philadelphia, PA 19131-1395 • ACRL

Montee Monty L. • Chief Catalog Librarian • Yale University Sterling Memorial Library • New Haven, CT 06520 • ACRL ALCTS

Montello Phyllis M. • Atlanta, GA 30340

Montes Cynthia A. • Librarian • Sacred Hearts Academy-High School • Honolulu, HI 96818 • AASL

Montgomery-Jenkins Helen • Palm Beach Gardens, FL 33418

Montgomery Ann • Media Coordinator • Glenbard East High School • Lombard, IL 60148 • AASL LAMA

Montgomery April L. • Librarian • Barrington Middle School Media Center • Barrington, IL 60010 • AASL RASD YALSA

Montgomery Barbara E. • Orland Park, IL 60462 • AASL

Montgomery Beatrice • Knoxville, TN 37919 • Continuing

Montgomery Christopher • Cataloger • Wesleyan University Olin Memorial Library • Middletown, CT 06459

Montgomery Dale L. • Director, Library & Media Serv. • University of Wisconsin Murphy Library • La Crosse, WI 54601 • ACRL

Montgomery James G. • Branch Head • Toronto Public Library • Toronto ON, Canada • PLA RASD EMIERT

Montgomery Jean C. • Roanoke, VA 24018

Montgomery Jean G. • Librarian • Bridgewater-Raritan High School • Bridgewater, NJ 08807 • AASL

Montgomery Judith R. • Assistant Librarian • Bowdoin College Library • Brunswick, ME 04011 • ACRL LITA

Montgomery Katherine C. • Assistant Librarian/Tech. Serv. • University of Science & Arts of Oklahoma • Chickasha, OK 73018

Montgomery Kimberly K. • Reference Librarian • University of Central Florida Library • Orlando, FL 32816-0666 • ACRL

Montgomery Linda • Compton Junior High School • Bakersfield, CA 93306 • AASL

Montgomery Martha B. Dr. • Trustee • Free Library of Philadelphia • Philadelphia, PA 19103 • ALTA

Montgomery Michael • Reference Librarian • Princeton University • Princeton, NJ 08544-2098 • SRRT

Montgomery Patricia A. • Library Director • Park City Public Library • Park City, UT 84060 • LAMA PLA

Montgomery Paula K. • Publisher • School Library Media Activities Monthly • Baltimore, MD 21230 • AASL ALSC

Montgomery Suzanne S. • New Bern, NC 28562

Montgomery Teresa • Head of Cataloging & Automation • Southern Oregon State Coll Library • Ashland, OR 97520 • ACRL ALCTS LITA

Montgomery Thomas M. • Media Specialist • Barrineau Park Elementary School • Cantonment, FL 32533

Montgomery Wanda • Librarian • Harwood Junior High School • Bedford, TX 76021 • AASL

Montgomery William J. • Leeds, MA 01053

Montiel Yvonne • Trustee • Phoenix Public Library • Phoenix, AZ 85004 • ALTA

Montori Carla J. • Head, Preservation Division • University of Michigan Libraries • Ann Arbor, MI 48109-1205 • ACRL ALCTS LAMA

Montoya Cynthia • Henderson, NV 89014-5910 • YALSA

Montoya Leopoldo M. • Coor. for Cataloging Services • Medical College of Pennsylvania F.A. Moore Library of Medicine • Philadelphia, PA 19129 • ALCTS

Montre John R. • Student • University of Missouri-Columbia School of Library & Informational Science • Columbia, MO 65211

Montviloff Natalia • Sr. Cataloger, Slavic Section • Library of Congress • Washington, DC 20541

Monty Vivienne • Head of Government & Business • York University Glendon Campus Leslie Frost Library • Toronto ON, M4N 3M6 Canada • ACRL LAMA RASD

Monyakula Phyllis A. • Library Media Specialist • Blue Valley High School • Stilwell, KS 66085 • AASL IRRT

Moody Ardis R. • Library Media Specialist • Lincoln Public Schools • Lincoln, NE 68502 • AASL

Moody Audrey J. • Documents Specialist • Contra Costa County Library • Pleasant Hill, CA 94523 • GODORT

Moody Aurelia • Chicago, IL 60615 • AASL ALSC *Life*

Moody Beverly J. • Branch Supervisor • Staff Association of the Dayton & Montgomery County Public Library • Dayton, OH 45402 • PLA EMIERT SRRT

Moody David • Cataloging Librarian • University of Detroit-Mercy Main Library • Detroit, MI 48221 • ACRL ALCTS

Moody Diane S. • Naperville, IL 60565 • AASL

Moody Eileen • Media Specialist • Greenwich High School • Greenwich, CT 06830 • AASL

Moody James H. • Librarian I • Lubbock City-County Library • Lubbock, TX 79401

Moody Karen W. • Student • San Jose State University Division of Library & Information Science • San Jose, CA 95192-0029 • ASCLA LITA IFRT NMRT SRRT

Moody Margaret M. • Librarian • Harvard Law School Library • Cambridge, MA 02138 • ACRL ALCTS GODORT

Moody Marilyn D. • Executive Director • Bucks County Free Library • Doylestown, PA 18901 • LAMA PLA

Moody Marilyn K. • Head Technical Services • Rensselaer Polytechnic Institute • Troy, NY 12180 • ACRL ALCTS LAMA LITA RASD GODORT IFRT MAGERT *Life*

Moody Myrtle A. • Assistant Librarian • Harvard Law School Library • Cambridge, MA 02138

Moody Regina B. • Librarian • Brennen Elementary School • Columbia, SC 29206 • AASL LIRT

Moody Roland H. • Winchester, MA 01890 • Continuing

Moody Wendy • Branch Librarian • Free Library of Philadelphia • Philadelphia, PA 19103

Moomaw Judith A. • Davis, CA 95616 • ALCTS

Moon Beverly W. • Phillipsburg Free Public Library • Phillipsburg, NJ 08865 • ALSC PLA IFRT SRRT

Moon Eric • Sarasota, FL 34243 • PLA IFRT *Honorary*

Moon Ilse • Sarasota, FL 34243 • RASD GODORT ILERT LRRT

Moon James H. • Librarian-Cataloger • University of Pittsburgh Hillman Library • Pittsburgh, PA 15260 • ACRL ALCTS

Moon Kyung-ah Gina • Librarian I • Miami-Dade Public Library System • Miami, FL 33130-1504 • YALSA

Moon Loretta M. • High School Media Specialist • Iowa Falls High School • Iowa Falls, IA 50126 • AASL

Moon Margaret K. • Librarian • Baker College of Muskegon • Muskegon, MI 49442 • ACRL

Moon Mary Lynn • Reference Librarian • Clemson University Robert Muldrow Cooper Library • Clemson, SC 29634-3001 • RASD

Moon Myra Jo • Preservation Librarian • Colorado State University William E. Morgan Library • Fort Collins, CO 80523 • ACRL ALCTS

Moon Peter S. • Manager • Hartford Steam Boiler • Hartford, CT 06102 • LAMA LITA

Moon Sylvia D. • Librarian • Atlanta-Fulton Public Library • Atlanta, GA 30303

Mooney Hollis • Logan Elemantary School • Dundalk, MD 21222 • AASL

Mooney Jennifer M. • Associate Manager • Bellcore • Piscataway, NJ 08854 • LITA

Mooney Margaret T. • Government Publications Ln • University of California Rivera Library • Riverside, CA 92517 • LITA GODORT

Mooney Martha T. • Editor of Book Review Digest • H. W. Wilson Company • Bronx, NY 10452 • ALCTS

Mooney Maryann A. • Ln • Haines Elementary School Library • New Lenox, IL 60451 • AASL

Mooney Sandra • Design Resource Center,Head • Louisiana State University Libraries • Baton Rouge, LA 70803 • ACRL RASD

Mooney Toni L. • Pasadena Public Library • Pasadena, TX 77506-4895

Moore-Evans Angela • Librarian • Foote, Cone, & Belding Information Specialist • San Francisco, CA 94111 • RASD

Moore-Jansen Cathy L. • Social Sciences Librarian • Wichita State University Ablah Library • Wichita, KS 67208 • ACRL RASD

Moore-Wright Tonilee A. • Medical Library Dir/Mgr. • Sentara Hampton General Hospital Library • Hampton, VA 23669 • AASL

Moore Alice • Robert L. William Public Library • Durant, OK 74701

Moore Anita S. • Media Specialist • Buffalo Gap High School • Swoope, VA 24479 • AASL

Moore Ann L. • Director • Fayetteville Free Library • Fayetteville, NY 13066 • PLA

Moore Ann M. • Parma, OH 44134

Moore Ann Marie • Head of Reference • Manhasset Public Library • Manhasset, NY 11030

Moore Ann R. • Head of Technical Services • Upper Arlington Public Library • Upper Arlington, OH 43221

Moore Anne Campbell • Catalog Librarian • Boston College O'Neill Library • Chestnut Hill, MA 02167 • ACRL ALCTS SRRT

Moore Anne L. • Librarian • Library of Congress • Washington, DC 20541

Moore Arline L • Serials Cataloger • Southern Methodist University • Dallas, TX 75275

Moore Audrey Dodds • Reference Services Manager • California State Library • Sacramento, CA 94237-0001 • ASCLA

Moore Barbara • Assistant Director of Libraries • University of Rochester Rush Rhees Library • Rochester, NY 14627 • LAMA LITA

Moore Barbara G. • Norman, OK 73069

Moore Barbara N. • PALS Customer Support • Unisys • Norcross, GA 30092 • LITA

Moore Barbara S. • Library Media Specialist • Butterfield Trail Elementary School • Fayetteville, AR 72703 • AASL

Moore Bessie Boehm • Trustee/Vice Chairperson • National Commission on Libraries & Information Science • Little Rock, AR 72201 • ALTA ASCLA PLA *Honorary*

Moore Betty Rose • Librarian • Columbia University Libraries • New York, NY 10027

Moore Beverly B. • Library Director • University of Southern Colorado • Pueblo, CO 81001 • ACRL LAMA

Moore Carole R. • Chief Librarian • University of Toronto Library System • Toronto ON, M5S 1A5 Canada • ACRL LAMA

Moore Carolyn A. • Deputy Librarian • City Hall Municipal Reference • Chicago, IL 60602 • RASD GODORT

Moore Carolyn M. • Head of Adult Services • Clearwater Public Library • Clearwater, FL 34623 • LAMA PLA RASD LRRT

Moore Catherine • Audio Visual Services • High Point Public Library • High Point, NC 27261 • PLA VRT

Moore Charlie L. Jr • Abbeville, SC 29620

Moore Cherrilynn G. • Catlgr • Glendale Public Library • Glendale, AZ 85302 • LITA

Moore Connie J. • Richmond Public Schools • Richmond, VA 23219 • AASL

Moore Curtis P. • Director • Lebanon County Library System • Lebanon, PA 17042 • PLA

Moore Cynthia • Librarian • Brantley Middle School • Selma, AL 36701

Moore Dale B. • Director of Distribution • James Agee Film Project • Johnson City, TN 37601 • VRT

Moore Deborah C. • Bristol Public Library • Bristol, VA 24201-4199 • LITA

Moore Debra K. • Crosby, TX 77532 • AASL ALSC IFRT SRRT

Moore Diane M. • Student • State University New York at Buffalo School of Inf. & Library Studies • Buffalo, NY 14260 • AASL

Moore Doris Helen • Granville, OH 43023 • ALSC *Life*

Moore Dorothy A. • Student • Catholic University of America School of Library and Information Science • Washington, DC 20064 • AASL

Moore Dorothy L. • Technical Information Specialist • National Library of Medicine • Bethesda, MD 20894

Moore Elaine E. • Reference Services Supervisor • Western Kentucky University Helm-Cravens Library • Bowling Green, KY 42101 • ACRL RASD LIRT MAGERT

Moore Eleanor DeWald • Clarion, PA 16214 • AASL ALSC *Life*

Moore Elizabeth • Greensboro, NC 27406 • ACRL LAMA *Life*

Moore Elizabeth Atkinson • Librarian • Van E. Blanton Elementary School • Miami, FL 33150 • AASL

Moore Everett L. • Palmdale, CA 93550

Moore Fred W. • Director • Ferguson Municipal Public Library • Ferguson, MO 63135

Moore Grace G. • Recorder of Documents • State Library of Louisiana • Baton Rouge, LA 70821-0131 • GODORT

Moore Hazel • New Orleans, LA 70126 • AASL YALSA

Moore Helga S. • Deputy Director • San Diego Public Library • San Diego, CA 92101 • LITA PLA

Moore Hilda E. • Director Emeritus • University of Maryland at Baltimore Health Sciences Library • Baltimore, MD 21201 • Life

Moore J. Terry • Director • Hibbing Public Library • Hibbing, MN 55746 • LAMA PLA

Moore Jackie • Trustee • San Juan Island Public Library • Friday Harbor, WA 98250

Moore Jane F. • Chief of Library Development • North Carolina State Library • Raleigh, NC 27601-2807 • ASCLA LAMA PLA

Moore Jane Ross • Chief Librarian & Professor Emer • City University of New York Graduate School Mina Rees Library • New York, NY 10036-8099 • ACRL ALCTS LAMA LITA RASD IRRT *Life*

Moore Janice A. • Head Librarian • Roland Park Country School • Baltimore, MD 21210 • AASL

Moore Jayne E. • Media Specialist • Saint Michaels High School • St. Michaels, MD 21663 • AASL

Moore Jean B. • Ridgewood, NJ 07450

Moore Jill L. • Student • University of California Los Angeles Graduate School of Library & Information Science • Los Angeles, CA 90024 • PLA

Moore Jo Anne M. • Director of Sch Lib Media Prog. • Dallas Independent School District Accounts Payable • Dallas, TX 75204 • AASL

Moore Joanne E. • Librarian • Cherry Hill Free Public Library • Cherry Hill, NJ 08034

Moore Joanne M. • Director Library Services, K-12 • Litchfield High School • Litchfield, CT 06759 • AASL

Moore John I. • Attorney • Taylor, Porter, Brooks & Phillips • Baton Rouge, LA 70821 • LITA

Moore Joyce W. • Director of Library Services • Jefferson Community College Library • Louisville, KY 40202 • ACRL

Moore Judy Carol • Serial Cataloger • East Carolina University Joyner Library • Greenville, NC 27858-4353 • ALCTS

Moore Karen C. • Regional Youth Services Ln • Saint Louis Public Library Macachek Branch • St. Louis, MO 63139

Moore Karen R. • Media Specialist • Olde Providence Communications Magnet • Charlotte, NC 28226 • AASL

Moore Kathryn H. • Reference Librarian • Cardinal Stritch College • Milwaukee, WI 53217

Moore Kathryn J. • Branch Manager • Love County • Marietta, OK 73448

Moore Kathryn Mihalcik • Librarian • Eyer Junior High School Library • Macungie, PA 18062 • AASL

Moore Kay Kirlin Mr. • Greenville, RI 02828 • Continuing

Moore Kelly M. • Reference Librarian • Clausen Miller Gorman Caffrey & Witous P.C. Library • Chicago, IL 60603

Moore Kerri A. • Student • University of California Los Angeles Graduate School of Library & Information Science • Los Angeles, CA 90024

Moore L. A. Mr. • N Plainfield, NJ 07060 • LAMA PLA *Life*

Moore La Vaunne • Trustee • Thomas Jefferson Library • Jefferson City, MO 65101 • ALTA

Moore Lana • Middle School Librarian • Ironton Middle School • Ironton, OH 45638 • AASL LIRT

Moore Laurel V. • Highland, CA 92346 • Continuing

Moore Lawrence A. • Ontario Library Association • Toronto ON, M5C 1M3 Canada • LITA

Moore Leslie A. • Student • University of Washington Graduate School of Library and Information Science • Seattle, WA 98195

Moore Linda L. • Waldorf, MD 20603 • AASL

Moore Lorraine • Cataloging Dept. Head • University of Kansas Library • Lawrence, KS 66045-2800 • ACRL ALCTS LITA

Moore M. Heather • Asst. to the Research Libn. • University of Texas Ransom Humanities Research Center • Austin, TX 78713 • ACRL

Moore Mae Frances Ed.D. • Instructor • Laney College Library • Oakland, CA 94607

Moore Margaret E. • Head Info. Management Education • University of North Carolina • Chapel Hill, NC 27599-3902 • ACRL RASD LIRT LRRT

Moore Maria • Fife Lake Public Library • Fife Lake, MI 49633

Moore Mary E. • Tulsa City-County Library System • Tulsa, OK 74103

Moore Mary E. • Librarian • Bailey Elementary School • Pasadena, TX 77502

Moore Mary G. • Chief of Technical Services • Los Alamos County Library • Los Alamos, NM 87544

Moore Mary L. • Branch Head • Oakdale Library • Oakdale, CA 95361

Moore Mary Lee • Director Media Services • Chatham County Schools • Pittsboro, NC 27312

Moore Mary Y. • Chief Statewide Planning & Devel • Washington State Library • Olympia, WA 98504-2470 • ASCLA

Moore MaryLouise • Detroit, MI 48228

Moore Maryann K. • Head of Catalog • Greenwich Library • Greenwich, CT 06830

Moore Matthew S. • Librarian II- Circulation • Clearwater Public Library • Clearwater, FL 34623 • LAMA PLA IFRT

Moore Mattie Ruth • San Antonio, TX 78227 • AASL ALSC *Continuing*

Moore May E. • Head Librarian • Unionville High School • Unionville, ON, L3R 8G5 Canada

Moore Merle • Clarksburg-Harrison Public Library • Clarksburg, WV 26301

Moore Milton C. • Edwardsville, IL 62025

Moore Nancy • Director • North Palm Beach Public Library • North Palm Beach, FL 33408

Moore Nancy H. • Director • Craft Memorial Library Mercer County Service Center • Bluefield, WV 24701 • LAMA PLA

Moore Pamela C. • Children's Program Librarian • Morgan Hill Public Library • Morgan Hill, CA 95037

Moore Pamela S. • Collier County Public Library Golden Gate Branch • Naples, FL 33999 • ALSC

Moore Pamela W. • Media Specialist • Stout Junior High School • Dearborn, MI 48124 • AASL IFRT

Moore Patricia S. • Birmingham, AL 35226

Moore Patsy Mrs • Associate Librarian • Saint Albans School • Washington, DC 20016

Moore Paula R. • Head, Youth Services • Arlington Heights Memorial Library • Arlington Heights, IL 60004-5966 • ALSC PLA

Moore Peter M. • Tech. Services Coord. • Mansfield-Richland County Public Library • Mansfield, OH 44902-1295

Moore R. Jonathan • Catlin, IL 61817

Moore Ralph L. • Trustee • East Cleveland Public Library • East Cleveland, OH 44112 • ALTA

Moore Rebecca C. • Student • University of North Carolina at Chapel Hill School of Information and Library Science • Chapel Hill, NC 27599-3360 • AASL

Moore Richard • Bolsa Grande High School • Garden Grove, CA 92644 • AASL YALSA

Moore Robert C Jr. • Waltham, MA 02154

Moore Rosa Lee • Tullahoma, TN 37388

Moore Russell S. • Library Director • Springfield Town Library • Springfield, VT 05156-2997 • LAMA PLA

Moore Sandra • Providence Day School • Charlotte, NC 28226 • AASL

Moore Sarah S. • Catlgr Instr Media Proc • DeKalb County School System • Atlanta, GA 30329 • ALCTS

Moore Sheridan P. • San Antonio Independent School District • San Antonio, TX 78210 • AASL

Moore Sheryl R. • Librarian • University of Southwestern Louisiana Libraries • Lafayette, LA 70503 • ACRL

Moore Sue N. • Librarian • John Rolfe Middle School • Richmond, VA 23223 • AASL

Moore Susan • Lexington, KY 40502

Moore Susan M. • Social Science/Science Catlgr • University of Arizona Library • Tucson, AZ 85721 • ACRL ALCTS MAGERT NMRT

Moore Teresa A. • Library Director • Archer Daniels Midland County Library • Decatur, IL 62526

Moore Thomas J. • Dean of Libraries • Central Michigan University Charles V. Park Library 315 • Mount Pleasant, MI 48859 • ACRL LAMA

Moore Thomas L. • Director • Wake County Public Library System • Raleigh, NC 27610 • ALCTS ALSC LAMA LITA PLA RASD

Moore Virginia B. • Librarian • Anacostia Senior High School • Washington, DC 20020 • AASL YALSA IFRT *Life*

Moore Wendy E. • Student • University of North Carolina at Chapel Hill School of Information and Library Science • Chapel Hill, NC 27599-3360 • IFRT LHRT SRRT

Moore William H. • Trustee • William Leonard Public Library District • Robbins, IL 60472 • ALTA

Moore de Diaz Laurita • Rio Salado Community College • Phoenix, AZ 85003

Moores Janet L. • Library Assistant III • University of California Rivera Library • Riverside, CA 92517

Moorhead Kenneth E. • Associate Librarian • Eastern Connecticut State University J. Eugene Smith Library • Willimantic, CT 06226 • ACRL EMIERT

Moorhouse Alice K. • H. M. McKemy Middle School • Tempe, AZ 85282 • AASL

Moorman John Allyn • City Librarian • Decatur Public Library • Decatur, IL 62523 • ASCLA LAMA PLA

Moorman Laura J. • Supervisor, Reference • Westerville Public Library • Westerville, OH 43081

Moorman Tonia Hull • Public Library of Cincinnati and Hamilton County • Cincinnati, OH 45202 • PLA IFRT SRRT

Moose Ruth M. • Albemarle, NC 28001

Morales Diana • Head Librarian • San Antonio Public Library Las Palmes Branch Library • San Antonio, TX 78237 • PLA

Morales Estela • Director • Centro Universitario de Investigaciones Bibliotecologica • Mexico D.F. 04510, Mexico

Morales Grace L. • Brooks County Library Ed Rachal Memorial Library • Falfurrias, TX 78355 • ACRL LITA

Morales Luz A. • Student • University of California Los Angeles Graduate School of Library & Information Science • Los Angeles, CA 90024 • ALCTS

Morales Milton • Trustee • Mid-Continent Public Library • Independence, MO 64050 • ALTA

Morales Nydia • Librarian • University of Puerto Rico • Rio Piedras, PR 00931

Moran Arlene D. • Community Relations Liaison • Brooklyn Public Library • Brooklyn, NY 11238 • PLA

Moran Barbara B. • Dean and Professor • University of North Carolina at Chapel Hill School of Information and Library Science • Chapel Hill, NC 27599-3360 • ACRL LAMA LRRT

Moran Darlene Freeman • Branch Librarian • Cleveland Public Library Martin Luther King Jr. Branch • Cleveland, OH 44106

Moran David L. • Ardmore, OK 73401

Moran Diane • Librarian • Marine Corps Logistics Base • Barstow, CA 92311

Moran Douglas John • Tukwila, WA 98188

Moran Elizabeth A. • Library Director • Camden Public Library • Camden, ME 04843

Moran Gerald D. • Head Librarian • Geneva College McCartney Library • Beaver Falls, PA 15010 • ACRL LAMA RASD

Moran Irene E. • Modesto, CA 95356 • LAMA *Continuing*

Moran John H. • Toledo-Lucas County Public Library Sanger Branch • Toledo, OH 43606 • PLA YALSA

Moran June • Media Specialist • Red Bank Middle School • Red Bank, NJ 07701 • ALSC

Moran Lynda A. • Trustee • East Islip Public Library • East Islip, NY 11730-2896

Moran Margaret M. • Director • Community Free Library • Holley, NY 14770

Moran Mary Agatha C.S.J. Sr. • Librarian • Saint Paul High School • Bristol, CT 06010

Moran Michael J. • Director • Asnuntuck Community College Learning Resource Center • Enfield, CT 06082 • ACRL

Moran Robert F. Jr • Director of Library Services • Indiana University Northwest Library • Gary, IN 46408 • LAMA

Moran Rosemary W. • Tulsa City-County Library Martin East Regional Library • Tulsa, OK 74129 • RASD YALSA

Moran Sandra Renee • Warren East High School • Bowling Green, KY 42101 • AASL

Moran Sharon • Director • Terryville Public Library • Terryville, CT 06786

Moran Sylvia J. Mrs. • Librarian • Erie Community College/North Library • Williamsville, NY 14221 • ACRL

Moran Teresita C. • Chief Librarian • Ateneo de Manila University Professional School Library • Makati, Metro Manila, Philippines • ACRL

Moran Thomas J. • Director • Moline Public Library • Moline, IL 61265

Moran William S. • Humanities/Social Sciences Lbrn. • Dartmouth College Library Baker Memorial Library • Hanover, NH 03755-3525 • ACRL LAMA

Morandi Edward P. • Sandy, UT 84092

Morano Kristin Janine • Long Branch, NJ 07740 • PLA

Morant Sandra Kelly • Student • North Carolina Central University • Durham, NC 27707 • LITA

Morante Rosemary • Department Serv Librarian K-12 • Windsor High School • Windsor, CT 06095 • AASL

Morchower Gail M. • International Game Fish Association • Pompono Beach, FL 33061

Mordini Lourdes N. • Head of Adult Services • Warren-Newport Public Library District • Gurnee, IL 60031 • RASD

Morehead Jeffrey D. • Monographic Cataloger • University of California-Los Angeles (UCLA) • Los Angeles, CA 90024-1450 • ALCTS MAGERT SRRT

Morehead Joe Dr. • Professor • State University of New York at Albany School of Information Science & Policy • Albany, NY 12222 • GODORT

Morehead Kelly K. • Media Specialist • North Fayette Community Schools • West Union, IA 52175 • AASL

Morehead Marilyn R. • Library Director • Mary E. Bartlett Memorial Library • Brentwood, NH 03833

Morehouse Eloise F. • Editor • H. W. Wilson Company • Bronx, NY 10452 • RASD

Morehouse Harold G. • Dean of Libraries • University of Nevada-Reno Noble H. Getchell Library • Reno, NV 89557 • ACRL

Morehouse Robert Stewart • Student • University of Kentucky • Lexington, KY 40506-0056 • RASD

Morehouse Valerie J. • District Information Specialist • Bismarck School District • Bismarck, ND 58501 • AASL ASCLA LITA RASD

Moreillon Judi L. • Librarian • Los Ninos School • Tucson, AZ 85706 • AASL

Morein P. Grady • Director of Libraries • University of West Florida John C. Pace Library • Pensacola, FL 32514 • ACRL LAMA

Moreland Curtis R. • Librarian • Technical Library • Pensacola, FL 32509-5700 • PLA FLRT

Moreland Virginia • Reference Librarian • Georgia State University Pullen Library • Atlanta, GA 30303-3081 • ACRL LAMA RASD LRRT SRRT

Morell D. Gary • Acquisitions Librarian • Teikyo-Westmar University • Le Mars, IA 51031-3429

Morelli Mary L. • Computer Progammer • State of Connecticut Office of Comptroller • Hartford, CT 06106 • ALCTS LITA

Morelock Molete • Mobile, AL 36606-1830 • Continuing

Moren Barbara J. • Reference Librarian • Stratford Library Association • Stratford, CT 06497

Moren Harold M. • Acquisitions Librarian • Harvard Law School Library • Cambridge, MA 02138 • ACRL ALCTS

Moreno Carmen Garcia • International Affairs Office • Ibby Mexico • Mexico City, Mexico • ALSC

Moreno Catherine H. • Assistant Head of Catalog Dept. • University of California-Berkeley University Library • Berkeley, CA 94720

Moreno Esperanza A. • Reference Librarian • University of Texas at El Paso Library • El Paso, TX 79968-0582 • ACRL RASD *Life*

Moreno Maria Pilar • Student • Spain Biblioteca Nacional • 28071 Madrid, Spain • LAMA IRRT

Moreno Mary Helen • Head, Interlibrary Loan • University of California-Davis Library • Davis, CA 95616 • RASD EMIERT

Moreno Nancy Quesada • Legislative Reference Librarian • Legislative Reference Library • Austin, TX 78711

Moreno Yolanda N. • Branch Supervisor • Orange Public Library El Modena Branch • Orange, CA 92669 • PLA

Morenon Sarah M. • Student • University of Rhode Island Graduate School of Library & Information Studies • Kingston, RI 02881-0815 • AASL

Morey David S. Jr. • Student • Rutgers University School of Communication Information & Library Studies • New Brunswick, NJ 08903 • LITA

Morey Elaine D. • Librarian • Wayland Junior High School • Wayland, MI 49348

Morey Helen E. • Librarian Cataloger • Central Florida Community College Library • Ocala, FL 32670 • ACRL ALCTS LITA RASD

Morey Jill Stanton • Director • Brighton Public Library • Brighton, MI 48116 • ASCLA

Morga Claire M. • Librarian • West Babylon Public Library • West Babylon, NY 11704

Morgan-Bungard Julianne • Harrisonburg, VA 22801 • ACRL

Morgan-Green Kathy M. • Student • University of Texas at Austin Graduate School of Library & Information Sciences • Austin, TX 78712-1276

Morgan-Landman Vickilynn • Student • Catholic University of America Library Science Library • Washington, DC 20064

Morgan Anne C. • Head of Technical Services • New Mexico State University Library • Las Cruces, NM 88003-0006 • ACRL ALCTS

Morgan Barbara L. • Reference Librarian • University of Massachusetts Library • Amherst, MA 01003 • ACRL SRRT

Morgan Betsy Susan • School Librarian • Cathedral Preparatory School • Erie, PA 16501 • AASL YALSA

Morgan Betty • Trustee • West Florida Regional Library • Pensacola, FL 32501

Morgan Bronwyn W. • Assistant Director • Mississippi County Library System and College Library • Blytheville, AR 72315

Morgan Candace D. • Deputy Director, Comm Lib. Serv. • Fort Vancouver Regional Library • Vancouver, WA 98663 • PLA IFRT

Morgan Carleton G. • Student • Orange Coast College • Costa Mesa, CA 92628-5005

Morgan Carolyn C. • Librarian • Hughes Research Labs, RL84 • Malibu, CA 90265

Morgan Dennis M. • District Media Coordinator • Riverview Junior High School • Murray, UT 84123 • AASL

Morgan Elinor W. • Pulaski County High School • Dublin, VA 24084 • AASL

Morgan Elizabeth M. • Librarian • Hempstead High School • Dubuque, IA 52001 • AASL

Morgan Elleene Jones • Branch Head • Lake Lanier Regional Library Lawrenceville Branch • Lawrenceville, GA 30245-4707

Morgan Eric L. • Systems Librarian • North Carolina State University • Raleigh, NC 27695 • ACRL LITA

Morgan Erma J. • Deputy Librarian Technical Serv. • King County Library System • Seattle, WA 98109-5191 • ALCTS LITA *Life*

Morgan Florence B. Miss • Fort Collins, CO 80521 • ACRL ALCTS *Continuing*

Morgan Gary W. • Student • University of Illinois Graduate School of Library and Information Science • Urbana, IL 61801

Morgan Heather C. • Library Director • North Castle Public Library • Armonk, NY 10504 • PLA

Morgan Ina K. • Media Director • Palatka High School Resource Center • Palatka, FL 32077 • AASL

Morgan James • O.H. Close School California Youth Authority • Stockton, CA 95213-9001 • ASCLA

Morgan James • Automation Librarian • Indiana University School of Medicine Library • Indianapolis, IN 46202-5121 • LITA

Morgan James E. • Director • Oregon Health Science University Library • Portland, OR 97207 • ACRL LAMA *Life*

Morgan James J. • Library Assistant • Brookline High School Burack Library • Brookline, MA 02146 • ACRL

Morgan Joan • Noblesville High School • Noblesville, IN 46060 • AASL

Morgan John M. • Reference Librarian • University of Toledo William S. Carlson Library • Toledo, OH 43606-3399 • ACRL ALCTS LAMA LITA RASD *Life*

Morgan Julia M. • Hennepin County Library Southdale-Hennepin Area Library • Edina, MN 55435 • PLA RASD SRRT

Morgan Karen F. • Student • Texas Woman's University School of Library & Information Studies • Denton, TX 76204 • YALSA EMIERT IFRT SRRT

Morgan Karen L. • Reference/Collection Devel. • University of Michigan-Dearborn Mardigian Library • Dearborn, MI 48128-1491 • ACRL RASD

Morgan Kathryn E. • Media Specialist • Brown Station Elementary School • Gaithersburg, MD 20878 • AASL

Morgan Kathryn N. • Associate Librarian • University of Virginia Alderman Library • Charlottesville, VA 22903-2498 • ACRL IRRT

Morgan Laurel A. • School Library Media Specialist • Chesterfield Heights Elementary Schools Norfolk Public Schools • Norfolk, VA 23504 • AASL

Morgan Linda E. • Delray Beach Public Library Association Inc. • Delray Beach, FL 33444

Morgan Lynn Kasner • Assistant Dean Inf. Resources • Mount Sinai Medical Center Levy Library • New York, NY 10029 • ACRL LAMA

Morgan Margaret H. • Head Technical Services Catlgr • Freeport Public Library • Freeport, IL 61032 • ALCTS GODORT

Morgan Marianne M. • Media Specialist • Leslie R. Fisher Elementary School • Oklahoma City, OK 73170

Morgan Marie A. • Head, Catalog Department • Tulane University Howard-Tilton Memorial Library • New Orleans, LA 70118 • ACRL ALCTS LAMA NMRT

Morgan Martha R. • Student • Syracuse University School of Information Studies • Syracuse, NY 13244-4100

Morgan Mary L. • Interlibrary Loan • South Carolina State Library • Columbia, SC 29211

Morgan Mendell D. • Library Director • Incarnate Word College Library Saint Pius X Library • San Antonio, TX 78209

Morgan Nancy T. • Cincinnati, OH 45421

Morgan Phyllis S. • Information Specialist • Reddy Communications, Inc. • Albuquerque, NM 87109

Morgan Robert C. • Cataloger • Library of Congress • Washington, DC 20541

Morgan Sally W. • Director • Hawaii State Library System Library for the Blind & Phys Hndcpd • Honolulu, HI 96815-3894 • ASCLA

Morgan Sheila E. • Librarian • Genesee District Library Davison Branch • Davison, MI 48423 • PLA

Morgan Susan M. • Reference Librarian • Jefferson College Library • Hillsboro, MO 63050 • ACRL ALCTS RASD GODORT

Morganstern Betty • Information/Prog/Outreach Ln • Annapolis & Anne Arundel County Public Library • Annapolis, MD 21401-7042 • LITA RASD

Morganti Deena J. • Head Librarian • Pennsylvania State University Berks Campus • Reading, PA 19610-6009 • ACRL LAMA RASD LIRT

Morganti Joseph W. • Chevron Park Technical Library • San Ramon, CA 94583 • ALCTS LITA

Moriarty Judith E. • Cataloging Coordinator • University of Wisconsin-Platteville Elton S. Karrmann Library • Platteville, WI 53818-3099 • ACRL ALCTS IFRT

Moriarty Paul V. • Assistant Director • University of Wisconsin-Platteville Elton S. Karrmann Library • Platteville, WI 53818-3099 • ACRL ALCTS IFRT

Moriearty Jill A. • Government Publications Ln • Northeastern Oklahoma State University John Vaughan Library-LRC • Tahlequah, OK 74464 • ACRL GODORT

Morimoto Hideyuki • University of Iowa Library • Iowa City, IA 52242 • ACRL ALCTS LITA IRRT

Morin Gerard R. • Librarian • Wisdom Junior-Senior High School • St Agatha, ME 04772 • AASL YALSA

Morin Jodie Y. • Reference Librarian • Buena Vista College Ballou Libray • Storm Lake, IA 50588 • ALCTS LITA RASD GODORT LIRT

Morin Louise E. • Newton Ctr, MA 02159 • Continuing

Morin Robert • Cataloger • University of New Hampshire Library • Durham, NH 03824 • ACRL ALCTS

Morisseau Caroline B. • New City, NY 10956 • AASL IFRT

Morita Ichiko T. • Head of Cataloging Department • Ohio State University Libraries • Columbus, OH 43210-1286 • ACRL ALCTS LITA

Morita Machiko • Librarian • County of Los Angeles Public Library • Downey, CA 90241-7400 • PLA

Morita Sharon N. • Medford, MA 02155 • ALCTS

Moritz Charles F. • Editor • H. W. Wilson Company • Bronx, NY 10452 • ACRL

Moritz Thomas D. • California Academy of Sciences • San Francisco, CA 94118 • ACRL IFRT IRRT MAGERT SRRT

Moritz William D. • Associate Director • University of Wisconsin-Milwaukee Golda Meir Library • Milwaukee, WI 53201

Morland Barbara R. • Supervisory Librarian • Library of Congress • Washington, DC 20541 • PLA RASD

Morland Dorothy L. • Pacific Palisades, CA 90272 • AASL

Morley Debby • Student • University of North Carolina at Chapel Hill School of Information and Library Science • Chapel Hill, NC 27599-3360 • LITA

Morman Edward T. • Institute of The History of Medicine • Baltimore, MD 21205-2169 • ACRL

Mormon Pauline H. • Burleson, TX 76028

Mormon Ruth A. • Librarian • Greenspun Junior High School • Henderson, NV 89014

Morner Claudia J. • Associate University Librarian • Boston College Libraries • Chestnut Hill, MA 02167 • ACRL LAMA LIRT

Morning Todd • Head of Youth Services • Schaumburg Township District Library • Schaumburg, IL 60194 • ALSC PLA YALSA

Moroney Mary J. • Coor of Auto & Tech Serv • Eastern Oklahoma District Library System • Muskogee, OK 74401 • PLA

Morr Lynell A. • Art Librarian • John & Mable Ringling Museum of Art, Art Research Library • Sarasota, FL 34243 • ACRL

Morra Sylvia T. • Middletown, PA 17057

Morrill Allen S. • Kansas City Art Institute Library • Kansas City, MO 64111 • ACRL LHRT

Morrill Billie A. • Head, Circulation Services • East Lyme Public Library • Niantic, CT 06357-1100

Morrill Kimberly C. • Student • University of South Carolina College of Library & Information Science • Columbia, SC 29208

Morrill Marcia S. • Trustee • Madison-Jefferson County Public Library • Madison, IN 47250 • ALTA

Morrill Walter D. • Library Director • Hanover College Duggan Library • Hanover, IN 47243-0287 • ACRL LITA

Morris-Dunkley Ramona M. • Goldsboro, NC 27530

Morris Ann Louise • Head Librarian • Hyannis Public Library Association • Hyannis, MA 02601

Morris Anne E. • Manager, Library Data Systems • Austin Public Library • Austin, TX 78768 • LITA PLA

Morris Annette S. • Georgetown University Law Center Edward Bennett Williams Library • Washington, DC 20001-1417 • ALCTS

Morris Betsy H. • Head, Computing Services • University of Rochester Edward G Miner Library • Rochester, NY 14642

Morris Betty J. • Associate Professor • Long Island University Palmer School of Library & Information Science • Greenvale, NY 11548 • AASL

Morris Bonnie • Media Generalist • Minnehaha Academy • Minneapolis, MN 55406 • AASL

Morris Caroline S. • Director • Pennsylvania Hospital Medical Library • Phildelphia, PA 19107 • ACRL ILERT

Morris Catherine D. • Library Director • Brown Deer Public Library • Brown Deer, WI 53223 • LAMA PLA

Morris Darlene S. • Senior Librarian • University of Minnesota-Duluth Library • Duluth, MN 55812-2495

Morris Dilys E. • Assistant Director • Iowa State University Library • Ames, IA 50011-2140 • ACRL ALCTS LITA

Morris Donna • Librarian • Venable Elementary School • Charlottesville, VA 22903 • AASL

Morris Donna L. • Director of Public Services • Metropolitan Library System • Oklahoma City, OK 73102 • LAMA PLA

Morris Dorothy • Wadsworth, OH 44281

Morris Dorothy • Media Specialist • Pine Street School Library • Thomson, GA 30824 • AASL ALSC YALSA

Morris Effie Lee • San Francisco, CA 94109 • ALSC ALTA PLA EMIERT SRRT *Continuing*

Morris Glenna E. • Head of Extensions Services • Wayne County Public Library • Wooster, OH 44691

Morris Hallie J. • Branch Librarian • Jefferson Parish Library Department • Metairie, LA 70010 • PLA

Morris Helen M. • Mary Jacobs Library • Rocky Hill, NJ 08503

Morris Howard W. • Reference Librarian • Spokane County Library District Valley Branch • Spokane, WA 99206

Morris Jacqueline G. • Indiana Department of Education Ctr for Sch Impro & Performance • Indianapolis, IN 46204 • AASL ALSC

Morris James A. • Lake City, FL 32055

Morris Janie C. • Librarian • Duke University William R. Perkins Library • Durham, NC 27706 • ACRL

Morris Jean L. • Student • University of Pittsburgh School of Library and Information Science • Pittsburgh, PA 15260

Morris Jennifer D. • Central Services Coordinator • Geneva Free Library • Geneva, NY 14456 • LITA PLA

Morris Joan L. • Head, Catalog Department • Carnegie Library of Pittsburgh • Pittsburgh, PA 15213-4080

Morris John • Walnut Creek, CA 94598-2608

Morris Joyce • School Librarian • McGuffey School District • Claysville, PA 15323 • AASL

Morris Judy B. • Greybull, WY 82426 • AASL

Morris Karen L. • Jefferson-Madison Regional Library • Charlottesville, VA 22901-5287

Morris Karen T. • Librarian • Okmulgee High School • Okmulgee, OK 74447 • AASL LIRT

Morris Leanna • Librarian • Marshall Public Library • Marshall, IL 62441

Morris Leslie A. • Curator of Books & Manuscripts • Rosenbach Museum and Library • Philadelphia, PA 19103 • ACRL

Morris Leslie R. • Director • Niagara University Library • Niagara University, NY 14109 • ACRL LITA RASD LRRT

Morris Linda A. • Media Specialist • Beavercreek Schools Shaw Elementary School • Beavercreek, OH 45431 • AASL ALSC

Morris Margarette A. • Media Librarian • Belfry High School • Belfry, KY 41514

Morris Mark H. • Sch L Media Spec • Irvington High School • Irvington, NY 10533

Morris Marlene B. • Media Specialist • Hewlett-Woodmere Public Schools • Hewlett, NY 11557

Morris Mary Ann • Acquisitions Librarian • Capital University Library • Columbus, OH 43209 • ACRL

Morris Mary B. • Atlanta, GA 30331

Morris Mary F. • Greenville, NC 27836 • ACRL

Morris Mary S. • Librarian/Dist Media Coordinator • Show Low Schools • Show Low, AZ 85901 • AASL

Morris Miriam L. • Head of Extension Services • Lane Public Library • Hamilton, OH 45011 • LAMA PLA

Morris Nancy E. • Cataloging Librarian • Phoenix Public Library • Phoenix, AZ 85004 • ACRL ALCTS LITA PLA RASD

Morris Pamela A. • Arlington, TX 76012 • GODORT

Morris Patricia S. • East Hanover Middle School • East Hanover, NJ 07936 • AASL LITA YALSA

Morris Patrick A. • Oak Park, IL 60304

Morris Peggy A. • Coordinator of Library Services • Metro-Nashville-Davidson County Public Schools • Nashville, TN 37204 • AASL

Morris R. Philip II Mr. • Assistant Director • High Point Public Library • High Point, NC 27261 • ALCTS LAMA LITA PLA

Morris Raymond • Trustee • Arapahoe Library District • Littleton, CO 80121 • PLA

Morris Richard W. • Student • San Jose State University Division of Library & Information Science • San Jose, CA 95192-0029 • RASD IFRT

Morris Sally E. • Reference Librarian • Glenview Public Library • Glenview, IL 60025 • RASD SRRT

Morris Sharon B. • Head Librarian • North Springs High School • Atlanta, GA 30328 • AASL

Morris Sonja • Instructional & Ref Libn • Diablo Valley College Library • Pleasant Hill, CA 94523 • ACRL LIRT

Morris Steve R. • Miami, FL 33143 • ACRL RASD

Morris Susan D. • Interloan Librarian • University of Georgia Libraries • Athens, GA 30602 • ACRL RASD IRRT

Morris Susan M. • Head, Technical Services • Cedar Falls Public Library • Cedar Falls, IA 50613 • ACRL ALCTS

Morris Teresa • Student • Salisbury State University Blackwell Library • Salisbury, MD 21801 • LITA

Morris Terry • Assistant Childrens Librarian • Payson Public Library • Payson, AZ 85541 • ALSC

Morris Thelma Ananias • Children's Librarian • Los Angeles Public Library Baldwin Hills Branch • Los Angeles, CA 90016

Morris Thelma J. • Head of Social Science Dept • Cleveland Public Library • Cleveland, OH 44114-1271 • RASD IFRT

Morris Theodora • Ventura, CA 93003 • AASL

Morris Timothy J. • Subject Cataloging • Library of Congress • Washington, DC 20541

Morris Trisha A. • Head Librarian • Pennsylvania State University • DuBois, PA 15801 • ACRL

Morris Tzvee • Program Officer • Metropolitan Library Service Agency (MELSA) • Saint Paul, MN 55104-3083 • LAMA PLA

Morris Victoria J. • Student • Wayne State University • Detroit, MI 48202

Morris William C. • Advertising Promotion Director • HarperCollins Publishers HarperCollins Children's Books • New York, NY 10022 • AASL ALSC YALSA

Morrisey Locke J. • University of California-Irvine Library • Irvine, CA 92713 • ACRL NMRT

Morrison-Morgan Julia E. • Pittsford, NY 14534 • AASL

Morrison Billy M. • Student • Southern Connecticut State University School of Libray Science & Instructional Technology • New Haven, CT 06515

Morrison Bobbie • Library Director • Pacific Grove Public Library • Pacific Grove, CA 93950 • PLA

Morrison Carol J. • Information Network Consultant • Dupage Library System • Geneva, IL 60134 • ASCLA LAMA PLA

Morrison Daryl • Special Collections Librarian • University of the Pacific • Stockton, CA 95211 • ACRL

Morrison David Lee • Documents Division Librarian • University of Utah Marriott Library • Salt Lake City, UT 84112-1179 • GODORT

Morrison Deborah L. • Sonoma County Library Sonoma Valley Regional Branch • Sonoma, CA 95476

Morrison Dorothy G. • Librarian • Bon Air Elementary School • Richmond, VA 23235 • AASL

Morrison Gary • Oakland, CA 94611 • YALSA

Morrison J. Michael • APO, AE 09162 • AFLRT

Morrison Jane B. • Librarian • Hampden Sydney College Eggleston Library • Hampden-Sydney, VA 23943

Morrison Jennifer C. • Coral Springs, FL 33065

Morrison Kimberly M. • Librarian • Fairview Elementary School • Waynesboro, PA 17268 • AASL

Morrison Lissa • Kingston, AR 72742

Morrison Louise • Olympia, WA 98502-6202

Morrison Margaret • Santa Ana, CA 92706 • ACRL LAMA *Continuing*

Morrison Margaret L. • University of Central Arkansas-Torreyson Library • Conway, AR 72035 • ACRL LITA RASD GODORT

Morrison Marian M. • Circulation/Reference Librarian • LeMoyne-Owen College Hollis F. Price Library • Memphis, TN 38126

Morrison Mary A. • Librarian • St. Mary's High School • Worcester, MA 01610

Morrison Mary L. • Extension Services • Findlay-Hancock County Public Library • Findlay, OH 45840 • ASCLA

Morrison Meris Elaine • Director • Brooks Memorial Library • Brattleboro, VT 05301

Morrison Pat • Reference & Public Servs Dir • Southern Missionary College McKee Library • Collegedale, TN 37315 • RASD

Morrison Patricia A. • Senior Librarian • Sonoma Cnty Library Northwest Regional Branch • Santa Rosa, CA 95401

Morrison Pauline • Resource Librarian • Anchorage School District • Anchorage, AK 99502 • AASL ALSC

Morrison Perry D. • Professor Emeritus • University of Oregon Library • Eugene, OR 97403-1299 • ACRL RASD *Life*

Morrison Ray L. • Library Director • Mid-America Nazarene College Mabee Library • Olathe, KS 66061 • ACRL

Morrison Rebecca H. • Reference Librarian • Kemp Public Library • Wichita Falls, TX 76301

Morrison Robert P. • Reference Librarian • Utah State University Merrill Library • Logan, UT 84322-3000 • ACRL RASD IFRT

Morrison Roberta E. • Head of Youth Services • Franklin Park Public Library District • Franklin Park, IL 60131 • ALSC

Morrison Samuel F. • Director • Broward County Division of Libraries Broward County Library • Fort Lauderdale, FL 33301 • LAMA PLA SRRT

Morrison Sheila T. • Technical Services Librarian • Wellesley College Library Margaret Clapp Library • Wellesley, MA 02181-8275 • LITA

Morrison Shirley R. • Children's Librarian • Santa Barbara Public Library System • Santa Barbara, CA 93102 • ALSC IFRT

Morriss Susan • Waynesville School District Media Center • Waynesville, MO 65583 • AASL

Morrissett Linda A. • Circulation Services Supervisor • Western Kentucky University Helm-Cravens Library • Bowling Green, KY 42101 • ACRL LAMA

Morrissette Patricia F. • Technical Services Librarian • Upper Dublin Public Library • Dresher, PA 19025 • ALCTS

Morrissey Eleanor • Nashville, TN 37205 • Continuing

Morrissey Leslie S. • Library Director • Holmes Public Library • Halifax, MA 02338-1394 • PLA

Morrissey William P. • Reference Librarian • Barry University Library • Miami Shores, FL 33161 • ACRL

Morrow-Schwab Ann • Student • University of North Carolina Department of Library & Information Studies • Greensboro, NC 27412-5001 • YALSA EMIERT IFRT SRRT

Morrow Carolyn • Harvard University • Cambridge, MA 02138 • ALCTS

Morrow Christina K. • Milwaukee Public Library • Milwaukee, WI 53233 • RASD

Morrow Claudia L. • Student • University of California-Berkeley School of Library & Information Studies • Berkeley, CA 94720 • ALSC EMIERT IFRT SRRT

Morrow Deborah • Automation Librarian • Grand Valley State University Zumberge Library • Allendale, MI 49401-9403 • ACRL ALCTS LITA

Morrow Jean A. • Director of Libraries • New England Conservatory of Music-Spaulding Library • Boston, MA 02115 • ACRL

Morrow Karen • Librarian • Lakewood School District • Hebron, OH 43025

Morrow Kathryn M. • Librarian • Meadowview Cedar Hills School • Oak Creek, WI 53154 • AASL ALSC

Morrow Linda D. • Assistant Library Director • Troy Public Library • Troy, MI 48084

Morrow Lydia A. • Governors State University University Library • University Park, IL 60466

Morrow M. H. • Wellesley, MA 02181

Morrow Maureen M. • Long Island University Palmer School of Library & Information Science • Greenvale, NY 11548

Morrow Patricia A. • Elementary Librarian • David Lipscomb Elementary School • Nashville, TN 37204 • AASL ALSC

Morrow Patricia J. • Student • Rutgers University School of Communication Information & Library Studies • New Brunswick, NJ 08903 • AASL

Morrow Wyndol J. Mr • Houston, TX 77071 • LAMA PLA *Life*

Morse-Kahn Deborah • Student • Hamline University • Saint Paul, MN 55104 • IFRT

Morse Alfred W. • Kennett Sq, PA 19348 • ACRL ALCTS *Life*

Morse Alicia Mrs. • Durham, CT 06422

Morse B Jo • Alaska State Library • Anchorage, AK 99503 • AASL ASCLA

Morse Barbara J. • Director • Southwick Public Library • Southwick, MA 01077

Morse Beatrice • Eight Mile, AL 36613

Morse Celia B. • Berkley Public Library • Berkley, MI 48072 • PLA

Morse David H. • Assoc. Dir. for Collection Res. • University of Southern California Norris Medical Library • Los Angeles, CA 90033-4582 • ACRL ALCTS LAMA LITA RASD

Morse Elizabeth E. • Head of Children's Services • Wallingford Public Library • Wallingford, CT 06492

Morse Joan E. • Lib Media Spec/H S Coor for Sys • Reading Memorial High School • Reading, MA 01867

Morse Linda R. • North York Public Library • North York ON, M2N 5N9 Canada

Morse Lori J. • Free Library of Philadelphia • Philadelphia, PA 19103 • PLA RASD NMRT

Morse Mark P. • Director • L.E. Phillips Memorial Public Library • Eau Claire, WI 54701 • LAMA PLA

Morse Pat Bastin • Gainesville, FL 32605

Morse Rick • Student • Wayne State University Library Science Program • Detroit, MI 48202 • ALSC SRRT

Morse Ruth N. • Reference Support Librarian • County of Los Angeles Public Library Norwalk Library 501 • Norwalk, CA 90650

Morse Susan Virginia • Director, LRC • DeVry Institute of Technology • Phoenix, AZ 85021 • ACRL

Morse Tenna • Technical Information Ctr Mgr • Computer Science Corp Technical Information Center • Silver Spring, MD 20910

Morse Yvonne • Director • Ringling School of Art & Design • Sarasota, FL 34234 • LAMA

Morshead Diana • Student • University of Michigan School of Information and Library Studies • Ann Arbor, MI 48109-1092 • LITA

Morsi Tracy M • Children's Librarian • Waterford Township Public Library • Waterford, MI 48329 • ALSC PLA

Morsman E Kimball Mr • Evanston, IL 60201 • ACRL *Life*

Morss Robert L. • Las Vegas-Clark County Library District Green Valley Library • Henderson, NV 89014

Mort Mary-Ellen M.L.S. • Principal • Alameda County Business Library • Oakland, CA 94612

Mort Sarah L. • Assistant Professor • University of Arizona Graduate Library School • Tucson, AZ 85721 • ACRL LAMA

Mortensen Kalleen • Access Services Librarian • University of Wisconsin Instructional Materials Center • Madison, WI 53706

Mortensen Vivian J. • Park Ridge Public Library • Park Ridge, IL 60068-4188 • PLA

Mortenson Kathleen E. • Falmouth Public Library • Falmouth, MA 02540

Mortenson Phyllis • Supervisor Reference Librarian • Alameda Free Library • Alameda, CA 94501

Mortimer Ruth • Rare Books Curator • Smith College William Allan Neilson Library • Northampton, MA 01063 • ACRL

Morton Bruce • Assistant Dean for Public Serv. • Montana State University • Bozeman, MT 59717-0332 • ACRL LAMA RASD GODORT

Morton Donald J. • Library Director • University of Massachusetts Medical School Medical Center Library • Worcester, MA 01655 • ACRL ALCTS LAMA LITA

Morton Ellen • Library Director • Peoples Library • New Kensington, PA 15239

Morton Katharine D. • Downers Grove, IL 60515 • ACRL

Morton Laura M. • Waterloo Public Library • Waterloo, IA 50701 • LAMA

Morton Marianne M. • Student • Dalhousie University School of Library & Inf. Studies • Halifax NS, B3H 4H8 Canada

Morton Sandra J. • Student • Towson State University • Towson, MD 21204 • AASL

Morton Susan D. • Adult Services Librarian • New Castle-Henry County Public Library • New Castle, IN 47362 • PLA RASD YALSA

Mosborg Stella F. • Residence Halls Librarian • University of Illinois Library • Urbana, IL 61801 • ACRL LAMA

Mosby Anne Page • Associate Professor • Georgia State University Pullen Library • Atlanta, GA 30303-3081 • ACRL ALCTS RASD

Mosby Barbara H. • Media Specialist • F. A. Toomer Elementary School • Atlanta, GA 30318

Mosby Elizabeth • Associate Project Director • National Medical Association • Washington, DC 20001

Moscatt Angeline • New York Public Library Donnell Library Center • New York, NY 10019 • ALSC PLA EMIERT SRRT

Moschetta Virginia M. • Supervisor,Electronic Services • AT&T Information Research Center • Bernardsville, NJ 07924 • LITA RASD

Moschetti Teresa • Student • University of Arizona Graduate Library School • Tucson, AZ 85721 • AASL

Moscoso Ana Isabel • Library Director • University of Puerto Rico Medical Sciences Campus • San Juan, PR 00936 • ACRL

Moseley Anne • Director • Cherokee County Public Library • Gaffney, SC 29340

Moseley Dorothy N. • Library Principal Associate • Atlanta-Fulton Public Library Southwest Regional Library • Atlanta, GA 30331 • PLA

Moseley Lisa S. • Burskirk, NY 12028
Moseley Molly • Student • University of Alabama School of Library & Information Studies • Tuscaloosa, AL 35487-0252 • PLA
Moseley Monica • Reference Librarian • New York Public Library Performing Arts • New York, NY 10023 • ACRL
Mosell Molaan K. • Student • University of Iowa School of Library & Information Science • Iowa City, IA 52242
Moseman Suzanne S. • Catonsville, MD 21228
Moser Jody A. • Reference Service Spec. • Orange County Public Library University Park Branch • Irvine, CA 92715 • PLA
Moser Judith E. • Head,Original Cataloging • Claremont Colleges Libraries Honnold/Mudd Library • Claremont, CA 91711 • ALCTS
Moser Katherine T. • Student • University of Michigan School of Information and Library Studies • Ann Arbor, MI 48109-1092
Moses Barbara • Holmes Beach, FL 34217-1245 • PLA
Moses Camelia T. • Library Media Specialist • Carthage Central School District West Carthage Elementary School • Carthage, NY 13619 • AASL
Moses Carolyn S. • Student • Queens College Graduate School of Library & Information Studies • Flushing, NY 11367
Moses D. James • Assistant Director • Hastings Public Library • Hastings, NE 68902
Moses Hanna • Assistant Head of Technical Serv • Skokie Public Library • Skokie, IL 60077-3680
Moses Lynn M. • Allentown, PA 18104
Moses Ruth E. Miss • Concord, NH 03301 • Continuing
Moses Stefan B. • Livingston, TX 77351-9300 • ACRL ASCLA PLA *Life*
Mosey Jeanette • Director of Support Services • Arapahoe Library District • Littleton, CO 80121 • ACRL ALCTS LITA
Moshen Virginia • Adult Services Librarian • Matawan-Aberdeen Public Library • Matawan, NJ 07747
Moshenberg Ellen R. • Orange, CT 06477
Mosher Paul H. • Vice Provost & Director of Libs • University of Pennsylvania Library Van Pelt-Dietrich Library Center • Philadelphia, PA 19104-6206 • ACRL ALCTS
Mosher Sharon • Teacher-Librarian • Beatty-Fleming School • Brampton, ON, L6U 2A1 Canada • AASL ALSC
Moshfegh Mahnaz K. • Indiana University School of Library and Information Science • Bloomington, IN 47405 • ALCTS NMRT
Moshfeghian Patricia E. • Brownsville, TX 78521 • AASL
Mosimann Elizabeth A. • Readen Services Librarian • University of Pennsylvania Library Van Pelt-Dietrich Library Center • Philadelphia, PA 19104-6206 • ACRL RASD
Moskal Arlene • School Media Specialist • Fort Lee Public Schools #1 • Fort Lee, NJ 07024 • AASL
Moskal Fredereike A. • Library Director • Lewis University Library • Romeoville, IL 60441 • ACRL
Moskal Judy K. • Arlington Hts., IL 60004 • ALSC
Moskal Robin • Reference Librarian • University of Maryland Baltimore County Kuhn Library • Catonsville, MD 21228 • ACRL
Moskal Stephen L. Sr. • Library Director • LaGrange Public Library • La Grange, IL 60525 • PLA
Moskin Hanna R. • Librarian • P.S. 87 • New York, NY 10024 • AASL
Moskos Peter N. • Student • University of Pittsburgh School of Library and Information Science • Pittsburgh, PA 15260
Moskovits Leah • Librarian • The Hillel Academy • Passaic, NJ 07055
Moskowitz Kathryn B. • Carondelet High School Library • Concord, CA 94518
Moskowitz May • Librarian • Gleen Schoenhals School • Southfield, MI 48076
Moskowitz Michael Ann • Director • Emerson College Library • Boston, MA 02116 • ACRL
Moslander Charlotte D. M. S. • Periodicals/BI Librarian • College of New Rochelle Gill Library • New Rochelle, NY 10805 • ACRL
Mosler J. Rona • Director • Hackettstown Public Library • Hackettstown, NJ 07840 • PLA
Mosley Gloria A. • High School Librarian • Snyder High School • Snyder, OK 73566
Mosley Ivan T. Sr. • Durham, NC 27704
Mosley Kathrine E. • Austin, TX 78703
Mosley Madison M. Jr • Saint Petersburg, FL 33733-0445 • ACRL
Mosley Mary F. • Regional Children's Librarian • District of Columbia Public Library Francis Gregory Regional Branch • Washington, DC 20020 • ALSC
Mosley Mary Mac • Director • Shorter College Livingston Library • Rome, GA 30165 • AASL ACRL ALCTS LAMA LITA YALSA
Mosley Mattie Jacks • Associate Prof of Lib Sci • Louisiana State University • Shreveport, LA 71115 • AASL ALSC
Mosley Rose E. • Maywood Public Library • Maywood, IL 60153 • ALTA
Moss Anne E. • University of Dayton • Dayton, OH 45469-1390 • ACRL LHRT LRRT
Moss Barbara J. • Cataloging & Classification • Glenview Public Library • Glenview, IL 60025
Moss Bruce • Trustee • Kanawha County Public Library • Charleston, WV 25301 • ALTA
Moss Carol • Huntington Beach, CA 92649
Moss Charmagne L. • Reference Librarian • NASA Headquarters • Washington, DC 20546
Moss Constance J. • Carrollton Public Library • Carrollton, TX 75006 • LITA PLA
Moss Debbie • Hd, Div. of Technical Support • Orange County Library System Orlando Public Library • Orlando, FL 32801-2471 • PLA IFRT
Moss Eugenie L. • Cynthiana, KY 41031 • RASD
Moss Joseph Fred • Student • University of North Carolina at Chapel Hill School of Information and Library Science • Chapel Hill, NC 27599-3360 • ACRL
Moss Josievet • Detroit, MI 48214-2959 • SRRT
Moss Laurence • Babson College • Babson Park, MA 02157
Moss Linda L. • Washington, DC 20008 • IRRT
Moss Loretta E. • Library Director • C A D E S • Olajuela, Costa Rica
Moss M Eugenia • Oneonta, NY 13820 • ACRL IFRT *Continuing*
Moss Margaret M. • Librarian • Brown Junior High School • Henderson, NV 89015
Moss Mary M. • Elmwood Park Public Library • Elmwood Park, IL 60635
Moss Wayne • Trustee • Indianapolis Marion County Public Library • Indianapolis, IN 46206 • ALTA PLA IFRT
Mostafa Javed • Student • University of Texas at Austin Graduate School of Library & Information Sciences • Austin, TX 78712-1276 • LITA
Mote A. Christine • Catalogue Management Librarian • Arizona State University Hayden Library • Tempe, AZ 85287-1006 • LAMA
Mote Marie T. • Reference Librarian • Bellaire City Library • Bellaire, TX 77401-4498 • IFRT
Moten Stella L. • Librarian • Superconducting Super Collider • Dallas, TX 75237-3946
Motomatsu Nancy R. • Olympia, WA 98502 • AASL YALSA *Life*
Motson David E. • Southwest Texas State University University Library • San Marcos, TX 78666-4604 • IFRT
Mott Lawrence V. • Savoy, IL 61874
Mott Schuyler L. • Hamlin Memorial Library • Paris, ME 04271 • PLA IFRT
Mott William R. • Director of Development • Vanderbilt University Library Jean & Alexander Heard Library • Nashville, TN 37240-0007 • ACRL LAMA
Motteler Marilynn R. • Los Osos, CA 93402
Mottin Barbara • Branch Supervisor • Saint Louis County Library • St. Louis, MO 63131
Motylewski Karen • Northeast Document Conservation Center • Andover, MA 01810-1494 • ALCTS
Motz Minne R. • New York, NY 10033 • ALSC *Continuing*
Motzer Lederle T. • Student • University of Washington Graduate School of Library and Information Science • Seattle, WA 98195
Moulden Carol M. • Reference Librarian • National-Louis University • Evanston, IL 60201-1796 • ACRL
Moulton Catherine A. • Head of Cataloging Department • Boston University Mugar Memorial Library • Boston, MA 02215 • ACRL ALCTS LAMA LITA
Moulton David A. • Librarian • Strayer College • Washington, DC 20005 • ACRL
Moulton Katherine E. • Student • State University of New York at Albany School of Information Science & Policy • Albany, NY 12222
Moulton P. L. • Marblehead, MA 01945 • ALSC *Continuing*
Mounce Clara B. • City Librarian • Bryan Public Library • Bryan, TX 77803
Mounce Marvin W. • State Library of Florida Division of Library & Information Services • Tallahassee, FL 32399-0250 • ASCLA LITA RASD
Mount Kathy • Librarian • Northshore High School Library • Slidell, LA 70461
Mount Patricia M. • Administrative Assistant • Lubbock City-County Library • Lubbock, TX 79401 • PLA RASD
Mountain Timothy H. • Library Tech. Asst. I • Fullerton Public Library • Fullerton, CA 92632
Mountfort Ruth A. • Young Adult Librarian • Melrose Public Library • Melrose, MA 02176 • ALSC
Mountney Sherry L. • Director-Librarian • Tamarack Public Library • Lakeview, MI 48850 • PLA
Mounts Mark S. • Student • Rutgers University School of Communication Information & Library Studies • New Brunswick, NJ 08903 • ACRL RASD
Moustafa Theresa-Ann • Head of Children's Dept. • Metuchen Public Library • Metuchen, NJ 08840
Mouw James R. • Head of Serials • University of Chicago Library • Chicago, IL 60637-1502 • ACRL ALCTS LAMA NMRT
Mouzon Evarnie • Librarian • Northern Senior High School • Detroit, MI 48202 • AASL
Mowen Mary B. • Assistant Librarian • Keyser-Mineral County Library Potomac Valley Regional Library • Keyser, WV 26726
Mowery David C. • Branch Librarian • Brooklyn Public Library Clinton Hill Branch • Brooklyn, NY 11238
Mowery Linda • Hutchenson Junior High School • Arlington, TX 76010
Mowery M. Kay • Branch Librarian • University of Georgia Georgia Experiment Station Library • Griffin, GA 30223-1797 • ACRL LITA
Mowery Robert L. • Humanities Librarian • Illinois Wesleyan University Sheean Library • Bloomington, IL 61702 • ACRL ALCTS
Mowrey Judy • Librarian • De Anza College • Cupentino, CA 95070 • ACRL
Mowry Clara B. Miss • Providence, RI 02906 • Life
Moxley Melody A. • Headquarters Supervisor • Rowan Public Library • Salisbury, NC 28144 • PLA
Moxness Mary J. • Reference Librarian • Saint Mary's College Fitzgerald Library • Winona, MN 55987
Moy Clarence T. • Milford, NY 13807 • ASCLA LAMA *Life*
Moy Naomi O. • Bibliographic Instruction Coord. • California State University-Dominguez Hills Library • Carson, CA 90747 • ACRL LIRT
Moya del Pino Anne C. • Libraian II • Napa City-County Library • Napa, CA 94559-3396
Moye Mary V. • Librarian • Atlanta-Fulton Public Library • Atlanta, GA 30303 • GODORT
Moye Stephanie W. • Cambridge, MA 02139 • SRRT
Moyer Alexander M. • Southeastern Louisiana University Linus A. Sims Memorial Library • Hammond, LA 70402 • ALCTS
Moyer Anna Jane • Readers' Services Librarian • Gettysburg College Musselman Library • Gettysburg, PA 17325-1493 • ACRL
Moyer Heidi • Bethlehem, MD 21212 • AASL
Moyer James M. • Public Library of Charlotte & Mecklenburg County • Charlotte, NC 28202
Moyer Michael • Librarian • United States Air Force Base Library FL2805 • Edwards AFB, CA 93523-5000 • PLA
Moyers Joyce C. • Librarian • Rockingham Public Library • Harrisonburg, VA 22801 • PLA
Moyle Kate • Acquistions Librarian • Santa Clara County Free Library • San Jose, CA 95112-4446
Moynahan Sharon A. • Exec Sec of SALALM • University of New Mexico General Library • Albuquerque, NM 87131 • ACRL
Moynihan Timothy • Trustee • Bridgeview Public Library • Bridgeview, IL 60455 • ALTA
Mozenter Frada L. • Charlotte, NC 28212 • ACRL RASD LIRT
Mozga John P. • Assistant Director • Joliet Public Library • Joliet, IL 60431 • LITA
Mozina Kara J. • Avon Lake Public Library • Avon Lake, OH 44012
Mozley Dorothy • Orange City, FL 32763-6181 • Continuing
Mraz Patricia B. • Librarian • Champlain Valley Union High School • Hinesburg, VT 05461 • AASL
Mraz Penelope A. • Student • Clark-Atlanta University School of Library & Information Studies • Atlanta, GA 30314-4391 • PLA
Mrazek Larry C. • Student • Louisiana State University School of Library & Information Science • Baton Rouge, LA 70803-3290
Mroz Marguerite S. • Assistant Materials Selection • Baltimore County Public Library • Towson, MD 21204 • PLA RASD
Mrozek Krystyna B. • Student • University of Chicago Graduate Library School • Chicago, IL 60637
Mrozoski Mary Ann • Gary Public Library • Gary, IN 46402
Muallem Miriam • Student • Texas Woman's University School of Library & Information Studies • Denton, TX 76204
Mucci Judith • Associate Director • Orange County Library System Orlando Public Library • Orlando, FL 32801-2471 • LAMA PLA RASD GODORT
Muccing Willie E. • Acquisitions Librarian • Broward County Division of Libraries Broward County Library • Fort Lauderdale, FL 33301 • ALCTS
Much Jeanne • University of Wisconsin • Oshkosh, WI 54901

Muchhala Carolyn J. • Menomonee Falls, WI 53051 • AASL

Muchmore Wendy M. • Technical Serv. Coordinator • Livermore Public Library • Livermore, CA 94550 • ALCTS LITA PLA

Muchoney Anne D. • Marshall, VA 22115

Muchoney Joanne V. • Librarian • Ingomar Elementary School • Ingomar, PA 15237

Muchow Michael D. • University of Missouri Libraries-Columbia Elmer Ellis Library • Columbia, MO 65201-5149 • ACRL

Muck Judith A. • St Joseph, MO 64506-3434

Mudd Isabelle G. • Fairbanks, AK 99707 • FLRT

Mudrak Angela K. • Technical Services Librarian • Youngstown State University William F. Maag Library • Youngstown, OH 44555

Mudrick Kristine E. • Cabrini College Library • Radnor, PA 19087-3699 • LITA

Mudrock Theresa A. • University of Washington Graduate School of Library and Information Science • Seattle, WA 98195 • ACRL LIRT

Mueck Vicki Byrd • Seguin, TX 78155 • AASL NMRT SRRT

Muellenbach Joanne M. • Librarian • Meriter Hospital Memorial Medical Library • Madison, WI 53715

Mueller Allen W. • Director • Wesley Theological Seminary Lib • Washington, DC 20016 • ACRL RASD

Mueller Barbara H. • Arlington Heights, IL 60005

Mueller Bonnie • Librarian • U. S. General Accounting Office • Washington, DC 20548 • LITA FLRT

Mueller Britt K. • Senior Catalog Librarian • University of Oregon Library • Eugene, OR 97403-1299 • LITA

Mueller Carol J. • Head of the Marc Dept. • University of Wisconsin-Madison Memorial Library • Madison, WI 53706 • ACRL ALCTS LAMA

Mueller Carolyn J. • Chair, Processing Services • Humboldt State University Library • Arcata, CA 95521 • ALCTS LITA

Mueller Elizabeth • Consultant • Suburban Library System • Burr Ridge, IL 60521 • PLA

Mueller Elizabeth J. • Joplin, MO 64804

Mueller Gertrude H. • Milwaukee, WI 53207 • PLA   *Life*

Mueller Joan M. • Assistant Director • Oshkosh Public Library • Oshkosh, WI 54901 • LAMA PLA RASD

Mueller John • Northbrook, IL 60062 • PLA

Mueller Julie Glienna • Librarian • Gottlieb Memorial Hospital Library • Melrose Park, IL 60160

Mueller Karen L. • Librarian • Highland Junior High School • Libertyville, IL 60048 • AASL YALSA

Mueller Kirstin R. • Seattle, WA 98105-5815

Mueller Margret A. • Richmond Public Library North Avenue Branch • Richmond, VA 23222

Mueller Marion B. • Librarian • Lakeview Elementary School • Neenah, WI 54956

Mueller Martha A. • Associate Catlgr & Ser Librarian • Alfred University College of Ceramics Library • Alfred, NY 14802-1297 • ACRL ALCTS

Mueller Mary M. • Director • Rhino Records • Santa Monica, CA 90404

Mueller Peggy • Staff Development Officer • University of Texas Libraries General Libraries • Austin, TX 78713-7330 • ACRL LAMA

Mueller Randall C. • Accountant • University of Texas at Austin Graduate School of Library & Information Sciences • Austin, TX 78712-1276 • ALSC

Mueller Randall L. • Student • University of Cincinnati Langsam Library • Cincinnati, OH 45221-0033 • IFRT

Mueller Raymond Lynn • Music Librarian • Wisconsin Conservatory of Music • Milwaukee, WI 53202 • ALCTS

Mueller Sharon L. • Student • Southern Connecticut State University School of Libray Science & Instructional Technology • New Haven, CT 06515

Mueller Stephanie A. • Cabrillo College Library • Aptos, CA 95003 • ALCTS

Mueller Susan M. • Director of Technical Services • University of Montana Library • Missoula, MT 59812 • ALCTS LITA

Mueller Troye Carolyn • Librarian • San Luis Obispo City-County Library South Bay Branch • Los Osos, CA 93402

Mueller Victoria • Columbus, OH 43017

Muellner John • Head Librarian • Schiller Park Public Library • Schiller Park, IL 60176-1699 • PLA

Muenz Mercedes • Notre Dame, IN 46556 • Continuing

Mugridge Rebecca L. • Library Specialist IV • University of Pittsburgh Hillman Library • Pittsburgh, PA 15260 • ALCTS MAGERT

Muhammad Suad M. • Washington University Olin Library • Saint Louis, MO 63130 • ACRL

Muhlemann Karin • CH-8053 Zurich, Switzerland

Muhlena David P. • Student • University of Iowa School of Library & Information Science • Iowa City, IA 52242 • SRRT

Muir Anne T. • Saint Patrick's Episcopal Day School • Washington, DC 20007 • AASL ALSC

Muir Camille S. • San Jose, CA 95108 • ACRL

Muir Gordon D. • Senior Asst. Reference Librarian • State Univ Coll Feinberg Library • Plattsburgh, NY 12901 • ACRL

Muir Helen • Trustee • Miami-Dade Public Library System • Miami, FL 33130-1504 • ALTA

Muir Holly J. • Student • University of Texas at Austin Graduate School of Library & Information Sciences • Austin, TX 78712-1276 • SRRT

Muir Scott P. • Systems Officer • University of Alabama Amelia Gayle Gorgas Library • Tuscaloosa, AL 35487-0266 • LITA

Muirhead Gail E. • System Librarian • Joint Computer Program for Libraries • Skokie, IL 60077 • LITA

Mulac Carolyn M. • Assistant Unit Head, Info. Ctr. • Chicago Public Library • Chicago, IL 60605 • RASD

Mulawka Chet • Manager • Atherton Library • Atherton, CA 94027 • PLA SRRT

Mulberg Lillian • Shaker Hts, OH 44122

Mulcahy Bryan L. • Reference Librarian • Lee County Library System • Fort Myers, FL 33901 • PLA

Mulcahy Daniel M. • Trustee • Dearborn Department of Libraries Henry Ford Centennial Library • Dearborn, MI 48126

Mulcahy Kevin P. • Rutgers University Libraries Archibald Stevens Alexander Library • New Brunswick, NJ 08903 • ACRL RASD IFRT

Mulcare Nancy • Librarian • Bishop Stang High School • North Dartmouth, MA 02747 • AASL

Mulder Christopher J. • University Librarian • Edith Cowan University • Churchlands, Australia • ACRL

Mulder Connie • Columbus, OH 43223 • IFRT SRRT

Mulder Craig A. • Asst. Director for Education • Johns Hopkins University Libraries William H Welch Medical Library • Baltimore, MD 21205 • ACRL LITA

Mulder James L. • Reference Librarian • Peru State College Library • Peru, NE 68421 • ACRL

Muldner June • George H. Nichols Elementary School • Endicott, NY 13760 • AASL

Muldoon James R. • Principal/President • Food for Thought • Coram, NY 11727

Mule Gabriel D.C. Sr • Provincial Librarian & AV Coor. • Seton Provincialate • Los Altos Hills, CA 94022 • AASL ASCLA LAMA

Mulford Martha G. • Student • Appalachian State University Department of Library Science & Educational Foundation • Boone, NC 28608 • AASL

Mulfort Ann L. • St. Paul, MN 55102 • IFRT NMRT SRRT

Mulgrew Patricia • Branch Manager • Prince George County Memorial Library System Hyattsville Branch • Hyattsville, MD 20782 • LAMA PLA

Mulhern Frank J. • Baton Rouge, LA 70806

Mulholland Connie M. • Library Systems Manager • Scottsdale Public Library • Scottsdale, AZ 85251 • PLA

Mulholland Mary L. • Annandale, VA 22003

Mulhollon Daniel P. • Chief, Government Division • Library of Congress • Washington, DC 20541

Mulia Gusti • Yonkers, NY 10701 • ALCTS LITA

Mulkey Jack C. • Associate Director • Arkansas State Library • Little Rock, AR 72201 • ASCLA PLA

Mulkey Marie B. • Park Forest, IL 60466

Mulkey Patricia P. • Library Coordinator • Plano Public School • Plano, TX 75023 • AASL

Mulks Gwendolyn A. • Legal Librarian • Ray, Quinney & Nebeker • Salt Lake City, UT 84145-0385

Mull Barbara • Interlibrary Loan • Mid-Continent Public Library • Independence, MO 64050

Mull Margaret M. • Minneapolis, MN 55401 • PLA   *Life*

Mullane Jane Ann • Librarian • Summitt Elementary School • Austin, TX 78727 • ALSC

Mullaney Beth J. • Pittsburgh, PA 15216-3149 • ACRL LAMA

Mullarkey Thomas • Rockville, MD 20850

Mullen Annette J. • New York, NY 10025

Mullen Donald • Library Director • Dover Public Library • Dover, NH 03820

Mullen Evelyn Day • Raleigh, NC 27605 • Continuing

Mullen Francis X. • Librarian • Ridley Township Public Library • Folsom, PA 19033 • LAMA PLA RASD

Mullen Gail • Director • Barrie Public Library • Barrie ON, L4M 3M2 Canada • PLA RASD

Mullen Gregory T. • Assistant City Librarian • Santa Monica Public Library • Santa Monica, CA 90401 • PLA

Mullen Helen Mae • Children's Coordinator • Free Library of Philadelphia • Philadelphia, PA 19103 • ALSC PLA

Mullen Joan M. • Librarian/Dept. Chair • Sparrows Point High School • Baltimore, MD 21219 • AASL

Mullendore Betty J. • Washington, DC 20011 • PLA RASD   *Life*

Mullens Susan • Flagstaff, AZ 86001

Muller-Oelrichs Gaby • Chief Librarian • German Historical Institute • Washington, DC 20009 • ACRL

Muller Alice B. • Phoenix, AZ 85044

Muller Charles W. Jr. • Librarian III Asst. Hd. of Tech. • Broward County Division of Libraries Broward County Library • Fort Lauderdale, FL 33301 • ALCTS LITA

Muller Claudya B. • Cuyahoga County Public Library • Cleveland, OH 44134-2792 • LAMA PLA

Muller Emily B. • Oak Harbor, WA 98277-8360

Muller Frederick B. • Halsted School Library • Newton, NJ 07860 • AASL LIRT

Muller Janet D. • John Handley High School • Winchester, VA 22601 • AASL

Muller Karen • ALCTS/LAMA Executive Director • American Library Association • Chicago, IL 60611-2795 • ALCTS LAMA   *Life*

Muller Lola IL • Long Point, IL 61333 • Continuing

Muller Mary M. • United States Embassy Ottawa • Ogdensburg, NY 13669-0430

Muller Patricia • Arlington County Department of Libraries • Arlington, VA 22201 • YALSA

Muller Robert H. Mr • Walnut Creek, CA 94595 • ACRL ALCTS LAMA   *Life*

Muller Susan K. • County of Los Angeles Public Library Rowland Heights Branch • Rowland Heights, CA 91740 • ALSC RASD

Muller William A. III • Director • Bristol Public Library • Bristol, VA 24201-4199 • LAMA LITA PLA

Mullican Dorothy C. • Trustee • Jefferson Parish Library • Metairie, LA 70010 • ALTA

Mulligan Anne-Marie • Reference Librarian • Lucius Beebe Memorial Library • Wakefield, MA 01880

Mulligan Helen • School Library Media Spec. • Cherry Lane School Library • Westbury, NY 11514 • AASL

Mulligan Thomas C. • School Librarian • San Francisco Unified School District • San Francisco, CA 94104

Mullin Joan • Media Specialist • Welcome Elementary School • Greenville, SC 29611 • AASL

Mullin Kalinski Carol A. • Librarian • Chrysler Corporation • Highland Park, MI 48288

Mullin Michael C. • Director • Watertown Regional Library • Watertown, SD 57201-0250 • PLA NMRT

Mullin Patrick J. • Asst. Univ. Libn. for Sys • University of North Carolina • Chapel Hill, NC 27599-3902 • ACRL LITA

Mullin Patrick M. • Youth Department Coordinator • Amarillo Public Library • Amarillo, TX 79189 • ALSC

Mullin Wayne • Head of Access Services • University of California McHenry Library • Santa Cruz, CA 95064 • ACRL ALCTS LAMA RASD

Mulliner Kent • Assistant to Director • Ohio University Vernon R. Alden Library • Athens, OH 45701-2978 • ACRL LITA IRRT

Mullins Betty R. • Assistant Law Librarian • Mississippi State Law Library • Jackson, MS 39215-1040 • GODORT

Mullins James L. • Director of Library Services • Indiana University at South Bend Franklin D. Schurz Library • South Bend, IN 46634 • ACRL LAMA

Mullins Linda • Rowan Public Library • Salisbury, NC 28144

Mullins Lynn S. • Director • Rutgers University John Cotton Dana Library • Newark, NJ 07102 • ACRL LAMA LITA SRRT

Mullins Rita S. • Central High School • Blountville, TN 37617 • AASL

Mullowney Joanne P. • Student • Rutgers University School of Communication Information & Library Studies • New Brunswick, NJ 08903

Mulready Alice T. • Library Director • The Tufts Library • Weymouth, MA 02188 • PLA

Mulroy Kathleen • Director • Holy Family College Library • Philadelphia, PA 19114 • ACRL LAMA RASD

Mulroy Kevin • Gene Autry Western Heritage Museum • Los Angeles, CA 90027-1462 • ACRL

Mulroy Mary • Director of Operations • Saint Louis Public Library • St. Louis, MO 63103-2389 • LAMA PLA

Mulvaney John P. • Mary Washington College Library Simpson Library • Fredericksburg, VA 22401-4664 • ACRL ALCTS LRRT

Mulvey Dennis • Administrator • Centre County Library & Historical Museum • Bellefonte, PA 16823 • PLA SRRT

Mulvihill JoAnn • Reference Librarian • Arizona State University Hayden Library • Tempe, AZ 85287-1006 • ACRL RASD

Mumby James R. • Associate/Architectural Design • TWP Associates, Inc. • Bloomfields Hills, MI 48302

Mumford John • Reference Librarian • Juniata College L A Beeghly Library • Huntingdon, PA 16652

Mumford Shaw • Student • University of Wisconsin-Milwaukee School of Library & Information Science • Milwaukee, WI 53201 • IFRT SRRT

Mumma Polly S. • University of North Alabama Collier Library • Florence, AL 35632 • ALCTS

Munasque Narcissa V. • Director • National Library of the Philippines • Manila, Philippines
Munch Vincent A. • Montville Township Public Library • Montville, NJ 07045 • LAMA PLA RASD
Mundell Jacqueline • Nebraska Library Commission • Lincoln, NE 68508 • ASCLA LAMA LITA
Munden Gail • Chicago, IL 60603
Mundle Todd M. • University of Regina • Regina SK, S4S 0A2 Canada • LITA
Mundy Catherine A. • Reference Librarian • University of Colorado At Colorado Springs Library • Colorado Springs, CO 80933-7150 • ACRL
Munger Lucinda M. • Student • University of South Carolina College of Library & Information Science • Columbia, SC 29208 • PLA
Munger Melinda • Librarian • Miami-Dade Public Library System • Miami, FL 33130-1504 • ALSC
Munger Sally L. • Library Assistant II • Minneapolis Public Library Franklin Branch • Minneapolis, MN 55404 • PLA
Mungovan Susan A. • Asst Mgr Business & Technology • Allen County Public Library • Fort Wayne, IN 46801-2270 • GODORT
Munkres Raymond • Trustee • Metropolitan Library System • Oklahoma City, OK 73102 • ALTA PLA
Munn R. Russell • Kelowna BC, V1W 1C2 Canada • LAMA PLA *Continuing*
Munnelly Ann M. • Paralegal • Playtex Family Products • Stamford, CT 06904
Munns Sunny Ellen • Cataloging/Reference • Casper College Goodstein Foundation Library • Casper, WY 82601 • ACRL EMIERT
Munoff Gerald J. • Deputy Director • University of Chicago Library • Chicago, IL 60637-1502 • ACRL ALCTS LAMA
Munoz-Sola Haydee S. • Director of Library System • University of Puerto Rico • Rio Piedras, PR 00931 • ACRL
Munoz Patricia A. • Librarian • Randolph Elementary School • Arlington, VA 22307 • AASL ALSC
Munoz Romeo S. • Student • Northern Illinois University Department of Library & Information Studies • DeKalb, IL 60115 • AASL
Munro Sharon C. • Student • Dalhousie University School of Library & Inf. Studies • Halifax NS, B3H 4H8 Canada • ACRL ASCLA PLA RASD YALSA
Munroe Mary H. • Business/Public & Urban Affairs • Georgia State University Pullen Library • Atlanta, GA 30303-3081 • ACRL ALCTS RASD
Munroe Michael C. • Dallas, TX 75230 • RASD
Muns Raleigh C. • University of Missouri-Saint Louis • St. Louis, MO 63121-4499 • GODORT IFRT
Munson Charles T. • Librarian • Wisconsin Clearinghouse • Madison, WI 53703 • SRRT
Munson Judith A. • Student • University of Rhode Island Graduate School of Library & Information Studies • Kingston, RI 02881-0815
Munson Kurt I. • Student • University of Illinois Graduate School of Library and Information Science • Urbana, IL 61801
Munson Sally L. • Branch Librarian • Long, Aldridge & Norman Law Library • Atlanta, GA 30328
Munson Sara C. • Orange Public Library • Orange, CT 06477
Munsterman Marilyn • Denver, CO 80218 • ALCTS
Munthali Eggineta C. • Virginia Bch, VA 23464 • ACRL
Muntz J. Richard • Head Librarian • Western Baptist College Library • Salem, OR 97301 • ACRL RASD
Munywoki Ben M. • Student • University of North Texas School of Library & Information Sciences • Denton, TX 76203
Murata Corey I. • Reference Librarian • University of Hawaii Thomas Hale Hamilton Library • Honolulu, HI 96822 • RASD
Murata Mabel Ms • Detroit, MI 48217
Murata Susan S. • University of Hawaii Thomas Hale Hamilton Library • Honolulu, HI 96822 • LITA
Murchison Nola • Branch Manager • Riverside City & County Library Desert Hot Springs Branch • Desert Hot Springs, CA 92240
Murden Steven H. • Assistant Department Head • Virginia Commonwealth University James Branch Cabell Library • Richmond, VA 23284-2033 • ALCTS SRRT
Murdoch Janice H. • Washington, PA 15301 • AASL
Murdoch Mary E. Mrs • S Pasadena, CA 91030 • Continuing
Murdoch Robert G. • Assoc. Dir. of Pub. & Tech. Serv • Utah State University Merrill Library • Logan, UT 84322-3000 • ACRL LAMA
Murdoch Sandra K. • Base Librarian • Base Library FL 4810 • APO, AA 34001-5000 • AFLRT FLRT *Life*
Murdock Doris M. • Chula Vista, CA 91910 • Continuing
Murdock J. Larry • Documents Coor. & Reference Libn • Purdue University Libraries • West Lafayette, IN 47907-1530 • ACRL RASD GODORT MAGERT
Murdock Jeanne M. • Student • University of North Texas School of Library & Information Sciences • Denton, TX 76203 • PLA
Murdock Sue • Head Librarian • Carnegie Library of Pittsburgh Library for the Blind & Phys Hndcpd • Pittsburgh, PA 15213-1389 • ASCLA
Murdough Wess-John • San Francisco, CA 94127 • ACRL IFRT SRRT
Murfin Marjorie E. • Reference Librarian • Ohio State University Libraries • Columbus, OH 43210-1286 • LAMA RASD
Murgai Sarla R. • University of Tennessee T Carter & M Rawlings Lupton Lib • Chattanooga, TN 37403
Muro Ernest A. • President • Vendor Relations • Annandale, NJ 08801-0040 • ACRL ALCTS LITA ERT ILERT *Life*
Muro Susan C. • Executive Director • Southern Connecticut Library Council • Hamden, CT 06518-3235
Muroi Linda S. • Reference Librarian • San Diego State University Library • San Diego, CA 92119-2120 • ACRL RASD LIRT
Muronaga Karen N. • School Librarian • Abraham Lincoln Elementary School • Honolulu, HI 96813 • AASL
Murphey Barbara Ann • Director • Largo Public Library • Largo, FL 34640 • LAMA LITA PLA
Murphy-Walters Angela • Curriculum Librarian • Western Carolina University Hunter Library • Cullowhee, NC 28723-9002 • IFRT
Murphy Ann B. • Commissioner • Massachusetts Board of Library Commissioners • Boston, MA 02215-2070
Murphy Anne Marie • Branch Manager • Sonoma County Library • Santa Rosa, CA 95404
Murphy Anne R. • Librarian • Saint Marys School • Rockville, MD 20852
Murphy Audrey S. • Automation Librarian • Southeastern Libraries Cooperating (SELCO) • Rochester, MN 55901 • LITA
Murphy Barbara • Information Services Information • Westport Public Library • Westport, CT 06880
Murphy Barbara B. • Librarian • Shaler Area Sch Dist • Pittsburgh, PA 15116 • ALSC
Murphy Becky • Syracuse, NY 13219
Murphy Beverly S. • Student • Indiana University School of Library and Information Science • Bloomington, IN 47405
Murphy Bobby J. • Librarian • Saint Vincent De Paul • Peoria, IL 60614 • AASL
Murphy Brenda K. • Head of Youth Services • Skokie Public Library • Skokie, IL 60077-3680 • ALSC
Murphy Carolyn N. • District Supervisor • Fayette County Public Schools • Lexington, KY 40502 • AASL
Murphy Catherine • Director of Library Media Servs • Three Village Central School District • Setauket, NY 11733 • AASL ALCTS
Murphy Charles G. • Librarian • Fuss & O'Neill, Inc. • Manchester, CT 06040 • ALCTS LITA RASD
Murphy David W. • Cambridge, MA 02139 • SRRT
Murphy Deborah A. • Reference Librarian • University of California McHenry Library • Santa Cruz, CA 95064 • ACRL RASD
Murphy Diana G. • Librarian • Penn Hills School District • Pittsburgh, PA 15235 • AASL LIRT
Murphy Diane E. • Library Media Specialist • Saint Mark's School • Southborough, MA 01772 • AASL
Murphy Dolores • Children's Librarian • Paramus Public Library • Paramus, NJ 07652 • YALSA
Murphy Elizabeth • Librarian • Solano County Library • Fairfield, CA 94533
Murphy Ellen M. • Special Collections Librarian • University of Wisconsin • Milwaukee, WI 53201 • ACRL
Murphy Eugenia K. • New Haven, IN 46774 • VRT
Murphy Evelyn S. • Head Technical Service • Public Library of Des Moines • Des Moines, IA 50308-1791 • LITA IRRT
Murphy Frances • Huntington Memorial Library • Oneonta, NY 13820
Murphy Georgina M. • Canisius College Andrew L. Bouwhuis Library • Buffalo, NY 14208-1098 • ACRL
Murphy Gerald E. • Director • Northeast Georgia Regional Library • Clarkesville, GA 30523
Murphy Harry R. • Reference Librarian • University of Washington Libraries Odegaard Undergraduate Library • Seattle, WA 98195 • ACRL ALCTS NMRT
Murphy Helen W. • Lewes, DE 19958
Murphy Jane E. • Data Base Manager • Bibliomation Inc. • Stratford, CT 06497 • ALCTS
Murphy Janet H. • University of San Diego Copley Library • San Diego, CA 92110 • ACRL RASD
Murphy Janet M. • Reference/Adult Services Ln. • Hastings-On-Hudson Public Library • Hastings-On-Hudson, NY 10706 • PLA
Murphy Janice M. • Reference Librarian • Library of Michigan • Lansing, MI 48909
Murphy Jean A. • Assoc Libr Director Public Serv. • Mesa Public Library • Mesa, AZ 85201-6768 • LAMA
Murphy Joan D. • Albuquerque, NM 87102
Murphy Joan M. • Outreach Librarian • Elkhart Public Library Osolo Branch • Elkhart, IN 46514
Murphy Joseph Patrick • Administrative Services Asst. • Marin County Free Library • San Rafael, CA 94903
Murphy Joyce A. • Librarian • Lakeshore Elementary School • Monroe, LA 71203 • AASL
Murphy Karen L. • Coquille Valley Middle School • Coquille, OR 97423 • AASL ALSC
Murphy Kathleen A. • Head of Technical Services • Elmhurst Public Library • Elmhurst, IL 60126 • ALCTS
Murphy Kathryn B. • School Media Specialist • Starr Elementary school • Starr, SC 29684 • AASL
Murphy Kathryn L. • Ref/Tech Services Librarian • Northwest Missouri State University Owens Library • Maryville, MO 64468 • ACRL
Murphy Kathryn W. • Pittsburgh, PA 15228
Murphy Kerri T. • Student • Rutgers University School of Communication Information & Library Studies • New Brunswick, NJ 08903 • AASL
Murphy Kristine L. • Head of Order Department • Southern Methodist University • Dallas, TX 75275 • ACRL ALCTS
Murphy LaVerne • High School Librarian • LaGrange I.S.D. • LaGrange, TX 78945 • IFRT
Murphy Lauren L.R. • Student • University of Washington Graduate School of Library and Information Science • Seattle, WA 98195 • NMRT
Murphy Linda K. • Boston Public Library • Boston, MA 02117 • ALSC
Murphy Lois M. • Extension Department Librarian • Waukegan Public Library • Waukegan, IL 60085 • ASCLA
Murphy Lucile L. • Librarian • University of the Ozarks Dobson Memorial Library • Clarksville, AR 72830 • Continuing
Murphy M. Jims • Watertown, MA 02172 • FLRT
Murphy Marilyn G. • Eureka, CA 95501
Murphy Mary A. • Librarian • United States Air Force Eglin Base Library • Eglin AFB, FL 32542
Murphy Mary Catherine • Teacher-Librarian • Mary Lyon School Library • Chicago, IL 60634 • AASL
Murphy Pamela H. • Student • University of South Florida School of Library & Information Science • Tampa, FL 33620 • AASL YALSA
Murphy Pamela J. • Cataloger • Greenfield Public Library • Greenfield, MA 01301
Murphy Patricia A. • Director • Palo Verde College • Blythe, CA 92225 • ACRL
Murphy Patricia M. • Library Director • Ohio University • Saint Clairsville, OH 43950 • ACRL
Murphy Paul • Trustee • Clinton Public Library • Clinton, IA 52732 • ALTA
Murphy Paul A. • Library Director • Messenger Public Library of North Aurora • North Aurora, IL 60542
Murphy Paul H. • Librarian • Vanderbilt University Science Library • Nashville, TN 37240-0007 • ACRL RASD *Life*
Murphy Paula • A-V Services Librarian • Loyola University • Chicago, IL 60611 • ACRL VRT
Murphy Peggy A. • Librarian • Roseville Public Library • Roseville, CA 95678
Murphy Pency G. • Dallas, TX 75238 • ALCTS
Murphy Richard W. • Library Director • Prince William County Public Library Central Branch • Prince William, VA 22192 • LAMA
Murphy Ronald • Montclair Free Public Library • Montclair, NJ 07042 • PLA
Murphy Ruth R. • San Antonio, TX 78240 • ALSC
Murphy Sarah M. • Media Coordinator • Lexington Senior High School • Lexington, NC 27292 • AASL
Murphy Sheila • Program Officer, Literary Arts • Lila Wallace-Reader's Digest Fund • New York, NY 10016
Murphy Susan • Bluepoint, NY 11715 • YALSA
Murphy Terri L. • Director, Corporate Services • CLSI, Inc. • Newtonville, MA 02160 • LITA
Murphy Thomas L. • Arlington, VA 22201
Murphy Virginia A. • Media Specialist • Maple Elementary School • Cambridge, MD 21613 • AASL
Murphy Virginia Sr. • Director of Library • Marian College of Fond du Lac Cardinal Meyer Library • Fond du Lac, WI 54935
Murphy Walter H. • Executive Director • Flint River Regional Library • Griffin, GA 30223
Murphy William D. • Chicago, IL 60657 • Continuing
Murphy William G. • East Islip Public Library • East Islip, NY 11730-2896 • ALTA
Murr Kenneth R. • Reference Librarian • Clemson University Robert Muldrow Cooper Library • Clemson, SC 29634-3001 • RASD
Murra Dieta J. • Asst. Dir. Technical Service • Medical College of Wiconsin Libraries • Milwaukee, WI 53226 • LITA

Murray William E. • Student • Syracuse University School of Information Studies • Syracuse, NY 13244-4100

Murray-Roe Joyce E. • Goldey Beacom College Library • Wilmington, DE 19808 • ACRL

Murray-Rust Catherine L. • Assistant University Librarian • Cornell University Library • Ithaca, NY 14853 • LAMA

Murray Audrey L. • Student • University of Saint Thomas • St. Paul, MN 55105 • AASL EMIERT NMRT

Murray Barbara J. • Adult Coordinator • Palm Springs Unified School District • Palm Springs, CA 92262

Murray Bruce C. • Glenn Dale, MD 20769 • ALSC PLA

Murray Carol F. • Student • University of Washington Graduate School of Library and Information Science • Seattle, WA 98195

Murray Christopher T. • Technical Services Librarian • Orangeburg-Calhoun Technical College • Orangeburg, SC 29115

Murray Classie M. • Referecen Librarian • Lincoln Library • Springfield, IL 62701

Murray Darice D. • Senior Librarian • Abilene Public Library • Abilene, TX 79601-5793

Murray Dawn M. • Student • Simmons College Graduate School of Library & Information Science • Boston, MA 02115 • LITA

Murray Diane • Tucson, AZ 85716 • MAGERT

Murray Diane E. • Director of Libraries • Grand Valley State University Zumberge Library • Allendale, MI 49401-9403 • ACRL LAMA

Murray Donald A. Jr • Circulation Librarian • University of Minnesota O. Meredith Wilson Library • Minneapolis, MN 55455-0414 • ACRL LAMA

Murray Edward A. • Audio-Visual Librarian • Steele Memorial Library • Elmira, NY 14901-2799 • PLA

Murray Elizabeth H. • Student • Simmons College Graduate School of Library & Information Science • Boston, MA 02115 • ACRL

Murray Florence B. • Professor Emeritus • University of Toronto Faculty of Library & Information Science • Toronto ON, M5S 1A1 Canada • ACRL RASD *Continuing*

Murray Ginger • Student • University of Oklahoma School of Library & Information Studies • Norman, OK 73019 • ALSC YALSA NMRT

Murray Grace • Sacramento, CA 95818 • Continuing

Murray Harris C. • Student • University of South Carolina College of Library & Information Science • Columbia, SC 29208 • AASL

Murray Hilary Ann • Acquisitions Librarian • Wheaton College Wallace Library • Norton, MA 02766 • ACRL ALCTS

Murray James B. • Birmingham Public Library • Birmingham, AL 35203

Murray James H. • Staff Specialist III • Maryland State Department of Education Division of Library Development & Services • Baltimore, MD 21201

Murray James L. • Trustee • Prince George's County Memorial Library System • Hyattsville, MD 20782-2098 • ALTA

Murray Janet A. • Teacher-Bug Dept.,Library Aide • LaSalle Academy • Providence, RI 02908 • AASL

Murray Janet P. • Librarian/Ed Media Specialist • Wilson High School • Portland, OR 97219 • AASL LITA

Murray John D. • Director • Westmont College Roger John Voskuyl Library • Santa Barbara, CA 93108-1099 • ACRL LITA

Murray Juanita • Southfield, MI 48075

Murray Judith L. • Student • University of Michigan School of Information and Library Studies • Ann Arbor, MI 48109-1092

Murray Kathleen R. • Assoc. Director for Ln Oper. • Lamar University Gray Library • Beaumont, TX 77710 • ACRL ALCTS IFRT

Murray Laura • Head of AV Department • Metro Toronto Reference Library • Toronto ON, M4W 2G8 Canada • AASL ASCLA LAMA PLA VRT

Murray Lee M. • Head,Science & Technology Libs • Syracuse University • Syracuse, NY 13244 • ACRL

Murray Lucia M. • Adult Reference Librarian • Corvallis-Benton County Public Library • Corvallis, OR 97330-4728 • PLA

Murray Margaret A. • Consultant • Southeast Missouri Library Asst Program • Poplar Bluff, MO 63901 • ASCLA

Murray Marijean • Supervisory Librarian • United States Army Valent Learning Resource Center • Fort Bliss, TX 79918-5000 • AFLRT

Murray Nadine A. • London, ON, N6G 3L3 Canada • PLA RASD YALSA

Murray Peggy E. • Library Director • Los Gatos Public Library • Los Gatos, CA 95032 • PLA

Murray Raymond • Multitype Development Consultant • Northern Illinois Library System • Rockford, IL 61108 • ACRL ASCLA PLA

Murray Robert B. • Reference Department • Orange County Library System Orlando Public Library • Orlando, FL 32801-2471

Murray Rochelle • Head of Children's Services • Davenport Public Library • Davenport, IA 52801 • ALSC

Murray Ruth C. Mrs. • Baton Rouge, LA 70808

Murray Theresa A. • Louisville, CO 80027

Murray Thomas • Trustee • Indian Trails Public Library District • Wheeling, IL 60090 • ALTA

Murray Timothy D. • Associate Librarian • University of Delaware Library • Newark, DE 19717-5267 • ACRL

Murray William A. • Aurora Public Schools • Aurora, CO 80011-9023 • AASL IFRT LIRT SRRT

Murrell Jeanette L. • Public Services Librarian • Casper College Goodstein Foundation Library • Casper, WY 82601 • ACRL

Murrell Paula R. • Media Specialist • Urbandale Community Schools • Urbandale, IA 50322 • AASL

Murrey Nancy L. • Student • University of South Florida College of Education • Tampa, FL 33620 • IFRT

Mursec Ljudmila T. • Milwaukee, WI 53219

Murten Holly T. • Dallas, TX 75228

Murtha Leslie • Student • Rutgers University School of Communication Information & Library Studies • New Brunswick, NJ 08903

Musante Patricia • Asst. Dir/Children's Lib • Potsdam Public Library • Potsdam, NY 13676

Muscardin Joann • Plainview, NY 11803

Muse Vonceil F. • Dallas, TX 75241 • Continuing

Muselman Brenda Jean • Bookkeeper/Tech Servs • Adair County Public Library • Kirksville, MO 63501

Muselman LaRae C. • Librarian • Pekin Community High School • Pekin, IL 61554 • AASL YALSA

Muser Jeanette • Librarian • West Windsor-Plainsboro High School • Princeton Junction, NJ 08550-0248 • AASL

Musgrave Mary H. • Director • DeSoto Public Library • DeSoto, TX 75115 • LAMA PLA

Mushakoji Nobukazu • Assistant Professor • Daito Bunka University • Tokyo, Japan • ACRL ALCTS ERT MAGERT

Mushel Susan A. • Information Access Librarian • Texas Tech University Libraries • Lubbock, TX 79409-0002 • GODORT

Mushenheim Cecilia A. • Research Assistant/Cataloger • University of Dayton • Dayton, OH 45469-1390 • ACRL ALCTS

Mushisky Nicole M. • Toledo-Lucas County Public Library Maumee Branch • Maumee, OH 43537

Mushko Richard A. • Elizabeth, NJ 07208

Musmann Klaus Ph.D. • Collection Development Librarian • University of Redlands Armacost Library • Redlands, CA 92374-3758 • ACRL LRRT

Musselman Barbara A. • Regional Genealogy Specialist • Cuyahoga County Public Library Fairview Park Regional Branch • Fairview Park, OH 44126-2189 • PLA RASD MAGERT

Musser E. Glenn Jr. • Head Technical/Building Sus. • Worcester Public Library • Worcester, MA 01608 • ALCTS LITA

Musser Linda R. • Pennsylvania State University Libraries • University Park, PA 16802 • ACRL MAGERT

Musser Nancy Thomas • Chief, Technical Services • San Francisco Public Library • San Francisco, CA 94102 • ALCTS PLA

Mussett Steven A. • Catalog Librarian • University of Evansville • Evansville, IN 47722 • ALCTS SRRT

Mustain-Wood Janice R. • Library Director • Fort Lupton Public & School Library • Ft Lupton, CO 80621 • PLA

Mustain John E. • Associate Librarian • Stanford University Libraries Cecil H. Green Library • Stanford, CA 94305-6004 • ACRL LHRT

Mustar Terry • Trustee • Clark County Public Library • Springfield, OH 45501-1080 • ALTA

Musto Frederick W. • Reference Librarian • Yale University Sterling Memorial Library • New Haven, CT 06520 • ACRL ALCTS RASD LHRT

Mustonen Karlo K. • Reference Librarian • Utah State University Merrill Library • Logan, UT 84322-3000 • ACRL GODORT

Muszynski-Compton Linda • Student • Clark-Atlanta University School of Library & Information Studies • Atlanta, GA 30314-4391

Mutale Elaine B. • Youth Services Librarian • San Diego Public Library Valencia Park Branch • San Diego, CA 92102 • ALSC NMRT

Muth Bell S. • Reference Librarian • Bowling Green Public Library • Bowling Green, KY 42101

Muth Irene C. • San Diego, CA 92123

Muth Melissa A. • Muncie, IN 47303 • ACRL

Muth Tom J. • Deputy Director • Topeka Public Library • Topeka, KS 66604-1374 • LAMA PLA RASD IFRT

Muthler Roberta J. • Librarian • Keystone Central School District • Lock Haven, PA 17745 • AASL

Muthoni Verna M. • Children's Coordinator • San Bernardino County Library • San Bernardino, CA 92415 • ALSC YALSA EMIERT

Mutschler Herbert F. • Bellevue, WA 98006 • ALTA LAMA LITA PLA *Life*

Muzzy Patsy A. • Reference Librarian • Portland Public Library • Portland, ME 04101 • PLA

Mwacalimba Hudwell • Univ Ln • University of Zambia Library Studies Department • Lusaka, Zambia • ACRL

Myall Carolynne • Head Technical Services • Eastern Washington University • Cheney, WA 99004 • ALCTS SRRT

Myer Catherine M. • Sylmar, CA 91342 • PLA RASD IFRT

Myer Elizabeth G. • Barrington, RI 02806 • Continuing

Myer Gail K. • Director • Benson Memorial Library • Titusville, PA 16354 • PLA

Myer Violet F. • Sykesville, MD 21784 • AASL PLA *Continuing*

Myers-Culver Margaret M. • Librarian • Eaton Rapids Middle School • Eaton Rapids, MI 48827

Myers-Hayer Jeffrey • Library of Congress • Washington, DC 20541 • ALCTS IRRT

Myers-Hayer Patricia A. • Assistant Section Head • Library of Congress • Washington, DC 20541

Myers Anne K. • Head of Technical Services • Boston University Pappas Law Library, School of Law • Boston, MA 02215 • LITA

Myers Ardie S. • Afro-American Reference Spec • Library of Congress • Washington, DC 20541 • RASD

Myers Barbara A. • Waco, TX 76710

Myers Barbara L. • Director • Fraser Public Library • Fraser, MI 48026 • LAMA LITA PLA

Myers Barbara S. • Librarian • Sunnyvale Public Library • Sunnyvale, CA 94088-3714

Myers Carol B. • Branch Services Director • Public Library of Charlotte & Mecklenburg County • Charlotte, NC 28202 • LAMA PLA

Myers Carolyn L. • Reference Media Services Ln • Northern Michigan University Lydia M. Olson Library • Marquette, MI 49855 • ACRL

Myers Carolyn W. • Serials Librarian • University of Nevada-Las Vegas James R. Dickinson Library • Las Vegas, NV 89154 • ACRL

Myers Charles J. • Science Librarian • Franklin & Marshall College Library • Lancaster, PA 17604-3003

Myers Christine B. • Las Cruces, NM 88005 • Continuing

Myers Diane D. • Director of Media Services • Fulton County Board of Education • Atlanta, GA 30315 • AASL

Myers Donald J. • Library Media Specialist • Newfield Central Schools Junior/Senior High School Library • Newfield, NY 14867 • AASL IFRT

Myers Dorian • Student • University of Texas at Austin Graduate School of Library & Information Sciences • Austin, TX 78712-1276 • AASL ALSC

Myers Dorothy S. • San Francisco, CA 94117

Myers Earleen H. • Librarian Technical Services • Skokie Public Library • Skokie, IL 60077-3680 • ALCTS LITA

Myers Elizabeth L. • Oakland, CA 94610 • Continuing

Myers Florence S. • University of Southern Mississippi Cook Memorial Library • Hattiesburg, MS 39406-5053 • NMRT

Myers Gay • Library Assistant • St. Paul's School • Baltimore, MD 21027 • AASL

Myers Harry J. • Jefferson County Public Library Standley Lake Library • Arvada, CO 80005

Myers James N. • Director • Temple University Paley Library • Philadelphia, PA 19122 • ACRL

Myers Jeane E. • Texas Woman's University School of Library & Information Studies • Denton, TX 76204

Myers Jennifer L. • Media Specialist • Spring Grove Middle School • Spring Grove, PA 17362

Myers Joan A. • Librarian • Hopkins Road Elementary School • Richmond, VA 23234 • AASL

Myers Joseph A. • Berkeley High School • Moncks Corner, SC 29461 • AASL

Myers Judy E. • Assistant to the Director • University of Houston Libraries • Houston, TX 77204-2091 • ACRL LAMA LITA RASD GODORT

Myers Judy L. • Cataloger • University of Northern Iowa Donald O. Rod Library • Cedar Falls, IA 50613-3675 • ACRL

Myers Kay A. • Children Subject Specialist • Anchorage Municipal Libraries Z. J. Loussac Library • Anchorage, AK 99503 • ALSC

Myers Kenneth R. • Delray Beach, FL 33445-6842 • ACRL RASD

Myers Kris L. • English Instructor • Granville Middle School • Granville, OH 43023

Myers Kurtz • Chicago, IL 60614 • ACRL PLA *Life*

Myers Leslie • Library Director • Josephine-Louise Public Library • Walden, NY 12586

Myers Marcia J. • Associate Dean • University of Tennessee Library • Knoxville, TN 37996-1000 • ACRL LAMA LITA RASD LRRT

Myers Margaret • OLPR Director • American Library Association • Chicago, IL 60611-2795 • CLENE FLRT ILERT SRRT

Myers Marilyn • Head of Collection Development • Arizona State University-West Fletcher Library • Phoenix, AZ 85069-7100 • ACRL ALCTS LAMA LRRT

Myers Marilyn J. • Student • University of Hawaii School of Library & Information Studies • Honolulu, HI 96822 • AASL

Myers Marsha A. • Elementary School Librarian • Vienna Elementary School • Vienna, WV 26105 • AASL

Myers Martha O. • Librarian • The Madeira School Inc. • McLean, VA 22102 • AASL LIRT

Myers Mary • Librarian • Oberlin Elementary School • Oberlin, KS 67749 • AASL

Myers Mary C. • Librarian • Lake Placid Memorial Library • Lake Placid, FL 33852 • PLA

Myers Maurine B. • Technical Services Librarian • Ottumwa Public Library • Ottumwa, IA 52501

Myers Melanie P. • Librarian • Ohio State University Libraries • Columbus, OH 43210-1286 • ALSC YALSA

Myers Nancy Lee • Acquisitions Librarian • University of South Dakota I.D. Weeks Library • Vermillion, SD 57069-2390 • LAMA

Myers Nancy S. • Head of Youth Services • Crystal Lake Public Library • Crystal Lake, IL 60014 • ALSC

Myers Norma J. • Asst Dir for Arch & Spec Coll • East Tennessee State University • Johnson City, TN 37614 • ACRL

Myers Patricia H. • Los Gatos, CA 95030

Myers Peggy • Director • Cape May County Library • Cape May, NJ 08204

Myers Penelope • Head, Access Services • Temple University Paley Library • Philadelphia, PA 19122 • ACRL LAMA

Myers R. David • Director • State Historical Society of Wisconsin Library • Madison, WI 53705 • ACRL LAMA LHRT

Myers Robert C. • Reference Librarian • Central Washington University • Ellensburg, WA 98926 • ACRL RASD

Myers Robert J. • Dir., Learning Resources Ctr. • Atlanta Metropolitan College • Atlanta, GA 30310 • ACRL EMIERT

Myers Roger W. • Student • University of Tennessee-Knoxville Graduate School of Library & Information Science • Knoxville, TN 37996-4330

Myers Rose E. • Librarian • University of Hawaii-West Oahu • Pearl City, HI 96782

Myers Sally L. • Librarian • Penn Hills School District John H. Linton Junior High • Pittsburgh, PA 15235 • AASL

Myers Sharon M. • Chicago, IL 60626

Myers Shirley D. • Librarian • Hilham Elementary School • Hilham, TN 38568

Myers Steven W. • Assistant Manager,Genealogy Dept • Allen County Public Library • Fort Wayne, IN 46801-2270

Myers Susan E. • Columbia, MD 21044 • AASL

Myers Susan L. • College Librarian • Austin College Abell Library • Sherman, TX 75090 • ACRL LAMA

Myers Victor C. • Temporary, Head of Cataloging • University of Missouri Libraries-Columbia Elmer Ellis Library • Columbia, MO 65201-5149 • ALCTS

Myers Victoria B. • Librarian • Wilmington College Library • New Castle, DE 19720 • ACRL

Myers Yvonne O. • Assistant Director • Public Library of Steubenville & Jefferson County • Steubenville, OH 43952

Myerson Susan S. • Head Cataloger • Harvard College Fine Arts Library • Cambridge, MA 02138

Myhre Margaret R. • Stu • University of California-Berkeley School of Library & Information Studies • Berkeley, CA 94720

Mykytiuk Lawrence J. • Student • University of Wisconsin School of Library & Information Studies • Madison, WI 53706 • LRRT NMRT

Myles Bobbie R. • Systems Librarian • Boston Public Library • Boston, MA 02117

Myles John A. • Library Media Specialist • Liberty Center Local SD • Liberty Center, OH 43532 • AASL

Mynatt Martha L. • John C. Fremont Junior High School • Las Vegas, NV 89104

Myoung Soon-Hee • Head Librarian • Sejong Institute Library • Songnamsi, Kyonggido, South Korea • ACRL IRRT

Myren Shirley • Trustee • East Chicago Public Library • E. Chicago, IN 46312 • PLA

Myrick Ada • Trustee • Bossier Parish Library • Bossier City, LA 71111

Myrick James R. • Assistant Director/Technical Ser • Flint River Regional Library • Griffin, GA 30223

Myrick John Paul • Director • Cullman County Public • Cullman, AL 35055 • PLA

Myrick Judy C. • Cataloging Librarian • Hinds Community College District Learning Resource Center • Raymond, MS 39154 • ALCTS

Myrick William J. Dr. • New York, NY 10022

Myron Vicki L. • Director • Spencer Public Library • Spencer, IA 51301

Mysliwiec Ronald P. • Trustee • Brooklyn Public Library • Brooklyn, NY 11238 • ALTA

Myton Marilyn • Librarian • East High School • Columbus, OH 43205 • AASL

Naar Anna M. • Butler, PA 16001 • ALSC

Nabity David R. Mr. • Trustee • Omaha Public Library • Omaha, NE 68102 • ALTA

Nachman Julie A. • Librarian • Georgetown University Joseph Mark Lauinger Library • Washington, DC 20057-1006 • IFRT

Nachod Katherine B. • Gov Doc/Microforms • Tulane University Monte M. Lemann Memorial Law Library • New Orleans, LA 70118-5600 • ACRL GODORT

Nacu Mary Z. • Children's Librarian • San Jose Public Library Evergreen Branch • San Jose, CA 95121

Nadanasabapathy V. • University Librarian • Murdoch University Library • Willeton 6155, Australia • ACRL ALCTS LITA

Nader Julie C. • Mountain View, CA 94043-2981

Nadeski Karen L. M. • Melrose, MA 02176-4731 • ALCTS

Nadler Barbara • Yonkers, NY 10710 • ACRL

Nadler Judith • Assistant Director • University of Chicago Library • Chicago, IL 60637-1502 • ALCTS

Naef Lisa H. • Assistant Director • Humboldt County Library • Eureka, CA 95501

Naeseth Gerhard B. • Madison, WI 53711 • ACRL ALCTS *Life*

Nafke Alexa J. • Liverpool, NY 13090-1624

Naftal Alison J. • New Brunswick, NJ 08901

Naftzger Karen S. • Rocky River, OH 44116

Nagai Gayle A. • Houston, TX 77063 • LITA

Nagaraja Jayashri Ms. • Head, Chemistry Library • Princeton University Library • Princeton, NJ 08544 • LITA

Nagata Hidekazu • Associate Professor • Asia University Library • Tokyo, Japan • ACRL

Nagel Kay M. • Reference Librarian • University of Georgia Libraries • Athens, GA 30602 • ACRL RASD

Nagel Rosemary A. • Eugene, OR 97405 • AASL YALSA

Nagler Nancy C. • Administrative Asst. Adult Servs • Dorchester County Public Library • Cambridge, MD 21613 • ALCTS

Nagolski Donald J. • Assoc. Dir. of Library Services • Dr. Wm. M. Scholl College of Podiatric Medicine Library • Chicago, IL 60610

Nagorske Erin M. • Manager, Library • USCEA Library • Washington, DC 20006 • LAMA

Nagy Jean • Library Board Secretary • Whiting Public Library • Whiting, IN 46394

Nagy Karen N. • Director • Stanford University • Stanford, CA 94305-6011 • ACRL ALCTS

Nagy Kathleen A. • Columbus Metropolitan Library • Columbus, OH 43215

Nagy Marcia J. • Extension Services Coordinator • Milwaukee Public Library • Milwaukee, WI 53233 • PLA

Nagy Marilyn • Fiske Free Library • Claremont, NH 03743 • PLA

Nahanni Kiatch J. • Edmonton AB, T6G 2C6 Canada

Nahinsky Beth A. • Queens Borough Public Library Jackson Heights Branch • Jackson Heights, NY 11372 • LIRT

Nahl-Jakobovits Diane • Instructor • University of Hawaii School of Library & Information Studies • Honolulu, HI 96822 • ACRL RASD

Nahley Mary • President Board of Directors • Danbury Public Library • Danbury, CT 06810 • ALTA LAMA PLA

Nahory Sarah D. • Librarian • South Mecklenburg H S • Charlotte, NC 28210 • AASL

Nahrwold Carol J. • Allen County Public Library • Fort Wayne, IN 46801 • RASD GODORT

Nails Claire M. • Branch Manager • Atlanta-Fulton Public Library Kirkwood Branch • Atlanta, GA 30317 • PLA

Nainis Linda • Bethesde, MD 20815 • ALCTS ILERT

Nair Vijay • Associate Librarian • Western Connecticut State University • Danbury, CT 06810 • ACRL RASD IFRT

Nairn Charles E. • Sault Sainte Marie, MI 49783 • Continuing

Naismith Patricia A. • Director • Springfield High School • Springfield, PA 19064 • AASL

Naismith Rachael • Reference Library Inst. Coor. • Carnegie-Mellon University • Pittsburgh, PA 15213 • RASD

Naito Bill • Trustee • Multnomah County Library • Portland, OR 97212 • ALTA

Naito Carol L. • Senior Librarian • Berkeley Public Library • Berkeley, CA 94704 • ALSC

Naito Eisuke • Professor • National Center for Science Information System • Tokyo 112, Japan • ALCTS

Naito Marilyn G. • Assistant Library Director • University of Hawaii-West Oahu • Pearl City, HI 96782 • ACRL LIRT LRRT

Naito Shirley S. • Oahu Children's Coordinator • Hawaii State Library • Honolulu, HI 96813 • ALSC

Najera Carlos L. • Branch Manager • Houston Public Library Flores Branch • Houston, TX 77003 • YALSA

Nakako Irene • Children's Librarian • Rock Springs Public Library • Rock Springs, WY 82901

Nakamura Margaret • Librarian • Moanalua Elementary School • Honolulu, HI 96819 • AASL

Nakamura Toyoko • Librarian • Anuenue Elementary School Library • Honolulu, HI 96822 • AASL

Nakano Kimberly L. • Mililani Twn, HI 96789

Nakarai Frances A. • Elizabethton, TN 37643

Nakashima Janice • Lubbock, TX 79416 • GODORT SRRT

Nakata Yuri • Tolovana Park, OR 97145

Nalewajka Anna Kay • Reed-Custer High School • Braidwood, IL 60408 • AASL

Nally Irene T. • Library Director • Gale Library • Newton, NH 03858

Nalwasky Celeste DiCarlo • Middle School Librarian • Peters Township School District • McMurray, PA 15317 • AASL ALSC YALSA

Nam Wonki K. • Ln • Central State University Hallie Q Brown Memorial Library • Wilberforce, OH 45384

Name Eniko Singer De • Library Director • Universidad de las Americas Puebla • 72820 Puebla, Mexico • ACRL

Namjoofard Javad • Banking Supervisior • Central Bank of Iran • Tehran, Iran

Namminga Barbara M. • Edmond, OK 73034 • RASD

Namsick Lynn Jo • Pima Community College West Campus LRC • Tucson, AZ 85709

Nance Lena L. • Branch Manager • Cuyahoga County Public Library • Cleveland, OH 44134-2792 • PLA

Nance Mildred M. • Librarian • District of Columbia • Washington, DC 20003 • ASCLA LAMA ILERT

Nandan Roletta L. • Glenview, IL 60025 • PLA

Nangle N. Paige • Youth Department Head • Cedar Falls Public Library • Cedar Falls, IA 50613 • ALSC

Nanji Razia • University of Florida • Gainesville, FL 32605 • ACRL RASD

Nanna Laura A. • Acquisitions Dept. • University of California UCSB Library • Santa Barbara, CA 93106-9010 • ACRL ALCTS LITA

Napier Judy A. • Reference Librarian • Schaumburg Township District Library • Schaumburg, IL 60194 • PLA

Naples Ronald J. • Trustee • Free Library of Philadelphia • Philadelphia, PA 19103 • ALTA

Napoli Donald J. • Director • Saint Joseph County Public Library • South Bend, IN 46601 • PLA

Napp John B. • Sylvania, OH 43560

Nappi Arno L. • Librarian I, Ref (Part-time) • San Mateo Public Library • San Mateo, CA 94402 • RASD IFRT

Nappi Sandra • Public School -#138 Queens-School Library • Rosedale, NY 11422

Napsha Cheryl A. • Director • Adams Memorial Library • Latrobe, PA 15650 • LAMA PLA YALSA

Naquin Lucy • Lafourche Parish Library Larose Cut Off Branch • Larose, LA 70373 • AASL

Naquin Terry • Trustee • West Baton Rouge Parish Library • Port Allen, LA 70767

Naqvi Nargis • Library Officer • Institute of Strategic Studies • Islamabad, Pakistan

Narang Sat P. • Associate Professor • Eastern Illinois University Booth Library • Charleston, IL 61920-3099

Nardelli Sharon A. • Upper Merion School District • King of Prussia, PA 19406 • AASL

Nardini Robert F. • Head Bibliographer • Yankee Book Peddler • Contoocook, NH 03229 • ACRL

Narsis Nancy • Librarian • Newington High School Library • Newington, CT 06111 • AASL

Naru Linda A. • Planning & Development Officer • Center for Research Libraries • Chicago, IL 60637 • ACRL

Narver Betty Jane • Trustee • Seattle Public Library • Seattle, WA 98104-1193 • ALTA PLA

Nary Linda Lee • Technical Services Manager • Plano Public Library System L.E.R. Schimelpfenig Library • Plano, TX 75023-5108 • ALCTS LITA PLA

Nasatir Marilyn • Berkeley, CA 94708 • LITA

Nascimento Janice M. • Training Coordinator • First Union Bank Training & Development FL0425 • Jacksonville, FL 32231-0010

Nasea Melissa M. • Serials Librarian • East Carolina University Health Sciences Library • Greenville, NC 27858-4354 • ACRL ALCTS ASCLA

Nash Beverly A. • Head of Reference Services • Broward County-South Regional Library • Pembroke Pines, FL 33024 • RASD

Nash Chrissie J. • Adm Offr • Library of Congress • Washington, DC 20541

Nash Elizabeth A. • Acquisitions Librarian • Bradford College Hemingway Library • Haverhill, MA 01835

Nash Harriet S. • Philadelphia, PA 19102 • AASL

Nash Jean L. • Director • West Warwick Public Library System • West Warwick, RI 02893 • LAMA

Nash Julie • Head Librarian • Upper Arlington Public Library Lane Road Branch • Upper Arlington, OH 43220

Nash Mary D. • Head of Reference • Creighton University Reinert-Alumni Memorial Library • Omaha, NE 68178 • ACRL RASD

Nash N. Frederick Mr. • Cura of Rare Bks/Assoc Prof • University of Illinois Library • Urbana, IL 61801 • ACRL RASD *Life*

Nash Robert P. • Collection Development Librarian • University of Nebraska at Omaha University Library • Omaha, NE 68182-0237 • ACRL

Nash Sally E. • Student • University of Washington Graduate School of Library and Information Science • Seattle, WA 98195 • SRRT

Nash Stanley D. • Humanities Resource Librarian • Rutgers University Libraries • New Brunswick, NJ 08903 • ACRL LIRT

Nash Stephen L. • Library Media Specialist • Greece Central School District Hoover Drive Middle School • Rochester, NY 14615 • AASL

Nashak Catherine Persico • Reference Librarian • Deer Park Public Library • Deer Park, NY 11729

Naslund Cheryl Terrass • Vestal, NY 13850 • ACRL ALCTS

Nasri William Z. • Assoc Prof • University of Pittsburgh School of Library and Information Science • Pittsburgh, PA 15260 • ACRL IRRT

Nass Gaylene R. • University of Iowa School of Library & Information Science • Iowa City, IA 52242

Nassar Nancy • Library Consultant • Aldine Independent School District • Houston, TX 77032 • AASL

Nasso Christine • Dir,Lit/Gen Ref Dev • Gale Research, Inc. • Detroit, MI 48226 • AASL PLA RASD

Nasta Patricia • Librarian • Sachem Public Library • Holbrook, NY 11741

Natale Barbara J. • Student • Kent State University School of Library & Information Science • Kent, OH 44242-0001 • AASL

Natale Joseph A. • Student • University of North Texas School of Library & Information Sciences • Denton, TX 76203 • ACRL RASD SRRT

Nathan Catherine A. • Branch Head • Memphis-Shelby County Public Library Bartlett Branch • Memphis, TN 38134 • IFRT

Nathan Phyllis J. • Manager Library Services • Rockford Memorial Hospital • Rockford, IL 61103

Nathans Judith I. • Manager, Library Resource Center • Arthur D. Little Inc. Cambridge Information Center • Cambridge, MA 02140 • LAMA

Natijehashem Lily • Archivist/Librarian • New York Association for New Americans • New York, NY 10004 • ACRL

Natividad Evelyn D. • The Adler Planetarium Library • Chicago, IL 60605 • ALCTS

Natke Nora Jane • Youth Services Coordinator • Riverside City & County Public Library Central Branch • Riverside, CA 92502 • ALSC PLA YALSA

Natoli Dorothy L. • Westford, MA 01886 • AASL

Natowitz Allen • Brooklyn, NY 11223

Natraj Sharadha • Farmington Hills, MI 48331

Natzke Barbara J. • Trustee • Warrenville Public Library District • Warrenville, IL 60555 • ALTA

Naudain Florence • Portland, OR 97209-1641

Naughton Dorothy • Waukesha, WI 53186 • Continuing

Nauman Ann K. Dr • Professor of Education & Lib Sci • Southeastern Louisiana University • Hammond, LA 70402 • AASL

Naumann Luisa M. • Librarian • Harlendale I.S.D. McCollum High School • San Antonio, TX 78221

Naumer Janet N. • Porterville, CA 93258 • LITA

Navari Leslie • Naval Postgraduate School Dudley Knox Library • Monterey, CA 93943-5002

Navarre Emily • Southeastern Library Services • Davenport, IA 52804-3026 • LAMA PLA

Navarrette Elena • Manager • Tucson Public Library Mission Branch • Tucson, AZ 85713

Navarro Anthony F. • Student • Polytechnic University • Brooklyn, NY 11201 • LITA

Navarro Frank A. • Senior Librarian • Los Angeles Public Library Panorama City Branch Library • Panorama City, CA 91402 • EMIERT

Navarro Sharon • Librarian • North High School • Riverside, CA 92507

Nayer Alice C. • Director • Elmont Public Library • Elmont, NY 11003 • ALSC LAMA PLA RASD

Naylor Alice P. • Professor • Appalachian State University Dept of Reading • Boone, NC 28608 • AASL ALSC YALSA IFRT SRRT

Naylor Melva L. • Youth Services/Outreach • Four County Library System • Vestal, NY 13850 • ALSC PLA

Naylor Richard J. • Assistant Director • William K. Sanford Town Library • Loudonville, NY 12211

Naylor Ronald P. • Assistant Director • University of Miami Libraries Richter Library • Coral Gables, FL 33124 • ACRL ASCLA LAMA

Nazari Jana C. • School Librarian • Armstrong Elementary School • Dallas, TX 75205 • AASL

Nazarian Anahid • Rutherford, CA 94573

Ndenga Viola • Director • McGregor Public Library • Highland Park, MI 48203 • ACRL ALCTS ASCLA LAMA LITA PLA RASD CLENE IFRT ILERT SRRT

Neal Anne • Branch Librarian • Frenso County Free Library Auberry Branch • Auberry, CA 93602

Neal Christina W. • Ann Arbor, MI 48104 • ACRL

Neal Clara B. • Media Specialist • Dunbar Senior High School • Washington, DC 20001 • AASL

Neal James G. • Indiana University • Bloomington, IN 47405 • ACRL LAMA RASD IRRT LHRT

Neal James P. • State Senator • Newark Free Library • Newark, DE 19711-7146 • ALTA LITA

Neal Jane M. • Media Specialist • Goodrich Junior High School • Lincoln, NE 68521 • AASL IFRT

Neal Janette • Reference & Information Libn. • Free Library of Philadelphia • Philadelphia, PA 19103 • RASD GODORT SRRT *Life*

Neal Janice A. • Marketing Manager • INLEX, Inc. • Monterey, CA 93942 • LITA

Neal John Vincent • Vice President • Neal-Schuman Publishers, Inc. • New York, NY 10013

Neal Kathryn • Media Specialist • Drake State Technical College • Huntsville, AL 35811

Neal M. • Librarian • University of North Carolina Walter Royal Davis Library • Chapel Hill, NC 27599-3924 • ALCTS

Neal Margaret D. • Adult Services Librarian • Champaign Public Library & Information Center • Champaign, IL 61820-5193 • PLA

Neal Myron E. • Reference Librarian II • Public Library of Cincinnati and Hamilton County • Cincinnati, OH 45202

Neal Peyton R. • President • PRN Associates • Washington, DC 20008 • ACRL LITA FLRT GODORT

Neal Robert L. • Director • Allegany County Library System • Cumberland, MD 21502-2981 • PLA

Neal Susan Lynn • Adult Services Librarian • Bedford Public Library • Bedford, TX 76021

Neale Marilee • Director • La Marque Public Library • La Marque, TX 77568-4195 • LAMA PLA

Neale Tim • McGraw-Hill Ryerson LTD • Whitby, ON, L1N 9B6 Canada • LITA

Nealon MaryEllen • Silver Spring, MD 20910 • LHRT

Near Janie Lamar Miss • Atlanta, GA 30319 • ACRL RASD *Continuing*

Neary Ann M. • Coordinator of Service • Southwestern Connecticut Library Council • Bridgeport, CT 06604 • ASCLA RASD CLENE IFRT SORT

Neary Coleen P. • Washington, DC 20009

Neary Mary Ann • Chief of Ref Serv • State Library of Massachusetts • Boston, MA 02133 • RASD GODORT

Neavill Gordon B. • Assoc Prof • University of Alabama School of Library & Information Studies • Tuscaloosa, AL 35487-0252 • ALCTS LHRT

Neavill Helen A. • Cataloger/Ref/I.L.L. • Winona State University • Winona, MN 55987 • ACRL

Nebehay E. H. Mrs. • New York, NY 10016 • Continuing

Nebeker Birte • Bloomfield College Library • Bloomfield, NJ 07003

Nebel Jean C. • Librarian • Riverside Unified School District Middle School • Riverside, CA 92506 • AASL IFRT

Nedderman Robert M. • Library Director • Hastings College Perkins Library • Hastings, NE 68901 • IFRT

Nedell Emily • Bloomington, IN 47408 • ACRL

Nedswick Robert • Young Adult Librarian • Maurice M. Pine Free Public Library • Fair Lawn, NJ 07410 • RASD YALSA

Nee Louise A. • Reference Coordinator • Rolling Meadows Library • Rolling Meadows, IL 60008

Needham Charlotte M. • Granada East Library • Phoenix, AZ 85017 • AASL

Needham George M. • Director of Communications • Ohio Library Association • Columbus, OH 43215-3840

Needham John R. Jr • Library Director • Roane State Community College Library • Harriman, TN 37748 • SRRT

Neegan Leone A. • Medical Librarian • Yuma Regional Media Center • Yuma, AZ 85364 • LAMA

Neel Kathrine F. • Raleigh, NC 27605 • LAMA PLA *Life*

Neel Patricia A. • Teacher • Cherry Creek School District • Englewood, CO 80110 • AASL LITA EMIERT

Neeley James D. • Head, Reference Department • University of Kansas Watson Library • Lawrence, KS 66045-2800 • ACRL ASCLA RASD

Neeley Kathleen L. • Head of the Science Libraries • University of Kansas Anschutz Science Library • Lawrence, KS 66045-2800 • ACRL

Neely Ann • Reference Librarian • Parkland College Library • Champaign, IL 61821 • ACRL RASD

Neely Betty • Director Literacy • Shawnee Library System • Carterville, IL 62918

Neely Bill • Library Advisory Board Chairman • Paris Public Library • Paris, TX 75460

Neely Eugene T. • Dean of Libraries • Adelphi University Swirbul Library • Garden City, NY 11530 • ACRL LAMA LITA

Neely Gail S. • Catalog Librarian • Cornell University Martin P. Catherwood Library • Ithaca, NY 14851-3901 • ACRL ALCTS LITA

Neely Gardner • Fayette County Margaret Mitchell Public Library • Fayetteville, GA 30214 • PLA

Neely Glenda S. • Professor-Reference Librarian • University of Louisville Ekstrom Library • Louisville, KY 40292 • ACRL RASD

Neely Susan P. • Student • Belpre City Schools • Belpre, OH 45714 • AASL

Neerman Sandra M. • Assistant Director • Greensboro Public Library • Greensboro, NC 27402 • PLA

Neese Janet A. • Acting Director • State University of New York (SUNY) College at Geneseo Milne Library • Geneseo, NY 14454-1498 • ACRL

Neff Beth W. • Director • Ellsworth Cmnty College Library • Iowa Falls, IA 50126 • ACRL LAMA LITA

Neff Dorothy C. • Branch Adult Services Librarian • Schenectady County Public Library • Schenectady, NY 12305

Neff Evaline B. • United States Department of Education Office of Educational Res & Improvement • Washington, DC 20208-5571 • ASCLA PLA

Neff Jerry W. • Executive Director • Wagnalls Memorial Library • Lithopolis, OH 43136 • LAMA

Neff John W. • Director-Policy Analysis • American Public Transit Association • Washington, DC 20005 • RASD

Neff Linda S. • Head of Caataloging • Pasco County Library System Processing Center • Port Richey, FL 34668

Neff Patricia S. • Library Systems Consultant • Innovative Interfaces, Inc. • Berkeley, CA 94710 • LAMA

Negaard Chere J. • Public Services Librarian • University of California • Los Angeles, CA 90024-1573 • ACRL LAMA LITA RASD

Negherbon Vincent Rev • Care Saint Francis College • Loretto, PA 15940

Negip Marilyn J. • Student • San Jose State University Division of Library & Information Science • San Jose, CA 95192-0029 • IFRT

Negro Antoinette • Media Specialist • Quince Orchard High School • Giathersburg, MD 20878 • AASL ALSC LITA YALSA

Negroni Italia A. • Media Specialist • Stamford High School • Stamford, CT 06902 • AASL

Negus Linda M. • Childrens Services • Swan Library • Albion, NY 14411

Nehlig Mary E. • Assistant Director • West Chester University Francis Harvey Green Library • West Chester, PA 19383 • ACRL

Neidhardt Kirk L. • Student • University of Kentucky College of Library & Information Science • Lexington, KY 40506-0391 • IFRT SRRT

Neidorf Iran L. • Foreman • Maintenance Coatings, Company • Addison, IL 60101 • ALTA

Neidrauer Paula Z. • APO, NY 09705

Neie Marilyn J. • Library Media Specialist • Klondike Elementary School • West Lafayette, IN 47906 • AASL

Neigel Barbara B. • Librarian • Morristown-Beard School • Morristown, NJ 07962-1999

Neighbarger Patricia A. • Cataloging Librarian • George Mason University Libraries • Fairfax, VA 22030 • ALCTS LITA

Neighbors Fred D. • Alabama Public Library Service • Montgomery, AL 36130 • ASCLA PLA

Neighbour Mary L. • Glen Mills, PA 19342

Neighbours Betty T. • Media Coordinator • Jesse Wharton Elementary School • Greensboro, NC 27405 • AASL

Neikirk-Seamans Marsha S. • University of Maryland Baltimore County Kuhn Library • Catonsville, MD 21228 • ACRL

Neikirk Harold D. • Director • Western Maryland College Hoover Library • Westminster, MD 21157-4390 • ACRL LAMA

Neill Marion • Sandusky, OH 44870 • ALSC PLA *Continuing*

Neill Priscilla • Ft. Wright, KY 41011 • ACRL LAMA

Neilson Janice V.K. • Halawa Correctional Facility • Aiea, HI 96701 • ASCLA

Neilson Susan H. • Mclean, VA 22102 • ALCTS

Neilson Susan Wolf • Student • University of North Carolina Department of Library & Information Studies • Greensboro, NC 27412-5001 • IFRT

Neis Catherine • Trustee • Grand Rapids Public Library • Grand Rapids, MI 49503-3093

Neis William B. • Student • Wayne State University Library Science Program • Detroit, MI 48202

Neitz Cordelia M. • Carlisle, PA 17013 • ACRL ALCTS
Life

Nekritz Leah K. • Dean of Learning Resources • Prince George's Community College Library Media Center • Largo, MD 20772 • ACRL

Nelms Willie • Director • Sheppard Memorial Library • Greenville, NC 27858 • PLA

Nelsen Alice R. • Bowie, MD 20715 • AASL

Nelsen Mary Y. • Student • Emporia State University School of Library & Information Management • Emporia, KS 66801

Nelson Anne G. • Chairperson,Library Media Center • Farmingdale High School • Farmingdale, NY 11735 • AASL

Nelson April L. • Librarian I • Los Angeles County Library Manhattan Beach Branch • Manhattan Beach, CA 90266

Nelson Barbara K. • Order Librarian • Auburn University Ralph Brown Draughon Library • Auburn, AL 36849-5606 • ACRL ALCTS

Nelson Barbara L. • Library Media Specialist • North High School • North Saint Paul, MN 55109 • AASL

Nelson Barbara L. • School Media Specialist • Manor Oaks-William R. Bowie • New Hyde Park, NY 11040

Nelson Barbara L. • Highland, IN 46322 • PLA RASD

Nelson Bennie • National City, CA 92050 • EMIERT

Nelson Bonnie Crotty • Librarian • Microelectronics Center of North Carolina John L. Reynolds Library • Research Triangle Pk, NC 27709

Nelson Bonnie R. • Deputy Chief Librarian • John Jay College of Criminal Justice • New York, NY 10019 • ACRL LITA RASD

Nelson Bruce J. • Librarian • Benito Juarez High School • Chicago, IL 60608 • AASL

Nelson C. Berit • Sales Support Specialist • Data Research Associates Inc. • Saint Louis, MO 63132

Nelson Carol A. • Libray Media Specialist • Aldine Independent School District • Houston, TX 77032 • IFRT

Nelson Carol Quissell • Director, Media Services • Eau Claire Board of Education Library Division • Eau Claire, WI 54701 • AASL

Nelson Carol R. • Munice, IN 47304 • ACRL ALCTS

Nelson Carolee K. • Reference Floor Supervisor • Anchorage Municipal Libraries Z. J. Loussac Library • Anchorage, AK 99503 • PLA

Nelson Catherine • Lafayette, IN 47901 • ACRL RASD
Continuing

Nelson Catherine Glick • Onan Corp Library MN01-1480 • Minneapolis, MN 55432

Nelson Catherine R. • Tulane University Howard-Tilton Memorial Library • New Orleans, LA 70118 • ACRL ALCTS NMRT

Nelson Cathy • Assistant Director • Berlin-Peck Memorial Library • Kensington, CT 06037 • ALSC

Nelson Cheryl A. • George Washington University Gelman Library • Washington, DC 20052 • ACRL

Nelson Cheryl S. • Media Specialist • Burrillville Middle School • Harrisville, RI 02830 • AASL

Nelson Christie • Technical Services Librarian • Everett Community College Library Media Center • Everett, WA 98201-1327 • LITA

Nelson Christine L. • Librarian • Crownpoint High School • Crownpoint, NM 87313 • AASL

Nelson Darlene J. • Mktg. Serv. Mgr. • Computype, Inc. • Saint Paul, MN 55113 • LAMA

Nelson David N. • Head Original Cataloging • Texas A & M University Sterling C. Evans Library • College Station, TX 77843-5000 • ACRL ALCTS LITA EMIERT GODORT IRRT

Nelson Elizabeth A. • Librarian II • Los Angeles Public Library Studio City Branch • Studio City, CA 91604

Nelson Elizabeth Beezley • Adult Reference • Medina County District Library • Medina, OH 44256

Nelson Elizabeth S. • Children's Librarian • Solano County Library Fairfield-Suisun Community Library • Fairfield, CA 94533

Nelson Florence K. • Librarian • Milwaukee Public Library • Milwaukee, WI 53233 • PLA

Nelson Frances S. • Student • Southern Connecticut State University School of Libray Science & Instructional Technology • New Haven, CT 06515 • ACRL

Nelson Frank M. • Public Library Consultant • Idaho State Library Eastern Field Office • Idaho Falls, ID 83405-0919 • LITA

Nelson Garet B. • Student • University of South Florida School of Library & Information Science • Tampa, FL 33620

Nelson Gene • Adminstrator • Las Vegas-Clark County Library District Charleston Heights Branch • Las Vegas, NV 89107 • ALSC LAMA PLA YALSA IFRT

Nelson Glee E. • Childrens Librarian • Columbus Public Library • Columbus, NE 68601

Nelson Harriet O. • Hd,Reference/Soc Serv/Sci Div • Catholic University of America John K. Mullen of Denver Memorial Library • Washington, DC 20064 • ACRL

Nelson Helen • Director • Oceanside Public Library • Oceanside, CA 92054 • LAMA PLA

Nelson James A. • State Librarian & Commissioner • Kentucky Department for Libraries & Archives • Frankfort, KY 40602-0537 • ASCLA PLA CLENE

Nelson James A. • Student • Kent State University School of Library & Information Science • Kent, OH 44242-0001 • SRRT

Nelson James B. • Missouri State Library • Jefferson City, MO 65102 • IFRT

Nelson Jeanne V. • Murrieta Valley Unified School District • Murrieta, CA 92362 • AASL

Nelson JoAnn • Library Director • Oldham Public Library • Oldham, SD 57051

Nelson Joanne C. • Student • University of California Science Library • Santa Cruz, CA 95064 • GODORT

Nelson John B. • San Francisco Public Library • San Francisco, CA 94102

Nelson Judith K. • Outreach Coordinator • Medina County District Library • Medina, OH 44256 • ASCLA

Nelson Judy M. • Owner • Mrs. Nelson's Toy & Book Shop • LaVerne, CA 91750

Nelson Judy T. • Children's Librarian • Bellevue Public Library • Bellevue, WA 98004 • YALSA

Nelson Karen R. • Director • Brevard County Library • Cocoa, FL 32922-7781 • ALCTS LAMA

Nelson Kathleen • Media Generalist • Wavasha-Kellogg High School • Wabasha, MN 55981

Nelson Kathleen E. • Student • University of Hawaii School of Library & Information Studies • Honolulu, HI 96822

Nelson Kenneth R. • Southgate, MI 48195 • SRRT

Nelson Kerry • Student • University of California-Berkeley School of Library & Information Studies • Berkeley, CA 94720

Nelson Kevin S. • Circulation • Port Arthur Public Library • Port Arthur, TX 77642-3136

Nelson LaDonna • Lincoln Grade School • Lincoln, KS 67455 • AASL

Nelson Linda • School Library Media Spec. • San Jose Episcopal Day School • Jacksonville, FL 32217 • AASL

Nelson Maggie E. • Public Relation Coordinator • Peoria Public Library • Peoria, IL 61602 • LAMA ERT NMRT

Nelson Margaret R. • Head Librarian • United States Enviromental Protection Agency Region I • Boston, MA 02203

Nelson Marie L. • Colorado Springs, CO 80919-2308 • AFLRT FLRT

Nelson Marietta L. • Information Specialist • National Institute of Standards & Technology • Gaithersburg, MD 20899

Nelson Marilyn • Student • State University of New York (SUNY) School of Information & Library Studies • Buffalo, NY 14260

Nelson Marion A. • Elizabethtown, KY 42701

Nelson Mark E. • Librarian • West Des Moines Public Library • West Des Moines, IA 50265 • PLA

Nelson Mary Lois • Head of Adult Services • Council Bluffs Free Public Library • Council Bluffs, IA 51503 • PLA

Nelson Mary M. • IRMS • University of Illinois Graduate School of Library and Information Science • Urbana, IL 61801

Nelson Maureen O. • Adult Services • Tucson Public Library Wilmot Branch • Tucson, AZ 85710 • PLA

Nelson Michael • Reference Librarian • University of Wyoming • Laramie, WY 82071 • RASD

Nelson Michael B. • Social Science Cataloger • Washington State University • Pullman, WA 99164-2112

Nelson Nancy Melin • Publishing • Meckler Publishing • Westport, CT 06880 • LITA ERT IRRT

Nelson Nancy R. • Asst. Libn. for Circulation/Res. • University of Delaware Library • Newark, DE 19717-5267 • LAMA IFRT NMRT

Nelson Naomi L. • Atlanta, GA 30322

Nelson Norman L. • Assistant University Librarian • Oklahoma State University Library • Stillwater, OK 74078-0375 • ACRL LAMA

Nelson Pat • Youth Services Director • Westmoor Elementary School • Northbrook, IL 60062 • AASL

Nelson Patricia Hickman • Troy, NY 12180 • AASL ALSC

Nelson Rachel W. • Cleveland, OH 44118 • PLA
Continuing

Nelson Rachelle R. • Asst. Head Shared Cataloging Dpt • University of Pennsylvania Library Van Pelt-Dietrich Library Center • Philadelphia, PA 19104-6206 • ALCTS

Nelson Robert B. • Asst. Dir. Memb. Services1234567 • American Library Association • Chicago, IL 60611-2795 • AASL ACRL ALCTS ALSC ALTA ASCLA LAMA LITA PLA RASD YALSA AFLRT CLENE EMIERT ERT FLRT GODORT IFRT ILERT IRRT LHRT LIRT LRRT MAGERT NMRT SORT SRRT VRT

Nelson Rosemary H. • Central Library Administrator • Phoenix Public Library • Phoenix, AZ 85004 • LAMA PLA

Nelson Roxanna A. • Hockton, CA 95219

Nelson Sandra S. • Asst. State Ln. & Archivist • Tennessee State Library & Archives • Nashville, TN 37243-0312 • ASCLA PLA CLENE

Nelson Sterling D. • Southport, ME 04576 • Continuing

Nelson Terri L. • Children's Librarian • Princeton Public Library • Princeton, NJ 08542 • ALSC PLA

Nelson Vaunda M. • Shady Side Academy • Pittsburgh, PA 15221 • AASL ALSC

Nelson William Neal • University Librarian • Samford University Library • Birmingham, AL 35229 • ACRL IRRT

Nelson Yvonne D. • Trustee • Newark Public Library • Newark, NJ 07101-0630 • ALTA PLA

Neman Caryl • Duncan Elementary School • Fort Hood, TX 76544 • AASL

Nemchek Lee Rachel • Inforamtion Resources Manager • Morrison & Foerster • Los Angeles, CA 90013-1024

Nemec Ida L. • Plum Lake Women's Club Library • Sayner, WI 54560

Nemechek Sharon L. • Student • University of California Los Angeles Graduate School of Library & Information Science • Los Angeles, CA 90024 • GODORT SRRT

Nemer Barbara J. • Director of Curriculum & Media • Robbinsdale Area Schools Independent School District #281 • Robbinsdale, MN 55422 • AASL

Nemer Ronna C. • Reference Librarian • San Jose Public Library • San Jose, CA 95113

Nemeth John • Cointrin GE, Switzerland • Continuing

Nemeth Mary H. • Media Specialist/Coordinator • Upper Arlington City Schools • Columbus, OH 43221 • AASL LITA

Nemeth Phyllis H. • Arcadia, CA 91007

Nemetz-Haussmann Gail • Osterville, MA 02655

Nemeyer Carol A. Dr. • Elkins Park, PA 19117 • ALCTS LAMA
Continuing

Nemoto Akira • Assistant Professor • University of Library and Information • Ibaraki, Japan

Nemoy Leon • Annenberg Research Institute for Judaic & Middle Eastern Studies • Philadelphia, PA 19106 • ACRL ALCTS
Continuing

Nepote Paul W. • Librarian • Burlingame High School • Burlingame, CA 94010 • AASL NMRT

Neprud Beulah G. • Norfolk, NE 68701 • Continuing

Nerboso Salvatore D. • Plymouth, MA 02360 • ACRL PLA
Life

Nergelovic Paul T. • United States Military Academy Library • West Point, NY 10996-1799 • AFLRT

Neri Joseph S. • Partner • Book Wholesales,Inc. • Lexington, KY 40511 • ALSC PLA YALSA

Nero Lutr • Student • University of Pittsburgh School of Library and Information Science • Pittsburgh, PA 15260 • ALSC LRRT SRRT

Neroda Edward W. • Director • Shasta College Library • Redding, CA 96099

Nersesian Florita G. • Senior Librarian • Wasco State Prison • Shafter, CA 93280

Nervig James • Trustee • West Des Moines Public Library • West Des Moines, IA 50265

Nesbeth Carmen L. • Library Technician • Ottawa-Carleton Health Department Library • Ottawa, ON, K2A 4A4 Canada

Nesbit Angus B. • Seattle, WA 98107

Nesbit Eva M. • Saint Petersburg Public Library • St. Petersburg, FL 33713 • ALSC

Nesbit Larry L. • Mansfield, PA 16933

Nesbitt Olive K. • Erie, PA 16502 • Continuing

Nesbitt Robin L. • Columbus, OH 43214

Nesmith E. DeForest • Reference Librarian • Union College Library • Lincoln, NE 68506-4386 • ACRL RASD

Nespeca Sue McCleaf • Youth Services Consultant • NOLA Regional Library System • Warren, OH 44483 • ALSC

Ness Amy L. • Student • University of North Texas School of Library & Information Sciences • Denton, TX 76203

Ness Charles Henry • State College, PA 16803 • ACRL

Ness Pamela M. • The Dalton School • New York, NY 10028 • AASL ALSC

Ness Twila Cavey • Media Specialist • Harmony Hills Elementary • Silver Springs, MD 20906 • AASL

Nesse Mark A. • Director • Everett Public Library • Everett, WA 98201 • PLA

Nesse Sheila P. • Librarian, Collection Devel. • Sno-Isle Regional Library • Marysville, WA 98271-9164

Nesta Angela • Librarian • Cuyamaca College • El Cajon, CA 92019

Nestell Clifford L. • Director of Library Services • Shawnee Mission Medical Center • Shawnee Mission, KS 66201 • ALCTS LITA

Nestfield Charles R. • Wayne State University Library Science Program • Detroit, MI 48202 • GODORT

Nestler Anthony G. • Evanston, IL 60202

Nestler Karen H. • Frankenberry, Laughlin & Constable Information Services • Milwaukee, WI 53202

Neth Jane • Cache La Pouder Junior High School • La Porte, CO 80535 • AASL

Nettleman James D. • Associate Librarian • Rutgers University Paul Robeson Library • Camden, NJ 08101-3990 • LITA GODORT

Neu Margaret J. • Head Librarian • Corpus Christi Caller Times Newspaper Library • Corpus Chrsti, TX 78469

Neubacher Eric • New York, NY 10021 • ACRL GODORT

Neubauer Janice • Library Director • Duxbury Free Library • Duxbury, MA 02332 • LITA

Neubauer Richard A. • Prof of Library Science • Bridgewater State College Program of Library Media Studies • Bridgewater, MA 02324

Neuburg Helen G. • Bookseller • Wit & Widsom Booksellers • Lawrenceville, NJ 08648 • ALSC

Neufang Ralf E. • Reference Librarian • University of Hawaii Thomas Hale Hamilton Library • Honolulu, HI 96822

Neufeld Judith B. • Asst Director • Long Island Library Resource Council • Stony Brook, NY 11794-3399 • ALCTS

Neufeld Robert S. • Adult & Branch Services Coor. • Asheville-Buncombe Library System • Asheville, NC 28801 • PLA RASD

Neugebauer Rhonda L. • Latin Amer. Area Specialist • Arizona State University Libraries • Tempe, AZ 85287-1006 • ACRL IRRT NMRT

Neuhedel Rebecca A.T. • Massapequa, NY 11758

Neuhofer M. Dorothy Sr • Librarian • St. Leo College Library • St Leo, FL 33574 • ACRL LAMA

Neuman Delia • Associate Professor • University of Maryland College of Library and Information Services • College Park, MD 20742-4345 • AASL

Neuman Jerry Mr. • Oakland, CA 94606-1631 • PLA

Neuman Richard J. • Director (Retired) • Salina Public Library • Salina, KS 67401 • Continuing

Neuman Susan G. • Director of Business Library • University of Pittsburgh • Pittsburgh, PA 15260 • ACRL LITA RASD *Life*

Neumann Darlene • Edgewood Middle School • Highland Park, IL 60035 • ALSC

Neumann Joan • Director • New York Metropolitan Reference & Research Library Agency (METRO) • New York, NY 10003 • ASCLA

Neumann Nancy A. • Sioux City, IA 51104

Neumeister Susan M. • Associate Librarian • State University of New York (SUNY) Central Technical Services • Buffalo, NY 14260 • ALCTS

Neumiller Marilyn C. • Librarian • North Central Regional Library • Wenatchee, WA 98821 • ALSC PLA

Neurohr Karen Mrs. • Poteau, OK 74953

Neuschaefer Hilda L. • Assistant Chief • Administrative Offices of the United States Courts • Washington, DC 20544 • FLRT

Neuschafer Harold • Director • Sussex County Library System • Newton, NJ 07860-0076

Neuser Paulette • Two Rivers, WI 54241

Neuville Lynn S. • Assistant Director • Paramus Public Library • Paramus, NJ 07652 • LAMA

Neuwirth Joan • Bolton Public Schools • Bolton, CT 06043 • AASL

Neve Alice R. • Supervisor of Youth Services • Saint Paul Public Library • St. Paul, MN 55102 • ALSC PLA

Neve Lois C. • Branch Librarian • Watertown Public Library • Watertown, MA 02172

Nevens Arlene • Assistant Director • Great Neck Library • Great Neck, NY 11024

Neverman Diane K. • Follett Software Company • McHenry, IL 60050-5589 • LITA

Neveu Estelle D. • Librarian • Castle College • Windham, NH 03087 • ACRL

Neville Ellen P. • Purdue University • West Lafayette, IN 47907 • ALCTS

Neville Linda • Library Media Specialist • Rafael de J Codero Public School #37 • Jersey City, NJ 07302 • AASL

Neville Merlene R. • Cannon Junior High School • Las Vegas, NV 89120

Neville Robert F. • Asst. Dean, Technical Services • College of Charleston Robert Scott Small Library • Charleston, SC 29424 • ALCTS LITA

Neville Sandra H. • Branch Manager • San Antonio Public Library • San Antonio, TX 78205 • PLA

Neville Sharon L. • Howard County Library • Columbia, MD 21044 • YALSA IFRT

Neville Tina M. • Instructor Librarian • University of South Florida • Saint Petersburg, FL 33701

Nevin Susanne • Head of Technical Services • Gustavus Adolphus College Folke Bernadotte Memorial Library • St Peter, MN 56082 • ACRL ALCTS

Nevins Janet O • Tucson, AZ 85715

Nevins Kate F. • V.P., Member Services • Online Computer Library Center (OCLC) • Dublin, OH 43017-3395 • ACRL ALCTS ASCLA LITA GODORT IRRT

Nevins Patrick F. • Head Librarian • Richton Park Public Library District • Richton Park, IL 60471 • ALSC PLA

Nevling Pamela M. • Student • Clarion University of Pennsylvania College of Library Science • Clarion, PA 16214

New Beverly C. • Rockville, MD 20852

New Frances Y. • Scottsdale, AZ 85258 • ACRL RASD LRRT

New Gregory R. • Asst Ed Dewey Decimal Class • Library of Congress • Washington, DC 20541 • AASL ALCTS PLA *Life*

Newbanks Beverly S. • Elementary Library Coordiantor • RE-1 Valley School District • Sterling, CO 80751 • AASL

Newberg Ellen J. • Director • Kitsap Regional Library • Bremerton, WA 98310

Newberg Pamela J. • Children's Librarian • Lake Bluff Public Library • Lake Bluff, IL 60044 • ALSC YALSA

Newburg James D. • Director • Point Loma Nazarene College Ryan Library • San Diego, CA 92106

Newbury Brenda • Media Specialist • Spirit Creek Middle School • Hepzibah, GA 30815 • AASL

Newby Gregory B. • Asst Prof • University of Illinois • Urbana, IL 61801 • LITA

Newby Jill • Yale University Engineering & Applied Science Library • New Haven, CT 06520 • ACRL RASD

Newcomb Jean A. • Nashua High School Media Center • Nashua, NH 03062 • AASL

Newcomb Margot D. • Minneapolis, MN 55409 • AASL

Newcomer Katharine • Cleveland Hts., OH 44118 • LAMA PLA *Continuing*

Newcomer Patricia R. • Director • Iowa Wesleyan College Chadwick Library • Mount Pleasant, IA 52641

Newcomer Stephen A. • Catalog Librarian • Los Angeles Public Library • Los Angeles, CA 90071 • IFRT IRRT MAGERT SRRT

Newell Bernadine • Trustee • Calumet City Public Library • Calumet City, IL 60409-4003 • ALTA

Newell Brian K. • Logansport, IN 46947-9675

Newell Debra L. • Librarian • Saint Joseph C. C. School District #169 • St. Joseph, IL 61873 • AASL

Newell Jane • Librarian • Franklin Public Library • Franklin, PA 16323 • PLA

Newell Jane K. • Local History Archivist/Ref Ln • Orange Public Library • Orange, CA 92666 • PLA

Newell Lynne H. • Director of Preservation • Connecticut State Library • Hartford, CT 06106 • ALCTS

Newell Rick K. • Interlibrary Loan Librarian • Western Library Network (WLN) • Lacey, WA 98503 • ALCTS LITA CLENE LIRT NMRT

Newell Ruth • Trustee • Fountaindale Public Library District • Bolingbrook, IL 60440 • ALTA SRRT

Newell Sandra O. • Library Program Specialist • State Library of Florida Division of Library & Information Services • Tallahassee, FL 32399-0250 • ASCLA PLA

Newell Thomas K. • Student • University of Texas at Austin Graduate School of Library & Information Sciences • Austin, TX 78712-1276 • LITA NMRT

Newhard Eleanor M. • Branch Librarian • Long Beach Public Library & Info Ctr El Dorado Branch • Long Beach, CA 90815

Newhard Robert D. • Torrance, CA 90505 • LAMA LITA PLA

Newhouse Gary • Director, Library & Television • Oakton Community College Library • Des Plaines, IL 60016 • ACRL RASD

Newhouse Margo J. • School Librarian K-6 • Ocotillo Elementary School • Phoenix, AZ 85017 • AASL

Newhouse Marilyn J. • K-12 Media Specialist • South Winneshiek Community Schools • Calmar, IA 52132 • AASL

Newins Nancy • Reference Librarian • Randolph-Macon College McGraw-Page Library • Ashland, VA 23005 • ACRL RASD LIRT

Newkirk Janice G. • Reference Librarian • State University of New York (SUNY) University Libraries • Albany, NY 12222 • ACRL LITA RASD

Newland Ida Raulins Mrs • Newton, MA 02158 • ACRL RASD *Life*

Newlen Robert R. • Library of Congress • Washington, DC 20541 • LAMA FLRT NMRT

Newlin Lyman W. • Lewiston, NY 14092 • ALTA PLA

Newling Mary H. • Head of A/YA Services • Piscataway Township Free Pub Library John F Kennedy Memorial Library • Piscataway, NJ 08854 • RASD

Newlon Eloise F. • Charleston, WV 25311 • Continuing

Newman Carol A. • Jenison, MI 49428-1944 • AASL ALSC

Newman Debbie • Tucson, AZ 85719-3235

Newman Donna K. • Supervisor AV Dept. • Monroe County Public Library • Bloomington, IN 47408

Newman Erna • Hd. of Reference • Half Hollow Hills Community Public Library • Dix Hills, NY 11746

Newman Evelyn D. • West Columbia, SC 29169 • AASL

Newman Frances • Cumberland Regional Library • Amherst NS, B4H 4B9 Canada

Newman George C. • Director,E.H. Butler Lib • State University of New York College at Buffalo, E. H. Butler Library • Buffalo, NY 14222-1095 • ACRL LAMA

Newman George P. III • Librarian • Duffield Primary School • Duffield, VA 24244 • AASL

Newman Gerald L. • Principal-Bibliographer • Loyola University E.M. Cudahy Memorial Library • Chicago, IL 60626 • ACRL ALCTS

Newman Irene M. • Madison, WI 53703 • AASL YALSA *Continuing*

Newman Linda D. • Asst. Dir. of Lib Systems • University of Cincinnati • Cincinnati, OH 45221-0033 • LITA

Newman Linda K. • Salt Lake City, UT 84102

Newman Linda P. • Mines & Map Librarian • University of Nevada-Reno • Reno, NV 89557 • MAGERT

Newman Lorna R. • Interlibrary Loan • Loyola University E.M. Cudahy Memorial Library • Chicago, IL 60626 • ACRL RASD

Newman Marianne L. • Greene County Public Library • Xenia, OH 45385 • IFRT

Newman Marilyn D. • Media Specialist • Park Springs Elementary School • Coral Springs, FL 33067 • AASL

Newman Mary T. • Media Specialist • Lakeview Elementary School • Miami, FL 33168 • AASL

Newman Michael L. • Information Consultant/Ln. • Stanford University Lane Medical Library • Stanford, CA 94305-5323 • ACRL IFRT

Newman Peggy L. • Head, Librarian • Ardmore Free Library • Ardmore, PA 19003 • YALSA

Newman Richard W. • Utlas International • Etobicoke, ON, M8X 2X2 Canada • LITA

Newman Ruth T. • Miami, FL 33193 • Continuing

Newman Shonra C. • Robeson Community College • Lumberton, NC 28359

Newman Susan T. • Chief Librarian • City University of New York Graduate School Mina Rees Library • New York, NY 10036-8099 • ACRL LAMA LITA RASD IRRT LRRT

Newmark-Kruger Barbara • Director • Upper Saddle River Public Library • Upper Saddle River, NJ 07458-1699 • LAMA PLA YALSA

Newmark Laura C. • Portola Valley, CA 94028 • RASD

Newmyer Joann • Acting Director • Eastern Connecticut State University J. Eugene Smith Library • Willimantic, CT 06226 • ACRL

Newsham John S. • Librarian/Media Technologist • Valley Park High School Library • Valley Park, MO 63088 • AASL

Newsom Liza C. • Brooks County Public Library • Quitman, GA 31643

Newsome James M. • Reference Librarian • College of Saint Catherine • Saint Paul, MN 55105 • ACRL IFRT

Newsome Karen Liston • Coor of II Res and Ref Ctr. • University of Illinois Library • Urbana, IL 61801 • ACRL ASCLA RASD

Newsome Walter L. • Documents Librarian • University of Virginia Alderman Library • Charlottesville, VA 22903-2498 • GODORT

Newson Susan L. • East Meadow, NY 11554 • RASD

Newstein Gail • Media Specialist • Wynnebrook Elementary School • West Palm Beach, FL 33414 • AASL

Newton Barbara I. • Chief Technical Library • United States Air Force Phillips Laboratory Technical Library • Kirtland AFB, NM 87117-6008 • AFLRT FLRT

Newton Charlotte • Athens, GA 30603-0992 • ALCTS *Continuing*

Newton David A. • Austin, TX 78703

Newton Deborah A. • Library Microsystems Specialist • California State Library Library Development Services Bureau • Sacramento, CA 95814-3324 • LITA

Newton Ellen S. • Librarian • United Food & Commercial Workers International Union • Washington, DC 20006 • RASD GODORT

Newton Francis L. Jr. Mr. • Librarian II • Cumberland County Public Library and Information Center • Fayetteville, NC 28301 • ALCTS PLA EMIERT

Newton Harriet A. • Senior Librarian • Los Angeles Public Library North Hollywood Regional Branch • North Hollywood, CA 91601 • PLA IFRT

Newton Joan E. • Chattanooga, TN 37415 • AASL

Newton Lyman F. Jr • Hd, Tech Svs./Auto. Sys. Mgr. • Aurora Public Library • Aurora, IL 60505-4299 • LITA

Newton Ruth • Assistant Branch Librarian • Howard County Library • Columbia, MD 21044

Newton Thela J. • Library Assistant • California State University-Chico • Chico, CA 95926

Ney Debbie • Southwest Christian School • Ft. Worth, TX 76133 • ALSC

Ney Michael V. • Student • Indiana University School of Library and Information Science • Bloomington, IN 47405 • LITA

Ney Neal J. • Director • Park Forest Public Library • Park Forest, IL 60466

Neyer Tommy C. • Media Specialist • Campbell County School District • Gillette, WY 82717 • Life

Neyerlin Celeste E. • Student • State University of New York (SUNY) School of Information & Library Studies • Buffalo, NY 14260 • PLA

Neyman Sandra B. • College Librarian • Marietta College Dawes Memorial Library • Marietta, OH 45750 • ACRL LAMA LITA LHRT

Ng H. Wen Mrs. • Librarian • Cutter Library & Information Services • Berkeley, CA 94701

Ng Hon Hung Philip • Center for Research Libraries • Chicago, IL 60637 • ACRL ALCTS NMRT

Ng Kok-Koon • National University of Singapore Central Library • Singapore 0511, Singapore • ACRL LAMA RASD

Ng Marilyn • Alameda, CA 94501

Ng Rebecca • Catalog Librarian • Loyola Law School • Los Angeles, CA 90015-1295 • ALCTS LITA

Ngan Winifred W. • Assistant Librarian • Saint Francis Episcopal Day School • Houston, TX 77024

Ngo-Nguidjol Emilie • Reference Librarian • University of Wisconsin-Madison Memorial Library • Madison, WI 53706 • ACRL EMIERT IRRT

Nguyen Janet C. • Catalog Librarian • National Library of Medicine • Bethesda, MD 20894

Nham Diana Y. • Library Technician • University of Hawaii Hilo Library • Hilo, HI 96720

Nibbelink Ellen • Madison, WI 53703

Nibley Elizabeth B. • Reference Librarian • The American University Library • Washington, DC 20016-8046 • ACRL RASD

Nichin Sheryl J. • Chicago, IL 60641 • ALCTS LITA PLA

Nichol Patricia • Oak Hill School • Nashville, TN 37220 • AASL ALSC

Nicholaou Mary P. • Director • Mohawk Valley Library Association • Schenectady, NY 12306 • PLA

Nicholas Myra J. • Library Services Manager • Santa Barbara Public Library System • Santa Barbara, CA 93102

Nicholas Pamela J. • Asst Head, Access Services • University of Notre Dame Theodore M. Hesburgh Library • Notre Dame, IN 46556 • LAMA

Nicholas Sylvia M. • Reference Librarian • Northwestern University Galter Health Sciences Library • Chicago, IL 60611

Nicholas Thomas P. • Dir of Library & Television Serv • Aurora Public Library • Aurora, CO 80012 • PLA

Nicholas Vera • Librarian • California State Library • Sacramento, CA 94237-0001

Nicholes Eleanor L. Dr • Salt Lk City, UT 84102

Nicholls Mary Lois • Children's Librarian • Smithtown Library • Smithtown, NY 11787 • ALSC

Nicholls Melinda • Librarian • Bellows Free Academy Media Center • St. Albans, VT 05478 • ALSC

Nicholls Pat • Associate Director, Automation • University of Manitoba Elizabeth Dafoe Library • Winnipeg MB, R3T 2N2 Canada • ACRL ALCTS LITA

Nichols Art • Trustee • Mid-Continent Public Library • Independence, MO 64050 • ALTA

Nichols Barbara • Honeoye Falls, NY 14472 • NMRT

Nichols Bernadine B. • Librarian/Media Specialist • Brookville High School • Brookville, OH 45309 • AASL

Nichols Betty M. • Supervisor of Continuing Edu. • Kansas City Public Library • Kansas City, MO 64106

Nichols Catherine J. • Student • San Jose State University Division of Library & Information Science • San Jose, CA 95192-0029 • ALSC

Nichols Danielle R. • Chicago, IL 60657

Nichols Danita R. • Librarian • New York Public Library Saint Agnes Branch • New York, NY 10024 • ALSC NMRT

Nichols Darlene P. • University of Michigan Libraries • Ann Arbor, MI 48109-1205 • ACRL NMRT

Nichols Doris E. • Apple Valley, CA 92307

Nichols Elizabeth D. • Technical Services Coordinator • Stockton-San Joaquin County Public Library • Stockton, CA 95202 • ALCTS LAMA LITA PLA SRRT *Life*

Nichols Gail J. • Edwardsville, IL 62025

Nichols Gail M. • Rodeo, CA 94572 • AASL ALCTS LAMA LITA GODORT MAGERT

Nichols Gerald D. • Director • Suffolk Cooperative Library System • Bellport, NY 11713 • LAMA

Nichols Holly R. • Student • University of Kentucky College of Library & Information Science • Lexington, KY 40506-0391

Nichols J. Gary • State Librarian • Maine State Library • Augusta, ME 04333 • ASCLA

Nichols Janet W. • Library Media Specialist • Cherry Creek High School • Englewood, CO 80111 • AASL

Nichols John V. • Director • Oshkosh Public Library • Oshkosh, WI 54901 • LAMA LITA PLA RASD YALSA

Nichols Judy • Youth Services Coor. • Wichita Public Library • Wichita, KS 67202 • ALSC LAMA PLA

Nichols Judy W. • Head, Technical Services • Chatham-Effingham-Liberty Regional Library (CEL) • Savannah, GA 31499-4301 • ALCTS

Nichols Kathleen • Creative Librarian • J. Walter Thompson • Chicago, IL 60611 • IFRT

Nichols Lee Ann • Sterling, CO 80751 • AASL ALSC

Nichols Linda A. • Coordinator • Steuben-Allegany BOCES SLS • Bath, NY 14810 • AASL

Nichols Lucy • Searsport, ME 04974 • Continuing

Nichols Lyn • Raleigh County Public Library • Beckley, WV 25802-1876

Nichols Madeleine M. • Curator, Dance Collection • The New York Public Library • New York, NY 10016 • ACRL

Nichols Margaret Irby • Denton, TX 76201 • RASD

Nichols Margaret M. • Tucson, AZ 85710 • ALSC

Nichols Marilyn L. • Mt. Berry, GA 30149

Nichols Mary Ellen • Strongsville, OH 44136 • SRRT

Nichols Olivia M. • Trustee • Farmers Branch Public Library • Farmers Branch, TX 75234 • ALTA

Nichols Paula • Treasurer & Vice-President • Friends of Walnut Creek • Walnut Creek, CA 94596

Nichols Paula J. • Student • University of Iowa School of Library & Information Science • Iowa City, IA 52242 • ALCTS

Nichols Stephen L. • Publisher • Free Trade Publications • San Antonio, TX 78248

Nichols Vicki A. • Librarian IV • Jefferson County Public Library • Lakewood, CO 80215 • LITA

Nicholsen Margaret E. • Evanston, IL 60201 • AASL *Continuing*

Nicholson Beth • Director • Upshur County Public Library Regional Library • Buckhannon, WV 26201 • PLA

Nicholson Dianne L. • Head of Support Services • Okanagan Regional Library • Kelowna, BC, V1Y 7X8 Canada • ALCTS LITA PLA

Nicholson Jewel • Jamaica, NY 11435 • LAMA

Nicholson Katharine R. • School Library Media Teacher • Monterey Peninsula Unified School District • Monterey, CA 93940 • AASL

Nicholson Myreen • Norfolk, VA 23507 • ACRL

Nicholson Nancy M. • Librarian • North Shore High School Library • Glen Head, NY 11545 • AASL YALSA

Nicholson Natalie N. • Director of Library/Emeritus • Massachusetts Institute of Technology Libraries (MIT) • Cambridge, MA 02139

Nichter Alan • Branch Librarian • Tampa-Hillsborough County Public Library, Lutz Branch • Lutz, FL 33549 • PLA

Nick Carole L. • Reference Librarian • Prince George's County Memorial Library Bowie Branch • Bowie, MD 20715

Nickel Bernie H. • Director • Emmett-HNK Inc. • Novato, CA 94947

Nickel Michael J. • Emmett-HNK Inc. • Novato, CA 94947

Nickel Mildred L. • Lansing, MI 48912 • Continuing

Nickel Robbie Leah • Elko, NV 89801-7006 • AASL

Nickels Anita B. • Grand Junction, CO 81501

Nickels Judith L. • Head Reference Dept. • Northbrook Public Library • Northbrook, IL 60062 • PLA RASD

Nickelsburg Marilyn M. • Iowa City, IA 52245 • ALSC

Nickerson D Arnold • Chatham, MA 02633

Nickerson Donald J. • Director • Coastal Plain Regional Library • Tifton, GA 31794 • LAMA LITA PLA

Nickerson Louann M. • West Regional Librarian • Kern County Library Southwest Bakersfield • Bakersfield, CA 93311

Nickerson Miriam • University of Arizona Library • Tucson, AZ 85721

Nickerson Susan L. • Director • Roseville Public Library • Roseville, CA 95678 • LAMA PLA

Nicklas Suzanne G. • Littleton, CO 80127

Nickles Mac Arthur • Library Director • Garfield Public Library • Garfield, NJ 07026 • PLA

Nicklin Susan M. • Student • University of Nebraska at Omaha University Library • Omaha, NE 68182-0237 • AASL

Nicodmeus Dorothy A. • Frederick, MD 21701 • LAMA PLA *Continuing*

Nicolas Catherine L. • Libray Director • Seward Community Library • Seward, AK 99664 • LAMA

Nicolayev Jennie • Burlingame, CA 94010 • ACRL RASD

Nicoles Richard H. • Conversion Project Manager • California State Library • Sacramento, CA 94237-0001

Nicolson Mary C. • Juneau, AK 99801-8676 • IRRT

Nida Jane B. • Arlington, VA 22207-2755 • Continuing

Nie Caroline Rong • Student • University of Illinois Graduate School of Library and Information Science • Urbana, IL 61801

Nie Geoffrey P. • Ajax Public Library • Ajax ON, L1S 2H8 Canada • LAMA

Nieball Mary L. Dr. • District Dean of Library Service • San Jacinto College • Pasadena, TX 77505 • ACRL

Niebuhr Gary • Director • Greendale Public Library • Greendale, WI 53129 • PLA

Niece Alice L. • Rocky Mount, NC 27804

Nieder Mary Frances • Oswego, NY 13126 • Continuing

Niederhoff Barbara M. • Hartwick College Stevens German Library • Oneonta, NY 13820

Niederlander Nicholas F. • Library Director • Richmond Heights Memorial Library • Richmond Hts, MO 63117

Niekamp Dorothy R. • Cataloging Dept. • Indiana University at Bloomington University Libraries • Bloomington, IN 47405 • ACRL ALCTS

Nielsen B.J. • Collection Development Librarian • Keene Public Library • Keene, NH 03431

Nielsen Brian • Asst. Univ. Librarian • Northwestern University Library • Evanston, IL 60208-2300 • ACRL LITA LRRT

Nielsen Carol S. • Program Officer/Ofc for the Pres • American Library Association • Chicago, IL 60611-2795

Nielsen Jacqualine • Librarian • Pueblo of Pojoaque Library • Santa Fe, NM 87501

Nielsen Joseph R. • Bookmobile Librarian • Weber County Library • Odgen, UT 84401 • PLA IFRT

Nielsen Katherine A. • Librarian • Marin Country Day School • Corte Madera, CA 94925 • ALSC

Nielsen Kristin A. • Reference Librarian • University of Georgia Libraries • Athens, GA 30602 • RASD

Nielsen Laura F. • Rochester, NY 14617

Nielsen Linda D. • Student • Our Lady of the Lake University • San Antonio, TX 78207-4666 • AASL

Nielsen Nancy J. • San Bernardino County Library Victorville Branch • Victorville, CA 92392 • YALSA EMIERT

Nielsen Sheila J. • Mt. Prospect, IL 60056-2879 • LITA

Nielsen Sonja M. • Library Director • Norwich Free Academy • Norwich, CT 06360 • AASL LAMA

Nielslen Steven • Assoc Dir of Library Services • East Carolina University Joyner Library • Greenville, NC 27858-4353

Nielson Kathleen V. • Librarian • Burlington High School • Burlington, VT 05401

Nielson Paula I. • Asst Univ Ln for Database Mgt • Loyola Marymount University Charles Von Der Ahe Library • Los Angeles, CA 90045

Niemann Bonnie C. • Student • Indiana University School of Library and Information Science • Bloomington, IN 47405 • AASL

Niemeyer Karen K. • Director of Media Services • Carmel Clay School • Carmel, IN 46033 • AASL

Niemeyer Kay Dr. • Media Services Manager • San Diego County Office of Education • San Diego, CA 92111 • AASL

Niemeyer Mollie D. • Coordinator of Technical Serv. • Central Missouri State University Ward Edwards Library • Warrensburg, MO 64093 • ACRL ALCTS NMRT

Niemi Peter G. • Director • Madison Public Library • Madison, WI 53703 • ASCLA LAMA LITA PLA RASD

Niemiec Nancy M. • Serials Librarian • Arlington County Department of Libraries • Arlington, VA 22201 • ACRL RASD

Niemira Margarita M. • Assistant Director • Monterey Public Library • Monterey, CA 93940 • PLA

Nienow Beth M. • Mankato State University Memorial Library • Mankato, MN 56002-8400 • ACRL NMRT

Nies Rebecca F. • Library Director • Endicott College • Beverly, MA 01915 • ACRL

Niesen Yvonne L. • Automation Coordinator/Cataloger • University of Wisconsin Center Fond du Lac • Fond Du Lac, WI 54935

Niesobecki Sara • Brookline, MA 02146 • PLA

Niewerth Debra S. • Lafayette, IN 47905

Nifong Arthur E. Jr. • Provo, UT 84604 • PLA SRRT

Niki Kenji • Clln Devel Ln • Saint John's University Library • Jamaica, NY 11439

Nikolai Norma C. • Trustee • Palatine Public Library • Palatine, IL 60067 • ALTA

Niles Carrie M. • Librarian • State University of New York College Daniel A. Reed Library • Fredonia, NY 14063

Niles Judith F. • Director, Office of Colln. Mgr. • University of Louisville Ekstrom Library • Louisville, KY 40292 • ACRL ALCTS

Niles Mary Ann • Londonderry, NH 03053 • ACRL

Nili Afshin M. • Student • Drexel University College of Information Studies • Philadelphia, PA 19104-2875

Nilles Virginia • Director • Georgetown County Memorial Library • Georgetown, SC 29440 • ALTA

Nilsen Kirsti S. • University of Toronto Faculty of Library & Information Science • Toronto ON, M5S 1A1 Canada • RASD GODORT

Nilsen Micheline C. • Swarthmore, PA 19081-2319 • ACRL

Nilson Julieann V. • Hd Mono Processing Services • Indiana University • Bloomington, IN 47405 • ACRL ALCTS LITA

Nilsson Edward O. • Architect • Edward O. Nilsson Associates Architects/Planners • Marblehead, MA 01945

Nilsson Frances S. • Manager, Collection Development • Babson College Horn Library • Babson Park, MA 02157-0901 • ACRL ALCTS RASD LIRT

Nimasang Patcharaporn • Student • Emporia State University School of Library & Information Management • Emporia, KS 66801

Nimec Michael M. • Student • University of Pittsburgh School of Library and Information Science • Pittsburgh, PA 15260 • AASL PLA

Nimitz Suzanne • Graduate Student • University of Arizona Graduate Library School • Tucson, AZ 85721 • ACRL RASD

Nimmer Ronald J. • Associate University Librarian • Wright State University University Library • Dayton, OH 45435 • ALCTS

Nimmo Kristin S. • Adult Services Librarian • Clarendon Hills Public Library • Clarendon Hills, IL 60514

Ninemire David E. • Student • University of Missouri-Columbia School of Library & Informational Science • Columbia, MO 65211

Nino Carrie P. • Reference Librarian • Lakeview Public Library • Rockville Center, NY 11570 • PLA RASD *Life*

Nino Mary • San Jose, CA 95110 • AASL

Nino Raul G. • Administrative Assistant • American Library Association • Chicago, IL 60611-2795

Nipp Deanna • Coordinator of Public Services • Tennessee Technological University • Cookeville, TN 38505 • ACRL RASD

Nipper Sheryl J. • Dir. of Software Appl. Devlp. • Allison-Ross Application Systems • Golden, CO 80401 • LITA PLA

Nipps Karen • Assistant Curator of Printed Bk. • Library Company of Philadelphia • Philadelphia, PA 19107 • ACRL

Niro Raymond C. • Manager, Tech Info Ctr • Raytheon Company Equipment Division • Sudbury, MA 01776 • LITA RASD

Nisby Dora R. • Director • Beaumont I.S.D. Admin Bldg. • Beaumont, TX 77706 • AASL YALSA

Nisenoff Sylvia • ACA Librarian • American Association for Counseling & Development • Alexandria, VA 22304

Nish Carol A. • Librarian • Saint Joan of Arc School • Omaha, NE 68124

Nishibu Yumi • Osaka American Center Library • Osaka, Japan

Nisinger Connie J. • Head Librarian • Normandy High School • St. Louis, MO 63133

Nisonger Thomas E. • Assistant Professor • Indiana University School of Library and Information Science • Bloomington, IN 47405 • ACRL ALCTS LITA IFRT

Nissen Ronda J. • Teacher/Librarian • Spring Bluff School • Winthrop Harbor, IL 60096

Nissen Susan K. • Law Librarian • Montana Power Company • Butte, MT 59701

Nissenbaum Robert J. • Director • Loyola Marymount University William M. Rains Library • Los Angeles, CA 90015-1295 • CLENE

Nissley Meta • Associate Librarian • California State University-Chico Meriam Library • Chico, CA 92929-0295 • ACRL ALCTS RASD

Nist Kathleen A. • Librarian • Algonac High Schoool • Algonac, MI 48001 • AASL

Nista Ann S. • Associate Director • Temple University Health Science Center Library • Philadelphia, PA 19140 • ACRL LAMA

Nistendirk Verna Ruth • Tallahassee, FL 32308-5745 • LAMA PLA *Life*

Niswanger Amy • Media Specialist • Eagle Valley High School • Gypsum, CO 81637 • LAMA PLA

Nitecki Danuta A. • Assoc. Dir. for Public Servs. • University of Maryland Libraries • College Park, MD 20742 • ACRL LAMA RASD *Life*

Nitecki Joseph • Delmar, NY 12054 • ACRL *Continuing*

Nitsch Lisa • El Monte, CA 91732

Nitschke Eric R. • Reference Librarian • Emory University Libraries Robert W. Woodruff Library • Atlanta, GA 30322-2870 • ACRL RASD

Nitschke Marie M. • Reference Librarian • Emory University Libraries Robert W. Woodruff Library • Atlanta, GA 30322-2870 • ACRL RASD LHRT

Nitz Andrew M. • Library Assistant • TeleSee Library Services • Wheaton, MD 20902

Nitz Michael L. • Collection Coordinator • Appleton Public Library • Appleton, WI 54911-4780 • ALCTS IFRT SRRT

Niu Shien H. • San Luis Obispo, CA 93401 • GODORT IRRT

Niven J. Eileen • Edmonds, WA 98020 • ALSC

Niven Moira • Chief Librarian • Alan Pittendrigh Library Technikon Natal • Durban 400, South Africa

Niver Betty • Tulsa, OK 74133

Nivison Patricia S. • Director • Franklin Township Public Library • Somerset, NJ 08873 • PLA

Nix Jeanne M. • Librarian • San Jose Public Library Evergreen Branch • San Jose, CA 95121

Nix Kemie • Director • Children's Literature for Children • Atlanta, GA 30327 • AASL ALSC

Nix Larry T. • Bureau Director • Wisconsin Division for Library Services • Madison, WI 53707 • ASCLA LAMA PLA

Nixdorff John S. • Venable Baetjer & Howard • Baltimore, MD 21201 • ACRL ALCTS LAMA LITA RASD GODORT

Nixie Kathy • Director • Calhoun County Library • Port Lavaca, TX 77979 • LAMA PLA MAGERT

Nixon Alice • Associate City Librarian • Bryan Public Library • Bryan, TX 77803

Nixon Alison M. • Student • University of Michigan School of Information and Library Studies • Ann Arbor, MI 48109-1092 • SRRT

Nixon Arless B. • Phoenix, AZ 85013

Nixon Arne • Prof Of Ch Lit • California State University • Fresno, CA 93740-0034

Nixon Brailsford • Librarian • The Bryn Mawr School • Baltimore, MD 21210 • AASL

Nixon Frances O. • Trustee • Central Arkansas Library System • Little Rock, AR 72201-4698 • ALTA

Nixon Helen E. • Peoria, IL 61614 • RASD YALSA

Nixon Judy M. • Consumer & Family Sci. Librarian • Purdue University • West Lafayette, IN 47907 • RASD

Nixon Madeline F. Dr. • Dir,Henry Barnard Sch Media Ctr • Rhode Island College • Providence, RI 02908 • AASL

Nixon Paul E. • Library Systems Manager • Apak Systems Limited • Etobicoke ON, M9C 5K6 Canada • LITA

Nixon Paul E. • Medical Librarian • Providence-Saint Margaret Health Center Library • Kansas City, KS 66112

Nixon Samuel A. • Librarian • Carver Middle School • Chesterfield, VA 23831 • AASL

Nixon Thomas Jones • Yale University Sterling Memorial Library • New Haven, CT 06520 • ACRL

Nizalowski Edward • Library Media Specialist • Newark Valley High School • Newark Valley, NY 13811

Nkabinde Thokozile • Student • Saint John's University Division of Library & Information Science • Jamaica, NY 11439 • AASL ALSC PLA

Nkansah Daniel D. • Children's Librarian • Queens Borough Public Library Hillcrest Branch • Flushing, NY 11366

Noa Patricia A. • Edgewater, MD 21037

Noah Carolyn B. • Children's Services Consultant • Central Massachusetts Regional Library System • Worcester, MA 01608-2074 • ALSC PLA

Noah Julia T. • Library Director • Dunedin Public Library • Dunedin, FL 34698-7998 • LAMA PLA

Nobari Nuchine • Library Alliance, Inc. • New York, NY 10016 • LITA

Nobel Steven A. • Supervising Librarian • Queens Borough Public Library • Jamaica, NY 11432

Noble A Ann • Head Technical Service • Houston Baptist University Moody Memorial Library • Houston, TX 77074 • ALCTS

Noble Amy S. • Middletown, CT 06457

Noble Barbara • Parkway School District • Chesterfield, MO 63017 • AASL

Noble Betsey M. • Director • Dalnd Memorial Library • Mt. Vernon, NH 03057 • PLA RASD

Noble Dave • Englewood, CO 80111 • LITA

Noble Hadley W. • Hd,Serials & Binding Dept. • University of Rochester Rhees Library • Rochester, NY 14627-0055

Noble Judith • Law Library Director • Capehart & Scatchard, P.A • Mount Laurel, NJ 08054 • ACRL SRRT

Noble Mary E. • Librarian II • University of Iowa Libraries • Iowa City, IA 52242-1379 • ALCTS

Noble Nancy A. • Special Collections/Ref Libn. • Portsmouth Public Library • Portsmouth, NH 03801

Noble Nancy C. • Director Librarian • South Lyon Public Library • South Lyon, MI 48178

Noble Richard C. • Rare Books Cataloger • Brown University John Hay Library, Box A • Providence, RI 02912 • ACRL ALCTS

Noble Wendy H. • Librarian • Kansas City Kansas Public Library • Kansas City, KS 66101

Nobler Ruth • Librarian • Koko Head Elementary School Library • Honolulu, HI 96825 • AASL

Nobles Augustine G. • Brandon, FL 33510

Nobriga Barbara • Librarian • Poway High School • Poway, CA 92064 • AASL YALSA

Noda Nancy E. • San Francisco State University J. Paul Leonard Library • San Francisco, CA 94132 • ACRL

Noe Michael J. • Science & Engineering Ref. Libn. • University of Utah Marriott Library • Salt Lake City, UT 84112-1179

Noel Celine • Science Cataloger • University of North Carolina • Chapel Hill, NC 27599-3902

Noel James D. • University of Rhode Island Library • Kingston, RI 02881-0803 • RASD GODORT

Noerr K. T. • Chief Executive Officer • Information Management & Engineering Ltd. (IME) • London EC1V 4JT, England • ACRL ALCTS LITA IRRT

Noetzold Shirley A. • Media Spec • Andover High School • Bloomfield Hills, MI 48013 • AASL

Nofcier Lena B. • Venice, FL 33595 • ALSC PLA *Continuing*

Noffsinger Donna M. • Reference/Serials Librarian • Mishawaka-Penn Public Library • Mishawaka, IN 46544 • ALCTS PLA RASD

Noffsinger Linda S. • Lakewood, CO 80226 • LITA

Nofsinger Mary M. • Head, Reference • Washington State University Library • Pullman, WA 99164-5610 • ACRL LAMA RASD LIRT

Noga Michael M. • University of California(UCLA) Geology-Geophysics Library • Los Angeles, CA 90024-1567 • ACRL MAGERT

Nogami Amy • Honolulu, HI 96818 • PLA AFLRT FLRT

Noguchi Sachie • Japanese Bibliographer/Cataloger • University of Pittsburgh Hillman Library • Pittsburgh, PA 15260 • ACRL LITA

Noiles James M. • Winthrop, MA 02152

Noiseux Walter F. • Librarian II • Onondaga County Public Library • Syracuse, NY 13202 • IFRT

Nolan Amy D. • Student • University of Texas at Austin Graduate School of Library & Information Sciences • Austin, TX 78712-1276

Nolan Barbara J. • School Librarian • West Irondequoit Central School Dist • Rochester, NY 14617 • AASL

Nolan Charlotte S. • Associate Dean • University of California-Berkeley School of Library & Information Studies • Berkeley, CA 94720 • ALCTS LITA

Nolan Christina B. • Director • Shorewood Public Library • Shorewood, WI 53211 • LAMA PLA

Nolan Christopher W. • Head of Reference • Trinity University • San Antonio, TX 78212 • ACRL RASD LIRT

Nolan Diana C. • Reference Librarian • Danbury Public Library • Danbury, CT 06810

Nolan Irene J. Ms. • Adult Services Librarian • Hamden Library • Hamden, CT 06518

Nolan Joan A. • Lansdale, PA 19446 • AASL

Nolan Kay • Killiney, Ireland

Nolan Lillian M. • Youth Libraian • Fond du Lac Public Library • Fond du Lac, WI 54935 • ALSC PLA

Nolan Marianne • Reference Coordinator • Cleveland State University Library • Cleveland, OH 44115 • RASD

Nolan Martha D. • Hartford, CT 06103 • ACRL RASD *Life*

Nolan Peggy H. • Librarian • Ascension Day School Library • Lafayette, LA 70501 • AASL

Nolan Susanne H. • Head, Ellettsville Branch • Monroe County Public Library • Bloomington, IN 47408 • PLA

Noles Judy H. • Library Supervisor • Webster Parish School Board • Minden, LA 71039 • AASL

Nolin Kelly A. • Student • University of Rhode Island Graduate School of Library & Information Studies • Kingston, RI 02881-0815 • ACRL ALCTS IRRT

Nollen Sheila H. • Documents Librarian • Western Illinois University Libraries • Macomb, IL 61455 • ACRL GODORT

Nonamaker Patricia A. • Reference Librarian • Bethlehem Public Library • Delmar, NY 12054

Noojin Donna A. • Extension & Outreach Libn • Huntsville-Madison County Public Library • Huntsville, AL 35804

Noonan John • Director Research Center • (AIG) Financial Products Corporation • Westport, CT 06880 • RASD ILERT *Subscribing*

Noonan Patricia K. • Head of Technical Services • Gail Borden Public Library • Elgin, IL 60120 • ALCTS LITA PLA

Noonan Patricia Q. • Librarian I • Prince William Library Potomac Branch • Woodbridge, VA 22191

Noonekozakiewicz Mary C. • Children's Librarian • East Brunswick Public Library • E. Brunswick, NJ 08816

Norberg Kerry J. Ms. • Librarian • Ventura High School • Ventura, CA 93001 • AASL

Norcross Jane M. • Atlanta, GA 30329 • ALTA

Nordberg Erik C. • Student • Wayne State University Library Science Program • Detroit, MI 48202 • SRRT

Nordberg Helen S. • Cataloger • Smithsonian Institution Libraries • Washington, DC 20540

Nordheden Holly Ewan • Assistant OCLC Cataloging Libn • University of Illinois Library • Urbana, IL 61801 • ACRL ALCTS FLRT

Nordland Cindy Lee • Akron, OH 44310 • ASCLA

Nordlie Kristen R. • Territory Manager • Faxon Company Inc. • Westwood, MA 02090 • LITA

Nordling Dianne L. • Student • University of Alaska Juneau Library • Juneau, AK 99801-9977

Nordmeyer Richerdine • Palatine Public Library • Palatine, IL 60067 • PLA

Nordstrom Gail • Stillwater Public Library • Stillwater, MN 55082

Nordstrom Kathryn A. • Librarian • Minnesota Correctional Facility Oak Park Heights-Library • Stillwater, MN 55082 • ASCLA

Nordstrom Virginia • Associate Professor • Bowling Green State University Jerome Library • Bowling Green, OH 43403 • AASL ACRL ALSC EMIERT

Nored Alverna E. • Librarian • Withrow Senior High School Library • Cincinnati, OH 45208 • AASL RASD YALSA

Nored Melissa H. • Student • University of Oklahoma School of Library & Information Studies • Norman, OK 73019

Norek Meryl • Bethlehem Public Library • Delmar, NY 12054 • RASD

Norell Irene P. • Associate Professor,Emerita • San Jose State University Division of Library & Information Science • San Jose, CA 95192-0029 • Continuing

Norem Monica Rabel • Branch Librarian • Harris County Public Library Bear Creek Branch • Houston, TX 77084

Norfolk Sandra L. • Fort Knox, KY 40121 • AASL ALSC

Norick Ronald Mayor • Trustee • Metropolitan Library System • Oklahoma City, OK 73102 • ALTA

Norkeliunas Sue A. • Librarian • Arlington High School South Campus • LaGrangeville, NY 12540 • AASL

Norland Barbara • Community Librarian • Montgomery County Public Library Aspen Hill Community Library • Rockville, MD 20853 • PLA IFRT

Norlin Dennis A. • Assistant Professor of Lib Admin • University of Illinois • Urbana, IL 61801 • ACRL LITA IFRT

Norlin Sandra K. • Assistant Director • Champaign Public Library & Information Center • Champaign, IL 61820-5193 • LAMA PLA

Norman Anita L. • Head, Reference Department • University of Nebraska at Kearney Library • Kearney, NE 68849

Norman Anne • Dover, DE 19901-7744 • ASCLA

Norman Audrey O. • Librarian • Baltimore County Public Library • Towson, MD 21204 • SRRT

Norman Carol G. • Technical Services Librarian • Beverly Hills Public Library • Beverly Hills, CA 90210 • LITA

Norman Carolyn F. • Coor. Lib & Learning Res. • California Community Colleges • Sacramento, CA 95814

Norman Elizabeth J. • Circulation/Reference Librarian • Oklahoma Baptist University • Shawnee, OK 74801-2590

Norman Jim • Phoenix Public Library • Phoenix, AZ 85004 • PLA

Norman Karla C. • Leavenworth, KS 66048 • ACRL FLRT

Norman Margaret • Manager • Boehringer Ingelheim Pharmaceuticals, Inc. • Ridgefield, CT 06877 • LITA

Norman Margaret Victoria • The Westminster Schools • Atlanta, GA 30327 • AASL

Norman Nita Vegamora • Branch Manager • Phoenix Public Library Harmon Branch • Phoenix, AZ 85003 • PLA

Norman O. Gene • Head, Reference Department • Indiana State University • Terre Haute, IN 47809 • ACRL LAMA RASD

Norman Ronald V. • Director • Kearney Public Library Information Center • Kearney, NE 68847-5397

Norman Steve R. • Director • Waupun Public Library • Waupun, WI 53963 • LAMA NMRT

Norman Sue K. • Librarian/Head Reference • Dickinson College Library Boyd Lee Spahr Library • Carlisle, PA 17013 • ACRL

Norman Wayne R. • Librarian • Mercer County Library Ewing Branch • Trenton, NJ 08628 • RASD

Norris Alice May • Director • Raritan Public Library • Raritan, NJ 08869

Norris Carol B. • Online Searching Librarian • East Tennessee State University • Johnson City, TN 37614 • ACRL RASD

Norris Catherine A. • Childrens Librarian • Janesville Public Library • Janesville, WI 53545-3971 • ALSC

Norris Cheryl L. • Library/Media Generalist • Matthew Thornton School • Londonderry, NH 03053 • AASL

Norris Cynthia Hurt • Cataloger, Librarian I • Amarillo Public Library • Amarillo, TX 79189

Norris Helen L. • Rockford, IL 61103 • Life

Norris Jerry • Student • University of North Texas School of Library & Information Sciences • Denton, TX 76203 • LITA

Norris Mary M. • Librarian • Solano County Library John F. Kennedy Branch • Vallejo, CA 94590

Norris Nancy • Associate Librarian • University of California-Los Angeles University Research Library • Los Angeles, CA 90024 • ACRL IFRT

Norris Paul W. • Technical Services Clerk • Duke University William R. Perkins Library • Durham, NC 27706

Norris Peggy A. • Adult/Technial Librarian • Joeten-Kiyu Public Library • Saipan, MP 96950 • ALSC

Norris Peggy W. • Woodcliff Lake, NJ 07675

Norrisey Susan M. • Information Access Librarian • Texas Tech University Texas Tech Library • Lubbock, TX 79409 • ACRL RASD GODORT LIRT

Norstedt Daniel A. • Reference Librarian • University of Wisconsin-Eau Claire William D. McIntyre Library • Eau Claire, WI 54702 • ACRL

Norstedt Marilyn L. • Head of Cataloging Department • Virginia Polytechnic Institute and State University, Newman Library • Blacksburg, VA 24061-0434 • ALCTS LITA

Norsworthy James A. Jr • Coor of Audovisual Servs. • C.B. Young, Jr. Service Center • Louisville, KY 40209

North Daniel L. • Hd, Acquisitions/Clln Devel. • University of West Florida John C. Pace Library • Pensacola, FL 32514 • ACRL ALCTS

North Gary W. • Asst Div Chief, Natl Mapping Div • United States Geological Survey • Reston, VA 22092 • MAGERT

North Lydia P. • Subject Systems Researcher • BBC Film & VT Library • Middx TW89NF, United Kingdom

North Robert Jr Mr • Buffalo, NY 14222 • Continuing

North Susan L. • Ames Public Library • Ames, IA 50010

North William D. • Arlington Hts, IL 60004 • IFRT

Northcutt Robert G • Lakewood, CA 90712 • SRRT

Northern B. Penny • Kansas City, KS 66102

Northington Jean W. • Student • Texas Woman's University School of Library & Information Studies • Denton, TX 76204 • RASD

Northover A. N. • Oxford OX1 3BG, United Kingdom • ACRL LAMA RASD

Northrop Janet Kahkonen • Worthington, OH 43085-3823 • LAMA

Northway Daria L. • Pleasant hill; CA 94523

Norton Alice • Keene Valley, NY 12943 • LAMA PLA *Life*

Norton Beverly J. • Gov't Information Data Manager • Brigham Young University • Provo, UT 84602 • GODORT

Norton Helen • Library-Media Specialist • Kettering Junior High School • Kettering, OH 45420 • AASL IFRT

Norton Joan R. • Student • University of Washington Graduate School of Library and Information Science • Seattle, WA 98195 • IFRT

Norton John D. • Student • State University of New York at Albany School of Information Science & Policy • Albany, NY 12222

Norton Kelley R. • La Mesa, CA 91942-1819

Norton Kristin E. • Graduate Student • Simmons College Graduate School of Library & Information Science • Boston, MA 02115

Norton Linda N. • Vineyard Hvn, MA 02568

Norton Margaret • Librarian • Sturgis Public Library • Sturgis, MI 49091

Norton Margaret W. • Librarian • Fenwick High School Library • Oak Park, IL 60302

Norton Meb • School Librarian • Metairie Park Country Day High School • Metairie, LA 70005 • AASL ALSC YALSA

Norton Muriel J. Miss • Fort Wayne, IN 46804 • Continuing

Norton Sue • Associate Director • Katy Independent School District • Katy, TX 77492 • AASL

Norton Wendy M. • Watertown Public Library • Watertown, MA 02172

Norvell Donna • Edmond, OK 74013 • ALSC PLA

Norvell LaNethea A. • Oklahoma City, OK 73119

Norwood Deborah A. • State Law Librarian • Washington State Law Library • Olympia, WA 98504 • LAMA LITA GODORT

Norwood Dorcuas • Student • Clark University School of Library & Info Science • Atlanta, GA 30314

Norwood Flint • Director • Iredell County Library • Statesville, NC 28677 • PLA

Norwood Jimmie C. • Librarian • East Elementary School Library • Greenwood, MS 38930 • AASL

Norwood Pamela Z. • Librarian in Adult Services • Rockford Public Library • Rockford, IL 61101-1061 • PLA

Norwood Scott M. • Base Librarian • United States Air Force Elmendorf Base Library • Elemendorf AFB, AK 99506-5000 • FLRT

Norwood Virginia • Media Specialist • Mount Airy Middle School • Mount Airy, MD 21771 • AASL

Nosanchuk Barbara J. • Media Specialist • Ithaca High School • Ithaca, NY 14850 • YALSA

Nosek Nancy E. • South Holland Public Library • South Holland, IL 60473 • RASD

Noselson Judith H. • New York, NY 10028

Nossett Denice A. • Los Angeles Public Library R. L. Stevenson Branch • Los Angeles, CA 90023

Notarnicola Dorothy L. • San Diego, CA 92111 • RASD

Notarstefano Vincent C. • Saint John's University Division of Library & Information Science • Jamaica, NY 11439

Notess Greg R. • Information Services Dept. • Montana State University • Bozeman, MT 59717-0332 • ACRL

Notestein Jeanne E. • Denville Free Public Library • Denville, NJ 07834

Nothacker Mimi J. • Librarian • Cabrini High School • New Orleans, LA 70119

Nothum Lynne • Branch Manager • Amherst Public Library Eggertsville-Snyder Branch • Amherst, NY 14226 • PLA

Notowitz Joshua D. • Baltimore, MD 21208 • RASD

Nottage Judith M. • Librarian • University of Maine at Orono University College Library • Bangor, ME 04401 • ACRL SRRT

Nottingham Gloria E. • Richmond, VA 23228 • ALSC YALSA *Life*

Nottingham Sharon • Head of Branches • Onondaga County Public Library • Syracuse, NY 13202 • PLA IFRT

Nourie Alan R. • Assoc Univ P Serv Ln For Clln Devel • Illinois State University Milner Library • Normal, IL 61761-0900 • ACRL

Nourse Mary Long • Athens, GA 30610 • ACRL PLA *Life*

Nousanen Diane L. • Director of LRC • Texas School For The Blind Learning Resource Center Library • Austin, TX 78756

Nousiainen George • Green Acres Elementary School • North Haven, CT 06473 • AASL ALSC

Novack Frances L. • Senior Young Adult • New York Public Library Jefferson Market Branch Library • New York, NY 10011 • YALSA

Novak Audrey T. • Assistant Director • Bibliomation Inc. • Stratford, CT 06497 • LITA

Novak Carol Ann Sister • Associate Professor • College of Saint Francis Library Science Program • Joliet, IL 60435 • ACRL RASD

Novak Denise D. • Pittsburgh, PA 15229 • IFRT

Novak Gail • Jane B. Cook Library • University of South Florida Library • Sarasota, FL 34243-2197 • ACRL IFRT

Novak Gloria J. • Nevada City, CA 95959 • LAMA

Novak Hille • Head of Acquisitions Department • University of San Francisco Richard A. Gleeson Library • San Francisco, CA 94117 • ACRL ALCTS

Novak Lorrine M. • Adminstration Librarian • Frankfort Public Library • Frankfort, IL 60423 • LAMA PLA

Novak Mary S. • Director • Franklin Public Library • Franklin, OH 45005

Novak Paul E. • Pittsburgh, PA 15229 • LITA

Novak Shirley • Director • Harlem Junior High School • Loves Park, IL 61111 • AASL

Novak Susan M. • Head of Children's Services • Stanislaus County Free Library • Modesto, CA 95354 • ALSC

Novak Vickie L. • Administrative Librarian • Calumet City Public Library • Calumet City, IL 60409-4003 • LAMA PLA

Novelli Jean L. • Director • Dolton Public Library District • Dolton, IL 60419-1091 • PLA

Novetsky Phyllis • Einstein School Media Center • Oak Park, MI 48237 • AASL

Novik Sandra M. • Co-op Projectr Director • Queensborough Community College Library • Bayside, NY 11364

Novo Maria T. • Student • Miami-Dade Public Library System • Miami, FL 33130-1504

Novotny Larry J. • Assistant Personnel Officer • Cleveland Public Library • Cleveland, OH 44114-1271 • LAMA

Novy Ronald A. • Director • Sampson-Clinton Public Library • Clinton, NC 28328

Nowacki Carol • Jr. High Librarian • Strong Junior High School • Melvindale, MI 48122

Nowacki John R. • Savannah, GA 31419

Nowak Edmund • Trustee • Calumet City Public Library • Calumet City, IL 60409-4003 • ALTA

Nowak Jane M. • History Department • Los Angeles Public Library • Los Angeles, CA 90071 • RASD

Nowak Kathleen Didan • Reference Librarian • Brewster School • Durham, CT 06427 • AASL

Nowak Maria J. • Student • University of Illinois Graduate School of Library and Information Science • Urbana, IL 61801

Nowak Patricia A. • Branch Librarian • Chicago Public Library Northtown Branch • Chicago, IL 60645 • PLA

Nowak Thomas J. • Student • Miami University Edgar W. King Library • Oxford, OH 45056 • ACRL RASD

Nowakowski Bernadette H. • Children's Librarian • Chicago Public Library Scottsdale Branch • Chicago, IL 60652 • ALSC

Nowakowski Frances • Reference Librarian • Dalhousie University Killam Library • Halifax NS, B3H 4H8 Canada • ACRL

Nowell Glenna G. • Librarian • Gardiner Public Library • Gardiner, ME 04345 • PLA

Nowicki Bruno • Trustee • Detroit Public Library • Detroit, MI 48202 • ALTA

Nowinski Barbara • Traverse Area District Library • Traverse City, MI 49684

Nowitz David A. • Systems Design Manager • AT&T Bell Laboratories • Murray Hill, NJ 07974 • LITA

Nowlan Gwendolyn Wright Dr • Prof. of Lib. Sci. & Inst. Tech. • Southern Connecticut State University School of Libray Science & Instructional Technology • New Haven, CT 06515

Nowlan Julia M. • Media Coordinator • McLeansville Middle School • McLeansville, NC 27301 • AASL

Nowlin Dorothy S. • Dallas, TX 75214

Noyce Sharon S. • Student • University of Maryland College Park Theodore R. McKeldin Library • College Park, MD 20742-7011

Noyes Claude C. • Head Collection & Development • University of Rochester Carlson Library • Rochester, NY 14627 • ACRL ALCTS LITA LRRT

Noyes J C. • Bridgeport National Bindery • Agawam, MA 01001 • ALCTS

Noyes Judy Gibson • University Librarian • Colgate University Everett Needham Case Library • Hamilton, NY 13346 • ACRL

Noyes Naomi • New York, NY 10011 • ALSC

Noyes Nicholas • Librarian • Maine Historial Society • Portland, ME 04101 • ACRL RASD

Noyes Pamela A. • Reference Librarian • Georgetown University Joseph Mark Lauinger Library • Washington, DC 20057-1006 • ACRL RASD LIRT

Nozick Sandy • Reference Librarian • Weld County Library District • Greeley, CO 80631

Nshaiwat Naila A. M. • Rocky Hill, CT 06067

Nuckles Patricia A. • Student • Clark-Atlanta University School of Library & Information Studies • Atlanta, GA 30314-4391 • PLA

Nuckolls Karen A. • Head of Technical Services • Skidmore College Lucy Scribner Library • Saratoga Springs, NY 12866 • ACRL

Nudelman Judith B. • Trustee • Ruth L. Rockwood Memorial Library • Livingston, NJ 07039 • ALTA

Nudo Donna L. • Chicago, IL 60656

Nuffer Roy A. • Librarian-Information Services • Schoolcraft College Library • Livonia, MI 48152-2696 • RASD

Nugent Barbara E. • New York, NY 10012

Nugent Carol • Youth Services Librarian • Prescott Public Library • Prescott, AZ 86303

Nugent Christine R. • Reference Head • Maryville College Lamar Memorial Library • Maryville, TN 37801

Nugent Ellen M. • Escuela Bella Vista • Miami, FL 33102-8537 • AASL

Nugent Sara C. • Student • University of South Florida School of Library & Information Science • Tampa, FL 33620 • AASL ALSC

Nuhn Elizabeth S. • Librarian • Potters Road Elementary School • West Seneca, NY 14224 • AASL

Null David • Head Reference • University of New Mexico General Library • Albuquerque, NM 87131 • ACRL RASD

Null David R. • High School Librarian • Wentzville R-4 School District Wentzville High School Library • Wentzville, MO 63385 • AASL

Null Robbin L. • Professional Librarian • Saint Louis Public Library Tesson Ferry Branch • St. Louis, MO 63123 • PLA

Null Wanda • Director • Acton Memorial Library • Acton, MA 01720 • PLA IFRT

Numon Kathy • Media Specialist • Adams Middle School • North Platte, NE 69101 • AASL

Nunan Edith M. • Philadelphia, PA 19136 • Continuing

Nunes Cynthia J. • Sierra Madre, CA 91024-1328 • LITA IFRT SRRT

Nunes Donald R. • Ref Ln • Alameda County Library Centerville Branch • Fremont, CA 94536 • PLA

Nunley Joanne K. • Librarian • S. Clemens High School Library • Schertz, TX 78154 • AASL

Nunnally Josephine Ms. • Richmond, VA 23225 • Continuing

Nuquist Reidun D. • Reference Specialist • University of Vermont Bailey Howe Library • Burlington, VT 05405-0036

Nurse Carol L. • New York Metropolitan Reference & Research Library Agency (METRO) • New York, NY 10003 • LITA

Nussbaum Lisa S. • Euclid Public Library • Euclid, OH 44123-2091

Nussbaum Ruth J. • Reference Librarian • Library of Congress Library for the Blind & Physically Handicapped • Washington, DC 20542 • ASCLA

Nute Anne B. • School Librarian • Gilford Elementary School • Gilford, NH 03246 • AASL

Nutt Anne B. • Newport Beach, CA 92660

Nuttall Harry D. • Subject Specialist Librarian • Jacksonville State University Library • Jacksonville, AL 36265 • ACRL RASD

Nutter Donald • Trustee • Alhambra Public Library • Alhambra, CA 91801

Nutter Mary Jane • Librarian, Adult Services • Prince George's County Memorial Library System New Carrollton Branch Library • New Carrollton, MD 20784 • PLA RASD

Nutter Susan K. • Director of Libraries • North Carolina State University • Raleigh, NC 27695-7111 • ACRL ALCTS LAMA LITA RASD

Nutting Anne C. • Berkeley, CA 94707

Nutty David J. • Asst Univ Libn for Public Serv • Loyola University E.M. Cudahy Memorial Library • Chicago, IL 60626 • ACRL

Nuzzo David J. • Williamsville, NY 14221 • LITA

Nwude Rebecca P. • Hd. of Circulation Servs. • University of Maryland College Park Theodore R. McKeldin Library • College Park, MD 20742-7011 • ACRL LAMA

Nyame Comfort Seiwah • Assistant Librarian • Ghana Institute of Management and Public Administration • Achimota, Ghana • LITA

Nyberg Sandra K. • Preservation Microfilm Serv Mgr. • Southeastern Library Network (SOLINET) • Atlanta, GA 30309-2955 • ACRL ALCTS

Nyce Louise • Library Director • Department of Defense Pentagon Library • Washington, DC 20310 • LAMA AFLRT FLRT

Nydegger-Paulitz Nancy • Student • McGill University Libraries • Montreal PQ, H3A 1Y1 Canada • PLA IFRT SRRT

Nye Diane M. • Berrien Springs Public Schools • Berrien Springs, MI 49103 • YALSA

Nye James H. • Library of Congress • Washington, DC 20541 • ACRL IRRT

Nyfeler Suzan E. • Central Texas Library System • Austin, TX 78768-2287 • ALSC

Nyhan Cathy • San Francisco Public Library • San Francisco, CA 94102 • YALSA

Nyhan Constance W. • Grad Advisor • University of California-Los Angeles (UCLA) • Los Angeles, CA 90024-1450 • ACRL IFRT LIRT

Nyitray Nancy • Public Service Librarian • Saint Clair County Community College • Port Huron, MI 48061-6015 • RASD

Nyland Fritz C. Mrs • Asheville, NC 28801 • Continuing

Nyland Nancy M. • Student • University of Maryland College of Library and Information Services • College Park, MD 20742-4345 • AASL LITA

Nylund Carol L. • Librarian • Longview High School • Longview, TX 75601 • AASL

Nyquist Corinne E. • Librarian • State University of New York College at New Paltz Sojourner Truth Library • New Paltz, NY 12561 • ACRL IRRT SRRT

Nyren Dorothy • Chief of Central Library • Brooklyn Public Library • Brooklyn, NY 11238 • RASD

Nystrom Kathleen A. • Manager of Cataloging • Saint Louis Public Library • St. Louis, MO 63103-2389 • ALCTS PLA

Nytes-Baron Barbara A. • Student • University of Houston Libraries • Houston, TX 77204-2091

Nytes M. Jacqueline • Associate Director • Indianapolis Marion County Public Library • Indianapolis, IN 46206 • LAMA PLA

Nzinga Moremi • Coordinator/Lib Tech Cert Prog • University of California Library • Los Angeles, CA 90024 • ACRL

O'Brian Bonnie J. • Supervisor Library Services • Los Angeles Unified School District • Los Angeles, CA 90017 • AASL

O'Brien-Brumley Colleen M. • Student • Wayne State University Library Science Program • Detroit, MI 48202

O'Brien Anne F. • Reference Librarian • Gulf Beaches Public Library • Madeira Beach, FL 33708

O'Brien Anne M. • Director • Pollard Memorial Library • Lowell, MA 01852 • PLA

O'Brien Bonnie L. • Library Director • Shrewsbury Public Library • Shrewsbury, MA 01545 • LAMA PLA

O'Brien Carmelina S. • Student • Southern Connecticut State University School of Libray Science & Instructional Technology • New Haven, CT 06515 • AASL

O'Brien Carolyn S. • Cave Creek, AZ 85331-5838 • AASL

O'Brien Chris J. • Library Automation Representive • Follett Software Company • McHenry, IL 60050-5589 • LRRT

O'Brien Christine M. • Director • Butler Public Library • Butler, NJ 07405 • PLA

O'Brien David J. • Hope College Van Wylen Library • Holland, MI 49423

O'Brien David W. Esq • Trustee • Free Library of Philadelphia • Philadelphia, PA 19103 • ALTA

O'Brien Debbie K. • Bradenton, FL 34207

O'Brien Deborah S. • Librarian • Sandwich High School • Sandwich, MA 02345 • AASL

O'Brien Diane R. • Director • Joint Free Public Library of The Chathams • Chatham, NJ 07928 • LAMA

O'Brien Dina McLean • Student • University of Arizona Graduate Library School • Tucson, AZ 85721

O'Brien Elizabeth • Director • Tarpon Springs Public Library • Tarpon Spring, FL 34689 • PLA

O'Brien Elizabeth H. • Bradford, MA 01835-8208

O'Brien Elmer J. • Dayton, OH 45459 • ACRL

O'Brien Gail • Librarian • Dover Plains Library • Dover Plains, NY 12522-0604

O'Brien Hyon • Head of Circulation Department • Teaneck Public Library • Teaneck, NJ 07666

O'Brien James M. • Executive Director • Suburban Library System • Burr Ridge, IL 60521 • LAMA PLA *Life*

O'Brien Jane • Librarian/Teacher • Creighton Preparatory School • Omaha, NE 68114 • AASL

O'Brien Jane D. • Head of Circulation • Schaumburg Township District Library • Schaumburg, IL 60194 • PLA

O'Brien Janina • Librarian • San Gorgonio High School • San Bernardino, CA 92404 • AASL

O'Brien Julie M. • Librarian • Wells Public Library • Wells, ME 04090-0699

O'Brien Katherine Lord • Philadelphia, PA 19128 • Continuing

O'Brien Kathleen • Library Media Specialist • Killingly High School • Danielson, CT 06268 • AASL

O'Brien Lee • Assistant Administrator • Cecil County Public Library • Elkton, MD 21921 • LAMA PLA

O'Brien Leonard R. • APO, AE 09058-0005 • AASL

O'Brien Leslie C. • Cataloger • Virginia Polytechnic Institute and State University, Newman Library • Blacksburg, VA 24061-0434 • ALCTS NMRT

O'Brien Loretta R. • Deputy Director • Carnegie Library of Pittsburgh • Pittsburgh, PA 15213-4080 • PLA

O'Brien Margaret R. • Arlington, VA 22201 • ACRL ERT NMRT

O'Brien Maria G. • Information Specialist • Enzon, Incorporation • South Plainfield, NJ 07080 • LAMA LITA

O'Brien Marlys H. • Director • Kitchigami Regional Library • Pine River, MN 56474-0084 • ALSC ALTA ASCLA PLA *Life*

O'Brien Mary Jo • Reference Area Supervisor • Olathe Public Library • Olathe, KS 66061

O'Brien Mary P. • Technical Librarian • Booz, Allen & Hamilton Inc. • Bethesda, MD 20814-4455 • ALCTS

O'Brien Michael G. • Chicago, IL 60657

O'Brien Nancy P. • University of Illinois Library • Urbana, IL 61801 • ACRL ALCTS LAMA *Life*

O'Brien Patrick • Director • Dallas Public Library • Dallas, TX 75201 • AASL ALSC LAMA PLA

O'Brien Philip M. Dr. • Whittier College Wardman Library • Whittier, CA 90608-9984 • ACRL

O'Brien Roberta Luther • Head Librarian • Greenhill School • Dallas, TX 75244-3698 • AASL

O'Brien Sherry A. • Reference Librarian • Wheaton College Wallace Library • Norton, MA 02766

O'Brien Susan C. • Downers Grove Public Library • Downers Grove, IL 60515 • PLA

O'Brien Susan M. • New York, NY 10009

O'Brien Terry M. • Bronx, NY 10466

O'Brien William • Administrator • Iowa Supreme Court • Des Moines, IA 50319 • ALTA

O'Connell Albert John • Media/Computers Teacher • Victos Mravlag Elementary School #21 • Elizabeth, NJ 07208-1058 • ALSC LITA LIRT

O'Connell Candyce A. • Library Media Specialist • Swallow School • Hartland, WI 53029 • AASL

O'Connell Catherine A. • Director • Free Public Library of Woodbridge • Woodbridge, NJ 07095 • LAMA PLA

O'Connell Courtenay B. • River Ridge Middle School • New Port Richey, FL 34654 • AASL

O'Connell Eileen M. • Trustee • Copiague Memorial Public Library • Copiague, NY 11726 • ALTA

O'Connell Rebecca B. • Student • University of Pittsburgh School of Library and Information Science • Pittsburgh, PA 15260
O'Connell Sharon K. • Skaneateles, NY 13152
O'Connell Susan • Director • Rushmore Memorial Public Library • Highland Mills, NY 10930
O'Connell Susan A. • Reference Librarian • Dayton & Montgomery County Public Library • Dayton, OH 45402-2103
O'Connell Thomas D. • Head's Inc. • Birmingham, AL 35203 • LAMA
O'Connell Thomas F. • Dover, MA 02030 • ACRL *Continuing*
O'Connell Ward • Mount Saint Joseph High School • Baltimore, MD 21229
O'Connor-Levy Linda L. • Assistant Director • Manatee County Public Library System • Bradenton, FL 34205
O'Connor Bonnie C. • Reference Library • Yale University Medical Library • New Haven, CT 06510 • ACRL
O'Connor Cheryl O. • Edison, NJ 08817
O'Connor Cindi E. • Student • University of Rhode Island Graduate School of Library & Information Studies • Kingston, RI 02881-0815 • ALSC PLA SRRT
O'Connor Daniel O. • Associate Professor • Rutgers University School of Communication Information & Library Studies • New Brunswick, NJ 08903 • LAMA LRRT
O'Connor Daragh I. • Cataloger • H.W. Wilson Company • Bronx, NY 10452 • ACRL
O'Connor Deborah F. • Director • Geauga County Public Library • Chardon, OH 44024 • LAMA PLA IFRT
O'Connor Dorothy M. • Clifton, NJ 07011
O'Connor Geraldine M. • Manager • Raytheon Company • Lexington, MA 02173 • LITA
O'Connor Grace • Children Librarian • Chicago Public Library Hegewisch Branch • Chicago, IL 60633 • ALSC
O'Connor Gwen • Librarian • Friends Seminary • New York, NY 10003 • AASL YALSA
O'Connor Joan B. • San Francisco, CA 94108 • RASD
O'Connor Karen R. • Head Outreach Services • Waterford Township Public Library • Waterford, MI 48329 • ASCLA PLA
O'Connor Kathleen M. • Coor. off Campus Library Servs. • Gonzaga University Crosby Library • Spokane, WA 99258 • ACRL
O'Connor Kevin • Milwaukee Public Library • Milwaukee, WI 53233 • ALTA
O'Connor Mary B. • Librarian I-Cataloger • Southern Methodist University DeGolyer Library & Fikes Hall • Dallas, TX 75275-0396
O'Connor Mary Lee • Librarian/K-6 & K-3 Teacher • Park Orchard Elementary School • Kent, WA 98031
O'Connor Mary Lou • North Andover, MA 01845
O'Connor Maryalice • Naples, FL 33962
O'Connor Michael D. • Periodicals Librarian • Harvard University Countway Library of Medicine • Boston, MA 02115 • ALCTS
O'Connor Paula • Director, Information Services • American Federation of Teachers • Washington, DC 20036 • RASD IFRT
O'Connor Stephen T. • University of Rochester Rush Rhees Library • Rochester, NY 14627
O'Connor Thomas A. • Trustee • Minneapolis Public Library & Information Center • Minneapolis, MN 55401-1992 • ALTA PLA
O'Connor Thomas F. Bro. • Bronx, NY 10471 • ACRL RASD LHRT
O'Connor Thomas H. • Librarian • Saint Scholastica High School • Chicago, IL 60645 • AASL
O'Connor Vivian M. • Librarian • Atlanta-Fulton Public Library Sandy Springs Branch • Sandy Springs, GA 30328
O'Dell Judith E. • Law/Reference Librarian • Central Michigan University Charles V. Park Library 315 • Mount Pleasant, MI 48859 • ACRL
O'Dell Lorraine I. • Assistant Director • Mount Vernon Public Library • Mt. Vernon, NY 10550 • LAMA PLA
O'Dell Lynn • Librarian • Carol Stream Public Library • Carol Stream, IL 60188 • LAMA
O'Doherty Kathleen • Director • Woburn Public Library • Woburn, MA 01801
O'Donnell Anne M. • Student • San Jose State University Division of Library & Information Science • San Jose, CA 95192-0029
O'Donnell Elizabeth M. • Head Circulation/Readers Serv. • Manchester City Library • Manchester, NH 03104-6199 • YALSA
O'Donnell Jim • Geology Librarian • California Institute of Technology • Pasadena, CA 91125 • MAGERT
O'Donnell John W. • Student • Southern Connecticut State University School of Libray Science & Instructional Technology • New Haven, CT 06515 • ACRL
O'Donnell Marian C. • San Francisco, CA 94123
O'Donnell Mary Ann • White Plains, NY 10606 • ACRL
O'Donnell Michael J. • Assistant Professor • College of Staten Island Saint George Campus Library • Staten Island, NY 10301 • ACRL LIRT
O'Donnell Nina D. • Branch Library Manager • Waimanalo Public & School Library • Waimanalo, HI 96795
O'Donnell Peggy • Port Hueneme, CA 93041 • PLA
O'Donnell Ruth E. • Consultant • State Library of Florida • Tallahassee, FL 32399-0250 • ASCLA
O'Donnell Teresa B. • Student • Clark University School of Library & Info Science • Atlanta, GA 30314 • LAMA
O'Donnell Veronica S. • Branch Manager • Fairfax County Public Library Patrick Henry Branch • Vienna, VA 22180 • PLA
O'Donoghue Laura K. • Loomis, CA 95650
O'Donoghue Patrice • Little Rock, AR 72207-4524
O'Farrell Jill • Trinity School of Texas • Longview, TX 75601
O'Field William R. Jr. • President • Roper Junior High School • Washington, DC 20019
O'Fiesh Terry • Librarian • Big Chimney Elementary School • Charleston, WV 25302
O'Glee Betty C. • Camden, AR 71701
O'Gorman Kathryn Chilson • Head, Acquisitions • University of Cincinnati • Cincinnati, OH 45221-0033 • ALCTS
O'Grady Erin J. • Branch Lib Mgr/Broad Channel • Queens Borough Public Library • Jamaica, NY 11432 • PLA IRRT NMRT
O'Grady James P. • Student • University of Washington Graduate School of Library and Information Science • Seattle, WA 98195
O'Hagan Alfred • Trustee • Brooklyn Public Library • Brooklyn, NY 11238 • ALTA
O'Hagan Dierdre R. • Youth Adult Specialist • Yonkers Public Library Will Branch • Yonkers, NY 10708 • RASD YALSA
O'Halloran A. Therese • Branch Librarian • Harris County Public Library Baldwin Boetteher Branch • Humble, TX 77338
O'Halloran Julia A. • Astoria, NY 11103 • IFRT
O'Hanlon Nancy • Head Ref/Undergraduate Library • Ohio State University • Columbus, OH 43210 • ACRL LITA RASD
O'Hara Edward J. • Director • Manhattanville College Library • Purchase, NY 10577-0560 • ACRL ALCTS LITA RASD
O'Hara Frederic J. Dr. • Prof. Emeritus • Long Island University Palmer School of Library & Info. Sci. • Brookville, NY 11548 • AASL ALSC GODORT *Life*
O'Hara Judith M. • St. Joan of Arc School • Chagrin Falls, OH 44022 • AASL
O'Hara Mary • Field Consultant • Onondaga County Public Library at the Galleries • Syracuse, NY 13202-2494 • LAMA PLA
O'Hare Earlene W. • Reference Librarian • Port Jefferson Free Library • Pt. Jefferson, NY 11777-1897
O'Hare Sandra • Childrens' Librarian • Derby Public Library • Derby, CT 06418
O'Hare William M. Jr. • Librarian • Yoakum High School Library • Yoakum, TX 77995 • LAMA LITA *Life*
O'Herron Virginia S. • Director • Florida State University System Extension Library • Tampa, FL 33617-2011 • ACRL LAMA
O'Keefe Ann M. • Student • Wayne State University Library Science Program • Detroit, MI 48202
O'Keefe Deborah M. • Librarian III • Phoenix Public Library • Phoenix, AZ 85004 • ALCTS LITA PLA
O'Keefe Jacqueline T. • Student • University of Texas at Austin Graduate School of Library & Information Sciences • Austin, TX 78712-1276
O'Keefe Sandra S. • Reference Librarian • Lloyd House Alexandria Library • Alexandria, VA 22314 • PLA
O'Keefe Sara • Children's Librarian • Santa Cruz City-County Library System Branciforte Branch • Santa Cruz, CA 95060 • ALSC
O'Keefe Tarnel A. • Children's Librarian • Richmond Public Library • Richmond, CA 94804
O'Keeffe Richard L. • University Librarian • Corpus Christi State University • Corpus Chrsti, TX 78412 • ACRL
O'Konek L. M. Lt. • Naval & Marine Corps Reserve Center • Augusta, GA 30909-3904 • AASL
O'Laughlin Sandra S. • Tampa, FL 33612
O'Leary Gerda M. • Student • University of Alabama School of Library & Information Studies • Tuscaloosa, AL 35487-0252 • AASL
O'Leary Kathleen A. • Reference Librarian • Olathe Public Library • Olathe, KS 66061
O'Leary Susan • Account Services Manager • EBSCO Subscription Services • Tenafly, NJ 07670 • ALCTS ALSC
O'Mahony Daniel P. • Assistant Govn Publ Librarian • University of Colorado-Boulder University Libraries • Boulder, CO 80309 • GODORT
O'Malley Carol M. • Anchorage, AK 99519-0975 • ILERT
O'Malley Dean A. • Anchorage, AK 99519-0975
O'Malley Elizabeth S. • Children's Librarian • Gaston-Lincoln Regional Library • Gastonia, NC 28054 • PLA
O'Malley Joan • Sherburne Elementary School • Killington, VT 05751 • AASL
O'Malley Judith Ann • Associate Editor General Publ. • H. W. Wilson Company • Bronx, NY 10452 • ALSC
O'Malley Margaret M. • Academy of Notre Dame High School Library • Tyngsboro, MA 01879
O'Malley Terrence J. • Serials Catalog Librarian • Cleveland State University Library • Cleveland, OH 44115 • ALCTS
O'Neal Anita J. Mrs. • Media Specialist • Anderson Park School • Atlanta, GA 30314 • AASL
O'Neal Celia M. • Cypress, TX 77429
O'Neal Francine I. • Media Specialist • Dr. James Craik Elementary School • Pomfret, MD 20675 • AASL
O'Neal Mary Alice • Pine Trail Elementary • Ormond Beach, FL 32174 • AASL *Life*
O'Neil B. Joseph • Roslindale, MA 02131
O'Neil Helen Sister • School of the Holy Child • Drexel Hill, PA 19026
O'Neil Marcia A. • Grover City, CA 93433
O'Neil Margaret M. • Adult Services Librarian • Penfield Public Library • Penfield, NY 14526
O'Neil Mary A. • University of Arizona Library • Tucson, AZ 85721
O'Neil Mary Ellen • Hamburg, NY 14075 • AASL
O'Neil Rosanna • Chief, Cataloging Dept. • Pennsylvania State University E506 Pattee Library • University Park, PA 16802 • ACRL ALCTS LAMA
O'Neil Sara L. • Tucson, AZ 85733 • ACRL ALSC IFRT
O'Neill-Lack Isabella • Reference Librarian • Bucknell University Bertrand Library • Lewisburg, PA 17837-2086 • ACRL GODORT
O'Neill Ann L. • Student • University of North Carolina at Chapel Hill School of Information and Library Science • Chapel Hill, NC 27599-3360 • ACRL LRRT
O'Neill Camille L. • Library Instruction Librarian • University of Arizona Library • Tucson, AZ 85721 • ACRL EMIERT LIRT
O'Neill Carmel T. • Director-Jeremy Richard Librar • University of Connecticut • Stamford, CT 06903 • ACRL RASD
O'Neill Diane J. • San Jose, CA 95125-1412
O'Neill Edward T. Dr. • OCLC Online Computer Library Center • Dublin, OH 43017-3395 • ACRL ALCTS LITA LRRT
O'Neill James C. • Library Associate • University of Wisconsin-Madison Memorial Library • Madison, WI 53706
O'Neill Janis A. • Clerk • Virginia Beach City Public Schools Office of Media and Technology • Virginia Beach, VA 23462
O'Neill John R. • Library Director • Cottonwood Public Library • Cottonwood, AZ 86326 • PLA
O'Neill Marta G. • Indianapolis, IN 46268
O'Neill Mary Ann • Warwick, RI 02888
O'Neill Nancy • Head of Adult Services • Santa Monica Public Library • Santa Monica, CA 90401 • PLA
O'Neill Sharon M. • Goshen, IN 46526
O'Polka Andrea M. • Student • University of Michigan School of Information and Library Studies • Ann Arbor, MI 48109-1092 • ASCLA LITA IFRT
O'Regan Sheila M. • School Librarian • Saint Catharine Academy Library • Bronx, NY 10469
O'Reilly Agnes M. Sr. • Librarian • Saint Michael's School • Poway, CA 92064
O'Reilly Dorcas M. • Principal Librarian • Black Gold Cooperative Library System • Ventura, CA 93003 • ALCTS LITA
O'Riley Jane R. • Serials/Audiovisual Librarian • Mansfield Independent School District • Mansfield, TX 76063
O'Rourke Beth A. • Literature Coordinator • The Galef Institute • Los Angeles, CA 90025
O'Rourke Kathryn • Technical Service & Acquistions • East Brunswick Public Library • E. Brunswick, NJ 08816
O'Rourke Kimberly E. • Chicago, IL 60614
O'Rourke Margaret J. • Science Librarian • Georgetown University • Washington, DC 20057-1006 • ACRL LAMA
O'Rourke Penny • Librarian • Byron Public Library District • Byron, IL 61010
O'Shea Cornelius M. • Assistant Director • Chicago Public Library Sulzer Regional Library • Chicago, IL 60625 • LAMA PLA RASD EMIERT
O'Shea Frances G. • Director • Rosebud County Public Library • Forsyth, MT 59327 • ALCTS ALSC PLA

O'Shea Margaret A. • Chicago, IL 60643 • AASL YALSA
O'Sullivan Curtis Hooper • Commissioner • Napa City-County Library • Napa, CA 94559-3396 • ALTA
O'Sullivan Gerald F. • Director • Stockton State College • Pomona, NJ 08240
O'Sullivan Lou H. Mrs. • Director • Clarence Dillon Public Library • Bedminister, NJ 07921 • PLA
O'Toole Carol P. • Reference Librarian • Lyons Township High School • LaGrange, IL 60525 • AASL
O'Toole Ellen E. • Pittsburgh, PA 15224 • PLA
O'mara Marie T. • Technical Information Spec. • Defense Technical Information Center • Alexandria, VA 22304-6145 • PLA AFLRT FLRT
Oade Penny Maedella • Reference Information Librarian • Hernando County Library System • Brooksville, FL 34601 • RASD IFRT
Oakes Cynthia • Student • Rosary College Graduate School of Library & Information Science • River Forest, IL 60305 • AASL EMIERT IFRT SRRT
Oakes Frank E. • St. Louis, MO 63112 • ACRL ALCTS *Life*
Oakes Mary G. • Librarian • Maricopa County Law Library • Phoenix, AZ 85003
Oakes Sharyn • Senior Librarian • Coronado Public Library • Coronado, CA 92118 • ALCTS RASD
Oakes Wayne • Student • Clarion University of Pennsylvania College of Library Science • Clarion, PA 16214
Oaklander Linda G. • Librarian • Flint Public Library • Flint, MI 48502 • RASD EMIERT
Oakley Adeline D. • Randolph, MA 02368 • ALSC *Continuing*
Oakley Moore Catherine Sue • Librarian • Lake Forest Montessori Magnet School • New Orleans, LA 70126 • AASL
Oakley Patricia C. • Roxboro, NC 27573-4918 • AASL
Oakley Robert L. • Board Member • Montgomery County Department of Public Libraries • Rockville, MD 20850 • ALTA PLA
Oakley Roy • Pine Plains, NY 12567 • AASL ALSC *Subscribing*
Oakley Sondra H. • Student • University of North Carolina at Chapel Hill School of Information and Library Science • Chapel Hill, NC 27599-3360
Oakley Valerie • Reference Librarian • Southbury Public Library • Southbury, CT 06488
Oaks Claire • Dir. Prog. Devel. & Fdn. Rel. • Chicago Public Library Harold Washington Library • Chicago, IL 60605 • IFRT
Oaks Deborah D'Elia • Franklin, PA 16323
Oaks Jean R. • Media Specialist • Monroe Comprehensive High School • Albany, GA 31707 • AASL YALSA IFRT
Oaks Robert K. • Latham & Watkins • Washington, DC 20004 • RASD
Oates Susan L. • Student • Rutgers University School of Communication Information & Library Studies • New Brunswick, NJ 08903 • AASL SRRT
Oatley Anna C. • El Paso, TX 79930 • AASL LIRT
Oatts Marlyn • Librarian • Stevens Forest Elementary School • Columbia, MD 21045 • AASL
Obenschain Beth • Media Specialist • Carver Elementary School • Wendell, NC 27591 • AASL
Ober Greta D. • Columbia Hospital for Women Reproductive Toxicology Center • Washington, DC 20037-1404 • ACRL
Oberc Susanne F. • Librarian Acquisitions & Catlgr • NASA Lewis Research Center Library • Cleveland, OH 44135 • ALCTS FLRT
Oberembt Kenneth J. • Director • American University in Cairo Library • Cairo, Egypt • ACRL
Oberg Diane • Trustee • Crestwood Public Library District • Crestwood, IL 60445
Oberg Dianne • Assistant Professor • University of Alberta Department of Elementary Education • Edmonton, AB, T6G 2G5 Canada • AASL
Oberg Larry R. • Director of Libraries • Albion College Stockwell-Mudd Libraries • Albion, MI 49224 • ACRL
Oberg Marilyn A. • Head,Acquisitions Department • California State University Hayward Library • Hayward, CA 94542
Oberheiser Susana M. • Miami-Dade Public Library West Kendall Regional Library • Miami, FL 33186
Oberholtzer Patrick B. • Librarian • Gallaudet University Library • Washington, DC 20002 • ACRL LAMA LITA
Oberla Janet L. • Librarian • Texas A & M University Sterling C. Evans Library • College Station, TX 77843-5000 • ACRL RASD GODORT
Oberlander Susan • Northern New Mexico Cmnty Coll Learning Resource Center • Espanola, NM 87532 • ACRL LAMA
Oberlin Richard J. • Anaheim, CA 92801 • LITA
Oberman Cerise • State University of New York at Plattsburgh (SUNY) • Plattsburgh, NY 12901 • ACRL
Oberman Tobi • Head of Circulation • Skokie Public Library • Skokie, IL 60077-3680
Obert Beverly J. • Mount Zion District Library • Mt. Zion, IL 62549 • NMRT
Obits Jeneane N. • Student • Central Michigan University • Mount Pleasant, MI 48859 • AASL
Obrecht Claire A. • Reference Librarian • Schaumburg Township District Library • Schaumburg, IL 60194 • PLA RASD
Obrian Parker • Applications Design Manager • International Library Systems • Vancouver, BC, V6H 3V3 Canada • LITA
Obringer David C. • Reference Librarian • Edinboro University of Pennsylvania Baron-Forness Library • Edinboro, PA 16444 • ACRL
Obringer Katy • Supervisor of Childrens Services • Palo Alto City Library Children's Library • Palo Alto, CA 94301 • ALSC PLA
Obst Mary • Librarian • Detroit Public Library Downtown Branch • Detroit, MI 48226-2284
Obuchan Peter G. • Director • Newbury College Mewshaw Library • Brookline, MA 02146 • ACRL
Obuchowski Rita • Library Trustee • Indian Trails Public Library District • Wheeling, IL 60090 • ALTA
Ocain Karen L. • Student • Rutgers University School of Communication Information & Library Studies • New Brunswick, NJ 08903 • ALSC
Ochs Mary A. • Reference/Instruction Coor. • Cornell University • Ithaca, NY 14853-5301 • ACRL
Ochs Phyllis E. • Librarian • Schenectady County Public Library • Schenectady, NY 12305 • Life
Ochsner Renata E. • Library Director • Green Hills Public Library • Palos Hills, IL 60465 • PLA
Ockene David L. • Supv Ln History & Social Sci Dept • New York Public Library Mid-Manhattan Branch • New York, NY 10016
Ocker Ralph • President & Conservation • Ocker & Trapp Library Bindery Inc. • Emerson, NJ 07630 • ALCTS
Ocon Benjamin O. • Branch Manager • Anderson-Foothill Library • Salt Lake City, UT 84108
Odahowski Kristine • Literacy Coordinator • Leon County Public Library System • Tallahassee, FL 32301
Odani Barbara • Children's Librarian • New Milford Public Library • New Milford, NJ 07646 • ALSC
Oddo Anthony J. • Yale University Sterling Memorial Library • New Haven, CT 06520
Oddo Jane A. • Head Librarian • Huntington Public Library • Huntington, NY 11743
Oddy Pat M. • Head, Catalogue Control • British Library • W Yorkshire LS23 7BQ, United Kingdom • ALCTS
Odean Kathleen F. • Barrington, RI 02806 • ALSC
Odegaard Gladys C. • Assistant Science Librarian • University of Illinois at Chicago • Chicago, IL 60680 • ALCTS RASD
Odell Charles • Belmont, MA 02178
Odell Gertrude D. • Sn Bernardino, CA 92405 • Continuing
Odell Karen • Erwin Vocational Technical • Tampa, FL 33610
Odenheim Claire E. • Librarian • Zia Middle School • Las Cruces, NM 88005 • AASL YALSA
Odenheim Pilar • Director • William E. Dermody Free Public Library • Carlstadt, NJ 07072 • PLA
Oderwald Sara M. • Reference Librarian • S.M.O. Associates • Belle Mead, NJ 08502
Odette Gladys • Essex-Hudson Regional Library Cooperative • Orange, NJ 07050 • ASCLA PLA
Odgen Barbara W. • Asst. Lawer Sch Libn • Wheeler School • Providence, RI 02906 • AASL IFRT
Odgen Stanley L. III • Information Conservation Inc Library Bindery Company of PA • Hatfield, PA 19440 • ALCTS
Odhner Carroll C. • Library Director • Academy of the New Church • Bryn Athyn, PA 19009 • ACRL
Odikpa Roberta • New York City Board of Education • Brooklyn, NY 11201
Odinov Alexis E. • Student • University of Pittsburgh School of Library and Information Science • Pittsburgh, PA 15260
Odle Janet • Columbia College Stafford Library • Columbia, MO 65202
Odlevak Therese A. • Student • University of Michigan School of Information and Library Studies • Ann Arbor, MI 48109-1092 • PLA RASD
Odofin Julie • Coordinator Children's Services • Oakland Public Library • Oakland, CA 94612 • ALSC
Odom Anne S. • Librarian • Smyrna Middle School • Smyrna, TN 37167 • ALSC
Odom Melanie A. • Reference Librarian • Venice Area Public Library • Venice, FL 34285
Odsen Elizabeth R. • Technical Services Librarian • Alaska Court Libraries • Anchorage, AK 99501 • ALCTS LITA *Life*
Odvarko Yaroslava • Librarian • Littler Mendelson Fastiff & Tichy • San Francisco, CA 94108
Ody Arnold D. • Trustee • Bucks County Free Library • Doylestown, PA 18901 • ALTA
Oedekoven Diana M • University of Arizona Library • Tucson, AZ 85721
Oefelein Vicki O. • Collin County Community College • McKinney, TX 75070 • ACRL
Oehler Eileen L. • Hastings, MI 49058-9106 • ACRL RASD *Life*
Oehlerts Donald E. Mr. • Decatur, GA 30033
Oehlerts Susan A. • Library Assistant • Georgia Institute of Technology • Atlanta, GA 30332
Oehlman Pamela J. • School Librarian • Garfield Elememtary School Long Beach Unified School District • Long Beach, CA 90805 • AASL
Oeljen Vicki L. • Hennepin County Library • Minnetonka, MN 55343 • PLA
Oelke Anne C. • Cambria-Friesland School District • Cambria, WI 53923 • AASL ALSC YALSA
Oelz Erling R. • Director of Public Service • University of Montana Library • Missoula, MT 59812
Oertli David L. • Librarian • Nebraska Library Commission • Lincoln, NE 68508
Oestreich Kathryn D. • Orange, CA 92666
Oestrich Carol R. • New York, NY 13903 • AASL
Oetling Melinda M. • Northlake Christian School • Covington, LA 70433 • AASL
Oettinger Catherine M. • Trustee • Port Jefferson Free Library • Pt. Jefferson, NY 11777-1897
Oettinger David • Director of Libraries • University of the Virgin Islands The Ralph M. Paiewonsky Library • Saint Thomas, VI 00802
Oettinger Margaret Anne • Librarian • Middle County School District Centereach High School • Centereach, NY 11720 • ALCTS YALSA IFRT LIRT
Offerman Mary Columba Sr • Dubuque, IA 52001 • YALSA
Offermann Glenn • Head Librarian • Concordia College Buenger Memorial Library • Saint Paul, MN 55104-5494 • ACRL ALCTS ALSC
Offutt Ava E. • Business Information Center • Bristol-Myers Squibb • Evansville, IN 47721
Ofstad Odessa L. • Special Collections Librarian • Northeast Missouri State University • Kirksville, MO 63501 • ACRL
Oftedahl Lenora A. • Coordinator, Technical Services • Northern State University • Aberdeen, SD 57401 • ALCTS IFRT
Ogan Leslie A. • Brooklyn, NY 11223 • ALSC
Ogasapian Nancy Hill • Tyngsboro Junior/Senior High School • Tyngsboro, MA 01879 • AASL
Ogbaa Clara K. • Reference Librarian • Atlanta University Center Robert W. Woodruff Library • Atlanta, GA 30314 • ACRL RASD SRRT
Ogbin Frances • Gilboa, NY 12076 • Continuing
Ogburn Dorothy M. • Mount Tabor High School Media Center • Wiston-Salem, NC 27106 • AASL
Ogburn Joyce L. • Yale University Sterling Memorial Library • New Haven, CT 06520 • ACRL ALCTS
Ogburn Patricia M. • Hawaiian Sugar Planters' Association Plantation Archives • Aiea, HI 96822
Ogden Barclay W. • Head, Conservation Dept. • University of California-Berkeley University Library • Berkeley, CA 94720 • ALCTS
Ogden Katherine L. • Clearwater, FL 34615
Ogden Lennie • Londonderry High School Library/Media Center • Londonderry, NH 03053 • AASL
Ogden Nina M. • Pierce, ID 83546
Ogden Patti D. • School Librarian • Berkeley Hall School • Los Angeles, CA 90049 • AASL YALSA
Ogden Raymond P. • Executive Director • Southeastern Libraries Cooperating (SELCO) • Rochester, MN 55901 • PLA
Ogden Suzanne M. • Manager Library Service • Frito-Lay, Inc. Corporate Library • Dallas, TX 75265 • LAMA RASD
Ogea Clara D. • Lake Charles, LA 70605
Ogea Patricia A. • Houston Public Library • Houston, TX 77002 • PLA
Ogg Harold • Chief Information Officer • Roosevelt University Library • Chicago, IL 60605
Ogg Marlene H. • Technical Services Manager • Evanston Public Library • Evanston, IL 60201
Ogilvie Eleanor M. • Librarian • University of Chicago Lab School Library • Chicago, IL 60637 • ALSC
Ogilvie Marilyn B. • Curator, Hist of Sci Cllns • University of Oklahoma History of Science Collection • Norman, OK 73019 • ACRL
Ogle Marie V. • Student • University of Kentucky College of Library & Information Science • Lexington, KY 40506-0391

Ogle Mary H. • Bookmobile Librarian • Wicomico County Free Library • Salisbury, MD 21801 • ASCLA

Ogle Oren • Cataloger • Portland State University Library • Portland, OR 97207 • ACRL ALCTS

Oglesby Mary E. • Assistant Youth Services • Alsip-Merrionette Park Library District • Alsip, IL 60658

Ogonek Donna L. • Neptune Twp, NJ 07753

Ogonji Jewel H. • Hd L Serv & Prog Off • District of Columbia Public Library Martin Luther King Memorial Library • Washington, DC 20001

Ogren Sandra L. • Children Librarian • Burien Community Library • Seattle, WA 98148 • ALSC

Oh Kyosik • Adult Reference Services • Chicago Public Library West Belmont Branch • Chicago, IL 60634 • PLA

Oh Soo Young • Head of Technical Services • West Islip Public Library • West Islip, NY 11795-3999

Ohanian-Chateauneuf Seta M. • Library Aide • Stone Hill School Cranston School Department • Cranston, RI 02920 • AASL

Ohashi Nobuko • Graduate Student • University of Washington Graduate School of Library and Information Science • Seattle, WA 98195 • ALSC

Ohles Janet A. • NN/LM, New England Region 8 • University of Connecticut Health Center Lyman Maynard Stowe Library • Farmington, CT 06032

Ohlrich Karen Browne • Library Media Specialist • Waterloo Elementary School • Columbia, MD 21045 • AASL

Ohnuki Masako • Occidental College Library • Los Angeles, CA 90041

Ohr Donna M. • Student • University of Washington Graduate School of Library and Information Science • Seattle, WA 98195 • IFRT LHRT

Ohr Grace Marion • Lacey, WA 98503 • ACRL ALCTS *Life*

Ohta Carol • Librarian • Punahou School • Honolulu, HI 96822 • AASL

Ohta Hitoshi • Student • University of Hawaii School of Library & Information Studies • Honolulu, HI 96822

Oishi Elsie J. • Senior Librarian • Jacksonville Public Libraries Main Library • Jacksonville, FL 32202 • RASD

Oistad David L. • Owner • Image Prints Incorporated • Lansing, MI 48910 • ALCTS

Oiye Julie Ann Y. • Librarian, Skyway Library • King County Library System • Seattle, WA 98109-5191 • PLA RASD YALSA EMIERT

Ojala Marydee • Park city, UT 84060-0770 • RASD ILERT

Oka Susan Y. • Assistant Librarian • Academy of Motion Picture Arts & Sciences Center for Motion Picture Study • Beverly Hills, CA 90211

Okabe Lorraine H. • Librarian • League of California Cities • Sacramento, CA 95814

Okada Connie • Art Librarian • University of Washington Art Library • Seattle, WA 98195 • ACRL

Okada Emily M. • Reference Librarian • Indiana University • Bloomington, IN 47405 • ACRL LIRT

Okahara Barbara E. • Librarian • Hilo Intermediate School • Hilo, HI 96720 • AASL YALSA

Okamoto Kyoko • Gaithersburg, MD 20879

Okarma Mary E. • Shongum School • Randolph, NJ 07869 • AASL

Okarma Susan • Saint Charles, IL 60174 • AASL

Okazaki Kiyo • Branch Librarian • Petaluma Regional Library • Petaluma, CA 94952

Okerson Ann • Washington, DC 20005-4404 • ACRL ALCTS

Okey Susan J Thorpe • Cataloger • Carmel Clay School • Carmel, IN 46033 • ALCTS

Okie Anne L. • Marketing Manager • Macmillan Library Services Division of Macmillan Publishing Company • New York, NY 10022 • AASL ALSC YALSA

Okimoto Jean K. • Branch Library Manager • Kahuku Public and School Library • Kahuku, HI 96731 • PLA

Okobi Elsie A. • Assistant Professor • Southern Connecticut State University School of Libray Science & Instructional Technology • New Haven, CT 06515 • LITA

Okonak Nancy F. • Assistant Director • Adams Memorial Library • Latrobe, PA 15650 • ALSC PLA

Okonek Mary Lynne • Head of Acquisitions • Cleveland Public Library • Cleveland, OH 44114-1271

Okrasa Maksymilian • Librarian/Technical Serv. • University of Toronto Robarts Library • Toronto ON, Canada • LITA

Okrent Marilyn T. • Personnel Director • Queens Borough Public Library • Jamaica, NY 11432 • LAMA PLA

Oktay Elizabeth J. • Acquistion Librarian • Vassar College Library • Poughkeepsie, NY 12601 • ACRL

Okuizumi Eizaburo • Japanese Librarian • University of Chicago Library • Chicago, IL 60637-1502 • ACRL EMIERT

Okuma Joanne M. • Assistant Librarian • United States Air Force HQ PACAF/MWOL • Hickam AFB, HI 96853-5301 • AFLRT FLRT

Olaves-Mullican Melinda K. • Librarian I • Leon County Public Library System • Tallahassee, FL 32301 • ALCTS

Olbrick Michelle J. • Peoria High School • Peoria, AZ 85345 • AASL YALSA

Oldach Linda R. • Director of Library Services • Mount Wachusett Community College Library • Gardner, MA 01440 • ACRL LAMA

Olden Anthony • Senior Lecturer • Dept of Information Studies & Technology Ealing College of Higher Education • Ealing London W5 5RF, United Kingdom

Older Priscilla D. • Mansfield University Library • Mansfield, PA 16933 • ACRL LHRT SRRT

Olderr Steven • Oak Park, IL 60304-1836

Oldfield Norma M. • Administrative Coordinator • Friends of the Selby Public Library • Sarasota, FL 34230

Oldfield William R. • Head Cataloging • University of Waterloo • Waterloo ON, N2L 3G1 Canada • LITA

Oldham Janet G. • Technical Services Assistant • Chemeketa Community College • Salem, OR 97309

Oldham Jenifer A. • University of Illinois at Chicago University Library • Chicago, IL 60680

Oldick John • Queens Borough Public Library • Jamaica, NY 11432 • ALCTS PLA

Oldja Diane E. • Student • University of South Florida School of Library & Information Science • Tampa, FL 33620 • AASL

Olds Sara Fant • Lawrenceville, GA 30243

Oleary Hester • Director • Osceola County Library System • Kissimmee, FL 32741 • PLA

Oleary Jennie L. • Coordinator of Library Services • Arizona Department of Corrections • Phoenix, AZ 85007 • ASCLA

Oleksowicz Verne D. • Deputy Director • Great River Regional Library • Saint Cloud, MN 56301

Olender Karen L. • Base Librarian • United States Air Force Base Library/FL5688 • APO, AE 09719 • LAMA PLA AFLRT FLRT

Olendzki Kenneth L. • Trustee • Arlington Heights Memorial Library • Arlington Heights, IL 60004-5966 • PLA

Olesak Kathryn A. • Librarian • Schenley High School • Pittsburgh, PA 15213 • AASL

Olesen Marti • Jasper School Library • Jasper, AR 72641

Olesen Rigmor • Brooklyn, NY 11209 • PLA RASD EMIERT

Olfert Lisa A. • Van Nuys, CA 91402

Olguin Cristina • Children's Librarian • Claymont Public Library • Claymont, DE 19703 • ALSC

Oliker Michael A. • Chicago, IL 60641 • ILERT

Oling Lori L. • Reference Librarian • University of Colorado at Denver Auraria Library • Denver, CO 80204 • ACRL NMRT

Olitsky Ida Roslyn • Elementary School Librarian • School District of Philadelphia John Hancock Demonstration School • Philadelphia, PA 19114 • AASL ALSC YALSA

Oliva Armida • City of Commerce Public Library • Commerce, CA 90040 • ALSC

Olive Cynthia M. • Reference Librarian • Niles Public Library • Niles, IL 60648

Olive J. Fred III • Hd,Educational Tech Services • University of Alabama at Birmingham • Birmingham, AL 35294 • ACRL LAMA LITA

Oliveira Marilda D. • Head Librarian • Brazil Unicamp-Biblioteca IMECC • Campinas S. Paulo, Brazil

Oliver Andrea L. • Emporia, KS 66801

Oliver Andrea M. • Librarian-Information Services • Oak Park Public Library • Oak Park, IL 60301

Oliver Barbara W. • Librarian • Benjamin Franklin High School • New Orleans, LA 70122 • AASL

Oliver Christine • Library Assistant • McGill University Libraries • Montreal PQ, H3A 1Y1 Canada • ACRL

Oliver Cyndy T. • Student • University of North Carolina Department of Library & Information Studies • Greensboro, NC 27412-5001

Oliver Donna B. • Student • Georgia State University Pullen Library • Atlanta, GA 30303-3081 • AASL

Oliver Gwendolyn L. • Library Director • Mountain View College Learning Resource Center • Dallas, TX 75211 • ACRL

Oliver James W. • Chemistry Librarian • Michigan State University Chemistry Library • East Lansing, MI 48824-1322

Oliver Janice C. • Elementary School Librarian • Hope P. Sullivan Elementary School • Southaven, MS 38671 • AASL ALSC LIRT

Oliver Jessie A. • Director of The Media Center • Andrews University James White Library • Berrien Springs, MI 49104-1400

Oliver John A. • Flint Public Library • Flint, MI 48502 • LAMA PLA *Life*

Oliver Kathleen D. • Library Media Specialist • Lee's Summit High School • Lee's Summit, MO 64063 • AASL

Oliver Kenton L. • Library Director • Olathe Public Library • Olathe, KS 66061 • PLA IFRT

Oliver Margaret K. • Chestertown, MD 21620 • ACRL *Life*

Oliver Patricia A. • Student • University of Rhode Island Graduate School of Library & Information Studies • Kingston, RI 02881-0815 • AASL EMIERT IFRT

Oliver Patricia F. • Children's Librarian • Portsmouth Public Library • Portsmouth, RI 02871 • ALSC

Oliver Patricia G. • Librarian • Alfredo Andrews School • Saint Croix, VI 00840 • AASL

Oliver Peter L. • Austin, TX 78765-9591 • ACRL

Oliver Rebecca B. • Director • Clifton-Greenlee County Public Library • Clifton, AZ 85533 • CLENE

Oliver Robert J.K. • Second Vice President • Chase Manhattan Bank • New York, NY 10081

Oliver Vickie L. • Student • Northern Illinois University Department of Library & Information Studies • DeKalb, IL 60115

Oliver Wanda E. • Librarian • Rhett Brown Memorial Library • Sandy Hook, KY 41171

Oliver Warren W. Jr. Mrs. • Lake Oswego, OR 97034

Olivere Barbara L. • Arlington, VA 22204 • AASL

Olivetti Lorenz J. • Arlington, VA 22204 • RASD

Olivier Evelyn R. • Asst. Library Director Adm. • University of Texas Health Science Center Briscoe Library • San Antonio, TX 78284-7940 • ACRL ALCTS LAMA LITA RASD LIRT LRRT

Olivier Lee J. • Branch Head • San Francisco Public Library Bayview-Waden Branch • San Francisco, CA 94124 • PLA

Olleman Colleen D. • Student • King County Library System Kent Regional Library • Kent, WA 98032 • ALSC

Ollendorff Monica A. • Reference Librarian • Saginaw Valley State University Melvin J. Zahnow Library • University Center, MI 48710

Oller A. Kathryn • Waynesboro, PA 17268 • Continuing

Olley Lorraine H. • Head, Preservation Dept. • Indiana University • Bloomington, IN 47405 • ACRL ALCTS

Ollinger John R. • Saint Peters Preparatory High School • Jersey City, NJ 07302

Olmstead Dorothy A. • Seward, NE 68434 • PLA *Continuing*

Olmstead Joanne • School Librarian • Andalucia Elementary School Library • Phoenix, AZ 85301 • AASL

Olmstead Joni L. • Sno-Isle Regional Library • Marysville, WA 98271-9164

Olmstead Rebecca • School Librarian • Springbrook High School • Silver Spring, MD 20904 • AASL YALSA

Olney Margaret G. • Media Services Director • Moore County Schools • Carthage, NC 28327 • AASL

Olsen Barbara B. • Reference • Augusta County Library • Fishersville, VA 22939

Olsen Cynthia M. • Children's Coordinator • San Bernardino Public Library • San Bernardino, CA 92410 • ALSC

Olsen Don • San Antonio, TX 78212 • ALCTS PLA *Life*

Olsen Doris A. • Everett, WA 98201

Olsen Janus F. • Director • Natrona County Public Library • Casper, WY 82601-2598 • LAMA PLA

Olsen Jennifer • Libray Media Specialist • Academy Street Elementary School • Bayport, NY 11705 • AASL

Olsen Jill • Librarian • Hewitt Associates Library • Newport Beach, CA 92658-6300

Olsen Judith J. • Reference Librarian • Villanova University Falvey Memorial Library • Villanova, PA 19085-1699 • ACRL

Olsen Judith M. • Librarian • Burlington County College Library • Pemberton, NJ 08068 • ACRL

Olsen Katherine Mills • Specialist, Library Media Ed. • Utah State Office of Education • Salt Lake City, UT 84111 • AASL

Olsen Kathryn • Librarian • Dakota County Library • Eagan, MN 55123

Olsen Paula C. • Children's Librarian • Providence Public Library • Providence, RI 02903-3283

Olsen Randy J. • Assistant University Librarian • Brigham Young University Harold B. Lee Library • Provo, UT 84602 • ACRL ALCTS LAMA RASD

Olsen Richard A. • Director • Rhode Island College James P. Adams Library • Providence, RI 02908 • ACRL

Olsen Rowena J. • Librarian • McPherson College Miller Library • McPherson, KS 67460-1402 • ACRL ALCTS RASD

Olsen Sarah G. • LRC Director • Community High School District 94 • West Chicago, IL 60185 • AASL

Olsen Sperry L. • Student • University of South Carolina College of Library & Information Science • Columbia, SC 29208

Olsen Thomas • Dist Media Generalist • Boise Schools IMC • Boise, ID 83702 • AASL

Olsen Wallace C. • Cornell University College of Agricultural & Life Science • Ithaca, NY 14853

Olsgaard John N. • Associate Provost • University of South Carolina • Columbia, SC 29208 • ACRL LRRT

Olshan Toni P. • Collection Development Lbrn. • Alfred University Herrick Memorial Library • Alfred, NY 14802 • ACRL
Olshen Toni A. • York University Libraries • North York ON, M3J 1P3 Canada • ACRL LAMA LITA RASD
Olshin Henry • Trustee • East Meadow Public Library • East Meadow, NY 11554-1700 • ALTA
Olson Anton J. • Head of Technical Services • Northwestern University Galter Health Sciences Library • Chicago, IL 60611 • ALCTS LITA
Olson Arden R. • Sales Manager • R. R. Bowker • New Providence, NJ 07974 • AASL LITA
Olson Carol A. • Adminstrative Librarian • Letterman Army Institute of Research • San Francisco, CA 94129 • AFLRT
Olson Catherine Cowen • Reference Librarian • Tomball College-North Harris Montgomery Community College District • Tomball, TX 77375
Olson Chalermsee • Student • Northern Illinois University Department of Library & Information Studies • DeKalb, IL 60115 • ACRL
Olson Charlotte C. • Sirsi Corporation • Huntsville, AL 35801
Olson Christel • Student • University of Hawaii School of Library & Information Studies • Honolulu, HI 96822
Olson Christine A. • Librarian • Chris Olson & Associates Information Services Marketing • Arnold, MD 21012 • ACRL LAMA PLA ILERT
Olson Cindy S. Miss • Central Middle School • East Grand Forks, MN 56721
Olson Daniel L. • Ohio University Vernon R. Alden Library • Athens, OH 45701-2978 • ACRL ALCTS
Olson David R. • Head of Public Service • University of South Dakota I.D. Weeks Library • Vermillion, SD 57069-2390 • ACRL
Olson Debra Gerard • Saint Louis Park, MN 55416 • GODORT
Olson Dennis H. • Library Director • Menomonie Public Library • Menomonie, WI 54751
Olson Douglas A. • Kirkland, WA 98034
Olson Elaine • Trustee • Western Plains Library System • Clinton, OK 73601
Olson Eric R. • The Cat's Pajamas • Anacortes, WA 98221
Olson Eva • Snata Rosa, CA 95409-3058 • Continuing
Olson Evelyn N. • Director • Roselle Free Public Library • Roselle, NJ 07203
Olson Gail A. • Children's Librarian • Schiller Park Public Library • Schiller Park, IL 60176-1699 • ALSC YALSA
Olson Gary L. • Park Falls, WI 54552
Olson Georgine N. • Corn Belt Library System • Normal, IL 61761 • ASCLA LAMA
Olson Helen C. • Reference • Katonah Village Library • Katonah, NY 10536 • RASD
Olson Hope A. • Assistant Professor • University of Alberta Library • Edmonton AB, T6G 2J8 Canada • ALCTS LRRT SRRT
Olson Ivy T. • Carol Stream, IL 60188 • Continuing
Olson Jan • Library Staff • United States Court Library • Seattle, WA 98104
Olson Joann Mrs • Public Library Consultant • South Carolina State Library • Columbia, SC 29211 • PLA
Olson John A. • University of Minnesota John R. Borchert Map Library • Minneapolis, MN 55455-0414 • MAGERT
Olson Judith L. • Head of Circulation • Barrington Public Library District • Barrington, IL 60010
Olson Kathleen Lemmer • Tacoma, WA 98499 • AASL YALSA *Life*
Olson Kenneth D. • Albuquerque, NM 87109 • ACRL ALCTS *Life*
Olson Lauris T. • Reference Librarian • University of Pennsylvania Library Van Pelt-Dietrich Library Center • Philadelphia, PA 19104-6206 • ACRL RASD GODORT LHRT MAGERT
Olson Linda M. • University of Wisconsin-River Falls Chalmer Davee Library • River Falls, WI 54022 • ACRL LITA
Olson Linda M. • Superior, WI 54880 • ALSC YALSA
Olson Lisa J. • Fort Worth, TX 76132,3233
Olson Lowell E. • Associate Professor • University of Minnesota • Minneapolis, MN 55455 • AASL YALSA *Life*
Olson Lucie • Director • Socorro Public Library • Socorro, NM 87801
Olson Marilyn A. • Children's Librarian • Johnson Free Public Library • Hackensack, NJ 07601 • ALSC PLA
Olson Mary Ann • Student • Dynix Incorporated • Provo, UT 84601 • LITA RASD LIRT
Olson MaryAnn • Media Specialist • Pine Tree Elementary School • Plainfield, IN 46167 • AASL
Olson Melinda P. • Trustee • Powells Books for Kids • Beaverton, OR 97005
Olson Michael P. • Germanic Studies Bibliographer • UCLA Library University Research Library • Los Angeles, CA 90024-1575 • ACRL
Olson Nancy B. • Professor • Mankato State University Memorial Library • Mankato, MN 56002-8400 • ACRL ALCTS LITA
Olson Raymond C. • Associate Editor, Booklist • American Library Association • Chicago, IL 60611-2795
Olson Regina K. • Library Specialist • University of Notre Dame Engineering Library • Notre Dame, IN 46556-5601 • ACRL
Olson Renee A. • Librarian • Reading Public Library • Reading, MA 01867-2550
Olson Robert J. • Asst Prof Librarian Catlg Div • University of Minnesota O. Meredith Wilson Library • Minneapolis, MN 55455-0414 • ACRL ALCTS
Olson Roberta • Director • Fremont County Library • Lander, WY 82520 • ALSC PLA
Olson Rue E. • Director of Lib Servs. • Illinois Agricultural Association IAA & Affiliated Companies Library • Bloomington, IL 61701 • LAMA LITA RASD GODORT
Olson Sharon K. • Reference Librarian • Evansville-Vanderburgh County Public Library • Evansville, IN 47708-1694 • RASD
Olson Sharon L. • Librarian • Palo Alto City Library • Palo Alto, CA 94303 • RASD
Olson Susan J. • Milwaukee, WI 53218
Olson Susan Mary • Director, Field Marketing Servs. • Online Computer Library Center (OCLC) • Dublin, OH 43017-3395
Olson Therese • Georgetown, TX 78626 • ALCTS
Olson Wayne K. • Reference Librarian • United States Department of Agriculture National Agricultural Library • Beltsville, MD 20705-2351 • RASD
Olsrud Lois • Reference Librarian • University of Arizona Library • Tucson, AZ 85721 • RASD
Olsson Margaret G. • Reference Librarian • University of Texas at Dallas University Library • Richardson, TX 75083-0643 • ACRL RASD LIRT
Olszak Lydia P. • East Carolina University Joyner Library • Greenville, NC 27858-4353 • RASD
Olszewski Lawrence J. • OCLC Library • Online Computer Library Center (OCLC) • Dublin, OH 43017-3395 • ACRL RASD
Olszewski Lela Jones • Champaign Public Library & Information Center • Champaign, IL 61820-5193 • PLA
Olszewski Rose Mary • Children's Librarian • Chicago Public Library Northtown Branch • Chicago, IL 60645 • ALSC
Olthoff Ada Phyllis • Minneapolis, MN 55412 • ALSC PLA RASD
Oltman Jerilyn K. • Galesburg, IL 61402-0065 • ALCTS IRRT
Oltmanns Gail V. • Personnel Director • University of Virginia Alderman Library • Charlottesville, VA 22903-2498 • ACRL LAMA
Oltmanns Judith • Assistant Director • Scottsbluff Public Library • Scottsbluff, NE 69361-2493 • LITA
Oltrogge Margaret N. • Library Media Specialist • Weber Elementary Jefferson County Schools • Arvada, CO 80005 • AASL
Olver Lynne M. • Reference Librarian • Morris County Free Library • Whippany, NJ 07981 • RASD
Olvey Lee Donne • Vice-President • OCLC Online Computer Library Center • Dublin, OH 43017-3395
Omdahl Ingjerd O. • Boonsboro, MD 21713
Omidsalar Teresa Portilla • Reference Instruction Librarian • University of California-Los Angeles (UCLA) • Los Angeles, CA 90024-1450
Omohundro Vicki E. • Librarian • Gayton Elementary School • Richmond, VA 23233
Omoike Isaac I. • Baton, LA 70820 • PLA SRRT
Omundsen Anne • Framingham, MA 01701
Omura Grace I. • Honolulu, HI 96818-3149 • AASL
Onalle Juan • Student • University of Texas-Pan American • Edinburg, TX 78539-2999
Oneal Frances • Southwood Junior High School • Anderson, SC 29624 • AASL
Ong Cynthia • Salt Lake City Public Library • Salt Lake City, UT 84111 • ALTA
Ong Megan E. • Keiser College of Technology • Fort Lauderdale, FL 33309
Ongley David C. • Glennallen, AK 99588 • ACRL LITA
Onieal Marty • Asst. Main Library Director • Broward County Division of Libraries Broward County Library • Fort Lauderdale, FL 33301 • ALCTS PLA SRRT
Oniewski Rose • Head, Doc. Serials, Microforms • University of South Alabama • Mobile, AL 36688 • ACRL GODORT IFRT
Onil Dupuis • Charge De Recherche • Crepup • Montreal PQ, Canada • ACRL
Onion Matthew W. • Assistant Director • Cabell County Public Library • Huntington, WV 25701 • LAMA PLA IFRT
Onkst Wayne • Head of Adult Services • Kenton County Public Library • Covington, KY 41011
Onn Shirley A. • Distance Education Librarian • University of Calgary Libraries • Calgary AB, T2N 1N4 Canada • ACRL
Ono Margaret • Tacoma, WA 98467 • PLA AFLRT FLRT
Ono Masao • Sakodo-Shi, 350-02, Japan • ACRL IRRT
Onsager Lawrence W. • Library Director • Still Memorial Library • Kirksville, MO 63501 • ACRL ASCLA LITA
Ontell Valerie • Mesa College Library • San Diego, CA 92111 • ACRL
Onufrak Paul N • Student • University of Iowa School of Library & Information Science • Iowa City, IA 52242
Onumbu Linda • Librarian I-Tech Services • Omaha Public Library • Omaha, NE 68102 • LITA
Oordt Jerry • Sales Representative • Quality Books Inc. • Lake Bluff, IL 60044-2204
Oordt Joleen • Sales Representative • Quality Books Inc. • Lake Bluff, IL 60044-2204
Oostdik Diana • Parkside Elementary School • Monroe, WI 53566
Opalack Paul • Noblestar Systems Corporation • Falls Church, VA 22042
Opalka Elaine T. • Adm. Asst. to Deputy Exec. Dir. • American Library Association • Chicago, IL 60611-2795
Oparanozie Teri • Reference Librarian • University of Bridgeport • Bridgeport, CT 06601
Opatow Dave • Director • Freeport Memorial Library • Freeport, NY 11520
Opem John D. • Manager, Information Services • Abbott Laboratories • Abbott Park, IL 60064 • LAMA LITA *Life*
Opinante Avril Lynn • Student • State University of New York College of Optometry • New York, NY 10010 • RASD IFRT NMRT
Opitz Patricia L. • Student • University of Oklahoma School of Library & Information Studies • Norman, OK 73019 • AASL
Oppenheim Linda R. • Librarian • Princeton University • Princeton, NJ 08544-2098
Oppenheim Michael R. • Clln Development Coordinator • California State University-Los Angeles John F. Kennedy Memorial Library • Los Angeles, CA 90032-8300 • ACRL ALCTS LITA RASD GODORT LIRT
Oppenheim Regina H. • Student • Rutgers University Libraries Livingston College Kilmer Area Library • Piscataway, NJ 08854
Oppenheimer Susan A. • Ln/Science & Tech Department • Los Angeles Public Library • Los Angeles, CA 90071 • RASD
Oppenheimer Trudy • Assistant to the President • Springfield Library/Museums Association • Springfield, MA 01103 • LITA
Oppenneer Bernard L. • Director • Des Plaines Public Library • Des Plaines, IL 60016 • LAMA PLA
Oppman Mary • Supervisor School Libraries • Portage Township Schools • Portage, IN 46368-5057 • AASL YALSA
Oram Richard W. • Public Services Librarian • University of Texas Ransom Humanities Research Center • Austin, TX 78713 • ACRL
Oram Robert W. • Austin, TX 78759 • ACRL LAMA *Life*
Orange Satia Marshall • Head, Children's Department • Forsyth County Public Library • Winston-Salem, NC 27101 • SRRT
Orcutt Linda S. • Multitype Cooperative Librarian • Wisconsin Valley Library Service • Wausau, WI 54401 • PLA
Orcutt Roberta K. • Reno, NV 89503 • Continuing
Orell Margery • Collection Development • Central Piedmont Cmnty College Library • Charlotte, NC 28235 • ACRL
Orellana Paula • Reference Librarian • Glencoe Public Library • Glencoe, IL 60022-1597 • RASD
Oren Annette J. • Gahanna, OH 43230
Orenstein Virginia • Librarian • Stanislaus County Free Library • Modesto, CA 95354
Oreskovic Carol • Fieldston School • Riverdale, NY 10583
Organ Jill A. • Media Specialist • Greenville Junior High School • Greenville, OH 45331 • AASL
Orgren Carl F. • Director • University of Iowa School of Library & Information Science • Iowa City, IA 52242 • ACRL RASD
Orlandi Jack • Senior Systems Analyst • Pennsylvania State University Pattee Library • University Park, PA 16802 • LITA
Orlando Alverda • Soquel, CA 95073
Orlando Julianne H. • School Librarian/Media Spec • Sunset Elementary School • Tacoma, WA 98466 • AASL
Orlando Marie C. • Youth Services Coordinator • Suffolk Cooperative Library System • Bellport, NY 11713 • ALSC PLA YALSA
Orlick Jody B. • Librarian III • Sonoma County Library • Santa Rosa, CA 95404 • RASD

Orlik Ralph R. • Inf. Technology Services • Library of Congress • Washington, DC 20541 • LITA
Orlin Bonnie M. • Senior Systems Analyst • Faxon Company Inc. • Westwood, MA 02090 • LITA
Orme William A. • Indiana University-Purdue University at Indianapolis Library (IUPUI) • Indianapolis, IN 46202 • ACRL IFRT LIRT
Ormes Janet D. • Head Librarian • Goddard Space Flight Center NASA • Greenbelt, MD 20771 • ACRL LITA FLRT
Ormond Sarah C. • Baldwin Public Library • Birmingham, MI 48012-3002
Ormond Suzanne • Trustee • New Orleans Public Library • New Orleans, LA 70140 • ALTA
Ormsbee F. Charles • Media Services Librarian • Randolph-Macon College McGraw-Page Library • Ashland, VA 23005 • VRT
Ormsbee Lisette • Adult Services Librarian • Henrico County Public Library Tuckahoe Area Library • Richmond, VA 23229 • PLA SRRT
Ormsby Rita J. • Student • University of Wisconsin-Madison School of Library & Information Studies • Madison, WI 53706 • GODORT IRRT
Ormston Ruth W. • Dunedin, FL 34698 • AASL *Continuing*
Orne Jerrold Dr. • Chapel Hill, NC 27514 • Continuing
Oronson Joyce Marie • Librarian • Baltimore County Public Library • Towson, MD 21204 • PLA
Oros Susan Robillard • Research Libraries Group Inc. (RLG) • Mountain View, CA 94041-1100
Orozco Julia M. • Library Director • Salinas Public Library • Salinas, CA 93901 • LAMA
Orozco Tenorio Jose • I.T.A.M./Library • 01000 Mexico D.F., Mexico • ACRL ALCTS
Orpinela Johnette K. • Librarian • Franklin High School Library • Stockton, CA 95205 • AASL
Orr Christine • Wasatch Middle School • Heber, UT 84032
Orr Christine J. • Student • University of California-Berkeley School of Library & Information Studies • Berkeley, CA 94720
Orr E. Jean • Bellaire, OH 43906
Orr Edna Dearth Miss • Kansas City, MO 64111 • Life
Orr Gloria J. • Off-Campus Coor./Archivist • University of Maryland Libraries • College Park, MD 20742 • ACRL
Orr Inez G. • Student • Clark-Atlanta University School of Library & Information Studies • Atlanta, GA 30314-4391
Orr Janine H. • Reference Librarian • Indiana University School of Medicine Library • Indianapolis, IN 46202-5121 • ACRL
Orr Joella A. • Director • Denton Public Library • Denton, TX 76201 • LAMA PLA
Orr Margaret H. • Ames, IA 50010 • ACRL ALCTS *Life*
Orr Monica • Trustee • Louisville Free Public Library • Louisville, KY 40203-2257 • ALTA
Orr Nancy Y. • Oxford, MD 21654 • Continuing
Orr Pamela M. • Media Specialist • Urbana Elementary School • Frederick, MD 21701 • AASL
Orr Philip E. • Champaign, IL 61820
Orr Sally I. • The Webb Schools • Claremont, CA 91711 • AASL
Orraca Sadako • Technical Service Librarian • Proskauer Rose Goetz and Mendelsohn Library • New York, NY 10036 • ALCTS
Orsburn Elizabeth C. • Head, Film & Video Center • Free Library of Philadelphia • Philadelphia, PA 19103 • PLA
Orser Frank W. • Assoc. University Librarian • University of Florida Libraries • Gainesville, FL 32611-2047 • ALCTS
Orser Lawan V. • Associate Librarian • University of Florida Libraries • Gainesville, FL 32611 • ACRL ALCTS LITA LRRT
Ortega Edna • Demarest Public Library • Demarest, NJ 07627
Ortega Felipe • Trustee • Center for Employment Training • Escondido, CA 92025 • ALTA
Ortega Patricia L. • Librarian • Catholic University of America John K. Mullen of Denver Memorial Library • Washington, DC 20064
Ortego Gilda Baeza • Doctoral Student • Texas Woman's University School of Library & Information Studies • Denton, TX 76204 • EMIERT
Orth Claire E. • Audubon Montessori School • New Orleans, LA 70118 • AASL
Orth Nancy M. • Department Head of Circulation • University of Connecticut Homer Babbidge Library • Storrs, CT 06269-1005 • ACRL LAMA LITA
Orth Sue Ann J. • Media Specialist • Southwest Middle School • Orlando, FL 32812 • AASL YALSA
Ortiz Cynthia • Librarian • United States Department of Energy Nevada Technical Library • Las Vegas, NV 89193-8518 • ACRL ALCTS LAMA LITA
Ortiz Daniel • Bayamon, PR 00959 • ACRL ALCTS LAMA LITA RASD EMIERT IRRT LRRT SRRT
Ortiz Diane • Mgt Analyst-Court Records Ln • City of Las Vegas Municipal Court • Las Vegas, NV 89101 • ACRL ALCTS LAMA LITA
Ortiz Maria E. • Student • University of California-Berkeley School of Library & Information Studies • Berkeley, CA 94720
Ortiz Oneida R. • Humacao University College Library • Humacao, PR 00661
Ortiz Raquel • Student • Harvard College Library Widener Memorial Library • Cambridge, MA 02138 • ALCTS
Ortiz Sylvia • Head,Reference Unit • New Mexico State University Library • Las Cruces, NM 88003-0006 • RASD
Ortner Jill W. • Student • Pratt Institute Graduate School of Library & Information Science • Brooklyn, NY 11205
Ortopan LeRoy D. • Librarian • University of California-Berkeley University Library • Berkeley, CA 94720
Ortwein Mary E. • Librarian • R. Guild Gray Elementary School • Las Vegas, NV 89102
Ortynsky Taras A. • Head of Technical Services • Villanova University Falvey Memorial Library • Villanova, PA 19085-1699 • ACRL ALCTS
Orvedahl Virginia • Director • Halifax County Library • Halifax, NC 27839 • PLA IFRT SRRT
Orwig Gail T. • Childrens Librarian • Fremont Main Library • Fremont, CA 94538
Orzel Dolores Sr • Saint Basil Academy • Philadelphia, PA 19111 • YALSA
Orzen Rickie L. • Librarian • The Meadows School • Las Vegas, NV 89128-7302 • YALSA
Osato Debra L. • Student • University of Arizona Graduate Library School • Tucson, AZ 85721 • LITA PLA EMIERT
Osberg Gail H. • Assistant Regional Manager • Reston Regional Library • Reston, VA 22090 • PLA
Osborn Andrew D. • Roseville NSW 2069, Australia
Osborn Anne • Senior Librarian • Youth Training School • Ontario, CA 91761
Osborn Cindy • Tucson, AZ 85715 • AASL
Osborn Dorothy H. • Durham, NC 27707
Osborn Lucie P. • Director • Laramie County Library System • Cheyenne, WY 82001-2799 • LAMA PLA
Osborn Susan J. • Student • Emporia State University Emporia in the Rockies • Denver, CO 80204
Osborn V. Jeanne Dr. • Iowa City, IA 52240 • ACRL ALCTS *Life*
Osborne Ann B. • Cataloger • Midlands Technical College • Columbia, SC 29202
Osborne Connie J. • Vice-President • Houchen Bindery Ltd. • Utica, NE 68456 • ALCTS
Osborne Gloria J. • Student • University of Michigan School of Information and Library Studies • Ann Arbor, MI 48109-1092
Osborne H Don • President • Houchen Bindery Ltd. • Utica, NE 68456
Osborne Jo • Ch Ln • Worthington Public Library • Worthington, OH 43085
Osborne Karen L. • Student • University of Arizona Graduate Library School • Tucson, AZ 85721 • ACRL ALSC PLA RASD IFRT SRRT
Osborne Larry N. • Assistant Professor • University of Hawaii Thomas Hale Hamilton Library • Honolulu, HI 96822 • ALCTS LITA
Osborne Michael J. • Librarian • Southern California University Washington Public Affairs Center • Washington, DC 20004 • ALCTS
Osborne Nancy Seale • Associate Librarian • State University of New York (SUNY) Penfield Library • Oswego, NY 13126-3514 • ACRL RASD IFRT LIRT SRRT
Osborne Pamela R. • Automation Coordinator • Alameda County Library System • Fremont, CA 94538 • LITA PLA
Osborne Robin • Student • Columbia University Library Service Library • New York, NY 10027
Osborne Taeh C. • Renton, WA 98058
Osborne Tim • Director of Media Services • Lee County School District Lee County Media Services • Fort Myers, FL 33901
Osborne Zelda L. • Houston, TX 77027-6308 • Continuing
Osburn Charles B. • Dean of Libraries • University of Alabama Amelia Gayle Gorgas Library • Tuscaloosa, AL 35487-0266 • ACRL ALCTS
Osburn Harriet S. • Middletown, CT 06457 • Continuing
Osegueda Laura M. • Head of Chemistry Library • University of California-Berkeley University Library • Berkeley, CA 94720 • ACRL
Osenga Sharon Lynn • Administrator • Meridian Library System • Kearney, NE 68847 • PLA
Oser Anita K. • Western Carolina University Hunter Library • Cullowhee, NC 28723-9002 • MAGERT
Oserman Steve • Reference Librarian • Skokie Public Library • Skokie, IL 60077-3680 • PLA
Oserman Stuart • Trustee • Morton Grove Public Library • Morton Grove, IL 60053 • ALTA
Osgood James B. • Assistant Librarian • Kennedy-King College Library • Chicago, IL 60621 • ACRL SRRT
Osheroff Shiela Keil • Serials Cataloger • Oregon State University William Jasper Kerr Library • Corvallis, OR 97331-4501 • ACRL EMIERT
Oshiro Luanne N. • Tracy, CA 95376 • ACRL ALCTS LITA
Oshiro Madelline E. • Librarian • Kamehameha Elementary School • Honolulu, HI 96817
Oshiro Michi C. • Student • University of Hawaii School of Library & Information Studies • Honolulu, HI 96822 • AASL ALSC YALSA
Osier Donald V. • Librarian & Assoc. Prof. • University of Minnesota O. Meredith Wilson Library • Minneapolis, MN 55455-0414 • ACRL
Osier Michele M. • Columbia, SC 29210
Osif Bonnie • Asst. Enginering Librarian • Pennsylvania State University Libraries • University Park, PA 16802 • ACRL
Oslizly Barbara H. • Community Librarian • United States Army Wildflecken • APO, AE 09026
Oslund Janet L. • Student • University of Arizona Graduate Library School • Tucson, AZ 85721 • ALCTS GODORT IRRT
Osmanski Paul S. • Washington, DC 20009-3376 • ALCTS
Osmer Elizabeth G. • Librarian • Woodside Elementary School • Topsham, ME 04086 • AASL
Osmun Curtis • Serials Cataloging Assistant • Northwestern University Library • Evanston, IL 60208-2300
Osmus Lori L. • Head, Serials Cataloging Section • Iowa State University Library • Ames, IA 50011-2140 • ACRL ALCTS
Osorio Nestor L. • Sci-Engrg. Subj. Spec. • Northern Illinois University University Libraries • DeKalb, IL 60115-2868 • ACRL
Ossen Virginia F. • Long Beach, CA 90807 • Continuing
Ossolinski Lynn • Librarian • Incline High School • Incline, NV 89450 • AASL LIRT
Ostar Lewis M. • Director • Raritan Valley Community College Libray • Somerville, NJ 08876 • LAMA
Ostaszewski Theodore • Lee's Summit, MO 64063
Ostby Lloyd • Head, Humanities Dept. • Memphis-Shelby County Public Library and Information Center • Memphis, TN 38104-4025 • IRRT
Ostdiek Janet A. • Librarian/Director • Gretna Public Library • Gretna, NE 68028
Osten Margaret E. • New York, NY 10027 • Continuing
Ostendorf JoEllen • Librarian • Georgia Department of Education Division of Public Library Services • Atlanta, GA 30303-3692
Ostendorf Paul John Brother • Head Librarian • Saint Mary's College Fitzgerald Library • Winona, MN 55987 • ACRL ALCTS RASD
Osteno Marie • Student • San Jose State University Division of Library & Information Science • San Jose, CA 95192-0029
Ostenso Ann • Librarian • Monte Vista Elementary School • Monterey, CA 93940 • AASL
Osterby Marian L. • Centralia, WA 98531
Ostergren Marilyn J. • Student • University of Washington Graduate School of Library and Information Science • Seattle, WA 98195 • IFRT
Ostermayer Lois M. • Cape May County Library • Cape May, NJ 08204
Ostermick Patricia D. • Student • University of Wisconsin-Milwaukee School of Library & Information Science • Milwaukee, WI 53201
Osterreich Shelley • Librarian • Central Connecticut State University • New Britain, CT 06050 • ACRL
Ostertag J. Keith • Student • Louisiana State University School of Library & Information Science • Baton Rouge, LA 70803-3290
Osthus Mary J. • Librarian • Lincoln High School • Sioux Falls, SD 57105 • AASL YALSA
Ostler Larry J. • Assistant University Librarian • Brigham Young University Harold B. Lee Library • Provo, UT 84602 • ACRL LAMA
Ostler Rosemarie • Reference Librarian • University of Oregon Library • Eugene, OR 97403-1299
Ostling Anne M. • Student • Queens College Grad Sch of Lib & Inf Studies • Flushing, NY 11367
Ostlund James • Director of User Services • University of Notre Dame • Notre Dame, IN 46556 • LITA
Ostovany Parkhideh • Librarian • New York Public Library • Bronx, NY 11201 • NMRT
Ostrander Molly K. • Student • University of California Science Library • Santa Cruz, CA 95064 • NMRT
Ostrander Richard E. • Director • Yakima Valley Regional Library • Yakima, WA 98901 • PLA
Ostrem Steve • Cedar Rapids Public Library • Cedar Rapids, IA 52401 • RASD
Ostrom Janice C. • Coordinator of Media Services • Instructional Media Center • Salina, KS 67401 • AASL LITA

Ostroski Sandra E. • Reference Librarian • Neptune Township Public Library • Neptune, NJ 07753 • NMRT

Ostroumov Tatiana • Senior Librarian • Oakland Public Library • Oakland, CA 94612 • Life

Ostrove Geraldine E. • Office of Cataloging Support • Library of Congress • Washington, DC 20541 • ALCTS

Ostrow Julie Ann • Corporate Librarian • Thermo King Corporation Library • Minneapolis, MN 55420

Ostrow Rona • Associate Dean, Public Services • Adelphi University Swirbul Library • Garden City, NY 11530 • ACRL LITA

Ostrowski Lawrence C. • Coordinator of Extension Service • Saint Joseph County Public Library • South Bend, IN 46601 • PLA

Ostrum Roxane M. • Librarian • Avalon Public Library • Avalon, PA 15202

Ostrye-Macdonald Anne T. • Fort Collins, CO 80525

Ostwald Mordecai • Philadelphia, PA 19131 • ACRL GODORT IFRT MAGERT

Osuala Kate O. Dr. • Librarian II • Free Library of Philadelphia • Philadelphia, PA 19103 • ACRL LRRT

Oswald David B. • Cataloger • Church of Jesus Christ of Latter-Day Saints • Salt Lake City, UT 84150

Oswald Diane M. • Student • University of North Texas School of Library & Information Sciences • Denton, TX 76203 • AASL

Oswald Dianne R. • San Jose, CA 95125

Oswald Tina A. • Librarian • Washington State University Library • Pullman, WA 99164-5610 • ACRL NMRT

Oswalt Paul K. • Librarian • Dallas Public Library • Dallas, TX 75201

Otchere Freda E. • Sr. Catlg. & Standards Libn. • Concordia University Libraries • Montreal PQ, H3G 1M8 Canada • ACRL ALCTS

Otero-Boisvert Maria • Head of Library • Loyola University Mallinckrodt Campus • Wilmette, IL 60091-1560 • ACRL

Otis Lynn Marie • Librarian • Hamilton Middle School • Long Beach, CA 90805 • AASL

Otis Perry W. • Student • University of Alabama School of Library & Information Studies • Tuscaloosa, AL 35487-0252

Ott Martha T. • Cumberland, ME 04021

Ott Pamela • Librarian (K-6) • McConnellsburg Elementary School • McConnellsburg, PA 17233

Ottaviano Doris Baginski • Head Reference Librarian • United States Naval War College Library • Newport, RI 02841 • ACRL RASD

Otte George • Trustee • State Library of Iowa • Des Moines, IA 50319 • ALTA

Otte Julie A. • Student • Brigham Young University School of Library & Information Sciences • Provo, UT 84602 • PLA

Otten Alice • Student • Syracuse University School of Information Studies • Syracuse, NY 13244-4100

Otten Jeanne C. • Library Systems Analyst • Western Library Network (WLN) • Lacey, WA 98503-0888 • ALCTS LITA SRRT

Ottenstein Matthew H. • Research Librarian • Federal Reserve Bank of New York • New York, NY 10045 • RASD

Ottenstein Susanne • Larchmont, NY 10538

Otteraaen Marion J. • Library Director • Longview Public Library • Longview, WA 98632-2993 • AASL ALCTS ALSC ALTA LAMA PLA RASD YALSA

Otterson Ron • Trustee • Minneapolis Public Library & Information Center • Minneapolis, MN 55401-1992 • ALTA PLA

Otteson M. Jeanne • Student • University of Wisconsin-Madison School of Library & Information Studies • Madison, WI 53706 • ALSC

Ottignon Susan A. • Reference Librarian • Villanova University Falvey Memorial Library • Villanova, PA 19085-1699 • ACRL

Otto Betty J. • Librarian • Boys Town Library Services • Boys Town, NE 68010 • RASD

Otto Kenneth C. • Azusa Pacific University Marshburn Memorial Library • Azusa, CA 91702

Otto Paul • Information Desk Librarian • Brooklyn Public Library • Brooklyn, NY 11238 • LITA

Otto Sondra K. • Branch Supervising Librarian • Tulsa City-County Library Skiatook Branch • Skiatook, OK 74070

Otto Theophil M. • Head of Public Services • Eastern Washington University • Cheney, WA 99004 • ACRL

Ottosen Terri J. • Colton, CA 92324 • PLA

Ottow Carolyn M. • Student • Oklahoma State University Library • Stillwater, OK 74078-0375

Ouchi Sharon S. • Cataloging Librarian • University of Hawaii Thomas Hale Hamilton Library • Honolulu, HI 96822 • ALCTS

Oudard Denis F. • Digi Press • Louisville, KY 40207 • ALCTS LITA

Ouderkirk Jane A. • Head, Cataloging Services • Harvard College Library Widener Memorial Library • Cambridge, MA 02138 • ASCLA LAMA LITA PLA GODORT

Ouellette Cheryl S. • Student • Simmons College Graduate School of Library & Information Science • Boston, MA 02115

Ouellette Janice A. • Fitchburg State College Library • Fitchburg, MA 01420

Ouida Andrea • Trustee • River Edge Public Library • River Edge, NJ 07661 • ALTA

Oukada Jennie • Librarian • Saint Richard's School Library • Indianapolis, IN 46208

Ouye Kathleen G. • City Librarian • San Mateo Public Library • San Mateo, CA 94402 • ALCTS ALSC LAMA LITA PLA RASD

Ovalle Maria E. • Student • University of Texas at Austin Graduate School of Library & Information Sciences • Austin, TX 78712-1276 • AASL

Over Elizabeth S. • Media Specialist • North East High School • North East, MD 21901

Overbeck James A. • Atlanta, GA 30307 • ACRL

Overby Mary E. • Documents Librarian • Ashland Community College • Ashland, KY 41101 • GODORT

Overcash Gina R. • Humanities Reference Librarian • Auburn University Ralph Brown Draughon Library • Auburn, AL 36849-5606 • ACRL RASD

Overeynder R. E. • Director • Nedbook International • 1003AC Amsterdam, Netherlands

Overgaard Lynn Hyde • Director • Penn Yan Public Library • Penn Yan, NY 14527

Overland Don • Trustee • Clinton Public Library • Clinton, IA 52732 • ALTA

Overman Joan D. • Librarian • Corning-Painted Post School District • Painted Post, NY 14870

Overmier Judith A. • University of Oklahoma School of Library & Information Studies • Norman, OK 73019 • ACRL ALCTS LHRT LRRT

Overmyer Elizabeth C. • Children's Librarian • Bay Area Library & Information System • Oakland, CA 94607 • ALSC RASD

Overstreet Allen J. • Florida Department of Corrections Library Service • Tallhassee, FL 32399-2500 • ASCLA

Overton Elizabeth • East Qougue, NY 11942 • ALTA PLA *Life*

Overton Linda J. • Librarian I • Sachem Public Library • Holbrook, NY 11741

Overwein Joseph H. Mrs • Dayton, OH 45415

Ow Pamela J. • Librarian I • San Francisco Public Library Eureka Valley-Harvey Milk Mem Branch • San Francisco, CA 94114

Owen Amy • Director • Utah State Library • Salt Lake City, UT 84115-2579 • ASCLA PLA

Owen Ann K. • New Hudson, MI 48165

Owen Barbara L. • Librarian • National Institute of Justice Library • Washington, DC 20531

Owen Carol A. • Technical Librarian • Radian Corporation • Research Triangle Pk, NC 27709 • LAMA LIRT

Owen Delores • Pikes Peak Library District • Colorado Springs, CO 80901

Owen Dolores B. • Lafayette, LA 70503

Owen Fran • Sevier County Schools • Sevierville, TN 37862 • AASL

Owen Gwen E. • Public Information Assistant • Dayton & Montgomery County Public Library • Dayton, OH 45402-2103

Owen M. Jeanne • Director • Plains & Peaks Regional Library System • Colorado Spgs, CO 80906-1967 • ALTA ASCLA LAMA PLA

Owen Mary D. • Student • Northern Illinois University Department of Library & Information Studies • DeKalb, IL 60115 • IFRT

Owen Mary J. • Youth Adult Librarian • Los Angeles Public Library West L.A. Rgnl. Branch • Los Angeles, CA 90025 • YALSA

Owen Rosemary S. • Bethesda, MD 20817

Owen Sandra E. • Branch Manager- Librarian II • Annapolis & Anne Arundel County Edgewater Branch • Edgewater, MD 21037 • PLA

Owen Suzanne Mrs. • Adult Services Librarian • Crown Point Community Library • Crown Point, IN 46307 • ALCTS

Owen Terry M. • Juneau, AK 99802 • ACRL

Owen Wiley C. Mr • Associate Director • Sara Hightower Regional Library • Rome, GA 30161 • LITA PLA

Owen Will • Systems Librarian • University of North Carolina • Chapel Hill, NC 27599-3902

Owens Anita G. • Librarian I • Chicago Public Library Harold Washington Library • Chicago, IL 60605 • IFRT

Owens Ann S. • Librarian • Sacramento Public Library • Sacramento, CA 95814

Owens Anne J. • Adult Programming Librarian • Glendale Public Library • Glendale, AZ 85302 • PLA RASD

Owens Barbara G. • Tiburon, CA 94920 • AASL ALSC *Life*

Owens Bea • Readers Advisor Library Assoc. • Kansas City Kansas Public Library • Kansas City, KS 66101

Owens Bette C. • Raleigh, NC 27606 • PLA

Owens Betty • Elm Street Elementary • Rome, GA 30161 • AASL

Owens Carl • Baylor School Library • Chattanooga, TN 37401

Owens Carolyn • High School Librarian • Ramona High School • Ramona, CA 92065 • AASL

Owens Deborah • Trustee • Ouachita Parish Public Library • Monroe, LA 71201 • ALTA

Owens Edward P. • Coordinator of Technical Serv • Montgomery College • Rockville, MD 20850 • ALCTS LITA

Owens Elizabeth S. • Librarian • California State Library • Sacramento, CA 94237-0001

Owens Genevieve S. • Acting Hd., Clln. Devel. • University of Missouri-Saint Louis • St. Louis, MO 63121-4499 • ACRL ALCTS

Owens Jacqueline A. • Student • State University of New York at Albany School of Information Science & Policy • Albany, NY 12222

Owens Janet • Trustee • Worcester County Library • Snow Hill, MD 21863 • PLA

Owens Jennifer M. • Chesterfield County Library • Chesterfield, VA 23832 • ALSC YALSA

Owens Julia C. • Ln. Business & Technology Dept. • Seattle Public Library • Seattle, WA 98104-1193

Owens Leann M. • Shelley Junior High School • Shelley, ID 83274 • AASL YALSA

Owens Lessie V. • Assistant Librarian • District of Columbia Public Library Martin Luther King Memorial Library • Washington, DC 20001 • PLA

Owens Lillian D. • Indianapolis, IN 46218 • Continuing

Owens Linda • Media Specialist • West Noble Middle School • Ligonier, IN 46767 • AASL

Owens Major • Washington, DC 20515 • PLA CLENE *Honorary*

Owens Margaret • Associate Director/Public Serv • Jefferson County Public Library • Lakewood, CO 80215 • LAMA

Owens Margaret Jean • Library Services Manager • Santa Ana Public Library • Santa Ana, CA 92701 • LAMA

Owens Marian C. • Branch Head • Cobb County Public Library Vinings Branch • Atlanta, GA 30339 • RASD

Owens Marsha • Student • University of Alabama School of Library & Information Studies • Tuscaloosa, AL 35487-0252 • PLA IFRT

Owens Nancy L. • Business Manager • Grand Rapids Public Library • Grand Rapids, MI 49503-3093 • PLA

Owens Patricia L. • Director • Connecticut State Library • Hartford, CT 06106 • ASCLA PLA

Owens Patrick A. • Reference Librarian • Central Washington University • Ellensburg, WA 98926 • ACRL RASD

Owens Sheryl B. • Head, Circulation Department • Ohio State University Libraries • Columbus, OH 43210-1286 • LAMA

Owens William D. III • Omaha, NE 68123

Owings Connie S. • Technical Services Manager • Davenport Public Library • Davenport, IA 52801 • LITA

Owings Cronon Priscilla A. • Media Specialist • Swain Elementary School • Plainville, GA 30733 • AASL

Owl Rebecca L. • Billings, MT 59101 • RASD

Ownby Joyce • New Children's Librarian • Deschutes County Library • Bend, OR 97701 • ALSC

Ownes Dorothy J. • Coor. Library Automation Servs. • University of Colorado at Denver Auraria Library • Denver, CO 80204 • ACRL ALCTS LAMA LITA NMRT

Owsley Betty J. • Indianapolis, IN 46208 • IRRT

Oxborrow M. R. • Reference Librarian • Marshall-Lyon County Library • Marshall, MN 56258 • PLA RASD

Oxenfeld Elizabeth E. • School Library Media Specialist • General Greene School Of Science & Technology • Greensboro, NC 27408

Oxley Amy L. • Librarian • Indianapolis Marion County Public Library • Indianapolis, IN 46206 • YALSA

Oxley Martha • Assistant Director • Cherry Hill Free Public Library • Cherry Hill, NJ 08034 • PLA

Oxley Philip M. • Systems Librarian • Ontario Legislative Library • Toronto ON, M7A 1A9 Canada • LITA

Oyama Caroline M. • Deputy Manager, Public Relations • New York Public Library • New York, NY 10018-2788 • LAMA

Oyer Charlotte • Reference Librarian • California State Univ • Northridge, CA 91330 • ACRL RASD GODORT

Oyer V. Christine • Learning Resources Center Dir. • Washington School Library • Decatur, IL 62521 • AASL ALSC

Oyler David K. • Director • University of San Francisco Richard A. Gleeson Library • San Francisco, CA 94117 • ACRL ALCTS LAMA LITA *Life*

Oyler Patricia G. • Associate Professor • Simmons College Graduate School of Library & Information Science • Boston, MA 02115 • ACRL ALCTS LAMA

Ozaki Toshio • Mgr. of Inf Tech Dept • Japan Systems Co., Ltd. • Tokyo 153, Japan

Ozinga Connie Jo • Library Director • Jackson County Public Library • Seymour, IN 47274

Ozolins Karl L. • St Paul, MN 55113

Ozubko Susan • Library Director • Mountain View Public Library • Mountain View, CA 94041 • LAMA PLA

Paar Paul • Bozeman Public Library • Bozeman, MT 59715

Pabbruwe Herman A. • Group Services Director • Kluwer Academic Publishers • 3300 AH Dordrecht, Netherlands

Paben Charlene M. • Director • Park County Library • Cody, WY 82414 • PLA

Pabey Angel • Trustee • Lake County Public Library • Merrillville, IN 46410-5382 • ALTA

Pabst Kathleen T. • Library Director • Mechanics Institute Library • San Francisco, CA 94104

Pace-Cannon Penny • Librarian • Indianapolis Marion County Public Library • Indianapolis, IN 46206 • PLA

Pace Cheryl S. • Head of Reference • University of Kansas Medical Center A.R. Dykes Library • Kansas City, KS 66103 • LITA RASD SRRT

Pace James T. • Student • University of Washington Graduate School of Library and Information Science • Seattle, WA 98195

Pace Julian H. • Reference Librarian • Southwest Missouri State University Library • Springfield, MO 65804-0095 • ACRL ALTA RASD

Pace Miriam M. • Chief,Network Division • Library of Congress Library for the Blind & Physically Handicapped • Washington, DC 20542 • ASCLA

Pace Patricia A. • Orlando, FL 32825

Pacey Brenda M. • Lincoln Trail Libraries System • Champaign, IL 61821-1068 • AASL ASCLA LAMA PLA

Pacheco Benjamin • Trustee • Brooklyn Public Library • Brooklyn, NY 11238 • ALTA

Pacheco E Diane • Director • East Bridgewater Public Library • East Bridgewater, MA 02333 • PLA

Pacheco Ernestina • Student • University of Texas at Austin Graduate School of Library & Information Sciences • Austin, TX 78712-1276

Pacheco Karen • Children's Librarian II • Alameda County Library Centerville Branch • Fremont, CA 94536

Pacheco Miguel M. • Reference Services • Louisiana State University Libraries Troy H. Middleton Library • Baton Rouge, LA 70803-3342

Pachman Frederic C. • Monmouth Medical Center Altschul Medical Library • Long Branch, NJ 07740 • ASCLA NMRT

Pachon Carrie W. • Assistant Director • City of Commerce Public Library • Commerce, CA 90040 • LAMA PLA

Pachta Bernadine CSJ • Brighton, MA 02135

Pacifici Sabrina I. • Dir. of Lib & Research Svs • Sidley & Austin • Washington, DC 20006

Pack Nancy C. • Tallahassee, FL 32304 • ASCLA PLA RASD *Life*

Packard Gwen K. • Highland Pk, IL 60035

Packard Jean L. • Baltimore Sun • Baltimore, MD 21278

Packard Merlin W. Mr • Washington, DC 20007 • ACRL ALCTS RASD *Life*

Packard Sarah R. • Westmont, IL 60559

Packard Sheila R. • Children's Services Consultant • Eastern Massachusetts Regional Library System • Boston, MA 02117 • ALSC PLA

Packer Donna • Head of Collection Services • Western Washington University Wilson Library • Bellingham, WA 98225 • ACRL ALCTS LITA

Packer Joan G. • Farmington, CT 06032 • ACRL

Packham Joanne • Student • Utah State University Merrill Library • Logan, UT 84322-3000 • AASL

Packwood Cyril O. • Hamilton HMCX, Bermuda • PLA

Padala Patricia • Washtenaw Intermediate School Library • Ann Arbor, MI 48106 • AASL

Padalecki Christy R. Mrs. • Luther Burbank High School • San Antonio, TX 78204 • AASL

Paddock Caroline Miss • El Paso, TX 79935-2522 • Continuing

Padersen Kara L. • Student • University of Missouri-Columbia School of Library & Informational Science • Columbia, MO 65211

Padgett Elizabeth • Librarian • Forest Lane Elementary School • Columbia, SC 29206 • ALSC

Padgett Frances B. • Macclenny, FL 32063 • Continuing

Padgitt Dorothy A. • Librarian • River Grove Public Library District • River Grove, IL 60171

Padilla Irene M. • Deputy Director • Harford County Library • Belcamp, MD 21017 • LAMA PLA

Padilla Pedro A. • Student • University of Michigan Libraries Information and Library Studies • Ann Arbor, MI 48109 • ACRL

Padilla Ramonita • Congers, NY 10920

Padilla Sue A. • Ida Long Goodman Memorial Library • St. John, KS 67576 • AASL PLA YALSA

Padley Pamela M. • Head, Adaptive Cataloging Sect. • University of California-Irvine Library • Irvine, CA 92713 • ALCTS NMRT

Padnos Mark • Reference Librarian • New York Public Library Fordham Library Center • Bronx, NY 10458

Paduchowski Joan • Trustee • Derry Public Library • Derry, NH 03038 • ALTA

Padway Janet G. • Asst Dir for Technical Servs. • University of Wisconsin-Milwaukee Golda Meir Library • Milwaukee, WI 53201 • ACRL ALCTS LAMA LITA

Paeth Carolyn R. • President Trustee Board • McCook Public Library • McCook, IL 60525

Paez Linda B. • Reference Librarian • Anne Arundel Community College Andrew G. Truxal Library • Arnold, MD 21012 • ACRL LIRT

Pagan Marian • Librarian • Chicago Public Library Harold Washington Library • Chicago, IL 60605 • LITA PLA EMIERT

Pagano Giac Mr • Librarian • Delbarton School • Morristown, NJ 07960 • AASL

Pagano Rosalie A. • Media Specialist • Lindberg Elementary School • Palisades Park, NJ 07650 • AASL ALSC

Page Betty B. • Guilford, CT 06437 • AASL

Page Charles Kim • Santa Rosa, CA 95404

Page Cheryl A. • Dist. Lib/Media Coordinator • Douglas County School District No.#4 Roseburg Pub Schs • Roseburg, OR 97470-1798 • AASL

Page Dennis N. • Director • Grand Forks Public Library • Grand Forks, ND 58201 • ASCLA PLA

Page Elsie P. • Albuquerque, NM 87105

Page Jacquelin M. • Pompano Beach, FL 33062 • LRRT

Page John S. Jr. • Dep Dir Learning Resources Div • University of the District of Columbia Learning Resources Division • Washington, DC 20008 • ACRL *Life*

Page Julie Allen • Preservation Librarian • University of California-San Diego Central University Library • La Jolla, CA 92093-0175 • ALCTS

Page Kathryn • Facilities Devel. Chief • San Francisco Public Library • San Francisco, CA 94102 • LAMA PLA RASD MAGERT

Page Leslie A. • Children's Librarian • Woonsocket Harris Public Library • Woonsocket, RI 02895 • ALSC NMRT

Page Lynda D. • District Lib/Media Director • Crandall Independent School District • Crandall, TX 75114 • AASL

Page Margaret C. • Head Adult Services • Saint Clair County Library System • Port Huron, MI 48060-4098 • Continuing

Page Mary S. • Head, Technical Services • Rutgers University Libraries Library of Science & Medicine • Piscataway, NJ 08855-1029 • ACRL ALCTS LAMA LITA

Page Penny B. • Librarian • Rutgers University Libraries Center of Alcohol Studies • Piscataway, NJ 08855-0969

Page Priscilla • Montpelier, VT 05601 • Continuing

Page Richard M. • Lib. Automation Devel. Group • University of Southern California Doheny Library • Los Angeles, CA 90089-0182 • LITA

Page William L. • Associate Dean • Drexel University W. W. Hagerty Library • Philadelphia, PA 19104 • ACRL

Pagel Doris B. • Mankato, MN 56001 • ALSC *Continuing*

Pagniucci Barbara A. • Head School Librarian • Notre Dame High School for Girls • Chicago, IL 60634 • AASL

Pagotto Sarah L. • Lehigh Elementary School • Walnutport, PA 18088 • AASL

Pahlmeyer Susan B. • Head of Reference Services • North Dakota State Library • Bismarck, ND 58505

Pai Edward Y. H. • Student • University of California Los Angeles Graduate School of Library & Information Science • Los Angeles, CA 90024 • LITA EMIERT LRRT SRRT

Paick Hea-Won • Student • University of Tennessee-Knoxville Graduate School of Library & Information Science • Knoxville, TN 37996-4330 • ACRL RASD IFRT SRRT

Paielli Carol J. • Troy, MI 48098

Paietta Ann C. • Circulation Librarian • Yale University Medical Library • New Haven, CT 06510 • ACRL LAMA NMRT

Paige M. Jean • Rockledge, FL 32955 • Continuing

Paige Susan C. • Head of Circulation • Rogers Memorial Library • Southampton, NY 11968

Paik Youngjoo • Senior Researcher • Korean Women's Development Institute • Seoul, South Korea • ACRL

Paine Cheryl M. • Alliance, OH 44601

Paine Merlyn L. • Student • University of California-Berkeley School of Library & Information Studies • Berkeley, CA 94720

Paine Ramona • Librarian • Hennessey Public School • Hennessey, OK 73742 • AASL

Paine William D. • Librarian • United States Forest Service Forest Products Laboratory • Madison, WI 53705-2398 • ALCTS

Painter Ann F. • Balmore Vic 3407, Australia • ACRL ALCTS LITA *Life*

Painter Christine L. • Bud Werner Memorial Library • Steamboat Spg, CO 80477 • PLA

Painter Frances O. • Virginia Polytechnic Inst & State Univ University Libraries • Blacksburg, VA 24062-9001 • ACRL LAMA

Painter John C. • Head Librarian • Delaware Technical & Community College • Georgetown, DE 19947 • ACRL

Painter Patricia A. • Student • Auburn University at Montgomery • Montgomery, AL 36117-3596 • ACRL RASD NMRT

Painter Sarah J. • Wooster, OH 44691

Painter Tina • Asst. Director • Bergenfield Free Public Library • Bergenfield, NJ 07621

Pair Jonathan Grant • Reference Librarian • University of Alabama Amelia Gayle Gorgas Library • Tuscaloosa, AL 35487-0266 • ACRL RASD

Paisley Serena • Ch Ln • Colonial Williamsburg Foundation • Williamsburg, VA 23187

Paiste Marsha Starr • Salem, NH 03079 • ACRL ALCTS

Pajak Susan A. • Media Specialist • W. Wilson School • Hammond, IN 46324 • AASL

Pak Teresa Cho • Lewisville, TX 75067

Pakozdi Diane K. • Library Media Specialist • Montgomery Elementary School • Cincinnati, OH 45242 • AASL LRRT SRRT

Pakula Lida M. • Dearborn, MI 48124

Pal Surekha • Chicago Heights, IL 60411

Paladino Paul H. • Library Director • Montrose District Library • Montrose, CO 81401 • PLA

Palalay Aurora L. • Downey, CA 90242

Palan Diane • Community Services Librarian • Waco-McLennan County Library • Waco, TX 76701

Palansky Kathleen • Park Ridge, IL 60068 • AASL YALSA *Life*

Palazzola Benedette A. • Senior Librarian Assistant • Duke University • Durham, NC 27708

Palazzolo Vivian F. • Children's Librarian • Queens Borough Public Library • Jamaica, NY 11432 • ALSC

Paldan Diane N. • Technical Services Librarian • Wayne State University Science & Engineering Library • Detroit, MI 48202 • ACRL ALCTS

Palen-Hernandez Edmee • Student • State University of New York (SUNY) Thomas E. Dewey Graduate Library • Albany, NY 12222

Palen Ann T. • Trustee • Laramie County Library System • Cheyenne, WY 82001-2799

Palen Jan • Buena Park, CA 90620

Palen Roberta R. • Chicago Public Library • Chicago, IL 60605 • PLA GODORT IFRT

Palenski Ruth J. • McLean, VA 22102

Palermo Patricia A. • Lutherville, MD 21093-1704

Palestrant Zelma G. • The Citadel • Charleston, SC 29409 • ACRL ALCTS RASD GODORT

Paletsas William S. • Librarian • Edison Junior High School • Los Angeles, CA 90001 • AASL EMIERT NMRT

Paliath Elsie G. • Librarian • Calvert Hall College • Towson, MD 21204 • AASL

Palko Joanne D. • Database Management Head • University of Connecticut Homer Babbidge Library • Storrs, CT 06269-1005 • ALCTS

Palkovic Candace E. • Red Oak, TX 75154-2019

Palladino Anita M. • Student • Long Island University Palmer School of Library & Information Science • Greenvale, NY 11548 • YALSA

Palladino Kathryn • Training Coordinator • Gaylord Information Systems • Liverpool, NY 13090 • LITA

Palladino Rosalina M. • Senior Librarian • Bedford Hills Correctional Facility • Bedford Hills, NY 10507 • ASCLA

Pallardy Judy S. • Engineering Librarian • University of Missouri-Columbia Engineering Library • Columbia, MO 65211-5149 • ACRL LAMA

Pallas Frieda E. • Library Asst./Children's Serv. • San Diego Public Library Point Loma Branch • San Diego, CA 92107 • ALSC

Pallechio Flora S. • McNeil Island Corrections Center • Steilcoom, WA 98388

Pallowick Richard • California Academy of Sciences • San Francisco, CA 94118 • ALCTS

Palm Miriam W. • Principal Acq. Librarian • Stanford University Libraries Cecil H. Green Library • Stanford, CA 94305-6004 • ACRL ALCTS

Palm Suzanne M. • Richfield, MN 55423

Palmateer Brenda • Library Media Specialist • Weber Junior High School • Sagniaw, MI 48601 • AASL

Palmatier Roxanne B. • Documents Coordinator • Northeastern University • Boston, MA 02115 • GODORT SRRT

Palme Lyn Hansen • Branch Librarian • Contra Costa County Library Orinda Branch Library • Orinda, CA 94563 • PLA RASD

Palmer Bruce W. • Northern Arizona University Cline Library • Flagstaff, AZ 86011-6022 • ACRL

Palmer Carole L. • Champaign, IL 61821-3247

Palmer Catherine C. • Normal, IL 61761

Palmer Catherine S. • Humanities Librarian • University of California-Irvine Library • Irvine, CA 92713 • ACRL RASD LIRT

Palmer David J. • Asst. Library Director • Chula Vista Public Library • Chula Vista, CA 91910 • PLA

Palmer David T. • Systems Librarian • University of Hong Kong • Hong Kong, Hong Kong • LITA

Palmer David W. • Flint, MI 48503-2811 • ACRL LAMA *Life*

Palmer Dottie • Librarian • Rochester Public Library District • Rochester, IL 62563

Palmer Eileen M. • Assistant Director • Health Sciences Libraries Consortium • Philadelphia, PA 19104

Palmer Ellen L. • Branch Librarian • Columbus Metropolitan Library Karl Road Branch • Columbus, OH 43229

Palmer Emily S. • Jefferson County Public Library • Lakewood, CO 80215

Palmer Foster M. • Watertown, MA 02172 • ACRL LITA *Life*

Palmer George E. • Illinois State University Milner Library • Normal, IL 61761-0900 • ACRL LAMA RASD

Palmer Helen H. • Head. Cataloging Department • University of California-Los Angeles (UCLA) • Los Angeles, CA 90024-1450 • ACRL ALCTS LITA YALSA IFRT SRRT

Palmer Independence • Librarian • Mill Creek Elementary School • Lenexa, KS 66215 • AASL

Palmer J. Stephan • Student • Clark-Atlanta University School of Library & Information Studies • Atlanta, GA 30314-4391

Palmer Joseph • Director • Mansfield-Richland County Public Library • Mansfield, OH 44902-1295 • PLA

Palmer Joseph W. • Associate Professor • State University of New York at Buffalo School of Information Library • Buffalo, NY 14260

Palmer Judith B. • Library Media Specialist • North Allegheny High School • Wexford, PA 15090 • AASL IFRT LIRT

Palmer Judith L. • Library Services Manager • Irving Public Library System • Irving, TX 75015-2288 • ALCTS LRRT

Palmer Julia R. • New York, NY 10028 • PLA

Palmer Katie • Information Systems Analyst • 3M Center • Saint Paul, MN 55144-1000 • LITA

Palmer Laura L. • Chester, NJ 07930

Palmer Lisa • Librarian • San Jose Public Library • San Jose, CA 95113

Palmer Marguerite • Technical Services • Kanawha County Public Library • Charleston, WV 25301

Palmer Mary • Kalamazoo Public Library • Kalamazoo, MI 49007-5270 • YALSA

Palmer Mary P. • Clarkston, GA 30021 • AASL

Palmer Patricia E. • Virginia Commonwealth University • Richmond, VA 23284-2033 • ALCTS

Palmer Patricia L. • Reference Librarian • Oak Lawn Public Library • Oak Lawn, IL 60453 • RASD

Palmer Ray A. • American Association of Immunologist • Bethesda, MD 20814

Palmer Renee G. • Student • University of Alabama School of Library & Information Studies • Tuscaloosa, AL 35487-0252

Palmer Richard • Trustee • Warren Public Library • Warren, MI 48092

Palmer Richard J. • Head Librarian • Macomb Intermediate School District • Mount Clemens, MI 48044-1497 • AASL

Palmer Robert B. • New York, NY 10024 • ACRL LAMA *Life*

Palmer Roberta Gaetz • Head Librarian • Glasgow Middle School • Alexandria, VA 22312 • AASL

Palmer Roger C. • Technical Manager • Getty Art History Info Prog Information Program • Santa Monica, CA 90401-1455 • ACRL ALCTS LAMA LITA LRRT

Palmer Sarah B. • Student • University of Maryland College of Library and Information Services • College Park, MD 20742-4345 • PLA

Palmer Shirley C. • San Diego, CA 92111-3841

Palmer Virginia Ellis • Middletown, OH 45042 • ACRL RASD

Palmer Zoe Ann • Librarian • Orono Middle School Library • Long Lake, MN 55356 • AASL ALSC *Life*

Palmerini John M. • Trustee • Gates Public Library • Rochester, NY 14624 • ALTA

Palmero Kristopher J. • Hamlin, NY 14464

Palmieri Immaculata A. • Whitestone, NY 11357 • ASCLA

Palmieri Suzanne H. • Groton, CT 06340

Palmin Nina • Slavic Cataloger • Library of Congress • Washington, DC 20541 • ACRL

Palmisano-Drucker Elsalyn P. • Library Director • West Long Branch Public Library • W. Long Branch, NJ 07764 • PLA

Palmore S. Norris • Head, Infoservices • Boston Consulting Group Research Library • Chicago, IL 60606 • RASD

Palmquist Larry E. • Automation Consultant • Northern Illinois Library System • Rockford, IL 61108 • LITA

Palmquist Marlene A. • Director • James Blackstone Memorial Library • Branford, CT 06405

Palo Eric E. • Librarian • Renton Technical College • Renton, WA 98056 • ACRL RASD

Palomo Ann E. • Applications Support Supervisor • Cleveland Public Library • Cleveland, OH 44114-1271 • ALCTS LITA NMRT

Pals Helen • Unity Christian High School • Orange City, IA 51041

Palsson Gerald D. • Associate University Librarian • San Diego State University Library • San Diego, CA 92119-2120 • ACRL

Palumbo Kristine M. • Bibliographic Servs. Mgr. • Cherry Creeks School • Denver, CO 80231 • ALCTS LITA

Palzer William F. • Reference Librarian • Winona State University • Winona, MN 55987 • ACRL RASD

Palzkill Lisa D. • Assistant Legislative Librarian • Gibson, Dunn & Crutcher • Washington, DC 20036 • PLA RASD

Pamintuan Celia • Librarian • Defense Language Institute Aiso Library • Presidio of Monterey, CA 93944 • AFLRT

Pan Jane H. • Children's Librarian • New York Public Library Seward Park Branch • New York, NY 10002 • ALSC

Panagopoulos Beata D. • Head of Technical Service • Harvard University JF Kennedy School of Government Library • Cambridge, MA 02138

Panares Kathryn M. • Social Sciences Head • Chicago Public Library Sulzer Regional Library • Chicago, IL 60625 • PLA

Pancerella Gina M. • Student • Drexel University College of Information Studies • Philadelphia, PA 19104-2875 • SRRT

Panchadsaram Madhuram K. • FPO, AE 09619-1022 • AFLRT FLRT

Panciuk Mircea Mr. • Head Librarian • Concordia College Library • Edmonton AB, T5B 4E4 Canada • ACRL

Panda Krushna C. Dr. • Asst. Librarian • Berhampur University Central Library • Orissa, 760007, India

Pande Amaravati • Documentation Officer • National Commission of Pop • Kathamandu, Nepal • LAMA

Pandelakis Helene S. • Union City, NJ 07087

Pandit Jyoti P. • Assistant Librarian • State University of New York (SUNY) • Stony Brook, NY 11794-2225 • GODORT

Pandolfo Barbara • East Memorial Mill Lane School • Farmingdale, NY 11735 • AASL LAMA

Pandolfo Steven P. • College Librarian • Mills College Library • Oakland, CA 94613 • ACRL

Pandya Robin T. • Student • Kent State University School of Library & Information Science • Kent, OH 44242-0001 • ACRL PLA

Pandya Roxanna G. • Student • University of Missouri-Columbia School of Library & Informational Science • Columbia, MO 65211 • ACRL ALCTS LITA LHRT

Panek Joan B. • Librarian • Warren Elementary School • Ashland, MA 01721 • AASL

Panella Deborah S. • Paul, Weiss, Rifkind, Wharton, & Garrison • New York, NY 10019 • ACRL ALCTS ASCLA LAMA LITA RASD GODORT IFRT IRRT LRRT SORT

Panella Nancy DLS • Librarian Director • Saint Luke's Hospital Bolling Library • New York, NY 10025

Panetta Linda S. • School Media Specialist • Waterbury Elementary School • Waterbury, CT 06704 • AASL

Panetta Rebecca L. • Computer Services Coordinator • Lake Lanier Regional Library Lawrenceville Branch • Lawrenceville, GA 30245-4707

Pang Shuo Mimi • Student • University of California-Berkeley School of Library & Information Studies • Berkeley, CA 94720

Pangburn Pamela C. • National Research Council Library • Washington, DC 20418

Paniagua Ernestine • Reference Librarian • College of New Rochelle Gill Library • New Rochelle, NY 10805

Paniagua Maria A. • United Nations Dag Hammarskjold Library • New York, NY 10017 • LITA LIRT

Panian Linda K. • Marquette County Historical Society • Marquette, MI 49855

Panigabutra-Roberts Anchalee • Cornell University Library • Ithaca, NY 14853 • ACRL IRRT SRRT

Panitz Barbara R. • Cataloger • Library of Congress • Washington, DC 20541

Pankake Marcia J. • Professor & Bibliographer • University of Minnesota Meredith Wilson Library • Minneapolis, MN 55455 • ACRL ALCTS *Life*

Pankiewicz Kate L. • Student • University of Washington Graduate School of Library and Information Science • Seattle, WA 98195 • AASL

Pankin Mary Faith • Cataloger • George Washington University Gelman Library • Washington, DC 20052 • ACRL ALCTS LAMA LITA

Pankow David P. • Cur Cary Graphic Arts Clln • Rochester Institute of Technology Wallace Memorial Library • Rochester, NY 14623-0887 • ACRL

Pankowsky Susan • Atlanta, GA 30328

Pannebaker Susan • Children's Librarian • Abington Free Library • Abington, PA 19001 • ALSC

Pannell Sarah Saltonstall • Union County Library • New Albany, MS 38652 • ALSC PLA

Panni Elizabeth M. • Children's Librarian • King County Library System • Seattle, WA 98109-5191

Panofsky Hans E. • Evanston, IL 60202 • Continuing

Pansch Detlev • Online Coordinator • North Suburban Library System Central Serials Services • Morton Grove, IL 60053

Panski Saul J. • Head Librarian/Assoc. Professor • Compton College • Compton, CA 90221 • SRRT

Pantages Sandra K. • Fremont Main Lib. Manager • Alameda County Library System • Fremont, CA 94538 • LAMA PLA

Pantano Richard • Library Director • New Hampshire College Shapiro Library • Manchester, NH 03104-1394 • ACRL ALCTS ASCLA LAMA LITA RASD CLENE GODORT

Panz Richard • Director • Rochester Public Library • Rochester, NY 14604 • PLA

Panza Cynthia S. • Shelby Township, MI 48315 • AASL

Panzera Donald P. • Coll Serv/Exec Officer • Library of Congress • Washington, DC 20541 • LAMA FLRT

Paolera Liz Della • Watertown, MA 02172 • AASL

Paolilli Almonte Louis • Branch Manager • North Orange Library • Apopka, FL 32703 • PLA

Paolillo Julia B. • Secretariat for Legal Affairs • Organization of American States (OAS) Chief Information Center • Washington, DC 20006-4499

Papa Deborah M. • Adult Services • Akron-Summit County Public Library • Akron, OH 44326-0001 • PLA

Papa Denise • Head of Technical Services • Dunedin Public Library • Dunedin, FL 34698-7998

Papa Stephanie M. • Baltimore, MD 21286

Papadakis Stella • Ames Public Library • Ames, IA 50010

Papademetriou George C. Rev. • Library Director • Hellenic College • Brookline, MA 02146 • ACRL EMIERT

Papai Beverly D. • Director • Farmington Community Library • Farmington Hills, MI 48334 • AASL ACRL ALCTS ALSC ALTA ASCLA LAMA LITA PLA RASD YALSA IFRT

Papazoglou Alexandra • Director of Libraries • Athens College • Athens 15410, Greece • AASL

Pape Sabrina L. • Vassar College Library • Poughkeepsie, NY 12601 • ACRL

Papietro Rocco • Trustee • Coalinga-Huron Library District • Coalinga, CA 93210

Pappademos Ella • Librarian • Percy Julian Junior High School Media Center • Oak Park, IL 60302 • AASL

Pappajohn Rhonda C. • Librarian • Eatonville Middle School • Eatonville, WA 98374 • AASL

Pappalardo Barbara A. • Information Services Librarian • Cmnty Coll of Allegheny County North Campus • Pittsburgh, PA 15237

Pappas Cheryl M. • Dir of L Serv K-12 • Stoughton High School Library • Stoughton, MA 02072 • AASL YALSA

Pappas Evan • Bronx, NY 10463 • ALCTS

Pappas Kathryn M. • Children's Librarian • Seattle Public Library Holly Park Library • Seattle, WA 98118 • ALSC PLA

Pappas Marjorie L. • Assistant Professor • Wright State University • Dayton, OH 45435 • AASL

Pappenfuss Jerilyn • District Library Media Director • Germantown School District • Germantown, WI 53022 • AASL NMRT

Pappenhagen Jill N.J. • Student • Kent State University School of Library & Information Science • Kent, OH 44242-0001 • ALSC PLA

Paprocki Robert • Hillside, IL 60162

Paque Diana M. • Head Librarian • Solano Community College • Suisun, CA 94585 • ACRL ALCTS LITA

Paquette-Terrian Angie R. • Concordia, KS 66901

Paquette Judith • Bibliographer • University of California McHenry Library • Santa Cruz, CA 95064 • ACRL ALCTS LAMA RASD

Paradis Daniel • Student • University of Montreal Ecole de Bibliotheconomie • Montreal PQ, H3C 3J7 Canada • ALCTS SRRT

Paradis Trudy R. • Reference Librarian • Reading Public Library • Reading, MA 01867-2550

Paradise Juleigh A. • Reader Advisor • Bristol Public Library • Bristol, CT 06010

Paradowski Jeama C.J. • Student • Wayne State University Library Science Program • Detroit, MI 48202

Paramore Pamela J. • Student • Texas Woman's University School of Library & Information Studies • Denton, TX 76204

Paranac Anne Marie • Library Director • National Association of Homebuilders Research Center • Upper Marlboro, MD 20772 • ACRL

Parang Elizabeth • University of Nevada-Las Vegas James R. Dickinson Library • Las Vegas, NV 89154 • ACRL ALCTS

Parascandola Louis J. • Pratt Institute Library • Brooklyn, NY 11205

Parchuck Jill A. • Business Librarian • Columbia University Libraries • New York, NY 10027 • ALCTS RASD

Pardaen Piia R. • Student • University of North Carolina Department of Library & Information Studies • Greensboro, NC 27412-5001

Pardee Eric • Trustee • Cleveland Heights-University Heights Public Library • Cleveland Heights, OH 44118

Pardee Kathleen • Student • University of Arizona Graduate Library School • Tucson, AZ 85721

Pardo Carol E. • Rare Book Cataloger • Columbia University Libraries Butler Library • New York, NY 10027 • ACRL ALCTS LAMA LITA IRRT

Pardo Leslie • Student • Kent State University School of Library & Information Science • Kent, OH 44242-0001 • IFRT SRRT

Pardoe Janice R • Rides for Bay Area Commuters • San Francisco, CA 94105-1512 • LITA SRRT

Pardue William J. • Student • University of Illinois Graduate School of Library and Information Science • Urbana, IL 61801

Pardyjak Robert S. • Head of Technical Services • Chester County Library & District Center • Exton, PA 19341-2496

Pare Ellen • Detroit, MI 48214

Pare Vicki A. • Culver, IN 46511 • AASL

Paredes-Ruiz Eudoxio B. • Head Bibliography Control Dept. • University of Saskatchewan Library • Saskatoon SK, S7N 0W0 Canada • ALCTS

Parent Anne T. • Regional Administrator • Central Massachusetts Regional Library System • Worcester, MA 01608-2074 • ACRL ASCLA PLA

Parent Roger H. • Deputy Executive Director • American Library Association • Chicago, IL 60611-2795 • LAMA

Parente Judy F. • Falls Church, VA 22044 • AASL

Parente Lois E. • Cranston, RI 02920

Parente Sharon C. • User Services Librarian • Middle Tennessee State University Library • Murfreesboro, TN 37132 • ACRL

Parentean Amy L. W. • Reference Librarian • Alverno College • Milwaukee, WI 53215

Parenti Pamela K • Library Assistant • Acton-Boxborough Regional High School • Acton, MA 01720 • AASL

Paretsky Mary E. • Children's Department Head • Lawrence Public Library • Lawrence, KS 66044 • ALSC

Parfrey Hilda W. • IMC Director • Sandburg Elementary School • Madison, WI 53704 • AASL ALSC

Parhad Bronwyn W. • Head of Youth Services • Winnetka Public Library District • Winnetka, IL 60093 • ALSC

Parham Judith S. • Librarian • James F. Byrnes High School • Duncan, SC 29334 • AASL

Parham Kay B. • Director of Libraries • Southeastern Oklahoma State University Bennett Memorial Library • Durant, OK 74701

Parham Myrtis Ann • Chief, Research & Inf Serv. • National Defense University • Washington, DC 20319 • LITA AFLRT FLRT

Parhamovich Mary M. • Assistant Librarian • Arizona State University Hayden Library • Tempe, AZ 85287-1006 • ACRL LAMA GODORT

Parikh Kaumudi H. • Librarian • Holy Cross High School Library • Waterbury, CT 06708 • AASL

Parikh Neel • Chief of Branches • San Francisco Public Library • San Francisco, CA 94102 • ALSC PLA RASD

Paringer William A. • Student • Rutgers University School of Communication Information & Library Studies • New Brunswick, NJ 08903

Parins Anita S. • CDR, USAITAC Attn: IAAII-PIL • Washington, DC 20374 • RASD AFLRT FLRT

Paris Janelle A. • Huntsville, TX 77340-3438 • AASL ALSC *Life*

Paris Marion • University of Alabama • Tuscaloosa, AL 35487-0266 • ACRL LAMA LRRT

Paris Sanford P. • Los Angeles Public Library • Los Angeles, CA 90071 • ALTA

Paris Terrance • Mount Saint Vincent University Library • Halifax NS, B3M 2J6 Canada

Parise Marina P. • Reference Librarian • Santa Monica College Library • Santa Monica, CA 90405

Parise Mary J. • Miami, FL 33161 • ALCTS

Parise Pierina • Portland, OR 97221

Pariseau Joanne L. • School Librarian • Newport Town School • Newport Ctr, VT 05857 • AASL

Parisi Mark J. • Student • Simmons College Graduate School of Library & Information Science • Boston, MA 02115 • LITA

Parisi Paul A. • President • Acme Bookbinding Company • Charlestown, MA 02129 • ALCTS

Park Amey L. • Head,Bibliographic Control Unit • Kent State University Libraries • Kent, OH 44242 • ALCTS

Park Anne G. • Coor. of Off-Campus Lib Servs. • Mercer University Main Library • Macon, GA 31207 • ACRL

Park Bruce L. • Senior Vice President • Geac Computers Inc. • Dallas, TX 75244 • LITA

Park Catherine S. • Director • Harris County Public Library • Houston, TX 77054 • PLA

Park Chung I. • Reference Libraian/Assoc. Prof. • Malcolm X College Library • Chicago, IL 60612 • ALCTS

Park Debra • Director of Development • University of Illinois Graduate School of Library and Information Science • Urbana, IL 61801 • ASCLA LAMA PLA

Park Elizabeth H. • Reference Department • Memphis State University Main Library • Memphis, TN 38152 • ACRL

Park Gemma R. • Head of Acquisitions • University of the District of Columbia Learning Resources Division • Washington, DC 20008

Park Geraldine B. • Authority Control Librarian • University of Maryland Libraries • College Park, MD 20742 • LITA

Park Leland M. Dr • Director • Davidson College Library • Davidson, NC 28036 • ACRL

Park Sarah K. • Audiovisual Librarian • Ypsilanti District Library • Ypsilanti, MI 48197 • PLA

Park Sue Y. • Student • University of California-Berkeley School of Library & Information Studies • Berkeley, CA 94720 • LITA

Park Taemin K. • Indiana University School of Library and Information Science • Bloomington, IN 47405 • ALCTS

Parke Carol R. • Assoc Univ Ln for Public Serv. • Syracuse University • Syracuse, NY 13244 • ACRL LAMA *Life*

Parke Kathryn E. • Black Mt, NC 28711-2532 • ACRL RASD *Continuing*

Parker Arlene Noble • Director • Springfield Free Public Library • Springfield, NJ 07081 • LAMA LITA PLA

Parker Barbara • Annapolis, MD 21403 • ACRL

Parker Blanche C. • Darien Library • Darien, CT 06820-4497

Parker Bret H. • Stanislaus County Free Library • Modesto, CA 95354 • ACRL

Parker Carol B. • Librarian • Gulfport Public Library • Gulfport, FL 33707 • ALCTS

Parker Catherine E. • Library Director • Charles County Community College • La Plata, MD 20646-0910 • ACRL ALCTS LAMA LITA

Parker Charles Estes • Director • State Library of Florida Division of Library & Information Services • Tallahassee, FL 32399-0250 • ASCLA PLA CLENE

Parker Cheryl A. • Librarian • District of Columbia Public Schools • Washington, DC 20020 • AASL

Parker D. Lee • Student • University of Rhode Island Graduate School of Library & Information Studies • Kingston, RI 02881-0815 • ALSC PLA SRRT

Parker David • Trustee • East Meadow Public Library • East Meadow, NY 11554-1700 • ALTA

Parker Deborah C. • Student • Drexel University College of Information Studies • Philadelphia, PA 19104-2875 • AASL

Parker Diane C. • Western Washington University Wilson Library • Bellingham, WA 98225 • ACRL

Parker Dorothy J. • Librarian • Atlanta-Fulton Public Library Sandy Springs Branch • Sandy Springs, GA 30328 • RASD IFRT

Parker Eleanor V. • Sales Consultant • Follett Software Company • Norman, OK 73070 • LITA

Parker Elisabeth Betz • Asst. Chief/Prints & Photos • Library of Congress • Washington, DC 20541 • ACRL ALCTS LITA

Parker Emelia M. • Librarian • Grace A. Dow Memorial Library • Midland, MI 48640 • ACRL ALCTS

Parker Eric C. • Student • University of Illinois Graduate School of Library and Information Science • Urbana, IL 61801

Parker Evelyn • Trustee • East Orange School District Curriculum Office • East Orange, NJ 07017

Parker Frances M. • Asst Dir for Public Serv • Colby College Libraries • Waterville, ME 04901 • ACRL

Parker J. Carlyle • University Archivist • California State Univ Stanislaus • Turlock, CA 95380 • RASD

Parker Jan F. • Fond du Lac, WI 54935 • AASL

Parker Jane C. • Media Evaluator • Wake County Public School System • Raleigh, NC 27611 • AASL YALSA IFRT

Parker Janet C. • Library Supervisor • Free Library of Philadelphia Haverford Branch • Philadelphia, PA 19153

Parker Jean M. • Assistant Library Director • Saint Olaf College Rolvaag Memorial Library • Northfield, MN 55057-1097 • ACRL LAMA

Parker Jean M. • Library Director • Pentwater Township Library • Pentwater, MI 49449

Parker Jewel Gray Mrs • Annandale, VA 22003-1513 • Continuing

Parker Jo Ann • Librarian Director • Crane County Library • Crane, TX 79731

Parker Joan W. • Ln • Palo Alto Unified School District • Palo Alto, CA 94306 • AASL

Parker Joy • Librarian • Willington Board of Education • West Willington, CT 06279 • AASL YALSA IFRT

Parker Judith B. • Supervisor • Yale University Cross Campus Library • New Haven, CT 06520 • LAMA

Parker June D. • Document Librarian • East Carolina University Joyner Library • Greenville, NC 27858-4353 • GODORT

Parker Kathy • Library Assistant • Bell, Boyd & Lloyd • Chicago, IL 60602

Parker Kimberly H. • Librarian • Miss Wade's Fashion Merchandising College • Dallas, TX 75258 • ACRL

Parker Kimberly J. • Science Bibliographer • Yale University Kline Science Library • New Haven, CT 06511-8142 • ACRL RASD MAGERT

Parker Lanny C. • Library Automation Coordinator • Wake County Public Library System • Raleigh, NC 27610 • LITA PLA

Parker Lillie • Fresno, CA 93704

Parker Linda L. • Chair, Central Reference Servs. • University of Nebraska-Lincoln University Libraries • Lincoln, NE 68588-0410 • ACRL LAMA RASD

Parker Lucille J. Miss • St Clairsvl, OH 43953 • AASL YALSA *Life*

Parker Malcolm G. • Shreveport, LA 71105 • ACRL ALCTS *Life*

Parker Marcia J. • Librarian • King County Library System • Seattle, WA 98109-5191 • ALSC YALSA

Parker Mary M. • Media Specials • North Drive School • Goldsboro, NC 27534 • AASL

Parker Mary M. D. • Coor. Reference Services • MINITEX Lib Info Network University of Minnesota • Minneapolis, MN 55455-0414 • PLA RASD

Parker Mildred M. • Library/Media Specialist • Prairie View Elementary School • Gainesville, FL 32601 • AASL

Parker Millie M. • Head Librarian • Paine College Collins-Callaway Library • Augusta, GA 30901 • ACRL

Parker Nancy • Librarian • Covington City School System Covington Elementary School • Covington, TN 38019

Parker Nathan • Chicago Public Library Damen Avenue Branch • Chicago, IL 60647

Parker Necia T. • Bibl Instruction Librarian • University of Arkansas Libraries • Fayetteville, AR 72701-1201 • ACRL LITA RASD IFRT NMRT

Parker Patricia D. • Children's Librarian • Torrance Public Library • Torrance, CA 90503

Parker Ralph E. • Cleveland Public Schools • Cleveland, OH 44114

Parker Richard M. • Assistant Director • Tulsa City-County Library System • Tulsa, OK 74103 • LAMA PLA

Parker Robert M. • Trustee • Saint Joseph County Public Library • South Bend, IN 46601 • ALTA

Parker Sandra L. • Coordinator/Instructor • Chabot College • Hayward, CA 94545

Parker Sandra S. • Summerville High School Gregg Campus • Summerville, SC 29483 • AASL

Parker Sara Ann • Commissioner of Libraries • State Library of Pennsylvania Department of Education • Harrisburg, PA 17105 • ASCLA LAMA

Parker Sidney B. Rev. • Board Member • Jacksonville Public Libraries Main Library • Jacksonville, FL 32202

Parker Susan E. • Circulation Services Librarian • Harvard Law School Library • Cambridge, MA 02138 • ACRL LAMA SRRT

Parker Suzanne M. • Tucson, AZ 85746

Parker Virginia E. • Flushing, NY 11355 • RASD *Continuing*

Parker Wayne • Lovett School • Atlanta, GA 30327

Parkhill John T. • Don Mills ON, M3B 2E5 Canada • Continuing

Parkhurst Carol A. • AUL for Systems Technical Srvs • University of Nevada-Reno Noble H. Getchell Library • Reno, NV 89557 • ACRL LAMA LITA

Parkin Arlene S. • Librarian • Our Lady of Lourdes School • Decatur, IL 62526 • AASL

Parkinson Diane R. • Microforms Librarian • Brigham Young University Harold B. Lee Library • Provo, UT 84602
Parkinson Nancy • Student • Rutgers University School of Communication Information & Library Studies • New Brunswick, NJ 08903 • ALCTS PLA EMIERT
Parkman Mary S. • Beverly, MA 01915
Parks Alta M. • Birmingham, MI 48009 • LAMA PLA *Life*
Parks Diane • Referene Librarian • Boston Public Library • Boston, MA 02117 • ALCTS PLA RASD
Parks Dora Ruth • Burlington, NC 27215 • Continuing
Parks Evelyn L. • Burlington, NC 27215 • Continuing
Parks George R. • University Librarian • University of Southern Maine • Portland, ME 04103 • ACRL LAMA MAGERT
Parks James F. Jr • Head Librarian • Millsaps College Millsaps-Wilson Library • Jackson, MS 39210 • ACRL ALCTS RASD GODORT
Parks Joan G. • Head, Reference Services • Southwestern University A. Frank Smith Junior Library Center • Georgetown, TX 78626
Parks Larry G. • Head Librarian • Wood Dale Public Library • Wood Dale, IL 60191
Parks Lethene • Hunters, WA 99137 • ASCLA PLA RASD CLENE SRRT *Continuing*
Parks Margaret E. • Student • Oregon State University William Jasper Kerr Library • Corvallis, OR 97331-4501
Parks Robert E. • Curator of Autograph Manuscripts • Pierpont Morgan Library • New York, NY 10016 • ACRL
Parks Sandra L. • Harrisonburg High School • Harrisonburg, VA 22801 • ALSC
Parks Thomas E. • Urbana, IL 61801 • ACRL *Life*
Parlee Phyllis • Trustee • Arlington Heights Memorial Library • Arlington Heights, IL 60004-5966 • PLA
Parman Pamela W. • Library Media Specialist • Maryville High School Library • Maryville, TN 37801 • AASL
Parmenter Mary Jane • Library Director • Hastings-On-Hudson Public Library • Hastings-On-Hudson, NY 10706 • PLA
Parmer Coleen K. • Bowling Green State University Jerome Library • Bowling Green, OH 43403 • GODORT
Parnell Ellen Green • Richmond Public Library Westover Hills Branch • Richmond, VA 23225
Parnell Gerald R. • Public Services Librarian • Gardner-Webb College • Boiling Springs, NC 28017
Parnell Marilyn H. • Librarian • Farmington High School Library • Farmington, CT 06032 • AASL
Parnell Nelson • Trustee • Springfield-Greene County Library • Springfield, MO 65801 • ALTA
Parnell Pat • Collections Librarian • University of Saskatchewan Library • Saskatoon SK, S7N 0W0 Canada • ACRL ALCTS RASD LIRT
Parnell William O. • Library Assistant • Claremont Colleges Libraries Honnold/Mudd Library • Claremont, CA 91711
Parnes Daria A. • Reference Librarian • Reston Regional Library • Reston, VA 22090
Parr Anne M. • Zwolle, LA 71486
Parr Caroline S. • Central Rappahannock Regional Library Wallace Memorial Library • Fredericksburg, VA 22401 • ALSC PLA IFRT SRRT
Parr Louise M. • Principal Librarian • Monmouth County Library Wall Township Branch • Wall, NJ 07719
Parr Mary Y. • Asst. Dean Technical Services • Saint John's University Library • Jamaica, NY 11439
Parr Virginia H. • Reference Libn/Bibliographer • University of Cincinnati • Cincinnati, OH 45221-0033 • ACRL RASD
Parra Claire E. • Palo Alto City Library • Palo Alto, CA 94303
Parravano Ellen A. • Executive Director • Southeastern New York Library Resources Council • Highland, NY 12528 • ASCLA LAMA RASD
Parret Janice E. • Librarian • Riddle High School • Riddle, OR 97469
Parrine Mary Jane • Menlo Park, CA 94025 • ACRL ALCTS IRRT
Parrish Darlene A. • Business Reference Librarian • Florida Atlantic University S.E. Wimberly Library • Boca Raton, FL 33431
Parrish Jerral R. Mr. • Library Media Services Director • Bethany Lutheran College Memorial Library • Mankato, MN 56001-4490 • ACRL LITA
Parrish Kirsten J. • Student • Rosary College Graduate School of Library & Information Science • River Forest, IL 60305
Parrish Leila Raven • Houston Public Library Robinson-Westchase Branch • Houston, TX 77042
Parrish Marcia L. • Librarian • Lois Lenski Elementary School • Littleton, CO 80121 • AASL
Parrish Marilyn McKinley • Consultant • Information Transfer • East Petersburg, PA 17520 • LAMA PLA ILERT
Parrish Nancy B. • High Point Public Library • High Point, NC 27261 • PLA RASD
Parrish Sharon E. • Children's Librarian • Boulder City Library • Boulder City, NV 89005
Parrott Joanne S. • Trustee • Hartford County Library Adminstration Office • Belcamp, MD 21017
Parrott M. • Greensboro, NC 27403-1414
Parry David R. • Director • Lake County Public Library • Leadville, CO 80461
Parsch Janet H. • Head, Technical Services • University of Arkansas Mullins Library • Fayetteville, AR 72701 • ACRL LAMA LITA IRRT
Parsh Laurietta G. • Library Media Specialist • Lake Forest Elementary District #67 Deer Path Middle School • Lake Forest, IL 60045 • AASL ALSC
Parsley Brantley H. • Director • Mobile College J.L. Bedsole Library • Mobile, AL 36663-0220 • ACRL
Parsley David E. • Technical Services Librarian • East Tennessee State University Sherrod Library • Johnson City, TN 37614 • ACRL
Parson Andrew R. • Student • University of Pittsburgh School of Library and Information Science • Pittsburgh, PA 15260 • ACRL RASD IFRT
Parson Calleen M. • Media Specialist • Hamilton High West • Trenton, NJ 08610
Parson Karen L. • Fox Valley Technical College Educational Resource Center • Appleton, WI 54913
Parson Lethiel C. Dr. • Library Director • Atlantic Union College G. Eric Jones Library • South Lancaster, MA 01561 • ACRL
Parsons A. Chapman • Executive Vice President • Ohio Library Foundation • Columbus, OH 43215 • Continuing
Parsons A. Lynette • Assistant City Librarian • Sterling Municipal Library • Baytown, TX 77520
Parsons Jane A. • Baltimore, MD 21204
Parsons John W.A. • Plymouth, IN 46563 • ALTA
Parsons Kathy A. • Reference Librarian • Iowa State University Library • Ames, IA 50011-2140 • ACRL RASD GODORT MAGERT
Parsons Larry • Library Media Specialist • Ocean Beach School District • Ilwaco, WA 98624 • AASL
Parsons Lora Nita • Chugiak High School • Eagle River, AK 99577
Parsons Lucy • Hd,Circulation & Deaf Svs. • Broward County Division of Libraries South Regional Branch • Hollywood, FL 33024 • ASCLA
Parsons Marian M. • Plano Public School • Plano, TX 75023 • AASL ALSC LIRT
Parsons Marilyn T. • School Librarian • Lake City Elementary School • Lake City, TN 37769
Parsons Mary Jane • Student • Dalhousie University School of Library & Inf. Studies • Halifax NS, B3H 4H8 Canada • ALSC
Parsons Mary P. Miss • Bryson City, NC 28713 • ACRL *Continuing*
Parsons Muriel W. • Ambler, PA 19002
Parsons Phil S. • Amos Memorial Public Library • Sidney, OH 45365 • LAMA PLA
Parsons Richard W. • Admin. Asst. to the Director • Baltimore County Public Library • Towson, MD 21204 • PLA
Partello Patricia L. • Student • University of Pittsburgh School of Library and Information Science • Pittsburgh, PA 15260 • ACRL IFRT
Partello Peggie • Interim Director • Keene State College Mason Library • Keene, NH 03431 • ACRL IFRT
Partin James R. • Student • Ohio Dominican College • Columbus, OH 43219
Partlow Penelope W. • Head Librarian • St. Paul's School • Brooklandville, MD 21022 • AASL ALSC
Partnoy Diane K. • Director • Rachel Kohl Community Library, Inc. • Concordville, PA 19331
Parto Babak • Head Librarian • College of Arts & Social Science Library Science Department • Shiraz, Iran • ACRL ALCTS ALSC LAMA LITA
Parton William A. • Arkansas Technical University Tomlinson Library • Russellville, AR 72801
Partovi Patricia L. • Regional Librarian • San Bernardino County Library Yucaipa Branch • Yucaipa, CA 92399
Partovi Ziaeddin • Student • University of Oklahoma School of Library & Information Studies • Norman, OK 73019
Partrick Joan Gallagher • Wilmington, NC 28405
Partridge Barbara • Natick, MA 01760 • Continuing
Partridge Cathleen F. • Director of Learning Resources • Salt Lake Community College Library • Salt Lake City, UT 84130-0808 • ACRL LAMA
Partridge Frances Jane • Rockville, MD 20852 • ACRL RASD *Life*
Partridge Marian M. • Vallejo, CA 94591
Partridge Sharon M. • Documents Librarian • Jefferson County Public Library • Lakewood, CO 80215 • GODORT IFRT
Parys Marie • Librarian • Nicholas A. Ferri Middle School • Johnston, RI 02919 • AASL
Parziale Lucian A. • Vice President Computer Svs • H. W. Wilson Company • Bronx, NY 10452 • AASL ACRL LAMA LITA PLA RASD LRRT
Pascale Linda • Student • Broward County Division of Libraries West Regional Branch • Plantation, FL 33324 • EMIERT IFRT SRRT
Paschall Freedonia • Texas Tech University Southwest Collection-106 Math • Lubbock, TX 79409
Pasco Carl E. • Coor of Instr Resources & Media • Glenbrook South High School • Glenview, IL 60025 • AASL
Pasco Rebecca J. • Library Media Specialist • Lincoln Public Schools Irving Junior High School • Lincoln, NE 68502 • AASL LITA YALSA
Pashkin Irwin • Assistant Director • Free Public Library of Woodbridge • Woodbridge, NJ 07095 • PLA
Pasicznyuk Robert W. • Staff Librarian • Baylor University School of Nursing • Waco, TX 76706
Pask Judith M. • Undergraduate Librarian • Purdue University Libraries • West Lafayette, IN 47907-1530 • ACRL RASD LIRT
Paske Sandra D. • Assoc Admin Prog Specialist • University of Wisconsin-Madison Memorial Library • Madison, WI 53706 • ALCTS
Pasnick Ann • Acquisitions/Cataloging Libn • Addison Public Library • Addison, IL 60101-2499 • ALCTS
Pasquale Ann E. • Head, Special Collections • New York Academy of Medicine Library • New York, NY 10029 • ACRL
Pasqualini Bernard F. • Hd Database & Newspaper Center • Free Library of Philadelphia • Philadelphia, PA 19103 • RASD *Life*
Pasquariella Susan Kingsley • New York, NY 10033 • LITA IRRT
Pasquinelli Rolando • Senior Librarian • Los Angeles Public Library • Los Angeles, CA 90071
Passalacqua Deborah • Director • Broward County Division of Libraries West Regional Branch • Plantation, FL 33324 • ASCLA PLA
Passalacqua Michael J. • Student • Wayne State University Library Science Program • Detroit, MI 48202 • SRRT
Passanese Lillian M. • Director/NCCC • Niagara County Community College Faculty Resource Center • Sanborn, NY 14132
Passante Anna • Library Media Specialist • South Division High School • Milwaukee, WI 53207
Passarelli Anne B. • Seattle, WA 98103 • RASD
Passarello Nancy H. • Resource Teacher/Media Services • Pinellas County Schools • Largo, FL 34649-2942
Passaro Terry J. • Head Librarian • Encyclopaedia Britannica • Chicago, IL 60604 • ACRL
Passe Walter • Wabasha, MN 55981
Passella Nancy J. • Children's Librarian • Young Readers • North Olmsted, OH 44070 • ALSC
Passet Joanne E. • Assistant Professor • Indiana University School of Library and Information Science • Bloomington, IN 47405 • LHRT
Passo Janice M. • Las Vegas-Clark County Library Spring Valley Library • Las Vegas, NV 89103 • YALSA
Paster Amy L. • Cataloger/Reference Librarian • Pennsylvania State University Libraries • University Park, PA 16802 • ACRL ALCTS
Paster Judith A. • Cranston, RI 02905
Paster Luisa • Database Management Librarian • Princeton University • Princeton, NJ 08544-2098 • SRRT
Pasternack Howard • Providence, RI 02906 • ACRL LITA
Pasternack Marcia A. • Senior Librarian • New York State Library State Education Department • Albany, NY 12230 • ALCTS
Pasternak Amy S. • Silver Spg, MD 20910
Pasternak Eve R. • Pierpont Morgan Library • New York, NY 10016 • ACRL
Pasternak Linda • Oakland, MI 48363 • AASL
Pastine Maureen D. • Director, Central Univ. Lib. • Southern Methodist University Fondren Library • Dallas, TX 75275-0135 • ACRL ALCTS ASCLA LAMA LITA RASD IRRT LIRT LRRT
Pastore Ellen G. • Coordinator • Monterey Bay Area Cooperative Library System • Monterey, CA 93940 • RASD
Pastucha Joy E. • Warren Wilson College Martha Ellison Library • Swannanoa, NC 28778 • ACRL ALCTS RASD
Paszamant Carol B. • Citation/Location Center • Rutgers University Libraries • New Brunswick, NJ 08903 • RASD
Pata Juliana C. • Student • Queens College Graduate School of Library & Information Studies • Flushing, NY 11367 • ACRL
Patanella Paul V. • Librarian • Art Institute of Philadelphia • Philadelphia, PA 19103 • ACRL IFRT

Pate Carolyn J. • Administrative Librarian • Community Library Div B1640 • Fort Sill, OK 73503-5100 • LAMA LITA AFLRT

Pate Deborah H. • Student • Emporia State University School of Library & Information Management • Emporia, KS 66801 • AASL ACRL ALSC PLA RASD YALSA NMRT SRRT

Pate Gaye • Head Circulation • Missouri Southern State College Library • Joplin, MO 64801 • ACRL RASD

Pate Louise C. • Marana Junior High School • Marana, AZ 85653 • AASL YALSA NMRT

Pate Patricia M. • Reference Librarian • University of Houston Clear Lake Neumann Library • Houston, TX 77058 • ACRL RASD

Patel Jashu P. • Professor • Chicago State University Department of Library Science & Communication Media • Chicago, IL 60628

Paterson Katherine W. • Barre, VT 05641 • ALSC

Pathak Susanna Bartmann • Resource Servs. Librarian • Johns Hopkins University Milton S. Eisenhower Library • Baltimore, MD 21218 • ACRL RASD

Patnychuk Stephanie L. • Information Specialist • Gunster, Yoakley and Stewart • West Palm Beach, FL 33401

Paton Jennie C. • Audio-Visual Coordinator • Georgia Southern University Library • Statesboro, GA 30460-8074

Paton John C. • Head of Reference • Statesboro Regional Library • Statesboro, GA 30458

Patout Gerald F. Jr. • Library Director • Domino Sugar Corporation Research Division • Brooklyn, NY 11211

Patric Laurel • Assistant Director of Libraries • Glendale Public Library • Glendale, CA 91205 • LAMA PLA

Patrick Berry W. • Library Program Manager • United States Navy Naval Air Station • Pensacola, FL 32508 • AFLRT

Patrick Beverly A. • Student • University of South Florida School of Library & Information Science • Tampa, FL 33620 • PLA

Patrick Carol A. • Reference Librarian • Cleveland State University Library • Cleveland, OH 44115 • ACRL ALCTS LAMA RASD EMIERT

Patrick Darlene J. • Acquisition Librarian • Northeastern Illinois University Library • Chicago, IL 60625 • ACRL

Patrick Jill • Director of Library Services • Ontario College of Art • Toronto ON, M5T 1W1 Canada • ACRL

Patrick Linnea R. • Salem Public Library • Salem, OR 97309-5020 • PLA

Patrick Lucia • Documents Librarian • Florida State University Robert M. Strozier Library • Tallahassee, FL 32306-2047 • ACRL GODORT MAGERT

Patrick Michael K. • Gifts Librarian • Boston College Libraries • Chestnut Hill, MA 02167 • ACRL

Patrick Patricia M. • Public Services Consultant • Upper Hudson Library System • Albany, NY 12206 • ALSC PLA

Patrick Retta B. • School Library Media Consultant • Little Rock, AR 72221 • AASL LAMA

Patrick Rita E • Cataloging Services Manager • AMIGOS Bibliographic Council,Inc. • Dallas, TX 75251-2104 • ALCTS

Patrick Ruth J. • University Librarian • University of British Columbia • Vancouver BC, V6T 1Z1 Canada • ACRL LAMA LITA CLENE

Patrick Sally M. • Training Coordinator • Salt Lake City Public Library • Salt Lake City, UT 84111 • LAMA PLA CLENE

Patrick Stephen Allan • Head, Documents/Law/Maps Dept. • East Tennessee State University • Johnson City, TN 37614 • ACRL GODORT

Patrick Violetta F. • Atlanta, GA 30324

Patron Susan H. • Sr.Children's Librarian • Los Angeles Public Library • Los Angeles, CA 90071 • ALSC

Patruccelli Maxine B. • Easton, CT 06612 • AASL LAMA LIRT LRRT

Patsiner Connie A. • Executive Director • Indiana Visual & Audio Network Library Services Authority • Indianapolis, IN 46220 • VRT

Pattee Alice P. • Sun City, AZ 85373 • ACRL ALCTS
Continuing

Pattee Sherrill A. • Information Specialist • Kansas State University Libraries • Manhattan, KS 66506-7166

Patten Kathryn B. • Assistant Librarian • Brentwood Academy • Brentwood, TN 37027

Patten Kathy L. • Library Media Specialist • Pleasant Ridge Elementary School • Saline, MI 48176 • AASL

Patterson Ann Eileen • Marquette, MI 49855 • PLA RASD
Life

Patterson Bobbie J. • Coordinator • Washington Superintendent of Public Instruction Educational Materials Center • Olympia, WA 98504

Patterson Carolyn A. • Bexley Public Library • Columbus, OH 43209

Patterson Charles D. Dr • Professor • Louisiana State University School of Library & Information Science • Baton Rouge, LA 70803-3290 • ACRL RASD IFRT LIRT

Patterson Christine A. • Student • Drexel University College of Information Studies • Philadelphia, PA 19104-2875 • LITA

Patterson Christine D. • Colorado Spring, CO 80909-5213 • PLA

Patterson Elizabeth • Head Reference Librarian • Emory University Libraries Robert W. Woodruff Library • Atlanta, GA 30322-2870 • ACRL LITA

Patterson Grace L. • Director • Hudson County Community College • Jersey City, NJ 07306

Patterson Janet D. • Monroe County Public Library • Bloomington, IN 47408 • RASD

Patterson Janet E. • Student • Chadron State College Reta E. King Library • Chadron, NE 69337 • PLA

Patterson Jeanne M. • Lyndhurst, OH 44124 • PLA

Patterson Jennifer B. • Student • University of Texas at Austin Graduate School of Library & Information Sciences • Austin, TX 78712-1276

Patterson Jill K. • Senior Librarian • Glendora Public Library • Glendora, CA 91740 • RASD IFRT

Patterson John W. • Trustee • Richmond Public Library • Richmond, VA 23219

Patterson Kathleen • Rhinebeck, NY 12572

Patterson Lillie G. • Spec. School Library Serv. • Baltimore City Department of Education • Baltimore, MD 21215

Patterson Linda S. • Media & Communication Coord • Walton County School District • DeFuniak Springs, FL 32433

Patterson Lisa L. • Coal City, IL 60416

Patterson Lotsee • Associate Professor • University of Oklahoma School of Library & Information Studies • Norman, OK 73019 • AASL EMIERT

Patterson M. Aimee • NASA Johnson Space Center • Houston, TX 77058

Patterson Margaret • Marc Communications Format Spec • Library of Congress • Washington, DC 20541 • ALCTS LITA
Life

Patterson Margaret H. Mrs. • Shepherdstown, WV 25443 • ACRL
Continuing

Patterson Michele E. • Reference/Technical Service • Beech Grove Public Library • Beech Grove, IN 46107 • RASD

Patterson Patricia • Dir of Legal Info Services • Schiff Hardin & Waite • Chicago, IL 60606

Patterson Patricia B. • Student • Florida State University School of Library and Information Studies • Tallahassee, FL 32306-2048

Patterson Patti R. • Head of Reference Department • United States Naval Academy Nimitz Library • Annapolis, MD 21402-5029 • ACRL LAMA RASD AFLRT

Patterson Robert D. • Houghton, MI 49931

Patterson Robert H. • Director of Libraries • University of Tulsa McFarlin Library • Tulsa, OK 74104-3189 • ACRL LAMA

Patterson Sandra W. • Librarian • Library of Congress • Washington, DC 20541 • GODORT

Patterson Shelley K. • Librarian • Perkins School for the Blind • Watertown, MA 02172

Patterson Thomas H. • Associate Director • University of North Carolina Walter Clinton Jackson Library • Greensboro, NC 27412-5201 • ACRL LAMA

Patterson Trudy J. • Librarian • Jefferson Davis Parish Library • Jennings, LA 70546

Patterson Vicki R. • Librarian • Bay County Public Library Association NW Regional Lib System • Panama City, FL 32401-2625

Pattie Ling-Yuh W. • Asst. Dir. for Technical Svs. • University of Kentucky Libraries • Lexington, KY 40506-0039 • ALCTS LITA

Pattillo Sharon B. • Educational Media Specialist • Hunterdon Central Regional High School • Flemington, NJ 08822 • AASL

Pattison Frederick • Librarian • American Journal of Nursing Co. • New York, NY 10019 • ACRL ASCLA
Life

Pattison Joanne • Bradenton, FL 34209-1143

Pattison Laura B. • Student • State University of New York at Albany School of Information Science & Policy • Albany, NY 12222 • ACRL SRRT

Patton Charlotte T. • Head Librarian • Darlington High School • Rome, GA 30161 • ILERT

Patton David G. • Project Architect • Phillips Swager Associates • Naperville, IL 60563 • LAMA

Patton Eddie Mr. • Trustee • Birmingham Public Library • Birmingham, AL 35203 • ALTA

Patton Frances G. • Student • Bloomfield Middle School • Bloomfield, NJ 07003 • AASL

Patton Glenn E. • Cataloging & Services Section • Online Computer Library Center (OCLC) • Dublin, OH 43017-3395 • ALCTS LITA

Patton Janice K. • Eden Webster Libraries • Saint Louis, MO 63119-9957 • NMRT

Patton JoAnna • E.C.S. School for Girls • Westmount PQ, H3Y 3H6 Canada

Patton John Jr. • Trustee • Glenview Public Library • Glenview, IL 60025

Patton Linda L. • Univ. Librarian/Reference • Florida State University Robert M. Strozier Library • Tallahassee, FL 32306-2047 • ACRL RASD

Patton Mary • Branch Head • Metropolitan Library System Warr Acres Branch • Oklahoma City, OK 73132-2401 • PLA

Patton Patricia R. • Paintsville, KY 41240 • PLA

Patton Rebecca B. • Public Library Consultant • Arrowhead Library System • Virginia, MN 55792 • PLA RASD

Patton Richard J. Jr. • Assistant to City Librarian • Denver Public Library • Denver, CO 80203-2165 • PLA

Patton Samuel • Trustee • Mid-Hudson Library System • Poughkeepsie, NY 12601

Patton Sandra • Coordinator of Media • Colorado Springs Public Schools • Colorado Springs, CO 80903 • AASL

Patwell Paul D. • Newark Public Library • Newark, NJ 07101-0630 • GODORT

Paul Barbara A. • Head Librarian • Chicago Heights Public Library • Chicago Heights, IL 60411 • ALCTS ALSC ASCLA LAMA PLA RASD

Paul Carol • District Media • Douglas Public Library District • Castle Rock, CO 80104

Paul Jacqueline R. • Asst. Librarian/Tech. Services • Widener University School of Law Library • Wilmington, DE 19803-0475 • ALCTS LITA

Paul Jeffrey H. • Interim Assoc. Director • San Jose State University Clark Library • San Jose, CA 95192-0028

Paul Joan Miller • Student • University of South Florida School of Library & Information Science • Tampa, FL 33620 • ALSC

Paul Nancy L. • Brandon Public Library • Brandon, WI 53919 • PLA

Paul Patricia J. • Information Coordinator • Univ of Wisconsin • Stevens Pt, WI 54481 • ACRL LAMA

Paul Paula • Orangeburg County Library • Orangeburg, SC 29115-1367 • LAMA PLA

Paul Sandra K. • SKP Associates • New York, NY 10010 • ALCTS LITA IRRT

Paul Sara • Librarian • Overbrook Educational Center • Philadelphia, PA 19151 • AASL

Paul Sheila T. • Columbia, MD 21044 • RASD NMRT

Paulaskas Linda C. • Director • South Milwaukee Public Library • S Milwaukee, WI 53172 • PLA

Paulette Elaine • Director • Wood County Dist Public Library • Bowling Green, OH 43402 • PLA IFRT

Pauley Patricia L. • Librarian • Anchorage Municipal Libraries Z. J. Loussac Library • Anchorage, AK 99503

Pauli David N. • Director • Missoula Public Library • Missoula, MT 59802 • PLA

Paulin Mary Ann • Media Specialist • Negaunee Public Schools • Negaunee, MI 49866 • AASL ALSC YALSA *Life*

Paulk Janet T. • Library Personnel Officer • Emory University Libraries Robert W. Woodruff Library • Atlanta, GA 30322-2870 • ACRL LAMA

Paulk Sara • Reference Librarian • Concord Public Library • Concord, NH 03301

Paullin William D. • Assistant Director • Atlantic County Library • Mays Landing, NJ 08336 • LAMA LITA PLA

Pauls Adonijah • Fresno, CA 93702 • ALCTS

Paulsen Dorothy A. • Files Section Head • Time Warner Inc. • New York City, NY 10021 • ALCTS LITA

Paulsen Elizabeth D. • Serial Supervisor • University of Idaho Library • Moscow, ID 83843

Paulsen Julie L. • Business Office Manager • Weber County Library • Odgen, UT 84401

Paulsen Marcia S. • Media Director • Buffalo Senior High School • Buffalo, MN 55313 • AASL

Paulsen Marian T. • Associate Director • Anoka County Library • Blaine, MN 55434

Paulson Avis M. • Librarian II • Moline Public Library • Moline, IL 61265

Paulson Barbara A. • Pres. & Assecc/802 • National Endowment for Humanities • Washington, DC 20506 • ACRL

Paulson Carl F. • Student • Rutgers University School of Communication Information & Library Studies • New Brunswick, NJ 08903

Paulson Lynn P. • Director • University of Wisconsin System Adminstration • Madison, WI 53706 • ACRL

Paulson Merle J. • Head Acquisitions • Wichita State University Ablah Library • Wichita, KS 67208 • ACRL ALCTS

Paulson Peter • Executive Director • Forest Press/OCLC • Albany, NY 12206-2082 • ASCLA ERT ILERT IRRT

Paulson Susan • Online Computer Library Center (OCLC) Pacific Network • Rancho Cucamonga, CA 91730

Paulson Sylvia B. Miss • Green Bay, WI 54301 • ALSC YALSA
Continuing

Paulus Mary C. • Baltimore County Public Library • Towson, MD 21204 • ALSC PLA

Paulus Renee S. • Reference Librarian • Berkeley Heights Public Library • Berkeley Hts, NJ 07922

Paulus Rita C. • Encino, CA 91436 • LITA RASD

Pauly Regina R. • Glassboro State College • Glassboro, NJ 08028 • AASL LRRT

Pausch Lois M. • Geology Librarian/Assoc. Prof. • University of Illinois • Urbana, IL 61801 • ACRL ALCTS LIRT

Pausley Alexander • Trustee • Cleveland Heights-University Heights Public Library • Cleveland Heights, OH 44118

Paustenbaugh Jennifer F. • Patent&Economic Develp. Libn • Oklahoma State University Edmon Low Library • Stillwater, OK 74078-0375 • ACRL LAMA LHRT

Paustenbaugh Richard T. • Reference Librarian • Indiana University School of Library and Information Science • Bloomington, IN 47405 • ACRL LAMA RASD

Paustian P. Robert • Director of Libraries • Lebanon Valley College • Annville, PA 17003-0501 • ACRL

Pautler Ward S. • Library Systems Coordinator • Buffalo & Erie County Public Library • Buffalo, NY 14203 • LITA PLA

Pautzsch Richard O. • Orlando, FL 32825 • Continuing

Pavalon Donna • Woodbury Junior High School • Las Vegas, NV 89121 • AASL

Paveglio Pat • Assistant Director • Marguerite deAngeli Library • Lapeer, MI 48446 • IFRT

Pavelko Charlotte A. • Librarian • Denair High School • Denair, CA 95316

Pavey Margaret • Avondale Ests, GA 30002

Pavia Marie C.P. • Student • University of Missouri-Columbia School of Library & Informational Science • Columbia, MO 65211

Pavitt Judith • Librarian • West Middle School • Plymouth, MI 48170 • AASL

Pavlak Anne • Director • Amityville Public Library • Amityville, NY 11701 • LAMA PLA

Pavon Ana-Elba • Student • University of California-Berkeley University Library • Berkeley, CA 94720

Pawlek Cynthia F. • Reference/Bibliographer • Dartmouth College Library Baker Memorial Library • Hanover, NH 03755-3525 • ACRL

Pawley Carolyn P. • Head, Cataloging Division • University of Guelph Library • Guelph ON, N1G 2W1 Canada • ACRL ALCTS LAMA

Pawlik Deborah A. • Director • Seton Hill College Reeves Memorial Library • Greensburg, PA 15601

Pawlocki Susan F. • Getty Center Resources Collections • Santa Monica, CA 90401 • ALCTS LITA NMRT

Pawson Robert D. • Assistant Director • Leonia Public Library • Leonia, NJ 07605

Paxman Jim • Nashville, TN 37221

Payanzo Jane S. • Williamsport, PA 17701

Paydar Margaret L B • Memphis, TN 38111

Payette Dolores • Librarian • Bartlett Public Library District • Bartlett, IL 60103 • LAMA PLA

Payette Patricia E. • Principal Librarian • Bayonne Public Library • Bayonne, NJ 07002 • PLA GODORT

Payette Richard J. • Assistant Director • West Warwick Public Library System • West Warwick, RI 02893

Payne Alfredda H. • Assistant to the Editor • National Association of Social Workers • Washington, DC 20002

Payne Altona • Trustee • Willingboro Public Library • Willingboro, NJ 08046 • ALTA

Payne Ann Marie • Student • University of Washington Graduate School of Library and Information Science • Seattle, WA 98195

Payne Beverly H. • Media Specialist • Brentwood Middle School • Brentwood, TN 37027 • AASL

Payne Carol A. • University of South Florida Library • Tampa, FL 33620-5600

Payne Charles T. • Assistant Director for Systems • University of Chicago Library • Chicago, IL 60637-1502 • ACRL ALCTS LITA

Payne David L. • Columbus, MS 39702 • Continuing

Payne David S.P. • Reference Librarian • Palm Beach County Library System • West Palm Beach, FL 33406

Payne Denise G. • Head of Adult Services • Geneva Public Library District • Geneva, IL 60134

Payne Douglass B. • Computer Systems Coordinator • Boston University Mugar Memorial Library • Boston, MA 02215 • LITA

Payne Elizabeth A. • Executive Director • Washington Research Library Consortium • Lanham, MD 20706 • ASCLA LITA

Payne Gale M. • Librarian • Brentwood Academy • Brentwood, TN 37027

Payne Gary • Seattle, WA 98125 • LITA

Payne Geoffrey J. • Executive Director • Caval Limited • Richmond VIC 3121, Australia • ACRL ALCTS LITA

Payne Jo Lynne • Cambridge, MA 02139-4723 • ALCTS

Payne John K. • Director of Library Services • Mars Hill College Memorial Library • Mars Hill, NC 28754 • IFRT SRRT

Payne John R. • Austin, TX 78703 • ACRL

Payne Laura S. • Madison, NC 27025

Payne Leila M. • Head, Database Management Div • Texas A & M University Sterling C. Evans Library • College Station, TX 77843-5000 • ACRL ALCTS LITA

Payne Leslie P. • Children's Librarian • Salinas Public Library • Salinas, CA 93901

Payne Linda M. • Lake Country Elementary School • Lake Placid, FL 33852 • AASL YALSA

Payne Lyn L. • Orange County Library System Windermere Branch • Windermere, FL 32786

Payne Martha N. • Coor Tech Serv and Automation • Haverford College James P. Magill Library • Haverford, PA 19041 • LITA

Payne Mary Louise • Morristown, NJ 07962 • AASL ALCTS EMIERT *Continuing*

Payne Patricia C. • Librarian • University of Massachusetts at Boston • Boston, MA 02116 • ACRL

Payne Phyllis C. • Special Collections Cataloger • Boston University Mugar Memorial Library • Boston, MA 02215 • ACRL

Payne Robin L. • Arkansas State University Dean B. Ellis Library • State University, AR 72467-2040 • ACRL

Payne Sally L. • Director • Papillion Public Library • Papillion, NE 68046 • LITA PLA

Payne Sandra • Young Adult Librarian • New York Public Library Branches Staten Island Borough Office • Staten Island, NY 10301 • YALSA

Payne Shirley F. • N Kingstown, RI 02852

Paynter David M. • Director • New Hanover County Library • Wilmington, NC 28401-3998 • LAMA PLA

Payson Evelyn H. • University of Wisconsin Library and Learning Resources • Whitewater, WI 53190 • ACRL

Payson Patricia L. • Librarian • Southwest Wisconsin Technical College Library • Fennimore, WI 53809 • ACRL RASD

Payton Barbara W. • Librarian • Philadelphia Public Schools • Philadelphia, PA 19126 • AASL

Pazelt Nancy S. • Reference Librarian • Cuyahoga County Public Library Parma Regional • Parma, OH 44129-3199 • PLA

Paznekas Susan J. • Public Library Consultant • Maryland State Department of Education Division of Library Development & Services • Baltimore, MD 21201 • PLA LIRT

Peabody Brewster E. • Library of Congress • Washington, DC 20541 • ACRL ALCTS *Life*

Peabody Diann • Director • Watseka Public Library • Watseka, IL 60970

Peabody Janet M. • Torrance, CA 90503 • LITA

Peabody Kenneth W. • AT&T Bell Laboratories • Murray Hill, NJ 07974 • LITA

Peach Janet S. • San Luis Obispo, CA 93401

Peach Janis K. • Librarian • Sullivan College • Louisville, KY 40205 • ACRL

Peacock Alma G. • Childrens Librarian • Mamie Doud Eisenhower Pub. Lib. • Broomfield, CO 80020 • ALSC

Peacock Diane H. • Media Specialist • Long County High School • Ludowici, GA 31316 • AASL

Peacock Gary D. • Reference Librarian • Delaware State College William C. Jason Library • Dover, DE 19901

Peacock Helen M. • Chapel Hill, NC 27514 • AASL YALSA

Peacock Jill E. • Student • Indiana University at Bloomington University Libraries • Bloomington, IN 47405-9998 • RASD IFRT

Peacock Phoebe B. • Sr. Processing Librarian • Library of Congress • Washington, DC 20541 • ACRL

Peaden Cecil L. • Student • University of Illinois Graduate School of Library and Information Science • Urbana, IL 61801 • ALCTS IFRT

Peak Jeanne • Media Specialist • Buena Vista Elementary School • Greer, SC 29650 • AASL

Peake Carolyn S. • Assistant Director • Lake Oswego Public Library • Lake Oswego, OR 97034 • PLA

Pearce Douglas A. • Director • Warwick Public Library • Warwick, RI 02886 • PLA

Pearce Ellen • Rolla, MO 65401

Pearce Jean • Reader's Services Librarian • Wheaton College Wallace Library • Norton, MA 02766 • ACRL LAMA RASD

Pearce Lillian E. Miss • Flushing, NY 11354 • PLA RASD *Continuing*

Pearce Patsy A. • Children's Specialist • Public Library of Des Moines North Side Library • Des Moines, IA 50313 • ALSC

Pearce Rosemary • Riverhead, NY 11901 • AASL ALSC

Pearl M. Beth • Librarian • Buckingham Elementary School • Bend, OR 97701 • AASL

Pearl Nancy L. • Resources Coordinator • Tulsa City-County Library System • Tulsa, OK 74103 • PLA RASD IFRT

Pearl Patricia D. • Richmond, VA 23226-1517

Pearl Ronna • Librarian • Carteret Free Public Library • Carteret, NJ 07008 • PLA

Pearlmutter Jane • Outreach Program Manager • University of Wisconsin-Madison School of Library & Information Studies • Madison, WI 53706

Pearlmutter Regina • New York, NY 10028 • IFRT

Pearsall Alice B. • Essexville, MI 48732 • AASL YALSA *Continuing*

Pearsall Patrice K. • Head of Technical Services • Algonquin Area Public Library District • Algonquin, IL 60102 • ALCTS

Pearsall Priscilla D. • Madison, WI 53705

Pearse Leslie B. • Section Manager, Doc Dept • Online Computer Library Center (OCLC) • Dublin, OH 43017-3395 • LITA

Pearson Anne C. • Henderson, KY 42420 • ALTA IFRT

Pearson Barbara L. • Library Director • El Segundo Public Library • El Segundo, CA 90245 • PLA RASD YALSA

Pearson Bruce • Church of Jesus Christ of Latter-Day Saints • Salt Lake City, UT 84150

Pearson Carolyn V. • Information Specialist • Alki Software Corporation • Seattle, WA 98109

Pearson Connie • Library Media Teacher • Rancho Cotate High School • Rohnert Park, CA 94928

Pearson Dana B. • Student • University of North Texas School of Library & Information Sciences • Denton, TX 76203

Pearson Deb • University of Nebraska Love Library • Lincoln, NE 68588-0410

Pearson Eddie C. • Head, Circulation Librarian • West Georgia College Library Media Program • Carrollton, GA 30118

Pearson Elizabeth R. • Librarian • Montreat-Anderson College Nelson Bell Library • Montreat, NC 28757

Pearson Evette • Northwestern State University Eugene P. Watson Library • Natchitoches, LA 71457 • LIRT NMRT

Pearson Glenda J. • Microforms/Newspaper Ln • University of Washington Suzzallo Library • Seattle, WA 98195

Pearson Gretchen E. • Head of Public Services • LeMoyne College • Syracuse, NY 13214 • ACRL RASD

Pearson Helen E. • Librarian/Media Specialist • Ben Hill Elementary School • Atlanta, GA 30311

Pearson Henrietta • Clinton Public Library • Clinton, IA 52732 • ALTA

Pearson Karen L. • Reference/Public Svs. Libn. • Saint Xavier University • Chicago, IL 60655 • ACRL LIRT

Pearson Lina H. • Library/Media Specialist • Brockington Elementary School • Darlington, SC 29532 • AASL

Pearson Lois R. • Chicago, IL 60657

Pearson M. Joyce • Student • University of South Carolina College of Library & Information Science • Columbia, SC 29208

Pearson Norma J. • Head Science & Technology Lib • University of Akron University Library & Learning Resource • Akron, OH 44325-1707 • ACRL LRRT

Pearson Norman R. • Head Technical Services • Wittenberg University Thomas Library • Springfield, OH 45501

Pearson Pamela J. • Houston Public Library Jungman Branch • Houston, TX 77057

Pearson Patricia H. • School Librarian • J.D. Smith Junior High School • North Las Vegas, NV 89030 • AASL

Pearson Penelope A. • Head, Undergraduate Library • Ohio State University Libraries • Columbus, OH 43210-1286 • ACRL

Pearson Peter D. • Executive Director • Friends of The Saint Paul Public Library • Saint Paul, MN 55101

Pearson Roger L. • Library Director • Naperville Public Libraries • Naperville, IL 60540 • PLA

Pearson Rosemary • Student • Rosary College Graduate School of Library & Information Science • River Forest, IL 60305 • PLA IFRT

Pearson Sara • Director • Urbandale Public Library • Urbandale, IA 50322

Pearson Wanda L. • Director • Brownsburg Public Library • Brownsburg, IN 46112

Pearson Waynn • City Librarian • Cerritos Public Library • Cerritos, CA 90701 • PLA

Pearsons Sheila M. • Branch Librarian • Bay County Library System South Side Branch • Bay City, MI 48706

Peart Gwendolyn B. • Media Specials • Touns Elementary School • Altanta, GA 30301 • AASL

Pease Barbara • Reference Librarian • California State University-Chico Meriam Library • Chico, CA 92929-0295 • ACRL RASD

Pease Elaine K. • Cataloger • Millersville University of Pennsylvania • Millersville, PA 17551-0302

Pease Lesley Daignault • Information Services • Syracuse University Library E. S. Bird Library • Syracuse, NY 13244-2010 • ACRL

Pease Susan V. • Lewiston Public Library • Lewiston, ME 04240 • ALSC

Peaseley Robert E. • Charlotte, NC 28227-4072 • AASL LITA IFRT LIRT LRRT SRRT

Peasley Rozelle F. • Coordinator, Library Media Serv • Empire Union School District • Modesto, CA 95354 • AASL

Peattie Noel • Librarian Humanities • University of California Shields Library • Davis, CA 95616 • ACRL ALCTS IFRT SRRT

Peavy Susan M. • Information Specialist • DeSoto Library • DeSoto, KS 66030

Pec Jean A. • Serials Specialist • University of Notre Dame • Notre Dame, IN 46556 • ACRL ALCTS LAMA

Pecarovich Kathleen • Asst Head of Tech Serv • University of California L.A. Library Law Library • Los Angeles, CA 90024-1302

Peccia Dorothy Baas • Librarian • Pocomoke Elementary School • Pocomoke City, MD 21851 • AASL

Pech Ann • Librarian • Autaugaville Junior Senior High School • Autaugaville, AL 36003 • AASL

Pecho-Murazzi Isaias J. • Rio Piedras, PR 00921

Peck Amory • Trustee • Tumwater Timberland • Tumwater, WA 98501 • ALTA

Peck Amy E. Miss • San Antonio, TX 78291-0121 • ALCTS   *Life*

Peck Ann D. • Chevy Chase, MD 20815

Peck Christine Morgan • Community Library Coordinator • Aberdeen Timberland Library • Aberdeen, WA 98520 • VRT

Peck David R. • Student • Clarion University of Pennsylvania College of Library Science • Clarion, PA 16214 • IFRT

Peck Elizabeth A. • Architecture Librarian • Roger Williams College Library • Bristol, RI 02809-2921 • ACRL

Peck Kathleen C. • Library Director • Westridge School for Girls Library • Pasadena, CA 91105 • AASL

Peck Laurie S. • Mountain View Public Library • Mountain View, CA 94041

Peck Nancy C • Middle School Librarian • Williams Middle School Alfred L. Wood Library • Longmeadow, MA 01106 • AASL

Peck Nancy R. • The Plains Public Library • The Plains, VA 22171 • PLA

Peck Penny • Children's Librarian • San Leandro Library • San Leandro, CA 94577 • ALSC

Peck Philip • Concord, MA 01742 • LAMA

Peck Robert M. • New Orleans, LA 70118 • ACRL

Peck Ruth M. • W Springfield, MA 01089 • AASL ALSC LITA PLA ERT GODORT LIRT LRRT MAGERT

Peck Shirley S. • Coordinator of Info Tech. • Catonsville Community College • Baltimore, MD 21228 • ACRL

Peck V. Jane • Nova Biomedical • Waltham, MA 02192

Peckham Susan M. • Cranston, RI 02905

Pecon Sally N. • Editorial Research & Development • Martindale-Hubbell Inc. • New Providence, NJ 07974 • ACRL ALCTS RASD

Pecone Carmela • Director, Education Dept. • Avon Books • New York, NY 10016

Pecoraro Sarah A. • Student • State University of New York (SUNY) School of Information & Library Studies • Buffalo, NY 14260 • AASL

Pecoul Ellen R. • New Orleans, LA 70118

Pedak-Kari Maria • Librarian • Montgomery County Department of Public Libraries • Rockville, MD 20850

Peden Robert M. • Partner • F1 Services • Dallas, TX 75207 • ILERT

Pedersen-Summey Terri L. • Emporia State University William Allen White Library • Emporia, KS 66801 • NMRT

Pedersen Barbara • Resource/AV Coordinator • Schaumburg School District # 54 • Schaumburg, IL 60195

Pedersen Carolyn • ARMD/2 • University of Washington Suzzallo Library • Seattle, WA 98195 • ALCTS LITA

Pedersen Karen T. • Assoc Mgr, Info Resource Center • South Carolina State Development Board • Columbia, SC 29202

Pedersen Nancy • Circulation Librarian • Bradford College Hemingway Library • Haverhill, MA 01835

Pedersen Sarah • Dean of Library Services • Evergreen State College • Olympia, WA 98505 • ACRL SRRT

Pedersen Sharon L. • Ballwin, MO 63011

Pedersen Susan • Children's & Young Adult Ln • Wicomico County Free Library • Salisbury, MD 21801

Pedersen Wayne A. • Iowa State University Library • Ames, IA 50011-2140 • LAMA LRRT

Pedersoli Heleni Marques • Bibl. Foreign Lang & Lit. • University of Maryland Libraries • College Park, MD 20742 • ACRL ALCTS IRRT NMRT

Pederson Ann • Educational Services Librarian • University of North Dakota Chester Fritz Library • Grand Forks, ND 58202-0175 • ACRL RASD LIRT

Pederson Claudia • Systems Administrator • Wakarusa Public Library • Wakarusa, IN 46573 • LITA PLA

Pederson Daniel E. • Minneapolis Public Library & Information Center • Minneapolis, MN 55401-1992 • SRRT

Pederson Randy L. • Computer Services Librarian • University of North Dakota Chester Fritz Library • Grand Forks, ND 58202-0175 • ACRL LAMA LITA RASD

Pederson Robert C. • Ames, IA 50010 • RASD NMRT

Pedigo Peggy • Mgr. Technical Services • Motorola • Phoenix, AZ 85008

Pedraza Ellen • Kenosha, WI 53142

Peduzzi Roberta E. • Acquisition Librarian • Belleville Area College Library • Belleville, IL 62221 • ACRL

Peebles Barbara N. • Oakland, OR 97462 • AASL

Peek Richard M. • Head, Preservation Dept. • University of Rochester Rush Rhees Library • Rochester, NY 14627-0055

Peek Robin P. • Assistant Professor • Simmons College Graduate School of Library & Information Science • Boston, MA 02115 • LITA LRRT

Peel Martha D. • Librarian • Hartsville High School • Hartsville, SC 29550 • AASL LRRT

Peel Richard C. • Arizona State Library Library for the Blind & Phys Hndcpd • Phoenix, AZ 85008 • ASCLA PLA   *Life*

Peele Marla H. • Seattle, WA 98107

Peeler Jean S. • Edgefield, SC 29824 • AASL

Peeling Lisa H. • Public Services Librarian II • Baltimore County Public Library • Towson, MD 21204 • ALSC

Peelle Jami E. • Special Collections • Kenyon College Olin Library • Gambier, OH 43022 • ACRL

Peelle Linda K. • Branch Supervisor • Willows Public Library Bayliss Branch • Glenn, CA 95943

Peeples Margaret C. • Tahlequah, OK 74464-3630

Peerson Ethel Miss • Florence, AL 35630 • ALTA PLA   *Continuing*

Peery Alice • Public Library of Charlotte & Mecklenburg County • Charlotte, NC 28202 • LAMA PLA RASD

Peete Gary Ronald • Government Documents Dept • University of California-Berkeley University Library • Berkeley, CA 94720 • ACRL GODORT

Peetz Deborah J. • Alexandria, VA 22302 • LITA

Peglow Catherine • Librarian • Keys School • Palo Alto, CA 94306 • AASL

Pegolotti James A. • Western Connecticut State University • Danbury, CT 06810

Pegues Laura T. • Librarian • Lee County Library System • Fort Myers, FL 33901

Peguese Charles R. • Asst. Dean for Instructional Res • Harrisburg Area Community College McCormick Library • Harrisburg, PA 17110 • ACRL LAMA

Pehe Jana • West Germany, Germany • ALCTS

Pehle Jane J. • Head of Youth Services • Hammond Public Library • Hammond, IN 46320 • ALSC PLA

Pei Xiaohua • Bellvue, WA 98008

Peiffer Jo Rae • Media Specialist • Fairfield High School • Fairfield, IA 52556 • AASL

Peins Maryann • Edison, NJ 08820 • ALSC ASCLA

Peipert Mary E. • Ft. Worth, TX 76107 • AASL

Peischl Thomas M. • Dean of Library Services • Mankato State University Memorial Library • Mankato, MN 56002-8400 • ACRL LAMA

Pejsa Pamela • Trustee • Thousand Oaks Library • Thousand Oaks, CA 91362

Pekala Reba L. • Librarian • shoreham Wading River High School • Shoreham, NY 11786 • AASL

Pekar Connie A. • Mentor, OH 44060

Pelak Patricia A. • Acting Director • Little Falls Free Public Library • Little Falls, NJ 07424

Pelavin Sol H. • President • Pelavin Associates,Inc. • Washington, DC 20036 • ACRL

Pelikan Margaret • Director • Harrison Memorial Library • Carmel By The Sea, CA 93921 • LAMA PLA

Pelkey Kimberly A. • Philadelphia, PA 19130

Pelkey Patricia • Trustee • Calumet City Public Library • Calumet City, IL 60409-4003 • ALTA

Pelki David • Trustee • Bridgeview Public Library • Bridgeview, IL 60455 • ALTA

Pell Claiborne • Washington, DC 20510 • AASL ACRL ALCTS ALSC ALTA ASCLA LAMA LITA PLA RASD YALSA   *Honorary*

Pelland Joan M. • Director/Tech Svs. • University of South Florida Library • Sarasota, FL 34243-2197 • ACRL ALCTS IFRT

Pelle Elizabeth • Librarian • Frederick County Public Library C. Burr Artz Library • Frederick, MD 21701 • LAMA PLA

Pellegrini Susan E. • Reference Librarian • Schaumburg Township District Library • Schaumburg, IL 60194 • PLA RASD

Pellen Rita • Asst. Director for Pub. Serv. • Florida Atlantic University S.E. Wimberly Library • Boca Raton, FL 33431 • ACRL LAMA

Pellerin Mary Ann Dr • Bristol, CT 06010 • AASL LITA LIRT

Pelletier Colleen A. • Technical Services Librarian • Plattsburgh Public Library • Plattsburgh, NY 12901

Pelletier Karen • Library Media Center Director • Jefferson Central School • Jefferson, NY 12093

Pelletier Mary H. • Forest Hills, NY 11375

Pelley Shirley • Director • Southern Nazarene Unuversity R T Williams • Bethany, OK 73008 • ACRL ALCTS LAMA LITA RASD

Pellington Mary Ellen • Director • Muskingum County Library System • Zanesville, OH 43701 • LAMA PLA SRRT

Pellowski Anne • New York, NY 10025 • ALSC

Pellusch Jana E. • Student • University of Texas at Austin Graduate School of Library & Information Sciences • Austin, TX 78712-1276 • EMIERT SRRT

Pelman Sue • Librarian/Cataloger • Thousand Oaks Library • Thousand Oaks, CA 91362 • ALCTS PLA

Peloquin Margaret I. • Head Librarian • Austin Community College Riverside Campus-LRS • Austin, TX 78741

Pelose Sandra J. • Reference Librarian • Sacramento Public Library • Sacramento, CA 95814

Peloso Mary A. • Webster, NY 14580

Pelsma Kimberlie H. • Librarian • Olathe Public Schools • Olathe, KS 66062 • AASL

Peltier Euclid J. • Boston, MA 02114-4303 • PLA

Peltola Bette J. • University of Wisconsin-Milwaukee School of Education • Milwaukee, WI 53201 • ALSC

Pelton James R. • Director • Shreve Memorial Library • Shreveport, LA 71120-1523 • LAMA PLA

Pember Janet S. • Librarian • Central Ninth High School • Beaumont, TX 77703 • AASL YALSA

Pemberton Eleanor F. • Librarian I • Atlanta-Fulton Public Library • Atlanta, GA 30303 • PLA SORT

Pemberton Sara R. • Children's Services Librarian • Downers Grove Public Library • Downers Grove, IL 60515

Penberthy Laura J. • Student • University of Washington Graduate School of Library and Information Science • Seattle, WA 98195 • SRRT

Pence Cheryl S. • Librarian • Illinois State Historical Library • Springfield, IL 62701

Penchansky Mimi B. • Associate Professor • Queens College Benjamin S. Rosenthal Library • Flushing, NY 11367-0904 • ACRL RASD SRRT

Pendergrass Margaret E. • Springfield, IL 62703

Pendergrass Robert • Assistant Media Director • Professional Resource Center • Taylor, MI 48180-3941

Pendlebury Theresa • Media Coordinator • Art Center College of Design • Pasadena, CA 91103

Pendleton Deborah E. • Trustee • Mobile Public Library • Mobile, AL 36602 • ALTA

Pendleton Mark A. • Reference Librarian • Thomas Branigan Memorial Library • Las Cruces, NM 88001 • RASD

Pendley Marcia R. • Head Outreach Services • Morrisson-Reeves Library • Richmond, IN 47374

Penfold Frances W. • Oklahoma Cty, OK 73134-6008 • Continuing

Peng Alex • Flushing, NY 11355

Pengelly Kenneth C. • Assoc Prof L Media Education • Mankato State University Library Media Education Department • Mankato, MN 56003 • AASL ALSC SRRT

Pengilly Nona I. • Student • University of California-Berkeley School of Library & Information Studies • Berkeley, CA 94720

Penhale Sara • Sci Ln & Asst Prof Of Biology • Earlham College Wildman Science Library • Richmond, IN 47374 • ACRL

Penick Hal W. • Librarian • Iowa City Public Library • Iowa City, IA 52240 • ALCTS

Penington Mary Judith • Branch Librarian • Blinn College Bryan Branch Library • Bryan, TX 77802 • AASL ACRL LITA

Peniston-Styles Shernette • Reference Librarian • Bermuda Library • Hamilton HM11, Bermuda • RASD EMIERT

Peniston William A. • Reference Librarian • Chili Public Library • Rochester, NY 14624

Penka Carol B. • University of Illinois Library • Urbana, IL 61801 • ACRL ALCTS RASD LIRT   *Life*

Penke Ann K. • Head Librarian • Lakeland College Library • Sheboygan, WI 53081 • Life

Penkowsky Peyton L. • Librarian III,Adult Services • Montgomery County Department of Public Libraries • Rockville, MD 20850 • PLA RASD IFRT

Penland Dawn R. • Student • University of North Carolina School of Library Science • Chapel Hill, NC 27599-3360 • ACRL

Penland Patrick R. Dr. • Professor • University of Pittsburgh School of Library and Information Science • Pittsburgh, PA 15260 • Life

Penn Carlton A. • Supervisor of Media Services • Pinelands Regional School District • Tuckerton, NJ 08087-0248 • AASL

Pennell Charles • Head, Cataloging Division • Memorial University of Newfoundland • St. John's, NF, A1B 3Y1 Canada • ACRL ALCTS LITA

Penner Elaine C. • Base Librarian • United States Air Force Goodfellow Base Library-SSL • Goodfellow AFB, TX 76908

Penniman W. David • President • Council on Library Resources • Washington, DC 20036-2117 • LRRT

Penninger Monica • Director • Santa Fe Springs City Library • Santa Fe Springs, CA 90670 • PLA

Pennington Billy • Library Director • Birmingham-Southern College Library C. A. Rush Learning Center • Birmingham, AL 35254 • ACRL LAMA

Pennington Jerry G. • Director • Appleton Public Library • Appleton, WI 54911-4780 • ALCTS ALTA LAMA LITA PLA

Pennington June V. • Librarian Cataloger • Manatee County Public Library System • Bradenton, FL 34205

Pennington Melinda S. • Education Catalog Libn • Western Kentucky University Helm-Cravens Library • Bowling Green, KY 42101 • ACRL ALCTS

Pennington Sharyn T. • Scottsdale Public Library Mustang Branch • Scottsdale, AZ 85258 • PLA VRT

Pennington Teresa L. • Librarian • Paris Carnegie Library • Paris, IL 61944

Penny Susan H. • Rivera School • El Paso, TX 79912 • AASL

Penprase Catherine J. • Port Hueneme, CA 93041

Penrod Karen L. • Student • Simmons College Graduate School of Library & Information Science • Boston, MA 02115 • LITA

Penrod Saundra K. • Media Teacher • Lakeside Middle School • Fort Wayne, IN 46805

Penrose Charles Dr • Assistant Librarian. • Clarkson University Educational Resources Center • Potsdam, NY 13699-5590 • Continuing

Penson Andrew • Reference & Info Specialist • South Carolina State College Miller F. Whittaker Library • Orangeburg, SC 29117 • ACRL

Penson Merryll S. • Director • Simon Schwob Memorial Library Columbus College • Columbus, GA 31993 • ACRL ALCTS LAMA LITA

Pensyl Ornella L. • Supervisory Info Serv Spec • Defense Intelligence Agency • Washington, DC 20340-3341 • AFLRT FLRT

Penta Vince L. P.S. • Longview, WA 98632

Pentecost Ann • Children's Librarian • Stockton-San Joaquin County Public Library • Stockton, CA 95202 • ALSC

Pentlicky Anne A. • Rutgers Preparatory Lower School Library • Somerset, NJ 08873 • AASL

Pentlin Floyd C. • Librarian/Media Specialist • Lee's Summit High School • Lee's Summit, MO 64063 • AASL SRRT

Penton Gvorja Miss. • Student • Washington Parish Library • Franklinton, LA 70438

Penton Sharon F. • Grace-Saint Lukes School • Memphis, TN 38104 • AASL

Penwarden Ann P. • Monroe Community College LeRoy V. Good Library • Rochester, NY 14623-0701 • IFRT LIRT NMRT

Pepchinski Gina Hardalo • Houston, TX 77025

Pepin E. Mc Kenney • Trustee • New Orleans Public Library • New Orleans, LA 70140 • ALTA

Peplinski Rebecca E. • Children's Librarian • Town of Tonawanda Public Library Brighton Branch • Tonawanda, NY 14150

Peplowski Celia • Mobile, AL 36609 • PLA *Continuing*

Pepper Jennifer G. • Student • Clarion University of Pennsylvania College of Library Science • Clarion, PA 16214

Pepper Larry • AV Service Director • Rolling Prairie Library System • Decatur, IL 62522 • VRT

Peppers Michele M. • South Huntington Public Library • Huntington Station, NY 11746 • ACRL

Perahia Linda S. • Librarian • Queens Borough Public Library • Jamaica, NY 11432

Percaccia Carole A. • New York City, NY 10012

Percelli Irene M. • Special Projects Coordinator • New York Public Library • New York, NY 10018-2788 • ACRL ALCTS

Percival Elaine B. • Media Specialist • Mary P. Douglas Elementary School • Raleigh, NC 27609 • AASL

Percoco Kathy • Reference Librarian • Westfield Memorial Library • Westfield, NJ 07090

Perdreau Michel S. • Athens, OH 45701 • ACRL IRRT

Perdue Charles O. • Kansas City, KS 66117 • LAMA PLA

Perdzock Donna L. • Director • Euclid Public Library • Euclid, OH 44123-2091

Perecman Carol J. • Tavy Stone Fashion Library The Detroit Historical Museum • Detroit, MI 48202

Pereira Asdrubal Belandria • Atizapan de Zaragoza, Mexico

Pereira Frank • Jamica, NY 11413

Pereira Monica A. • Student • University of Wisconsin-Madison School of Library & Information Studies • Madison, WI 53706 • LITA PLA

Perentesis Stephanie C. • Librarian • Michigan State University Libraries • East Lansing, MI 48824-1048

Perer Harriet S. • David Posnack Day School • Plantation, FL 33313 • AASL

Peresich Mary Giles Sr • Catalog Librarian • University of South Alabama • Mobile, AL 36688 • ACRL ALCTS

Peretz Annette • New Hyde Pk, NY 11040 • ACRL

Perez-Snyder Gioconda • Student • University of Pittsburgh School of Library and Information Science • Pittsburgh, PA 15260 • AASL

Perez Alice J. • Reference Specialist • University of California-San Diego Central University Library • La Jolla, CA 92093-0175 • ACRL RASD NMRT

Perez Andres E. • National Sutonomous University of Honduras • Tegucigalpa, Honduras • IRRT

Perez Denise • Assistant Director Tech. Serv. • University of Puerto Rico • Rio Piedras, PR 00931 • LAMA

Perez Estrella • Chief of Selection & Acquisition • Intevep Cit Biblioteca • Caracas 1070-A, Venezuela

Perez Evangelina • Head Librarian • University of Puerto Rico • Rio Piedras, PR 00931 • ACRL

Perez Evelyn • Librarian/Hd Technical Servs. • University of Puerto Rico Aguadilla Regional College • Aguadilla, PR 00604

Perez Ligia D. • Student • University of California Los Angeles Graduate School of Library & Information Science • Los Angeles, CA 90024

Perez Maria L. • Branch Manager • Miami-Dade Public Library Miami Beach Branch • Miami, FL 33139

Perez Sarai • Library Director • Universidad Adventista de las Antillas • Mayaquez, PR 00709-0118 • ACRL ALCTS LITA

Perez-Lopez Rene • Director • Virginia Wesleyan College • Norfolk, VA 23502

Perez-Stable Maria A. • Social Sciences Librarian • Western Michigan University Libraries • Kalamazoo, MI 49008

Perillo Emilie L. • Woodhaven, NY 11421 • ALTA PLA *Life*

Perilloux Rose Marie • Trustee • Saint John the Baptist Parish Library • LaPlace, LA 70068 • ALTA

Peristiani Koula A. • Nicosia, Cyprus • ACRL

Perk Lawrence J. • Ohio State University Libraries • Columbus, OH 43210-1286

Perkins-Rolnick Jane L. • Student, MLS • University of North Carolina Department of Library & Information Studies • Greensboro, NC 27412-5001

Perkins David L. • California State Univ • Northridge, CA 91330

Perkins Denise M. • Librarian • Owen County Elementary School • Owenton, KY 40359 • AASL LITA

Perkins Edna M. • Trustee • Las Vegas-Clark County Library District • Las Vegas, NV 89101 • ALTA

Perkins Gay H. Dr. • Business Reference Librarian • Western Kentucky University Helm-Cravens Library • Bowling Green, KY 42101

Perkins Helen • Evanston, IL 60204 • ACRL RASD *Continuing*

Perkins Jill T. • Assistant Librarian • State University of New York Bartle Library • Binghamton, NY 13902-6012

Perkins Leon • Temple, TX 76503-0089

Perkins Linda A. • Children's Librarian • Berkeley Public Library • Berkeley, CA 94704 • ALSC LAMA PLA

Perkins Linda Hall • Media Specialist • Kenwood Elementary School • Louisville, KY 40214

Perkins Michael J. • Business Librarian • San Diego State University Library • San Diego, CA 92182-0511 • ACRL RASD LIRT

Perkins Priscilla L. • Head of Technical Services • Alma College • Alma, MI 48801 • ALCTS

Perkins Roxanne R. • Senior Librarian • Palo Alto City Library Downtown Branch • Palo Alto, CA 94301 • RASD IFRT VRT

Perkins Ruth M. • Student • River Bluffs Regional Library • Saint Joseph, MO 64501 • ALCTS PLA

Perkins Sandra A. • Librarian • Okinawa Christian School • Okinawa 901-21, Japan

Perkis Barbara L. • Assistant Director • Illinois Regional Library for The Blind & Physically Handicapped • Chicago, IL 60608 • ASCLA *Life*

Perkus Paul C. • Librarian • City University of New York • New York, NY 10021 • ACRL

Perla Carole • Librarian (K-8) • Uxbridge Public Schools Whiten Middle School • Uxbridge, MA 01569 • AASL

Perlee Gail M. • Librarian III • Phoenix Public Library Ocotillo Branch • Phoenix, AZ 85041 • PLA

Perlett Patricia J. • Mendham Township Middle School • Brookside, NJ 07926

Perlman-Stites Janice • Director • Seton Medical Center Library • Daly City, CA 94015

Perlman Carol W. • Wilmette, IL 60091

Perloff Evelyn • Director • Behavioral Measurement Database • Pittsburgh, PA 15232-0787 • ACRL

Perlow Mitchell L. • Director • Millis Public Library • Millis, MA 02054

Perlstein Adele A. • Lindenhurst, NY 11757-3534 • PLA RASD *Continuing*

Perlungher Jane R. • Director • Keene Public Library • Keene, NH 03431 • LAMA PLA *Life*

Permahos Susan L. • Assistant Director • Essex-Hudson Regional Library Cooperative • Orange, NJ 07050

Pernice Jeanne • Librarian • Winslow High School Library • Winslow, ME 04902 • AASL

Pernicone Eileen • Florida State University School of Library and Information Studies • Tallahassee, FL 32306-2048

Pernicone Joyce • Broward County-South Regional Library • Pembroke Pines, FL 33024

Pernotto Kathy • Student • Kent State University School of Library & Information Science • Kent, OH 44242-0001

Pero Marie C. • Library Assistant • Emmanuel College Library • Boston, MA 02115 • IFRT LRRT

Perone Karen L. • Systems Librarian • Canisius College Andrew L. Bouwhuis Library • Buffalo, NY 14208-1098

Perrault Anna H. • Librarian • Louisiana State University Libraries Troy H. Middleton Library • Baton Rouge, LA 70803-3342 • ACRL ALCTS RASD

Perrera Margaret M. • Librarian • Osceola County Library System BVL Library • Kissimmee, FL 34743

Perrier Janice W. • Oak Ridge, NJ 07438 • RASD

Perrin Elizabeth A. • Children's Librarian • Wethersfield Public Library • Wethersfield, CT 06109 • ALSC IFRT

Perrin June M. • Spokane, WA 99207 • LITA

Perrin Margaret B. • John Jay College of Criminal Justice • New York, NY 10019

Perrin Richard E. • Head, Interloans/Online Services • Ferris State University • Big Rapids, MI 49307 • ACRL RASD

Perrine Donna C. • Olivet, MI 49076

Perrine Richard H. • Honolulu, HI 96815 • ACRL RASD *Life*

Perrino John A • Middletown Junior High School Library • Middletown, NY 10940 • AASL

Perritt Patsy H. • Professor • Louisiana State University School of Library & Information Science • Baton Rouge, LA 70803-3290 • AASL ALSC YALSA

Perrone Jeanne Munroe • Branch Supervisor • U S Dept of Energy Library • Washington, DC 20585 • ACRL LITA RASD FLRT

Perroni Mary B. • Reference Librarian • Friendswood Public Library • Friendswood, TX 77546

Perrotta Lorraine M. • Head of Serials • Getty Center Resources Collections • Santa Monica, CA 90401 • ALCTS

Perry-Lube Linda • Northville, MI 48167 • PLA

Perry Andrew H. • Assistant Director • State University of New York at Binghamton Libraries (SUNY) • Binghamton, NY 13902-6012

Perry Annette Lutnesky • Genealogical Consultants Ltd • San Jose, CA 95112

Perry Barbara J. • Librarian • Jefferson Elementary School • Wyandotte, MI 48192

Perry Barbara M. • Librarian • Chaparral Elementary School • Phoenix, AZ 85029 • AASL

Perry Beth I. • Chief, Regional Library • Rhode Island Department of State Library Services • Providence, RI 02903-4222

Perry Betty P. • Library Media Spec • W. E. Cottle Elementary School • Eastchester, NY 10707 • AASL

Perry Beverly A. • Librarian • Park View High School • Sterling, VA 22170 • YALSA

Perry Carole Mrs. • Library/Media Specialist • Jessup Elementary School Library • Jessup, MD 20794 • AASL

Perry Charles E. • East Central University Linscheid Library • Ada, OK 74820-6899 • ACRL

Perry Claudia A. • State University of New York College of Optometry • New York, NY 10010 • ACRL

Perry Debra L. • Branch Manager • Atlanta-Fulton Public Library Anne Wallace Branch • Atlanta, GA 30313 • ALSC SRRT

Perry Douglas F. • Director • Hampton Public Library • Hampton, VA 23669-3596 • LAMA PLA

Perry Edward C. • Northampton, MA 01060 • Continuing

Perry Emma B. • Baton Rouge, LA 70808 • ACRL

Perry Helen Ann • El Toro, CA 92630 • AASL YALSA
Continuing

Perry Helen L. • Library Service Director • Neill Public Library • Pullman, WA 99111 • ALSC PLA IFRT LRRT

Perry Jane M. • School Library Media Specialist • Tooker Avenue School • West Babylon, NY 11704 • AASL

Perry Janet M. • Manager, Higher Edu. Programs • Novell • Walnut Creek, CA 94596 • ACRL LITA

Perry Jimmie M. • Reference Librarian • United States Army Waterways Express Station • Vicksburg, MS 39180-0631

Perry Joan E. • St Clair Shores, MI 48080 • AASL

Perry June L. • Tarentum, PA 15084

Perry Karen M. • Media Coordinator • High Point Central High School • High Point, NC 27262 • AASL ALSC YALSA

Perry L. Stephen • Fayettville, AR 72701-3444 • ACRL

Perry Margaret • University Librarian • Valparaiso University Moellering Memorial Library • Valparaiso, IN 46383 • ACRL RASD   *Life*

Perry Martha Reed • Student • University of Kentucky College of Library & Information Science • Lexington, KY 40506-0391

Perry Michael A. • Children's Librarian • Indianapolis-Marion County Public Library Warren Branch • Indianapolis, IN 46229 • ALSC YALSA

Perry Myrna G. Miss • Catalog Librarian • David Lipscomb University University Library • Nashville, TN 37204-3951 • ACRL ALCTS

Perry Pat • Arapahoe Library District • Littleton, CO 80121 • ALTA

Perry Patricia M. • Children's Librarian II • Cumberland County Public Library and Information Center • Fayetteville, NC 28301 • ALSC

Perry Patricia Malone • Administrative Librarian • Boston Public Library • Boston, MA 02117

Perry Patrick M. • Director • Bovey Public Library • Bovey, MN 55709 • PLA

Perry Paula J. • Chief Catalog Records • Cassidy Cataloging Services • New York, NY 10038 • ALCTS

Perry Rhonda G. • Student • North Carolina Central University • Durham, NC 27707 • AASL EMIERT

Perry Ruth Wilcox • Rancho Palos Verdes, CA 90274 • Continuing

Perry Sarah W. • Library Director • Eagle Pass Public Library • Eagle Pass, TX 78852

Perry Scott T. • Asst Head Acquisitions Dept. • University of Chicago Library • Chicago, IL 60637-1502 • ALCTS

Perry Sharon K. • Assoc Librarian-Public Services • California State University • Fullerton, CA 92634

Perry Sonia S. • Cataloging Librarian • National Institutes of Health Library • Bethesda, MD 20892 • ALCTS

Perry Susan L. • Director, Department Systems Grp • Stanford University • Stanford, CA 94305-6011 • ACRL SRRT

Perry Vivian E. • Branch Manager • Washington County Library Park Grove Branch • Cottage Grove, MN 55016 • ALSC

Perryman Wayne R. • Head Librarian Acquisitions • University of Texas Libraries General Libraries • Austin, TX 78713-7330 • ALCTS

Persak Susan W. • Director • Chester Library • Chester, NJ 07930 • PLA

Perschbacher Virginia Brady • Head, Ref/Adult Services • Chickasaw Library Systems • Ardmore, OK 73401 • PLA SRRT

Pershing Gwen • Reference Librarian • Indiana University • Bloomington, IN 47405

Persico Thomas M. • Student • University of Rhode Island Graduate School of Library & Information Studies • Kingston, RI 02881-0815

Persily Gail L. • Coordinator, Instructional Res • University of California San Francisco Library • San Francisco, CA 94143-0840 • LITA

Persing Robert D. • Belmont, MA 02178 • IFRT

Persky Gail M. • University Librarian • Fogelman Library New School for Social Research • New York, NY 10003 • ALCTS LITA

Persky Terrill A. • Division Head,Library Services • Henry Ford Community College • Dearborn, MI 48128-1495 • PLA

Person Diane • Brooklyn, NY 11201 • AASL YALSA

Person Ellen M. • Director • Baker College Library • Flint, MI 48507 • ACRL LAMA LITA RASD

Person Roland C. • Carbondale, IL 62901 • ACRL

Person Ruth J. • Associate Vice Chancellor • University of Missouri-Saint Louis • St. Louis, MO 63121-4499 • ACRL LAMA   *Life*

Person Wilhelmina E. • Spvr Sr Lib Asst • Newark Public Library • Newark, NJ 07101-0630

Persons Jerry C. • Head System Office • Stanford University • Stanford, CA 94305-6011

Persons Nancy A. • Library Assistant • Deerfield Academy • Deerfield, MA 01342 • ACRL

Persson Dorothy M. • Head,Psychology Library • University of Iowa Libraries • Iowa City, IA 52242-1379 • ACRL LAMA RASD

Persson Lauralyn • Head of Childrens Services • Wilmette Public Library • Wilmette, IL 60091 • ALSC

Persyn Mary G. • Law Librarain • Valparaiso University Law Library • Valparaiso, IN 46383

Perushek D. E. • Associate Dean • University of Tennessee John C. Hodges Library • Knoxville, TN 37996-1000 • ACRL ALCTS IRRT

Pesaitis Patricia A. • Name Authority Ed • H. W. Wilson Company • Bronx, NY 10452 • LITA

Peschel Robyn G. • Student • State University of New York (SUNY) Thomas E. Dewey Graduate Library • Albany, NY 12222

Pesheck Susan D. • Cedarburg, WI 53012 • ALSC

Peskorz Adela Z. • Minneapolis Public Library & Information Center • Minneapolis, MN 55401-1992

Pester Carol R. • Pawnee Elementary School • Omaha, NE 68157 • AASL

Pestun Aloysius J. Fr. • Trustee • St. John Bosco High School Library • Bellflower, CA 90706

Petek Theresa A. • Student • Kent State University School of Library & Information Science • Kent, OH 44242-0001 • LITA RASD

Petelchuk-Lutz Patricia • Librarian • Bergenfield High School Media Center Library • Bergenfield, NJ 07621 • AASL

Peter-Cherneff Brigitte • Director of Student Services • Kwantlen College Libraries • Surrey, BC, V3T 5H8 Canada • ACRL ALCTS LAMA LITA

Peterman Annis • Pinot Point, TX 76258

Peterman Hedra L P • Asst. Children's Coordinator • Free Library of Philadelphia • Philadelphia, PA 19103 • ALSC

Peterman Jacques R. • Hd, Central Lending Library • Free Library of Philadelphia • Philadelphia, PA 19103-1189 • PLA

Peters Andy • Automation Coordinator • Pioneer Library System • Norman, OK 73069

Peters Anne C. • Director of Development • Social Law Library • Boston, MA 02108 • LAMA

Peters Bennie J. • Librarian • Northeast High School • Kansas City, MO 64124 • AASL

Peters Christopher A. • Student • Syracuse University School of Information Studies • Syracuse, NY 13244-4100

Peters Dion P. • Student • Iowa State University Library • Ames, IA 50011-2140

Peters Evelyn G. • New Orleans, LA 70115 • AASL YALSA   *Life*

Peters Helen V. • Director • Sinclair Community College Learning Resource Center • Dayton, OH 45402-1421 • ACRL ALCTS LITA RASD LIRT

Peters Janet E. • Librarian • Hinsdale South High School • Darien, IL 60559 • AASL

Peters Jean R. • Library Journal Cahners Publishing Company • New York, NY 10011 • ACRL RASD

Peters John A. • Government Pubs. Librarian • State Historical Society of Wisconsin • Madison, WI 53706 • GODORT

Peters John E. • Children Librarian • New York Public Library Epiphany Branch • New York, NY 10010 • ALSC

Peters Karla Wayner • Erlangen Elementary School Library Media Center • APO, AE 09066-0005 • AASL

Peters Kenneth M. • Student • Black Hills State University • Spearfish, SD 57799-9548

Peters Marion C. • Head, Chemistry Library • University of California-Los Angeles (UCLA) • Los Angeles, CA 90024-1450 • ACRL

Peters Marjorie A. • Reference Librarian • College of DuPage Learning Resources Center • Glen Ellyn, IL 60137 • ACRL

Peters Mary Jane • Mc Henry, IL 60050-3765 • AASL

Peters Michele • Children's Librarian • Albuquerque Public Library Juan Tabo Branch • Albuquerque, NM 87111 • ALSC

Peters Paul Evan • Coalition for Networked Information • Washington, DC 20036 • LITA

Peters Priscilla S. • Serials/Systems Librarian • California State Univ Stanislaus • Turlock, CA 95380 • ACRL ALCTS LITA GODORT

Peters Sarah G. • Student • University of Rhode Island Graduate School of Library & Information Studies • Kingston, RI 02881-0815

Peters Stephen H. • Cataloger • Northern Michigan University Lydia M. Olson Library • Marquette, MI 49855 • ACRL ALCTS LITA

Peters Steve • Trustee • Tucson Pima Library • Tucson, AZ 85726 • ALTA

Peters Susan L. • Stone Mountain, GA 30083 • ACRL

Peters Thomas A. • Collection Devel Coordinator • Mankato State University Memorial Library • Mankato, MN 56002-8400 • ACRL ALCTS LITA LRRT

Peters Timothy J • Coor. of Library Services • Southwestern Michigan College Fred L. Mathews Library • Dowagiac, MI 49047

Peters Todd C. • Student • University of Texas at Austin Graduate School of Library & Information Sciences • Austin, TX 78712-1276

Peters Victoria M. • Student • University of Arizona Graduate Library School • Tucson, AZ 85721 • LITA PLA IFRT SRRT

Peters William • Trustee • Suffolk Cooperative Library System • Bellport, NY 11713 • ALTA

Peters William T. • Director Emeritus • Grosse Pointe Public Library Central Branch • Grosse Pointe, MI 48236

Peters William Wilson Jr. • Reference Librarian • Coronado Public Library • Coronado, CA 92118

Petersen Barbara • Interarts Ltd. • Cambridge, MA 02138

Petersen Catherine J. • Librarian • Perry Community High School • Perry, IA 50220 • AASL

Petersen Christina M. • Media Specialist • Westhampton Beach Junior High School Library • Westhampton Beach, NY 11978

Petersen Elizabeth J. • Librarian • Spaulding School • Waukegan, IL 60087 • AASL

Petersen Elizabeth M. • Minneapolis, MN 55401-1829

Petersen Elizbeth G • Librarian,Reading Room • National Oceanic & Atomospheric Administration US Government/Dept. of Commerce • Camp Spring, MD 20748

Petersen Everett N. • Chief • Unesco Library & Document Service • Paris, France • Continuing

Petersen Jean L. • Chicago Public Library • Chicago, IL 60605 • SRRT

Petersen Karen • Librarian • Novato High School Library • Novato, CA 94947 • SRRT

Petersen Karla D. • Asst Univ Libn for Tech Serv • Loyola University E.M. Cudahy Memorial Library • Chicago, IL 60626 • ACRL ALCTS

Petersen Lois A. • Northwest Arctic School District • Kotzebue, AK 99752 • AASL YALSA

Petersen Marie T. • Student • University of Maryland College of Library and Information Services • College Park, MD 20742-4345 • ALSC

Petersen Nancy Anne • Cataloger • Portland Public Schools • Portland, OR 97208-3107 • AASL ALCTS LITA IFRT

Petersen Raleigh C. • Reference Librarian • Central Arkansas Library System • Little Rock, AR 72201-4698 • RASD

Petersen Toni • Art & Architecture Thesaurus • Williamstown, MA 01267 • ALCTS LITA

Peterson Agnes F. • Curator • Stanford University • Stanford, CA 94305-6011 • ACRL

Peterson Alma H. • Nathan Hale School • New London, CT 06320

Peterson Andrea • Student • Indiana University School of Library and Information Science • Bloomington, IN 47405

Peterson Anita R. • City of Inglewood Public Library • Inglewood, CA 90301-1771 • PLA

Peterson Betty Jo • Children's Literature Specialist • California State University,Fresno Henry Madden Library • Fresno, CA 93740-0034 • ALSC

Peterson Billie R. • Reference Librarian • Baylor University Moody Memorial Library • Waco, TX 76798-7148 • ACRL LITA RASD LIRT

Peterson Bob D. • Student • University of Wisconsin-Madison School of Library & Information Studies • Madison, WI 53706 • PLA SRRT

Peterson Bonnie J. • Senior Librarian • Denver Public Library Ross-University Hills • Denver, CO 80222

Peterson Carla A. • Yuma, AZ 85364 • AASL YALSA EMIERT NMRT

Peterson Carole M. • Head Librarian • Bowlby Public Library • Waynesburg, PA 15370 • ALSC LAMA PLA IFRT

Peterson Carolyn R. • Head Librarian • Midlothian Public Library • Midlothian, IL 60445

Peterson Carolyn Y. • Reference Librarian • James E. Cheek Learning Resource Center • Raleigh, NC 27611

Peterson Carroll E. • Red Oak, IA 51566

Peterson Charlene E. • Director of Youth Services • Rolling Meadows Library • Rolling Meadows, IL 60008

Peterson Charles B. III • Sr Map Catlgr • Library of Congress • Washington, DC 20541 • MAGERT

Peterson Christina A. • Reference Librarian • San Jose State University Clark Library • San Jose, CA 95192-0028 • ACRL RASD LIRT

Peterson Christine C. • Branch Librarian • Boston Public Library West Roxbury Branch • West Roxbury, MA 02132 • PLA

Peterson Cynthia L. • Head of Cataloging • University of Texas Southwestern Medical Center at Dallas Library • Dallas, TX 75235-9049

Peterson David R. • Senior Librarian • Burbank Public Library • Burbank, CA 91502

Peterson Deb • School Media Specialist • Glenwood High School • Glenwood, IA 51534 • AASL
Peterson Debra D. • Library Director • Sedro Woolley Public Library • Sedro-Wooley, WA 98284 • PLA
Peterson Denise D. • Assistant Director • Wake County Public Library System • Raleigh, NC 27610 • LAMA PLA
Peterson Dennis R. • Director • Palmer College of Chiropractic Palmer Health Science Library • Davenport, IA 52803 • ACRL
Peterson Diane • Marathon County Public Library • Wausau, WI 54401
Peterson Donna L. • Dir. of Lib Media Services • Lincoln Public Schools Library Media Services • Lincoln, NE 68510 • AASL
Peterson Donna Mae • Librarian • Cornelia Elementary School • Edina, MN 55435 • AASL
Peterson Eddy L.S. • Park Village Elementary School • San Antonio, TX 78218-4199 • AASL ALSC
Peterson Elaine • Asst. Dean for Technical Servs. • Montana State University • Bozeman, MT 59717-0332 • ACRL
Peterson Ellen L. • Asst Director-Adm Servs • Free Public Library of Woodbridge • Woodbridge, NJ 07095 • PLA
Peterson Erin K. • Student • University of Arizona Graduate Library School • Tucson, AZ 85721 • PLA
Peterson Esther • Edina, MN 55435 • ACRL ALCTS *Life*
Peterson Fran • K-12 Librarian • Wessington Springs High School • Wessington Springs, SD 57382 • AASL
Peterson Francine • Librarian • M Lynn Bennion School • Salt Lake Cty, UT 84102 • AASL
Peterson Fred M. • University Librarian • Illinois State University Milner Library • Normal, IL 61761-0900 • ACRL ALCTS LAMA CLENE LIRT *Life*
Peterson Gail F. • Branch Coordinator • Palm Beach County Library System • West Palm Beach, FL 33406
Peterson Harold P. • Librarian • Minneapolis Institute of Arts • Minneapolis, MN 55404
Peterson Jane L. • Student • University of Washington Graduate School of Library and Information Science • Seattle, WA 98195
Peterson Jean • Supervising Branch Librarian • New York Public Library Mid-Manhattan Branch • New York, NY 10016 • RASD SORT SRRT
Peterson Jennifer G. • Reference/Adult Serv Librarian • Springfield Public Library • Springfield, OR 97477 • RASD
Peterson Jerry L. • Davie, FL 33314-2556
Peterson Joan C. • Box Elder High School • Brigham City, UT 84302 • AASL
Peterson Julia C. • Manager • Cargill Information Center • Minneapolis, MN 55440 • LAMA
Peterson Julie • Online Computer Library Center (OCLC) • Dublin, OH 43017-3395 • ACRL ALCTS
Peterson June M. • Librarian • Fremont Public Library District • Mundelein, IL 60060 • LAMA PLA
Peterson Kenneth • School Librarian • Oscar Mayer Elementary School • Chicago, IL 60614
Peterson Kenneth G. • Carbondale, IL 62901 • Continuing
Peterson Kim • Head of Technical Services • Saint Louis Public Library • St. Louis, MO 63103-2389 • ALCTS
Peterson Levi S. • Trustee • Weber County Library • Odgen, UT 84401 • ALTA
Peterson Lisa • Santa Cruz, CA 95062-2640 • ALCTS
Peterson Lorna • Assistant Professor • State University of New York at Buffalo • Buffalo, NY 14260 • ACRL RASD
Peterson Marcy F. • Student • University of North Texas School of Library & Information Sciences • Denton, TX 76203 • PLA
Peterson Marilyn Goodrich • Librarian • Rolling Ridge Elem Sch • Olathe, KS 66061 • AASL
Peterson Mary S. • Student • Simmons College Graduate School of Library & Information Science • Boston, MA 02115 • AASL ALSC
Peterson Max P. • Director-Library & Info. Servs. • Utah State University Merrill Library • Logan, UT 84322-3000 • ACRL
Peterson Mildred Othmer • Chicago, IL 60637 • ACRL PLA IRRT *Continuing*
Peterson Miriam E. • Niles, IL 60648 • AASL ALSC *Continuing*
Peterson Nancy E. • Sheridan, WY 82801
Peterson Patricia • Librarian • University of Southern Mississippi McCain Library & Archives • Hattiesburg, MS 39406-5148 • ACRL
Peterson Patricia E. • Director • Central Minnesota Library Exchange • St. Cloud, MN 56301 • ASCLA
Peterson Sandra • Media Director • Hastings Public Schools • Hastings, NE 68901 • AASL
Peterson Sandra K. • Documents Librarian • Yale University Seeley G. Mudd Library • New Haven, CT 06520 • ACRL LAMA RASD GODORT MAGERT
Peterson Sharon G. • Interfaith Medical Center Jewish Hospital Division • Brooklyn, NY 11238
Peterson Sonia M. • Reference Librarian • Cook Memorial Library • Libertyville, IL 60048
Peterson Susan M. • Grafton, MA 01519 • ALCTS
Peterson Susan R. • Newton, NH 03858 • AASL
Peterson Susan V. • Elementary School Librarian • Centennial Elementary • Lawrence, KS 66046 • AASL
Peterson Suzanne • Librarian • John Adams Middle School • Santa Monica, CA 90405 • AASL
Peterson Suzanne M. • Jefferson Middle School • St. Clair Shores, MI 48081
Peterson Thomas J. • Supervisor-Media Services • Sioux Falls Public School District 49-5 • Sioux Falls, SD 57104 • AASL
Peterson Vivian • Fremont, NE 68025 • Continuing
Peterson William D. • Washington, DC 20011
Petersons Metra E. • Chief Ln & Record Mgmt Branch • National Labor Relations Board Library-900 • Washington, DC 20570 • ALCTS
Petherick Susan M. • Lancaster, NY 14086 • PLA YALSA
Petosa Francine • Librarian • Bristol Public Library • Bristol, CT 06010 • ALCTS ALSC ALTA LAMA LITA PLA RASD YALSA IFRT
Petra Ross A. • Student • University of Iowa School of Library & Information Science • Iowa City, IA 52242
Petre Suzanne • Grosse Ile, MI 48138-1023
Petresky Shari L. • Director of Lib & Media Services • Redondo Beach Public Library • Redondo Bch, CA 90277 • LAMA PLA
Petrie Nancy Evalyn • Study Center Supervisor • Tempe Public Library • Tempe, AZ 85282 • LAMA PLA
Petrino Jennifer D. • Administrator Library Services • Mercer County Library Lawrence Branch • Lawrenceville, NJ 08648-4132 • ALCTS ALSC LAMA PLA RASD
Petrisko Adrienne L. • Wayne, PA 19087 • EMIERT
Petro Mary M. • Director • Cherry Valley District Library • Cherry Valley, IL 61016
Petroff Loumona J. • Cataloger • Boston University School of Theology Library • Boston, MA 02215 • ALCTS
Petroskey Melanie T. • Hammond, IN 46323-1742
Petrou Judith E. • Portage, IN 46368-1021 • ALTA
Petrovic Alex • Trustee • Kansas City Public Library • Kansas City, MO 64106 • ALTA
Petrowski Joseph • V-P Marketing • Lawrence Erlnaum Associate • Hillsdale, NJ 07642 • ACRL
Petrowski Mary J. • Assistant Undergrad. Librarian • University of Illinois • Champaign, IL 61801 • ACRL LAMA LITA RASD LIRT
Petrulis Robert C. • Trustee • Cleveland Public Library • Cleveland, OH 44114-1271 • ALTA
Petrus Bonita G. • Systems Analyst • AT&T Network Services • Atlanta, GA 30309
Petruzzi Heidi Ann • Librarian/Indexer • USA Today • Arlington, VA 22209
Petry Bonnie L. • Adjunct Librarian • San Diego City College • San Diego, CA 92101 • ACRL
Petry Sherry L. • Librarian • Atlanta-Fulton Public Library • Atlanta, GA 30303 • RASD
Pettengill George E. • Arlington, VA 22203 • ACRL LAMA LITA *Life*
Pettengill Mary C. • Library Assistant III • University of Texas • Austin, TX 78712-1276
Pettengill Richard • Assistant Professor • Oakland University • Rochester, MI 48309-4401 • ACRL ALCTS LAMA LITA RASD LRRT
Pettengill Susan S. • Freehold, NJ 07728
Petterchak Louis D. • Denver, CO 80203 • SRRT
Petterson Anne H. • Librarian • Stoughton Public Library • Stoughton, MA 02072
Petterson Mary F. • Director Emeritus • Weber County Library • Odgen, UT 84401 • PLA
Pettigrew Sophie Beth • Bodega Bay, CA 94923
Pettit Daille G. • Arlington, VA 22201 • RASD
Pettit Shirley • Program Specialist • Orange County Public Schools • Orlando, FL 32801 • AASL
Pettitt Richard N. Jr. Dr. • Head of Access & Admin Services • Miami University Edgar W. King Library • Oxford, OH 45056 • ACRL
Pettus Eloise S. • Abilene, TX 79606
Petty Jenny B. • Ouachita Baptist University • Arkadelphia, AR 71998-0001 • AASL EMIERT
Petty Johnese G. • Director • Springdale Public Library • Springdale, AR 72764 • ALSC PLA YALSA IFRT
Petty Mary E. • Serials Acquisitions Librarian • Gonzaga University Crosby Library • Spokane, WA 99258
Petty Sue A. Wright • Library Director • Mary Lou Johnson-Hardin County District Library • Kenton, OH 43326 • PLA
Petursdottir Kristin • Director of Public & School Libs • Ministry of Education • Reykjavik, 150, Iceland
Petz Roberta A. • Oak Brook, IL 60521-2350
Petzold Mary E. • Circulation Librarian • Mead Public Library • Sheboygan, WI 53081
Peverada Mary Catherine • Children's Librarian • Portland Public Library • Portland, ME 04101 • ALSC
Peyton Ann F. • Graduate School • Westwood Elementary School Memphis City Schools • Memphis, TN 38109 • AASL
Peyton Janice Lucas • LRC Director • North Harris County College Learning Resources Center • Tomhall, TX 77377-1969 • ACRL
Pezzulo Judy • Computer/Tech. Coordinator • Riverside Beaver County Schools • Ellwood City, PA 16117 • AASL
Pfaff Caryl Anne • Lco Ojibwa College Community Library • Hayward, WI 54843
Pfahl Brabara • Reference Librarian • Ella M. Everhard Public Library • Wadsworth, OH 44281
Pfahler Sandra J. • Associate Director • University of Wisconsin-Madison Memorial Library • Madison, WI 53706 • ACRL LAMA
Pfahlert Jean M. • Rochester Hills Public Library • Rochester, MI 48307
Pfander Jeanne L. • Science Reference Librarian • University of Arizona Library • Tucson, AZ 85721 • ACRL IRRT
Pfannenstiel Cynthia S. • Special Services Librarian • Pittsburg State University Leonard Axe Library • Pittsburg, KS 66762 • RASD
Pfannenstiel William J. • Reference Librarian • Northeastern Oklahoma A&M College Learning Resources Center • Miami, OK 74354 • ACRL IRRT
Pfau Dixie E. • Yakima, WA 98902
Pfeffer Marcia • Library Director • Ardsley Public Library • Ardsley, NY 10502 • PLA
Pfefferle Marilyn E. • Student • Bridgewater State College Program of Library Media Studies • Bridgewater, MA 02324 • AASL
Pfefferle R A. • Jamaica Estates, NY 11432 • Continuing
Pfeifer Dorothy M. • Librarian • La Plata Middle School • Silver City, NM 88061 • AASL
Pfeiffer Carol M. • Assoc. Univ. Ln. for Tech. Servs • University of Virginia Alderman Library • Charlottesville, VA 22903-2498 • ACRL ALCTS LAMA LITA
Pfeiffer Cindy • Librarian • Pittsburg High School • Pittsburg, KS 66762 • AASL
Pfeiffer Elizabeth D. • Student • University of Washington Graduate School of Library and Information Science • Seattle, WA 98195 • SRRT
Pfeiffer Jane • Librarian • Lewes Public Library • Lewes, DE 19958 • PLA
Pfeiffer Janet M. • School Librarian • Fairfax County Public Schools • Alexandria, VA 22307 • AASL
Pfeiffer Robert M. • Circulation • Milwaukee Public Library • Milwaukee, WI 53233 • LAMA PLA
Pfeifle Barbara E. • Student • University of Kentucky College of Library & Information Science • Lexington, KY 40506-0391
Pfeil Barbara • Librarian • Hilltop School • Mendham, NJ 07945 • AASL
Pfeuffer Deborah L. • Seaucus, NJ 07094 • AASL ALSC EMIERT IFRT
Pfingsten Thomas • Portland, OR 97229 • ACRL
Pfister Fred • Professor • University of South Florida Library • Tampa, FL 33620-5600 • AASL
Pfister Jack O. • Trustee • Downers Grove Public Library • Downers Grove, IL 60515 • ALTA
Pflueger Kenneth E. • Director • California Lutheran University Pearson Library • Thousand Oaks, CA 91360 • ACRL ALCTS LAMA LITA RASD EMIERT GODORT IRRT LIRT SRRT
Pflug Amy J. • Redford, MI 48239 • IFRT
Pfluger Anita • Library Media Specialist • Stratford High School • Stratford, CT 06497 • AASL
Pflum Glenn D. • Longmont, CO 80501 • ACRL
Pfohl Daniel M. • Cataloger • 196th Station Hospital • APO, AE 09705 • ALCTS
Pfotenhauer Susan • Saint Charles Public Library • St. Charles, IL 60174
Phalan Mary A. • Asst Dept. Head, Acq Dept. • Free Library of Philadelphia • Philadelphia, PA 19103
Pham Thuan T. Mrs. • La Crosse, WI 54601
Phan Henry • Canberra City, Australia
Phares Abner J. • Librarian • Lockhart Elementary School • St Thomas, VI 00801
Pharis Mary M. • Garfield Heights, OH 44125
Pharo Mollie M. • Librarian • Evansville-Vanderburgh County Oaklyn Branch Library • Evansville, IN 47711 • PLA SRRT
Phebus Ruth A. • Librarian • San Jose Public Library • San Jose, CA 95113
Phelan Carolyn G • Librarian/Book Reviewer • Northbrook Public Library • Northbrook, IL 60062 • ALSC

Phelan Daniel F. • Distance Support Services, Head • Ryerson Polytechnical Institute • Toronto ON, M5B 2K3 Canada • ACRL

Phelan James F. • Controller • H. W. Wilson Company • Bronx, NY 10452 • ACRL ASCLA LAMA LITA RASD

Phelps Catherine • Syracuse University School of Information Studies • Syracuse, NY 13244-4100 • ALCTS

Phelps Charles V. • Student • University of Southern California • University Pk, CA 90089-0182 • ACRL LITA

Phelps Connie L. • Assistant Librarian • University of New Orleans Earl K. Long Library • New Orleans, LA 70148 • ACRL NMRT SRRT

Phelps Doug • Asst. Dir. for Resource Svs. • Vanderbilt University Library • Nashville, TN 37240-0007 • ACRL ALCTS LAMA IRRT   *Life*

Phelps Helen S. • Student • University of North Texas School of Library & Information Sciences • Denton, TX 76203 • AASL LITA RASD

Phelps Holly A. • Cherry Hill, NJ 08034 • ACRL LHRT

Phelps Jennifer • Children's Librarian • H.P. Wright Library • Ventura, CA 93003

Phelps Jonathan O. • Cataloger • University of Massachusetts Medical School Medical Center Library • Worcester, MA 01655 • ACRL ALCTS

Phelps Lena D. • Senior Clerk • D. Stenstrom Elementary • Oviedo, FL 32765 • AASL

Phelps Lillie Mae • Rosenberg, TX 77471

Phelps Nancy • School Media Specialist • Window Rock High School • Fort Defiance, AZ 86504

Phelps Neil R. • Librarian III • Arlington County Department of Libraries • Arlington, VA 22201

Phelps Sandra J. • Regional Reference Office • Iowa City Public Library • Iowa City, IA 52240 • RASD GODORT

Phelps Sharon M. • Children's Librarian • Indiana University School of Library and Information Science • Bloomington, IN 47405 • ALSC

Phelps Thomas C. • National Endowment for Humanities • Washington, DC 20506 • ACRL LAMA PLA LHRT

Phend Steven L. • Materials Manager • Goshen Public Library • Goshen, IN 46526

Phenix Katharine J. • Boulder, CO 80304-1935 • SRRT

Phetteplace Brenda L. • Burnsville, NC 28714 • AASL

Phifer Kenneth O. Dr • Librarian • Montgomery County Department of Public Libraries • Rockville, MD 20850

Phifer Marchita • Reference Librarian • University of South Carolina Coastal Carolina College Kimbel Library • Conway, SC 29526 • LIRT

Philbin Margaret • Media Cataloger • Marywood College Library Learning Resources Center • Scranton, PA 18509

Philbin Paul P. • Reference Librarian • University of Vermont Dana Medical Library • Burlington, VT 05405 • RASD

Philbrick John A. III • Trustee • Free Library of Philadelphia • Philadelphia, PA 19103 • ALTA

Philbrick Linda B. • Trustee • Cumberland County Public Library and Information Center • Fayetteville, NC 28301

Philbrick Marcia • Nemaha Valley High School • Seneca, KS 66538 • AASL

Philibosian Stephen • Assistant Librarian • California State University Hayward Library • Hayward, CA 94542 • ACRL

Philipp Fred A. • President & CEO • Corporate Library Blackwell North America • Lake Oswego, OR 97035 • PLA

Philippi Grace • Austin, TX 78703 • PLA YALSA
                                                        Continuing

Philipps E. Jane • Science Librarian • Queens University • Kingston, ON, K7L 3N6 Canada • ACRL

Philippsen Lola Mae • Collection Development ILL Ln. • Saint Mary's College Cushwa-Leighton Library • Notre Dame, IN 46556 • RASD

Philips Christopher Lee • Chief, Inf. Resources Mgt. • The Washington Post • Washington, DC 20071 • ACRL

Philips Sarah M. • University of North Florida Thomas G. Carpenter Library • Jacksonville, FL 32245-7605

Phillip Cynthia A Jones • Library Media Specialist • Grand Haven Public Schools • Grand Haven, MI 49417 • AASL

Phillips-Hamblett Harriette • Librarian • Lake Region Union High School • Orleans, VT 05860 • AASL

Phillips Ann • Scottsdale, AZ 85253

Phillips Anne • Denver Public Library • Denver, CO 80204-2602

Phillips Beulah V. • Supervisory Librarian • Lackland Air Force Base Officer Training Group Library • Lackland AFB, TX 78236-5000 • AFLRT

Phillips Carl D. • Student • University of Washington Libraries Odegaard Undergraduate Library • Seattle, WA 98195 • ACRL LIRT

Phillips Carol K. • Head of Children's Serv • East Brunswick Public Library • E. Brunswick, NJ 08816 • ALSC PLA

Phillips Carole C. • City Island, NY 10464 • AASL ALSC RASD

Phillips Carroll R. • Adult Services Librarian • Contra Costa County Library Walnut Creek Branch • Walnut Creek, CA 94596

Phillips Casey R. • Reference Librarian • University of Southern Mississippi Cook Memorial Library • Hattiesburg, MS 39406-5053 • ACRL

Phillips Clare • East Perth WA 6004, Australia

Phillips Clarence M. • Librarian I • College of Charleston Robert Scott Small Library • Charleston, SC 29424 • ACRL RASD LIRT LRRT NMRT

Phillips Cynthia • Brighton, MA 02135

Phillips Dennis J. • Library Director • Pennsylvania State Univ • Fogelsville, PA 18051 • ACRL

Phillips Earl Jr. • Librarian • J.W. Lilley School Library • Sicklerville, NJ 08094 • AASL

Phillips Edith • Southfield, MI 48034 • ALCTS IFRT
                                                        Continuing

Phillips Elnora F. • Branch Librarian • Mid-Continent Public Library Raytown Branch • Raytown, MO 64133

Phillips Faye • Special Collections • Louisiana State University Libraries • Baton Rouge, LA 70803 • ACRL

Phillips Gary • Oklahoma Department of Libraries • Oklahoma Cy, OK 73105-3298 • PLA

Phillips Gary L. • Quality Control Engineer • NOTIS Systems, Inc. • Evanston, IL 60201-3622 • LITA SRRT

Phillips Harry M. • Pennsauken, NJ 08110 • PLA SRRT

Phillips Heather • Cataloger • Rice University Fondren Library • Houston, TX 77251-1892

Phillips Jackson Julianne • Manager,Circulation Division • Columbus Metropolitan Library • Columbus, OH 43215 • LAMA PLA

Phillips James M. • Brewster School • Edinburg, TX 78540 • AASL

Phillips Janet A. • Oakland, CA 94610 • ACRL ALCTS GODORT   *Continuing*

Phillips Jocelyn E. • Student • University of Western Ontario School of Library & Information Science • London ON, N6G 1H1 Canada • LITA

Phillips John B. • Documents Librarian • Oklahoma State University Library • Stillwater, OK 74078-0375 • GODORT
                                                        Life

Phillips John C. • Map Librarian • University of Toledo William S. Carlson Library • Toledo, OH 43606-3399 • MAGERT

Phillips Joyce • Trustee • Prince William Public Library System Administrative Support Center • Prince William, VA 22192-5073

Phillips Juanita B. • Librarian • Stella Worley Junior High • Westwego, LA 70094

Phillips Judith Z. • Director • Minerva Public Library • Minerva, OH 44657 • PLA

Phillips June • Library Director • Livingston Public Library • Livingston, MT 59047 • ALSC PLA

Phillips Karen J. • Head Librarian • Brentwood School • Los Angeles, CA 90024

Phillips Kathleen P. • A.D. Harris High School • Panama City, FL 32401 • AASL LIRT

Phillips Linda A. • Reference Coordinator • North Bay Cooperative • Santa Rosa, CA 95404

Phillips Linda L. • Head, Cooperative Info. Servs. • University of Tennessee John C. Hodges Library • Knoxville, TN 37996-1000 • ACRL

Phillips Linda L. • Librarian • University School of Jackson • Jackson, TN 38305

Phillips Linda R. • Young Adult Specialist • Contra Costa County Library • Pleasant Hill, CA 94523 • YALSA IFRT

Phillips Lori J. • Reference Librarian • University of Wyoming Coe Library • Laramie, WY 82071-3334

Phillips Lorna • Asst Chief Ext Servs Dept • Queens Borough Public Library • Jamaica, NY 11432

Phillips LuOuida Vinson • Waco, TX 76710 • Continuing

Phillips M. B. • Springfield, MA 01103 • Continuing

Phillips Mabel Gaye • Director • Christian County Library • Ozark, MO 65721 • LAMA PLA

Phillips Margaret M. • San Francisco, CA 94110

Phillips Marie A. • Manager/Adult Services • Rockford Public Library • Rockford, IL 61101-1061 • RASD

Phillips Marilyn P. • Children's Librarian • University City Public Library • University City, MO 63130 • ALSC

Phillips Marion Miss • Minneapolis, MN 55405 • Continuing

Phillips Martha J. • Asst for Pub Serv Operations • University of Texas Libraries General Libraries • Austin, TX 78713-7330 • ACRL

Phillips Mary • Young Adult Librarian • New City Library • New City, NY 10956 • YALSA

Phillips Melissa K. • Reference Librarian • Seminole County Library System Central Branch • Casselberry, FL 32707 • LITA PLA RASD

Phillips Pat J. • Library Media Coordinator • Columbia School District • Burbank, WA 99323 • AASL

Phillips Patricia A. • Coor of Tech Serv • University of the South Jessie Ball duPont Library • Sewanee, TN 37375-4005 • ALCTS

Phillips Richard F. • Boulder, CO 80306-1851

Phillips Rosalyn M. • Roswell, GA 30076

Phillips Ruth F. • Phoenix, AZ 85016 • ACRL ALCTS
                                                        Continuing

Phillips Ruth H. • Columbus, OH 43215 • Life

Phillips Ruth M. • Berkeley Heights, NJ 07922-2459 • Continuing

Phillips S. Bernadette A. • Librarian • Saint Francis Preparatory School • Fresh Meadows, NY 11365

Phillips Shawn K. • San Francisco, CA 94102

Phillips Susan K. • Asst Dir for Technical Serv • University of Texas Libraries General Libraries • Austin, TX 78713-7330 • ALCTS LITA

Phillips Susan Kay • Assistant Librarian • Ohio University Chillicothe Library • Chillicothe, OH 45601 • ACRL

Phillips Teresa C. • Plano, TX 75025 • AASL

Phillips Thaddeus J. • Library Services Manager • Huntington Beach Library Info. & Cultural Resource Center • Huntington Beach, CA 92648 • LAMA LITA SRRT

Phillips Thelma M. • Fort Worth, TX 76112

Phillips Theresa E. • Bloomington, IN 47401 • ALSC

Phillips Tom • Chicago, IL 60643 • ASCLA

Phillips Vicki W. • Science and Engineering Division • Oklahoma State University Library • Stillwater, OK 74078-0375 • ACRL GODORT

Phillips Virginia • Asst Director Branch Services • University of Texas Libraries General Libraries • Austin, TX 78713-7330 • ACRL RASD   *Life*

Phillips Zeph IV • Senior Research Officer • Australian Trade Commission • Los Angeles, CA 90004

Phillips Zlata F. • Library School Research Assoc. • State University of New York at Albany School of Information Science & Policy • Albany, NY 12222

Phinney Hartley K. Jr. • Chief Librarian • Institute of Paper Science & Technology • Atlanta, GA 30318 • ACRL LAMA

Phinney Jeannette C. • Librarian • Daughters of the Republic of Texas Library at the Alamo • San Antonio, TX 78295-1401

Phinney Mary R. • Director • Morrill Memorial Library • Norwood, MA 02062

Phinney Nadine L. • Media Librarian • Truckee Meadows Community College Learning Resources Center • Reno, NV 89512

Phipps Maria E. • President • M.E. Phipps & Associates Inc Library & Information Consultants • Guelph ON, N1H 4J7 Canada

Phipps Michael • Director • Omaha Public Library • Omaha, NE 68102 • PLA

Phipps Shelley E. • Asst Univ Ln for Br Serv • University of Arizona Library • Tucson, AZ 85721 • ACRL LAMA

Phoenix Kathie A. • Oceanside, CA 92056

Phornsuwan Saangsri • Ramkhamhaeng University Department of Library Science Faculty of Humanites • Bangkok 10240, Thailand

PiRoman Rafael • Trustee • Queens Borough Public Library • Jamaica, NY 11432 • ALTA PLA

Piala Vanessa J. • Humanities Adminstrator • National Endowment for Humanities • Washington, DC 20506 • ALCTS

Piane Mimi • Media Specialist • The Stanley Clark School Media Center • South Bend, IN 46614 • AASL

Pianko Trudy M. • Director • South River Public Library • South River, NJ 08882 • PLA

Piascik Jeanne M. • Student • Kent State University School of Library & Information Science • Kent, OH 44242-0001

Piatz Carolyn R. • Cataloger • Lewis & Clark College Aubrey R. Watzek Library • Portland, OR 97219

Piazza Julia E. • School Library Media Spec. • Llewellyn Elementary School • Portland, OR 97202 • AASL

Picard Gail • Atlanta-Fulton Public Library Cleveland Avenue Branch • Atlanta, GA 30315 • PLA

Picardini Grace H. • Ripley, NY 14775 • Continuing

Piccininni James C. • Library Director • University of Saint Thomas • Houston, TX 77006 • ACRL

Piccinino Rocco • Science Libraran • Smith College William Allan Neilson Library • Northampton, MA 01063 • ACRL LAMA

Picha Charlotte G. • Branch Supervisor • Lorain Public Library Avon Branch • Avon, OH 44011 • PLA

Piche Patricia A. • Boulder, CO 80304-1906 • ACRL ALCTS ALSC

Picheloup Charlene R. • Librarian • Loreauville High School • Loreauville, LA 70552 • AASL

Pichette William H. • Professor/Chairman • Sam Houston State University Department of Library Science • Huntsville, TX 77341-2236 • AASL

Pick Sue • Hamilton Public Library • Hamilton, New Zealand • PLA

Pickard Patricia W. • Library Media Specialist • Sequoyah Junior High School • Doraville, GA 30340 • AASL

Pickard Sallie H. • Jacksonville Public Library Beaches Branch • Neptune Beach, FL 32266

Pickell Barbara J. • Library Director • Lompoc Public Library • Lompoc, CA 93436 • PLA IFRT

Picken Gilbert G. • Librarian • Martin County Library • Fairmont, MN 56031

Pickenpaugh Treva A. • Branch Manager • Dayton & Montgomery County Public Library Huber Heights Branch • Huber Heights, OH 45424 • ALSC

Pickens Lynne R. • Youth Librarian • Atlanta-Fulton Public Library • Atlanta, GA 30303 • ALSC PLA

Pickens Terry L. • Assistant Director • Mesa County Public Library • Grand Junction, CO 81502 • PLA

Pickering James H. • Asheville, NC 28803 • Continuing

Pickering Margaret A. • Manager,Lib Personnel & Payroll • University of California-Los Angeles (UCLA) • Los Angeles, CA 90024-1450 • ACRL LAMA

Pickering Sharon S. • Trustee • Crestwood Public Library District • Crestwood, IL 60445

Pickett Ellen • Director • Liberty Municipal Library • Liberty, TX 77575-4796 • PLA

Pickett Joanne H. • Librarian • Sabine Parish Library • Many, LA 71449 • ALTA PLA

Pickett Mary Joyce • Director of Library Services • Illinois Benedictine College Lownik Library • Lisle, IL 60532 • ACRL ALCTS LAMA LITA

Pickett Sean A. • Student • University of California-Berkeley University Library • Berkeley, CA 94720 • LITA

Pickette Charles B. • Burke, VA 22015 • LITA

Pickthorn Barbara L. • Asst. Director of Public Servs. • Cameron University • Lawton, OK 73505 • ACRL

Pickworth Hannah S. • Baltimore, MD 21210 • AASL

Pidgeon Alice • Coordinator of Technical Servs • Pace University School of Law Library • White Plains, NY 10603-3796

Piehl Ann R. • Whitefish Bay Public Library • Milwaukee, WI 53217 • ALSC

Piehl Kathleen K. • Reference/Education Librarian • Mankato State University Memorial Library • Mankato, MN 56002-8400

Piele Linda J. • Associate Director • Univ of Wisconsin-Parkside L Library • Kenosha, WI 53141 • ACRL IRRT

Pien Shui-Hsien • Acquisitions/Serials Librarian • Mansfield University Library • Mansfield, PA 16933 • ACRL

Piepenburg Scott R. • Follett Software Company • McHenry, IL 60050-5589 • ALCTS

Pieper Aurora A. • Reference Librarian • Chippewa Falls Public Library • Chippewa Falls, WI 54729 • IFRT NMRT

Piepho Patricia E. • Park Ridge, IL 60068

Pierce Alice F. • Coordinator of Children's Serv. • Lexington Public Library • Lexington, KY 40507

Pierce Anton R. • SNR Auto Plan Spec • Library of Congress • Washington, DC 20541 • LITA

Pierce Connie M. • Library Director • Signal Mountain Public Library • Signal Mt., TN 37377 • LITA PLA

Pierce Constance W. • Cataloging Editor • Library of Congress • Washington, DC 20541

Pierce Cynthia • Chevy Chase, MD 20815

Pierce Darlene M. • Librarian • Northern Michigan University Lydia M. Olson Library • Marquette, MI 49855 • GODORT IFRT

Pierce Elizabeth • Student • Kent State University School of Library & Information Science • Kent, OH 44242-0001

Pierce Frances B. • Librarian • Grossmont College Library • El Cajon, CA 92020 • ACRL ALCTS   *Life*

Pierce Ilona Dr. • Jordan School District • Sandy, UT 84070 • AASL

Pierce Janell D. • Student • University of Arizona Graduate Library School • Tucson, AZ 85721 • RASD IFRT SRRT

Pierce Jeannette E. • Student • University of Illinois Graduate School of Library and Information Science • Urbana, IL 61801 • SRRT

Pierce JoAnne B. • Director • Simsbury Public Library • Simsbury, CT 06070 • PLA

Pierce Linda I. • Gonzaga University Crosby Library • Spokane, WA 99258 • ACRL SRRT

Pierce Marjorie W. • Brewster, MA 02631

Pierce Mary Edith • San Antonio, TX 78218-6105 • ALCTS   *Life*

Pierce Mildred • Hawthorne, NV 89415 • AASL RASD *Life*

Pierce Nancy S. • Director • Nottoway County Library • Nottoway, VA 23955 • PLA

Pierce Patricia J. M.L.S. • Library Automation Products, Inc. • San Diego, CA 92126

Pierce Ranae • Librarian • Salt Lake City Public Library Chapman Branch • Salt Lake City, UT 84104 • PLA YALSA

Pierce Renee • Genealogy Collection Manager • Miami-Dade Public Library System • Miami, FL 33130-1504 • RASD

Pierce Sally K. • Librarian • Jackson Public Library • Jackson, MO 63755 • PLA

Pierce Samuel • Trustee • Bucks County Free Library • Doylestown, PA 18901 • ALTA

Pierce Sommers • Manager of Technical Services • American Bankers Association Library • Washington, DC 20036 • LITA

Pierce Suzanne W. • Trustee • Akron-Summit County Public Library • Akron, OH 44326-0001 • ALTA

Pierce Sydney J. • University of Oklahoma School of Library & Information Studies • Norman, OK 73019 • RASD LRRT

Pierce William S. • State College, PA 16801 • LAMA

Pierce William S. • Student • University of Pittsburgh School of Library and Information Science • Pittsburgh, PA 15260

Pieri Nancy L. • Director • Lee Memorial Library • Allendale, NJ 07401 • PLA

Pierik Marilyn A. • Reference Librarian • Mount Hood Community College • Gresham, OR 97030 • ACRL

Piernan Nancy K. • Public Services Librarian • University of Detroit-Mercy Main Library • Detroit, MI 48221 • ACRL

Pierre-Lys Sandra • Exhibits Assistant • Association of American University Presses • New York, NY 10012

Pierre Zenata W. • Librarian • Madison High Sch Lib • Portland, OR 97220

Pierret Linda • Youth Librarian-Part Time • Tippecanoe County Public Library • Lafayette, IN 47901

Pierschalla Linda A • Information/Reference Ln. • Illinois Benedictine College Lownik Library • Lisle, IL 60532 • RASD

Piersma Mary L. • Chair, Dept of Education • University of Alabama in Huntsville Library • Huntsville, AL 35899 • AASL

Piersol Lawrence L. • Trustee • Sioux Falls Public Library • Sioux Falls, SD 57102

Pierson Betty • Manager Technical Services • Lexington Public Library • Lexington, KY 40507 • ALCTS

Pierson Brenda W. • Indianapolis, IN 46260

Pierson Diana • Director • Mitchell Public Library • Hillsdale, MI 49242

Pierson Mary K. • Clarmont, CA 91711 • ALSC

Pierson Robert M. • Santa Fe, NM 87505 • ACRL ALCTS RASD   *Life*

Pierson Steve • Library Director • Covina Public Library • Covina, CA 91722 • PLA

Piesco Eileen • W. Plam Beach, FL 33415 • ALSC

Pieszak Anne E. • Prescott Unified School Dist. #1 • Prescott, AZ 86303

Pietila Linda • Librarian • Mountain View High School • Bend, OR 97701 • AASL

Pietrala Marcia • New Alexandria, PA 15670 • ACRL

Pietris Mary K Dewees • Chief, Off for Subj Catlg Policy • Library of Congress • Washington, DC 20541 • ALCTS LITA   *Life*

Pietrobono Judy M. • Reference Librarian • South Brunswick Public Library • Monmouth Junction, NJ 08852 • RASD YALSA

Pietrow Arthur • Trustee • East Islip Public Library • East Islip, NY 11730-2896

Pietsch Laura L. • Bellevue, NE 68005 • AASL

Pietsch Sara R. • Student • University of Texas at Austin Graduate School of Library & Information Sciences • Austin, TX 78712-1276 • AASL

Piette Mary • Logan, UT 84321-4722 • ACRL RASD IFRT LIRT

Piety Jean Z. • Head, Science & Technology Dept • Cleveland Public Library • Cleveland, OH 44114-1271 • PLA RASD

Piety John S. • Director • John Carroll University Grasselli Library • University Heights, OH 44118 • ACRL

Pietzak Stephen D. • Pittsburgh, PA 15210

Piggford Roland R. • Shrewsbury, MA 01545

Pignatora Jeffrey J. • Student • State University of New York (SUNY) School of Information & Library Studies • Buffalo, NY 14260

Pike Karen Measell Mrs. • Wilson, NC 27893 • AASL

Pike Lee E. • Head, Business Library • University of Alabama • Tuscaloosa, AL 35487-0266 • ACRL RASD

Pike Martha L. • Technical Services Librarian • Woodbury University Library • Burbank, CA 91510-7846

Pike Nancy M. • Head Librarian • Venice Area Public Library • Venice, FL 34285 • LAMA PLA IFRT

Pike Susan • Director • Matawan-Aberdeen Public Library • Matawan, NJ 07747 • LAMA PLA SORT

Pike Susan S. • Information Services Manager • Riverside Public Library • Riverside, IL 60546 • RASD

Pikul Diane M. • Assistant Director for P. S. • Norwalk Community College Learning Resource Center • Norwalk, CT 06854-1655 • ACRL

Pikul Marie T. • Trustee • Cicero Public Library • Cicero, IL 60650 • ALTA PLA

Pilachowski David M. • Denison University Library • Granville, OH 43023 • ACRL RASD

Pilaroscia Margaret M. • Rochester, NY 14625

Pilarski James P. • Director, Information Services • United States Army Corps of Engineers • Chicago, IL 60606-7206 • IFRT SRRT

Pilch Monica M. • Trustee • McCook Public Library • McCook, IL 60525

Pilecky-Dekajlo Adriana M. • Center for Research Libraries • Chicago, IL 60637 • ALCTS

Pilette Roberta S. • New York Historical Society Library • New York, NY 10024-5194 • ACRL

Pilgrim Artis • Librarian III • Chicago Public Library • Chicago, IL 60605 • PLA

Pilkington Laura A. • Student • State University of New York at Albany School of Information Science & Policy • Albany, NY 12222 • SRRT

Pillado Elvia • Assistant Librarian • Houston Public Library Tuttle Branch • Houston, TX 77020

Pillans Judith H. • Media Specialist • Riverside Presbyterian Day School • Jacksonville, FL 32204 • AASL ALSC

Pillard Vicki • Marysville Jr/Sr High School • Marysville, KS 66508

Pillet Sylvaine M. • Paris 75017, France

Pilling Stella • British Library Document Supply Center • West Yorkshire, England

Pillow Martha S. • Roanoke, VA 24019

Pillow Robert E. • User Services Librarian • Virginia Polytechnic Institute and State University, Newman Library • Blacksburg, VA 24061-0434 • ACRL LAMA

Pillow Robert G. • Technical Services Librarian • University of Saint Thomas • St. Paul, MN 55105 • ALCTS

Pillsbury Penelope D. • Director • Brownell Library • Essex Junction, VT 05452

Piloto Maribel • Miami, FL 33135 • IFRT SRRT

Pilsitz June • Newport Beach Public Library • Newport Beach, CA 92660 • RASD

Pilvin Barbara J. • Social Science & History Dept. • Free Library of Philadelphia • Philadelphia, PA 19103 • ACRL RASD LHRT LIRT

Pilzer Cecily R. • Children's Librarian I • Montgomery County Public Library Silver Spring Branch • Silver Spring, MD 20910-4390 • ALSC PLA YALSA IFRT

Pinamont James C. • Student • Emporia State University Emporia in the Rockies • Denver, CO 80204

Pinches Mary F. • Assoc Prof Emer & Ln • Case Western Reserve Univ Freiberger Library • Cleveland, OH 44106-7151 • Life

Pinckard Mara • Head, Science Reference • Arizona State University Libraries • Tempe, AZ 85287-1006 • ACRL

Pinckney Cathey L. • Director Library • Saint Johns Hospital & Health Center • Santa Monica, CA 90404 • ERT

Pinckney Kay • Atlanta Journal Constitution • Atlanta, GA 30302 • RASD GODORT

Pinckney Louise S. • Librarian • Hammond Lower School • Columbia, SC 29209 • PLA

Pincock Rulon D. Mr. • Santa Ana, CA 92705 • AASL YALSA   *Life*

Pincus Joan Mrs. • Trustee • Yonkers Public Library • Yonkers, NY 10701 • ALTA

Pincus Lena M. • Librarian • South California Psychoanalytic Institute F. Alexander Library • Beverly Hills, CA 90211 • ASCLA

Pindell Alvetta S. • Coordinator, Info. Programs • National Agricultural Library • Beltsville, MD 20705 • RASD

Pindell Nancy • Franklin School Library • Keene, NH 03431 • AASL

Pinder Jane L. • Student • State University of New York at Albany School of Information Science & Policy • Albany, NY 12222 • LITA PLA

Pinder Jo Ann • Director • Lake Lanier Regional Library Lawrenceville Branch • Lawrenceville, GA 30245 • LAMA PLA CLENE

Pine Nancy M. • Systems Librarian • Barry University Library • Miami Shores, FL 33161

Pine Susan J. • The New York Public Library • New York, NY 10016 • ALSC

Pineda Conchita J. • Assistant Vice President • Citibank, N.A. • New York, NY 10043

Pingel Carol Jean • Librarian • Hamilton High School • Milwaukee, WI 53220 • AASL YALSA

Pingitore Janet • Pittsburgh, PA 15217

Pings Joan Gilmore • Plant City, FL 33567 • ALCTS RASD   *Life*

Pings Vern M. Mr. • Plant City, FL 33567 • ACRL LITA *Life*

Pini Paula • Reference Librarian • University of New Haven Marvin K Peterson Library • West Haven, CT 06516

Pinkerman Loren L. • Reference Librarian • Wofford College Sandor Teszler Library • Spartanburg, SC 29303-3663 • ACRL ALCTS

Pinkerton Marjorie J. • Library Director • William Woods College Dulany Memorial Library • Fulton, MO 65251 • ACRL

Pinkett Sylvia D. • Denton, MD 21629

Pinkham Eleanor H. • Head Librarian • Kalamazoo College Library • Kalamazoo, MI 49007-3285 • ACRL

Pinkowski Patricia E. • Alzheimer's Association • Chicago, IL 60611 • LITA IRRT

Pinkston Beverly J. • Head Branch Librarian • Toledo-Lucas County Public Library Sylvania Branch • Sylvania, OH 43560 • PLA RASD

Pinkston Dawn B. • Librarian • Cypress Springs Elementary School • Ruston, LA 71270 • AASL

Pinnell-Stephens June A. • Collection Development Libn • Fairbanks North Star Borough Public Library & Regional Center-Noel Wien Library • Fairbanks, AK 99701 • ALCTS IFRT

Pinnell Elizabeth J. • Computer Sciences Corporation • U.S. Enviromental Protection Agency ERL Library • Gulf Breeze, FL 32561 • ALCTS LITA RASD GODORT

Pinnell Julie M. • Librarian • Johnson County Community College Library • Overland Park, KS 66210 • ACRL LITA

Pinsmore Mary A. • Lakeland, FL 33803

Pinson Annie Katherine • Jackson, MS 39209

Pinson Leah F. • Philadelphia, PA 19103 • Continuing

Pinter Aimee • Reference/Govt. Doc. • Franklin-Johnson County Public Library • Franklin, IN 46131 • RASD GODORT

Pinto David E. • Director • Mercyhurst College Hammermill Library • Erie, PA 16546 • ACRL

Pinto Trudy • Trustee • Livonia Public Library • Livonia, MI 48154-3045 • ALTA

Pintozzi Chestalene • Reference Librarian • University of Arizona Library • Tucson, AZ 85721 • ACRL RASD LIRT

Pinzelik Barbara P. • Int. Assoc. Dean for Pub Svs • Purdue University Libraries • West Lafayette, IN 47907-1530 • ACRL

Pionessa Geraldine F. • Microforms Librarian, C118 • University of Arizona Library • Tucson, AZ 85721 • ACRL

Piotrowicz Lynn M. • Student • University of Pittsburgh School of Library and Information Science • Pittsburgh, PA 15260 • ACRL RASD

Piotter Ginger • Librarian • The Community School • Ketchum, ID 83340 • AASL

Piper Dave • Head of Microcomputer Services • University of Arizona Arizona Health Sciences Center Library • Tucson, AZ 85724 • LITA

Piper Elizabeth Martin • Glen Arm, MD 21057 • AASL

Piper James J. • Head Librarian • Pioneer High School • Ann Arbor, MI 48103

Piper Michael C. • Executive Director • Kansas Library Network Board • Topeka, KS 66612

Piper Virginia M. • Library Media Specialist • Cyril Public Schools • Cyril, OK 73029 • AASL ALSC LAMA YALSA EMIERT IFRT NMRT

Piper Wayne W. • Mgr. Automation & Technical Serv • Toledo-Lucas County Public Library • Toledo, OH 43624

Pipkin Joyce J. • Cataloger • Laughlin Library • Laughlin, NV 89028-2225

Pipkin Pamela N. • Kilgore, TX 75662

Pippin Karma • Doctoral Student • University of California-Berkeley School of Library & Information Studies • Berkeley, CA 94720 • ACRL

Piquet Jeanette Moore • Assistant Manager • Saint Louis Public Library Buder Branch • St. Louis, MO 63109 • PLA ERT

Piquett Charles D. • Corvallis, OR 97330-3279

Pires Priscilla • Adult Services Librarian • Fondulac District Library • East Peoria, IL 61611

Pirie Suzanne L. • Lake Zurich, IL 60047

Pirkle Lauren S. • Adult Reference Librarian • Champaign Public Library & Information Center • Champaign, IL 61820-5193 • PLA

Pirodsky Nancy E. • Librarian II Children's Dept Hd • Garden City Public Library • Garden City, NY 11530

Pirog Karen • Periodicals Dept. Supervisor • Springfield City Library • Springfield, MA 01103

Pirone Mary Ann • Hd. Reader's Advisory Young Ad. • Aurora Public Library • Aurora, IL 60505-4299 • YALSA

Pirsch Carol McBride • Trustee • Omaha Public Library • Omaha, NE 68102 • ALTA

Pirtle Constance P. • Milwaukee Public Library • Milwaukee, WI 53233 • ALCTS

Pirtle Cynthia Pulliam • Trustee • Pirtle Gallery • Tyler, TX 75701 • ALTA

Pisa Maria G. • Asst Director Policy & Planning • United States Department of Agriculture National Agricultural Library • Beltsville, MD 20705-2351 • ACRL FLRT

Pisani Assunta S. • Assoc. Ln. for Clln. Devel. • Harvard College Library Widener Memorial Library • Cambridge, MA 02138 • ACRL ALCTS

Pisano Silvia L. • Auxiliar Procesos Tecnicos • Argentina UBA Facultad de Arquitectura-Bca. • Capital Federal, Argentina • LAMA RASD IRRT

Pisano Vivian M. • Supv Ln Technical Services • Oakland Public Library • Oakland, CA 94612 • ALCTS LITA RASD

Piscitelli Aimee C. • Documents/Microtext Librarian • Texas A & M University Sterling C. Evans Library • College Station, TX 77843-5000 • ACRL GODORT IFRT

Piscitelli Felicia A. • Audio-Visual Cataloger • Texas A & M University • College Station, TX 77843-5000 • ALCTS MAGERT

Piscuskas Barbara A. • Director • Lawrenceville School • Lawrenceville, NJ 08648

Piselli Kathy • Environmental Protection Agency Records Center/LA I • Atlanta, GA 30365 • ALCTS GODORT

Piserchia Susan M. • Ocean Grove, NJ 07756 • NMRT

Pisha Louis J. • Long Island University B. Davis Schwartz Memorial Library • Greenvale, NY 11548 • LHRT

Pitalo Tamalane B. • Nichols Middle School • Biloxi, MS 39530

Pitard Susan M. • Student • University of San Diego • San Diego, CA 92110 • LHRT NMRT SRRT

Pitcher Ellen M. • Anderson, IN 46012

Pitcher John B. • Bloomsburg University Harvey A. Andruss Library • Bloomsburg, PA 17815 • LITA

Pitchford Martha • Tech. Servs./Automation Ln. • Addison Public Library • Addison, IL 60101-2499 • ALCTS LITA

Pitel Vonna • Director • Cedarburg High School • Cedarburg, WI 53012 • AASL

Pitell Lynetta S. • Saint Helens Public Library • St. Helens, OR 97051 • PLA

Piternick George • Prof Emeritus • University of British Columbia Library Archives & Information Studies • Vancouver BC, Canada • ACRL RASD *Life*

Pitet Lynn T. • Student • University of Findlay Shafer Library • Findlay, OH 45840

Pitkin Gary M. • Director of University Libraries • University of Northern Colorado James A. Michener Library • Greeley, CO 80639 • ACRL ALCTS LAMA

Pitkin Patricia A. • Library Director • Rochester Institute of Technology • Rochester, NY 14623 • LITA

Pitman Randy • Librarian • Kitsap Regional Library • Bremerton, WA 98310 • VRT

Pitman Ronnie A. • Librarian • North Carolina State University D. H. Hill Library • Raleigh, NC 27695-7111

Pitney Barbara • Library Adminstrator • Plainfield Public Library District • Plainfield, IL 60544 • PLA

Pitschmann Louis A. • University of Wisconsin-Madison Memorial Library • Madison, WI 53706 • ACRL ALCTS

Pitsikoulis Toni V. • Children's Department Manager • Charlotte & Mecklenburg Public Library Morrison Regional Library • Charlotte, NC 28211 • ALSC

Pitt Janine E. • Westlake Village, CA 91361 • PLA

Pitt Judith Mrs. • Librarian • Mount Saint Agnes Academy • Hamilton HMDX, Bermuda • AASL

Pitt Marcia • Media Specialist • Avocado Elementary School • Homestead, FL 33030 • AASL

Pitt Mary V • Savannah, GA 31419

Pitti Daniel V. • University California-Berkeley • Berkeley, CA 94720 • ALCTS LITA

Pittman Ann • Reference/Interlibrary Loan Ln. • Fairbanks North Star Borough Public Library & Regional Center-Noel Wien Library • Fairbanks, AK 99701 • PLA

Pittman Dorothy E. • Coodinator of Adult Services • Harford County Library • Ben Camp, MD 21017 • PLA RASD

Pittman Margaret R. • Lake Orion, MI 48362

Pittman Wanda M. • Cataloger • University of Chicago Library • Chicago, IL 60637-1502 • ACRL ALCTS

Pitto Mark W. • Bibl. Database Librarian • Clemson University R. M. Cooper Library • Clemson, SC 29634-3001 • ALCTS NMRT

Pitts Clara D. • Mingo School • Tulsa, OK 74115

Pitts Elizabeth • Student • University of Washington Graduate School of Library and Information Science • Seattle, WA 98195 • EMIERT IFRT SRRT

Pitts Elizabeth M. • Media Coor • David D. Jones Elementary School • Greensboro, NC 27406 • AASL ALSC

Pitts Jayne M. • School Librarian (K-5) • Northern Elementary School Scott County • Georgetown, KY 40324 • ALSC

Pitts Judy M. • Student • Florida State University School of Library and Information Studies • Tallahassee, FL 32306-2048 • AASL YALSA LIRT LRRT

Pitts Loretta J. • Collection Mgr., Librarian • University of Houston Law Libraries • Houston, TX 77204-6390 • AASL

Pitts Roberta L. • Head, Personnel Operations • Texas A & M University Sterling C. Evans Library • College Station, TX 77843-5000 • LAMA

Pittsley Kate A. • Asst. Librarian-Reference • University of Michigan Kresge Business Adm Library • Ann Arbor, MI 48109-1234 • RASD IFRT SRRT

Pittson Cynthia • Assoc Ed • H. W. Wilson Company • Bronx, NY 10452 • LITA

Pixley Colleen A. • Student • University of Arizona Graduate Library School • Tucson, AZ 85721 • IFRT SRRT

Pixley Karen M. • Librarian • Auburndale Public Library • Auburndale, FL 33823

Pizzo-Cloutier Daria • Librarian I Youth Services • Lee County Library System • Fort Myers, FL 33901

Pizzuto Heather L. • Orange County Public Library San Clemente Branch • San Clemente, CA 92672 • PLA

Pla Ricardo E. • Student • Queens College Grad Sch of Lib & Inf Studies • Flushing, NY 11367 • SRRT

Place Philip A. • Director • Harford County Library • Belcamp, MD 21017 • LAMA PLA *Life*

Pladera Lucretia • Library District Administrator • Hilo Public Library • Hilo, HI 96720 • LAMA PLA

Plaine Anne P. • Student • Syracuse University School of Information Studies • Syracuse, NY 13244-4100

Plair Norman V. • Coordinator • Dayton & Montgomery County Public Library • Dayton, OH 45402-2103 • PLA

Plaisted Barbara • Elementary Librarian • King Street School Library • Port Chester, NY 10573 • AASL ALSC *Life*

Plaisted Glen L. • Director • Northeast Kansas Library System • Shawnee Mission, KS 66204-2217 • PLA

Planas Hortensia M. • Librarian II • Miami-Dade Public Library System • Miami, FL 33130-1504

Plank David M. • Prof Indexer • H. W. Wilson Company • Bronx, NY 10452

Plank Marietta A. • Assoc Dir for Technical Serv. • University of Maryland Libraries • College Park, MD 20742 • ALCTS LITA

Plante Jean Mr. • Conseiller • Federation des cegeps • Montreal PQ, H2P 1E7 Canada • LAMA LITA

Planton Stanley P. • Head Librarian • Ohio University Chillicothe Library • Chillicothe, OH 45601

Plantz Elizabeth J. • African Cataloger • Boston College • Chestnut Hill, MA 02167 • ACRL ALCTS

Plaso Kathy A. • Sipesville, PA 15561

Platoff Paula L. • Studio City, CA 91604

Platt Carol • Assistant • Queens Borough Public Library • Jamaica, NY 11432 • ALSC ASCLA

Platt J.T. • Trustee • Calcasieu Parish Public Library • Lake Charles, LA 70601 • LAMA

Platt John H. Jr. • Executive Director • Masonic Library & Museum of Pennsylvania • Philadelphia, PA 19107-2520 • ACRL

Platt Judith • Catlg Ln • Federal Reserve Bank of Philadelphia • Philadelphia, PA 19106 • ACRL

Platt Mary E. • Asst. Public Servs. Librarian • Kennesaw State College • Marietta, GA 30061 • ACRL

Platt Mary L. • Reference Librarian • Chappaqua Library • Chappaqua, NY 10514

Platt Susan • Calgary Public Library • Calgary AB, T2G 2M2 Canada

Platt Suzy • CRS-CRD • Library of Congress • Washington, DC 20541 • RASD FLRT

Platte Edna H. • Coor. of Collection Development • Fort Bend County Library System • Richmond, TX 77469 • PLA RASD

Platz Nancy L. • Librarian • Madison Central School • Madison, NY 13402

Platz Valerie A. • Assistant Manager • Bell Atlantic NSI • Arlington, VA 22201 • LAMA NMRT *Life*

Plavan Marilyn • Saint Louis, MO 63109

Player Bobby • Head of Serials • Howard University Libraries Founders Library • Washington, DC 20059

Plaza Janet E. • Library Director • Aurora Public Library • Aurora, IL 60505-4299 • LAMA PLA

Plazek Annette D. • Bay Village, OH 44140 • AASL ALSC NMRT

Pleasants Margaret L. • Librarian Gr. 7-12 • Pulaski Academy • Little Rock, AR 72212

Plenge Sindi • Student • Syracuse University School of Information Studies • Syracuse, NY 13244-4100 • ACRL LITA IFRT NMRT SRRT

Plesser Frances L. • Young Adult Librarian • East Meadow Public Library • East Meadow, NY 11554-1700 • PLA

Plessner Joan • Riverside City & County Public Library • Riverside, CA 92502-0468

Pletcher Kathy • University of Wisconsin-Green Bay Library Learning Center • Green Bay, WI 54311 • ACRL

Pletsch Ellen J. • Collection Devel. Librarian • United States Department of Agriculture National Agricultural Library • Beltsville, MD 20705-2351 • ALCTS RASD

Pletscher Josephine M. • Librarian • Rio Hondo Community College Library • Whittier, CA 91101

Plettner Martha A. • Student • Simmons College Graduate School of Library & Information Science • Boston, MA 02115

Pletzke Chester J. • Director of LRC • Uniformed Service University • Bethesda, MD 20814

Pletzke Linda M. • Library of Congress • Washington, DC 20541 • ALCTS

Pleune Joyce • Grnd Rapids, MI 49505 • LAMA PLA *Life*

Plevak Linda L. • Student • University of Texas at Austin Graduate School of Library & Information Sciences • Austin, TX 78712-1276 • ALSC PLA

Plisch Sandra L. • Librarian • Rayovac Technical Center Library • Madison, WI 53744-4960 • RASD

Plitt Jeanne G. Mrs • Library Director • Alexandria Library • Alexandria, VA 22314 • LAMA

Plizga Brenda A. • Brighton Public Library • Brighton, MI 48116 • PLA

Plodinec Louise R. • Millbrook Elementary School • Aiken, SC 29803 • AASL

Ploeg Thomas A. • Library Programs Coordinator • Georgia Department of Education Division of Public Library Services • Atlanta, GA 30303-3692 • ASCLA LAMA PLA

Ploeger Nancy M. • High School Librarian • Hays Consolidated Indp Sch Dist • Buda, TX 78610 • AASL

Ploeger Pamela I. • Circulation Services Librarian • Dartmouth College Library Baker Memorial Library • Hanover, NH 03755-3525 • ACRL ALCTS

Ploetz Patricia • Media Specialist • Minnetonka Intermediate School • Excelsior, MN 55331 • AASL YALSA

Ploetz Susan M. • Librarian Grade 3 • Milwaukee Public Library • Milwaukee, WI 53233

Ploss Helen L. • Assoc Head of Catalog Department • Massachusetts Institute of Technology Libraries (MIT) • Cambridge, MA 02139 • ALCTS

Ploszaj Stanley J. • Automation Specialist • Westchester Library System • Elmsford, NY 10523 • LITA

Plotkin Elaine S. • Adult Specialist • Harris County Public Library • Houston, TX 77054 • PLA

Plotkin Mark A. • Serials Librarian • Supreme Court of U.S. Library • Washington, DC 20543 • FLRT

Plotnick Rosemary T. • Cataloger/Librarian • Yale University Sterling Memorial Library • New Haven, CT 06520 • ALCTS

Plotnik Arthur • Associate Publisher • American Library Association • Chicago, IL 60611-2795

Plotzke Robert F. • Executive Director • Rolling Prairie Library System • Decatur, IL 62522 • LAMA PLA

Ploughman Jane E. • Acting Public Serv. Librarian • Green Mountain College Griswold Library • Poultney, VT 05764

Plourde Jacqueline A. • Media Spec • Madison Junior High School • Naperville, IL 60565 • AASL

Plucinsky Marie F. • Director • John F. Kennedy Memorial Library • Wallington, NJ 07057 • ALTA

Pluemer Bonnie J. • Northwest Regional Library Systems • Sioux City, IA 51102 • PLA

Plum Dorothy A. Miss • Keene Valley, NY 12943-0046 • ACRL YALSA *Continuing*

Plum Stephen H. • Reference Librarian • University of Connecticut Homer Babbidge Library • Storrs, CT 06269-1005 • ACRL RASD

Plumb Carolyn Ginell • Marshall/Plumb Research Associates • Burbank, CA 91505

Plumer Irene • Holbrook, NY 11741

Plumley Boyd F. • Fredricksburg, VA 22401-0782

Plummer-Raphael Richard A. • Marketing Manager • Valley Record Distributors Inc. • Woodland, CA 95695

Plummer Diane D. • Librarian • Saline Middle School • Saline, MI 48176

Plummer John H. • Reference Librarian • Franklin Park Public Library District • Franklin Park, IL 60131 • RASD

Plummer Sue J. • Children's Librarian • Sebastopol Regional Branch Library • Sebastopol, CA 95472 • ALSC LIRT

Plunkett Donna N. • Media Spec. • Savannah Country Day Sch • Savannah, GA 31419 • AASL

Plunkett Wilson T. • Federal Documents Librarian • Louisiana State University Libraries Middleton Library • Baton Rouge, LA 70803-3342 • ACRL ALCTS GODORT LHRT LRRT

Pluscauskas Martha M. • Assistant Coordinator • East York Board of Education Professional Library • Toronto ON, M4C 2V3 Canada • AASL ALSC

Pluster Irma M. • Supervisory Children's Ln • Mesa Public Library • Mesa, AZ 85201-6768 • PLA

Plute-Santos Rachel D. • Inverness Heights, MN 55077 • ALSC PLA SRRT

Plyler Ruth E. • Student • University of South Carolina College of Library & Information Science • Columbia, SC 29208

Poage Larry • Trustee • Tucson Pima Library • Tucson, AZ 85726 • ALTA

Poarch Erma R. • Fairfax, VA 22031

Poarch Margaret E. • Santa Rosa, CA 95403 • ALSC *Continuing*

Pobanz Becky • Youth Services Consultant • Corn Belt Library System • Normal, IL 61761 • ALSC

Pober Stacy • Smithtown, NY 11787

Pober Susan J. • Head of Children's Services • Millburn Public Library • Millburn, NJ 07041 • ALSC PLA IFRT

Pobutsky Olga N. • Chief • Detroit Public Library Edison Branch Library • Detroit, MI 48228

Poche Susan A. • Student • Our Lady of the Lake University • San Antonio, TX 78207-4666

Pochi Alan • Coordinator of Cataloging • Ferris State University • Big Rapids, MI 49307 • ACRL ALCTS LITA

Pocius Kristine • Abington Heights Middle School • Clarks Summit, PA 18411 • AASL

Podd Juliana • Cataloging • Suffolk Cooperative Library System • Bellport, NY 11713 • LITA

Podell Penny E. • Vice President • Milwaukee County Federated Library System • Milwaukee, WI 53233 • ALTA

Podesva Jerome R. • Trustee • East Alton Public Library • East Alton, IL 62024 • ALTA

Podgajny Stephen J. • Brunswick Public Library Association • Brunswick, ME 04011 • PLA

Podnos Selim S. • Trustee • Montgomery County Department of Public Libraries • Rockville, MD 20850 • ALTA PLA

Podoll Darryl B. • Director • Valley City State University Allen Memorial Library • Valley City, ND 58072 • ACRL

Podrygula Susan G. • Technical Services Librarian • Minot State University Memorial Library • Minot, ND 58701 • ACRL

Poe Mya Thanda • Library of Congress • Washington, DC 20541 • IRRT

Poe Philippa Howard • Aztec, NM 87410 • ALTA

Poehlmann Christian H. • Seattle, WA 98145-2144 • ACRL RASD

Poehlmann Nancy E. • Principal Cataloger • University of Washington Suzzallo Library • Seattle, WA 98195

Poel Elizabeth E. • Associate Historian • U. S. General Accounting Office • Washington, DC 20548

Poer Rebecca Susan • Coor. of Media Services • The Education Center • Lenoir, NC 28645 • AASL

Poertner Marilyn • Asst Director • Boise Public Library • Boise, ID 83702-0715

Poff Doug • University of Alberta Cameron Library • Edmonton AB, T6G 2J8 Canada • ACRL LAMA LITA

Pohl Gunther E. • Great Neck, NY 11020 • RASD

Pohl Janet M. • Librarian • International School of Duesseldorf, e.v • 4000 Duesseldorf 31, Germany • AASL ALCTS YALSA

Pohl L. Frederick Jr. • Cataloger • Cornell University Albert R. Mann Library • Ithaca, NY 14853-4301 • ALCTS

Pohl Linda M. • Librarian I • Milwaukee Public Library Zablocki Branch • Milwaukee, WI 53215

Pohl Robert K. Mr • Ephraim, WI 54211 • LAMA PLA *Life*

Poindexter Marilyn • Boston, MA 02115 • PLA

Poinsett Margaret J. • Trenton, NJ 08610

Poirier Gayle A. • BI Libn./Reference Services • Louisiana State University Libraries Troy H. Middleton Library • Baton Rouge, LA 70803-3342 • ACRL LIRT

Poisson Richard D. • Dracut, MA 01826 • ACRL

Pokorney Perri Michele • Librarian • Benjamin Foulois Traditional Academy • Suitland, MD 20746 • AASL

Polach Frank • Deputy Univ Librarian • Rutgers University Libraries • New Brunswick, NJ 08903 • ACRL LAMA

Polacheck Dem • Massillon, OH 44646 • Continuing

Polacheck Janet G. • Massillon, OH 44646 • YALSA *Continuing*

Polan Morris • Emeritus • California State University-Los Angeles John F. Kennedy Memorial Library • Los Angeles, CA 90032-8300

Poland Jean A. • Asst. Engineering Librarian • Purdue University Libraries • West Lafayette, IN 47907 • ACRL

Polansky Patricia A. • Russian Bibl • University of Hawaii Thomas Hale Hamilton Library • Honolulu, HI 96822 • ACRL

Pole Kathryn M. • Denton, TX 76201

Polelle Mark R. • Student • Rutgers University School of Communication Information & Library Studies • New Brunswick, NJ 08903

Polentz Patricia A. • Original Catlgr/Asst Prof. • Virginia Polytechnic Inst & State Univ University Libraries • Blacksburg, VA 24062-9001 • ACRL

Polep Jan • Reference • Crystal Lake Public Library • Crystal Lake, IL 60014 • RASD

Polette Nancy J. • Book Lures, Inc • O'Fallon, MO 63366 • AASL

Polewchak Jane • Indexer • H. W. Wilson Company • Bronx, NY 10452 • RASD

Polhemus Georgia • Somerville, NJ 08876

Polhill Rachel W. • Ln • Montevallo University Carmichael Library • Montevallo, AL 35115 • ACRL

Poli Rosario • Assistant Professor • Case Western Reserve Univ Freiberger Library • Cleveland, OH 44106-7151 • ACRL RASD LIRT

Polich Deborah J. • Head of Adult Services • Oceanside Public Library • Oceanside, CA 92054 • PLA

Polidori Amy E. • Student • Wayne State University Library Science Program • Detroit, MI 48202

Polirer Sarah A. • Archivist • Office of Court Adminstration • New York, NY 10013 • ACRL

Polit Carlos E. • Bloomington, IN 47408

Politakis Michael L. • Chief Information Officer • Quality Books Inc. • Lake Bluff, IL 60044-2204

Polites Bente L. • Reference Librarian • Villanova University Falvey Memorial Library • Villanova, PA 19085-1699 • ACRL

Politi Mary A. • Student • State University of New York at Albany School of Information Science & Policy • Albany, NY 12222

Politzer Lisa I. • Encinitas, CA 92024 • AASL

Polk Diana D. • Reference Librarian • Deere & Company Library • Moline, IL 61265 • ACRL

Polk Elizabeth A. • Administrative Supervisor LRC • Austin Independent School District • Austin, TX 78752 • AASL ALSC

Polk Ruth Lynch • Reference Librarian • University of Maryland-Eastern Shore Frederick Douglass Library • Princess Anne, MD 21853

Polkingharn Anne T. • Librarian K-8 • Harbor Day School • Corona del Mar, CA 92625 • AASL

Pollach Karen • Reference Librarian • Multnomah County Library Gresham Branch • Gresham, OR 97030

Pollack Miriam • System Development Officer • North Suburban Library System • Wheeling, IL 60090 • ASCLA PLA CLENE

Pollak Marsha L. • Supervising Librarian • Sunnyvale Public Library • Sunnyvale, CA 94088-3714 • ALCTS LITA PLA

Pollakoff Stanley R. • Student • Rutgers University School of Communication Information & Library Studies • New Brunswick, NJ 08903

Pollard Alan P. • Hd, Slavic and Europeau Div. • University of Michigan Libraries • Ann Arbor, MI 48109-1205 • ACRL ALCTS

Pollard Charyl C. • Poughkeepsie, NY 12603 • ACRL LITA RASD GODORT

Pollard Frances M. • Executive Assistant for L Serv. • Eastern Illinois University Booth Library • Charleston, IL 61920-3099 • ACRL ALCTS LAMA LITA RASD

Pollard Frances S. • Head, Reference Librarian • Virginia Historical Society Lib • Richmond, VA 23221-0311

Pollard H. Jeannette • Teacher-ESL • Boston Public Schools • Boston, MA 02108 • AASL ALCTS LITA EMIERT

Pollard Larry • Coor. of Reference Services • Radford University John P. McConnell Library • Radford, VA 24142 • RASD

Pollard Margaret E. • Reference Librarian • Pellissippi State Technical Community College • Knoxville, TN 37933 • ACRL RASD LIRT

Pollard Richard • Assistant Professor • University of Tennessee-Knoxville Graduate School of Library & Information Science • Knoxville, TN 37996-4330 • LITA

Pollard Richard C. • University Librarian • California State University • Fullerton, CA 92634 • ACRL ALCTS LAMA LITA

Pollard Russell O. • Head of Technical Services • Harvard University Andover-Harvard Theological Library • Cambridge, MA 02138

Pollastro Michael • University of Idaho Library • Moscow, ID 83843 • LITA RASD

Pollitz John H. • Reference Librarian • Augustana College Library • Rock Island, IL 61201 • ACRL LITA NMRT

Pollock Ann H. • Reference Librarian • University of Wisconsin-Madison Memorial Library • Madison, WI 53706 • ACRL RASD

Pollock Carol J. • Public Service • Lynchburg College • Lynchburg, VA 24501

Pollock Ethel L. • Learning Resources Coordinator • Eastern Virginia Medical School Moorman Memorial Library • Norfolk, VA 23501

Pollock James A. • Reference Librarian • Central Virginia Cmnty Coll • Lynchburg, VA 24502 • RASD

Pollock Jean • Children's Librarian • Oakland Public Library Diamond Branch • Oakland, CA 94602

Pollock Kimberly K. • Student • Wayne State University Library Science Program • Detroit, MI 48202 • ACRL ALCTS LITA

Pollock Margaret M. • Akron, OH 44313 • Continuing

Pollock Nancy B. • Librarian • Taylor Community Library • Taylor, MI 48180 • LAMA PLA

Pollock Sara Rutkowski • Research Librarian • Walt Disney World Epcot Outreach Epcot Ctr • Lk Buena Vis, FL 32830 • LITA RASD

Pollok Karen E. • Librarian • Naval Air Station Oceana • Virginia Bch, VA 23460 • AFLRT FLRT

Polly Jean Armour • Assistant Director of Pub. Serv. • Liverpool Public Library • Liverpool, NY 13088 • LITA PLA

Polmanteer Rose K. • Prescott, AZ 86301

Polomski Linda • Teacher/Lib Media Specialist • Farm Hill School Library and Spencer School Library • Middletown, CT 06457 • AASL

Pols Wendell B. • Ref & Spec Clln Ln Archivist • Roger Williams College Library • Bristol, RI 02809-2921

Polson Billie M. • Head Catalog Librarian • University of Nevada-Las Vegas James R. Dickinson Library • Las Vegas, NV 89154 • ACRL ALCTS

Polson Jerilyn H. • Law Librarian • Fairfax Law Library • Fairfax, VA 22030

Poma Michael A. • Reference/Instruction Librarian • Creighton University Reinert-Alumni Memorial Library • Omaha, NE 68178 • ACRL LIRT

Pomazal Priscilla F. • Student • Clark-Atlanta University School of Library & Information Studies • Atlanta, GA 30314-4391

Pomerantz Bruce F. • Ad Serv Coor • Clermont County Public Library • Batavia, OH 45103-3192 • LAMA PLA

Pomerantz Karyn L. • User Education Librarian • George Washington University Himmelfarb Health Sciences Library • Washington, DC 20037 • LIRT

Pomerantz Susan J. • Wyandot Elemetary School • Dublin, OH 43017

Pomeroy Beth A. • Head of Bookmobile Department • Elkhart Public Library • Elkhart, IN 46516-3184 • PLA

Pomes Stephen V. • Librarian I • Jefferson Parish Library • Metairie, LA 70010

Ponce Barbara S. • Pinellas Park Public Library • Pinellas Park, FL 34665 • PLA

Ponczak Lydia • Trustee • Acorn Public Library District • Oak Forest, IL 60452 • ALTA

Pond Arthur T. • Senior Librarian • Los Angeles Public Library Hyde Park Branch • Los Angeles, CA 90043 • LAMA PLA

Pond Kathleen Kouba • Library/Media Specialist • Mount Ogden Middle School • Ogden, UT 84403 • AASL

Pond Patricia • Beaverton, OR 97007 • Life

Ponemon Richard D. • Trustee • The Bryant Library • Roslyn, NY 11576

Pong Connie K.L. • New Orleans Baptist Theological Seminary John T Christian Library • New Orleans, LA 70126 • ALCTS

Ponis Roberta • Coord.,Library Media Services • Jefferson County School District Professional Library Media Center • Golden, CO 80401 • AASL

Ponnappa Biddanda P. • Asst. Professor/Coordinator, ILS • University of Tennessee John C. Hodges Library • Knoxville, TN 37996-1000

Ponsell Mary Lou • Director • Wilmington College Library • New Castle, DE 19720 • ACRL LAMA

Ponsford Bennett Claire • Austin, TX 78731

Pontau Donna Z. • Livermore, CA 94550 • ACRL ASCLA RASD

Pontiff Donovan • Trustee • Saint Mary Parish Library • Franklin, LA 70538 • ALTA IFRT

Pontius Jack E. • Microforms & Periodical Ln • Pennsylvania State University Libraries • University Park, PA 16802 • ALCTS

Ponville Myra A. • Student • Louisiana State University School of Library & Information Science • Baton Rouge, LA 70803-3290 • PLA RASD

Pool Dorothy S. • Dallas County Community College District District Service Center • Mesquite, TX 75150-2095 • CLENE

Pool James W. • Asst. Librarian • University of Tulsa McFarlin Library • Tulsa, OK 74104-3189 • ALCTS

Pool Jeraldine B. • Media Specialist • Oak Street School • Basking Ridge, NJ 07920 • AASL

Poole-Jones Christine W. • Supervisor Elementary Libraries • Portland Public Schools • Portland, OR 97208-3107 • AASL

Poole Barbara • Saint Agnes Saint Stephen's School • Alexandria, VA 22302 • AASL

Poole Deborah • Government Documents Dept. • Loyola University Library • New Orleans, LA 70118 • GODORT

Poole Eva D. • Manager of Library Services • Emily Fowler Public Library • Denton, TX 76201 • PLA

Poole Frazer G. • Library of Congress • Washington, DC 20541 • ACRL LAMA *Life*

Poole Jay Martin • Assistant Director • Texas A & M University Sterling C. Evans Library • College Station, TX 77843-5000 • ACRL ALCTS LAMA

Poole Jeanne • Toledo-Lucas County Public Library • Toledo, OH 43624 • ALCTS

Poole Jocelyn • Student • University of Pittsburgh School of Library and Information Science • Pittsburgh, PA 15260 • SRRT

Poole Katherine K. • Visual Collections Librarian • Massachusetts Inst of Technolgy Physics Reading Room, 26-152 • Cambridge, MA 02139

Poole Kinuye J. • Ser Catlg Ln • University of Washington Suzzallo Library • Seattle, WA 98195

Poole Martha A. • School Media Specialist • Hopewell Elementary School • Glastonbury, CT 06033 • AASL

Poole Mary E. • Troy, NC 27371 • GODORT

Poole Paula R. • Library Assistant • Chemeketa Community College • Salem, OR 97309

Poole Rebecca S. • Media Supervisor • Fountain-Ft. Carson School District • Fountain, CO 80817 • AASL

Pooler Margaret M. • Kalamazoo, MI 49009

Poon Cecilia Siu-Wah • Sioux City, IA 51102 • ACRL

Poon Grace K. N. • Student • University of Toronto Faculty of Library & Information Science • Toronto ON, M5S 1A1 Canada

Poon Pak K. • Lib. Specifications Specialist • H. W. Wilson Company • Bronx, NY 10452 • LITA

Poon Sau Ping • Student • University of Toronto Faculty of Library & Information Science • Toronto ON, M5S 1A1 Canada • LITA

Poon Wei Chi • Head Librarian • University of California-Berkeley Asian American Studies Library • Berkeley, CA 94720 • EMIERT

Poor Allen J. • University of Chicago Library • Chicago, IL 60637-1502 • ALCTS LITA

Poore Linda M. • Accokeek, MD 20607 • NMRT SRRT

Poore Nancy S. • Fairfax, VA 22033 • AASL

Poore William S. • King County Library System • Seattle, WA 98109-5191

Popa Opritsa A. • University of California Shields Library • Davis, CA 95616 • IRRT

Pope Andrew T. • Librarian • University of New Brunswick • Fredericton NB, E3B 5H5 Canada • ACRL LITA

Pope Edwina M. Sr. • Wichita, KS 67213

Pope Karen Osborne • Government Publications Lib. • University of Wisconsin-Eau Claire William D. McIntyre Library • Eau Claire, WI 54702 • ACRL GODORT LIRT

Pope Laura M. • Librarian • Polytechnic University • Brooklyn, NY 11201 • LITA SRRT

Pope Nancy N. • Systems Librarian • Louisiana State University Libraries Troy H. Middleton Library • Baton Rouge, LA 70803-3342 • LITA SRRT

Pope Nolan F. • Assoc Dir Auto; General Lib Sys • University of Wisconsin-Madison Memorial Library • Madison, WI 53706 • ALCTS LITA

Pope Tony Lee • Kingston, GA 30145

Popecki Jeanne M. • Library Director • Champlain College Library • Burlington, VT 05401 • ACRL

Popecki Joseph T. • Winooski, VT 05401 • Continuing

Popek Teresa R. • Media Specialist • West Springfield Public Library • West Springfield, MA 01089

Popescu Constantin C. • Associate Director • Milwaukee School of Engineering Schroeder Library • Milwaukee, WI 53201 • ACRL ALCTS

Popit Ellen H. • Project Coordinator • Shawnee Library System • Carterville, IL 62918 • ALSC

Popko John • Asst Dir for Tech Serv • University of Missouri-Kansas City Library • Kansas City, MO 64110-2499 • ALCTS LAMA LITA

Popkoff Robert B. • Student • University of Wisconsin-Milwaukee School of Library & Information Science • Milwaukee, WI 53201

Poplack Laura P. • Reference Librarian • New Haven Free Public Library • New Haven, CT 06510 • YALSA

Poplawski Judith A. • Central Catholic School • Lecanto, FL 32661

Popma Paula J. • Asst. Univ. Libn. Access Service • Santa Clara University Michel Orradre Library • Santa Clara, CA 95053 • ACRL

Popnik Marlene A. • Librarian • Susquehanna Township Middle School • Harrisburg, PA 17109 • AASL

Popovic Tanya V. • Cataloging Librarian • Le Moyne College • Syracuse, NY 13214 • ACRL ALCTS

Popovich Charles J. • Ohio State University Business Library • Columbus, OH 43210-1395 • ACRL RASD

Popovitch-Krekic Ruzica • Reference Librarian • Mount Saint Mary's College • Los Angeles, CA 90049 • ACRL

Popp Lisa M. • Student • Wayne State University Library Science Program • Detroit, MI 48202

Popp Mary • Head, Library Instruction • Indiana University at Bloomington University Libraries • Bloomington, IN 47405 • ACRL RASD CLENE LIRT

Popper Sue • Trustee • Daniel Boone Regional Library • Columbia, MO 65205-1267 • ALTA

Poquette Cindy Lou • Petoskey, MI 49770

Porcella Luisa • Technical Services Librarian • Millburn Public Library • Millburn, NJ 07041

Pore Sally G. • Student • Simmons College Graduate School of Library & Information Science • Boston, MA 02115 • RASD

Pores Jeanne • Trustee • The Bryant Library • Roslyn, NY 11576

Porfiri Lois M. • Minneapolis, MN 55407

Porfirio Dawn • Library Specialist • University of Arizona • Tucson, AZ 85721

Poris Florence • Librarian • Haworth School Library • Haworth, NJ 07641 • AASL

Pormen Paul E. • School Media Director • Austintown Local Sch • Youngstown, OH 44484 • AASL

Porras Valentin • Assistant Library Director • Daly City Public Library • Daly City, CA 94015

Porta Maria A. • Assistant Agriculture Librarian • University of Illinois at Urbana Champaign • Urbana, IL 61801 • ACRL RASD

Porta Mary DePaul Sr • Librarian • Bishop McCort High School Library • Johnstown, PA 15905

Portela Thomas • Trustee • Merrick Public Library • Merrick, NY 11566 • PLA IFRT

Porter Barry L. • Littleton, CO 80123

Porter Betsy S. • Head of Reference • University of Wyoming Coe Library • Laramie, WY 82071-3334 • ACRL LAMA RASD

Porter Betty Ann • Head, Lodge Learning Lab. • Xavier University • Cincinnati, OH 45207 • ACRL

Porter Cathy A. • Librarian • Northern Trust Company • Chicago, IL 60675

Porter Cheryl • Bergenfield Free Public Library • Bergenfield, NJ 07621 • ALTA

Porter Cynthia • Catalog Librarian • Walt Disney Imagineering • Glendale, CA 91221 • ALCTS

Porter Don • Assoc. Dir. Info. Technology • Rensselaer Polytechnic Institute • Troy, NY 12180 • LITA

Porter Dorothy • Trustee • Birmingham Area Library Service • Birmingham, AL 35203 • ALTA PLA

Porter Ellen R. • Librarian I/Rover • Columbus Metropolitan Library Main Library Branch • Columbus, OH 43215 • PLA RASD

Porter Esther • Librarian • Ontario High School • Mansfield, OH 44905 • AASL

Porter Exa Lynn R • Public Service Librarian • North Harris College • Houston, TX 77073 • ACRL

Porter G. Margaret • Associate Librarian • University of Notre Dame Theodore M. Hesburgh Library • Notre Dame, IN 46556 • ACRL RASD

Porter Gayle • University of Arizona • Tucson, AZ 85721 • EMIERT

Porter George S. • Engineering Reference Librarian • North Carolina State University • Raleigh, NC 27695-7111 • ACRL

Porter Jean F. • Consultant • CMP Associates Inc • Grosse Pointe Park, MI 48230-1853 • ACRL LAMA PLA RASD ILERT SRRT

Porter Jean M. • Head Documents Dept. • North Carolina State University • Raleigh, NC 27695-7111 • ACRL GODORT

Porter Jill L. • Reference Librarian • Chadbourne & Parke • New York, NY 10112 • GODORT IFRT

Porter Lee W. • Systems Librarian • Department of Defense Pentagon Library • Washington, DC 20310 • LITA AFLRT FLRT

Porter Linda • Senior Librarian • Richmond Public Library Ginter Park Branch • Richmond, VA 23227

Porter Maria • Saint Joseph County Public Library • South Bend, IN 46601 • LAMA PLA

Porter Richard D. • Library Automation Consultant • Unisys, Corporation • Lombard, IL 60148 • LITA

Porter Rozanne A. • Algonquin Area Public Library District • Algonquin, IL 60102 • ALSC

Porter Samuel A. • Trustee • Columbus Metropolitan Library • Columbus, OH 43215 • ALTA PLA

Porter Stuart T. Jr. • Director • Russell Library • Middletown, CT 06457 • PLA

Porterfield Paul C. • University of Richmond • Richmond, VA 23173 • ACRL VRT

Portice Linda E. • Ann Arbor, MI 48104

Portis Juanita W. • Deputy Director • Howard University Libraries Founders Library • Washington, DC 20059

Portman Marquitta M. • Marietta, GA 30067 • AASL

Portnick Phillip • Trustee • Cuyahoga County Public Library • Cleveland, OH 44134-2792

Portnowitz Patricia A. • Director • Palm Bay Public Library • Palm Bay, FL 32905 • LAMA PLA

Portugal Rhoda E. • Director • Lyndhurst Free Public Library • Lyndhurst, NJ 07071

Portwood Helen Gail • Honolulu, HI 96847 • ALSC PLA *Continuing*

Posamentier Evelyn J. • San Francisco, CA 94114

Posel Frances R. • Seattle, WA 98119 • SRRT

Posel Nancy R. • Director • Abington Free Library • Abington, PA 19001 • PLA

Posey Jasmine Y. • Head Children's Services • Greenwich Library • Greenwich, CT 06830 • ALSC
Posey Linda L. • Headquarters Branch Manager • Jackson-George Regional Library System • Pascagoula, MS 39567 • PLA
Posey Susann F. • Mercersburg Academy Albert M Swank Library • Mercersburg, PA 17236
Poske Jo Ann M. • Detroit, MI 48228 • EMIERT SRRT
Posner Frances A. • Chicago, IL 60660 • Continuing
Posniak John R. • Senior Reference Librarian • United States Department of the Treasury Comptroller of the Currency Library • Washington, DC 20219 • FLRT IRRT
Possner Roger D. • South Pasadena Public Library • South Pasadena, CA 91030
Post Glen • Libraian • Maret School • Washington, DC 20008 • AASL
Post Mary M. • St Paul, MN 55107 • Continuing
Post Mary M. • U S Navy Lieutenant • United States Navy Service School Command Code 011 • Great Lakes, IL 60086-5243 • AFLRT CLENE
Post Phyllis C. • Head of Technical Services • Capital University Law Library • Columbus, OH 43215 • ALCTS
Post William E. • Dir of Library Collecfilms • California State University-Chico • Chico, CA 95926 • ACRL
Postal Justine • Reference Department • Palm Beach County Library System • West Palm Beach, FL 33406 • PLA RASD GODORT
Poste Leslie • Geneseo, NY 14454-0068 • ACRL PLA *Life*
Postelnek Rosanne • Reference Librarian • R C Miller Memorial Library • Beaumont, TX 77706 • ALCTS IFRT
Postema Beth E. • Fargo Public Library • Fargo, ND 58102
Poster Susan E. • Reference Librarian • Pasadena Public Library • Pasadena, CA 91101 • PLA
Posteraro Catherine H. • Reference Librarian • Saint Joseph College Library • West Hartford, CT 06117 • ACRL
Postlethwaite Bonnie S. • Tufts University Nils Yngve Wessell Library • Medford, MA 02155 • LITA
Poston Sandy W. • Durham, NC 27712-9285 • AASL
Poteet Susan S. • Catalog Librarian • Southern Illinois University Delyte W. Morris Library • Carbondale, IL 62901-6632 • ACRL ALCTS LITA PLA
Potelicki Athalene O. • Branch Manager • Cuyahoga County Public Library Garfield Heights Branch • Garfield Heights, OH 44125-3299 • PLA
Potempa Vicki A. • Livonia, MI 48150
Potenza Philip A. • Branch Library Manager • Queens Borough Public Library • Jamaica, NY 11432
Potenziani Jo Ann • Director • Des Plaines Valley Public Library District • Lockport, IL 60441 • PLA
Potmesil Elaine R. • Alliance, NE 69301 • AASL
Potok Chaim • Trustee • Free Library of Philadelphia • Philadelphia, PA 19103 • ALTA
Potter Barbara J. • Sci Tech Subject Specialist • Contra Costa County Library • Pleasant Hill, CA 94523
Potter Corinne J. • Director • Saint Ambrose University McMullen Library • Davenport, IA 52803 • ACRL
Potter Cresa • Lake Jackson, TX 77566
Potter Daphne Fallieros • Student • Simmons College Graduate School of Library & Information Science • Boston, MA 02115 • LITA
Potter Dorothy F. • Pasadena, CA 91107
Potter Elaine G. • A/V Cataloger • Johnson County Public Library • Franklin, IN 46131
Potter Janet S. • San Diego, CA 92126-1129
Potter Jo K. • Director • Alpha Park Public Library District • Bartonville, IL 61607 • PLA
Potter Karen • Director of Library Services • Maitland Public Library • Maitland, FL 32751
Potter Robert Ellis • Head of Adult Services • Dunedin Public Library • Dunedin, FL 34698-7998 • RASD
Potter Steven V. • Mid-Continent Public Library Blue Springs Branch • Blue Springs, MO 64015 • PLA IFRT
Potter Susan • Assistant Director • Regis University Dayton Memorial Library • Denver, CO 80221-1099 • ACRL
Potter T. Linda • Student • Emporia State University School of Library & Information Management • Emporia, KS 66801 • AASL
Potter William Gray Dr. • Director of Libraries • University of Georgia Libraries • Athens, GA 30602 • ACRL LITA LRRT
Pottle Connie • Coordinator of Youth Services • Memphis-Shelby County Public Library and Information Center • Memphis, TN 38104-4025 • ALSC PLA
Potts Donald • Galveston, TX 77554-6101
Potts Esther T. • Tucson, AZ 85718 • Continuing
Potts Joseph C. • Sys & Operations Anly • University of Utah Marriott Library • Salt Lake City, UT 84112-1179
Potts Kenneth J. • Librarian • Northern Illinois University University Libraries • DeKalb, IL 60115-2868 • ACRL LHRT LRRT
Potts Loretta S. • Childrens's Librarian • Henderson County Public Library • Hendersonville, NC 28739
Potts Sandra L. • Head of Technical Services • White Pine Library Cooperative • Saginaw, MI 48602-5590 • ALCTS PLA
Potvin Barbara D. • Librarian • Pomerene Elementary School • Pomerene, AZ 85627 • AASL
Poulin Jeffrey M. • Trustee • Prince William Public Library System Administrative Support Center • Prince William, VA 22192-5073
Poulin Maryjane • Science & Engineering Librarian • University of Maine Raymond H. Fogler Library • Orono, ME 04469
Pouliott Marianne K. • Librarian • G.E. Silicones Library & Information Center • Waterford, NY 12188 • ASCLA LAMA LITA
Poulsen Elizabeth A. • Highland Beach Library • Highland Beach, FL 33487
Poultney Judy J. • Normal Public Library • Normal, IL 61761 • RASD
Pouncey Lorene • Houston, TX 77005 • ACRL
Pound Beverley Anne • Seattle, WA 98115 • ACRL LAMA RASD MAGERT
Pounds Virginia M. • Library Specialist • Roosevelt Elementary School • Spokane, WA 99204 • AASL
Poundstone Sally H. • Director • Westport Public Library • Westport, CT 06880 • LAMA PLA
Pourciau L J. • Assoc. V.P. Academic Affairs • Memphis State University Main Library • Memphis, TN 38152 • ACRL LAMA
Pourron Eleanor K. • Chief,Materials Management Div. • Arlington County Department of Libraries • Arlington, VA 22201 • ALCTS LAMA PLA RASD YALSA
Pourzadeh-Boushehri Nobuko • Student • University of Florida Libraries • Gainesville, FL 32611-2047
Povilaitis Leanna J. • Assistant Director • Randolph Township Free Public Library • Randolph, NJ 07869 • PLA IFRT
Povilonis Louise Eunice • Hartford, CT 06106
Povsic Frances • Bowling Green, OH 43402 • ALSC
Powell Anice C. • Director • Sunflower County Library • Indianola, MS 38751
Powell Antoinette M. • Student • Carnegie Mellon University Hunt Institute • Pittsburgh, PA 15213
Powell Ashley B. • Circulation Librarian • Connecticut College • New London, CT 06320-4196 • ACRL
Powell Bettie B. • Library Director • Page Public Library • Page, AZ 86040 • PLA
Powell Bobby R. • Gainesville, FL 32605-5304
Powell Candace A. • Technical Services Librarian • Angelina College • Lufkin, TX 75902
Powell Cheryl • Assistant Branch Librarian • Brooklyn Public Library Canarsie Branch Library • Brooklyn, NY 11236 • ALSC
Powell Daisy W. • Washington, DC 20002
Powell Doris D. • Children's Librarian • Lee County Library System • Sanford, NC 27330
Powell Frances F. • Student • East Carolina University Department of Library & Information Studies • Greenville, NC 27858-4353
Powell Gloria • Belton, MO 64012
Powell HT • New York, NY 10457 • ACRL
Powell Jan • Woodland Park High School Library • Woodland Park, CO 80866 • AASL
Powell Jean • Media Spec • Public Schs-Unit 3 • Harrisburg, IL 62946 • AASL
Powell Jill H. • Reference Librarian • Cornell University Engineering Library • Ithaca, NY 14853-2201 • ACRL
Powell Joan • Data Processing Manager • County of Los Angeles Public Library • Hawthorne, CA 90250 • LITA PLA
Powell John M. • Reference Librarian • Widener University Wolfgram Library • Chester, PA 19013 • ACRL ALCTS LIRT
Powell Katherine L. • Library Media Specialist • Dumas Junior High School • Dumas, AR 71639 • AASL
Powell Kathleen • Childrens Librarian • Brunswick-Glynn County Regional Library • Brunswick, GA 31523-0901 • ALSC
Powell Katrina N. • Keck, Mahin & Cate • Chicago, IL 60601
Powell Lawrence Clark • Tucson, AZ 85718 • AASL ACRL ALCTS ALSC ALTA ASCLA LAMA LITA PLA RASD YALSA *Honorary*
Powell Lillian • Children's Reference Librarian • San Francisco Public Library Parkside Branch • San Francisco, CA 94116 • PLA
Powell Lisa M. • Director of Reference • Rock Island Public Library • Rock Island, IL 61201-8143
Powell Lynnie G. • Trustee • Cleveland Public Library • Cleveland, OH 44114-1271 • ALTA
Powell Margaret K. • Assistant Curator • Trinity College Library • Hartford, CT 06106 • ACRL RASD
Powell Margaret S. • Documents/Reference Librarian • College of Wooster Andrews Library • Wooster, OH 44691 • ACRL ALCTS LITA RASD GODORT IFRT MAGERT
Powell Mary • Director • Indian River County Library • Vero Beach, FL 32960 • LAMA
Powell Mary Beth • Little Rock, AR 72205 • Continuing
Powell Michael E. • Director LRC • Washington University • St Louis, MO 63130 • ACRL
Powell Nancy N. • Albany, OR 97321 • ACRL LAMA
Powell Patricia J. • Technical Services Librarian • Roanoke College Library • Salem, VA 24153
Powell Patricia Kay • Coordinator • Clear Creek Independent School District • League City, TX 77573 • AASL
Powell Phillip P. • Assistant Reference Librarian • College of Charleston Robert Scott Small Library • Charleston, SC 29424 • ACRL LIRT
Powell Ronald R. • University of Missouri-Columbia School of Library & Informational Science • Columbia, MO 65211 • ACRL LRRT
Powell Ruth Ann • Tech Servs Ln • Fairmont State College Library • Fairmont, WV 26554
Powell Teresa G. • Serials Acquisitions Librarian • University of Arizona Library • Tucson, AZ 85721
Powell Wayne E. • Branch Manager • Miami-Dade Public Library System Key Biscayne Branch • Key Biscayne, FL 33149
Power Colleen J. • Coor. of Rgnl. Serv./Sci. Libn. • California State University-Chico Meriam Library • Chico, CA 92929-0295 • ACRL
Power Florence M. • Pasadena, CA 91105 • Continuing
Power Harold Trent • Oakland Public Library Asian Branch • Oakland, CA 94607
Power Hattie L. • Regional Library Director • Illinois Regional Library for The Blind & Physically Handicapped • Chicago, IL 60608 • ASCLA IFRT IRRT
Power Margaret C. • Reference Librarian • DePaul University Libraries • Chicago, IL 60614 • ACRL RASD
Power Mary T. • Public Services Librarian II • Baltimore County Public Library • Towson, MD 21204 • PLA
Power Penelope • Librarian • Garrison Forest School • Garrison, MD 21055 • AASL
Powers Anne • Computer/Audiovisual Librarian • DeLand Area Public Library • DeLand, FL 32724 • RASD
Powers Anthony E. • First Assistant • Chicago Public Library Carl Roden Branch • Chicago, IL 60631
Powers Carol • University of Central Arkansas-Torreyson Library • Conway, AR 72035 • ACRL
Powers Carol • Morristown, IN 46161
Powers Carolyn • Library Director • Arkansas State University Beebe Branch • Beebe, AR 72012 • ACRL LITA VRT
Powers Elaine G. • Librarian • Hughston Sports Medicine Foundation • Columbus, GA 31995
Powers James C. • Resident Historian • Boyd County Public Library • Ashland, KY 41101 • PLA RASD
Powers James E. Mrs • Macon, GA 31210 • Continuing
Powers Janet E • Librarian • John G. Shedd Aquarium • Chicago, IL 60605
Powers Joan C. • Student • State University of New York School of Information & Library Sci • Albany, NY 12203
Powers Judith • Nantucket, MA 02554 • AASL
Powers Kathleen M. • Student • State University of New York at Buffalo School of Information Library • Buffalo, NY 14260 • IFRT
Powers L Jeanne • Refernce Librarian • Bristol Public Library • Bristol, VA 24201-4199
Powers Linda M. • Rockford, IL 61108 • AASL
Powers Mary A. • Library Media High School • Windsor High School • Windsor, VT 05089 • AASL
Powers Nancy M. • Librarian III • Atlanta-Fulton Public Library • Atlanta, GA 30303 • LAMA
Powers R. William • District Librarian • Lake & Peninsula School District • King Salmon, AK 99613 • AASL
Powers Sandra L. • Library Director • Society of the Cincinnati Library • Washington, DC 20008 • ACRL
Powers Shirley • Trustee • Thomas Jefferson Library System • Jefferson Cty, MO 65102 • ALTA
Powis Katherine • Librarian • Horticultural Society of New York Inc. Library • New York, NY 10019
Poynter Susan C. • University of California Rivera Library • Riverside, CA 92517
Pozar Diane C. • Library Media Specialist • Wallkill High School • Wallkill, NY 12589 • AASL
Pozezanac Edita A. • Greenfield Park, PQ, J4V 2M9 Canada
Prabha Chandra • OCLC Online Computer Library Center • Dublin, OH 43017-3395 • ALCTS LITA LRRT
Prachick Toni • Watauga, TX 76148
Prado Ruben D. G. • Rice University Fondren Library • Houston, TX 77251-1892

Praedor Wayne • Chief Information Officer • Eastern Washington University • Cheney, WA 99004 • LITA
Prager George A. • Chief Cataloger • Brooklyn Law School Library • Brooklyn, NY 11201
Praino Silvestra • Reference Librarian • Mahwah Free Public Library • Mahwah, NJ 07430
Pranger Karen L. • Morgan Hill, CA 95037
Prasek Margaret A. • Reference Librarian • Columbia University Health Sciences Library • New York, NY 10032
Prassel Ann H. • Head of Reference • University of Arkansas Libraries • Fayetteville, AR 72701-1201
Prather Susan K. • Krames Communications Library & Resource Center • San Bruno, CA 94066-3030 • LITA *Subscribing*
Prather Terry B. • Charles A Cannon Memorial Library Kannapolis Branch • Kannapolis, NC 28081
Prather Virginia • Parsons, KS 67357 • PLA RASD
Prats Mario A. • University of California-Berkeley University Library • Berkeley, CA 94720
Pratt Allan D. • Tempe, AZ 85284 • LITA
Pratt Barbara D. • Librarian • First Presbyterian Day School • Jackson, MS 39202
Pratt Barbara F. • Longboat Key, FL 34228
Pratt Carolyn • Law Librarian • Mitchell, Silberberg & Knupp Law Library • Los Angeles, CA 90064
Pratt Charles A. • Assistant Director,Catalyst • Jersey City State College • Jersey City, NJ 07305 • AASL LITA
Pratt Dianne P. • Librarian III • Milwaukee Public Library Atkinson Branch • Milwaukee, WI 53209
Pratt Elizabeth G. • Student • University of Michigan School of Information and Library Studies • Ann Arbor, MI 48109-1092 • IFRT SRRT
Pratt Florine E. • Chicago, IL 60619 • PLA *Continuing*
Pratt Jana E. • Children's Librarian • Newport Beach Public Library Corona del Mar Branch • Corona del Mar, CA 92625 • PLA
Pratt Jennifer S. • John Curtis Free Library • Hanover, MA 02339
Pratt Mary L. • Asst. Head of Reference Dept. • Cabell County Public Library • Huntington, WV 25701 • PLA RASD GODORT
Pratt Mary S. • Los Angeles, CA 90020 • RASD
Pratt Melonie S. • Student • East Carolina University Department of Library & Information Studies • Greenville, NC 27858-4353 • AASL
Pratt Susan S. • Student • Catholic University of America School of Library and Information Science • Washington, DC 20064 • NMRT
Pratt Sylvia K. • Public Relations Officer • Nicolet Federated • Green Bay, WI 54301-5194 • PLA
Pratt Virginia • Berkeley, CA 94708 • ACRL
Pray Barbara A. • Covington, KY 41011 • PLA IFRT SRRT
Pray Barbara P. • Librarian • Downers Grove High School South • Downers Grove, IL 60516 • AASL
Preacher Catherine A. • Arnold, MD 21012
Precht Janet L. • Cataloger-Central Processing • Independent School District #279 • Maple Grove, MN 55369-6605 • ALCTS
Prechtel John M. • Athens, GA 30603-9999
Preddy Leslie Burton • Student • Indiana State University • Terre Haute, IN 47809 • AASL
Preece Barbara G. • Cataloger • Southern Illinois University Delyte W. Morris Library • Carbondale, IL 62901-6632 • ACRL ALCTS
Preer Jean L. • Associate Dean • Catholic University of America School of Library and Information Science • Washington, DC 20064 • IFRT LHRT
Preiss Margaret A. • Head Children's Services • Saint Charles City-County Library • St. Peters, MO 63376-0529 • ALSC LAMA
Prendergast Amy C. • Librarian I • University of Missouri-Rolla Curtis Laws Wilson Library • Rolla, MO 65401
Prendergast Kathleen • Chicago, IL 60613
Prendergast Kevin W. • Reference Librarian • Montclair State College Harry A Sprague Library • Upper Montclair, NJ 07043-1699
Prendeville Jet M. • Houston, TX 77098 • ACRL
Prensky Tina B. • Reference Librarian • Pittsford Community Library • Pittsford, NY 14534 • RASD
Prentice Ann E. • Assoc Vice-Pres. for Info. Res. • University of South Florida Library • Tampa, FL 33620-5600 • ACRL ALTA LAMA LHRT LRRT
Prentice Anna M. • Fabens, TX 79838 • AASL
Prentice Barbara S. Dr. • Tucson, AZ 85719 • ALTA PLA
Prentiss Susan M. • Pittsburgh, PA 15208
Prescott Joan C. • Director • Rogers Free Library • Bristol, RI 02809 • PLA SRRT
Prescott Katherine • Lakewood, OH 44107 • ASCLA *Continuing*
Prescott Margaret A. • Baltimore County Public Library Randallstown Area Branch • Randallstown, MD 21133 • PLA
Preshell Linda • Media Specialist • Ramseur School • Ramseur, NC 27316 • AASL
Preslan Bruce • Director • OCLA Pacific Network • Rancho Cucamonga, CA 91730
Presley-Clark Lynn • Liberty Middle Magnet School • Madison, AL 35758 • AASL LITA
Presley Ann M • Media Center Director • Pulaski County Special School District • Little Rock, AR 72216
Presley Beverly • Clark University • Worcester, MA 01610 • MAGERT
Presley Paula • Assistant Editor • Thomas Jefferson University Press • Kirksville, MO 63501 • ACRL LITA
Presley Roger • Head Acquisition Department • Georgia State University Pullen Library • Atlanta, GA 30303-3081
Presnell Jenny L. • Soc Sci & Humanities Ref Libn • Miami University Edgar W. King Library • Oxford, OH 45056
Press Nancy Ottman • Resource Sharing Coordinator • University of Washington Pacific Northwest • Seattle, WA 98195 • ALCTS CLENE
Press Richard L. Dr • Sacramento, CA 95826 • ACRL
Presser Carolynne • Director • University of Manitoba Elizabeth Dafoe Library • Winnipeg MB, R3T 2N2 Canada • ACRL ALCTS LAMA LITA
Pressman Sylvia • Trustee • Dearborn Department of Libraries Henry Ford Centennial Library • Dearborn, MI 48126
Pressnall Patricia E. • Librarian • Albany Unified School District • Albany, CA 94706
Prestegard Renee M. • American Library Association • Chicago, IL 60611-2795 • IFRT NMRT
Preston Alfred L. • Fort Greely Army Post Library • APO, AP 96508 • PLA AFLRT FLRT
Preston Barbara Ann • Librarian • Gatesville Elementary Library • Gatesville, TX 76528
Preston Bonita J. • Bibliographic Instruction Libn. • Catonsville Community College • Baltimore, MD 21228 • ACRL LIRT
Preston Cecilia M. • Student • University of California-Berkeley School of Library & Information Studies • Berkeley, CA 94720 • LITA
Preston Gregor A. • Cataloger • University of California-Davis Library • Davis, CA 95616 • ALCTS
Preston Jane M. • Library Media Specialist • Masuk High School • Monroe, CT 06468 • AASL IFRT
Preston Laurie A. • Asst. Reference Librarian • University of South Carolina • Columbia, SC 29208 • ACRL LITA RASD NMRT
Preston Mary Alice • Librarian/Media Specialist • Payson Junior High School Library • Payson, AZ 85541
Preston N. J. • Librarian • Lorain Public Library South Branch • Lorain, OH 44055 • ASCLA
Preston Nancy R. • Assistant Director • ERIC Clearinghouse on Information Resources Syracuse University • Syracuse, NY 13244
Preston Susan B. • Renfroe Middle School • Decatur, GA 30030 • AASL
Prether Jonelle L. • Pottsville, PA 17901
Pretlow Delores Z. • Director of Media Services • Richmond Public Schools • Richmond, VA 23219 • AASL LAMA YALSA
Pretorius Marycarol F. • Library/Media Specialist • Dayton Public Schools Patterson Career Center • Dayton, OH 45402 • AASL
Pretzer Dale H. • Director • Hackley Public Library • Muskegon, MI 49440 • PLA
Preuss Karen L. • Children's Librarian • J. Lewis Crozer Library • Chester, PA 19013 • ALSC PLA YALSA
Preusz Janet H. • Vigo County Public Library • Terre Haute, IN 47807 • ALCTS
Preuthun Paula • Grosse Pointe, MI 48230 • ALSC PLA *Life*
Prevetti Christine A. • Milwaukee Public Library • Milwaukee, WI 53233 • YALSA
Prewitt Claudia C. • Leland, MS 38756
Prewitt Marja G. • Dist Librarian/Media Coordinator • Saint Mary's School District • Saint Mary's, AK 99658
Prhys Lloyd D. • Tech. Servs. Ln/Sys. Admin. • University of the Virgin Islands The Ralph M. Paiewonsky Library • Saint Thomas, VI 00802 • ALCTS CLENE IFRT IRRT
Price Anita L. • Student • Howe Military School • Howe, IN 46746
Price Anna L. • Catalog Librarian • Montana State University • Bozeman, MT 59717-0332 • ACRL ALCTS
Price Bennett J. Dr • System Analyst • University of California San Francisco Library • San Francisco, CA 94143-0840 • LITA
Price Bernadette B. • Mahopac, NY 10541 • NMRT SRRT
Price Carol C. • Assistant Director • Levittown Public Library • Levittown, NY 11756-1292
Price Carole M. • Student • University of Pittsburgh School of Library and Information Science • Pittsburgh, PA 15260
Price Carolyn P. • Adult Service Librarian • Clemmons Branch Library • Clemmons, NC 27012 • RASD
Price Cheryl A. • Wheaton, IL 60187 • ACRL LRRT
Price Clement A. Dr. • Trustee • Newark Public Library • Newark, NJ 07101-0630 • ALTA PLA
Price Darlene • Head, Circulation Dept. • Air University Library • Maxwell AFB, AL 36112
Price David M. • Assistant State Librarian • California State Library • Sacramento, CA 94237-0001 • PLA
Price Elaine F. • Media Specialist • Rome Middle School • Rome, GA 30161 • AASL
Price Grace E. • Public Affairs Specialist • Library of Congress • Washington, DC 20541 • AASL
Price Helen L. • Topeka, KS 66611 • Continuing
Price Jean • Pikes Peak Library District • Colorado Springs, CO 80901
Price Jeffrey S. • Student • San Jose State University Division of Library & Information Science • San Jose, CA 95192-0029
Price Judith A. • Administrator-Acquistions-Serial • Public Service Electric & Gas Company Library • Newark, NJ 07101
Price LaJean • Media Specialist • Culler Junior High School • Lincoln, NE 68504 • AASL
Price Larry C. • Librarian • Ingram Library Services Inc. • La Vergne, TN 37086-1986 • AASL ACRL ALCTS ALSC ASCLA LAMA LITA PLA CLENE ERT FLRT
Price Linda J. • Librarian • Hine Junior High School • Washington, DC 20003 • AASL NMRT
Price Lisa M. • Elroy, PA 18964
Price Lisa R. • Student • University of California Los Angeles Graduate School of Library & Information Science • Los Angeles, CA 90024 • ALSC PLA RASD SRRT
Price Louise C. • Deputy Director • Manchester City Library Carpenter Memorial Building • Manchester, NH 03104-6199
Price Lydia • Youth Services Librarian • North Riverside Public Library • North Riverside, IL 60546
Price Lydia • Berkeley, IL 62163
Price M. Consuelo Sr. • Librarian • Bishop Walsh High School Library • Cumberland, MD 21502 • AASL
Price M. Elaine • Branch Head • Providence Branch Library • Providence, KY 42450 • PLA NMRT
Price Marty G. • Mary Holmes College Barr Library • West Point, MS 39773
Price Mary Jo Mrs. • San Antonio, TX 78213
Price Mary Sauer • Director for Acquisition • Library of Congress • Washington, DC 20541 • ALCTS
Price Michael • Director • Providence Athenaeum • Providence, RI 02903
Price Millicent R. • Supervisory Librarian • San Bernardino Public Library • San Bernardino, CA 92410
Price Neil V. • Associate Professor & Chair • University of North Dakota Department of Library Science & Audiovisual Instruction • Grand Forks, ND 58202 • AASL
Price Olive B. • Chairman, Advisory Committee • O'Connor Foundation • Hobart, NY 13788
Price Pamela A. • Director of Library Services • Mercer County Community College Library • Trenton, NJ 08690 • ACRL LIRT
Price Patricia A. • Warren, MI 48081 • ALSC YALSA
Price Paul S. Dr. • Director,Learning Resources • Thames Valley State Technical College • Norwich, CT 06360 • ACRL
Price Robbin J. • Children's Librarian • Half Moon Bay Branch Library SMCO Library • Half Moon Bay, CA 94019
Price Susan P. • Student • Rutgers University School of Communication Information & Library Studies • New Brunswick, NJ 08903
Price Virginia A. • Technical Librarian • Arthur D. Little, Inc. • North Charleston, SC 29418 • GODORT
Pricer Wayne F. Jr. • Hays, KS 67601
Prichard Frances D. • Library Media Specialist • Voorhees Middle School • Voorhees, NJ 08043 • AASL YALSA
Prichard Hazel W. • Hope, AR 71801 • Continuing
Prichard Phyllis Ms. • Alief Independent School District • Houston, TX 77099
Pride Lula H. • Assistant Director • Indian Prairie Public Library District • Willowbrook, IL 60517 • ASCLA
Pridgen Pamela S. • Director • Hattiesburg, Petal & Forrest County, The Library • Hattiesburg, MS 39401 • PLA
Pridham Sherman • Library Director • Portsmouth Public Library • Portsmouth, NH 03801
Priesing Patricia L. • Supervisor Media Services • Hopewell Valley Regional Schools Central High School • Pennington, NJ 08534 • AASL YALSA

Priestly Beatrice J. • Senior Librarian • Long Branch Public Lib • Long Branch, NJ 07740 • PLA

Prilliman Jack L. • Conway Spgs, KS 67031

Prime Lynn F. • Children's Librarian • Sonoma County Library • Santa Rosa, CA 95404 • AASL ALSC

Primm E. Russell • Childrens Press • Chicago, IL 60656 • ALSC

Primus Carol J. • Mesa County Public Library • Grand Junction, CO 81502

Primus David M. • Marmot Project Mesa State College Library • Grand Junction, CO 81502 • LITA

Primus Donna P. • Supervising Librarian • Brooklyn Public Library Crown Heights Branch • Brooklyn, NY 11225

Prince Barbara Ann • Student • North Carolina Central University • Durham, NC 27707

Prince Teresa L. • Student • University of Michigan School of Information and Library Studies • Ann Arbor, MI 48109-1092 • RASD

Prince Timothy C. • Reference Librarian • Saskatchewan Legislative Library • Regina SK, S4S 0B3 Canada • RASD

Prince William W. • Reference Librarian • University of Tennessee T Carter & M Rawlings Lupton Lib • Chattanooga, TN 37403

Prindiville Sue • Asst. Head of Reference • Naperville Public Libraries • Naperville, IL 60540 • PLA RASD

Prine Cynthia J. • Spauldings Library • District Heights, MD 20747

Prine Stephen • Network Consultant • Library of Congress Library for the Blind & Physically Handicapped • Washington, DC 20542 • ASCLA

Pringle Dawn • Library Director • Jordan Valley District Library • East Jorden, MI 49727 • PLA RASD

Pringle Julie D. • Coordinator, Collection Devel. • Fairfax County Public Library • Fairfax, VA 22033-1909 • ALCTS LAMA

Pringle Terry L. • San Juan Capistrano, CA 92675 • LITA RASD

Printz Mike L. • Librarian • Topeka West High School • Topeka, KS 66604 • AASL YALSA

Prisender Kathleen J. • Queens College Graduate School of Library & Information Studies • Flushing, NY 11367 • IRRT

Pristasch Carol • Principal Librarian • Elizabeth Public Library • Elizabeth, NJ 07202 • ALCTS LITA

Pritchard Cicely J. G • Assistant to the Librarian • University of Regina Library • Regina SK, S4S 0A2 Canada • ACRL

Pritchard Clara B. • Phoenix, AZ 85018

Pritchard Donna • Peoria, IL 61614-5157 • RASD

Pritchard Eileen • Science Librarian • California Polytechnic State University Robert E. Kennedy Library • San Luis Obispo, CA 93407 • ACRL LIRT

Pritchard Elsie T. • Acquisitions Librarian • Morehead State University Camden-Carroll Library • Morehead, KY 40351 • ALCTS

Pritchard John A. • Director • Catawba County Library • Newton, NC 28658 • LAMA LITA PLA IFRT NMRT

Pritchard Patricia A. • Technical Service • Fondulac District Library • East Peoria, IL 61611 • ALCTS

Pritchard Sarah M. • Director of Library • Smith College William Allan Neilson Library • Northampton, MA 01063 • ACRL ALCTS LAMA RASD LRRT SRRT

Pritchard Sharon • Librarian • Kirksville Upper Elementary School • Kirksville, MO 63501

Pritchett Jane E. • Bibl. Instruction Librarian • Delaware State College William C. Jason Library • Dover, DE 19901 • ACRL FLRT IFRT

Pritchett John C. • Library Director • Columbia College J. Drake Edens Library • Columbia, SC 29203 • LAMA

Pritchett Mebane M. • Trustee • Atlanta-Fulton Public Library • Atlanta, GA 30303 • PLA

Pritts Susan A. • Assistant Librarian • University of Michigan Kresge Business Adm Library • Ann Arbor, MI 48109-1234 • ALCTS LITA

Pritzker Marian F. • Board President • Chicago Public Library • Chicago, IL 60605 • ALTA

Probasco Thomas L. • Student • Indiana University School of Library and Information Science • Bloomington, IN 47405

Proces Stephen L. • Director • Neenah Public Library • Neenah, WI 54957-0569

Prochazka Richard J. • Student • Clarion University of Pennsylvania College of Library Science • Clarion, PA 16214

Proctor Deborah K. • Secondary Lib Media Specialist • Campbell County School District • Gillette, WY 82717 • AASL IFRT

Proctor Drew L. • Costabile Associates Inc • Bethesda, MD 20814

Proctor Edward • Asst. Prof/Asst. Ref. Librarian • University of Illinois at Chicago University Library • Chicago, IL 60680

Proctor Ellen R. • United Medical Center Library Services • Moline, IL 61265

Proctor Irene Adams Mrs. • Nashville, TN 37211

Proctor Joanne M. • Topeka, KS 66604 • AASL ALSC

Proctor Judy C. • Brazil, IN 47834

Proctor Lynne A. • Children's Librarian • Pikes Peak Library District • Colorado Springs, CO 80901-1579

Proctor Marsha W. • Durham, NC 27707

Proctor Martha Jane • Regional Branch Head • Charleston County Library Dorchester Road Regional • North Charleston, SC 29418

Proctor Pamela A. • Media Specialist • Dearborn Public Schools • Dearborn, MI 48126 • AASL

Proctor Sandra J. • Student • University of North Carolina at Chapel Hill School of Information and Library Science • Chapel Hill, NC 27599-3360 • SRRT

Proctor Thomas C. • Director of Library Services • Fort Belknap College Library • Harlem, MT 59526 • ACRL

Prodrick R Gerald • Oakville ON, L6J 3M7 Canada • ACRL

Profeta Catherine Cherry • Student • University of North Carolina at Chapel Hill School of Information and Library Science • Chapel Hill, NC 27599-3360

Profeta Patricia C. • Metuchen, NJ 08840

Proffitt David S. • Student • North Carolina Central University • Durham, NC 27707

Progar Dorothy • Waco, TX 76710 • LAMA PLA

Progar Therese L. • Children's Specialist • Orange County Public Library University Park Branch • Irvine, CA 92715 • YALSA

Promen Peter J. • Librarian • Johns Hopkins University School of Advanced International Studies • Washington, DC 20036 • LITA

Promis Patricia A. • Acquisitions Librarian • University of Arizona Library • Tucson, AZ 85721 • ACRL ALCTS RASD EMIERT NMRT

Promos Marianne • Assistant Division Chief • Free Library of Philadelphia • Philadelphia, PA 19103 • LAMA PLA

Pronevitz Gregory • Asst. Dir. for Member Services • OHIONET • Columbus, OH 43221 • ALCTS ASCLA

Propes Terri L. • San Jacinto College Lee Davis Library • Pasadena, TX 77505-2007 • ACRL

Prophater Susan L. • Alexandria, VA 22306 • PLA

Prophett Bonnie L. • East Elementary School • Sharon, MA 02324 • AASL ALSC

Prorak Diane • Librarian • University of Idaho Library • Moscow, ID 83843 • ACRL LIRT SRRT

Proseus Linda S. • Media Coordinator • Forest Hills Middle School • Wilson, NC 27893 • AASL

Prosser Elizabeth L. • Media Specialist • White Oak Elementary School • Indianapolis, IN 46234 • AASL

Prosser Judith M. • Library Consultant • West Virginia Library Commission • Charleston, WV 25305

Protopappas Frederic P. • Ln.-Program Officer • Library of Congress • Washington, DC 20541

Proudfit Claribel • Des Moines, IA 50316-3704 • Continuing

Proudfoot Anne L. • Senior Librarian • San Jose Public Library • San Jose, CA 95113 • PLA

Proudfoot Linda • Chief Cataloging Section • Joint Bank-Fund Library • Washington, DC 20431 • ALCTS LAMA LITA   *Life*

Proudfoot William S. • Student • San Jose State University Division of Library & Information Science • San Jose, CA 95192-0029

Proulx Adeline • Omaha, NE 68114 • ALSC PLA
                                                                    Continuing

Prouty Sharman E. • Assistant Librarian • Memorial Libraries Flynt Library of Historic Deerfield & Pocumtuck Asn Library • Deerfield, MA 01342-0053 • ACRL ALCTS
                                                                    Life

Provine Rick E. • Media Librarian • University of Virginia Clemons Library • Charlottesville, VA 22904-0100 • VRT

Provis William H. Jr. • Chicago Public Library Harold Washington Library • Chicago, IL 60605 • RASD

Provow Cynthia J. • Library Media Services • BOCES Albany • Latham, NY 12110

Prucha Cristine L. • Circulation Librarian • University of Wisconsin Murphy Library • La Crosse, WI 54601 • ACRL LAMA

Prudden Margaret M. • Federal Government Document Ln. • Montgomery County Department of Public Libraries • Rockville, MD 20850 • GODORT

Pruett Barbara Jean • Library Director • United States International Trade Commission • Washington, DC 20436 • FLRT SRRT

Pruett Diane M. • Fairfax County Public Library John Marshall Branch • Alexandria, VA 22310

Pruett Nancy J. • Reference Librarian • Sandia National Laboratories • Albuquerque, NM 87185 • MAGERT

Pruitt Laura E. • Librarian • Fox Senior High School • Arnold, MO 63010 • AASL

Pruitt Lynne E. • Acquisition Librarian • Milwaukee Public Library • Milwaukee, WI 53233 • PLA

Pruitt Nina • Librarian • Tangier School Library • Tangier, VA 23440 • AASL ALSC

Pruitt William R. • Student • University of North Texas School of Library & Information Sciences • Denton, TX 76203 • LRRT SRRT

Prusha Anne B. • Project Coordinator • Geauga County Public Library • Chardon, OH 44024 • LAMA YALSA

Prussing Anne S. • University of California-San Diego Biomedical Library • La Jolla, CA 92093 • ACRL ALCTS

Pryce Clyde E. • Regional Library Officer • United States Information Agency (USIA) • Washington, DC 20547

Prygoski Vincent W. • Thomas Cooley Law School Library • Lansing, MI 48901

Pryor Carol • Service High School • Anchorage, AK 99507

Pryor Helen F. • Student • University of Michigan School of Information and Library Studies • Ann Arbor, MI 48109-1092 • ACRL IRRT NMRT

Pryor Nona Ann • Media Specialist • Archdale-Trinity Middle School • Trinity, NC 27370 • AASL YALSA

Przepasniak James R. • Head of Technical Services • Oak Park Public Library • Oak Park, IL 60301 • PLA

Przybylo Ted • Trustee • Niles Public Library • Niles, IL 60648 • ALTA

Ptacek William H. • Director • King County Library System • Seattle, WA 98109-5191 • LAMA PLA

Puacz Mira • Chicago, IL 60618

Puccetti Robin L • City Librarian • Independence Public Library • Independence, OR 97351 • PLA

Pucci Rosemarie J. • Sea Cliff, NY 11579

Puccio Joseph A. • Public Service Officer • Library of Congress • Washington, DC 20541 • ALCTS RASD

Pucheu Mary Lynn • Ville Platte, LA 70586 • ALSC YALSA   *Life*

Puckett Marianne • Associate Director • Louisiana State University School of Medicine • Shreveport, LA 71130-3932

Puderbaugh Velma Elaine • Librarian • Seattle Public Library • Seattle, WA 98104-1193 • ALCTS ALSC

Pudewell Jeff • Student • University of California-Berkeley School of Library & Information Studies • Berkeley, CA 94720

Puerto Cecilia P. • Bakersfield, CA 93306 • ACRL EMIERT IRRT

Puffer Karen J. • Lancaster, CA 93535

Puffer Yvonne L. • Head Librarian • Newark Free Library • Newark, DE 19711-7146 • LAMA PLA

Puffinbarger Kay • Joplin, MO 64804

Pugh Belinda • Librarian • Kings Bay Base Library • Kings Bay, GA 31547 • AFLRT FLRT

Pugh Ellen T. • Lacey, WA 98503 • ACRL ALCTS   *Life*

Pugh Margaret M. • Student • Florida State University School of Library and Information Studies • Tallahassee, FL 32306-2048

Pugh Quincy • Richland County Public Library • Columbia, SC 29201

Pugh Richard J. • Student • State University of New York at Albany School of Information Science & Policy • Albany, NY 12222 • LITA

Pugh Stephen • Western Regional Sales Manager • Yankee Book Peddler • Contoocook, NH 03229 • ALCTS

Pugliese Paul J. • Director • Duquesne University Library • Pittsburgh, PA 15282 • ACRL LITA

Puhek Esther L. • Head of Southwest Library • Kenosha Public Library • Kenosha, WI 53142-5799 • PLA

Puhek Sheila • Board Member • Whiting Public Library • Whiting, IN 46394

Pukkila Marilyn R. • Refrence Librarian • Colby College Libraries • Waterville, ME 04901 • ACRL SRRT

Pukl Joseph M. Jr. • Head,Acquistions Dept. • University of South Carolina • Columbia, SC 29208

Pulikonda Ella • Director • Tipton County Public Library • Tipton, IN 46072

Pullen Geneva B. • Manager of Extension Services • Lexington Public Library • Lexington, KY 40507 • LAMA PLA

Pullen June W. • Cartersville High School Library • Cartersville, GA 30120 • AASL YALSA

Puller Maryam W. • Assistant Director of Libraries • Township of Lower Merion • Ardmore, PA 19003

Pulliam Linda M. • Tallahassee, FL 32301 • PLA

Pullin Mary S. • Main Library & Adult Servs Dir • Reuben McMillan Free Library Association Youngstown & Mahoning Cnty P L • Youngstown, OH 44503

Pulsipher Susan E. • Director of Library Services • Methodist College • Fayetteville, NC 28311-1499 • ACRL ALCTS

Pulver A. Issac • Student • Wayne State University Library Science Program • Detroit, MI 48202 • IFRT SRRT

Pulver Beth A. • Student • Wayne State University • Detroit, MI 48202 • AASL

Puma DeDe • Santa Rosa, CA 95403
Puma Michael J. • Director of Library Services • Perma-Bound Books Hertzberg-New Method, Inc. • Jacksonville, IL 62650 • ALCTS ALSC YALSA
Pumphrey Mark E. • Assistant Director/Adult Serv. • Transylvania County Library • Brevard, NC 28712 • RASD
Puncke Rose Marie V. • Librarian • Pearl Harbor Elementary School • Honolulu, HI 96818
Pung Patricia M. • Assistant Head Catalog Dept. • University of California UCSB Library • Santa Barbara, CA 93106-9010 • ALCTS
Pungitore Verna L. • Indiana University School of Library and Information Science • Bloomington, IN 47405 • ASCLA LAMA PLA IFRT LRRT
Puniello Francoise S. • Director • Rutgers University Libraries Mabel Smith Douglass Library • New Brunswick, NJ 08903-0270 • ACRL
Punshon Bette • Wayne, NJ 07470
Purcell Cheryl • Library Director • Eastern Mississippi Community College Golden Triangle Campus Library • Mayhew, MS 39753
Purcell Ellen C. • Assistant Librarian • P.K. Yong Laboratory School Mead Library • Gainesville, FL 32611 • AASL
Purcell Kathleen V. • Chief, Human Resources • Annapolis & Anne Arundel County Public Library • Annapolis, MD 21401-7042 • PLA
Purcell Marcia L. • Director of Library Promotion • Random House, Inc. • New York, NY 10022 • PLA RASD YALSA
Purcell Muriel M. • Librarian & Teacher • Crane School • Santa Barbara, CA 93108
Purcell Nadine • Tech Serv Ln & Automation Coor. • Jackson County Library System • Medford, OR 97501 • ALCTS LITA
Purcell Shawn • New York State Library • Albany, NY 12230
Purdue Sandy • Children's Librarian • Minneapolis Public Library Linden Hills Branch • Minneapolis, MN 55410 • ALSC
Purdy Betsy F. • Librarian I-Children's Services • Broward County Library Imperial Point Branch • Fort Lauderdale, FL 33308 • ALSC YALSA
Purdy Victor • Assistant Professor • Brigham Young University School of Library & Information Sciences • Provo, UT 84602
Purins Sandra A. • Meadowbrook Elementary School • East Meadow, NY 11554 • AASL
Purinton Judith S. • Assistant Reference Librarian • Huntsville-Madison County Public Library • Huntsville, AL 35804
Purnell Jean M. • Assoc. Dean of Public Services • University of the Pacific • Stockton, CA 95211 • ACRL LAMA RASD
Pursch Lenore D. • Director • United States Air Force • Wright-Patterson AFB, OH 45433 • AFLRT
Pursley Lisa D. • Georgia Southern University Henderson Library • Statesboro, GA 30460
Purtill Diane • Social Sciences Division • Chicago Public Library • Chicago, IL 60605 • PLA
Purtill Mary L. • Student • University of North Carolina Department of Library & Information Studies • Greensboro, NC 27412-5001 • AASL
Purucker Mary I. • Head Librarian • Santa Monica High School • Santa Monica, CA 90405 • AASL ALSC YALSA
Purvis Brenda S. • Director • Gainesville College John Harrison Hosch Library • Gainesville, GA 30503 • ACRL
Purvis Laurel T. • Ragsdale High School • Jamestown, NC 27407 • AASL
Puryear Charlene E. • Student • University of South Carolina College of Librarianship • Columbia, SC 29208
Puryear Dorothy S. • Nassau Library System • Uniondale, NY 11553 • ASCLA PLA EMIERT SRRT
Puryear Rebecca S. • Media Specialist • Anson Senior High School Anson County Schools • Wadesboro, NC 28170 • AASL YALSA
Puterko Susan M. • Librairan I • Chicago Public Library • Chicago, IL 60605
Putnam Carolyn D. • Library Media Specialist • Millwood Elementary School • Sumter, SC 29154 • AASL
Putnam Cheryl L. • Saginaw, MI 48603
Putnam Eleanor Ann • Librarian • Chugach Optional Elementary School • Anchorage, AK 99504 • AASL
Putnam Mary Ann • Holton Arms School Inc. • Bethesda, MD 20817 • AASL
Putnam Miriam • Andover, MA 01810 • Continuing
Putnam Nancy J. • Rutgers University Libraries • New Brunswick, NJ 08903
Putney Marie-Louise F. • Charleston, SC 29412
Putney Patricia E. • Student • Brown University Rockefeller Library • Providence, RI 02912
Putz Paul D. • Chugiak, AK 99567
Puvogel J. Cole • Director • LaRoche College John J. Wright Library • Pittsburgh, PA 15237 • ACRL ALCTS RASD LHRT
Puziak Kathleen M. • Dallas, TX 75230-5659
Pye Linda • Southwestern Oklahoma State University Al Harris Library • Weatherford, OK 73096
Pyke Carol J. • Jamestown Elementary School • Arlington, VA 22207 • AASL
Pyle Connie J. • Kensington, CA 94708
Pyle Linda A. • Philadelphia, PA 19145
Pyle Martha • San Bruno Public Library • San Bruno, CA 94066
Pyonteck William P. • Library Director • Hunterdon County Library • Flemington, NJ 08822 • LAMA
Pyroth Elisabeth • Head Librarian • Goethe House New York Library • New York, NY 10028
Pytlik Jean D. • Castro Valley, CA 94546
Qaissaunee Barbara F. • Head of Technical Services • Delaware State College William C. Jason Library • Dover, DE 19901 • ACRL ALCTS
Qi Yalan • Student • University of South Carolina College of Library & Information Science • Columbia, SC 29208
Qian Jin • Student • Saint John's University Division of Library & Information Science • Jamaica, NY 11439
Qin Jian • Student • University of Illinois Graduate School of Library and Information Science • Urbana, IL 61801 • LRRT
Qin Minmin • Student • University of Maryland College of Library and Information Services • College Park, MD 20742-4345
Qiu Jing • Student • University of Illinois Graduate School of Library and Information Science • Urbana, IL 61801 • ACRL
Qiu Kui • Student • Ohio State University • Columbus, OH 43210
Qiu Xinmu • Student • Emporia State University School of Library & Information Management • Emporia, KS 66801
Quade Nancy C. • Brooklyn Public Library • Brooklyn, NY 11238
Quadri Nancy J. • Branch Manager • Anne Arundel County Public Library Provinces Branch • Severn, MD 21144
Quaglieri Maureen L. • Manchester, NH 03104-1771
Quah Swee-Lan • Cataloger • Ohio University Vernon R. Alden Library • Athens, OH 45701-2978 • ALCTS IRRT
Qualls Betty N. • Student • Indiana University School of Library and Information Science • Bloomington, IN 47405 • ACRL RASD
Qualls June M. • Findlay, OH 45840-6068 • ALCTS
Qualters Roger B. • Branch Librarian • Aurora Hills Branch Library • Arlington, VA 22202
Quam Alison • Librarian • Heckscher Foundation Resource Center Lincoln Center Institute • New York, NY 10023 • ALSC
Quamme Beverly J. • Media Specialist • Carl Ben Eielson Elementary School • Fargo, ND 58103 • AASL
Quammen Teva J. • Personnel Manager • Internal Revenue Service • Richmond, VA 23229
Quan Alix Minton • Computer Systems Librarian • Somerville Public Library • Somerville, MA 02143 • PLA
Quan Leon Anna S. • Student • University of Arizona Graduate Library School • Tucson, AZ 85721
Quan Sharon L. • Student • University of California Los Angeles Graduate School of Library & Information Science • Los Angeles, CA 90024 • RASD
Quan Shirley N. • Children's Librarian • Orange County Public Library Fountain Valley Branch • Fountain Valley, CA 92708 • ALSC PLA
Quanbeck Beth Marie • Director of Library Development • South Dakota State Library • Pierre, SD 57501-2294 • ASCLA PLA
Quarles Barbara V. • Librarian Grade 2 • Phoenix Public Library • Phoenix, AZ 85004 • ALSC
Quartz Beatrice M. • Palmetto, FL 34221 • Continuing
Quast Emilie J. • University of Minnesota • Minneapolis, MN 55455 • ALCTS LITA
Quattlebaum M. V. • Arlington, VA 22202 • Continuing
Quay Richard H. • Head, Humanities/Social Sciences • Miami University Edgar W. King Library • Oxford, OH 45056 • ACRL
Queinnec Young-Hee • Chief Canadian Marc Off • National Library of Canada Information Technical Services • Ottawa ON, K1A 0N4 Canada
Quelland Nancy • Monterey Public Library • Monterey, CA 93940
Quement Shirley • New York, NY 10014 • RASD
Quenon Evan • Head Librarian • Brown McCarroll & Oaks Hartline • Austin, TX 78701
Query Eunice • Hudson, NC 28638 • AASL ALSC *Continuing*
Query Lance D. • Assistant University Librarian • Northwestern University Library • Evanston, IL 60208-2300
Queyquep Tess G. • Cataloger • Houston Public Library • Houston, TX 77002 • ALCTS EMIERT
Quiatkowski Sandra E. • Indianapolis, IN 46219-2506
Quick Janet • Library Media Specialist • South Woods Middle School • Syosset, NY 11791 • AASL IFRT
Quick Mary Beth • Rock Hill, SC 29732 • Continuing
Quick Richard C. • Geneseo, NY 14454 • ACRL
Quick Theresa J. • University of Illinois • Urbana, IL 61801
Quicksall Sandra K. • Publications Coordinator • Hercules Incorporated Aerospace Division • McGregor, TX 76657
Quigg Agnes B. • Preservation Officer • University of Hawaii Library • Honolulu, HI 96822 • ALCTS
Quigley Amy E. • Westford, MA 01886 • ALSC
Quigley Loretta M. • Student • Southern University in New Orleans Leonard S. Washington Library • New Orleans, LA 70126 • ACRL ALCTS NMRT
Quigley Margaret C. • Children's Librarian • Upper Dublin Public Library • Dresher, PA 19025 • ALSC PLA
Quigley Michael B. • Media Specialist • New Fairfield Junior and Senior High School • New Fairfield, CT 06812 • AASL
Quillin Judy W. • Assistant Administrator • Wicomico County Free Library • Salisbury, MD 21801 • PLA
Quilling Mary L. • Director • Marymount College Library • Rancho Palos Verdes, CA 90274 • ACRL LAMA RASD LIRT
Quimby Dorothy W. Ms • Head Librarian • Unity College Library • Unity, ME 04988
Quimby Harriet B. • West Falmouth, MA 02574 • ALSC PLA *Continuing*
Quin Mary E. • Louisville Free Public Library • Louisville, KY 40203-2257 • RASD GODORT
Quine Maryclaire M. • Albuquerque, NM 87194-7822 • ALSC YALSA IFRT
Quinlan Barbara M. • Director-Branch Services Div. • Mississauga Public Library System • Mississauga ON, L5B 3Y3 Canada • LAMA PLA
Quinlan Cheryl J. • Student • Wayne State University • Detroit, MI 48202 • AASL
Quinlan Colleen M. • Bloomingdale Public Library • Bloomingdale, IL 60108 • ALSC
Quinlan Judith B. • Head of Reference Department • University of Georgia Libraries • Athens, GA 30602 • ACRL LAMA LITA RASD
Quinlan Melitta • Trustee • Mid-Wisconsin Federated Library System • Fond du Lac, WI 54935-5510 • ALTA
Quinlan Nora J. • Hollywood, FL 33020 • ACRL
Quinlivan Kathleen • Orchard Park, NY 14127
Quinn-Wisniewski Karen A. • Student • University of Maryland College of Library and Information Services • College Park, MD 20742-4345
Quinn Amy A. • Houston, TX 77079
Quinn Bridget E. • Student • Middle Country Public Library • Centereach, NY 11720 • NMRT SRRT
Quinn Carol J. • Coordinator of Reference • Western Maryland College Hoover Library • Westminster, MD 21157-4390 • ACRL
Quinn Cheryl • Trustee • Mount Prospect Public Library • Mount Prospect, IL 60056
Quinn David J. Dr. • Campus Head Librarian • Suffolk County Community College Western Campus Library • Brentwood, NY 11717 • ACRL
Quinn Elizabeth A. • Student • Florida State University School of Library and Information Studies • Tallahassee, FL 32306-2048
Quinn Judy A. • Senior Editor • Library Journal Magazine • New York, NY 10011
Quinn Kelly • Long Beach, CA 90815
Quinn Marie C. • Baltimore County Public Library • Towson, MD 21204 • PLA
Quinn Mary A. • Director • Monroe County Public Library • Key West, FL 33040
Quinn Mary Ellen • Director,Collection Development • Chicago Public Library Harold Washington Library • Chicago, IL 60605 • ALCTS RASD
Quinn Mary Lee • Media Specialist • Hampton Elementary School • Hampton, CT 06247 • AASL
Quinn Mary R. • Head of Circulation • Winchester Public Library • Winchester, MA 01890 • ASCLA RASD
Quinn Mary R. Mrs. • Radford, VA 24141
Quinn Michael • Reference Department Head • Ames Public Library • Ames, IA 50010 • RASD
Quinn Sharon E. • Head, Original Cataloging • University of Maine Raymond H. Fogler Library • Orono, ME 04469 • LITA
Quinn Susan C. • Student • Rosary College Graduate School of Library & Information Science • River Forest, IL 60305 • AASL
Quinn Vicky L. • Student • Clark-Atlanta University School of Library & Information Studies • Atlanta, GA 30314-4391

Rainwater Jean M. • Reader Services Librarian • Brown University Library • Providence, RI 02912 • ACRL

Rais Shirley M. • Chino, CA 91710

Raiteri Stephen L. • Beavercreek, OH 45434

Raithel Frederick J. • Head of Circulation • Daniel Boone Regional Library • Columbia, MO 65205-1267

Rajec Elizabeth M. • Head Acquisitions • City College of New York (CUNY) • New York, NY 10031 • ACRL ALCTS IRRT

Rake Anthony I. • Librarian • Wauconda High School Library • Wauconda, IL 60084 • AASL

Rake Judith A. • Literacy Program Coordinator • Secretary of State Literacy Office • Springfield, IL 62701

Rake Patricia T. • Gulfport, MS 39501

Raker Joseph W. • Head of Acquisitions • Boston Public Library • Boston, MA 02117 • ALCTS LAMA

Rakestraw Marsha K. • Student • Emporia State University School of Library & Information Management • Emporia, KS 66801

Rakowitz Beverly W. • Technical Information Specialist • U.S. Army Health Care Studies & Clinical Inv. Acty. • Ft. Sam Houston, TX 78218 • LITA RASD AFLRT FLRT

Raley Patricia Fortner • Media Specialist • Mandarin Oaks Elementary School • Jacksonville, FL 32223 • AASL

Rall Julie A • Findlay, OH 45840

Ralli Richard A. • Deputy Librarian • Australian Defence Force Academy • Campbell ACT 2600, Australia • ACRL ALCTS LAMA LITA

Ralls Robert O. • Systems Analyst • Library of Congress • Washington, DC 20541 • LITA

Ralph Johnnie Ann • Associate University Librarian • California State University • San Bernardino, CA 92407 • ACRL

Ralston Carl E. • Bowling Green, OH 43402 • LITA PLA RASD

Ralston Marilyn Joan • Cataloger-Database Management • Villanova University Falvey Memorial Library • Villanova, PA 19085-1699 • ACRL

Ralya Kelyn L. • Student • University of Alabama School of Library & Information Studies • Tuscaloosa, AL 35487-0252

Ramage Kathryn L. • Emporia, KS 66801

Ramage Patricia G. • Systems Librarian • University of South Alabama Library • Mobile, AL 36688 • LITA LRRT

Ramaty Vera M. • Librarian • Montgomery County Public Library White Oak Branch • Silver Spring, MD 20904

Ramberger Vernon W. • Librarian • Hillendale Elementary School • Chadds Ford, PA 19317 • AASL ALSC   *Life*

Rambler Linda K. Dr. • Middletown, PA 17057

Rambo Gloria P. • Library Director • Lasalle Parish Library • Jena, LA 71342 • LAMA PLA

Rambo Helen M. • Catalog Librarian • Northwest Nazarene College Riley Library • Nampa, ID 83686

Rambo Marjorie • Newport News, VA 23602 • LAMA PLA AFLRT FLRT   *Life*

Rambo Neil • Associate Director • University of Washington Health Science Library & Info Center • Seattle, WA 98195

Rambo Patricia A. • Asst. Children's Librarian • Poplar Creek Public Library Dist • Streamwood, IL 60107 • ALSC

Ramey Marsha • Supervisor • Saint Louis County Library Grand Glaze Branch • St. Louis, MO 63011

Ramin Nerissa • Indexer • H. W. Wilson Company • Bronx, NY 10452 • LITA

Ramirez Anthony L. • Oxnard, CA 93030-2343

Ramirez Art • Librarian III • Chicago Public Library Toman Branch • Chicago, IL 60623

Ramirez Diana • Social Sciences Ref. Librarian • Texas A & M University Sterling C. Evans Library • College Station, TX 77843-5000 • ACRL

Ramirez Esmirna G. • Librarian II • Forsyth County Public Library • Winston-Salem, NC 27101 • GODORT

Ramirez Jennii L. • Student • San Jose State University Division of Library & Information Science • San Jose, CA 95192-0029

Ramirez Luis Antonio • Community Library Manager • Los Angeles County Public Library El Monte Branch • El Monte, CA 91731

Ramirez Marianne S. • Northern Valley Regional High School • Old Tappan, NJ 07675 • AASL YALSA IFRT

Ramirez Martha A. • Bibliographer • University of California McHenry Library • Santa Cruz, CA 95064 • ACRL

Ramirez Oscar • Librarian • University of Nuevo Leon Unidad Linares • Linares NL 67700, Mexico • LITA IRRT

Ramirez Rudy • Librarian • City Unified Sch Dist-Balboa H S • San Francisco, CA 94112 • AASL

Ramm Dorothy V. • Periodicals Reference Libn • Northwestern University Library Transportation Library • Evanston, IL 60208 • ACRL RASD

Ramnath Prema • Bolingbrook, IL 60440

Ramos Karen R. • Librarian II-Branch Librarian • Stockton-San Joaquin County Public Library • Stockton, CA 95202 • YALSA

Ramos Luis Raul • Delaware State College William C. Jason Library • Dover, DE 19901

Ramos Mario S. • Student • University of South Carolina College of Library & Information Science • Columbia, SC 29208

Ramos Mary A. • Asst. Dir. of Admissions • University of Maryland Baltimore County Kuhn Library • Catonsville, MD 21228 • LITA NMRT

Ramos Monserrat • Director of Library • ITESM-CEM Biblioteca • Mexico C.P. 54766, Mexico • ACRL

Ramp Ellen M. • Library Media Specialist • Eldridge Park Elementary Lawrenceville Elementary • Lawrenceville, NJ 08648 • AASL

Rampey Leslie C. • Student • University of South Carolina College of Library & Information Science • Columbia, SC 29208

Ramsaur Barbara Meyer • Information Services • Cecil County Public Library • Elkton, MD 21921 • RASD

Ramsay Diana O. • Stephens County High School • Toccoa, GA 30577 • AASL

Ramsay Ellen E. • A-1030 Vienna, Austria • AASL YALSA

Ramsay Penne A. • Substitute Librarian • Westminster Public Library • Westminster, CO 80030-4970

Ramsdell Kristin R. • Bibliographic Instruction Ln • California State University Hayward Library • Hayward, CA 94542 • ACRL LIRT

Ramsey Ann • Director • Chester County Library • Chester, SC 29706 • LAMA PLA

Ramsey Ann-Marie C. • Librarian I • Prince George's Cnty Memorial Lib Surratts-Clinton Branch • Clinton, MD 20745 • PLA IFRT SRRT

Ramsey Caroline • Vice President • Gateway Productions Inc • New Orleans, LA 70115

Ramsey Denora • Trustee • Nantahala Regional Library • Murphy, NC 28906 • ALTA

Ramsey Donna Epps • El Paso, TX 79906 • ACRL AFLRT FLRT SORT SRRT

Ramsey Elizabeth L. • Lodi High School • Lodi, CA 95240

Ramsey Jack A. • Glendale, CA 91208 • Continuing

Ramsey Keitha Y. • Manager, Automated Cataloging • University of Houston Libraries • Houston, TX 77204-2091 • ALCTS NMRT

Ramsey Marilyn • Head of Acquistions • University of San Diego Copley Library • San Diego, CA 92110 • ALCTS

Ramsey Pamela Kelley • Emporia State University School of Library & Information.Management • Emporia, KS 66801

Ramsey Wendy G. • Hilliard, OH 43026 • ALSC PLA

Ranalli Barbara A. • Newark, DE 19702 • ACRL ALCTS LAMA

Rancilio James M. • Library Director • Bullard Sanford Memorial Library • Vassar, MI 48768 • ALSC LAMA PLA

Rancour Carolyn M. • Seattle, WA 98116

Rancurello Carmella M. • Children's Librarian • Dayton & Montgomery County Public Library Kettering-Moraine Branch • Kettering, OH 45429

Rand Duncan D. • Director • Lethbridge Public Library • Lethbridge AB, T1J 4C4 Canada • ALSC PLA

Rand Roena • Trustee • Gary Public Library • Gary, IN 46402 • ALTA

Randall Ann K. • Director • Howard University Libraries Founders Library • Washington, DC 20059 • ACRL ALCTS LAMA   *Life*

Randall J. Parke • Architect/Consultant • Pecsok Jelliffe & Randall Library Architects • Indianapolis, IN 46240 • ALTA LAMA PLA ERT

Randall Kevin M. • Chicago, IL 60625 • ALCTS

Randall Lynn E. • Director • Caldwell College Library • Caldwell, NJ 07006-6195 • ACRL LAMA RASD LIRT

Randall Mary R. • Student • University of Washington Graduate School of Library and Information Science • Seattle, WA 98195 • AASL

Randall Michael H. • Assistant Head of Serials Dept. • University of California-Los Angeles (UCLA) • Los Angeles, CA 90024-1450 • ALCTS

Randall Michelle • Episcopal School of Dallas • Dallas, TX 75229 • AASL IFRT

Randall Sara L. • Project Manager • NOTIS Systems, Inc. • Evanston, IL 60201-3622 • LITA

Randelia Gool B. • Director • Indiana Vocational Technical College • Sellersburg, IN 47172

Randi Judi • Orange, CT 06477

Randle Rose Marie • Rice University Fondren Library • Houston, TX 77251-1892

Randles R. Jeffrey • Programmer/Analyst • Washington University Olin Library • Saint Louis, MO 63130 • ALCTS LITA

Randolph Anne • Denver Public Library Friends Foundation • Denver, CO 80204

Randolph Anne C. • Director • Derby Public Library • Derby, KS 67037 • ALTA LAMA PLA

Randolph Dena • Coor. of Multicultural Affairs • Fieldston School Tate Library • Bronx, NY 10471

Randolph Susan E. • Washington, DC 20007 • ALSC

Randolph Virginia S. • Head Librarian Public Service • Pepperdine University Payson Library • Malibu, CA 90263 • ACRL LIRT

Randolph William • Riverside, CA 92516 • AASL

Randorf Debra A. • State University of New York (SUNY) College at Old Westbury Library • Old Westbury, NY 11568

Raney Carol K. • Greensboro, NC 27410 • AASL ALSC

Raney Doris K. • Manager • Lexington Public Library Southside Branch • Lexington, KY 40503 • LAMA PLA

Raney Hollaman M. • Trustee • Jackson-Hinds Library System • Jackson, MS 39201 • ALTA

Raney Leon • Dean of Libraries • South Dakota State University Briggs Library • Brookings, SD 57007 • ACRL

Ranger Kim L. • Government Documents Librarian • Grand Valley State University Zumberge Library • Allendale, MI 49401-9403 • GODORT SRRT

Rangoon Betty G. • West Hartford, CT 06107

Ranhand Jori L. • Hunter College Library • New York, NY 10021 • ACRL

Ranier Raymond P. • Student • Indiana University School of Library and Information Science • Bloomington, IN 47405

Ranieri Ann E. • Head of Technical Services • Beaver College • Glenside, PA 19038 • ACRL

Rankeillor Robert M. • Library Director • Santa Fe Community College Library • Gainesville, FL 32602

Rankin-Grams Kathleen A. • Librarian II • Detroit Public Library • Detroit, MI 48202 • PLA RASD

Rankin Allison R. • Student • University of North Carolina At Wilmington Randall Library • Wilmington, NC 28403-3297

Rankin Barbara E. • Avon, CT 06001

Rankin Carol • Highland Public Library • Highland, NY 12528

Rankin Juliann E. • Periodicals Librarian • California State University-Chico Meriam Library • Chico, CA 92929-0295

Rankin Karen M. • Glendale, CA 91206

Rankin Katherine L. • Las Vegas, NV 89109 • ACRL ALCTS MAGERT

Rankin Kathy D. • School Librarian • Washington Episcopal School • Washington, DC 20016 • ALSC

Rankin Mary K. • Butler, PA 16001

Rankin Priscilla • Gainesville College John Harrison Hosch Library • Gainesville, GA 30503 • ACRL

Rankin Rachel E. • Student • University of Wisconsin School of Library & Information Studies • Madison, WI 53706

Rankin Rachel M. • Media Specialist • Damascus High School • Damascus, MD 20872 • AASL

Rankin Virginia • School Librarian • Tillicum Middle School • Bellevue, WA 98008 • AASL LIRT

Rannie Patricia M. • Indexer CBI • H.W. Wilson Company • Bronx, NY 10452 • ALSC

Ransil M. Michele Cdp • Dir of Lib Automated Sys • Ball State University Bracken Library • Muncie, IN 47306-0160 • ACRL LITA

Ransom Charles G. • Diversity Librarian • University of Michigan Graduate Library Reference • Ann Arbor, MI 48109 • ACRL

Ransom Helen E. • West Bloomfield, MI 48324 • ASCLA LITA   *Life*

Ransom Joan M. Ms. • Philadelphia, PA 19148 • Life

Ransom Marcia J. • Director • Winfield Public Library • Winfield, KS 67156 • LAMA PLA

Ransom Margaret A. • Queen Annes County Free Library • Stevensville, MD 21666

Ransom Stanley A. Jr. • Plattsburgh, NY 12901 • ALCTS PLA   *Life*

Ranta Judith A. • Queens Borough Public Library • Jamaica, NY 11432 • ALCTS PLA

Rantala Donald O. • LRC Specialist • WITC • Superior, WI 54880

Ranum Mark L. • Reference Services Coordinator • East Central Regional Library • Cambridge, MN 55008 • PLA RASD IFRT

Rao B. V. R. Dr. • Bangalore 560 069, India • Continuing

Rao Geetha A. • Corporate Inf. Specialist • Promega Corporation • Madison, WI 53711 • ACRL

Rao Jan S. • School Library Media Specialist • Geneva High School • Geneva, NY 14456 • AASL

Rao Kathleen H. • Framingham, MA 01701 • ALSC

Rao Narsu Revathi • Barrington, RI 02806

Rao Pal V. Dr. • Dean of Library Services • Central Missouri State University Ward Edwards Library • Warrensburg, MO 64093 • ACRL LAMA LITA

Rapczynski Mary L. • Ascension Church • Bowie, MD 20719 • AASL ALSC

Raph Theresa E C • Los Angeles, CA 90045-0975

Raphael Joan L. • Student • San Diego Public Library • San Diego, CA 92101 • ALSC PLA

Raphael Mary E. (Molly) • Executive Asst to Director • District of Columbia Public Library Martin Luther King Memorial Library • Washington, DC 20001 • LAMA LITA PLA IFRT

Rapoport Barbara J. • Authority Control Libn/Map Catlg • University of California-Los Angeles (UCLA) • Los Angeles, CA 90024-1450 • ALCTS LITA MAGERT

Rapp Brigid • Info. Services Branch Chief • Environmental Protection Agency Headquarters Library • Washington, DC 20460 • PLA FLRT

Rapp Gerald D. • Librarian • Lutheran High School South • Saint Louis, MO 63123 • AASL

Rapp Gerald D. • Corporate Legal Counsel • Dayton & Montgomery County Public Library • Dayton, OH 45402-2103 • ALTA

Rapp Jessica S. • Student • Simmons College Graduate School of Library & Information Science • Boston, MA 02115 • LITA

Rapp Joan G. • Director of Libraries • University of Missouri-Saint Louis • St. Louis, MO 63121-4499 • ACRL LAMA

Rapp Marie A. • Professor Emerita • University of Illinois at Chicago University Library • Chicago, IL 60680 • Life

Rapp Marilyn A. • Br Hd • Chicago Public Library Jefferson Park Branch • Chicago, IL 60630 • PLA

Rapp Robert Franz • System Operations Librarian • Maude Shunk Public Library • Menomonee Falls, WI 53051 • LITA IFRT

Rappaport Ellen C. • Freelancer • Ameritech Information Systems • Albany, NY 12206 • LITA

Rappaport Ellen Diane • Barton Avenue Elementary School • Patchogue, NY 11772 • AASL

Rappelt John F. • Northport, NY 11768 • AASL YALSA *Life*

Rappoport Avi • Berkeley, CA 94703-1839 • LITA

Raquet J. Robin • Science Librarian • Trinity University • San Antonio, TX 78212 • ACRL RASD

Rardin Barbara A. • Ericson Public Library • Boone, IA 50036

Raresheid Cynthia L. • Director • World Almanac Education • Cleveland, OH 44113 • AASL

Rarus Marcia • Librarian • Lincoln-Sudbury Regional High School • Sudbury, MA 01776

Rasbold Virginia A. • Technical Serv./Reference Ln. • Allegany Community College • Cumberland, MD 21502-2596 • ACRL ALCTS

Rasche Richard R. • Galveston, TX 77550 • ACRL

Raschke Susan Doughty • Extened Campus Librarian • Regis University Dayton Memorial Library • Denver, CO 80221-1099

Raschkow Elenka B. • Reference Librarian • Lansing Community College • Lansing, MI 48901 • ACRL LAMA

Rasimus Edward J. • Trustee • Pikes Peak Library District • Colorado Springs, CO 80901

Rask Stephen • Library Director • Rockport Public Library • Rockport, MA 01966

Raske Collen R. • Project Manager/Librarian • Zimmerman Associates, Inc. Department of Interior Library • Herndon, VA 22070 • ALCTS

Raskin Howard B. • Head of Circulation • Cornell University Albert R. Mann Library • Ithaca, NY 14853-4301

Raskin Susan R. • Supervisor of Children's Serv • Newton Free Library • Newton, MA 02159 • ALSC

Rasmus Sherry Ms. • West Point Junior Senior High School • West Point, NE 68788

Rasmussen Dorothy • Chicago, IL 60626 • RASD

Rasmussen Dorothy • Trustee • Schaumburg Township District Library • Schaumburg, IL 60194

Rasmussen Gordon E. • De Kalb, IL 60115

Rasmussen Lisa • Student • McGill University Libraries • Montreal PQ, H3A 1Y1 Canada

Rasmussen Phyllis • Librarian • Library of Congress • Washington, DC 20541 • FLRT IRRT

Rasmussen Rosemary • Director of Children's Services • White Plains Public Library • White Plains, NY 10601 • ALSC

Rasmussen Ruth J. • Library Director • Dartmouth College Dana Biomedical Library • Hanover, NH 03755-3881 • ACRL

Rasmussen Virginia M. • Associate Librarian • Weber County Library • Odgen, UT 84401

Rast Elaine K. • Head Cataloging Auto Rec Dept. • Northern Illinois University University Libraries • DeKalb, IL 60115-2868 • ACRL ALCTS

Ratchford Amy L. • Student • Catholic University of America School of Library and Information Science • Washington, DC 20064 • RASD

Rathbone Cathy • Librarian • Valley Regional Library • Yakima, WA 98901

Rathbone Marjorie • Head of Technical Services • Saint Josephs University Drexel Library • Philadelphia, PA 19131-1395 • ALCTS

Rathbone May C. • University of Washington Suzzallo Library • Seattle, WA 98195

Rathbun Gail P • Senior Librarian • Tempe Public Library • Tempe, AZ 85282 • PLA

Rathburn Linda J. • Savannah, GA 31401 • ACRL

Rathe Bette D. • Media Librarian • Augustana College Mikkelsen Library • Sioux Falls, SD 57197 • ACRL ALSC

Rather Barbara A. • Union Public School • Tulsa, OK 74134 • AASL

Rather John Carson • Kensington, MD 20895 • ACRL RASD *Life*

Rather Lucia J. • Kensington, MD 20895 • ALCTS LITA *Life*

Rathgeber Jo • Alberto Culver Research Library • Melrose Park, IL 60160

Rathje Roberta D. • Librarian III • University of Nebraska Love Library • Lincoln, NE 68588-0410 • NMRT

Rathke Mary Kay • University of Maryland-Eastern Shore Frederick Douglass Library • Princess Anne, MD 21853 • ACRL SRRT

Rathvon David A. • Dallas Public Library Forest Green Branch • Dallas, TX 75243-4114

Ratkin Annette Levy • Nashville, TN 37205

Ratledge Julia J. • Library Clerk III • Atlanta-Fulton Public Library Buckhead Branch • Atlanta, GA 30305

Ratliff Louise M. • Library Information Systems • University of California-Los Angeles (UCLA) • Los Angeles, CA 90024-1450 • ALCTS LITA NMRT

Ratner Pam • General Librarian • Long Beach Public Library Bret Harte Branch • Long Beach, CA 90810

Ratner Rhoda S. • Chief Librarian • Smithsonian Institution Libraries Natural Museum of American History • Washington, DC 20560 • ACRL ALCTS

Rattunde Karen • Librarian • Carnegie-Stout Public Library • Dubuque, IA 52001 • ALCTS LITA

Ratzlaff Arlene M. • Haakon School District 27-I • Philip, SD 57567

Ratzlaff Marcella J. • Hutchinson Public Library • Hutchinson, KS 67501 • PLA CLENE NMRT

Rau Brenda • Librarian • Doldy Elementary School • Lake Charles, LA 70605 • AASL

Rau Elizabeth M. • Washington, DC 20036 • SRRT

Rau Kirk • Assistant Director for Lib. Serv • University of Maine at Augusta Learning Resources Center • Augusta, ME 04330 • ACRL LIRT

Rauch Cindy • Children's Librarian • Homewood Public Library District • Homewood, IL 60430 • ALSC

Rauch Doris E. • Librarian • University of New Brunswick • Fredericton NB, E3B 5H5 Canada • ALCTS

Rauch Ellen C. • Asst. Reg Adm for Member Serv. • Boston Public Library Copley Square • Boston, MA 02117 • LAMA PLA CLENE

Rauch Marguerite C. • Acquisitions Librarian • United States Naval War College Library • Newport, RI 02841 • ACRL LITA AFLRT GODORT

Rauchwerger Diane • Sunnyvale, CA 94087 • AASL ALSC EMIERT

Raue Philip E. • Saint Philip's College LRC • San Antonio, TX 78203

Rauenbuehler Linda L. • Student • University of North Carolina School of Library Science • Chapel Hill, NC 27599-3360 • MAGERT

Rauer Andrea M. • K-5 Media Specialist • Hoover Elementary School • West Branch, IA 52358 • AASL

Raught Floramae D. • Tacoma, WA 98407 • AASL YALSA *Life*

Rauh Edwin D. • Director • Jackson County Library • Ripley, WV 25271 • PLA

Rauh Richard • Architect • Richard Rauh & Associates • Atlanta, GA 30305 • LAMA

Rauhala Barbara • Administrative Librarian • Marin County Free Library Novato Branch • Novato, CA 94947

Raulerson Joan • Librarian • Marist School • Atlanta, GA 30319 • AASL YALSA

Raum Elizabeth • Fardo, ND 58102

Raum Hans L. Jr. • Librarian • Middlebury College • Middlebury, VT 05753-6062 • ACRL

Rausch Sally J. • Bloomington, IN 47401 • ACRL ALCTS LAMA LITA

Rauschenbach Richard R. • President • Rauschbach, Casini & Urban Architects and Engineers • Independence, OH 44131 • LAMA

Rauschenberger D. B. • Director • Haddonfield Public Library • Haddonfield, NJ 08033

Rausen Ruth G. • New York, NY 10024

Rausert Karin • Student • University of Illinois Graduate School of Library and Information Science • Urbana, IL 61801

Rauth Eileen M. • Burlington County Library Pinelands Branch • Medford, NJ 08055

Rave David A. • Director • A. Mitchell Library • Aberdeen, SD 57401

Ravenholt Amy L. • Regional Lib Community Coor • Yakima Valley Regional Library • Yakima, WA 98901

Ravenhorst Johanna • Buena Vista, VA 24416-0762 • AASL

Ravenscroft Donna F. • Bethesda, MD 20814 • AASL PLA RASD

Raver Patsy J. • Director • Monon Town & Township Library • Monon, IN 47959-0305

Ravvin Linda M. • Lexington, KY 40502 • ACRL LAMA RASD IFRT LIRT

Rawan Atifa R. • Documents Librarian • University of Arizona Library • Tucson, AZ 85721 • ACRL GODORT

Rawles-Heiser Carolyn • Director • Douglas County Library • Minden, NV 89423

Rawley Wayne • Director, Inst. & Research Serv. • University of Iowa Libraries • Iowa City, IA 52242-1379 • ACRL LAMA IFRT

Rawlings Mary H. • Rocky River, OH 44116 • AASL

Rawlings Sharon • Adult Seervices Librarian • Metuchen Public Library • Metuchen, NJ 08840 • RASD VRT

Rawlins Barbara • Loyola-Notre Dame Library, Inc. • Baltimore, MD 21212

Rawlinson Helen Ann • Deputy Director • Richland County Public Library • Columbia, SC 29201 • LAMA PLA

Rawlinson Pamela • Deputy Director • Plymouth District Library • Plymouth, MI 48170 • ALSC LITA YALSA

Rawnsley Virgilia I. • Preservation Consultant • Conservation Center for Art & Historic Artifacts • Philadelphia, PA 19102 • ACRL ALCTS

Rawson Nancy A. • Director of Human Resources • Denver Public Library • Denver, CO 80204-2602 • LAMA PLA CLENE

Rawson Nancy B. • Reference Librarian • Wellesley Free Library • Wellesley, MA 02181-5989 • LITA

Rawson William • Bookmobile Librarian • Monterey County Free Library Prunedale Branch • Salinas, CA 93907

Ray Barbara J. • Jenks High School Library • Jenks, OK 74037 • ALSC

Ray Becky A. • Public Services Librarian • Vanderbilt University Central Library • Nashville, TN 37240-0007 • ACRL RASD SRRT

Ray Betty K. • Book Coordinator • Lake County Public Library • Merrillville, IN 46410-5382

Ray Dee Ann • Library Director • Western Plains Library System • Clinton, OK 73601

Ray Diane E. • Student • Northern Illinois University Department of Library & Information Studies • DeKalb, IL 60115

Ray Donald L. • Head of Reference • Mercy College Libraries • Dobbs Ferry, NY 10522 • ACRL

Ray Ellen G. • Baltimore County Public Library Arbutus Branch • Baltimore, MD 21227-2598

Ray Gillian B. • Librarian I, Children's • County of Los Angeles Libraries Diamond Bar • Diamond Bar, CA 91764 • ALSC IFRT

Ray Gloria • Asst Ln for Prog & Tech Servs • East Bonner County Library District • Sandpoint, ID 83864

Ray Gordon L. • Executive Director • Fraser Valley Regional Library • Abbotsford BC, V2S 5Y1 Canada • ALCTS ALSC LAMA PLA RASD IFRT

Ray H Annette Miss • Fort Polk, LA 71459 • LAMA PLA *Life*

Ray Jean Meyer • Somerville, MA 02143 • ACRL MAGERT *Continuing*

Ray Jennifer Sue • Berrien Springs High School • Berrien Springs, MI 49301

Ray John G. • Assistant Director • Loyola-Notre Dame Library, Inc. • Baltimore, MD 21212 • ACRL

Ray John L. • Trustee • Kanawha County Public Library • Charleston, WV 25301 • ALTA

Ray Josphine • Trustee • Bellwood Public Library • Bellwood, IL 60104 • ALTA

Ray Kathryn C. • Branch Librarian • District of Columbia Public Library Tenley Friendship Branch • Washington, DC 20016 • PLA MAGERT

Ray Lorraine A. • Librarian I • Santa Clara Public Library • Santa Clara, CA 95051 • NMRT

Ray Melinda J. • Librarian • Oakwoods School • Granbury, TX 76049 • AASL ALSC LITA YALSA IFRT NMRT

Ray Nancy C. • Director • Southern Pines Public Library • Southern Pines, NC 28387 • LAMA PLA

Ray Phyllis B. • Librarian • Dallas Public Library • Dallas, TX 75201 • ALSC PLA

Ray Ron L. • Acquisition Dept. • Rutgers University Libraries • Piscataway, NJ 08855-1179 • ACRL ALCTS

Ray Sally R. • Plano, TX 75075

Ray Sheila J. • Librarian • Base Library FL4819 • Tyndall AFB, FL 32403 • AFLRT

Ray Tom H. • Adaptive Cataloging • Louisiana State University Libraries Troy H. Middleton Library • Baton Rouge, LA 70803-3342 • ALCTS LITA RASD

Raybon Jean • Arkadelphia, AR 71923

Rayburn Michael E. • Bay Area Representative • Audio Graphic Syatems • San Bernaridino, CA 92402 • AASL

Rayfield Patricia • Reference Librarian • Ludington Library • Bryn Mawr, PA 19010 • RASD

Rayle Ruth • Adult Services • Cuyahoga County Public Library Olmsted Falls Branch • Olmsted Falls, OH 44138 • RASD IFRT

Raymaker Catherine B. • Narraguagus High School • Harrington, ME 04643 • AASL IFRT

Rayment Peter W. • Director • Toledo Public Library • Toledo, OR 97391 • LAMA

Raymer Anne C. • Manager • Saint Joseph County Public Library Roger B. Francis Branch • South Bend, IN 46635 • YALSA

Raymond Barbara J. • Technical Info. Specialist • Niagara Mohawk Power Corporation • Syracuse, NY 13202 • ACRL LITA GODORT NMRT

Raymond Chadwick T. • Executive Librarian • Northbrook Public Library • Northbrook, IL 60062 • LAMA PLA

Raymond Joan Bieri • Assistant Librarian • Mount Lebanon Public Library • Mount Lebanon, PA 15228 • RASD

Raymond Mary Sister • Librarian • Catherine McAuley High School • Brooklyn, NY 11203 • AASL

Raymond Mimi • Reference • Vernon Area Public Library • Prairie View, IL 60069

Raynal Maryse • Paris, 75015, France • LITA

Raynis Patti • Head Librarian/Director • Patagonia Public Library • Patagonia, AZ 85624 • VRT

Rayson Jenny M. • Cataloger • University of Texas at El Paso Library • El Paso, TX 79968-0582 • ALCTS

Rayward W. Boyd • University of New South Wales • Kensington NSW 2033, Australia • ACRL ALCTS LITA PLA

Raz Robert E. • Director • Grand Rapids Public Library • Grand Rapids, MI 49503-3093 • LAMA PLA

Razer Bob • Assistant Director Support Serv. • Central Arkansas Library System • Little Rock, AR 72201-4698 • LAMA PLA

Razewski Carol A. • Anchorage, AK 99502

Raznick Barbara J. • Head Librarian • Saul Brodsky Jewish Community Library • Saint Louis, MO 63146-0020

Razumny Aja Markel • Southeast Regional Coordinator • Alaska State Library • Juneau, AK 99811-571 • PLA

Razzaghi Farzaneh • Student • Texas Woman's University School of Library & Information Studies • Denton, TX 76204

Rea Ann • Librarian • Beal College Library • Bangor, ME 04401

Rea Hazel • Buffalo, MO 65622 • Continuing

Rea Jay Weston • Hd, Collection Development • Eastern Washington University • Cheney, WA 99004 • ACRL ALCTS

Rea Linda M. • Director • Hastings-Adams County Library • Hastings, NE 68901 • PLA

Rea Nancy B. • Edgewater Library • Edgewater, MD 21037

Rea Patricia A. • Iuka, MS 38852-6118

Rea Zhita Elvord • Library Consultant • Los Angeles County Office of Education • Downey, CA 90242 • AASL

Read Glenn F. Jr. • Ln for Latin Amer Studies • Indiana University • Bloomington, IN 47405 • ACRL ALCTS *Life*

Read Helen F. • Shorewood Hills Elementary School • Madison, WI 53705 • AASL

Read Steven D. • Director • McPherson Public Library • McPherson, KS 67460 • PLA

Reader Evan A. • Associate Director • California State University Office of the Chancellor • Los Alamitos, CA 90720

Reader Nicole • Student • University of California-Berkeley University Library • Berkeley, CA 94720 • ALSC

Reading Barbara A. • Children's Librarian • Thomas Jefferson Library System • Jefferson Cty, MO 65102 • PLA

Reading Dorothy • Northbrook, IL 60062 • Continuing

Reading Kenneth M. • Coordinator • Umatilla County Library Special Library District • Pendleton, OR 97801-0530

Readinger Michael H. • University of Kansas Spencer Research Library • Lawrence, KS 66045-2800

Readman Samuel N. • Asst. Gov't Docs Librarian • New Orleans Public Library • New Orleans, LA 70140 • GODORT

Ready Sandra • Assistant Dean • Mankato State University Memorial Library • Mankato, MN 56002-8400 • ACRL ASCLA LAMA LIRT

Reagan Agnes L. • Rogers, AR 72756 • RASD GODORT

Reagan Fannie • Lake Lanier Regional Library Lawrenceville Branch • Lawrenceville, GA 30245-4707

Reagan Janice B. • Berkley, MI 48072 • Continuing

Reagan M. Reilly Mrs. • Cookeville, TN 38501-3755

Reagan Michael J. • Circulation Unit Coordinator • California State University Oviatt Library • Northridge, CA 91328-1289 • LAMA

Reagan Randolph L. • Student • Kent State University School of Library & Information Science • Kent, OH 44242-0001 • ALCTS LITA IFRT

Reagan Sandra K. • Librarian • Broken Bow High School • Broken Bow, OK 74728 • AASL

Reagor Melinda Ann • Hd, Copy Cataloging/Recon Coor. • Rutgers University Libraries Technical & Automated Services • Piscataway, NJ 08855 • ALCTS LAMA

Ream Daniel L. • Head Reference Services • Virginia Commonwealth University • Richmond, VA 23284-2033 • ACRL LAMA RASD

Ream Deana • Mid-Michigan Library League • Cadillac, MI 49601

Ream Judith K. • Director, Interlibrary Loan • North Suburban Library System • Wheeling, IL 60090 • LITA RASD SRRT

Ream Leslie M. • Kutztown, PA 19530 • AASL

Ream Sally • Library Director • Miami-Dade Community College Medical Center Campus Library • Miami, FL 33127 • ACRL LITA

Reames Sally • Library Trustee • Kalamazoo Public Library • Kalamazoo, MI 49007-5270 • ALTA PLA

Reams Bernard D. Jr. Dr. • Law Librarian • Washington University Libraries Freund Law Library • St. Louis, MO 63130 • ACRL ALCTS LAMA RASD GODORT

Reandeau Julie A. • Student • University of Wisconsin-Madison School of Library & Information Studies • Madison, WI 53706 • LHRT

Reandeau Patricia K. • LMC Elementary Coordinator • Sun Prairie Schools • Sun Prairie, WI 53590 • AASL

Reandeau Walter E. • Director • Sun Prairie Public Library • Sun Prairie, WI 53590

Rearden Phyllis • Associate Professor • Eastern Illinois University Booth Library • Charleston, IL 61920-3099 • ACRL ALCTS LITA LIRT

Reardon Ann L. • Allen County Public Library • Fort Wayne, IN 46801

Reardon Barbara M. • Reference Librarian • Bettendorf Public Library • Bettendorf, IA 52722 • PLA

Reardon Elizabeth M. • Head Librarian • Mc Callie School • Chattanooga, TN 37404 • AASL

Reardon Siobhan A. • Budget & Planning Advisor • The New York Public Library • New York, NY 10016 • PLA

Rearick Carol • Brighton, MI 48116 • AASL

Reason Joseph Henry • Tallahassee, FL 32308 • ACRL ALTA *Life*

Reason Louise E. • Librarian • Conant Public Library • Winchester, NH 03470

Reason Sudie M. • Librarian • Williamston High School • Williamston, NC 27892

Reasoner Lynne U. • Associate Librarian • University of California Rivera Library • Riverside, CA 92517 • GODORT

Reasoner Roberta Craig • Media Generalist • Brooklyn Center High School • Brooklyn Center, MN 55430 • AASL YALSA

Reaume Rose M. • Farmington Hl, MI 48335

Reaves Alice F. • Savannah, TN 38372 • AASL ALSC

Rebarcak Pamela Zager • Head,Mongraphs Acq. Section • Iowa State University Library • Ames, IA 50011-2140 • ALCTS

Rebeck Robbyn G. • Administrative Librarian • Worth Public Library District • Worth, IL 60482 • LAMA PLA RASD IFRT

Rebenack John H. • Akron, OH 44313 • LAMA PLA IFRT MAGERT *Continuing*

Rebman Elisabeth H. • Ref. Librarian/Lecturer • University of California-Berkeley School of Library & Information Studies • Berkeley, CA 94720 • ACRL ALCTS

Rebuldela Harriet • Head, Acquisitions Department • University of Colorado-Boulder University Libraries • Boulder, CO 80309 • ACRL ALCTS LRRT

Rech Suzanne Maley • Children's Librarian • Ocean County Library Barnegat Branch • Barnegat, NJ 08005 • AASL

Reck Alice • Coordinator IMC • Instructional Materials Center • Terre Haute, IN 47803 • AASL

Recker Perry D. • Special Collections Assistant • University of Pittsburgh School of Library and Information Science • Pittsburgh, PA 15260 • ALCTS ALSC RASD

Reckner Joyce D. • Head Technical Services • Kenton County Public Library • Covington, KY 41011

Recktenwald Ann • San Jose, CA 95127 • LAMA RASD

Record Nancy • Kilgour School Library • Cincinnati, OH 45208

Record Pauline L. • Orange City, FL 32763

Rector Carol • Trustee • Prince William Public Library System Administrative Support Center • Prince William, VA 22192-5073

Rector S. • Winfield Scott Elementary School • Fort Scott, KS 66701 • AASL

Rector Wendell H. • Librarian • John Read Middle Sch • West Redding, CT 06896 • AASL

Reda Anna • Head of Circulation/Bookkeeper • Worth Public Library District • Worth, IL 60482

Redalje Susanne J. • Head Chemistry Library • University of Washington Chemistry Library • Seattle, WA 98195 • ACRL RASD

Redden Camille J. • Reference Librarian • Southern University Shreveport-Bossier City Campus • Shreveport, LA 71107

Redden Catherine M. • Director • Leach Library • Londonderry, NH 03053

Reddick Mary J. • General Reference Librarian • University of Utah Marriott Library • Salt Lake City, UT 84112-1179 • ACRL IRRT

Redding Faye S. • Ln • Baltimore Police Department Library Education & Training Division • Baltimore, MD 21202 • ASCLA RASD

Redding Joan • Adult Services Libraian • Upper Arlington Public Library • Upper Arlington, OH 43221

Redding Linda L. • School Media Specialist • Plymouth Community Intermediate School • Plymouth, MA 02360 • AASL ALSC

Reddoch Barbara S. • Little Rock, AR 72221

Reddy Eileen A. • Pittsburgh, PA 15217

Reddy Himabindu B. • Glenview, IL 60025 • IFRT

Reddy Joan L. • Director • Minnehaha County Library • Crooks, SD 57020 • PLA

Reddy Marlita A. • Editoral Code & Data, Inc. • Detroit, MI 48226 • GODORT

Redfearn Caroline • Director/Head Librarian • West Memphis Public Library • West Memphis, AR 72301 • ACRL ASCLA

Redfearn E. Patricia • Swansea, MA 02777 • ALCTS

Redfern Bernice I. • Associate Librarian • San Jose State University Clark Library • San Jose, CA 95192-0028 • ACRL

Redfern Laurie • Santa Rita, GU 96915

Redfield Dale E. • Supervising Librarian • Ventura Cnty Lib Serv Agency Simi Valley Library • Simi Valley, CA 93063

Redfield Jay H. • Long Island University Brooklyn Center • Brooklyn, NY 11201 • ACRL RASD LIRT

Reding Susan M. • Geneva Free Library • Geneva, NY 14456

Redington Deirdre E. • Collections Services Librarian • Bradley University Cullom-Davis Library • Peoria, IL 61625 • ACRL ALCTS

Redman Betsy J. • Acquisitions Librarian • Arizona State University Hayden Library • Tempe, AZ 85287-1006 • ACRL ALCTS LAMA SRRT

Redman Dee Ann F. • Student • Parmly Billings Library • Billings, MT 59101 • PLA RASD

Redmond Angela Dierking • Austin, TX 78720-2185

Redmond Ann P. • Media Librarian • Southern Middle School Library • Lexington, KY 40503 • AASL

Redmond John O. • Chief,Technical Processing Sect • United States Nuclear Regulatory Commission • Washington, DC 20555 • ALCTS

Redmond Mary • Librarian • New York State Library State Education Department • Albany, NY 12230 • ACRL ASCLA LAMA RASD GODORT IFRT

Redo James A. • Adm Asst • Remar Enterprises • Loganville, GA 30244

Reeb Richard C. • Interim Asst. Dir. for Tech Serv • University of Wisconsin-Madison Memorial Library • Madison, WI 53706 • ALCTS

Reece Motoko B. Dr. • Cleveland Public Library • Cleveland, OH 44114-1271 • ACRL

Reece Sue Abrams • Librarian • Ferris High School • Ferris, TX 75125

Reed-Lowery Mary • Memphis, TN 38134

Reed-Scott Jutta • Senior Program Officer • Association of Research Libraries (ARL) • Washington, DC 20036 • ACRL ALCTS

Reed Ada Dorothy • Arlington, VA 22205-1502 • ALSC PLA *Life*

Reed Ann C. • Media Specialist • Richardson High School • Federalsburg, MD 21632 • AASL

Reed Ann M. • Corvallis, OR 97330 • SRRT

Reed Barbara Ann • Cos Cob, CT 06807

Reed Barbara D. • Graduate Student • University of South Carolina College of Library & Information Science • Columbia, SC 29208

Reed Barbara E. • Dartmouth College Sherman Art Library • Hanover, NH 03755-3570 • ACRL RASD IRRT

Reed Bette J. • Grand Priarie, TX 75052

Reed Betty M. Miss • Dallas City Community Unit 336 • Dallas City, IL 62330 • AASL

Reed Bonnie • Lubback, TX 79424-3328

Reed Brenda • Head Librarian • Bishop's College School • Lennoxville PQ, J1M 1Z8 Canada • AASL

Reed Bruce • Sales Representative • Quality Books Inc. • Lake Bluff, IL 60044-2204

Reed Carol A. • Science Subject Specialist • University of Toledo William S. Carlson Library • Toledo, OH 43606-3399 • ACRL

Reed Carol A. • Student • University of Alabama School of Library & Information Studies • Tuscaloosa, AL 35487-0252

Reed Caroline • University of the Virgin Islands The Ralph M. Paiewonsky Library • Saint Thomas, VI 00802

Reed Catherine A. • Bayside, WI 53217

Reed Cathie • Librarian • Montessoir Society of Central Maryland • Baltimore, MD 21093 • AASL

Reed Claudia A. • Director of Libraries • Mount Saint Mary's College • Los Angeles, CA 90049 • ACRL

Reed Donald A. • Los Angeles, CA 90037

Reed Elaine Paez • County Librarian • Auburn-Placer County Library • Auburn, CA 95603-3789 • PLA

Reed Elizabeth M. • Branch Librarian • Arkron-Summit County Public Library Richfield Branch • Richfield, OH 44286 • YALSA

Reed Ellen B. • Assistant Administrator • Las Vegas-Clark County Library District East Las Vegas Branch • Las Vegas, NV 89121

Reed Emily • Cockeysville, MD 21030 • Continuing

Reed Helen I. • Dir of Access Service & Budgets • University of Northern Colorado James A. Michener Library • Greeley, CO 80639 • ACRL ALCTS LAMA LITA *Life*

Reed Jeannine L. • Librarian-Adult Services/Ref • Rockford Public Library • Rockford, IL 61101-1061

Reed John H. • Houston, TX 77025 • LITA

Reed Joy A. • Manager Serials Operations • University Microfilms International • Ann Arbor, MI 48106-1346 • ALCTS LITA RASD

Reed Judy Diane • Lake Worth Public Library • Lake Worth, FL 33460

Reed Kathlyn L. • Houston, TX 77074-5003 • ACRL

Reed Lawrence L. • Reference/Instructional Ln • Moorhead State University Livingston Lord Library • Moorhead, MN 56563-2989 • ACRL

Reed Lola N. • Miami, FL 33176

Reed Marcia C. • Curator of Rare Books • Getty Center Resources Collections • Santa Monica, CA 90401 • ACRL

Reed Maria A. • Manager, Reference Services • Illinois State Library • Springfield, IL 62701-1796 • RASD

Reed Marianne • University of Kansas Anschutz Science Library • Lawrence, KS 66045-2800 • LITA

Reed Moncella • Reference Librarian • Rogers-Hough Memorial Library • Rogers, AR 72756

Reed Pamela B. • Saint Vincent College & Archabbey Libraries • Latrobe, PA 15650-2690 • NMRT

Reed Phyllis • Media Librarian • Panola College • Carthage, TX 75633

Reed Renee • Butler University Irwin Library • Indianapolis, IN 46208

Reed Renee S. • Acting Hd, Lang & Lit Dept. • Minneapolis Public Library & Information Center • Minneapolis, MN 55401-1992 • SRRT

Reed Sally G. • Director • Ilsley Public Library • Middlebury, VT 05753 • LAMA PLA IFRT

Reed Suzanne U. • Duxbury, MA 02332

Reed Virginia R. • Science Librarian • Northeastern Illinois University Library • Chicago, IL 60625 • ACRL

Reeder-Tinsley Yvon • Media Specialist • Floris Elementary School • Herndon, VA 22071

Reeder Geneva N. • Librarian • Lower Dauphin Junior High School Library • Hummelstown, PA 17036 • AASL

Reeder Lanell M. • Student • Brigham Young University School of Library & Information Sciences • Provo, UT 84602 • ALSC

Reeder Maureen A. • Reference Librarian • Torrance Public Library • Torrance, CA 90503 • GODORT

Reeder Nancy P. • Librarian • Heathwood Hall Episcopal School • Columbia, SC 29201 • AASL

Reeder Norman • Branch Librarian • Torrance Public Library • Torrance, CA 90503 • LAMA LITA

Reeder Pamela K. • Asst Tech Serv Lib Bldg Mgr • Missouri Valley College Library • Marshall, MO 65340

Reeds Elizabeth • Mission Viejo, CA 92691 • ACRL LIRT

Reedy Lucie S. • Ann Arbor, MI 48105 • ACRL

Reedy Ruth Clark • Lake Charles, LA 70605 • Continuing

Reedy V. Dianne • Manager, Acquisitions Dept. • Houston Public Library • Houston, TX 77002

Reeling Patricia A. • Associate Professor • Rutgers University School of Communication Information & Library Studies • New Brunswick, NJ 08903 • ACRL RASD GODORT LRRT *Life*

Reelitz Janice B. • Director of School Libraries • Cranbrook Schools • Bloomfield Hills, MI 48303 • AASL YALSA

Rees Larry M. • Director • Jefferson Community College-SW Campus • Louisville, KY 40272

Rees Louise B. • Serials Cataloger • University of Pennsylvania Library Van Pelt-Dietrich Library Center • Philadelphia, PA 19104-6206 • ALCTS

Rees Maureen • Librarian • North Brunswick Free Public Library • North Brunswick, NJ 08902

Rees Trevor L. • Student • State University of New York at Albany School of Information Science & Policy • Albany, NY 12222 • GODORT

Rees Virginia F. • Albany, NY 12203

Reese Boyd • Presbyterian Historical Society Library • Philadelphia, PA 19147 • LAMA

Reese Celia A. • Librarian • Loretto Academy Library • El Paso, TX 79903

Reese Cher L. • Reference Clerk • John Marshall Law School Library • Chicago, IL 60604

Reese Diana • Salida, CO 81201-9508 • ASCLA LAMA

Reese Gary F. • Managing Librarian • Tacoma Public Library • Tacoma, WA 98402

Reese Gregory L. • Director • East Cleveland Public Library • East Cleveland, OH 44112 • LAMA PLA

Reese Laurie B. • Young Adult Librarian • Los Angeles Public Library Fairfax Branch • Los Angeles, CA 90036 • RASD YALSA

Reese Lynna B. • Monroe, MI 48161 • ACRL PLA RASD

Reese Margaret T. • Head Information Services • Vanderbilt University George Peabody College • Nashville, TN 37203

Reese Pamela L. • Public Relations Coordinator • Public Library of Nashville and Davidson County • Nashville, TN 37203-3585

Reeser Lana D. • Student • Indiana University School of Library and Information Science • Bloomington, IN 47405 • SRRT

Reeske Chris • Head of Technical Services • Escondido Public Library • Escondido, CA 92025 • ALCTS

Reetz Latricia Ann • Shelby Twp, MI 48315 • RASD IFRT

Reeve Angelica • Brooke Elementary School • Austin, TX 78702 • AASL

Reeves Cathy L. • Learning Resources Center Dir. • Dodge City Community College • Dodge City, KS 67801 • ACRL LAMA GODORT

Reeves Janice S. • Appleton, WI 54911-2138

Reeves Joan Ress • Providence, RI 02906 • ALTA

Reeves Judy • Library Media Specialist • Daleville City Schools • Daleville, AL 36322 • AASL

Reeves Lois H. • Librarian • Nations Bank Corporate Library • Norfork, VA 23510

Reeves Marc D. • Head Conservation Office • New York Public Library • New York, NY 10018-2788 • ACRL ALCTS

Reeves Roberta A. • Brighton, MI 48116

Reeves Roger L. • Curator of History/Director • Historical Society of Douglas County • Omaha, NE 68111

Reeves Sarah B. • University of Alabama Amelia Gayle Gorgas Library • Tuscaloosa, AL 35487-0266 • ACRL ALCTS RASD GODORT IFRT SRRT

Regal Carol A. • Librarian • Torrance Unified School District Torrance High School • Torrance, CA 90501 • AASL LITA EMIERT LRRT

Regan A. Alexandra • Oakland, CA 94610

Regan Dione • Norcross Public Library • Norcross, GA 30071

Regan Eda M. • Reference Librarian & Instr. • Mills College Library • Oakland, CA 94613 • ACRL

Regan Harold J. • Vice President • H. W. Wilson Company • Bronx, NY 10452 • ACRL ALCTS LAMA LITA RASD

Regan Lynne Cochran • Head,General Information Dept. • Free Library of Philadelphia • Philadelphia, PA 19103 • PLA RASD

Regan Sally • Art/Audiovisual Librarian • Portland Public Library • Portland, ME 04101

Regazzi John J. • President • Engineering Information Inc • New York, NY 10017 • ALCTS LITA

Regens Nancy L. • High School Librarian • Tucson High School • Tucson, AZ 85705 • AASL YALSA

Regent Heeseop • 75013 Paris, France

Regis Kate A. • Librarian • Lawrence Academy • Groton, MA 01450 • AASL YALSA

Register Judith D. • Library Manager • Scottsdale Public Library Mustang Branch • Scottsdale, AZ 85258

Regli Esther • Eau Claire, WI 54703 • Continuing

Regner Erlinda J. • Reference Librarian • Chicago Public Library • Chicago, IL 60605 • PLA RASD

Regnier Flora D. • Arlington, VA 22207-3024

Rego Sylna M. • Head of Branch Services • Peabody Institute Library • Peabody, MA 01960-9998

Rehbach Jeffrey R. • Systems Librarian • Middlebury College Egbert Starr Library • Middlebury, VT 05753-6007 • LITA

Rehbein Linda M. • Washington County Library • Woodbury, MN 55125 • PLA

Rehder Denise R. • School Library Media Spec. • Kings Highway Elementary School • Westport, CT 06880 • AASL

Rehder Patricia A. • Community Services Specialist • Public Library of Des Moines • Des Moines, IA 50308-1791

Reherman Mary Ann • Library Media Director • Putnam City North Senior High School • Oklahoma City, OK 73132 • AASL

Rehling Abbey-jo • Livonia, MI 48154-2911 • ALSC YALSA

Rehmar Marie • Reference Service Librarian • Cleveland State University Joseph Bartunek III Law Library • Cleveland, OH 44115-2403 • ACRL ALCTS LITA RASD GODORT

Rehmke Denise M. • Media Specialist • West High School Library IMC • Iowa City, IA 52246 • AASL

Rehnberg Marilyn • Reference Librarian • Saint Paul Public Library • St. Paul, MN 55102 • PLA RASD EMIERT

Rehnquist-Rosazza Trudi S. • Director, Volunteer Program • University of Iowa Hospitals and Clinics • Iowa City, IA 52242

Rehor Lois • Palo Alto City Library • Palo Alto, CA 94303 • PLA

Rehring Margaret C. • Cincinnati, OH 45208 • AASL YALSA *Life*

Reibach Lois R. • Lutheran Theological Seminary Krauth Memorial Library • Philadelphia, PA 19119-1794 • ALCTS SRRT

Reibel Dorothy E. • Pomeroy, OH 45769

Reiber James T. • Library Supervisor I • Free Library of Philadelphia • Philadelphia, PA 19103 • RASD IRRT

Reich Barbara S. • Rahway, NJ 07065 • ASCLA LITA RASD

Reich Nancy • Coordinating Librarian • Los Angeles Unified School District • Los Angeles, CA 90017 • AASL YALSA

Reich Phyllis • Chief Reference Librarian • University of Minnesota Saint Paul Campus Libraries • Saint Paul, MN 55108 • ACRL

Reich Steven R. • Librarian • Houston Public Library Flores Branch • Houston, TX 77003

Reich Victoria A. • Serials and Acquisitions Dept. • Stanford University • Stanford, CA 94305-6011 • ALCTS

Reichel Jill Mrs • Director • North Syracuse Free Library • Syracuse, NY 13212

Reichel Mary • Asst. Univ Librn-Central Servs. • University of Arizona Library • Tucson, AZ 85721 • ACRL LAMA RASD

Reichenbach Delores M. • Librarian/Media Specialist • Martin Elementary School • Martin, KY 41649 • AASL

Reichenback Miriam J. • Student • Drexel University College of Information Studies • Philadelphia, PA 19104-2875 • AASL ALSC

Reicher Leslie • Preservation Officer • Brandeis University Main Library • Waltham, MA 02254-9110 • ALCTS

Reicher Nancy • Media Specialist • Lincoln College Prep Academy • Kansas City, MO 64108 • AASL

Reichert Shirley M. • Library Director • East Syracuse Free Library • East Syracuse, NY 13057 • PLA IFRT

Reichhardt John M. • Technical Librarian • Computer Sciences Corporation • Dayton, OH 45414

Reichwein Berniece • Assistant Librarian Emerita • University of Cincinnati Central Library • Cincinnati, OH 45221-0033 • ACRL ALCTS *Life*

Reid Annis Rae • Director of Branch Service • New Orleans Public Library • New Orleans, LA 70140

Reid Bonnie • Reference Librarian • Downers Grove Public Library • Downers Grove, IL 60515 • PLA

Reid Carol E. • Bloomington, IL 61704 • ALSC PLA

Reid Carol S. • Library Clerk II • New York State Library State Education Department • Albany, NY 12230 • IFRT SRRT

Reid Carolyn Anne • Associate Director • Cornell University Medical College Library • New York, NY 10021-4896 • ACRL LAMA

Reid Carrie A. • Student • San Jose State University Division of Library & Information Science • San Jose, CA 95192-0029 • LITA

Reid Carrol • Dean, Learning Resources & Servs • Utah Valley Community College • Orem, UT 84058 • ACRL

Reid Charles E. • Trustee • National Commission on Library & Information Science (NCLIS) • Washington, DC 20036 • ALTA PLA

Reid Gail R. • Fayetteville, NC 28303-4915

Reid Grace • Librarian • Vestavia Hills Library • Vestavia Hills, AL 35216 • ALSC PLA

Reid Grace • Student • University of Alabama Graduate School of Library Science • Moundville, AL 35474

Reid Heather J. • Harvard College Library Widener Memorial Library • Cambridge, MA 02138

Reid Jeanne K. • Ardsley, NY 10502

Reid John C. • Library Services Director • West Bend Community Memorial Library • West Bend, WI 53095 • ALSC PLA RASD

Reid Joyce A. • Assistant Executive Director • Lewis & Clark Library System • Edwardsville, IL 62025 • LAMA PLA YALSA

Reid Judith P. • Reference Librarian • Library of Congress • Washington, DC 20541 • RASD

Reid L Anne • Maude Shunk Public Library • Menomonee Falls, WI 53051 • RASD

Reid Margaret Bachman • Librarian • Briggs Lawrence County Public Library • Ironton, OH 45638 • LAMA PLA

Reid Margaret C. • Southwest District Chief • Chicago Public Library Beverly Branch • Chicago, IL 60643

Reid Marion T. • Director of Library Services • California State University San Marcos • San Marcos, CA 92096 • ACRL ALCTS LAMA IFRT LRRT

Reid Martha L. • Russell Library • Middletown, CT 06457

Reid Mary • Trustee • Brentwood Public Library • Brentwood, NY 11717 • PLA

Reid Meta L. • Troy, NY 12180 • LITA PLA

Reid Michele M. • Director of Public Services • South Dakota State Library • Pierre, SD 57501-2294 • ACRL

Reid Nancy A. Dr. • Trustee • Free Library of Philadelphia • Philadelphia, PA 19103 • ALTA

Reid Pauline • Assistant Librarian • Sills Cummis, et al. • Newark, NJ 07102-5400

Reid Rebecca F. • Head Media Specialist • Albany High School • Albany, GA 31708-2601 • AASL

Reid Robert H. • Cuyahoga County Public Library • Cleveland, OH 44134-2792 • ALCTS

Reid Thelma • San Diego, CA 92103 • AASL ALSC *Life*

Reid W. Mike • Aquisitions Manager • Dialog Information Service Inc. • Palo Alto, CA 94304

Reid Winnifred Mrs • New Haven, CT 06509 • Continuing

Reida Linda K. • Western Carolina University Hunter Library • Cullowhee, NC 28723-9002 • ACRL LAMA CLENE

Reider Carole A. • Librarian • Linden Free Public Library Sunnyside Branch • Linden, NJ 07036

Reidinger Betsy • Periodicals Librarian • New Jersey Institute of Technology Van Houten Library • Newark, NJ 07102 • ALCTS

Reidy Donna C. • Westchester, IL 60154 • IFRT

Reidy Marie S. • Children's Librarian • Long Beach Public Library & Info Ctr El Dorado Branch • Long Beach, CA 90815 • ALSC

Reierson Carolyn J. • Chagrin Fall, OH 44022 • LITA

Reif Allan H. • Director of Purchasing • Queens Borough Public Library • Jamaica, NY 11432

Reif Kathleen S. • Coordinator, Marketing & Prog • Baltimore County Public Library • Towson, MD 21204 • ALSC PLA

Reif Lenore S. • Direcctor, Resource Center • Loyola Academy Resource Center • Wilmette, IL 60091 • AASL IFRT

Reif Valerie • Student • Emporia State University School of Library & Information Management • Emporia, KS 66801

Reifel Louie E. Mrs • Houston, TX 77024 • Continuing

Reiff Harry B. • North/South Area Adminstrator • Free Library of Philadelphia • Philadelphia, PA 19103 • LAMA PLA *Life*

Reiff Marianne E. • Catalog Librarian • State Services Organization Library • Washington, DC 20001 • ALCTS

Reiffenberger Linda • Ray High School • Kearney, AZ 85237 • AASL

Reik Constance • Ref. Librarian/Coor. Online Serv • Tufts University Arts & Sciences Library • Medford, MA 02155 • ACRL RASD

Reiling Lois M. • Tucson, AZ 85718

Reilley Mildred A • Trustee • Kutztown University Rohrbach Library • Kutztown, PA 19530-0721 • ACRL

Reilly Barbara D. • Shreve Memorial Library • Shreveport, LA 71120-1523

Reilly Carol H. • I & R/Outreach Librarian • Wake County Public Library System • Raleigh, NC 27610 • PLA

Reilly Catherine R. • Trustee • Massepequa Public Library • Massapequa, NY 11758 • ALTA PLA

Reilly Dayle A. • Novato, CA 94947

Reilly Deborah D. • Librarian • Kent County Public Library • Chestertown, MD 21620 • PLA

Reilly Dina M. • Deer Park Public Library • Deer Park, NY 11729 • PLA

Reilly Elizabeth F. • Hillside Elementary School • Berwyn, PA 19312 • AASL ALSC

Reilly Jennifer L. • Asst Ln I, Children's Services • Nashua Public Library • Nashua, NH 03060

Reilly Jonathan • Trustee • Sachem Public Library • Holbrook, NY 11741

Reilly Karen E. • Owner • Northern Archival Copy • Shoreview, MN 55126 • ALCTS

Reilly Karen J. • Associate Librarian • College of the Holy Cross Dinand Library • Worcester, MA 01610 • ACRL LAMA LITA

Reilly Karen R. • Librarian • Eastern Maine Technical College Library • Bangor, ME 04401 • ACRL

Reilly Linda A. • Librarian • Plymouth-Carver Intermediate School Library • Plymouth, MA 02360 • AASL ASCLA LITA

Reilly Lois L. • Rochester Hills, MI 48307-1369 • ACRL

Reilly Maureen • Media Specialist • Lewis Mills High School • Burlington, CT 06013 • AASL

Reilly Rebecca S. • Serials Librarian • Saint Josephs University Drexel Library • Philadelphia, PA 19131-1395 • ACRL ALCTS

Reilly Susan M. • Director • Miracle Valley Regional Library System City-County Public Library • Moundsville, WV 26041 • ALSC LAMA PLA

Reilly Violet M. • Catalog Department Head • Lakewood Public Library • Lakewood, OH 44107

Reiman Anthony Clare Sr. • Audio-Visual Coordinator • Saint John the Baptist Diocesan High School Library • West Islip, NY 11795

Reiman David A. • Automation Coordinator • University of Toledo William S. Carlson Library • Toledo, OH 43606-3399 • ACRL

Reiman Diane Joslyn • Librarian • University of Rochester Carlson Library • Rochester, NY 14627 • ACRL

Reiman Lorraine A. • Instructor/Ref Librarian • East Carolina University Health Sciences Library • Greenville, NC 27858-4354

Reiman Mary G. • Media Specialist • Southeast High School • Lincoln, NE 68506 • AASL

Reimann Amy M. • Circulation Supervisor • Mountain View Public Library • Mountain View, CA 94041

Reimer Ann • Trustee • Everett Public Library • Everett, WA 98201

Reimer Dorthy N. • Reader Service Department Head • W C Bradley Library • Columbus, GA 31906

Reimer Elizabeth A. • Head Technical Services • Northbrook Public Library • Northbrook, IL 60062 • ALCTS

Reimer Sylvia D. • Washburn University of Topeka Mabee Library • Topeka, KS 66621 • NMRT

Reinbach Edna Miss • Spokane, WA 99208 • ALCTS *Continuing*

Reinecker Nancy C. • Technical Services Librarian • West Georgia Regional Library • Carrollton, GA 30117 • ALCTS

Reiner Julie S. • Information Access Consultant • Lewis & Clark Library System • Edwardsville, IL 62025 • ALCTS LAMA LITA

Reiner Lee E. • Information Manager/Librarian • SME Consulting Engineers Inc. • Rockville, MD 20852

Reinert Margaret Ann • Reference Librarian • Mid-Continent Public Library North Independence Branch • Independence, MO 64050 • ALCTS PLA RASD

Reinhardt Elizabeth P. • Head Librarian • Catholic High School Library • Baton Rouge, LA 70806 • AASL

Reinhardt N. S. • Rare Book Cataloger; Lecturer • Harvard College Houghton Library-Rare Books & Manuscripts • Cambridge, MA 02138 • ACRL

Reinhart Arthur D. • Supervising Librarian • New Haven Free Public Library • New Haven, CT 06510

Reinhart Billie J. • Science/Engineering Librarian • Cleveland State University Library • Cleveland, OH 44115 • ACRL RASD IFRT LIRT

Reinhart Miriam • Santa Monica, CA 90404

Reinhart Scott • Carroll County Public Library • Westminster, MD 21157 • LITA

Reinhart Zelda Z. • Student • Rutgers University School of Communication Information & Library Studies • New Brunswick, NJ 08903

Reinhold Edna J. • Manager, Collection Development. • Saint Louis Public Library • St. Louis, MO 63103-2389 • PLA

Reinicke Sally • Elementary Librarian • Long Meadow Elementary • Rochester, MI 48309 • AASL

Reinke Bernett G. • Library Director • Dickinson State University Stoxen Library • Dickinson, ND 58601 • ACRL

Reinke Carol R. • Head Librarian • Public Libraries of Saginaw Zauel Branch • Saginaw, MI 48603 • LAMA PLA

Reinke Vicky H. • Asst. Director, Student Services • University of Maryland College of Library and Information Services • College Park, MD 20742-4345 • RASD

Reinker Melode G. • Student • University of Hawaii School of Library & Information Studies • Honolulu, HI 96822 • SRRT

Reinmiller James • Director • Hazleton Area Public Library • Hazleton, PA 18201

Reinstein Julia • Trustee • Cheektowaga Public Library Reinstein Branch • Cheektowaga, NY 14225 • ALTA PLA FLRT

Reis Cynthia • Library Technician • University of Hawaii Hilo Library • Hilo, HI 96720

Reis Tovah • Library Director • C. Sheba Medical Center • Tel-Hashoner 52621, Israel

Reiser Jane F. • Reference Librarian • Ela Area Public Library District • Lake Zurich, IL 60047 • YALSA

Reiser William D. • Monroe County Library System • Monroe, MI 48161

Reisinger Jane M. • Children's Information Assistant • North Carroll Library • Hampstead, MD 21074

Reisinger Paul • Trustee • Northbrook Public Library • Northbrook, IL 60062 • ALTA

Reisman Susan K. • Library Trustee • Southington Public Library • Southington, CT 06489 • ALTA

Reisner Rosalind C. • Lincroft, NJ 07738

Reisner Susan • Head Youth Services • Northbrook Public Library • Northbrook, IL 60062 • ALSC YALSA

Reiss Edith M. • Circulation Services Librarian • Carrollton Public Library • Carrollton, TX 75006 • PLA IFRT NMRT

Reiss Robert • Head of Catalog Dept. • Albert Einstein College of Medicine Gottesman Library • Bronx, NY 10461

Reist Paul A. • Reference Librarian • Stanford University Jackson Library • Stanford, CA 94305

Reit Janet W. • Reference Librarian • University of Vermont Bailey Howe Library • Burlington, VT 05405-0036 • ACRL RASD LIRT

Reiter Denise E. • Student • Florida State University School of Library and Information Studies • Tallahassee, FL 32306-2048 • IFRT

Reiter Elizabeth A. • Mystic, CT 06355

Reiter Helmut • Head of Cataloging • Illinois Institute of Technology Chicago Kent College of Law Library • Chicago, IL 60661-3901 • ALCTS

Reiter Jane • Student • Drexel University College of Information Studies • Philadelphia, PA 19104-2875 • ACRL PLA RASD LRRT SRRT

Reiter Mary Lee • Evening/Weekend Reference Libn. • North Idaho College Library • Coeur d'Alene, ID 83814

Reith Louis J. Dr • Rare Book Librarian • Georgetown University Joseph Mark Lauinger Library • Washington, DC 20057-1006 • ACRL IRRT LHRT

Reitman Irene • Part-Time Reference Librarian • Glencoe Public Library • Glencoe, IL 60022-1597 • RASD

Reitman Jo • Manager/News Information Ctr. • Journal/Sentinel Inc. News Information Center • Milwaukee, WI 53201 • IFRT

Reitsma Richard • Reference Librarian • Northwestern College • Orange City, IA 51041

Reitz Joan M. • Student • University of Washington Graduate School of Library and Information Science • Seattle, WA 98195

Reitz Margaret • Louisa, VA 23093 • IFRT

Reitz Mary Lyn • Library Coordinator • Paris Gibson Middle School • Great Falls, MT 59401 • AASL ALSC LITA

Rejebian William K. • Adult Services • Phoenix Public Library Mesquite Branch • Phoenix, AZ 85032 • PLA IFRT

Rekowski Richard G. • Director • Mary H. Weir Public Library • Weirton, WV 26062-4690 • PLA

Relkin Dolly • Trustee • Great Neck Library • Great Neck, NY 11024 • ALTA

Remak Elisabeth M. • Senior Librarian • Radio Free Europe Radio Liberty Library • Munich, 8000, 67, Germany • ACRL NMRT

Rembert Shirley G. • Student • Kent State University School of Library & Information Science • Kent, OH 44242-0001

Remer Robert • Deputy Com/Fin and Adm. • Chicago Public Library • Chicago, IL 60605

Remick Katherine G. • Librarian/Bookstore Owner • Edward T Rabbit & Co • Richmond, VA 23226 • ALSC

Remington David Gray • Deputy State Libn. • Washington State Library • Olympia, WA 98504 • AASL ACRL ASCLA LITA PLA

Remington Tracy L. • Library Assistant/Librarian • California State University-Sacramento Library • Sacramento, CA 95819-6039

Remissong Carol J. • Trustee • Aurora Public Library • Aurora, IL 60505-4299 • ALTA

Remmel Mary W. • Pittsburgh, PA 15210

Remmenga Kent W. • Circulation Librarian • Lincoln City Libraries • Lincoln, NE 68508

Remmert-Loud Maryellen • Director • Robbins Library Junior Library • Arlington, MA 02174 • PLA

Remnek Miranda Beaven • Slavic Bibl • University of Minnesota Walter Library • Minneapolis, MN 55455 • ACRL

Remsberg Helen Miss • Seattle, WA 98101 • Continuing

Ren Juan • Student • Brandeis University Goldfarb Library • Waltham, MA 02254-9110
Ren Wen H. • East Brunswick, NJ 08816
Renaud Robert • Director, Support Services • Markham Public Libraries • Unionville, ON, L3R 5C4 Canada
Rendell Douglas W. • Director • Peabody Institute Library • Danvers, MA 01923
Rendler Richard E. • Deputy City Librarian • San Jose Public Library • San Jose, CA 95113
Reneker Maxine H. • Palo Alto, CA 94306 • ACRL LAMA LRRT
Renfro Carol C. • Technical Services Librarian • Anderson County Library • Anderson, SC 29622-4047 • ALCTS
Renfro Patricia E. • Associate Director of Libraries • University of Pennsylvania Library Van Pelt-Dietrich Library Center • Philadelphia, PA 19104-6206 • ACRL
Reng Jodi • Director • Pend Oreille County Library District • Newport, WA 99156-1708 • PLA
Renkosik Debbie G. • Peru, IL 61354
Renner Charlene E. • Dean of Libraries • Western Michigan University Libraries Dwight B. Waldo Library • Kalamazoo, MI 49008 • ACRL ALCTS LITA
Renninger Karen • Rockville, MD 20850 • GODORT
Reno Ramona L. • Tucson, AZ 85712
Renshaw Marita M. • Catalog Librarian • Northern Illinois University University Libraries • DeKalb, IL 60115-2868 • ACRL ALCTS
Rentof Beryl L. • New York, NY 10017 • ACRL LITA RASD CLENE LIRT
Renton Jeanne E. • Lake Placid, FL 33852-9651 • AASL
Renton Margaret A. • Librarian • University of California Government Publication Department Library • Irvine, CA 92713 • ACRL GODORT
Rentschler Cathy D. • Editor Library Literature • H. W. Wilson Company • Bronx, NY 10452 • LAMA LITA PLA LHRT LRRT
Rentschler Joanne • East Middle School • Farmington Hills, MI 48386 • AASL
Rentz James F. • Head-Techincal Services • Rockford Public Library • Rockford, IL 61101-1061 • ALCTS
Renyer E. Sue • Reference Librarian • Los Angeles County Public Library Las Virgenes Library 116 • Agoura, CA 91301
Renzema Judy • Branch Supervisor • Sacramento Public Library • Sacramento, CA 95814 • PLA
Repasky J. Stephan • Reference Librarian • Friends of San Francisco Public Library • San Francisco, CA 94102
Repasky Linda K. • Youngstown, OH 44512-1125
Repella Alexia D. • Student • Honigman Miller Schwartz & Cohn • Detroit, MI 48226
Repetto Ann M. • Librarian • Veterans Adminstration Medical Center • Saint Louis, MO 63125
Repice Sheila • Info Res Mgr/Corporarte Ln • NAC Re Corporation • Greenwich, CT 06836 • LITA
Repman Denise C. • Cataloging Coordinator • Delgado Community College Moss Memorial Library • New Orleans, LA 70119
Repman Judi • Assistant Professor • Texas Tech University Libraries • Lubbock, TX 79409-0002 • AASL
Repman Martha A. • Philadelphia, PA 19118 • PLA
Repp Laurie A. • Reference Librarian • DePaul University Library • Chicago, IL 60604-2287
Reppert Louise • Sandy Springs, MD 20860 • ALSC PLA *Continuing*
Requena Adele S. • New York, NY 10031 • Continuing
Requena Marilyn A. • T A M C, HI 96859-5000 • LITA AFLRT FLRT
Resch Peter T. • Science Librarian • University of Regina • Regina SK, S4S 0A2 Canada • ACRL LITA
Rescigno Dolores • Staff Librarian • Port Authority of NY & NJ Library • New York, NY 10048 • ALCTS
Resciniti Karen P. • Children's Librarian • Temple Terrace Public Library • Temple Terrace, FL 33617
Resco Carol S. • Head, Physical Sciences Library • University of California • Riverside, CA 92517-5900 • ACRL
Resende Maria Isabel • Catalog Librarian • Brown University Rockefeller Library • Providence, RI 02912 • ACRL ALCTS
Reser David W. • Library of Congress • Washington, DC 20541 • ACRL ALCTS
Resetar Donna R.R. • Valparaiso University Moellering Memorial Library • Valparaiso, IN 46383 • ACRL
Resnick N. Janeen • Asst Rgnl Admin • Western Massachusetts Regional Library System • Hatfield, MA 01038
Reszetar Maryalice Hedge • Associate Executive Director • National Commission on Library & Information Science (NCLIS) • Washington, DC 20036 • LAMA IRRT
Retcho Carol A. • Dept. Head/ Main Periodicals • Broward County Division of Libraries Broward County Library • Fort Lauderdale, FL 33301
Retrum Rose • Learning Center Director • School District #118 • Wauconda, IL 60084 • AASL
Retseck Christine E. • Adult Services Librarian • Lake County Public Library • Merrillville, IN 46410-5382
Rettberg Daniel J. • Duke University William R. Perkins Library • Durham, NC 27706 • ACRL ALCTS
Rettberg Paul A. • Trustee • Elk Grove Village Public Library • Elk Grove Village, IL 60007 • ALTA
Rettew Robert H. • Reference Librarian • Salve Regina University Library • Newport, RI 02840
Rettig James R. • Asst. Ln. for Ref. & Info. Serv. • College of William & Mary Earl Gregg Swem Library • Williamsburg, VA 23187-8794 • ACRL LAMA RASD
Rettig Marcia S. • Student • Clarion University of Pennsylvania College of Library Science • Clarion, PA 16214 • ACRL LAMA IFRT
Rettig Mildred M. • Evansville, IN 47714 • PLA *Continuing*
Rettig William L. • Children's YA Consultant • Madison School District • Madison, WI 53714
Retzer Cathy E. • Elementary Librarian • Medford Area Elementary School • Medford, WI 54451 • AASL
Retzer Elizabeth Dr. • Sarasota, FL 34235 • Continuing
Retzlaff Karen E. • Student • Mayville State University Library • Mayville, ND 58257 • AASL IFRT
Retzlaff Robert R. • Trustee • Union Springs Public Library • Union Springs, AL 36089
Reuben Sandra • Director • County of Los Angeles Public Library • Hawthorne, CA 90250 • PLA
Reuland Anne C. • Reference Librarian • Vanderbilt University Central Library • Nashville, TN 37240-0007 • ACRL RASD IFRT
Reuland Mary S. • Student • Simmons College Graduate School of Library & Information Science • Boston, MA 02115 • PLA
Reuther David L. • Editor-in-Chief • William Morrow & Company,Inc. • New York, NY 10019 • ALSC
Revay Maria Ioona • Student • Rutgers University School of Communication Information & Library Studies • New Brunswick, NJ 08903
Reveal Arlene H. • Bridgeport, CA 93517 • AASL
Revelle Keith • Anchorage, AK 99507
Revercomb Pamela • Altmar-Parish-Williamstown Middle School • Parish, NY 13131 • AASL
Reville Frances C. • Senior Librarian • Brooklyn Public Library • Brooklyn, NY 11238
Rew Alice • Librarian • Atascadero High School Library • Atascadero, CA 93422 • AASL
Rewakowicz Maria G. • Slavic Cataloger • New York Public Library Annex • New York, NY 10036-4396 • ACRL
Rewers Marion • Trustee • Calumet City Public Library • Calumet City, IL 60409-4003 • ALTA
Rewerts Kathryn M. • Media Services Consultant • Waterloo Community Schools • Waterloo, IA 50702 • AASL
Rex Heather • University of New Mexico Centennial Science & Engineering Library • Albuquerque, NM 87131 • ACRL MAGERT
Rex Janet Beth • Public Service Librarian • University of North Dakota Chester Fritz Library • Grand Forks, ND 58202-0175 • ACRL
Rex Syl • Le Claire, IA 52753
Rexford Victoria L. • Student • University of North Texas School of Library & Information Sciences • Denton, TX 76203 • PLA IFRT
Rey Anna • Farmers Branch, TX 75244
Rey Justo • Chief Operating Officer • Distribuidora del Libro, Inc. (D.D.L. Book Inc.) • Miami, FL 33166
Reyes Awilda • Librarian • University of Puerto Rico Graduate School of Librarianship • Rio Piedras, PR 00931 • ACRL
Reyes Caroline M. • Manager, Index Development • NewsBank, Inc. • New Canaan, CT 06840 • ALCTS LITA
Reyes Helen M. • Med Ln • John Muir Medical Center • Walnut Creek, CA 94598-3194
Reyes Joan • Resident Librarian • New York University Library of the School of Law • New York, NY 10012-1099 • LAMA NMRT
Reyes Karen N. • Student • San Jose State University Division of Library & Information Science • San Jose, CA 95192-0029
Reyff Candace I. • Beelman Learning Center Director • Somonauk Grade School • Somonauk, IL 60552
Reynolds Ann • Trustee • Kanawha County Public Library • Charleston, WV 25301 • ALTA
Reynolds Anne L. • Director • Wellesley Free Library • Wellesley, MA 02181-5989 • ALCTS ALSC LAMA LITA PLA RASD
Reynolds Brian A. • Siskiyou County Library • Yreka, CA 96097 • PLA
Reynolds David B. • Librarian • University of Rochester Rush Rhees Library • Rochester, NY 14627-0055 • ACRL
Reynolds David P. • Catalog Librarian/Monographs • Arizona State University Hayden Library • Tempe, AZ 85287-1006 • ALCTS
Reynolds Debra E. • Pittsburgh, PA 15221
Reynolds Dennis J. • Capcon Library Network • Washington, DC 20036 • ACRL ASCLA LAMA LITA PLA CLENE LRRT
Reynolds Donald B. Jr. • Assistant Administator • Central Kansas Library System • Great Bend, KS 67530-4090 • AASL ALSC ASCLA LAMA PLA YALSA CLENE SRRT
Reynolds Elizabeth M. Mrs. • Portland, OR 97221 • Continuing
Reynolds Elizabeth W. • Part-time Reference Librarian • Diablo Valley College Library • Pleasant Hill, CA 94523 • ACRL LITA
Reynolds Ellen • Library Director • Ontario Public Library • Ontario, NY 14519 • PLA
Reynolds Flora E. • Berkeley, CA 94707 • ACRL ALSC *Life*
Reynolds Flora L. • Winson-Salem, NC 27107
Reynolds Gladys N. • Portsmouth, OH 45662 • AASL ALSC
Reynolds Glenna A. • Dayton & Montgomery County Public Library • Dayton, OH 45402-2103
Reynolds Gloria H. • Asst. to the Univ. Ln. • Brown University Library • Providence, RI 02912
Reynolds Holly S. • Circulation Coordinator • New Mexico State University • Las Cruces, NM 88003-0006
Reynolds Jamie G. • Acquisitions Librarian • Edison Community College Univ. of S Florida Learning Resources Center • Fort Myers, FL 33906-6210
Reynolds Jean • President • Millbrook Press Inc. • Brookfield, CT 06804
Reynolds Judith A. • Cataloger • Kenosha Public Library • Kenosha, WI 53142-5799 • PLA
Reynolds Judy • Coordinator of Library Instr • San Jose State University Clark Library • San Jose, CA 95192-0028 • ACRL LRRT
Reynolds Kathy J. • Middle School Media Specialist. • Midview Middle School Library Midview Local Schools • Grafton, OH 44044 • AASL
Reynolds Lynda • Stillwater, OK 74075 • ALSC PLA
Reynolds Mara C. • Community Librarian • Fort Vancouver Regional Library Stevenson Library • Stevenson, WA 98648
Reynolds Martha G. • Managing Librarian • State University of New York (SUNY) College at Geneseo Milne Library • Geneseo, NY 14454-1498 • ACRL RASD LIRT
Reynolds Martha L. • Director • Frederick County Public Library C. Burr Artz Library • Frederick, MD 21701 • PLA
Reynolds Mary Cay • Arizona State University Hayden Library • Tempe, AZ 85287-1006 • ACRL
Reynolds Maryan • Lacey, WA 98503 • Continuing
Reynolds Michael M. • Professor • University of Maryland College of Library and Information Services • College Park, MD 20742-4345 • ACRL RASD *Life*
Reynolds Monique B. • Children's Librarian • Glen Rock Public Library • Glen Rock, NJ 07452-1795 • ALSC
Reynolds Nancy M. • Providence, RI 02908 • AASL
Reynolds Penny F. • Senior Librarian/Adult Reference • Tyler Public Library • Tyler, TX 75702 • RASD
Reynolds Regina R. • Asst Sect Hd Natl Ser Data Prog • Library of Congress • Washington, DC 20541 • ALCTS
Reynolds Rose • Librarian • Fort Madison Public Libraries • Fort Madison, IA 52627
Reynolds Stephen R. • Marion, IA 52302 • AASL ALSC IFRT
Reynosa Rachel • Trustee • San Antonio Public Library • San Antonio, TX 78205
Reyome James D. • Trustee • Lake County Public Library • Merrillville, IN 46410-5382 • ALTA
Rezabek Charlene Boyer • University of Oklahoma Libraries University Libraries • Norman, OK 73019
Rezabek Frankie B. • Librarian • Cooper Intermediate School • Mc Lean, VA 22101
Reznick Carolyn H. • Chappaqua, NY 10514 • ACRL
Reznick Evi • Media Spec • The Epstein School Solomon Schechter School • Atlanta, GA 30328
Rhea Norma L. • Plainfield, IN 46168
Rhea Simms • Librarian • Hutchinson School • Memphis, TN 38119
Rheay Mary Louise • Atlanta, GA 30342
Rhee Byung Mock • Professor • Yonsei University Department of Library Science • Seoul 120-749, South Korea • ACRL LAMA IRRT
Rhee Kun M. • Simi Valley, CA 93063
Rhee Margaret Sue • Director • Northwest Christian College Learning Resource Center • Eugene, OR 97401
Rhein Donna E. • West Brook, CT 06498
Rhein Janie P. • Reference Librarian • Wilton Library Association Inc. • Wilton, CT 06897 • NMRT
Rhein Jean F. • Director • Seminole County Library System Seminole County Services Building • Sanford, FL 32771 • LAMA PLA IRRT

Rhim Choonhee L. • Student • University of California Los Angeles Graduate School of Library & Information Science • Los Angeles, CA 90024

Rhine Cynthia • System Librarian • University of North Carolina • Chapel Hill, NC 27599-3902 • ACRL LITA

Rhinehart Patricia • Adult Reference • Livonia Public Library Alfred Noble Branch • Livonia, MI 48150

Rhines Linda S. • Lakeside School Library • Seattle, WA 98125

Rhoades Alice J. • Technical Services Librarian • Texas A & M University at Galveston • Galveston, TX 77553-1675 • ALCTS

Rhoades Connie A. • Student • University of North Texas School of Library & Information Sciences • Denton, TX 76203 • AASL IFRT

Rhoads Carol A. • Materials Processing Librarian • Montana College of Mineral Science & Technology • Butte, MT 59701

Rhoads Spencer L. • Product Planning Specialist • Gaylord Information Systems • Liverpool, NY 13090

Rhoads Susan • Highland Park High School • Dallas, TX 75205

Rhoda Nancy L. • Student • San Jose State University Division of Library & Information Science • San Jose, CA 95192-0029 • PLA

Rhodd Monica • Branch Library Manager • Queens Borough Public Library South Ozone Park Branch • South Ozone Park, NY 11420 • RASD

Rhoden Linda • Macclenny, FL 32063

Rhodes Clayton E. • Oldtown, MD 21555 • RASD YALSA *Life*

Rhodes Deborah L. • Public Library Branch Manager • Enoch Pratt Free Library Northwood Branch • Baltimore, MD 21218

Rhodes Debra S. • Director • Palm Harbor Library • Palm Harbor, FL 34683

Rhodes Glenda T. • Oxford, OH 45056-2317 • PLA RASD

Rhodes JoAnn M. • Trustee • William Leonard Public Library District • Robbins, IL 60472 • ALTA

Rhodes Kathleen C. • Media Specialist • Hialeah Middle School • Hialeah, FL 33181 • AASL

Rhodes Robin S. • Miller's Creek, NC 28651 • AASL IFRT

Rhodes Sala M. • Circulation/Reference • Darton College Harold B. Wetherbee Library • Albany, GA 31707

Rhodes Saralinda A. • Reference Librarian • University of Kansas Watson Library • Lawrence, KS 66045-2800

Rhodes Sharon A. • Festus, MO 63028

Rhodes Trish • Librarian • Wolthrap Elementary School • Vienna, VA 22203 • AASL

Rholes Julia M. • Reference Division • Texas A & M University Sterling C. Evans Library • College Station, TX 77843-5000 • RASD

Rhone Virginia S. • Port Neches, TX 77651 • PLA

Rhoten Kendra H. • Librarian • Coles Elementary School • Manassaa, VA 22111-3699 • AASL

Rhymes Sara • Elgin, IL 60120

Rhyne Phyllis L. • District Librarian • Mathis Independent School Dist. • Mathis, TX 78368 • AASL

Rials Alison C • Media Center Director • South Broward High School • Hollywood, FL 33020 • AASL

Rialubin Florescita R. • College Librarian • Pamantasan Ng Lungsod • Manila, Philippines

Ribarchak Marian • Shaler Area High School • Pittsburgh, PA 15209 • AASL

Ribbens Dennis • Director • Lawrence University Seeley G. Mudd Library • Appleton, WI 54911 • ACRL RASD *Life*

Ribek Peter • Trustee • Suffolk Cooperative Library System • Bellport, NY 11713 • ALTA

Ribnicky Karen Ferraris • Director • Library Display Design Systems • Berlin, CT 06037 • LAMA PLA

Ricard Richard J. Jr • Team Lead.,Hispanic His & Lit • Library of Congress • Washington, DC 20541 • ALCTS

Ricards Margery A. • Librarian • Rio Mesa High School • Oxnard, CA 93030 • AASL

Riccobene Patricia • Franklin Lake, NJ 07417 • AASL

Rice Alice M. • Librarian • Frontier Elementary School • Angleton, TX 77515 • AASL

Rice Anna Carolyn • Elizabeth, NJ 07202 • Continuing

Rice Carolyn C. • Librarian • Eastside High School • Taylors, SC 29687 • AASL ILERT

Rice Connie • Librarian • Southgate Elementary Blatt & Evergreen St. • Southgate, KY 41071 • AASL

Rice Cynthia • Trustee • Greensboro Public Library • Greensboro, NC 27402 • ALTA

Rice Cynthia N. • Reference Dept. • King County Library System • Seattle, WA 98109-5191

Rice D. Douglas • Trustee • Sioux City Public Library • Sioux City, IA 51101-1203 • ALTA

Rice Elwood A. • Librarian • Tillicum Middle School • Bellevue, WA 98008 • AASL ALSC

Rice Jacqueline A. • Librarian • Blue Ridge School • Dyke, VA 22935 • AASL

Rice Jan L. • Lafayette, LA 70503-4756 • RASD

Rice Jeanne M. • Head Librarian • Tomah Public Library • Tomah, WI 54660 • PLA

Rice Jessica M. • Syracuse Newpapers • Syracuse, NY 13221-4915 • PLA

Rice Joseph Philip • Librarian II • Chicago Public Library • Chicago, IL 60605 • LAMA PLA

Rice Karen • Head, Cataloging Dept. • Western Washington University Wilson Library • Bellingham, WA 98225 • LITA

Rice Mary L. • Milwaukee, WI 53207

Rice Mary Lois • Gaithersburg, MD 20877 • Continuing

Rice Natalee E. • Student • University of Washington Graduate School of Library and Information Science • Seattle, WA 98195 • PLA IFRT

Rice Patricia O. • Documentation & Training Ln. • Pennsylvania State University Pattee Library • University Park, PA 16802 • ACRL

Rice Robert H. • Trustee • Pueblo Library District McClelland Library • Pueblo, CO 81004-1997 • PLA

Rice Robin C. • Student • University of Wisconsin-Madison School of Library & Information Studies • Madison, WI 53706 • IFRT SRRT

Rice Rosamond H. • Northern Marianas College • Saipan, MP 96950 • GODORT

Rice Rosemary D. • Bridgeport, MI 48722

Rice Sally E. • Coordinator Adult Services • East Orange Public Library • East Orange, NJ 07018 • PLA RASD

Rice Sherwin • Elizabethtown, NC 28337 • PLA

Rice Suzanne S • Ball State University Bracken Library • Muncie, IN 47306-0160 • ACRL IRRT

Riceman Anne S. • Madison, WI 53705

Rich David M. • Catalog Librarian • Brown University Rockefeller Library • Providence, RI 02912 • ACRL ALCTS

Rich Elizabeth L. • Director • Needham Free Public Library • Needham, MA 02194 • RASD

Rich Evelyn J. • Publisher • Careers & Colleges • New York, NY 10018 • AASL PLA YALSA

Rich Janine • Tallahassee, FL 32304

Rich Paul John • University of Western Australia • Nedlands W A 6009, Australia • ACRL LHRT

Rich Sandra S. • Santa Clara, CA 95051 • AASL

Rich Susan • North Caldwell, NJ 07006 • ALSC

Rich Zelda R. • Trustee/Board of Lib Trustee • Skokie Public Library • Skokie, IL 60077-3680 • ALTA PLA SRRT

Richard-Onn Lynne E. • School Librarian • London and Middlesex R.C.S.S. Board • London, ON, N6A 4X5 Canada • AASL

Richard Ethel P. • East Orange, NJ 07018 • AASL ALSC *Life*

Richard Gwendolyn Potier • Campus Librarian • Houston Community College Library Westchester Branch • Houston, TX 77079 • SORT

Richard Harris M. • Head Librarian • San Juan College Library • Farmington, NM 87401 • ACRL

Richard Marc • Orginial Cataloging Librarian • McGill University McLennan Library • Montreal PQ, Canada • AFLRT

Richard Peggy J. • Systems Librarian • University of Miami Libraries Richter Library • Coral Gables, FL 33124 • LITA

Richard Stephen G. • Associate Librarian • Glasgow University Library • Glasgow, A12 8QE United Kingdom • ACRL LRRT

Richards Anne S. • Assistant Director • Henrietta Public Library • Rochester, NY 14623 • PLA

Richards Barbara G. • Associate Director • Carnegie-Mellon University Libraries Hunt Library • Pittsburgh, PA 15213 • ACRL ALCTS LITA LRRT

Richards Benjamin B. • Walnut Creek, CA 94595-3648 • Continuing

Richards Berry G. • Director of Libraries • Lehigh University Libraries Fairchild-Martindale Library • Bethlehem, PA 18015 • ACRL ALCTS LAMA LITA

Richards Brett A. • Terre Haute, IN 47803 • PLA AFLRT

Richards Carine F. • Student • San Jose State University Division of Library & Information Science • San Jose, CA 95192-0029 • PLA

Richards Carol J. • Librarian • State University of New York College at Buffalo, E. H. Butler Library • Buffalo, NY 14222-1095 • ACRL RASD

Richards Daniel T. • Dartmouth College Dana Biomedical Library • Hanover, NH 03755-3881 • ACRL ALCTS LAMA

Richards Diane • Business Librarian • North Dakota State University Library • Fargo, ND 58105-5599 • ACRL RASD

Richards Dorothy K. Mrs. • Media Serv/AV/Library Supv. • Lisbon Central School Library • Lisbon, CT 06351

Richards Freda E. • Birmingham, MI 48009

Richards James H. Jr • Las Cruces, NM 88005 • Life

Richards Jane G. • Automation Support Adminstrator • Dekalb County Public Library • Decatur, GA 30032 • LITA

Richards Katherine M. • Director of Library Services • Woodbury University Library • Burbank, CA 91510-7846 • ACRL

Richards N. Kay • Student • University of Washington Graduate School of Library and Information Science • Seattle, WA 98195 • ACRL

Richards P. Craig • Sioux City, IA 51102

Richards Pamela C. • Media Specialist • Hastings Middle School • Columbus, OH 43220 • AASL ALSC *Life*

Richards Pamela S. • Professor • Rutgers University School of Communication Information & Library Studies • New Brunswick, NJ 08903 • LHRT

Richards R. J. • Collection Development Manager • Greene County Public Library • Xenia, OH 45385 • PLA

Richards Ruth • Librarian • Kinsman Free Public Library • Kinsman, OH 44428

Richards Ruth N. • Surry Central High School • Dobson, NC 27041 • AASL

Richards Susan D. • Iowa City, IA 52240 • AASL

Richards Susan L. • Assistant Dir for Clln Mgmt • University of Vermont Bailey Howe Library • Burlington, VT 05405-0036

Richards Timothy F. • Director • University of Michigan-Dearborn Mardigian Library • Dearborn, MI 48128-1491 • ACRL ALCTS LAMA LITA RASD IFRT LIRT LRRT

Richards Vicki • Student • Kent State University School of Library & Information Science • Kent, OH 44242-0001 • ALSC

Richards William A. • North Georgia College Stewart Library • Dahlonega, GA 30597-3001 • ACRL

Richardson Bernard E. • Reno, NV 89503 • ACRL *Life*

Richardson Betty • Staff Development Coordinator • King County Library System • Seattle, WA 98109-5191 • LAMA CLENE EMIERT IRRT

Richardson Cecelia G. • Florence, SC 29505

Richardson Christine K. • Academic • Curtin University of Technology • Perth, Australia

Richardson Cynthia S. • Sound Recordings Cataloger • King County Library System • Seattle, WA 98109-5191

Richardson Deborah M. • Librarian • Lake Travis Middle School • Austin, TX 78734

Richardson Donald G. • Bibl. Instr & Tech Reports Ln. • Worcester Polytechnical Institute George C Gordon Library • Worcester, MA 01609-2280 • ACRL

Richardson Dorothy W. • Library Media Specialist • Odom Elem Sch Colquitt Cnty Board of Education • Moultrie, GA 31768 • AASL ALSC

Richardson Edna S. Mrs • Librarian • Marshall County High Scool Library • Guntersville, AL 35976 • Life

Richardson Gail • La Mesa, CA 91942 • Continuing

Richardson Gay A. • Richmond, VA 23235 • Continuing

Richardson Gregg M. • Reference Librarian • University of Minnesota Library • St Paul, MN 55108 • ACRL IFRT

Richardson Heidi B. • Librarian • Harford County Public Library Whiteford Branch • Whiteford, MD 21160

Richardson Helen • Children's Librarian • Orange Public Library Santiago Branch • Orange, CA 92669 • PLA

Richardson James T. • Senior Assistant Cataloger • University of Delaware Library • Newark, DE 19717-5267 • NMRT

Richardson Jan Hester • Maint. Tech. Support Ctr. • United States Postal Service • Norman, OK 73070-6708

Richardson Joan • Jesuit High School Library • New Orleans, LA 70119 • AASL LITA YALSA

Richardson John A. • Suffolk Cooperative Library System • Bellport, NY 11713 • ALCTS LITA PLA

Richardson John V. Jr Dr. • Associate Professor • Southern California University School of Library Science • Los Angeles, CA 90089-0182 • ACRL RASD GODORT LHRT LRRT

Richardson Jon A. • Student • University of Iowa School of Library & Information Science • Iowa City, IA 52242 • AASL

Richardson Karen Lee • United States Court of Appeals Library -3rd Circuit • Philadelphia, PA 19106 • ACRL GODORT

Richardson Laura • McCracken Middle School • Hilton Head, SC 29926 • AASL

Richardson Linda B. • Reference Librarian • Virginia Polytechnic Inst & State Univ University Libraries • Blacksburg, VA 24062-9001 • ACRL RASD LIRT

Richardson Lori • Head of Children's • La Porte County Public Library • La Porte, IN 46350

Richardson M Gayle • Children's Librarian • Seattle Public Library North East Branch • Seattle, WA 98115 • PLA

Richardson Margaret • West Palm Beach, FL 33401

Richardson Margie A. • Coordinator, Information Svs. • Richland County Public Library • Columbia, SC 29201

Richardson Mark L. • Student • University of Western Ontario School of Library & Information Science • London ON, N6G 1H1 Canada

Richardson Martha L. • Southeastern Library Network (SOLINET) • Atlanta, GA 30309-2955
Richardson Mary E. • Sausalito Public Library • Sausalito, CA 94965 • PLA
Richardson Molly • Los Angeles, CA 90066
Richardson Nancy • Circulation, Dept. Head • Bloomfield Township Public Library • Bloomfield Hills, MI 48302-2437
Richardson Robert • Reference Librarian • Montclair State College Harry A Sprague Library • Upper Montclair, NJ 07043-1699
Richardson Ruth Ann Miss • Vinton, IA 52349 • PLA RASD *Life*
Richardson Selma K. • Professor • University of Illinois Graduate School of Library and Information Science • Urbana, IL 61801 • AASL ALSC
Richardson Sharon M. • Librarian I • Finney Library • Milwaukee, WI 53208 • PLA AFLRT FLRT GODORT
Richardson Smith W. • Mountain Home, AR 72653 • ACRL
Richardson Susan • Children's Librarian • Red Wing Public Library • Red Wing, MN 55066
Richardson Sylvia • Media Processing Supervisor • Gwinnett County Public Schools • Lawrenceville, GA 30245 • AASL LITA
Richardson Teresa E. • Head Librarian • Chaminade College Prep • West Hills, CA 91304 • YALSA
Richardson Timothy A. Mr. • Trustee • Omaha Public Library • Omaha, NE 68102 • ALTA
Richardson Virginia H. • Librarian III • University of Hawaii Library • Honolulu, HI 96822 • GODORT
Richardson Wilma R. • Reference/Vertical File Ln • University of Texas at Tyler • Tyler, TX 75701
Richburg Verdie • Branch Supervisor • Jefferson Parish Library Department • Metairie, LA 70010 • NMRT
Richer Linda S. • Oberlin College Library • Oberlin, OH 44074 • ACRL
Richeson Mary Karin • Student • Texas Medical Association Library • Austin, TX 78701
Richey Cynthia K. • Children's Librarian • Mount Lebanon Public Library • Mount Lebanon, PA 15228 • ALSC
Richey Naomi A. • La Habra, CA 90631
Richgruber Karen W. • Librarian/Youth Outreach • Duluth Public Library • Duluth, MN 55802
Richie Richard P. • Student • University of California-Berkeley School of Library & Information Studies • Berkeley, CA 94720 • NMRT
Richins Aleene R. • Librarian • Bella Vista High School • Fair Oaks, CA 95628
Richling Joann T. • Nova Scotia Department of Labour Library • Halifax NS, B3J 2T8 Canada
Richman Ethel • Asst. Director • Cattermole Memorial Library • Fort Madison, IA 52627
Richman Sue C. • Asst. Univ. Librarian Cataloger • Florida Atlantic University S.E. Wimberly Library • Boca Raton, FL 33431
Richmond Alice S. • Librarian • North Carolina Central University • Durham, NC 27707
Richmond Bertha • Trustee • Western Plains Library System • Clinton, OK 73601
Richmond Carolyn Allen • Librarian • Otken Elementary-McComb School District • McComb, MS 39648
Richmond Diane A. • Head, Science & Tech. Info. • Chicago Public Library • Chicago, IL 60605 • SRRT
Richmond Elizabeth B. • Consultant • Rick Richmond Information Systems • Eau Claire, WI 54701 • ACRL GODORT
Richmond Gail A. • Librarian • Point Loma High School • San Diego, CA 92106 • AASL ALSC YALSA IFRT LIRT
Richmond Ginny • Public Library of Des Moines • Des Moines, IA 50308-1791 • YALSA
Richmond Joyce • Medical Librarian • Anne Arundel General Hospital Memorial Library • Annapolis, MD 21401 • ASCLA LITA
Richmond Patricia S. • Pepperdine University Payson Library • Malibu, CA 90263 • ALCTS
Richmond Phyllis A. • Chagrin Falls, OH 44022-2806 • ACRL ALCTS LITA *Continuing*
Richmond Sharon L. • College Sta, TX 77845
Richmond Stephen M. • Branch Manager • Dayton & Montgomery County Public Library Northmont Branch • Engelwood, OH 45322 • YALSA SRRT
Richner Jo • Director • Mount Pulaski District Library • Mt. Pulaski, IL 62548
Richter Bertina • Librarian • California State University,Fresno Henry Madden Library • Fresno, CA 93740-0034
Richter Carole J. • Student • Northern Kentucky University Steely Library • Highland Heights, KY 41099-6101 • ACRL
Richter Dorothy S. • Camp Hill, PA 17011-1347
Richter Elizabeth B. • Student • Southern Connecticut State University School of Libray Science & Instructional Technology • New Haven, CT 06515 • PLA
Richter Heddy A. • Landenberg, PA 19350 • ACRL
Richter Kathleen A. • Assistant Director • Riverhead Free Library • Riverhead, NY 11901
Richter Linda • Mankato State University Memorial Library • Mankato, MN 56002-8400
Richter Mary Jean • L'Anse Creuse High School Library • Mount Clemens, MI 48045 • AASL
Richvalsky Neil F. • School Lib Development Advisor • Pennsylvania Dept of Education State Library of Pennsylvania • Harrisburg, PA 17126-0333 • AASL IFRT
Richwine Eleanor • Associate Librarian • Western Maryland College Hoover Library • Westminster, MD 21157-4390 • ACRL ALCTS IFRT
Ricigliano Lorraine • Associate Director • University of Puget Sound Collins Memorial Library • Tacoma, WA 98416 • ACRL LITA LIRT
Rick Jean A. • Head of Reference • West Texas State University Cornette Library • Canyon, TX 79016-0748
Rick Scott • Student • University of Wisconsin-Milwaukee School of Library & Information Science • Milwaukee, WI 53201 • PLA IFRT SRRT
Rickelton Esther G. • King County Library System • Seattle, WA 98109-5191 • LAMA PLA
Rickenberg Lee • Trustee • Paramus Public Library • Paramus, NJ 07652 • ALTA PLA
Ricker Alison Scott • Science Librarian • Oberlin College Library • Oberlin, OH 44074 • ACRL
Ricker Cheri D. • Librarian • Phoenix Christian High School • Phoenix, AZ 85015 • AASL
Ricker Eleanor L. • Gilford, NH 03246 • Continuing
Ricker Kendra D. • Media Specialist • Duval County School Board Pinedale Elementary School #93 • Jacksonville, FL 32205 • AASL
Rickerson Carla • Special Collections Division • University of Washington • Seattle, WA 98195 • ACRL RASD
Rickerson George T. • Director • University of Missouri Office of Library Systems • Columbia, MO 65211 • LITA
Rickerson Judith E. • Branch Librarian • Stockton-San Joaquin County Public Library Fair Oaks • Stockton, CA 95205
Rickert Carol • Newark Public Library Emerson R. Miller Branch • Newark, OH 43055 • ALSC ASCLA LAMA PLA RASD IFRT NMRT SRRT
Rickert Warren W. • Patillas, PR 00723
Rickett Katherine • Chesapeake General Hospital • Chesapeake, VA 23320
Ricketts Betty J. • Exhibit Manager • OCLC Online Computer Library Center • Dublin, OH 43017-3395 • ERT
Ricketts Elizabeth L. • Trustee • Akron-Summit County Public Library • Akron, OH 44326-0001 • ALTA
Ricketts Mary • Grand Falls, A2A 1Y7 Canada
Ricklefs Dale L. • Library Director • Round Rock Public Library • Round Rock, TX 78664 • PLA
Rickles Suzanne R. • Branch Manager • Houston Public Library Ring Branch • Houston, TX 77055 • PLA
Rickner Bettie Estes • Director • Oklahoma State Dept of Education Library Media Section • Oklahoma City, OK 73105-4955 • AASL
Ricks Bonnie B. • Delta Junction, AK 99737
Ricks E. Suzanne • Librarian • Iona Elementary School • Iona, ID 83427 • AASL
Ricks Thomas W. • Science Reference Librarian • University of Colorado At Colorado Springs Library • Colorado Springs, CO 80933-7150 • ACRL
Ridder Dale • Trustee • Zion-Benton Public Library District • Zion, IL 60099
Riddick Joseph • University of Tennessee Library • Knoxville, TN 37996-1000
Riddick Norma F. • Catalog Librarian • Vanderbilt University Library • Nashville, TN 37240-0007 • ACRL ALCTS
Riddle Cecilia • Principal Librarian • Los Angeles Public Library • Los Angeles, CA 90071
Riddle Laura M. • Head Librarian • Slaton City Library • Slaton, TX 79364 • PLA
Riddles James A. • Stockton, CA 95204 • ACRL LAMA *Life*
Ridenhour Mary Helen • Jackson Park Elementary School • Kannapolis, NC 28081 • AASL
Ridenour Alice M. • Assoc Ln & Hd Tech Proc • Montana State University • Bozeman, MT 59717-0332 • ACRL ALCTS *Life*
Ridenour Lisa R. • Interlibrary Loan Coordinator • Clemson University Robert Muldrow Cooper Library • Clemson, SC 29634-3001
Rider Jeanne M. • Prospect Heights, IL 60070-1730
Rider Lillian M. • Reference Dept. • McGill University • Montreal PQ, H3A 1Y1 Canada • ACRL RASD
Ridgdell Brenda S. • Middle School Librarian • Harry M. Hurst Middle School • Destrehan, LA 70047
Ridgeway Hazel L. • Senior Librarian/Children Servs • City of Inglewood Public Library • Inglewood, CA 90301-1771 • ALSC
Ridgeway Merrilyn S. • Program Development Coor. • University of Arizona Graduate Library School • Tucson, AZ 85721 • AASL LAMA
Ridgeway Trish • Head, Technical Services • Handley Library • Winchester, VA 22601 • ACRL RASD LIRT
Ridgley-Nalley Tamara J. • Media Specialist • Sedgefield Elementary School • Charlotte, NC 28209
Ridgway Barbara B. • District Lib. Media Coordinator • Helena School District #1 • Helena, MT 59601 • AASL
Ridinger Robert B. Marks • Northern Illinois University University Libraries • DeKalb, IL 60115-2868 • ACRL SRRT
Ridings Elisabeth W. • Cincinnati, OH 45220 • Continuing
Ridings Jacqueline • Media Spec • Greenwood High School • Greenwood, SC 29646 • AASL YALSA IFRT
Ridley A. Michael • Associate Librarian, Systems • University of Waterloo • Waterloo ON, N2L 3G1 Canada • ACRL LITA
Ridley Christy • Bethesda, MD 20817
Ridley Naomi K. • Savannah, GA 31420
Ridnour Susan • Manager of Library Services • Haynes & Boone Law Firm • Dallas, TX 75202
Riebel Ellis F. • East Stroudburg, PA 18301
Riechel Rosemarie • Research & Online Search Spec. • Queens Borough Public Library • Jamaica, NY 11432 • ALCTS PLA RASD
Riechers Jeannette E. • Head, Reader's Services • Arlington Heights Memorial Library • Arlington Heights, IL 60004-5966 • PLA
Riedel Susan H. • Sr Automation Planning Spec • Library of Congress • Washington, DC 20541 • ALCTS LITA
Riedesel Laureen F. • Director • Beatrice Public Library • Beatrice, NE 68310 • LAMA PLA
Riedl Jeann N. • Student • State University of New York at Albany School of Information Science & Policy • Albany, NY 12222
Riedy Allen J. • Cornell University Libraries John M. Echols Collections • Ithaca, NY 14853-5301 • ACRL IRRT
Rieffel Robert • Head, Catalog Department • Enoch Pratt Free Library • Baltimore, MD 21201-4484 • ALCTS
Riegel Donna L. • Construction Coordinator • Broward County Division of Libraries Broward County Library • Fort Lauderdale, FL 33301 • LAMA PLA SORT
Riegel Janet S. • Claremont, CA 91711 • AASL ALSC LITA IFRT LRRT SRRT
Riegel Jo A. • Librarian • Wagnalls Memorial Library • Lithopolis, OH 43136 • LITA PLA RASD
Riegel Tamara E. • Cataloger • Lutheran Theological Seminary A.R. Wentz Library • Gettysburg, PA 17325 • ACRL ALCTS
Riegelsberger Sally C. • Sales Support • Data Research Associates Inc. • Saint Louis, MO 63132
Rieger Kathy B. • Student • Emporia State University School of Library & Information Management • Emporia, KS 66801
Rieger Margaret A. • Extension Supervisor • Public Library of Cincinnati & Hamilton County Miami Twnshp Branch • Cleves, OH 45002
Riehl Sallie K. • Library Director • Wheeler Basin Regional Library • Decatur, AL 35602 • PLA
Riehl Sandy • Estancia High School Library • Costa Mesa, CA 92627
Riehm Susan M. • Allen County Public Library • Fort Wayne, IN 46801 • PLA RASD
Rieke Judith L. • Special Projects Librarian • University of North Dakota Chester Fritz Library • Grand Forks, ND 58202-0175 • ALCTS
Riel Steven J. • Amherst College Robert Frost Library • Amherst, MA 01002 • ALCTS
Rielly Loretta J. • Bibliographic Instr. Coor. • Oregon State University William Jasper Kerr Library • Corvallis, OR 97331-4501 • ACRL RASD LIRT
Rieman Phyllis • Niles West High School • Skokie, IL 60076
Riemenschneider Beth • General Reference Librarian • Columbus Metropolitan Library Main Library Branch • Columbus, OH 43215
Riemenschneider Jackie B. • Hinkle Elementary School • Springtown, TX 76082 • AASL ALSC YALSA IFRT
Riemer John J. • Head of Serials Cataloging • University of Georgia Libraries • Athens, GA 30602 • ALCTS LITA GODORT IFRT SRRT
Riemer Louise B. • Coord of Cmnty Lib & Vol Servs • Howard County Library • Columbia, MD 21044 • ASCLA
Riemschussel Christiee • Director • American Fork City Library • American Fork, UT 84003 • PLA
Rienerth Sharon L. • Catalog Librarian • Edinboro University of Pennsylvania Baron-Forness Library • Edinboro, PA 16444 • ACRL ALCTS

Riepe Jeanette B. • Head of Technical Services • Urbandale Public Library • Urbandale, IA 50322

Riepma Helen • West Texas State University Cornette Library • Canyon, TX 79016-0748 • ACRL LITA

Riesberg Eunice L. • Northeastern Iowa Regional Library System • Waterloo, IA 50701 • PLA

Riese Rebecca L. • Ed. Asst. • Rockrimmon Press • Colorado Springs, CO 80918

Riesenman Patricia • Reference Librarian • Indiana University • Bloomington, IN 47405 • ACRL RASD IFRT IRRT

Riester Leslie C. • Ann Arbor, MI 48103-1606

Rietstra Edith J. • Librarian • Orange Coast College • Costa Mesa, CA 92628-5005 • ACRL IFRT LIRT

Rife Wilma S. • University Library Director • Washburn University of Topeka Mabee Library • Topeka, KS 66621 • ACRL

Riffe John V. • Cataloger • Pueblo Library District McClelland Library • Pueblo, CO 81004-1997

Riffer Diane L. • Librarian • Timber Lane Elementary School • Falls Church, VA 22046 • AASL

Rift Leo R. • Ithaca, NY 14850 • Continuing

Rigby Paul • Director • Atlantic Community College Daniel Leeds Library • Mays Landing, NJ 08330 • ALCTS

Riger Robert P. • Managing Director • Market Partners International • New York, NY 10016 • LITA

Rigg Alice • Student • San Jose State University Clark Library • San Jose, CA 95192-0028 • PLA

Riggen Jennie • Head Technical Services • Alaska State Library • Juneau, AK 99811-571 • ALSC

Riggin Thomas E. • Manager Govermment Sales • Baker & Taylor Books • Charlotte, NC 28217 • AFLRT

Riggins Anita E. • Library Clerk V • Indianapolis Marion County Public Library • Indianapolis, IN 46206

Riggle Judy • Director • Avon Lake Public Library • Avon Lake, OH 44012 • LAMA PLA

Riggs Colby M. • University of California-Irvine Library • Irvine, CA 92713 • ALCTS LITA

Riggs Dean E. • Acquisition Librarian • University of Toledo William S. Carlson Library • Toledo, OH 43606-3399 • ACRL ALCTS

Riggs Donald E. • Dean, University Library • University of Michigan Libraries • Ann Arbor, MI 48109-1205 • ACRL LAMA LITA *Life*

Riggs E Louisa Miss • Vallejo, CA 94590 • ALSC PLA *Continuing*

Riggs John I. • Buffalo, NY 14223

Righetti Mary Ann • Corvallis, OR 97330

Rightmyer Sandra P. • Director • New Providence Memorial Library • New Providence, NJ 07974 • LAMA PLA

Rights Edith A. • Librarian • Montclair Art Museum LeBrun Library • Montclair, NJ 07042 • ACRL

Rigler Malia Ann • Seattle, WA 98103

Rigney Larry R. • Librarian • Grant Foreman Elementary School • Muskogee, OK 74403 • AASL

Rigoulot Lois M. • Director • Millbrook Library • Millbrook, NY 12545-0286 • ALSC PLA

Rigsby John Michael Jr. • Librarian II • Free Library of Philadelphia Northeast Regional Library • Philadelphia, PA 19149 • ALSC

Rihani Rushdi F. • Student • Wayne State University Library Science Program • Detroit, MI 48202 • ACRL

Rike Galen E. • Head, Central Reference Serv. • Western Michigan University Libraries • Kalamazoo, MI 49008 • ACRL RASD LRRT

Riker Ross • Audio-Visual Services Librarian • Kendallville Public Library • Kendallville, IN 46755

Rile Elizabeth B. • Idea Center • Columbus, IN 47201 • IFRT

Riley Ann Campion • Head Cataloging • Maryville University • St. Louis, MO 63141 • ALCTS

Riley Betty S. • Library Coordinator • State Department of Education • Oklahoma City, OK 73105 • AASL

Riley Cheryl A. • Catalog Maintenance Unit Head • Central Missouri State University Ward Edwards Library • Warrensburg, MO 64093 • ALCTS IFRT NMRT

Riley Elaine • Montowese Elementary School Library Media Center • North Haven, CT 06473 • AASL

Riley Gordon D. • Student • Wayne State University Library Science Program • Detroit, MI 48202 • ACRL IFRT

Riley Jacquelene W. • Cincinnati, OH 45220 • ALCTS

Riley Jacqueline • Louisiana Universities Marine Consortium Library • Chauvin, LA 70344 • ACRL

Riley Josephine • Trustee • East Saint Louis Public Library • East St. Louis, IL 62201 • ALTA

Riley Juanita • Central High School Library • Milton, FL 32570 • AASL

Riley Kathleen • School Librarian/Media Spec. • Beachwood Schools • Beachwood, OH 44122 • ALSC NMRT

Riley Leslie S W • Director • Cornwall Public Library • Cornwall Hudson, NY 12520 • ALCTS ALSC ALTA LAMA LITA PLA RASD

Riley Margaret F. • Circulation Librarian • Worcester Polytechnical Institute George C Gordon Library • Worcester, MA 01609-2280

Riley Margie • School Library Media Specialist • Weatherless Elementary School • Washington, DC 20019 • AASL

Riley Mary H. • Arlington, VA 22207

Riley Mary L. • Supervisor • Grand Rapids Public Library • Grand Rapids, MI 49503-3093

Riley Melinda J. • Student • Whitehall Elementary School • Anderson, SC 29625 • ALSC

Riley Melissa J. • Librarian • San Francisco Public Library • San Francisco, CA 94102 • IFRT SRRT

Riley Oliva P. • Columbus, OH 43201

Riley Paul D. • Seattle University Lemieux Library • Seattle, WA 98122

Riley Randy J. • East Lansing, MI 48823

Riley Richard K. • Administrative Services Ln. • Southwest Texas State University • San Marcos, TX 78666 • LAMA

Riley Sandra • Columbus, NE 68601

Riley Sheila M. • Washington, DC 20008 • ALCTS LITA FLRT

Rilke Elna S. • Student • State University of New York at Albany School of Information Science & Policy • Albany, NY 12222 • AASL

Rill Teresa L. • Tucson, AZ 85719

Rimmel Jan E. • Public Library of Charlotte & Mecklenburg County • Charlotte, NC 28202

Rinaldo Constance • Collection Dev. Librarian • Dartmouth College Dana Biomedical Library • Hanover, NH 03755-3881 • ACRL ALCTS LAMA

Rinard Virginia • La Verne, CA 91750 • PLA YALSA *Continuing*

Rinas Mary E. • Chief Librarian • United States Air Force • Wright-Patterson AFB, OH 45433 • PLA AFLRT ERT FLRT IFRT LHRT

Rinderknecht Deborah L. • Coor., Humanities Reference • University of Tennessee John C. Hodges Library • Knoxville, TN 37996-1000 • LAMA

Rine Joseph L. • Minneapolis Community College • Minneapolis, MN 55403 • Life

Rineer Paula J. • Dallastown Area High School • Dallastown, PA 17313

Rinehart Constance • Ann Arbor, MI 48106 • ACRL ALCTS *Life*

Rinehart Julia R. • Administrator • Berks County Public Library System • Leesport, PA 19533 • ALSC LAMA LITA PLA RASD

Rinehart Marcia • Trustee • Johnson County Library • Shawnee Mission, KS 66201 • ALTA

Rines Allen R. • Emmanuel College Library • Boston, MA 02115 • LITA

Riney Judith N. Sr. • Director of Library Sevice • Brescia College Library • Owensboro, KY 42301 • ACRL

Ring-Nelson Marilyn • Seattle Public Library • Seattle, WA 98104-1193 • PLA

Ring Anne M. • Head Librarian • Winchester House Library • Libertyville, IL 60048

Ring Constance • School Library Media Specialist • North Bellmore U. Fr. Dist • North Bellmore, NY 11710 • AASL

Ring Diane • Denver, CO 80210

Ring Douglas • Trustee • Los Angeles Public Library • Los Angeles, CA 90071 • ALTA

Ring Jeffery R. • Automation Librarian • University of Texas-Brownsville • Brownsville, TX 78520-4994 • ACRL LITA

Ring Richard R. • Collection Development Librarian • University of Kansas Watson Library • Lawrence, KS 66045-2800 • ACRL ALCTS

Ringer Barbara • Washington, DC 20024

Ringer Sarah • Princeton, NJ 08540

Ringer Susan Gillis • Assistant Ref Libn./Gov Doc Libn • Fond du Lac Public Library • Fond du Lac, WI 54935

Ringering Leona H. • Park Forest, IL 60466

Ringland Inez I. • Director • Rosary College • River Forest, IL 60305-1066 • AASL ACRL ALCTS ALTA ASCLA LAMA LITA PLA RASD YALSA FLRT GODORT LRRT

Ringler Rebecca R. • Catalog Librarian • University of California-San Diego • La Jolla, CA 92093-0175 • ALCTS LITA

Ringquist Lois S. • Children's Services Librarian • Minneapolis Public Library & Information Center • Minneapolis, MN 55401-1992 • ALSC

Ringsdorf Carolyn • Director • Upper Darby Township & Sellers Free Public Library • Upper Darby, PA 19082

Rink Thomas E. • Student • University Center at Tulsa • Tulsa, OK 74106 • ALCTS LAMA LITA RASD EMIERT FLRT IFRT SRRT

Rinke Karen S. • Teacher • Saint John School • Lawrence, KS 66044 • AASL ALSC

Rinkel Gene K. • Librarian • University of Illinois Library • Urbana, IL 61801 • ACRL

Rinker Miriam B. • Librarian • Stonewall Jackson High School Library • Mount Jackson, VA 22842 • AASL

Rinker Nancy A. • Student • University of North Carolina at Chapel Hill School of Information and Library Science • Chapel Hill, NC 27599-3360

Rinn Martha A. • Texas Lutheran College Blumberg Memorial Library • Seguin, TX 78155

Rinne Nancy C. • Librarian • Louisburg High School • Louisburg, KS 66053 • AASL YALSA

Rinne Teri A. • Student • University of California-Berkeley School of Library & Information Studies • Berkeley, CA 94720 • LITA

Rion Jean A. • Mount Pleasant, SC 29464-9476 • PLA ILERT

Riordan Dale Bartle • University of North Carolina at Charlotte J. Murrey Atkins Library • Charlotte, NC 28223

Rioux Margaret A. • Acquisitions Librarian • Woods Hole Oceanographic Institution • Woods Hole, MA 02543 • ALCTS IFRT

Ripley Cynthia • Architect Librarian • Ripley Associates • San Francisco, CA 94115-2215 • LAMA

Ripley Hugh W. • Dean Library Services/Librarian • Barry University Library • Miami Shores, FL 33161 • ACRL IFRT

Ripley Kathy E. • Media Specialist • Fayette County Sr H S • Fayetteville, GA 30214 • AASL

Rippel Jeffrey A. • Director • Lubbock City-County Library • Lubbock, TX 79401 • PLA

Ripple Eleanor F. • Clements, MD 20624 • AASL ALSC *Life*

Riquelmy Christina A. • Monographic Cataloger • Louisiana State University Libraries Troy H. Middleton Library • Baton Rouge, LA 70803-3342 • ACRL ALCTS EMIERT IRRT

Risch Carolyn M. • Butterfield Elementary School • Tucson, AZ 85741

Risch E. • Ramapo College of New Jersey Library • Mahwah, NJ 07430

Riseley Jerry B. • Director • Authentic Press Mandan Indian Library • North Hills, CA 91343

Risen Dennis • Project Manager • Case Western Reserve University • Cleveland, OH 44106 • LITA

Riser Rosalind • Coordinator of Instr. Materials • Osceola District Instruction Media Center • Kissimmee, FL 34744 • AASL ALSC

Rishel Marguerite E. • South Pasadena, FL 33707 • Continuing

Rishworth Susan K. • History Librarian • American College of Obstetricians and Gynecologists Resource Center • Washington, DC 20024 • ACRL RASD SRRT

Rising Maxine L. • Librarian Adult Services • Harford County Library Joppa Branch • Joppa, MD 21085 • PLA

Riskind Mary J.L. • Montclair Free Public Library • Montclair, NJ 07042 • ALSC PLA

Risko Terence W. • Director • Cape Girardeau Public Library • Cape Girardeau, MO 63701 • PLA

Rismiller Anne B. • Trustee • Omaha Public Library • Omaha, NE 68102 • ALTA

Risner Kevin R. • Librarian • University of Georgia Libraries • Athens, GA 30602

Risser Barbara A. • Fayettville, NC 28314 • RASD FLRT

Risser Irene K. • Curriculum Librarian • Millersville University of Pennsylvania • Millersville, PA 17551-0302 • ACRL

Rissinger Michael • Head, Database Mgt. • New York University Frederick Ehrman Medical Library • New York, NY 10016-6450 • ACRL ALCTS LITA

Rissman John Bloomberg • University of California Rivera Library • Riverside, CA 92517 • ACRL ALCTS

Rist Julianne F. • Miami, FL 33190

Risto Thomas • Library Director • Northwood Institute Library • Midland, MI 48640 • ACRL ALCTS LAMA LITA

Ristow Rebecca Gitlin • Information Services Manager • Indiana Youth Institute • Indianapolis, IN 46204 • YALSA

Ristroph Elizabeth P. • Charleston County Library • Charleston, SC 29403 • PLA

Ritch Alan W. • Librarian • University of California-Santa Cruz Library • Santa Cruz, CA 95064 • ACRL LITA IFRT LIRT

Ritcheson Arleen • Pona City, OK 74601

Ritchey Susan • Carpenter Middle School • Plano, TX 75023

Ritchie Barbara J. • Library Systems Manager • University of San Diego Department of Library Science • San Diego, CA 92110 • ALCTS LITA

Ritchie Catherine J. • Young Adult Librarian • Decatur Public Library • Decatur, IL 62523 • YALSA

Ritchie Eleanor N. • Branch Head • Charlotte Hall Branch Library • Charlotte Hall, MD 20622 • RASD

Ritchie Pamela R. • Rockwell, NC 28138 • AASL

Ritchot-Russell Sharon E. • Student • McGill University Graduate School of Library & Information Studies • Montreal PQ, H3A 1Y1 Canada • ACRL ALCTS IFRT SRRT

Ritsema Irene • Librarian • Washington Christian School • Silver Spring, MD 20902 • AASL

Ritt Lee G. • Instructional Specialist Media • Virginia Beach City Public Schools Office of Media and Technology • Virginia Beach, VA 23462 • AASL LITA

Rittel Mary Ellen • Worthington, OH 43235

Ritten Karla J. • Stu • Lewis & Clark Library • Helena, MT 59601

Ritter Audrey • North Ferrisburg, VT 05473-9604

Ritter Helen • Student • Saint John's University Division of Library & Information Science • Jamaica, NY 11439 • LITA

Ritter Linda B. • Director of Learning Resources • Dakota Wesleyan University Layne Library • Mitchell, SD 57301-4398 • ACRL LAMA

Ritter Philip W. • Director • Gaston-Lincoln Regional Library • Gastonia, NC 28054 • LAMA PLA

Ritter Sally K. • Brooklyn, NY 11201

Ritterhouse Kathy L. • Director • Grand Prairie Memorial Library • Grand Prairie, TX 75051 • LAMA PLA

Rittinger Barbara • Manassas, VA 22110

Rittmeyer Deborah G. • Byron, NY 14422-9718 • AASL YALSA

Ritz Maura P. • Head Reference • Darien Library • Darien, CT 06820-4497 • RASD

Ritz Paul S. • Librarian • Clearwater Public Library North Greenwood Branch • Clearwater, FL 34615-5329

Ritz Susan V. • Student • University of North Carolina Department of Library & Information Studies • Greensboro, NC 27412-5001 • ALCTS LITA RASD

Rivenburgh Edwin F. • Library Director • Community College of the Finger Lakes Library • Canandaigua, NY 14424 • ACRL

River Sandra A. • Current Periodicals/Micro Lns • Texas Tech University Texas Tech Library • Lubbock, TX 79409 • ACRL ALCTS RASD

Rivera-Aguilera Alma B. • Automation Officer • Universidad Centsoamericana Jose Simeon Canas • San Salvador, El Salvador

Rivera-Camacho Ketty • Student • University of Puerto Rico Graduate School of Librarianship • Rio Piedras, PR 00931

Rivera Alicia • Trustee • Hillcrest School • Oakland, CA 94618 • ALSC

Rivera Heather • Newark Public Library • Newark, NJ 07101-0630

Rivera Jodi L. • Balboa Island, CA 92662

Rivera Katherine A. • Tech. Servs. Librarian • Daly City Public Library • Daly City, CA 94015 • LITA

Rivera Linda R. • Head Librarian • El Paso High School • El Paso, TX 79902 • AASL YALSA IFRT

Rivera Mary M. • Technical Services Coordinator • New York Metropolitan Reference & Research Library Agency (METRO) • New York, NY 10003 • ACRL ALCTS LITA

Rivera Mildred I. • Acquisitions/Clln Development • University of the Sacred Heart • Santurce, PR 00914

Rivera Rita S. • Student • Clarion University of Pennsylvania College of Library Science • Clarion, PA 16214 • PLA

Rivera Tina J. • Schiller Park Public Library • Schiller Park, IL 60176-1699

Rivera Vilma R. • Student • Catholic University of Puerto Rico Encarnacion Valdes Library • Ponce, PR 00732

Rivers Susan E. • Armada Free Public Library • Armada, MI 48005

Rivers Vickie • Charleston County Library James Island Branch • Charleston, SC 29412

Rives Lydia L. • Springfield, VA 22153 • AFLRT FLRT ILERT

Rivetti Anthony • Davis Markel & Edwards • New York, NY 10017

Riviello Barbara Jo • H. W. Wilson Company • Bronx, NY 10452 • ALCTS

Rizer Sally A. • Librarian • Clark County Public Library • Springfield, OH 45501-1080 • ALSC

Rizzo John R. • Professor of Management • Western Michigan University Libraries • Kalamazoo, MI 49008 • LAMA

Rizzotti Dana J. • Program Development Analyst • Boston Public Library • Boston, MA 02117

Rizzutto Doris M. • Baton Rouge, LA 70810-5144

Roach Celeste C. • Resident Intern • Cornell University • Ithaca, NY 14853-5301 • LAMA

Roach Darlene S. • Student • Central State University Library • Edmond, OK 73034-0193 • AASL ALSC LITA IFRT LHRT SRRT

Roach Elizabeth • Reference Librarian • King County Library System • Seattle, WA 98109-5191 • PLA

Roach Helen • Student • Texas Woman's University School of Library & Information Studies • Denton, TX 76204

Roach Jacqueline L. • Neumann College Library • Aston, PA 19014 • ACRL

Roach Jeanne S. • University of North Carolina Department of Library & Information Studies • Greensboro, NC 27412-5001 • AASL IFRT

Roach Julie A. • Biomedical Info. Specialist • Glaxo Inc. • Research Tri. Pk., NC 27709

Roach Laura L. • Branch Librarian • San Bernardino County Library Fontana Branch • Fontana, CA 92335

Roach Mary K. • Asst. Head -- Cataloging • University of Kansas Watson Library • Lawrence, KS 66045-2800 • ACRL ALCTS LITA

Road Rachel • West Lafayette, IN 47906 • Life

Roake Barbara J. • Trustee • Lisle Library District • Lisle, IL 60532 • ALTA

Roark Barbara • Spies Public Library • Menominee, MI 49858

Roark Derrie B. • Assoc. V-P of LRC • Hillsborough Community College Ybor City Campus • Tampa, FL 33675-5096 • ACRL LAMA

Roark William N. • Madison, WI 53715

Roat Ruth I. • Director • New Harmony Working Mens Institute • New Harmony, IN 47631

Roatch Mary A. • Phoenix, AZ 85015 • ASCLA

Roay Barbara A. • San Bruno, CA 94066

Roback Jean M. • Carleton College Library • Northfield, MN 55057-4097

Robar Terri J. • Head, Reference Department • University of Miami Libraries Richter Library • Coral Gables, FL 33124 • LAMA

Robare Lori P. • Student • Willamette University Mark O Hatfield Library • Salem, OR 97301

Robarts Andrea L. • London, ON, N6G 3H1 Canada • ACRL IRRT LRRT SRRT

Robarts Cathy L. • Flint Public Library • Flint, MI 48502

Robb Adalin Mayes • Jenkintown, PA 19046 • Continuing

Robb Alison A. • Woods Hole, MA 02543 • Continuing

Robb Elizabeth G. • Chapel Hill, NC 27514 • ACRL ALCTS *Life*

Robb Gaylord G. • Bonita Springs, FL 33923 • MAGERT

Robb James A. • Administrator • North Arkansas Regional Library • Harrison, AR 72601 • LAMA IFRT

Robb Margaret • Oxford 0X4 3NP, England

Robbana Jeanne • Program Development Coordinator • South Jersey Regional Library Midway Professional Center • Hammonton, NJ 08037 • CLENE

Robbers Sandra M. • Indianhead Library System • Eau Claire, WI 54701 • PLA

Robbian Michael K. • Cataloger • Livingstone College • Salisbury, NC 28144

Robbins Anne K. • Cheshire, CT 06410 • RASD

Robbins Bruce C. • Carmel, IN 46032-4163 • LITA

Robbins Catherine L. • Student • Savannah College of Art & Design • Savannah, GA 31401

Robbins Corinne L. • Educationl Media Specialist • North Miami Beach Senior High School • North Miami Beach, FL 33162 • AASL

Robbins Curtis G. • Student • University of Pittsburgh School of Library and Information Science • Pittsburgh, PA 15260 • ACRL LITA PLA RASD IFRT MAGERT NMRT SRRT

Robbins Emma B. • Saint Paul, MN 55102

Robbins Jane • Library Educator • University of Wisconsin School of Library & Information Studies • Madison, WI 53706 • ACRL PLA LRRT

Robbins Linda Miller • Director • Jefferson County Public Law Library • Louisville, KY 40202 • LITA

Robbins Louise S. • Assistant Professor • University of Wisconsin-Madison College Library Helen C. White Hall • Madison, WI 53706 • ACRL LAMA IFRT LRRT

Robbins Ortha D. • Minneapolis, MN 55406 • PLA RASD *Life*

Robbins Rachel H. • Interlibrary Services Librarian • University of Texas Libraries • Austin, TX 78713 • ACRL LAMA RASD IFRT NMRT

Robbins Rita E. • Resource Media Teacher • Fort Wayne Community Schools Anthis Career Center/Rm 215 • Fort Wayne, IN 46802 • AASL

Robbins Ronald E. • Head of Public Services • Lafayette College Skillman Library • Easton, PA 18042-1797 • ACRL LAMA SORT

Robbins Sara • Law Librarian • Brooklyn Law School Library • Brooklyn, NY 11201 • LAMA

Robbins Sybil C. • Houston, TX 77081

Robenson Pamela J. • Library Media Specialist • Chino High School • Chino, CA 91710 • AASL LIRT

Robers Terry E. • Student • University of Wisconsin-Milwaukee School of Library & Information Science • Milwaukee, WI 53201 • LITA

Roberson Gloria • Adelphi University Swirbul Library • Garden City, NY 11530

Roberson Janie • Elementary School Librarian • Cub Run Elementary School • Cub Run, KY 42729 • AASL

Roberson Janis L. • Director • Grapevine Public Library • Grapevine, TX 76051 • ALCTS ALSC LAMA PLA RASD

Roberson Jean Mrs. • Temple, TX 76502 • Continuing

Roberson Kip M. • Student • Indiana University School of Library and Information Science • Bloomington, IN 47405 • RASD SRRT

Robert Connie M. • School Librarian • Juanita Gardine School • Christiansted, VI 00820 • AASL

Roberto Clare • Bronxville Middle/High School • Bronxville, NY 10708 • AASL

Roberton Terri-Lane K. • Student • McGill University Libraries • Montreal PQ, H3A 1Y1 Canada • ASCLA

Roberts Alice L. • Branch Librarian • Boston Public Library Jamaica Plain Branch • Jamaica Plain, MA 02136

Roberts Andrea • Merion Mercy Academy • Merion Station, PA 19066 • AASL

Roberts Ann D. • Adult Services Librarian • Prince William Public Library Chinn Park Regional Library • Prince William, VA 22192

Roberts Barbara S. • Librarian • Miami Christian College Library • Miami, FL 33101 • ACRL

Roberts Barbara S. • Reference Science Division • District of Columbia Public Library Martin Luther King Memorial Library • Washington, DC 20001 • LITA PLA RASD

Roberts Beverly Mrs. • Librarian • Jonas Salk Elementary School • Mesa, AZ 85207

Roberts Bickie C. • High School Librarian • Presidio Independent School District • Presidio, TX 79845

Roberts Bobby L. • Director • Central Arkansas Library System • Little Rock, AR 72201-4698 • PLA

Roberts Carolyn D. • Trustee • Palatine Public Library • Palatine, IL 60067 • ALTA

Roberts Catherine W. • Head of Cataloging Dept. • Berea College Hutchins Library • Berea, KY 40404 • LITA

Roberts Cecile • Levittown, NY 11756 • Continuing

Roberts Celia A. • Reference Librarian • Simsbury Public Library • Simsbury, CT 06070

Roberts Cheryl D. • Librarian II-Children's Services • Phoenix Public Library Yucca Branch • Phoenix, AZ 85015 • PLA

Roberts Constance F. • Principal Cataloger • University of Connecticut Homer Babbidge Library • Storrs, CT 06269-1005 • ALCTS

Roberts Cynthia H. • Head, Collection Development • Catonsville Community College • Baltimore, MD 21228 • ACRL ALCTS

Roberts David • Library Director • Wissahickon Valley Public Library • Ambler, PA 19002 • PLA

Roberts Delno M. • Abilene, TX 79601

Roberts E. Frank • Readers' Services Librarian • Indian River Correctional Institution Library • Vero Beach, FL 32968 • ASCLA IFRT LIRT

Roberts Edward G. • Director of Libraries • Georgia Institute of Technology • Atlanta, GA 30332 • Continuing

Roberts Elizabeth A. • The Colony Public Library • The Colony, TX 75056-1219 • SRRT

Roberts Elizabeth L. • Chapel Hill, NC 27516 • ALSC SRRT

Roberts Faye C. • Assistant Director • Suwannee River Regional Library • Live Oak, FL 32060 • PLA

Roberts Frances L. • Director/Librarian • Grant County Library • Ulysses, KS 67880 • PLA

Roberts Gail E. • Young Adult Librarian • Farmington Community Library • Farmington Hills, MI 48334 • YALSA

Roberts Geralyn Z. • Children's Librarian • Plumb Memorial Library Huntington Branch • Shelton, CT 06484 • PLA

Roberts Jane G. • Huntsville-Madison County Public Library • Huntsville, AL 35804

Roberts Jayare • Ancestral File & Coorp Spec. • Family History Library • Salt Lake City, UT 84150 • LITA RASD

Roberts Jean A. • Supervisor, Outreach Services • Lorain Public Library • Lorain, OH 44052 • PLA IFRT

Roberts Jessica A. • Librarian • Broward County Division of Libraries South Regional Branch • Hollywood, FL 33024 • PLA

Roberts John C • Media Specialist • Willow Springs School • Menomonee Falls, WI 53051 • AASL

Roberts John H. • Head, Music Library • University of California-Berkeley Music Library • Berkeley, CA 94720 • ACRL

Roberts John Storm • Original Music • Tivoli, NY 12583

Roberts Joni • Librarian • Willamette University Mark O Hatfield Library • Salem, OR 97301

Roberts Joseph W. • New York, NY 10021 • Continuing

Roberts Josie Mrs. • Library-Media Director • Purvis High School • Purvis, MS 39475 • AASL

Roberts Justine • Mill Valley, CA 94941 • ACRL ALCTS LAMA LITA LRRT *Continuing*
Roberts Katherine M. • Correctional Librarian • DRDC Library • Denver, CO 80239-8004 • ASCLA
Roberts Kathryn E. • Charlotte, NC 28226 • AASL SRRT
Roberts Kenneth H. • Paris 75015, France • IRRT *Continuing*
Roberts LaDonne • Gifts & Exchange Librarian • Mississippi State University Mitchell Memorial Library • Mississippi State, MS 39762 • ACRL ALCTS
Roberts Leila-Jane • Livingston, NJ 07039 • Continuing
Roberts Linda A. • School Library Media Spec. • Northeast High School • Arma, KS 66712 • AASL
Roberts Linda K. • Student • Kent State University School of Library & Information Science • Kent, OH 44242-0001 • ALSC PLA
Roberts Lisa C. • Student • University of North Texas School of Library & Information Sciences • Denton, TX 76203
Roberts Lois • Oakland, CA 94605 • AASL
Roberts Lucille • Trustee • Evansville-Vanderburgh County Public Library • Evansville, IN 47708-1694 • ALTA
Roberts Marceline • Branch Manager • Milwaukee Public Library • Milwaukee, WI 53233 • ALSC
Roberts Margaret • Hd/Per., Art & Recreation • New Orleans Public Library • New Orleans, LA 70140 • PLA
Roberts Margarette June • Hackettstown, NJ 07840
Roberts Matt T. Mr • Binding Officer • Library of Congress • Washington, DC 20541 • ACRL ALCTS *Life*
Roberts Pamela M. • Reference • Montgomery County Public Library Aspen Hill Community Library • Rockville, MD 20853 • PLA RASD IRRT
Roberts Pamela S. • Librarian • Brooklyn Public Library • Brooklyn, NY 11238
Roberts Patricia A B • Program Officer • Montana Dept of Commerce • Helena, MT 59620-0535 • GODORT
Roberts Paul R. • Library Director • Clarke College Schrup Library • Dubuque, IA 52001 • ACRL
Roberts Peter J. • Archivist/Asst. Professor • Georgia State University Pullen Library • Atlanta, GA 30303-3081
Roberts Rodney W. • School Librarian • Eagle Mountain-Saginaw I.S.D. W. E. Boswell High School • Ft. Worth, TX 76179 • AASL
Roberts Ronald L. • San Antonio, TX 78239 • Continuing
Roberts Sallie H. • Assistant Professor • Ohio State University College of Education • Columbus, OH 43210 • AASL YALSA
Roberts Scott • Librarian • Grosse Pointe North High School • Grosse Pointe Woods, MI 48236 • AASL
Roberts Sharon A. • Assistant Dean of Lib Tech Servs • Ball State University Bracken Library • Muncie, IN 47306-0160 • ALCTS
Roberts Sherrill • Librarian • Service Employees International Union • Washington, DC 20005
Roberts Susan P. • Program Coordinator • Carroll County Public Library • Westminster, MD 21157 • ALSC PLA
Roberts Susanne F. • Humanities Bibliographer • Yale University Sterling Memorial Library • New Haven, CT 06520 • ACRL
Roberts Tena • Director of the Library • Wesleyan College Willet Memorial Library • Macon, GA 31297 • ACRL
Roberts Teresa L. • Circulation Supervisor • Lafayette Parish Public Library • Lafayette, LA 70502-3427 • PLA SORT
Roberts Tina M. • Elementary School Media Spec. • Hampton Schools Kraft Elementary School • Hampton, VA 23666
Roberts Vann R. • Decatur, GA 30033 • PLA
Roberts Victoria Mosty • Director • Butt-Holdsworth Memorial Library • Kerrville, TX 78028
Roberts William H. • Director • Forsyth County Public Library • Winston-Salem, NC 27101 • ALTA LAMA PLA IFRT NMRT
Robertson Ann M. • Access Information Associates Inc. • Bellaire, TX 77401 • ACRL LAMA ILERT *Life*
Robertson Barbara A. • Dayton, OH 45426
Robertson Betty L. • Librarian • Mary Esther Public Library • Mary Esther, FL 32569
Robertson Billy O. • Library Director • Union University • Jackson, TN 38305 • ACRL ALCTS LAMA LITA RASD LIRT
Robertson Carol D. • Library Media Specialist • Dumbarton Middle School • Baltimore, MD 21212 • AASL
Robertson Christine A. • Student • Wayne State University Library Science Program • Detroit, MI 48202 • LITA IFRT NMRT SRRT
Robertson Craig A. • Chemistry/Physics Librarian • University of Vermont Bailey Howe Library • Burlington, VT 05405-0036 • LITA RASD
Robertson Deborah Anne • Director of Public Programs • American Library Association • Chicago, IL 60611-2795
Robertson Debra E.J. • Librarian III • Fresno County Free Library Cedar Clinton Library • Fresno, CA 93703 • ALSC
Robertson Earl • Peoria Public Schools • Peoria, IL 61614 • AASL
Robertson Ellen • University of Colorado Norlin Library • Boulder, CO 80309-0184 • ACRL RASD EMIERT
Robertson Helen Lee • Resource Center Librarian • Karby Center Resource Center for Aging Family • Calgary AB, T2P 1B2 Canada • ACRL
Robertson Howard W. • Slavic Catalog Librarian/Bibl. • University of Oregon Library • Eugene, OR 97403-1299 • ACRL
Robertson Joan E. • Cataloger • H. W. Wilson Company • Bronx, NY 10452 • ALCTS
Robertson Judith E. • Cataloger • School Dist-1 • Seattle, WA 98115 • ALCTS
Robertson Karen A. • Director of Library Services • Morgan State University Soper Library • Baltimore, MD 21239-4098 • ACRL
Robertson Kayla W. • Plainfield, NJ 07060
Robertson Marian P. • Director • Manhasset Public Library • Manhasset, NY 11030 • ALSC LAMA LITA PLA RASD YALSA
Robertson Marie S. • Lexington, KY 40593
Robertson Marilyn N. • Los Angeles Unified School District • Los Angeles, CA 90017 • AASL
Robertson Martha L. • Librarian • Kalaheo High School Library Media Center • Kailua, HI 96734
Robertson Marylett R. • Knoxville, TN 37909 • ALSC *Continuing*
Robertson May Rose • Falls Church, VA 22041
Robertson Meg Lloyd • St. Paul, MN 55116
Robertson Nancy • Library Microfilms • Sunnyvale, CA 94086 • ALCTS
Robertson Nancy A. • Norwell Public Library • Norwell, MA 02061
Robertson Nancy Maltby • Librarian • Lacey Timberland Regional Library • Lacey, WA 98503 • AASL
Robertson Nancy R. • Student • Library Company of Philadelphia • Philadelphia, PA 19107 • ACRL
Robertson Patsy • Library Media Specialist • Olympia High School • Rochester, NY 14612 • AASL
Robertson R. Bruce • Spec. Collections Cataloger • Historical Society of Pennsylvania Library • Philadelphia, PA 19107 • MAGERT
Robertson Sandra D. • Director of Library Services • Prestonsburg Community College • Prestonburg, KY 41653-9502 • ACRL
Robertson Sandra V. • Librarian • Pearisburg Public Library • Pearisburg, VA 24134 • PLA
Robertson Shirley M. • Burlingame, CA 94010 • ALSC
Robertson Susan • Student • University of Rhode Island Graduate School of Library & Information Studies • Kingston, RI 02881-0815 • AASL
Robertson Susan E. • Head, Copy Cataloging • University of Maine Raymond H. Fogler Library • Orono, ME 04469
Robertus Debbie E. • University of Oklahoma Press • Norman, OK 73019 • PLA AFLRT
Robey Linda F. • Coast Episcopal Schools • Pass Christian, MS 39571 • AASL
Robichaux Anne K. • Associate Dir. of Libraries • Medical University of South Carolina Library • Charleston, SC 29425 • LITA
Robie Katherine T. • Cataloger • Amherst College Robert Frost Library • Amherst, MA 01002 • ALCTS
Robien Eleanor A. • Librarian • Grayslake Community High School Library • Grayslake, IL 60030 • AASL
Robillard Marie T. • Library Director • Clarence Public Library • Clarence, NY 14031 • PLA
Robin David P. • Kalamazoo, MI 49006 • IFRT NMRT
Robins Eleanor R. • Lithonia, GA 30058
Robins Nora D.S. • Collectons Coordinator • University of Calgary Libraries • Calgary AB, T2N 1N4 Canada • ACRL
Robins William M. • Director • Dunellen Public Library • Dunellen, NJ 08812
Robinson Ann A. • Director • Plainville Public Library • Plainville, MA 02762
Robinson Arthur • Trustee • Atlanta-Fulton Public Library • Atlanta, GA 30303 • PLA
Robinson Ashley • McLean High School Library • McLean, VA 22101 • AASL
Robinson Barbara Jean • Librarian • Houston Public Library W.L.D. Johnson Branch • Houston, TX 77051
Robinson Barbara M. • Washington, DC 20008 • ASCLA LAMA PLA ILERT
Robinson Bennie P. • University of Akron Bierce Library • Akron, OH 44325-1706 • ACRL
Robinson Bernetta D. • Reference Librarian • La Salle University Connelly Library • Philadelphia, PA 19141 • ACRL
Robinson Carol S. • Librarian • Massachusetts Institute of Technology Barker Eng. Lib. Room 10-500 • Cambridge, MA 02139 • ACRL ALCTS LITA NMRT
Robinson Carol W. • Librarian • Mount Vernon Public Library • Mt. Vernon, NY 10550
Robinson Carrie C. • Montgomery, AL 36117 • Continuing
Robinson Cathy A. • Manager • Arlington County Department of Libraries Westover Branch • Arlington, VA 22205 • ALSC PLA
Robinson Charles W. • Director • Baltimore County Public Library • Towson, MD 21204 • ALCTS ALSC ALTA ASCLA LAMA LITA PLA RASD YALSA
Robinson Christine M. • Transylvania University Library • Lexington, KY 40508 • ACRL LITA
Robinson Connie S. • Student • University of Southern Mississippi School of Library Science • Hattiesburg, MS 39406-5146
Robinson Cynthia K. • Madison, WI 53711-2121 • LITA RASD
Robinson Cynthia L. • School Librarian • Fountain Hills Junior Senior High School • Fountain Hills, AZ 85268 • AASL
Robinson Daniel L. • Editorial Specification Spec. • H. W. Wilson Company • Bronx, NY 10452 • AASL ALCTS LITA RASD
Robinson David E. • Hammond, IN 46324
Robinson David G. • Automation Librarian • Middle Tennessee State University Library • Murfreesboro, TN 37132
Robinson David L. Jr. • Acquisitions Librarian • East Central University Linscheid Library • Ada, OK 74820-6899 • ACRL RASD NMRT
Robinson Deborah • Lafayette, IN 47904 • LAMA PLA
Robinson Deborah P. • Student • University of South Florida School of Library & Information Science • Tampa, FL 33620 • AASL SRRT
Robinson Doris J. • Regional Children's Serv Manager • Cuyahoga County Public Library Fairview Park Regional Branch • Fairview Park, OH 44126-2189 • ALSC
Robinson Dwight W. • Seville, OH 44273
Robinson Elizabeth A. • Original Cataloger • University of California-San Diego Central University Library • La Jolla, CA 92093-0175
Robinson Ellen N. • Brooklyn, NY 11218 • ASCLA LITA
Robinson Evelyn B. Miss • Glen Cove, NY 11542 • PLA RASD *Continuing*
Robinson Gayle N. • Foley Intermediate School • Foley, AL 36535 • AASL ALSC
Robinson Gleniece A. Ph.D. • Branch Libraries Administrator • Dallas Public Library • Dallas, TX 75201 • PLA IFRT LRRT
Robinson Gregory C. • Head of Access Services • Ithaca College Library • Ithaca, NY 14850 • ACRL LAMA
Robinson Hanne • Auburn, CA 95603
Robinson Hazel M. • Media Serv Supv • Arthur Hamilton Elementary School • Phoenix, AZ 85009 • AASL ALSC
Robinson Irene A. • Media Service Librarian • Azusa Pacific University Marshburn Memorial Library • Azusa, CA 91702
Robinson Irma A. • President • I. Robinson Design • Chicago, IL 60604
Robinson J. Carmen • Reference Librarian • Lower Columbia College Alan Thompson Library • Longview, WA 98632
Robinson Jacalyn • Delta Correctional Center • Delta, CO 81401 • AASL ASCLA
Robinson Jane E. • Pittsburgh, PA 15228 • Continuing
Robinson Janet A. • NCR Corporation • Wichita, KS 67226-1397
Robinson Janet Lee • Branch Manager • Lake Lanier Regional Library Peachtree Corners Branch • Norcross, GA 30092
Robinson Janis M. • Library/Media Specialist • James M. Bennett Sr. High School • Salisbury, MD 21801 • AASL
Robinson Jay L. • System Librarian • Newton Public Library • Newton, IA 50208
Robinson Joel M. • Director • Tippecanoe County Public Library • Lafayette, IN 47901
Robinson Joyce W. • Librarian • Istrouma High School • Baton Rouge, LA 70805
Robinson Julia A. • Student • University of Maryland College of Library and Information Services • College Park, MD 20742-4345
Robinson Julia I. • Plattsburgh, NY 12901
Robinson Julie A. • Student • University of California Los Angeles Graduate School of Library & Information Science • Los Angeles, CA 90024 • LHRT
Robinson Kara L. • Reference Librarian • Kent State University Libraries • Kent, OH 44242 • ACRL RASD
Robinson Karen G. • Children's Librarian • North Regional Library • Raleigh, NC 27615
Robinson Kate W. • Sales Representative • Information Access Company • Foster City, CA 94404

Robinson Kathryn • Dept. Head, Social Science • Orange County Library System Orlando Public Library • Orlando, FL 32801-2471 • RASD

Robinson Kathryn A. • Student • Lincoln Library • Springfield, IL 62701 • RASD

Robinson Kathy M. • Librarian • North Brook Elementary School • Vale, NC 28168 • AASL ALSC

Robinson Kay L. • Mountain Lakes, NJ 07046 • ASCLA NMRT

Robinson Linda J. • Cataloging Services Sections Mgr • OCLC Online Computer Library Center • Dublin, OH 43017-3395 • ALCTS LITA

Robinson Mary H. • Collection Development Manager • Tucson Pima Library • Tucson, AZ 85726 • PLA IFRT

Robinson Mary-Ann • Student • University of Oklahoma School of Library & Information Studies • Norman, OK 73019

Robinson Mercier C. • Head of Children's Services • East Cleveland Public Library • East Cleveland, OH 44112 • ALSC

Robinson Michael C. • Student • Florida State University School of Library and Information Studies • Tallahassee, FL 32306-2048

Robinson Michael J. • Student • Long Island University Palmer School of Library & Information Science • Greenvale, NY 11548 • ACRL

Robinson Mitchell L. • United States Navy Naval Regional Contacting Center • Philadelphia, PA 19112

Robinson Phyllis • Librarian • Archie Morrison Elementary School • Braintree, MA 02184 • AASL YALSA IFRT NMRT

Robinson Quinn C. • Library Technician • Library of Congress • Washington, DC 20541 • IFRT

Robinson Rae F. • White Plains, NY 10604 • ACRL ALCTS *Continuing*

Robinson Rebecca L. • Media Specialist • Lordstown Junior/Senior High School • Warren, OH 44481 • AASL

Robinson Regan • Editor • Librarian's Collection Letter • Keller, WA 99140

Robinson Rick • Glen Ellyn, IL 60137-5700 • LAMA LITA NMRT

Robinson Ruth Ann • Gulph Mills, PA 19428 • Continuing

Robinson Sandra N. • Kramer Junior High School • Washington, DC 20020 • AASL

Robinson Sharon E. • Black Studies Librarian I • Atlanta-Fulton Public Library • Atlanta, GA 30303 • ACRL EMIERT

Robinson Shelley W. • Librarian • South College of Tennessee • Knoxville, TN 37917

Robinson Tracey • Head,Production Services • Harvard University Library • Cambridge, MA 02138-2901 • LITA

Robinson William C. • Associate Professor • University of Tennessee-Knoxville Graduate School of Library & Information Science • Knoxville, TN 37996-4330 • ALCTS

Robinson William J. • Fairborn, OH 45324

Robison Carolyn • Associate University Librarian • Georgia State University Pullen Library • Atlanta, GA 30303-3081 • ACRL LAMA SORT *Life*

Robison David F.W. • Student • University of California-Berkeley School of Library & Information Studies • Berkeley, CA 94720 • LITA SRRT

Robison Dennis E. • University Librarian • James Madison University Carrier Library • Harrisonburg, VA 22807 • ACRL ALCTS LITA *Life*

Robison Emily A. • Librarian • Jefferson Elementary School • Westfield, NJ 07092 • AASL ALSC

Robison Janet W. • Library Media Specialist • Towers High School • Decatur, GA 30032 • AASL

Robison Philip I. • White Oak, TX 75693-2626 • ACRL ERT

Roblee Martha N. • Assoc Dir/Network Coordinator • Indiana State Library • Indianapolis, IN 46204-2296 • ASCLA PLA

Robles Daniel O • District Librarian • Blanchard Community Library • Santa Paula, CA 93060-2784 • PLA

Robles Jane M. • Student • University of California • Santa Cruz, CA 95064 • SRRT

Robles Kimberley D. • Student • University of California Los Angeles Graduate School of Library & Information Science • Los Angeles, CA 90024 • RASD EMIERT IFRT IRRT NMRT

Robles Lisa A. • Asst. Medical Librarian • Kaiser Permanente Medical Center • Panorama City, CA 91402

Robles Patricia A. • Student • University of California Los Angeles Graduate School of Library & Information Science • Los Angeles, CA 90024

Robling John S. • Beulah, MI 49617 • Continuing

Robnett Bill • Vanderbilt University Central Library • Nashville, TN 37240-0007 • ACRL ALCTS

Robrock David P. • Special Collection Librarian • University of Nevada-Las Vegas James R. Dickinson Library • Las Vegas, NV 89154 • ACRL

Robrock Janice A. • Henderson, NV 89015

Robson Elizabeth A. • Librarian • Danville Correctional Center • Danville, IL 61834 • ASCLA

Robson Elizabeth D. • Librarian Outreach Section • Cleveland Public Library • Cleveland, OH 44114-1271 • ACRL LAMA *Life*

Robson John M. • Director • Rose-Hulman Institute of Technology • Terre Haute, IN 47803 • ACRL LAMA

Robson Timothy D. • Asst Director for Tech Services • Case Western Reserve Univ Freiberger Library • Cleveland, OH 44106-7151 • ACRL ALCTS LITA SRRT

Roby Beth B. • Co-Owner • Texas Furniture • Brownwood, TX 76801

Roby Mary D. • Shorter College Livingston Library • Rome, GA 30165

Roby Sandra G. • Director Library/Media Services • Waltham Public Schools • Waltham, MA 02154

Roca Joan • Systems Analyst • Mankato State University Memorial Library • Mankato, MN 56002-8400 • LITA

Rocca Josephine A. • Sheboygan, WI 53081 • PLA *Continuing*

Rocchio Eileen M. • Student • University of Rhode Island Graduate School of Library & Information Studies • Kingston, RI 02881-0815 • AASL

Rocco M. Catherine • Cary, NC 27513-2446

Roch Margaret E. • Librarian III • Memphis-Shelby County Public Library and Information Center • Memphis, TN 38104-4025 • PLA

Rocha Sinai P. • Reference • Baylor University Moody Memorial Library • Waco, TX 76798-7148 • RASD GODORT

Roche Phyllis M. • Educational Media Specialist • H. L. Bonsall • Camden, NJ 08104 • AASL

Roche Richard G. • Brookfield, IL 60513

Roche Sally H. • Head of Access Services • University of Rochester Rush Rhees Library • Rochester, NY 14627-0055 • ACRL

Rocheleau Barbara S. • Library Media Specialist • Fairfield High School • Fairfield, CT 06430 • IFRT

Rocheleau Kathleen D. • Shrewsbury, MA 01545

Rocheleau Margaret K. Mrs • Lehighton, PA 18235 • ACRL ALCTS *Continuing*

Rochell Carlton C. • Dean • New York University Elmer Holmes Bobst Library • New York, NY 10012 • ACRL IRRT

Rochelle Patricia • Reference Librarian • Arlington Heights Memorial Library • Arlington Heights, IL 60004-5966 • RASD

Rochen Phyllis • Akiva Hebrew Day School • Lathrup Village, MI 48076 • AASL

Rochester Maxine Dr. • Associate Professor • Charles Sturt University Riverina • Wagga Wagga NSW 2650, Australia • IRRT

Rochman Hazel P. • Asst. Ed., Books for Youths • American Library Association • Chicago, IL 60611-2795

Rock Noeme S. • Tracy Joint Union High School • Tracy, CA 95376 • AASL

Rocke Reve P. • Librarian • University of California-Davis Library • Davis, CA 95616

Rockefeller-MacArthur Elizabeth E. • Student • San Jose State University Division of Library & Information Science • San Jose, CA 95192-0029 • SRRT

Rockefeller Monica J. • W Hartford, CT 06119

Rockershousen Lee A. • Wheaton, IL 60187

Rockman Connie C. • Children Services Supervisor • Ferguson Library • Stamford, CT 06904 • ALSC ILERT IRRT

Rockman Ilene F. • Associate Dean (Interim) • California Polytechnic State University Robert E. Kennedy Library • San Luis Obispo, CA 93407 • ACRL LAMA LITA RASD EMIERT LIRT LRRT SRRT *Life*

Rockmore Janice P. • Cataloger • Lawrence Headquarters • Lawrenceville, NJ 08648

Rockom Melissa • Library Aide • Isom Intermediate School • Lynden, WA 98264

Rockwell Ford A. • Wichita, KS 67208 • LAMA PLA *Life*

Rockwell Kenneth W. • Technical Services Division • University of Utah Marriott Library • Salt Lake City, UT 84112-1179 • MAGERT

Rockwell Virginia • Trustee • Denver Public Library • Denver, CO 80204-2602 • ALTA PLA

Rockwood Arlene R. • Union Christian College • La Union, Philippines • AASL ACRL LIRT

Rockwood Ruth H. • Tallahassee, FL 32308-5859 • Continuing

Rod Catherine M. • Reader Services Librarian • Grinnell College • Grinnell, IA 50112-0811 • ACRL GODORT LIRT

Rod Donald C. • Ames, IA 50010 • Continuing

Rodabaugh Edna H. • Long Beach, CA 90804 • ACRL *Continuing*

Rodak Valerie A. • Librarian • Nevada County Library • Nevada City, CA 95959 • ALCTS LAMA LITA PLA

Rodarte Antonio • Cataloger • University of Texas at El Paso Library • El Paso, TX 79968-0582

Rodd Noreen M. • Franklin, MA 02038

Roddy Carol Lynn • Section Manager • Ameritech Information Systems • Dublin, OH 43017

Roddy Kevin M. • Librarian II • University of Hawaii Hilo Library • Hilo, HI 96720

Roddy Mary Ruth Sr • Librarian • Saint Joseph School Library • Martinsburg, WV 25401

Rode Jill Rosenthal • Director • Ocean Springs Public Library • Ocean Springs, MS 39564 • PLA YALSA

Rode Joanne O. • Student • San Jose State University School of Business • San Jose, CA 95192-0070 • YALSA

Rode Mia J. • Head, OMC Section, SUL • Stanford University • Stanford, CA 94305-6011 • ALCTS LAMA

Rodean Trudy O. • Borman Elementary Library • Denton, TX 76205 • AASL

Roden Jean D. • Acquisitions Librarian • Shoreline Community College Ray W Howard Library Media Center • Seattle, WA 98133 • ACRL IRRT

Rodenberger Jackie • Selma Elementary School • Selma, IN 47383 • AASL

Rodenschmit Carol • Order Clerk • Madison Public Library • Madison, WI 53703 • ACRL ALCTS ALSC ALTA ASCLA LAMA LITA PLA RASD YALSA

Roderer Karoline E. • Student • University of Pittsburgh School of Library and Information Science • Pittsburgh, PA 15260 • EMIERT IRRT SRRT

Roderer Nancy K. • Medical Library Director • Yale University Medical Historical Library • New Haven, CT 06510 • ACRL LITA

Roderick Elizabeth • Literacy Consultant • Virginia State Library & Archives • Richmond, VA 23219 • ASCLA NMRT

Roderick Mary P. • El Paso, TX 79902

Rodes Virginia I. • Sales Representative • Book House • Jonesville, MI 49250 • ACRL ALCTS IFRT

Rodger Eleanor J. • PLA Executive Director • American Library Association • Chicago, IL 60611-2795 • PLA *Life*

Rodgers Frank • Director • University of Miami Libraries Richter Library • Coral Gables, FL 33124 • ACRL ALCTS ASCLA *Life*

Rodgers Helen E. • Torrance, CA 90503 • Continuing

Rodgers Jeanne M. • Librarian • Union High School • Tolleson, AZ 85353 • AASL

Rodgers Judith E. • Instructor/Librarian • University of North Alabama Collier Library • Florence, AL 35632 • AASL

Rodgers Linda • Trustee • Metropolitan Library System • Oklahoma City, OK 73102 • ALTA PLA

Rodgers Marguerite • Oakland, CA 94610 • ACRL RASD *Continuing*

Rodgers Marie E. • Student • Queens College Grad Sch of Lib & Inf Studies • Flushing, NY 11367 • EMIERT IFRT SRRT

Rodgers Marilyn L. • Student • Southern Connecticut State University School of Libray Science & Instructional Technology • New Haven, CT 06515

Rodgers Patricia A. • St. Helena Public Library • St Helena, CA 94574

Rodgers Patricia M. • Coordinator Technical Services • University of South Alabama • Mobile, AL 36688 • ALCTS

Rodgers Ronald C. Dr • Trustee • Wilmette Public Library • Wilmette, IL 60091 • ALTA

Rodgers Sara E. • Student • Pratt Institute Graduate School of Library & Information Science • Brooklyn, NY 11205 • LITA

Rodgers Siegel Jane • Rare Books/Manuscript Ln • Columbia University Libraries Butler Library • New York, NY 10027 • ACRL

Rodich-Hodges Nancy Ann • Technical Services Librarian • Mid-Mississippi Regional Library System • Kosciusko, MS 39090 • ALCTS PLA

Rodkewich Patricia J. • Reference/Bibliographer Doc Libn • University of Minnesota Library • St Paul, MN 55108 • ACRL GODORT

Rodman Janis M. • Reference Services Supervisor • Monterey Public Library • Monterey, CA 93940 • PLA

Rodman Ruey L. • Columbus, OH 43202

Rodne Mary E. • Administrative Librarian • Bloomingdale Public Library • Bloomingdale, IL 60108 • PLA

Rodney Mae L. • Director • Winston-Salem State University • Winston-Salem, NC 27110 • ACRL RASD

Rodning Claudia A. • Edmonton, AB, T6G 0R8 Canada

Rodrigues Helena F. • Bibliographic Control Librarian • Roger Williams College Library • Bristol, RI 02809-2921 • ACRL LITA

Rodrigues Kevin J. • Student • Rutgers University School of Communication Information & Library Studies • New Brunswick, NJ 08903

Rodrigues Linda • Trustee • Newark Public Library • Newark, NJ 07101-0630 • ALTA PLA

Rodriguez-Buckingham Antonio • Professor • University of Southern Mississippi School of Library Science • Hattiesburg, MS 39406-5146

Rodriguez-Collazo Angel A. • Student • I C P R Junior College • Hato Rey, PR 00919 • ACRL

Rodriguez Ann Milagros • San Juan, PR 00901 • FLRT

Rodriguez Christine A. • Los Angeles, CA 90031 • PLA

Rodriguez Corene T. • Loomis, CA 95650

Rodriguez Elena • Student • University of Maryland College of Library and Information Services • College Park, MD 20742-4345 • AASL ALSC EMIERT SRRT

Rodriguez Eliezer • Student • Simmons College Graduate School of Library & Information Science • Boston, MA 02115 • ACRL

Rodriguez Ginger G. • Public Relations Office • East Chicago Public Library • E. Chicago, IN 46312

Rodriguez Harmony • Associate Librarian • Oxnard College Library • Oxnard, CA 93030

Rodriguez Ines F. • Head Librarian • Saint Johns School • Santurce, PR 00907-1560 • AASL

Rodriguez Jill P. • Bensenville Community Public Library • Bensenville, IL 60106 • LAMA PLA

Rodriguez Judith • Libraian • New York Public Library Inwood Regional Branch • New York, NY 10034 • YALSA

Rodriguez Ketty • Denton, TX 76201-1002 • ALCTS

Rodriguez Luis F. • Asst Dir for Public Servs • Stockton State College • Pomona, NJ 08240 • ACRL GODORT

Rodriguez Marisela • Cummings Media Center • APO, AP 96319-0005

Rodriguez Marisol Gutierrez • Assistant Librarian • University of Puerto Rico Graduate School of Librarianship • Rio Piedras, PR 00931

Rodriguez Miriam J. • Student • University of North Texas School of Library & Information Sciences • Denton, TX 76203

Rodriguez Robert S. • Library Technical Services • College of The Mainland Learning Resources Center • Texas City, TX 77591 • ACRL ALCTS LITA RASD LIRT SRRT

Rodriguez Ronald • Coordinator/Librarian • California State University • Fullerton, CA 92634 • ACRL

Rodstein Frances M. • Adminstrative Services Libn • Manatee County Public Library System • Bradenton, FL 34205

Roe Constance D. • School Library Media Specialist • Putnam High School • Putnam, CT 06260 • AASL YALSA

Roe Eunice • Rutgers University School of Communication Information & Library Studies • New Brunswick, NJ 08903 • ACRL LAMA RASD

Roe Grace C. Miss • Dunedin, FL 33528 • PLA RASD
Continuing

Roe Nancy P. • Cataloger • University of Maine at Presque Isle Library • Presque Isle, ME 04769-2888 • MAGERT

Roebuck Edith • Abilene, TX 79605 • Continuing

Roebuck Jarrett Margaret A. • Librarian • University of Washington Gallagher Law Library • Seattle, WA 98105 • ACRL LAMA LITA

Roeckel Alan G. • Director • Garden City Public Library • Garden City, NY 11530

Roecker Fred A. • User Education Librarian • Ohio State University Libraries • Columbus, OH 43210-1286 • LITA

Roedder Kathleen • Gloucester, MA 01930

Roeder Catherine G. • Systems & Bibliographic Ln • Southeast Missouri State Univ Kent Library • Cpe Girardeau, MO 63701 • ACRL ALCTS LITA

Roeder Christine S. • Director,LRC • DeVry Institute of Technology • Columbus, OH 43209 • ACRL

Roeder Randall • Coe College Stewart Memorial Library • Cedar Rapids, IA 52402-5092

Roehling Steven R. • Head , Reference Deparment • Charleston County Library • Charleston, SC 29403

Roehm Frances E. • Bloomington, IL 61701 • RASD IFRT

Roelants Josiane • Professor • Free University of Brussels • Brussels 1050, Belgium • ACRL ALCTS LITA

Roelofs Merry Lynn • Baxter, MN 56401

Roelse Lois A. • Student • University of Kentucky College of Library & Information Science • Lexington, KY 40506-0391

Roese Madeleine A. • Morristown, NJ 07960

Roesler Karen Mrs. • Co-Director • Wallingford Public Library • Wallingford, CT 06492

Roess Anne C. • Librarian • People Gas Light & Coke Co • Chicago, IL 60603 • LITA

Roest James Vander • Library Trustee • Kalamazoo Public Library • Kalamazoo, MI 49007-5270 • ALTA PLA

Roets Lois F. Ed. D • Des Moines, IA 50310-2801

Roettgen Kathleen M. • Student • University of Missouri-Kansas City Library • Kansas City, MO 64110-2499 • PLA IFRT

Roff Donna W. • Asst. Manager Community Libs • Ventura County Library Services Agency • Ventura, CA 93003

Roff Sandra S. • Assistant Professor in Library • Baruch College Library • New York, NY 10010 • ACRL

Rogaliner Susan Wehling • Geneva, IL 60134

Rogalla Michael A. • Youth Services & Outreach Coor. • Scott County Library System • Eldridge, IA 52748 • ALSC

Rogalsky Virginia • Librarian • Las Virgenes Unified School District • Agoura, CA 91361

Rogan Mary Ellen W. • Archivist/Manuscripts Libn • New York Public Library Billy Rose Theatre Collection • New York, NY 10023 • ACRL

Rogenmoser Debra • Saint Mary's College of California • Moraga, CA 94575 • ACRL

Roger Mae Durham • Senior Lecturer • University of California-Berkeley School of Library & Information Studies • Berkeley, CA 94720 • AASL ALSC PLA YALSA IFRT
Continuing

Rogero Thomas T. • Asst. Dir. for Public Servs. • University of Miami Libraries Richter Library • Coral Gables, FL 33124 • ACRL LAMA RASD

Rogers Alfred E. • Catalog Librarian • University of Texas Libraries General Libraries • Austin, TX 78713-7330

Rogers Ann M. • Pine, CO 80470 • AASL IFRT

Rogers Anne M. • Director • Paris-Bourbon County Library • Paris, KY 40361 • PLA

Rogers Barbara A. • Children's Librarian • Carnegie Library of Pittsburgh South Side Branch • Pittsburgh, PA 15203 • PLA

Rogers Barbara J. • Technical Librarian • Fina Oil & Chemical Company • Deer Park, TX 77536

Rogers Betty J. • Head of Reference • Coe College Stewart Memorial Library • Cedar Rapids, IA 52402-5092 • ACRL RASD LIRT

Rogers Brian D. • Director • Connecticut College • New London, CT 06320-4196 • ACRL

Rogers Cheryl M. • Marketing Representative • Southeastern Library Network (SOLINET) • Atlanta, GA 30309-2955 • LITA

Rogers Curtis R. • Graduate Student/Assistant • University of South Carolina College of Library & Information Science • Columbia, SC 29208 • ACRL

Rogers Donna L. • Student • Concord College Library • Athens, WV 24712 • IFRT

Rogers Dorothy S. • Head of Catalog • Carleton University Library • Ottawa ON, K1S 5J7 Canada • LITA

Rogers Earl M. • Cura of Archives • University of Iowa Library • Iowa City, IA 52242 • ACRL ALCTS   *Life*

Rogers Elizabeth D. • Tustin, CA 92680

Rogers Elizabeth Dee • University of North Texas • Denton, TX 76203 • IRRT NMRT

Rogers Ellen A. • Bronx, NY 10462

Rogers Glen M. • Trustee • Montclair Free Public Library • Montclair, NJ 07042

Rogers Gloria H. • Catalog Librarian • San Diego State University Library • San Diego, CA 92119-2120 • ALCTS

Rogers H. Carton III • Associate Dir of Lib-Tech Serv • University of Pennsylvania Library Van Pelt-Dietrich Library Center • Philadelphia, PA 19104-6206

Rogers Helen C. • Indianapolis, IN 46205

Rogers Helen M. • Librarian • University of Hawaii Hilo Library • Hilo, HI 96720

Rogers Irene • Assistant Director • Yonkers Public Library • Yonkers, NY 10701 • ALCTS LAMA PLA

Rogers Janet B. • Tate Woods Elementary School • Lisle, IL 60532 • AASL

Rogers Janet F. • Media Director • Board of Education • Griffin, GA 30224 • AASL

Rogers Jean • Southern Education Baptist Center • Olive Branch, MS 38654 • AASL

Rogers Jean C. • Juneau, AK 99801 • ALSC

Rogers Jeanne M. • Youth & Adult Services Librarian • Daniel Boone Regional Library • Columbia, MO 65205-1267 • YALSA

Rogers Jo Ann V. • Lexington, KY 40503-2125 • LITA

Rogers Jo Ann W. • Librarian • Fort Worth Academy • Fort Worth, TX 76133 • NMRT

Rogers Joan M. • Head of Adult Services • Waterford Township Public Library • Waterford, MI 48329 • PLA RASD

Rogers Juanita B. • Children's Librarian • Choctawhatchee Regional Library Troy Public Branch • Troy, AL 36081 • ALSC

Rogers Kathleen A. • Gathiersburg, MD 20882 • ALSC

Rogers Linda C. • Janesville Public Library • Janesville, WI 53545-3971 • RASD

Rogers M. Maggie • Director of Inf & Doc Service • Northwest Regional Education Laboratory Library • Portland, OR 97204 • AASL YALSA

Rogers Marcia L. • Collection Management Librarian • Arlington Heights Memorial Library • Arlington Heights, IL 60004-5966 • PLA RASD

Rogers Margaret J N • Acquisitions Librarian • First Regional Library • Hernando, MS 38632

Rogers Margaret N. • Administrative Supervisor • Cornell University Library • Ithaca, NY 14853 • ACRL

Rogers Marilyn L. • Head Serials Dept. • University of Arkansas Libraries • Fayetteville, AR 72701-1201

Rogers Marjorie L. • Cincinnati, OH 45220

Rogers Martha • Librarian II • Miami-Dade Public Library West Kendall Regional Library • Miami, FL 33186

Rogers Martha J. • Fort Wayne, IN 46805

Rogers Mary E. • University Librarian • Sacred Heart University Library • Fairfield, CT 06432-1023 • LITA

Rogers Michael E. • Asst. News Editor • Library Journal Cahners Publishing Company • New York, NY 10011

Rogers Nan S. • Library Director • Bethel Public Library • Bethel, CT 06801

Rogers Patricia J. • Assoc. Libn. for Book Cllns • Harvard University Fine Arts Library • Cambridge, MA 02138 • ACRL ALCTS LAMA LITA PLA

Rogers Patricia P. • Media Specialist • Middleton High School Media Center • Charleston, SC 29407 • AASL

Rogers Peggy V. • Magnolia, AR 71753

Rogers Ruth M. • Alameda County Library System • Fremont, CA 94538 • ALCTS IRRT LRRT

Rogers Rutherford D. • Hamden, CT 06517 • Life

Rogers Sally A. • Hd,Serials,Non-Bk,Thesis Catlg • Ohio State University Libraries • Columbus, OH 43210-1286 • ACRL ALCTS LAMA LITA

Rogers Seleta J. • Education Coordinator • Georgia Department of Education • Atlanta, GA 30334 • AASL LITA

Rogers Sharon J. • Assoc. Vice President • George Washington University • Washington, DC 20052 • ACRL LAMA RASD   *Life*

Rogers Shelley L. • Authority/Online • Kent State University Libraries • Kent, OH 44242 • ACRL

Rogers Shirley A. • Mohegan Lake, NY 10547

Rogers Stephen • Ohio State University Libraries • Columbus, OH 43210-1286 • ACRL RASD

Rogers Susan L. • Manitoba Department of Education & Training • Winnipeg MB, R3G 0T3 Canada • ALCTS

Rogers Timothy H. • Director • Oneida Public Library • Oneida, NY 13421 • PLA

Rogers William Ted • Serials Librarian • Brown & Root Inc., Information Resource Center • Houston, TX 77020

Rogers Wyma J. • Systems • Santa Barbara Public Library System • Santa Barbara, CA 93102

Rogerson Mary Frances • Director • Casey Memorial Library • Ft Hood, TX 76541 • PLA FLRT

Rogge Rena W. • Assistant Director • Kean College of New Jersey Library • Union, NJ 07083 • ACRL ALCTS LITA RASD GODORT

Rogge Stephen L. • Director • Rapides Parish Library • Alexandria, LA 71301 • LAMA PLA RASD

Roggenbuck Mary June • Associate Professor • Catholic University of America School of Library and Information Science • Washington, DC 20064

Roggenstein Carol A. • Branch Manager • Palm Beach County Public Library System Palm Beach Gardens Branch • Palm Beach Gardens, FL 33410 • RASD

Roggia Sally • Acting Assistant Professor • University of Hawaii Thomas Hale Hamilton Library • Honolulu, HI 96822 • ACRL ALCTS

Roggow Judith • Library Adminstrator • Minnegasco, Inc. • Minneapolis, MN 55402 • RASD

Rogoff June B. • Head Central Library • Rochester Public Library • Rochester, NY 14604 • LAMA PLA RASD

Rogson Lorraine P. • Arlington, TX 76013 • ALCTS SRRT

Rohde Kathy L. • Evansville, WI 53536 • AASL

Rohde Nancy J. • Assistant Professor • University of Minnesota • Minneapolis, MN 55455 • LITA PLA RASD CLENE IFRT

Rohdy Margaret A. • Hd Shared Catlg Dept • University of Pennsylvania Library Van Pelt-Dietrich Library Center • Philadelphia, PA 19104-6206 • ACRL ALCTS LITA

Rohe Terry Ann • Portland State University Library • Portland, OR 97207 • ACRL

Rohlf Robert H. • Director • Hennepin County Library • Minnetonka, MN 55343 • LAMA PLA ERT   *Life*

Rohm Yvonne • Librarian • Aid Association for Luthrans (AAL) • Appleton, WI 54919 • LITA

Rohmann Gloria P. • Asst. Chief Sci. Tech. Div. • New York Public Library • New York, NY 10018-2788 • ACRL LAMA LITA

Rohr Judy A. • Adult Services Manager • Fullerton Public Library • Fullerton, CA 92632 • PLA

Rohrbaugh Ann S. • Assistant Dir for Lib Operations • Kalamazoo Public Library • Kalamazoo, MI 49007-5270

Rohrbaugh Janet M. • Clackamas County Library • Oak Grove, OR 97267

Rohrbaugh Pat • Librarian • John Marshall High School • Rochester, MN 55901 • AASL

Rohrbough Wanda Sue • Reference Librarian • Ohio University Libraries • Athens, OH 45701-2978 • ACRL

Rohrer Elizabeth P. • Senior Librarian • Palo Alto City Library Downtown Branch • Palo Alto, CA 94301

Rohrer Lorie J. • Assistant Children's Librarian • Lake Forest Library • Lake Forest, IL 60045

Rohrer Richard L. • Director • University of Minnesota Saint Paul Campus Libraries • Saint Paul, MN 55108 • ACRL LAMA

Rohrig Thomas T. • Texas Tech University Libraries • Lubbock, TX 79409-0002 • ACRL LAMA RASD GODORT *Life*

Roig Barbara Yeutter • Librarian-Assistant • Boulder Public Library • Boulder, CO 80306 • ALSC

Rojas-Leon Octavio G. • Bogota DE, Colombia • ACRL LAMA LITA PLA ILERT IRRT SRRT

Rojas Eunice M. • Cataloger • Emory University Pitts Theology Library • Atlanta, GA 30322

Rojtas-Milliner Mary Cay • Steel Valley High School • Munhall, PA 15120 • AASL

Rokicki Betty A. • Library Aid • Greenfield School • Milwaukee, WI 53215

Roland Barbara • Norfolk, VA 23505 • Continuing

Roland Daniel R. • Cottonwood Falls, KS 66845 • ACRL IFRT SRRT

Roland Lisa L. • Student • Appalachian State University Department of Library Science & Educational Foundation • Boone, NC 28608 • AASL ALSC SRRT

Roland Sharon L. • Head Librarian • Billings Senior High School • Billings, MT 59102 • YALSA

Rolater Cholly J. • Discovery Store, Inc. • Dallas, TX 75380-0498

Rolen Helen T. • Manager • ALZA Corp., Research Library • Palo Alto, CA 94303-0802 • ALCTS LITA

Rolen Rhonda B. • Springhill, LA 71075

Rolfes Amy E. • Cincinnati, OH 45209 • PLA

Rolich Andrea • Collection Preservation • University of Wisconsin-Madison Memorial Library • Madison, WI 53706

Roling Sharon Voshell • Morristown, NJ 07960 • ACRL ALCTS LAMA LITA RASD

Roll Kelly L. • Library Specialist III • Stanford University Lane Medical Library • Stanford, CA 94305-5323 • NMRT

Roll Maureen • San Jose, CA 95110-2220 • PLA

Rollett Ginny C. • Sno-Isle Regional Library Edmonds Branch • Edmonds, WA 98020

Rollins Alden M. • Documents and Reference Ln. • University of Alaska • Anchorage, AK 99508

Rollins Arline M. • Columbus, OH 43214

Rollins Brenda L. • Library Media Specialist • Country Parkway Elementary School • Williamsville, NY 14221 • AASL

Rollins Deborah V. • Reference • University of Maine Raymond H. Fogler Library • Orono, ME 04469 • ACRL NMRT

Rollins Debra C. • Media Specialist • Rapides High School • Lecompte, LA 71346 • AASL LIRT

Rollins Gene • Chief of Technical Services • Houston Public Library • Houston, TX 77002 • LAMA LITA

Rollins Jacqueline A. • University of South Carolina at Spartanburg-Library • Spartanburg, SC 29303 • ALSC YALSA *Life*

Rollins JoAnn M. • South Windsor, CT 06074 • AASL

Rollins Joseph W. • President • Charlemae Hill Rollins Foundation • Chicago, IL 60605 • ALSC

Rollins Linda K. • Librarian • Morgan Elementary School Library • Paducah, KY 42003 • AASL *Life*

Rollins Ottilie H. • Potsdam, NY 13676 • Continuing

Rollins Peggy J. • Vacaville, CA 95687

Rollins Rebecca R. • Librarian I • Memphis-Shelby County Public Library and Information Center • Memphis, TN 38104-4025 • PLA IFRT

Rollman Mary • Ann Arbor, MI 48105 • Continuing

Rollock Barbara T. • Brooklyn, NY 11203 • ALSC PLA SRRT

Roloff Joyce P. • Librarian • Kellogg Middle School • Seattle, WA 98155 • AASL YALSA *Life*

Rolsma Greg A. • Board of Trustees Member • Pierce County Rural Library District • Tacoma, WA 98446 • ALTA PLA

Rolstad Gary O. • Associate State Librarian • State Library of Louisiana • Baton Rouge, LA 70821-0131

Rolston Darrell • Trustee • Kanawha County Public Library • Charleston, WV 25301 • ALTA

Rom Pat • Wooster, OH 44691 • ACRL IFRT SRRT

Romaine Paul W. • Columbia University Library Service Library • New York, NY 10027 • ACRL ALCTS

Romalis Carl • Senior Librarian • Arthur Kill Correctional Facility Library • Staten Island, NY 10309 • ASCLA

Roman Anne M. • Assistant Director • Piscataway Public Library Westergard Branch • Piscataway, NJ 08854 • PLA

Roman Dorothy J. • Trustee • Connetquot Public Library • Bohemia, NY 11716 • ALTA

Roman Marjorie Ross • Chesterfield, MO 63017 • ALSC

Roman Susan • ALSC/ALTA Executive Director • American Library Association • Chicago, IL 60611-2795 • ALSC ALTA

Romanansky Marcia C. • Vice President • Blackwell North America • Blackwood, NJ 08012 • ACRL ALCTS PLA

Romanelli Catherine • Library Director • Sachem Public Library • Holbrook, NY 11741 • PLA

Romani Dorothy P. • Troy, MI 48084 • Continuing

Romaniuk Elena • Coordinator, Serials Mgt. Unit • University of Victoria McPherson Library • Victoria BC, V8W 3H5 Canada

Romanko Karen A. • Reference Librarian • Southwestern University Law Library • Los Angeles, CA 90005

Romano Anne • Librarian • Taft School • Watertown, CT 06795 • AASL

Romano Beatrice E. • Librairian • Saddle Brook Public Library • Saddle Brook, NJ 07662 • PLA ERT

Romano Donna • Maspeth, NY 11378 • PLA

Romano Pia M. • Student • Simmons College Graduate School of Library & Information Science • Boston, MA 02115

Romano Rosina • Carmel, NY 10512 • AASL EMIERT IFRT

Romano Wendy J. • Chief, Technical Services • County of Los Angeles Public Library • Hawthorne, CA 90250 • LAMA LITA PLA

Romans Caroline Ward • Chief Children's Svs Consultant • Nassau Library System • Uniondale, NY 11553 • ALSC

Romans Larry • Information Services Librarian • Vanderbilt University Library • Nashville, TN 37240-0007 • ACRL GODORT

Romanski Consuelo B. • Trustee • Oregon State Library • Salem, OR 97310-0640 • ALTA

Romary Michael • Ref Bibl Instruction Coord • University of Maryland • Baltimore, MD 21228 • ACRL LAMA LITA LIRT

Rome Alan • Saint Mary Seminary • Wickliffe, OH 44092 • ACRL LAMA

Romelczyk Gerald J. • Director • Walpole Public Library • Walpole, MA 02081

Romeo Richard • Student • Pratt Institute Graduate School of Library & Information Science • Brooklyn, NY 11205

Romer Frances M. • Young Adult Librarian • Northport-East Northport Public Library • Northport, NY 11768

Romer James W. • University of North Carolina Walter Clinton Jackson Library • Greensboro, NC 27412-5201 • ACRL ALCTS

Romer Karen E. • High School Librarian • Redwood Chrisitan Schools, Inc • San Leandro, CA 94579 • AASL

Romerin Judith S. • Student • University of Rhode Island Graduate School of Library & Information Studies • Kingston, RI 02881-0815 • ACRL

Romero Carmen G. • Librarian II • Caribbean Regional Library • San Juan, PR 00931 • ACRL

Romero Catherine S. • Columbia, MD 21044

Romero Elizabeth A. • Pioneer Library System Moore Public Library Branch • Moore, OK 73160

Romero Georg L. • Customer Services • Dialog Information Service Inc. • Palo Alto, CA 94304 • RASD

Romero Joe • Trustee • Westchester Public Library • Westchester, IL 60154 • ALTA

Romero Lisa A. • Graduate Assistant • University of Illinois Library • Urbana, IL 61801

Romero Nancy L. • Head, Rare Book & Special Clln. • University of Illinois Library • Urbana, IL 61801 • ACRL

Romeu Raquel Dr. • Professor • Le Moyne College • Syracuse, NY 13214 • Continuing

Romig Ronald E. • RLDS Church Library-Archives • Independence, MO 64051

Romito David • Student • University of Illinois Graduate School of Library and Information Science • Urbana, IL 61801 • PLA RASD IFRT SRRT

Romito Meredith A. • Librarian • Highland Elementary School • Mesa, AZ 85213 • AASL LIRT

Romm Linda S. • Student • University of North Carolina Department of Library & Information Studies • Greensboro, NC 27412-5001 • AASL SRRT

Romo Jose Leon • Library Director • Saint Vincent DePaul Regional Seminary Library • Boynton Beach, FL 33436 • ACRL

Romoser Ruth • Librarian • Thurston Middle School • Springfield, OR 97478 • AASL

Romweber Margaret Toll • Boca Raton, FL 33433 • Continuing

Ronayne Betty Lee • Reference Librarian • California State University-Sacramento Library • Sacramento, CA 95819-6039 • ACRL

Ronberg Dennis • Owner • Linden Tree Children's Records & Books • Los Altos, CA 94022

Ronchetti Ann L. • Bibl, English & Comparative Lit • University of Pittsburgh Hillman Library • Pittsburgh, PA 15260 • ACRL

Rondeau Margaret K. • Sebastian, FL 32958 • ALTA PLA

Rondestvedt Helen F. • Issaquah, WA 98027

Ronen Naomi • Reference Librarian • Harvard Law School Library • Cambridge, MA 02138 • ACRL LITA

Roney Raymond G. • Dean, Instructional Services • El Camino College Library and Media Services • Torrance, CA 90506 • ACRL

Roney Susan E. • Student • University of Wisconsin-Milwaukee School of Library & Information Science • Milwaukee, WI 53201 • AASL

Ronnback Janet • Branch Librarian • Aitkin Public Library • Aitkin, MN 56431

Ronney Darlene • Reference Librarian • East Cleveland Public Library • East Cleveland, OH 44112

Ronning Harriet • Library Board Trustee • Sioux Falls Public Library • Sioux Falls, SD 57102

Roochvarg Lynn Weber • Lansdale, PA 19446

Roochvarg Myron • Director • Commack Public Library District • Commack, NY 11725 • LAMA LITA PLA

Rood Joanna K. • Network Adminstrator • Clackamas County Library • Oak Grove, OR 97267 • PLA

Rook Paulette N. • Student • University of North Texas School of Library & Information Sciences • Denton, TX 76203 • RASD

Rooks Cindy • Novi, MI 48050 • ALSC

Rooks Dana C. • Assistant Director for Admin. • University of Houston Libraries • Houston, TX 77204-2091 • ACRL LAMA RASD

Roome Barbara C. • St Paul, MN 55105 • PLA YALSA *Continuing*

Rooney Eugene M. S.J. Rev • Washington, DC 20007 • ACRL

Rooney Merilyn H. • Gary, IN 46403 • AASL

Rooney Paul M. • Buffalo, NY 14222

Rooney Sieglinde E. H. • Associate Librarian • University of Alberta Library • Edmonton AB, Canada • ACRL

Roop Donna K. • Allegan Public Library • Allegan, MI 49010

Roorda Jayne • Intel Corp • Chandler, AZ 85226

Roos Jean Carolyn Miss • Kissimmee, FL 32741 • PLA YALSA *Continuing*

Roos Marianne L. • Library Director • Handley Library • Winchester, VA 22601 • LAMA PLA

Roos Tedine J. • Director • Rochester Public Library • Rochester, NH 03867

Roosa Mark S. • University of Delaware Library • Newark, DE 19717-5267 • ALCTS

Roosa Mary D. • Sarasota, FL 34277

Roose Tina • Automation Consultant • North Suburban Library System • Wheeling, IL 60090 • RASD EMIERT SRRT

Root Ann • Student • Queens College Graduate School of Library & Information Studies • Flushing, NY 11367 • AASL YALSA

Root Dick Lisa A. • Lexington, KY 40517-2959

Root Eileen M. • Reference Librarian • Kaneohe Regional Library • Kaneohe, HI 96744

Root Elizabeth A. • Head, Technical Services • United States International Trade Commission • Washington, DC 20436 • FLRT

Root Jennifer A. • Gleason Public Library • Carlisle, MA 01741

Root Mary F. • Interlibrary Cooperation Spec. • River Bend Library System • Coal Valley, IL 61240

Root Nina J. • Director of Library Services • American Museum of Natural History Library • New York, NY 10024 • ACRL ALCTS LAMA LITA RASD IFRT

Root Patricia S. • Reference/Young Adult • Bronxville Public Library • Bronxville, NY 10708 • YALSA

Root Ronald W. • Librarian • Tulsa Junior College • Tulsa, OK 74115

Root Susan P. • Reference Librarian • Eastern Loudon Regional Library • Sterling, VA 22170

Rootenberg Barbara • President • B & L Rootenberg Rare Books • Sherman Oaks, CA 91403 • ACRL

Rooth Catherine L. • Library Media Coordinator • Monmouth Elementary School • Monmouth, OR 97361 • AASL

Roozen Nancy • Waukesha School District • Waukesha, WI 53186 • AASL

Roper Dewitt F. • Reference Librarian • Roosevelt Public Library • Roosevelt, NY 11575 • PLA

Roper Diann • Student • University of Pittsburgh School of Library and Information Science • Pittsburgh, PA 15260

Roper Fred W. • Dean • University of South Carolina College of Library & Information Science • Columbia, SC 29208

Roppolo Frances W. • Librarian • Saint Charles Parish Library • Luling, LA 70070

Roquet Judy R. • Library Coordinator • Polk Education Service District • Dallas, OR 97338 • AASL ALCTS

Rorer Christina H. • North Wales, PA 19454 • ACRL

Rorick Janice • Turlock, CA 95380-2991 • AASL

Rorlich Hari S. Ph.D • Head-Micrographics • University of Southern California Doheny Library • Los Angeles, CA 90089-0182 • ALCTS

Rory Carolyn M. • Librarian II-Reference • Whittier Public Library • Whittier, CA 90602

Rosa Helene C. • Holland, PA 18966

Rosa Lucille M. • Head, Technical Services Div. • United States Naval War College Library • Newport, RI 02841 • ALCTS

Rosa R. Mark • Student • University of Wisconsin School of Library & Information Studies • Madison, WI 53706

Rosado Tove H. • Acquisitions Dept./Monograph Sec • University of Connecticut Homer Babbidge Library • Storrs, CT 06269-1005 • ALCTS

Rosania Elizabeth D. • Nazareth, PA 18064 • ALSC

Rosapepe Diana L. • Assistant Director • Roanoke County Public Library Hollins Branch Library • Roanoke, VA 24019 • PLA

Rosar Virginia W. • Library Media Specialist • Smithtown Elementary School Lib. • Smithtown, NY 11787 • AASL

Rosaschi Jim P. • Sonoma County Library • Santa Rosa, CA 95404 • LITA

Rosato Lynn M. • Library Director • Monroe Public Library Monroe Center Green • Monroe, CT 06468 • PLA

Rosauer Rita • Adult Services Head • Bettendorf Public Library • Bettendorf, IA 52722 • RASD

Roscello Frances R. • Associate in School Library Serv • State Education Department Bureau of School Library/ Media Programs • Albany, NY 12234 • AASL

Roscoe Gladys Mrs • Staten Island, NY 10301

Rose Alison Yvonne • Pawhuska, OK 74056

Rose Anne • Children's Librarian • Independence Township Library • Clarkston, MI 48346 • ALSC IFRT

Rose Beverly L. • Phillipsburg Free Public Library • Phillipsburg, NJ 08865 • RASD YALSA

Rose Calvin Dunlap • Librarian/Cataloger • Naval Postgraduate School Dudley Knox Library • Monterey, CA 93943-5002 • AFLRT

Rose David L. • Director of Curriculum • Claremont Unified School District • Claremont, CA 91711 • AASL

Rose Diana F. • Deputy Chief Provincial Libn • Newfoundland Public Library Service • St. Johns NF, Canada

Rose Dorothy • Trustee • Half Hollow Hills Community Public Library • Dix Hills, NY 11746 • ALTA

Rose Elizabeth L. • Director • Pine Manor College Annenberg Lib & Commun Ctr • Chestnut Hill, MA 02167

Rose Emily C. • Peekskill, NY 10566 • RASD

Rose Frances E. • Government Document Librarian • University of Victoria McPherson Library • Victoria BC, V8W 3H5 Canada • GODORT

Rose Frances Elinor • Cincinnati, OH 45226 • Continuing

Rose Gwendolyn H. • West Linn, OR 97068-3528

Rose J. Martin • Head of Cataloging • Cumberland Regional Library • Amherst NS, B4H 4B9 Canada

Rose Jacqueline C. • Children's Librarian • Wake County Public Libraries Southeast Regional Library • Garner, NC 27529

Rose Jane R. • School Library Media Specialist • Stonehedge Elementary West Genesee Central Schools • Camillus, NY 13031 • ALSC

Rose Jennifer J. • Head of Acquisitions • Getty Center Resources Collections • Santa Monica, CA 90401

Rose Lois D. • Library of Congress • Washington, DC 20541

Rose Louise • Librarian/Media Specialist • West Las Vegas High School • Las Vegas, NM 87701 • AASL

Rose Mary Sue • Manager, Literature Services • Marion Merell Dow Inc • Kansas City, MO 64114

Rose Merilyn K. • Student • Kent State University School of Library & Information Science • Kent, OH 44242-0001 • PLA

Rose Robert F. • Asst. Dir. Inf. & Instr. Servs. • University of Northern Iowa Donald O. Rod Library • Cedar Falls, IA 50613-3675 • ACRL LAMA RASD

Rose Ronda • Temple Emanuel Community Day School • Beverly Hills, CA 90211 • AASL ALSC

Rose Terence L. • Speedway, IN 46224-1726 • ACRL RASD NMRT

Rose Vicky L. • Indianapolis-Marion County Public Library Southport Branch • Indianapolis, IN 46227-8899 • ALSC

Rosedale Jeff H. • Head, Access & Tech Support • Columbia University Leaman/Social Work Library • New York, NY 10027 • ACRL LITA IFRT IRRT SRRT

Roselius Sherry R. • Children's Services Specialist • King County Library System • Seattle, WA 98109-5191

Roselle Ann M. • Student • University of Illinois Graduate School of Library and Information Science • Urbana, IL 61801

Roselle William C. • Thiensville, WI 53092-1334 • ACRL LAMA   *Life*

Rosemary Patricia A. • John R. Downes School • Newark, DE 19711

Rosen-Share Barbara • Silver Spring, MD 20910

Rosen Amy L. • Student • Saint John's University Division of Library & Information Science • Jamaica, NY 11439 • AASL IFRT NMRT

Rosen Bonita Maky • Cleveland, OH 44124-1610

Rosen Elizabeth M. • Dr. Howard School Champaign Unit 4 • Champaign, IL 61821 • AASL ALSC YALSA   *Life*

Rosen Gwen • Librarian • Hebrew Academy of Indianapolis • Indianapolis, IN 46260 • AASL

Rosen Harvey S. • Librarian • Scotsdale Elementary School Library • El Paso, TX 79925

Rosen Janice F. • District of Columbia Public Library Martin Luther King Memorial Library • Washington, DC 20001 • ACRL PLA NMRT

Rosen Joan G. • Librarian • Cheltenham High School • Wyncote, PA 19095 • AASL YALSA

Rosen Lawrence Dr. • Trustee • Birmingham Public Library • Birmingham, AL 35203 • ALTA

Rosen Leslie • Head Librarian • American Foundation for the Blind • New York, NY 10011 • ASCLA

Rosen Martha A. • Columbia, MD 21045

Rosen Martha D. • Library Media Specialist • Edgewood School Library • Scarsdale, NY 10583 • AASL IFRT

Rosen Nathan A. • Assistant Director • Proskauer Rose Goetz and Mendelsohn Library • New York, NY 10036 • LITA RASD

Rosen Rhonda • Coor. Media & Reserve Services • Loyola Marymount University Charles Von Der Ahe Library • Los Angeles, CA 90045 • ACRL VRT

Rosen Roberta N. • Irvington Public Library • Irvington, NJ 07111 • LITA PLA

Rosen Scott J. • Student • San Jose State University Division of Library & Information Science • San Jose, CA 95192-0029 • ACRL

Rosen Vicki • Off. Campus Services Librarian • University of San Francisco Richard A. Gleeson Library • San Francisco, CA 94117 • ACRL

Rosen Wendy L. • Plainview-Bethpage Public Library • Plainview, NY 11803 • ASCLA RASD

Rosenbaum David • Royal Oak, MI 48067-2489 • Continuing

Rosenbaum Marilyn S. • Plainview, NY 11803

Rosenberg Alissa L. • Reference Librarian • Minnesota Historical Society • Saint Paul, MN 55102 • RASD IFRT

Rosenberg Betty • Malibu, CA 90265 • Continuing

Rosenberg Eileen R. • Park Ridge Public Library • Park Ridge, IL 60068-4188 • ALSC

Rosenberg Elizabeth • Haworth, NJ 07641

Rosenberg Florence H. • Franconia, NH 03580

Rosenberg Gail L. • Executive Director • Union Middlesex Regional Library Cooperative • Piscataway, NJ 08854 • ACRL ALSC ASCLA LAMA LITA PLA RASD

Rosenberg Gayle S. • Reference Librarian • Wilmette Public Library • Wilmette, IL 60091

Rosenberg Harlene Z. • Media Specialist • Hunterdon Central Regional High School • Flemington, NJ 08822 • AASL

Rosenberg Heidi M. • Institute for Psychoanalysis • Chicago, IL 60601 • ACRL

Rosenberg Jane A. • Assistant Director • National Endowment for Humanities • Washington, DC 20506 • ACRL ALCTS LITA LHRT LRRT

Rosenberg John E. • Washington, DC 20008

Rosenberg Jupith Campbell • Youth Services Coordinator • Akron-Summit County Public Library • Akron, OH 44326-0001 • ALSC

Rosenberg Kathy • Father Flanagan High School • Omaha, NE 68131 • AASL

Rosenberg Kenyon C. • Assoc Dir Natl Tech Inf Serv • National Tech Inf Serv • Springfield, VA 22161

Rosenberg Melvin H. • Los Angeles, CA 90042

Rosenberg Phyllis E. • Director • Branch District Library • Coldwater, MI 49036 • LAMA PLA

Rosenberg Rona S. • Librarian-Adult Services • Tucson Pima Library • Tucson, AZ 85726 • PLA

Rosenberg Susan L. • Head Reference Librarian • Brookdale Community College • Lincroft, NJ 07738 • ACRL LITA RASD

Rosenberg Victor • Associate Professor • University of Michigan School of Information and Library Studies • Ann Arbor, MI 48109-1092 • LITA ERT LRRT

Rosenberger H Stephen • Reference/Circulation Ln I • Fashion Institute of Technology Library • New York, NY 10001 • ACRL

Rosenberger Joan • Librarian • Wilder Elementary School • Littleton, CO 80123 • AASL

Rosenberger Merry G. • Reference Librarian • Montgomery County Community College Learning Resource Center • Blue Bell, PA 19422-0758 • ACRL

Rosenberry Connie • Librarian • Clair-Mel Elementary School • Tampa, FL 33619

Rosenblatt Connie L. • Student • Auburn University Ralph Brown Draughon Library • Auburn, AL 36849-5606 • AASL ALSC

Rosenblatt Liane S. • Children's Librarian • District of Columbia Public Library Martin Luther King Memorial Library • Washington, DC 20001

Rosenblatt Susan F. • Associate University Librarian • University of California-Berkeley University Library • Berkeley, CA 94720 • ACRL ALCTS LITA

Rosenbloom Buena • Highland Park, NJ 08904 • Continuing

Rosenbloom Elizabeth L. • Coldwater, MI 49036

Rosenbloom Mary M. • Reference Department • University of Kansas Watson Library • Lawrence, KS 66045-2800 • ACRL LHRT

Rosenblum Marylyn • Owner • Interactive Learning Materials • Katonah, NY 10536

Rosenblum Rachel S. • Jupiter, FL 33458-8101

Rosenblum Sarah W. • Reference Librarian • Millburn Public Library • Millburn, NJ 07041

Rosenblum Susan F. • Librarian • Port Richmond High School • Staten Island, NY 10302 • AASL

Rosendall Glynis M. • Branch Librarian • Evansville-Vanderburgh County Public Library • Evansville, IN 47708-1694 • PLA

Rosenfeld Edward L. • Assoc Dir for Clln Servs • Johns Hopkins University Milton S. Eisenhower Library • Baltimore, MD 21218 • ACRL ALCTS

Rosenfeld Elena • Children's Librarian • Mount Prospect Public Library • Mount Prospect, IL 60056 • LITA YALSA

Rosenfeld Ellen A. • Overland Park, KS 66212

Rosenfeld Jane B. • Adult Services Librarian • Buffalo & Erie County Public Library • Buffalo, NY 14203

Rosenfeld Joel C. • Director • Rockford Public Library • Rockford, IL 61101-1061 • LAMA PLA

Rosenfeld Louis B. • University of Michigan School of Information and Library Studies • Ann Arbor, MI 48109-1092

Rosenfield Sandra • Supervisor of Technical Services • Caroline County Public Library • Denton, MD 21629

Rosenior Ian D. • Student • Pratt Institute Graduate School of Library & Information Science • Brooklyn, NY 11205

Rosenkoetter Susan J. • Branch Head Librarian • Rochester Public Library Charlotte Branch • Rochester, NY 14612 • AASL YALSA

Rosenkranz Adam C. • Reference Librarian/ Bibl • Claremont Colleges Libraries Honnold/Mudd Library • Claremont, CA 91711 • ACRL

Rosenkranz Baiba • Head of Technical Services • Deerfield Public Library • Deerfield, IL 60015

Rosenkranz Wilbur K. • Head Librarian • Niles North High School • Skokie, IL 60077 • AASL

Rosenquist-Buhler Carla • Education Librarian • University of Nebraska-Lincoln University Libraries • Lincoln, NE 68588-0410 • ACRL

Rosenshield Jill K. • University of Wisconsin-Madison Memorial Library • Madison, WI 53706 • ACRL

Rosensteel J Randal • Adminstrator Assistant to Dir. • Free Library of Philadelphia • Philadelphia, PA 19103 • PLA

Rosenstein Frederick J. • Indexer • H. W. Wilson Company • Bronx, NY 10452

Rosenstein Linda L. • Technical Processing • University of Pennsylvania Libraries Biomedical Library • Philadelphia, PA 19104-6060 • ACRL ALCTS LITA

Rosenthal Andrea M. • Librarian • Yankee Group • Boston, MA 02114

Rosenthal Avram • Division Head Library Service • Henry Ford Community College • Dearborn, MI 48128-1495 • ACRL LAMA   *Life*

Rosenthal Barbara • Media Specialist • Riverside Middle School • Watertown, WI 53094 • AASL

Rosenthal Dorothy B. • Access Services • University of Miami Libraries Richter Library • Coral Gables, FL 33124 • ACRL LITA

Rosenthal Freda M. • Student • North Carolina Central University • Durham, NC 27707

Rosenthal Joseph A. • San Francisco, CA 94117 • ACRL LAMA   *Life*

Rosenthal Marilyn G. • Reference Librarian • Nassau Community College Library • Garden City, NY 11530 • ACRL

Rosenthal Marjorie N. • Assistant Professor • Long Island University Palmer School of Library & Information Science • Greenvale, NY 11548 • AASL ALSC IRRT

Rosenthal Myron M. Prof • Boca Raton, FL 33433

Rosenthal Phyllis T. • Director • New Milford Public Library • New Milford, NJ 07646 • LAMA PLA IFRT

Rosenthal Rich • Operations Director • Public Library of Charlotte & Mecklenburg County • Charlotte, NC 28202

Rosenthal Ruth • Trustee • Brentwood Public Library • Brentwood, NY 11717 • PLA

Rosenthal Sonya M. • Cataloger • Carnegie Mellon University Libraries • Pittsburgh, PA 15213 • ACRL SRRT

Rosenthal Stuart A. • Asst. Chief, Tech. Servs. Dept. • Queens Borough Public Library • Jamaica, NY 11432 • LAMA

Rosenthal William E. • AT&T Bell Laboratories • Murray Hill, NJ 07974 • LITA

Rosenwald Peter Joseph • Librarian III • County of Los Angeles Public Library Duarte Library • Duarte, CA 91010

Rosenzweig Mark C. • LaGuardia Community College • Long Island City, NY 11101 • ACRL RASD IFRT IRRT SRRT

Rosenzweig Susan • Lincoln, RI 02865 • AASL ALSC PLA YALSA ILERT

Rosett Ann D. • Head Librarian • Northwest College of The Assemblies Of God Hurst Library • Kirkland, WA 98033 • ACRL RASD LIRT

Rosett Barbara M. • Stamford, CT 06905

Rosetti Margaret • Supervisor Children's Services • Boyden Library • Foxboro, MA 02035

Rosier William T. • Business Manager • Indiana Cooperative Library Services Authority (INCOLSA) • Indianapolis, IN 46278 • LAMA

Rosinia James M. • Dir. of Information Services • University of North Carolina Center for Early Adolescence • Carrboro, NC 27510 • YALSA

Rosinski Donna M. • Support Assistant • INLEX, Inc. • Monterey, CA 93942 • LRRT

Rosinski Geraldine • Reference & Technical Svs. Libn • Pearl River Public Library • Pearl River, NY 10965

Roske Peggy L. • Public Services Librarian • College of Saint Benedict Library • Saint Joseph, MN 56374

Roskoski Laura M. • Librarian • Southeastern Louisiana Area Health Education Center • Covington, LA 70434 • LITA NMRT

Rosman Fran Morris • University Synagogue Library • Los Angeles, CA 90049

Rosolanko Janet C. • Children's Librarian • Somerset County Library Bridgewater Branch • Bridgewater, NJ 08807 • ALSC

Ross-Parris Negla V. • Assistant Branch Librarian • Brooklyn Public Library New Lots Branch • Brooklyn, NY 11238

Ross-Plant Delanie M. • Clearwater Public Library East Branch • Clearwater, FL 34625

Ross Alexander D. • Head Art Librarian • Stanford University • Stanford, CA 94305-6011 • ACRL

Ross Ann L. • Librarian • Woodland Heights Elementary School • Spartanburg, SC 29301 • AASL LIRT

Ross Anne H. • Fine Arts Department Librarian • Tampa-Hillsborough County Public Library • Tampa, FL 33602

Ross Barbara M. • Librarian/Branch Supervisor • Elk Grove Unified School District Samuel Jackman Middle School • Sacramento, CA 95823 • AASL YALSA IFRT

Ross Carol W. • Naperville, IL 60540

Ross Carole L. • Technical Services Supervisor • New Haven Free Public Library • New Haven, CT 06510

Ross Carr • University of Southern Maine • Portland, ME 04103

Ross Charles • President • FMS Publishing Company • Atlanta, GA 30316

Ross David J. • Systems Specialist • H.W. Wilson Company • Bronx, NY 10452 • LITA

Ross Gail C. • Public Services Librarian • Baltimore County Public Library Woodlawn Branch • Baltimore, MD 21207

Ross Gary M. • University of South Carolina • Columbia, SC 29208 • ACRL ALCTS

Ross Gertrude A. • Pittsburgh, PA 15213 • Continuing

Ross Jamie S. • Asheville, NC 28806 • AASL IFRT

Ross Janet N. • National Automobile Museum • Reno, NV 89501

Ross Jean E. • Librarian • Columbus Metropolitan Library • Columbus, OH 43215 • PLA

Ross Jean Lindsay • New Milford, CT 06776-2510 • ACRL RASD   Continuing

Ross Jennifer L. • Graduate Student • University of Illinois Graduate School of Library and Information Science • Urbana, IL 61801 • LIRT

Ross John B. • Head, Systems Department • Georgia Institute of Technology Price Gilbert Memorial Library • Atlanta, GA 30332-0900 • LITA

Ross John M. • University Librarian • California State University-Los Angeles John F. Kennedy Memorial Library • Los Angeles, CA 90032-8300 • GODORT

Ross Judith D. • Reference Librarian • Middle Georgia Regional Library • Macon, GA 31201 • PLA

Ross Julie M. • Student • Catholic University of America School of Library and Information Science • Washington, DC 20064 • LITA

Ross Kent C. • Director • Arcadia Public Library • Arcadia, CA 91007 • ALCTS ALSC LAMA PLA RASD GODORT IFRT

Ross Kim • Librarian • Cedar Valley College Library • Lancaster, TX 75146-3799

Ross Lora B. • Norfolk, VA 23508

Ross Lyman B. • Reference Librarian • University of Vermont Bailey Howe Library • Burlington, VT 05405-0036 • ACRL RASD

Ross Marc • Consultant • Rosewood Partnership • Allentown, PA 18105

Ross Margaret M. • Library Media Specialist • Tri-Cities High School • East Point, GA 30344 • AASL

Ross Marie H. • Albuquerque, NM 87123 • ALCTS

Ross Pamela A. • Middlesex School • Concord, MA 01742

Ross Pamela G. • Ref Libn Microcomputer Coor. • Bucknell University Bertrand Library • Lewisburg, PA 17837-2086 • SRRT

Ross Pamela J. • Iowa Wesleyan College Chadwick Library • Mount Pleasant, IA 52641 • ACRL LAMA RASD LIRT

Ross Patricia A. • Sacramento, CA 95815-2403

Ross Patricia Molloy • Reference & Adult Services Ln • Westerville Public Library • Westerville, OH 43081

Ross Patsy S. • Library Director • Marshall Public Library • Marshall, TX 75670

Ross Philip R. • Director • Lonoke/Prairie County Regional Library • Lonoke, AR 72086 • PLA

Ross Phyllis • Technical Information • Mobil Research & Development Corp. • Dallas, TX 75381

Ross Raymond • Trustee • Pine Bluff & Jefferson County Library System • Pine Bluff, AR 71601

Ross Regene C. • Assistant Chief • Library of Congress • Washington, DC 20541 • ALCTS

Ross Robert • Trustee • Free Library of Philadelphia • Philadelphia, PA 19103 • ALTA

Ross Robert D. • Director • Ridgewood Public Library • Ridgewood, NJ 07450

Ross Rosemary • Head, Cataloging Dept. • Central Washington University • Ellensburg, WA 98926 • ALCTS EMIERT

Ross Rosemary • Baltimore County Public Library White Marsh Branch • Baltimore, MD 21236 • ALSC PLA

Ross Ruth M. • Reference Librarian • Olympic College Learning Resources Center • Bremerton, WA 98310

Ross Saundra L. • Student • Indiana University School of Library and Information Science • Bloomington, IN 47405 • LITA

Ross Shirley D. • School Media Specialist • Lexington Middle School Library • Lexington, MO 64067 • AASL

Ross Shirley L. • Director of Media Services • John Glenn High School • Walkerton, IN 46574 • AASL

Ross Sidnie • Librarian • Cargill Information Center • Minneapolis, MN 55440 • RASD

Ross Theresa A. • Oak Park, IL 60302

Ross Virginia H. • San Diego, CA 92116-2237 • ALSC
                                        Continuing

Ross Yvonne H. • San Antonio, TX 78230 • Continuing

Rossbach Doris E. • Seattle, WA 98116 • Continuing

Rosselet Stuart F. • Bemidji State University A. C. Clark Library • Bemidji, MN 56601-2699 • ACRL LAMA LITA RASD   Life

Rossell Glenora E. • Pittsburgh, PA 15235-5002 • Continuing

Rosselli Nicholas D. • Systems Librarian • Indiana University Northwest Library • Gary, IN 46408 • ACRL SRRT

Rosselot Barbara L. • Library Media Specialist • North Adams Libraries • Seaman, OH 45679 • AASL

Rossi Gary J. • Head, Audiovisual Section • University of California-Irvine Library • Irvine, CA 92713 • ACRL ALCTS LITA

Rossi Geraldine R. • Librarian • Suffern Free Library • Suffern, NY 10901-5694

Rossi Pat • Charlotte, NC 28262

Rossini Adriana C. • Student • University of Toronto Faculty of Library & Information Science • Toronto ON, M5S 1A1 Canada

Rossman Muriel J. • Assistant Director • MINITEX Lib Info Network University of Minnesota • Minneapolis, MN 55455-0414 • ALCTS LITA RASD

Rossmann Phyllis A. • Government Documents Librarian • Seton Hall University Law Library • Newark, NJ 07102

Rossoff Judith H. • Liverpool Public Library • Liverpool, NY 13088 • ALCTS LAMA PLA

Rosson Michael L. • Director of Media Services • Kingsborough Community College Library • Brooklyn, NY 11235 • LITA

Rosswurm K. M. • Asst. Director • New City Library • New City, NY 10956

Rostamizadeh Suzanne • Senior Librarian • San Jose Public Library • San Jose, CA 95113 • ALCTS PLA

Rosten Patricia E. • Librarian • Brooklyn Public Library Sheepshead Bay Branch • Brooklyn, NY 11235

Rostkowski Georgene • School Lib Media Asst • John Muir Elementary School • Martinez, CA 94553

Rotch Susan R. • Bedford Public Library • Bedford, NH 03102 • PLA

Roth Alison C. • Regional Services Manager • Faxon Company Inc. • Westwood, MA 02090

Roth Alvin R. • Asst Supv Instr Media • Saint Paul Public Schools • St Paul, MN 55108 • AASL

Roth Eris E. Mrs • Whittier, CA 90603

Roth Harvey • Trustee • Roth Publishing Inc. • Great Neck, NY 11021

Roth Karen L. • Largo, FL 34641 • ILERT

Roth Kelly • Pittsburgh, PA 15205 • AASL

Roth Lester • Trustee • Marin County Free Library • San Rafael, CA 94903

Roth Lynne Pettys • Alexandria, KY 41001

Roth Sandra F. • Solon, OH 44139 • PLA

Rothal Jeffrey N • Juneau, AK 99802-2096 • ACRL IFRT

Rothberg Marilyn F. • Stonehurst Hills Elementary School • Upper Darby, PA 19082 • AASL

Rothberg Ryna H. • Garden Grove, CA 92640 • ALSC PLA

Rothe Kurt B. • Exec Dir of Learning Resources • University of Wisconsin-Green Bay Library Learning Center • Green Bay, WI 54311 • ACRL

Rothenberg Dianne • Ph. D. Candidate • ERIC Clearinghouse on Elementary & Eary Childhood Education • Urbana, IL 61801 • PLA LHRT LRRT

Rothenberg Mark H. • Suffolk Cooperative Library System • Bellport, NY 11713 • ASCLA LAMA PLA RASD EMIERT IRRT LRRT MAGERT

Rothenberg Patricia • Reference Librarian • Camden County Library Echelon Urban Center • Voorhees, NJ 08043

Rothenberger Gregory J. • Saint Elizabeth Hospital Medical Center Bannon Health Science Library • Lafayette, IN 47903 • SRRT

Rothenfluh Julie • Naperville Public Libraries • Naperville, IL 60540 • ALSC

Rother Jeffrey A. • Kent, OH 44240 • RASD

Rothfarb Anne L. • Belmont, MA 02178 • ACRL SRRT

Rothfarb Lee A. • Associate Prof. Music Theory • Harvard University Library • Cambridge, MA 02138-2901 • ACRL LITA NMRT

Rothfuss Joan • LRC Director • Robert Morris College • Springfield, IL 62704 • ACRL

Rothhaar Janet A. • Catalog Librarian • Broward Community College • Fort Lauderdale, FL 33314 • ALCTS

Rothlein Barbara • Branch Librarian • Ocean County Library System Plvmsted Branch • New Egypt, NJ 08533

Rothlisberg Allen P. • Head Librarian • Northland Pioneer College • Holbrook, AZ 86025

Rothman Jonathan • System Librarian • Harvard University • Cambridge, MA 02138 • LITA

Rothman Marilyn R. • Reference Librarian • Mental Health Center of Boulder County • Boulder, CO 80302

Rothman Ruth S. • Circulation Librarian • Portland Public Library • Portland, ME 04101 • LAMA LITA PLA

Rothstein Pauline M. • Director of Information Servs. • Russell Sage Foundation Library • New York, NY 10021 • ACRL

Rothstein Samuel Dr • Prof Emeritus,Sch of Lib Archv • University of British Columbia • Vancouver BC, Canada • Continuing

Rothwell James B. • F.D. Roosevelt Elementary School • Hyde Park, MA 02136 • AASL YALSA

Rothwell Roberta B. • Technical Services Librarian • Weston Public Library • Weston, MA 02193 • ALCTS LITA

Rothwell Webb B. Mrs • Charlottesville, VA 22901 • AASL YALSA   Continuing

Rotsaert Stefanie C. • Elementary School Librarian • Essex Fells School Library • Essex Fells, NJ 07021 • AASL

Rott William D. • Branch Manager • Town of Tonawanda Public Library • Kenmore, NY 14217 • PLA

Rottmann Clara Thoren Dr. • Lincoln, NE 68516

Rottmann Frances K. • Student • University of Missouri-Columbia School of Library & Informational Science • Columbia, MO 65211

Roualet Sharon M • School Librarian • Edgewood Junior High School • Ellettsville, IN 47429 • AASL

Roubal Michelle Y. • Student • Northern Illinois University Department of Library & Information Studies • DeKalb, IL 60115 • IFRT

Rouch Lawrence L. • Ft. Collins, CO 80526 • ACRL

Roudebush Lawanda C. • Human Resources Coor/ Business L. • Thomas Ford Memorial Library • Western Springs, IL 60558 • LAMA

Roudman Leonard D. • Youth Services Librarian • San Ramon Library • San Ramon, CA 94583

Rougeau Laskie M. • Vinton, LA 70668 • AASL

Rougeot Renee L. • Youth Services Coordinator • Watertown Library Association • Watertown, CT 06795 • ALSC

Rougeux Debora A. • Goverment Doc Tech Serv Libn • University of Pittsburgh Hillman Library • Pittsburgh, PA 15260 • ACRL GODORT

Rough Allan C. • Department Head • University of Maryland Hornbake Library • College Park, MD 20742 • ACRL

Rough Marianne C. • Acquisitions Librarian • Prince George Community College Library Media Center • Largo, MD 20772 • ACRL

Roughton Anne • San Francisco Public Library • San Francisco, CA 94102

Rouke Linda D. • Editor • Copycat Press • Racine, WI 53408-1546

Roulhac Nellie ED.D. • Trustee • Free Library of Philadelphia • Philadelphia, PA 19103 • ALTA

Roullard Josephine D. • Reference Librarian • Stanislaus County Free Library • Modesto, CA 95354

Rouls Charles • Research Analyst • Michigan Department of Civil Rights Library • Detroit, MI 48226

Roumani Vivienne R. • Head, Document Delivery • University of California-Berkeley University Library • Berkeley, CA 94720 • ACRL LITA RASD

Roumillat Judy C. • Media Specialist • Saint Andrews Elementary School • Charleston, SC 29405 • AASL

Rounds Joseph B. • Buffalo, NY 14209 • LAMA PLA *Life*

Rounds Sandra M. • APO, AP 96205 • PLA

Roundtree Elizabeth • Head Technical Services • Saint Tammany Parish Library • Covington, LA 70433 • ALCTS PLA GODORT

Roundy Tamara • Cataloger • Georgia State University • Atlanta, GA 30303-3083 • ALCTS SRRT

Rountree Brenda B. • Copycat Press • Racine, WI 53408-1546

Rountree Elizabeth • Library Director • Saint Tammany Parish Library • Covington, LA 70433

Roupp Constance • Librarian • Harlan Rowe Middle School • Athens, PA 18810 • AASL

Rourke Cynthia A. • Algonac, MI 48001 • ACRL LAMA

Rourke Eileen Elizabeth • Manager, Corporate Library Serv • Fannie Mae • Washington, DC 20008

Rousch Ann • Trustee • Warren Public Library • Warren, MI 48092

Rouse Carol S. • Palm Beach County Library System • West Palm Beach, FL 33406

Rouse Charlie Lou Mrs. • Stillwater, OK 74074 • AASL

Rouse David A. • Librarian • Chicago Public Library • Chicago, IL 60605 • RASD SRRT

Rouse Michael R. • County Librarian • Saint Johns County Public Library • St Augustine, FL 32095 • PLA IFRT

Rouse Roscoe Dr. • University Library Historian • Oklahoma State University Library • Stillwater, OK 74078-0375 • ACRL LAMA LHRT *Life*

Roush Suanne B. • Saint Petersburg, FL 33702

Rousseau Janice C. • Student • Simmons College Graduate School of Library & Information Science • Boston, MA 02115

Routh Spencer J. • Principal Librarian Clln. Devel. • University of Queensland Library • St. Lucia, QLD 4072, Australia • ACRL ALCTS RASD

Roux Yvonne R. • Rutland, VT 05701 • YALSA

Rouzier Michael • Montreal PQ, H3W 2E6 Canada

Rovelli Beverly E. • School Library Media Specialist • Broadllin-Perth Middle School • Amsterdam, NY 12010

Rovelstad Howard • Director Emeritus • University of Maryland College Park Theodore R. McKeldin Library • College Park, MD 20742-7011 • ACRL LAMA *Life*

Rovelstad Mathilde V. Dr. • Professor Emeritus • Catholic University of America School of Library and Information Science • Washington, DC 20064

Rovenger Judith • Chair Consultant • Westchester Library System • Elmsford, NY 10523 • ALSC

Rovira Carmen • Washington, DC 20008 • IRRT *Continuing*

Row Jane S. • Coordinator Social Sciences • University of Tennessee John C. Hodges Library • Knoxville, TN 37996-1000 • ACRL RASD

Row Stephanie • Head, Acquisitions Dept. • San Francisco Public Library Order Department • San Francisco, CA 94102 • ALCTS

Rowan Dawn C. • Albany, NY 12202 • ACRL

Rowan Diane M. • Hawthorne, NY 10532

Rowan Melena A. • Network Liaison Officer • State University of New York OCLC Library Network • Albany, NY 12246 • LITA RASD

Rowden Dorothea H. • Santa Rosa, CA 95401-5833

Rowe-Jackson Valerie • Branch Team Manager • Atlanta-Fulton Public Library • Atlanta, GA 30303 • LAMA PLA

Rowe Caroline E. • Reference Librarian • University of West Florida John C. Pace Library • Pensacola, FL 32514

Rowe Dorothy B. • Medical Librarian • Central DuPage Hospital Medical Library • Winfield, IL 60190

Rowe Glenda Smith • Library Media Specialist • Saranac Central School Library • Saranac, NY 12981 • AASL

Rowe Glenn N. • Director Library Archive • Church of Jesus Christ of Latter-Day Saints • Salt Lake City, UT 84150 • ACRL ALCTS LAMA LITA

Rowe Jane Culler • Placerville, CA 95667 • Continuing

Rowe John • Sales & Marketing Director • Filmakers Library • New York, NY 10016 • VRT *Subscribing*

Rowe Judith S. • Manager of Research Services • Princeton University • Princeton, NJ 08544-2098 • ACRL ALCTS RASD GODORT

Rowe Katherine S. • Birmingham, AL 35206

Rowe Lena L. • Student • Kent State University School of Library & Information Science • Kent, OH 44242-0001 • AASL

Rowe Lois • Saratoga Senior High School • Saratoga Springs, NY 12866

Rowe Mary Jane • Overland High School • Aurora, CO 80012 • AASL

Rowe Mercedes L. • New Rochelle, NY 10801 • AASL YALSA EMIERT

Rowe Richard R. • President • Faxon Company Inc. • Westwood, MA 02090 • Life

Rowe Robert • Trustee • Palos Verdes Library District • Pls Vrd Pnsla, CA 90274 • ALTA PLA

Rowe Sylvia N. • Director • Colleton County Memorial Library • Walterboro, SC 29488 • PLA

Rowell Ada D. • Bloomington, MN 55438 • ACRL ALCTS *Continuing*

Rowell Barbara F. • Anniston, AL 36201-5968

Rowell Gordon A. • South Chatham, MA 02659 • Continuing

Rowell Nancy A. • Librarian • Chico Senior High School Chico ISD • Chico, CA 95926 • AASL

Rowland-Rhodes Diane • Assistant Director • North Bergen Free Public Library • North Bergen, NJ 07047-5097

Rowland A Ray • Librarian Emeritus • Augusta College Reese Library • Augusta, GA 30910 • ACRL ALCTS RASD *Life*

Rowland Barbara S. • Falls Church, VA 22046 • MAGERT

Rowland David • Shepherdstown, WV 25443

Rowland Eileen • Sherman, CT 06784

Rowland Gerry E. • Special Populations Coor. • State Library of Iowa • Des Moines, IA 50319 • ASCLA PLA

Rowland Janet M. • Winston-Salem, NC 27103-4221

Rowland Patricia A. • Oakboro, NC 28129-0183

Rowley Gordon S. • Asst. Director for Collections • Iowa State University Library • Ames, IA 50011-2140 • ACRL ALCTS LAMA *Life*

Rowley Keith • Librarian • Utah Valley Community College • Orem, UT 84058 • ACRL

Roxburgh Stephen • Vice Pres & Publ Bks Yng Readers • Farrar Straus Giroux Inc • New York, NY 10003 • YALSA

Roxbury Sherry L. • Bronx, NY 10462 • PLA

Roy Alice R. • Hampton, VA 23669-5518 • AFLRT

Roy Anjana • Anchorage Municipal Libraries Z. J. Loussac Library • Anchorage, AK 99503

Roy Babette L. • Irving, TX 75062

Roy Barbara • Ln • Miami-Dade Public Library System Coral Reef Branch • Miami, FL 33165

Roy Coleen Hudson • Cuyahoga Community College Western Campus Library • Parma, OH 44130

Roy Loriene • University of Texas at Austin Graduate School of Library & Information Sciences • Austin, TX 78712-1276 • ALSC PLA RASD CLENE

Roy Mary E. • Student • University of Kentucky College of Library & Information Science • Lexington, KY 40506-0391

Roy Terry K. • Information Services Coor. • Lafayette Parish Public Library • Lafayette, LA 70502-3427 • RASD

Royal Henrietta • Librarian • Statesboro Regional Library • Statesboro, GA 30458

Royal Selvin W. • Chair • University of Central Arkansas Department of Educational Media & Library Science • Conway, AR 72032-5001 • AASL

Royalty Alice J • Librarian • Clute Intermediate School Brazosport ISD • Freeport, TX 77541

Royce Carol E. • Librarian • Ponus Ridge Middle School • Norwalk, CT 06854 • AASL ALSC

Royce Carolyn S. • Chief Librarian • Ocean County Library System • Toms River, NJ 08753 • LAMA PLA

Royer Susan B. • Assistant Director • Huntsville-Madison County Public Library • Huntsville, AL 35804 • PLA

Roylance Susan R. • Auckland, New Zealand

Royo Dawne • Library Media Specialist • Guilford Elementary School • Columbia, MD 21046 • AASL

Royo Tammy • Library Media Specialist • Bollman Bridge Elementary School • Jessup, MD 20794 • AASL

Roys Carolyn R. • Davenport, IA 52803 • AASL IFRT

Roysdon Christine • Head Reference Division • Lehigh University Libraries Linderman Library 30 • Bethlehem, PA 18015-3067 • ACRL LITA RASD

Royse Molly Pitts • Kansas State University Farrell Library • Manhattan, KS 66506-1200 • ACRL

Royston Mary G. • Librarian • H. L. Bourgeois High School • Gray, LA 70359 • AASL ALTA YALSA

Rozanski Barbara • Administrative Librarian • Prospect Heights Public Library District • Prospect Heights, IL 60070 • LAMA PLA

Rozarie Vera J. • Supervisor Lib Serv • Lordship School • Stratford, CT 06497 • AASL EMIERT

Rozek Jane M. • Schaumburg Township District Library • Schaumburg, IL 60194

Rozell Norine G. • Assistant Librarian • Richton Park Public Library District • Richton Park, IL 60471 • PLA

Rozensky Patti L. • Highland Park, IL 60035 • AASL ALSC

Rozett Jean A. • Director • Science Park Development Corporation • New Haven, CT 06511

Rozgonyi Timothy D. • Library Manager • Pittsburgh Press • Pittsburgh, PA 15230

Rozman Phyllis • Kensington, MD 20895

Rozum Marjorie B. • Woolridge Elementary School • Midlothian, VA 23112 • AASL

Rubacha Edmund • Reference Librarian • Wesleyan University Olin Memorial Library • Middletown, CT 06459 • ACRL

Rubalcava Hortencia • Trustee • City of Commerce Public Library • Commerce, CA 90040 • ALTA

Rubel Evelyn K. • Media Specialist • Rippling Woods Elementary School • Glen Burnie, MD 21061 • AASL

Ruben Jacqelen S. • Librarian • Los Angeles Public Library • Los Angeles, CA 90071 • PLA

Ruben Roberta L. • Assistant Professor • Western Illinois University Department of Media & Educational Technology • Macomb, IL 61455 • LIRT

Rubendall Elizabeth • Lincoln, NE 68510 • Continuing

Rubens Charlotte C. • Head Technical Operations • University of California Northern Regional Library Facility • Richmond, CA 94804 • ACRL ALCTS LAMA LITA SRRT

Rubenstein Nancy F. • Reference Librarian • Heidelberg College Beeghly Library • Tiffin, OH 44883 • ACRL RASD

Rubery Nancy M. • Children's Consultant • Wayne County Library System • Newark, NY 14513 • ALSC PLA

Rubey Daniel • Humanities Librarian • Lehman College Library • Bronx, NY 10468 • ACRL

Rubi Martha E. • Student • University of Missouri-Columbia School of Library & Informational Science • Columbia, MO 65211

Rubin Alice Fisher Esq. • Trustee • Brooklyn Public Library • Brooklyn, NY 11238 • ALTA

Rubin Angela B. • Humanities Librarian • Southern Illinois University Delyte W. Morris Library • Carbondale, IL 62901-6632 • ACRL RASD

Rubin Anna R. • University of South Florida School of Library & Information Science • Tampa, FL 33620

Rubin Arlene • Library • Winsor School Library • Boston, MA 02215 • AASL YALSA

Rubin Audrey A. • Somers, NY 10589

Rubin Catherine P. • Librarian • Department of Labor Library • Raleigh, NC 27601

Rubin Deborah Eve • Bethesda, MD 20817-1541

Rubin Ellen • Library Media Specialist • Wallkill High School • Wallkill, NY 12589 • AASL

Rubin James M. • Chicago, IL 60657-2707

Rubin Katharine Evans • New Orleans, LA 70119

Rubin Michael • Project Manager • Evaluation and Training Institute • San Francisco, CA 94110

Rubin Rhea J. • Oakland, CA 94618 • ASCLA PLA CLENE IFRT ILERT SRRT

Rubin Richard E. • Cuyahoga Falls, OH 44223-1945 • LAMA RASD IFRT

Rubin Roberta L. • Chestnut Hill, MA 02167

Rubin Susan D. • Chappaqua, NY 10514

Rubin William D. • Collection Development Manager • Medina County District Library • Medina, OH 44256 • ALCTS LAMA PLA

Rubner Robert J. • E. Northport, NY 11731

Rubush Sarah H. • Branch Librarian • Roanoke City Public Library Williamson Road Branch • Roanoke, VA 24012

Ruby Carmela M. • Sacramento, CA 95819

Ruby Edith A. • Media Specialist • Coalgate High School • Coalgate, OK 74538

Ruby Irple P. • Director • McCook Community College von Riesen Library • McCook, NE 69001 • ACRL

Ruby Lois F. • Wichita, KS 67206 • YALSA
Ruby Patricia A. • Student • Florida State University School of Library and Information Studies • Tallahassee, FL 32306-2048
Ruck Kathy S. • Reference Assistant-Youth Serv. • Schaumburg Township District Library • Schaumburg, IL 60194
Rucker Cheryl Hylton • Teacher • District of Columbia Public Schools • Washington, DC 20019
Rucker Linda • Co-Owner • Musi & Key & Musi & Key Publishing • Tucson, AZ 85737 • PLA
Rucker Ronald E. • Librarian • Middlebury College Egbert Starr Library • Middlebury, VT 05753-6007 • ACRL LITA
Ruckman Stanley • Director of Learning Services • New Mexico State University at Alamogordo Library • Alamogordo, NM 88310-0477 • ACRL
Ruda Sharon • Head of Information Services • Fountaindale Public Library Dist • Romeoville, IL 60441
Rudasill Lynne P. • Eureka College Melick Library • Eureka, IL 61530 • ACRL RASD GODORT
Rudd Jane • Librarian • Watson Junior High School • Muleshoe, TX 79347 • AASL
Rudden Kathleen A. • Rye Public Library • Rye, NH 03870 • LITA
Rudder Lorna A. • Manager Customer Relations Dept. • H. W. Wilson Company • Bronx, NY 10452 • LITA
Rudder Margo • Student • University of North Texas School of Library & Information Sciences • Denton, TX 76203 • AASL
Ruddick Brian P. • Technical Services Asst Director • Cleveland State University Library • Cleveland, OH 44115 • LAMA
Ruddick Patsy • Director Library Services • Garden City Community Junior College Library • Garden City, KS 67846 • ACRL
Ruddy Margaret Sr. • Cardinal Stritch College • Milwaukee, WI 53217 • ACRL
Rudeen Marlys E. • Head, Acquisitions Department • Center for Research Libraries • Chicago, IL 60637 • ALCTS
Rudell-Betts Linda M. • Los Angeles, CA 90024
Ruder Clarice M. • Branch Librarian • Tampa-Hillsborough County Public Library Peninsular Branch • Tampa, FL 33629
Rudie Helen M. • Curriculum Librarian • Concordia College Carl B. Ylvisaker Library • Moorhead, MN 56562 • AASL ALSC IFRT
Rudin Claire • Bayside, NY 11360
Rudisell Carol A. • Associate Librarian • University of Delaware Library • Newark, DE 19717-5267 • ACRL
Rudisill Sharon • YA Librarian • Enoch Pratt Free Library Reistertown Road Branch • Baltimore, MD 21215
Rudloff Diana • Trustee • Upper Perkiomen Valley Library Association • Red Hill, PA 18076 • ALTA
Rudner Judy M. • Student • University of California Los Angeles Graduate School of Library & Information Science • Los Angeles, CA 90024 • NMRT
Rudnick Corrine • Wayazata, MN 55391-1639
Rudolph Evan E. • Vice President • Southern School Media • Bowling Green, KY 42104 • PLA
Rudolph N. Janell • Instructor Librarian • Memphis State University Libraries • Memphis, TN 38152 • ACRL
Rudy Olga I. • Plano, TX 75093
Rudyk Martha • New Haven, CT 06515
Rue Nancy • Head,Reference Department • Ohio University Libraries • Athens, OH 45701-2978 • ACRL RASD
Ruebel Tamara L. • Reference Librarian • Highland Park Public Library • Highland Park, IL 60035 • PLA RASD SRRT
Rueby Cheryl R. • Director, Library Services • Matthews Medical & Scientific Books • St. Louis, MO 63043 • ALCTS LITA
Ruediger Claudia • DePauw University Roy O. West Library • Greencastle, IN 46135-0037 • ACRL RASD
Rueff Mary Z. • Youth Services Librarian • Hussey-Mayfield Memorial Public Library • Zionsville, IN 46077 • ALSC PLA YALSA
Rueth Marion U. • Saint Petersburg, FL 33710 • LAMA
Rueveni Ron • Philadelphia, PA 19136
Ruezinsky Robert • Trustee • Free Public Library of Woodbridge • Woodbridge, NJ 07095 • AASL ALTA PLA
Ruf Walter • Director • Unification Theological Seminary Library • Barrytown, NY 12507 • ACRL ALCTS LAMA LITA RASD
Rufalo Betty S. • Trustee • Newark Public Library • Newark, NJ 07101-0630 • ALTA PLA
Ruff David C. • Reference Librarian • Schaumburg Township District Library • Schaumburg, IL 60194 • LAMA PLA
Ruff Luise C. • Student • San Jose State University Division of Library & Information Science • San Jose, CA 95192-0029
Ruff Martha R. • Librarian • National Association for the Advancement of Colored People (NAACP) • Baltimore, MD 21215 • ACRL EMIERT SRRT
Ruff Merle B. • Johannesburg Public Library • Johannesburg, South Africa • LITA
Ruff Rosalie A. • Head of Information Services • Hammond Public Library • Hammond, IN 46320
Ruff Virginia F. • Bedford, VA 24523 • Continuing
Ruffin Francis E. Jr. • Piedmont College E. Louise Patten Library • Demorest, GA 30535 • ACRL ALCTS SRRT
Ruffin Helen H. • Library Media Specialist • Sky Haven Elementary School • Atlanta, GA 30311
Ruffin Ida E. • Library Supervisor • Free Library of Philadelphia Queen Memorial Branch • Philadelphia, PA 19146 • EMIERT
Ruffing Joan D. • Librarian Media Specialist • Cardinal Mooney High School • Youngstown, OH 44507 • AASL
Ruffino Peggy P. • Librarian • Pine View Middle School • Covington, LA 70434 • AASL
Ruffle Kathryn P. • Prince George, BC, V2K 2E2 Canada • SRRT
Ruffner Frederick G. Jr. • Omnigraphics Inc. • Detroit, MI 48226 • Honorary
Ruffner James A. • Academic Services Officer • Wayne State University • Detroit, MI 48202 • ACRL LIRT LRRT
Rufsvold Margaret • Naples, FL 33962 • AASL ACRL *Life*
Rugeley Barbara K. • Reference Librarian • Citrus College Hayden Memorial Library • Glendora, CA 91740-1899
Rugeley Virginia H. • Trustee • Kanawha County Public Library • Charleston, WV 25301 • ALTA
Rugelis Rasma • Associate University Librarian • York University Libraries • North York ON, M3J 1P3 Canada • ALCTS LITA
Rugen Frances J. • Oxnard, CA 93031 • PLA AFLRT FLRT
Rugg Claire T. • Librarian • United States Naval Station Base Library • FPO, AE 09593-0114 • ACRL AFLRT
Rugg John D. • Genealogist • Ohio Roots • Granville, OH 43023
Rugge Sae • Oakland, CA 94611 • ILERT
Ruggere Christine A. • Curator Special Collections • University of Pennsylvania Library Van Pelt-Dietrich Library Center • Philadelphia, PA 19104-6206 • ACRL
Rugheimer Virginia • Charleston, SC 29401 • Continuing
Ruhl Taylor D. • Director of Library Service • Pacific Union College W.E. Nelson Memorial Library • Angwin, CA 94508 • ACRL RASD MAGERT
Ruhlin Michele T. • Crystal Lake, IL 60012-1715 • ACRL GODORT
Ruhman Emma • Los Angeles, CA 90034
Ruhnke Charm • Resource Development Consultant • Lewis & Clark Library System • Edwardsville, IL 62025 • PLA
Ruiz-Valera Phoebe • Head of Technical Services • Association of The Bar Of The City of New York Library • New York, NY 10036
Ruiz Cora Mrs. • Trustee • City of Commerce Public Library • Commerce, CA 90040 • ALTA
Ruiz Deborah • Public Services Librarian • Monterey Peninsula College • Monterey, CA 93940 • ACRL EMIERT
Ruiz Jose A. • Professional Academic Librarian • Ohio State University Libraries • Columbus, OH 43210-1286 • ACRL
Ruiz Oralia R. • Associate Librarian • Southwest Research Institute Thomas Baker Slick Memorial Library • San Antonio, TX 78284
Rukhman Inna • Cataloging Librarian • RFE/RL Research Institute Library • 8000 Munchen 22, Germany
Rule Amy E. • Archv., Ctr for Creative Photo- • University of Arizona Library • Tucson, AZ 85721 • ACRL
Rule Esther T. • Elementary School Librarian • Stanton Elementary School • Stanton, KY 40380 • ALSC
Rule Judy K. • Cabell County Public Library • Huntington, WV 25701 • LAMA LITA PLA IFRT
Rule Sylvia S. • Asst. Ln. Collection Devel. Ref • Indiana University East Library Learning Resources Center • Richmond, IN 47374-1289
Rulon Belinda • Media Specialist • Hamilton Heights High School • Arcadia, IN 46030 • AASL
Rumbaugh Paula K. • Data Acquistions & Creation • Online Computer Library Center (OCLC) • Dublin, OH 43017-3395 • RASD
Rumble Lucy Kepler Mrs • Fort Collins, CO 80521 • Life
Rumbold Sherry W. • Sch. Lib. Media Specialist • Montgomery County Schools West Middle School • Mt. Gilead, NC 27306
Rumer Karen S. • Euless, TX 76039
Rumery Joyce V. • Head, Access Services • University of Maine Raymond H. Fogler Library • Orono, ME 04469 • ACRL LAMA LITA
Rumman Eman G. • Medical Librarian • Episcopal Hospital Medical Library • Philadelphia, PA 19125
Rumme Dennis A. • Director of Media Services • Irvington Public Schools • Irvington, NJ 07111 • AASL
Rumph Deanna M. • Student • University of California-Berkeley School of Library & Information Studies • Berkeley, CA 94720 • ALSC
Rumph Virginia A. • Serials Librarian • Butler University Irwin Library • Indianapolis, IN 46208 • IFRT
Rumple Carol A. • Southwestern High School • Shelbyville, IN 46167
Rumps Andrea J. • Director • Milan Public Library • Milan, MI 48160 • PLA
Rumsa Phyllis M. • Children's Librarian • Algonquin Area Public Library District • Algonquin, IL 60102 • ALSC
Runchey Judy • Children's Librarian • Richmond Public Library • Richmond BC, V6X 2E3 Canada • YALSA
Runevitch Denise E. • Berea, OH 44017 • AASL PLA
Runge Kay K. • Director • Davenport Public Library • Davenport, IA 52801 • LAMA PLA ERT *Life*
Runge Lois Jean • Paynesville, MN 56362 • AASL ALSC
Rungren Lawrence • Reference Librarian • Bedford Public Library • Bedford, MA 01730
Runkle Martin • Director • University of Chicago Library • Chicago, IL 60637-1502 • ACRL
Runser Robert E. • Okemos, MI 48864 • AASL ACRL *Life*
Runyan Carolyn R. • Fort Collins, CO 80525-3209
Runyon Robert S. • Director • University of Nebraska at Omaha University Library • Omaha, NE 68182-0237 • ACRL LITA
Ruoff Sandra • Director • Guilford Free Library • Guilford, CT 06437 • PLA
Ruoff Susan K. • Student • Drexel University College of Information Studies • Philadelphia, PA 19104-2875
Rupert E A. • Clarion University of Pennsylvania College of Library Science • Clarion, PA 16214
Rupert Elizabeth A. • Librarian • Palmetto Public Library • Palmetto, FL 34221
Rupert Mary Ann • Amherst, NH 03031 • ERT
Rupp-Serrano Karen J. • University of Oklahoma Libraries University Libraries • Norman, OK 73019 • ACRL RASD
Rupp Cynthia R. • Lake Elsinore, CA 92530
Rupp Nancy F. • Librarian • Saint John's School • Houston, TX 77019 • AASL
Rupp Nancy J. • Children's Librarian • Santa Clara County Free Library • San Jose, CA 95112-4446
Ruppe Carol V. • Tempe, AZ 85282 • ACRL
Ruppersberger Kay • Library/Media • Warren Elementary School • Cockeysville, MD 21030 • AASL
Ruppert Ann T. • Reference Librarian • Point Loma Nazarene College Ryan Library • San Diego, CA 92106 • ACRL
Ruppert Nancy L. • Librarian • Heritage Book Shop • Los Angeles, CA 90035 • ACRL
Rupprecht Leslie P. • E Orange, NJ 07018 • Continuing
Rusaw Sally E. • Head Librarian • Mater Dei College Library • Ogdensburg, NY 13669 • ACRL
Ruscella Phyllis L. • Coor. of Bibliographic Instr. • University of Central Florida Library • Orlando, FL 32816-0666 • ACRL
Rusch-Feja Diann D. • Max Planck Institute for Human Development & Education • D-1000 Berlin, 33, Germany • GODORT IRRT
Rusch Leona M. • Youth Services Librarian • Bartlett Public Library District • Bartlett, IL 60103 • ALSC PLA
Ruschin Siegfried • Librarian for Collection Dev • Linda Hall Library • Kansas City, MO 64110 • ACRL
Ruschoff Carlen M. • Head Cataloging Department • Georgetown University Joseph Mark Lauinger Library • Washington, DC 20057-1006 • ACRL ALCTS LITA
Rush Barbara M. • Library Media Specialist • Wood Park Primary School U.F.S.D.10 • Commack, NY 11725 • AASL
Rush Carol L. • Pasadena, CA 91107-4440
Rush N. Orwin • Director Emeritus • Florida State University Robert M. Strozier Library • Tallahassee, FL 32306-2047 • Continuing
Rush Wayne C. • Grover Cleveland Middle School • Caldwell, NJ 07960 • AASL
Rushing Darla H. • Head of Cataloging • Loyola University Library • New Orleans, LA 70118 • ACRL ALCTS LITA
Rushing Fran • Librarian • Wentworth Military Academy Sellers-Coombs Library • Lexington, MO 64067 • ACRL
Rushing Naomi J. • Washington, DC 20005 • ACRL ALCTS *Continuing*
Rusiewski Charles • Media Director • Nashville Community High School District #99 • Nashville, IL 62263 • AASL YALSA
Rusin Nancy M. • Student • Wayne State University • Detroit, MI 48202
Rusinek Carol S. • Valparaiso, IN 46383
Rusk-Foushee Amy • Tucson, AZ 85705

Rusk Alice C. • Baltimore, MD 21214 • AASL   *Continuing*
Rusk Cherie B. • Oregon State University William Jasper Kerr Library • Corvallis, OR 97331-4501
Russ Beverly S. • Children's Librarian • Brooklyn Public Library Bay Ridge Branch • Brooklyn, NY 11209 • ALSC
Russ Kennetta P. • Library Media Specialist • Loudoun County High School • Leesburg, VA 22075 • AASL
Russ Ronald S. • Student • State University of New York at Buffalo School of Information Library • Buffalo, NY 14260 • ACRL ALCTS LITA
Russell-Mackwood Sharon • Teacher Librarian • David Branklin Elementary School • Surrey BC, V3W 3V4 Canada • AASL ALSC
Russell Alison M. • Paradise Valley, AZ 85253
Russell Ann • Northeast Document Conservation Center • Andover, MA 01810-1494 • ALCTS
Russell Anna Loe • Hermitage, TN 37076 • ACRL RASD   *Continuing*
Russell Barbara • Coordinator • Unified School District #233 • Olathe, KS 66062
Russell Brenda C. • Library Director • T.L.L. Temple Memorial Library • Diboll, TX 75941 • PLA
Russell Bruce L. • Long Beach, CA 90814-3073
Russell Cara L. • Student • University of Texas at Austin Graduate School of Library & Information Sciences • Austin, TX 78712-1276
Russell Clara Y. • Branch Manager • Houston Public Library Dixon Branch Library • Houston, TX 77021
Russell David A. • Librarian • Southern Oregon State Coll Library • Ashland, OR 97520
Russell Elizabeth • Providence, RI 02909 • Continuing
Russell F. Adele • Stanly County Public Library • Albemarle, NC 28001 • PLA
Russell Fern J. • University of Alberta • Edmonton AB, T6G 2J8 Canada
Russell Flora L. • Asst Dean of Learning Resources • Cmnty Coll of Allegheny County North Campus • Pittsburgh, PA 15237
Russell Gwendolyn C. • Librarian • Beverly Hills Middle School • Huntington, WV 25705 • AASL
Russell Janice M. • Librarian II • Phoenix Public Library • Phoenix, AZ 85004
Russell John F. • Houston, TX 77061 • IFRT
Russell John W. • Librarian • Johnson County Community College Library • Overland Park, KS 66210 • ACRL LAMA
Russell Judith C. • Dir., Library Programs Service • United States Government Printing Office • Washington, DC 20401 • GODORT
Russell Judy A. • Carlisle Community Schools • Carlisle, IA 50047
Russell Judy C. • Administrative Librarian • Joeten-Kiyu Public Library • Saipan, MP 96950 • ALCTS PLA
Russell Julia • Amityville, NY 11701 • Continuing
Russell Karen Brickett • Educational Media Specialist • Maryland School for the Deaf Columbia Campus • Columbia, MD 21044 • AASL
Russell Karen L. • Librarian III/Branch Librarian • Alexandria Public Library Duncan Branch • Alexandria, VA 22301 • LAMA
Russell Kathleen E. • Public Service Librarian • Curry College Library • Milton, MA 02186 • ACRL
Russell Keith W. • United States Department of Agriculture National Agricultural Library • Beltsville, MD 20705-2351 • ACRL LITA
Russell Kirk A. • Acquisition Dept. • Brigham Young University • Provo, UT 84602
Russell Leland E. • Dean, Learning Resources • MiraCosta College • Oceanside, CA 92056
Russell Lottye W. • Trustee • Kanawha County Public Library • Charleston, WV 25301 • ALTA
Russell Lynda • Corbett Middle/High School Library • Corbett, OR 97019
Russell Marilyn L. Ph.D. Dr • Fine Arts Librarian • University of Minnesota-Duluth Library • Duluth, MN 55812-2495 • ACRL
Russell Martha A. • Library Media Specialist • West Bridgewater Junior Senior High School • West Bridgewater, MA 02379 • AASL YALSA
Russell Mary A. • Lacey, WA 98503
Russell Mary E. • Exeter, NH 03833 • ALSC PLA   *Continuing*
Russell Maureen Ann • Cataloger • University of California-Los Angeles (UCLA) • Los Angeles, CA 90024-1450
Russell Nan • Trustee • Manatee County Public Library System • Bradenton, FL 34205
Russell Pamella A. • Student • Rutgers University • Camden, NJ 08102 • ALCTS LAMA PLA IRRT
Russell Patrick J. • Rare Book Cataloger • University of California-Berkeley Bancroft Library • Berkeley, CA 94720 • ACRL ALCTS LITA

Russell Paula • Tyler Junior College Vaughn Library & Learning Res Ctr • Tyler, TX 75711-9020
Russell Phyllis • Trustee • Rockford Public Library • Rockford, IL 61101-1061 • ALTA
Russell Ralph E. • University Librarian • Georgia State University Pullen Library • Atlanta, GA 30303-3081 • ACRL LAMA
Russell Rhoda C. • Public Information Officer • Lake Lanier Regional Library • Duluth, GA 30245 • LAMA IFRT
Russell RoseMarie S. • Librarian • Loyola-Blakefield School • Towson, MD 21204 • AASL
Russell Sandra • Truckee, CA 96162 • AASL
Russell Sara L. • Assistant Director • Kinchafoonee Regional Library • Dawson, GA 31742
Russell Sara S. • Director • Kinchafoonee Regional Library • Dawson, GA 31742
Russell Scott R. • Marketing Director • Salt Lake County Library System • Salt Lake City, UT 84121-3188
Russell Susan J. • Library Assistant • Alameda County Library Dublin Branch • Dublin, CA 94568 • ALSC
Russell Thyra K. • Order Librarian • Southern Illinois University Delyte W. Morris Library • Carbondale, IL 62901-6632 • ACRL ALCTS
Russell Tracy C. • Head, Doc., Microforms & Media • Iowa State University Library • Ames, IA 50011-2140 • ACRL
Russell Victoria L. • Library Media Specialist • Queen Bee Elementary School • Glendale Heights, IL 60139 • AASL
Russell Virginia Ann • Pittsburgh, PA 15213 • Continuing
Russell Virginia Miss • Brookfield, IL 60513 • AASL YALSA   *Continuing*
Russman Penny A. • Science Reference Librarian • Wesleyan University • Middletown, CT 06457 • ACRL LITA LIRT
Russo Christina T. • Academic Librarian • Manhattanville College Library • Purchase, NY 10577-0560
Russo Edward J. • Head,Sangamon Valley Collection • Lincoln Library • Springfield, IL 62701 • RASD
Russo Joy • Library Media Specialist • Kennebunk High School • Kennebunk, ME 04043 • AASL
Russo Michele C. • Ref Ln/coor Of Bibl Instr • Indiana University at South Bend Franklin D. Schurz Library • South Bend, IN 46634 • ACRL RASD LIRT
Russo Roseanne A. • Alachua, FL 32615 • ALSC YALSA
Russo Stephen • Director • Long Branch Public Lib • Long Branch, NJ 07740 • LAMA PLA RASD
Russov Olga • Library Assistant-Serials • Institute of Paper Science & Technology • Atlanta, GA 30318
Rust Margaret B. • University of Michigan Libraries • Ann Arbor, MI 48109-1205 • ALCTS LAMA LITA
Rust Roxy J. • Westvaco Corporation Forest Science Laboratory Library • Sammerville, SC 29484
Rusthoven Cherie • Olde Creek Elementay School • Fairfax, VA 22032 • AASL
Rusthoven Christine D. • Youth Services Librarian • Oak Lawn Public Library • Oak Lawn, IL 60453 • AASL
Rustomfran Perveen K. • Memphis-Shelby County Public Library and Information Center • Memphis, TN 38104-4025
Rutan Janet M. • Head of Cataloging • Harvard University Countway Library of Medicine • Boston, MA 02115
Rutemiller Annette M. • Martin Marietta Air Traffic Systems • Washington, DC 20024
Ruth Anne • Fort Walton Beach, FL 32547
Ruth Donna R. • Houston, TX 77025-2414
Ruth Grace W. • Children's Book Selection Spec. • San Francisco Public Library • San Francisco, CA 94102 • ALSC PLA EMIERT
Ruth Lindsay D. • Reference/Young Adult Librarian • Geneva Free Library • Geneva, NY 14456 • PLA
Ruthenberg Donnell L. • Librarian I • University of California California Newspaper Project • Sacramento, CA 94257-0001 • ALCTS
Rutherford Ann • Librarian • Moorcroft Elementary School • Moorcroft, WY 82721 • AASL
Rutherford Carmen Maureen • Elementary Librarian • Normandy Elementary Library Office • Saint Louis, MO 63121
Rutherford Christine A. • Reference Librarian • Northwest Regional Library System • Sioux City, IA 51101
Rutherford Jane A. • Library System Analyst • Gallaudet University Library • Washington, DC 20002
Rutherford John D. • Systems Librarian • Central Connecticut State University Elihu Burritt Library • New Britain, CT 06050 • ACRL LITA
Rutherford Mark • Library Media • Damasuus-Union School District • Boring, OR 97009 • AASL
Rutherford Marla J. • Indianapolis, IN 46201-1276
Ruthruff Katheryn A. • John H. Wood Middle School • San Antonio, TX 78233-4498 • AASL
Rutimann Hans • New York, NY 10024

Rutkovskis Gunars • Boston Public Library • Boston, MA 02117 • ACRL ALCTS LITA
Rutkowski Barbara J. • Student • Wayne State University Library Science Program • Detroit, MI 48202
Rutkowski Hollace A. • Vice President, Info Services • QVC Network • West Chester, PA 19380 • LITA
Rutledge John B. • Bibl West European Resources • The University of North Carolina Collection Development Department • Chapel Hill, NC 27599-3918 • ACRL
Rutledge Marcia • Head of Adult Services • Troy Public Library • Troy, MI 48084 • PLA RASD
Rutmayer Eileen C. • Library Media Director • Rialto High School • Rialto, CA 92376
Rutsch Marion Hanes • Silver Spring, MD 20906 • ALSC
Rutstein Joel S. • Colorado State University William E. Morgan Library • Fort Collins, CO 80523 • ALCTS
Rutter Kathleen Hunter • Cataloger/Shelflisting Sec. Head • Harvard College Library Widener Memorial Library • Cambridge, MA 02138 • ACRL LITA
Rutter Suzanne L. • Technical Services Librarian • Yale University Beinecke Rare Book & Manuscript Library • New Haven, CT 06520 • ACRL ALCTS
Ruttle Mary Lou • Librarian • Carrick High School Library • Pittsburgh, PA 15210 • AASL
Rutz Deanna • Eastwood Middle School • Indianapolis, IN 46220 • AASL
Rutz Rochelle R. • Elm Grove Public Library • Elm Grove, WI 53122-0906 • ALCTS ALSC PLA YALSA
Rutzel Doris C. • Librarian • Saint Matthew School Library • Seattle, WA 98125
Rutzen A Ruth Miss • Northville, MI 48167 • Continuing
Ruys Alberta Ann Sr • Director of Library • Fontbonne College Library • Saint Louis, MO 63105 • ACRL
Ryan-Zeugner Kathryn M. • Interlibrary Loan • University of Notre Dame Theodore M. Hesburgh Library • Notre Dame, IN 46556 • ACRL RASD IFRT
Ryan Amy • Minneapolis Public Library & Information Center • Minneapolis, MN 55401-1992
Ryan Anne • Librarian • Minneapolis Community College • Minneapolis, MN 55403 • ACRL
Ryan Audrey Honig • Librarian • Miami-Dade Public Library System • Miami, FL 33130-1504 • ASCLA
Ryan Barbara Sr. • Vanier ON, K1L 7K3 Canada • Continuing
Ryan Beverly • Systems Librarian • California State University John M. Pfau Library • San Bernardino, CA 92407 • LITA
Ryan Bonnie • Head Access Services • Syracuse University Library E. S. Bird Library • Syracuse, NY 13244-2010 • ACRL LAMA RASD
Ryan Daniel H. • Trustee • Northbrook Public Library • Northbrook, IL 60062 • ALTA
Ryan Diane M. • Assoc Cura. Prints & Photographs • Chicago Historical Society • Chicago, IL 60614 • LITA
Ryan Donald L. • Director Libraries • Russell Sage College Library • Troy, NY 12180 • ACRL ALCTS   *Life*
Ryan Elizabeth • Albany, NY 12209
Ryan Evelyn O. • MacArthur Junior High School • Prospect Heights, IL 60070 • AASL
Ryan Felicia M. • Peoria, IL 61615 • ALSC PLA *Continuing*
Ryan Gail K. • West Simsbury, CT 06092 • ALSC
Ryan George • Illinois State Library • Springfield, IL 62701-1796 • ASCLA
Ryan Holly J. • Canfield, OH 44406
Ryan Jenny L. • Library Manager • Laubach Literacy International Library • Syracuse, NY 13210 • PLA
Ryan Joe • Student • Syracuse University School of Information Studies • Syracuse, NY 13244-4100 • LITA LRRT SRRT
Ryan Kenneth W. • Reference Librarian • California State University-Los Angeles John F. Kennedy Memorial Library • Los Angeles, CA 90032-8300 • ACRL RASD LIRT
Ryan L Dolores • Lakewood, OH 44107 • IFRT *Continuing*
Ryan Margaret A. • Student • University of Oklahoma Libraries University Libraries • Norman, OK 73019 • PLA IFRT LHRT NMRT SRRT
Ryan Marianne P. • General Documents Librarian • University of Iowa Libraries • Iowa City, IA 52242-1379 • GODORT
Ryan Marilyn P. • Assistant Administrator • Villa Park Public Library • Villa Park, IL 60181 • RASD
Ryan Mary A. • Head of Reference Services • University of Missouri Libraries-Columbia Elmer Ellis Library • Columbia, MO 65201-5149 • ACRL LAMA RASD
Ryan Mary A. Miss • Librarian • Cedar Rapids Public Library • Cedar Rapids, IA 52401 • Life
Ryan Mary F. • Escondido, CA 92029
Ryan Mary J. • Marina Del Re, CA 90292 • Continuing
Ryan Mary O. • Gaithersburg, MD 20878-2739
Ryan Mary Patricia • Librarian • Niles College of Loyola University College of Arts & Sciences Library • Chicago, IL 60631 • ACRL

Ryan Mary S. • Children's Librarian • King County Library System Burien Branch • Seattle, WA 98166 • ALSC
Ryan Nancy R. • Student • University of North Carolina at Chapel Hill School of Information and Library Science • Chapel Hill, NC 27599-3360
Ryan Patricia A. • Shelby Twp, MI 48316
Ryan Patricia H. • Huntsville, AL 35801
Ryan Patricia M. • Lower Merion Library Association • Ardmore, PA 19003 • LAMA PLA
Ryan Richard A. • Librarian • Public Library of Cincinnati and Hamilton County • Cincinnati, OH 45202
Ryan Richard W. • Curator of Rare Books • University of Michigan William L Clements Library • Ann Arbor, MI 48109 • ACRL LITA
Ryan Ronald S. • Hd of Intergrated Library System • Case Western Reserve Univ Freiberger Library • Cleveland, OH 44106-7151 • ACRL
Ryan Susan K. • Library Assistant • Chemeketa Community College • Salem, OR 97309
Ryan Susan M. • Government Documents Librarian • Stetson University DuPont-Ball Library • De Land, FL 32720-3769 • ACRL GODORT
Ryan Theresa C. • Library Administration Office • University of California-Los Angeles (UCLA) • Los Angeles, CA 90024-1450 • ALCTS LITA
Ryan William L. • Director of Library Services • Lamar University • Orange, TX 77630 • ACRL LAMA LITA LIRT
Rybarczyk Barclay • Kenmore, NY 14217
Rybarczyk James J. • Librarian • Buffalo & Erie County Public Library • Buffalo, NY 14203
Ryberg H. Theodore • Sugar Grove, PA 16350 • ACRL LAMA *Life*
Rychlik Wilma M. • Kenmore, NY 14223
Rycombel Judith T. • Head Reference Librarian • DePaul University Library • Chicago, IL 60604-2287 • RASD
Rycroft Barbara • Librarian • Fairview Developmental Center Staff Library • Costa Mesa, CA 92626
Ryczek Marianne • Youth Services Librarian • Bellwood Public Library • Bellwood, IL 60104 • ALSC
Ryden John • Librarian • Legal Assistance Foundation • Chicago, IL 60604
Ryden Yvonne • Trustee • Morton Grove Public Library • Morton Grove, IL 60053 • ALTA
Ryder Laura • Head Librarian • Wertheim Schroder & Company • New York, NY 10019
Ryder Olive M. Miss • Los Angeles, CA 90020 • Continuing
Ryder Rebecca J. • Student • University of Kentucky College of Library & Information Science • Lexington, KY 40506-0391 • ALCTS
Ryer Jeanne M. • Reference/Adult Svs Librarian • Norwell Public Library • Norwell, MA 02061 • RASD
Ryhanen Susan • Librarian • Van Cortlandtville Elementary School • Mohegan Lake, NY 10547 • AASL NMRT
Rylander Carolyn S. • Cataloger • Central State University Library • Edmond, OK 73034-0193 • ALCTS LITA *Life*
Ryley Alison M. • New York Public Library • New York, NY 10018-2788 • ACRL
Rynders Kathryn C. • Director • Red Wing Public Library • Red Wing, MN 55066 • ACRL RASD
Rynkiewicz Robert P. • Atlantic City Free Public Library • Atlantic City, NJ 08401
Rynn Midori Y. Dr. • Scranton, PA 18510 • ACRL LITA *Life*
Rys Judith Elaine • Librarian • Holy Spirit School • Saint Paul, MN 55105 • AASL YALSA
Rystrom Barbara B. • Reference Librarian • Aiken Technical College • Aiken, SC 29802 • ACRL
Ryszka Deborah A. • Coor., Copy Cataloging Unit • University of Delaware Morris Library • Newark, DE 19717-5267 • ACRL ALCTS
Ryus Joseph E. • Richmond, CA 94806-2617 • ACRL ALCTS LITA *Life*
Ryus Phyllis K. • Richmond, CA 94806
Rzepecki Arnold M. • Sacred Heart Major Seminary • Sacred Heart Major Seminary • Detroit, MI 48206
Saab Nina • Student • San Jose State University Division of Library & Information Science • San Jose, CA 95192-0029
Saario Barbara • Tahoma High School • Kent, WA 98042
Saavedra Shawna L. • Student • University of California Los Angeles Graduate School of Library & Information Science • Los Angeles, CA 90024 • IFRT SRRT
Saba Bettye M. • Evansville, IN 47712-5034 • Continuing
Saban Mike M. • Trustee • McCook Public Library • McCook, IL 60525
Sabatini Joseph D. • Head Librarian • Albuquerque Public Library • Albuquerque, NM 87102 • PLA
Sabatino Susan A. • Librarian • Kean College of New Jersey Library • Union, NJ 07083 • ACRL LIRT
Sabatiuk Ludmila K. • Miami Beach, FL 33140 • Continuing
Sabbach Lisette W. • Thesaurus Librarian • Predicasts • Cleveland, OH 44106 • ALCTS RASD
Sabeh Diane J. • Saint Edmunds Academy • Pittsburgh, PA 15217 • AASL ALSC
Sabella Pam • Newland, NC 28657
Sabia Jill A. • Student • Long Island University Palmer School of Library & Info. Sci. • Brookville, NY 11548 • ACRL
Sabin Barbara B. • Apollo Middle School • Hollywood, FL 33024 • AASL
Sabin Robert G. • Science & Engineering Libn • Rice University Fondren Library • Houston, TX 77251-1892 • ACRL
Sabine Julia E. • New Hartford, NY 13413 • ACRL *Continuing*
Sable John A. • Student • State University of New York at Buffalo School of Information Library • Buffalo, NY 14260 • PLA NMRT SRRT
Sabol Laurie • Reference Librarian • Bowling Green State University William Jerome Library • Bowling Green, OH 43403-0175 • ACRL LAMA IRRT SRRT
Sabosik Patricia E. • Editor/Publisher • Choice Magazine • Middleton, CT 06457 • ACRL
Sabransky F. Allen • Library Board President • Josephine County Library System • Grants Pass, OR 97526
Sabric Georgianne S. • Punxsutawney, PA 15767 • AASL
Sabsay David • Director • Sonoma County Library • Santa Rosa, CA 95404 • LAMA LITA PLA
Saccardi Marianne • Whitby School Library Fairfield-Westchester • Greenwich, CT 06831 • ALSC
Saccheus Marelda • Village Librarian • Elim Community Library • Elim, AK 99739
Sacco Concetta N. • Librarian • West Haven Public Library • West Haven, CT 06516 • PLA RASD
Sacco Gail Alter • Director • Voorheesville Public Library • Voorheesville, NY 12186 • LAMA PLA RASD
Sachar Steven R. • Queens Borough Public Library • Jamaica, NY 11432 • ACRL IRRT
Sachdeva Marion H. • Head of Technical Services • University of New Haven Marvin K Peterson Library • West Haven, CT 06516 • ALCTS IRRT
Sachs Kathie B. • School Librarian • Shady Grove Elementary School • Ambler, PA 19002 • AASL
Sachse Gladys M. • Dardanelle, AR 72834-9802 • AASL GODORT *Continuing*
Sachse Renate B. • Catalog Librarian • Franklin and Marshall College • Lancaster, PA 17604 • ACRL
Sack Jean C. • Librarian • John Archer School • Bel Air, MD 21014 • AASL YALSA
Sack Nancy • Resident Librarian • University of Illinois at Chicago University Library • Chicago, IL 60680
Sackett Judy A. • Head, Preservation Department • University of Kentucky Libraries • Lexington, KY 40506-0039 • ACRL ALCTS
Sackett Susan M. • Information Services Librarian • Washington County Library • Cottage Grove, MN 55016
Sackler Jessie B. • Dallas, TX 75230
Sacknoff Judith • Lexington, MA 02173
Sacks Lorraine I. • Librarian • Salvation Army School For Officers Training Brengle Memorial Library • Suffern, NY 10901 • ACRL
Sacks Pamela • Co-owner • Cheshire Cat Book Store • Washington, DC 20015
Sacks Patricia Ann • Director of Libraries • Muhlenberg College Trexler Library • Allentown, PA 18104-5586 • ACRL ALCTS LAMA LITA GODORT
Sacks Patti Paris • Port Washington, NY 11050 • ALSC
Sadak Luz • Vienna, VA 22180 • ACRL
Sader Marion • R. R. Bowker • New Providence, NJ 07974 • AASL ACRL RASD FLRT
Sadler Alyssa A. • Lakeside, CA 92040-4547 • ALSC PLA YALSA EMIERT IFRT
Sadler Catherine E. • Librarian • Charleston Library Society • Charleston, SC 29401
Sadler Cynthia • Librarian • Texas State Technical Institute Amarillo Library • Amarillo, TX 79111-0002 • ACRL
Sadler Graham H. • Director • Henrico Public Library • Richmond, VA 23223 • LAMA PLA *Life*
Sadler Julia F. • Medical Librarian • Billings Clinic • Billings, MT 59107-5100
Sadler Philip • Assoc. Prof. Ch. & Yng. Ad. Lit. • Central Missouri State University Ward Edwards Library • Warrensburg, MO 64093 • AASL ALSC YALSA IFRT
Sadler Richard Dr. • Trustee • Weber County Library • Ogden, UT 84401 • PLA
Sadler Shirley L. • Chicago, IL 60620
Sadlier Mary A. • Lima, OH 45805
Sadow Sandy • Widener University School of Law Library • Wilmington, DE 19803-0475 • ALCTS
Sadowski Frank E. Jr. • Head Catalog Department • University of Rochester Rush Rhees Library • Rochester, NY 14627-0055 • ALCTS
Sadowski Lynda • Mentor High School • Mentor, OH 44060 • AASL
Saecker Tasha • Coord. of Children's Services • Cape Girardeau Public Library • Cape Girardeau, MO 63701 • ALSC
Saenz Rose Marie • Auto-Graphics Inc. • Pomona, CA 91768 • LITA
Safar Michal • Information Specialist • IIT Research Institute Manufacturing Tech Info Anly Ctr • Chicago, IL 60616 • LITA
Safarli Linda F. • Reference/Young Adult Librarian • Newport Library • Bellevue, WA 98006
Saferite Linda • Library Director • Scottsdale Public Library • Scottsdale, AZ 85251 • LAMA LITA PLA
Saffady William K. • Delmar, NY 12054
Safford Barbara R. • Adjunct Asst Prof of Lib Science • University of Northern Iowa Donald O. Rod Library • Cedar Falls, IA 50613-3675 • AASL ALSC
Safford Herbert D. Dr. • Director • University of Northern Iowa Donald O. Rod Library • Cedar Falls, IA 50613-3675 • ACRL
Safford Hildred • Norway, ME 04268 • Continuing
Safford Mary F. • Colorado School of Mines Arthur Lakes Library • Golden, CO 80401 • GODORT
Saffran Mary Jane • New York, NY 10017
Safley Ellen Derey • Librarian • University of Texas at Dallas University Library • Richardson, TX 75083-0643 • LAMA RASD
Safran Franciska • State University of New York College Daniel A. Reed Library • Fredonia, NY 14063
Safranek Sarah M. • Clinical Librarian • University of Texas Medical Branch Moody Medical Library • Galveston, TX 77555-1035
Safratowich Michael • Grand Forks, ND 58201-8725 • ALCTS
Saft Roger A. • Reference Librarian • Pine Bluff & Jefferson County Library System • Pine Bluff, AR 71601 • PLA
Sagat Judith S. • Children's Librarian • Ossining Public Library • Ossining, NY 10562 • AASL
Sage Gail M. • Sonoma County Library • Santa Rosa, CA 95404 • ALSC
Sage Katharine Miss • Meriden, CT 06450 • Continuing
Sage Mona K • Library Media Director • Ponca City High School • Ponca City, OK 74601 • AASL YALSA
Sage Norman D. • Reference Librarian • College of Lake County Learning Resource Center • Grayslake, IL 60030 • ACRL RASD
Sager Donald J. • Publisher • Highsmith Co., Inc. • Fort Atkinson, WI 53538-0800 • LAMA LITA PLA
Sager Harvey M. • Reference Librarian • Arizona State University Libraries • Tempe, AZ 85287-1006 • ACRL
Sager Lynn S. • State Coordinator • Wisconsin Library Association • Madison, WI 53704 • ALSC
Sager Philip E. • Librarian • University of Louisville Ekstrom Library • Louisville, KY 40292 • LITA RASD
Sager Rochelle • Dir., Lib & Media Services • Fashion Institute of Technology Library • New York, NY 10001 • ACRL LAMA LITA RASD *Life*
Sager SuAnn • Western Middle School • Parma, MI 49269 • AASL YALSA
Saginor Karen L. • Catalog Librarian • City College of San Francisco • San Francisco, CA 94112 • SRRT
Sagraves Barbara R. • Hd, Presv Assessment & Replmnt • Northwestern University Library • Evanston, IL 60208-2300 • ALCTS
Sague Virginia M. • Kodiak, AK 99615
Sahak Judy Harvey • Assistant Director • Claremont Colleges Scripps College • Claremont, CA 91711 • ACRL
Sahd Beth Ann E. • Elementary Librarian • Denver Elementary School Cocalico School District • Denver, PA 17517 • AASL
Sahling Margaret E. • Coshocton, OH 43812 • Continuing
Sahraie Arlene • Director • Fairview Public Library • Fairview, NJ 07022
Sahukhan Samina • Columbus, OH 43221
Saile Cherrie J. • Library Associate • University of Kansas Library • Lawrence, KS 66045-2800 • RASD
Sain Azalee B. • Acquisitions Head • North Carolina Department of Community Colleges Library • Raleigh, NC 27603
Saindon Shelley R. • Student • University of Illinois Graduate School of Library and Information Science • Urbana, IL 61801
Saines Sherri B. • Student • Thiel College • Greenville, PA 16125
Saint John Nancy • Public Relations Coordinator • San Diego County Library • San Diego, CA 92123

Sainz Yolanda • Tucson, AZ 85702
Saira Yasmin • New York, NY 10025
Saitis Paula W. • Librarian IV • Chicago Public Library • Chicago, IL 60605
Saito Masaei • Professor • Tohoku Fukushi University • Miyagi 981, Japan • ACRL IFRT IRRT
Saix Austin Sr. • Librarian • Saint Vincent de Paul School • Phoenix, AZ 85031
Sak Ludmila • Senior Catalog Librarian • Rutgers University Libraries Technical & Automated Services • Piscataway, NJ 08855 • ACRL
Sakai Charlotte T. • San Jose Public Library • San Jose, CA 95113 • PLA
Sakai Cora • Coordinator of Childrens Servs. • Hilo Public Library • Hilo, HI 96720
Sakai Diane H. • Librarian • Honolulu Community College Library • Honolulu, HI 96817-4598 • ACRL LITA *Life*
Sakalas Cristine A. • Reference Consultant • Suburban Library System • Oak Lawn, IL 60453
Sakamoto Kyoko • Nara 634, Japan • ACRL
Sakash Deborah F. • Student • Brodart Company • Williamsport, PA 17705 • ACRL ALCTS LITA NMRT
Sakellarios Mary H. • Children's Librarian • Palm Springs Public Library • Palm Springs, FL 33461
Sakey Joseph G. • Commissioner Off. Of Cable TV • Cambridge Public Library • Cambridge, MA 02138 • PLA
Sakmar Michael G. • Supervisor of Public Services • Bartow County Public Library • Cartersville, GA 30120
Sakuma Bernice E. • Mending Clerk • Palo Alto City Library • Palo Alto, CA 94303
Sala Chris M. • Student • Rutgers University School of Commun Info & Library Studies • New Brunswick, NJ 08903 • ACRL
Sala Nola K. • Librarian • Salt Lake County Library Systems Sandy Library • Sandy, UT 84092
Salabiye Velma S. • Librarian • University of California Los Angeles American Indian Studies Library • Los Angeles, CA 90024-1548
Salahuddin Bilal d. • Student • University of Illinois Graduate School of Library and Information Science • Urbana, IL 61801
Salahuddin Naimah J. • Student • University of Illinois Graduate School of Library and Information Science • Urbana, IL 61801 • SRRT
Salak Phylis A. • Trustee • Fairfax County Public Library • Fairfax, VA 22033-1909
Salamone Cheryl A. • Student • University of California Los Angeles Graduate School of Library & Information Science • Los Angeles, CA 90024 • LITA
Salas Joanne • Librarian I • Milwaukee Public Library • Milwaukee, WI 53233 • YALSA
Salas Juanita • Trustee • City of Commerce Public Library • Commerce, CA 90040 • ALTA
Salas Laura E. • Student • University of Oklahoma School of Library & Information Studies • Norman, OK 73019 • NMRT
Salazar David R. • Washington, DC 20003-3017
Salazar Joy B. • Wasatch High School • Heber City, UT 84032 • AASL
Salazar Theresa A. • Rare Book Librarian • University of Arizona Library • Tucson, AZ 85721 • ACRL EMIERT
Sale Josephine W. • East Hartford, CT 06118 • Continuing
Salecki Cynthia A. • Trustee • Bedford Park Public Library District • Bedford Park, IL 60501 • ALTA PLA
Saleeby Willie Mrs. • Trustee • South Carolina State Library • Columbia, SC 29211 • ALTA
Salerno Henry M. • Coordinator of Libraries • Brentwood District Instructional Media Center • Brentwood, NY 11717 • AASL IFRT
Salesses Peter P. • LMC Director • Edwin O. Smith High School Library Media Center • Storrs, CT 06268
Salfrank Nancy • Adukt Services Specialist • River Bluffs Regional Library • Saint Joseph, MO 64501 • ALCTS
Salibi-Cripe Laila S. • Monographic Cataloger • Indiana University School of Library and Information Science • Bloomington, IN 47405
Saliers Jane F. • Atlanta-Fulton Public Library Ponce De Leon Branch • Atanta, GA 30306 • ALSC
Salih Heidi M. • Youth Services Librarian • Mercer County Library System Twin Rivers Branch • East Windsor, NJ 08520
Salik Felicia • Co-Chairperson • Enoch Pratt Free Library • Baltimore, MD 21201-4484 • Continuing
Salika Catherine I. • Assistant Director • University of Illinois • Urbana, IL 61801 • LITA
Salinger Florence A. • Head of Technical Services • Penn State Harrisburg • Middletown, PA 17057 • ACRL ALCTS
Salisbury Faith Miss • Seattle, WA 98115 • PLA RASD *Continuing*
Salisbury Jane S • Youth Librarian • Multnomah County Library Hollywood Branch • Portland, OR 97212 • PLA SRRT
Salisbury Susan J. • Administrator, Information Serv. • California Medical Association • San Francisco, CA 94120-7690
Salistean John C. • Manager • Houchen Bindery Ltd. • Utica, NE 68456
Salit-Mischel Barbara • Buffalo, NY 14216
Salita Christine T. • Director • Half Hollow Hills Community Library • Dix Hills, NY 11746 • LAMA PLA
Saljooghi Shohreh • Assistant Librarian • Los Angeles College of Chiropractic • Whittier, CA 90604 • LRRT
Salk Judith E. • Trustee • R. R. Bowker • New Providence, NJ 07974 • ALCTS LITA
Sallack Donna J. • Technical Services Librarian • Scranton Public Library Albright Memorial Library • Scranton, PA 18509-3248 • ALCTS
Salle Ellen M. • Emporia State University Emporia in the Rockies • Denver, CO 80204 • YALSA
Sallee Desiree D. • Student • Indiana University School of Library and Information Science • Bloomington, IN 47405
Sallee Sandra D. • School Librarian • Whigham School • Whigham, GA 31797
Saller Joan A. • Operations Librarian • County of Los Angeles Public Library • Hawthorne, CA 90250
Salley John T. • Librarian • Oak Hills Bible College • Bemidji, MN 56601 • ACRL
Sallstrom Marilee A. • Adult Librarian • Long Beach Public Library • Long Beach, CA 90802-4482
Salluzzo Sharon • Children's Librarian • Penfield Public Library • Penfield, NY 14526 • ALSC
Salmon Glenee L. • InterLibrary Loan Supervisor • Minneapolis Public Library & Information Center • Minneapolis, MN 55401-1992
Salmon Jo-An C. • Honolulu, HI 96822 • ALSC
Salmon Joyce • Assoc Ln • Punahou School • Honolulu, HI 96822 • LIRT
Salmon Kay L. • Gorrie Elementary School • Tampa, FL 33606 • AASL
Salmon Linda • Librarian • Clymer Library Association • Pocono Pines, PA 18350
Salmon Michael W. • Librarian • Amateur Athletic Foundation • Los Angeles, CA 90018
Salmon Sheila • Director, Library Power Project • American Reading Council • New York, NY 10016 • AASL
Salmon Stephen R. • Chairman of the Board • Carlyle Systems Inc. • San Mateo, CA 94608 • LITA
Salmon Virginia L. • Student • University of Kentucky College of Library & Information Science • Lexington, KY 40506-0391 • IFRT
Salner Gwendolyn K. • Government Publications Ln • Bemidji State University A. C. Clark Library • Bemidji, MN 56601-2699 • ACRL RASD GODORT
Salo Annette C. • Area Librarian • Saint Paul Public Library Lexington Branch • Saint Paul, MN 55104 • PLA
Salo Kristine E. • Librarian • Brown & Caldwell • Atlanta, GA 30346
Salomon Kathleen E. • Getty Center for the History of Art Humanities Library • Santa Monica, CA 90401-1455 • ACRL RASD
Salony Mary F. • Student • Clarion University of Pennsylvania College of Library Science • Clarion, PA 16214 • RASD IFRT SRRT
Salovon Muriel • Young Adult Librarian • Cuyahoga County Public Library Orange Branch • Pepper Pike Village, OH 44124
Salpeter Michael S. • Brooklyn, NY 11224
Salt Bonnie B. • Project Cataloguer • Harvard University • Cambridge, MA 02138 • ACRL
Salt Elizabeth A. Ms • Catalog Librarian • Otterbein College Courtright Memorial Library • Westerville, OH 43081
Saltalamachia Joyce D. • Library Director • New York Law School • New York, NY 10013 • ACRL LITA
Salter Audrey S. • Burke, VA 22015
Salter Billie I. • Social Science Librarian • Yale University Social Science Library • New Haven, CT 06520 • IRRT
Salter Doris Z. • Bakersfield, CA 93306
Salter Jeffrey L. • Assistant Director • Shreve Memorial Library • Shreveport, LA 71120-1523
Salter Nellie C. • Media Specialist • Cherokee County Board of Education Ball Ground School • Ball Ground, GA 30107 • AASL
Saltman Judith M. • Associate Professor • University of British Columbia School of Library, Archival & Information Studies • Vancouver BC, V6T 1Z1 Canada • ALSC YALSA
Saltzer Linda M. • Library Director • Daly City Public Library • Daly City, CA 94015 • LAMA PLA
Saltzman Alice B. • Nicholls State University Allen J. Ellender Memorial Library • Thibodaux, LA 70310
Salvador Bo-Gay Tong • UCLA Library University Research Library • Los Angeles, CA 90024-1575 • ALCTS LITA
Salvador Fermina M. • Librarian • Palau Public Library • Koror Palau, GU 96940 • NMRT
Salvadore Maria B. • Children's Servs. Coordinator • District of Columbia Public Library Martin Luther King Memorial Library • Washington, DC 20001 • ALSC PLA
Salvadori Theodore • Blackwood, NJ 08012 • IFRT SRRT
Salvati Janet Sue • Librarian • Fairmont State College Library • Fairmont, WV 26554 • ACRL RASD *Life*
Salvesen Susan E. • Salt Lake City Public Library • Salt Lake City, UT 84111 • ALCTS ALSC LAMA PLA RASD YALSA
Salyer Anna C. • Instructional Servs. Librarian • University of Alaska Egan Library • Juneau, AK 99801-9977
Salyers Catherine A. • Director • Saint Josephs College Library • Rensselaer, IN 47978-0410 • ACRL ALCTS RASD GODORT LIRT
Salyers Connie E. • Associate Dir. of Pub. Services • Shawnee State University Library • Portsmouth, OH 45662-4303 • ACRL LITA
Salzer Elizabeth • University Librarian • Santa Clara University Michel Orradre Library • Santa Clara, CA 95053 • ACRL LAMA LITA LRRT
Salzer Melodie A. • Middletown, CT 06457
Salzer Nancy J. • Rochester, NY 14622
Salzman Scott D. • Systems Librarian • University of Southern Mississippi Cook Memorial Library • Hattiesburg, MS 39406-5053 • LITA
Sam Sherrie • Head, of Access Services • University of Mississippi John Davis Williams Library • University, MS 38677 • ACRL
Samad Margaret Evelyn • Mulberry, IN 46058
Samdahl Don H. • Serials Catalog Librarian • University of Alabama Amelia Gayle Gorgas Library • Tuscaloosa, AL 35487-0266 • ALCTS
Samek Antonia HD • Student • University of Wisconsin-Madison School of Library & Information Studies • Madison, WI 53706 • IFRT LHRT LRRT
Samelson Audrey • Associate • Broward County Library Coral Springs Library • Coral Springs, FL 33065
Samet Janet • Northwestern State University Watson Memorial Library • Natchitoches, LA 71497 • ALCTS
Sammakia Katherine Erwin • Boulder, CO 80301-3637
Sammataro John A. • President • Advanced Library Systems Inc • Andover, MA 01810
Sammataro Linda J. • Reference Librarian • University of Tennessee John C. Hodges Library • Knoxville, TN 37996-1000 • ACRL RASD LIRT SRRT
Sammons Christa • Librarian • Yale University Beinecke Rare Book & Manuscript Library • New Haven, CT 06520 • ACRL
Samore Theodore • Professor • University of Wisconsin-Milwaukee School of Library & Information Science • Milwaukee, WI 53201 • ACRL ALCTS GODORT *Continuing*
Samp Rollyn H. • Trustee • Sioux Falls Public Library • Sioux Falls, SD 57102
Sampier Judith M. • Librarian • Oak Valley Elementary • Omaha, NE 68144 • AASL
Sample Elizabeth J. • Media Specialist • Millard North High School • Omaha, NE 68154 • AASL
Sample Judith A. • Reference-Adult Services Head • Amarillo Public Library • Amarillo, TX 79189 • RASD
Sample Rick A. • Head Librarian • American Psychologial Assn Arthur W. Melton Library • Washington, DC 20036 • ACRL ASCLA ILERT
Sample Teresa A. • Student • University of Maryland College of Library and Information Services • College Park, MD 20742-4345 • LITA
Samples Margaret B. • Public Services Coordinator • Nicholson Memorial Library • Garland, TX 75040-6365
Sampson Ellanie • Director • Truth or Consequences Public Library • Truth or Cons, NM 87901 • PLA IFRT
Sampson Lynda M. • Systems Coordinator • Cerritos College Library • Norwalk, CA 90650 • ACRL EMIERT
Sampson Shirley M. • Penn Valley, CA 95946
Sampson Zora J. • Student • University of Oklahoma School of Library & Information Studies • Norman, OK 73019 • SRRT
Samson Mary Ann • Circulation Manager • Saint Louis University Omer Poos Law Library • St. Louis, MO 63108-3478 • RASD
Samson Michael • Technical Services Librarian • Wayne State University Library Science Program • Detroit, MI 48202 • ALCTS LITA NMRT
Samson Robert C. • Assistant Director of Libraries • University of Texas at Arlington • Arlington, TX 76019-0497 • LITA
Samuel Cynthia • Christiansted, VI 00820-4519 • AASL
Samuel Jerrold M. • Trustee • Montgomery County Department of Public Libraries • Rockville, MD 20850 • ALTA PLA

Samuels Alan R. Dr. • Genreal Services Consultant • Ramapo Catskill Library System • Middletown, NY 10940 • ASCLA
Samuels Gertrude Miss • Clearwater, FL 34616 • Continuing
Samuelson Eileen • Free Library of Philadelphia Falls of Schuylkill Branch • Philadelphia, PA 19129
Samuelson Howard • Camarillo, CA 93010 • Continuing
Samuelson Valerie A. • Bibl. & Interlibrary Loan Ctr. • Chicago Public Library • Chicago, IL 60605 • LAMA RASD
San Agustin Frank R. • Nieves M. Flores Memorial Library • Agana, GU 96910 • LAMA LITA YALSA GODORT SORT
Sanborn F M. Mrs • Carmel, CA 93921 • Continuing
Sanborn Karen L. • Student • Church of Jesus Christ of Latter-Day Saints • Salt Lake City, UT 84150
Sanborn LaVonne K. • Assistant Professor • Western Illinois University Libraries • Macomb, IL 61455 • AASL ALSC
Sanchez-Vegas Saadia • Student • University of California-Berkeley University Library • Berkeley, CA 94720
Sanchez Alexander J. • Milwaukee Public Library Zablocki Branch • Milwaukee, WI 53215 • ALSC
Sanchez Dolores • Librarian • Arrowview Middle School • San Bernardino, CA 92407
Sanchez M. Ellsabeth • University of South Carolina Libraries • Columbia, SC 29208 • ACRL
Sanchez Theresa D. • Student • Pratt Institute Graduate School of Library & Information Science • Brooklyn, NY 11205 • IFRT NMRT
Sanchez Wanda • School Librarian • Bell Vista Adventist Academy • Mayaguez, 00709 Puerto Rico • AASL
Sand Mary R. • Mgr.,Nursing Learning Res Lab • University of North Dakota College of Nursing • Grand Forks, ND 58202 • NMRT
Sand Nanette O. • Berkeley, CA 94705
Sandberg-Fox Ann M. Dr. • Colcester, VT 05446 • ALCTS LITA
Sandberg Carol A. • Library Media Specialist • Kenyon-Wanamingo High School • Kenyon, MN 55946 • AASL YALSA
Sandberg Diana J. • Apple Valley, MN 55124 • RASD
Sandberg Elaine E. • Columbia, SC 29210
Sandberg Jennie Saisakorn • Asst. Humanities Libn. • Massachusetts Institute of Technology Libraries (MIT) • Cambridge, MA 02139 • ACRL
Sande Lisa • Student • Florida State University School of Library and Information Studies • Tallahassee, FL 32306-2048
Sanden Adrienne • Editor • Arizona State Library Association • Phoenix, AZ 85032
Sander Harold J. • Indianapolis, IN 46220 • LAMA PLA *Life*
Sanderbeck Beth E. • Library Supervisor • University of Tennessee MTAS Library • Knoxville, TN 37996-4105
Sanderford Marianna • Director • Kaneville Public Library District • Kaneville, IL 60144
Sanderlin Rebecca J. • Librarian Grade 4 • Phoenix Public Library Mesquite Branch • Phoenix, AZ 85032 • PLA
Sanders Ann Marie • Government Pubs Librarian • Tennessee Technological University • Cookeville, TN 38505 • GODORT MAGERT
Sanders Anna M. • Student • University of South Carolina College of Library & Information Science • Columbia, SC 29208
Sanders Anne S. • Director • East Albemarle Regional Library • Elizabeth Cty, NC 27909
Sanders Barbara Ann • Lamar Elementary School • Sinton, TX 78387 • AASL
Sanders Beverly J. • Saint Louis, MO 63114
Sanders Charlene R. • Administrative Librarian • West Chicago Public Library District • West Chicago, IL 60185 • PLA
Sanders Elizabeth H. • Librarian • Brewster Academy Kenison Library • Wolfeboro, NH 03894 • AASL
Sanders Elizabeth S. • Greensboro, NC 27410 • AASL ALSC
Sanders Emily C. • Charleston, SC 29401 • Continuing
Sanders Jacqueline C. • Head Librarian • The Bryn Mawr School • Baltimore, MD 21210 • AASL LAMA
Sanders Jan W. • Library Director • Bartlesville Public Library • Bartlesville, OK 74003 • LAMA PLA
Sanders Jean S. • Assistant Librarian • Ross & Hardies • Chicago, IL 60601
Sanders Kathleen M. • Student • Emporia State University School of Library & Information Management • Emporia, KS 66801 • SRRT
Sanders Kathy A. • Assistant Director Pub Services • University of Arkansas at Little Rock Ottenheimer Library • Little Rock, AR 72204 • ACRL LAMA
Sanders Lawrence • Saint Thomas ON, N5R 3E5 Canada
Sanders Lou Helen Dr. • Dir. of Libraries Assoc Prof • Jackson State University • Jackson, MS 39217 • ACRL LAMA RASD LIRT
Sanders Lylah A. • Santa Barbara, CA 93111 • Continuing
Sanders Marcia • Wilmington, DE 19809 • Continuing
Sanders Mark M. • Vice President, Library Division • Roswell Bookbinding • Phoenix, AZ 85009 • ALCTS
Sanders Melodie • University of Tulsa Ls • Tulsa, OK 74104
Sanders Mildred W. • Charlotte, NC 28216
Sanders Minda M. • Lancaster, PA 17603 • Continuing
Sanders Patricia D. • Coordinator of Reference Serv • Montclair State College Harry Sprague Library • Upper Montclair, NJ 07043 • ACRL
Sanders Richard R. • Doraville Public Library • Doraville, GA 30340
Sanders Robert B. • Student • DePauw University Roy O. West Library • Greencastle, IN 46135-0037
Sanders Ronald T. • Student • University of Southern Mississippi School of Library Science • Hattiesburg, MS 39406-5146
Sanders Rosann • Librarian • Brainerd Public Library • Brainerd, MN 56401 • PLA
Sanders Thomas Ray • Auburn University Ralph Brown Draughon Library • Auburn, AL 36849-5606 • ACRL ALCTS
Sanders Vickie A. • Librarian • Failure Analysis Associates • Menlo Park, CA 94025 • ACRL YALSA
Sanderson Harlan G. • Media Librarian • Luther College • Decorah, IA 52101 • VRT
Sandfaer Mogens • Cern AS-SI Scientific Information Service • CH-1211 Geneva 23, France • LITA
Sandfelder Paula M. • Dunwoody, GA 30338 • RASD ILERT
Sandford Betsy Ross • Librarian • NASA/Ames Research Center • Moffett Field, CA 94035-1000
Sandham Valerie J. • Union, OH 45322 • PLA
Sandhu Roop K. • Senior Cataloger • Oklahoma State University Library • Stillwater, OK 74078-0375
Sandidge Pat • Managing Director • Friends of Santa Cruz Public Libraries • Santa Cruz, CA 95063
Sandilands Mark L. • Assoc Prof of Psychology • University of Lethbridge Library • Lethbridge AB, T1K 3M4 Canada
Sandine Margaret A. • Cataloger • South Dakota School of Mines & Technology • Rapid City, SD 57701
Sandique-Owens Amelia • Chief, Cataloging & Bibl Access • The American University Library • Washington, DC 20016-8046 • LITA
Sandler Arlene D. • Branch Librarian • Saint Louis Public Library Kingshighway Branch • St. Louis, MO 63110
Sandler Claire R. • Media Program Manager • University of Michigan • Ann Arbor, MI 48109-1205
Sandler Gary D. • Xerox • Fairport, NY 14450
Sandler Mark S. • Coordinator,Graduate Lib Selec. • University of Michigan Libraries • Ann Arbor, MI 48109-1205 • ACRL ALCTS
Sandlian Pamela K. • Librarian • Denver Public Library • Denver, CO 80203-2165 • ALSC PLA
Sandlin Carolyn • Coordinator of Media Services • Clayton County Board of Education Morrow Annex • Morrow, GA 30260 • AASL
Sandlin Cynthia • Archdale, NC 27263
Sandness Susan S. • Director • Rapid City Public Library • Rapid City, SD 57701-3630 • AASL ALCTS ALSC LAMA LITA PLA RASD YALSA CLENE SORT
Sandoe Mildred W. • Xenia, OH 45385 • Continuing
Sandore Beth • Asst. Automated Servs. Ln. • University of Illinois Library • Urbana, IL 61801 • LITA
Sandretto Rebecca • Assistant Branch Librarian • Livonia Public Library Alfred Noble Branch • Livonia, MI 48150 • LAMA PLA RASD
Sands Bryan W. • Operations Manager • Computer Services Division of Glendale/Pasadena Public Library • Pasadena, CA 91101
Sands George A. Jr • Director • Caroline County Public Library • Denton, MD 21629 • LAMA LITA PLA RASD
Sands Kathy A. • DeSoto, TX 75115-4674 • ALCTS
Sands Kathy A. • Branch Manager • Jeffersonville Township Public Library • Jeffersonville, IN 47131-1548
Sands Kim L. • Librarian • Souhegan Cooperative High School • Amherst, NH 03031 • AASL YALSA
Sands Margaret • Oneida County BOCES • Utica, NY 13501 • ALCTS VRT
Sands Rita • Librarian • Peter Kiewit Middle School • Omaha, NE 68118 • AASL
Sandstedt Carl R. • Director • Saint Charles City-County Library • St. Peters, MO 63376-0529 • PLA
Sandstrom John C. • Asst Adult Selection Librarian • Houston Public Library • Houston, TX 77002 • PLA SRRT
Sandstrom Judith • Serials Librarian • Illinois Institute of Technology Paul V. Galvin Library • Chicago, IL 60616
Sandstrom Judy • Intermediate School Librarian • Beaverton School District 48 • Beaverton, OR 97075 • AASL
Sandstrom Lorriane E. • Branch Manager • Springfield-Greene County Library Kickapoo Prairie Branch • Springfield, MO 65807
Sandstrom Pamela E. • Doctoral Student • Indiana University School of Library and Information Science • Bloomington, IN 47405
Sandstrum John D. • Acquisitions Librarian • Mobile Public Library • Mobile, AL 36604-3273
Sandvik Karin • Collection Developer • University of Wisconsin Murphy Library • La Crosse, WI 54601 • ACRL IRRT
Sandy Catherine E. • Port Washington, NY 11050 • Continuing
Sandy Marjorie M. • Head of Adult Reading Department • Bloomfield Township Public Library • Bloomfield Hills, MI 48302-2437 • LAMA PLA RASD YALSA
Sandys Peter N. • President • Enem Systems Inc. • Waunakee, WI 53597-9586
Sanentz Shahe' N. • Systems/Reference Librarian • Pace University Library New York Civic Center • New York, NY 10038
Saner Eileen K. • Library Director • Associated Mennonite Biblical Seminaries Library • Elkhart, IN 46517 • ACRL ALCTS
Sanford Anastasia Sister • Librarian • Josephinum High School Library • Chicago, IL 60622 • YALSA LIRT
Sanford Catherine • Children's Librarian • Boston Public Library Hyde Park Branch • Hyde Park, MA 02136
Sanford Clarke • Director Media Services • California State University • Bakersfield, CA 93311 • LAMA
Sanford Janet T. • Baltimore County Public Library Perry Hall Branch • Baltimore, MD 21136 • PLA
Sanford Jaspyr B. • Sam Houston State University Newton Gresham Library • Huntsville, TX 77341-2281 • ACRL
Sanford Marion R. • Student • Florida State University School of Library and Information Studies • Tallahassee, FL 32306-2048 • AASL
Sanford Peg • 7-12 School Librarian • Saugatuck Public Schools • Saugatuck, MI 49453 • AASL
Sanger Brenda M. • Student • Northern Illinois University Department of Library & Information Studies • DeKalb, IL 60115
Sanger Helen • Librarian • Frick Art Reference Library • New York, NY 10021 • ACRL ALCTS
Sanger Stephanie K. • Brookfield, IL 60513 • AASL
Sani Martha Jo • Assistant Librarian • University of Colorado Wm. White Bus Library • Boulder, CO 80309-0419 • ACRL RASD GODORT LIRT
Sanko Anna M. • Design Manager • DuBose Associated, Inc. • Hartford, CT 06105
Sanko Shannon J. • Student • University of Illinois Graduate School of Library and Information Science • Urbana, IL 61801 • RASD
Sankot Janice M. • Roseville, MN 55113 • ACRL
Sannino Mark A. • Librarian • Trenton Free Public Library • Trenton, NJ 08608 • ACRL
Sannwald William • Director • San Diego Public Library • San Diego, CA 92101 • ACRL ALCTS ALSC ASCLA LAMA LITA PLA RASD YALSA
Sans Sue Ellen • Librarian (K-5) • Heritage Oak Elementary School • Roseville, CA 95678
Sansobrino Jean C. • Corporate Librarian • PACCAR Inc. • Bellevue, WA 98009
Sansone Laurie D. • Wallington, NJ 07057
Santa Vicca Edmund F. • Head, Reference Services • Arizona State University Libraries • Tempe, AZ 85287-1006 • ACRL RASD SRRT
Santangelo Mark • Trustee/Treasurer • Newark Public Library • Newark, NJ 07101-0630 • ALTA PLA
Santasier Loretta A. • East Setauket, NY 11733 • AASL ALSC LITA RASD
Santavicca Maria E. • Mount Clemens, MI 48044 • PLA
Santella Robert A. • Student • University of South Carolina College of Library & Information Science • Columbia, SC 29208 • ALSC PLA IFRT SRRT
Santharam Setti S. • Assistant Editor • H. W. Wilson Company • Bronx, NY 10452 • ACRL
Santiago Raymond • Assistant Director • Miami-Dade Public Library System • Miami, FL 33130-1504
Santizo Nedria A. • Head of Cataloging • University of Oklahoma Libraries University Libraries • Norman, OK 73019 • ACRL ALCTS
Santo Linda L. • A-V Librarian • Burlingame Public Library • Burlingame, CA 94010
Santoliquido Judy L. • Student • State University of New York at Albany School of Information Science & Policy • Albany, NY 12222

Santos Mary Jane • Student • Delaware County District Library • Delaware, OH 43015
Santos Stephanie F. • Chicago, IL 60630
Santosuosso Joseph P. • EDI Analyst • Faxon Company Inc. • Westwood, MA 02090 • ACRL LITA
Santrock John • Trustee • Kanawha County Public Library • Charleston, WV 25301 • ALTA
Sanudo Manuel • Reference Librarian • Queens College Benjamin S. Rosenthal Library • Flushing, NY 11367-0904 • ACRL
Sanville Thomas J. • Executive Director • Ohio Library & Information Network • Columbus, OH 43212 • ASCLA LAMA LITA
Sanzone Donna S. • Executive Editor, Library Ref. • G. K. Hall & Company • Boston, MA 02111 • ACRL LITA
Saper Alvin • Board Member • Lincolnwood Public Library District • Lincolnwood, IL 60646
Sapio Nancy M. • Smithtown, NY 11787
Sapir Jeanne A. • Chesterland, OH 44026 • PLA IFRT NMRT SRRT
Sapon-White Richard E. • Virginia Polytechnic Inst & State Univ University Libraries • Blacksburg, VA 24062-9001 • ACRL
Saporito Don L. • Director of Libraries • University of Southwestern Louisiana Libraries • Lafayette, LA 70503
Sapp Gregg E. • Head Access Services • Montana State University • Bozeman, MT 59717-0332 • ACRL LAMA
Sapp Lauren B. • Duke University William R. Perkins Library • Durham, NC 27706 • ACRL RASD GODORT
Sapp Mildred S. • Media Specialist • Mandarin High School • Jacksonville, FL 32258
Sappington Sharon C. • Birmingham, AL 35210 • AASL
Saracevic Blanka R. • New Brunswick Free Public Library • New Brunswick, NJ 08901 • ALSC
Saragnese Mary T. • Library Media Specialist • Turtle Hook Junior High School • Uniondale, NY 11553 • AASL PLA RASD YALSA EMIERT
Saraidaridis Susan • Reading, MA 01867
Sarangapani Chetluru • Head Serials • University of the District of Columbia Learning Resources Division • Washington, DC 20008 • ACRL
Sarath Carol A. • Library Media Specialist • Gallup-McKinly County Schools • Gallup, NM 87301 • AASL
Saravis Judith A. • Reference Librarian • EPA Region I Library • Boston, MA 02203
Sarber Mary A. • Main Library Adminstration • El Paso Public Library • El Paso, TX 79901 • PLA
Sardella Wendy J. • Student • State University of New York School of Information & Library Studies • Amherst, NY 14260 • PLA IFRT SRRT
Sarff JoEllen E. • Librarian II • Prince George's County Memorial Library System /Largo-Kettering Branch • Largo-Kettering, MD 20772 • ALSC PLA
Sarff Margaret R. • Manager Public Services • Davenport Public Library • Davenport, IA 52801 • RASD
Sargeant Doris Lewis • Library Director • Brentwood Public Library • Brentwood, NY 11717 • AASL ACRL ALSC ASCLA LAMA LITA PLA RASD YALSA CLENE EMIERT ERT GODORT LRRT SORT
Sargent Anne M. • Assoc. Dir. Technical Serv Sys • University of Detroit-Mercy Outer Drive Library • Detroit, MI 48219-3599 • LAMA CLENE IRRT
Sargent Constance • Library Aide III • Loudoun County Public Library • Leesburg, VA 22075
Sargent Dency • Executive Director • Capitol Region Library Council • Windsor, CT 06095 • ASCLA IFRT
Sargent Elizabeth K. • Student • Rosary College Graduate School of Library & Information Science • River Forest, IL 60305
Sargent Frank C. • Fletcher, NC 28732-9402
Sargent Judith P. • Head Librarian • Chittenden Public Library • Chittenden, VT 05737
Sargent Kathleen T. • Fort Washington, MD 20744 • AASL LRRT
Sargent Wilford R. III • Librarian III • Miami-Dade Public Library System North Dade Regional • Miami, FL 33056 • PLA YALSA IFRT SRRT
Sari JoAnn • Cincinnati, OH 45239 • AASL
Saricks Joyce • Hd of Literature & AV Svs • Downers Grove Public Library • Downers Grove, IL 60515 • PLA IFRT
Sarkies Ina H. Mrs. • Librarian • New Iberia Senior High School • New Iberia, LA 70560 • AASL
Sarkodie-Mensah Kwasi • Bibliographic Instruction Coor. • Northeastern University • Boston, MA 02115 • ACRL IRRT LIRT
Sarkozy Ilona Eszter • Detroit, MI 48226 • AASL
Sarlin Nadine E. • Locust Valley High School • Locust Valley, NY 11560 • AASL
Sarnese Phyllis J. • Elizabeth Williams Public Library • Snellville, GA 30278 • RASD
Sarno Susan J. • Palos Verdes Library District • Pls Vrd Pnsla, CA 90274
Sarnoff Stephanie • Director • Mount Kisco Public Library • Mount Kisco, NY 10549 • PLA IFRT
Sarratt Janet P. • Media Specialist • Ewing Junior High School Library • Gaffney, SC 29340 • AASL ALSC YALSA
Sarris Shirley C. • Publishing Consultant • Sarris Bookmarketing Service Inc. • New York, NY 10011 • AASL PLA RASD YALSA
Sarsfield Virginia G. • Library Product Specialist • Computer Management & Development Services • Harrisonburg, VA 22801 • LITA
Sartin Margaret L. • Lukachukai, AZ 86507 • AASL
Sartor Gladys J. • Arvada, CO 80003
Sartori Eva • Development Officer • University of Nebraska Love Library • Lincoln, NE 68588-0410 • ACRL
Sartori Judy R. • Kings Park Psychiatric Center Health Science Library • Kings Park, NY 11717 • ASCLA RASD
Sartorius Joel • Children's Librarian • Free Library of Philadelphia Richmond Branch • Philadelphia, PA 19134
Sarver Betty A. • Middle School Librarian • Jason Lee Middle School Tacoma Public School • Tacoma, WA 98023 • AASL
Sarver Garry L. • School Librarian • Decatur High School Federal Way Public Schools • Federal Way, WA 98023
Sarver Maryann • Head of Children's Services • Rockford Public Library • Rockford, IL 61101-1061 • ALSC PLA
Sasges Judy • Coordinator of Young Adult Serv • Santa Clara County Free Library • San Jose, CA 95112-4446 • YALSA
Saskowski Ronald E. Jr. • Student • State University of New York (SUNY) School of Information & Library Studies • Buffalo, NY 14260 • IFRT LHRT SRRT
Sass Rivkah K. • Consultant • Washington State Library • Olympia, WA 98504-2470 • ALSC LITA CLENE IRRT
Sass Susan V. • Student • University of Missouri-Columbia School of Library & Informational Science • Columbia, MO 65211
Sassani Mary Louise • Librarian • Saint Clement Mary Hofbauer • Baltimore, MD 21237 • AASL
Sassano Jean E. • Trustee • Commack Public Library District • Commack, NY 11725 • ALTA
Sasse Margo L. • Head of Catalog Dept. • Colorado State University William E. Morgan Library • Fort Collins, CO 80523 • ACRL ALCTS
Sassen Catherine J. • Senior Monographs Catlg Libn • University of North Texas • Denton, TX 76203 • ACRL ALCTS LITA LRRT
Sasso Maureen D. • Dir., Information Serv. Div. • Duquesne University Library • Pittsburgh, PA 15282 • ACRL LITA RASD LIRT
Sasso Robert • Trustee • Brentwood Public Library • Brentwood, NY 11717 • PLA
Sata Chiyono • Washington, DC 20008
Satchwell Ruth • Millburn, NJ 07041-1314 • Continuing
Sater Analya • Los Angeles, CA 90024
Satermoen Carol A. • Denver, CO 80229
Sathi Katherine G. • Humanities Librarian • Saint Louis Public Library • St. Louis, MO 63103-2389
Sathrum Robert L. • Humboldt State University Library • Arcata, CA 95521 • ACRL MAGERT
Sato Terri C. • Assistant Librarian • Yokota Base Library • APO, AP 96328-5000
Sato Yuko • Canon City, CO 81212
Satrom Janet S. • O'Fallon, IL 62269
Satsky Maynard A. • Library Director • San Francisco Base Library • APO San Francisco, CA 96264-5000 • PLA AFLRT
Satterfield Jacqueline C. • Seabrook, TX 77586
Satterfield Virginia • Augusta, GA 30901-2333 • Life
Satterthwaite Rebecca K. • Associate Director, Public Serv. • University of Nebraska Medical Ctr McGoogan Library of Medicine • Omaha, NE 68198-6705 • ACRL
Satterwhite Robin R. • Head of Public Services • Colorado College Tutt Library • Colorado Springs, CO 80903 • ACRL
Sattley Helen R. • Farmington, CT 06032-2978 • AASL ALSC IFRT *Continuing*
Satya Sarina • Student • Baylor University Library • Waco, TX 76798-7026 • RASD
Satyasai-Crimmin Panit • Librarian IV-Cataloger • University of Massachusetts at Boston Joseph P. Healey Library • Boston, MA 02125-3393 • ACRL
Satyendra-Holland Gita S. • Librarian • Saddleback College • Mission Viejo, CA 92692 • ACRL EMIERT LIRT
Sauage Marilyn A. • Media Generalist • Robbinsdale Area Schools Independent School District #281 • Robbinsdale, MN 55422 • AASL
Saucier Marci W. • Kenner, LA 70065
Saudargas Thomas A. • Library Application Specialist • College Center for Library Automation • Tallahassee, FL 32304 • ALCTS LITA LIRT
Sauer Arlene • Children's Librarian • Passaic Public Library • Passaic, NJ 07055 • ALSC
Sauer David A. • Head Librarian • Boston University College of Liberal Arts • Boston, MA 02215 • ACRL MAGERT SRRT
Sauer Greg • Student • Southern Connecticut State University School of Libray Science & Instructional Technology • New Haven, CT 06515
Sauer Janice A. • Mobile, AL 36608 • ACRL LIRT
Sauer Jeffrey K. • Director • Anderson Public Library • Lawrenceburg, KY 40342 • PLA IFRT
Sauer Jeffrey T. • Trustee • West Florida Regional Library • Pensacola, FL 32501
Sauer Laurie A. • Student • University of Wisconsin-Madison School of Library & Information Studies • Madison, WI 53706
Sauer Mary L. • SAC Command Librarian • United States Air Force Strategic Air Command Library • Offutt AFB, NE 68113 • AFLRT FLRT
Sauer Patrick J. • National Information Center for Educational Media (NICEM) • Albuquerque, NM 87196
Saul J. Muriel • Librarian • Michigan State University Libraries • East Lansing, MI 48824-1048
Saul Marion J. • Allentown, PA 18102
Saul Susan F. • Systems Librarian • Minuteman Library Network • Framingham, MA 01701 • ALCTS LITA
Saule Mara R. • Executive Asst. to President • University of Vermont President's Office • Burlington, VT 05405-0036 • ACRL
Saulmon Sharon A. • Head Librarian • Rose State College Learning Resources Center • Midwest City, OK 73110 • ACRL ALTA PLA
Saulsbury Margie M. • Library Director • Jasper Public Library • Jasper, TX 75951 • PLA
Saunders Dawn M. • Computer Serv Coor • New York Public Library • New York, NY 10018 • LITA
Saunders E. Stewart • Collection Development Coor. • Purdue University • West Lafayette, IN 47907 • ACRL LHRT
Saunders Elinor P. • Branch Head • Public Libraries of Saginaw Butman-Fish Branch • Saginaw, MI 48602 • PLA
Saunders Joseph Mrs • Boston, MA 02130
Saunders Judith A. • Artist • Marathon Sportswear • Chicago, IL 60643 • NMRT
Saunders Kay C. • Student • Texas Woman's University School of Library & Information Studies • Denton, TX 76204 • ALSC PLA IFRT NMRT SORT
Saunders L. Jane • Weber County Library North Branch • Ogden, UT 84414 • PLA IFRT
Saunders Laverna M. • A.U.L. for Technical Services • University of Nevada-Las Vegas James R. Dickinson Library • Las Vegas, NV 89154 • ACRL ALCTS LAMA
Saunders Lelia B. • Alexandria, VA 22314
Saunders Linda L. • Media Specialist/Elem. Library • Whittier Elementary • Muskogee, OK 74403 • AASL
Saunders Linda M. • Student • University of North Carolina Department of Library & Information Studies • Greensboro, NC 27412-5001
Saunders Marjorie D. • Lakeland, FL 33813 • AASL ALSC
Saunders Phyllis E. • Librarian • New York Public Library • Bronx, NY 10458 • YALSA
Saunders Susan M. • Charlotte Country Day School • Charlotte, NC 28226 • AASL
Saunter Robert E. • Director • Clark County Public Library • Springfield, OH 45501-1080 • PLA
Saur Cindy S. • Info. Res. Libn./Coordinator • Gallaudet University Library • Washington, DC 20002 • ACRL
Sauro Ricardo H. • Library Director • Tipton Public Library • Tipton, IA 52772-1753 • PLA
Savage Carol S. • Barringer Elementary School • Charlotte, NC 28208 • AASL
Savage Carroll S. • Media Specialist • Swift Creek Elementary • Midlothian, VA 23112 • AASL
Savage Daniel A. • Chief Librarian • Redeemer College • Ancaster ON, L9G 3N6 Canada • ACRL ALCTS LAMA RASD
Savage Deborah A. • Reference • County of Los Angeles Public Library A. C. Bilbrew Branch • Los Angeles, CA 90061 • PLA RASD
Savage Elaine A. • Administrative Librarian • Palos Heights Public Library • Palos Heights, IL 60463 • LAMA PLA
Savage Janis T. • District Media Director • Sauk-Prairie Schools • Sauk City, WI 53583 • AASL
Savage Jean • Racine, WI 53402 • PLA
Savage John Dr. • Trustee • New Orleans Public Library • New Orleans, LA 70140 • ALTA
Savage Judith G. • Xavier High School • Middletown, CT 06457 • AASL YALSA IFRT
Savage Kathleen M. • Infoplace Librarian • Cuyahoga County Public Library Maple Heights Regional Branch • Maple Heights, OH 44137 • PLA RASD
Savage Linda • Carson, CA 90746

Savage Shannon • Director • Argonne National Laboratory Technical Information Services Division • Argonne, IL 60439-4801 • LITA

Savage Stephen M. • University of Kentucky Libraries • Lexington, KY 40506-0039 • SRRT

Savage William E. • Production Development • University Microfilms International • Ann Arbor, MI 48106-1346 • ALCTS

Savalli Toni E. • Coordinator of Collection Devel • Spokane Public Library Comstock Building Library • Spokane, WA 99201-0976

Savard Rejean • Professor of Library Science • Universite De Montreal Ebsi C.P. 6128, Succ. A • Montreal PQ, H3C 3J7 Canada • PLA

Savaro Josephine • Philadelphia, PA 19106 • Continuing

Savas Nancy J. • Reference Librarian • South Huntington Public Library • Huntington Station, NY 11746

Savedow K. Paul • Free Library of Philadelphia • Philadelphia, PA 19103 • PLA

Savela Marcia G. • Director • Kasson Public Library • Kasson, MN 55944

Saveleva Melinda • West Lafayette, IN 47906-0561

Savery Virginia R. • Director • Royal Oak Public Library • Royal Oak, MI 48068 • Continuing

Saviano Diana M. • San Francisco, CA 94118 • AASL ACRL YALSA

Savido Linda D. • School Librarian • Banksville Middle Gifted Center • Pittsburgh, PA 15206 • AA3L

Saville Amanda J. • Librarian • Saint John's College University of Cambridge • Cambridge CB2 1TP, United Kingdom • ACRL

Savoie Brietta D. • Asst. Ref & Circulation Libn • River Edge Public Library • River Edge, NJ 07661

Savoie Edmond • Glen Rock, NJ 07452 • RASD

Savoit Helen • Trustee • Mid-Hudson Library System • Poughkeepsie, NY 12601

Sawa Anne • Calgary Public Library • Calgary AB, T2G 2M2 Canada • LITA

Sawa Yoshiko T. • Technical Services • University of Toronto Robarts Library • Toronto ON, Canada • ACRL ALCTS LITA

Sawatani Toshiko • Echigun, Shiga-ken, Japan • ALSC PLA

Sawczuk Anita • Education Media Specialist • Old Turnpike School • Califon, NJ 07830 • AASL

Sawicki Norma Jean • Publisher • Houghton Mifflin Company • New York, NY 10003 • ALSC ERT IFRT

Sawin Philip Jr • University of Wisconsin-Stout Library Learning Center • Menomonie, WI 54751 • ACRL

Sawina Jodie A. • Student • Chula Vista Public Library • Chula Vista, CA 91910

Sawka Barbara J. • Head, Music Library & Archive • Stanford University • Stanford, CA 94305-6011

Sawusch Ann Mina • Research Institute on Alcoholism Library • Buffalo, NY 14203 • ACRL LITA RASD GODORT

Sawyer-Burleson Suzanne L. • Lansing, MI 48910 • SRRT

Sawyer Jeanne C. • Tandem Computers • Cupertino, CA 95014 • LITA

Sawyer Kate • Information Specialist • Sawyer School • Pittsburgh, PA 15222

Sawyer Marian W. • Student • Montana State University • Bozeman, MT 59717-0332 • AASL

Sawyer Mary H. • Adult Services Assistant Dir • Williamsburg Regional Library • Williamsburg, VA 23185

Sawyer Rebecca Benet • Millburn, NJ 07041

Sawyer Ruth M. • Austin, TX 78705 • Continuing

Sawyers Elizabeth J. • Assistant to the Director • Ohio State University Libraries • Columbus, OH 43210-1286 • ACRL LITA

Sax Connie A. • Media Specialist • Ruben Dario Middle School • Miami, FL 33172 • AASL ALSC SRRT

Saxe Minna C. • Chief Tech Svs Librarian • City University of New York Graduate School Mina Rees Library • New York, NY 10036-8099 • ALCTS

Saxman Susan E. • Amity, PA 15311

Saxton Elna L. • Rochester, NY 14626

Saxton Jennifer • Miami-Dade Community College North Campus Library • Miami, FL 33167

Saye Jerry D. • Associate Professor • University of North Carolina at Chapel Hill School of Information and Library Science • Chapel Hill, NC 27599-3360 • ALCTS LITA

Sayer Mimi • Head of Acquisitions Department • San Francisco State University J. Paul Leonard Library • San Francisco, CA 94132

Sayers Agnes C. • Irvine, CA 92715

Sayers Ann C. • School Librarian • Farnsworth Middle School • Guilderland, NY 12084 • ALSC

Sayers John E. • Head Librarian • Forest Park Public Library • Forest Park, IL 60130 • PLA

Sayles Jeremy W. • Off-Campus Lib Serv. Coor. • Georgia College Ina Dillard Russell Library • Milledgeville, GA 31061 • ACRL

Sayles Lydia C. • Circulation Library Assistant • Mary Vinson Memorial Library Baldwin/Milledgeville Pub Lib • Milledgeville, GA 31061

Saylor John M. • Head Librarian • Cornell University Engineering Library • Ithaca, NY 14853-2201 • ACRL LITA

Saylor Patricia M. • Children's Librarian • Akron-Summit County Public Library Mogadore Branch • Mogadore, OH 44260 • ACRL

Saylor Priscilla Chris • Librarian • Columbus Public Schools Department of Library Media Services • Columbus, OH 43211 • AASL ALSC

Saylor V. Louise • Dean of Libraries • Eastern Washington University • Cheney, WA 99004 • ACRL ALCTS LAMA LITA LRRT

Sayre James K. • Student • College of San Mateo Library • San Mateo, CA 94402

Sayre John L. • Director of University Libraries • Phillips University Zollars Memorial Library • Enid, OK 73702 • Continuing

Sayre John R. • Director • Phillips University Zollars Memorial Library • Enid, OK 73702 • AASL ACRL ALCTS RASD YALSA IRRT LIRT

Sayre William C. • Coor. for Budgets & Facilities • University of Iowa Libraries • Iowa City, IA 52242-1379 • ACRL LAMA

Sbacchi Margareta • South Lancaster, MA 01561 • ACRL ALCTS

Scaer Paul J. • Philadelphia, PA 19144

Scales Burley J. • Student • University of Kentucky College of Library & Information Science • Lexington, KY 40506-0391

Scales Pamela H. • Tulsa, OK 74114 • ACRL

Scales Pat R. • Librarian • Greenville Middle School Library • Greenville, SC 29607 • AASL ALSC

Scalessa Rosemary • Media Specialist • Montgomery School • Atlanta, GA 30319

Scamack Anita M. • Student • University of Kentucky College of Library & Information Science • Lexington, KY 40506-0391

Scamara Susan E. • Library Associate • San Bernardino County Library Rialto Branch • Rialto, CA 92376 • ALSC

Scamman Carol J. • Humanities Librarian • Stephen F. Austin State University Steen Library • Nacogdoches, TX 75962 • RASD LIRT

Scanio Ellen • Librarian • Warminster Township Free Library • Warminster, PA 18974

Scank Janet M. • Head Librarian • Peabody Library • Columbia City, IN 46725 • PLA

Scanlon Donna L. • Lancaster County Library • Lancaster, PA 17602 • ALSC IFRT

Scanlon Joanne M. • Washington, DC 20016-2920

Scanlon Kathleen • Serials Librarian • La Guardia Community College • Long Island, NY 11101

Scanlon Kaval K. • Serials & Documents Coordinator • George Washington University Gelman Library • Washington, DC 20052

Scanlon Mary E. • Reference Librarian • West Islip Public Library • West Islip, NY 11795-3999

Scannell Henry F. • Reference Librarian II • Boston Public Library • Boston, MA 02117 • LITA RASD

Scannell Kristine M. • Reference Librarian • National Library of Medicine • Bethesda, MD 20894 • RASD

Scannell Mariann • Media Coordinator • Carver Public Schools • Carver, MA 02330 • AASL

Scarborough Ruth • Hackettstown, NJ 07840 • Continuing

Scarbrough S Jean • Librarian • Montague Area Public Schools • Montague, MI 49437 • AASL

Scarbrough William P. • Library Manager • Kirkland & Ellis • Los Angeles, CA 90071

Scardina Nancy • Westtown School • Westtown, PA 19395 • AASL

Scarinci Florence • Acquisition Librarian /Unit Head • Nassau Community College Library • Garden City, NY 11530

Scarlatelli Virginia • Director • Washington Township Free Public Library • Long Valley, NJ 07853 • PLA

Scarlett Richard A. • Senior Librarian • Hennepin County Library Southdale-Hennepin Area Library • Edina, MN 55435 • PLA RASD

Scarnecchia Sally A. • Director • University Microfilms International • Ann Arbor, MI 48106-1346 • ALCTS

Scarry Patricia A. • Marketing Manager • University of Chicago Press Journals Division • Chicago, IL 60637 • ALCTS

Scattergood Augusta R. • Ln • Kent Place School • Summit, NJ 07902-0308 • AASL

Scaun Anatole • Catawissa, PA 17820-9730 • ACRL

Scepanski Jordan M. • Dir, Lib & Learning Resources • California State University-Long Beach University Library & Learning Resources • Long Beach, CA 90840-1901 • ACRL LAMA IRRT

Schaad Gerrianne • Student • University of South Florida School of Library & Information Science • Tampa, FL 33620

Schaaf Robert W. • Senior Documents Specialist • Library of Congress • Washington, DC 20541 • ACRL RASD FLRT GODORT IRRT

Schaafsma Carol • Head,Serials Department • University of Hawaii Thomas Hale Hamilton Library • Honolulu, HI 96822 • ACRL ALCTS LITA

Schaafsma Roberta • Powder Springs, GA 30073 • ACRL

Schaap Jeanne • Des Plaines, IL 60016 • AASL

Schabel Donald J. • Assistant Director • Lexington Public Library • Lexington, KY 40507 • LAMA LITA PLA

Schaber Dale • Elementary Media Specialist • Franklin Elementary School • Appleton, WI 54911 • AASL

Schacher Betty C. • Director • Ridgefield Public Library • Ridgefield, NJ 07657 • LAMA PLA

Schacht John N. • Librarian • University of Iowa Libraries • Iowa City, IA 52242-1379 • ACRL LHRT LIRT

Schacht Katherine G. • Amigos Bibliographic Council • Dallas, TX 75251

Schacht Lenore A. • Director • Indian Prairie Public Library District • Willowbrook, IL 60517 • LAMA PLA

Schachter Judith S. • School Library Media Specialist • Lapham Elementary School • Madison, WI 53703 • AASL IFRT

Schachter June • Bibliographer/Reference Libn. • McGill University Libraries • Montreal PQ, H3A 1Y1 Canada • ACRL

Schachter Randi Michelle • Student • University of Rhode Island Graduate School of Library & Information Studies • Kingston, RI 02881-0815

Schad Jasper G. • Dean of Libraries • Wichita State University Ablah Library • Wichita, KS 67208 • ACRL ALCTS LAMA

Schade Barbara L. • LRC Director • Crowder College • Neosho, MO 64850 • ACRL

Schade Carolyn • ABC News • Washington, DC 20036 • RASD

Schader Freddy • Little Rock, AR 72207 • Continuing

Schadlich Thomas P. • Acting Director • Prosser Public Library • Bloomfield, CT 06002

Schadt Audrey • Salisbury State University Blackwell Library • Salisbury, MD 21801

Schadt Deborah L. • Kirkland, WA 98033

Schaefer Barbara • George Eastman House • Rochester, NY 14607 • ALCTS

Schaefer Betty • Reference Librarian • Dwight Foster Public Library • Fort Atkinson, WI 53538 • PLA

Schaefer Carol E. • Student • Saint John's University Division of Library & Information Science • Jamaica, NY 11439 • ALSC PLA

Schaefer Elizabeth K. • Elmwood Park, IL 60635-4224 • Continuing

Schaefer Joan G. • Technical Service Librarian • Barrington Public Library • Barrington, RI 02806

Schaefer Julie L. • Student • Wayne State University • Detroit, MI 48202 • PLA

Schaefer Karl R. • Student • University of Oklahoma School of Library & Information Studies • Norman, OK 73019

Schaefer Leslie C. • Assistant Librarian • Valparaiso University Law Library • Valparaiso, IN 46383 • ACRL GODORT NMRT

Schaefer Martin • Trustee • Schaumburg Township District Library • Schaumburg, IL 60194

Schaefer Patricia • Library Director • Muncie-Center Township Public Library • Muncie, IN 47305 • PLA

Schaefer Patricia D. • Librarian • Polytechnic School • Pasadena, CA 91106 • ALSC

Schaefer Steve W. • Director • Uncle Remus Regional Library System • Madison, GA 30650 • LAMA PLA

Schaefer Victor A. • Professor Emeritus • University of Notre Dame Libraries • Notre Dame, IN 46556 • ACRL ALCTS *Life*

Schaeffer-Hirsh Sheila • Wilmette, IL 60091 • AASL ALSC YALSA

Schaeffer Alice M. • New York, NY 10040 • AASL SRRT

Schaeffer Deanna M. • Library Media Specialist • Christa McAuliffe Elementary School • Woodbridge, VA 22193 • AASL

Schaeffer Deborah L. • Reference-Instructional Lib • California State University-Los Angeles John F. Kennedy Memorial Library • Los Angeles, CA 90032-8300 • ACRL LAMA RASD LIRT

Schaeffer Gretchen B. • Director LRC • Briar Cliff College Library • Sioux City, IA 51104-2100 • LITA

Schaeffer Robert L. • Vice President-Sales • R. R. Donnelley & Sons • Chicago, IL 60616

Schaer Martha • Director • Newton Public Library • Newton, IA 50208 • PLA

Schaetzel Thomson Mrs • University of Colorado Health Science Center, Denison Mem Lib • Denver, CO 80262 • ALCTS

Schaetzke Elizabeth A. • Rochester Public Library Wheatley Branch • Rochester, NY 14608

Schafer Diane M. • Head Librarian • Crystal Lake South High School • Crystal Lake, IL 60014 • AASL YALSA

Schafer Gerald J. • Coor. of Collection Develp • University of Colorado at Denver Auraria Library • Denver, CO 80204 • ALCTS LAMA RASD

Schafer Jessica • Special Services Librarian • Grand Rapids Public Library • Grand Rapids, MI 49503-3093 • ASCLA RASD

Schafer Judith M. • La Habra, CA 90631 • ALCTS

Schafer Patricia A. • Deputy Director, OLIN Library • Cornell University 213 Olin Library • Ithaca, NY 14853-5301 • ACRL LAMA

Schafer Patricia A. • Children's Librarian • Ventura County Library Services Agency Camarillo Library • Camarillo, CA 93010 • ALSC

Schaff Cynthia C. • Library Director • Williston Community Library • Williston, ND 58801

Schaffer Lynne F. • Smithsonian Institution Libraries National Air & Space Museum Library • Washington, DC 20560

Schaffner Amy G. • Dallas, TX 75214

Schaffner Ann C. • Science Library Assistant Dir • Brandeis University Gerstenzang Science Library • Waltham, MA 02254 • ACRL ALCTS LITA

Schaffner Bradley L. • University of Kansas Watson Library • Lawrence, KS 66045-2800 • ACRL

Schaffner Della • Librarian • Leola Public Library • Leola, SD 57456

Schaffner Jeanette K. • University of Pittsburgh • Pittsburgh, PA 15260 • ACRL RASD

Schaffner Judith • New York, NY 10034 • AASL IFRT SRRT

Schaffner Wendy A. • Student • Clarion University of Pennsylvania • Clarion, PA 16214 • PLA SRRT

Schafrick Anita M. • Student • University of South Carolina College of Library & Information Science • Columbia, SC 29208

Schaich Barbara E. • Head Audio-Visual Services • Troy Public Library • Troy, MI 48084 • PLA

Schaleger Paul C. • Student • University of Wisconsin-Milwaukee School of Library & Information Science • Milwaukee, WI 53201 • NMRT

Schalk-Greene Katherine • Gloucester County College Library Media Center • Sewell, NJ 08080 • LITA CLENE

Schall Jane A. • Maude Shunk Public Library • Menomonee Falls, WI 53051 • ALCTS

Schallert Ruth F. • Assistant Natural History Ln • Smithsonian Institution Libraries • Washington, DC 20560

Schalow John M T • Head of Cataloging Department • Northeastern University Libraries • Boston, MA 02115 • ACRL ALCTS LITA

Schamberg Giovanna C. • Los Angeles, CA 90064 • Continuing

Schambow Karen H. • Library Consultant • Follett Library Books Company • Crystal Lake, IL 60014 • AASL ALCTS ALSC

Schankman Lawrence H. • Reference Librarian • Valdosta State College Library • Valdosta, GA 31698-0001 • ACRL GODORT

Schano Donna J. • Librarian • Fox Chapel Area School District • Pittsburgh, PA 15238 • AASL

Schanot John B. • Student • University of North Texas School of Library & Information Sciences • Denton, TX 76203

Schantz Katherine Ruth • Orrville, OH 44667 • Continuing

Schanz Yvonne • Trustee • Livonia Public Library • Livonia, MI 48154-3045 • ALTA

Schaperkotter Dorothy L. • Saint Louis, MO 63118 • PLA RASD *Continuing*

Schapira Elyse • Librarian II • New York Public Library Public Relations Office • New York, NY 10018 • ACRL

Schapiro Benjamin H. • Customer Support Coordinator • NOTIS Systems, Inc. • Evanston, IL 60201-3622 • LITA LRRT

Schapiro Monte • Thesaurus Developer • U.S. Holocaust Memorial Museum Library • Washington, DC 20036-4907

Schaplowsky Alan • Books & Serials Acquisitions Hd • Columbia University Libraries Butler Library • New York, NY 10027 • ALCTS

Schappert Catherine • Coor., Automated & Tech Svs • Marywood College Library Learning Resources Center • Scranton, PA 18509

Schappert David G. • Director of Learning Resources • Luzerne County Community College Library • Nanticoke, PA 18634 • ACRL LAMA LITA LRRT

Schappert Linda G. • Director LRC/Library • University of New Mexico-Los Alamos • Los Alamos, NM 87544 • ACRL

Schara Rita M. • Lexington, KY 40503

Scharding Nancy N. • Elmore, OH 43416-0353 • YALSA

Scharf Davida • Director • Engineering Societies Library • New York, NY 10017 • ACRL ALCTS LAMA LITA

Scharf Margaret K. • Reference Librarian • University of Central Florida Library • Orlando, FL 32816-0666 • ACRL LAMA

Scharf Phyllis E. • Student • State University of New York at Albany School of Information Science & Policy • Albany, NY 12222 • AASL ALSC PLA EMIERT IFRT NMRT SRRT

Scharfenberg George E J • Whitewater, WI 53190

Scharniger Patricia A. • Aiken, SC 29803

Schatz Cindy A. • Harvard University Countway Library of Medicine • Boston, MA 02115 • ACRL LITA RASD LIRT

Schatz Martha M. • Director • Rutherford County Library • Spindale, NC 28160

Schatz Natalie M. • Director • Tufts University-Fletcher School of Law & Diplomacy • Medford, MA 02155-7082 • ACRL

Schau David A. • Branch Librarian • Kanawha County Public Library • Dunbar, WV 25064 • PLA

Schaub Theresa F. • Children's Librarian • Traverse Area District Library • Traverse City, MI 49684 • ALSC

Schaubman Debbi F. • Government Documents Library • Michigan State University Libraries • East Lansing, MI 48824-1048 • GODORT

Schauman Claudia • Public Library of Nashville and Davidson County • Nashville, TN 37203-3585 • PLA

Schaus Margaret C. • Reference Librarian II • Haverford College James P. Magill Library • Haverford, PA 19041 • ACRL

Schdel Mavis W. • Buffalo, NY 14216 • ACRL

Sche Josephine Yu • Associate Professor • Southern Connecticut State University School of Libray Science & Instructional Technology • New Haven, CT 06515 • ACRL ALCTS LITA

Schear Thomas W. • Passaic, NJ 07055

Schebora John C. • Broward County Division of Libraries Broward County Library • Fort Lauderdale, FL 33301 • SRRT

Schechter Ann Binder • Wynnewood, PA 19096

Schechter Frederick M. • La Mesa, CA 91941 • ALCTS

Schechter Gary • Brooklyn, NY 11215

Schechter Ilene R. • Reference Services Supervisor • Library of Michigan • Lansing, MI 48909

Schechter Janis O Driscoll • Coordinator of Children's Svs. • Santa Cruz City-County Library System • Santa Cruz, CA 95060 • ALSC YALSA IFRT

Schechter Roberta E. • Old Bridge, NJ 08857 • RASD

Scheck Gail I. • School Library Media Spec • Greenfield Middle School • Phoenix, AZ 85040 • AASL

Scheckter Stella J. • Concord, NH 03301

Schecter Lori • Executive Director • Laurel County Public Library • London, KY 40741 • LAMA IFRT

Scheel Marti • Librarian • United States Postal Services Library • Washington, DC 20260-1641 • LITA FLRT SRRT

Scheer Cheryl L. • Renton, WA 98055

Scheer John C. • Willard Public Library • Evansville, IN 47710

Scheer Malcolm E. • Library Director • New York School of Interior Design Library • New York, NY 10022 • ACRL ALCTS *Life*

Scheer William K. • Librarian III • Adams County Public Library Administration • Thornton, CO 80229 • PLA

Scheeren William • School Librarian • Hempfield Area Senior High School Library • Greensburg, PA 15601 • AASL

Scheetz George H. • Director • Champaign Public Library & Information Center • Champaign, IL 61820-5193 • LAMA PLA RASD LHRT

Scheffel Marie L. • Niagara-on-Lake ON, L0S 1J0 Canada • ACRL

Scheffer Ann H. • Librarian • Clearwater Public Library • Clearwater, FL 34623 • PLA

Scheffler Kay C. Mrs • Librarian • Salem Lutheran School Library • Gretna, LA 70053 • AASL

Scheffler Phyllis J. • Branch Manager • Newport Beach Public Library Balboa Branch • Balboa, CA 92661 • PLA

Scheib Charlene • Schuylkill Intermediate Unit 29 • Marlin, PA 17951 • AASL

Scheibe Margaret H. • Administrative Program Coor • College of Saint Scholastica Library • Duluth, MN 55811 • AASL

Scheiber Hazel A. • Lincoln, NE 68508 • Continuing

Scheid Alice B. • Venice, FL 33595 • Continuing

Scheidt Nancy • Children's Librarian • Fresno County Free Library • Fresno, CA 93721-2285

Schein Lorraine • Library Manager • Polytechnic University L.I. Campus Library • Farmingdale, NY 11735 • ACRL ALCTS

Scheines Patricia E. • Library Media Specialist • Tappan Zee High School • Orangeburg, NY 10962 • AASL IFRT

Schell Allan H. • Cataloger • University of Notre Dame Libraries • Notre Dame, IN 46556 • ALCTS

Schell Catherine • Earlton, FL 32631-0082

Schell Deborah Ann • Head Librarian • Chesaning Public Library • Chesaning, MI 48616

Schell Harold B. • Prof. Emeritus of Library Adm. • University of Cincinnati Central Library • Cincinnati, OH 45221-0033 • ACRL LAMA *Life*

Schell Irene I. • Woodbury, NJ 08096

Schell Joan B. • St. Petersburg Times • St. Petersburg, FL 33701 • RASD

Schell Kate M. • Senior Software Engineer • CLSI, Inc. • Newtonville, MA 02160 • LITA

Schell William H. • Director • Martin Memorial Library • York, PA 17401

Schellerup Patrica • Librarian • Bellarmine-Jefferson High School • Burbank, CA 91501

Schellhase Dorothy • Media Director • Westwood High School • Ishpeming, MI 49849

Schellhorn Mary • Director • Columbia College Library • Chicago, IL 60605 • ACRL LAMA LITA

Schellinger Merry B. • Minneapolis, MN 55406 • ACRL ALCTS LITA IRRT

Schenck William Z. • Falls Church, VA 22042 • ACRL ALCTS

Schendel Joy M. • Library Director • Lyon County Library • Yerington, NV 89447 • ALSC LAMA PLA CLENE LIRT

Schene Carol • Supervising Librarian K-8 • Taunton Public Schools • Taunton, MA 02780 • AASL

Schepis Frank J. III • Director • Kirkland Public Library • Kirkland, WA 98033

Schepis Sandra K. • Asst. Professor/Librarian • Westchester Community College • Valhalla, NY 10595

Schepmoes Rita • Librarian • L. E. Smoot Memorial Library • King George, VA 22485

Scheppke James B. • State Librarian • Oregon State Library • Salem, OR 97310-0640 • PLA

Scheps Susan • Children's Service • Shaker Heights Public Library Bertram Woods Branch • Shaker Hts., OH 44122 • ALSC PLA

Scher Rita S. • Readers Services Asst Director • East Tennessee State University Sherrod Library • Johnson City, TN 37614 • ACRL

Scheraga Miriam K. • Associate Librarian • Cornell University Library • Ithaca, NY 14853-5301 • ACRL

Scherb-Clift Marie • Los Angeles County Public Library Extention Services 900 • Lancaster, CA 93534

Scherba Sandra A. • Director • Cromaine Library • Hartland, MI 48353-0950 • LAMA PLA YALSA

Scherdin Mary Jane • Collection Access Librarian • University of Wisconsin Center for Health Sciences Library • Madison, WI 53706 • ACRL

Scherer-Holt Angela M. • Library Syustems Coordinator • Orange County Library System Orlando Public Library • Orlando, FL 32801-2471

Scherer Jeffrey A. • Partner • Meyer Scherer & Rockcastle Ltd. • Minneapolis, MN 55401 • LAMA PLA

Scherer Leslie C A • Director • Wallingford Public Library • Wallingford, CT 06492

Scherer Linda D. • Baltimore County Public Library • Towson, MD 21204

Scherger Louise M. SMD Sister • Student • Kent State University School of Library & Information Science • Kent, OH 44242-0001 • PLA

Scherma Ann H. • Supv., Publications Research • Faxon Company Inc. • Westwood, MA 02090 • ALCTS

Scherma Jan R. • System Administrator Cataloger • Seekonk Public Library • Seekonk, MA 02771 • PLA

Schermer Dora Miss • Holland, MI 49423 • Continuing

Schermerhorn Steve • Systems Librarian • Stockton-San Joaquin County Public Library • Stockton, CA 95202 • NMRT

Scherr Brenda M. • Business Information Specialist • Georgetown University Joseph Mark Lauinger Library • Washington, DC 20057-1006 • ACRL LAMA RASD

Scherr Jean W. • Columbus, OH 43221 • Continuing

Scherrei Rita A. • AUL- Admin. & Personnel • University of California-Los Angeles (UCLA) • Los Angeles, CA 90024-1450 • ACRL LAMA SRRT

Scherrer Peggy • Librarian • Boone Trail Elementary School • Wentzville, MO 63385

Scheschy Virginia M. • Asst. Director for Tech. Serv. • Marquette University Memorial Library • Milwaukee, WI 53233 • ACRL LITA

Scheu James W. • Plymouth, MN 55441-4834 • IFRT

Scheu Jean W. • Media Specialist • Pilgrim Lane Elementary School • Plymouth, MN 55441 • AASL IFRT

Scheu John M. • Librarian II • University of Missouri-Saint Louis • St. Louis, MO 63121-4499 • IFRT SRRT

Scheuermann Joan M. • Kenilworth, NJ 07033 • Continuing

Schiavone Dorothea A. • Suffern, NY 10901
Schick Carla J. • Reynoldsburg, OH 43068
Schick Lynne A. • Head of Youth Services • Ela Area Public Library District • Lake Zurich, IL 60047 • ALSC
Schick Wendy M. • Chief Librarian • Burlington Public Library • Burlington ON, L7R 1J4 Canada • PLA
Schickler Clairann G. • Serials Cataloger Grade 3 • University of Washington Suzzallo Library • Seattle, WA 98195 • ALCTS
Schieber Philip M. • Public Relations Director • OCLC Online Computer Library Center • Dublin, OH 43017-3395
Schieberl Yvonne • Montclair State College Harry Sprague Library • Upper Montclair, NJ 07043
Schiefelbein Daniel C. • Ocala, FL 32675-6706
Schiefer JoAnne Basar • Reference Librarian • Heidelberg College • Tiffin, OH 44883
Schieferstein Grace A. • Reading, PA 19601
Schiek Mary E. • Library Media Specialist • Utica Elementary Schools Utica City School District • Utica, NY 13501 • AASL
Schierling Ingrid • Head of Technical Services • University of Colorado At Colorado Springs Library • Colorado Springs, CO 80933-7150 • ACRL ALCTS LITA
Schiff Adam L. • Assoc. Librarian/User Services • California Academy of Sciences • San Francisco, CA 94118 • ACRL RASD SRRT
Schiff Margaret M. • Director • Garden City Library • Garden City, ID 83714-1429 • PLA IRRT
Schiff Nancy Buck • Outreach Coordinator • Central Rappahannock Regional Library Wallace Memorial Library • Fredericksburg, VA 22401
Schiffhauer Sharon M. • Library Budget Officer • State University of New York (SUNY) at Buffalo • Buffalo, NY 14260 • LAMA
Schiffhauer Truth H. • Newark, DE 19711 • ASCLA
Schild Betty • Children's Librarian • Lake Blackshear Regional Library • Americus, GA 31709
Schild F. D. PhD • Bakersfield, CA 93307 • AASL ACRL *Life*
Schild Marion • Brooklyn, NY 11201 • ALCTS *Continuing*
Schildhauer Edward W. • Student • Simmons College Graduate School of Library & Information Science • Boston, MA 02115 • LITA
Schilesman Megan J. • Student • University of Wisconsin School of Library & Information Studies • Madison, WI 53706 • PLA
Schiller Anita R. • La Jolla, CA 92037 • ACRL LITA RASD GODORT LRRT SRRT *Continuing*
Schiller Theoma J. • District Elementary Librarian • Alvord Unified School District • Riverside, CA 92505 • AASL
Schilling Raymond L. • Trustee • Maywood Public Library • Maywood, IL 60153 • ALTA
Schilling Sally B. • Federal Documents Librarian • University of Missouri Libraries-Columbia Elmer Ellis Library • Columbia, MO 65201-5149 • GODORT
Schilling William J. • Business Librarian • Albany Public Library • Albany, NY 12210 • RASD
Schiltz Katherine E. • Hd Ln • Timberland North Mason • Belfair, WA 98525 • PLA
Schimek Brigitte • Cataloger • York University Libraries • North York ON, M3J 1P3 Canada
Schimizzi Anthony J. • Cataloger • University of Alabama at Birmingham Mervyn H. Sterne Library • Birmingham, AL 35294-0014 • ALCTS
Schimizzi James A. J. • Pinon Unified School District #4 • Pinon, AZ 86510
Schimmel Louise S. • Librarian • Norfolk Library • Norfolk, CT 06058
Schimmelpfeng Richard H. • Storrs, CT 06268 • ACRL ALCTS
Schindler Dudy L. • Media Specialist/Librarian • Boonton High School Leslie Booth Library • Boonton, NJ 07005 • AASL
Schingeck Candace • Service Acquisitions Manager • University Microfilms International • Ann Arbor, MI 48106-1346 • ALCTS LITA
Schioldan Trine E. Ms. • Student • McGill University Graduate School of Library & Information Studies • Montreal PQ, H3A 1Y1 Canada • ALSC PLA
Schipper Rachel A. • Student • University of Maryland College of Library and Information Services • College Park, MD 20742-4345
Schipul Elizabeth V. • Periodicals Librarian • Incarnate Word College • San Antonio, TX 78209-9367 • NMRT
Schiraldi Francis • Reference Librarian • Massepequa Public Library • Massapequa, NY 11758
Schirmer Robert W. • Director • University of Findlay Shafer Library • Findlay, OH 45840 • ACRL LITA RASD
Schirtzinger Dorothy M. • Library Director • Lee County Library System • Fort Myers, FL 33901 • PLA
Schiwek Joseph A. Jr. • Librarian • Bassist College • Portland, OR 97201
Schizer Zevie B. • Trustee • Brooklyn Public Library • Brooklyn, NY 11238 • ALTA
Schlabach Martin L. • Information Literacy Specialist • Cornell University Albert R. Mann Library • Ithaca, NY 14853-4301 • ACRL LITA RASD
Schlabach Robert L. • Acquisitions/Gifts Librarian • George Mason University Fenwick Library • Fairfax, VA 22030
Schlachter Gail A. • President • Reference Services Press • San Carlos, CA 94070 • ACRL RASD EMIERT ILERT
Schlaeger Susan K. • Tustin, CA 92680
Schlaf Suzanne S. • Schaumburg Township District Library • Schaumburg, IL 60194 • PLA
Schlaff Donna • East Boston, MA 02128
Schlafly Thomas F. • Board President • Saint Louis Public Library • St. Louis, MO 63103-2389 • ALTA
Schlageter Barbara E. • Student • North Carolina Central University • Durham, NC 27707 • SRRT
Schlather Mary A. • Asst. Dir. Head of Children Serv • East Alton Public Library • East Alton, IL 62024 • ALSC PLA YALSA
Schlegel Wendy E. • Student • Saint Louis Public Library • St. Louis, MO 63103-2389 • ALCTS NMRT
Schleifer Harold B. • Director, University Library • California State Polytech University • Pomona, CA 91768 • ACRL
Schleifer James T. • Director • College of New Rochelle Gill Library • New Rochelle, NY 10805 • ACRL ALCTS LAMA RASD
Schlein Susan • School Librarian • Fort Bend Independent School District E A Jones Elementary School • Sugar Land, TX 77487 • AASL ALSC YALSA
Schlekau Linda C. • Upi Elementary School • Agana, GU 96910 • AASL YALSA
Schlesinger Daniel Mrs. • Trustee • Hammond Public Library • Hammond, IN 46320 • ALTA PLA
Schlesinger Deborah L. • Director • Lewis & Clark Library • Helena, MT 59601 • ALSC LAMA LITA PLA RASD
Schlesinger E. B. • Burbank, CA 91505 • Continuing
Schlesinger Frances C. • Documents Librarian • University of Massachusetts at Boston Joseph P. Healey Library • Boston, MA 02125-3393 • GODORT MAGERT
Schlesinger Kenneth • Student • Pratt Institute Library • Brooklyn, NY 11205
Schley Ruth • Cornwall, PA 17016 • Continuing
Schlichter Ashley R. • Student • University of Texas at Austin Graduate School of Library & Information Sciences • Austin, TX 78712-1276
Schlichter Marcus • Wayne State College U S Conn Library • Wayne, NE 68787 • ACRL ALCTS RASD
Schlichting Helen • Sac City, IA 50583 • AASL YALSA
Schlichting Mark • Designer Living Books • Broderbund Software • Novato, CA 94948-6121
Schlicker Susan L. • Head of Youth Services • South Holland Public Library • South Holland, IL 60473 • ALSC
Schlidt Barbara A. • Student • University of North Carolina Department of Library & Information Studies • Greensboro, NC 27412-5001 • AASL
Schlief Ruth J. • Librarian • Alhambra Traditional School • Phoenix, AZ 85019 • AASL
Schlimm Chrysostom V. Rev. • Director • Saint Vincent College & Archabbey Libraries • Latrobe, PA 15650-2690 • ACRL ALCTS
Schling Margret J. • Venice, CA 90291 • NMRT SRRT
Schlipf Frederick A. • Executive Director • Urbana Free Library • Urbana, IL 61801-3283 • LAMA PLA
Schlipf June P. • Cincinnati, OH 45224
Schlissel Betty K. • Librarian In Charge • Murray Bergtraum High School Library • New York, NY 10038
Schloegel Josephine • High School Librarian • Sacred Heart Academy • New Orleans, LA 70115 • AASL
Schloman Barbara F. • Head, Ref. & Inf. Servs Ln. • Kent State University Library • Kent, OH 44242 • ACRL RASD
Schlosser Catherine T. • Librarian • Louise S. McGehee School • New Orleans, LA 70130 • AASL
Schlosser Sue Ann • Library Director • White County Public Library System • Searcy, AR 72143 • PLA
Schlotter Theresa C. • Media Specialist • Power Middle School • Farmington Hills, MI 48335 • AASL
Schlotzhauer Vernon • Huntingdon, PA 16652 • ACRL
Schluckebier Carol J. • Librarian • Arthur Hill Senior High School • Saginaw, MI 48602 • AASL
Schlueter Kay • Director • Texas State Law Library • Austin, TX 78711 • RASD GODORT
Schlueter Kay C. • Northfield Falls, VT 05664 • RASD
Schlup Leonard • Akron, OH 44314
Schmader Janice E. • Pickerington, OH 43147
Schmalberg Aaron • Teacher • Miami University Acq Dept. • Oxford, OH 45056 • AASL
Schmalenberger J. • Library/Media Technician • Martin Elementary School • Santa Ana, CA 92707 • AASL ALSC
Schmalz Beverly J. • Madison, WI 53705-3566 • PLA
Schmalz Rochelle P. • Director of Library Services • Saint Mary's Hospital & Medical Center Medical Library • San Francisco, CA 94117
Schmeer David L. • Dayton, OH 45419
Schmeiser Edith • Librarian • Curtis High School • Staten Island, NY 10301 • AASL
Schmeling Victoria A. • Librarian • New York Public Library Branches Staten Island Borough Office • Staten Island, NY 10301 • YALSA
Schmelz-Keil Lynne M. • Librarian • Harvard University Tozzer Library • Cambridge, MA 02138 • ACRL
Schmelzer Beth W. • Student • University of Maryland College of Library and Information Services • College Park, MD 20742-4345 • AASL
Schmid Jean T. • Librarian • Salt Lake City Public Library • Salt Lake City, UT 84111 • ALSC PLA
Schmid Joycelyn H. • Reference Librarian • Austin College Abell Library • Sherman, TX 75090
Schmid Judith L. • Notre Dame High School for Boys Library • Niles, IL 60648 • AASL
Schmidlin Ann C. • Librarian-Fine Arts/AV • Tampa-Hillsborough County Public Library • Tampa, FL 33602
Schmidt A. Anne • Cataloger • Unified School District • Shawnee Mission, KS 66205 • AASL ALCTS
Schmidt Alesandra M. • Suffield, CT 06078 • ACRL
Schmidt Arline J. • Kings Park Elementary School • Springfield, VA 22151 • AASL
Schmidt Beatrix • Farmington, NM 87499
Schmidt Beth E. • Library Media Specialist • Colgate Elementary School • Baltimore, MD 21224 • AASL
Schmidt C. James • University Librarian • San Jose State University Clark Library • San Jose, CA 95192-0028 • ACRL ALCTS LAMA LITA RASD *Life*
Schmidt Carol K. • Librarian • Bullis School • Potomac, MD 20854 • AASL
Schmidt Carole Y. • Circulation/Reference Libn. • Moorhead State University Livingston Lord Library • Moorhead, MN 56563-2989 • ACRL
Schmidt Charles J. • Director • Middle Georgia Regional Library • Macon, GA 31201 • PLA
Schmidt Christine M. • Library Media Specialist • Hales Corners Elementary School • Hales Corners, WI 53130 • AASL
Schmidt Diane • Librarian • University of Illinois • Urbana, IL 61801 • ACRL
Schmidt Donna Cheryl • School Librarian/Teacher • Westview Elementary School C-6 • Neosho, MO 64850 • AASL
Schmidt Ford • Associate Librarian • Willamette University Mark O Hatfield Library • Salem, OR 97301 • ACRL
Schmidt Fred C. • Head of Government Document Dept • Colorado State University William E. Morgan Library • Fort Collins, CO 80523 • GODORT MAGERT
Schmidt Geri • Vail, CO 81657-5163
Schmidt Holly H. • Marc Consultant • Blackwell North America • Lake Oswego, OR 97034 • LITA YALSA
Schmidt Joanne M. • Asst Dir for Bibl. Servs. • Emerson College Library • Boston, MA 02116 • ACRL ALCTS LAMA LITA IFRT LIRT LRRT
Schmidt Judith • Librarian • Clague Middle School • Ann Arbor, MI 48105
Schmidt Kara • Student • San Jose State University Division of Library & Information Science • San Jose, CA 95192-0029
Schmidt Karen A. • Acquisitions Librarian • University of Illinois Library • Urbana, IL 61801 • ACRL ALCTS LITA LRRT
Schmidt Martha M. • Assistant City Librarian • Santa Clara Public Library • Santa Clara, CA 95051 • LAMA PLA IFRT
Schmidt Martha R. Miss • Huntington, WV 25702-9627 • ACRL ASCLA *Life*
Schmidt Mary Anne • Director • First Baptist Church Truett Library • Dallas, TX 75201
Schmidt Mary Jane • Director • Newburgh Free Library • Newburgh, NY 12550 • AASL ALCTS ALSC ALTA ASCLA LAMA LITA PLA RASD CLENE EMIERT ERT GODORT IFRT LIRT LRRT MAGERT SORT SRRT
Schmidt Mary M. • West Babylon Public Library • West Babylon, NY 11704
Schmidt Nancy J. • Librarian • Indiana University • Bloomington, IN 47405 • ACRL
Schmidt Oscar R. • South Lancaster, MA 01561
Schmidt Phyllis A. • Reference Librarian • Fort Hays State University Forsyth Library • Hays, KS 67601 • ACRL
Schmidt Rita Ann • Great Fls, MT 59401 • AASL IFRT
Schmidt Sallie • The Colony, TX 75056
Schmidt Sally L. • Colorado Springs, CO 80910

Schmidt Sandra L. • User Services Librarian • NOTIS Systems, Inc. • Evanston, IL 60201-3622 • ALCTS LITA ILERT

Schmidt Sharon A. • Librarian • Harcourt Brace Jovanovich • Orlando, FL 32821

Schmidt Sherrie • Dean of University Libraries • Arizona State University Hayden Library • Tempe, AZ 85287-1006 • ACRL ALCTS LITA

Schmidt Steven J. • Circulation/ILS Librarian • Indiana University-Purdue University at Indianapolis Library (IUPUI) • Indianapolis, IN 46202 • ACRL LRRT

Schmidt Susan H. • Business & Circulation Librarian • Loyola University • Chicago, IL 60611 • LAMA NMRT

Schmidt Susan K. • Branch Manager • Public Library of Annapolis & Anne Arundel County Severna Park Branch • Severna Park, MD 21146

Schmidt Susan M. • Student • Emporia State University Emporia in the Rockies • Denver, CO 80204

Schmidt Suzy • San Marino Toy & Book Shop • San Marino, CA 91108 • ALSC

Schmidt Ted • Director • Loveland Public Library • Loveland, CO 80537 • PLA

Schmidt Theresa B. • Glenwood Public Library • Glenwood, MN 56334

Schmidt Vincent P. • Santa Barbara, CA 93105 • ASCLA

Schmidtke David R. • Marshfield, WI 54449

Schmidtke Laurie • San Jose Public Library • San Jose, CA 95113

Schmidtke Sheila C. • Student • Drexel University College of Information Studies • Philadelphia, PA 19104-2875

Schmidtman Kathleen M. • Resource Librarian • Anchorage School District • Anchorage, AK 99502 • AASL ALSC IFRT

Schmidtmann Nancy K. • Library Media Specialist • East Meadow Public Schools George H. McVey School • East Meadow, NY 11554

Schmiedl Keith S. • President • Coutts Library Services • Lewiston, NY 14092-1797 • LITA

Schmierer Helen F. • Library Systems/Planning Analyst • Brown University Rockefeller Library • Providence, RI 02912 • ACRL ALCTS LITA

Schmierer Sandra J. • Student • Catholic University of America School of Library and Information Science • Washington, DC 20064 • AASL YALSA

Schmit Lynn B. • Library Director • Mahomet Township Public Library • Mahomet, IL 61853

Schmitt-Marsteller Jackie I. • Reference Librarian • Parkersburg & Wood County Public Library • Parkersburg, WV 26101

Schmitt Damaris A. • Reference Librarian • Saint Louis Community College at Meramec • St Louis, MO 63122 • ACRL

Schmitt John F. • Trustee • Suffolk Cooperative Library System • Bellport, NY 11713 • ALTA

Schmitt John P. • Reference Librarian • Colorado State University William E. Morgan Library • Fort Collins, CO 80523 • ACRL RASD

Schmitt Madelaine • Cataloger & Science Bibl • University of Wisconsin-Platteville Elton S. Karrmann Library • Platteville, WI 53818-3099 • SRRT

Schmitt Margaret S. • Library Director • Alsip-Merrionette Park Library District • Alsip, IL 60658 • PLA

Schmittel Barbara L. • Chicago, IL 60626

Schmittroth John Jr. • Director,New Publication Dev • Gale Research, Inc. • Detroit, MI 48226 • ACRL RASD

Schmitz Cecilia M. • Auburn University Ralph Brown Draughon Library • Auburn, AL 36849-5606 • ACRL ALCTS NMRT

Schmitz Eugenia E. Dr. • Grand Rapids, MI 49503 • ALCTS RASD   *Continuing*

Schmitz Kathleen M. • Columbia, MO 65203 • PLA

Schmitz Sandra M. • Librarian • Berkeley Public Library • Berkeley, CA 94704 • PLA

Schmitz Theresa M. • Bookseller • The Children's Bookshop • Brookline, MA 02146 • ALSC

Schmoll Donavon M. • Director • Wartburg College Engelbrecht Library • Waverly, IA 50677-9987 • ACRL

Schmottlach Beth A. • Children's Librarian • Flint Memorial Library • North Reading, MA 01864 • ALSC

Schmuch Joseph J. • Reading, MA 01867 • Continuing

Schmuckal Christine • Detroit Free Press Library • Detroit, MI 48226

Schmudde Jan E. • Northlake Public Library District • Melrose Park, IL 60164 • PLA

Schnabel Jerry • Media Director • Harmony Area Schools • Harmony, MN 55939 • AASL

Schnack Patricia E. • Iowa City, IA 52240

Schnaitter A. F. Ms • Santa Fe, NM 87505 • ACRL ALCTS   *Life*

Schnapf Susan E. • Librarian • Brooklyn Public Library Brooklyn Heights Branch • Brooklyn, NY 11201

Schnare Mary Kay W. • Student • University of Rhode Island Graduate School of Library & Information Studies • Kingston, RI 02881-0815 • AASL ALSC

Schnare Robert E. • Director • United States Naval War College Library • Newport, RI 02841 • ACRL ALCTS LAMA LITA RASD AFLRT FLRT GODORT MAGERT

Schneberger Lois I. • Original Catlg & Spec Lang Ln • Arizona State University Libraries • Tempe, AZ 85287-1006 • ACRL ALCTS LAMA LITA

Schneck Steven M. • Englewood, CO 80151-0362 • IFRT

Schneeweis Joseph E. • Student • Louisiana State University School of Library & Information Science • Baton Rouge, LA 70803-3290 • NMRT

Schnegg Sally A. • Project Manager • Getty Center Resources Collections • Santa Monica, CA 90401 • ALCTS

Schneider Alys E. • Des Plaines, IL 60016 • PLA RASD

Schneider Anne M. • Director of Reader Services • South Carolina State Library • Columbia, SC 29211

Schneider Annella M. • Student • Texas Woman's University School of Library & Information Studies • Denton, TX 76204 • AASL ALSC

Schneider D. W. • Associate Dean • Louisiana State University Libraries Middleton Library • Baton Rouge, LA 70803-3342 • ACRL LAMA

Schneider Denise Mortensen • East Troy, WI 53120 • RASD

Schneider Elizabeth • Asst Dir for Clln/Sys Mgmt • Massachusetts General Hospital Treadwell Library • Boston, MA 02114 • ACRL LITA

Schneider Evelyn J. • Louisville, KY 40205 • ACRL LAMA   *Continuing*

Schneider Evelyn Ruth Sr. • Bowling Green, OH 43402-3448 • AASL

Schneider Francisca • Librarian • Berkeley Public Library North Branch • Berkeley, CA 94707

Schneider Hennie R. • Rockville, MD 20852-4753 • Continuing

Schneider Holle E. • Hollins College • Hollins, VA 24020

Schneider Jacqueline D. • Asstistant Director of the Libr. • Davis & Elkins College Library • Elkins, WV 26241

Schneider Jan • Ed. Consultant • SOITA • Franklin, OH 45324 • AASL

Schneider Janet M. • Schoolcraft College Library • Livonia, MI 48152-2696 • GODORT

Schneider Jayne B. • School Librarian • Lassiter Middle School • Louisville, KY 40214 • AASL

Schneider Joan C. • Director • Southeastern Connecticut Library Association • Groton, CT 06340-6097 • ASCLA LITA AFLRT

Schneider Judith A. • Cataloger/Serials Librarian • U. S. General Accounting Office • Washington, DC 20548

Schneider Julia T. • Director • Missouri Western State College Hearnes Learning Resources Center • Saint Joseph, MO 64507 • ACRL

Schneider Karen G. • Student • University of Illinois Graduate School of Library and Information Science • Urbana, IL 61801 • ALSC PLA YALSA IFRT SRRT

Schneider Lois E. • Coor of Instructional Services • Queens College Benjamin S. Rosenthal Library • Flushing, NY 11367-0904 • ACRL LIRT

Schneider Marcia G. • Community Relations Librarian • San Francisco Public Library • San Francisco, CA 94102 • LAMA PLA

Schneider Rose Ellen • River Valley High School • Spring Green, WI 53588 • AASL ALSC YALSA

Schneider Stewart P. • Faculty • University of Rhode Island Graduate School of Library & Information Studies • Kingston, RI 02881-0815 • GODORT

Schneider Susan J. • Washington, DC 20008

Schneider Ted M. • Orwigsburg, PA 17961

Schneiderman Lynn A. • Student • Creighton University Reinert-Alumni Memorial Library • Omaha, NE 68178 • SRRT

Schneier Alfred Jr • Trustee • Denville Free Public Library • Denville, NJ 07834

Schneiter Thomas E. • Access Services • Indiana University • Bloomington, IN 47405 • ACRL

Schnelle Cindy • Hoxie High School • Hoxie, KS 67740 • AASL

Schneller William D. • New Bedford Free Public Library • New Bedford, MA 02740

Schnoor Craig • Trustee • Rockford Public Library • Rockford, IL 61101-1061 • ALTA

Schnuttgen Hildegard • Head Reference Librarian • Youngstown State University William F. Maag Library • Youngstown, OH 44555 • ACRL

Schober Mary E. Mrs • Branch Librarian • Lorain Public Library Sheffield Lake-Domonkas Branch • Sheffield Lake, OH 44054 • PLA

Schober Trudy J. • Wayne, IL 60184

Schobernd Elizbeth M. • Normal, IL 61761

Schoch Lavonne L. • Librarian • Wrightwood Elementary • Wrightwood, CA 92397 • ALSC

Schoch Marjorie R. • Asst. Director Emeritus • University of Indianapolis Krannert Memorial Library • Indianapolis, IN 46227 • AASL RASD   *Life*

Schock Richard G. • Librarian • Moody Bible Institute Library • Chicago, IL 60610 • ACRL ALCTS RASD LRRT

Schock Theo Mrs • Children's Librarian • Stanislaus County Free Library • Modesto, CA 95354 • IFRT

Schockmel Richard B. • Collection Development Librarian • Utah State University Merrill Library • Logan, UT 84322-3000 • ACRL

Schoeler-Urch Diane • Assistant Director Tech. Serv. • University of Wisconsin • Oshkosh, WI 54901 • ACRL ALCTS LAMA LITA

Schoen David M • Reference Librarian • Niagara University Library • Niagara University, NY 14109

Schoen Dena J. • Slavic Catalog Librarian • Hoover Institution on War, Revolution & Peace Library • Stanford, CA 94305-6010 • ACRL

Schoen Kenneth N • Manager • Kenneth Schoen Bookseller • Eastampton, MA 01027

Schoenblum Lynne • Children's Librarian • Yonkers Public Library • Yonkers, NY 10701

Schoenbrun Cyndi • Philadelphia, PA 19151

Schoeneman Lori S. • Charlotte, NC 28269 • AASL PLA

Schoenfield Patty • Cartersville, GA 30120

Schoenhaar Cheryl A. • Asst. Professor/BR Librarian • University of Wisconsin-Superior Jim Dan Hill Library • Superior, WI 54880 • ACRL IFRT LIRT

Schoenhardt Richard E. • Simsbury, CT 06070

Schoenly Richard D. • Student • University of Pittsburgh School of Library and Information Science • Pittsburgh, PA 15260

Schoenrock Victoria Jean • Youth Services Librarian • Waukegan Public Library • Waukegan, IL 60085

Schoenthal Carla S. • Marin County Free Library Novato Branch • Novato, CA 94947

Schoenung James G. • President • Library Technologies, Inc. • Abington, PA 19001

Schofer Yvonne • Humanities Bibliographer • University of Wisconsin-Madison Memorial Library • Madison, WI 53706 • ACRL

Schofield Edward T. Dr • Chapel Hill, NC 27514 • Continuing

Schofield Pamela W. • Legislative Reference Librarian • State Library of Massachusetts • Boston, MA 02133

Schofield Ruth A. • Quality Control Analyst • University Microfilms International • Ann Arbor, MI 48106-1346 • LITA RASD NMRT

Schofield Tammy J. • Student • University of Alabama School of Library & Information Studies • Tuscaloosa, AL 35487-0252 • IFRT SRRT

Scholl Lisa M. • Reference/Program Librarian • Illinois Regional Library for The Blind & Physically Handicapped • Chicago, IL 60608 • ASCLA

Scholten Frances • Frederick, MD 21701 • YALSA   *Life*

Scholtz James C. • Rockford, IL 61109-2534 • VRT

Scholtz Mary P. • CCE Academic Support • Embry-Riddle Aeronautical University • Daytona Beach, FL 32114 • ACRL LITA IFRT

Scholz Ann Margaret • Racine, WI 53403

Schomberg Janie R. • Media Specialist • Leal School • Urbana, IL 61801 • AASL ALSC

Schomer Charles D. • Media Specialist • Seminole High School • Sanford, FL 32771

Schomp Katherine W. • Trustee • Denver Public Library • Denver, CO 80204-2602 • ALTA PLA

Schon Isabel • Professor-Director • California State University San Marcos • San Marcos, CA 92069-0001 • AASL

Schonbrun Michael • Trustee • Boulder Public Library • Boulder, CO 80306

Schondelmayer Barbara K. • Hastings Public Library • Hastings, MI 49058

Schone Christine A. • Saint Charles Borromeo Seminary Ryan Memorial Library • Overbrook, PA 19096-3012 • ALCTS

Schoneman Ruth E. Miss • Chicago, IL 60637 • ACRL ALCTS   *Life*

Schoolfield D B. • Research Department Cataloger • Mobil Research & Development Corp. • Dallas, TX 75381 • ALCTS MAGERT

Schoon Marion • Head Reference Division • Harvard College Library Widener Memorial Library • Cambridge, MA 02138 • ACRL

Schoonmaker Dina B. • Head, Special Clln & Presv. • Oberlin College Library • Oberlin, OH 44074 • ACRL ALCTS

Schoonmaker Nancy E. • Director of Marketing • Gaylord Brothers • Syracuse, NY 13221

Schoonover Mary Jo • Oconomowoc Junior High School Library Media Center • Oconomowoc, WI 53066 • AASL

Schopp Lily K. • Hemet, CA 92343 • PLA RASD   *Continuing*

Schor Abby R. • Collection Development Librarian • Evanston Public Library • Evanston, IL 60201 • RASD

Schormann M T. Mrs • De Kalb, IL 60115 • ALSC YALSA   *Life*

Schormann Victor • Gifts and Exchange Librarian • Northern Illinois University University Libraries • DeKalb, IL 60115-2868 • ACRL ALCTS LAMA LITA RASD   *Life*

Schorr Steven G. • Trustee • Las Vegas-Clark County Library District Flamingo Library • Las Vegas, NV 89119 • ALTA

Schorrig Claudia • Boca Raton, FL 33432

Schott Faye-Ann • Library of Congress • Washington, DC 20541 • IRRT

Schott Ken • Librarian • University of Nevada-Las Vegas James R. Dickinson Library • Las Vegas, NV 89154 • RASD GODORT

Schott Michael • Trustee • San Antonio Public Library • San Antonio, TX 78205

Schottlaender Brian E. • Asst. Univ. Ln. for Tech. Serv. • UCLA Library University Research Library • Los Angeles, CA 90024-1575 • ALCTS LITA   *Life*

Schrader Aileen R. • Newport Beach, CA 92660 • ALTA PLA

Schrader Alvin M. • Associate Professor • University of Alberta • Edmonton, AB T6G 2J4 Canada • IFRT

Schrader Martha N. • Canby, OR 97013 • AASL

Schrader Mary E. • Oakland, CA 94619 • AI SC

Schrader Susan I. • Coordinator of Reference • Heartland Area Education Agency • Johnston, IA 50131-1603 • AASL LITA

Schrag Dwayne D. • Central Library Reference Head • University of Texas at Arlington • Arlington, TX 76019-0497 • ACRL RASD

Schrag Sandra K. • Texas Christian University Mary Couts Burnett Library • Fort Worth, TX 76129

Schrager Carole • Richmond Hill Public School #62 • Richmond Hill, NY 11419 • AASL

Schram Judy • Library Media Specialist • Lamphere High School • Madison Heights, MI 48071 • AASL

Schramm Daniel I. • Fort Wayne, IN 46807

Schramm Mary M. • Part-time Reference • Northbrook Public Library • Northbrook, IL 60062

Schraner Frank D. • Student • Wayne State University Library Science Program • Detroit, MI 48202

Schrank H. Paul Jr • Raleigh, NC 27614

Schraufnagel Nancy E. • Reference Librarian • Wisconsin Reference & Loan Library • Madison, WI 53716 • ACRL

Schraut Debra • Catalog Librarian • Missouri Historical Society • Saint Louis, MO 63112-0040

Schreck Susan Brill • Trustee • Skokie Public Library • Skokie, IL 60077-3680 • ALTA PLA

Schreffler Lynne W. • Eastern Lancaster County School District • New Holland, PA 17557-0609

Schreiber June P. • West Nyack Free Library • West Nyack, NY 10994 • PLA

Schreiber Mae N. • University of Akron Bierce Library • Akron, OH 44325-1706

Schreiber Meredith • Powell's Books • Portland, OR 97209

Schreiber Robert Edwin • Kingston, IL 60145

Schreier Rose • Juneau, AK 99802

Schreiner Elke M. • Children's Librarian • Orange County Public Library La Habra Branch • La Habra, CA 90631 • ALSC

Schreiner Leo W. • New York Public Library Branches Staten Island Borough Office • Staten Island, NY 10301 • YALSA

Schremser Donna Barrett • Director • Huntsville-Madison County Public Library • Huntsville, AL 35804 • LAMA PLA

Schremser Robert F. • Huntsville, AL 35801 • ASCLA PLA EMIERT LHRT

Schreyer Alice D. • Curator of Special Collections • University of Chicago Library • Chicago, IL 60637-1502 • ACRL LHRT

Schriek Robert W. • Reference Librarian • Rutgers the State University Justice Henry Ackerson Law Library • Newark, NJ 07102 • ACRL

Schrift Leonard B. • President • Ballen Booksellers Intl Inc • Hauppauge, NY 11788 • ACRL ALCTS LITA ERT

Schrimmer Jean A. • Librarian I • Art Institute of South California • Laguna Beach, CA 92651

Schritter Linda S. • College of Saint Mary • Omaha, NE 68124 • RASD FLRT LIRT

Schrock Kathleen Beck • Librarian • Cape Cod Museum of Natural History • Brewster, MA 02631

Schrock Nancy Carlson • Winchester, MA 01890 • ALCTS

Schrodt Paul • United Theological Seminary • Dayton, OH 45406 • ACRL IFRT

Schroeder Alan T. • Student • University of California Los Angeles Graduate School of Library & Information Science • Los Angeles, CA 90024

Schroeder Anne-Marie • Bibliographer • Encyclopaedia Britannica • Chicago, IL 60604

Schroeder Beverly • Sales Representative • Quality Books Inc. • Lake Bluff, IL 60044-2204

Schroeder Carol • Reference Librarian • Adelphi University Swirbul Library • Garden City, NY 11530 • RASD

Schroeder Edwin C. • Rare Book Team/Proc. Serv. Dept. • Yale University Sterling Memorial Library • New Haven, CT 06520 • ACRL

Schroeder Edwin M. • Director • Florida State University Law Library • Tallahassee, FL 32306-1034 • ACRL ALCTS LITA RASD GODORT

Schroeder Eileen E. • State College, PA 16801-5222 • ACRL

Schroeder Eunice M. • Student • Emporia State University School of Library & Information Management • Emporia, KS 66801 • PLA

Schroeder Jan K. • Director • Duluth Public Library • Duluth, MN 55802 • LAMA PLA

Schroeder Jean S. • Teacher • Unified School District • Tucson, AZ 85717-0400 • ALSC

Schroeder Judy L. • Medical Librarian • Sharon Regional Health System • Sharon, PA 16146

Schroeder Linda E. • Librarian • Thorne Middle School • Port Monmouth, NJ 07758 • AASL

Schroeder Marilyn D. • Head of Acquistions • Georgetown University Law Center Edward Bennett Williams Library • Washington, DC 20001-1417 • LAMA

Schroeder Penelope Mrs. • Librarian • Saint James Episcopal School • Los Angeles, CA 90005 • AASL

Schroeder Randall L. • Reference Librarian • Augustana College Library • Rock Island, IL 61201

Schroeder Rianne L. • Librarian I • Lincoln City Libraries • Lincoln, NE 68508

Schroeder Susan • Dunckel Middle School • Farmington Hills, MI 48009 • AASL

Schroer Craig B. • Student • University of Texas at Austin Graduate School of Library & Information Sciences • Austin, TX 78712-1276 • RASD NMRT

Schroer Muffet S. • Technology Librarian • Glenview Public Library • Glenview, IL 60025 • ALCTS LITA

Schroether Marian Ruth • Waukegan, IL 60087 • ALSC
                                                                    Continuing

Schroth Angela • Library Manager • Washington County Library Lake Elmo Branch • Lake Elmo, MN 55042

Schroth Margaret B. • Hd, Reference & Bibliography • State Library of Louisiana • Baton Rouge, LA 70821-0131 • RASD IFRT

Schroyer Helen Q. • Head of Special Collections • Purdue University Libraries • West Lafayette, IN 47907-1530 • ACRL

Schryba William K. • Matko Company • Mountainside, NJ 07092

Schual Nora • Director • Amityville Public Library • Amityville, NY 11701 • LAMA PLA

Schub Helen Sue • Reference Librarian • New York University Elmer Holmes Bobst Library • New York, NY 10012 • ACRL IRRT LIRT

Schubel Maura Dolan • Woodbridge, VA 22192

Schubert-Davis Roselinde V. • Director of Special Services • Rolling Meadows Library • Rolling Meadows, IL 60008 • PLA IFRT

Schubert Irene K. • Head, Reference Section • Library of Congress • Washington, DC 20541 • LITA RASD FLRT

Schubert Leda • Vermont Department of Education • Montpelier, VT 05602 • AASL ALSC

Schubert Lucia J. • Mercer Island High School • Mercer Island, WA 98040 • AASL

Schubert Patricia S. • Student • Selby Public Library • Sarasota, FL 33577 • LITA PLA RASD IFRT

Schuck Alan H. • Librarian • Arizona State University-West Fletcher Library • Phoenix, AZ 85069-7100

Schuck Brian R. • Asst. Librarian, Reference • Indiana University at South Bend Franklin D. Schurz Library • South Bend, IN 46634 • LITA

Schuckel Sally • Librarian • Kellogg Community College Learning Resource Center • Battle Creek, MI 49017-3397 • ACRL LITA RASD

Schuckett Sandy • School Librarian • Eastman Avenue School Library • Los Angeles, CA 90023 • AASL ALSC

Schudel Cheryl L. • Middletown, OH 45044 • AASL IFRT SRRT

Schuessler Jane C. • Cataloging Manager • Multnomah County Library • Portland, OR 97212 • ALCTS

Schuettich Patricia • Librarian • Saint John's University Library • Jamaica, NY 11439 • ACRL

Schuetze-Coburn Marje K. • Los Angeles, CA 90066 • ACRL

Schuh Judith Weese • Media Specialist • Ramstein Jr High School Library Media Center • APO, AE 09094 • AASL

Schuhl Edith S. • Library Media Specialist • Hartford Board of Education • Hartford, CT 06106 • AASL

Schuitema Joan E. • Music Technical Servs. Librarian • Northwestern University Library • Evanston, IL 60208-2300 • LITA

Schule Diane P. • Head Librarian • Paul VI High School • Fairfax, VA 22030 • AASL YALSA

Schule K. Lynn • Baltimore County Public Library • Towson, MD 21204 • LAMA PLA

Schuler Carolyn • Children's Service Consultant • Monroe County Library System • Rochester, NY 14604 • ALSC PLA

Schull Diantha D. • Executive Director • French-American Foundation • New York, NY 10014 • PLA EMIERT ERT IRRT

Schuller Carla N V • Director • San Benito Public Library • San Benito, TX 78586 • ALSC LAMA PLA

Schuller Kathleen M. • Public Service Manager • Washington County Library • Woodbury, MN 55125 • PLA

Schuller Ruta • Racine, WI 53402 • ACRL

Schulman Donna L. • Librarian • Cornell University (ILR) Lenz Library • New York, NY 10010 • ACRL RASD SORT SRRT

Schulman Rhonda • Part-time Librarian • Great Neck Library • Great Neck, NY 11024

Schulman Sylvia Wolf • Librarian • Westport Public Library • Westport, CT 06880 • PLA RASD LIRT

Schulte-Albert H. G. Dr. • Associate Professor • University of Western Ontario • London ON, N6G 1H1 Canada • ALCTS EMIERT LHRT

Schulte Marilyn J. • Grapevine, TX 76051 • LITA PLA

Schulte Stephanie L. • Head of Adult Services • Cedar Rapids Public Library • Cedar Rapids, IA 52401 • RASD

Schultheis Constance • Cleveland Heights, OH 44121

Schultheiss L. A. • La Grange, IL 60525

Schultz Alison J. • Middle School Librarian • Robidoux Middle School • St. Joseph, MO 64505

Schultz Barbara • Plummer-Worley Joint School District • Plummer, ID 83851

Schultz Carole L. • Director, Library Services • Central Piedmont Cmnty College Library • Charlotte, NC 28235 • ACRL LAMA

Schultz Cathern Joan • Librarian • East High School • Madison, WI 53704 • AASL

Schultz Dorothy M. • Elem. School Library-Teacher • Cloud Elementary School USD #59 • Wichita, KS 67204 • AASL

Schultz Elizabeth J. • Trustee • Anaheim Public Library • Anaheim, CA 92805 • ALTA

Schultz Gail • Trustee • Oregon State Library • Salem, OR 97310-0640 • ALTA

Schultz Gary J. • Director • Fargo Public Library • Fargo, ND 58102 • LAMA PLA

Schultz Katharine • Head Librarian • College Preparatory School • Oakland, CA 94618

Schultz Kim E. • Central Michigan University • Troy, MI 48084 • ACRL

Schultz Linda A. • Children's Librarian • Parlin-Ingersoll Library • Canton, IL 61520

Schultz Lois B. • Suburban Library System • Burr Ridge, IL 60521 • AASL ALSC PLA

Schultz Lois M. • Head of Technical Services • Northern Kentucky University Steely Library • Highland Heights, KY 41099-6101 • ACRL ALCTS

Schultz Ruth D. • Assistant Director • American Dental Association Bureau of Library Services • Chicago, IL 60611

Schultz Susan N. • Student • Emporia State University School of Library & Information Management • Emporia, KS 66801 • PLA YALSA EMIERT IFRT

Schultz Susan Walker • Wallingford, CT 06492

Schultz Sydney O. • Clearwater, FL 34616

Schultz Virginia G. • Student • San Jose State University Division of Library & Information Science • San Jose, CA 95192-0029

Schultze Salvatrice G. • Coordinator of Children's Serv • Hartford Public Library • Hartford, CT 06103-3003 • ALSC

Schulz Catherine • Director • North Shore Library • Glendale, WI 53217 • LAMA PLA

Schulz Clair A. Mr • Librarian • Tir-County Area School District • Plainfield, WI 54966

Schulz Elizabeth L. • Children's Librarian • Boston Public Library • Boston, MA 02117

Schulz Kathleen M • Humanities Librarian • Wittenberg University Thomas Library • Springfield, OH 45501 • ACRL LIRT

Schulz Mike • Library Director • Western Montana College Lucy Carson Library • Dillon, MT 59725 • AASL ACRL RASD

Schulz Richard J. • Assoc. Librarian Tech. Servs. • Princeton University • Princeton, NJ 08544-2098

Schulz Stanley D. • Library Director • Kilgore Memorial Library • York, NE 68467 • PLA
Schulz Ursula • University of Rochester Rhees Library • Rochester, NY 14627-0055 • ALCTS LITA
Schulze Anita Inskip • East Berlin, PA 17316 • Continuing
Schulze Mildred • Cincinnati, OH 45224 • Continuing
Schulzetenberg A. C. Dr. • Professor Emeritus • Saint Cloud State University Centennial Hall LRC • St. Cloud, MN 56301-4498 • AASL ACRL *Life*
Schumacher Andrea • Hampton, NH 03842 • PLA
Schumacher Barbara R. • Reference Librarian • Broward County Division of Libraries Broward County Library • Fort Lauderdale, FL 33301
Schumacher Claudia A. • Reference Department , Head • Stratford Library Association • Stratford, CT 06497 • RASD
Schumacher Mark • University of North Carolina Walter Clinton Jackson Library • Greensboro, NC 27412-5201
Schumacher Mary J. • Wichita, KS 67207 • AASL
Schumacher Mary M. • Children's Librarian • Middle Country Public Library • Centereach, NY 11720 • ALSC PLA
Schuman Patricia Glass • President • Neal-Schuman Publishers, Inc. • New York, NY 10013 • AASL ACRL ALCTS ALSC LAMA LITA PLA RASD GODORT IFRT SRRT
Schumann Linda B. • Media Specialist • Northeastern Local School District • Springfield, OH 45502 • AASL
Schumann Robert E. • Trustee • Lake County Public Library • Merrillville, IN 46410-5382 • ALTA
Schumm Robert W. • Denton, TX 76201
Schuneman Anita • Monographic Cataloger • University of Colorado Norlin Library • Boulder, CO 80309-0184 • ACRL ALCTS
Schur Barbara S. • Venice, FL 34285
Schurter James L. • Dean of Academic Support Prog. • University of Wisconsin-Stevens Point Albertson Learning Resource Center • Stevens Point, WI 54481 • LAMA
Schuster Bonnie • System Administrator • University of Montana Library • Missoula, MT 59812 • ACRL LITA
Schuster David • Student • Missouri University School of Library Science • Columbia, MO 65211
Schuster Janice G. • Head of Public Services • Providence College Phillips Memorial Library • Providence, RI 02918 • GODORT
Schuster Lois • Bedford, MA 01730
Schusterich Jo Ann M. • Outreach Librarian • Elmhurst Public Library • Elmhurst, IL 60126
Schut Grace • Director • Saint Peter's College Theresa & Edward O'Toole Library • Jersey City, NJ 07306 • ACRL ALCTS LITA RASD
Schutt Dedre A. • Williamsville, NY 14221 • ALCTS
Schverak Frankie V. • System Coordinator/Cataloger • United States Air Force Wright Labotatory Technical Library • WPAFB, OH 45433-6523 • ALCTS LITA AFLRT FLRT
Schwab Jean Solin • Cupertino, CA 95014
Schwab Linda J. • Elmhurst Public Library • Elmhurst, IL 60126
Schwab Ruth S. • Education & Job Inf Ctr Ln • Ossining Public Library • Ossining, NY 10562 • PLA
Schwabacher Betty C. • San Francisco, CA 94116 • ALSC
Schwadron Marlene • East Williston, NY 11596 • AASL YALSA
Schwager Emanuel • Montgomery County Community College Learning Resource Center • Blue Bell, PA 19422-0758
Schwahn Caron • Literacy Coordinator • Las Vegas-Clark County Library District Las Vegas Library • Las Vegas, NV 89101
Schwalbe Marietta • Saint Louis, MO 63129 • AASL LITA NMRT
Schwalen Wayne • Trustee • Rockford Public Library • Rockford, IL 61101-1061 • ALTA
Schwalm Wynette D. • Branch Manager • Fort Worth Public Library Meadowbrook Branch • Fort Worth, TX 76112
Schwamberger Jane M. • Santa Cruz, CA 95061-7646 • PLA IFRT
Schwanz Kathleen A. • Seattle, WA 98102-4969
Schwark Suzanne C. • Librarian • Lompoc High School • Lompoc, CA 93436 • AASL
Schwartz Ada E. Miss • Boonsboro, MD 21713 • LAMA PLA *Life*
Schwartz Allen D. • Library Services Director • Santa Fe Public Library • Santa Fe, NM 87501 • LAMA PLA
Schwartz Amy J. • Technical Services Librarian • Peoria Public Library • Peoria, IL 61602
Schwartz Barbara L. • Non-Salaried Librarian • Pratt Institute Graduate School of Library & Information Science • Brooklyn, NY 11205
Schwartz Barbara R. • Costa Mesa Library • Costa Mesa, CA 92627 • ALSC PLA YALSA
Schwartz Charles A. • Social Sciences Bibliographer • Rice University Fondren Library • Houston, TX 77251-1892 • ACRL LRRT
Schwartz Diane • Media Specialist • Hindley School • Darien, CT 06820 • AASL
Schwartz Diane • Bergenfield, NJ 07621 • AASL
Schwartz Elisheva • Preservation Cataloging Supv. • State University of New York College at Buffalo, E. H. Butler Library • Buffalo, NY 14222-1095 • ALCTS
Schwartz Frederick E. • Manager, EDI Dept. • Faxon Company Inc. • Westwood, MA 02090 • ALCTS LITA
Schwartz Hannah Y. • Children's Book Store Owner • Children's Book World • Haverford, PA 19041 • ALSC
Schwartz Helen F. • Philadelphia, PA 19149 • AASL ALCTS ALSC
Schwartz Irving L. • Trustee • Dayton & Montgomery County Public Library • Dayton, OH 45402-2103 • ALTA
Schwartz Lawrence S. • Theatre/Film Librarian • Southern Methodist University • Dallas, TX 75275 • ACRL ALCTS IFRT LIRT
Schwartz Lynda • Librarian • Porter Junior High School • Granada Hills, CA 91344 • AASL
Schwartz Marla J. • Chief, Acq. & Serials Dept. • Washington College of Law Library • Washington, DC 20016 • ALCTS LITA
Schwartz Martin J. • Librarian • United States Department of Justice Criminal Division Library • Washington, DC 20531
Schwartz Mary B. • Reference Librarian • University of Baltimore Langsdale Library • Baltimore, MD 21201 • ACRL RASD
Schwartz Modest • Trustee • Alhambra Public Library • Alhambra, CA 91801
Schwartz Nancy E. • Director Advertising & Promoton • H. W. Wilson Company • Bronx, NY 10452 • RASD ERT
Schwartz Patricia Sister • Librarian • Saint Hugh School • Miami, FL 33133
Schwartz Philip J. • Educational Librarian • University of Texas Libraries General Libraries • Austin, TX 78713-7330
Schwartz Raymond P. • National Library of Medicine • Bethesda, MD 20894
Schwartz Renee • Assistant to the University Ln. • University of Illinois at Chicago University Library • Chicago, IL 60680 • ACRL LAMA IFRT SRRT
Schwartz Renee • Media Specialist • School Board of Broward County Learning Resources Department • Fort Lauderdale, FL 33312-7533 • AASL
Schwartz Roberta B. • Asst. Dir. for Bibl. Records • Suffolk University Sawyer Library • Boston, MA 02108 • ACRL ALCTS SRRT
Schwartz Roberta S. • Van Wyck Junior High School • Wappingers Falls, NY 10516 • AASL
Schwartz Ruth S. • Director of Libraries • Fairleigh Dickinson University Weiner Library • Teaneck, NJ 07666 • ACRL
Schwartz S Arlene • Auto Circ Sys. Tech Advisor • County of Los Angeles Public Library • Downey, CA 90241-7400 • ALCTS LAMA LITA PLA
Schwartz Sarah E. • Asst. Dir. for Support Services • Sno-Isle Regional Library • Marysville, WA 98271-9164
Schwartz Steve A. • Director, Professional Council • Service Employees International Union • Washington, DC 20005
Schwartz Vanette M. • Social Science & Maps Librarian • Illinois State University • Normal, IL 61761 • ACRL LITA RASD LIRT MAGERT
Schwartz Virginia C. • Humanities Coordinator • Milwaukee Public Library • Milwaukee, WI 53233 • PLA RASD
Schwartz-Monroe Shula • City Librarian • National City Public Library • National City, CA 92050 • PLA
Schwartzbauer Eileen T. • Sociology Department Head • Minneapolis Public Library & Information Center • Minneapolis, MN 55401-1992 • RASD
Schwartzburg Selma • Junior High School Librarian • Nathan Hale I.S. 239K • Brooklyn, NY 11201 • AASL
Schwartzkopf Rebecca • Serials Librarian • Mankato State University Memorial Library • Mankato, MN 56002-8400 • RASD MAGERT
Schwarz Amy E. • Pompton Lake High School • Pompton Lakes, NJ 07442
Schwarz Ann E. • Librarian • Wm. E. DeLuca Jr. Elementary Sch • North Babylon, NY 11703 • AASL
Schwarz Betsy • Adult Services Librarian • Red Wing Public Library • Red Wing, MN 55066 • RASD SRRT
Schwarz Davine • Treasurer • West Islip Public Library • West Islip, NY 11795-3999 • ACRL ALTA PLA
Schwarz Donna • Curriculum Materials Librarian • Oklahoma State University Edmon Low Library • Stillwater, OK 74078-0375 • AASL ACRL
Schwarz Herbert J. Jr • New York, NY 10022 • ACRL
Schwarz Janet • Richmond, VA 23229
Schwarz June L. • Librarian • UFT Educational Center Library • Brooklyn, NY 11201
Schwarz Sara C. • Reference Librarian • Northeastern Illinois University Library • Chicago, IL 60625
Schwarz Susan • Director • Moses Greeley Parker Library • Dracut, MA 01826 • PLA
Schwarz Vera M. • Associate Librarian • La Sierra University Library • Riverside, CA 92515
Schwarzkopf L. C. • Greenbelt, MD 20770 • ACRL RASD GODORT MAGERT *Life*
Schwarzlose Sally Frye • Librarian I • Evanston Public Library • Evanston, IL 60201 • ALSC
Schwarzmann Diane D. • Assistant Director • Yorba Linda Public Library • Yorba Linda, CA 92686 • PLA
Schwegler Jean M. • Marion, IA 52302 • AASL
Schwehm Roblyn W. • Reference Librarian • State Library of Louisiana • Baton Rouge, LA 70821-0131
Schweickart Ruth Louise • Oxford, OH 45056 • ACRL ALCTS *Continuing*
Schweid Jean M. • Reference Librarian • Groton Public Library • Groton, CT 06340
Schweinsberg Catherine J. • Director • Brevard County Library • Cocoa, FL 32922-7781 • PLA RASD
Schweitzberger Kathleen A. • Head of Cataloging • University of Missouri-Kansas City Library • Kansas City, MO 64110-2499 • ACRL ALCTS
Schweizer Linda S. • University of Maryland College Park Theodore R. McKeldin Library • College Park, MD 20742-7011 • IRRT
Schwenger Frances S. • Director • Metropolitan Toronto Reference Library • Toronto ON, M4W 2G8 Canada • LAMA LITA PLA RASD
Schwenn Janet Marilyn • ECC/USF Learning Resources • Fort Myers, FL 33906-6210 • ACRL LITA RASD *Life*
Schwerner Nancy H. • Head Librarian • Clark State Community College • Springfield, OH 45501 • ACRL
Schwind Penelope • Asst Dir for Tech Services • Bryn Mawr College Canaday Library • Bryn Mawr, PA 19010 • ACRL ALCTS LAMA LITA
Schwotzer Pamela G. • Library Director • North Hampton Public Library • North Hampton, NH 03862
Schyndel Malka • Florida Atlantic University Library • Boca Raton, FL 33431 • ALCTS ILERT
Sciacca Joseph T. • Lincoln Trail Libraries System • Champaign, IL 61821-1068 • PLA IRRT
Scialdo Rudolph F. • Chairman & President • Library Bureau Inc. • Herkimer, NY 13350 • ERT
Scigliano Marisa Anna • Head Cataloger • Trent University Thomas J. Bata Library • Peterborough ON, K9J 7B8 Canada • ALCTS LITA
Scigulinsky Cynthia A. • Librarian II • New Jersey State Library Department of Education • Trenton, NJ 08625-0520
Scilken Marvin H. • Director • Orange Public Library • Orange, NJ 07050 • ACRL ALCTS LAMA LITA PLA RASD EMIERT ILERT LHRT SRRT *Life*
Scime Joy P. • Stoner Prairie Elementary School • Madison, WI 53711 • AASL
Scobell Elizabeth H. • Director of Library • West Virginia State College Drain-Jordan Library • Institute, WV 25112-1002 • ACRL
Scobey Sarah E. • Student • Emporia State University School of Library & Information Management • Emporia, KS 66801
Scofield Constance V. • Director • University of Wisconsin Center Marinette County Campus Library • Marinette, WI 54143
Scofield Sandra D. • Whitesboro, NY 13492-1246
Scoles Clyde S. • Executive Director • Toledo-Lucas County Public Library • Toledo, OH 43624 • LAMA PLA
Scolman Sheryl J. • Asst. Librarian • Pierce County Rural Library Peninsula Branch • Gig Harbor, WA 98335
Sconyers Debra A. • Serials Cataloger • Old Dominion University Library • Norfolk, VA 23529-0256
Scorza Joseph C. • Executive Director • Health Sciences Libraries Consortium • Philadelphia, PA 19104 • ACRL LITA
Scott-Zaleski Linda • Product Specialist • NOTIS Systems, Inc. • Evanston, IL 60201-3622 • LITA
Scott Alice H. • Assistant Commissioner • Chicago Public Library Harold Washington Library • Chicago, IL 60605 • ASCLA PLA LRRT
Scott Anne F. • Student • Simmons College Graduate School of Library & Information Science • Boston, MA 02115
Scott Anne M. • Dawson College • Westmount, PQ, H3Z 1A4 Canada
Scott Barbara G. • Managing Librarian • Tacoma Public Library Grace R Moore Branch • Tacoma, WA 98409 • PLA
Scott Bertha • Federal Bureau of Investigation FBI Academy Library • Quantico, VA 22135

Scott Bettie H. • CUNY Law School • Flushing, NY 11367 • ACRL GODORT

Scott Clare • Head Librarian • CLASP • San Francisco, CA 94118

Scott Darryl A. • Government Documents Librarian • Gary Public Library • Gary, IN 46402 • GODORT

Scott David A. • Ann Arbor, MI 48108 • PLA RASD

Scott Deborah K. • Overland Park, KS 66212 • ALCTS LITA

Scott Dorothea • Exeter Devon EX 24TJ, United Kingdom • Continuing

Scott Edward A. • Director of Library • Furman University • Greenville, SC 29613-0600 • ACRL LAMA *Life*

Scott Elizabeth O. • School Librarian • Rappahannock County High School • Sperryville, VA 22740

Scott Elizabeth Richman • Adult Services Librarian • Ocean County Library System • Toms River, NJ 08753 • ALCTS PLA CLENE

Scott Elnora S. • APO San Francisco, CA 96224-0074 • LAMA AFLRT

Scott Evelyn D. • Student • Emporia State University Emporia in the Rockies • Denver, CO 80204

Scott Frances E. • Mendon, MA 01756-0366

Scott Heather E. • Student • University of British Columbia School of Library, Archival & Information Studies • Vancouver BC, V6T 1Z1 Canada • ALSC PLA

Scott Helen • Wilkerson Group • New York, NY 10017

Scott Helen V. • Tucson, AZ 85716 • Continuing

Scott Ianthia L. • Media Specialist • Ursula Collins Elementary School • Augusta, GA 30901

Scott Jack W. • Head Music Library • Kent State University Library • Kent, OH 44242

Scott James E. • Student • University of Iowa School of Library & Information Science • Iowa City, IA 52242 • EMIERT

Scott Janice • Media Specialist • West Vigo Middle School • West Terre Haute, IN 47885 • AASL

Scott John E. • West Virginia State College Drain-Jordan Library • Institute, WV 25112-1002

Scott John P. • American School in Switzerland • Montagnola-Lugano, Switzerland • AASL YALSA

Scott Joy Whitney • Librarian • Center for Advanced Study in the Behavioral Sciences • Stanford, CA 94305

Scott Karen M. • Student • Kent State University School of Library & Information Science • Kent, OH 44242-0001 • PLA RASD

Scott Kathryn S. • International Monetary Fund & World Bank • Washington, DC 20433 • ALCTS LITA

Scott Kenneth J. • Head Librarian • Goodall Memorial Library Sanford Public Library • Sanford, ME 04073 • GODORT

Scott Lani P. • Head Librarian • Maui Library District Kahului Library • Kahului, HI 96732 • PLA

Scott Laura E. • Ferndale, MI 48220

Scott Laurie J. • Manager, Information Resources • AECL Candu • Mississauga, ON, L5K 1B2 Canada • LITA

Scott Lisa A. • Student • Wayne State University Library Science Program • Detroit, MI 48202 • IFRT NMRT

Scott Louise M. • President Board of Trustee • A.K. Smiley Public Library • Redlands, CA 92373 • PLA

Scott Margaret Gethers • School Librarian • Greendale Elementary School • New Ellenton, SC 29809 • AASL

Scott Margaret J. • Davenport Public Library • Davenport, IA 52801

Scott Margaret W. • Coordinator of Collection Mgt • Middle Tennessee State University Library • Murfreesboro, TN 37132 • ACRL ALCTS

Scott Marguerite A. • Birmingham Public Library • Birmingham, AL 35203 • LAMA LITA PLA EMIERT LRRT

Scott Marian Herr • Tualatin, OR 97062-8757 • ALSC PLA *Continuing*

Scott Marilynn S. • Anchorage, AK 99511 • Continuing

Scott Mark • Assistant Science Librarian • Massachusetts Institute of Technology Libraries (MIT) • Cambridge, MA 02139 • ACRL YALSA

Scott Mary E. • Mattoon, IL 61938 • ACRL ALCTS *Life*

Scott Melissa C. • University of Texas Southwestern Medical Center Library • Dallas, TX 75235-9049 • LAMA

Scott Nancey T. • Library Director • Central Mississippi Regional Library System • Pearl, MS 39208 • LAMA

Scott Nancy G. • Children's Librarian • Durham County Public Library North Durham Branch Library • Durham, NC 27704

Scott Ralph • Associate Professor Lib Serv • East Carolina University Joyner Library • Greenville, NC 27858-4353 • GODORT

Scott Ramsey Faber • Senior Librarian • Georgia Department of Corrections Hays Correctional Institution • Trion, GA 30753

Scott Rosalind • Media Specialist • Buechel Metro High School • Louisville, KY 40216 • AASL

Scott Rosemary D. • Englewood, CO 80110

Scott Sally J. • University of Wyoming • Laramie, WY 82071 • ACRL

Scott Sandra • Director • Three Rivers Library System • Glenwood Springs, CO 81602-1429 • ALCTS ASCLA LAMA CLENE

Scott Sharon K. • Head,Serials Dept. • University of Nevada-Reno Noble H. Getchell Library • Reno, NV 89557 • ACRL ALCTS

Scott Shirley • Media Specialist • Lady's Island Elementary School • Beaufort, SC 29902 • AASL

Scott Shirley F. • Media Coordinator • New Bern High School • New Bern, NC 28562 • EMIERT

Scott Shirley R. • Head of Research Services • Oregon State University William Jasper Kerr Library • Corvallis, OR 97331-4501 • ACRL LAMA LRRT

Scott Susan L. • Librarian • Marshall Elementary School • Modesto, CA 95350 • AASL

Scott Sylvia R. • Laurel, MD 20707

Scott Thelma J. • Assistant Librarian • Waynesburg College Library • Waynesburg, PA 15370

Scott Thomas L. • System Director • Plum Creek Library System • Worthington, MN 56187 • PLA

Scott Wendy L. • Library Personnel Officer • North Carolina State University • Raleigh, NC 27695 • LAMA

Scott Willodene A. • Nashville, TN 37205 • Continuing

Scotto Barbara • Teacher • Brookline Public Schools Michael Driscoll School • Brookline, MA 02146 • ALSC IFRT

Scranton Carrol • Student • University Center at Tulsa • Tulsa, OK 74106

Scribner Mary E. • Librarian • Westwood High School • Austin, TX 78750 • AASL

Scribner Ronda L. • Broken Arrow, OK 74014 • AASL

Scribner Ruth Brisso • Librarian • Florin High School Library Media Center • Sacramento, CA 95828 • AASL

Scrimgeour Andrew D. • Student • Drexel University College of Information Studies • Philadelphia, PA 19104-2875 • ACRL LAMA

Scriven Esther L. • School Library Media Specialist • Roy H. Mann I. S. 78 • Brooklyn, NY 11234 • AASL YALSA

Scrivener Laurie L. • Student • University of Oklahoma School of Library & Information Studies • Norman, OK 73019 • RASD NMRT

Scrivner Mary B. • Reference Librarian • Palatine Public Library • Palatine, IL 60067 • PLA

Scro Suzanne • Lakehurst, NJ 08733 • ALSC

Scroggins Deborah • Elementary Librarian • Marked Tree Elementary School • Marked Tree, AR 72365

Scroggs Sandra Jane • San Antonio, TX 78212 • AASL ALSC

Scruggs Teresa • Tucson, AZ 85745

Scruggs Welta C. • El Paso, TX 79922

Scudder Judith Bauer • Librarian • Sacred Heart Cathedral Preparatory • Sn Francisco, CA 94109 • AASL

Scudder Mary Ms. • Director • Lynchburg College • Lynchburg, VA 24501 • ACRL

Scullock Sheila • Systemwide Services Adm • Dallas Public Library • Dallas, TX 75201 • LAMA PLA

Scully Edward G. • Trustee • Macomb County Library • Mount Clemens, MI 48044 • ALTA

Scully Elizabeth • Head of Technical Services • Marathon County Public Library • Wausau, WI 54401

Scully Jean M. • System Manager • Saint Charles Public Library • St. Charles, IL 60174 • ALCTS

Scully Mark F. • Dir of Info Dissemination Policy • Government Printing Office • Washington, DC 20401 • ALCTS

Scully Thomas F. • Director • Beverly Public Library • Beverly, MA 01915

Scurr J. W. Reginald Mr. • Gilman, IA 50106 • Continuing

Scurry James A. • Fayetteville, NC 28303-2632

Seabock Janet E. • Librarian I, Collection Dev. • Fairfax County Public Library • Fairfax, VA 22033-1909

Seaboldt Lora L. • Student • Saint Joseph Mercy Hospital • Pontiac, MI 48341-2985

Seabright Virginia H. • Waterford, VA 22190 • Continuing

Seach Rachel R. • Idabel, OK 74745

Seacord Laura F. • Levittown, NY 11756 • ALSC

Seago George H. • Trustee • South Carolina State Library • Columbia, SC 29211 • ALTA

Seagraves Helen • Westside School Library • Hood River, OR 97031 • AASL

Seagren Jeannine V. • Library Media Specialist • Wilmore-Davis Elementary School • Wheat Ridge, CO 80033 • AASL

Seal Robert A. • University Librarian • University of Texas at El Paso Library • El Paso, TX 79968-0582 • ACRL LAMA IRRT

Seale Clifton C. • Extension Services Div. • Queens Borough Public Library • Jamaica, NY 11432 • PLA

Seale Colleen • University of Florida Libraries • Gainesville, FL 32611-2047 • ACRL RASD LIRT LRRT

Seale Linda N. • Science Cataloger • University of Alberta Cameron Library • Edmonton AB, T6G 2J8 Canada • ALCTS MAGERT

Sealor Margaret A. • Herndon, VA 22071-2546 • ALCTS LITA

Sealy Brian H. • Assistant Librarian • University of Michigan Libraries • Ann Arbor, MI 48109-1205 • LAMA LITA

Seaman Barbara Wahls • Adminstrative Services Libn. • Barrington Public Library District • Barrington, IL 60010

Seaman Helen Denyse • Assistant Law Librarian • Baylor University Law Library • Waco, TX 76798-7128

Seaman Jacquelyn A. • Winnetka, IL 60093 • AASL

Seaman Martha A. • Deputy Director • Baldwin Public Library • Birmingham, MI 48012-3002 • LAMA PLA

Seaman Sally G. • Librarian II • Schaumburg Township District Library • Schaumburg, IL 60194 • ALCTS

Seaman Sheila L. Ms • Asst. Dean for Public Services • College of Charleston Robert Scott Small Library • Charleston, SC 29424 • LITA

Seamans James E. • Technical Services Librarian • Saint Mary's Seminary & University The Knott Library • Baltimore, MD 21210 • ALCTS

Seamans Nancy H. • Director • College of Health Sciences Learning Resources Center • Roanoke, VA 24016

Searcy David L. • Head Branch Librarian • Atlanta-Fulton Public Library East Atlanta Branch • Atlanta, GA 30316 • PLA RASD EMIERT SRRT

Searcy Fred Jr. • Florida State University School of Library and Information Studies • Tallahassee, FL 32306-2048 • ACRL

Searcy Herbert • Tucson, AZ 85712 • ACRL ALCTS *Life*

Searing Susan E. • Acting Deputy Director • University of Wisconsin-Madison Memorial Library • Madison, WI 53706 • ACRL LAMA RASD EMIERT SRRT

Searle Colleen D. • Mt. Shasta, CA 96067

Searles Judith • Staff Director • Southern Methodist University Colophon,Friends of the SMU Libraries • Dallas, TX 75275 • LAMA

Searls Eileen H. • Law Librarian • Saint Louis University Omer Poos Law Library • St. Louis, MO 63108-3478 • ACRL LITA

Sears Amy E. • Brooklyn Public Library Clinton Hill Branch • Brooklyn, NY 11238 • ALSC IFRT SRRT

Sears Carlton A. • Director • Broome County Public Library • Binghamton, NY 13901 • LAMA

Sears Debra J. • State Library of Florida Division of Library & Information Services • Tallahassee, FL 32399-0250 • RASD

Sears Gloria • Houston, TX 77092

Sears Jean L. • Head Document Librarian • Miami University Edgar W. King Library • Oxford, OH 45056 • GODORT

Sears Julienne K. • Regional Librarian • Environmental Protection Agency EPA Region 10 Library • Seattle, WA 98101 • FLRT

Sears Linda M. • Branch Administrator • Mishawaka-Penn Public Library Bittersweet Branch • Mishawaka, IN 46544

Sears Linda W. • Kissimmee, FL 34746 • AASL

Sears Lynn E. • Law Librarian • Deuel Vocational Institute • Tracy, CA 95376

Sears Robert E. • Director • Oakland City College • Oakland City, IN 47660 • ACRL NMRT

Sears Robert W. • Business Librarian • Tulsa City-County Library System • Tulsa, OK 74103 • RASD

Sears Russell L. • Reference Librarian • Glendale Community College Library/Media Center • Glendale, AZ 85302 • RASD

Sears William T. • Library Media Specialist • Mesa Verde High School • Citrus Heights, CA 95621 • AASL LITA

Searson Mike T. • Student • University of Nebraska-Lincoln Libraries • Lincoln, NE 68588 • ACRL

Sease Sandra S. • Butler, PA 16001-1664

Seaton Ruth Ann • Winnona Park School • Decatur, GA 30030

Seaver Maryann T. • Oklahoma State University Edmon Low Library • Stillwater, OK 74078-0375

Seavey Charles A. • University of Arizona Graduate Library School • Tucson, AZ 85721 • PLA GODORT LHRT MAGERT

Seavey Patricia A. • Technical Services Librarian • Antelope Valley College • Lancaster, CA 93536 • ACRL ALCTS

Seawell Mary R. Miss • Cary, NC 27511 • ACRL RASD *Continuing*

Seay Catherine L. • Clayton County Library System • Jonesboro, GA 30236 • ALSC

Seay Jerry G. • Student • University of South Carolina College of Library & Information Science • Columbia, SC 29208

Seay John L. • Reference Librarian • Winter Park Public Library • Winter Park, FL 32789

Sebastian Jacquelyn • Children's Librarian • E. P. Foster Library • Ventura, CA 93001

Sebesta Karen J. • Librarian • Highlands High School • San Antonio, TX 78210 • AASL

Sechrest Sandra L. • Government Document Librarian • Wisconsin University • La Crosse, WI 54601 • GODORT MAGERT VRT

Secor Glen M. • Chief Financial Officer • Yankee Book Peddler • Contoocook, NH 03229 • IFRT

Secor John R. • Yankee Book Peddler • Contoocook, NH 03229 • ALCTS

Secord Anne Marie • University Librarian • National University Library • San Diego, CA 92108 • ACRL

Secord William R. • Library Media Specialist • East Hartford High School Penney Alumni Library • East Hartford, CT 06118 • AASL

Secoy Myra L. • DR, IL 61761 • Continuing

Secrest Lang F. • School Librarian • Huachuca Mountain Elementary School • Sierra Vista, AZ 85635 • AASL

Secter Ann L. • Children's Librarian • The Bryant Library • Roslyn, NY 11576 • ALSC

Secter Charles W. • Adjunct Reference Librarian • Hofstra University Libraries • Hempstead, NY 11550

Sedenquist Susan • Grand Forks, ND 58201 • PLA

Sedgwick Alice J. • Library Director • F L Weyenberg Public • Mequon, WI 53092 • LAMA PLA

Sedlock Barbara J. • Assistant Technical Serv Ln • Defiance College Anthony Wayne Library • Defiance, OH 43512

Sedney Frances V. • Children's Coordinator • Harford County Library • Belcamp, MD 21017 • AASL ALSC PLA YALSA LHRT

See Bill D. • Director of Library Services • Springfield School District 186 • Springfield, IL 62704 • AASL

See Constance M. • Alexandria, VA 22307 • RASD

See Judith S. • Trustee • Monroe County Library System • Monroe, MI 48161 • ALTA

Seeburger Charles L. • Reference Librarian • Holy Family College Library • Philadelphia, PA 19114

Seecharan Bonita M • Student • Wayne State University Library Science Program • Detroit, MI 48202 • PLA

Seeger Barbara • Public School 68 • Ridgewood, NY 11385 • AASL

Seeger Nancy J. • Washington, DC 20008

Seegert Lynda C. • Head Technical Services/Ref. • Granite City Public Library District • Granite City, IL 62040 • ALCTS

Seehusen Maren • Librarian • Dubuque Senior High School • Dubuque, IA 52001 • AASL

Seekamp Linda Wobbe • Information Services Librarian • Saint Mary's College of California • Moraga, CA 94575 • ACRL ALCTS RASD LIRT

Seel Jeanne L. • School Library Media Specialist • Ticonderoga Elementary School • Ticonderoga, NY 12883

Seele Carl D. • San Jose, CA 95112 • RASD

Seeley Ann M. • Kensington, MD 20795 • Continuing

Seeley Priscilla • Library Media Specialist • Farley Elementary School • Huntsville, AL 35803 • AASL

Seelig Joan M. • Cataloger • Springfield City Library • Springfield, MA 01103 • ALCTS

Seelig Katharine • Information Services Director • Lisle Library District • Lisle, IL 60532 • RASD

Seely Barbara L. • Student • Kutztown University Library Science Department • Kutztown, PA 19530 • AASL

Seely Doris J. • University of Minnesota O. Meredith Wilson Library • Minneapolis, MN 55455-0414 • ACRL ALCTS IRRT

Seely Edward • Technical Services Head • Cleveland Public Library • Cleveland, OH 44114-1271 • ALCTS PLA

Seely Ella M. • Humanities Department Manager • Multnomah County Library Central Branch • Portland, OR 97205 • LAMA PLA RASD

Seeman Janis • Cataloger • Richmond Public Library • Richmond, VA 23219

Seeman Kris A. • Student • Miami University Acq Dept. • Oxford, OH 45056

Seetoo Amy D. • Directory Products Manager • University Microfilms International • Ann Arbor, MI 48106-1346 • ACRL ALCTS LITA RASD EMIERT GODORT

Sefcik Ann M. • L. W. Fox Tech High School • San Antonio, TX 78205 • AASL

Sefcik Delphine M. • Hawthorn Center Medical Library • Northville, MI 48167

Sefcik Rosalie M. • Children's Librarian-Supv. • Linden Free Public Library • Linden, NJ 07036 • ACRL ILERT IRRT

Segal Jane D. • Reference/Collection Devel Ln. • Rice University Fondren Library • Houston, TX 77251-1892 • ACRL LIRT

Segal JoAn S. • Associate Exec. Dir., Programs • American Library Association • Chicago, IL 60611-2795 • ACRL

Segal Judith Dr. • Director • Hollins College Fishburn Library • Roanoke, VA 24020 • ACRL LAMA

Segal Robert B. • Trustee • Southeastern Public Library System of Oklahoma • McAlester, OK 74501

Segall Jo-Ann • Head Librarian • Sidwell Friends School Library • Washington, DC 20016

Segawa Laura • Jefferson County Public Library Golden Branch • Golden, CO 80401 • NMRT

Segel Bernard J. • Head of Technical Services • Pepperdine University • Malibu, CA 90263 • ACRL ALCTS LITA

Segel Judith D. • System Director • Black Gold Cooperative Library System • Ventura, CA 93003 • ASCLA LAMA PLA CLENE

Seger Robert M. • Director • Clinton Public Library • Clinton, IA 52732 • PLA

Segesta James E. • Librarian • California State University • Bakersfield, CA 93311

Seghetti Michael R. • Trustee • Peoria Public Library • Peoria, IL 61602 • ALTA

Segor Phyllis Lee • School Librarian • G. Holmes Braddock Senior High School • Miami, FL 33186 • AASL YALSA

Segura-Langton Elvira • Young Adult Services Librarian • Santa Fe Public Library Oliver LaFarge Branch • Santa Fe, NM 87505 • YALSA

Seher Mary Ann • School Librarian • Skyline Elementary School • Tacoma, WA 98406 • AASL

Seibel Marie B. • Miami Lakes Technical Education Center • Miami Lakes, FL 33014-6785 • AASL

Seibert Ellen • Technical Writer • Goal Systems International • Columbus, OH 43235

Seibert Karen S. • Assoc. University Librarian • Northern Arizona University Cline Library • Flagstaff, AZ 86011-6022 • ACRL LAMA

Seibert Royleen K. • Coordinator of Circulation Serv. • Northern Kentucky University Steely Library • Highland Heights, KY 41099-6101 • ACRL

Seid Ruth E. • Children's Librarian • Los Angeles Public Library Panorama City Branch Library • Panorama City, CA 91402 • ALSC SRRT

Seidel Diana J. • Manager Northside Branch • Lexington Public Library • Lexington, KY 40507

Seiden Beverly B. • Tamarac, FL 33319

Seiden Peggy A. • Head Librarian • Pennsylvania State University New Kensington • New Kensington, PA 15068 • ACRL LITA RASD

Seidenberg Edward • Director Library Development • Texas State Library • Austin, TX 78711 • ASCLA

Seidensticker Susan S. • Assistant Manager • Houston Public Library Collier Branch • Houston, TX 77092 • PLA RASD

Seidl James C. • Director • Woodlands Library Cooperative • Albion, MI 49224 • PLA

Seidler Yvonne • Materials Selection Coor • Timberland Regional Library • Olympia, WA 98501 • VRT

Seidman Rose-Shoshanah • Skokie, IL 60076

Seidman Ruth K. • Hd. Engineering & Science Lib • Massachusetts Institute of Technology Barker Eng. Lib. Room 10-500 • Cambridge, MA 02139 • ACRL LAMA

Seifert Betty R. • Branch Librarian • Public Library Woods Branch • Grosse Pointe, MI 48236 • PLA RASD *Life*

Seifert Sally F. • Dir.of Public Relations/Programs • Deerfield Public Library • Deerfield, IL 60015 • LAMA

Seiffer Nancy • Library Media Specialist • Dansville Primary School • Dansville, NY 14437

Seighman Eli • Director • Swan Library Wayland Academy • Beaver Dam, WI 53916 • AASL YALSA

Seigler Janet • Media Specialist • Nash Middle School • Smyrna, GA 30080

Seigler Michael E. • Assistant Director • Pine Mountain Regional Library • Manchester, GA 31816

Seik Jo E. • Library Relations Representative • H. W. Wilson Company • Bronx, NY 10452 • LITA

Seiler Carol • Copperas Cove, TX 76522 • LITA IFRT

Seiler Jeff L. • Student • Kent State University School of Library & Information Science • Kent, OH 44242-0001 • IFRT SRRT

Seiler Mary Jessica • Assistant Librarian • Atlanta College of Art Library • Atlanta, GA 30309

Seiler Patricia A. • Hernando, FL 32642

Seim Joan E. • Principal Ln. Tech. Svcs • Sonoma County Library • Santa Rosa, CA 95404 • LITA

Seim Mary R. • Madison, WI 53705 • PLA

Sein Jacqueline J. • Acquisitions Specialist • National Rehabilitation Information Center • Silver Spring, MD 20910-3319 • SRRT

Seiner Nancy • Librarian • Carnegie Library of Pittsburgh Squirrel Hill Branch • Pittsburgh, PA 15217 • ALSC PLA IFRT

Seipp Michele A. • Lafayette Public Library • Lafayette, CO 80026 • ALSC PLA

Seiser Virginia • Associate to the Dean • University of New Mexico General Library • Albuquerque, NM 87131 • ACRL LHRT

Seitz Evelyn M. • East Side Union High School District • San Jose, CA 95133 • AASL YALSA

Seitzer Deborah L. • Springfield Catholic High School • Springfield, MO 65809 • AASL YALSA

Seiz H. Alberta Miss • Bloomington, MN 55438 • Continuing

Sekely Maryann • Assistant Editor • Public Affairs Information Service • New York, NY 10036-4396

Selander Lucy • Minneapolis Public Library Nokomis Community Library • Minneapolis, MN 55417 • ALSC

Selbe Cheryl A. • Exhibit Coordinator • Online Computer Library Center (OCLC) • Dublin, OH 43017-3395 • ERT

Selbe Mary E. • Librarian • Glenview Public Library • Glenview, IL 60025

Selbert Daphne G. • Associate Director • Principia College Marshall Brooks Library • Elsah, IL 62028 • ACRL

Selby Barbara S. • Government Documents • University of Virginia Alderman Library • Charlottesville, VA 22903-2498 • GODORT

Selby Janet • Clln. Devlp./Instr. Supp. Tech. • State University of New York College at Cortland • Cortland, NY 13045 • ALCTS

Seldin Daniel T. • Head Geography & Map Library • Indiana University • Bloomington, IN 47405 • ACRL ALCTS GODORT MAGERT

Seleb David John • Reference Librarian • South Holland Public Library • South Holland, IL 60473 • RASD

Self George Anah Mrs. • Librarian • Carson-Newman College Library • Jefferson City, TN 37760 • ACRL GODORT

Self James R. • University of Virginia Clemons Library • Charlottesville, VA 22904-0100 • ACRL ALCTS RASD VRT

Self Phyllis C. • Wyoming, OH 45215

Self Sara Jane • Reference Librarian • Orange County Public Library Laguna Beach Branch • Laguna Beach, CA 92651 • ALSC PLA RASD

Self Sharon W. • Media Specialist Librarian • Hardaway High School • Columbus, GA 31995 • AASL ACRL

Self Steven E. • Reference Librarian • Austin Community College Riverside Campus-LRS • Austin, TX 78741 • ACRL SRRT

Seligsohn Selma • New York, NY 10021

Seling Kathy A. • Resource Center Instructor • Clover Park Research Center • Tacoma, WA 98499 • ALCTS LITA LIRT

Selkowitz Harriet J. • Assoc Dir of Libs for Tech Servs • University of Washington • Seattle, WA 98195 • ALCTS LAMA LITA

Sell Daniel • Director • Jamestown Community College Hultquist Library • Jamestown, NY 14702-0020

Sellberg Roxanne J. • Librarian • University of Washington Suzzallo Library • Seattle, WA 98195 • ACRL ALCTS LAMA LITA

Selle Donna M. • Director • Jefferson-Madison Regional Library • Charlottesville, VA 22901-5287 • ALCTS ALSC ASCLA LAMA LITA PLA RASD YALSA IFRT LRRT SORT

Selle Mary Ann • Librarian • Brandon School Library • Brandon, WI 53919 • AASL

Selleck Roberta G. • Librarian • Harvard College Library Widener Memorial Library • Cambridge, MA 02138 • ACRL

Sellen Betty-Carol • Silver Spring, MD 20901 • IFRT ILERT IRRT SRRT

Sellen Mary K. • Chapman College Clarke Memorial Library • Orange, CA 92666 • ACRL

Sellers David A. • Student • Pratt Institute Graduate School of Library & Information Science • Brooklyn, NY 11205 • ACRL RASD IFRT NMRT SRRT

Sellers Frances T. • Librarian • Carlisle Area School District IU 15 • Carlisle, PA 17013 • AASL YALSA

Sellers Judith M. • Gaston, SC 29053

Sellers Linda E. • Southern Methodist University Fondren Library • Dallas, TX 75275-0135 • ACRL LAMA LITA RASD

Sellers Minna D. • Reference Librarian • Rush University Library • Chicago, IL 60612 • ACRL

Sellers Ruth E. • Children's Librarian • Montgomery County Department of Public Libraries Kensington Branch • Kensington, MD 20895 • ALSC

Sellers Wayne C. • Palestine, TX 75801 • ALTA

Sellers Wendy S. • West Des Moines Public Library • West Des Moines, IA 50265 • ALCTS IFRT

Selles-Roney Johanna M. • Student • Southern Connecticut State University School of Libray Science & Instructional Technology • New Haven, CT 06515

Sellgren Judith A. • Media Specialist • Rochester Community Schools Adams High School • Rochester Hills, MI 48066 • AASL

Sellman Norma G. • Librarian • Monroe College • Bronx, NY 10468

Sells Rosemary A. • Student • Portland State University School of Education • Portland, OR 97207 • AASL ALSC

Selsinger Susan • Trustee • Phoenix Public Library • Phoenix, AZ 85004 • ALTA

Seltzer Ada M. • Director • University of Mississippi Medical Center • Jackson, MS 39216-4505 • ACRL RASD *Life*

Seltzer Miriam • Reference Librarian • Tufts University-Fletcher School of Law & Diplomacy • Medford, MA 02155-7082 • ACRL

Selvar Jane Cumming • Director • Bronxville Public Library • Bronxville, NY 10708 • LAMA RASD

Selverstone Harriet S. • Media Specialist • Norwalk High School • Norwalk, CT 06851 • AASL IFRT

Selvitella Barbara A. • Director of Media Services • Foxboro High School • Foxboro, MA 02035 • AASL ALSC ALTA YALSA IFRT

Selzer John C. • Manager, Fine Arts Department • Toledo-Lucas County Public Library • Toledo, OH 43624 • PLA

Selzer Michael I. • Gt. Burlington, MA 01230 • ACRL

Seman Rhoda R. • Librarian • Washington Elementary School • Evanston, IL 60646

Semchyshen Marion • Trustee • Dearborn Department of Libraries Henry Ford Centennial Library • Dearborn, MI 48126

Semeniuk Iris E. • University of Alberta Cameron Library • Edmonton AB, T6G 2J8 Canada

Semenza Jenny Lynne • Student • Brigham Young University School of Library & Information Sciences • Provo, UT 84602

Semertzaki-Koutras Eva • 115 28 Athens, Greece • ACRL ALCTS

Seminara Eleanor • Lewiston, NY 14092 • Continuing

Semmes Jean K. • Ann Arbor, MI 48104

Semoneit Joyce G. • Media Specialist • Brookdale Community College • Lincroft, NJ 07738 • ACRL

Sempell Pennie • Author • Songs & Company • San Francisco, CA 94102

Semper Claudia M. • Head of Media Dept • Boston College O'Neill Library • Chestnut Hill, MA 02167 • ACRL SRRT VRT

Semrau Jeannine Aragon • County Librarian • Madera County Library • Madera, CA 93637 • PLA IFRT

Semrau Ruth • Librarian • Lovejoy Independent School District • Allen, TX 75002 • AASL ALSC

Senack Julie • Ventnor, NJ 08406

Senator Rochelle B. • Middle School Librarian • Public Schools • New Canaan, CT 06840 • AASL

Sendek Irene • Asst. Director, Admin Svs. • Concordia University • Montreal PQ, Canada

Senden Julie • Director • John A. Stahl Library • West Point, NE 68788 • PLA

Sender Michelle V. • Washington, DC 20008 • AASL ALSC *Life*

Sender Ruth E. • Head Administrator • Itasca Community Library • Itasca, IL 60143 • PLA

Sendi Karen A. • Head of Reference Services • University of Toledo William S. Carlson Library • Toledo, OH 43606-3399 • ACRL RASD

Senecal Kristin S. • Librarian • Dickinson College Library Boyd Lee Spahr Library • Carlisle, PA 17013 • ACRL ALCTS

Senezak Christina • Head Librarian • Patterson Belknap Webb & Tyler • New York, NY 10112

Seng Ann E. • Evansville-Vanderburgh County Public Library • Evansville, IN 47708-1694 • PLA

Seng Mary A. • Assistant Director • University of Texas Libraries General Libraries • Austin, TX 78713-7330 • ACRL LAMA LITA

Senkevitch Judith J. • Assistant Professor • University of Wisconsin-Milwaukee School of Library & Information Science • Milwaukee, WI 53201 • ACRL LAMA PLA

Senkus Linda J. • Technical Librarian • Torrington Company • Torrington, CT 06790-4942

Senner Rachel • Freeman, SD 57029 • PLA

Sensale Maria T. • Reading Room Manager • MIT Laboratory for Computer Science • Cambridge, MA 02139 • ACRL LITA

Sensi Karen E. • Allentown, NJ 08501 • AASL

Senter James B. • Reference Clerk • Glendora Public Library • Glendora, CA 91740

Sentz Christine H. • Librarian II • Milwaukee Public Library North Milwaukee Branch • Milwaukee, WI 53209 • PLA YALSA

Senzig Donna • Director • University of Wisconsin-Madison College Library Helen C. White Hall • Madison, WI 53706 • ACRL LAMA LITA RASD *Life*

Seo Michelle W. • Assistant Librarian • Judge's Library • Washington, DC 20001

Sepahpour Suzy • School Librarian • Eagle Valley Junior High School • Carson City, NV 89701

Sepin Gladys S. • Hamilton, OH 45013 • LAMA PLA *Continuing*

Sepkoski Sally • Assistant Director • Sparta Public Library • Sparta, NJ 07871

Sepp Frederick C. Jr • Senior Assistant Librarian • Pennsylvania State University Pattee Library • University Park, PA 16802 • ACRL RASD

Seppala-Holtzman Anne M. • Librarian III • New York Public Library • New York, NY 10018-2788 • ALCTS

Sequenzia Sofia • Librarian • Brooklyn Public Library Brooklyn Heights Branch • Brooklyn, NY 11201

Sequirea Yvonne D. • Student • Simmons College Graduate School of Library & Information Science • Boston, MA 02115

Serafin Donna • Preservation Officer • State University of New York at Buffalo • Buffalo, NY 14260 • ALCTS

Serafin Traci L. • Champaign, IL 60820

Serafini Laura • Occidental College Library • Los Angeles, CA 90041

Seraphin Bonnie • Upland, CA 91786

Seraphine M. Sr • Librarian • Flintridge Sacred Heart Academy Library • La Canada-Flintridge, CA 91011 • AASL

Serban William M. • Asst. Professor-Political Sci. • Xavier University • New Orleans, LA 70125 • ACRL

Sercan Cecilia S. • Romance Language Cataloger • Cornell University • Ithaca, NY 14853-5301 • ACRL ALCTS

Serchuk Barnett • Head of Technical Services • Hofstra University Libraries • Hempstead, NY 11550 • ACRL

Serebnick Judith • Associate Professor • Indiana University School of Library and Information Science • Bloomington, IN 47405 • ACRL ALCTS IFRT LRRT

Serebrin Ray • Coodinator • Seattle Public Library • Seattle, WA 98104-1193

Serenyi Peg • Librarian • Georgetown Day High School • Washington, DC 20016 • AASL

Serex S Emily • Jamaica Pln, MA 02130 • ALCTS *Continuing*

Serge Allard • Librarian • College De Rouyn-Noranda • Rouyn-Noranda PQ, J9X 5M5 Canada • ACRL ALCTS LAMA LITA

Sergeant Clare H. • Jackson, MI 49202 • LAMA RASD *Continuing*

Sergent Lana Turner • Librarian • Lee High School Library • Jonesville, VA 24263 • AASL

Sergent Tina A. • Librarian • Miami Institute of Psychology Library • Miami, FL 33166-6612

Sergo Raymond M. • Trustee • Lyons Public Library • Lyons, IL 60534

Serice Janet C. • Austin, TX 78731

Serikaku Laurie R. • Hum & Social Sci Divisions • Library of Congress • Washington, DC 20541 • ACRL RASD EMIERT

Serine Virginia A. • Mansfield, PA 16933

Serio Carla J • Student • University of North Texas School of Library & Information Sciences • Denton, TX 76203

Seris Eileen J. • Media Specialist • West High School • Greeley, CO 80634 • AASL

Serna Hortensia G. • San Diego, TX 78384

Serpico Margaret Ann • Piscataway, NJ 08854 • ALSC

Serrato Richard • Audio-Visual Manager • Alameda County Library System • Fremont, CA 94538

Serreau Elizabeth M.H. • Cannon Beach, OR 97110 • ASCLA SRRT

Servaes-Aiad Brita • Student • Long Island University Palmer School of Library & Information Science • Greenvale, NY 11548

Servais Carolyn • Library Media Specialist • Little Chute High School • Little Chute, WI 54140 • AASL

Serynek William P. • Director • Massepequa Public Library • Massapequa, NY 11758

Serzan Sharon L. • Program Manager • Defence Technical Information Center • Alexandria, VA 22304 • ALCTS

Seskin Ann H. • Cataloging Librarian II • Boston University Mugar Memorial Library • Boston, MA 02215 • ACRL

Sessa Jane T. • Library Director • Securities & Exchange Commission • Washington, DC 20549 • LITA FLRT

Sessions Deborah S. • Librarian • Vermont College Gary Memorial Library • Montpelier, VT 05602

Sessions Judith A. • Dean • Miami University Acq Dept. • Oxford, OH 45056 • ACRL LAMA LITA *Life*

Sessions Tracy A. • Assistant Director • Georgetown County Memorial Library • Georgetown, SC 29440

Seter Faye M. • Grafton, ND 58237 • AASL

Sethi Bali Mr. • International Press Publications Incorporation • Willowdale, ONT, M2R 3G6 Canada

Setlak Kathryn M. • Chicago, IL 60609 • AASL

Setliff Margaret H. • Law Librarian • Supreme Court Law Library • Honolulu, HI 96808 • Continuing

Setnick Sandra B. • Reference Librarian • Southern Methodist University • Dallas, TX 75275

Settler Leo H. Jr. • Library of Congress • Washington, DC 20541

Settles Cheryl L. • Lakewood, CO 80226 • IFRT

Settles Rosayle A. • Student • Columbia University School of Library Service • New York, NY 10027

Setzer Patricia S. • Acquisitions Librarian • Wayne County Public Library • Goldsboro, NC 27530 • PLA

Setzler Marilyn F. • Media Generalist • Lakeview Elementary School • Robbinsdale, MN 55422 • AASL ALSC

Seu Claire SK • Student • University of Hawaii School of Library & Information Studies • Honolulu, HI 96822 • AASL

Seufert Edward C. • Head Librarian • Lindsey Wilson College Katie Murrell Library • Columbia, KY 42728 • ACRL LAMA

Seufert William J. • Librarian • New York Public Library High Bridge Branch • Bronx, NY 10452 • MAGERT

Severance Robert • Chapel Hill, NC 27514 • ACRL PLA FLRT *Life*

Severance Rosemary • East Lansing, MI 48823

Severns Hannah Miss • Moorestown, NJ 08057 • PLA *Continuing*

Severns Tiffany L. • Libertyville, IL 60048 • ACRL

Severs Mary L. • Cataloging Librarian • William Rainey Harper College Learning Resources Center • Palatine, IL 60067 • ALCTS

Severson Richard J. • Lake Oswego, OR 97035

Severt Lois C. • Head, Online Records Cataloging • University of Louisville Ekstrom Library • Louisville, KY 40292 • ACRL ALCTS LAMA CLENE

Severtson Susan M.Q. • President • Chadwyck-Healey Inc. • Alexandria, VA 22314 • ACRL ALCTS *Subscribing*

Severy Marion • Technical Services Librarian • Genentech Inc • So. San Francisco, CA 94080 • ALCTS

Sevetson Andrea L. • Government Documents Librarian • University of California-Berkeley University Library • Berkeley, CA 94720 • ACRL GODORT

Sevier Jennifer L. • Pekin, IL 61554

Sevigny Phyllis • Palatine Public Library • Palatine, IL 60067 • PLA RASD

Sevilla Judy C. • La Mirada, CA 90638 • RASD SRRT

Sevillano Suzette M Montaner • Baldwin School of Puerto Rico • Guaynalbo, PR 00657

Sevold Louise A. • Shaker Heights Public Library • Shaker Heights, OH 44120 • ALCTS PLA

Seward Virginia R. • C. Berger & Company • Wheaton, IL 60189

Sewell Jack R. • Kalamazoo, MI 49007

Sewell Robert G. • Assoc Univ Ln for Clln Devl Mgt • Rutgers University Libraries • New Brunswick, NJ 08903 • ACRL ALCTS

Sewell Winifred • Cabin John, MD 20818 • ACRL ALCTS ASCLA LITA RASD LIRT *Continuing*

Seweryn Natalie A. • Asst. Dir for Acquisitions • New York Public Library • New York, NY 10018-2788 • ALCTS

Sewill Edna H. • Program Manager, Curriculum • San Jose Unified School District • San Jose, CA 95126 • AASL

Sexton-Cooley Susan D. • Circulation Libn/Sys Admin • Sara Hightower Regional Library • Rome, GA 30161

Sexton Anna M. • Albany, NY 12206 • Continuing

Sexton Ellen • Indexer • H. W. Wilson Company • Bronx, NY 10452 • ACRL

Sexton Irwin • San Antonio, TX 78216

Sexton Mark • Advisory Board • College of New Rochelle Gill Library • New Rochelle, NY 10805

Sexton Pat • Student • University of Hawaii School of Library & Information Studies • Honolulu, HI 96822 • SRRT

Sexton Ron J. • Librarian • Carnegie Corporation of New York • New York, NY 10022 • AASL ALCTS NMRT

Sexton Sara C. • Ashtabula, OH 44004 • Continuing

Sexton Stephen L. • Documents/Reference Librarian • University of Texas at San Antonio-Library • San Antonio, TX 78249 • ACRL GODORT

Sexty Suzanne • Bibl. Instr. Coordinator • Memorial University Queen Elizabeth II Library • St Johns NF, A1B 3Y1 Canada • ACRL LIRT

Seymore Vanessa Hicks • Queens, NY 11411

Seymour-Ford Janice E. • Student • University of Wisconsin School of Library & Information Studies • Madison, WI 53706 • ALCTS

Seymour-Green Marie A. • Library Tech. • Oakland University • Rochester, MI 48309-4401 • NMRT

Seymour Celene L. • Head Librarian • Indiana Free Library • Indiana, PA 15701

Seymour Gary F. • Homer Junior High School • Homer, NY 13077 • AASL

Seymour Jill R. • Phoenix, AZ 85021-6030

Seymour Joanna P. • Program Librarian • Santa Clara County Free Library Campbell Public • Campbell, CA 95008 • PLA RASD

Seymour Lynn • Fort Worth Public Library • Fort Worth, TX 76102

Seymour Sharon • Librarian I • Harold Washington Library Center Chicago Public Library • Chicago, IL 60605 • IFRT LRRT

Seymour Viveca • Librarian • Stanford University • Stanford, CA 94305-6011 • ACRL ALCTS

Sgambati Filomena Ms. • Dearborn Heights, MI 48127

Sgritta Verna L. • Fullerton, CA 92631

Sgro Larry • Director, Learning Res. Center • Horry-Georgetown Tech • Conway, SC 29526 • ACRL

Shaaban Marian T. • International Document Librarian • Indiana University at Bloomington University Libraries • Bloomington, IN 47405 • GODORT

Shabb Cynthia H. • Vanderbilt University Science Library • Nashville, TN 37240-0007 • ACRL MAGERT

Shaben Helen M. • Technical Services Librarian • Clarke College Schrup Library • Dubuque, IA 52001 • ALCTS

Shabowich Stanley A. • Grulla Junior High School • La Grulla, TX 78548 • AASL

Shachter Linda M. • English Librarian • Hillel Torah North Suburban Day School • Skokie, IL 60077 • AASL

Shackelford-McLinn Claudette • Coordinating Librarian • Los Angeles Unified School District • Los Angeles, CA 90017 • AASL

Shackelford Eileen R. • Library Director • Arizona Western College Library • Yuma, AZ 85366-0929 • ACRL LAMA

Shackelford Joan H. • Reference Librarian • Randolph Public Library • Asheboro, NC 27203 • PLA

Shackelford Marilyn L. • Regional Librarian • Hardesty South Regional Library • Tulsa, OK 74133 • RASD

Shacklette Nancy S. • Springfield Free Public Library • Springfield, NJ 07081 • ALSC

Shadbolt Sally • Simi Valley, CA 93065 • Continuing

Shade Lucinda C. • Whiteman AFB, MO 65305

Shade Ronald H. • Librarian • United States Department of Defense Intelligence Agency • Washington, DC 20301 • RASD AFLRT FLRT

Shadle Paula M. • Student • Kent State University School of Library & Information Science • Kent, OH 44242-0001

Shadle Steven C. • ISDS Cataloger • Library of Congress • Washington, DC 20541 • LITA

Shady Jean M. • Serials Project Librarian • Harvard Law School Library • Cambridge, MA 02138 • ALCTS

Shaevel Evelyn • Dir. of Marketing-Publishing • American Library Association • Chicago, IL 60611-2795 • YALSA

Shaevel Shirley • Griffith, IN 46319

Shafa Zary M. Dr. • Associate Library Director • University of Dallas William A. Blakley Library • Irving, TX 75062 • LAMA LITA IRRT LRRT

Shafer Anne Elise • Resource Center Librarian • Evanston Township High School • Evanston, IL 60204 • AASL

Shafer Cathy L. • AV/Reference Librarian • County of Los Angeles Public Library Lynwood Branch • Lynwood, CA 90262 • ILERT

Shafer Dale R. • Director Library • Court Saint Christian Church • Salem, OR 97301

Shafer Marcia • Gwynedd Valley, PA 19437 • ALSC PLA IFRT

Shafer Ruth • Children & Youth Serials • Fort Vancouver Regional Library • Vancouver, WA 98663 • ALSC

Shafer Scott L. • Lima Public Library • Lima, OH 45801 • ACRL

Shaffer Carolyn R. • Science Librarian • Illinois State University Milner Library • Normal, IL 61761-0900

Shaffer Dallas Y. • County Librarian • Monterey County Free Libraries • Salinas, CA 93901 • LAMA PLA

Shaffer Deborah A. • Librarian • Kaukauna High School Library • Kaukauna, WI 54130

Shaffer Faye Hylton • Media Specialist • Alamance Elementary School • Greensboro, NC 27406 • AASL

Shaffer Jodi • Media Specialist • Albion Middle School • Albion, NY 14411

Shaffer Kay L. • Slavic Biblographer & Cataloger • State University of New York (SUNY) University Libraries • Albany, NY 12222 • ACRL ALCTS

Shaffer Kenneth M. Jr • Director • Brethren Historical Library & Archives • Elgin, IL 60120

Shaffer Margaret • Director • Terrebonne Parish Library • Houma, LA 70360 • PLA

Shaffer Margaret • Media Specialist • Easton High School • Easton, MD 21601 • AASL

Shaffer Mary Ann Ms. • Assistant Public Services Dir • Timberland Regional Library • Olympia, WA 98501

Shaffer Norman J. • Chief Photoduplication Serv • Library of Congress • Washington, DC 20541 • ALCTS

Shaffer Patricia A. • Librarian • Waterford Township Public Library • Waterford, MI 48329 • ALSC PLA

Shaffner Winifred C. • Teacher • Marion County Schools Kendall Elementary School • Marion, IN 46952 • ALSC

Shaftel Roberta • Librarian • Solano County Library John F. Kennedy Branch • Vallejo, CA 94590

Shah Aruna C. • Beckley, WV 25801

Shah Nishat M. • Assistant Editor • H. W. Wilson Company • Bronx, NY 10452 • ACRL

Shah Sushila R. • Cataloging Librarian • DeWitt Wallace Library MacAlester College • Saint Paul, MN 55105 • ACRL ALCTS LITA

Shah Syed M. • Ed., Biol. & Agricultural Index • H. W. Wilson Company • Bronx, NY 10452 • LITA

Shaheen Linda S. • Student • Kent State University School of Library & Information Science • Kent, OH 44242-0001

Shahegh Mahvash H. • Student-LTA III • Enoch Pratt Free Library • Baltimore, MD 21201-4484 • LITA

Shahinian Katherine S. • Librarian • Woodbury Elementray School • Shaker Heights, OH 44120

Shahmir Caroline G. • Bowling Green, KY 42103

Shain Lee Ann • Director • Fitzgerald-Ben Hill County Library • Fitzgerald, GA 31750-2591

Shair Sondra • Associate Librarian • University of California-Berkeley University Library • Berkeley, CA 94720 • ACRL RASD

Shalat Harriet T. • Supervising Librarian • New York Public Library Mid-Manhattan Branch • New York, NY 10016

Shaller Ann Smith • Walt Disney Imagineering • Glendale, CA 91221

Shaller Antoinette • Newton, MA 02168

Shallit Barbara • Aberdeen, NJ 07747 • ALSC

Shama Carol • Reference Librarian • Wood Library • Canandaigua, NY 14424-1295 • YALSA

Shamalla Michael R. • Manager • Newport Beach Public Library • Newport Beach, CA 92660 • LAMA

Shamel Cynthia L. • Hourly Reference Librarian • Mesa College Library • San Diego, CA 92111 • ACRL ALCTS

Shamp B Kathleen • Fine Arts Librarian • Cleveland Public Library • Cleveland, OH 44114-1271

Shams Marie-Lise A. • Madison Heights, MI 48071 • SRRT

Shamy Salwa M. • East Brunswick Public Library • E. Brunswick, NJ 08816 • RASD SRRT

Shan Millie M. • Editor • Routledgê • London EC4P 4EE, England • RASD

Shanafelt Ellen M. • Trustee • Macomb County Library • Mount Clemens, MI 48044 • ALTA

Shanafelt Nancy F. • Catalog Librarian • McMurry University Jay-Rollins Library • Abilene, TX 79697

Shands Alice M. • Director of Volunteer Services • Arkansas Childrens Hospital • Little Rock, AR 72202 • ALSC ASCLA

Shane Charlotte J. • Partner • Shane-Armstrong Information Systems • Fayetteville, AR 72702

Shane Dorothy C. • Syracuse, NY 13202 • ACRL RASD *Continuing*

Shane Jackie G. • Student • University of Illinois Graduate School of Library and Information Science • Urbana, IL 61801

Shane Yvette L. • Head, Youth Services • Baldwin Public Library • Birmingham, MI 48012-3002 • ALSC

Shang Stella I-Hua • Regional Librarian • New York Public Library Baychester Branch • New York, NY 10475 • PLA EMIERT

Shank Lora • Reference Librarian • Burlingame Public Library • Burlingame, CA 94010

Shank Russell • Assistant Vice Chancellor • University of California-Los Angeles (UCLA) • Los Angeles, CA 90024-1450 • ACRL ALCTS LAMA LITA RASD IFRT LHRT *Life*

Shankie Robert A. • Trustee • Warren Public Library • Warren, MI 48092

Shankle Clarinda J. • Pensacola, FL 32503

Shanley Dennis M. • Director • Anoka Public Library • Anoka, MN 55303 • LAMA PLA

Shanley Lorraine W. • Managing Director • Market Partners International • New York, NY 10016

Shanley Patricia C. • Library Media Specialist • Pearl River High School • Pearl River, NY 10965 • AASL

Shannon Amy W. • Reference Librarian • University of Oklahoma Libraries University Libraries • Norman, OK 73019 • ACRL IFRT

Shannon Donna M. • Student • University of North Carolina School of Library Science • Chapel Hill, NC 27599-3360 • AASL ALSC

Shannon Dwight W. • Chico, CA 95926

Shannon Jerry B. Ms. • All Levels Librarian • Ropes Independent School District • Ropesville, TX 79358

Shannon Jill K. • Tuscaloosa, AL 35401-5914 • ACRL ALCTS

Shannon Kathleen L. • Thornwood High School • South Holland, IL 60473 • AASL *Life*

Shannon Marcia • Special Project Consultant • Massachusetts Board of Library Commissioners • Boston, MA 02215-2070 • LAMA PLA

Shannon Michael • Acting Chief Librarian • Lehman College Library • Bronx, NY 10468 • ACRL GODORT

Shannon Patrick • Trustee • Hennepin County Library • Minnetonka, MN 55343 • ALTA

Shannon Zella J. • Minneapolis Public Library & Information Center • Minneapolis, MN 55401-1992 • LAMA PLA

Shao Hsi-Ping • Dean • University of Wisconsin Library and Learning Resources • Whitewater, WI 53190

Shapera Gladys S. • Asst. Dir.,Main Lib & Tech Svs • Carnegie Library of Pittsburgh • Pittsburgh, PA 15213-4080 • ALCTS LAMA LITA PLA RASD

Shapiro Barbara • Great Neck, NY 11021

Shapiro Barbara B. • Coor. of Adult Services • New York Public Library Mid-Manhattan Branch • New York, NY 10016 • LAMA PLA RASD CLENE

Shapiro Barbara G. • Library Director • Cherry Hill Free Public Library • Cherry Hill, NJ 08034 • LAMA PLA

Shapiro Beth J. • University Librarian • Rice University Fondren Library • Houston, TX 77251-1892 • ACRL ALCTS LAMA

Shapiro Carol Schor • Head Cataloger • Fordham Law School Library • New York, NY 10023 • ALCTS

Shapiro Debra S. • Librarian I • Labat-Anderson Inc • Chicago, IL 60604

Shapiro Ezra D. • Student • State University of New York at Albany School of Information Science & Policy • Albany, NY 12222 • RASD IFRT LHRT

Shapiro June R. • Director • Greece Public Library • Rochester, NY 14626

Shapiro Leila C. • Regional Librarian • Montgomery County Department of Public Library/ Bethesda Regional Library • Bethesda, MD 20814 • LAMA PLA RASD IFRT

Shapiro Leonard • Shelter Rock Public Library • Albertson, NY 11507 • ALTA

Shapiro Marjorie S. • Glen Cove, NY 11542 • ACRL

Shapiro Martin P. • The American University Library • Washington, DC 20016-8046 • ACRL IFRT IRRT

Shapiro Mary L. • VP, Product Planning & Commun • Baker & Taylor Books • Bridgewater, NJ 08807-0920 • PLA

Shapiro Nancy A. • Needham, MA 02194

Shapland Bonnie D. • Librarian • Hawthorne Brook Middle School • Townsend, MA 01469 • AASL

Shapton Gregory B. • Principal Librarian • Pomona Public Library • Pomona, CA 91769-2271 • PLA

Share Barbara B. • Teacher • W.R. Thomas Middle School • Miami, FL 33175

Sharik Shirley • Whistler, AL 36612

Sharka Jane A. • Library Media Specialist • Naperville Central High School • Naperville, IL 60540 • AASL

Sharkey Paulette Bochnig • Madison, WI 53711

Sharman Linda • Trustee • Spokane County Library District • Spokane, WA 99212-1853 • ALTA

Sharp Anita • Palco High School • Palco, KS 67657 • AASL

Sharp Avery T. Dr • University Librarian • Baylor University Moody Memorial Library • Waco, TX 76798-7143 • LAMA

Sharp Brenda H. • Motion Picture-Vidio Librarian • Boeing Support Services • Seattle, WA 98124-2207

Sharp Gary L. • Assistant Librarian • North Bend Public Library • North Bend, OR 97459 • PLA

Sharp Kay • DeSoto, TX 75115 • AASL

Sharp Linda • Reference Librarian • University of Notre Dame Libraries • Notre Dame, IN 46556 • ACRL

Sharp Michele N. • Maharishi International University Library • Fairfield, IA 52556-2091

Sharp Patricia C. • North Palm Beach, FL 33408 • ACRL

Sharp Rebekah A. • Student • University of Missouri-Columbia School of Library & Informational Science • Columbia, MO 65211 • ALSC PLA

Sharp S. Celine • Asst. Circulation Dpt Head • Brigham Young University • Provo, UT 84602

Sharp Sharon • Norcross Public Library • Norcross, GA 30071

Sharp Sue • President • Belleville Public Library • Belleville, IL 62220

Sharpe Mary H. • U S Corporation Research Center • Libertyville, IL 60048

Sharpe Sharon S. • Head Library Media Specialist • Deever Administrative Center • Junction City, KS 66441 • AASL ALSC IFRT

Sharples Mary E. • Hinsdale Public Library • Hinsdale, IL 60521 • LAMA PLA

Sharpless Dorothy E. • Sevierville, TN 37862 • Continuing

Sharpley Barbara G. • Librarian • Albany High School • Albany, NY 12208

Sharps Sandy • Librarian • Williams High School • Plano, TX 75074 • AASL YALSA

Sharretts Cristina W. • University of Virginia Library • Charlottesville, VA 22903

Sharrow Marilyn J. • University Librarian • University of California-Davis Library • Davis, CA 95616

Shasteen Ruth H. • Director • Elizabeth Titus Memorial Library • Sullivan, IL 61951

Shattuck Marian L. • Palo Alto, CA 94304

Shauck Stephanie Mareck • Joppa, MD 21085 • AASL ALSC

Shaughnessy Anita F. • Student • University of Pittsburgh School of Library and Information Science • Pittsburgh, PA 15260

Shaughnessy Anne V. • Springfield, IL 62704

Shaughnessy Joel A. • Foreign Broadcast Information Service • Washington, DC 20013

Shaughnessy Jospeh X. • Associate Business Director • Waco-McLennan County Library • Waco, TX 76701

Shaughnessy Patti Mrs. • Fremont, CA 94539 • PLA

Shaughnessy Thomas Dr. • University Librarian • University of Minnesota O. Meredith Wilson Library • Minneapolis, MN 55455-0414 • ACRL

Shaup Joy A. • Coordinator, Library Services • Cucamonga School District • Rancho Cucamonga, CA 91730 • AASL ALSC

Shaver Dorothy M. • Director • Beaverton City Library • Beaverton, OR 97005 • ALCTS ALSC ALTA LAMA LITA PLA RASD YALSA IFRT

Shaver Lolly L. • Librarian • East Central Arkansas Regional Library Cross Counry Library • Wynne, AR 72396 • PLA

Shaver Marilyn H. • Assistant Librarian • Indiana University • Bloomington, IN 47405 • ACRL LAMA

Shavit David • Associate Professor • Northern Illinois University Department of Library & Information Studies • DeKalb, IL 60115

Shavlik Rebecca R. • Saint Paul, MN 55110-6532

Shaw Amy • Southwest Public Libraries • Grove City, OH 43123

Shaw Barbara A. • Palo Alto, CA 94301 • ALSC

Shaw Betty B. • California, PA 15419

Shaw Beverly • Trustee • Rapid City Public Library • Rapid City, SD 57701-3630

Shaw Charlotte A. • Royal Oak, MI 48073 • LAMA PLA *Continuing*

Shaw Craig S. • Non-Salaried Librarian • Maharishi International University Library • Fairfield, IA 52556-2091

Shaw Debora • Associate Professor • Indiana University School of Library and Information Science • Bloomington, IN 47405 • ALCTS LITA

Shaw Deborah L. • Serials Librarian • Oklahoma State University Edmon Low Library • Stillwater, OK 74078-0375

Shaw Debra H. • Brazil Public Library • Brazil, IN 47834

Shaw Debra Sue • Columbus, OH 43202

Shaw Diane • St. Paul, MN 55117

Shaw Doris G. • Church Farm School • Paoli, PA 19301

Shaw Gail E. • Chicago, IL 60646

Shaw Georgann K. • Greenville College Ruby E. Dare Library • Greenville, IL 62246 • ACRL

Shaw James T. • Government Documents Librarian • California State University • Fullerton, CA 92634 • ACRL GODORT LIRT

Shaw Jan T. • United States Courts Library Lafayette Branch • Lafayette, LA 70501

Shaw Jane B. • Director • Lisle Library District • Lisle, IL 60532 • ALCTS ALTA ASCLA LAMA LITA PLA RASD YALSA IFRT

Shaw Joyce M. • Librarian • Lincoln Park Zoo Society • Chicago, IL 60614

Shaw Judith H. • Librarian II (Cataloger) • Redwood City Public Library • Redwood City, CA 94063-1868 • ALCTS

Shaw Kathleen T. • Mount Verono, WA 98273

Shaw Linda K. • Student • University of Washington Graduate School of Library and Information Science • Seattle, WA 98195 • ACRL

Shaw Linda S. • Librarian • University of Indianapolis Krannert Memorial Library • Indianapolis, IN 46227

Shaw Mabel W. • Reference Librarian • Tallahassee Community College • Tallahassee, FL 32304 • ACRL RASD LIRT

Shaw Mary M. • Honolulu, HI 96822

Shaw Matt • Student • University of North Carolina Department of Library & Information Studies • Greensboro, NC 27412-5001 • SRRT

Shaw Richard N. • Director • Technical College of the Low Country • Beaufort, SC 29902 • ACRL

Shaw Roberta F. • Library Director • Flagler County Public Library • Palm Coast, FL 32037

Shaw Ronald W. • Student • State University of New York (SUNY) School of Information & Library Studies • Buffalo, NY 14260

Shaw Ruth Jean • Director of Library Resources • Anchorage School District Purchasing Dept • Anchorage, AK 99517 • AASL ACRL ALCTS ALSC ASCLA LAMA LITA PLA RASD YALSA EMIERT IFRT LIRT SORT

Shaw Sarah J. • Catalog Librarian (Music) • Brown University Rockefeller Library • Providence, RI 02912 • ACRL ALCTS

Shaw Spencer G. • Professor Emeritus • University of Washington Graduate School of Library and Information Science • Seattle, WA 98195 • AASL ALSC ALTA ASCLA LAMA PLA RASD YALSA CLENE EMIERT IRRT *Honorary*

Shaw Stewart A. • Oakland, CA 94610 • EMIERT

Shaw Susan H. • South Dakota State University Briggs Library • Brookings, SD 57007 • ACRL ALCTS IRRT MAGERT

Shaw Suzanne J. • Automation Librarian • University of Florida Libraries • Gainesville, FL 32611-2047 • ACRL LITA

Shaw Trinket F. • Student • University of Alabama School of Library & Information Studies • Tuscaloosa, AL 35487-0252

Shaw W. Lawrence Mr. • John F. Kennedy University • Orinda, CA 94563 • ACRL ALCTS *Life*

Shaw William T. • Trustee • Topeka Public Library • Topeka, KS 66604-1374

Shawkey Dallas R. • Catalog Department Coordinator • Brooklyn Public Library • Brooklyn, NY 11238 • ALCTS ASCLA LAMA

Shawl Jeannette P. • Reference Librarian • Lawrence Public Library • Lawrence, KS 66044 • PLA RASD EMIERT

Shayne Mette • Northwestern University Library • Evanston, IL 60208-2300 • ACRL IRRT

Shea Elizabeth A. • Law Librarian • Baker, Manock & Jensen • Fresno, CA 93704 • LAMA LITA

Shea Frances C. • Rumson-Fairhaven Regional High School • Rumson, NJ 07760

Shea Regina Kram • Jenkintown, PA 19046-2740 • RASD

Sheaffer Marc L. • Manager,Vendor Conversion Serv. • Brodart Company • Williamsport, PA 17705 • ALCTS

Shealy Mark W. • Dallas, TX 75214

Shear Joan A. • Reference Librarian • Boston College Law Library • Newton Center, MA 02159 • RASD

Shearer Hallie I. Miss • Evanston, IL 60201 • Life

Shearer John Allen Jr • Staff Librarian • West Liberty State College Elbin Library • West Liberty, WV 26074 • ACRL LIRT

Shearer Kenneth D. Jr • Professor • North Carolina Central University • Durham, NC 27707 • PLA IRRT LRRT

Shearer Martha A. • Reference Librarian • Alexandrian Public Library • Mount Vernon, IN 47620 • PLA

Shearer Mary I. • Government Documents Librarian • University of Houston Law Libraries • Houston, TX 77204-6390 • GODORT

Sheares Ora Myles • Olympia Fields, IL 60461

Shearin Roberta B. • Reference Librarian • United States Department of Army Army Corp of Engr Hd Library • Washington, DC 20314-1000 • PLA

Shearman Suzanne • Student • State University of New York at Buffalo School of Information Library • Buffalo, NY 14260 • AASL

Shears Jesse • Trustee • William Leonard Public Library District • Robbins, IL 60472 • ALTA

Sheary Edward J. • Director • Asheville-Buncombe Library System • Asheville, NC 28801 • ALCTS ALSC PLA RASD

Sheble Mary Ann • Librarian II • University of Alabama • Tuscaloosa, AL 35487-0266 • ALCTS LAMA LHRT

Shechtman Dorothy • Library Director • Tappan Library • Tappan, NY 10983 • PLA

Shedd-Driskel Meredith A. • Library of Congress • Washington, DC 20541

Shedd Carol J. • Outreach Librarian • Harvard University Center for International Affairs Library • Cambridge, MA 02138

Shedden David B. • Archivist • Poynter Institute for Media Studies • St Petersburg, FL 33701 • ACRL RASD

Shedlock James • Chicago, IL 60613 • ACRL RASD

Sheehan Amy J. • Student • University of Texas at Austin Graduate School of Library & Information Sciences • Austin, TX 78712-1276 • NMRT

Sheehan Anne • Children's Librarian • Wellesley Free Library • Wellesley, MA 02181-5989 • YALSA

Sheehan Connie • New Berlin, WI 53151 • PLA

Sheehan Margaret M. • Librarian IV-Catlog Spec. • Toledo-Lucas County Public Library • Toledo, OH 43624 • ALCTS

Sheehan Mary Ann • Reg. Info. Services Librarian • Fairfax County Public Library Fairfax City Regional Branch • Fairfax, VA 22030 • RASD

Sheehan Michael G. • Student • Indiana University School of Library and Information Science • Bloomington, IN 47405

Sheehan Patricia K. • Assistant Coordinator, HALS • Houston Public Library • Houston, TX 77002 • PLA

Sheehan Shirley A. • Branch Librarian • Mobile Public Library Monte L Moorer Branch • Mobile, AL 36608-1827

Sheehan Virginia M. • Shrewsbury, MA 01545

Sheehan William J. Rev. • Biblioteca Apostolica Vaticana • 00120 Vatican City, Vatican

Sheehey Teresa • Reference Librarian • County of Los Angeles Public Library • Downey, CA 90241-7400

Sheehy Carolyn A. • Director of Library Services • North Central College Oesterle Library • Naperville, IL 60540 • ACRL LAMA RASD

Sheehy Helen M • International Documents Ln. • Pennsylvania State University Pattee Library • University Park, PA 16802 • ACRL GODORT

Sheehy Louis G. • Assistant Director • Trumbull Library • Trumbull, CT 06611

Sheel Frieda E. • Director • Mineola Memorial Library • Mineola, TX 75773 • PLA

Sheeley Laurence E. • Columbus Metropolitan Library Main Library Branch • Columbus, OH 43215

Sheely Dorothea • Newport Beach, CA 92663 • Continuing

Sheeran Carole A. • Alexandria, VA 22302

Sheerin Vivian • Librarian • Lakeland Regional High School • Wanaque, NJ 07465 • AASL

Sheerin William Dr. • Trustee • Yonkers Public Library • Yonkers, NY 10701 • ALTA

Sheesley Deborah F. • Design Arts/BI Librarian • Drexel University W. W. Hagerty Library • Philadelphia, PA 19104 • ACRL

Sheets Angela F. • Student • Westminster College Reeves Memorial Library • Fulton, MO 65251-1299

Sheets Barbara J. • Librarian • Madison Public Library Sequoya Branch • Madison, WI 53705

Sheets Carol • Trustee • Wyoming Library • Wyoming, MI 49509 • ALSC PLA RASD

Sheets Shirley H. • Associate Director Admin. Servs. • University of Texas at Arlington • Arlington, TX 76019-0497 • LAMA

Sheffer Carol L. • Consultant • New York State Library State Education Department • Albany, NY 12230 • ASCLA PLA

Sheffer Karen M. • Rockville, MD 20853 • ALSC

Sheffield Diana • Reference,Government Doc. • New York Law School • New York, NY 10013 • ACRL LITA RASD GODORT

Sheffield Joanne W. • Potomac Community Library • Potomac, MD 20854 • RASD

Sheffield Rebecca S. • Muncie, IN 47302

Sheffner Margot F. • Student • San Jose State University Division of Library & Information Science • San Jose, CA 95192-0029

Sheffo Belinda M. • Technical Services Librarian • Westmoreland County Cmnty College • Youngwood, PA 15697

Sheffold Donetta A. • Management Assistant • Oregon State University William Jasper Kerr Library • Corvallis, OR 97331-4501 • NMRT SORT

Shehan Carol K. • Student • University of Maryland College of Library and Information Services • College Park, MD 20742-4345 • AASL

Shehan Kay • Assistant Business Librarian • Washington University Libraries • Saint Louis, MO 63130-4899 • ACRL RASD LIRT

Sheil Joan Sr • Director • Teikyo Marycrest University Cone Library • Davenport, IA 52804 • ACRL

Sheinwald Fran • Senior Librarian • New York State Department of Law • New York, NY 10271

Shelden Lucinda D. • Hillyard Branch Library • Spokane, WA 99207 • ALSC

Sheldon Brooke E. • Dean • University of Texas at Austin Graduate School of Library & Information Sciences • Austin, TX 78712-1276 • PLA

Sheldon Janis I. • Kingwood, TX 77345 • ALSC

Sheldon L. Scott • Admin Libn for Lib Development • New Mexico State Library • Santa Fe, NM 87503

Sheldon Susan M. • Catalog Librarian • New Mexico State Library • Santa Fe, NM 87503 • ALCTS

Sheldon Susan W. • Poway, CA 92064 • AASL PLA

Sheldon Ted P. • Director • University of Missouri-Kansas City Library • Kansas City, MO 64110-2499 • ACRL RASD

Sheley Marie D. • Public Services Librarian • Nicholls State University Allen J. Ellender Memorial Library • Thibodaux, LA 70310 • ACRL

Shelfer Katherine M. • Business Reference Librarian • Florida State University • Tallahassee, FL 32306-2047 • LITA RASD LRRT

Shelkrot Elliot • President & Director • Free Library of Philadelphia • Philadelphia, PA 19103 • ALTA LAMA PLA

Shell Kathy • Trustee • Newnan-Coweta Public Library • Newnan, GA 30263

Shell Suzanne L. • Reference Librarian • United States Marine Corps Air Station Library • Cherry Point, NC 28533 • RASD AFLRT FLRT

Shellaby Suzanne • Head, Library Task Force • University of California-Los Angeles (UCLA) • Los Angeles, CA 90024-1450 • ACRL LAMA

Shellenbarger Linda K. • Middleburgh Heights, OH 44130 • AASL VRT

Sheller Cate • Academic Computer Ctr Director • Mount Mercy College J. Edward Lundy Library • Cedar Rapids, IA 52402

Sheller John F. • Reference Librarian • McChord Air Force Base • Tacoma, WA 98438 • ACRL PLA AFLRT EMIERT IRRT NMRT

Shelley Anne T. • Senior Benefit Assistant • Kimberly-Clarke Corporation • Neenah, WI 54956 • ALCTS RASD

Shelley Carolyn J. • Elkhart, IN 46514

Shelley Kathleen M. • Reference Librarian • Enoch Pratt Free Library • Baltimore, MD 21201-4484

Shelley Michael H. • Special Projects • Library of Congress • Washington, DC 20541 • LAMA

Shelley Tru • Long Beach, CA 90813

Shellinger Mark E. • Principal • Weller Elementary School • Fairbanks, AK 99701

Shellman Richard • Gibson City, IL 60936 • RASD

Sheltman Richard A. • Library Trustee • Zion-Benton Public Library District • Zion, IL 60099

Shelton Cynthia • Bibliographer • University of California-Los Angeles University Research Library • Los Angeles, CA 90024 • ACRL ALCTS

Shelton Diana W. • Assistant Director Inf. Serv. • University of Wyoming • Laramie, WY 82071 • ACRL

Shelton Diane E. • Director • Graceland College Frederick Madison Smith Library • Lamoni, IA 50140 • ACRL LAMA

Shelton Elease B. • Librarian • Luthersville Elementary School • Luthersville, GA 30251 • AASL YALSA

Shelton Gregory A. • Assistant Librarian • United States Naval Observatory • Washington, DC 20392-5100 • ALCTS AFLRT FLRT

Shelton John L. • Lawrenceville, GA 30246

Shelton Kathryn H. • Librarian/Historical Library • Alaska State Library • Juneau, AK 99811-571 • ACRL ALCTS

Shelton Melinda G. • Student • Birmingham Public Library • Birmingham, AL 35203

Shelton Richard L. • Lake Lanier Regional Library Peachtree Corners Branch • Norcross, GA 30092 • RASD

Shelton Thomas C. • Student • Drexel University College of Information Studies • Philadelphia, PA 19104-2875

Shelver Elizabeth • Minneapolis, MN 55403 • LAMA PLA *Life*

Shemberg Marian H. • Bowling Green, OH 43402 • IFRT

Shen Alice • Pace University Law Library • White Plains, NY 10603-3796

Shen Emily Chung-Yi • Monographer/Acqusitions Ln • University of Texas at Arlington • Arlington, TX 76019-0497 • ACRL IRRT

Shen Jean L. • New York, NY 10010

Shen Li-chun • Student • Rutgers University School of Communication Information & Library Studies • New Brunswick, NJ 08903 • ALCTS LITA RASD

Shen Margaret Y. • Head of Catalog Department • Cleveland Public Library • Cleveland, OH 44114-1271 • ALCTS LITA

Shen Shirley • Manager, Cataloging • County of Los Angeles Public Library • Hawthorne, CA 90250

Shen Teresa C. • South Holland Public Library • South Holland, IL 60473 • ALCTS

Shen Wei • Bronx, NY 10469

Shen Xiaoyan • University of the Pacific • Stockton, CA 95211 • LITA

Shen Ying • Student • Rutgers University School of Communication Information & Library Studies • New Brunswick, NJ 08903

Shen Zhijia • Student • University of Illinois Graduate School of Library and Information Science • Urbana, IL 61801

Shencavitz Susan • Librarian • Richmond Elementary School • Richmond, VT 05477 • AASL

Shenette Cynthia A. • Librarian • Clark University Robert Hutchings Goddard Library • Worcester, MA 01610 • ACRL

Shepard Aaron • Davis, CA 95617

Shepard Barbara • Automated Services Librarian • Occidental College Library • Los Angeles, CA 90041 • ACRL LITA SRRT

Shepard Beatrice G. • Indianapolis, IN 46240

Shepard Caroline L. • Youth Services Consultant • North Carolina State Library • Raleigh, NC 27601-2807 • ALSC YALSA

Shepard Jean E. • Brooksville, ME 04614 • AASL IFRT LRRT SRRT

Shepard Josephine • Denver, CO 80227 • Continuing

Shepard Julianne • Tacoma, WA 98403

Shepard L Phelps • Tacoma, WA 98405

Shepard Martha • Victoria BC, V8t 5B5 Canada

Shepard Nancy • Weed, CA 96094 • ACRL

Shepard Susan E. • Student • University of Western Ontario School of Library & Information Science • London ON, N6G 1H1 Canada • IFRT LHRT

Shepherd-Shlechter Rae C. • Louisville, KY 40214 • PLA GODORT

Shepherd Antoinette • Assistant Director • Helen Hall Public Library • League City, TX 77573 • LITA PLA

Shepherd Gay W. • Reference Bibliographic Ln • Greensboro College James Addison Jones Library • Greensboro, NC 27401 • ACRL LIRT

Shepherd Jane B. • Wilkesboro, NC 28697 • ALSC NMRT

Shepherd Murray C. • University Librarian • University of Waterloo Library • Waterloo ON, N2L 3G1 Canada • ACRL

Shepherd Odette F. • Head of Serials Department • Indiana University at Bloomington University Libraries • Bloomington, IN 47405 • ALCTS LITA *Life*

Shepherd Sandra S. • Media Coordinator • Sylvan Elementary School • Snow Camp, NC 27349 • AASL

Sheppard Dawn F. • Librarian • Ohio Township Public Library System • Newburgh, IN 47630

Sheppard Deann A. • Library Media Specialist • Lorraine Academy #72 Library Media Center • Buffalo, NY 14220 • AASL

Sheppard Jan • Sales Rep • NOTIS Systems • Raleigh, NC 27609 • LITA

Sheppard Jocelyn A. • Catalog Librarian • Bethany College Phillips Memorial Library • Bethany, WV 26032 • ACRL

Sheppard Kathryn Ann • Technical Services Coordinator • Glendale Public Library • Glendale, CA 91205 • ALCTS

Sheppard Sandra F. • Acquisitions Librarian • Lincoln Land Community College Learning Resource Center • Springfield, IL 62794-9256 • ACRL SRRT

Sherby Louise S. • Assistant Director Public Servs. • University of Missouri Miller-Nichols Library • Kansas City, MO 64110 • ACRL LITA RASD

Shereff Susan • Trustee • Cumberland County Public Library and Information Center • Fayetteville, NC 28301

Sherer Beverly R. • Admin Asst to Head of EDP • Illinois Department of Energy and Natural Resources Library • Springfield, IL 62704-1892

Sherer Elaine R. • Research Librarian • Massachusetts Bay Community College Learning Resource Center • Wellesley, MA 02181 • ACRL

Sherer Ree • Vice President • Ebsco Subscription Services • Birmingham, AL 35202 • ACRL ALCTS

Sheridan Amy A. • San Diego, CA 92122-2625

Sheridan Clare • Library Director • Warner Baird Spring Lake Township Library • Spring Lake, MI 49456

Sheridan Diane L. • Student • Indiana University-Purdue University at Indianapolis Library (IUPUI) • Indianapolis, IN 46202 • RASD

Sheridan Donna L. • Student • Catholic University of America School of Library and Information Science • Washington, DC 20064 • AASL IFRT NMRT SRRT

Sheridan Elizabeth A. • Youth Services Librarian • Upper Arlington Public Library • Upper Arlington, OH 43221

Sheridan John • Head Librarian • Colorado College Tutt Library • Colorado Springs, CO 80903 • ACRL SRRT

Sheridan Leslie W. • Director of Libraries • University of Toledo William S. Carlson Library • Toledo, OH 43606-3399 • ACRL

Sheridan Margaret G. Mrs • Altoona, PA 16601 • Continuing

Sheridan Robert N. • Ronkonkoma, NY 11779 • PLA RASD *Life*

Sheridan Susan M. • Head of Technical Services • Amherst College Robert Frost Library • Amherst, MA 01002 • ACRL ALCTS

Sherif Sue • Public Services Librarian • Fairbanks North Star Borough Public Library & Regional Center-Noel Wien Library • Fairbanks, AK 99701 • ALSC PLA

Sheriff Judith Anne • Children's & Young Adult Ln • Duluth Public Library • Duluth, MN 55802 • YALSA IFRT

Sherk Jeffrey L. • Student • University of Missouri-Columbia School of Library & Informational Science • Columbia, MO 65211

Sherlock John • Assistant Librarian • University of California-Davis Library • Davis, CA 95616 • ACRL LIRT SRRT

Sherlock Katy A. • University of Illinois Graduate School of Library and Information Science • Urbana, IL 61801 • LAMA

Sherman-Peterson Ronald • Head Cataloger • Bellevue Public Schools • Bellevue, WA 98009-9010 • ALCTS LITA

Sherman Ajno T. • Saint Louis, MO 63130

Sherman Arthur E. • Acquisitions Librarian • Saint John's University Library • Jamaica, NY 11439 • ACRL ALCTS MAGERT

Sherman Barbara A. • Student • Redan Library • Redan, GA 30074

Sherman Barbara Hope • Circulation Librarian • DePaul University Libraries • Chicago, IL 60614

Sherman Betty C. • Librarian/Media Director • Eureka Senior High School • Eureka, CA 95501

Sherman Deborah A. • Childern's Coordinator • Medina County District Library • Medina, OH 44256 • ALSC PLA

Sherman Eileen • Boston, MA 02114

Sherman Gale W. • Early Childhood Librarian • Pocatello Public Library • Pocatello, ID 83201 • ALSC

Sherman Janice E. • Morton, IL 61550 • PLA

Sherman Leslye J. • Coordinator Ch. & YA • Lane Public Library • Hamilton, OH 45011 • ALSC YALSA

Sherman Louise L. • Library Media Specialist • Anna C. Scott School • Leonia, NJ 07605 • AASL ALSC

Sherman Madeline R. • Librarian • Proctor Junior-Senior High School Library • Proctor, VT 05765 • AASL

Sherman Mary A. • Director • Pioneer Library System • Norman, OK 73069 • LAMA PLA IRRT

Sherman Maxine • Tech. Librarian I/Cataloger • Cuyahoga County Public Library Parma-Snow Branch • Parma, OH 44134-2789

Sherman Natalie E. • Children's Specialist • Orange County Public Library Cypress Branch • Cypress, CA 90630 • ALSC EMIERT

Sherman Roger S. • Information Specialist • SRI International Research Information Services • Menlo Park, CA 94025

Sherman Sarah • Head of Womens Collections • Northwestern University Library • Evanston, IL 60208-2300 • Life

Sherod Martha C. • Reference Librarian • Davenport Public Library • Davenport, IA 52801

Sherrard Karen L. • Director • Albion Public Library • Albion, MI 49224 • LAMA

Sherrer Johannah • Head of Reference • Duke University William R. Perkins Library • Durham, NC 27706 • ACRL LAMA RASD

Sherrod Bobbie C. • Library Assistant • Kettleson Memorial Library • Sitka, AK 99835

Sherrod Marge T. • Trustee • New Orleans Public Library • New Orleans, LA 70140

Sherrod Ruth L. • Ijamsville, MD 21754

Sherry Candice S. • Asbury College • Wilmore, KY 40390

Sherry Joan • Upper Saddle River Public Library • Upper Saddle River, NJ 07458-1699 • ALSC

Sherry Timothy • Trustee • Pierce County Rural Library District • Tacoma, WA 98446 • ALTA PLA

Sherwin Margaret • Librarian • Southern Illinois University • Edwardsville, IL 62026

Sherwin Nancy H. • Public Services Librarian • Porter Public Library • Westlake, OH 44145 • PLA RASD

Sherwin Phyllis L. • Assistant Branch Manager • Allen County Public Library • Fort Wayne, IN 46801 • YALSA

Sherwood Arlyn K. • Map Librarian • Illinois State Library • Springfield, IL 62701-1796 • GODORT MAGERT

Sherwood Janice W. • York, PA 17404 • Continuing

Sherwood Judith • Supv Librn Technical Services • San Diego Public Library • San Diego, CA 92101 • LITA

Sherwood Julie D. • Children's Librarian • Stockton-San Joaquin Public Lib Tracy Branch • Tracy, CA 95376 • ALSC

Sherwood Mary Frances • McNeese State University Lether E. Frazar Memorial Library • Lake Charles, LA 70609

Sherwood Nancy • Head Technical Services • Garden City Public Library • Garden City, NY 11530

Sherwood Pamela A • Student • University of Washington Graduate School of Library and Information Science • Seattle, WA 98195

Sherwood Shelia H. • Children's Librarian • Queens Borough Public Library Fresh Meadows Branch • Fresh Meadows, NY 11365

Shestack Jerome J. Esq • Trustee • Free Library of Philadelphia • Philadelphia, PA 19103 • ALTA

Shetler Diane L. • Robbins Library Junior Library • Arlington, MA 02174 • ALSC

Sheviak Jean K. • Systems Librarian • Union College Schaffer Library • Schenectady, NY 12308 • ALCTS LITA

Shewmake Connie L. • Public Services Librarian • Lake Land College • Mattoon, IL 61938

Shewmaker Julia McClure • Information Specialist • Science Applocations International Corporation (S.A.I.C.) • Oak Ridge, TN 37831 • RASD EMIERT ERT NMRT

Shiao Julia I. • Branch Librarian • Mercy College Libraries Yorktown Campus • Yorktown, NY 10598 • ACRL GODORT

Shiau Ian-Lih Mary • Senior Librarian • Grumman Melbourne Systems Division • Melbourne, FL 32902 • LITA

Shiban Janet R. • Student • University of California Los Angeles Graduate School of Library & Information Science • Los Angeles, CA 90024

Shieh Frances • Branch Library Manager • Queens Borough Public Library Auburndale-Clearview Branch • Flusing, NY 11358

Shiel Penny J. • Tallmadge, OH 44278

Shields Brigid F. • Librarian • Minnesota Historical Society • Saint Paul, MN 55102

Shields Caryl L. • Librarian • United States Geological Survey • Denver, CO 80225 • ACRL FLRT

Shields Catherine C. • Jewett City, CT 06351

Shields Dorothy Huntwork • Associate Librarian • University of Michigan Libraries • Ann Arbor, MI 48109-1205 • ACRL RASD SRRT

Shields Dorothy M. • Associate Professor • Brigham Young University School of Library & Information Sciences • Provo, UT 84602 • ALCTS ALSC

Shields Gerald R. • Leland, IL 60531 • PLA

Shields Joseph E. • Trustee • West Islip Public Library • West Islip, NY 11795-3999 • ALTA ASCLA PLA

Shields Mark W. • Student • Pratt Institute Graduate School of Library & Information Science • Brooklyn, NY 11205 • PLA RASD LRRT

Shields Mary Lynn • Librarian • Lake Forest Park Elementary School • SEattle, WA 98155

Shields Maureen R. • Head Adult Services • New City Library • New City, NY 10956 • PLA IFRT

Shiery Floyd W. • Humanities Cataloger • University of Utah Marriott Library • Salt Lake City, UT 84112-1179 • ACRL ALCTS

Shiff Joel • Trustee • Peninsula Public Library • Lawrence, NY 11559

Shiffler Marguerite I. • School Librarian • Stafford Senior High School • Falmouth, VA 22405

Shiflett Lee • Louisiana State University School of Library & Information Science • Baton Rouge, LA 70803-3290 • ACRL GODORT LHRT LRRT

Shiflett Mary Ellen • J. B. Martin Middle School • Paradis, LA 70080 • AASL

Shih Cherie • Librarian • Long Beach Public Library North Branch • Long Beach, CA 90815

Shih Diana • Senior Cataloging Librarian • American Museum of Natural History Library • New York, NY 10024

Shih Mei Yuh • Associate Researcher • Science & Technology Information Center National Science Council • Taipei, Taiwan

Shih Philip C. • Director • Logansport Cass County Public Library Logansport Public Library • Logansport, IN 46947

Shih Win-Yuan • Student • University of Illinois Graduate School of Library and Information Science • Urbana, IL 61801 • LAMA

Shiiba Motoko • Associate Librarian • Tokyo Womans Christian University • Mitaka Tokyo, Japan • ACRL ALCTS

Shilcutt Mary C. • High School Librarian • Richland High School Birdville Independent School District • Fort Worth, TX 76180 • AASL

Shill Harold B. • Head of Library & Info Services • Pennsylvania State University Heindel Library • Middletown, PA 17057 • ACRL LAMA LITA RASD GODORT

Shill Vickie B. • Student • University of Alabama School of Library & Information Studies • Tuscaloosa, AL 35487-0252

Shilling-Koh Caren A. • Flushing, NY 11357-3436

Shilling Natalie J. • Youth Librarian • Multnomah County Library Woodstock Branch • Portland, OR 97206

Shilling Wynne • Trustee • Half Hollow Hills Community Public Library • Dix Hills, NY 11746 • ALTA

Shimabukuro K. T. • Librarian • United States Information Agency Library Program (USIA) • Washington, DC 20547 • LITA

Shimamura Dayle Y. • Eli Lilly & Company Tippcoanoe Laboratories DC TL13 • Lafayette, IN 47902 • LITA

Shimel Charlotte • Librarian • Agawam High School Library • Agawam, MA 01001 • AASL

Shimer James F. • Librarian • Avon Grove High School • West Grove, PA 19390 • AASL YALSA

Shimko Florence • N Brunswick, NJ 08902 • PLA RASD *Life*

Shimkus Beverly W. • Savannah, GA 31405

Shimoguchi Wayne • Catalog Librarian • San Diego State University Library • San Diego, CA 92119-2120

Shimojima Anne L. • Childrens Services • Braeside School • Highland Park, IL 60035 • AASL ALSC

Shimon Louise G. • Media Specialist • United Community School • Boone, IA 50036 • AASL

Shimp Andrew G. • Reference Librarian • University of Bridgeport Magnus Wahlstrom Library • Bridgeport, CT 06601 • ACRL SRRT

Shimrock Dana K. • Garrett Community College • McHenry, MD 21541

Shin K. Soon • Medical Librarian • National Library of Medicine • Bethesda, MD 20894

Shindel Maxine • Library Media Specialist • Chase Elementary School Baltimore County Board of Education • Baltimore, MD 21220 • AASL IFRT

Shindell Ingrid C. • Networking Specialist • Auto-Graphics Inc. • Phoenix, MD 21131 • ALCTS

Shiner Elaine P. • Rare Book Cataloger • John Carter Brown Library • Providence, RI 02912 • ACRL ALCTS IFRT

Shing C. • Coos Bay, OR 97420

Shingler Joyce • DeFuniak Springs, FL 32433

Shinn Carla Henry • Asheboro, NC 27203-4450

Shinn Isabella E. • Seattle, WA 98119-3779 • Continuing

Shipe Susan A. • Student • Kent State University School of Library & Information Science • Kent, OH 44242-0001 • PLA

Shipe Timothy • Coor. Humanities Division • University of Iowa Libraries • Iowa City, IA 52242-1379 • ACRL

Shipley Cynthia K. • Media Specialist • S. Lanham Elementary School • FPO, AP 96306-005 • ALSC

Shipley John G. • Business & Science Reference Ln. • Miami-Dade Public Library System • Miami, FL 33130-1504 • LITA NMRT

Shipley Paula T. • Assistant Librarian • Ransom Everglades School • Miami, FL 33157 • AASL

Shipman George W. • University Librarian • University of Oregon Library • Eugene, OR 97403-1299 • ACRL LITA *Life*

Shipman Kelly R. • Student • University of Tennessee-Knoxville Graduate School of Library & Information Science • Knoxville, TN 37996-4330

Shipp Carol • Children's Librarian • Chicago Public Library Martin Luther King Jr Branch • Chicago, IL 60616

Shipp Ruth E. • Seattle, WA 98125

Shippert Paul A. • Lusby, MD 20657 • AASL

Shippey Susan S. • Science Librarian • Rochester Public Library • Rochester, NY 14604

Shipps Anthony W. • Librarian Emeritus • Indiana University School of Library and Information Science • Bloomington, IN 47405 • ACRL RASD

Shirato Linda • Eastern Michigan Univ • Ypsilanti, MI 48197 • ACRL LIRT

Shiren Leslie B. • Wilmette, IL 60091

Shires Jill • University of Southern Mississippi • Hattiesburg, MS 39406-5053 • ALCTS

Shires Leslyn M. • Assistant Superintendent • Wisconsin Division for Library Services • Madison, WI 53707 • ASCLA

Shires Nancy P. • Reference Librarian • East Carolina University Joyner Library • Greenville, NC 27858-4353 • LITA RASD

Shirey Stewart C. • Financial Analyst • Consolidated Fianacial Resources • Greenville, TX 75401

Shirk Gary M. • Bow, NH 03304 • ALCTS LAMA

Shirk John C. • Library Director • North Central Bible College T. J. Jones Memorial Library • Minneapolis, MN 55404 • ACRL PLA LIRT

Shirky Martha H. • Language & Literature Librarian • University of Missouri-Columbia Ellis Library • Columbia, MO 65201

Shirley Elender K. • Student • University of Oklahoma School of Library & Information Studies • Norman, OK 73019 • EMIERT NMRT SRRT

Shirley Elizabeth Rae • Winston-Salem, NC 27104

Shirley Iris C. • Librarian • Fairwold School Media Center • Columbia, SC 29203 • AASL

Shirley Jonathan Y. • Librarian-Teacher • Shanksville-Stony Creek School Library • Shanksville, PA 15560 • AASL ALSC LITA YALSA

Shirley Lisa E. • Toronto ON, M6R 1R2 Canada • IFRT

Shirley Norma • Poughkeepsie, NY 12603 • AASL

Shiroma Susan G. • Government Documents Librarian • New York University Elmer Holmes Bobst Library • New York, NY 10012 • ACRL LAMA RASD GODORT IRRT

Shisler Shirley • Head of Reference Department • Public Library of Des Moines • Des Moines, IA 50308-1791 • PLA RASD GODORT

Shiu Pei-Jung • Government Publications Libn • University of California-Irvine Library • Irvine, CA 92713 • ACRL GODORT

Shive Ed • Sales Manager • Midwest Library Sales • Indianapolis, IN 46224

Shively Daniel Mr. • Cataloging Coordinator • Patrick J. Stapleton Library Indiana University of Pennsylvania • Indiana, PA 15705 • ACRL LITA *Life*

Shivers Rebecca R. • Student • University of North Texas School of Library & Information Sciences • Denton, TX 76203 • PLA AFLRT NMRT

Shklanka Olga • Chairman of Library Services • Regional College • Grande Prairie AB, Canada • ALCTS LAMA

Shlaes Nancy • Professor of Library Science • Governors State University University Library • University Park, IL 60466 • ACRL

Shlensky Nancy • Youth Service Coordinator • East Chicago Public Library • E. Chicago, IN 46312

Shnay Zipporah D. • Executive Director • Jewish Public Library • Montreal, PQ, H3W 1M6 Canada • LAMA PLA

Shneiderman Dee • Student • University of North Carolina • Greensboro, NC 27412-5001 • ALCTS LITA PLA RASD IFRT NMRT SRRT

Shoaf Eric C. • Preservation Officer • Duke University William R. Perkins Library • Durham, NC 27706 • ALCTS

Shoar Shahin • Sr. Assistant Librarian • State University of New York at Plattsburgh (SUNY) • Plattsburgh, NY 12901 • ACRL IRRT NMRT

Shoch Trudy • Cataloging Librarian • Lake Forest Library • Lake Forest, IL 60045

Shocket Eileen • Chief Librarian • Saint Edwards University Scarborough Phillips Library • Austin, TX 78704 • ACRL ALCTS LAMA LITA RASD GODORT IFRT LIRT

Shockley Doris T. • Atlanta, GA 30331

Shoemake Peggy C. • Director of Learning Resources • John Wood Community College • Quincy, IL 62301 • ACRL LAMA

Shoemaker Jane E. • North High School • Sheboygan, WI 53083 • AASL

Shoemaker Joel • Library Media Specialist • Southeast Junior High School • Iowa City, IA 52240 • YALSA

Shoemaker Karen J. • Portland, OR 97210-3625

Shoemaker Kellie M. • Clementon, NJ 08021-5851 • IFRT

Shoemaker Margot M. • Children's Librarian • Lee Memorial Library • Allendale, NJ 07401 • ALSC

Shoffner Ralph M. • Ringgold Management Systems Inc. • Beaverton, OR 97075-0368 • ACRL ALCTS LITA PLA LRRT

Shoffstall Betsy Ann • District Librarian • Ridgemont Local Schools • Ridgeway, OH 43345 • AASL

Shogren Martha S. • Sebastopol, CA 95472 • ALSC

Shogren William S. • Sturgeon Bay, WI 54235 • ACRL LAMA PLA

Shold Rosemary • Division Chief • Washington State Library • Olympia, WA 98504-2479 • ALCTS LAMA

Sholund Elizabeth G. • Reference Librarian • Timberland Regional Library Lacey Branch • Lacey, WA 98503 • RASD

Shoniker Fintan R. Rev. • Saint Vincent College & Archabbey Libraries • Latrobe, PA 15650-2690

Shonrock Diana D. • Assistant Library Instr Prof • Iowa State University Library • Ames, IA 50011-2140 • ACRL LIRT

Shontz David E. • Head of Access Services • University of Texas Health Science Center Briscoe Library • San Antonio, TX 78284-7940 • ACRL LAMA SRRT

Shontz Marilyn L. • Assistant Professor • University of North Carolina Department of Library & Information Studies • Greensboro, NC 27412-5001 • AASL

Shook Bruce Anne P • Media Specialist • Mendenhall Middle School • Greensboro, NC 27408 • AASL YALSA

Shook Persis • Trustee • Tacoma Public Library • Tacoma, WA 98402 • ALTA

Shope Grace E. • Instructional Materials Supv • Abington School District • Abington, PA 19001 • AASL

Shorb Betsy • Yng Ad Spec • Prince George's County Memorial Library Bowie Branch • Bowie, MD 20715 • YALSA

Shorb Stephen R. • Student • University of Iowa School of Library & Information Science • Iowa City, IA 52242 • ACRL LAMA LITA PLA

Shore Elliott • History Librarian • Institute For Advanced Studies Library • Princeton, NJ 08543-0631 • ACRL ALCTS SRRT

Shore John R. • Dir. of Media & Technology • Winston-Salem Forsyth County School • Winston-Salem, NC 27102 • AASL

Shore Karen M. • Library Media Specialist • Cumberland High School Library • Cumberland, RI 02864 • AASL

Shore Marilee • Administrator • Lanier Library Association, Inc. • Tryon, NC 28782

Shore Marshall A. • Brooklyn, NY 11223 • ALSC SRRT

Shorstein Sylvia • Foundation Board/end • Jacksonville Public Libraries Main Library • Jacksonville, FL 32202

Short Bradley H. • Creative Arts Librarian • Brandeis University Goldfarb Library • Waltham, MA 02254-9110 • ACRL

Short Eleanor P. • Technical Services Librarian • Frederick County Public Library C. Burr Artz Library • Frederick, MD 21701 • ALCTS PLA

Short John T. • Avon, CT 06001 • AASL ALTA VRT

Short Judith A. • Joppatowne High School • Joppa, MD 21085 • AASL

Short Mary H. • New York, NY 10014 • Continuing

Short Nancy J. • Student • Sussex County Department of Libraries • Georgetown, DE 19947 • ALSC

Short Thomas M. • Clerk • Indianapolis Marion County Public Library • Indianapolis, IN 46206

Short Virginia • Librarian • University of California Shields Library • Davis, CA 95616 • ACRL RASD

Short William M. • Coordinator of Public Services • Rhodes College Burrow Library • Memphis, TN 38112 • ACRL

Shorten Anne Charlene • Owego Free Academy Library • Owego, NY 13827 • AASL

Shortreed Vivian H. • Worcester, MA 01602 • ACRL

Shotola Carol A. • Administrative Assistant • Berwyn Public Library • Berwyn, IL 60402

Shoup Robin J • School Librarian • Fort Couch Middle School Upper Saint Clair School District • Upper St. Clair, PA 15241 • AASL ALSC

Shouse Daniel L. • Student • Indiana University School of Library and Information Science • Bloomington, IN 47405 • LITA

Shouse Richard • San Francisco, CA 94115 • ILERT

Shove Raymond H. • Professor Emeritus • University of Minnesota • Minneapolis, MN 55414 • ACRL RASD *Life*

Showalter-Moore Katherine A. • APO, AA 34037

Showalter Ruth • Trustee • Calvert County Public Library • Prince Frederick, MD 20678 • ALTA

Showman Kathy • Media Specialist • West Friendship Elementary School • West Friendship, MD 21794 • AASL

Shoyinka Patricia H. • Librarian • Internal Revenue Services District Library • Boston, MA 02203 • ACRL

Shrack Patricia R. • Student • University of Maryland College of Library and Information Services • College Park, MD 20742-4345 • AASL ALSC

Shrader Juanita Jay • Librarian • Fort Myers Christian School • Ft. Myers, FL 33907

Shreeves Edward • Asst. Univ Librarian Collection • University of Iowa Library • Iowa City, IA 52242 • ACRL ALCTS

Shreffler Barbara A. • Rice University Fondren Library • Houston, TX 77251-1892

Shreffler John R. • Chicago, IL 60615

Shreve Doris L. Mrs. • Chesterfield, MO 63017 • ASCLA YALSA *Continuing*

Shreve Lillian S. • Ft. Myers, FL 33901

Shrewsbury Lynn D. • Manager • Southeastern Library Network (SOLINET) • Atlanta, GA 30309-2955

Shreyer Andrew D. • Serials Cataloger • University of California UCSB Library • Santa Barbara, CA 93106-9010

Shrier Jean H. • Peoria Public Library • Peoria, IL 61602

Shrive Anita • Librarian • Old Forge Elementary School • Old Forge, PA 18518

Shriver Elizabeth A. • Roxboro Middle School • Cleveland Heights, OH 44106 • AASL YALSA

Shriver Jane A. • Head,Copy Cataloging • University of Minnesota • Minneapolis, MN 55455 • ACRL ALCTS NMRT

Shriver Margaret A. • Appleton, WI 54914

Shroder Emelie J. • Assistant Commissioner • Chicago Public Library • Chicago, IL 60605 • LAMA PLA

Shropshire Kathy • Head of Branch • Greensboro Public Library Guilford College Branch • Greensboro, NC 27410 • PLA

Shropshire Marybeth • Media Generalist • Bishop Kelly High School • Boise, ID 83709 • AASL

Shropshire Sandra • Idaho State University Eli M. Oboler Library • Pocatello, ID 83209-8089

Shrote Stanley C. • Louisville, KY 40203

Shtern Avrom David • Archival Researcher • Canadian Jewish Congress National Archives • Montreal PQ, H3G 1C5 Canada

Shu Evena • Reference Librarian • Bruggemeyer Memorial Library City of Monterey Park • Monterey Park, CA 91754

Shuart James M. • Hofstra University Libraries • Hempstead, NY 11550 • ACRL ASCLA LAMA

Shubeck Elizabeth A. • Reference Librarian • Addison Public Library • Addison, IL 60101-2499

Shubert Joseph F. • State Librarian • New York State Library State Education Department • Albany, NY 12230 • ASCLA PLA

Shubert Steven B. • Toronto, M4K 2Z3 Canada • ALCTS LHRT

Shuchman Marilyn • Assistant Branch Librarian • Brooklyn Public Library Sheepshead Bay Branch • Brooklyn, NY 11235

Shuck Robert L. • Head of Circulation • University of Colorado At Colorado Springs Library • Colorado Springs, CO 80933-7150

Shuey Andrea L. • Branch Manager • Dallas Public Library Pleasant Grove Branch • Dallas, TX 75217-4399 • LAMA PLA *Life*

Shufeldt Patricia S. • Coordinator, Technical Services • Greenville County Library • Greenville, SC 29601 • ALCTS LITA PLA *Life*

Shugar Candace L. • Library Media Specialist • Jones Junior High School • Toledo, OH 43609 • AASL

Shugars Jacqueline B. • Assistant Director • Spencer Public Library • Spencer, IA 51301

Shuh Barbara A. • Asst. Mgr. Cataloging Section • Canada Institute for Scientific & Technical Information National Research Council • Ottawa ON, K1A 0S2 Canada • LITA

Shukitt Pamela A • Wilmington College Library • New Castle, DE 19720 • ACRL

Shuldiner Richard M. • Student • Queens College Graduate School of Library & Information Studies • Flushing, NY 11367 • IFRT SRRT

Shuler Jackye W. • Library Assistant • Alabama Public Library Service • Montgomery, AL 36130

Shuler John A. • Dept. Hd od Documents, Maps Mirc • Colgate University Everett Needham Case Library • Hamilton, NY 13346 • GODORT

Shulman Marian P. • Saint John's University School of Law Library • Jamaica, NY 11439 • ACRL

Shulski Marilyn • Business Personnel Manager • Dupage Library System • Geneva, IL 60134

Shults Charlene H. • Reference Librarian • Rutgers University Libraries • New Brunswick, NJ 08903 • ACRL RASD

Shumaker Calvin • Trustee • Spokane Public Library Comstock Building Library • Spokane, WA 99201-0976 • ALTA

Shumaker Lois • Carmichael, CA 95608 • LITA IRRT

Shuman Bruce A. • Wayne State University Library Science Program • Detroit, MI 48202 • RASD IFRT

Shuman Elizabeth S. Mrs • Philadelphia, PA 19118 • ALSC PLA *Continuing*

Shuman Margaret G. • La Gomera, Canary Islands Spain • Continuing

Shumate Christel • Literacy Coordinator • Sussex County Department of Libraries • Georgetown, DE 19947 • PLA

Shumer Barbara L. • West Bloomfield, MI 48322 • ALSC

Shumway Audrey H. • Director • Dixie College Library • Saint George, UT 84770

Shumway Jean M. • Student • University of Iowa School of Library & Information Science • Iowa City, IA 52242

Shunn Phyllis J. • Librarian • Walsh College of Accountancy Business Administration • Troy, MI 48007-7006

Shupe Barbara A. • Chair, Library Dept. • Nassau Community College Library • Garden City, NY 11530 • ACRL MAGERT

Shupe Marjorie E. Miss • Dublin, OH 43017 • Continuing

Shupe Mary S. • Librarian • Sachse Public Library • Sachse, TX 75048

Shuping Elizabeth K. • Youth Services Librarian • Florence County Library • Florence, SC 29501 • YALSA

Shupp Doris L. • Saint Margaret Mary School • Harrisburg, PA 17103

Shurgot Gail S. • Boeing Support Services • Seattle, WA 98124-2207 • LITA

Shurman Richard L. • Administrator • Cooperative Computer Services • Wheeling, IL 60090 • ASCLA LITA

Shurtz Sally A. • Student • Louisiana State University School of Library & Information Science • Baton Rouge, LA 70803-3290 • ACRL RASD IFRT

Shuster Helen M. • Acting Director • Worcester Polytechnical Institute George C Gordon Library • Worcester, MA 01609-2280 • ACRL

Shuster Marilyn • University of North Carolina at Charlotte J. Murrey Atkins Library • Charlotte, NC 28223

Shutkin Sara A. • Archivist/Records Manager • Alverno College Library Media Center • Milwaukee, WI 53234-3922 • ACRL IFRT

Shutt Christopher C. • Lexington Herald-Leader Company • Lexington, KY 40508

Shutters Joan • Trustee • Michigan City Public Library • Michigan City, IN 46360 • ALTA

Shwonek Victoria L. • Student • University of California-Berkeley School of Library & Information Studies • Berkeley, CA 94720 • ALSC NMRT

Shyam Winnie • Librarian • Southern Connecticut State University Hilton C. Buley Library • New Haven, CT 06515

Siano Edna A. • Woodland Presbyterian School • Memphis, TN 38119 • AASL

Siarny William D. Jr. • Library Director • National Live Stock & Meat Board • Chicago, IL 60611

Sias Alice M. • Midland, MI 48640

Siatra Eleni • Teaching Fellow • Miami University Acq Dept. • Oxford, OH 45056 • ACRL IRRT

Sibai Mohamed Makki Dr • Assistant Library Science Prof • King Saud University College of Arts • Riyakh, Saudi Arabia • AASL ACRL ALCTS ALSC ALTA ASCLA LAMA LITA PLA RASD YALSA CLENE ERT GODORT IFRT ILERT IRRT LHRT LIRT LRRT MAGERT SORT SRRT

Sibley Carol Hanson • Cur Ln • Moorhead State University Livingston Lord Library • Moorhead, MN 56563-2989 • ALSC

Sibley Elizabeth A. • University of California-Berkeley Moffitt Undergraduate Library • Berkeley, CA 94720 • ACRL SRRT

Sibley Joan M. • Special Collections • University of Texas Ransom Humanities Research Center • Austin, TX 78713 • ACRL

Sibley Marjorie H. • Augsburg College George Sverdrup Library • Minneapolis, MN 55454 • ACRL *Continuing*

Sibley Melissa J. • Librarian • Hennepin County Library Champlin Library • Champlin, MN 55316 • PLA ERT

Sicherman Robbin M. • Inwood School #4 • Inwood, NY 11696 • AASL ALSC

Siciliano Anthony J. • Head of Technical Services • Indian Trails Public Library District • Wheeling, IL 60090

Sick Karlan K. • Young Adult Specialist • New York Public Library • Bronx, NY 10458 • YALSA

Sickles Linda • Director • Orion Twp. Public Library • Lake Orion, MI 48362 • LAMA PLA IFRT

Sicklesteel Laurel A. • Detroit, MI 48224

Siddall Jean M. • Library Director • Wilson Free Library • Wilson, NY 14172

Siddiqui Moid Ahmad • Reference Specialist • King Fahd University of Petroleum & Minerals Library • Dhahran-31261, Saudi Arabia

Siddoway Richard M. • Director of Library Media Serv. • Davis County School District • Farmington, UT 84025 • AASL NMRT

Sidell Charlotte B. • Needham, MA 02192

Sider Sonya M. • University of Washington UW Extension Office • Seattle, WA 98195 • LITA

Sides Rochelle S. • YA Librarian • Birmingham Public Library Springville Road Branch • Birmingham, AL 35215 • YALSA

Sidman Margaret • Assistant Director • Montville Township Public Library • Montville, NJ 07045 • ALSC YALSA

Sidnell Pamela L. • Children's Librarian • Paris Public Library • Paris, TX 75460

Sidorsky Phyllis G. • Librarian-Lower School • National Cathedral School • Washington, DC 20016 • AASL ALSC

Sidwell Sydney R. • Information Specialist • John D. & Catherine T. MacArthur Foundation • Chicago, IL 60603 • LAMA RASD NMRT

Siebenmorgen Ruth • Berkeley, CA 94705 • LAMA PLA *Life*

Siebens Laura J. • Ln • Explorer Jr. High School • Everett, WA 98204

Siebert Brenda S. • North Whidbey Middle School • Oak Harbor, WA 98277 • AASL

Siebert Evita A. • Assistant Librarian • Kadena AB Library • APO, AP 96368-5135 • ALCTS LAMA RASD AFLRT

Siebert Mary Kay • Chicago, IL 60625-3771 • LITA GODORT

Siebert Roger D. • Reference Librarian • California State University Hayward Library • Hayward, CA 94542 • ACRL RASD MAGERT

Siebert Sara L. • Cockeysville, MD 21030 • Continuing

Sieburth Janice F. • Reference Librarian • University of Rhode Island Pell Marine Science Library • Narragansett, RI 02882 • ACRL RASD

Sieg Julia • Librarian • Central Florida Regional Library • Ocala, FL 32671 • LAMA

Siegal Isabel • Arrington Middle School • Birmingham, AL 35211 • AASL

Siegel Alison B. • Student • Georgia State University • Atlanta, GA 30303-3083 • AASL IFRT

Siegel Ben • Trustee • Lincolnwood Public Library District • Lincolnwood, IL 60646

Siegel Bette L. • Documents Librarian • State Library of Massachusetts • Boston, MA 02133 • ASCLA GODORT

Siegel Gretta • Librarian • Washington State University • Vancouver, WA 98663 • ACRL SRRT

Siegel Leora O. • Urbana, IL 61801

Siegel Lori M. • St. Louis, MO 63130

Siegel Mara H. • Trinity College • Burlington, VT 05401

Siegel Naomi L. • Pittsburgh, PA 15215

Siegel Susan N. • Student • San Jose State University Division of Library & Information Science • San Jose, CA 95192-0029

Siegelbaum Leena • Librarian • Michigan State University Libraries • East Lansing, MI 48824-1048 • ACRL

Siegemund-Broka Barbara G. • Associate Editor • University of Oklahoma Press • Norman, OK 73019

Siegenthaler Myra V. • Head Librarian • Boston University School of Theology Library • Boston, MA 02215 • ACRL LAMA

Sieger Charles F. Jr. • Director • Fairleigh Dickinson University Messler Library • Rutherford, NJ 07070-2299

Siegfried Chris • The American School in London • London NW8 ONP, England • AASL YALSA

Siegfried Patricia S. • Student • Public Library of Charlotte & Mecklenburg County • Charlotte, NC 28202 • ALSC PLA

Siegler Marla • Part-time Librarian • University of Minnesota • Minneapolis, MN 55455

Siegman Gita • Proprietor • GS Associates • Silver Spring, MD 20902

Siegmann Starla C. • Librarian • Wisconsin Lutheran College • Milwaukee, WI 53226 • ACRL

Siegmund Michelle N. • President • RARE Paper & Preservation Services • High Point, NC 27263

Siegrist Edith B. • Professor Emerita • University of South Dakota I.D. Weeks Library • Vermillion, SD 57069-2390 • Continuing

Sielaff B. McKinley • Student • Rutgers University School of Communication Information & Library Studies • New Brunswick, NJ 08903

Siemaszkiewicz Wojciech J. • Librarian • New York Public Library • New York, NY 10018-2788 • ACRL ALCTS EMIERT

Siemens Bessie M. Mrs • Library Director • Universidad De Montemorelos • Montemorelos, Mexico

Siemer Patricia A. • Greene County Public Library • Xenia, OH 45385 • PLA

Siemers Lynne K. • Director • Washington Hospital Center Library Media Services • Washington, DC 20010-2975 • ASCLA LAMA LITA

Sieminski Veronica • Las Cruces, NM 88005 • Continuing

Siemon Jeff • Student • Christian Theological Seminary • Indianapolis, IN 46208 • LITA

Sierka Ann • Brooking-Harbor School District • Brookings, OR 97415

Sierra Michael • Branch Manager • Spokane Public Library Manito Branch • Spokane, WA 99203-2556 • PLA

Siever Robert A. • Books & Monographs Librarian • Franklin & Marshall College Library • Lancaster, PA 17604-3003 • ALCTS

Sievers Arlene M. • Case Western Reserve Univ Freiberger Library • Cleveland, OH 44106-7151 • ACRL ALCTS CLENE IRRT

Sievers Thomas W. • Reference Librarian • Northbrook Public Library • Northbrook, IL 60062

Sieving Pamela C. • Librarian • Kellogg Eye Center L • Ann Arbor, MI 48105 • ACRL RASD IFRT

Siewert Sue • Public Services Manager • Kenosha Public Library • Kenosha, WI 53142-5799

Sifling Donna M. • Part-time Reference Librarian • Indian Prairie Public Library District • Willowbrook, IL 60517

Sifnakis Debbie L. • Student • State University of New York (SUNY) School of Information & Library Studies • Buffalo, NY 14260

Siga Sharon • Peace Library System • Grande Prairie AB, T8W 6T2 Canada

Sigafoos Mary L.J. • Law Librarian • Jackson, Tufts, Cole & Black • San Francisco, CA 94108

Sigala Stephanie C. • Head Librarian • Saint Louis Art Museum Richardson Memorial Library • St. Louis, MO 63110 • ACRL LAMA

Sigborn Rose Ann • Swansea, MA 02777 • AASL

Sigg Rhonda M. • Media Center Specialist • Lincoln Elementary School • Iola, KS 66749 • AASL

Siggins Jack A. • Yale University Sterling Memorial Library • New Haven, CT 06520 • ACRL LAMA

Siggins Linda D. • Regional Collection Coordinator • County of Los Angeles Public Library East County Region 800 • West Covina, CA 91790 • PLA

Sigl Doris M. • North Carolina State University D. H. Hill Library • Raleigh, NC 27695-7111 • ACRL LITA

Sigler Judy • Librarian I • Mobile Public Library • Mobile, AL 36602 • PLA

Sigler Lorraine • Librarian • La Puente High School Library • La Puente, CA 91744 • YALSA

Sigler Marcia • Eugene, OR 97401 • Continuing

Sigler Ronald Dr. • Library Consultant • Dr. Ron Sigler and Associates • Rowland Heights, CA 91748 • LITA PLA IFRT ILERT VRT

Sigmond Phyllis Abbott • Delafield, WI 53018 • AASL

Signorelli Penny J. • Fullerton, CA 92635 • RASD

Signori Dolores A. Dr • Toronto ON, M5R 2M6 Canada • ACRL

Signori Donna L. • Librarian • University of Victoria McPherson Library • Victoria BC, V8W 3H5 Canada • ACRL ALCTS

Sigwald John • Librarian • Unger Memorial Library • Plainview, TX 79072-7235 • ALSC PLA IFRT

Siitonen Leena M. • Associate Professor • University of Rhode Island Graduate School of Library & Information Studies • Kingston, RI 02881-0815 • ACRL IRRT LRRT

Sikes Janice W. • Manager, Special Collections • Atlanta-Fulton Public Library • Atlanta, GA 30303 • ACRL CLENE

Sikes Linda E. • Lorman, MS 39096 • AASL

Sikora Barbara Jean • Director • Livingston Free Public Library • Livingston, NJ 07039 • ALTA LAMA

Sikora Judith • Reference Librarian • Genesee Community College Alfred O'Connell Library • Batavia, NY 14020 • LAMA LITA

Sikora Walter S. • Student • Indiana University School of Library and Information Science • Bloomington, IN 47405

Silan Cleone • Woodland, CA 95695

Silberg Adah • Director • Peninsula Public Library • Lawrence, NY 11559 • LAMA PLA

Silberger Katy • Head Reference Librarian • Marist College Library • Poughkeepsie, NY 12601 • ACRL LITA RASD LIRT

Silberstein Stephen M. • President • Innovative Interfaces, Inc. • Berkeley, CA 94710 • ACRL ALCTS LITA

Silcox Nancy V. • John Adams Elementary School • Alexandria, VA 22311 • AASL YALSA

Silcox Tinsley E. • Director, Hammon Arts Library • Southern Methodist University • Dallas, TX 75275

Silence Lynn K. • Technical Services Supervisor • Saint Louis County Library • St. Louis, MO 63131 • PLA IFRT

Sileo Helena E • Head Librarian • The Ellis School • Pittsburgh, PA 15206 • AASL ALSC

Siler Freddie Bush • Cumberland County Public Library and Information Center • Fayetteville, NC 28301 • ACRL AFLRT FLRT

Siler Sherry Daniel • Chief Librarian • LTV Aerospace & Defense Co. • Dallas, TX 75265-0003

Siler Sue Asher • Student • Catholic University of America School of Library and Information Science • Washington, DC 20064

Silk Bonita J. • Kernersville, NC 27284 • PLA

Silk Eleana S. • Librarian • Saint Vladimir's Seminary Library • Crestwood, NY 10707 • ACRL

Silk Susan L. • President • Media Strategies Inc. • Chicago, IL 60610 • IFRT

Sill Laura A. • University of Notre Dame Theodore M. Hesburgh Library • Notre Dame, IN 46556 • LAMA NMRT

Sill Lois P. • Reference Librarian • Clemson University Robert Muldrow Cooper Library • Clemson, SC 29634-3001 • ACRL RASD

Silletto Suzanne M. • Glendale, CA 91202-2345 • NMRT

Silliman Alice M. • Grand Haven, MI 49417 • PLA RASD *Continuing*

Silloway Mary H. • Mendon, VT 05701 • ACRL ALTA PLA

Silva Betty D. • Fairfield High School • Fairfield, CA 94533 • AASL

Silva Donald A. • El Cajon, CA 92020

Silva Elizabeth Talbot • Community Relations Coordinator • Alameda County Library System • Fremont, CA 94538 • LAMA PLA IFRT

Silver Barbara C. • Librarian • University of California UCSB Library • Santa Barbara, CA 93106-9010 • GODORT

Silver Carole K. • Library Media Specialist • Long Beach Middle School Library Media Center • Long Beach, NY 11561 • AASL YALSA

Silver Cy H. • Facilities Planner • California State Library • Sacramento, CA 94237-0001 • LAMA

Silver Dale • Richmond, VA 23220

Silver Dorcas L. • Librarian I • High Point Public Library • High Point, NC 27261 • ALCTS PLA

Silver Gary L. • Mid-Peninsula Library Cooperative • Iron Mountain, MI 49801 • LAMA CLENE

Silver Hallie Yundt • Public Services Coordinator • Manitowoc Public Library • Manitowoc, WI 54220 • PLA RASD

Silver Lenoa • Lacey, WA 98503 • Continuing

Silver Susan L. • Reference Librarian • University of South Florida College of Education • Tampa, FL 33620

Silverberg Solange • Associate Librarian Tech Serv • University of Toronto Library • Toronto ON, Canada • ALCTS LAMA LITA

Silverblatt Cheryl • Director • Port Townsend Public Library • Port Townsend, WA 98368 • LAMA PLA

Silveria Janie Barnard • San Jose State University Monterey County Campus Library • Salinas, CA 93902

Silveria Steven • Supervising Librarian • Monterey County Library Seaside Branch • Seaside, CA 93955 • PLA

Silverman Alan J. • Original Cataloging • University of Pennsylvania Library Van Pelt-Dietrich Library Center • Philadelphia, PA 19104-6206 • ALCTS

Silverman Barbara • Central Elementary School Library • Corpus Christi, TX 78410 • AASL ALSC VRT

Silverman Joan A. • Reference Librarian • New Haven Free Public Library • New Haven, CT 06510

Silverman Judith Mrs. • Librarian • Del Mar Pines School • San Diego, CA 92130 • AASL

Silverman Karen Sandlin • Information Services Manager • Robert Morris Associates • Philadelphia, PA 19103-7398 • ALCTS RASD

Silverman Sandra • Librarian III • Houston Public Library • Houston, TX 77002

Silverman Scott H. • Head,Cataloging Division • Bryn Mawr College Canaday Library • Bryn Mawr, PA 19010 • LITA

Silvernail J. E. • Mobile Public Library • Mobile, AL 36602 • LITA

Silverrod Nancy A. • Novi Public Library • Novi, MI 48375 • ALSC IFRT

Silvers Carol A. • State Documents Coordinator • Idaho State Library • Boise, ID 83702 • GODORT

Silversteen Sophy • Cataloger • Rice University Fondren Library • Houston, TX 77251-1892 • ACRL ALCTS

Silverstein Bruce K. • Student • Long Island University Palmer School of Library & Information Science • Greenvale, NY 11548 • ACRL RASD

Silverstein Ellen R. • Head Librarian • Morgan, Lewis & Bockius Library Counselors At Law • Philadelphia, PA 19103 • ACRL IFRT

Silverstein Elyse • Law Librarian • New York Power Authority • New York, NY 10019 • LAMA LITA

Silverstein Grant M. • Mansfield, PA 16933

Silverstein Louis H. • Literary Anthropologist • Yale University Sterling Memorial Library • New Haven, CT 06520 • ACRL

Silverthorn Mary E. • Professor Emeritus • University of Toronto Faculty of Library & Information Science • Toronto ON, M5S 1A1 Canada • Continuing

Silvester E. Mrs. • Collections Librarian • McGill University Humanity & Social Science Area Library • Montreal PQ, Canada • ACRL ALCTS RASD

Silvestre Melissa • Student • University of California-Los Angeles Graduate School of Library & Information Science • Los Angeles, CA 90024-1520

Silvey Anita • Horn Book Inc. • Boston, MA 02108 • ALSC

Silvia Michael V. • Student • University of Rhode Island Graduate School of Library & Information Studies • Kingston, RI 02881-0815 • IFRT SRRT

Silvis-Milton Eleanor M. • Librarian • Westmoreland County Cmnty College • Youngwood, PA 15697

Siman Esther • Branch Manager • San Diego Public Library San Carlos Branch • San Diego, CA 92119 • PLA YALSA

Sime Judith • Librarian • Miami Country Day School Library • Miami, FL 33161 • AASL

Simek Ione Mrs. • Bottineay, ND 58318 • AASL YALSA *Life*

Simeone Henrietta • Librarian • Solvay High School • Solvay, NY 13209 • Continuing

Simington Faithe • Bay City, OR 97107 • AASL YALSA

Siminitus Jacquelyn E. • Public Sector Dir. Lbns Edu. • Pacific Bell • San Francisco, CA 94107 • LITA PLA

Simkin Faye • New York, NY 10023 • IFRT

Simkin Janice E. • Metuchen, NJ 08840

Simkins Elizabeth • Goldsboro, NC 27530-1652 • ACRL *Continuing*

Simkins Joyce A. • Librarian • Holy Names High Sch Lib • Oakland, CA 94618 • AASL

Simmen Sheri L. • Director • Fondulac District Library • East Peoria, IL 61611 • PLA

Simmons-Welburn Janice D. • Head of Reference • University of Iowa Libraries • Iowa City, IA 52242-1379 • ACRL RASD

Simmons Alma W. • Detroit, MI 48210

Simmons Barbara Trippel • Brookfield, MA 01506 • ACRL

Simmons Beverley J. • Director of Libraries • Sunnyvale Public Library • Sunnyvale, CA 94088-3714 • ASCLA LAMA LITA PLA

Simmons Brian • Medical Librarian • Blodgett Memorial Medical Center Richard R Smith Medical Library • Grand Rapids, MI 49506

Simmons Bryan • Hudson, FL 34667-2948

Simmons Carol • Librarian • Thornell Road School • Pittsford, NY 14534

Simmons David S. • Director • Mideastern Ohio Library Organization (MOLO) • Louisville, OH 44641 • ASCLA PLA

Simmons Edna H. • Brooklyn, NY 11238

Simmons Edwin D. • Reference Librarian • Atlanta-Fulton Public Library Southwest Regional Library • Atlanta, GA 30331 • PLA

Simmons Eileen D. • Reference/Adult Service Lbrn. • Wichita Public Library • Wichita, KS 67202 • IFRT

Simmons Elizabeth • Student • University of South Florida School of Library & Information Science • Tampa, FL 33620 • YALSA

Simmons Elizabeth M. • Youth Services Librarian • Kirkwood Highway Library • Wilimington, DE 19808-4817 • ALSC YALSA

Simmons Emma Jo • Acquistions Librarian • Corpus Christi State University • Corpus Chrsti, TX 78412

Simmons Fannie R. • Branch Coordinator • Dekalb County Public Library • Decatur, GA 30032 • PLA RASD

Simmons Jamie O. • Senior Cataloger • Stark County District Library • Canton, OH 44702 • ALCTS

Simmons Jean W. • New Haven, VT 05472 • ACRL

Simmons Joe L. Dr. • Trustee • Thomas Jefferson Library System • Jefferson Cty, MO 65102 • ALTA

Simmons Joseph M. • Fairfield, CT 06430 • Continuing

Simmons Juanita G. • Director • T.C. Simmons Library Learning Center • Detroit, MI 48204 • AASL ALSC ASCLA

Simmons Kitty J. • Technical Services Librarian • La Sierra University Library • Riverside, CA 92515 • ALCTS

Simmons Lorene • Wichita State University Library • Wichita, KS 67208

Simmons Marilyn • Anthony Elementary School • Leavenworth, KS 66048 • AASL

Simmons Marion L. • Williamsburg, VA 23185 • Continuing

Simmons Marsha T. • Librarian • Grand Caillou Middle School • Houma, LA 70363 • AASL

Simmons Michael R. • Ozone Park, NY 11417

Simmons Peter • Professor • University of British Columbia School of Library, Archival & Information Studies • Vancouver BC, V6T 1Z1 Canada • LITA

Simmons Priscilla S. • Coordinator of Special Services • Boulder Public Library • Boulder, CO 80306 • ASCLA

Simmons R. Daniels Rev. • Librarian • Simmons Theological Library • Williamstown, WV 26187-1353 • PLA

Simmons Randall C. • Director • Northwest Nazarene College Riley Library • Nampa, ID 83686 • ACRL

Simmons Rebecca A. • Associate Librarian • George Eastman House • Rochester, NY 14607

Simmons Rita M. • Detroit Public Library • Detroit, MI 48202

Simmons Robert M. • Curriculum Librarian • Bridgewater State College Clement C. Maxwell Library • Bridgewater, MA 02325 • ACRL

Simmons Robert R. • Head, Interlibrary Loan Dept. • Mid-Hudson Library System • Poughkeepsie, NY 12601

Simmons Susan P. • Trustee • East Islip Public Library • East Islip, NY 11730-2896

Simmons Wendy A. • Silver Springs, MD 20910 • ALCTS

Simms Gloria C. • Media Specialist • Hilton Head Primary School • Hilton Head Island, SC 29926 • AASL

Simms Sheila • Trustee • Peninsula Public Library • Lawrence, NY 11559

Simon Anne E. • Hawley, PA 18428

Simon Bradley A. • Talihina, OK 74571 • Continuing

Simon Carolyn G. • Green Valley, AZ 856142715

Simon Charlotte • Huntington Woods, MI 48070

Simon D. H. • Peapack, NJ 07945 • PLA

Simon Dale • Account Manager • Corporate Library Blackwell North America • Lake Oswego, OR 97035 • LITA

Simon David A. • Reference Librarian • Polytechnic University • Brooklyn, NY 11201 • LITA

Simon David P. • Serials Librarian • New Haven Free Public Library • New Haven, CT 06510 • ACRL

Simon Janelle Q. • Versailles, KY 40383 • AASL

Simon Janet A. • Abington Senior High Library • Abington, PA 19001 • AASL

Simon Jeanne H. • Washington, DC 20024

Simon Jeffrey J. • Technical Staff • AT&T Bell Laboratories • Murray Hill, NJ 07974 • LITA

Simon Lorraine A. • Washington, MI 48094

Simon Marie-Louise • Saint Laurent PQ, H4R 1B1 Canada • PLA

Simon Marjorie B. • Readers' Services Librarian • Goucher College Julia Rogers Library • Towson, MD 21204 • ACRL LIRT

Simon Matthew J. • Chief Librarian • Queens College Benjamin S. Rosenthal Library • Flushing, NY 11367-0904 • ACRL LAMA LRRT

Simon Patricia B. • Suffern, NY 10901 • RASD CLENE IFRT SRRT

Simon Ralph R. • Cleveland, OH 44122-7521 • AASL SRRT

Simon Rose A. Dr • Director of Libraries • Salem College Gramley Library • Winston-Salem, NC 27108-0548 • ACRL LAMA

Simon Samuel L. • Finkelstein Memorial Library • Spring Valley, NY 10977 • LAMA PLA IFRT   *Life*

Simon Vaughn L. • Director • Inland Library System • San Bernardino, CA 92405 • PLA

Simonds Michael J. • Executive Director • Bibliomation Inc. • Stratford, CT 06497 • ASCLA LAMA

Simone Debby L. • Librarian • Alachua County Library District • Gainesville, FL 32601 • LAMA PLA

Simoneau Karin • Staff Research Associate • University of California-Los Angeles (UCLA) • Los Angeles, CA 90024-1450

Simonetti Karen L. • Chicago, IL 60605

Simonis James J. • Director • Le Moyne College • Syracuse, NY 13214 • ACRL LAMA LITA

Simons Barbara A. • Collecton's Development Ln. • Goucher College Julia Rogers Library • Towson, MD 21204 • ACRL ALCTS RASD GODORT   *Life*

Simons Joy V. Miss. • Milwaukee, WI 53202 • Continuing

Simons Kevin E. • Texas A & M University Sterling C. Evans Library • College Station, TX 77843-5000 • RASD NMRT

Simons Linda Keir • Information Services Coordinator • University of Dayton Roesch Library • Dayton, OH 45469 • RASD

Simons Marilyn J. • Children's Librarian • Mill Valley Public Library • Mill Valley, CA 94941

Simons Michael F. • Reference Librarian • University of Nevada-Reno Noble H. Getchell Library • Reno, NV 89557 • ACRL

Simons Nancy R. • Reference/Catalog Librarian • University of Arizona Library • Tucson, AZ 85721 • ACRL LITA

Simonsen J. Doreen • Student • University of Michigan School of Information and Library Studies • Ann Arbor, MI 48109-1092

Simonson Cathy • Middleton, OH 45042

Simonton Melissa A. • Student • Emporia State University School of Library & Information Management • Emporia, KS 66801 • AASL

Simonton Wesley C. Mr • Minneapolis, MN 55424 • ALCTS LITA   *Life*

Simovich Susan K. • Jefferson Township Public Library • Oak Ridge, NJ 07438 • LAMA PLA

Simowski Joyce M. • Detroit Area Agency On Aging • Detroit, MI 48226 • IFRT

Simpfendorfer Linda R. • Student • Passaic Public Library • Passaic, NJ 07055 • ALSC

Simplicio Marion M. • Cataloging Librarian • Nazareth College of Rochester • Rochester, NY 14618

Simpson-Holz Linda • Project Manager • Administrative Offices of the United States Courts • Washington, DC 20544

Simpson Alice H. • Oberlin, OH 44074 • ACRL ALCTS
Continuing

Simpson Ann • Public Services Librarian • Metropolitan Library System at Del City • Oklahoma City, OK 73102

Simpson Arlene B. • Assistant Director • Falls Church Public Library • Falls Church, VA 22046

Simpson Barbara • Director • Kean College of New Jersey Library • Union, NJ 07083 • ACRL LAMA LITA LIRT

Simpson Barbara D. • Elementary Librarian • Rapid City School District • Rapid City, SD 57701 • YALSA

Simpson Betty J. • Galesburg, IL 61401 • PLA IFRT

Simpson Carol • Director • North Babylon Public Library • North Babylon, NY 11703 • PLA

Simpson Carol Mann • Facilitator Lib. Technology • Mesquite Independent School District • Mesquite, TX 75149 • AASL

Simpson Charles W. • State University of New York (SUNY) • Stony Brook, NY 11794-2225 • ACRL ALCTS LAMA LITA

Simpson Claire D. • Educational Media Specialist • South Valley School • Moorestown, NJ 08057 • AASL

Simpson Dian • Burton Adventist Academy • Arlington, TX 76017 • AASL

Simpson Donald B. • President • Center for Research Libraries • Chicago, IL 60637 • ACRL

Simpson Elizabeth Y. • Tilton, NH 03276

Simpson Ernestine • President, Board of Trustees • Atlantic City Free Public Library • Atlantic City, NJ 08401 • PLA

Simpson Imogene • Bowling Green, KY 42101 • Continuing

Simpson Jane L. • Librarian • Saltars Point Elementary School • Steilacoom, WA 98388

Simpson Janice M. • Director • Cullman County Public • Cullman, AL 35055 • LAMA PLA RASD

Simpson Karen L. • Periodicals Librarian • Brevard Community College • Cocoa, FL 32922

Simpson Margaret D. • School & Library Liaison • A Clean Well-Lighted Place for Books • Larkspur, CA 94939 • ALSC SRRT

Simpson Martha F. • Student • Southern Connecticut State University School of Libray Science & Instructional Technology • New Haven, CT 06515 • ALSC

Simpson Megan • J. O. Davis Elementary School • Irving, TX 75061

Simpson Nancy J. • Librarian • East Palestine Memorial Public Library • East Palestine, OH 44413 • PLA

Simpson Paula Ann • Director • Monterey Public Library • Monterey, CA 93940

Simpson Raymond D. • Sun City Center, FL 33573

Simpson Stephen Robert • Assoc. V.P./University Librarian • Hawaii Pacific University Meader Library • Honolulu, HI 96813-3192 • ACRL RASD

Simpson Sue C. • Circulation Librarian • Hoover Public Library • Birmingham, AL 35216

Simpson Susan M. • Director • Albany County Public Library • Laramie, WY 82070 • PLA YALSA

Simpson Valrie G. • Assistant Regional Librarian • Broward County-South Regional Library • Pembroke Pines, FL 33024

Simpson Virginia M. • Champaign, IL 61820

Sims-Wood Janet L. • Asst Chief Librarian/Reference • Howard University Libraries Founders Library • Washington, DC 20059 • ACRL EMIERT

Sims Carmen M. • Student • University of Alabama School of Library & Information Studies • Tuscaloosa, AL 35487-0252 • PLA RASD

Sims Jacqueline T. • Head of Library Inf. Services • Catawba College Library • Salisbury, NC 28144

Sims Lana • Librarian • San Jacinto Intermediate School • Pasadena, TX 77504 • AASL

Sims Martha J. • Director • Dept of Public Library Muncipal Ctr • Virginia Beach, VA 23456 • AASL ALSC ASCLA

Sims Mary E. • Kirksville, MO 63501

Sims Oscar L. • Henderson, NV 89014 • ACRL

Simton Chester • Library/Media Specialist • Palmer High School Library • Palmer, AK 99645

Simutis Len • Executive Director • Ohio Library & Information Network • Columbus, OH 43212

Sinche Shery • Gayle Middle School • Falmouth, VA 22405

Sinclair Caryn M. • Adult Reference Dept., Head • Plainfield Public Library District • Plainfield, IL 60544

Sinclair Dorothy • Professor Emeritus • Case Western Reserve University • Cleveland, OH 44106-7151 • Continuing

Sinclair Jean E. • Teacher/Librarian • Washington High School • Chicago, IL 60617 • AASL

Sinclair Marianne R. • Student • Wayne State University Library Science Program • Detroit, MI 48202 • AASL

Sinclair Regina A. • Head, Preservation Dept. • John Hopkins University • Baltimore, MD 21218 • ACRL ALCTS

Sinclair Rose • Librarian • W. C. Cunningham Middle School • Houston, TX 77049 • AASL ALSC IFRT

Sindel Amy C. • Gales Ferry, CT 06335

Sineath Timothy W. • University of Kentucky College of Library & Information Science • Lexington, KY 40506-0391 • ACRL LITA LRRT

Sinex Joan M. • Santa Cruz, CA 95060

Singelton Joan • Bartlesville Public Library • Bartlesville, OK 74003

Singer Andrea • Associate Librarian • Indiana University at Bloomington University Libraries • Bloomington, IN 47405 • ACRL GODORT IRRT

Singer Dona • Professor-Acting Director • Bergen Community College Library & Learning Resource Center • Paramus, NJ 07652-1595 • ACRL LAMA

Singer Helen R. • Student • Pratt Institute Graduate School of Library & Information Science • Brooklyn, NY 11205 • LITA

Singer Linda A. • Trustee • Fairfax County Public Library • Fairfax, VA 22033-1909 • AASL

Singer Marilyn • Librarian • Thornton Fractional Township HSD 215 • Calumet City, IL 60409 • AASL IFRT

Singer Phyllis • Librarian • Beach Channel High School • Rockaway Park, NY 11694 • RASD YALSA

Singer William M. • Designer • Gruzen Samton Steinglass Architects & Planners • New York City, NY 10010 • IFRT

Singh Diljit • Student • Florida State University School of Library and Information Studies • Tallahassee, FL 32306-2048

Singh Harcharan • Acquisitions & Serials Librarian • Brooklyn Law School Library • Brooklyn, NY 11201

Singh Haymwantee P. • Student • State University of New York at Albany School of Information Science & Policy • Albany, NY 12222

Singh Jasjit K. • Head Librarian • Davenport College of Business Library Lansing Branch • Lansing, MI 48901 • ACRL LAMA

Singh Jaswant Dr. • Librarian • Grand Ledge High School • Grand Ledge, MI 48837 • AASL

Singh Rosemary Anne • Special Project Assistant • University of Wisconsin Center Manitowoc Library • Manitowoc, WI 54220

Singh Sharon R. • Librarian/Associate Director • Public Library of Cincinnati and Hamilton County • Cincinnati, OH 45202 • PLA

Singh Tribhuvan • President • International Book Company • Absecon Highlands, NJ 08201 • PLA

Singletary Robyn P. • Librarian Trainee • Loudoun County Public Library • Leesburg, VA 22075

Singleton Cynthia • Head, Reader Service Dept. • University of Windsor Leddy Library • Windsor ON, N9B 3P4 Canada • ACRL

Singleton David W. • Library Director • Transylvania County Library • Brevard, NC 28712 • PLA RASD NMRT

Singleton Janet B. • Plevna, KS 67568 • AASL LITA

Singleton Jeanette P. • Awendaw, SC 29429

Singleton Kenneth B. • Camden, SC 29020

Singleton Sandra A. • School Library Media Specialist • Huntington Place Elementary School • Northport, AL 35476 • AASL ALSC NMRT

Singleton Sheri Lynn • Montgomery, AL 36117 • IFRT

Sinha Reeta • Student • Houston Academy of Medicine Texas Medical Center Library • Houston, TX 77030

Sinha Vaswati R. • Biblo Instr & Outreach Coor. • Lafayette College Skillman Library • Easton, PA 18042-1797

Sink Joanne F. • Media Specialist • Alamance Elementary School • Greensboro, NC 27406 • AASL

Sink Robert • Archivist Record Manager • New York Public Library Division P • New York, NY 10163-2240 • ACRL LHRT

Sink Thomas • Marcy Hospital Library • Toledo, OH 43624

Sinkankas George M. • Associate Professor • University of Tennessee-Knoxville Graduate School of Library & Information Science • Knoxville, TN 37996-4330 • ALCTS LITA

Sinko Agnes M. • Director • Irvington Public Library Guiteau Foundation Library • Irvington, NY 10533 • PLA

Sinkule Karen L. • National Library of Medicine • Bethesda, MD 20894

Sinnott Elisabeth • Student • Columbia University Libraries Butler Library • New York, NY 10027 • ACRL ALCTS

Sinnott Wendy R. • Media Specialist • Kinnelon High School Library • Kinnelon, NJ 07405

Sinnreich Naomi B. • Trustee • Lowenthal, Landau & Fischer • New York, NY 10177 • ACRL

Sinofsky Esther R. Dr • Frost Junior High School • Granada Hills, CA 91344 • AASL

Sinsheimer Florence E. • Reference Librarian • Scarsdale Public Library • Scarsdale, NY 10583

Sintes Mac • New Orleans Public Library Latter Branch • New Orleans, LA 70115 • IFRT

Sintz Edward F. • Charlotte, NC 28215

Sinwell Carol A. • Branch Manager • Fairfax County Public Library Kings Park Library • Burke, VA 22015

Sipe Lynn F. • Asst. Univ. Librn for Clln Devel • University of Southern California Doheny Library • Los Angeles, CA 90089-0182 • ACRL ALCTS LAMA

Sipe Vicki L. • Student • University of Maryland College of Library and Information Services • College Park, MD 20742-4345 • ALCTS

Sipher Ann • School Library Media Spec. • Albany School of Humanities • Albany, NY 12209

Sipos Caryn G. • Co-Ordinator Young Adult Serv. • Alameda County Library System • Fremont, CA 94538 • YALSA

Sipos Laszlo • Asst Tech Serv Librarian • Somerset County Library Bridgewater Branch • Bridgewater, NJ 08807

Sippen Kathi H. • AV Librarian • Durham County Library • Durham, NC 27701

Sir Carol S. • Elmhurst, IL 60126

Sirene Walt • Trustee • Prince William Public Library System Administrative Support Center • Prince William, VA 22192-5073

Sirkin Benita • Golden Valley, MN 55416

Sirls Barbara D. • Director • Marshall County Public Library • Benton, KY 42025

Sirmans Barbara C. • Associate Dir/Extension Serv. • Birmingham Public & Jefferson County Free Library • Birmingham, AL 35203 • LAMA PLA EMIERT IFRT

Sirois Laura A. • Nashua, NH 03060 • AASL

Siry Kathleen A. • Administrative Assistant • Campbell County Public Library • Cold Spring, KY 41076 • ACRL PLA IRRT

Sisak Kathleen A. • Senior Serials Associate • City University of New York Graduate School Mina Rees Library • New York, NY 10036-8099 • LITA

Sischo Julia • Seattle, WA 98177

Sisco Linda M. • Jones, OK 73049

Sisneros B. Caroline • Santa Monica, CA 90404 • NMRT

Sison D. Ruth • Long Beach, CA 90815 • EMIERT IFRT LRRT SRRT

Sisson Ginger A. • Student • Wayne State University Library Science Program • Detroit, MI 48202 • AASL

Sisson Helen L. • Dearborn, MI 48126 • Life

Sisson John E. III • Biology Librarian • University of California-Irvine Library • Irvine, CA 92713 • ACRL IFRT

Sisson Lorene R. • Media Curriculum • San Jose State University Clark Library • San Jose, CA 95192-0028 • ACRL ALCTS MAGERT SORT

Sisson Marion A. • Librarian Grade III • Milwaukee Public Library Mill Road Branch • Milwaukee, WI 53223 • ALSC

Sisson Norma A. • Media Specialist • Ames High School • Ames, IA 50010 • AASL

Sit Agatha • Cataloging/Reference Librarian • Hong Kong University of Science & Technology Library • Kowloon, Hong Kong • ACRL ALCTS ALSC LITA RASD CLENE LRRT

Sites Katherine P. • Colonial Heights, VA 23834 • AFLRT FLRT

Sitkin John H. • Assistant Catalog Head Librarian • Boston University Mugar Memorial Library • Boston, MA 02215 • ACRL ALCTS LITA

Sitter Clara L. • Curriculum/Reference Librarian • University of Alaska • Anchorage, AK 99508

Sittig William J. • Director, Collections Develp • Library of Congress • Washington, DC 20541 • ALCTS

Sittler-Matz Beatrice • Student • Simmons College Graduate School of Library & Information Science • Boston, MA 02115 • ACRL ALCTS RASD

Sitton Eva W. • Oxford, GA 30267

Sitton Karen Liptzin • Director • Hebrew University of Jerusalem Bloomfield Library • Jerusalem 91905, Israel

Sitts Maxine K. • Program Officer • Commission on Preservation & Access • Washington, DC 20036 • ALCTS LITA IFRT

Siudzinski Anne-Marie C. • Hinsdale, IL 60521

Sivak Marie R. • School Supervisor • Illinois State Board of Education • Springfield, IL 62777 • AASL AFLRT

Sivak Patrick • Librarian • Greater Latrobe Junior High School • Latrobe, PA 15650 • AASL

Sivaram Swaraj L. • Information Analyst • Shell Oil Company Library Processing Center • Houston, TX 77210-4302 • ALCTS

Siviter-Assadourian Norma • Head Special Collections • Southwestern University A. Frank Smith, Jr. Library Center • Georgetown, TX 78626

Sivulich Kenneth G. • Deputy Director • Queens Borough Public Library • Jamaica, NY 11432 • LAMA PLA *Life*

Sixta James A. • Administrator • Northeastern Iowa Regional Library System • Waterloo, IA 50701

Sizemore Mary M. • Asst. Branch Head/Children's Ln • Charleston County Library Mount Pleasant Branch • Mount Pleasant, SC 29464

Sizemore W. C. Dr • President • Alderson-Broaddus College • Philippi, WV 26416

Sjoblom Liisa M. • Student • University of Texas at Austin Graduate School of Library & Information Sciences • Austin, TX 78712-1276 • ACRL IFRT

Sjodin Debbie E. • Cataloger • Seattle Public Library • Seattle, WA 98104-1193

Sjogren Linda K. • Graduate Student • University of Hawaii School of Library & Information Studies • Honolulu, HI 96822

Sjolin Scott D. • Student • Emporia State University School of Library & Information Management • Emporia, KS 66801 • IFRT NMRT SRRT

Skaar Suzan • Moorhead, MN 56560-5734 • AASL

Skaggs Guelda T. • Librarian • Cave Spring Junior High School Library • Roanoke, VA 24018 • AASL

Skaggs Joan D. • Claremont, NC 28610

Skaggs Sandy Mrs • Trustee • Mid-Continent Public Library • Independence, MO 64050 • ALTA

Skaja Patricia S. • A. T. Kearney Inc. • Chicago, IL 60606 • NMRT

Skallerup Harry R. • Boca Raton, FL 33486 • ACRL *Life*

Skalstad Doris • Minneapolis, MN 55403 • PLA RASD *Life*

Skaptason Trish • Senior Administrative Lbrn. • United States Department of Education Office of Educational Res & Improvement • Washington, DC 20208-5571 • ASCLA PLA

Skapura Robert J. • Librarian • Clayton Valley High School • Concord, CA 94521 • AASL LIRT

Skarbek Valeria Madden • Riviera Beach, MD 21122 • AASL YALSA *Life*

Skarzynski George • Director of Libraries • Nepean Public Library • Nepean ON, K2G 5K7 Canada • LAMA PLA

Skau Dorothy B. • New Orleans, LA 70124 • ACRL FLRT *Continuing*

Skeele Lillian • Columbus, OH 43214 • Continuing

Skeen Wallace Reeves • Trustee • Horry County Memorial Library • Conway, SC 29526 • ALTA

Skeers Timothy M. • Government Publications Libn • Northern Illinois University University Libraries • DeKalb, IL 60115-2868 • GODORT MAGERT

Skehan Patricia A. • Elementary-Junior High School Ln • Los Angeles Unified School District • Los Angeles, CA 90017 • AASL

Skelding Thomas G. • Humanities Librarian • Mansfield University Library • Mansfield, PA 16933

Skellenger Shirley A. • Librarian II • San Jose Public Library • San Jose, CA 95113 • IFRT

Skelley Cornelia • Instructional Materials Services • Bellevue, WA 98005 • AASL

Skelley Grant T. • Associate Professor • University of Washington Graduate School of Library and Information Science • Seattle, WA 98195 • ACRL RASD *Life*

Skellie Karen S. • Branch Manager • Avis G. Williams Library Stone Mountain Regional Library • Decatur, GA 30033 • PLA

Skelton L. Wayne • Manager Litigation • Baker & Botts Law Firm • Houston, TX 77002

Skelton William E. • Newnan-Coweta Public Library • Newnan, GA 30263 • PLA RASD GODORT IRRT

Skemer Don C. • Hd. Spec. Collections & Archives • Princeton University Library • Princeton, NJ 08544 • ACRL

Skene Ann L. • Media Specialist • Crooked Creek Elementary School • Indianapolis, IN 46208 • AASL

Skerrett Claire M. Dr. • Bala Cynwd, PA 19004 • LRRT

Skewis Charles A. • Acquisitions Librarian • University of Alabama Amelia Gayle Gorgas Library • Tuscaloosa, AL 35487-0266 • ACRL ALCTS LITA

Skibell Harris • Muze, Inc. • Brooklyn, NY 11211

Skidmore Felecia A. • Lakeland, FL 33813 • AASL

Skidmore Gail • Cataloger • Pacific Grove Public Library • Pacific Grove, CA 93950

Skidmore Larry R. • Church of Jesus Christ of Latter-Day Saints • Salt Lake City, UT 84150

Skidmore Lottie M. • Wichita, KS 67218 • Continuing

Skidmore Stephen C. • City Librarian • Ponca City Library • Ponca City, OK 74601 • PLA

Skiff Gail J. • Adult Services Librarian • F L Weyenberg Public • Mequon, WI 53092 • RASD

Skiffington Frances W. • University of New Orleans Earl K. Long Library • New Orleans, LA 70148 • GODORT

Skifstad Nancy J. • Assistant Librarian • Kimberly-Clark Corporation • Roswell, GA 30076 • ACRL ALCTS LRRT

Skiles Patricia N. • Librarian • Windson Oaks Elementary School • Virginia Beach, VA 23452 • AASL

Skillen David R. • Vice President/DCA • Diversified Consultants Association • Atlanta, GA 30303 • LAMA

Skinner Diana • Ashland, OH 44805

Skinner Diane H. • Media Specialist • Springfield Elementary School • Springfield, GA 31329 • AASL

Skinner Jean E. • Catlgr Ser & Microforms • New York University Elmer Holmes Bobst Library • New York, NY 10012

Skinner Pamela A. • Associate Reference Librarian • Smith College William Allan Neilson Library • Northampton, MA 01063 • ACRL RASD

Skinner Robert • Asst. Head Ref. Services Div. • University of California-San Diego Central University Library • La Jolla, CA 92093-0175 • ACRL LITA

Skinner Robert E. • University Librarian • Xavier University • New Orleans, LA 70125 • LAMA

Skinner Thomas E. • Birmingham, AL 35216 • ACRL ALCTS RASD IFRT

Skinner Vicki F. • Austin, TX 78735 • LITA

Skiple Jacqueline J. • University City, MO 63130

Skipper Andria D. • Chattanooga-Hamilton County Bicentennial Library • Chattanooga, TN 37402

Skipper Barbara • Student • University of North Texas School of Library & Information Sciences • Denton, TX 76203 • AFLRT

Skipper James E. • Ithaca, NY 14850-6368 • ACRL RASD *Life*

Skipper Nancy S. • Reference Libn-Bibliographer • Cornell University Library • Ithaca, NY 14853 • ACRL

Skipsna Alvin • Saratoga Spgs, NY 12866

Sklansky Laura R. • University of Illinois At Chicago Library of the Health Sciences • Chicago, IL 60612 • RASD

Sklar Hinda F. • Head of Technical Services • Harvard University Frances L Loeb Library • Cambridge, MA 02138 • ACRL LITA

Sklensky Anne L. • Librarian II-Ref. Supervisor • Santa Clara Public Library • Santa Clara, CA 95051 • RASD

Skolmen Robert L. • Palo Alto City Library • Palo Alto, CA 94303

Skop Vera • Head, Information & Readers Serv • Greenwich Library • Greenwich, CT 06830 • PLA

Skorupski Diane C. • Librarian • Liberty Elementary School • Tucson, AZ 85706 • AASL

Skotnicki Peggy A. • Librarian II • Buffalo & Erie County Public Library System Serials Dept. • Buffalo, NY 14203

Skousen Diana N. • Reference Librarian • Johnson C. Smith University James B.Duke Memorial Library • Charlotte, NC 28216 • ACRL

Skowronski Joan • Librarian • Tampa-Hillsborough County Public Library • Tampa, FL 33602 • PLA VRT

Skramovsky Mary C. • Librarian • Linden Free Public Library • Linden, NJ 07036 • ACRL

Skrine James A. • Learning Center Director • Washington Junior High School • Naperville, IL 60540 • AASL

Skrivanek Richard F. • Mendota Heights, MN 55120-1313 • AASL ALSC *Life*

Skruck Alicia M. • Student • Southern Connecticut State University School of Libray Science & Instructional Technology • New Haven, CT 06515

Skruck Eileen • Media Specialist • Orchard Hills • Milford, CT 06460 • AASL

Skrzeszewski Stan E. • Deputy CEO • Southern Ontario Library Service • London, ON, N6A 1V8 Canada • LAMA LITA PLA EMIERT

Skubish Barbara E. • Head of Information Services • Dunedin Public Library • Dunedin, FL 34698-7998 • RASD

Skufca A. Marie • North Platte, NE 69101

Skuja Lucija • Grand Rapids, MI 49503 • Continuing

Skullerud Karen • Library Media Specialist • Helix High School • La Mesa, CA 92041

Skuster Charlotte W. • Norwich, NY 13815

Skutnik John S. • Cleveland Heights, OH 44106

Skvarla Donna J. • Administrator/Off. of Lib Devel. • Oklahoma Department of Libraries • Oklahoma City, OK 73105-3298 • PLA

Slack Marion J. • Reference Librarian • Framingham State College Henry Whittemore Library • Framingham, MA 01701

Slade Alexander L. • Coord of Extension Lib Svs • University of Victoria McPherson Library • Victoria BC, V8W 3H5 Canada • ACRL

Slade Elizabeth G. • Digital Equipment Corporation Maynard Area Information Services • Maynard, MA 01754-2571 • ALCTS LITA RASD

Slade Kent • Purchasing Agent • Weber County Library • Odgen, UT 84401

Slade Linda Mrs. • Bossier City, LA 71111

Slade Rod • Vice President • Saztec International • Eugene, OR 97401 • LITA

Sladetz Janice • Trustee • Stickney-Forest View Library • Stickney, IL 60402 • ALTA

Slagle Kennith L. • Cataloger • Center for Research Libraries • Chicago, IL 60637 • ALCTS

Slane Anne C. • Cataloger • Worthington Public Library • Worthington, OH 43085 • ALCTS LITA

Slane Maureen E. • West Hartford, CT 06107

Slaney Jennifer A • Librarian • Taylorville Public Library • Taylorville, IL 62568 • PLA

Slaney Sharon • Library Media Specialist • Lakeland Senior High School • Rathdrum, ID 83858 • AASL NMRT

Slanicky John M. • Fossil Ridge Public Library • Braidwood, IL 60408

Slanker Barbara O. • Champaign, IL 61820 • ACRL PLA *Life*

Slate Ted • Director of Research Services • Newsweek Inc. • New York, NY 10022

Slater Bill G. • Acquisitions Dept. Chair • Brigham Young University Harold B. Lee Library • Provo, UT 84602

Slater David M. • Media Librarian • Ocean County Library System • Toms River, NJ 08753 • LITA PLA

Slater Frank • Asst. Director/Admin. & OP • University of North Dakota Chester Fritz Library • Grand Forks, ND 58202-0175 • ALCTS

Slater James R. • Branch Librarian • Free Public Library of Woodbridge • Woodbridge, NJ 07095 • RASD YALSA *Life*

Slater Ronald J. • Chair, Technical Services Dept. • Laurentian University • Sudbury ON, P3E 2C6 Canada • ACRL ALCTS LITA

Slating Beth A. • Head, Technical Processing Dept. • Montgomery County Norristown Public Library • Norristown, PA 19401

Slatko Adele • West Bloomfield, MI 48322

Slaton Gwendolyn C. • Director of Library • Essex County College • Newark, NJ 07102 • ACRL

Slattery Carole C. • Elementary School Librarian • Newton Public Schools • Newton, MA 02159 • AASL ALSC

Slattery Charles E. • Subject Bibl./Reference Libn • Central Missouri State University Ward Edwards Library • Warrensburg, MO 64093 • ACRL

Slattery Kathleen G. • Pacific Palisades, CA 90272

Slaughter Elizabeth • Student • Brigham Young University School of Library & Information Sciences • Provo, UT 84602

Slaughter Mary W. • Wrightsville, GA 31096 • Continuing

Slaughter Vera Miss • Oakland, CA 94612 • ACRL RASD *Life*

Slavens Cara L. • Student • University of Michigan School of Information and Library Studies • Ann Arbor, MI 48109-1092

Slavens Mary V. • Library Media Specialist • Marvell Primary School • Marvell, AR 72366 • AASL

Slavens Thomas P. • Professor • University of Michigan School of Information and Library Studies • Ann Arbor, MI 48109-1092

Slavik Carol • Children's Librarian • Douglas County Library • Minden, NV 89423

Slavin Suzy M. • Reference Librarian • McGill University McLennan Library • Montreal PQ, Canada

Slaybaugh Nancy • Pennsylvania State University Pattee Library • University Park, PA 16802 • LAMA

Slayton Sharon L. • Librarian • David Douglas High School • Portland, OR 97233 • AASL

Slebodnick Patricia R. • County Librarian • Tehama County Library • Red Bluff, CA 96080-3383 • PLA

Sled Jill D. • Renton, WA 98056

Sleeman Allison M. • Monographic Cataloger • University of Virginia Library • Charlottesville, VA 22903 • ACRL ALCTS

Sleeman John K. • Systems Librarian • University of Virginia Alderman Library • Charlottesville, VA 22903-2498 • LITA

Sleeman Linda E. • Cuyahoga County Public Library Bedford Branch • Bedford, OH 44146 • ALSC YALSA

Sleeman William E. • Law Librarian • Aspen Systems Corporation • Rockville, MD 20850-3172 • GODORT

Sleeth James G. • Director • Steele Memorial Library • Elmira, NY 14901-2799

Sleicher Barbara A. • Warwick, RI 02886 • AASL

Sleight Wicky • Library Director • Marshall Public Library • Marshall, MO 65340 • ALSC LAMA PLA RASD

Slezak Regina E. • Asst. Adm. for Public Services • Fall River Public Library • Fall River, MA 02720 • PLA RASD

Slick Myrna H. Dr • Holsopple, PA 15935

Sliekers Hendrik • Director of Library Services • Trinity Christian College Library • Palos Heights, IL 60463 • ACRL

Sliepcevich Natalie • Anaconda, MT 59711

Slife Joye D. P. • Gainesville, GA 30507

Slight-Gibney Nancy • Head, Aquisitions Department • Santa Clara University Michel Orradre Library • Santa Clara, CA 95053 • ACRL ALCTS LAMA IFRT

Slightam Julie A. • Student • University of Wisconsin-Milwaukee School of Library & Information Science • Milwaukee, WI 53201

Sliker Shirley • Lansing, MI 48910

Slinger Michael J. • Director • Suffolk University Law Library • Boston, MA 02114 • ACRL LAMA

Slipsky Mary Jane Pietila • South Ogden, UT 84403-3015

Slive Daniel J. • Reference Librarian • John Carter Brown Library • Providence, RI 02912 • ACRL IFRT

Slivka Krystal K. • Chemical Science Librarian • Case Western Reserve University Sears Library • Cleveland, OH 44106

Slivka Regina K. • Director of Media Services • Bishop Gallagher High School • Harper Woods, MI 48225 • AASL

Slivken David E. • Senior Librarian • Public Library of Des Moines • Des Moines, IA 50308-1791

Sloan Bernard G. • Director • Illinois Library Computer System Office • Champaign, IL 61820 • ACRL LITA

Sloan Brenda D. • Special Collections Librarian • Mary Washington College Library Simpson Library • Fredericksburg, VA 22401-4664

Sloan Elaine F. • New York, NY 10027 • ACRL

Sloan Frances • Trustee • Kanawha County Public Library • Charleston, WV 25301 • ALTA

Sloan James Jr Mr • Librarian • Warsaw Community Public Library • Warsaw, IN 46580 • ALTA PLA *Life*

Sloan James W. • Los Angeles, CA 90008 • Continuing

Sloan Jane E. • Rutgers University Libraries Mabel Smith Douglass Library • New Brunswick, NJ 08903-0270 • ACRL

Sloan Margaret D. • School Librarian • Willowridge High School • Sugarland, TX 77487 • AASL

Sloan Marion J. Mr. • Encyclopaedia Britannica • Chicago, IL 60604 • AASL PLA

Sloan Martha • Head, Readers Service • Deerfield Public Library • Deerfield, IL 60015

Sloan Mary J. • Atlanta, GA 30306

Sloan Maureen G. • Library Director • Oregon Graduate Institute Library • Beaverton, OR 97006 • ACRL

Sloan Patricia K. • Legislative Reference Librarian • Legislative Reference Library • Lincoln, NE 68509 • GODORT

Sloan Phyllis • Serials Assistant • CUNY Law School • Flushing, NY 11367

Sloan Robert C. Jr. • Reference Librarian • Saint Mary's College of Maryland Library • St. Mary's City, MD 20686 • ACRL LITA

Sloan Ruth C. • Director • Waldwick High School Library • Waldwick, NJ 07463 • YALSA

Sloan Tom W. • Director and State Librarian • State Librarian Delaware Division of Libraries • Dover, DE 19901 • ALCTS ASCLA GODORT

Sloane Robert J. • Art Librarian • Chicago Public Library Harold Washington Library • Chicago, IL 60605

Sloat Elisabeth E. • Student • University of Rhode Island Graduate School of Library & Information Studies • Kingston, RI 02881-0815 • IFRT SRRT

Slocum Grace P. • Wilmington, NC 28401

Slocum Hannah R. • Administration • San Jose Public Library • San Jose, CA 95113 • LAMA PLA

Slocum Maureen • Library Aide • Eanes Elementary School Eanes Independant School Dist • Austin, TX 78746 • AASL

Slocum Robert B. • Dryden, NY 13053 • Continuing

Sloderbeck Mary Jane Sr. • Marian High School • Mishawaka, IN 46544

Sloma Susan A. • Student • Rosary College Graduate School of Library & Information Science • River Forest, IL 60305 • PLA

Slone Debra J. • Librarian I • Berkeley Public Library South Branch • Berkeley, CA 94703 • ALSC

Slone Eugenia F. • Library Media Specialist • Brookfield High School Library • Brookfield, CT 06804 • AASL

Slone Nancy C. • Student • San Jose State University Division of Library & Information Science • San Jose, CA 95192-0029

Slone Tommye F. • Learning Resource Specialist • George Junior High School • Rosenberg, TX 77471 • AASL ALSC

Slotte Vicki A. • Library Media Specialist • Kemmerer Junior Senior High School Library • Diamondville, WY 83116 • AASL

Slough Eileen M. • Reference Librarian • Hilo Public Library • Hilo, HI 96720

Slovasky Stephen • Manager, Bibliographic Control • Research Publications • Woodbridge, CT 06525

Slowik George • New York, NY 10011

Sluk John M. • Head, Cataloging Department • Oberlin College Library • Oberlin, OH 44074 • ACRL ALCTS

Slusar Linda • Winfield Public Library • Winfield, IL 60190

Sluss Sara B. • Assoc. Libn. for Readers Servs. • Baruch College Library • New York, NY 10010 • ACRL LAMA LITA

Sluter Catherine C. • Periodicals Supervisior • California State University Oviatt Library • Northridge, CA 91328-1289

Slutsky Bruce • Science Librarian • Saint John's University Library • Jamaica, NY 11439 • ACRL

Slutz Mark J. • Student • Kent State University School of Library & Information Science • Kent, OH 44242-0001 • PLA

Sly Janice R. • Library Media Specialist • Shiever School • Pelham, GA 31779 • AASL

Sly Margery N. • College Archivist • Smith College William Allan Neilson Library • Northampton, MA 01063 • ACRL

Slyfield Donna C. • Head,Readers Service Dept • Helen M. Plum Memorial Library • Lombard, IL 60148 • PLA SORT

Slygh Gyneth • Highsmith Co., Inc. • Fort Atkinson, WI 53538-0800 • AASL LITA

Slyhoff Merle J. • Media & Doc Delivery Servs Ln • University of Pennsylvania Libraries Biddle Law Library • Philadelphia, PA 19104-6279 • ACRL ALCTS LAMA RASD VRT

Smailes Suzanne A. • Student • Kent State University School of Library Science/Columbus Program • Columbus, OH 43210

Smaldone Paul • Brooklyn Public Library Brooklyn Heights Branch • Brooklyn, NY 11201

Smalkin Celeste M. • Lutherville, MD 21093 • AASL IFRT

Small Amy K. • Public Relations Specialist • Westchester Library System • Elmsford, NY 10523 • LAMA

Small Ann H. • Parks Middle School • Atlanta, GA 30310

Small Betti D. • College Station, TX 77845 • ALCTS RASD SRRT

Small Robert C. Jr. • Dean Coll of Edu & Human Devel • Radford University College of Education & Human Development • Radford, VA 24142 • YALSA IFRT

Small Wendell G. Jr. • APO, AE 09154

Smalley Sandia L. • Senior Cataloger • Harvard College Library Widener Memorial Library • Cambridge, MA 02138 • ALCTS

Smalley Topsy N. • Public Services Librarian • Cabrillo College Library • Aptos, CA 95003

Smalls Mary L. • Collections Organization Coord. • South Carolina State College Miller F. Whittaker Library • Orangeburg, SC 29117 • ACRL

Smart Anne M. • Children's Librarian • Boston Public Library Charleston Branch • Charleston, MA 02129 • ALSC

Smart Donna T. • Trustee • Salt Lake City Public Library • Salt Lake City, UT 84111 • ALTA

Smart Doris M. • Engineering Research Librarian • Sundstrand Data Control, Inc. • Redmond, WA 98073-9701 • ACRL

Smart Margaret • Westminster, CO 80030 • ACRL RASD *Life*

Smart Patricia K. • Burbank, CA 91501

Smead Harold G. • South Plainfield Free Public Library • South Plainfield, NJ 07080 • PLA

Smetana Lucinda M. • Greeley, CO 80631 • AASL

Smets Kristine AJ • Cataloger • Center for Research Libraries • Chicago, IL 60637

Smid Marcelyn J. • George, IA 51237 • ACRL ALCTS RASD

Smiley Grace • Saint Louis, MO 63123 • Continuing

Smiley Joseph E. Jr • Non-Salaried • University of South Florida Library • Tampa, FL 33620-5600

Smiley Julie • Sales Representative • The Heckman Bindery Inc. • North Manchester, IN 46962 • ACRL ALCTS

Smillie James B. • Acquisitions Librarian • Susquehanna University • Selinsgrove, PA 17870

Smiloff Debbie • Librarian • Hicksville Free Public Library • Hicksville, NY 11801

Smilow Jill • Sales & Marketing Mgr. Sch. L. • Candlewick Press • Cambridge, MA 02140 • ALSC YALSA

Smink Anna R. • Head Librarian • Holton Arms School Inc. • Bethesda, MD 20817 • AASL

Smink Nancy J. • Director • Pottsville Free Public Library • Pottsville, PA 17901 • PLA

Smiraglia Richard P. • Assistant Professor • Columbia University School of Library Service • New York, NY 10027 • ALCTS LITA LRRT

Smirensky Helen K. • New York State Library • Albany, NY 12230

Smith-Edwards Beverly A. • Student • University of Oklahoma School of Library & Information Studies • Norman, OK 73019 • AASL

Smith-Epps E. Paulette • Project Manager • Atlanta-Fulton Public Library • Atlanta, GA 30303 • LAMA PLA IFRT SRRT

Smith-Freeman Patricia M. • Branch Librarian • College of New Rochelle Brooklyn Campus • Brooklyn, NY 11208 • ACRL

Smith-Nickles Suzanne R. Mrs. • Hands Down The Exchange • Greenwood, SC 29646

Smith Aaron S. • Network Librarian • Michigan Library Consortium • Holt, MI 48842 • ALCTS

Smith Adeline M. • Amelia, VA 23002

Smith Alice G. Dr. • Emeritus Professor • University of South Florida School of Library & Information Science • Tampa, FL 33620 • ASCLA YALSA

Smith Alice K. • Library Media Specialist • Brighton Central Schools Library Media Services • Rochester, NY 14618 • AASL LIRT

Smith Alice Reviere • Black Studies/Women Studies Libn • Cleveland State University Library • Cleveland, OH 44115 • ACRL

Smith Alison McManus • Linden, MI 48451-9033 • AASL YALSA

Smith Alma D. • DeQuincy High School • DeQunicy, LA 70633

Smith Amy S. • Fresno, CA 93704-3709 • LITA ILERT

Smith Angus J. • Lake Mary, FL 32746 • RASD

Smith Ann F. • Libraries Staff Personnel Ofc • Rutgers University Libraries • New Brunswick, NJ 08903 • LAMA

Smith Ann M. • Branch Manager • Enoch Pratt Free Library Hamilton Branch • Baltimore, MD 21214 • PLA

Smith Ann M. • Augustana College Mikkelsen Library • Sioux Falls, SD 57197 • RASD GODORT LIRT

Smith Ann Montgomery • Wentworth Institute of Technology • Boston, MA 02115 • ACRL

Smith Ann Mrs. • Trustee • Topeka Public Library • Topeka, KS 66604-1374

Smith Anne P. • Head, Preservation Dept. • Ohio University Vernon R. Alden Library • Athens, OH 45701-2978 • ALCTS

Smith Anne P. • Director • Georgia Historical Society Library • Savannah, GA 31499

Smith Annie Laurie • Lincoln, NE 68510 • Continuing

Smith Ava M. • Waco, TX 76708

Smith Barbara E. • Saratoga Springs, NY 12866 • GODORT

Smith Barbara F. • Head Librarian • Austin Memorial Library • Cleveland, TX 77327

Smith Barbara G. • Section Chief • Maryland State Department of Education Division of Library Development & Services • Baltimore, MD 21201 • ASCLA PLA

Smith Barbara J. • Orton ON, L0N 1N0 Canada • Continuing

Smith Barbara J. • Director • Smithsonian Institution Libraries • Washington, DC 20560 • ACRL LAMA

Smith Barbara Jane • Sabine Pass I.S.D. • Sabine Pass, TX 77655 • AASL RASD CLENE IRRT VRT

Smith Barbara L. • Librarian • Georgetown Day School • Washington, DC 20007 • AASL YALSA

Smith Barbara L. • Automation Librarian • Marist College Library • Poughkeepsie, NY 12601 • LITA

Smith Barbara W. • Branch Head • Charles County Public Library P.D. Brown Memorial Branch • Waldorf, MD 20601

Smith Beryl J. • Reference Librarian • Niagara University Library • Niagara University, NY 14109

Smith Beryl K. • Acting Head • Rutgers University Libraries Archibald Stevens Alexander Library • New Brunswick, NJ 08903 • ACRL ALCTS

Smith Bessie • Goldsboro, NC 27534

Smith Bettye F. • Manager of Lib Acq & Accounts • Covington & Burling Law Library • Washington, DC 20004

Smith Bettye L. • Regional Children's Librarian • District of Columbia Public Library Woodridge Regional Branch • Washington, DC 20018 • ALSC SRRT

Smith Bobbie J. • Director of Library • Long Beach City College • Long Beach, CA 90808

Smith Bobbye T. • Librarian • West Yadkin School Media Center • Hamptonville, NC 27020

Smith Brenda H. • Assistant Editor • H. W. Wilson Company • Bronx, NY 10452

Smith Carol • Interlibrary Loan Ln/Acq • Nogales/Santa Cruz County Library • Nogales, AZ 85621

Smith Carol P. • Reference Librarian • Kalamazoo College Library • Kalamazoo, MI 49007-3285 • ACRL RASD LIRT

Smith Caroline L. • Ann Arbor, MI 48105 • LITA

Smith Carolyn • Rare Books Librarian • Johns Hopkins University Milton S. Eisenhower Library • Baltimore, MD 21218 • ACRL

Smith Carolyn L. • Director • Penfield Public Library • Penfield, NY 14526 • PLA

Smith Carolyn M. • Director of Library/Media Svs • Rush-Henrietta Central School District • Henrietta, NY 14467 • AASL

Smith Carolyn Shelor • Librarian • J.R. Tucker High School • Richmond, VA 23294 • AASL

Smith Catherine A. • Reference Librarian • Northwestern University Galter Health Sciences Library • Chicago, IL 60611 • RASD

Smith Charles L. • Trustee • Council Bluffs Free Public Library • Council Bluffs, IA 51503

Smith Charles R. • Coor. Science & Technology • Texas A & M University Sterling C. Evans Library • College Station, TX 77843-5000 • ACRL ALCTS LAMA

Smith Chris Tina • Student • University of California Los Angeles Graduate School of Library & Information Science • Los Angeles, CA 90024

Smith Clifford D. • Head Extension Service Division • Salem Public Library • Salem, OR 97309-5020

Smith Craig A. • Reference Div. Admin. • Oregon State Library • Salem, OR 97310-0640

Smith Cristen J. • Student • University of Oklahoma School of Library & Information Studies • Norman, OK 73019 • AASL

Smith Cynthia W. • Elementary School Librarian • Elko Grammar School • Elko, NV 89801 • AASL

Smith Dana E. • Parks Library • Iowa State University Library • Ames, IA 50011-2140 • LAMA

Smith David A. • Library of Congress • Washington, DC 20541 • ACRL ALCTS

Smith David C. • Student • Wayne State University Library Science Program • Detroit, MI 48202 • MAGERT

Smith David Rexford • Hopkins, MN 55343 • LAMA PLA *Life*

Smith Dean Phillip • New York Public Library Tremont Branch • Bronx, NY 10457 • ALSC IFRT NMRT SRRT

Smith Deborah L. • Student • University of Arizona Library • Tucson, AZ 85721 • RASD

Smith Deborah M. • Student • Rutgers University School of Communication Information & Library Studies • New Brunswick, NJ 08903 • PLA ERT

Smith Denis J. • Ameriscribe • Chicago, IL 60661

Smith Dennis E. • Director-Library Affairs • University of California • Oakland, CA 94612-3550 • ACRL ALCTS LAMA

Smith Dennis R. • Assistant Librarian • University of Pittsburgh • Pittsburgh, PA 15260 • ACRL RASD

Smith Dentye M. • Library Media Specialist • West Fulton High School • Atlanta, GA 30318 • AASL

Smith Diane • Arts & Design Librarian • Ryerson Polytech Institute • Toronto ON, M5B 2K3 Canada • ACRL

Smith Diane B. • High School Librarian • Hazelwood Central High School • Florissant, MO 63031 • AASL

Smith Diane Green • Assistant Professor • Northeast Louisana University • Monroe, LA 71209-0720 • AASL ALSC

Smith Diane Harvey • Librarian • Pennsylvania State University Pattee Library • University Park, PA 16802 • ACRL LAMA RASD GODORT

Smith Diane J. • Bibliographic Services Supvr • Orange County Public Library • Santa Ana, CA 92705 • ALCTS LITA PLA

Smith Diane L. • Trustee • Christian County Library • Ozark, MO 65721 • ALTA

Smith Diane L. • United States Department of Justice Criminal Library • Washington, DC 20530 • RASD

Smith Diane R. • Adult Services Librarian • Onondaga County Public Library Betts Branch • Syracuse, NY 13205

Smith Dinah L. • Mansfield Public Library • Mansfield, MA 02048 • PLA

Smith Donald R. • Assoc Dir for General Services • University of Tulsa McFarlin Library • Tulsa, OK 74104-3189 • ACRL

Smith Donald T. • Eugene, OR 97405-2803 • ACRL ALCTS LAMA LITA RASD *Life*

Smith Donde H. • Prince George County Memorial Library • Oxon Hill, MD 20745 • PLA YALSA

Smith Donna B. • Fort Mitchell, KY 41017

Smith Donna C. • Student • University of Southern Mississippi School of Library Science • Hattiesburg, MS 39406-5146

Smith Donna Ridley • Tahoe City, CA 96145

Smith Dorcas B. • Onalaska, TX 77089 • ALCTS MAGERT

Smith Doris A. • Bedford Public Schools Lane School/ Davis School • Bedford, MA 01730 • AASL

Smith Doris J. • Chicago, IL 60619 • AASL

Smith Dorman H. • Director of Public Services • Central Michigan University Charles V. Park Library 315 • Mount Pleasant, MI 48859 • LAMA

Smith Dorothy B. • Librarian/ Learning Res. Spec. • Galindo Elementary School • Austin, TX 78704 • AASL ALSC

Smith Dorothy C. • Schenectady, NY 12309 • Continuing

Smith Dorothy D. • Computer-Based Services Ln. • University of Washington • Seattle, WA 98195 • ACRL RASD

Smith Dorothy Lockaby • Saint Joseph's Hospital • Lowell, MA 01854

Smith Duncan F. • Faculty • North Carolina Central University • Durham, NC 27707 • PLA CLENE

Smith E Marjorie • Catalog Specialist • Iowa State University Library • Ames, IA 50011-2140 • ACRL ALCTS *Life*

Smith Earl C. • North Carolina State University • Raleigh, NC 27695 • LITA

Smith Edward H L III • Menands, NY 12204

Smith Edward R. • Law Librarian • Morris County Law Library • Morristown, NJ 07963-0900

Smith Eleanor • Trustee • Loudoun County Public Library • Leesburg, VA 22075 • ALTA

Smith Eleanor T. • San Francisco, CA 94109 • Continuing

Smith Eleanor T. • Cohasset, MA 02025 • Continuing

Smith Elizabeth H. • Assoc. Dir. for Technical Servs • East Carolina University Joyner Library • Greenville, NC 27858-4353

Smith Elizabeth M. • Student • University of North Carolina at Chapel Hill School of Information and Library Science • Chapel Hill, NC 27599-3360 • RASD

Smith Elizabeth Martinez • City Librarian • Los Angeles Public Library • Los Angeles, CA 90071 • AASL ACRL ALCTS ALSC ALTA ASCLA LAMA LITA PLA RASD YALSA CLENE EMIERT GODORT IFRT IRRT SORT SRRT

Smith Elizabeth S. • Head of Library • Pennsylvania State University Behrend College Library • Erie, PA 16563-0902 • ACRL LAMA LIRT LRRT SORT

Smith Elizabeth W. • Gifts Librarian • Georgetown University Joseph Mark Lauinger Library • Washington, DC 20057-1006

Smith Ella Gray • Trustee • Davie County Public Library • Mocksville, NC 27028-2115 • ALTA

Smith Ellyn K. • Librarian • Pittsfield Public Library • Pittsfield, ME 04967

Smith Emma C. • Greenville, SC 29611-1622 • Continuing

Smith Eric J. • Engineering Librarian • Duke University • Durham, NC 27708 • ACRL LITA

Smith Evelyn J. • Trustee • Saint Charles Parish Library • Luling, LA 70070 • ALTA

Smith Evelyn L. • Chief Tech Servs Librarian • University of Michigan Law Library • Ann Arbor, MI 48109-1210 • ALCTS LITA

Smith Evelyn Z. Mrs • Pacific Palisades, CA 90272 • ACRL RASD *Life*

Smith Faith A. • Librarian • West Springfield Junior High School Library • West Springfield, MA 01089 • AASL

Smith Floda V. • Salmon, ID 83467 • Continuing

Smith Frances N. Mrs. • Des Moines, WA 98198 • Continuing

Smith Frances W. Mrs • Bordentown, NJ 08505 • LAMA PLA *Continuing*

Smith Frederick E. • Lib Devel Specialist II • New York State Library State Education Department • Albany, NY 12230 • ALCTS LITA *Life*

Smith Fredrica C. • Circulation Librarian • Withers Memorial Public Library • Nicholasville, KY 40356

Smith Gail D. • Regional Manager • Memphis-Shelby County Public Library and Information Center • Memphis, TN 38104-4025 • LAMA PLA RASD IFRT

Smith Genevieve W. • Morgantown, WV 26505 • AASL ACRL IFRT LIRT SRRT

Smith Geoffrey D. • Curator, Charvat Collection • Ohio State University Libraries • Columbus, OH 43210-1286 • ACRL

Smith George V. • Acting Director • Alaska State Library • Juneau, AK 99811-571

Smith Geraldine E. • Catlg & Database Mgmt Librarian • University of North Texas • Denton, TX 76203 • ACRL ALCTS LITA IFRT LIRT

Smith Gloria E. • Adult Librarian • Los Angeles Public Library Brentwood Branch • Los Angeles, CA 90049

Smith Gloria L. • Tucson, AZ 85710 • ACRL RASD IRRT

Smith Gordon W. • Associate Director • California State University • Seal Beach, CA 90740 • ACRL LITA

Smith Grace F. • Richmond, VA 23229

Smith Gwendolyn • Windsor ON, N9A 6W8 Canada • Continuing

Smith Hal Haynes • Johnson City, TN 37601 • Continuing

Smith Hannis S. • Saint Paul, MN 55101 • ASCLA PLA *Life*

Smith Harold F. • Parkville, MO 64152 • ACRL RASD *Continuing*

Smith Heidi • Alexander, NY 14005

Smith Helen • Trustee • Kanawha County Public Library • Charleston, WV 25301 • ALTA

Smith Helen F. • Pennsylvania State University Libraries • University Park, PA 16802 • ACRL RASD LIRT

Smith Henrietta M. • Associate Professor • University of South Florida School of Library & Information Science • Tampa, FL 33620 • AASL ALSC YALSA SRRT

Smith Howard • Trustee • Brooklyn Public Library • Brooklyn, NY 11238 • ALTA

Smith Howard M. • City Librarian • Richmond Public Library • Richmond, VA 23219 • Continuing

Smith Irene C. • Miami-Dade Public Library System South Miami Branch • South Miami, FL 33143 • ALSC

Smith Isabel F. • Trustee • Bloomfield Township Public Library • Bloomfield Hills, MI 48302-2437 • ALTA

Smith Ivan R. • McKinley Senior High School • Washington, DC 20002

Smith J. Christina • Reference Ln Bibliographer • Boston University Mugar Memorial Library • Boston, MA 02215 • ACRL RASD IRRT NMRT SRRT

Smith Jacqueline • Head of Learning Resources • Philadelphia College of Pharmacy & Science-Joseph W. England Library • Philadelphia, PA 19104-4491 • ACRL LITA VRT

Smith James L. • Library Consultant • Alabama Public Library Service • Montgomery, AL 36130 • ASCLA

Smith James L. • Buena Regional High School • Buena, NJ 08310 • AASL

Smith James Patrick • Nonprint Librarian • Adelphi University Swirbul Library • Garden City, NY 11530 • AASL VRT

Smith James R. • Asst. Head, Louisiana Division • New Orleans Public Library • New Orleans, LA 70140

Smith Jane Bandy • Education Specialist • Alabama Department of Education • Montgomery, AL 36130 • AASL

Smith Jane E. • Continuing Education Coordinator • Utah State Library • Salt Lake City, UT 84115-2579 • CLENE

Smith Janel M. • Children's Librarian • Allen Public Library • Allen, TX 75002 • ALSC PLA

Smith Janet • Trustee • Palos Verdes Library District • Pls Vrd Pnsla, CA 90274

Smith Janet E. • Branch Librarian • Lucedale-George County Library • Lucedale, MS 39452 • PLA

Smith Janet S. • Referene Librarian • Klamath County Public Library System • Klamath Falls, OR 97603 • NMRT

Smith Janice • Administrator • School District 12 Media Center • Northglenn, CO 80221 • AASL

Smith Janice E. • Librarian/Media Specialist • Arnold Elementary School • Arnold, MD 21012 • AASL

Smith Janice L. • Teacher • Osawatomie Unified School District 37 • Osawatomie, KS 66064 • AASL YALSA NMRT

Smith Janis J. • Proctor R. Hug High School • Reno, NV 89512

Smith Jean A. • Encinitas, CA 92024

Smith Jean M. Dr. • Associate Dean for Library Serv. • Lower Columbia College Alan Thompson Library • Longview, WA 98632 • ACRL LAMA

Smith Jean Matthew O.P. Sister • School Librarian • Saint James Elementary School • San Francisco, CA 94110

Smith Jeanette C. • Head, Government Documents • New Mexico State University Library • Las Cruces, NM 88003-0006 • YALSA GODORT

Smith Jeanette J. • Librarian • Saint Louis Public Library Julia Davis Branch • St. Louis, MO 63115 • PLA

Smith Jeanette M. • Media Services Director • Forsyth Country Day School • Lewisville, NC 27023 • AASL YALSA

Smith Jennifer • Milford, OH 45150 • ALSC

Smith Jessie C. • Head Librarian • Fisk University Library & Media Center • Nashville, TN 37208 • ACRL

Smith Jessie Cottman • Director of Library Services • University of Maryland-Eastern Shore Frederick Douglass Library • Princess Anne, MD 21853 • ACRL

Smith Jewell G. • Springfield, MO 65807

Smith Jimmy Neil • Executive Director • NAPPS • Jonesborough, TN 37659

Smith Joan C. • Director Special Projects • Library of Michigan • Lansing, MI 48909 • AASL ASCLA PLA CLENE

Smith Joan Elise Sister • Catholic Central High School • Springfield, OH 45505

Smith John B. • Director of Libraries • State University of New York (SUNY) Frank Melville Jr. Memorial Library • Stony Brook, NY 11794-3300 • ACRL

Smith Jolene • Senior Librarian • Ocean County Library System • Toms River, NJ 08753 • PLA

Smith Joy A. • Media Specialist • John Heard Elementary School • Macon, GA 31206 • AASL

Smith Joyce W. • Babylon, NY 11702

Smith Juanita J. • Muncie, IN 47304-2132 • Life

Smith Judith A. • Circulation/Periodicals Libn • Mission College LRS • Santa Clara, CA 95054 • ACRL

Smith Judith L. • Student • University of South Carolina College of Library & Information Science • Columbia, SC 29208

Smith Judith P. • Student • University of Illinois Graduate School of Library and Information Science • Urbana, IL 61801

Smith Judy B. • Library Media Specialist • Asbell Elementary School • Fayetteville, AR 72703 • AASL

Smith Judy B. • Librarian • Dolvin Elementary School Library • Alpharetta, GA 30201 • AASL ALSC

Smith Judy R. • Cleveland, TN 37312 • AASL

Smith Judy R. • Director of Development • Library Foundation of San Francisco • San Francisco, CA 94104

Smith June B. • Resource Center Director • Johnson & Wales University • Charleston, SC 29403

Smith K. Wayne Dr. • President & CEO • OCLC Online Computer Library Center • Dublin, OH 43017-3395

Smith Karel A. Mrs • Saint Louis, MO 63104 • AASL

Smith Karen E. • Library Media Specialist • Hill View Elementary School • Sylvania, OH 43560

Smith Karen E. • Student • University of Illinois Graduate School of Library and Information Science • Urbana, IL 61801 • IFRT

Smith Karen F. • Reference Coordinator • State University of New York (SUNY) at Buffalo • Buffalo, NY 14260 • ACRL RASD GODORT

Smith Karen J. • Ottumwa, IA 52501

Smith Karen P. • Assistant Professor • Queens College Benjamin S. Rosenthal Library • Flushing, NY 11367-0904 • AASL ALSC PLA LHRT SRRT

Smith Karla U. • Student • University of Wisconsin-Milwaukee School of Library & Information Science • Milwaukee, WI 53201

Smith Karol Loraine • Muir John Junior High School • Burbank, CA 91504

Smith Kathryn L. • City Librarian • Winter Haven Public Library • Winter Haven, FL 33880 • LAMA PLA

Smith Kent L. • Wyncote, PA 19095

Smith Kevin • Executive Director • Literacy Volunteers of America New York State • Buffalo, NY 14225

Smith Kevin J. • Division Head • Dayton & Montgomery County Public Library • Dayton, OH 45402-2103

Smith Kimberly A. • Librarian • San Diego County Library Poway Branch Library • Poway, CA 92064-4687

Smith Kitty • Assistant Professor • University of North Carolina Department of Library & Information Studies • Greensboro, NC 27412-5001 • LAMA CLENE

Smith Lamar R. • Reno, NV 89503 • ACRL YALSA *Life*

Smith Lary • Bloomington, IN 47401

Smith Laura • Trustee • Roosevelt Public Library • Roosevelt, NY 11575 • ALTA

Smith Laura F. • Student • Northern Illinois University Department of Library & Information Studies • DeKalb, IL 60115

Smith Laura L. • Library Assistant • John Peter Smith Hospital Medical Library • Fort Worth, TX 76104

Smith Leah-Jay • Cincinnati, OH 45220 • IFRT

Smith Ledell B. • Baton Rouge, LA 70805

Smith Lena Denham • School Librarian • Barret T. Middle School • Louisville, KY 40206 • AASL

Smith Leroy D. • Media Specialist • Mitchell High School • Colorado Springs, CO 80909 • LITA

Smith Leslie E. • Student • University of Missouri-Columbia School of Library & Informational Science • Columbia, MO 65211 • PLA

Smith Lesly M. • Manager • Dallas Public Library Forest Green Branch • Dallas, TX 75243-4114

Smith Linda A. • Librarian • Palmdale Traditional School • Phoenix, AZ 85040 • AASL EMIERT

Smith Linda D. • Kingsport, TN 37664

Smith Linda L. • Cataloging • University of North Florida • Jacksonville, FL 32216 • ACRL ALCTS *Life*

Smith Lindner • Board Member • Jacksonville Public Libraries Main Library • Jacksonville, FL 32202

Smith Lisa M. • Fort Worth, TX 76103

Smith Lois Dehaan • Geisler Learning Resource Center • Pella, IA 50219 • ALCTS LITA

Smith Lori L. • Government Documents • Southeastern Louisiana University Linus A. Sims Memorial Library • Hammond, LA 70402 • GODORT

Smith Lorraine K. • Eanes Elementary School • Austin, TX 78746 • AASL

Smith Lorre B. • Hd. of Media Microforms, Per • State University of New York (SUNY) University Libraries • Albany, NY 12222 • ACRL ALCTS LAMA LITA

Smith Louann • Reference Librarian • Anoka County Library • Blaine, MN 55434

Smith Louise • Saint Petersburg, FL 33707 • Continuing

Smith Lucy O. • Reference Librarian • Triton College Library • River Grove, IL 60171

Smith Lynn M. • Milwaukee, WI 53216

Smith Lynn R. • Trustee • Newnan-Coweta Public Library • Newnan, GA 30263

Smith Lynne Dr. • Dean of Library Services • University of South Carolina Coastal Carolina College Kimbel Library • Conway, SC 29526

Smith Mackenzie • Systems Librarian • Harvard University • Cambridge, MA 02138 • LITA

Smith Margaret • Administrative Librarian • Evergreen Park Public Library • Chicago, IL 60642 • LAMA PLA

Smith Margaret N. • Branch Library Supervisor • Jacksonville Public Libraries Main Library • Jacksonville, FL 32202 • PLA

Smith Margaret O. • Reference, Circulation • Glencoe Public Library • Glencoe, IL 60022-1597 • PLA

Smith Margery E. • Technical Services Librarian • Edwin A Bemis Public Library Littleton Public Library • Littleton, CO 80120 • ALCTS LITA

Smith Margit J. • Cataloging Librarian • University of San Diego Copley Library • San Diego, CA 92110 • IRRT

Smith Margo • Louisville, KY 40205-1656 • ALCTS

Smith Margo W. • Library Technician • Pacific Beach High School • San Luis Obispo, CA 93401 • YALSA

Smith Marilee • Software Analyst • Wang Laboratories • Irving, TX 75039

Smith Marilyn E. • Senior Librarian • Farmington Branch Library • Farmington, MI 48335 • PLA

Smith Marilyn J. • Librarian • Navy Supply Corps School Library • Athens, GA 30606-5000 • AFLRT FLRT

Smith Marion T. • Cheshire, CT 06410

Smith Marjorie N. • Reference Librarian • University of Hawaii Thomas Hale Hamilton Library • Honolulu, HI 96822 • RASD

Smith Mark A. • Student • State University of New York (SUNY) School of Information & Library Studies • Buffalo, NY 14260 • NMRT

Smith Mark L. • Library Systems Administrator • Texas State Library • Austin, TX 78711

Smith Martha Eszes • Head of Reference Department • Claremont Colleges Libraries Honnold/Mudd Library • Claremont, CA 91711 • ACRL RASD

Smith Martha M. • Director • Saint Mary's College S. G. Kenan Library • Raleigh, NC 27603-1689 • ACRL IFRT LHRT LRRT

Smith Martha W. • Media Specialist • Rankin School • Greensboro, NC 27405 • AASL

Smith Martin A. • Head, Ctrl. Research Serv Dept • Smithsonian Institution Libraries • Washington, DC 20560

Smith Marvin E. • Thousand Oaks Library • Thousand Oaks, CA 91362 • LAMA PLA IFRT

Smith Mary • Trustee • Maywood Public Library • Maywood, IL 60153 • ALTA

Smith Mary A. • Library Manager • Southwest Public Libraries • Grove City, OH 43123 • PLA

Smith Mary Alice • Harvey, IL 60426 • Continuing

Smith Mary Alice • Head of Reference/Adult Services • West Des Moines Public Library • West Des Moines, IA 50265

Smith Mary Ann C. • Librarian • Thomas J. Watson School • Endicott, NY 13760 • AASL

Smith Mary Ellen • Lakewood, CA 90713 • ALCTS *Continuing*

Smith Mary Jane • Educational Media Specialist • East Brunswick High School Medical Center • East Brunswick, NJ 08816 • AASL

Smith Mary Jo • Student • Kent State University School of Library & Information Science • Kent, OH 44242-0001 • ALSC

Smith Mary L. • Library Director • O'Fallon Public Library • O'Fallon, IL 62269 • PLA

Smith Mary Margaret • Librarian • McGill-Toolen High School Library • Mobile, AL 36604 • AASL

Smith Mary Morgan • Coor. of Children's Services • Northland Public Library • Pittsburgh, PA 15237 • ALSC PLA

Smith Mary Paige • Technical Services Librarian • University of Baltimore Law Library • Baltimore, MD 21201 • ACRL SRRT

Smith Maude M. • San Francisco, CA 94109

Smith Maureen E. • Student • Simmons College Graduate School of Library & Information Science • Boston, MA 02115

Smith Maureen Millea • Public Library of Cincinnati and Hamilton County • Cincinnati, OH 45202 • ALSC

Smith Maurya M. • Student • University of Arizona Graduate Library School • Tucson, AZ 85721 • VRT

Smith McNeale T. • Doswell, VA 23047

Smith Merna L. • Associate Director • Salt Lake City Public Library • Salt Lake City, UT 84111 • LAMA PLA

Smith Merrill F. • Vendor • Yankee Book Peddler • Contoocook, NH 03229 • ALCTS IFRT

Smith Merrily A. • Preservation Program Officer • Library of Congress • Washington, DC 20541 • ALCTS

Smith Michael D. • Student • University of Arizona Graduate Library School • Tucson, AZ 85721 • ALSC PLA

Smith Michael R. • Automation Specialist • Dynix, Incorporated • Forest Grove, OR 97116 • LITA

Smith Mindy • Fireside Elementary Library • Louisville, CO 80027 • AASL

Smith Miriam S. • Springfield, PA 19064

Smith Mitchell R. • Chicago, IL 60649 • ALSC PLA SRRT

Smith Monica Jill • Information Services Librarian • Pepperdine University Plaza Library • Culver City, CA 90230 • ACRL EMIERT ILERT IRRT LIRT LRRT

Smith Myron J. Jr. • Director • Tusculum College Library • Greeneville, TN 37743 • ACRL

Smith Nancy • Director • Waterford Township Public Library • Waterford, MI 48329 • LAMA PLA CLENE SORT

Smith Nancy • Systems Librarian • Medical University of South Carolina Library • Charleston, SC 29425

Smith Nancy J. • Senior Descriptive Cataloger • Library of Congress • Washington, DC 20541 • ALCTS LITA

Smith Nancy J. • Westerville Public Library • Westerville, OH 43081 • ALSC PLA

Smith Nancy L. • Librarian • Dixon Correctional Center Illinois Department of Corrections • Dixon, IL 61021 • ASCLA

Smith Nancy Laura • Student • East Carolina University Department of Library & Information Studies • Greenville, NC 27858-4353 • AASL

Smith Nancy M. • Director • Belleville Public Library • Belleville, IL 62220 • PLA

Smith Nancy P. • Issaquah, WA 98027-8543 • PLA

Smith Nathan M. Dr • Brigham Young University School of Library & Information Sciences • Provo, UT 84602 • LRRT

Smith Newland F. III • Collection Management Librarian • Garrett-Evangelical Seabury Western Theological Seminaries • Evanston, IL 60201 • ACRL

Smith Norma M. • Director-Serials Operations • University Microfilms International • Ann Arbor, MI 48106-1346

Smith Norma S. • Student • Kent State University School of Library & Information Science • Kent, OH 44242-0001 • LITA EMIERT NMRT

Smith Pamela R. • Dir., National Customer Serv. • Baker & Taylor Books • Charlotte, NC 28217 • AASL ALCTS LITA PLA

Smith Parker K. Jr. • Trustee • Kanawha County Public Library • Charleston, WV 25301 • ALTA

Smith Patience M. • Student • University of Pittsburgh School of Library and Information Science • Pittsburgh, PA 15260 • LITA

Smith Patricia A. • Libn.-Head Campus Librarian • City College of San Francisco John Adamds Campus • San Francisco, CA 94117

Smith Patricia A. • Head Acquisitions • Colorado State University William E. Morgan Library • Fort Collins, CO 80523 • ACRL ALCTS LITA

Smith Patricia D. • Pace Academy • Atlanta, GA 30327

Smith Patricia F. • Branch Librarian • New York Public Library Division P • New York, NY 10163-2240 • PLA YALSA

Smith Patricia H. • Executive Director • Texas Library Association • Austin, TX 78746 • PLA ERT

Smith Patricia Luken • Bloomington, IL 61704

Smith Patricia M. • Library Media Specialist • Joliet Central High School • Joliet, IL 60432 • YALSA

Smith Paula V. • Assistant Director • Rochester Public Library • Rochester, NY 14604 • LAMA PLA

Smith Peggy Brooks • Director • Doane College Perkins Library • Crete, NE 68333 • ACRL IFRT *Life*

Smith Peter A. • Online Services Coordinator • Western Washington University Wilson Library • Bellingham, WA 98225 • ACRL LITA RASD

Smith Philip M. • Head of Catalog Department • Memphis State University Main Library • Memphis, TN 38152 • ACRL ALCTS LITA

Smith Phillip C. • Reference Librarian • Brigham Young University Hawaii Campus • Laie, HI 96762

Smith Phyllis Allen • Program Administrator • Marblehead High School Library • Marblehead, MA 01945

Smith Phyllis B. • Children's Librarian • Lane Public Library • Hamilton, OH 45011 • ALSC PLA

Smith Phyllis D. • Student • Clark-Atlanta University School of Library & Information Studies • Atlanta, GA 30314-4391 • EMIERT LRRT SRRT

Smith Rachel H. • Acting Head • Mississippi College Speed Library • Clinton, MS 39056 • LITA

Smith Randolph N. • Enoch Pratt Free Library • Baltimore, MD 21201-4484

Smith Randolph R. • Boulder Public Library • Boulder, CO 80306 • LAMA LITA SRRT

Smith Rebecca A. • Curator of Research Materials • Historical Museum of Southern Florida • Miami, FL 33130

Smith Rey E. • Coor. Library Automation Proj. • University of Puerto Rico • San Juan, PR 00936-4898

Smith Richard D. • President • Wei T'o Associates • Matteson, IL 60443 • ACRL ALCTS

Smith Richard J. • Asst. Dir. for Tech. Services • University of Southwestern Louisiana Libraries • Lafayette, LA 70503 • ACRL ALCTS LITA

Smith Rise L. • Technical Services Librarian • Dakota State University Karl E. Mundt Library • Madison, SD 57042-1799 • ACRL

Smith Rita H. • Reference Librarian • University of Tennessee John C. Hodges Library • Knoxville, TN 37996-1000 • ACRL

Smith Rita J. • Program Director • University of Florida Libraries Baldwin Library • Gainesville, FL 32611

Smith Rita Louise • Administrative Librarian • White Sands Missile Range Post Library • White Sands MR, NM 88002

Smith Rita P. • Ref. & Bibl. Instr. Librarian • Brigham Young University Hawaii Campus • Laie, HI 96762 • ACRL LIRT

Smith Robert B. • Air Products & Chemicals • Allentown, PA 18195-1501 • LITA

Smith Robert C. • Associate Professor • Western Kentucky University Library Media Education • Bowling Green, KY 42101 • AASL

Smith Robert D. • Librarian • Vista Community College • Berkeley, CA 94704 • ACRL

Smith Robert Norton • Director • International Library Service • Northants, NN13 5JS, England • IRRT

Smith Robert S. • Director • Medina County District Library • Medina, OH 44256 • LAMA PLA IFRT

Smith Robyn H. • Fairbanks North Star Borough Public Library & Regional Center-Noel Wien Library • Fairbanks, AK 99701 • YALSA

Smith Ronnie • Student • University of Alabama School of Library & Information Studies • Tuscaloosa, AL 35487-0252

Smith Rosemary • Utlas International • Etobicoke, ON, M8X 2X2 Canada • LITA

Smith Ruby Anne • Reference Librarian • Public Library of Johnston County & Smithfield • Smithfield, NC 27577 • PLA IFRT

Smith Ruth M. • Student • Dalhousie University School of Library & Inf. Studies • Halifax NS, B3H 4H8 Canada

Smith Sally Decker • Reference Librarian • Indian Trails Public Library District • Wheeling, IL 60090 • PLA

Smith Sally Gildea • Western Library Network (WLN) • Lacey, WA 98503-0888 • AASL ALCTS LITA

Smith Sally Porter • Collection Development Ln. • King County Library System • Seattle, WA 98109-5191 • PLA

Smith Sallye W. • Denver, CO 80222-3830 • ACRL LITA EMIERT GODORT LIRT LRRT SORT

Smith Sandra • Librarian • Wilson Elementary School • Imperial, PA 15126 • AASL

Smith Sandra D. • Union County Schools • Monroe, NC 28112 • AASL

Smith Sandra K. • Financial Management Analyst • San Diego County Office of Finanical Management • San Diego, CA 92101

Smith Sandra L. • Catalog/Automation Librarian • Fullerton College William T. Boyce Library • Fullerton, CA 92634 • ALCTS

Smith Sandra S. • Assistant Adult Serv Librarian • Lodi Public Library • Lodi, CA 95240 • RASD

Smith Sara L. • Student • Indiana University School of Library and Information Science • Bloomington, IN 47405 • RASD

Smith Scott A. • Regional Sales Manager • Blackwell's • Portland, OR 97214 • ACRL ALCTS LITA ERT NMRT

Smith Sharon E. • Los Alamos National Lab Lib • Los Alamos, NM 87545-0020 • LITA

Smith Sharon K. • Student • Northwestern University Library • Evanston, IL 60208-2300

Smith Sharon L. • Portland, OR 97219 • ACRL EMIERT LRRT

Smith Sharron L. • Manager of Public Schools • Kitchener Public Library • Kitchener ON, N2H 2H1 Canada • SORT

Smith Sharyl G. • Associate Director • Granite School District • Salt Lake City, UT 84115 • AASL ALSC LAMA

Smith Sharyll A. • Librarian • Hennepin County Library Ridgedale-Hennepin Area Library • Minnetonka, MN 55343 • PLA CLENE

Smith Sherrill L. • Assistant to the Director • Public Libraries of Saginaw • Saginaw, MI 48605 • LAMA PLA EMIERT

Smith Shirley • Media Specialist • G.A. Treakle Elementary School • Chesapeake, VA 23323 • AASL

Smith Sieglinde K. • Oregon Historial Society • Portland, OR 97205 • NMRT

Smith Sirleine • Administrator • Eckhart Public Library • Auburn, IN 46706

Smith Starr E. • APO, AE 09213-7900 • ACRL RASD IFRT

Smith Stephanie D.L. • Boone, NC 28607

Smith Stephen C. • Reference Services Librarian • Spartanburg County Public Library • Spartanburg, SC 29304

Smith Stephen E. • Senior Associate/Project Arch. • TWP Associates, Inc. • Bloomfields Hills, MI 48302

Smith Stephen J. • Student • University of Illinois Graduate School of Library and Information Science • Urbana, IL 61801

Smith Steven Escar • Student • University of South Carolina College of Library & Information Science • Columbia, SC 29208

Smith Susan A. • Head of Acquisitions • West Georgia College Irvine Sullivan Ingram Library • Carrollton, GA 30118 • ACRL LITA LRRT

Smith Susan H. • Head, Catalog Librarian • University of Mississippi John Davis Williams Library • University, MS 38677 • ALCTS

Smith Susan K. • Senior Research Librarian • National Steel Corporation R & D Technical Library • Trenton, MI 48183 • ACRL

Smith Susan P. • Serials Section Head • University of Connecticut Homer Babbidge Library • Storrs, CT 06269-1005 • ALCTS

Smith Susan R. • Acquisitions • Gannon University Nash Library • Erie, PA 16541 • IFRT

Smith Susan S. • Youth Services Librarian • Orland Park Public Library • Orland Park, IL 60462 • ALSC NMRT

Smith Susan S. • Student • University of North Carolina Department of Library & Information Studies • Greensboro, NC 27412-5001

Smith Susan S. Dr. • Lakeview Center Inc. • Pensacola, FL 32501-1857 • ASCLA

Smith Susan V. • University of South Carolina Union Library • Union, SC 29379 • ACRL RASD LIRT

Smith Susan W. • Carmel, CA 93921 • LITA

Smith Suzanne W. • Coffee County Lannom Memorial Library • Tullahoma, TN 37388

Smith Suzette M. • Blasdell, NY 14219

Smith Sweetman R. • Lee County Library System • Fort Myers, FL 33901

Smith Sylvia • Director • Burnham Library • Bridgewater, CT 06752

Smith Tammy U. • Snellville, GA 30278 • AASL YALSA

Smith Ted D. • Student • University of California-Los Angeles (UCLA) • Los Angeles, CA 90024-1450 • ACRL GODORT NMRT

Smith Ted J. • Director • Norfolk Public Library • Norfolk, NE 68701 • PLA

Smith Teresa A. • Librarian • Cleveland Public Library • Cleveland, OH 44114-1271 • PLA

Smith Terry M. • AV Cataloger • University of Oregon Library • Eugene, OR 97403-1299

Smith Thelma P. • Librarian • Alamo Heights Junior School • San Antonio, TX 78209 • AASL

Smith Thomas E. • Clln/Facilities Manager • United States Nuclear Regulatory Commission • Washington, DC 20555 • LAMA

Smith Thomas J. • Las Vegas, NV 89121 • PLA NMRT

Smith Timothy D. • Librarian • Ohio University Vernon R. Alden Library • Athens, OH 45701-2978 • ACRL RASD LIRT

Smith Timothy Ray • Coordinator • Hawaii Prevention Resource Center • Honolulu, HI 96814 • ACRL RASD

Smith Tracy L. • Student • Catholic University of America Library Science Library • Washington, DC 20064 • SRRT

Smith Trina • Santa Ana, CA 92701 • PLA

Smith Valerie A. • Glen Morgan, WV 25847 • AASL

Smith Valerie M. • Supervisor, Adult Services • Lorain Public Library • Lorain, OH 44052 • PLA RASD

Smith Veronica F. • Student • Emporia State University Emporia in the Rockies • Denver, CO 80204

Smith Vicki L. • Cataloger • University Microfilms International • Ann Arbor, MI 48106-1346

Smith Vicki L. • Assistant Librarian • Mabel C. Fry Public Library • Yukon, OK 73099

Smith Vincent Jr. • Head of Cataloging Department • California State University,Fresno Henry Madden Library • Fresno, CA 93740-0034

Smith Virginia • Trustee • Conyer-Rockdale Library Systems • Conyers, GA 30207

Smith Virginia C. • Assistant Director • Gloucester County Library • Sewell, NJ 08080 • PLA

Smith Virginia R. • Head • State Library of Louisiana • Baton Rouge, LA 70821

Smith W. K. • Coordinator of Development • Western Michigan University Libraries • Kalamazoo, MI 49008

Smith William H. • Information Librarian • University of Alaska Elmer E. Rasmuson Library • Fairbanks, AK 99775-1005 • ACRL ALCTS RASD

Smith William Howard • Trustee • Jefferson County Public Library • Lakewood, CO 80215 • ALTA

Smith Zelda • Beaver Country Day School • Chestnut Hill, MA 02167 • AASL

Smith-Wood Kathy Johnson • Trustee • Montclair Free Public Library • Montclair, NJ 07042

Smithee Jeannette P. • Central New York Library Resources Council • Syracuse, NY 13208 • ASCLA LAMA LITA PLA GODORT

Smithers Anne B. • Health Science Cataloger • University of Alberta Cameron Library • Edmonton AB, T6G 2J8 Canada • ACRL ALCTS

Smithers Judie G. • Des Plaines, IL 60018 • ACRL FLRT GODORT IFRT

Smithson L Rebecca • Elementary Librarian • Will Rogers Elementary School • McAlester, OK 74501 • AASL

Smithson Paul G. • Associate Director • Kalamazoo College Library • Kalamazoo, MI 49007-3285 • ACRL LITA

Smithson Sandra • Lavaca, AR 72941

Smoak Carolyn B. • Media Specialist • Hand Middle School • Columbia, SC 29205 • AASL

Smoak Nancy B. • Media Coordinator • New London Elementary School • New London, NC 28127 • AASL

Smock Mildred K. • Director • Council Bluffs Free Public Library • Council Bluffs, IA 51503 • LAMA PLA

Smode Joan E. • President • JES Library Automation Consulting Services Inc. • Coquitlam BC, V3K 4H3 Canada • LITA

Smokey Sheila C. • Supervisor Librarian • FMC Corporation GSD Library-PO5 • Santa Clara, CA 95052

Smokonich Paula • Mount Lebanon Public Library • Mount Lebanon, PA 15228

Smoot Leroy • New York, NY 10032-7841 • ALCTS ALSC PLA RASD

Smoot Mabel • Trustee • McGregor Public Library • Highland Park, MI 48203 • ALTA

Smorch Thomas M. • Library Automation Supervisor • Black Gold Coop Library System • San Luis Obispo, CA 93403 • LITA

Smothers Joyce W. • Chief Librarian • Monmouth County Library Eastern Branch • Shrewsbury, NJ 07702

Smoyer Catherine L. • Monrovia, CA 91016

Smoyer Charles E. • Student • University of North Texas School of Library & Information Sciences • Denton, TX 76203 • PLA NMRT

Smuda Janice D. • Early Childhood Specialist • Cuyahoga County Public Library Parma-Snow Branch • Parma, OH 44134-2789 • ALSC

Smurlo Gloria C. • Student • Kutztown University Library Science Department • Kutztown, PA 19530 • ALSC SRRT

Smutko Charlotte S. • Asst. to the Coordinator • District of Columbia Public Library Martin Luther King Memorial Library • Washington, DC 20001 • ALSC IFRT

Smyers Richard P. • Reference Librarian • East Chicago Public Library Robert A Pastrick Branch • East Chicago, IN 46312

Smykla Evelyn Ortiz • Birmingham, AL 35244-1724 • RASD

Smyth Carol B. • Wayne Township Library • Richmond, IN 47374 • PLA

Smyth Cathryn H. • Clarion University of Pennsylvania College of Library Science • Clarion, PA 16214

Smyth Elaine B. • Head, Rare Books Collection • Louisiana State University Libraries • Baton Rouge, LA 70803 • ACRL ALCTS

Smyth May • Student • Long Island University Palmer School of Library & Info. Sci. • Brookville, NY 11548

Smyth Sheila A. • Associate Director • Nazareth College of Rochester • Rochester, NY 14618 • ALCTS

Smythe Victor N. • Librarian/Archivist • New York Public Library Schomburg Center for Research in Black Culture • New York, NY 10037 • ACRL

Smythe Wiebke • Student • University of Toronto Faculty of Library & Information Science • Toronto ON, M5S 1A1 Canada

Snair Dale S. • Director • Georgia Regional Library for the Blind & Physically Handicapped • Atlanta, GA 30310 • ASCLA

Snape Roger • Hamilton 5, Bermuda

Snapp Elizabeth M. • Director of Libraries • Texas Woman's University Mary Evelyn Blagg-Huey Library • Denton, TX 76204-1715 • ACRL ALCTS LAMA LITA RASD

Snapp Suellen • Adult Services Librarian • Warren Library Association • Warren, PA 16365

Snauffer Nancy L. • Librarian • Houston Public Library Carnegie Branch • Houston, TX 77009 • PLA RASD EMIERT

Snavely Loanne L. • Reference /Documents Librarian • Bloomsburg University Harvey A. Andruss Library • Bloomsburg, PA 17815 • ACRL

Snead Esther • John Knox Retirement Village • Orange City, FL 32763

Snead Marie E. • Indiana, PA 15701 • Continuing

Sneberger Ellen • Supervising Librarian • San Diego Public Library • San Diego, CA 92101 • RASD

Sneed Joanne M. • Granville County Library System • Oxford, NC 27565

Sneed Martha Crockett • United States Patent & Trademark Office Library Programs • Washington, DC 20231 • FLRT GODORT

Sneed Pearl Jean Miss • Librarian Emeritus • Jackson Municipal Library • Jackson, MS 39206 • LAMA PLA Continuing

Sneed Rebecca • Wolfe City, TX 75496

Snell Marion T. • Tierra del Sol Middel School • Lakeside, CA 92040 • AASL

Snell Mary Kay • Director • Amarillo Public Library • Amarillo, TX 79189 • LAMA PLA

Snell Maryann E. • Pittsburgh, PA 15239

Snell Patricia P. • Albuquerque, NM 87110 • ACRL ALCTS LITA Life

Snell Sandra Kay • Head,Reference Services • University of Missouri-Saint Louis • St. Louis, MO 63121-4499 • ACRL RASD

Snelling Bradley K. • Student • Indiana University School of Library and Information Science • Bloomington, IN 47405 • ALCTS IFRT

Snelson Pamela • Assistant Director • Drew University • Madison, NJ 07940-4007 • ACRL LITA LRRT

Snezek P Paul • Director • Wheaton College Buswell Memorial Library • Wheaton, IL 60187 • ACRL ALCTS LITA

Snider C. Elaine • Kyrene School District Waggoner Elementary School • Tempe, AZ 85284 • AASL ALSC

Snider Daniel B. • Library Director • Lovett Memorial Library • Pampa, TX 79065

Snider David P. • Director • Casa Grande Public Library • Casa Grande, AZ 85222 • PLA YALSA SRRT

Snider Edith E. • Librarian • Tennessee Department of Economic & Community Development • Nashville, TN 37243-0405

Snider Larry C. • Associate Librarian/Scie & Tech • California State University-Long Beach University Library & Learning Resources • Long Beach, CA 90840-1901 • ACRL LITA

Snider Lois A. • Librarian • King County Library System Kingsgate Library • Kirkland, WA 98034 • YALSA

Snider Ron • Trustee • Alabama Public Library Service • Montgomery, AL 36130 • ALTA PLA

Snider Susan C. • Curriculum Supervisor • New Hampshire Department of Education • Concord, NH 03301 • AASL

Snider Virginia L. • Librarian • United States Government Printing Office • Washington, DC 20401 • RASD FLRT GODORT

Snitow Emily L. • Librarian • Westfield High School Library • Westfield, NJ 07090 • AASL

Snodgras Janice L. • Phoenix, AZ 85032 • ALSC PLA

Snodgrass Isabelle S. • New Orleans, LA 70115 • Continuing

Snodgrass Linda J. • Reference Librarian • Worcester State College • Worcester, MA 01602 • ACRL

Snodgrass Wilson D. • Associate Director • Southern Methodist University • Dallas, TX 75275 • ACRL ALCTS

Snodgrasse Elaine • Lake Villa Public Library District • Lake Villa, IL 60046

Snoeyenbos Ann P. • Reference Librarian • New York University Elmer Holmes Bobst Library • New York, NY 10012 • ACRL GODORT IFRT IRRT NMRT

Snoke Elizabeth R. • Librarian • United States Army Command General Staff College • Fort Leavenworth, KS 66027-6900 • AFLRT FLRT

Snoke Helen Lloyd • Santa Fe, NM 87501 • AASL ALSC IFRT

Snook Glenn • Trustee • Metropolitan Library System • Oklahoma City, OK 73102 • ALTA PLA

Snow Christine A. • Reference Librarian • Dayton & Montgomery County Public Library • Dayton, OH 45402-2103 • PLA

Snow David E. • Fox Island, WA 98333

Snow Lucile • Logansport, IN 46947 • LAMA PLA Continuing

Snow Lucile D. • Salem, VA 24153 • Continuing

Snow Marilyn R. • Head, Reference Department • University of Central Florida Library • Orlando, FL 32816-0666 • ACRL RASD

Snow Richard • Head Librarian • Clarion University of Pennsylvania Venango Campus • Oil City, PA 16301 • ACRL ALCTS

Snow Richard • Loyola University Library • New Orleans, LA 70118 • ACRL ALCTS

Snow Sharon K. • Librarian • San Jose Public Library Pearl Avenue Branch • San Jose, CA 95136 • ALSC

Snow Susan W. • Miami, FL 33157

Snowden Carol S. • Librarian • Columbus Metropolitan Library • Columbus, OH 43215

Snowden Deanna • Administrator • Kaskaskia Library System • Smithton, IL 62285

Snowden Nancy G. • Adult Services Librarian • Henderson County Public Library • Hendersonville, NC 28739

Snowhill Lucia • Department Head, Gov't Pubn Dept • University of California Library • Santa Barbara, CA 93106 • ACRL LITA RASD GODORT

Snowman Paul A. III • Lakehurst, NJ 08733

Snowten Renee • Philadelphia, PA 19102

Snure Karen R. • Ohio State University Libraries • Columbus, OH 43210-1286 • ACRL RASD

Snyder Ann M. • Retrospective Conversion Ln. • Eastman School of Music Sibley Music Library • Rochester, NY 14604

Snyder Candace • De Witt High School • De Witt, MI 48820

Snyder Carol I. • Oregon State Hospital • Salem, OR 97310

Snyder Carolyn A.W. • Dean of Library Affairs • Southern Illinois University Delyte W. Morris Library • Carbondale, IL 62901-6632 • ACRL LAMA LITA IRRT

Snyder Charlotte • Baltimore County Public Library • Towson, MD 21204

Snyder Christie • Elementary Library Media Spec. • Ida Long Goodman Memorial Library • St. John, KS 67576 • AASL

Snyder Clifford H. AIA • Architect • Snyder Szantner & Peters Architects • Farmington Hill, MI 48331 • ACRL LAMA

Snyder Cynthia Cobb • Reference • Claremont Colleges Libraries Honnold/Mudd Library • Claremont, CA 91711

Snyder David A. • Systems Librarian • Boston University Mugar Memorial Library • Boston, MA 02215 • LITA Life

Snyder Debora S. • Sunnyvale, CA 94089 • PLA

Snyder Dolores G. • Hd. of the Reference Dept. • Homewood Public Library District • Homewood, IL 60430 • RASD

Snyder Gerald E. • Programmer Analyst Manager • Florida Center for Library Automation • Gainesville, FL 32609

Snyder Grace O. • Northport, MI 49670 • AASL

Snyder Helen Mary • South Bend, IN 46617 • Continuing

Snyder Henry L. • Professor/Director • University of California • Riverside, CA 92517-5900 • ACRL

Snyder Jane V. • Prospect Associates • Rockville, MD 20852

Snyder Janice M. • Olegon City, OR 97045 • AASL ALSC LITA IFRT

Snyder Jean F. • Librarian • Mershon Sawyer Johnston Dunwoody & Cole • Miami, FL 33131

Snyder Jill A. • Asst. Head, Reference Department • New York Academy of Medicine Library • New York, NY 10029 • ASCLA RASD

Snyder Judith • Media Specialist • Lafayette School Corporation • Lafayette, IN 47905

Snyder Laura M. • Eastman School of Music Sibley Music Library • Rochester, NY 14604 • ALCTS

Snyder Lillian H. • Community Librarian • Germantown Library • Germantown, MD 20874 • PLA

Snyder Lisa S. • Assistant Librarian • Landon School • Bethesda, MD 20817 • RASD

Snyder Lise S. • University of California College Library • Los Angeles, CA 90024 • ACRL RASD LIRT

Snyder Louise • Sterling College Kelsey Library • Sterling, KS 67579-0098 • ACRL ALCTS LITA RASD

Snyder Luella • Trustee • Franklin Parish Library • Winnsboro, LA 71295 • ALTA

Snyder Lynn • Student • Santa Clara University Heafey Law Library • Santa Clara, CA 95053

Snyder Margaret M. • Western European Cataloter • Hoover Institution on War, Revolution & Peace Library • Stanford, CA 94305-6010 • ACRL ALCTS

Snyder Mary Groves • Sanger, TX 76266 • AASL ALSC LRRT

Snyder Mary M. • Librarian • Reynoldsville Public Library • Reynoldsville, PA 15851 • ALSC PLA

Snyder Michael G. • Director • West Allis Public Library • West Allis, WI 53214

Snyder Richard L. • Wallingford, PA 19086 • Continuing

Snyder Robert C. • Trustee • Lincoln Parish Library • Ruston, LA 71270 • ALTA

Snyder Robert D. • Circulation Manager • Columbus Metropolitan Library Karl Road Branch • Columbus, OH 43229 • LIRT

Snyder Sherrie E. • Westerville, OH 43081 • CLENE

Snyder Shirley A. • Head Librarian • Pennsylvania State University Shenango Campus • Sharon, PA 16146 • ACRL

Snyder Susan E. • Columbiana Public Library • Columbiana, OH 44408

Snyder Suzanne J. • Media Specialist • Bloomfield Hills Schools Pine Bloomfield El • Orchard Lake, MI 48323 • AASL

Snyder Sylvia B. • Coral Ridge Elementary School • Fairdale, KY 40118 • AASL

Snyder Virginia B. • Collegeville, PA 19426

Snyder William • Director • Henderson County Public Library • Hendersonville, NC 28739

Snyder William E. • Newark, OH 43055

Snyderwine L. Thomas • Staff Librarian • Gannon University Nash Library • Erie, PA 16541 • ACRL

Snydes Kristen L. • Student • University of Washington Graduate School of Library and Information Science • Seattle, WA 98195

So Henry K. • University of California-Berkeley Law Library • Berkeley, CA 94720-2499 • LITA

Soares Richard E. • Map/Geology/Geography Libn. • Brigham Young University • Provo, UT 84602

Soash Richard • Head Cataloger • Library Technical Services School Service Center • Wichita, KS 67219-3399 • AASL ALCTS

Sobba Andrea • Director • Garnett Public Library • Garnett, KS 66032 • PLA

Sober Marc C. • Head, Audio-Visual Dept. • Enoch Pratt Free Library • Baltimore, MD 21201-4484 • PLA VRT

Sobiech Caroline K. • Student • Indiana University School of Library and Information Science • Bloomington, IN 47405 • AASL ALSC PLA IFRT

Sobieski Lou Ann • Librarian • Sequoyah School • Pasadena, CA 91105

Sobin Maryann D. • Librarian • Engelhard Corporation Technical Information Center • Edison, NJ 08818 • ALCTS

Sobon Juliette L. • Director • Washington Township Public Library • Westwood, NJ 07675

Sobus Charles • Trustee • McCook Public Library • McCook, IL 60525

Sochran Sara E. • Librarian • Valley Stream Unified School District No. 13 • Valley Stream, NY 11582-3002

Soderbloom Betsy K. • Student • Wayne State University Library Science Program • Detroit, MI 48202 • AASL

Soderholm Dorothy J. • Serials Cataloger • University of Nebraska • Lincoln, NE 68588 • ACRL ALCTS LITA *Life*

Soderland Kenneth W. • Assistant Administrative Dir • University of Chicago Library • Chicago, IL 60637-1502 • ALCTS LITA *Life*

Soderstrum Constance J. • Head, Technical Services • Mount Prospect Public Library • Mount Prospect, IL 60056 • ALCTS

Sodol Petro R. • Bayside, NY 11361

Sodowsky Kay M. • Green Hills Public Library • Palos Hills, IL 60465 • PLA RASD IFRT

Soekefeld Elisabeth • Student • North Carolina Central University • Durham, NC 27707 • SRRT

Soenksen Shirley • Friends of the Lincoln Park Lib • Weld Library District Lincoln Park Branch • Greeley, CO 80631 • PLA RASD IFRT

Sofer Bat Ami • Director • Whitman Public Library • Whitman, MA 02382 • PLA

Sofko Carol J. • Librarian • Bishop Verot High School • Fort Myers, FL 33919

Sogge Neil • Bellingham, WA 98225

Sogunro Abi O. • Librarian • Montgomery College Germantown Campus Library • Germantown, MD 20874 • LAMA RASD

Sohl Marjorie A. • Highland, IN 46322 • PLA RASD *Life*

Sohn Jeanne G. • Director Library Services • Central Connecticut State University • New Britain, CT 06050 • ACRL ALCTS LAMA

Soifer Libby P. • Reference/Interlibrary Loan Libn • University of Maine Raymond H. Fogler Library • Orono, ME 04469 • RASD SORT SRRT

Sokalski Marcel OFM Conv. Fr. • Kolbe-Cathedral High School • Bridgeport, CT 06604

Sokol Christina • Quality Control Librarian • Western Library Network (WLN) • Lacey, WA 98503 • ACRL ALCTS SRRT

Sokol Christopher John • Ipswich Suffolk, England • ACRL

Sokol Elizabeth P. • Librarian • Adams Junior High School • Youngstown, OH 44502

Sokolov Barbara J. • Director • University of Alaska • Anchorage, AK 99508 • ACRL LAMA

Sokolove Robbe S. • Jefferson County Public Library Villa Regional Branch • Lakewood, CO 80226 • LAMA PLA IFRT SRRT

Sokolowski Denise • Librarian • University of Maryland • APO, AE 09102 • ACRL

Solanes Maria E. • Larchmont, NY 10538 • LITA

Solberg Judy L. • Collection Management • University of Maryland College Park Theodore R. McKeldin Library • College Park, MD 20742-7011 • ACRL ALCTS SRRT

Solberg Norma S. • Library Media Specialist • Avery Coonley School • Downers Grove, IL 60515 • AASL IFRT

Soldner Dean • Collection Development Coor. • Mobile Public Library • Mobile, AL 36602 • ALCTS PLA RASD

Soldner Nancy C. • Director, Library Media Services • Hutchinson Public Schools • Hutchinson, KS 67504-1908 • AASL

Solomon Alan C. • Head Reference Librarian • Yale University Sterling Memorial Library • New Haven, CT 06520

Solomon Christy • Trustee • Daniel Boone Regional Library • Columbia, MO 65205-1267 • ALTA

Solomon Deborah A. • Student • State University of New York at Albany School of Information Science & Policy • Albany, NY 12222

Solomon Diane M. • Program Coordinator • Northwest Regional Library Cooperative • Chester, NJ 07930 • ASCLA

Solomon Dorothy C. • Orchard Park, NY 14127

Solomon Fern Rice • Senior Librarian • Montgomery County Department of Public Libraries • Rockville, MD 20850 • LITA PLA RASD IFRT

Solomon Gail D. • Alexandria, VA 22312

Solomon Gerry K. • Media Coordinator • New Hope Elementary School • Chapel Hill, NC 27514 • AASL ALSC

Solomon Harriet • Administrative Assistant • Syosset Public Library • Syosset, NY 11791

Solomon Janet G. • Atlanta, GA 30324 • ALSC

Solomon Liz Linton • Circulation/Serials • Elon College Iris Holt McEwen Library • Elon College, NC 27244-0187 • ACRL

Solomon Todd • Joint Free Library of Morristown & Morris Township • Morristown, NJ 07960

Solove Daniel M. • Director • Whitehall Township Public Library • Whitehall, PA 18052 • PLA

Soloven Diane W. • Fort Lauderdale, FL 33312 • AASL

Solt Jerry A. • Trustee • Wagnalls Memorial Library • Lithopolis, OH 43136

Soltan Simone • Librarian • Palm Valley School Library • Palm Springs, CA 92264

Soltermann Donna • Assistant Professor • Saint Louis Community College at Meramec • St Louis, MO 63122

Soltesz David S. • Public Services Librarian • Cuyahoga County Public Library Fairview Park Regional Branch • Fairview Park, OH 44126-2189 • SRRT

Soltis Laura W. • Director • Newton County Library Systems • Covington, GA 30209 • PLA

Soltysiak Caren L. • Head of Technical Services • Vernon Area Public Library • Prairie View, IL 60069 • PLA

Solvick Shirley B. • Chief Art & Literature • Detroit Public Library Acq Dept • Detroit, MI 48202-4093

Solyom Gwen E. • Lynchburg, VA 24503-0620

Somerlot Judith A. • Library Media Specialist • Johnson Elementary School • Warrenville, IL 60555 • AASL

Somers Herbert A. • Hd, Govt. Publications & Map • Northwestern University Library • Evanston, IL 60208-2300 • GODORT MAGERT

Somers Jeanne M. • Director of Library Services • Kent State University Libraries • Kent, OH 44242 • LITA

Somers Michael A. • Kansas State University Farrell Library • Manhattan, KS 66506-1200

Somers Sally W. • Asst. Univ. Libn/Technical Svs. • Tulane University Howard-Tilton Memorial Library • New Orleans, LA 70118 • ACRL ALCTS

Somerscales Patricia V. • Schenectady County Community College Library Resources Center • Schenectady, NY 12305 • ACRL

Somerville Arleen N. • Head of Sci & Engr Libraries • University of Rochester Carlson Library • Rochester, NY 14627 • ACRL RASD

Somerville Mary R. • Asst. Director, Br. & Spec. Serv • Miami-Dade Public Library System • Miami, FL 33130-1504 • ALSC LAMA PLA

Sommer Carol A. • Clark Memorial Library • Los Angeles, CA 90018 • ACRL ALCTS

Sommer Deborah • University of California-Berkeley University Library • Berkeley, CA 94720 • ALCTS LAMA

Sommer June • Saint Louis County Library • St. Louis, MO 63131

Sommer Valerie • South San Francisco Public Library • South San Francisco, CA 94080

Sommerfield Elizabeth H. • School Librarian • J. William Leary Junior High School Library • Massena, NY 13662 • AASL

Sommers Jo E. • Librarian • Latin School of Chicago • Chicago, IL 60610 • AASL

Sommers Katherine L. • Library Media Specialist • Running Brook Elementary School • Columbia, MD 20755 • AASL

Sommerville James L. III • Reference Librarian • Somerville Public Library • Somerville, NJ 08876

Somvanshi Kalavati A. • Senior Associate • Hardy Holzman Pfeiffer • New York, NY 10010 • ACRL

Sondheim John W. • Manager Special Collections • Enoch Pratt Free Library • Baltimore, MD 21201-4484 • LAMA LITA PLA RASD IFRT LHRT LRRT

Sondrol Helen L. • Lincoln University Langston Hughes Memorial Library • Lincoln University, PA 19352

Soneberg Sadie • Director • Big Bend Village Library • Big Bend, WI 53103

Song Jizhong • Student • University of Pennsylvania • Philadephia, PA 19104

Song Yun • Alhambra, CA 91803

Songe Alberta A. • Student • Louisiana State University School of Library & Information Science • Baton Rouge, LA 70803-3290 • AASL

Sonn Lark Lee • Serials Librarian • Ferris State University • Big Rapids, MI 49307 • ALCTS LITA

Sonnenberg Barbara H. • Cincinnati, OH 45208 • Continuing

Sonnenburg Reinhart • Classics & German Librarian • Ohio State University Libraries • Columbus, OH 43210-1286 • ACRL

Sonobe Masuko • Librarian • Institute of Developing Economies • Shinjuku, Tokoyo 162, Japan • LITA

Sontag Eleanor A. • Rockville, MD 20850 • AASL ALSC NMRT

Soofi Janet R. • Librarian • F L Weyenberg Public • Mequon, WI 53092

Soong Eileen M. Mrs • Honolulu, HI 96817 • ACRL LITA *Life*

Soong Samson C. • Belle Mead, NJ 08502 • ACRL ALCTS

Soong Xualin • Student • Saint John's University Division of Library & Information Science • Jamaica, NY 11439

Sopalsky Donna L. • Assistant Director • Haverstraw Kings Daughters Public Library • Haverstraw, NY 10927 • RASD

Soper Marley H. • Director • Andrews University James White Library • Berrien Springs, MI 49104-1400 • AASL ACRL ALCTS LAMA LITA RASD YALSA

Soper Mary Ellen • Assistant Professor • University of Washington Graduate School of Library and Information Science • Seattle, WA 98195 • ALCTS

Sophos Patricia Ellen • San Bruno Public Library • San Bruno, CA 94066

Sopko Marvin • Librarian • Sioux Falls Lutheran School • Sioux Falls, SD 57105 • AASL

Sorensen Holly Richards • Bensenville, IL 60106

Sorensen Jane E. • Chicago, IL 60641-3517 • ALSC

Sorensen Joan A. • Deputy Director • Greenville County Library • Greenville, SC 29601

Sorensen Marilou R. • Associate Professor • University of Utah Marriott Library • Salt Lake City, UT 84112-1179 • ALSC

Sorensen Rebecca A. • Assistant Librarian • University of Michigan Libraries • Ann Arbor, MI 48109-1205 • ACRL

Sorensen Richard J. • School Library Supervisor • Department of Public Instruction Division for Library Services • Madison, WI 53707 • AASL

Sorensen Stephen L. • Head Catalog Department • University of Texas at San Antonio-Library • San Antonio, TX 78249 • ACRL ALCTS LITA

Sorenson Barbara • Library Director • Amery Public Library • Amery, WI 54001

Sorenson David W. • Schenectady, NY 12309 • ACRL

Sorenson Liene S. • Ref./AV Servs Libn • Oak Park Public Library • Oak Park, IL 60301 • RASD EMIERT IRRT

Sorenson Lillian R. • Librarian • Dickinson State University Stoxen Library • Dickinson, ND 58601

Sorenson Lynette E. • Student • University of Washington Graduate School of Library and Information Science • Seattle, WA 98195

Sorenson Lynn Kathleen • Clarksburg, MD 20871 • PLA

Sorenson Marla • Serials Librarian • Amery Public Library • Amery, WI 54001

Soret Judith E. • Head Librarian • Penn Wynne Library • Wynnewood, PA 19096

Sorg Elizabeth A. • Librarian • Norristown State Hospital • Norristown, PA 19401

Sorge Celia E. • Librarian • King County Library System • Seattle, WA 98109-5191 • ALSC SRRT

Sorgenfrei Robert K. • Colorado School of Mines Arthur Lakes Library • Golden, CO 80401 • ALCTS

Soriano Doris J. • Associate Director-Branch Libs. • Long Beach Public Library • Long Beach, CA 90802-4482 • LAMA LITA PLA

Sorkin David E. • John Marshall Law School Library • Chicago, IL 60604

Sornsin Kathleen • Shanley High School • Fargo, ND 58102 • AASL

Soroka Marguerite C. • Lunenburg, MA 01462-1433 • ACRL ALCTS *Life*

Sorokin Florence • Palatine, IL 60067

Sorrentino Robert L. • Cherry Hill, NJ 08003-4720

Sorrier Isabel • Director • Statesboro Regional Library • Statesboro, GA 30458 • ALTA LAMA PLA

Sorury Kathryn L. • Assistant Librarian • Indiana University • Bloomington, IN 47405 • ACRL ALCTS CLENE NMRT

Sosa Jorge F. • Miami, FL 33186 • IFRT

Sosinske Adrienne A. • Cataloger • University of Wisconsin-Oshkosh • Oshkosh, WI 54901 • ACRL ALCTS

Sosnicki Sheila • Trustee • Palos Heights Public Library • Palos Heights, IL 60463

Sosnik Nancy L. • Raleigh, NC 27615 • ACRL RASD

Sosnowski Mark J. • Bridgeport, CT 06665

Sossa Magda • Branch Team Manager • Atlanta-Fulton Public Library • Atlanta, GA 30303 • PLA

Soto-Barra Laura • Librarian Supervisor • Metro Toronto Reference Library • Toronto ON, M4W 2G8 Canada • LAMA

Soto Patricia S. • Trustee • Ramapo Catskill Library System • Middletown, NY 10940

Sottilaro Barbara • Library Media Specialist • Mauger Middle School • Middlesex, NJ 08846 • AASL

Sottile Donna • Trustee • Monroe County Library System • Monroe, MI 48161 • ALTA

Souby Anne R. • Editor • Steck-Vaughn Publishing Co. • Austin, TX 78759-8364 • AASL ALSC

Soucy Jeannine • Mexico, NY 13114 • RASD

Souder Gloria • Assistant Director • Upper Perkiomen Valley Library • Red Hill, PA 18076

Souders Marilyn • Head, Technical Processes • Newsweek Inc. • New York, NY 10022 • RASD

Souders Sue • Librarian • Upper Perkiomen Middle School • East Greenville, PA 18041 • AASL

Souffront Blanche L. • Assistant Director • Division of Libraries, Museums & Archaeological Services • Charlotte Amalie, VI 00802 • LAMA PLA

Soule Maria J. • Extension Services Coordinator • Monroe County Public Library • Key West, FL 33040 • ACRL PLA

Soules Aline E. • Manager, Tech Services & Auto • University of Michigan Kresge Business Adm Library • Ann Arbor, MI 48109-1234 • ACRL ALCTS LAMA LITA

Soundararajan Uma S. • Student • Rosary College Graduate School of Library & Information Science • River Forest, IL 60305 • LITA

Sounders Catherine F. • Media Coordinator • Mills Road Elementary School • Jamestown, NC 27282 • AASL

Soupiset Kathryn A. • Trinity University • San Antonio, TX 78212 • ALCTS

Sours Katherine M. • Head of General Collections • Broward County Division of Libraries Broward County Library • Fort Lauderdale, FL 33301 • LITA PLA

Sousa Antoinette L. • Heldsburg, CA 95448 • AASL IFRT SRRT

Soutar Joan • Fairbanks, AK 99708

Souter Thomas A. • Dean of Library Services • Troy State University Library • Troy, AL 36082 • ACRL

South Jean-Anne M. • Assistant Department Head • Baltimore County Public Library • Towson, MD 21204 • LAMA PLA

South Sharon M. • Media Specialist • Millard South High School Library • Omaha, NE 68137 • AASL

South William E. • Clayton, AL 36016

Southard Sally • Librarian • Middlesex Middle School • Darien, CT 06820 • AASL

Southerland Carol A. • South Lenoir High School • Deep Run, NC 28525 • AASL

Southers Carla • Reference Librarian • Briggs Lawrence County Public Library • Ironton, OH 45638 • AASL

Southon Priscilla J. • Vice Pres. for Human Resources • New York Public Library • New York, NY 10018 • ACRL LAMA

Southwick Amy • Systems Research Analyst • Library of Congress • Washington, DC 20541 • LITA

Southwick Jean M. • Student • Syracuse University School of Information Studies • Syracuse, NY 13244-4100

Southwood Natalie • Information Services Specialist • Defense Intelligence Agency • Washington, DC 20340-3341 • ALCTS

Souto Saul H. • Universidad de Monterrey • Garza Garcia NL, Mexico

Souza Margaret A. • Head of Technical Services • Santa Cruz City-County Library System • Santa Cruz, CA 95060 • ALCTS

Souza Mary Beth • Reference Librarian • Emory University Libraries Robert W. Woodruff Library • Atlanta, GA 30322-2870 • ACRL SRRT

Souza Sandra • Grants Manager • Massachusetts Board of Library Commissioners • Boston, MA 02215-2070 • ASCLA PLA

Sova Harry Dr. • Regent University • Virginia Beach, VA 23464-9875

Sovanski Vincent G. • Librarian • Gail Borden Public Library • Elgin, IL 60120 • ALSC

Soverly Alex E. • Outreach Librarian • East Chicago Public Library • E. Chicago, IN 46312

Soverly Ronald A. • Trustee • Lake County Public Library • Merrillville, IN 46410-5382 • ALTA

Sowards Janet • Westland, MI 48185

Sowards Steven W. • Swarthmore College Library • Swarthmore, PA 19081 • LHRT

Sowden Mary Louise • Asst. Director Technical & Clln. • State Library of Pennsylvania • Harrisburg, PA 17101 • ACRL LITA GODORT

Sowell Cary L. • Head Librarian • Austin Community College Northridge Library • Austin, TX 78714 • ACRL LIRT

Sowers Barbara J. • Youth Services Librarian • Freeport Public Library • Freeport, IL 61032 • ALSC

Sowers Marilyn A. • Union County High School • Liberty, IN 47353 • AASL YALSA

Soy Susan K. • Associate Director • Austin Public Library • Austin, TX 78768 • LITA PLA *Life*

Sozansky Basil W. • Serials Management Division • University of Minnesota O. Meredith Wilson Library • Minneapolis, MN 55455-0414 • ALCTS LAMA

Spack Katheryn A. • Student • Emporia State University Emporia in the Rockies • Denver, CO 80204 • ACRL

Spadaro Joseph • Student • University of Wisconsin School of Library & Information Studies • Madison, WI 53706

Spagnoli Ronald B. • Assistant Librarian • Cleveland Public Library • Cleveland, OH 44114-1271 • RASD

Spahr Janet E. • Government Documents Librarian • Virginia Polytechnic Institute and State University, Newman Library • Blacksburg, VA 24061-0434 • ACRL GODORT

Spain Frances L. • Schenectady, NY 12309 • Continuing

Spake Deanna • Mgr. Dowd Film & Sound Library • Public Library of Charlotte & Mecklenburg County • Charlotte, NC 28202

Spala Jeanne • Library Relations Rep. • H. W. Wilson Company • Cerritos, CA 90701

Spalding C. Sumner • Fort Washington, MD 20744 • ALCTS *Life*

Spalding Helen H. • Associate Director of Libraries • University of Missouri-Kansas City Library • Kansas City, MO 64110-2499 • ACRL LAMA

Spalsbury Jeff R. • Livermore, CA 94550 • ACRL

Spangenberger Darlean D. • Student • Texas Woman's University School of Library & Information Studies • Denton, TX 76204 • NMRT

Spangle Kathryn M. • Pharr Memorial Library • Pharr, TX 78577-4806 • RASD

Spangler Katherine L. • Student • University of California-Berkeley School of Library & Information Studies • Berkeley, CA 94720 • ALSC EMIERT

Spanhoff Elisabeth D. • Student • Louisiana State University School of Library & Information Science • Baton Rouge, LA 70803-3290 • ALCTS IFRT

Spanier Florence W. • Deerfield Beach, FL 33442-7659

Spaniol Susan F. • Library Media Specialist • Northville Public Schools Cooke Middle School • Northville, MI 48167 • AASL

Spann Carol S. • Children's Materials Coor. • Fort Worth Public Library • Fort Worth, TX 76102 • ALSC

Spann Gayle • Dallas, TX 75218

Spanne Joan A. • Whitworth College Library • Spokane, WA 99251 • ACRL

Spanogle Juanita L. • Head Librarian • Winfield Public School • Winfield, IL 60190 • AASL

Spanos-Telsing Kim T. • Youth Services Coordinator • York County Library System • York, PA 17402-9004 • ALSC

Sparanese Ann C. • Young Adult Librarian • Englewood Public Library • Englewood, NJ 07631 • YALSA EMIERT

Sparkman Allen • Trustee • Boulder Public Library • Boulder, CO 80306

Sparkman Kathy • Head Catalog Librarian • Baylor University Library • Waco, TX 76798-7026 • ACRL ALCTS

Sparkman Mickey M. • Hd, Central Ref. Services • Waco-McLennan County Library • Waco, TX 76701

Sparks Carla • Assistant Head of Youth Services • Bloomfield Township Public Library • Bloomfield Hills, MI 48302-2437 • ALSC

Sparks Claud G. • Professor • University of Texas at Austin Graduate School of Library & Information Sciences • Austin, TX 78712-1276 • ACRL LAMA LHRT

Sparks Helen A. • Children's Services Supervisor • Carroll County Public Library Taneytown Branch • Taneytown, MD 21787 • ALSC

Sparks James J. • Student • University of Missouri-Columbia School of Library & Informational Science • Columbia, MO 65211

Sparks Jane M. Dr • Librarian • Knox County Schools • Knoxville, TN 37901 • AASL

Sparks Joan E. • Reference Librarian • Jackson Community College Library • Jackson, MI 49201 • ACRL

Sparks Kenneth J. • Library Technical Assistant I • Chuckawalla Valley State Prison • Blythe, CA 92225 • ASCLA

Sparks Martha E. • Duke University Law Library • Durham, NC 27706

Sparks Robert W. • Gift Books/Reference Librarian • Gannon University Nash Library • Erie, PA 16541

Sparks Ronald L. • Special Collections-Archives Ln • California State University Hayward Library • Hayward, CA 94542 • ACRL

Sparr Linda K. • Childern's Librarian • Harris County Public Library Aldine Library • Houston, TX 77037 • ALSC

Spartz Arlyn Mary • Milwaukee, WI 53222 • Continuing

Spaulding Amy E. • Associate Professor • Saint John's University Division of Library & Information Science • Jamaica, NY 11439 • AASL ALSC ASCLA

Spaulding Barbara J. • Data Base Management Coordinator • Brown University Rockefeller Library • Providence, RI 02912 • ACRL ALCTS LITA IFRT

Spaulding Diana B. • Richmond, CA 94805-2325

Spaulding Frank H. • Piscataway, NJ 08854 • LAMA IRRT

Spaulding Nancy Jo • Dir. of Library & Media Serv • Round Rock Independent School District • Austin, TX 78729 • AASL

Spawn Carol M. • Librarian • Academy of Natural Sciences of Philadelphia • Philadelphia, PA 19103-1195 • ACRL ALCTS

Spayd Cynthia J. • Reading Hospital School of Nursing • Reading, PA 19612-6052

Spaziani Carol • Cmnty Srvs/Audio Visual Coord • Iowa City Public Library • Iowa City, IA 52240 • ASCLA PLA

Spear Linda A. • Head of Extension Services • Euclid Public Library • Euclid, OH 44123-2091 • PLA

Spear Martha J. • Berkley High School • Berkley, MI 48072 • AASL

Spearing Edwina • Head of Public Services • Beaconsfield Public Library • Beaconsfield PQ, H9W 4A7 Canada • PLA

Spearman Donna G. • Reference Librarian • Jefferson County Public Library Arvada Branch • Arvada, CO 80002

Spears Dixie J. • Fort Smith, AR 72903 • AASL

Spears Shirley K. • Library Director • B B Comer Memorial Lib • Sylacauga, AL 35150 • IFRT

Specht Alice W. • Director of Univ. Libraries • Hardin-Simmons University Richardson Library • Abilene, TX 79698

Specht Joe W. • Library Director • McMurry University Jay-Rollins Library • Abilene, TX 79697

Specht Rita K. • Librarian • Davenport Public Library • Davenport, IA 52801
Specian Ginger • School Librarian • Southfield School Library • Shreveport, LA 71106 • AASL
Speck Michele A. • Hacienda Heights, CA 91745-4790
Spector Joel M. • Madison, WI 53705 • ACRL
Spector Maya • Children's Librarian • Palo Alto City Library Children's Library • Palo Alto, CA 94301
Speer Jack A. • Buckmaster Publishing • Mineral, VA 23117
Speer Jean A. • Library Media Specialist • Heath Junior High School • Greeley, CO 80631 • AASL
Speights Faye D. • Carson, MS 39427
Speights Joan B. • Student • Auburn University Ralph Brown Draughon Library • Auburn, AL 36849-5606 • AASL
Speirs Gilmary Sr. • Librarian • Marywood College Library Learning Resources Center • Scranton, PA 18509 • ACRL
Speirs Katherine Sally • Student • University of Western Ontario School of Library & Information Science • London ON, N6G 1H1 Canada
Spell Cynthia L. • University of Massachusetts Library • Amherst, MA 01003 • ALCTS
Speller Benjamin F. Jr. • Professor & Dean • North Carolina Central University • Durham, NC 27707 • ALCTS LAMA LITA *Life*
Spence Addie F. • Nashville, TN 37207-4220 • Continuing
Spence Dennis R. • Stillwater, NJ 07875 • PLA RASD *Life*
Spence Dwayne R. • Trustee • Wagnalls Memorial Library • Lithopolis, OH 43136
Spence Karen J. • Coor., Children's Services • Yakima Valley Regional Library • Yakima, WA 98901
Spence Karen J. • Branch Chief User Services • United States Department of Energy Office of Scientific & Technical Info. • Oak Ridge, TN 37831
Spence Marcia A. • Branch Coordinator • Monroe County Library System • Monroe, MI 48161
Spence Marilyn • Asst. Head Catalog Department • Cleveland Public Library • Cleveland, OH 44114-1271
Spence Melville R. • Perrysburg, OH 43551 • Continuing
Spence Paul H. • Professor Emeritus • University of Alabama at Birmingham Mervyn H. Sterne Library • Birmingham, AL 35294-0014 • ACRL *Continuing*
Spence Rethia C. • Media Specialist • Valley Point Elementary School • Dalton, GA 30720 • AASL
Spence Roger F. • Adult Services Librarian • Shaker Heights Public Library • Shaker Heights, OH 44120
Spence Theresa S. • Access Services Coordinator • Michigan Technological University Library • Houghton, MI 49931 • ACRL LAMA LITA
Spencer Barbara L. • Lower School Librarian • Saint Mark's School of Texas • Dallas, TX 75230 • AASL ALSC
Spencer Carol L. • Children's Librarian • Derby Public Library • Derby, KS 67037 • ALSC YALSA
Spencer Caroline • Director • Hawaii State Library • Honolulu, HI 96813 • PLA
Spencer Catherine K. • Plano, TX 75075-7301
Spencer Dorothy A. Ph.D. • Librarian • California School Professional Psychology Library • Fresno, CA 93721 • ACRL LRRT
Spencer Frances K. • Librarian • Community Unit School District #220 • Barrington, IL 60010 • AASL YALSA
Spencer Geneva C. • Cataloger • Greensboro Public Schools • Greensboro, NC 27402
Spencer Helen • Redondo Beach Public Library • Redondo Bch, CA 90277 • PLA RASD
Spencer Janice S. • Media Specialist • District of Columbia Public Schools • Washington, DC 20020 • AASL
Spencer Joan M. • Darien, IL 60559
Spencer John S. • Reference Librarian • University of the South Jessie Ball duPont Library • Sewanee, TN 37375-4005 • ACRL LIRT NMRT
Spencer Katherine • Brandon, MS 39042 • Continuing
Spencer Kathleen M. • Franklin and Marshall College • Lancaster, PA 17604 • ACRL LAMA
Spencer Linda A. • Librarian • North Carolina State University D. H. Hill Library • Raleigh, NC 27695-7111
Spencer Marita L. • Blackstone Public Library • Blackstone, MA 01504 • PLA
Spencer Martha B. • Marine Corps Base General Library • Camp Lejeune, NC 28542
Spencer Pamela G. • Librarian • Thomas Jefferson High School for Science & Technology • Alexandria, VA 22312 • AASL ALSC YALSA IFRT
Spencer Patricia O. • Social Science Librarian • Los Angeles Public Library • Los Angeles, CA 90071 • GODORT
Spencer Robert W. • Trustee • Bloomfield Township Public Library • Bloomfield Hills, MI 48302-2437 • ALTA
Spencer Sue R. • Randolph County Schools • Asheboro, NC 27203 • AASL ALSC
Spencer Valerie C. • Sacramento, CA 95822 • EMIERT IFRT
Spengler Mary M. • Anchorage Municipal Libraries Z. J. Loussac Library • Anchorage, AK 99503
Spensley Malcolm C. Mr • New York, NY 10027 • Life
Sperber Edith W. • Coordinator of Libraries • Lincoln Public Schools Brooks School • Lincoln, MA 01730 • AASL
Sperber G. Matthew • Director • Upper Hudson Library System • Albany, NY 12206 • LAMA PLA
Sperber Jeffrey C. • New York Public Library Stapleton Branch • Staten Island, NY 10304 • RASD
Sperl V. R. • Sayville, NY 11782-2702 • Continuing
Sperling Robert B. • Head, Public Services • University of Texas School of Public Health Library • Houston, TX 77225 • ACRL MAGERT
Spernoga Margaret I. • Senior Library Systems Analyst • Ameritech Information Systems • Dublin, OH 43017
Sperrazza Karen A. • Library Media Specialist • Clayville Library Association • Clayville, NY 13322
Sperring Beverly A. • Assistant Head of Reference • University of Chicago Library • Chicago, IL 60637-1502 • RASD
Sperry George A. IV • Government Sales Representative • The Baker & Taylor Company • Stafford, VA 22554 • AFLRT FLRT
Sperry Janeth H. • Cleveland Heights, OH 44106
Spetland Charles G. • Assistant Librarian • University of Minnesota • Minneapolis, MN 55455 • ACRL RASD
Spetter Allan • Trustee • Dayton & Montgomery County Public Library • Dayton, OH 45402-2103 • ALTA
Spicer Caroline T. • Cornell University Library • Ithaca, NY 14853 • ACRL
Spicer Cheryl • Librarian • Correia Junior High School • San Diego, CA 92107 • AASL
Spicer Orlin C. • Kansas City, MO 64152 • ACRL RASD *Life*
Spicknell Nancy K. • Student • University of Michigan School of Information and Library Studies • Ann Arbor, MI 48109-1092
Spiegel Barry • North Tonawanda, NY 14120 • SRRT
Spiegel Emily B. • Media Specialist • Southside Fundamental Middle School • St. Petersburg, FL 33713 • AASL YALSA
Spielman C R. • Trustee • Jefferson County Public Library • Lakewood, CO 80215 • ALTA
Spielman Patricia A. • Student • Our Lady of the Lake University • San Antonio, TX 78207-4666 • AASL ALSC SRRT
Spielman Rozelin • Director • Flint Memorial Library • North Reading, MA 01864
Spiers Bonnie E. • Student • University of North Carolina at Chapel Hill School of Information and Library Science • Chapel Hill, NC 27599-3360
Spiers KaeLi • Librarian • Amos Press • Sidney, OH 45365 • LRRT
Spies Phyllis B. • OCLC Online Computer Library Center • Dublin, OH 43017-3395 • LITA RASD
Spiess Patricia L. • Librarian • La Crosse Public Library • La Crosse, IN 46348
Spigai Frances G. • President • Database Services Intl • Gleneden Beach, OR 97388
Spigner Christine E. • Trustee • Queens Borough Public Library • Jamaica, NY 11432 • ALTA PLA
Spikes Edgar L. • Trustee • East Chicago Public Library • E. Chicago, IN 46312 • PLA
Spilker Kay • Program Specialist Media • Winston Salem/Forsythe County School • Winston Salem, NC 27102 • AASL
Spiller Deborah J. • Chicago, IL 60614 • LAMA PLA ILERT
Spiller Jean F. • Librarian • Chaparral High School • Las Vegas, NV 89121 • AASL YALSA
Spillers Lisa D. • User Services Librarian • Edith Cowan University Library • Mount Lawley WA 6050, Australia • ACRL IRRT
Spillers Roger E. • Director • Nobles County Library and Information Center • Worthington, MN 56187
Spillios Nicholas G. • Trustee • Edmonton Public Library • Edmonton AB, T5J 2V4 Canada • ALTA PLA
Spilman Donnadine • Librarian • Carroll County Board of Education • Westminster, MD 21157 • AASL
Spindler Timothy J. • University of Wisconsin School of Library & Information Studies • Madison, WI 53706
Spink Christine L. • Student • University of Pittsburgh School of Library and Information Science • Pittsburgh, PA 15260 • LITA PLA RASD
Spink Edward T. • Director Media Services • Lansing School District • Lansing, MI 48911
Spinks Paul • Director of Libraries • Naval Postgraduate School Dudley Knox Library • Monterey, CA 93943-5002 • ACRL AFLRT
Spino Victoria B. • Student • University of Pittsburgh School of Library and Information Science • Pittsburgh, PA 15260
Spires Michael J. • Daily Chronicle • DeKalb, IL 60115 • ACRL LAMA SRRT
Spiro Gail L. • Merced, CA 95348 • ASCLA
Spirt Diana L. • Bayville, NY 11709 • AASL ALSC *Continuing*
Spisak Richard • Trustee • Hammond Public Library • Hammond, IN 46320 • ALTA SORT
Spitalniak Vicky L. • Brookfield, CT 06804
Spitler Karen R. • Librarian • Lansing Middle School Unified School District #469 • Lansing, KS 66043
Spitzer Kathy • Sch Lib & Info Specialist • North Syracuse Junior High School • North Syracuse, NY 13212 • AASL
Spivak Howard • Director Library Systems • Brooklyn College Library • Brooklyn, NY 11210 • LITA
Spivey Barbara L. • Albuquerque Academy Library • Albuquerque, NM 87109 • ACRL ALCTS NMRT
Spivey J. Allen • Library Director • Brunswick Junior College Library • Brunswick, GA 31523-5101 • ACRL
Spivey Jeanie • Director • Olney Community Library • Olney, TX 76374
Spivey Mark A. • Librarian in General Reference • University of Utah Marriott Library • Salt Lake City, UT 84112-1179 • ACRL RASD
Spivey Mary • Plantation, FL 33317 • NMRT SRRT
Spiles Carolyn J. • Student • University of Wisconsin-Madison School of Library & Information Studies • Madison, WI 53706
Spodick Edward F. • Asst. Ln. Media Resources Ctr. • Hong Kong University of Science & Technology University Library • Kowloon, Hong Kong • ACRL LITA IFRT IRRT SRRT
Spohn Richard A. • University of Cincinnati Geology Physics Library • Cincinnati, OH 45221-0153 • ACRL MAGERT
Spohrer James H. • Librarian for Germanic Cllns • University of California-Berkeley University Library • Berkeley, CA 94720 • ACRL
Spollen Marie • Librarian • Tompkins Cortland Community College • Dryden, NY 13053
Sponheim Ruth • Librarian • Fort Dodge High School • Ft Dodge, IA 50501 • AASL YALSA
Sponseller Laura J. • Kent State University School of Library & Information Science • Kent, OH 44242-0001 • IFRT
Spooner Gloria A. • Library Consultant • State Library of Louisiana • Baton Rouge, LA 70821-0131 • ASCLA
Spooner Pam • Reference Librarian • Southwest Texas State University • San Marcos, TX 78666 • RASD GODORT LIRT NMRT
Spoor Richard D. • Director • Union Theological Seminary Library The Burke Library • New York, NY 10027 • ACRL ALCTS LITA
Spore Stuart • Hd,Cataloging & Automated Sys • New York University Library of the School of Law • New York, NY 10012-1099 • ALCTS LAMA LITA SRRT
Sporing Suzi • Technical Services Librarian • Litton Industries, Incorporation • Beverly Hills, CA 90210
Sporn Anne • Bethesda, MD 20817 • AASL ALSC FLRT
Spornick Charles D. • Lilburn, GA 30247-4865 • ACRL
Spotkov Leslie J. • Assisant Director • North Olympic Library System • Port Angeles, WA 98362
Spradling Mary Mace • Kalamazoo, MI 49007 • Continuing
Sprague Linda B. • Elementary Media Specialist • Bishop Elementary School • Topeka, KS 66614 • AASL
Sprague Mary W. • Instructor • Ohio State University Health Sciences Library • Columbus, OH 43210 • ACRL
Sprague Nancy R. • Tucson, AZ 85711
Sprague Olive Miss • Jersey City, NJ 07302 • Continuing
Sprague Ora Ann • Spring Arbor, MI 49283 • ACRL ALCTS *Continuing*
Sprain Mara L. • Sci & Engineering Bibilographer • University of Colorado at Denver Auraria Library • Denver, CO 80204 • ACRL LITA RASD
Sprandel Barbara • Student • University of Michigan School of Information and Library Studies • Ann Arbor, MI 48109-1092 • PLA
Sprang Betty • Newport Beach Public Library • Newport Beach, CA 92660
Sprauer Linda J. • Director • Woodburn Public Library • Woodburn, OR 97071 • LAMA PLA
Sprauge Joanne • Trustee • Sachem Public Library • Holbrook, NY 11741
Spray Constance R. • Metairie, LA 70005
Sprehe Beverly J. • Head of Catalog Department • Metropolitan Library System Capitol Hill Branch • Oklahoma City, OK 73109 • ALCTS LITA
Sprenkle Peter R. • Student • University of Illinois Graduate School of Library and Information Science • Urbana, IL 61801

Spriestersbach Barbara • State Department of Education • Oklahoma City, OK 73105 • AASL

Sprimont Jonnie B. • Director of Instructional Media • Pasco County School Board • Land O Lakes, FL 34639 • AASL LITA

Sprince Leila Joy • Children's/Young Adult Librarian • Broward County Division of Libraries West Regional Branch • Plantation, FL 33324 • ALSC YALSA

Spring Donald P. • Librarian • University of California • Los Angeles, CA 90024-1573 • ACRL RASD CLENE IFRT SRRT

Spring Elizabeth P. • Rochester, NY 14619

Spring Martha K. • Student • University of Michigan Graduate Library Reference • Ann Arbor, MI 48109

Springborn Janice T. • Children's Librarian • Cary Public Library • Cary, IL 60013 • ALSC

Springer Camille • Mario Gallegos Elementary School • Houston, TX 77011

Springer Jay • Los Angeles, CA 90066 • IFRT SRRT

Springer Joe • Curator • Goshen College • Goshen, IN 46526 • ACRL

Springer John A. • Lonesome Pine Regional Library • Wise, VA 24293

Springer Judith M. • Librarian • New Trier High School • Winnetka, IL 60093 • AASL

Springer Linda N. • Branch Coordinator • Johnson County Library • Shawnee Mission, KS 66201 • LAMA PLA

Springer Mary Patricia • Mark Keppel High School • Alhambra, CA 91801 • AASL LIRT

Springer Susan • Library Media Specialist • Marysville Elementary School • Marysville, KS 66508 • AASL

Springstubb Tricia • Trustee • Cleveland Heights-University Heights Public Library • Cleveland Heights, OH 44118

Sprinkle-Hamlin Sylvia Y. • Associate Director • Forsyth County Public Library • Winston-Salem, NC 27101 • LAMA PLA EMIERT

Sprinkle Michael Doss • Executive Director • Wake Forest University Bowman Gray School of Medicine • Winston Salem, NC 27157-1069 • ACRL ALCTS LAMA LITA RASD

Sproat Barbara L. • Library Spec/Children's Servs • Orange County Public Library Garden Grove Regional Branch • Garden Grove, CA 92640 • ALSC

Sproat Mary Lou M. • Director of Media Services • Merrillville Community School Corp. • Merrillville, IN 46410 • AASL

Sproat Rebeccah L. • Gig Harbor, WA 98332

Sproles Sharon B. • Knoxville, TN 37909 • AASL

Sprott Mary C. • Supervising Librarian • Sunnyvale Public Library • Sunnyvale, CA 94088-3714 • PLA RASD GODORT

Sprowls Pat W. • Elk City, OK 73644

Spruds Biruta A. • Librarian Material Selection • Hennepin County Library • Minnetonka, MN 55343

Spurgeon Kathy R. • University of Tennessee-Knoxville Graduate School of Library & Information Science • Knoxville, TN 37996-4330

Spurling Loretta A. • Student • University of Tennessee-Knoxville Graduate School of Library & Information Science • Knoxville, TN 37996-4330 • LITA

Spurlock Sandra E. • Honeywell, Defense Auionics Systems Division • Albuquerque, NM 87113

Spurrier Suzanne F. • Library Director • Harding University • Searcy, AR 72149-0928

Spyers-Duran Mary V. • Cardinal Stritch College • Milwaukee, WI 53217 • LITA

Spyers-Duran Peter • Dean of Libraries & Library Sci. • Wayne State University • Detroit, MI 48202 • ACRL LITA
Life

Spyers-Duran Kimberly • Social Sciences Ref Ln • University of Houston Libraries • Houston, TX 77204-2091 • ACRL LAMA RASD NMRT

Spyros Marsha L. • Administrative Librarian • New York Public Library Ninety-Sixth Street Branch • New York, NY 10028 • ALCTS PLA RASD

Square Gregory J. • Mgr. of Information Services • Great Lakes Technology Transfer Center • Cleveland, OH 44070-5310 • LITA RASD FLRT GODORT

Squier Laura N. • Minot State University Memorial Library • Minot, ND 58701

Squire Deborah L. • Library Media Specialist • Pelham Memorial High School • Pelham, NY 10803 • AASL

Squires Richard D. • Rochester Institute of Technology Wallace Memorial Library • Rochester, NY 14623-0887

Squires Susan H. • Media Specialist • Pontiac Central High School • Pontiac, MI 48341 • AASL

Squires Susan McClintock • Reference Librarian • Meredith College Carlyle Campbell Library • Raleigh, NC 27607 • ACRL

Sracic Karen K. • Westminster College McGill Library • New Wilmington, PA 16172-0001 • ALCTS

Sreebny Oren • Director,Database Development • Maxwell Online • McLean, VA 22102 • LITA SRRT

Sridaran Geetha • Student • Clark-Atlanta University School of Library & Information Studies • Atlanta, GA 30314-4391

Srisuro Anne A. • Evanston, IL 60201

Srivastava Nirmala NS • Librarian I • Chicago Public Library Harold Washington Library • Chicago, IL 60605 • ALCTS

Srygley Judith A. • Dallas Baptist University Vance Memorial Library • Dallas, TX 75211 • ALCTS

Srygley Sara K. • Tallahassee, FL 32312-3547 • Continuing

St Aubin Kendra Peterson • USNP Project Coordinator • Rhode Island Historical Society Library • Providence, RI 02906 • ACRL RASD GODORT

St. Amand Norma P. • Librarian/Media Specialist • Cranbrook Schools • Bloomfield Hills, MI 48303 • AASL SRRT

St. Andre Kenneth E. • Librarian I • Phoenix Public Library Saguaro Branch • Phoenix, AZ 85008

St. Aubin Arleen K. • Slavic Cataloger-Classifier • Boston Public Library • Boston, MA 02117 • ACRL ALCTS

St. Cavish Mary E. • Coral Spring, FL 33071 • AASL IFRT SRRT

St. Clair Ann G. • Head of Catalog Division • Mobile Public Library • Mobile, AL 36604-3273 • ALCTS LITA PLA

St. Clair Catherine L. • Anaheim Public Library • Anaheim, CA 92805

St. Clair Gloriana • Asst. Dean and Head • Information Access Services • University Park, PA 16802 • ACRL ALCTS LAMA LITA LRRT

St. Clair Guy L. • OPL Resources Ltd • New York, NY 10156

St. Clair Jean W. • Jamaica, NY 11433 • ALSC

St. Clair Linda C. • Asst. Director, Caps • University of New Mexico Zimmerman Library • Albuquerque, NM 87131-1466 • ACRL LIRT

St. Clair Mary • Lower School Librarian • Santa Catalina School Library • Monterey, CA 93940

St. Germain Jane A. • Information Manager • Hewlett-Packard, Inc. • Fort Collins, CO 80525

St. Germain Mary S. • Slavic/South Asia Cataloger • University of Washington Suzzallo Library • Seattle, WA 98195

St. Hilaire Sharon E. • Library Director • Seekonk Public Library • Seekonk, MA 02771 • LAMA LITA PLA

St. John John Mary Sr. • Mary Louis Academy • Jamaica, NY 11432

St. John Leslie A. • Youth Librarian • Atlanta-Fulton Public Library • Atlanta, GA 30303 • ALCTS ALSC PLA

St. Julien Betsy A. • Baton Rouge, LA 70808

St. Martin Dora J. • Assistant Mgr. Sci & Tech Dept. • Toledo-Lucas County Public Library • Toledo, OH 43624 • PLA RASD SRRT

St. Onge Barbara S. • Library Media Specialist • Bristol Board of Education • Bristol, CT 06010 • AASL

St. Pierre Valerie • Cataloging Librarian • University of Alabama at Birmingham • Birmingham, AL 35294

Staack Katherine • Associate Librarian • Tufts University Arts & Sciences Library • Medford, MA 02155 • ACRL ALCTS

Staas Gretchen L. • Consultant for Lib & Media Servs • Garland Independent School District • Garland, TX 75040 • AASL ALSC

Staats Christine • Oakland, CA 94610 • Continuing

Staatz Evelyn R. • Director • Longview Community College Library • Lee's Summit, MO 64081 • ACRL LAMA

Stabler Elizabeth F. • Head Librarian • The Day School • New York, NY 10024 • AASL YALSA

Stabler Karen Chittick • Head of Information Services • New Mexico State University Library • Las Cruces, NM 88003-0006 • ACRL LAMA LITA RASD LIRT

Stabo Kristine Blum • Youth Librarian • Maude Shunk Public Library • Menomonee Falls, WI 53051 • ALSC

Stacey Carolyn M. • Student • University of Michigan School of Information and Library Studies • Ann Arbor, MI 48109-1092 • SRRT

Stacey Kathleen M. • Staff Development Coordinator • Annapolis & Anne Arundel County Public Library • Annapolis, MD 21401-7042

Stach Marilee A. • Reference Librarian • Waubonsee Community College • Sugar Grove, IL 60556

Stachacz John C. • Chairperson • Dickinson College Library Boyd Lee Spahr Library • Carlisle, PA 17013 • ACRL

Stachelczyk Marilyn I. • Annapolis, MD 21401

Stachnik Charlene M. • University of Michigan Museum Library • Ann Arbor, MI 48109-1079

Stachura David C. • Trustee • Schiller Park Public Library • Schiller Park, IL 60176-1699 • ALTA

Stack Bill • Queens Borough Public Library Far Rockaway Branch • Far Rockaway, NY 11691 • YALSA SRRT

Stack Bryan L. • Documents Librarian • University of Nebraska at Omaha University Library • Omaha, NE 68182-0237 • GODORT

Stack John J. • Pittsburgh, PA 15206 • AASL NMRT

Stack Kathleen • Librarian/Industry Analyst • First National Bank of Chicago Corporate Information Center • Chicago, IL 60670

Stack May E. • Director • Western New England College D'Amour Library • Springfield, MA 01119 • ACRL LAMA LITA

Stack Robert J. • Granite City Public Library District • Granite City, IL 62040 • LAMA PLA

Stacknick Mary Theresa • Library Media Specialist • Clearwater Central Catholic High School • Clearwater, FL 34620 • AASL

Stackpole Laurie S. • Chief Librarian • Naval Research Laboratory • Washington, DC 20375 • ACRL ALCTS LAMA LITA FLRT

Staerkel Kathleen A. • Head of Young Peoples Services • Indian Trails Public Library District • Wheeling, IL 60090 • ALSC

Staffaroni Kathy M. • Student • Rutgers University School of Communication Information & Library Studies • New Brunswick, NJ 08903 • IFRT ILERT IRRT LHRT SRRT

Staffeldt Darlene M. • Information Resources • Montana State Library • Helena, MT 59620

Stafford-Vaughan Beth • Womens Studies Librarian • University of Illinois Library • Urbana, IL 61801 • ACRL RASD EMIERT SRRT

Stafford Audrey A. • Administrative Services Manager • Anaheim Public Library • Anaheim, CA 92805

Stafford Brian P. • Pitman, NJ 08071 • AASL

Stafford Cecilia D. • Asst. Libn. for Public Services • Tulane University Howard-Tilton Memorial Library • New Orleans, LA 70118 • ACRL LAMA LIRT

Stafford Flora M. • Asst. Dir. Public Services • Florida State University Robert M. Strozier Library • Tallahassee, FL 32306-2047 • ACRL LAMA RASD

Stafford I E. Miss • Brattleboro, VT 05301 • AASL ALSC
Continuing

Stafford Marian R. • Abingdon, VA 24210 • Continuing

Stafford Peyton W. • Portland, OR 97219

Stafford R. M. • Bexley Public Library • Columbus, OH 43209

Stafford Sandra J. • Woodbridge, VA 22192-6414 • ALSC

Stafford Vera Kay • Jefferson County Public Library • Lakewood, CO 80215 • ALTA

Stagg Kathleen M. • Librarian • Evangeline Parish Library • Ville Platte, LA 70586

Staggs Judith A. • Friendship Christian School • Lebanon, TN 37087

Stahl Barry • Alexandria Library • Alexandria, VA 22314 • IFRT SRRT

Stahl Freda D. • Cullman, AL 35055-4840

Stahl Joan R. • National Museum of American Art • Washington, DC 20560 • ACRL

Stahl Ritarose Sister • Library Aide • Silver Lake College Library • Manitowoc, WI 54220

Stahl Wilson M. • University of North Carolina at Charlotte J. Murrey Atkins Library • Charlotte, NC 28223 • ACRL LITA

Stahlman Cherry S. • Media Specialist/Librarian • Curundu Elementary School • APO, AA 34002

Stahlschmidt Agnes • Tucson, AZ 85718

Stahly Patricia L. • Cape Girardeau, MO 63701

Stainbrook Lynn M. • Director • Orrville Public Library • Orrville, OH 44667 • LAMA PLA RASD

Staines Gail M. • Coor. of Bibl. Instruction • Niagara County Community College Faculty Resource Center • Sanborn, NY 14132 • ACRL

Staino Rocco A. • Director • Ulster BOCES School Library System • New Paltz, NY 12561 • AASL ALSC IFRT

Stalder Robert P. • Children's Librarian • Lacey Timberland Library • Lacey, WA 98503

Staley Donna L. • Forsyth County Public Library • Winston-Salem, NC 27101 • ALTA

Staley Laura A. • City University Library • Mercer Island, WA 98040

Staley Merton • President Board of Trustees • Rolling Meadows Library • Rolling Meadows, IL 60008

Staley Valeria H. • Trustee • Orangeburg County Library • Orangeburg, SC 29115-1367 • ALTA

Stalker Dianne S. • Stony Brook, NY 11790-1931 • ACRL ALCTS LRRT

Stalker John • Head of Information Services • Ohio State University • Columbus, OH 43210 • ACRL IRRT

Stalker Kathleen K. • Darien, CT 06820 • PLA

Stalker Laura • Asst. Dir/Center for Bibl Study • University of California • Riverside, CA 92517-5900 • ACRL ALCTS IFRT

Stallinga Sid • Trustee • Sioux Falls Public Library • Sioux Falls, SD 57102
Stallings Alice • Media Specialist • Cary Reynolds School • Dorvallie, GA 30340
Stallmann Diane • Trustee • Ramsey County Public Library Adminstrative Offices • Shoreview, MN 55126-5800 • ALTA
Stalteri Lori L. • Beverly Public Library Beverly Farms Branch • Beverly, MA 01915-2208
Stalzer Rita M. Sr • Bibliographer • Loyola University E.M. Cudahy Memorial Library • Chicago, IL 60626 • ACRL
Stam David H. • University Librarian • Syracuse University • Syracuse, NY 13244 • ACRL ALCTS
Stam Deirdre C. • Catholic University of America School of Library and Information Science • Washington, DC 20064
Stam Julian J. • Binding Librarian • Harvard University Library • Cambridge, MA 02138-2901
Stamatoplos Anthony C. • Associate Reference Librarian • Butler University Irwin Library • Indianapolis, IN 46208 • ACRL
Stambaugh Laine • Personnel Librarian • University of Oregon Library • Eugene, OR 97403-1299 • LAMA NMRT
Stamelos Ellen • Cat. Dir. Manager • Dallas Public Library • Dallas, TX 75201 • LITA
Stamguts Candice • Enon, OH 45323 • AASL
Stamison Christine M. • Student • Rosary College Graduate School of Library & Information Science • River Forest, IL 60305
Stamm Andrea L • Head Monographic Cataloging • Northwestern University Library • Evanston, IL 60208-2300
Stampfl Barbara A. • Assistant City Librarian • Lakeland Public Library • Lakeland, FL 33801 • PLA
Stamps-Etheredge Crystal L. • Director • Magnolia Bar Association • Jackson, MS 39205-0648
Stamps Hazel C. • Director of Personnel Services • Harvard College Library Widener Memorial Library • Cambridge, MA 02138 • ACRL LAMA EMIERT
Stan Susan M. • Editor • The Five Owls, Inc. • Minneapolis, MN 55405 • YALSA
Stanbery-Cotney Gilda E. • Director • Peach Public Libraries • Fort Valley, GA 31030 • PLA
Stancel Nancy D. • Cataloging Librarian • University of Missouri-Kansas City Library • Kansas City, MO 64110-2499 • ALCTS
Stancin Sandra J. • United State Navy Station Library • Kings Bay, GA 31547
Stancl Bethanne B. • Librarian • Silver Creek Central School • Silver Creek, NY 14137 • AASL
Stancliff June M. • Head of Technical Services • St. Joseph Public Library • St Joseph, MO 64501 • ALCTS
Stancliff Susan J. • Student • Wayne State University Library Science Program • Detroit, MI 48202
Stancliffe Andrew J. • Acting Head, Acquisitions Dept. • UCLA Library University Research Library • Los Angeles, CA 90024-1575 • ALCTS
Standard Lisa G. • Children's Librarian • Harris County Public Library Crosby Branch • Crosby, TX 77532 • PLA
Standefer Steven R. • Director • Natchitoches Parish Library • Natchitoches, LA 71457 • PLA
Standifer Anna Wallace • Trustee • Fountaindale Public Library District • Bolingbrook, IL 60440 • ALTA
Standifer Hugh • Owner • Justan Information Management Group • Carrollton, TX 75006-6807
Standifird Vance B. • Church of Jesus Christ of Latter-Day Saints • Salt Lake City, UT 84150
Standland Nadine P. • Media Specialist • Marianna Middle School • Marianna, FL 32446 • ALCTS
Stanfield Vicki T. • Media Coordinator • Piney Grove Elementary School • Kernersville, NC 27284 • AASL ALSC
Stanford Edward B. • Saint Paul, MN 55108 • ACRL LAMA *Life*
Stang Christine S. • Librarian • East High School • Salt Lake City, UT 84102 • AASL
Stange Mary Ann • Media Specialist • Chippewa Valley High School • Mount Clemens, MI 480414 • AASL
Stanger Keith J. • Coordinator,Access Services • Eastern Michigan Univeristy • Ypsilanti, MI 48197 • ACRL LITA RASD
Stanger Mary H. • Bloomington, IN 47401 • Continuing
Stangl Peter • Director • Stanford University Lane Medical Library • Stanford, CA 94305-5323 • LITA
Stangohr Margaret K. • Head of Cataloging Department • East Carolina University Health Sciences Library • Greenville, NC 27858-4354 • ALCTS
Stangroom Scott A. • Student • Simmons College Graduate School of Library & Information Science • Boston, MA 02115 • ACRL
Stanhope Charles V. • Administrative Librarian • Library of Congress • Washington, DC 20541 • LAMA RASD
Stanhope Sara C. • Baltimore County Public Library Parkville-Carney Branch • Baltimore, MD 21234 • PLA
Staninger Steven W. • Reference Librarian • University of San Diego Copley Library • San Diego, CA 92110
Stanke Carol D. • District Media Coordinator • Sheboygan Area School District • Sheboygan, WI 53081 • AASL
Stanke Nicola K. • Director • Carnegie-Stout Public Library • Dubuque, IA 52001 • LAMA PLA
Stanko Emily A. • Southfield, MI 48075 • PLA YALSA *Life*
Stankus-Saulaitis Algirdas A. • Silas Bronson Library • Waterbury, CT 06702-1981 • ALCTS RASD
Stanley-Dunham Janine • Assistant Editor • H. W. Wilson Company • Bronx, NY 10452 • ASCLA YALSA
Stanley C Vaughan • Library Director/Historian • Stratford Hall Plantation Jessie Ball duPont Memorial Library • Stratford, VA 22558
Stanley David H. • Pittsburgh, PA 15203
Stanley E. H. Jr. • Trustee • South Carolina State Library • Columbia, SC 29211 • ALTA
Stanley Ellen • Reference Librarian • Dartmouth Public Libraries Southworth Library • South Dartmouth, MA 02748
Stanley Emma L. • Branch Manager • Atlanta-Fulton Public Library Southwest Regional Library • Atlanta, GA 30331 • LAMA PLA IFRT SRRT
Stanley Jane • Library Director • Highland Park Public Library • Highland Park, NJ 08904
Stanley Janet L. • Chief Librarian • Smithsonian Institution Libraries Museum of African Art Branch Library • Washington, DC 20560 • ACRL LITA RASD IRRT
Stanley John H. • Head Librarian of Special Cllns • Brown University Rockefeller Library • Providence, RI 02912 • ACRL
Stanley Karen • Head of Children's Servs Dept • Rosenberg Library Adult Services • Galveston, TX 77550 • ALSC
Stanley Kathi L. • Interlibrary Loan Unit • New York State Library • Albany, NY 12230
Stanley Kathleen • Program Coordinator/Librarian • Western Arizona Area Health Education Center, Incorporation • Bullhead City, AZ 86442
Stanley Laurel • Library Director • Lyndon State College Samuel Read Hall Library • Lyndonville, VT 05851 • ACRL ALCTS LITA RASD
Stanley Mary J. • Bibliographic Instruction Coor • Indiana University-Purdue University at Indianapolis Library (IUPUI) • Indianapolis, IN 46202 • ACRL
Stanley Nancy M. • Head, Acquisitions Receiving • Pennsylvania State University E506 Pattee Library • University Park, PA 16802 • ACRL ALCTS
Stanley Retha • Lindale, TX 75771
Stanley Sharon F. • Student • University of Texas at Austin Graduate School of Library & Information Sciences • Austin, TX 78712-1276
Stanley Sharon L. • USAF Officer • Base Library Fl 4488 • Pope AFB, NC 28308
Stanley Sydney • Advanced Marketing Services • San Diego, CA 92101
Stanley William P. • San Francisco, CA 94121 • ACRL *Life*
Stanmyre Josie • Student • Catholic University of America School of Library and Information Science • Washington, DC 20064
Stann Patsy Haley • Hd. of Lib. & Inf Sci Library • Catholic University of America Library Science Library • Washington, DC 20064 • ACRL
Stano Elaine • Plymouth State College Lamson Library • Plymouth, NH 03264 • LITA
Stansell Shelvia M. • Bookmobile Assistant • Tensas Parish Library • Saint Joseph, LA 71366
Stansifer Glenna • Library Director • Inyo County Free Library • Independence, CA 93526 • PLA
Stanton Anne G. • Associate Librarian • Louisiana State University Libraries Troy H. Middleton Library • Baton Rouge, LA 70803-3342 • ALCTS MAGERT
Stanton Gary G. • Garrett County Board of Education • Oakland, MD 21550 • AASL
Stanton Hope C. • Technical Information Spec. • United States Department of Agriculture National Agricultural Library • Beltsville, MD 20705-2351 • ALSC
Stanton Lee W. • Principal Librarian • New York State Library State Education Department • Albany, NY 12230 • ACRL ASCLA
Stanton Mary M. • Director • Auburn Public Library • Auburn, WA 98002 • LAMA
Stanton Robert E. • Auburn, WA 98002 • LITA RASD
Stanton Vida C. Mrs • University of Wisconsin-Milwaukee School of Library & Information Science • Milwaukee, WI 53201 • AASL ALSC
Staples Alice P. • University of Arizona Library • Tucson, AZ 85721
Staples Gail S. • Librarian Reference • Cochise College Libraries • Sierra Vista, AZ 85635
Staples Loretta T. • Amherst, NH 03031
Staples Robert H. Mr. • Island Heights, NJ 08732 • LAMA PLA *Life*
Stapleton Diana L. • Assistant Periodicals Librarian • Eastern Kentucky University John Grant Crabbe Library • Richmond, KY 40475-3121
Stapleton Margaret M. • Tampa-Hillsborough County Library System Ruskin Branch • Ruskin, FL 33570
Stapley Polly • LSW SLS • Mt. Morris, NY 14510
Star Michelle P. • Student • Clarion University of Pennsylvania College of Library Science • Clarion, PA 16214 • LAMA
Starbuck Edith M. • Student • Indiana University School of Library and Information Science • Bloomington, IN 47405 • ALCTS NMRT
Starbuck Philip N. • Mountain Home, AR 72653 • Continuing
Starck Lorelei • Marketing Specialist • Milwaukee Public Library • Milwaukee, WI 53233 • LAMA PLA
Starck Martha • Milwaukee, WI 53218 • ACRL NMRT
Starck Mary I. • Atlanta-Fulton Public Library • Atlanta, GA 30303 • PLA
Starck William L. • Collections Services • Library of Congress • Washington, DC 20541
Stark Caroline • Director • Public Library of Nashville and Davidson County • Nashville, TN 37203-3585 • PLA
Stark Li S. • Bronxville, NY 10708 • ALSC IFRT
Stark Linda A. • Librarian • Florida Christian College • Kissimmee, FL 34744 • ACRL LAMA RASD
Stark Marcella L. • Instructional Servs. Coordinator • Syracuse University Library E. S. Bird Library • Syracuse, NY 13244-2010 • ACRL RASD LIRT
Stark Peter L. • Head Map Librarian • University of Oregon Library • Eugene, OR 97403-1299 • MAGERT SRRT
Stark Susan • Trustee • Long Beach Public Library • Long Beach, NY 11561 • ALTA RASD
Stark Suzanne W. • School Librarian • Easto Baton Rouge Parish Schools Dufrocg Elementary School • Baton Rouge, LA 70806
Stark Ted • Asst. Administration • Central Iowa Regional Library • Des Moines, IA 50312
Starkey Edward D. • University Librarian • University of San Diego Copley Library • San Diego, CA 92110 • ACRL RASD
Starkey Flo • L & Media Coor • Roswell Independent School District Materials Center • Roswell, NM 88201 • ALSC
Starkey R. F. • Ravenswood, WV 26164-1521
Starkey S. Elizabeth • Reference Librarian • DeKalb County Public Library Wesley Chapel Branch • Decatur, GA 30034 • RASD NMRT
Starks Thomas E. • Oxford High School • Oxford, MI 48051 • AASL
Starkus Kristina • Slavic & E. European Bibl. • Ohio State University Libraries • Columbus, OH 43210-1286
Starkweather Catherine M. • Student • University of Kentucky College of Library & Information Science • Lexington, KY 40506-0391 • LRRT
Starkweather Wendy M. • Asst. Univ. Lbn. for Pub. Servs. • University of Nevada-Las Vegas James R. Dickinson Library • Las Vegas, NV 89154 • ACRL LAMA LITA
Starling Betsy K. • Library Media Specialist • Memorial High School • Madison, WI 53719 • AASL
Starling Dorothy G. • Bristol, TN 37620
Starling Jean W.S. • Student • University of Arizona Graduate Library School • Tucson, AZ 85721 • ACRL ALCTS LAMA LITA PLA RASD SRRT
Starnes Jane K. • Library Systems Admin. • Intel Corporation • Hillsboro, OR 97124-6497 • LITA
Starnes Shannan L. • Lynchburg, VA 24502
Starr-Young Catherine • Information Specialist • Amdahl Corporation Corporate Marketing Library • Sunnyvale, CA 94088-3470
Starr Carol • Library Director • Benicia Public Library • Benicia, CA 94510 • LAMA PLA YALSA IFRT SRRT *Life*
Starr Glenn Ellen • Reference & Instruction Ln • Appalachian State University Carol Grotnes Belk Library • Boone, NC 28608 • ACRL RASD LIRT
Starr Jeanne • Orange Elementary School • Glenwood, IN 46133
Starr Karen J. • Idaho State Library • Boise, ID 83702 • LITA IRRT
Starr Marilyn E. • Chairperson of Library Res. • Spring Arbor College Library • Spring Arbor, MI 49283 • ACRL
Starr Susan S. • Librarian • University of California-San Diego Central University Library • La Jolla, CA 92093-0175 • ACRL LITA RASD GODORT
Starratt Joseph A. • Dir of Tech & Auto Services • Southern Illinois University Delyte W. Morris Library • Carbondale, IL 62901-6632 • ACRL LAMA LITA

Starrett Mary Jo • Media Supervisor • Shawnee High School • Medford, NJ 08055 • AASL

Start Nancy E. • Assistant Librarian • State University of New York (SUNY) Health Sciences Library • Buffalo, NY 14214

Staskus Linda • Children's Librarian • Cuyahoga County Public Library Parma Ridge Branch • Parma, OH 44129

Stasser Jane • Director • Bound Brook Memorial Library • Bound Brook, NJ 08805

Staszak Kathie • Children's Librarian III • Milwaukee Public Library Llewellyn Branch • Milwaukee, WI 53207 • ALSC

Stathakis Kleo • Trustee • Anderson County Library • Anderson, SC 29622-4047

Staton Evelyn V. • Head Librarian • Woodrow Wilson High School • San Francisco, CA 94134 • AASL

Staton Susan T. • Media Specialist • Sullivan Middle School Media Center • Rock Hill, SC 29730 • AASL YALSA

Staub Jacquelyn A. Sr. • Media Specialist • Delone Catholic High School • McSherrystown, PA 17344

Staubach Cristine A. • Storrs, CT 06268

Stauble Margaret Jane • Student • University of Southern Mississippi School of Library Science • Hattiesburg, MS 39406-5146 • LITA MAGERT

Stauderman Helen M. • Director • Mark Twain Library Association • Redding, CT 06875 • PLA YALSA

Staudigel Elizabeth M. • Librarian (Part-time) • Saddleback College • Mission Viejo, CA 92692

Staudt Cecilia • Saint Louis, MO 63043 • ALCTS LITA PLA RASD

Staudt Emily • Burleson, TX 76028-7505 • ACRL RASD *Continuing*

Stauffer Isabel • Weston ON, M9P 3A6 Canada • Continuing

Stauffer Suzanne H. • Reference Assistant • Tuscarawas County Public Library • New Phila, OH 44663-2634

Staum-Kuniej Sonja • Museum Librarian • Museum of Contemporary Art • Chicago, IL 60611

Stautland Tamara • Instructional Materials Spec. • San Diego Public Schools Instructional Media Center • San Diego, CA 92123 • AASL

Stavash Patricia • Most Sacred Heart of Jesus Elementary School • Wallington, NJ 07057

Stave Christopher D. • University of California Los Angeles Graduate School of Library & Information Science • Los Angeles, CA 90024

Stavis Ruth L. • Newtonville, MA 02160

Stavn Virginia B. • Science & Business Librarian • Saint Paul Public Library • St. Paul, MN 55102 • PLA

Stavovy Patricia B. • Public Library Director • Avella Area Public Library Center • Avella, PA 15312 • PLA

Stavrolakis Rachel G. • Marietta, GA 30060 • AASL

Stavrou Fotini • Aristotle University of Thessaloniki • Thessaloniki 540 06, Greece • ACRL

Stawski Nina • Milwaukee, WI 53211-3533 • ACRL ALCTS

Steadman Kathryn G. • Kalamazoo, MI 49009

Steadman Susan M. • Peachtree City, GA 30269

Steadman Vincent • Branch Manager • Enoch Pratt Free Library Reistertown Road Branch • Baltimore, MD 21215 • PLA

Stear Edward B. • Student • CW Post Palmer Grad L Sch • Brookville, NY 11548 • LITA

Stearns Harriet C. • Moorestown, NJ 08057

Stearns Judy • Adult Technical Services Lib • Ketchikan Public Library • Ketchikan, AK 99901

Stearns Megan • Seattle Public Library • Seattle, WA 98104-1193 • FLRT GODORT

Stearns Melissa M. • Technical Services Librarian • Franklin Pierce College Library • Rindge, NH 03461-0060 • ALCTS NMRT

Stearns Sandra L. • Walterboro, SC 29488 • AASL

Stearns Susan M. • Vice-President • Faxon Research Services Inc • Cambridge, MA 02142 • ACRL LITA ERT

Stebbins Peggy L. • Student • Texas Woman's University School of Library & Information Studies • Denton, TX 76204

Stebelman Scott D. • Reference Librarian • George Washington University Gelman Library • Washington, DC 20052 • ACRL RASD

Steben Florence W. • Naperville, IL 60563

Stebleton Dorothy • Mason Middle School • Mason, MI 48854

Steck Melinda Kay • Student • University of South Carolina College of Library & Information Science • Columbia, SC 29208 • AASL

Stecking Susan E. • Milwaukee, WI 53211-3446

Steckler Irene M. • Special Asst to the Librarian • Library of Congress • Washington, DC 20541

Steckler Phyllis B. • President • Oryx Press • Phoenix, AZ 85012-3397 • RASD

Steckler Ron R. • School Library Media Specialist • Jackson Junior High School • Jackson, WY 83001

Stecyk George E. • Director of Marketing • Dawson Subscription Service • Mt. Morris, IL 61054 • LITA

Steeb Roger D. • Assistant Reference Librarian • New Mexico State University Library • Las Cruces, NM 88003-0006 • RASD

Steeby Carolyn Sue • Head of Children Services • Willard Public Library • Battle Creek, MI 49017 • ALSC

Steed Sharonne A. • Student • Emory University Libraries Robert W. Woodruff Library • Atlanta, GA 30322-2870

Steel Rebecca Dierdre • Librarian • Kalamazoo Institute of Arts Library • Kalamazoo, MI 49007-5102

Steel Virginia • Head, Access Services • University of California-San Diego Library 0175A • La Jolla, CA 92093-0175 • ACRL ALCTS LAMA

Steele Anitra T. • Children's Specialist • Mid-Continent Public Library • Independence, MO 64050 • ALSC

Steele Beth K. • Homewood, AL 35209

Steele Carl L. • Director • Rock Valley College Educational Resources Center • Rockford, IL 61111 • ACRL ALCTS RASD

Steele Elsa B. • Student • University of Washington Graduate School of Library and Information Science • Seattle, WA 98195 • LITA PLA

Steele Jean • Media Specialist • Saint Joseph Grade School • Cuyahoga Falls, OH 44221

Steele Kirstin A. • Technical Services Director • Williamsburg Regional Library • Williamsburg, VA 23185

Steele M. Susan • Head of Access Services • University of Texas Medical Branch Moody Medical Library • Galveston, TX 77555-1035 • ACRL

Steele Margaret E. • Director Systems Office • University of Louisville Ekstrom Library • Louisville, KY 40292

Steele Martha • Head of Access • University of Houston Libraries • Houston, TX 77204-2091 • ACRL LAMA RASD

Steele Nancy K. • Library Director • Blue Earth Community Library • Blue Earth, MN 56073

Steele Patricia A. • Acting Assoc. Dean for Pub. Serv • Indiana University • Bloomington, IN 47405 • ACRL LAMA

Steele Patrick N. • Head of Technical Services • Euclid Public Library • Euclid, OH 44123-2091 • ALCTS SRRT

Steele Richard J. • President • Minicomputer Systems, Inc. • Boulder, CO 80302-5653 • LITA

Steele Sue • Systems Librarian • Monash University Library • Clayton VIC 3168, Australia • LITA

Steele U. M. • Dover, DE 19903-0944 • ASCLA LAMA *Life*

Steele Victoria L. • Head of Special Collections • University of Southern California Doheny Library • Los Angeles, CA 90089-0182 • ACRL

Steelman R. M. • Monticello, AR 71655 • ACRL ALCTS RASD *Continuing*

Steelman Terry D. • Design Director • Ballinger • Philadelphia, PA 19106 • ACRL

Steen Carol • Mountain Lakes, NJ 07046 • ACRL LAMA RASD

Steen Judith • Head, Interlibrary Loan • University of California-Santa Cruz Library • Santa Cruz, CA 95064 • ACRL RASD

Steen K. Carol • Longview, WA 98632 • EMIERT IFRT LHRT SRRT

Steenberg Gerald W. • Director • Saint Paul Public Library • St. Paul, MN 55102 • LAMA PLA

Steenbergen James A. • Assistant Librarian • Riverdale Public Library • Riverdale, IL 60627 • ASCLA PLA

Steenbergen Pat • Librarian • Board of Education for the City of York • City of York, M6M 4A8 Canada • LITA

Steensland Ronald P. • Director • Lexington Public Library • Lexington, KY 40507 • ACRL ALCTS ALSC ALTA ASCLA LAMA LITA PLA RASD YALSA

Steensma Rom V. • Commercial Director • Nedbook International • 1003AC Amsterdam, Netherlands • ACRL ALCTS

Steep Melinda K. • Children's Librarian • Monrovia Public Library • Monrovia, CA 91016 • ALSC

Steepleton Judith • Fairfield Glade, TN 38557

Steere Paul J. • Regional Library Officer • American Embassy, Bangkok (USIS) • APO San Francisco, CA 96346-0001 • ACRL ASCLA LAMA PLA FLRT IFRT IRRT *Life*

Steere Peter L. • Special Collections • University of Arizona Library • Tucson, AZ 85721

Stefanak Margaret • Executive Director • Lewis & Clark Library System • Edwardsville, IL 62025 • ASCLA LAMA

Stefancic Emil J. • Euclid, OH 44117 • Continuing

Stefani Carolyn R. • Cambridge Public Library • Cambridge, MA 02138 • PLA

Stefani Joann • Head, Acq. & Serials Dept. • University of Mississippi John Davis Williams Library • University, MS 38677 • ACRL ALCTS

Stefansson Jody • Director of High School Library • Polytechnic School • Pasadena, CA 91106 • AASL YALSA

Steffe Mary Ellen • Trustee • Calumet City Public Library • Calumet City, IL 60409-4003 • ALTA

Steffee Barbara • Assistant Librarian • Salt Lake City Public Library • Salt Lake City, UT 84111

Steffen Ruth S. • Assistant Professor • University of Wisconsin-Stevens Point Library • Stevens Point, WI 54481 • ACRL ALCTS

Steffen Susan Swords • Northwestern University Joseph Schaffner Library • Chicago, IL 60611 • ACRL RASD

Steffens Katherine • Assistant to Director • Secaucus Free Public Library • Secaucus, NJ 07094

Steffensen Elizabeth • Student • Rosary College Graduate School of Library & Information Science • River Forest, IL 60305 • LITA PLA

Steffensen Jean • Law Librarian • Contra Costa County Law Library • Martinez, CA 94553

Steffer Erika K. • Editor • Women's Inter-Church Council of Canada • Toronto ON, Canada • FLRT IFRT NMRT SRRT

Steffes Leslie J. • Librarian • Phoenix Public Library • Phoenix, AZ 85004 • ALCTS LAMA LITA PLA

Stegman Jill • Library Media Specialist • Atascadero High School Library • Atascadero, CA 93422 • AASL

Stegman Richard • Las Vegas-Clark County Library District Charleston Heights Branch • Las Vegas, NV 89107 • ALCTS PLA

Stehle Dorothy • Cataloger • Library of Congress • Washington, DC 20541 • Continuing

Stehlik Romack Jane E. • Director, LRC • Creighton University Health Sciences Library • Omaha, NE 68178

Steigner Mary A. • Franklin Institute of Boston • Boston, MA 02116 • ACRL

Stein Barbara • Media Specialist • Roosevelt Elementary School • Iowa City, IA 52246 • AASL

Stein Barbara L. • Associate Professor • University of North Texas School of Library & Information Sciences • Denton, TX 76203 • AASL ALSC

Stein Barbara S. • Librarian • Pittsburgh Public Schools • Pittsburgh, PA 15213 • AASL

Stein Dennis • Minneaplois, MN 55438

Stein Gael B. • Director • Saint Johnsbury Athenaeum • St. Johnsbury, VT 05819

Stein Gordon S. • Cranston, RI 02920 • ACRL

Stein Jay W. • John Marshall Law School Library • Chicago, IL 60604 • Life

Stein Johanna M. • Cleveland, OH 44112

Stein Josephine M. • School Librarian • Saint Peter and Paul Schools • St. Thomas, VI 00803

Stein Linda Lawrence • Associate Librarian • University of Delaware Morris Library • Newark, DE 19717-5267

Stein Maria L. • Rochester Public Library • Rochester, NY 14604

Stein Marianne M.B. • Children's Librarian • Mahwah Free Public Library • Mahwah, NJ 07430 • ALSC

Stein Mary H. • Adult Services Librarian • East Baton Rouge Parish Library • Baton Rouge, LA 70806-7699

Stein Merrill D. • Wilmington, DE 19803 • ACRL

Stein Rachelle • Supervising Branch Librarian • New York Public Library Division P • New York, NY 10163-2240

Stein Sarah D. • Student • Emporia State University Emporia in the Rockies • Denver, CO 80204 • LITA

Stein Shari • Student • Rutgers University School of Communication Information & Library Studies • New Brunswick, NJ 08903 • RASD GODORT MAGERT

Stein Sheila • Director • Syosset Public Library • Syosset, NY 11791 • PLA

Stein Sheila B. • Assistant Branch Manager • Queens Borough Public Library Fresh Meadows Branch • Fresh Meadows, NY 11365 • PLA

Steinberg David L. • Director • Shenandoah County Library • Edinburg, VA 22824 • PLA

Steinberg Eileen • Librarian • Austin Meehan Middle Sch • Philadelphia, PA 19152 • YALSA

Steinberg Elaine E. • Librarian • Saint Xavier High School Library • Louisville, KY 40217 • YALSA

Steinberg Judith • Skokie, IL 60076 • AASL

Steinberg Marilyn H. • Northeastern University • Boston, MA 02115 • ACRL LITA

Steinberg Marion • Francis Lewis High School • Fresh Meadows, NY 11365 • IFRT

Steinberg Mimi L. • Database Management Unit Head • Temple University Paley Library • Philadelphia, PA 19122 • ALCTS

Steinberg Raymond • Learning Resources Specialist • Bethel School District Frontier Junior High School • Tacoma, WA 98445 • AASL

Steinberger Erica J. • General Research Corporation Library Systems • Santa Barbara, CA 93160-6770

Steindler C. Nicole • Ch. Rel./Memb.--Admin. Secy. • American Library Association • Chicago, IL 60611-2795

Steiner Dorothy • Part-time Librarian • Temple Akiba Library • Culver City, CA 90230

Steiner Edna V. • Red Wing, MN 55066 • Continuing

Steiner Janet E. • Executive Director • South Central Research Library Council • Ithaca, NY 14850 • ASCLA LAMA

Steiner Karen F. • Akron-Summit County Public Library • Akron, OH 44326-0001

Steiner Karl R. • Systems Administrator • Saginaw Valley State University Melvin J. Zahnow Library • University Center, MI 48710

Steiner Laurel A. • Reference/Young Adult • King County Library System Burien Branch • Seattle, WA 98166

Steiner Mary L. • Cataloger • DeWitt Wallace Library MacAlester College • Saint Paul, MN 55105 • ALCTS LITA

Steiner Nita • Douglas County Library System Reedsport Branch Library • Reedsport, OR 97467 • ALSC

Steiner Ronald A. Mr • Associate Library Director • Patrick J. Stapleton Library Indiana University of Pennsylvania • Indiana, PA 15705 • Life

Steiner Sandra S. • Youth Librarian • Contra Costa County Library Martinez Library • Martinez, CA 94553

Steinfeld Michael • Director • Brookline Public Library • Brookline, MA 02146 • LAMA PLA

Steinfirst Susan • Associate Professor • University of North Carolina at Chapel Hill School of Information and Library Science • Chapel Hill, NC 27599-3360 • ALSC

Steinfort Judith C. • Librarian/Writing Teacher • Saint Joseph High School • Frederiksted, VI 00840 • AASL EMIERT

Steinhagen Elizabeth N. • Humboldt State University Library • Arcata, CA 95521 • ALCTS IRRT

Steinhart Sydnae M. • Sci Ref Libn/Catalog Librarian • Bowdoin College Library • Brunswick, ME 04011 • ACRL

Steinhoff Cynthia K. • Acquisitions Librarian • Anne Arundel Community College Andrew G. Truxal Library • Arnold, MD 21012

Steinhoff Nancy C. • La Crosse Public Library • La Crosse, WI 54601

Steiniger Karen • Student • University of California Los Angeles Graduate School of Library & Information Science • Los Angeles, CA 90024

Steinke Cynthia A. • Assoc. Univ. Ln. for Clln. • University of Minnesota Meredith Wilson Library • Minneapolis, MN 55455 • ACRL ALCTS LAMA

Steinke Eleanor G. • Nashville, TN 37215 • Continuing

Steinke Susan A. • Dayton & Montgomery County Public Library • Dayton, OH 45402-2103 • RASD

Steinkraus Ann M. • Racine, WI 53405

Steinman Debbie J. • Support Services Librarian • Springfield Public Library • Springfield, OR 97477

Steins Janet L. • Head, Chemistry Library • State University of New York (SUNY) Chemistry Library • Stony Brook, NY 11794-3425 • ACRL SRRT

Steinway Susan Z. • Cambridge, MA 02140-3601

Steinweg Hilda • Madison, WI 53704 • Continuing

Steitz Rosanne T. • School Librarian • Myers Elementary School • Elkins Park, PA 19117 • AASL

Stelbrink Mary H. • Librarian • Jacksonville Country Day School • Jacksonville, FL 32245 • AASL

Stelk Roger E. • Student • Virginia Polytechnic Institute and State University, Newman Library • Blacksburg, VA 24061-0434 • ACRL IFRT LIRT

Stell Kate • District Librarian • Shell Lake Schools • Shell Lake, WI 54871

Stelling Jerry J. • Librarian • Lakeshore High School • Stevensville, MI 49127 • AASL YALSA

Stelling Prue • Curriculum Librarian • State University of New York at Binghamton Libraries (SUNY) • Binghamton, NY 13902-6012 • ACRL

Stellman Judy • Student • Towson State University • Towson, MD 21204 • AASL

Stelmasik Barbara A. • Head, Book Acquisitions • University of Minnesota O. Meredith Wilson Library • Minneapolis, MN 55455-0414

Stelter Linda • Media Coordinator/Cataloger • Eau Claire Board of Education Library Division • Eau Claire, WI 54701 • AASL

Steltjes Julie • Student • Queens College Graduate School of Library & Information Studies • Flushing, NY 11367 • ALCTS PLA

Stelzer Stuart P. • Clarksville, AR 72830 • ACRL CLENE IFRT IRRT LIRT SRRT *Life*

Stembal Mary Ellen • Technical Services Librarian • Cook Memorial Library • Libertyville, IL 60048 • ALCTS LAMA PLA

Stembridge Karen M. • Student • Clarion University of Pennsylvania • Clarion, PA 16214 • PLA IFRT SRRT

Stemke Paul B. • Computer & Technical Serv Ln • Middle Country Public Library • Centereach, NY 11720

Stemler Adele • Marketing Manager • Attaintment Company Inc. • Verona, WI 53593-0160 • ASCLA

Stemme Virginia L. • Perham, MN 56573 • AASL ALSC

Stemmer Katherine R. • Director • Bridgeport Hospital Reeeves Memorial Library • Bridgeport, CT 06610 • ASCLA LAMA

Stempel Ellen K. • Section Head, Federal Documents • Hawaii State Library • Honolulu, HI 96813 • ACRL RASD GODORT

Stempel William J. • Honolulu, HI 96826

Stempinski Christine A. • New Haven, CT 06515 • ALSC

Sten Linda S. • Librarian • Atlanta-Fulton Public Library Northside Branch • Atlanta, GA 30327

Stengel Mark G. • Lewis-Clark State College Library • Lewiston, ID 83501 • ACRL RASD

Stenstrom Joe Ann Mrs. • Bethesda, MD 20817 • ALSC

Stenstrom Patricia F. • Library & Inf. Sci. Librarian • University of Illinois Library • Urbana, IL 61801 • ACRL LAMA LHRT LRRT

Stenzel Elaine M. • Reference Librarian • Northbrook Public Library • Northbrook, IL 60062

Stepanian Ellen M. • Library Media Director • Shaker Heights City School • Shaker Hts, OH 44120 • AASL ALCTS ALSC YALSA *Life*

Stepanovich Mitch M. • University of Texas at Arlington • Arlington, TX 76019-0497 • LIRT

Stephan Sandra S. • Public Lib Serv Section Chief • Maryland State Department of Education Division of Library Development & Services • Baltimore, MD 21201 • ASCLA LAMA PLA CLENE

Stephanoff Kathryn • Director • Allentown Public Library • Allentown, PA 18102 • ACRL ALCTS ALSC LITA RASD GODORT

Stephans Hildegard • Associate Administrative Ln • American Philosophical Society Library • Philadelphia, PA 19106 • ACRL

Stephany Patricia A. • Circulation Manager • Conyer-Rockdale Library Systems • Conyers, GA 30207

Stephen Carol • Pittsburgh, PA 15214 • Continuing

Stephen Diane I. • Big Rapids, MI 49307 • AASL

Stephen Ross G. • Rider College • Lawrenceville, NJ 08648-3099 • ACRL LAMA LITA RASD

Stephens Alice G. • Head of Library Operations • Alabama Public Library Service • Montgomery, AL 36130 • ASCLA LITA

Stephens Alice M. • Reference InterLibrary Loan Ln • Hammond Public Library • Hammond, IN 46320

Stephens Ann E. • Director • Keene Memorial Library • Fremont, NE 68025 • PLA

Stephens Annabel K. • University of Alabama School of Library & Information Studies • Tuscaloosa, AL 35487-0252 • Life

Stephens Arial A. • Granville County Library System • Oxford, NC 27565 • PLA

Stephens Betsy J. • Information Supervisor • Lake Lanier Regional Library Lawrenceville Branch • Lawrenceville, GA 30245-4707

Stephens Brenda Wilson • County Librarian • Orange County Public Library • Hillsborough, NC 27278

Stephens Catherine L. • Student • University of Pittsburgh School of Library and Information Science • Pittsburgh, PA 15260

Stephens Dennis J. • Collections Development Officer • University of Alaska Elmer E. Rasmuson Library • Fairbanks, AK 99775-1005 • ACRL ALCTS IFRT

Stephens Doris G. • Director • Alexander County Library • Taylorsville, NC 28681

Stephens J. T. • Trustee • EBSCO Subscription Service • Birmingham, AL 35201 • LITA

Stephens Janet A. • Head, Science/Technology/AV • Aurora Public Library • Aurora, IL 60505-4299 • PLA

Stephens Jennifer S. • Dresser Industries • Dallas, TX 75221

Stephens Jerry W. • Director • University of Alabama at Birmingham Mervyn H. Sterne Library • Birmingham, AL 35294-0014 • ACRL

Stephens Joan M. • Serials/Microforms Librarian • Georgia State University Pullen Library • Atlanta, GA 30303-3081

Stephens John H. • Librarian • Grosse Pointe South High School • Grosse Pointe Farms, MI 48236 • AASL

Stephens Kathy L. • Reference Librarian • University of Southern Mississippi Cox Library • Long Beach, MS 39560 • ACRL RASD

Stephens Krista K. • Blue Island, IL 60406 • PLA

Stephens Larry D. • Public Services Librarian • Bartow County Public Library • Cartersville, GA 30120

Stephens Louise • Glendale Public Library • Glendale, AZ 85302 • PLA

Stephens Marianne Deal • Student • Simmons College Graduate School of Library & Information Science • Boston, MA 02115

Stephens Mary L. • County Librarian • Yolo County Library • Woodland, CA 95695 • ALSC LAMA LITA PLA RASD IFRT IRRT

Stephens Phyllis L. • Rye Free Reading Room • Rye, NY 10580 • YALSA

Stephens Susan M. • Librarian • Mount Sterling-Montgomery Cnty P L • Mt Sterling, KY 40353

Stephenson Bill • Chief Telephone Reference • District of Columbia Public Library Martin Luther King Memorial Library • Washington, DC 20001

Stephenson Carrie C. • Reference-Public Serv. Libn • Union College Abigail E. Weeks Memorial Library • Barbourville, KY 40906-1499

Stephenson Christie D. • Asst Fine Arts Ln • Univ of Virginia Library • Charlottesvll, VA 22903 • ACRL LITA

Stephenson Doris F. • Catalog Librarian • Manchester College • North Manchester, IN 46962 • ACRL ALCTS LITA

Stephenson Emogene C. • Children's Librarian • Cincinnati & Hamilton Public Library Sycamore Branch • Cincinnati, OH 45242

Stephenson Helen • Reference Librarian • London Public Libraries • London ON, N6B 3L7 Canada • YALSA

Stephenson Hester • Sr Ch Ln • Somerset County Library System • Bridgewater, NJ 08807 • ALSC

Stephenson James E. • Society of the Cincinnati Library • Washington, DC 20008 • ACRL

Stephenson Janet • Ida Rupp Public Library • Port Clinton, OH 43452

Stephenson Margaret Abigail • Covington, GA 30209 • AASL

Stephenson Midji G. • Managing Librarian • Tucson Public Library Pima/River Center Branch • Tucson, AZ 85715 • PLA YALSA

Stephenson Nina Kay • Reference Librarian • University of New Mexico Zimmerman Library • Albuquerque, NM 87131-1466 • ACRL

Stephenson Phyllis M. • Tech. Processing • Andrews County Library • Andrews, TX 79714 • PLA LRRT

Stepien Matthew • Trustee • Summit Public Library District • Summit, IL 60501

Stepka Susan A. • Student • University of Wisconsin-Milwaukee School of Library & Information Science • Milwaukee, WI 53201

Stepp Barbara B. • Librarian/Media Specialist • Blacksburg High School • Blacksburg, VA 24060

Sterba Josephine S. • Park Ridge, IL 60068 • YALSA

Sterchi Teresa P. • Student • University of Tennessee-Knoxville Graduate School of Library & Information Science • Knoxville, TN 37996-4330

Sterlein Marie Frances • Senior Infor. Specialist • Bethlehem Steel Corporation Corporate Information Center • Bethlehem, PA 18016-7699

Sterling Harold G. • Vice President/Sales • Quality Books Inc. • Lake Bluff, IL 60044-2204 • PLA NMRT

Sterling Judith K. • Assoc. Director Technical Servs. • University of Maryland Baltimore County Kuhn Library • Catonsville, MD 21228 • ACRL ALCTS LAMA

Sterling Judith L. • Librarian • Pennoyer School District #79 • Norridge, IL 60656 • AASL

Sterling Richard • Plymouth Public Library • Plymouth, MA 02360 • ACRL

Sterling Sofia G. • Wilton, CT 06897

Sterling Stephanie L. • Reference Librarian • University of California-Los Angeles (UCLA) • Los Angeles, CA 90024-1450 • NMRT

Sterling Terry • Librarian • Koelbel Public Library • Littleton, CO 80121 • NMRT

Stern Alice F. • Yount Adult Librarian • Boston Public Library • Boston, MA 02117 • YALSA

Stern Barbara • Los Angeles County Law Library • Los Angeles, CA 90012 • ALCTS NMRT

Stern Claire • Jewish Public Library • Montreal, PQ, H3W 1M6 Canada

Stern Joan F. • Librarian • Martin Luther King Elementary School • Cambridge, MA 02139

Stern Judith L. • Student • Queens College Grad Sch of Lib & Inf Studies • Flushing, NY 11367

Stern Kerry C. • Director • Mount San Antonio College • Walnut, CA 91789 • LAMA

Stern Marilyn • Librarian • Dream Lake Elementary School • Apopka, FL 32712 • AASL

Stern Marilyn • Technical Services Librarian • United States Merchant Marine Academy • Kings Point, NY 11024-1699 • ACRL

Stern Marjorie G. • Sn Francisco, CA 94109

Stern Peter • Director • Checkpoint Systems Inc • Thorofare, NJ 08086

Stern Raya • Trustee • Watertown Public Library • Watertown, MA 02172 • ALTA

Stern Richard E. • Reference Librarian • Seton Hall University • South Orange, NJ 07079-2690 • ACRL RASD LRRT

Sternberg Hilary • State University of New York College at Buffalo, E. H. Butler Library • Buffalo, NY 14222-1095 • ACRL

Sternberger Milton • Trustee • Memphis-Shelby County Public Library and Information Center • Memphis, TN 38104-4025

Sterner Constance C. • St. Thomas, VI 00802

Sterner Janice M. • Reference Coordinator • Timberland Regional Library Olympia Branch • Olympia, WA 98501 • PLA RASD

Sterner Kathleen B. • Student • University of Maryland College of Library and Information Services • College Park, MD 20742-4345

Sterner Susan D. • Manager,Bibliographic Control • Denver Public Library • Denver, CO 80204-2602 • LITA

Sternheim Karen • Reference/Public Services Ln • University of California-Los Angeles (UCLA) • Los Angeles, CA 90024-1450 • ACRL RASD

Sternlieb Michael • Student • Queens College Graduate School of Library & Information Studies • Flushing, NY 11367 • ACRL LITA RASD LIRT NMRT

Stetina James P. • Director • Marathon County Public Library • Wausau, WI 54401 • PLA

Stetson Catherine • Librarian • Walker School • Needham, MA 02192

Stetson Deanie • Librarian • Falmouth High School • Falmouth, ME 04105 • AASL YALSA

Stetson William H. • South Hadley, MA 01075

Stettner Victoria A. • Collections Assistant • Massachusetts Institute of Technology Dewey Library • Cambridge, MA 02139 • ACRL NMRT

Steuart Bradley W. • President • American Genealogical Lending Library • Bountiful, UT 84010 • PLA RASD

Steuben Raymond L. • Columbia College Library • Columbia, CA 95310 • ACRL

Steuer Bonnie • Trustee • Indian Trails Public Library District • Wheeling, IL 60090 • ALTA

Stevelman Sharon R. • San Diego, CA 92127

Stevens-Becksvoort Margaret A. • Student • Clarion University of Pennsylvania College of Library Science • Clarion, PA 16214 • AASL SRRT

Stevens-Jones Eloise • Media Specialist • Clifton Elementary School • Atlanta, GA 30316 • AASL

Stevens Alice K. • Librarian • Kalamazoo Public Library • Kalamazoo, MI 49007-5270 • ALSC *Life*

Stevens Arla • Monte Vista High School • Danville, CA 94526 • AASL

Stevens Barbara R. • Coordinator Bibliographic Inst. • University of Wisconsin-Eau Claire William D. McIntyre Library • Eau Claire, WI 54702 • ACRL SRRT

Stevens Deborah Lynn • Media Specialist • South Wayne Junior High School • Indianapolis, IN 46241 • AASL

Stevens Dixie L. • Dir • Long Beach Public Library • Long Beach, MS 39560

Stevens Donna H. • West Bend, WI 53095

Stevens Doreen F. • Cleburne, TX 76031-5910 • PLA IFRT

Stevens Florence H. • Children's Librarian • John C Hart Mem Library • Shrub Oak, NY 10588 • ALSC

Stevens Frank A. • Director • United States Department of Education Office of Educational Res & Improvement • Washington, DC 20208-5571 • EMIERT

Stevens Hannah • Asst. to AUL Tech Serv. • Yale University Sterling Memorial Library • New Haven, CT 06520 • ACRL LAMA SRRT

Stevens Helen M. • Boone, IA 50036 • Continuing

Stevens J Pheetta • Reference Librarian • Lansing Public Library • Lansing, MI 48933 • ACRL LAMA LRRT

Stevens Jay L. • Lead Programmer Analyst • Northern Kentucky University • Highland Heights, KY 41099-6101 • LITA

Stevens Liv J. • Phoenix, AZ 85021-7911 • AASL

Stevens Marian A. • Librarian • Tredyffrin Public Library • Strafford, PA 19087

Stevens Mary F. • Technical Service Librarian • Wellesley Free Library • Wellesley, MA 02181-5989 • ALCTS

Stevens Michael L. • Supervisor of Technical Svs. • Springfield City Library • Springfield, MA 01103 • LITA

Stevens Norman D. • University Librarian • University of Connecticut Homer Babbidge Library • Storrs, CT 06269-1005 • ACRL LITA *Life*

Stevens Patricia T. • Library Media Specialist • Long Beach Unified School District • Long Beach, CA 90813

Stevens Patricia W. • Product Manager/BRS Onsite • Maxwell Online • McLean, VA 22102 • ACRL LITA RASD *Subscribing*

Stevens Patrick J. • Head, Copy Cataloging Section • Cornell University Library • Ithaca, NY 14853-5301 • ALCTS

Stevens Rebecca • School Media Coordinator • William Lenoir Middle School • Lenoir, NC 28645 • AASL

Stevens Robert D. • Professor Emeritus • University of Hawaii School of Library & Information Studies • Honolulu, HI 96822 • ACRL ALCTS *Life*

Stevens Rolland E. • Professor • University of Illinois Library • Urbana, IL 61801 • ACRL RASD *Life*

Stevens Stanley D. • Map Librarian • University of California-Santa Cruz Library • Santa Cruz, CA 95064 • MAGERT

Stevens Susan O. • Librarian • Socastee High School • Myrtle Beach, SC 29577 • AASL

Stevens Teresa L. • Winters, CA 95694

Stevenson Andrew K. • Librarian • Brooklyn Public Library • Brooklyn, NY 11238

Stevenson Condict G. • Student • Catholic University of America Library School Library • Washington, DC 20064

Stevenson David A. • Owner • Le Duc's Books • Laurel, MT 59044

Stevenson Evelyn W. • Library Media Teacher • Will C. Wood High School • Vacaville, CA 95688

Stevenson Grace T. • Imperial Beach, CA 91932 • PLA RASD *Life*

Stevenson John A. • Coor Government Publications • University of Delaware Library • Newark, DE 19717-5267 • GODORT IFRT MAGERT NMRT

Stevenson Julie • Teacher • San Francisco School • San Francisco, CA 94110 • ALSC

Stevenson Marsha J. • Head of Reference • University of Notre Dame Theodore M. Hesburgh Library • Notre Dame, IN 46556 • ACRL LAMA RASD SRRT

Stevenson Mary Jane • Director • Farmers Branch Public Library • Farmers Branch, TX 75234 • ALCTS LAMA LITA PLA RASD YALSA

Stevenson Maxine • Alton, IL 62002 • AASL

Stevenson Michael I. • Business Information Analyst • Harvard Business School Baker Library • Boston, MA 02163

Stevenson Milton W. • Head Librarian • Virginia Intermont College J. F. Hicks Library • Bristol, VA 24201 • ACRL LAMA IFRT

Stevenson Nanette • Art Director • Putnam Sons • New York, NY 10016 • ALSC

Stevenson Roberta • Davis, CA 95616 • ACRL ALCTS *Continuing*

Stevenson Rosemary M. • Asst Prof/afro Americana Bibl • University of Illinois Library • Urbana, IL 61801 • ACRL ALTA

Stevenson Sheila • Adult Collection Coordinator • Oak Park Public Library • Oak Park, IL 60301 • IRRT

Steward Celeste F. • Castro Valley, CA 94546 • PLA

Stewart-Murphy Charlotte A. • Research Collections Director • McMaster University Library • Hamilton ON, L8S 4L6 Canada • ACRL

Stewart Alice K. • Student • Kansas City Public Library • Kansas City, MO 64106 • YALSA AFLRT

Stewart Anna C. • Librarian, Chief • United States Air Force Academy Community Center Library • Colorado Springs, CO 80840-5731 • ALCTS PLA AFLRT FLRT

Stewart Anne C. • Librarian • Hatboro-Horsham School District Crooked Billet School • Hatboro, PA 19040 • AASL

Stewart Audrey K. • Library Coordinator, Librarian • Alexander Local Schools • Albany, OH 45710

Stewart Barbara • Govt. Doc./Reference Librarian • Rice University Fondren Library • Houston, TX 77251-1892 • GODORT

Stewart Barbara L. • Director, Documentation Center • CRIES • Managua, Nicaragua • LITA

Stewart Betty F. • Library Director • John C Hart Mem Library • Shrub Oak, NY 10588 • LAMA PLA RASD YALSA

Stewart Byron • Documents Librarian • Southwest Missouri State University Library • Springfield, MO 65804-0095 • GODORT

Stewart Carol J. • Library Director • Clayton County Library System • Jonesboro, GA 30236 • LAMA PLA

Stewart Charles C. • Chief, Technical Services • City College of New York (CUNY) • New York, NY 10031 • ACRL ALCTS LAMA GODORT IFRT IRRT LHRT SORT SRRT

Stewart Cherilyn C. • Chicago, IL 60657

Stewart Christopher P. • Information Specialist • University of California • Berkeley, CA 94709 • ACRL LITA CLENE GODORT IFRT ILERT IRRT LIRT LRRT MAGERT NMRT SRRT

Stewart Clara J. • Librarian • Kellogg Community College Learning Resource Center • Battle Creek, MI 49017-3397

Stewart D. Michael • Trustee • Salt Lake County Library System • Salt Lake City, UT 84121-3188

Stewart David • Treasurer • Kanawha County Public Library • Charleston, WV 25301 • ALTA

Stewart David Marshall • Nashville, TN 37205 • Continuing

Stewart Deborah E. • Delaware County Library System • Brookhaven, PA 19015 • ALSC

Stewart Dodie Ms. • Branch Librarian • Adams County Public Library Administration • Thornton, CO 80229

Stewart Donald E. • Evanston, IL 60201

Stewart Duncan R. • Student • Indiana University School of Library and Information Science • Bloomington, IN 47405

Stewart George E. • Librarian/Media Specialist • Highland Park High School • Amarillo, TX 79107 • AASL YALSA

Stewart George R. • Director • Birmingham Public Library • Birmingham, AL 35203 • LAMA PLA

Stewart Henry R. Jr • Director • Emporia State University William Allen White Library • Emporia, KS 66801 • ACRL LAMA ERT

Stewart James A. • Librarian III,Hd History Dept. • Chicago Public Library • Chicago, IL 60605 • RASD

Stewart James B. • Director • Victoria Public Library • Victoria, TX 77901 • LAMA LITA PLA

Stewart Janet • Head of Reference • University of Massachusetts at Boston Joseph P. Healey Library • Boston, MA 02125-3393 • ACRL RASD

Stewart Jeanne Elizabeth • Field Supervisor • Watauga Regional Library Center • Johnson City, TN 37601

Stewart Jessie M. • Librarian-District Coordinator • Burkburnett Junior High School • Burkburnett, TX 76354 • AASL

Stewart Jim • San Antonio, TX 78230

Stewart Jo • Coor. of Instr. Materials • North Little Rock Schools • North Little Rock, AR 72115-0687 • AASL

Stewart Joan G. • Wilmette, IL 60201

Stewart Joanne R. • Reference & Serials Librarian • Waukegan High School Library • Waukegan, IL 60085 • AASL YALSA

Stewart John D. • Assistant Library Director • Dept of Public Library Muncipal Ctr • Virginia Beach, VA 23456

Stewart Karen • Colorado Legislative Council Joint Legislative Library • Denver, CO 80203 • LITA

Stewart Kathleen • Granbury, TX 76048

Stewart Kathryn A. • Library Services Director • Brevard County Library • Cocoa, FL 32922-7781 • ALTA PLA

Stewart Linda B. • Librarian • Hebrew Day School of Fort Lauderdale • Ft. Lauderdale, FL 33304 • AASL ALSC YALSA IFRT

Stewart Linda L. • Teacher • Lehigh Elementary School • Walnutport, PA 18088

Stewart Louise B. • Retro Link Associates • Provo, UT 84601 • AASL ACRL LITA

Stewart Marianna • Technical Librarian • Corning Incorp. • Corning, NY 14831 • ALCTS LITA

Stewart Marilyn L. • Assistant Director • Saint Charles Public Library • St. Charles, IL 60174

Stewart Marsha • Librarian • Ancona School • Chicago, IL 60615 • AASL ALSC

Stewart Marsha G. • McCormick Elementary School • Mullins, SC 29574 • AASL

Stewart Mary C. • Media Services Administrator • Edgewood Independent School District • San Antonio, TX 78237-1399 • AASL IFRT

Stewart Mary Rita • Marketing Representative • General Research Corporation Library Systems • Santa Barbara, CA 93160-6770 • AASL LITA PLA

Stewart Nettie M. • Trustee • Mobile Public Library • Mobile, AL 36602 • ALTA

Stewart Norma V. Mrs. • Denver, CO 80231 • AASL ALSC *Life*

Stewart Robert W. • Director • Asbury Park Free Public Library • Asbury Park, NJ 07712 • ACRL ALCTS ASCLA LAMA LITA PLA RASD GODORT MAGERT

Stewart Sharon L. • Senior Librarian • University of Alabama McLure Education Library • Tuscaloosa, AL 35487-0266 • LAMA LIRT

Stewart Susan A. • Chattooga County Library • Summerville, GA 30747 • PLA

Stewart Susan L. • Life & Health Physical Sci Libn • University of Nevada-Reno • Reno, NV 89557 • ACRL

Stewart Suzanne K. • Pittsburgh, PA 15238 • ACRL IFRT LHRT

Stewart Theresa G. • Media Specialist • Country Isles Elementary School • Fort Lauderdale, FL 33326 • AASL ALSC

Stewart Volker F. • University of Baltimore Langsdale Library • Baltimore, MD 21201

Stewart William H. • Director • Lubbock City-County Library • Lubbock, TX 79401

Stewig John Warren • Glendale, WI 53217 • ALSC

Stiber Barbara • Branch Manager • Cuyahoga County Public Library Parma Ridge Branch • Parma, OH 44129 • LAMA PLA

Stich Clare R. • Santa Clara Public Library • Santa Clara, CA 95051 • ALSC

Stich Julie M. • International Foundation of Employee Benefit Plans • Brookfield, WI 53008-0069

Sticha Philip E. • President • VIS Consultants, Inc. • Columbia, MD 21044 • LITA EMIERT

Stichler Richard N. • Student • Drexel University College of Information Studies • Philadelphia, PA 19104-2875 • ACRL IFRT NMRT SRRT

Stick Dorothy J. • Head of Administrative Servs. • Public Library of Des Moines • Des Moines, IA 50308-1791 • LAMA PLA

Stickford Mary D. • Youth Services Librarian • Roswell Public Library • Roswell, NM 88201 • ALSC

Stickley Marcia E. • Library Media Specialist • Hedgesville Elementary School • Hedgesville, WV 25427 • AASL ALSC

Stickman James • Head, Serials Division • University of Washington Suzzallo Library • Seattle, WA 98195 • ALCTS LITA   *Life*

Stickney Ruth C. • Supervising Librarian • Central California Conference of S.D.A Office of Education • Clovis, CA 93612 • AASL

Stief Janet Reber • Student • University of Maryland College of Library and Information Services • College Park, MD 20742-4345 • ALSC

Stieg Margaret F. • Professor • University of Alabama School of Library & Information Studies • Tuscaloosa, AL 35487-0252 • ACRL RASD LHRT   *Life*

Stielow Frederick J. • Executive Director • Tulane University Amistad Research Center • New Orleans, LA 70118-5698 • IFRT LHRT

Stielstra Julie • Assistant Librarian • MacNeal Hospital Health Sciences Resource Center • Berwyn, IL 60402 • ASCLA RASD

Stien Arlene M. • Librarian • Ionia High School • Ionia, MI 48846 • AASL

Stier Rosalina A. • Branch Manager • Allen County Public Library Little Turtle Branch • Ft. Wayne, IN 46825 • PLA

Stierholz Katrina L. • Interlibrary Loan L.A. • University of Missouri-Saint Louis • St. Louis, MO 63121-4499 • LITA

Stierman Jeanne Koekkoek • Macomb, IL 61455 • RASD

Stierman John • Assistant Professor/References • Western Illinois University Libraries • Macomb, IL 61455

Stievater Susan M. • Associate Librarian • State University of New York College at Buffalo, E. H. Butler Library • Buffalo, NY 14222-1095 • ACRL RASD

Stiewe Sherlyn • Trustee • Mid-Wisconsin Federated Library System • Fond du Lac, WI 54935-5510 • ALTA

Stiff Renee F. • North Carolina Central University James E. Shepard Memorial Library • Durham, NC 27707 • GODORT

Stiffler Barbara Lee • Librarian • Niagra-Wheatfield Senior High School • Sanborn, NY 14094 • AASL YALSA

Stiffler Michael D. • Student • Indiana University School of Library and Information Science • Bloomington, IN 47405 • RASD LRRT

Stiffler Rose Marie • Assistant Director • Johnson County Public Library • Franklin, IN 46131 • LAMA LITA PLA

Stigge Lawrence L. • Union City, CA 94587

Stigleman Sue E. • Asheville, NC 28814-8074 • ACRL LITA LIRT

Stiles Muriel H. • Beaman Memorial Public Library • West Boylston, MA 01583

Stiles Rebecca E. • Bloomington, IN 47401

Stiles Ruth M. • Reference Librarian • North Harris College • Houston, TX 77073 • ACRL GODORT IFRT

Stiles Virginia F. Ms. • McCarthy Middle School • Chelmsford, MA 01824 • AASL LIRT

Still Julie M. • Reference Librarian Part-time • Widener University Wolfgram Library • Chester, PA 19013 • ACRL IRRT

Stilley Cynthia S. • Children's Services Librarian • Flint Public Library • Flint, MI 48502 • ALSC

Stillman June S. • Reference Librarian • University of Central Florida Library • Orlando, FL 32816-0666 • ACRL

Stillman Mary E. Dr • Special Asst to the President • Albright College • Reading, PA 19612-5234 • LAMA RASD   *Life*

Stillman Minna Miss • Palo Alto, CA 94301 • Continuing

Stillwagon Rebecca • Branch Manager • Cobb County Public Library System Lewis A. Ray Branch • Smyrna, GA 30080

Stillwater Fraida Joy • Southfield, MI 48034

Stillwell Elizabeth J. • Children's Librarian • Baldwinsville Public Library • Baldwinsville, NY 13027-2485 • ALSC

Stillwell Kamala D. • Director • Maricopa County Library District • Phoenix, AZ 85032 • ALCTS ALSC LAMA LITA PLA RASD YALSA

Stillwell Stephen J. Jr. • Librarian • Harvard University • Cambridge, MA 02138 • ACRL SRRT

Stilson Deborah J. • Young Adult Services Coor. • Yakima Valley Regional Library • Yakima, WA 98901 • YALSA

Stilwell Martha Johnson • Kellogg Community College Learning Resource Center • Battle Creek, MI 49017-3397

Stimatz Lisa R. • Student • Indiana University School of Library and Information Science • Bloomington, IN 47405 • ACRL

Stimpson Gloria P. Ms. • Librarian • Donoghue Elementary School • Chicago, IL 60653

Stimson Andrew W. • Executive Director • Waukegan Public Library • Waukegan, IL 60085 • LAMA LITA PLA

Stimson Nancy F. • Student • University of California Los Angeles Graduate School of Library & Information Science • Los Angeles, CA 90024 • PLA RASD IFRT NMRT SRRT

Stinchcomb Maxine • Chicago, IL 60614 • ALSC

Stine Diane • Librarian • Northeastern Illinois University Library • Chicago, IL 60625 • ACRL

Stine Nancy • Salisbury, NC 28144

Stine Walter D. • Head of Reserves & Circulation • Harvard University Library • Cambridge, MA 02138-2901 • LITA

Stines Joe • Acting Director • Tampa-Hillsborough County Public Library • Tampa, FL 33602 • ALSC YALSA

Stinnett Hubert • Trustee • Breckinridge County Public Library • Hardinsburg, KY 40143 • PLA

Stipa Virginia • Head of Circulation • Cherry Hill Free Public Library • Cherry Hill, NJ 08034 • PLA

Stipe Shannon Cynthia • Linda Hall Library • Kansas City, MO 64110

Stipek Kathleen • Reference Librarian • Alachua County Library District • Gainesville, FL 32601 • PLA

Stipo Ellen J. • Student • Queens College Graduate School of Library & Information Studies • Flushing, NY 11367 • ASCLA

Stirling Isabel A. • Head, Science Library • University of Oregon Library • Eugene, OR 97403-1299 • ACRL IRRT LIRT

Stites Barbara J. • Executive Director • Tampa Bay Library Consortium • Tampa, FL 33619 • ASCLA LAMA LITA CLENE

Stith Janet • Asst Dir • University of Kentucky Libraries • Lexington, KY 40506-0039

Stith Kay Ann • Librarian • Dodge City High School Library • Dodge City, KS 67801

Stith Linda A. • Regional Librarian • Bluegrass South Regional Library Office • Nicholasville, KY 40356 • LAMA PLA

Stitt Margaret L. • Gates Mills, OH 44040-0043 • ALSC PLA   *Life*

Stitt Theresa J. • School Librarian • Fulton Junior High School • Fulton, NY 13069 • AASL

Stitt Walter • Director • Attleboro Public Library Sweet Memorial • Attleboro, MA 02703 • ALCTS

Stivers M J • Library Relations Representative • H. W. Wilson Company • Bronx, NY 10452 • ALSC

Stluka Thomas H. • Director of Member Services • American Acad of Dermatolgy • Evanston, IL 60201

Stoan Stephen K. • Asst Dir for Public Services • University of Texas at Arlington • Arlington, TX 76019-0497 • RASD

Stobbe Anne • Texas Panhandle Library System • Amarillo, TX 79189 • PLA

Stober Carlene M. • Student • Rutgers University School of Communication Information & Library Studies • New Brunswick, NJ 08903 • RASD

Stober Paula J. • Student • San Jose State University Division of Library & Information Science • San Jose, CA 95192-0029

Stoch Ronald V. • Library Director • Eisenhower Public Library District • Harwood Heights, IL 60656 • LAMA PLA

Stock Barbara A. • Lockhart, TX 78644

Stock Jonathan C. • Fairfield, CT 06430

Stock Mildred • Teacher of Library • Public School 205 • Brooklyn, NY 11204 • AASL

Stock Norman • Head, Acquisitions Department • Montclair State College Harry Sprague Library • Upper Montclair, NJ 07043 • ALCTS

Stock Theron P. • Associate Director • Weber County Library • Odgen, UT 84401

Stockard Joan • Research Services Librarian • Wellesley College Library Margaret Clapp Library • Wellesley, MA 02181-8275 • ACRL

Stocker Erik Bradford • Librarian • Redwood Library & Athenaeum • Newport, RI 02840-3292 • ACRL LAMA LHRT

Stocker Jean N. • Librarian • Phoenix Public Library Yucca Branch • Phoenix, AZ 85015 • PLA IFRT SRRT

Stocker Patricia M. • Outreach Coordinator • Wayne County Library System • Newark, NY 14513 • PLA

Stocker Randi L. • Reference Librarian • Indiana University-Purdue University at Indianapolis Library (IUPUI) • Indianapolis, IN 46202 • ACRL ALSC LAMA

Stockey Edward A. • Library Automation Officer • Indiana University at Bloomington University Libraries • Bloomington, IN 47405-9998 • ACRL

Stockham Lyn H. • Librarian • Childersburg Middle School • Childersburg, AL 35044 • AASL

Stocking Carolyn J. • Storrs, CT 06268 • GODORT

Stockinger Jill F. • Chief Librarian • Port Arthur Public Library • Port Arthur, TX 77642-3136

Stockland Deborah J. • Hazeltine Corporation • Greenlawn, NY 11740 • LITA

Stockland Karen L. • Graduate Student • University of Kentucky College of Library & Information Science • Lexington, KY 40506-0391

Stockman Cheryl A. • Branch Librarian • Manchester City Library West Manchester Branch • Manchester, NH 03102 • LAMA PLA

Stockmon Milrean Ph.D. • Head Librarian • Arkansas Baptist College Library • Little Rock, AR 72202

Stockner Patricia G. • Director • Warrenville Public Library District • Warrenville, IL 60555 • LAMA PLA RASD YALSA

Stockton David A. • Oglethorpe University Library • Atlanta, GA 30319

Stockton Gloria J. • Director • University of California Northern Regional Library Facility • Richmond, CA 94804 • ACRL ALCTS ASCLA LAMA LITA RASD IRRT LRRT

Stockton Melissa • Marketing Representative • AMIGOS Bibliographic Council,Inc. • Dallas, TX 75251-2104 • ASCLA LITA LRRT

Stoddard Jewell K. • Co-owner & Manager • Cheshire Cat Book Store • Washington, DC 20015 • ALSC

Stoddart Linda • Dir. of Information Services • Switzerland Library International Institute of Management Development • Lausanne 1001, Switzerland • ACRL LAMA RASD

Stodola Bernard • Trustee • Hammond Public Library • Hammond, IN 46320 • ALTA

Stoebenau June B. • Branch Librarian • Reading Public Library Southeast Branch • Reading, PA 19602

Stoebner Sue C. • Library IV • University of California • Santa Cruz, CA 95064

Stoeckenius Kai W. • Technical Services • Boise State University Library • Boise, ID 83725 • ACRL ALCTS

Stoeker Joan Ms • Library Director • Garfield Memorial Library Clare Public Library • Clare, MI 48617 • PLA

Stoenner Sharon A. • District Manager • SVE • Jacksonville, FL 32241 • AASL PLA

Stoering Ann T. • Student • University of Wisconsin-Milwaukee School of Library & Information Science • Milwaukee, WI 53201

Stoessl Elizabeth F. • Head of Selection & Acquisitions • Arlington County Department of Libraries • Arlington, VA 22201 • ALCTS PLA

Stoffel Ann • Serials Librarian • Louisville Public Library • Louisville, CO 80027 • ALCTS

Stoffel Lester L. • Downers Grove, IL 60515 • ASCLA LAMA PLA   *Continuing*

Stoffle Carla J. • University Librarian • University of Arizona Library • Tucson, AZ 85721 • ACRL LAMA LITA RASD   *Life*

Stogner Shirlene • Reference Librarian • University of Southern Mississippi Cook Memorial Library • Hattiesburg, MS 39406-5053 • LIRT

Stoicovy Monica R. • Director • Brentwood Library • Pittsburgh, PA 15227

Stoke Linda B. • Pompano Beach, FL 33069 • AASL

Stoker Jerome L. • Research Libraries Systems Coord • New York Public Library • New York, NY 10016 • LITA

Stokes Aileen • Trustee • Horry County Memorial Library • Conway, SC 29526 • ALTA

Stokes Alfred • Trustee • New Orleans City Hall • New Orleans, LA 70112 • ALTA

Stokes Edith I. • New York University Elmer Holmes Bobst Library • New York, NY 10012 • RASD YALSA   *Continuing*

Stokes Helena Olivia • Houston, TX 77021

Stokes Jayme L. • Librarian K-12 • Ouachita Christian School • Monroe, LA 71203

Stokes Judith E. • Rhode Island College James P. Adams Library • Providence, RI 02908 • GODORT

Stokes Mike S. • Lombard, IL 60148

Stokes Stephanie • Friends of San Francisco Public Library • San Francisco, CA 94102

Stokes Susan A. • Assistant Department Director • Broward County Library Florida Center for the Book • Fort Lauderdale, FL 33301 • PLA

Stokes Susan A. • Student • Lincoln Elementary School • Schenectady, NY 12304 • AASL

Stokes Thomas E. • Librarian • Emmanuel School of Religion Library • Johnson City, TN 37601-9989 • ACRL LAMA

Stokesberry Brent A. • Head of Adults Services • Kokomo Howard County Public Library • Kokomo, IN 46901

Stokke Terrence L. • Student • University of Wisconsin-Milwaukee School of Library & Information Science • Milwaukee, WI 53201

Stoksik Pamela V. • Head of Technical Services • Ontario Legislative Library • Toronto ON, M7A 1A9 Canada • LAMA LITA

Stolaas Mary J. • Norland, WA 98358 • AASL

Stoll Emma A. • Rogers, AR 72756

Stolleis Patrick E. • Library Principal Associate • Atlanta-Fulton Public Library • Atlanta, GA 30303 • RASD

Stoller Irene • Walnut Creek, CA 94595 • LAMA PLA *Life*
Stoller Joshua • Librarian • South Side Middle School • Rockville Center, NY 11570
Stollwerk Susan • Hofstra University Axinn Library • Hempstead, NY 11550
Stolt Wilbur A. • Norman, OK 73019 • ACRL
Stoltz Dorothy M. • Reinholds, PA 17569-9053
Stolz Jim • Information Services Supervisor • Pikes Peak Library District • Colorado Springs, CO 80901 • PLA
Stomberg Lisa B. • Student • University of North Carolina at Chapel Hill School of Information and Library Science • Chapel Hill, NC 27599-3360
Stombres Debra S. • Aurora Christian School • Aurora, IL 60506
Stommel Barbara O. • Student • University of Maryland College Park Theodore R. McKeldin Library • College Park, MD 20742-7011
Stone Alva T. • Head of Cataloging • Florida State University Law Library • Tallahassee, FL 32306-1034 • ALCTS LITA
Stone Ann F. • Personnel Librarian • Duke University William R. Perkins Library • Durham, NC 27706 • ACRL LAMA
Stone Anne F. • Belmont, MA 02178
Stone Ava L. • Director • Flagstaff City-Coconino County Public Library • Flagstaff, AZ 86001 • ALCTS ASCLA LITA PLA RASD YALSA
Stone C. Walter Dr. • Alameda, CA 94501 • AASL PLA *Life*
Stone Carl • Director • Anderson County Library • Anderson, SC 29622-4047 • LAMA PLA RASD
Stone Carol • Adult Services Supervisor • Alhambra Public Library • Alhambra, CA 91801 • LITA PLA RASD
Stone Carol A. • Serials Librarian • Miami-Dade Public Library System • Miami, FL 33130-1504 • PLA
Stone Christine • Pittsburgh, PA 15213
Stone Christine R. • Student • Drexel University College of Information Studies • Philadelphia, PA 19104-2875 • AASL
Stone Dana • Knoxville, TN 37919
Stone Elise J. • Gahanna, OH 43230
Stone Elizabeth W. • Dean Emerita • Catholic University of America School of Library and Information Science • Washington, DC 20064 • AASL ACRL ALCTS ALSC ALTA ASCLA LAMA LITA PLA RASD YALSA CLENE FLRT ILERT IRRT LHRT *Honorary*
Stone Ellen C. • Old Mystic, CT 06372
Stone Evelyn P. Miss • Marathon, NY 13803 • LAMA *Life*
Stone Glenice W. • Baton Rouge, LA 70810 • AASL
Stone Herbert M. • Vice President/Trustee • Brown, Healey, Stone & Sauer • Cedar Rapids, IA 52402
Stone Howard P. • Catalog Librarian • Brown University Rockefeller Library • Providence, RI 02912 • ACRL ALCTS MAGERT
Stone J.S. Mrs. • Library Board Trustee • Houston Public Library • Houston, TX 77002
Stone Jason R. • Assistant Director • East Brunswick Public Library • E. Brunswick, NJ 08816 • LAMA
Stone Jean Evelyn Leah • Library Associate • Brooks Free Library • Harwich, MA 02645
Stone Joyce L. • Desert Hot Springs, CA 92240 • PLA YALSA *Life*
Stone Laura G. • University of Kentucky • Lexington, KY 40506-0056
Stone Linda D. • Public Service Librarian • Baltimore County Public Library • Towson, MD 21204 • PLA
Stone Lucie H. • Chesapeake, VA 23325 • IRRT *Continuing*
Stone Lysbeth Kaye • Santa Fe, NM 87501 • AASL YALSA IFRT LIRT
Stone Marilyn • Media Director • Hickman High School • Columbia, MO 65203 • AASL
Stone Nelda Jeanne • Library Assistant • Orange County Public Library Laguna Beach Branch • Laguna Beach, CA 92651
Stone Philip J. Mr • Washington, DC 20008 • Life
Stone Richard L. • Cataloger • H. W. Wilson Company • Bronx, NY 10452 • ALCTS
Stone Robert H. • Lebanon, TN 37088-0542 • ACRL ALCTS LITA RASD *Life*
Stone S. Kaye • Livingston, AL 35470
Stone Steven A. • Librarian • Bradley University Cullom-Davis Library • Peoria, IL 61625 • ACRL LITA
Stone Susan • Berkeley, CA 94703-1012 • LITA
Stone Susan Owens • Head of Young Adult Services • The Bryant Library • Roslyn, NY 11576
Stone Toby G. • Librarian • American University of Paris • Paris, France • ACRL LAMA RASD CLENE
Stone Vicki • Assistant Librarian • Fort Stockton Public Library • Fort Stockton, TX 79735
Stonebrook Margaret • Library Director • Brevard County Library • Cocoa, FL 32922-7781
Stonehewer Judith E. • Chief Librarian • Marianopolis College • Motreal, PQ, H3H 1W1 Canada • ACRL
Stoneking Linda • Nacogdoches, TX 75961 • AASL IFRT
Stoner Jeanette B. • Trustee • Monroe County Library System • Monroe, MI 48161 • ALTA
Stoner Robert J. • Climax Springs, MO 65324
Stoner Ronald P. • Head of Information Services • Evanston Public Library • Evanston, IL 60201
Stonestreet Robert D. • Director • Public Library of Cincinnati and Hamilton County • Cincinnati, OH 45202
Stooksbury Stanley F. • School Librarian • Knox County Schools • Knoxville, TN 37901 • AASL ALSC
Stopka Christina K. • Buffalo Bill Historical Center Harold McCracken Research Libray • Cody, WY 82414 • ACRL
Stoppe Rebecca D. • El Dorado, AR 71730 • AASL ALSC
Stoppel William A. • Director of Library • Drake University Cowles Library • Des Moines, IA 50311 • ACRL ALCTS *Life*
Storaekre Linda C. • Student • CW Post Palmer Grad L Sch • Brookville, NY 11548 • IFRT SRRT
Storck Bernadette R. • Library Administrator • Pinellas Public Library Cooperative • Clearwater, FL 34624 • LAMA PLA
Storck John N. • Bluffton, OH 45817 • Continuing
Storck John W P • Director • Martins Ferry Public Library • Martins Ferry, OH 43935
Storer Charlotte • Trustee • Des Plaines Public Library • Des Plaines, IL 60016 • ALTA PLA
Storey-Ewoldt Veronica L. • Consultant • Plains & Peaks Regional Library System • Colorado Spgs, CO 80906-1967 • AASL ACRL PLA SRRT
Storey Gloria • Library Assistant • Fullerton College William T. Boyce Library • Fullerton, CA 92634
Storey Lorraine A. • Student • Syracuse University School of Information Studies • Syracuse, NY 13244-4100 • AASL
Stork Lenora P. • Columbia, SC 29206
Storm Tamara S. • Shelbyville Cmnty Sch Dist 4 • Shelbyville, IL 62565
Stormont Samuel R. • Coord. Computerized Ref. Serv. • Temple University Paley Library • Philadelphia, PA 19122
Storms Kate • Rensselaerville, NY 12147 • LAMA IFRT ILERT
Storrs James • Waco, TX 76710-1355
Storrs Jean E. S. • Baltimore, MD 21218 • IFRT
Storsteen Linda L. • Palmdale City Library • Palmdale, CA 93550 • LAMA PLA
Stortz Rose Marie • Head Librarian • Midland Senior High School • Midland, TX 79701 • AASL
Storwick Michael E. • Beaverton, OR 97005-5883
Story-Huffman Mary L. • Student • Emporia State University School of Library & Information Management • Emporia, KS 66801 • SRRT
Story Angela S. • Media Specialist • Oak Ridge High School • Orlando, FL 32809 • AASL
Story Dawn R. • Graduate Student • University of Iowa School of Library & Information Science • Iowa City, IA 52242
Stott Judith A. • Shaker Junior High School • Latham, NY 12110 • AASL
Stott Leisa • Librarian 1 • Church of Jesus Christ of Latter-Day Saints • Salt Lake City, UT 84150 • ACRL
Stottlemyer Gary L. • Systems Librarian • Shawnee State University Library • Portsmouth, OH 45662-4303 • ACRL LITA
Stotts Jolene • Vista, CA 92084
Stouffer Richard C. • Trustee • Rochester Hills Public Library • Rochester, MI 48307 • ALTA
Stoughton Judith M L • Head of Children's Services • Russell Library • Middletown, CT 06457
Stout-Mitchell TaJaun • Trustee • Memphis-Shelby County Public Library and Information Center • Memphis, TN 38104-4025
Stout Betty J. • Senior Librarian • Mountain View Public Library • Mountain View, CA 94041
Stout Don • Sale Representative • Quality Books Inc. • Lake Bluff, IL 60044-2204
Stout Mary A. • Community Campus Librarian • Pima Community College West Campus LRC • Tucson, AZ 85709 • ACRL ALCTS LITA
Stout Mary Ann • Lexington, KY 40508
Stout Mary J. • Library Director • Ohio University Southern Campus • Ironton, OH 45638-2296 • ACRL CLENE
Stout Paul W. • Map Librarian • Ball State University Bracken Library • Muncie, IN 47306-0160 • MAGERT
Stout Ruth • Branch Manager • San Mateo County Library Millbrae Branch • Millbrae, CA 94030
Stoutenburg Brian H. • Cherokee Regional Library Lafayette-Walker County Library • Lafayette, GA 30728
Stovall Naomi • Executive Assistant • Iowa Library Association • Des Moines, IA 50309
Stovel Madeleine D. • Research Libraries Group Inc. (RLG) • Mountain View, CA 94041-1100 • LITA
Stover Barbara • Goshen, NY 10924
Stover Elizabeth M. • Trustee • Vernon Area Public Library • Prairie View, IL 60069 • ALTA
Stover Lauren • Cataloging Librarian • Enoch Pratt Free Library • Baltimore, MD 21201-4484
Stover Mark • Library Director • The Library California Family Study Center • North Hollywood, CA 91607 • ACRL RASD
Stover Sarah Anna • Serial Cataloger • University of Southern California Doheny Library • Los Angeles, CA 90089-0182 • ALCTS
Stover Sherry K. • New Carrollton, MD 20784 • RASD
Stowe Fern E. • Sandy Spring, MD 20860 • ALCTS RASD *Life*
Stowe Jennifer • Nashua, NH 03063 • LAMA
Stowe Melinda S. • Head of Local Systems • University of Rochester Rush Rhees Library • Rochester, NY 14627 • LITA
Stowell Michael C. • Library Director • Tulare Public Library • Tulare, CA 93274 • PLA
Stowell Patricia K. • Librarian • Elmhurst Public Library • Elmhurst, IL 60126
Stowers Joel A. • Library Director • University of Tennessee at Martin Paul Meek Library • Martin, TN 38238-5047 • ACRL
Stowers Kim B. • School Librarian • Midland Independent School District • Midland, TX 79701 • AASL
Stowers Marianne W. • Cataloger-Librarian • Lincoln Library • Springfield, IL 62701 • ALCTS
Strable Edward G. • Chicago, IL 60637
Strable Jane S. • Weekend Reference Librarian • University of Chicago D'Angelo Law Library • Chicago, IL 60637 • ACRL GODORT
Strachan Elizabeth • District Media Director • Menomonie Area School District • Menomonie, WI 54751 • AASL
Strachan Evelyn A. • Children's Services Coordinator • Indianapolis Marion County Public Library • Indianapolis, IN 46206 • ALSC PLA *Life*
Strachman Esther A. • Librarian • Center for the Disabled • Albany, NY 12202 • AASL ASCLA
Strack Nancy • Student • Northern Illinois University Department of Library & Information Studies • DeKalb, IL 60115
Strader Bill • Head of Library Development • Nevada State Library & Archives • Carson City, NV 89710 • ASCLA LAMA LITA
Strader Jean • Student • Texas Woman's University School of Library & Information Studies • Denton, TX 76204
Strader Richard H. • Battle Creek Public Schools • Battle Creek, MI 49017 • AASL
Strader Thomas E. • Ponce Inlet, FL 32127 • ACRL LAMA *Life*
Strahan Michael F. • Computer Reference Services Ln. • Northern Michigan University Lydia M. Olson Library • Marquette, MI 49855 • LITA
Strahler Clytie E. • Associate Director Emeritus • Wittenberg University Thomas Library • Springfield, OH 45501 • Continuing
Straight Lana R. • Head of Branch Library • Ann Arbor Public Library • Ann Arbor, MI 48104
Straiton T. Harmon Jr. • Document & Microforms Dept Head • Auburn University Ralph Brown Draughon Library • Auburn, AL 36849-5606 • ACRL RASD GODORT
Straka Kathy Umbricht • Librarian • Southern New England Telephone Company • New Haven, CT 06511 • LITA
Straley Dona S. • Middle East Librarian • Ohio State University Libraries • Columbus, OH 43210-1286 • ACRL ALCTS
Strammiello Rosemary • Associate Editor • H. W. Wilson Company • Bronx, NY 10452 • LITA
Strand Myrtle L. Miss • Menomonie, WI 54751 • Continuing
Strand Ruth H. • Batavia, IL 60510
Strandtmann Sandra A. • Children's Librarian • Juneau Public Libraries • Juneau, AK 99801 • ALSC YALSA
Strange Christy • District Librarian • Storey County School District • Virginia City, NV 89440 • AASL PLA YALSA SRRT
Strange Michele M. • Columbia, MO 65203 • GODORT
Strange Thomas R. • Daniel Boone Regional Library • Columbia, MO 65205-1267 • LAMA PLA
Stratford Jean • Head Librarian • University of California-Davis Library • Davis, CA 95616 • GODORT
Stratford Juri • University of California-Davis Library • Davis, CA 95616 • GODORT
Stratford Sandra K. • Media Services Coordinator • Columbus College • Columbus, GA 31993

Stratford Vaughn M. • Director • San Rafael Public Library • San Rafael, CA 94901 • LAMA

Stratton Cynthia L. • Clarion, PA 16214 • PLA

Stratton Diane S. • Yuma County Library District • Yuma, AZ 85364

Stratton Elizabeth Gayle Mason • Princeton Public Library • Princeton, NJ 08542 • RASD

Stratton Eudocia Miss • Librarian • Jackson District Library • Jackson, MI 49201 • LAMA PLA *Life*

Stratton George • Director • North Olympic Library System • Port Angeles, WA 98362 • ALSC ALTA PLA GODORT

Stratton John B. • Stillwater, OK 74074 • Continuing

Stratton John M. • Bethany College Wallerstedt Library • Lindsborg, KS 67456-1896 • ACRL

Stratton June R. • Chicago, IL 60647

Stratton Margaret • Trustee • Nantahala Regional Library • Murphy, NC 28906 • ALTA

Stratton Sandra I. • Chesapeake, VA 23320 • ALSC

Stratton Stephen E. • Detroit, MI 48208 • RASD

Strauch Katina • Head of Collection Development • College of Charleston Robert Scott Small Library • Charleston, SC 29424 • ACRL ALCTS LITA RASD GODORT IRRT LRRT

Straughter Monica L. • Houston, TX 77057 • RASD

Straus Leslie S. • Innovative Interfaces, Inc. • Berkeley, CA 94710 • LITA

Strauss Amy E. • Director • Prospect Park Free Library • Philadelphia, PA 19076

Strauss Anita Phillips • The Library Power Project c/o Reader's Digest • New York, NY 10016 • AASL

Strauss Barbara J. • Product Support Specialist • OCLC Online Computer Library Center • Dublin, OH 43017-3395 • ACRL ALCTS LITA

Strauss Beverly V. • Library Teacher • Martin High School • Jamaica, NY 11434 • Continuing

Strauss Diane C. • Assoc. Univ. Librn. of Pub Servs • University of North Carolina Walter Royal Davis Library • Chapel Hill, NC 27599-3924 • ACRL LAMA RASD GODORT LIRT

Strauss Jill R. • Student • University of Wisconsin School of Library & Information Studies • Madison, WI 53706 • PLA

Strauss Kathleen G. • San Antonio Public Library • San Antonio, TX 78205 • LITA PLA

Strauss Michael E. • Senior Vice President, Marketing • Baker & Taylor Books • Bridgewater, NJ 08807-0920 • PLA

Strauss Richard F. • Librarian • Bucks County Free Library Pennwood Branch • Langhorne, PA 19047

Strauss Robert F. • Asst Tech Serv Ln/Assist Prof • University of North Carolina-Asheville D Hiden Ramsey Library • Asheville, NC 28804-3299

Strautman Ann E. • Student • University of Texas at Austin Graduate School of Library & Information Sciences • Austin, TX 78712-1276 • ALSC

Strautman Randolph B. • Assistant Director • Flint River Regional Library • Griffin, GA 30223 • LAMA PLA RASD

Stravinski Ceasar • Trustee • Saint Joseph County Public Library • South Bend, IN 46601 • ALTA

Straw Joseph G. • Student • Kent State University School of Library & Information Science • Kent, OH 44242-0001 • RASD

Strawder Maxine S. • Memphis, TN 38106 • EMIERT IRRT

Strawn Gary L. • Authority Ln, Catlgr.& Sys Anly. • Northwestern University Library • Evanston, IL 60208-2300 • ALCTS LITA SRRT *Life*

Strawn Jack Alton • Sul Ross Middle School • San Antonio, TX 78228

Strawn Patricia Ann • Librarian • John Jay High School • San Antonio, TX 78227

Strayer Jean-Jacques L. • Hunter College Library • New York, NY 10021 • ACRL

Strazer Michelle • Reference Librarian • College of Lake County Learning Resource Center • Grayslake, IL 60030

Straziuso Louisa • Reference Librarian • Shawnee State University Library • Portsmouth, OH 45662-4303 • LIRT

Strbak Ellen J. • Head, Technical Services Dept. • Onondaga County Public Library at the Galleries • Syracuse, NY 13202-2494 • ALCTS

Strecher Christine E. • Austin, TX 78751 • IFRT ILERT

Strecker Eleanor J. • Lawrence, KS 66049

Street Margery M. • Special Projects Librarian • Warringah Shire Library • New South Wales, Australia • PLA

Streeter Daniel D. • Cashier • University Book Store • Seattle, WA 98105

Streeter David • Supervisor/Special Collections • Pomona Public Library • Pomona, CA 91769-2271 • RASD SRRT

Strege Karen • Idaho State Library • Boise, ID 83702

Strehl Susan J. • Catalog/Reference Librarian • Southeastern Libraries Cooperating (SELCO) • Rochester, MN 55901 • PLA RASD

Streicher Selma B • Adult Reference Librarian • Los Angeles Public Library San Pedro Regional Branch • San Pedro, CA 90731

Streiff Jane • Delmar, NY 12054 • AASL

Streightiff W.A. Nancy • Volunteer Supervisor • Northome City Library • Northome, MN 56661

Streimer Marie J. • Harbor School • New London, CT 06320 • AASL

Streit Marla M. • Bourbonnais, IL 60914 • AASL

Streit Samuel A. • Asst Univ Ln For Spec Clln • Brown University Rockefeller Library • Providence, RI 02912 • ACRL

Streitfeld Shirley • Library Assistant III • Miami-Dade Public Library System • Miami, FL 33130-1504

Strelioff Kathleen S. • Senior Librarian • Los Angeles Public Library Angeles Mesa Branch • Los Angeles, CA 90043 • PLA

Strern Jane R. • Director/Trustee • Dorado Community Library • Dorado, PR 00646 • ALTA PLA

Streusand Alan L. • Trustee • Wilton Library Association Inc. • Wilton, CT 06897 • ALCTS LAMA LITA PLA RASD YALSA

Strever Diane E. • Shelton, CT 06484

Stricke Stella • Los Angeles, CA 90064

Strickland Elaine V. • Dodds-Med • Ankara, Turkey • AASL LITA

Strickland Elizabeth H. • Media Specialist • Buchholz High School • Gainesville, FL 32606 • AASL

Strickland Jane • Media Specialist • Cy-Fair Independent School District • Houston, TX 77041 • AASL

Strickland Martha E. • Director • Universal City Public Library • Universal City, TX 78148-4150 • LAMA PLA

Strickland Regina • Reference/ILL • Horseshoe Bend Regional Library • Dadeville, AL 36853

Strickland Robert L. • Media Specialist • Mayport Junior High School • Atlantic Beach, FL 32233

Strickland Stephanie A. • Liliha Public Library • Honolulu, HI 96817 • PLA IFRT

Strickland William C. • Reference Librarian • Tulane University Howard-Tilton Memorial Library • New Orleans, LA 70118 • ACRL

Strickler David M. • University of Southern California • Los Angeles, CA 90033 • LITA RASD

Strickler Richard L. • Toms River, NJ 08753 • Life

Strickler Sally A. • General Reference Librarian • Western Kentucky University Helm-Cravens Library • Bowling Green, KY 42101 • ACRL RASD

Stricoff Frances • Coor. Main Library Services • Smithtown Library • Smithtown, NY 11787 • PLA

Stricoff Roberta R. • Glen Head, NY 11545 • AASL

Striedieck Suzanne S. • Asst. Dir. ,Tech Svs & Clln Mgt • North Carolina State University D. H. Hill Library • Raleigh, NC 27695-7111 • ACRL ALCTS LAMA LITA LHRT LRRT

Striegel Mary Jane • Reference/ILL Librarian • Southwest State University • Marshall, MN 56258 • ACRL RASD *Life*

Strife Mary L. • Coordinator for Public Services • SUNY College of Technology Library • Utica, NY 13504 • ACRL

Strife Nancy Ralston • Crescent School • Waldwick, NJ 07463

Striman Brian D. • Head of Technical Services • University of Nebraska-Lincoln Libraries • Lincoln, NE 68588 • ACRL IFRT

Strimple Brenda Kay • South Ripley Jr-Sr High School • Versailles, IN 47042 • AASL

Striner Sara J. • Library of Congress • Washington, DC 20541

Stringer-Hye Richard S. • Student • Texas A & M University Sterling C. Evans Library • College Station, TX 77843-5000 • ACRL IRRT

Stringer Barbara J. • Rochester Hills, MI 48306 • ALSC

Stripling Barbara K. • Library Media Specialist • Fayetteville High School EC • Fayetteville, AR 72701 • AASL YALSA LIRT

Stripling Janet A. • Cataloging • H.W. Wilson Company • Bronx, NY 10452 • ALCTS

Stris Ellen C. • University of North Texas • Denton, TX 76203

Strobel Tracy R. • Student • State University of New York (SUNY) School of Information & Library Studies • Buffalo, NY 14260 • ACRL GODORT IFRT SRRT

Strober Katherine M. • Senior Assistant Librarian • California State University • San Bernardino, CA 92407 • ACRL

Stroberger Katherine Ann • Librarian II • Sonoma County Library • Santa Rosa, CA 95404 • PLA RASD YALSA IFRT SRRT

Stroble Janice A. • Ferguson Municipal Public Library • Ferguson, MO 63135

Strode Joanna M. • Director • Wabash Carnegie Public Library • Wabash, IN 46992 • PLA

Stroehlein Iola R. • Tucson, AZ 85719

Stroh Ann W. • Media Director • Pingry Elementary School Short Hills Campus • Short Hills, NJ 07078 • AASL

Strohecker Edwin C. • Horse Cave, KY 42749 • Continuing

Strohl Bonnie • Asst. Director for Public Serv. • University of Scranton Harry & Jeanette Weinberg Memorial • Scranton, PA 18510-4700 • ACRL LAMA RASD LIRT LRRT SRRT

Strohl LeRoy S. III • Director • Mary Washington College Library Simpson Library • Fredericksburg, VA 22401-4664 • ACRL LAMA

Strohl Mary P. • Regional Supervisor • Martin Luther King Branch Lib • Sacramento, CA 95831 • PLA

Strohmeyer Kristin L. • Reference Librarian • Hamilton College Burke Library • Clinton, NY 13323 • ACRL LIRT

Strom Kelly S. • Champaign, IL 61821 • PLA

Stroman Rosalie Holmes • Chief Readers Services Section • National Institutes of Health Library • Bethesda, MD 20892 • ACRL LITA

Stromberg Patricia R. • Library Media Specialist • Peiffer Elementary School • Littleton, CO 80127 • AASL

Stromgren Alice A. • Riverside, CA 92507 • AASL ILERT

Strommer Anne R. • College Coordinator,Tech Servs. • North Harris Montgomery Cmnty Coll Learning Resources Technical Center • Houston, TX 77060 • ACRL ALCTS LITA IFRT

Stromquist Frances L. • Chicago, IL 60640

Stromquist John • Assistant Manager • Westchester Cnty of Dept Plng County Data Processing • White Plains, NY 10601-3370 • LITA

Strong Bonnie J. • Director • Sharon Public Library • Sharon, MA 02067 • ALCTS ALSC LAMA LITA PLA RASD

Strong Bryce Y. • Head Librarian • Port Isabel Public Library • Port Isabel, TX 78578

Strong Gary E. • State Librarian • California State Library • Sacramento, CA 94237-0001 • ASCLA LAMA PLA *Life*

Strong Janet M. • Orientation Librarian • Boise State University Library • Boise, ID 83725 • ACRL

Strong Judith L. • Trenton, NJ 08618

Strong Judith T. • Coordinator of Children's Servs. • Chatham-Effingham-Liberty Regional Library (CEL) • Savannah, GA 31499-4301

Strong Marjorie J. • Student • McGill University Libraries • Montreal PQ, H3A 1Y1 Canada • NMRT

Strong Nancy E. • Library Media Specialist • Ellington High School • Ellington, CT 06029 • AASL YALSA

Strong Sandra S. • Director • Norwich City School • Norwich, NY 13815 • AASL

Strong Stacy • Springville, UT 84663-2171

Strong Sunny A. • Children's Services Coordinator • Sno-Isle Regional Library • Marysville, WA 98271-9164 • ALSC LAMA PLA YALSA CLENE LRRT

Strother Garland • Director • Saint Charles Parish Library • Luling, LA 70070

Stroud Lois C. • Media Specialist • Pelham Road Elementary School • Greenville, SC 29615 • AASL

Stroup Betty A. • Pittsburgh, PA 15227

Stroup Elizabeth F. • Director • Seattle Public Library • Seattle, WA 98104-1193 • ASCLA LAMA PLA RASD GODORT

Stroup Ruth Marie • Pittsburgh, PA 15227-1419 • Continuing

Strouse Roger L. • MMI Companies Inc. Resource Center • Deerfield, IL 60015 • ASCLA

Strowd Elvin E. • Durham, NC 27705

Stroyan Susan E. • University Librarian • Illinois Wesleyan University Sheean Library • Bloomington, IL 61702 • LAMA

Strozik Teresa F. • Director, Technical Services • Hamilton College Burke Library • Clinton, NY 13323 • ACRL ALCTS LAMA LITA

Strubbe Lisa Aren • Cincinnati, OH 45226

Strube Randy L. • Dubuque, IA 52001-8623 • AASL

Strubel Tamara K. • Children's Librarian • Rochester Public Library Wheatley Branch • Rochester, NY 14608

Struble Jacquelyn A. • Mountain View North School • Flanders, NJ 07836 • AASL

Struble Patricia J. • Librarian • Reorganized Church of Jesus Church • Independence, MO 64051 • RASD

Strunk Barbara C. • Librarian • Oneida Elementary Library • Oneida, TN 37841 • AASL

Strupp Sybil A. • Cataloger • University of Wisconsin-Stevens Point Library • Stevens Point, WI 54481

Struthers Donna G. • Head, Cataloging Department • Florida International University • Miami, FL 33199 • ALCTS LITA

Struthers Helen • Branch Manager • DeKalb County Library System Covington Library • Decatur, GA 30032

Struthers Lisa A. • Breckville, OH 44141 • ACRL
Struthers Sue A. • Riverside City & County Public Library • Riverside, CA 92502-0468 • ALSC
Struzik John F. • Student • University of Rhode Island Graduate School of Library & Information Studies • Kingston, RI 02881-0815 • ACRL IRRT NMRT
Stryer Andrea S. • New Spectrum • Stanford, CA 94305 • AASL
Strzelecki Kathleen • Worth School District #127 • Worth, IL 60482
Strzempka Mary Ellen • Librarian • Incarnation School Library • Sarasota, FL 34239
Stuart Crit • Asst. Dir. for Public Services • Georgia Institute of Technology Price Gilbert Memorial Library • Atlanta, GA 30332-0900 • ACRL LITA RASD
Stuart Gail W. • Assistant Librarian • Northern Esses Community College • Haverhill, MA 01830 • ACRL
Stuart Jeanne I • Student • Wayne State University Library Science Program • Detroit, MI 48202
Stuart Lynne M. • State College, PA 16801 • RASD
Stuart Mary H. MD • Trustee • State Library of Iowa • Des Moines, IA 50319 • ALTA
Stuart Mavis B. • Charlotte, NC 28209 • AASL
Stuart-Stubbs Basil • Vancouver BC, V6R 3K4 Canada
Stubbings Hilda U. • Bloomington, IN 47408-4215 • ACRL
Stubbins Sara L. • Librarian/Asst. Professor • Southwest Missouri State University Library • Springfield, MO 65804-0095 • AASL
Stubblefield Jane C. • Belmont Abbey College Library • Belmont, NC 28012
Stubbles Beverly A. • Director of Library Services • Sioux Falls College Norman B. Mears Library • Sioux Falls, SD 57105-1699
Stubbs Deborah L. • Bronx, NY 10475
Stubbs Janis T. • Head of Technical Services • Delaware County Library System • Brookhaven, PA 19015
Stubbs Judith A. • Technical & Computer Serv Assoc • Oral Roberts University Library • Tulsa, OK 74171
Stubbs Linda T. • Librarian • Library of Congress • Washington, DC 20541 • ALCTS
Stubbs Walter O. • Adminstrative Librarian • Opelousas-Eunice Public Library • Opelousas, LA 70570
Stuckert Jewell S. • Director • Katonah Village Library • Katonah, NY 10536
Stuckey Angie • Adult Services Coordinator • Dekalb County Public Library • Decatur, GA 30032 • PLA
Stuckey Janet H. • Asst Access/Admin Svs Libn. • Miami University Edgar W. King Library • Oxford, OH 45056 • ACRL LAMA
Stuckey Lindalee • Glen Ellyn, IL 60137
Stuckey Michele M. • Librarian • United States Patent & Trademark Office Scientific & Technical Information Center • Arlington, VA 22304
Stucki Curtis W. • Reference Librarian • Washington State Library • Olympia, WA 98504-2470 • ACRL ALCTS *Life*
Stuckman Elizabeth • Library Trustee • DeKalb County Public Library • Decatur, GA 30030 • ALTA
Stuckwish Chris E. • AV Librarian • Jefferson Parish Library Department • Metairie, LA 70010
Stucky Gail N. • Public Services Librarian • Bethel College Library • North Newton, KS 67117 • RASD
Stucky John C. • Head-Interlibrary Lending • Stanford University Libraries Cecil H. Green Library • Stanford, CA 94305-6004 • ACRL
Stucky Martha L. • North Newton, KS 67117 • ALSC *Continuing*
Studdard Fran • Librarian • Clear Lake High School Annex • Houston, TX 77058
Studdard Paul W. • Student • Clark-Atlanta University School of Library & Information Studies • Atlanta, GA 30314-4391
Studdert Ron Dr. • Media Serv/AV/Library Supv. • Carrollton Farmers Branch Independent School District • Carrollton, TX 75006 • AASL
Studdiford Abigail M. • Director • Middlesex County College Library • Edison, NJ 08818-3050 • ACRL ALCTS LITA
Studemeister Margarita S. • Publications Coordinator • National Security Archive • Washington, DC 20036
Studer Margaret A. • SNO Isle Regional Library System Arlington Public Library • Arlington, WA 98223 • YALSA
Studer William J. Dr. • Director of Libraries • Ohio State University Libraries • Columbus, OH 43210-1286 • ACRL
Studley Jeanette A. • Special Services Manager • Fairfax County Public Library Sherwood Regional Branch • Alexandria, VA 22306 • ASCLA LITA PLA
Studt Lindy • Media Specialist • Cicero School • Cicero, IL 60650 • AASL LIRT
Studwell William E. • Head Cataloger • Northern Illinois University University Libraries • DeKalb, IL 60115-2868 • ACRL ALCTS
Stueart Chris F. • Librarian • Charles River Associates • Boston, MA 02116 • LAMA LITA
Stueart Robert D. • Dean • Simmons College Graduate School of Library & Information Science • Boston, MA 02115 • AASL ACRL ALCTS ALSC LAMA PLA YALSA IFRT IRRT
Stuelpe Bonnie Dr. • Dir Interdisciplinary Studies • Fort Wayne Community Schools • Ft. Wayne, IN 46802 • AASL
Stuempfle Carol Denise • Brooklyn, NY 11226
Stueve Portia D. • Librarian • Community Unit School District 3 • Valmeyer, IL 62295 • AASL PLA
Stuff Marjorie A. • Lincoln, NE 68504 • Continuing
Stuhlman Daniel D. • Chicago, IL 60645
Stuivenga William J. • Database Reference Librarian • Southern Methodist University Fondren Library • Dallas, TX 75275-0135 • ACRL IFRT LIRT NMRT
Stukel Tony J. • Assistant Dir for Automation • University of Wisconsin • Milwaukee, WI 53201 • LITA
Stull Ann Marie • Seattle, WA 98105
Stull Nina F. • Fremont, CA 94539 • YALSA
Stull S. Louise • Fresno, CA 93710 • Continuing
Stumbaugh Colleen R.C. • Senior Processing Librarian • Library of Congress • Washington, DC 20541 • ACRL
Stumberg M. Sue • Highland, CA 92346
Stump Ron • Branch Manager • Riverside City & County Library • Moreno Valley, CA 92553
Stump Sandra L. • Acquisitions Librarian • Albright College • Reading, PA 19612-5234 • ACRL LITA
Stump Sheryl L. • Delta State University • Cleveland, MS 38733 • ALCTS
Stumpf Frances F. • Serials Librarian • Saint Louis University Pius XII Memorial Library • St. Louis, MO 63108 • ALCTS GODORT
Stunz Joan Betsy • Library Administrator • Tucson Pima Library • Tucson, AZ 85726 • PLA
Sturcken Rodney A. • Jefferson Parish Library Department • Metairie, LA 70010
Sturdivant Nan • Children's Servs. Coordinator • Tulsa City-County Library System • Tulsa, OK 74103 • ALSC PLA
Sturgell Sally S. • Librarian • Indian Creek Middle School Library • Trafalgar, IN 46181
Sturgeon C. Michael • Student • Palm Beach Atlantic College Library • W Palm Beach, FL 33401 • IFRT SRRT
Sturgeon Mary Lou • Librarian • Pick Elementary School • Fort Leonard Wood, MO 65473
Sturges Denyse K. • Student • University of Illinois at Chicago University Library • Chicago, IL 60680
Sturges Michelle M. • Cataloger • Kapiolani Community College Library • Honolulu, HI 96816 • IFRT NMRT
Sturgis Carl • Library Director • Richard Salter Storrs Library • Longmeadow, MA 01106 • PLA IFRT
Sturgis Jennifer L. • Science Reference Librarian • George Mason University Fenwick Library • Fairfax, VA 22030 • ACRL
Sturr Natalie O. • System Librarian • State University of New York (SUNY) Penfield Library • Oswego, NY 13126-3514
Sturtevant Anne F. • Cockeysville, MD 21030 • Continuing
Sturtevant Carolyn R. • LC Intern • Library of Congress Preservation Office • Washington, DC 20540 • ALCTS NMRT
Sturz John E. • Media Specialist • William Rainey Harper College Learning Resources Center • Palatine, IL 60067
Sturzl Alice A. • Instructional Media Specialist • Edith Evans Community Library • Laona, WI 54541 • AASL PLA
Stussman Barak R. • Student • University of Maryland College of Library and Information Services • College Park, MD 20742-4345 • LITA SRRT
Stussy Susan A. • Student • Washburn University of Topeka Mabee Library • Topeka, KS 66621 • ACRL LAMA
Stuter Janice C. • Principal Librarian • California Department of Corrections Education & Inmate Programs Unit • Sacramento, CA 94283-0001 • ASCLA
Stutts Corinne F. • Bow, NH 03304 • ACRL RASD
Stutts Shirley • School Librarian • Gattis Junior High School • Clovis, NM 88101 • AASL
Stutz Mary Hardee • A.W. Edwards Elementary School • Havelock, NC 28532 • AASL
Stwalley Louise T. • Government Documents Librarian • Auraria Higher Education Library • Denver, CO 80204 • GODORT
Stwodah M. Ibrahim • Head of Readers Services • Longwood College Library Dabney S Lancaster Library • Farmville, VA 23901
Stype Lynne • Librarian • Republic Middle School • Republic, MO 65738 • AASL
Su Jie • Student • Florida State University School of Library and Information Studies • Tallahassee, FL 32306-2048
Su Julie C. • Serials Cataloger • Indiana University-Purdue University at Indianapolis Library (IUPUI) • Indianapolis, IN 46202 • ALCTS
Su Mila C. • Sr. Assistant Librarian • Pennsylvania State University Robert E. Eiche Library • Altoona, PA 16601-3760 • ACRL RASD
Su Shiao-Feng • Student • University of Illinois Graduate School of Library and Information Science • Urbana, IL 61801 • LITA
Su Siew-Phek T. • Acquisition Librarian • University of Florida Libraries • Gainesville, FL 32611-2047 • ACRL ALCTS
Su Valerie L. • Deputy Dir & Hd of Pub Svs • Stanford University Lane Medical Library • Stanford, CA 94305-5323 • ACRL LAMA
Suber Catharine • Dayton, OH 45420 • PLA RASD *Continuing*
Subler Joyce Anne • San Antonio, TX 78250
Subrahmanyam Bhagirathi • University of California Los Angeles Graduate School of Library & Information Science • Los Angeles, CA 90024 • LITA
Subramania Ramya • Elizabeth, NJ 07201 • RASD
Subramanian Jane M. • Staff Associate • State Univ of NY Coll at Potsdam Frederick W. Crumb Memorial Library • Potsdam, NY 13676 • ALCTS
Suchy Mary Jo • Fred C. Fischer Library • Belleville, MI 48111
Suda Jane T. • San Francisco, CA 94115 • ACRL IFRT NMRT SRRT
Suda Rullie A. • Shoreham, NY 11786 • AASL
Sudall Arthur D. • Director • Rahway Public Library • Rahway, NJ 07065
Sudderth Christy L. • Ardmore, OK 73401 • AASL
Suddeth Paula F. • Director • Elbert County Library • Elberton, GA 30635
Sudduth Elizabeth • Head of Technical Services • Randolph-Macon College McGraw-Page Library • Ashland, VA 23005 • ACRL ALCTS LAMA LITA
Sudduth Gary Neill • Trustee • Minneapolis Public Library & Information Center • Minneapolis, MN 55401-1992 • ALTA PLA
Sudduth William E. • Ref. Ln/Coor. of Govt. Documents • University of Richmond • Richmond, VA 23173 • ACRL RASD GODORT
Sudekum Katharine • Annandale, NJ 08801 • LITA
Suderman Robert C. • Director of LRC • Bethel College • Saint Paul, MN 55112 • ACRL ALCTS LAMA LITA RASD
Sudmalis Linda M. • Kent, OH 44240 • EMIERT IFRT SRRT
Sudo Minako • Assistant Professor • Yamawaki-Gaknen Junior College • Minato-ku, Tokyo 107, Japan • ACRL
Suelflow Sara C. • Student • University of Illinois Graduate School of Library and Information Science • Urbana, IL 61801 • LITA PLA
Suemnicht Allen • Head, Adult Services • Belleville Public Library • Belleville, IL 62220 • IFRT
Suess Mary • Librarian • Milwaukee Public Library • Milwaukee, WI 53233
Suessmuth Charles • Deer Park Public Library • Deer Park, TX 77536 • LAMA PLA
Suever Sharon C. • Huntsville, AL 35802
Suffecool Tracy A. • Conrwall-on-Hudson, NY 12520
Sugar William A • Bloomington, IN 47401 • ACRL
Sugden Barbara L. • Head Librarian • Barrington Public Library District • Barrington, IL 60010 • LAMA
Sugden Martin D. • Reference Librarian • Jacksonville Public Libraries Main Library • Jacksonville, FL 32202 • LAMA RASD
Sugg Espert A. • San Francisco, CA 94112
Suggs Michelle • Trustee • Lincoln Library • Springfield, IL 62701 • ALTA
Suggs Sharon A J • Asst. Coor. Adult Services • District of Columbia Public Library Martin Luther King Memorial Library • Washington, DC 20001 • RASD YALSA
Suggs Wayne L. • Library Supervisor • Richland Public Library • Richland, WA 99352-3539 • LAMA PLA RASD
Sugimura Sue S. • Librarian • Hawaii State Library System Library for the Blind & Phys Hndcpd • Honolulu, HI 96815-3894 • ASCLA
Sugnet Christopher • Acquisitions Librarian • University of Arizona Library • Tucson, AZ 85721 • ALCTS
Sugranes Maria R. • Manager, Automation Services • California State University-Long Beach University Library & Learning Resources • Long Beach, CA 90840-1901 • LITA
Suhrweier C. V. • Toledo, OH 43606 • ASCLA YALSA *Continuing*
Sui May • San Francisco, CA 94122
Suitch Susan L. • Student • Drexel University W. W. Hagerty Library • Philadelphia, PA 19104 • ACRL RASD
Sujka Debra Jo • Ryerson Polytech Institute • Toronto ON, M5B 2K3 Canada

Sukiennik Adelaide Weir • Asst. Director for Collections • University of Pittsburgh Hillman Library • Pittsburgh, PA 15260 • ACRL ALCTS SRRT

Sukovich John E. • Jalis Inc. Management Systems • Newberry, SC 29108 • ACRL

Sukut Joyce • Branch Librarian • Lakes Region Library • Inverness, FL 32652-4507 • PLA

Sulenski Toby V. Mrs • Reference Librarian • Las Vegas-Clark County Library District Flamingo Library • Las Vegas, NV 89119 • RASD GODORT

Sulerud Grace K. • Acquisitions & Reference Ln • Augsburg College George Sverdrup Library • Minneapolis, MN 55454 • ACRL

Sulik Cinde • St Thomas More High School • Lafayette, LA 70508 • AASL

Sullenger Lee W. • Head of Reference • Stephen F. Austin State University Steen Library • Nacogdoches, TX 75962 • ACRL

Sullenger Paula • Student • University of North Carolina at Chapel Hill School of Information and Library Science • Chapel Hill, NC 27599-3360 • ALCTS IFRT IRRT

Sullewsky Marianne • Huntington, NY 11743-1127 • SRRT

Sulli Cathleen P. • Director • North Salem Free Library • North Salem, NY 10560 • NMRT

Sulli Gerard • Media Specialist • Uriah Hill Elementary School • Peekskill, NY 10566

Sullivan Ann B. • Librarian • Sadie Saulter Elementary School • Greenville, NC 27834 • AASL

Sullivan Barbara A. • Extension Services Coordinator • Oceanside Public Library • Oceanside, CA 92054 • LAMA

Sullivan Becky L. • Meridian, MS 39305

Sullivan BenDell Miss • Fort Worth, TX 76103 • AASL ALSC   *Life*

Sullivan Beverly M. • Somerset, MA 02726

Sullivan Bud M. Jr. • Trustee • Lodi Public Library • Lodi, CA 95240

Sullivan Calista S. • Supervisor, Technical Services • Humboldt County Library • Eureka, CA 95501

Sullivan Carol Wood • Systems Librarian • United States Air Force Academic Library Institute of Technology • Wright-Patterson AFB, OH 45433 • LITA AFLRT

Sullivan Catherine M. • Reference Librarian • South Orange Public Library • South Orange, NJ 07079 • PLA RASD NMRT

Sullivan Cecil G. • Bronx, NY 10462 • RASD   *Continuing*

Sullivan Christine P. • Peahala Park, NJ 08008-3302

Sullivan Clare M. • Librarian • Saint Joseph High School Library • Trumbull, CT 06611

Sullivan Constance • Costabile Associates Inc • Bethesda, MD 20814 • ALCTS

Sullivan David • Rare Book Librarian • Stanford University Libraries Cecil H. Green Library • Stanford, CA 94305-6004 • ACRL

Sullivan Edith E. • Essex RM2-5BA, England

Sullivan Eileen M. • Children's Services Director • Cook Memorial Library • Libertyville, IL 60048

Sullivan Ellen • Tylertown, MS 39667

Sullivan Frances Anna • Wichita, KS 67212 • ALSC PLA
Continuing

Sullivan James L. • Librarian • Braircliff College • Miami, FL 33165

Sullivan Jane G. • Branch Head • South Cobb Branch • Mableton, GA 30059 • ALSC PLA

Sullivan Janice • Jesuit Preparatory School • Dallas, TX 75244 • AASL

Sullivan Jeanne M. • Chesterfield, MO 63017-4910

Sullivan Jennifer B. • Newburgh, IN 47630

Sullivan Joan B. • Outreach Librarian • Dane County Library Service • Madison, WI 53703

Sullivan Karen Collamore • Student • University of Michigan School of Information and Library Studies • Ann Arbor, MI 48109-1092

Sullivan Kate A. • Project Manager • University Microfilms International • Ann Arbor, MI 48106-1346

Sullivan Kathleen A. • Thousand Oaks Library • Thousand Oaks, CA 91362 • RASD IFRT

Sullivan Kathleen S. • Managing Libn.,Traveling Lib. • King County Library System • Seattle, WA 98109-5191 • PLA RASD

Sullivan Kathryn • Periodicals Librarian • Winona State University • Winona, MN 55987 • LITA

Sullivan Kathy • Student • California State University-Long Beach University Library & Learning Resources • Long Beach, CA 90840-1901

Sullivan Kelley • Librarian • Massac County High School • Metropolis, IL 62960 • AASL

Sullivan Kelli A. • Elementary School Librarian • Unified School District Tecumseh North Elementary School • Tecumseh, KS 66542 • AASL

Sullivan Kenneth A. • Medical Informatics Specialist • University of Florida Health Science Center Library • Gainesville, FL 32610 • PLA

Sullivan Larry E. • Chief, Rare Bk & Spec Clln Div • Library of Congress • Washington, DC 20541 • ACRL LHRT

Sullivan Laura A. • Reference Librarian • Northern Kentucky University Steely Library • Highland Heights, KY 41099-6101 • ACRL

Sullivan Laura T. • Library Administrator • Tucson Pima Library • Tucson, AZ 85726 • LAMA PLA

Sullivan Leonard • San Francisco, CA 94118 • Continuing

Sullivan Louise B. • New Britain, CT 06053

Sullivan Lucia F. • Columbus School for Girls • Columbus, OH 43209

Sullivan M. Ann Cornelia Sr. • Holy Name Academy • Seattle, WA 98112 • AASL

Sullivan Margaret M. • West Lafayette, IN 47906 • ACRL ALCTS   *Life*

Sullivan Marian L. • Trustee • Oak Lawn Public Library • Oak Lawn, IL 60453 • ALTA

Sullivan Mary S. • Tampa, FL 33604

Sullivan Maureen • New Haven, CT 06511 • ACRL LAMA CLENE

Sullivan Michael V. • Librarian • University of California-Los Angeles (UCLA) • Los Angeles, CA 90024-1450 • ACRL

Sullivan Michele F. • Palo Alto, CA 94306

Sullivan Nancy J. • Branch Manager • Columbus Metropolitan Library • Columbus, OH 43215 • PLA

Sullivan Peggy • Executive Director • American Library Association 60611-2795 • ACRL ALSC • Life

Sullivan Peter G. • Patient Education Librarian • Veteran Administration Medical Center • Dayton, OH 45428

Sullivan Philip L. • Adult Services Coor. • Madison Public Library • Madison, WI 53703

Sullivan Rebecca W. • Director • Terrell Public Library • Terrell, TX 75160 • LAMA PLA

Sullivan Robert • Trustee • Clark County Public Library • Springfield, OH 45501-1080 • ALTA

Sullivan Robert C. • Huntingtown, MD 20639 • ACRL ALCTS   *Life*

Sullivan Robert J. Jr • Reference Librarian • Reed, Smith, Shaw and McClay • Pittsburgh, PA 15219 • RASD

Sullivan Sharon A. • Personnel Librarian • Ohio State University Libraries • Columbus, OH 43210-1286 • ACRL

Sullivan Sharon G. • Northeast Sales Manager • Yankee Book Peddler • Contoocook, NH 03229 • ACRL ALCTS

Sullivan Suzanne • Assistant Librarian • Goodall Memorial Library Sanford Public Library • Sanford, ME 04073 • PLA GODORT

Sullivan Thomas E. • Pittsboro, NC 27312-8549

Sullivant Jean A. • Assistant Director for Info Serv • Mount Sinai Medical Center Levy Library • New York, NY 10029 • ACRL SRRT

Sulman Gail M. • Treasure Island Elementary School • North Bay Village, FL 33141 • AASL

Sulouff Patricia T. • Syracuse University School of Information Studies • Syracuse, NY 13244-4100 • ACRL RASD

Sultana John G. • Student • Pratt Institute Graduate School of Library & Information Science • Brooklyn, NY 11205 • RASD SRRT

Sultemeier Susan A. • Adult Reference Librarian • Albuquerque Public Library Juan Tabo Branch • Albuquerque, NM 87111 • RASD

Sulzbach Deborah E. • Librarian • Public Library of Des Moines • Des Moines, IA 50308-1791

Sulzer John H. • Head, General Reference Sections • Pennsylvania State University Libraries • University Park, PA 16802 • ACRL GODORT

Sumberg Alfred D. • Associate General Secretary • American Association of University Professors (AAUP) • Washington, DC 20005

Sumerford Steve • Branch Librarian • Greensboro Public Library Vance H. Chavis Lifelong • Greensboro, NC 27405 • LAMA PLA

Sumler Claudia B. • Camden County Library Echelon Urban Center • Voorhees, NJ 08043 • LAMA PLA CLENE

Summa James D. • Queensbury, NY 12804

Summer Morton J. • Trustee • Finkelstein Memorial Library • Spring Valley, NY 10977

Summer Penelope • Student • University of South Carolina College of Library & Information Science • Columbia, SC 29208

Summer Susan Cook • Original Monographs Catlg Dept. • Columbia University Libraries • New York, NY 10027 • ACRL ALCTS IFRT

Summerfield Carol J. • Editorial Director • Ferguson Publishing Company • Chicago, IL 60606

Summerhill Craig A. • Systems Coordinator • Coalition for Networked Information • Washington, DC 20036 • ACRL LITA

Summerhill Karen Storin • Education Services Coordinator • Georgetown University Law Center • Washington, DC 20001 • ACRL LIRT

Summers Carol J. • Oxnard Public Library • Oxnard, CA 93030 • RASD

Summers F. William • Dean • Florida State University School of Library and Information Studies • Tallahassee, FL 32306-2048 • ASCLA PLA LRRT

Summers George V. Dr. • Director • East Stroudsburg University Kemp Library • East Stroudsburg, PA 18301 • ACRL LRRT

Summers Linda E. • Librarian • Greenburgh Public Library • Elmsford, NY 10523

Summers Lorraine S. • Assistant State Librarian • State Library of Florida Division of Library & Information Services • Tallahassee, FL 32399-0250 • ASCLA

Summers Michael • Librarian • Queens Borough Public Library • Jamaica, NY 11432 • NMRT

Summers Ruth O. • Director • Pittsford Community Library • Pittsford, NY 14534 • LAMA PLA

Summerville F. Lovenia • Cataloging Unit Head • University of North Carolina at Charlotte J. Murrey Atkins Library • Charlotte, NC 28223 • ACRL ALCTS LAMA LITA LRRT

Sumner Ellen L. • Athens, GA 30606 • LHRT

Sumner William • Personnel Assistant • Civil Services Commission City of San Francisco • San Francisco, CA 94103

Sumners William M. • Chicago Public Library • Chicago, IL 60605

Sump Gretchen • Library Director • Clarinda Public Library • Clarinda, IA 51632 • LAMA PLA RASD

Sumpter Ethel L. • Rdr Adv Hist Div • District of Columbia Public Library Martin Luther King Memorial Library • Washington, DC 20001

Sumpter Martha K. • Base Librarian • United States Air Force • Kirtland AFB, NM 87115

Sumrall Annette • Irving Public Schools Bowie Junior High School • Irving, TX 75060

Sumrall Richard M. • Library Director • Lincoln Public Library • Lincoln, IL 62656 • PLA

Sun Bob H. T. • Head of Catalog Dept. • University of West Florida John C. Pace Library • Pensacola, FL 32514 • ACRL ALCTS

Sun Frank H. • Serials Dept. • University of Nebraska Love Library • Lincoln, NE 68588-0410 • ALCTS

Sun Hongyi • Student • Saint John's University School of Law Library • Jamaica, NY 11439

Sunanda Susan • Albany, NY 12208

Sund Carole S. • Information Specialist • The Network, Inc. • Andover, MA 01810 • ACRL

Sund Cheryl L. • Librarian • United States Geological Survey • Denver, CO 80225 • FLRT MAGERT

Sundaram Anita • Director of Technical Service • National University Library • San Diego, CA 92108

Sundberg Debra • Trustee • Sioux City Public Library • Sioux City, IA 51101-1203 • ALTA

Sundberg Mary P. • Holland Patent Free Library • Holland Patent, NY 13354

Sunde Esther • Student • University of Washington Graduate School of Library and Information Science • Seattle, WA 98195

Sundell Jonathan D. • Children's Librarian • Rural Hall Stanleyville Branch Library • Rural Hall, NC 27045

Sunderman Joanne • Director • Pioneer Memorial Library • Colby, KS 67701 • PLA

Sunderman John Mr. • Trustee • Summit Public Library District • Summit, IL 60501

Sundin Kimberley K. • Student • University of Arizona Graduate Library School • Tucson, AZ 85721

Sundstrom Donna G. • Director • Winnetka Public Library District • Winnetka, IL 60093 • PLA

Sung Carolyn H. • Exec. Officer Constituent Serv. • Library of Congress • Washington, DC 20541 • ACRL

Sung Lop-Choi L.C. • Student • University of Wisconsin-River Falls Chalmer Davee Library • River Falls, WI 54022 • ALCTS

Sung Wei-Nee • Flushing, NY 11367 • ACRL NMRT

Suni Julie • Longmont, CO 80503

Suniga Cynthia R. • Austin, TX 78752

Suopis Mary Jean • Student • Rutgers University School of Communication Information & Library Studies • New Brunswick, NJ 08903

Suozzi Patricia A. • Director • Chatham College • Pittsburgh, PA 15232 • ACRL LAMA RASD

Supler Nancy B. • Elementary School Librarian • Sudley Elementary School • Manassas, VA 22110 • AASL

Suput Ray R. • Ball State University Department of Library & Information Science • Muncie, IN 47306-1099 • ACRL   *Continuing*

Surato Edward J. • New Haven, CT 06512 • PLA

Surface Laurie • Director • Tazewell County Public Library • Tazewell, VA 24651 • PLA

Surles Judith C. • Director • Allerton Public Library • Monticello, IL 61856 • PLA

Suruda Anne R. • Student • University of Washington Graduate School of Library and Information Science • Seattle, WA 98195 • IFRT

Sus Maryann • Head of Library • Lake County Public Library Highland Branch • Highland, IN 46322

Susinos Pablo • Student • University of Texas at Austin Graduate School of Library & Information Sciences • Austin, TX 78712-1276

Sussman Marge • Children's Librarian • Berkeley Public Library West Branch • Berkeley, CA 94702 • ALSC EMIERT SRRT

Suter Cindy E. • Memphis, TN 38104

Suter Jean M. • Student • Rosary College Graduate School of Library & Information Science • River Forest, IL 60305

Suter Marcia • Learning Resources Ctr Dir. • University of Toledo Scott Park Campus • Toledo, OH 43606 • ACRL ILERT

Suter Millie • Conservator & Manager • Ocker & Trapp Library Bindery Inc. • Emerson, NJ 07630 • ALCTS

Sutherland Helen G. • School Librarian • Cedar Grove School Evergreen Sch Dist • San Jose, CA 95148 • AASL

Sutherland Iva M. • University Presbyterian Church • Seattle, WA 98105 • ASCLA LITA

Sutherland Jacqueline K. • Student • University of South Florida Library • Tampa, FL 33620-5600

Sutherland Jamie D. • Adult Literacy Coordinator • City of Commerce Public Library • Commerce, CA 90040

Sutherland Laurie • Head of Serials Acquisitions • University of Washington Suzzallo Library • Seattle, WA 98195 • ALCTS

Sutherland Louise V. • Administrative Librarian • U S Department of Education • Washington, DC 20208-5571 • AASL ACRL ALCTS LITA FLRT

Sutherland Mary K. • Illinois Library Computer System Office • Champaign, IL 61820 • ALCTS SRRT

Sutherland Mary-Morag • Office of Development • University of Chicago • Chicago, IL 60637 • ACRL RASD

Sutherland Monika • Owner • Unicorn Books • Tarboro, NC 27886

Sutherland Peter B • Student • Long Island University Palmer School of Library & Information Science • Greenvale, NY 11548 • LITA

Sutherland Richard R. • Librarian,Instruction • Foothill College Library • Los Altos Hills, CA 94022-4599 • ACRL LIRT SRRT

Sutherland Susan • Trustee • Yankee Book Peddler • Contoocook, NH 03229 • ALCTS

Sutherland Thomas A. • Director • Paducah Public Library • Paducah, KY 42001 • LAMA PLA

Sutherland Timothy L. • Research Librarian • Indiana University Northwest Library • Gary, IN 46408 • GODORT

Sutherland Zena B. • University of Chicago Graduate Library School • Chicago, IL 60637 • ALSC

Suttell Katherine H. • Librarian III, Information Line • Atlanta-Fulton Public Library • Atlanta, GA 30303 • PLA

Sutter Sem C. • W. European Bibliographer • University of Chicago Library • Chicago, IL 60637-1502 • ACRL IFRT SRRT

Suttersield Debra A. • Director • White River Regional Library • Batesville, AR 72501 • PLA

Suttle George • Student • Montana State University • Bozeman, MT 59717-0332

Suttle Jacqueline A. • Saint Pius X High School • Albuquerque, NM 87110

Sutton Anne G. • Library Director • Riviera Beach Public Library • Riviera Beach, FL 33404 • AASL LAMA PLA YALSA EMIERT ILERT

Sutton Carolyn P. • Librarian • Hanahan High School • Charleston, SC 29406 • AASL

Sutton Clara • Media Specialist • Washington-Wilkes Comprehensive High School • Washington, GA 30673 • AASL

Sutton Ellen D. • Anthropology & Psych Subj Spec • University of Illinois Library • Urbana, IL 61801 • ACRL RASD

Sutton J. Brett • Assistant Professor • University of Illinois Graduate School of Library and Information Science • Urbana, IL 61801 • LITA IFRT

Sutton James E. • Director • Morse Inst Library • Natick, MA 01760 • LAMA

Sutton Joann F. • San Francisco, CA 94116 • IFRT

Sutton Joanna • Supervisor • Hughes Aircraft Company Space & Communications Group • Los Angeles, CA 90009

Sutton Joanne • Library Director • Moscow Public Schools • Moscow, ID 83843 • AASL

Sutton Judith K. • Deputy Director • Public Library of Charlotte & Mecklenburg County • Charlotte, NC 28202 • LAMA PLA IFRT

Sutton Lynn Sorensen • Director • Wayne State University Science & Engineering Library • Detroit, MI 48202 • ACRL

Sutton Robert F. • Plymouth Meeting, PA 19462 • Continuing

Sutton Roger • Executive Editor • Bulletin of the Center for Children's Books • Chicago, IL 60637 • ALSC YALSA

Sutton Sandra A. • Librarian • Washington Elementary School • Phoenix, AZ 85051

Sutton Sandra K. • Adjunct Librarian • Medgar Evers College Library • Brooklyn, NY 11225

Sutton Sandra Kellogg • Helena, AL 35080 • ALCTS RASD *Life*

Sutton Stuart A. • Lecturer • University California-Berkeley • Berkeley, CA 94720

Sutton Suzanne D. • Reference Librarian • Palm Springs Public Library • Palm Springs, CA 92262 • PLA RASD

Suvak Daniel S. • Director • Walsh College Library • North Canton, OH 44720-3396 • ACRL

Suyat Patsy H. • Librarian • Mckinley High Sch Lib • Honolulu, HI 96814 • AASL

Suzuki Hiroaki • Librarian • Aoyama Gakuin University Library • Tokyo, Japan • ACRL ALCTS

Suzuki Yukihisa • President • Kyoto University of Foreign Studies • Kyoto, Japan • ACRL ALCTS *Life*

Svang Marie A. • Library Aide III • Minneapolis Public Library Washburn Branch • Minneapolis, MN 55419

Svee Beth • Director • Santa Clara Public Library • Santa Clara, CA 95051 • ALCTS ALSC LAMA PLA RASD YALSA

Sveinsson Joan L. • Director • The Colony Public Library • The Colony, TX 75056-1219

Svengalis Kendall F. • State Law Librarian • Rhode Island Supreme Court State Law Library • Providence, RI 02906

Svenonius Elaine F. • Professor • University of California Los Angeles Graduate School of Library & Information Science • Los Angeles, CA 90024 • ALCTS

Svibruck Jonathan • Blauvelt, NY 10913 • AASL ALSC LIRT

Swade Susanna • Elementary Principal • Columbus City Public Schools Olde Orchard Elementary School • Columbus, OH 43213 • AASL ALSC

Swadley Victoria D. • Student • University of Missouri-Columbia School of Library & Informational Science • Columbia, MO 65211 • ALSC

Swafford Carolyn J. • Librarian • Groton Public Library • Groton, CT 06340

Swafford William M A • State Documents Department • Riverside City & County Public Library • Riverside, CA 92502-0468 • GODORT IFRT

Swaim Carolyn S. • Media Specialist • Randleman High School Media Center • Randleman, NC 27317 • AASL

Swaim Elinor H. • Salisbury, NC 28144 • ALTA

Swaim Elizabeth A. • Special Collections Librarian • Wesleyan University Olin Memorial Library • Middletown, CT 06459 • ACRL LITA *Life*

Swaim Glendora R. • Bloomington, IN 47404-1865

Swaim Tracy N. • Acting Head of Technical Serv. • Alaska State Library • Juneau, AK 99811-571 • ALCTS PLA

Swain Barbara C. • Home Economics Librarian • University of Illinois • Urbana, IL 61801 • ACRL

Swain Michelle R. • Student • Southern Illinois University Dept. of Curriculum & Instr. • Carbondale, IL 62901 • ALSC PLA

Swain Trudi G. • Haverford College James P. Magill Library • Haverford, PA 19041 • ACRL

Swaine Cynthia Wright • Instruction Librarian • Old Dominion University Library • Norfolk, VA 23529-0256 • LIRT

Swaine Lynne E. • Librarian • Rockingham County Public Library Eden Branch • Eden, NC 27288 • PLA IFRT

Swalboski Marlys • Director • Buckham Memorial Library • Faribault, MN 55021

Swalley Linda S. • Houston Public Library Jungman Branch • Houston, TX 77057

Swallow Lanny T. • Head, Reference Department • Palos Verdes Library District • Pls Vrd Pnsla, CA 90274

Swallow Robin T. • Librarian • Hermosa Beach School District • Hermosa Beach, CA 90254

Swalwell Lila L. • Seattle, WA 98103 • AASL

Swan Elaine C. • Director • Stickney-Forest View Library • Stickney, IL 60402 • LAMA

Swan Frank J. • Director • Uinta County Library Evanston Branch • Evanston, WY 82930

Swan James A. • Director • Central Kansas Library System • Great Bend, KS 67530-4090 • LAMA PLA

Swan John C. • Director • Bennington College Crossett Library • Bennington, VT 05201 • ACRL IFRT SRRT

Swan Martha E. • Periodicals & Microforms Lbrn. • University of Mississippi John Davis Williams Library • University, MS 38677 • ACRL

Swan Sally A. • Post Librarian • Robert F. Barrick Memorial Library • Fort Ritchie, MD 21719

Swan Sandra J. • Wichita, KS 67208-1609 • RASD SRRT

Swanbeck Jan B. • Head of Document Division • University of Florida Libraries • Gainesville, FL 32611-2047 • GODORT

Swanekamp Joan • Head, Original Monographs Catlg. • Columbia University Libraries Butler Library • New York, NY 10027 • ALCTS LITA

Swank Laurie • Student • Northern Illinois University Department of Library & Information Studies • DeKalb, IL 60115 • AFLRT SRRT

Swank Raynard C. • Professor Emeritus • University of California-Berkeley School of Library & Information Studies • Berkeley, CA 94720 • ACRL LITA *Life*

Swank Rebecca J. • Librarian • Advanced Information Consultants • Canton, MI 48187

Swank Sallie E. • Student • Texas Woman's University School of Library & Information Studies • Denton, TX 76204

Swanker Esther M. • Schenectady, NY 12308

Swann James T. • Media Coordinator • Jacksonville High School • Jacksonville, NC 28540 • AASL

Swansen Cynthia N. • Women's History Research Center • Washington, DC 20036

Swanson Ann • Administrator • North Central Regional Library • Mason City, IA 50401 • PLA

Swanson Audrey E. • Minneapolis, MN 55423

Swanson Barbara • Director • Portland Community College Library • Portland, OR 97219

Swanson Barbara • Head of Support Services • Kern County Library System • Bakersfield, CA 93301

Swanson Carl O. • Chicago, IL 60646 • Continuing

Swanson Charleen M. • Librarian II-Branch Head • Riverside City & County Public Library Arlington Branch • Riverside, CA 92563 • PLA

Swanson Claire • Librarian • Cedar Grove High School Memorial Middle School • Cedar Grove, NJ 07009 • AASL

Swanson Coral S. • Arrowhead Library System • Janesville, WI 53545 • LAMA PLA

Swanson Cynthia • Sn Francisco, CA 94109

Swanson Dawn C. • Library Branch Supervisor • Chesterfield County Public Library Bon Air Branch • Richmond, VA 23235 • PLA

Swanson Dawn J. • Librarian II • Berkeley Public Library • Berkeley, CA 94704

Swanson Dorothy A. • Head of Branch Services • Hillsboro Public Library Tanasbourne Branch • Portland, OR 97229

Swanson Edward • Principal Cataloger • Minnesota Historical Society • Saint Paul, MN 55102 • ACRL ALCTS LITA GODORT IRRT MAGERT *Life*

Swanson Eleanor K. • Head of Technical Services • Saint Charles Public Library • St. Charles, IL 60174

Swanson Grace B. Mrs • Minneapolis, MN 55436 • Life

Swanson Jean R. • Technical Services Librarian • University of Redlands Armacost Library • Redlands, CA 92374-3758 • ACRL ALCTS

Swanson Joanne • Learning Center Director • Nelson Elementary School • Batavia, IL 60510 • AASL

Swanson Karen A. • Coordinator • Mesa County School District #51 • Grand Junction, CO 81503 • AASL

Swanson Kenneth G. • Administrative Librarian • Indian Trails Public Library District • Wheeling, IL 60090 • LAMA PLA

Swanson Linda • Circulation Manager • Concordia College Carl B. Ylvisaker Library • Moorhead, MN 56562

Swanson M Corrine Miss • Librarian • Ramsey Jr High School Library • Minneapolis, MN 55441 • AASL YALSA *Life*

Swanson Mary L. • Library Media Specialist • Normandy Elementary School • Littleton, CO 80123 • AASL IFRT

Swanson Patricia K. • Assistant Director • University of Chicago Library John Crerar Library • Chicago, IL 60637-1403 • ACRL

Swanson Ron • Fort Vancouver Regional Library • Vancouver, WA 98663 • LITA

Swanson Sandra E. • Staff Librarian • Butterworth Hospital Health Science Library • Grand Rapids, MI 49503-2599 • GODORT

Swanson Stanley S. • Corvallis, OR 97330 • Continuing

Swanson Susan E. • Winchester, MA 01890

Swanson Winifred L. • Coordinator of Adult Services • Sonoma County Library • Santa Rosa, CA 95404 • PLA RASD

Swantko Karen M. • Ansonia, CT 06401

Swarbrick Maria • Student • University of Alberta • Edmonton, AB T6G 2J4 Canada

Swarlis Linda • Sewickley Academy • Sewickley, PA 15143 • AASL

Swarthout Betsy S. • Reference Librarian • Western Carolina University Hunter Library • Cullowhee, NC 28723-9002 • LIRT NMRT

Swartout Deborah B. • Director: Academic Support Serv. • Antioch/New England Graduate School • Keene, NH 03431 • ACRL LITA RASD SRRT

Swartz-Truesdell Linda • Hd,Publicity Programming, Sys Sv • Kenosha Public Library • Kenosha, WI 53142-5799 • PLA

Swartz Marie • Trustee • San Antonio Public Library • San Antonio, TX 78205

Swartz Patrice • Librarian • The Morning Call-Library • Allentown, PA 18105 • LAMA LITA

Swartz Penny • Deerfield, IL 60015 • AASL

Swartz Renee Becker • Trustee • Monmouth County Library • Manalapan, NJ 07726 • ALTA

Swartz Vicki • Walter Panas High School • Peekskill, NY 10566 • AASL

Swartz William D. • Librarian • Old Dominion Animal Hosp • Mc Lean, VA 22101

Swartzbaugh Roger G. • Medical Reference Librarian • Saint John's Hospital Health Sciences Library • Springfield, IL 62769

Swartzburg Susan G. • Preservation Specialist • Rutgers University Libraries • New Brunswick, NJ 08903 • ACRL ALCTS IRRT LHRT

Swartzel Judith K. • Director • Rowley Free Public Library • Rowley, MA 01969

Swartzell Ann G. • Associate Librarian • University of California-Berkeley Conservation Department • Berkeley, CA 94720 • ACRL ALCTS

Swartzentruber Julie M. • School Library Media Specialist • Canaseraga Central School • Canaseraga, NY 14822 • AASL

Swatos Priscilla • Illini Hospital Perlmutter Library • Silvis, IL 61282

Swatuck Marilyn • Librarian • Brooklyn Public Library • Brooklyn, NY 11238 • PLA RASD *Life*

Swaty Mary A. • Catalog Librarian • Arizona State University Libraries • Tempe, AZ 85287-1006 • ALCTS

Swayze Janet E. • Librarian • Capa Junior-Senior High School • Capac, MI 48014 • AASL

Swe Thein • Assistant Director of Libraries • University of Maryland College of Library and Information Services • College Park, MD 20742-4345

Swearengin Jami • Student • Pratt Institute Graduate School of Library & Information Science • Brooklyn, NY 11205

Swearingen Wilba • Associate Director • Louisiana State University Medical Center Library • New Orleans, LA 70112-2223 • ALCTS RASD

Sweat Mary Lee • University Librarian • Loyola University Library • New Orleans, LA 70118 • ACRL

Sweberg Mark R. • Reference Librarian • Providence Public Library • Providence, RI 02903-3283

Swecker Ruby H. • Media Librarian • Stratton Junior High School • Beckley, WV 25801 • AASL

Swedberg Donna J. • Librarian II • Santa Cruz City-County Library • Santa Cruz, CA 95060 • RASD

Sweedler Ulla S. • Associate Librarian • University of California-San Diego • La Jolla, CA 92093-0175 • ACRL

Sween Patricia A. • Media Generalist • Twin Bluff Middle School • Red Wing, MN 55066 • AASL IFRT

Sween Roger D. • Library Cooperation Specialist • Office of Library Development & Services • Saint Paul, MN 55101 • ASCLA PLA

Sweeney Elizabeth P. • Catalog Librarian • Boston College Libraries • Chestnut Hill, MA 02167 • NMRT

Sweeney John F. • Student • University of California-Berkeley School of Library & Information Studies • Berkeley, CA 94720

Sweeney Mary-Jo • Manager of Library Services • Department of Correction • Boston, MA 02202 • ASCLA

Sweeney Richard T. • Library Information Dean • Polytechnic University • Brooklyn, NY 11201 • LITA

Sweeney Robert J. • Student • Rutgers University School of Communication Information & Library Studies • New Brunswick, NJ 08903

Sweeney Suzanne • Auto. Coor/Faculty Servs Mgr. • Stanford University Jackson Library • Stanford, CA 94305 • ACRL ALCTS LITA *Life*

Sweeney Thomas F. • Trustee • Baldwin Public Library • Birmingham, MI 48012-3002

Sweeney Virginia • Reference Librarian • Albertus Magnus College Library • New Haven, CT 06511

Sweeny Donald N. III • Friends of the Grosse Pointe Public Library • Southfield, MI 48037-2007 • PLA

Sweet Donald G. • Library Director • University of Arkansas at Little Rock Ottenheimer Library • Little Rock, AR 72204 • ACRL LAMA IFRT IRRT

Sweet Doris Ann • Reference Coordinator • Boston University Mugar Memorial Library • Boston, MA 02215 • ACRL ALCTS LAMA LITA RASD GODORT LIRT

Sweet Freddy • President • Live Wire Video Publishers • San Francisco, CA 94118 • YALSA

Sweet Linda Z. • Technical Services Librarian • Sussex County Department of Libraries • Georgetown, DE 19947 • ALCTS

Sweet Marianne F. • Berwyn, IL 60402

Sweet Mary Ann • Library Media Specialist • Vernon Elementary School • Portland, OR 97211 • AASL

Sweet Sharon E. • Manager of Information Serv. • Warner & Stackpole • Boston, MA 02109 • LAMA

Sweetland James H. • University of Wisconsin-Milwaukee School of Library & Information Science • Milwaukee, WI 53201 • ACRL RASD

Sweetland Karen K. • Student • Saint Anselm College Geisel Library • Manchester, NH 03102-1310

Sweetland Loraine F. • Rebok Memorial Library • Silver Spring, MD 20904

Sweetnam Nancy C. • Elementary Librarian • Manchester Board of Education • Manchester, CT 06040 • AASL ALSC

Swei Ay-chuen • Taichung, Taiwan • ALSC LITA VRT

Sweigart Mary L. • Library Media Specialist • Freshman School • Del Rio, TX 78840 • AASL

Swem E. G. III • Louisville Free Public Library • Louisville, KY 40203-2257

Swenarton Hope R. Mrs • Glen Cove, NY 11542 • Continuing

Swensen Dale S. • Assistant Head,Catalog Dept. • Brigham Young University Harold B. Lee Library • Provo, UT 84602 • ALCTS LITA

Swensen Rolf H. • Darien, CT 06820 • ACRL RASD LHRT

Swenson Evelyn • Pope Elementary School • Puyallup, WA 98374

Swenson Gail • Librarian • Chico Junior High School • Chico, CA 95926

Swenson Jacqueline H. • Student • University of Hawaii School of Library & Information Studies • Honolulu, HI 96822 • SRRT

Swenson Karen C. • Lake Lanier Regional Library Lawrenceville Branch • Lawrenceville, GA 30245-4707

Swenson Mary Lou • Media Specialist • Saint Thomas More School • Decatur, GA 30030 • AASL

Swerczek Christine O. • Student • University of Washington Graduate School of Library and Information Science • Seattle, WA 98195 • LITA RASD

Swerdlove Dorothy L. • New York, NY 10019

Swetman Barbara E. • Hamilton College Burke Library • Clinton, NY 13323 • ALCTS

Swett Veronica P. • Tech Inf Mgr/Collection Devel. • Queens Borough Public Library • Jamaica, NY 11432 • RASD NMRT

Swiatek Janice • Student • Yale University School of Management • New Haven, CT 06520

Swibold Gretchen V. • Media Specialist • Canton Elementary School • Collinsville, CT 06022 • AASL ALSC

Swicegood Mary R. • Arlington Public Schools Media Processing Center • Arlington, VA 22207 • ALCTS

Swidan Eleanor A. • Reference Librarian • Enoch Pratt Free Library • Baltimore, MD 21201-4484 • RASD

Swier Terrill K. • Davison, MI 48423 • AASL IFRT

Swift Ardyce • Redmond Branch Library • Redmond, OR 97756 • YALSA

Swift Elizabeth E. • Student • Florida State University School of Library and Information Studies • Tallahassee, FL 32306-2048

Swift Janet M. • Library Director • University of Connecticut at Waterbury • Waterbury, CT 06710-2288 • ACRL

Swift Julie • Detroit, MI 48207-2946

Swigart Phyllis A. • Media Specialist • North Platte High School • North Platte, NE 69101 • AASL

Swigger Keith • Professor, Dean • Texas Woman's University School of Library & Information Studies • Denton, TX 76204 • ACRL

Swindells Geoffrey D. • Queens Borough Public Library Steinway Branch • Long Island City, NY 11105 • ALCTS LITA PLA RASD LHRT SRRT

Swindler Luke • Social Sciences Bibliographer • The University of North Carolina Collection Development Department • Chapel Hill, NC 27599-3918 • ACRL ALCTS IFRT SRRT

Swinehart David • Cataloger • Lake County Public Library • Merrillville, IN 46410-5382 • ALCTS

Swinehart Denise J. • Head of Children's Services • Lake County Public Library • Merrillville, IN 46410-5382 • ALSC

Swinehart J J. Mrs • Columbus, OH 43214 • LAMA PLA *Life*

Swinger Nancy Russell • Asst. Mgr/Magazines Newspapers • Columbus Metropolitan Library • Columbus, OH 43215

Swink Esther • Director • Metro Nashville Public Schools • Nashville, TN 37204 • AASL

Swink Sue Ellen • Professional • GDS Associates, Inc. • Austin, TX 78757

Swinney Jacquelyn • Reference Librarian • Azusa Pacific University Marshburn Memorial Library • Azusa, CA 91702

Swinney Sara Carter • Director • South Mississippi Regional Library • Columbia, MS 39429 • LAMA

Swinney Victoria K. • Reference Librarian • Cameron University • Lawton, OK 73505 • ACRL IRRT

Swinson William • Director • Millburn Public Library • Millburn, NJ 07041 • LAMA PLA

Swinton Cordelia W. • Head Lending Services • Pennsylvania State University E506 Pattee Library • University Park, PA 16802 • ACRL LAMA

Swirsky Sandy • Overfelt High School • San Jose, CA 95122

Swisher Susan K. • Reference Coordinator • Serra Research Center • San Diego, CA 92101 • RASD

Swistock Phyllis • Don Bosco Technical Institute • Rosemead, CA 91770 • LITA

Switzer Amy • Cleveland Hts, OH 44106 • YALSA

Switzer Catherine M. • School Library Services Coor • Kaukauna Area Schools • Kaukauna, WI 54130 • AASL YALSA

Switzer Jo Ann H. • Medical Reference Librarian • Indiana University School of Medicine Library • Indianapolis, IN 46202-5121 • ACRL

Switzer Patricia Stinson • Head, ISB Libraries • University of North Texas • Denton, TX 76203 • ACRL

Switzer Peri I. • Acquisitions/Document Delivery • United States Air Force Wright Laboratory Technical Library • Wright-Patterson AFB, OH 45433-6523 • ACRL ALCTS LAMA AFLRT FLRT

Switzer Teri R. • Personnel Librarian • Colorado State University William E. Morgan Library • Fort Collins, CO 80523 • ACRL LAMA

Swofford Lyndal Miss • Chicago Ridge, IL 60415 • ACRL *Continuing*

Swope Carla J. • Librarian • Basehor Community Library • Basehor, KS 66007

Swope Cynthia D. • Indianapolis, IN 46260

Swope Melanie J. • Carson, CA 90745 • AASL

Swope Paula J. • H. W. Wilson Company • Bronx, NY 10452 • RASD

Swora Tamara • Presv Microfilming Offr. • Library of Congress • Washington, DC 20541 • ALCTS LITA FLRT

Sword Donna M. • CLSI • Las Vegas-Clark County Library District • Las Vegas, NV 89101 • LITA

Sworsky Felicia G. • Reference Supervisor • Illinois Valley Library System • Pekin, IL 61554 • ASCLA PLA RASD

Sy Karen J. • Seattle, WA 98115 • GODORT

Sybrowsky Paul K. • President • DYNIX Inc. • Provo, UT 84606 • PLA

Sydelko Bette S. • Student • Guthrie Medical Center Robert Packer Hospital Library • Sayre, PA 18840

Syfert Samuel R. • Unit Librarian • Community Unit 301 • Bethany, IL 61914 • AASL

Sykas Anna • Springfield, VT 05156 • RASD LRRT

Sykes Arthur I.M. • Technical Services Coordinator • Brampton Public Library • Brampton ON, Canada • PLA

Sykes Carol S. • Director • Laconia Public Library • Laconia, NH 03246 • ALCTS PLA

Sykes Jacqueline E. • Branch Librarian • Atlanta-Fulton Public Library College Park Branch • College Park, GA 30337 • PLA RASD SRRT

Sykes Kaye • Librarian • Lewiston Junior High School Library • Lewiston, ME 04240 • AASL

Sykes Vivian M. • Student • University of Michigan • Ann Arbor, MI 48109-1205 • ACRL ALSC RASD EMIERT LIRT

Sylvester-Jose Marsha L. • Student • University of Hawaii at Manoa Catalog Dept. • Honolulu, HI 96822 • PLA

Sylvester Jane M. • Student • State University of New York at Albany School of Information Science & Policy • Albany, NY 12222

Sylvester Melvin R. • Head of Periodicals • Long Island University B. Davis Schwartz Memorial Library • Greenvale, NY 11548 • ACRL

Sylvester Virginia R. • Head Access Service • Arizona State University Libraries • Tempe, AZ 85287-1006 • ACRL

Sylvia Margaret J. • Librarian/Acquisitions • St. Mary's University Academic Library • San Antonio, TX 78228 • ALCTS

Symes Dal Ph.D. • Humanities Librarian • Western Washington University Wilson Library • Bellingham, WA 98225 • ACRL

Symington Nancy • Librarian • Dennis Memorial Library Association • Dennis, MA 02638

Symonds Lynn • Palo Alto City Library Downtown Branch • Palo Alto, CA 94301 • PLA IRRT

Symons Ann K. • Juneau-Douglas High School Library Juneau School District • Juneau, AK 99801 • AASL ALSC YALSA LIRT

Symons John W. • Juneau, AK 99801

Sypert Clyde F. Dr • San Pablo, CA 94806 • LITA

Syrdahl Peter M. • Trustee • Brooklyn Public Library • Brooklyn, NY 11238 • ALTA

Syrek Tammy A. • Student • Rutgers University School of Communication Information & Library Studies • New Brunswick, NJ 08903 • LITA NMRT

Syrett Matthew • Painted Post, NY 14870

Syring Millie L. • Interlibrary Loan Librarian • Nevada State Library & Archives • Carson City, NV 89710

Sysol Karen E. • Student • DePaul University Bookstore • Chicago, IL 60614

Syverson Shirley W. • Portland, OR 97220-4441

Sywak Esther • Librarian • North Bellmore Public Library • N. Bellmore, NY 11710

Sywak Myron • Associate Professor • Long Island University Palmer School of Library & Information Science • Greenvale, NY 11548

Sywetz Elizabeth J. • Director • Herkimer County BOCES • Herkimer, NY 13350-1499 • AASL

Syzek Timothy J. • Newark Public Library • Newark, NJ 07101-0630

Szabo Charlotte Hope • Assistant Director • White Plains Public Library • White Plains, NY 10601

Szabo John F. • Director • Robinson Township Public Library District • Robinson, IL 62454 • IRRT

Szabo Susan G. • Librarian • Hawken School • Lyndhurst, OH 44124 • AASL

Szafranski Sandra L. • Director of Instruction • School District of Cambridge • Cambridge, WI 53523 • AASL

Szalai Valerie M. • Chicago, IL 60659

Szalkowski Barbara H. • Catalog Librarian • South Texas College of Law Library • Houston, TX 77002 • ACRL ALCTS

Szambelan Carol • Business Reference Specialist • University of Notre Dame Theodore M. Hesburgh Library • Notre Dame, IN 46556

Szarejko Celia M. • Systems Librarian • East Tennessee State University • Johnson City, TN 37614 • LITA LRRT

Szarmach Janet E. • Cataloger • Library of Congress • Washington, DC 20541 • ALCTS LITA

Szasz Susan Marie • Cornell University Library • Ithaca, NY 14853-5301 • ACRL ALCTS

Szatek Pearl • Associate Librarian • University of Massachusetts-Dartmouth Library • North Dartmouth, MA 02747 • ALCTS

Szatkowski Dea Kay • OCLC Services Representative • Incolsa/OCLC • Indianapolis, IN 46278 • ACRL ALCTS LITA

Szczerban Marbeth K. • School Librarian • Hanby School • Wilmington, DE 19810

Szczesiak Halina W. • Watsonville, CA 95076

Sze Melanie C. • Supervisor,Technical Library • GAF Chemicals Corporation • Wayne, NJ 07470 • LITA

Szeberenyi Betty H. • Harwich Port, MA 02646

Szeliga Gail • Librarian • Union-Endicott School District • Endicott, NY 13760 • AASL

Szemraj Edward R. • Trustee • Cheektowaga Public Library North Branch • Cheektowaga, NY 14225 • AASL

Szeto Dorcas C. • Serials Librarian • Azusa Pacific University Marshburn Memorial Library • Azusa, CA 91702 • ACRL

Szivos Maria • Sechelt BC, V0N 3A0 Canada • Continuing

Szkorla Joanne C. • Chicago, IL 60645 • PLA

Szlapak Amy S. • Student • State University of New York (SUNY) School of Information & Library Studies • Buffalo, NY 14260

Szmuk Szilvia E. • Saint John's University Library • Jamaica, NY 11439 • ACRL

Szofran Nancy C. • Systems Administrator • Eastern Montana College Library • Billings, MT 59101-0298 • LITA

Szombathy Anges L. • Head of Cataloging Department • City College of San Francisco • San Francisco, CA 94112

Szpila Jerome S. • Reference Information Librarian • Free Library of Philadelphia • Philadelphia, PA 19103

Szudy Lois Francis • Library Director • Otterbein College Courtright Memorial Library • Westerville, OH 43081 • ACRL LAMA LITA GODORT IFRT

Szudy Thomas A. • Library Consultant • State Library of Ohio • Columbus, OH 43266-0334

Szydlo Eileen K. • College of Saint Francis Library Science Program • Joliet, IL 60435 • RASD

Szymanski Frances M. • Head Librarian • Amundsen High School • Chicago, IL 60625 • AASL

Szymanski Sheri S. • Library Assistant • Monroe Public Library Monroe Center Green • Monroe, CT 06468

Szymczak Ralph J. • Senior Reference Librarian • Brandeis University Goldfarb Library • Waltham, MA 02254-9110 • GODORT

Szymula Susan E. • Library Director • South Mainland Library Micco • Barefoot Bay, FL 32976 • LAMA NMRT

Szynaka Edward M. • Director • Pasadena Public Library • Pasadena, CA 91101 • PLA

Ta Kiem-Dung T. • Student • Laredo Public Library • Laredo, TX 78040

Taback Aili C. • Reference Librarian • Contra Costa County Library • Pleasant Hill, CA 94523

Tabar Margaret E. • Breck School • Minneapolis, MN 55422 • Life

Tabas Betsy R. • Librarian • Temple University College of Engineering CS ARCH • Philadelphia, PA 19122 • ACRL

Tabb Bruce • Student • University of Oregon • Eugene, OR 97403

Tabb Winston • Associate Librarian Collections • Library of Congress • Washington, DC 20541 • ACRL ALCTS RASD

Tabeling Michael T. • Beck & Tabeling Architects, Inc. • Bath, OH 44210 • LAMA

Taben Eva • Special Service Consultant • Westchester Library System • Elmsford, NY 10523

Taber Jennifer H. • Wheaton Public Library • Wheaton, IL 60187-5376

Taber Sharon A. • Director • Fort Lewis College Library • Durango, CO 81301 • ACRL CLENE

Tabler Elaine A. • Librarian • Marietta High School • Marietta, OK 73448 • AASL YALSA

Tabor Harold • Library Director • Florida College Chatlos Library • Temple Terrace, FL 33617-5578 • ACRL LAMA LITA RASD

Tabor Jean M. • Director • Canton Public Library • Canton, MI 48188 • LAMA LITA PLA

Tabor Karel L. • Head of Public Services • Farmers Branch Public Library • Farmers Branch, TX 75234

Tabor Lauren D. • Lawndale, CA 90260

Tabor Linda M. • Clearwater, FL 34624

Tabor Roberta K. • Media Specialist • Hope High School • Providence, RI 02906

Tabor Stephen R. • Cataloger • University of California Rivera Library • Riverside, CA 92517 • ACRL

Taborsky Theresa • Director • Widener University Wolfgram Library • Chester, PA 19013 • ACRL LAMA

Tabuchi DeAnn A. • Student • San Jose State University Division of Library & Information Science • San Jose, CA 95192-0029 • ALSC PLA

Tacchi Mary Jane • Assistant Coordinator • The New York Public Library • New York, NY 10016 • YALSA

Tacha Karolyn K. • Manhattan, KS 66502 • AASL

Tachihata Chieko • Hawaiian Curator • University of Hawaii Thomas Hale Hamilton Library • Honolulu, HI 96822 • ACRL RASD   *Life*

Tack Carol Ann • Cushman & Wakefield • New York, NY 10036 • LAMA

Tackett Sarilda E. • Children's Librarian • Hunterdon County Library North County Branch • Annandale, NJ 08801 • ALSC

Taeuber Sandra H. • Burbank, IL 60459 • AASL

Taff Tanya M. • Skokie, IL 60077

Taft Ann F. • Librarian • Orange County Library System Orlando Public Library • Orlando, FL 32801-2471 • RASD

Tag Sylvia G. • Student • University of Iowa School of Library & Information Science • Iowa City, IA 52242 • PLA

Taggart Charlotte C. • Librarian • Gilman Middle School Media Center • Baltimore, MD 21210 • AASL

Taggart Thoburn Jr. • Assistant Professor • Wichita State University Ablah Library • Wichita, KS 67208 • ACRL

Tagler John • Director • Elsevier Science Publishing Company Inc. • New York, NY 10010 • ACRL ALCTS

Taguchi Yoko • Kyoto Seika University • Kyoto 606, Japan • ACRL IFRT SRRT

Tague-Sutcliffe Jean M. • Dean • University of Western Ontario School of Library & Information Science • London ON, N6G 1H1 Canada

Taha Karen T. • Librarian • Elmdale Elementary School • Springdale, AR 72764 • AASL

Tahir Peggy • California Pacific Medical Center Health Sciences Library • San Francisco, CA 94120-7999

Taillon Marilyn G. • Librarian • Arthur Andersen & Company • St. Charles, IL 60174

Tainton Madeleine • Media Services Director • Nazareth College of Rochester • Rochester, NY 14618 • SRRT

Tait Phyllis M. • Oakland, CA 94609

Tait Susan F. • Coordinator, Young Adult Servs. • Seattle Public Library • Seattle, WA 98104-1193 • ASCLA YALSA IFRT

Tajiri Elizabeth Z. • Student • University of North Carolina at Chapel Hill School of Information and Library Science • Chapel Hill, NC 27599-3360

Tajudin Mary R. • Librarian I • Newport Beach Public Library Mariners Branch • Newport Beach, CA 92660 • PLA LIRT

Takacs Sherlyn M. • Student • San Jose State University Division of Library & Information Science • San Jose, CA 95192-0029

Takahashi Annabelle T. • Humanities Reference Librarian • University of Hawaii Thomas Hale Hamilton Library • Honolulu, HI 96822 • ACRL

Takaki Sue • Trustee • Pueblo Library District McClelland Library • Pueblo, CO 81004-1997 • PLA

Takakoshi Gay B. • Arlington, VA 22202

Takata C Christine • Branch Librarian • Contra Costa County Library Pittsburg Branch • Pittsburg, CA 94565 • ALSC PLA YALSA

Takawashi Tadayoshi • Associate Professor • Shizouka Prefectural College • Hamamathsu, Japan • ACRL ALCTS ALSC LITA RASD

Takemura Lillian • Librarian • Waiakea Elementary School • Hilo, HI 96720 • AASL

Takeuchi Betty G. • President • San Marino Toy & Book Shop • San Marino, CA 91108 • ALSC YALSA

Takeuchi Satoru • Vice President • University of Library and Information Science • Tsukuba-shi, 305, Japan • ALSC EMIERT IRRT

Talar Anita Sister • Reference Librarian • Seton Hall University • South Orange, NJ 07079-2690 • ACRL RASD LIRT LRRT

Talbert Christine C. • Lynbrook Elementary School • Springfield, VA 22150 • AASL

Talbert Edward J. • Washington, DC 20023 • Continuing

Talbert Valerie • Manager,Main Children's Room • Dayton & Montgomery County Public Library • Dayton, OH 45402-2103 • ALSC

Talbert Versie Barnes • Librarian • Chicago Public Library • Chicago, IL 60605

Talbot Dawn E. • Information Manager • Center for Magnetic Recording Research University of California • San Diego, CA 92093 • ACRL LITA

Talbot Dixie B. • Marysville, KS 66508

Talbot Faye Hoffman • School Librarian • Park Forest Middle School • Baton Rouge, LA 70814 • AASL

Talbot Gregory F. • Westfield, NJ 07090 • ACRL

Talbot Kathleen • Stilwell Junior High School • West Des Moines, IA 50265

Talbot Philip R. • Student • San Jose State University Division of Library & Information Science • San Jose, CA 95192-0029

Talbot Richard J. • Director of Libraries • University of Massachusetts Library • Amherst, MA 01003 • ACRL

Talchik Rita • Librarian • Christ Church School • Fort Lauderdale, FL 33308 • AASL

Talcott Ann W. • Short Hills, NJ 07078 • LAMA ILERT

Talcott Anne E. • Librarian • Huron Public Library • Huron, OH 44839 • PLA

Taleb Mohamed A. • Systems Librarian • University of Arizona Library • Tucson, AZ 85721 • LITA

Talentino William • Goodnow Library • Sudbury, MA 01776-2383 • LAMA

Taliaferro Helen A. • Chief, Reader Services • United States Air Force Air University Library • Maxwell AFB, AL 36112-5564 • AFLRT

Talip Clay Sariya • Asst Dept Head, Govt Doc Dept • Broward County Division of Libraries Broward County Library • Fort Lauderdale, FL 33301 • LAMA

Talis Ross M. • City Librarian • Oak Creek Public Library • Oak Creek, WI 53154

Talladay Beverly W. • Kenmore, NY 14223 • AASL ALSC

Tallau Adeline • Librarian • Rutgers University Libraries Library of Science & Medicine • Piscataway, NJ 08855-1029 • ACRL ALCTS RASD

Tallent Edward P. • Reference Librarian • Harvard College Library Lamont Library • Cambridge, MA 02138 • ACRL RASD IFRT LIRT

Talley Arleen E. • Librarian • Enoch Pratt Free Library Herring Run Branch • Baltimore, MD 21213

Talley Brenda T. • Student • University of North Texas School of Library & Information Sciences • Denton, TX 76203

Talley Doris • Asheboro, NC 27203 • AASL

Talley Jay • Assistant Librarian • University of Arizona Library • Tucson, AZ 85721

Talley Kaye M. • Serials Librarian • University of Central Arkansas Torreyson Library • Conway, AR 72032

Talley Loretta K. • Librarian • Elk Run School • Elk Run Heights, IA 50707 • YALSA

Talley Marcia D. • Manager, Technical Services • U. S. General Accounting Office • Washington, DC 20548 • LAMA LITA

Talley Mary C. • Library Consultant/Owner • Library Management Systems • Sherman Oaks, CA 91423 • LAMA LITA ILERT

Talley Patsy L. • Supervisor Library Services • Federal Home Loan Bank Dallas • Dallas, TX 75261

Talley Sarah E. • Student • State University of New York at Albany School of Information Science & Policy • Albany, NY 12222

Tallmadge Mary Mother • Librarian Emeritus • Barat College Library • Lake Forest, IL 60045 • ACRL LAMA
Continuing

Tallman Helen J. • Media Specialist • MAST Academy • Virginia Key, FL 33149 • AASL YALSA

Tallman Johanna E. • La Canada, CA 91011 • ACRL

Tallman Julie I. • Asst Prof • University of Iowa School of Library & Information Science • Iowa City, IA 52242 • AASL YALSA IFRT IRRT

Tallman Marna C. • Deschutes County Library • Bend, OR 97701 • RASD

Talma Elaine • Director/Trustee • Sir Charles Hayward Library • Freeport, Bahamas

Talmadge Linda L. • Media Specialist • Our Lady of Peace School • Columbus, OH 43214

Talty Catherine E. • Sawyer Free Library • Gloucester, MA 01930

Tam Ching-fan • Dalhousie University Library • Halifax NS, B3H 4H8 Canada

Tam Miriam • Asst. Dir. Technical Service • American Museum of Natural History Library • New York, NY 10024

Tam Vernon • Hd, Art Music Recreation/AV • Hawaii State Library • Honolulu, HI 96813

Tamblyn Eldon W. • Head Cataloger • Portland State University Library • Portland, OR 97207 • ACRL ALCTS

Tambo David C. • Head, Special Collections • University of California UCSB Library • Santa Barbara, CA 93106-9010 • ACRL IRRT

Tamburello Victor • Reference Librarian • Ocean County College-LRC • Toms River, NJ 08753

Tames Beverly W. • Student • Emporia State University School of Library & Information Management • Emporia, KS 66801

Tamimi Judith Ann • Reference Librarian • California State Univ Stanislaus • Turlock, CA 95380

Taminiau Julia A. • McGill University Graduate School of Library & Information Studies • Montreal PQ, Canada • LITA

Tamlyn Brenda • Media Servs/AV Library Supv. • Wyndmere School Library • Wyndmere, ND 58081

Tamlyn Heidi J. • Student • University of Wisconsin-Milwaukee School of Library & Information Science • Milwaukee, WI 53201

Tammany Rosina M. • Librarian,Acquisitions • Eastern Michigan Univeristy • Ypsilanti, MI 48197 • ACRL ALCTS LRRT

Tamminga Tim • Director, Network Sales • CD Plus, Inc. • New York, NY 10036 • LITA

Tan Leticia Banada • Reference Librarian • County of Los Angeles Public Library Norwalk Library 501 • Norwalk, CA 90650

Tan Limin • Student • Queens College Graduate School of Library & Information Studies • Flushing, NY 11367

Tanaka Nancy N. • Library Technicion VII • Hawaii State Public Library System Centralized Processing Center • Honolulu, HI 96813

Tancin Charlotte A. • Librarian • Carnegie Mellon University Hunt Institute • Pittsburgh, PA 15213 • ACRL ALCTS

Tandler Adriana Acauan • Head, New American Project • Queens Borough Public Library • Jamaica, NY 11432 • PLA EMIERT IRRT

Tandowsky Eleanor • Reference Librarian • Fremont Main Library • Fremont, CA 94538

Tane Judith • Library Media Specialist • Old Westbury School of the Holy Child • Old Westbury, NY 11568

Tanenbaum Frances • Jenkintown, PA 19046

Tang Chui Yan C. • Student • University of Pittsburgh School of Library and Information Science • Pittsburgh, PA 15260 • ACRL EMIERT SRRT

Tang Donna Taxco • Assistant to the Provost • Pima Community College Downtown Campus • Tucson, AZ 85703-0027 • ACRL IRRT

Tang Eugenia G. C. • Documents/Microtext Ref Libn • Texas A & M University Sterling C. Evans Library • College Station, TX 77843-5000 • GODORT

Tang Heng-Yuan • Snyder, NY 14226 • ACRL RASD

Tang Klairon K.L • Catalog Librarian • Bellaire City Library • Bellaire, TX 77401-4498 • ALCTS IRRT

Tang Lorna Y. • Head of Technical Services • University of Chicago D'Angelo Law Library • Chicago, IL 60637 • ALCTS

Tang Maria M. • Bibliographic Access Manager • County of Los Angeles Public Library • Downey, CA 90241-7400 • ALCTS LITA

Tang Sherman Dr. • Manager, Central Library • Queens Borough Public Library • Jamaica, NY 11432

Tang Stella S. • SRI International Research Information Services • Menlo Park, CA 94025 • LITA

Tang Thomas S. • Student • Clark-Atlanta University School of Library & Information Studies • Atlanta, GA 30314-4391

Tang Vitus C. • Cataloging • Stanford University • Stanford, CA 94305-6011 • ALCTS

Tangeman Sharon M. • Library Media Specialist • Redemptorist High School • Baton Rouge, LA 70805 • AASL

Tangney Robert L. • Student • University of Washington Graduate School of Library and Information Science • Seattle, WA 98195

Tango Carmen • Librarian II • Boynton Beach City Library • Boynton Beach, FL 33435 • ALSC

Taniguchi Marilyn J. • Los Angeles, CA 90064

Tanis James Dr • Director of Libraries • Bryn Mawr College Canaday Library • Bryn Mawr, PA 19010

Tanis Norman E. • Chatsworth, CA 91311

Tanji Lorelei A. • Fine Arts Librarian • University of California-Irvine Library • Irvine, CA 92713 • ACRL LITA NMRT

Tankersley Heather L. • Librarian III • Memphis-Shelby County Public Library Millington Branch Library • Millington, TN 38053

Tanksley Carol B. • Assistant Professor • Duquesne University Library • Pittsburgh, PA 15282 • ACRL EMIERT IFRT

Tannenbaum Harve A • Director • Ohio County Public Library • Wheeling, WV 26003 • LAMA PLA

Tannenbaum Jerry Y. • Director, Technical Services • H.W. Wilson Company • Bronx, NY 10452 • LITA

Tanner Ann R. • Library Media Specialist • Dundalk Middle School • Dundalk, MD 21222 • AASL

Tanner Anne B. • Assistant Dean • Drexel University College of Information Studies • Philadelphia, PA 19104-2875

Tanner Betty L. • ATLAS Coordinator • Scottsdale Public Library • Scottsdale, AZ 85251 • LITA

Tanner Elizabeth • Librarian • Seaforth College of Tafe • Seaforth NSW 2092, Australia

Tanner Linda L. • Library Director • Montello Public Library • Montello, WI 53949 • PLA

Tanner Sally • Librarian • Bossier Parish School System • Bossier City, LA 71112

Tanner Thomas M. • Library Director • Lincoln Christian College and Seminary • Lincoln, IL 62656 • ACRL

Tanno John W. • Associate University Librarian • University of California Rivera Library • Riverside, CA 92517 • ACRL ALCTS LAMA LITA

Tanselle G. Thomas • Vice President • Guggenheim Memorial Foundation • New York, NY 10016 • ACRL

Tao Dorothy S. • Information Specialist • State University of New York at Buffalo • Buffalo, NY 14260 • ACRL

Taormina Anthony P. • Library Director • Lodi Memorial Library • Lodi, NJ 07644

Tapiero Judith • Director • The Organized Library • Princeton, NJ 08543-7403

Tapley Bridgette M. • University of North Carolina at Charlotte J. Murrey Atkins Library • Charlotte, NC 28223

Tapley Janet H. • Central Library Manager • Newport Beach Public Library • Newport Beach, CA 92660 • PLA RASD

Taplin Franklin P. • South Hadley, MA 01075 • Continuing

Tappana Kathy A. • Online Info. Services Libn. • Springfield-Greene County Library • Springfield, MO 65801 • ACRL ALSC RASD LRRT

Tappe Anthony • President • Anthony Tappe and Associate Inc. • Boston, MA 02111 • ACRL LAMA

Tapper Margaret M. • Library Systems Specialist • University of California-Irvine Library • Irvine, CA 92713 • ALCTS LITA NMRT

Taraba M. Susan • Head, Rare Materials Cataloging • Duke University William R. Perkins Library • Durham, NC 27706 • ACRL SRRT

Tarakan Sheldon L. • President • Visible Ink Incorporated • East Hills, NY 11577 • LAMA

Taran Nadia P. • Branch Manager • Fairfax County Public Library John Marshall Branch • Alexandria, VA 22310 • PLA

Taranko Walter • Media Coordinator • Maine State Library • Augusta, ME 04333 • AASL

Tarbell Susan A. • Technical Services Librarian • United States Air Force • Scott Air Force Base, IL 62265-0001 • FLRT

Tarbox Margaret A. • Library Consultant • Wolff, Lang, Christopher Architects • Rancho Cucamonga, CA 91730 • PLA

Tarbox Ruth • Chicago, IL 60610 • AASL ALSC *Continuing*

Tardie Joseph J. • Ebsco Subscription Services • Shrewsbury, NJ 07702

Tardiff Kristine A. • Student • Florida State University School of Library and Information Studies • Tallahassee, FL 32306-2048

Tareski Nancy L. • Library Assistant • University of Iowa School of Library & Information Science • Iowa City, IA 52242

Tarlton Martha K. • Head, General Reference Services • University of North Texas • Denton, TX 76203 • ACRL RASD

Tarlton Shirley M. • Charlotte, NC 28226 • ACRL ALCTS   *Life*

Tarpley Margaret J. • Ogbomoso, Oyo, Nigeria W. Africa

Tarpley N. Joanne • Supervisor, Reference & Research • University of Guam • Mangilao, GU 96923

Tarr Anna M. Miss • Franklin, PA 16323 • Continuing

Tarr Susan M. • Library of Congress • Washington, DC 20541 • LAMA LITA

Tarsitano Carol A. • Branch Head • Chicago Public Library Portage-Cragin Branch • Chicago, IL 60641 • ALSC PLA

Tarver Charle P. • Tuskegee, AL 36083

Tarver Elizabeth Miss • Librarian Emeritus • Louisiana State University Libraries Troy H. Middleton Library • Baton Rouge, LA 70803-3342 • Continuing

Tarwater Barbara H. • Cedar Rapids, IA 52402 • AASL YALSA

Tasa Koichi • Columbia University East Asian Library • New York, NY 10027

Taschner Andrea J. • Librarian I • Arapahoe Library District • Littleton, CO 80121

Tasevoli Barbara • Library Media Specialist • Buck Lodge Middle School • Adelphi, MD 20783 • AASL

Tashima Marie • Lake View Terrace, CA 91342-7218 • ACRL LITA   *Life*

Tashjian Sharon A. • Librarian • North Bend Public Library • North Bend, OR 97459

Tashjian Virginia • City Librarian • Newton Free Library • Newton, MA 02159 • ACRL ALSC PLA

Taslitz Florence • Covina South Hills High School Library • Covina, CA 91723

Tassia Margaret R. • Professor • Millersville University • Millersville, PA 17551 • AASL ALSC

Tassios Carolann • Director • Yorba Linda Public Library • Yorba Linda, CA 92686 • ALCTS ALSC PLA RASD

Tastad Shirley A. • University of Wyoming • Laramie, WY 82071

Taste Sharon A. • Reference Librarian • Dayton & Montgomery County Public Library • Dayton, OH 45402-2103

Tatalias Jean • Mitre Corp Library • Mc Lean, VA 22102 • LITA

Tate Albert III • Dir. of Library • Notre Dame Seminary • New Orleans, LA 70118 • ACRL ALCTS LAMA

Tate David • Director • Van Buren District Library • Decatur, MI 49045

Tate Elaine A. • Tacoma, WA 98405

Tate Janet A. • Student • University of Washington Graduate School of Library and Information Science • Seattle, WA 98195

Tate Julie VanMetre • Henry Clay Elementary School • Ashland, VA 23005

Tate Marsha • Director • Musser Public Library • Muscatine, IA 52761 • PLA

Tate Marsha A. • Documents Operations Supervisor • Pennsylvania State University Pattee Library • University Park, PA 16802 • GODORT

Tate Suzanne • Reference Librarian • Randolph Public Library • Asheboro, NC 27203 • ALCTS RASD

Tate Teresa Rohrabaugh • Salem, OR 97304 • ALSC

Tate Thelma H. • Reference Librarian • Douglass College Library • New Brunswick, NJ 08854 • ACRL RASD EMIERT IRRT LIRT LRRT

Tateoka Fumie • Librarian • Library of Congress • Washington, DC 20541 • ACRL ALCTS LAMA FLRT SORT

Tatom Syble E. Miss • Stamps, AR 71860 • Continuing

Tatum Brenda L. • Trustee • Pine Bluff & Jefferson County Library System • Pine Bluff, AR 71601

Tatum Elsie B. • Sun City, AZ 85373-1460 • ACRL   *Life*

Tatum Fred • Hattiesburg, MS 39401 • ALTA

Tatum George M. Mr • Collection Development Librarian • George Mason University Libraries • Fairfax, VA 22030 • ACRL ALCTS   *Life*

Tatum Patricia T. • Berwick Elementary School • Berwick, LA 70342 • AASL

Tatum W. Barnes • Greensboro College • Greensboro, NC 27401 • ACRL

Taub Barbara C. • Manager, Technical Services • Babson College Horn Library • Babson Park, MA 02157-0901 • ALCTS

Taub Robert • Trustee • Dearborn Department of Libraries Henry Ford Centennial Library • Dearborn, MI 48126

Taube John E. • Minneapolis, MN 55413 • ACRL RASD IFRT

Tauber Kathleen • Librarian • Eagleville Elementary School Library • Eagleville, PA 19403

Tauber Paula R. • Brooklyn, NY 11229

Taucher Judith H. • Young Adult Librarian • Cuyahoga County Public Library Solon Branch • Solon, OH 44139 • YALSA

Tauriello Carol Z. • Director • Erie 1 BOCES School Library System • Lancaster, NY 14086 • AASL

Tausky Janice Semler • Reference • University of Massachusetts Labor Relations & Research Center • Amherst, MA 01003 • RASD

Tavares Cecelia M. • Asst. Dir. for Tech. Servs. • Suffolk University Law Library • Boston, MA 02114 • ALCTS LITA

Tavares Claudia C. • Librarian • Augusta Technical Institute • Augusta, GA 30906

Tavaska John R. • Manager Technical Support • H.W. Wilson Company • Bronx, NY 10452 • LITA RASD

Tavill Kay • Public Services/Bibl. • Loyola University • Chicago, IL 60611 • ACRL RASD

Taviss Patricia A. • Carmel, IN 46032-5272

Tawarahara Jan Y. • Federal Documents Librarian • Hawaii State Public Library • Honolulu, HI 96813

Taylor Anita K. • Student • University of Missouri-Columbia School of Library & Informational Science • Columbia, MO 65211

Taylor Anne C. • Principal Librarian/Branch Head • Free Public Library of Woodbridge • Woodbridge, NJ 07095 • PLA SRRT

Taylor Anne E. • Public Services Librarian • El Paso Community College • El Paso, TX 79998 • ACRL

Taylor Arlene G. • Associate Professor • Columbia University Library Service Library • New York, NY 10027 • ALCTS LITA LRRT

Taylor Audrey J. • Reference Librarian • University of Houston Libraries • Houston, TX 77204-2091 • ACRL RASD GODORT

Taylor Barbara • Sony Corporation • Cypress, CA 90630

Taylor Barbara J.H. • UNESCO • Washington, DC 20044 • ACRL ALTA LAMA IRRT

Taylor Betty Jo • Library Media Coordinator • Con Sch Dist No 2 • Raytown, MO 64133 • AASL

Taylor Caro • Branch Librarian • Cuba Circulating Library • Cuba, NY 14727 • PLA

Taylor Carol A. • Librarian • Atlanta-Fulton Public Library Sandy Springs Branch • Sandy Springs, GA 30328

Taylor Carol P. • Birmingham, AL 35216 • ALCTS

Taylor Carole R. • Director • Fort Valley State College H.A. Hunt Memorial Library • Ft. Valley, GA 31030 • ACRL CLENE

Taylor Catherine O. • Peace Dale, RI 02883 • AASL

Taylor Cathey A. • Head of Technical Services • Harnett County Public Library System • Lillington, NC 27546

Taylor Celianna I. • Columbus, OH 43221 • ALCTS LITA
Life

Taylor Chip • Owner • Chip Taylor Communications • Derry, NH 03038 • AASL

Taylor Christine M. • Bayboro, NC 28515 • PLA

Taylor Christine M. • Assistant Manager • Columbus Metropolitan Library • Columbus, OH 43215

Taylor Clark H. Ms. • Student • Memphis-Shelby County Public Library and Information Center • Memphis, TN 38104-4025 • PLA

Taylor David C. • Undergraduate Librarian • University of North Carolina • Chapel Hill, NC 27599 • ACRL

Taylor Deborah D. • Young Adult Services Specialist • Enoch Pratt Free Library • Baltimore, MD 21201-4484 • YALSA

Taylor Dennis S. • University Archivist • Clemson University Robert Muldrow Cooper Library • Clemson, SC 29634-3001 • ACRL

Taylor Diana R. • Student • University of Oklahoma School of Library & Information Studies • Norman, OK 73019 • AASL YALSA

Taylor Donna M. • Director • Sewickley Public Library • Sewickley, PA 15143 • PLA

Taylor E. Gilbert • Reference Librarian • Smithsonian Institution Libraries • Washington, DC 20540

Taylor Edith P. Mrs. • Assistant Librarian • Nicholls State University Allen J. Ellender Memorial Library • Thibodaux, LA 70310 • GODORT

Taylor Elizabeth A. • Student • University of Arizona Graduate Library School • Tucson, AZ 85721 • ACRL

Taylor Elizabeth G. • Reference Librarian • Westfield Memorial Library • Westfield, NJ 07090 • RASD

Taylor Elizabeth J. • Librarian I • University of Michigan-Dearborn Mardigian Library • Dearborn, MI 48128-1491 • ALCTS

Taylor Elizabeth P. • Youth Materials Selection Spec. • Chicago Public Library Harold Washington Library • Chicago, IL 60605 • ALSC

Taylor Evelyn • Children's Librarian • Los Angeles County Public Library La Canada Flintridge Branch • La Canada Flintridge, CA 91011 • ALSC

Taylor Heather M. • Student • San Jose State University Division of Library & Information Science • San Jose, CA 95192-0029 • PLA

Taylor Helen S. Mrs • Union, NJ 07083 • LAMA
Continuing

Taylor Jacqulyn J. • Norman Public Library • Norman, OK 73069

Taylor Janice P. • Titusville, FL 32781-1231 • AASL

Taylor Jeanie M. • Library Media Specialist • Pearl-Cohn High School • Nashville, TN 37208 • AASL

Taylor Jimminzine B. • Reference Librarian • Prairie View A & M University • Prairie View, TX 77446 • RASD

Taylor Joan H. • Student • Clark-Atlanta University School of Library & Information Studies • Atlanta, GA 30314-4391

Taylor Joan R. • Technical Information Specialist • United States Information Agency (USIA) • Washington, DC 20547 • FLRT

Taylor Jody R. • Asst Dir, Reference/Online Serv • Saint Josephs College Library • Rensselaer, IN 47978-0410 • ACRL

Taylor Joie L. • Columbus, NE 68601 • AASL

Taylor Joyce G. • Librarian • Indiana University-Purdue University at Indianapolis Library (IUPUI) • Indianapolis, IN 46202 • LAMA NMRT

Taylor Jr. James A. • Librarian • Atlanta-Fulton Public Library • Atlanta, GA 30303 • PLA IFRT

Taylor Judith Keller • Director • Rochester Public Library • Rochester, MN 55904-3777 • LAMA PLA CLENE

Taylor K Renee • Catalog Librarian • Millsaps College Millsaps-Wilson Library • Jackson, MS 39210 • ALCTS LITA

Taylor Katherine M. • Cincinnati, OH 45226 • IFRT SRRT

Taylor Kathryn T. • Director • Littleton Public Library • Littleton, NH 03561

Taylor Kay P. • Head, Community & Outreach Serv. • Durham County Library • Durham, NC 27702 • PLA

Taylor Kenneth I. • Millersville, PA 17551 • AASL   *Life*

Taylor Kevin • Trustee • East Saint Louis Public Library • East St. Louis, IL 62201 • ALTA

Taylor Kimberly K. • Director • Colorado State Library Center for the Book • Denver, CO 80203

Taylor Larry D. • Manager, Library Services • Wyeth-Ayerst Research • Princeton, NJ 08543-8000 • ACRL

Taylor Lisa C. • Outreach Librarian • San Bernardino County Library • San Bernardino, CA 92415

Taylor Lorraine N • Mesa, AZ 85204

Taylor Lynn M. • Senior Librarian • Denver Public Library • Denver, CO 80203-2165 • PLA

Taylor Margaret Haseltine • Moab, UT 84532

Taylor Margaret L. • Whittier, CA 90601-1035 • NMRT

Taylor Margaret L. Miss • Greensboro, NC 27408 • Continuing

Taylor Margaret T. • Lecturer • University of Michigan School of Information and Library Studies • Ann Arbor, MI 48109-1092 • RASD YALSA LRRT SRRT

Taylor Marilynn A. • Librarian • Public Schools Osterholz Elementary School • APO New York, NY 09355-0005 • AASL

Taylor Marion • Librarian • Rapides Parish Library • Alexandria, LA 71301 • Continuing

Taylor Marion E. • Head, Collection Development • University of California-Santa Cruz Library • Santa Cruz, CA 95064 • ACRL ALCTS IFRT SRRT

Taylor Marion E. • Preservation Review Librarian • Harvard College Library Widener Memorial Library • Cambridge, MA 02138 • ALCTS

Taylor Mark A. • London ON, N6G 2E4 Canada • ALSC PLA

Taylor Marlene • Administrative Manager • National Agricultural Library • Beltsville, MD 20705-2351

Taylor Martha K. • Student • University of Southern Mississippi School of Library Science • Hattiesburg, MS 39406-5146

Taylor Martha M. • Trustee • South Carolina State Library • Columbia, SC 29211 • ALTA

Taylor Marvin J. • Special Collections • Columbia University Health Sciences Library • New York, NY 10032 • ACRL

Taylor Mary • ACRL, Publications Prog Officer • American Library Association • Chicago, IL 60611-2795

Taylor Mary Lu • Branch Librarian • East Oahu Library District Waikiki-Kapahulu Public Lib • Honolulu, HI 96815

Taylor Mary P. • Burns High School • Lawndale, NC 28090 • AASL

Taylor Melanie A. • Student • University of Rhode Island Graduate School of Library & Information Studies • Kingston, RI 02881-0815

Taylor Merrily E. • University Librarian • Brown University Rockefeller Library • Providence, RI 02912 • ACRL LAMA

Taylor Merwin E. • Cataloging Librarian, Monographs • University of North Texas • Denton, TX 76203 • ACRL ALCTS LITA

Taylor Michael Y. • Director • Pender County Library • Burgaw, NC 28425

Taylor Nancy L. • Reference Librarian • Earlham College Lilly Library • Richmond, IN 47374 • ACRL

Taylor Nettie B. • Baltimore, MD 21207 • ASCLA LAMA PLA CLENE
Continuing

Taylor Patricia A. • Asst to the Asst Commr Res & Ref • Chicago Public Library • Chicago, IL 60605

Taylor Patricia A. • Southeast Community College Whitesburg Center • Whitesburg, KY 41858 • ACRL

Taylor Patricia Little • Technical Cataloger • AT&T Bell Laboratioris • Holmdel, NJ 07733 • ALCTS RASD

Taylor Prudence A. • Athens, GA 30605 • RASD

Taylor Rebecca A. • Librarian • St Tammany Parish Library Slidell Branch • Slidell, LA 70458 • LAMA PLA RASD

Taylor Reginald • Trustee • Roosevelt Public Library • Roosevelt, NY 11575 • ALTA

Taylor Renda D. • Ashley River Creative Arts Elementary School • Charleston, SC 29407

Taylor Rhonda Harris • Bullard, TX 75757 • ACRL

Taylor Rita J. • Consultant • Emory University • Atlanta, GA 30329 • LITA

Taylor Robert N. • Cataloger • University of Texas Libraries General Libraries • Austin, TX 78713-7330

Taylor Robert S. • Syracuse, NY 13215 • Continuing

Taylor Sally H. • Oppenheimer, Rosenberg, Kelleher • San Antonio, TX 78205

Taylor Sandy • Trustee • River Bluffs Regional Library • Saint Joseph, MO 64501

Taylor Sheryl Sheeres • Sioux City, IA 51250

Taylor Susan D. • McPherson College Miller Library • McPherson, KS 67460-1402 • ACRL LIRT

Taylor Suzanne N. • Documents Librarian • Colorado State University William E. Morgan Library • Fort Collins, CO 80523 • GODORT IFRT MAGERT

Taylor Teri • Coordinator Library Services • Windward School • White Plains, NY 10605

Taylor Thurston • W. Vancouver BC, V7T 1X5 Canada • Life

Taylor Tom • Manager,Dist. Info. Service • Fort Vancouver Regional Library • Vancouver, WA 98663 • RASD

Taylor Vera • Des Moines, IA 50314

Taylor William Buck • Trustee • Mobile Public Library • Mobile, AL 36602 • ALTA

Taylor William F. • Chairman, Board of Trustees • Asheville-Buncombe Library System • Asheville, NC 28801 • ALTA

Taylor William R. • Information Service Librarian • Vanderbilt University Management Library • Nashville, TN 37203 • ACRL LAMA RASD

Taylor Wilma W. • Director • Sulphur Springs Public Library • Sulphur Springs, TX 75482 • PLA

Taylor Zada Miss • Newport Beach, CA 92660 • Continuing

Taylorson Jane • University California-Berkeley • Berkeley, CA 94720 • ACRL SRRT

Taysom Daniel B. • University of California Hastings College of the Law Library • San Francisco, CA 94102 • ACRL

Tayyara Joy • Craig, CO 81625

Tayyeb Rashid • Head of Technical Services • St. Mary's University Patrick Power Library • Halifax NS, B3H 3C3 Canada • ALCTS

Tchiyuka Evelyn • Ellicott City, MD 21043-0002

Teachworth Judy M. • Head, Youth Services • Canton Public Library • Canton, MI 48188 • ALSC PLA

Teague Cynthia M. • Documents/Maps Librarian • University of Vermont Bailey Howe Library • Burlington, VT 05405-0036 • GODORT MAGERT

Teague Teresa R. • Cataloger • Sunhealth Corporation Sunhelath Resource Center • Charlotte, NC 28266-8800

Teaney Carol • Librarian • Lashly & Baer, P.C. • Saint, MO 63101 • PLA

Teather Linda M. • Head of Catalog Section • University of Waterloo Library • Waterloo ON, Canada • ACRL ALCTS LITA

Tebbetts Diane R. • Associate Director • University of New Hampshire Library • Durham, NH 03824 • ACRL LAMA LITA

Tebbetts Don S. • Director Technical Services • Idaho State University Eli M. Oboler Library • Pocatello, ID 83209-8089 • ACRL

Tebbetts Letha F. • Northwest Crossing Elementary • San Antonio, TX 78250 • AASL

Tebo Marlene K. • University of California-Davis Library • Davis, CA 95616 • ACRL

Tedder Mary E. • Media Coordinator • Lincoln Middle School • Greensboro, NC 27408 • AASL

Tedei Mary • Trustee • Schiller Park Public Library • Schiller Park, IL 60176-1699 • ALTA

Tedford Judy • Lansing Elementary School • Lansing, NC 28643 • AASL

Tedford Laila • Librarian • Marie Drake Middle School • Juneau, AK 99801 • AASL

Teefy Jennifer A. • Student • Drexel University College of Information Studies • Philadelphia, PA 19104-2875

Teel Katherine R. • Cataloger • New York University Elmer Holmes Bobst Library • New York, NY 10012 • ALCTS

Teeson Elizabeth F. • Librarian • Orangewood Elementary School • Phoenix, AZ 85021 • AASL

Teeter Enola Jane N. • Librarian • Longwood Gardens Library • Kennett Square, PA 19348-0501 • ALCTS

Teeter Gladys W. • Children's Librarian • Akron-Summit County Public Library West Hill Branch • Akron, OH 44303 • ALSC

Teeter Nancy E. • Pittsburgh, PA 15212-5222 • LITA

Teeter Robert J. • Librarian • Alameda County Library System • Fremont, CA 94538

Teets Carin L. • Dayton, VA 22821-9501

Teeven Barbara L. • Librarian • Washington Community High School Library • Washington, IL 61571

Tefft Carol L. • Head Librarian • Los Altos Public Library • Los Altos, CA 94022 • PLA

Tegeler Regina • Librarian • Stirling Central School • Stirling, NJ 07980 • AASL

Teger Nancy L. • Cooper City, FL 33026 • AASL LITA YALSA

Tegler Patricia • Librarian • Freeborn & Peters • Chicago, IL 60603 • ACRL ALCTS RASD

Tehrani Farideh • Head of Access Servs • Rutgers University Libraries Archibald Stevens Alexander Library • New Brunswick, NJ 08903 • ALCTS IRRT

Teigen Philip • Deputy Chief, History of Med. • National Library of Medicine • Bethesda, MD 20894 • ACRL LHRT

Teisberg Daniel P. • Book Selection Librarian • Minneapolis Public Library & Information Center • Minneapolis, MN 55401-1992 • LAMA

Teixeira Lauren S. • Fremont, CA 94536

Telatnik George M. • Librarian • Canisius College Andrew L. Bouwhuis Library • Buffalo, NY 14208-1098 • ACRL ALCTS LAMA LITA LIRT

Telegdy Maryll I. • Head, Technical Services • Napa City-County Library • Napa, CA 94559-3396

Telerski R. Michele • Student • Kent State University School of Library & Information Science • Kent, OH 44242-0001 • ACRL

Telford Cheryl Jones • Anne Arundel County Public Library Riviera Beach Branch • Pasadena, MD 21122 • PLA

Tellefson H. J. • Librarian II • San Jose Public Library • San Jose, CA 95113

Teller Carol J. • Librarian • Marin Catholic College Preparatory • Kentfield, CA 94904

Tellier Raymond E. • Pascoag, RI 02859

Tellman Jennalyn W. • Catalog Librarian • University of Arizona Library • Tucson, AZ 85721 • ACRL ALCTS LIRT

Tema William John • Director • Altadena Library District • Altadena, CA 91001 • LAMA

Temanson Elizabeth • Librarian • Kindred School District #2 • Kindred, ND 58051 • AASL

Temp Beatrice J • Manager of Humanities Dept • Houston Public Library • Houston, TX 77002 • PLA RASD

Temple Gretchen A. • Stockton-San Joaquin County Public Library • Stockton, CA 95202

Temple Harold L. • Cataloger • College of Dupage Learning Resources Center • Glen Ellyn, IL 60137 • ALCTS

Temple Patricia • Librarian • Henrico Public Library • Richmond, VA 23223 • PLA

Temple Patricia A. • Head Librarian/Media Specialist • Miami Senior High School • Miami, FL 33135

Temple Sharon S. • Librarian • Bammel Middle School Library • Houston, TX 77090 • AASL

Temple William Byron • Administrative Librarian • Tensas Parish Library • Saint Joseph, LA 71366 • PLA

Temples James R. • Student • University of Illinois Graduate School of Library and Information Science • Urbana, IL 61801 • PLA

Temsky Miriam C. • Boston Public Library • Boston, MA 02117 • YALSA

Ten Have Elizabeth Davis • Library Systems Consultant • Michigan State University Libraries • East Lansing, MI 48824-1048 • ACRL ALCTS LITA

TenBrink Charles J. • University of Chicago D'Angelo Law Library • Chicago, IL 60637 • ACRL IFRT

Tenenbaum Jeffrey M. • Reference Librarian • University of Massachusetts Library • Amherst, MA 01003 • ACRL RASD IFRT

Tenhoff Melody L. • Media Generalist • Tilden Elementary School • Hastings, MN 55033 • AASL

ten Hoor Joan • Preservation Librarian • Newberry Library • Chicago, IL 60610 • ACRL ALCTS

Teninty Ruth • Detroit, MI 48205 • ACRL ALCTS ASCLA RASD EMIERT IFRT NMRT SRRT

Tennant Roy • Public Services Automated Sys • University of California-Berkeley University Library • Berkeley, CA 94720 • ACRL LITA

Tennen Judith J. • Ed • Book Smart • New York, NY 10011

Tennen Nancy • Book Smart • New York, NY 10011

Tennison Joy E. • Library Consultant • JR Professionals • Lafayette, CA 94549 • ILERT

Tennyson Judy • Library Consultant • York Region Board of Education • Aurora ON, L4G 3H2 Canada • AASL

Tennyson Melanie • Student • Louisiana State University School of Library & Information Science • Baton Rouge, LA 70803-3290

Tenofsky Deborah G. • University of Illinois at Chicago University Library • Chicago, IL 60680 • ACRL IFRT SRRT

Tenopir Carol • Honolulu, HI 96825 • RASD LRRT

Tenpas Cynthia • Career Resources Specialist • University of California • Riverside, CA 92517-5900 • ACRL

Tenzis Virginia • Director • Sipley School • Woodridge, IL 60517 • AASL

Teo Elizabeth • Librarian • Moraine Valley Community College Library • Palos Hills, IL 60465 • ACRL

Teoh George M. • Campus Librarian • Houston Community College Northwest Campus • Houston, TX 77041 • ACRL

Tepe Ann E. • Mgr, Library Training Services • Follett Software Company • McHenry, IL 60050-5589 • AASL

Teplitskaia Helen • Asst. Reference Librarian • University of Illinois At Chicago Library of the Health Sciences • Chicago, IL 60612

Tepner Warren L. • Pasadena, CA 91102-0354

Tepper Krysta A. • Head of Marketing • Bloomington Public Library • Bloomington, IL 61702-3308 • PLA

Tepper Laurie C. • Student • University of North Carolina at Chapel Hill School of Information and Library Science • Chapel Hill, NC 27599-3360

TerHaar Linda K. • Coor., Collection Development • University of Michigan • Ann Arbor, MI 48109-1205 • ACRL RASD

Teramoto Diane T. • Student • University of Hawaii School of Library & Information Studies • Honolulu, HI 96822 • ALSC

Terbille Charles • Reference Librarian • University of Toledo William S. Carlson Library • Toledo, OH 43606-3399 • ACRL LHRT

Terca Barbara J. • Elementary Librarian • Lyman Middle School • Kennebec, SD 57544 • AASL

Teresinski Sally S. • Librarian • Winneconne High School • Winneconne, WI 54986

Terhorst George • Board Member • Kent County Library System • Grand Rapids, MI 49503

Terhune Joy E. • Associate Professor • University of Kentucky College of Library & Information Science • Lexington, KY 40506-0391 • AASL ALSC

Terhune Linda L. • St. Louis, MO 63134 • NMRT SRRT

Terpanjian Danila • Cataloging Librarian • Harvard University Littauer Library • Cambridge, MA 02138

Terpstra Judith A.K. • Eagle River, AK 99577 • LITA

Terrell-Collymore Francine • Berwyn Public Library • Berwyn, IL 60402

Terrell Joan • Dallas, TX 75230-2502

Terrell Joy • Motorbooks International • Osceola, WI 54020

Terrill Henry • Automated Systems Librarian • Harding University • Searcy, AR 72149-0928 • ACRL LITA GODORT

Territo Patty A. • Student • Louisiana State University School of Library & Information Science • Baton Rouge, LA 70803-3290

Terry Carol • Technical Services Librarian • Norman Public Schools • Norman, OK 73069

Terry Carol D. • Project Consultant • Gonzaga University Crosby Library • Spokane, WA 99258 • LAMA

Terry Carol S. • Rhode Island School of Design Library • Providence, RI 02903 • ACRL ALCTS LAMA LITA RASD

Terry Frank W. • Trustee • Los Angeles Public Library • Los Angeles, CA 90071 • ALTA

Terry Franni J. • Clifford Johnson School • Aurora, IL 60505

Terry Helen • Milwaukee, WI 53202 • Continuing

Terry James L. • Head, Access Services • New York University Elmer Holmes Bobst Library • New York, NY 10012 • ACRL

Terry Jane • Librarian • Chadwick School Leavenworth Library • Palos Verdes Peninsu, CA 90274 • YALSA

Terry Josephine R. • Director • Butte County Library • Oroville, CA 95966 • LAMA PLA IFRT MAGERT

Terry Juanita • Reference Librarian,Emerita • Williams College Sawyer Library • Williamstown, MA 01267 • ACRL RASD *Continuing*

Terry L. Faye • Brownsburg, IN 46112 • AASL

Terry Lonny Wayne • Cataloger • Vestavia Hills Library • Vestavia Hills, AL 35216 • ACRL ALCTS LAMA PLA RASD YALSA ILERT LHRT MAGERT

Terry Michael • Library Director • Spertus College of Judaica Asher Library • Chicago, IL 60605 • ACRL

Terry Robert D • Library Trustee • DeKalb County Public Library Adminstration Building • Decatur, GA 30030 • ALTA

Terry Susan Noalani • Librarian • World Resources Institute Library • Washington, DC 20006 • ALSC IRRT

Terry William L. • Trustee • Central Arkansas Library System • Little Rock, AR 72201-4698 • ALTA

Terryberry Ann B. • Acting Director, Lib & Media Svs • North Adams State College • North Adams, MA 01247 • ACRL ALCTS

Tertell Susan M. • Department Head • Minneapolis Public Library & Information Center • Minneapolis, MN 55401-1992 • PLA

Terwillegar Jane C. • Palm Beach County Schools H. L. Johnson School • Royal Palm Beach, FL 33411 • AASL ALCTS ALSC

Terwilliger Cynthia • Director • Mackinac Island Public Library • Mackinac Island, MI 49757

Terwilliger Gail • Coordinator, Children's Service • Cumberland County Public Library and Information Center • Fayetteville, NC 28301 • ALSC PLA

Tesarek Lutisha • Kauai Library District • Lihue, HI 96766

Tesdell Angelin E. Miss • Everett, WA 98201-1320 • ACRL ALCTS *Life*

Tesdell Kate • Hoyt Library Supervisor • Public Libraries of Saginaw • Saginaw, MI 48605 • PLA

Teshima-Miller A. Lani • Student • University of Hawaii School of Library & Information Studies • Honolulu, HI 96822

Teske Boris A. • Reference Librarian • Montana State University • Bozeman, MT 59717-0332 • ACRL

Teskey John D. Mr • Director • University of New Brunswick • Fredericton NB, E3B 5H5 Canada • ACRL LAMA

Tesovnik Mary E. • Milwaukee, WI 53213-2567 • ALCTS PLA *Continuing*

Tess Mark J. • Student • Clarion University of Pennsylvania • Clarion, PA 16214 • SRRT

Tessema Legesse N. • Student • Clark-Atlanta University School of Library & Information Studies • Atlanta, GA 30314-4391

Tessman Nancy • Deputy Director • Salt Lake City Public Library • Salt Lake City, UT 84111 • ACRL ALSC LAMA PLA RASD YALSA CLENE IFRT

Testa Barbara E. • Children's Librarian • Los Angeles Public Library Goldwyn-Hollywood Regional Branch • Los Angeles, CA 90028

Testa Jo Ann • Librarian • Saint Mary Regional High School • South Amboy, NJ 08879 • AASL

Testa Philip A. • Devlp. & Comm Svs Dir • City of Chandler • Chandler, AZ 85225

Tester Ronald L. • Cataloger • Grapevine Public Library • Grapevine, TX 76051 • Life

Tetove Judith • Senior Librarian • Los Angeles Public Library Sun Valley Branch • Sun Valley, CA 91352

Tetu Thomas • Schenck High School • East Millinocket, ME 04430

Teubert Lola H. • YA Libn./Literacy Libn. • Evansville-Vanderburgh County Public Library • Evansville, IN 47708-1694

Teubert Susan E. • District Media Director • River Rouge District Media Office • River Rouge, MI 48218 • AASL

Teuton Luella B. Dr. • Head Librarian • South Florida Community College • Avon Park, FL 33825 • ACRL

Teutsch Yitzhak • Serials Cataloger • Harvard Law School Library • Cambridge, MA 02138

Teval Charles B. • Branch Librarian • Stockton-San Joaquin County Public Library Southeast Neighborhood • Stockton, CA 95206 • PLA IFRT

Tevis Jean A. • Manager, Red Carpet Serv. • Topeka Public Library • Topeka, KS 66604-1374 • ASCLA PLA RASD

Tevis Raymond H. • Director,Research Division • Arizona State Library Department of Library Archives & Public Records • Phoenix, AZ 85007

Tewell K. M. • Assistant Branch Manager • Dolley Madison Library • McLean, VA 22101 • PLA

Tews Thomas E. • Student • University of Wisconsin-Madison School of Library & Information Studies • Madison, WI 53706

Tezla Kathy E. • Collection Mgr. for Social Sci. • Emory University Libraries Robert W. Woodruff Library • Atlanta, GA 30322-2870 • ACRL ALCTS

Thabit Hassan J. • Assistant Professor • King Abdulaziz Univ • Median Munawwara, Saudi Arabia

Thacker Angela • North Vancouver, V7N 3L2 Canada

Thacker Elizabeth L. • San Francisco, CA 94118

Thacker Kyle • Media Coordinator • Brown Summit Elementary School • Browns Summit, NC 27214 • AASL

Thacker Nadine L. • Student • Wayne State University Library Science Program • Detroit, MI 48202 • IFRT SRRT

Thackery David T. • Curator of Local & Family Hist. • Newberry Library • Chicago, IL 60610 • RASD

Thackston Frances • Durham, NC 27707 • ACRL ALCTS FLRT

Thadathil Goerge V. • Assistant College Librarian • Bishop College Zale Library • Dallas, TX 75241

Thal Ileane L. • Reference Librarian II • Baldwin Public Library • Birmingham, MI 48012-3002
Thaman Betty Jo • Librarian • Ben Franklin School • Franklin, WI 53132 • AASL
Thames Beth • Librarian • Sammons Elementary School • Houston, TX 77038 • AASL
Thamm Suanne Z. • Asst. Exec. Offc.,Collection Svs • Library of Congress • Washington, DC 20541 • ALCTS LAMA
Thampi-Regy Usha R. • Principal Librarian • Paterson Free Public Library Danforth Memorial Library • Paterson, NJ 07501
Thane Beverly J. • Southwester Vermont Medical Center Medical Library • Bennington, VT 05342
Tharp James A. • Librarian • Longview Community College Blue Springs • Blue Springs, MO 64105 • RASD
Tharp Julie • Assistant Reference Librarian • Arizona State University Hayden Library • Tempe, AZ 85287-1006
Tharp Tari S. • Children's Librarian • Oxford Lane Library • Oxford, OH 45056
Thatcher Anne B. • Coor., Business Technology • Seattle Public Library • Seattle, WA 98104-1193 • RASD
Thatcher Mary E. • Humanities Bibliographer • University of Connecticut Homer Babbidge Library • Storrs, CT 06269-1005
Thatcher Roland N. • Cataloging Supervisor • Family History Library • Salt Lake City, UT 84150 • RASD
Thau Richard • Boonton-Holmes Public Library • Boonton, NJ 07005 • PLA
Thauberger Marianne T. • Coordinator of Reference Serv • University of Regina Education Library • Regina SK, S4S 0A2 Canada • ACRL LITA RASD
Thaxter Pamela J. • Bibliographer for Social Science • Temple University Paley Library • Philadelphia, PA 19122 • ACRL ALCTS RASD IFRT
Thaxton Carlton J. • Americus, GA 31709
Thayer Alix J. • High School Librarian • Charlotte Amalie High School • St. Thomas, VI 00801 • YALSA
Thayer Helen M. Miss • Plymouth, MA 02360-3401 • PLA *Continuing*
Thayer Marlene P. • Grand Ledge, MI 48837
Thayer Martha B. • Reference Librarian • King County Library System Shoreline Branch • Seattle, WA 98155 • RASD
Thayer Pamela R. • Head, Special Collections • Queens University Douglas Library • Kingston, ON, K7L 5C4 Canada • ACRL ALCTS
Thayer Richard • Reference Librarian • Janesville Public Library • Janesville, WI 53545-3971 • RASD
Thayer Shirley • Trustee • Escondido Public Library • Escondido, CA 92025 • ALTA
Thebaud Laura L. • Librarian • Meade County Public Lib • Brandenburg, KY 40108 • PLA RASD
Thebo Bill • Board President • North Kansas City Public Library • North Kansas City, MO 64116-3399 • ALTA
Theeke Tina M. • Branch Librarian • Farmington Community Library • Farmington Hills, MI 48334 • LAMA
Theinert Leo J. • Asst. Professor Library • Borough of Manhattan Community College Randolph Memorial Library • New York, NY 10007 • RASD
Theis Ann C. • Chesterfield County Library • Chesterfield, VA 23832 • YALSA
Thelin Sonya R. • Assistant Manager • Columbus Metropolitan Library • Columbus, OH 43215 • RASD
Then Mary Beth • Student • Catholic University of America School of Library and Information Science • Washington, DC 20064 • ACRL
Thenell Janice C. • Coordinator, Public Relations • Multnomah County Library • Portland, OR 97212 • LAMA PLA
Theobald Julia OP Sr. • Rosary High School • Aurora, IL 60506 • AASL
Theobald Kathleen T. • Student • State University of New York at Albany School of Information Science & Policy • Albany, NY 12222
Therriault Lynne K. • Librarian • Pinole Valley High School • Pinole, CA 94564
Thevenote Theresa • Director • Avoyelles Parish Library • Marksville, LA 71351 • LAMA PLA
Thews Dorothy D. • St. Paul, MN 55112 • ACRL IRRT
Thibault Melissa R. • Boca Raton, FL 33428 • EMIERT IFRT SRRT
Thibodeau Patricia L. • Director • Mountain Area Health Education Center Information & Media Services • Asheville, NC 28801-4686
Thibodeaux Annette B. • High School Librarian • Archbishop Chapelle High School • Metairie, LA 70003 • AASL
Thiede Beverly J. • Area Library Division Manager • Hennepin County Library • Minnetonka, MN 55343 • LAMA PLA
Thiegs Francis J. • Head of Bibliographic Control • New York University Frederick Ehrman Medical Library • New York, NY 10016-6450 • ACRL ALCTS
Thiel Sarah G. • Student • University of Missouri-Columbia School of Library & Informational Science • Columbia, MO 65211 • IFRT SRRT
Thiele Barbara J. • Scotch Plains, NJ 07076 • PLA
Thiele Gloria D. • Nevada City, CA 95959
Thiele Kay C. • Student • Texas Woman's University School of Library & Information Studies • Denton, TX 76204
Thieling Kaileen R. • Head of Branch Services • Central Mississippi Regional Library System • Pearl, MS 39208 • PLA
Thierry Lynn • Venice, FL 34285 • PLA RASD
Thies Arlene • Trustee • Wayne Public Library • Wayne, NJ 07470 • ALTA
Thiesen Barbara A. • Technical Services Librarian • Bethel College • North Newton, KS 67117 • ACRL
Thiesse Carol J. • Student • University of Southern Mississippi School of Library Science • Hattiesburg, MS 39406-5146
Thiessen Lois M. • Elementary Librarian • Unified School District 460 • Hesston, KS 67062 • AASL
Thigpen Elizabeth M. • Media Specialist • Incirlik Elementary School • APO, AE 09824 • IRRT
Thigpen Geraldine • School Library Media Specialist • Emerson Junior High School • Los Angeles, CA 90024 • AASL
Thigpen Rosie Meadows • Young Adult Librarian • Atlanta-Fulton Public Library West End Branch • Atlanta, GA 30310 • ALSC PLA YALSA
Thigpen Sara C. • Student • University of South Carolina College of Library & Information Science • Columbia, SC 29208
Third Bettie Jane • Ridgefield, CT 06877
Thirlwall David E. • Head, Woods Education Library • University of Manitoba D.S. Woods Education Library • Winnipeg MB, R3T 2N2 Canada
Thiry Christopher J.J. • Student • University of Michigan School of Information and Library Studies • Ann Arbor, MI 48109-1092 • MAGERT
Thistle Dawn R. • Reader Services Librarian • College of the Holy Cross Dinand Library • Worcester, MA 01610 • ACRL LAMA RASD
Thomann Carolyn N. • Librarian • Palmyra High School Library • Palmyra, WI 53156 • AASL
Thomas Albertha Clark • Executive Director • Literacy Volunteers of Westchester • Elmsford, NY 10523 • EMIERT
Thomas Ann • Librarian • Challenger Middle School-LMC • Colorado Springs, CO 80920 • AASL
Thomas Anne • Rexham Corporation • Matthews, NC 28106-7003
Thomas Barbara • Co-owner • Toad Hall Bookstore • Austin, TX 78705 • ALSC
Thomas Barbara C. • Texas A & M University Medical Sciences Library • College Station, TX 77843
Thomas Barbara J. • Student • State University of New York (SUNY) School of Information & Library Studies • Buffalo, NY 14260 • PLA
Thomas Bernadette Sr. • Librarian • Holy Cross High School • Delran, NJ 08075 • AASL ALCTS YALSA NMRT
Thomas Beverly • Trustee • Peoria Public Library • Peoria, IL 61602 • ALTA
Thomas Bobbi • Student • University of Maryland College of Library and Information Services • College Park, MD 20742-4345 • AASL
Thomas Brenda H. • Media Specialist, AV Department • Public Schools • Pittsfield, MA 01201
Thomas Byron • Trustee • East Central Regional Library • Cedar Rapids, IA 52401
Thomas Carol M. • Kalamazoo, MI 49006
Thomas Carol Mrs. • Trustee • Detroit Public Library • Detroit, MI 48202 • ALTA
Thomas Caroline M. • Principal Accounting Clerk • Atlanta-Fulton Public Library • Atlanta, GA 30303
Thomas Carolyn • Reference Librarian • Merced County Library • Merced, CA 95340
Thomas Carolyn W. • Putnam County School System • Cookeville, TN 38501 • AASL
Thomas Carren A. • Educational Media Specialist • Voorhees High School Library • Glen Gardner, NJ 08826 • AASL
Thomas Catherine • Morton High School • Morton, TX 79346 • AASL
Thomas Catherine M. • Librarian • Columbia University Libraries • New York, NY 10027 • LITA
Thomas Charles W. • Baltimore County Public Library • Towson, MD 21204 • ALTA PLA IFRT
Thomas Christopher A. • Student • University of California Los Angeles Graduate School of Library & Information Science • Los Angeles, CA 90024
Thomas Dale A. • Director of Education • University of Kansas Medical Center A.R. Dykes Library • Kansas City, KS 66103
Thomas David H. • Head, Technical Services • Michigan Technological University Library • Houghton, MI 49931 • ACRL ALCTS LITA
Thomas David L. Jr. Mr. • Trustee • Mobile Public Library • Mobile, AL 36602 • ALTA
Thomas Deborah • Head of Public Services • North Carolina University Ramsey Library • Asheville, NC 28804 • RASD
Thomas Diana M. Dr. • Associate Professor • University of California-Los Angeles (UCLA) • Los Angeles, CA 90024-1450 • ACRL ALCTS RASD EMIERT IRRT
Thomas Diane D. • Hilliard Station School • Hilliard, OH 43026 • AASL
Thomas Donald L. • Director, Financial Services • Harris County Public Library • Houston, TX 77054 • PLA
Thomas Dorothy M. • Janesville, WI 53546 • Continuing
Thomas Ernestine • Environmental Protection Agency • Washington, DC 20460 • LITA
Thomas Fannette H. • Reference Librarian • Essex Community College James A. Newpher Library • Baltimore, MD 21237 • ALSC RASD
Thomas Fran • Student • Rutgers University School of Communication Information & Library Studies • New Brunswick, NJ 08903
Thomas Frankie T. Mrs. • Northport, AL 35476 • RASD IFRT *Continuing*
Thomas Gail C. • Librarian • Churchland Academy Elementary School • Portsmouth, VA 23703 • AASL
Thomas Gail S. • Owner • Computer Wizard Professional Building • Long Beach, CA 90813
Thomas Glynys R. • Public Services, Bibliographic • Emerson College Library • Boston, MA 02116 • ACRL
Thomas Grace H. • Associate Librarian • University of California UCSB Library • Santa Barbara, CA 93106-9010 • ALCTS
Thomas Gregory S. • Assistant Dir, Library Services • Amarillo Public Library • Amarillo, TX 79189 • ALCTS
Thomas Hannah C. • Head,Special Collections Catlg • Ohio State University Libraries • Columbus, OH 43210-1286 • ACRL ALCTS
Thomas Helen F. • Munich International School Library • Starnberg, 8130 Germany • AASL
Thomas Helen J Lind • Charleston, WV 25312 • AASL ALSC
Thomas Jacquelyn H. • Academy Librarian • Phillips Exeter Academy Library • Exeter, NH 03833-1104 • AASL ACRL ALCTS LITA
Thomas James M. • Sr. Prog/Analyst • Carl Systems, Inc. • Denver, CO 80210 • LITA
Thomas Janet K. • Cataloger • Florida Southern College Roux Library • Lakeland, FL 33801
Thomas Janice • Media Coordinator • Manchester High School • Akron, OH 44319 • AASL
Thomas Janice M. • Head, Circulation Division • University of Washington Suzzallo Library • Seattle, WA 98195 • ACRL LAMA LITA IRRT
Thomas Jean F. • Green Mountain, IA 50637
Thomas Joan M. • Rochester, NY 14619
Thomas Johanna V. • Student • Queens College Graduate School of Library & Information Studies • Flushing, NY 11367
Thomas John B. • Dean, Learning Resources • Davidson County Community College Learning Resource Center • Lexington, NC 27293 • ACRL
Thomas John B. III • Chief, Rare Book Cataloging • University of Texas Ransom Humanities Research Center • Austin, TX 78713 • ACRL
Thomas Jonathan R. • Collection Development Librarian • Boston College Law Library • Newton Center, MA 02159 • ACRL ALCTS
Thomas Josephine • Technical Services Librarian • Calumet City Public Library • Calumet City, IL 60409-4003 • ALCTS
Thomas Juanita S. • Library Media Specialist • Clear Spring Elementary School • Clear Spring, MD 21722
Thomas Judy M. • Media Specialist • Portland Public Schools • Portland, OR 97208-3107 • AASL
Thomas Julia W. • Littlton, CO 80120
Thomas Julie A. • Technical Services Librarian • Drake University Cowles Library • Des Moines, IA 50311 • ALCTS LITA
Thomas Karen I. • Librarian • Glorietta Elementary School • Orinda, CA 94563 • ALSC
Thomas Karen L. • Reference Librarian • Muskogee Public Library • Muskogee, OK 74401 • PLA RASD
Thomas Karol Jean • Librarian • San Mateo County Office of Education • Redwood City, CA 94065-1064 • AASL
Thomas Katherine M. • Student • University of Western Ontario School of Library & Information Science • London ON, N6G 1H1 Canada
Thomas Kathryn O. • School Media Specialist • Greenville High School • Greenville, SC 29650

Thomas Kathy S. • Librarian • Public Library of Des Moines North Side Library • Des Moines, IA 50313

Thomas Kenneth C. • Staten Island, NY 10301

Thomas Kristi S. • Student • University of Texas at Austin Graduate School of Library & Information Sciences • Austin, TX 78712-1276

Thomas L. Jack • Trustee • Euclid Public Library • Euclid, OH 44123-2091 • ALTA

Thomas Laura L. • Student • University of Texas at Austin Graduate School of Library & Information Sciences • Austin, TX 78712-1276

Thomas Lawrence E. • University Librarian • Seattle Univ Library • Seattle, WA 98122 • Life

Thomas Linda C. • Townsend, DE 19734 • ACRL

Thomas Louise • Kent County Library System • Grand Rapids, MI 49503 • ALTA

Thomas Lucille C. • Brooklyn, NY 11225 • AASL ALSC YALSA EMIERT IRRT SRRT *Life*

Thomas Lucinda A. • Front Royal, VA 22630

Thomas Lucy B. • Library Director • Santa Barbara Cottage Hospital David L. Reeves Medical Library • Santa Barbara, CA 93102

Thomas Lucy L. • Pittsburgh, PA 15210

Thomas Lynda H. • Shaker Heights, OH 44122

Thomas M. Rosemary • Kerrville, TX 78028

Thomas Mabel L. • Librarian • Department of Defense Pentagon Library • Washington, DC 20310

Thomas Marcia L. • Director • Eureka Public Library • Eureka, IL 61530 • LAMA PLA

Thomas Margaret F. Miss • Hermitage, TN 37076 • Continuing

Thomas Margaret Miller • Orangeburg County Library • Orangeburg, SC 29115-1367 • ALSC

Thomas Margie J. • Librarian • NEWSBANK, Incorporation • Naples, FL 33942 • AASL

Thomas Margo A. • Media Specialist • Tzouanakis Elementary School • Greencastle, IN 46135 • AASL

Thomas Marie T. • Reference Librarian • Barrington Area Library • Barrington, IL 60010

Thomas Mark A. • Director • Johnson City Public Library • Johnson City, TN 37601-5771 • LAMA PLA

Thomas Mark A. • Reference Librarian • Texas A & M University Sterling C. Evans Library • College Station, TX 77843-5000 • GODORT MAGERT

Thomas Mark E. • Cook Christian Training School • Tempe, AZ 85281 • ALCTS RASD

Thomas Martin E. • Sacramento, CA 95818 • Continuing

Thomas Mary Alma • Mitchell, SD 57301 • AASL PLA *Continuing*

Thomas Mary Augusta • Assistant Dir Planning & Adm. • Smithsonian Institution Libraries • Washington, DC 20560 • LAMA

Thomas Mary C. • Library of the American Women's Club • 2587 AB Den Haag, Netherlands

Thomas Mary Sr • Librarian • Mary Immaculate Academy Library • New Britain, CT 06053

Thomas Matthew Jr. • Trustee • Jackson-Hinds Library System • Jackson, MS 39201 • ALTA

Thomas Melanie • User's Service Librarian • Middle Tennessee State University Andrew L. Todd Library • Murfreesboro, TN 37132

Thomas Michael C. • Reference Librarian • Indian Trails Public Library District • Wheeling, IL 60090

Thomas Nan E. • Director • Albert L. Scott Public Library • Alabaster, AL 35007

Thomas Nancy P • Student • Rutgers University Libraries • New Brunswick, NJ 08903 • AASL

Thomas Nell M. • Public Services Librarian • Thomas Jefferson Junior High School • Beeville, TX 78102

Thomas Nena Virginia • Student • University of Illinois Graduate School of Library and Information Science • Urbana, IL 61801 • NMRT

Thomas P. Steven • Instructor/Reference Librarian • Washburn University of Topeka Mabee Library • Topeka, KS 66621

Thomas Patricia • Director • Plymouth Public Library • Plymouth, MI 48170 • ALTA LAMA LITA PLA

Thomas Patricia M. • Head Cataloger • Stockton-San Joaquin County Public Library • Stockton, CA 95202 • ALCTS PLA

Thomas Patricia Q. • Librarian • Derby Elementary School • Derby Line, VT 05830 • AASL

Thomas Paul H, • Head, Catalog Dept. • Hoover Institution on War, Revolution & Peace Library • Stanford, CA 94305-6010 • ACRL ALCTS LAMA LITA

Thomas Paulette S. • Head of Technical Services • Virginia Historical Society Lib • Richmond, VA 23221-0311

Thomas Rebecca L. • Librarian • Shaker Heights City School District • Shaker Heights, OH 44120 • ALSC

Thomas Robert D. Sr. • Coordinator • Sauk Valley Community College Learning Resource Center • Dixon, IL 61021 • ACRL ALTA

Thomas Robert M. • Coordinator Librarian • New York Public Library Mid-Manhattan Branch • New York, NY 10016

Thomas Rosa A. • Dothan, AL 36303 • Continuing

Thomas Sandra • Trustee • Kanawha County Public Library • Charleston, WV 25301 • ALTA

Thomas Sarah E. • Director for Cataloging • Library of Congress • Washington, DC 20541 • ACRL ALCTS LITA *Life*

Thomas Sarah K. • Director,Library Services • Embry-Riddle Aeronautical University • Prescott, AZ 86301 • ACRL

Thomas Scott E. • Reference Department • Scranton Public Library Albright Memorial Library • Scranton, PA 18509-3248

Thomas Sharon • Librarian • Goddard ILC/JH • Goddard, KS 67052 • AASL

Thomas Sherilyn • Director of Development • Library Foundation of San Francisco • San Francisco, CA 94104

Thomas Shirley R. • Head, Circulation & Reserves • Virginia Commonwealth University • Richmond, VA 23284-2033 • LAMA

Thomas Stacie L. • Information Specalist • Dialog Information Service Inc. • Palo Alto, CA 94304

Thomas Steve R. • University of Tennessee John C. Hodges Library • Knoxville, TN 37996-1000

Thomas Suzanne L. • Technical Specialist • University of Pittsburgh Hillman Library • Pittsburgh, PA 15260 • ALCTS *Life*

Thomas Tamela M. • Coordinator of Adult Services • Uncle Remus Regional Library System • Madison, GA 30650

Thomas Thelma Ruffin • New York, NY 10001 • YALSA

Thomas Toy • Librarian • Kennedy Elementary School • Texarkana, TX 75503

Thomas Vanrea M. • Student • Pratt Institute Graduate School of Library & Information Science • Brooklyn, NY 11205 • ACRL LAMA LITA

Thomas Victoria L. • Student • University of Washington Graduate School of Library and Information Science • Seattle, WA 98195

Thomas Vivian • Palo Alto, CA 94306

Thomas Wendy M. • Public Service Librarian • Radcliffe College Schlesinger Library • Cambridge, MA 02138 • ACRL SRRT

Thomas Willamae D. • Scottsdale, AZ 85260-7505

Thomasian Belinda F. • Library Director • Rutland Free Public Library • Rutland, MA 01543 • PLA

Thomason Cathy R. • Technical Services Librarian • Oxnard Public Library • Oxnard, CA 93030 • ACRL ALCTS

Thomason Helen C. • Librarian • Chattanooga Public Schools • Chattanooga, TN 37421 • AASL

Thomason Lynn A. • Medical Librarian • United States Veterans Administration Medical Center • Louisville, KY 40206

Thomason Mary Jean • Technical Services Librarian • Samford University Library • Birmingham, AL 35229

Thomasson Raymond F. • Charleston, WV 25302 • ALSC YALSA *Life*

Thome Helen E. • Librarian • Flint Public Library Cody Branch • Flint, MI 48507-1595 • PLA RASD *Life*

Thomes Katherine • Student • University of Wisconsin-Madison School of Library & Information Studies • Madison, WI 53706

Thommasson Alan A. • Branch Library Manager • Queens Borough Public Library • Jamaica, NY 11432

Thompson-Joyner Rita S. • Hd. Tech. Servs. Dept. • District of Columbia Public Library Martin Luther King Memorial Library • Washington, DC 20001 • ALCTS PLA

Thompson-Schmidt Margaret • Director of Media Services • Farmington Public Schools • Farmington, MI 48336 • AASL

Thompson-Stiles Mary • Daisy Elementary School • Loris, SC 29569

Thompson Ann • Associate University Librarian • University of Cincinnati • Cincinnati, OH 45221-0033 • ACRL ALCTS LAMA RASD

Thompson Ann R. • Director, Research • Special Libraries Association • Washington, DC 20009

Thompson Annie F. • Professor • University of Puerto Rico Graduate School of Librarianship • Rio Piedras, PR 00931 • ACRL LIRT

Thompson Antoinette Ms. • Library Assistant • Ferguson Municipal Public Library • Ferguson, MO 63135

Thompson Barbara E. • Information Technician • DIA/ RTS-2B • Washington, DC 20340 • ALCTS FLRT

Thompson Barbara F. • Head Librarian • Forsyth County Public Library Rual Hall Branch • Winston-Salem, NC 27045

Thompson Betsy J. • Assistant Director • Sioux City Public Library • Sioux City, IA 51101-1203 • PLA

Thompson Bette M. • Reference Librarian • Ann Arbor Public Library • Ann Arbor, MI 48104 • PLA RASD EMIERT

Thompson Betty J. • Library of Congress • Washington, DC 20541

Thompson C. Dawn • Copyright Cataloger • Library of Congress • Washington, DC 20541 • LITA

Thompson Carol L. • Rochester, NY 14612 • ALSC

Thompson Carol L. • Parma, OH 44134

Thompson Carrie K. • Reference Librarian • Paine College Collins-Callaway Library • Augusta, GA 30901

Thompson Christine • Dakota County Library System Burnsville Branch Library • Burnsville, MN 55337

Thompson Christine E. • Assistant Professor • University of Wisconsin-Milwaukee School of Library & Information Science • Milwaukee, WI 53201 • ALCTS

Thompson Cindy • Student • Northeast Louisiana University Library Science Program-College of Education • Monroe, LA 71209

Thompson Connie • Assistant Librarian • Fort Stockton Public Library • Fort Stockton, TX 79735

Thompson D Lynn • Assistant Director • Southern Pines Public Library • Southern Pines, NC 28387 • RASD

Thompson Dale • Director • Providence Public Library • Providence, RI 02903-3283 • ACRL ALCTS LAMA LITA PLA RASD EMIERT IFRT SRRT

Thompson Deborah L. • Student • University of Oklahoma School of Library & Information Studies • Norman, OK 73019

Thompson Denise A. • Librarian • Corvallis-Benton County Public Library • Corvallis, OR 97330-4728

Thompson Diane G. • Greensboro, NC 27403-1868

Thompson Diane M. • System Expansion Program Manager • Pierce County Rural Library District • Tacoma, WA 98446 • LAMA PLA

Thompson Dixie • Phoenix, AZ 85021 • AASL ALSC *Continuing*

Thompson Don K. • Preservation Librarian • University of Southern California Doheny Library • Los Angeles, CA 90089-0182 • ACRL ALCTS SRRT

Thompson Dorothea M. • Reference Librarian • Carnegie-Mellon University Libraries Hunt Library • Pittsburgh, PA 15213 • ACRL RASD LIRT

Thompson Dot S. • Bucknell University Bertrand Library • Lewisburg, PA 17837-2086 • ACRL LIRT

Thompson Douglas M. • Student • University of California Los Angeles Graduate School of Library & Information Science • Los Angeles, CA 90024 • ACRL

Thompson Edna May • Bennington, VT 05201 • AASL ALSC *Continuing*

Thompson Elizabeth A. • Adminstrative Assistant • American College of Radiology • Reston, VA 22091 • LAMA

Thompson Elizabeth M. • Washington, DC 20007 • ACRL

Thompson Ellen • Riverside, CA 92507

Thompson Ellen C. • Young Adult Librarian • Westminster Public Library • Westminster, CO 80030-4970 • YALSA

Thompson Ellen P. • Reference Librarian • Wheaton Public Library • Wheaton, IL 60187-5376 • RASD

Thompson Elsa Smith • Albuquerque, NM 87108 • PLA *Continuing*

Thompson Evan • Orwell, VT 05760

Thompson Florence E. • Branch Librarian • Public Library of Cincinnati and Hamilton County Mount Washington Branch • Cincinnati, OH 45230

Thompson Frances M. • Leander, TX 78641 • AASL ALSC

Thompson Gary • University of California-Los Angeles (UCLA) • Los Angeles, CA 90024-1450 • LITA

Thompson Gary B. • Head of Information Serv. • Cleveland State University Library • Cleveland, OH 44115 • ACRL ILERT

Thompson Glenda P. • Information Supervisor • Lake Lanier Regional Library System Lilburn Public Library • Lilburn, GA 30247

Thompson Glenn J. Dr. • Professor • University of Wisconsin-Eau Claire William D. McIntyre Library • Eau Claire, WI 54702 • ALCTS RASD *Life*

Thompson Helen R. Mrs. • Washington, DC 20037 • RASD *Continuing*

Thompson Hubert J. • Chicago Public Library Sulzer Regional Library • Chicago, IL 60625 • ACRL PLA RASD IFRT SRRT

Thompson J. A. • John Wiley & Sons, Inc. • New York, NY 10158

Thompson J. Rebecca • Associate Librarian • State Univ of NY Coll at Potsdam Frederick W. Crumb Memorial Library • Potsdam, NY 13676 • ACRL ALCTS LAMA LITA

Thompson Jacque D. • Librarian • Paseo Academy of the Arts • Kansas City, MO 64108 • AASL

Thompson James C. • University of California Rivera Library • Riverside, CA 92517 • ACRL

Thompson Jane M. • Librarian • Ludlow High School Library • Ludlow, MA 01056 • AASL

Thompson Janet • Rice University Fondren Library • Houston, TX 77251-1892

Thompson Janet C. • Librarian • Hamilton Park Pacesetter Elementary School • Dallas, TX 75243 • AASL

Thompson Jean A. • Falmouth, ME 04105-1127

Thompson Jean T. • Assistant Director • University of Wisconsin-Madison Memorial Library • Madison, WI 53706 • ACRL RASD

Thompson Jennifer G. • Director • Chillicothe & Ross County Public Library • Chillicothe, OH 45601

Thompson John H. • Brooklyn, NY 11201

Thompson John T. • Baraboo, WI 53913-2530 • ALSC PLA

Thompson Jolyn K. • Student • Rutgers University School of Communication Information & Library Studies • New Brunswick, NJ 08903 • SRRT

Thompson Judith • St Johnsbury, VT 05819 • AASL

Thompson Judith A. • San Diego, CA 92101 • ACRL

Thompson Judith E. • Student • Berry College Memorial Library • Mount Berry, GA 30149 • SRRT

Thompson Judy L. • Parsons, KS 67357 • AASL

Thompson Julia C. • Librarian II • Santa Clara County Free Library Cupertino Public Library • Cupertino, CA 95014 • YALSA

Thompson Julia M. • Mt. Pleasant, SC 29464 • PLA IFRT

Thompson Katherine • Trustee • Wheeler Basin Regional Library • Decatur, AL 35602 • ALTA

Thompson Katherine • Kansas State University Libraries • Manhattan, KS 66506-7166

Thompson Katherine Jean • Sanborn, NY 14132

Thompson Kathleen L. • Director • Chapel Hill Public Library • Chapel Hill, NC 27514 • LAMA

Thompson Kathy P. • Carrollton Public Library • Carrollton, TX 75006 • RASD

Thompson Larry A. • University of Nebraska • Lincoln, NE 68588 • ACRL

Thompson Laura I. • Austin, TX 78703 • ACRL *Continuing*

Thompson Laurie L. • Assistant Director • George Washington University Himmelfarb Health Sciences Library • Washington, DC 20037

Thompson Leone B. • Library Media Specialist • H. D. Woodson Senior High School • Washington, DC 20019 • AASL

Thompson Linda • Librarian • Spring Lake Earth School District • Earth, TX 79031

Thompson Linda D. • Librarian • Thomas Haley Elementary School • Irving, TX 75062 • AASL

Thompson Linda L. • Assistant Director, Bibl Service • University of Houston Libraries • Houston, TX 77204-2091 • ALCTS LAMA LITA RASD

Thompson Linda L. • Children's Outreach Librarian • Joliet Public Library • Joliet, IL 60431 • ALSC

Thompson Lisa C. • Index Editor • National Security Archive • Washington, DC 20036 • GODORT IRRT

Thompson Lois J. • Director • Marion County Public Library • Fairmont, WV 26554 • PLA

Thompson Lois M. • Toledo, OH 43612-1657 • RASD YALSA *Life*

Thompson Lola R. • Waco, TX 76710 • ALSC *Continuing*

Thompson Lucille W. • Reference Librarian • Montana State University • Bozeman, MT 59717-0332 • ACRL

Thompson Lynn H. • Hope Valley, RI 02832 • PLA YALSA

Thompson M. G. • Orangeburg, SC 29115 • Continuing

Thompson Marianne M. • Head of Information Services • Fountaindale Public Library District • Bolingbrook, IL 60440

Thompson Marilyn L. • Newport Public Library • Newport, OR 97365 • ASCLA RASD

Thompson Marilyn M. • Media Center Clerk • Cameron Elementary School West Covina Unified School District • West Covina, CA 91790

Thompson Mary Agnes E • Secretary/Treasurer • Council on Library Resources • Washington, DC 20036-2117 • LAMA

Thompson Mary E. • Lafayette, IN 47905 • Continuing

Thompson Mary S. • Student • North Carolina Central University • Durham, NC 27707

Thompson Matilda E. • Chevy Chase, MD 20815 • AASL

Thompson Matt F. • Roanoke, VA 24015

Thompson Michele K. • Student • University of Rhode Island Graduate School of Library & Information Studies • Kingston, RI 02881-0815 • LITA

Thompson Miriam E. • Preston, CT 06365

Thompson Miriam H. • Librarian II • Detroit Public Library Downtown Branch • Detroit, MI 48226-2284

Thompson Nena • Trustee • Anderson County Library • Anderson, SC 29622-4047

Thompson Neva P. • Library Media Specialist • Humboldt Unified School District • Dewey, AZ 86327 • AASL

Thompson Paige L. • Boca Raton, FL 33434

Thompson Patricia A. • Junior High Librarian/ Computers • Churchill Junior High School • Galesburg, IL 61401 • LRRT

Thompson Patricia T. • Michigan State University Libraries • East Lansing, MI 48824-1048

Thompson Paulette R. • Librarian • McCornack Library • Eugene, OR 97405 • AASL ALSC

Thompson Richard • Beloit Memorial High School Library • Beloit, WI 53511 • AASL

Thompson Richard E. • Director • Wilmette Public Library • Wilmette, IL 60091 • LAMA LITA PLA RASD

Thompson Robert • Manager, Library Computing Serv. • York University Libraries • North York ON, M3J 1P3 Canada

Thompson Ronelle K. H. • Director • Augustana College Mikkelsen Library • Sioux Falls, SD 57197 • ACRL LAMA

Thompson Rosalind R. • King County Library System Valley View Library • Seattle, WA 98188 • ALSC

Thompson Rosanne T. • Children's Librarian • Timberland Regional Library Olympia Branch • Olympia, WA 98501 • ALSC

Thompson Rosemary • Coordinator of Library Services • Dufferin-Peel RCSS Board • W. Mississauga, ON, L5R 1C5 Canada • AASL

Thompson Russell E. • Manager, Technical Support • Brodart Company • Williamsport, PA 17705 • LITA

Thompson Ruth C. • San Francisco, CA 94123 • ALCTS

Thompson Ruth L. • New Orleans, LA 70115-6450

Thompson Sally Anne M. • Librarian • Orangedale School • Phoenix, AZ 85008 • AASL ALSC YALSA

Thompson Sally L. • Librarian • The New York Public Library • New York, NY 10016 • PLA

Thompson Sandra M. • Temple University Ambler Campus Library • Philadelphia, PA 19002-3993 • ACRL LIRT

Thompson Sara • Acquisitions Librarian • Stanislaus County Free Library • Modesto, CA 95354

Thompson Sarah B. • Librarian • Bates Elementary School • Fayetteville, AR 72701 • AASL

Thompson Stephen L. • Humanities/Reference Librarian • Brown University Library • Providence, RI 02912

Thompson Steven E. • Head, Serials Department • Brown University Library • Providence, RI 02912 • ALCTS

Thompson Sue Ann • Librarian • Casa Grande Public Library • Casa Grande, AZ 85222 • ALSC PLA

Thompson Susan • Senior Librarian • Los Angeles Public Library Systems Little Tokyo Branch • Los Angeles, CA 90013

Thompson Susan J. • Head Science Librarian • Indiana State University • Terre Haute, IN 47809 • ACRL LITA

Thompson Susan M. • Assistant Director • Mercyhurst College Hammermill Library • Erie, PA 16546 • ACRL LITA

Thompson Susan O. • New York, NY 10025

Thompson Suzanne E. • Head of Ref & Inf Services • Portland Public Library • Portland, ME 04101 • PLA

Thompson Sybil J. • Librarian • Phillips Junior College • Clovis, CA 93612 • AASL ACRL NMRT

Thompson Sylvia • Library Coordinator • Pasadena Unified School District Sierra Madre Elementary School Library • Sierra Madre, CA 91024 • AASL

Thompson Theresa R. • Student • Saint John's University Division of Library & Information Science • Jamaica, NY 11439

Thomsen Elizabeth B. • Database Manager • North of Boston Library Exchange (NOBLE) • Beverly, MA 01915

Thomson Andros • East Millstone, NJ 08875

Thomson Gary A. • Systems Librarian • Tarleton State University • Stephenville, TX 76402 • ACRL

Thomson Gordon R. • Deputy Director • North York Public Library • North York ON, M2N 5N9 Canada • LAMA PLA

Thomson Kristin K. • St. George, UT 84771

Thomson Mary Beth • University of Houston Libraries • Houston, TX 77204-2091 • ALCTS LAMA

Thomson Ralph D. • Director Emeritus/Professor Emer • University of Utah Marriott Library • Salt Lake City, UT 84112-1179 • Continuing

Thomson Sarah C. • Branch Librarian • Pinelands Branch Library • Medford, NJ 08055

Thomson Sarah E. • Cataloging Dept. • University of Massachusetts University Library • Amherst, MA 01003 • ACRL ALCTS SRRT

Thomson Sarah K. Dr • Librarian • Bergen Community College Library & Learning Resource Center • Paramus, NJ 07652-1595 • ACRL ALCTS RASD *Life*

Thomson William M. Jr. • Naples, FL 33942

Thoner Jane T. • North Brunswick Free Public Library • North Brunswick, NJ 08902

Thor Angela M. • Syracuse, NY 13210 • ACRL

Thorburn Colleen M. • Gainesville, FL 32608 • ACRL ALCTS

Thoreen Bonnie Vikan • Asst Dean, LR & Staff Devel • Napa Valley College Library • Napa, CA 94558-6236

Thorin Suzanne E. • Chief of Staff • Library of Congress • Washington, DC 20541 • ACRL

Thorisch Thomas • Ref. & Bibl. Instruction • Central State University Library • Edmond, OK 73034-0193

Thorkildson Terry A. • Adult Services Librarian • Alachua County Library District • Gainesville, FL 32601 • PLA RASD

Thorn-Olson Cecelia J. • Director • United States Army Armament, Munitions & Chem. Cmd. • Rock Island, IL 61299-6000 • LITA AFLRT

Thornburg Barbara J. • Albany, OR 97321-3050

Thornburg Marilyn W. • Librarian Media Specialist • Chesapeake Public Schools Truitt Middle School • Chesapeake, VA 23324

Thornbury Donald R. • Head, Catalog Division • Princeton University • Princeton, NJ 08544-2098 • ACRL ALCTS

Thorndike Nicholas S. • Reference Librarian • East Chicago Public Library • E. Chicago, IN 46312 • RASD IFRT SRRT

Thorne Bonnie B. • Professor • Sam Houston State University Department of Library Science • Huntsville, TX 77341-2236 • AASL ACRL ALCTS LHRT LRRT *Life*

Thorne Larry R. • Head Librarian • Alva Public Library • Alva, OK 73717 • PLA

Thorne Marco G. • San Diego, CA 92115

Thorne Rosemary • Head/Reference Department • San Jose State University Clark Library • San Jose, CA 95192-0028 • ACRL LAMA RASD IFRT

Thorngren Barbara P. • Eaglecrest High School • Aurora, CO 80015 • AASL IFRT

Thornhill Robert E. • Siskiyou County Library • Yreka, CA 96097 • PLA IRRT LRRT

Thornley Katherine A. • Student • University of California-Berkeley School of Library & Information Studies • Berkeley, CA 94720

Thornton Eileen • Librarian Emerita • Oberlin College Library • Oberlin, OH 44074 • ACRL LAMA *Life*

Thornton Elizabeth E. • Library Director • Bentley Memorial Library • Bolton, CT 06043

Thornton Glenda Ms. • Associate Director for Lib Svs • University of Colorado at Denver Auraria Library • Denver, CO 80204 • ACRL LAMA

Thornton Joyce K. • Executive Assistant • Texas A & M University • College Station, TX 77843-5000 • ACRL LAMA LRRT

Thornton Linda L. • Interlibrary Loan Librarian • Auburn University Ralph Brown Draughon Library • Auburn, AL 36849-5606 • ACRL RASD

Thornton Madge M. Dr • Library Media • Original Providence • Chicago, IL 60644

Thornton Pamela C. • Assistant Director • Kean College of New Jersey Library • Union, NJ 07083 • ACRL LAMA

Thornton Ruth L. • Burlington, NY 13315

Thornton Sheila F. • Head State Library Service • California State Library • Sacramento, CA 94237-0001 • ASCLA LAMA LITA RASD GODORT

Thornton Susan K. • Assistant Base Librarian • Offutt Air Force Base Library • Offutt AFB, NE 68113-4004 • YALSA

Thorp H Arlene Ms • Weare, NH 03281 • ALSC *Continuing*

Thorpe Andrea L. • Director • Richards Free Library • Newport, NH 03773 • PLA

Thorpe Diantha • Editor/Publisher • The Shoe String Press • Hamden, CT 06514 • AASL ALSC

Thorpe Frederick A. • Managing Director & Chairman • Ulverscroft Large Print Books Ltd. Publications • Leicestershire, England • ASCLA PLA

Thorpe Roberta C. • Wyld Database Manager • Wyoming State Library • Cheyenne, WY 82002

Thorrat Lori • Student • Kent State University School of Library & Information Science • Kent, OH 44242-0001

Thorsen Don D. • Assistant Librarian • Rantoul Public Library • Rantoul, IL 61866 • PLA

Thorsen Jeanne M. • Manager, Community Relations • King County Library System • Seattle, WA 98109-5191 • LAMA PLA

Thorseth Liv M. • Reference/Collections Librarian • University of Regina Education Library • Regina SK, S4S 0A2 Canada • ACRL LITA PLA RASD LIRT

Thorson Connie C. • Acquisitions Librarian • University of New Mexico General Library • Albuquerque, NM 87131 • ACRL

Thorson Shirley M. • Director • Southbury Public Library • Southbury, CT 06488 • VRT

Thrash Blanche C. • Student • Georgia State University Pullen Library • Atlanta, GA 30303-3081

Thrash Sarah M. • Director • Seaford District Library • Seaford, DE 19973 • PLA

Thrasher Jerry A. • Director • Cumberland County Public Library and Information Center • Fayetteville, NC 28301 • ALTA LAMA LITA PLA

Thrasher Margaret L. • Branch Manager • Prince George's County Memorial Library System New Carrollton Branch Library • New Carrollton, MD 20784

Thrasher Ray E. Mrs • Director of Library Services • Trevecca Nazarene College • Nashville, TN 37210 • AASL ACRL LITA RASD YALSA LIRT

Thrasher Ross • Catalog Librarian • University of Colorado At Colorado Springs Library • Colorado Springs, CO 80933-7150 • ACRL LITA

Thrasher Susan E. • Substitute Librarian I • Urbana Free Library • Urbana, IL 61801-3283

Threadgill Catherine H. • Branch Librarian • Harris County Public Library Tomall Branch • Tomball, TX 77375

Threats Deborah A. • Ann Arbor, MI 48105

Threatt Doris • Trustee • Kansas City Public Library • Kansas City, MO 64106 • ALTA

Threatt Helen K. • Head Reference/Librarian • Atlanta University Center Robert W. Woodruff Library • Atlanta, GA 30314

Threlkeld Jean • Head Librarian • Newport Way Library • Bellevue, WA 98006 • PLA

Thresher Jacquelyn E. • Director • Princeton Public Library • Princeton, NJ 08542 • LAMA PLA SRRT

Thrift Gale • Oceanfront Library • Virginia Beach, VA 23451

Thro Mary Ellen • Cary Public Library • Cary, IL 60013 • RASD

Thrower-Dowdell Dorcel D. • Manager • Toledo-Lucas County Public Library • Toledo, OH 43624 • PLA

Thrower Anne E. • Regional Assistant Director • Sandhill Regional Library System • Rockingham, NC 28379-4995 • LAMA PLA

Thrush Pinkie • Head Librarian • North Davidson Public Library • Welcome, NC 27374

Thubauville Jeanine M. • Acting Head, Reference Dept. • University of Wisconsin-Madison Memorial Library • Madison, WI 53706 • ACRL RASD

Thuesen Mary W. • Hiddenite Elementary School • Hiddenite, NC 28636 • AASL ALSC

Thurman Elizabeth D. • Director • Oldham County Public Library • LaGrange, KY 40031 • LAMA PLA

Thurman Glenda B. • University of Central Arkansas Department of Educational Media & Library Science • Conway, AR 72032-5001 • AASL LITA

Thurman Patricia • North Pole, AK 99705-6665 • Continuing

Thurston Charles B. • Education/Reference Librarian • University of Texas at San Antonio-Library • San Antonio, TX 78249 • ACRL RASD

Thurston Ella M. • Learning Center Director • Mundelein School District #75 Carl Sandburg Middle School • Mundelein, IL 60060 • AASL

Thurston Janice • Trustee • Bedford Park Public Library District • Bedford Park, IL 60501 • PLA

Thurston Patricia K. • Student • University of Texas at Austin Graduate School of Library & Information Sciences • Austin, TX 78712-1276 • ACRL

Thurston Shirley B. • Lakeport, CA 95453

Thurston Tobey M. • Edgewater, FL 32132

Thwaits Susan • Library Assistant • Contra Costa County Library • Pleasant Hill, CA 94523

Thweatt Elizabeth A. • Spokane, WA 99202 • Life

Thweatt Virginia B. • Assistant Cataloging Department • Lockwood Memorial Library • Buffalo, NY 14260 • ACRL ALCTS *Life*

Thwing Valerie L. • Interlibrary Loan Librarian • Central Arkansas Library System • Little Rock, AR 72201-4698 • PLA RASD

Tiarks Pearl R. • Print Media Supervisor • Loess Hills AEA 13 • Council Bluffs, IA 51502

Tibbals Alicia J. • Reference Librarian • Collin Cnty Cmnty Coll Dist Central Campus Library • Mc Kinney, TX 75069 • ACRL RASD LIRT LRRT

Tibbets Celeste • Atlanta-Fulton Public Library • Atlanta, GA 30303 • PLA RASD SRRT

Tibbetts Caroline J. • Associate Librarian • University of Delaware Morris Library • Newark, DE 19717-5267 • ACRL

Tibbetts Robert A. • Columbus, OH 43214 • ACRL

Tibbits George D. Jr. • Cataloger (Librarian I) • Chicago Public Library • Chicago, IL 60607 • Life

Tibbits Randolph K. • Information Specialist • Rice University Fondren Library • Houston, TX 77251-1892

Tibbitts Connie • Paulding County High School Library Media Center • Dallas, GA 30132 • AASL

Tibbo Helen R. • University of North Carolina at Chapel Hill School of Information and Library Science • Chapel Hill, NC 27599-3360 • RASD LRRT

Tibbs Jo Ann Winkelman • Clearwater, FL 34616-2327 • ASCLA LAMA LITA RASD ILERT LRRT

Tiblin Mariann E. • Scandinavian Bibliographer • University of Minnesota O. Meredith Wilson Library • Minneapolis, MN 55455-0414 • Life

Tibollo Gail • Student • State University of New York (SUNY) School of Information & Library Studies • Buffalo, NY 14260 • AASL

Tice Margaret E. • Supervising Librarian • Brooklyn Public Library Flatlands Branch • Brooklyn, NY 11234 • ALSC

Tichenor Irene • Brooklyn History Society • Brooklyn, NY 11201 • ACRL

Tickerhoof Donna • Cobb County Public Library System Powder Springs Branch • Powder Springs, GA 30073

Tickner Dooney • The Destin Library • Destin, FL 32540

Tidal Angelina R. • Head Librarian • Letcher County Public Library • Whitesburg, KY 41858

Tieberg-Bailie John • Trustee • Mount Prospect Public Library • Mount Prospect, IL 60056 • LAMA

Tiedemann Mary Jane • Commander • Pearl Habor Naval Shipyard • Pearl Harbor, HI 96860-5350 • AFLRT

Tiefel Virginia M. • Director, Library User Education • Ohio State University Libraries • Columbus, OH 43210-1286 • ACRL LITA LIRT

Tieger Helen • Tivoli, NY 12583

Tieken Sandra C. • Student • Louisiana State University School of Library & Information Science • Baton Rouge, LA 70803-3290 • PLA

Tien Sieu Mai C. Mrs. • Associate Professor • Natl Taiwan University • Taipei 10764 ROC, Taiwan • ALSC PLA

Tiernan Marylee • Librarian • Crescenta Valley High School • La Crescenta, CA 91214

Tierney Carol J. • Levittown, NY 11756

Tierney Catherine M. • San Carlos, CA 94070-4631 • ACRL ALCTS LITA

Tiessen Robert J. • Reference Librarian • Carroll College Corette Library • Helena, MT 59625 • ACRL GODORT

Tietjen Linda D. CRM • Coordinator of Access Services • University of Colorado at Denver Auraria Library • Denver, CO 80204 • ACRL LAMA LITA RASD LRRT NMRT

Tietjen Mildred C. • Plains, GA 31780

Tietz Kathy • Director • Hudson Public Library • Hudson, WI 54016

Tietze Phyllis S. • Media Specialist • Pendleton High School • Pendleton, SC 29670

Tiffany Constance J. • Glendora Public Library • Glendora, CA 91740 • ALTA LAMA LITA PLA RASD YALSA IFRT

Tiffany Linda L. • Children's Libn./Asst. Mgr. • Columbus Metropolitan Library • Columbus, OH 43215

Tifft Rosamond E. • Reference Librarian • Bethlehem Public Library • Delmar, NY 12054 • PLA ERT

Tikovt Ene M. • Carleton University Library • Ottawa ON, K1S 5J7 Canada • LITA

Tilch David Michael • Trustee • Prince George's County Memorial Library System • Hyattsville, MD 20782-2098 • ALTA

Tilden Roberta M. • Collection Development Coor. • Durham County Library • Durham, NC 27702 • PLA

Tileston Nancy B. • United States Fish & Wildlife Services • Anchorage, AK 99503 • LAMA LITA FLRT

Tilghman Cynthia C. • Student • University of Alabama in Birmingham School Library Media Program • Birmingham, AL 35294 • AASL ALSC

Tilghman Levin H. • Free Library of Philadelphia • Philadelphia, PA 19103

Tilitz Robert R. Mr. • Trustee • Queens Borough Public Library • Jamaica, NY 11432 • ALTA PLA

Tilker Barbara • Director, Instruction • Wichita Falls Independent School District • Wichita Falls, TX 76301

Tillberg Joann W. • Librarian • Salem High School • Virginia Beach, VA 23464

Tiller Glen Gordon • Associate Director Tech. Serv. • Central Arizona College • Coolidge, AZ 85228

Tillery Christine A. • Garland, TX 75043

Tillery Theresa A. • Euless, TX 76039 • PLA

Tilles E Doris • Corvallis, OR 97330 • ACRL

Tillett Barbara B. • Head of Catalog Department • University of California-San Diego Central University Library • La Jolla, CA 92093-0175 • ACRL ALCTS LITA

Tillett Ellen L. • Technical Services Coordinator • University of South Carolina at Spartanburg-Library • Spartanburg, SC 29303 • RASD

Tillett Janine • Bowman Gray School of Medicine Carpenter Library • Winston-Salem, NC 27157

Tilley Marilyn • Media Specialist • Atlanta Public Schools • Atlanta, GA 30315 • AASL

Tilley Patricia • Librarian • Alameda County Library Newark Branch • Newark, CA 94560

Tillia Joan M. • Student • Kent State University School of Library & Information Science • Kent, OH 44242-0001 • SRRT

Tillin Alma • Albany, CA 94706 • Continuing

Tillinghast Nancy • Student • University of South Carolina College of Library & Information Science • Columbia, SC 29208 • ALSC PLA YALSA

Tillis Jennifer M. • Coor. of Collection Management • University of Wisconsin-Green Bay Library Learning Center • Green Bay, WI 54311

Tillman Ann • Librarian • Crockett Memorial Library • Alamo, TN 38001

Tillman Caroline S. • Ln • Springfield High School • Springfield, IL 62704 • AASL

Tillman Hope N. • Director of Libraries • Babson College Horn Library • Babson Park, MA 02157-0901 • ACRL LAMA LITA RASD

Tillman Janet L. • Coordinator of Public Services • Master's College, The • Santa Clarita, CA 91322 • ACRL

Tillman Michael L. • Librarian • State University of New York College at Cortland • Cortland, NY 13045 • ACRL

Tillotson Noreen T. • Student • State University of New York (SUNY) School of Information & Library Studies • Buffalo, NY 14260 • RASD

Tillotson Willie L. • Trustee • East Chicago Public Library • E. Chicago, IN 46312 • PLA

Tilman Della • North Manchester, IN 46962-1198 • PLA YALSA *Continuing*

Tilmanis Agate J. • Library of Congress • Washington, DC 20541

Tilner J. S. • Librarian • Franklin High School • Seattle, WA 98144 • AASL YALSA

Tilson Koleta S. • Librarian • Sullivan Central High School • Blountville, TN 37617

Tilson Marie • Senior Reference Librarian • Chevron Corporation Library • San Francisco, CA 94104 • LAMA RASD *Life*

Tilton Christine Shama • Columbus, OH 43214

Tilton Kathleen • Virginia Beach, VA 23462

Tilton Loretta • Librarian • Norwalk Public Library • Norwalk, IA 50211

Timberlake Cynthia Mrs • Aiea, HI 96701

Timberlake Mary E. • Clemson, SC 29631 • ACRL GODORT IRRT *Continuing*

Timberlake Patricia P. • Head,Journalism Library • University of Missouri-Columbia Journalism Library • Columbia, MO 65203 • ACRL RASD

Timberlake Phoebe • Serial Librarian • University of New Orleans Earl K. Long Library • New Orleans, LA 70148 • ACRL ALCTS

Timko Georgene A. • Director • Northwest Missouri State University Owens Library • Maryville, MO 64468 • ACRL LAMA

Timlin Peggy M. • Curator of Manuscripts & Books • Pilgrim Society • Plymouth, MA 02360-3891

Timm Helen • Trustee • Timberland Regional Library • Olympia, WA 98501 • ALTA

Timmens Patricia S. • Branch Librarian • Lake Tahoe Branch Library • Zephyr Cove, NV 89448 • PLA

Timmerman Donna • Minooka, IL 60447

Timmerman Jennifer Ruth • Florence, KY 41042-9100

Timmermann Robert V. • Librarian • Carson Regional Library • Carson, CA 90745

Timmons Lizz • Librarian • Sagamore Hill Elementary School • Ft. Worth, TX 76103 • AASL ALSC

Timmons Rose L. • District of Columbia Public Library Martin Luther King Memorial Library • Washington, DC 20001 • ALSC EMIERT

Timms Marilyn H. • Librarian • Hurffville School • Sewell, NJ 08080 • AASL

Timothy Jean Sr • Bishop Kearney High School Library • Brooklyn, NY 11204 • YALSA

Tims Glenn • Senior Librarian Technical Serv • Tyler Public Library • Tyler, TX 75702 • ALCTS

Tincher Tina M. • Student • University of Michigan Libraries Information and Library Studies • Ann Arbor, MI 48109

Ting Eunice C. • Cataloger/Collection Dev. Libn. • University of California-Los Angeles Biomedical Library • Los Angeles, CA 90024-1798 • ACRL ALCTS GODORT

Ting-I Li • Student • State University New York at Buffalo School of Inf. & Library Studies • Buffalo, NY 14260

Tingelstad Gertrude • Cataloging Librarian • Oregon State University William Jasper Kerr Library • Corvallis, OR 97331-4501 • Continuing

Tinker Roslyn M. Mrs. • Saddle River Day School Library • Saddle River, NJ 07458

Tinnin Nathan D. • Head Librarian • Austin Community College Northridge Library • Austin, TX 78714

Tino Carmela N. • Stratford, CT 06497 • ACRL

Tinsley Pamela S. • Librarian • Midlothian Middle School • Midlothian, VA 23113 • AASL

Tinsman Ann F. • Librarian • James Wood High School • Winchester, VA 22601 • AASL YALSA

Tinsman Carole • Trustee • Johnson County Library • Shawnee Mission, KS 66201 • ALTA

Tomlianovich Julie A. • Children's Librarian • Hutchinson Public Library • Hutchinson, KS 67501 • ALSC

Tomlin Marsha A. • Library Consultant • Clinton Memorial Hospital • Wilmington, OH 45177

Tomlin Robbin L. • Librarian I • Memphis-Shelby County Public Library and Information Center • Memphis, TN 38104-4025

Tomlin Shirley W. • Nashville, TN 37205 • AASL ALSC

Tomlinson Carl M. • Associate Professor • Northern Illinois University • DeKalb, IL 60115-2854 • ALSC

Tomlinson Eleanor B. • Student • North Carolina Central University • Durham, NC 27707

Tomlinson Helen I. • Wales Center, NY 14169 • SRRT VRT

Tomlinson Liza • Trainer & Liaison • Gaylord Information Systems • Liverpool, NY 13090 • LITA

Tomomitsu Julie K. • Ln • Manoa Elementary School • Honolulu, HI 96822 • AASL

Tomoyasu Christine F. • Head Librarian • Leeward Community College Library • Pearl City, HI 96782 • ACRL

Tompkins Carol L. • Librarian II • Forsyth County Public Library • Winston-Salem, NC 27101 • ALSC

Tompkins Ernie • Librarian • Palo Alto City Library Mitchell Park Branch Library • Palo Alto, CA 94303 • PLA IFRT VRT

Tompkins Louise • Social Science Reference Ln • Princeton University • Princeton, NJ 08544-2098 • ACRL RASD GODORT

Tompkins Melba • Technical Services Department • East Cleveland Public Library • East Cleveland, OH 44112

Tompkins T. Philip • Director Information Svs. • Estrella Mountain Community College Center • Litchfield Park, AZ 85340 • ACRL LITA EMIERT SRRT

Tomposki Philip • Reference Librarian • United States Navy Naval Education & Training Center Main Library • Newport, RI 02841-5002 • ACRL

Toms Elaine G. • Assistant Professor • Dalhousie University School of Library & Inf. Studies • Halifax NS, B3H 4H8 Canada • LITA

Tonascia Sallie S. • Children's Librarian • San Luis Obispo City-County Library South County Branch • Arroyo Grande, CA 93420

Toner Valerie M. • Librarian • East Providence Public Library Central Library • East Providence, RI 02914

Toney Bernard J. • Assoc Prof Dept of Lib Sci • Shippensburg University Lehman Memorial Library • Shippensburg, PA 17257-2299

Toney Pendilita S. • Fay Herron Elementary School • North Las Vegas, NV 89030 • ALSC

Toney Stephen R. • President, Systems Planning • Systems Planning • Las Vegas, NV 89119 • LITA

Tong Josie S. • Curriculum Librarian • University of Alberta • Edmonton AB, T6G 2J8 Canada • ACRL

Tong Tong • Student • University of Oklahoma School of Library & Information Studies • Norman, OK 73019

Tong Wai-Ling Margaret • Benicia, CA 94510

Tong Wei-Jin • Librarian • George Washington University Gelman Library • Washington, DC 20052 • ALCTS

Tongate John T. • Head Reference Librarian • University of Texas Libraries Perry-Castaneda Library • Austin, TX 78713-7730

Tonn Elizabeth C. • Vermont College Gary Memorial Library • Montpelier, VT 05602

Tonner Shawn • Marietta, GA 30066 • ACRL

Tonsing Janice P. • Librarian • Parkway Central High School • Chesterfield, MO 63017 • AASL

Tonta Yasar A. • Student • University of California-Berkeley School of Library & Information Studies • Berkeley, CA 94720 • LITA LRRT

Tontar Silvia M. • Assistant Director • Pollard Memorial Library • Lowell, MA 01852

Tooey M. J. • Asst. Dir., Information Servs. • University of Maryland at Baltimore Health Sciences Library • Baltimore, MD 21201

Toohey Lynnette M. • Children's Librarian • Holmes Public Library • Halifax, MA 02338-1394

Tooker Anna Lisa • Cannon Falls, MN 55009

Tooker Kathleen A. • Eastern Library System • Omaha, NE 68144 • PLA

Tooker Peggy J. • Director • Woolworth Community Library • Jal, NM 88252 • AASL PLA YALSA

Toole Linda A. • Costabile Associates Inc • Bethesda, MD 20814

Toole Maureen A. • Monmouth County Library • Manalapan, NJ 07726 • YALSA

Toombs Kenneth E. • Director-Emeritus • University of South Carolina • Columbia, SC 29208 • ACRL LAMA *Life*

Toomer Clarence • Library Director • Greensboro College James Addison Jones Library • Greensboro, NC 27401 • ACRL

Toomey Alice F. • Clemson, SC 29631 • Continuing

Toomey Julianne M. • Winchester, MA 01890-3138 • AASL ALSC

Toomey Mary Alice • Library Supervisor • Glendale Public Library Grandview Branch • Glendale, CA 91201 • PLA

Toon Kathy • Manager, Children's Center • Dallas Public Library • Dallas, TX 75201 • ALSC LAMA PLA

Toor Jay W. • Publisher • Library Learning Resources, Inc. • Berkeley Hts, NJ 07922 • AASL ERT

Toor Ruth • Media Specialist • Southern Boulevard School Library • Chatham, NJ 07928 • AASL ALSC

Toor Saira A. • Burr Ridge, IL 60521

Topcik Evelyn • Louisville Collegiate School Library • Louisville, KY 40204

Topel A. Robert • Administrative Librarian • Grayslake Area Public Library District • Grayslake, IL 60030-1590 • PLA

Topham Dorothy P. • Fresno, CA 93726-4202 • PLA *Life*

Topham Elsie M. • Green Valley, AZ 85614-2733

Topham Karen P. • Public Services Asst./LRC • Brookdale Community College • Lincroft, NJ 07738 • ACRL

Toplicar Joan M. • Plano, TX 75074

Toplon James E. • Nashville, TN 37215

Topolski Deborah A. • Vermont College Gary Memorial Library • Montpelier, VT 05602

Topp Barbara H. • Administrator • Northwest Indiana Area Library Services Authority (NIALSA) • Merrillville, IN 46410

Topp Marvalyn • Rockford, IL 61107

Topp Victoria A. • University of Wisconsin-Whitewater Harold Andersen Library • Whitewater, WI 53190 • ACRL RASD

Topping Russell J. • Gainesville, FL 32605

Toppler Terri A. • Media Specialist • Walcott School • Walcott, IA 52773

Torbet Janice E. • Documents Librarian • San Francisco Public Library • San Francisco, CA 94102 • GODORT

Torchia Evelyn R. • Kankakee, IL 60901

Torgerson Richard B. • Student • Indiana University School of Library and Information Science • Bloomington, IN 47405

Torgeson Mary Jo • King County Library System Valley View Library • Seattle, WA 98188 • PLA SRRT

Torgeson Paula L. • Director • Dunlap Public Library District • Dunlap, IL 61525 • PLA

Toribara Lynne • Head of Cataloging • Santa Clara University Michel Orradre Library • Santa Clara, CA 95053 • ALCTS

Torige Anne E. • Student • University of Hawaii School of Library & Information Studies • Honolulu, HI 96822 • AASL

Torkelson Jon A. • Senior Librarian • Auburn-Placer County Library • Auburn, CA 95603-3789 • PLA IFRT

Tormey Patricia S. • Riverhead, NY 11901

Tormey Robert J. • Public Information Coordinator • Pioneer Library System • Norman, OK 73069 • PLA

Torney Kay J. • Director • Henry Stephens Memorial Library • Almont, MI 48003-0517 • PLA

Tornquist Kristi M. • Magnolia, AR 71753

Torok Sarah T. • Fairfield, CT 06430

Torr Lydia M. Mrs • Librarian • Meredith Public Library • Meredith, NH 03253

Torrence Barbara • Librarian • Adams High School • Rochester, MI 48064

Torrence Bernice M. • Burwell, NE 68823 • PLA
Continuing

Torrens Carol E. • Reference Librarian • Salem Public Library • Salem, OR 97309-5020

Torrens Miguel A. • Asst. MARC Coordinator • University of Toronto Library System • Toronto ON, M5S 1A5 Canada • LITA

Torres-Blank Sheila A. • Media & Special Projects Catlg • Wichita State University Library • Wichita, KS 67208

Torres-Zayas Adalin I. • Long Beach, CA 90802-5618 • LAMA EMIERT SRRT

Torres Alfredo O. • Assistant Editor • Viva America Media Group Micasa Magazine • Miami, FL 33145

Torres Edith M. • Student • Long Island University Palmer School of Library & Information Science • Greenvale, NY 11548 • LITA

Torres Ema E. • Librarian II • Houston Public Library Park Place Branch • Houston, TX 77017 • EMIERT

Torres Leida I. • Howard University Libraries Founders Library • Washington, DC 20059

Torres Rita A. • Senior Librarian • San Jose Public Library • San Jose, CA 95113 • EMIERT

Torres Susan • Novato Unified School District • Novato, CA 94945

Torrey Elizabeth C. • Simmons College Graduate School of Library & Information Science • Boston, MA 02115

Torstad Julie Kae • Acquisitions Librarian • Plano Public Library System L.E.R. Schimelpfenig Library • Plano, TX 75023-5108 • ALCTS PLA

Tortorello Deborah A. • Trustee • Mesa Public Library • Mesa, AZ 85201-6768 • ALTA

Toscan Joyce S. • Asst. Univ. Ln. for Public Servs • University of Southern California Doheny Library • Los Angeles, CA 90089-0182 • ACRL LIRT

Toschik Joseph C. • San Jose, CA 95111

Toth-Chernin Janice • Ann Arbor, MI 48104 • AASL

Toth Alexander B. • Bethesda, MD 20816 • Continuing

Toth Carolyn A. • Library Director • Community Library of Castle Shannon • Castle Shannon, PA 15234 • PLA

Toth Cindy K. • Librarian • Hot Springs Community High School • Thermopolis, WY 82443

Toth George S. • Slavic & East European Catlgr • Library of Congress • Washington, DC 20541 • ACRL IRRT

Toth Luann • Associate Book Review Editor • School Library Journal • New York, NY 10011 • ALSC YALSA

Toth Margaret K. • Rochester, NY 14621-3010 • ACRL ALCTS
Continuing

Toth Robert W. • Menominee County Library • Stephenson, MI 49887

Toth Sally B. • All Saints Episcopal School • Ft. Worth, TX 76108

Totten Herman L. • Professor • University of North Texas School of Library & Information Sciences • Denton, TX 76203 • ACRL ALCTS LITA *Life*

Totten Jennifer • E. Walpole, MA 02032

Tottori Shelli L. S. • School Librarian • Roosevelt High School • Honolulu, HI 96822 • AASL

Tou Yen-yi • Student • University of Wisconsin-Madison School of Library & Information Studies • Madison, WI 53706

Touchard Wolfhard • Collection Development Librarian • Andrews University James White Library • Berrien Springs, MI 49104-1400

Touchet Dianne M. • Librarian • Paul Breaux Middle School • Lafayette, LA 70501 • AASL

Touchstone Lana L. • John F. Kennedy Library • Vallejo, CA 94590 • PLA IFRT SRRT

Touhy Patricia A. • Coordinator • Central Texas Library System • Austin, TX 78768-2287

Toups Brenda W. • Prof/Resource Devel Spec • Saint Charles Parish School • Luling, LA 70070 • AASL IFRT

Toups Danelle L. • Student • University of Southern Mississippi School of Library Science • Hattiesburg, MS 39406-5146

Toups Patricia T. • Life Office Management Association Inc Information Center • Atlanta, GA 30327

Touraine Linda S. • Special Service Librarian/Ref. • Denton Public Library • Denton, TX 76201

Tousley-Escalante Joanna • Head of Tech Serv & Automation • Austin Community College Northridge Library • Austin, TX 78714 • ACRL

Tovar Albert • Asst. Library Adminstrator • County of Los Angeles Public Library Montebello Library 601 • Montebello, CA 90640 • PLA

Tow Mary E. • Student • University of Rhode Island Graduate School of Library & Information Studies • Kingston, RI 02881-0815 • AASL

Towar Carolyn A. • Cataloging Specialist • Kent County Library System • Grand Rapids, MI 49503

Towe Susan J. • Student • University of North Carolina at Chapel Hill School of Information and Library Science • Chapel Hill, NC 27599-3360

Tower Karen G. • Children's Librarian • Canton Public Library • Canton, MI 48188

Tower Kathleen R. • Special Collection Librarian • Mesa State College Library • Grand Junction, CO 81501 • ACRL GODORT

Tower Mary L. • Head, Extension Department • Monroe County Library System • Rochester, NY 14604 • ASCLA

Tower Michelle M. • Phoenix, AZ 85028

Towers Suellen M. • McLean, VA 22101 • ACRL

Towery James G. Mr • West Des Moines, IA 50265-4477 • ACRL
Life

Towery Margaret G. • Platersvle, MS 38862 • ALCTS PLA
Life

Towery Stephen • Librarian • Walla Walla Public Library • Walla Walla, WA 99362 • ALCTS LITA PLA

Towey Cathleen A. • Floral Park, NY 11001-2825

Towle Jean Ann • District Consultant • Pottsville Free Public Library • Pottsville, PA 17901

Towler Jeannine • Librarian • Albemarle County Schools Henley Junior High School • Crozet, VA 22932 • AASL

Towles Julie D. • Rockville, MD 20853-2211

Towles Karen B. • Washington, DC 20017

Town Karen K. • Trustee • East Central Regional Library • Cedar Rapids, IA 52401 • ALTA

Towne Marjorie F. • Librarian • Nathaniel Rochester Community School • Rochester, NY 14608 • AASL

Towne Rebecca J. • Lakes Region Library • Inverness, FL 32652-4507 • LAMA PLA RASD IFRT LRRT SRRT

Towne Susan G. • Branch Libn.& Hd, Tech Serivces • Mid-Columbia Library • West Richland, WA 99352 • PLA

Trezza Alphonse F. • Professor • Florida State University School of Library and Information Studies • Tallahassee, FL 32306-2048 • ACRL ASCLA LAMA PLA CLENE GODORT *Life*

Trezza Mildred • Tallahassee, FL 32308

Triandafilou Mary R. • Branch Supervisor • Harford County Public Library Whiteford Branch • Whiteford, MD 21160

Tribble Judith E. • Brazil, IN 47834 • ACRL LAMA

Tribby Michael L. • Student • University of Iowa School of Library & Information Science • Iowa City, IA 52242 • EMIERT IFRT SRRT

Triber Beverly Finlayson • Librarian • Virginia Pack Elementary School Library • Columbia, SC 29204 • AASL ALSC

Tribit Donald K. • Periodicals-Microfilms Librarian • Millersville University of Pennsylvania • Millersville, PA 17551-0302 • ACRL

Tricarico Mary Ann Dr • Director • Peabody Institute Library • Peabody, MA 01960-9998 • LAMA PLA

Trice Thomas G. • Director • Napa City-County Library • Napa, CA 94559-3396 • LAMA PLA

Triche Charles W. • Assoc Prof • University of Southwestern Louisiana Libraries • Lafayette, LA 70503 • ACRL

Trichtinger Mary Jo • Children's Librarian • Pittsburgh Public Schools • Pittsburgh, PA 15213 • ALSC

Trickey Katherine M. • Reference Librarian • Pittsburg State University Leonard Axe Library • Pittsburg, KS 66762 • RASD

Tricoles Rosanne • San Jose, CA 95129 • RASD YALSA

Tricsko Mary Ann • Children's Librarian • Cleveland Public Library West Park Branch • Cleveland, OH 44111 • ALSC

Trienens Roger J. • Saratoga Springs, NY 12866-2219 • ACRL ALCTS *Life*

Trieschmann Mary H. Sr. • Cataloging Department • Jefferson Parish Library Department • Metairie, LA 70010

Trieschmann Ruth Ann • Manchester, CT 06040-8190

Triffleman Sarah A. • Student • University of Rhode Island Graduate School of Library & Information Studies • Kingston, RI 02881-0815 • EMIERT SRRT

Triggs Alice • School Librarian • Seven Trees School • San Jose, CA 95111 • AASL

Triggs Patricia A. • Elkhorn, WI 53121 • PLA

Trimble Essie Elizabeth • Media Specialist • Redan High School Dekalb County Board of Education • Stone Mtn, GA 30088 • AASL

Trimble Gail D. • Albuquerque, NM 87109

Trimble Jeffrey • Catalog Librarian • University of Alabama • Tuscaloosa, AL 35487-0266 • NMRT

Trimble M. Elizabeth • Houston, TX 77040 • AASL

Trimble Theron L. Dr. • Chairman, Library Advisory Bd. • Collier County Public Library • Naples, FL 33940 • ALTA LAMA PLA

Trimby Susan L. • Wilmington, IL 60481 • YALSA

Trimingham Robert • Acquisitions Librarian • California State University-Sacramento Library • Sacramento, CA 95819-6039

Trimmer Keith R. • Head Catalog Department • University of Southern California Doheny Library • Los Angeles, CA 90089-0182 • ACRL ALCTS LAMA SRRT *Life*

Triner Jeanne E. • Student • Rosary College Graduate School of Library & Information Science • River Forest, IL 60305 • AASL

Trinkaus-Randall Gregor • Cllns Mgmt/Presv Specialist • Massachusetts Board of Library Commissioners • Boston, MA 02215-2070 • ACRL ALCTS

Triolo Victor A. • Associate Professor Libn Sci. • Southern Connecticut State University School of Libray Science & Instructional Technology • New Haven, CT 06515

Tripicchio Teresa A. • Children's Librarian • Deer Park Public Library • Deer Park, NY 11729

Tripp Richard C. • Trustee • Indian Trails Public Library District • Wheeling, IL 60090 • ALTA

Tripplett M. Glenn • Director • Okaloosa-Walton Junior College Learning Resources Center • Niceville, FL 32578

Tripuraneni Vinaya L. • Claremont, CA 91711

Trishman Judith S. • Capital Projects Administrator • Columbus Metropolitan Library • Columbus, OH 43215 • LAMA

Trivett Martha S. • Manager • Johnson City Medical Center Hospital Hospital Library • Johnson City, TN 37604-6094

Trivison Margaret A. • Librarian • Pilgrim Library • Los Angeles, CA 91020 • AASL YALSA

Trkla Janis L. • Head of Circulation • Lake Forest Library • Lake Forest, IL 60045

Troche Peter • Law Librarian • Bower & Gardner • New York, NY 10022

Troese Carol Blair • Director • Cranberry Public Library • Mars, PA 16046

Troia Terri S. • Chesapeake, VA 23323 • AASL

Troisi Barbara • Teacher • Kingsburg Elementary School • Kingsburg, CA 93631 • AASL

Trojanowski James D. • Metropolitan Community College • Omaha, NE 68103

Trojanowski Julia Q. • Creighton University Reinert-Alumni Memorial Library • Omaha, NE 68178 • ACRL

Troke Margaret K. • Stockton, CA 95209-4851 • LAMA PLA *Life*

Troll Denise A. • Researcher/Library Automation • Carnegie-Mellon University Libraries Hunt Library • Pittsburgh, PA 15213 • LITA

Trolley Jacqueline H. • Manager, Corp. Communications • Institute for Scientific Information • Philadelphia, PA 19104 • LITA ERT

Tromater Raymond B. • Southwest Arkansas Regional Library • Hope, AR 71801 • PLA

Trombley Lois A. • Supervisor Children's • Dearborn Department of Libraries Henry Ford Centennial Library • Dearborn, MI 48126

Trompler John • Lubbock, TX 79416

Tron Michael • Trustee • Evansville-Vanderburgh County Public Library • Evansville, IN 47708-1694

Troncale Anthony T. • New York, NY 10011 • LITA RASD IFRT NMRT

Tronier Suzanne • Librarian • University of Washington Suzzallo Library • Seattle, WA 98195 • ACRL SRRT

Trop Darcy K. • Emmaus, PA 18049

Troselius Renee A. • Librarian • Minnehaha Academy • Minneapolis, MN 55406 • AASL

Trosper Penny L. • Student • Texas Woman's University School of Library & Information Studies • Denton, TX 76204

Trost Theresa K. • Texas Tech University Libraries • Lubbock, TX 79409-0002 • ACRL RASD GODORT LIRT

Trotsky Lila • Librarian • Laura Sprague Elementary School • Prairie View, IL 60069 • AASL

Trotta Marcia • Assistant Director • Meriden Public Library • Meriden, CT 06450

Trotter Jacqueline Leanne • Student • Western Illinois University Department of Learning Resources • Macomb, IL 61455

Trotter Tracy • University of Pittsburgh School of Library and Information Science • Pittsburgh, PA 15260

Trotti Jonny B. • Wadesboro Central School • Wadesboro, NC 28170 • AASL

Troublefield Cathy • Student • University of North Carolina Department of Library & Information Studies • Greensboro, NC 27412-5001 • AASL

Troudt Michael J. • Waukesha Public Library • Waukesha, WI 53186

Trout Anita M. • Old Charles Town Library • Charles Town, WV 25414 • YALSA

Trout Anne • Audio-Visual Librarian • Midland County Public Library • Midland, TX 79702 • VRT

Trout Carolyn • Director • Joplin Public Library • Joplin, MO 64801 • PLA

Trout Linda S. • Omaha Public Library • Omaha, NE 68102 • GODORT

Trout Mary-Ellen • Carlsbad, NM 88220

Troutman Christine L. • Erie, PA 16502

Troutman Patsy H. • Media Coordinator • Providence Senior High School • Charlotte, NC 28226

Troutner Joanne • Tippecanoe School Corp. • Lafayette, IN 47905 • AASL ALSC

Trowell Amy U. • Acting Librarian • Charleston County Library Edisto Branch • Edisto Island, SC 29438 • PLA

Troxclair Deborah • Assistant Branch Supervisor • Jefferson Parish Library Department • Metairie, LA 70010

Troxel Wilma • Evanston, IL 60201 • Continuing

Troy Lynda A. • Librarian • Washington Senior High School • Washington C.H., OH 43160 • AASL YALSA

Troy Margaret E. • Lawrence, MA 01841 • PLA

Troy Timothy • Librarian • University of Arizona Center for Creative Photography • Tucson, AZ 85721 • ACRL

Troyer Alice K. • Librarian/Media Specialist • Charles Sahs School District 110 • Chicago, IL 60638 • AASL

Trubiano Frank M. • Maspeth, NY 11378 • AASL YALSA

Trubowitz Ethel • Reference & Circulation Libn. • Jewish Community Library of The JEA of Metro West New Jersey • Fairfield, NJ 07004-1615 • RASD

Truck Lorna • Coordinator of Extension Servs • Public Library of Des Moines • Des Moines, IA 50308-1791

Trucksis Theresa A. • Director • Reuben McMillan Free Library Association Youngstown & Mahoning Cnty P L • Youngstown, OH 44503 • LAMA PLA

Trudell Robert J. • Director • Greenburgh Public Library • Elmsford, NY 10523 • PLA

Trudicks Patricia • Learning Center Director • Elm School • Burr Ridge, IL 60521 • AASL

True Elizabeth • Minneapolis, MN 55422 • AASL ALSC IFRT

True Helen C. • Detroit, MI 48207 • PLA RASD *Life*

Truesdale Sandy • Trustee • Mount Prospect Public Library • Mount Prospect, IL 60056 • PLA

Truesdell Eugenia • Westchester, PA 19380 • Continuing

Truesdell Walter G. Rev • Librarian • Reformed Episcopal Seminary Library • Philadelphia, PA 19104 • ACRL ALCTS *Life*

Truett Carol Dr. • Director • Whiting Public Library • Whiting, IN 46394 • AASL PLA YALSA

Truett Margaret I. • Student • Florida State University School of Library and Information Studies • Tallahassee, FL 32306-2048

Truex Nina E. • North Hollywood, CA 91617

Truhart Debra L. • Public Information Officer • District of Columbia Public Library Martin Luther King Memorial Library • Washington, DC 20001 • LAMA

Truitt Charlotte A. • Patient Health Education Ln. • Bay Pines Veteran Medical Center • Bay Pines, FL 33504

Truitt Marc • Princeton University Firestone Library • Princeton, NJ 08544 • ALCTS

Trulio Virginia Lucey • Media Specialist • Montgomery County Public Schools • Rockville, MD 20850 • AASL IFRT

Trumble Bruce M. • Senior Cataloger • Harvard College Library Widener Memorial Library • Cambridge, MA 02138 • ACRL ALCTS

Trumbly Shona Mrs. • Educational Media Specialist • Hainesport Township School • Hainesport, NJ 08036 • AASL

Trump Kathryn R. • Boeing Technical Libraries • Renton, WA 98055

Trumpler Elisabeth • Head of the Cataloging Dept. • Drexel University W. W. Hagerty Library • Philadelphia, PA 19104 • ALCTS LITA

Trupiano Rose • Marquette University Memorial Library • Milwaukee, WI 53233

Trupiano Victoria A. • Student • North Central College Oesterle Library • Naperville, IL 60540 • SRRT

Trupkiewicz Kelly J. • Student • Emporia State University William Allen White Library • Emporia, KS 66801 • ILERT

Trutwin Judith K. • Reference & Adult Svs. Libn. • Broward County Public Library Margate Branch • Margate, FL 33063

Tryon Jonathan S. • Associate Professor • University of Rhode Island Graduate School of Library & Information Studies • Kingston, RI 02881-0815 • ACRL IFRT

Tryon Lucia M. • Pensacola, FL 32503 • ALSC YALSA *Continuing*

Trzeciak William J. • Glendale Public Library • Glendale, CA 91205 • IFRT LHRT

Trzicky Richard F. • Director • Gilbert Junior High School L.M.C. • Gilbert, AZ 85234-3477 • AASL YALSA

Tsai Betty L. • Langhorne, PA 19047 • ACRL

Tsai Bor-sheng • Assistant Professor • Wayne State University Library Science Program • Detroit, MI 48202

Tsai Elizabeth H. • Technical Services Librarian • Solano Community College • Suisun, CA 94585 • ACRL LITA

Tsai Fu-Mei • Farmington Hl, MI 48331

Tsai Kathyrn • San Jose, CA 95123 • ALCTS

Tsai Maurice • Library Director • Harlingen Public Library Lon C Hill Memorial Library • Harlingen, TX 78550 • LAMA PLA LRRT

Tsai Rui-Hung • Ijamsville, MD 21754-9120 • AASL

Tsai Sheh-gni • Assistant Librarian • California Academy of Sciences • San Francisco, CA 94118 • ACRL ALCTS LITA

Tsai Yungpei • Hays, KS 67601

Tsang Daniel C. • University of California-Irvine Library • Irvine, CA 92713 • ACRL RASD IFRT SRRT

Tsang Lau Foon • Student • University of Iowa School of Library & Information Science • Iowa City, IA 52242

Tschanz Virginia A. • Reference Librarian • University of Denver Penrose Library • Denver, CO 80208 • LITA RASD

Tschekaloff C. S. Mrs • Bellevue, WA 98009-3233 • ALSC YALSA *Continuing*

Tscherny Elena • Coordinator Exhibits and Prog. • District of Columbia Public Library Martin Luther King Memorial Library • Washington, DC 20001

Tschudy Karen D. • Director • Twinsburg Public Library • Twinsburg, OH 44087 • LAMA PLA

Tschudy William • Trustee • Johnson County Library • Shawnee Mission, KS 66201 • ALTA

Tse Linda L. • Cultural Minorities Librarian • Montgomery County Public Library Silver Spring Branch • Silver Spring, MD 20910-4390 • PLA EMIERT

Tseng Li-hwa • Baton Rouge, LA 70816

Tseng Louisa • Librarian • Glover Memorial Hospital Medical Library • Needham, MA 02192 • ACRL

Tseng Sally C. • Principal Serials Cagaloger • University of California-Irvine Library • Irvine, CA 92713 • ACRL ALCTS LITA IRRT

Tseng Winnie W M • Kettering, OH 45429

Tso Pak Suet • Unionville, ON, L3R 3M1 Canada • LITA
Tso Petrina • Northbrook Public Library • Northbrook, IL 60062
Tsoi Wing Sze Michelle • Serials/Cataloging Librarian • Wake Forest University School of Law Library • Winston-Salem, NC 27109 • ALCTS
Tsou Judy S. • Assistant Head • University of California-Berkeley Music Library • Berkeley, CA 94720 • ACRL
Tsui Chih-Yi • Student • Syracuse University School of Information Studies • Syracuse, NY 13244-4100 • LITA
Tsui Josephine • Manager, Bibliographic Services • Metropolitan Toronto Reference Library • Toronto ON, M4W 2G8 Canada • ALCTS LAMA LITA
Tsui Susan L. • Bibl. Cont. Coordinator • University of Dayton Roesch Library • Dayton, OH 45469 • EMIERT
Tsujita Izumi • Los Angeles, CA 90042 • LITA
Tsukahara Hiroshi • Tokyo 115, Japan • ALSC LAMA PLA IFRT
Tsukamoto Jack T. • Periodicals Librarian • Ball State University Library Department of Library Services • Muncie, IN 47306 • ACRL IRRT
Tsuneishi Warren M. • Chief, Asian Division • Library of Congress • Washington, DC 20541 • ACRL ALCTS LITA RASD IRRT *Life*
Tsusaki Edna K. • Pearl City, HI 96782 • Continuing
Tsutsumi Carole K. • Librarian • Waiakea High School • Hilo, HI 96720 • AASL
Tu Feili Brenda • Associate Researcher • Information & Computing Library • Tiapei 10636, Taiwan • ALCTS LAMA RASD
Tu Kuang-Pei • Librarian • Los Angeles Public Library • Los Angeles, CA 90071 • ACRL LHRT LRRT
Tu Shu-Chen H. • Assistant Librarian • Bridgewater State College Clement C. Maxwell Library • Bridgewater, MA 02325
Tu Wen-Huei • Student • University of Wisconsin-Madison School of Library & Information Studies • Madison, WI 53706 • LITA RASD
Tubb Sara A. • Collection Management Spec. • Mississippi Library Commission • Jackson, MS 39209 • ALCTS ASCLA RASD
Tubbs Sibyl O. Miss • Omaha, NE 68106 • PLA *Continuing*
Tubbs William J. • Director • Washington College Clifton M. Miller Library • Chestertown, MD 21620 • ACRL ALCTS LAMA LITA RASD IFRT
Tubby Ruth P. • Medford, NJ 08055-2213 • ALSC PLA *Continuing*
Tubesing Nancy Loving • Duluth, MN 55804-2023 • AASL
Tubman Marianna S. • Tech. Services Librarian • Nueva Center for Learning • Hillsborough, CA 94010 • LIRT
Tubolino Karen M. • Providence Hospital Medical Library • Southfield, MI 48037
Tuceling William F. • Reference Librarian • United States General Accounting Office Library System Off Of Lib Serv • Washington, DC 20548
Tucey Richard K. • Supervisor,Non-Public Services • Pueblo Library District McClelland Library • Pueblo, CO 81004-1997 • LITA
Tuchman Helene L. • Director • Watertown Public Library • Watertown, MA 02172 • ALTA LAMA LITA PLA RASD YALSA GODORT IFRT LHRT SORT
Tuchman Maurice S. • Librarian • Hebrew College • Brookline, MA 02146 • ACRL
Tuchrello William P. • Field Director • Library of Congress • APO, AE 09839-4900
Tuck Barbara L. • University of North Florida • Jacksonville, FL 32216
Tuck Sherrie A. • Acquisitions Librarian • Episcopal Divinity School Weston School of Theology Libraries • Cambridge, MA 02138
Tucker-Miller Veronica E. • St Thomas, VI 00801 • AASL
Tucker Ben R. • Chief Off for Descriptive Catlg • Library of Congress • Washington, DC 20541 • ALCTS MAGERT
Tucker Betty E. • Louisiana State University School of Medicine • Shreveport, LA 71130-3932
Tucker Christine L. • Southern Maryland Regional Library Association • Charlotte Hall, MD 20622
Tucker Cornelia A. • Head Acquisitions Department • Temple University Paley Library • Philadelphia, PA 19122 • ACRL ALCTS LITA
Tucker Florence R. • Assoc Dir for Support Serv • Detroit Public Library Acq Dept • Detroit, MI 48202-4093 • ALCTS LAMA LITA PLA RASD
Tucker James • Trustee • Escondido Public Library • Escondido, CA 92025 • ALTA
Tucker James M. • Assoc Librarian Audio-Visual • Santa Fe Springs City Library • Santa Fe Springs, CA 90670 • PLA VRT
Tucker Jan L. • Trustee • Arlington Heights Memorial Library • Arlington Heights, IL 60004-5966 • ALTA
Tucker Joan • Iowa City, IA 52245
Tucker John B. • Bristol, England
Tucker Lynda J. • Librarian • Elementary School • Montgomery, TX 77356 • AASL
Tucker Mae S. • Mt Holly, NC 28120 • RASD *Continuing*
Tucker Marcia L. • Cataloging Assistant • Institute For Advanced Studies Library • Princeton, NJ 08543-0631
Tucker Mark • Purdue University • West Lafayette, IN 47907 • ACRL LHRT LRRT
Tucker Marsha • Media Consultant • West Bloomfield High School • West Bloomfield, MI 48033 • AASL EMIERT
Tucker Mary Ellen • Systems Librarian • Barnard College • New York, NY 10027 • LITA
Tucker Nancy • Librarian • Aragon High School • San Mateo, CA 94402 • AASL
Tucker Nancy E. • Automated Library Systems Spec. • Jefferson County Public Schools • Lakewood, CO 80215 • LITA
Tucker Pamela S. • Assistant Librarian • Horace W. Sturgis Library • Marietta, GA 30061 • ACRL RASD
Tucker Phillip H. • Coordinator of the LRC • Perry County School District • Perryville, MO 63775 • LITA
Tucker Rhonda J. • Louisville, KY 40216
Tucker Richard B. • President • The Tucker Co • Londonderry, NH 03053
Tucker Robert C. • Greenville, SC 29609 • Continuing
Tucker Rosalie G. Miss • Reader Services Librn. Emeritus • Vassar College Library • Poughkeepsie, NY 12601 • Continuing
Tucker Ruth W. • Boston College O'Neill Library • Chestnut Hill, MA 02167 • ACRL ALCTS LITA
Tucker Sandra L. • Research Librarian • Texas A & M University Texas Transportation Insitute • College Station, TX 77843-3135 • ACRL RASD
Tucker Susan B. • Catalog Librarian, Preservation • Yale University Sterling Memorial Library • New Haven, CT 06520 • ACRL ALCTS
Tucker Toni L. • Director • BroMenn Health Care • Normal, IL 61761 • LAMA
Tucker Yema J. • Coordinator, Adult Services • District of Columbia Public Library Martin Luther King Memorial Library • Washington, DC 20001 • PLA RASD
Tuckwood Dwight O. • Columbia, MO 65201 • ALCTS LITA *Life*
Tuckwood Jo Ann • Columbia, MO 65201 • ACRL RASD *Life*
Tudiver Lillian • Brooklyn, NY 11238 • ACRL RASD *Life*
Tudor Dean • Ryerson Polytech Institute • Toronto ON, M5B 2K3 Canada
Tudor Dodie B. • Agency Head, Avenues Branch • Salt Lake City Public Library Avenues Branch • Salt Lake City, UT 84103 • ALSC
Tudor Jan D. • Reference Librarian • Willamette University Mark O Hatfield Library • Salem, OR 97301 • ACRL LIRT
Tudor Joann M. • Clermont County Public Library Goshen Branch • Goshen, OH 45122
Tudor John Jeffrey • Instructional Technology Spec. • Guilford County Schools • Greensboro, NC 27401 • AASL
Tufano Anne Louise Sr. • Library Services Director • Molloy College James Edward Tobin Library • Rockville Ctr, NY 11570
Tuffs David W. • Interlibrary Loan Librarian • Ohio State University Libraries • Columbus, OH 43210-1286
Tufts Cindy • Technical Services Manager • Loudoun County Public Library • Leesburg, VA 22075
Tufts Margaret L. • Librarian • Houston Public Library Kendall Branch • Houston, TX 77079 • PLA
Tugby Svea A. • Librarian in Charge • Gilford Middle High • Gilford, NH 03246 • AASL ALCTS NMRT
Tuggle Dorene D. • Los Angeles, CA 90018
Tuggle Pamela C. • Media Coordinator • Prince George County School Board • Prince George, VA 23875 • AASL *Life*
Tugwell Helen M. • Media Services Director • Guilford County Schools • Greensboro, NC 27401 • AASL
Tugwell Patricia P. • Reference Librarian • Department of Defense Pentagon Library • Washington, DC 20310 • AFLRT FLRT
Tulberg Gordon • Trustee • Hennepin County Library • Minnetonka, MN 55343 • ALTA
Tuleya Linda M. • Cherry Hill, NJ 08034 • AASL ALSC EMIERT IFRT NMRT SRRT
Tulis Susan E. • Document Librarian • University of Virginia • Charlottesville, VA 22901 • ACRL GODORT MAGERT
Tulk Gwendolyn R. • Librarian • South Junior High School • Kalamazoo, MI 49008
Tull Laura • Asst Director of Automation • Kentucky State University Blazer Library • Frankfort, KY 40601 • LITA GODORT SRRT
Tullis Sarah H. • Information & Programming Head • Baltimore County Public Library Pikesville Branch • Baltimore, MD 21208 • PLA
Tully Carol M. • San Antonio, TX 78209
Tully Sharon • Bibliographical/Reference Libn • University of Manitoba Elizabeth Dafoe Library • Winnipeg MB, R3T 2N2 Canada • ACRL LITA
Tuma Deborah • Supervisor • Lincoln City Library Victor E. Anderson Branch • Lincoln, NE 68507-1698 • YALSA IFRT NMRT
Tumarkin Peter • Owner • Peter Tumarkin Fine Books • New York, NY 10021 • ACRL
Tumey Ronald C. • Director • Tangipahoa Parish Library • Amite, LA 70422 • ALTA LAMA LITA PLA IFRT ILERT SRRT
Tumino Elizabeth • Children's Librarian • Queens Borough Public Library • Jamaica, NY 11432 • PLA
Tumlin Markel D. • University of San Diego Copley Library • San Diego, CA 92110 • ACRL
Tumulty Patricia A. • Executive Director • New Jersey Library Association • Trenton, NJ 08607 • ASCLA
Tung Cecilia L. • Librarian • Texas Instruments Incorporated • Plano, TX 75086 • ALCTS LAMA LITA
Tunis Catharine M. • Reference Librarian • Board of Governors of the Federal Reserve System • Washington, DC 20551
Tunison Janice A. • Lincoln, NE 68516 • AASL LITA
Tunnell Enrica H. Mrs • New York, NY 10027 • Continuing
Tunnell Juanita • Supervisor, Indian Trails Branch • Saint Louis County Library • St. Louis, MO 63131
Tunnell Michael O. • Dept of Cirrculum & Instruction • Brigham Young University • Provo, UT 84602 • ALSC
Tunney Deborah M. • Student • Queens College Graduate School of Library & Information Studies • Flushing, NY 11367 • IFRT
Tunsoy Donna M. • Coor of Library Operations • Martin County Public Library • Stuart, FL 33494-2374 • PLA
Tunstall Margaret H. • Texas Southern University • Houston, TX 77004
Tuohy Eileen M. Sr • Librarian • Marymount High School Library • Los Angeles, CA 90077 • AASL
Tuohy Judith • University of Wisconsin-Madison Memorial Library • Madison, WI 53706 • RASD NMRT
Tuomi Margaret A. • Student • University of North Carolina Department of Library & Information Studies • Greensboro, NC 27412-5001
Tupin Jane L. • Senior Librarian • State Librarian Delaware Division of Libraries • Dover, DE 19901 • ACRL ALCTS ASCLA GODORT NMRT
Turbak Michelle A. • Stroudsburg, PA 18360
Turbyfill Dorothy K. • Tampa, FL 33612 • Continuing
Turchi Marilyn Lindgren • Resource Center Director • Crow Island School • Winnetka, IL 60093 • AASL
Turchyn Andrew Dr. • Professor & Librarian Emeritus • Indiana University at Bloomington University Libraries • Bloomington, IN 47405-9998 • ACRL *Continuing*
Turchyn Sylvia J. • Assistant Head of Cataloging • Indiana University • Bloomington, IN 47405 • ACRL ALCTS IFRT
Tureski Diane M • Bronx Project Librarian • New York Public Library Parkchester Branch Library • Bronx, NY 10462 • ALSC NMRT
Tureski Tim P. • Bronx, NY 10461 • IFRT NMRT SRRT
Turhollow C Anne • Science Reference Librarian • San Diego State University Library • San Diego, CA 92182-0511 • ACRL RASD LIRT
Turiel David • Mt Kisco, NY 10549-2120 • ACRL ALCTS RASD *Life*
Turitz Mitchell L. • Serials Librarian • San Francisco State University J. Paul Leonard Library • San Francisco, CA 94132 • ALCTS LITA
Turk Elizabeth Ann • Student • Columbia University Libraries Butler Library • New York, NY 10027
Turk James • Trustee • Waukegan Public Library • Waukegan, IL 60085
Turk Muriel S. • Asst. to the Director • Great Neck Library • Great Neck, NY 11024 • PLA
Turk Susan C. • Media Spec • Hialeah Elementary School • Hialeah, FL 33010 • AASL
Turkalo David M. • Collection Develpment Librarian • Social Law Library • Boston, MA 02108
Turkel Robert • Student • Florida State University School of Library and Information Studies • Tallahassee, FL 32306-2048 • RASD
Turknett Marilyn J. • Martinez, GA 30907
Turko Karen A. • Head Preservation Service • University of Toronto Library • Toronto ON, M5S 1A5 Canada
Turley Richard E. Jr. • Managing Director • Church of Jesus Christ of Latter-Day Saints • Salt Lake City, UT 84150 • ACRL ALTA LAMA
Turnbull Fiona M. • Cataloger • Missouri Botanical Garden Library • Saint Louis, MO 63166
Turnbull Mildred B. • Tryon, NC 28782 • Continuing
Turnbull Patricia B. • Library Development Consultant • Lincoln Trail Libraries System • Champaign, IL 61821-1068 • AASL ASCLA IFRT

Turner Ann • Head, Catalogue Records Div. • University of British Columbia • Vancouver BC, V6T 1Z1 Canada • ALCTS LAMA LITA

Turner Ann C. • Brewton-Parker College • Mount Vernon, GA 30445

Turner Anne M. • Santa Cruz City-County Library System • Santa Cruz, CA 95060 • LAMA PLA

Turner Audrey Jean • Part-time Reference Librarian • Eastern Washington University Spokane Center Library • Spokane, WA 99204 • ACRL ASCLA RASD

Turner Barbara • Librarian • Bushnell Public Library • Bushnell, IL 61422 • PLA

Turner Beatrice J. • Palmer, AK 99645

Turner Bonnie L. • Reference/Clln. Devel. Librarian • Bradley University Cullom-Davis Library • Peoria, IL 61625 • RASD

Turner Brenda G. • Public Services Librarian • Lexington Community College Library • Lexington, KY 40506-0235 • ACRL

Turner Camille A. • Madera County Library • Madera, CA 93637

Turner Carol A. • Assistant Dir. for Public Servs. • University of Florida Libraries • Gainesville, FL 32611-2047 • ACRL LAMA LITA GODORT MAGERT

Turner Carolyn C. • Assistant Librarian • A.M. Barbe High School • Lake Charles, LA 70605 • AASL

Turner Charlotte E. • Librarian • Chelsea School • Silver Spring, MD 20910

Turner Cheryl • Administrator • Jefferson County Public Library • Monticello, FL 32344 • ASCLA PLA RASD IRRT

Turner Christine N. • Student • Simmons College Graduate School of Library & Information Science • Boston, MA 02115 • ALCTS IFRT SRRT

Turner Diane J. • Science/Engineering Liaison • University of Colorado at Denver Auraria Library • Denver, CO 80204

Turner Diane Young • Dir, Library Personnel Svs • Yale University Sterling Memorial Library • New Haven, CT 06520 • ACRL LAMA

Turner Elizabeth W. • Head Librarian • DeKalb College North Campus Learning Resources Center • Dunwoody, GA 30338 • ACRL

Turner Frank L. Jr. Dr. • Professor of Library Science • Texas Woman's University School of Library & Information Studies • Denton, TX 76204 • LHRT

Turner Gayne • Susitna Valley High School Library • Willow, AK 99688

Turner Gurley • Meridale, NY 13806

Turner Helen E. • Bradenton, FL 33507 • ACRL YALSA *Continuing*

Turner Helen W. • Assistant Children's Department • Williamsburg Regional Library • Williamsburg, VA 23185 • YALSA IFRT

Turner James E. • YA/AV Librarian • Patchogue-Medford Library • Patchogue, NY 11772

Turner James H. • Magnolia, KY 42757 • YALSA

Turner Jamie Louise • Branch Librarian • Oakland Public Library Elmhurst Branch • Oakland, CA 94621 • ACRL PLA RASD YALSA EMIERT IRRT VRT

Turner Joan B. • Ridgefield, CT 06877

Turner Judith E. • Linn-Benton Community College Learning Resource Center • Albany, OR 97321 • ACRL RASD LIRT NMRT

Turner Karen A. • Director • Bowling Green Public Library • Bowling Green, KY 42101

Turner Kathy • Community Librarian • Sno-Isle Regional Library Edmonds Branch • Edmonds, WA 98020 • PLA IRRT

Turner Kathy A. • Reference Librarian • Florida Institute of Technology Library • Melbourne, FL 32901

Turner Kathy M. • Technical Services Librarian • Elizabeth City State University • Elizabeth City, NC 27909 • ALCTS

Turner Lawrence D. • Matthews, NC 28105 • RASD

Turner Lillie J.W. • Asst. LRC Coor. • Saint Philip's College • San Antonio, TX 78203 • ACRL ALCTS LAMA

Turner Lucile Miss • Winchester, VA 22601-8628 • ALCTS ASCLA *Continuing*

Turner Mabel A. • Spokane, WA 99201 • Continuing

Turner Marcellus • Library Instruction Librarian • East Tennessee State University Sherrod Library • Johnson City, TN 37614 • ACRL LIRT

Turner Marilyn S. • Kansas State University Farrell Library • Manhattan, KS 66506-1200 • ALCTS

Turner Martha A. • River Oaks Baptist School • Houston, TX 77027 • AASL ALSC

Turner Merriam B. • Librarian • Dundalk Elementary School • Baltimore, MD 21222 • AASL

Turner Michael G. • Trustee • East Meadow Public Library • East Meadow, NY 11554-1700 • ALTA

Turner Nancy B. • Student • Clark-Atlanta University School of Library & Information Studies • Atlanta, GA 30314-4391 • SRRT

Turner Nancy K. • Head, Archives & Special Clln. • Ball State University Bracken Library • Muncie, IN 47306-0160 • ACRL ERT IFRT

Turner Nancy R. • Librarian Grade 3 Adult Serv. • Montgomery County Department of Public Libraries • Rockville, MD 20850

Turner Pat W. • Library Media Specialist • Cartersville Middle School • Cartersville, GA 30120

Turner Patricia • Bibliographer • University of Minnesota O. Meredith Wilson Library • Minneapolis, MN 55455-0414 • ACRL RASD

Turner Patricia • Library Assistant • Boston Consulting Group Research Library • Chicago, IL 60606

Turner Patricia F. • Baltimore County Public Library • Towson, MD 21204 • ALTA PLA

Turner Philip M. • Dean • University of Alabama School of Library & Information Studies • Tuscaloosa, AL 35487-0252 • AASL ACRL ALCTS ALSC ASCLA PLA RASD

Turner Ray • Librarian • Southeast Area Health Education Center • Hazard, KY 41701

Turner Ruth N. Miss • Walnut Creek, CA 94595 • Continuing

Turner Sandra D. • Head Librarian • Denver Public Library Montbello Library • Denver, CO 80239 • LITA

Turner Sharon L. • Director • Morgantown Public Library • Morgantown, WV 26505 • PLA

Turner Sue E. • Bowlby Public Library • Waynesburg, PA 15370

Turner Susan • Canton, CT 06019 • ALCTS

Turner Susan S. • Greensboro, NC 27403 • AASL

Turner Susanna J. • Coor. Reference Department • Mississippi State University Mitchell Memorial Library • Mississippi State, MS 39762 • ACRL RASD LIRT

Turner Theoso-D Rejean L. • Consultant/Information Research • TGS Information Services • Edmonton, T6E 4B8 Canada • LITA ILERT NMRT

Turner Tom A. • University Branch Librarian • Skidaway Institute of Oceanography Library • Savannah, GA 31416-0687 • SRRT

Turner Virginia S. • Dir. of Libs. & Instrc. Resource • Alexandria City School District • Alexandria, VA 22302 • AASL

Turner William A. • Plattsburgh, NY 12901-3904

Turney Martha K. • Director • Thomas Hackney Braswell Memorial Library • Rocky Mount, NC 27804 • LAMA PLA

Turoci Esther M. • Supervisor/Technical Services • Westerville Public Library • Westerville, OH 43081 • PLA

Turock Betty J. • Chair & Director LIS • Rutgers University School of Communication Information & Library Studies • New Brunswick, NJ 08903 • ASCLA LAMA PLA RASD LIRT LRRT SRRT

Turpen Doreen • LSCA Project Manager • Washington State Library • Olympia, WA 98504-2470 • ASCLA LAMA

Turrell Susan W. • Head Librarian • Tunkhannock Public Library • Tunkhannock, PA 18657

Turse Cynthia G. • Elementary Librarian • Saint Andrew's Priory • Honolulu, HI 96813 • AASL

Turton Katherine M. • Indiana, PA 15701

Turula Margaret • Lake George, NY 12845 • Continuing

Turvold Nelda J. • Mankato, MN 56001

Tusa Bobs M. • Birmingham, AL 35213 • ACRL

Tusa Sarah D. • Serials Acquisitions Librarian • Lamar University Gray Library • Beaumont, TX 77710 • ALCTS

Tuss Joan • Student • Saint John's University Division of Library & Information Science • Jamaica, NY 11439 • ACRL

Tuszynski Thomas M. • Junior Fellow • Library of Congress • Washington, DC 20541 • NMRT

Tuten Jane H. • Head of Technical Services • University of South Carolina at Aiken Gregg-Graniteville Library • Aiken, SC 29801

Tuten Peggy S. • Crownsville, MD 21032-2137

Tuteur Civia M. • Children's Librarian • Chicago Public Library Jefferson Park Branch • Chicago, IL 60630 • ALSC

Tutt Bennett Celestine C. • Oakland, CA 94612

Tuttle Claire H. • Rochester, NY 14618 • GODORT

Tuttle Dorothy • Librarian • Chamberlin Free Public Library • Greenville, NH 03048

Tuttle George W. • Branch Head • New Orleans Public Library Gentilly Branch • New Orleans, LA 70122

Tuttle Helen W. • Princeton, NJ 08540 • ACRL ALCTS *Life*

Tuttle Joseph C. • Librarian • Pasquotank-Camden Library • Elizabeth City, NC 27909 • LITA

Tuttle Judith • Trustee • Horry County Memorial Library • Conway, SC 29526 • ALTA

Tuttle Judith A. • Head, User Services • University of Wisconsin-Madison Memorial Library • Madison, WI 53706 • ACRL LAMA

Tuttle Kathy • Seattle University Lemieux Library • Seattle, WA 98122

Tuttle Marcia L. • Head, Serials Department • University of North Carolina • Chapel Hill, NC 27599 • ACRL

Tuttle Margaret P. • Findlay, OH 45840 • Continuing

Tuttle Merrie B. • Cataloger • Joint Free Library of Morristown & Morris Township • Morristown, NJ 07960 • ALCTS

Tuttle Nancy L. • Olmsted Falls, OH 44138

Tuttle Robin E. • Lycoming College Library • Williamsport, PA 17701-5192 • ACRL RASD

Tuttle Walter Alan • Librarian • National Humanities Center • Resrch Tr Pk, NC 27709-2256 • ACRL ALCTS LITA RASD

Tutty Joy Miss • District Librarian • Masterton Public Library • Masterton, New Zealand • PLA

Tuytschaevers Mary A. • Reference Librarian • Lake County Public Library • Merrillville, IN 46410-5382 • ACRL PLA

Tuzinski Jean H. • State Library of Pennsylvania Department of Education • Harrisburg, PA 17105 • AASL

Tweed Marie • Air Products & Chemicals • Allentown, PA 18195-1501 • LITA

Tweedie Catherine • Asst to Dir for Space Planning • Colorado State University • Fort Collins, CO 80523 • ACRL

Tweedie Sally Bersey • Devon, PA 19333 • AASL

Twigg Janet F. • Student • University of Kentucky College of Library & Information Science • Lexington, KY 40506-0391

Twiss-Brooks Andrea B. • Reference Librarian • Lamar University Gray Library • Beaumont, TX 77710

Twist Angela M. • Student • Saint John's University Division of Library & Information Science • Jamaica, NY 11439

Twogood A. Eliane • Library Media Specialist • Tacoma Public Schools Mason Public School • Tacoma, WA 98407 • AASL

Twogood Kay • Director • Kaysville City Library • Kaysville, UT 84037 • PLA

Twombly John Fogg IV • Senior Librarian • Richmond Public Library Hull Street Branch • Richmond, VA 23224 • PLA IRRT

Tyagi K. G. • Director • Social Sci Doc Centre • New Dehli 110001, India • ALCTS LAMA LITA

Tyce Richard S. • Head Librarian • Pennsylvania State University Hazleton Campus Library • Hazleton, PA 18201 • ACRL LITA GODORT

Tychnowicz Susan A. • Holbrook, NY 11741 • PLA

Tyckoson David A. • Head, Reference Department • University at Albany Libraries • Albany, NY 12222 • ACRL ALCTS RASD GODORT *Life*

Tyer A. Lois • Head, Reference Department • Quincy Public Library • Quincy, IL 62301 • PLA RASD

Tyer Travis E. • Executive Director • Great River Library System • Quincy, IL 62301-3997 • AASL ACRL ALTA ASCLA LAMA LITA PLA RASD CLENE IFRT

Tygett Mary G. • Central Missouri State University Ward Edwards Library • Warrensburg, MO 64093 • RASD

Tyler Anne • Spanaway Lake High School • Spanaway, WA 98387

Tyler Audrey Q. • Director of Projects • Fulton County Superior Court • Atlanta, GA 30310

Tyler Carolyn • Librarian • University of South Carolina • Columbia, SC 29208

Tyler Effie B. • Libn/Edu Material Specialist • Dawson Technical Institute • Chicago, IL 60609

Tyler Kim E. • Professional Library • Sacred Heart General Hospital • Eugene, OR 97440 • LITA

Tyler Linda C. • Associate Library Director • Charleston Southern University L Mendel Rivers Library • Charleston, SC 29411 • ACRL

Tyler Marcia M. • Librarian • T. E. Baxter School • Midlothian, TX 76065

Tyler Onie Mrs. • Creighton Community Schools • Creighton, NE 68729 • AASL

Tyler Robert R. • President • Spring Independent School District Salyers Elementary • Spring, TX 77373

Tyler Sara E. • Bowling Green, KY 42101 • Continuing

Tyler Thomas G. • Associate Director • University of Denver Penrose Library • Denver, CO 80208 • ACRL ALCTS LAMA LITA RASD GODORT LIRT LRRT SORT

Tymciurak Olya Tatiana • Naperville, IL 60567-4476

Tynan Carolyn M. • Assistant Librarian • Indiana University • Bloomington, IN 47405 • ACRL LAMA LIRT

Tynan Elizabeth R. • Reference Librarian • Santa Rosa Junior College • Santa Rosa, CA 95401

Tynan Laurie F. • Executive Director • Montgomery County Norristown Public Library • Norristown, PA 19401 • LAMA PLA

Tynan Mary A. • Turner Free Library • Randolph, MA 02368

Tyndall Lucy A. • Student • Neil F. Austin Public Library • High Point, NC 27261

Tyndall Pamela A. • Student • Simmons College Graduate School of Library & Information Science • Boston, MA 02115 • RASD

Tynemouth Brian W. • Medford, MA 02155

Tyner Dail • Adm Offr Exchange & Gift Div • Library of Congress • Washington, DC 20541

Tyner Sue • Technical Services Asst Director • University of Texas at San Antonio-Library • San Antonio, TX 78249 • LITA

Tyree-Rose Carmen • Librarian II • Free Library of Philadelphia • Philadelphia, PA 19103

Tyree Stephen M. • Head of Interlibrary Loan Dept. • University of Wisconsin-Milwaukee Golda Meir Library • Milwaukee, WI 53201 • NMRT SRRT

Tyrrell Kenie M. • Librarian • Fort Gibson High School • Fort Gibson, OK 74403 • AASL

Tyrrell Mary Ann S • Librarian • Michigan State University Libraries • East Lansing, MI 48824-1048 • ACRL ALCTS LAMA

Tyrrell Michele • Media Specialist • Arundel Middle School • Odenton, MD 21113 • AASL

Tysinger Barbara R. • University of North Carolina • Chapel Hill, NC 27599 • ACRL ALCTS LITA SRRT

Tyson Christy • Seattle Public Library Southwest Branch • Seattle, WA 98126 • YALSA IFRT

Tyson John C. • State Librarian • Virginia State Library & Archives • Richmond, VA 23219 • ACRL ASCLA PLA LIRT

Tyson Ruby U. • Librarian • American Federation of Labor Congress of Ind Org (AFL-CIO) • Washington, DC 20006 • ALCTS LAMA RASD SRRT

Tzovaras Joyce Smith • Brooklyn, NY 11230 • AASL IFRT

Ubel James A. • Director • Shawnee Library System • Carterville, IL 62918 • ASCLA PLA

Ubysz Priscilla M. • Senior Librarian • United Technologies Otis Elevator • Farmington, CT 06032

Uchitelle Daniel J. • Director Center Inf. Serv. • Modern Language Association • New York, NY 10003 • ACRL LAMA

Uchtorff Barbara J. • Customer Liaison • Gaylord Information Systems • Liverpool, NY 13090 • ACRL LAMA LITA

Uddin Shantha C. • Encyclopaedia Britannica • Chicago, IL 60604 • LITA

Udstuen Christine M. • Trustee • Crystal Lake Public Library • Crystal Lake, IL 60014 • ALTA LAMA SRRT

Uebelacker Susan • Branch Manager • Prince George's County Memorial Library System /Largo-Kettering Branch • Largo-Kettering, MD 20772 • LAMA PLA YALSA

Uebele Dorothy M. • Gardnerville, NV 89410

Uesugi Isao • Head, Cataloging Services • Claremont Colleges Libraries Honnold/Mudd Library • Claremont, CA 91711 • LITA

Ufer Sharon J. • Tacoma, WA 98405 • PLA

Ugorowski Michael W. • Student • University of Texas at Austin Graduate School of Library & Information Sciences • Austin, TX 78712-1276 • SRRT

Uhden Felicia D. • Catalog Librarian • Corvallis-Benton County Public Library • Corvallis, OR 97330-4728 • ALCTS PLA IFRT

Uhl Catherine G. • Director • Puyallup Public Library • Puyallup, WA 98371

Uhl Edna • Trumbull, CT 06611 • Continuing

Uhl Rebecca S. • Asst. Libn./Catalog Lib for Sci. • Arizona State University Hayden Library • Tempe, AZ 85287-1006 • ACRL IRRT

Uhleman Judith A. • Coordinator • Erie County Library System • Erie, PA 16501

Uhlhorn Ivanka • De Laura-Satellite Research Center • Satellite Beach, FL 32937 • AASL

Uhlhorn Melissa A. • Student • University of Texas at Austin Graduate School of Library & Information Sciences • Austin, TX 78712-1276 • ALCTS NMRT

Uhlmann Douglas D. • Assistant Librarian • William Penn Charter School • Philadelphia, PA 19144 • YALSA

Uhrenholdt Ruth F. • Librarian • Rochester City School District #16 Library • Rochester, NY 14619

Uibel Barbara • Salnave Elementary School • Cheney, WA 99004

Uknalis Irena S. • Librarian II/Children's Libn. • Free Library of Philadelphia Katharine Drexel Branch • Philadelphia, PA 19154-3516 • ALSC

Ukwu Dele C. • Student • Loyola Marymount University William M. Rains Library • Los Angeles, CA 90015-1295

Ulbrecht Vera N. • Rockville, MD 20850 • ALCTS

Ulbrich David Earl • Circulation/Reference Librarian • Danville Public Library • Danville, VA 24541 • PLA

Ulgaran Lillian L. • Aiea, HI 96701 • PLA

Ulicny Linda L. • Student • University of Wisconsin School of Library & Information Studies • Madison, WI 53706

Ulincy Loretta D. • Medical Reference Librarian • National Library of Medicine • Bethesda, MD 20894

Ullin Albert • Little Bookroom Childrens Bookshop • Melbourne VIC, Australia • YALSA

Ullman Donald • Trustee • Peoria Public Library • Peoria, IL 61602 • ALTA

Ullman Scott H. • Alameda County Library Castro Valley Branch • Castro Valley, CA 94546

Ulloa Clara I. • Laguna Hills, CA 92653

Ulm Sandra W. • Administrator School L Media • Florida Department of Education • Tallahassee, FL 32399 • AASL

Ulmer Anne Christine • Student • Wayne State University Library Science Program • Detroit, MI 48202 • ALSC

Ulmschneider John E. • Asst. Dir. for Library System • North Carolina State University • Raleigh, NC 27695 • LAMA LITA

Ulrey Patricia D. • Lighthouse Pt, FL 33064

Ulrich Fred W. • Central Library Manager • Santa Cruz City-County Library System • Santa Cruz, CA 95060

Ulrich Jennifer • Catalog Librarian • Eastern Mennonite Coll • Harrisonburg, VA 22801

Ulrich Kathleen M. • School Library Media Spec. • Curry Elementary School • Tempe, AZ 85282 • AASL IRRT

Ulrich Pamela L. • Spanaway Lake High School • Spanaway, WA 98387

Ulrich Paul S. • Head Automated Circulation Sys. • Amerika Gedenkbibliothek • 1000 Berlin 61, Germany • ACRL LITA

Ulrich S. Jane • Director • Southwest Regional Library Systems • Durango, CO 81301 • ASCLA PLA

Ulrich Susan • Support Services Manager • Monterey Public Library • Monterey, CA 93940

Ulrich Tina J. • Reference Librarian • Elkhart Public Library • Elkhart, IN 46516-3184

Ulrich Ursula W. • Reference Librarian • Wheaton Public Library • Wheaton, IL 60187-5376 • RASD IFRT

Umana Christine J. • Library Media Specialist • Fontbonne Academy • Milton, MA 02186 • AASL

Umbach Stephanie • Assistant Librarian • Valparaiso University Moellering Memorial Library • Valparaiso, IN 46383

Umberson Donna • Tempe, AZ 85282 • ACRL

Umfress Marilyn • Librarian I • Memphis-Shelby County Public Library and Information Center • Memphis, TN 38104-4025 • PLA RASD

Umoh Linda K. • Cataloging Librarian • Southern Methodist University • Dallas, TX 75275

Umpleby Elisabeth A. • Student • Syracuse University School of Information Studies • Syracuse, NY 13244-4100 • PLA

Umstead Daniel Brian • Student • Syracuse University School of Information Studies • Syracuse, NY 13244-4100

Unaeze Felix Eme • Assistant Professor • Ferris State University • Big Rapids, MI 49307 • ACRL RASD

Underbrink Robert L. • Carlinville, IL 62626 • ACRL LAMA   *Life*

Underdue William H. • Binding Officer • Library of Congress • Washington, DC 20541 • ALCTS

Underwood Irene H. • Collection Development Mgr. • Louisville Free Public Library • Louisville, KY 40203-2257 • PLA

Underwood Jennifer S. • Student • Long Island University Palmer School of Library & Info. Sci. • Brookville, NY 11548

Underwood Kathleen E. • District Librarian • Oak Grove School District • San Jose, CA 95119 • AASL

Underwood Willis H. • Trustee • Anderson County Library • Anderson, SC 29622-4047

Ungar Albert J. • Trustee • Queens Borough Public Library • Jamaica, NY 11432 • ALTA PLA

Ungar Janice T. • Farmington Community Library • Farmington Hills, MI 48334

Ungarelli Louis D. • Director • Concord Public Library • Concord, NH 03301 • PLA YALSA

Unger Bigelane A. • King County Library System Issaquah Branch • Issaquah, WA 98027 • ALSC

Unger Carol D. • Assistant Head Preservation Sect • National Library of Medicine • Bethesda, MD 20894 • ALCTS FLRT

Unger Dorothy K. • Oshkosh, WI 54901 • Continuing

Unger Myron • Trustee • Mid-Hudson Library System • Poughkeepsie, NY 12601

Unger Steven • Institute of Public Administration Library • New York, NY 10036 • ACRL LAMA PLA

Ungurait Karen W. • Associate University Librarian • Florida State University Robert M. Strozier Library • Tallahassee, FL 32306-2047 • ACRL CLENE GODORT IFRT

Union Bunni • Children's Services • Geauga West Library • Chesterland, OH 44026 • YALSA

Union Terri S. • Fayetteville, NC 28303 • PLA IFRT

Unkles Sally Alice • Student • University of South Florida School of Library & Information Science • Tampa, FL 33620

Unmacht Diane L. • Librarian • Lake Washington High School • Kirkland, WA 98033 • AASL YALSA

Unmuth-Shelley Judean A. • Fond du Lac, WI 54935

Unpingco Elizabeth • Trustee • Nieves M. Flores Memorial Library • Agana, GU 96910 • ALTA

Unruh Jennifer K. • Student • Emporia State University School of Library & Information Management • Emporia, KS 66801 • SRRT

Unterholzner Dennis L. • Carthage College John Mosheim Ruthrauff Library • Kenosha, WI 53141 • ACRL

Unver Amira V. • George Washington University Himmelfarb Health Sciences Library • Washington, DC 20037 • ALCTS

Upchurch Sharon Kay • Director of Library • Culver-Stockton College Car Johann Memorial Library • Canton, MO 63435 • ACRL LAMA

Upell Joan M. • IMC Director • Ravinia School • Highland Park, IL 60035 • AASL

Upham Karen • Genesee District Library • Flint, MI 48504

Upham Lois N. • Lithonia, GA 30058 • ALCTS LRRT

Uppgard Jeannine • Director, Library • Westfield State College Ely Memorial Library • Westfield, MA 01086 • ACRL LAMA

Upshaw Dorothy • Trustee • Macomb County Library • Mount Clemens, MI 48044 • ALTA

Upson Gail E. • Arnold & Porter Library • Washington, DC 20036

Uptigrove Kenneth R. • Director • Owosso Public Library • Owosso, MI 48867 • LAMA PLA IFRT

Upton Jodi • Rome, GA 30161

Urbajs Alojz • Institute of Information Sciences • Maribor 62000, Yugoslavia

Urban Cheryl L. • Public Services Librarian III • Baltimore County Public Library Randallstown Area Branch • Randallstown, MD 21133 • PLA

Urban Ilsabe L. • Librarian • Telesec Temporary Services • Kensington, MD 20895

Urban Jean M. • Automation Coordinator • Rochester Public Library • Rochester, MN 55904-3777 • LITA

Urbanic Allan • Librarian for Slavic Collection • University of California-Berkeley University Library • Berkeley, CA 94720 • ACRL

Urbanik Elizabeth S. • Danville, VA 24540

Urbanski Ruth I. • Student • Pasco County Library System Processing Center • Port Richey, FL 34668

Urbanski Verna P. • University Librarian • University of North Florida Thomas G. Carpenter Library • Jacksonville, FL 32245-7605 • ALCTS

Urbizagastegui Shelley G. • Arkansas College • Batesville, AR 72501

Urias-Barker Zelina • Denton, TX 76203

Uricchio William J. • Bibliographic Control Dept. • University of Connecticut Homer Babbidge Library • Storrs, CT 06269-1005 • LITA

Urka Mary Ann T. • Takoma Park, MD 20912

Urness Carol Dr • Assistant Curator • University of Minnesota O. Meredith Wilson Library • Minneapolis, MN 55455-0414 • ACRL LRRT

Urquhart Mary K. • Baltimore, MD 21239

Urquiza Belinda Dunford • Librarian • Library of Congress • Washington, DC 20541 • ACRL ALCTS LITA

Urr Clifford H. • Director • James Martin Associates • Reston, VA 22091 • LITA ILERT

Urrizola Manuel M. • Cataloging Librarian • Loyola Marymount University Charles Von Der Ahe Library • Los Angeles, CA 90045

Ursel Darlene M. • Librarian • Plymouth District Library • Plymouth, MI 48170

Urtz Nancy • Head of Public Services • Saint Anselm College Geisel Library • Manchester, NH 03102-1310

Usher Caroline P. • Durham, NC 27705

Usher Donna Bush • Bartlett, IL 60103

Usher Esther • Danvers, MA 01923 • Continuing

Usher Phyllis Land • Senior Officer • Indiana Department of Education Ctr for Sch Impro & Performance • Indianapolis, IN 46204 • AASL

Ushizaki Susumu • Cataloger • Rikkyo University • Tokyo, 171 Japan • ALCTS LITA

Usovicz Eileen • Maps the Micrographic Preservation Service • Bethlehem, PA 18017

Utasi Michael G. • Director, National Sales Admin. • Baker & Taylor Books • Charlotte, NC 28217

Uthmann Edith L. • Technical Service Librarian • Longview Public Library • Longview, WA 98632-2993 • ALCTS

Utigard Phyllis R. • Librarian/Media Specialist • Richford Junior Senior High School • Richford, VT 05476 • AASL

Utterback Martha • Acting Director • Daughters of the Republic of Texas Library at the Alamo • San Antonio, TX 78295-1401

Utuk Efiong S. Dr. • Willingboro, NJ 08046

Utz William H. III • West Virginia Graduate College Library Services • Institute, WV 25112 • ACRL LITA

Utzinger Orchard • Librarian • Raymond Elementary School • Franksville, WI 53126 • ALSC

Uva Peter A. • Head, Public Services • State University of New York Health Science Center Library • Syracuse, NY 13210 • ACRL ALCTS LITA RASD
Uyehara Cynthia M. • Student • University of Hawaii School of Library & Information Studies • Honolulu, HI 96822 • AASL ALSC LITA
Uyehara Harry Y. • University of Guam • Mangilao, GU 96923 • AASL ALSC
Uzdavinis Maria C. • Student • State University of New York at Albany School of Information Science & Policy • Albany, NY 12222
Uzman Betty • Conway, AR 72032 • ACRL
Vaaler Nan Stormont • Napa, CA 94558
Vacca Susan M. • Career Resources Librarian • Harvard University Career Reference Library • Cambridge, MA 02138
Vaccaro Beth • Account Services Manager • EBSCO Subscription Services • Springfield, VA 22151-4148 • LITA IFRT
Vaccaro William J. • Librarian • Chicago Public Library Sulzer Regional Library • Chicago, IL 60625 • LITA PLA
Vachss Lynn • Keene, NH 03431
Vachta Rosemary • Trustee • Elmhurst Public Library • Elmhurst, IL 60126 • ALTA PLA
Vaeth Helen L. • Milwaukee, WI 53222 • Continuing
Vago Marianne • National Starch & Chemical Corp. • Bridgewater, NJ 08807 • LITA
Vail Althea L. • Blackwood, NJ 08012 • AASL
Vail James • Trustee • Cleveland Heights-University Heights Public Library • Cleveland Heights, OH 44118
Vaillancourt Anna M. • Van Nuys, CA 91401-2548
Vaillancourt P. M. Dr. • Albany, NY 12208 • ACRL RASD *Life*
Vainstein Rose • Professor Emeritus • University of Michigan School of Information and Library Studies • Ann Arbor, MI 48109-1092 • ACRL PLA RASD *Life*
Vajda Rosemary • East Gwillimbury Public Library • Holland Landing, ON, L0G 1H0 Canada
Vakili Mary Jane • Iowa State University Library • Ames, IA 50011-2140 • ACRL LAMA RASD GODORT
Valadie Elizabeth M. • Head of Technical Services • Loyola University Loyola Law School Library • New Orleans, LA 70118 • LAMA
Valance Marsha J. • Regional Librarian • Wisconsin Rgnl L for the Blind & Physically Handcpd • Milwaukee, WI 53233 • PLA YALSA SRRT
Valauskas Edward J. • Head Library Public Services • Superconducting Super Collider • Dallas, TX 75237-3946 • ACRL ALCTS LITA
Valdez Esteban • Student • University of Arizona Graduate Library School • Tucson, AZ 85721 • ACRL RASD
Valdez Jesus • 14050 Mexico D.F., Mexico • LRRT
Valdez Karen J. • Literature Specialist • Toys That Teach • Sacramento, CA 95841
Valdez Melba E. • Student • University of Texas at Austin Graduate School of Library & Information Sciences • Austin, TX 78712-1276 • ACRL
Valdez Roberto • Branch Librarian • Oakland Public Library • Oakland, CA 94612
Valdez Roseanna O. • Student • Indiana University School of Library and Information Science • Bloomington, IN 47405
Valduga Kathy • Product Manager • Quality Books Inc. • Lake Bluff, IL 60044-2204 • VRT
Valen Linda M. • Children's Librarian • Saint Paul Public Library • St. Paul, MN 55102 • PLA
Valente Colleen A. • Catalog Librarian • University of Vermont Bailey Howe Library • Burlington, VT 05405-0036
Valente Elda C. • Springfield, OH 45504 • Continuing
Valentijn Nico F. • Elkhart, IN 46514 • AASL
Valentin-Marty Jeannette • Head Puerto Rican Collection • University of Puerto Rico • Mayaguez, PR 00708
Valentin Yolanda • Student • University of Alabama School of Library & Information Studies • Tuscaloosa, AL 35487-0252
Valentine-Jakublak Eleanor • Student • Indiana University School of Library and Information Science • Bloomington, IN 47405
Valentine Barbara B. • Reference • Linfield College Northup Library • McMinnville, OR 97128 • ACRL
Valentine Christine R. • Davenport College Magaret D. Sneden Library • Grand Rapids, MI 49306 • RASD
Valentine Diana • Childrens Librarian • Enoch Pratt Free Library Waverly Branch • Baltimore, MD 21218 • ALSC
Valentine Karen Gerdetz • Amesbury Public Library • Amesbury, MA 01913
Valentine Patrick M. Dr. • Director • Wilson County Public Library • Wilson, NC 27893 • PLA RASD LHRT
Valentine Phyllis A. • Senior Associate Librarian • University of Michigan Libraries • Ann Arbor, MI 48109-1205
Valentine Wayne • North Dover Elementary School • Dover, NJ 07801 • AASL
Valentino Rose • Lyndhurst, OH 44124 • ALSC
Valenzuela Paul R. • Student • State University of New York at Albany School of Information Science & Policy • Albany, NY 12222
Valeria Sr. M. • Librarian • St Bernard High Sch Lib • Playa Del Rey, CA 90291
Valerio Lisa L. • Student • Macomb County Library • Mount Clemens, MI 48044 • IFRT SRRT
Valeski Janet L. • Reference Librarian • Quinnipiac College • Hamden, CT 06518 • ACRL LIRT
Valino Nenita M. • Head, Catalog Dept. • Anne Arundel Community College Andrew G. Truxal Library • Arnold, MD 21012
Valk Judy P. • Coordinator Technical Services • Pollard Memorial Library • Lowell, MA 01852
Vallar Cynthia L. • Hannah More Center School • Reistertown, MD 21136 • AASL ALSC
Vallely John R. • Associate Librarian • Siena College • Loudonville, NY 12211-1462 • ACRL ALCTS
Vallone Richard W. • New England Conservatory of Music-Spaulding Library • Boston, MA 02115 • ACRL
Valovich Diane E. • Coordinator of Media Service • The University School of Nova University • Fort Lauderdale, FL 33314 • AASL
Valukas Salomeja • New Haven, CT 06511 • Continuing
Valunas Madelyn • System Librarian • Shippensburg University Lehman Memorial Library • Shippensburg, PA 17257-2299 • ACRL ALCTS LAMA LITA RASD
Vammen Anna N. • Librarian • Capitol City Junior College of Business • Little Rock, AR 72204 • ACRL NMRT
Van Antwerp Karen M. • Student • University of Detroit-Mercy Main Library • Detroit, MI 48221
Van Auken Barbara • Trustee • Peoria Public Library • Peoria, IL 61602 • ALTA
Van Auken Carol C. • Student • Long Island University Palmer School of Library & Information Science • Greenvale, NY 11548 • AASL ALSC
Van Auken Nancy O. • Richmond, VA 23235
Van Auker Rosalind • Assistant Education Librarian • California State University-Sacramento Library • Sacramento, CA 95819-6039 • ACRL
Van Balen John • Head of Public Services • University of South Dakota I.D. Weeks Library • Vermillion, SD 57069-2390
Van Bergen Gayle E. • Solon, OH 44139 • ALSC
Van Berkel John C. • Director • Manatee County Public Library System • Bradenton, FL 34205 • PLA
Van Bockstaele Beatrice M. • U. S. Correspondent • Bibliotheque De France • Paris 75013, France • LITA
Van Bradt John C. • Student • Emporia State University Emporia in the Rockies • Denver, CO 80204
Van Cura Mary Ann E. • Head of Technical Service • Hamline University School of Law • St. Paul, MN 55104 • ALCTS LITA LRRT
Van Cutsem Eveline J. • San Francisco, CA 94131
Van De Ven Anne K. • Student • Thomas Ford Memorial Library • Western Springs, IL 60558
Van DeMoortell Raymond • Curator • San Francisco State University • San Francisco, CA 94132
Van Der Meer Rebecca • Student • University of South Carolina College of Library & Information Science • Columbia, SC 29208
Van DerWoude Gladys A. • Silver Spring, MD 20904 • AASL
Van Deusen Nancy • Head of Technical Services • State University of New York Agricultural & Technical College • Cobleskill, NY 12043 • ACRL
Van Diest Raymond G. • Librarian • Foothill High School Library • Redding, CA 96001 • AASL
Van Dreel Mary Gabriel Sr. • Director • Silver Lake College Library • Manitowoc, WI 54220 • ACRL
Van Dyk David J. • Retrospective Conversion Spec • Online Computer Library Center (OCLC) • Dublin, OH 43017-3395 • ALCTS LITA
van Dyke Aase S. • Children's Services Div. Chief • Norwalk Public Library • Norwalk, CT 06850 • ALSC
Van Dyke Flora • Childrens Services Coordinator • New Haven Free Public Library • New Haven, CT 06510 • ALSC PLA
Van Dyke Marilyn • Assistant Librarian • Geneva College McCartney Library • Beaver Falls, PA 15010 • ACRL ALCTS ALSC LIRT
Van Dyke Susan Bridges • Charlotte, NC 28211-4135
Van Eenam Carol J. • Music/AV Cataloger • University of Utah Marriott Library • Salt Lake City, UT 84112-1179 • ACRL ALCTS
Van Fleet Connie J. • Assistant Professor • Louisiana State University School of Library & Information Science • Baton Rouge, LA 70803-3290 • PLA RASD IFRT
Van Fleet Nancy S. • Director • Sheridan Junior High School • Sheridan, WY 82801 • AASL
Van Fleet Ron • General Manager • Brodart Company • Williamsport, PA 17705 • LITA
Van Fossen Michael G. • International Documents Libn. • University of North Carolina Davis Library CB#3922 • Chapel Hill, NC 27599 • GODORT
Van Garsse Yvan Dr. • Bibl Voor • Hedendaasse Dokumentatie • Sint Niklaas, ZZ 00004 • GODORT
Van Gesen Daniel J. • Snowflake High School • Snowflake, AZ 85937 • AASL YALSA
Van Goethem Geraldine • Head, Acquisitions/Serials Dept. • Duke University William R. Perkins Library • Durham, NC 27706 • ALCTS LITA
Van Hamersveld Christine E. • Houston, TX 77090-2402 • AASL
Van Heck III Charles • Asst. Librarian Public Services • University of the South Jessie Ball duPont Library • Sewanee, TN 37375-4005 • ACRL
van Heyst Janet S. • Librarian • T.W. Browne Middle School • Dallas, TX 75233 • AASL IFRT
Van Hoeck Michele K. • Inter-Biodiversity Res. Ctr. • California Academy of Sciences • San Francisco, CA 94118
Van Hook Beverly • Holderby & Bierce Publishers • Rock Island, IL 61201
Van Horn James • Trustee • Lincoln City Libraries • Lincoln, NE 68508 • ALTA
Van Horn Miranda P. • Westmont, NJ 08108-2002 • AASL LIRT
Van Horne Geneva T. • Professor • University of Montana Library • Missoula, MT 59812 • AASL YALSA
Van Houlen Lynn M. • Librarian • Spinal Cord Injury Information Center • Santa Rosa, CA 95405 • ASCLA
Van House Nancy • Dean • University of California-Berkeley School of Library & Information Studies • Berkeley, CA 94720 • PLA LRRT
Van Houten Patricia O. • Miami-Dade Public Library System Coral Gables Branch • Coral Gables, FL 33134 • PLA
Van Hoy Catherine S. • Cumberland County Public Library and Information Center, Bordeaux Branch • Fayetteville, NC 28304 • LAMA
Van Hoy David C. • Principal Serials Cataloger • Massachusetts Institute of Technology Libraries (MIT) • Cambridge, MA 02139 • ALCTS SRRT
Van Kirk Elizabeth J. • Library Assistant • Phoenix Public Library Cholla Branch • Phoenix, AZ 85051-1598 • YALSA
Van Kirk Shannon E. • Head Librarian • Immaculate Heart High School • Los Angeles, CA 90028 • AASL ALSC YALSA EMIERT IFRT SRRT
Van Lancker Anita K. • Moline, IL 61265-1430
Van Laningham Ruth P. • Librarian • Costabile Associates • Bethesda, MD 20814 • ALCTS
Van Meter Joyce • Library Media Specialist • Rocky Mountain Elementary • Westminster, CO 80030 • AASL
Van Metre Linda • Librarian • Saint Joseph Catholic School Library • Brandenton, FL 34205
Van Note Roy N. • Tucson, AZ 85712 • ACRL ALCTS *Life*
Van Opdorp Beth McMenamin • Student • Northern Illinois University Department of Library & Information Studies • DeKalb, IL 60115 • SRRT
Van Orden Phyllis Jeanne • Professor • Wayne State University Library Science Program • Detroit, MI 48202 • AASL ALCTS ALSC LRRT
Van Orden Richard D. • Prog Dir,Res & Acad Libs • OCLC Online Computer Library Center • Dublin, OH 43017-3395 • ACRL RASD
Van Orden Susan • Pocatello, ID 83201 • AASL
Van Pelt Martha A. • Operations Manager • Clermont County Public Library • Batavia, OH 45103-3192
Van Pelt Richard S. • Vienna, VA 22180 • AASL
Van Pelt Robbie A. • Dhahran Airpt 31932, Saudi Arabia
Van Pulis Noelle • Authorities Librarian • Ohio State University Libraries • Columbus, OH 43210-1286 • ACRL ALCTS LITA RASD LIRT
Van Riddle Martha B. • Director • Avon Public Library • Avon, MA 02322 • PLA
Van Sicklen Lindsay L. • Librarian • Commonwealth College Library • Richmond, VA 23235 • ACRL
Van Wert Sally B. • Greeley, CO 80634
Van Willigen Anne • Student • University of Kentucky College of Library & Information Science • Lexington, KY 40506-0391
Van Woerkom Barbara J. • Reference Librarian • National Press Club • Washington, DC 20045
Van Wormer Lee • Media Specialist • Union Park Middle School Orange County Public Schools • Orlando, FL 32817 • AASL
Van Wynen Dieke • New Media Manage • Wolters Kluwer Academic • Holland, Netherlands
Van Zanten Judith E. • Librarian • Clarendon Hills Public Library • Clarendon Hills, IL 60514
Van Zile Joan E. • Pentwater, MI 49449 • PLA

Van de Voorde Philip • Government Publications Spec. • Iowa State University Library • Ames, IA 50011-2140 • ACRL GODORT

Van de Vyver Katia A. • Student • University of Texas at Austin Graduate School of Library & Information Sciences • Austin, TX 78712-1276 • RASD

Van de Water Julia C. Dr. • Library Media Specialist • Great Neck North High School • Great Neck, NY 11023 • AASL

Van der Meulen Ann E. • Student • State University of New York (SUNY) School of Information & Library Studies • Buffalo, NY 14260 • AASL

VanAlyea Pat • Owner • Book Bay • Milwaukee, WI 53211 • ALSC

VanAntwerp Thomas • Houston, TX 77004

VanArsdale Dennis G. • Technical Services Librarian • Westark Community College • Fort Smith, AR 72913

VanAusdal Karl • Music Librarian • Appalachian State University Carol Grotnes Belk Library • Boone, NC 28608 • ACRL RASD LHRT

VanAvery Annalisa R. • Senior Assistant Librarian • State University of New York (SUNY) University Libraries • Albany, NY 12222 • ACRL ALCTS

VanBaars Jen W. • Student • Catholic University of America School of Library and Information Science • Washington, DC 20064

VanBiema Mary E. • Cataloger • Mannes College of Music Harry Scherman Library • New York, NY 10024 • ALCTS

VanBlair Betty A. • Director of Library Services • Southwest Baptist University Estep Library • Bolivar, MO 65613 • ACRL LAMA

VanBuren Mary • Associate Librarian • Cornell University N.Y. State Agriculture Experiment • Ithaca, NY 14456-0462 • ACRL

VanBuskirk Elisabeth L. • Associate Director, Research • New Jersey Education Association • Trenton, NJ 08608 • RASD

VanCleve Nancy J. • Athens, GA 30606 • ALCTS

VanCura Joyce Bennett • Director, Learning Resources Ctr • Morton College • Cicero, IL 60656 • ACRL LAMA LITA RASD

VanDeCarr Janet • Park Ridge Public Library • Park Ridge, IL 60068-4188 • ALSC PLA

VanDeWalle Cindy K. • Media Specialist K-6 • Alan Shepard Elementary School North Scott Community School District • Long Grove, IA 52756 • AASL

VanDelinder Bonnie L. • Librarian • Lutheran Theological Seminary A.R. Wentz Library • Gettysburg, PA 17325

vandenHeuvel Elizabeth T. • Atlanta, GA 30306 • PLA IFRT LHRT SRRT

VanDerBellen Liana • Chief Rare Books Librarian • National Library of Canada Information Technical Services • Ottawa ON, K1A 0N4 Canada • Continuing

VanDerBogert Virginia • Appalachian State University Carol Grotnes Belk Library • Boone, NC 28608

vanderDoes Jill J. • Librarian • Vanderbilt University Management Library • Nashville, TN 37203 • RASD

VanDerVoorn Neal • Branch Librarian • Washington State Library Services Western State Hospital • Fort Steilacoom, WA 98494 • ASCLA

VanDeroef Helena M. • Technical Cataloger • Bellcore • Piscataway, NJ 08854 • ALCTS LITA

VanDeusen Jessie • Schenectady, NY 12308 • Continuing

VanDeventer Barbara • Chicago, IL 60610 • ACRL ALCTS

VanDusen Sandy M. • Student • Sterling Public Library • Sterling, CO 80751 • RASD

VanDussen Margaret G. • Pt Angeles, WA 98362 • LAMA PLA *Continuing*

VanEpps Sharyn Lynn • Library Media Coordinator • Department of Defense Dependent Schools • APO New York, NY 09641 • AASL ALSC LIRT LRRT

VanFleet Marie E. • Br Ln • Trails Regional Library • Warrensburg, MO 64093

VanFossan Kathryn R. • Head of Technical Services • Olivet Nazarene University Benner Library & Resource Center • Kankakee, IL 60901-0592 • ACRL ALCTS

VanGemert Edward V. • Media & Micro Computer Ctr Libn • University of Wisconsin-Madison College Library Helen C. White Hall • Madison, WI 53706 • ACRL

VanGiesen Linda D. • East York Elementary School • York, PA 17402 • AASL ALSC YALSA

VanGieson Marilyn J. • Library Branch Manager • Pearl City Public Library • Pearl City, HI 96782 • PLA

VanGilder Louise • Head of Tech. Servs/Ref. Ln. • Berkeley Heights Public Library • Berkeley Hts, NJ 07922 • ALCTS RASD

VanGundy Amelia C. • Asst. Director for Tech. Servs • Clinch Valley College John Cook Wyllie Library • Wise, VA 24293 • ALCTS

VanHandel Ralph A. • Lafayette, IN 47905 • LAMA PLA *Life*

VanHelden Charlotte M. • Setauket, NY 11733 • AASL

VanHorn Carole J. • Assistant Professor Univ. Ln • University of Wisconsin-Stevens Point Library • Stevens Point, WI 54481 • LITA

VanHouten Michael A. • Head of Public Services • Albion College Stockwell-Mudd Libraries • Albion, MI 49224 • ACRL

VanKeuren Linda A. • Student • University of Pittsburgh School of Library and Information Science • Pittsburgh, PA 15260

VanKirk Karen I. • Head Technical Service • Corpus Christi Public Library • Corpus Christi, TX 78401 • LITA

VanLeer Jerilyn M. • Library Media Teacher • Sedgwick Middle School • West Hartford, CT 06107 • AASL

VanMeter Vandelia • Chair, Dept Lib & Info Sci • Spalding University • Louisville, KY 40203 • AASL YALSA

VanNortwick Barbara L. • Associate Professor • Skidmore College Lucy Scribner Library • Saratoga Springs, NY 12866 • ACRL GODORT

VanOgtrop Stefanie • Sr Br Ln • Contra Costa County Library Danville Branch • Danville, CA 94526 • PLA

VanOrsdol Mary F. • San Juan Capistrano, CA 92675

VanPielt Gordon • Cataloging Librarian • Georgetown University Law Center Edward Bennett Williams Library • Washington, DC 20001-1417 • ALCTS IFRT

VanRiper-Geibig Claire • Student • Wayne State University Library Science Program • Detroit, MI 48202 • IFRT LHRT SRRT

VanSickle Charlotte Mrs • Trustee • Parlin-Ingersoll Library • Canton, IL 61520

VanSonnenberg Catherine • San Diego Public Library • San Diego, CA 92101 • PLA RASD MAGERT

VanStraten Daniel G. • Technical Services Manager • Mead Public Library • Sheboygan, WI 53081

VanSyckle Georgiana • Online Computer Library Center (OCLC) • Dublin, OH 43017-3395

VanSyoc Edna E. • Milo, IA 50166 • Continuing

VanVliet Lucille W. • Pinehurst, NC 28374 • AASL

VanWaart Ellen • Student • Emporia State University William Allen White Library • Emporia, KS 66801

VanWhy Carol B. • Department Head • Minneapolis Public Library & Information Center • Minneapolis, MN 55401-1992 • GODORT

VanWiemokly Jane G. • Principal Librarian • Morris County Free Library • Whippany, NJ 07981

VanWilligen Jacqueline • School Librarian • Paul Laurence Dunbar Senior High School • Kentucky, KY 40502 • AASL YALSA

VanWingen Peter M. • Spec. Rare Bk & Spec Clln Doc • Library of Congress • Washington, DC 20541 • ACRL

VanWingen Rachel Senner • Intl. Data Sharing Program Mgr. • Environmental Protection Agency • Washington, DC 20460 • LAMA GODORT

VanWinkle Betty J. • Elementary Media Specialist • Edwardsville School District No. 7 • Edwardsville, IL 62025 • AASL

VanWinkle Elva Young • Gaithersburg, MD 20879-3029 • ALSC PLA

VanYoung Sayre • Reference Librarian • Berkeley Public Library • Berkeley, CA 94704

VanZanten Frank V. • Mid-Hudson Library System • Poughkeepsie, NY 12601 • PLA IFRT SRRT

VanZee Gertrude Maude • Kalamazoo, MI 49007 • Continuing

VanZoeren Joan • Library Trustee • Kalamazoo Public Library • Kalamazoo, MI 49007-5270 • ALTA PLA

VanZwalenburg Joyce • Paia, HI 96779 • PLA IFRT

Vana Clara M. • Assistant Librarian • University of Pittsburgh at Greensburg • Greensburg, PA 15601 • ALCTS

Vanca Lynn K. • Children's Librarian • Akron-Summit County Public Library • Akron, OH 44326-0001 • ALSC PLA IFRT

Vance Barbara E. • Santa Clara Public Library • Santa Clara, CA 95051 • LITA

Vance Elizabeth J. • Librarian • Woodrow Wilson High School • Beckley, WV 25801 • AASL

Vance Kenneth E. • Professor Emeritus • University of Michigan School of Information and Library Studies • Ann Arbor, MI 48109-1092 • IRRT *Continuing*

Vance Mary-Louise H. • Biloxi, MS 39531 • Continuing

Vance Pamela J. • Head of Technical Services • Gary Public Library • Gary, IN 46402 • LAMA

Vance Pamela S. • Assistant Director Adm Servs • University of Pittsburgh • Pittsburgh, PA 15260 • LAMA LITA

Vance Sally M. • Librarian • Bromenn Health Care Health Sciences Library • Bloomington, IL 61701-2850

Vance Sharon K. • Library System Manager • Wheaton College • Wheaton, IL 60187 • LITA

Vance Susan • Atlantic County Library • Atlantic County Library • Mays Landing, NJ 08336

Vance V. Ellis • Director, Instructional Media • Fresno County Office of Education Library • Fresno, CA 93721-2000 • AASL

Vancil David E. • Terre Haute, IN 47802 • ACRL

Vande Vusse Mary Ann • C/YA Coordinator • Minnesota Valley Regional Library • Mankato, MN 56002-3446 • ALSC

VandeKamp Margaret G. • Librarian • Clinton High School • Clinton, IA 52732 • YALSA

VandeWater Nina W. • Franklin, TN 37064-5333

Vandefifer Teddy Mrs. • Coordinator of Media Service • Carman-Ainsworth Community Schools • Flint, MI 48507 • AASL

Vandegrift J R. Rev • Librarian • Dominican House of Studies Dominican College Library • Washngton, DC 20017-1584 • ALCTS LAMA LITA

Vandenberge Mary E. • Reference & Information Ln • Free Library of Philadelphia • Philadelphia, PA 19103

Vandenburgh Anne • Madison, WI 53715

Vander Ark Lorraine • Librarian • West Side Christian School • Grand Rapids, MI 49504

Vander Hart Robert J. • Iowa City, IA 52245

Vander Ploeg Pamela A. • Coor. of Youth Services • Kent County Library System • Grand Rapids, MI 49503 • ALSC YALSA

Vander Ven Jack T. • Cincinnati, OH 45223-1704

VanderLinde Mary K. • Librarian • Rochester Hills Public Library • Rochester, MI 48307 • PLA

VanderVall Ethel • School Librarian • Sir Francis Drake Elementary School • San Francisco, CA 94124 • AASL

Vanderbeck Maria Sister • Head Librarian • Queen of Holy Rosary College Library • Fremont, CA 94539

Vanderbeck Susan • Los Angeles, CA 90068 • NMRT

Vanderberg Patricia S. • Richmond, CA 94805 • ALCTS LIRT

Vanderberg Thelma • Community Information Spec. • New York Public Library • New York, NY 10016 • PLA

Vanderbrook Jane H. • Nuernberg Middle School • APO, AE 09222 • AASL AFLRT

Vandercook Sharon • Reference Coordinator • San Joaquin Valley Library System • Fresno, CA 93721

Vandergrift Kay E. • Rutgers University School of Communication Information & Library Studies • New Brunswick, NJ 08903 • AASL ALSC PLA

Vanderhoff Barbara Ann • Acquisitions Librarian • Arizona State University Libraries • Tempe, AZ 85287-1006 • ACRL ALCTS

Vanderhooft Eloise G. • Sandy, UT 84070 • ACRL ALCTS PLA RASD

Vanderhorst Sheila K. • Princeton, MA 01541 • ALSC

Vanderkooy Mary E. • Student • Kent State University School of Library & Information Science • Kent, OH 44242-0001

Vanderlaan Robert J. • Cataloger • Muskegon Community College Allen G Umbreit Library • Muskegon, MI 49442 • ACRL ALCTS ALSC LAMA LITA RASD EMIERT ERT GODORT IFRT IRRT LIRT SRRT

Vandermark Sondra • Deputy State Librarian • State Library of Ohio • Columbus, OH 43266-0334 • ASCLA LAMA LITA PLA

Vandermeer Lynne • Children's Librarian • Loutit Library • Grand Haven, MI 49417-1298 • ALSC

Vandermeer Rita K. • Student • Wayne State University Library Science Program • Detroit, MI 48202 • AASL

Vanderoef Shirley A. • Director • Westhampton Beach Free Library • Westhampton Beach, NY 11978-0051

Vanderpol Diane L. • Student • Syracuse University School of Information Studies • Syracuse, NY 13244-4100

Vanderpoorten Mary B. • General Manager • EBSCO Subscription Service • Birmingham, AL 35201 • ALCTS RASD ILERT

Vanderryst June • Reference Librarian • Plano Public Library System • Plano, TX 75086-0356 • PLA IFRT

Vandersall Lloyd K. • Orrville, OH 44667 • Continuing

Vandersluis Helen A. • Librarian Young Adults • Miami-Dade Public Library System • Miami, FL 33130-1504 • YALSA

Vandersteen Elizabeth K. • Assistant Director • Rapides Parish Library • Alexandria, LA 71301

Vanderwagen Sheryl A. • Director • Georgetown Township Public Library • Jenison, MI 49428 • PLA RASD

Vanderwiel Judy L. • Stockholm, NJ 07460 • AASL ALSC

Vanderwilt Kim E. • Adult Reference Librarian • Indianapolis Marion County Public Library • Indianapolis, IN 46206

Vandett Nancy M. • Trustee • Arkansas Department of Higher Education • Little Rock, AR 72201-3818 • ACRL LIRT

Vandiver Beth • Media Specialist • Franklin County Junior High School • Carnesville, GA 30521 • YALSA

Vandivier Elizabeth L. • Washington, DC 20003 • ACRL RASD GODORT

Vanek Andrea • Oakland, CA 94610
Vanek Edna V. • Chicago, IL 60611
Vanghn Doris H. • Trustee • Conyer-Rockdale Library Systems • Conyers, GA 30207
Vanke Judith P. • Children's Librarian • Cuyahoga County Public Library North Olmsted Branch • North Olmsted, OH 44070-3186 • ALSC
Vanko Lillian • Sarasota, FL 34234 • Continuing
Vanlandinghan Diana • School Librarian • Sapula High School • Sapula, OK 74066 • AASL
Vann J. Daniel III • Dean of Library Services • Bloomsburg University Harvey A. Andruss Library • Bloomsburg, PA 17815 • ACRL ALCTS LAMA LITA RASD *Life*
Vann Sarah K. • Professor Emeritus • University of Hawaii School of Library & Information Studies • Honolulu, HI 96822 • IRRT *Continuing*
Vannet David H. • Librarian • Juanita High School • Kirkland, WA 98034 • AASL
Vannorsdall Mildred May • Cincinnati, OH 45220 • ASCLA *Continuing*
Vanpatten Margaret A. • Reference/Adult Service Ln • Baldwinsville Public Library • Baldwinsville, NY 13027-2485 • PLA RASD IFRT
Vansickle Sharon L. • Norcross High School • Norcross, GA 30071 • AASL
Varela Anita M. • Student • San Jose State University Division of Library & Information Science • San Jose, CA 95192-0029 • LITA EMIERT
Varela D. Isabela • Student • University of Iowa School of Library & Information Science • Iowa City, IA 52242
Varenhorst Karen A. • Student • University of Texas at Austin Graduate School of Library & Information Sciences • Austin, TX 78712-1276 • AASL
Varga Carol • Director • Burton Public Library • Burton, OH 44021
Varga Lisa N. • Kenmore Middle School • Arlington, VA 22204
Varga Terese M. • Victoria Public Library • Victoria, TX 77901
Vargas Ezequiel • Trustee • Rockford Public Library • Rockford, IL 61101-1061 • ALTA
Vargas Patricia H. • Assistant Director • Groton Public Library • Groton, CT 06340 • PLA
Vargason Jo-an C. • Library Assistant • Polk Community College • Winter Haven, FL 33881
Vargha Rebecca B. • Associate Librarian • National Humanities Center • Resrch Tr Pk, NC 27709-2256 • LITA RASD
Vargo Jacqueline M. • Student • University of Pittsburgh School of Library and Information Science • Pittsburgh, PA 15260 • LITA
Varieur Normand L. • Administrative Librarian • U S Army ARDEC Sci & Tech Inf Br. • Picatinny Arsenal, NJ 07806 • LAMA LITA *Life*
Varjabedian Kathryn • Cataloger • Los Alamos National Lab Lib • Los Alamos, NM 87545-0020
Varjao-Atkinson Jaqueline • Washington, DC 20016 • ACRL
Varki Mariamma • Reference Librarian • Widener University Wolfgram Library • Chester, PA 19013 • ACRL
Varlejs Jana • Dir Prof Devel L Inf Sci • Rutgers University School of Communication Information & Library Studies • New Brunswick, NJ 08903 • YALSA CLENE LRRT SRRT
Varma Valsamani • Research Librarian • Youngstown State University William F. Maag Library • Youngstown, OH 44555 • ACRL
Varme Angela S. • Student • University of Northern Iowa Purchasing Off • Cedar Falls, IA 50614 • ALSC
Varnado Kay L. Dr. • Assoc Professor-LRD • Miami-Dade Public Library System Coral Reef Branch • Miami, FL 33165
Varner Carroll H. • Associate University Librarian • Illinois State University Milner Library • Normal, IL 61761-0900 • ACRL LITA IRRT
Varner Joyce M. • Jess Dunn Correctional Center Leisure Library • Taft, OK 74463 • ASCLA
Varnes Jennifer A. • Librarian • Camden County Library Echelon Urban Center • Voorhees, NJ 08043
Varnes Oliver C. Jr. • Acquisitions Librarian • Mount San Antonio College • Walnut, CA 91789 • ACRL LIRT
Varnet Harvey Dr. • Director • Governors State University University Library • University Park, IL 60466 • ACRL LAMA LITA
Varnon Dianne P. • Reference Services Head (LAIII) • Washoe County Library Sierra View Branch • Reno, NV 89502 • PLA NMRT
Varona Esperanza B. • Assistant Head Librarian • University of Miami Libraries Richter Library • Coral Gables, FL 33124
Vartanian Rita • Student • University of Washington Graduate School of Library and Information Science • Seattle, WA 98195
Vartuli Janice M. • Library Director • Sidney Memorial Public Library • Sidney, NY 13838 • PLA
Varughese Lola • Louisiana State University Libraries Troy H. Middleton Library • Baton Rouge, LA 70803-3342 • ALCTS
Vasaturo Ronald L. • Greenbelt, MD 20770-3004 • ALCTS LITA
Vasi John J. • Associate University Librarian • University of California UCSB Library • Santa Barbara, CA 93106-9010 • ACRL LAMA
Vasilakis Nancy • School Librarian • Tower School • Marblehead, MA 01945 • ALSC
Vasilik Patricia M. • Childrens Coordinator • Clifton Public Library • Clifton, NJ 07011 • ALSC
Vasquez Leslie E. • RONDAC Coordinator • OCLC Online Computer Library Center • Dublin, OH 43017-3395
Vasquez Linda P. • Austin Public Library • Austin, TX 78768
Vasquez Teresa M. • Coordinator, SEL Cataloging • University of Alberta • Edmonton AB, T6G 2J8 Canada • ALCTS
Vass Mary M. • University of Kentucky Education Library • Lexington, KY 40506 • ACRL
Vassallo Benita Weber • Chief of Library Services • Inter-American Development Bank Felipe Herrera Library • Washington, DC 20577
Vassallo Paul • Annapolis, MD 21401 • ACRL ALCTS *Life*
Vasse Sarah J. • Clln Development Librarian • Orange County Community College • Middletown, NY 10940 • ACRL ALCTS LIRT
Vassilakos Marion • Assistant City Librarian • San Bernardino Public Library • San Bernardino, CA 92410
Vassolo Karen K. • Acquisitions Librarian • Palos Park Public Library • Palos Park, IL 60464 • PLA
Vastine James P. • Acting Assoc Dir for Pub Servs • University of South Florida Library • Tampa, FL 33620-5600 • ACRL
Vastine Susan M. • Associate Librarian • University of South Florida Library • Tampa, FL 33620-5600 • ALCTS RASD *Life*
Vastine Thomas J. • Trustee • Villa Park Public Library • Villa Park, IL 60181 • ALTA IFRT
Vath Deborah • Librarian • Los Ranchitos School Library • Tucson, AZ 85710 • AASL
Vathis Alma Christine • Technical Librarian • Intel Corp • Chandler, AZ 85226 • RASD
Vaughan Carol C. • Rosenberg, TX 77471 • PLA
Vaughan Carol M. • Head of Technical Services • University of Missouri Libraries-Columbia Elmer Ellis Library • Columbia, MO 65201-5149 • ALCTS LITA
Vaughan Carolyn R. • Assistant Director • Henderson County Public Library • Hendersonville, NC 28739
Vaughan Carolyn R. • Media Speicalist • Ahfachekee School • Clewiston, FL 33440
Vaughan Charles L. • Information Specialist • Martin Marietta Energy Systems Fusion Energy Library • Oak Ridge, TN 37831-8074 • LITA
Vaughan Doris W. • Reference/Acquisitions Librarian • Central State University Hallie Q Brown Memorial Library • Wilberforce, OH 45384
Vaughan F Richard • Indiana University School of Law Library • Bloomington, IN 47405
Vaughan James M. • Head of Access Services • University of Chicago Library John Crerar Library • Chicago, IL 60637-1403 • ACRL
Vaughan Janet E. • Librarian • Columbia Heights High School • Columbia Hts, MN 55421 • AASL LITA
Vaughan Linda K. • Peachtree City, GA 30269
Vaughan Linda S. • School Librarian • Hampton Elementary School • Greensboro, NC 27410
Vaughan Marilyn • Irving, TX 75062 • PLA
Vaughan Mary • Dir.,Learning Resources Ctr • University of Tennessee-Martin School of Education Adminstration • Martin, TN 38238-5029 • AASL
Vaughan Ruth • Halifax NS, B3H 2J5 Canada
Vaughan Valerie • Amherst, MA 01002 • PLA
Vaughn Anita S. • Student • University of South Carolina College of Library & Information Science • Columbia, SC 29208
Vaughn Dawn P. • Cherry Creeks School • Denver, CO 80231 • AASL LITA
Vaughn Florence E. • Tyler, TX 75702 • AASL YALSA *Continuing*
Vaughn Frances • Director of Library • University of Texas-Brownsville • Brownsville, TX 78520-4994 • ACRL ALCTS LAMA LITA PLA RASD YALSA LIRT LRRT
Vaughn Jean R. • De Kalb High School Library Media Center • DeKalb, IL 60115
Vaughn Judith • Chatham Elementary School • Chatham, IL 62629 • AASL
Vaughn Kenneth R. • Librarian • Costabile Associates Inc • Bethesda, MD 20814
Vaughn Nada A. • Interlibrary Loan Supervisor • Washington University Libraries • Saint Louis, MO 63130 • ACRL RASD
Vaughn Priscilla • Assistant Director • Billerica Public Library • Billerica, MA 01821
Vaughn Robert V. Dr. • Information Broker • Aye-Aye Press • St. Croix, VI 00821 • Life
Vaughn Sarah C. • Extension Librarian • University of Kentucky Libraries • Lexington, KY 40506-0039 • ACRL NMRT
Vaughn Sherri • Librarian • Farmington Community Library • Farmington Hills, MI 48334
Vaughn Susan J. • Collection Development Librarian • Brooklyn College Library • Brooklyn, NY 11210 • ACRL ALCTS RASD SRRT
Vaughn Tzu-Hsiu • Student • Central Missouri State University Ward Edwards Library • Warrensburg, MO 64093
Vaught Jennifer L. • Librarian • Marshall High School Portland Public Schools • Portland, OR 97266 • AASL
Vavrek Bernard F. Dr. • Professor • Clarion University of Pennsylvania College of Library Science • Clarion, PA 16214 • PLA
Vavricka D. Karen • Associate Director • Tom Green County Library • San Angelo, TX 76903-5834 • LAMA
Vazakas Susan M. • Science Librarian • Boston University • Boston, MA 02215 • ACRL
Veach Daniel L. • Atlanta, GA 30307 • GODORT
Veach Grace L. • Cataloger • Decatur Public Library • Decatur, IL 62523
Veal Robin E. • Student • College of Saint Catherine • Saint Paul, MN 55105
Vean Julia • Trustee • Pueblo Library District McClelland Library • Pueblo, CO 81004-1997 • PLA
Veaner Allen B. • Tucson, AZ 85751-0786 • ACRL LAMA ILERT LHRT *Life*
Veatch James R. Jr Mr • Head of Technical Services • Nashville State Technical Institute Educational Resource Center • Nashville, TN 37209 • ALCTS GODORT
Veatch Lamar • Director • Irving Public Library System • Irving, TX 75015-2288 • LAMA PLA CLENE IFRT
Veccia Rose • Astoria, NY 11106
Vedder Harvey B. • Systems Engineer • Bell of Pennsylvania Marketing • Harrisburg, PA 17101 • LITA
Vedder Marion H. • Schenectady, NY 12301 • ASCLA PLA *Continuing*
Veenstra Geraldine B. • Battle Ground, WA 98604 • ALSC
Veenstra John G. Dr. • Cali, Colombia • ACRL ALCTS *Life*
Veeser Rozanne C. • Reference Librarian • Texas Tech University Libraries • Lubbock, TX 79409-0002 • ACRL RASD
Vega Marilyn D. • Library Commissioner • City of Commerce Public Library • Commerce, CA 90040 • ALTA
Vega S. A. • Student • University of Iowa School of Library & Information Science • Iowa City, IA 52242 • RASD EMIERT LRRT SRRT
Vehre John L. Jr. • Director • Greenville Public Library • Greenville, OH 45331 • LITA RASD
Veihman Robert A. • Associate Dean • College of DuPage Learning Resources Center • Glen Ellyn, IL 60137
Veit Fritz • Chicago, IL 60615 • ACRL ALCTS *Life*
Veitch Carol J. • Director • Montgomery-Floyd Rgnl Library • Christianbrg, VA 24073 • LAMA PLA
Vejzovic Laila M. • Pullman, WA 99163
Vela-Creixell Mary I. • Librarian • Fulbright & Jaworski • San Antonio, TX 78205
Vela Leonor G. • Professor of Bibliography • Escola University of Bibliografia Document • 08028, Barcelona, Spain • LITA RASD
Velante Cynthia G. • Librarian • Saint Hilda School • Edmonton AB, T6K 2N2 Canada • ALCTS
Velarde James A. • System Manager/Cataloger • Stanislaus County Free Library • Modesto, CA 95354
Velazquez-Santos Maria E. • Fort Bragg, NC 28307
Velde John E. Jr • Omaha, NE 68114 • ALTA IRRT
Velez Sara B. • Librarian • New York Public Library Performing Arts • New York, NY 10023 • IRRT
Velicer Lloyd F. • Asst Govt Pubn Ln • State Historical Society of Wisconsin • Madison, WI 53706 • ALCTS GODORT
Vella Barbara J. • Trustee • Rockford Public Library • Rockford, IL 61101-1061 • ALTA
Vella Sandra A. • Academic Personnel Coordinator • University of California-Davis Library • Davis, CA 95616 • ACRL
Velligas Robert M. • Native Hawaiian Library Project • Honolulu, HI 96819-4429 • IFRT SRRT
Vellucci Margaret M. • Edison Public Library North Edison Branch • Edison, NJ 08820 • ALSC

Vellucci Sherry L. • Saint John's University Division of Library & Information Science • Jamaica, NY 11439 • ACRL ALCTS LITA
Velnich Doreen • Head Librarian • Philadelphia School District Pedagogical Library • Philadelphia, PA 19103 • AASL LITA YALSA
Veltema John H. • Director Media Services • Jenison Public School District • Jenison, MI 49428 • AASL
Veltfort Susan M. • King County Library System Maple Valley Library • Maple Valley, WA 98038 • ALSC PLA YALSA IFRT
Veltze Linda A. • Asst. Professor • Appalachian State University Department of Library Science & Educational Foundation • Boone, NC 28608 • AASL
Venable Andrew A. Jr. • Director • Gary Public Library • Gary, IN 46402 • PLA
Venable Rosemary H. • Ft Washington, MD 20744 • AASL
Venant Maria-Elena • New York, NY 11435
Venard Tamara L. • Johnstown, OH 43031 • AASL
Venburg Cynthia A. • Plainview Elementary School • Plainview, MN 55964 • AASL
Venetis Mary Jo • Rockwall, TX 75087 • ALCTS
Veneziano Velma D. • Librarian Emeritus • Northwestern University Library • Evanston, IL 60208-2300 • LITA
Venkat Hema • Student • Clark-Atlanta University School of Library & Information Studies • Atlanta, GA 30314-4391
Vent Marilyn • Los Vegas, NV 89170-2218 • ACRL ALCTS
Ventgen Carol • Director • Coos Bay Public Library • Coos Bay, OR 97420 • LAMA PLA
Ventresca Jordy L. • Coor of User Serv & Phys Plant • Worthington Public Library • Worthington, OH 43085 • LAMA PLA RASD
Ventrone Carl P. • LRC Director • Cincinnati Technical College • Cincinnati, OH 45223 • ACRL LITA
Venturella Karen M. • Student • Queens Borough Public Library • Jamaica, NY 11432 • SRRT
Veomett Colleen M. • Yakima Indian Nation Library • Toppenish, WA 98948
Veon Mary L. • Student • Kent State University School of Library & Information Science • Kent, OH 44242-0001
VerVoort Heather • Student • University of Wisconsin-Madison School of Library & Information Studies • Madison, WI 53706 • ALSC
Vera Patricia A. • Librarian • Crowley Public Library • Crowley, TX 76036 • NMRT
Veracka Peter G. • Librarian • Pontifical Coll Josephinum A.T. Wehrle Memorial Library • Columbus, OH 43235 • ACRL
Verbesey J. Robert • Mastics-Moriches-Shirley Community Library • Shirley, NY 11967 • ALTA LAMA PLA
Verbesey Kevin E. • Setauket, NY 11733
Verble Frances H. • Cataloging Unit • University of Tennessee-Memphis Health Sciences Center Library • Memphis, TN 38163 • ALCTS
Verchot Martha E. • Science Librarian • Illinois State University Milner Library • Normal, IL 61761-0900 • ACRL LITA
Verdini James M. • New Haven, CT 06511 • ACRL
Veress Eugene S. • Albion Correctional Facility • Albion, NY 14411
Vergara Stephanie A. • Villa Vergara Vintage Books • Saint Louis, MO 63116
Verge Colleen • Librarian • Ann Arbor Public Library • Ann Arbor, MI 48104
Verges Bruni • Assistant Director • Westchester Library System • Elmsford, NY 10523 • PLA IFRT
Verheyen Carol Y. • Student • University of California Los Angeles Graduate School of Library & Information Science • Los Angeles, CA 90024 • ACRL
Verhoef Rae • Reference Librarian • Yolo County Library • Woodland, CA 95695
Verhoff Patricia A. • Eastern Idaho Technical College • Idaho Falls, ID 83401 • ACRL
Verich Thomas M. • University Archivist • University of Mississippi John Davis Williams Library • University, MS 38677 • ACRL
Verkade Vanessa M. • Northeastern University • Boston, MA 02115 • LITA
Verlinde Gary • Midland Public Schools • Midland, MI 48640 • AASL
Vermaaten Roberta • Reference/Inf. Substitute • Jackson District Library • Jackson, MI 49201 • RASD
Vermandois Nancy • Librarian • East Hampton High School Libarary • East Hampton, NY 11937 • AASL YALSA
Vermillion Terry • Student • Texas Woman's University School of Library & Information Studies • Denton, TX 76204
Vermouth Paul C. Jr • Massachusetts Institute of Technology Libraries (MIT) • Cambridge, MA 02139 • ACRL RASD IFRT
Vernerder Gloria J. • Head of Youth Services • Hinsdale Public Library • Hinsdale, IL 60521 • ALSC PLA
Vernon Christie D. • Tidewater Librarian • Saint Leo College • Langley AFB, VA 23665 • ACRL AFLRT
Vernon Elizabeth • Cambridge, MA 02238 • ACRL
Vernon Elizabeth V. • Orlando, FL 32808
Vernon Joan M. • Student • San Jose State University Division of Library & Information Science • San Jose, CA 95192-0029
Vernon Nancy Singleton • Director • Madison Public Library • Madison, NJ 07940 • LAMA PLA RASD YALSA
Verret Brenda • Belle Chasse, LA 70037
Verrette Irma • Funeral Director • Pointe Coupee Parish Library • New Road, LA 70760 • ALTA
Verruso Cynthia L. • Librarian I/Agency Head • Port Washington Public Library • Port Washington, NY 11050
Vertrees Linda S. • Head Acquistions Division • Chicago Public Library • Chicago, IL 60607 • ALCTS LAMA PLA
Veryha Wasyl Dr. • Head-Slavic Catalog Unit • University of Toronto • Toronto ON, M5S 1A5 Canada • Continuing
Vespa David J. • Catholic University of America Libraries • Washington, DC 20064 • ACRL RASD CLENE SRRT VRT
Vespo Martin J. • Persident • Grolier Educational Corporation • Peekskill, NY 10566 • AASL
Vest Stephen C. • Director • Botetourt County Library • Roanoke, VA 24012
Vestal Jeanne G. • Franklin Watts Inc. • New York, NY 10016 • AASL ALSC
Vestal Lucille • Children's Librarian • Los Angeles Public Library Expositition Park Branch • Los Angeles, CA 90007 • ALSC
Vestling Christina • Tucson, AZ 85704-2066
Veth Terry R. • Librarian • Minneapolis Public Library & Information Center • Minneapolis, MN 55401-1992 • LITA
Vetter Alta C. • Kansas City, MO 64151
Vezina Elizabeth A. • Lunenburg, MA 01462 • NMRT
Via Barbara J. • Reference Librarian • University at Albany Libraries • Albany, NY 12222 • ACRL
Via Cynthia K. • Pioneer Hi-Bred International Inc. • Des Moines, IA 50309
Via John E. • Assistant Director • Wake Forest University Z Smith Reynolds Library • Winston Salem, NC 27109-7777 • ACRL ALCTS LAMA LITA RASD
Viacava Lillian D. • Associate Chief Librarian • Iona College Ryan Library • New Rochelle, NY 10801 • ACRL ALCTS LITA RASD
Viator Van P. • Reference Librarian • Northeast Louisiana University Sandel Library • Monroe, LA 71209-0720 • ACRL RASD
Vicarel Jo Ann • Cleveland Heights-University Heights Public Library • Cleveland Heights, OH 44118
Vicari Joan • Library Director • Ocean City High School • Ocean City, NJ 08226
Vicchiarelli Caroline F. • Rgnl Services Children's Mgr • Cuyahoga County Public Library Mayfield Regional Branch • Mayfield Village, OH 44143-2179 • ALSC
Vickers Ann J. • Catalog Librarian • Elon College Iris Holt McEwen Library • Elon College, NC 27244-0187 • ALCTS
Vickers Charles R. • Lewes, DE 19958
Vickers Lucile F. • Security National Bank • Sioux City, IA 51102 • LITA RASD *Continuing*
Vickery Ethel A. • Reference Librarian • Mount Olive Public Library • Budd Lake, NJ 07828 • PLA RASD
Vickery George W. • Director • Bay County Public Library Association NW Regional Lib System • Panama City, FL 32401-2625
Vickrey William • Trustee • West Florida Regional Library • Pensacola, FL 32501 • ALTA PLA
Vicoli Sharon Beth • Student • University of Maryland College of Library and Information Services • College Park, MD 20742-4345 • LITA RASD SRRT
Victor Barbara H. • Childern's Librarian • Indian Trails Public Library District • Wheeling, IL 60090
Victor Michele S. • Law Librarian • Cullen and Dykman • Brooklyn, NY 11201
Victoria Van R. • Reference Librarian • Kent Free Library • Kent, OH 44240
Victoria Vicki R. • Assistant Director/Hd of Info. • Stow Public Library • Stow, OH 44224 • RASD
Victorson Kenneth J. • Professional Services Consultant • NOTIS Systems, Inc. • Evanston, IL 60201-3622 • ACRL
Victorson Patricia L. • Woodbridge, VA 22192
Vidaeus Eva-Maria • Reference Librarian • University of the District of Columbia Learning Resources Division • Washington, DC 20008
Vidmanis Visvaldis E. • Becker College • Worcester, MA 01615-0071 • ACRL RASD
Vidor Ann B. • Head Catalog Department • Emory University Libraries Robert W. Woodruff Library • Atlanta, GA 30322-2870 • ALCTS LITA
Vidor David L. • Business Librarian • Emory University Libraries Robert W. Woodruff Library • Atlanta, GA 30322-2870 • RASD
Vielbig Richard J. • Librarian • Rio Linda Senior High School Grant Joint Union High School District • Rio Linda, CA 95673 • AASL
Viele George B. • Director • Greensboro Public Library • Greensboro, NC 27402 • AASL ACRL ALCTS ALSC ALTA ASCLA LAMA LITA PLA RASD IFRT
Viera Ann R. • University of Tennessee • Knoxville, TN 37996-4500 • ACRL SRRT
Vierck Marcia • Branch Librarian • Elkhart Public Library Pierre Morgan Branch • Elkhart, IN 46517 • LAMA PLA
Vieregger Mary Anne • Assistant Librarian/Teacher • Creighton Preparatory School • Omaha, NE 68114 • AASL
Viertel Linda M. • Librarian • Queens Borough Public Library • Jamaica, NY 11432 • NMRT
Vietri Linda S. • Harleysville, PA 19438 • AASL
Viets Lola • Librarian • Winfield High School Library • Winfield, KS 67156 • AASL
Vigil Annette D. • Reference Librarian • Tempe Public Library • Tempe, AZ 85282
Viglierchio Mario • Grebyd • 1424 Buenes Aires, Argentina • ACRL LITA PLA
Vignovich Ray L. • Administration • Appleton Public Library • Appleton, WI 54911-4780
Vigo-Cepeda Luisa • Professor • University of Puerto Rico Graduate School of Library and Information Science • Rio Piedras, PR 00920 • ACRL ALCTS
Vikor Desider L. • Assoc Dir for Clln Mgt • University of Maryland College Park Theodore R. McKeldin Library • College Park, MD 20742-7011 • ACRL ALCTS
Vikor Marlene W. • Contract Librarian II • University of Maryland College Park Theodore R. McKeldin Library • College Park, MD 20742-7011 • LITA
Vilaro Annette Buurstra • Des Plaines, IL 60016 • Continuing
Viles Ann • Music Librarian • Memphis State University Music Library • Memphis, TN 38152 • LAMA LHRT
Villar Susanne P. • Library Director • Colby-Sawyer College • New London, NH 03257
Villarreal Guadalure • Rice University Fondren Library • Houston, TX 77251-1892
Villavecchia Marie • Director • Union City Free Public Library • Union City, NJ 07087 • PLA
Villemaire Maureen L. • Burlington, VT 05401 • AASL YALSA
Vilmanis Andrew • Reference Librarian • Seminole County Public Library System North Branch Library • Sanford, FL 32771
Vilnins Raita • Assistant Administrative Libn. • Elmhurst Public Library • Elmhurst, IL 60126 • LAMA PLA
Viloria Oliva • Head of Card Section • University of Southern California Doheny Library • Los Angeles, CA 90089-0182
Vincent Beth A. • Student • Clarion University of Pennsylvania Rena M. Carlson Library • Clarion, PA 16214
Vincent Donald E. Dr. • Durham, NH 03824 • Continuing
Vincent Katharine H. • Bethesda, MD 20814
Vincent Linda S. • Librarian II • Milwaukee Public Library • Milwaukee, WI 53233 • RASD
Vincent Nancy • Assistant Director • Keene Public Library • Keene, NH 03431 • PLA
Vincent Paula E. • Chief, Cataloging Branch • Department of Defense Pentagon Library • Washington, DC 20310 • ALCTS FLRT
Vincent Steven • Dickinson College Library Boyd Lee Spahr Library • Carlisle, PA 17013 • IFRT
Vincent Susan R. • Board of Governors of the Federal Reserve System • Washington, DC 20551
Vincze Margaret B. • Honolulu, HI 96830-0386 • AASL
Vine Rita • Head, Reference Department • University of Toronto Robarts Library • Toronto ON, Canada • ACRL RASD
Viner Mamie N. • Director • Knoxville Public Library • Knoxville, IA 50138-2296
Vinerts Nancy Medland • Newark, CA 94560
Vinh Alphonse N. • Reference Librarian • Yale University Sterling Memorial Library • New Haven, CT 06520 • ACRL ALCTS
Vinnes Norman M. • Director • Ramsey County Public Library Adminstrative Offices • Shoreview, MN 55126-5800 • LAMA PLA
Vinson BJ • Library Director • Great Falls Clinic • Great Falls, MT 59405
Vinson Paul Everett • Cataloger • San Antonio Public Library • San Antonio, TX 78205 • LITA
Vinsonhaler Chris • Student • University of Southern Mississippi School of Library Science • Hattiesburg, MS 39406-5146
Vint Patricia A. • Dearborn Heights, MI 48127 • ACRL LITA

Votaw Floyd M. • Seminary Librarian • The Masters Seminary • Sun Valley, CA 91352
Votaw Paul L. • Jacksonville Public Libraries Main Library • Jacksonville, FL 32202 • ALCTS
Voth Eileen • Librarian • Ellinwood School Community Library • Ellinwood, KS 67526 • PLA
Votisek Judith A. • Fremont, CA 94539
Vough Audrey A. • Lexington, KY 40502
Voulgarelis Evelyn • Head of Children's Services • Riverhead Free Library • Riverhead, NY 11901 • ALSC
Vowels Heidi J. • University of Wisconsin-Oshkosh • Oshkosh, WI 54901
Voyles Jeanne F. • Head, Loan Librarian • University of Arizona Library • Tucson, AZ 85721
Voyles Judson • Long Beach, CA 90815 • ALCTS PLA LHRT *Continuing*
Vozel Linda A. • Cataloger for Biblio Database • Case Western Reserve University • Cleveland, OH 44106-7151 • ACRL ALCTS
Vrabel Mark E. • Student • University of Pittsburgh School of Library and Information Science • Pittsburgh, PA 15260
Vrantsidis Bill V. • Social Sciences & Humanities Ln • Toronto Public Library Northern District-Professional Library • Toronto ON, M4R 1B9 Canada • PLA RASD IFRT SRRT
Vratny-Watts Janet • Senior Information Specialist • Apple Computer, Inc. Library • Cupertino, CA 95014 • LITA
Vrattos Constance • Lesley College Library • Cambridge, MA 02138
Vreeland Martha A. • Traverse Area District Library • Traverse City, MI 49684
Vrenios Diane • Phoenix, AZ 85068 • LAMA LITA
Vretos Linda Aird • Head Librarian • West Springfield High School • Springfield, VA 22152 • AASL YALSA
Vriesacker Jane • Director • Reedsburg Public Library • Reedsburg, WI 53959 • LITA
Vronay Tim R. • Student • University of Southern Mississippi School of Library Science • Hattiesburg, MS 39406-5146 • ACRL RASD
Vuckovich C. Y. • Library Director • Community College of Beaver County Library • Monaca, PA 15061-2587 • ACRL
Vukas Rachel R. • Reference Librarian • Washburn University of Topeka Mabee Library • Topeka, KS 66621 • ACRL
Vuylsteke Leslie V. • Serials Cataloging Librarian • University of Cincinnati Langsam Library • Cincinnati, OH 45221-0033 • ACRL ALCTS
Vychodil Boris M. • System Analyst • Duke University William R. Perkins Library • Durham, NC 27706
Vyhnanek Kay E. • Head, Circulation & Interlib. • Washington State University Library • Pullman, WA 99164-5610 • ACRL LAMA RASD
Vyhnanek Louis A. • Librarian III • Washington State University Library • Pullman, WA 99164-5610 • ACRL RASD GODORT
WU Hongyu • Montgomery, WV 25136 • IFRT
Waagner Sharon F. • Long Lake, NY 12847
Waanders Judith N. • DeKalb Central High School • Waterloo, IN 46793 • AASL
Wachel Kathleen B. • Head Acquisitions Department • University of Iowa Library • Iowa City, IA 52242 • ACRL
Wachsmann-Linnan Ute • Columbia, SC 29205-3334
Wachstein Harry R. • Regional Library Coordinator • Free Library of Philadelphia Northeast Regional Library • Philadelphia, PA 19149
Wachter-Nelson Ruth • Librarian • Saint Joseph's Hospital LRC • Marshfield, WI 54449
Wachter Sarah A. • Rolling Prairie Library System • Decatur, IL 62522 • AASL ALSC YALSA
Wacker Nancy J. B. • Richland, WA 99352
Wacker Patricia L. • Librarian • Sunnyside School District Mission Manor School • Tucson, AZ 85706
Wackerman Ellie • Catlgr Assoc Libn II • University of Maryland Libraries • College Park, MD 20742 • ALCTS VRT
Wada Sandra M. • Librarian • Maui Community Correctional Center • Wailuku, HI 96793 • ASCLA
Waddell Richard E. • Library Director • Embry-Riddle Aeronautical University • Daytona Beach, FL 32114 • ACRL LAMA
Waddington Elizabeth R. • Billings, MT 59102
Waddle Linda L. • Deputy Executive Director • American Library Association • Chicago, IL 60611-2795 • AASL YALSA
Wade Anne D. • Senior Market Analyst • Chubb & Son Inc. • Warren, NJ 07059 • ALCTS LAMA RASD
Wade Anne K. • Head, Tech Processes Division • East Baton Rouge Parish Library • Baton Rouge, LA 70806-7699 • PLA
Wade Betty Jane • Salem, WV 26426 • Continuing
Wade Eric D. • United States Court of Appeals Ninth Circuit Library • San Francisco, CA 94119-3939 • LAMA NMRT
Wade Gordon S. • Library Director • Carroll Public Library • Carroll, IA 51401 • PLA
Wade Helen M. Sr. • Media Center Director • Convent of the Sacred Heart • Greenwich, CT 06831 • AASL LIRT
Wade Kathleen M. • Los Angeles, CA 90049 • AASL ALSC LAMA YALSA LHRT LRRT
Wade Kelly • Student • Fresno Pacific College Hiebert Library • Fresno, CA 93702
Wade Marianne R. • Librarian • Shining Mountain Elementary School • Spanaway, WA 98387
Wade Maureen J. • Los Angeles Public Library • Los Angeles, CA 90071
Wade Nancy L. • Children's Librarian • Public Library of Cincinnati and Hamilton County Mariemont Branch • Cincinnati, OH 45227 • ALSC
Wade Patricia M. B. • Saint Mary's College of California • Moraga, CA 94575 • ACRL LIRT NMRT
Wade Sherry A. • Librarian/Families for Literacy • Kern County Library System • Bakersfield, CA 93301 • ALSC
Wadham Timothy R. • Dallas Public Library Dallas West Branch • Dallas, TX 75212-3790 • ALSC
Wadle Christine M. • Librarian • Midstate College • Peoria, IL 61602 • ACRL
Wadleigh Linda J. • Student • University of Georgia Department of Instructional Technolgy • Athens, GA 30602 • AASL
Wadler Karen E. • Fremont School Dist 79 • Mundelein, IL 60060 • AASL
Wadsworth Carol E. • New York, NY 10024 • IFRT SRRT
Wadsworth Jill • Library Media Specialist • Algonkian Elementary School • Sterling, VA 22170 • AASL
Wagar Catherine J. • Librarian II • New Orleans Public Library • New Orleans, LA 70140
Wagar David E. • Director, Instructional Media • Edmonds School District • Lynnwood, WA 98036-7400 • AASL
Wagar Elsa A. • Bellevue, OH 44811
Wagar Joanna M. • Clln. Devlp. Librarian • Northern Michigan University Lydia M. Olson Library • Marquette, MI 49855 • ACRL ALCTS SRRT
Wagar Joyce A. • Librarian • King County Library System • Seattle, WA 98109-5191 • ALSC
Wagenknecht Kristina Mrs. • Gladstone, OR 97027
Wagenknecht Robert E. • Director • Chesterfield County Library • Chesterfield, VA 23832 • ASCLA LAMA LITA PLA RASD IRRT LRRT
Wager Gerald R. • Librarian-Cataloger • Library of Congress • Washington, DC 20541
Wager Judy • Librarian • Saint Clair County Library System • Port Huron, MI 48060-4098
Waggener Linda R. • Reference Librarian • Natrona County Public Library • Casper, WY 82601-2598
Waggoner Ann S. • Chair, Public Services • California State University • Northridge, CA 91330 • ACRL
Waggoner Mary H. • Reference/Documents Librarian • Mississippi University for Women Fant Memorial Library • Columbus, MS 39701
Wagh Sulbha • Silver Cross Hospital Health Science Library • Joliet, IL 60432
Wagle Iqbal N. • Head, Microtext Section & Serv • University of Toronto John Robarts Library • Toronto ON, M5S 1A5 Canada • ASCLA
Wagman Frederick H. • Ann Arbor, MI 48105 • ACRL ALCTS *Life*
Wagman Gerald H. • Manager, Library Inf. Center • Schering-Plough Research Institute • Bloomfield, NJ 07003
Wagner-Birkner Robin • Automation Librarian • Franklin & Marshall College Library • Lancaster, PA 17604-3003
Wagner-Mees Drue • Young Adult Librarian • Los Angeles Public Library Brentwood Branch • Los Angeles, CA 90049 • YALSA
Wagner Barbara L. • Regional EPA Librarian • Environmental Protection Agency Region VIII Library • Denver, CO 80202-1087 • LITA FLRT GODORT SRRT
Wagner Betty L. • Hd Architecture-Urban Planning • University of Washington • Seattle, WA 98195 • ACRL
Wagner Bryan L. • Federal Information Center • Cumberland, MD 21502
Wagner Christina M. • Reference Librarian • Lincoln Library • Springfield, IL 62701
Wagner Claudia C. • Sales Support Specialist • Data Research Associates Inc. • Saint Louis, MO 63132
Wagner Clinton C. • Cataloger • Family History Library • Salt Lake City, UT 84150
Wagner Colette A. • Coord of Academic Computing • City University of New York • New York, NY 10021 • ACRL LITA
Wagner Cynthia A. • Childrens Librarian • Milwaukee Public Library Capitol Branch • Milwaukee, WI 53216 • ALSC
Wagner Dietmar U. • Reference Librarian • Ann Arbor Public Library • Ann Arbor, MI 48104 • PLA
Wagner E Patricia • West Point, NY 10996-1706 • AASL ALSC
Wagner Ernest C. • Washington, DC 20011 • ACRL
Wagner Evelyn M. • Akron, OH 44313 • ALSC
Wagner George L. • Assistant Director • Westport Public Library • Westport, CT 06880 • LAMA PLA
Wagner Gulten Dr. • Lecturer • Curtin University of Technology Library and Information Studies • Perth WA 6001, Australia
Wagner Jane E. • Cincinnati, OH 45238 • Continuing
Wagner Janet • Youth Serv Ln • Oak Park & River Forest High School • Oak Park, IL 60302 • AASL
Wagner Janet S. • Reference Librarian • Hofstra University Axinn Library • Hempstead, NY 11550 • ACRL LAMA GODORT
Wagner January • Detroit Public Library Downtown Branch • Detroit, MI 48226-2284 • RASD
Wagner Judith B. • Reference Librarian • College of DuPage Learning Resources Center • Glen Ellyn, IL 60137 • ACRL
Wagner Karen P. • Librarian • James Bowie Elementary School • Dallas, TX 75248 • AASL ALSC
Wagner Leah M. • Children's Librarian • Monroe Township Public Library • Jamesburg, NJ 08831 • ALSC PLA
Wagner Leonard J. • Librarian • University of Oklahoma Robert M Bird Health Sciences Library • Oklahoma City, OK 73190
Wagner Lois C. • Auburn Public Library • Auburn, ME 04210 • RASD
Wagner Mary M. • Chair,Dept of Information Mgmnt • College of Saint Catherine • Saint Paul, MN 55105 • LITA IRRT
Wagner Meg L. • Student • Texas Woman's University School of Library & Information Studies • Denton, TX 76204
Wagner Paige G. • Youth Sevice Librarian • East Routt Library District • Steamboat Spring, CO 80477 • ALSC
Wagner Ralph D. • University of Illinois Graduate School of Library and Information Science • Urbana, IL 61801 • ACRL IFRT
Wagner Robert L. • Director of Libraries • The Episcopal Academy • Merion, PA 19066
Wagner Robin O. • Assistant Librarian • Stickney-Forest View Library • Stickney, IL 60402 • PLA
Wagner Rod • Director • Nebraska Library Commission • Lincoln, NE 68508 • ASCLA
Wagner Rose M. • Dir., Coor. Clln. Devel. Proj. • Chicago Public Library Harold Washington Library • Chicago, IL 60605 • RASD
Wagner Sabina H. • Reference Librarian • King County Library System Burien Branch • Seattle, WA 98166 • IFRT
Wagner Sharon Lee • Community Library Manager • West Hollywood Library • West Hollywood, CA 90069
Wagner Stephen S. • Acting Curator, Pforzheimer Clln • New York Public Library • New York, NY 10018-2788 • ACRL
Wagner Sylvia B. • Trustee • Omaha Public Library • Omaha, NE 68102 • ALTA
Wagnitz Ann • Goodyear Middle School • Akron, OH 44308
Wagoner Betty L. • Medical Records Administrator • University of Illinois College of Veterinary Medicine • Urbana, IL 61801
Wagoner Lori L. • Student • Catholic University of America School of Library and Information Science • Washington, DC 20064
Wagoner Margaret A. • Libn./Asst Mgr Extension Svs • Indianapolis-Marion County Pubilc Library • Indianapolis, IN 46202
Wahab Shaista • Special Collection Cataloger • University of Nebraska at Omaha University Library • Omaha, NE 68182-0237
Wahl Doris M. • Librarian II • Saint Paul Public Library • St. Paul, MN 55102
Wahl Phyllis A. • Dillingham Middle School/High School Library • Dillingham, AK 99576 • AASL YALSA
Wahl Richard • Charles Town, WV 25414 • LITA IRRT
Wahlgren C. David • Hoisington, KS 67544
Wahlmark Carolyn C. • Ada, OH 45810 • ACRL
Wahoski Helen I. • Oshkosh, WI 54901 • ACRL LAMA *Life*
Wahrenbrock Mark • Student • Data Research Associates Inc. • Saint Louis, MO 63132
Wahrman Jo A. • Librarian • Goodland High School • Goodland, KS 67735 • AASL
Waibel Grace T. • Inf Analyst, Popualtion Div. • United States Bureau of Census • Washington, DC 20233 • FLRT GODORT

Waickman Anna M. I.H. M. • Director • Marygrove College Library • Detroit, MI 48221 • ACRL ALCTS ALSC LITA RASD

Waidelich Kimberley R. • APO, AE 09130

Waindle Barbara A. • Serials Assistant • John Marshall Law School Library • Chicago, IL 60604 • ALCTS

Wainwright A. D. Mr. • Princeton, NJ 08540 • Continuing

Wainwright Frances M. • Seattle, WA 98107

Wair Donna C. • Tennessee State Law Library • Nashville, TN 37243-0609

Waite Amy • Youth Services Librarian • Wasilla Public Library • Wasilla, AK 99654-7085 • ALSC PLA IFRT

Waite Ellen J. • Director of Libraries • Loyola University E.M. Cudahy Memorial Library • Chicago, IL 60626 • ACRL LAMA

Waite Inga M. • College Librarian • Saint John's College Library • Santa Fe, NM 87501 • ACRL

Waite Nancy L. • Jefferson Elementary School • Fayetteville, AR 72701 • AASL

Waitman Lorraine Pellicano • Description Librarian • United Nations Dag Hammarskjold Library • New York, NY 10163 • ALCTS GODORT

Waity Gloria A. • Madison, WI 53716 • AASL PLA YALSA CLENE ILERT

Wajenberg Arnold S. • Principal Cataloger • University of Illinois Library • Urbana, IL 61801 • ALCTS LITA

Wakashige Benjamin T. • Head Librarian • Western New Mexico University • Silver City, NM 88062 • ACRL

Wakefield Carol A. • Assistant Library Director • Hillsboro Public Library • Hillsboro, OR 97123 • PLA

Wakefield Kathleen A. • Student • Nebraska Library Commission • Lincoln, NE 68508 • ASCLA LITA PLA IFRT LIRT NMRT SRRT

Wakefield Virginia T. • Librarian • Garnet Valley High School • Concordville, PA 19331 • AASL

Wakeley Mary F. • Norfolk, NE 68701 • AASL

Wakeman Veronica N. • Associate Librarian/Slavic Catlg • University of California-Berkeley University Library • Berkeley, CA 94720 • ALCTS

Waker Alesia S. • Vienna, VA 22180 • ALSC PLA YALSA IFRT NMRT

Wakil F. A. • Cataloger • University of Saskatchewan Library • Saskatoon SK, S7N 0W0 Canada • ALCTS

Wakulchik Linda Darlene • Librarian • Indianapolis Marion County Public Library • Indianapolis, IN 46206

Walbert Barbara G. • Normal, IL 61761

Walbridge Sharon • Access Services Administrator • Oregon State Library • Salem, OR 97310-0640 • LITA

Walch David B. • University Librarian • California Polytechnic State University Robert E. Kennedy Library • San Luis Obispo, CA 93407 • ACRL

Walchak Nancy M. • Director of Public Services • Hill School Library • Pottstown, PA 19464 • AASL RASD

Walcher Marilyn • Director • Scott County Library • Scott City, KS 67871

Walchle Barbara A. • Assistant Cataloger • Emporia State University William Allen White Library • Emporia, KS 66801 • NMRT

Walcott Barbara • Hilldale, NJ 07642 • RASD

Walcott M. Alena • Fort Myers, FL 33908 • Continuing

Walcott Rosalind • Biology Librarian • State University of New York Biology Library • Stony Brook, NY 11794-5260 • ACRL ALCTS

Wald Malcolm D. • St. Laurent, PQ, H4M 1R9 Canada • ACRL

Wald Marlena M. • Coor., of Collection Devel. • University of Georgia Science Library • Athens, GA 30602 • ACRL ALCTS LAMA LIRT VRT

Walde Florence • Superior, WI 54880 • AASL ACRL *Continuing*

Waldemar David L. • Librarian • Hennepin County Library • Minnetonka, MN 55343 • PLA

Walden Amy L. • South River Public Library • South River, NJ 08882 • ALSC

Walden Barbara L. • History Bibliographer • University of Minnesota • Minneapolis, MN 55455 • ACRL

Walden Beth L. • Reference Department • Kern County Library System • Bakersfield, CA 93301

Walden Charles F. Jr. • Student • University of Tennessee-Knoxville Graduate School of Library & Information Science • Knoxville, TN 37996-4330

Walden Graham R. • Reference Librarian • Ohio State University • Columbus, OH 43210 • ACRL RASD GODORT

Walden John M. • Historical Librarian • Kern County Library System • Bakersfield, CA 93301

Walden Judith A. • Public Services Manager • Metropolitan Library System • Oklahoma City, OK 73102 • PLA

Walden Winston A. • Director • Tennessee Technological University • Cookeville, TN 38505 • ACRL LAMA

Walder Antoinette Lynn • Director • Wright Memorial Public Library • Oakwood, OH 45419-2598 • PLA IFRT

Waldera Katherine A. • Reference/Information Serv Libn • Bismarck Veterans Memorial Public Library • Bismarck, ND 58501 • PLA

Waldhart Thomas James • Dean, Associate Professor • University of Kentucky College of Library & Information Science • Lexington, KY 40506-0391 • ACRL RASD

Waldman Brett • Operations Manager • The Bookmen Inc • Minneapolis, MN 55401

Waldman Robert • Director • University of Michigan Residence Hall Libraries • Ann Arbor, MI 48109-1372

Waldron Esther C. • Pittsburgh, PA 15232 • ALCTS LITA

Waldron Karen M. • Librarian • Schuylkill Valley Primary School Library • Leesport, PA 19535 • AASL

Waldrop Laura • Librarian • Anahuac Elementary School • Anahuac, TX 77514 • ALSC

Waldrop Ruth • Tuscaloosa, AL 35406 • ERT *Continuing*

Wallan Josette S. • Information Access Company • Foster City, CA 94404

Waligora Dawn K. • Student • State University of New York (SUNY) School of Information & Library Studies • Buffalo, NY 14260

Walk Mary E. • Children's Librarian • Spencer Public Library • Spencer, IA 51301 • ALSC

Walke Martha M. • Librarian • Thomas Jefferson Middle School • Arlington, VA 22204 • ALSC

Walker Alberta • Pomona, CA 91767 • ACRL ALCTS LAMA LITA

Walker Alice O. • Community Service/Local Hist Ln • East Central Georgia Regional Library Augusta-Richmond County • Augusta, GA 30901

Walker Barbara A. • Head of Technical Services • WC RESA (Wayne Cnyt Reg Ed Serv) • Wayne, MI 48184

Walker Barbara L. • Redmond, WA 98053 • ALSC

Walker Barbara Lee • Librarian Media Specialist • Paul J Gelinas Junior High School • Setauket, NY 11733

Walker Billie E. • Student • University of Southern Mississippi School of Library Science • Hattiesburg, MS 39406-5146

Walker Bonnie M. • Abilene Christian University Margaret & Herman Brown Library • Abilene, TX 79699

Walker Brooke S. • Student • Judson College • Marion, AL 36756

Walker Camilla L. • Student • Emporia State University School of Library & Information Management • Emporia, KS 66801

Walker Candace E. • Dominican Santa Cruz Hospital Medical Library • Santa Cruz, CA 95065 • LITA

Walker Charlotte G. • Charlottesville, VA 22903

Walker Constance • Saluda, NC 28773

Walker Dana G. • Library Clerk • Atlanta-Fulton Public Library • Atlanta, GA 30303 • PLA

Walker Dana M. • University of Georgia Libraries • Athens, GA 30602

Walker Debbie S. • County of Los Angeles Public Library Clifton M. Brakensiek Library 505 • Bellflower, CA 90706

Walker Denise A. • Prince William Public Library Chinn Park Regional Library • Prince William, VA 22192 • YALSA

Walker Diane L. • Media Coordinator • Franklinville School • Franklinville, NC 27248 • AASL

Walker Diane Parr • Music Librarian • University of Virginia Music Library • Charlottesville, VA 22903

Walker Doris T. • Assistant Library Director • East Orange Public Library • East Orange, NJ 07018 • PLA

Walker Elaine M. • Serial Librarian • Cornell University Library • Ithaca, NY 14853 • ACRL ALCTS *Life*

Walker Elinor • Springdale, AR 72764 • Continuing

Walker Elizabeth A. • Pasadena Public Library • Pasadena, CA 91101

Walker Evelyn C. • Director • Alexandrian Public Library • Mount Vernon, IN 47620 • ALSC PLA YALSA

Walker Flora W. • Reference Coordinator • Lake Lanier Regional Library Lawrenceville Branch • Lawrenceville, GA 30245-4707 • RASD SRRT

Walker Gail J. • Student • University of Alberta Faculty of Library Science • Edmonton AB, Canada

Walker Hannah M. • Systems Librarian • University of California (UCLA) ORION Users Services Office • Los Angeles, CA 90024 • ACRL LITA

Walker Heather C. • Principia • Lower-Middle School • Saint Louis, MO 63131-1099

Walker James J. • Cataloger Librarian • La Sierra University Library • Riverside, CA 92515 • ALCTS

Walker Jean • Library Media Specialist • Seymour High School • Seymour, CT 06483 • AASL

Walker Jennifer • Information Services Librarian • Richland County Public Library • Columbia, SC 29201

Walker Joe L. • Catalog & Reference Librarian • Saint Clair Shores Public Library • St. Clair Shores, MI 48081 • ACRL ALCTS PLA RASD

Walker John R. • Reference Librarian • Pottsville Free Public Library • Pottsville, PA 17901

Walker Jon K. • Manager, Technical Services • Tulsa City County Library System • Tulsa, OK 74103

Walker Juanita C. • Student • Prairie View A & M University • Prairie View, TX 77446

Walker Judith A. • Curriculum Materials Librarian • University of North Carolina at Charlotte J. Murrey Atkins Library • Charlotte, NC 28223 • AASL ACRL

Walker Judith A. • United States Navy Naval Air Station Library • NAS Pensacola, FL 32508-5000 • AFLRT

Walker Judy • Burlington ON, L7R 3L6 Canada

Walker Julie A. • Librarian • Old Town Elementary School • Round Rock, TX 78683 • AASL

Walker Karen E. • Librarian • Vigo County Public Library • Terre Haute, IN 47807 • PLA VRT

Walker Katherine • De Kalb, IL 60115 • ACRL LAMA *Continuing*

Walker Kathryn A. • Reference Librarian • Atlanta Journal Constitution • Atlanta, GA 30302

Walker Kent M. • Tampa, FL 33635

Walker Laura P. • Librarian Director • The Brookings Institution Library • Washington, DC 20036 • ACRL ALCTS LAMA

Walker Lee P. • Director • Chicot County Library • Lake Village, AR 71653 • LAMA

Walker Libby • Technical Services Librarian • Bowling Green Public Library • Bowling Green, KY 42101

Walker Lisa K. • Secretary/Receptionist • Oregon Council for the Humanties • Portland, OR 97205

Walker Louise Miss • W. Barnstable, MA 02668 • ASCLA RASD *Continuing*

Walker Lucile A. • Public Services Librarian • Baltimore County Public Library Randallstown Area Branch • Randallstown, MD 21133

Walker Lucinda H. • Brooklyn, NY 11217 • SRRT

Walker Madge B • Librarian • Greeneville-Greene County Library • Greeneville, TN 37743 • PLA

Walker Margaret A. • Lansing, IL 60438 • AASL

Walker Margaret S. • Government Documents Librarian • Florida Atlantic University S.E. Wimberly Library • Boca Raton, FL 33431 • GODORT

Walker Margaret V. • Sterling, VA 22170

Walker Margo L. • Omaha, NE 68104-1248 • SRRT

Walker Mary Louise • Harrisburg, PA 17111 • ALCTS

Walker MaryAnn E. • Coordinator of Library Systems • University of Dayton Roesch Library • Dayton, OH 45469 • ACRL LITA

Walker Michael C. • Reference Librarian • Virginia Commonwealth University • Richmond, VA 23284-2033 • ACRL

Walker Nancy A. • Director of the Library • Berkshire Community College • Pittsfield, MA 01201

Walker Patricia • Richmond High School District #16 • Richmond, MO 64085 • AASL

Walker Patricia A. • Senior Librarian • Los Angeles Public Library Wilshire Branch • Los Angeles, CA 90004

Walker Patricia O. • Asst. University Librarian • Wright State University University Library • Dayton, OH 45435 • ACRL ALCTS

Walker Paula M. • Assistant Director • University of Washington Libraries Odegaard Undergraduate Library • Seattle, WA 98195 • ACRL

Walker Phyllis G. • Media Specialist • Palmetto Elementary School • Miami, FL 33156 • AASL

Walker Ray • Teacher-Librarian • Skeena Junior Secondary School • Terrace, BC, V8G 3C1 Canada

Walker Richard D. • Professor • University of Wisconsin School of Library & Information Studies • Madison, WI 53706 • ACRL LRRT MAGERT *Life*

Walker Robin Gay • Tualatin, OR 97062-9722

Walker Rosemary • Wentworth Institute of Technology • Boston, MA 02115 • ACRL

Walker Stephen • Warrensburg, MO 64093 • ACRL SRRT

Walker Sue Albertson • Director of Curriculum • Lancaster School District • Lancaster, PA 17603 • AASL

Walker Sue E. • Penn Yan, NY 14527

Walker Susan J. • Branch Librarian • Jacksonville Public Library Willow Branch Library • Jacksonville, FL 32205

Walker Suzannah • Director • Indianapolis Program for Literacy and Citizenship • Indianapolis, IN 46202

Walker Terri L. • Regional Director • Screven-Jenkins Regional Library • Sylvania, GA 30467 • LAMA PLA

Walker Thomas D. • Urbana, IL 61801-4270 • LHRT

Walker Tommy L. • Student • University of North Texas School of Library & Information Sciences • Denton, TX 76203

Walker Walter D. • Acquistions of Catologing Dept. • Huntington Library • San Marino, CA 91108

Walker William B. • Chief Librarian • Metropolitan Museum of Art Library • New York, NY 10028 • ACRL LAMA *Life*

Walker William D. • Associate Director • New York Public Library • New York, NY 10018-2788 • ACRL

Walker William E. • Librarian I • Stockton-San Joaquin County Public Library • Stockton, CA 95202

Walkonen Helvi • Marquette, MI 49855 • Life

Wall Barbara • Jamesville, NY 13078-9786 • AASL YALSA

Wall Carol • Youngstown State University William F. Maag Library • Youngstown, OH 44555 • ACRL

Wall Dennis • Cataloger • Jefferson Parish Library Department • Metairie, LA 70010

Wall H. Duncan • Interim Director • Yardstick Associates • Watertown, MA 02172 • ACRL ALCTS LHRT LRRT

Wall James M. • Editor • Christian Century Foundation • Chicago, IL 60605 • ALTA PLA

Wall Jan D. • Librarian • Glen Oaks Middle School • Baton Rouge, LA 70811 • AASL

Wall Katharine • Ouachita Parish Public Library • Monroe, LA 71201

Wall L. A. Jr. Mrs. • Hattiesburg, MS 39401 • LAMA

Wall Margaret E. • Reference Librarian • La Salle University Connelly Library • Philadelphia, PA 19141 • ACRL LAMA RASD

Wall Norma B. • District Dir of Lib & Med Serv • Hinds Community College District Learning Resource Center • Raymond, MS 39154 • ACRL LAMA LITA

Wall Thomas B. • Public Services Librarian • University of Pittsburgh School of Library and Information Science • Pittsburgh, PA 15260 • ACRL PLA RASD

Wallace Alan Hugh • University of Tennessee Library • Knoxville, TN 37996-1000 • ACRL LIRT

Wallace Anne V. • Rowland Elementary School • Stone Mountain, GA 30083 • AASL

Wallace Barbara R. • Director • Bacon Memorial Public Library • Wyandotte, MI 48192 • AASL

Wallace Barbara T. • Media Specialist • Winter Park High School • Winter Park, FL 32792 • AASL NMRT

Wallace Catherine S. • Indanapolis, IN 46208 • ALTA

Wallace Constance M. • Charlotte Memorial Medical Center • Charlotte, NC 28232 • LITA

Wallace Danny P. • Associate Dean • Louisiana State University School of Library & Information Science • Baton Rouge, LA 70803-3290 • RASD LRRT

Wallace Harriet E. • Geology Librarian • University of Illinois Library • Urbana, IL 61801 • Life

Wallace James O. • Director Emeritus • San Antonio College Library • San Antonio, TX 78212 • ACRL ALCTS LITA   *Life*

Wallace Jean • Clinton Junior High School • Clinton, IL 61727 • AASL

Wallace Julia F. • Head, Govt. Pubn. Library • University of Minnesota Meredith Wilson Library • Minneapolis, MN 55455 • ACRL GODORT

Wallace Karen L. • Children's Librarian • Watauga County Library • Boone, NC 28607 • ALSC IFRT

Wallace Linda • Media Specialist • Starmont Schools • Strawberry Point, IA 52076

Wallace Linda E. • Media Specialist • Quarterfield Elementary School • Severn, MD 21144

Wallace Linda K. • PIO Director • American Library Association • Chicago, IL 60611-2795

Wallace Lynn • Librarian • Montecito Elementary School • Santa Barbara, CA 93108

Wallace Madeline • Student • Kent State University School of Library & Information Science • Kent, OH 44242-0001

Wallace Mary K. • Student Assistant • Huntsville-Madison County Public Library • Huntsville, AL 35804 • ACRL

Wallace Mary-Ann • Supervisor • Santa Clara County Free Library Cupertino Public Library • Cupertino, CA 95014 • PLA

Wallace Patricia E. • Bibliographic Control Center Ln • Enoch Pratt Free Library • Baltimore, MD 21201-4484 • ALCTS LITA

Wallace Patricia M. • Head Serials Department • University of Colorado-Boulder University Libraries • Boulder, CO 80309 • LITA

Wallace Paula • Coordinator of Reference Svs. • New Bedford Free Public Library • New Bedford, MA 02740 • PLA

Wallace Paula E. • Highland Media Center • Ewing, MO 63440 • AASL

Wallace Paula R. • Media Specialist • Sullivan's Island Elementary School • Sullivan's Island, SC 29482 • AASL

Wallace Phyllis M. • Childrens Librarian • Bloomington Public Library • Bloomington, IL 61702-3308 • ALSC

Wallace Richard E. • A. E. Staley Manufacturing Company • Decatur, IL 62525 • ACRL ALCTS LAMA RASD GODORT

Wallace Robin A. • Wm S. Hart Union High School District Arroyo Seco Junior High • Santa Clarita, CA 91354 • AASL

Wallace Shirley A. • Library Assistant • Southgate Veterans Memorial Library • Southgate, MI 48195

Wallace Victoria • Hilton Head Island, SC 29926 • LAMA PLA   *Life*

Wallace Virginia • Media Specialist • Mauldin High School • Mauldin, SC 29662 • AASL

Wallace Wendy L. • Sparta, NJ 07871

Wallace William J.L. Dr • Trustee • Kanawha County Public Library • Charleston, WV 25301 • ALTA

Wallace Wilma E. • Bartlett, TN 38135

Wallach John S. • Director • Dayton & Montgomery County Public Library • Dayton, OH 45402-2103 • LAMA PLA

Wallach Joyce B. • K-8 Media Coordinator • Northridge Local Schools • Dayton, OH 45414 • AASL ALSC

Wallach Ruth • Torrance, CA 90505 • ACRL

Walle David C. • Computer Assistant • University of North Texas School of Library & Information Sciences • Denton, TX 76203 • ASCLA

Wallen Joyce M. • Library Director • Miami Public Library • Miami, OK 74354 • PLA

Wallen Regina T. • Director of Technical Services • Santa Clara University Heafey Law Library • Santa Clara, CA 95053 • ALCTS

Wallender Martha L. • Schenectady, NY 12309 • ALSC

Waller Andrew B. • Student • University of British Columbia Library Archives & Information Studies • Vancouver BC, Canada

Waller Carol A. • Librarian • Park Ridge Public Library • Park Ridge, IL 60068-4188 • PLA

Waller Hope C. • Director • Sherman Public Library • Sherman, TX 75090-5975 • LAMA PLA

Waller J. Earl • System Designer • INLEX, Inc. • Monterey, CA 93942 • LITA

Waller Joshua • Reference Librarian • Fashion Institute of Technology Library • New York, NY 10001

Waller Judith • Librarian • Boulder Public Library • Boulder, CO 80306 • RASD

Waller Michael M. • Student • Southern Connecticut State University School of Libray Science & Instructional Technology • New Haven, CT 06515

Waller Pamela Ann • Lubbock, TX 79417

Waller Theodore Mr. • Southbury, CT 06488 • AASL ALTA   *Life*

Wallette Mavice Mrs. • Chairman of the Board • Shreve Memorial Library • Shreveport, LA 71120-1523

Walley Lynn • Media Specialist • Henderson High School • Chamblee, GA 30341 • AASL

Wallick Lillie F. • Librarian • Saint Bartholomew Consolidated School • Cincinnati, OH 45231 • AASL

Wallin Camille Clark • Henderson, NV 89014 • ACRL LAMA NMRT

Wallin Irene H. • Library Director • Mary M. Campbell Public Library • Marcus Hook, PA 19061

Walling Carolyn • Winter Haven, FL 33884

Walling Linda Lucas • Professor • University of South Carolina College of Library & Information Science • Columbia, SC 29208 • ASCLA RASD

Walling Ruth • Decatur, GA 30030 • Continuing

Wallis C Lamar • Memphis, TN 38112 • LAMA PLA   *Life*

Wallis Roberta J. • Student • New York Public Library • New York, NY 10018-2788 • LITA

Wallish Ruth Ann • Youth Services Librarian • Dolton Public Library District • Dolton, IL 60419-1091

Wallmann Mary W. • Albany, CA 94707 • AASL YALSA

Walls Esther J. • New York, NY 10023 • IRRT *Continuing*

Walls Nina • Ridley Pk, PA 19078

Walsack Eileen • Media Specialist • Hudson Regional Junior Senior High School • Highlands, NJ 07732

Walsdorf John J. • Blackwell North America • Lake Oswego, OR 97034 • ACRL

Walser Marianna Long • Media Specialist • Chattahoochee Elementary School • Duluth, GA 30136 • AASL

Walsh-Koci Patricia J. • Learning Resoures Specialist • Pasadena Independent School District Parks Elementaru School • Pasadena, TX 77503 • AASL

Walsh-Rock Gloria C. • Children's Services Librarian • Downers Grove Public Library • Downers Grove, IL 60515 • ALSC

Walsh Amy E. • Fairleigh Dickinson University Weiner Library • Teaneck, NJ 07666 • ACRL ALCTS

Walsh Carol Jean • Reference Librarian • New Milford Public Library • New Milford, NJ 07646 • ASCLA RASD

Walsh Christine A. • Westminster, CO 80020

Walsh E Elizabeth • Havertown, PA 19083 • AASL CLENE

Walsh Frances E. • Professor • Slippery Rock University of Pennsylvania • Slippery Rock, PA 16057 • AASL ALSC

Walsh Frank W. Mr • Saint Mary of the Woods College Library • St Mary of the Woods, IN 47876 • ACRL ALCTS   *Life*

Walsh Jan • Consultant • Washington State Library • Olympia, WA 98504-2470 • LAMA PLA

Walsh Jeanne M. • Dover Free Library • East Dover, VT 05341-0267

Walsh Jim • Hd. of Govt. Doc. & Microforms • Boston College O'Neill Library • Chestnut Hill, MA 02167 • ACRL GODORT MAGERT

Walsh Joan E. • Media Librarian • Flossmoor Public Library • Flossmoor, IL 60422

Walsh Joanna • Lexington, MA 02173 • ACRL ALCTS LITA CLENE ILERT

Walsh John S. • Trustee • Portsmouth Public Library • Portsmouth, OH 45662

Walsh Julie • Library/Media Specialist • South Side Middle School • Rockville Center, NY 11570

Walsh Katherine E. • Student • Long Island University Palmer School of Library & Information Science • Greenvale, NY 11548

Walsh Kathleen A. • Student • Northern Illinois University Department of Library & Information Studies • DeKalb, IL 60115 • ACRL GODORT IFRT SRRT

Walsh Kathleen M. • Anna M. McCabe School • Smithfield, RI 02917 • AASL

Walsh Lea • Coordinator of Network Services • South Carolina State Library • Columbia, SC 29211

Walsh Leona Sr • Librarian • Saint Mary of the Woods College Library • St Mary of the Woods, IN 47876

Walsh Lynn R. • Library Director • North Indian River County Library • Sebastian, FL 32958 • PLA YALSA

Walsh Margaret J. • San Francisco, CA 94121

Walsh Margaret M. • Denver, CO 80231-3136

Walsh Mary Jane • Ref/Bibl Instr Ln • Colgate University Everett Needham Case Library • Hamilton, NY 13346 • ACRL IFRT

Walsh Michael A. • Automation Coordinator • Enoch Pratt Free Library • Baltimore, MD 21201-4484

Walsh Michael K. • Supervisory Librarian • Library of Congress • Washington, DC 20541

Walsh Molly • Montreal Children's Library • Montreal PQ, H3Z 1X4 Canada

Walsh Nancy Ballard • Arlington, VA 22204 • PLA

Walsh Nina May • Mississauga, ON, L5M 4Y8 Canada

Walsh Robert R. • Library Building Consultant • Virginia State Library & Archives • Richmond, VA 23219 • ACRL LAMA ILERT

Walshak Mary Lynn • Hd,Government Documents Dept. • Georgia Southern University Henderson Library • Statesboro, GA 30460 • ACRL GODORT

Walster Dian E. • Asst. Prof. Lib. Media • University of Colorado at Denver School of Education • Denver, CO 80217 • AASL LITA LIRT LRRT

Walston Claude E. • Dean • University of Maryland College of Library and Information Services • College Park, MD 20742-4345 • ACRL LITA LRRT

Walstrom Jon L. • Map Curator • Minnesota Historical Society • Saint Paul, MN 55102 • MAGERT

Walter Candace K. • Library Director • Wood River Public Library • Wood River, IL 62095 • ALTA PLA

Walter Craig A. • Tulsa, OK 74112 • ACRL RASD NMRT

Walter Janice L. • Louisville, KY 40213-1043

Walter Jo Ann M • Director • McKune Memorial Library • Chelsea, MI 48118 • CLENE

Walter John • Director • New Castle Public Library • New Castle, PA 16101 • PLA

Walter Judy G. • AE, NY 09146 • AASL

Walter Katherine L. • Chair. Serials Department • University of Nebraska Love Library • Lincoln, NE 68588-0410 • ACRL ALCTS LAMA

Walter Kenneth G. • Director of Library Service • Southern Connecticut State University Hilton C. Buley Library • New Haven, CT 06515 • ACRL ALCTS   *Life*

Walter Robert A. • Library Director • Pittsburg State University Leonard Axe Library • Pittsburg, KS 66762 • ACRL LAMA GODORT   *Life*

Walter Valyrie A. • Software Support Librarian • Hawaii State Public Library System • Honolulu, HI 96813

Walter Viola I. • Grand Rapids, MN 55744 • Continuing

Walter Virginia A. • Assistant Professor • University of California Los Angeles Graduate School of Library & Information Science • Los Angeles, CA 90024 • ALSC PLA SRRT

Walters Carol G. • Director • Montgomery County Public Library • Troy, NC 27371 • ALSC LAMA PLA

Walters Catherine F. • Coor. of Children's & YA Serv. • Chattanooga-Hamilton County Bicentennial Library • Chattanooga, TN 37402 • ALSC

Walters Christine H. • Iowa City, IA 52240 • PLA RASD IFRT NMRT SRRT

Walters Clarence R. • Prog. Dir. for State & Pub. Libs • Online Computer Library Center (OCLC) • Dublin, OH 43017-3395 • ASCLA PLA

Walters Corky • Wyoming State Library • Cheyenne, WY 82002-0650

Walters Daniel L. • Library Director • Spokane Public Library Comstock Building Library • Spokane, WA 99201-0976 • ALTA LAMA PLA SRRT

Walters Frances M. • Branch Manager • Saint Joseph County Public Library Western Branch Library • South Bend, IN 46619 • ALSC PLA

Walters Jaclyn A. • APO, AE 09138-3584

Walters John R. Dr. • Asbury Theological Seminary B. L. Fisher Library • Wilmore, KY 40390 • LITA

Walters Laura R. • Social Sciences Bibliographer • Tufts University • Medford, MA 02155 • ACRL

Walters Lowell A. • Student • Clarion University of Pennsylvania College of Library Science • Clarion, PA 16214

Walters Mary Anne • Reference Librarian • Mitre Corp Library • Mc Lean, VA 22102

Walters Mary D. • Los Angeles, CA 90047

Walters Pamela L. • Library Consultant • Archdiocese Of San Antonio • San Antonio, TX 78284 • AASL CLENE SRRT

Walters Patricia • Children's Librarian • Santa Clara County Free Library Campbell Public • Campbell, CA 95008 • ALSC

Walters Patsy • Medical Librarian • Methodist Medical Center Library • Peoria, IL 61636

Walters Phyllis E. • Cataloger • Plainfield Public Library • Plainfield, IN 46168

Walters Roberta J. • Houston, TX 77005-3110 • LAMA

Walters Sharon A. • Student • Saint Mary's College of California • Moraga, CA 94575 • EMIERT ERT IFRT NMRT SRRT

Walters Sheila • Hd, Interlibrary Loan & Doc Svs • Arizona State University Libraries • Tempe, AZ 85287-1006 • ACRL

Walters Suzanne • President • Walters & Associates Strategic Marketing & Development Consultants • Denver, CO 80222 • LAMA

Walth Laura A. • Public Library of Des Moines • Des Moines, IA 50308-1791

Walthall Shirley • Trustee • Everett Public Library • Everett, WA 98201

Walther Helen L. • McKinsey and Company • Houston, TX 77010 • RASD

Walther James H. • Milwaukee, WI 53202 • GODORT NMRT

Walther Peg • Director of Library Services • City University Library • Mercer Island, WA 98040 • ACRL

Walther Robert E. • Reference Librarian • University of Pennsylvania Library Van Pelt-Dietrich Library Center • Philadelphia, PA 19104-6206 • ACRL

Waltmire Theodore V. • Library Director • McCook Public Library • McCook, IL 60525 • LAMA PLA

Walton Carol G. • Acting Asst. Chair/Catlg. Dept. • University of Florida Libraries • Gainesville, FL 32611-2047 • ACRL ALCTS LITA

Walton Clyde C. • Timonium, MD 21093 • ACRL RASD *Life*

Walton Deedra J. • Orlando, FL 32806

Walton Homer J. Jr. • Head of Cataloging Dept. • University of South Carolina • Columbia, SC 29208 • ACRL ALCTS LITA

Walton Jacquelyn M. • Library Director • Hancock County Public Library • Hawesville, KY 42348-0249

Walton Judy M. • Technical Services Supervisor • Mobile Public Library • Mobile, AL 36602 • ALCTS PLA

Walton Kathleen Endres • Congressional Quarterly Library • Washington, DC 20037 • ACRL GODORT

Walton Lonita M. • Deputy Director • Atlanta-Fulton Public Library • Atlanta, GA 30303 • LAMA PLA RASD

Walton Nancy Kay • San Jose Public Library • San Jose, CA 95113

Walton Robert A. • President • CLSI, Inc. • Newtonville, MA 02160

Walton Terence M. • Coor. Clln. Devel. & Mgt. • Lee County Library System Processing Center • Fort Myers, FL 33912 • ALCTS RASD

Walton Victoria A. • Media Specialist • Horace Mann School • Iowa City, IA 52245 • AASL

Walton Virginia • Helena, MT 59601-1927 • YALSA *Life*

Waltos Rosemary • Director • Millbury Public Library • Millbury, MA 01527

Waltz Mary Anne L. • Geog/Anthropology/Maps Bibl • Syracuse University Library E. S. Bird Library • Syracuse, NY 13244-2010 • ALCTS GODORT MAGERT

Walz Jennifer L. • Asst. Ref Librarian • King's College • Wilkes Barre, PA 18711 • ACRL RASD

Walzer Helen S. • Atlanta, GA 30305

Walzer Joyce • Upper Montclair, NJ 07043

Wampler Dorris M. • Bridgewater, VA 22812

Wamsley Patricia A. • Library Media Specialist • Houston Junior Senior High School Library • Big Lake, AK 99652 • AASL YALSA

Wan William W. • Coordinator Technical Services • Texas Woman's University Mary Evelyn Blagg-Huey Library • Denton, TX 76204-1715 • ACRL ALCTS LITA

Wand Patricia A. • University Librarian • The American University Library • Washington, DC 20016-8046 • ACRL IFRT IRRT *Life*

Wanden Joy A. • User Support Coordinator • Online Computer Library Center (OCLC) Pacific Network • Rancho Cucamonga, CA 91730

Wanderman Miriam • Cataloger • Adelphi University Swirbul Library • Garden City, NY 11530

Wang Andrew H. • Dir., Asia Pacific & Tech Servs • OCLC Online Computer Library Center • Dublin, OH 43017-3395

Wang Ann C. • Librarian,Cataloging Division • Library of Congress • Washington, DC 20541

Wang Anna K. • Strong Museum • Rochester, NY 14607 • VRT

Wang Anna M. • Systems Librarian • Ohio State University Libraries • Columbus, OH 43210-1286 • ACRL ALCTS LAMA LITA LRRT

Wang Catherine Y. • Asst Dept Hd Catlg Dept • Drexel University W. W. Hagerty Library • Philadelphia, PA 19104 • ACRL ALCTS

Wang Chi • Hd of Chinese & Korean Sect • Library of Congress • Washington, DC 20541 • ACRL IRRT

Wang Chih • University of Guam • Mangilao, GU 96923 • ACRL LITA

Wang Christina S. • Collection Development • Baker & Taylor Books • Bridgewater, NJ 08807 • ACRL

Wang Christine C. • Regional Manager • Queens Borough Public Library • Jamaica, NY 11432

Wang Dujiang • Student • University of North Texas School of Library & Information Sciences • Denton, TX 76203

Wang Fawn Zefang • Student • Haskins Laboratories • New Haven, CT 06511

Wang Feng • Graduate Assistant • Southern Connecticut State University School of Libray Science & Instructional Technology • New Haven, CT 06515

Wang Gary Y. Dr • Transtech International Corp. • Natick, MA 01760

Wang Guo-hua • Search Unit Coordinator • Boston University Mugar Memorial Library • Boston, MA 02215

Wang Hazel Ho • Branch Services Manager • Orange Public Library El Modena Branch • Orange, CA 92669 • PLA

Wang Hui-Jung • Lake Hiawatha, NJ 07034-1255

Wang Hung I. • New York, NY 10027 • Continuing

Wang J.P. • San Diego, CA 92126-5750

Wang Jianrong • Student • State University of New York (SUNY) School of Information & Library Studies • Buffalo, NY 14260 • ALCTS IFRT

Wang Jin • Student • Louisiana State University School of Library & Information Science • Baton Rouge, LA 70803-3290 • ALCTS

Wang Joanna • Children's Librarian • Clark Public Library • Clark, NJ 07066

Wang Jun • Student • Northern Illinois University Department of Library & Information Studies • DeKalb, IL 60115 • IFRT SRRT

Wang Kwang-Mei • Student • University of Hawaii School of Library & Information Studies • Honolulu, HI 96822 • ALSC MAGERT

Wang Linda H.Y. • Reference Librarian • University of South Alabama Library • Mobile, AL 36688

Wang Ling • Student • Southern Connecticut State University School of Libray Science & Instructional Technology • New Haven, CT 06515

Wang Margaret K. • Coordinator of Original Catalog • University of Delaware Morris Library • Newark, DE 19717-5267 • ACRL EMIERT

Wang Mei-Chih • Tainan Hsien, Taiwan

Wang Ming • Student • State University New York at Buffalo School of Inf. & Library Studies • Buffalo, NY 14260

Wang Molly M. • Indexer • H. W. Wilson Company • Bronx, NY 10452 • ACRL

Wang Pei-Han • Student • University of Pittsburgh School of Library and Information Science • Pittsburgh, PA 15260

Wang Pei-Ying • Student • Rutgers University School of Communication Information & Library Studies • New Brunswick, NJ 08903 • LITA PLA

Wang Peiling • College Park, MD 20742

Wang Rong • Student • Historical Society of Pennsylvania • Voorhees, NJ 08043 • ALCTS

Wang Rui • DeKalb, IL 60115

Wang Selina • Metairie, LA 70006 • ALCTS

Wang Sing-Wu • Fisher Act 2611, Australia • ALCTS *Continuing*

Wang Su-Yueh S. • Los Alamitos, CA 90720-4814

Wang Susana C. • Librarian • Navy Department Library • Washington, DC 20374-0571 • ALCTS AFLRT

Wang Teresa C. • Head, Govt Pubs & Maps Dept • University of Texas at Arlington • Arlington, TX 76019-0497 • GODORT MAGERT

Wang Weiban • Student • University of Michigan School of Information and Library Studies • Ann Arbor, MI 48109-1092 • RASD EMIERT IFRT

Wang Weiwei • Student • University of Illinois Graduate School of Library and Information Science • Urbana, IL 61801

Wang Xin • Student • Kent State University School of Library & Information Science • Kent, OH 44242-0001

Wang Yongming • Student • Rutgers University School of Communication Information & Library Studies • New Brunswick, NJ 08903

Wang Yubai • Graduate Student • Simmons College Graduate School of Library & Information Science • Boston, MA 02115

Wang Yuh-Ching • North Potomac, MD 20878

Wang Zheng • Student • Dalhousie University School of Library & Inf. Studies • Halifax NS, B3H 4H8 Canada

Wanggaard Janice H. • Drew University • Madison, NJ 07940-4007 • GODORT

Wangsgard Lynnda M. • Director • Weber County Library • Odgen, UT 84401

Waniewski Margaret E. • Good Hope School Library • St. Croix, VI 00840

Wankmiller Madelyn Mrs. • Westboro, MA 01581-1418 • ALSC PLA *Continuing*

Wannamaker Lois Marie • Des Moines, IA 50312

Wanner Gail A. • Senior Library Consultant • DYNIX Inc. • Provo, UT 84606 • LITA

Wanninger Patricia Dwyer • Assistant Director • Janesville Public Library • Janesville, WI 53545-3971 • LITA PLA

Wanser Jeffery C. • Hd of Ref & Gov Doc • Hiram College Teachout-Price Memorial Library • Hiram, OH 44234 • ACRL RASD GODORT

Wantz Michael R. • Director • Perry County District Library • New Lexington, OH 43764 • PLA

Wappat Martha Mrs • Ft Lauderdale, FL 33305 • Continuing

Waraksa Raymond P. • Media Specialist • Bristol Central High School • Bristol, CT 06010 • AASL

Waranius Kathleen F. • Librarian II • Houston Public Library • Houston, TX 77002 • SRRT

Warburg Helena F. • Collection Development Librarian • Williams College Sawyer Library • Williamstown, MA 01267 • ACRL

Warby Marian • Librarian II • San Antonio Public Library Las Palmes Branch Library • San Antonio, TX 78237

Warchol Melissa A. • Gahanna, OH 43230

Ward Ann Baker • Reference Department • North Carolina State University D. H. Hill Library • Raleigh, NC 27695-7111 • Life

Ward Barbara Pyle • Librarian • Burley Jr. High School Library • Burley, ID 83318-2444

Ward Betty C. • Decatur, TN 37322 • AASL

Ward Cheryl L. • Tucson Pima Library • Tucson, AZ 85726

Ward Chris • Las Vegas-Clark County Library District Sunrise Branch • Las Vegas, NV 89110 • PLA

Ward Cindy A. • University of Detroit-Mercy Outer Drive Library • Detroit, MI 48219-3599

Ward Clayton • Trustee • Western Plains Library System • Clinton, OK 73601

Ward Deborah A. • Elementary School Teacher • Lawndale Academy • Chicago, IL 60623 • ALSC IFRT IRRT

Ward Dilys M. • Student • University of Western Ontario School of Library & Information Science • London ON, N6G 1H1 Canada • ALSC

Ward Dorothy A. • Library Aide II • Minneapolis Public Library & Information Center • Minneapolis, MN 55401-1992

Ward Edith • Mahwah, NJ 07430 • ALCTS LITA IRRT

Ward Evelyn M. • Head of Literature Department • Cleveland Public Library • Cleveland, OH 44114-1271 • RASD

Ward Gerald F. • Sacramento Public Library Carmichael Regional Branch • Carmichael, CA 95608 • ACRL RASD

Ward Grace L. • Ferndale, MI 48220 • ALSC

Ward Holly • Trustee • Romeo District Library • Romeo, MI 48065

Ward James E. • Director • David Lipscomb University University Library • Nashville, TN 37204-3951 • ACRL LIRT

Ward Jane C. • Metro Christian Academy • Tulsa, OK 74136 • AASL ALSC

Ward Janet A. • Wilmington, NC 28409

Ward Jeannette A. • Techinical Service • University of Central Florida Library • Orlando, FL 32816-0666 • ACRL

Ward Jennifer A. • Orlando, FL 32825 • AASL

Ward Joyce M. • Orlando College South Campus • Orlando, FL 32806

Ward Karin E. • TRW Inc. • Redondo Beach, CA 90278 • ALCTS

Ward Kelly M. • Library Assistant • University California-Berkeley • Berkeley, CA 94720

Ward Lois H. • Head, Technical Services • Ohio Wesleyan University • Delaware, OH 43015 • ACRL ALCTS LAMA LITA RASD GODORT IFRT LIRT MAGERT SRRT

Ward Louise Miss • Biloxi, MS 39531 • ACRL RASD *Life*

Ward Lucinda • Techincal Service Librarian • Fond du Lac County Library • Fond du Lac, WI 54935-4220

Ward Lucy • Trustee • Metropolitan Library System • Oklahoma City, OK 73102 • ALTA PLA

Ward Marcia • Reference Librarian • Sumter County Library • Sumter, SC 29150

Ward Margaret T. • Detroit, MI 48214

Ward Marian E. • Annapolis East Elementary School Library • Middleton NS, B0S 1P0 Canada • AASL ALSC

Ward Maribeth • Vice President-Customer Services • NOTIS Systems, Inc. • Evanston, IL 60201-3622 • ACRL LITA

Ward Marilyn J. • Asst. Prof. of Education • Carthage College John Mosheim Ruthrauff Library • Kenosha, WI 53141 • ALSC

Ward Marsha Lee • Falls Church, VA 22044

Ward Michael A. • Trustee • Downers Grove Public Library • Downers Grove, IL 60515 • ALTA

Ward Nan • Librarian • Gay Avenue Primary School • Gladewater, TX 75647

Ward Nellie C. • Maryvale High School • Phoenix, AZ 85033 • YALSA LIRT

Ward Richard O. • Student • San Jose State University Division of Library & Information Science • San Jose, CA 95192-0029

Ward Robert • Library Director • Horry County Memorial Library • Conway, SC 29526 • PLA

Ward Sandra N. • Science Librarian • Mount Holyoke College Miles-Smith Science Library • South Hadley, MA 01075-1493 • ACRL LITA LIRT

Ward Sherry A. • Library Specialist II • New Mexico State University Library • Las Cruces, NM 88003-0006

Ward Shirlene A. • Evanston, IL 60202 • LITA

Ward Suzanne M. • Information Specialist • Purdue University Libraries • West Lafayette, IN 47907

Ward Troy Faith • Student • West Georgia College Library Media Program • Carrollton, GA 30118 • AASL EMIERT IFRT SRRT

Ward Ursula A. • Government Documents Librarian • Metropolitan Library System Capitol Hill Branch • Oklahoma City, OK 73109 • ALCTS GODORT

Ward Valerie G. • Reference/Information • Towers Perrin • Calgary AB, T2P 3Y7 Canada

Warde Mary V. • Senior Administrator/Librarian • Municipal Bond Investors Assurance • Armonk, NY 10504

Wardell Margaret • Northfield, MN 55057 • ACRL RASD *Continuing*

Warden Margaret S. • Helena, MT 59601 • ALTA

Wardle Leslie • Salt Lake City Public Library • Salt Lake City, UT 84111

Ware Dorothy W. • Director of Group Services • Public Library of Charlotte & Mecklenburg County • Charlotte, NC 28202

Ware Jennifer D. • Serials Librarian • California State University-Sacramento Library • Sacramento, CA 95819-6039 • ACRL ALCTS

Ware Linda K. • Library Technican II • Kern County Library Rathbun Branch • Bakersfield, CA 93308

Ware Lucinda Frances • Baltimore County Public Library • Towson, MD 21204 • ALSC PLA

Ware Mary K. • Librarian 6-12 • Mount Vernon Community Schools • Mt. Vernon, IA 52314 • AASL

Ware Michael L. • Reference Librarian • Greenville County Library • Greenville, SC 29601

Ware Nola S. • Northeastern Oklahoma State University John Vaughan Library-LRC • Tahlequah, OK 74464

Wareham Karen Ann • Librarian • Westlake School for Girls Westlake School Library • Los Angeles, CA 90077 • AASL

Wares Michael • Head Cataloger • Fordham University Libraries • Bronx, NY 10458

Warf Margaret A. • Media Specialist • Moss Street Elementary School • Reidsville, NC 27320 • AASL

Warfel Pauline L. Mrs • Bethel Park, PA 15102 • PLA RASD *Continuing*

Warfield Elizabeth T. • Rochester Public Library • Rochester, MN 55904-3777 • AASL ALSC

Wargo Peggy M. • Assistant Town Librarian • Fairfield Public Library • Fairfield, CT 06430 • ALCTS PLA

Warheit Deborah A. • Los Angeles, CA 90025 • ALSC

Warhit Peter A. • Student • San Jose State University Division of Library & Information Science • San Jose, CA 95192-0029 • PLA RASD

Warhol Jennifer B. • Student • Texas Instruments, Inc. Library/Research Center • Austin, TX 78769

Wark Jonathan Peter • Student • University of Rhode Island Graduate School of Library & Information Studies • Kingston, RI 02881-0815

Warkentin Cheryl J. • Hutchinson Community College • Hutchinson, KS 67501

Warkentin Katherine • Documents Librarian • Shippensburg University Lehman Memorial Library • Shippensburg, PA 17257-2299

Warling Brian N. • University of California Los Angeles Biomedical Library (UCLA) • Los Angeles, CA 90024 • ACRL

Warmann Carolyn • Hutchinson, KS 67502 • ACRL

Warmington Sandra K. • Sacramento, CA 95820 • LITA SRRT

Warmkessel Marjorie M. • Coor. of Library Instruction • Millersville University of Pennsylvania • Millersville, PA 17551-0302 • ACRL LIRT

Warmund Solange • Librarian • United Nations International School • New York, NY 10010 • AASL

Warncke Ruth • Chicago, IL 60611 • Continuing

Warne Shaaron M. • Student • University of Washington Graduate School of Library and Information Science • Seattle, WA 98195 • ACRL

Warner-Wilson Margaret J. • Librarian I • Southwest Texas State University • San Marcos, TX 78666

Warner Alice Sizer • Lexington, MA 02173 • ILERT

Warner Beth A. • Head, Libray Systems Office • University of Michigan • Ann Arbor, MI 48109-1205 • ACRL ALCTS LITA RASD

Warner Claudia • Co-Director • Algona Public Library • Algona, IA 50511

Warner Earleen J. • Head Librarian • Pioneerland Library System • Willmar, MN 56201

Warner Edward S. • Library Director • Defiance College Anthony Wayne Library • Defiance, OH 43512 • ACRL

Warner Elaine • Librarian • Friends Seminary • New York, NY 10003 • AASL YALSA

Warner Elaine • OSU-OKC OK State University-OK City Campus • Oklahoma City, OK 73107

Warner Elizabeth R. • Education Services Librarian • Thomas Jefferson University Scott Memorial Library • Philadelphia, PA 19107 • ACRL ASCLA LITA RASD LIRT LRRT

Warner Frances Miss • Chicago, IL 60622 • ACRL *Continuing*

Warner Gail P. • Director • Oxnard Public Library • Oxnard, CA 93030 • LAMA PLA SRRT

Warner Izella W. • Chinook, MT 59523

Warner Joyce E. • Librarian • Linapuni El School Library • Honolulu, HI 96822 • AASL ALSC

Warner Julaine P. • Librarian • Phoenix Public Library Palo Verde Branch • Phoenix, AZ 85031 • PLA

Warner Karen R. • Coordinator of Services • Northeast Community College • Norfolk, NE 68702-0469 • ACRL

Warner Mara • Chicago, IL 60626

Warner Marnie • Law Library Coordinator • Trial Court Law Libraries • Boston, MA 02108 • ASCLA LAMA SRRT *Life*

Warner Robert M. • Dean • University of Michigan School of Information and Library Studies • Ann Arbor, MI 48109-1092

Warner Wayne G. Dr • North Columbia Elementary School • Appling, GA 30802 • AASL ALSC

Warnken Paula N. • Director • Xavier University McDonald Memorial Library • Cincinnati, OH 45207 • ACRL LAMA LITA

Warnock Rita H. • Curator of Broadsides • Brown University Library • Providence, RI 02912 • ACRL IFRT

Warpeha Rita C. • Silver Spring, MD 20901

Warren-Wenk Peggy • Reference Librarian • York University Glendon Campus Leslie Frost Library • Toronto ON, M4N 3M6 Canada • ACRL LAMA RASD

Warren Bonnie L. • Student • University of Washington Graduate School of Library and Information Science • Seattle, WA 98195

Warren Caroline C. • Durham, NC 27701

Warren Catherine • Headquarters Librarian • First Regional Library • Hernando, MS 38632 • PLA

Warren Catherine • Educational Services Librarian • Cornell University Medical College Library • New York, NY 10021-4896 • ACRL EMIERT

Warren Charles David • Director • Richland County Public Library • Columbia, SC 29201 • LAMA PLA

Warren Craig M. • Librarian • Choate Rosemary Hall Foundation Inc. • Wallingford, CT 06492 • ACRL RASD

Warren Debra E. • Chatham, NY 12037

Warren Dorthea A. • Library Assistant • University of California-Los Angeles (UCLA) • Los Angeles, CA 90024-1450

Warren Emma A. • Director • Rutgers University Libraries Livingston College Kilmer Area Library • Piscataway, NJ 08854 • ACRL LAMA LITA

Warren Gary L. • Student • University of Kentucky College of Library & Information Science • Lexington, KY 40506-0391 • ACRL

Warren Harold K. • Trustee • Cumberland County Public Library and Information Center • Fayetteville, NC 28301

Warren Janet B. • Librarian • Goodland Public Library • Goodland, KS 67735 • PLA

Warren John W. • Subject Specialist • University of Alabama in Huntsville Library • Huntsville, AL 35899 • ACRL

Warren Julia B. • Tyler, TX 75702

Warren Katherine • Western New Mexico University • Silver City, NM 88062 • ACRL

Warren Kenneth A. • Director • Lakewood Public Library • Lakewood, OH 44107 • PLA

Warren Kimberly A. • Information Specialist • BNR Incorporation • Research Triangle Pk, NC 27709 • ALSC

Warren Lola N. • Head of Reference • Johnson County Library • Shawnee Mission, KS 66201 • PLA RASD

Warren Lynda Reid • Librarian • Timberlane Regional High School • Plaistow, NH 03865 • AASL YALSA

Warren Nora C. • Information Resources Manager • Northwestern Regional Library • Elkin, NC 28621 • ALCTS

Warren Robert O. • Executive Editor • Harper Collins Publishers • New York, NY 10022 • ALSC

Warren Ruth M. • Librarian • Douglas County Public Library • Douglasville, GA 30134

Warren Sherry • Youth Services Librarian • Tempe Public Library • Tempe, AZ 85282 • ALSC

Warren Susan S. • Reference Supervisor • Newport Beach Public Library • Newport Beach, CA 92660 • PLA

Warren Taylor K. • Williamsburg, VA 23185-4012 • AFLRT FLRT

Warren Yolanda • Reference Librarian • Washington & Lee University • Lexington, VA 24450

Warrick Vera A. • Technical Services Supv. • Burlingame Public Library • Burlingame, CA 94010

Warrington David R. • Librarian for Special Cllns • Harvard Law School Library • Cambridge, MA 02138 • ACRL LHRT

Warrington John • Media Specialist • Carlisle High School • Carisle, OH 45005

Warro Edward A. • Loyola University E.M. Cudahy Memorial Library • Chicago, IL 60626 • ACRL ALCTS

Warth L Terry • Special Collections Cataloger • University of Kentucky Libraries • Lexington, KY 40506-0039 • ACRL ALCTS LITA IFRT

Warth Martha Neal Mrs. • Trustee • Nantahala Regional Library • Murphy, NC 28906 • ALTA

Wartinbee Kathleen • Student • University of Michigan Libraries Information and Library Studies • Ann Arbor, MI 48109 • AASL

Wartluft David J. Rev • Director of the Library • Lutheran Theological Seminary Krauth Memorial Library • Philadelphia, PA 19119-1794 • ACRL

Wartman William B. III • Director • Roanoke Rapids Public Library • Roanoke Rapids, NC 27870 • PLA

Warton Jennifer L. • Student • Emporia State University School of Library & Information Management • Emporia, KS 66801 • AASL

Wartzok Susan • Hd, Cataloging & Tech Proc. • Eden Webster Libraries • Saint Louis, MO 63119-9957 • ACRL ALCTS IFRT

Warwick James F. • Director • Rock Island Public Library • Rock Island, IL 61201-8143 • ALCTS ALSC ASCLA LAMA LITA PLA RASD

Warwick Margaret E. • Seattle, WA 98125

Warwick Robert T. • Bibliographic Database Man • Rutgers University Libraries Technical & Automated Services • Piscataway, NJ 08855 • ALCTS LITA CLENE NMRT

Warwick Rochelle • Student • Queens College Grad Sch of Lib & Inf Studies • Flushing, NY 11367 • LITA

Warzala Martin L. • Manager • Baker & Taylor Books • Bridgewater, NJ 08807-0920 • ACRL ALCTS LITA

Wash Melba Wilson • Director • Reelfoot Regional Library Center • Martin, TN 38237 • PLA

Washburn Keith E. • Executive Director • Central New York Library Resources Council • Syracuse, NY 13208 • ACRL ASCLA IFRT

Washburn Wanda L. Mrs. • Head of Technical Processing • Jackson-Madison County Library • Jackson, TN 38301

Washington Alice H. • Trustee • Atlanta-Fulton Public Library • Atlanta, GA 30303 • PLA

Washington Alice M. • Librarian • Big Valley Christian School • Modesto, CA 95356 • AASL

Washington Barbara G. • Library Faculty • Kennedy-King College Library • Chicago, IL 60621 • ACRL RASD LRRT

Washington Dorothy A. • Montclair, NJ 07042-1715 • ACRL ALCTS

Washington George Jr. • Houston, TX 77288-0087

Washington Idella A. • Librarian • Phillips Elementary School Library • New Orleans, LA 70122 • AASL

Washington Marquita M. • Children Librarian • Atlanta-Fulton Public Library • Atlanta, GA 30303 • ALSC

Washington Nancy • Assistant Director • University of South Carolina • Columbia, SC 29208 • ACRL ALCTS

Washington Penny C. • Branch Library Manager • Dallas Public Library Audelia Road Branch • Dallas, TX 75238-1999 • PLA

Washington Rowena C. • Librarian • Sante Fe School Unified School District • Oakland, CA 94608 • AASL ALSC LIRT

Washington Sigrid M. Mrs. • Regional Branch Librarian • District of Columbia Public Library Woodridge Regional Branch • Washington, DC 20018

Washkevich Peter D. • Student • Princeton University Firestone Library • Princeton, NJ 08544

Wasick Jennifer L. • Student • Florida State University School of Library and Information Studies • Tallahassee, FL 32306-2048

Wasielewski Terry L. • Head of Technical Services • Russell Sage College Library • Troy, NY 12180

Wasiewicz Ann • School Library Media Specialist • Jordan-Elbridge School District Elbridge Elementary School • Elbridge, NY 13060 • AASL ALSC

Wasilick Michael J. • Branch Supervisor • Wake County Public Library System • Raleigh, NC 27610

Waskow Sharon R. • New York, NY 10002 • AASL

Wasowicz Laura E. • Worcester, MA 01609

Wassell Merrill L. • Canton Public Library • Canton, MI 48188

Wassenich Red • Austin Community College Rio Grande Campus • Austin, TX 78701 • ACRL LIRT

Wasser Janice L. • School Librarian • Banff Private School • Houston, TX 77069

Wasserman Diane • LMC Director • Sugar Creek Elementary School • Verona, WI 53593 • AASL

Wasserman Paul • Professor • University of Maryland Hornbake Library • College Park, MD 20742 • RASD

Wasserman Safari C. • Fairfax, VA 22032

Wasserman Scott E. • Trustee • Johnson County Library • Shawnee Mission, KS 66201 • ALTA

Wasserman Sherry • Librarian Grade 2 • Oak Park Public Library • Oak Park, MI 48237

Wasserman Susan K. • Student • Wayne State University Library Science Program • Detroit, MI 48202

Wasserstrom Leslie K. • Southfield, MI 48034-5450

Wassink Donald B. • Head of Library Systems • Hong Kong University of Science & Technology University Library • Kowloon, Hong Kong • LITA IFRT

Wasson Patricia • Assistant Librarian • Illinois State Geological Survey • Champaign, IL 61820

Wasylenko Lydia W. • Associate Librarian • Syracuse University Library E. S. Bird Library • Syracuse, NY 13244-2010 • ACRL ALCTS

Wasylyshyn James J. • San Francisco, CA 94115

Watanabe Jean E. • Librarian • John F. Kennedy Library • Vallejo, CA 94590 • ALSC

Watanabe Lynn B. • Madison, FL 32340-2738

Watanabe Nagisa • Student • University of Hawaii School of Library & Information Studies • Honolulu, HI 96822 • IRRT

Waterbury Ann E. • Albany, NY 12204

Waterhouse Colleen A. • St. Catharines, ON, L2T 3P4 Canada

Waterman Blaine • San Francisco Public Library Park Branch • San Francisco, CA 94117 • SRRT

Waterman Kathleen • Chatham, NJ 07928 • PLA *Continuing*

Waterman Roberta A. • Student • West Virginia University Evansdale Library • Morgantown, WV 26506-6105 • AASL YALSA IFRT LRRT SRRT

Waters Barbara A. • Director/Librarian • Fryeburg Public Library • Fryeburg, ME 04037

Waters Donald J. • Head, Systems Office • Yale University Sterling Memorial Library • New Haven, CT 06520 • ACRL LITA

Waters Joseph M. • Chicago Public Library Wrightwood Branch • Chicago, IL 60652

Waters Keith R. • Director/Operations • Fast Forward Video Distributions • Clearwater, FL 34625 • VRT

Waters Lily A. • Army Management Staff College Library • Alexandria, VA 22311 • ACRL RASD AFLRT FLRT

Waters Marie B. • Librarian • University of California-Los Angeles (UCLA) • Los Angeles, CA 90024-1450 • ACRL RASD IFRT IRRT

Waters Nancy • Yonkers Public Library • Yonkers, NY 10701

Waters Patricia A. • Hamburg Township Library • Hamburg, MI 48139

Waters Richard L. • Library Consultant • H.B.W. Associates, Inc. • Denton, TX 76201 • AASL ACRL ALTA ASCLA LAMA LITA PLA RASD

Waters W. Robin • Manager, Medical Library • Porter Memorial Hospital Medical Library • Denver, CO 80210-5876 • LITA

Waterson Carrie E. • Indianapolis-Marion County Public Library Nora Branch • Indianapolis, IN 46240-1835

Waterson Jennifer K. • Reference/Children's Librarian • Monterey County Free Library Prunedale Branch • Salinas, CA 93907

Watford Jacquelynn • Darlington County Library • Darlington, SC 29532

Watkins Anna S. • Student • University of Tennessee-Knoxville Graduate School of Library & Information Science • Knoxville, TN 37996-4330 • ALSC

Watkins Carolyn K. • Library Director • Walker Memorial Library • Westbrook, ME 04092

Watkins Cynthia • Las Cruces, NM 88001

Watkins Donna • Librarian II Branch Librarian • Pasadena Public Library • Pasadena, CA 91101

Watkins Donna J. • Henderson, NV 89014 • LAMA

Watkins Jan S. • Head of Ref Youth Serv. • Schaumburg Township District Library • Schaumburg, IL 60194 • ALSC PLA

Watkins Joyce • Trustee • McGregor Public Library • Highland Park, MI 48203 • ALTA

Watkins Julia • Librarian • Harford Day School • Bel Air, MD 21014 • AASL

Watkins Julie E. • Library Assistant • Richardson Public Library • Richardson, TX 75080

Watkins Karen J. • State Librarian • New Mexico State Library • Santa Fe, NM 87503 • ASCLA

Watkins Lucinda • New Port Richey Public Library • New Port Richey, FL 34652

Watkins Margie L. • Memphis, TN 38114

Watkins Mary L. • Assistant Director • Gary Public Library • Gary, IN 46402

Watkins Michael P. • Student • University of Tennessee-Knoxville Graduate School of Library & Information Science • Knoxville, TN 37996-4330 • RASD

Watkins Robert L. • Assoc. Dir. Bibliographic Res Ct • AMIGOS Bibliographic Council,Inc. • Dallas, TX 75251-2104 • ALCTS LITA IFRT

Watkins Steven G. • Asst Head, Science Library • University of California-Santa Cruz Library • Santa Cruz, CA 95064 • ACRL LITA

Watkins Susan J. • Librarian • Eastern Nazarene College Nease Library • Wollaston, MA 02170 • ACRL

Watkins Vicki A. • Lincoln University Inman E. Page Library • Jefferson City, MO 65102-0029 • LITA IFRT

Watkyns-Batchelor Joanna B. • Children's Librarian • Los Angeles Public Library Sunland Tujunga Branch • Tujunga, CA 91042

Watman Celeste • Director • Hicksville Free Public Library • Hicksville, NY 11801 • LAMA

Watrous Lyle C. • Reference Librarian • Arizona State University Hayden Library • Tempe, AZ 85287-1006

Watrous Mary A. • Librarian • Mohave County Library Charles C. Royall Memorial Library • Lake Havasu City, AZ 86403 • PLA

Watson-Boone Peter G. • Director of the Library • University of Wisconsin-Milwaukee Golda Meir Library • Milwaukee, WI 53201 • ACRL LAMA RASD LRRT

Watson-Boone Rebecca • Mequon, WI 53092 • ACRL RASD LRRT *Life*

Watson-Phillips Anita • Library Board Commissioner • Grand Rapids Public Library • Grand Rapids, MI 49503-3093

Watson Andrea • Monograph Cataloger • University of Alabama Amelia Gayle Gorgas Library • Tuscaloosa, AL 35487-0266 • ALCTS LITA

Watson Anne L. • Librarian • Mary Ann Binford Elementary School • Albuquerque, NM 87121-8311 • AASL

Watson Barbara L. • Indianapolis, IN 46208

Watson Benjamin • Rare Books Librarian • University of San Francisco Richard A. Gleeson Library • San Francisco, CA 94117 • ACRL

Watson Carol F. • Librarian • Huntington High School • Huntington, WV 25701 • AASL

Watson Carolyn R. • Information Services Libn. • Loudoun County Public Library • Leesburg, VA 22075 • PLA

Watson Cynthia Cummings • Director • Ericson Public Library • Boone, IA 50036

Watson Cynthia Post • Reference Librarian • Phoenix Public Library Juniper Branch • Phoenix, AZ 85027 • RASD

Watson Dana • University of Alabama School of Library and Information Studies • Tuscaloosa, AL 35487 • AASL ALSC

Watson Duane A. • Assoc. Librarian • New York Historical Society Library • New York, NY 10024-5194 • ACRL ALCTS LAMA MAGERT

Watson Elizabeth S. • Chief Librarian • Fitchburg Public Library • Fitchburg, MA 01420 • ALSC

Watson Ellen I. • Director • Bradley University Cullom-Davis Library • Peoria, IL 61625 • ACRL LAMA LITA

Watson Gail H. • Librarian • Franklin County South Junior High School • Cowan, TN 37318 • AASL

Watson Gaye G. • Director • A. H. Meadows Library • Midlothian, TX 76065

Watson Halbert • City Librarian • Pomona Public Library • Pomona, CA 91769-2271 • ALCTS LAMA LITA PLA RASD YALSA EMIERT IFRT SRRT

Watson Jerry J. • Professor of Children's Lit. • University of Iowa Libraries • Iowa City, IA 52242-1379

Watson Joyce Frank • Building Planning Coor. • University of Hawaii Thomas Hale Hamilton Library • Honolulu, HI 96822 • LAMA

Watson Judy E. • Burlington, IA 52601

Watson Justine P. • Assistant Librarian • Sioux Falls Public Library • Sioux Falls, SD 57102 • PLA

Watson Kathy Cox • Media Librarian • Ewing Elementary School • Wallingford, KY 41093 • AASL

Watson LeAnn Rugland • Reference Librarian • Montgomery County Library System • Conroe, TX 77301 • RASD IFRT

Watson Linda • Student • San Jose State University Division of Library & Information Science • San Jose, CA 95192-0029

Watson Linda A. • Director • University of Virginia Medical Center Claude Moore Health Sciences Library • Charlottesville, VA 22908 • ACRL ALCTS LAMA LITA RASD

Watson Linda J. • Archivist • Colorado State Archives • Denver, CO 80203 • ACRL

Watson Margaret • Trustee • Dearborn Department of Libraries Henry Ford Centennial Library • Dearborn, MI 48126

Watson Marie L. • Library Supervisor • Free Library of Philadelphia West Oak Lane Branch Library • Philadelphia, PA 19138

Watson Marilyn A. • Zuni Elementary • Scottsdale, AZ 85260

Watson Mark • Assistant to Dean • Southern Illinois University Delyte W. Morris Library • Carbondale, IL 62901-6632 • ACRL LAMA IRRT LIRT

Watson Mark R. • Head, Catalog Dept. • University of Oregon Library • Eugene, OR 97403-1299 • ALCTS LITA NMRT

Watson Marlys A. • Student • University of Kentucky College of Library & Information Science • Lexington, KY 40506-0391 • ALCTS

Watson MaryFrances E. • Rosary College Graduate School of Library & Information Science • River Forest, IL 60305

Watson Maureen E. • Optometry Librarian • Ferris State University • Big Rapids, MI 49307

Watson Merlyn Mrs • Badgett Elementary School • Little Rock, AR 72206 • AASL

Watson Natalie A. • St. Petersburg Times • St. Petersburg, FL 33701

Watson Patricia L. • Director • Knox County Public Library System • Knoxville, TN 37902 • LAMA PLA

Watson Paula D. • Acting Director, General Serv. • University of Illinois Library • Urbana, IL 61801 • ACRL LAMA LITA RASD GODORT

Watson R. A. • Springfield, IL 62703 • ACRL

Watson Robert E. • Executive Director • Franklin Park Public Library District • Franklin Park, IL 60131 • PLA

Watson Ron • Cataloging Dept.- URL • University of California-Los Angeles (UCLA) • Los Angeles, CA 90024-1450 • ACRL ALCTS ALSC LAMA LITA RASD ERT GODORT IFRT IRRT LHRT LIRT LRRT MAGERT SORT SRRT

Watson Sarah • Librarian • Omaha Public Library • Omaha, NE 68102 • AASL ALSC PLA YALSA

Watson Virginia • Student • Brigham Young University School of Library & Information Sciences • Provo, UT 84602 • RASD

Watson Warren • Director of Libraries • Crane Public Library • Quincy, MA 02169 • LAMA LITA PLA

Watstein Sarah Barbara • Assoc Libn for Pub Svs • Hunter College Library • New York, NY 10021 • ACRL RASD SRRT

Watt John R. • Stockton, CA 95219

Watt Lois B. • Stanford, CA 94305 • AASL ALSC *Life*

Watt Marcia A. • Preservation Librarian • Yale University Sterling Memorial Library • New Haven, CT 06520 • ACRL ALCTS

Watt Nona K. • Head of Technical Services • Indiana University School of Law Library • Bloomington, IN 47405 • ACRL

Wattenberg Julie M. • Asst. Head, Info. Processing Dpt • University of Massachusetts Library • Amherst, MA 01003 • ACRL ALCTS LITA

Watters Cynthia • Catalog Librarian • Middlebury College Egbert Starr Library • Middlebury, VT 05753-6007 • ALCTS LITA MAGERT

Watters Lisa D. • Clermont County Public Library • Batavia, OH 45103-3192 • LAMA

Watts Adalyn S. • University of La Verne • La Verne, CA 91750 • ACRL

Watts Anne • Coordinator, Downtown Branch • Saint Louis Public Library • St. Louis, MO 63103-2389 • LAMA PLA GODORT

Watts Coaline • Librarian • Chicago Board of Education • Chicago, IL 60620

Watts Janet W. • Student • San Jose State University Division of Library & Information Science • San Jose, CA 95192-0029

Watts Melanie M. • Student • University of Alabama School of Library & Information Studies • Tuscaloosa, AL 35487-0252 • NMRT

Watts Richard S. • Coordinator of Technical Process • San Bernardino County Library • San Bernardino, CA 92415 • ALCTS PLA

Watts Rita J. • St. Charles, MO 63303 • AASL ALSC

Watts Thomas J. • Student • Indiana State University • Terre Haute, IN 47809 • ACRL

Wattson Marcia • Hennepin County Library Ridgedale-Hennepin Area Library • Minnetonka, MN 55343

Wauchter Edward CSC Bro • Lakewood, OH 44107 • AASL

Waugh Charles L. • Student • University of South Florida School of Library & Information Science • Tampa, FL 33620

Waugh Katharine A. • Reference Librarian • Vassar College Library • Poughkeepsie, NY 12601 • ACRL

Waxman Lowell T. • Librarian Branch Manager • San Diego Public Library College Heights Branch • San Diego, CA 92115 • PLA

Way Colleen M. • Reference Services Rep. • OCLC Online Computer Library Center • Dublin, OH 43017-3395 • LITA

Way Harold E. • Account Executive-Electronic Sys • University Microfilms Int. • Overland Park, KS 66210 • RASD

Way Melinda S • Associate Librarian • Mount Saint Mary College Curtin Memorial Library • Newburgh, NY 12550-3598

Way Olivia R. • Tenants Harbor, ME 04860 • AASL ALSC   *Life*

Way Sue • Librarian • Calcasiev Parish Nelson Elementary School • Lake Charles, LA 70605 • AASL

Wayland-Merryweather Illa • Fredonia, NY 14063 • AASL

Wayland April Halprin • Los Angeles, CA 90049

Wayman Richard • Kent County Library System East Grand Rapids Branch • East Grand Rapids, MI 49506

Wayne Alesia M. • Student • Syracuse University School of Information Studies • Syracuse, NY 13244-4100

Wayne Elena • Films Incorporated • Chicago, IL 60640-1199 • VRT

Wayte Nancy F. • Media Specialist • Five Forks Middle School • Lawrenceville, GA 30244

Waznis Betty • Librarian III • San Diego County Library • San Diego, CA 92123

Weakland Pete D. • Trustee • Tucson Pima Library • Tucson, AZ 85726 • ALTA

Weakley Carolyn A. • Librarian • Phillips College • Louisville, KY 40216

Weakley Laurie L. • Systems Librarian • University of North Carolina • Chapel Hill, NC 27599 • LITA

Weant Rebecca E. • Salisbury, NC 28144

Weas Andrea T. • Automation Services Librarian • State University of New York (SUNY) College at Geneseo Milne Library • Geneseo, NY 14454-1498 • ACRL LITA

Weaser Angela L. • Geneva, IL 60134-2349

Weatherall Barbara • Champaign, IL 61821 • ACRL MAGERT

Weatherbee Marjorie • Care Public Library • Fall River, MA 02726 • Continuing

Weatherell Betty R. • Pittsburgh, PA 15228

Weatherholt Virginia • Librarian • Spencer County Library System • Grandview, IN 47615

Weatherly C. Diann • Gov Doc Ln & Ref Ln • University of Alabama at Birmingham Mervyn H. Sterne Library • Birmingham, AL 35294-0014 • ACRL GODORT

Weatherly Walter • Trustee • Alabama Public Library Service • Montgomery, AL 36130 • ALTA PLA

Weatherman Lesley Mrs. • Librarian • North Star Elementary School • Nikiski, AK 99635

Weathers Barbara H. • Upper School Librarian • Duchesne Academy of the Sacred Heart High School • Houston, TX 77024 • AASL

Weathers Judy K. • Part-time Reference Librarian • King County Library System • Seattle, WA 98109-5191

Weathers Marganne M. • Librarian • Fort Lewis Library System • Fort Lewis, WA 98433-5000

Weathers Virginia W. • Reference Librarian • University of South Carolina • Columbia, SC 29208 • ACRL RASD

Weaver-Meyers Pat L. • Head of Access Services • University of Oklahoma Libraries University Libraries • Norman, OK 73019 • ACRL LAMA CLENE

Weaver-Stern Phoebe J. • Tuscaloosa, AL 35487

Weaver Alice O. • Reference Librarian • University of Toledo William S. Carlson Library • Toledo, OH 43606-3399 • ACRL RASD LHRT

Weaver Barbara F. • Director • Rhode Island Department of State Library Services • Providence, RI 02903-4222 • AASL ASCLA

Weaver Barlow • San Mateo, CA 94402

Weaver Bruce A. • Ohio State University • Columbus, OH 43210 • ACRL

Weaver Carolyn G. • Associate Director for Adm. • University of Washington Health Science Library & Info Center • Seattle, WA 98195 • ACRL

Weaver Clarence L. • Grand Rapids, MI 49503 • Continuing

Weaver Connie J. • Student • Shippensburg University Lehman Memorial Library • Shippensburg, PA 17257-2299 • PLA

Weaver Dorothy M. • Teacher • Lake Bluff Junior High School Library • Lake Bluff, IL 60044 • AASL

Weaver Eris • Circulation Technician • Sonoma County Library • Santa Rosa, CA 95404 • PLA

Weaver Gail • Lavaca Public Schools • Lavaca, AR 72941 • AASL

Weaver Gladys L • Head Librarian • Navasota Public Library • Navasota, TX 77868 • PLA

Weaver Gwendolyn N. • Director of Information Resource • Harvard Business School Baker Library • Boston, MA 02163 • LITA

Weaver Jamie Lyn • Glenview, IL 60025 • AASL

Weaver Janice H. • Indiana State Library • Indianapolis, IN 46204-2296

Weaver Josephine E. • United States Army Davis Library • Fort Devens, MA 01433 • LAMA PLA   *Life*

Weaver Judith W. • Student • Simmons College Graduate School of Library & Information Science • Boston, MA 02115 • PLA YALSA EMIERT IFRT NMRT SRRT

Weaver LeeAnna R. • Student • University of Oklahoma School of Library & Information Studies • Norman, OK 73019 • IFRT

Weaver Lynne K. • Student • State University of New York at Albany School of Information Science & Policy • Albany, NY 12222

Weaver Monica K. • Student • University of Illinois Graduate School of Library and Information Science • Urbana, IL 61801

Weaver Patricia J.S. • Reference Librarian • Saint Joseph's University Libraries Drexel Library • Philadelphia, PA 19131-1395 • RASD

Weaver Ronald D. • FPO, AP 96321-0008 • AASL FLRT LIRT

Weaver Ruby • Covington, LA 70433

Weaver Shari L. • Yale University Sterling Memorial Library • New Haven, CT 06520 • LITA

Weaver Susan • Kent State University East Liverpool Campus • East Liverpool, OH 43920 • ACRL

Weaver Thomas M. • Director • Hist Society of the Militia & National Guard • Washington, DC 20001 • LAMA LITA

Weaver Virginia H. • Atlanta, GA 30305

Webb-Metz Gina • Coord of Training & Doc • BCCLS Computer Consortium Inc. • Hackensack, NJ 07601

Webb-Ozmun Marybeth • Assistant • Eastern Oklahoma District Library System • Muskogee, OK 74401 • YALSA

Webb A Marvin Jr • Librarian • Baltimore City Public Schools • Baltimore, MD 21218 • AASL ALSC

Webb Barbara • Associate Director • Fairfax County Public Library • Fairfax, VA 22033-1907 • PLA

Webb Ellen L. • Office of Attorney General State House Annex • Concord, NH 03301

Webb Frances • Circulation Librarian • Miami Public Library • Miami, OK 74354

Webb Frances E. • Reference Librarian • Ranndolph-Macon Woman's College Lipscomb Library • Lynchburg, VA 24503-1526 • ACRL

Webb Gisela M. • Asst. to the Dean of Libs. • Arizona State University Hayden Library • Tempe, AZ 85287-1006 • LAMA

Webb Gloria • Kansas City, MO 64109

Webb Harriet R. • Student • University of North Texas School of Library & Information Sciences • Denton, TX 76203 • ALSC PLA

Webb John P. • Asst. Dir. for Lib. Automation • Washington State University • Pullman, WA 99164-2112 • ACRL ALCTS LITA

Webb Kathleen W. • Princeton Day School • Princeton, NJ 08542 • AASL

Webb Lois • Comfort, TX 78013 • ALTA

Webb Loretta L. • Librarian • Castlemont High School • Oakland, CA 94605

Webb Lynda A. • Cataloger • Memphis-Shelby County Public Library and Information Center • Memphis, TN 38104-4025 • Life

Webb Margaret H. • Urbana, IL 61801

Webb Marion L. • Reference Librarian • King County Library System • Seattle, WA 98109-5191

Webb Nancy L. • Head, Government Documents Dept. • University of Arkansas Mullins Library • Fayetteville, AR 72701 • ACRL LITA GODORT MAGERT

Webb Nancy S. • Library Aide • The Grammer School at Stony Hill • Wilbraham, MA 01095 • AASL

Webb Rebecca H. • Senior Librarian • Salt Lake City Public Library Rose Park Branch • Salt Lake City, UT 84116 • PLA

Webb Sara S. • Assistant Libraries Director • Selby Public Library • Sarasota, FL 33577 • LAMA PLA

Webb Thomasina • President • Twinc • New York, NY 10012

Webb Tyrone T. • Director of Learning Resources • Bevill State Community College Walker Camus • Sumiton, AL 35148

Webb Walter • Editor • H. W. Wilson Company • Bronx, NY 10452

Webb Wendy • Youngstown Board of Education • Youngstown, OH 44503 • AASL

Webb William H. • Phoenix, AZ 85018 • ACRL LITA   *Life*

Webber Barbara • Media Specialist • Holland High School • Holland, MI 49423 • AASL

Webber Clara J. Miss • Claremont, CA 91711 • ALSC PLA   *Continuing*

Webber Cynthia J. • Bridgewater State College Clement C. Maxwell Library • Bridgewater, MA 02325

Webber Denise M. • Director • Acorn Public Library District • Oak Forest, IL 60452 • PLA

Webber Ruth A. • Cataloger • Worcester State College • Worcester, MA 01602 • IFRT

Webber Steve • Virginia Intermont College J. F. Hicks Library • Bristol, VA 24201

Webbert Charles A. • Stone Ridge, NY 12484 • ACRL RASD   *Life*

Webbink Helen L. • McLean, VA 22102-2912 • ACRL ALCTS LITA

Webby Ernest J. Jr. • Director • Brockton Public Library • Brockton, MA 02401 • LAMA PLA   *Life*

Webekind Janet • Librarian • Wedgwood School • Sewell, NJ 08080 • AASL

Weber Anita M. • Kent, OH 44240

Weber Ann T. • Catalog Librarian • University of North Carolina at Charlotte J. Murrey Atkins Library • Charlotte, NC 28223 • ALCTS

Weber Arlene A • Student • Long Island University Palmer School of Library & Information Science • Greenvale, NY 11548 • AASL

Weber Barbara • Bookmobile Coordinator • Fullerton Public Library • Fullerton, CA 92632

Weber Charlotte • Librarian • Pittsburgh Public Schools • Pittsburgh, PA 15213 • AASL

Weber David C. • Stanford University • Stanford, CA 94305-6011 • ACRL LAMA   *Life*

Weber Donald John • Florida Bureau of Library Services for the Blind and Physically Handicapped • Daytona Beach, FL 32119 • ASCLA

Weber Ellenjoy • Head of Childrens Services • Coronado Public Library • Coronado, CA 92118

Weber Field G. Ms. • Playa del Rey, CA 90293

Weber Helen I. • Student • State University of New York at Albany School of Information Science & Policy • Albany, NY 12222

Weber Janet L. • Librarian • Kansas Department Of Corrections Ellsworth Correctional Facility • Ellsworth, KS 67439

Weber Janice E. • Student • University of Northern Iowa Department of Library Science • Cedar Falls, IA 50613-0462 • AASL

Weber Joan • Branch Manager • Spokane Public Library Shadle Branch • Spokane, WA 99205 • PLA

Weber Joseph E. • Student • University of Kentucky College of Library & Information Science • Lexington, KY 40506-0391 • SRRT

Weber Judith E. • Madison, WI 53717

Weber Julie A. • Reference Librarian • Homewood Public Library District • Homewood, IL 60430

Weber Kathleen A. • Reference Librarian • University of Missouri-Kansas City Library • Kansas City, MO 64110-2499

Weber La Donna Riddle • School Librarian • The Mary Erskine School • Scotland EH4 3NT, United Kingdom

Weber Laura R. • Coordinator Young Adult Serv. • Los Angeles Public Library • Los Angeles, CA 90071 • PLA YALSA

Weber Linda C. • Librarian • University of Southern California Doheny Library • Los Angeles, CA 90089-0182 • ACRL

Weber Lisa A. • University of Texas at El Paso Library • El Paso, TX 79968-0582

Weber Lisa B. • Archives Specialist • National Historical Publications and Records Commission (NHPRC) • Washington, DC 20408 • ALCTS LITA

Weber Louise E. • Librarian • Franklin High School • Franklin, WI 53132 • AASL

Weber Mark W. • Director of Staff Services • Kent State University • Kent, OH 44242 • LAMA

Weber Michael A. • Asst Dir & Catalog Librarian • Alvernia College • Reading, PA 19607 • ALCTS

Weber Nancy J. • Student • University of Iowa School of Library & Information Science • Iowa City, IA 52242 • AASL

Weber Nola S. • Reference Librarian • Central Oregon Community College • Bend, OR 97701 • AASL ACRL PLA

Weber Roberta L. • Head of Youth Services • Dunedin Public Library • Dunedin, FL 34698-7998 • ALSC

Weber Ruth A. • E. Windsor, NJ 08520 • ASCLA PLA *Life*

Weber Sandra R. • Graduate Student • Texas Woman's University School of Library & Information Studies • Denton, TX 76204 • ALCTS PLA RASD NMRT

Weber Tamera L. • Student • Florida State University School of Library and Information Studies • Tallahassee, FL 32306-2048

Webermier Sandra L. • Ft. Collins, CO 80526

Webert Jane T. • Assistant Librarian • Nicholls State University Allen J. Ellender Memorial Library • Thibodaux, LA 70310 • ACRL

Webster Alma • Edmonton AB, T5K 2A3 Canada • Continuing

Webster Andrea L. D. • Student • Syracuse University School of Information Studies • Syracuse, NY 13244-4100 • ALSC PLA EMIERT IFRT SRRT

Webster Anne C. • Student • State University of New York (SUNY) School of Information & Library Studies • Buffalo, NY 14260

Webster Connie L. • Director of Technical Services • Dauphin County Library System • Harrisburg, PA 17101 • ALCTS

Webster Deborah K. • Reference Librarian • University of North Carolina Law Library • Chapel Hill, NC 27599 • RASD

Webster Della • Trustee • Warren Public Library • Warren, MI 48092

Webster Heidi P. • Library Media Specialist • Indian River School • Canaan, NH 03741 • AASL

Webster Janet G. • Oregon State University Hartfield Marine Science Center • Newport, OR 97365 • ACRL IFRT

Webster Janice E. • Troy, MI 48084 • AASL

Webster Judith D. • Head, Acquisitions Department • University of Tennessee Library • Knoxville, TN 37996-1000 • ACRL ALCTS

Webster Kirsten N. • High School Librarian (7-12) • Neodesha High School • Neodesha, KS 66757 • AASL YALSA

Webster Lawrence • State Library of Florida Division of Library & Information Services • Tallahassee, FL 32399-0250 • ALTA ASCLA PLA

Webster Margaret C. • Documentation Officer • National Archives of Canada Canadian Postal Archives • Ottawa ON, K1A 0N3 Canada • RASD

Webster Marilyn J. • Senior Librarian Serials Div. • Los Angeles Public Library Serials Division • Los Angeles, CA 90033 • ALCTS

Webster Marva C. • Librarian/Popular Library Dept. • Atlanta-Fulton Public Library • Atlanta, GA 30303 • PLA YALSA

Webster Michael G. • Las Vegas, NV 89119 • RASD

Webster Patricia B. • Assoc Bureau Sch Lib Media Prog • State Education Department Bureau of School Library/ Media Programs • Albany, NY 12234 • AASL

Webster Sarah A. • Volusia County Public Library • Daytona Beach, FL 32124 • LITA

Wechtler Stephen R. • Director • Tenafly Public Library • Tenafly, NJ 07670-2087 • ALSC LAMA RASD IFRT

Wecker Charlene D. • Systems Department • Wayne State University • Detroit, MI 48202 • ACRL ALCTS LITA

Weddell Jeanette • Trustee • White Lake Township Library • White Lake, MI 48383 • ALTA

Wedding Mary Ann • Library Coordinator Elementary • Franklin Community School Corporation • Franklin, IN 46131 • AASL

Weddle Georgia Moe • Orange County Public Library • Santa Ana, CA 92705

Wedge Nancy L. • LTA III • University of South Carolina • Columbia, SC 29208 • AASL

Wedgeworth Robert • Dean • Columbia University School of Library Service • New York, NY 10027 • ACRL ALCTS LITA *Life*

Wedig Eric M. • Head Gov Documents & Micrform • Tulane University Howard-Tilton Memorial Library • New Orleans, LA 70118 • ACRL GODORT MAGERT

Wee Lily K. • Associate Librarian • Quincy College Brenner Library • Quincy, IL 62301-2699

Weech Terry L. • Associate Professor • University of Illinois Graduate School of Library and Information Science • Urbana, IL 61801 • PLA GODORT LRRT *Life*

Weed-Brown Roberta E. • Adult Services Coordinator • Newport Beach Public Library • Newport Beach, CA 92660 • PLA RASD

Weed Joe K. • EBSCO Subscription Service • Birmingham, AL 35201 • LAMA ERT

Weed Katherine S. • Librarian, Office of Counsel • University of Alabama at Birmingham • Birmingham, AL 35294

Weed Lois A. • Assistant Librarian • Taylor University Zondervan Library • Upland, IN 46989 • ACRL

Weed Sarah Stanley • Director • George Hail Free Library • Warren, RI 02885 • PLA

Weedman Judith • Oakland, CA 94611-4719 • AASL ALSC

Weedman Karen L. • Colorado State University William E. Morgan Library • Fort Collins, CO 80523 • LITA

Weedon John • Director • Mifflin County Library • Lewistown, PA 17044

Weeg Barbara E. • Reference Librarian • University of Northern Iowa Donald O. Rod Library • Cedar Falls, IA 50613-3675 • ACRL ASCLA RASD

Weekley Barbara • Shiloh High School • Lithonia, GA 30058 • AASL

Weekly Suzann M. • Director • Saint Thomas Aquinas College Library Lougheed Library • Sparkill, NY 10976 • ACRL EMIERT IRRT

Weeks Ann C. • AASL/YALSA Executive Director • American Library Association • Chicago, IL 60611-2795 • AASL YALSA

Weeks Arnold D. Jr. • Director • Clay County Public Library • Green Cove Springs, FL 32043 • PLA

Weeks Art • Director • Finger Lakes Library System • Ithaca, NY 14850 • PLA

Weeks Barbara K. • Head Librarian • Claymont Public Library • Claymont, DE 19703 • LAMA PLA

Weeks Carolyn L. • Reference Librarian • Pennsylvania State University Heindel Library • Middletown, PA 17057 • ACRL RASD NMRT

Weeks Diane M. • Catalog Librarian • Anoka County Library • Blaine, MN 55434

Weeks Elizabeth H. • Claremont, CA 91711 • Continuing

Weeks Patsy L. • Director • Howard Payne University • Brownwood, TX 76801 • ALSC YALSA

Weeks Thomas E. • Student • Memphis-Shelby County Public Library and Information Center • Memphis, TN 38104-4025 • PLA NMRT

Weems Cheryl M. • Children's Librarian • Palos Verdes Library District • Pls Vrd Pnsla, CA 90274

Weerts Mary Jane • Branch Supervisor • Kern County Library System Eleanor N. Wilson Branch • Bakersfield, CA 93304-5696

Weese Dwain • Richmond, BC, V6Y 1V8 Canada

Weese Florence K. • Coor. of Library Services • Triton College Library • River Grove, IL 60171 • ACRL RASD LIRT

Weessies Paula K. • Asst. Director-Children's Libn. • Georgetown Township Public Library • Jenison, MI 49428

Weglarz Catherine R. • New Brunswick, NJ 08901

Wegley Alberta J. • Pittsburgh, PA 15236

Wegman-French Lysa • Boulder, CO 80302

Wegman Robert L. • Library Administrator • Normal Public Library • Normal, IL 61761

Wegner Lucy • Head, Lib Automation Devlp • University of Southern California Doheny Library • Los Angeles, CA 90089-0182 • ACRL LITA

Wegner Myrna M. • Dir of Lib Med Services • Topeka Public Schools • Topeka, KS 66611 • AASL

Wegner Sandra S. • County Librarian • Midland County Public Library • Midland, TX 79702

Wegscheid Maria • Adult Services Librarian • Bellwood Public Library • Bellwood, IL 60104 • PLA RASD

Wehmeyer Christy • Shell Oil Company • Houston, TX 77001-0587 • ALCTS LITA

Wehmeyer Lillian M. Dr. • Director,Adminstrative Svs. • Norwalk-La Mirada Unified School District • Norwalk, CA 90650 • AASL

Wehner Karey L. • Senior Children's Librarian • San Francisco Public Library • San Francisco, CA 94102 • ALSC

Wehr Sally A. • Piscataway, NJ 08854 • ALSC

Wehrman Basil C. • Nebraska Wesleyan University Cochrane-Woods Library • Lincoln, NE 68504 • IFRT

Wehrmeister Andrea E. • Bloomington, IN 47408-4339

Wei Anna L. • Head Technical Services Dept. • Santa Monica Public Library • Santa Monica, CA 90401 • ALCTS

Wei Betty L. • Trustee • Coudersport Public Library • Coudersport, PA 16915

Wei Karen T. • University of Illinois Library • Urbana, IL 61801

Wei Wei • Science Reference Librarian • University of California Science Library • Santa Cruz, CA 95064 • ACRL

Weibel Kathleen • Delaware, OH 43015 • SRRT

Weibel Marguerite • Instructor/Librarian • Ohio State University Health Sciences Library • Columbus, OH 43210

Weible Arlene A. • Asst. Documents Librarian • Yale University Seeley G. Mudd Library • New Haven, CT 06520 • ALCTS GODORT

Weible Evelyn B. • IMC Director • Northside School • Middleton, WI 53562 • AASL ALSC IFRT

Weiblen Katharine B. • Assistant Dept. Head • Minneapolis Public Library & Information Center • Minneapolis, MN 55401-1992

Weick Jacquolyn • Trustee • Morton Grove Public Library • Morton Grove, IL 60053 • ALTA

Weick Robert J. • Ln. & Media Center Director • Wayne High School Media Center • Fort Wayne, IN 46819 • AASL

Weide Janice • Reference Librarian • Salem Public Library • Salem, OR 97309-5020

Weidman Jeffrey Dr • Art Librarian • Oberlin College Library • Oberlin, OH 44074 • ACRL IFRT

Weidman Julia H. • Lake Bluff, IL 60044

Weigand L. Ann • Extensions Div. Clerk • Anderson Public Library • Anderson, IN 46016

Weigel James • Librarian • Killingly Intermediate School The Cutler Library • Dayville, CT 06241 • AASL RASD

Weigel Jill • Branch Head • Chicago Public Library Hamlin Park Branch • Chicago, IL 60618 • PLA

Weigl Robert W. • Reference Librarian • Avon Lake Public Library • Avon Lake, OH 44012

Weihs Jean • Toronto ON, M4W 2A9 Canada • ALCTS

Weikart Natalie W. • Community Relations Specialist • Prince George's County Memorial Library System • Hyattsville, MD 20782-2098 • LAMA

Weikel Lisa J. • Milwaukee, WI 53211

Weikum James M. • Director • Arrowhead Library System • Virginia, MN 55792 • PLA

Weil Ben H. • Warren, NJ 07059

Weil Beth T. • Head Librarian • University of California-Berkeley Biosciences Library • Berkeley, CA 94720 • ACRL LAMA

Weil Christine • Librarian • Locust Valley Intermediate School Library • Locust Valley, NY 11560 • AASL

Weil Jami L. • Consultant/Continuing Education • Sampson-Clinton Public Library • Clinton, NC 28328 • AASL LITA CLENE LRRT

Weil Kenneth S. • Director • Great Neck Library • Great Neck, NY 11024 • LAMA PLA

Weil Martha S. • Humanities Bibliographer • Humboldt State University Library • Arcata, CA 95521 • ACRL LIRT

Weiland Karen B. • Director • Valdez Consortium Library • Valdez, AK 99686

Weiland Susan D. • Wichita State University Ablah Library • Wichita, KS 67208

Weilant Edward • Science Reference Librarian • Bowling Green State University William Jerome Library • Bowling Green, OH 43403-0175 • ACRL

Weilerstein Deborah E. • Arlington, VA 22204 • ALSC *Continuing*

Weill Marianne C. • Readers Services Coordinator • Greenwich Library • Greenwich, CT 06830 • PLA

Weimar Mary Kennedy • Youth Services Librarian • Alsip-Merrionette Park Library District • Alsip, IL 60658 • ALSC PLA

Weimer Ferne L. • Director • Billy Graham Center Library • Wheaton, IL 60187 • ACRL ALCTS LITA

Weimer Jane C. • Regional Librarian • Port Orange Regional Library Darrel Kreighbaum Memorial Branch • Port Orange, FL 32119-4144 • LAMA PLA

Weimer Linda A. • Portland, OR 97213

Weimer Sally Willson • Library Reference Department • University of California UCSB Library • Santa Barbara, CA 93106-9010 • ACRL LITA RASD

Weimer Susan K. • Greensboro, NC 27408 • LITA

Weimerskirch Philip J. • Providence Public Library • Providence, RI 02903-3283 • ACRL

Weinberg-Kinsey David W. • Executive Director • Switch • Milwaukee, WI 53217 • LITA

Weinberg Bella H. • Professor • Saint John's University Division of Library & Information Science • Jamaica, NY 11439 • ALCTS LITA

Weinberg Belle • Senior Librarian • New York Public Library • New York, NY 10018-2788 • RASD

Weinberg Jo-Anne T. • Young Adult Librarian • Greenburgh Public Library • Elmsford, NY 10523 • YALSA

Weinberg Linda • Cataloger • Adelphi University Swirbul Library • Garden City, NY 11530

Weinberg Pamela M. • Branch Head • Chicago Public Library Oriole Park Branch • Chicago, IL 60656 • PLA

Weinberg Wanda J. • Reference Department • Ohio University Vernon R. Alden Library • Athens, OH 45701-2978

Weinberger Leslie A. • American Family Mutual Insurance Group • Madison, WI 53783

Weinberger Marc S. • Madison, WI 53705 • IFRT

Weindel Kenneth J. • Saint Louis, MO 63116

Weiner Barbara S. • Staff Librarian • Hazelden Foundation • Center City, MN 55012

Weiner Eva • Library Trustee • Skokie Public Library • Skokie, IL 60077-3680 • ALTA PLA EMIERT IFRT

Weiner Herbert • Director • Franklin Square Public Library • Franklin Sq, NY 11010

Weiner Irene C. • Reference Librarian • Pennsylvania State University Pattee Library • University Park, PA 16802

Weiner J. L. • Librarian • Aptakisic Junior High School • Buffalo Grove, IL 60089 • AASL

Weiner Judy Getler • Business,Economics & Law Div. • New York State Judicial Department Appellate Division Law Library • Rochester, NY 14614-2182 • AASL

Weiner Martha J. • Champaign, IL 61821 • ALCTS

Weiner Max • Trustee • Brooklyn Public Library • Brooklyn, NY 11238 • ALTA

Weiner Paula • Library Programs Administrator. • Torrance Public Library • Torrance, CA 90503 • PLA

Weiner Seymour S. • Prof • French Italian • Amherst, MA 01002 • Continuing

Weiner Shelly • Adult Public Services Librarian • Southfield Public Library David Stewart Memorial Library • Southfield, MI 48037-2055 • ALCTS PLA RASD

Weinert Marian • Librarian • United Nations International School • New York, NY 10010 • AASL

Weingand Darlene E. Dr. • University of Wisconsin School of Library & Information Studies • Madison, WI 53706 • PLA CLENE IRRT

Weingart Doris • Head Circulation Services • University of California Rivera Library • Riverside, CA 92517 • ACRL LAMA

Weingart Sandra J. • Student • University of Kentucky College of Library & Information Science • Lexington, KY 40506-0391

Weingarth Darlene • Agana, GU 96910

Weinhaus Judith Kornblum • LMS • Louis Armstrong IS 227 • East Elmhurst, NY 11369 • AASL

Weinheimer James L. • Slavic/Germanic Cataloger • Princeton University • Princeton, NJ 08544-2098 • ACRL

Weinhold David J. • Director • Eastern Shores Library System • Sheboygan, WI 53081 • ALTA LAMA PLA

Weinhold Karin S. • Science & Technology Specialist • Cuyahoga County Public Library Parma Regional • Parma, OH 44129-3199 • PLA RASD SRRT

Weinhold Siegfried • Parma, OH 44130 • GODORT

Weinkauf Rebecca L. • Carson City, NV 89704 • AASL EMIERT IRRT

Weinland Judith K. • Student • Simmons College Graduate School of Library & Information Science • Boston, MA 02115

Weins Leo M. • President • H. W. Wilson Company • Bronx, NY 10452 • ACRL ALCTS LAMA LITA PLA RASD

Weinschenk Andrea • Coordinator of Computer Services • Boston University Mugar Memorial Library • Boston, MA 02215 • ACRL RASD

Weinshenker Ruby B. • Student • Dalhousie University School of Library & Inf. Studies • Halifax NS, B3H 4H8 Canada

Weinstein Carol R. • Toledo, OH 43617

Weinstein Carolyn R. • Student • Queens College Graduate School of Library & Information Studies • Flushing, NY 11367 • NMRT

Weinstein Eileen • Librarian • Midwood High School • Brooklyn, NY 11210 • AASL

Weinstein Ellen B. • Head, Library School Library • Long Island University Palmer School of Library & Information Science • Greenvale, NY 11548

Weinstein Judith L. • Summit, NJ 07901

Weinstein Robert J. • Head Technical Service • Yonkers Public Library • Yonkers, NY 10701

Weinstock Carl • Trustee • Long Beach Public Library • Long Beach, NY 11561 • ALTA PLA

Weinston Irwin S. • Librarian • Queens Borough Public Library Fresh Meadows Branch • Fresh Meadows, NY 11365

Weintraub Benjamin • Highland Park, NJ 08904 • Continuing

Weintraub D. Kathryn • Chicago, IL 60637 • ACRL ALCTS LITA

Weintraub Denise M. • Personnel Officer • University of Chicago Library • Chicago, IL 60637-1502 • ACRL LAMA

Weintraub Fran Greeley • Student • Catholic University of America School of Library and Information Science • Washington, DC 20064 • AASL

Weintraub Frouin Tamara S. • Head,Cataloging Services • University of California-San Diego Biomedical Library • La Jolla, CA 92093 • ALCTS

Weintraub Irwin • Rutgers University Libraries Library of Science & Medicine • Piscataway, NJ 08855-1029 • ACRL IFRT SRRT

Weintraub Janet • Librarian • Jericho Public Library • Jericho, NY 11753 • RASD

Weintraub Susan • Coordinator of Library Services • The Park School • Brooklandville, MD 21022 • AASL

Weintrop Jane • Student • State University of New York (SUNY) School of Information & Library Studies • Buffalo, NY 14260

Weir Barbara J. • Serials Librarian • Swarthmore College Library • Swarthmore, PA 19081

Weir Birdie O. • Director of LRC • Alabama A&M University J.F. Drake Memorial LRC • Normal, AL 35762 • ACRL LIRT SORT

Weir Daryl K. • Hudson, OH 44236

Weir Gail • Product Marketing Manager • GEAC • Markham, ON, L3R 44T5 Canada • LITA

Weir Gay Marie • Boonville High School • Boonville, IN 47601

Weir Janet K. • Asst. Dir. of Public Services • Central Arizona College • Coolidge, AZ 85228 • NMRT

Weir Janice C. • Director of LCR • Missouri Valley College Library • Marshall, MO 65340 • ACRL

Weir Judith • Broward Community College North Campus • Coconut Creek, FL 33066

Weir Katherine M. • Business & Social Sciences Ln. • Illinois State University Milner Library • Normal, IL 61761-0900 • ACRL

Weirich-Faris Crystal L. • Children's Librarian • Indianapolis-Marion County Library Brightwood Branch • Indianapolis, IN 46218-3852 • ALSC

Weirich Nancy • West Lafayette, IN 47906

Weisbard Phyllis Holman • Acting Women's Studies Ln. • University of Wisconsin-Madison Memorial Library • Madison, WI 53706 • ACRL

Weisblatt Maureen • Branch Head • Cleveland Heights-University Heights Public Library University Heights Branch • University Heights, OH 44118 • PLA

Weisbrod David L. • Assistant Professor • Columbia University School of Library Service • New York, NY 10027 • ALCTS LITA LRRT

Weisbrod Elizabeth J. • Auburn University Ralph Brown Draughon Library • Auburn, AL 36849-5606

Weisbroth Stephanie P. • Trustee • Montgomery County Department of Public Libraries • Rockville, MD 20850 • ALTA PLA IFRT

Weisburg Hilda K. • Library Media Special • Sayreville High School Library • Parlin, NJ,08859 • AASL YALSA

Weischedel Elaine Fort • Assistant Director • Turner Free Library • Randolph, MA 02368 • ALSC PLA

Weisel Juanita • Coor. of Reference Services • Lamar University Gray Library • Beaumont, TX 77710 • RASD

Weisenberg Renee • Branch Librarian • Los Angeles Public Library Palisades Branch • Pacific Palisades, CA 90272 • RASD IFRT SRRT

Weisenfels Marjorie A. • St. Louis, MO 63119

Weiser Joan • Student • University of Iowa School of Library & Information Science • Iowa City, IA 52242

Weiser Linda J. • Student • University of Iowa School of Library & Information Science • Iowa City, IA 52242

Weiser Virginia R. • Goleta, CA 93117 • Life

Weisgram Stefanie OSB Sr. • Librarian • College of Saint Benedict Library • Saint Joseph, MN 56374 • RASD

Weiskel Timothy C. Prof. • Harvard Divinity School • Cambridge, MA 02138 • ACRL IRRT NMRT

Weislak Susan L. • Wylie Senior High School • Wylie, TX 75098 • AASL

Weisman Brenda A. • Director of Information Service • Brooklyn Bothanic Garden • Brooklyn, NY 11225 • ACRL

Weisman JoAnne B. • Chelmsford, MA 01824 • AASL

Weisman Kathryn M. • Librarian • Willowbrook School Library Media Center • Glenview, IL 60025 • ALSC

Weisman Shirley • Coordinating Field Librarian • Los Angeles Unified School District • Los Angeles, CA 90017 • AASL

Weisman Suzy • Milwaukee Art & Museum Library • Milwaukee, WI 53202

Weisman Zelda W. • Librarian • William M. Meredith Elementary School • Philadelphia, PA 19147 • AASL

Weismiller David • Trustee • Winnipeg Public Library • Winnipeg MB, R3C 3P5 Canada • ALTA

Weiss Annette B. • Librarian • Baldwin Public Library • Birmingham, MI 48012-3002 • AASL

Weiss Barbara L. • Director • Fallon County Library • Baker, MT 59313 • ALSC PLA IFRT

Weiss Bernice C. • Head Cataloger • Harvard University Countway Library of Medicine • Boston, MA 02115 • ALCTS IFRT

Weiss Beth • Head, Librarian • Yavneh Academy • Paramus, NJ 07652

Weiss Carla A. • Reference Librarian • Rhode Island College • Providence, RI 02908 • RASD

Weiss Cynthia A. • Director • Kendall Young Library • Webster City, IA 50595

Weiss Daniel • Reference Librarian • Bernards Township Library • Basking Ridge, NJ 07920 • RASD IFRT SRRT

Weiss Egon • Carlsbad, CA 92009-7855 • Continuing

Weiss Eleanor • Milford, NH 03055

Weiss Gloria A. • Trustee • North Bellmore Public Library • N. Bellmore, NY 11710 • ALTA

Weiss Henry • Librarian • Palm Springs Public Library • Palm Springs, CA 92262 • PLA

Weiss Howard K. • Cambridge, MA 02138 • RASD LIRT

Weiss Jack • Dean L.R.C. • Elgin Community College • Elgin, IL 60123 • ACRL LAMA LITA

Weiss Janet C. • Librarian • Rider College • Lawrenceville, NJ 08648-3099 • ACRL LIRT

Weiss Jeff J. • A/V Librarian • Muncie-Center Township Public Library • Muncie, IN 47305

Weiss Joan T. • Reference Librarian • Irvington Public Library • Irvington, NJ 07111 • PLA

Weiss Joanne • Librarian • Grove School • Northbrook, IL 60062 • AASL

Weiss Kay • Burlington Public Library • Burlington, IA 52601 • PLA RASD YALSA

Weiss Kristin L. • Newark, OH 43055 • ACRL

Weiss M. Jerry • Trustee • Montclair Free Public Library • Montclair, NJ 07042 • ALTA YALSA IFRT

Weiss Mary S. • Librarian • Dearborn Board of Education • Dearborn, MI 48126 • AASL LITA YALSA

Weiss Miriam R. • New York Public Library Conservation Division • New York, NY 10018 • ALCTS NMRT

Weiss Paul J. • Systems Librarian • National Library of Medicine • Bethesda, MD 20894 • ACRL ALCTS LITA SRRT

Weiss Paula K. • Director • Pekin Public Library • Pekin, IL 61554 • PLA

Weiss Randy • Trustee • Greathall Productions • Benicia, CA 96510

Weiss Ronnie B. • Student • Queens College Graduate School of Library & Information Studies • Flushing, NY 11367

Weiss Stephen C. • Documents/Reference Librarian • Utah State University Merrill Library • Logan, UT 84322-3000 • ACRL GODORT MAGERT

Weiss Susan A. • Librarian • Ballard High School • Seattle, WA 98117 • AASL YALSA

Weiss Wynne E. • Trustee • Indian Trails Public Library District • Wheeling, IL 60090 • ALTA IFRT

Weisse Leah H. • Sheboygan Falls, WI 53085 • ACRL

Weisser Teresa A. • Serials Librarian • Lafayette College Skillman Library • Easton, PA 18042-1797 • ALCTS

Weissinger Nancy J. • Reference Librarian • Teachers College-Columbia University Milbank Memorial Library • New York, NY 10027 • ACRL RASD SRRT

Weissinger Thomas • Africana Center Librarian • Cornell University Library • Ithaca, NY 14853 • ACRL

Weisskopf Vera J. • Head of Circulation Services • Washington University Libraries • Saint Louis, MO 63130-4899 • ACRL LAMA

Weissman Edward S. • Catalog Librarian • Cornell University Library • Ithaca, NY 14853 • ALCTS LITA

Weitendorf Nancy A. • Oxford Lane Library • Oxford, OH 45056 • YALSA

Weitz Jay N. • Quality Control Librarian • Online Computer Library Center (OCLC) • Dublin, OH 43017-3395 • ALCTS LITA IFRT SRRT

Weitzel William Townsend • Ithaca, NY 14850 • Continuing

Weitzen Betty W. • Teacher-Librarian • Steuben Junior High School Library • Milwaukee, WI 53216 • AASL

Welborn Evelyn • Trustee • Anderson County Library • Anderson, SC 29622-4047

Welborn Lynda B. • School Lib Media Consultant • Colorado State Library Department of Education • Denver, CO 80203 • AASL YALSA

Welborn Ronny V. • Student • University of North Carolina Department of Library & Information Studies • Greensboro, NC 27412-5001 • RASD

Welborn Victoria • Head,Science Library • University of California-Santa Cruz Library • Santa Cruz, CA 95064 • ACRL

Welbourne James C. • Assistant Director • Carnegie Library of Pittsburgh • Pittsburgh, PA 15213-4080 • PLA SRRT

Welbourne Penny A.J. • Ln. Clln Devel & Bibl Control • University of Pittsburgh Libraries Falk Library of the Health Sciences • Pittsburgh, PA 15261 • ALCTS LITA

Welburn William C. • Diversity/Spec Servs Librarian • University of Iowa Libraries • Iowa City, IA 52242-1379 • ACRL LITA

Welch Charlotte L. • Head of Technical Services • Bennington College Crossett Library • Bennington, VT 05201 • LITA

Welch Cindy C. • Student Liaison Librarian • Cumberland County Public Library and Information Center • Fayetteville, NC 28301 • YALSA

Welch Donald A. • Bell Helicopter Textron • Fort Worth, TX 76101

Welch Douglas • Assistant Librarian • State University of New York College of Technology • Canton, NY 13617 • ACRL

Welch Eileen L. • Librarian • United States Department of Agriculture APHIS Library • Hyattsville, MD 20782 • ACRL ASCLA LAMA FLRT

Welch Elizabeth Skip • Deer Park, WA 99006

Welch Eric C. • Freeport, IL 61032 • ACRL IFRT

Welch Frances P. • Assistant, Library Automation • Chemeketa Community College • Salem, OR 97309

Welch Isaac • Branch Manager • Alachua County Library District Alachua Branch • Alachua, FL 32615

Welch Janet E. • Coor. of Library User Education • Bowling Green State University William Jerome Library • Bowling Green, OH 43403-0175 • ACRL LIRT

Welch Janet M. • Executive Director • Rochester Regional Library Council • Rochester, NY 14607 • ASCLA LAMA

Welch Jeanie • Reference Librarian • University of North Carolina at Charlotte J. Murrey Atkins Library • Charlotte, NC 28223 • ACRL RASD

Welch Jim C. • Director of System Operations • Metropolitan Library System Capitol Hill Branch • Oklahoma City, OK 73109 • LITA

Welch Jimmie L. • Librarian • Chickasha Public Library • Chickasha, OK 73018 • ALCTS PLA

Welch John D. • Reference Librarian • Virginia Western Community College • Roanoke, VA 24015

Welch John T. II • Assistant State Librarian • North Carolina Department of Cultural Resources State Library • Raleigh, NC 27601-2807

Welch Kate M. • Midwest Sales Manager • R. R. Bowker • New Providence, NJ 07974 • PLA

Welch Linda Hays • Koogler Middle School • Aztec, NM 87410 • AASL

Welch Lynn E. • Student • San Jose State University Division of Library & Information Science • San Jose, CA 95192-0029 • PLA SRRT

Welch Mary H. • Head, Serials Control Unit • University of Kentucky Libraries • Lexington, KY 40506-0039 • ALCTS LITA

Welch Maureen M. • Student • University of Wisconsin School of Library & Information Studies • Madison, WI 53706 • RASD NMRT

Welch Mozelle • Dallas, TX 75235 • AASL

Welch Natalie D. • Ann Arbor, MI 48104

Welch Patricia H • M-Link Librarian • University of Michigan Graduate Library Reference • Ann Arbor, MI 48109

Welch Steven J. • Director • Paterson Free Public Library Danforth Memorial Library • Paterson, NJ 07501 • PLA

Welch Theodore F. • Professor of Japanese Studies • Northern Illinois University • DeKalb, IL 60115-2854 • ACRL LAMA *Life*

Welchman Nicholas • Ref/ser Ln • Eastern Connecticut State University J. Eugene Smith Library • Willimantic, CT 06226 • ACRL

Weld Eleanor V. • Medford, NJ 08055 • Life

Weldon Jean • Serials Cataloger • Duke University William R. Perkins Library • Durham, NC 27706

Weldon Susan L. • Hd, Inf Delivery Svs • Wright State University Paul Laurence Dunbar Library • Fairborn, OH 45435 • ACRL RASD

Weliver Evelyn R. • Interlochen Center for The Arts Academic Library • Interlochen, MI 49643 • AASL

Welken Marion L. • Austin, MN 55912 • Continuing

Welker Betty E. • New York, NY 10024

Welker Beverly J. • Portland, OR 97206

Welker Carol L. • Media Technician • Del Paso Manor School • Sacramento, CA 95821

Welkie Joyce Mrs. • Westville Elementary School • Westville, IN 46391 • AASL ALSC

Weller Ann C. • Deputy Libn. for the Health Sci. • University of Illinois At Chicago Library of the Health Sciences • Chicago, IL 60612 • ACRL LAMA

Weller Cindy Beck • Pillsbury, Madison & Sutro Library • San Francisco, CA 94104 • ACRL

Weller LeAnn C. • Engineering Librarian • University of Kansas • Lawrence, KS 66045-2121 • ACRL LITA RASD

Weller Mary P. • Amherst, NH 03031

Weller Quinn E. • Librarian • Foote, Cone, & Belding • Chicago, IL 60611

Welles Gordon S. • Administration Librarian • Grande Prairie Public Library District • Hazel Crest, IL 60429 • ALCTS LAMA PLA RASD YALSA

Wellheiser Johanna G. • Mgr., Preservation Servs. Dept. • Metro Toronto Reference Library • Toronto ON, M4W 2G8 Canada • ALCTS

Welling Renee S. • Sr. Administrative Librarian • Orange County Public Library Crown Valley Branch • Laguna Niguel, CA 92677

Wellington James K. • Scottsdale, AZ 85257 • PLA

Wellman Gail E. • Roosevelt Elementary School • Binghamton, NY 13901 • AASL

Wellman Joanna S. • Chief Selector • Springfield City Library • Springfield, MA 01103

Wellman Marc G. • Librarian • Louisiana State Penitentiary • Angola, LA 70712

Wellman Vivian D. • Reference Librarian • Church of Jesus Christ of Latter-Day Saints • Salt Lake City, UT 84150

Wellons Pamela R. • Coordinator of Acquisitions Svrs • Radford University John P. McConnell Library • Radford, VA 24142

Wells-Young Jean • Documents Librarian • Winthrop College Ida Jane Dacus Library • Rock Hill, SC 29733 • GODORT

Wells Amy Tracy • Student • University of South Florida School of Library & Information Science • Tampa, FL 33620 • LITA

Wells Catherine A. • East Cleveland, OH 44112 • RASD

Wells Cheryl J. • Media Specialist • Central Middle School • Broken Arrow, OK 74012 • AASL

Wells Corri E.V. • Student • University of North Texas School of Library & Information Sciences • Denton, TX 76203 • ACRL YALSA IFRT SRRT

Wells David B. • Hd Ref Dept & Microcomputer Ctr. • Las Vegas-Clark County Library District Flamingo Library • Las Vegas, NV 89119 • RASD

Wells Doris K. • Branch Librarian • Dekalb County Public Library Scott Candler Branch • Decatur, GA 30032

Wells Dorothy V. • Los Angeles, CA 90024-0711 • ACRL

Wells Elray P. • Librarian • Edison Middle School • Houston, TX 77011

Wells Frances D. • El Paso, TX 79912 • Continuing

Wells James L. • President • Washington County Library • Woodbury, MN 55125 • LAMA LITA PLA

Wells John W. • Garland County Library • Hot Spring National, AR 71901

Wells Karen K. • Sr. Research Analyst • EG & G Rocky Flats • Golden, CO 80402

Wells Kathleen L. • Head, Serials Cataloging Section • Louisiana State University Libraries Troy H. Middleton Library • Baton Rouge, LA 70803-3342 • ALCTS

Wells L. Ada • Napoleon, OH 43545

Wells Lea H • Long Beach, CA 90815 • ACRL LAMA IRRT

Wells Linda Bennett • Keller, TX 76248

Wells Lisa L. • Lindsay, OK 73052 • NMRT

Wells Margaret F. • Reference Librarian • Orange County Library System Orlando Public Library • Orlando, FL 32801-2471 • ALSC PLA

Wells Margaret R. • State University of New York (SUNY) Silverman Undergraduate Library • Buffalo, NY 14260 • ACRL LAMA LIRT

Wells Maria X. Dr. • Curator • University of Texas Ransom Humanities Research Center • Austin, TX 78713 • ACRL IRRT LHRT

Wells Marjan • San Mateo, CA 94403

Wells Mary Kay • Coord. TX Pan Handle Lib System • Amarillo Public Library • Amarillo, TX 79189 • ASCLA PLA

Wells Mary M. • Cataloger • Saint Edwards University Scarborough Phillips Library • Austin, TX 78704

Wells Nancy E. • Assistant Librarian • Price Waterhouse Library • Toronto ON, Canada

Wells Richard T. • Director • Randolph Public Library • Asheboro, NC 27203 • LAMA PLA

Wells Sharon B. • Chicago, IL 60619

Wells Stephanie • Chestatee Regional Library • Gainesville, GA 30505-2399

Wells Stewart L. • Director • Worcester County Library • Snow Hill, MD 21863 • ASCLA PLA

Wells Thomas R. • Course Reserve Librarian • Brigham Young University Harold B. Lee Library • Provo, UT 84602

Wellsman Jennifer A. • AT&T Consumer Products Marketing Information Resource Center • Parsippany, NJ 07054 • RASD

Wellvang James K. • Head of Preservation Department • University of Texas at Arlington • Arlington, TX 76019-0497 • ACRL ALCTS

Welmaker Roland B. • Adjunct Professor • Clark-Atlanta University School of Library & Information Studies • Atlanta, GA 30314-4391 • AASL

Welscher Catherine • Milford, OH 45150

Welsh Barbara W. • Placement Director • Drexel University College of Information Studies • Philadelphia, PA 19104-2875

Welsh Catherine E. • Library Director • Siena College • Loudonville, NY 12211-1462 • ACRL LAMA

Welsh Catherine M. • Librarian • Thomas Dale High School • Chester, VA 23831 • AASL

Welsh Harry E. • Director • Manhattan College Cardinal Hayes Library • Bronx, NY 10471

Welsh Helen C. • Albany, NY 12208

Welsh Lorraine • Hanover, MA 02339

Welsh Sharon L. • Cataloger • Wilmington Area Health Education Center • Wilmington, NC 28402 • ALCTS

Welsh William J. • Bethesda, MD 20814

Welt Gerald • Board Attorney • Las Vegas-Clark County Library District Flamingo Library • Las Vegas, NV 89119 • ALTA

Welter Gloria J. • Media Specialist • South Middle School • Waltham, MA 02154 • AASL YALSA *Life*

Welter Nancy A. • Bothell, WA 98011

Welton Ann I. • Auburn, WA 98001 • YALSA

Welty Barbara Jean • Librarian • West Geauga Middle School • Chesterland, OH 44026

Weltyk Donna M. • Assistant Head of Ad Services • Elmhurst Public Library • Elmhurst, IL 60126

Welzenbach Sandra L. • San Antonio, TX 78250

Wemett Lisa C. • Young Adult Librarian • Fairport Public Library • Fairport, NY 14450 • Life

Wen Sheila • Naperville, IL 60540 • SRRT

Wenberg Lisle • Microform Librarian • California State University Oviatt Library • Northridge, CA 91328-1289

Wendel Clara E. • Orlando, FL 32804 • ALTA PLA *Continuing*

Wendell Dennis C. • Special Materials Cataloger • Iowa State University Library • Ames, IA 50011-2140 • ALCTS

Wendell Diana • Medical Librarian • Community-General Hospital of Greater Syracuse Staff Library • Syracuse, NY 13215

Wender Ruth W. • Norman, OK 73072

Wendlandt Nancy • Sr Hs Ln • Bemidji Public Schools • Bemidji, MN 56601 • AASL YALSA

Wendler Anne V J • Automation Consultant • Lincoln Trail Libraries System • Champaign, IL 61821-1068 • ASCLA LITA

Wendler Robin R. • Harvard University • Cambridge, MA 02138 • ALCTS LITA

Wendling Kathleen A. • Swisher, IA 52338-9726

Wendorf Richard • Librarian • Harvard College Houghton Library-Rare Books & Manuscripts • Cambridge, MA 02138 • ACRL

Wendroff Catriona • Director of General Library • Golden Gate University • San Francisco, CA 94105 • ACRL ALCTS LITA RASD IRRT LIRT

Wendt James M. • Chattanooga-Hamilton County Bicentennial Library • Chattanooga, TN 37402

Wendt Mary Elizabeth • Assoc. Director • New York Public Library • Bronx, NY 10458 • LAMA PLA YALSA SRRT *Life*

Wendt Penny S. • Media Specialist • Spring Valley High School • Columbia, SC 29223 • AASL

Wendtland Frances • Head, Children's & Ext. Servs. • Eugene Public Library • Eugene, OR 97401

Weng Ai-Wei • Student • Indiana University School of Library and Information Science • Bloomington, IN 47405

Weng Cathy • Hd. of Ser. Catlg. Unit • Temple University Paley Library • Philadelphia, PA 19122 • ACRL ALCTS

Weng Yanqiu Florence • Medical Librarian • Jane Phillips Medical Center • Bartlesville, OK 74006

Wenger Carol • Librarian-Aide • Canyon Elementary School Library c/o Lincoln County School District #1 • Diamondville, WY 83116 • AASL

Wenger Jean M. • Chicago, IL 60645

Wenger Larry B. • Law Librarian • University of Virginia • Charlottesville, VA 22901 • ACRL ALCTS LITA RASD GODORT

Wenglin Barbara N. • Adult Services Librarian • White Plains Public Library • White Plains, NY 10601

Wennersten Barbara A. • Goshen Intermediate School • Goshen, NY 10924 • AASL

Wensink Dot • New England Aquarium Library • Boston, MA 02110 • ALCTS ASCLA LAMA

Wentling Mary M. Mrs. • Wilmington Christian School • Hockessin, DE 19707

Wentroth Mary Ann • Oklahoma City, OK 73134 • Continuing

Wentworth Priscilla G. • Clemson University Robert Muldrow Cooper Library • Clemson, SC 29634-3001 • ACRL RASD LIRT

Wentz Deleyne A.R. • Utah State University Merrill Library • Logan, UT 84322-3000 • ACRL

Wenz Robert E. • Member Services Coordinator • Ohio Net • Columbus, OH 43221-3978 • ALCTS LITA LIRT

Wenzel Anne M. • Librarian Pre K-12 • International School of Panama • APO, AA 34002 • AASL YALSA

Wenzel Duane E. • Head Librarian • Bernice P. Bishop Museum Library • Honolulu, HI 96817-0916

Wenzel Kirsten L. • Information Services Librarian • Fountaindale Public Library District • Bolingbrook, IL 60440

Wenzel Lizbeth D. • Hutchison, KS 67504 • AASL LITA

Wenzel Marilyn • Asst. Librarian • Concordia University Klinck Memorial Library • River Forest, IL 60305-1499 • AASL ACRL ALCTS

Wepking Mary A. • Student • University of Wisconsin-Milwaukee School of Library & Information Science • Milwaukee, WI 53201 • RASD IFRT SRRT

Werber Paula F. • Librarian • Gilmour Academy Thomas More Library • Gates Mills, OH 44040 • AASL

Werdine Pamela • Trustee • Michigan City Public Library • Michigan City, IN 46360 • ALTA

Werft Sandra • Osprey, FL 34229-9538

Werking Beth • Children's Services Librarian • Columbus Metropolitan Library • Columbus, OH 43215

Werking Richard Hume • Librarian & Associate Dean • United States Naval Academy Nimitz Library • Annapolis, MD 21402-5029 • ACRL LAMA LHRT

Werley Elaine J • Orefield, PA 18069

Werlin Caryn • Lexington, MA 02173 • AASL

Werling Anita L. • Georgetown, IN 47122

Wermager Paul N. • Honolulu, HI 96825

Wern Katherine A. • Chief Librarian • Chitedze Research Station Library • Lilongwe, Malawi

Werne Kenneth L. • Librarian I • Anaheim Public Library • Anaheim, CA 92805

Werner Christine M. • Fairfax, VA 22032 • FLRT

Werner Edward C. Mr • Librarian • Western New Mexico University • Silver City, NM 88062 • ACRL LAMA *Life*

Werner Elizabeth • Associate Director • Clearwater Christian College Library • Clearwater, FL 34619 • ACRL

Werner Fajardo L. H. • Davis, CA 95616 • ACRL

Werner Gloria • University Librarian • UCLA Library University Research Library • Los Angeles, CA 90024-1575 • ACRL ALCTS LITA

Werner Hedy L. • Branch Manager • Cuyahoga County Public Library Parma Heights Branch • Parma Heights, OH 44130-3086 • PLA

Werner Laura L. • Librarian • Oakland Junior High School • Columbia, MO 65202 • AASL

Werner Susan • Children's Librarian • Maui Library District • Wailuku, HI 96793

Werner Valeria Ines • Student • Univ De Buenos Aires • Buenos Aires, Argentina

Wernimont-Bodnar Alice M. • Student • University of Wisconsin-Madison School of Library & Information Studies • Madison, WI 53706 • IFRT SRRT

Werrell Emily L. • Reference Librarian • Northern Kentucky University Steely Library • Highland Heights, KY 41099-6101 • ACRL

Wert Gary L. • President • Wert Bookbinding, Inc. • Grantville, PA 17028 • ALCTS

Wert Lucille M. Dr • Champaign, IL 61820 • ACRL LAMA *Continuing*

Wertan Theresa L. • Film Cataloger • National Geographic Society Library • Washington, DC 20036 • ALCTS IFRT IRRT

Wertheim Alice H. • Librarian • The Epstein School • Atlanta, GA 30328 • AASL

Wertheim Stephen C. • Trustee • Cleveland Heights-University Heights Public Library • Cleveland Heights, OH 44118

Wertheimer Marilyn L. • Assistant Professor Ref Bibliogr • University of Colorado-Boulder University Libraries • Boulder, CO 80309 • ACRL

Wertsman Vladimir • Senior Librarian • New York Public Library Mid-Manhattan Branch • New York, NY 10016 • EMIERT

Wertz Paula J. • Tulsa Area Library Cooperative • Tulsa, OK 74103 • PLA YALSA NMRT

Wertz Ramonda S. • Trustee • West Hartford Public Library • W. Hartford, CT 06107 • ALTA PLA

Wertz Virginia • Washington, DC 20015

Wesley Gary L. • Elecronic Product Analyst • University Microfilms International • Ann Arbor, MI 48106-1346 • LITA

Wesley Phillip • Los Angeles, CA 90039

Wesley Threasa L. • Reference Librarian • Northern Kentucky University Steely Library • Highland Heights, KY 41099-6101 • ACRL

Wesling Angela G. • Director • El Camino Hospital Library • Mountain View, CA 94039-7025 • ASCLA

Wessells Robert S. • Reference Librarian • United States Navy Naval Education & Training Center Main Library • Newport, RI 02841-5002 • AFLRT FLRT

Wessenberg Kristi L. • Library Supervisor • Regional Audio Visual Department • Oakland, CA 94612 • VRT

Wessing Virginia M. R.N. Med. • Student • Central Missouri State University Library Science & Information Services • Warrensburg, MO 64093 • PLA

Wessling Julie E. • Colorado State University William E. Morgan Library • Fort Collins, CO 80523 • ACRL LITA

Wesson Ruby • Head Librarian • Trinity Bible College Fred Graham Library • Ellendale, ND 58436 • ACRL

Wesson Shirley B. • Valley Park High School Library • Valley Park, MO 63088

West-Twitero Sharilyn I. • Head of Reference • Rapid City Public Library • Rapid City, SD 57701-3630 • PLA GODORT

West Andrew E. • Catalog Librarian • Saint Michael's College • Toronto ON, M5S 1J4 Canada • ACRL ALCTS

West Barbara G. • Oswego Public Library District • Oswego, IL 60543 • PLA

West Camille S. • Student • University of Tennessee-Knoxville Graduate School of Library & Information Science • Knoxville, TN 37996-4330

West Carrie L. • Librarian • AT&T • Brookfield, WI 53005

West Deborah • Head of Reference • Gannon University Nash Library • Erie, PA 16541 • ACRL

West Debra J. • Auburn University at Montgomery • Montgomery, AL 36117-3596 • NMRT

West Diane • Assistant Cataloger • Seton Hall University Law Library • Newark, NJ 07102

West Donna Lynn • Manager, Information Research • Morrison, Haney & Dowd • Columbia, SC 29224-5218 • LITA

West Dorothea C. • Librarian • Agassiz Middle School • Fargo, ND 58102 • AASL

West Elizabeth A. • Cataloger • Costabile Associates Inc • Bethesda, MD 20814 • ALCTS

West Jacqueline W. • Coordinator Learning Resources • Highline School District • Seattle, WA 98166 • AASL LITA EMIERT IFRT LIRT

West Jenifer K. • Georgia College Ina Dillard Russell Library • Milledgeville, GA 31061 • ALCTS

West Jennifer A. • Student • Wayne State University Library Science Program • Detroit, MI 48202 • PLA IFRT

West Jo Rita • Library Assistant • Abilene Public Library • Abilene, TX 79601-5793

West John R. • Assistant Librarian • Austin College Abell Library • Sherman, TX 75090 • ACRL LITA

West Juanita M. • Librarian • Williams Middle School • St. Louis, MO 63113

West Juliet M. • Student • Clarion University of Pennsylvania College of Library Science • Clarion, PA 16214

West Kathy • Business & Economics Ln • University of Alberta • Edmonton AB, Canada • ACRL LAMA RASD

West Linda G. • Assoc. Libn Clln and Cataloging • Harvard University • Cambridge, MA 02138 • ALCTS LITA

West Linda H. • Technical Service Director • Northeastern Oklahoma State University John Vaughan Library-LRC • Tahlequah, OK 74464 • ACRL ALCTS LITA

West Linda L. • West Covina, CA 91791

West Louis G. • Business Librarian • Texas Southern University • Houston, TX 77004 • EMIERT

West Lynn S. • Flower Mound, TX 75067-8435

West Mable A. • Breckenridge Junior High School • Breckenridge, TX 76424 • AASL

West Marian S. • Ann Arbor, MI 48105 • AASL

West Marjory H. • Adult Services Librarian • Phoenix Public Library • Phoenix, AZ 85004 • PLA

West Mark A. • Administrative Librarian • Elk Grove Village Public Library • Elk Grove Village, IL 60007 • LAMA LITA PLA

West Marsha L. • Athens, GA 30605 • AASL NMRT

West Mary B. • Colorado Spring, CO 80909

West Mary L. • Student • University of Kentucky College of Library & Information Science • Lexington, KY 40506-0391 • PLA

West Melanie J. • Librarian II • New Smyrna-Brannon Library • New Smyrna Beach, FL 32168

West Nevenka • Head, Salvic Collections • University of Manitoba Libraries Elizabeth Dafoe Library • Winnipeg MB, R3T 2N2 Canada • ACRL EMIERT

West Sharon M. • Associate Professor/Science Lib • University of Alaska Elmer E. Rasmuson Library • Fairbanks, AK 99775-1005 • ACRL RASD

West Stanley L. • Gainesville, FL 32607 • ACRL *Life*

West Susan J. • M&M/Mars Library Research Services • Hackettstown, NJ 07840-1552 • ASCLA

West Thomas J. • Director • Crawfordsville District Public Library • Crawfordsville, IN 47933 • LIRT

West Timothy J. • Technical Services Librarian • Greenville Public Library • Greenville, MI 48838 • IFRT

Westall John C. • Technical Services Librarian • Illinois Wesleyan University Sheean Library • Bloomington, IL 61702 • ACRL ALCTS

Westberg Susan K. • Quality Control Supervisor • OCLC Online Computer Library Center • Dublin, OH 43017-3395 • ALCTS

Westbrook Betty J. • Bay City, TX 77414 • AASL

Westbrook Bradley D. • Reference Librarian • Columbia University Libraries • New York, NY 10027 • ACRL ALCTS LHRT LRRT

Westbrook Jo Lynn • Coord for Ref & Instr Undergrad • University of Michigan Libraries • Ann Arbor, MI 48109-1205 • ACRL SRRT

Westbrook Leslie Ann • Benicia, CA 94510

Westbrook Mary S. • Central Rappahannock Regional Library Wallace Memorial Library • Fredericksburg, VA 22401 • ALCTS

Westbrooks Allegra M. • Charlotte, NC 28216 • Continuing

Westbury Winnie G. • Director • Calhoun County Public Library • St. Matthews, SC 29135

Westby Barbara M. • Bethesda, MD 20817 • ACRL ALCTS *Life*

Westcott Nancy D. • Head of Technical Services • University of Hawaii William S. Richardson • Honolulu, HI 96822 • ALCTS

Westen Louise M. • Santa Fe, NM 87501-2144 • ASCLA *Continuing*

Westendorf Vicki L. • Scottsdale, AZ 85251 • RASD

Wester Marilyn D. • Portland, OR 97202 • ALCTS *Continuing*

Westerman Jody C. • Youth Services Librarian • Tigard Public Library • Tigard, OR 97223 • IFRT SRRT

Westerman Judy G. • Director of Library & Media Serv • Pittsburgh Public Schools Division of Library Services • Pittsburgh, PA 15226 • AASL

Westerman Robert C. • Seattle, WA 98104

Westermann Mary L. • Assistant Professor • CW Post Palmer Grad L Sch • Brookville, NY 11548 • ACRL

Westermeier Kathryn • Library Media Specialist • W.G. Rice Elementary School • Mt. Holly Springs, PA 17065 • AASL

Westermeyer Beverly R. • SISIS Manager • Smithsonian Institution Libraries • Washington, DC 20540 • LITA

Western Dorothea • Sun City, AZ 85351 • Continuing

Westerveet Catherine C. • Student • University of Pittsburgh School of Library and Information Science • Pittsburgh, PA 15260 • ALSC

Westfall Gloria D. • Foreign Documents Librarian • Indiana University at Bloomington University Libraries • Bloomington, IN 47405 • GODORT

Westfall Marsha • Director • Peoria Heights Public Library • Peoria Heights, IL 61614

Westfall Martha L. • Lebanon, IN 46052

Westfall Michelle C. • Student • State University of New York (SUNY) School of Information & Library Studies • Buffalo, NY 14260 • AASL

Westfall Rebecca A. • Student • University of Oklahoma School of Library & Information Studies • Norman, OK 73019 • PLA

Westfall Sarah E. • Librarian • Washington Elementary School • Kingsport, TN 37660 • AASL NMRT

Westfall Susanne • Director • University of Wisconsin Center Sheboygan Battig Memorial Library • Sheboygan, WI 53081 • ALCTS RASD

Westley Donna • Southwest Michigan Library Coop • Paw Paw, MI 49079 • ACRL LITA CLENE

Westling Ellen R. • Associate Director • Harvard University Countway Library of Medicine • Boston, MA 02115 • ACRL LAMA LITA

Westman Stephen R. • Information/Systems Librarian • Georgia College Ina Dillard Russell Library • Milledgeville, GA 31061 • LITA RASD LIRT

Westmoreland Donald • Computer Sys. Specialist • Jefferson Parish Library • Metairie, LA 70010 • LITA

Westmoreland Kathy W. • School Librarian • Goldsmith Elementary School • Louisville, KY 40220 • AASL

Westmoreland Mary Ellen R. • Director • Oconee County Library • Walhalla, SC 29691

Westmoreland Pat • Trustee • Metropolitan Library System • Oklahoma City, OK 73102 • ALTA PLA

Westneat Helen C. • Yellow Springs, OH 45387

Weston Ann B. • Head, Circulation • Northbrook Public Library • Northbrook, IL 60062 • PLA

Weston Claudia V. • National Agricultural Library • Beltsville, MD 20705-2351

Weston E. Paige • Library Systems Coordinator • University of Illinois at Chicago • Chicago, IL 60680 • ACRL LITA RASD

Weston Eileen E. • Assistant Librarian • University of Delaware Library • Newark, DE 19717-5267

Weston Karen A. • Government Publications Libraria • University of Wisconsin Library and Learning Resources • Whitewater, WI 53190 • GODORT

Weston Ruth E. • Assistant Librarian • District of Columbia Public Library Benning Branch • Washington, DC 20019

Westover Keith R. • Serials Librarian • Brigham Young University School of Library & Information Sciences • Provo, UT 84602 • ALCTS

Westover Nancy W. • School Librarian • Miller Avenue School • Shoreham, NY 11786 • AASL

Westphal Angela J. • Adult Services Librarian • Zion-Benton Public Library District • Zion, IL 60099

Westrum Jane Ann • Head Librarian • Ottawa University Myers Library • Ottawa, KS 66067-3399

Westwood Debra A. • Coor. Deaf & Hard of Hearing • Seattle Public Library • Seattle, WA 98104-1193 • ASCLA

Westwood Karen E. • Outreach Services • University of Minnesota Library • St Paul, MN 55108 • ASCLA

Weswig Kathleen L. • Librarian • Memorial Middle School Library • Albany, OR 97321 • AASL

Wethal Joan H. • Library Director • Oregon Public Library • Oregon, WI 53575

Wetherall Robert • Library Director • Dover Public Library • Dover, DE 19901 • PLA

Wetherbee Louella V. • Dallas, TX 75229-6207 • ACRL ASCLA LITA IRRT

Wetherell Karen S. • Orinda, CA 94563

Wetherill Julie M. • Systems Librarian • Harvard University Library • Cambridge, MA 02138-2901 • LITA

Wetmore Margaret • Reference Librarian • Corvallis-Benton County Public Library • Corvallis, OR 97330-4728 • RASD

Wettig Joan E. • Director of the Library • Bellarmine College Library • Louisville, KY 40205-0671 • ACRL ALCTS LAMA LITA RASD

Wettstein Eric John • Reference Librarian • Valdosta State College Library • Valdosta, GA 31698-0001 • ACRL

Wetzel Bettina Mrs • Myersville, MD 21773 • AASL YALSA *Life*

Wetzel Bonnie • Assistant Catalog Librarian • New Mexico State University Library • Las Cruces, NM 88003-0006

Wetzel Shirley H. • Rice University Fondren Library • Houston, TX 77251-1892

Weweler Johanna P. • Information Librarian • Mount Royal College Library • Calgary AB, T3E 6K6 Canada • ACRL RASD

Wexler Elinor • Media Specialist • Franklin School • East Orange, NJ 07040 • AASL

Wexler Kay F. • Asst Chief, Enhanced Cataloging • Library of Congress • Washington, DC 20541 • ALCTS LAMA RASD

Wexler Lynne S. • Head Librarian • Mother Guerin High School • River Grove, IL 60171 • AASL YALSA IFRT

Weyant Charles E. • Public Services Librarian • Linn-Benton Community College Learning Resource Center • Albany, OR 97321 • ACRL

Weyhe Joan Monica • Juneau, AK 99802-1633

Weymouth Gail • Sherburne Memorial Library • Killington, VT 05751 • PLA

Weymouth Laura H. • Lincoln, NE 68510

Weymuller Margaret A. • Omaha, NE 68114 • Continuing

Whalen Kevin J. • Clinton, NJ 07013 • LITA NMRT

Whalen Margaret E. • Librarian • Saint John Vianney High School • Holmdel, NJ 07733 • AASL

Whalen Mary Grace • Head, of Film Lib & Media Servs • Metropolitan Museum of Art, The Robert Goldwater Library • New York, NY 10028-9962

Whalen Michael B. • Law Librarian • Mayer, Brown, and Platt • Los Angeles, CA 90071-1563 • LITA RASD

Whaley Ingrid E. • Librarian I • Henrico County Public Library Tuckahoe Area Library • Richmond, VA 23229 • PLA RASD

Whaley Janet P. • Marketing Manager/BRS Software • Maxwell Online • McLean, VA 22102 • LITA *Subscribing*

Whaley Janie • Media Specialist • Floyd Central Junior Senior High School • Floyds Knobs, IN 47119 • AASL

Whaley John H. • Head, Special Clln. & Archives • Virginia Commonwealth University • Richmond, VA 23284-2033 • ACRL LITA

Whaley Joyce K. • Brook, IN 47922

Whalin Kathleen D. • Director • Belfast Free Library • Belfast, ME 04915

Wharff Sherrill • Northern Virginia Community College Manassas Campus Library • Manassas, VA 22110

Wharram Polly • Director of Library Services • West London Institute of Higher Education • Middlesex, TW7 5DU, England • ACRL

Wharton Judith A. • Librarian • Allen I. S. D. Vaughan Elementary • Allen, TX 75002 • AASL NMRT

Wharton Mary E.K. • Baltimore, MD 21201-5223 • ACRL ALCTS RASD

Wharton Susan E. • Documents/Reference Librarian • Smith College William Allan Neilson Library • Northampton, MA 01063 • ACRL NMRT

Whatley Shirley G. • Librarian • Wilshire Elementary School • San Antonio, TX 78218

Whealton Frances M. • Director • Kershaw County Library • Camden, SC 29020-3595 • PLA

Wheat Carolyn C. • Trustee • Chalmette Middle School • Chalmette, LA 70043

Wheat Kimberley • Arlington, VA 22204

Wheat Stella I. • Collection Development Librarian • Pine Forest Regional Library • Richton, MS 39476

Wheat Valerie J. • Student • University of Missouri-Columbia School of Library & Informational Science • Columbia, MO 65211 • EMIERT

Wheatley Beverly Glenn • Librarian • Carroll Elementary School • Bernalillo, NM 87004 • AASL ALSC IFRT LIRT

Wheatley Danielle M. • Adult Librarian • San Jose Public Library Rosegarden Branch • San Jose, CA 95126

Wheaton Patricia A. • Librarian • Palo Alto City Library Mitchell Park Branch Library • Palo Alto, CA 94303

Wheeler Albert D. Jr. • Director of Library Services • Georgia Department of Corrections • Atlanta, GA 30303

Wheeler Allison S. • St. Lawrence-Lewis BOCES • Norwood, NY 13668 • AASL

Wheeler Barbara J. • Student • University of Alabama School of Library & Information Studies • Tuscaloosa, AL 35487-0252 • PLA

Wheeler Beverly J. • High School Library Specialist • Roosevelt High School • Washington, DC 20011 • AASL

Wheeler Carol L. • Government Documents Ref Ln • University of Georgia Libraries • Athens, GA 30602 • ACRL GODORT

Wheeler Carolyn J. • Admin Asst Pers Serv • Indianapolis Marion County Public Library • Indianapolis, IN 46206

Wheeler Claudia J. • Downers Grove, IL 60516 • ACRL

Wheeler Deborah J. • Baltimore County Public Library Pikesville Branch • Baltimore, MD 21208 • PLA

Wheeler Fred Barry • Student • Catholic University of America Library Science Library • Washington, DC 20064 • LITA LIRT

Wheeler Genevieve S. • Library Administrator • Saint Bernard Parish Community College Library • Chalmette, LA 70043 • ACRL

Wheeler James M. • Director • Volusia County Public Library • Daytona Beach, FL 32124 • ALCTS ALSC ALTA LAMA LITA PLA RASD YALSA GODORT SRRT

Wheeler Karen E. • School Media Specialist • Central Elementary School • Kissimmee, FL 32743

Wheeler Kathleen S. • Media Specialist • Gardner Road Elementary School library • Horseheads, NY 14845

Wheeler Kathy P • Student • Louisiana State University School of Library & Information Science • Baton Rouge, LA 70803-3290 • PLA RASD

Wheeler Marcella L. • Associate Librarian • Pennsylvania College of Straight Chiropractic • Horsham, PA 19044

Wheeler Mary Ann • School Media Specialist • Livonia Public Schools • Livonia, MI 48154-5474

Wheeler Maurice B. • Staff Devel. & Ln. Recruitment • University of Pittsburgh School of Library and Information Science • Pittsburgh, PA 15260

Wheeler Patricia • Librarian • Kreuzberg Elementary School • APO, AE 09052

Wheeler Robert L. • Naples, FL 33942

Wheeler Susan M. • Baltimore, MD 21213

Wheeler Susan R. • Documents Librarian • King County Library System • Seattle, WA 98109-5191 • GODORT

Wheeler Wayne R. • Nogales/Santa Cruz County Library • Nogales, AZ 85621

Wheelock Anne • Student • University of California Los Angeles Graduate School of Library & Information Science • Los Angeles, CA 90024 • LITA NMRT

Wheelock Elisabeth M. • Reference Librarian • Frederick County Public Library C. Burr Artz Library • Frederick, MD 21701 • PLA RASD

Wheelwright Jessie C. • Honolulu, HI 96816 • Continuing

Whelan Jean A. • Lafayette, CO 80046 • ACRL

Whelan Mary H. • Assoc. Lbrn. & Dir. Tech. Serv. • Wheaton College Wallace Library • Norton, MA 02766 • ACRL ALCTS LITA

Whelan Patricia J. • Saint Clair Shores Public Library • St. Clair Shores, MI 48081 • ALTA

Whelstone Kathryn A. • Media Specialist • Mineral County Schools • Keyser, WV 26726 • AASL

Whenry Jack • Trustee • Metropolitan Library System • Oklahoma City, OK 73102 • ALTA PLA

Wherry Timothy Lee • Head, Librarian • Pennsylvania State University Robert E. Eiche Library • Altoona, PA 16601-3760

Whetzel Sheila A. • Library Branch Manager • Middleburg Library • Middleburg, VA 22117 • PLA IFRT

Whiddon Renee M. • High School Librarian • Merryville High School • Merryville, LA 70653 • AASL

Whiddon Valerie J. • Media Specialist • Hutto Middle School • Bainbridge, GA 31717 • YALSA

Whiffin Jean I. • Preservation Officer • University of Victoria McPherson Library • Victoria BC, V8W 3H5 Canada • ALCTS

Whildin Sara Lou • Head Librarian • Pennsylvania State University Delaware County Campus • Media, PA 19063 • ACRL ALCTS LAMA RASD

Whinihan Jacqueline M. • Troy, MI 48098

Whinnery Linda • Library Media Teacher • Marvin Elementary School • San Diego, CA 92120 • AASL

Whipple Beth • Librarian • Mount View Elementary School • Las Vegas, NV 89115

Whipple Caroline Becker • Director • University of Wisconsin Center Barron County • Rice Lake, WI 54868 • ACRL LAMA

Whipple Helen M. • Head of Technical Services • Minnesota Legislative Reference Library • Saint Paul, MN 55155 • LITA

Whisenant David A. • ILL Coordinator • Tampa Bay Library Consortium • Tampa, FL 33619 • LITA

Whisennand Cynthia S. • Librarian • Irving Independent School District McLivley Elementary School • Irving, TX 75061 • AASL NMRT

Whishant J. Jeanne • Spruce Pine, NC 28444 • RASD

Whisler John A. • Head Periodicals Public Services • Eastern Illinois University Booth Library • Charleston, IL 61920-3099 • ACRL

Whisler Karen L. • Reference • Eastern Illinois University Booth Library • Charleston, IL 61920-3099 • ACRL LITA RASD GODORT

Whisman Linda A. • Director • Southwestern University Law Library • Los Angeles, CA 90005 • ACRL IFRT

Whisner Mary • University of Washington Gallagher Law Library • Seattle, WA 98105

Whistler Alice E. • Asst Ln/Reference & User Edu • Santa Clara University Michel Orradre Library • Santa Clara, CA 95053 • ACRL LAMA RASD

Whitacre Ann • Student • Texas Woman's University School of Library & Information Studies • Denton, TX 76204

Whitacre Cynthia Marie • Mgr., Tech Processing Sect. • Online Computer Library Center (OCLC) • Dublin, OH 43017-3395 • ALCTS *Life*

Whitacre Kathryn L. • Librarian II-Children's • Free Library of Philadelphia • Philadelphia, PA 19103 • ALSC

Whitacre Linda H. • Calhoun, GA 30701-4655 • AASL

Whitacre Randy • Media Specialist • Charlotte High School • Punta Gorda, FL 33950 • AASL

Whitaker Catherine Seitz • University of Pittsburgh Buhl Social Work Library • Pittsburgh, PA 15260 • ACRL

Whitaker Charlene • Student • San Jose State University Division of Library & Information Science • San Jose, CA 95192-0029

Whitaker Diane • Director • Annie Halenbake Ross Library • Lock Haven, PA 17745-1298

Whitaker Dianne • Student • University of Maryland College of Library and Information Services • College Park, MD 20742-4345 • RASD ILERT NMRT

Whitaker Dorothy S. • Floyd Elementary School • Floyd, VA 24091

Whitaker Douglas A. • Deputy Director • Wayne Oakland Library Federation • Wayne, MI 48184 • ASCLA

Whitaker Elaine C. • Head Librarian • Knapp, Petersen & Clarke • Glendale, CA 91203

Whitaker Eleanor • Springfield, MO 65804

Whitaker Jeanne E. • Student • Emporia State University School of Library & Information Management • Emporia, KS 66801

Whitaker Rebecca J. • Information Retrieval Specialist • Indiana Cooperative Library Services Authority (INCOLSA) • Indianapolis, IN 46278 • LITA RASD CLENE

Whitbeck George W. • Indiana University School of Library and Information Science • Bloomington, IN 47405 • ACRL GODORT LRRT

Whitcomb Laurie Ann • Reference Librarian • Pasadena Public Library • Pasadena, CA 91101

Whitcomb Marjorie • Lakewood, OH 44107

Whitcraft Margaret • Lititz, PA 17543

White Aisha • Pittsburgh, PA 15221 • ALSC EMIERT SRRT

White Ann T. • Director • Spartanburg School District #3 • Glendale, SC 29346 • AASL LIRT

White Anne B. • Media Specialist • Southern Elementary School • Greensboro, NC 27406 • AASL

White Barbara • Librarian • Akron-Summit County Public Library McDowell Branch • Akron, OH 44313 • ALSC

White Barbara • Library Director • Coweta Public Library • Coweta, OK 74429

White Barbara B. • Children's Librarian • Frederick County Public Library C. Burr Artz Library • Frederick, MD 21701 • ALSC PLA

White Beryl Elaine • Librarian • Wilson,Elser,Moskowitz et al • New York, NY 10170

White Beverly C. • Belmont Senior High School • Los Angeles, CA 90026 • AASL

White Billie K. • Assistant Librarian • District of Columbia Public Library Martin Luther King Memorial Library • Washington, DC 20001 • PLA YALSA NMRT

White Brenda H. • Coordinator Library Media • Danbury Public Schools • Danbury, CT 06810 • AASL

White Bryant Prudence • Librarian • Alabama A&M University J.F. Drake Memorial LRC • Normal, AL 35762

White Candace K. • Ann Arbor, MI 48103 • ALCTS

White Candice Wagner • Anson County Schools • Wadesboro, NC 28170

White Carol A. • Reference Librarian • Georgia Institute of Technology Price Gilbert Memorial Library • Atlanta, GA 30332-0900 • ACRL RASD

White Carol J. • Head Cataloger • University of Wyoming • Laramie, WY 82071 • ALCTS LITA

White Carol M. • Student • University of Washington Graduate School of Library and Information Science • Seattle, WA 98195 • LITA RASD IFRT ILERT SRRT

White Carolyn H. • Chapel Hill, NC 27516

White Cecil R. • Director • Saint Patrick's Seminary • Menlo Park, CA 94025 • ACRL SRRT

White Charles R. • Edu Cons Library Media • State Department Education Vocational Technical Schools • Middletown, CT 06457 • AASL IFRT IRRT

White Charlotte • Washington, DC 20016

White Cheryl B. • Student • San Jose State University Division of Library & Information Science • San Jose, CA 95192-0029

White Cheryl D. • Children's Librarian • Mililani Public Library • Mililani, HI 96789

White Cindy • Novi Meadows Elementary School • Novi, MI 48374

White Civia A. • Charlotte, NC 28270-5943

White Cynthia • Head Librarian • East Point Public Library • East Point, GA 30344

White Deborah H. • School Media Specialist • Waterville Junior Senior High School • Waterville, NY 13480 • AASL YALSA

White Don B. • Manager General Reference • Public Library of Charlotte & Mecklenburg County • Charlotte, NC 28202 • PLA RASD

White E. Carolyn • INT Dir Instr Media Services • Gettysburg College Musselman Library • Gettysburg, PA 17325-1493 • ACRL

White Earle • Trustee • Prince George's County Memorial Library System • Hyattsville, MD 20782-2098 • ALTA

White Eda • Children's Services Coordinator • Los Angeles Public Library • Los Angeles, CA 90071 • ALSC

White Edna Mae • Librarian • Cedar Valley College Library • Lancaster, TX 75146-3799 • ACRL

White Edwin C. Jr. • Information Specialist • Rutland County Solid Waste District • Rutland, VT 05701-5915 • ACRL

White Elaine N. • Gig Harbor, WA 98332-9129

White Elaine Raybon • Mahomet, IL 61853

White Elizabeth • Dir., Historical Res. Ctr. • Houston Academy of Medicine Texas Medical Center Library • Houston, TX 77030 • ACRL LAMA

White Emilie C. • Government Documents Librarian • Mississippi State University Mitchell Memorial Library • Mississippi State, MS 39762 • GODORT

White Eric H. • Chief AV Division • District of Columbia Public Library Martin Luther King Memorial Library • Washington, DC 20001 • VRT

White Frank • Automation Librarian • University of Windsor • Windsor ON, N9B 3P4 Canada • LITA

White Helen I. • Director of LRC • Glenbard South High School Library • Glen Ellyn, IL 60137 • AASL

White Herbert S. • Distinguished Professor • Indiana University School of Library and Information Science • Bloomington, IN 47405 • ACRL LRRT

White Howard D. • Professor • Drexel University College of Information Studies • Philadelphia, PA 19104-2875

White Howard S. • Editor, LTR • American Library Association • Chicago, IL 60611-2795

White Jacqueline R. • Media Specialist • Mercer County High School • Harrodsburg, KY 40330 • AASL

White James William • Director • La Crosse Public Library • La Crosse, WI 54601 • ALCTS ALTA LAMA LITA PLA RASD YALSA

White Jane G. • Bement, IL 61813

White Janet F. • Ann Arbor, MI 48105 • ACRL RASD *Life*

White Janice S. • Librarian • Ritchie County Public Library • Harrisville, WV 26362 • PLA

White Jeffery S. • Longmont, CO 80501

White John B. • Dir of Learning Resources • Gadsden State Community College • Gadsden, AL 35999 • ACRL

White Joyce G. • John A. Shaw Elementary School • New Orleans, LA 70117

White Judy B. • Roseville, MN 55113 • AASL

White Julia F. • Library Director • Beals Memorial Library • Winchendon, MA 01475

White Kathy Lynn • Dearborn Department of Libraries Henry Ford Centennial Library • Dearborn, MI 48126 • LAMA PLA

White Katsue • Student • University of California-Los Angeles (UCLA) • Los Angeles, CA 90024-1450

White Kristen M. • Alexandria, VA 22302 • SRRT

White Laurel L. • Hd, Circulation & Automation • Boise Public Library • Boise, ID 83702-0715

White Lawrence A. • Brazoria County Library System Alvin Branch • Alvin, TX 77511

White Lely K. • Cataloger • University of Dallas William A. Blakley Library • Irving, TX 75062 • IRRT

White Lisa M. • Branch Supervisor • Ontario City Library South Ontario Branch • Ontario, CA 91761-6479 • PLA YALSA NMRT

White Loisann Dowd • Assistant Librarian • Getty Center Resources Collections • Santa Monica, CA 90401 • ACRL RASD

White Louise S. • Cataloger • Atlanta-Fulton Public Library • Atlanta, GA 30303 • LITA

White Luella Evelyn • Kent, WA 98031

White Lynda S. • Assistant Fine Arts Librarian • University of Virginia Fine Arts Library • Charlottesville, VA 22903 • ACRL

White Margaret L. • Student • University of Alabama School of Library & Information Studies • Tuscaloosa, AL 35487-0252 • PLA RASD

White Margaret S. • Reference & Systems Ln. • Columbia College Library • Chicago, IL 60605

White Marianne D. • Librarian • Henrico County Public Library Tuckahoe Area Library • Richmond, VA 23229 • PLA

White Marianne Swanson • Head Librarian • Coopersville District Library • Coopersville, MI 49404

White Marion I. • Dallas, TX 75240 • ACRL LIRT NMRT

White Marsha • Gainesville, FL 32604

White Martha L. • Whittle Communications • Knoxville, TN 37902 • IFRT

White Martha Murray • Librarian • Indian River High School • Frankford, DE 19945

White Marvin G. • President • Plastic Window Products Company • Highland Park, IL 60035 • AASL ALCTS

White Mary H. • Robbins Library Junior Library • Arlington, MA 02174

White Mary Lou • Wright State University College of Education & Human Services • Dayton, OH 45435 • AASL ALSC IFRT IRRT

White Maureen • University of Houston at Clear Lake Learning Resources Specialist Program • Houston, TX 77058 • AASL ALSC YALSA IRRT

White Meryl • Reference Librarian • Cornell University • Ithaca, NY 14853-5301

White Myra • Acting Assisting Director • California State Polytech University • Pomona, CA 91768 • ACRL ALCTS

White Pam • Science Reference Librarian • University of Oregon • Eugene, OR 97403

White Patrice S. • FPO, AE 09645

White Patricia A. • Ithaca, NY 14850 • ACRL RASD

White Patricia H. • St. Charles, MO 63301 • PLA

White Paul A. • Assistant Director • Mid-Continent Public Library • Independence, MO 64050 • LAMA PLA

White Philip C. • Business Librarian • Durham County Library • Durham, NC 27701

White Phillip M. • San Diego State University Library • San Diego, CA 92182-0511 • LIRT

White Priscilla Moxom • Los Angeles, CA 90039 • ALSC

White Robert L. • Assistant Director • University of California-Santa Cruz Library • Santa Cruz, CA 95064 • LAMA

White Robert W. • Executive Director • BCCLS Computer Consortium Inc. • Hackensack, NJ 07601 • ALCTS LAMA LITA PLA

White Ruth M. • Asheville, NC 28803 • RASD YALSA *Life*

White Sandra G. • Librarian • Rippon Elementary School • Woodbridge, VA 22193 • AASL

White Sharon • Media Specialist • Northwest High School • Indianapolis, IN 46224 • AASL

White Sherry J. • Head Public Services • Boynton Beach City Library • Boynton Beach, FL 33435

White Sumner Mr. • City Librarian • New Haven Free Public Library • New Haven, CT 06510 • LAMA LITA PLA

White Teresa G. • Law Library Manager • O'Melveny & Myers Law Library • Los Angeles, CA 90071-2899 • LAMA LITA

White Tiffany C. • Student • San Jose State University Division of Library & Information Science • San Jose, CA 95192-0029 • ASCLA

White Timothy E. • Worth, IL 60482

White Trudy W. • Librarian • E.G. Ross Elementary School • Albuquerque, NM 87109 • AASL ALSC

White Velma M. • Prichard, AL 36610

White Vivian B. • Alabama Department of Corrections • Montgomery, AL 36130 • ASCLA PLA

White Wallace W. • Director • Flesh Public Library • Piqua, OH 45356 • PLA

White Wendolyn A. • Hopkinsville, KY 42240

White William C. • Assistant Librarian • Lindbergh High School John Dressel Library • Saint Louis, MO 63126 • AASL

White Wilma E. • Franklin Elementary School • Junction City, KS 66441 • AASL

Whited Diane D. • Librarian • Samford University Library • Birmingham, AL 35229

Whited Jane Kathryn • Librarian • Manchester High School • North Manchester, IN 46962 • AASL

Whitehair David E. • Product Support Specialist • OCLC Online Computer Library Center • Dublin, OH 43017-3395 • LITA

Whitehead James M. • Reference Librarian • University of Georgia Libraries • Athens, GA 30602

Whitehead Jennifer • Head Librarian • Wesley Privette Memorial Library • Bailey, NC 27807

Whitehead Marcia E. • Reference Librarian • University of Richmond Boatwright Library • Richmond, VA 23173 • ACRL IFRT LIRT

Whitehead Margaret J. • Brooksville, KY 41004 • PLA YALSA

Whitehead Olive F. • Philadelphia, PA 19139 • Continuing

Whitehill Margaret E. • Base Librarian • Langley Air Force Base • Langley AFB, VA 23665 • AFLRT FLRT

Whitehouse Barbara • Librarian • Missisquoi Valley High School • Swanton, VT 05488 • AASL

Whitehouse Lynn K. • Branch Manager • San Diego Public Library La Jolla Branch • La Jolla, CA 92037-4802 • PLA

Whitehouse Peggy D. • Gretna, LA 70056 • ALCTS LITA

Whitehurst Nancy K. • Student • University of South Florida School of Library & Information Science • Tampa, FL 33620 • ALCTS LITA

Whiteley Sandra • Editor, Reference Books Bulletin • American Library Association • Chicago, IL 60611-2795

Whiteman D. Bruce • Head of Rare Books & Spec Cllns • McGill University Libraries • Montreal PQ, H3A 1Y1 Canada • ACRL

Whitener Betty Lynn • Librarian HSRC • University of North Carolina • Chapel Hill, NC 27599-3902

Whitesell David R. • Student • Columbia University School of Library Service • New York, NY 10027 • ACRL

Whiteside Jane M. • Head of Children's Services • Fountaindale Public Library District • Bolingbrook, IL 60440 • ALSC

Whitesides William L. • Consultant • Virginia State Library & Archives • Richmond, VA 23219 • ASCLA PLA CLENE   *Continuing*

Whitfield Mary W. • E.A. Poe Intermediate School • Annandale, VA 22003

Whitford Robert H. • New York, NY 10033 • ACRL RASD   *Continuing*

Whitham Bruce Alan • Student • University of Western Ontario School of Library & Information Science • London ON, N6G 1H1 Canada • ACRL RASD NMRT

Whiting Elaine M. • Branch Director • Somerset County Library Peapack-Gladstone Branch • Peapack, NJ 07977

Whiting Eleanor M. • Washington, DC 20009

Whiting Elizabeth J. • Librarian • National Institute of Standards & Technology • Gaithersburg, MD 20899 • ALCTS

Whiting James H. • Richmond, VA 23226

Whiting Peter C. • Student • Rosary College Graduate School of Library & Information Science • River Forest, IL 60305 • ALCTS GODORT

Whiting Ralph L. • Supervisor of Media Ed. • School District of La Crosse • La Crosse, WI 54601 • AASL

Whitlatch Jo Bell • Interim Library Director • San Jose State University Clark Library • San Jose, CA 95192-0028 • ACRL LAMA RASD LRRT

Whitley Bernice • Grand Rapids Community College Library • Grand Rapids, MI 49503 • ACRL LAMA LITA

Whitley Ellen L. • Library Media Specialist • Chelsea High School • Chelsea, MA 02150 • AASL

Whitley Katherine M. • Reference Librarian • University of Arizona Library • Tucson, AZ 85721 • ACRL LITA RASD

Whitlock Cheryl I. • Librarian • University of Saskatchewan Library • Saskatoon SK, S7N 0W0 Canada • ACRL

Whitlock Donna L. • Librarian • Wando High School Media Center • Mount Pleasant, SC 29464 • AASL YALSA

Whitlow Charles G. • Boonton, NJ 07005 • LITA IFRT SRRT

Whitlow Cherrill M. • Librarian/Films Director • Rio Grande High School Library • Albuquerque, NM 87105 • LAMA

Whitman M. Janice • Library Media Coordinator • Shawnee Heights Unified School District #450 • Tecumseh, KS 66452-9797 • AASL

Whitman Mary Beth • Media Specialist • Burtsfield Elementary School • Lafayette, IN 47906 • AASL
Whitmer Sandra L. • Chestatee Regional Library Blackshear Place Library • Gainesville, GA 30507
Whitmill Glenna • Librarian • Shiawassee County Library • Corunna, MI 48817 • PLA
Whitmire Joan • School Librarian • Cullen Middle School • Corpus Christi, TX 78412 • AASL
Whitmore Marilyn P. • Coor. of Library Instruction • University of Pittsburgh Hillman Library • Pittsburgh, PA 15260 • ACRL RASD LIRT
Whitmore Menandra M. • Librarian • Department of Defense Pentagon Library • Washington, DC 20310 • AFLRT
Whitmore Sharon S. • Rougemont, NC 27572
Whitnah Wendy L. • Westlake, OH 44145 • ALSC
Whitney Byron V. • Head of Bibliographic Control • Clarkson University Educational Resources Center • Potsdam, NY 13699-5590 • ACRL ALCTS LITA GODORT
Whitney Dorotha L. • Elyria, OH 44035 • Continuing
Whitney Gretchen • Assistant Professor • University of Arizona • Tucson, AZ 85721 • ALCTS LITA IFRT
Whitney Karen A. • Librarian • Agua Fria Union High School Library • Avondale, AZ 85323 • AASL YALSA IFRT LIRT
Whitney Katie M. • Student • Louisiana State University School of Library & Information Science • Baton Rouge, LA 70803-3290 • RASD SRRT
Whitney Loretta A. • Homewood, IL 60430
Whitney M. Jane • Assistant Librarian • University of Wisconsin Center Baraboo-Sauk County Library • Baraoo, WI 53913 • ASCLA
Whitney Marla J. • Systems Librarian • University of Hawaii Thomas Hale Hamilton Library • Honolulu, HI 96822 • LITA IFRT SRRT
Whitney Rebecca • Student • Southern Connecticut State University School of Libray Science & Instructional Technology • New Haven, CT 06515
Whitney Roberta H. • Co-Head, Children's Services • J.V. Fletcher Library • Westford, MA 01886
Whitney Rosemary R. • Reference Librarian • Simsbury Public Library • Simsbury, CT 06070 • RASD
Whitney Sharron • Stanley County School District School District 57-1 • Fort Pierre, SD 57532 • AASL
Whitney Virginia • Blue Hill, ME 04614 • ACRL
Whitney William T. • Yorba Linda, CA 92686
Whitson Donna L. • Assistant Professor • University of Wyoming • Laramie, WY 82071 • AASL ACRL LAMA LITA PLA
Whitson Joyce G. • Library Media Specialist • Manhattan High School • Manhattan, KS 66502 • AASL YALSA
Whitson Katharine A. • Student • University of Washington Graduate School of Library and Information Science • Seattle, WA 98195
Whitson Kathryn A. • Librarian • Westfield High School • Westfield, IN 46074 • AASL
Whitson Randolph L. • Assistant Director • Tennessee University Library at Chattanooga • Chattanooga, TN 37403 • ACRL LAMA
Whitson William L. • Acting Head, Ref./Clln Devlp. • University of California-Berkeley Moffitt Undergraduate Library • Berkeley, CA 94720 • ACRL LITA
Whitt Alisa J. • Computer Assisted User Serv Ln • Emory University Libraries Robert W. Woodruff Library • Atlanta, GA 30322-2870 • LITA SRRT
Whitt Kathleen M. • Circulation Librarian • Beloit Public Library • Beloit, WI 53511
Whitt Nancy S. • Head of Cataloging • University of Texas at Dallas University Library • Richardson, TX 75083-0643 • ALCTS LITA
Whitt Susan F. • Lumberton, NC 28358
Whittaker Brenda L. • Collection Development Librarian • National Library of Medicine • Bethesda, MD 20894 • ALCTS
Whittaker Edward L. • Assistant Director • Bucks County Free Library • Doylestown, PA 18901 • LAMA LITA PLA
Whittaker Joan E. • Curator • Queens Borough Public Library • Jamaica, NY 11432
Whittaker Martha A. • Marketing Manager • Colorado Alliance of Research Libraries • Denver, CO 80210 • LITA
Whittaker Martha E. • Student • University of California-Berkeley School of Library & Information Studies • Berkeley, CA 94720 • IFRT
Whittaker Mary Silva • Librarian • Boeing Support Services • Seattle, WA 98124-2207 • ACRL
Whittaker Scott • Long Beach, NY 11561
Whitten Joseph N. Dr • Madison, MS 39110-9452 • ACRL ALCTS *Life*
Whitten Robin • Trustee • Portland Public Library • Portland, ME 04101
Whitten Virginia W. • Austin, TX 78705
Whittenburg Robert • Morristown Hamblen High School West Library • Morristown, TN 37814

Whittier Margaret G. • Interlibrary Services Coor. • Emory University Libraries Robert W. Woodruff Library • Atlanta, GA 30322-2870 • ACRL RASD
Whittier Ruth E. • Concord, NH 03301 • Continuing
Whittinghill JoEllen • Student • Sam Houston State University Department of Library Science • Huntsville, TX 77341-2236
Whittington Becky • Library Associate II • Lorain Public Library South Branch • Lorain, OH 44055 • ALSC
Whittington Christine A. • Hum & Soc Sciences Ref Ln • University of Maine Raymond H. Fogler Library • Orono, ME 04469 • ACRL RASD GODORT
Whittington Erma P. • Durham, NC 27705 • ACRL *Continuing*
Whittle Ann Harding • Northern Kentucky University Steely Library • Highland Heights, KY 41099-6101 • ACRL
Whittle Susan S. • Director • Southwest Georgia Regional Library Gilbert H Gragg Library • Bainbridge, GA 31717 • PLA
Whittlesey-First Karen L. • Hd., Copy Catlg/Database Mgr. • Harvard Law School Library • Cambridge, MA 02138 • ACRL ALCTS SRRT
Whitton Lynda F. • Counselor (Lib. II) • Corpus Christi Public Library • Corpus Christi, TX 78401 • PLA
Whitwell Helen • Director • St. Joseph High School Library • Lakewood, CA 90713
Whitworth E. Andra • Student • University of Texas at Austin Graduate School of Library & Information Sciences • Austin, TX 78712-1276
Whorton Barbie • Advisory Board Member • Anaheim Public Library • Anaheim, CA 92805 • ALTA PLA IFRT
Whyte Dee • Librarian • Foothills Elementary School • Buckley, WA 98321 • AASL
Whyte John P. Jr. • Acting Director of Library Media • Watertown High School • Watertown, MA 02172 • AASL
Whyte Susan • Linfield College Northup Library • McMinnville, OR 97128 • ACRL
Wibbens John P. • Trustee • Saint Joseph County Public Library • South Bend, IN 46601 • ALTA
Wibbing William H. • Acquisition Librarian • Washington University Libraries • Saint Louis, MO 63130-4899 • ALCTS LAMA
Wiberley Stephen E. Jr • University of Illinois at Chicago University Library • Chicago, IL 60680 • ACRL ALCTS LRRT
Wicher Linda J. • Director of Youth Serrvices • Highland Park Public Library • Highland Park, IL 60035 • ALSC YALSA
Wick Constance S. • Librarian • Harvard College Kummel Library of Geological Sciences • Cambridge, MA 02138 • ACRL MAGERT
Wick Kristen • Lib. Supv., Head of Reference • Contra Costa County Library • Pleasant Hill, CA 94523 • PLA RASD SRRT
Wick Robert L. • University of Colorado at Denver Auraria Library • Denver, CO 80204 • LITA NMRT
Wick Sharon L. • Ann Arbor, MI 48104
Wick Susan K. • Atlantic County Library Brigantine Branch • Brigantine, NJ 08203
Wickberg Sandra W. • Reference Librarian • University Center at Tulsa • Tulsa, OK 74106 • NMRT
Wicke Robert E. • Detroit, MI 48202 • IFRT
Wickens Alan E. • Young Adult Librarian • Manoa Public Library • Honolulu, HI 96822 • YALSA
Wicker Leonora I. • Merritt Island High School • Merritt Island, FL 32952 • AASL
Wicker Maxine • Northwest Regional Library Systems • Sioux City, IA 51102 • ALTA
Wicker W. Walter • Library Director • Louisiana Technical University Prescott Memorial Library • Ruston, LA 71270-9985 • ACRL
Wickersham M. Ann • Proj Coor Family Res Oppor Guide • Clearwater Public Library • Clearwater, FL 34623 • PLA
Wickey Eva M. • Librarian • West Elementary School • Arcadia, FL 33821 • ALSC
Wickey Marjorie J. • Bakersfield, CA 93306 • AASL
Wickham Irene • Tahlequah, OK 74465
Wickham Jane M. • Southfield, MI 48034 • PLA RASD *Continuing*
Wickham Myrtice M. • Port Jervis, NY 12771 • Continuing
Wickizer Alice F. • Document Librarian • Indiana University • Bloomington, IN 47405 • ACRL GODORT
Wicklund Bonnie • Glenallen Elementary School • Silver Spring, MD 20902 • AASL
Wicklund Joyce J. • Minneapolis, MN 55403 • AASL YALSA *Life*
Wicklund Martha J. • Minneapolis, MN 55427
Wicklund Shirley P. • Director • Pima Community College • Tucson, AZ 85709
Wickremeratne Swarna • Cataloging Librarian • Loyola University E.M. Cudahy Memorial Library • Chicago, IL 60626 • ALCTS

Wicks Charlene T. • Library Department Chairman • Baltimore County Schools Pikesville High School • Baltimore, MD 21208 • AASL
Wicks Charlotte M. • Media Specialist • West Junior High School West Memphis School District • West Memphis, AR 72301 • AASL
Wicks Jerry R. • Administration • Glenbrook North High School • Northbrook, IL 60062 • AASL
Wicks Scott • Cornell University Library • Ithaca, NY 14853-5301
Wickwire Peggy L. • Children's Services • Canby Public Library • Canby, OR 97013 • ALSC
Widden Nancy • Library Assistant • Phoenix Public Library Palo Verde Branch • Phoenix, AZ 85031 • PLA
Widder Agnes Haigh • Reference Librarian • Michigan State University Libraries • East Lansing, MI 48824-1048 • ACRL ALCTS RASD
Widdicombe Richard P. • Director • Stevens Institute of Technology S.C. Williams Library • Hoboken, NJ 07030
Widem Barbara D. • Children's Librarian • Montgomery County Department of Public Libraries Twinbrook Branch • Rockville, MD 20851-1598 • ALSC PLA EMIERT *Continuing*
Widener Michael • Archivist/Rare Books Librarian • University of Texas Tarlton Law Library • Austin, TX 78705-5799 • ACRL
Widener Sarah A. • Austin, TX 78746 • Continuing
Widenmann Elizabeth • Assistant • Columbia University Libraries Butler Library • New York, NY 10027 • ACRL ALCTS GODORT IRRT SRRT
Widera Michele A. • Documents Librarian • University of Utah Marriott Library • Salt Lake City, UT 84112-1179 • GODORT SORT
Widhu Sarah • Harrington School Lexington Public School • Lexington, MA 02173 • AASL
Widman Rudy • Director of LRC • Indian River Community College • Fort Pierce, FL 34981-5599 • ACRL LAMA LIRT NMRT
Widmer Susan Louise • Librarian • Honolulu Community College Library • Honolulu, HI 96817-4598
Widner Jack • Edinboro University of Pennsylvania Baron-Forness Library • Edinboro, PA 16444
Widner Michael L. • Indianapolis, IN 46201 • RASD
Widom Rodeane L. • Director • Glendale Public Library • Glendale, AZ 85302 • PLA
Widrich Marlene R. • Coral Springs, FL 33071 • ACRL PLA RASD FLRT
Wiebe Margaret A. • Hesston College • Hesston, KS 67062 • ACRL
Wieben Sue A. • Coordinator • Indianhead Library System • Eau Claire, WI 54701 • RASD
Wiecking Emma • Mankato, MN 56001 • Continuing
Wieczorek Valeria • Librarian • Saint David Catholic School • Davie, FL 33328 • AASL
Wiedenhoefer Joyce C. • Branch Librarian • Cleveland Public Library Eastman Branch • Cleveland, OH 44111
Wieder Judith • Lake Lanier Regional Library Peachtree Corners Branch • Norcross, GA 30092
Wiederhorn-Baltrunas Wendy • BHA-Getty Art History Information Program • Williamstown, MA 01267
Wiedower Madeline C. • Library Asst./Circulatior Supv. • University of San Diego Copley Library • San Diego, CA 92110
Wiegand Robert H. • Reference Librarian • Long Beach City College • Long Beach, CA 90808
Wiegand Wayne A. • Professor • University of Wisconsin • Madison, WI 53706 • IFRT LHRT LRRT SRRT
Wieghorst-Warden Mary • Barber Elementary School • Phillipsburg, NJ 08865 • AASL
Wiehn John F. • Librarian • General Datacomm Inc. Engineering Library • Middlebury, CT 06762-1299 • LAMA
Wielage Beth P. • Reference Librarian • DeKalb College Central Campus Library • Clarkston, GA 30021-2396
Wieland Fred J. • Selden, NY 11784 • AASL
Wieland Margaret A. • Valley City State University Allen Memorial Library • Valley City, ND 58072
Wielenberg Peggy L. • Director of Information Services • Prairie School • Racine, WI 53402 • LAMA LITA ILERT SORT
Wielhorski Karen H. • Texas A & M University Sterling C. Evans Library • College Station, TX 77843-5000 • ACRL LAMA RASD
Wieman Jean M. • Director Continuing Education • Fullerton Union High School • Fullerton, CA 92634 • AASL IFRT
Wieman Lisa B. • Student • University of Maryland College of Library and Information Services • College Park, MD 20742-4345 • AASL YALSA IFRT
Wiemann Gail • Acting Reference Coordinator • Alameda County Library System • Fremont, CA 94538 • PLA RASD
Wiemers Eugene L. • Asst Univ Libn for Clln Mgmt • Northwestern University Library • Evanston, IL 60208-2300 • ACRL ALCTS

Wiencek Maria • Director, Devel & PR • Rutgers University Libraries Archibald Stevens Alexander Library • New Brunswick, NJ 08903

Wiencke Patricia M. • Reference Librarian • Kaneohe Public Library • Kaneohe, HI 96744

Wiener Sylvia B. • Forest Hills, NY 11375

Wiersma Nancy L. • Board Member • Crestwood Public Library District • Crestwood, IL 60445

Wierum Ann R. • Cannon Beach, OR 97110-0807

Wiese Claudette C. • Parkwood Senior High School • Monroe, NC 28170 • AASL

Wiest Natalie H. • Library Director • Texas A & M University at Galveston • Galveston, TX 77553-1675 • ACRL

Wiggaert Thea C. • Student • University of Maryland College of Library and Information Services • College Park, MD 20742-4345

Wiggin Frances M. • Director • Bedford Public Library • Bedford, NH 03102

Wiggin Kendall F. • State Librarian • New Hampshire State Library • Concord, NH 03301

Wiggins Beacher J. E. • Chief, Shared Cataloging Div. • Library of Congress • Washington, DC 20541 • ALCTS

Wiggins Carol A. • Supervisor Media Services • Lane Education Service District • Eugene, OR 97402 • AASL ALSC

Wiggins Catherine • Librarian • Chapin Memorial Library • Myrtle Beach, SC 29577 • LAMA PLA

Wiggins Christine Barwick • Librarian • Neuse Regional Library System • Kinston, NC 28501

Wiggins Emilie V. • Washington, DC 20008 • Continuing

Wiggins Janet K. • Librarian • Oakland Public Library • Oakland, CA 94612

Wiggins Karen A. • Manager, Science-Technology Dept • Toledo-Lucas County Public Library • Toledo, OH 43624 • PLA

Wiggins Mary Lou • Dallas, TX 75205

Wiggins Sarah A. • Student • University of Pittsburgh School of Library and Information Science • Pittsburgh, PA 15260

Wiggins Theresa S. • Assoc. Ln. for the Med. Coll. • Medical College of Pennsylvania F.A. Moore Library of Medicine • Philadelphia, PA 19129 • ACRL ALCTS LITA RASD *Life*

Wight Barbara L. • Los Angeles, CA 90008 • ALTA *Continuing*

Wightman Clifford B. Mr. • Tucson, AZ 85710 • LAMA PLA *Continuing*

Wighytman Konda • Media Director • Simle Junior High School Media Center • Bismarck, ND 58501 • LITA

Wigley Mary Lou • City Librarian • South Pasadena Public Library • South Pasadena, CA 91030 • LAMA PLA

Wiig Linda • Honolulu, HI 96816 • ACRL

Wiist Stephen • Head of Access Serv. & Technical • Columbia University Libraries • New York, NY 10027 • ACRL ALCTS

Wiita Mae M. • Phoenix, AZ 85015

Wikander Lawrence E. • Williamstown, MA 01267 • Continuing

Wikoff Ruth S. • Associate Director Emerita • University of Houston Libraries • Houston, TX 77204-2091 • Continuing

Wiktorowicz Paula • Children's Librarian • Boston Public Library Roslindale Branch • Roslindale, MA 02131-2517 • ALSC

Wilbarger Jeannine L. • Manager Circulation Center • Toledo-Lucas County Public Library • Toledo, OH 43624 • PLA

Wilber Mary D. • Librarian • Zula B. Wylie Library • Cedar Hill, TX 75104 • PLA RASD

Wilbert Gail Beth • Milwaukee, WI 53215

Wilbur Helen L. • New York, NY 10036 • LITA

Wilbur Janice A. • Jefferson, MA 01522

Wilbur Sharon Faye • Librarian • United States Army Commander, HQ, TEXCOM • Fort Hood, TX 76544-5065 • FLRT *Life*

Wilburn Hugh • Head of Public Services • Harvard University Lorb Design Library • Cambridge, MA 02115 • ACRL RASD SRRT

Wilburn Lou Mrs. • Trustee • South Carolina State Library • Columbia, SC 29211 • ALTA

Wilburn Marion • Sheridan College of Applied Arts and Technology • Oakville ON, L6H 2L1 Canada • ALCTS LITA

Wilburn Robert C. • President Board of Trustees • Carnegie Library of Pittsburgh • Pittsburgh, PA 15213-4080

Wilburne Karlynn • Student • Wayne State University Library Science Program • Detroit, MI 48202

Wilcha Rhea • Delaware Valley Middle School • Milford, PA 18337-9441

Wilcher-Roberts Easter • Fort Lauderdale, FL 33313-2249 • PLA RASD

Wilcox-Owens Amy • Brown County Junior High School • Nashville, IN 47448 • AASL

Wilcox Barbara E. • West Branch, IA 52358 • AASL ALSC

Wilcox Connie D. • Branch Librarian • Patrick County Library • Stuart, VA 24171 • LAMA PLA

Wilcox Donald L. • University of Michigan Libraries • Ann Arbor, MI 48109-1205

Wilcox Dorothy • Librarian • Lichen Year Round Elementary • Citrus Heights, CA 95621

Wilcox Elizabeth A. • Librarian • Philadelphia Maritime Museum Library • Philadelphia, PA 19106 • ALCTS

Wilcox Janet M. • Student • Emporia State University School of Library & Information Management • Emporia, KS 66801

Wilcox John G. • University of Georgia Libraries • Athens, GA 30602 • GODORT

Wilcox Lynn • Senior Law Cataloger • University of Maine School of Law Donald L. Garbrecht Library • Portland, ME 04102

Wilcox Margaret C. • Rochester, NY 14618 • Continuing

Wilcox Nancy L. • Managing Ed., Highsmith Press • Highsmith Co., Inc. • Fort Atkinson, WI 53538-0800 • PLA ILERT

Wilcox Susan R. • Student • University of Tennessee-Knoxville Graduate School of Library & Information Science • Knoxville, TN 37996-4330 • AASL ALSC YALSA

Wilcox Terry L. • Interlibrary Loan Librarian • Wisconsin Reference & Loan Library • Madison, WI 53716

Wilcoxen Patricia L. • Head of Circulation Services • University of Chicago Library • Chicago, IL 60637-1502 • LAMA

Wild Cynthia D. • Student • University of Arizona Graduate Library School • Tucson, AZ 85721 • ALSC PLA IFRT NMRT

Wild Judith W. • Deputy, Head Tech Services • Brooklyn College Library • Brooklyn, NY 11210

Wild Larry • Head Librarian • Providence College & Seminary • Otterburne, MB, R0A 1G0 Canada • ACRL ALCTS LAMA RASD

Wild Valerie G. • St. Louis Park, MN 55416 • RASD

Wildberger Mary E. • Mountain View, CA 94040 • AASL ALSC

Wilde John H. • Erskine College Library McCain Library • Due West, SC 29639

Wilde Lucy E. • Reference Librarian • Kansas State University Libraries • Manhattan, KS 66506-7166 • ACRL RASD

Wilde Miriam E. • Hillyard Branch Library • Spokane, WA 99207

Wilder Alison H. • Rochester, NY 14617

Wilder Charlotte P. • Director of Media Services • Irmo High School Library • Columbia, SC 29212 • AASL YALSA

Wilder David T. • Medford, NJ 08055 • ACRL ALSC IRRT *Life*

Wilder Duane E. • Partner • Wilder Deem Associates • New York, NY 10014 • ACRL ALTA *Life*

Wilder Katherine Miss • Ashtabula, OH 44004 • Continuing

Wilder Lee • Computer Resource Specialist • Virgin Islands Dept. of Education District of St. Croix (MLS Office) • Christiansted, VI 00821 • AASL ACRL AFLRT

Wilder Nancy S. • Video Librarian • Electronic Data Sys Corp • Dallas, TX 75230

Wilder Roberta B. • Assistant Technical Serv Chief • East Central Georgia Regional Library Augusta-Richmond County • Augusta, GA 30901 • ALCTS

Wilder Shirley K. • Safety Harbor Public Library • Safety Harbor, FL 34695 • ALSC RASD

Wilder Stanley J • A.D. Administrative Services • Louisiana State University Libraries • Baton Rouge, LA 70803 • LAMA RASD

Wildin Nancy Y. • Librarian • Seattle Public Library • Seattle, WA 98104-1193 • LITA

Wilding Richard • Mid-Continent Public Library • Independence, MO 64050

Wilding Thomas L. • Associate Director • Massachusetts Institute of Technology Libraries (MIT) • Cambridge, MA 02139 • ACRL LAMA SRRT

Wildman Lana D. • Williamsport, IL 62693-0404

Wildman Linda • Periodical Librarian • Andrews University James White Library • Berrien Springs, MI 49104-1400

Wile Raymond R. • Flushing, NY 11358 • ACRL RASD *Life*

Wilen Rosamond L. • Senior Librarian • Teaneck Public Library • Teaneck, NJ 07666 • LITA

Wilensky Sharon R. • Librarian • San Francisco Public Library Richmond Branch • San Francisco, CA 94118 • EMIERT

Wiler Linda L. • Florida Atlantic University Library • Boca Raton, FL 33431

Wiles-Young Sharon • Serials Manager • Lehigh University Libraries Linderman Library 30 • Bethlehem, PA 18015-3067 • ACRL

Wiles E. M. • Oklahoma City, OK 73114 • Life

Wiles Timothy J. • Reference Librarian • University of Northern Iowa Donald O. Rod Library • Cedar Falls, IA 50613-3675

Wiley Cathy J. • Technical Librarian • United States Navy Research Lab • Washington, 20375-0000 • LITA

Wiley Helen Cannon • Librarian • Katherine Burke School • San Francisco, CA 94121 • ALSC

Wiley Jim • Trustee • Thomas Jefferson Library • Jefferson City, MO 65101 • ALTA

Wiley Judy E. • Librarian • San Jose Unified Schools • San Jose, CA 95126

Wiley Lynn • Head of Circulation • Boston College O'Neill Library • Chestnut Hill, MA 02167 • ACRL LAMA LITA

Wiley Neata • Librarian • Russellville High School • Russellville, KY 42276 • AASL

Wilford Jane M. • London SW5 0ET, England

Wilford Valerie J. • Executive Director • Illinois Valley Library System • Pekin, IL 61554 • AASL ASCLA LAMA CLENE

Wilgus Anne B. • Assoc. Dir., Head of Reference • North Carolina Wesleyan College Elizabeth Braswell Pearsall Library • Rocky Mount, NC 27804

Wilhelm Diane • System Automation Manager • Suburban Library System • Burr Ridge, IL 60521 • PLA

Wilhelm Diane B. • Chatham-Effingham-Liberty Regional Library (CEL) • Savannah, GA 31499-4301

Wilhelm Judith L. • Librarian • Forcey Christian School • Silver Spring, MD 20904 • AASL

Wilhelm Kristen M. • Student • State University New York at Buffalo School of Inf. & Library Studies • Buffalo, NY 14260 • ACRL RASD GODORT IFRT LHRT

Wilhelm Rebecca C. • Librarian Media Specialist • Tillamook School District #9 • Tillamook, OR 97141 • IFRT

Wilhelme Judith A. • Head, Serials Acquisitions • University of Michigan Libraries • Ann Arbor, MI 48109-1205

Wilhelmi Ilse Miss • Columbus, OH 43212 • Continuing

Wilhite Flora R. • Director • Sterling Municipal Library • Baytown, TX 77520 • LAMA PLA

Wilhite Jeffrey M. • Student • University of Oklahoma Libraries University Libraries • Norman, OK 73019 • SRRT

Wilhite Marjorie G. • Serials Librarian • University of Iowa Library • Iowa City, IA 52242 • ACRL ALCTS LITA

Wilhite R. Margaret • Saint Charles Parish Library • Luling, LA 70070

Wilhoit Karen H. • Head of Cataloging • Wright State University College of Education & Human Services • Dayton, OH 45435 • ALCTS NMRT

Wilinski Grant W. • Atlantic Community College Daniel Leeds Library • Mays Landing, NJ 08330 • ACRL

Wilke Diane • Head Librarian • Ottawa Township High School • Ottawa, IL 61350

Wilke Ekkehard-Teja P. • Director • Institute for the Study of 19th Century Europe (ISNCE) • Riverside, IL 60546

Wilke Janet Stoeger • Head of Curriculum/Nonbook • University of Nebraska at Kearney Library • Kearney, NE 68849 • ACRL

Wilke Mary • Chicago, IL 60618 • PLA

Wilken Ann J. • Everly, IA 51338-0300

Wilkens Carol D. • Chicago, IL 60634

Wilkens Elizabeth B. • Assistant Executive Director • Capitol Region Library Council • Windsor, CT 06095 • PLA

Wilker Garnetta K. • Eugene, OR 97405

Wilkerson Warner B. • Librarian • California State University Hayward Library • Hayward, CA 94542 • ALCTS

Wilkes Adeline W. • Professor Associate. • Texas Woman's University School of Library & Information Studies • Denton, TX 76204 • ACRL ALCTS LITA LRRT

Wilkes Helen H. • University of Georgia Libraries • Athens, GA 30602 • ACRL ALCTS LITA

Wilkes Lilly C. • Titusville, FL 32781 • Continuing

Wilkes Pamela • Dialog Information Service Inc. • Palo Alto, CA 94304 • ACRL RASD

Wilkie Sandra M. • Coordinator, Children's Services • Farmington Community Library • Farmington Hills, MI 48334 • ALSC LAMA PLA

Wilkie Wilma K. • Hawaii Legislative Reference Bureau Library • Honolulu, HI 96813 • GODORT

Wilkin Binnie Tate • Los Angeles, CA 90043 • AASL ALSC EMIERT

Wilkin Phillip W. • Social Science Bibliographer • University of Pittsburgh Hillman Library • Pittsburgh, PA 15260 • ACRL

Wilkin Refna M. • Executive Editor Children's Bks. • Putnam & Grosset Book Group • New York, NY 10016 • ALSC YALSA IFRT

Wilkins Alice L. • Director of Library Services • Sandhills Community College • Pinehurst, NC 28374 • ACRL LAMA

Wilkins Barratt • Director • State Library of Florida Division of Library & Information Services • Tallahassee, FL 32399-0250 • ASCLA LAMA PLA

Wilkins Carla L. • Librarian • Gibbs Memorial Library • Mexia, TX 76667

Wilkins Cary • Clemson University • Clemson, SC 29632 • ACRL IFRT

Wilkins Jonathan C. • Dept. Hd., Circulation • Orange County Library System Orlando Public Library • Orlando, FL 32801-2471

Wilkins Katherine G. • Student • Rosary College Graduate School of Library & Information Science • River Forest, IL 60305 • PLA RASD NMRT SRRT

Wilkins Lois E. • Media Serv/AV/Library Supv. • Sussex County Vocational Tech. Keller Library • Sparta, NJ 07871 • AASL

Wilkins M. Lesley • Hd,Rare Bks, Spec Clln, Archives • American University in Cairo Library • Cairo, Egypt • ACRL ALCTS LITA IRRT LHRT

Wilkins Patricia A. • Branch Manager • Bucks County Free Library Lower County Branch • Levittown, PA 19057 • PLA

Wilkins Rebecca A. • Children's Book Buyer-Manager • W.W. Wickel Book Company Anderson Bookshops • Naperville, IL 60563 • ALSC

Wilkins Walter R. • Asst. Health Sciences Librarian • University of Illinois at Chicago College of Medicine • Peoria, IL 61656 • RASD LIRT LRRT

Wilkinson Billy R. • Baltimore, MD 21201 • ACRL LAMA *Life*

Wilkinson Carroll Wetzel • Interim Head, Circulation Servs. • West Virginia University Charles C. Wise Jr. Library • Morgantown, WV 26506 • ACRL LAMA SRRT

Wilkinson Catherine L. • Head of Cataloging Librarian • Appalachian State University Carol Grotnes Belk Library • Boone, NC 28608 • ALCTS LITA *Life*

Wilkinson David W. • Coordinator Comp. Aided Ref. • California State University-Los Angeles John F. Kennedy Memorial Library • Los Angeles, CA 90032-8300

Wilkinson E. H. • Turramurra NSW 2074, Australia • LITA

Wilkinson Fleeta M. • Media Coordinator • Merrick-Moore Elementary School • Durham, NC 27704

Wilkinson Frances C. • University of New Mexico General Library • Albuquerque, NM 87131

Wilkinson Gayle T. • School Librarian • Travis Junior High School 1600 Finley Rd. • Irving, TX 75062 • AASL

Wilkinson Helen • Ypsilanti, MI 48197 • Continuing

Wilkinson Holley • Corona Del Mar, CA 92625 • ALTA

Wilkinson J. P. Dr. • Professor • University of Toronto Faculty of Library & Information Science • Toronto ON, M5S 1A1 Canada • LRRT

Wilkinson Patrick J. • Documents & Maps Librarian • University of Northern Iowa Donald O. Rod Library • Cedar Falls, IA 50613-3675 • ACRL RASD GODORT MAGERT SRRT

Will Barbara H. • Network Coordinator • California State Library Library Development Services Bureau • Sacramento, CA 95814-3324 • ASCLA

Will Donna Riley • Librarian • Jackson Intermediate School • Falls Church, VA 22042 • AASL

Will Marie • Chicago, IL 60641 • ALSC *Continuing*

Will Mary-Kay • Atlanta, GA 30315 • ALSC PLA YALSA

Willard Anne H. • Killingworth, CT 06417

Willard Beth R. • Los Angeles, CA 90025

Willard Jeffrey A. • Evanston, IL 60202

Willard Louis Charles • Librarian • Harvard University Andover-Harvard Theological Library • Cambridge, MA 02138 • ACRL ALCTS

Willard Robert S. • Director Government Markets • Mead Data Central Inc. • Dayton, OH 45401 • LITA RASD FLRT GODORT

Willard Roxanne J. • Student • State University of New York at Buffalo School of Information Library • Buffalo, NY 14260 • AASL ALSC IFRT SRRT

Willard Sylvia J. • Branch Manager • San Luis Obispo City-County Library Atascadero Branch • Atascadero, CA 93422

Willard Wallace Mrs. • Librarian • Trinity Episcopal Day School • Natchez, MS 39120

Willeford Norma J. • Trustee • Chicago Ridge Public Lib • Chicago Ridge, IL 60415

Willems Wanda • Laramie, WY 82070 • AASL

Willemse Jean D. • Head-Adult Serv & A-V Serv • Dearborn Department of Libraries Henry Ford Centennial Library • Dearborn, MI 48126 • PLA

Willemse John • University Librarian • University of South Africa Library • Pretoria, South Africa • ACRL

Willenbrink Angela S. • Children's Assistant • Public Library of Cincinnati & Hamilton County-Bonham Branch • Wyoming, OH 45215 • ALSC

Willer Kenneth H. • Medical Resource Facility of Los Gatos • Los Gatos, CA 95030

Willerson Pamela J. • Adairsville, GA 30103

Willes Karen D. • Administrative Librarian • Sunnyvale Public Library • Sunnyvale, CA 94088-3714 • PLA

Willett Charles • Gainesville, FL 32608 • ACRL ALCTS RASD IFRT IRRT SRRT

Willett Charles Perry • Reference Librarian • Indiana University at Bloomington University Libraries • Bloomington, IN 47405-9998 • ACRL

Willett Dorothy S. Jr • Vice-Chair Board of Trustees • Durham Public Library • Durham, CT 06422 • ALTA LAMA PLA

Willett Holly G. • Texas Woman's University School of Library & Information Studies • Denton, TX 76204 • ALSC PLA LHRT LRRT

Willett Mary A. • Clearwater, FL 34616 • Continuing

Willett Suzanne N. • Library-Media Specialist • Francis Junior High School • Washington, DC 20037 • AASL

Willey Darro C. • Deputy Director • Broward County Division of Libraries Broward County Library • Fort Lauderdale, FL 33301 • LAMA PLA

Willey Heather M. • New York, NY 10021-3994 • LITA RASD

Willey Kayla • Library Automation Coordinator • Brigham Young University Harold B. Lee Library • Provo, UT 84602 • ACRL

Willey Sharon • Director • Cass County Public Library • Harrisonville, MO 64701 • LAMA PLA

Willhite Kathleen • Head Librarian • Vicksburg District Library • Vicksburg, MI 49097

Willhite Sherry • University of California-San Diego • La Jolla, CA 92093-0175 • ACRL

Willhoff Jacquelyn L. • Reference Librarian • Highland Park Public Library • Highland Park, IL 60035 • RASD

Williams-Capone Dayna L. • Student • Austin College Abell Library • Sherman, TX 75090 • ACRL

Williams-Garner Dolores B. • Public Services Librarian • Houston Community College • Houston, TX 77004 • ACRL RASD LIRT

Williams-Henry Rhonda K.C. • Media Cataloger • Alabama A&M University J.F. Drake Memorial LRC • Normal, AL 35762

Williams-Jenkins Barbara • Dean • South Carolina State College Miller F. Whittaker Library • Orangeburg, SC 29117 • ACRL LITA

Williams-Stewart Gladys • Bronx Community College • Bronx, NY 10453

Williams-Zivkovich Jean Diane • Librarian • Hennepin County Library Edina Library • Edina, MN 55424 • ALSC LAMA PLA RASD CLENE IRRT

Williams Ada M. • Augusta, GA 30906 • Continuing

Williams Allyson • Adult Services Librarian • Campbell County Public Library • Rustburg, VA 24588 • RASD

Williams Amanda • Berkeley, CA 94702 • ALTA *Continuing*

Williams Andrea L. • Curriculum Materials Librarian • Midwestern State University George Moffett Library • Wichita Fls, TX 76308 • ALSC LHRT

Williams Angela K. • Colorado Springs, CO 80907

Williams Anita L. • Media Specialist • DuBose Middle School • Summerville, SC 29483 • AASL ALSC

Williams Ann • Fort Lauderdale, FL 33301 • ERT

Williams Ann E. • Cataloger • University of Kansas Library • Lawrence, KS 66045-2800 • ACRL ALCTS

Williams Ann Lemke • Plano, TX 75024

Williams Ann W. • Director • Alachua County Library District • Gainesville, FL 32601 • PLA

Williams Ann W. • Student • University of California-Los Angeles (UCLA) • Los Angeles, CA 90024-1450 • ALCTS RASD LHRT

Williams Annette M. • State University of New York at Buffalo School of Information Library • Buffalo, NY 14260 • ACRL

Williams Armina E. Crosby • Cornwells Heights, PA 19020 • Continuing

Williams Arthur C. • Library Principle Associate • Atlanta-Fulton Public Library West Hunter Branch • Atlanta, GA 30314

Williams Avery W. • Chicago, IL 60649 • Continuing

Williams Barbara A. • Program Manager • MAXIMA Corporation • Lanham, MD 20706 • ACRL ALCTS LITA

Williams Barbara L. • Director of Library Services • Tarrant County Jr College Library NW Campus • Fort Worth, TX 76179 • ACRL

Williams Barbara O. • Librarian • Queens Borough Public Library • Jamaica, NY 11432

Williams Benjamin D. • Student • Ashtabula County District Library Geneva Branch Library • Geneva, OH 44041

Williams Benjamin R. Ph.D. • Director • Beaver College • Glenside, PA 19038

Williams Betty H. • Reference Librarian • Lander College Jackson Library • Greenwood, SC 29649

Williams Billee C. • Librarian II • Phoenix Public Library Saguaro Branch • Phoenix, AZ 85008 • PLA

Williams Bonnie E. • Principal Librarian • New York Public Library Donnell Library Center • New York, NY 10019 • PLA

Williams Brian K. • Automated Systems Manager • Multnomah County Library Central Branch • Portland, OR 97205 • LITA

Williams Brian R. • Student • Wayne State University Arthur Neef Law Library • Detroit, MI 48202

Williams Brian W. • Wichita, KS 67208 • ACRL

Williams Carol • Instructional Materials Center • Vacaville, CA 95688 • AASL ALSC

Williams Carole L. • Branch Libraries Mgr. • Saint Paul Public Library • St. Paul, MN 55102 • LAMA PLA

Williams Carole Spahn • Director • Reuben Hoar Library • Littleton, MA 01460 • PLA

Williams Catherine L. • Interlibrary Loan/Reference Ln. • Siena College • Loudonville, NY 12211-1462 • ACRL LIRT NMRT

Williams Charles M. • Technical Services Librarian • American Dietetic Association Natl Ctr for Nutrition & Diet. • Chicago, IL 60600-0995 • LITA

Williams Cherry • Sheridan County Fulmer Public Library • Sheridan, WY 82801

Williams Claibourne George • Bluefield State College Hardway Library • Bluefield, WV 24701

Williams Clarica • Morehead, KY 40351 • Continuing

Williams Connie H. • Kenilworth Junior High School Library • Petaluma, CA 94952

Williams Cynthia D. • Madison, CT 06443 • ALSC

Williams Danby O. • Director • Clark County Public Library • Winchester, KY 40391 • LAMA PLA

Williams David L. • Reference Librarian • Chicago Public Library • Chicago, IL 60605 • IFRT IRRT SRRT

Williams Dawn • Jefferson Parish Library Department • Metairie, LA 70010

Williams Delmus E. • Dean of Univ. Libraries • University of Akron Bierce Library • Akron, OH 44325-1706 • ACRL ALCTS LAMA

Williams Diana B. • Delafield, WI 53018

Williams Diana D. • Public Services Support Div. • Wichita Public Library • Wichita, KS 67202 • ALCTS

Williams Diane • Syracuse, NY 13203

Williams Diane N. • University of South Alabama • Mobile, AL 36688 • LITA

Williams Dinah H. • Trustee • Ouachita Parish Public Library • Monroe, LA 71201 • ALTA

Williams Donna M. • Student • Lake Bluff Public Library • Lake Bluff, IL 60044

Williams Doris • Setauket, NY 11733 • ACRL

Williams Doris V. • AV Librarian • Lisle Library District • Lisle, IL 60532 • VRT

Williams Dorothy J. • Children's Librarian • Peabody Library • Columbia City, IN 46725 • ALSC

Williams Dorothy L. • Assistant Director • Philadelphia School District Pedagogical Library • Philadelphia, PA 19103

Williams Douglas E. • Retrospecitive Conversion Spec • OCLC Incorporation • Dublin, OH 43017 • ALCTS

Williams Eddie A. • Director of Automated Serv. • University of Southern Mississippi Cook Memorial Library • Hattiesburg, MS 39406-5053 • ACRL LAMA LITA

Williams Edna J. • Miami, FL 33150

Williams Edna L. • Library Director • Tuskegee University • Tuskegee Institute, AL 36088 • ACRL LAMA

Williams Edwin E. • Cambridge, MA 02138 • ACRL ALCTS

Williams Edwin E. • Naval Regional Librarian • Naval Regional Library • Groton, CT 06349-5052 • PLA AFLRT FLRT

Williams Eleanor H. • Lecturer/Instructor • South Mountain Community College Library • Phoenix, AZ 85040 • ACRL EMIERT

Williams Elizabeth A. • Student • Kent State University School of Library & Information Science • Kent, OH 44242-0001 • PLA

Williams Elizabeth C. • Librarian • Atlanta-Fulton Public Library • Atlanta, GA 30303 • PLA SRRT

Williams Elizabeth O. • Malibu, CA 90265 • Continuing

Williams Esther • Science Reference Librarian • Vassar College Library • Poughkeepsie, NY 12601 • ACRL

Williams Eve A. • Student • Dalhousie University School of Library & Inf. Studies • Halifax NS, B3H 4H8 Canada • RASD EMIERT SRRT

Williams Fabienne J. • Sr. Conversion Specialist • OCLC Incorporation • Dublin, OH 43017

Williams Faith • Student • Catholic University of America School of Library and Information Science • Washington, DC 20064 • SRRT

Williams Faye M. • Library Media Specialist • Ruth Fyfe Elementary School • Las Vegas, NV 89106 • AASL EMIERT

Williams Gary D. • Reference Librarian • Aiken County Public Library Nancy Carson Library • North Augusta, SC 29841

Williams Gene Mrs. • Orion Twp. Public Library • Lake Orion, MI 48362

Williams Gordon R. • Napa, CA 94558 • ALCTS

Williams Greta A. • Serial Librarian • Radford University John P. McConnell Library • Radford, VA 24142

Williams Gretchen C. • Miami, FL 33157 • Continuing

Williams Gwendolyn H. • Librarian • Lindblom Technical High School Library • Chicago, IL 60636

Williams H L. Mrs • Cambridge, MA 02138 • ACRL RASD *Continuing*

Williams Harriet J. • Student • University of North Texas School of Library & Information Sciences • Denton, TX 76203

Williams Harry Roger III • Library Director • Jacob Edwards Library • Southbridge, MA 01550

Williams Hazel A. • Edmore, MI 48829

Williams Helen E. • Librarian IV/Instructor • Morehead State University Camden-Carroll Library • Morehead, KY 40351

Williams Helene C. • Information/Reference • Michigan State University Libraries • East Lansing, MI 48824-1048 • ACRL

Williams Hugh Edwin Jr • Librarian • Stoneham Public Library • Stoneham, MA 02180

Williams Ianthee M. • Brooklyn, NY 11210 • PLA

Williams Ida Sutton • Ardmore, OK 73402

Williams J. Linda • Consultant • Maryland State Department of Education Division of Library Development & Services • Baltimore, MD 21201 • AASL LAMA *Life*

Williams J. Randolf • Student • University of Western Ontario School of Library & Information Science • London ON, N6G 1H1 Canada • AASL

Williams James • Asst. Ed. & Social Sci. Ln. • University of Illinois Library • Urbana, IL 61801 • ACRL ALCTS LHRT LRRT SRRT

Williams James F. II • Dean • University of Colorado-Boulder University Libraries • Boulder, CO 80309 • ACRL LITA

Williams Jane • Silver Spring, MD 20904

Williams Janet • Director Lib. & Reference Serv. • Educational Testing Service • Princeton, NJ 08541 • AASL YALSA

Williams Janet A. • Director • Scott County Library System • Shakopee, MN 55379 • PLA

Williams Janet A. • Media Specialist • Charlotte County School Board • Punta Gorda, FL 33950 • AASL

Williams Janet L. • Head, Technical Services • Wyoming State Library • Cheyenne, WY 82002-0650

Williams Jean B. • Reference Librarian • Cambridge Public Library Central Square Branch • Cambridge, MA 02139

Williams Jean E. • Library Media Specialist • Green Street School • Cazenovia, NY 13035 • AASL IFRT

Williams Jean F. • Cataloger • Mohawk Valley Community College Library • Utica, NY 13501 • ACRL

Williams Jean F. • North Carolina Agricultural & Technical State University • Greensboro, NC 27411

Williams Jeanne S. • Student • University of South Florida School of Library & Information Science • Tampa, FL 33620

Williams Jeffie R. • Student • University of Alabama School of Library & Information Studies • Tuscaloosa, AL 35487-0252 • ACRL

Williams Jerilynn A. • Coordinator • Houston Public Library • Houston, TX 77002 • PLA

Williams Joan B. • Strafford, VT 05072

Williams Joan Frye • INLEX, Inc. • Monterey, CA 93942 • LITA

Williams John E. • Director of Library Services • Mesquite Public Library • Mesquite, TX 75149

Williams John T. Dr. • Ann Arbor, MI 48107 • Continuing

Williams Juanita A. • Librarian • Hillsborough Community College Dale Mabry Campus • Tampa, FL 33630

Williams Judith L. • Director of Libraries • Jacksonville Public Libraries Main Library • Jacksonville, FL 32202 • LAMA PLA

Williams Judy A. • Vienna, VA 22180 • ALSC PLA

Williams Judy R. • Old Greenwich, CT 06870 • AASL LIRT

Williams June B. • Crofton, MD 21114-2614

Williams Karen A. • Head, Central Reference • University of Arizona Library • Tucson, AZ 85721 • ACRL RASD

Williams Karen J. • Oval Librarian • Ohio University Vernon R. Alden Library • Athens, OH 45701-2978

Williams Karen J. • Resource Center Manager • Westwood Elementary School • Stillwater, OK 74075 • LITA

Williams Katherine G. Dr • Cary, NC 27511 • ACRL

Williams Kathryn J. • Los Cerros Middle School • Danville, CA 94526 • AASL

Williams Leroy D. • President,Library Board of Ctrl • Saint John the Baptist Parish Library • Laplace, LA 70068 • ALTA

Williams Lesley A. • Skokie Public Library • Skokie, IL 60077-3680 • RASD IFRT NMRT SRRT

Williams Lila E. • Systems/Cataloging Librarian • University of Richmond • Richmond, VA 23173 • LITA

Williams Lisa B. • Assistant Director • Lake Lanier Regional Library Lawrenceville Branch • Lawrenceville, GA 30245-4707 • PLA

Williams Lolita • Librarian • Elgin High School • Elgin, IL 60120 • AASL

Williams Lydia S. • Branch Head • Public Library of Charlotte & Mecklenburg County • Charlotte, NC 28202 • PLA RASD IFRT

Williams Lynda • Head Reference & Adult Services • Marion Public Library • Marion, OH 43302 • PLA

Williams Lynn Barstis • Humanities Reference Librarian • Auburn University Ralph Brown Draughon Library • Auburn, AL 36849-5606 • ACRL

Williams Lynne A. • Solano County Library • Fairfield, CA 94533 • ALCTS IFRT SRRT

Williams M. Yvonne • Trustee • Portland Community College Cascade Center • Portland, OR 97211 • ALTA

Williams MLou • Hermiston Public Library • Hermiston, OR 97838

Williams Marc • Trustee • Jefferson County Public Library • Lakewood, CO 80215 • ALTA

Williams Margaret K. • Adm. Instructional Media Servs. • Stockton Unified School District • Stockton, CA 95205 • AASL

Williams Margaret N. • Marshall, TX 75671 • ACRL LITA EMIERT SRRT

Williams Mariane K. • Valley City, ND 58072

Williams Marjorie • Director • Arab Public Library • Arab, AL 35016

Williams Martha L. • Periodicals/Serials Librarian • Minot State University Memorial Library • Minot, ND 58701

Williams Marvin Jr. • Serials Cataloger • University of West Florida John C Pace Library • Pensacola, FL 32514-5750 • ACRL ALCTS GODORT

Williams Mary A. • Computer Teacher • Saint Michael School • Wheaton, IL 60181 • AASL ALSC

Williams Mary D. • Branch Librarian • Chugiak-Eagle River Library • Eagle River, AK 99577

Williams Mary S. • Director • Graduate Theological Union Library • Berkeley, CA 94709 • ACRL ALCTS LAMA RASD

Williams Mary W. • Director • Central High School • Pageland, SC 29728 • AASL

Williams Maurvene D. • Program Officer • Library of Congress Center for the Book • Washington, DC 20540 • FLRT

Williams Michael B. • Berkeley, CA 94709

Williams Mitzi R. • Huntington, WV 25701 • RASD

Williams Muriel • Montclair, NJ 07042

Williams Nadine L. • Head of Adult Services • Eugene Public Library • Eugene, OR 97401

Williams Nanci L. • Children's Services Coordinator • Huntington Beach Library Info. & Cultural Resource Center • Huntington Beach, CA 92648 • ALSC YALSA

Williams Nancy L. • Ln/Assistant Chair Catlg Dept. • University of Florida Libraries • Gainesville, FL 32611-2047 • ALCTS LITA

Williams Novella E. • Media Specialist • Louis Sheffield Elementary School • Jacksonville, FL 32226

Williams Nyal Z. • Music Librarian • Ball State University Bracken Library • Muncie, IN 47306-0160

Williams Opal Miss • Sulphur Spring, TX 75482 • Continuing

Williams Pamela S. • Head Reference Dept. • Frostburg State University Lewis J. Ort Library • Frostburg, MD 21532 • ACRL

Williams Pamella K. • Director • West Linn Public Library • West Linn, OR 97068 • PLA

Williams Patricia A. • Asst. Head Cataloging • University of Chicago Library • Chicago, IL 60637-1502 • ALCTS LITA

Williams Patricia A. • Library Media Specialist • Atlanta Public Schools Downtown Learning Center • Atlanta, GA 30307 • AASL LIRT LRRT

Williams Patricia A. • Durant, OK 74701 • LITA PLA NMRT SRRT

Williams Patricia B. • Librarian • Cummings High School • Burlington, NC 27215 • AASL YALSA

Williams Patricia D. • School Librarian • Kingsport City Schools Lincoln Elementary • Kingsport, TN 37664 • AASL

Williams Patricia D. • St. Louis, MO 63135 • ACRL

Williams Patricia F. • Library Media Specialist • Sparkman High School • Toney, AL 35773 • AASL YALSA LIRT

Williams Paul • Librarian • Newark Public Library • Newark, NJ 07101-0630

Williams Paulette • Teacher Resource Librarian • Shelby County Board of Education • Alabaster, AL 35007 • AASL

Williams Pauline C. • Head, Public Services • Montevallo University Carmichael Library • Montevallo, AL 35115 • ACRL

Williams Philip N. • Student • Indiana University School of Library and Information Science • Bloomington, IN 47405

Williams Rebecca • Student • North Carolina Central University • Durham, NC 27707 • AASL EMIERT LRRT SRRT

Williams Reginald • Trustee • Atlanta-Fulton Public Library • Atlanta, GA 30303 • PLA

Williams Richard C. • New York, NY 10023

Williams Robert B. • Director • Kennesaw State College • Marietta, GA 30061 • ACRL LAMA

Williams Robert C. • Reference Librarian • Anchorage Municipal Libraries Z. J. Loussac Library • Anchorage, AK 99503

Williams Robert L. • Automation Librarian • South Texas Library System • Corpus Christi, TX 78401 • LITA

Williams Robert V • Associate Professor • University of South Carolina College of Library & Information Science • Columbia, SC 29208 • GODORT IRRT LHRT LRRT

Williams Roberta S. • Librarian • Mars Hill College Memorial Library • Mars Hill, NC 28754

Williams Rosemarie • Orange, CA 92666 • ALCTS LITA PLA RASD

Williams Rosemary M. • Educational Resource Librarian • Ball State University Bracken Library • Muncie, IN 47306-0160

Williams S. Jean • High School Librarian • Kalamazoo Public Schools • Kalamazoo, MI 49006

Williams Sally F. • Boston, MA 02118 • ACRL ALCTS RASD

Williams Sandra A. • Plano, TX 75023

Williams Sandra L. • Madison, NC 27025

Williams Sandra Q. • Librarian • St. Cloud State University • Saint Cloud, MN 56301 • AASL LITA

Williams Sara E. • Tulane University Howard-Tilton Memorial Library • New Orleans, LA 70118 • ACRL RASD LIRT SRRT

Williams Sara R. • Preservation Librarian • State University of New York (SUNY) University Libraries • Albany, NY 12222 • ACRL ALCTS

Williams Sean L. • Lake Lanier Regional Library Peachtree Corners Branch • Norcross, GA 30092

Williams Shannon H. • Birmingham Public & Jefferson County Free Library • Birmingham, AL 35203 • RASD NMRT

Williams Sharon K. • Lexington, KY 40502

Williams Sharon O. • Information Research Analyst • Hewlett-Packard Company • Corvallis, OR 97330

Williams Sheila L. • Asst. Library Manager • Euless Public Library • Euless, TX 76039 • ALCTS

Williams Sheryl du Roy • President • California Systems Design, Inc. • Pasadena, CA 91101 • AASL

Williams Shirley A. • Technical Services Librarian • Harding University Brackett Library • Searcy, AR 72143

Williams Sue • Trustee • San Jose Public Library • San Jose, CA 95113 • ALTA

Williams Sue Darden • Director • Norfolk Public Library • Norfolk, VA 23510-1776 • ALTA LAMA PLA

Williams Sue H. • Librarian • Saint George's Day School • Germantown, TN 38138 • AASL

Williams Susan D. • Head Librarian • Blue Ridge Community College • Flat Rock, NC 28731

Williams Susan M. • Collection Development Libn • University of Colorado-Boulder University Libraries • Boulder, CO 80309 • ALCTS

Williams Susan M. • Reference/Extension Librarian • Pinal County Library District • Florence, AZ 85232

Williams Suzanne • Kinkaid School • Houston, TX 77024 • AASL YALSA

Williams Suzanne • Asheville-Buncombe Library System • Asheville, NC 28801 • ALSC

Williams Sylvia J. • Branch Librarian • Phoenix Public Library Century Branch • Phoenix, AZ 85016 • PLA

Williams Tamatha R. • Children's Librarian • Cumberland County Public Library and Information Center, Cliffdale Branch • Fayetteville, NC 28303 • YALSA

Williams Telva G. • Librarian • Arcola Public Library • Arcola, IL 61910

Williams Tina G. • Student • Southwestern Oklahoma State University Al Harris Library • Weatherford, OK 73096 • AASL ALSC LAMA LITA YALSA EMIERT IFRT LHRT NMRT SRRT

Williams Trudy L. • Student • Catholic University of America School of Library and Information Science • Washington, DC 20064 • ALCTS FLRT

Williams Wallace D. • Head Librarian • Saint Croix Public Libraries • St. Croix, VI 00820 • LAMA LITA

Williams Wilda W. • Associate Editor, Lib Journal • Cahners Publshing • New York, NY 10011

Williams Wiley J. • Chapel Hill, NC 27516 • RASD GODORT *Continuing*

Williamschen Jodi L. • Student • University of Wisconsin-Milwaukee School of Library & Information Science • Milwaukee, WI 53201

Williamsen Audrey Sr • Librarian • Saint Catharine College Library • St. Catharine, KY 40061

Williamson Ann E. • Teacher • Lyman Trumball School • Chicago, IL 60619 • AASL

Williamson Dale A. • Business Reference • Lancaster County Library • Lancaster, PA 17602 • RASD

Williamson Edgar • University of Delaware Morris Library • Newark, DE 19717-5267 • ACRL RASD

Williamson Elizabeth A. • Springfield, OH 45503 • SRRT

Williamson Georgie G. • Treasure Island, FL 33706 • AASL YALSA *Life*

Williamson Gwen C. • Ridgecrest, CA 93555

Williamson Jane • Director & Archivist • Historical Foundation C P Church • Memphis, TN 38104

Williamson Janet A. • Reference/Collections Librarian • University of Alberta Rutherford Library North • Edmonton AB, T6G 2J4 Canada • RASD

Williamson Janie • Rose Hill High School • Rose Hill, KS 67133 • AASL

Williamson Jeanine M. • Student • University of Alabama School of Library & Information Studies • Tuscaloosa, AL 35487-0252 • SRRT

Williamson Josephine • University of Delaware Library • Newark, DE 19717-5267 • ACRL ALCTS LAMA

Williamson Judy • Librarian/Teacher • Point Pleasant High School • Point Pleasant, WV 25550 • AASL

Williamson Karin L. • Student • University of Michigan School of Information and Library Studies • Ann Arbor, MI 48109-1092 • AASL IFRT

Williamson Kathy J. • Grand Forks, ND 58201-6257 • ACRL RASD NMRT

Williamson Laurence T. • Managing Librarian • Seattle Public Library • Seattle, WA 98104-1193

Williamson Leann • Student • Indiana State University Department of Library Science • Terre Haute, IN 47809 • AASL

Williamson Linda • Windsor, VT 05089

Williamson Linda E. • U. S. Studies Librarian • Rhodes House Library • Oxford, 0X1 3RG, England • GODORT IRRT

Williamson Linda S. • Columbia, MD 21044

Williamson Lydia J. • Phoenix, AZ 85008

Williamson Mary L. • University of Wisconsin-Madison Memorial Library • Madison, WI 53706 • ACRL RASD

Williamson Mary Lou • Director, Media Center • Academy of the New Church • Bryn Athyn, PA 19009 • AASL

Williamson Nancy J. • Professor • University of Toronto Faculty of Library & Information Science • Toronto ON, M5S 1A1 Canada • ACRL ALCTS LITA

Williamson Phyllis B. • Supervisor of Library Services • Great Falls Public School Administration Library • Great Falls, MT 59403 • AASL ALSC LAMA LITA IFRT

Williamson Roger O. • Little Rock, AR 72209

Williamson Sandra A. • Saint Francis College • Loretto, PA 15940 • ACRL

Williamson Susan G. • Head Librarian • University of Pennsylvania Libraries Annenberg School for Communication • Philadelphia, PA 19104-6220 • ACRL

Williamson Veera K. • Technical Services Librarian • Hughes Hubbard & Reed Library • New York, NY 10005

Williamson William L. • Professor Emeritus • University of Wisconsin School of Library & Information Studies • Madison, WI 53706 • ACRL IFRT IRRT LHRT *Life*

Williangham-Taylor Nancy • Library Media Specialist • Northbrook School District No. 28 • Northbrook, IL 60062-5497 • AASL

Willich Carolyn S. • Student • East Texas State University Library • Commerce, TX 75428 • EMIERT

Williford Hubert • Trustee • West Florida Regional Library • Pensacola, FL 32501

Williford Paul S. • Reference Librarian • G. Pillow Lewis Memorial Library Memphis College of Art • Memphis, TN 38112

Williford Randall J. • Trustee • Weber County Library • Odgen, UT 84401 • ALTA

Willis Barbara H. • Student • University of Arizona Graduate Library School • Tucson, AZ 85721 • ALCTS PLA

Willis Carl • Trustee • Daniel Boone Regional Library • Columbia, MO 65201

Willis Carla A. • School Librarian • John Muir Middle School • San Jose, CA 95118 • AASL ALSC

Willis Deborah J. • Associate Director, CAPS • University of New Mexico General Library • Albuquerque, NM 87131 • ACRL

Willis Don • Director Advanced Technology • University Microfilms International • Ann Arbor, MI 48106-1346 • ALCTS

Willis Donald C. • Reference Librarian • Seattle Public Library • Seattle, WA 98104-1193 • PLA RASD IFRT

Willis Dorothy B. • Director of Library Service • Bishop Clarkson College • Omaha, NE 68131-3799 • LAMA IFRT

Willis E. Sue • Head Reference • Central Rappahannock Regional Library Wallace Memorial Library • Fredericksburg, VA 22401

Willis Eileen B. • Winter Park, FL 32792 • Continuing

Willis Eleanor • Branch Librarian • New Haven Public Library Fair Haven Branch • New Haven, CT 06513

Willis Elizabeth I. • Englewood, CO 80112 • ACRL RASD

Willis Emily Pispeky • Librarian • Culpeper Middle School • Culpeper, VA 22701 • AASL

Willis Gail E. • Seattle, WA 98105 • IFRT LHRT SRRT

Willis Glee M. • Engineering Librarian • University of Nevada-Reno Engineering Library • Reno, NV 89557-0044 • ACRL

Willis Ione P. • Head of Technical Services • Madison-Jefferson County Public Library • Madison, IN 47250 • ALCTS

Willis Joan K. • Oregon Institute of Technology Library • Klamath Falls, OR 97601 • GODORT

Willis Joyce • Administrative Librarian • Matteson Public Library • Matteson, IL 60443 • LAMA PLA IFRT

Willis Laura M. • Administrative Officer • Howard University Libraries Founders Library • Washington, DC 20059 • LAMA

Willis Maria Clara B. • Cataloger • University of the District of Columbia Learning Resources Division • Washington, DC 20008

Willis Mark R. • Public Information Officer • Dayton & Montgomery County Public Library • Dayton, OH 45402-2103

Willis Paul A. • Director of Library • University of Kentucky Libraries • Lexington, KY 40506-0039

Willis Robin K. • Chapel Hill, NC 27514

Willis Roni L. • Assistant Director • West Georgia Regional Library • Carrollton, GA 30117 • LAMA PLA

Willis Scott A. • Librarian II • County of Los Angeles Public Library Culver City Library 330 • Culver City, CA 90230

Willison Maureen I. • Manager, Public Services • Richmond Public Library • Richmond BC, V6X 2E3 Canada

Williss Sally J. • Librarian Trainee • Glen Cove Public Library • Glen Cove, NY 11542 • PLA RASD IFRT SRRT

Williams Karen M. • Student • University of North Texas School of Library & Information Sciences • Denton, TX 76203

Willman Timothy S. • Ferguson, MO 63135 • SRRT

Willmer Maria C. • Assistant Librarian • Dykema, Gossett Law Library • Detroit, MI 48243

Willmering William J. • Hd Serial Records Section • National Library of Medicine • Bethesda, MD 20894

Willms Bruce C. • Head of Technical Services • DeWitt Wallace Library MacAlester College • Saint Paul, MN 55105 • ACRL ALCTS

Willoughby Ethel B. • Pine Bluff, AR 71603

Willoughby Nona C. • Walnut Creek, CA 94595-4031

Willows Gwen L. • Student • San Jose State University Division of Library & Information Science • San Jose, CA 95192-0029 • SRRT

Wills Elizabeth A. • Library Assistant III • University of Alabama at Birmingham • Birmingham, AL 35294

Wills Lynda J. • Director • Winchester Public Library • Winchester, MA 01890 • PLA

Willson-Metzger Alicia C. • Ref/Bibl Instruction Librarian • Montana College of Mineral Science & Technology • Butte, MT 59701

Willson Elizabeth A. • Washington, DC 20009 • PLA

Willson Ray L. • Director • Southeast Kansas Library System • Iola, KS 66749

Willson Richard E. • Executive Director • Starved Rock Library System • Ottawa, IL 61350 • ASCLA LAMA PLA

Wilmesherr Jon P. • Student • Mayland Community College • Spruce Pine, NC 28777 • ALCTS SRRT

Wilmot Edwin G. • Connecticut Correctional Institution • Enfield, CT 06082 • ASCLA

Wilmoth Sally A. • School Book Fairs Services • Pinellas, FL 34666

Wilmoth Susan E. • Tucson, AZ 85741

Wilner A Isabel • Towson, MD 21204 • Continuing

Wilsey Jayne A. • Student • San Jose State University Division of Library & Information Science • San Jose, CA 95192-0029

Wilson-Lingbloom Evie • Mill Creek Library • Mill Creek, WA 98012 • ALSC LAMA PLA YALSA

Wilson-Smith Catherine • Records Management Supervisor • Orange County Transit Authority Resource Center • Garden Grove, CA 92640-5208 • RASD

Wilson Alane • University of Calgary Library Sciences/ Professions Area • Calgary, AB, T2N 1N4 Canada • LITA CLENE

Wilson Alden P. • Pittsboro, NC 27312-8547 • Continuing

Wilson Alida F. • San Rafael, CA 94901 • AASL

Wilson Andrea H. • Collection Develpment Assistant • Broward County Division of Libraries Broward County Library • Fort Lauderdale, FL 33301 • VRT

Wilson Ann • Reference Services Coordinator • Wright Memorial Public Library • Oakwood, OH 45419-2598 • PLA RASD

Wilson Anthony M. • Coordinator of Lib Tech Programs • Highline College Library 25-ID Coord. Library Tech. Program • Des Moines, WA 98198-9800 • ACRL LITA CLENE LIRT

Wilson Ashby S. Jr. • Division Director • Virginia State Library & Archives • Richmond, VA 23219

Wilson Barbara • Adult Services Librarian • Cuyahoga County Public Library Parma-Snow Branch • Parma, OH 44134-2789

Wilson Barbara L. • Lincoln, RI 02865

Wilson Barbara L. • Central Middle School • Riverside, CA 92506

Wilson Betsy • Assoc. Dir. of Libs/Pub. Servs. • University of Washington • Seattle, WA 98195 • ACRL LAMA LITA RASD LIRT

Wilson Bette J. • Library Media Specialist • Auke Bay Elementary School • Juneau, AK 99801 • AASL

Wilson Betty Jean • Periodicals Librarian • Morehead State University Camden-Carroll Library • Morehead, KY 40351 • ACRL

Wilson Betty-Ruth • Assistant Catalog Librarian • Southern Illinois University • Carbondale, IL 62901-6632 • ACRL ALCTS *Life*

Wilson Bonnie K. • Media Specialist/Elementary • Hilltop Elementary School • Glen Burnie, MD 21061 • AASL

Wilson Bradford L. • Student • University of Illinois Graduate School of Library and Information Science • Urbana, IL 61801

Wilson Bruce Alan • Charlotte, NC 28202-1600

Wilson C. Daniel Jr. • City Librarian • New Orleans Public Library • New Orleans, LA 70140 • LAMA PLA

Wilson Candace B. • Librarian • Russell County Junior High School • Russell Springs, KY 42642-4010 • AASL

Wilson Carol Ann • Assistant Director • Westfield Memorial Library • Westfield, NJ 07090 • ALSC PLA

Wilson Carol R. • Librarian • National Center for Manufacturing Sciences • Ann Arbor, MI 48108 • ALCTS GODORT

Wilson Carole • San Diego State University General Reference Division • San Diego, CA 92182-0511 • ACRL

Wilson Caroline Rich • Furlong, PA 18925 • ALSC PLA CLENE

Wilson Carolyn T. • Acquisitions Librarian • David Lipscomb University University Library • Nashville, TN 37204-3951

Wilson Cheryl • Head of Special Collections • New Mexico State University Library • Las Cruces, NM 88003-0006 • ACRL MAGERT

Wilson Craig A. • Assistant Director • Oregon State University William Jasper Kerr Library • Corvallis, OR 97331-4501 • ACRL ALCTS LAMA LHRT

Wilson Danee A. • Media Center Director • Walter Johnson High Sch • Bethesda, MD 20878 • AASL

Wilson Daniel T. • Asst. Dir. for Access Services • University of Virginia Medical Center Claude Moore Health Sciences Library • Charlottesville, VA 22908

Wilson David C. • Director • Ocmulgee Regional Library System • Eastman, GA 31023

Wilson David E. • Deputy Director • Salt Lake County Library System • Salt Lake City, UT 84121-3188

Wilson Diana • Trustee • Las Vegas-Clark County Library District • Las Vegas, NV 89101 • ALTA

Wilson Donna Dake • Head of Technical Services • Kenyon College • Gambier, OH 43022 • ALCTS

Wilson Doris E. • Tacoma, WA 98408 • Continuing

Wilson Dorothy • San Antonio, TX 78233

Wilson E. Lynn Mrs • Tennessee Prison for Women McCall School • Nashville, TN 37219-5256

Wilson Elaine F. Mrs • Librarian/Director • Siloam Springs Public Library • Siloam Spgs, AR 72761

Wilson Eleanor E. • Wooster, OH 44691

Wilson Eleanor L. • Cataloger • Bristol Public Library • Bristol, CT 06010

Wilson Eleanor S. • Student • Southern Connecticut State University School of Libray Science & Instructional Technology • New Haven, CT 06515 • ACRL

Wilson Enid • Catalog Librarian • Boston University Mugar Memorial Library • Boston, MA 02215 • ACRL ALCTS *Life*

Wilson Evelyn R. • Student • University of South Carolina College of Library & Information Science • Columbia, SC 29208 • SRRT

Wilson F. W. • Pierpont Morgan Library • New York, NY 10016

Wilson Florabelle • Librarian • Indiana Central University Library • Indianapolis, IN 46208 • Continuing

Wilson Florence I. • Denver, CO 80212 • ALCTS PLA *Life*

Wilson Florence J. • Associate Director • Vanderbilt University Library • Nashville, TN 37240-0007 • ACRL ALCTS LAMA LITA

Wilson Fran • Media Specialist • Conant Elementary School • Bloomfield Hills, MI 48302 • AASL

Wilson Gertrude H. • Louisville, KY 40203 • AASL YALSA *Continuing*

Wilson Guy W. • Librarian • United States Catholic Conference • Washington, DC 20017 • ACRL

Wilson Helen T. • Media Coordinator • Granville County Schools • Oxford, NC 27565 • YALSA

Wilson Holly J. • Reference Librarian • U.S Army Intelligence& Threat Analysis Center • Washington, DC 20374-5085 • AFLRT

Wilson Jacqueline • Coor, Information Services • University of California San Francisco Library • San Francisco, CA 94143-0840 • ACRL

Wilson James D. • Student • East Carolina University Department of Library & Information Studies • Greenville, NC 27858-4353 • PLA

Wilson Jane • San Francisco, CA 94109 • ACRL IRRT *Life*

Wilson Jane A. • Reference Librarian • Gale Free Library • Holden, MA 01520 • PLA RASD

Wilson Jane A. Dr. • School Media Specialist • Emerald

Junior High School • Greenwood, SC 29646 • AASL IFRT

Wilson Janice M. • Librarian • California School of Professional Psychology Los Angeles Campus Library • Alhambra, CA 91803-1360 • ACRL RASD LIRT

Wilson Jenni L. • Student • University of Illinois Graduate School of Library and Information Science • Urbana, IL 61801

Wilson JoAnn • Library Media Specialist • Raytown South Middle School • Raytown, MO 64138

Wilson Joan B. • Media Specialist • Wellesley Public Schools Bates School • Wellesley, MA 02181

Wilson John J. • Assistant Librarian • Cate School McBean Library • Carpinteria, CA 93014-5005

Wilson John P. • Serials Librarian • Vanderbilt University Library Jean & Alexander Heard Library • Nashville, TN 37240-0007 • ALCTS

Wilson John S. • Documents Librarian • Baylor University Moody Memorial Library • Waco, TX 76798-7148

Wilson Joyce • Trustee • Central Arkansas Library System • Little Rock, AR 72201-4698 • ALTA

Wilson June E. • Chief • Ontario Library Service-Escarpment • Hamilton ON, L8K 1N7 Canada

Wilson Karen A. • Assistant Director • Stanford University Jackson Library • Stanford, CA 94305 • ACRL LAMA

Wilson Karen S. • Asst Dir for State & Fed Prog • Virginia State Library & Archives • Richmond, VA 23219

Wilson Katherine H. • The Futures Group • Glastonbury, CT 06033-4409 • RASD

Wilson Katherine S. • Student • University of Illinois Graduate School of Library and Information Science • Urbana, IL 61801 • RASD SRRT

Wilson Kathleen I. • Librarian • St. Stephen's Episcopal School • Austin, TX 78767 • AASL

Wilson Keith • Dynix Incorporated • Provo, UT 84601

Wilson Laura S. • Advertising & Promotion Mgr. • ABC-CLIO Inc. • Santa Barbara, CA 93116-1911 • AASL

Wilson Letitia A. • Coor. of Children's Service • Dayton & Montgomery County Public Library • Dayton, OH 45402-2103 • ALSC PLA

Wilson Leuretta W. • Library Manager • Salt Lake County Library System South Salt Lake Branch • Salt Lake City, UT 84115 • PLA

Wilson Lillian M. • Minot, ND 58701 • Continuing

Wilson Linda G. • Sales Representative • CLSI, Inc. • Gladstone, MO 64119 • PLA

Wilson Linda J. • Education Librarian • Virginia Polytechnic Institute and State University, Newman Library • Blacksburg, VA 24061-0434 • ACRL ALSC RASD YALSA LIRT

Wilson Linda L. • Merced County Library • Merced, CA 95340 • LAMA PLA YALSA

Wilson Linda L. • Hilton Head Island, SC 29926 • ALCTS LRRT

Wilson Linda M. • Head Librarian • Saint John's School • Houston, TX 77019 • AASL YALSA LIRT

Wilson Lucy • College Librarian • University of Cincinnati Raymond Walters College • Cincinnati, OH 45236 • ACRL

Wilson Lynda J. • Student • State University of New York at Albany School of Information Science & Policy • Albany, NY 12222 • SRRT

Wilson Mareth • Librarian • National University Library • Sacramento, CA 95826 • ACRL RASD

Wilson Margaret F. • University Librarian • Florida A&M University S.H. Coleman Memorial Library • Tallahassee, FL 32307 • ACRL

Wilson Marian S. • Librarian • Syracuse Elementary School • Syracuse, KS 67878 • AASL

Wilson Marie K. • Resource Coordinator • The Calhoun School • New York City, NY 10024 • AASL

Wilson Marijo S. • Monograph Cataloger/Editor • Cornell University Albert R. Mann Library • Ithaca, NY 14853-4301 • ACRL ALCTS LITA

Wilson Marilyn J. • San Diego, CA 92127

Wilson Marjorie • SRI International Research Information Services • Menlo Park, CA 94025 • LAMA LITA RASD

Wilson Mary A. • Librarian • Southern California College • Costa Mesa, CA 92626 • ACRL

Wilson Mary C. • Cataloging Librarian • Labat-Anderson Incorporated • Arlington, VA 22201 • ALCTS NMRT

Wilson Mary Dabney • Head, Bibliographic Ctrl. Dept • University of Texas at Arlington • Arlington, TX 76019-0497 • ALCTS LITA

Wilson Mary E. • School Librarian • Erie Elementary School • Chandler, AZ 85224 • AASL

Wilson Mary Ellen • Acquisitions Supervisor • Vanderbilt University Library Jean & Alexander Heard Library • Nashville, TN 37240-0007

Wilson Mary L. • Director of Libraries • Charlotte Country Day School • Charlotte, NC 28211 • AASL

Wilson Memory A. • Director of Technical Operations • Amos Memorial Public Library • Sidney, OH 45365 • SRRT

Wilson Mildred L. • Library Media Specialist • Unites States Air Force Academy Air Academy High School •

Colorado Springs, CO 80840 • AASL

Wilson Myoung Chung • Reference Librarian • Rutgers University Libraries Archibald Stevens Alexander Library • New Brunswick, NJ 08903 • ACRL

Wilson Myra J. • Coordinator of Library Services • Delta State University • Cleveland, MS 38733 • ACRL LAMA

Wilson Myrtle V. • Librarian • Orange Public Schools • Orange, NJ 07050

Wilson Nancy C. • Librarian/Media Specialist • Newport Middle School • Newport, OR 97365 • AASL

Wilson Nina M. • Principal Librarian • Los Angeles Public Library • Los Angeles, CA 90071

Wilson Patricia • Senior Librarian • Inter-Community School-Zurich Attn: Library • Zumikon, Switzerland • AASL LAMA PLA IRRT

Wilson Patricia • Reference Librarian • Brock University • St. Catharines ON, L2S 3A1 Canada • ACRL

Wilson Patricia Jane • Assistant Professor of LRC • University of Houston at Clear Lake Learning Resources Specialist Program • Houston, TX 77058 • ALSC

Wilson Patricia S. • Public Services Librarian • University of Kentucky Libraries Agriculture Department • Lexington, KY 40546-0091 • ACRL

Wilson Phillis M. • Head Children's Services • Niles Public Library • Niles, IL 60648 • ALSC

Wilson Rebecca A. • Assistant Director • Susquehanna University • Selinsgrove, PA 17870 • ACRL LAMA

Wilson Richard • Senior Anaylst, Prod Mgmt • Utlas International • Etobicoke, ON, M8X 2X2 Canada • LITA

Wilson Robert K. • Head of Reader Services • Winona State University • Winona, MN 55987 • ACRL

Wilson Robert R. • Librarian • Ashland Public Library • Ashland, OR 97520 • YALSA

Wilson Robert W • Haverhill Public Library • Haverhill, MA 01830 • RASD

Wilson Sandra E. • F.J. Burke Elementary School • Medway, MA 02053

Wilson Sandra L. • Lake Agassiz Regional Library • Moorhead, MN 56560 • LAMA PLA

Wilson Sandra L. • Educational/Library Assistant • Josephine County Schools • Cave Junction, OR 97523

Wilson Savan Wilby • Director Tech Learning Res Ctr • University of Southern Mississippi • Hattiesburg, MS 39406-5053 • AASL

Wilson Steven L. • School Librarian • Tacoma Public Schools Truman Middle School • Tacoma, WA 98406 • AASL

Wilson Sue Ellen • Childrens Services Coordinator • Spokane County Library District • Spokane, WA 99212-1853

Wilson Sue L. • Audio-Visual Head • Kalamazoo Public Library • Kalamazoo, MI 49007-5270 • ACRL PLA

Wilson Therese M. • Student • University of Wisconsin-Milwaukee School of Library & Information Science • Milwaukee, WI 53201 • AASL ALSC YALSA

Wilson Thomas C. • Head of Systems • University of Houston Libraries • Houston, TX 77204-2091 • ACRL LITA

Wilson Virginia G. • Wilmington, MA 01887 • Life

Wilson Virginia H. • Director • Bessemer Public Library • Bessemer, AL 35020

Wilson W. Randall • Director • Parlin-Ingersoll Library • Canton, IL 61520 • LAMA PLA

Wilson Wayne V. • Library Director • Amateur Athletic Foundation • Los Angeles, CA 90018

Wilson William • Base Librarian • United States Air Force RAF Upper Heyford, U.K. • APO, AE 09466 • AFLRT

Wilson William G. • Librarian & Lecturer • University of Maryland College of Library and Information Services • College Park, MD 20742-4345 • ACRL ALCTS RASD CLENE

Wilson William J. • Director • Milwaukee County Federated Library System • Milwaukee, WI 53233 • LAMA PLA IFRT

Wilson Yvonne M. • Associate Librarian • University of California-Irvine Library • Irvine, CA 92713 • ACRL GODORT

Wilt Catherine C. • Assoc Dir Lib & Info Svs • AMIGOS Bibliographic Council,Inc. • Dallas, TX 75251-2104 • ASCLA PLA

Wilt Charles F. • Student • Texas Woman's University School of Library & Information Studies • Denton, TX 76204

Wilt Larry J. M. • University of Maryland Baltimore County Kuhn Library • Catonsville, MD 21228 • ACRL ALCTS IFRT

Wilt Louise C. • Librarian/Media Specialist • Most Holy Redeemer School • Tampa, FL 33612

Wilts Joan J. • Assistant Director • Waukegan Public Library • Waukegan, IL 60085 • LAMA

Wiltse Helen Citron • Associate Director • Georgia Institute of Technology Price Gilbert Memorial Library • Atlanta, GA 30332-0900 • ACRL ALCTS LAMA LITA

Wiltshire Denise A. • Reston, VA 22091 • FLRT

Wiltshire Kathleen M. • Columbia University Libraries

Butler Library • New York, NY 10027

Wimble Erica S. • Student • Indiana University School of Library and Information Science • Bloomington, IN 47405

Win May Kyi • Curator, SEA Collection • Northern Illinois University University Libraries • DeKalb, IL 60115-2868 • ACRL

Winans Diane • Manager/Support Services • Geauga County Public Library • Chardon, OH 44024 • ALCTS LITA

Winar Martin P. • Director • Mercer County Library Lawrence Branch • Lawrenceville, NJ 08648-4132 • LAMA *Life*

Winberry Carolyn J. • Science Librarian • University of South Carolina • Columbia, SC 29208 • ACRL

Winchel Michele J. • Muskegon County Library Norton Shores Branch • Muskegon, MI 49441

Winchell Carol A. • Reference Librarian • Ohio State University Libraries • Columbus, OH 43210-1286

Winchell Rob • Las Vegas-Clark County Library District Flamingo Library • Las Vegas, NV 89119 • LITA

Winchester David E. • Serials/Reference Librarian • Washburn University Library • Topeka, KS 66621 • ACRL ALCTS

Winckler Paul A. • Glen Cove, NY 11542-3415

Winder Sylvia A. • Santa Cruz County Schools • Santa Cruz, CA 95010

Windorf Carol • Deputy Director • Library Cooperative of Macomb • Mount Clemens, MI 48044-3198

Windsor Elizabeth A. • Ames, IA 50010 • ACRL RASD *Life*

Windsor Kay M. • Pembroke Hill School • Kansas City, MO 64112 • AASL

Windsor Laura L. • Reference Librarian • Embry-Riddle Aeronautical University • Daytona Beach, FL 32114

Winecoff Sandra R. • Visiting Assistant Professor • University of South Carolina • Columbia, SC 29208 • AASL ALSC IFRT

Winegarden Jack R. • Trustee • Genesee District Library • Flint, MI 48504

Winer Arnold M. • Valley High School Library • Santa Ana, CA 92704 • AASL YALSA

Winer Elaine S. • Teacher • Portola Valley School District • Portola Valley, CA 94028

Winfree Barbara S. • Youth Services Coordinator • Timberland Regional Library • Olympia, WA 98501 • ALSC

Wing Caroline H. • Wytheville, VA 24382

Wing Elaine K. • Librarian I • Maricopa County Sheriff Department Madison Facility • Phoenix, AZ 85003

Wing Judith G. • Senior Assistant Librarian • University at Albany Libraries • Albany, NY 12222 • ACRL ALCTS

Wing Melinda B. • Children's Librarian • Palo Alto City Library Children's Library • Palo Alto, CA 94301 • PLA

Wing Susan E. • Librarian I-Young Adult Services • Barrington Public Library District • Barrington, IL 60010 • ALSC

Wingard Mary S. • Media Specialist • Oak Ridge Elementary School • Oak Ridge, NC 27310 • AASL
Wingate Elaine K. • Chicago, IL 60610
Wingate Jeaneen • Librarian • Calvert School • Baltimore, MD 21210 • AASL
Wingate Jeanne Anne • Elementary Librarian • Hurst-Euless-Bedford Independent School District • Bedford, TX 76022 • AASL
Wingenroth Janet L. • Librarian • Spokane Falls Community College • Spokane, WA 99214-5288 • LIRT
Winger Howard W. • North Manchester, IN 46962
Winger Margaret A. • Chicago, IL 60625-3301
Wingfield Tommie J. • Business Librarian • University of Texas at Arlington • Arlington, TX 76019-0497
Wingfield Valerie • Manuscripts Specialist • New York Public Library • New York, NY 10016
Wingo Carl • Student • University of California-Berkeley University Library • Berkeley, CA 94720 • LITA
Winkel Lois • Bethesda, MD 20817 • AASL ALCTS ALSC YALSA
Winkels Evelyn H. • Librarian • Fairfax County Public Library Pohick Regional Branch • Burke, VA 22015 • LAMA PLA
Winkle Melody J. • Student • University of Washington Graduate School of Library and Information Science • Seattle, WA 98195 • IFRT SRRT
Winkle Sharon L. • Library Director • Mead Public Library • Sheboygan, WI 53081 • ALCTS ALSC LAMA LITA PLA RASD
Winkleblack Carole B. • Director • LeGrand Pioneer Heritage Library • LeGrand, IA 50142
Winklebleck Mary Walsh • Reference Librarian/Adult Svs • Sunnyvale Public Library • Sunnyvale, CA 94088-3714
Winkler-Worley Mary E. • Student • University of Wyoming • Laramie, WY 82071
Winkler Carol K. • Librarian • Nerinx Hall • Webstergrove, MO 63119 • AASL
Winkler Jean J. • Director • Basalt Regional Library District • Basalt, CO 81621-0470
Winkler Joseph M. • Co-ordinator/Research Cllns. • Saint Louis Public Library • Saint Louis, MO 63103-2389 • PLA MAGERT
Winkler Michael • University of Massachusetts at Boston Joseph P. Healey Library • Boston, MA 02125-3393 • LITA
Winkler Paul Walter • Arlington, VA 22204 • ALCTS
Winkler Richard A. • Library Media Specialist • T. Roosevelt Elementary School • Manhattan, KS 66502
Winn Betsy S. • Librarian • Saint Francis Episcopal Day School • Houston, TX 77024 • AASL
Winn Patricia S. • Librarian • Clarksville High School • Clarksville, TN 37043 • AASL
Winne Brian W. • Partner • Arthur Andersen Company • Chicago, IL 60603 • LITA
Winner Marian C. • Director • Northern Kentucky University Steely Library • Highland Heights, KY 41099-6101 • ACRL LAMA
Winner Ronald • Assistant Director • Western Illinois Library System • Galesburg, IL 61401 • AASL ALCTS ALTA LAMA PLA *Life*
Winnick Pauline • Boston, MA 02110 • Continuing
Winnicki Amanda V. • General Reference • Flint Public Library • Flint, MI 48502 • GODORT
Winninger Diana • Head-Monographs Cataloging • Canada Institute for Scientific & Technical Information • Ottawa ON, Canada • ALCTS
Winowich Nicholas • Charleston, WV 25314
Winowski Maria Puszkar • North Arlington Public Library • North Arlington, NJ 07032 • ALTA LAMA PLA
Winroth Elizabeth W. • Librarian • Oregon Historial Society • Portland, OR 97205
Winrow John • Liverpool L3 8EW, England
Winsche Elizabeth • Director • Muskegon County Library • Muskegon, MI 49442-1094
Winship Laurie Reith • Syracuse, NY 13224
Winske Elaine M. • Documents Librarian • Florida International University North Miami Campus • North Miami, FL 33181 • ACRL ALCTS LITA GODORT
Winslow Carol M. • Librarian • McGary Middle School Media Center • Evansville, IN 47714 • AASL
Winslow Ernestine • Trustee • San Antonio Public Library • San Antonio, TX 78205
Winslow Jane • Executive Director • Friends of San Francisco Public Library • San Francisco, CA 94102 • PLA
Winslow Mildred M. • Kalamazoo, MI 49006-1900 • Continuing
Winslow Theresa • Head,Technical Services • Somerset County Library • Bridgewater, NJ 08807 • ALCTS LITA
Winsmore Gail A. • Assistant Director • Noblesville-Southeastern Public Library • Noblesville, IN 46060
Winsor Karen J. • Highland Park School District 108 Library • Highland Park, IL 60035 • AASL
Winstandley Virginia • Clarksville, IN 47129 • ACRL *Continuing*
Winstead Jean D. • Saint Raphael Elementary School • Crystal, MN 55428 • AASL
Winstead Susan L. • Charlotte, NC 28212 • AASL
Winston Heidi Martin • Indexer • H. W. Wilson Company • Bronx, NY 10452 • ACRL
Winston Lorenzo • Saint Louis County Library Natural Bridge Branch • St. Louis, MO 63121
Winston Mark D. • Student • University of Pittsburgh School of Library and Information Science • Pittsburgh, PA 15260 • PLA IFRT SRRT
Winter Anna Belle • Forestville, MD 20747 • Continuing
Winter Arn Ellsworth • Director • Mason County Public Library • Point Pleasant, WV 25550 • PLA
Winter Bernadette G. • Rockford, IL 61107 • AASL
Winter Dorothy M. • Las Vegas, NV 89121
Winter Eugenia B. • Collection Development Coord. • California State University • Bakersfield, CA 93311 • ACRL
Winter Frances • Riverside, IL 60546
Winter Frank • Associate Librarian • University of Saskatchewan Library • Saskatoon SK, S7N 0W0 Canada • ALCTS LAMA LITA
Winter Mary E. • Librarian III • Milwaukee Public Library • Milwaukee, WI 53233 • ALCTS
Winter Neva • Milton Elementary • Rye, NY 10580
Winter Theodore G. • Special Cataloger • Union Theological Seminary in Virginia Library • Richmond, VA 23227 • ALCTS LITA
Winters Barbara A. • Associate University Librarian • Wright State University University Library • Dayton, OH 45435 • ALCTS LITA
Winters Colleen • Director • Forest Grove City Library • Forest Grove, OR 97116 • IFRT
Winters Linda S. • Glendale Community College Library • Glendale, CA 91208
Winters Tere • Library Director • Naropa Institute Library • Boulder, CO 80302
Wintersteen Theodora R. • Librarian • Kuskokwim Consortium Library Bethel Public Library • Bethel, AK 99559
Winzer Kathleen M. • Costabile Associates Inc • Bethesda, MD 20814 • ALCTS
Wion Linda R. • Crater High School • Central Point, OR 97502 • AASL
Wiren Eleanor L. • West Lafayette, IN 47906 • Continuing
Wiren Harold N. Mr • Seattle, WA 98115 • ACRL LITA *Life*
Wirig Joan S. • Library A-V Coordinator • Summit-Argo Public Schools • Summit, IL 60501 • AASL
Wirkus Janice E. • Student • Brigham Young University School of Library & Information Sciences • Provo, UT 84602
Wirsching Bridgett F. • Library Tech. • Puget Sound Naval Shipyard Leisure Library • Bremerton, WA 98314-5000 • NMRT
Wirstrom Sandra E. • Librarian • Wilmington High School • Wilmington, VT 05363 • AASL
Wirt Michael J. • Director • Spokane County Library District • Spokane, WA 99212-1853 • PLA
Wirtanen James • Pub. Svs. Libn./Computer Coor. • Loyola University Mallinckrodt Campus • Wilmette, IL 60091-1560 • ACRL
Wirthlin Virginia S. • Carousel Book Fair • Salt Lake City, UT 84109
Wirtz Ronald L. • Library Director • American Institute of Baking • Manhattan, KS 66502 • LITA
Wirtz Theresa M. • Yankee Book Peddler • Contoocook, NH 03229
Wischhusen Loring Miss • Cleveland, OH 44110 • ALSC LAMA *Life*
Wisdom Sara J. • Senior Librarian • Public Library of Des Moines East Side Branch • Des Moines, IA 50317 • PLA
Wise Carolyn • Pelion, SC 29123
Wise Elaine A. • Librarian I • Broward County Library Imperial Point Branch • Fort Lauderdale, FL 33308 • PLA
Wise Flossie E. • Reference Librarian • University of Tennessee John C. Hodges Library • Knoxville, TN 37996-1000 • ACRL
Wise Ina M. • Chicago, IL 60629
Wise Judy L. • Librarian • Pembroke Hill School • Kansas City, MO 64112 • AASL
Wise Leona L. • Gift Librarian & German Lit Bibl • University of Southern California Doheny Library • Los Angeles, CA 90089-0182 • ACRL ALCTS IRRT
Wise Lisa • Technical Services Librarian • Three Rivers Library System • Glenwood Springs, CO 81602-1429
Wise M Suzanne • Documents Librarian • Appalachian State University Carol Grotnes Belk Library • Boone, NC 28608 • ACRL RASD GODORT
Wise Martha Kay • Libn/Educational Media Spec • Brown Middle School • Ravenna, OH 44266 • AASL
Wise Matthew W. • Music Cataloger • New York University Elmer Holmes Bobst Library • New York, NY 10012 • ALCTS
Wise Maxine • School Library Media Coordinator • East Wake Middle School • Raleigh, NC 27604 • AASL YALSA
Wise Nell Carole • Media Specialist • South Aiken High School • Aiken, SC 29801 • AASL
Wise Ronnie W. • Director • Bolivar County Library Robinson-Carpenter Memorial Library • Cleveland, MS 38732
Wise Rosalie • Preservation Vendor • Micro Media • Mineola, NY 11501 • ALCTS
Wise Virginia J. • Lecturer on Law • Harvard Law School Library • Cambridge, MA 02138 • ACRL GODORT IFRT
Wisel Lee Marie • Cataloging Librarian • Columbia Union College Theofield G. Weis Library • Takoma Park, MD 20912-7796 • ACRL ALCTS IFRT
Wiselogel Barbara J. • Reference Librarian • Louisville Public Library • Louisville, CO 80027 • LITA RASD IFRT
Wiseman Mary Jane • University of Wisconsin School of Library & Information Studies • Madison, WI 53706 • ALSC PLA *Life*
Wiseman Robert • Trustee • Lexington Public Library • Lexington, KY 40507 • ALTA
Wisener Joanne C. • Trustee • Yuma County Library District • Yuma, AZ 85364 • ALTA
Wiser Patricia L. • Media Serv/AV/Library Supr. • School Administrative Unit 21 Media Center • Hampton, NH 03842 • AASL
Wishart H. Lynn • Director • Yeshiva University Cardozo School of Law Library • New York, NY 10003-3299 • ACRL LAMA LITA RASD GODORT *Life*
Wisher Doris J. • Student • Simmons College Graduate School of Library & Information Science • Boston, MA 02115
Wishner Dorothy • Haverford, PA 19041
Wishnetsky Susan • Serials/Acquisitions Ln • Northwestern University Galter Health Sciences Library • Chicago, IL 60611 • ACRL ALCTS
Wislinski Barbara L. • Librarian • Southwestern High School Library • Detroit, MI 48209-2976 • YALSA
Wismer Donald • Trustee • Cary Memorial Library • Wayne, ME 04284
Wisner Edwin A. • Trustee • Wagnalls Memorial Library • Lithopolis, OH 43136
Wisnewski Mary M. • Student • University of Illinois Graduate School of Library and Information Science • Urbana, IL 61801 • ALSC
Wisnieski Mary • Library Tech Asst. II • University of Florida Libraries • Gainesville, FL 32611-2047
Wisniewski Deb M. • Livonia, MI 48150
Wisniewski E Mrs • Asst Dir For Ext Serv • Burlington County Library • Mount Holly, NJ 08060-1394
Wisniewski Julia L. • Librarian • University of Maryland College Park Theodore R. McKeldin Library • College Park, MD 20742-7011
Wisniewski Michelle McTeer • Librarian I/Outreach Services • Rochester Hills Public Library • Rochester, MI 48307
Wisotzki Lila B. • Baltimore County Public Library • Towson, MD 21204 • ALSC PLA SRRT
Wissemann Nancy W. • Library Director • West Springfield Public Library • West Springfield, MA 01089 • PLA
Wissman Marie • Trustee • Bossier Parish Library • Bossier City, LA 71111
Wistner Robert • Trustee • Columbus Metropolitan Library • Columbus, OH 43215 • ALTA PLA
Wit Linda G. • Student • Northern Illinois University • DeKalb, IL 60115-2854 • AASL
Witcher Curt B. • Manager/Genealogy Department • Allen County Public Library • Fort Wayne, IN 46801-2270 • RASD
Witcher Patricia • Data Management Analyst • PRC Inc. • Arlington, VA 22202 • RASD LRRT
Witherell Elizabeth H • Curator of Manuscripts • University of California UCSB Library • Santa Barbara, CA 93106-9010 • ACRL
Withers Beth • Branch Manager • Atlanta-Fulton Public Library Buckhead Branch • Atlanta, GA 30305 • ALSC
Withers Carol M. • Student • San Jose State University Division of Library & Information Science • San Jose, CA 95192-0029
Witherspoon Elizabeth A. • Library Supervisor • Purdue University Black Cultural Center Library • W Lafayette, IN 47906
Withington Rebecca Z. • Pewaukee, WI 53072 • ACRL
Withoff Alan B. • Mgr. of Branches & Extension • Muskingum County Library System • Zanesville, OH 43701 • LAMA PLA VRT
Withrow Lillian C. • Law Librarian • Gibson, Ochsner & Adkins Law Library • Amarillo, TX 79101

Witkower M. T. • Systems Manager • J. Paul Getty Trust • Santa Monica, CA 90401 • LITA

Witschi Laura L. • Librarian, Acting Director • Schriener College W.M Logan Library • Kerrville, TX 78028

Witsenhausen Helen • Mgr. Corporate Information Ctr. • John Wiley & Sons, Inc. • New York, NY 10158 • ACRL ALCTS LITA

Witt Carolyn • Library Director • Washington Public Library • Washington, MO 63090

Witt John M. • Director • Arkansas City Public Library • Arkansas City, KS 67005-2695

Witt Marcia A. • Network Librarian • Michigan Library Consortium • Lansing, MI 48911

Witt Susan T. • Librarian • Union East School Library • Cheektowaga, NY 14225 • AASL

Witte Deborah A. • Reference Librarian (part-time) • Portland Public Library • Portland, ME 04101

Witte Dianne L. • New England, ND 58647

Witte Sandra J. • Media Generalist Librarian • Eagle Point Elementary • Oakdale, MN 55128 • AASL

Witte Victoria B. • Head Reference & Inf. Services • Washington University Libraries • Saint Louis, MO 63130-4899 • ACRL RASD

Wittekind Anne M. • Cincinnati, OH 45231-4709

Witten Dana M. • Student • Northwestern State University Eugene P. Watson Library • Natchitoches, LA 71457

Witten Jane Daley • Student • University of North Carolina at Chapel Hill School of Information and Library Science • Chapel Hill, NC 27599-3360 • ALCTS RASD

Witten Rochelle G. • Reference Librarian • Paradise Valley Community College • Phoenix, AZ 85032 • ACRL RASD

Wittenbach Stefanie A. • Assistant Head,Reference Dept. • University of New Mexico General Library • Albuquerque, NM 87131 • ACRL LITA

Wittenborg Karin • Assoc. Univ Ln. for Clln Devel. • University of California-Los Angeles (UCLA) • Los Angeles, CA 90024-1450 • ACRL ALCTS

Witthus Rutherford W. • Coor. of Lib Develp Spec Cllns • University of Colorado at Denver Auraria Library • Denver, CO 80204 • ACRL

Wittig Alice S. • Medocino, CA 95460 • AASL

Wittig Constance M. • University of Wisconsin-Milwaukee School of Library & Information Science • Milwaukee, WI 53201 • LITA

Wittig Pamela Horak • Children's Services • Madison Public Library • Madison, WI 53703 • ASCLA *Life*

Wittig Teressa M. • Wilkinsburg, PA 15221 • ACRL

Wittkopf Barbara J. • Librarian • Louisiana State University Libraries Troy H. Middleton Library • Baton Rouge, LA 70803-3342 • ACRL LAMA RASD LIRT

Wittlin Denise M. • West Palm Beach, FL 33415

Wittock Paul J. • Student • University of North Texas School of Library & Information Sciences • Denton, TX 76203

Wittorf Robert H. • Asst Dir For Sys & Admin Svs • University of Notre Dame Libraries • Notre Dame, IN 46556 • ACRL LAMA

Witucke A. Virginia • Central Michigan University Off-Campus Library Services • Fairfax, VA 22031 • ACRL RASD IFRT LIRT

Witus Gillian Winston • Los Angeles, CA 90024 • ALSC

Witwer Kathryn A. • Branch Manager/Juvenile Bibl. • Allen County Public Library Georgetown Branch Library • Ft. Wayne, IN 46815

Wiwcharuk Tom S. • Toronto ON, M6H 2W3 Canada • LITA

Wixom Sharen E-L S • Reference Librarian • Chatham-Effingham-Liberty Regional Library (CEL) • Savannah, GA 31499-4301 • RASD EMIERT

Wiza Judith M. • Dir.,Bus & Economics Inf Ctr • University of Kentucky Libraries • Lexington, KY 40506-0039 • ACRL LITA RASD

Wladis Beth E. • Asst Dept Hd, Art & Literature • The New York Public Library • New York, NY 10016 • PLA RASD IFRT

Wlodarczyk Katherine L. • Library Media Specialist • Clarkston Senior High School Media Center • Clarkston, MI 48346 • AASL YALSA

Wlodkoski Carol A. • Middle School Librarian • Norwood Junior High School • Norwood, MA 02062 • AASL

Wobbe Jean • Director Library Media • School District • Tracy, CA 95376 • AASL

Wodarczyk Ann • Librarian • Main Road School • Newfield, NJ 08344

Wodrich Schmidt Kathy • Serials Coordinator • University of Wisconsin Murphy Library • La Crosse, WI 54601 • ALCTS LRRT

Woeckel Allan J. • Administrative Director • Reddick Library • Ottawa, IL 61350

Woelfel Barry • Student • University of California-Berkeley School of Library & Information Studies • Berkeley, CA 94720

Woerner Karen • Colorado Territorial Correction Facility • Canon City, CO 81212

Wogaman Mariol R. • Oregon State University William Jasper Kerr Library • Corvallis, OR 97331-4501 • ACRL RASD

Wogenstahl Curtis C. • Student • University of Oklahoma School of Library & Information Studies • Norman, OK 73019

Wogoman Rebecca • Clearwater Public Library • Clearwater, FL 34623

Wohl Lauren L. • Marketing Dir • Disney Publishing • New York, NY 10011 • AASL ALSC

Wohlberg Cynthia • Children's Librarian • Los Angeles Public Library System Atwater Branch • Los Angeles, CA 90039 • ALSC

Wohlford Carol L. • Principal • Paideia Academy • Wichita, KS 67218 • ALSC

Wohlmuth Sonia R. • University of South Florida School of Library & Information Science • Tampa, FL 33620

Wohlschlag Sarah A. • Branch Librarian • Bay County Library System Sage Branch • Bay City, MI 48706 • PLA RASD

Wohnrade Ruth M. • Learning Center Director • Canterbury School • Crystal Lake, IL 60014 • AASL

Wohrley Andrew J. • Student • Indiana University School of Library and Information Science • Bloomington, IN 47405

Woike Glenn V. • Head Librarian • Daemen College Marian Library • Amherst, NY 14226-3592 • ACRL

Woitte Susan L. • Librarian I • Norfolk Public Library • Norfolk, VA 23510-1776

Woizeschke Kristin A. • Champlin, MN 55316 • IFRT

Wojcik James • Trustee • Poplar Creek Public Library Dist • Streamwood, IL 60107 • ALTA

Wojcik Joan • Saint Bernard High School Library Media Center • Uncasville, CT 06382 • AASL

Wojcikiewicz Sophia • Chicago, IL 60635 • AASL YALSA *Life*

Wojewodzki Catherine W. • Associate Librarian • University of Delaware Library • Newark, DE 19717-5267 • ACRL LIRT

Wojnaroski Janet B. • Librarian/Media Specialist • Roosevelt High School • Kent, OH 44240 • AASL

Wolbers Dennis M. • Student • San Jose State University Division of Library & Information Science • San Jose, CA 95192-0029

Wolcott Debbie A. • Supervisor • City of Virginia Beach Extension Services • Virginia Beach, VA 23452

Wolcott Laurie J. • Technical Serivces Librarian • Taylor University Zondervan Library • Upland, IN 46989 • ACRL ALCTS

Wolcott Mary E. • Library Assistant I • University of Texas Libraries General Libraries • Austin, TX 78713-7330

Wolcott Merlin D. • Sandusky, OH 44870 • LAMA PLA *Life*

Wold Jill S. • Waubonsee Community College Library • Sugar Grove, IL 60554

Wold Mary I. • Heber Springs, AR 72543 • ALTA PLA

Wold Shelley T. • Documents/Reference Librarian • University of Arkansas at Little Rock Ottenheimer Library • Little Rock, AR 72204 • ACRL GODORT

Wolf Bonnie J. • High School Librarian • Dodgeville High School • Dodgeville, WI 53533 • AASL ALSC YALSA

Wolf Carol J. • Public Service Librarian • Metropolitan Library System Village Branch • Oklahoma City, OK 73120-4110

Wolf Carolyn E. • Head of Public Services • Hartwick College Stevens German Library • Oneonta, NY 13820

Wolf Catharine D. • Library Media Specialist • Macedon Elementary School • Macedon, NY 14502 • AASL

Wolf Diane S. • Englewood, NJ 07631

Wolf Dorothy L. • Branch Librarian • Carroll County Public Library Eldersburg Branch • Eldersburg, MD 21784

Wolf Edward G. • Indiana, PA 15701 • ACRL ALCTS *Life*

Wolf Jay F. • Incline Villege, NV 89450

Wolf Joy G. • Children & Young Adult Librarian • Northfield Public Library • Northfield, MN 55057 • ALSC LAMA RASD IFRT *Life*

Wolf Kathleen M. • Supervising Librarian • Pierce County Rural Library District • Tacoma, WA 98446

Wolf Lois G. • Librarian-Technical Services • Eastern Connecticut State University J. Eugene Smith Library • Willimantic, CT 06226 • ACRL LITA

Wolf Louise B. • Librarian • Lombard Junior High School • Galesburg, IL 61401

Wolf Margaret M. • Exton, PA 19341-1484

Wolf Melinda J. • Decatur, GA 30033

Wolf Milton T. • Head of Collection Development • University of Nevada-Reno Noble H. Getchell Library • Reno, NV 89557 • LITA LIRT

Wolf Otto • Trustee • Mid-Hudson Library System • Poughkeepsie, NY 12601

Wolf Richard E. • Richard E. Wolf and Associates • Arlington, VA 22216

Wolf Rochelle G. • St Louis, MO 63130 • AASL

Wolfe Barbara • District Chairperson Libraries • Plainview-Old Bethpage Schools • Plainview, NY 11803 • AASL

Wolfe Carl F. • Project Leader • Dow USA Applied Information Sciences • Freeport, TX 77541-3259 • ACRL ALCTS LITA *Life*

Wolfe Charlotte • Senior Associate Librarian • University of Michigan Libraries • Ann Arbor, MI 48109-1205 • ACRL ALCTS

Wolfe Cynthia A. • Midland, TX 79705

Wolfe D Jane • Fort Lee, VA 23801

Wolfe Deborah A. • Reference Librarian • Midland County Public Library • Midland, TX 79702

Wolfe Gary D. • Director,Library Development Div • State Library of Pennsylvania • Harrisburg, PA 17101 • ASCLA PLA

Wolfe Joanne • Trustee • Farmers Branch Public Library • Farmers Branch, TX 75234 • ALTA

Wolfe Kimberly A. • Children's Librarian • Jackson County Library System • Medford, OR 97501

Wolfe Lisa A. • Public Information Office • Spokane Public Library Comstock Building Library • Spokane, WA 99201-0976 • LAMA

Wolfe Lynne M. • Columbus Metropolitan Library • Columbus, OH 43215 • ALSC YALSA

Wolfe Marcelle B. • Chalmette, LA 70043

Wolfe Marcia G. • Amsterdam School • Belle Mead, NJ 08502 • AASL

Wolfe Marion C. • Phoenix, AZ 85006 • Continuing

Wolfe Martha K. • Reader Service Librarian • University of Windsor Leddy Library • Windsor ON, N9B 3P4 Canada • ACRL ASCLA MAGERT

Wolfe Meg • Phoenix Public Library Century Branch • Phoenix, AZ 85016 • PLA YALSA

Wolfe Michele B. • West Chester, PA 19380 • ACRL

Wolfe N. J. • Associate Director for Info Serv • New York University Medical Library • New York, NY 10016 • ACRL LAMA RASD

Wolfe Patricia • Trustee • San Jose Public Library • San Jose, CA 95113 • ALTA

Wolfe Susan J. • Chief. Lawbooks Sections • Administrative Offices of the United States Courts • Washington, DC 20544 • ALCTS

Wolff Cynthia J. • Government Documents Ref Libn • University of Oklahoma Libraries University Libraries • Norman, OK 73019 • GODORT

Wolff Kimberly P. • Reference Librarian • Saint Petersburg Junior College Clearwater Campus Library • Clearwater, FL 34625 • ACRL

Wolford Betty • Library Automation Specialist • Princeton Technical Service Center • Cincinnati, OH 45246 • AASL

Wolford Larry E. • Delanco, NJ 08075

Wolford Linda • Adult Services Supervisor • Kansas City Kansas Public Library • Kansas City, KS 66101

Wolford Valerie Eslyn • Library Manager • Rhone-Poulenc AG Company • Research Triangle Pk, NC 27709 • LAMA

Wolfram Mary S. • Librarian • Norman High School • Norman, OK 73072 • AASL

Wolfson Linda • Trustee • Bucks County Free Library • Doylestown, PA 18901 • ALTA

Wolke Dorothy C. • Bronx, NY 10461 • ACRL ASCLA

Wolkenbreit Janis • Crocker Farm Elementary School • Amherst, MA 01002 • AASL

Woll Christina B. • Palacios, TX 77465 • AASL ALSC

Wollam Kathy L. • Columbia, SC 29201 • ALSC PLA

Wollam Martha D. • Laurel, MD 20707 • IFRT

Wollenweber Mark • City Manager • City of Saint Clair Shores • St. Clair Shores, MI 48081 • ALTA

Wollrab Lou • Information Coordinator • World Education • Boston, MA 02111 • IFRT

Wolner Roberta C. • San Jose Public Library • San Jose, CA 95113

Wolper Janet E. • East Brunswick, NJ 08816

Wolpert Louise A. • Toledo-Lucas County Public Library • Toledo, OH 43624

Wolter Anne M. • Instructional Materials Ctr Dir • Richmond School • Sussex, WI 53089 • AASL

Wolter Billie J. • Arvada Junior High School • Arvada, CO 80002 • AASL

Wolter John A. • Columbia, MD 21044 • MAGERT

Wolter Virginia L. • Student • Toledo-Lucas County Public Library Holland Branch Library • Holland, OH 43528 • IFRT

Wolters Nancy E. • Chair of Student Chapter • State University of New York at Albany School of Information Science & Policy • Albany, NY 12222

Woltz Martha • Assistant Librarian Public Serv • University of Science & Arts of Oklahoma • Chickasha, OK 73018

Wolven Eleanor H. • Assistant Director • Finkelstein Memorial Library • Spring Valley, NY 10977

Wolven Robert A. • Assistant Director Bibl Control • Columbia University Libraries Butler Library • New York, NY 10027 • ALCTS LITA

Wolverton Carol L. • Librarian II/ Reference • Montgomery County Department of Public Libraries Long Branch Community • Silver Springs, MD 20901-3898

Wolz Carolyn W. • Elementary School Media Spec. • Saugerties Central School District • Saugerties, NY 12477 • AASL

Womack Anne G • Reference Librarian • Plano Public Library System Gladys Harrington Library • Plano, TX 75074-6000 • IFRT

Womack Carol Z. • Business Librarian • University of California-Irvine Library • Irvine, CA 92713 • ACRL LAMA RASD LIRT

Womack James R. • Student • University of Southern Mississippi School of Library Science • Hattiesburg, MS 39406-5146

Womack John P. • Econ. Newspaper & Ser. Bibl. • University of Texas Libraries General Libraries • Austin, TX 78713-7330 • ALCTS

Womack Sharon G. • State Librarian • Arizona State Library Department of Library Archives & Public Records • Phoenix, AZ 85007

Womack Sharon Kay • Head of Reference Department • University of Louisville Ekstrom Library • Louisville, KY 40292 • ACRL RASD

Womble Kathryn • Student • University of Washington Suzzallo Library • Seattle, WA 98195 • MAGERT

Womeldorf Jack • Descriptive Cataloger • Library of Congress • Washington, DC 20541 • ACRL ALCTS *Life*

Wonak Gerald J. • Trustee • Wonak & Associates, Inc. • Elk Grove Village, IL 60007 • ALTA

Wondrack Carol A. • Children's Librarian • Robert Fulton Elementary School • North Bergen, NJ 07047 • YALSA

Wondriska Rebecca S. • Government Publication Librarian • Trinity College Library • Hartford, CT 06106 • GODORT

Wong Amy A. • Student • University of Washington Graduate School of Library and Information Science • Seattle, WA 98195

Wong Carol Y. • U.S Army Intelligence& Threat Analysis Center • Washington, DC 20374-5085 • Life

Wong Clark C. • Asst. Director of Libraries • California State University Oviatt Library • Northridge, CA 91328-1289

Wong Cynthia J. • Cataloger • University of Texas Libraries General Libraries • Austin, TX 78713-7330 • IRRT

Wong Deborah J. • Baltimore County Public Library • Towson, MD 21204 • PLA

Wong Eugenia J. K. • Technical Services Manager • Orange Public Library • Orange, CA 92666 • LITA

Wong Gail • Pennington, NJ 08534

Wong Jean L. • University Microfilms International • Ann Arbor, MI 48106-1346 • ALCTS

Wong Katherine C. • Student • University of Oklahoma School of Library & Information Studies • Norman, OK 73019

Wong Kelley M. • Student • State University of New York at Albany School of Information Science & Policy • Albany, NY 12222

Wong Kwai-ying • Librarian • Hong Kong University of Science & Technology • Kowloon, Hong Kong

Wong Lana • Hd. of Ref. & Outline Services • Chapman University Thurman Clarke Memorial Library • Orange, CA 92666 • ACRL RASD

Wong Linda • Aloha, OR 97007 • AASL

Wong Lok-Kuen • Student • Southern Connecticut State University School of Libray Science & Instructional Technology • New Haven, CT 06515

Wong Margaret C. • Chief of Public Service • County of Los Angeles Public Library • Hawthorne, CA 90250 • LAMA PLA

Wong Marilynn M L • Maui Memorial Hospital Medical Library • Wailuku, HI 96793 • ASCLA

Wong Mary J. • Glendale, AZ 85302 • AASL

Wong Ming K. Mr. • Ohio State University Libraries • Columbus, OH 43210-1286 • ALCTS LITA MAGERT

Wong Monica C. • Collection Devlp Libn • El Paso Community College • El Paso, TX 79998 • LITA IRRT

Wong Nancy Chao • Editor • H. W. Wilson Company • Bronx, NY 10452 • ALCTS

Wong Patricia M. • Supervising Librarian • Berkeley Public Library South Branch • Berkeley, CA 94703 • ALSC LAMA PLA EMIERT

Wong Smay L. • Deerfield, IL 60015 • ACRL ALCTS

Wong Solomon H.M. • Sr. Reference Librarian • United States Information Service (USIS) Library • FPO, AP 96522-0002 • PLA

Wong Susan A. • Student • University of California-Berkeley School of Library & Information Studies • Berkeley, CA 94720

Wong William Sheh • East Asian Librarian • University of California-Irvine Library • Irvine, CA 92713 • ACRL IRRT

Wonsek Pamela L. • Head, Access Services • Hunter College Library • New York, NY 10021 • ACRL LAMA

Wonsever Eithne C. • East Rockaway, NY 11518

Woo Janet C. • Branch Librarian • Los Angeles Public Library Memorial Branch • Los Angeles, CA 90019 • EMIERT

Woo Janice • Student • University of California-Berkeley School of Library & Information Studies • Berkeley, CA 94720 • ACRL LITA IFRT LRRT SRRT

Woo Jensa • Librarian • San Francisco Public Library Chinatown Branch • San Francisco, CA 94108 • ALSC PLA

Woo Kathleen • Periodicals Librarian • University of San Francisco Richard A. Gleeson Library • San Francisco, CA 94117

Woo Linda C. • Ln • University of Washington Suzzallo Library • Seattle, WA 98195 • ACRL

Woo Stella W. • Student • Rutgers University School of Communication Information & Library Studies • New Brunswick, NJ 08903

Wood-Davis Carol • Newport Beach, CA 92660

Wood Alberta Auringer • Map Librarian • Memorial University of Newfoundland • St. John's, NF, A1B 3Y1 Canada • MAGERT

Wood Ann F. • Shelby, OH 44875 • PLA

Wood Ann L. • Reference Librarian • University of Massachusetts Library • Amherst, MA 01003 • ACRL IRRT *Life*

Wood Arline L. • Librarian • Harrison Elementary Schools • Harrison, NY 10528 • AASL

Wood Audrey R. • San Francisco, CA 94107 • ALSC SRRT

Wood Bonnie Bess • Librarian • Trinity Episcopal School Edith Aiken Library • New Orleans, LA 70130 • AASL IFRT VRT

Wood Brenda • Holland, KY 42153

Wood Camille D. • Asst. Director • Nampa Public Library • Nampa, ID 83651 • NMRT

Wood Carol L. • Essex, MA 01929

Wood Charlotte L. • Library Consultant • Career Devel & Assessment Ctr • Seattle, WA 98125

Wood Christine L. • Student • University of Missouri-Kansas City Library • Kansas City, MO 64110-2499 • RASD

Wood Cooper D. • University of Colorado Health Science Center, Denison Mem Lib • Denver, CO 80262 • LITA

Wood Cynthia J. • Student • Catholic University of America School of Library and Information Science • Washington, DC 20064 • AASL

Wood Darlis A. • Reference Librarian • Chevron Corporation Library • San Francisco, CA 94104

Wood David A. • Head of Hum. & Social Sci. • University of Washington • Seattle, WA 98195 • ACRL

Wood Dianne M. • Reference Librarian • Findlay-Hancock County Public Library • Findlay, OH 45840 • RASD

Wood Dora Nelle • Media Specialist • John Will Elementary School • Mobile, AL 36608 • AASL

Wood Dorothy L. • Librarian • Orange County Public Library Chapman Branch • Garden Grove, CA 92641 • PLA

Wood Elizabeth • Trustee • Huntington Public Library • Huntington, NY 11743 • ALTA

Wood Elizabeth J. • Business Librarian • Bowling Green State University William Jerome Library • Bowling Green, OH 43403-0175 • LAMA

Wood Ethel M. • Oak Ridge, TN 37830 • Continuing

Wood Floris W. • Science Ln. & Data Archivist • Bowling Green State University William Jerome Library • Bowling Green, OH 43403-0175 • ACRL

Wood Gail • Dir. Edu Supporty Service • Montgomery College Germantown Campus • Germantown, MD 20874 • ACRL LAMA RASD

Wood Gayle E. • Library Systems Coordinator • Illinois Library Computer System Office • Champaign, IL 61820

Wood Irene D. • Editor, Nonprint Materials • American Library Association • Chicago, IL 60611-2795 • VRT

Wood Johanna S. Mrs • Washington, DC 20015 • AASL ALSC YALSA *Life*

Wood John B. • Reference Librarian • California State University-Los Angeles John F. Kennedy Memorial Library • Los Angeles, CA 90032-8300 • ACRL ALCTS IFRT

Wood Julienne L. • Shreveport, LA 71104 • ACRL RASD FLRT

Wood Kalthleen A. • Head Librarian • District of Columbia Public Library • Washington, DC 20001

Wood Karen Ann • Special Asst to Librarian of Con • Library of Congress • Washington, DC 20541

Wood Kathryn L. • Head of Technical Services • Nyack Library • Nyack, NY 10960 • ALSC

Wood Kincaid M. • Student • University of Central Arkansas Department of Educational Media & Library Science • Conway, AR 72032-5001 • LITA IFRT SRRT

Wood Leslie J. • Student • Wake Forest University Z Smith Reynolds Library • Winston Salem, NC 27109-7777 • IFRT SRRT

Wood Linda • Reference Librarian • Columbus Metropolitan Library Main Library Branch • Columbus, OH 43215 • RASD GODORT

Wood Linda M. • Library Director • Alameda County Library System • Fremont, CA 94538 • LAMA PLA

Wood Linda P. • Library Media Specialist • South Kingstown High School • Wakefield, RI 02879 • AASL

Wood Loretta • Secondary Media Coordinator • Olathe Public Schools • Olathe, KS 66062 • AASL LITA IFRT

Wood Lou Anne • Media Specialist • Takoma Academy Library • Takoma Park, MD 20912

Wood Madeline L. • Fowler, CO 81039 • ALSC NMRT

Wood Marilyn R. • Media Specialist • East Marshall Community Schools • LeGrand, IA 50142 • AASL

Wood Mary W. • University of California Shields Library • Davis, CA 95616

Wood Michael B. • Dean • Ball State University Library Department of Library Services • Muncie, IN 47306 • ACRL LAMA

Wood Monica H. Sr. • Librarian • Saint John's University Library • Staten Island, NY 10301 • ACRL

Wood Norma W. • Eastland, TX 76448 • ALCTS LITA *Life*

Wood Olivia K. • Reference Librarian • Samford University Library • Birmingham, AL 35229

Wood Patricia • Librarian II • District of Columbia Public Library Martin Luther King Memorial Library • Washington, DC 20001 • RASD

Wood Patrick W. • Administrator • Clarion District Library • Clarion, PA 16214 • ACRL RASD

Wood Raymund F. Dr. • Encino, CA 91316 • Continuing

Wood Richard J. • Sam Houston State University Newton Gresham Library • Huntsville, TX 77341-2281 • ACRL

Wood Robert D. • Eastland, TX 76448 • LAMA PLA *Life*

Wood Robert T. • Student • Louisiana State University School of Library & Information Science • Baton Rouge, LA 70803-3290

Wood Ruthmary J. • Asst Dept Hd Tech Serv Dept • Aurora Public Library • Aurora, IL 60505-4299 • Life

Wood Sandra L. • Taylor Elementary School • Brooksville, KY 41004 • AASL

Wood Sandra L. • Student • San Jose State University Division of Library & Information Science • San Jose, CA 95192-0029

Wood Stephen D. • Director • Cleveland Heights-University Heights Public Library • Cleveland Heights, OH 44118 • PLA

Wood Susan Cheryl • Technical Systems Librarian • Burroughs-Wellcome Company Technical Information Department • Research Triangle Pk, NC 27709 • LITA

Wood Susan M. • Student • Catholic University of America School of Library and Information Science • Washington, DC 20064 • ALSC PLA

Wood Wendy D. • Northern Kentucky University Steely Library • Highland Heights, KY 41099-6101 • NMRT

Wood William Bliss • Gresham, OR 97030 • ACRL RASD *Continuing*

Woodall Nancy C. • Librarian • Fairfax County Public Library • Fairfax, VA 22033-1907 • LAMA PLA

Woodall Nancy K. • Student • University of Richmond • Richmond, VA 23173 • LITA

Woodard Beth Ellen • State Reference Center, Head • Arizona State Library Department of Library Archives & Public Records • Phoenix, AZ 85007 • PLA

Woodard Beth S. • Central Information Serv Ln • University of Illinois Library • Urbana, IL 61801 • ACRL RASD

Woodard Frances H. • Huntsville-Madison County Public Library • Huntsville, AL 35804

Woodard Gloria Lewis • Assistant Director • Nichols P. Sims Library • Waxahachie, TX 75165

Woodard Virginia W. • Student • State University of New York (SUNY) University Libraries • Albany, NY 12222 • AASL

Woodburn David M. • Executive Director • Mississippi Library Commission • Jackson, MS 39209 • PLA

Woodbury Ella M. • Online Research Services Ln • Florida Department of Education • Tallahassee, FL 32399 • RASD

Woodbury Linda L. • New Orleans Public Library • New Orleans, LA 70140 • ALSC

Woodcock Alexandra • Glendora Public Library • Glendora, CA 91740

Woodcock Vickie C. • Director • Farmington Public Library District • Farmington, IL 61531

Wooddell Wendy • Clay Senior High School Library • Oregon, OH 43616

Woodford Arthur M. • Director • Saint Clair Shores Public Library • St. Clair Shores, MI 48081 • LAMA PLA

Woodford Susanne L. • Assistant Managing Librarian • King County Library System • Seattle, WA 98109-5191 • PLA RASD EMIERT

Woodfork Suewilla I. • Librarian • Marks Meadow School • Amherst, MA 01002 • AASL

Woodhams Caroline M. • Pierce County Rural Library District Lakewood Branch • Tacoma, WA 98499

Woodhouse Diane • School Library Media Spec. • Broadway Elementary School • Elmira, NY 14904 • AASL

Wooding Rochelle • Teacher-Librarian • DeWitt Clinton Elementary School • Chicago, IL 60659

Woodle Miriam T. • Southfield, MI 48075 • Continuing

Woodlee Rick G. • Librarian • Tennessee Valley Authority Technical Library • Chattanooga, TN 37402-2801

Woodley Mary S. • Sr. Cataloging Asst. • Getty Center for the History of Art Humanities Library • Santa Monica, CA 90401-1455 • ALCTS

Woodmansee James • Student • University of California-Berkeley School of Library & Information Studies • Berkeley, CA 94720 • LITA

Woodrow Ann C. • Portola Valley, CA 94028 • AASL

Woodruff Camille • Fort Gorden, GA 30905-0341

Woodruff Cindy E. • Cataloging Department • Niagara University Library • Niagara University, NY 14109 • ALCTS SRRT

Woodruff Cynthia • Gilman Lower School Library • Baltimore, MD 21210 • AASL ALSC

Woodruff Evelyn L. • Librarian II • San Mateo Public Library • San Mateo, CA 94402

Woodruff Hertha J. • W. Bloomfield, MI 48322

Woodruff Laura C. • Librarian • Northern High School • Detroit, MI 48202

Woodruff M Joan • Monroe, MI 48161

Woodrum Frances L. • Director • Jacksonville Public Library • Jacksonville, IL 62650 • LAMA PLA

Woodrum Pat • Director • Tulsa City-County Library System • Tulsa, OK 74103 • PLA

Woods Andrea L. • Student • University of Missouri-Columbia School of Library & Informational Science • Columbia, MO 65211 • ALSC PLA

Woods Barbara J. • Student • Rutgers University School of Communication Information & Library Studies • New Brunswick, NJ 08903 • PLA SRRT

Woods Catharine C. • Boulder, CO 80303

Woods Cheryl A. • Student • San Jose State University Division of Library & Information Science • San Jose, CA 95192-0029 • LITA

Woods Cynthia B. • Librarian • Senseny Road School • Winchester, VA 22601 • AASL ALSC

Woods Elaine W. • Arlington, VA 22202 • ALCTS LITA

Woods Frances B. • Chief Cataloger • Yale University Law Library • New Haven, CT 06520 • ACRL ALCTS

Woods Janice T. • East Northport, NY 11731

Woods Julia A. • Director • Mesa State College Library • Grand Junction, CO 81501 • ACRL LAMA

Woods Lawrence A. • Dir. of Information Systems • University of Iowa Libraries • Iowa City, IA 52242-1379 • ACRL ALCTS LITA

Woods Lawrence J. • Assistant Executive Director • Public Affairs Information Service • New York, NY 10036-4396 • ACRL

Woods Marian Mrs. • Librarian • Birmingham Public Library Southside Branch • Birmingham, AL 35211

Woods Marilyn • Librarian • Minot Forest School • Wareham, MA 02571

Woods Marla K. • Student • Texas Woman's University School of Library & Information Studies • Denton, TX 76204 • AASL

Woods Mary • Assistant Librarian • Avila College Hooley-Bundschu Library • Kansas City, MO 64145 • ALCTS PLA RASD

Woods Mary B. • Falls Church, VA 22044 • AASL ALSC

Woods Muriel K. • School Library Media Specialist • Northview Elementary School • Manhattn, KS 66502 • AASL

Woods Patricia W. • Librarian • Benjamin Franklin Information Center Sussex Technical High School • Georgetown, DE 19947 • AASL LAMA LITA IFRT LIRT

Woods Phyllis J. • Teacher-Librarian • Whitney M. Young Magnet High School • Chicago, IL 60607 • AASL

Woods Richard F. • Executive Director • Marmot Project Mesa State College Library • Grand Junction, CO 81502 • ASCLA LAMA LITA

Woods Selina J. • Winchester, MA 01890 • AASL ALSC

Woodson-Marks Sue M. • Student • Simmons College Graduate School of Library & Information Science • Boston, MA 02115 • LITA

Woodson Almeta G. • Librarian • Clark-Atlanta University School of Library & Information Studies • Atlanta, GA 30314-4391 • ACRL

Woodstrom Ruy K. • District Children's Librarian • Minneapolis Public Library Walker Community Library • Minneapolis, MN 55408

Woodstrup Wendi • Young Adult Librarian • Ewa Beach Public and School Library • Ewa Beach, HI 96706

Woodsworth Anne • Dean • Long Island University Palmer School of Library & Info. Sci. • Brookville, NY 11548 • ACRL ASCLA LAMA PLA

Woodward Ann • Atlanta, GA 30307 • ALTA   *Continuing*

Woodward Jeannette • College of Santa Fe Library • Santa Fe, NM 87501 • ACRL

Woodward Joanne M. • Chestnut Hill Elementary School • Midland, MI 48640 • AASL

Woodward Lawrence W. • Librarian • Government Printing Office • Washington, DC 20401 • ALCTS RASD FLRT GODORT LHRT MAGERT

Woodward Neil • President • Category Six Books, Inc. • Denver, CO 80218 • ACRL

Woodward Phyllis K. • Head of Reference Service • Lake County Public Library • Merrillville, IN 46410-5382 • RASD

Woodward Sallie • Librarian • Crockett Public Library • Crockett, TX 75835

Woodward Wade M. • Director of Library • Northern State University Williams Library • Aberdeen, SD 57401-7198 • LRRT

Woodworth Patricia J. • Head, Circulation Services • Quincy Public Library • Quincy, IL 62301

Woodworth Patricia K. • Librarian • John Wood Community College • Quincy, IL 62301

Woody Jacqueline B. • Upper Marlboro, MD 20772

Woody Janet C. • Head of Automated Services Dept. • Virginia Commonwealth University • Richmond, VA 23284-2033 • LITA

Woody Thomas J. • Student • Clark-Atlanta University School of Library & Information Studies • Atlanta, GA 30314-4391

Wool Gregory J. • Asst. Prof. Cataloging • Iowa State University Library • Ames, IA 50011-2140 • ACRL ALCTS EMIERT LRRT NMRT

Wool Susan E. • Book Cataloger • H. W. Wilson Company • Bronx, NY 10452 • ACRL

Wooldridge Betty M. • Director • Blue Ridge Regional Library • Martinsville, VA 24115 • LAMA PLA RASD YALSA

Wooldridge Steven M. • Media Librarian • University of Michigan Libraries Information and Library Studies • Ann Arbor, MI 48109

Woolf Monica • Acting Ln./Supervisory work • H. E. Finger Learning Res. Center • Houston, TX 77096 • AASL ALSC

Woolf-Ivory Jonalyn R. • Assistant Director Public Servs • Sno-Isle Regional Library • Marysville, WA 98271-9164 • PLA

Woolley Helen • Head of Moore County Libraries • Killgore Memorial Library • Dumas, TX 79029 • PLA CLENE

Woolley Jeanette • Library Media • Jackson Elementary School • Salt Lake City, UT 84116

Woolls E. Blanche • Professor • University of Pittsburgh School of Library and Information Science • Pittsburgh, PA 15260 • AASL ALSC ASCLA LITA YALSA IFRT   *Life*

Woolsey George M. • Homewood, IL 60430 • ALCTS

Woolston Elliott K. • Oak Ridge High School • El Dorado Hills, CA 95630

Woolverton Debbie S. • Research Librarian • Marie Selby Botanical Garden • Sarasota, FL 34236 • ACRL

Woolverton Phil T. • University of Oklahoma School of Library & Information Studies • Norman, OK 73019 • AASL IFRT

Woon Lillian W. • Instructor/Student Serv Office • University of Hawaii School of Library & Information Studies • Honolulu, HI 96822 • NMRT

Wooster Linda I. • APO, AE 09175 • LITA AFLRT FLRT GODORT IFRT

Wooster Martha F. • Librarian • Harvard University • Cambridge, MA 02138 • ACRL ALCTS LAMA LITA

Wooten Jimmi • Reference Librarian • Maywood Public Library • Maywood, IL 60153

Wooten Toni L. • Student • University of North Carolina at Chapel Hill School of Information and Library Science • Chapel Hill, NC 27599-3360 • ALSC

Wootton-Milhander Nancy • Student • Indiana University School of Library and Information Science • Bloomington, IN 47405

Wootton M. Norris Ms • Director of Lib/Media Services • Flint River Technical Institute • Thomaston, GA 30286

Worden Catherine Mrs. • Ventura, CA 93001 • Continuing

Worden David M. • Reference Librarian • Hernando County Library System West Hernando Branch • Brooksville, FL 34613

Wordinger Debra L. • Assistant Director • Indian Prairie Public Library District • Willowbrook, IL 60517

Workman Gaylord E. • Chicago, IL 60632 • LITA

Workman Judith B. • Elementary Librarian • Mount Vernon Community Schools • Mount Vernon, IA 52314 • AASL ALSC

Works Theresa A. • Jackson, CA 95642

Worley Barbara M. • Librarian • Hill Country M. S. Library • Austin, TX 78746 • AASL

Worley Jean N. • Media Specialist • Redland Elementary School • Homestead, FL 33031 • AASL

Worley Joan H. • Director • Maryville College Lamar Memorial Library • Maryville, TN 37801 • ACRL ALCTS LAMA RASD IFRT

Worley Larry • Head Acquisitions • University of Dallas William A. Blakley Library • Irving, TX 75062 • ACRL

Worley Nelson • Director • Appomattox Regional Library • Hopewell, VA 23860

Worman R. C. • Knoxville, TN 37918

Wormer Grace • Iowa City, IA 52240 • ACRL   *Life*

Woroby Maria K. • St. Paul, MN 55112 • LIRT

Worrell Diane F. • Reference Librarian • Appalachian State University Carol Grotnes Belk Library • Boone, NC 28608 • ACRL RASD

Worrell Donald E. Jr • Director • Mount Clemens Public Library • Mount Clemens, MI 48043 • AASL LAMA

Worrell Felissa L. • Information Specialist • Independent Project Analyst, Inc. • Reston, VA 22090 • ASCLA LAMA ILERT LRRT NMRT

Worrell Placida • University of Southern California Doheny Library • Los Angeles, CA 90089-0182

Worsham Carol E. • Apex Middle School • Apex, NC 27502 • AASL

Worthing Richard L. • Librarian • California State Library • Sacramento, CA 94237-0001 • ALCTS

Worthington Nancy E. • Manhattan, KS 66502

Wortman Barbara S. • Head of Children's Services • Public Library of Mount Vernon & Knox County • Mount Vernon, OH 43050 • ALSC IFRT NMRT

Wortman Irene B. • Trustee • Harnett County Public Library System • Lillington, NC 27546

Wortman Lois H. • Director • Cumberland College • Williamsburg, KY 40769 • ACRL

Wortman William A. • Miami University Edgar W. King Library • Oxford, OH 45056 • ACRL ALCTS

Wortzel Murray N. • New York, NY 10010 • ACRL

Wosika Karen • Children's Librarian • San Bernardino County Library Barstow Branch • Barstow, CA 92311 • ALSC

Wostel June H. • Branch Supervisor • Multnomah County Library Gregory Heights Branch • Portland, OR 97213

Wou Kan Wong • Branch Head • New York Public Library Huguenot Park Branch Library • Staten Island, NY 10312 • PLA CLENE

Woukonish Nancy C. • Library Assistant • Manchester City Library • Manchester, NH 03101

Woy James B. • Philadelphia, PA 19102 • RASD

Woycik Janet M. Mrs. • Director • Cyrenius H Booth Library • Newtown, CT 06470

Wozniak Gayle G. • Lib Tech Asst Supervisor • University of South Florida Library • Tampa, FL 33620-5600

Wozniak Linda A. • Children's Librarian • Dewitt Community Library • Dewitt, NY 13214 • PLA

Wozniak Sherrill Weaver • Student • Indiana University School of Library and Information Science • Bloomington, IN 47405 • ACRL ALCTS LITA EMIERT GODORT IFRT SRRT

Wozny Jay • Executive Director • Corn Belt Library System • Normal, IL 61761 • LAMA PLA

Wray Douglas J. • Student • Simmons College Graduate School of Library & Information Science • Boston, MA 02115

Wray Stanley Tanner III • Takoma Park, MD 20912 • SRRT

Wray Wendell L. • Professor Emeritus • University of Pittsburgh School of Library and Information Science • Pittsburgh, PA 15260 • PLA

Wreath April I. • Systems Librarian • University of North Carolina Walter Clinton Jackson Library • Greensboro, NC 27412-5201 • ALCTS LITA

Wrege Ann S. • Director • Cheshire Public Library • Cheshire, CT 06410 • PLA

Wren Janice C. • Cumberland College • Willamsburg, KY 40769 • ACRL GODORT

Wren Jill R. • Adams and Ambrose Publishing • Madison, WI 53715 • ACRL LITA GODORT LIRT LRRT

Wrenn Mildred B. • Library Director • Marshall County Library • Holly Springs, MS 38635 • PLA NMRT

Wright-Sedan Rebecca S. • Student • State University of New York (SUNY) Thomas E. Dewey Graduate Library • Albany, NY 12222

Wright Amy L. • School Services Librarian • Elmhurst Public Library • Elmhurst, IL 60126 • AASL ALSC

Wright Arlene D. • Public Services Coordinator • Northern State University • Aberdeen, SD 57401 • ACRL RASD GODORT LIRT

Wright Arthuree R.M. • Acting Assistant Director • Howard University Libraries Founders Library • Washington, DC 20059 • ACRL ALCTS

Wright Barbara W. • Librarian • Peter Thacher Middle School • Attleboro, MA 02307 • AASL

Wright Betsy V. • Wisconsin State Law Library • Madison, WI 53707-7881 • GODORT

Wright Brenda L. • Librarian I • Atlanta-Fulton Public Library • Atlanta, GA 30303 • ALCTS LITA PLA

Wright Brenda M. • Florida A&M University • Tallahassee, FL 32307

Wright Carol A. • Reference Librarian • Pennsylvania State University Pattee Library • University Park, PA 16802 • ACRL

Wright Carolyn R. • High School Librarian • McAlester High School Library • McAlester, OK 74501 • AASL

Wright Catherine • San Rafael Public Library • San Rafael, CA 94901

Wright Catherine A. • General Information Dept. • Multnomah County Library Central Library • Portland, OR 97205 • PLA

Wright Cheryl S. • Branch Manager • Indianapolis-Marion County Public Library Prospect Branch • Indianapolis, IN 46203-2088

Wright Christopher • Chief-Loan Division • Library of Congress • Washington, DC 20541 • ALCTS

Wright Deborah L. • Automation Consultant • Follett Software Company • McHenry, IL 60050-5589 • AASL

Wright Deborah L. • Children Services Supervisor • Prince William Library Potomac Branch • Woodbridge, VA 22191 • ALSC

Wright Denise Anton • Bloomington, IL 61701 • ALSC

Wright Denna • Children's Librarian • Park City Public Library • Park City, UT 84060 • ALSC

Wright Dian A. • Media Specialist • Roosevelt Middle School • Cedar Rapids, IA 52405 • AASL

Wright Donald E. • Director • Niles Public Library • Niles, IL 60648 • LAMA PLA   *Life*

Wright Dorothy W. • Preservation Librarian • Cornell University Albert R. Mann Library • Ithaca, NY 14853-4301 • ALCTS LITA

Wright Eleanor M. • Littleton, CO 80122

Wright Ethel C. Miss • La Jolla, CA 92037 • Continuing

Wright Frances V. • Seattle, WA 98155

Wright Geraldine Murphy • Camillus, NY 13031

Wright Gretchen S. • Reference Librarian • Catonsville Community College • Baltimore, MD 21228

Wright Helen H. • Head Librarian • Pittsfield Public Library • Pittsfield, IL 62363

Wright Helen K. • Chicago, IL 60643

Wright Janet K. • Arts & Humanities Librarian • Portland State University Library • Portland, OR 97207

Wright Janette D. • Director, Public Libraries • State Library of New South Wales • Sydney NSW, Australia • LAMA LITA PLA

Wright Jasper H. • South Bend, IN 46615 • LAMA PLA   *Life*

Wright Jaye C. • Library Assistant I • University of Missouri Libraries-Columbia Elmer Ellis Library • Columbia, MO 65201-5149 • RASD

Wright Jean Acker • Library Systems • Vanderbilt University Library Jean & Alexander Heard Library • Nashville, TN 37240-0007 • ACRL ALCTS LITA GODORT

Wright Jerry T. • Reference Librarian • University of South Alabama Library • Mobile, AL 36688

Wright Jill D. • Technical Services Manager • Franklin-Johnson County Public Library • Franklin, IN 46131 • ALCTS LITA PLA

Wright Joanna S. • Librarian I • Hudson Area Branch Library • Hudson, FL 34667

Wright John • Toledo, OH 43606

Wright John A. • Head Librarian • Pine Crest Upper School Library • Ft Lauderdale, FL 33308 • AASL ACRL

Wright John B. • Authority Control Librarian • Brigham Young University • Provo, UT 84602 • ALCTS

Wright John G. • Edmonton AB, T6G 1P9 Canada • AASL YALSA

Wright John L. • Branch Manager • Cuyahoga County Public Library North Royalton Branch • North Royalton, OH 44133 • LAMA

Wright John N. • Atlanta, GA 30307 • ACRL

Wright Johnna M. • El Paso, TX 79902 • AASL

Wright Kathleen • Student • Syracuse University School of Information Studies • Syracuse, NY 13244-4100 • SRRT

Wright Kathryn F. • Librarian • Dallas County Library • Fordyce, AR 71742

Wright Kathryn S. • Cataloger • Indiana State University Cunningham Memorial Library • Terre Haute, IN 47809 • ACRL ALCTS LITA

Wright Katie H. Dr. • Trustee • East Saint Louis Public Library • East St. Louis, IL 62201 • ALTA

Wright Kieth C. • Faculty • University of North Carolina Department of Library & Information Studies • Greensboro, NC 27412-5001 • LAMA LITA

Wright Laura M. • Childrens Librarian I • Marin Country Day School • Corte Madera, CA 94925

Wright Lauri L. • Augusta College Reese Library • Augusta, GA 30910

Wright Leona C. • Coor. Children/Young Adult Serv. • Washoe County Library Sierra View Branch • Reno, NV 89502 • ALSC YALSA

Wright Leslie J. • Seattle, WA 98115-6940

Wright Linda A. • Librarian • Columbia Public School • Columbia, MS 39429 • AASL

Wright Linda B. • Houston, TX 77059

Wright Linda D. • Circulation Supervisior • Greensboro Public Library • Greensboro, NC 27402

Wright Linda G. • Director • Kanawha County Public Library • Charleston, WV 25301 • LAMA PLA

Wright Linda M. • Musser Public Library • Muscatine, IA 52761 • ACRL RASD

Wright Linda M. • Marine City, MI 48039

Wright Madeleine G. • Pallot Librarian • Suffolk University Law Library • Boston, MA 02114 • GODORT

Wright Marcia L. • Director • Campbell County Public Library • Gillette, WY 82716 • LAMA PLA RASD YALSA
Life

Wright Margaret C. • Savannah Elementary School • Savannah, GA 31401

Wright Marie H. Ms. • Oakland Park, FL 33334

Wright Marie Turner • Librarian • Indiana University-Purdue University at Indianapolis Library (IUPUI) • Indianapolis, IN 46202 • ACRL ALSC RASD GODORT

Wright Marjorie E. • Children's Program Librarian • Los Altos Public Library • Los Altos, CA 94022 • ALSC

Wright Marjorie P. • Chair • Volusia County Public Library • Daytona Beach, FL 32124 • ALTA

Wright Marlene Mrs • Branch Librarian • Loudoun County Public Library System • Sterling, VA 22170 • ACRL ALCTS ALSC LAMA PLA RASD   *Life*

Wright Mary M. • Education Librarian • Western Kentucky University Library Media Education • Bowling Green, KY 42101 • ACRL

Wright Michelle M. • Clear Lake High School Clear Creek Independent School District • Houston, TX 77058

Wright Myrna F. • Librarian • Minnesota Library for the Blind and Physically Handicapped • Faribault, MN 55021

Wright Nancy L. • Palm Springs, FL 33461

Wright Olie • Ln Assistant-Special Displays • Edgewater Public Library • Edgewater, FL 32132

Wright Patrick D. • University of Manitoba • Winnipeg MB, R3T 2N2 Canada • ACRL RASD LIRT

Wright Paul R. • Reference Department • Miami University Edgar W. King Library • Oxford, OH 45056 • RASD

Wright Pauline W. • Librarian • Gurdon Primary School • Gurdon, AR 71743 • AASL

Wright Phyllis M. • Interlibrary Loans/Supv Ref • Brock University • St. Catharines ON, L2S 3A1 Canada

Wright Raymond S. III • Family History Coordinator • Brigham Young University • Provo, UT 84602 • RASD

Wright Robert A. • Reference Librarian • Whittier College School of Law • Los Angeles, CA 90020

Wright Sara Sue • Reference Services Supervisor • Kanawha County Public Library • Charleston, WV 25301 • PLA

Wright Sue Edmonds • Trustee • Cabell County Public Library • Huntington, WV 25701 • ALTA PLA

Wright Susan • Mobile Services Librarian • Sno-Isle Regional Library • Marysville, WA 98271-9164 • ASCLA LAMA PLA

Wright Susan • Trustee • Montgomery County Department of Public Libraries • Rockville, MD 20850 • ALTA PLA

Wright Susan Dulaney • Library Media Specialist • Oak Hall Episcopal School • Ardmore, OK 73401 • AASL YALSA

Wright Susan L. • Branch Head • Orange County Library Systems Southwest Branch Library • Orlando, FL 32819

Wright Thomas C. • Student • Brigham Young University School of Library & Information Sciences • Provo, UT 84602

Wright Trellis C. • Special Projects • Library of Congress • Washington, DC 20541 • LAMA

Wright Vennetta • Student • University of Maryland College of Library and Information Services • College Park, MD 20742-4345

Wright William F. • Information Specialist • AT&T Bell Laboratories • Murray Hill, NJ 07974 • ACRL LITA RASD

Wrighten Mary G. • Multicultural Servs Ref. Ln. • Bowling Green State University Jerome Library • Bowling Green, OH 43403 • ACRL EMIERT

Wrightington Lucy • So. Otselic, NY 13155

Wrightson Denelle C. • Hidell Architects • Dallas, TX 75204 • LAMA

Wrigley E. S. • Director • Francis Bacon Library • Claremont, CA 91711-3979 • ACRL

Wrinkle Barbara D. • Director • United States Air Force Base Library • Hanscom AFB, MA 01731-5000 • AFLRT FLRT

Wrisley Carole J. • Johnson County Community College Library • Overland Park, KS 66210 • ACRL

Writz Jacklyn M. • Texas Woman's University School of Library & Information Studies • Denton, TX 76204

Wroclawski Patricia T. • Children's Marketing Manager • Kroch's & Brentano's Books • Chicago, IL 60603 • ALSC

Wrona Michael J. • Librarian • Detroit College of Business Warren Campus Library • Warren, MI 48092-5209

Wronka Gretchen M. • Senior Librarian • Hennepin County Library • Minnetonka, MN 55343 • ALSC PLA

Wronsky Marilyn • Children's Librarian • Marin County Library • Corte Madera, CA 94925

Wrotenbery Carl R. • Director of Libraries • Southwestern Baptist Theological Seminary Roberts Library • Fort Worth, TX 76122 • ACRL ALCTS LAMA RASD LIRT

Wsol Sharon E. • Administrative Librarian • Crete Public Library District • Crete, IL 60417 • LAMA PLA

Wu Anna C. • Physical Sciences Ref Librarian • George Mason University Fenwick Library • Fairfax, VA 22030

Wu Daisy T. • Head Basic Sci & Engr Library • University of Michigan • Ann Arbor, MI 48109-1205 • ACRL IFRT

Wu Diana Yuhfen H. • San Jose State University Clark Library • San Jose, CA 95192-0028 • LRRT SRRT

Wu Edith Y. K. Miss • Assistant Librarian • Chinese University of Hong Kong • Shatin NT, Hong Kong • LITA

Wu Ginger Y. • Student • Emporia State University School of Library & Information Management • Emporia, KS 66801

Wu Harry P. • Director • Saint Clair County Library System • Port Huron, MI 48060-4098 • LAMA PLA

Wu Hong • Student • Northern Illinois University Department of Library & Information Studies • DeKalb, IL 60115

Wu Hsiao-Chuan • Edison, NJ 08817 • ACRL

Wu Hui-lan C. • Madison, WI 53705-1529 • ALCTS ALSC PLA RASD

Wu Jean • School Librarian • Milby Senior High School • Houston, TX 77012 • AASL

Wu Jennifer L. • Librarian • Seattle Central Community College • Seattle, WA 98122 • LIRT

Wu Jing • Flushing, NY 11366

Wu Julia L. • Librarian • Virgil Junior High School • Los Angeles, CA 90004 • AASL

Wu Lisa C. • Chief Technical Service Section • National Institutes of Health Library • Bethesda, MD 20892

Wu May S. • Buffalo, NY 14230 • LITA

Wu Pei-Ling • Coordinator Technical Services • DePauw University Roy O. West Library • Greencastle, IN 46135-0037 • ALCTS LITA

Wu Shaoping • Student • Simmons College Graduate School of Library & Information Science • Boston, MA 02115 • ACRL

Wu Tony C. • Science Indexer • H. W. Wilson Company • Bronx, NY 10452 • PLA

Wu Wen-Hui • Wheelock College Library • Boston, MA 02215

Wu Xian Connie • Rutgers University Libraries Library of Science & Medicine • Piscataway, NJ 08855-1029 • ACRL

Wuehler Anne • Senior Reference Consultant • Family History Library • Salt Lake City, UT 84150

Wuertele Laura M. • Student • San Jose State University Division of Library & Information Science • San Jose, CA 95192-0029 • IFRT

Wuertz Eva L. • Librarian • University of Southern California Doheny Library • Los Angeles, CA 90089-0182 • ACRL RASD

Wuest Ruth • Swiss National Library • 3003 Bern, Switzerland

Wulf Kathryn • Librarian • Ell-Saline High School • Brookville, KS 67425

Wulf Werner A. • E.C. Weber Fraser Public Library • Fraser, MI 48026 • ALTA

Wulfekoetter Gertrude • Seattle, WA 98101 • ACRL ALCTS   *Continuing*

Wulff L. Yvonne • Assistant Director • University of Michigan Libraries • Ann Arbor, MI 48109-1205 • ACRL ALCTS

Wullert Diana M. • Librarian • Cascade High School • Turner, OR 97392 • AASL

Wullner Julie E. • Reference Librarian • Lincoln Library • Springfield, IL 62701 • PLA RASD

Wulwick Dorine • Roslyn, NY 11576 • AASL

Wunder Richard D. • Librarian • Westminster College of Salt Lake City • Salt Lake City, UT 84105 • ACRL ALCTS SRRT

Wunderlich Clifford S. • Cataloger • Harvard University Andover-Harvard Theological Library • Cambridge, MA 02138

Yaughn Valerie E. • Librarian • South College Library • Savannah, GA 31406

Yavarkovsky Jerome • Director • New York State Library State Education Department • Albany, NY 12230 • ACRL ASCLA LITA LRRT

Yax Margaret E. • Student • University of Illinois Graduate School of Library and Information Science • Urbana, IL 61801 • ACRL

Yazgoor Donald • Library Director • Norwalk Public Library • Norwalk, CT 06850 • LITA PLA

Ybanez Anthony • Trustee • Phoenix Public Library • Phoenix, AZ 85004 • ALTA

Ye Ding • Student • University of Hawaii School of Library & Information Studies • Honolulu, HI 96822 • ACRL

Yeager Gerry • Automated Services Librarian • Harford Community College • Bel Air, MD 21015 • ACRL ALCTS

Yeager Janice Skinner • Associate Director • Monroe County Public Library • Bloomington, IN 47408 • LAMA PLA

Yeager Mary M. • Clarks Suummit, PA 18411 • EMIERT IFRT SRRT

Yeager Rhoda M. • Alice Smith Elementary School Library • Reno, NV 89506 • AASL GODORT

Yealy Gretchen S. • Serial Cataloger • Brown University Rockefeller Library • Providence, RI 02912 • ACRL ALCTS

Yeargain Eloisa Gomez • Head of Public Services • University of California-Los Angeles (UCLA) • Los Angeles, CA 90024-1450

Yeates Elizabeth J. • Chief Public Document Room • United States Nuclear Regulatory Commission • Washington, DC 20555 • GODORT

Yeaton Evelyn H. Miss • Asheville, NC 28804 • PLA RASD *Continuing*

Yeck William S. Mrs • Trustee • Washington Township Public Library • Centerville, OH 45459

Yecny Dick • Director • The Dalles School District #12 Ram Center • The Dalles, OR 97058

Yee Bonnie J. • Senior Librarian • Burbank Central Library • Burbank, CA 91502 • Life

Yee Florence H. • Managing Librarian • East Oahu Library District • Honolulu, HI 96816 • PLA IFRT

Yee Helen W. • Public Utilities Counsel • California Public Utilities Comm • San Francisco, CA 94102

Yee Janice A. • Deputy Co. Librarian • Santa Clara County Free Library • San Jose, CA 95112-4446 • ALSC LAMA PLA EMIERT

Yee Martha M. • Cataloger • University of California Los Angeles Film & Television Archive (UCLA) • Los Angeles, CA 90038 • ALCTS LITA

Yee Sandra • Dept. Head Univ Library • Eastern Michigan Univ • Ypsilanti, MI 48197 • ACRL

Yee Vivian H. • Librarian • Sleepy Hollow Elementary School • Orinda, CA 94563 • AASL ALSC

Yegerlehner Shirley • Assistant to Director • Indiana University-Purdue University at Indianapolis Library (IUPUI) • Indianapolis, IN 46202 • ACRL

Yeh Daniel J. • Subject Coor • West Chester University Francis Harvey Green Library • West Chester, PA 19383 • ACRL

Yeh Helen S. C. • Asst. Director for Tech. Serv. • Prairie View A & M University • Prairie View, TX 77446 • ACRL LITA

Yeh Mengi • Student • Drexel University College of Information Studies • Philadelphia, PA 19104-2875

Yeh Pauline P. • Assistant Director for Tech Serv • Montclair State College Harry Sprague Library • Upper Montclair, NJ 07043 • LITA

Yeh Shih-Ting • Youth Services Librarian • San Diego Public Library Linda Vista Branch • San Diego, CA 92111 • ALSC

Yeh Thomas Yen-Ran • Prof & Hd Docs Dept • Central Washington University • Ellensburg, WA 98926 • ACRL GODORT MAGERT

Yeh Yi Y. • Library Media Specialist • West Middle School • Binghamton, NY 13905

Yela Gary E. • Senior Assistant Librarian • University of Delaware Morris Library • Newark, DE 19717-5267 • ACRL NMRT

Yeldell Catherine C. • Bastrop, LA 71220-3467

Yelich Hope H. • Reference Librarian • College of William and Mary Earl Gregg Swem Library • Williamsburg, VA 23187-8794 • ACRL RASD

Yelich Nolan T. • Librarian • Virginia State Library & Archives • Richmond, VA 23219 • LAMA PLA *Life*

Yellin Carol-Lynn • Trustee • Memphis-Shelby County Public Library and Information Center • Memphis, TN 38104-4025

Yellock Belinda B. • Branch Manager • Atlanta-Fulton Public Library Thomasville Heights Branch • Atlanta, GA 30315 • ALSC PLA NMRT

Yelverton John R. • Associate Director • University of Georgia Libraries • Athens, GA 30602 • ACRL ALCTS RASD

Yen Cynthia D. • Hawaii State Public Library • Honolulu, HI 96813 • ASCLA

Yensen Sandra C. • Assistant Director • Chelmsford Public Library • Chelmsford, MA 01824-3088 • PLA

Yeo-Tang Isabel • Nanyang Technological University Library • Singspore, 2263, Singapore

Yeomans Danielle E. • Ravena, NY 12143 • AASL

Yerkes Deborah L. • Assistant Documents Librarian • University of South Carolina • Columbia, SC 29208 • GODORT MAGERT

Yerkovich Marilee • Backman Elementary • Salt Lake City, UT 84116 • AASL

Yerman Roslyn F. • Head Reference Librarian • Madison Heights Public Library • Madison Heights, MI 48071

Yerxa Catharine M. Miss • Winchester, MA 01890 • ASCLA PLA *Continuing*

Yesner Bernice L. • School Library Media Teacher • Beecher Road School • Woodbridge, CT 06525 • AASL ALSC

Yetter Cathleen L. • Pacific Lutheran University Mortvedt Library • Tacoma, WA 98447

Yeung Andrew Yue-Yan Dr. • Hong Kong Baptist College Library • Kowloon, Hong Kong

Yeung Esther Y L • Head of Tech Serv/Catlg Ln • Fuller Theological Seminary • Pasadena, CA 91182 • ACRL ALCTS LAMA RASD

Yeung Wing-Yee • Bibliographical Center for Research • Denver, CO 80222 • LITA

Yi Cindy K. • Research Librarian • Boston Consulting Group Research Library • Chicago, IL 60606 • RASD

Yianakulis Georgia L. Sr. • Librarian • Bellarmine Prep High School • Tacoma, WA 98405 • AASL

Yick Patricia • Teacher Center Coordinator • Western Arkansas Education Co-op • Branch, AR 72928

Yingling Ann • Sunnyvale Public Library • Sunnyvale, CA 94088-3714 • ALCTS LAMA PLA

Yip Susan Young • Librarian • Morgan Hill Public Library • Morgan Hill, CA 95037

Yiu Dorothy L.S. • Student • University of California-Berkeley School of Library & Information Studies • Berkeley, CA 94720 • ALSC

Yliniemi Hazel A. • Director of Inst Resources • Fargo Public Schools • Fargo, ND 58103 • AASL YALSA

Yoakum Barbara Bebber • Librarian • U S Naval Academy Nimitz Library • Annapolis, MD 21402 • ACRL FLRT

Yoakum Cynthia C. • Cary, NC 27511

Yochelson Abby L. • Library of Congress • Washington, DC 20541

Yockey Judith K. • Hamilton, MT 59840 • AASL

Yockey Michael • Head of Technical Services • Holt Labor Library • San Francisco, CA 94102 • ALCTS

Yocum Patricia B. • Coor. Collection Devel. • University of Michigan • Ann Arbor, MI 48109-1205 • ACRL

Yoder Carol Rempel • Colorado Springs, CO 80904 • ACRL

Yoder David R. • Beaver, PA 15009

Yoder Devon J. • Library Director • Goshen College • Goshen, IN 46526 • ACRL LAMA

Yoder Eunice M. • La Verne, CA 91750 • ACRL RASD *Life*

Yoder Jane P. • Library Media Specialist • Thomas Jefferson Junior High School • Waukegan, IL 60085 • AASL IFRT

Yogmour Olga • Librarian, Asst. Director • Akron-Summit County Public Library • Akron, OH 44326-0001 • LAMA PLA

Yohannes Gebregeoris T. • Student • University of Texas at Austin Graduate School of Library & Information Sciences • Austin, TX 78712-1276 • IRRT SRRT

Yohe Paula • Library Media Specialist • J.U. Martin Jr High School • Dillon, SC 29536 • AASL

Yoke John S. Jr. • Technical Servs Liaison/Circ. • Greenwich Library • Greenwich, CT 06830

Yokote Gail • University of California-Los Angeles Biomedical Library • Los Angeles, CA 90024-1798 • LITA

Yonan Mary J. • School Librarian • Dennis Elementary School Decatur School District # 61 • Decatur, IL 62522 • AASL

Yonce Barbara • Branch Supervisor • Greenville County Library • Greenville, SC 29601 • PLA

Yonemura Lucille T. • Head Acquisitions • San Jose State University Division of Library & Information Science • San Jose, CA 95192-0029 • ALCTS NMRT

Yonezawa Pearl M. • Senior Librarian • Los Angeles Public Library R. L. Stevenson Branch • Los Angeles, CA 90023

Yongue Tina A. • Goldsboro, NC 27534 • RASD

Yonke Louis L. • Davenport College of Business Library Lansing Branch • Lansing, MI 48901 • ACRL LAMA GODORT LRRT

Yonki Mary Ann W • District Consultant • Osterhout Free Library • Wilkes Barre, PA 18701 • PLA

Yonovich Cindy L. • Wayne County Community College • Taylor, MI 48180

Yontz Elaine • University of Florida Libraries • Gainesville, FL 32611 • ACRL ALCTS NMRT VRT

Yoo Tae J. • Head Law Librarian • Lum Hoens Abeles Conant & Danzis Law Library • Roseland, NJ 07068-1049

Yoon Chong Y. • Cataloging Librarian • State University of New York (SUNY) College at Old Westbury Library • Old Westbury, NY 11568 • ACRL ALCTS LITA GODORT

Yoon Sandra G. • Libn II/Br Supv./Childrens Libn. • Kern County Library System • Bakersfield, CA 93301

York Charlene C. • Reference Librarian • State Library of Ohio • Columbus, OH 43266-0334 • ACRL

York Edwin G. • Middlesex County College Library • Edison, NJ 08818-3050

York Grace A. • Coor Government Info Services • University of Michigan Libraries • Ann Arbor, MI 48109-1205 • ACRL GODORT

York Helen P. • Administration District Libn. • Yonkers School Library System • Yonkers, NY 10704 • AASL

York Henry E. • Head, Collections Management • Cleveland State University Library • Cleveland, OH 44115

York Janice L. • Cuyahoga Falls, OH 44221

York Linda S. • Librarian • Dallas School System Adelle Turner School • Dallas, TX 75231 • AASL

York Mark • Emporia State University School of Library & Information Management • Emporia, KS 66801

York Mary Ellen • Monmouth College Guggenheim Memorial Library • West Long Branch, NJ 07764 • ACRL

York Maurice C. • North Carolina Librarian • East Carolina University Joyner Library • Greenville, NC 27858-4353

York Michael C. • University Librarian • University of New Hampshire Library • Durham, NH 03824 • ACRL

York Sam • Trustee • Pierce County Rural Library District • Tacoma, WA 98446 • ALTA PLA

York Vicky • Head Govt. Information • Montana State University • Bozeman, MT 59717-0332 • GODORT

Yorks Melissa • Gaithersburg, MD 20877

Yorks Pamela F. • Engineering Librarian • University of Washington Engineering Library • Seattle, WA 98195 • ACRL RASD

Yoshida Claire S. • Systems Librarian • University of Maryland Libraries • College Park, MD 20742 • LITA

Yoshida Tadashi Mr • New York, NY 10011 • ACRL ALCTS *Life*

Yoshimoto Eileen K. • Branch Inf. Services Manager • Cumberland County Public Library and Information Center, Eutaw Branch • Fayetteville, NC 28314-1936

Yoshimura Katherine E. • Librarian III • University of Hawaii Thomas Hale Hamilton Library • Honolulu, HI 96822

Yoshimura Lani • Director • Santa Clara County Free Library Gilroy Public • Gilroy, CA 95020

Yoshimura Miles • Social Science Bibliographer • Rutgers University Libraries Archibald Stevens Alexander Library • New Brunswick, NJ 08903 • ACRL RASD

Yoshimura Yoshiko • Area Specialist-Japan • Library of Congress • Washington, DC 20541 • ACRL

Yoshina Joan M. • School Librarian • Moanalua Intermediate School • Honolulu, HI 96819 • AASL

Yoshino Laureen Y. • Verona, WI 53593

Yost Barbara J. • Jefferson County Public Library • Lakewood, CO 80215 • LAMA

Yost Brian K. • Student • University of Illinois Graduate School of Library and Information Science • Urbana, IL 61801

Yost Dee R. • Adminstrator • Republican Valley Library System • Hastings, NE 68901-4663

Youles Kathryn E • Extension Services Librarian • Pine Mountain Regional Library • Manchester, GA 31816 • PLA

Young-Lie Magdalene • Library Media Specialist • Singapore American School • Singapore 1026, Singapore • AASL LIRT

Young Amanda M. • Head Media/Serials Div. • Northwestern State University Watson Memorial Library • Natchitoches, LA 71497

Young Anne J. • Student • Mayville State University Library • Mayville, ND 58257 • AASL IFRT SRRT

Young Antionette K. • Newark, OH 43055

Young Arthur P. • Dean of Libraries • University of South Carolina • Columbia, SC 29208 • ACRL ALCTS LAMA RASD LHRT LRRT *Life*

Young Barbara N. • Special Serv Supervisor Art Serv • Miami-Dade Public Library System • Miami, FL 33130-1504

Young Bertha T. Miss • Staten Island, NY 10301 • PLA *Continuing*

Young Besty F. • Student • University of Hawaii School of Library & Information Studies • Honolulu, HI 96822 • AASL

Young Betty I. • Head of East Campus Library • Duke University William R. Perkins Library • Durham, NC 27706 • ACRL LHRT

Young Carmilla B. • Albert Wicker Elementary School • New Orleans, LA 70112

Young Carolyn • Library Media Specialist • Lee's Summit School District #7 • Lee's Summit, MO 64063 • AASL NMRT

Young Cecil T. • Friends of Oberlin Public Library • Oberlin, OH 44074

Young Cecilia A. • Head of Technical Services • Yuma County Library District • Yuma, AZ 85364 • PLA

Young Christina C. • Washington, DC 20017 • AASL ALSC RASD

Young Christine • Haverhill Public Library • Haverhill, MA 01830

Young Claryce T. • Library Principal Assoc. • Atlanta-Fulton Public Library Adamsville Collier Heights Branch • Atlanta, GA 30331 • ALSC ASCLA

Young Colette F. H. • Hd, Soc Sci & Philosophy Sect • Hawaii State Library • Honolulu, HI 96813 • PLA *Life*

Young Dana M. • Student • Texas Woman's University School of Library & Information Studies • Denton, TX 76204 • PLA

Young Diana D. • Director, Network Operations • North Carolina Department of Cultural Resources State Library • Raleigh, NC 27601-2807 • ALSC ASCLA LAMA PLA YALSA

Young Dong-Shiuh • President • Library Automation Products • New York, NY 10001 • LITA

Young E Lorene • Leavenworth, WA 98826

Young Elizabeth M. • Catalog Librarian • New York Institute of Technology • Old Westbury, NY 11568 • ALCTS

Young Eris L. • Trustee • Hennepin County Library • Minnetonka, MN 55343 • ALTA

Young Evelyn G. • Shawnee Mission, KS 66205-2817

Young Frances O. • Associate Director • University of Detroit Mercy Library • Detriot, MI 48219-3599 • ACRL

Young Gary Rev. • Librarian • Weber High School Library • Chicago, IL 60639

Young Heartsill H. • Mason, TX 76856 • Continuing

Young Helen A. • Minneapolis, MN 55408-1980 • LAMA PLA *Life*

Young J. Bradford • University of Pennsylvania • Philadelphia, PA 19104 • ALCTS

Young Janet E. • University of Alabama at Birmingham Mervyn H. Sterne Library • Birmingham, AL 35294-0014

Young Jennifer C. • Columbus Metropolitan Library Livingston Branch • Columbus, OH 43227

Young Jerry F. • Director • Anoka County Library • Blaine, MN 55434 • PLA

Young John P. • Director • William Jewell College Curry Library • Liberty, MO 64068 • LAMA

Young John Robert • Williamsburg County Library • Kingstree, SC 29556 • ALSC PLA

Young Juana R. • Associate Director of Libraries • University of Arkansas Mullins Library • Fayetteville, AR 72701 • ACRL

Young Juanita M. • Los Osos, CA 93402

Young Judith E. • Tallahassee, FL 32308

Young Judith W. • Cleveland, MS 38732

Young Judy K. • The Baldwin School • Bryn Mawr, PA 19010 • AASL YALSA

Young Katherine A. • Boulder, CO 80303 • AASL

Young Laura C. • Media Specialist • Lakeland Senior High School • Lakeland, FL 33801

Young Linda L. • Librarian • Jefferson County Public Schools Western Middle School • Louisville, KY 40212

Young Lorna J. • Music Cataloger/Selector • University of Saskatchewan Library • Saskatoon SK, S7N 0W0 Canada • ACRL ALCTS

Young Lura A. • Cosmos Club Library • Washington, DC 20008

Young Lynne Marie • Director • Northfield Public Library • Northfield, MN 55057 • PLA

Young M. Jane • Reference Librarian • Minnesota Legislative Reference Library • Saint Paul, MN 55155

Young M. Patricia • Librarian IV • Chicago Public Library Harold Washington Library • Chicago, IL 60605 • PLA RASD

Young Marcelyn A. • Highland Park, NJ 08904 • AASL

Young Margaret • Coppell Independent School District Coppell Middle School • Coppell, TX 75019 • AASL

Young Margaret • Asst. Dir of Instr. Services • Deerfield Public Schools • Deerfield, IL 60015 • AASL

Young Margo • University of Alberta • Edmonton AB, T6G 2J8 Canada • ACRL ALCTS LITA RASD

Young Martha • Vanderbilt University Central Library • Nashville, TN 37240-0007

Young Mary E. • Branch Librarian • Charles A Cannon Memorial Library Kannapolis Branch • Kannapolis, NC 28081 • PLA IFRT

Young Mary Elizabeth • Bernards High School • Bernardsville, NJ 07924 • AASL

Young Mary L. • Head Librarian • Institute of American Indian Arts • Santa Fe, NM 87504 • EMIERT

Young Mary R. • Shreveport, LA 71105

Young Melissa L. • AT&T Bell Laboratories • Holmdel, NJ 07733-1988

Young Nancy J. • Administrative Librarian • Dekalb County Public Library • Decatur, GA 30032 • LAMA PLA

Young Nancy J. • Library Media Center • Gregory Middle School • Naperville, IL 60564 • AASL

Young Nancy J. • Reference Librarian • Cornell University School of Hotel Administration Library • Ithaca, NY 14853-6902 • ACRL

Young Nicole • Senior Library Assistant • Escondido Public Library • Escondido, CA 92025

Young Noel D. • Librarian • Central Missouri State University Ward Edwards Library • Warrensburg, MO 64093 • ACRL IFRT IRRT SRRT

Young Pat C. • Texas Wesleyan University West Library • Fort Worth, TX 76105

Young Patricia A. • Brooklyn, NY 11201-1942 • ACRL ALCTS

Young Peter R. • Executive Director • National Commission on Library & Information Science (NCLIS) • Washington, DC 20036 • LAMA LITA

Young Philip H. • Director • University of Indianapolis Krannert Memorial Library • Indianapolis, IN 46227 • ACRL

Young Phyllis • Collection Coodinator • County of Los Angeles Public Library • Hawthorne, CA 90250 • ALCTS PLA RASD

Young Phyllis M. • Asst. Dir. for Public Serv. • Virginia State Library & Archives • Richmond, VA 23219 • ACRL

Young Richard F. • Dir.,Off. of Consv./Presv. • United States Senate • Washington, DC 20510-7124 • ALCTS

Young Robert N. • Williamsburg, VA 23185

Young Sally • Principal Librarian • Pasadena Public Library • Pasadena, CA 91101 • PLA

Young Sally J. • Education Media Specialist • Parsippany Hills High School • Parsippany, NJ 07054 • AASL

Young Sandra C. • Sr. Tech. Info. Res. Analyst • Ashland Oil Technical Reference Center • Lexington, KY 40512

Young Sarah L. • Library Assistant • Benesch, Friedlander, Coplan & Aronoff-Law Firm • Columbus, OH 43215

Young Stephen R. • Rare Book Team Leader • Yale University Sterling Memorial Library • New Haven, CT 06520 • ACRL ALCTS SRRT

Young Terrence E. Jr. • Instructor of Library Science • University of New Orleans College of Education-Program in Library Science • New Orleans, LA 70148 • AASL

Young Timothy G. • Archivist • Yale University Beinecke Rare Book & Manuscript Library • New Haven, CT 06520 • IFRT

Young Verna H F • Government Documents Librarian • University of Hawaii Thomas Hale Hamilton Library • Honolulu, HI 96822 • ALCTS GODORT

Young Victoria • Head of Reader Services • Xavier University McDonald Memorial Library • Cincinnati, OH 45207 • ACRL

Young Virginia E. • Student • University of Alabama School of Library & Information Studies • Tuscaloosa, AL 35487-0252

Young Virginia G. • Trustee • Daniel Boone Regional Library • Columbia, MO 65205-1267 • ACRL ALTA ASCLA LAMA PLA *Honorary*

Young Wendy L. • Student • University of Wisconsin-Milwaukee School of Library & Information Science • Milwaukee, WI 53201

Young William H. • Auberry, CA 93602 • IFRT

Young William L. • Faculty • West Virginia Library Commission • Charleston, WV 25305 • ALTA IFRT

Youngberg Rosalin A. • Librarian/Reading Specialist • Saint Francis de Sales School • Lake Zurich, IL 60047 • AASL ALSC

Youngblut Cindi L. • Director • Sage Public Library • Osage, IA 50461

Youngck Marlys • Curriculum Laboratory Librarian • Winona State University • Winona, MN 55987 • ACRL

Younger Jennifer A. • Asst. Dir. for Technical Servs. • Ohio State University Libraries • Columbus, OH 43210-1286 • ACRL ALCTS LAMA LITA IRRT LRRT MAGERT

Younger Melinda M. • Media Librarian • Sandusky Middle School • Lynchburg, VA 24502 • AASL

Younger Mildred L. • Fairhaven, NJ 07704 • AASL

Younghaus Ellen L. • Student • University of South Florida School of Library & Information Science • Tampa, FL 33620

Youngholm Philip • Library Systems Consultant • Innovative Interfaces, Inc. • Berkeley, CA 94710 • ACRL ALCTS LITA

Youngs Marian A. • Kalamazoo, MI 49009 • Life

Younkin Constance • Everett Public Library • Everett, WA 98201

Yount Anna L. • Head, Central Adult Services • Asheville-Buncombe Library System • Asheville, NC 28801 • RASD

Youree Beverly B. • Professor • Middle Tennessee State University Library • Murfreesboro, TN 37132 • AASL YALSA

Yourman Madeline C. Mrs • Stanford, CA 94305 • ACRL RASD *Life*

Youse Elizabeth C. • Baltimore, MD 21212

Yousef Annetta • Las Vegas-Clark County Library District • Las Vegas, NV 89101 • PLA RASD

Yozgat Susan • Head of Circulation • Volusia County Library Center • Daytona Beach, FL 32114

Yrastroza Kathleen S. • Library Media Clerk • Cupertino Union School District DeVargas Elementary School • San Jose, CA 95129 • ALSC

Yribar Rita • Regional Branch Supervising Ln. • Monterey County Free Library Prunedale Branch • Salinas, CA 93907 • PLA NMRT

Ysturiz Margaret • Sn Francisco, CA 94123 • ALSC

Yturralde Victoria • Davis, CA 95616 • PLA

Yu Abraham J. • Catalog Librarian • University of California General Library • Irvine, CA 92713

Yu Bing • Student • Southern Connecticut State University School of Libray Science & Instructional Technology • New Haven, CT 06515

Yu Chin-Wen C. • Student • Wake Forest University Z Smith Reynolds Library • Winston Salem, NC 27109-7777 • LITA RASD

Yu Lixin • Student • State University of New York (SUNY) Thomas E. Dewey Graduate Library • Albany, NY 12222

Yu Oi Ling C. • Aspen Systems Corporation • Rockville, MD 20850-3172

Yu Priscilla C. • Acting Asst. to the Dir. • University of Illinois Library • Urbana, IL 61801 • ACRL LAMA IRRT LHRT

Yu Sy-Wei • Bibliographic Instruction Ln. • Delaware State College William C. Jason Library • Dover, DE 19901

Yu Yuet-Fai R. • Assistant Manager Info Services • Coopers & Lybrand • Causeway Bay, Hong Kong • RASD

Yuan Barbara • Head, Technical Services • Winchester Public Library • Winchester, MA 01890

Yuan James • Acquisitions Librarian • Morgan State University Soper Library • Baltimore, MD 21239-4098

Yuan Patricia • Head of Catalog Division • Dayton & Montgomery County Public Library • Dayton, OH 45402-2103

Yucht Alice H. • Joyce Kilmer School Library • Milltown, NJ 08850 • AASL ALSC

Yucht Donald J. • Librarian for Technology • New York University Elmer Holmes Bobst Library • New York, NY 10012

Yueh Norma N. • Prof. & Dir. of Library Services • Ramapo College of New Jersey Library • Mahwah, NJ 07430 • ACRL

Yuen-Lo Carrie • District Resource Centre School District #57 • Prince George BC, V2M 1L7 Canada • AASL ALCTS LAMA LITA RASD YALSA

Yuen Audrey A. • Head Technical Service • Geneva Public Library District • Geneva, IL 60134 • ALCTS

Yuengling Fred • Science Librarian • University of California Science Library • Santa Cruz, CA 95064 • ACRL RASD

Yugo Susan • Library Technical Assistant • Waukegan Public Library • Waukegan, IL 60085

Yuille W. Kelly • Washington Suburban Sanitary Commission Engineering Library • Laurel, MD 20707

Yukawa Masako • Head Libn.,Gov't. Docs. Dept. • Long Island University B. Davis Schwartz Memorial Library • Greenvale, NY 11548 • ACRL GODORT

Yungmeyer Elinor • Chicago, IL 60611 • AASL PLA *Life*

Yunker Beverley B. • Rockwall, TX 75087

Yurcaba Ann Campbell • OCLC Services Coordinator • Palinet & Union Library Catalogue of Pennsylvania • Philadelphia, PA 19104

Yurczyk Judith J. • Student • University of Wisconsin-Milwaukee School of Library & Information Science • Milwaukee, WI 53201 • LITA

Yurenka Katrina • West Topsham, VT 05086

Yurgaites Christine • Librarian at Large • Genesee District Library • Flint, MI 48504

Yurisic Virginia B. • School Librarian • West End Elementary School • Meadville, PA 16335 • AASL

Yursik M. Pamela • School Library Media Specialist • Woodbrook Elementary School • Charlottesville, VA 22901 • AASL

Yurth Helene • Bemus Point, NY 14712

Yuschak Donna • Evansville-Vanderburgh County Oaklyn Branch Library • Evansville, IN 47711 • PLA

Yuster Leigh C. • R. R. Bowker • New Providence, NJ 07974 • ALCTS LITA

Yusuke Kihara • Preident • Kihara Shosando Coop LTD • Tokyo, Japan • LAMA

Yuuji Nabet • Chief Librarian • Aoyama Gakuin University Library • Tokyo, Japan • ACRL ALCTS LITA ILERT
Zabel Diane M. • Social Science Ref. Librarian • Pennsylvania State University Pattee Library • University Park, PA 16802 • ACRL RASD
Zabel Linda L. • North Harrison High School • Ramsey, IN 47166 • AASL
Zabel Patricia L. • Fort Smith Public Library • Fort Smith, AR 72901 • RASD YALSA
Zabkowicz Robert • Student • East Chicago Public Library • E. Chicago, IN 46312 • PLA RASD
Zaborski Jacqueline M. • Librarian • South College • West Palm Beach, FL 33409
Zacharda Judith H. • Student • Inglemoor High School • Bothell, WA 98011 • AASL
Zachariah Gail • Ohio Valley Area Libraries (OVAL) • Wellston, OH 45692 • ALSC PLA IFRT
Zachary Patricia A. • Media Specialist • Walters Public Schools • Walters, OK 73572 • AASL
Zachert M. J. K. Dr. • Tallahassee, FL 32312 • Continuing
Zachowski Julie A. • Director • Beaufort County Library • Beaufort, SC 29902 • PLA
Zack Daniel G. • Director • Borden Public Library District • Elgin, IL 60120 • PLA
Zack John J. • Trustee • Monroe County Library System • Monroe, MI 48161 • ALTA
Zack Kristina L. • Student • Louisiana State University School of Library & Information Science • Baton Rouge, LA 70803-3290
Zack Miriam B. • Tampa, FL 33629 • AASL
Zack Shirley A. • St Paul, MN 55105 • ACRL ALCTS
Zackheim Michael R. • Serials-Gov. Docs. Librarian • State University of New York College at New Paltz Sojourner Truth Library • New Paltz, NY 12561 • LRRT
Zackrison Linda M. • Librarian • Sterne, Kessler, Goldstein & Fox • Washington, DC 20036 • LITA
Zadner Paul A. • Librarian • State University of New York College at Buffalo, E. H. Butler Library • Buffalo, NY 14222-1095 • ACRL LITA *Life*
Zaenger Kathleen L. • Director • Howell Carnegie Disrict Library • Howell, MI 48843-2195 • LAMA PLA
Zafren Herbert C. • Director of Libraries • Hebrew Union College Library • Cincinnati, OH 45220 • ACRL LAMA *Life*
Zager Daniel • Oberlin College Library • Oberlin, OH 44074
Zagon Eileen • Senior Assistant Librarian • Penn State Harrisburg • Middletown, PA 17057
Zaheer Naheed R. • Student • University of California-Berkeley School of Library & Information Studies • Berkeley, CA 94720 • IFRT
Zahn Patricia L. • Branch Manager • Alameda County Library Newark Branch • Newark, CA 94560
Zahner Jane E. • Reference/Government Document Ln • Valdosta State College Library • Valdosta, GA 31698-0001 • LIRT
Zahorbenski Steven W. • Library of Science & Medicine • Rutgers University Libraries Library of Science & Medicine • Piscataway, NJ 08855-1029
Zahrfeld Sharon M. • Clerk • South Lyon Public Library • South Lyon, MI 48178
Zaidman Anna • Librarian • Saint Louis University Pius XII Memorial Library • St. Louis, MO 63108 • ACRL
Zais-Gabbert Harriet Dr • Head, VIC Library • VIC Library • Vienna A-1400, Austria • LAMA LITA IRRT
Zajanc Jacqueline R. • Renton, WA 98055
Zajic Lois • Lower School Librarian • Friends School • Baltimore, MD 21210
Zajkowski Maureen C. • Coordinator of Database • State University of New York Bartle Library • Binghamton, NY 13902-6012 • ACRL ALCTS LITA
Zaklad Loretta • Librarian • Rose Valley School • Moylan, PA 19065
Zaklan Gerri • Librarian • Saint Andrew's Episcopal School • Bethesda, MD 20817 • AASL YALSA ILERT
Zald Anne E. • Reference Librarian • University of Washington Suzzallo Library • Seattle, WA 98195 • ACRL GODORT SRRT
Zalecki Melinda N. • Director • Pulaski County Library • Pulaski, VA 24301 • PLA
Zales Dorothy • Hickory Creek School • Frankfort, IL 60423 • AASL
Zaleski Daniel • New York, NY 10014
Zaleski Ilene H. • Assistant Director • North Miami Public Library • North Miami, FL 33161
Zaleski Joan C. • School Librarian • Ann M. MacArthur School • Locust Valley, NY 11560 • AASL ALSC
Zaleski Joan P. • Director • Connetquot Public Library • Bohemia, NY 11716 • PLA
Zaleski Mary A. • John R. Rogers Elementary School • Vancouver, WA 98661 • AASL
Zall Elisabeth W. • Rare-Book Cataloger • Huntington Library • San Marino, CA 91108 • ALCTS IFRT SRRT
Zambella BethAnn • Bibliogrpahic Inst. Coor. • Rutgers University Libraries • New Brunswick, NJ 08903
Zambusi William J. • C.E.O. • The Ontario Library Services Center • Waterloo, ON, N2J 4N5 Canada • ALCTS PLA
Zamora Mary U. • Hephzibah, GA 30815 • SRRT
Zamouri Ali • Assistant Librarian • Yale University Ornithology Peabody Museum of Natural History • New Haven, CT 06511 • ACRL ALCTS LITA *Life*
Zanarini Linda S. • Dakota Dunes, SD 57049
Zander Nancy C. • Branch Librarian • Oak Park Public Library • Oak Park, IL 60301
Zandieh Shohreh • Student • San Jose State University Division of Library & Information Science • San Jose, CA 95192-0029 • NMRT
Zange Cathleen C. • Ref./Periodicals Librarian • Judson College Library • Elgin, IL 60123 • ACRL LITA RASD LIRT
Zankel Jeanne • Children's Reference Librarian • Westfield Memorial Library • Westfield, NJ 07090
Zanoni Jean R. • Cataloger • University of Wisconsin-Milwaukee Golda Meir Library • Milwaukee, WI 53201 • ALCTS
Zanotti Carla • Dir. of Sales & Mktg. Support • BlueFeather Communications, Inc. • Lake Forest, IL 60045 • NMRT
Zapatos Craig S. • Main Library Supervisior • San Antonio Public Library • San Antonio, TX 78205 • LAMA PLA
Zaplitny Paul • Branch Librarian • Brooklyn Public Library • Brooklyn, NY 11238 • EMIERT
Zaporozhetz Laurene E. • Director • Louisiana State University • Shreveport, LA 71115 • ACRL ALCTS LAMA LITA RASD CLENE GODORT LIRT SORT SRRT
Zappas Elise T. • Catalog Librarian • Drew University • Madison, NJ 07940-4007
Zappen Susan • Rensselaer Polytechnic Institute • Troy, NY 12180 • ALCTS
Zappone William F. • Librarian • Edward R. Murrow High School • Brooklyn, NY 11230 • AASL *Life*
Zar Kathleen A. • Librarian • University of Chicago Library John Crerar Library • Chicago, IL 60637-1403 • ACRL LAMA LITA RASD
Zaragoza-Goode Lois M. • Department Head • Pensacola Junior College Learning Resource Center • Pensacola, FL 32504-8998
Zarem Janet • Pacific Palisades, CA 90272
Zaremba John • Cataloger • Newark Public Library • Newark, NJ 07101-0630
Zarkin Joyce G. • Bookmobile/Outreach/YA • Bugbee Memorial Library • Danielson, CT 06239
Zarlenga Cecelia • Melrose Park Public Library • Melrose Park, IL 60160
Zarnosky Margaret R. • Granada Hills, CA 91344-4010 • IFRT
Zarobila Charles • Head of Periodicals • John Carroll University Grasselli Library • University Heights, OH 44118 • ACRL
Zarriello Margaret • Assistant to Library Director • Kent State University Ashtabula Campus Library • Ashtabula, OH 44004
Zartner Norma • Milwaukee, WI 53225 • YALSA *Continuing*
Zartner Rebecca • Library Director • Miami University Hamilton Campus Rentschler Library • Hamilton, OH 45011 • ACRL
Zaslavsky Judith M. • Wynnewood, PA 19096 • AASL ALSC *Life*
Zastaury Jane Ryder • Children's Librarian • Memphis-Shelby County Public Library Randolph Branch • Memphis, TN 38122 • ALSC
Zastrow Ed J. • East Central Regional Library • Cedar Rapids, IA 52401 • ALTA PLA
Zastrow Louise M. • Trustee • Lodi Public Library • Lodi, CA 95240
Zatterberg Helen • Chicago, IL 60640 • Continuing
Zatz Norma L. • Trustee • Skokie Public Library • Skokie, IL 60077-3680 • ALTA PLA
Zauha Janelle M. • Student • University of Iowa School of Library & Information Science • Iowa City, IA 52242 • ACRL LITA PLA RASD IFRT
Zavilinsky Vicky • Media Specialist • Somerset Elementary School • Chevy Chase, MD 20815 • AASL
Zavish Gloria G. • Librarian • North Miami Public Library • North Miami, FL 33161 • LAMA PLA RASD YALSA
Zavortink David W. • Palmer Public Library • Palmer, AK 99645 • ALCTS PLA
Zawacki Maria E. • Director • Johnsburg Public Library • McHenry, IL 60050 • PLA
Zazueta Victor • AV Librarian/Reference Librarian • Los Angeles County Library Leland R. Weaver Library • South Gate, CA 90208
Zbornik Doris • Oberlin College Library • Oberlin, OH 44074 • LAMA
Zdon Elizabeth A. • Systems Reference Librarian • Dakota County Library • Eagan, MN 55123 • RASD
Zeager Lloyd • Librarian • Lancaster Mennonite Hist Society • Lancaster, PA 17602
Zebos Jacquelyn E. • Student • University of South Florida School of Library & Information Science • Tampa, FL 33620 • SRRT
Zebrowski Judy • Reference Librarian • Pennsylvania State University Berks Campus • Reading, PA 19610-6009 • ACRL RASD
Zeccardi Michele K. • Newton Square, PA 19073
Zecharias Meseratch • Reference Media Librarian • Syracuse University Library E. S. Bird Library • Syracuse, NY 13244-2010 • ACRL IRRT
Zechel Robert D. • Trustee • Downers Grove Public Library • Downers Grove, IL 60515 • ALTA
Zedney Francis L. • Librarian • Weber County Library • Odgen, UT 84401
Zeh Dawn E. • Student • San Jose State University Division of Library & Information Science • San Jose, CA 95192-0029 • SRRT
Zeidberg David S. • Special Collections • University of California-Los Angeles University Research Library • Los Angeles, CA 90024 • ACRL
Zeiger Carrie • Director • Newnan-Coweta Public Library • Newnan, GA 30263 • PLA
Zeiger Hanna B. • Chestnut Hill, MA 02167 • AASL ALSC
Zeigler Susan A. • Children's Librarian • New York Public Library Baychester Regional Branch • Bronx, NY 10475 • ALSC
Zeiher Lynne • Head of Reference • Mid-Columbia Library Kennewick Branch • Kennewick, WA 99336
Zeind Samir M. • Head Librarian • Huntington Memorial Hospital Health Sciences Library • Pasadena, CA 91105
Zeitler Carolyn R. • Student • San Jose State University Division of Library & Information Science • San Jose, CA 95192-0029
Zeitlin Bonnie • Wheeling, IL 60090
Zeitlin Eugenia F. • Woodland Hills, CA 91364
Zeitschik Marc • President • Archival Survival Inc. • Brooklyn, NY 11215 • ALCTS
Zelaya Silvia Priscila • Director • Biblioteca Empresarios Juveniles • San Salvador, El Salvador
Zelenka Bernadine JLM • Student • University of California Los Angeles Graduate School of Library & Information Science • Los Angeles, CA 90024 • ACRL LHRT
Zelenski Judy Kulp • Assistant Director • Central Colorado Library System • Wheat Ridge, CO 80033 • LITA
Zeljak Cathy M. • Reference • George Washington University Gelman Library • Washington, DC 20052 • ACRL LITA RASD
Zella Renee E. • Thornton, CO 80229-1220
Zellar Carol A. • Children's Librarian • Oswego City Library • Oswego, NY 13126
Zeller Doreen M. • Wauwatosa, WI 53213
Zeller Florence • Student • Fairfield University Gustav & Dagmar Nyselius Library • Fairfield, CT 06430-7524 • LITA
Zellers Joanne M. • Area Spec African Sect • Library of Congress • Washington, DC 20541 • ACRL LITA RASD ILERT IRRT
Zellmer Arlys • Librarian • Beloit Memorial High School Library • Beloit, WI 53511 • AASL
Zellmer Linda R. • University of Wyoming • Laramie, WY 82071 • ACRL MAGERT
Zelman Elaine • Teacher of Library • High School for the Humanities • New York, NY 10011 • AASL
Zelman Jacqueline M. • Director, Univ Computer Serv. • Florida International University • Miami, FL 33199 • LAMA LITA
Zelnick Lisa Mrs. • Dayton, KY 41074 • LITA RASD
Zelter Bonnie Clayton • San Mateo, CA 94402-3635 • ERT
Zelter Judith A. • Adult Services Head • Niles Public Library • Niles, IL 60648 • PLA
Zembicki Christine • Branch Librarian • Clifton Public Library Allwood Branch • Allwood, NJ 07012 • ACRL LAMA
Zembrosky Kathryn S. • Student • University of Wisconsin-Milwaukee School of Library & Information Science • Milwaukee, WI 53201
Zenan Joan S. • Director/Savitt Medical Libn. • University of Nevada-Reno • Reno, NV 89557 • ACRL
Zendzian Lynda K. • Catalog Librarian • Bowdoin College Library • Brunswick, ME 04011 • ACRL LITA
Zenelis John G. • Associate Director • Temple University Paley Library • Philadelphia, PA 19122 • ACRL
Zenk Margaret L. • Pittsburgh, PA 15218 • Continuing
Zenor Stanley D. • Executive Director • Association Education Communication & Technology • Washington, DC 20005 • AASL

Zeringue Gayle C. • Student • Louisiana State University School of Library & Information Science • Baton Rouge, LA 70803-3290

Zerkow Syma • Librarian • Houston Public Library • Houston, TX 77002 • PLA

Zerwas Maria A. • Plano, TX 75075

Zerwekh Charles E. Jr. • Castle Creek, NY 13744-9710 • ACRL LITA   *Life*

Zeugner Lorenzo A. Jr • Head of Acquisition Department • University of Notre Dame Theodore M. Hesburgh Library • Notre Dame, IN 46556 • ALCTS LAMA

Zevnik Lawrence G. • Student • Northern Illinois University Department of Library & Information Studies • DeKalb, IL 60115 • PLA

Zhan Haixia • Student • Rosary College Graduate School of Library & Information Science • River Forest, IL 60305

Zhang Dongming • Elect. Res. & Monograph Catlgr. • Cornell University Albert R. Mann Library • Ithaca, NY 14853-4301

Zhang Foster Jia • System Analyst • Research Libraries Group Inc. (RLG) • Mountain View, CA 94041-1100

Zhang Kaiping • Student • State University of New York at Albany School of Information Science & Policy • Albany, NY 12222 • IFRT

Zhang Limin • Librarian I • Chicago Public Library Chinatown Branch • Chicago, IL 60616

Zhang Meng • Student • Catholic University of America School of Library and Information Science • Washington, DC 20064

Zhang Ping • Student • University of Kentucky College of Library & Information Science • Lexington, KY 40506-0391

Zhang Sha Li • Student • Univ of Kentucky Southeast Cmnty College • Cumberland, KY 40823 • ACRL IFRT

Zhang Tian X. • Student • Saint John's University Division of Library & Information Science • Jamaica, NY 11439

Zhang Wei • Serials Librarian • Northwestern University Library • Evanston, IL 60208-2300

Zhang Wei-Ping • Cataloging/Processing Librarian • Kent State University School of Library & Information Science • Kent, OH 44242-0001 • ALCTS

Zhang Wenxian • Ansonia Library • Ansonia, CT 06401

Zhang Xiaoyan • Assistant Cataloger • University of Southern Mississippi Cook Memorial Library • Hattiesburg, MS 39406-5053

Zhang Xiaoyin • Technical Services Librarian • University of Maryland Baltimore County Kuhn Library • Catonsville, MD 21228

Zhang Yingting • Student • Rutgers University School of Communication Information & Library Studies • New Brunswick, NJ 08903 • ACRL

Zhang Zhibin • Student • University of Alabama School of Library & Information Studies • Tuscaloosa, AL 35487-0252

Zhao Er-Pin • Student • University of Texas at Austin Graduate School of Library & Information Sciences • Austin, TX 78712-1276

Zhao Jiyuan • Assistant Professor • Wuhan University Library • Hubei Province Wuhan, China

Zhao Lingzhen • Honolulu, HI 96814

Zhao Xiaoli • Student • State University of New York at Albany School of Information Science & Policy • Albany, NY 12222

Zhao Yilan • Poplar Creek Public Library Dist • Streamwood, IL 60107

Zheng Ting • Graduate Student • University of Wisconsin-Whitewater Harold Andersen Library • Whitewater, WI 53190 • LITA

Zhezhko Irina • Student • Simmons College Graduate School of Library & Information Science • Boston, MA 02115 • ACRL

Zhong Jiecheng J C • Student • Texas Woman's University School of Library & Information Studies • Denton, TX 76204

Zhou Jian-Zhong • Science Librarian • University of Delaware Library • Newark, DE 19717-5267 • LITA

Zhou Lianhong • Bloomington, IN 47408

Zhou Peter Xinping • Student • University of Illinois Graduate School of Library and Information Science • Urbana, IL 61801

Zhou Yan • Student • University of Pittsburgh School of Library and Information Science • Pittsburgh, PA 15260

Zhou Yuan • University of Minnesota John R. Borchert Map Library • Minneapolis, MN 55455-0414

Zhou Zehao • Student • Kent State University School of Library & Information Science • Kent, OH 44242-0001

Zhu Quan-Vui Snow • East Brunswick, NJ 08854

Zhu Xiaofeng • Student • Gettysburg College Musselman Library • Gettysburg, PA 17325-1493 • LITA LRRT

Ziauddin Tasneem F. • Bolingbrook, IL 60440

Zibell Hazel M. • Jacksonville, FL 32217

Ziccardi Gerald J. • Philadelphia, PA 19145-4814

Zich Joanne A. • Gov Doc & Non-Print Media Ln • The American University Library • Washington, DC 20016-8046 • ACRL GODORT

Zickefoose Gordon T. • Library Media Specialist • Berea City Schools • Berea, OH 44017 • AASL

Zidar Judith A. • National Agricultural Library • Beltsville, MD 20705-2351

Ziebarth Maxine K. • San Clemente, CA 92672-2464

Ziebell Peggy L. • Ironwood Elmentary School • Tucson, AZ 85741

Ziegenfus Susan Bromer • Curriculum Materials Librarian • East Stroudsburg University Kemp Library • East Stroudsburg, PA 18301 • ACRL

Ziegler Beth • Branch Head, Temecula • Temecula Library • Temecula, CA 92590 • LAMA PLA

Ziegler David R. • Eisenhower Public Library District • Harwood Heights, IL 60656 • ALSC YALSA

Ziegler Judith • Grozer Chester Medical Center • Upland, PA 19013

Ziegler Rebecca L. • Reference Librarian • Georgia Southern University Henderson Library • Statesboro, GA 30460 • ACRL RASD

Ziegler Ronald M. • Reference Librarian • Washington State University Library • Pullman, WA 99164-5610

Ziegler Roy A. • Serials Librarian • Southeast Missouri State University • Cape Girardeau, MO 63701 • ALCTS GODORT

Ziegman Bruce • Librarian • Fort Vancouver Regional Library • Vancouver, WA 98663

Zielinska Marie F. • Chief, Multilingual Biblserv. • National Library of Canada • Ottawa, ON, K1A 0N4 Canada • PLA EMIERT

Zielinski Denise M. • Helen M. Plum Memorial Library • Lombard, IL 60148 • ALSC

Zielke Evelyn R. • Student • Brigham Young University School of Library & Information Sciences • Provo, UT 84602 • ACRL

Zielke Frank L. • High School Librarian • Greybull High School Library • Greybull, WY 82426 • AASL LITA YALSA IFRT LIRT SRRT

Ziemianski Annette T. • School Library Media Specialist • Jacob Gunther Elementary School • North Bellmore, NY 11710

Zieselman Paula M. • Fulbright & Jaworski • New York, NY 10103 • ALCTS LITA

Ziessman Yolan • Clearwater, FL 34623 • Continuing

Zietlow Ruth A. • Student • University of Minnesota • Minneapolis, MN 55455 • GODORT IRRT

Zietz Stephen J. • PACSCL Coordinator • University of Pennsylvania • Philadelphia, PA 19104 • ACRL ALCTS

Ziglar Fran • Public Library of Nashville & Davidson County/WPLN Talking Library • Nashville, TN 37210

Ziglin Janice A. • School Librarian • Elmbrook Middle School • Elm Grove, WI 53122 • AASL

Zika John R. • Head Librarian • Person County Public Library • Roxboro, NC 27573 • PLA

Zikas Patricia J. • Circulation Supervisor • Geneva Public Library District • Geneva, IL 60134

Zilka David • Collection Development Ln • Monessen Public Library • Monessen, PA 15062-1182 • PLA

Zilla Karin Bornmann • Manager • Martin Marietta Corporation Business Information Center • Bethesda, MD 20817 • LITA

Zillman Joanne C. • Youth Services Librarian • Bedford Park Public Library District • Bedford Park, IL 60501 • ALSC YALSA

Zilonis Mary Frances Dr. • Director of Educational Media • Cambridge Public Schools • Cambridge, MA 02138 • AASL EMIERT LIRT

Ziman Loreen H. • County of Los Angeles Public Library Valencia Library 113 • Valenica, CA 91355 • PLA RASD

Zimmer Connie W. • Assistant Professor • Arkansas Tech University School of Education • Russellville, AR 72801 • AASL

Zimmer Nancy • Librarian • Mounds View Senior High School Library • St. Paul, MN 55112 • AASL

Zimmerle Arleen A. • Media Services Librarian • La Salle University Connelly Library • Philadelphia, PA 19141 • ACRL

Zimmerman Ann S. • United States Fish & Wildlife Service National Fisheries Research Center • Ann Arbor, MI 48105 • FLRT

Zimmerman Carla B. • Marlboro Psychiatric Hospital • Marlboro, NJ 07746

Zimmerman Charlotte • Rochester Hills, MI 48309

Zimmerman Diana J. • Librarian • Center for Migration Studies Library/Archives • Staten Island, NY 10304 • ACRL EMIERT

Zimmerman Elaine • Director • Cheektowaga Public Library • Cheektowaga, NY 14225 • LAMA PLA

Zimmerman Gerald A. • Hd,Spec Proj,Visual & Perf Arts • Chicago Public Library Harold Washington Library • Chicago, IL 60605

Zimmerman Glen A. • Dir for Tech Processes Research • Library of Congress • Washington, DC 20541 • ALCTS LAMA   *Life*

Zimmerman Irene • Gainesville, FL 32609 • ASCLA PLA   *Life*

Zimmerman Irene E. • Head, CTS Social Science Dept. • University of Wisconsin-Madison Memorial Library • Madison, WI 53706 • ACRL ALCTS LAMA

Zimmerman Jill M. • Automation Librarian • Saint Philip's College LRC • San Antonio, TX 78203 • LITA IFRT

Zimmerman Karen P. • Archivist • University of South Dakota I.D. Weeks Library • Vermillion, SD 57069-2390 • ACRL EMIERT

Zimmerman Kay D. • Emporia, KS 66801

Zimmerman Lee F. • Hendersonvle, NC 28739 • Continuing

Zimmerman Marian A. • Reference Libn/Professor • College of Dupage Learning Resources Center • Glen Ellyn, IL 60137 • ACRL RASD IRRT

Zimmerman Martha • West Florida Regional Library • Pensacola, FL 32501

Zimmerman Michael C. • Research Librarian • Federal Reserve Bank of Dallas • Dallas, TX 75222 • ALCTS LITA

Zimmerman Nancy P. • Doctoral Grad/Teaching Assoc. • Texas Woman's University School of Library & Information Studies • Denton, TX 76204 • AASL ALSC LITA YALSA LRRT

Zimmerman Robert D. • Architect • Harry Weese & Associates • Chicago, IL 60610 • ACRL LAMA

Zimmermann Carole R. • Librarian • Library of Congress • Washington, DC 20541 • ACRL ALCTS

Zimmermann R. Marie • Library Director • Highline Community College • Des Moines, WA 98198-9800 • ACRL LAMA LITA

Zimmers Rob • Sales Representative • Quality Books Inc. • Lake Bluff, IL 60044-2204 • PLA

Zimmeth Margaret E. • Detroit Public Library • Detroit, MI 48202

Zindars Sharon • Assistant Director • Sun Prairie Public Library • Sun Prairie, WI 53590

Zink Lois C. • Sparks Middle School • Sparks, NV 89431 • AASL

Zink Steven D. • University of Nevada-Reno • Reno, NV 89557 • ACRL LAMA RASD GODORT

Zink Thomas Karen K. • Student • Ball State University Department of Library & Information Science • Muncie, IN 47306-1099

Zinkel Marcia L. • Librarian • Twin Valley High School Library • Elverson, PA 19520 • AASL

Zinn Nancy Whitten • Head of Special Collection • University of California San Francisco Library • San Francisco, CA 94143-0840 • ACRL

Zinnato Diana • Assoc Director Collection Mgt. • Thomas Jefferson University Scott Memorial Library • Philadelphia, PA 19107 • LITA

Zins Martha Lee • Media Generalist • Katherine Curren Elementary School Media Center • Hopkins, MN 55343 • AASL IFRT LRRT   *Life*

Zinsley June M. • Head Technical Services • Sachem Public Library • Holbrook, NY 11741 • ALCTS

Zintz Linda S. • Plano, IA 52581-9708

Ziolko Joseph F. • Director • Mississippi County Library System and College Library • Blytheville, AR 72315 • ACRL PLA

Ziolkowski Darlene M. • Personnel Librarian • University of Illinois at Chicago University Library • Chicago, IL 60680 • ACRL LAMA

Zipkowitz Fay • University of Rhode Island Graduate School of Library & Information Studies • Kingston, RI 02881-0815 • ACRL ALCTS ASCLA PLA LRRT

Zipp Louise S. • Geology Librarian • University of Iowa Libraries • Iowa City, IA 52242-1379 • ACRL MAGERT

Zirps Christina C. • Asst. to the Executive Director • Library of Congress • Washington, DC 20541 • FLRT

Zisk Janet M. • Midkiff Learning Center Kamehameha Schools • Honolulu, HI 96817

Ziskind Sylvia • Los Angeles, CA 90010 • Continuing

Zito Valerie • Reference Librarian • Contra Costa County Library • Pleasant Hill, CA 94523 • PLA

Zitterkopf Marilyn R. • Cataloger • California State University • Fresno, CA 93740-0034 • ALCTS RASD

Zlatnik Judith R. • Fremont, CA 94536

Zlatos Christy L. • Reference/Collection Devel Ln • Washington State University Library • Pullman, WA 99164-5610 • ACRL RASD LRRT

Zlendich Janice • Chair, Technical Services Dept. • California State University • Fullerton, CA 92634

Zmrazek Donna • Librarian • Berea High School • Berea, OH 44017 • AASL

Zobel Miriam • President • Zobel Book Service • Clintondale, NY 12515 • ACRL

Zoerb Carol J. • University Librarian • University of Nebraska • Omaha, NE 68182 • ACRL

Zogg Thomas R. • Reference Librarian • University of Minnesota-Duluth Library • Duluth, MN 55812-2495 • ACRL LRRT MAGERT

Zogott Howard O. • Urban Librarian • Free Library of Philadelphia • Philadelphia, PA 19103 • LAMA PLA RASD

Zolno Ann L. • Massasoit Community College Blue Hills • Canton, MA 02021

Zollars Scotty M. • Librarian • Twin Lakes Technical College • Harrison, AR 72602 • NMRT

Zoller Jean G. • Library Director • Wyoming Middle Sch • Wyoming, OH 45215 • AASL

Zolyniak Henrietta • Oak Ridge High School • Oak Ridge, TN 37830 • AASL

Zone Beth • Trustee • Cuyahoga County Public Library • Cleveland, OH 44134-2792

Zonghi Roberta • Curator of Rare Books • Boston Public Library • Boston, MA 02117 • ACRL

Zonligt Martin J. • Reference Librarian • Stanislaus County Free Library • Modesto, CA 95354

Zook Joy • Librarian • Tell City Middle School • Tell City, IN 47586 • AASL

Zoppa Linda • School Media Specialist • Pablo Casals Middle School • Bronx, NY 10475 • AASL ALSC

Zoppel Carol A. • Assistant to the Director • Massachusetts Institute of Technology Libraries (MIT) • Cambridge, MA 02139 • ACRL LAMA NMRT

Zorbas Elaine R. • Librarian III-Reference • Pasadena Public Library • Pasadena, CA 91101 • RASD

Zoretich Josie • Community Library Manager • County of Los Angeles Public Library Culver City Library 330 • Culver City, CA 90230 • PLA

Zorn Marcia • Youth Services Librarian • Bedford Public Library • Bedford, TX 76021 • ALSC

Zou Qiong • Student • Kutztown University Library Science Department • Kutztown, PA 19530

Zsigmondi Eva Mrs. • Student • City College of New York (CUNY) • New York, NY 10031

Zsoldos Theresia • Beauty, KY 41203 • AASL *Continuing*

Zubatsky David S. • Lancaster, PA 17603 • ACRL ALCTS

Zubiri Raymond J. • Trustee • Coalinga-Huron Library District • Coalinga, CA 93210

Zubritzky Paul G. • Branch Librarian • Ocean County Library Jackson Branch • Jackson, NJ 08527

Zuck Gregory J. • Winfield, KS 67156-2423 • LITA

Zucker Barbara F. • Carbondale, IL 62901

Zucker Blanche M. • Las Vagas, NV 89102

Zucker Faye • Faye Zucker Editorial Service • New York, NY 10002-4703

Zuckerman Arline • University Research Librarian • University of California-Los Angeles (UCLA) • Los Angeles, CA 90024-1450 • ACRL ALCTS LITA

Zuckerman Jack J. • Accountant • East Meadow Public Library • East Meadow, NY 11554-1700 • PLA

Zuckerman Judy E. • New York Public Library • Bronx, NY 10458 • ALSC

Zuege Mary Lou • Librarian • Menomonee Falls High School • Menomonee Falls, WI 53051 • AASL

Zuelke Elizabeth Hatton • Reference Librarian • Washington Township Public Library • Dayton, OH 45459 • RASD

Zugby Lillian C. • Takoma Park, MD 20912 • ACRL *Continuing*

Zuger Christine F. • Cataloger • Cameron University • Lawton, OK 73505 • ALCTS

Zuhr Mary K. • Librarian • Grand Oaks Elementary School • Clinton, TN 37716

Zuidema Kristina S. • Elementary Librarian • Edna Libby School • Sebago Lake, ME 04075

Zuiderveld Sharon R. • Catalog Librarian • Bound to Stay Bound Books Inc. (BTSB) • Jacksonville, IL 62650 • AASL ALCTS

Zukas Nora L. • Reference Librarian • University of Illinois at Chicago University Library • Chicago, IL 60680

Zuke Janice E. • Librarian • Belleville Area College Granite City Center • Granite City, IL 62040 • ACRL

Zukoski Pamela J. • Student • Indiana University School of Library and Information Science • Bloomington, IN 47405

Zula Floyd M. • Head, Monographs-Acquisitions • Tulane University Howard-Tilton Memorial Library • New Orleans, LA 70118 • ACRL ALCTS

Zullig Marlene A. • Niskayuna, NY 12309

Zullo Vincent R. • Manager User Services • H. W. Wilson Company • Bronx, NY 10452 • LITA

Zulu Itibari M. • Reference Librarian • California State University,Fresno Henry Madden Library • Fresno, CA 93740-0034

Zumalt Joseph R. • Student • Kansas City Kansas Public Library • Kansas City, KS 66101

Zumbo Stephen M. • Asst. Adm./Head of Reference • Chicago Ridge Public Lib • Chicago Ridge, IL 60415 • PLA RASD

Zumbro Catherine Lee • Gainesville, FL 32604-1118 • GODORT

Zummak Rosemary • Jesup, IA 50648

Zumsteg Laurie P. • Graduate Student • University of Washington Graduate School of Library and Information Science • Seattle, WA 98195

Zundel Karen M. • Director • McKeesport Hospital Health Science Library • McKeesport, PA 15132

Zunder Marjorie D. • Lib. Info Serv. Coodinator • Vermont Department of Libraries • Montpelier, VT 05609

Zupko Janet • Chicago, IL 60626

Zuppa Theodore C. • Cataloger • Francis Marion University James A. Rogers Library • Florence, SC 29501 • ALCTS LITA *Life*

Zuraw Cathy • Director, LRC • Sheridan College of Applied Arts and Technology • Oakville ON, L6H 2L1 Canada • LAMA

Zurcher Susan R. • Public Service Librarian • Hampshire Public Library District • Hampshire, IL 60140 • ALTA PLA

Zurflieh Virginia A. • Tampa-Hillsborough County Public Library • Tampa, FL 33602

Zuriff Susan Rom • Head, Serials Cataloging • University of Minnesota • Minneapolis, MN 55455 • ACRL ALCTS

Zurkammer Michael D. • Germantown, TN 38139

Zurrow Mary J. • Saint Theresa School • Coral Gables, FL 33134 • AASL ALSC

Zussy Nancy L. • State Librarian • Washington State Library • Olympia, WA 98504 • ACRL ASCLA LAMA PLA *Life*

Zvirin Stephanie H. • Associate Editor, Booklist • American Library Association • Chicago, IL 60611-2795 • YALSA

Zvolanek F J Jr • Milwaukee, WI 53210 • ACRL ALCTS *Life*

Zvonkin Judith F. • Librarian II • District of Columbia Public Library Martin Luther King Memorial Library • Washington, DC 20001

Zwanziger Marie • Librarian • The New York Public Library • New York, NY 10016 • RASD

Zweiback Allen T. • Flushing, NY 11354

Zweig Barbara L. • Reference Librarian • Alsip-Merrionette Park Library District • Alsip, IL 60658

Zweizig Douglas L. • University of Wisconsin School of Library & Information Studies • Madison, WI 53706 • ASCLA PLA LRRT *Life*

Zwemer Diane • Reference/Instruction Librarian • University of California Library • Los Angeles, CA 90024 • ACRL LIRT

Zwer Susan G. • Librarian Reference Department • Orange County Library System Orlando Public Library • Orlando, FL 32801-2471 • PLA

Zwick Beverly A. • Information Specialist • Lake Lanier Regional Library Lawrenceville Branch • Lawrenceville, GA 30245-4707

Zwick Erica A. • Librarian • Garvey Schubert & Barer • Seattle, WA 98104

Zwick Louise Y. • Branch Manager & Children's Ln • Houston Public Library Stanaker Branch • Houston, TX 77011 • EMIERT

Zwickel Nancy A. • Student • University of Oklahoma School of Library & Information Studies • Norman, OK 73019 • AASL

Zwiefler Irving • Trustee • Peninsula Public Library • Lawrence, NY 11559

Zwierski Michele • Unit Coordinator • Southwest Texas State University • San Marcos, TX 78666 • ALCTS

Zwinggi Eda A. • St Peter, MN 56082 • ACRL ALCTS *Continuing*

Zych Marie J. • Teacher-Librarian • Perry Traditional Academy • Pittsburgh, PA 15214 • AASL YALSA

Zydek Ann M. • Director • Warsaw Community Public Library • Warsaw, IN 46580 • LAMA PLA

Zynda Fisher Nancy • Oklahoma City, OK 73107

Zyroff Ellen Slotoroff • Principal Librarian • San Diego County Library • San Diego, CA 92123 • ALCTS PLA LIRT

Zysk Larry W. • Librarian • Aquinas College Learning Resource Center • Grand Rapids, MI 49506-1799 • ACRL RASD

Zyskowski Douglas A. • City Librarian • Southfield Public Library David Stewart Memorial Library • Southfield, MI 48037-2055 • LAMA LITA PLA

Zyzik Ursula Z. • Reference/Public Serv Librarian • Saint Xavier University • Chicago, IL 60655 • IRRT

Organization Members

A. B. Shepard High School • Palos Heights, IL 60463 • AASL

A. Mitchell Library • David A. Rave • Aberdeen, SD 57401 • ALCTS ALSC LAMA PLA RASD

A.H. Johnson Memorial Library • Barbara Rudio • Kodiak, AK 99615 • PLA

ABT Associates, Inc. • Sharon Christenson • Cambridge, MA 02138 • Subscribing

Aberdeen Timberland Library • Christine Morgan Peck • Aberdeen, WA 98520 • ALTA PLA

Abilene Christian University Margaret & Herman Brown Library • Marsha Harper • Abilene, TX 79699 • ACRL ALCTS LAMA LITA RASD YALSA

Abington Community Library • Mary Tuthill • Clarks Summit, PA 18411 • LAMA PLA

Abu Dhabi Men's College Higher Colleges of Technology • Felicity F. Hajjar • Abu Dhabi, United Arab Emirates • AASL ACRL LITA

Acad of Amer Franciscan Hist • Stephen Cavin • Berkeley, CA 94709 • ACRL

Academia San Jose High School • Ana Mayo • Guaynabo, PR 00966

Academic Press • Tara Catogge • San Diego, CA 92101 • ACRL   Subscribing

Academy of Art College Library • James E. Van Buskirk • San Francisco, CA 94133

Academy of the Holy Cross • Judith Bradley • Kensington, MD 20895 • AASL

Acadia University Library • Iain J. Bates • Wolfville NS, B0P 1X0 Canada • ACRL ALCTS LAMA LITA

Ada County District Library • Dian Hoffpauir • Boise, ID 83709 • ALSC ALTA LAMA PLA RASD YALSA

Ada Public Library • Jennifer K. Greenstreet • Ada, OK 74820

Adams County School District #14 Instructional Materials Center • Roberta Altenbern • Commerce Cty, CO 80022 • AASL ALSC YALSA

Adath Jeshurun Congregation Gottlieb Memorial Library • Barbara Steinberg • Elkins Park, PA 19117 • AASL PLA

Addison-Wesley Publ Co • Anne Dulligan • Reading, MA 01867 • Subscribing

Addison Trail High School • Charles Citrano • Addison, IL 60101

Adelanto School District • Don Balick • Adelanto, CA 92301

Adelphi University Swirbul Library • Eugene T. Neely • Garden City, NY 11530 • ACRL ALCTS LITA RASD

Adirondack Community College • William B Martin • Queensbury, NY 12801 • ACRL RASD LIRT

Adler Sch of Prof Psych • Karen Drescher • Chicago, IL 60601 • ACRL LRRT

Administrative College of Papua New Guinea • Kwamala Kalo • Papua, New Guinea

Adrian Sr High Sch Lib • Adrian, MI 49221

Aerospace Corporation • Susan B. Crowe • Los Angeles, CA 90080-0966 • ACRL ALCTS LAMA LITA RASD GODORT   Subscribing

African Books Collective Ltd. • Hans M. Zell • Oxford OX1 1HU, England • ACRL EMIERT   Subscribing

Ainsworth Public Library • Gail J. Irwin • Ainsworth, NE 69210

Akron-Summit Cnty Pub Lib • Steven Hawk • Akron, OH 44326-0001 • AASL ALCTS ALSC ALTA ASCLA LAMA LITA PLA RASD YALSA

Alabama A&M University J.F. Drake Memorial LRC • Birdie O. Weir • Normal, AL 35762 • ACRL ALCTS ALSC ALTA ASCLA LAMA LITA RASD YALSA CLENE EMIERT GODORT IFRT IRRT LHRT LIRT LRRT SORT

Alabama Library Association • Barbara F. Black • Montgomery, AL 36104

Alabama Southern Cmnty Coll John D. Forte Library • Angela C. Lee • Monroeville, AL 36461-2000 • ACRL

Alabama State University Levi Watkins Learning Ctr Lib • John L. Buskey • Montgomery, AL 36195-0301 • ACRL ALCTS ALSC LAMA LITA RASD LIRT SORT

Alameda Cnty Off of Edu LRS Curriculum Library • Jim Fryer • Hayward, CA 94541-1198 • AASL

Alameda County Library System • Linda M. Wood • Fremont, CA 94538 • AASL ALCTS ALSC ALTA ASCLA LAMA LITA PLA RASD YALSA

Alaska Library Association • Audrey P. Kolb • Valdez, AK 99686

Alaska State Library • Karen R. Crane • Juneau, AK 99811-571 • AASL ACRL ALCTS ALSC ALTA ASCLA LAMA LITA PLA RASD YALSA FLRT GODORT IFRT SRRT

Albany Public Library • Edward B. House • Albany, OR 97321

Albert Wisner Public Library • Karen Bash Romaner • Warwick, NY 10990

Alberta Culture & Multicultural Libs & Cmnty Devel • Joseph Forsyth • Edmonton, AB, T5M 2M2 Canada • ALTA ASCLA LAMA PLA

Alberta Vocational College • Vickiilin M. Nicholson • Edmonton AB, T5J 1L6 Canada • ACRL RASD

Albertson College of Idaho N.L. Terteling Library • Dale Corning • Caldwell, ID 83605 • ACRL ALCTS LITA RASD

Albion College Stockwell-Mudd Libraries • Larry R. Oberg • Albion, MI 49224 • ACRL

Albuquerque Public Library • Alan B. Clark • Albuquerque, NM 87102 • AASL ALCTS LAMA LITA PLA

Alcorn State University Library • Margaret P. Frazier • Lorman, MS 39096 • AASL ACRL ALCTS ALSC ASCLA LAMA LITA PLA RASD YALSA EMIERT GODORT IFRT LIRT LRRT VRT

Alexander City State Jr Coll Thomas D. Russell Library • Alexander City, AL 35010 • ACRL ASCLA

Alfred Dickey Free Library • Jamestown, ND 58401

Alg Hogeschool Amsterdam Fac Informatie/Communicatie • 1001 EW Amsterdam, Netherlands

Algonquin Area Pub Lib Dist • Randall Vlcek • Algonquin, IL 60102

Alice E. Chatlos Library Practical Bible Training School • Gerald Franz • Bible School Park, NY 13737-0612 • ACRL

Alice L. Pendleton Library • Louise MacKenzie • Isleboro, ME 04848

Allen County Public Library • Jeffrey R. Krull • Fort Wayne, IN 46801-2270 • AASL ACRL ALCTS ALSC ALTA LAMA LITA PLA RASD YALSA

Allen University J. S. Flipper LRC • Annie H. Coleman • Columbia, SC 29204

Alpine County Library • Dianne Brigham • Markleeville, CA 96120 • PLA

Altadena Library District • William John Tema • Altadena, CA 91001 • PLA

Altoona Public Library • Kim Smith • Altoona, IA 50004

Altschul Group Corporation • Eileen A. Cronin • Evanston, IL 60201 • Subscribing

Alva Public Library • Larry R. Thorne • Alva, OK 73717 • ALSC PLA

Alverno Coll Lib Media Ctr • Jean E. DeLauche • Milwaukee, WI 53234-3922 • ACRL ALCTS ASCLA LAMA LITA RASD EMIERT GODORT LIRT SORT

Alverno High School Library • Marianne S. Newman • Sierra Madre, CA 91024 • AASL

Amber University Library Resource Center • Charles Hickox • Garland, TX 75041

Amdahl Corporation Technical Research Cntr. • Susan McTague • Sunnyvale, CA 94086 • LITA

Amer Assn of Law Libs • Judith L. Genesen • Chicago, IL 60604

Amer Schs of Prof Psych • Eleanor Hill • Chicago, IL 60604 • LITA

Amer Soc for Inf Sci • Richard B. Hill • Silver Spring, MD 20910-3602

Amer Univ in Cairo Lib • Lamia Eid • Linden, NJ 07036 • ACRL ALCTS LAMA LITA RASD

American Arbitration Association Eastman Arbitration Library • New York, NY 10020

American College of Greece Deree College Library • Maria Stergiou • Aghia Paraskevi, Greece • ACRL ALCTS

American Dental Association Bureau of Library Services • Aletha Kowitz • Chicago, IL 60611

American Educational Complex • Killeen, TX 76540 • ACRL ALCTS LAMA RASD

American Embassy • Angela K. Titone • APO New York, NY 09080

American Federation of State Cnty & Muncipal Employees • William R. Wilkinson • Washington, DC 20036 • SORT SRRT

American Institute of Aero and Astro Inc • New York, NY 10019 • LITA

American Institute of Commerce • Davenport, IA 52807 • ACRL

American Medical Association • Arthur W. Hafner • Chicago, IL 60610

American Overseas School of Rome • APO New York, NY 09794-0007

American Philosophical Society Library • Philadelphia, PA 19106 • ACRL ALCTS RASD

American School Foundation, AC • Cynthia A. Christie de Muhlbach • Mexico DF, 01120, Mexico • AASL

American School of Bilboa • Newburgh, NY 12550

American School of Paris Upper School Library • Barbara Kamm • Saint Cloud 92210, France • AASL

American Studies Research Centre • Sreenidhi Iyengar • Hyderabad 500 007, India • ACRL ALCTS RASD

American University of Beirut Univ Lib-Ser Dept. • Lilian Vitale • Valley Stream, NY 11581 • ACRL ALCTS LITA RASD

Ameritech Information Systems Information Resource Center • Indrani Embar • Chicago, IL 60661 • ALCTS LAMA RASD   Subscribing

Ames Free Library • Barbra N. Katz • North Easton, MA 02356 • PLA

Amity Rgnl Sr High Sch • Woodbridge, CT 06525 • YALSA

Amphitheater Public Schools • Tucson, AZ 85737-7599 • AASL YALSA

Amphitheater Public Schools Croos-Harelson Library • Karen Heusted • Tucson, AZ 85704 • AASL YALSA

An Chomhairle Leabharlanna • Thomas Armitage • Dublin 2, Ireland • AASL ALCTS ALSC ASCLA LAMA LITA PLA RASD

Anchorage Municipal Libraries Z. J. Loussac Library • Mary H. McGee • Anchorage, AK 99503 • ALTA

Andalusia Public Library • Howard Strevel • Andulisa, AL 36420 • PLA

Anderson College Library Johnston Memorial Library • Kent Millwood • Anderson, SC 29621 • ACRL

Anderson County Library • Carl Stone • Anderson, SC 29622-4047 • ALTA

Anderson Public Library • David A. Bucove • Anderson, IN 46016 • ACRL ALCTS ASCLA LAMA LITA PLA RASD YALSA

Andover Public Library • Tom Newman • Andover, CT 06232 • ALSC

Andrew College Pitts Library • Karan Ann Berryman • Cuthbert, GA 31740 • ACRL

Anglo-American Moscow • Apo, AE 09721 • AASL

Ann May School of Nursing Library & Media Center • Darlene A. Robertelli • Neptune, NJ 07754

Anne Arundel Cnty Pub Schs • A. Brian Helm • Annapolis, MD 21401 • AASL ALCTS LAMA LITA YALSA

Anne Arundel Community College Andrew G. Truxal Library • Harry E. Foster • Arnold, MD 21012 • ACRL ALCTS LAMA LITA RASD

Annenberg/CPB Project • Lynn M. Smith • Washington, DC 20004 • Subscribing

Anniston-Calhoun Cnty Pub Lib • Anninston, AL 36202 • ALSC LAMA PLA

Anoka-Ramsey Community College Library • Lorraine Bangoure • Coon Rapids, MN 55433 • ACRL

Anoka County Library • Jerry F. Young • Blaine, MN 55434

Anoka Public Library • Loretta Vail • Anoka, MN 55303 • ALCTS ALSC PLA RASD

Anthony Public Library • Sandy Trotter • Anthony, KS 67003

Antigo Public Library • Antigo, WI 54409 • ALSC LAMA PLA

Antilles School, Inc. • Carol Wax • St Thomas, VI 00801

Antioch Public Library District • Kathy D. Labuda • Antioch, IL 60002 • ALSC PLA RASD

Antique Auto Club of America Library & Research Center • Hershey, PA 17033 • ACRL ALCTS

Apollo Moving Specialist • Michael J. Dick • Minneapolis, MN 55413 • LAMA   Subscribing

Appalachian State University Carol Grotnes Belk Library • Richard T. Barker • Boone, NC 28608 • AASL ACRL ALCTS LAMA LITA PLA RASD

Apple Computer, Inc. Library • Monica E. Ertel • Cupertino, CA 95014 • Patron

Appleton Senior High School East Library • Appleton, WI 54915 • AASL YALSA

Aquinas Jr College Library • Milton, MA 02186 • ACRL

Aquinas Junior College Library • Peggy Chance • Nashville, TN 37205 • ACRL

Archbishop Carroll H S • Washington, DC 20017 • AASL YALSA EMIERT

Archbishop Rummel High School Library • Deborah Kettenring Lobrano • Metairie, LA 70001 • AASL

Argo Community High School Media Center • Carolyn Hobaugh • Summit, IL 60501 • AASL

Arizona State Lib Assn • Ellen E. Ramsay • Phoenix, AZ 85032

Arizona State Library Dept of Lib Archv & Public Rcds • Sharon Turgeon • Phoenix, AZ 85007 • AASL ACRL ALCTS ALSC ALTA ASCLA LAMA LITA PLA RASD YALSA CLENE GODORT ILERT LIRT MAGERT

Arkansas Library Association • Sherry Price Walker • Little Rock, AR 72207-6344 • AASL ACRL ALCTS ALSC ALTA PLA RASD GODORT IFRT NMRT

Arkansas State Library • John A. Murphey • Little Rock, AR 72201 • AASL ACRL ALCTS ALSC ALTA ASCLA LAMA LITA PLA RASD YALSA CLENE EMIERT ERT FLRT GODORT IFRT ILERT IRRT LHRT LIRT LRRT MAGERT NMRT SORT SRRT

Arkansas State University Dean B. Ellis Library • Bill Hansard • State University, AR 72467-2040 • AASL ACRL ALCTS ALSC LAMA LITA PLA RASD

Arkansas Technical University Tomlinson Library • Bill Parton • Russellville, AR 72801 • ACRL ALCTS LAMA LITA

Arkansas Valley Voc Tech Sch Resource Center • Ozark, AR 72949

Armada Free Library • Armada, MI 48005

Arrowhead High School • Sara Larsen • Hartland, WI 53029 • AASL YALSA IFRT

Arrowhead Library System • Kenneth R. Nielsen • Virginia, MN 55792 • ALTA LITA PLA

Arthur Temple Sr Mem Lib • Florene Hall • Pineland, TX 75968

Arvilla E Diver Memorial Library • Jane Daurio • Schaghticoke, NY 12154 • PLA

Ascension Parish Library • Earline M. Decoteau • Donaldsonville, LA 70346-2535 • LAMA PLA RASD YALSA

Ashgate Publishing Company • Tawnya K. Quiet • Brookfield, VT 05036 • ACRL   *Subscribing*

Ashland College Library • Darwyn J. Batway • Ashland, OH 44805 • ACRL ALCTS RASD GODORT

Ashtabula Cnty Dist Pub Lib • William J. Tokarczyk • Ashtabula, OH 44004 • ALTA PLA

Asia University Library • Hidekazu Nagata • Tokyo, Japan • AASL ALCTS LITA RASD

Asian Pacific Amer Lns Association • Ichiko T. Morita • Chicago, IL 60660

Asotin County Library • Clarkston, WA 99403

Assn for Lib & Inf Sci Edu (ALISE) • Raleigh, NC 27607

Assn of Amer Univ Presses • Peter C. Grenquist • New York, NY 10012

Assn of Res Libs (ARL) • Duane Webster • Washington, DC 20036 • ACRL ALCTS LITA

Astoria High School Library • Michael W. Foster • Astoria, OR 97103 • AASL ERT

Astoria Public Library • Bruce R. Berney • Astoria, OR 97103

Astoria Public Library District • Astoria, IL 61501

Athabasca University Library • Patricia Appavoo • Athabasca AB, T0G 2R0 Canada • ACRL ALCTS LAMA LITA RASD

Athenaeum of Ohio • Deborah Harmeling • Cincinnati, OH 45230 • ACRL ALCTS

Atkinson Public Library District • Sarah A. Patton • Atkinson, IL 61235-0633

Atlanta-Fulton Public Library • Atlanta, GA 30303 • ALCTS ALSC ASCLA LAMA LITA PLA RASD YALSA

Atlanta Hist Soc Lib • Anne Salter • Atlanta, GA 30305 • ACRL

Atlanta Public Library • Lee Ann Hamilton • Atlanta, TX 75551 • PLA

Atlanta University Center Robert W. Woodruff Library • Joseph E. Troutman • Atlanta, GA 30314 • ACRL ALCTS LAMA LITA RASD

Atlantic City Fr Pub Lib • Maureen Sherr Frank • Atlantic City, NJ 08401

Auburn University Learning Resources Center • Auburn, AL 36849 • AASL

Auburn University Ralph Brown Draughon Library • William C. Highfill • Auburn, AL 36849-5606 • AASL ACRL ALCTS ALTA ASCLA LAMA LITA PLA RASD YALSA

Auckland Public Library • Auckland, New Zealand • RASD

Audio Editions • Grady Hesters • Auburn, CA 95604 • Subscribing

Augusta Public Library • Maggie Tarelli-Falcon • Augusta, KS 67010

Aurora Public Schools • William A. Murray • Aurora, CO 80011-9023

Aurora University Library • Susan L. Craig • Aurora, IL 60506

Australian National University Library Menzies • C. Steele • Canberra ACT 2600, Australia • ACRL ALCTS LAMA LITA RASD

Auto-Graphics Inc. • Joel M. Lee • Pomona, CA 91768 • ALCTS PLA GODORT   *Subscribing*

Avec Technical Services Inc. • Joan Rataic-Lang • Mississauga, ON, LSJ 1K5 Canada • ACRL ERT
                                                      Subscribing

Avoca Elementary School District 37 • Barbara Entin • Wilmette, IL 60091 • AASL

B.C. Archv and Rcds Serv Library • Victoria BC, V8V 1X4 Canada • ACRL ALCTS

BC Inventar, Inc. • V. Kenneth Olsen • Houston, TX 77032 • Subscribing

BOCES-NERPC • Carle Place, NY 11514

Babbitt Public Library • Janet Kivisto • Babbitt, MN 55706

Bailey & Gardner A.I.A. • Judson M. Gardner • Orange, VA 22960 • Subscribing

Baker & Taylor Books • Mary L. Shapiro • Bridgewater, NJ 08807 • AASL ACRL ALCTS ALSC ALTA ASCLA LAMA LITA PLA RASD YALSA ERT NMRT   *Patron*

Baker & Taylor Video • Carl Mann • Morton Grove, IL 60053 • VRT   *Subscribing*

Baker County Public Library • Aletha G. Bonebrake • Baker, OR 97814

Bakersfield City School District Professional Library • Joslin Kessler • Bakersfield, CA 93305 • AASL

Bakersfield College Grace Van Dyke Bird Library • Fred Rue Jacobs • Bakersfield, CA 93305-1229 • ACRL

Baldwin-Wallace College • Berea, OH 44017 • ACRL ALCTS LAMA RASD

Banaras Hindu University Library • Varanasi-221 005, India • ACRL ALCTS LITA RASD

Bancroft Memorial Library • Elanie Malloy • Hopedale, MA 01747

Bank Street Coll of Edu Lib • Eleanor R. Kulleseid • New York, NY 10025 • ACRL ALCTS LAMA

Baptist Missionary Association Theo Sem /Kellar Lib • James C. Blaylock • Jacksonville, TX 75766-5414

Barat College Library • Alan F. Barney • Lake Forest, IL 60045 • ACRL RASD

Barberton Public Library • Barbara L. Kirbawy • Barberton, OH 44203-2458 • ALSC PLA RASD

Baruch College Library • Kristin A. McDonough • New York, NY 10010 • ACRL ALCTS LAMA LITA RASD

Basehor Community Library • Carla J. Swope • Basehor, KS 66007

Bassist College • Norma Bassist • Portland, OR 97201 • ACRL

Bastrop Public Library • Belinda Boon • Bastrop, TX 78602-0670 • PLA ERT IFRT

Bay City Public Schools • Colleen Kazmierski • Bay City, MI 48706 • AASL

Bay Path College • Barbara Feret • Longmeadow, MA 01106 • ACRL

Bay Shore Sr High Sch Lib • Helen F. Flowers • Bay Shore, NY 11706 • AASL ALSC

Bay State College The Library • Carol Fitzpatrick • Boston, MA 02116

Bayliss Public Library • Janus Storey • Sault Sainte Marie, MI 49783

Baylor University Library • S. M. Hughes • Waco, TX 76798-7151 • AASL ACRL ALCTS ALSC ALTA ASCLA LAMA LITA PLA RASD YALSA CLENE EMIERT ERT FLRT GODORT IFRT ILERT IRRT LHRT LIRT LRRT MAGERT NMRT SORT SRRT

Bayonne Public Library • Sneh Bains • Bayonne, NJ 07002 • AASL ACRL ALCTS ALSC ALTA ASCLA LAMA LITA PLA RASD YALSA GODORT LIRT

Bayport Blue Point Pub Lib • Anna M. Davis • Blue Point, NY 11715

Bayville Free Library • Lorna L. Bertino • Bayville, NY 11709

Bd of Coop Edu Serv OCM BOCES-Sch Lib Sys • Judith A. Jerome • Syracuse, NY 13221 • AASL ALSC ASCLA IFRT

Beacham Publishing, Inc. • Deborah M Beacham • Washington, DC 20008 • Subscribing

Beaver College • Benjamin R. Williams • Glenside, PA 19038 • ACRL ALCTS LITA RASD

Beaverton Schools Professional Library • Beaverton, OR 97075 • AASL LITA

Bedford Free Library • Susan K. McMahon • Bedford, NY 10506

Bedford Public Library • Susan A. Miller • Bedford, IN 47421 • ASCLA LAMA PLA

Beekman Library • Lee Eaton • Poughquag, NY 12570

Beirut University College Stoltzfus Library • New York, NY 10115-0065

Bell Canada Inf Resource Centre • Montreal, PQ, H2Z 1S4 Canada • ALCTS LAMA LITA RASD

Bellaire Public Library • John T. Kniesner • Bellaire, OH 43906 • PLA

Bellevue Public Library • Theodore R. Allison • Bellevue, OH 44811 • ALCTS LAMA PLA YALSA

Bellingham Public Library • Claudia J. McCain • Bellingham, WA 98227 • ALCTS ALSC ALTA LAMA LITA PLA RASD

Belmont Hill School Library Byrnes Library • Carolyn Thomas • Belmont, MA 02178

Beloit Public Library • Alan M. Tollefson • Beloit, WI 53511

Bemis Public Library • Littleton, CO 80120

Benedictine College North Campus Library • Anna L. Cairney • Atchison, KS 66002 • ACRL

Benet Academy Library • Deborah Sola • Lisle, IL 60532 • AASL

Bentley Memorial Library • Elizabeth E. Thornton • Bolton, CT 06043 • PLA

Bergen-Passaic Rgnl Lib Coop • Anne C. Ciliberti • Hawthorne, NJ 07506 • AASL ASCLA PLA RASD

Bergen Community College Lib & Learning Resource Ctr • Dona Singer • Paramus, NJ 07652-1595 • ACRL ALCTS LIRT

Berkeley Business College • Ewa Leszkiewicz • New York, NY 10017 • ACRL

Berkeley Public Library • Regina U. Minudri • Berkeley, CA 94704 • ALCTS ALSC ALTA LAMA LITA PLA RASD YALSA

Berkshire School Library Berkshire School • Susan B. Young • Sheffield, MA 01257

Bermuda Library • Cyril O. Packwood • Hamilton HM11, Bermuda • ALSC LITA PLA

Berrien Springs Public Schools • Diane M. Nye • Berrien Springs, MI 49103 • AASL ALSC

Berry College Memorial Library • Ondina S. Gonzalez • Mount Berry, GA 30149 • ACRL LAMA RASD GODORT

Berwick Public Library • Ann F. Diseroad • Berwick, PA 18603

Bessemer State Technical College • Ralph Bearse • Bessemer, AL 35021

Bethalto Public Library • Mary-Ellen Grisham • Bethalto, IL 62010

Bethel Theo Sem Lib • Saint Paul, MN 55112

Bethlehem Public Library • Barbara P. Mladinov • Delmar, NY 12054

Bethune-Cookman College Swisher Library • B. R. Henderson • Daytona Beach, FL 32115 • ACRL LAMA LITA

Bevill State Community College Walker Camus • Tyrone T. Webb • Sumiton, AL 35148 • ACRL LIRT

Bibl Ctr for Res • David H. Brunell • Denver, CO 80222

Bibl Tech Hogeschool • J. Zandvliet • South Holland, Netherlands • ACRL ALCTS RASD

Biblio Ecole Des Hautes Commerciales • Montreal PQ, H3T 1V6 Canada • ACRL ALCTS LITA RASD

Biblio Municipale de Montreal Section des Acquisitions • Jacques Panneton • Montreal PQ, H2G 3E4 Canada • AASL ACRL ALCTS ALSC ALTA ASCLA LAMA LITA PLA RASD YALSA

Bibliocentre E Division of Centennial College • Scarborough ON, Canada • ALCTS LITA ERT

Bibliotekstjanst AB Referensbiblioteket • Goran Eliasson • S-221 00 Lund, Sweden • ALCTS ALSC LITA RASD

Bibliotheque Nationale Du Quebec • Philipee Sauvageau • Montreal PQ, H2X 1X4 Canada • ACRL ALCTS

Bibliotheque de bibliotheconomie Universite de Montreal • Arlette Joffe-Nicodeme • Montreal PQ, H3C 3J7 Canada • AASL ACRL ALCTS ALSC LAMA LITA PLA RASD YALSA CLENE EMIERT ERT FLRT GODORT IFRT ILERT IRRT LHRT LIRT LRRT MAGERT NMRT SORT SRRT

Bienville Parish Library • Joyce S. Lilly • Arcadia, LA 71001 • PLA

Big Ben Cmnty Coll Lib • Moses Lake, WA 98837 • ACRL ALCTS LITA

Billings Farm & Museum Library • Esther Munroe Swift • Woodstock, VT 05091 • ACRL ALCTS

Birch Lane School Library • Ruth Lessinger • Massapequa, NY 11762 • AASL NMRT

Birmingham-Southern Coll Lib C. A. Rush Learning Center • Billy Pennington • Birmingham, AL 35254 • ACRL ALCTS ASLC LAMA LITA RASD YALSA

Birmingham Central Library Serials Section • B. H. Baumfield • Birmingham B3 3H, England

Birmingham Polytechnic Main Library • M. M. Hadcroft • Birmingham B42 2SU, England • ACRL ALSC LITA PLA RASD

Birmingham University Library • Birmingham B15 2TT, England • ACRL LITA

Bishop State Community College Minnie Slade Bishop Library • Robert L. Parker • Mobile, AL 36603-5898 • ACRL

Bishops University Library • William Curran • Lennoxville PQ, J1M 1Z7 Canada • ACRL ALCTS LAMA RASD

Bismark State College Library • Marcella Schmaltz • Bismarck, ND 58501 • ACRL GODORT

Black Hawk College • Kewanee, IL 61443

Black Hawk College Library Research Center • M. Andereck • Moline, IL 61265 • ACRL ALCTS RASD

Black Mountain Library, CSIRO • Canberra ACT 2601, Australia • ACRL ALCTS LITA RASD

Bladen Community College Library • Dublin, NC 28332

Bladen County Public Library • Jamie S. Hansen • Elizabethtown, NC 28337 • PLA

Blair Public Library • Anne T. Keenan • Blair, NE 68008

Blanchester Public Library • Blanchester, OH 45107

Blanton & Moore Company • Richard E. Sansom • Barium Springs, NC 28010 • Subscribing

Bleyhl Community Library • Grandview, WA 98930

Bloomfield Twp Pub Lib • Stephen A. Kershner • Bloomfield Hills, MI 48302-2437 • ALSC ALTA PLA IFRT

Bloomingdale Free Public Library • Bloomingdale, NJ 07403 • ALTA LAMA PLA

Blue Cloud Abbey Library • Rev J. McMullen • Marvin, SD 57251 • ACRL ALCTS

Blue Grass Rgnl Lib Ctr • Columbia, TN 38401 • ALSC ALTA LAMA PLA

Blue Island Public Library • Rosemary Robinson • Blue Island, IL 60406 • ALCTS RASD YALSA

Blue Mountain Cmnty Coll Lib • Darcy Dauble • Pendleton, OR 97801 • ACRL ALCTS

Bluefield College Easley Library • Henry S. Whitlow • Bluefield, VA 24605-9986 • ACRL LIRT

Bluffton-Wells Cnty Pub Lib • Barbara Jean Elliott • Bluffton, IN 46714

Bogazici University Library • Ender Altug • Istanbul, Turkey

Boise State University Library • Timothy A. Brown • Boise, ID 83725 • AASL ACRL ALCTS ASCLA LITA RASD YALSA GODORT

Bolivar-Harpers Ferry Library • Candace R. Schmidt • Harpers Ferry, WV 25425

Book Group, The Utah Humanites Resource Center • Helen A. Cox • Salt Lake City, UT 84111-2908

Book It ! • Eunice Ellis • Wichita, KS 67201 • Subscribing

Books on Tape • Newport Beach, CA 92660 • PLA *Contributing*

Boone-Madison Public Library • Mitch Casto • Madison, WV 25130

Boothbay Harbor Memorial Library • Barbara Harvey • Boothbay Harbor, ME 04538

Borroughs Manufacturing Corp • Jerry Norman • Kalamazoo, MI 49007 • AASL ACRL ASCLA LAMA PLA *Subscribing*

Boston Conservatory of Music Lib • Reg Didham • Boston, MA 02215

Boston Edison • Lisa McDonough • Boston, MA 02199 • Subscribing

Boston University Alumni Medical Library • Irene Christopher • Boston, MA 02118 • ACRL ALCTS ASCLA LAMA LITA RASD

Boston University Mugar Memorial Library • John P. Laucus • Boston, MA 02215 • ACRL ALCTS ASCLA LAMA LITA RASD

Bound Brook Memorial Library • Jane Stasser • Bound Brook, NJ 08805

Bound to Stay Bound Books Inc. (BTSB) • Sharon R. Zuiderveld • Jacksonville, IL 62650 • AASL ALCTS ALSC PLA *Subscribing*

Boundary County Library • Beverly Docherty • Bonners Ferry, ID 83805

Bourbonnais Pub Lib Dist • Karen Burden • Bourbonnais, IL 60914 • PLA

Bowdoin College Library • Brunswick, ME 04011 • ACRL ALCTS LITA RASD GODORT

Bowie Public Library • Virginia Harrington • Bowie, TX 76230

Bowling Green Public Library • Karen A. Turner • Bowling Green, KY 42101 • AASL LAMA PLA RASD YALSA

Bowling Green State University William Jerome Library • Rush G. Miller • Bowling Green, OH 43403-0175 • AASL ACRL ALCTS ALSC ASCLA LAMA LITA PLA RASD YALSA GODORT

Boy Scouts of America • Dorothy D. Edwards • Irving, TX 75015-2079

Boyden Public Library • Boyden, IA 51234

Bozeman Sr High Sch Lib • Bozeman, MT 59715 • AASL

Bradford Area H S Lib • Bradford, PA 16701 • AASL

Bradley Public Library • Ruth Drassler • Bradley, IL 60915

Brandon Academy • Brandon, FL 33509-1027

Brandon University John E. Robbins Library • Richard J. Bazillion • Brandon MB, R7A 6A9 Canada • ACRL ALCTS LAMA RASD

Branford Intermediate School • Branford, CT 06405 • AASL YALSA

Brazil Universidade Federal Do Rio Grande Do Sul • Heloisa B. Schreiner • 90040 Porto Alegre, Brazil • ACRL ALCTS LITA RASD

Brentwood Public Library • Tedgina N Bradford • Brentwood, TN 37027

Brevard College James A. Jones Library • Karen Woods • Brevard, NC 28712 • ACRL

Briar Cliff College Library • Bernice Schuetz • Sioux City, IA 51104-2100 • ACRL

Bridgeport Engineering Institute • Fairfield, CT 06430 • ACRL

Bridgeport Public Library • Patricia Stegall • Bridgeport, TX 76026

Bridgeport Public Library • Bridgeport, NE 69336

Bridgewater State College Clement C. Maxwell Library • Owen T. P. McGowan • Bridgewater, MA 02325 • AASL ACRL ALCTS LAMA LITA RASD YALSA

Brielle Public Library • Evalina S. Erbe • Breille, NJ 08730

Brigham Young University Harold B. Lee Library • Sterling J. Albrecht • Provo, UT 84602

Bristol Community College LRC • Shirley C. Wyker • Fall River, MA 02720 • ACRL ALCTS LAMA LITA RASD

British Columbia Legis Lib • Sheila J. Gann • Victoria BC, V8V 1X4 Canada • ACRL ALCTS RASD GODORT

British Library Information Sciences (BLISS) • London, England • AASL ACRL ALCTS ALSC ALTA ASCLA LAMA LITA PLA RASD YALSA CLENE EMIERT ERT FLRT GODORT IFRT ILERT IRRT LHRT LIRT LRRT MAGERT NMRT SORT SRRT

British Library of Political & Economic Science • London WC2A 2HD, Great Britain • ACRL

Brock University • Patricia Wilson • St. Catharines ON, L2S 3A1 Canada • AASL ACRL ALCTS LAMA LITA RASD

Brodart Company • Cassandra Brush • San Diego, CA 92127-1798 • Patron

Brook Avenue School • Bay Shore, NY 11706

Brookline Public Library • Michael Steinfeld • Brookline, MA 02146 • AASL ACRL ALCTS ALSC ALTA ASCLA LAMA LITA PLA RASD YALSA

Brooklyn History Society • Irene Tichenor • Brooklyn, NY 11201

Brooklyn Public Library • Larry Brandwein • Brooklyn, NY 11238 • ALCTS ALTA LAMA LITA PLA RASD

Brooks School • Gunta Vittands • North Andover, MA 01845

Brother Rice High School Library • Sara Daniel • Birmingham, MI 48301-4045 • AASL

Broward Cnty Div of Libs Broward County Library • Samuel F. Morrison • Fort Lauderdale, FL 33301 • AASL ACRL ALCTS ALSC ALTA ASCLA LAMA LITA PLA RASD YALSA

Broward Pub Lib Foundation, Inc. • Kay Harvey • Fort Lauderdale, FL 33301

Brown County Public Library • Nashville, IN 47448 • ALTA LAMA PLA

Brown University Rockefeller Library • Merrily E. Taylor • Providence, RI 02912 • AASL ACRL ALCTS ALTA ASCLA LAMA LITA PLA RASD YALSA

Brunswick Public Library Association • Stephen J. Podgajny • Brunswick, ME 04011

Buckingham Browne & Nichols Sch Upper School Library • Elizabeth H. Bronnert • Cambridge, MA 02138 • AASL

Buckley School, The • New York, NY 10021 • YALSA

Buffalo & Erie Cnty Pub Lib • Donald H. Cloudsley • Buffalo, NY 14203 • AASL ACRL ALCTS ALSC ALTA ASCLA LAMA LITA PLA RASD YALSA

Buffalo & Erie Cnty Pub Lib Sys Serials Dept. • Donald H. Cloudsley • Buffalo, NY 14203 • ACRL ALCTS LITA

Bullfrog Films • Winifred Scherrer • Oley, PA 19547 • AASL ALSC *Subscribing*

Buncombe County Schools • Carolyn Andrade • Asheville, NC 28806 • AASL

Bur Oak Library System • Shorewood, IL 60436 • ALCTS ALSC ALTA LAMA LITA PLA RASD YALSA

Burgundy Farm Country Day School Library • Ann Van Deusen • Alexandria, VA 22303 • AASL

Burlington County Library • Charles E. Carr • Mount Holly, NJ 08060-1394 • ALCTS ASCLA LAMA LITA PLA RASD ERT GODORT IFRT

Burlington Public Library • Patricia A. Chevis • Burlington, WI 53105-1491 • PLA

Burlington Public Library • Anne Walluk • Burlington, CT 06013

Burnham Library • Margaret Golden • Bridgewater, CT 06752

Burnt Hills-Ballston Lake Dist Library Office • Mary J. Egan • Burnt Hills, NY 12027 • YALSA LIRT

Burnt Hills-Ballstone Lake Community Library • Patricia McCarty • Burnt Hills, NY 12027 • PLA

Burton Public Library • Carol Varga • Burton, OH 44021 • ALSC LAMA PLA YALSA IFRT

Business One Irwin • Carol DeSelm • Homewood, IL 60430 • ACRL PLA RASD *Subscribing*

Butler County Community College L. W. Nixon Library • El Dorado, KS 67042 • ACRL ALCTS RASD

Butler University Irwin Library • John P. Kondelik • Indianapolis, IN 46208 • ACRL ALCTS ALSC LAMA LITA RASD GODORT IFRT LIRT

C S I R Library Periodical Sections • B. Fouche • 0001 Pretoria, South Africa • ACRL ALCTS LITA RASD

CBIS • Chris Hill • Norcross, GA 30092 • LITA *Subscribing*

CLSI, Inc. • Susan M. Stearns • Newtonville, MA 02160 • LITA PLA *Subscribing*

CNIB Library for the Blind • Barbara Freeze • Toronto ON, M4G 3EB Canada • ASCLA LITA

CRC Press, Incorporation • Wesley Lawton • Boca Raton, FL 33431 • ACRL PLA *Subscribing*

CSIRO The Manager Serials Acquisitions • John Thawley • E Melbourne VIC 3002, Australia • ACRL ALCTS LAMA LITA RASD

Cabarrus Mem Hosp Lib • Concord, NC 28025

Cabrillo College Library • Aptos, CA 95003 • ACRL LITA IFRT LIRT

Cabrini College Library • Kristine E. Mudrick • Radnor, PA 19087-3699 • ACRL ALCTS RASD

Calgary Board of Education Professional Library • M. Jane Webb • Calgary AB, T3E 4M2 Canada • AASL ACRL ALCTS ALSC LITA RASD

Calgary Public Library • Calgary AB, T2G 2M2 Canada • ACRL ALCTS ALSC LITA PLA YALSA EMIERT ILERT

Calhoun County Public Library • Winnie G. Westbury • St. Matthews, SC 29135

Calif Inst of Integral Studies • Bruce A. Flath • San Francisco, CA 94117 • ACRL

Calif State Univ-Long Beach Univ Lib & Learning Resources • Jordan M. Scepanski • Long Beach, CA 90840-1901 • AASL ACRL ALCTS ASCLA LAMA LITA RASD YALSA

Calif State Univ-Los Angeles John F. Kennedy Memorial Library • JoAn D. Kunselman • Los Angeles, CA 90032-8300 • ACRL ALCTS ASCLA LAMA LITA RASD YALSA

California Library Association • Mary Sue Ferrell • Sacramento, CA 95814

California State Library • Gary E. Strong • Sacramento, CA 94237-0001 • AASL ACRL ALCTS ALSC ALTA ASCLA LAMA LITA PLA RASD YALSA FLRT GODORT MAGERT

Camargo Township Public Library • Nancy Jones • Villa Grove, IL 61956

Camberwell City Libraries • L. Ellis • Camberwell VIC 3124, Australia • ALCTS LITA PLA

Cambridge Public Lib Dist • Eleanor Sponsel • Cambridge, IL 61238

Cambridge University Press • Joan Schwartz • New York, NY 10022

Camden Cnty Voc & Tech School IMC • R. McDivitt • Sicklerville, NJ 08081

Camden County Library • Carrie Ruggles • Camdenton, MO 65020-1320 • ALSC PLA

Camden County Library Echelon Urban Center • Karen Avenick • Voorhees, NJ 08043 • ALCTS ALSC ALTA LAMA LITA PLA RASD YALSA

Camp Verde Public Library • Phyllis Hazekamp • Camp Verde, AZ 86322 • PLA

Campbellsville College • Barbara N. Bishop • Campbellsville, KY 42718 • AASL ACRL ALCTS LAMA LITA RASD

Canada Ctr for Inland Waters Lib • Eve Dowie • Burlington ON, L7R 4A6 Canada

Canada Department of Agriculture Library • Ottawa ON, K1A 0C5 Canada • ACRL ALCTS LAMA LITA RASD

Canada Inst for Sci & Tech Inf National Research Council • Ottawa ON, K1A 0S2 Canada • ACRL ALCTS LAMA LITA RASD FLRT GODORT

Canadian Library Association • Jane Hanson Cooney • Ottawa ON, K2P 1L5 Canada

Canadian Union College Library • Keith H. Clouten • College Heights AB, T0C 0Z0 Canada • ACRL

Canadien D Architecture Bibliotheque/Library • Murray Waddington • Montreal PQ, H3H 2S6 Canada • ACRL ALCTS

Cannon Falls Library • Leona Livingston • Cannon Falls, MN 55009 • PLA

Cape Breton Regional Library • Ian R. Mac Intosh • Sydney NS, B1P 6X9 Canada

Cape Cod Community College • West Barnstable, MA 02668 • ACRL ALCTS LITA RASD

Cape Girardeau Public Library • Terence W. Risko • Cape Girardeau, MO 63701 • ALTA LITA

Cape Lib Automation Materials Sharing (CLAMS) • Hyannis, MA 026101 • ALCTS LITA

Cape Town City Libraries • H. C. Heymann • Cape Town, 8000, South Africa • ALSC PLA

Capital District Library Council • Charles D. Custer • Albany, NY 12206-2027 • AASL ACRL ALSC ALTA ASCLA LAMA LITA PLA RASD YALSA GODORT IFRT LHRT LIRT LRRT SORT

Carbondale Public Library • Ann M. Muldoon • Carbondale, PA 18407

Cardinal Spellman High School Library • Brockton, MA 02402

Caribbean Center for Advanced Studies Library • Nilsa R. Vargas • San Juan, PR 00902-3711

Carl Sandburg College LRC • Frederick Visel • Galesburg, IL 61401 • ACRL RASD

Carlinville Public Library • Iris M. Zimmer • Carlinville, IL 62626

Carnegie Free Library • Julia Allen • Connellsville, PA 15425

Carnegie Library of Eufaula • Eufaula, AL 36027

Carnegie Library of Pittsburgh • Robert B. Croneberger • Pittsburgh, PA 15213-4080 • GODORT

Carnegie Public Library • Elisabeth Stewart • Angola, IN 46703

Carnegie Public Library • Fay Willis • Washington, IN 47501

Carnegie Public Library • Sid F. Graves • Clarksdale, MS 38614 • PLA

Carnegie Public Library • Ann Kaiser • Las Vegas, NM 87701

Carnegie Public Library District • Martha Miller • La Harpe, IL 61450

Caroline Library Inc. • Kay D. Brooks • Bowling Green, VA 22427 • PLA

Carroll College Library • Russel C. Evans • Waukesha, WI 53186 • ACRL ALCTS ALSC LITA RASD GODORT IFRT LIRT

Carroll County Public Library • Jarrett Boyd • Carrollton, KY 41008 • PLA

Carter Lake Public Library • Darlene Beaver • Carter Lake, IA 51510

Carthage Central High School Library • Carthage, NY 13619 • AASL YALSA

Carthage College John Mosheim Ruthrauff Library • Eugene A. Engeldinger • Kenosha, WI 53141 • AASL ACRL ALCTS ASCLA LAMA LITA RASD YALSA

Casa Grande Public Library • David P. Snider • Casa Grande, AZ 85222

Caseyville Public Library • Diana LeBlanc • Caseyville, IL 62232

Casper College Goodstein Foundation Library • Lynnette Anderson • Casper, WY 82601 • ACRL ALCTS RASD IFRT LIRT

Catahoula Parish Library • Una S. Paul • Harrisonburg, LA 71340 • PLA

Catawba College Library • Evelina M. Tseng • Salisbury, NC 28144 • ACRL ALCTS LAMA LITA RASD GODORT LIRT LRRT

Catherine Booth Bible College • Adrian B. Dalwood • Winnipeg MB, R3B 2P2 Canada • ACRL

Catholic Univ of Puerto Rico Encarnacion Valdes Library • Antonio Matos • Ponce, PR 00732

Catholic University of America Library Science Library • Patsy Haley Stann • Washington, DC 20064 • AASL ACRL ALCTS ALSC ASCLA LAMA LITA PLA RASD YALSA CLENE FLRT GODORT IFRT IRRT LHRT LIRT LRRT MAGERT NMRT SORT SRRT

Cazenovia College Library • Stanley J. Kozaczka • Cazenovia, NY 13035 • ACRL

Cecil County Board of Education • H Fred Thomas • Elkton, MD 21921-5684

Cedar Mill Community Library • Marjan Wazeka • Portland, OR 97229

Cedar Park Public Library • Pauline Lam • Cedar Park, TX 78613

Cedar Valley College Library • Carol Barrett • Lancaster, TX 75146-3799 • ACRL SORT

Centenary College of Louisiana • James W. Marcum • Shreveport, LA 71134-1188 • ACRL ALCTS LAMA LITA RASD

Center Library • Richard H. Peiser • Des Plaines, IL 60018 • EMIERT

Center Moriches Free Public Library • Nan Peel • Center Moriches, NY 11934-5024

Center School • East Hampton, CT 06424 • AASL

Center for Early Education • Lucy E. Greene • Los Angeles, CA 90048 • AASL ALSC

Center for Research Libraries • Donald B. Simpson • Chicago, IL 60637 • ACRL ALCTS ASCLA LAMA LITA RASD

Centerville & Center Township Public Library • Marie N. Bunch • Centerville, IN 47330 • ALSC PLA

Centerville Public Library Association • Centerville, MA 02632

Central Arkansas Library System • Bobby L. Roberts • Little Rock, AR 72201-4698 • ACRL ALCTS ALSC ALTA ASCLA LAMA LITA PLA RASD YALSA IFRT SORT

Central Baptist Theological Seminary Library • Larry Blazer • Kansas City, KS 66102-3964

Central Maine Library District • Peggy A. Stewart • Augusta, ME 04333 • PLA

Central New York Library Resources Council • Keith E. Washburn • Syracuse, NY 13208 • AASL ACRL ALCTS ALTA ASCLA LITA RASD IFRT

Central State University Library • John Lolley • Edmond, OK 73034-0193 • AASL ACRL ALCTS ALSC ALTA ASCLA LAMA LITA PLA RASD YALSA ERT FLRT GODORT IFRT IRRT LHRT LIRT LRRT MAGERT NMRT SORT SRRT

Centro De Informacion Academica • Puebla 7200, Mexico

Chadron State College Reta E. King Library • Terrence F. Brennan • Chadron, NE 69337 • AASL ACRL ALCTS ALSC LITA RASD

Chaminade High School Library • Hollywood, FL 33021

Champanville Public Library • Champanville, WV 25508

Chanute Public Library • Susan J. Willis • Chanute, KS 66720 • PLA

Charles A Ramson Dist Lib • Janice Park • Plainwell, MI 49080-1896

Charles Stark Draper Inc Technical Information Center • M. Hope Coffman • Cambridge, MA 02139 • LAMA LITA

Charleston County Library • Brenda A. Johnson • Charleston, SC 29403

Charleston County School • Cynthia H. Ritoch • Charleston, SC 29401

Charlestown-Clark Cnty Lib • Tamsie Meurer • Charlestown, IN 47111

Charlotte Latin School • Judy Kennedy • Charlotte, NC 28207

Charlotte Public Library • Lou Ann Boone • Charlotte, MI 48813 • LAMA

Chatham-Effingham-Liberty Regional Library (CEL) • Irma Harlan • Savannah, GA 31499-4301 • ALSC ALTA LAMA LITA PLA RASD GODORT

Chatham Area Library District • Gene Wilken • Chatham, IL 62629

Chattanooga-Hamilton County Bicentennial Library • Jane E. McFarland • Chattanooga, TN 37402 • ALCTS ALSC ALTA ASCLA LAMA LITA PLA RASD YALSA GODORT IFRT SORT SRRT

Chattanooga State Tech Cmnty College Library • Victoria P. Leather • Chattanooga, TN 37406 • ACRL RASD

Chattooga County Library • Susan A. Stewart • Summerville, GA 30747 • PLA

Cherokee High School • Nancy W. Donohue • Marlton, NJ 08053 • AASL YALSA

Cherokee Regional Library Lafayette-Walker County Library • Brian H. Stoutenburg • Lafayette, GA 30728

Cherry Hill High School West • Denise Wiltsee • Cherry Hill, NJ 08002 • AASL

Chesapeake College Library • Kay L. Brodie • Wye Mills, MD 21679 • ACRL

Chesterfield County Library • Robert E. Wagenknecht • Chesterfield, VA 23832 • AASL ALCTS ALSC ALTA ASCLA LAMA LITA PLA RASD

Chestnut Hill College • Mary J. Larkin • Philadelphia, PA 19118 • ACRL LIRT

Chiang Mai University Library • Rujaya Abhakorn • Chaing Mai, Thailand • AASL ACRL ALCTS ALSC LAMA LITA PLA RASD

Chicago Coll of Osteopathic Med Alumni Memorial Library • Sandra A. Worley • Downers Grove, IL 60515 • ACRL

Chicago One Stop, Inc. Browser Display Systems • Howard M. Rosen • Chicago, IL 60610 • Subscribing

Chicago Public Library Harold Washington Library • John B. Duff • Chicago, IL 60605

Chicago Public Library Professional Library • Mary A. Bonhomme • Chicago, IL 60605 • AASL ACRL ALCTS ALSC ALSA LITA LAMA LITA PLA RASD YALSA AFLRT CLENE EMIERT ERT FLRT GODORT IFRT ILERT IRRT LHRT LRRT MAGERT NMRT SORT SRRT VRT

Chicago Women in Publishing • Chicago, IL 60611 • Subscribing

Chickasaw Library Systems • Joel M. Robinson • Ardmore, OK 73401

Children's Memorial Hospital Brennemann Library • Meg Ward • Chicago, IL 60614

Chinese-Amer Lns Assn • Chang Lee • Denver, CO 80204

Chinese Inf & Culture Ctr • David Lu • New York, NY 10020-1579 • ACRL IRRT

Chinese Univ of Hong Kong Lib • Hong Kong BCC, Hong Kong • ACRL ALCTS LITA RASD

Choate Mental Health & Devel Ctr Library • Anna, IL 62906

Christ The King Seminary Library • Rev. Bonaventure Hayes • E Aurora, NY 14052

Christ the King School • Omaha, NE 68114

Christian Heritage Coll • Mona Hsu • El Cajon, CA 92021

Christian Theological Seminary • David Bundy • Indianapolis, IN 46208 • ACRL

Christopher Newport College Captain John Smith Library • Wendell A. Barbour • Newport News, VA 23606 • ACRL ALCTS ALSC ALTA LAMA LITA RASD

Chronicle Books • Victoria M. Rock • San Francisco, CA 94103 • Subscribing

Chulalongkorn University • Prachak Poomvises • Bangkok 10330, Thailand • AASL ACRL ALCTS ASCLA LAMA LITA PLA RASD YALSA

Churchill Films • Los Angeles, CA 90025 • VRT
Subscribing

Cincinnati Hist Soc Lib • Laura L. Chace • Cincinnati, OH 45203 • ACRL ALCTS LAMA LITA RASD

Cincinnati Law Lib Assn • Cincinnati, OH 45202 • ACRL ALCTS LAMA LITA FLRT LRRT

City Coll of New York (CUNY) • Wilson C. Luquire • New York, NY 10031 • AASL ACRL ALCTS LAMA LITA RASD

City of Signal Hill Library • Carole Molloy • Signal Hill, CA 90806 • PLA

Clapp Memorial Library • Owen Maloney • Belchertown, MA 01007

Claremont Colleges Libraries Honnold/Mudd Library • Bonnie Jackson Clemens • Claremont, CA 91711 • ACRL ALCTS ASCLA LAMA LITA RASD YALSA GODORT IFRT LHRT LIRT SORT SRRT

Clarion Univ of Pennsylvania Rena M. Carlson Library • Gerard B. McCabe • Clarion, PA 16214 • AASL ACRL ALCTS ALSC ALTA ASCLA LAMA LITA PLA RASD CLENE GODORT SRRT

Clark-Atlanta University Sch of Lib & Inf Studies • Lorene B. Brown • Atlanta, GA 30314-4391 • AASL ACRL ALCTS ALSC ALTA ASCLA LAMA LITA PLA RASD YALSA CLENE EMIERT ERT FLRT GODORT IFRT ILERT IRRT LHRT LIRT LRRT MAGERT NMRT SORT SRRT

Clark University Robert Hutchings Goddard Library • Susan S. Baughman • Worcester, MA 01610 • ACRL ALCTS LAMA LITA RASD LIRT MAGERT

Claymont Sch Dist Pub Lib • Mary Lee Smith • Dennison, OH 44621

Clemson University Robert Muldrow Cooper Library • Joseph F. Boykin • Clemson, SC 29634-3001 • ACRL ALCTS LAMA LITA RASD

Cleveland Chiropractic College • Marcia Thomas • Kansas City, MO 64131 • ACRL

Cleveland County Library • Lorene Terry • Rison, AR 71665

Cleveland Hts-Univ Hts Pub Lib • Stephen D. Wood • Cleveland Heights, OH 44118 • ACRL ALCTS LAMA LITA PLA RASD YALSA

Cleveland Institute of Art • Cristine C. Rom • Cleveland, OH 44106 • ACRL ALCTS LAMA RASD

Cleveland Public Library • Marilyn Gell Mason • Cleveland, OH 44114-1271 • AASL ACRL ALCTS ALSC ALTA ASCLA LAMA LITA PLA RASD YALSA CLENE EMIERT ERT FLRT GODORT IFRT ILERT IRRT LHRT LIRT LRRT MAGERT NMRT SORT SRRT

Clinch Valley College John Cook Wyllie Library • Robin Paul Benke • Wise, VA 24293 • AASL ACRL ALCTS LITA RASD YALSA

Clinton High School Library • Joan Strang • Clinton, MA 01510 • AASL

Clintonville Public Library • Clintonville, WI 54929 • ALSC PLA

Clover Township Public Library • Coralie Null • Woodhull, IL 61490

Clymer Library Association • Charlotte J. Mitchell • Pocono Pines, PA 18350

Cmnty Coll of Allegheny Cnty Allegheny Campus Library • Christina Russell • Pittsburgh, PA 15212 • ACRL ALCTS LAMA LITA RASD LIRT

Cmnty Coll of Philadelphia Educational Resource Center • Donald Jones • Philadelphia, PA 19130 • ACRL ALCTS LITA RASD

Cmnty Coll of Rhode Island • Charles D Arezzo • Warwick, RI 02886 • ACRL ALCTS LAMA LITA RASD LIRT

Cmnty Coll of Rhode Island • Robrt Aspri • Lincoln, RI 02865-4585 • ACRL LITA RASD

Cnty of Los Angeles Pub Lib • Sandra Reuben • Downey, CA 90241-7400 • AASL ACRL ALCTS ALSC ALTA ASCLA LAMA LITA PLA RASD YALSA CLENE EMIERT ERT FLRT GODORT IFRT ILERT IRRT LHRT LIRT LRRT MAGERT NMRT SORT SRRT

Cnty of Los Angeles Pub Lib • Sandra Reuben • Hawthorne, CA 90250 • RASD

Cnty of Los Angeles Pub Lib A. C. Bilbrew Branch • Cora B. Forcell • Los Angeles, CA 90061

Cnty of Los Angeles Pub Lib Angelo M. Iacoboni Branch • Linda Larsen • Lakewood, CA 90712 • ALSC RASD

Cnty of Los Angeles Pub Lib Bell Library 630 • Beth S. Krupsaw • Bell, CA 90201 • ALSC RASD

Cnty of Los Angeles Pub Lib Carson Library 301 • Carson, CA 90745 • ALSC PLA RASD

Cnty of Los Angeles Pub Lib Central County Region 600 • West Hollywood Library • Montebello, CA 90640 • ALSC LAMA LITA PLA RASD

Cnty of Los Angeles Pub Lib Compton Library 531 • Joanne Nyota Eldridge • Compton, CA 90220 • ALSC RASD

Cnty of Los Angeles Pub Lib Culver City Library 330 • Culver City, CA 90230 • ALSC RASD

Cnty of Los Angeles Pub Lib Gardena Library 313 • Julie L W Fu • Gardena, CA 90247 • PLA

Cnty of Los Angeles Pub Lib Hacienda Heights Library 815 • Hacienda Heights, CA 91745 • ALSC RASD

Cnty of Los Angeles Pub Lib Huntington Park Library 633 • Evelyn Escatiola Baca • Huntington Park, CA 90255 • ALSC LITA PLA RASD

Cnty of Los Angeles Pub Lib Lancaster Library 101 • Paula C. Hock • Lancaster, CA 93534 • PLA RASD

Cnty of Los Angeles Pub Lib Lomita Library 317 • Linda Shimane • Lomita, CA 90717 • ALSC PLA

Cnty of Los Angeles Pub Lib Montebello Library 601 • Montebello, CA 90640 • ALSC RASD

Cnty of Los Angeles Pub Lib North County Region Office 108 • Kathryn Ginoza • Valencia, CA 91355 • ALSC LAMA RASD

Cnty of Los Angeles Pub Lib Norwalk Library 501 • Norwalk, CA 90650 • GODORT

Cnty of Los Angeles Pub Lib Rosemead Library 624 • Rosemead, CA 91770 • ALSC RASD

Cnty of Los Angeles Pub Lib South County Region 500 • Richard J. Beebe • Norwalk, CA 90650 • ALSC PLA RASD

Cnty of Los Angeles Pub Lib South El Monte Branch • South El Monte, CA 91733

Cnty of Los Angeles Pub Lib Valencia Library 113 • Valenica, CA 91355 • ALSC PLA RASD GODORT

Cnty of Los Angeles Pub Lib West County Region 300 • Carson, CA 90745 • ALSC PLA RASD IFRT

Cnty of Los Angeles Pub Lib West Covina Library 801 • Joan Livingston • West Covina, CA 91790 • ALSC PLA RASD

Cochise College • Catherin Lincer • Douglas, AZ 85607 • ACRL

Cogswell Coolege Library • Lorna Corbetta-Noyes • Cupertino, CA 95014 • ACRL

Coker College J.L. Coker III Memorial Library • Neal A. Martin • Hartsville, SC 29550 • ACRL ALCTS LITA RASD YALSA

Colby Community College Davis Memorial Library • Judith E. Agnew • Colby, KS 67701 • ACRL GODORT

Colegio Puertorriqueno De Ninas • Ana Rita Betancourt • Caparra Heights, PR 00920

Colegio Regional de las Montana Learning Resources Center • Ivellisse Rodriguez • Utuado, PR 00641 • ACRL

Colegio San Jose • Emerida Rivera • Rio Piedras, PR 00928 • AASL

Coleman Library • Charlene J. Cole • Tougaloo, MS 39174 • ACRL ALCTS LAMA RASD EMIERT

Colgate University Everett Needham Case Library • Emily Hutton • Hamilton, NY 13346 • ACRL ALCTS LAMA LITA RASD

College Misericordia • Dallas, PA 18612 • AASL ACRL ALCTS ASCLA LAMA LITA RASD YALSA

College of Associated Arts • Mary Beth Frasczak • Saint Paul, MN 55102 • ACRL

College of Charleston Robert Scott Small Library • David J. Cohen • Charleston, SC 29424 • ACRL ALCTS ASCLA LAMA LITA RASD GODORT IFRT LIRT LRRT

College of Great Falls Library • Great Falls, MT 59405 • ACRL RASD

College of Mount Saint Vincent Elizabeth Seton Library • Kathleen Cassidy • Bronx, NY 10471 • ACRL ALCTS

College of New Caledonia • Katherine Plett • Prince George BC, V2N 1P8 Canada • ACRL ALCTS LAMA LITA RASD

College of Saint Catherine Saint Mary's Campus Library • M. Rocky Ralebipi • Minneapolis, MN 55454

College of Saint Mary • Omaha, NE 68124 • ACRL

College of Saint Rose Neil Hellman Library • Barbara J. Clune • Albany, NY 12203 • ACRL ALCTS RASD

College of Southern Idaho Library Media Center • William Beale • Twin Falls, ID 83303-1238 • ACRL ALCTS RASD

College of West Virginia Library • Franklin D. Roberts • Beckley, WV 25801 • ACRL

College of William and Mary Earl Gregg Swem Library • Nancy H. Marshall • Williamsburg, VA 23187-8794 • AASL LAMA

College of the Bahamas Library • Vanrea Rolle • Nassau, Bahamas • ACRL ALCTS LAMA LITA RASD ERT LIRT

Collegiate School Reed Library • Allen Chamberlain • Richmond, VA 23229 • AASL ALSC YALSA IFRT

Collinsville Mem Public Lib • Collinsville, IL 62234 • PLA

Colonie Central High School • L. Fox • Albany, NY 12205 • AASL

Colorado College Tutt Library • John Sheridan • Colorado Springs, CO 80903 • ACRL ALCTS LAMA LITA RASD

Colorado Library Association • Rogers Bakes • Pine Cliffe, CO 80471

Colorado Springs Sch Dist 11 Professional Library • Sandra Patton • Colorado Springs, CO 80903 • AASL ALSC

Colorado State Library Department of Education • Nancy M. Bolt • Denver, CO 80203 • AASL ACRL ALCTS ALTA ASCLA LAMA LITA PLA RASD GODORT LRRT

Colorado State University William E. Morgan Library • Joan L. Chambers • Fort Collins, CO 80523 • AASL ACRL ALCTS LAMA LITA PLA RASD

Columbia College Library • Mary Schellhorn • Chicago, IL 60605 • ACRL ALCTS LAMA LITA RASD

Columbia Pacific University • San Rafael, CA 94901 • ASCLA

Columbia Public Library • Columbia, IL 62236 • PLA

Columbia University Library Service Library • New York, NY 10027 • AASL ACRL ALCTS ALSC ALTA ASCLA LAMA LITA PLA RASD YALSA CLENE EMIERT ERT FLRT GODORT IFRT ILERT IRRT LHRT LIRT LRRT MAGERT NMRT SORT SRRT

Columbus Academy Library • Gohanna, OH 43230 • AASL

Columbus Metropolitan Library • Larry D. Black • Columbus, OH 43215

Columbus State Community College Educational Resources Center • Linda Landis • Columbus, OH 43215 • ACRL

Colusa County Free Library • Joyce Becker • Colusa, CA 95932 • AASL ALSC YALSA

Commercial Appeal News Library • Virginia Everett • Memphis, TN 38103 • LAMA IFRT

Commodore Business Machines • John DiLullo • West Chester, PA 19380 • AASL ACRL ASCLA PLA
Subscribing

Community College of Vermont • Eileen A Chalfoun • Brattleboro, VT 05301-9127

Community Consolidated School District #21 • Tom O'Brien • Wheeling, IL 60090 • AASL

CompCare Publishers • Bob Morris • Minneapolis, MN 55441 • Subscribing

Comstock Township Library • Comstock, MI 49041 • LAMA PLA YALSA

Concord Academy Library • Concord, MA 01742 • AASL

Concord College Library • Thomas M. Brown • Athens, WV 24712 • AASL ACRL ALCTS LAMA LITA YALSA

Concordia College • Kurt Bodling • Bronxville, NY 10708 • ALCTS LITA

Concordia College Library • Kevin Brandon • Ann Arbor, MI 48105 • ACRL

Concordia Parish Library • Amanda Taylor • Ferriday, LA 71334 • PLA

Concordia Teachers College Link Library • Myron D. Boettcher • Seward, NE 68434 • AASL ACRL ALCTS LAMA RASD

Concordia University • Louis Vagianos • Montreal PQ, H3G 1M8 Canada • ACRL ALCTS LAMA LITA RASD

Congressional Quarterly Incorp. • Linda M. Futato • Washington, DC 20037 • AASL ACRL PLA RASD ERT
Subscribing

Connecticut College • Brian D. Rogers • New London, CT 06320-4196 • ACRL ALCTS LITA RASD GODORT

Connecticut Library Association • Suzanne C. Berry • Hartford, CT 06105

Connecticut State Library • Hartford, CT 06106 • AASL ACRL ALCTS ALSC ALTA ASCLA LAMA LITA PLA RASD YALSA

Contra Costa County Library • Ernest Siegel • Pleasant Hill, CA 94523 • ALCTS ASCLA LAMA LITA PLA RASD YALSA IFRT

Converse College Mickel Library • Vivian C. Jones • Spartanburg, SC 29302-0006 • ACRL ALCTS LAMA LITA RASD

Conway Public Library • M. Marschner • Conway, NH 03818 • PLA YALSA

Conyer-Rockdale Lib Sys • Deborah S. Manget • Conyers, GA 30207 • PLA

Cook Hill School Library • Mindy Sohcot • Wallingford, CT 06492 • AASL

Cook Memorial Library • Frederick H. Byergo • Libertyville, IL 60048 • ALCTS ALSC ALTA LAMA LITA PLA RASD YALSA

Coop Lib Agency for Sys & Serv (CLASS) • Robert A. Drescher • San Jose, CA 95112-4698 • ACRL ASCLA LITA PLA ERT

Copiah-Jefferson Rgnl Lib • Joe A. Tynes • Hazlehurst, MS 39083

Copiah-Lincoln Junior College Evelyn W. Owsalt Library • Kendall P. Chapman • Wesson, MS 39191 • ACRL

Coppin State College Library • Baltimore, MD 21216 • ACRL ALCTS RASD

Coquille Public Library • Molly Barrett • Coquille, OR 97423 • LAMA PLA

Cordova Public Library • Corrine A. Erickson • Cordova, AK 99574

Corn Belt Library System • Jay Wozny • Normal, IL 61761

Cornell University Library • Herbert Finch • Ithaca, NY 14853-5301 • AASL ACRL ALCTS ALSC ALTA ASCLA LAMA LITA PLA RASD YALSA

Corporate Library Blackwell North America • Fred A. Philipp • Lake Oswego, OR 97035 • ACRL ALCTS LITA PLA
Subscribing

Corydon Public Library • Corydon, IN 47112 • ALSC RASD

Cote Saint-Luc Public Library • Cote Saint-Luc PQ, H4W 2X8 Canada • LAMA LITA PLA RASD YALSA

Council Bluffs Fr Public Lib • Mildred K. Smock • Council Bluffs, IA 51503 • ALCTS ALSC ALTA ASCLA LAMA LITA PLA RASD YALSA

Council Rock School District Library-Media Services • Ellen M. Short • Richboro, PA 18954 • AASL

Council for Bibliographic and Information Technologies (CoBIT) • Sondra L. Plymire • Columbus, OH 43221-2112 • LITA
Subscribing

Council on Library/Media Tech (COLT) • Beverly Patton • Oxon Hill, MD 20750

Countryside Montessori School • Angela Fornaro • Largo, FL 34644

Coutts Library Services, Inc • Keith S. Schmiedl • Lewiston, NY 14092-1797 • Subscribing

Coventry High School • Coventry, CT 06238 • AASL YALSA

Crawford County Public Library • Janice Holzbog • English, IN 47118

Crawfordsville Dist Pub Lib • Thomas J. West • Crawfordsville, IN 47933 • ALSC ALTA LAMA PLA

Cresskill High School Library • Cresskill, NJ 07626 • AASL YALSA LIRT

Crete Public Library District • Sharon E. Wsol • Crete, IL 60417

Crichton College Oscar White Memorial Library • Deborah D. Mabbott • Memphis, TN 38175-7830 • ACRL

Criswell College, The Wallace Library • Dawn Pilcher • Dallas, TX 75246

Crittenden County Library • Sherry Tinsley • Marion, KY 42064

Croton Free Library • Mary Donnery • Croton Hudson, NY 10520 • LAMA

Crown Pt Ctrl Media Proc • Crown Point, IN 46410 • AASL

Crystal Falls District Community Library • Winnefred A. Lesandrini • Crystal Falls, MI 49920

Ctrl Connecticut State Univ • New Britain, CT 06050 • AASL ACRL ALCTS ALSC LAMA LITA RASD

Ctrl Intelligence Agency Lib (C.I.A.) • Washington, DC 20505

Ctrl Islip High Sch Lib • Central Islip, NY 11722 • AASL YALSA

Ctrl Maine Voc Tech Inst • Robert Kirchherr • Auburn, ME 04210 • ACRL CLENE

Ctrl States Inst of Addiction Training & Education Program • Chicago, IL 60610

Cudahy Middle School • Rose Ann Dieck • Cudahy, WI 53110 • AASL YALSA

Cumberland Cnty Coll Lib • Vineland, NJ 08360 • ACRL

Cumberland Regional High School • Edward J. Foster • Seabrook, NJ 08302 • AASL

Cupeyville School • Elsa E. Gonzalez-Ruiz • Rio Piedras, PR 00928

Curley Publishing Inc. • Paul Jobling • South Yarmouth, MA 02664 • Contributing

Custom Manufacturing Inc. • Michael Waters • Wmmitsburg, MD 21727 • Subscribing

Cuyahoga County Public Library • Cleveland, OH 44134-2792 • ALTA

Cyrenius H Booth Library • Janet M. Woycik • Newtown, CT 06470

D. Bob Henson Memorial Library • Brenda Griffin Warren • Nederland, TX 77627 • PLA

D. S. Limited • J. H. Tickle • Nottingham NG2 6AP, England • LITA PLA   *Subscribing*

DYNIX Inc. • Paul K. Sybrowsky • Provo, UT 84606 • LITA PLA ERT   *Subscribing*

Dakota State University Karl E. Mundt Library • Ethelle S. Bean • Madison, SD 57042-1799 • AASL ACRL ALCTS LAMA LITA RASD YALSA

Dakota Wesleyan University Layne Library • Linda B. Ritter • Mitchell, SD 57301-4398

Dalkey Archive Press • Suzanne Henert • Naperville, IL 60540 • ACRL   *Subscribing*

Dallas Public Library • Patrick O'Brien • Dallas, TX 75201 • AASL ACRL ALCTS ALSC ALTA ASCLA LAMA LITA PLA RASD YALSA CLENE EMIERT ERT GODORT LIRT MAGERT NMRT SRRT

Damascus Community School c/o Amer Embassy Damascus Syria • Washington, DC 20521-6110 • AASL

Daniel Boone Regional Library • Thomas R. Strange • Columbia, MO 65205-1267 • ALCTS

Danvers High School Library • Betsy Stine • Danvers, MA 01923 • AASL

Danville Area Community College • Danville, IL 61832 • ACRL ALCTS RASD LIRT

Danville Public Library • Roberta D. Allen • Danville, IL 61832

Darby Free Library • Audrey Childs • Darby, PA 19023 • PLA

Dartmouth College Library Baker Memorial Library • Margaret A. Otto • Hanover, NH 03755-3525 • ACRL ALCTS LITA RASD

Darton College Harold B. Wetherbee Library • Edward L. Philbin • Albany, GA 31707 • ACRL

Data Research Associates Inc. • Carl Grant • Saint Louis, MO 63132 • Subscribing

Data Trek, Inc. • Kimberly Gates • Carlsbad, CA 92008 • LITA   *Subscribing*

Dauphin County Library System • Richard A. Bowra • Harrisburg, PA 17101

Davenport College of Business Library • Kenneth Fitzhugh • Grand Rapids, MI 49502

Davenport Public Library • Kay K. Runge • Davenport, IA 52801

David Lipscomb University University Library • James E. Ward • Nashville, TN 37204-3951 • ALCTS LAMA RASD

Davidson College Library • Davidson, NC 28036 • ACRL ALCTS LAMA LITA RASD

Davis & Elkins College Library • Clarence L. Coffindaffer • Elkins, WV 26241 • ACRL IFRT SRRT

Davis & Henderson Ltd. • Susan Siddle • Toronto, ON, M4B 3E5 Canada • Subscribing

Davis County Library • Pete J. Giacoma • Farmington, UT 84025 • ALSC LAMA PLA

Davis School Library • Camden, NJ 08105 • AASL EMIERT

Dawson College Library Periodicals Department • Ronald E. Spivock • Westmount PQ, H3Z 1A4 Canada • ACRL ALCTS RASD

Dawson Community College • Glendive, MT 59330 • ACRL

Dawson County High School Media Center • Glendive, MT 59330 • AASL

Dawson Technical Institute • Effie B. Tyler • Chicago, IL 60609 • ACRL ALCTS LAMA LITA RASD

Dayton & Montgomery Cnty Pub Library • John S. Wallach • Dayton, OH 45402-2103 • AASL ACRL ALCTS ALSC ALTA ASCLA LAMA LITA PLA RASD YALSA

Daytona Beach Community College • Yvonne Newcomb Doty • Daytona Beach, FL 32015 • ACRL LITA RASD

De Kalb High School Library Media Center • Christa Even • DeKalb, IL 60115 • AASL YALSA

DeKalb College Library • Gretchen H. Neill • Clarkston, GA 30021 • ACRL ALCTS LAMA RASD

DePaul University Libraries • Doris R. Brown • Chicago, IL 60614 • ACRL ALCTS LAMA LITA RASD

Dean Junior College • Jerald K. Dachs • Franklin, MA 02038-1994 • ACRL ALCTS LAMA LITA RASD

Dearborn Trade • Charles A. Lilly • Chicago, IL 60610 • Subscribing

Decatur Public Library • Joyce A. Iliff • Decatur, IN 46733

Decatur Public Library • James C. Seidl • Decatur, IL 62523 • ALCTS LAMA LITA PLA RASD YALSA

Deerfield Community School • Joan C. Bilodeau • Deerfield, NH 03037

Deerfield Public Library • Jack Alan Hicks • Deerfield, IL 60015 • ACRL ALCTS ALSC ALTA LAMA LITA RASD YALSA

Defence Information Services D/Director Network Services • Canberra ACT 2600, Australia • ALCTS

Defiance College Anthony Wayne Library • Edward S. Warner • Defiance, OH 43512

Del Norte Library District • Christin McCollum • Crescent City, CA 95531

Delaware County District Library • Patricia Ebbatson • Delaware, OH 43015

Delaware Library Association • Wilmington, DE 19899

Delaware State College William J. Jason Library • Richard Bradberry • Dover, DE 19901 • ACRL ALCTS LAMA LITA RASD EMIERT ERT GODORT LIRT

Delaware Valley College Sci & Agr Krauskopf Memorial Library • Constance R. Shook • Doylestown, PA 18901

Delaware Valley High School • Carla Daniel • Milford, PA 18337

Delgado Community College Moss Memorial Library • Lenora C. Lockett • New Orleans, LA 70119 • ACRL

Delhi Public Library • J. C. Mehta • Delhi 110006, India • ALCTS

Delhi University Library System Central Library • Susheel Kaur • Delhi, India • ACRL ALCTS LAMA LITA RASD

Delphi Public Library • Martha Lou Miller • Delphi, IN 46923 • PLA

Delsea Regional Middle School • Franklinville, NJ 08322 • AASL

Delta Community Library • Delta Junction, AK 99737 • PLA

Delta Lithograph Company • Kenneth W. Hoffmann • Valencia, CA 91355-1111 • Subscribing

Delta Public Library • Delta, CO 81416 • LAMA PLA

Delta State University • Myra Macon • Cleveland, MS 38733 • AASL ACRL ALCTS ALSC LAMA LITA RASD ERT FLRT GODORT IFRT LIRT LRRT

Demco Inc. • Patrick Wall • Madison, WI 53707 • AASL ACRL ASCLA PLA ERT   *Subscribing*

Deming Public Library • Robert D. Schalau • Deming, NM 88030 • PLA

Demopolis Public Library • A. Denise Milton • Demopolis, AL 36732

Denison University Library • Charles B. Maurer • Granville, OH 43023 • ACRL LAMA LITA RASD

Denmark Technical College Learning Resource Center • Imogene I. Book • Denmark, SC 29042 • ACRL

Denver Public Library • Denver, CO 80204-2602 • AASL ACRL ALCTS ALSC ALTA ASCLA LAMA LITA PLA RASD YALSA

Department of External Affairs Library Acl • Ruth M.F. Thompson • Ottawa ON, K1N 5A1 Canada • ACRL ALCTS GODORT

Department of Public Instruction Division for Library Services • Kay M. Ihlenfeldt • Madison, WI 53707 • AASL ACRL ALCTS ALSC ALTA ASCLA LAMA LITA PLA RASD

Departmental Library Indian & Northern Affairs • Ottawa ON, K1A 0H4 Canada • ALCTS LAMA LITA RASD

Derby Public Library • Karen A. Higginson • Derby, CT 06418 • PLA

Detroit College of Business • Dearborn, MI 48126 • ACRL

Detroit College of Business • Carolyn Stingel • Flint, MI 48504

Detroit College of Business Warren Campus Library • Michael J. Wrona • Warren, MI 48092-5209 • ACRL

Detroit Public Library • Jean T. Curtis • Detroit, MI 48202 • AASL ACRL ALCTS ALTA ASCLA LAMA LITA PLA RASD YALSA

Deutsche Buecherei • Helmut Roetzsch • Leipzig, Germany • ACRL ALCTS LITA

Deutsches Bibliotheks • D Hoffmann • 1000 Berlin 31, Germany • AASL ACRL ALCTS ASCLA LITA RASD YALSA

Devel Res & Analysts Lib • Robert G. Millar • Philadelphia, PA 19104-6285 • LAMA

Dillard University Library • Emma B. Perry • New Orleans, LA 70122

Dillingham Public Library • A. L. Levinson • Dillingham, AK 99576 • PLA

Dillsburg Area Public Library • Emily Geschwindt • Dillsburg, PA 17019

Disclosure Incorporated • Michael Rittmann • New York, NY 10106 • ACRL RASD   *Subscribing*

Dist of Columbia Lib Assn (DCLA) • Susan Fifer Canby • Washington, DC 20044

Dist of Columbia Pub Lib Martin Luther King Mem Lib • Hardy R. Franklin • Washington, DC 20001 • ALSC ALTA ASCLA LAMA LITA PLA RASD YALSA EMIERT GODORT IFRT

Dixie College Library • Audrey H. Shumway • Saint George, UT 84770 • ACRL

Dixon Homestead Library • Elizabeth Stewart • Dumont, NJ 07628 • ALSC ALTA LAMA PLA RASD

Dobbs Ferry High School Library • Ann Horrigan • Dobbs Ferry, NY 10522 • AASL YALSA

Documents Index • Laurie Andriot • McLean, VA 22101 • Subscribing

Dodge Center Public Library • Lorraine Reha • Dodge Center, MN 55927

Donald C. Brace Library • Barrett B. McCandless • Pearl Harbor, HI 96860

Donnelly College Library • Greg Erickson • Kansas City, KS 66102 • ACRL

Donovan Publishing Company • Jo May • Newport Beach, CA 92663 • Patron

Dorado Community Library • Jane R. Strern • Dorado, PR 00646

Douglas College Libraries • Virginia Chisholm • New Westminster BC, V3L 582 Canada • ACRL ALCTS RASD

Douglas County Library System • Betty J. Hazel • Roseburg, OR 97470 • ALCTS ALSC RASD

Douglas Public Library • Anita Dodd • Ava, MO 65608

Dover Public Library • Robert Wetherall • Dover, DE 19901

Dover-Eyota Elementary Schools • Sue Wilmes • Eyota, MN 55934 • AASL NMRT

Dow Chemical USA Research & Development Library • Plaquemine, LA 70764

Dowagiac Public Library • Jacqueline S. Baker • Dowagiac, MI 49047

Dowdell Library of South Amboy • W. Keith McCoy • South Amboy, NJ 08879 • ALSC ALTA LAMA RASD

Dowling College • Philip Y. Blue • Oakdale, NY 11769

Downers Grove High School South • B. Pray • Downers Grove, IL 60516 • AASL YALSA

Downey City Library • Victoria L. Jenkins • Downey, CA 90241 • ALTA

Dr Eugene Clark Library • Rose Aleta Laurell • Lockhart, TX 78644 • PLA

Drake Public Library • Lisa Pope • Centerville, IA 52544

Drake State Technical College • Kathryn Neal • Huntsville, AL 35811 • ACRL

Drake University Cowles Library • Des Moines, IA 50311 • ACRL ALCTS LITA RASD

Drexel University W. W. Hagerty Library • William L. Page • Philadelphia, PA 19104 • AASL ACRL ALCTS ALSC ALTA ASCLA LAMA LITA PLA RASD YALSA ERT FLRT GODORT IFRT IRRT LHRT LIRT LRRT NMRT SRRT

Drury College Library • Springfield, MO 65802 • ACRL ALCTS LITA RASD

DuBois Public Library • DuBois, PA 15801

DuPage Library System • Pamela P. Feather • Geneva, IL 60134 • AASL ACRL ALCTS ALSC ALTA ASCLA LAMA LITA RASD YALSA IFRT LRRT

Dudley-Tucker Library • Sherry Brox • Raymond, NH 03077-0382 • PLA

Duluth Public Library • Duluth, MN 55802 • ALSC LITA RASD GODORT

Duncan Systems Specialist Inc. • Margot Keuper • Oakville, ON, L6J 7J8 Canada • Subscribing

Dundee Township Library • Dundee, IL 60118 • ALSC ALTA LAMA RASD

Dunedin Public Library • Dobbie Allison • Dunedin, New Zealand

Duneland School Corporation Inc. Instructional Materials Center • John A. Corso • Chesterton, IN 46304 • AASL ALCTS

Dunkirk Public Library • Gay Ann Rife • Dunkirk, IN 47336

Dunn Library Simpson College • Cynthia M. Dyer • Indianola, IA 50125 • ACRL ALCTS LAMA RASD

Dunsmuir High School Library • Paul Melo • Dunsmuir, CA 96025 • ALSC NMRT

Durban Municipal Library • Durban 4000, South Africa • ALSC PLA RASD

Durham Academy Library • Dorothy H. Osborn • Durham, NC 27705 • AASL LIRT

Dwight D. Eisenhower Library • Joan A. Krautheim • Totowa Borough, NJ 07512 • PLA

Dyer Library Association • Maureen Oppenheim-Golub • Saco, ME 04072 • PLA

Dyke College • Donna Trivison • Cleveland, OH 44115 • ACRL ALCTS LAMA RASD

Dymaxion Research Limited • Peter Mason • Halifax, NS, B3J 1R2 Canada • AASL ALCTS LITA *Subscribing*

E Griffith Opportunity • Denver, CO 80204

EZ-Reader, Incorporation • Jonathan R. Cato • St. Petersburg, FL 33711 • AASL ASCLA LITA PLA *Subscribing*

East-West University • Ekkehard-Teja P. Wilke • Chicago, IL 60605

East Bonner Cnty Lib Dist • Gloria Ray • Sandpoint, ID 83864

East Brunswick Public Library • Sharon M. Karmazin • E. Brunswick, NJ 08816 • PLA

East Carolina University Joyner Library • Marilyn E. Miller • Greenville, NC 27858-4353 • AASL ACRL ALCTS ALSC ASCLA LAMA LITA PLA RASD EMIERT GODORT IRRT LIRT MAGERT

East Central University Linscheid Library • Charles E. Perry • Ada, OK 74820-6899

East Chicago Public Library • Theodore D. Mason • E. Chicago, IN 46312 • PLA

East Cleveland Public Library • Gregory L. Reese • East Cleveland, OH 44112

East Georgia College • Swainsboro, GA 30401-2699 • ACRL

East Lansing Public Library • James O. Langmo • East Lansing, MI 48823 • ALSC LAMA PLA RASD

East Longmeadow High School • Patricia A. Kokoszka • East Longmeadow, MA 01028 • AASL

East Moline Public Library • Patricia A. Hudson • East Moline, IL 61244 • ALSC PLA

East Orange Public Library • Marc M Eisen • East Orange, NJ 07018 • AASL ACRL ALSC ALTA ASCLA LAMA LITA PLA RASD YALSA EMIERT GODORT SRRT

East Ridge Middle School • Ridgefield, CT 06877 • AASL

East Smithfield Public Library • Esmond, RI 02917

East Stroudsburg University Kemp Library • George V. Summers • East Stroudsburg, PA 18301

Eastern Book Company • Richard J. Coyne • Portland, ME 04112 • ACRL ALCTS LITA PLA *Contributing*

Eastern Connecticut Lib Assn • Marietta W. Johnson • Willimantic, CT 06226 • AASL ACRL ASCLA LITA PLA YALSA CLENE

Eastern Indiana ALSA • Harold W. Boyce • Anderson, IN 46016-2701

Eastern Kentucky University John Grant Crabbe Library • Ernest E. Weyhrauch • Richmond, KY 40475-3121 • AASL ACRL ALCTS ASCLA LAMA LITA RASD YALSA

Eastern Michigan Univ Lib Center of Educational Resources • Morell D. Boone • Ypsilanti, MI 48197 • AASL ACRL ALCTS LITA RASD

Eastern Montana College Library • Edward W. Neroda • Billings, MT 59101-0298 • AASL ACRL ALCTS ALSC LITA RASD GODORT

Eastern New Mexico Univ LRC • Rollah A. Aston • Roswell, NM 88201 • ACRL ALCTS LAMA

Eastern Oklahoma District Library System • Marilyn L. Hinshaw • Muskogee, OK 74401

Eastern Oklahoma State College Library • Joyce Shelton • Wilburton, OK 74578 • ACRL

Eastern Paralyzed Vet Assn Library • Angela L. Wu • Jackson Heights, NY 11370

Eau Claire District Library • Eau Claire, MI 49111

Ecole Polytechnique La Bibliotheque • Olivier Paradis • Montreal PQ, H3C 3A7 Canada • ACRL ALCTS LAMA LITA

Edgecombe Cnty Mem Lib Pinetops Branch • Susan C. Webb • Pinetops, NC 27864 • ALSC PLA

Edgecombe County • Jackie Beach • Tarboro, NC 27886 • ALSC ALTA LAMA PLA RASD YALSA

Edgewater Public Library • Eileen Kopczynski • Edgewater, NJ 07020 • PLA

Edinboro Univ of Pennsylvania Baron-Forness Library • Saul Weinstein • Edinboro, PA 16444 • ACRL GODORT LIRT LRRT

Edinburgh-Wright-Hagman Lib • Cathy Hamm • Edinburgh, IN 46124 • PLA

Edison State Community College • Mary Beth Aust-Keefer • Piqua, OH 45356

Edith Belle Libby Mem Lib • Barbara P. Howard • Old Orch Bch, ME 04064

Edmonds Community College Library • Gregory Golden • Lynnwood, WA 98036 • ACRL LITA

Edmund Burke School • Amy Breaux • Washington, DC 20008 • AASL

Educational Communications Inc. • Paul Krouse • Lake Forest, IL 60045 • *Subscribing*

Educational Media Centre • Carole Gilman • Ancaster ON, L9G 4B7 Canada

Edward Lowe Foundation • Rita Pusey • Cassopolis, MI 49031 • ALCTS LAMA LITA PLA RASD VRT

Einstein Middle School Library • Jean S. Farris • Seattle, WA 98177

El Paso Public Library • Carolyn F. Tankersley • El Paso, TX 79901 • ACRL ALCTS ASCLA LAMA PLA RASD

Eldorado Mem Pub Lib Dist • Brenda K. Funkhouser • Eldorado, IL 62930

Elk Grove High School Library • Esther P. Perica • Elk Grove Village, IL 60007 • AASL RASD

Elk Grove Village Public Library • Mark A. West • Elk Grove Village, IL 60007 • ALSC ALTA PLA RASD YALSA

Elk Township Library • Janet L. Dyki • Peck, MI 48466-0268 • PLA

Elkhart Public Library • George M. Brich • Elkhart, IN 46516-3184 • AASL ACRL ALCTS ALSC ALTA LAMA LITA PLA RASD YALSA

Elko County Library • Hailie Tomingas Gunn • Elko, NV 89801

Ellsworth Public Library • Margaret Levenhagen • Ellsworth, WI 54011

Elm Place Middle School • Diana H. Ball • Highland Park, IL 60035

Elmhurst College A. C. Buehler Library • Melvin J. Klatt • Elmhurst, IL 60126 • ACRL ALCTS LAMA LITA RASD YALSA

Elmhurst Public Library • Marilyn H. Boria • Elmhurst, IL 60126 • ALCTS ALSC ALTA LAMA LITA PLA RASD YALSA

Elmira College Gannett-Tripp Library • James D. Gray • Elmira, NY 14901 • ACRL ALCTS LAMA LITA RASD GODORT LIRT

Elmwood Park Public Library • Albert J. Korbel • Elmwood Park, IL 60635

Elon College Iris Holt McEwen Library • Plummer A. Jones • Elon College, NC 27244-0187 • AASL ALSC GODORT

Elsevier Sci Publ Co Inc. • Mary Fugle • New York, NY 10010 • *Subscribing*

Elyria Public Library • Donald H. Burrier • Elyria, OH 44035 • ALSC LAMA PLA RASD

Emery-Pratt Company • Avery Weaver • Owosso, MI 48867-1372 • *Subscribing*

Emma Willard School Library • Barbara Wiley • Troy, NY 12180 • AASL

Emmanuel College Library • Boston, MA 02115 • ACRL ALCTS LAMA RASD

Employment & Immigration • Ottawa ON, K1A 0J9 Canada • ALCTS LAMA LITA

Emporia State University William Allen White Library • Henry R. Stewart • Emporia, KS 66801 • AASL ACRL ALCTS ALTA ASCLA LAMA LITA PLA RASD YALSA

Endicott College • Rebecca F. Duschatko • Beverly, MA 01915

Enem Systems Inc. • Peter N. Sandys • Waunakee, WI 53597-9586 • *Subscribing*

Enid M. Baa Library • Jeannette B. Allis • Saint Thomas, VI 00802 • ALCTS ASCLA LITA YALSA

Enoch Pratt Free Library • Anna A. Curry • Baltimore, MD 21201-4484 • ACRL ALCTS ASCLA PLA GODORT SORT

Enrique S Kiki Camerena Memorial Library • Sandra Tauler • Calexico, CA 92231 • PLA

Ephrata Public Library • Jennifer Raimo • Ephrata, PA 17522

Episcopal Cathedral School Library • Magda E. Habeeb • Santurce, PR 00908 • AASL

Erie Public Library District • Erie, IL 61250

Erik Ramstad Junior High School Library • Minot, ND 58701 • AASL YALSA

Erskine College Library McCain Library • Due West, SC 29639

Escambia Cnty Coop Lib System • Jane E. Jackson • Atmore, AL 36502 • PLA

Escambia County School Board Professional Library • Mary E. Gregory • Pensacola, FL 32503 • AASL YALSA

Essex Free Library • Susan Overfield • Essex, VT 05451

Essex Institute Library • William T. La Moy • Salem, MA 01970 • ACRL

Estes Park Pub Lib Dist • Judy A. Hoxsey • Estes Park, CO 80517

Estey Co. • Dickson, TN 37055 • *Subscribing*

Estherville Public Library • Esthersville, IA 51334

Ethical Culture School • Mary Jane Cahill • New York, NY 10023 • AASL

Etobicoke Public Libraries • Jennifer Milne • Etobicoke ON, M9C 5G1 Canada • ACRL ALCTS ALSC ASCLA LITA PLA RASD EMIERT

Eugene School Dist 4J Cataloging Dept. • Sheryl B. Steinke • Eugene, OR 97402 • AASL ALCTS LITA

Eunice Public Library • Peggy Suter • Eunice, NM 88231

Eureka College Melick Library • Ralph D. Wagner • Eureka, IL 61530 • ACRL RASD

Evan Terry Associate P. C. Architects • James L. Terry • Birmingham, AL 35209 • LAMA *Subscribing*

Evangeline Parish Library • Lisa K. Brasher • Ville Platte, LA 70586

Evanston Public Library • Donald E. Wright • Evanston, IL 60201 • ALCTS ALSC ALTA LAMA LITA PLA RASD YALSA

Evart Public Library • Lilas VanScoyoc • Evart, MI 49631

Everett Community College Library Media Center • Margaret C. Landrum • Everett, WA 98201-1327 • ACRL ALCTS RASD

Everett School District Instructional Material Center • Everett, WA 98201 • AASL ALSC

Evergreen Park Public Library • Margaret Smith • Chicago, IL 60642

Ewing High School Library • Sue McDonald • Trenton, NJ 08618 • AASL LIRT

Ezra H. Baker School Library • Constance P. Andrews • West Dennis, MA 02670 • AASL

FENCO, Div of U. Hosp Supply Corporation • Matthew Lyons • Burlington, NJ 08016 • Subscribing

Fachhochschule Fur Bibl Dokumentationswesen • Koln, D-5000, Germany • ACRL ALCTS LITA RASD

Fachhoohschule Fur • P. Vodosek • 7000 Stuttgart 1, Germany • PLA LHRT

Facts on File • James Warren • New York City, NY 10016 • AFLRT *Subscribing*

Fairfax County Public Library • Edwin S. Clay • Fairfax, VA 22033-1909 • AASL ACRL ALCTS ALSC ASCLA LAMA LITA PLA RASD YALSA

Fairfield Cnty Dist Lib • Rosemary S. Martin • Lancaster, OH 43130 • AASL ALSC ALTA LAMA LITA PLA RASD

Fairfield Public Library • Erma Lou Warren • Fairfield, IL 62837

Fairmont State College Library • Robert G. Masters • Fairmont, WV 26554 • AASL ACRL ALCTS RASD YALSA

Fairview Heights Public Library • Deborah M. Owen • Fairview Heights, IL 62208 • ALSC ALTA PLA

Fairview South School • Sandra L. Julian • Skokie, IL 60077 • AASL

Fanlight Productions • Ben Achtenberg • Boston, MA 02130 • VRT *Subscribing*

Fanwood Memorial Library • Fanwood, NJ 07023

Far West Data Control Inc. • Dave Roberts • Astoria, OR 97103 • AASL ACRL ALCTS LITA *Subscribing*

Faulkner University Alabama Christian College • Bernice C. Weaver • Montgomery, AL 36193 • AASL ACRL YALSA

Faxon Company Inc. • Richard R. Rowe • Westwood, MA 02090 • ACRL ALCTS LAMA LITA *Sustaining*

Fayetteville Free Library • Ann L. Moore • Fayetteville, NY 13066 • LAMA YALSA

Federal Bureau of Investigation • John Tully • Quantico, VA 22135 • ACRL ALCTS LAMA RASD

Felician College Library • Stephen Karetzky • Lodi, NJ 07644 • ACRL ALCTS LAMA LITA RASD EMIERT IRRT LIRT LIRT SRRT

Ferdinand Postma Library • Noordburg 2522, South Africa • AASL ACRL ALCTS ASCLA LAMA LITA PLA RASD YALSA

Ferguson Library • Ernest A. DiMattia • Stamford, CT 06904 • AASL ALCTS ALSC ALTA ASCLA LITA RASD GODORT

Films Incorporated • Elena Wayne • Chicago, IL 60640-1199 • VRT *Subscribing*

First Presbyterian Church • Pat Robinson • Greensboro, NC 27401

Fisk University Library & Media Center • Jessie C. Smith • Nashville, TN 37208 • ACRL ALCTS RASD

Five Towns College Library • Mildred Gardner • Dix Hills, NY 11746-6055

Fla Keys Cmnty Coll Lib • Lawrence S. Berk • Key West, FL 33040 • ACRL ALCTS LITA LIRT

Fla Mental Health Res Lib Univ of S Fla Libs • Ardis Hanson • Tampa, FL 33612 • ACRL

Flagg-Rochelle Pub Lib Dist • Rochelle, IL 61068 • PLA

Flinders Univ of S Australia • Adelaide 5001, Australia • ACRL ALCTS LITA RASD YALSA

Flint Public Library • Gloria J. Coles • Flint, MI 48502 • PLA

Flint Public Library • Shirley M. Raynard • Middleton, MA 01949

Floral Park Mem Junior/Senior High School • Madeline Hendrix • Floral Park, NY 11001 • AASL YALSA

Florida Community College at Jacksonville • Judith J. Johnson • Jacksonville, FL 32202

Florida Library Association • Marjorie J. Stealey • Winter Park, FL 32789

Florida Southern College Roux Library • Theodore Haggard • Lakeland, FL 33801 • AASL ACRL ALCTS LITA RASD

Florida State University Robert M. Strozier Library • Charles E. Miller • Tallahassee, FL 32306-2047 • ACRL ALCTS ALSC ALTA ASCLA LAMA PLA RASD YALSA CLENE EMIERT ERT FLRT GODORT IFRT ILERT IRRT LHRT LIRT LRRT MAGERT NMRT SORT SRRT

Florida Theological College • Graceville, FL 32440 • ACRL

Floyd County Public Library • Homer L. Hall • Prestonsburg, KY 41653 • PLA

Fluvanna County Library • Lilli Tuttle • Fork Union, VA 23055

Follett Software Company • Charles R. Follett • McHenry, IL 60050-5589 • AASL LITA *Subscribing*

Fondulac District Library • Sheri L. Simmen • East Peoria, IL 61611

Forbes Library • Blaise Bisaillon • Northampton, MA 01060 • ALSC

Fordham Prep School Library • August A. Stellwag • Bronx, NY 10458

Fordham University Libraries • James McCabe • Bronx, NY 10458 • ACRL RASD

Forest House Publishing Company • Dianne L. Spahr • Lake Forest, IL 60045-0738 • Subscribing

Forest Press/OCLC • Albany, NY 12206-2082 • AASL ALCTS ASCLA PLA ERT IRRT

Forman School Library • Jamie Severy Dwan • Litchfield, CT 06759-0080

Forrest Public Library District • Forrest, IL 61741

Fort Branch Public Library • Ft. Branch, IN 47648

Fort McPherson Library • Helen T. Kiss • Ft. McPherson, GA 30330 • ALCTS LAMA LITA PLA RASD AFLRT

Fort Meade Public Library • Fort Meade, FL 33841

Fort Valley State College H.A. Hunt Memorial Library • Bernice Eaton • Ft. Valley, GA 31030 • ALSC

Fort Wayne Community Schools • Bonnie Stuelpe • Ft. Wayne, IN 46802 • AASL ALSC YALSA

Fortville-Vernon Twp Pub Lib • Fortville, IN 46040

Fossil Ridge Public Library • John M. Slanicky • Braidwood, IL 60408 • LAMA PLA

Foster Parent Plan Internation • Chaichin W. Chen • East Greenwich, RI 02818 • LITA

Four Rivers ALSA • Ida L. McDowell • Evansville, IN 47708 • PLA

Fox Lake District Library • Harry J. Bork • Fox Lake, IL 60020

Fox Lane High School • David G. Cook • Bedford, NY 10506

Fox River Grove Public Lib Dist • Sue Sandeer • Fox River Grove, IL 60021 • ALSC PLA AFLRT

Fox Valley Technical College Educational Resource Center • Karen L. Parson • Appleton, WI 54913 • ACRL LIRT

Fr Lib of Springfield Twnshp • Philadelphia, PA 19118

Francis C. Hammond Library Junior High School Library • Jacquelin McDonald • Alexandria, VA 22304 • AASL YALSA

Frankfort Public Library • Frankfort, IL 60423

Frankfort Public Library • Claude W. Caddell • Frankfort, IN 46041

Franklin County Libarary • David Bass • Rocky Mount, VA 24151 • PLA

Franklin Institute Library • Irene D. Coffey • Philadelphia, PA 19103 • LAMA

Frederick Community College Learning Resources Center • Edward I. Campbell • Frederick, MD 21702 • ACRL RASD

Free Library of Philadelphia • Elliot Shelkrot • Philadelphia, PA 19103 • AASL ACRL ALCTS ALSC ALTA ASCLA LAMA LITA PLA RASD YALSA ERT SORT SRRT

Freed-Hardeman Univ Lib • Henderson, TN 38340-2399 • ACRL

Freehold Public Library • Barbara Greenberg • Freehold, NJ 07728 • PLA

Freeport Public Library • John F. Locascio • Freeport, IL 61032

Freline Inc. • Mary T. Rowland • Hagerstown, MD 21741 • AASL ALSC ALTA PLA YALSA ERT *Subscribing*

Fremont Public Library District • E. M. Maiden • Mundelein, IL 60060

Fresno Cnty Off of Edu Library • V. Ellis Vance • Fresno, CA 93721-2000 • AASL ALSC

Fresno County Free Library • John K. Kallenberg • Fresno, CA 93721-2285 • AASL ALCTS ALTA ASCLA LAMA LITA PLA RASD

Friends Fr Lib of Germantown • Helen Eigabroadt • Philadelphia, PA 19144 • AASL ALCTS ALSC PLA MAGERT

Friends of Libs USA (FOLUSA) • Sandy F. Dolnick • Philadelphia, PA 19107

Friends of The Library of Los Altos & Community, Inc. • Los Altos, CA 94023-0212

Friends of the Chicago Pub Lib • Chicago, IL 60602

Frontier Community College • Fairfield, IL 62837 • ACRL LITA

Frontier Press Company • Columbus, OH 43216 • Subscribing

Ft Lauderdale Friends of Lib • Ft. Lauderdale, FL 33338

Fugazzi College • Patricia Jones • Nashville, TN 37211

Fugazzi College • Sarah Wilkins • Lexington, KY 40502

Fuller Public Library • Tamara McClure • Hillsboro, NH 03244

Fulton-Montgomery Cmnty Coll Library • JoAnn O. McCreight • Johnstown, NY 12095 • ACRL

Gale Research Inc. • Karen Bratton • Detroit, MI 48226-4094 • AASL ACRL ALSC PLA RASD YALSA AFLRT ERT *Patron*

Galena Public Library District • Maren Coates • Galena, IL 61036 • ALSC

Galesburg High School • K. Callison • Galesburg, IL 61401

Galva Public Library District • Galva, IL 61434 • PLA

Garces Memorial High School • Bakersfield, CA 93305

Garden City Public Library • Garden City, NY 11530 • AASL ALSC LAMA PLA RASD YALSA

Gardiner School Library Districts 7 & 4 • Gardiner, MT 59030 • AASL

Garrett-Evangelical Seabury Western Theological Seminaries • Alva R. Caldwell • Evanston, IL 60201 • ACRL ALCTS LITA RASD

Gary Public Library • Mary L. Watkins • Gary, IN 46402 • PLA

Gavilan College Library • S.C. Au-Yeung • Gilroy, CA 95020

Gaylord Bros. • Chris Nicely • Syracuse, NY 13221-4901 • AASL ACRL ALCTS ALSC ASCLA LAMA LITA PLA RASD YALSA ILERT *Subscribing*

Gene Autry Western Heritage Museum • Kevin Mulroy • Los Angeles, CA 90027-1462 • ACRL

General Automation Incorporation • David Hall • Anaheim, CA 92805 • LITA *Subscribing*

General Society of Mechanics & Tradesman Library • New York, NY 10036

Geneseo Public Library District • Nancy K. Buikema • Geneseo, IL 61254

Geneva Public Library • Donna L. Shearer • Geneva, NE 68361 • PLA

George F. Cram Company • Bryan D. Hollingsworth • Indianapolis, IN 46206 • Subscribing

George G. White Elem Sch Media Center • Hillsdale, NJ 07642 • AASL ALSC

George Stone Center for Childrens Books • Doty Hale • Claremont, CA 91711-6188 • AASL ALSC EMIERT IRRT

Georgetown Public Library • Rena Latoz • Georgetown, IL 61846

Georgetown Visitation Prep Sch • Diana J. Berry • Washington, DC 20007 • AASL

Georgia Dept of Archv & Hist • Steven W. Engerrand • Atlanta, GA 30334 • ACRL ALCTS LAMA LITA RASD

Georgia Historical Society • Anne P. Smith • Savannah, GA 31499 • ACRL

Georgia Library Association • Sharon W. Self • Young Harris, GA 30582 • PLA

Georgian Court College Farley Memorial Library • Barbara J. Hutchinson • Lakewood, NJ 08701 • ACRL ALCTS LAMA RASD

German-Masontown Pub Lib • Gail Cunningham • Masontown, PA 15461

Gilbert Public Library • Pat Casteneda • Gilbert, AZ 85234 • LAMA

Gladstone Area Sch & Public Lib • Melva Jean Goodman • Gladstone, MI 49837 • PLA

Glasgow City-County Library • James F. Jondrow • Glasgow, MT 59330

Glass High School Library • Lynchburg, VA 24501

Glassboro State College • Sandor Szilassy • Glassboro, NJ 08028 • AASL ACRL ALCTS LAMA LITA RASD ERT FLRT GODORT IFRT LIRT LRRT

Glen Crest Junior High School • Glen Crest, IL 60137

Glenbard S High Sch Lib • H. White • Glen Ellyn, IL 60137 • AASL YALSA

Glenbard W High Sch Lib • Judy Ala • Glen Ellyn, IL 60137 • AASL YALSA

Glenbrook North High School • Jerry R. Wicks • Northbrook, IL 60062 • AASL LITA YALSA LIRT

Glendale Community College Library/Media Center • Glendale, AZ 85302 • ACRL LAMA LITA RASD

Globe Pequot Press • Anna C. Clifford • Chester, CT 06412 • Subscribing

Godwins Inc Frank B. Hall Consulting Company • Frank J. Fimmano • New York, NY 10016 • Contributing

Goethe Institute • John C. Schroeder • Beverly Hills, CA 90211 • ACRL

Gold Beach Union High School Library • Patricia Renner • Golden Beach, OR 97444 • AASL YALSA

Gonzaga College High School Attn: Library • Michael B. Finnerty • Washington, DC 20001 • AASL

Gonzales Public Library • Barbara Gorden • Gonzales, TX 78629

Goshen Public Library • Rose M. Chenoweth • Goshen, IN 46526 • ALSC ALTA PLA RASD

Goteborgs Universitet • Paul Hallberg • Goteborg S-402 22, Sweden • ACRL ALCTS

Goucher College Julia Rogers Library • Nancy L. Magnuson • Towson, MD 21204 • ACRL ALCTS LAMA LITA

Gould Evans Architects, P.A. • Robert E. Gould • Kansas City, MO 64112 • LAMA PLA *Subscribing*

Governors State University University Library • Harvey Varnet • University Park, IL 60466 • ACRL LAMA

Govt Employees Insurance Co (GEICO) • Charles Irons • Washington, DC 20076 • Patron

Graland Country Day School Lib • Denver, CO 80220 • AASL ALSC

Grambling State University A. C. Lewis Memorial Library • Pauline W. Lee • Grambling, LA 71245 • AASL ACRL ALCTS ALSC ALTA ASCLA LAMA LITA PLA RASD YALSA

Granby Free Public Library • Patricia Kislo • Granby, MA 01033

Grand Rapids Baptist Coll & Sem Library • David S. Slusher • Grand Rapids, MI 49505 • ACRL

Grandville Branch Library • Janet S. Hook • Grandville, MI 49418 • PLA

Grant MacEwan Community College Technical Services-Room 138 • Edmonton AB, T5B 0R8 Canada • AASL ACRL ALCTS ALSC LAMA LITA RASD

Gray-New Gloucester High School Library • Susan M. Chapman • Gray, ME 04039 • AASL

Great Books Foundation • Alice Letvin • Chicago, IL 60601-2298

Great Lakes Junior College • Saginaw, MI 48607

Great River Library System • Travis E. Dunn • Quincy, IL 62301-3997 • AASL ACRL ALCTS ALSC ALTA ASCLA LAMA LITA PLA RASD YALSA CLENE IFRT NMRT

Great River Regional Library • Kenneth E. Behringer • Saint Cloud, MN 56301 • ALCTS ALTA LAMA PLA RASD YALSA

Greater New Haven State Technical College • Alba Reynaga • North Haven, CT 06473 • ACRL

Green County Public Library • Evelyn J. Givens • Greensburg, KY 42743

Green Mountain College Griswold Library • Katharine Reichert • Poultney, VT 05764 • ACRL ALCTS LAMA LITA RASD IFRT

Green River Cmnty Coll Lib • Auburn, WA 98002 • ACRL ALCTS LAMA RASD

Greenburgh Public Library • Robert J. Trudell • Elmsford, NY 10523

Greenfield Community College Library • Carol G. Letson • Greenfield, MA 01301 • ACRL ALCTS LAMA RASD

Greenfield Public Library • John M McConagha • Greenfield, IN 46140

Greenhaven Press • David Bender • San Diego, CA 92128-9009 • ERT IFRT *Subscribing*

Greensboro Day School • Carol M. Garlington • Greensboro, NC 27429-0361

Greensburg Public Library • Alice Rust • Greensburg, IN 47240 • ALSC PLA

Greentown Public Library • Marjorie I. Bontrager • Greentown, IN 46936

Greenville County Library • Greenville, SC 29601 • AASL ALCTS ALSC ALTA LAMA LITA PLA RASD YALSA GODORT IFRT

Greenville Technical College Learning Resources Center • Lloyd Gene Elliott • Greenville, SC 29606 • ACRL

Greenwich Academy • Marilyn Musser • Greenwich, CT 06830 • AASL YALSA

Greenwood Publishing Group • Nora F. Kisch • Westport, CT 06881 • ACRL *Subscribing*

Gressco Ltd. • George Histed • Waunakee, WI 53597-0339 • Subscribing

Griffin Technology Inc. • Frank Ault • Victor, NY 14564-0998 • Subscribing

Grinnell College • Grinnell, IA 50112-0811 • ACRL ALCTS LAMA LITA RASD

Grolier Educational Corporation • Jennifer I. Rux • Danbury, CT 06816 • AASL *Sustaining*

Guam Library Association • GMF, GU 96921
Guilford College Library • Herbert Poole • Greensboro, NC 27410 • ACRL ALCTS LITA RASD
Gulliver Academy Library • Coral Gables, FL 33156 • AASL ALSC YALSA
Guyton Library • Mountain, MS 38610 • ACRL
H. B. Beal Secondary School • Barbara J. Graham • London ON, N6B 1W5 Canad⌐ • AASL
H. W. Wilson Company • Bronx, NY 10452 • AASL ACRL ALCTS ALSC ALTA ASCLA LAMA LITA PLA RASD YALSA ERT SRRT
Patron
HRD Group • Carol-Ann Haycock • Vancouver BC, V5Z 4C9 Canada • AASL IRRT
Subscribing
Haagse Hogeschool Library B.D.I. • 2585 GL The Hague, Netherlands • ACRL ALCTS PLA RASD
Hackettstown High School Library • Hackettstown, NJ 07840 • AASL YALSA
Hagerstown Jr Coll Lib • Jane V. Humbertson • Hagerstown, MD 21742-6590
Hagley Museum & Library • Glenn Porter • Wilmington, DE 19807 • ACRL ALCTS
Haledon Public Library • Marilyn Schwerdt • Haledon, NJ 07508 • PLA
Half Hollow Hills High Sch East • Jaylene Chin • Dix Hills, NY 11746 • AASL YALSA
Hall Fowler Memorial • Ionia, MI 48846
Hall High School • Barbara E. Fulara • Spring Valley, IL 61362 • AASL LITA IFRT IRRT
Hallenbook • Leo Hallen • Chatham, NY 12037 • ALCTS ASCLA RASD
Subscribing
Hallym University Library • Young Woon Choi • Kangwon Do 200, North Korea
Halton Board of Education • Burlington ON, L7R 3Z2 Canada • AASL
Hamburg Public Library • Daniel La Rue • Hamburg, PA 19526
Hamilton-Fulton-Montgomery School Library System • Deborah Booth • Johnstown, NY 12095 • AASL
Hamilton College Burke Library • Clinton, NY 13323 • ACRL ALCTS LAMA LITA RASD
Hamilton Public Library • Hamilton ON, L8N 4E4 Canada • AASL ACRL ALCTS ALSC ALTA ASCLA LAMA LITA PLA RASD YALSA EMIERT GODORT IFRT LRRT MAGERT
Hamlin-Lincoln Cnty Pub Lib • David Burch • Hamlin, WV 25523
Hamline University Bush Memorial Library • Jack King • Saint Paul, MN 55104 • ACRL ALCTS LITA RASD
Hammond Public Library • Arthur S. Meyers • Hammond, IN 46320 • ALCTS ALSC ALTA RASD
Hammondsport Public Library • Judith Garrison • Hammondsport, NY 14810 • PLA
Hampden-Booth Theatre Library • Raymond Wemminger • New York, NY 10003
Hampden Sydney College • David J. Norden • Hampden Sydney, VA 23943 • ACRL ALCTS LAMA LITA
Hampshire Cnty Library • J. C. Beard • Winchester Hants, England • ACRL ALCTS LITA PLA RASD
Hampshire Rgnl High Sch Lib • Anita L. Goddard • Westhampton, MA 01027 • AASL
Hamtramck Public Library Albert J. Zak Memorial Library • Carol M. Sterling • Hamtramck, MI 48212
Hancock County Library System Headquarters • Prima Wusnack • Bay Saint Louis, MS 39520
Hancock Shaker Village Library • Robert F. W. Meader • Pittsfield, MA 01201
Hannibal-LaGrange College L.A. Foster Library • Julie A. Dothager • Hannibal, MO 63401 • LIRT
Hannibal Free Public Library • Ann Sundermeyer • Hannibal, MO 63401
Hanover College Duggan Library • Hanover, IN 47243-0287 • AASL ACRL ALCTS RASD GODORT
Harcourt Brace Jovanovich Publishers • Louise Howton • San Diego, CA 92101 • ALSC YALSA
Subscribing
HarperCollins Publishers HarperCollins Children's Books • William C. Morris • New York, NY 10022 • ERT
Contributing
Harrie P. Woodson Mem Lib • Pat Beavers • Caldwell, TX 77836
Harriette Person Mem Lib • Nancy S. Batton • Port Gibson, MS 39150 • PLA NMRT
Harry Lundeberg School of Seamanship-Library • Piney Point, MD 20674 • AASL ACRL ALCTS RASD
Hartford City Public Library • Jane Miller • Hartford City, IN 47348 • PLA
Hartford Graduate Center • Hartford, CT 06120 • ACRL LAMA
Hartford Public Library • Michael J. Gelhausen • Hartford, WI 53027-1596 • PLA
Hartford Public Library • John S. Burgan • Hartford, CT 06103-3003 • SORT

Hartley Public Library • Merna R. Menke • Hartley, IA 51346
Harvard College Library Widener Memorial Library • Yen Tsai Feng • Cambridge, MA 02138 • ACRL ALCTS LAMA LITA RASD
Hattiesburg, Petal & Forrest County, The Library • Pamela S. Pridgen • Hattiesburg, MS 39401
Havana Public Library District • Nancy I. Glick • Havana, IL 62644 • PLA
Haverford College James P. Magill Library • Michael S. Freeman • Haverford, PA 19041 • ACRL ALCTS LAMA LITA RASD GODORT LIRT
Havre-Hill County Library • Bonnie Williamson • Havre, MT 59501 • PLA IFRT LIRT
Hawaii Library Association • Floriana Cofman • Honolulu, HI 96813 • IFRT
Hawaii Med Library Inc • Honolulu, HI 96813
Hawaii State Pub Lib Sys Office of the State Librarian • Bart Kane • Honolulu, HI 96813 • ASCLA
Haworth Municipal Library • Elizabeth Rosenberg • Haworth, NJ 07641
Hayden Consol Fr Lib Dist • John W. Hartung • Hayden, ID 83835
Hayes Presidential Ctr Lib • Barbara A. Paff • Fremont, OH 43420
Hayner Public Library District • Alton, IL 62002 • LITA RASD
Hazleton Area Public Library • James Reinmiller • Hazleton, PA 18201 • PLA
Health Sci Libs Consortium • Joseph C. Scorza • Philadelphia, PA 19104 • LITA
Hebrew Union College Library • Cincinnati, OH 45220
Hebron Elementary School • Deborah B. Salewski • Hebron, CT 06248 • AASL
Heidelberg College • Ed M. Krakora • Tiffin, OH 44883 • AASL LAMA
Helen K. Furness Free Library • Steve Marrone • Wallingford, PA 19086
Helena Township Library • Billie Jo Johnson • Alden, MI 49612
Helsinki University Library • 00171 Helsinki, Finland • ACRL ALCTS LITA RASD
Hemlock High School Library • Hemlock, MI 48626
Henderson-Wilder Library Upper Iowa University • Becky S. Wadian • Fayette, IA 52142 • ACRL
Henderson Cmnty Coll Lib University of Kentucky • Henderson, KY 42420 • ACRL
Henderson County Public Library • Donald Wathen • Henderson, KY 42420
Hendersonville Public Library • Virginia Duffett • Hendersonville, TN 37075 • PLA
Hennepin County Library • Robert H. Rohlf • Minnetonka, MN 55343 • AASL ACRL ALCTS ALSC ALTA ASCLA LAMA LITA PLA RASD YALSA
Henrico Public Library • Graham H. Sadler • Richmond, VA 23223 • ALCTS ALSC ALTA LAMA LITA PLA RASD YALSA IFRT
Henry Ford Hospital Library Sladen Library • Nardina L. Nameth • Detroit, MI 48202
Henry Holt and Company • Audrey D. Melkin • New York, NY 10011 • AASL ALSC PLA YALSA ERT
Subscribing
Herbert Norman Library Canadian Academy • Kobe 658, Japan
Herrick Public Library • Robert L. Sherwood • Holland, MI 49423 • ALSC LAMA PLA
Herrin County Library • Herrin, IL 62948
Hester Junior High School District 84 • Franklin Park, IL 60131 • ALSC YALSA
Hicksville Free Public Library • Kenneth S. Barnes • Hicksville, NY 11801 • PLA
Hidell Architects • William Hidell • Dallas, TX 75204 • LAMA
Subscribing
Highland High School Library • Hardy, AR 72542 • AASL YALSA
Highlights for Children Inc. • Garry C. Myers • Columbus, OH 43216-0269 • AASL ALSC YALSA
Subscribing
Hilbert College McGrath Library • Thaddeus J. Ciambor • Hamburg, NY 14075 • ACRL
Hill Junior College Library • Hillsboro, TX 76645 • ACRL ALCTS LITA
Hillier Group, The • Joseph Rizzo • Princeton, NJ 08540 • Contributing
Hillsboro Public Library • Emma E. Cress • Hillsboro, IL 62049
Hillsdale College Mossey Learning Resources Center • Dan Joldersma • Hillsdale, MI 49242 • ACRL ALCTS LAMA LITA RASD
Hillside Free Public Library • Hillside, NJ 07205
Hillwood Museum • Jeannette Harper • Washington, DC 20008

Hobart & William Smith Colleges Warren H. Smith Library • Paul W. Crumlish • Geneva, NY 14456 • ACRL ALCTS LAMA RASD
Hofstra University Axinn Library • Charles Andrews • Hempstead, NY 11550 • ACRL ALCTS LAMA RASD YALSA GODORT
Hogskolan I Boras • Louise Freden • S-50115 Boras, Sweden • AASL ACRL ALCTS ASCLA LAMA LITA PLA RASD YALSA
Hollins College Fishburn Library • Richard E. Kirkwood • Rpample, VA 24020 • ACRL ALCTS LAMA LITA RASD GODORT
Holmes Public Library • Leslie S. Morrissey • Halifax, MA 02338-1394
Holy Cross College • Raymond Dufresne • Notre Dame, IN 46556 • ACRL
Holy Cross High School Library • Pauline E. DiCicco • Flushing, NY 11358
Holyoke Public Library • Paul H. Normand • Holyoke, MA 01040
Homer Township Public Library District • Regetta Meyers • Lockport, IL 60441
Homewood-Flossmoor High School Library • Judith M. Soltis • Flossmoor, IL 60422 • AASL
Homochitto Valley Lib Serv • Elizabeth Roderick • Natchez, MS 39120 • PLA
Hong Kong Academy for Performing Arts Library • Jospehine Hung • Wanchai, Hong Kong • ACRL LRRT
Hong Kong Baptist College Library • Kowloon, Hong Kong • ACRL ALCTS LITA
Hong Kong International School • Natalie Choy • Tai Tam, Hong Kong • AASL YALSA
Hong Kong Polytech Library • Kowloon, Hong Kong • ACRL ALCTS LITA RASD
Hood College J.H. Apple Library • Charles L. Kuhn • Frederick, MD 21701 • ACRL LITA
Hoopeston Public Library • Lou Graham • Hoopeston, IL 60942
Hope Welty Pub Lib Dist • Norabel J. Baker • Cerro Gordo, IL 61818
Hopkins Cnty-Madisonville Public Library • Madisonville, KY 42431
Hopkinsville Community College Library • Cynthia F. Atkins • Hopkinsville, KY 42241-2100
Horace W. Porter School • Barbara Jezek • Columbia, CT 06237 • AASL
Hortonville Public Library • Carolyn Habeck • Hortonville, WI 54944
Hot Springs Public Library • Hot Springs, SD 57747
Hotchkiss Library of Sharon • Gail Mirabile • Sharon, CT 06069
Hotho and Company • Donna Hotho • Fort Worth, TX 76147 • Subscribing
Houghton Mifflin Company • Jennifer E. Roberts • Boston, MA 02108
Housatonic Valley Rgnl High Sch • Kathleen K. Mera • Falls Village, CT 06031 • AASL YALSA LIRT
Houston-Tillotson Coll Lib Downs-Jones Library • Patricia Quaterman • Austin, TX 78702 • ACRL ALCTS
Houston Public Library • David M. Henington • Houston, TX 77002
Howard College at Big Spring Library • David R. Drake • Big Spring, TX 79720 • ACRL
Howard Hughes Medical Institute Investment Library • Cathy E. Harbert • Bethesda, MD 20817 • RASD
Hudson County Community College • Grace L. Patterson • Jersey City, NJ 07306 • ACRL
Hudson High School Library • Hudson, NY 12534
Hudson Valley Community College Dwight Marvin Library • Brenda E. Twiggs • Troy, NY 12180 • ACRL RASD
Humacao Univ Coll Lib • Oneida R. Ortiz • Humacao, PR 00661 • ACRL ALCTS ASCLA LAMA LITA RASD YALSA
Humana Hospital Michael Reese Florsheim Library • Chicago, IL 60616-3390
Humphreys County Library System • Shirley H. Keenum • Belonzi, MS 39038 • PLA
Hunter College Library • New York, NY 10021 • ACRL ALCTS ASCLA LAMA LITA RASD
Huntingdon College Houghton Memorial Library • Eric A. Kidwell • Montgomery, AL 36106 • ACRL ALCTS LAMA
Hurlbutt Elementary School • Barbara W. Allen • Weston, CT 06883 • AASL
Hustisford Library • Candace Graulich • Hustisford, WI 53034
Hutchinson Community College • Patricia B. Vierthaler • Hutchinson, KS 67501 • ACRL
Hutchinson Public Library • Leroy M. Gattin • Hutchinson, KS 67501
Hyrum City Library • Linda Andersen • Hyrum, UT 84319

IBM ACIS • Caryl K. McAllister • Milford, CT 06460 • Patron

Ibnkhuldoon National School • Gillian Howells • Manama Bahrain, Arabian Gulf • AASL

Ida Grove Public Library • Lois Segerstrom • Ida Grove, IA 51445

Ida Public Library • Belvidere, IL 61008

Idaho Library Association • Camille D. Wood • Moscow, ID 83843

Idaho Power Company • Denise Saunders • Boise, ID 83707 • Subscribing

Idaho State Library • Charles A. Bolles • Boise, ID 83702 • AASL ACRL ALCTS ALSC ALTA ASCLA LAMA LITA PLA RASD YALSA GODORT

Idea House Publishing Company • Christopher Largent • Wilmington, DE 19806 • Subscribing

Ideals Publishing Corporation • Janet H. Fairchild • Nashville, TN 37214 • AASL ALSC   *Subscribing*

Illinois Benedictine College Lownik Library • Mary Joyce Pickett • Lisle, IL 60532 • ACRL GODORT

Illinois College Schewe Library • Martin H. Gallas • Jacksonville, IL 62650-2299 • ACRL ALCTS RASD

Illinois Institute of Technology Paul V. Galvin Library • David R. Dowell • Chicago, IL 60616 • ACRL ALCTS LAMA LITA RASD GODORT LIRT MAGERT SORT

Illinois Library Association • Barbara A. Cunningham • Chicago, IL 60610-4306 • GODORT IFRT

Illinois State Hist Lib • Jill Blessman • Springfield, IL 62701 • ACRL ALCTS RASD

Illinois State Library • Bridget Later Lamont • Springfield, IL 62701-1796 • AASL ACRL ALCTS ALSC ALTA ASCLA LAMA LITA PLA RASD YALSA AFLRT CLENE EMIERT ERT FLRT GODORT IFRT ILERT IRRT LHRT LIRT LRRT MAGERT NMRT SORT SRRT

Illinois State University Milner Library • Fred M. Peterson • Normal, IL 61761-0900 • AASL ACRL ALCTS ALSC ASCLA LAMA LITA PLA RASD GODORT

Illinois Valley Library System • Valerie J. Wilford • Pekin, IL 61554 • AASL ACRL ALCTS ALSC ALTA ASCLA LAMA LITA PLA RASD YALSA

Immaculata College • Florence Marie • Immaculata, PA 19345 • ACRL LAMA

Immaculate Heart High School • Miriam Claire • Tucson, AZ 85704

Immaculate High School Library • Danbury, CT 06810

Incarnate Word College • Mendell D. Morgan • San Antonio, TX 78209-9367

Independent School District #535 Educational Service Center • Ann Thomas • Rochester, MN 55904 • AASL

Indian Institute of Management • Bangalore 560 076, India • ACRL ALCTS LITA

Indian River Community College • Fran Mimms • Fort Pierce, FL 34981-5599 • AASL

Indiana Coop Lib Serv Authority (INCOLSA) • Barbara E. Markuson • Indianapolis, IN 46278 • ALCTS LAMA LITA PLA

Indiana Library Federation • Linda D. Kolb • Indianapolis, IN 46202

Indiana State Library • Charles Ray Ewick • Indianapolis, IN 46204-2296 • AASL ACRL ALCTS ALSC ALTA ASCLA LAMA LITA PLA RASD YALSA CLENE GODORT

Indiana State University Department of Library Science • Terre Haute, IN 47809 • AASL ACRL ALCTS ALSC ALTA ASCLA LAMA LITA PLA RASD YALSA CLENE FLRT GODORT IFRT ILERT IRRT LHRT LIRT LRRT SRRT

Indiana Univ Southeast Lib Southeastern Campus Library • New Albany, IN 47150-6405 • AASL ACRL ALCTS LAMA LITA RASD

Indiana Univ at Bloomington University Libraries • James G. Neal • Bloomington, IN 47405-9998 • AASL ACRL ALCTS ALSC ALTA ASCLA LAMA LITA PLA RASD YALSA

Indiana University East Library Learning Resources Center • Gordon Lynn Hufford • Richmond, IN 47374-1289 • ACRL RASD

Indiana University School of Law Library • James F. Bailey • Indianapolis, IN 46202 • ACRL ALCTS LAMA LITA RASD GODORT IFRT LIRT

Indiana University School of Library and Information Science • Bloomington, IN 47405 • AASL ACRL ALCTS ALSC ALTA ASCLA LAMA LITA PLA RASD YALSA GODORT IFRT IRRT LIRT LRRT NMRT SRRT

Indiana University at Kokomo Learning Resources Center • Kokomo, IN 46904-9003 • AASL ACRL LAMA RASD YALSA GODORT LIRT NMRT

Indianapolis Marion Cnty Pub Lib • Raymond E. Gnat • Indianapolis, IN 46206 • AASL ACRL ALCTS ALSC ALTA ASCLA LAMA LITA PLA RASD YALSA

Indianapolis Museum of Art Lib • Carolyn Metz • Indianapolis, IN 46208 • ACRL

Indianapolis Public School Media Services • Barbara J. Stevens • Indianapolis, IN 46202 • AASL ALSC

Infocentre Corporation • Saint Laurent PQ, H4R 2B8 Canada • ACRL ALCTS ALTA LAMA LITA PLA   *Subscribing*

Information Access Company • Ron Puchir • Foster City, CA 94404 • AASL ACRL ALCTS LAMA LITA RASD   *Sustaining*

Ingram Library Services Inc. • La Vergne, TN 37086-1986 • Subscribing

Innovative Interfaces, Inc. • Gerald M. Kline • Berkeley, CA 94710 • Subscribing

Insdoc-National Science Library • T. Viswanathan • New Delhi-110067, India • ACRL ALCTS LITA RASD

Inst of Amer Indian Arts • Susan D. Gilroy • Santa Fe, NM 87504 • ACRL

Inst of Intl Edu Library Communications • W Richard Heyer • New York, NY 10017

Inst of Transpersonal Psych Library • Peter I. Hirose • Menlo Park, CA 94025

Institute of Technology Library • E. M. Dunphy • Aberdeen AB11HG, Scotland

Instituto Brasileiro de Informacao Ciencia e Tecnologia • E. C. Principe de Oliveria • 70.070 Brasilia, Brazil • ACRL ASCLA LAMA PLA

Instituto Juan March Biblioteca • 28006 Madrid, Spain • RASD

Internal Revenue Service • Darlene Carter • Washington, DC 20224 • Subscribing

International Academy Library • Richard G. Racheter • Tampa, FL 33609 • ACRL

International Brotherhood of Teamsters Library • Theresa A. Fritz • Washington, DC 20001

International College, Inc. • Jacquelyn Barr • Naples, FL 33962 • ACRL ALCTS

International School of Beijing American Embassy-Beijing • Richard Chesley • FPO San Francisco, CA 96655-0001 • ALSC YALSA

International Youth Library • Andreas Bode • Munich 60, Germany • ALSC

Intertec Publishing Corporation • Dutch Sadler • Overland Park, KS 66212 • Subscribing

Interweave Press • Loveland, CO 80537 • Subscribing

Intevep Cit Biblioteca • Caracas 1070-A, Venezuela • ACRL ALCTS ASCLA LAMA LITA

Intl Amer Univ of Puerto Rico • Hato Rey, PR 00919 • ACRL ALCTS ASCLA LAMA LITA RASD CLENE LIRT SORT

Intl Christian Univ Library • Masako Kito • Tokyo, Japan • ACRL ALCTS LITA

Intl Civil Aviation Org Library • M. C. Tuduri • Montreal PQ, H3A 2R2 Canada • LITA

Intl Falls Public Lib • International Falls, MN 56649 • PLA

Intl Lib Archv Museum of Optometry • Bridget Kowalczyk • St Louis, MO 63141 • ALCTS ASCLA LAMA LITA RASD

Intl Sch Media Serv • Maria Luz Cayabyab • Metro Manila 3117, Philippines • AASL

Intl Sch of Amsterdam • Margaret Armstrong-Law • NL1008 AD Amsterdam, Netherlands • AASL ACRL ALCTS ALSC LAMA LITA YALSA

Iola Public Library • Iola, KS 66749

Iola Village Library • Elizabeth Berkholtz • Iola, WI 54945

Iolani School Library • Janine S. Volkmar • Honolulu, HI 96826

Iona College Elizabeth Seton School Library • Marian M. Sullivan • Yonkers, NY 10701

Iowa Library Association • Naomi Stovall • Des Moines, IA 50309

Ira J. Taylor Library • Denver, CO 80210 • ACRL ALCTS RASD

Iredell County Library • Flint Norwood • Statesville, NC 28677 • PLA

Ireland Univ Coll Lib Periodicals Dept. • S. Phillips • Dublin 4, Ireland • AASL ACRL ALCTS LITA

Irene Ingle Public Library • Michelle Kay Jabusch • Wrangell, AK 99929-0679

Irish Times, Ltd. • Brenda Mc Niff • Dublin 2, Ireland • Subscribing

Irmo Middle School R Library Media Center • Columbia, SC 29210

Irving Public Library System • Irving, TX 75015-2288 • ALCTS ALSC ALTA LAMA LITA PLA RASD YALSA GODORT IFRT

Irvington Public Library • Lorelei C. McConnell • Irvington, NJ 07111

Isidore Newman School Library • Laura A. Covington • New Orleans, LA 70115

Islamic Resource Institute • Shabbir Mansuri • Tustin, CA 92680

Island Free Library • Sandra Gaffett • Block Island, RI 02807 • PLA

Island Trees High School Library • Susan Mendelson • Levittown, NY 11756-5799 • AASL

Islip Public Library • Ann Geddes • Islip, NY 11751 • PLA YALSA

Isothermal Community College • Susan Vaughan • Spindale, NC 28160

Istanbul Intl Cmnty Sch Library • Mary Berkmen • Istanbul, Turkey • AASL

Italy Johns Hopkins University • Bologna, Italy • ACRL

Ithaca College Library • W. Robert Woerner • Ithaca, NY 14850 • ACRL ALCTS LAMA LITA RASD

Ivoryton Public Library • Ivoryton, CT 06442

J. B. Conant High School Professional Library • Carol Dering • Hoffman Estates, IL 60194 • AASL

J.C. Holliday Memorial Library • Ronald A. Novy • Clinton, NC 28328

JD Store Equipment, Inc. • Donald Ross • Los Angeles, CA 90021 • Subscribing

Jackson County Public Library • Connie Jo Ozinga • Seymour, IN 47274 • LAMA PLA RASD

Jackson Parish Library • Faye R. Hood • Jonesboro, LA 71251

Jacksonville Public Libraries Main Library • Judith L. Williams • Jacksonville, FL 32202

Jacksonville University Carl S. Swisher Library • Thomas H. Gunn • Jacksonville, FL 32211 • AASL ACRL ALCTS RASD

Jamaica Library Service • Sybil M. Iton • Kingston 5, Jamaica • ALCTS LAMA LITA RASD

James Cook Univ of N Queensland Library • J. McKinlay • Townsville Q.4811, Australia • ACRL ALCTS LITA

James J. Shea Sr Mem Lib American International College • F. Knowlton Utley • Springfield, MA 01109 • ACRL ALCTS LAMA

Jamestown Community College Cattaraugus Campus Lib. Business Office • Tony Bisignano • Olean, NY 14760-2662 • ACRL RASD

Jamestown Community College Hultquist Library • Daniel Sell • Jamestown, NY 14702-0020 • ACRL LAMA RASD

January Productions • Allan W. Peller • Hawthorne, NJ 07507-0066 • AASL   *Subscribing*

Jasper County Public Library • Lynn Daugherty • Rensselaer, IN 47978

Jasper Public Library • Lori Galbreath • Jasper, IN 47546 • ALSC PLA

Jefferson Community College Library • Louisville, KY 40202 • ACRL ALCTS LAMA LITA RASD

Jefferson County Library • Judith B. Gunter • Hadlock, WA 98339 • LAMA PLA

Jefferson County Library • Dorothy B. Gill • Beaumont, TX 77705

Jefferson County Public Library • William A. Knott • Lakewood, CO 80215 • ALTA PLA

Jefferson County School District Prof Lib Media Ctr • Roberta Ponis • Golden, CO 80401 • AASL ALCTS LITA RASD

Jefferson Prsh Lib Dept • Metairie, LA 70010 • AASL ACRL ALCTS ALSC ALTA ASCLA LAMA LITA PLA RASD YALSA

Jefferson W High Sch Lib • Lois Malm • Meriden, KS 66512

Jeffersonville Twp Public Lib • William F. Bolte • Jeffersonville, IN 47131-1548 • ALCTS LAMA PLA RASD YALSA

Jennings County Public Library • Larry L. Cunningham • North Vernon, IN 47265-1596 • PLA

Jennings Public Library • Jennings, LA 70546

Jersey City Public Library • Dennis J. Hayes • Jersey City, NJ 07302-3499

Jessica L. Bramley Free Library • Shirley H. Drummond • Jordan, NY 13080

Jesuit-Krauss-McCormick Library • Mary R. Bischoff • Chicago, IL 60615 • ACRL ALCTS LITA RASD

Jewish Theo Sem of America Library • Naomi Steinberg • New York, NY 10027 • ACRL ALCTS LITA

Jippro Research Library • Tokyo 176, Japan • AASL ACRL ALCTS ALSC LITA RASD EMIERT GODORT IRRT LIRT

Joeten-Kiyu Public Library • Judy C. Russell • Saipan, MP 96950 • ALSC PLA RASD

Johannesburg Public Library • Dawn Evender • Johannesburg, South Africa

John Carroll High School Library • Carolyn White • Bel Air, MD 21014 • AASL

John Carroll University Grasselli Library • John S. Piety • University Heights, OH 44118 • ACRL ALCTS RASD GODORT LIRT

John Jay College of Criminal Justice • Eileen Rowland • New York, NY 10019 • ACRL ALCTS ASCLA LAMA LITA RASD

John Mosser Pub Lib Dist • J Davis • Abingdon, IL 61410-1451

John de la Howe School • Joanne Gokey • McCormick, SC 29835

Johnson County Library • Shawnee Mission, KS 66201 • LAMA

Johnson County Public Library • Beverly A. Martin • Franklin, IN 46131 • ALSC LAMA PLA IFRT

Johnston Public Library • Muriel Burrows • Baxter Springs, KS 66713

Joliet Catholic Academy Library • Joanne Schwenke • Joliet, IL 60435 • AASL

Joliet Public Library • James R. Johnston • Joliet, IL 60431 • ACRL ALCTS ALTA LAMA LITA PLA RASD YALSA

Joplin High School Library Central Library Office • Joplin, MO 64804 • AASL

Jordaan Memorial Library • Margaret Larson • Larned, KS 67550 • PLA

Juneau Public Libraries • Donna B. Pierce • Juneau, AK 99801 • LAMA PLA

Justice Public Library • Jeanne Glowacki • Justice, IL 60458

K.R. Montgomery & Assoc. Inc. Architecture & Interior Design • Shirley Montgomery • Anderson, IN 46016 • Subscribing

Kaiser Hospital Medical Library • Leeni I. Balogh • Santa Rosa, CA 95403

Kalamazoo Public Library • Saul J. Amdursky • Kalamazoo, MI 49007-5270 • ALCTS LAMA LITA PLA RASD

Kansas City Art Institute Library • Allen S. Morrill • Kansas City, MO 64111 • ACRL ALCTS LITA RASD

Kansas Hist Soc Lib • David A. Haury • Topeka, KS 66612-1291 • ACRL ALCTS GODORT

Kansas Library Association • Hutchinson, KS 67501

Kansas State Library • Duane F. Johnson • Topeka, KS 66612-1593 • ACRL ALCTS ASCLA LAMA LITA PLA RASD CLENE GODORT SORT

Kansas State University-Salina Tullis Library Resource Center • Beverlee Kissick • Salina, KS 67401

Kansas Wesleyan University Memorial Library • Sandra H. Keist • Salina, KS 67401 • GODORT

Kapiolani Cmnty Coll Lib • Terry D. Webb • Honolulu, HI 96816 • ACRL

Karch & Associates Inc. • Addie M. Brown • Washington, DC 20006 • ACRL

Kasetsart University • Rewat Garnpojana • Bangkok 10900, Thailand • ACRL ALCTS LAMA LITA

Katharine Gibbs School • Karen Schulhoff • New York, NY 10017

Kean College of New Jersey Library • Barbara Simpson • Union, NJ 07083 • AASL ACRL ALCTS ASCLA LAMA LITA RASD YALSA GODORT LIRT

Kearny Public Library • Gail E. Colure • Kearny, NJ 07032

Keene Junior High School • M. L. St John • Keene, NH 03431

Keio University School Sch of Lib & Inf Sci • Hiroko Kameoka • Tokyo, 108, Japan • AASL ACRL ALCTS LAMA LITA PLA RASD YALSA

Keiser College of Technology • Marilyn Jordan • Fort Lauderdale, FL 33309

Kellogg Community College Learning Resource Center • Battle Creek, MI 49017-3397 • ACRL ALCTS RASD

Kendallville Public Library • Doris A. Goins • Kendallville, IN 46755 • ALSC PLA

Kenilworth Free Public Library • Adriana Bennett Bernstein • Kenilworth, NJ 07033 • PLA

Kenilworth Pub Lib Dist • Scott Bates • Kenilworth, IL 60043

Kennebec Valley Tech Coll • Janet Sibley • Fairfield, ME 04937 • ACRL

Kennebunk Free Library • Natalie R. Savage • Kennebunk, ME 04043

Kenosha Unified Sch Dist #1 Instructional Media Center • Henry J. Wellner • Kenosha, WI 53144 • AASL ALCTS ALSC LITA

Kensington Central Library • London W8 7NX, England • ALCTS LITA RASD

Kent Adhesive Product Company (KAPCO) • Bill Minnich • Kent, OH 44240-0011 • AASL ACRL ALCTS PLA   *Contributing*

Kent School Library • Marel E. Rogers • Kent, CT 06757 • AASL

Kent State University Libraries • Don L. Tolliver • Kent, OH 44242 • AASL ACRL ALCTS ALSC ALTA ASCLA LAMA LITA PLA RASD YALSA ERT FLRT GODORT IFRT IRRT LHRT LRRT NMRT SORT

Kent State University Sch of Lib Science/ Columbus Prog • Mary T. Kim • Columbus, OH 43210 • ACRL ALCTS ALSC LAMA LITA PLA RASD

Kentland Public Library • Roberta Dewing • Kentland, IN 47951 • PLA

Kentucky Dept for Libs & Archv • James A. Nelson • Frankfort, KY 40602-0537 • AASL ACRL ALCTS ALSC ALTA ASCLA LAMA LITA PLA RASD YALSA

Kentucky Library Association • John T. Underwood • Frankfort, KY 40601

Kentucky State University Blazer Library • Karen C. McDaniel • Frankfort, KY 40601 • AASL ACRL ALCTS LAMA LITA RASD EMIERT

Kenyon College • Ralph W. Holibaugh • Gambier, OH 43022 • ACRL ALCTS LAMA LITA RASD GODORT LIRT

Kershaw Elementary School • Bernice W. Connor • Chicago, IL 60621 • ALSC

Kettering Foundation Library • Dayton, OH 45459-2799 • RASD

Kewanee Public Library • Kewanee, IL 61443 • PLA

Keystone Junior College Miller Library • Narda Tafuri • La Plume, PA 18440 • ACRL LAMA

Kilgore High School • Marion Dovel • Kilgore, TX 75662 • AASL

Kilgore Public Library • Kilgore, TX 75662

Kinchafoonee Regional Library • Sara S. Russell • Dawson, GA 31742

King County Library System • William H. Ptacek • Seattle, WA 98109-5191 • ACRL ALCTS ALSC ALTA LAMA LITA PLA RASD YALSA EMIERT GODORT IFRT LRRT NMRT SORT SRRT

King Fahd National Library • Yahya M. Sa ati • Riyadh 11472, Saudi Arabia • ACRL ALCTS ASCLA LAMA LITA PLA RASD IFRT IRRT LRRT MAGERT

King Fahd Univ of Petroleum & Minerals Library • Dhahran-31261, Saudi Arabia • ACRL ALCTS LAMA LITA RASD CLENE IRRT LIRT LRRT SORT

King Saud University Libraries • S. A. Al-Rashid • Riyadh-11495, Saudi Arabia

King's College • Wilkes Barre, PA 18711 • ACRL ALCTS LAMA LITA RASD

Kingman-Millcreek Pub Lib • Delores Sunderman • Kingman, IN 47952

Kingman Carnegie Public Library • Linda Slack • Kingman, KS 67068

Kings College Library • Briarcliff Manor, NY 10510 • ACRL ALCTS RASD

Kingsborough Cmnty Coll Lib • John R. Clune • Brooklyn, NY 11235 • ALCTS LITA RASD

Kingsley Lib Equipment Co • Eleanor V. Kingsley • Pomona, CA 91768 • SRRT   *Subscribing*

Kintronics Inc • Neal Allen • Elmsford, NY 10523 • AASL ACRL LAMA LITA PLA   *Subscribing*

Knox Cnty Pub Lib Sys • Patricia L. Watson • Knoxville, TN 37902 • ALCTS ALTA LAMA LITA PLA RASD GODORT IFRT

Knox College Henry W. Seymour Library • Douglas L. Wilson • Galesburg, IL 61402 • ACRL RASD

Kokagakuin University Library • Tokyo 150, Japan • AASL ACRL ALCTS LITA RASD YALSA

Kungl Biblioteket Ut/s • Birgit Antonsson • Stockholm, Sweden • ACRL

Kuskokwin Consortium Library • Bethel, AK 99559

Kuwait Soc for the Advancement of Arab Children • Safat 13100, Kuwait • AASL ALSC YALSA

L'Anse Creuse Dist Media Ctr • Mary Cantoni • Mount Clemens, MI 48043-1184 • AASL ALSC LAMA

L. E. Smoot Memorial Library • Rita Schepmoes • King George, VA 22485 • ALTA PLA

L.E. Phillips Mem Pub Lib • Eau Claire, WI 54701 • ALCTS ALSC ALTA LAMA LITA PLA RASD YALSA

La Grange Asssociation Library • Rosemary E. Detrich • Poughkeepsie, NY 12603

La Joie Parles Livres • Paris F 75004, France

La Jolla Country Day School • La Jolla, CA 92037 • AASL YALSA IFRT

La Porte County Public Library • Judy R. Hamilton • La Porte, IN 46350 • ALSC PLA RASD YALSA

La Reina High School • Eileen DeBruno • Thousand Oaks, CA 91360 • AASL

La Salle Public Library • La Salle, IL 61301 • PLA YALSA

La Sierra Academy Library • Madalyn Lathrop • Riverside, CA 92505

La Trobe University • Bundoora VIC, Australia • ACRL ALCTS LITA RASD GODORT

Lackawanna Trail High School Library • Factoryville, PA 18419 • YALSA

Lafourche Parish Public Library • Kathleen M. Kilgen • Thibodaux, LA 70301

Lake-Sumter Community College • Dianne P. McComas • Leesburg, FL 32788 • ACRL ALCTS

Lake City Public Library • Kathleen A. Durand • Lake City, MN 55041

Lake County Public Library • Carol A. Derner • Merrillville, IN 46410-5382 • ACRL ALCTS LAMA LITA PLA RASD

Lake Erie College Lincoln Learning Resource Center • Christopher K. Bennett • Painesville, OH 44077 • ACRL ALCTS

Lake Forest Library • Kaye A. Grabbe • Lake Forest, IL 60045 • PLA

Lake Geneva Public Library • Barbara Davis • Lake Geneva, WI 53147 • ALTA

Lake Linden-Hubbell Pub Sch Library • Kathleen Johnson • Lake Linden, MI 49945

Lake MacQuarie Municipal Library • Boolaroo NWS 2284, Australia

Lake Park High School-X West • Roselle, IL 60172 • AASL YALSA

Lake Region High School Library • Deborah G. Canavan • Bridgton, ME 04009 • AASL YALSA

Lakehead University • Thunder Bay ON, P78 5E1 Canada

Lakehead University Library • Fred McIntosh • Thunder Bay ON, P7B 5E1 Canada • AASL ACRL ALCTS ASCLA LAMA LITA RASD

Lakeside School Library • Brenda Brock • Seattle, WA 98125 • AASL LITA LIRT

Lakeview Public Library • Seymour W. James • Rockville Center, NY 11570 • PLA EMIERT

Lamar University-Port Arthur Gates Library • Jimmet Giron Lawrence • Port Arthur, TX 77640 • ACRL ALCTS LAMA RASD ERT IFRT LIRT LRRT

Lancaster Central School • Patricia A. Easton • Lancaster, NY 14086 • AASL

Lancaster Public Library • Richard Meldrom • Kilmarnock, VA 22482 • PLA

Lane Public Library • Mary Pat Essman • Hamilton, OH 45011

Langdon Public Library • Newington, NH 03801

Langston University G. Lamar Harrison Library • Alberta G. J. Mayberry • Langston, OK 73050 • ACRL ALCTS LAMA RASD EMIERT GODORT

Lansing Public Library • Joyce H. Thomas • Lansing, MI 48933 • AASL ALCTS ALSC ALTA LAMA LITA PLA RASD YALSA

Las Vegas-Clark Cnty Lib Dist Flamingo Library • Charles W. Hunsberger • Las Vegas, NV 89119 • ALCTS ALSC ALTA LAMA LITA PLA RASD GODORT IFRT SORT

Lasell College Brennan Library • Allyson Gray • Auburndale, MA 02166 • ACRL LAMA LITA

Latin School of Chicago Lower School Library • Leslie Rumney • Chicago, IL 60610

Laubach Literacy Intl Lib • Jenny L. Ryan • Syracuse, NY 13210 • RASD

Laurel Public Library • Elizabeth B. Strange • Laurel, DE 19956

Lauren Rogers Museum of Art • Tammy Atkinson • Laurel, MS 39440

Lawrence Memorial Library • Bristol, VT 05443

Lawrenceville School • Barbara A. Piscuskas • Lawrenceville, NJ 08648 • AASL ACRL LITA YALSA LIRT

Lebanon Public Library • Betty D. Amico • Lebanon, IL 62254

Lebanon Union High School • Andrea Arlington • Lebanon, OR 97355

Lectorum Publications Inc. • New York, NY 10011 • Subscribing

Ledyard Board of Education • Ledyard, CT 06339

Lee College Learning Resources Center • Kenneth Roach • Baytown, TX 77520-4703 • ACRL ALCTS ASCLA LAMA LITA RASD GODORT

Lee County Library System • Dorothy M. Schirtzinger • Fort Myers, FL 33901 • AASL ACRL ALCTS ALSC ALTA ASCLA LAMA LITA PLA RASD YALSA CLENE EMIERT GODORT IFRT LHRT LRRT SORT SRRT

Lee County Public Library • Bishopville, SC 29010 • PLA NMRT

Lees-McRae College Carson Library • Richard Jackson • Banner Elk, NC 28604 • ACRL

Legis Lib of Saskatchewan • Marian J. Powell • Regina SK, S4S 0B3 Canada

Legislative Library of Manitoba • Susan E. Bishop • Winnipeg MB, R3C 1T5 Canada • ACRL ALCTS LAMA LITA RASD GODORT IFRT

Lehighton Memorial Library • Lehighton, PA 18235

Lenoir-Rhyne College Carl A. Rudisill Library • A. Curtis Paul • Hickory, NC 28603 • ACRL CLENE ILERT LIRT

Lesley College Library • Nancy B. Isaacs • Cambridge, MA 02138 • AASL ACRL ALCTS YALSA

Leslie County Public Library • Mason T. Collett • Hyden, KY 41749 • PLA

Levi E. Coe Library • Karen Smith • Middlefield, CT 06455-0458 • ALSC PLA YALSA

Lewis & Clark Library System • Margaret Stefanak • Edwardsville, IL 62025 • ACRL ALTA LITA RASD

Lewis-Clark State College Library • Paul Krause • Lewiston, ID 83501 • ACRL ALCTS GODORT

Lewiston Auburn College Library • Evelyn A. Greenlaw • Lewiston, ME 04240 • ACRL

Lexecon • Mary A. Peyovich • Chicago, IL 60604 • NMRT *Subscribing*

Lexington High School Library • Molly Pellicciaro • Lexington, VA 24450-9807 • YALSA IFRT

Lib Assn of Warehouse Pt • Vincent J. Bologna • East Windsor, CT 06088

Lib Dept Bee Cnty Coll • Charles P. Thomas • Beeville, TX 78102 • ACRL

Lib Design & Equipment Co • Library, PA 15129 • LAMA

Lib Equipment Dealers Assn • Jim Malise • Allentown, PA 18102

Liberty County Library • Cindy Rooley • Chester, MT 59522 • PLA

Liberty High School Media Center • Karen L. Bertel • Colorado Springs, CO 80920 • AASL

Libertyville High School Library • Anna Marie Kelly • Libertyville, IL 60048

Libraries Online Inc • William Edge • Middletown, CT 06457

Library Binding Institute • Sally Grauer • Edina, MN 55439 • AASL ACRL ALCTS *Subscribing*

Library Board of West Australia Alexander Library • Lynn Allen • Perth WA 6000, Australia • ACRL

Library Bureau Inc. • Rudolph F. Scialdo • Herkimer, NY 13350 • Subscribing

Library Conservatorium of Music • Joanna Parkes • Sydney NSW 2000, Australia • ACRL RASD

Library of Congress • James H. Billington • Washington, DC 20541 • AASL ACRL ALCTS ALSC ALTA ASCLA LAMA LITA PLA RASD YALSA

Library of Congress Prof. Guild AFSCME Local 2910 • Washington, DC 20540

Library of Michigan • James W. Fry • Lansing, MI 48909 • AASL ACRL ALCTS ALSC ALTA ASCLA LAMA LITA PLA RASD YALSA CLENE EMIERT ERT FLRT GODORT IFRT ILERT IRRT LHRT LIRT LRRT MAGERT NMRT SORT

Lima Public Library • James F. Bouchard • Lima, OH 45801

Lincoln-Lawrence-Franklin Regional Library • Brookhaven, MS 39601 • PLA

Lincoln City Libraries • Carol J. Connor • Lincoln, NE 68508 • AASL ACRL ALCTS ALSC ALTA ASCLA LITA PLA RASD YALSA

Lincoln College McKinstry Library • June Burke • Lincoln, IL 62656 • ACRL LIRT LRRT

Lincoln County Library System • Mary Lynn Corbett • Kemmerer, WY 83101 • ALCTS ALSC LAMA PLA RASD

Lincoln Elementary School • Ann Marlow • Monticello, IL 61856 • AASL

Lincoln High School Lib • Margaret J. England • Stockton, CA 95207 • AASL

Lincoln Land Community College Learning Resource Center • Mike Davis • Springfield, IL 62794-9256 • ACRL ALCTS RASD IFRT LIRT SRRT

Lincoln Library • Carl W. Volkmann • Springfield, IL 62701 • ALCTS ALSC ALTA ASCLA LAMA LITA PLA RASD YALSA

Lincoln Orens School Library • Martha Manz • Island Park, NY 11558 • AASL

Lincoln Parish Library • Julia King Avant • Ruston, LA 71270 • PLA

Lincoln Public Schools • Josephine Sheffield • Lincoln, NE 68502 • AASL LITA YALSA

Lincoln Public Schools Library Media Services • Donna L. Peterson • Lincoln, NE 68510 • AASL LITA YALSA

Lincoln Trail Libraries System • Janice Beck Ison • Champaign, IL 61821-1068 • AASL ACRL ALCTS ALTA ASCLA LAMA LITA PLA RASD YALSA AFLRT CLENE EMIERT ERT FLRT GODORT IFRT ILERT IRRT LHRT LIRT LRRT MAGERT NMRT SORT SRRT VRT

Lincoln University Inman E. Page Library • Jefferson City, MO 65102-0029 • AASL ACRL ALCTS ALSC LAMA LITA RASD YALSA

Lincoln University Langston Hughes Memorial Library • Lincoln University, PA 19352 • ACRL

Lincolnwood Pub Lib Dist • Cynthia A. Josephs • Lincolnwood, IL 60646

Linda Hall Library • Louis E. Martin • Kansas City, MO 64110 • ACRL ALCTS LAMA RASD

Lindenhurst Memorial Library • Lindenhurst, NY 11757 • ALCTS ALSC LAMA PLA RASD YALSA

Lindenwold Public Library • Lindenwold, NJ 08021

Linfield College Northup Library • Lynn K. Chmelir • McMinnville, OR 97128 • AASL ACRL ALCTS LAMA RASD GODORT LIRT

Lisbon Village Library • Patricia L. de Belloy Williams • Lisbon, ME 04250

Literacy Volunteers of America • Helen Crouch • Syracuse, NY 13214

Lithuanian Library Association of America • Kristina M. Mengeling • Woodstock, IL 60098

Little Chute High School • Carolyn Servais • Little Chute, WI 54140

Little Silver Public Library • Susan Edwards • Little Silver, NJ 07739

Live Oak County Library • Opal Miller • George West, TX 78022

Logan College of Chiropractic Learning Resources Center • Rosemary E. Buhr • Chesterfield, MO 63006-1065 • ACRL

London Board of Education Professional Library • London, ON, N6A 5L1 Canada • AASL ACRL ALSC YALSA

London Public Libraries • R. Osborne • London ON, N6B 3L7 Canada • ACRL ALCTS ALSC LAMA LITA PLA RASD YALSA

Lonesome Pine Regional Library • Richardia S. Johnson • Wise, VA 24293

Long Beach Public Library • Cordelia Howard • Long Beach, CA 90802-4482 • ACRL ALCTS ALSC LAMA LITA RASD YALSA EMIERT GODORT IFRT LRRT MAGERT SORT SRRT

Long Island University Brentwood Campus Library • Joong Suk Kim • Brentwood, NY 11717 • ACRL

Long Island University Library School Library • Ellen B. Weinstein • Greenvale, NY 11548 • AASL ACRL ALCTS ALSC ALTA ASCLA LAMA PLA RASD YALSA EMIERT FLRT GODORT IFRT ILERT IRRT LIRT LRRT MAGERT NMRT SORT SRRT

Loogootee Public Library • Vicky Doyle • Loogootee, IN 47553

Lorain Cnty Cmnty Coll Lib • Leslie Z. Loranth • Elyria, OH 44035 • ACRL

Lorain Public Library • Pauline Demaree • Lorain, OH 44052

Los Alamos High School Library • Los Alamos, NM 87544 • AASL YALSA

Los Angeles County Law Library • Richard T. Iamele • Los Angeles, CA 90012 • ACRL LITA RASD

Los Angeles Public Library • Los Angeles, CA 90033 • AASL ALSC PLA

Los Angeles Public Library • Elizabeth Martinez Smith • Los Angeles, CA 90071 • AASL ACRL ALCTS ALSC ALTA LAMA LITA PLA RASD YALSA

Los Angeles Public Library • Robert Reagan • Los Angeles, CA 90033 • LAMA PLA

Los Medanos College • A. Donatelli • Pittsburg, CA 94565

Loudonville Public Library • Susan L. Vermilya • Loudonville, OH 44842 • LAMA PLA YALSA

Louise Adelia Read Mem Lib • Hancock, NY 13783

Louisiana Baptist Convention Mae Lee Mem Library/Archives • Kathy L. Sylvest • Alexandria, LA 71309

Louisiana Library Association • Baton Rouge, LA 70821

Louisiana State Univ Libs Middleton Library • D. W. Schneider • Baton Rouge, LA 70803-3342 • AASL ACRL ALCTS ALSC ALTA LAMA LITA PLA RASD YALSA ERT FLRT GODORT NMRT SRRT

Louisiana State Univ Libs Troy H. Middleton Library • October R. Ivins • Baton Rouge, LA 70803-3342 • ACRL ALCTS

Louisiana State University James C. Bolton Library • Anna Burns • Alexandria, LA 71302-9633 • ACRL ALCTS LITA RASD

Louisville Free Public Library • Harriet Henderson • Louisville, KY 40203-2257 • ACRL ALCTS ALSC ALTA ASCLA LAMA LITA PLA RASD SORT

Louisville High School • Woodland Hls, CA 91364 • AASL

Lourdes College Library • Sylvania, OH 43560 • ACRL

Lowell Public Library • Virginia Maravilla • Lowell, IN 46356

Lower Moreland High Sch Lib • J. Tumas • Huntingdon Valley, PA 19006 • AASL

Loyola Marymount University Charles Von Der Ahe Library • Los Angeles, CA 90045 • ACRL ALCTS LAMA RASD

Loyola University E.M. Cudahy Memorial Library • Ellen J. Waite • Chicago, IL 60626 • ACRL ALCTS LAMA LITA RASD

Loyola University Library • Mary Lee Sweat • New Orleans, LA 70118 • ACRL ALCTS LAMA LITA RASD GODORT LIRT SORT

Lubbock City-County Library • Jeffrey A. Rippel • Lubbock, TX 79401 • AASL ACRL ALCTS ALSC LAMA LITA PLA RASD YALSA

Lufkin Sr High Sch Lib • Mary Goodwin • Lufkin, TX 75901 • AASL

Luther Burbank High Sch Lib • Marian Kan • Sacramento, CA 95823 • AASL

Luther Northwestern Seminary Library • Norman G. Wente • Saint Paul, MN 55108 • ACRL

Lydia Bruun Woods Mem Lib • Hope Schawang • Falls City, NE 68355 • PLA

Lynchburg College • Mary Scudder • Lynchburg, VA 24501 • ACRL LAMA LITA RASD

Lyons Public Library • Winifred Koukol • Lyons, IL 60534

M. Alice Chapin Memorial Library • Mary K. Downing • Marion, MI 49665

M. D. Anderson Hospital Research Medical Library • Houston, TX 77030

M.J. Industries, Inc. • Gerard L. Blanchet • Georgetown, MA 01833 • Subscribing

M.S. Biesecker Public Library • Eleanor L. Schrock • Somerset, PA 15501

MPI Home Video • Sam Citro • Oak Forest, IL 60452 • VRT *Subscribing*

MacCormac Junior College Library • Barbara Walters • Chicago, IL 60604

Macmillan Library Services Div of Macmillan Publ Co • Harriet Thomas • New York, NY 10022 • Subscribing

Macomb County Library • Carol F. Goodwin • Mount Clemens, MI 48044 • AASL ACRL ALCTS ALSC ASCLA LAMA PLA RASD GODORT

Macomb Library for the Blind & Physically Handicapped • Linda Champion • Mount Clemens, MI 48044

Macon Cnty-Tuskegee Pub Lib • Annie M. Lucas • Tuskegee, AL 36083 • PLA

Macon College Library • James R. Macklin • Macon, GA 31297 • ACRL

Macquarie University Library Serials Section • B. Mitcheson • NSW 2109, Australia • ACRL ALCTS LAMA LITA RASD

Madison Business College Library • Suellen S. Briggs • Madison, WI 53705 • ACRL LIRT LRRT

Madison Parish Library • Gay C. Yerger • Tallulah, LA 71282 • PLA

Madison Public Library • Nancy Sabbe • Madison, SD 57042 • PLA

Madison Public Library • Louise Kern • Madison, IL 62060

Madisonville Community College • Jacquelyn Beeler Calvert • Madisonville, KY 42431 • ACRL LITA

Madrid-Waddington Ctrl Sch • Madrid, NY 13660 • AASL YALSA LIRT

Mahidol University Library & Information Center • Vipa Goysookho • Nakorpathom 73170, Thailand • ACRL ALCTS LAMA RASD

Mahoning Law Library Association • Youngstown, OH 44503 • ACRL ALCTS LAMA LITA RASD

Mahwah High School • Ronald Bennett • Mahwah, NJ 07430 • AASL

Maine Library Association • Cathy Callahan • Augusta, ME 04330

Maitland Public Library • Dusty S. Gres • Maitland, FL 32751 • ALCTS ALSC ALTA LAMA PLA RASD

Malmo Staobibl • Suen Nilsson • Malmo, 221 42, Sweden • LAMA RASD

Malta High School Library • Barbara J. Galt • Malta, MT 59538

Manchester Polytechnic • I. Rogerson • Manchester M15 6BH, England • ACRL ALCTS LITA RASD

Manchester Township Library • Dorothy Davies • Manchester, MI 48158

Manchester Twp Middle Sch • Lakehurst, NJ 08733 • AASL

Manhattan College Cardinal Hayes Library • Harry E. Welsh • Bronx, NY 10471 • ACRL

Manhattan Pub Lib Dist • Judy Bunting • Manhattan, IL 60442

Manitoba Culture, Heritage Public Library Services • Sylvia Nicholson • Brandon MB, R7A 7A1 Canada • ALCTS ASCLA LAMA PLA YALSA

Manitoba Education Library • Winnipeg MB, R3G 0T3 Canada • AASL

Mankato State University Memorial Library • Dale K. Carrison • Mankato, MN 56002-8400 • AASL ACRL ALCTS ALSC ALTA ASCLA LAMA LITA PLA RASD YALSA GODORT LIRT MAGERT SORT

Maple Shade School • Vicki Alfano • Maple Shade, NJ 08052 • AASL

Maplewood Public Library • Michele A. Seipp • Maplewood, MO 63143

Marburger Stempel-Erzeugung • Marburg 3550, Germany • Subscribing

Marengo-Union Elem Dist #165 • Marengo, IL 60152 • AASL

Margaret Cooper Public Library • Susanne Robb • Linton, IN 47441

Minkler Library Education Centre • Willowdale ON, M2N 5N8 Canada • AASL ACRL ALCTS RASD YALSA

Minneapolis Pub Lib & Inf Ctr • Swan Goldberg • Minneapolis, MN 55401-1992 • AASL ALCTS ALSC ALTA ASCLA LAMA LITA PLA RASD YALSA GODORT

Minnesota Ctr for Arts Edu • Golden Valley, MN 55422

Minnesota Library Association • JoAnne Kelty • Minneapolis, MN 55411

Minnesota Sch of Prof Psych • Clare F. Lee • Minneapolis, MN 55414-1589 • ACRL LITA

Minnie Cline Elementary School Library • Deborah Lymer • Savannah, MO 64485

Mishawaka-Penn Public Library • David J. Eisen • Mishawaka, IN 46544

Mississauga Public Library • Donald M. Mills • Mississauga ON, L5B 2N6 Canada • LAMA PLA RASD YALSA

Mississippi Library Association • Sharon Buchanan • Jackson, MS 39289-1448 • GODORT

Mississippi State University Mitchell Memorial Library • George R. Lewis • Mississippi State, MS 39762 • AASL ACRL ALCTS ALSC ASCLA LAMA LITA PLA RASD

Mississippi University for Women Fant Memorial Library • David L. Payne • Columbus, MS 39701

Missouri Baptist College • Nitsa S. Hindeleh • Creve Coeur, MO 63141 • ACRL ALCTS LAMA

Missouri Library Association • Jean Ann McCartney • Columbia, MO 65201 • ERT IFRT

Missouri Library Network Corp. • Mary Mercante • Saint Louis, MO 63141 • ALCTS LITA

Missouri State Library • Monteria Hightower • Jefferson City, MO 65102 • AASL ACRL ALCTS ALSC ALTA ASCLA LAMA LITA PLA RASD EMIERT GODORT IFRT SRRT

Mitchell Public Library • Jacqueline L. Traut • Mitchell, SD 57301-2596 • LITA

Mitchell Public Library • Susan Medland • Mitchell, IN 47446 • PLA

Mobile Public Library • Ann G. St. Clair • Mobile, AL 36604-3273 • ALCTS ALSC ALTA ASCLA LAMA LITA PLA RASD LAMA GODORT SORT

Modern Language Association • Daniel J. Uchitelle • New York, NY 10003 • ACRL LAMA LITA RASD

Moffat Library • Julie M. Baxter • Washingtonville, NY 10992

Mohegan Community College • Mary Kao • Norwich, CT 06360 • ACRL LAMA RASD LIRT

Mokena Community Public Library District • Beth M. Mitchell • Mokena, IL 60448

Moline Public Library • Sherrie E. Snyder • Moline, IL 61265

Monash Univ Coll Gippsland Library • J. Martin • Churchill VIC, Australia • AASL ACRL ALCTS ALSC LITA RASD

Monash University Library • E.H. T. Lim • Clayton VIC 3168, Australia • ACRL ALCTS LITA RASD

Monmouth College Library • Gillian S. Gremmels • Monmouth, IL 61462-9989 • ACRL

Monmouth Junction School • Nathan Levy • Monmouth Junction, NJ 08852 • AASL

Monroe Cnty Cmnty Coll Lib • Susan Moore • Monroe, MI 48161 • ACRL ALCTS LITA RASD

Monroe County Library System • Gordon M. Conable • Monroe, MI 48161 • PLA

Monroe County Library System • Richard Panz • Rochester, NY 14604 • ACRL ALCTS ALSC ALTA LAMA LITA PLA CLENE

Monroe County Public Library • Robert A. Trinkle • Bloomington, IN 47408 • AASL ALCTS PLA RASD

Montana Library Association • Deborah L. Schlesinger • Helena, MT 59601

Montana Off of Public Instr Resource Center • Cheri Y. Bergeron • Helena, MT 59602 • AASL ALSC

Montana State Library • Richard T. Miller • Helena, MT 59620 • AASL ACRL ALCTS ALSC ALTA ASCLA LAMA LITA PLA RASD YALSA

Montauk Library • Karen Rade • Montauk, NY 11954 • ALTA PLA

Monterey County Free Libraries • Dallas Y. Shaffer • Salinas, CA 93901

Montgomery Cnty Dept of Pub Libs • Agnes M. Griffen • Rockville, MD 20850 • PLA

Montgomery College • Lynda B. Logan • Rockville, MD 20850

Montgomery College Germantown Campus Library • Gail Wood • Germantown, MD 20874

Montgomery College Takoma Park Campus Edu Supp Serv • Nancy J. Nuell • Silver Spring, MD 20912

Montgomery County Library System • Conroe, TX 77301 • LAMA PLA

Monticello High School • Lois Doherty • Monticello, IL 61856 • AASL ALSC

Montpelier-Harrison Pub Lib • Nancy S. Neff • Montpelier, IN 47359

Montreat-Anderson College Library • Elizabeth Pearson • Montreat, NC 28757 • ACRL ALCTS RASD

Montrose County School District RE-1J • Roger H. Lake • Montrose, CO 81402 • AASL ALSC YALSA

Montvale Free Public Library • Susan J. Ruttenber • Montvale, NJ 07645 • RASD YALSA

Moon Township Public Library • Kathy Woodruff • Coraopolis, PA 15108 • PLA

Moonbeam Publications, Inc. • Grosse Pointe, MI 482236 • Subscribing

Moore College of Art Library • Paula A. Feid • Philadelphia, PA 19103 • ACRL ALCTS LAMA RASD IFRT LIRT

Moore Free Library • Cynthia W. Nau • Newfane, VT 05345

Moorestown High Sch Media Ctr • Selena H. Berdosh • Moorestown, NJ 08057 • AASL YALSA

Moorestown Library • Ethel Klingerman • Moorestown, NJ 08057 • ALCTS ALSC ALTA LAMA LITA RASD

Mooresville Public Library • Patricia A. Vahey • Mooresville, IN 46158 • PLA

Moorpark College Library • Edward F. Tennen • Moorpark, CA 93021 • ACRL

Moravian Coll & Theo Sem Reeves Library • Bethlehem, PA 18018 • ACRL ALCTS RASD LIRT

Morgan County Public Library • Wanda R. Allen • Martinsville, IN 46151

Morongo Community Library • Katharine E. Weiner • Banning, CA 92220 • EMIERT

Morrisson-Reeves Library • Richmond, IN 47374 • ALSC LAMA RASD

Mother McAuley Liberal Arts High School Library • Patricia McGreal • Chicago, IL 60642 • AASL

Mounds Park Academy • Elizabeth Chmelik • St Paul, MN 55109 • AASL YALSA

Mount Allison University Ralph Pickard Bell Library • Tom Eadie • Sackville NB, E0A 3C0 Canada • ACRL ALCTS RASD

Mount Aloysius College Library • Eileen M. Bentsen • Cresson, PA 16630-1999 • ACRL ALCTS ASCLA RASD

Mount Angel Abbey • Hugh Feiss • St. Benedict, OR 97373 • ACRL ALCTS LITA

Mount Holyoke College Williston Memorial Library • South Hadley, MA 01075-1493 • ACRL ALCTS LAMA LITA RASD

Mount Mary College Haggerty Library • E. Joan Korsmeyer • Milwaukee, WI 53222 • ACRL

Mount Mercy College J. Edward Lundy Library • Marilyn Murphy • Cedar Rapids, IA 52402 • ACRL ALCTS RASD

Mount Morris Consolidated • Mt Morris, MI 48458

Mount Morris Public Library • Rebecca McCanse • Mt Morris, IL 61054

Mount Olive High School • John A. Young • Flanders, NJ 07836 • AASL YALSA LIRT LRRT

Mount Pleasant Public Library • Lesley M. Sandlin • Mt. Pleasant, TX 75455 • PLA

Mount Prospect Public Library • Marilyn G. Genther • Mount Prospect, IL 60056 • ALCTS ALSC ALTA LAMA LITA PLA RASD

Mount Pulaski District Library • Jo Richner • Mt. Pulaski, IL 62548 • PLA

Mount Saint Vincent Univ Lib • Lucien Bianchini • Halifax NS, B3M 2J6 Canada • ACRL ALCTS LAMA RASD

Mount Zion District Library • Beverly J. Obert • Mt. Zion, IL 62549 • PLA

Mountain Plains Lib Assn c/o I.D. Weeks Library • Joseph R. Edelen • Vermillion, SD 57069-2390

Msgr Kelly High School • Beaumont, TX 77707 • AASL

Mt Wachusett Cmnty Coll Lib • Linda R. Oldach • Gardner, MA 01440 • ACRL

Muehl Public Library • Virginia Trost • Seymour, WI 54165

Mulder's Red Carpet Moving & Storage • Richard Benthin • Kalamazoo, MI 49004 • ACRL LAMA PLA *Subscribing*

Multnomah County Library • Ginnie Cooper • Portland, OR 97212 • ALTA PLA

Multnomah Press • Dick Sleeper • Portland, OR 97266 • ERT *Subscribing*

Muncie-Ctr Twp Pub Lib • Patricia Schaefer • Muncie, IN 47305

Municipal Ref Library • Wilma J. Dewey • Los Angeles, CA 90012 • ACRL LAMA

Munson Medical Center • N. L. Powers • Traverse City, MI 49684-2386 • ASCLA

Murphy Public Library • Doris Carrington • Murphy, NC 28906 • PLA NMRT

Museum of Modern Art Library • Clive Phillpot • New York, NY 10019-5498 • ACRL ALCTS LAMA LITA RASD ERT IFRT IRRT SRRT

Museum of Science Library • Boston, MA 02114-1099 • AASL ALSC

Music Library Association • A. Ralph Papakhian • Bloomington, IN 47405

Muskegon County Library • Elizabeth Winsche • Muskegon, MI 49442-1094 • ALSC ALTA PLA RASD

N C Ctrl Univ • Benjamin F. Speller • Durham, NC 27707 • AASL ACRL ALCTS ALSC ALTA ASCLA LAMA LITA PLA RASD YALSA EMIERT ERT FLRT GODORT IFRT ILERT IRRT LHRT LIRT LRRT MAGERT NMRT SORT SRRT

N C Dept of Cultural Resources State Library • Howard F. McGinn • Raleigh, NC 27601-2807 • AASL ACRL ALCTS ALSC ALTA ASCLA LAMA LITA PLA RASD YALSA

N Georgia Tech Inst Library • Dawn Adams • Clarkesville, GA 30523

N Harris Montgomery Cmnty Coll Learning Resources Tech Ctr • Anne R. Strommer • Houston, TX 77060 • ACRL ALCTS LAMA LITA RASD GODORT

N Hennepin Cmnty Coll Lib • Lawrence R. Cullen • Brooklyn Park, MN 55445 • ACRL ALCTS LAMA LITA RASD

NB Kinokuniya Co. Ltd. • Yasushi Sakai • Hongo Tokyo 113(KIN), Japan • ACRL ALCTS LITA RASD

NELINET Inc. • Marshal Keys • Newton, MA 02162 • AASL ACRL ALCTS ASCLA LAMA LITA RASD CLENE EMIERT GODORT

Nantahala Regional Library • Murphy, NC 28906 • ALTA PLA

Nanuet Public Library • Patricia Brunsman • Nanuet, NY 10954

Nanyang Tech Univ Lib • Singpore, 2263, Singapore • ALCTS LITA

Napa City-County Library • Thomas G. Trice • Napa, CA 94559-3396 • ALCTS RASD

Naples Library • Elizabeth Warner • Naples, NY 14512 • PLA

Naples Public Library • Diane AM Rhein • Naples, ME 04055

National-Louis University Division of Learning Resources • Marilyn A. Lester • Evanston, IL 60201-1796 • AASL ACRL ALCTS ALSC LAMA LITA RASD

National Archives, The • Washington, DC 20408 • ACRL ALCTS LITA RASD

National Assembly Library • Hyo Soon Song • Seoul 150-703, North Korea

National Central Library • Chi-chun Tseng • Taipei, 100, Taiwan • AASL ACRL ALCTS ASCLA LAMA LITA PLA RASD YALSA GODORT

National Defense University • Sarah A. Mikel • Washington, DC 20319 • AFLRT

National Gallery of Art Library • Neal T. Turtell • Washington, DC 20565 • ACRL ALCTS ALTA LAMA LITA RASD FLRT LRRT SORT

National Institute Dev Admin Library & Information Center • Navanit Intrama • Bangkok 24, Thailand • ACRL ALCTS LAMA LITA

National Institutes of Health Clinic Center Library • Carolyn P. Brown • Bethesda, MD 20892 • ASCLA

National Judicial College Law Library • Reno, NV 89557

National Librarians Association • Alma, MI 48801

National Library • Hedwig Anuar • Singapore, Singapore • AASL ACRL ALCTS ALSC ALTA ASCLA LAMA LITA PLA RASD YALSA ERT FLRT IRRT LIRT LRRT MAGERT SRRT

National Library Mulitlingual Biblio Service • Marie F. Zielinska • Ottawa ON, K1A 0N4 Canada • ALCTS IRRT

National Library Service • Papua, New Guinea

National Library of Australia • H. Bryan • Canberra ACT 2600, Australia • AASL ACRL ALCTS ALTA ASCLA LAMA LITA PLA RASD YALSA CLENE ERT FLRT GODORT IRRT LHRT LIRT MAGERT

National Library of Canada Information Technical Services • Ottawa ON, K1A 0N4 Canada • AASL ACRL ALCTS ALSC ALTA ASCLA LAMA LITA PLA RASD YALSA ERT FLRT GODORT IRRT LHRT LIRT LRRT NMRT SORT

National Library of Medicine • Bethesda, MD 20894 • ACRL ALCTS LAMA LITA RASD

National Library of New Zealand • Elaine N. Hall • Wellington, 6001, New Zealand • AASL ACRL ALCTS ALSC ALSC LAMA LITA PLA RASD

National Library of Scotland • I. McGowan • Edinburgh EH1 1EW, Scotland • ACRL ALCTS LAMA RASD

National Library of Wales • Aberystwyth SY23 3BU, England

National Security Archive • Washington, DC 20036

National Sporting Library,Inc. • Middleburg, VA 22117

National Taiwan Normal University Library • Taipei, Taiwan • AASL ACRL ALCTS ALSC LAMA LITA RASD YALSA LRRT

National University of Singapore Central Library • Peggy Wai Chee Hochstadt • Singapore 0511, Singapore • ACRL ALCTS LAMA LITA RASD

Natl Ctr for Social Policy and Practice Information Center • Charlotte Perry • Silver Spring, MD 20910 • RASD

Natl Inst of Environmental Health Science Library (NIEHS) • W. Davenport Robertson • Research Triangle Pk, NC 27709 • LITA FLRT

Natl Register Publ Co • Ida M. Teverbaugh • Wilmette, IL 60091 • LITA PLA RASD *Patron*

Natl Taiwan Univ Lib Serials Section D • Zu-Zan Yang • Taipei 10764 ROC, Taiwan

Natrona County Public Library • Janus F. Olsen • Casper, WY 82601-2598 • ALCTS LAMA LITA PLA RASD

Natrona County School District 1 Library Service Coordinator • Casper, WY 82601 • AASL

Naval Construction Bn Ctr (NCBC) • Eleanor V. Manos • Port Hueneme, CA 93043-5000 • AFLRT

Naval Weapons Station • Yorktown, VA 23691 • PLA AFLRT

Naval Weapons Support Center • Crane, IN 47522-5011

Nazareth Academy Library • La Grange Park, IL 60525

Neal Junior High School • No Chicago, IL 60064 • ALSC IFRT

Nebraska Library Association • Fiona M. Turnbull • Bellevue, NE 68005

Nebraska Library Commission • Rod Wagner • Lincoln, NE 68508 • AASL ACRL ALCTS ALSC ALTA LAMA LITA PLA RASD YALSA CLENE EMIERT ERT FLRT GODORT IFRT ILERT IRRT LHRT LIRT LRRT MAGERT NMRT SORT SRRT

Neosha County Community Junior College Library • Dan W. Viergever • Chanute, KS 66720 • ACRL LAMA

Nesbitt Memorial Library • Ruth Poncik • Columbus, TX 78934

Nevada Library Association • Duncan McCoy • Boulder City, NV 89005

Nevada State Library & Archives • Joan G. Kerschner • Carson City, NV 89710 • AASL ACRL ALCTS ASCLA LAMA LITA RASD FLRT GODORT IFRT SRRT

Nevins Memorial Library • Methuen, MA 01844

New Age Publishing & Retailing Alliance (NAPRA) • Marilyn McGuire • Eastsound, WA 98245 • Subscribing

New Albany-Floyd Cnty Pub Lib • Stephen T. Day • New Albany, IN 47150 • LAMA PLA RASD

New Berlin Public Library • New Berlin, WI 53151 • LAMA PLA

New Brunswick Community College • Campbellton NB, E3N 3G7 Canada • ACRL

New Canaan Country Sch Lib • New Canaan, CT 06840

New Carlisle & Olive Township Public Library • Stephen Boggs • New Carlisle, IN 46552

New England Historic Genealogical Society • Lynne Burke • Boston, MA 02116 • ACRL ALCTS LITA

New England Inst of Tech Learning Resources Center • Sharon J. Charette • Warwick, RI 02886 • ACRL

New Fairfield Consol Sch • Judy Suchy • New Fairfield, CT 06812

New Hampshire State Library Technical Services Section • Kendall F. Wiggin • Concord, NH 03301 • AASL ACRL ALCTS ALSC ALTA ASCLA LAMA LITA PLA RASD YALSA GODORT

New Haven Free Public Library • Sumner White • New Haven, CT 06510 • ACRL ALCTS ALSC ALTA ASCLA LAMA LITA PLA RASD YALSA ILERT

New Holland Community Library • Pamela A. Snelgrove • New Holland, PA 17557

New Jersey Library Association • Patricia A. Tumulty • Trenton, NJ 08607 • ACRL PLA

New Jersey State Library Department of Education • Barbara F. Weaver • Trenton, NJ 08625-0520 • AASL ACRL ALCTS ALSC ALTA ASCLA LAMA LITA PLA RASD YALSA FLRT GODORT LRRT SRRT

New Mexico Highlands University Donnelly Library • Raul C. Herrera • Las Vegas, NM 87701 • AASL ACRL ALCTS LAMA LITA RASD YALSA GODORT LIRT LRRT MAGERT

New Mexico Library Association • Albuquerque, NM 87112

New Mexico State Library • Virginia D. Hendley • Santa Fe, NM 87503 • AASL ACRL ALSC ALTA ASCLA LAMA LITA PLA RASD YALSA

New Mexico State University at Alamogordo Library • Stanley Ruckman • Alamogordo, NM 88310-0477

New Mexico State University at Carlsbad Library-(LRC) • Julia White • Carlsbad, NM 88220 • ACRL LAMA LITA CLENE ERT

New Milford High School Library • New Milford, CT 06776 • ASCLA

New Orleans Public Library • C. Daniel Wilson • New Orleans, LA 70140 • AASL ACRL ALSC ALTA ASCLA LAMA LITA PLA RASD YALSA

New River Cmnty Coll Lib • Roberta White • Dublin, VA 24084

New Westminster Public Library • New Westminster BC, V3M 2B3 Canada • LAMA PLA RASD

New York Chiropractic Coll Lib • Daniel L. Kanaley • Seneca Falls, NY 13148-0800 • ACRL ALCTS LAMA LITA CLENE LIRT

New York Library Association • Susan Lehman Keitel • Albany, NY 12210-1802

The New York Public Library • Edwin S. Holmgren • New York, NY 10016 • AASL ACRL ALCTS ALSC ALTA LAMA LITA PLA RASD YALSA

New York Public Library Division P • Paul J. Fasana • New York, NY 10163-2240 • LITA RASD FLRT GODORT MAGERT

New York Public Library Office of Children's Services • New York, NY 10016 • AASL ALSC PLA

New York Public Library Office of Special Services • Mario M. Gonzalez • New York, NY 10016 • ASCLA EMIERT IFRT SRRT

New York Public Library Office of Technical Services • New York, NY 10016 • ACRL LAMA LITA PLA

New York Public Library Office of Young Adult Services • Mary Foggleson • New York, NY 10016 • AASL YALSA

New York Public Library Parkchester Branch Library • Wendy D. Caldiero • Bronx, NY 10462 • PLA

New York Society Library • Virginia Hass • New York, NY 10021 • ACRL

New York State Library State Education Department • Joseph F. Shubert • Albany, NY 12230 • AASL ACRL ALCTS ALSC ALTA ASCLA LAMA LITA PLA RASD YALSA CLENE EMIERT ERT FLRT GODORT IFRT IRRT IRRT LHRT LIRT LRRT MAGERT NMRT SORT SRRT

New York Tech Coll Lib • Darrow C. Wood • Brooklyn, NY 11201 • ACRL ALCTS LAMA LITA RASD EMIERT ERT SRRT

New York Times • New York, NY 10036

New York University Elmer Holmes Bobst Library • Carlton C. Rochell • New York, NY 10012 • AASL ACRL ALCTS ALSC ASCLA LAMA LITA RASD

Newark Public Library • Alex Boyd • Newark, NJ 07101-0630 • ACRL ALCTS ALSC ALTA ASCLA LAMA LITA PLA RASD YALSA CLENE EMIERT ERT GODORT IFRT LHRT LRRT MAGERT SORT SRRT

Newburgh Free Academy • Sue Delpup • Newburgh, NY 12550 • AASL YALSA

Newbury College Mewshaw Library • Brookline, MA 02146 • ACRL ALCTS LAMA LITA RASD

Newcastle Polytechnic • NE1 8ST, England • AASL ACRL ALCTS ALSC LITA PLA RASD

Newcomen Society of the U.S. Thomas Newcomen Library • Nancy Arnold • Exton, PA 19341

Newfoundland Pub Lib Serv Arts & Culture Centre • Pearce J. Penny • St. John's NF, A1B 3A3 Canada • ALTA LAMA PLA RASD

Newton North High School Library • Dorothy Powdermaker • Newton, MA 02160

Newton Public Library/Museum • Barbara Swearingen • Newton, IL 62448

Niagara Public Schools Library • Thomas J. Bugni • Niagara, WI 54151

Nicholls State University Allen J. Ellender Mem Lib • Randall A. Detro • Thibodaux, LA 70310 • AASL ACRL ALCTS LAMA LITA PLA RASD YALSA GODORT LIRT MAGERT

Nichols College Conant Library • Kay Lee • Dudley, MA 01571 • ACRL LAMA

Nicolet Area Technical College Learning Resources Center • Allan A. Mussehl • Rhinelander, WI 54501 • ACRL ALCTS LAMA LITA RASD

Niedersaechsische Staats- und Universitaetsbibliothek • V. Vogt • D-3400 Goettingen, Germany • AASL ACRL ALCTS ASCLA LAMA LITA PLA RASD YALSA LHRT

Niherst School of Languages • Judy Whilby • Port of Spain, Trinidad • ACRL

Niles Community Library • Anne Frese • Niles, MI 49120 • ALCTS ALSC ALTA LAMA LITA PLA RASD YALSA IFRT

Noblesville-Southeastern Public Library • Noblesville, IN 46060 • ALTA RASD YALSA

Nocona Public Library • Nocona, TX 76255

Nogales/Santa Cruz Cnty Lib • Helen G. Maul • Nogales, AZ 85621 • ALCTS ALSC ALTA LAMA LITA PLA RASD YALSA EMIERT IFRT IRRT

Norelius Community Library • Patricia Champman • Denison, IA 51442

Norfolk Public Library • Norfolk, VA 23510-1776 • ACRL ALCTS ALSC ALTA LAMA LITA PLA RASD YALSA

Normal Public Library • Robert L. Wegman • Normal, IL 61761 • ALSC LAMA

Norman Ross Publishing Inc. • Norman A. Ross • New York, NY 10019 • ACRL ALCTS *Subscribing*

North Adams Public Library • North Adams, MA 01247

North Adams State College Eugene L. Freel Library • Gary A. Lewis • North Adams, MA 01247 • ACRL ALCTS LITA RASD

North American Baptist Seminary Kaiser-Ramker Library • George W. Lang • Sioux Falls, SD 57105-1599 • ALCTS RASD

North Babylon Public Library • Carol Simpson • North Babylon, NY 11703 • PLA

North Bay Branch Library • Lynn Haven, FL 32444

North Bend Public Library • North Bend, OR 97459 • ALSC ALTA LAMA PLA

North Branch Township • Karen Lambert • North Branch, MI 48461 • PLA NMRT

North Carolina Agricultural & Technical State University • Alene C. Young • Greensboro, NC 27411 • ACRL ALCTS LITA RASD IFRT LRRT SORT

North Carolina Biotechnology Ctr • Nancy G. Bruce • Research Triangle Pk, NC 27709

North Carolina Ctrl Univ James E. Shepard Mem Lib • Floyd C. Hardy • Durham, NC 27707 • ACRL ALCTS LAMA LITA RASD

North Carolina Lib Assn • Raleigh, NC 27601-1023

North Carolina State University D. H. Hill Library • Susan K. Nutter • Raleigh, NC 27695-7111 • ACRL ALCTS LAMA LITA RASD MAGERT

North Country Lib Coop • Virginia, MN 55792 • ASCLA PLA

North Dakota Library Association • Betty A. Gard • Grand Forks, ND 58202-0175 • NMRT

North Dakota State Library • Bismarck, ND 58505 • AASL ACRL ALCTS ALTA LAMA LITA PLA RASD CLENE GODORT IFRT LIRT NMRT

North Dakota State University Library • John W. Beecher • Fargo, ND 58105-5599 • ACRL ALCTS LAMA LITA RASD GODORT

North Iowa Area Cmnty Coll Library • Donald Kamps • Mason City, IA 50401 • ACRL ALCTS RASD

North Middle School Library • Maryanne Beninati • Great Neck, NY 11023 • AASL YALSA

North Platte Public Library • Wilma L. McFarland • North Platte, NE 69101

North Shore Community College Learning Shore Community College • Anne M. Johnsen • Danvers, MA 01923-4017 • ACRL ALCTS LITA RASD LIRT

North Shore Country Day School • Leslie Trainer • Winnetka, IL 60093 • AASL LITA

North Smithfield Public Library • Carol H. Brouwer • Slatersville, RI 02876

North Suburban Library System • Sarah Ann Long • Wheeling, IL 60090 • AASL ACRL ALCTS ALSC ALTA ASCLA LAMA LITA PLA RASD YALSA CLENE EMIERT ERT FLRT GODORT IFRT ILERT IRRT LHRT LIRT LRRT MAGERT NMRT SORT SRRT

North Syracuse Free Library • Jill Reichel • Syracuse, NY 13212

North Tonawanda Public Library • Daniel R. Killian • North Tonawanda, NY 14120 • ALSC PLA

Northampton Area Public Library • Mary Beller • Northampton, PA 18067 • PLA

Northampton Cnty Public Schs • Nancy H. Lecato • Eastville, VA 23347 • AASL

Northampton County Area Community College-LRC • Bethlehem, PA 19103 • ACRL LITA RASD

Northeast Harbor Library • Robert R. Pyle • Northeast Hbr, ME 04662 • ALTA

Northeast Missouri State • Kirksville, MO 63501 • AASL ACRL ALCTS ALSC ASCLA LAMA LITA RASD GODORT LIRT

Northeast Texas Cmnty Coll Learning Resource Center • William L. Dey • Mount Pleasant, TX 75455 • ACRL ALCTS RASD

Northeastern Illinois Univ Lib • Bradley F. Baker • Chicago, IL 60625 • AASL ACRL ALCTS ASCLA LAMA LITA PLA RASD YALSA

Northeastern Junior College Library • Francis E. Medaris • Sterling, CO 80751-2399 • ACRL

Northern British University • Patricia Appavoo • Prince George BC, V2L 5P2 Canada • ACRL ALCTS LAMA LITA RASD

Northern Highlands Rgnl High Sch Library • Patricia Ricconbene • Allendale, NJ 07401 • AASL

Northern Illinois Library System • Rockford, IL 61108 • AASL ACRL ALCTS ALSC ALTA ASCLA LAMA LITA PLA RASD YALSA ILERT LIRT

Northern Illinois University Dept of Lib & Inf Studies • Cosette Kies • DeKalb, IL 60115

Northern Illinois University University Libraries • Norman E. Vogt • DeKalb, IL 60115-2868 • AASL ACRL ALCTS ALSC ASCLA LAMA LITA PLA RASD YALSA CLENE FLRT GODORT IFRT IRRT LIRT MAGERT NMRT SORT SRRT

Northern Nevada Cmnty Coll • Juanita P. Karr • Elko, NV 89801 • ACRL LAMA LITA

Northern State Prison Library • Gail Gillespie • Newark, NJ 07114

Northern Waters Library Service • Mike Cross • Ashland, WI 54806

Northwest Christian College Learning Resource Center • Margaret Sue Rhee • Eugene, OR 97401 • ACRL ALCTS LAMA LITA LIRT

Northwest College John Taggart Hinckley Library • Jerome H. Halpin • Powell, WY 82435 • ACRL

Northwest Nazarene College Riley Library • Randall C. Simmons • Nampa, ID 83686 • ACRL ALCTS LAMA RASD

Northwest Ohio Literacy Council • Rose Marie Duffy • Lima, OH 45801

Northwestern Connecticut Community College Library • Arthur Pethybridge • Winisted, CT 06098 • ALCTS

Northwestern University Library • John P. McGowan • Evanston, IL 60208-2300 • ACRL ALCTS LAMA LITA RASD YALSA GODORT IRRT MAGERT

Norton Memorial Library • Landrum Salley • Pineville, LA 71360

Norwalk Community College Learning Resource Center • Carmen L. Bayles • Norwalk, CT 06854-1655 • ACRL RASD

Notre Dame Academy for Girls • Gloria A. Lukacovic • Los Angeles, CA 90064 • AASL

Notre Dame College of Ohio • Sandra Harris • Cleveland, OH 44121 • ACRL

Notre Dame Seminary Library • Jules A. Tate • New Orleans, LA 70118

Notre Dame Womens College • Mary Michael • Kyoto, Japan • ACRL ALCTS LAMA LIRT

Nottingham High School • Trenton, NJ 08619 • AASL YALSA

Nova Scotia Provincial Library • Marion L. Pape • Halifax NS, B3L 4S4 Canada • AASL ACRL ALSC ALTA LAMA LITA PLA RASD IFRT SRRT

Nova University Einstein Library • Fort Lauderdale, FL 33314 • ACRL

Nutley Free Public Library • Cynthia C. Chamberlin • Nutley, NJ 07110 • PLA RASD YALSA

Nutley High Sch Lib • Jo Ann A. Tropiano • Nutley, NJ 07110 • AASL YALSA

Nyack College Library • Donald E. Keeney • Nyack, NY 10960 • ACRL ALCTS LAMA LITA RASD LIRT LRRT SRRT

Nyack Library • James J. Mahoney • Nyack, NY 10960 • LAMA PLA YALSA

Oakland City College • Robert E. Sears • Oakland City, IN 47660 • ACRL

Oakland Community College Central Warehouse • Judy Murray • Auburn Hills, MI 48326-2671 • LITA

Oakland Park City Library • Alicia McHugh • Oakland, FL 33334 • LAMA PLA

Oakland Unified School District Professional Library • Mildred H. Caver • Oakland, CA 94606 • AASL

Oakton Community College Library • Des Plaines, IL 60016 • ACRL ALCTS LAMA LITA RASD GODORT LIRT

Oakville Public Library • Eleanor James • Oakville ON, L6J 2Z4 Canada • ALCTS ALSC ALTA LITA PLA RASD

Oakwood School Library • Poughkeepsie, NY 12601 • AASL

Oberlin College Library • William A. Moffett • Oberlin, OH 44074 • ACRL ALCTS ASCLA LAMA LITA RASD

Oberlin Public Library • Oberlin, OH 44074-1626

Oblate Sch of Theo Lib • Clifford Dawdy • San Antonio, TX 78216 • ACRL ALCTS RASD

Occidental College Library • Jacquelyn A. McCoy • Los Angeles, CA 90041 • ACRL LITA RASD ALCTS

Ocean City Free Public Library • Michael Lamott Mason • Ocean City, NJ 08226-3071 • PLA

Oceanside Public Library • Helen Nelson • Oceanside, CA 92054 • ALCTS ALSC ALTA LAMA PLA RASD YALSA GODORT

Off of Lib Devel & Serv • William G. Asp • Saint Paul, MN 55101 • AASL ACRL ALCTS ALSC ALTA ASCLA LAMA LITA PLA RASD CLENE FLRT GODORT IFRT IRRT LIRT SORT SRRT

Ohio Bell Library • Jessie Martin • Cleveland, OH 44114

Ohio Bus Sales, Inc. • Thomas A. Lockshin • Canton, OH 44706 • PLA   *Subscribing*

Ohio County Public Library • Hartford, KY 42347

Ohio Dominican College • Tina Butler • Columbus, OH 43219

Ohio Library Association • Lynda Murray • Columbus, OH 43215-3840 • ERT NMRT

Ohio Public Library District • Cheryl Norden • Ohio, IL 61349 • PLA

Ohio State University Libraries • William J. Studer • Columbus, OH 43210-1286 • AASL ACRL ALCTS ALSC ALTA ASCLA LAMA LITA PLA RASD YALSA CLENE EMIERT ERT FLRT GODORT IFRT ILERT IRRT LHRT LIRT LRRT MAGERT NMRT SORT SRRT

Ohio University • David A. Wright • Zanesville, OH 43701 • ACRL ALCTS LAMA LITA RASD LIRT

Oil City Library • Kay Ensle • Oil City, PA 16301 • PLA

Oil City Sr High Sch Lib • Chris Sullivan • Oil City, PA 16301

Oil Spill Pub Inf Ctr • Mary H. McGee • Anchorage, AK 99501 • ACRL ALCTS RASD

Okaloosa-Walton Junior College Learning Resources Center • Lucy Warren • Niceville, FL 32578 • ACRL ALCTS LAMA LITA

Okanagan College Library • G. Zilm • Kelowna BC, V1Y 4X8 Canada • ACRL

Okanagan Regional Library • Lesley Dieno • Kelowna, BC, V1Y 7X8 Canada • LAMA PLA RASD YALSA

Oklahoma Baptist University • Betsy B. Aldridge • Shawnee, OK 74801-2590 • ACRL ALCTS LAMA LITA RASD GODORT

Oklahoma Christian College Library • Oklahoma City, OK 73136-1100 • ACRL RASD

Oklahoma City Schools Media Center • Oklahoma City, OK 73106 • AASL ALCTS

Oklahoma City University Dulaney-Browne Library • Danelle Hall • Oklahoma City, OK 73106 • ACRL LAMA GODORT

Oklahoma Department of Libraries • Robert L. Clark • Oklahoma City, OK 73105-3298 • AASL ACRL ALCTS ALSC ALTA ASCLA LAMA LITA PLA RASD YALSA CLENE EMIERT ERT FLRT GODORT IFRT ILERT IRRT LHRT LIRT LRRT MAGERT NMRT SORT SRRT

Oklahoma Historical Society • Edward Connie Shoemaker • Oklahoma City, OK 73105

Oklahoma Junior College • Janet S. Riggs • Tulsa, OK 74133

Oklahoma Library Association • Kay A. Boies • Edmond, OK 73013 • NMRT

Oklahoma State Univ Tech Okmulgee Learning Resource Ctr • Rebecca M. Kirkbride • Okmulgee, OK 74447-0088 • ACRL

Okmulgee Public Library • Patricia Doan • Okmulgee, OK 74447

Olathe Public Library • Kenton L. Oliver • Olathe, KS 66061

Olive Free Library Association • Rosalie Burgher • West Shokan, NY 12494

Oliver Ames High School • Kathryn A. Kenney • North East, MA 02356 • AASL YALSA

Oliver Wolcott Library • Patricia L. Joy • Litchfield, CT 06759 • ALSC PLA IFRT

Olivet College Library • Todd S. Trevorrow • Olivet, MI 49076 • ACRL ALCTS LAMA RASD LIRT

Olympic College Learning Resources Center • Ruth M. Ross • Bremerton, WA 98310 • ACRL ALCTS RASD

Omaha Home for Boys Library • Doug McElwain • Omaha, NE 68104 • AASL NMRT

Omaha Public Library • Michael Phipps • Omaha, NE 68102 • LAMA

Omnigraphics Inc. • Barbara D. Cooper • Fort Lauderdale, FL 33301 • AASL ACRL ALCTS ALSC ALTA LAMA LITA PLA RASD   *Patron*

Online Computer Lib Ctr (OCLC) • David J. Van Dyk • Dublin, OH 43017-3395 • ACRL ALCTS ASCLA LAMA LITA PLA RASD GODORT IRRT LRRT MAGERT

Ontario Institute for Studies • Toronto ON, M5S 1V6 Canada • ACRL ALCTS LAMA LITA RASD

Ontario Ministry of Education Inf Serv & Resources Unit • Roy Hilary • Toronto ON, M7A 1L2 Canada • ALCTS LAMA LITA RASD

Opelousas-Eunice Pub Lib • Walter O. Stubbs • Opelousas, LA 70570

Orange County Library System Orlando Public Library • Kuang-Pei Tu • Orlando, FL 32801-2471 • LAMA PLA

Orangeburg Library • Jack Linden • Orangeburg, NY 10962 • PLA

Orcas Island Library District • Jay Rozendaal • Eastsound, WA 98245 • ALTA YALSA

Orchard Books Division of Franklin Watts • New York, NY 10016 • AASL ALSC PLA YALSA ERT IFRT   *Subscribing*

Oregon Library Association • Salem, OR 97301

Oregon State Library • James B. Scheppke • Salem, OR 97310-0640 • AASL ACRL ALCTS ALSC ALTA ASCLA LAMA LITA PLA RASD YALSA CLENE GODORT IFRT LHRT LRRT MAGERT NMRT SORT

Oregon State University William Jasper Kerr Library • Melvin R. George • Corvallis, OR 97331-4501 • AASL ACRL ALCTS ASCLA LAMA LITA PLA RASD YALSA MAGERT

Oryx Press • Phyllis B. Steckler • Phoenix, AZ 85012-3397 • ERT   *Subscribing*

Oskaloosa Public Library • Randy L. Bellinger • Oskaloosa, IA 52577 • LAMA

Ossipee Public Library • Lindalee Lambert • Center Ossipee, NH 03814

Osterhout Free Library • Joan M. Costello • Wilkes Barre, PA 18701 • ALCTS ALSC LAMA RASD YALSA

Osterreichische Nationalbibliothek • Vienna A1014, Austria • ACRL

Otago University Library • M. J. Wooliscroft • Dunedin, New Zealand • ACRL ALCTS LITA

Otani Joshi Tanki Dai Library 942-1 • Osaka 584, Japan

Otisville Correctional Facility Library • D. Drewett • Otisville, NY 10963 • ASCLA

Ouachita Baptist University • Ray Granade • Arkadelphia, AR 71923 • ACRL

Ouachita Parish Public Library • Agnes A. Harris • Monroe, LA 71201

Our Lady Queen of Heaven School • Jacqueline Bohdan • Lake Charles, LA 70605 • AASL

Outagamie Waupaca Library System • Richard W. Krumwiede • Appleton, WI 54911 • ALSC ALTA LAMA PLA

Owens Technical College Library • Nancy Emrick • Toledo, OH 43699 • ACRL RASD

Owensboro-Daviess Cnty Pub Library • Alice Gene Lewis • Owensboro, KY 42301

Owensville Carnegie Library • Peggy Callis • Owensville, IN 47665

Oxford College O'Kelley Memorial Library • Mary McNeill • Oxford, GA 30267 • ACRL

Oxford Public Library • Jane O. Gallagher • Oxford, CT 06483

Oxford University Bodleian Library • Oxford 0X1 3BG, England • ACRL ALCTS LITA GODORT

Oxnard Public Library • Gail P. Warner • Oxnard, CA 93030

Ozark Regional Library • Ironton, MO 63650 • ALSC PLA RASD

Ozarka Technical College • Mary Ellen Hawkins • Melbourne, AR 72556 • ACRL

Ozarks Regional Library • Karen M. Duree • Fayetteville, AR 72701

Pacific NW Library Association • Carol Hilderbrand • Billings, MT 59101-0747

Packer Collegiate Institute Main Library • Brooklyn, NY 11201 • AASL YALSA LIRT

Paine College Collins-Callaway Library • Millie M. Parker • Augusta, GA 30901 • ACRL ALCTS LAMA RASD

Palisades High School Library • Nancy Leed • Kintnersville, PA 18930 • AASL

Palm Beach County Library System • Jerry W. Brownlee • West Palm Beach, FL 33406 • ACRL ALSC LAMA PLA IFRT

Palo Alto City Library • Mary Jo Levy • Palo Alto, CA 94303 • AASL ACRL ALSC LAMA LITA PLA RASD YALSA IFRT

Palo Alto College • Gloria E. Hilario • San Antonio, TX 78224

Pan Asian Pubn (USA) Inc. • Union City, CA 94587 • Subscribing

Paramus Catholic High Sch Lib • Alma J. Henderson • Paramus, NJ 07652

Paris Junior College • LuLane Caraway • Paris, TX 75460 • ACRL LAMA LITA

Parish Day School • Cheron Adams • Dallas, TX 75240 • AASL ALSC

Parkway School District • Barbara Noble • Chesterfield, MO 63017 • AASL LAMA LITA ILERT

Parmly Billings Library • William M. Cochran • Billings, MT 59101

Pasco County Library System Processing Center • Linda Allen • Port Richey, FL 34668 • ACRL ALCTS ALSC ALTA LAMA LITA PLA RASD YALSA

Passaic Township Public Library • Catherine McErlean • Stirling, NJ 07980

Passaic Valley High School • Jan Mazza • Little Falls, NJ 07424 • AASL

Patrick Henry High School • Robert A. Hall • Hamler, OH 43524

Patrick J. Stapleton Library Indiana Univ of Pennsylvania • Indiana, PA 15705 • ACRL ALCTS LAMA LITA RASD GODORT

Patten College Library • Patricia Bauer • Oakland, CA 94601

Paul D. West Prof Lib Fulton County Board of Education • East Point, GA 30344 • AASL ALSC RASD

Paul VI High School • Diane Schule • Fairfax, VA 22030

Paw Paw Public Library • Mildred H. Pritchard • Paw Paw, MI 49079

Payson Jr High Sch Lib • Irene L. Schwartzbauer • Payson, AZ 85541 • AASL IFRT

Payson Public Library • Edward P. Miller • Payson, AZ 85541

Pegasus Publishing Company, Inc. • Michael Comley • Louisville, KY 40202-1004 • Subscribing

Peirce Junior College Library • Debra Schrammel • Philadelphia, PA 19102 • ACRL

Peninsula Library System • Linda D. Crowe • San Mateo, CA 94402

Pennsylvania Library Association • Margaret S. Bauer, CAE • Harrisburg, PA 17110 • ERT

Pennsylvania State University E506 Pattee Library • Nancy M. Cline • University Park, PA 16802 • AASL ACRL ALCTS LAMA LITA PLA RASD YALSA EMIERT GODORT LIRT MAGERT SRRT

Peoria Public Library • Margareth Gibbs • Peoria, IL 61602 • ACRL ALCTS ALSC LAMA LITA PLA RASD YALSA

Pepperdine University Payson Library • Joseph McDonald • Malibu, CA 90263 • ACRL ALCTS LAMA LITA RASD

Pequot Library • Mary F. Freedman • Southport, CT 06490

Perma-Bound Books Hertzberg-New Method, Inc. • Ben Mangum • Jacksonville, IL 62650 • ALSC YALSA
Contributing

Perth Amboy Public Library • Patricia Gandy • Perth Amboy, NJ 08861

Peterson's • Carole L. Cushmore • Princeton, NJ 08543-2123 • PLA RASD
Contributing

Pettigrew Regional Library • Martha S. Smith • Plymouth, NC 27962

Philadelphia Museum of Art Library • Philadelphia, PA 19101 • ACRL

Philippi Public Library • Mary Ellen Weekley • Philippi, WV 26416 • PLA NMRT

Phillips Academy Oliver Wendell Holmes Library • Susan Noble • Andover, MA 01810 • AASL ACRL ALCTS

Phillips Cnty Cmnty Coll Library • Helena, AR 72342 • ACRL ALCTS LITA

Phillips Junior College • Gulf Port, MS 39501 • ACRL

Phillips Junior College • Nancy D. Milliken • Fayetteville, NC 28301 • ACRL

Phillips Junior College Library Condie Campus • Valeh Dabiri • Campbell, CA 95008 • ACRL

Phillips Junior College of the Mississippi Gulf Coast • Cynthia Bouchard • Gulfport, MS 39507 • ACRL

Phillips Memorial Library • Edgar C. Bailey • Providence, RI 02918 • ACRL ALCTS LAMA LITA RASD LIRT

Philo Public Library District • June E. Highsmith • Philo, IL 61864

Phoenix College Library • Georgia M. Dillard • Phoenix. AZ 85013 • ACRL ALCTS LITA RASD LIRT

Phoenix Country Day Sch Lib • Phoenix, AZ 85060

Phoenix Elem Sch Dist. 1 • Dee Deihl • Phoenix, AZ 85006-2152

Phoenixville Public Library • Joan McIntyre • Phoenixville, PA 19460

Pickard Cicero Free Library • Lois Perry • Cicero, NY 13039

Piedmont College E. Louise Patten Library • John F. Camp • Demorest, GA 30535 • ACRL

Pierce Cnty Rural Lib Dist • Carolyn J. Else • Tacoma, WA 98446 • ALCTS ALSC ALTA ASCLA LAMA LITA PLA RASD YALSA

Pike-Amite-Walthall Lib Sys • Mc Comb, MS 39648 • PLA IFRT

Pikes Peak Library District • Bernard A. Margolis • Colorado Springs, CO 80901

Pine Crest Upper School Library • John A. Wright • Ft Lauderdale, FL 33308 • AASL YALSA

Pinkerton Academy Library • Sally E. Hartikka • Derry, NH 03038 • AASL

Pioneer Library System • Mary A. Sherman • Norman, OK 73069

Pitkin County Library • Kathleen Chandler • Aspen, CO 81611

Pittsburgh Rgnl Lib Ctr • H. E. Broadbent • Pittsburgh, PA 15221 • ALCTS ASCLA LAMA LITA PLA

Pittsfield Public Library • Pittsfield, IL 62363

Pittston Library Association • Pittston, PA 18640

Placentia Library District • Elizabeth D. Minter • Placentia, CA 92670 • PLA

Plainfield Cmnty Consol Sch Dist 202, Media Serv • Eileen Diercks • Plainfield, IL 60544

Plainfield High School Library • Louise J. Oliver • Central Village, CT 06332 • AASL

Plainfield Public Library • Charr L. Skirvin • Plainfield, IN 46168 • ALCTS ALSC ALTA LAMA LITA PLA RASD YALSA

Plainfield Public Library • Karen J. Thorburn • Plainfield, NJ 07060 • ACRL ALCTS LITA PLA RASD YALSA

Plains & Peaks Rgnl Lib Sys • M Jeanne Owen • Colorado Spgs, CO 80906-1967

Plainsboro Free Public Library • Virginia V W Baeckler • Plainsboro, NJ 08536 • ALTA

Planned Parenthood Resource Ctr • Lisa DeVuono • Philadelphia, PA 19107-5740

Pleasant Company • Middleton, WI 53562 • AASL ALSC PLA
Subscribing

Plymouth Public Library • Thelma M. Kruse • Plymouth, MA 02360 • ALCTS ALSC LAMA PLA RASD

Plympton Public Library • Plympton, MA 02367

Point Loma Nazarene College Ryan Library • James D. Newburg • San Diego, CA 92106 • ACRL ALCTS LAMA LITA RASD LIRT

Pointe Claire Public Library • C. Cote • Pt. Claire PQ, H9R 4V1 Canada • ALSC PLA

Polish Welfare Association Learning Center • Joanna K. Borowiec • Chicago, IL 60641 • LITA RASD EMIERT

Polk County Public Library • Barbara Brewer • Columbus, NC 28722 • PLA

Pomperaug High School • Richard Boston • Southbury, CT 06488 • AASL IFRT LIRT

Pope John XXIII National Seminary Library • Weston, MA 02193

Popular Culture Inc. • Patricia A. Curtis • Ann Arbor, MI 48106 • PLA RASD
Subscribing

Port Arthur Indp Sch Dist Media Center • Groves, TX 77619

Port Washington Public Library • Edward de Sciora • Port Washington, NY 11050 • ALCTS ALSC ALTA LAMA LITA PLA RASD YALSA IFRT

Portage County Public Library • Leonard W. Swift • Stevens Point, WI 54481 • ALCTS ALSC PLA RASD

Porter County Public Library • Don Johnson • Valparaiso, IN 46383

Porter Memorial Hospital Medical Library • W. Robin Waters • Denver, CO 80210-5876

Portland Cmnty Coll Lib • Barbara Swanson • Portland, OR 97219 • ACRL

Portland Public Library • Sheldon B. Kaye • Portland, ME 04101 • ALCTS ALSC ALTA ASCLA LAMA LITA PLA RASD YALSA GODORT IFRT

Portland Public Schools • Richard Gilkey • Portland, OR 97208-3107 • AASL ALCTS LITA RASD YALSA

Poseyville Carnegie Pub Lib • Carol Renee Lamar • Poseyville, IN 47633

Post Elementary School • Maury Shiver • Post, TX 79356 • ALSC

Pottawatomie-Wabaunsee Regional Library • Freda J. Dobbins • Saint Marys, KS 66536 • PLA

Prairie State College • Chicago Hts, IL 60411 • ACRL

Prentice Hall General Reference Library Marketing Department • Linda Parise • New York, NY 10023 • ACRL ALCTS PLA RASD YALSA
Subscribing

Presbyterian College Library Processing Center • Lennart Pearson • Clinton, SC 29325 • AASL ACRL ALCTS RASD YALSA LIRT

Presbyterian Hist Soc Lib • Philadelphia, PA 19147 • ACRL ALCTS

Prevention Resource Center • Mary O'Brien • Springfield, IL 62704 • ASCLA

Price City Library • Pat Brown • Price, UT 84501

Price Elementary Library • Mary Achziger • Garland, TX 75043 • AASL

Prince Edward Island Prov Lib • Donald Scott • Charlottetown, PE, C1A 8T8 Canada • AASL ALCTS LITA PLA YALSA

Prince Edward Island University • C. Merritt Crockett • Charlottetown PEI, C1A 4P3 Canada • ACRL ALCTS RASD

Prince George Public Library • June Huggins-Chan • Prince George BC, V2L 5L1 Canada • ALCTS ALSC ALTA LAMA LITA PLA RASD YALSA

Prince George's Cmnty Coll Library Media Center • Leah K. Nekritz • Largo, MD 20772 • ACRL ALCTS LAMA LITA

Prince George's County Memorial Library System • William R. Gordon • Hyattsville, MD 20782-2098 • ALTA LAMA PLA

Prince Memorial Library • M. B Pawle • Cumberland Center, ME 04021

Prince William Cnty Public Lib Central Branch • Richard W. Murphy • Prince William, VA 22192 • ALCTS ALSC LAMA LITA PLA RASD YALSA

Princeton Public Library • Jacquelyn E. Thresher • Princeton, NJ 08542 • ALCTS ALSC ALTA LAMA LITA PLA RASD YALSA

Princeton Theological Seminary • James F. Armstrong • Princeton, NJ 08542 • ACRL ALCTS LAMA LITA RASD

Princeton University • Donald W. Koepp • Princeton, NJ 08544-2098 • ACRL ALCTS ASCLA LAMA LITA RASD

Private Library c/o Notre Dame-Howard • Ray Turner • South Bend, IN 46601

Professional Risk Management of California • Bernard J. Halliwell • Oakland, CA 94612

Prometheus Research Library • New York, NY 10013

Prosser Public Library • Thomas P. Schadlich • Bloomfield, CT 06002 • ALCTS ALSC PLA RASD

Provincetown Public Library • Joseph A. Poire • Provincetown, MA 02657

Proviso East High School Library • Eva B. Lewis • Maywood, IL 60153 • AASL

Proviso West High School Library • Douglas Duechler • Hillside, IL 60162

Pryor Public Library • Thomasine L. Ward • Pryor, OK 74361

Pub Affairs Inf Serv • Barbara M. Preschel • New York, NY 10036-4396 • ACRL LITA PLA RASD GODORT IRRT
Subscribing

Public Library of Charlotte & Mecklenburg County • Robert E. Cannon • Charlotte, NC 28202 • ACRL ALCTS LAMA PLA RASD YALSA

Public Library of Cincinnati & Hamilton Cnty Staff Assn • Melinda K. Caldwell • Cincinnati, OH 45202-2071

Public Library of Cincinnati and Hamilton County • James Robert Hunt • Cincinnati, OH 45202 • AASL ACRL ALCTS ALSC ALTA ASCLA LAMA LITA PLA RASD YALSA

Public Library of Des Moines • Elaine Graham Estes • Des Moines, IA 50308-1791 • ACRL ALCTS ALSC LITA RASD

Public Library of Nashville and Davidson County • Caroline Stark • Nashville, TN 37203-3585

Puerto Rico Assn of Sch Lns • Carmencita Leon • Hato Rey, PR 00919-1559

Puerto Rico Junior College • Carolina, PR 00628 • LAMA IFRT LIRT

Puget Sound Christian College • Ann Emery • Edmonds, WA 98020 • ACRL

Pulaski County Public Library • Winamac, IN 46996

Puskarich Public Library • Saundra Tate • Cadiz, OH 43907

Puyallup Public Library • Catherine G. Uhl • Puyallup, WA 98371

Quality Books Inc. • James E. Hickey • Lake Bluff, IL 60044-2204 • Subscribing

Queens Borough Public Library • Constance Cooke • Jamaica, NY 11432 • ALTA PLA RASD YALSA

Queens College Benjamin S. Rosenthal Library • Matthew J. Simon • Flushing, NY 11367-0904 • AASL ACRL ALCTS LAMA LITA PLA RASD EMIERT GODORT LIRT SRRT

Queens College Everett Library • Rosemary H. Arneson • Charlotte, NC 28274 • ACRL ALCTS LAMA LITA RASD

Queens University Douglas Library • Sheila A. Johnson • Kingston, ON, K7L 5C4 Canada • LITA

Queensborough Community College Library • Daniel Davila • Bayside, NY 11364 • ACRL ALCTS LAMA LIRT

Quincy College • Sandra Neal • Quincy, MA 02169 • ACRL

Quogue Library • L. Pastore • Quogue, NY 11959

Quogue Library Inc • Anne Realmuto • Quogue, NY 11959

R. J. Reynolds Tobacco Co. • Nellie W. Sizemore • Winston-Salem, NC 27102 • LAMA LITA
Subscribing

R.C.G. BOCES Sch Lib Sys • Renee A. Silber • Castleton, NY 12033 • AASL IFRT LIRT

REI America, Incorporation • Javier Castro • Miami, FL 33166 • ACRL PLA
Subscribing

RMIT Central Library • D. Schauder • Melbourne Vic 3000, Australia • ACRL ALCTS LAMA LITA RASD

Rachel Kohl Cmnty Lib, Inc. • Diane K. Partnoy • Concordville, PA 19331

Radio Free Europe Reference Library • Irene Dutikow • New York, NY 10019 • ACRL EMIERT

Rainy River Cmnty Coll Lib • Larry Oveson • International Falls, MN 56649 • ACRL

Ramsey County Public Library Adminstrative Offices • Norman M. Vinnes • Shoreview, MN 55126-5800 • AASL ACRL ALCTS ALTA LAMA LITA PLA RASD YALSA

Ramsey High School Library • Ramsey, NJ 07446 • AASL YALSA

Rand Afrikaans University H.F. Verwoerd Library • P. Aucamp • Johannesburg 2000, South Africa • AASL ACRL ALCTS ASCLA LITA PLA

Randwick Mun Lib Serv • Vonnie Young • Maroubra NSW 2035, Australia • ALSC

Ranken Technical College • Barbara Edwards • Saint Louis, MO 63113 • ACRL

Raquette Lake Free Library • Cheryl Morales-Frese • Raquette Lake, NY 13436

Ravenswood Hosp Mem Ctr Nursing Library • Chicago, IL 60640

Reading Area Community College • Linda C. Lawrence • Reading, PA 19603 • ACRL LAMA

Reber Memorial Library • Norma Cole • Raymondville, TX 78580

Red Bank Public Library • Gertrude Hooker • Red Bank, NJ 07701

Red River Community College Library • Patricia Bozyk • Winnipeg MB, R3H 0J9 Canada • AASL ACRL ALCTS LAMA LITA RASD

Reddick Library • Allan J. Woeckel • Ottawa, IL 61350

Redwood Falls Public Library • Redwood Falls, MN 56283

Redwood Library & Athenaeum • Erik Bradford Stocker • Newport, RI 02840-3292 • ALCTS

Reference Press, Incorporated • Patrick J. Spain • Austin, TX 78723 • PLA RASD *Subscribing*

Regina Public Library • Ken Jensen • Regina SK, S4P 3Z5 Canada • ALCTS ALSC ALTA ASCLA LAMA LITA PLA RASD

Rehoboth Beach Public Library • Margaret LaFoud • Rehoboth Beach, DE 19971

Rend Lake College Learning Resource Center • Jana Smith-Caldwell • Ina, IL 62846

Republican Valley Library System • Dee R. Yost • Hastings, NE 68901-4663

Res Libs Group Inc. (RLG) • Jennifer Hartzell • Mountain View, CA 94041-1100 • ACRL ALCTS LAMA LITA RASD IFRT IRRT MAGERT

Research Institute on Alcoholism Library • Diane Augustino • Buffalo, NY 14203 • ACRL

Retro Link Associates • Thomas W. MacDonald • Provo, UT 84601 • LITA PLA *Subscribing*

Rgnl Council Pub Libs Room 2410-12 • Wood Tin Tse • Kowloon, Hong Kong • ALCTS PLA RASD

Rhode Island College James P. Adams Library • Richard A. Olsen • Providence, RI 02908 • AASL ACRL ALCTS LAMA LITA RASD GODORT

Rhode Island Department of State Library Services • Barbara Weaver • Providence, RI 02903-4222 • AASL ACRL ALCTS ALSC ASCLA LAMA LITA PLA RASD YALSA CLENE GODORT IFRT

Rhode Island Library Association • Providence, RI 02903

Rhodes University Library • Cape Province, South Africa • ACRL ALCTS LITA RASD

Richard Bland College Library • Eike Hueter • Petersburg, VA 23805 • ACRL RASD

Richland Northeast High School • Evlyn Julian King • Columbia, SC 29223 • AASL

Richmond Hill Public Library • Jane Horrocks • Richmond Hill ON, L4C 5E5 Canada

Ridgefield High School Library • Ridgefield, CT 06877 • AASL IFRT

Ridgewood Public Library • Robert D. Ross • Ridgewood, NJ 07450 • PLA

Rijkshogeschool Studierichting b.d.i./o.c. • 9704 C M Groningen, Netherlands

Riley Family Library • Indianapolis, IN 46202-5200 • ALSC YALSA

Rio Grande College • Rio Grande, OH 45674 • ACRL ALCTS LAMA

Rittenhouse Financial Serv Inc. • Deborah D. Manning • Philadelphia, PA 19103 • Patron

River Bend Library System • Robert W. McKay • Coal Valley, IL 61240 • ALCTS ALSC ASCLA LITA PLA RASD

River Forest Public Library • Barbara Hall • River Forest, IL 60305 • ALTA LAMA PLA

Riverdale School Library • Kathleen Fritts • Portland, OR 97219 • AASL

Riverside Brookfield High School Media Services • Riverside, IL 60546 • AASL

Riverside City & County Public Library • Judith M. Auth • Riverside, CA 92502-0468 • ACRL ALCTS ALSC ALTA LAMA LITA PLA RASD YALSA EMIERT GODORT SORT

Robey Memorial Library • Katrinka Sieber • Waukon, IA 52172

Robins Air Force Base Library • Rosalind J. Jackson • Robins AFB, GA 31098-5000 • LAMA AFLRT

Robinson Twp Pub Lib Dist • Shirley A. Wakefield • Robinson, IL 62454

Rochester Public Library • Charlotte M. Dawson • Rochester, PA 15074

Rock Rapids Public Library • Linda McCormack • Rock Rapids, IA 51246

Rockaway Free Public Library • Joyce L. Wener • Rockaway, NJ 07866

Rockford Public Library • Joel C. Rosenfeld • Rockford, IL 61101-1061

Roddenbery Memorial Library • Cairo, GA 31728

Roger Williams College Library • Carol K. DiPrete • Bristol, RI 02809-2921 • ACRL ALCTS LAMA LITA RASD

Rogers State College Thunderbird Library • J. Alan Lawless • Claremore, OK 74017 • ACRL

Rolling Prairie Library System • Robert F. Plotzke • Decatur, IL 62522 • AASL ACRL ALCTS ALSC ALTA ASCLA LAMA LITA PLA RASD YALSA

Roman Catholic High Sch Lib • Alice Dowling • Philadelphia, PA 19107 • AASL

Rondout School District • David Broman • Lake Forest, IL 60045

Roosevelt Public Library • Jeanne Mayernik • Roosevelt, NY 11575 • ALTA

Rosemont College Library • C. Danial Elliott • Rosemont, PA 19010-1699 • ACRL ALCTS LAMA LITA RASD

Rosenberg Library Adult Services • John D. Hyatt • Galveston, TX 77550 • ALTA LITA PLA GODORT

Roseville High School • Julie Estridge • Roseville, CA 95678

Rosicrucian Research Library • San Jose, CA 95191

Roslyn High School Library • Roslyn Heights, NY 11577 • AASL YALSA

Roslyn Middle School Library • Roslyn Heights, NY 11577 • AASL

Rossford Public Library • Michael F. French • Rossford, OH 43460 • ALSC PLA RASD

Rostraver Public Library • Judith E. Yoskosky • Belle Vernon, PA 15012

Roswell Indp Sch Dist Materials Center • Flo Starkey • Roswell, NM 88201 • AASL IFRT

Routledge, Chapman & Hall • Donald O'Connor • New York, NY 10001 • ACRL RASD *Subscribing*

Roxbury Community College Learning Resource Center • Monica P. Bond • Boston, MA 02120 • ACRL ALCTS LAMA LITA RASD EMIERT

Royal Library • Erland Kolding Nielsen • Copenhagen, Denmark

Royal School of Librarianship • DK 2300 Copenhagen, Denmark • AASL ACRL ALCTS ALSC ALTA ASCLA LAMA LITA PLA RASD YALSA

Royal University Library of Oslo • N-0255 Oslo 2, Norway • ACRL ALCTS LAMA LITA RASD

Rushford Public Library • Gladys E. Iverson • Rushford, MN 55971

Rusk County Library • Henderson, TX 75652

Rusk State Hospital • Judy Vermillion • Rusk, TX 75785

Russ Bassett Company • Jerome A. Goodall • Whittier, CA 90606 • Subscribing

Russell Library • Stuart T. Porter • Middletown, CT 06457 • ALSC ALTA LAMA PLA RASD YALSA

Rutgers University Libraries Archibald Stevens Alexander Lib • Joanne R. Euster • New Brunswick, NJ 08903 • AASL ACRL ALCTS ALSC ASCLA LAMA LITA PLA RASD YALSA CLENE EMIERT ERT FLRT GODORT IFRT ILERT IRRT LHRT LIRT LRRT MAGERT NMRT SORT SRRT

Rutgers University Sch of Commun Inf & Lib Studies • Richard W. Budd • New Brunswick, NJ 08903

Rye Country Day School • Amy Perlman • Rye, NY 10580

S African Med Res Council • Steve F. Rossouw • Tygerberg 7505, South Africa • LITA

S Ctrl Kansas Lib Sys • Leroy M. Gattin • Hutchinson, KS 67501

S Puget Sound Cmnty Coll Library • Susan Perkins • Olympia, WA 98502-6292 • ACRL

S. Edward & Gertrude (Godfrey) Ronk Memorial Library • Robert F. Sennholz • Spring Mills, PA 16875

SAS Institute Technical Library • Cary, NC 27513

SVS, Inc. • Wendy Glickman • New York, NY 10019 • Subscribing

Sabah State Library • Sabah, Malaysia

Sacramento County Office of Education • Penny G. Kastanis • Sacramento, CA 95827 • AASL YALSA IFRT

Sacramento Public Library • Sacramento, CA 95814 • AASL ACRL ALCTS ALSC ASCLA LAMA LITA PLA RASD YALSA

Sacred Heart School of Montreal • Joan Maclellan • Montreal PQ, H3H 1Y4 Canada • AASL

Sage Publications, Inc. • David McCune • Newbury Park, CA 91320 • ACRL *Subscribing*

Saguaro High School Library • Carol R. Barclay • Scottsdale, AZ 85250 • AASL YALSA

Saint Ambrose University McMullen Library • Corinne J. Potter • Davenport, IA 52803 • LAMA LITA RASD

Saint Anthony Medical Center Hardymon Medical Library • Pamela L. Caruzzi • Columbus, OH 43205-1546 • ASCLA LITA

Saint Augustine High School • Wilbur J. Atwood • New Orleans, LA 70119 • AASL ILERT

Saint Catharines Public Library • M. Rossetto • St. Catharines ON, L2R 7K2 Canada • ALCTS ALTA LAMA LITA PLA RASD

Saint Catherine School Turner Hall Library • Howard L. Pugh • Richmond, VA 23226 • AASL IFRT

Saint Charles Borromeo Seminary Ryan Memorial Library • Lorena A. Boylan • Overbrook, PA 19096-3012 • ACRL ALCTS LITA RASD

Saint Charles Public Library • Diana Mignery Brown • St. Charles, IL 60174 • ALCTS ALSC LAMA PLA RASD YALSA

Saint Clair College Library • Windsor ON, N9A 6S4 Canada • ACRL RASD

Saint Croix Country Day School • Sylvina M. Trout • St. Croix, VI 00850 • ALSC

Saint Frances High School Instr Materials Ctr Lib • Susanne Bogdon • St. Frances, WI 53207 • AASL YALSA

Saint Francis College • Patricia B. Aughinbaugh • Loretto, PA 15940 • ACRL LAMA RASD

Saint Francis College McGarry Library • Joan Torrone • Brooklyn Heights, NY 11201 • ACRL

Saint Francis Hospital • Evanston, IL 60202

Saint Georges School Nathaniel P. Hill Library • Newport, RI 02840

Saint Gregory's College James Kelly Library • Patrick McCool • Shawnee, OK 74801-2403 • ACRL

Saint Jerome's College Library • D. Gary Draper • Waterloo, ON, N2L 3G3 Canada • ACRL RASD

Saint John Preparatory High School Library • Astoria, NY 11105 • YALSA

Saint John Regional Library • Mary Ellen Travis • Saint John NB, E2L 4Z6 Canada • LAMA PLA

Saint John Vianney College Seminary Library • Maria Martinez Rodriguez • Miami, FL 33165

Saint John's College Library • Kathryn P. Kinzer • Annapolis, MD 21404 • ACRL ALCTS LAMA

Saint John's University Library • Marie F. Melton • Jamaica, NY 11439 • AASL ACRL ALCTS ALSC ALTA LAMA LITA PLA RASD GODORT SORT

Saint John's Villa Academy • A. Alexander • Staten Island, NY 10305

Saint Joseph Academy Library • Cleveland, OH 44111

Saint Joseph Seminary College Pere Rouquette Library • Timothy J. Burnett • Saint Benedict, LA 70457 • ALCTS

Saint Joseph's College Library • S. Teresa Ryan • Brooklyn, NY 11205 • ACRL LIRT

Saint Joseph's College Library Wellehan Library • Fleurette Kennon • North Windham, ME 04062-1198 • ACRL

Saint Louis Christian College Library • Christian D. Schink • Florissant, MO 63033

Saint Louis Public Library • Glen E. Holt • St. Louis, MO 63103-2389 • ALTA

Saint Louis University Library • Amelia LL. Manalo • 2600 Baguio City, Philippines • ACRL ALCTS LAMA

Saint Luke's Hospital Medical Health Science Library • Donald Pohnl • Cedar Rapids, IA 52402 • ALCTS LITA RASD

Saint Mary Seminary • Alan Rome • Wickliffe, OH 44092

Saint Mary's College Alumni Memorial Library • Sylvia M. Chang • Orchard Lake, MI 48324 • ACRL

Saint Mary's College Cushwa-Leighton Library • M. Bernice Hollenhorst • Notre Dame, IN 46556 • ACRL ALCTS LAMA RASD

Saint Mary's College S. G. Kenan Library • Martha M. Smith • Raleigh, NC 27603-1689 • ACRL ALCTS RASD

Saint Mary's College of Maryland Library • John G. Williamson • St. Mary's City, MD 20686 • ACRL ALCTS LAMA LITA RASD

Saint Mary's Hospital Patients Library • Ardis C. Sawyer • Rochester, MN 55902 • LAMA

Saint Mary's University Patrick Power Library • Halifax NS, B3H 3C3 Canada • ACRL ALCTS LAMA LITA RASD

Saint Marys High School Library • Julianne M. Irwin • Annapolis, MD 21401

Saint Michael High School • Nathalee Bryant • St. Michaels, AZ 86511 • AASL

Saint Norbert College Todd Wehr Library • De Pere, WI 54115 • ACRL ALCTS LAMA LITA RASD

Saint Patrick High School • Kathleen Gerhardstein • Chicago, IL 60634 • AASL

Saint Paul High School Library • Angela M. Nolan • Santa Fe Springs, CA 90671 • AASL

Saint Paul Public Library • Gerald W. Steenberg • St. Paul, MN 55102 • ALCTS ALSC LAMA LITA PLA RASD YALSA EMIERT ILERT

Saint Paul's Episcopal School • Mobile, AL 36608 • AASL

Saint Paul's School Ohrstrom Library • Concord, NH 03301

Saint Pauls School Library • Mimi Krystel • Clearwater, FL 34624 • AASL

Saint Stephens Episcopal School Library • Caril M. Baker • Bradenton, FL 34209 • AASL

Saint Tammany Parish Library • Elizabeth Rountree • Covington, LA 70433

Saint Thomas Public Library • Carolyn Kneeshaw • St. Thomas ON, N5P 3Z7 Canada

Saint Xavier High School • Julie Conlon • Cincinnati, OH 45224 • AASL LITA LIRT

Saint Xavier University • Jo Ann Ellingson • Chicago, IL 60655 • ACRL ALCTS LAMA LITA RASD

Salamanca Public Library • Thomas L. Sharbaugh • Salamanca, NY 14779 • PLA

Salem-Teikyo University Benedum Library • Phyllis D. Freedman • Salem, WV 26426 • ACRL ALCTS GODORT

Salem Central High School Library • Denna Patzer • Salem, WI 53168 • AASL

Salem Press, Inc • Ken Burles • Pasadena, CA 91101 • AASL ACRL PLA RASD   *Patron*

Salem Public Library • Salem, OH 44460

Salem State College Library • Neil B. Olson • Salem, MA 01970 • ACRL ALCTS RASD

Salem Township Public Library • Jerri A. Short • Morrow, OH 45152 • PLA

Salesianum School Library • Elizabeth E. Diemer • Wilmington, DE 19802 • AASL

Salinas Public Library • John Gross • Salinas, CA 93901

Salt Lake City Public Library • J. Dennis Day • Salt Lake City, UT 84111 • AASL ACRL ALCTS ALSC ALTA ASCLA LAMA LITA PLA RASD YALSA

Salt Lake Community College Library • Salt Lake City, UT 84130-0808 • ACRL LAMA

Salvation Army School Hicks Memorial Library • Renee K. Burrell • Atlanta, GA 30310 • ACRL ALCTS RASD

Salzmann Library Saint Francis Seminary • S. Colette Zirbes • Saint Francis, WI 53235 • ACRL ALCTS LAMA RASD

Samford University Library • Birmingham, AL 35229 • ACRL ALCTS ALTA LAMA LITA RASD GODORT LIRT

San Bernardino County Library • Barbara L. Anderson • San Bernardino, CA 92415

San Diego Railroad Museum Lib • Roy Pickering • San Diego, CA 92101 • ALCTS

San Francisco Public Library • Elizabeth Hope Hayes • San Francisco, CA 94102

San Joaquin Memorial High School Library • Fresno, CA 93703 • YALSA

San Jose Public Library • James H. Fish • San Jose, CA 95113 • AASL ACRL ALCTS ALSC ALTA ASCLA LAMA LITA PLA RASD YALSA

San Jose State University Clark Library • Ruth Hafter • San Jose, CA 95192-0028 • AASL ACRL ALCTS ALSC ASCLA LAMA LITA PLA RASD YALSA

San Jose State University Monterey County Campus Library • Janie Barnard Silveria • Salinas, CA 93902 • AASL ACRL LITA RASD

San Juan Island Public Library • Kathleen M. McHarg • Friday Harbor, WA 98250 • PLA

San Mateo County Library • Nancy L. Lewis • San Mateo, CA 94402 • AASL ACRL ALCTS ALSC ALTA ASCLA LAMA LITA PLA RASD YALSA

Sandusky Public Library • Harriet Eagle • Sandusky, MI 48471

Sanibel Public Library • Patricia J. Allen • Sanibel, FL 33957

Santa Ana Public Library • Robert J. Richard • Santa Ana, CA 92701 • ALCTS ALTA LAMA LITA PLA RASD EMIERT GODORT IFRT

Santa Clara University Michel Orradre Library • Elizabeth Salzer • Santa Clara, CA 95053 • ACRL ALCTS LAMA LITA RASD

Santa Fe Cmnty Coll Lib • Robert M. Rankeillor • Gainesville, FL 32602 • ACRL

Santa Monica Public Library • Winona Allard • Santa Monica, CA 90401 • ALCTS ALSC LITA PLA RASD YALSA

Sapulpa Public Library • Spaula, OK 74066

Saskatchewan Inst of Sci & Tech Palliser Campus Library • Allan E. Wallbridge • Moose Jaw SK, S6H 4R4 Canada • ACRL

Saskatchewan Provincial Library • Regina SK, S7P 3V7 Canada • AASL ACRL ALCTS ALTA ASCLA LAMA LITA PLA RASD YALSA

Saskatoon Public Library • Saskatoon SK, SN5 OJ6 Canada • ALCTS ALSC LAMA LITA PLA RASD YALSA

Satya Wacana University • Rosella Kameo • Saltiga,Jateng 50711, Indonesia • ACRL ALCTS LAMA RASD

Saudi-S.A.I.S. • Jeddah 21231, Saudi Arabia • AASL

Saugatuck Douglas Dist Lib • Deborah Torres • Douglas, MI 49406 • PLA

Sauk City Public Library • Sauk City, WI 53583

Sauk Valley Community College Learning Resource Center • Robert D. Thomas • Dixon, IL 61021 • ACRL

Sault College Library • Liz Hansen • Sault Ste Marie ON, P6A 5L3 Canada • ACRL LAMA LIRT

Sault Sainte Marie Pub Lib • Brian R. Ingram • Sault Ste. Marie ON, P6A 3C3 Canada

Saunders Secondary School • Shirley Gladwell • London ON, N6K 1H5 Canada • AASL YALSA

Savanna Library District • Savanna, IL 61074

Savannah Country Day Sch • Donna N. Plunkett • Savannah, GA 31419 • AASL

Savery Library Talladega College • France Dates • Talladega, AL 35160 • ACRL ALCTS LAMA

Saxton B. Little Fr Lib, Inc. • Janice M. Benda • Columbia, CT 06237

Scarborough Board of Education Professional Library 2 • Rowan Amott • Scarborough ON, M1P 4N6 Canada

Scarborough Public Library Board • P. Bassnett • Scarborough, ON, M1P 4P4 Canada • ACRL ALCTS ALSC LAMA PLA RASD YALSA

Scarecrow Press, Inc. • Albert W. Daub • Metuchen, NJ 08840 • Contributing

Scenic Regional Library • Union, MO 63084 • LAMA PLA

Schiller Intl Univ • Cathy Eberhart • W-6900 Heidelberg, Germany • ACRL

Schiller Park Public Library • John Muellner • Schiller Park, IL 60176-1699

Scholastic Inc. • Lucy Evankow • New York, NY 10003 • YALSA

School District of Elmbrook District Media Center • Daryl Wunrow • Brookfield, WI 53005-1730 • AASL

Schoolcraft College Library • Jeanne Bonner • Livonia, MI 48152-2696 • ACRL LAMA LITA

Schweitzer Sortiment • Thomas Emig • D-8000 Munchen 2, Germany • ACRL ALCTS PLA   *Contributing*

Sci and Tech Inf Ctr National Science Council • Tao-Hsing Ma • Taipei10636, Taiwan

Scott County Public Library • Scottsburg, IN 47170

Scott County Sr High • Georgetown, KY 40324 • AASL YALSA

Scottish Rite Supreme Council Library • Washington, DC 20009

Scottsbluff Public Schools • Scottsbluff, NE 69361

Scottsboro Jr High Sch Lib • Scottsboro, AL 35768 • AASL ALSC

Scranton Public Library Albright Memorial Library • Jack Finnerty • Scranton, PA 18509-3248 • LAMA PLA GODORT

Scurry County Library • Noreen E. Taylor • Snyder, TX 79549 • ALSC PLA

Seattle Ctrl Cmnty Coll • Seattle, WA 98122 • ACRL ALCTS LAMA LITA RASD

Seattle Public Library • Elizabeth F. Stroup • Seattle, WA 98104-1193 • AASL ACRL ALCTS ALSC ALTA ASCLA LAMA LITA PLA RASD EMIERT FLRT IFRT LIRT SRRT

Secaucus Free Public Library • Margaret Grazioli • Secaucus, NJ 07094 • PLA SORT

Sedalia Public Library • Sedalia, MO 65301 • PLA

Sedona Public Library • Joan A R Duke • Sedona, AZ 86336

Seguin High School Library • Marge Panterrmuel • Seguin, TX 78155

Selma and Dallas Cnty Public Lib • Patricia Blalock • Selma, AL 36701

Sem of the Immaculate Conception • Huntington, NY 11743 • ALCTS GODORT

Seminary Library • Helen Kenik Mainelli • Oak Brook, IL 60521 • ACRL ALCTS

Seminole Junior College Boren Library • Jonna Bunyan • Seminole, OK 74818 • ACRL LAMA

Seminole Library Association • Patricia T. Bartell • Seminole, FL 34642 • PLA

Seminole Public Library • Seminole, OK 74868

Semmes-Murphey Clinic • Patricia P. Irby • Memphis, TN 38103 • ASCLA LRRT

Seneca College Library Resource Center • Tanis Fink • North York ON, M2J 2X5 Canada • ACRL LAMA RASD

Seneca Nation Library • Salamanca, NY 14779

Seneca Public Library • Louise G. Hogan • Seneca, IL 61360 • ALTA

Seton Hall University • Robert A. Jones • South Orange, NJ 07079-2690 • ACRL ALCTS LAMA LITA RASD GODORT LIRT

Seymour Public Library • Wayne Gudzinkas • Seymour, CT 06483

Shabonee School • Gail M. Gertson • Northbrook, IL 60062 • AASL

Shaker High School Library • Joyce D. Horsman • Latham, NY 12110 • AASL ALSC YALSA IFRT

Sharon School Library • D. N. Donoher • Robbinsville, NJ 08691

Shattuck Saint Mary's School The Hirst Library • Faribault, MN 55021

Shawnee Library System • James A. Ubel • Carterville, IL 62918 • ASCLA LAMA PLA

Shelbyville Public Library • Shelley Koehler • Shelbyville, IL 62565

Sheldon Jackson College Library • Evelyn K. Bonner • Sitka, AK 99835

Sheldon Public Library • Ruth Rodvik • Sheldon, IA 51201 • PLA

Shelter Island Public Library • Janet Olinkiewicz • Shelter Island, NY 11964

Shelton State Community College Junior College Division Library • Deborah J. Grimes • Tusacaloosa, AL 35405 • ACRL

Shenandoah University Howe Library • Christopher Bean • Winchester, VA 22601 • ACRL ALCTS LAMA LITA RASD

Shepherd High School • Shephered, MT 59079 • AASL

Sherborn Library • M. Elizabeth Johnston • Sherborn, MA 01770

Sherburne Memorial Library • Gail Weymouth • Killington, VT 05751

Sherman College of Straight Chiropractic, Bahon Library • Spartanburg, SC 29304 • ACRL

Sherman Library Association • Deborah Lang-Froggatt • Sherman, CT 06784 • PLA

Shipley Upper School Library • Judith N. Williams • Bryn Mawr, PA 19010

Shortgrass Library System • Colleen Swift • Medicine Hat AB, T1A 8G2 Canada • ALCTS LAMA PLA

Showbest Fixture Company • Reinhard J. Heidfeld • Hillside, NJ 07205 • Contributing

Shreve Memorial Library • James R. Pelton • Shreveport, LA 71120-1523 • ALTA ASCLA LAMA PLA RASD

Sidwell Friends School Library • Jo-Ann Segall • Washington, DC 20016 • AASL YALSA LIRT

Signature Books • Brent Corcoran • Salt Lake City, UT 84111 • Subscribing

Silo Music • Ann Tangney • Waterbury, VT 05676 • Subscribing

Silverton Public Library • Jackie L. Leithauser • Silverton, CO 81433

Simmons College Beatley Library • Artemis M. G. Kirk • Boston, MA 02115 • ACRL ALCTS LAMA LITA RASD

Simmons College Grad Sch of Lib & Inf Sci • Robert D. Stueart • Boston, MA 02115 • AASL ACRL ALCTS ALSC ALTA LAMA LITA RASD YALSA ERT FLRT GODORT IFRT IRRT LHRT LIRT LRRT NMRT SORT SRRT

Simon & Schuster Books for Young Readers • Dagmar Greve • New York, NY 10023 • AASL ALSC   *Subscribing*

Simon Fraser University Library • Jayme L. Stokes • Burnaby BC, V5A 1S6 Canada • ACRL ALCTS LAMA LITA RASD

Simon Wiesenthal Center Library • Adaire Klein • Los Angeles, CA 90035

Simon's Rock of Bard Coll Lib • Joan C. Goodkind • Great Barrington, MA 01230 • ACRL LITA RASD

Simpson College Library • Miles S. Compton • Redding, CA 96003 • ACRL ALCTS RASD

Simsbury High School Library • Noreen R. Michaud • Simsbury, CT 06070 • YALSA

Sioux Falls College Norman B. Mears Library • Beverly A. Stubbles • Sioux Falls, SD 57105-1699 • ACRL ALCTS RASD

Siskiyou Cnty Off of Edu Library • Kathy Graves • Yreka, CA 96097 • AASL IFRT LIRT

Sisson Public Library Upper San Juan Library District • Lenore Bright • Pagosa Springs, CO 81147

Skidompha Library • Ellen Welsh • Damariscotta, ME 04543

Skokie Public Library • Carolyn Anthony • Skokie, IL 60077-3680 • ACRL ALCTS ALSC ALTA ASCLA LAMA LITA PLA RASD YALSA CLENE EMIERT IFRT IRRT SORT

Skolaskrifstofa Reykjavikur v/ Bokasafns • Margret Bjornsdottir • 101 Reykjavik, Iceland • AASL ALSC LIRT

Smith Vocational High School • Anne Russell • Northampton, MA 01060 • AASL

Smithsonian Institution Archives of American Art • Ellen A Nollman • Washington, DC 20560 • FLRT

Smoky Hill High School • Su A Eckhardt • Aurora, CO 80015 • AASL

Smyrna Public Library • Smyrna, DE 19977

Smyrna Public Library • Laurel S. Best • Smyrna, GA 30080 • PLA

Sno-Isle Regional Library • Thomas R. Mayer • Marysville, WA 98271-9164 • ALCTS ALSC ALTA LAMA LITA PLA RASD YALSA

Snowflake Public Library • Cathryn McDowell • Snowflake, AZ 85937 • PLA

Soc for Visual Education, Inc. • Julie McCallion • Chicago, IL 60614 • AASL   *Subscribing*

Sociedad de Bibliotecarios de Puerto Rico • Digan Escalare • Rio Piedras, PR 00931

Society of Librarians • Aura Jimenez de Panepinto • Pio Piedras, PR 00931 • ASCLA LAMA

Society of the Four Arts Library • Joanne Rendon • Palm Beach, FL 33480

Software AG of N America, Inc. • James J. Kopp • Reston, VA 22091 • ACRL LITA PLA   *Subscribing*

Sogang University Library • Seoul 121-742, South Korea • ACRL ALCTS LITA RASD

Soka University Library • Tokyo 192, Japan

Soldotna Public Library • Dorothy J. Bishop • Soldotna, AK 99669

Solvay Public Library • Daniel W. Casey • Solvay, NY 13209 • PLA

Somers Public Library • Frances C. Lee • Somers, NY 10589 • PLA

Somerset Cmnty Coll Lib University of Kentucky • James P. Miller • Somerset, KY 42501 • ACRL ALCTS LAMA RASD

Somersworth Public Library • Debora J.G. Longo • Somersworth, NH 03878

Sonoma County Library • David Sabsay • Santa Rosa, CA 95404

Sophia University Library • Tokyo 102, Japan • ACRL ALCTS LAMA LITA RASD

South Africa State Library • Pretoria 0001, South Africa • ALCTS ASCLA LAMA LITA RASD GODORT SRRT

South Africa University • Pretoria, South Africa

South Beloit Public Library • Vickie Ruthe Cogswell • South Beloit, IL 61080

South Carolina State College Miller F. Whittaker Library • Barbara Williams-Jenkins • Orangeburg, SC 29117 • ACRL ALCTS LAMA LITA RASD GODORT LIRT LRRT SORT

South Carolina State Library • Betty E. Callaham • Columbia, SC 29211 • AASL ACRL ALCTS ALTA ASCLA LAMA LITA PLA RASD YALSA

South Central Library System • Peter G. Hamon • Madison, WI 53704 • ASCLA LAMA PLA

South College Library • Valerie E. Yaughn • Savannah, GA 31406

South Dakota Library Association • Leon Raney • Pierre, SD 57501

South Dakota State Library • Jane Kolbe • Pierre, SD 57501-2294 • AASL ACRL ALCTS ALSC ALTA ASCLA LAMA LITA PLA RASD YALSA GODORT

South Dakota State University Briggs Library • Leon Raney • Brookings, SD 57007 • ACRL ALCTS LITA RASD

South Gerogia Regional Library • Roddelle B. Folsom • Valdosta, GA 31602 • ALTA PLA

South Glastonbury Library • Nancy St. Clair • South Glastonbury, CT 06073

South Lyon Public Library • Nancy C. Noble • South Lyon, MI 48178

South Middle School Library • Ruth Fox • Great Neck, NY 11020 • AASL ALSC

South Milwaukee Public Library • Linda C. Paulaskas • S Milwaukee, WI 53172 • PLA

South Suburban College Learning Resources Center • South Holland, IL 60473 • ACRL LAMA GODORT LIRT

South Windsor Public Library • Mary J. Dymek • South Windsor, CT 06074

Southampton Free Library • Patricia Harrington • Southampton, PA 18966

Southeast Community College • C. Barringer • Beatrice, NE 68310

Southeast Kansas Library System • Iola, KS 66749 • PLA

Southeast Voc Tech Inst • Sioux Falls, SD 57107 • ACRL

Southeastern Community College • W Burlington, IA 52655 • ACRL RASD

Southeastern Illinois Coll Lib • Melba Patton • Harrisburg, IL 62946

Southeastern Library Association • Claudia Medori • Tucker, GA 30085-0987

Southeastern Library Network (SOLINET) • Frank P. Grisham • Atlanta, GA 30309-2955 • ACRL ALCTS ASCLA LITA PLA RASD CLENE ERT   *Subscribing*

Southeastern Louisiana Univ Linus A. Sims Memorial Library • F. Landon Greaves • Hammond, LA 70402 • AASL ACRL ALCTS ALSC LITA RASD

Southeastern Public Library System of Oklahoma • McAlester, OK 74501 • PLA

Southern Alberta Inst of Tech Educational Resources-Library • R. Thornborough • Calgary AB, T2M 0L4 Canada • AASL ACRL ALCTS LAMA LITA RASD

Southern Arkansas University Library Media Center • Marilyn Sewell • El Dorado, AR 71730 • ACRL

Southern Calif Inst of Arch Arch-Urban Planning Lib • Kevin McMahon • Santa Monica, CA 90404 • ACRL

Southern Connecticut State Univ Hilton C. Buley Library • Kenneth G. Walter • New Haven, CT 06515

Southern Connecticut State Univ Sch of Libray Sci & Instr Tech • Emanuel Prostano • New Haven, CT 06515

Southern Illinois University • Gary N. Denue • Edwardsville, IL 62026 • AASL ACRL ALCTS LAMA LITA PLA RASD GODORT

Southern Illinois University Delyte W. Morris Library • Kenneth G. Peterson • Carbondale, IL 62901-6632 • AASL ACRL ALCTS ALSC ALTA LAMA LITA PLA RASD YALSA FLRT GODORT LIRT SRRT

Southern Maine Technical College Library • Don Bertsch • South Portlnd, ME 04106 • ACRL

Southern Ohio College Library • Elizabeth M. Naish • Cincinnati, OH 45237

Southern Ontario Library Service • Gabriele Lundeen • Ottawa ON, K1G 0N1 Canada • AASL ALCTS LAMA LITA PLA RASD YALSA

Southern Truck Body Corp. • Jerry W. Pebbles • Tampa, FL 33607 • LAMA

Southern Univ in New Orleans Leonard S. Washington Library • Eddiemae W. Young • New Orleans, LA 70126

Southern University • Baton Rouge, LA 70813

Southern Utah University Library • Ling Wang • Cedar City, UT 84720 • AASL ACRL ALCTS

Southington Public Library • Audrey Brown • Southington, CT 06489

Southport High School • Indianapolis, IN 46627 • AASL

Southwest Missouri State Univ Library • John M. Meador • Springfield, MO 65804-0095 • AASL ACRL ALCTS LAMA LITA RASD YALSA

Southwest Ohio Rgnl Lib Sys SWORL • Corinne Johnson • Wilmington, OH 45177

Southwest Public Libraries • Frances P. Black • Grove City, OH 43123 • ALCTS ALSC ALTA ASCLA LAMA LITA PLA RASD YALSA CLENE IFRT SORT SRRT

Southwest Regional Library • Deanna Fish • Bolivar, MO 65613

Southwest Virginia Cmnty Coll Library • Richlands, VA 24641

Southwest Wisconsin Lib Sys • James Wroblewski • Fennimore, WI 53809

Southwestern Christian College • Doris H. Johnson • Terrell, TX 75160

Southwestern College • Alice Eickmeyer • Phoenix, AZ 85032

Southwestern College • Lois I. Marriott • Chula Vista, CA 91910

Southwestern Connecticut Library Council • Ann M. Neary • Bridgeport, CT 06604 • LAMA PLA

Southwestern University A. Frank Smith Jr Lib Ctr • Lynne M. Brody • Georgetown, TX 78626 • ACRL ALCTS LAMA RASD

Southwick Public Library • Barbara J. Morse • Southwick, MA 01077 • LAMA PLA RASD YALSA

Spacesaver Corporation • Ann Schroedl • Fort Atkinson, WI 53538 • Subscribing

Sparta Public Library • Brenda Foote • Sparta, IL 62286

Spartan Sch of Aeronautics Lib • Emma Robertson • Tulsa, OK 74151

Speedway Public Library • Joan Masterson • Speedway, IN 46224 • PLA RASD

Spokane Public Library Comstock Building Library • Daniel L. Walters • Spokane, WA 99201-0976 • AASL ALCTS ALSC ALTA LAMA LITA PLA RASD YALSA EMIERT GODORT IFRT SORT SRRT

Spokane School District 81 Professional Library • Spokane, WA 99201 • AASL YALSA

Spoken Arts, Inc. • B. Holmes • Pinellas Park, FL 34666 • Subscribing

Spoon River College Learning Resources Center • Pat Russell • Canton, IL 61520 • ACRL

Spring Arbor College Library • Delores Knapp • Spring Arbor, MI 49283 • ACRL RASD

Spring Indp Sch Dist Wells Middle School • Sara C Howard • Houston, TX 77068 • AASL

Springfield College Babson Library • Gerald F. Davis • Springfield, MA 01109 • ACRL ASCLA LAMA LITA RASD

Springfield College of Illinois • Springfield, IL 62702 • ACRL

Springfield Tech Cmnty Coll Library • Tamson M. Ely • Springfield, MA 01101-9000 • ACRL ALCTS RASD

Springs Public Library • F. C. Coetzee • Springs 1560, South Africa • ALCTS

St Bonaventure Univ Lib • John A. Macik • St. Bonaventure, NY 14778 • ACRL ALCTS ALSC LITA RASD GODORT

St Brendan High Sch Lib • Mildred A. Copeland • Miami, FL 33165

St Clair Shores Pub Lib • Arthur M. Woodford • St. Clair Shores, MI 48081 • ALCTS ALSC ALTA LAMA LITA PLA RASD IFRT

St Joseph Cnty Pub Lib • Donald J. Napoli • South Bend, IN 46601

St Joseph by the Sea High Sch Library • Kathleen Delaney • Staten Island, NY 10312 • AASL

St Lawrence Coll St-Laurent • Kingston ON, K7L 5A6 Canada

St Louis Coll Pharmacy Lib • Judith A. Longstreth • St. Louis, MO 63110 • ACRL

St Louis Mercantile Lib Assn • Judith R. Friedrich • Saint Louis, MO 63101 • ALCTS

St Paul Acad & Summit Sch • Louise Rosel • St. Paul, MN 55105 • YALSA

St Petersburg Beach Pub Lib • William L. BarNett • St. Petersburg, FL 33706

St Pius X Catholic High Sch Flannery O'Connor Library • Mary D. O'Neil • Atlanta, GA 30345 • AASL

St Sebastians Country Day Sch Library • Needham, MA 02192 • AASL

St. Columbkille School • Papillion, NE 68046

Staatsburg Public Library • Staatsburg, NY 12580-0397

Stadt und Universitatsbibliothek • 6000 Frankfurt Am, Germany

Stanford University • David C. Weber • Stanford, CA 94305-6011 • AASL ACRL ALCTS ALSC ALTA ASCLA LAMA LITA RASD YALSA GODORT

Stark County District Library • Nan Johnston • Canton, OH 44702 • ALSC ALTA ASCLA LAMA PLA RASD IFRT

Starved Rock Library System • Richard E. Willson • Ottawa, IL 61350 • AASL ACRL ALCTS ALSC ALTA ASCLA LAMA LITA PLA RASD YALSA

State College Area School Library Processing Center • State College, PA 16803 • YALSA

State Historical Society of Iowa • Nancy Kraft • Iowa City, IA 52240 • ALCTS RASD

State Librarian Delaware Division of Libraries • Tom W. Sloan • Dover, DE 19901 • GODORT

State Library Northern Territory • Darwin NT 0801, Australia

State Library of Florida Div of Lib & Inf Serv • Barratt Wilkins • Tallahassee, FL 32399-0250 • AASL ACRL ALCTS ALSC ALTA ASCLA LAMA LITA PLA RASD YALSA

State Library of Iowa • Sharman B. Smith • Des Moines, IA 50319 • AASL ACRL ALCTS ALSC ALTA ASCLA LAMA LITA PLA RASD YALSA CLENE GODORT IFRT LRRT SORT

State Library of Louisiana • Thomas Francis Jaques • Baton Rouge, LA 70821 • AASL ACRL ALCTS ALTA ASCLA LAMA LITA PLA RASD YALSA

State Library of New South Wales • Sydney NSW 2000, Australia • ACRL ALCTS ASCLA LAMA LITA PLA RASD

State Library of Ohio • Richard Cheski • Columbus, OH 43266-0334 • AASL ACRL ALCTS ASCLA LAMA PLA RASD CLENE GODORT

State Library of Pennsylvania Department of Education • Sara Ann Parker • Harrisburg, PA 17105 • AASL ACRL ALCTS ALSC ASCLA LAMA LITA PLA RASD YALSA

State Library of Queensland • Melloy • S. Brisbane QLD 4101, Australia • AASL ACRL ALCTS ALTA ASCLA LAMA LITA PLA RASD YALSA

State Library of Tasmania • W. L. Brown • Hobart Tasmania 7000, Australia • ACRL ALCTS LITA RASD YALSA

State Library of Victoria Serials Section • W. M. Horton • Melbourne VIC 3000, Australia • AASL ACRL ALCTS ASCLA LAMA LITA RASD YALSA

State Univ of New York (SUNY) Central Technical Services • Barbara A. von Wahlde • Buffalo, NY 14260 • AASL ACRL ALCTS ALSC ALTA ASCLA LAMA LITA PLA RASD YALSA SRRT

State Univ of New York (SUNY) Frank Melville Jr. Mem Lib • John B. Smith • Stony Brook, NY 11794-3300 • ACRL ALCTS LITA RASD

State University of New York Agricultural & Technical College • Eleanor Carter • Cobleskill, NY 12043 • ACRL ALCTS ALSC LAMA LITA RASD

State University of New York Coll of Agr & Tech • Colleen Stella • Morrisville, NY 13408 • ACRL ALCTS RASD

State University of New York Office of Library Services • Glyn T. Evans • Albany, NY 12246 • ACRL ASCLA

Staten Bibliotekogskole • Stephanie S. Pedersen • Oslo 5, Norway • ACRL ALCTS LAMA LITA PLA

Statens Bibliotekstjeneste • Morten Laursen Vig • DK-1051 Copenhagen K, Denmark • ALCTS LITA PLA

Statewide Citizens Group Council for Florida Libraries • Barbara D. Cooper • Fort Lauderdale, FL 33301-1529 • ALTA

Statistics Canada Library • Mary Jane Maffini • Ottawa ON, K1A 0T6 Canada • LITA

Statsbiblioteket Tidsskr • Niels Mark • DK-8000 Aarhus C, Denmark • AASL ACRL ALCTS LITA RASD

Steck-Vaughn Company • Steven Korte • Austin, TX 78759 • Subscribing

Steger-South Chicago Heights Public Library District • Jane Schulten • Steger, IL 60475

Sterling Public Library • Sterling, CO 80751 • PLA

Steven J. Nash Publishing • Pattie Penegor • Highland Park, IL 60035 • Subscribing

Stewart, Tabori & Chang • Claudia Guerra • New York, NY 10012-3230 • AASL ALSC YALSA   *Subscribing*

Stockholm Stadsbibliotek • Bo Lund • S-117 94 Stockholm, Sweden • RASD

Stockton Township Public Library • M. J. O'Boyle • Stockton, IL 61085

Stoneham High School Library • Patricia M. Di Pietro • Stoneham, MA 02180 • AASL

Stonington Free Library • Stonington, CT 06378

Stoughton Public Library • Anne H. Petterson • Stoughton, MA 02072

Stratton Veterans Medical Center Library 142D • Albany, NY 12208

Stuart County Day School • Chigusa Hayashi • Princeton, NJ 08540 • AASL

Sturgis Public Library • Rita Schwartz • Sturgis, SD 57785

Sublette County Library • Daphne D. Platts • Pinedale, WY 82941 • PLA

Suburban Library System • James M. O'Brien • Burr Ridge, IL 60521 • AASL ACRL ALCTS ALSC ALTA ASCLA LAMA LITA PLA RASD YALSA

Suffield Academy • Suffield, CT 06078 • AASL

Sugar Grove Public Library District • Beverly S. Holmes • Sugar Grove, IL 60554 • ALTA PLA YALSA

Sukhothai Thammathirat Open Univ Off of Doc and Inf • Sompit Cusripituck • Nonthaburi 11120, Thailand • ALCTS RASD

Sultan Qaboos University Library • Moosa N. Al-Mufaraji • Muscat, Sultanate, Oman

Summit Public Library District • Jennifer Johnstone • Summit, IL 60501

Summit Public Schools • Jane A. Martinez • Summit, NJ 07901 • AASL ALSC

Summit School Library • Eileen Frost • Winston-Salem, NC 27106 • AASL

Sumpter Township Public Library Courthouse Square • Toledo, IL 62468

Sumter Area Technical College • Chris Bruggman • Sumter, SC 29150 • ACRL

Sun City Library • Sun City, AZ 85351 • LAMA PLA

Sundown High School • Sundown, TX 79372

Sunflower County Library • Anice C. Powell • Indianola, MS 38751 • LAMA PLA

Suomi College Library • Ellen Y. Seidel • Hancock, MI 49930 • ACRL

Surrey Public Library • Stan Smith • Surrey BC, V3X 3A2 Canada • ALTA LAMA YALSA

Susquehanna University • Peter V. Deekle • Selinsgrove, PA 17870 • ACRL ALCTS LITA RASD

Swarthmore College Library • Michael J. Durkan • Swarthmore, PA 19081 • ACRL ALCTS LAMA LITA RASD LIRT

Sweetwater Cnty Lib Sys • Helen E. Higby • Green River, WY 82935

Sweetwater County-City Library • Bonnie McSweeney • Sweetwater, TX 79556

Swisher County Library • Jo Alice Garrett • Tulia, TX 79088

Sylvania Schools • Peggy Rabideau • Sylvania, OH 43560 • AASL

Syracuse University Library E. S. Bird Library • David H. Stam • Syracuse, NY 13244-2010 • AASL ACRL ALCTS ALSC ASCLA LAMA LITA RASD YALSA

Syracuse University School of Information Studies • Donald A. Marchand • Syracuse, NY 13244-4100 • ACRL LITA

TPS Electronics • Palo Alto, CA 94303 • ALCTS LITA   *Subscribing*

Talladega Public Library • Lucinda Quinn • Talladega, AL 35160 • LITA

Talman Company, The • Marilee Talman • New York, NY 10011 • ACRL YALSA EMIERT MAGERT *Subscribing*

Tamanend Middle School • Judith A. Sheridan • Warrington, PA 18976 • AASL YALSA

Taneyhills Community Library • Norma Root • Branson, MO 65616-2712

Tangipahoa Parish Library • Ronald C. Tumey • Amite, LA 70422 • ALCTS ALSC ALTA LAMA PLA RASD YALSA GODORT IFRT SORT

Taylor County Public Library • Campbellvle, KY 42718

Taylor University Zondervan Library • David C. Dickey • Upland, IN 46989 • ACRL

Tech Serv Legis Lib • Joanne Robertson • Toronto ON, M7A 1A9 Canada • ACRL ALCTS LAMA LITA RASD FLRT GODORT

Tech Univ of Nova Scotia Library • Mohammad R. Hussain • Halifax NS, B3J 2X4 Canada • ACRL

Temple University Japan • G. David Green • Tokyo 192-03, Japan • ACRL

Tennessee Library Association • Betty L. Nance • Nashville, TN 37215-8417

Tennessee State Lib & Archv • Edwin S. Gleaves • Nashville, TN 37243-0312 • ACRL ALCTS ALTA ASCLA LAMA LITA PLA RASD GODORT IFRT LHRT LRRT MAGERT

Tennessee State University Brown-Daniel Library • Yildiz B. Binkley • Nashville, TN 37203 • ACRL RASD

Tennessee Temple University Cierpke Memorial Library • Edwin B. Fountain • Chattanooga, TN 37404 • ACRL ALCTS LAMA RASD

Terra Technical College Library • Mary K. Broestl • Fremont, OH 43420 • LAMA LITA

Terrebonne Parish Library • Margaret Shaffer • Houma, LA 70360 • ALSC ALTA

Teton County Library • Nancy E. Effinger • Jackson, WY 83001 • PLA

Tewsbury Public Schools Tewksbury High School • Hope Place • Tewksbury, MA 01876 • AASL YALSA

Texarkana Public Library • Alice L. Coleman • Texarkana, TX 75501

Texas A & I University James C Jernigan Library • Paul K. Goode • Kingsville, TX 78363 • ACRL

Texas A & M University Sterling C. Evans Library • Irene B. Hoadley • College Station, TX 77843-5000 • AASL ACRL ALCTS LITA PLA RASD YALSA

Texas Library Association • Patricia H. Smith • Austin, TX 78746 • NMRT

Texas State Library • William D. Gooch • Austin, TX 78711 • AASL ACRL ALSC ALTA ASCLA LAMA LITA PLA RASD

Texas State Technical College Library • Linda S. Koepf • Waco, TX 76705

Texas Tech University Libraries • E. Dale Cluff • Lubbock, TX 79409-0002 • AASL ACRL ALCTS ALSC ALTA LAMA LITA RASD YALSA LIRT SORT

Texas Water Commission Library • Sylvia Von Fange • Austin, TX 78711 • LAMA

Texas Wesleyan University West Library • Douglas M. Ferrier • Fort Worth, TX 76105 • ACRL ALCTS ALSC LAMA LITA RASD

Texas Woman's University Mary Evelyn Blagg-Huey Library • Elizabeth M. Snapp • Denton, TX 76204-1715 • AASL ACRL ALCTS ALSC ALTA ASCLA LAMA LITA PLA RASD YALSA CLENE EMIERT ERT FLRT GODORT IFRT ILERT LIRT MAGERT NMRT SORT SRRT

Texwood Furniture Corporation • Austin, TX 78702 • ERT   *Subscribing*

Thaddeus Stevens State School of Technology • George Friedline • Lanscaster, PA 17602

Thammasat University Library • Phakaivan Chiamcharoen • Bangkok 10200, Thailand • AASL ACRL ALCTS ALSC LITA RASD

Theatre Library Association Headquarters • Richard M. Buck • New York, NY 10023

Thomas Cnty Pub Lib Sys • Sandra O. Newell • Thomasville, GA 31792 • LAMA PLA

Thomas Hackney Braswell Mem Lib • Martha K. Turney • Rocky Mount, NC 27804 • ALTA IFRT

Thomas Jefferson Library System • Doris Jean Athy • Jefferson Cty, MO 65102 • ALSC LITA PLA RASD

Thomas More College Library • James M. McKellogg • Crestview Hills, KY 41017 • ACRL ALCTS RASD

Thorndike Press • Mary Kee • Thorndike, ME 04986 • PLA   *Subscribing*

Thrall Library • Mattie B. Gaines • Middletown, NY 10940

Three Rivers Center for Independent Living Library • Pittsburgh, PA 15208

Three Rivers Community College Rutland Library • Mark L. Daganaar • Poplar Bluff, MO 63901

Tidewater Community College Virginia Beach Campus Library • John W. Zwick • Virginia Beach, VA 23456 • ACRL LITA

Tiffin University Pfeiffer Library • Frances A. Fleet • Tiffin, OH 44883

Time Being Books • Jerry Call • Saint Louis, MO 63131 • Subscribing

Tippecanoe County Public Library • Joel M. Robinson • Lafayette, IN 47901 • ALCTS ALSC LAMA PLA RASD YALSA

Tiskilwa Township Library • Julie Marcum • Tiskilwa, IL 61368

Toccoa Falls College Seby Jones Library • Sarah M. Patterson • Toccoa Falls, GA 30598 • ACRL LIRT

Tokyo Toritsu Chuo • Haru Sadaka • Tokyo 106, Japan • RASD

Toledo-Lucas Cnty Pub Lib • Clyde S. Scoles • Toledo, OH 43624 • AASL ACRL ALCTS ALSC ALTA ASCLA LAMA LITA PLA RASD YALSA CLENE GODORT LIRT SRRT

Tolono Public Library • Theresa Montgomery • Tolono, IL 61880

Tomlinson College Library • Gayla L. Cassidy • Cleveland, TN 37320-3030

Toronto Public Library • Les Fowlie • Toronto ON, M5A 4L2 Canada • ALCTS ALTA ASCLA LAMA PLA RASD YALSA

Toronto Public Library Northern Dist-Prof Lib • Gwen Liu • Toronto ON, M4R 1B9 Canada

Torrington High School Library • Karen Shaffer • Torrington, CT 06790 • AASL

Torrington Library • Karen Worrall • Torrington, CT 06790

Torrington Middle School • Ginger McLaughlin • Torrington, WY 82240 • AASL YALSA

Toshokan Joho Daigaku Library • Ibaraki-Yen 305, Japan • LITA

Town of Crawford Free Library • James F. McIntyre • Pine Bush, NY 12566 • LAMA PLA

Towson State University • Towson, MD 21204 • AASL ACRL ALCTS ALSC LAMA LITA RASD YALSA GODORT

Towson State University Dept of Instr Tech • Towson, MD 21204 • AASL ALSC RASD

Transvaalse Onderwysmediadiens • Pretoria 0001, South Africa • ACRL ALSC

Transylvania University Library • Kathleen C. Bryson • Lexington, KY 40508 • ACRL ALCTS LITA RASD LIRT

Traverse Area District Library • Michael L. McGuire • Traverse City, MI 49684

Traverse des Sioux Lib Sys • John D. Christenson • Mankato, MN 56002-0608 • ALCTS LAMA PLA RASD

Trent University Thomas J. Bata Library • Murray W. Genoe • Peterborough ON, K9J 7B8 Canada • ACRL ALCTS LITA RASD MAGERT

Trenton Public Library • Mary Williams • Trenton, IL 62293 • PLA

Trevorton Public Library • Naomi Troutman • Trevorton, PA 17881

Tri-Valley Schools #49-6 • Lyons, SD 57041 • AASL

Trident Technical College Learning Resources Center LD-M • Marion L. Vogel • Charleston, SC 29411 • ACRL LAMA LITA RASD

Trigg County Library • M. Newby • Cadiz, KY 42211

Trinity College • Mark R. Yerburgh • Burlington, VT 05401 • ACRL

Trinity College Library • Thom Morris • Deerfield, IL 60015 • ACRL ALCTS RASD

Trinity College Library • Dublin 2, Ireland • ACRL ALCTS LITA

Trinity School Library • Atlanta, GA 30327 • AASL LIRT

Trinity School Library • Rebecca M. Zeren • Menlo Park, CA 94025 • ALSC

Triton College Library • John H. Frye • River Grove, IL 60171 • ACRL LITA RASD

Troll Associates • Marvin Schecter • Mahwah, NJ 07430 • Subscribing

Troy State University Library • Thomas A. Souter • Troy, AL 36082 • ACRL ALCTS LAMA LITA RASD

Trujillo Alto Municipal Library • Milagros Rodriguez • Trujillo Alto, PR 00977 • ALCTS PLA RASD

Trumbull High Sch Media Ctr • Edward Farrell • Trumbull, CT 06611 • AASL LITA YALSA IFRT LIRT

Tsurumi University • Toranosuke Takeda • Yokohama 230, Japan • RASD

Tucson Pima Library • Liz R. Miller • Tucson, AZ 85726 • ACRL ALCTS ALSC ALTA ASCLA LAMA LITA PLA RASD YALSA IFRT

Tufts University Nils Yngve Wessell Library • David R. McDonald • Medford, MA 02155 • ACRL ALCTS LAMA LITA RASD GODORT LIRT SRRT

Tulane University Howard-Tilton Memorial Library • Philip E. Leinbach • New Orleans, LA 70118 • ACRL ALCTS LAMA LITA RASD

Tulare County Library System • Brian G. Lewis • Visalia, CA 93277 • ALSC PLA RASD GODORT IFRT

Tulare Public Library • Michael C. Stowell • Tulare, CA 93274

Tulsa City-Cnty Lib Sys • Pat Woodrum • Tulsa, OK 74103 • ACRL ALCTS ALSC ASCLA LITA PLA

Tundra Books/Livres Toundra • C. Mitchell • Montreal, PQ, H3Z 2N2 Canada • ALSC *Subscribing*

Tunxis Community College Library • Farmington, CT 06032 • ACRL

Twin Falls Public Library • Arlan Call • Twin Falls, ID 83301 • ALSC ALTA LAMA PLA

Twin Falls Sr High Sch Lib • Shirley Ann Thorpe • Twin Falls, ID 83301 • AASL

Twp High Sch Lib Dist 214 Technical Processing Center • Ann Marie Wurster • Arlington Heights, IL 60005 • AASL ALCTS

U S Off of Surface Mining Dept of The Interior/ Library • Carmelita Lavayna Portugal • Pittsburgh, PA 15220 • FLRT

U. Nations Dag Hammarskjold Lib • Jakob VanHeijst • New York, NY 10163 • ACRL ALCTS LAMA LITA RASD GODORT IRRT MAGERT

U. S. Army Corps of Engineers Attn: Dist Lib R.M. Serbu • Baltimore, MD 21201 • LITA FLRT

U. S. Army Med Res Inst of Infectious Diseases Library • Anna Linton • Frederick, MD 21702

U. S. Def Communications Agency Library & Information Center • Arlington, VA 22204-2199 • LAMA LITA FLRT

U. S. Dept of Agr National Agricultural Library • Joseph H. Howard • Beltsville, MD 20705-2351 • ACRL ALCTS LITA RASD

U. S. Equal Employment Oppor Commission Library • Susan Taylor • Washington, DC 20507 • ALCTS LAMA LITA

U. S. Merchant Marine Acad • George J. Billy • Kings Point, NY 11024-1699 • ACRL ALCTS LAMA ERT FLRT GODORT LIRT

U. S. Naval Submarine Base NLON • Groton, CT 06349-5000 • PLA

U. S. Patent & Trademark Off Library Programs • Amanda M A Putnam • Washington, DC 20231

U. S. Soldiers Airmen Home Main Library • Edward M. Underwood • Washington, DC 20317 • ALCTS ASCLA AFLRT FLRT

U.S. Holocaust Memorial Museum Library • Elizabeth Koeing • Washington, DC 20036-4907

UMS-Wright Preparatory School • Joan D. Crawford • Mobile, AL 36607

USA Today • Barbara R. Ellenbogen • Arlington, VA 22209 • Subscribing

Umpqua Community College Library • Freda R. Munger • Roseburg, OR 97470 • ACRL ALCTS

Uniformed Service University • Bethesda, MD 20814 • ACRL ALCTS ASCLA LAMA LITA PLA RASD FLRT NMRT

Union Carbide/Nova Tran • Bruce Humphrey • Clear Lake, WI 54005 • Subscribing

Union City Public Library • Virginia M. Hiatt • Union City, IN 47390

Union County College MacKay Library-LRC • Cranford, NJ 07016 • ACRL LRRT

Union County Public Library • Daniel S. MacNeill • Monroe, NC 28110 • ALCTS ALSC PLA RASD YALSA

Union Fr Sch Dist 30 Lib • M. Mathews • Valley Stream, NY 11582 • AASL

Union Theo Sem Lib The Burke Library • Milton McC. Gatch • New York, NY 10027 • ACRL ALCTS LAMA LITA RASD IFRT

Union Theo Sem in Virginia Library • John B. Trotti • Richmond, VA 23227 • ACRL

United Federation of Teachers Library • Christine P. Carter • New York, NY 10010 • AASL ACRL RASD YALSA IFRT

United States Air Force Base Central Funds Library • Sharron P. Cooper • Nellis AFB, NV 89110 • FLRT

United States Air Force Base Luke Library • M Cecilia Rothschild • Luke AFB, AZ 85309-5725 • AFLRT

United States Air Force Castle Air Force Base • Caroline M. Cantillas • Castle, CA 95342-5000 • PLA

United States Air Force Holbrook Library • Louise S. Engelstad • Ellsworth AFB, SD 57706 • PLA

United States Army Command & General Staff College • C. Suzanne Stephens • Fort Leavenworth, KS 66027-6900

United States Army Corps of Engineers • Ann Scott • Wilmington, NC 28402 • LITA RASD

United States Army Judge Advocate General's School • Daniel C. Lavering • Charlottesville, VA 22903-1781 • ACRL

United States Army USDB Library • Ft. Leavenworth, KS 66027

United States Coast Guard Acad Library (d1) • Patricia A. Daragan • New London, CT 06320-4195 • ACRL ALCTS LAMA LITA RASD FLRT GODORT

United States Naval Academy Nimitz Library • Richard A. Evans • Annapolis, MD 21402-5029 • AASL ACRL ALCTS LAMA LITA RASD AFLRT

United States Navy Bahrain • Margo Cannonier • FPO New York, AE 09834-5400 • AFLRT

United States Sports Academy Library • Jeffrey D. Calametti • Daphne, AL 36526 • ACRL ALCTS RASD

Univ Coll of Cape Breton • Julia Schneider • Sydney, NS, B1P 6L2 Canada • ACRL

Univ of Arkansas at Little Rock Ottenheimer Library • Kathy A. Sanders • Little Rock, AR 72204 • AASL ACRL ALCTS ALSC ALTA ASCLA LAMA LITA PLA RASD YALSA

Univ of Arkansas for Med Sci Lib • Audrey Newcomer • Little Rock, AR 72205-7186 • ACRL ALCTS ASCLA LAMA LITA RASD

Univ of British Columbia Lib Central Serials • Ann Turner • Vancouver BC, V6B 3T5 Canada • AASL ACRL ALCTS LITA PLA RASD YALSA

Univ of Calif-Berkeley University Library • Joseph A. Rosenthal • Berkeley, CA 94720 • AASL ACRL ALCTS ALSC LAMA LITA PLA RASD MAGERT SORT SRRT

Univ of Calif-Los Angeles (UCLA) • Christopher D G Coleman • Los Angeles, CA 90024-1450 • AASL ACRL ALCTS ALSC ASCLA LAMA LITA PLA RASD YALSA

Univ of Calif-Los Angeles Afro-American Studies • Gladys P. Lindsay • Los Angeles, CA 90024-1545 • ACRL

Univ of Calif-Santa Cruz Library • Geraldine Sweet • Santa Cruz, CA 95064

Univ of California-Irvine Library • Calvin J. Boyer • Irvine, CA 92713 • ACRL ALCTS LAMA LITA RASD GODORT LIRT LRRT

Univ of California-San Diego Library 0175A • Dorothy Gregor • La Jolla, CA 92093-0175 • ACRL ALCTS LAMA LITA RASD

Univ of California Los Angeles Grad Sch of Lib & Inf Sci • Beverly P. Lynch • Los Angeles, CA 90024 • AASL ACRL ALCTS ALSC ASCLA LAMA LITA PLA RASD YALSA CLENE IFRT IRRT NMRT SRRT

Univ of Hong Kong Libs • H. Anthony Rydings • Hong Kong B00 041, Hong Kong • ACRL ALCTS

Univ of Kansas Sch of Med Medical Library • Wichita, KS 67214 • ACRL LAMA

Univ of Maine at Presque Isle Library • Anna McGrath • Presque Isle, ME 04769-2888 • ACRL ALCTS LITA RASD

Univ of Maryland-Eastern Shore Frederick Douglass Library • Jessie Cottman Smith • Princess Anne, MD 21853 • ACRL LITA

Univ of Mass Lib • Richard J. Talbot • Amherst, MA 01003 • AASL ACRL ALCTS ALSC ALTA ASCLA LAMA LITA RASD YALSA

Univ of Missouri-Columbia Sch of Lib & Inf Sci • Ruth Dalman • Columbia, MO 65211

Univ of Missouri Libs-Columbia Elmer Ellis Library • Martha A. Bowman • Columbia, MO 65201-5149 • AASL ACRL ALCTS ALSC ALTA ASCLA LAMA LITA PLA RASD YALSA

Univ of Montreal Bibliotheques • Arlette Joffe-Nicodeme • Montreal, PQ, H3C 3J7 Canada • ALCTS LAMA LITA PLA RASD LRRT

Univ of N C at Chapel Hill Sch of Inf and Lib Sci • Barbara B. Moran • Chapel Hill, NC 27599-3360 • AASL ACRL ALCTS ALSC LAMA LITA PLA RASD YALSA CLENE EMIERT FLRT GODORT ILERT IRRT LHRT LIRT LRRT MAGERT NMRT SORT SRRT

Univ of N C at Charlotte J. Murrey Atkins Library • Raymond A. Frankle • Charlotte, NC 28223 • AASL ACRL ALCTS ASCLA LAMA LITA RASD YALSA EMIERT GODORT LIRT LRRT MAGERT

Univ of Nebraska at Kearney Library • John K. Mayeski • Kearney, NE 68849 • AASL ACRL ALCTS ALSC ASCLA LAMA LITA RASD YALSA GODORT

Univ of New Hampshire Lib • Terri-Leigh Hinkle • Durham, NH 03824 • AASL ACRL ALCTS ALSC ASCLA LAMA LITA PLA RASD YALSA

Univ of New Mexico Gen Lib • Paul Vassallo • Albuquerque, NM 87131 • AASL ACRL ALCTS LAMA LITA PLA RASD YALSA

Univ of Papua New Guinea Lib Michael Somare Library • Papua, New Guinea

Univ of Pennsylvania Lib Van Pelt-Dietrich Lib Ctr • Paul R. Mosher • Philadelphia, PA 19104-6206 • ACRL ALCTS LAMA LITA RASD LIRT LRRT

Univ of S Alabama Lib • James A. Damico • Mobile, AL 36688 • AASL ACRL ALCTS ALSC ALTA ASCLA LAMA LITA PLA RASD YALSA

Univ of S C-Lancaster Medford Library • Shari L. Lohela • Lancaster, SC 29720

Univ of S Carolina Libs • Linda K. Allman • Columbia, SC 29208

Univ of S Carolina at Aiken Gregg-Graniteville Library • Frankie H. Cubbedge • Aiken, SC 29801 • ACRL ALCTS LAMA LITA RASD GODORT LIRT

Univ of S Fla Lib • Althea H. Jenkins • Sarasota, FL 34243-2197 • AASL ACRL ALCTS LAMA LITA RASD YALSA

Univ of S Fla Lib • Samuel Y. Fustukjian • Tampa, FL 33620-5600 • AASL ACRL ALCTS LITA PLA RASD YALSA

Univ of SW Louisiana Libs • Don L. Saporito • Lafayette, LA 70503 • AASL ACRL ALCTS ASCLA LAMA LITA PLA RASD YALSA

Univ of Saskatchewan Lib • Frank Winter • Saskatoon SK, S7N 0W0 Canada • AASL ACRL ALCTS LAMA LITA RASD GODORT IFRT SORT

Univ of Southern California Doheny Library • Los Angeles, CA 90089-0182 • ACRL ALCTS LAMA LITA RASD ERT GODORT SORT

Univ of Southern Mississippi Cook Memorial Library • James R. Martin • Hattiesburg, MS 39406-5053 • AASL ACRL ALCTS ALSC ALTA ASCLA LAMA LITA RASD YALSA CLENE EMIERT FLRT IRRT LIRT LRRT MAGERT NMRT SORT

Univ of Southern Mississippi Cox Library • Elaine DeSmith • Long Beach, MS 39560 • ACRL

Univ of Southern Mississippi School of Library Science • Jeannine L. Laughlin-Porter • Hattiesburg, MS 39406-5146 • AASL ACRL ALCTS ALSC LITA PLA RASD YALSA

Univ of Strathclyde Lib • A. Harrison • Glasgow G4 ONS, Scotland • ACRL ALCTS ALSC LITA RASD

Univ of Tennessee-Knoxville Grad Sch of Lib & Inf Sci • Glenn E. Estes • Knoxville, TN 37996-4330 • AASL ACRL ALCTS ALSC LAMA LITA PLA RASD YALSA GODORT LHRT LIRT LRRT

Univ of Texas Med Br Moody Medical Library • Brett A. Kirkpatrick • Galveston, TX 77555-1035 • ACRL ALCTS LAMA LITA RASD GODORT

Univ of Texas at El Paso Lib • Carol M. Kelley • El Paso, TX 79968-0582 • AASL ACRL ALCTS ALSC ASCLA LAMA LITA RASD EMIERT GODORT LIRT MAGERT SRRT

Univ of Toronto Lib Sys • Carole R. Moore • Toronto ON, M5S 1A5 Canada • ACRL ALCTS LITA RASD

Univ of Toronto Lib Sys Trinity College Library • Linda W. Corman • Toronto ON, M5S 1H8 Canada • ACRL ALCTS RASD

Univ of Wisconsin-Madison Memorial Library • Madison, WI 53706 • ACRL ALCTS LAMA LITA RASD FLRT GODORT SRRT

Univ of Wisconsin-Milwaukee Sch of Lib & Inf Sci • Mohammed Aman • Milwaukee, WI 53201

Univ of Wisconsin-Stevens Pt Library • Arne Arneson • Stevens Point, WI 54481 • AASL ACRL ALCTS ALSC LAMA LITA RASD GODORT LIRT

Univ of Wisconsin-Superior Jim Dan Hill Library • Bob D. Carmack • Superior, WI 54880 • AASL ACRL ALCTS LAMA LITA RASD YALSA GODORT LIRT

Univ of the Dist of Columbia Learning Resources Division • Albert J. Casciero • Washington, DC 20008 • ACRL ALCTS LAMA LITA RASD

Univ of the West Indies-Mona Department of Library Studies • Daphne Douglas • Kingston, Jamaica • AASL ACRL ALCTS LITA RASD YALSA

Universidad Metropolitana • Rio Piedras, PR 00928 • ACRL ALCTS

Universidad de Costa Rica Biblioteca,Documentacion e Info • Maria Julia Vargas Bolanos • San Jose, Costa Rica

Universidad de Puerto Rico Colegio Universitario Tec • Bayamon, PR 00959-1919 • ACRL ALCTS

Universita di Genova Facolta di Scirnze Politiche • Gaetano Ferro • 16124 Genova, Italy • ACRL

Universitabibliothek • Joachim Felix Leonhard • D-7800 Tubingen, Germany • ACRL LAMA

Universitaet Konstanz Die Bibliothek • 7750 Konstanz, Germany • ACRL ALCTS

Universitaets-Bibliothek • 2800 Bremen 33, Germany • ACRL ALCTS

Universitatsbibliothek Hannover und Technische Informationsbibl. • G. Schlitt • D-3000 Hannover, Germany • ACRL ALCTS ALSC

Universitatsbiliothek • Bielefeld, Germany • ACRL ALCTS LITA

Universite De Moncton • M. Albert Levesque • Moncton NB, E1A 3E9 Canada • ALCTS

Universite Du Quebec a Montreal Bibliotheque • M. Jean Pierre Cote • Montreal, PQ, H3C 3P3 Canada • ACRL ALCTS LAMA LITA RASD GODORT LIRT

Universite de Sherbrooke (G) Bibliotheque Generale • Jules Chasse • Sherbrooke PQ, J1K 2R1 Canada • ACRL ALCTS LAMA LITA RASD

Universitesbibliotheek • J. Roegiers • B3000 Lueven, Belgium • ALCTS LAMA LITA RASD

Universiti Kebangsaan Malaysia Perpustakaan Tun Seri Lanang • Selangor, Malaysia • ACRL ALCTS LAMA LITA ERT LIRT LRRT SORT

University Club of Chicago Library • Despina Damolaris • Chicago, IL 60603 • IFRT IRRT

University College London • F. J. Friend • London WC1E 6BT, England • ACRL ALCTS LITA

University of Adelaide Barr Smith Library • Adelaide 5001, Australia • ACRL ALCTS LITA PLA RASD

University of Alaska Elmer E. Rasmuson Library • Paul H. McCarthy • Fairbanks, AK 99775-1005 • AASL ACRL ALCTS ALSC ALTA ASCLA LAMA LITA PLA RASD YALSA

University of Alberta Library • Ernie B. Ingles • Edmonton AB, T6G 2J8 Canada • AASL ACRL ALCTS ALSC ASCLA LAMA LITA PLA RASD YALSA ERT GODORT IFRT IRRT LIRT LRRT SORT SRRT

University of Alberta Library Serials Section • Ernie B. Ingles • Edmonton AB, T6G 2J8 Canada • AASL ALCTS

University of Arizona Library • W. David Laird • Tucson, AZ 85721 • AASL ACRL ALCTS ALSC ASCLA LITA RASD YALSA SRRT

University of Arkansas Libraries • John A. Harrison • Fayetteville, AR 72701-1201 • AASL ACRL ALCTS ASCLA LAMA LITA PLA RASD YALSA

University of Auckland Library • P. B. Durey • Auckland, New Zealand • ACRL ALCTS LITA RASD

University of Baltimore Langsdale Library • Wanda G. Breitenbach • Baltimore, MD 21201 • ACRL ALCTS LAMA LITA RASD GODORT IFRT LIRT SORT

University of Bombay • Bombay 400 098, India • ACRL ALCTS

University of British Columbia Library • Ann Turner • Blaine, WA 98230-8076 • ACRL ALCTS ALTA LITA RASD YALSA

University of Calgary Libraries • A. H. McDonold • Calgary AB, T2N 1N4 Canada • AASL ACRL ALCTS LAMA LITA RASD YALSA

University of California UCSB Library • Joseph A. Boisse • Santa Barbara, CA 93106-9010 • ACRL ALCTS LAMA LITA RASD

University of Canberra • Lois Jennings • Belconnen ACT 2616, Australia • AASL ACRL ALCTS ALSC LAMA LITA PLA RASD

University of Canterbury Library • Richard Hlavac • Christchurch 1, New Zealand • ACRL ALCTS LAMA LITA RASD

University of Cape Town Carleton Harrison Edu Lib • A. S. C. Hooper • Rondebosch 7700, South Africa • ACRL ALCTS LAMA LITA RASD

University of Central Arkansas Torreyson Library • Willie Hardin • Conway, AR 72032 • AASL ACRL ALCTS ALSC ASCLA LAMA LITA PLA RASD GODORT

University of Charleston Andrew Thomas Memorial Library • Sandra A. Williamson • Charleston, WV 25304 • ACRL ALCTS LITA RASD

University of Chicago Library • K Jane Ciacci • Chicago, IL 60637-1502 • AASL ACRL ALCTS ALSC ALTA ASCLA LAMA LITA PLA RASD YALSA CLENE EMIERT ERT FLRT GODORT IFRT ILERT IRRT LHRT LIRT LRRT MAGERT NMRT SORT SRRT

University of Cincinnati Central Library • Cincinnati, OH 45221-0033 • AASL ACRL ALCTS ALSC ASCLA LAMA LITA RASD YALSA

University of Colorado-Boulder University Libraries • James F. Williams • Boulder, CO 80309 • AASL ACRL ALCTS ALSC ALTA ASCLA LAMA LITA PLA RASD YALSA

University of Connecticut Homer Babbidge Library • Norman D. Stevens • Storrs, CT 06269-1005 • AASL ALCTS LITA RASD YALSA

University of Connecticut at Avery Point Library • Constance B. Cooke • Groton, CT 06340-6097 • ACRL

University of Delaware Library • Susan Brynteson • Newark, DE 19717-5267 • AASL ACRL ALCTS ALSC ALTA ASCLA LAMA LITA RASD YALSA GODORT IFRT LIRT MAGERT

University of Evansville • R. N. Sharma • Evansville, IN 47722 • ACRL ALCTS LITA RASD

University of Florida Libraries • Dale B. Canelas • Gainesville, FL 32611-2047 • AASL ACRL ALCTS ASCLA LAMA LITA PLA RASD YALSA SORT

University of Georgia Costal Plain Experim St Lib • Patricia M Griffin • Tifton, GA 31793 • ACRL

University of Georgia Libraries • William Gray Potter • Athens, GA 30602 • AASL ACRL ALCTS ALSC ALTA ASCLA LAMA LITA PLA RASD YALSA CLENE EMIERT ERT FLRT GODORT IFRT ILERT IRRT LHRT LIRT LRRT MAGERT NMRT SORT SRRT

University of Haifa Library • Shmuel Sever • Haifa 3199, Israel • AASL ACRL ALCTS ALSC LAMA LITA PLA RASD

University of Hawaii Thomas Hale Hamilton Library • John R. Haak • Honolulu, HI 96822 • AASL ACRL ALCTS ALSC ALTA ASCLA LAMA LITA PLA RASD YALSA ERT MAGERT

University of Houston Libraries • Robin N. Downes • Houston, TX 77204-2091 • AASL ACRL ALCTS ALSC ALTA ASCLA LAMA LITA PLA RASD YALSA

University of Illinois Library • Michael J. Gorman • Urbana, IL 61801 • AASL ACRL ALCTS ALSC ALTA ASCLA LAMA LITA PLA RASD YALSA CLENE EMIERT ERT FLRT GODORT IFRT ILERT IRRT LHRT LIRT LRRT MAGERT NMRT SORT SRRT

University of Iowa Libraries • Sheila D. Creth • Iowa City, IA 52242-1379 • AASL ACRL ALCTS ALSC ALTA ASCLA LAMA LITA PLA RASD YALSA CLENE EMIERT ERT FLRT GODORT IFRT ILERT IRRT LHRT LIRT LRRT MAGERT NMRT SORT SRRT

University of Leicester Library • Leicester LEI 7RH, England • ACRL ALCTS

University of Lethbridge Library • Barbara Marshalsay • Lethbridge AB, T1K 3M4 Canada • ACRL ALCTS LITA RASD

University of London Library • W.G. Simpson • London, England • ACRL ALCTS

University of Maine Raymond H. Fogler Library • Elaine M. Albright • Orono, ME 04469

University of Malawi Library Chancellor College • Zomba, Malawi

University of Manitoba Libraries Elizabeth Dafoe Library • Carolynne Presser • Winnipeg MB, R3T 2N2 Canada • AASL ACRL ALCTS LAMA LITA RASD YALSA GODORT

University of Mary Library • Cheryl M. Bailey • Bismarck, ND 58504 • LAMA LITA

University of Maryland Coll of Lib and Inf Serv • Claude E. Walston • College Park, MD 20742-4345 • AASL ACRL ALCTS ALSC ALTA ASCLA LAMA LITA PLA RASD YALSA CLENE EMIERT ERT FLRT GODORT IFRT ILERT IRRT LHRT LIRT LRRT MAGERT NMRT SORT SRRT

University of Melbourne Baillieu Library • W. D. Richardson • Melbourne VIC 3052, Australia • ACRL ALCTS LITA

University of Melbourne Institute of Education • G. Murphy • Carlton VIC 3053, Australia • AASL ACRL ALCTS ALSC LITA RASD

University of Miami Libraries Richter Library • Frank Rodgers • Coral Gables, FL 33124 • AASL ACRL ALCTS ALSC ALTA ASCLA LAMA LITA PLA RASD YALSA

University of Michigan Libraries Information and Library Studies • Ann Arbor, MI 48109 • AASL ACRL ALCTS ALSC ALTA ASCLA LAMA LITA PLA RASD CLENE EMIERT ERT FLRT GODORT IFRT ILERT IRRT LHRT LIRT LRRT MAGERT NMRT SORT SRRT

University of Minnesota O. Meredith Wilson Library • Basil W. Sozansky • Minneapolis, MN 55455-0414 • AASL ACRL ALCTS ALSC ALTA ASCLA LAMA LITA PLA RASD YALSA ERT IRRT SORT SRRT

University of Mississippi John Davis Williams Library • Jean Major • University, MS 38677 • ACRL ALCTS LITA RASD GODORT

University of Montana Library • Ruth J. Patrick • Missoula, MT 59812 • AASL ACRL ALCTS LITA RASD GODORT MAGERT

University of Natal Library • F. Scholtz • Durban 4001, South Africa • AASL ACRL ALCTS LAMA LITA RASD

University of New Brunswick • John D. Teskey • Fredericton NB, E3B 5H5 Canada • LAMA

University of New Brunswick Ward Chipman Library • K. M. Duff • Saint John NB, E2L 4L5 Canada • ACRL ALCTS LITA RASD

University of New England • K. G. Schmude • Armidale NSW, Australia • ACRL ALCTS LITA RASD

University of New England Jack S. Ketchum Library • Andrew J. Golub • Biddeford, ME 04005 • ACRL

University of New Mexico Native American Studies • Albuquerque, NM 87131 • ACRL

University of New Mexico Valencia Campus • Kris Warmoth • Los Lunas, NM 87031 • ACRL

University of New Orleans Earl K. Long Library • Jill B. Fatzer • New Orleans, LA 70148 • AASL ACRL ALCTS ALSC ASCLA LAMA LITA PLA RASD GODORT

University of New South Wales Social Sciences Library • Allan Horton • Kensington 2033, Australia • AASL ACRL ALCTS LITA RASD

University of Newcastle Auchmuty Library • William Linklater • Newcastle NSW, 2308, Australia • ACRL ALCTS LAMA LITA RASD

University of North Dakota Chester Fritz Library • Frank A. D'Andraia • Grand Forks, ND 58202-0175 • ACRL ALCTS LAMA LITA

University of North Dakota Dept of Lib Sci & AV Instr • Neil V. Price • Grand Forks, ND 58202 • AASL ACRL ALCTS ALSC PLA RASD IFRT LIRT

University of North Texas • B. Donald Grose • Denton, TX 76203 • AASL ACRL ALCTS ALSC ALTA ASCLA LAMA LITA PLA RASD FLRT GODORT IRRT LHRT LIRT NMRT SORT SRRT

University of Northern Colorado James A. Michener Library • Gary M. Pitkin • Greeley, CO 80639 • AASL ACRL ALCTS ALSC ASCLA LAMA LITA PLA RASD YALSA

University of Oklahoma Libraries University Libraries • Nancy E. Larsen • Norman, OK 73019 • AASL ACRL ALCTS ALSC ALTA ASCLA LAMA LITA PLA RASD YALSA FLRT LIRT SORT SRRT

University of Phoenix • Judyth Lessee • Tucson, AZ 85711 • ACRL RASD

University of Pittsburgh Hillman Library • Lisa Mitten • Pittsburgh, PA 15260 • ACRL ALCTS LAMA LITA RASD

University of Pittsburgh Sch of Lib and Inf Sci • Toni Carbo Bearman • Pittsburgh, PA 15260 • AASL ACRL ALCTS ALSC ALTA ASCLA LAMA LITA PLA RASD YALSA CLENE EMIERT GODORT LIRT MAGERT NMRT SRRT

University of Portland Clark Memorial Library • Joseph P. Browne • Portland, OR 97203-5798 • AASL ACRL ALCTS LITA RASD

University of Puerto Rico • Mayaguez, PR 00708 • AASL ACRL ALCTS LAMA LITA RASD CLENE LIRT

University of Puerto Rico Biblioteca Ciencias • Vilma Bayron • San Juan, PR 00931-3302 • AASL ACRL ALCTS ASCLA LAMA RASD CLENE ERT FLRT GODORT IFRT IRRT LHRT LIRT LRRT NMRT SORT SRRT

University of Queensland • F. D. O. Fielding • Brisbane Queensland, Australia • AASL ACRL ALCTS ALTA ASCLA LAMA LITA RASD

University of Redlands Armacost Library • Fred E. Hearth • Redlands, CA 92374-3758 • ACRL ALCTS LAMA LITA RASD

University of Rhode Island Coll of Continuing Edu Lib • Jean Sheridan • Providence, RI 02908 • ACRL RASD

University of Rhode Island Grad Sch of Lib & Inf Studies • Elizabeth Futas • Kingston, RI 02881-0815 • AASL ACRL ALCTS LAMA LITA PLA RASD YALSA LRRT

University of Richmond • Judith L. Hunt • Richmond, VA 23173 • AASL ACRL ALCTS LAMA LITA RASD YALSA

University of Ryukyu Library • Okinawa 901-24, Japan

University of San Carlos Library • Nela D. Serrato • Cebu City, Philippines • ACRL ALCTS RASD

University of Scranton Harry & Jeanette Weinberg Mem • Bonnie Strohl • Scranton, PA 18510-4700 • ACRL ALCTS LAMA LITA RASD LIRT

University of Sheffield Library • M. Hannon • Sheffield S10 2TN, England • ACRL ALCTS ASCLA LAMA LITA RASD

University of South Australia Library Serials • Underdale 5032, Australia • AASL ACRL ALCTS ALSC LITA RASD

University of South Carolina • Arthur P. Young • Columbia, SC 29208

University of South Carolina Coastal Carolina Coll Kimbel Lib • Lynne Smith • Conway, SC 29526 • ACRL ALCTS RASD GODORT

University of South Carolina Salkehatchie Campus Library • Marvin J. Light • Allendale, SC 29810 • ACRL RASD SRRT

University of South Dakota I.D. Weeks Library • Imre Meszaros • Vermillion, SD 57069-2390 • ACRL ALCTS LAMA LITA RASD

University of Stellenbosch University Library • Stellenbosch, 7600, South Africa • ACRL ALCTS LAMA LITA RASD

University of Sydney Fisher Library • Joanne Threlfall • Sydney NSW, Australia • ACRL ALCTS LITA RASD GODORT

University of Tampere Library • Hannele Soini • 33101 Tampere, Finland • AASL ACRL ALCTS LITA LHRT LRRT

University of Tasmania Morris Miller Library • Christine Crecker • Hobart Tasmania 7001, Australia • AASL ACRL ALCTS LITA RASD YALSA

University of Technology Library • M. Hopkins • Leicestershire, England • ACRL ALCTS RASD

University of Technology, Sydney Library • Steve O'Connor • Broadway NSW 2007, Australia • ACRL ALCTS LITA RASD

University of Technology/Sydney Kuring-Gai Campus Muir Library • Susan Edwards • Lindfield NSW 2070, Australia

University of Tennessee Library • Paula T. Kaufman • Knoxville, TN 37996-1000 • AASL ACRL ALCTS ALSC LAMA LITA PLA RASD YALSA GODORT IRRT LIRT MAGERT NMRT SORT SRRT

University of Texas Libraries • Harold Billings • Austin, TX 78713 • AASL ACRL ALCTS ALSC ALTA ASCLA LAMA LITA PLA RASD YALSA

University of Texas Libraries General Libraries • Harold Billings • Austin, TX 78713-7330 • AASL ACRL ALCTS ALSC ALTA ASCLA LAMA LITA PLA RASD YALSA CLENE EMIERT ERT FLRT GODORT IFRT ILERT IRRT LHRT LIRT LRRT MAGERT NMRT SORT SRRT

University of Texas School of Public Health Library • Stephanie L. Normann • Houston, TX 77225 • ACRL LAMA LITA GODORT

University of Tokyo Center for American Studies • Tokyo, Japan • ACRL RASD GODORT

University of Toronto Faculty of Lib & Inf Sci • Diane Henderson • Toronto ON, M5S 1A1 Canada • AASL ACRL ALCTS ALSC ASCLA LAMA LITA PLA RASD YALSA EMIERT ERT FLRT GODORT IFRT IRRT LIRT MAGERT NMRT SORT SRRT

University of Tulsa McFarlin Library • Robert H. Patterson • Tulsa, OK 74104-3189 • ACRL ALCTS LAMA LITA RASD GODORT

University of Utah Marriott Library • Salt Lake City, UT 84112-1179 • AASL ACRL ALCTS ALSC ALTA ASCLA LAMA LITA PLA RASD YALSA

University of Victoria McPherson Library • Dean W. Halliwell • Victoria BC, V8W 3H5 Canada • AASL ACRL ALCTS LITA RASD YALSA MAGERT

University of Washington Suzzallo Library • Betty G. Bengtson • Seattle, WA 98195 • AASL ACRL ALCTS ALSC ALVA ASCLA LAMA LITA PLA RASD EMIERT ERT FLRT GODORT IFRT IRRT LHRT LIRT MAGERT NMRT SORT SRRT

University of Washington Tacoma Branch Campus Library • Tacoma, WA 98402 • ACRL

University of Waterloo • M. C. Shepherd • Waterloo ON, N2L 3G1 Canada • ACRL ALCTS LAMA LITA RASD

University of West Indies Main Library • Michael Gill • Bridgetown-Barbados, West Indies • ACRL ALCTS LITA

University of Western Cape • Peter E. September • Bellville, 7535, South Africa • AASL ACRL ALCTS LAMA LITA YALSA

University of Western Ontario Sch of Lib & Inf Sci • Jean M. Tague-Sutcliffe • London ON, N6G 1H1 Canada • AASL ACRL ALCTS ALSC ALTA ASCLA LAMA LITA PLA RASD YALSA ERT FLRT GODORT IFRT IRRT LHRT LIRT LRRT MAGERT NMRT SORT SRRT

University of Windsor • Windsor ON, N9B 3P4 Canada • ACRL ALCTS LAMA LITA RASD ERT IRRT LRRT SORT

University of Winnipeg Library • William Converse • Winnipeg MB, B3B 2E9 Canada • ACRL

University of Wisconsin Sch of Lib & Inf Studies • Madison, WI 53706 • AASL ACRL ALCTS ALSC ALTA ASCLA LAMA LITA PLA RASD YALSA EMIERT ERT FLRT GODORT IFRT ILERT IRRT LHRT LIRT LRRT MAGERT NMRT SORT SRRT

University of Witwatersrand • R. Musiker • Braamfontein, South Africa • ACRL ALCTS RASD

University of Wyoming • Keith M. Cottam • Laramie, WY 82071 • AASL ACRL ALCTS ALSC ALTA ASCLA LAMA LITA PLA MAGERT

University of the Pacific • Thomas W. Leonhardt • Stockton, CA 95211 • AASL ACRL ALCTS ALSC LAMA LITA PLA RASD

University of the Philippines Inst of Lib Sci Lib • Quezon City 3004, Philippines

University of the Virgin Islands The Ralph M. Paiewonsky Library • David Oettinger • Saint Thomas, VI 00802 • ACRL GODORT

University of the West Indies • O. O. Ogundipe • Saint Augustine, Trinidad • ACRL ALCTS LAMA LITA RASD GODORT LIRT LRRT

University of the West Indies Library • Mona, Jamaica • ACRL ALCTS LITA

Upland Public Library • Linda Yao • Upland, CA 91786 • ALCTS ALSC LAMA LITA PLA RASD

Upper Arlington Public Library • John M. Brooks-Barr • Upper Arlington, OH 43221

Upper Merion Area Sch Dist Professional Library • Margaret T. McCaskey • King of Prussia, PA 19406 • AASL

Upper Perkiomen High School • W. Harner Jr. • Pennsburg, PA 18073 • AASL YALSA

Upsala College Wirths Campus Library • Sally Capobianco • Sussex, NJ 07461 • ACRL LAMA RASD

Urban Libraries Council • Keith Doms • State College, PA 16801

Ursinus College Library • Charles A. Jamison • Collegeville, PA 19426 • ACRL ALCTS LAMA LITA RASD

Ursuline Academy • Lana McFarland • Dallas, TX 75229 • AASL

Ursuline Academy Danny Hurtig Memorial Library • Sylvia Probst • New Orleans, LA 70118

Utah Library Association • Donald Trottier • Salt Lake City, UT 84115

Utah State University Merrill Library • Kenneth E. Marks • Logan, UT 84322-3000 • AASL ACRL ALCTS ALSC ALTA LAMA LITA PLA RASD ERT FLRT GODORT IFRT IRRT LHRT LRRT SORT SRRT

VTLS Inc. • Bruce Heterick • Blacksburg, VA 24060 • Subscribing

Valdosta State College Library • George R. Gaumond • Valdosta, GA 31698 • ACRL ALCTS ALSC LAMA LITA RASD YALSA

Valencia Community College Learning Resources Center • Donna Carver • Orlando, FL 32802 • ACRL ALCTS LAMA LITA RASD LIRT

Valley City State University Allen Memorial Library • Darryl B. Podoll • Valley City, ND 58072 • AASL ALCTS LAMA LITA RASD YALSA GODORT IFRT LIRT

Valley Cottage Library • Vly Cottage, NY 10989 • PLA RASD IFRT

Valley Stream Mem High Sch Library • Valley Stream, NY 11580

Valley Stream North High School • Harvey Brody • Franklin Square, NY 11010 • AASL

Valleyview School • Betty Stanton • Denville, NJ 07834 • AASL

Vancouver Community College Langara Campus Library • Judith Neamtan • Vancouver BC, V5Y 2Z6 Canada • ACRL ALCTS ASCLA LAMA LITA RASD

Vancouver Public Library • Madeleine Aalto • Vancouver BC, V6Z 1X5 Canada • ACRL ALCTS ALSC LAMA LITA PLA RASD YALSA EMIERT IFRT MAGERT

Vanderbilt University Library Jean & Alexander Heard Library • Malcolm Getz • Nashville, TN 37240-0007 • ACRL ALCTS LAMA LITA RASD

Vandercook College of Music Harry Ruppel Memorial Library • Marguerite J. Krynicki • Chicago, IL 60616

Varian Associates Technical Library • Joan Frances Murphy • Palo Alto, CA 94304

Vassar College Library • Charles Henry • Poughkeepsie, NY 12601 • ACRL ALCTS LAMA LITA RASD GODORT

Ventura Cnty Lib Serv Agency • Dixie D. Adeniran • Ventura, CA 93002 • ACRL ALCTS ALSC ALTA ASCLA LAMA LITA RASD YALSA CLENE EMIERT FLRT GODORT IFRT LHRT LIRT NMRT SORT

Vermont College Gary Memorial Library • Montpelier, VT 05602 • ACRL

Vermont Department of Libraries • Patricia E. Klinck • Montpelier, VT 05609 • AASL ACRL ALCTS ALSC ALTA LAMA LITA PLA RASD YALSA CLENE EMIERT ERT FLRT GODORT IFRT ILERT IRRT LHRT LIRT LRRT MAGERT NMRT SORT SRRT

Vermont Library Association • Paula J. Baker • Burlington, VT 05402-0803 • ALTA

Vernon Area Public Library • Allen Meyer • Prairie View, IL 60069 • ALCTS ALSC LAMA LITA PLA RASD

Victoria Public Library • Lee Teal • Victoria BC, V8W 3H2 Canada • ALCTS LAMA PLA RASD YALSA

Victoria University • R. C. Brandeis • Toronto ON, M5S 1K7 Canada • ACRL ALCTS LAMA RASD

Victoria University Library Periodicals • Wellington, New Zealand • ACRL ALCTS ASCLA LITA RASD

Video Trend, Inc. • Mary Zack • Livonia, MI 48150 • Subscribing

Vienna International Centre Library • S. R. Khan • A-1400 Vienna, Austria • ACRL ALCTS LAMA LITA

Villa Duchesne High Sch Lib • Saint Louis, MO 63131 • AASL

Villa Julie College Library • Peter H. Curtis • Stevenson, MD 21153 • ACRL LAMA RASD

Viola Public Library District • Viola, IL 61486

Virgin Islands Dept of Edu #108 Curriculum, Instr & Libs • Saint Thomas, VI 00802 • AASL

Virginia Commonwealth University • William J. Judd • Richmond, VA 23284-2033

Virginia Library Association • Deborah Trocchi • Alexandria, VA 22314-4109

Virginia Public Library • Catherine S. Liptak • Virginia, MN 55792 • ALSC PLA RASD YALSA

Virginia State Lib & Archv • Ella G. Yates • Richmond, VA 23219

Virginia State University Johnston Memorial Library • Catherine V. Bland • Petersburg, VA 23803 • AASL ACRL ALCTS ALSC LAMA LITA RASD YALSA LIRT

Virginia Theological Seminary • Jack Goodwin • Alexandria, VA 22304-5201 • ACRL ALCTS LITA

Virginia Union University • Vonita W. Dandridge • Richmond, VA 23220 • ACRL EMIERT

Voorheesville Public Library • Gail Alter Sacco • Voorheesville, NY 12186 • ALTA

W Chicago Pub Lib Dist • Charlene R. Sanders • West Chicago, IL 60185 • ALCTS ALTA PLA

W Va Lib Assn • Charleston, WV 25305

Wabash Carnegie Public Library • Joanna M. Strode • Wabash, IN 46992 • LAMA PLA

Wabash College • Larry J. Frye • Crawfordsville, IN 47933 • ACRL ALCTS RASD

Wabash Valley Library Network • Dennis C. Lawson • Lafayette, IN 47901-1470 • AASL ALTA ASCLA LAMA PLA RASD

Wabasha Public Library • Judith Schierts • Wabasha, MN 55981

Wagner College Lib and Learning Resources Ctr • Y John Auh • Staten Island, NY 10301 • ACRL ALCTS LITA RASD GODORT

Wagner Free Institute of Science • Philadelphia, PA 19121 • ALCTS

Wakpala High School • Jack T. Shillingstad • Wakpala, SD 57658-0111 • AASL EMIERT

Wakulla Middle School • Joy L. Lewis • Crawfordville, FL 32327 • AASL YALSA

Wales, College of Librarianship Inf & Lib Studies Lib • Aberystwyth SY233AS, Wales • AASL ACRL ALCTS ALSC ALTA ASCLA LAMA LITA PLA RASD YALSA ERT FLRT ILERT IRRT LHRT LIRT LRRT MAGERT NMRT SORT SRRT

Walker & Company • Penny Rosenthal • New York, NY 10019 • ASCLA *Subscribing*

Walker School District 181 Instructional Material Center • Donna Witt • Clarendon Hills, IL 60514 • AASL LITA YALSA

Walla Walla Community College Library • Sandra L. Blackaby • Walla Walla, WA 99362 • ACRL LITA RASD

Walt Disney Company, The • Cathryn C. Girard • Burbank, CA 91521 • Subscribing

Walter Reed Army Medical Center Medical Library • Hoyt Galloway • Washington, DC 20307-5001 • AFLRT FLRT

Walworth-Seeley Public Library • Mary Perry • Walworth, NY 14568

Warren County Community College • Lynea Anderman • Washington, NJ 07882-9605 • ACRL ALCTS PLA RASD IFRT LIRT

Warren Library Association • Ann Lesser • Warren, PA 16365 • ALSC LITA RASD

Warsaw Community Public Library • Warsaw, IN 46580 • PLA

Warsaw Public Library • Warsaw, IL 62379

Wartburg Theological Seminary Reu Memorial Library • Joel L. Samuels • Dubuque, IA 52003-7797 • ACRL

Warwick Valley Middle School Library • Patricia Juliano • Warwick, NY 10990 • AASL ALSC

Washburn University Library • Topeka, KS 66621 • ACRL ALCTS ASCLA LAMA LITA RASD GODORT

Washington & Jefferson College Memorial Library • Robert Connell • Washington, PA 15301 • ACRL ALCTS RASD

Washington County Free Library • Charles S. Blank • Hagerstown, MD 21740

Washington County Library • Dorothy A. Lore • Potosi, MO 63664-1998

Washington Library Association • Barbara Tolliver • Bellevue, WA 98007

Washington Parish Library • Anita R. Ruble • Franklinton, LA 70438 • ALTA PLA

Washington State Library • Nancy L. Zussy • Olympia, WA 98504-2470 • AASL ACRL ALCTS ALSC ALTA ASCLA LAMA LITA RASD YALSA CLENE GODORT IRRT SORT

Washington State Univ Lib • Maureen D. Pastine • Pullman, WA 99164-5610 • ACRL ALCTS ALSC ASCLA LAMA LITA PLA RASD GODORT IFRT IRRT LIRT

Washington Township Library • Barbara A. Marine • Washington, IL 61571

Washington University Libraries • Saint Louis, MO 63130-4899 • ACRL ALCTS LAMA LITA RASD GODORT

Watauga Regional Library Center • Joy A. Mowery • Johnson City, TN 37601 • ALTA PLA

Water Department of Philadephia Library • Raymond Frank Roedell • Philadelphia, PA 19107

Waterford Public Library • Vincent Juliano • Waterford, CT 06385 • ALCTS LITA PLA RASD

Waterford Twp Public Lib • Steven Fleisher • Atco, NJ 08004

Waterloo Public Library • Beverly F. Lind • Waterloo, IA 50701 • ALCTS ALSC ALTA ASCLA LAMA LITA PLA RASD

Waterloo Public Memorial Library • Joel R. Zibell • Waterloo, WI 53594 • PLA

Watertown Regional Library • Michael C. Mullin • Watertown, SD 57201-0250 • PLA

Watseka Public Library • Watseka, IL 60970 • PLA

Watterson College • Amy Morris Lain • Louisville, KY 40218

Wauseon Exempted Sch Dist Lib Wauseon Public Library • Francita L. Gasche • Wauseon, OH 43567 • ALTA PLA

Waverley City Libraries • Charles Emerton • Mt Waverley, 3149, Australia • ALCTS LITA PLA RASD YALSA

Waverly Public Library • Patricia R. Coffie • Waverly, IA 50677 • RASD

Wayland Baptist Univeristy Van Howeling Library • Mary P. Fox • Plainview, TX 79072

Wayne Community College Learning Resource Center • Goldsboro, NC 27533

Wayne County Community College Library • James Flaherty • Detroit, MI 48226 • ACRL

Wayne Oakland Library Federation • Malcolm K. Hill • Wayne, MI 48184 • ALCTS ALSC ALTA ASCLA LAMA LITA PLA RASD YALSA

Wayne Public Library • Wayne, NE 68787

Wayne State University • Detroit, MI 48202 • AASL ACRL ALCTS ALSC ALTA ASCLA LAMA LITA PLA RASD YALSA

Wayne State University Libraries • Peter Spyers-Duran • Detroit, MI 48202

Waynesburg College Library • Suzanne Wylie • Waynesburg, PA 15370

Webb Inst of Naval Arch Library • David J. Zaehringer • Glen Cove, NY 11542 • ACRL

Webb School of Knoxville Library • Tena Litherland • Knoxville, TN 37923 • AASL YALSA

Webber College Library G & R Babson Learning Center • Jeanne Tillman • Babson Park, FL 33827 • ACRL LITA

Weber County Library • Lynnda M. Wangsgard • Odgen, UT 84401 • PLA

Webster Parish Library • Barbara E. Slack • Minden, LA 71055 • ALSC PLA

Webster University Library • St Louis, MO 63119 • AASL ACRL ALCTS RASD

Weld County Library District • Luella Kinnison • Greeley, CO 80631

Wellesley College Library Margaret Clapp Library • Barbara S. St. Onge • Wellesley, MA 02181-8275 • ACRL ALCTS LAMA LITA RASD GODORT

Wells College Library • Jeri L. Vargo • Aurora, NY 13026 • ACRL

Wells High School Library • Sharleen A. Ober • Wells, ME 04090 • AASL

Wellsburg Public Library • Betty Lindaman • Wellsburg, IA 50680

Wellsville Central Schools • Carol Brown • Wellsville, NY 14895

Wenatchee High School • Wenatchee, WA 98801

Wenham Public Library • Wenham, MA 01984

Wernersville Public Library • Philippa McKee • Wernersville, PA 19565 • PLA

Wesleyan College Willet Memorial Library • Tena Roberts • Macon, GA 31297 • AASL ACRL ALCTS ALSC LITA RASD

West Babylon Public Library • Anne Marie Dolan • West Babylon, NY 11704 • ALTA LAMA LITA PLA RASD YALSA

West Baton Rouge Parish Library • Frances D. Cole • Port Allen, LA 70767

West Caldwell Public Library • West Caldwell, NJ 07006

West Carroll Parish Library • Mary Ann Brennan • Oak Grove, LA 71263

West Chester Public Library • West Chester, PA 19380

West Frankfort Public Library • Sarah Jane Alexander • West Frankfort, IL 62896 • PLA CLENE

West Lafayette Public Library • W Lafayette, IN 47906

West Leyden High School West Media Center • M. Bruscate • Northlake, IL 60164

West Linn Public Library • Pamella K. Williams • West Linn, OR 97068 • ALSC PLA

West Nyack Free Library • Lorette M. Adams • West Nyack, NY 10994 • ALTA

West Palm Beach Public Library • Sally Bailey • West Palm Beach, FL 33401 • PLA

West Shore Public Library • Roberta E. Greene • Camp Hill, PA 17011

West Virginia Inst of Tech Vining Library • Victor C. Young • Montgomery, WV 25136 • ACRL ALCTS LAMA

West Virginia Library Commission • Frederic J. Glazer • Charleston, WV 25305 • ALTA LAMA LITA PLA

Westborough Sr High Sch Lib • Diane Libbey • Westborough, MA 01581 • AASL

Westbrook College Library • Roberta C. Gray • Portland, ME 04103

Westbrook Public Library • Lewis Daniels • Westbrook, CT 06498

Western Albemarle High School • Janet C. Frieden • Crozet, VA 22901 • AASL

Western Conservative Baptist Sem Cline-Tunnell Library • Robert A. Krupp • Portland, OR 97215-3399 • ACRL ALCTS RASD

Western District Public Library • Orion, IL 61273

Western Illinois Library System • Sherwood Kirk • Galesburg, IL 61401 • AASL ALCTS ALSC ALTA ASCLA LAMA LITA PLA RASD YALSA GODORT

Western Kentucky University Helm-Cravens Library • Michael B. Binder • Bowling Green, KY 42101 • AASL ACRL ALCTS ALSC ALTA ASCLA LAMA LITA PLA RASD YALSA

Western Maryland College Hoover Library • George T. Bachmann • Westminster, MD 21157-4390 • AASL ACRL ALCTS ALSC LAMA LITA RASD GODORT IFRT LIRT SORT

Western Michigan Univ Libs Dwight B. Waldo Library • Charlene E. Renner • Kalamazoo, MI 49008 • AASL ACRL ALCTS LAMA LITA RASD

Western New Mexico University • Benjamin T. Wakashige • Silver City, NM 88062 • ACRL ALCTS LAMA RASD GODORT LIRT

Western New York Library Resources Council • Mary W. Ghikas • Buffalo, NY 14203

Western Oklahoma State College W.C. Burris LRC • Julie Ann Ligon • Altus, OK 73521 • ACRL

Western Publishing Company Golden Press • Joyce Stein • New York, NY 10022 • Subscribing

Western Theological Seminary Beardslee Library • Holland, MI 49423 • ACRL ALCTS

Western Wyoming Cmnty Coll • Robert L. Kalabus • Rock Springs, WY 82902 • ACRL ALCTS

Westminster Choir College Talbott Library • Mary Benton • Princeton, NJ 08540 • ACRL ALCTS LITA

Westminster College Reeves Memorial Library • Lorna K. Mitchell • Fulton, MO 65251-1299 • ACRL ALCTS LAMA

Weston Public Library • Jane W. Atkinson • Weston, CT 06883-0146

Westover School Library • Charles Thompson • Middlebury, CT 06762

Westport Public Library • Sally H. Poundstone • Westport, CT 06880 • ALCTS LAMA LITA PLA RASD YALSA

Westridge School for Girls Library • Pasadena, CA 91105 • AASL

Westville Correctional Center Library Services • Janice Coffeen • Westville, IN 46391 • ASCLA

Westwood First Presbyterian Church Library • Cincinnati, OH 45211

Wethersfield Public Library • Om P. Wadhwa • Wethersfield, CT 06109 • LITA PLA RASD YALSA

Wharton County Junior College Hodges Learning Center • Patsy G. Norton • Wharton, TX 77488 • ACRL

Wheeling Jesuit College Library • Veronica Steiner • Wheeling, WV 26003 • ACRL ALCTS LITA

Whitaker Library Chowan College • Alice L. Hassell • Murfreesboro, NC 27855 • ACRL ALCTS

Whiting Public Library • Carol Truett • Whiting, IN 46394 • PLA

Whitinsville Social Library • Whitinsville, MA 01588

Whitman College • Walla Walla, WA 99362 • ACRL ALCTS LAMA LITA RASD GODORT LIRT LRRT

Whittier College Wardman Library • Philip M. O'Brien • Whittier, CA 90608-9984

Whittle Springs Middle School • Norma S. Kelley • Knoxville, TN 37917 • ERT IFRT   Subscribing

Wicomico County Free Library • Salisbury, MD 21801

Wiley College Thomas Winston Cole Sr. Library • Frank Francis • Marshall, TX 75670

Wilfrid Laurier Univ Lib • Erich Schultz • Waterloo ON, N2L 3C5 Canada • ACRL ALCTS LAMA RASD GODORT LIRT

Will Rogers Library • Margaret Guffey • Claremore, OK 74017

Willard Public Library • William A. Goodrich • Evansville, IN 47710

William B. Ogden Free Library • Anne R. Turner • Walton, NY 13856

William Carey Intl Univ Kenneth Scott Latourette Library • LeRoy L. Judd • Pasadena, CA 91104 • ACRL

William E. Dermody Fr Pub Lib • Pilar Odenheim • Carlstadt, NJ 07072

William K. Kohrs Mem Lib • June E. Lyman • Deer Lodge, MT 59722

William Leonard Pub Lib Dist • Maude Johnson • Robbins, IL 60472

William Paterson College Library • Robert L. Goldberg • Wayne, NJ 07470 • ACRL ALCTS LAMA RASD ERT GODORT LIRT LRRT

William Penn College Wilcox Library • Julie Ellen Hansen • Oskaloosa, IA 52577 • ACRL ALCTS LAMA RASD

Williamsburg County Library • Kingstree, SC 29556

Willmar Technical College • Yvonne Johnson • Willmar, MN 56201 • AASL

Willoughby-Eastlake Pub Lib • Dolly Gundersen • Willoughby, OH 44094 • ALCTS ALSC ALTA LAMA LITA PLA RASD YALSA

Willowbrook High Sch Lib • Catherine Jugle • Villa Park, IL 60181 • AASL

Wilmette Public Library • Richard E. Thompson • Wilmette, IL 60091

Wilmington College Watson Library • James T. Nichols • Wilmington, OH 45177 • ACRL RASD

Wilson College • Susan Matusak • Chambersburg, PA 17201 • ACRL

Winchester Community Library • Jenny Stonerock • Winchester, IN 47394

Windham Free Library Association • Windham, CT 06280

Windsor-Serverance Lib Dist • Kathleen P. Murphy • Windsor, CO 80550

Windsor Public Library • Fred C. Israel • Windsor ON, N9A 4M9 Canada • ALCTS ALSC ASCLA LAMA LITA PLA RASD

Windward School • Los Angeles, CA 90066 • AASL YALSA

Winfield Public Library • Linda Slusar • Winfield, IL 60190

Winnacunnet High School • Maureen D. Cullen • Hampton, NH 03842 • AASL

Winnebago Public Library • Phyllis Kasnick • Winnebago, IL 61088-0081 • PLA

Winnebago Software Corporation • Bob Engen • Caledonia, MN 55921 • AASL LAMA LITA PLA   Subscribing

Winnipeg Centennial Library • David Weismiller • Winnipeg, MB, R3C 3P5 Canada • LAMA

Winston-Salem State University • Mae L. Rodney • Winston-Salem, NC 27110 • ACRL ALCTS LAMA RASD LIRT

Winterthur Museum Library • Katharine Martinez • Winterthur, DE 19735 • ACRL ALCTS LAMA LITA RASD

Wisconsin Library Association • Larry Martin • Madison, WI 53704

Wisconsin Valley Library Service • Heather A. Eldred • Wausau, WI 54401 • ALSC ALTA LAMA PLA RASD

Witherle Memorial Library • Patricia M. Fowler • Castine, ME 04421 • ALTA LAMA PLA

Wofford College Sandor Teszler Library • Joyce Arthur • Spartanburg, SC 29303-3663 • ACRL ALCTS RASD

Wood-Ridge Memorial Library • Carol Beyer • Wood-Ridge, NJ 07075 • PLA

Woodbury University Library • William T. Stanley • Burbank, CA 91510-7846

Woodmere Academy Lower School Library • Woodmere, NY 11598 • AASL ALSC

Worcester Academy Nelson Wheeler Library • Janet Shainheit • Worcester, MA 01604 • AASL YALSA

Worcester Country School • Denny H Sepe-Snyder • Berlin, MD 21811

Workman Publishing Company, Inc. • Kathleen DeBoer • New York, NY 10003 • AASL RASD YALSA   Subscribing

World Book Publishing • William H. Nault • Chicago, IL 60661 • AASL ACRL ALCTS LAMA LITA PLA RASD   Sustaining

Worth Public Library District • Robbyn G. Rebeck • Worth, IL 60482 • ALCTS ALSC YALSA

Worthington Public Library • Meribah H. Mansfield • Worthington, OH 43085 • ALTA LAMA PLA RASD YALSA GODORT

Wyoming Library Association • Laura Grott • Cheyenne, WY 82003

Wyoming State Library • Suzanne J. Lebarron • Cheyenne, WY 82002-0650 • AASL ACRL ALCTS ALSC ALTA ASCLA LAMA LITA PLA RASD YALSA GODORT IFRT LIRT MAGERT

Wyomissing Library Association • Joan S. Eby • Wyomissing, PA 19610 • ALSC PLA

Xaiver University Library • Cincinnati, OH 45207 • ACRL ALCTS LAMA LITA RASD

Yonkers Public Library • Jacqueline E. Miller • Yonkers, NY 10701 • ALSC PLA

Yonsei University Library • Seung-Doo Yang • Seoul, South Korea • ACRL ALCTS LAMA LITA RASD

York High School Library • Betty Boyd • Elmhurst, IL 60126 • AASL

York Township Public Library • Julia Meade • Raub, IN 47976 • PLA

York University Libraries • Ellen Hoffmann • North York ON, M3J 1P3 Canada • ACRL ALCTS LAMA LITA RASD

Zentralbibliothek Zurich • Zurich, Switzerland • ACRL ALCTS RASD

Zion-Benton Twp High Sch Lib Instructional Materials Center • Margaret Schmude • Zion, IL 60099